2010 Standard Catalog of®

Collectibles publication partner of
Major League Baseball

BASEBALL CARDS

19th Edition

Edited by
Don Fluckinger
and the editors of Sports Collectors Digest® /Tuff Stuff®

*"The way a team plays as a whole determines its success.
You may have the greatest bunch of individual stars
in the world, but if they don't play together,
the club won't be worth a dime."*
—Babe Ruth

Published by

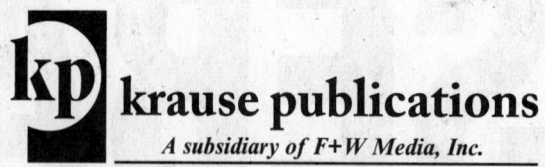

kp krause publications
A subsidiary of F+W Media, Inc.

700 East State Street • Iola, WI 54990-0001
715-445-2214 • 888-457-2873
www.krausebooks.com

Our toll-free number to place an order or obtain
a free catalog is (800) 258-0929.

ISSN 1935-0546

ISBN-13: 978-1-4402-0360-2
ISBN-10: 1-4402-0360-1

Designed by Stacy Bloch
Edited by Joe Clemens

Printed in the United States of America

ACKNOWLEDGMENTS

Hundreds of individuals have made countless valuable contributions that have been incorporated into the *Standard Catalog of Baseball Cards*. While all cannot be acknowledged, special appreciation is extended to the following principal contributors who have exhibited a special dedication by creating, revising or verifying listings and technical data, reviewing market valuations or providing cards to be illustrated.

Rob Adesso • Ken Agona • Gary Agostino • Lisa Albano • Dan Albaugh • Will Allison • Mark Anker • Ellis Anmuth • Steve Applebaum • Bill Atkinson

Rand Bailey • Bill Ballew • Andy Baran • Gary Bartolett • Judy Bartolett • Bob Bartosz • John Beisiegel • Karen Bell • Dr. Charles E. Belles • Dave Berman • Cathy Black • Jerry A. Blum • Ralph Blunt Jr. • Mike Bodner • Jeff Bossak • Bill Bossert • Bob Bostoff • Brian Boston • Jim Boushley • Mark Bowers • Mike Boyd • Roland Bracken • John Brigandi • Scott Brockelman • Lou Brown • Dan Bruner • Greg Bussineau

Billy Caldwell • Len Caprisecca • Tony Carrafiell • Brian Cataquet • Lee Champion • Dwight Chapin • Lou Chericoni • Ryan Christoff • Jim Clarke • Shane Cohen • Rich Cole • Paul Conan Jr. • Charles Conlon • Eric Cooper • Bill Cornell • Bryan Couling • Bob Crabill • Clyde Cripe • Al Cristafulli • Jim Cumpton • Robert Curtiss

Pete D'Luhosch • Tom Daniels • Stuart Dansinger • James Davis • Dick DeCourcy • Ken Degnan • Dan DeKing • Mike Del Gado • Bill Diebold • Larry Dluhy • Brett Domue • John Dorsey

Curtis Earl • Eric Eichelkraut • Mark Elliott • Jeff Emerson • Brian Engles • Shirley Eross • John B. Esch • Joe Esposito • Dan Even • Doak Ewing

Julian Fernandez • David Festberg • Robert Fisk • Jay Finglass • Nick Flaviano • Rick Fleury • Jeff Fritsch • Larry Fritsch

Gary Gagen • Richard Galasso • Tom Galic • Richard R. Gallagher • Chris Gallutia • Tony Galovich • Phillip Garrou • Gary Gatanis • Frank Giffune • Richard Gilkeson • Gerald J. Glasser • Philip Glazer • Keith David Goldfarb • Jack Goodman • Bill Goodwin • Dick Goddard • Howard Gordon • Mike Gordon • Sean Gottlieb • Bob Gray • Wayne Grove • Gerry Guenther • Don Guilbert • Tom Guilfoile

David Hall • Joel Hall • Walter Hall • Gary Hamilton • Tom Harbin • Michael Harrington • Don Harrison • Rich Hawksley • Herbert Hecht • Bill Henderson • Mike Henderson • Kathy Henry • Pete Henrici • Steve Hershkowitz • Bob Hicks • Gregg Hitesman • John Hoffman • Dennis Hollenbeck • Jack Horkan • Jim Horne • Brent Horton • Ron Hosmer • Marvin Huck • Brad Hudecek

Bob Ivanjack

Robert Jacobsen • David Jenkins • Donn Jennings • Scott Jensen • Andrew Jerome • Jim Johnston • Stewart Jones • Larry Jordan

Judy Kay • Allan Kaye • Michael Keedy • Frank Keetz • Mark Kemmerle • Rick Keplinger • John King • John Kitleson • Terry Knouse • Bob Koehler • David Kohler • A.F. Kokol • Dan Kravitz

Steve Lacasse • Jason Lange • Mark K. Larson • Lee Lasseigne • William Lawrence • Scott Lawson • Richard Leech • Morley Leeking • Tom Leon • Don Lepore • Rod Lethbridge • Scott Letts • David Levin • Stuart Leviton • Howie Levy • Hal Lewis • Rob Lifson • Lew Lipset • Jeff Litteral • Dick Lloyd • Chuck Lobenthal • Leon Luckey

Mark Macrae • Paul Marchant • Robert Marek • Bob Marotto • Art Martineau • Bob Marquette • Richard Masson • Bill Mastro • Ralph Maya • Dan McKee • Fred McKie • Tony McLaughlin • Don McPherson • Doug McWilliams • John Mehlin • Bill Mendel • H. Dexter • Joe Merkel • Blake Meyer • Louis Middleton • Bob Miller • Jay Miller • Keith Mitchell • J.A. Monaco • Robert Montgomery • Joe Moreno • Brian Morris • Mike Mosier • Scott Mosley • Mike Mowrey • Peter Mudavin • Mark Murphy • David Musser

Frank Nagy • Steve Neimand • Roger Neufeldt • Tim Newcomb • Joe Newman • Bill Nicolls • Chuck Nobriga • Mark Nochta • Wayne Nochta

Bud Obermeyer • Jeff Obermeyer • Keith Olbermann

D.J. Panaia • Joe Pasternack • Marty Perry • Tom Pfirrman • Dan Piepenbrok • Stan Pietruska • Paul Pollard • Harvey Poris • Don "Barefoot" Post

Pat Quinn

Ed Ranson • Fred Rapaport • Jim Resseque • Steve Rice • Mike Rich • Bob Richardson • Al Richter • Gavin Riley • Mark Rios • Ron Ritzler • Tom Reid • Bob Robles • Mike Rodell • Scott Roemer • Mike Rogers • Chris Ronan • Rocky Rosato • Alan Rosen • John Rumierz • Bob Rund • Moe Ryan

Len Samworth • Jon Sands • Kevin Savage • Stephen Schauer • Allan Schoenberger • Dave Schwartz • Robert Scott • Larry Serota • 707 Sports Cards • Jim Sexton • Corey Shanus • Max Silberman • Al Simeone • Paul Sjolin • Barry Sloate • Joe Smith • Mark Soltan • John Spalding • Kevin Spears • Gene Speranza • Nigel Spill • Jerry Spillman • David Spivack • Dana Sprague • Don Steinbach • Paul Stewart • Dan Stickney • Larry Stone • Ken Stough • Al Strumpf • Doug Stultz • Jim Suckow • Rich Suen • Joe Szeremet

J.J. Teaparty • Erik Teller • Lee Temanson • K.J. Terplak • Mark Theotikos • Dick Tinsley • Gary Tkac • Bud Tompkins • Joseph Tonely • Scott Torrey • Dan Tripper

Rich Unruh • Jack Urban • Glen Van Aken • Frank Van Damme • Brian Van Horn

Geno Wager • Frank Wakefield • Pete Waldman • Eric Waller • Tony Walls • Gary Walter • Frank Ward • Adam Warshaw • Dave Weber • Ken Weimer • Jeff Weiss • Richard Weiss • Dale Weselowski • E.C. Wharton-Tigar • Charles Williamson • Jay Wolt • Frank Wozny • Bill Wright

Rhett Yeakley • Rhys Yeakley • Kit Young

Ted Zanidakis

2010 Standard Catalog of
Baseball Cards

HOW TO USE THIS CATALOG

This catalog has been uniquely designed to serve the needs of collectors and dealers at all levels from beginning to advanced. It provides a comprehensive guide to more than 140 years of baseball card issues, arranged so that even the most novice hobbyist can consult it with confidence and ease.

The following explanations summarize the general practices used in preparing this catalog's listings. However, because of specialized requirements which may vary from card set to card set, these must not be considered ironclad. Where these standards have been set aside, appropriate notations are usually incorporated.

ARRANGEMENT

The most important feature in identifying and pricing a baseball card is its set of origin. Therefore the main body of this catalog, covering cards issued from 1863-date, has been alphabetically arranged within specific eras of issue according to the name by which the set is most popularly known to collectors, or by which it can be most easily identified by a person examining a card.

Previous editions of this catalog relied heavily upon card set identification numbers originated in Jefferson Burdick's pioneering "American Card Catalog." However, since that work was last updated over 40 years ago its numbering system has become arcane and is little used by the present generation of hobbyists. Where practical, sets which were listed in previous editions by their ACC designations have been reclassified alphabetically by a more readily identifiable signpost, such as manufacturer's name. Most of those sets however continue to bear the ACC catalog number in the set heading.

Among card issuers that produced sets for more than a single year, their sets are then listed chronologically, from earliest to most recent, again within specific eras.

Within each set, the cards are listed by their designated card number, or in the absence of card numbers, alphabetically according to the last name of the player pictured. Listing numbers found in parentheses indicate the number does not appear on the card. Certain cards which fall outside the parameters of the normal card numbering for a specific set may be found at the beginning or end of the listings for that set.

Listings are generally arranged in two major sections – major league and minor league issues.

MAJOR LEAGUE ISSUES

The main body of the book details major league baseball card issues from 1863 through the first half of 2008, divided into two sections: Vintage (1863-1980) and Modern (1981-2000). Issues released (2001-date) are available on the enclosed CD. In general, prior to about 1990, this will include issues that picture one or more baseball players, usually contemporary with their playing days, printed on paper or cardboard in a variety of shapes and sizes and given away as a premium with the purchase of another product or service. After 1990 or so the definition is broadened to remove the restriction of the card as an ancillary product and to include those printed on plastic, wood, metal, etc.

Included within each era's listings are related non-card collectibles featuring baseball players which do not fit under the definition previously given for baseball cards. These include many items on which players are depicted on materials other than paper or cardboard, such as pins, coins, silks, leathers, patches, felts, pennants, metallic ingots, statues, figurines, limited-edition artworks and others.

Also presented herein are foreign issues, one of the growth areas of the baseball card hobby in recent years. These encompass the various issues from countries outside of North America, particularly Latin America. Since the 1920s a variety of baseball cards, stamps and stickers have emanated from the Caribbean, South America and elsewhere chronicling the various winter baseball leagues that have flourished there, often stocked with former and future major league stars and, in the early years, providing the only contemporary cards of many U.S. and Latin Negro Leagues players.

Incorporated into the listings are some modern collectors' issues. There exists within the hobby a great body of cards known as "collectors' issues" (sometimes generically known as "broders") by virtue of their nature of having been produced solely for the hobby card market. These cards and sets are distinguished from "legitimate" issues in not having been created as a sales promotional item for another product or service – bubble gum, soda, snack cakes, dog food, cigarettes, gasoline, etc. This distinction, however, is no longer so easy to make since the early 1990s, when many baseball card issues by even the major national companies began to be sold without an accompanying product.

By their nature, and principally because the person issuing them was always free to print and distribute more of the same if they should ever attain any real value, collectors' issues were generally regarded by the hobby as having little or no premium value. Since the leagues and players' union began to enforce licensing restrictions in the early 1990s, the nature of collector's issues changed dramatically. The sets that were the work of an individual catering to the hobby market with an issue of relatively limited numbers and basic technology have given way to more sophisticated productions, often marketed to the general public, as well as the hobby.

The distinction between "collectors" and "legitimate" cards may be barely perceptible but is noted whenever possible. Generally, those collectors' emissions share some or all of these characteristics: 1) Prior to around 1990 they were not licensed by the players depicted, nor by their teams or leagues. 2) They were sold as complete sets rather than by pack or as singles. 3) The issue was marketed almost exclusively to the card collecting hobby audience through advertising in trade papers and public sporting press, and within the hobby's dealer network. 4) The cards were sold on a stand-alone basis, that is, not as a premium or adjunct to the sale of another product or service.

MINOR LEAGUE ISSUES (1867-1969)

Prior to 1970 virtually all minor league baseball cards were issued as single cards rather than as complete sets. Like contemporary major league cards they were usually intended as premiums given away with the purchase of goods and services.

The listings which follow offer individual card prices in three grades of preservation to allow accurate valuations of superstar and other special interest cards, along with cards that were short-printed or otherwise are scarce.

IDENTIFICATION

While most modern baseball cards are well identified on front, back or both, as to date and issue, such has not always been the case. In general, the back of the card is more useful in identifying the set of origin than the front. The issuer or sponsor's name will usually appear on the back since, after all, baseball cards were first produced as a promotional item to stimulate sales of other products. As often as not, that issuer's name is the name by which the set is known to collectors and under which it will be found listed in this catalog.

In some difficult cases, identifying a baseball card's general age, if not specific year of issue, can usually be accomplished by studying the biological or statistical information on the back of the card. The last year mentioned in either the biography or stats is usually the year which preceded the year of issue.

Over the years there have been many cards issued that bear no identification features at all with which to pinpoint the issuer. In such cases, they are cataloged by the names under which they are best known in the hobby. Many of the strip-card issues of the 1920s, for example, remain listed under the "W" catalog number where they were originally enumerated in the "American Card Catalog."

It is the ultimate goal, through the use of cross listings and more detailed indexes, to allow a person holding a card in his hand to find the catalog listing for that card with the greatest ease.

PHOTOGRAPHS

Wherever possible a photograph of the front and (prior to 1981) back of at least one representative card from most of the sets listed in this catalog has been incorporated into the listings to assist identification. (Persons who can provide sample cards for photography purposes for those sets which are missing photos in this volume are encouraged to contact the editor.)

Photographs have been printed in reduced size. The actual size of cards in each set is usually given in the introductory text preceding its listing, unless the card is the current standard size (2.5" by 3.5").

DATING

The dating of baseball cards by year of issue on the front or back of the card itself is a relatively new phenomenon. In most cases, to accurately determine a date of issue for an unidentified card, it must be studied for clues. As mentioned, the biography, career summary or statistics on the back of the card are the best way to pinpoint a year of issue. In most cases, the year of issue will be the year after the last season mentioned on the card.

Luckily for today's collector, earlier generations have done much of the research in determining year of issue for those cards that bear no clues. The painstaking task of matching the players' listed and/or pictured team against their career records often allowed an issue date to be determined.

In some cases, particular card sets were issued over a period of more than one calendar year, but since they are collected together as a single set, their specific year of issue is not important. Such sets will be listed with their complete known range of issue years.

There remain some early issues for which an exact year of issue cannot be reliably pinpointed. In those cases a "best guess" date or one in the middle of the possible range has been used to identify the issue; such cases are usually noted in the introductory text.

NUMBERING

While many baseball card issues as far back as the 1880s have featured card numbers assigned by the issuer to facilitate the collecting of a complete set, the practice has by no means been universal. Even today, not every set bears card numbers.

Logically, those baseball cards that were numbered by their manufacturer are presented in that numerical order within the listings of this catalog whenever possible. In a few cases, complete player checklists were obtained from earlier published sources that did not note card numbers, and so numbers have been arbitrarily assigned. Many other unnumbered issues have been assigned catalog numbers to facilitate their universal identification within the hobby, especially when buying and selling by mail. Among some issues for which the complete checklist remains unknown and for which new discoveries are still being reported, gaps have been left in the assigned numbering to facilitate future additions.

In all cases, numbers that have been assigned, or which otherwise do not appear on the card through error or by design, are shown in this catalog within parentheses. In virtually all cases, unless a more natural system suggested itself by the unique matter of a particular set, the assignment of numbers by the cataloging staff has been done by alphabetical arrangement of the players' last names or the card's principal title.

Significant collectible variations for any particular card are noted within the listings by the application of a suffix letter. In instances of variations, the suffix "a" is assigned to the variation which was created first, when it can be so identified.

NAMES

The identification of a player by full name on the front of his baseball card has been a common practice only since the 1920s. Prior to that, the player's last name and team were the usual information found on the card front.

As a general – though not universally applied – practice, the listings in this volume present the player's name exactly as it appears on the front of the card. If the player's full name only appears on the back, rather than on the front of the card, the listing may correspond to that designation.

A player's name checklisted in **bold italic** type indicates a rookie card as defined later in this introduction.

Cards that contain misspelled first or last names, or even wrong initials, will usually have included in their listings the incorrect information, with a correction accompanying in parentheses. This extends also to cases where the name on the card does not correspond to the player actually pictured.

In some cases, to facilitate efficient presentations, to maintain ease of use for the reader, or to allow for proper computer sorting of data, a player's name or card title may be listed other than as it actually appears on the card.

GRADING

It is necessary that some sort of card grading standard be used so that buyer and seller (especially when dealing through the Internet or by mail) may reach an informed agreement on the value of a card.

Pre-1981 cards are generally priced in the three grades of preservation in which those cards are most commonly encountered in the daily buying and selling in the hobby marketplace. They are listed in grades of Near Mint (NR MT), Excellent (EX) and Very Good (VG), reflecting the basic fact that few cards were able to survive for 25, 50 or even 100 years in close semblance to the condition of their issue.

The pricing of cards in these three conditions will allow readers to accurately price cards which fall in intermediate grades, such as EX-MT, or VG-EX.

Although grades below Very Good are not generally priced in this volume, close approximations of low-grade card values may be figured on the following formula: Good condition cards are valued at about 50 percent of VG price, with Fair cards about 50 percent of Good.

Cards in Poor condition have little or no market value except in the cases of the rarest and most expensive cards. In such cases, value has to be negotiated individually.

Modern (1981-date) issues, which have been preserved in top condition in considerable numbers, are listed only in the grade of Near Mint-to-Mint (NM/M). Earlier editions of this book priced such cards under the heading of Mint condition. However, the rise of independent grading services in the past decade and their use of the NM/M designation to describe the vast majority of new card specimens has influenced the marketplace to the extent that only a small percentage of cards, even fresh from the pack, can meet the strict standards for a true Mint example. The switch to a NM/M designation is part of the catalog's commitment to accurately reflect the current conditions of the card market.

As with older cards, values for lower-grade cards from 1981-date may be generally figured by using a figure of 75 percent of the NM/M price for Near Mint specimens, and 40 percent of the Mint price for Excellent cards.

For the benefit of the reader, we present herewith the grading guide which was originally formulated in 1981 by *Baseball Cards* magazine and *Sports Collectors Digest*, and has been continually refined since that time.

These grading definitions have been used in the pricing of cards in this book, but they are by no means a universally-accepted grading standard.

The potential buyer of a baseball card should keep that in mind when encountering cards of nominally the same grade, but at a price which differs widely from that quoted in this book.

Ultimately, the collector must formulate his/her own personal grading standards in deciding whether cards available for purchase meet the needs of their collection.

No collector is required to adhere to the grading standards presented herewith – nor to any other published grading standards.

Mint (MT): A perfect card. Well-centered, with parallel borders that appear equal to the naked eye. Four sharp, square corners. No creases, edge dents, surface scratches, paper flaws, loss of luster, yellowing or fading, regardless of age. No imperfectly printed card – out of register, badly cut or ink flawed – or card stained by contact with gum, wax or other substances can be considered truly Mint, even if new out of the pack. Generally, to be considered in Mint condition, a card's borders must exist in a ratio of no greater than 60/40 side to side and top to bottom.

Near Mint/Mint (NM/M): A nearly perfect card. Well-centered, with at least three sharp, square corners. No creases, edge dents, surface scratches, paper flaws, loss of luster, yellowing or fading, regardless of age. No imperfectly printed card – out of register, badly cut or ink flawed – or card stained by contact with gum, wax or other substances can be considered Near Mint/ Mint, even if new out of the pack. Generally, to be considered in NM/M condition, a card's borders must exist in a ratio of no greater than 65/35 side to side and top to bottom.

Near Mint (NR MT): At first glance, a Near Mint card appears perfect; upon closer examination, however, a minor flaw will be discovered. On well-centered cards, at least two of the four corners must be perfectly sharp; the others showing a minor imperfection upon close inspection. A slightly off-center card with one or more borders being noticeably unequal – no worse than in a ratio of 70/30 S/S or T/B – would also fit this grade.

Excellent (EX): Corners are still fairly sharp with only moderate wear. Card borders may be off-center as much as 80/20. No creases. May have very minor gum, wax or product stains, front or back. Surfaces may show slight loss of luster from rubbing across other cards.

Very Good (VG): Show obvious handling. Corners rounded and/ or perhaps showing minor creases. Other minor creases may be visible. Surfaces may exhibit loss of luster, but all printing is intact. May show major gum, wax or other packaging stains. No major creases, tape marks or extraneous markings or writing. All four borders visible, though the ratio may be as poor as 95/5. Exhibits honest wear.

Good (G): A well-worn card, but exhibits no intentional damage or abuse. May have major or multiple creases and/or corners rounded well beyond the border. A Good card will generally sell for about 50 percent the value of a card in Very Good condition.

Fair (F or Fr.): Shows excessive wear, along with damage or abuse. Will show all the wear characteristics of a Good card, along with such damage as thumb tack holes in or near margins, evidence of having been taped or pasted, perhaps small tears around the edges, or creases so heavy as to break the cardboard. Backs may show minor added pen or pencil writing, or be missing small bits of paper. Still, basically a complete card. A Fair card will generally sell for 50 percent the value of a Good specimen.

Poor (P): A card that has been tortured to death. Corners or other areas may be torn off. Card may have been trimmed, show holes from a paper punch or have been used for BB gun practice. Front may have extraneous pen or pencil writing, or other defacement. Major portions of front or back design may be missing. Not a pretty sight.

In addition to these terms, collectors may encounter intermediate grades, such as VG-EX or EX-MT. These cards usually have characteristics of both the lower and higher grades, and are generally priced midway between those two values.

With the rise in popularity of third-party authentication/grading services since the mid-1990s, it must be stressed that the grades and corresponding values presented in this book are for "raw" cards – cards which have not been independently graded. Depending on the reputation of the certification firm, cards that have been graded and encased in plastic slabs may sell for a significant premium over the values found here. This is especially true of high-grade specimens of vintage cards that in certified grades of Near Mint/Mint, Mint or Gem Mint may bring multiples of "catalog" value. Even collector-grade vintage cards can command a premium when authenticated, graded and slabbed because potential buyers may feel more secure in such cards' authenticity and freedom from tampering.

ROOKIE CARDS

While the status (and automatic premium value) that a player's rookie card carries has fluctuated in recent years, and though the hobby still has not reached a universal definition of a rookie card, many significant vintage-era rookie cards are noted in this catalog's listings by the use of *bold italic* type. Conversely, many significant modern-era rookie cards are noted in this catalog's listings by the use of **RC** or **(RC)**. Beginning with products issued in 2006, cards with an **(RC)** logo indicate the featured player has a rookie card issued prior to that year. For purposes of this catalog, a player's rookie card is considered to be any card in a nationally distributed, licensed Major League base (non-insert) set from a major manufacturer in the first year in which that player appears on a card, regardless of whether that player has yet appeared in a Major League game or is technically a rookie according to MLB definition.

VALUATIONS

Values quoted in this book represent the current retail market at the time of compilation (Summer, 2006). The quoted values are the result of a unique system of evaluation and verification created by the catalog's editors. Utilizing specialized computer analysis and drawing upon recommendations provided through their daily involvement in the publication of the hobby's leading sports collectors' periodicals, as well as the input of consultants, dealers and collectors, each listing is, in the final analysis, the interpretation of that data by one or more of the editors.

It should be stressed, however, that this book is intended to serve only as an aid in evaluating cards; actual market conditions are constantly changing. This is especially true of the cards of current players, whose on-field performance during the course of a season can greatly affect the value of their cards – upwards or downwards. Because of the extremely volatile nature of new card prices, especially high-end issues, we have chosen not to include the very latest releases from the major companies, feeling it is better to have no listings at all for those cards than to have inaccurate values in print. For the same reasons, many 21st century cards and sets are presented here without pricing. Extremely limited-production (or even unique) cards, often autographs and game-used equipment cards, may not be seen in the hobby market with enough frequency to establish realistic "book" values.

Because this volume is intended to reflect the national market, users will find regional price variances caused by demand differences. Cards of Astros slugger Jeff Bagwell will, for instance, often sell at prices greater than quoted herein at shops and shows in the Houston area. Conversely, his cards may be acquired at a discount from these valuations when purchased on the East or West Coast.

Publication of this book is not intended as a solicitation to buy or sell the listed cards by the editors, publisher or contributors.

Again, the values here are retail prices – what a collector can expect to pay when buying a card from a dealer. The wholesale price, that which a collector can expect to receive from a dealer when selling cards, will be significantly lower.

Many dealers operate on a 100 percent mark-up, generally paying about 50 percent of a card's retail value for cards that they are purchasing for inventory. On some high-demand cards, dealers will pay 100 percent or more of retail value, anticipating continued price increases. Conversely, for many low-demand cards, such as common (non-star) players' cards, dealers may pay as little as 10 percent or even less of retail with many base-brand cards of recent years having no resale value at all.

SET PRICES

Collectors may note that the complete set prices for newer issues quoted in these listings are usually significantly lower than the total of the value of the individual cards that comprise the set. This reflects two factors in the baseball card market. First, a seller is often willing to take a lower composite price for a complete set as a "volume discount" and to avoid carrying in inventory a large number of common-player or other lower-demand cards.

Second, to a degree, the value of common cards can be said to be inflated as a result of having a built-in overhead charge to justify the dealer's time in sorting cards, carrying them in stock and filling orders. This accounts for the fact that even brand new base-brand baseball cards, which cost the dealer around two cents each when bought in bulk, carry individual price tags of five cents or higher.

Some set prices shown, especially for vintage cards in top condition, are merely theoretical in that it is unlikely that a complete set exists in that condition. In general among older cards the range of conditions found in even the most painstakingly assembled complete set make the set values quoted useful only as a starting point for price negotiations.

ERRORS/VARIATIONS

It is often hard for the beginning collector to understand that an error on a baseball card, in and of itself, does not necessarily add premium value to that card. It is usually only when the correcting of an error in a subsequent printing creates a variation that premium value attaches to an error.

Minor errors, such as wrong stats or personal data, misspellings, inconsistencies, etc. – usually affecting the back of the card – are very common, especially in recent years. Unless a corrected variation was also printed, these errors are not noted in the listings of this book because they are not generally perceived by collectors to have premium value.

On the other hand, major effort has been expended to include the most complete listings ever for collectible variation cards. Many scarce and valuable variations are included in these listings because they are widely collected and often have significant premium value.

In the boom years of the early 1990s, some card companies produced their basic sets at more than one printing facility. This frequently resulted in numerous minor variations in photo cropping and back data presentation. Combined with a general decline in quality control from the mid-1980s through the early 1990s, which allowed unprecedented numbers of uncorrected error cards to be released, this caused a general softening of collector interest in errors and variations. Despite the fact most of these modern variations have no premium value, they are listed here as a matter of record.

COUNTERFEITS/REPRINTS

As the value of baseball cards has risen in the past 25+ years, certain cards and sets have become too expensive for the average collector to obtain. This, along with changes in the technology of color printing, has given rise to increasing numbers of counterfeit and reprint cards.

While both terms describe essentially the same thing – a modern-day copy that attempts to duplicate as closely as possible an original baseball card – there are differences that are important to the collector.

Generally a counterfeit is made with the intention of deceiving somebody into believing it is genuine, and thus paying large amounts of money for it. The counterfeiter takes every pain to try to make their fakes look as authentic as possible.

A reprint, on the other hand, while it may have been made to look as close as possible to an original card, is made with the intention of allowing collectors to buy them as substitutes for cards they may never be otherwise able to afford. The big difference is that a reprint is generally marked as such, usually on the back of the card.

In other cases, like the Topps 1952 reprint set and later Archives issues, the replicas are printed in a size markedly different from the originals, or utilizing current technology that differs from that available in the past. Collectors should be aware, however, that unscrupulous persons will sometimes cut off or otherwise obliterate the distinguishing word – "Reprint," "Copy," – or modern copyright date on the back of a reprint card in an attempt to pass it as genuine.

A collector's best defense against reprints and counterfeits is to acquire a knowledge of the look and feel of genuine baseball cards of various eras and issues.

UNLISTED CARDS

Persons encountering cards which are not listed in this reference should not immediately infer that they have something rare and/or valuable. With hundreds of thousands of baseball cards issued over the past century and thousands more being issued each year, this catalog's comprehensiveness will always remain relative. This is especially true in the area of modern cards and sets released regionally, and the vast universe of foreign and collectors' issues for which coverage has only recently begun. Readers who have cards or sets that are not covered in this edition are invited to correspond with the editor for purposes of adding to the compilation work now in progress. A photocopy or scan of the card's front and back will assist in determining its status. **For questions relating to modern-era cards, contact: Joe Clemens, *Standard Catalog of Baseball Cards*, 700 E. State St., Iola, Wis. 54990; e-mail Joseph.Clemens@fwpubs.com. For questions relating to vintage era cards, contact: Don Fluckinger, *Prospect HIll Publishing*, 32 Montgomery Ave., Nashua, NH 03060-5008; email tuffstuff@prospecthillpub.com.** Major contributions will be acknowledged in future editions.

NEW ISSUES

Because new baseball cards are being issued all the time, the cataloging of them remains an on-going challenge. The editors will attempt to keep abreast of new issues so that they may be added to future editions of this book. Readers are invited to submit news of new issues, especially limited-edition or regionally issued cards, to the editor at the address above.

Abbreviation Key

IS: Interleague Showdown

OPS: Overprinted "Promotional Sample"

ED: Expansion Draft

AS: All-Star

HL: Hit List

RC: Rookie Class

RC or (RC): Rookie Card

UPT: Unlimited Potential/Talent

SF: Star Factor

SP: Short Print

DT: Double Team

GLS: Gold Leaf Stars

CC: Curtain Calls

GLR: Gold Leaf Rookies

TP: Top Performers

FF: Future Foundation

DK: Diamond King

RR: Rated Rookie

DP: Double Print

IA: In Action

PC: Promo Card

SR: Star Rookie

HOW TO USE THE CD

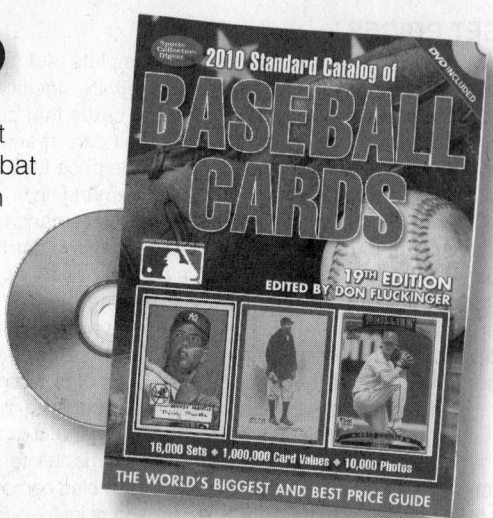

This CD is PC and Macintosh® compatible when used with Adobe Acrobat Reader® version 6.0 or later. A step-by-step free download of Adobe Acrobat Reader® 8 is available at www.adobe.com. Adobe Reader® 8 was used in creating the instructions that follow.

To help you successfully navigate through the PDF document, several types of searches are available.

USING BOOKMARKS

Click on the Bookmarks icon to open the Bookmarks window. Use these links to go to specific points of interest. To scroll through pages in each section, use the arrows at the top of the screen (see next page for instructions to find page navigators).

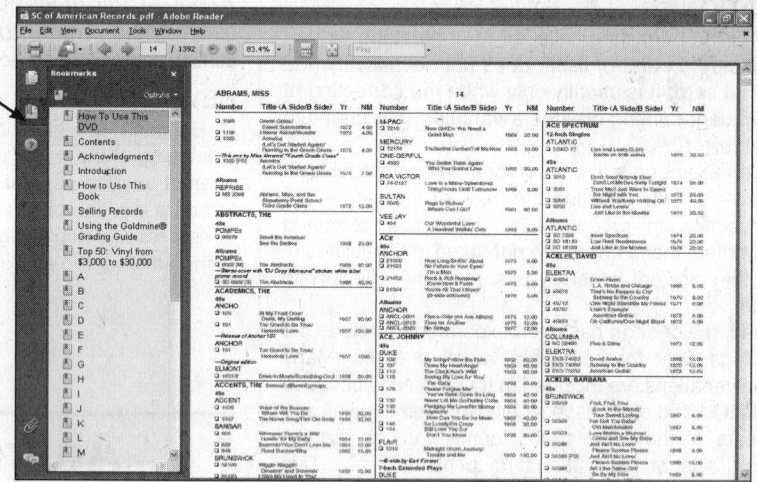

USING THE FIND BOX

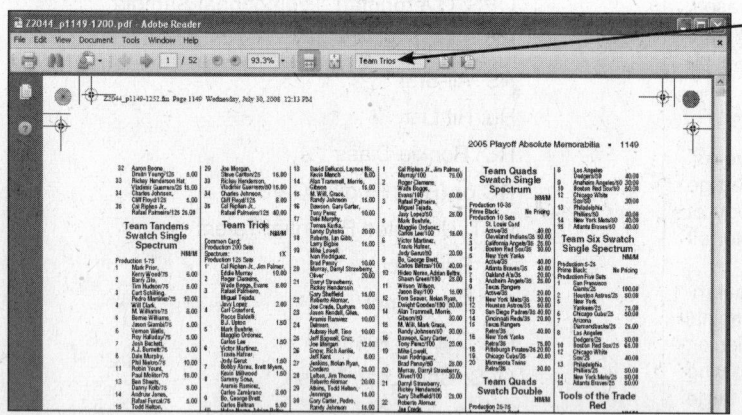

Locate the find box in the tool bar and enter the word(s) you are searching for.

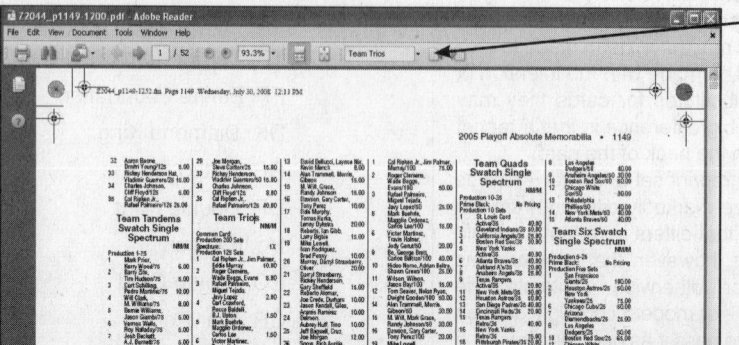

To navigate through the results of your search, use the Find Next icon.

USING THE SEARCH OPTION

Locate the Search button by choosing Customize Toolbars in the Tools pull-down menu. Check Search (binocular icon) to have the Search option available in the toolbar.

Click on the Search icon to open the Search dialog box.

In the Search dialog box, enter the word(s) you are searching for and click on the Search button.

The list of results will appear in the dialog box. Click on the listings to view each page that contains your searched word(s).

To begin a new word search, click on the New Search button.

USING PAGE NAVIGATORS

Activate the Page Navigator Toolbar by choosing Customize Toolbars in the Tools pull-down menu. Check each tool as shown at right. You are now able to page through the PDF document by using the arrows at the top of the screen or by entering a page number you wish to view.

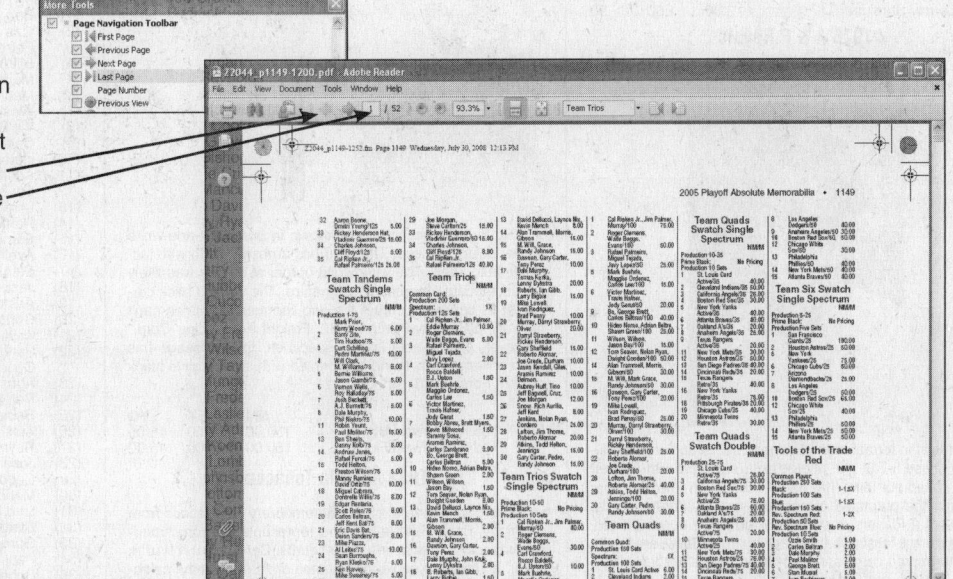

VINTAGE MAJOR LEAGUE CARDS (1869-1980)

The vast majority of cards and collectibles listed in this section were issued between 1869 and 1980 and feature major league players only. The term "card" is used rather loosely as in this context it is construed to include virtually any cardboard or paper product, of whatever size and/or shape, depicting baseball players and issued to stimulate the sales of another product or service.

A

1976 A & P Brewers

The Aaron and Yount cards from this regional issue support the set price. The set was issued by the A & P grocery chain. Oversize - 5-7/8" x 9" - cards (actually printed on semi-gloss paper) were given out at the stores in 1976 in series of four with the purchase of select weekly grocery specials. Players are pictured in tight capless portraits. Each photo has a black facsimile autograph; backs are blank. The unnumbered cards are checklisted here in alphabetical order.

		NM	EX	VG
Complete Set (16):		35.00	17.50	10.50
Common Player:		3.00	1.50	.90
(1)	Henry Aaron	20.00	10.00	6.00
(2)	Pete Broberg	3.00	1.50	.90
(3)	Jim Colborn	3.00	1.50	.90
(4)	Mike Hegan	3.00	1.50	.90
(5)	Tim Johnson	3.00	1.50	.90
(6)	Von Joshua	3.00	1.50	.90
(7)	Sixto Lezcano	3.00	1.50	.90
(8)	Don Money	3.00	1.50	.90
(9)	Charlie Moore	3.00	1.50	.90
(10)	Darrell Porter	3.00	1.50	.90
(11)	George Scott	3.00	1.50	.90
(12)	Bill Sharp	3.00	1.50	.90
(13)	Jim Slaton	3.00	1.50	.90
(14)	Bill Travers	3.00	1.50	.90
(15)	Robin Yount	10.00	5.00	3.00
(16)	County Stadium	3.00	1.50	.90

1976 A & P Royals

Identical in format to the Brewers' set issued around Milwaukee, these 5-7/8" x 9" photos picture players without their caps in posed portraits. The cards were given away four per week with the purchase of selected grocery item specials. Cards have a Players Association logo in the upper-left corner, and a black facsimile autograph on front. Backs are blank. The unnumbered cards are checklisted here alphabetically.

	NM	EX	VG
Complete Set (16):	40.00	20.00	12.00

Common Player:		3.00	1.50	.90
(1)	Doug Bird	3.00	1.50	.90
(2)	George Brett	20.00	10.00	6.00
(3)	Steve Busby	3.00	1.50	.90
(4)	Al Cowens	3.00	1.50	.90
(5)	Al Fitzmorris	3.00	1.50	.90
(6)	Dennis Leonard	3.00	1.50	.90
(7)	Buck Martinez	3.00	1.50	.90
(8)	John Mayberry	3.00	1.50	.90
(9)	Hal McRae	4.50	2.25	1.25
(10)	Amos Otis	4.50	2.25	1.25
(11)	Fred Patek	3.00	1.50	.90
(12)	Tom Poquette	3.00	1.50	.90
(13)	Mel Rojas	3.00	1.50	.90
(14)	Tony Solaita	3.00	1.50	.90
(15)	Paul Splittorff	3.00	1.50	.90
(16)	Jim Wohlford	3.00	1.50	.90

1968 Aamco Roger Maris Postcard

 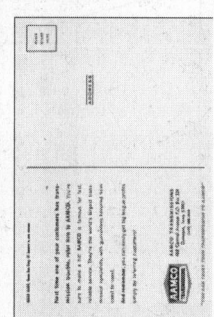

The cited date is approximate on this large-format (about 6" x 9") postcard. The borderless front has a color pose of the reigning home run king with the legend, "It's a real pennant winner!" The postcard format back is directed at auto service professionals, encouraging them to refer transmission problems to a local Aamco facility. A color Aamco logo is at bottom-left.

	NM	EX	VG
Roger Maris	150.00	75.00	45.00

1954 ABC Freight Postcard

So far only one player is known in this black-and-white glossy postcard issue. The front has a posed photo with facsimile autograph. The wide white border at bottom was likely to accomodate an authentic signature. The divided back carries in its upper-left corner the two-line message "You can't miss by playing ball with / ABC Freight Forwarding Corp." However, on the sole known specimen, that message has been obliterated by being overprinted with a decorative black design. Format is 3-1/2" x 5-7/16".

		NM	EX	VG
(1)	Ted Kluszewski/Btg	150.00	75.00	45.00
(2)	Ted Kluszewski/Fldg	150.00	75.00	45.00

1932 Abdulla Tobacco

Along with several other contemporary card issues from Germany, Babe Ruth is the lone representative from American baseball in this series of 200 cards. Cards are 1-11/16" x 2-1/2" and feature sepia-tone photos on front, with the celebrity's name and nation printed in the white border at bottom. Backs are in German and include a card number.

Babe Ruth, Amerika

		NM	EX	VG
196	Babe Ruth	1,750	875.00	525.00

1949-1950 Acebo y Cia

These small (about 1-1/2" x 1-3/4") Cuban cards were issued in matchboxes, probably over more than one season, as some players are known in photo variations. Fronts have a black-and-white or duotone photo, bordered, with the player name in plain type. Backs have player information presented in one of several different styles, or are blank-backed. It is likely this checklist, which includes a significant contingent of American players, is not complete.

		NM	EX	VG
Common Player:		100.00	50.00	30.00
(1)	Bob Addis	100.00	50.00	30.00
(2)	Luis Aloma	100.00	50.00	30.00
(3)	Ferrel (Ferrell) Anderson	100.00	50.00	30.00
(4)	Bill Antonello	100.00	50.00	30.00
(5)	Mario Arencibia	100.00	50.00	30.00
(6)	Maurice Atwright	100.00	50.00	30.00
(7)	Wesley Bailey	100.00	50.00	30.00
(8)	Vic Barnhart	100.00	50.00	30.00
(9)	Carlos Blanco	100.00	50.00	30.00
(10)	Herberto Blanco	100.00	50.00	30.00
(11)	Adolfo Cabrera	100.00	50.00	30.00
(12)	Emilio Cabrera	100.00	50.00	30.00
(13)	Lorenzo "Chiquitin" Cabrera	100.00	50.00	30.00
(14)	Rafael Villa Cabrera	100.00	50.00	30.00
(15)	Samuel Calderone	100.00	50.00	30.00
(16)	Avelino Canizares	100.00	50.00	30.00
(17)	Clemente "Sungo" Carreras	100.00	50.00	30.00
(18)	Jack Cassini	100.00	50.00	30.00
(19)	Aristonico Cocorreoso	100.00	50.00	30.00
(20)	Carlos Colas	100.00	50.00	30.00
(21)	Kevin (Chuck) Connors	450.00	225.00	135.00
(22)	Sandalio "Potrellilo" Consuegra	125.00	62.00	37.00
(23)	Agustin Cordeiro	100.00	50.00	30.00
(24)	Reinaldo Cordeiro	100.00	50.00	30.00
(25)	Reinaldo Cordeiro	100.00	50.00	30.00
(26)	Alejandro Crespo	100.00	50.00	30.00
(27)	Raymond "Talua" Dandridge	500.00	250.00	150.00
(28)	Jose "Pipo" de la Noval	100.00	50.00	30.00
(29)	Carlos "Yiqui" De Souza	100.00	50.00	30.00
(30)	Mario Diaz	100.00	50.00	30.00
(31)	Lino Donoso	100.00	50.00	30.00
(32)	Claro Duany	100.00	50.00	30.00
(33)	Gumersindo Elba	100.00	50.00	30.00
(34)	Paul (Al) Epperly	100.00	50.00	30.00
(35)	Roberto "Tarzan" Estalella	125.00	65.00	35.00
(36)	Jose Ma. Fernandez	100.00	50.00	30.00
(37)	Jose Ma. Fernandez Jr.	100.00	50.00	30.00

(38)	Rodolfo Fernandez	100.00	50.00	30.00
(39)	Thomas Fine	100.00	50.00	30.00
(40)	Andres Fleitas	100.00	50.00	30.00
(41)	Pedro Formental	100.00	50.00	30.00
(42)	"Sojito" Gallardo	100.00	50.00	30.00
(43)	Chicuelo Garcia	100.00	50.00	30.00
(44)	Manuel "Cocaina" Garcia	150.00	75.00	45.00
(45)	Pablo Garcia	100.00	50.00	30.00
(46)	Silvio Garcia	100.00	50.00	30.00
(47)	Lloyd Gearhart (Reverse image.)	100.00	50.00	30.00
(48)	Lloyd Gearhart (Corrected)	100.00	50.00	30.00
(49)	(Al) Gerheauser	100.00	50.00	30.00
(50)	Albert Gionfrido (Gionfriddo)	125.00	65.00	35.00
(51)	Leonardo Goicochea	100.00	50.00	30.00
(52)	Enrique Gonzalez	100.00	50.00	30.00
(53)	Hiram Gonzalez	100.00	50.00	30.00
(54)	Miguel Angel Gonzalez	125.00	65.00	35.00
(55)	Fermin Guerra	100.00	50.00	30.00
(56)	Wes Hamner	100.00	50.00	30.00
(57)	Eugene Handley	100.00	50.00	30.00
(58)	Rollie Hemsley	100.00	50.00	30.00
(59)	Salvador Hernandez	100.00	50.00	30.00
(60)	Clarence Hicks	100.00	50.00	30.00
(61)	Manuel "Chino" Hidalgo	100.00	50.00	30.00
(62)	Bob Hooper	100.00	50.00	30.00
(63)	Amado Ibanez	100.00	50.00	30.00
(64)	Don Lenhardt	100.00	50.00	30.00
(65)	Vicente Lopez	100.00	50.00	30.00
(66)	Raul Lopez	100.00	50.00	30.00
(67)	"Tony" Lorenzo	100.00	50.00	30.00
(68)	Adolfo Luque	150.00	75.00	45.00
(69)	John Bill Maldovan	100.00	50.00	30.00
(70)	Max Manning	250.00	125.00	75.00
(71)	Conrado Marrero	125.00	65.00	35.00
(72)	Rogelio "Limonar" Martinez/ Pitching	100.00	50.00	30.00
(73)	Rogelio "Limonar" Martinez/ Portait	100.00	50.00	30.00
(74)	Agapito Mayor	100.00	50.00	30.00
(75)	Lester McCrabb	100.00	50.00	30.00
(76)	Guillermo "Willy" Miranda	125.00	65.00	35.00
(77)	Rene Monteagudo	100.00	50.00	30.00
(78)	Julio "Jiqui" Moreno	100.00	50.00	30.00
(79)	Ernesto Morrilla	100.00	50.00	30.00
(80)	Howie Moss	100.00	50.00	30.00
(81)	Rafael Sam Noble	100.00	50.00	30.00
(82)	Regino Otero	100.00	50.00	30.00
(83)	Oliverio Ortiz	100.00	50.00	30.00
(84)	Roberto Ortiz/Btg	100.00	50.00	30.00
(85)	Roberto Ortiz/Potrait	100.00	50.00	30.00
(86)	Pedro Pages	100.00	50.00	30.00
(87)	Leonard Pearson	250.00	125.00	75.00
(88)	Eddie Pellagrin (Pellagrini)	100.00	50.00	30.00
(89)	Conrado Perez	100.00	50.00	30.00
(90)	Damon Phillips	100.00	50.00	30.00
(91)	Jose "Pototo" Piloto	100.00	50.00	30.00
(92)	William Powell	100.00	50.00	30.00
(93)	Al Prendergast	100.00	50.00	30.00
(94)	Napoleon Reyes (Holding bat.)	100.00	50.00	30.00
(95)	Napoleon Reyes (No bat.)	100.00	50.00	30.00
(96)	Donald Richmond	100.00	50.00	30.00
(97)	Hector Rodriguez	100.00	50.00	30.00
(98)	Oscar Rodriguez	100.00	50.00	30.00
(99)	Julio Rojo	100.00	50.00	30.00
(100)	Octavio Rubert	100.00	50.00	30.00
(101)	Arturo Seijas	100.00	50.00	30.00
(102)	Raymond Shore (Arms crossed.)	100.00	50.00	30.00
(103)	Raymond Shore (Pose unrecorded.)	100.00	50.00	30.00
(104)	Ford Smith	100.00	50.00	30.00
(105)	Rene Solis	100.00	50.00	30.00
(106)	Roberto Fernandez Tapanes	100.00	50.00	30.00
(107)	Don Thompson	100.00	50.00	30.00
(108)	Gilberto Torres	100.00	50.00	30.00
(109)	Quincy Trouppe	150.00	75.00	45.00
(110)	Christian Van Cuyk	100.00	50.00	30.00
(111)	John Van Cuyk	100.00	50.00	30.00
(112)	Ben Wade	100.00	50.00	30.00
(113)	Archie Wilson	100.00	50.00	30.00
(114)	Edward Wright	100.00	50.00	30.00
(115)	Adrian Zabala	100.00	50.00	30.00

1970 Action Cartridge

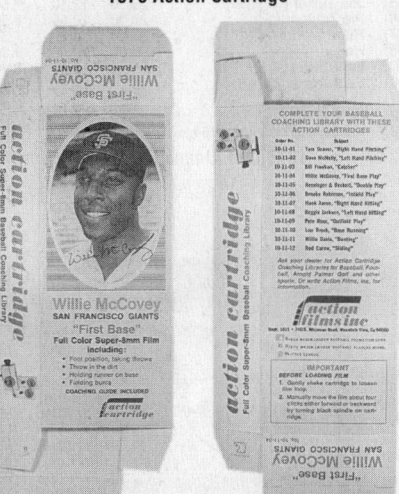

This set of boxes with baseball players' pictures on them was issued by Action Films Inc. of Mountain View, Calif., in 1970-71. The boxes, measuring 2-5/8" x 6" x 1" deep, contained 8mm film cartridges of various professional athletes demonstrating playing tips. The movie series include 12 baseball players. (Other sports represented were football, golf, tennis, hockey and skiing, a total of 40, in all). Boxes feature color player portraits inside an oval and include a facsimile autograph. The values listed are for complete boxes or player panels, without the movie cartridge.

		NM	EX	VG
Complete Set (12):		275.00	135.00	85.00
Common Player:		7.50	3.75	2.25
Box w/Cartridge: 2X				
Viewer:		60.00	30.00	20.00
1	Tom Seaver	40.00	20.00	12.00
2	Dave McNally	7.50	3.75	2.25
3	Bill Freehan	7.50	3.75	2.25
4	Willie McCovey	25.00	12.50	7.50
5	Glenn Beckert, Don Kessinger	7.50	3.75	2.25
6	Brooks Robinson	30.00	15.00	9.00
7	Hank Aaron	60.00	30.00	18.00
8	Reggie Jackson	45.00	22.50	13.50
9	Pete Rose	50.00	25.00	15.00
10	Lou Brock	25.00	12.50	7.50
11	Willie Davis	7.50	3.75	2.25
12	Rod Carew	25.00	12.50	7.50

1933-1934 Adams Hat Stores

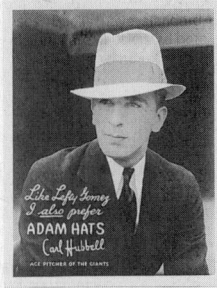

In the early 1930s a men's haberdasher issued a series of colorized 8" x 10" portrait photos of baseball players and other celebrities dressed in suit-and-tie and wearing a hat. Above a facsimile autograph on front is a testimonial for Adams Hats. Backs are stamped, "Property of Adams Hat Stores, Inc." The location of the issuing store or stores in unknown. Only the ballplayers are listed here.

		NM	EX	VG
Complete Set (3):		1,750	875.00	525.00
Common Player:		600.00	300.00	180.00
(1)	Carl Hubbell	600.00	300.00	180.00
(2)	Lefty Gomez	600.00	300.00	180.00
(3)	John McGraw	600.00	300.00	180.00

1910 A Fan For A Fan

These cardboard novelties were produced by the American Tobacco Co. About 7-1/4" in diameter, the bursting baseball and portrait are printed in color with a facsimile autograph. The handle is about 5" long. The back is blank. The known fans are listed here alphabetically; the checklist is likely incomplete.

		NM	EX	VG
Complete Set (5):		30,000	16,000	9,750
Common Player:		2,400	1,200	725.00
(1)	Frank Baker	4,500	2,250	1,350
(2)	Hal Chase	3,600	1,800	1,100
(3)	Ty Cobb	15,000	7,500	4,500
(4)	Larry Doyle	2,400	1,200	725.00
(5)	Christy Mathewson	5,500	2,750	1,650

1939 African Tobacco

The unlikely venue of the "other" U.S.A. (Union of South Africa) is the provenance of this rare Babe Ruth card. The African Tobacco Co. issued a set of 100 cards in a series titled "The World of Sport." The cards were issued in both a large (2-1/4" x 3-1/4") and small (1-3/4" x 2-1/2") format. Fronts have a black-and-white photo of Ruth, with a white border all around. Backs are printed in both English and Afrikaner.

		NM	EX	VG
34	Babe Ruth (Large)	1,250	625.00	375.00
34	Babe Ruth (Small)	1,250	625.00	375.00

1924-1925 Aguilitas Segundas

 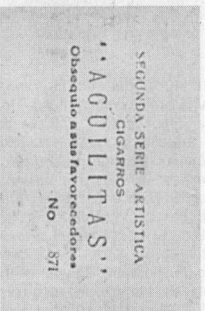

This set is known to collectors as Aguilitas Segundas for the top line of the ad on back. In reality, this second series cigarette card issue was issued several years before the Aguilitas first series counterpart. About 1-1/2" x 2-3/8", the cards have round black-and-white player portrait photos in a debossed rectangular area on glossy stock. Beneath the photo is a player name or nickname, with "BASE BALL" below. The ballplayers are a subset of a 900-card issue which included movie and stage stars, soccer players, boxers and other subjects. All baseball players are known within the numerical range of 841 through 899, though only four cards are known above #880, and none between #880-895. The known ballplayers comprise 44, many of whom were stars of the Negro Leagues, including several Hall of Famers and some who appear on no other career-contemporary cards. Cards are checklisted with the name as shown on the card, further identification, where necessary, is listed. parenthetically. Many surviving specimens show evidence of having been glued into an album which largely accounts for their survival in the area's hot, humid climate. Examples are rarely seen in condition approaching Excellent.

		NM	EX	VG
Common Player:		220.00	120.00	65.00
841	(Pablo "Champion") Mesa	220.00	120.00	65.00
842	A. (Armando) Marsans	250.00	125.00	75.00
843	C. (Cristobal) Torriente	7,500	2,250	1,350
844	Merito Acosta	220.00	120.00	65.00
845	Cheo Ramos	220.00	120.00	65.00
846	Joe (John Henry "Pop") Lloyd	10,000	2,750	1,650
847	(Herman Matias) Rios	220.00	120.00	65.00
848	(Lucas) Boada	220.00	120.00	65.00
849	(Jose) Mendez	6,000	1,750	1,000
850	(Valentin) Dreke	350.00	175.00	100.00
851	(Eugenio) Morin	220.00	120.00	65.00
852	Mayari (Esteban "Mayari" Montalvo)	250.00	125.00	75.00
853	(Valentin) Dreke	350.00	175.00	105.00
854	(Julio) Rojo	220.00	120.00	65.00
855	(Rafael) Almeida	250.00	125.00	75.00
856	(Emilio) Palmero	220.00	120.00	65.00
857	(Adolfo) Luque	800.00	250.00	150.00
858	(Isidro) Fabre	250.00	125.00	75.00
859	(Manuel) Cueto	220.00	120.00	65.00
860	Dibu (Pedro Dibut)	220.00	120.00	65.00
861	Cheo Ramos	220.00	120.00	65.00
862	(Jesse) Hubbard	750.00	375.00	225.00
863	Kakin (Gonzalez)	220.00	120.00	65.00
864	(Jose Maria) Fernandez	220.00	120.00	65.00
865	(Snake) Henry	450.00	225.00	135.00
866	Cruje (Ernie Krueger)	450.00	225.00	135.00
867	(Manuel) Parrado	220.00	120.00	65.00
868	(Chuck) Dressen	250.00	125.00	75.00
869	(Oscar) Charleston	10,000	3,500	2,150
870	Sam (John Henry "Pop") Lloyd	10,000	2,750	1,650
871	Mc. Key (Raleigh "Biz" Mackey)	6,000	2,250	1,350

		NM	EX	VG
872	P. (Eusebio "Papo") Gonzalez	220.00	120.00	65.00
873	(Clint) Thomas	600.00	300.00	180.00
874	(Dobie) Moore	600.00	300.00	180.00
875	(Frank) Duncan	600.00	300.00	180.00
876	O. (Oscar) Rodriguez	220.00	120.00	65.00
877	Lopito (Jose "Lopito" Lopez)	200.00	100.00	60.00
878	E. (Eustaquio "Bombin") Pedroso	1,000	500.00	300.00
879	(Dick) Lundy	6,000	1,375	825.00
880	Sirike (Valentin "Sirique" Gonzalez)	220.00	120.00	65.00
895	(Oscar) Tuero	220.00	120.00	65.00
897	(Alejandro) Oms	1,200	600.00	360.00
898	Peter (Jesse Petty)	250.00	125.00	75.00
899	(Danny) Clark	220.00	120.00	65.00

1926-1927 Aguilitas

 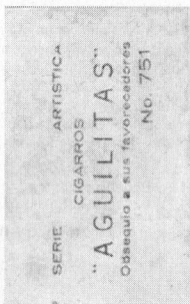

Uniforms worn by some of the players indicate this set was produced after the related series known as "Segundas," or Second Series. The baseball players - all Cuban nationals - are among 100 athletes (including soccer players and boxers) in a 900-card multi-subject set issued in packs of Aguilitas cigarettes. The cards are printed in black-and-white on glossy stock. On front is a large square portrait or action pose. In the bottom border is "BASE-BALL" with the player name and position below. Names as shown on the cards are presneted in this checklist, with further identification as necessary provided parenthetically. Several of the cards are duplicated in the series with different card numbers. Like most contemporary Latin American issues, surviving examples are seldom found in high-grade and often with evidence of having been mounted in an album.

		NM	EX	VG
	Common Player:	165.00	85.00	50.00
751	Cheo Hernandez	165.00	85.00	50.00
752	(Jose Maria) Fernandez	200.00	100.00	60.00
756	R. (Ricardo) Torres	165.00	85.00	50.00
759	Jacinto Calvo	165.00	85.00	50.00
761	E. (Emilio) Palmero	165.00	85.00	50.00
763	Champion (Pablo) Mesa	250.00	125.00	75.00
769	C. (Carlos) Zarza	165.00	85.00	50.00
771	Fernando Rios	165.00	85.00	50.00
772	J. (Joseito) Rodriguez	165.00	85.00	50.00
774	(Juanelo) Mirabal (Same as #824.)	250.00	125.00	75.00
776	L. (Lalo) Rodriguez	165.00	85.00	50.00
777	A. (Adolfo) Luque	350.00	175.00	100.00
778	Alejandro Oms	3,500	1,250	750.00
779	(Armando) Marsans (Same as #829.)	375.00	185.00	110.00
782a	A. (Alfredo) Cabrera	165.00	85.00	50.00
782b	Daniel Blanco (Same as #832.)	165.00	85.00	50.00
787	B. (Bartolo) Portuando	250.00	125.00	75.00
791	A. (Agustin) Navarro	165.00	85.00	50.00
796	R. (Raphael "Busta") Quintana	165.00	85.00	50.00
797	(Roberto) Puig (Same as #847.)	165.00	85.00	50.00
817	(Oscar) Levis	165.00	85.00	50.00
819	Raul Atan	165.00	85.00	50.00
821	(Jose) Pepin Perez	165.00	85.00	50.00
822	(Isidro) Fabre	200.00	100.00	60.00
823	(Bienvenido "Hooks") Jimenez	250.00	125.00	75.00
824	(Juanelo) Mirabal (Same as #774.)	250.00	125.00	75.00
825	Tomas Calvo	165.00	85.00	50.00
826	(Pelayo) Chacon	250.00	125.00	75.00
829	(Armando) Marsans (Same as #779.)	375.00	185.00	110.00
832	Daniel Blanco (Same as #782.)	165.00	85.00	50.00
836	(Valentin) Dreke	250.00	125.00	75.00
838	(Jose) Echarri	165.00	85.00	50.00
839	Miguel Angel (Gonzalez)	300.00	150.00	90.00
841	(Oscar) Estrada	300.00	150.00	90.00
846	Acostica (Jose Acosta)	300.00	150.00	90.00
847	(Roberto) Puig (Same as #797.)	165.00	85.00	50.00
849	(Cesar) Alvarez	165.00	85.00	50.00

1954 Alaga Syrup Willie Mays Postcard

The year of issue on this one-card set is approximate. In 3-1/4" x 5-1/2" format the black-and-white card has a borderless portrait on front with a facsimile autograph. Back has an ad for Alaga Syrup, along with standard postcard elements.

		NM	EX	VG
(1)	Willie Mays	300.00	150.00	90.00

1944-45 Albertype Hall of Fame Plaque Postcards - Type 1

From 1944-1952, Albertype was the official producer of the Baseball Hall of Fame's postcards available for public sale. The 3-1/2" x 5-1/2" black-and-white cards depict the bronze plaque of each inductee. Fronts have a white border. Postcard-style backs have a bit of player data and identification of the specific producer. In the first type of Albertype plaque postcards, issued 1944-45, the line of type beneath the photo has an abbreviation for the state name. Later Albertypes spelled out the state name. The unnumbered cards are checklisted here alphabetically.

		NM	EX	VG
	Complete Set (38):	800.00	400.00	240.00
	Common Player:	20.00	10.00	6.00
(1)	G.C. Alexander	25.00	12.50	7.50
(2)	Adrian Anson	20.00	10.00	6.00
(3)	Roger Bresnahan	20.00	10.00	6.00
(4)	Dan Brouthers	20.00	10.00	6.00
(5)	Morgan Bulkeley	20.00	10.00	6.00
(6)	Alexander Cartwright	20.00	10.00	6.00
(7)	Henry Chadwick	20.00	10.00	6.00
(8)	Fred Clarke	20.00	10.00	6.00
(9)	Ty Cobb	40.00	20.00	12.00
(10)	Eddie Collins	20.00	10.00	6.00
(11)	Jimmy Collins	20.00	10.00	6.00
(12)	Charles A. Comiskey	20.00	10.00	6.00
(13)	Candy Cummings	20.00	10.00	6.00
(14)	Ed Delahanty	20.00	10.00	6.00
(15)	Hugh Duffy	20.00	10.00	6.00
(16)	Buck Ewing	20.00	10.00	6.00
(17)	Lou Gehrig	50.00	25.00	15.00
(18)	Rogers Hornsby	20.00	10.00	6.00
(19)	Hughie Jennings	20.00	10.00	6.00
(20)	Ban Johnson	20.00	10.00	6.00
(21)	Walter Johnson	30.00	15.00	9.00
(22)	Willie Keeler	20.00	10.00	6.00
(23)	King Kelly	20.00	10.00	6.00
(24)	Nap Lajoie	20.00	10.00	6.00
(25)	Kenesaw Landis	20.00	10.00	6.00
(26)	Connie Mack	20.00	10.00	6.00
(27)	Christy Mathewson	30.00	15.00	9.00
(28)	John McGraw	20.00	10.00	6.00
(29)	Jim O'Rourke	20.00	10.00	6.00
(30)	Chas. Radbourn	20.00	10.00	6.00
(31)	Wilbert Robinson	20.00	10.00	6.00
(32)	Babe Ruth	65.00	32.00	19.50
(33)	George Sisler	20.00	10.00	6.00
(34)	Al Spalding	20.00	10.00	6.00
(35)	Tris Speaker	20.00	10.00	6.00
(36)	Honus Wagner	30.00	15.00	9.00
(37)	George Wright	20.00	10.00	6.00
(38)	Cy Young	30.00	15.00	9.00

1946-52 Albertype Hall of Fame Plaque Postcards - Type 2

From 1944-1952, Albertype was the official producer of the Baseball Hall of Fame's postcards available for public sale. The 3-1/2" x 5-1/2" black-and-white cards depict the bronze plaque of each inductee. Fronts have a white border. Postcard-style backs have a bit of biographical data and identification of the specific issuer. In the second series of Albertype plaque postcards, issued 1946-52, the line of type beneath the plaque photo spells out the New York state name. The unnumbered cards are checklisted here alphabetically.

Those cards found only in this series are noted with an asterisk. Because the Foxx and Ott cards were first issued in 1951, and the Paul Waner, Heilmann and 1864 Knickerboker Nine in 1952, they are scarcer than those issued earlier.

		NM	EX	VG
	Complete Set (63):	1,325	675.00	425.00
	Common Player:	20.00	10.00	6.00
(1)	G.C. Alexander	25.00	12.50	7.50
(2)	Adrian Anson	20.00	10.00	6.00
(3)	Roger Bresnahan	20.00	10.00	6.00
(4)	Dan Brouthers	20.00	10.00	6.00
(5)	Mordecai Brown	25.00	12.50	7.50
(6)	Morgan Bulkeley	20.00	10.00	6.00
(7)	Jesse Burkett (*)	25.00	12.50	7.50
(8)	Alexander Cartwright	20.00	10.00	6.00
(9)	Henry Chadwick	20.00	10.00	6.00
(10)	Frank Chance (*)	25.00	12.50	7.50
(11)	Jack Chesbro (*)	25.00	12.50	7.50
(12)	Fred Clarke	20.00	10.00	6.00
(13)	Ty Cobb	40.00	20.00	12.00
(14)	Mickey Cochrane (*)	25.00	12.50	7.50
(15)	Eddie Collins	20.00	10.00	6.00
(16)	Jimmy Collins	20.00	10.00	6.00
(17)	Charles A. Comiskey	20.00	10.00	6.00
(18)	Candy Cummings	20.00	10.00	6.00
(19)	Ed Delahanty	20.00	10.00	6.00
(20)	Hugh Duffy	20.00	10.00	6.00
(21)	Johnny Evers (*)	25.00	12.50	7.50
(22)	Buck Ewing	20.00	10.00	6.00
(23)	James E. (Jimmy) Foxx (*)	45.00	22.00	13.50
(24)	Frankie Frisch (*)	25.00	12.50	7.50
(25)	Lou Gehrig	50.00	25.00	15.00
(26)	Charlie Gehringer (*)	25.00	12.50	7.50
(27)	Clark Griffith (*)	25.00	12.50	7.50
(28)	Lefty Grove (*)	25.00	12.50	7.50
(29)	Harry Heilmann (*)	40.00	20.00	12.00
(30)	Rogers Hornsby	20.00	10.00	6.00
(31)	Carl Hubbell (*)	25.00	12.50	7.50
(32)	Hughie Jennings	20.00	10.00	6.00
(33)	Ban Johnson	20.00	10.00	6.00
(34)	Walter Johnson	30.00	15.00	9.00
(35)	Willie Keeler	20.00	10.00	6.00
(36)	King Kelly	20.00	10.00	6.00
(37)	Nap Lajoie	20.00	10.00	6.00
(38)	Kenesaw Landis	20.00	10.00	6.00
(39)	Connie Mack	20.00	10.00	6.00
(40)	Christy Mathewson	30.00	15.00	9.00
(41)	Tommy McCarthy (*)	25.00	12.50	7.50
(62)	Joe McGinnity (*)	25.00	12.50	7.50
(43)	John McGraw	20.00	10.00	6.00
(44)	Kid Nichols (*)	25.00	12.50	7.50
(45)	Jim O'Rourke	20.00	10.00	6.00
(46)	Mel Ott (*)	35.00	17.50	10.50
(47)	Herb Pennock (*)	25.00	12.50	7.50
(48)	Ed Plank (*)	25.00	12.50	7.50
(49)	Chas. Radbourn	20.00	10.00	6.00
(50)	Wilbert Robinson	20.00	10.00	6.00
(51)	Babe Ruth	65.00	32.00	19.50
(52)	George Sisler	20.00	10.00	6.00
(53)	Al Spalding	20.00	10.00	6.00
(54)	Tris Speaker	20.00	10.00	6.00
(55)	Joe Tinker (*)	25.00	12.50	7.50
(56)	Pie Traynor (*)	25.00	12.50	7.50
(57)	Rube Waddell (*)	25.00	12.50	7.50
(58)	Honus Wagner	30.00	15.00	9.00
(59)	Ed Walsh (*)	25.00	12.50	7.50
(60)	Paul Waner (*)	35.00	17.50	10.50
(61)	George Wright	20.00	10.00	6.00
(62)	Cy Young	30.00	15.00	9.00
(63)	Knickerbocker Nine 1864	35.00	17.50	10.50

1970 Carl Aldana Orioles

Belanger

Little is known about the distribution or origin of this 12-card regional set, which was available in 1970 in the Baltimore area. Measuring 3-1/4" x 2-1/8", the unnumbered cards picture members of the Baltimore Orioles and include two poses of Brooks Robinson. The cards feature line drawings of the players surrounded by a plain border. The player's last name appears below the portrait sketch. The set was named after Carl Aldana, who supplied the artwork for the cards.

		NM	EX	VG
Complete Set (12):		125.00	65.00	40.00
Common Player:		12.00	6.00	3.50
(1)	Mark Belanger	12.00	6.00	3.50
(2)	Paul Blair	12.00	6.00	3.50
(3)	Mike Cuellar	12.00	6.00	3.50
(4)	Ellie Hendricks	12.00	6.00	3.50
(5)	Dave Johnson	12.00	6.00	3.50
(6)	Dave McNally	12.00	6.00	3.50
(7)	Jim Palmer	45.00	22.50	13.50
(8)	Boog Powell	25.00	12.50	7.50
(9)	Brooks Robinson (Diving - face showing.)	40.00	20.00	12.00
(10)	Brooks Robinson (Diving - back showing.)	40.00	20.00	12.00
(11)	Frank Robinson	60.00	30.00	18.00
(12)	Earl Weaver	15.00	7.50	4.50

1971 Carl Aldana

Devoid of any indication of when produced or by whom, this set of obscure players of the 1940s and 1950s was a collectors' issue from Carl Aldana circa 1971. The cards are blank-backed, about 2-1/8" x 2-3/4". Fronts have a red background with an artwork player portrait in blue. The player's last name and card number are in dark blue, his first name in white. For a few of the players, this is their only known baseball card.

		NM	EX	VG
Complete Set (16):		125.00	60.00	37.50
Common Player:		10.00	5.00	3.00
1	Wally Hood	10.00	5.00	3.00
2	Jim Westlake	10.00	5.00	3.00
3	Stan McWilliams	10.00	5.00	3.00
4	Les Fleming	10.00	5.00	3.00
5	John Ritchey	10.00	5.00	3.00
6	Steve Nagy	10.00	5.00	3.00
7	Ken Gables	10.00	5.00	3.00
8	Maurice Fisher	10.00	5.00	3.00
9	Don Lang	10.00	5.00	3.00
10	Harry Malmburg (Malmberg)	10.00	5.00	3.00
11	Jack Conway	10.00	5.00	3.00
12	Don White	10.00	5.00	3.00
13	Dick Lajeskie	10.00	5.00	3.00
14	Walt Judnich	10.00	5.00	3.00
15	Joe Kirrene	10.00	5.00	3.00
16	Ed Sauer	10.00	5.00	3.00

1940s Alerta Antonio Alcalde Premium Pictures

There are still gaps in the hobby's knowledge of this late-1940s/early-1950s Cuban issue. Evidently a premium used in a contest conducted by a newspaper or sports periodical, these pictures are printed on semi-gloss paper in an 8" x 11" format. Featured on front are black-and-white posed action or portrait photos. The team name and symbol are above and a portrait, presumably of Antonio, is at bottom. Pictures are highlighted with color graphics: blue for Almendares, green for Cienfuegos, red for Havana and orange for Marianao. Backs are blank, but are sometimes seen with a round rubber-stamped "Alerta" logo or red boxed "ANTONIO, ALCALDE."

The unnumbered pictures are listed here alphabetically within team. The pictures include many American players and those who spent time in the major leagues.

		NM	EX	VG
Complete Set (70):		2,000	1,000	400.00
Common Player:		30.00	15.00	6.00

ALMENDARES SCORPIONS
(1)	Bill Antonello	35.00	17.50	7.00
(2)	Francisco Campos	35.00	17.50	7.00
(3)	Avelino Canizares	30.00	15.00	6.00
(4)	Yiqui De Souza	30.00	15.00	6.00
(5)	Rodolfo Fernandez	30.00	15.00	6.00
(6)	Andres Fleitas	30.00	15.00	6.00
(7)	Al Gionfriddo	35.00	17.50	7.00
(8)	Fermin Guerra	35.00	17.50	7.00
(9)	Bob Hooper	35.00	17.50	7.00
(10)	Vincente Lopez	30.00	15.00	6.00
(11)	Conrado Marrero	35.00	17.50	7.00
(12)	Agapito Mayor	30.00	15.00	6.00
(13)	Willy Miranda	35.00	17.50	7.00
(14)	Rene Monteagudo	35.00	17.50	7.00
(15)	Roberto Ortiz	35.00	17.50	7.00
(16)	Hector Rodriguez	35.00	17.50	7.00
(17)	Octavio Rubert	30.00	15.00	6.00
(18)	Rene Solis	30.00	15.00	6.00

CIENFUEGOS ELEPHANTS
(1)	Bob Addis	35.00	17.50	7.00
(2)	Sam Calderone	35.00	17.50	7.00
(3)	Jack Cassini	35.00	17.50	7.00
(4)	Alejandro Crespo	35.00	17.50	7.00
(5)	Paul (Al) Epperly	35.00	17.50	7.00
(6)	Thomas Fine	35.00	17.50	7.00
(7)	Pedro Formental (Formenthal)	30.00	15.00	6.00
(8)	Francisco Gallardo	30.00	15.00	6.00
(9)	Lloyd Gearhart	35.00	17.50	7.00
(10)	Leonardo Goicochea	30.00	15.00	6.00
(11)	Salvador Hernandez	35.00	17.50	7.00
(12)	Clarence (Buddy) Hicks	35.00	17.50	7.00
(13)	Max Manning	45.00	22.00	9.00
(14)	San (Ray) Noble	35.00	17.50	7.00
(15)	Regino Otero	35.00	17.50	7.00
(16)	Pedro Pages	30.00	15.00	6.00
(17)	Napoleon Reyes	35.00	17.50	7.00
(18)	Ernie Shore	35.00	17.50	7.00
(19)	Adrian Zabala	35.00	17.50	7.00

HAVANA LIONS
(1)	Ferrell Anderson	35.00	17.50	7.00
(2)	Wess Bailey	30.00	15.00	6.00
(3)	Vic Barnhart	35.00	17.50	7.00
(4)	Herberto Blanco	30.00	15.00	6.00
(5)	Emilio Cabrera	30.00	15.00	6.00
(6)	Pedro Formental (Formenthal)	30.00	15.00	6.00
(7)	Al Gerheauser	35.00	17.50	7.00
(8)	Miguel Angel Gonzalez	60.00	30.00	12.00
(9)	Chino Hidalgo	30.00	15.00	6.00
(10)	Jimmy Lenhart	30.00	15.00	6.00
(11)	Adolfo Luque	60.00	30.00	12.00
(12)	Max Manning	45.00	22.50	9.00
(13)	Julio Moreno	35.00	17.50	7.00
(14)	Lenox Pearson	45.00	22.50	9.00
(15)	Don Richmond	35.00	17.50	7.00
(16)	John Ford Smith	30.00	15.00	6.00
(17)	Don Thompson	35.00	17.50	7.00
(18)	Gilberto Torres	35.00	17.50	7.00

MARIANAO TIGERS
(1)	Mario Arencibia	30.00	15.00	6.00
(2)	Carlos Blanco	30.00	15.00	6.00
(3)	Chiquitin Cabrera	30.00	15.00	6.00
(4)	Sandalio Consuegra	35.00	17.50	7.00
(5)	Reinaldo Cordeiro	30.00	15.00	6.00
(6)	Talua (Ray) Dandridge	350.00	175.00	75.00
(7)	Mario Diaz	30.00	15.00	6.00
(8)	Claro Duany	35.00	17.50	7.00
(9)	Roberto Estalella	35.00	17.50	7.00
(10)	Chicuelo Garcia	30.00	15.00	6.00
(11)	Wesley Hamner	35.00	17.50	7.00
(12)	Rollie Hemsley	35.00	17.50	7.00
(13)	Amado Ibanez	30.00	15.00	6.00
(14)	Limonar (Rogelio) Martinez	35.00	17.50	7.00
(15)	Don Phillips	30.00	15.00	6.00
(16)	Bartholomew (Jim) Prendergast	35.00	17.50	7.00
(17)	John Trouppe	35.00	17.50	7.00

1904 Allegheny Card Co.

By definition the rarest card issue of the early 20th Century is this baseball game set featuring only National League players. It is thought that the sole known boxed set was produced as a prototype and never actually reached distribution. The issue contains 104 player cards and a "Ball Counter" card for each team. Cards are in playing-card format, about 2-1/2" x 3-1/2" with rounded corners. Backs are printed in red with

baseball equipment pictured. Fronts are printed in blue with a circular player portrait at center. Team name is at top, with player's last name (occasionally with initials and occasionally misspelled) beneath. The unique boxed set was discovered in the late 1980s. It was sold at auction in 1991 for $26,400, and again in 1995 for $11,000, after which it was broken up for individual card sales. The checklist is presented here in alphabetical order. All cards appear to have been hand-cut.

		NM	EX	VG
Common Player:		1,500	750.00	450.00
(1)	Ed Abbaticchio	1,500	750.00	450.00
(2)	Harry Aubrey	1,500	750.00	450.00
(3)	Charlie Babb	1,500	750.00	450.00
(4)	George Barclay	1,500	750.00	450.00
(5)	Shad Barry	1,500	750.00	450.00
(6)	Bill Beagen (Bergen)	1,500	750.00	450.00
(7)	Ginger Beaumont	1,500	750.00	450.00
(8)	Jake Beckley	2,500	875.00	525.00
(9)	Frank Bowerman	1,500	750.00	450.00
(10)	Dave Brain	1,500	750.00	450.00
(11)	Kitty Bransfield	1,500	750.00	450.00
(12)	Roger Bresnahan	2,500	875.00	525.00
(13)	Mordecai Brown	2,500	875.00	525.00
(14)	George Browne	1,500	750.00	450.00
(15)	Al Buckenberger	1,500	750.00	450.00
(16)	Jimmy Burke	1,500	750.00	450.00
(17)	Fred Carisch	1,500	750.00	450.00
(18)	Pat Carney	1,500	750.00	450.00
(19)	Doc Casey	1,500	750.00	450.00
(20)	Frank Chance	3,000	875.00	525.00
(21)	Fred Clarke	2,500	875.00	525.00
(22)	Dick Cooley	1,500	750.00	450.00
(23)	Bill Dahlen	1,750	875.00	450.00
(24)	Tom Daly	1,500	750.00	450.00
(25)	Charlie Dexter	1,500	750.00	450.00
(26)	Johnny Dobbs	1,500	750.00	450.00
(27)	Mike Donlin	1,500	750.00	450.00
(28)	Patsy Donovan	1,500	750.00	450.00
(29)	Red Dooin	1,500	750.00	450.00
(30)	Klondike Douglas (Douglass)	1,500	750.00	450.00
(31)	Jack Doyle	1,500	750.00	450.00
(32)	Bill Duggleby	1,500	750.00	450.00
(33)	Jack Dunn	1,500	750.00	270.00
(34)	Johnny Evers	3,000	875.00	525.00
(35)	John Farrel (Farrell)	1,500	750.00	450.00
(36)	Tim Flood	1,500	750.00	450.00
(37)	Chick Fraser	1,500	750.00	450.00
(38)	Ned Garver	1,500	750.00	450.00
(39)	Doc Gessler	1,500	750.00	450.00
(40)	Billy Gilbert	1,500	750.00	450.00
(41)	Kid Gleason	2,500	875.00	525.00
(42)	Ed Greminger (Gremminger)	1,500	750.00	450.00
(43)	Jim Hackett	1,500	750.00	450.00
(44)	Noodles Hahn	1,500	750.00	450.00
(45)	Ed. Hanlon	2,500	875.00	525.00
(46)	Jack Harper	1,500	750.00	450.00
(47)	Rudy Hulswitt	1,500	750.00	450.00
(48)	Fred Jacklitsch	1,500	750.00	450.00
(49)	Davy Jones	1,500	750.00	450.00
(50)	Oscar Jones	1,500	750.00	450.00
(51)	Bill Keister	1,500	750.00	450.00
(52)	Joe Kelley	2,500	875.00	525.00
(53)	Brickyard Kennedy	1,500	750.00	450.00
(54)	Johnny Kling	1,500	750.00	450.00
(55)	Otto Kruger (Krueger)	1,500	750.00	450.00
(56)	Tommy Leach	1,500	750.00	450.00
(57)	Sam Leever	1,500	750.00	450.00
(58)	Bobby Lowe	1,750	875.00	525.00
(59)	Carl Lundgren	1,500	750.00	450.00
(60)	Christy Mathewson	8,000	2,000	1,200
(61)	Tom McCreery	1,500	750.00	450.00
(62)	Chappie McFarland	1,500	750.00	450.00
(63)	Dan McGann	1,500	750.00	450.00
(64)	Iron Man McGinnity	2,500	875.00	525.00
(65)	John McGraw	2,500	875.00	525.00
(66)	Jock Menefee	1,500	750.00	450.00
(67)	Sam Mertes	1,500	750.00	450.00
(68)	Fred Mitchell	1,500	750.00	450.00
(69)	Pat Moran	1,500	750.00	450.00
(70)	Ed Murphy	1,500	750.00	450.00
(71)	Jack O'Neill	1,500	750.00	450.00
(72)	Mike O'Neill	1,500	750.00	450.00
(73)	Heinie Peitz	1,500	750.00	450.00
(74)	Ed Phelps	1,500	750.00	450.00
(75)	Deacon Phillippe	1,500	750.00	450.00
(76)	Togie Pittinger	1,500	750.00	450.00
(77)	Ed Poole	1,500	750.00	450.00
(78)	Tommy Raub	1,500	750.00	450.00
(79)	Bill Reidy	1,500	750.00	450.00
(80)	Claude Ritchie	1,500	750.00	450.00
(81)	Lew Ritter	1,500	750.00	450.00
(82)	Frank Roth	1,500	750.00	450.00
(83)	Jack Ryan	1,500	750.00	450.00
(84)	Jimmy Scheckard (Sheckard)	1,500	750.00	450.00
(85)	Jimmy Sebring	1,500	750.00	450.00
(86)	Frank Selee	7,500	2,000	1,200
(87)	Cy Seymour	1,500	750.00	450.00
(88)	Harry Smith	1,500	750.00	450.00
(89)	Homer Smoot	1,500	750.00	450.00
(90)	Tully Sparks	1,500	750.00	450.00
(91)	Joe Stanley	1,500	750.00	450.00
(92)	Harry Steinfeldt	1,500	750.00	450.00
(93)	Sammy Strang	1,500	750.00	450.00
(94)	Jack Suthoff (Sutthoff)	1,500	750.00	450.00
(95)	Jack Taylor	1,500	750.00	450.00
(96)	Luther Taylor	1,750	875.00	525.00
(97)	Roy Thomas	1,500	750.00	450.00
(98)	Joe Tinker	1,750	875.00	525.00
(99)	Fred Tinney (Tenney)	1,500	750.00	450.00
(100)	Honus Wagner	10,000	2,000	1,200
(101)	Jack Warner	1,500	750.00	450.00
(102)	Jake Weimer	1,500	750.00	450.00
(103)	Vic Willis	1,750	875.00	525.00
(104)	Harry Wolverton	1,500	750.00	450.00

(105) Boston Ball Counter	165.00	80.00	50.00
(106) Brooklyn Ball Counter	165.00	80.00	50.00
(107) Chicago Ball Counter	165.00	80.00	50.00
(108) Cincinnati Ball Counter	165.00	80.00	50.00
(109) New York Ball Counter	165.00	80.00	50.00
(110) Philadelpia Ball Counter	165.00	80.00	50.00
(111) Pittsburgh Ball Counter	165.00	80.00	50.00
(112) St. Louis Ball Counter	165.00	80.00	50.00

1888 Allen & Ginter World's Champions (N28)

This 50-card set was titled "The World Champions" and includes 10 baseball players and 40 other sports personalities such as John L. Sullivan and Buffalo Bill Cody. The approximately 1-1/2" x 2-3/4" cards were inserted in boxes of Allen & Ginter cigarettes. The card fronts are color lithographs on white card stock, and are considered among the most attractive cards ever produced. All card backs have a complete checklist for this unnumbered set, which includes six eventual Hall of Famers.

	NM	EX	VG
Complete Set (10):	16,750	8,250	5,500
Common Player:	850.00	425.00	250.00
(1) Adrian C. Anson	7,500	3,750	2,250
(2) Chas. W. Bennett	850.00	425.00	255.00
(3) R.L. Caruthers	850.00	425.00	255.00
(4) John Clarkson	2,500	925.00	550.00
(5) Charles Comiskey	2,750	1,375	825.00
(6) Capt. John Glasscock	850.00	425.00	255.00
(7) Timothy Keefe	2,500	875.00	500.00
(8) Mike Kelly	4,000	1,500	900.00
(9) Joseph Mulvey	850.00	425.00	255.00
(10) John Ward	2,500	875.00	500.00

1888 Allen & Ginter World's Champions Album (A16)

By redeeming 50 of the coupons found in boxes of A&G cigarettes, a lithographed album could be obtained in which to house the 50 cards of The World's Champions, Series 1 (N28). About 6" x 8", the album features an ornately decorated cover reproducing the cards of the day's top athletes, John L. Sullivan and Monte Ward. The back cover is blank. Inside, secured by means of string ties at three places, are 12 dual-sided color pages on which to glue the cards in the series. The album had its own designation in the American Card Catalog, A16.

	NM	EX	VG
World's Champions Album (A16)	4,500	2,500	1,250

1888 Allen & Ginter World's Champions (N29)

Building on the success of its first series of tobacco cards, Allen & Ginter issued a second series of "World Champions" in 1888. Once again, 50 of these approximately 1-1/2" x 2-3/4" color cards were produced, in virtually the same format. Only six baseball players are included in this set. The most obvious difference from the first series cards is the absence of the Allen & Ginter name on the card fronts.

	NM	EX	VG
Complete Set (6):	9,350	4,675	2,750
Common Player:	900.00	400.00	300.00
(1) Wm. Ewing	3,000	1,100	850.00
(2) Jas. H. Fogarty (Middle initial actually G.)	900.00	400.00	300.00
(3) Charles H. Getzin (Getzien)	900.00	400.00	300.00
(4) Geo. F. Miller	900.00	400.00	300.00
(5) John Morrell (Morrill)	1,150	450.00	325.00
(6) James Ryan	900.00	400.00	300.00

1888 Allen & Ginter World's Champions Album (A17)

By redeeming 50 of the coupons found in boxes of A&G cigarettes, a lithographed album could be obtained in which to house the 50 cards of The World's Champions, Series 2 (N29). About 6" x 8", the album features a handsomely decorated cover of a trumpeteer. The back cover is also in color with A&G's pipe-smoking man logo. Inside, secured by means of string ties at three places, are 12 dual-sided color pages on which to glue the cards in the series. The album had its own designation in the American Card Catalog, A16.

	NM	EX	VG
World's Champions Album (A17)	4,000	2,000	1,000

1888 Allen & Ginter World's Champions (N43)

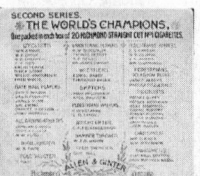

Presumably issued in a larger-than-standard cigarette package, the 50 cards designated N43 in the "American Card Catalog" are enhanced versions of the Allen & Ginter World's Champions (N29) series of 1888. As with the N29 set, six of the athletes in N43 are baseball players. The larger cards measure about 3-1/4" x 2-7/8" compared to the 1-1/2" x 2-3/4" size of the N29s. The larger format allows for the use of baseball-related color lithography to the right and left of the central player portrait. Like the N29 cards, backs of the N43 A&Gs present the entire "Series Two" checklist along with advertising of the Richmond tobacco company. Only the baseball players are cataloged here.

	NM	EX	VG
Complete Set (6):	26,400	14,000	7,700
Common Player:	3,850	1,500	1,000
(1) Wm. Ewing	8,500	3,825	2,375
(2) Jas. H. Fogarty (Middle initial actually G.)	3,850	1,500	1,000
(3) Charles H. Getzin (Getzien)	3,850	1,500	1,000
(4) Geo. F. Miller	3,850	1,500	1,000
(5) John Morrell (Morrill)	4,000	1,800	1,125
(6) James Ryan	3,850	1,500	1,000

1888 Allen & Ginter Girl Baseball Players (N48, N508)

At least three different brands of cigarette advertising can be found on the several different styles of photographic cards depicting women in baseball uniforms. About 1-1/2" x 2-5/8",

the cards picture models, rather than real ballplayers. The sepia-toned full-length photos are usually captioned with a position and a number and have a small square or other device advertising a particular brand. Some Dixie- and Virginia Brights-brand cards are known with advertising on back but most cards are blank-backed. As many as 36 different photos are thought to exist.

	NM	EX	VG
Ad Backs: 2X			
Common Player	650.00	325.00	200.00

1946-1947 Almanaque Deportivo

Former and future Major Leaguers mix with Negro Leaguers and Caribbean stars in this issue. Apparently sold in sheets of four, well-cut examples of these cards measure a nominal 1-7/8" x 2-1/2" and are printed in color on thin paper. Player identification is on the back of the card, usually with career notes and a large advertisement from one of many different sponsors. A colorful album was issued to house the set. Like all Cuban cards of the era, specimens surviving in grades of VG or better are scarce.

	NM	EX	VG
Complete Set (160):	6,000	3,000	1,800
Common Player:	35.00	17.50	10.00
Album:	400.00	200.00	120.00
A-1 Adolfo Luque	60.00	30.00	20.00
A-2 Tomas de la Cruz	35.00	17.50	10.00
A-3 Roberto Ortiz	45.00	22.50	13.50
A-4 Evelio Martinez	35.00	17.50	10.00
A-5 Jess Jessup	90.00	45.00	27.50
A-6 Santos Amaro	35.00	17.50	10.00
A-7 Rene Gonzalez	35.00	17.50	10.00
A-8 Buck O'Neil	625.00	310.00	185.00
A-9 J. (Lefty) Gaines	90.00	45.00	27.50
A-10 Max Lanier	45.00	22.50	13.50
A-11 George Hausmann	35.00	17.50	10.00
A-12 Avelino Canizares	35.00	17.50	10.00
A-13 Calampio Leon	35.00	17.50	10.00
A-14 Conrado Marrero	50.00	25.00	15.00
A-15 Alberto Leal	35.00	17.50	10.00
A-16 Lloyd Davenport	90.00	45.00	27.50
A-17 Teodoro Oxamendi	35.00	17.50	10.00
A-18 Santiago Ulrich	35.00	17.50	10.00
A-19 Lazaro Salazar	100.00	50.00	30.00
A-20 Cheo Ramos	35.00	17.50	10.00
A-21 Jorge Comellas	35.00	17.50	10.00
A-22 Agapito Mayor	35.00	17.50	10.00
A-23 Hector Rodriguez	45.00	22.50	13.50
A-24 Joe Williams	35.00	17.50	10.00
A-25 Andres Fleitas	35.00	17.50	10.00
C-1 Martin Dihigo	500.00	250.00	150.00
C-2 Alejandro Carrasquel	35.00	17.50	10.00
C-3 Adrian Zabala	35.00	17.50	10.00
C-4 Jimmy Roy	35.00	17.50	10.00
C-5 Napoleon Reyes	80.00	40.00	25.00
C-6 Stanislas Bread	35.00	17.50	10.00
C-7 Roland Gladu	35.00	17.50	10.00
C-8 Roy Zimmerman	35.00	17.50	10.00
C-9 Max Manning	125.00	62.50	37.50
C-10 Myron Hayworth	35.00	17.50	10.00
C-11 Pedro Miro	35.00	17.50	10.00
C-12 Jose Luis Colas	35.00	17.50	10.00
C-13 Conrado Perez	35.00	17.50	10.00
C-14 Luis Tiant Sr.	45.00	22.50	13.50
C-15 Ramon Heredia	35.00	17.50	10.00
C-16 Vinicio Garcia	35.00	17.50	10.00
C-17 (Walt) Nothe	35.00	17.50	10.00
C-18 Danny Gardella	35.00	17.50	10.00
C-19 Alejandro Crespo	60.00	30.00	20.00
C-20 Ray Noble	35.00	17.50	10.00
C-21 Pedro Pages	35.00	17.50	10.00

F-1	Napoleon y C. Blanco/Action	35.00	17.50	10.00
F-2	Chanquilon y H. Rodriguez/Action	35.00	17.50	10.00
F-3	Estalella y Fleitas/Action	35.00	17.50	10.00
F-4	Castano y Kimbro/Action	35.00	17.50	10.00
H-1	Miguel Angel Gonzalez	55.00	27.50	16.50
H-2	Pedro (Natilla) Jimenez	35.00	17.50	10.00
H-3	Fred Martin	35.00	17.50	10.00
H-4	James Lamarque	80.00	40.00	25.00
H-5	Salvador Hernandez	35.00	17.50	10.00
H-6	S. (Hank) Thompson	50.00	25.00	15.00
H-7	Antonio Ordenana	35.00	17.50	10.00
H-8	Manuel Garcia	35.00	17.50	10.00
H-9	Alberto Hernandez	35.00	17.50	10.00
H-10	Terry McDuffie	45.00	22.50	13.50
H-11	Louis Frank Klein	35.00	17.50	10.00
H-12	Herberto Blanco	35.00	17.50	10.00
H-13	H.(Henry) Kimbro	150.00	75.00	45.00
H-14	Rene Monteagudo	35.00	17.50	10.00
H-15	Lennox Pearson	100.00	50.00	30.00
H-16	Carlos Blanco	35.00	17.50	10.00
H-17	Pedro Formental	55.00	27.50	16.50
H-18	William Bell	35.00	17.50	10.00
H-19	Raul Navarro	35.00	17.50	10.00
H-20	Lazaro Medina	35.00	17.50	10.00
L-1	Julio Moreno	35.00	17.50	10.00
L-2	Daniel Parra	35.00	17.50	10.00
L-3	Rogelio Martinez	35.00	17.50	10.00
L-4	J. Antonio Zardon	35.00	17.50	10.00
L-5	Julian Acosta	35.00	17.50	10.00
L-6	Orlando Suarez	35.00	17.50	10.00
L-7	Manuel Hidalgo	35.00	17.50	10.00
L-8	Fermin Guerra	35.00	17.50	10.00
L-9	Regino Otero	35.00	17.50	10.00
L-10	Jorge Juan Torres	35.00	17.50	10.00
L-11	Valeriano Fano	35.00	17.50	10.00
L-12	Amado Ibanez	35.00	17.50	10.00
L-13	"Atares" Garcia	35.00	17.50	10.00
L-14	Armando Gallart	35.00	17.50	10.00
L-15	Perdo Dunabeitia	35.00	17.50	10.00
L-16	Oscar del Calvo	35.00	17.50	10.00
L-17	Johnny Davis	100.00	50.00	30.00
L-18	Emilio Cabrera	35.00	17.50	10.00
L-19	Lee Holleman	35.00	17.50	10.00
L-20	Antonio Napoles	35.00	17.50	10.00
L-21	Pedro Diaz	35.00	17.50	10.00
L-22	Lazaro Bernal	35.00	17.50	10.00
L-23	Hector Arago	35.00	17.50	10.00
L-24	Oscar Garmendia	35.00	17.50	10.00
L-25	Barney Serrell	90.00	45.00	27.50
L-26	Armando Marsans	55.00	27.50	16.50
L-27	Mario Diaz	35.00	17.50	10.00
L-28	Raymond Dandridge	350.00	175.00	105.00
L-29	Leon Tredway	35.00	17.50	10.00
L-30	Orestes Perera	35.00	17.50	10.00
L-31	Armando Vazquez	35.00	17.50	10.00
L-32	Cleveland Clark	50.00	25.00	15.00
L-33	Johnny Williams	90.00	45.00	27.50
L-34	Clarence Iott	35.00	17.50	10.00
L-35	Gilberto Torres	35.00	17.50	10.00
L-36	George Brown	35.00	17.50	10.00
L-37	Wayne Johnson	35.00	17.50	10.00
L-38	Miguel Angel Carmona	35.00	17.50	10.00
L-39	Leovigildo Xiques	35.00	17.50	10.00
L-40	Rafael Rivas	35.00	17.50	10.00
L-41	Joaquin Gutierrez	35.00	17.50	10.00
L-42	Miguel Lastra	35.00	17.50	10.00
L-43	Francisco Quicutis	35.00	17.50	10.00
L-44	Silvio Garcia	90.00	45.00	27.50
L-45	Angel Fleitas	35.00	17.50	10.00
L-46	Eddy Chandler	35.00	17.50	10.00
L-47	Gilberto Castillo	35.00	17.50	10.00
L-48	Isidoro Leon	35.00	17.50	10.00
L-49	Antonio Rodriguez	35.00	17.50	10.00
L-50	Laniel Hooker	90.00	45.00	27.50
L-51	Charles Perez	35.00	17.50	10.00
L-52	Ruben Garcia	35.00	17.50	10.00
L-53	Raquel Antunez	35.00	17.50	10.00
L-54	Claro Duany	45.00	22.50	13.50
L-55	Bucker (Booker) McDaniels	90.00	45.00	27.50
L-56	Francisco Jimenez	35.00	17.50	10.00
L-57	Luis Minsal	35.00	17.50	10.00
L-58	Rogelio Linares	35.00	17.50	10.00
L-59	Isasio Gonzalez	35.00	17.50	10.00
L-60	Manolo Parrado	35.00	17.50	10.00
L-61	Jose Maria Fernandez	35.00	17.50	10.00
L-62	Rogelio Valdes	35.00	17.50	10.00
L-63	R. Franco	35.00	17.50	10.00
L-64	J. Cedan	35.00	17.50	10.00
L-65	Jacinto Roque	35.00	17.50	10.00
L-66	Pablo Garcia	35.00	17.50	10.00
M-1	Pipo de la Noval	35.00	17.50	10.00
M-2	J. Valenzuela	35.00	17.50	10.00
M-3	Oliverio Ortiz	35.00	17.50	10.00
M-4	Antonio Castanos	35.00	17.50	10.00
M-5	Sandalio Consuegra	45.00	22.50	13.50
M-6	(Jim) Lindsey	35.00	17.50	10.00
M-7	Roberto Estalella	35.00	17.50	10.00
M-8	Lino Donoso	35.00	17.50	10.00
M-9	Paul Calvert	35.00	17.50	10.00
M-10	Gilberto Valdivia	35.00	17.50	10.00
M-11	Orestes Minoso	125.00	65.00	37.50
M-12	J. Cabrera	35.00	17.50	10.00
M-13	Manuel Godinez	35.00	17.50	10.00
M-14	Frank Casanovas	35.00	17.50	10.00
M-15	Roberto Avila	60.00	30.00	20.00
M-16	Pedro Orta	35.00	17.50	10.00
M-17	Feliciano Castro	35.00	17.50	10.00
M-18	Mario Arencibia	35.00	17.50	10.00
M-19	Antonio Diaz	35.00	17.50	10.00
M-20	Aristonico Correoso	35.00	17.50	10.00
M-21	Angel Gonzalez	35.00	17.50	10.00
M-22	Murray Franklin	35.00	17.50	10.00
M-23	Francisco Campos	35.00	17.50	10.00
M-24	Angel Castro	35.00	17.50	10.00

1910 All-Star Base-Ball

This rare set was issued circa 1910 by candy maker J.H. Dockman & Son. The cards, measuring approximately 1-7/8" x 3-3/8", were printed on the front and back of boxes of candy sold as "All Star Base-Ball Package." There are two players on each box; one on front (with a thumbnail notch at top), the other on back. The cards consist of drawings that bear no resemblance to the player named. In fact, the artwork on these cards crudely reproduces the images from the T3 Turkey Red cabinet series, giving a different player's name to each of the borrowed images. Many are found which were cut from the box immediately below the "PACKAGE" line, while others were cut to the full size of the panel. Values shown here presume the latter format.

		NM	EX	VG
	Complete Set (24):	50,000	25,000	12,500
	Common Player:	2,000	1,200	600.00
(1)	Johnny Bates	2,000	1,200	600.00
(2)	Heinie Beckendorf	2,000	1,200	600.00
(3)	Joe Birmingham	2,000	1,200	600.00
(4)	Roger Bresnahan	4,000	2,500	1,200
(5)	Al Burch	2,000	1,200	600.00
(6)	Donie Bush	2,000	1,200	600.00
(7)	Frank Chance	4,000	2,500	1,200
(8)	Ty Cobb	10,000	5,000	3,000
(9)	Wid Conroy	2,000	1,200	600.00
(10)	Jack Coombs	2,000	1,200	600.00
(11)	George Gibson	2,000	1,200	600.00
(12)	Dick Hoblitzel	2,000	1,200	600.00
(13)	Johnny Kling	2,000	1,200	600.00
(14)	Frank LaPorte	2,000	1,200	600.00
(15)	Ed Lennox	2,000	1,200	600.00
(16)	Connie Mack	4,000	2,500	1,200
(17)	Christy Mathewson	4,500	2,750	1,500
(18)	Matty McIntyre	2,000	1,200	600.00
(19)	Al Schweitzer	2,000	1,200	600.00
(20)	Jimmy Sheckard	2,000	1,200	600.00
(21)	Bill Sweeney	2,000	1,200	600.00
(22)	Terry Turner	2,000	1,200	600.00
(23)	Hans Wagner	9,000	4,500	2,700
(24)	Harry Wolter	2,000	1,200	600.00

1950 All-Star Baseball "Pin-Ups"

This set of 10 7" diameter black-and-white player photos was issued in the form of a booklet, with the individual pictures perforated to be punched out. Each picture has a hole at the top for hanging. The front and back cover of the book are identical and picture Ted Williams, along with a list of the players inside. Backs of each player picture have how-to tips for playing a specific position, hitting, base stealing, etc. Published by Garden City Publishing Co., Inc., the book carried a cover price of 50 cents. The unnumbered pictures are checklisted here alphabetically.

		NM	EX	VG
	Complete Book:	1,250	625.00	375.00
	Complete Set, Singles (10):	800.00	400.00	240.00
	Common Player:	25.00	12.50	7.50
(1)	Joe DiMaggio	200.00	100.00	60.00
(2)	Jim Hegan	25.00	12.50	7.50
(3)	Gil Hodges	75.00	37.50	22.50
(4)	George Kell	35.00	17.50	10.00
(5)	Ralph Kiner	45.00	22.50	13.50
(6)	Stan Musial	100.00	50.00	30.00
(7)	Mel Parnell	25.00	12.50	7.50

(8)	Phil Rizzuto	75.00	37.50	22.50
(9)	Jackie Robinson	150.00	75.00	45.00
(10)	Ted Williams	150.00	75.00	45.00

1954 All-Star Photo Pack

The complete checklist for this series of 6" x 8-3/4" blank-back, black-and-white player photos is unknown. The method of distribution is also speculative, though it is most likely they were sold in photo packs at concession stands. Photos, mostly posed action shots, are bordered in white and have the player name in a white strip near the bottom.

		NM	EX	VG
	Complete Set (24):	400.00	200.00	120.00
	Common Player:	10.00	5.00	3.00
(1)	Bobby Avila	10.00	5.00	3.00
(2)	Ernie Banks	25.00	12.50	7.50
(3)	Larry "Yogi" Berra	25.00	12.50	7.50
(4)	Ray Boone	10.00	5.00	3.00
(5)	Roy Campanella	25.00	12.50	7.50
(6)	Alvin Dark	10.00	5.00	3.00
(7)	Mike Garcia	10.00	5.00	3.00
(8)	Al Kaline	20.00	10.00	6.00
(9)	Ralph Kiner	15.00	7.50	4.50
(10)	Ted Kluszewski	15.00	7.50	4.50
(11)	Harvey Kuenn	10.00	5.00	3.00
(12)	Mickey Mantle	90.00	45.00	27.50
(13)	Ed Mathews	20.00	10.00	6.00
(14)	Willie Mays	50.00	25.00	15.00
(15)	Orestes Minoso	12.50	6.25	3.75
(16)	Stan Musial	35.00	17.50	10.00
(17)	Don Newcombe	12.50	6.25	3.75
(18)	Allie Reynolds	12.50	6.25	3.75
(19)	Robin Roberts	15.00	7.50	4.50
(20)	Eddie Robinson	10.00	5.00	3.00
(21)	Jackie Robinson	45.00	22.50	13.50
(22)	Al Schoendienst	15.00	7.50	4.50
(23)	Duke Snider	20.00	10.00	6.00
(24)	Ted Williams	80.00	40.00	24.00

1949 All-Stars Photo Pack

This set of "American and National League All Stars" player pictures is comprised of 6-1/4" x 9" black-and-white photos bordered in white with a simulated signature printed on front. Backs are blank. The set came in a red, black and white paper envelope with several of the pictures shown on front and red stars for decoration. The unnumbered pictures are listed here alphabetically.

		NM	EX	VG
	Complete Set (20):	375.00	185.00	110.00
	Common Player:	12.50	6.00	4.00
(1)	Luke Appling	17.50	9.00	5.00
(2)	Lou Boudreau	17.50	9.00	5.00
(3)	Dom DiMaggio	15.00	7.50	4.50
(4)	Joe DiMaggio	60.00	30.00	18.00
(5)	Bobby Doerr	17.50	9.00	5.00
(6)	Bob Feller	25.00	12.50	7.50
(7)	Joe Gordon	12.50	6.00	4.00
(8)	Tommy Henrich	12.50	6.00	4.00
(9)	George Kell	17.50	9.00	5.00
(10)	Ralph Kiner	17.50	9.00	5.00
(11)	Bob Lemon	17.50	9.00	5.00
(12)	Marty Marion	12.50	6.00	4.00
(13)	Stan Musial	35.00	17.50	10.00
(14)	Don Newcomb (Newcombe)	17.50	9.00	5.00
(15)	Pee Wee Reese	25.00	12.50	7.50
(16)	Phil Rizzuto	25.00	12.50	7.50
(17)	Jackie Robinson	45.00	22.50	13.50

		NM	EX	VG
(18)	Enos Slaughter	17.50	9.00	5.00
(19)	Vern Stephens	12.50	6.00	4.00
(20)	Ted Williams	45.00	22.50	13.50

1971 Allstate Insurance

This four-card series was distributed as part of an internal sales promotion for Allstate Insurance. Graphic artist Ray Lending, an Allstate employee, created the 2-1/2" x 3-1/4" cards in duo-tone black and green on white. Card fronts show the players in batting stance, with the player name in one of the upper corners and the "Hall of Fame Series" logo printed across the bottom of the card. The card backs carry the player's full name and position, followed by a brief career summary, biography, and Career Highlights chart listing major league totals. "1971 Charger" and "Hall of Fame Series" are printed at the bottom of the card back. 8,000 sets were distributed.

		NM	EX	VG
Complete Set (4):		400.00	200.00	120.00
Common Player:		50.00	25.00	15.00
(1)	Ty Cobb	50.00	25.00	15.00
(2)	Stan Musial	50.00	25.00	15.00
(3)	Babe Ruth	200.00	100.00	60.00
(4)	Ted Williams	150.00	75.00	45.00

1894 Alpha Photo-Engraving Baltimore Orioles

The rarest baseball card set of the 1890s (each card is known in only a single example) is the Baltimore Orioles team set issued by The Alpha Photo-Engraving Co. of that city. The round-corner 2-3/8" x 3-7/16" cards feature black-and-white photos of the National League champions in formalwear. Last-name identification is in a strip below the photo and a white border surrounds both. On the red-and-white backs a large ad for the producer is at center, while small baseball batter figures are in each corner surrounded by a leafy background. The unnumbered cards are checklisted here alphabetically, though the list may not be complete; one glaring omission is Hall of Fame outfielder Willie Keeler. In early 2006 the set was sold and broken up. Each card was authenticated and graded by SGC, with grades ranging from Fair to Very Good.

		NM	EX	VG
Common Player:				7,500
(1)	Frank Bonner			7,500
(2)	Steve Brodie			7,500
(3)	Dan Brouthers			37,500
(4)	Duke Esper			7,500
(5)	Kid Gleason			7,500
(6)	Ned Hanlon			32,500
(7)	Bill Hawke			7,500
(8)	George Hemming			7,500
(9)	Hughie Jennings			32,500
(10)	Joe Kelley			62,500
(11)	John McGraw			62,500
(12)	Sadie McMahon			7,500
(13)	Heinie Reitz			7,500
(14)	Wilbert Robinson			32,500

1916 Altoona Tribune

This Pennsylvania daily newspaper was one of several regional advertisers to use this black-and-white, 1-5/8" x 3" 200-card set for promotional purposes. The Altoona issue shares the checklist of the 1916 M101-4 Blank Backs. Type card and superstar collectors will pay a significant premium for a Tribune version of a specific card.

PREMIUM:
Common Player: 4-6X
Hall of Famer: 2-4X
(See 1916 M101-4 Blank Backs for checklist and base card values.)

1948 American Association Babe Ruth

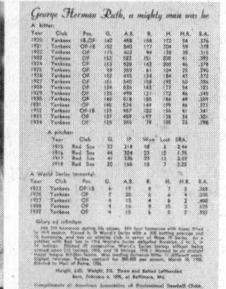

According to the credit line at bottom back (a version of the card is known without the credit line), this card was produced by the Midwestern AAA minor league known as the American Association. Recent discoveries also indicate that this card was probably both produced and issued by Pacific Coast Publishing Co. about a month after Ruth's death. The black and white card measures 4" x 5-11/16".

	NM	EX	VG
Babe Ruth	200.00	100.00	60.00

1909-11 American Beauty Cigarettes

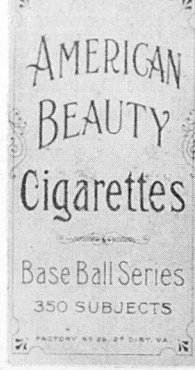

Two versions of the American Beauty Cigarettes advertising on the backs of T206 can be found; with and without a decorative border surrounding the typography, which is printed in green. All "350 Subjects" American Beauty cards originated from Factory No. 25 in Virginia. Because of the size of the original cigarette packaging in which they were a premium insert, American Beauty T206s may be a bit narrower than the standard 1-7/16". While the "350 Subjects" series is designated here as a 1910 issue, it is possible some cards were actually issued in 1909 or 1911. Among T205, AB backs may be found printed in either black or green, the latter somewhat scarcer.

PREMIUM:
T205: 2X
T206 350 Series: 1.5-2X
T206 460 Series: 2-2.5X
(See T205, T206 for checklists and base card values. Note: Cards with American Beauty backs may be somewhat narrower than standard 1-7/16" due to smaller original cigarette packaging.)

1908 American Caramel (E91, Set A)

Issued by Philadelphia's American Caramel Co., 1908-1910, the E91 set of Base Ball Caramels has limited popularity

with collectors because many of the color drawings show "generic" players rather than the named major leaguers; the same artwork was used to depict two or three different players. The player's name, position and team appear in the white border at bottom. The cards measure approximately 1-1/2" x 2-3/4" and were issued in three separate series. They can be differentiated by their backs, which checklist the cards. Set A lists the Athletics in the upper-left, the Giants at upper-right and the Cubs below. Set B lists the Cubs and Athletics on top with the Giants below, and Set C list Pittsburg and Washington on top with Boston below. A line indicating the cards were "Manufactured Only by the American Caramel Co." appears at the bottom.

		NM	EX	VG
Complete Set (33):		10,000	4,000	2,500
Common Player:		200.00	75.00	40.00
(1)	Charles Bender	425.00	175.00	100.00
(2)	Roger Bresnahan	425.00	175.00	100.00
(3)	Albert Bridwell	200.00	75.00	45.00
(4)	Mordecai Brown	425.00	175.00	100.00
(5)	Frank Chance	425.00	175.00	100.00
(6)	James Collins	425.00	175.00	100.00
(7)	Harry Davis	200.00	75.00	40.00
(8)	Arthur Devlin	200.00	75.00	40.00
(9)	Michael Donlin	200.00	75.00	40.00
(10)	John Evers	425.00	175.00	100.00
(11)	Frederick L. Hartsel	200.00	75.00	40.00
(12)	John Kling	200.00	75.00	40.00
(13)	Christopher Matthewson (Mathewson)	1,750	785.00	435.00
(14)	Joseph McGinnity	425.00	175.00	100.00
(15)	John J. McGraw	425.00	175.00	100.00
(16)	Daniel F. Murphy	200.00	75.00	40.00
(17)	Simon Nicholls	200.00	75.00	40.00
(18)	Reuben Oldring	200.00	75.00	40.00
(19)	Orvill Overall (Orval)	200.00	75.00	40.00
(20)	Edward S. Plank	750.00	325.00	185.00
(21)	Edward Reulbach	200.00	75.00	40.00
(22)	James Scheckard (Sheckard)	200.00	75.00	40.00
(23)	Osee Schreckengost (Ossee)	200.00	75.00	40.00
(24)	Ralph O. Seybold	200.00	75.00	40.00
(25)	J. Bentley Seymour	200.00	75.00	40.00
(26)	Daniel Shay	200.00	75.00	40.00
(27)	Frank Shulte (Schulte)	200.00	75.00	40.00
(28)	James Slagle	200.00	75.00	40.00
(29)	Harry Steinfeldt	200.00	75.00	40.00
(30)	Luther H. Taylor	400.00	160.00	100.00
(31)	Fred Tenney	200.00	75.00	40.00
(32)	Joseph B. Tinker	425.00	175.00	100.00
(33)	George Edward Waddell	425.00	175.00	100.00

1909 American Caramel (E91, Set B)

		NM	EX	VG
Complete Set (33):		9,500	4,000	2,400
Common Player:		200.00	75.00	40.00
(1)	James Archer	200.00	75.00	40.00
(2)	Frank Baker	425.00	175.00	100.00
(3)	John Barry	200.00	75.00	40.00
(4)	Charles Bender	425.00	175.00	100.00
(5)	Albert Bridwell	200.00	75.00	40.00
(6)	Mordecai Brown	425.00	175.00	100.00
(7)	Frank Chance	425.00	175.00	100.00
(8)	Edw. Collins	425.00	175.00	100.00
(9)	Harry Davis	200.00	75.00	40.00
(10)	Arthur Devlin	200.00	75.00	40.00
(11)	Michael Donlin	200.00	75.00	40.00
(12)	Larry Doyle	200.00	75.00	40.00
(13)	John Evers	425.00	175.00	100.00
(14)	Robt. Ganley	200.00	75.00	40.00

(15)	Frederick L. Hartsel	200.00	75.00	40.00
(16)	Arthur Hoffman (Hofman)	200.00	75.00	40.00
(17)	Harry Krause	200.00	75.00	40.00
(18)	Rich. W. Marquard	425.00	175.00	100.00
(19)	Christopher Matthewson (Mathewson)	1,100	450.00	275.00
(20)	John J. McGraw	425.00	175.00	100.00
(21)	J.T. Meyers	200.00	75.00	40.00
(22)	Dan Murphy	200.00	75.00	40.00
(23)	Jno. J. Murray	200.00	75.00	40.00
(24)	Orvill Overall (Orval)	200.00	75.00	40.00
(25)	Edward S. Plank	750.00	325.00	185.00
(26)	Edward Reulbach	200.00	75.00	40.00
(27)	James Scheckard (Sheckard)	200.00	75.00	40.00
(28)	J. Bentley Seymour	200.00	75.00	40.00
(29)	Harry Steinfeldt	200.00	75.00	40.00
(30)	Frank Shulte (Schulte)	200.00	75.00	40.00
(31)	Fred Tenney	200.00	75.00	40.00
(32)	Joseph B Tinker	425.00	175.00	100.00
(33)	Ira Thomas	200.00	75.00	40.00

1910 American Caramel (E91, Set C)

		NM	EX	VG
Complete Set (33):		11,000	4,400	2,850
Common Player:		200.00	75.00	40.00
(1)	W.J. Barbeau	200.00	75.00	40.00
(2)	Geo. Browne	200.00	75.00	40.00
(3)	Robt. Chech (Charles)	200.00	75.00	40.00
(4)	Fred Clarke	425.00	175.00	100.00
(5)	Wid Conroy	200.00	75.00	40.00
(6)	James Delehanty (Delahanty)	200.00	75.00	40.00
(7)	Jon A. Donohue (Donahue)	200.00	75.00	40.00
(8)	P. Donahue	200.00	75.00	40.00
(9)	Geo. Gibson	200.00	75.00	40.00
(10)	Robt. Groom	200.00	75.00	40.00
(11)	Harry Hooper	425.00	175.00	100.00
(12)	Tom Hughes	200.00	75.00	40.00
(13)	Walter Johnson	1,000	400.00	250.00
(14)	Edwin Karger	200.00	75.00	40.00
(15)	Tommy Leach	200.00	75.00	40.00
(16)	Sam'l Leever	200.00	75.00	40.00
(17)	Harry Lord	200.00	75.00	40.00
(18)	Geo. F. McBride	200.00	75.00	40.00
(19)	Ambr. McConnell	200.00	75.00	40.00
(20)	Clyde Milan	200.00	75.00	40.00
(21)	J.B. Miller	200.00	75.00	40.00
(22)	Harry Niles	200.00	75.00	40.00
(23)	Chas. Phillipi (Phillippe)	200.00	75.00	40.00
(24)	T.H. Speaker	650.00	275.00	125.00
(25)	Jacob Stahl	200.00	75.00	40.00
(26)	Chas. E. Street	200.00	75.00	40.00
(27)	Allen Storke	200.00	75.00	40.00
(28)	Robt. Unglaub	200.00	75.00	40.00
(29)	C. Wagner	200.00	75.00	40.00
(30)	Hans Wagner	2,900	1,250	575.00
(31)	Victor Willis	425.00	175.00	100.00
(32)	Owen Wilson	200.00	75.00	40.00
(33)	Jos. Wood	300.00	125.00	75.00

1909-11 American Caramel (E90-1)

The E90-1 set was issued by the American Caramel Co. from 1909 through 1911, with the bulk of the set being produced in the first year. The cards, which nominally measure 1-1/2" x 2-3/4" (with the usual tolerances for original cutting variations), were issued with sticks of caramel candy. They are color renderings of photographs. Backs state that 100 subjects are included in the set though more actually do exist.

There are several levels of scarcity in the set, those levels being mostly determined by the year the cards were issued. For the reader's convenience, the players' first names have been added in the checklist that follows. The complete set price includes all variations.

		NM	EX	VG
Complete Set (120):		150,000	75,000	40,000
Common Player:		400.00	125.00	40.00
(1)	Bill Bailey	400.00	125.00	40.00
(2)	Home Run Baker	1,500	350.00	125.00
(3)	Jack Barry	600.00	200.00	60.00
(4)	George Bell	500.00	175.00	60.00
(5)	Harry Bemis	1,000	350.00	150.00
(6)	Chief Bender	1,500	350.00	150.00
(7)	Bob Bescher	1,000	350.00	150.00
(8)	Cliff Blankenship	500.00	175.00	60.00
(9)	John Bliss	500.00	175.00	60.00
(10)	Bill Bradley	400.00	125.00	40.00
(11)	Kitty Bransfield ("P" on shirt.)	400.00	125.00	40.00
(12)	Kitty Bransfield (No "P.")	800.00	250.00	80.00
(13)	Roger Bresnahan	1,500	350.00	125.00
(14)	Al Bridwell	400.00	125.00	40.00
(15)	Buster Brown (Boston)	2,000	500.00	200.00
(16)	Mordecai Brown (Chicago)	800.00	250.00	80.00
(17)	Donie Bush	400.00	125.00	40.00
(18)	John Butler	500.00	175.00	60.00
(19)	Howie Camnitz	500.00	175.00	60.00
(20)	Frank Chance	1,500	350.00	125.00
(21)	Hal Chase	1,000	200.00	90.00
(22)	Fred Clarke (Philadelphia)	1,500	350.00	125.00
(23)	Fred Clarke (Pittsburgh)	5,000	1,250	500.00
(24)	Wally Clement	1,000	350.00	150.00
(25)	"Ty" Cobb	10,000	4,000	1,500
(26)	Eddie Collins	1,500	350.00	125.00
(27)	Frank Corridon	400.00	125.00	40.00
(28)	Sam Crawford	1,500	350.00	125.00
(29)	Lou Criger	400.00	125.00	40.00
(30)	George Davis	2,500	700.00	350.00
(31)	Harry Davis	400.00	125.00	40.00
(32)	Ray Demmitt	800.00	250.00	80.00
(33)	Mike Donlin	600.00	200.00	70.00
(34)	Wild Bill Donovan	500.00	175.00	60.00
(35)	Red Dooin	400.00	125.00	40.00
(36)	Patsy Dougherty	1,000	350.00	150.00
(37)	Hugh Duffy	5,000	1,250	500.00
(38)	Jimmy Dygert	400.00	125.00	40.00
(39)	Rube Ellis	400.00	125.00	40.00
(40)	Clyde Engle	500.00	175.00	60.00
(41)	Art Fromme	800.00	250.00	80.00
(42)	George Gibson (Back view.)	1,000	350.00	150.00
(43)	George Gibson (Front view.)	600.00	200.00	70.00
(44)	Peaches Graham	6,000	2,750	1,550
(45)	Eddie Grant	600.00	200.00	70.00
(46)	Dolly Gray	600.00	200.00	70.00
(47)	Bob Groom	400.00	125.00	40.00
(48)	Charley Hall	1,750	805.00	455.00
(49)	Roy Hartzell/Fldg	400.00	125.00	40.00
(50)	Roy Hartzell/Btg	600.00	200.00	70.00
(51)	Heinie Heitmuller	400.00	125.00	40.00
(52)	Harry Howell (Follow-through.)	400.00	125.00	40.00
(53)	Harry Howell (Wind-up.)	800.00	250.00	80.00
(54)	Tex Irwin (Erwin)	600.00	200.00	70.00
(55)	Frank Isbell	400.00	125.00	40.00
(56)	Joe Jackson	80,000	35,000	21,000
(57)	Hughie Jennings	1,500	350.00	125.00
(58)	Buck Jordon (Jordan)	400.00	125.00	40.00
(59)	Addie Joss/Portrait	1,500	690.00	125.00
(60)	Addie Joss/Pitching	6,000	2,750	1,550
(61)	Ed Karger	1,500	500.00	200.00
(62)	Willie Keeler/Portrait (Pink background.)	1,200	550.00	310.00
(63)	Willie Keeler/Portait (Red background.)	5,000	1,250	500.00
(64)	Willie Keeler/Throwing	4,000	1,000	400.00
(65)	John Knight	600.00	200.00	70.00
(66)	Harry Krause	400.00	125.00	40.00
(67)	Nap Lajoie	2,500	700.00	300.00
(68)	Tommy Leach/Throwing	1,000	350.00	150.00
(69)	Tommy Leach/Btg	600.00	200.00	70.00
(70)	Sam Leever	600.00	200.00	70.00
(71)	Hans Lobert	1,500	500.00	200.00
(72)	Harry Lumley	400.00	125.00	40.00
(73)	Rube Marquard	1,500	400.00	150.00
(74)	Christy Matthewson (Mathewson)	7,500	2,500	1,200
(75)	Stuffy McInnes (McInnis)	400.00	125.00	40.00
(76)	Harry McIntyre	400.00	125.00	40.00
(77)	Larry McLean	1,000	350.00	150.00
(78)	George McQuillan	400.00	125.00	40.00
(79)	Dots Miller	500.00	175.00	60.00
(80)	Fred Mitchell (New York)	400.00	125.00	40.00
(81)	Mike Mitchell (Cincinnati)	16,500	7,600	4,300
(82)	George Mullin	400.00	125.00	40.00
(83)	Rebel Oakes	800.00	250.00	80.00
(84)	Paddy O'Connor	800.00	250.00	80.00
(85)	Charley O'Leary	400.00	125.00	40.00
(86)	Orval Overall	800.00	250.00	80.00
(87)	Jim Pastorius	400.00	125.00	40.00
(88)	Ed Phelps	400.00	125.00	40.00
(89)	Eddie Plank	2,000	920.00	520.00
(90)	Lew Richie	600.00	200.00	70.00
(91)	Germany Schaefer	500.00	175.00	60.00
(92)	Biff Schlitzer	800.00	250.00	80.00
(93)	Johnny Seigle (Siegle)	1,500	500.00	200.00
(94)	Dave Shean	1,500	500.00	200.00
(95)	Jimmy Sheckard	600.00	200.00	70.00
(96)	Tris Speaker	10,000	2,000	800.00
(97)	Jake Stahl	6,000	2,750	1,550
(98)	Oscar Stanage	400.00	125.00	40.00
(99)	George Stone (No hands visible.)	400.00	125.00	40.00
(100)	George Stone (Left hand visible.)	600.00	200.00	70.00
(101)	George Stovall	500.00	175.00	60.00
(102)	Ed Summers	1,500	690.00	390.00
(103)	Bill Sweeney (Boston)	5,000	1,200	700.00
(104)	Jeff Sweeney (New York)	400.00	125.00	40.00
(105)	Jesse Tannehill (Chicago A.L.)	400.00	125.00	40.00
(106)	Lee Tannehill (Chicago N.L.)	400.00	125.00	40.00
(107)	Fred Tenney	800.00	250.00	80.00
(108)	Ira Thomas (Philadelphia)	400.00	125.00	40.00
(109)	Roy Thomas (Boston)	400.00	125.00	40.00
(110)	Joe Tinker	1,100	505.00	285.00
(111)	Bob Unglaub	400.00	125.00	40.00
(112)	Jerry Upp	1,500	500.00	200.00
(113)	Honus Wagner /Btg	10,000	4,000	2,000
(114)	Honus Wagner/Throwing	15,000	7,500	3,000
(115)	Bobby Wallace	1,500	350.00	125.00
(116)	Ed Walsh	10,000	2,000	800.00
(117)	Vic Willis	1,500	400.00	150.00
(118)	Hooks Wiltse	600.00	200.00	70.00
(119)	Cy Young (Cleveland)	8,000	2,000	800.00
(120)	Cy Young (Boston)	6,000	1,750	600.00

1910 American Caramel Pirates (E90-2)

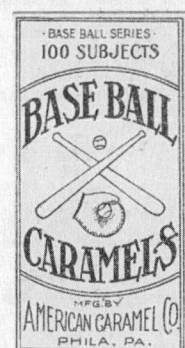

Closely related to the E90-1 American Caramel set, the E90-2 set consists of 11 cards featuring members of the 1909 champion Pittsburgh Pirates. The cards measure a nominal 1-1/2" x 2-5/8", though tolerances must be allowed for original cutting variations common to the era. They display a color lithograph on front set upon a solid color background of either red, green blue or pink. The player's name and "Pittsburg" appear in blue capital letters in the border beneath the portrait. The backs are identical to those in the E90-1 set, depicting a drawing of a ball, glove and crossed bats with the words "Base Ball Caramels" and a reference to "100 Subjects." The set includes Hall of Famers Honus Wagner and Fred Clarke.

		NM	EX	VG
Complete Set (11):		30,000	13,500	7,000
Common Player:		1,200	550.00	250.00
(1)	Babe Adams	1,200	550.00	250.00
(2)	Fred Clarke	2,000	900.00	400.00
(3)	George Gibson	1,200	550.00	250.00
(4)	Ham Hyatt	1,200	550.00	250.00
(5)	Tommy Leach	1,200	550.00	250.00
(6)	Sam Leever	1,200	550.00	250.00
(7)	Nick Maddox	1,200	550.00	250.00
(8)	Dots Miller	1,200	550.00	250.00
(9)	Deacon Phillippe	1,200	550.00	250.00
(10)	Honus Wagner	17,500	7,875	3,800
(11)	Owen Wilson	1,200	550.00	250.00

1910 American Caramel White Sox/Cubs (E90-3)

Similar in size (nominally 1-1/2" x 2-3/4", but with the usual tolerances for cutting variations on cards of the era) and style to the more popular E90-1 set, the E90-3 set was issued by the American Caramel Co. in 1910. The 20-card, color lithograph set includes 11 Chicago Cubs and nine White Sox. The fronts of the cards have a similar design to the E90-1 set, although different pictures were used. The backs can be differentiated by two major changes: The bottom of the card indicates the American Caramel Co. of "Chicago," rather than Philadelphia, and the top of the card contains the phrase "All The Star Players," rather than "100 Subjects."

		NM	EX	VG
Complete Set (20):		30,000	13,500	6,750
Common Player:		1,700	850.00	425.00
(1)	Jimmy Archer	1,700	850.00	350.00

(2)	Lena Blackburne	1,700	850.00	350.00
(3)	Mordecai Brown	3,000	1,500	550.00
(4)	Frank Chance	3,000	1,500	550.00
(5)	King Cole	1,700	850.00	350.00
(6)	Patsy Dougherty	1,700	850.00	350.00
(7)	Johnny Evers	3,000	1,500	550.00
(8)	Chick Gandil	4,500	2,250	900.00
(9)	Ed Hahn	1,700	850.00	425.00
(10a)	Solly Hofman	1,700	850.00	350.00
(10b)	Solly Hofman (Broken "m" in last name gives appearance of "Hofnlan.")	3,600	1,750	900.00
(11)	Orval Overall	1,700	850.00	350.00
(12)	Fred Payne	1,700	850.00	425.00
(13)	Billy Purtell	1,700	850.00	350.00
(14)	Wildfire Schulte	1,700	850.00	350.00
(15)	Jimmy Sheckard	1,700	850.00	350.00
(16)	Frank Smith	1,700	850.00	350.00
(17)	Harry Steinfeldt	1,700	850.00	350.00
(18a)	Joe Tinker (Blue background.)	3,000	1,500	550.00
(18b)	Joe Tinker (Green background.)	3,000	1,500	550.00
(19)	Ed Walsh	3,000	1,500	550.00
(20)	Rollie Zeider	1,700	850.00	350.00

1910 American Caramel Die-Cuts (E125)

Issued circa 1910 by the American Caramel Co., this set of die-cut cards is so rare that it wasn't even known to exist until the late 1960s. Apparently inserted in boxes of caramels, these cards, which are die-cut figures of baseball players, vary in size but are all relatively large - some measuring 7" high and 4" wide. Players from the Athletics, Red Sox, Giants and Pirates are known with a team checklist appearing on the back.

		NM	EX	VG
Common Player:		3,000	1,375	905.00
(1)	Babe Adams (Arms at sides.)	3,000	1,375	905.00
(2)	Red Ames (Throwing)	3,000	1,375	905.00
(3)	Home Run Baker	5,000	2,250	1,500
(4)	Jack Barry (Fielding)	3,000	1,375	905.00
(5)	Chief Bender	5,625	2,530	1,690
(6)	Al Bridwell (Fielding)	3,000	1,375	905.00
(7)	Bobby Byrne (Throwing)	3,000	1,375	905.00
(8)	Bill Carrigan (Catching)	3,000	1,375	905.00
(9)	Ed Cicotte (Throwing)	3,000	1,375	905.00
(10)	Fred Clark (Clarke)(Fielding)	5,000	2,250	1,500
(11)	Eddie Collins	5,000	2,250	1,500
(12)	Harry Davis (Fielding)	3,000	1,375	905.00
(13)	Art Devlin (Fielding)	3,000	1,375	905.00
(14)	Josh Devore	3,000	1,375	905.00
(15)	Larry Doyle (Throwing)	3,000	1,375	905.00
(16)	John Flynn (Running)	3,000	1,375	905.00
(17)	George Gibson (Hands in glove.)	3,000	1,375	905.00
(18)	Topsy Hartzell (Hartsel) (Fielding)	3,000	1,375	905.00
(19)	Harry Hooper (Throwing)	5,000	2,250	1,500
(20)	Harry Krause	3,000	1,375	905.00
(21)	Tommy Leach (Fielding)	3,000	1,375	905.00
(22)	Harry Lord (Throwing)	3,000	1,375	905.00
(23)	Christy Mathewson (Wind-up.)	18,750	8,440	5,625
(24)	Amby McConnell (Fielding)	3,000	1,375	905.00
(25)	Fred Merkle	3,000	1,375	905.00
(26)	Dots Miller (Throwing)	3,000	1,375	905.00
(27)	Danny Murphy	3,000	1,375	905.00
(28)	Red Murray (Fielding)	3,000	1,375	905.00
(29)	Harry Niles (Fielding)	3,000	1,375	905.00
(30)	Rube Oldring	3,000	1,375	905.00
(31)	Eddie Plank (Throwing)	18,750	8,440	5,625
(32)	Cy Seymour (Fielding)	3,000	1,375	905.00
(33)	Tris Speaker (Batting)	11,250	5,065	3,375
(34)	Tris Speaker (Fielding)	11,250	5,065	3,375
(35)	Jake Stahl (Fielding)	3,000	1,375	905.00
(36)	Ira Thomas	3,000	1,375	905.00
(37)	Heinie Wagner (Throwing)	3,000	1,375	905.00
(38)	Honus Wagner (Batting)	25,000	11,250	7,500
(39)	Honus Wagner (Throwing)	25,000	11,250	7,500
(40)	Art Wilson	3,000	1,375	905.00
(41)	Owen Wilson (Throwing)	3,000	1,375	905.00
(42)	Hooks Wiltse (Throwing)	3,000	1,375	905.00

1915 American Caramel (E106)

This 48-card set, designated E106 by the American Card Catalog, was produced by the American Caramel Co., of York, Pa., in 1915 and includes players from the National, American and Federal Leagues. Cards measure 1-1/2" x 2-3/4". The set is related to the E90-1 and E92 sets, from which the artwork is taken, but this issue has a glossy coating on front, which makes the cards very susceptible to cracking.

Chase, 1b. Buffalo Feds

This card is one of a set of forty-eight leading Baseball Players in the National, American and Federal Leagues. One card is given with every piece of Baseball Caramel manufactured by the

AMERICAN CARAMEL CO.

YORK PA

UNDER THE FAMOUS BRAND OF THE

P. C. W.

		NM	EX	VG
Complete Set (48):		40,000	20,000	12,500
Common Player:		700.00	350.00	200.00
(1)	Jack Barry	700.00	350.00	200.00
(2)	Chief Bender (White hat.)	1,300	650.00	400.00
(3)	Chief Bender (Striped hat.)	1,300	650.00	400.00
(4)	Bob Bescher	700.00	350.00	200.00
(5)	Roger Bresnahan	1,300	650.00	400.00
(6)	Al Bridwell	700.00	350.00	200.00
(7)	Donie Bush	700.00	350.00	200.00
(8)	Hal Chase (Portrait)	700.00	350.00	200.00
(9)	Hal Chase (Catching)	700.00	350.00	200.00
(10)	Ty Cobb (W/bat, facing front.)	9,000	4,500	2,700
(11)	Ty Cobb (Batting, facing to side.)	8,500	4,250	2,250
(12)	Eddie Collins	1,300	650.00	400.00
(13)	Sam Crawford	1,300	650.00	400.00
(14)	Ray Demmitt	700.00	350.00	200.00
(15)	Wild Bill Donovan	700.00	350.00	200.00
(16)	Red Dooin	700.00	350.00	200.00
(17)	Mickey Doolan	700.00	350.00	200.00
(18)	Larry Doyle	700.00	350.00	200.00
(19)	Clyde Engle	700.00	350.00	200.00
(20)	Johnny Evers	1,300	650.00	400.00
(21)	Art Fromme	700.00	350.00	200.00
(22)	George Gibson (Catching, back view.)	700.00	350.00	200.00
(23)	George Gibson (Catching, front view.)	700.00	350.00	200.00
(24)	Roy Hartzell	700.00	350.00	200.00
(25)	Fred Jacklitsch	700.00	350.00	200.00
(26)	Hugh Jennings	1,300	650.00	400.00
(27)	Otto Knabe	700.00	350.00	200.00
(28)	Nap Lajoie	1,300	650.00	400.00
(29)	Hans Lobert	700.00	350.00	200.00
(30)	Rube Marquard	1,300	650.00	400.00
(31)	Christy Matthewson (Mathewson)	4,450	2,200	1,330
(32)	John McGraw	1,300	650.00	400.00
(33)	George McQuillan	700.00	350.00	200.00
(34)	Dots Miller	700.00	350.00	200.00
(35)	Danny Murphy	700.00	350.00	200.00
(36)	Rebel Oakes	700.00	350.00	200.00
(37)	Eddie Plank	1,500	750.00	450.00
(38)	Germany Schaefer	700.00	350.00	200.00
(39)	Tris Speaker	1,800	900.00	550.00
(40)	Oscar Stanage	700.00	350.00	200.00
(41)	George Stovall	700.00	350.00	200.00
(42)	Jeff Sweeney	700.00	350.00	200.00
(43)	Joe Tinker (Portrait)	1,300	650.00	400.00
(44)	Joe Tinker (Batting)	1,300	650.00	400.00
(45)	Honus Wagner (Batting)	13,040	6,250	3,750
(46)	Honus Wagner (Throwing)	13,040	6,250	3,750
(47)	Hooks Wiltse	700.00	350.00	200.00
(48)	Heinie Zimmerman	700.00	350.00	200.00

1921 American Caramel Series of 80 (E121)

JOHN GRANEY
Util. O. F.—Cleveland Americans

This set consists of pictures of eighty of the leading BASE BALL STARS —of the— AMERICAN AND NATIONAL LEAGUES —Made only by— AMERICAN CARAMEL COMPANY, LANCASTER AND YORK, PENNA.

Issued circa 1921, the E121 Series of 80 is designated as such because of the card reverses which indicate the player pictured is just one of 80 baseball stars in the set. The figure of 80 supplied by the American Caramel Co. is incorrect as over 100 different pictures do exist. The unnumbered cards, which measure about 2" x 3-1/4", feature black and white photos. Two different backs exist for the Series of 80. The common back variation has the first line ending with the word "the," while the scarcer version ends with the word "eighty." The complete set price does not include the variations.

		NM	EX	VG
Complete Set (121):		52,500	21,500	10,000
Common Player:		150.00	60.00	30.00
(1)	G.C. Alexander (Arms above head.)	750.00	300.00	150.00
(2)	Grover Alexander (Right arm forward.)	1,500	600.00	300.00
(3)	Jim Bagby	150.00	60.00	30.00
(4a)	J. Franklin Baker	400.00	160.00	80.00
(4b)	Frank Baker	400.00	160.00	80.00
(5)	Dave Bancroft (Batting)	400.00	160.00	80.00
(6)	Dave Bancroft (Leaping)	400.00	160.00	80.00
(7)	Ping Bodie	150.00	60.00	30.00
(8)	George Burns	150.00	60.00	30.00
(9)	Geo. J. Burns	150.00	60.00	30.00
(10)	Owen Bush	150.00	60.00	30.00
(11)	Max Carey (Batting)	400.00	160.00	80.00
(12)	Max Carey (Hands at hips.)	400.00	160.00	80.00
(13)	Cecil Causey	150.00	60.00	30.00
(14)	Ty Cobb (Throwing, looking front.)	1,800	725.00	360.00
(15a)	Ty Cobb (Throwing, looking right, Mgr. on front.)	1,800	725.00	360.00
(15b)	Ty Cobb (Throwing, looking right, Manager on front.)	1,800	725.00	360.00
(16)	Eddie Collins	400.00	160.00	80.00
(17)	"Rip" Collins	150.00	60.00	30.00
(18)	Jake Daubert	150.00	60.00	30.00
(19)	George Dauss	150.00	60.00	30.00
(20)	Charles Deal (Dark uniform.)	150.00	60.00	30.00
(21)	Charles Deal (White uniform.)	150.00	60.00	30.00
(22)	William Doak	150.00	60.00	30.00
(23)	Bill Donovan	150.00	60.00	30.00
(24)	"Phil" Douglas	150.00	60.00	30.00
(25a)	Johnny Evers (Manager)	400.00	160.00	80.00
(25b)	Johnny Evers (Mgr.)	400.00	160.00	80.00
(26)	Urban Faber (Dark uniform.)	400.00	160.00	80.00
(27)	Urban Faber (White uniform.)	400.00	160.00	80.00
(28)	William Fewster (First name actually Wilson.)	150.00	60.00	30.00
(29)	Eddie Foster	150.00	60.00	30.00
(30)	Frank Frisch	400.00	160.00	80.00
(31)	W.L. Gardner	150.00	60.00	30.00
(32a)	Alexander Gaston (No position on front.)	150.00	60.00	30.00
(32b)	Alexander Gaston (Position on front.)	150.00	60.00	30.00
(33)	"Kid" Gleason	150.00	60.00	30.00
(34)	"Mike" Gonzalez	150.00	60.00	30.00
(35)	Hank Gowdy	150.00	60.00	30.00
(36)	John Graney	150.00	60.00	30.00
(37)	Tom Griffith	150.00	60.00	30.00
(38)	Heinie Groh	150.00	60.00	30.00
(39)	Harry Harper	150.00	60.00	30.00
(40)	Harry Heilman (Heilmann)	400.00	160.00	80.00
(41)	Walter Holke (Portrait)	150.00	60.00	30.00
(42)	Walter Holke (Throwing)	150.00	60.00	30.00
(43)	Charles Hollacher (Hollocher)	150.00	60.00	30.00
(44)	Harry Hooper	400.00	160.00	80.00
(45)	Rogers Hornsby	1,100	450.00	225.00
(46)	Waite Hoyt	400.00	160.00	80.00
(47)	Miller Huggins	400.00	160.00	80.00
(48)	Wm. C. Jacobson	150.00	60.00	30.00
(49)	Hugh Jennings	400.00	160.00	80.00
(50)	Walter Johnson (Throwing)	1,350	550.00	275.00
(51)	Walter Johnson (Hands at chest.)	1,425	575.00	285.00
(52)	James Johnston	150.00	60.00	30.00
(53)	Joe Judge	150.00	60.00	30.00
(54)	George Kelly	400.00	160.00	80.00
(55)	Dick Kerr	150.00	60.00	30.00
(56)	P.J. Kilduff	150.00	60.00	30.00
(57a)	Bill Killifer (Incorrect name.)	150.00	60.00	30.00
(57b)	Bill Killefer (Correct name.)	150.00	60.00	30.00
(58)	John Lavan	150.00	60.00	30.00
(59)	"Nemo" Leibold	150.00	60.00	30.00
(60)	Duffy Lewis	150.00	60.00	30.00
(61)	Al. Mamaux	150.00	60.00	30.00
(62)	"Rabbit" Maranville	400.00	160.00	80.00
(63a)	Carl May (Mays)	200.00	80.00	40.00
(63b)	Carl Mays (Correct name.)	200.00	80.00	40.00
(64)	John McGraw	400.00	160.00	80.00
(65)	Jack McInnis	150.00	60.00	30.00
(66)	M.J. McNally	150.00	60.00	30.00
(67)	Emil Muesel (Photo is Lou DeVormer.)	150.00	60.00	30.00
(68)	R. Meusel	150.00	60.00	30.00
(69)	Clyde Milan	150.00	60.00	30.00
(70)	Elmer Miller	150.00	60.00	30.00
(71)	Otto Miller	150.00	60.00	30.00
(72)	Guy Morton	150.00	60.00	30.00
(73)	Eddie Murphy	150.00	60.00	30.00
(74)	"Hy" Myers	150.00	60.00	30.00
(75)	Arthur Nehf	150.00	60.00	30.00
(76)	Steve O'Neill	150.00	60.00	30.00
(77a)	Roger Peckinbaugh (Incorrect name.)	150.00	60.00	30.00
(77b)	Roger Peckinpaugh (Correct name.)	150.00	60.00	30.00
(78a)	Jeff Pfeffer (Brooklyn)	150.00	60.00	30.00
(78b)	Jeff Pfeffer (St. Louis)	150.00	60.00	30.00
(79)	Walter Pipp	250.00	100.00	50.00
(80)	Jack Quinn	150.00	60.00	30.00
(81)	John Rawlings	150.00	60.00	30.00
(82)	E.C. Rice	400.00	160.00	80.00
(83)	Eppa Rixey, Jr.	400.00	160.00	80.00
(84)	Robert Roth	150.00	60.00	30.00
(85a)	Ed. Roush (C.F.)	400.00	160.00	80.00
(85b)	Ed. Roush (L.F.)	400.00	160.00	80.00
(86a)	Babe Ruth	17,500	7,000	3,500
(86b)	"Babe" Ruth	17,500	7,000	3,500
(86c)	George Ruth	19,000	7,600	3,800
(87)	"Bill" Ryan	150.00	60.00	30.00
(88)	"Slim" Sallee (Glove showing.)	150.00	60.00	30.00
(89)	"Slim" Sallee (No glove showing.)	150.00	60.00	30.00

		NM	EX	VG
(90)	Ray Schalk	400.00	160.00	80.00
(91)	Walter Schang	150.00	60.00	30.00
(92a)	Fred Schupp (Name incorrect.)	150.00	60.00	30.00
(92b)	Ferd Schupp (Name correct.)	150.00	60.00	30.00
(93)	Everett Scott	150.00	60.00	30.00
(94)	Hank Severeid	150.00	60.00	30.00
(95)	Robert Shawkey	150.00	60.00	30.00
(96a)	Pat Shea	150.00	60.00	30.00
(96b)	"Pat" Shea	150.00	60.00	30.00
(97)	George Sisler (Batting)	400.00	160.00	80.00
(98)	George Sisler (Throwing)	400.00	160.00	80.00
(99)	Earl Smith	150.00	60.00	30.00
(100)	Frank Snyder	150.00	60.00	30.00
(101a)	Tris Speaker (Mgr.)	800.00	325.00	160.00
(101b)	Tris Speaker (Manager - large projection.)	800.00	325.00	160.00
(101c)	Tris Speaker (Manager - small projection.)	800.00	325.00	160.00
(102)	Milton Stock	150.00	60.00	30.00
(103)	Amos Strunk	150.00	60.00	30.00
(104)	Zeb Terry	150.00	60.00	30.00
(105)	Chester Thomas	150.00	60.00	30.00
(106)	Fred Toney (Trees in background.)	150.00	60.00	30.00
(107)	Fred Toney (No trees.)	150.00	60.00	30.00
(108)	George Tyler	150.00	60.00	30.00
(109)	Jim Vaughn (Dark hat.)	150.00	60.00	30.00
(110)	Jim Vaughn (White hat.)	150.00	60.00	30.00
(111)	Bob Veach (Glove in air.)	150.00	60.00	30.00
(112)	Bob Veach (Arms crossed.)	150.00	60.00	30.00
(113)	Oscar Vitt	150.00	60.00	30.00
(114)	W. Wambsganss (Photo actually Fred Coumbe.)	150.00	60.00	30.00
(115)	Aaron Ward	150.00	60.00	30.00
(116)	Zach Wheat	400.00	160.00	80.00
(117)	George Whitted	150.00	60.00	30.00
(118)	Fred Williams	150.00	60.00	30.00
(119)	Ivy B. Wingo	150.00	60.00	30.00
(120)	Joe Wood	300.00	125.00	60.00
(121)	"Pep" Young	150.00	60.00	30.00

1922 American Caramel Series of 120 (E121)

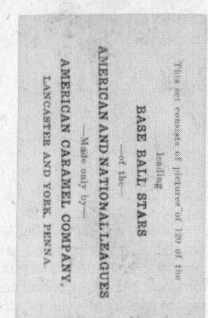

Produced by American Caramel Co. the E121 Series of 120 has back advertising that claims that the set contained 120 subjects. Identical in design to the E121 Series of 80 set except for the card backs, the black-and-white cards measure about 2" x 3-1/4". Numerous variations are found in the set, most involving a change in the player's name, team or position. The complete set price does not include variations.

		NM	EX	VG
Complete Set (127):		60,000	24,000	12,000
Common Player:		100.00	40.00	15.00
(1)	Chas. "Babe" Adams	100.00	40.00	15.00
(2)	G.C. Alexander	750.00	300.00	150.00
(3)	Jim Bagby	100.00	40.00	15.00
(4)	Dave Bancroft	400.00	160.00	80.00
(5)	Turner Barber	100.00	40.00	15.00
(6a)	Carlson L. Bigbee	100.00	40.00	15.00
(6b)	L. Bigbee	100.00	40.00	15.00
(7)	"Bullet Joe" Bush	100.00	40.00	15.00
(8)	Max Carey	400.00	160.00	80.00
(9)	Cecil Causey	100.00	40.00	15.00
(10)	Ty Cobb (Batting)	2,500	1,000	500.00
(11)	Ty Cobb (Throwing)	2,250	900.00	450.00
(12)	Eddie Collins	400.00	160.00	80.00
(13)	A. Wilbur Cooper	100.00	40.00	15.00
(14)	Stanley Coveleskie (Coveleski)	400.00	160.00	80.00
(15)	Dave Danforth	100.00	40.00	15.00
(16)	Jake Daubert	100.00	40.00	15.00
(17)	George Dauss	100.00	40.00	15.00
(18)	Dixie Davis	100.00	40.00	15.00
(19)	Lou DeVormer (Photo actually Irish Meusel.)	100.00	40.00	15.00
(20)	William Doak	100.00	40.00	15.00
(22)	Phil Douglas	100.00	40.00	15.00
(23)	Urban Faber	400.00	160.00	80.00
(24)	Bib Falk (Bibb)	100.00	40.00	15.00
(25)	Wm. Fewster (First name actually Wilson.)	100.00	40.00	158.00
(26)	Max Flack	100.00	40.00	15.00
(27)	Ira Falgstead (Flagstead)	100.00	40.00	15.00
(28)	Frank Frisch	400.00	160.00	80.00
(29)	W.L. Gardner	100.00	40.00	15.00
(30)	Alexander Gaston	100.00	40.00	15.00
(31)	E.P. Gharrity	100.00	40.00	15.00
(32)	George Gibson	100.00	40.00	15.00
(33)	Chas. "Whitey" Glazner	100.00	40.00	15.00
(34)	"Kid" Gleason	100.00	40.00	15.00
(35)	Hank Gowdy	100.00	40.00	15.00
(36)	John Graney	100.00	40.00	15.00
(37)	Tom Griffith	100.00	40.00	15.00
(38)	Chas. Grimm	100.00	40.00	15.00
(39)	Heine Groh	100.00	40.00	15.00
(40)	Jess Haines	400.00	160.00	80.00
(41)	Harry Harper	100.00	40.00	15.00
(43)	Harry Heilmann (Name correct, batting.)	600.00	240.00	120.00
(44)	Clarence Hodge	100.00	40.00	15.00
(45)	Walter Holke (Portrait)	100.00	40.00	15.00
(47)	Charles Hollocher	100.00	40.00	15.00
(48)	Harry Hooper	400.00	160.00	80.00
(49a)	Rogers Hornsby (2B.)	1,100	450.00	225.00
(49b)	Rogers Hornsby (O.F.)	1,100	450.00	225.00
(50)	Waite Hoyt	400.00	160.00	80.00
(51)	Miller Huggins	400.00	160.00	80.00
(52)	Walter Johnson	1,350	550.00	275.00
(53)	Joe Judge	100.00	40.00	15.00
(54)	George Kelly	400.00	160.00	80.00
(55)	Dick Kerr	100.00	40.00	15.00
(56)	P.J. Kilduff	100.00	40.00	15.00
(57)	Bill Killifer (Killefer) (Batting)	100.00	40.00	15.00
(58)	Bill Killifer (Killefer) (Throwing)	100.00	40.00	15.00
(59)	John Lavan	100.00	40.00	15.00
(60)	Walter Mails	100.00	40.00	15.00
(61)	"Rabbit" Maranville	400.00	160.00	80.00
(62)	Elwood Martin	100.00	40.00	15.00
(63)	Carl Mays	200.00	80.00	40.00
(64)	John J. McGraw	400.00	160.00	80.00
(65)	Jack McInnis	100.00	40.00	15.00
(66)	M.J. McNally	100.00	40.00	15.00
(67)	Emil Meusel (Photo actually Lou DeVormer.)	100.00	40.00	15.00
(68)	R. Meusel	100.00	40.00	15.00
(69)	Clyde Milan	100.00	40.00	15.00
(70)	Elmer Miller	100.00	40.00	15.00
(71)	Otto Miller	100.00	40.00	15.00
(72)	Johnny Mostil	100.00	40.00	15.00
(73)	Eddie Mulligan	100.00	40.00	15.00
(74a)	Hy Myers	100.00	40.00	15.00
(75)	Earl Neale	300.00	120.00	60.00
(76)	Arthur Nehf	100.00	40.00	15.00
(77)	Leslie Nunamaker	100.00	40.00	15.00
(78)	Joe Oeschger	100.00	40.00	15.00
(80)	Steve O'Neill	100.00	40.00	15.00
(81)	D.B. Pratt	100.00	40.00	15.00
(82a)	John Rawlings (2B.)	100.00	40.00	15.00
(82b)	John Rawlings (Utl.)	100.00	40.00	15.00
(83)	E.S. Rice (Initials actually E.C.)	400.00	160.00	80.00
(84)	Eppa J. Rixey	400.00	160.00	80.00
(86)	Wilbert Robinson	400.00	160.00	80.00
(87)	Tom Rogers	100.00	40.00	15.00
(88a)	Ed Rounnel (Rommel)	100.00	40.00	15.00
(88b)	Ed. Rommel	100.00	40.00	15.00
(89)	Ed Roush	400.00	160.00	80.00
(90)	"Muddy" Ruel	100.00	40.00	15.00
(91)	Walter Ruether	100.00	40.00	15.00
(92)	"Babe" Ruth (Photo montage.)	10,000	4,000	2,000
(93)	"Babe" Ruth (Holding bird.)	10,000	4,000	2,000
(94)	"Babe" Ruth (Holding ball.)	10,000	4,000	2,000
(95)	Bill Ryan	100.00	40.00	15.00
(96)	Ray Schalk (Catching)	400.00	160.00	80.00
(97)	Ray Schalk (Batting)	400.00	160.00	80.00
(98)	Wally Schang	100.00	40.00	15.00
(100)	Everett Scott	400.00	160.00	80.00
(101)	Joe Sewell	400.00	160.00	80.00
(102)	Robert Shawkey	100.00	40.00	15.00
(103)	Pat Shea	100.00	40.00	15.00
(104)	Earl Sheely	100.00	40.00	15.00
(105)	Urban Schocker	100.00	40.00	15.00
(106)	George Sisler (Batting)	400.00	160.00	80.00
(108)	Earl Smith	100.00	40.00	15.00
(109)	Elmer Smith	100.00	40.00	15.00
(110)	Frank Snyder	100.00	40.00	15.00
(111)	Bill Southworth	100.00	40.00	15.00
(112)	Tris Speaker (Small projection.)	600.00	240.00	120.00
(113)	Milton J. Stock	100.00	40.00	15.00
(114)	Amos Strunk	100.00	40.00	15.00
(115)	Zeb Terry	100.00	40.00	15.00
(116)	Fred Toney	100.00	40.00	15.00
(117)	George Topocer (Toporcer)	100.00	40.00	15.00
(118)	Bob Veach	100.00	40.00	15.00
(119)	Oscar Vitt	100.00	40.00	15.00
(120)	Curtis Walker	100.00	40.00	15.00
(121)	W. Wambsganss (Photo actually Fred Coumbe.)	100.00	40.00	15.00
(122)	Aaron Ward	100.00	40.00	15.00
(123)	Zach Wheat	400.00	160.00	80.00
(124)	George Whitted (Pittsburgh)	100.00	40.00	15.00
(125)	Fred Williams	100.00	40.00	15.00
(126)	Ivy B. Wingo	100.00	40.00	15.00
(127)	Ross Young (Youngs)	400.00	160.00	80.00

1922 American Caramel Series of 80 (E122)

Known as E122 in the American Card Catalog, this set is actually a parallel of the E121 American Caramel set. The cards are nearly identical to E121's "Series of 80," except the player's name, position and team are printed inside a gray rectangle at the bottom of the card, and the photos have a more coarse appearance. At 2" x 3-1/4", the E122s are slightly shorter than E121s.

		NM	EX	VG
Complete Set (81):		30,000	12,000	6,000
Common Player:		100.00	40.00	25.00
(1)	Grover Alexander	750.00	300.00	150.00
(2)	Jim Bagby	150.00	60.00	30.00
(3)	J. Franklin Baker	400.00	160.00	80.00
(4)	Dave Bancroft	400.00	160.00	80.00
(5)	Ping Bodie	150.00	60.00	30.00
(6)	George Burns	150.00	60.00	30.00
(7)	Geo. J. Burns	150.00	60.00	30.00
(8)	Owen Bush	150.00	60.00	30.00
(9)	Max Carey	400.00	160.00	80.00
(10)	Cecil Causey	150.00	60.00	30.00
(11)	Ty Cobb	1,900	760.00	380.00
(12)	Eddie Collins	400.00	160.00	80.00
(13)	Jake Daubert	150.00	60.00	30.00
(14)	George Dauss	150.00	60.00	30.00
(15)	Charles Deal	150.00	60.00	30.00
(16)	William Doak	150.00	60.00	30.00
(17)	Bill Donovan	150.00	60.00	30.00
(18)	Johnny Evers	400.00	160.00	80.00
(19)	Urban Faber	400.00	160.00	80.00
(20)	Eddie Foster	150.00	60.00	30.00
(21)	W.L. Gardner	150.00	60.00	30.00
(22)	"Kid" Gleason	150.00	60.00	30.00
(23)	Hank Gowdy	150.00	60.00	30.00
(24)	John Graney	150.00	60.00	30.00
(25)	Tom Griffith	150.00	60.00	30.00
(26)	Sam Harris (Stan "Bucky")	400.00	160.00	80.00
(27)	Harry Heilman (Heilmann)	400.00	160.00	80.00
(28)	Walter Holke	150.00	60.00	30.00
(29)	Charles Hollacher (Hollocher)	150.00	60.00	30.00
(30)	Harry Hooper	400.00	160.00	80.00
(31)	Rogers Hornsby	600.00	240.00	120.00
(32)	Wm. C. Jacobson	150.00	60.00	30.00
(33)	Walter Johnson	1,100	450.00	225.00
(34)	James Johnston	150.00	60.00	30.00
(35)	Joe Judge	150.00	60.00	30.00
(36)	George Kelly	400.00	160.00	80.00
(37)	Dick Kerr	150.00	60.00	30.00
(38)	P.J. Kilduff	150.00	60.00	30.00
(39)	Bill Killefer	150.00	60.00	30.00
(40)	John Lavan	150.00	60.00	30.00
(41)	Duffy Lewis	150.00	60.00	30.00
(42)	Perry Lipe	150.00	60.00	30.00
(43)	Al. Mamaux	150.00	60.00	30.00
(44)	"Rabbit" Maranville	400.00	160.00	80.00
(45)	Carl May (Mays)	200.00	80.00	40.00
(46)	John McGraw	400.00	160.00	80.00
(47)	Jack McInnis	150.00	60.00	30.00
(48)	Clyde Milan	150.00	60.00	30.00
(49)	Otto Miller	150.00	60.00	30.00
(50)	Guy Morton	150.00	60.00	30.00
(51)	Eddie Murphy	150.00	60.00	30.00
(52)	"Hy" Myers	150.00	60.00	30.00
(53)	Steve O'Neill	150.00	60.00	30.00
(54)	Roger Peckinbaugh (Peckinpaugh)	150.00	60.00	30.00
(55)	Jeff Pfeffer	150.00	60.00	30.00
(56)	Walter Pipp	175.00	70.00	35.00
(57)	E.C. Rice	400.00	160.00	80.00
(58)	Eppa Rixey, Jr.	400.00	160.00	80.00
(59)	Babe Ruth	9,000	3,600	1,800
(60)	"Slim" Sallee	150.00	60.00	30.00
(61)	Ray Schalk	400.00	160.00	80.00
(62)	Walter Schang	150.00	60.00	30.00
(63a)	Fred Schupp (Name incorrect.)	150.00	60.00	30.00
(63b)	Ferd Schupp (Name correct.)	150.00	60.00	30.00
(64)	Everett Scott	150.00	60.00	30.00
(65)	Hank Severeid	150.00	60.00	30.00
(66)	George Sisler (Batting)	400.00	160.00	80.00
(67)	George Sisler (Throwing)	400.00	160.00	80.00
(68)	Tris Speaker	750.00	300.00	150.00
(69)	Milton Stock	150.00	60.00	30.00
(70)	Amos Strunk	150.00	60.00	30.00
(71)	Chester Thomas	150.00	60.00	30.00
(72)	George Tyler	150.00	60.00	30.00
(73)	Jim Vaughn	150.00	60.00	30.00
(74)	Bob Veach	150.00	60.00	30.00
(75)	Oscar Vitt	150.00	60.00	30.00
(76)	W. Wambsganss	150.00	60.00	30.00
(77)	Zach Wheat	400.00	160.00	80.00
(78)	Fred Williams	150.00	60.00	30.00
(79)	Ivy B. Wingo	150.00	60.00	30.00
(80)	Joe Wood	150.00	60.00	30.00
(81)	Pep Young	150.00	60.00	30.00

1922 American Caramel Series of 240 (E120)

One of the most popular sets of the 1920s candy cards, the 1922 E120s were produced by the American Caramel Co. and distributed with sticks of caramel candy. The unnumbered cards measure 2" x 3-1/2". Cards depicting players from the American League are printed in brown ink on cream cardboard; National Leaguers are printed in green on blue-green stock. Backs carry team checklists. Many of the E120 photos were used in other sets of the era. A pair of 11-1/2" x 10-1/2" albums, holding 120 each and stamped American or National League were also issued.

WALTER JOHNSON
PITCHER, WASHINGTON AMERICANS

WASHINGTON AMERICANS
"SENATORS"
MANAGER—CLYDE MILAN

WALTER JOHNSON	PITCHER
TOM PHILLIPS	PITCHER
GEORGE MOGRIDGE	PITCHER
HARRY COURTNEY	PITCHER
J. T. ZACHARY	PITCHER
ED GHARRITY	CATCHER
VAL PICINICH	CATCHER
JOE JUDGE	FIRST BASE
STANLEY HARRIS	SECOND BASE
ROGER PECKINPAUGH	SHORT STOP
HOWARD SHANKS	THIRD BASE
LEON GOSLIN	OUTFIELD
SAM RICE	OUTFIELD
CLYDE MILAN	OUTFIELD
EARL SMITH	OUTFIELD

THIS PICTURE IS ONE OF A SERIES OF 240 PICTURES OF BASEBALL STARS—15 PLAYERS IN EACH OF THE 16 MAJOR LEAGUE TEAMS. WE SUPPLY HANDSOME BLANK ALBUMS TO HOLD 120 PICTURES—ONE FOR AMERICAN LEAGUE, ONE FOR NATIONAL LEAGUE—FOR 14 CENTS EACH POSTPAID.

AMERICAN CARAMEL CO.
LANCASTER, PA.   YORK, PA.

		NM	EX	VG
	Complete Set (240):	70,000	27,500	14,500
	Common Player:	110.00	50.00	30.00
	Album:	300.00	150.00	90.00
(1)	Charles (Babe) Adams	175.00	70.00	35.00
(2)	Eddie Ainsmith	175.00	70.00	35.00
(3)	Vic Aldridge	175.00	70.00	35.00
(4)	Grover C. Alexander	900.00	360.00	180.00
(5)	Jim Bagby	175.00	70.00	35.00
(6)	Frank (Home Run) Baker	500.00	200.00	100.00
(7)	Dave (Beauty) Bancroft	500.00	200.00	100.00
(8)	Walt Barbare	175.00	70.00	35.00
(9)	Turner Barber	175.00	70.00	35.00
(10)	Jess Barnes	175.00	70.00	35.00
(11)	Clyde Barnhart	175.00	70.00	35.00
(12)	John Bassler	175.00	70.00	35.00
(13)	Will Bayne	175.00	70.00	35.00
(14)	Walter (Huck) Betts	175.00	70.00	35.00
(15)	Carson Bigbee	175.00	70.00	35.00
(16)	Lu Blue	175.00	70.00	35.00
(17)	Norman Boeckel	175.00	70.00	35.00
(18)	Sammy Bohne	400.00	160.00	80.00
(19)	George Burns	175.00	70.00	35.00
(20)	George Burns	175.00	70.00	35.00
(21)	"Bullet Joe" Bush	175.00	70.00	35.00
(22)	Leon Cadore	175.00	70.00	35.00
(23)	Marty Callaghan	175.00	70.00	35.00
(24)	Frank Calloway (Callaway)	175.00	70.00	35.00
(25)	Max Carey	500.00	200.00	100.00
(26)	Jimmy Caveney	175.00	70.00	35.00
(27)	Virgil Cheeves	175.00	70.00	35.00
(28)	Vern Clemons	175.00	70.00	35.00
(29)	Ty Cob (Cobb)	3,500	1,400	700.00
(30)	Bert Cole	175.00	70.00	35.00
(31)	Eddie Collins	500.00	200.00	100.00
(32)	John (Shano) Collins	175.00	70.00	35.00
(33)	T.P. (Pat) Collins	175.00	70.00	35.00
(34)	Wilbur Cooper	175.00	70.00	35.00
(35)	Harry Courtney	175.00	70.00	35.00
(36)	Stanley Coveleskie (Coveleski)	500.00	200.00	100.00
(37)	Elmer Cox	175.00	70.00	35.00
(38)	Sam Crane	175.00	70.00	35.00
(39)	Walton Cruise	175.00	70.00	35.00
(40)	Bill Cunningham	175.00	70.00	35.00
(41)	George Cutshaw	175.00	70.00	35.00
(42)	Dave Danforth	175.00	70.00	35.00
(43)	Jake Daubert	175.00	70.00	35.00
(44)	George Dauss	175.00	70.00	35.00
(45)	Frank (Dixie) Davis	175.00	70.00	35.00
(46)	Hank DeBerry	175.00	70.00	35.00
(47)	Albert Devormer (Lou DeVormer)	175.00	70.00	35.00
(48)	Bill Doak	175.00	70.00	35.00
(49)	Pete Donohue	175.00	70.00	35.00
(50)	"Shufflin" Phil Douglas	175.00	70.00	35.00
(51)	Joe Dugan	175.00	70.00	35.00
(52)	Louis (Pat) Duncan	175.00	70.00	35.00
(53)	Jimmy Dykes	175.00	70.00	35.00
(54)	Howard Ehmke	175.00	70.00	35.00
(55)	Frank Ellerbe	175.00	70.00	35.00
(56)	Urban (Red) Faber	500.00	200.00	100.00
(57)	Bib Falk (Bibb)	175.00	70.00	35.00
(58)	Dana Fillingim	175.00	70.00	35.00
(59)	Max Flack	175.00	70.00	35.00
(60)	Ira Flagstead	175.00	70.00	35.00
(61)	Art Fletcher	175.00	70.00	35.00
(62)	Horace Ford	175.00	70.00	35.00
(63)	Jack Fournier	175.00	70.00	35.00
(64)	Frank Frisch	500.00	200.00	100.00
(65)	Ollie Fuhrman	175.00	70.00	35.00
(66)	Clarance Galloway	175.00	70.00	35.00
(67)	Larry Gardner	175.00	70.00	35.00
(68)	Walter Gerber	175.00	70.00	35.00
(69)	Ed Gharrity	175.00	70.00	35.00
(70)	John Gillespie	175.00	70.00	35.00
(71)	Chas. (Whitey) Glazner	175.00	70.00	35.00
(72)	Johnny Gooch	175.00	70.00	35.00
(73)	Leon Goslin	500.00	200.00	100.00
(74)	Hank Gowdy	175.00	70.00	35.00
(75)	John Graney	175.00	70.00	35.00
(76)	Tom Griffith	175.00	70.00	35.00
(77)	Burleigh Grimes	500.00	200.00	100.00
(78)	Oscar Ray Grimes	175.00	70.00	35.00
(79)	Charlie Grimm	175.00	70.00	35.00
(80)	Heinie Groh	175.00	70.00	35.00
(81)	Jesse Haines	500.00	200.00	100.00
(82)	Earl Hamilton	175.00	70.00	35.00
(83)	Gene (Bubbles) Hargrave	175.00	70.00	35.00
(84)	Bryan Harris (Harriss)	175.00	70.00	35.00
(85)	Joe Harris	175.00	70.00	35.00
(86)	Stanley Harris	500.00	200.00	100.00
(87)	Chas. (Dowdy) Hartnett	500.00	200.00	100.00
(88)	Bob Hasty	175.00	70.00	35.00
(89)	Joe Hauser	225.00	90.00	45.00
(90)	Clif Heathcote	175.00	70.00	35.00

(91)	Harry Heilmann	500.00	200.00	100.00
(92)	Walter (Butch) Henline	175.00	70.00	35.00
(93)	Clarence (Shovel) Hodge	175.00	70.00	35.00
(94)	Walter Holke	175.00	70.00	35.00
(95)	Charles Hollocher	175.00	70.00	35.00
(96)	Harry Hooper	500.00	200.00	100.00
(97)	Rogers Hornsby	900.00	360.00	180.00
(98)	Waite Hoyt	500.00	200.00	100.00
(99)	Wilbur Hubbell (Wilbert)	175.00	70.00	35.00
(100)	Bernard (Bud) Hungling	175.00	70.00	35.00
(101)	Will Jacobson	175.00	70.00	35.00
(102)	Charlie Jamieson	175.00	70.00	35.00
(103)	Ernie Johnson	175.00	70.00	35.00
(104)	Sylvester Johnson	175.00	70.00	35.00
(105)	Walter Johnson	1,600	650.00	325.00
(106)	Jimmy Johnston	175.00	70.00	35.00
(107)	W.R. (Doc) Johnston	175.00	70.00	35.00
(108)	"Deacon" Sam Jones	175.00	70.00	35.00
(109)	Bob Jones	175.00	70.00	35.00
(110)	Percy Jones	175.00	70.00	35.00
(111)	Joe Judge	175.00	70.00	35.00
(112)	Ben Karr	175.00	70.00	35.00
(113)	Johnny Kelleher	175.00	70.00	35.00
(114)	George Kelly	500.00	200.00	100.00
(115)	Lee King	175.00	70.00	35.00
(116)	Wm (Larry) Kopff (Kopf)	175.00	70.00	35.00
(117)	Marty Krug	175.00	70.00	35.00
(118)	Johnny Lavan	175.00	70.00	35.00
(119)	Nemo Leibold	175.00	70.00	35.00
(120)	Roy Leslie	175.00	70.00	35.00
(121)	George Leverette (Leverett)	175.00	70.00	35.00
(122)	Adolfo Luque	175.00	70.00	35.00
(123)	Walter Mails	175.00	70.00	35.00
(124)	Al Mamaux	175.00	70.00	35.00
(125)	"Rabbit" Maranville	500.00	200.00	100.00
(126)	Cliff Markle	175.00	70.00	35.00
(127)	Richard (Rube) Marquard	500.00	200.00	100.00
(128)	Carl Mays	200.00	80.00	40.00
(129)	Hervey McClellan (Harvey)	175.00	70.00	35.00
(130)	Austin McHenry	175.00	70.00	35.00
(131)	"Stuffy" McInnis	175.00	70.00	35.00
(132)	Martin McManus	175.00	70.00	35.00
(133)	Mike McNally	175.00	70.00	35.00
(134)	Hugh McQuillan	175.00	70.00	35.00
(135)	Lee Meadows	175.00	70.00	35.00
(136)	Mike Menosky	175.00	70.00	35.00
(137)	Bob (Dutch) Meusel	175.00	70.00	35.00
(138)	Emil (Irish) Meusel	175.00	70.00	35.00
(139)	Clyde Milan	175.00	70.00	35.00
(140)	Edmund (Bing) Miller	175.00	70.00	35.00
(141)	Elmer Miller	175.00	70.00	35.00
(142)	Lawrence (Hack) Miller	175.00	70.00	35.00
(143)	Clarence Mitchell	175.00	70.00	35.00
(144)	George Mogridge	175.00	70.00	35.00
(145)	Roy Moore	175.00	70.00	35.00
(146)	John L. Mokan	175.00	70.00	35.00
(147)	John Morrison	175.00	70.00	35.00
(148)	Johnny Mostil	175.00	70.00	35.00
(149)	Elmer Myers	175.00	70.00	35.00
(150)	Hy Myers	175.00	70.00	35.00
(151)	Roliene Naylor (Roleine)	175.00	70.00	35.00
(152)	Earl "Greasy" Neale	175.00	70.00	35.00
(153)	Art Nehf	175.00	70.00	35.00
(154)	Les Nunamaker	175.00	70.00	35.00
(155)	Joe Oeschger	175.00	70.00	35.00
(156)	Bob O'Farrell	175.00	70.00	35.00
(157)	Ivan Olson	175.00	70.00	35.00
(158)	George O'Neil	175.00	70.00	35.00
(159)	Steve O'Neill	175.00	70.00	35.00
(160)	Frank Parkinson	175.00	70.00	35.00
(161)	Roger Peckinpaugh	175.00	70.00	35.00
(162)	Herb Pennock	500.00	200.00	100.00
(163)	Ralph (Cy) Perkins	175.00	70.00	35.00
(164)	Will Pertica	175.00	70.00	35.00
(165)	Jack Peters	175.00	70.00	35.00
(166)	Tom Phillips	175.00	70.00	35.00
(167)	Val Picinich	175.00	70.00	35.00
(168)	Herman Pillette	175.00	70.00	35.00
(169)	Ralph Pinelli	175.00	70.00	35.00
(170)	Wallie Pipp	175.00	70.00	35.00
(171)	Clark Pittenger (Clarke)	175.00	70.00	35.00
(172)	Raymond Powell	175.00	70.00	35.00
(173)	Derrill Pratt	175.00	70.00	35.00
(174)	Jack Quinn	175.00	70.00	35.00
(175)	Joe (Goldie) Rapp	175.00	70.00	35.00
(176)	John Rawlings	175.00	70.00	35.00
(177)	Walter (Dutch) Reuther (Ruether)	175.00	70.00	35.00
(178)	Sam Rice	500.00	200.00	100.00
(179)	Emory Rigney	175.00	70.00	35.00
(180)	Jimmy Ring	175.00	70.00	35.00
(181)	Eppa Rixey	500.00	200.00	100.00
(182)	Charles Robertson	175.00	70.00	35.00
(183)	Ed Rommel	175.00	70.00	35.90
(184)	Eddie Roush	500.00	200.00	100.00
(185)	Harold (Muddy) Ruel (Herold)	175.00	70.00	35.00
(186)	Babe Ruth	15,000	6,000	3,000
(187)	Ray Schalk	500.00	200.00	100.00
(188)	Wallie Schang	175.00	70.00	35.00
(189)	Ray Schmandt	175.00	70.00	35.00
(190)	Walter Schmidt	175.00	70.00	35.00
(191)	Joe Schultz	175.00	70.00	35.00
(192)	Everett Scott	175.00	70.00	35.00
(193)	Henry Severeid	175.00	70.00	35.00
(194)	Joe Sewell	500.00	200.00	100.00
(195)	Howard Shanks	175.00	70.00	35.00
(196)	Bob Shawkey	175.00	70.00	35.00
(197)	Earl Sheely	175.00	70.00	35.00
(198)	Will Sherdel	175.00	70.00	35.00
(199)	Ralph Shinners	175.00	70.00	35.00
(200)	Urban Shocker	175.00	70.00	35.00
(201)	Charles (Chick) Shorten	175.00	70.00	35.00
(202)	George Sisler	500.00	200.00	100.00
(203)	Earl Smith (N.Y. Giants)	175.00	70.00	35.00
(204)	Earl Smith (Washington)	175.00	70.00	35.00
(205)	Elmer Smith	175.00	70.00	35.00
(206)	Jack Smith	175.00	70.00	35.00
(207)	Sherrod Smith	175.00	70.00	35.00

(208)	Colonel Snover	175.00	70.00	35.00
(209)	Frank Snyder	175.00	70.00	35.00
(210)	Al Sothoron	175.00	70.00	35.00
(211)	Bill Southworth	175.00	70.00	35.00
(212)	Tris Speaker	900.00	360.00	180.00
(213)	Arnold Statz	175.00	70.00	35.00
(214)	Milton Stock	175.00	70.00	35.00
(215)	Amos Strunk	175.00	70.00	35.00
(216)	Jim Tierney	175.00	70.00	35.00
(217)	John Tobin	175.00	70.00	35.00
(218)	Fred Toney	175.00	70.00	35.00
(219)	George Toporcer	175.00	70.00	35.00
(220)	Harold (Pie) Traynor	500.00	200.00	100.00
(221)	George Uhle	175.00	70.00	35.00
(222)	Elam Vangilder	175.00	70.00	35.00
(223)	Bob Veach	175.00	70.00	35.00
(224)	Clarence (Tillie) Walker	175.00	70.00	35.00
(225)	Curtis Walker	175.00	70.00	35.00
(226)	Al Walters	175.00	70.00	35.00
(227)	Bill Wambsganss	175.00	70.00	35.00
(228)	Aaron Ward	175.00	70.00	35.00
(229)	John Watson	175.00	70.00	35.00
(230)	Frank Welch	175.00	70.00	35.00
(231)	Zach Wheat	500.00	200.00	100.00
(232)	Fred (Cy) Williams	175.00	70.00	35.00
(233)	Kenneth Williams	175.00	70.00	35.00
(234)	Ivy Wingo	175.00	70.00	35.00
(235)	Joe Wood	400.00	160.00	80.00
(236)	Lawrence Woodall	175.00	70.00	35.00
(237)	Russell Wrightstone	175.00	70.00	35.00
(238)	Everett Yaryan	175.00	70.00	35.00
(239)	Ross Young (Youngs)	500.00	200.00	100.00
(240)	J.T. Zachary	175.00	70.00	35.00

1927 American Caramel Series of 60 (E126)

Issued in 1927 by the American Caramel Co., of Lancaster, Pa., this obscure 60-card set was one of the last of the caramel card issues. Measuring 2" x 3-1/4", the cards differ from most sets of the period because they are numbered. The back of each card includes an offer for an album to house the set which includes players from all 16 major league teams. The set has the American Card Catalog designation E126.

		NM	EX	VG
	Complete Set (60):	36,500	14,500	7,250
	Common Player:	125.00	55.00	30.00
1	John Gooch	200.00	80.00	40.00
2	Clyde L. Barnhart	200.00	80.00	40.00
3	Joe Busch (Bush)	200.00	80.00	40.00
4	Lee Meadows	200.00	80.00	40.00
5	E.T. Cox	200.00	80.00	40.00
6	"Red" Faber	600.00	240.00	120.00
7	Aaron Ward	200.00	80.00	40.00
8	Ray Schalk	600.00	240.00	120.00
9	"Specks" Toporcer ("Specs")	200.00	80.00	40.00
10	Bill Southworth	200.00	80.00	40.00
11	Allen Sothoron	200.00	80.00	40.00
12	Will Sherdel	200.00	80.00	40.00
13	Grover Alexander	1,000	400.00	200.00
14	Jack Quinn	200.00	80.00	40.00
15	C. Galloway	200.00	80.00	40.00
16	"Eddie" Collins	600.00	240.00	120.00
17	"Ty" Cobb	3,800	1,550	775.00
18	Percy Jones	200.00	80.00	40.00
19	Chas. Grimm	200.00	80.00	40.00
20	"Bennie" Karr	200.00	80.00	40.00
21	Charlie Jamieson	200.00	80.00	40.00
22	Sherrod Smith	200.00	80.00	40.00
23	Virgil Cheeves	200.00	80.00	40.00
24	James Ring	200.00	80.00	40.00
25	"Muddy" Ruel	200.00	80.00	40.00
26	Joe Judge	200.00	80.00	40.00
27	Tris Speaker	1,000	400.00	200.00
28	Walter Johnson	2,000	800.00	400.00
29	E.C. "Sam" Rice	600.00	240.00	120.00
30	Hank DeBerry	200.00	80.00	40.00
31	Walter Henline	200.00	80.00	40.00
32	Max Carey	600.00	240.00	120.00
33	Arnold J. Statz	200.00	80.00	40.00
34	Emil Meusel	200.00	80.00	40.00
35	T.P. "Pat" Collins	200.00	80.00	40.00
36	Urban Shocker	200.00	80.00	40.00
37	Bob Shawkey	200.00	80.00	40.00
38	"Babe" Ruth	15,000	6,000	3,000
39	Bob Meusel	200.00	80.00	40.00
40	Alex Ferguson	200.00	80.00	40.00
41	"Stuffy" McInnis	200.00	80.00	40.00
42	"Cy" Williams	200.00	80.00	40.00
43	Russel Wrightstone (Russell)	200.00	80.00	40.00
44	John Tobin	200.00	80.00	40.00
45	Wm. C. Jacobson	200.00	80.00	40.00

46	Bryan "Slim" Harriss	200.00	80.00	40.00
47	Elam Vangilder	200.00	80.00	40.00
48	Ken Williams	200.00	80.00	40.00
49	Geo. R. Sisler	800.00	325.00	160.00
50	Ed Brown	200.00	80.00	40.00
51	Jack Smith	200.00	80.00	40.00
52	Dave Bancroft	600.00	240.00	120.00
53	Larry Woodall	200.00	80.00	40.00
54	Lu Blue	200.00	80.00	40.00
55	Johnny Bassler	200.00	80.00	40.00
56	"Jakie" May	200.00	80.00	40.00
57	Horace Ford	200.00	80.00	40.00
58	"Curt" Walker	200.00	80.00	40.00
59	"Artie" Nehf	200.00	80.00	40.00
60	Geo. Kelly	600.00	240.00	120.00

1908 American League Pub. Co. Postcards

This set of black-and-white postcards was produced by the American League Publishing Co., Cleveland. The 3-1/2" x 5" cards have a large player posed-action photo against a white background and a smaller oval portrait photo in one of the top corners. A box at bottom contains some biographical data. The otherwise blank back has postcard indicia printed in black. The set carries an American Card Catalog designation of PC770. As might be expected, all but two of the players in the known checklist were contemporary members of the Cleveland ballclub.

		NM	EX	VG
Complete Set (16):		10,000	5,000	3,000
Common Player:		350.00	175.00	100.00
(1)	Harry Bay	350.00	175.00	100.00
(2)	Harry Bemis	350.00	175.00	100.00
(3)	Charles Berger	350.00	175.00	100.00
(4)	Joseph Birmingham	350.00	175.00	100.00
(5)	W. Bradley	350.00	175.00	100.00
(6)	Tyrus R. Cobb	2,500	1,250	750.00
(7)	Walter Clarkson	350.00	175.00	100.00
(8)	Elmer Flick	600.00	300.00	180.00
(9)	C.T. Hickman	350.00	175.00	100.00
(10)	William Hinchman	350.00	175.00	100.00
(11)	Addie Joss	750.00	375.00	225.00
(12)	Glen Liebhardt (Glenn)	350.00	175.00	100.00
(13)	Nap Lajoie	750.00	375.00	225.00
(14)	George Nill	350.00	175.00	100.00
(15)	George Perring	350.00	175.00	100.00
(16)	Honus Wagner	1,800	900.00	540.00

1950 American Nut & Chocolate Pennants (F150)

Although there is nothing on these small (1-7/8" x 4") felt pennants to identify the issuer, surviving ads show that the American Nut & Chocolate Co. of Boston sold them as a set of 22 for 50 cents. The pennants of American League players are printed in blue on white, while National Leaguers are printed in red on white. The pennants feature crude line-art drawings of the players at left, along with a facsimile autograph. A 10% variation in the size of the printing on the Elliott and Sain pennants has been noted, and may exist on others, as well. An approximately 17" x 7" version of the Ted Williams pennant is known and was available as a mail-in premium. Other players may also exist in that format. The checklist here is arranged alphabetically.

		NM	EX	VG
Complete Set (22):		1,800	900.00	550.00
Common Player:		65.00	32.50	20.00
(1)	Ewell Blackwell	65.00	32.50	20.00
(2)	Harry Brecheen	65.00	32.50	20.00
(3)	Phil Cavarretta	65.00	32.50	20.00
(4)	Bobby Doerr	100.00	50.00	30.00
(5)	Bob Elliott	65.00	32.50	20.00
(6)	Boo Ferriss	65.00	32.50	20.00
(7)	Joe Gordon	65.00	32.50	20.00
(8)	Tommy Holmes	65.00	32.50	20.00
(9)	Charles Keller	65.00	32.50	20.00

(10)	Ken Keltner	65.00	32.50	20.00
(11)	Ralph Kiner	100.00	50.00	30.00
(12)	Whitey Kurowski	65.00	32.50	20.00
(13)	Johnny Pesky	65.00	32.50	20.00
(14)	Pee Wee Reese	130.00	65.00	40.00
(15)	Phil Rizzuto	130.00	65.00	40.00
(16)	Johnny Sain	65.00	32.50	20.00
(17)	Enos Slaughter	100.00	50.00	30.00
(18)	Warren Spahn	100.00	50.00	30.00
(19)	Vern Stephens	65.00	32.50	20.00
(20)	Earl Torgeson	65.00	32.50	20.00
(21)	Dizzy Trout	65.00	32.50	20.00
(22)	Ted Williams	260.00	130.00	80.00
(22)	Ted Williams (17" x 7")	900.00	450.00	275.00

1968 American Oil Sweepstakes

One of several contemporary sweepstakes run by gas stations, this game required matching right- and left-side game pieces of the same athletic figure (or sporty auto) to win the stated prize. Naturally one side or the other was distributed in extremely limited quantities to avoid paying out too many prizes. Cards were given away in perforated pairs with a qualifying gasoline purchase. Uncut pairs carry a small premium over single cards. Data on which card halves were the rare part needed for redemption is incomplete and would have an effect on the collector value of surviving specimens. Individual game pieces measure 2-9/16" x 2-1/8" and are printed in color. Only the baseball players in the set are listed here.

		NM	EX	VG
(1a)	Mickey Mantle (Action, left side, $10.)	40.00	20.00	12.00
(1b)	Mickey Mantle (Portrait, right side, $10.)	30.00	15.00	9.00
(2a)	Willie Mays (Action, left side, $10.)	40.00	20.00	12.00
(2b)	Willie Mays (Portrait, right side, $10.)	25.00	12.50	7.50
(3a)	Babe Ruth (Action, left side, $1.)	40.00	20.00	12.00
(3b)	Babe Ruth (Portrait, right side, $1.)	25.00	12.50	7.50

1910 American Sports Candy and Jewelry

(See 1910 Orange Borders.)

1962 American Tract Society

These full-color cards, which carry religious messages on the back, were issued in 1962 by the American Tract Society, an interdenominational, non-sectarian publisher of Christian literature in the United States since 1825. Known as "Tra-cards," the cards measure 2-3/4" x 3-1/2" and feature color photographs on the fronts. The set includes religious scenes along with photos of various celebrities and sports stars, including baseball players Felipe Alou, Bobby Richardson, Jerry Kindall and Al Worthington. (There are two poses each of Alou and Kindall.) The backs carry rather lengthy, first-person religious testimonials from the players. The cards are numbered on the back in the lower right corner.

		NM	EX	VG
Complete Set (6):		70.00	35.00	20.00
Common Player:		10.00	5.00	3.00
43	Bobby Richardson	25.00	12.50	7.50
51a	Jerry Kindall (Cleveland)	10.00	5.00	3.00
51b	Jerry Kindall (Minnesota)	10.00	5.00	3.00
52a	Felipe Alou (Kneeling)	15.00	7.50	4.50
52b	Felipe Alou (Batting)	15.00	7.50	4.50
66	Al Worthington	10.00	5.00	3.00

1973 John B. Anderson Former Greats

This set of postcard-sized black-and-white cards features the artwork of John B. Anderson, a New York collector. Each card includes a facsimile autograph on front; backs are blank. The unnumbered cards are checklisted here in alphabetical order.

		NM	EX	VG
Complete Set (12):		30.00	15.00	9.00
Common Player:		4.00	2.00	1.25
(1)	Ty Cobb	6.00	3.00	1.75
(2)	Mickey Cochrane	4.00	2.00	1.25
(3)	Roberto Clemente	10.00	5.00	3.00
(4)	Lou Gehrig	10.00	5.00	3.00
(5)	Frank Frisch	4.00	2.00	1.25
(6)	Gil Hodges	6.00	3.00	1.75
(7)	Rogers Hornsby	4.00	2.00	1.25
(8)	Connie Mack	4.00	2.00	1.25
(9)	Christy Mathewson	6.00	3.00	1.75
(10)	Jackie Robinson	10.00	5.00	3.00
(11)	Babe Ruth	10.00	5.00	3.00
(12)	Pie Traynor	4.00	2.00	1.25

1977 John B. Anderson Aaron-Mays

This set of postcard size, black-and-white drawings is a collectors issue. Cards are blank-backed.

		NM	EX	VG
Complete Set (4):		5.00	2.50	1.50
Common Card:		2.00	1.00	.60
(1)	Hank Aaron (Arm in air.)	2.00	1.00	.60
(2)	Hank Aaron (Portrait)	2.00	1.00	.60
(3)	Willie Mays (Giants)	2.00	1.00	.60
(4)	Willie Mays (Mets)	2.00	1.00	.60

1977 John B. Anderson New York Teams

Stars and local favorites of the three New York teams of the 1940s and 1950s are featured in this set of collectors cards. The 3-1/2" x 5-1/2" blank-back, black-and-white cards feature artwork by John B. Anderson. The unnumbered cards are checklisted here in alphabetical order.

		NM	EX	VG
Complete Set (24):		45.00	27.50	13.50
Common Player:		4.00	2.00	1.25
(1)	Yogi Berra	6.00	3.00	1.75
(2)	Ralph Branca	4.00	2.00	1.25
(3)	Dolf Camilli	4.00	2.00	1.25
(4)	Roy Campanella	6.00	3.00	1.75
(5)	Jerry Coleman	4.00	2.00	1.25
(6)	Frank Crosetti	4.00	2.00	1.25
(7)	Bill Dickey	4.00	2.00	1.25
(8)	Joe DiMaggio	15.00	7.50	4.50
(9)	Sid Gordon	4.00	2.00	1.25
(10)	Babe Herman	4.00	2.00	1.25
(11)	Carl Hubbell	4.00	2.00	1.25
(12)	Billy Johnson	4.00	2.00	1.25
(13)	Ernie Lombardi	4.00	2.00	1.25
(14)	Willard Marshall	4.00	2.00	1.25
(15)	Willie Mays	10.00	5.00	3.00
(16)	Joe McCarthy	4.00	2.00	1.25
(17)	Joe Medwick	4.00	2.00	1.25
(18)	Joe Moore	4.00	2.00	1.25
(19)	Andy Pafko	4.00	2.00	1.25
(20)	Jackie Robinson	10.00	5.00	3.00
(21)	Red Ruffing	4.00	2.00	1.25
(22)	Bill Terry	4.00	2.00	1.25
(23)	Hoyt Wilhelm	4.00	2.00	1.25
(24)	Gene Woodling	4.00	2.00	1.25

1904 Anonymous Studio Cabinets

The origins of this series of cabinet photos are unknown, as is the full entent of the issue. It is known that the portraits are the uncredited work of Boston photographer Carl Horner. Sixteen pieces were sold in the 1991 Copeland Auction, though only the players listed here have been reliably checklisted. The cabinets measure about 5-3/8" x 6-7/8" and have black or dark gray borders. Some pieces are reported to have slate-blue blank backs. The player's last name is presented in the lower-left corner in black or white outline scrip. The unnumbered cards are checklisted here in alphabetical order.

		NM	EX	VG
Common Player:		750.00	375.00	225.00
(1)	Jake Beckley	750.00	375.00	225.00
(2)	Roger Bresnahan	750.00	375.00	225.00
(3)	Jimmy Collins	750.00	375.00	225.00
(4)	Lave Cross	600.00	300.00	180.00
(5)	Hugh Duffy	600.00	300.00	180.00
(6)	Clark Griffith	750.00	375.00	225.00
(7)	Danny Hoffman	600.00	300.00	180.00
(8)	Connie Mack	750.00	375.00	225.00
(9)	Iron Man McGinity (McGinnity)	750.00	375.00	225.00
(10)	John McGraw	750.00	375.00	225.00
(11)	Matty McIntyre	600.00	300.00	180.00

1912 Anonymous T207

While most T207s are found with one of five different cigarette brands advertised on back, there is a less commonly encountered type with no such ad. They are known as Anonymous backs. Two types are known, one originating from Factory 3 in Louisiana and one from Virginia's Factory 25. The latter is much scarcer though commands little additional premium.

(See 1912 T207 for checklist and price guide.)

1925 Anonymous Postcards

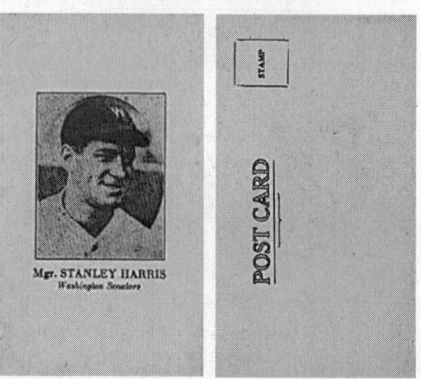

Mgr. STANLEY HARRIS
Washington Senators

POST CARD

STAMP

The date attributed is speculative based on the limited number of known subjects. These 3-1/4" x 5-1/2" cards have a square portrait photo at center in black-and-white. With the exception of Babe Ruth, all known subjects were managers in 1925. The subject is identified by name (in either all-caps or upper- and lower-case, team, and, sometimes, title "Mgr." At least two styles of undivided backs have been found, with an ornate "POST CARD" device at top and a stamp box. The cards are printed on low-grade cardboard. Collector uncertainty as to the origins of the cards and the potential supply has kept market prices down.

	NM	EX	VG
Common Player:	300.00	150.00	90.00
Tyrus Cobb	400.00	200.00	120.00
Mgr. Tyrus Cobb	400.00	200.00	120.00
Stanley Harris	200.00	100.00	60.00
Walter Johnson	300.00	150.00	90.00
John McGraw	200.00	100.00	60.00
"Bill" McKechnie	200.00	100.00	60.00
Wilbert Robinson	200.00	100.00	60.00
Babe Ruth	600.00	300.00	180.00

1940s-50s Anonymous Premium Photos

Harry Heilman

There is no indication on these 8" x 10" black-and-white photos as to who produced them or for what purpose. The blank-backed, white-bordered pictures have the player identified with a sometimes-misspelled script signature. It is not known if this checklist is complete.

		NM	EX	VG
Complete Set (12):		300.00	150.00	90.00
Common Player:		20.00	10.00	6.00
(1)	Ty Cobb	40.00	20.00	12.00

(2)	Dizzy Dean	25.00	12.50	7.50
(3)	Bob Feller	25.00	12.50	7.50
(4)	Lou Gehrig	40.00	20.00	12.00
(5)	Harry Heilman (Heilmann)	20.00	10.00	6.00
(6)	Roger (Rogers) Hornsby	25.00	12.50	7.50
(7)	Walter Johnson	25.00	12.50	7.50
(8)	Christy Mathewson	30.00	15.00	9.00
(9)	Bob Meusel	20.00	10.00	6.00
(10)	Irish Emil Meusel	20.00	10.00	6.00
(11)	Babe Ruth	50.00	25.00	15.00
(12)	Zack Wheat	20.00	10.00	6.00

1949-1950 Ansco Almendares Scorpions

This set of the Cuban Professional League champions of the 1949-50 season was sponsored by Ansco Cameras and Film, whose logo appears on front. Some cards have on back a rubber-stamp with the name of an Havana photo studio, which may have distributed the cards. The cards are actual black-and-white photos on glossy photo paper, measuring about 3" x 3-7/8". The Scorpions had many former and future major leaguers on their roster. Cards are listed alphabetically here.

		NM	EX	VG
Complete Set (20):		3,250	1,625	975.00
Common Player:		150.00	60.00	40.00
(1)	Bill Antonello	175.00	70.00	45.00
(2)	Zungo Cabrera	150.00	60.00	40.00
(3)	Tony Castanos	150.00	60.00	40.00
(4)	Avelino Canizares	150.00	60.00	40.00
(5)	Kevin (Chuck) Connors	450.00	180.00	110.00
(6)	Andres Fleitas	150.00	60.00	40.00
(7)	Al Gionfriddo	175.00	70.00	45.00
(8)	Fermin Guerra	150.00	60.00	40.00
(9)	Gene Handley	150.00	60.00	40.00
(10)	Bob Hooper	150.00	60.00	40.00
(11)	Vincente Lopez	150.00	60.00	40.00
(12)	Conrado Marrero	175.00	70.00	45.00
(13)	Agapito Mayor	150.00	60.00	40.00
(14)	Willie Miranda	175.00	70.00	45.00
(15)	Rene Monteagudo	150.00	60.00	40.00
(16)	Roberto Ortiz	150.00	60.00	40.00
(17)	Hector Rodriguez	150.00	60.00	40.00
(18)	Octavio Rubert	150.00	60.00	40.00
(19)	Rene Solis	150.00	60.00	40.00
(20)	Ed Wright	150.00	60.00	40.00

1961-62 Apple Fresh Milk Minnesota Twins

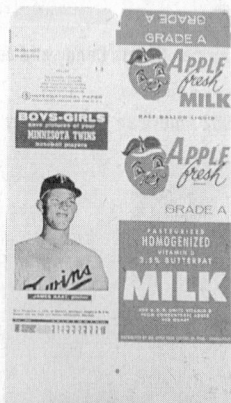

(See 1961, 1962 Cloverleaf Dairy Minnesota Twins.)

1971 Arco

 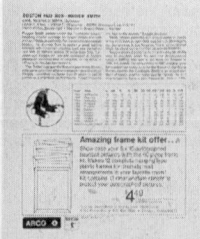

In 1971, players from four major league teams in the east were featured in a set of facsimile autographed color photos in a gas station giveaway program. Following the promotion,

leftover pictures were sold directly to collectors in the pages of the existing hobby media. The photos share an 8" x 10" format, with virtually all of the players being pictured without caps. Red, white and blue stars flank the player name in the bottom border. Black-and-white backs have career summary and stats, personal data, team sponsor and union logos and an ad for frames for the pictures. The unnumbered photos are listed here alphabetically within team.

		NM	EX	VG
Complete Set (49):		175.00	90.00	50.00
Common Player:		3.00	1.50	.90
RED SOX TEAM SET:		60.00	30.00	18.00
(1)	Luis Aparicio	10.00	5.00	3.00
(2)	Ken Brett	4.00	2.00	1.25
(3)	Billy Conigliaro	4.00	2.00	1.25
(4)	Ray Culp	4.00	2.00	1.25
(5)	Doug Griffin	4.00	2.00	1.25
(6)	Bob Montgomery	4.00	2.00	1.25
(7)	Gary Peters	4.00	2.00	1.25
(8)	George Scott	5.00	2.50	1.50
(9)	Sonny Siebert	4.00	2.00	1.25
(10)	Reggie Smith	5.00	2.50	1.50
(11)	Ken Tatum	4.00	2.00	1.25
(12)	Carl Yastrzemski	15.00	7.50	4.50
YANKEES TEAM SET:		65.00	32.50	20.00
(1)	Jack Aker	6.00	3.00	1.75
(2)	Stan Bahnsen	6.00	3.00	1.75
(3)	Frank Baker	6.00	3.00	1.75
(4)	Danny Cater	6.00	3.00	1.75
(5)	Horace Clarke	6.00	3.00	1.75
(6)	John Ellis	6.00	3.00	1.75
(7)	Gene Michael	6.00	3.00	1.75
(8)	Thurman Munson	12.00	6.00	3.50
(9)	Bobby Murcer	7.50	3.75	2.25
(10)	Fritz Peterson	6.00	3.00	1.75
(11)	Mel Stottlemyre	6.00	3.00	1.75
(12)	Roy White	7.50	3.75	2.25
PHILLIES TEAM SET:		40.00	20.00	12.00
(1)	Larry Bowa	3.00	1.50	.90
(2)	Jim Bunning	10.00	5.00	3.00
(3)	Roger Freed	3.00	1.50	.90
(4)	Terry Harmon	3.00	1.50	.90
(5)	Larry Hisle	3.00	1.50	.90
(6)	Joe Hoerner	3.00	1.50	.90
(7)	Deron Johnson	3.00	1.50	.90
(8)	Tim McCarver	5.00	2.50	1.50
(9)	Don Money	3.00	1.50	.90
(10)	Dick Selma	3.00	1.50	.90
(11)	Chris Short	3.00	1.50	.90
(12)	Tony Taylor	3.00	1.50	.90
(13)	Rick Wise	3.00	1.50	.90
PIRATES TEAM SET:		65.00	32.50	20.00
(1)	Gene Alley	3.00	1.50	.90
(2)	Steve Blass	3.00	1.50	.90
(3)	Roberto Clemente	30.00	15.00	9.00
(4)	Dave Giusti	3.00	1.50	.90
(5)	Richie Hebner	3.00	1.50	.90
(6)	Bill Mazeroski	7.50	3.75	2.25
(7)	Bob Moose	3.00	1.50	.90
(8)	Al Oliver	4.50	2.25	1.25
(9)	Bob Robertson	3.00	1.50	.90
(10)	Manny Sanguillen	3.00	1.50	.90
(11)	Willie Stargell	7.50	3.75	2.25
(12)	Luke Walker	3.00	1.50	.90

1980-81 Argus Publishing Reggie Jackson

Some of the cars from Reggie Jackson's collection of hot rods and vintage vehicles were featured on a series of promotional cards issued by the publisher of Hot Rodding and Super Chevy magazines. The standard-size color cards have photos of Jackson with his cars on front, along with magazine and other logos. Backs have information on Jackson's cars. It was reported 10,000 of each were produced for distribution at automotive trade shows and a California drag strip.

		NM	EX	VG
Complete Set (3):		40.00	20.00	12.00
(1)	1980 SEMA Show (Reggie Jackson) (1932 Ford highboy)	20.00	10.00	6.00
2	1981 SEMA (Reggie Jackson) (1932 Ford 5-window)	10.00	5.00	3.00
3	1981 Super Chevy Sunday (Reggie Jackson) (1955 Chevrolet)	10.00	5.00	3.00

1955 Armour Coins

In 1955, Armour inserted a plastic "coin" into packages of hot dogs. A raised profile of a ballplayer is on front along with the player's name and team. On back, between a diamond diagram and crossed bats are name, team, position, birthdate and date, batting and throwing preference, and 1954 hitting or pitching record. The coins measure 1-1/2" in diameter and are unnumbered. They can be found in a variety of colors, some of which are much scarcer than others and elicit higher prices from Armour specialists who have studied their relative scarcities. Values shown are for coins in the most common colors (aqua, blue, green, orange and red). Each 1955 coin can be found in two different "bust tilts" in which the tip of the cap and back point of the bust point to distinctly different areas of the rim. These variations are too arcane for the average collector. The complete set price includes only the most common variations.

		NM	EX	VG
Complete Set (24):		700.00	350.00	210.00
Common Player:		15.00	6.00	3.75
(1a)	John "Johnny" Antonelli ("New York Giants" on back.)	80.00	40.00	25.00
(1b)	John "Johnny" Antonelli ("N.Y. Giants" on back.)	15.00	7.50	4.50
(2)	Larry "Yogi" Berra	25.00	12.50	7.50
(3)	Delmar "Del" Crandall	15.00	7.50	4.50
(4)	Lawrence "Larry" Doby	25.00	12.50	7.50
(5)	James "Jim" Finigan	15.00	7.50	4.50
(6)	Edward "Whitey" Ford	40.00	20.00	12.00
(7a)	James "Junior" Gilliam ("bats L or R,")	60.00	30.00	18.00
(7b)	James "Junior" Gilliam ("bats L - R," thick lips, wide gap between "BROOKLYN" and "DODGERS")	35.00	17.50	10.00
(7c)	James "Junior" Gilliam ("bats L - R," thin lips, narrow gap between "BROOKLYN" and "DODGERS")	45.00	22.50	13.50
(8)	Harvey "Kitten" Haddix	15.00	7.50	4.50
(9a)	Ranson "Randy" Jackson (Ransom) ("nfielder" on back)	30.00	15.00	9.00
(9b)	Ranson "Randy" Jackson (Ransom) ("Infielder" on back.)	50.00	25.00	15.00
(10a)	Jack "Jackie" Jensen ("Boston Reb Sox")	60.00	30.00	18.00
(10b)	Jack "Jackie" Jensen ("Boston Red Sox")	20.00	10.00	6.00
(11)	Theodore "Ted" Kluszewski	20.00	10.00	6.00
(12a)	Harvey E. Kuenn (Widely spaced letters in name; last line on back is bats/throws.)	30.00	15.00	9.00
(12b)	Harvey E. Kuenn (Widely spaced letters in name; last line on back is 1954 average.)	100.00	50.00	30.00
(12c)	Harvey E. Kuenn (Condensed letters in name; last line on back is 1954 average.)	70.00	35.00	20.00
(13a)	Charles "Mickey" Mantel (Incorrect spelling.)	115.00	55.00	35.00
(13b)	Charles "Mickey" Mantle (Corrected) ("bats L or R")	400.00	200.00	120.00
(13c)	Charles "Mickey" Mantle (Corrected) ("bats L - R")	400.00	200.00	120.00
(14)	Donald "Don" Mueller (SP)	30.00	15.00	9.00
(15)	Harold "Pee Wee" Reese	25.00	12.50	7.50
(16)	Allie P. Reynolds	15.00	7.50	4.50
(17)	Albert "Flip" Rosen	20.00	10.00	6.00
(18)	Curtis "Curt" Simmons	20.00	10.00	6.00
(19)	Edwin "Duke" Snider	100.00	50.00	30.00
(20)	Warren Spahn	40.00	20.00	12.00
(21)	Frank Thomas (SP)	25.00	12.50	7.50
(22a)	Virgil "Fire" Trucks (WHITESOX)	25.00	12.50	7.50
(22b)	Virgil "Fire" Trucks (WHITE SOX)	50.00	25.00	15.00
(23)	Robert "Bob" Turley	25.00	12.50	7.50
(24)	James "Mickey" Vernon	15.00	7.50	4.50

1958 Armour S.F. Giants Tabs

In the Giants' first season on the West Coast, packages of Armour hot dogs in the Bay Area could be found with a small (about 2" x 1-5/8") lithographed tin player "tab" enclosed. In team colors of black, white and orange the tabs have black-and-white portraits at center, around which is a

round, square or diamond shaped device bearing the team name and other graphic touches. At the sides are wings with baseballs or caps printed thereon. A 1/2" tab is at top with a slotted panel at bottom. The tab of one piece could be inserted into the slot of another to create a chain of these pieces, or the top tab could be folded over a shirt pocket to wear the item as a badge. The unnumbered pieces are checklisted here alphabetically. NM values quoted are for unbent pieces only.

		NM	EX	VG
Complete Set (10):		2,700	1,350	825.00
Common Player:		250.00	125.00	75.00
(1)	Johnny Antonelli	250.00	125.00	75.00
(2)	Curt Barclay	250.00	125.00	75.00
(3)	Ray Crone	250.00	125.00	75.00
(4)	Whitey Lockman	250.00	125.00	75.00
(5a)	Willie Mays (Portrait in circle.)	450.00	225.00	135.00
(5b)	Willie Mays (Portrait in diamond.)	450.00	225.00	135.00
(6)	Don Mueller	250.00	125.00	75.00
(7)	Danny O'Connell	250.00	125.00	75.00
(8)	Hank Sauer	250.00	125.00	75.00
(9)	Daryl Spencer	250.00	125.00	75.00
(10)	Bobby Thomson	250.00	125.00	75.00

1959 Armour Bacon K.C. Athletics

Not so much a baseball card set as a handful of related single-card issues used at player promotional appearances, a total of four cards are currently known of this issue. Measuring either 5-1/2" x 3-1/4" or 5-1/2" x 4", the horizontal-format cards are printed in black-and-white on paper stock and are blank-backed. A posed player photo appears at left, with an ad for Armour bacon at right. Cards were given out at player appearances at local supermarkets. To date, all known specimens have been found autographed and are priced as such.

		NM	EX	VG
Complete Set (4):		900.00	450.00	275.00
Common Player:		75.00	37.00	22.00
(1)	Harry Chiti	75.00	37.50	22.50
(2)	Whitey Herzog	90.00	45.00	27.50
(3)	Roger Maris (Photo to waist.)	600.00	300.00	180.00
(4)	Roger Maris (Hands on knees.)	600.00	300.00	180.00

1959 Armour Coins

After a three-year layoff, Armour again inserted plastic "coins" into its hot dog packages. The coins retained their 1-1/2" size but did not include as much detailed information as in 1955. Missing from the coins' backs is information such as birthplace and date, team, and batting and throwing preference. The fronts contain the player's name and, unlike 1955, only the team nickname is given. The set consists of 20 coins which come in a myriad of colors. Common colors are navy blue, royal blue, medium green, orange and red. Many other colors are known, many of them scarce and of extra value to Armour specialists. In 1959 Armour had a mail-in offer of 10 coins for $1, which accounts for half of the coins in the set being much more plentiful than the others.

		NM	EX	VG
Complete Set (20):		400.00	200.00	120.00
Common Player:		15.00	7.50	4.50
(1)	Hank Aaron	30.00	15.00	9.00
(2)	John Antonelli	15.00	7.50	4.50
(3)	Richie Ashburn	30.00	15.00	9.00
(4)	Ernie Banks	30.00	15.00	9.00
(5)	Don Blasingame	15.00	7.50	4.50
(6)	Bob Cerv	15.00	7.50	4.50
(7)	Del Crandall	15.00	7.50	4.50
(8)	Whitey Ford	25.00	12.50	7.50
(9)	Nellie Fox	20.00	10.00	6.00
(10)	Jackie Jensen	20.00	10.00	6.00
(11)	Harvey Kuenn	30.00	15.00	9.00
(12)	Frank Malzone	20.00	10.00	6.00
(13)	Johnny Podres	30.00	15.00	9.00
(14)	Frank Robinson	30.00	15.00	9.00
(15)	Roy Sievers	15.00	7.50	4.50
(16)	Bob Skinner	15.00	7.50	4.50
(17)	Frank Thomas	15.00	7.50	4.50
(18)	Gus Triandos	15.00	7.50	4.50
(19)	Bob Turley	20.00	10.00	6.00
(20)	Mickey Vernon	15.00	7.50	4.50

1960 Armour Coins

The 1960 Armour coin issue is identical in number and style to the 1959 set. The unnumbered coins, 1-1/2" in diameter, once again came in a variety of colors. Common colors for 1960 are pale blue, royal blue, red, red-orange, light green, dark green and yellow. Values shown are for common-colored pieces. Scarcer colors exist and may be of premium value to specialists. The Bud Daley coin is very scarce, although it is not known why. Theories for the scarcity center on broken molding equipment, contract disputes, or that the coin was only inserted in a test product that quickly proved to be unsuccessful. As in 1959, a mail-in offer for 10 free coins was made available by Armour. The complete set price includes only the most common variations. Many 1960 Armour coins are found with only partial rims on back (Mantle is particularly susceptible to this condition). Coins without full back rims can grade no higher than VG.

		NM	EX	VG
Complete Set (20):		1,100	550.00	325.00
Common Player:		12.50	6.25	3.75
(1a)	Hank Aaron (Braves)	25.00	12.50	7.50
(1b)	Hank Aaron (Milwaukee Braves)	40.00	20.00	12.00
(2)	Bob Allison	20.00	10.00	6.00
(3)	Ernie Banks	30.00	15.00	9.00
(4)	Ken Boyer	12.50	6.25	3.75
(5)	Rocky Colavito	35.00	17.50	10.50
(6)	Gene Conley	12.50	6.25	3.75
(7)	Del Crandall	12.50	6.25	3.75
(8)	Bud Daley	750.00	375.00	225.00
(9a)	Don Drysdale (L.A condensed.)	35.00	17.50	10.50
(9b)	Don Drysdale (Space between L. and A.)	25.00	12.50	7.50
(10)	Whitey Ford	20.00	10.00	6.00
(11)	Nellie Fox	15.00	7.50	4.50
(12)	Al Kaline	20.00	10.00	6.00
(13a)	Frank Malzone (Red Sox)	12.50	6.25	3.75
(13b)	Frank Malzone (Boston Red Sox)	20.00	10.00	6.00
(14)	Mickey Mantle	75.00	37.50	22.50
(15)	Ed Mathews	20.00	10.00	6.00
(16)	Willie Mays	50.00	25.00	15.00
(17)	Vada Pinson	12.50	6.25	3.75
(18)	Dick Stuart	12.50	6.25	3.75
(19)	Gus Triandos	12.50	6.25	3.75
(20)	Early Wynn	12.50	6.25	3.75

1908 Art Post Card Co. Our Home Team

This set of team post cards presents players from five Midwestern teams in a foldout format. The cover of the accordian-fold novelty is in orange and green. A 3-1/2" x 5-1/2" postcard depicts a ballfield and various pieces of baseball equipment. Printed on a large baseball is "Our Home Team." Folded inside are a number of 2" x 2-1/4" panels with one or two player photos printed on each side. Each player is identified, though misspelled names are common.

	NM	EX	VG
Complete Set (5):	5,500	2,750	1,650
Common Team Card:	800.00	400.00	250.00

		NM	EX	VG
(1)	Chicago Cubs (Three Finger Brown, Frank Chance, Johnny Evers, Chick Fraser, Solly Hofman, Johnny Kling, Carl Lundgren, Pat Moran, Jake Pfeister, Ed Reulbach, Wildfire Schulte, Jimmy Sheckard, Jimmy Slagle, Harry Steinfeldt, Joe Tinker, Heinie Zimmerman)	1,200	600.00	360.00
(2)	Chicago White Sox (Nick Altrock, John Anderson, Jake Atz, George Davis, Jiggs Donohue (Donahue), Patsy Dougherty, Eddie Hahn, Frank Isbell, Fielder Jones, Frank Owen, George Rohe, Billy Sullivan, Lee Tannehill, Ed Walsh, Doc White)	1,850	925.00	550.00
(3)	Detroit Tigers (William Caughlin (Coughlin), Ty Cobb, Sam Crawford, Wild Bill Donovan, Red Downs, Hughie Jennings, Davy Jones, Red Killifer, Ed Killian, Matty McIntyre, George Mullin, Charley O'Leary, Fred Payne, Claude Rossman, Germany Schaefer, Boss Schmidt, George Suggs, Ed Summers, Ira Thomas, George Winter, Ed Willett)	2,000	1,000	600.00
(4)	St. Louis Browns (Bob Bailey, Bert Blue, Dode Criss, Bill Dinneen, Hobe Ferris, Bill Graham, Roy Hartzell, Danny Hoffman, Harry Howell, Charlie Jones, Tom Jones, Jimmy McAleer, Jack O'Connor, Barney Pelty, Jack Powell, Al Schweitzer, Tubby Spencer, George Stone, Rube Waddell, Bobby Wallace, Jimmy Williams, Joe Yeager)	950.00	475.00	285.00
(5)	St. Louis Cardinals	800.00	400.00	240.00

1953-55 Artvue Hall of Fame Plaque Postcards - Type 1

From 1953-1963, Artvue was the official producer of the Baseball Hall of Fame's postcards available for public sale. The 3-1/2" x 5-1/2" black-and-white cards depict the bronze plaque of each inductee. Fronts have a white border. Postcard-style backs have a bit of player data and identification of the specific producer. On Type 1 Artvue cards, issued 1953-55, the bolt holes in the four corners of the plaque are open. The Type 2 Artvues have baseball bolts in each corner of the plaque. The unnumbered cards are checklisted here alphabetically.

		NM	EX	VG
	Complete Set (79):	2,000	1,000	600.00
	Common Player:	30.00	15.00	9.00
(1)	G.C. Alexander	30.00	15.00	9.00
(2)	Adrian Anson	30.00	15.00	9.00
(3)	Frank Baker	30.00	15.00	9.00
(4)	Ed Barrow	30.00	15.00	9.00
(5)	Chief Bender	30.00	15.00	9.00
(6)	Roger Bresnahan	30.00	15.00	9.00
(7)	Dan Brouthers	30.00	15.00	9.00
(8)	Mordecai Brown	30.00	15.00	9.00
(9)	Morgan Bulkeley	30.00	15.00	9.00
(10)	Jesse Burkett	30.00	15.00	9.00
(11)	Alexander Cartwright	30.00	15.00	9.00
(12)	Henry Chadwick	30.00	15.00	9.00
(13)	Frank Chance	30.00	15.00	9.00
(14)	Jack Chesbro	30.00	15.00	9.00
(15)	Fred Clarke	30.00	15.00	9.00
(16)	Ty Cobb	80.00	40.00	24.00
(17)	Mickey Cochrane	30.00	15.00	9.00
(18)	Eddie Collins	30.00	15.00	9.00
(19)	Jimmy Collins	30.00	15.00	9.00
(20)	Charles Comiskey	30.00	15.00	9.00
(21)	Tom Connolly	30.00	15.00	9.00
(22)	Candy Cummings	30.00	15.00	9.00
(23)	Dizzy Dean	30.00	15.00	9.00
(24)	Ed Delahanty	30.00	15.00	9.00
(25)	Bill Dickey	30.00	15.00	9.00
(26)	Joe DiMaggio	80.00	40.00	24.00
(27)	Hugh Duffy	30.00	15.00	9.00
(28)	Johnny Evers	30.00	15.00	9.00
(29)	Buck Ewing	30.00	15.00	9.00
(30)	Jimmie Foxx	30.00	15.00	9.00
(31)	Frankie Frisch	30.00	15.00	9.00
(32)	Lou Gehrig	90.00	45.00	27.50
(33)	Charlie Gehringer	30.00	15.00	9.00
(34)	Clark Griffith	30.00	15.00	9.00
(35)	Lefty Grove	30.00	15.00	9.00
(36)	Gabby Hartnett	30.00	15.00	9.00
(37)	Harry Heilmann	30.00	15.00	9.00
(38)	Rogers Hornsby	30.00	15.00	9.00
(39)	Carl Hubbell	30.00	15.00	9.00
(40)	Hughie Jennings	30.00	15.00	9.00
(41)	Ban Johnson	30.00	15.00	9.00
(42)	Walter Johnson	60.00	30.00	18.00
(43)	Willie Keeler	30.00	15.00	9.00
(44)	King Kelly	30.00	15.00	9.00
(45)	Bill Klem	30.00	15.00	9.00
(46)	Nap Lajoie	30.00	15.00	9.00
(47)	Kenesaw Landis	30.00	15.00	9.00
(48)	Ted Lyons	30.00	15.00	9.00
(49)	Connie Mack	30.00	15.00	9.00
(50)	Rabbit Maranville	30.00	15.00	9.00
(51)	Christy Mathewson	60.00	30.00	18.00
(52)	Tommy McCarthy	30.00	15.00	9.00
(53)	Joe McGinnity	30.00	15.00	9.00
(54)	John McGraw	30.00	15.00	9.00
(55)	Kid Nichols	30.00	15.00	9.00
(56)	Jim O'Rourke	30.00	15.00	9.00
(57)	Mel Ott	30.00	15.00	9.00
(58)	Herb Pennock	30.00	15.00	9.00
(59)	Ed Plank	30.00	15.00	9.00
(60)	Chas. Radbourn	30.00	15.00	9.00
(61)	Wilbert Robinson	30.00	15.00	9.00
(62)	Babe Ruth	120.00	60.00	35.00
(63)	Ray Schalk	30.00	15.00	9.00
(64)	Al Simmons	30.00	15.00	9.00
(65)	George Sisler	30.00	15.00	9.00
(66)	Al Spalding	30.00	15.00	9.00
(67)	Tris Speaker	30.00	15.00	9.00
(68)	Bill Terry	30.00	15.00	9.00
(69)	Joe Tinker	30.00	15.00	9.00
(70)	Pie Traynor	30.00	15.00	9.00
(71)	Dazzy Vance	30.00	15.00	9.00
(72)	Rube Waddell	30.00	15.00	9.00
(73)	Honus Wagner	60.00	30.00	18.00
(74)	Bobby Wallace	30.00	15.00	9.00
(75)	Ed Walsh	30.00	15.00	9.00
(76)	Paul Waner	30.00	15.00	9.00
(77)	George Wright	30.00	15.00	9.00
(78)	Harry Wright	30.00	15.00	9.00
(79)	Cy Young	60.00	30.00	18.00

1956-63 Artvue Hall of Fame Plaque Postcards - Type 2

From 1953-1963, Artvue was the official producer of the Baseball Hall of Fame's postcards available for public sale. The 3-1/2" x 5-1/2" black-and-white cards depict the bronze plaque of each inductee. Fronts have a white border. Postcard-style backs have a bit of player data and identification of the specific producer. On Type 2 Artvue cards, issued 1956-63, there are baseball bolts in each corner of the plaque. The unnumbered cards are checklisted here alphabetically. Players unique to Type 2 are noted with an asterisk.

		NM	EX	VG
	Complete Set (94):	2,000	1,000	600.00
	Common Player:	25.00	12.50	7.50
(1)	G.C. Alexander	25.00	12.50	7.50
(2)	Adrian Anson	25.00	12.50	7.50
(3)	Frank Baker	25.00	12.50	7.50
(4)	Ed Barrow	25.00	12.50	7.50
(5)	Chief Bender	25.00	12.50	7.50
(6)	Roger Bresnahan	25.00	12.50	7.50
(7)	Dan Brouthers	25.00	12.50	7.50
(8)	Mordecai Brown	25.00	12.50	7.50
(9)	Morgan Bulkeley	25.00	12.50	7.50
(10)	Jesse Burkett	25.00	12.50	7.50
(11)	Max Carey (*)	25.00	12.50	7.50
(12)	Alexander Cartwright	25.00	12.50	7.50
(13)	Henry Chadwick	25.00	12.50	7.50
(14)	Frank Chance	25.00	12.50	7.50
(15)	Jack Chesbro	25.00	12.50	7.50
(16)	Fred Clarke	25.00	12.50	7.50
(17)	John Clarkson (*)	25.00	12.50	7.50
(18)	Ty Cobb	60.00	30.00	18.00
(19)	Mickey Cochrane	25.00	12.50	7.50
(20)	Eddie Collins	25.00	12.50	7.50
(21)	Jimmy Collins	25.00	12.50	7.50
(22)	Charles Comiskey	25.00	12.50	7.50
(23)	Tom Connolly	25.00	12.50	7.50
(24)	Sam Crawford (*)	25.00	12.50	7.50
(25)	Joe Cronin (*)	25.00	12.50	7.50
(26)	Candy Cummings	25.00	12.50	7.50
(27)	Dizzy Dean	25.00	12.50	7.50
(28)	Ed Delahanty	25.00	12.50	7.50
(29)	Bill Dickey	25.00	12.50	7.50
(30)	Joe DiMaggio	80.00	40.00	24.00
(31)	Hugh Duffy	25.00	12.50	7.50
(32)	Johnny Evers	25.00	12.50	7.50
(33)	Buck Ewing	25.00	12.50	7.50
(34)	Bob Feller (*)	25.00	12.50	7.50
(35)	Elmer Flick (*)	25.00	12.50	7.50
(36)	Jimmie Foxx	25.00	12.50	7.50
(37)	Frank Frisch	25.00	12.50	7.50
(38)	Lou Gehrig	80.00	40.00	24.00
(39)	Charlie Gehringer	25.00	12.50	7.50
(40)	Hank Greenberg (*)	25.00	12.50	7.50
(41)	Clark Griffith	25.00	12.50	7.50
(42)	Lefty Grove	25.00	12.50	7.50
(43)	Billy Hamilton (*)	25.00	12.50	7.50
(44)	Gabby Hartnett	25.00	12.50	7.50
(45)	Harry Heilmann	25.00	12.50	7.50
(46)	Rogers Hornsby	25.00	12.50	7.50
(47)	Carl Hubbell	25.00	12.50	7.50
(48)	Hughie Jennings	25.00	12.50	7.50
(49)	Ban Johnson	25.00	12.50	7.50
(50)	Walter Johnson	40.00	20.00	12.00
(51)	Willie Keeler	25.00	12.50	7.50
(52)	King Kelly	25.00	12.50	7.50
(53)	Bill Klem	25.00	12.50	7.50
(54)	Nap Lajoie	25.00	12.50	7.50
(55)	Kenesaw Landis	25.00	12.50	7.50
(56)	Ted Lyons	25.00	12.50	7.50
(57)	Connie Mack	25.00	12.50	7.50
(58)	Rabbit Maranville	25.00	12.50	7.50
(59)	Christy Mathewson	40.00	20.00	12.00
(60)	Joe McCarthy (*)	25.00	12.50	7.50
(61)	Tommy McCarthy	25.00	12.50	7.50
(62)	Joe McGinnity	25.00	12.50	7.50
(63)	John McGraw	25.00	12.50	7.50
(64)	Bill McKechnie (*)	25.00	12.50	7.50
(65)	Kid Nichols	25.00	12.50	7.50
(66)	Jim O'Rourke	25.00	12.50	7.50
(67)	Mel Ott	25.00	12.50	7.50
(68)	Herb Pennock	25.00	12.50	7.50
(69)	Ed Plank	25.00	12.50	7.50
(70)	Charles Radbourn	25.00	12.50	7.50
(71)	Sam Rice (*)	25.00	12.50	7.50
(72)	Eppa Rixey (*)	25.00	12.50	7.50
(73)	Jackie Robinson (*)	40.00	20.00	12.00
(74)	Wilbert Robinson	25.00	12.50	7.50
(75)	Edd Roush (*)	25.00	12.50	7.50
(76)	Babe Ruth	120.00	60.00	35.00
(77)	Ray Schalk	25.00	12.50	7.50
(78)	Al Simmons	25.00	12.50	7.50
(79)	George Sisler	25.00	12.50	7.50
(80)	Albert Spalding	25.00	12.50	7.50
(81)	Tris Speaker	25.00	12.50	7.50
(82)	Bill Terry	25.00	12.50	7.50
(83)	Joe Tinker	25.00	12.50	7.50
(84)	Pie Traynor	25.00	12.50	7.50
(85)	Dazzy Vance	25.00	12.50	7.50
(86)	Rube Waddell	25.00	12.50	7.50
(87)	Honus Wagner	40.00	20.00	12.00
(88)	Bobby Wallace	25.00	12.50	7.50
(89)	Ed Walsh	25.00	12.50	7.50
(90)	Paul Waner	25.00	12.50	7.50
(91)	Zack Wheat (*)	25.00	12.50	7.50
(92)	George Wright	25.00	12.50	7.50
(93)	Harry Wright	25.00	12.50	7.50
(94)	Cy Young	40.00	20.00	12.00

1967 Ashland Oil Grand Slam Baseball

These baseball player folders were issued in conjunction with a sweepstakes conducted at Ashland gas stations. The cards were originally issued in the form of a sealed tri-fold. When opened to 7-1/2" x 2", a black-and-white player photo is pictured at center. Back of the panel offers contest rules. The unnumbered panels are listed here in alphabetical order. (Note: The existence of the Jim Maloney card is now in question.)

		NM	EX	VG
	Complete Set (12):	375.00	185.00	110.00
	Common Player:	20.00	10.00	6.00
(1)	Jim Bunning	30.00	15.00	9.00
(2)	Elston Howard	25.00	12.50	7.50
(3)	Al Kaline	50.00	25.00	15.00
(4)	Harmon Killebrew	30.00	15.00	9.00
(5)	Ed Kranepool	20.00	10.00	6.00
(6)	Jim Maloney (SP) (Existence now in question.)	75.00	37.00	22.00
(7)	Bill Mazeroski	30.00	15.00	9.00
(8)	Frank Robinson	40.00	20.00	12.00
(9)	Ron Santo	25.00	12.50	7.50
(10)	Joe Torre	25.00	12.50	7.50
(11)	Leon Wagner	20.00	10.00	6.00
(12)	Pete Ward	20.00	10.00	6.00

1895 Ashman Studio Cabinets

The date attributed is speculative and about at the mid-point of the sole known subject's tenure with the Baltimore Orioles of the National League. In typical cabinet format, about 4-1/2" x 6-1/2", the card features a sepia-toned portrait photo attached to a blank-back, cream-colored thick cardboard mount bearing the advertising at bottom of the Baltimore photographer's studio. It is unknown whether cabinets of any of McGraw's teammates or adversaries were also produced.

	NM	EX	VG
John McGraw	10,000	5,000	3,000

1933 Astra Margarine

One of several "foreign" Babe Ruth cards issued during his prime was included in a 112-card set produced as premiums for Astra Margarine in Germany. Ruth is the only major league ballplayer in the issue. Cards are in full color, measuring 2-3/4" x 4-1/8". Backs of the unnumbered cards are printed in German. Three types of backs can be found on the Ruth card. Type 1, has the Astra name nearly centered. The Type 2 back has the brand name printed closer to the bottom of the card, with only four lines of type under it. Type 3 is a variation of Type 2 on which the appropriate page number (83) of the accompanying album is mentioned on the line immediately above "Handbuch des Sports" near the top. One card was given with the purchase of each 1/2 pound of margarine and the album could be ordered by mail. See also Sanella Margarine.

	NM	EX	VG
Type 1 Babe Ruth (Astra centered.)	1,500	750.00	450.00
Type 2 Babe Ruth (Astra at bottom.)	1,750	875.00	525.00
Type 3 Babe Ruth	3,500	1,750	1,000
(Astra at bottom w/83.)			

1978 Atlanta Nobis Center

In conjunction with a May 1978 card show to benefit the training/rehabilitation center supported by Hall of Fame linebacker Tommy Nobis, this collectors' set was issued. Most of the players on the 2-1/2" x 3-1/2" cards are former stars of the Boston, Milwaukee or Atlanta Braves, though players from a few other teams and footballer Nobis are also included; several of the players appeared at the show as autograph guests. The cards are in the style of 1959 Topps, with black-and-white player photos in a circle at center and a light green background. The career summary on back is in black-and-white. The unnumbered cards are checklisted here in alphabetical order.

	NM	EX	VG
Complete Set (24):	25.00	12.50	7.50
Common Player:	1.50	.70	.45
(1) Hank Aaron	6.00	3.00	1.75
(2) Joe Adcock	1.50	.70	.45
(3) Felipe Alou	1.50	.70	.45
(4) Frank Bolling	1.50	.70	.45
(5) Orlando Cepeda	2.00	1.00	.60

		NM	EX	VG
(6)	Ty Cline	1.50	.70	.45
(7)	Tony Cloninger	1.50	.70	.45
(8)	Del Crandall	1.50	.70	.45
(9)	Fred Haney	1.50	.70	.45
(10)	Pat Jarvis	1.50	.70	.45
(11)	Ernie Johnson	1.50	.70	.45
(12)	Ken Johnson	1.50	.70	.45
(13)	Denny Lemaster	1.50	.70	.45
(14)	Eddie Mathews	2.00	1.00	.60
(15)	Lee Maye	1.50	.70	.45
(16)	Denis Menke	1.50	.70	.45
(17)	Felix Millan	1.50	.70	.45
(18)	Johnny Mize	2.00	1.00	.60
(19)	Tommy Nobis	1.50	.70	.45
(20)	Gene Oliver	1.50	.70	.45
(21)	Johnny Sain	1.75	.90	.50
(22)	Warren Spahn	2.00	1.00	.60
(23)	Joe Torre	2.00	1.00	.60
(24)	Bob Turley	1.75	.90	.50

1968 Atlantic Oil Play Ball Game Cards

Because some of the cards were redeemable either alone or in combination for cash awards, and thus were issued in lesser quantities, completion of this game issue was difficult from Day 1. Fifty different players are known in the issue, along with a number of variations. The majority of the cards can be found with card backs either explaining the game rules or picturing a pitcher throwing to a batter. The cards were issued in two-card panels, designed to be separated into a pair of 2-1/2" x 3-1/2" cards. For lack of an MLB license, the color player photos at center have the uniform logos removed. Printed at top is the face value of the particular card, while the player's name, team and league are printed in the bottom border. A large player number is printed in a white circle at bottom-right. American Leaguers' cards are bordered in red, while the National League cards have blue borders.

		NM	EX	VG
Complete Set (Non-winners.) (40):		350.00	175.00	100.00
Common Player:		6.00	3.00	1.50
Instant Winner Card:		30.00	15.00	9.00
AMERICAN LEAGUE				
1a	Tony Oliva	6.00	3.00	1.75
1b	Brooks Robinson	15.00	7.50	4.50
1c	Pete Ward	6.00	3.00	1.75
2a	Max Alvis	6.00	3.00	1.75
2b	Campy Campaneris	6.00	3.00	1.75
2c	Jim Fregosi	6.00	3.00	1.75
2d	Al Kaline	20.00	10.00	6.00
2e	Tom Tresh	6.00	3.00	1.75
3	Bill Freehan ($2,500 winner)	300.00	150.00	90.00
4	Tommy Davis ($100 winner)	100.00	50.00	30.00
5a	Norm Cash	7.50	3.75	2.25
5b	Frank Robinson	15.00	7.50	4.50
5c	Carl Yastrzemski	25.00	12.50	7.50
6a	Joe Pepitone	7.50	3.75	2.25
6b	Boog Powell	10.00	5.00	3.00
6c	George Scott	6.00	3.00	1.75
6d	Fred Valentine	6.00	3.00	1.75
7	Tom McCraw ($10 winner)	75.00	37.00	22.00
8	Andy Etchebarren ($5 winner)	50.00	25.00	15.00
9a	Dean Chance	6.00	3.00	1.75
9b	Joel Horlen	6.00	3.00	1.75
9c	Jim Lonborg	6.00	3.00	1.75
9d	Sam McDowell	6.00	3.00	1.75
10	Earl Wilson ($1 winner)	35.00	17.50	10.50
11	Jose Santiago	6.00	3.00	1.75
NATIONAL LEAGUE				
1a	Bob Aspromonte	6.00	3.00	1.75
1b	Lou Brock	12.00	6.00	3.50
1c	Johnny Callison	6.00	3.00	1.75
1d	Pete Rose	25.00	12.50	7.50
1e	Maury Wills	7.50	3.75	2.25
2	Tommie Agee ($2,500 winner)	300.00	150.00	90.00
3a	Felipe Alou	7.50	3.75	2.25
3b	Jim Hart	6.00	3.00	1.75
3c	Vada Pinson	7.50	3.75	2.25
4a	Hank Aaron	25.00	12.50	7.50
4b	Orlando Cepeda	10.00	5.00	3.00
4c	Willie McCovey	12.00	6.00	3.50
4d	Ron Santo	9.00	4.50	2.75
5	Ernie Banks ($100 winner)	450.00	225.00	135.00
6	Ron Fairly ($10 winner)	75.00	37.50	22.50
7a	Roberto Clemente	75.00	37.50	22.50
7b	Roger Maris	25.00	12.50	7.50
7c a	Ron Swoboda	6.00	3.00	1.75
	(Collect w/ N.L. #6, win $10.)			
7c b	Ron Swoboda	45.00	22.00	13.50
	(Collect w/ N.L. #8, win $5.)			
8	Billy Williams ($5 winner)	95.00	47.00	28.00
9a	Jim Bunning	9.00	4.50	2.75
9b	Bob Gibson	12.00	6.00	3.50
9c	Jim Maloney	6.00	3.00	1.75
9d	Mike McCormick	6.00	3.00	1.75
10	Milt Pappas	6.00	3.00	1.75
11	Claude Osteen ($1 winner)	35.00	17.50	10.00

1969 Atlantic-Richfield Boston Red Sox

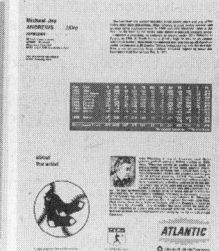

One of many larger-format (8" x 10") baseball premiums sponsored as gas station giveaways in the late 1960s and early 1970s was this set of Boston Red Sox player pictures by celebrity artist John Wheeldon sponsored by the Atlantic-Richfield Oil Co. Done in pastel colors, the pictures feature large portraits and smaller action pictures of the player against a bright background. A facsimile autograph is pencilled in beneath the pictures, and the player's name is printed in the white bottom border. Backs are printed in black-and-white and include biographical and career data, full major and minor legaue stats, a self-portrait and biography of the artist and the logos of the team, players' association and sponsor. The unnumbered pictures are checklisted here alphabetically.

		NM	EX	VG
Complete Set (12):		75.00	35.00	25.00
Common Player:		6.00	3.00	1.75
(1)	Mike Andrews	6.00	3.00	1.75
(2)	Tony Conigliaro	10.00	5.00	3.00
(3)	Ray Culp	6.00	3.00	1.75
(4)	Russ Gibson	6.00	3.00	1.75
(5)	Dalton Jones	6.00	3.00	1.75
(6)	Jim Lonborg	8.00	4.00	2.50
(7)	Sparky Lyle	8.00	4.00	2.50
(8)	Syd O'Brien	6.00	3.00	1.75
(9)	George Scott	8.00	4.00	2.50
(10)	Reggie Smith	8.00	4.00	2.50
(11)	Rico Petrocelli	8.00	4.00	2.50
(12)	Carl Yastrzemski	25.00	12.50	7.50

1962 Auravision Records

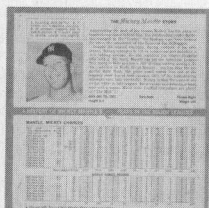

Similar in design and format to the 16-record set which was issued in 1964, this test issue can be differentiated by the stats on the back. On the 1962 record, Mantle is shown in a right-handed batting pose, as compared to a follow-through on the 1964 record. Where Gentile and Colavito are shown in the uniform of K.C. A's on the 1964 records, they are shown as a Tiger (Colavito) and Oriole (Gentile) on the earlier version. The set is checklisted here alphabetically.

		NM	EX	VG
Complete Set (8):		300.00	150.00	90.00
Common Player:		15.00	7.50	4.50
(1)	Ernie Banks	30.00	15.00	9.00
(2)	Rocky Colavito	25.00	12.50	7.50
(3)	Whitey Ford	30.00	15.00	9.00
(4)	Jim Gentile	15.00	7.50	4.50
(5)	Mickey Mantle	100.00	50.00	30.00
(6)	Roger Maris	35.00	17.50	10.50
(7)	Willie Mays	50.00	25.00	15.00
(8)	Warren Spahn	30.00	15.00	9.00

1964 Auravision Records

Never a candidate for the Billboard "Hot 100," this series of baseball picture records is popular with collectors due to the high-quality photos on front and back. On the grooved front side of the 6-3/4" x 6-3/4" plastic-laminated cardboard record is a color player photo with facsimile autograph, Sports Record trophy logo and 33-1/3 RPM notation. A color border surrounds the photo and is carried over to the unrecorded back side. There is another photo on back, along with a career summary and complete major and minor league stats and instructions for playing the record. In the bottom border is a copyright notice by Sports Champions Inc., and a notice that the Auravision Record is a product of Columbia Records. A hole at center of the record could be punched out for playing and the records featured a five-minute interview with the player by sportscaster Marty Glickman. The records were originally a mail-in premium available through an offer on Milk Dud candy boxes. Large quantities of the records made their way into the hobby as remainders. For early-1960s baseball items they remain reasonably priced today. The unnumbered records are checklisted here alphabetically. The Mays record is unaccountably much scarcer than the others.

		NM	EX	VG
Complete Set (16):		150.00	75.00	45.00
Common Player:		6.00	3.00	1.75
(1)	Bob Allison	6.00	3.00	1.75
(2)	Ernie Banks	9.00	4.50	2.75
(3)	Ken Boyer	6.00	3.00	1.75
(4)	Rocky Colavito	7.50	3.75	2.25
(5)	Don Drysdale	9.00	4.50	2.75
(6)	Whitey Ford	10.00	5.00	3.00
(7)	Jim Gentile	6.00	3.00	1.75
(8)	Al Kaline	10.00	5.00	3.00
(9)	Sandy Koufax	20.00	10.00	6.00
(10)	Mickey Mantle	25.00	12.50	7.50
(11)	Roger Maris	12.50	6.25	3.75
(12)	Willie Mays	75.00	37.50	22.50
(13)	Bill Mazeroski	9.00	4.50	2.75
(14)	Frank Robinson	9.00	4.50	2.75
(15)	Warren Spahn	9.00	4.50	2.75
(16)	Pete Ward	6.00	3.00	1.75

1945 Autographs Game

Politicians, movie stars and athletes are among the celebrities featured in this game from Leister Game Co. The 2-1/2" x 3-1/2" cards are printed in red and black on white and were issued in pairs. The celebrity whose signature was reproduced on the card was seen in a photograph and top, while his paired partner was shown at bottom in an artist's depiction. Only two baseball players are included in the set.

		NM	EX	VG
Complete Boxed Set (55):		650.00	325.00	195.00
9A	Joe DiMaggio, Babe Ruth (DiMaggio signature.)	75.00	37.50	22.50
9A	Babe Ruth, Joe DiMaggio (Ruth signature.)	125.00	62.50	37.50

B

1949 Baas Cheri-Cola

 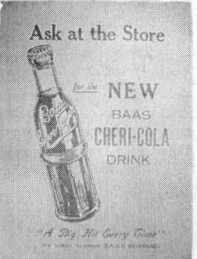

Only five of these premium issues have ever been cataloged so it's unknown how many comprise a set. The 7-5/8" x 9-1/2" pictures feature black-and-white player photos on front, with the player's name printed in white script. On back, printed in red, is an ad for Baas Cheri-Cola Drink. The unnumbered pictures are checklisted in alphabetical order.

		NM	EX	VG
Common Player:		125.00	65.00	40.00
(1)	Bobby Doerr	150.00	75.00	45.00
(2)	Bob Feller	250.00	125.00	75.00
(3)	Ken Keltner	125.00	65.00	40.00
(4)	John Sain	125.00	65.00	40.00
(5)	Ted Williams	600.00	300.00	180.00

1930 Baguer Chocolate

This rare Cuban issue was apparently current between the start of the 1930 season and the redemption expiration date of Jan. 31, 1931. The set consists of 90 black-and-white player photos, about 5/8" x 7/8". The pictures have white bor-

 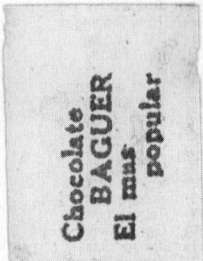

ders and a white strip at the bottom of photo with some form of the player's name. Backs are printed in red, "Chocolate BAGUER El mas popular." An album was issued to collect the pictures and when full it could be exchanged for baseball equipment, toys or candy. The unnumbered cards are checklisted here in alphabetical order.

		NM	EX	VG
Complete Set (90):		5,500	3,750	2,200
Common Player:		30.00	20.00	12.00
Album:		75.00	52.00	30.00
(1)	George Bancroft (Dave)	65.00	45.00	25.00
(2)	Clyde Beck	30.00	20.00	12.00
(3)	Larry Benton	30.00	20.00	12.00
(4)	Max Bishop	30.00	20.00	12.00
(5)	Clarence Blair	30.00	20.00	12.00
(6)	Fred Blake	30.00	20.00	12.00
(7)	Mitchell Blake (SP)	80.00	55.00	30.00
(8)	Joe Boley	30.00	20.00	12.00
(9)	Jim Bottomley	65.00	45.00	25.00
(10)	George Burns	30.00	20.00	12.00
(11)	Guy Bush	30.00	20.00	12.00
(12)	Mickey Cochrane	75.00	50.00	30.00
(13)	Eddie Collins	75.00	50.00	30.00
(14)	Kiki Cuyler	65.00	45.00	25.00
(15)	Jimmy Dikes (Dykes)	30.00	20.00	12.00
(16)	Leo Dixon	30.00	20.00	12.00
(17)	Pete Donohue	30.00	20.00	12.00
(18)	Taylor Douthit	30.00	20.00	12.00
(19)	George Earnshaw	30.00	20.00	12.00
(20)	R. Elliot (Jumbo Elliott)	30.00	20.00	12.00
(21)	Joe (Woody) English	30.00	20.00	12.00
(22)	Urban Faber	65.00	45.00	25.00
(23)	Lewis Fonseca	30.00	20.00	12.00
(24)	Jimmy Foxx	275.00	190.00	110.00
(25)	Walter French	30.00	20.00	12.00
(26)	Frankie Frisch	75.00	50.00	30.00
(27)	Lou Gehrig	600.00	420.00	240.00
(28)	Walter Gerber	30.00	20.00	12.00
(29)	Miguel A. Gonzalez	65.00	45.00	25.00
(30)	Goose Goslin	65.00	45.00	25.00
(31)	W. Grampp (Henry)	30.00	20.00	12.00
(32)	Burleigh Grimes	65.00	45.00	25.00
(33)	Charlie Grimm	30.00	20.00	12.00
(34)	Lefty Grove	75.00	50.00	30.00
(35)	Geo. Haas	30.00	20.00	12.00
(36)	(Bill) Hallahan	30.00	20.00	12.00
(37)	Stanley Harris	65.00	45.00	25.00
(38)	Geo. (Charles "Gabby") Hartnett	65.00	45.00	25.00
(39)	Cliff Heathcote	30.00	20.00	12.00
(40)	Babe Herman	30.00	20.00	12.00
(41)	Andy High	30.00	20.00	12.00
(42)	Rogers Hornsby	100.00	70.00	40.00
(43)	Dan Howley	30.00	20.00	12.00
(44)	Travis Jackson	65.00	45.00	25.00
(45)	Walter Johnson	250.00	175.00	100.00
(46)	Fred Lindstrom	65.00	45.00	25.00
(47)	Alfonso Lopez	75.00	50.00	30.00
(48)	Red Lucas	30.00	20.00	12.00
(49)	(Dolf) Luque	65.00	45.00	25.00
(50)	Pat Malone	30.00	20.00	12.00
(51)	Harry (Heinie) Manush	65.00	45.00	25.00
(52)	Fred Marberry	30.00	20.00	12.00
(53)	Joe McCarthy	65.00	45.00	25.00
(54)	J.J. McGraw	65.00	45.00	25.00
(55)	G. Mc. Millan (Norman McMillan)	30.00	20.00	12.00
(56)	Bing Miller	30.00	20.00	12.00
(57)	J. (Johnny) Moore	30.00	20.00	12.00
(58)	Buddy Myers (Myer)	30.00	20.00	12.00
(59)	Bob O'Farrell	30.00	20.00	12.00
(60)	Melvin Ott	75.00	50.00	30.00
(61)	Herb Pennock	65.00	45.00	25.00
(62)	Cy Perkins	30.00	20.00	12.00
(63)	Jack Quinn	30.00	20.00	12.00
(64)	Chas. Rhen (Rhem)	30.00	20.00	12.00
(65)	Harry Rice	30.00	20.00	12.00
(66)	Sam Rice	65.00	45.00	35.00
(67)	Lance Richbourg	30.00	20.00	12.00
(68)	W. (Wilbert) Robinson	65.00	45.00	25.00
(69)	Eddie Rommell (Rommel)	30.00	20.00	12.00
(70)	Charles Root	30.00	20.00	12.00
(71)	Muddy Ruel	30.00	20.00	12.00
(72)	Babe Ruth	900.00	630.00	360.00
(73)	Wally Schang	30.00	20.00	12.00
(74)	Bill Shores	30.00	20.00	12.00
(75)	Al Simmons	65.00	45.00	25.00
(76)	Geo. Sisler	75.00	50.00	30.00
(77)	Earl Smith	30.00	20.00	12.00
(78)	Riggs Stephenson	30.00	20.00	12.00
(79)	Joe (Walter "Lefty") Stewart	30.00	20.00	12.00
(80)	H. Summa	30.00	20.00	12.00
(81)	Bill Terry	65.00	45.00	25.00
(82)	Fresco Thompson	30.00	20.00	12.00
(83)	Charley Tolson	30.00	20.00	12.00
(84)	'Pie' Traynor	65.00	45.00	25.00
(85)	Dazzy Vance	65.00	45.00	25.00
(86)	Rube Walberg	30.00	20.00	12.00
(87)	'Hack' Wilson	65.00	45.00	25.00
(88)	Jimmy Wilson	30.00	20.00	12.00
(89)	Glenn Wright	30.00	20.00	12.00
(90)	Tom Zachary	30.00	20.00	12.00

1950s-70s Mel Bailey Player Postcards

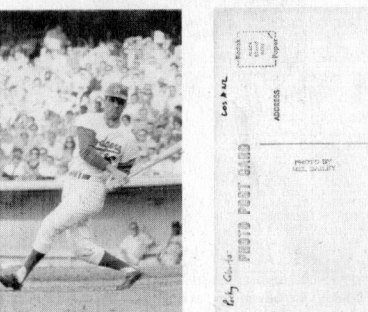

Photographer and hobbyist Mel Bailey was a prolific baseball photographer who produced many player postcards for their use in responding to fan requests for pictures and autographs. Several different formats of back design may be found. No checklist has been promulgated.

(Typical players $3-5; stars and Hall of Famers $10-30.)

1941 Ballantine Coasters

National League pitcher-catcher pairs are featured on this set of drink coasters issued by Ballantine Ale & Beer. The 4-1/2" diameter composition coasters are printed in black with orange, blue or red highlights. Fronts have line drawings of the batterymates and a few words about the previous or coming season. Backs have a Ballantine's ad. It is unknown whether there are more than these three coasters in the series.

		NM	EX	VG
Common Coaster:		35.00	17.50	10.00
(1)	Bob Klinger, Virgil Davis (Pirates)	35.00	17.50	10.00
(2a)	Lon Warneke, Gus Mancuso (Cardinals)("AT THE GAME IT'S . . ." above portraits.)	35.00	17.50	10.00
(2b)	Lon Warneke, Gus Mancuso (Cardinals)("At the Game it's" below portraits.)	35.00	17.50	10.00
(3)	Whit Wyatt, Mickey Owen (Dodgers)	35.00	17.50	10.00

1911 Baltimore News Newsboys Series

This scarce version of E94 carries on its back the notation, "Baltimore News Newsboy Series" and offers $1 to the first 35 boys completing the full set. Unlike the Close Candy Co. cards, the newspaper version is found only with the light blue background on front. The issue was designated M131 in the American Card Catalog.

		NM	EX	VG
Complete Set (30):		85,000	42,500	25,000
Common Player:		3,000	1,500	1,000
(1)	Jimmy Austin	3,000	1,500	1,000
(2)	Johnny Bates	3,000	1,500	1,000
(3)	Bob Bescher	3,000	1,500	1,000
(4)	Bobby Byrne	3,000	1,500	1,000
(5)	Frank Chance	7,500	3,750	2,250
(6)	Ed Cicotte	6,000	3,000	1,800
(7)	Ty Cobb	75,000	37,500	22,500
(8)	Sam Crawford	7,500	3,750	2,250
(9)	Harry Davis	3,000	1,500	1,000

		NM	EX	VG
(10)	Art Devlin	3,000	1,500	1,000
(11)	Josh Devore	3,000	1,500	1,000
(12)	Mickey Doolan	3,000	1,500	1,000
(13)	Patsy Dougherty	3,000	1,500	1,000
(14)	Johnny Evers	7,500	3,750	2,250
(15)	Eddie Grant	3,000	1,500	1,000
(16)	Hugh Jennings	7,500	3,750	2,250
(17)	Red Kleinow	3,000	1,500	1,000
(18)	Joe Lake	3,000	1,500	1,000
(19)	Nap Lajoie	9,000	4,500	2,700
(20)	Tommy Leach	3,000	1,500	1,000
(21)	Hans Lobert	3,000	1,500	1,000
(22)	Harry Lord	3,000	1,500	1,000
(23)	Sherry Magee	3,000	1,500	1,000
(24)	John McGraw	11,250	5,625	3,375
(25)	Earl Moore	3,000	1,500	1,000
(26)	Red Murray	3,000	1,500	1,000
(27)	Tris Speaker	13,500	6,750	4,050
(28)	Terry Turner	3,000	1,500	1,000
(29)	Honus Wagner	55,500	27,750	16,650
(30)	"Old" Cy. Young	22,500	11,250	6,750

1914 Baltimore News Terrapins

Players from both of Baltimore's professional baseball teams are included in this set of schedule cards from the local newspaper. That season fans could support the Orioles of the International League or the Terrapins of the Federal League. The newspaper's cards are 2-5/8" x 3-5/8", monochrome printed in either red or blue with a wide border. Players are pictured in full-length posed action photos with the backgrounds erased in favor of a few artificial shadows. The player name, position and league are shown on front. Backs have a schedule "AT HOME" and "ABROAD" of the appropriate team with an ad for the paper at top and a curious line at bottom which reads, "This Card is Given to," with space for a signature. The unnumbered cards are checklisted here in alphabetical order, though it is presumed the checklist is incomplete. Only the Federal Leaguers' cards are listed here; the Orioles will be found in the minor league section of this catalog. This scarce version of E94 carries on its back the notation, "Baltimore Newsboy Series." Unlike the Close Candy Co. cards, the newspaper version is found only with the light blue background on front.

		NM	EX	VG
Common Player:		8,800	4,400	2,640
(1)	Neal Ball	8,800	4,400	2,640
(2)	Mike Doolan	8,800	4,400	2,640
(3)	Happy Finneran	8,800	4,400	2,640
(4)	Fred Jacklitch (Jacklitsch)	8,800	4,400	2,640
(5)	Otto Knabe	8,800	4,400	2,640
(6)	Benny Meyers (Meyer)	8,800	4,400	2,640
(7)	Jack Quinn	8,800	4,400	2,640
(8)	Hack Simmons	8,800	4,400	2,640
(9)	Frank Smith	8,800	4,400	2,640
(10)	George Suggs	8,800	4,400	2,640
(11)	Harry (Swats) Swacina	8,800	4,400	2,640
(12)	Ducky Yount	8,800	4,400	2,640
(13)	Guy Zinn	8,800	4,400	2,640

1954 Baltimore Orioles Picture Pack

This appears to be a team-issued photo pack in the O's first season after moving from St. Louis. The black-and-white poses are 6" x 8" in format, bordered in white and blank-backed. Pictures have a facsimile autograph on front. At least three versions of the photo pack were issued over the course of the season to reflect roster changes. It is unknown whether this checklist is complete.

		NM	EX	VG
Complete Set (33):		600.00	300.00	180.00
Common Player:		20.00	10.00	6.00
(1)	Cal Abrams	20.00	10.00	6.00
(2)	Neil Berry	20.00	10.00	6.00
(3)	Vern Bickford	20.00	10.00	6.00
(4)	Jim Brideweser	20.00	10.00	6.00
(5)	Bob Chakales	20.00	10.00	6.00
(6)	Gil Coan	20.00	10.00	6.00
(7)	Joe Coleman	20.00	10.00	6.00
(8)	Clint Courtney	20.00	10.00	6.00
(9)	Chuck Diering	20.00	10.00	6.00
(10)	Jim Dyck	20.00	10.00	6.00
(11)	Howie Fox	20.00	10.00	6.00
(12)	Jim Fridley (Batting)	20.00	10.00	6.00
(13)	Jim Fridley (Portrait)	20.00	10.00	6.00
(14)	Jehosie Heard	25.00	12.50	7.50
(15)	Bill Hunter	20.00	10.00	6.00
(16)	Darrell Johnson	20.00	10.00	6.00
(17)	Dick Kokos	20.00	10.00	6.00
(18)	Lou Kretlow	20.00	10.00	6.00
(19)	Dick Kryhoski	20.00	10.00	6.00
(20)	Don Larsen	40.00	20.00	12.00
(21)	Don Lenhardt	20.00	10.00	6.00
(22)	Dick Littlefield	20.00	10.00	6.00

		NM	EX	VG
(23)	Sam Mele	20.00	10.00	6.00
(24)	Les Moss	20.00	10.00	6.00
(25)	Ray Murray	20.00	10.00	6.00
(26)	Billy O'Dell	20.00	10.00	6.00
(27)	Duane Pillette	20.00	10.00	6.00
(28)	Vern Stephens	20.00	10.00	6.00
(29)	Marlin Stuart	20.00	10.00	6.00
(30)	Bob Turley	40.00	20.00	12.00
(31)	Eddie Waitkus	20.00	10.00	6.00
(32)	Vic Wertz	25.00	12.50	7.50
(33)	Bob Young	20.00	10.00	6.00

1958 Baltimore Orioles Team Issue

CLIFFORD CONNIE JOHNSON
(CONNIE)

These blank-backed, black-and-white cards are approximately postcard size at 3-1/4" x 5-1/2" and feature posed portraits of the players printed on semi-gloss cardboard. The unnumbered cards are checklisted here alphabetically.

		NM	EX	VG
Complete Set (16):		165.00	82.00	49.00
Common Player:		12.00	6.00	3.50
(1)	Bob Boyd	12.00	6.00	3.50
(2)	Harry Brecheen	12.00	6.00	3.50
(3)	Hal Brown	12.00	6.00	3.50
(4)	Jim Busby	12.00	6.00	3.50
(5)	Foster Castleman	12.00	6.00	3.50
(6)	Billy Gardner	12.00	6.00	3.50
(7)	Connie Johnson	12.00	6.00	3.50
(8)	Ken Lehman	12.00	6.00	3.50
(9)	Willie Miranda	12.00	6.00	3.50
(10)	Bob Nieman	12.00	6.00	3.50
(11)	Paul Richards	12.00	6.00	3.50
(12)	Brooks Robinson	36.00	18.00	11.00
(13)	Gus Triandos	12.00	6.00	3.50
(14)	Dick Williams	12.00	6.00	3.50
(15)	Gene Woodling	18.00	9.00	5.50
(16)	George Zuverink	12.00	6.00	3.50

1970 Baltimore Orioles Traffic Safety

DAVE JOHNSON
2ND BASE

Baltimore
Orioles

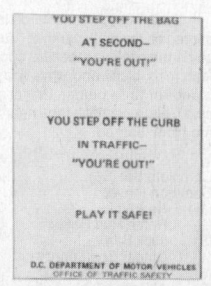

YOU STEP OFF THE BAG
AT SECOND—
"YOU'RE OUT!"

YOU STEP OFF THE CURB
IN TRAFFIC—
"YOU'RE OUT!"

PLAY IT SAFE!

D.C. DEPARTMENT OF MOTOR VEHICLES
OFFICE OF TRAFFIC SAFETY

Similar in concept and design to the much more common Washington Senators safety issue of the same year, the Orioles cards are printed on yellow paper in 2-1/2" x 3-7/8" format. Fronts have player photo, name, and position; backs have a safety message and notice of sponsorship by the D.C. Department of Motor Vehicles Office of Traffic Safety.

		NM	EX	VG
Complete Set (10):		25.00	12.50	7.50
Common Player:		2.50	1.25	.75
(1)	Mark Bellanger (Belanger)	2.50	1.25	.75
(2)	Paul Blair	2.50	1.25	.75
(3)	Don Buford	2.50	1.25	.75
(4)	Mike Cuellar (Back in Spanish.)	4.00	2.00	1.25
(5)	Dave Johnson	2.50	1.25	.75
(6)	Dave McNally	2.50	1.25	.75
(7)	Boog Powell	5.00	2.50	1.50
(8)	Merv Rettenmund	2.50	1.25	.75
(9)	Brooks Robinson	10.00	5.00	3.00
(10)	Earl Weaver	3.50	1.75	1.00

1971 Bank of Montreal Rusty Staub

This 4" x 6" color card was issued by the Bank of Montreal, probably in conjunction with an autograph appearance by the popular Expos slugger. The front has a photo of the player working on his war club. The team and sponsor's logo are at top-right. On back are the player's stats.

	NM	EX	VG
Rusty Staub	32.50	16.00	10.00

1913 Tom Barker Game (WG6)

Nearly identical in format to "The National Game" card set, this issue features a different back design of a red-and-white line art representation of a batter. Fronts of the round-cornered, 2-1/2" x 3-1/2" cards have a black-and-white player pose, or game action photo, along with two game scenarios used when playing the card game. There are nine action photos in the set. Player cards are checklisted here alphabetically. The set originally sold for 50 cents. The set was reprinted in the 1980s.

		NM	EX	VG
Complete Set (54):		6,155	2,760	1,530
Common Player:		48.00	24.00	15.00
Game Box:		78.00	36.00	18.00
(1)	Grover Alexander	360.00	162.00	90.00
(2)	Frank Baker	120.00	54.00	30.00
(3)	Chief Bender	120.00	54.00	30.00
(4)	Bob Bescher	48.00	24.00	15.00
(5)	Joe Birmingham	48.00	24.00	15.00
(6)	Roger Bresnahan	120.00	54.00	30.00
(7)	Nixey Callahan	48.00	24.00	15.00
(8)	Bill Carrigan	48.00	24.00	15.00
(9)	Frank Chance	120.00	54.00	30.00
(10)	Hal Chase	78.00	36.00	19.00
(11)	Fred Clarke	120.00	54.00	30.00
(12)	Ty Cobb	810.00	360.00	210.00
(13)	Sam Crawford	120.00	54.00	30.00
(14)	Jake Daubert	48.00	24.00	15.00
(15)	Red Dooin	48.00	24.00	15.00
(16)	Johnny Evers	120.00	54.00	30.00
(17)	Vean Gregg	48.00	24.00	15.00
(18)	Clark Griffith	120.00	54.00	30.00
(19)	Dick Hoblitzel	48.00	24.00	15.00
(20)	Miller Huggins	120.00	54.00	30.00
(21)	Joe Jackson	1,920	870.00	480.00
(22)	Hughie Jennings	120.00	54.00	30.00
(23)	Walter Johnson	420.00	180.00	110.00
(24)	Ed Konetchy	48.00	24.00	15.00
(25)	Nap Lajoie	120.00	54.00	30.00
(26)	Connie Mack	120.00	54.00	30.00
(27)	Rube Marquard	120.00	54.00	30.00
(28)	Christy Mathewson	420.00	180.00	110.00
(29)	John McGraw	120.00	54.00	30.00
(30)	Chief Meyers	48.00	24.00	15.00
(31)	Clyde Milan	48.00	24.00	15.00
(32)	Marty O'Toole	48.00	24.00	15.00
(33)	Nap Rucker	48.00	24.00	15.00
(34)	Tris Speaker	160.00	75.00	40.00
(35)	George Stallings	48.00	24.00	15.00
(36)	Bill Sweeney	48.00	24.00	15.00
(37)	Joe Tinker	120.00	54.00	30.00
(38)	Honus Wagner	720.00	330.00	180.00
(39)	Ed Walsh	120.00	54.00	30.00
(40)	Zach Wheat	120.00	54.00	30.00
(41)	Ivy Wingo	48.00	24.00	15.00
(42)	Joe Wood	72.00	33.00	18.00
(43)	Cy Young	420.00	180.00	100.00
(---)	Rules card	48.00	24.00	15.00
(---)	Score card	48.00	24.00	15.00

ACTION PHOTO CARDS

		NM	EX	VG
(A1)	Batter swinging, looking forward.	18.00	8.10	4.50
(A2)	Batter swinging, looking back.	18.00	8.10	4.50
(A3)	Runner sliding, fielder at bag.	18.00	8.10	4.50
(A4)	Runner sliding, umpire behind.	48.00	24.00	15.00
(A5)	Runner sliding, hugging base.	18.00	8.10	4.50
(A6)	Sliding play at plate, umpire at left.	18.00	8.10	4.50

		NM	EX	VG
(A7)	Sliding play at plate, umpire at right.	18.00	8.10	4.50
(A8)	Play at plate, runner standing.	18.00	8.10	4.50
(A9)	Runner looking backwards.	18.00	8.10	4.50

1974-80 Bob Bartosz Postcards

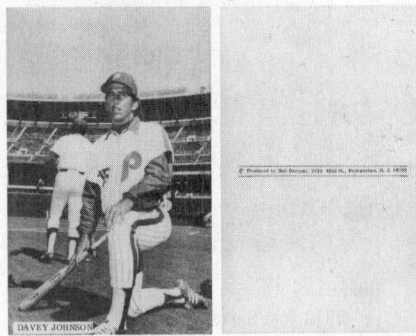

Through the last half of the 1970s, Bob Bartosz, who was a photographer covering the Phillies for a New Jersey daily newspaper, produced a series of player postcards. Most cards were produced at the request of the players for use in handling fan requests. Generally, no more than 500 cards of each player were ever produced. Most of the cards are in black-and-white with player name in a white stripe. Three cards were done in color. Size varies, but averages about 3-5/8" x 5-1/2". Back designs also vary, with most simply having Bartosz' credit line vertically at center. The unnumbered cards are checklisted here in alphabetical order.

		NM	EX	VG
	Complete Set (32):	3.00	1.50	.90
	Common Player:			
	BLACK-AND-WHITE POSTCARDS			
(1)	Hank Aaron (16th career grand slam)	7.50	3.75	2.25
(2)	Richie Ashburn (5th Delaware Valley Show)	3.00	1.50	.90
(3)	James Cool Papa Bell	3.00	1.50	.90
(4)	Bob Boone	4.00	2.00	1.25
(5)	Jimmie Crutchfield	3.00	1.50	.90
(6)	Barry Foote	3.00	1.50	.90
(7)	Steve Garvey	4.00	2.00	1.25
(8)	Tommy Hutton (Phillies)	3.00	1.50	.90
(9)	Tommy Hutton (Blue Jays)	3.00	1.50	.90
(10)	Dane Iorg	3.00	1.50	.90
(11)	Davey Johnson	3.00	1.50	.90
(12)	Jay Johnstone	3.00	1.50	.90
(13)	Dave Kingman (Stadium background.)	3.00	1.50	.90
(14)	Dave Kingman (Black background.)	3.00	1.50	.90
(15)	Greg Luzinski (Both feet show.)	3.00	1.50	.90
(16)	Greg Luzinski (Only left foot shows.)	3.00	1.50	.90
(17)	Jerry Martin (Phillies)	3.00	1.50	.90
(18)	Jerry Martin (Cubs)	3.00	1.50	.90
(19)	Tim McCarver	4.00	2.00	1.25
(20)	John Montefusco	3.00	1.50	.90
(21)	Jerry Mumphrey	3.00	1.50	.90
(22)	Phil Niekro	4.00	2.00	1.25
(23)	Robin Roberts (Hall of Fame induction.)	3.00	1.50	.90
(24)	Robin Roberts (4th Delaware Valley Show)	3.00	1.50	.90
(25)	Steve Swisher	3.00	1.50	.90
(26)	Tony Taylor (Uniform number visible.)	3.00	1.50	.90
(27)	Tony Taylor (Number is covered.)	3.00	1.50	.90
(28)	Tom Underwood	3.00	1.50	.90
(29)	Billy Williams (N.L. umpire.)	3.00	1.50	.90
(30)	1974 National League All-Stars	4.00	2.00	1.25
	COLOR POSTCARDS			
(1)	Greg Luzinski	7.50	3.75	2.25
(2)	Bill Madlock	7.50	3.75	2.25
(3)	Jason Thompson	6.00	3.00	1.75

1978 Bob Bartosz Baseball Postcards

Newspaper photographer Bob Bartosz produced a book of postcards in 1978 combining player poses, action shots and stadium photos. Two dozen cards are printed in 4" x 5-1/2"

black-and-white format and perforated on pages of four in the 8-1/2" x 11" book. Backs have standard postcard indicia and are numbered with a "BB" prefix and titled, all printing in black.

		NM	EX	VG
	Complete Book (24):	30.00	15.00	9.00
	Common Player:	1.50	.70	.45
1	25th anniversary of the 1950 Phillies (Group photo at old-timers game.)	1.50	.70	.45
2	Aaron and Mays at Cooperstown (Hank Aaron, Willie Mays)	4.00	2.00	1.25
3	Willie Mays	7.50	3.75	2.25
4	Aaron signing autographs (Hank Aaron)	3.00	1.50	.90
5	Dizzy Dean (Old-timers action sequence.)	2.50	1.25	.70
6	Jack Russell Stadium, Clearwater, Fla.	1.50	.70	.45
7	Paddy Livingston	1.50	.70	.45
8	Bob Feller (Old-timers game.)	2.50	1.25	.70
9	Hall of Fame Game at Doubleday Field	1.50	.70	.45
10	Doubleday Field at Cooperstown, N.Y.	1.50	.70	.45
11	Three Rivers Stadium, Pittsburgh	1.50	.70	.45
12	Hall of Fame Game at Doubleday Field	1.50	.70	.45
13	Shibe Park from the air	1.50	.70	.45
14	Olympic Stadium, Montreal	1.50	.70	.45
15	A tree grows at home plate (Shibe Park - 1974)	1.50	.70	.45
16	The Bleachers, Wrigley Field	1.50	.70	.45
17	Another Home Run (Hank Aaron)	2.50	1.25	.70
18	Home Run King (Hank Aaron)	2.25	1.25	.70
19	Autograph Time - 1950 (Phillies signing balls.)	1.50	.70	.45
20	The Champs (1976 Phillies)	1.50	.70	.45
21	Last Day - Shibe Park, 1977	1.50	.70	.45
22	Connie Mack Stadium, Philadelphia	1.50	.70	.45
23	Shibe Park	1.50	.70	.45
24	Shibe Park	1.50	.70	.45

1911 Baseball Bats

Issued circa 1911, cards in this rare 47-card issue were printed on the back panel of "Baseball Bats" penny candy. The cards themselves measure approximately 1-3/8" x 2-3/8" and feature a black-and-white player photo surrounded by an orange or white border. Player's name and team are printed in small, black capital letters near the bottom of the photo. Cards are blank-backed.

		NM	EX	VG
	Complete Set (50):	40,000	20,000	12,000
	Common Player:	550.00	275.00	165.00
(1)	Red Ames	550.00	275.00	165.00
(2)	Home Run Baker	1,100	550.00	330.00
(3)	Jack Barry	550.00	275.00	165.00
(4)	Ginger Beaumont	550.00	275.00	165.00
(5)	Chief Bender	1,100	550.00	330.00
(6)	Al Bridwell	550.00	275.00	165.00
(7)	Mordecai Brown	1,100	550.00	330.00
(8)	Bill Corrigan (Carrigan)	550.00	275.00	165.00
(9)	Frank Chance	1,100	550.00	330.00
(10)	Hal Chase	850.00	425.00	250.00
(11)	Ed Cicotte	925.00	460.00	275.00
(12)	Fred Clark (Clarke)	1,100	550.00	330.00
(13)	Ty Cobb	6,000	4,000	2,000
(14)	King Cole	550.00	275.00	165.00
(15)	Eddie Collins	1,100	550.00	330.00
(16)	Sam Crawford	1,100	550.00	330.00
(17)	Lou Criger	550.00	275.00	165.00
(18)	Harry Davis	550.00	275.00	165.00
(19)	Jim Delehanty	550.00	275.00	165.00
(20)	Art Devlin	550.00	275.00	165.00
(21)	Josh Devore	550.00	275.00	165.00
(22)	Wild Bill Donovan	550.00	275.00	165.00
(23)	Larry Doyle	550.00	275.00	165.00
(24)	Johnny Evers	1,100	550.00	330.00
(25)	John Flynn	550.00	275.00	165.00
(26)	George Gibson	550.00	275.00	165.00
(27)	Solly Hoffman (Hofman)	550.00	275.00	165.00
(28)	Walter Johnson	2,200	1,100	660.00
(29)	Johnny Kling	550.00	275.00	165.00
(30)	Nap Lajoie	1,100	550.00	330.00
(31)	Christy Mathewson	3,000	2,000	1,000
(32)	Matty McIntyre	550.00	275.00	165.00
(33)	Fred Merkle	550.00	275.00	165.00
(34)	Danny Murphy	550.00	275.00	165.00
(35)	Tom Needham	550.00	275.00	165.00
(36)	Harry Niles	550.00	275.00	165.00
(37)	Rube Oldring	550.00	275.00	165.00
(38)	Wildfire Schulte	550.00	275.00	165.00
(39)	Cy Seymour	550.00	275.00	165.00
(40)	Jimmy Sheckard	550.00	275.00	165.00
(41)	Tris Speaker	2,400	1,600	1,000
(42)	Oscar Stanage (Batting - front view.)	550.00	275.00	165.00
(43)	Oscar Stanage (Batting - side view.)	550.00	275.00	165.00
(44)	Ira Thomas	550.00	275.00	165.00
(45)	Joe Tinker	1,100	550.00	330.00
(46)	Heinie Wagner	550.00	275.00	165.00
(47)	Honus Wagner	4,500	2,250	1,350
(48)	Ed Walsh	1,100	550.00	330.00
(49)	Art Wilson	550.00	275.00	165.00
(50)	Owen Wilson	550.00	275.00	165.00

1887-1893 Baseball Currency

Because of their similarity in size (about 7-3/4" x 3-3/8"), design and color to then-circulating U.S. paper money, this form of advertising flyer was thought to catch the attention of the general public. The notes were printed in black-and-green (some 1889 Chicago notes are printed in black-and-red) on white. Fronts have at left a large oval portrait of the team's president or manager. At right on the Chicago and Detroit notes is a full-figure rendering of an unnamed Cap Anson. On the St. Louis notes, there is a picture of the Wilman Trophy indicative of the team's 1886 World's Championship. On the 1893 note, National League President N.E. Young is pictured at left, with a grouping of baseball equipment at right. In the center is a large ornate date with either "National Base Ball League" or "National / Base Ball Association" at top in gothic typography. Backs have black-and-white woodcuts of the team's players on a decorative green (or red) background. The notes were originally printed with large open spaces on front and back so that advertising messages could be over-printed by local merchants. The value of the notes can be affected by the location of a specific advertiser and/or the content of his message. Sports collectors compete with numismatists for examples of these advertising pieces.

	NM	EX	VG
1887 Chicago White Stockings (Front: Pres. A.G. Spalding. Back: Cap Anson, Mark Baldwin, John Clarkson, Tom Daily (Daly), Dell Darling, Silver Flint, Lou Hardie, Fred Pfeffer, Jimmy Ryan, Marty Sullivan, Billy Sunday, Ed Williamson.)	2,300	1,150	750.00
1887 Detroit Wolverines (Front: Manager Bill Watkins. Back: Lady Baldwin, Charlie Bennett, Fatty Briody, Dan Brouthers, Fred Dunlap, Charlie Ganzel, Ned Hanlon, Hardy Richardson, Jack Rowe, Sam Thompson, Stump Weidman (Wiedman), Deacon White.)	2,600	1,300	775.00
1887 St. Louis Browns (Front: Pres. Chris Von Der Ahe. Back: Jack Boyle, Doc Bushong, Bob Caruthers, Charlie Comiskey, Dave Foutz, Bill Gleason, Arlie Latham, Tip O'Neil (O'Neill), Yank Robinson, Curt Welch.)	4,000	2,000	1,200
1888 Chicago White Stockings (Front: Pres. A.G. Spalding. Back: Cap Anson, Mark Baldwin, John Clarkson, Tom Daily (Daly), Dell Darling, Silver Flint, Lou Hardie, Fred Pfeffer, Jimmy Ryan, Marty Sullivan, Billy Sunday, Ed Williamson.)	2,600	1,300	750.00
1888 Detroit Wolverines (Front: Manager Bill Watkins. Back: Lady Baldwin, Charlie Bennett, Fatty Briody, Dan Brouthers, Fred Dunlap, Charlie Ganzel, Ned Hanlon, Hardy Richardson, Jack Rowe, Sam Thompson, Stump Weidman (Wiedman), Deacon White.)	2,600	1,300	775.00
1889 Chicago White Stockings (Front: Pres. A.G. Spalding. Back: Cap Anson, Mark Baldwin, Tom Burns, Tom Daily (Daly), Dell Darling, Silver Flint, Bob Pettit, Fred Pfeffer, Jimmy Ryan, Marty Sullivan, George Van Haltren, Ed Williamson.)	2,600	1,300	750.00
1893 National League All-Stars (Front: Pres. N.E. Young. Back: Bob Allen, Cap Anson, Mark Baldwin, John Clarkson, Charles Comiskey, Dave Foutz, King Kelly, Billy Nash, Jim O'Rourke, Fred Pfeffer, George Van Haltren, John Ward.) (Value Undetermined)			

1979 Baseball Favorites "1953 Bowman"

This collectors' series was designed to represent an extension of the 64-card 1953 Bowman black-and-white card issue. This series uses the same design on its 2-1/2" x 3-3/4" format. Fronts have a black-and-white player photo with no

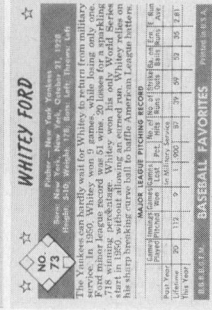

extraneous graphics. Backs are printed in red and black and offer career highlights, stats and biographical data, written as if in 1953. Many of the players in this collectors' edition originally appeared in Bowman's 1953 color series. Issue price was about $7.

	NM	EX	VG
Complete Set (16):	25.00	12.50	7.50
Common Player:	.75	.40	.25
65 Monte Irvin	.75	.40	.25
66 Early Wynn	.75	.40	.25
67 Robin Roberts	.75	.40	.25
68 Stan Musial	3.00	1.50	.90
69 Ernie Banks	1.50	.75	.45
70 Willie Mays	4.50	2.25	1.25
71 Yogi Berra	2.25	1.25	.70
72 Mickey Mantle	9.00	4.50	2.75
73 Whitey Ford	1.25	.60	.40
74 Bob Feller	.75	.40	.25
75 Ted Williams	4.50	2.25	1.25
76 Satchel Paige	3.00	1.50	.90
77 Jackie Robinson	3.00	1.50	.90
78 Ed Mathews	.75	.40	.25
79 Warren Spahn	.75	.40	.25
80 Ralph Kiner	.75	.40	.25

1964 Baseball Greats Postcard

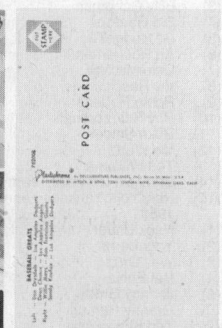

Four of California's star players are pictured on this standard-format (5-1/2" x 3-1/2") color postcard in a pair of two-player poses. Each player's facsimile autograph appears on front. Back is in typical postcard format with player identification, a stamp box and vertical center divider with publisher and distributor information. (See also Baseball Stars - Present and Future.)

	NM	EX	VG
Don Drysdale, Dean Chance, Willie Mays, Sandy Koufax	40.00	20.00	12.00

1910-57 Baseball Magazine Player Posters

Beginning shortly after its 1908 debut, Baseball Magazine produced a lengthy series of player posters which it offered as premiums to readers. Ranging in size from 9" x 12-1/4" to 9" x 20" (and a series of super-size 1957s), the posters feature poses of top players in sepia tones bordered in white. In the bottom border over the years appeared various formats of player identification, copyright information and promotion for the magazine. The unnumbered posters are listed here alphabetically by year. Some posters were reprinted over the years and there may exist pose variations as well as posters which have escaped this list. Names shown here may not coincide with the form in which they actually appear on the

posters. Inaccuracies in, or incompleteness of, the checklist is the likely result of its having been compiled from ads appearing in the magazine.

		NM	EX	VG
1910				
(1)	Ty Cobb	350.00	175.00	105.00
(2)	Johnny Evers	150.00	75.00	45.00
(3)	Hughie Jennings	100.00	50.00	30.00
(4)	Honus Wagner	300.00	150.00	90.00
1912				
(1)	Babe Adams	60.00	30.00	18.00
(2)	Howie Camnitz	60.00	30.00	18.00
(3)	Frank Chance	125.00	62.00	37.00
(4)	Claude Hendrix	60.00	30.00	18.00
(5)	Marty O'Toole	60.00	30.00	18.00
(6)	Boston Red Sox Team	250.00	125.00	75.00
(7)	New York Giants Team	250.00	125.00	75.00
1913				
(1)	Jimmy Archer	60.00	30.00	18.00
(2)	Jack Barry	60.00	30.00	18.00
(3)	Joe Bush	60.00	30.00	18.00
(4)	Sam Crawford	100.00	50.00	30.00
(5)	Eddie Collins	125.00	62.00	37.00
(6)	Jake Daubert	60.00	30.00	18.00
(7)	Larry Doyle	60.00	30.00	18.00
(8)	Art Fletcher	60.00	30.00	18.00
(9)	Joe Jackson	1,000	500.00	300.00
(10)	Walter Johnson	250.00	125.00	75.00
(11)	Nap Lajoie	200.00	100.00	60.00
(12)	Connie Mack	100.00	50.00	30.00
(13)	Fritz Maisel	60.00	30.00	18.00
(14)	Rube Marquard	100.00	50.00	30.00
(15)	Christy Mathewson	250.00	125.00	75.00
(16)	John McGraw	125.00	62.00	37.00
(17)	Stuffy McInnis	60.00	30.00	18.00
(18)	"Chief" Meyers	60.00	30.00	18.00
(19)	Red Murray	60.00	30.00	18.00
(20)	Eddie Plank	125.00	62.00	37.00
(21)	"Nap" Rucker	60.00	30.00	18.00
(22)	Reb Russell	60.00	30.00	18.00
(23)	Tris Speaker	125.00	62.00	37.00
(24)	Ed Walsh	100.00	50.00	30.00
(25)	Smokey Joe Wood	75.00	37.00	22.00
(26)	Boston Braves Team	250.00	125.00	75.00
(27)	Philadelphia Athletics Team	250.00	125.00	75.00
1914				
(1)	Home Run Baker	100.00	50.00	30.00
(2)	Larry Cheney	60.00	30.00	18.00
(3)	Joe Connolly	60.00	30.00	18.00
(4)	Hank Gowdy	60.00	30.00	18.00
(5)	Bill James	60.00	30.00	18.00
(6)	Jimmy Lavender	60.00	30.00	18.00
(7)	Rabbit Maranville	100.00	50.00	30.00
(8)	Dick Rudolph	60.00	30.00	18.00
(9)	Wally Schang	60.00	30.00	18.00
(10)	Bob Shawkey	60.00	30.00	18.00
(11)	Jimmy Sheckard	60.00	30.00	18.00
(12)	Charles Schmidt	60.00	30.00	18.00
(13)	Wildfire Schulte	60.00	30.00	18.00
(14)	Lefty Tyler	60.00	30.00	18.00
(15)	Boston Braves Team	200.00	100.00	60.00
(16)	Chicago Cubs Team	200.00	100.00	60.00
(17)	Chicago Whales Team	250.00	125.00	75.00
(18)	Cincinnati Reds Team	200.00	100.00	60.00
(19)	Cleveland Indians Team	200.00	100.00	60.00
(20)	Detroit Tigers Team	200.00	100.00	60.00
(21)	New York Yankees Team	200.00	100.00	60.00
(22)	St. Louis Browns Team	200.00	100.00	60.00
(23)	Washington Senators Team	200.00	100.00	60.00
1915				
(1)	Grover Alexander	125.00	62.00	37.00
(2)	Chief Bender	100.00	50.00	30.00
(3)	Harry Hooper	100.00	50.00	30.00
(4)	Duffy Lewis	60.00	30.00	18.00
(5)	Tris Speaker	100.00	50.00	30.00
(6)	Boston Red Sox Team	200.00	100.00	60.00
(7)	Chicago White Sox Team	200.00	100.00	60.00
(8)	Philadelphia Athletics Team	200.00	100.00	60.00
(9)	Philadelphia Phillies Team	200.00	100.00	60.00
(10)	St. Louis Cardinals Team	200.00	100.00	60.00
1916				
(1)	Larry Gardner	50.00	25.00	15.00
(2)	Buck Herzog	50.00	25.00	15.00
(3)	Rogers Hornsby	75.00	37.00	22.00
(4)	Walter Johnson	160.00	80.00	48.00
(5)	Fielder Jones	50.00	25.00	15.00
(6)	Benny Kauff	50.00	25.00	15.00
(7)	Dave Robertson	50.00	25.00	15.00
(8)	Babe Ruth (Pitching)	300.00	150.00	90.00
(9)	George Sisler	75.00	37.00	22.00
(10)	Zack Wheat	75.00	37.00	22.00
(11)	Boston Red Sox Team	150.00	75.00	45.00
(12)	Brooklyn Dodgers Team	100.00	50.00	30.00
(13)	Philadelphia Phillies Team	100.00	50.00	30.00
1917				
(1)	George Burns	50.00	25.00	15.00
(2)	Ed Cicotte	150.00	75.00	45.00
(3)	Art Fletcher	50.00	25.00	15.00
(4)	Red Faber	150.00	75.00	45.00
(5)	Happy Felsch	150.00	75.00	45.00
(6)	Ferd Schupp	50.00	25.00	15.00
(7)	Ray Schalk	50.00	25.00	15.00
(8)	Buck Weaver	150.00	75.00	45.00
(9)	Boston Red Sox Team	150.00	75.00	45.00
(10)	New York Giants Team	150.00	75.00	45.00
1918				
(1)	Home Run Baker	75.00	37.00	22.00
1919				
(1)	Ed Cicotte	75.00	37.00	22.00
(2)	Chicago White Sox Team	400.00	200.00	120.00
(3)	Cincinnati Reds Team	125.00	62.00	37.00
1920				
(1)	Jim Bagby	30.00	15.00	9.00
(2)	Dave Bancroft	45.00	22.00	13.50
(3)	Max Carey	45.00	22.00	13.50
(4)	Harry Coveleski	45.00	22.00	13.50
(5)	Hod Eller	30.00	15.00	9.00

		NM	EX	VG
(6)	Burleigh Grimes	45.00	22.00	13.50
(7)	Heinie Groh	30.00	15.00	9.00
(8)	Rogers Hornsby	45.00	22.00	13.50
(9)	Walter Johnson	75.00	37.00	22.00
(10)	Dick Kerr	30.00	15.00	9.00
(11)	Pat Moran	30.00	15.00	9.00
(12)	Duster Mails	30.00	15.00	9.00
(13)	Hy Myers	30.00	15.00	9.00
(14)	Steve O'Neill	30.00	15.00	9.00
(15)	Edd Roush	45.00	22.00	13.50
(16)	Dutch Ruether	30.00	15.00	9.00
(17)	Babe Ruth (Batting, no stands in background.)	700.00	350.00	210.00
(18)	Ray Schalk	45.00	22.00	13.50
(19)	Earl Smith	30.00	15.00	9.00
(20)	Sherrod Smith	30.00	15.00	9.00
(21)	Tris Speaker	45.00	22.00	13.50
(22)	Hippo Vaughn	30.00	15.00	9.00
(23)	Bobby Veach	30.00	15.00	9.00
(24)	Bill Wambsganss	30.00	15.00	9.00
(25)	Brooklyn Dodgers Team	125.00	62.00	37.00
(26)	Cleveland Indians Team	125.00	62.00	37.00
1921				
(1)	Dave Bancroft	45.00	22.00	13.50
(2)	Wilbur Cooper	30.00	15.00	9.00
(3)	Phil Douglas	30.00	15.00	9.00
(4)	Frank Frisch	50.00	25.00	15.00
(5)	Harry Heilmann	45.00	22.00	13.50
(6)	Waite Hoyt	45.00	22.00	13.50
(7)	George Kelly	45.00	22.00	13.50
(8)	Carl Mays	45.00	22.00	13.50
(9)	Mike McNally	30.00	15.00	9.00
(10)	Irish Meusel	30.00	15.00	9.00
(11)	Bob Meusel	30.00	15.00	9.00
(12)	Art Nehf	30.00	15.00	9.00
(13)	Wally Schang	30.00	15.00	9.00
(14)	Walter Schmidt	30.00	15.00	9.00
(15)	Frank Snyder	30.00	15.00	9.00
(16)	Aaron Ward	30.00	15.00	9.00
(17)	Ross Youngs	45.00	22.00	13.50
(18)	New York Giants Team	100.00	50.00	30.00
(19)	New York Yankees Team	300.00	150.00	90.00
(20)	Pittsburgh Pirates Team	100.00	50.00	30.00
1922 - NONE				
1923				
(1)	New York Giants Team	90.00	45.00	27.00
(2)	New York Yankees Team	200.00	100.00	60.00
1924				
(1)	Johnny Bassler	30.00	15.00	9.00
(2)	Jim Bottomley	45.00	22.00	13.50
(3)	Kiki Cuyler	45.00	22.00	13.50
(4)	Joe Dugan	30.00	15.00	9.00
(5)	Bibb Falk	30.00	15.00	9.00
(6)	Jack Fournier	30.00	15.00	9.00
(7)	Goose Goslin	45.00	22.00	13.50
(8)	Sam Harris	30.00	15.00	9.00
(9)	Gabby Hartnett	45.00	22.00	13.50
(10)	Travis Jackson	45.00	22.00	13.50
(11)	Baby Doll Jacobson	30.00	15.00	9.00
(12)	Charlie Jamieson	30.00	15.00	9.00
(13)	Herb Pennock	45.00	22.00	13.50
(14)	Sam Rice	45.00	22.00	13.50
(15)	Eppa Rixey	45.00	22.00	13.50
(16)	Muddy Ruel	30.00	15.00	9.00
(17)	Hollis Thurston	30.00	15.00	9.00
(18)	Pie Traynor	45.00	22.00	13.50
(19)	Dazzy Vance	45.00	22.00	13.50
(20)	Kenny Williams	30.00	15.00	9.00
(21)	New York Giants Team	90.00	45.00	27.00
(22)	Washington Senators Team	90.00	45.00	27.00
1925				
(1)	Vic Aldridge	30.00	15.00	9.00
(2)	Mickey Cochrane	45.00	22.00	13.50
(3)	Ted Lyons	45.00	22.00	13.50
(4)	Eddie Rommel	30.00	15.00	9.00
(5)	Al Simmons	45.00	22.00	13.50
(6)	Glenn Wright	30.00	15.00	9.00
(7)	Pittsburgh Pirates Team	90.00	45.00	27.00
(8)	Washington Senators Team	90.00	45.00	27.00
1926				
(1)	Les Bell	30.00	15.00	9.00
(2)	George H. Burns	30.00	15.00	9.00
(3)	Hughie Critz	30.00	15.00	9.00
(4)	Henry (Lou) Gehrig (Portrait)	250.00	125.00	75.00
(5)	Ray Kremer	30.00	15.00	9.00
(6)	Bob O'Farrell	30.00	15.00	9.00
(7)	Tommy Thevenow	30.00	15.00	9.00
(8)	George Uhle	30.00	15.00	9.00
(9)	Hack Wilson	45.00	22.00	13.50
(10)	New York Yankees Team	250.00	125.00	75.00
(11)	St. Louis Cardinals Team	90.00	45.00	27.00
1927				
(1)	Carmen Hill	30.00	15.00	9.00
(2)	Tony Lazzeri	45.00	22.00	13.50
(3)	Fred Lindstrom	45.00	22.00	13.50
(4)	Charlie Root	30.00	15.00	9.00
(5)	Lloyd Waner	45.00	22.00	13.50
(6)	Paul Waner	45.00	22.00	13.50
(7)	New York Yankees Team	200.00	100.00	60.00
(8)	Pittsburgh Pirates Team	90.00	45.00	27.00
1928				
(1)	Jimmie Foxx	60.00	30.00	18.00
1929				
(1)	Guy Bush	30.00	15.00	9.00
(2)	Lefty Grove	45.00	22.00	13.50
(3)	Chicago Cubs Team	125.00	62.00	37.00
(4)	Philadelphia Athletics Team	90.00	45.00	27.00
1930				
(1)	George Earnshaw	30.00	15.00	9.00
(2)	Wes Ferrell	30.00	15.00	9.00
(3)	Charley Gelbert	30.00	15.00	9.00
(4)	Babe Herman	30.00	15.00	9.00
(5)	Chuck Klein	45.00	22.00	13.50
(6)	Philadelphia Athletics Team	90.00	45.00	27.00
(7)	St. Louis Cardinals Team	90.00	45.00	27.00
1931				
(1)	Earl Averill	45.00	22.00	13.50
(2)	Ed Brandt	30.00	15.00	9.00

(3)	Ben Chapman	30.00	15.00	9.00
(4)	Joe Cronin	45.00	22.00	13.50
(5)	Bill Hallahan	30.00	15.00	9.00
(6)	Pepper Martin	40.00	20.00	12.00
1932 - NONE				
1933				
(1)	Dizzy Dean	75.00	37.00	22.00
(2)	Lou Gehrig (Batting)	225.00	110.00	67.00
(3)	Carl Hubbell	60.00	30.00	18.00
(4)	Heinie Manush	45.00	22.00	13.50
(5)	Mel Ott	45.00	22.00	13.50
(6)	Babe Ruth (Batting, stands in background.)	250.00	125.00	75.00
(7)	Hal Schumacher	30.00	15.00	9.00
(8)	Lon Warneke	30.00	15.00	9.00
(9)	New York Giants Team	90.00	45.00	27.00
(10)	Washington Senators Team	90.00	45.00	27.00
1934				
(1)	Dick Bartell	30.00	15.00	9.00
(2)	Paul Dean	45.00	22.00	13.50
(3)	Lefty Gomez	45.00	22.00	13.50
(4)	Rogers Hornsby	45.00	22.00	13.50
(5)	Ducky Medwick	45.00	22.00	13.50
(6)	Van Lingle Mungo	30.00	15.00	9.00
(7)	Schoolboy Rowe	30.00	15.00	9.00
(8)	Arky Vaughan	45.00	22.00	13.50
(9)	Lloyd Waner	45.00	22.00	13.50
(10)	Paul Waner	45.00	22.00	13.50
(11)	Detroit Tigers Team	100.00	50.00	30.00
1935				
(1)	Wally Berger	30.00	15.00	9.00
(2)	Ripper Collins	30.00	15.00	9.00
(3)	Charley Gehringer	45.00	22.00	13.50
(4)	Hank Greenberg	60.00	30.00	18.00
(5)	Mel Harder	30.00	15.00	9.00
(6)	Billy Herman	45.00	22.00	13.50
(7)	Buddy Myer	30.00	15.00	9.00
(8)	Al Simmons	45.00	22.00	13.50
(9)	Bill Terry	45.00	22.00	13.50
(10)	Joe Vosmik	30.00	15.00	9.00
(11)	Chicago Cubs Team	100.00	50.00	30.00
(12)	Detroit Tigers Team	90.00	45.00	27.00
1936				
(1)	Luke Appling	45.00	22.00	13.50
(2)	Frank Demaree	30.00	15.00	9.00
(3)	Paul Derringer	30.00	15.00	9.00
(4)	Joe DiMaggio	80.00	40.00	24.00
(5)	Vern Kennedy	30.00	15.00	9.00
(6)	Ernie Lombardi	45.00	22.00	13.50
(7)	Joe Moore	30.00	15.00	9.00
(8)	Terry Moore	30.00	15.00	9.00
(9)	Moose Solters	30.00	15.00	9.00
(10)	Hal Trosky	30.00	15.00	9.00
(11)	Bill Werber	30.00	15.00	9.00
(12)	New York Giants Team	100.00	50.00	30.00
(13)	New York Yankees Team	200.00	100.00	60.00
1937				
(1)	Cy Blanton	30.00	15.00	9.00
(2)	Dolph Camilli	30.00	15.00	9.00
(3)	Joe Cronin	45.00	22.00	13.50
(4)	Bill Dickey	50.00	25.00	15.00
(5)	Bob Feller	50.00	25.00	15.00
(6)	Stan Hack	30.00	15.00	9.00
(7)	Buddy Hassett	30.00	15.00	9.00
(8)	Bill Lee	30.00	15.00	9.00
(9)	Buddy Lewis	30.00	15.00	9.00
(10)	Johnny Mize	45.00	22.00	13.50
(11)	Jimmy Ripple	30.00	15.00	9.00
(12)	Charles Ruffing	45.00	22.00	13.50
(13)	Cecil Travis	30.00	15.00	9.00
(14)	Gee Walker	30.00	15.00	9.00
1938				
(1)	Ethan Allen	30.00	15.00	9.00
(2)	Clay Bryant	30.00	15.00	9.00
(3)	Harlond Clift	30.00	15.00	9.00
(4)	Frank Crosetti	35.00	17.50	10.50
(5)	Harry Danning	30.00	15.00	9.00
(6)	Bobby Doerr	45.00	22.00	13.50
(7)	Augie Galan	30.00	15.00	9.00
(8)	Ival Goodman	30.00	15.00	9.00
(9)	Joe Gordon	30.00	15.00	9.00
(10)	Tommy Henrich	35.00	17.50	10.50
(11)	Mike Kreevich	30.00	15.00	9.00
(12)	Frank McCormick	30.00	15.00	9.00
(13)	Babe Phelps	30.00	15.00	9.00
(14)	Johnny Rizzo	30.00	15.00	9.00
(15)	Red Rolfe	30.00	15.00	9.00
(16)	Johnny Vander Meer	35.00	17.50	10.50
(17)	Rudy York	30.00	15.00	9.00
1939				
(1)	Morrie Arnovich	30.00	15.00	9.00
(2)	Jimmie Foxx	45.00	22.00	13.50
(3)	Luke Hamlin	30.00	15.00	9.00
(4)	Bob Johnson	35.00	17.50	10.50
(5)	Charlie Keller	35.00	17.50	10.50
(6)	Ken Keltner	35.00	17.50	10.50
(7)	Emil "Dutch" Leonard	30.00	15.00	9.00
(8)	Bobo Newsom	30.00	15.00	9.00
(9)	Don Padgett	30.00	15.00	9.00
(10)	Bucky Walters	30.00	15.00	9.00
(11)	Ted Williams	120.00	60.00	36.00
1940 (9-1/2" x 12")				
(1)	George Case	20.00	10.00	6.00
(2)	Babe Dahlgren	20.00	10.00	6.00
(3)	Elbie Fletcher	20.00	10.00	6.00
(4)	Cookie Lavagetto	20.00	10.00	6.00
(5)	Barney McCosky	20.00	10.00	6.00
(6)	Bill McGee	20.00	10.00	6.00
(7)	Ducky Medwick	40.00	20.00	12.00
(8)	Eddie Miller	20.00	10.00	6.00
(9)	Hugh Mulcahy	20.00	10.00	6.00
(10)	Claude Passeau	20.00	10.00	6.00
(11)	Rip Radcliff	20.00	10.00	6.00
(12)	Jim Tabor	20.00	10.00	6.00
(13)	Eugene "Junior" Thompson	20.00	10.00	6.00
(14)	Mike Tresh	20.00	10.00	6.00
(15)	Roy Weatherly	20.00	10.00	6.00
(16)	Norm "Babe" Young	20.00	10.00	6.00
1941 (9-1/2" x 12")				
(1)	Sam Chapman	20.00	10.00	6.00
(2)	Ty Cobb	60.00	30.00	18.00
(3)	Mort Cooper	20.00	10.00	6.00
(4)	Dom DiMaggio	40.00	20.00	12.00
(5)	Jeff Heath	20.00	10.00	6.00
(6)	Thornton Lee	20.00	10.00	6.00
(7)	Danny Litwhiler	20.00	10.00	6.00
(8)	Al Lopez	40.00	20.00	12.00
(9)	Christy Mathewson	60.00	30.00	18.00
(10)	Joe McCarthy	40.00	20.00	12.00
(11)	Bill Nicholson	20.00	10.00	6.00
(12)	Pete Reiser	20.00	10.00	6.00
(13)	Elmer Riddle	20.00	10.00	6.00
(14)	Phil Rizzuto	60.00	30.00	18.00
(15)	Johnny Rucker	20.00	10.00	6.00
(16)	Hans Wagner	60.00	30.00	18.00
1942 (9-1/2" x 12")				
(1)	Jim Bagby	20.00	10.00	6.00
(2)	Ernie Bonham	20.00	10.00	6.00
(3)	Lou Boudreau	40.00	20.00	12.00
(4)	Tommy Bridges	20.00	10.00	6.00
(5)	Jimmy Brown	20.00	10.00	6.00
(6)	Dolph Camilli	20.00	10.00	6.00
(7)	Walker Cooper	20.00	10.00	6.00
(8)	Bob Elliott	20.00	10.00	6.00
(9)	Lou Gehrig (Batting)	100.00	50.00	30.00
(10)	Tex Hughson	20.00	10.00	6.00
(11)	Eddie Joost	20.00	10.00	6.00
(12)	Don Kolloway	20.00	10.00	6.00
(13)	Phil Marchildon	20.00	10.00	6.00
(14)	Clyde McCullough	20.00	10.00	6.00
(15)	George McQuinn	20.00	10.00	6.00
(16)	Cliff Melton	20.00	10.00	6.00
(17)	Lou Novikoff	20.00	10.00	6.00
(18)	Mickey Owen	20.00	10.00	6.00
(19)	Pee Wee Reese	50.00	25.00	15.00
(20)	Stan Spence	20.00	10.00	6.00
(21)	Vern Stephens	20.00	10.00	6.00
(22)	Virgil Trucks	20.00	10.00	6.00
(23)	Fred "Dixie" Walker	20.00	10.00	6.00
(24)	Max West	20.00	10.00	6.00
1943 (9-1/2" x 12")				
(1)	Hiram Bithorn	20.00	10.00	6.00
(2)	Spud Chandler	20.00	10.00	6.00
(3)	Al Javery	20.00	10.00	6.00
(4)	Bill Johnson	20.00	10.00	6.00
(5)	Kenesaw Landis	40.00	20.00	12.00
(6)	Tony Lupien	20.00	10.00	6.00
(7)	Marty Marion	25.00	12.50	7.50
(8)	Stan Musial	60.00	30.00	18.00
(9)	Bobo Newsom	20.00	10.00	6.00
(10)	Babe Ruth (Portrait)	80.00	40.00	24.00
(11)	Rip Sewell	20.00	10.00	6.00
(12)	Joe Schultz	20.00	10.00	6.00
(13)	Dizzy Trout	20.00	10.00	6.00
(14)	Mickey Vernon	20.00	10.00	6.00
(15)	Dick Wakefield	20.00	10.00	6.00
(16)	Mickey Witek	20.00	10.00	6.00
(17)	Early Wynn	40.00	20.00	12.00
(18)	New York Yankees Team	90.00	45.00	27.00
(19)	St. Louis Cardinals Team	90.00	45.00	27.00
1944 (9-1/2" x 12")				
(1)	Augie Galan	20.00	10.00	6.00
(2)	Johnny Hopp	20.00	10.00	6.00
(3)	Jack Kramer	20.00	10.00	6.00
(4)	Johnny Lindell	20.00	10.00	6.00
(5)	Ray Mueller	20.00	10.00	6.00
(6)	Hal Newhouser	40.00	20.00	12.00
(7)	Nelson Potter	20.00	10.00	6.00
(8)	Ray Sanders	20.00	10.00	6.00
(9)	"Snuffy" Stirnweiss	20.00	10.00	6.00
(10)	Jim Tobin	20.00	10.00	6.00
(11)	Thurman Tucker	20.00	10.00	6.00
(12)	Bill Voiselle	20.00	10.00	6.00
(13)	Ted Wilks	20.00	10.00	6.00
(14)	Detroit Tigers Team	90.00	45.00	27.00
(15)	St. Louis Browns Team	90.00	45.00	27.00
(16)	St. Louis Cardinals Team	90.00	45.00	27.00
1945 (9-1/2" x 12")				
(1)	Phil Cavarretta	20.00	10.00	6.00
(2)	Russ Christopher	20.00	10.00	6.00
(3)	Tony Cuccinello	20.00	10.00	6.00
(4)	Boo Ferriss	20.00	10.00	6.00
(5)	Hal Gregg	20.00	10.00	6.00
(6)	Steve Gromek	20.00	10.00	6.00
(7)	Ducky Medwick	40.00	20.00	12.00
(8)	George Myatt	20.00	10.00	6.00
(9)	Frank Overmire	20.00	10.00	6.00
(10)	Andy Pafko	25.00	12.50	7.50
(11)	Red Schoendienst	40.00	20.00	12.00
(12)	Chicago Cubs Team	90.00	45.00	27.00
(13)	Detroit Tigers Team	75.00	37.00	22.00
1946				
(1)	Joe Beggs	20.00	10.00	6.00
(2)	Johnny Berardino	25.00	12.50	7.50
(3)	Bill Bevens	20.00	10.00	6.00
(4)	Harry Brecheen	20.00	10.00	6.00
(5)	Mickey Harris	20.00	10.00	6.00
(6)	Kirby Higbe	20.00	10.00	6.00
(7)	Dave Koslo	20.00	10.00	6.00
(8)	Whitey Kurowski	20.00	10.00	6.00
(9)	Vic Lombardi	20.00	10.00	6.00
(10)	Phil Masi	20.00	10.00	6.00
(11)	Mike McCormick	20.00	10.00	6.00
(12)	Johnny Mize	40.00	20.00	12.00
(13)	Hal Newhouser	40.00	20.00	12.00
(14)	Johnny Pesky	20.00	10.00	6.00
(15)	Howie Pollett	20.00	10.00	6.00
(16)	Jerry Priddy	20.00	10.00	6.00
(17)	Aaron Robinson	20.00	10.00	6.00
(18)	Enos Slaughter	40.00	20.00	12.00
(19)	Eddie Stanky	20.00	10.00	6.00
(20)	Hal Wagner	20.00	10.00	6.00
(21)	Rudy York	20.00	10.00	6.00
(22)	Boston Red Sox Team	75.00	37.00	22.00
(23)	St. Louis Cardinals Team	75.00	37.00	22.00
1947				
(1)	Ewell Blackwell	20.00	10.00	6.00
(2)	Ralph Branca	20.00	10.00	6.00
(3)	Billy Cox	20.00	10.00	6.00
(4)	Bob Dillinger	20.00	10.00	6.00
(5)	Joe Dobson	20.00	10.00	6.00
(6)	Joe Gordon	20.00	10.00	6.00
(7)	Hank Greenberg	45.00	22.00	13.50
(8)	Clint Hartung	20.00	10.00	6.00
(9)	Jim Hegan	20.00	10.00	6.00
(10)	Larry Jansen	20.00	10.00	6.00
(11)	George Kell	40.00	20.00	12.00
(12)	Ken Keltner	20.00	10.00	6.00
(13)	Ralph Kiner	40.00	20.00	12.00
(14)	Willard Marshall	20.00	10.00	6.00
(15)	Walt Masterson	20.00	10.00	6.00
(16)	"Red" Munger	20.00	10.00	6.00
(17)	Don Newcombe	25.00	12.50	7.50
(18)	Hal Newhouser	40.00	20.00	12.00
(19)	Joe Page	20.00	10.00	6.00
(20)	Babe Ruth (Portrait)	100.00	50.00	30.00
(21)	Warren Spahn	40.00	20.00	12.00
(22)	Harry Taylor	20.00	10.00	6.00
(23)	Harry "The Hat" Walker	20.00	10.00	6.00
(24)	Brooklyn Dodgers Team	100.00	50.00	30.00
(25)	New York Yankees Team	150.00	75.00	45.00
1948				
(1)	Richie Ashburn	40.00	20.00	12.00
(2)	Rex Barney	20.00	10.00	6.00
(3)	Gene Bearden	20.00	10.00	6.00
(4)	Lou Brissie	20.00	10.00	6.00
(5)	Alvin Dark	20.00	10.00	6.00
(6)	Larry Doby	40.00	20.00	12.00
(7)	Carl Furillo	25.00	12.50	7.50
(8)	Frank Gustine	20.00	10.00	6.00
(9)	Fred Hutchinson	20.00	10.00	6.00
(10)	Sheldon Jones	20.00	10.00	6.00
(11)	Bob Lemon	40.00	20.00	12.00
(12)	Hank Majeski	20.00	10.00	6.00
(13)	Barney McCosky	20.00	10.00	6.00
(14)	Mel Parnell	20.00	10.00	6.00
(15)	Carl Scheib	20.00	10.00	6.00
(16)	Al Zarilla	20.00	10.00	6.00
(17)	Boston Braves Team	75.00	37.00	22.00
(18)	Cleveland Indians Team	75.00	37.00	22.00
1949				
(1)	Hoot Evers	20.00	10.00	6.00
(2)	Bob Feller	40.00	20.00	12.00
(3)	Billy Goodman	20.00	10.00	6.00
(4)	Sid Gordon	20.00	10.00	6.00
(5)	Gil Hodges	40.00	20.00	12.00
(6)	Art Houtteman	20.00	10.00	6.00
(7)	Dale Mitchell	20.00	10.00	6.00
(8)	Vic Raschi	20.00	10.00	6.00
(9)	Robin Roberts	40.00	20.00	12.00
(10)	Ray Scarborough	20.00	10.00	6.00
(11)	Duke Snider	50.00	25.00	15.00
(12)	Vic Wertz	20.00	10.00	6.00
(13)	Ted Williams	75.00	37.00	22.00
(14)	Brooklyn Dodgers Team	90.00	45.00	27.00
(15)	New York Yankees Team	90.00	45.00	27.00
1950				
(1)	Hank Bauer	15.00	7.50	4.50
(2)	Yogi Berra	30.00	15.00	9.00
(3)	Walt Dropo	12.00	6.00	3.50
(4)	Del Ennis	12.00	6.00	3.50
(5)	Johnny Groth	12.00	6.00	3.50
(6)	Granny Hamner	12.00	6.00	3.50
(7)	Ted Kluszewski	15.00	7.50	4.50
(8)	Johnny Lipon	12.00	6.00	3.50
(9)	Hank Sauer	12.00	6.00	3.50
(10)	Earl Torgeson	12.00	6.00	3.50
(11)	New York Yankees Team	50.00	25.00	15.00
(12)	Philadelphia Phillies Team	35.00	17.50	10.50
1951				
(1)	Grover Alexander	15.00	7.50	4.50
(2)	Chico Carrasquel	15.00	7.50	4.50
(3)	Bubba Church	12.00	6.00	3.50
(4)	Alvin Dark	12.00	6.00	3.50
(5)	Luke Easter	12.00	6.00	3.50
(6)	Carl Erskine	15.00	7.50	4.50
(7)	Ned Garver	12.00	6.00	3.50
(8)	Rogers Hornsby	15.00	7.50	4.50
(9)	Walter Johnson	25.00	12.50	7.50
(10)	Tony Lazzeri	15.00	7.50	4.50
(11)	Whitey Lockman	12.00	6.00	3.50
(12)	Ed Lopat	15.00	7.50	4.50
(13)	Sal Maglie	12.00	6.00	3.50
(14)	Willie Mays	150.00	75.00	45.00
(15)	Gil McDougald	20.00	10.00	6.00
(16)	Irv Noren	12.00	6.00	3.50
(17)	Eddie Robinson	12.00	6.00	3.50
(18)	Jackie Robinson	125.00	62.00	37.00
(19)	Red Rolfe	12.00	6.00	3.50
(20)	Tris Speaker	20.00	10.00	6.00
(21)	Eddie Stanky	12.00	6.00	3.50
(22)	Clyde Vollmer	12.00	6.00	3.50
(23)	Wes Westrum	12.00	6.00	3.50
(24)	Cy Young	25.00	12.50	7.50
(25)	New York Giants Team	40.00	20.00	12.00
(26)	New York Yankees Team	60.00	30.00	18.00
1952				
(1)	Bobby Avila	12.00	6.00	3.50
(2)	Lou Boudreau	20.00	10.00	6.00
(3)	Jim Busby	12.00	6.00	3.50
(4)	Roy Campanella	30.00	15.00	9.00
(5)	Gil Coan	12.00	6.00	3.50
(6)	Walker Cooper	12.00	6.00	3.50
(7)	Al Corwin	12.00	6.00	3.50
(8)	Murry Dickson	12.00	6.00	3.50
(9)	Leo Durocher	20.00	10.00	6.00
(10)	Bob Elliott	12.00	6.00	3.50
(11)	Ferris Fain	12.00	6.00	3.50
(12)	Jimmie Foxx	20.00	10.00	6.00
(13)	Mike Garcia	12.00	6.00	3.50
(14)	Hank Greenberg	25.00	12.50	7.50
(15)	Solly Hemus	12.00	6.00	3.50
(16)	Monte Irvin	20.00	10.00	6.00

(17)	Sam Jethroe	12.00	6.00	3.50
(18)	Ellis Kinder	12.00	6.00	3.50
(19)	Dick Kryhoski	12.00	6.00	3.50
(20)	Clem Labine	15.00	7.50	4.50
(21)	Mickey Mantle	200.00	100.00	60.00
(22)	Connie Marrero	12.00	6.00	3.50
(23)	Cass Michaels	12.00	6.00	3.50
(24)	Minnie Minoso	15.00	7.50	4.50
(25)	Don Mueller	12.00	6.00	3.50
(26)	Mel Parnell	12.00	6.00	3.50
(27)	Allie Reynolds	15.00	7.50	4.50
(28)	"Preacher" Roe	15.00	7.50	4.50
(29)	Saul Rogovin	12.00	6.00	3.50
(30)	Al Rosen	15.00	7.50	4.50
(31)	Red Schoendienst	20.00	10.00	6.00
(32)	Andy Seminick	12.00	6.00	3.50
(33)	Bobby Shantz	12.00	6.00	3.50
(34)	Duke Snider	25.00	12.50	7.50
(35)	Gerry Staley	12.00	6.00	3.50
(36)	Gene Stephens	12.00	6.00	3.50
(37)	Max Surkont	12.00	6.00	3.50
(38)	Bobby Thomson	12.00	6.00	3.50
(39)	Elmer Valo	12.00	6.00	3.50
(40)	Eddie Waitkus	12.00	6.00	3.50
(41)	Gene Woodling	15.00	7.50	4.50
(42)	Eddie Yost	12.00	6.00	3.50
(43)	Gus Zernial	12.00	6.00	3.50
(44)	Brooklyn Dodgers Team	50.00	25.00	15.00
(45)	New York Yankees Team	75.00	37.00	22.00
1953				
(1)	Joe Black	15.00	7.50	4.50
(2)	Billy Cox	12.00	6.00	3.50
(3)	Billy Loes	12.00	6.00	3.50
(4)	Billy Martin	15.00	7.50	4.50
(5)	Eddie Mathews	25.00	12.50	7.50
(6)	George Shuba	12.00	6.00	3.50
(7)	Hoyt Wilhelm	20.00	10.00	6.00
1954				
(1)	Joe Adcock	12.00	6.00	3.50
(2)	Johnny Antonelli	12.00	6.00	3.50
(3)	Gus Bell	12.00	6.00	3.50
(4)	Jim Greengrass	12.00	6.00	3.50
(5)	Bob Grim	12.00	6.00	3.50
(6)	Frank House	12.00	6.00	3.50
(7)	Jackie Jensen	12.00	6.00	3.50
(8)	Al Kaline	25.00	12.50	7.50
(9)	Harvey Kuenn	15.00	7.50	4.50
(10)	Willie Miranda	12.00	6.00	3.50
(11)	Wally Moon	12.00	6.00	3.50
(12)	Ray Moore	12.00	6.00	3.50
(13)	Don Mossi	12.00	6.00	3.50
(14)	Stan Musial	30.00	15.00	9.00
(15)	Hal Naragon	12.00	6.00	3.50
(16)	Chet Nichols	12.00	6.00	3.50
(17)	Billy Pierce	12.00	6.00	3.50
(18)	Arnie Portocarrero	12.00	6.00	3.50
(19)	James "Dusty" Rhodes	12.00	6.00	3.50
(20)	Babe Ruth	50.00	25.00	15.00
(21)	Dean Stone	12.00	6.00	3.50
(22)	Bob Turley	15.00	7.50	4.50
(23)	Jim Wilson	12.00	6.00	3.50
(24)	New York Giants Team	50.00	25.00	15.00
1955				
(1)	Gene Conley	12.00	6.00	3.50
(2)	Elston Howard	15.00	7.50	4.50
(3)	Hank Sauer	12.00	6.00	3.50
1956				
(1)	Hank Bauer	15.00	7.50	4.50
(2)	Yogi Berra	25.00	12.50	7.50
(3)	Ray Boone	12.00	6.00	3.50
(4)	Ken Boyer	15.00	7.50	4.50
(5)	Tom Brewer	12.00	6.00	3.50
(6)	Bob Buhl	12.00	6.00	3.50
(7)	Nellie Fox	20.00	10.00	6.00
(8)	Bob Keegan	12.00	6.00	3.50
(9)	Don Larsen	15.00	7.50	4.50
(10)	Jim Lemon	12.00	6.00	3.50
(11)	Danny O'Connell	12.00	6.00	3.50
(12)	Jim Pendleton	12.00	6.00	3.50
(13)	Bob Rush	12.00	6.00	3.50
(14)	Roy Sievers	12.00	6.00	3.50
(15)	Gus Zernial	12.00	6.00	3.50
1957				
(1)	Hank Aaron	30.00	15.00	9.00
(2)	Joe Adcock	12.00	6.00	3.50
(3)	Luis Arroyo	12.00	6.00	3.50
(4)	Ed Bailey	12.00	6.00	3.50
(5)	Ernie Banks	25.00	12.50	7.50
(6)	Roy Campanella	20.00	10.00	6.00
(7)	Billy Cox	12.00	6.00	3.50
(8)	Del Crandall	12.00	6.00	3.50
(9)	Whitey Ford	25.00	12.50	7.50
(10)	Bob Friend	12.00	6.00	3.50
(11)	Carl Furillo	15.00	7.50	4.50
(12)	Granny Hamner	12.00	6.00	3.50
(13)	Gil Hodges	15.00	7.50	4.50
(14)	Billy Hoeft	12.00	6.00	3.50
(15)	Walter Johnson	25.00	12.50	7.50
(16)	George Kell	20.00	10.00	6.00
(17)	Ted Kluszewski	20.00	10.00	6.00
(18)	Johnny Kucks	12.00	6.00	3.50
(19)	Harvey Kuenn	12.00	6.00	3.50
(20)	Clem Labine	12.00	6.00	3.50
(21)	Vern Law	12.00	6.00	3.50
(22)	Brooks Lawrence	12.00	6.00	3.50
(23)	Bob Lemon	20.00	10.00	6.00
(24)	Sherman Lollar	12.00	6.00	3.50
(25)	Billy Martin	15.00	7.50	4.50
(25)	Eddie Mathews	20.00	10.00	6.00
(26)	Charlie Maxwell	12.00	6.00	3.50
(27)	Willie Mays	60.00	30.00	18.00
(28)	Gil McDougald	15.00	7.50	4.50
(29)	Willie Miranda	12.00	6.00	3.50
(30)	Jimmy Piersall	12.00	6.00	3.50
(31)	Pee Wee Reese	25.00	12.50	7.50
(32)	"Rip" Repulski	12.00	6.00	3.50
(33)	Robin Roberts	20.00	10.00	6.00
(34)	Frank Robinson	30.00	15.00	9.00

(35)	Al Rosen	12.00	6.00	3.50
(36)	Babe Ruth	60.00	30.00	18.00
(37)	Herb Score	15.00	7.50	4.50
(38)	Enos Slaughter	20.00	10.00	6.00
(39)	Warren Spahn	20.00	10.00	6.00
(40)	Johnny Temple	12.00	6.00	3.50
(41)	Mickey Vernon	12.00	6.00	3.50
1957 (17-1/2" x 20")				
(1)	Johnny Antonelli	30.00	15.00	9.00
(2)	Hank Bauer	45.00	22.00	13.50
(3)	Frank House	30.00	15.00	9.00
(4)	Jackie Jensen	35.00	17.50	10.00
(5)	Al Kaline	45.00	22.00	13.50
(6)	Bob Lemon	35.00	17.50	10.00
(7)	Chet Nichols	30.00	15.00	9.00
(8)	Al Rosen	30.00	15.00	9.00
(9)	Dean Stone	30.00	15.00	9.00
(10)	Bob Turley	35.00	17.50	10.00
(11)	Mickey Vernon	30.00	15.00	9.00

1915 Baseball Magazine Premium

A special "Park Edition" of the April "Baseball Magazine," produced for sale at major league ballparks, was published in 1915. The cover features a J.F. Kernan portrait of Walter Johnson. Bound inside was a Kernan portrait of Christy Mathewson, printed on heavy, slick paper designed to be removed for display.

	NM	EX	VG
Complete Magazine:	3,500	2,500	1,500
Christy Mathewson (Premium)	2,000	1,000	600.00

1913 Baseball Managers Scorecard/Fan

This novelty souvenir item was presumable made for sale or as a giveaway promotion which could be customized with sponsors' advertising on the back. The body of the fan is a heavy cardboard ovoid about 9-1/2" x 9". At center is a scorecard. Printed in color around the scoring section are colorful caricatures of each National and American League manager either in a costume representing the team nickname or holding a mascot, etc. The piece is stapled to a 6" wooden stick. Local advertising may or may not appear on the back.

	NM	EX	VG
Joe Birmingham, Nixey Callahan, Frank, Chance, Fred Clarke, Bill Dahlen, Red, Dooin, Jonny Evers, Clark Griffith,, Miller Huggins, Hughie Jennings, Connie, Mack, John McGraw, Jake Stahl, George, Stallings, George Stovall, Joe Tinker	1,150	575.00	345.00

1950 Baseball Player Charms

The date of issue for this novelty item is conjectural, based on known player selection. Packaged in plastic bubbles for sale in vending machines, these charms are found in several different shapes - rectangle, octagon, etc. - and colors of plastic. A black-and-white photo appears at center with a loop at top for hanging. Size also varies but is about 3/4" x 1-1/4". Players are not identified on the charm and there is no number. The checklist here is in alphabetical order, and likely not complete.

		NM	EX	VG
Common Player:		20.00	10.00	6.00
(1)	Yogi Berra	45.00	22.00	13.50
(2)	Ewell Blackwell	20.00	10.00	6.00
(3)	Roy Campanella	45.00	22.00	13.50
(4)	Joe DiMaggio	75.00	37.00	22.00
(5)	Carl Erskine	20.00	10.00	6.00
(6)	Bob Feller	25.00	12.50	7.50
(7)	Carl Furillo	22.50	11.00	6.75
(8)	Lou Gehrig	65.00	32.00	19.50
(9)	Ralph Kiner	20.00	10.00	6.00
(10)	Stan Musial	55.00	27.00	16.50
(11)	Andy Pafko	20.00	10.00	6.00
(12)	Pee Wee Reese	35.00	17.50	10.50
(13)	Phil Rizzuto	30.00	15.00	9.00
(14)	Jackie Robinson	65.00	32.00	19.50
(15)	Babe Ruth	95.00	47.00	28.00
(16)	Duke Snider	35.00	17.50	10.50
(17)	Wally Westlake	20.00	10.00	6.00
(18)	Ted Williams	60.00	30.00	18.00

1952 Baseball Player Doubleheader Charms

These vending machine prizes were probably issued in the early 1950s, though pinning down a date via player selection is imprecise. About 7/8" in diameter, these novelties have black-and-white player photos on front and back, with the player's name in script beneath his portrait. A clear plastic dome covers the photos and is wrapped with a looped band for hanging. The unnumbered charms are listed here in alphabetical order.

		NM	EX	VG
Complete Set (31):		550.00	275.00	175.00
Common Player:		25.00	12.50	7.50
(1)	Richie Ashburn, Phil Masi	30.00	15.00	9.00
(2)	Hank Bauer, Johnny Pesky	25.00	12.50	7.50
(3)	Yogi Berra, Duke Snider	45.00	22.00	13.50
(4)	Ewell Blackwell, "Big" Jim Konstanty	25.00	12.50	7.50
(5)	Lou Boudreau, Allie Reynolds	27.50	13.50	8.25
(6)	Leland Brissie, Albert Schoendienst	27.50	13.50	8.25
(7)	Roy Campanella, Bob Elliott	30.00	15.00	9.00
(8)	Phil Cavarretta, Virgil Stallcup	25.00	12.50	7.50
(9)	Sam Chapman, Larry Jansen	25.00	12.50	7.50
(10)	Jerry Coleman, George Kell	27.50	13.50	8.25
(11)	Billy Cox, Junior Thompson	25.00	12.50	7.50
(12)	Walt Dropo, Myron McCormick	25.00	12.50	7.50
(13)	Al Evans, Wes Westrum	25.00	12.50	7.50
(14)	Walter Evers, Cliff Mapes	25.00	12.50	7.50
(15)	Bob Feller, Phil Rizzuto	35.00	17.50	10.50
(16)	Gordon Goldsberry, Stan Musial	30.00	15.00	9.00
(17)	Clint Hartung, Don Kolloway	25.00	12.50	7.50
(18)	Grady Hatton, Tommy Holmes	25.00	12.50	7.50
(19)	Tommy Henrich, Ted Kluszewski	27.50	13.50	8.25
(20)	Gene Hermanski, Hal Newhouser	25.00	12.50	7.50
(21)	Art Houtteman, Jackie Robinson	45.00	22.00	13.50
(22)	Sid Hudson, Andy Pafko	25.00	12.50	7.50
(23)	Ed Kazak, Bob Lemon	27.50	13.50	8.25
(24)	Ellis Kinder, Gus Zernial	25.00	12.50	7.50
(25)	Ralph Kiner, Joe Page	27.50	13.50	8.25
(26)	Ed Lopat, Paul Trout	25.00	12.50	7.50
(27)	Don Newcombe, Vic Wertz	25.00	12.50	7.50
(28)	Dave Philley, Aaron Robinson	25.00	12.50	7.50
(29)	Vic Raschi, Enos Slaughter	27.50	13.50	8.25
(30)	Pee Wee Reese, Gene Woodling	30.00	15.00	9.00
(31)	George Tebbetts, Eddie Yost	25.00	12.50	7.50

1961 Baseball Player Key Chains

The maker of these postage-stamp size (1-1/8" x 1-1/2") black-and-white, blank-back "cards" is unknown. From the inclusion of numerous journeyman Pirates players in the set, it probably has a Pittsburgh origin. Possibly intended for sale at stadium souvenir counters, they were made to be inserted into clear plastic key chain novelties, and have a semi-gloss front surface. Unnumbered, they are checklisted here alphabetically.

		NM	EX	VG
Complete Set (69):		400.00	200.00	120.00
Common Player:		5.00	2.50	1.50
(1)	Hank Aaron	15.00	7.50	4.50
(2)	Bob Allison	5.00	2.50	1.50
(3)	George Altman	5.00	2.50	1.50
(4)	Luis Aparicio	7.50	3.75	2.25
(5)	Richie Ashburn	7.50	3.75	2.25
(6)	Ernie Banks	10.00	5.00	3.00
(7)	Earl Battey	5.00	2.50	1.50
(8)	Hank Bauer	6.00	3.00	1.75
(9)	Gus Bell	5.00	2.50	1.50
(10)	Yogi Berra	10.00	5.00	3.00
(11)	Ken Boyer	6.00	3.00	1.75
(12)	Lew Burdette	5.00	2.50	1.50
(13)	Smoky Burgess	5.00	2.50	1.50
(14)	Orlando Cepeda	7.50	3.75	2.25
(15)	Gino Cimoli	5.00	2.50	1.50
(16)	Roberto Clemente	20.00	10.00	6.00
(17)	Del Crandall	5.00	2.50	1.50
(18)	Dizzy Dean	9.00	4.50	2.75
(19)	Don Drysdale	7.50	3.75	2.25
(20)	Sam Esposito	5.00	2.50	1.50
(21)	Roy Face	5.00	2.50	1.50
(22)	Nelson Fox	7.50	3.75	2.25
(23)	Bob Friend	5.00	2.50	1.50
(24)	Lou Gehrig	12.50	6.25	3.75
(25)	Joe Gibbon	5.00	2.50	1.50
(26)	Jim Gilliam	6.00	3.00	1.75
(27)	Fred Green	5.00	2.50	1.50
(28)	Pumpsie Green	5.00	2.50	1.50
(29)	Dick Groat	6.00	3.00	1.75
(30)	Harvey Haddix	5.00	2.50	1.50
(31)	Don Hoak	5.00	2.50	1.50
(32)	Glen Hobbie	5.00	2.50	1.50
(33)	Frank Howard	6.00	3.00	1.75
(34)	Jackie Jensen	5.00	2.50	1.50
(35)	Sam Jones	5.00	2.50	1.50
(36)	Al Kaline	9.00	4.50	2.75
(37)	Harmon Killebrew	7.50	3.75	2.25
(38)	Harvey Kuenn	5.00	2.50	1.50
(39)	Norm Larker	5.00	2.50	1.50
(40)	Vernon Law	5.00	2.50	1.50
(41)	Mickey Mantle	30.00	15.00	9.00
(42)	Roger Maris	12.00	6.00	3.50
(43)	Eddie Mathews	7.50	3.75	2.25
(44)	Willie Mays	12.00	6.00	3.50
(45)	Bill Mazeroski	7.50	3.75	2.25
(46)	Willie McCovey	7.50	3.75	2.25
(47)	Lindy McDaniel	5.00	2.50	1.50
(48)	Roy McMillan	5.00	2.50	1.50
(49)	Minnie Minoso	6.00	3.00	1.75
(50)	Danny Murtaugh	5.00	2.50	1.50
(51)	Stan Musial	12.00	6.00	3.50
(52)	Rocky Nelson	5.00	2.50	1.50
(53)	Bob Oldis	5.00	2.50	1.50
(54)	Vada Pinson	6.00	3.00	1.75
(55)	Vic Power	5.00	2.50	1.50
(56)	Robin Roberts	7.50	3.75	2.25
(57)	Pete Runnels	5.00	2.50	1.50
(58)	Babe Ruth	20.00	10.00	6.00
(59)	Ron Santo	6.00	3.00	1.75
(60)	Dick Schofield	5.00	2.50	1.50
(61)	Bob Skinner	5.00	2.50	1.50
(62)	Hal Smith	5.00	2.50	1.50
(63)	Duke Snider	9.00	4.50	2.75
(64)	Warren Spahn	7.50	3.75	2.25
(65)	Dick Stuart	5.00	2.50	1.50
(66)	Willie Tasby	5.00	2.50	1.50
(67)	Tony Taylor	5.00	2.50	1.50
(68)	Bill Virdon	5.00	2.50	1.50
(69)	Ted Williams	17.50	9.00	5.00

1978 Baseball Player Patches

These card-size (about 2-1/2" x 3-1/4") cloth patches feature embroidered player portraits on a white background with a color border. Uniform logos are not present. The patches originally sold for $2.50 apiece from the Penn Emblem Co., Philadelphia, though the company's name is not found on the patches. The unnumbered patches are listed here in alphabetical order.

		NM	EX	VG
Complete Set (103):		350.00	175.00	100.00
Common Player:		3.00	1.50	.90
(1)	Buddy Bell	3.00	1.50	.90
(2)	Johnny Bench	10.00	5.00	3.00
(3)	Vida Blue	3.00	1.50	.90
(4)	Bobby Bonds	3.00	1.50	.90
(5)	Bob Boone	3.00	1.50	.90
(6)	Larry Bowa	3.00	1.50	.90
(7)	George Brett	12.00	6.00	3.50
(8)	Lou Brock	9.00	4.50	2.75
(9)	Rick Burleson	3.00	1.50	.90
(10)	Jeff Burroughs	3.00	1.50	.90
(11)	Bert Campaneris	3.00	1.50	.90
(12)	John Candelaria	3.00	1.50	.90
(13)	Rod Carew	9.00	4.50	2.75
(14)	Steve Carlton	9.00	4.50	2.75
(15)	Gary Carter	7.50	3.75	2.25
(16)	Dave Cash	3.00	1.50	.90
(17)	Cesar Cedeno	3.00	1.50	.90
(18)	Ron Cey	3.00	1.50	.90
(19)	Chris Chambliss	3.00	1.50	.90
(20)	Jack Clark	3.00	1.50	.90
(21)	Dave Concepcion	3.00	1.50	.90
(22)	Cecil Cooper	3.00	1.50	.90
(23)	Jose Cruz	3.00	1.50	.90
(24)	Andre Dawson	3.00	1.50	.90
(25)	Dan Driessen	3.00	1.50	.90
(26)	Rawly Eastwick	3.00	1.50	.90
(27)	Dwight Evans	3.00	1.50	.90
(28)	Mark Fidrych	4.50	2.25	1.25
(29)	Rollie Fingers	7.50	3.75	2.25
(30)	Carlton Fisk	9.00	4.50	2.75
(31)	George Foster	3.00	1.50	.90
(32)	Steve Garvey	6.00	3.00	1.75
(33)	Rich Gossage	3.00	1.50	.90
(34)	Bobby Grich	3.00	1.50	.90
(35)	Ross Grimsley	3.00	1.50	.90
(36)	Ron Guidry	3.00	1.50	.90
(37)	Mike Hargrove	3.00	1.50	.90
(38)	Keith Hernandez	3.00	1.50	.90
(39)	Larry Hisle	3.00	1.50	.90
(40)	Bob Horner	3.00	1.50	.90
(41)	Roy Howell	3.00	1.50	.90
(42)	"Catfish" Hunter	7.50	3.75	2.25
(43)	Reggie Jackson	12.00	6.00	3.50
(44)	Tommy John	4.00	2.00	1.25
(45)	Jim Kern	3.00	1.50	.90
(46)	Chet Lemon	3.00	1.50	.90
(47)	Davey Lopes	3.00	1.50	.90
(48)	Greg Luzinski	3.00	1.50	.90
(49)	Fred Lynn	3.00	1.50	.90
(50)	Garry Maddox	3.00	1.50	.90
(51)	Bill Madlock	3.00	1.50	.90
(52)	Jon Matlack	3.00	1.50	.90
(53)	John Mayberry	3.00	1.50	.90
(54)	Lee Mazzilli	3.00	1.50	.90
(55)	Rick Monday	3.00	1.50	.90
(56)	Don Money	3.00	1.50	.90
(57)	Willie Montanez	3.00	1.50	.90
(58)	John Montefusco	3.00	1.50	.90
(59)	Joe Morgan	9.00	4.50	2.75
(60)	Thurman Munson	7.50	3.75	2.25
(61)	Bobby Murcer	3.00	1.50	.90
(62)	Graig Nettles	3.00	1.50	.90
(63)	Phil Niekro	7.50	3.75	2.25
(64)	Al Oliver	3.00	1.50	.90
(65)	Amos Otis	3.00	1.50	.90
(66)	Jim Palmer	9.00	4.50	2.75
(67)	Dave Parker	3.00	1.50	.90
(68)	Fred Patek	3.00	1.50	.90
(69)	Tony Perez	7.50	3.75	2.25
(70)	Lou Piniella	4.00	2.00	1.25
(71)	Biff Pocoroba	3.00	1.50	.90
(72)	Darrell Porter	3.00	1.50	.90
(73)	Rick Reuschel	3.00	1.50	.90
(74)	Jim Rice	6.00	3.00	1.75
(75a)	Pete Rose (Red border.)	12.00	6.00	3.50
(75b)	Pete Rose (Blue border.)	12.00	6.00	3.50
(76)	Joe Rudi	3.00	1.50	.90
(77)	Rick Reuschel	3.00	1.50	.90
(78)	Nolan Ryan	15.00	7.50	4.50
(79)	Manny Sanguillen	3.00	1.50	.90
(80)	Mike Schmidt	12.00	6.00	3.50
(81)	George Scott	3.00	1.50	.90
(82)	Tom Seaver	9.00	4.50	2.75
(83)	Ted Simmons	3.00	1.50	.90
(84)	Reggie Smith	3.00	1.50	.90
(85)	Willie Stargell	9.00	4.50	2.75
(86)	Rennie Stennett	3.00	1.50	.90
(87)	Jim Sundberg	3.00	1.50	.90
(88)	Bruce Sutter	7.50	3.75	2.25
(89)	Frank Tanana	3.00	1.50	.90
(90)	Garry Templeton	3.00	1.50	.90
(91)	Gene Tenace	3.00	1.50	.90
(92)	Jason Thompson	3.00	1.50	.90
(93)	Luis Tiant	3.00	1.50	.90
(94)	Joe Torre	4.50	2.25	1.25
(95)	Ellis Valentine	3.00	1.50	.90
(96)	Bob Watson	3.00	1.50	.90
(97)	Frank White	3.00	1.50	.90
(98)	Lou Whitaker	3.00	1.50	.90
(99)	Bump Wills	3.00	1.50	.90
(100)	Dave Winfield	9.00	4.50	2.75
(101)	Butch Wynegar	3.00	1.50	.90
(102)	Carl Yastrzemski	12.00	6.00	3.50
(103)	Richie Zisk	3.00	1.50	.90

Fantasy Baseball Player Pencil Clips

This series of modern (circa late 1990s) pencil clips features old-time baseball stars. The pieces feature enameled round buttons in various sizes attached to a steel frame designed to be slipped over a pencil, ostensibly for use with a scorecard during a ball game. These are often sold on eBay and at flea markets by persons purporting them to be old.

NO COLLECTIBLE VALUE
Ty Cobb
Christy Mathewson
Satchel Paige (St. Louis Browns)
Babe Ruth (Champions)
Honus Wagner
1959 World Series White Sox

1913 Baseball Player Stamps

The extent of this issue and the exact date and manner of its issue are not known. The large-format (about 1-13/16" x 2-1/2") stamps have color artwork of the players on a baseball diamond background. A solid colored frame with art deco detailing separates the picture from the white border. Backs are, of course, blank.

	NM	EX	VG
Chief Bender	200.00	100.00	60.00
Ty Cobb	1,750	875.00	525.00
Joe Jackson	2,250	1,125	675.00
Christy Mathewson	475.00	235.00	140.00
Tris Speaker	200.00	100.00	60.00

1892 Base Ball Scenes (N360)

The N360 American Card Catalog designation covers the several tobacco manufacturers who issued this type of card to advertise various brands. Obviously, the cards do not picture actual ballplayers, but rather have on their fronts color lithographs of attractive women in baseball uniforms and in game action. Approximately 2-3/16" x 3-15/16" most cards have a tiny line of type at bottom carrying a Donaldson Bros., N.Y., copyright. Those cards issued to promote the Little Rhody Cut Plus brand have a script ad message on front and a monthly schedule of the 12-team National League on back. Advertising for the various brands of tobacco companies may be printed directly on the card back, on a paper label pasted over another ad or overprinted on a previously printed ad. Cards are known with these manufacturers and brands. S.W. Venable: Cockade, Gay Head, Helmet, Ideal and Pluck; G.F. Young & Bro.: Little Rhody, and M.T. Coffey. Nine different poses are known for the card fronts.

	NM	EX	VG
Common Card:	600.00	300.00	180.00

1913 Base Ball Series Notebooks

The issue date cited is conjectural, based on writing found in a surviving specimen of this child's notebook. The 8" x 10" notebook has on its cover a baseball diamond and bleachers drawing in white on a beige background. Printed above and below the artwork are full-color reproductions of five baseball cards from the Philadelphia Caramel issues of 1909 (E95) and 1910 (E96). The cover is printed on thinner stock the original cards and has no printing on the reverse side. This has led to cut copies of these cards being misidentified as proofs. Because similar blank-back, thin stock cards are known of other players, it is possible other notebook covers may exist.

	NM	EX	VG
Complete Notebook:	750.00	375.00	225.00
Fred Clark (Clarke)(E96), Nap Lajoie (E96), Jake Pfeister (E96), Honus Wagner (E95), Ed Willetts (Willett)(E95)			
OBSERVED SINGLES			
Harry Krause (E95)	100.00	40.00	20.00

1911 Baseball Scorecard Fan

This unusual player collectible is a combination fan and scorecard published circa 1911. The cardboard scorecard is about 10-1/2" x 9" and stapled to an approximately 11" long wooden handle. Printed in black-and-white, there are 16 player portraits at top, separated by a baseball. At center is the portrait of young lady and at bottom is a ball-in-mitt photo. The fans can be found with various local advertising overprinted on front or back: Barton's Barber Shop, Ira P. File Ice Cream and Confectionery, Maine's Bliss School of Business, Poole Pianos, Kemper pharmacy, etc. The players are identified by last name and for lack of uniform details, specific identification of a few of them is speculative.

	NM	EX	VG
Germany Schaeffer (Schaefer), Bobby Wallace, Billy Sullivan, Hal Chase, George Moriarty, Harry Lord, Harry Davis, Nap Lajoie, Mickey Doolan, Clark Griffith, Bill Dahlen, Jeff Sweeney, Frank Chance, Art Devlin, Fred Clark (Clarke), Roger Bresnahan	1,500	750.00	400.00

1964 Baseball Stars - Present and Future Photocard

This large-format (11" x 8-1/2") color card features three group photos of top stars of the day. In addition to the photos, there are facsimile autographs of each player on the bright yellow background. Back is blank. (See also Baseball Greats Postcard.)

	NM	EX	VG
Sheet:	25.00	12.50	7.50
Dean Chance, Don Drysdale, Dick Farrell, Jim Fregosi, Sandy Koufax, Willie Mays, Joe Pepitone, Dick Radatz			

1912 Base Ball Stars Series

This set of blank-backed, black-and-white 6" x 9" pictures features the contestants of the 1912 World Series - the Red Sox and Giants. It is possible these pictures were sold at the ballparks during the Series. The checklist here is probably incomplete. The unnumbered pictures have been listed alphabetically within team.

	NM	EX	VG
Common Player:	450.00	225.00	135.00
BOSTON RED SOX			
(1) Hugh Bedient	450.00	225.00	135.00
(2) Joe Wood	480.00	240.00	145.00
N.Y. GIANTS			
(1) Rube Marquard	525.00	260.00	150.00
(2) Christy Mathewson	1,050	525.00	315.00
(3) Jeff Tesreau	450.00	225.00	135.00

1938 Baseball Tabs

The issuer and manner of distribution for these baseball tabs is unknown. About 3/4" diameter, with bendable wings at each side, the points of which could be stuck through fabric and thus attached to a cap or jacket, the tabs have black-and-white player portraits on a baseball-style background in one of several colors. Most of the player first names have parentheses around them. The team tabs have a large nickname at center and the city and league at bottom. The inclusion of American Association teams argues for distribution in the upper Midwest. The unnumbered tabs are listed here in alphabetical order.

	NM	EX	VG
Complete Set (53):	3,000	1,500	900.00
Common Player:	50.00	25.00	15.50
Common Team:	50.00	25.00	15.00
(1) Luke Appling	75.00	37.00	22.00
(2) Earl Averill	75.00	37.00	22.00
(3) Phil Cavarretta	50.00	25.00	15.00
(4) Dizzy Dean	100.00	50.00	30.00
(5) Paul Derringer	50.00	25.00	15.00
(6) Bill Dickey	90.00	45.00	27.00
(7) Joe DiMaggio	450.00	225.00	135.00
(8) Bob Feller	75.00	37.00	22.00
(9) Lou Fette	50.00	25.00	15.00
(10) Jimmie Foxx	100.00	50.00	30.00
(11) Lou Gehrig	375.00	185.00	110.00
(12) Charley Gehringer	75.00	37.00	22.00
(13) Lefty Gomez	75.00	37.00	22.00
(14) Hank Greenberg	90.00	45.00	27.00
(15) Lefty Grove	75.00	37.00	22.00
(16) Mule Haas	50.00	25.00	15.00
(17) Gabby Hartnett	75.00	37.00	22.00
(18) Rollie Hemsley	50.00	25.00	15.00
(19) Carl Hubbell	75.00	37.00	22.00
(20) Chuck Klein	75.00	37.00	22.00
(21) Red Kress	50.00	25.00	15.00
(22) Push-Em-Up-Tony Lazzeri	75.00	37.00	22.00
(23) Ted Lyons	75.00	37.00	22.00
(24) Joe Medwick	75.00	37.00	22.00
(25) Van Lingle Mungo	50.00	25.00	15.00
(26) Rip Radcliff	50.00	25.00	15.00
(27) Schoolboy Rowe	50.00	25.00	15.00
(28) Al Simmons	75.00	37.00	22.00
(29) Little Poison Waner	75.00	37.00	22.00
(30) Athletics (Philadelphia)	50.00	25.00	15.00
(31) Bees (Boston)	50.00	25.00	15.00
(32) Blues (Kansas City)	50.00	25.00	15.00
(33) Brewers (Milwaukee)	50.00	25.00	15.00
(34) Browns (St. Louis)	50.00	25.00	15.00
(35) Cardinals (St. Louis)	50.00	25.00	15.00
(36) Colonels (Louisville)	50.00	25.00	15.00
(37) Cubs (Chicago)	50.00	25.00	15.00
(38) Dodgers (Brooklyn)	50.00	25.00	15.00
(39) Giants (New York)	50.00	25.00	15.00
(40) Indians (Cleveland)	50.00	25.00	15.00
(41) Indians (Indianapolis)	50.00	25.00	15.00
(42) Millers (Minneapolis)	50.00	25.00	15.00
(43) Mud-Hens (Toledo)	50.00	25.00	15.00
(44) Nationals (Washington)	50.00	25.00	15.00
(45) Phillies (Philadelphia)	50.00	25.00	15.00
(46) Pirates (Pittsburgh)	50.00	25.00	15.00
(47) Red Birds (Columbus)	50.00	25.00	15.00
(48) Reds (Cincinnati)	50.00	25.00	15.00
(49) Red Sox (Boston)	50.00	25.00	15.00
(50) Saints (St. Paul)	50.00	25.00	15.00
(51) Tigers (Detroit)	50.00	25.00	15.00
(52) White Sox (Chicago)	50.00	25.00	15.00
(53) Yankees (New York)	65.00	32.00	19.50

1934-36 Batter-Up (R318)

National Chicle's 192-card "Batter-Up" set was issued over a three-year period. The blank-backed cards are die-cut, enabling collectors of the era to fold the top of the card over so that it could stand upright on its own support. The cards can be found in black-and-white or a variety of color tints. Card numbers 1-80 measure 2-3/8" x 3-1/4" in size, while the high-numbered cards (#81-192) measure 2-3/8" x 3" (1/4" smaller in height). The high-numbered cards are significantly more difficult to find than the lower numbers. The set's ACC designation is R318.

	NM	EX	VG
Complete Set (192):	33,000	13,000	6,500
Common Player (1-80):	125.00	50.00	25.00
Common Player (81-192):	240.00	95.00	45.00
1 Wally Berger	225.00	90.00	45.00
2 Ed Brandt	125.00	50.00	25.00
3 Al Lopez	400.00	160.00	80.00
4 Dick Bartell	125.00	50.00	25.00
5 Carl Hubbell	425.00	170.00	85.00
6 Bill Terry	400.00	160.00	80.00
7 Pepper Martin	125.00	50.00	25.00
8 Jim Bottomley	400.00	160.00	80.00
9 Tommy Bridges	125.00	50.00	25.00
10 Rick Ferrell	400.00	160.00	80.00
11 Ray Benge	125.00	50.00	25.00
12 Wes Ferrell	125.00	50.00	25.00
13 Bill Cissell	125.00	50.00	25.00
14 Pie Traynor	400.00	160.00	80.00
15 Roy Mahaffey	125.00	50.00	25.00
16 Chick Hafey	400.00	160.00	80.00
17 Lloyd Waner	400.00	160.00	80.00
18 Jack Burns	125.00	50.00	25.00
19 Buddy Myer	125.00	50.00	25.00
20 Bob Johnson	125.00	50.00	25.00
21 Arky Vaughn (Vaughan)	400.00	160.00	80.00
22 Red Rolfe	125.00	50.00	25.00
23 Lefty Gomez	400.00	160.00	80.00
24 Earl Averill	400.00	160.00	80.00
25 Mickey Cochrane	400.00	160.00	80.00
26 Van Mungo	125.00	50.00	25.00
27 Mel Ott	550.00	220.00	110.00
28 Jimmie Foxx	700.00	280.00	140.00
29 Jimmy Dykes	125.00	50.00	25.00
30 Bill Dickey	400.00	160.00	80.00
31 Lefty Grove	400.00	160.00	80.00
32 Joe Cronin	400.00	160.00	80.00
33 Frankie Frisch	400.00	160.00	80.00
34 Al Simmons	400.00	160.00	80.00

35	Rogers Hornsby	625.00	250.00	125.00
36	Ted Lyons	400.00	160.00	80.00
37	Rabbit Maranville	400.00	160.00	80.00
38	Jimmie Wilson	125.00	50.00	25.00
39	Willie Kamm	125.00	50.00	25.00
40	Bill Hallahan	125.00	50.00	25.00
41	Gus Suhr	125.00	50.00	25.00
42	Charlie Gehringer	400.00	160.00	80.00
43	Joe Heving	125.00	50.00	25.00
44	Adam Comorosky	125.00	50.00	25.00
45	Tony Lazzeri	400.00	160.00	80.00
46	Sam Leslie	125.00	50.00	25.00
47	Bob Smith	125.00	50.00	25.00
48	Willis Hudlin	125.00	50.00	25.00
49	Carl Reynolds	125.00	50.00	25.00
50	Fred Schulte	125.00	50.00	25.00
51	Cookie Lavagetto	125.00	50.00	25.00
52	Hal Schumacher	125.00	50.00	25.00
53	Doc Cramer	125.00	50.00	25.00
54	Si Johnson	125.00	50.00	25.00
55	Ollie Bejma	125.00	50.00	25.00
56	Sammy Byrd	125.00	50.00	25.00
57	Hank Greenberg	550.00	220.00	110.00
58	Bill Knickerbocker	125.00	50.00	25.00
59	Billy Urbanski	125.00	50.00	25.00
60	Ed Morgan	125.00	50.00	25.00
61	Eric McNair	125.00	50.00	25.00
62	Ben Chapman	125.00	50.00	25.00
63	Roy Johnson	125.00	50.00	25.00
64	"Dizzy" Dean	825.00	330.00	165.00
65	Zeke Bonura	125.00	50.00	25.00
66	Firpo Marberry	125.00	50.00	25.00
67	Gus Mancuso	125.00	50.00	25.00
68	Joe Vosmik	125.00	50.00	25.00
69	Earl Grace	125.00	50.00	25.00
70	Tony Piet	125.00	50.00	25.00
71	Rollie Hemsley	125.00	50.00	25.00
72	Fred Fitzsimmons	125.00	50.00	25.00
73	Hack Wilson	400.00	160.00	80.00
74	Chick Fullis	125.00	50.00	25.00
75	Fred Frankhouse	125.00	50.00	25.00
76	Ethan Allen	125.00	50.00	25.00
77	Heinie Manush	400.00	160.00	80.00
78	Rip Collins	125.00	50.00	25.00
79	Tony Cuccinello	125.00	50.00	25.00
80	Joe Kuhel	165.00	66.00	33.00
81	Thomas Bridges	240.00	96.00	48.00
82	Clinton Brown	240.00	96.00	48.00
83	Albert Blanche	240.00	96.00	48.00
84	"Boze" Berger	240.00	96.00	48.00
85	Goose Goslin	550.00	220.00	110.00
86	Vernon Gomez	600.00	240.00	120.00
87	Joe Glen (Glenn)	240.00	96.00	48.00
88	Cy Blanton	240.00	96.00	48.00
89	Tom Carey	240.00	96.00	48.00
90	Ralph Birkhofer	240.00	96.00	48.00
91	Frank Gabler	240.00	96.00	48.00
92	Dick Coffman	240.00	96.00	48.00
93	Ollie Bejma	240.00	96.00	48.00
94	Leroy Earl Parmalee	240.00	96.00	48.00
95	Carl Reynolds	240.00	96.00	48.00
96	Ben Cantwell	240.00	96.00	48.00
97	Curtis Davis	240.00	96.00	48.00
98	Wallace Moses, Billy Webb	525.00	210.00	105.00
99	Ray Benge	240.00	96.00	48.00
100	"Pie" Traynor	550.00	220.00	110.00
101	Phil. Cavarretta	240.00	96.00	48.00
102	"Pep" Young	240.00	96.00	48.00
103	Willis Hudlin	240.00	96.00	48.00
104	Mickey Haslin	240.00	96.00	48.00
105	Oswald Bluege	240.00	96.00	48.00
106	Paul Andrews	240.00	96.00	48.00
107	Edward A. Brandt	240.00	96.00	48.00
108	Dan Taylor	240.00	96.00	48.00
109	Thornton T. Lee	240.00	96.00	48.00
110	Hal Schumacher	240.00	96.00	48.00
111	Minter Hayes, Ted Lyons	600.00	240.00	120.00
112	Odell Hale	240.00	96.00	48.00
113	Earl Averill	550.00	220.00	110.00
114	Italo Chelini	240.00	96.00	48.00
115	Ivy Andrews, Jim Bottomley	700.00	280.00	140.00
116	Bill Walker	240.00	96.00	48.00
117	Bill Dickey	800.00	320.00	160.00
118	Gerald Walker	240.00	96.00	48.00
119	Ted Lyons	550.00	220.00	110.00
120	Elden Auker (Eldon)	240.00	96.00	48.00
121	Wild Bill Hallahan	240.00	96.00	48.00
122	Freddy Lindstrom	550.00	220.00	110.00
123	Oral C. Hildebrand	240.00	96.00	48.00
124	Luke Appling	550.00	220.00	110.00
125	"Pepper" Martin	400.00	160.00	80.00
126	Rick Ferrell	550.00	220.00	110.00
127	Ival Goodman	240.00	96.00	48.00
128	Joe Kuhel	240.00	96.00	48.00
129	Ernest Lombardi	550.00	220.00	110.00
130	Charles Gehringer	550.00	220.00	110.00
131	Van L. Mungo	260.00	105.00	52.00
132	Larry French	240.00	96.00	48.00
133	"Buddy" Myer	240.00	96.00	48.00
134	Mel Harder	240.00	96.00	48.00
135	Augie Galan	240.00	96.00	48.00
136	"Gabby" Hartnett	550.00	220.00	110.00
137	Stan Hack	240.00	96.00	48.00
138	Billy Herman	550.00	220.00	110.00
139	Bill Jurges	240.00	96.00	48.00
140	Bill Lee	240.00	96.00	48.00
141	"Zeke" Bonura	240.00	96.00	48.00
142	Tony Piet	240.00	96.00	48.00
143	Paul Dean	350.00	140.00	70.00
144	Jimmy Foxx	925.00	370.00	185.00
145	Joe Medwick	550.00	220.00	110.00
146	Rip Collins	240.00	96.00	48.00
147	Melo Almada	240.00	96.00	48.00
148	Allan Cooke	240.00	96.00	48.00
149	Moe Berg	675.00	270.00	135.00
150	Adolph Camilli	240.00	96.00	48.00
151	Oscar Melillo	240.00	96.00	48.00
152	Bruce Campbell	240.00	96.00	48.00

153	Lefty Grove	675.00	270.00	135.00
154	John Murphy	240.00	96.00	48.00
155	Luke Sewell	240.00	96.00	48.00
156	Leo Durocher	550.00	220.00	110.00
157	Lloyd Waner	550.00	220.00	110.00
158	Guy Bush	240.00	96.00	48.00
159	Jimmy Dykes	240.00	96.00	48.00
160	Steve O'Neill	240.00	96.00	48.00
161	Gen. Crowder	240.00	96.00	48.00
162	Joe Cascarella	240.00	96.00	48.00
163	"Bud" Hafey	240.00	96.00	48.00
164	"Gilly" Campbell	240.00	96.00	48.00
165	Ray Hayworth	240.00	96.00	48.00
166	Frank Demaree	240.00	96.00	48.00
167	John Babich	240.00	96.00	48.00
168	Marvin Owen	240.00	96.00	48.00
169	Ralph Kress	240.00	96.00	48.00
170	"Mule" Haas	240.00	96.00	48.00
171	Frank Higgins	240.00	96.00	48.00
172	Walter Berger	240.00	96.00	48.00
173	Frank Frisch	550.00	220.00	110.00
174	Wess Ferrell (Wes)	240.00	96.00	48.00
175	Pete Fox	240.00	96.00	48.00
176	John Vergez	240.00	96.00	48.00
177	William Rogell	240.00	96.00	48.00
178	"Don" Brennan	240.00	96.00	48.00
179	James Bottomley	550.00	220.00	110.00
180	Travis Jackson	550.00	220.00	110.00
181	Robert Rolfe	240.00	96.00	48.00
182	Frank Crosetti	325.00	130.00	65.00
183	Joe Cronin	550.00	220.00	110.00
184	"Schoolboy" Rowe	260.00	105.00	52.00
185	"Chuck" Klein	550.00	220.00	110.00
186	Lon Warneke	240.00	96.00	48.00
187	Gus Suhr	240.00	96.00	48.00
188	Ben Chapman	240.00	96.00	48.00
189	Clint. Brown	260.00	105.00	52.00
190	Paul Derringer	260.00	105.00	52.00
191	John Burns	260.00	105.00	52.00
192	John Broaca	475.00	190.00	95.00

1958 Bazooka "My Favorite Team" Patches

These screen-printed felt patches were available via a mail-in offer found in Topps baseball cards. Approximately 5" in diameter, they were intended to be sewn on jackets, caps, etc.

		NM	EX	VG
Complete Set (16):		450.00	225.00	135.00
Common Patch:		30.00	15.00	9.00
(1)	Baltimore Orioles	30.00	15.00	9.00
(2)	Boston Red Sox	35.00	17.50	10.50
(3)	Chicago Cubs	45.00	22.00	13.50
(4)	Chicago White Sox	30.00	15.00	9.00
(5)	Cincinnati Reds	30.00	15.00	9.00
(6)	Cleveland Indians	30.00	15.00	9.00
(7)	Detroit Tigers	30.00	15.00	9.00
(8)	Kansas City A's	30.00	15.00	9.00
(9)	Los Angeles Dodgers	40.00	20.00	12.00
(10)	Milwaukee Braves	35.00	17.50	10.50
(11)	New York Yankees	50.00	25.00	15.00
(12)	Philadelphia Phillies	30.00	15.00	9.00
(13)	Pittsburgh Pirates	30.00	15.00	9.00
(14)	San Francisco Giants	40.00	20.00	12.00
(15)	St. Louis Cardinals	30.00	15.00	9.00
(16)	Washington Senators	35.00	17.50	10.50

1959 Bazooka

The 1959 Bazooka set, consisting of 23 full-color, unnumbered cards, was printed on boxes of one-cent Topps bubble gum. The blank-backed cards measure 2-13/16" x 4-15/16", when properly cut. Nine cards were first issued, with 14 being added to the set later. The nine more plentiful cards are #'s 1, 5, 8, 9, 14, 15, 16, 17 and 22. Complete boxes would command double the price shown.

		NM	EX	VG
Complete Set (23):		8,500	4,250	2,500
Common Player:		100.00	50.00	30.00
(1a)	Hank Aaron (Name in white.)	500.00	250.00	150.00
(1b)	Hank Aaron (Name in yellow.)	485.00	240.00	145.00
(2)	Richie Ashburn (SP)	450.00	225.00	135.00
(3)	Ernie Banks (SP)	500.00	250.00	150.00
(4)	Ken Boyer (SP)	250.00	125.00	75.00
(5)	Orlando Cepeda	200.00	100.00	60.00
(6)	Bob Cerv (SP)	250.00	125.00	75.00
(7)	Rocky Colavito (SP)	375.00	187.50	93.75
(8)	Del Crandall	100.00	50.00	30.00
(9)	Jim Davenport	100.00	50.00	30.00
(10)	Don Drysdale (SP)	450.00	225.00	112.50
(11)	Nellie Fox (SP)	450.00	225.00	135.00
(12)	Jackie Jensen (SP)	250.00	125.00	75.00
(13)	Harvey Kuenn (SP)	200.00	100.00	60.00
(14)	Mickey Mantle	1,200	600.00	300.00
(15)	Willie Mays	650.00	325.00	162.50
(16)	Bill Mazeroski	225.00	110.00	65.00
(17)	Roy McMillan	100.00	50.00	30.00
(18)	Billy Pierce (SP)	250.00	125.00	75.00
(19)	Roy Sievers (SP)	250.00	125.00	75.00
(20)	Duke Snider (SP)	750.00	375.00	225.00
(21)	Gus Triandos (SP)	250.00	125.00	75.00
(22)	Bob Turley	200.00	100.00	60.00
(23)	Vic Wertz (SP)	250.00	125.00	75.00

1959 Bazooka Pennants

These screen-printed felt pennants were available via a mail-in offer found in Topps baseball cards. Approximately 15" long and 5" wide, they have a "COPYRIGHT BAZOOKA" bar near the wide end.

		NM	EX	VG
Complete Set (16):		600.00	300.00	180.00
Common Team:		40.00	20.00	12.00
(1)	Baltimore Orioles	40.00	20.00	12.00
(2)	Boston Red Sox	40.00	20.00	12.00
(3)	Chicago Cubs	40.00	20.00	12.00
(4)	Chicago White Sox	45.00	22.50	13.50
(5)	Cincinnati Redlegs	40.00	20.00	12.00
(6)	Cleveland Indians	40.00	20.00	12.00
(7)	Detroit Tigers	40.00	20.00	12.00
(8)	Kansas City A's	40.00	20.00	12.00
(9)	Los Angeles Dodgers	45.00	22.50	13.50
(10)	Milwaukee Braves	40.00	20.00	12.00
(11)	New York Yankees	50.00	25.00	15.00
(12)	Philadelphia Phillies	40.00	20.00	12.00
(13)	Pittsburgh Pirates	40.00	20.00	12.00
(14)	San Francisco Giants	40.00	20.00	12.00
(15)	St. Louis Cardinals	40.00	20.00	12.00
(16)	Washington Senators	40.00	20.00	12.00

1960 Bazooka

Three-card panels were printed on the bottoms of Bazooka bubble gum boxes in 1960. The blank-backed set is comprised of 36 cards with the card number located at the bottom of each full-color card. Individual cards measure 1-13/16" x 2-3/4"; the panels measure 2-3/4" x 5-1/2".

		NM	EX	VG
Complete Panel Set (12):		2,200	1,100	650.00
Complete Singles Set (36):		2,000	1,000	600.00
Common Player:		15.00	7.50	4.50
	Panel (1)	125.00	62.00	37.00
1	Ernie Banks	90.00	45.00	27.00
2	Bud Daley	15.00	7.50	4.50
3	Wally Moon	15.00	7.50	4.50
	Panel (2)	200.00	100.00	60.00
4	Hank Aaron	150.00	75.00	45.00
5	Milt Pappas	15.00	7.50	4.50
6	Dick Stuart	15.00	7.50	4.50
	Panel (3)	325.00	160.00	97.00

#	Player	NM	EX	VG
7	Roberto Clemente	200.00	100.00	60.00
8	Yogi Berra	90.00	45.00	27.00
9	Ken Boyer	25.00	12.50	7.50
	Panel (4)	100.00	50.00	30.00
10	Orlando Cepeda	50.00	25.00	15.00
11	Gus Triandos	15.00	7.50	4.50
12	Frank Malzone	15.00	7.50	4.50
	Panel (5)	200.00	100.00	60.00
13	Willie Mays	150.00	75.00	45.00
14	Camilo Pascual	15.00	7.50	4.50
15	Bob Cerv	15.00	7.50	4.50
	Panel (6)	125.00	62.00	37.00
16	Vic Power	15.00	7.50	4.50
17	Larry Sherry	15.00	7.50	4.50
18	Al Kaline	75.00	37.00	22.00
	Panel (7)	200.00	100.00	60.00
19	Warren Spahn	75.00	37.00	22.00
20	Harmon Killebrew	75.00	37.00	22.00
21	Jackie Jensen	25.00	12.50	7.50
	Panel (8)	175.00	87.00	52.00
22	Luis Aparicio	50.00	25.00	15.00
23	Gil Hodges	50.00	25.00	15.00
24	Richie Ashburn	50.00	25.00	15.00
	Panel (9)	125.00	62.00	37.00
25	Nellie Fox	50.00	25.00	15.00
26	Robin Roberts	50.00	25.00	15.00
27	Joe Cunningham	15.00	7.50	4.50
	Panel (10)	200.00	100.00	60.00
28	Early Wynn	50.00	25.00	15.00
29	Frank Robinson	75.00	37.00	22.00
30	Rocky Colavito	50.00	25.00	15.00
	Panel (11)	750.00	375.00	225.00
31	Mickey Mantle	500.00	250.00	150.00
32	Glen Hobbie	15.00	7.50	4.50
33	Roy McMillan	15.00	7.50	4.50
	Panel (12)	60.00	30.00	18.00
34	Harvey Kuenn	15.00	7.50	4.50
35	Johnny Antonelli	15.00	7.50	4.50
36	Del Crandall	15.00	7.50	4.50

1960 Bazooka Hot Iron Transfers

Team logo transfers were available via a mail-in offer found on cards inserted into packs of 1960 Topps. Varying in size and shape, but generally about 5" square, the transfers were packaged in a colorful envelope which provided instructions for ironing the logo to a t-shirt or other cloth surface. Unlike earlier Bazooka mail-in premiums, the gum is not named on the transfers. Values shown are for transfers without the envelope. Envelopes, which carried the name and logo of the team inside, are valued about the same as the transfer itself.

		NM	EX	VG
	Complete Set (16):	300.00	150.00	90.00
	Common Team:	20.00	10.00	6.00
	Envelope: 1X			
(1)	Baltimore Orioles	20.00	10.00	6.00
(2)	Boston Red Sox	20.00	10.00	6.00
(3)	Chicago Cubs	20.00	10.00	6.00
(4)	Chicago White Sox	20.00	10.00	6.00
(5)	Cincinnati Redlegs	20.00	10.00	6.00
(6)	Cleveland Indians	20.00	10.00	6.00
(7)	Detroit Tigers	20.00	10.00	6.00
(8)	Kansas City A's	20.00	10.00	6.00
(9)	Los Angeles Dodgers	22.50	11.00	6.75
(10)	Milwaukee Braves	20.00	10.00	6.00
(11)	New York Yankees	25.00	12.50	7.50
(12)	Philadelphia Phillies	20.00	10.00	6.00
(13)	Pittsburgh Pirates	22.50	11.00	6.75
(14)	San Francisco Giants	20.00	10.00	6.00
(15)	St. Louis Cardinals	20.00	10.00	6.00
(16)	Washington Senators	20.00	10.00	6.00

1961 Bazooka

TED KLUSZEWSKI — LOS ANGELES ANGELS 1st base — NO. 18 OF 36 CARDS

Similar in design to the 1960 Bazooka set, the 1961 edition consists of 36 cards printed in panels of three on the bottom of Bazooka bubble gum boxes. The full-color cards, which measure 1-13/16" x 2-3/4" individually and 2-3/4" x 5-1/2" as panels, are numbered 1 through 36. The backs are blank.

#	Player	NM	EX	VG
	Complete Set, Panels (12):	1,500	750.00	450.00
	Complete Set, Singles (36):	1,200	600.00	350.00
	Common Player:	12.00	6.00	3.50
	Panel (1)	750.00	375.00	225.00
1	Art Mahaffey	12.00	6.00	3.50
2	Mickey Mantle	350.00	187.50	93.75
3	Ron Santo	25.00	12.50	7.50
	Panel (2)	225.00	110.00	65.00
4	Bud Daley	12.00	6.00	3.50
5	Roger Maris	100.00	50.00	30.00
6	Eddie Yost	12.00	6.00	3.50
	Panel (3)	75.00	37.50	22.50
7	Minnie Minoso	15.00	7.50	4.50
8	Dick Groat	13.50	7.00	4.00
9	Frank Malzone	12.00	6.00	3.50
	Panel (4)	100.00	50.00	30.00
10	Dick Donovan	12.00	6.00	3.50
11	Ed Mathews	45.00	22.50	13.50
12	Jim Lemon	12.00	6.00	3.50
	Panel (5)	75.00	37.50	22.50
13	Chuck Estrada	12.00	6.00	3.50
14	Ken Boyer	15.00	7.50	4.50
15	Harvey Kuenn	12.00	6.00	3.50
	Panel (6)	100.00	50.00	30.00
16	Ernie Broglio	12.00	6.00	3.50
17	Rocky Colavito	25.00	12.50	7.50
18	Ted Kluszewski	25.00	12.50	7.50
	Panel (7)	250.00	125.00	75.00
19	Ernie Banks	100.00	50.00	30.00
20	Al Kaline	45.00	22.50	13.50
21	Ed Bailey	12.00	6.00	3.50
	Panel (8)	250.00	125.00	75.00
22	Jim Perry	12.00	6.00	3.50
23	Willie Mays	100.00	50.00	30.00
24	Bill Mazeroski	40.00	20.00	12.00
	Panel (9)	100.00	50.00	30.00
25	Gus Triandos	12.00	6.00	3.50
26	Don Drysdale	45.00	22.50	13.50
27	Frank Herrera	12.00	6.00	3.50
	Panel (10)	100.00	50.00	30.00
28	Earl Battey	12.00	6.00	3.50
29	Warren Spahn	45.00	22.50	13.50
30	Gene Woodling	12.00	6.00	3.50
	Panel (11)	100.00	50.00	30.00
31	Frank Robinson	45.00	22.50	13.50
32	Pete Runnels	12.00	6.00	3.50
33	Woodie Held	12.00	6.00	3.50
	Panel (12)	100.00	50.00	30.00
34	Norm Larker	12.00	6.00	3.50
35	Luis Aparicio	35.00	17.50	10.00
36	Bill Tuttle	12.00	6.00	3.50

1962 Bazooka

KEN BOYER — ST. LOUIS CARDINALS 3rd base

In 1962, Bazooka increased the size of its set to 45 full-color cards. The set is unnumbered and was printed in panels of three on the bottoms of bubble gum boxes. Individual cards measure 1-13/16" x 2-3/4" in size, with panels at 2-3/4" x 5-1/2". In the checklist that follows the cards have been numbered alphabetically, using the name of the player who appears on the left end of the panel. Panels (1), (11) and (15) were issued in much shorter supply and command a higher price.

	Player	NM	EX	VG
	Complete Set, Panels (15):	4,000	2,000	1,200
	Complete Set, Singles (45)	3,750	1,850	1,100
	Common Player:	12.50	6.25	3.75
	Panel (1)	850.00	425.00	255.00
(1)	Bob Allison	160.00	80.00	45.00
(2)	Ed Mathews	400.00	200.00	120.00
(3)	Vada Pinson	200.00	100.00	60.00
	Panel (2)	100.00	50.00	30.00
(4)	Earl Battey	12.50	6.25	3.75
(5)	Warren Spahn	45.00	22.50	13.50
(6)	Lee Thomas	12.50	6.25	3.75
	Panel (3)	75.00	40.00	25.00
(7)	Orlando Cepeda	30.00	15.00	9.00
(8)	Woodie Held	12.50	6.25	3.75
(9)	Bob Aspromonte	12.50	6.25	3.75
	Panel (4)	200.00	100.00	60.00
(10)	Dick Howser	12.50	6.25	3.75
(11)	Roberto Clemente	125.00	65.00	35.00
(12)	Al Kaline	45.00	22.50	13.50
	Panel (5)	125.00	65.00	35.00
(13)	Joey Jay	12.50	6.25	3.75
(14)	Roger Maris	85.00	42.50	25.00
(15)	Frank Howard	15.00	7.50	4.50
	Panel (6)	175.00	90.00	50.00
(16)	Sandy Koufax	125.00	65.00	35.00
(17)	Jim Gentile	12.50	6.25	3.75
(18)	Johnny Callison	12.50	6.25	3.75
	Panel (7)	50.00	25.00	15.00
(19)	Jim Landis	12.50	6.25	3.75
(20)	Ken Boyer	13.00	6.50	4.00
(21)	Chuck Schilling	12.50	6.25	3.75
	Panel (8)	575.00	285.00	175.00
(22)	Art Mahaffey	12.50	6.25	3.75
(23)	Mickey Mantle	300.00	150.00	75.00
(24)	Dick Stuart	13.50	6.75	4.00
	Panel (9)	100.00	50.00	30.00
(25)	Ken McBride	12.50	6.25	3.75
(26)	Frank Robinson	45.00	22.50	13.50
(27)	Gil Hodges	30.00	15.00	9.00
	Panel (10)	175.00	85.00	50.00
(28)	Milt Pappas	12.50	6.25	3.75
(29)	Hank Aaron	125.00	65.00	35.00
(30)	Luis Aparicio	30.00	15.00	9.00
	Panel (11)	900.00	450.00	275.00
(31)	Johnny Romano	160.00	80.00	50.00
(32)	Ernie Banks	500.00	250.00	150.00
(33)	Norm Siebern	160.00	80.00	50.00
	Panel (12)	75.00	35.00	25.00
(34)	Ron Santo	20.00	10.00	6.00
(35)	Norm Cash	15.00	7.50	4.50
(36)	Jimmy Piersall	15.00	7.50	4.50
	Panel (13)	175.00	85.00	50.00
(37)	Don Schwall	12.50	6.25	3.75
(38)	Willie Mays	125.00	65.00	35.00
(39)	Norm Larker	12.50	6.25	3.75
	Panel (14)	110.00	55.00	35.00
(40)	Bill White	12.50	6.25	3.75
(41)	Whitey Ford	50.00	25.00	15.00
(42)	Rocky Colavito	30.00	15.00	9.00
	Panel (15)	750.00	375.00	225.00
(43)	Don Zimmer	200.00	100.00	60.00
(44)	Harmon Killebrew	350.00	175.00	100.00
(45)	Gene Woodling	160.00	80.00	50.00

1963 Bazooka

FRANK ROBINSON — CINN. REDS OF — NO. 31 OF 36 CARDS

The 1963 Bazooka issue reverted to a 12-panel, 36-card set, but saw a change in the size of the cards. Individual cards measure 1-9/16" x 2-1/2", while panels are 2-1/2" x 4-11/16". The card design was altered also, with the player's name, team and position situated in a white oval at the bottom of the card. The full-color, blank-backed set is numbered 1-36. The complete set was counterfeited circa 2002, with many cards sold in "FGA" certified slabs, depressing the value of cards not graded by a major certification company.

#	Player	NM	EX	VG
	Complete Set, Panels (12):	1,750	875.00	525.00
	Complete Set, Singles (36):	1,200	600.00	350.00
	Common Player:	10.00	5.00	3.00
	Panel (1)	450.00	225.00	135.00
1	Mickey Mantle (Batting righty.)	325.00	160.00	100.00
2	Bob Rodgers	10.00	5.00	3.00
3	Ernie Banks	60.00	30.00	18.00
	Panel (2)	95.00	50.00	30.00
4	Norm Siebern	10.00	5.00	3.00
5	Warren Spahn (Portrait)	35.00	17.50	10.00
6	Bill Mazeroski	25.00	12.50	7.50
	Panel (3)	175.00	90.00	50.00
7	Harmon Killebrew (Batting)	50.00	25.00	15.00
8	Dick Farrell (Portrait)	10.00	5.00	3.00
9	Hank Aaron (Glove in front.)	90.00	45.00	27.50
	Panel (4)	150.00	75.00	45.00
10	Dick Donovan	10.00	5.00	3.00
11	Jim Gentile (Batting)	10.00	5.00	3.00
12	Willie Mays (Bat in front.)	90.00	45.00	22.50
	Panel (5)	125.00	65.00	35.00
13	Camilo Pascual (Hands at waist.)	10.00	5.00	3.00
14	Roberto Clemente (Portrait)	90.00	45.00	22.50
15	Johnny Callison (Pinstriped uniform.)	10.00	5.00	3.00
	Panel (6)	150.00	75.00	45.00
16	Carl Yastrzemski (Kneeling)	60.00	30.00	18.00
17	Don Drysdale	35.00	17.50	10.00
18	Johnny Romano (Portrait)	10.00	5.00	3.00
	Panel (7)	45.00	22.50	13.50
19	Al Jackson	10.00	5.00	3.00
20	Ralph Terry	10.00	5.00	3.00
21	Bill Monbouquette	10.00	5.00	3.00
	Panel (8)	150.00	75.00	45.00
22	Orlando Cepeda	35.00	17.50	10.00
23	Stan Musial	75.00	40.00	25.00
24	Floyd Robinson (No pinstripes.)	10.00	5.00	3.00
	Panel (9)	45.00	22.50	13.50
25	Chuck Hinton (Batting)	10.00	5.00	3.00

		NM	EX	VG
26	Bob Purkey	10.00	5.00	3.00
27	Ken Hubbs	12.50	6.25	3.75
	Panel (10)	75.00	40.00	25.00
28	Bill White	10.00	5.00	3.00
29	Ray Herbert	10.00	5.00	3.00
30	Brooks Robinson (Glove in front.)	40.00	20.00	12.00
	Panel (11)	100.00	50.00	30.00
31	Frank Robinson (Batting)	40.00	20.00	12.00
32	Lee Thomas	10.00	5.00	3.00
33	Rocky Colavito (Detroit)	30.00	15.00	9.00
	Panel (12)	90.00	45.00	27.50
34	Al Kaline (Kneeling)	45.00	22.50	13.50
35	Art Mahaffey	10.00	5.00	3.00
36	Tommy Davis (Follow-through.)	10.00	5.00	3.00

1963 Bazooka All-Time Greats

Consisting of 41 cards, the Bazooka All-Time Greats set was issued as inserts (five per box) in boxes of Bazooka bubble gum. A black-and-white portrait photo of the player is placed inside a gold plaque within a white border. Card backs contain a brief biography of the player. The numbered cards measure 1-9/16" x 2-1/2". Cards can be found with silver fronts instead of gold; the silver are worth double the values listed.

		NM	EX	VG
	Complete Set (41):	675.00	335.00	200.00
	Common Player:	13.50	6.75	4.00
	Silver: 2.5X	.00	.00	.00
1	Joe Tinker	13.50	6.75	4.00
2	Harry Heilmann	13.50	6.75	4.00
3	Jack Chesbro	13.50	6.75	4.00
4	Christy Mathewson	30.00	15.00	9.00
5	Herb Pennock	13.50	6.75	4.00
6	Cy Young	30.00	15.00	9.00
7	Ed Walsh	13.50	6.75	4.00
8	Nap Lajoie	13.50	6.75	4.00
9	Eddie Plank	13.50	6.75	4.00
10	Honus Wagner	35.00	17.50	10.00
11	Chief Bender	13.50	6.75	4.00
12	Walter Johnson	30.00	15.00	9.00
13	Three-Fingered Brown	13.50	6.75	4.00
14	Rabbit Maranville	13.50	6.75	4.00
15	Lou Gehrig	60.00	30.00	18.00
16	Ban Johnson	13.50	6.75	4.00
17	Babe Ruth	65.00	32.50	20.00
18	Connie Mack	13.50	6.75	4.00
19	Hank Greenberg	20.00	10.00	6.00
20	John McGraw	13.50	6.75	4.00
21	Johnny Evers	13.50	6.75	4.00
22	Al Simmons	13.50	6.75	4.00
23	Jimmy Collins	13.50	6.75	4.00
24	Tris Speaker	13.50	6.75	4.00
25	Frank Chance	13.50	6.75	4.00
26	Fred Clarke	13.50	6.75	4.00
27	Wilbert Robinson	13.50	6.75	4.00
28	Dazzy Vance	13.50	6.75	4.00
29	Grover Alexander	16.00	8.00	4.75
30	Kenesaw Landis	13.50	6.75	4.00
31	Willie Keeler	13.50	6.75	4.00
32	Rogers Hornsby	16.00	8.00	4.75
33	Hugh Duffy	13.50	6.75	4.00
34	Mickey Cochrane	13.50	6.75	4.00
35	Ty Cobb	60.00	30.00	18.00
36	Mel Ott	13.50	6.75	4.00
37	Clark Griffith	13.50	6.75	4.00
38	Ted Lyons	13.50	6.75	4.00
39	Cap Anson	13.50	6.75	4.00
40	Bill Dickey	13.50	6.75	4.00
41	Eddie Collins	13.50	6.75	4.00

1964 Bazooka

The 1964 Bazooka set is identical in design and size to the previous year's effort. However, different photographs were used from year to year. The 1964 set consists of 36 full-color, blank-backed cards numbered 1 through 36. Individual cards measure 1-9/16" x 2-1/2"; three-card panels measure 2-1/2" x 4-11/16". Sheets of 10 full-color baseball stamps were inserted in each box of bubble gum.

		NM	EX	VG
	Complete Set, Panels (12):	1,400	700.00	425.00
	Complete Set, Singles (36):	950.00	475.00	275.00
	Common Player:	10.00	5.00	3.00
	Panel (1)	225.00	110.00	70.00
1	Mickey Mantle (Bat on shoulder.)	200.00	100.00	60.00
2	Dick Groat	10.00	5.00	3.00
3	Steve Barber	10.00	5.00	3.00
	Panel (2)	75.00	37.00	22.00
4	Ken McBride	10.00	5.00	3.00
5	Warren Spahn (Cap to waist.)	35.00	17.50	10.50
6	Bob Friend	10.00	5.00	3.00
	Panel (3)	150.00	75.00	45.00
7	Harmon Killebrew (Portrait)	35.00	17.50	10.50
8	Dick Farrell (Hands above head.)	10.00	5.00	3.00
9	Hank Aaron (Glove to left.)	75.00	37.50	22.50
	Panel (4)	150.00	75.00	45.00
10	Rich Rollins	10.00	5.00	3.00
11	Jim Gentile (Portrait)	10.00	5.00	3.00
12	Willie Mays (Looking to left.)	75.00	37.50	22.50
	Panel (5)	150.00	75.00	45.00
13	Camilo Pascual (Follow-through.)	10.00	5.00	3.00
14	Roberto Clemente (Throwing)	75.00	37.50	22.50
15	Johnny Callison (Batting, screen showing.)	10.00	5.00	3.00
	Panel (6)	125.00	62.00	37.00
16	Carl Yastrzemski (Batting)	40.00	20.00	12.00
17	Billy Williams (Kneeling)	30.00	15.00	9.00
18	Johnny Romano (Batting)	10.00	5.00	3.00
	Panel (7)	65.00	32.50	20.00
19	Jim Maloney	10.00	5.00	3.00
20	Norm Cash	12.50	6.25	3.75
21	Willie McCovey	30.00	15.00	9.00
	Panel (8)	40.00	20.00	12.00
22	Jim Fregosi (Batting)	10.00	5.00	3.00
23	George Altman	10.00	5.00	3.00
24	Floyd Robinson (Pinstriped uniform.)	10.00	5.00	3.00
	Panel (9)	40.00	20.00	12.00
25	Chuck Hinton (Portrait)	10.00	5.00	3.00
26	Ron Hunt (Batting)	10.00	5.00	3.00
27	Gary Peters (Pitching)	10.00	5.00	3.00
	Panel (10)	90.00	45.00	27.00
28	Dick Ellsworth	10.00	5.00	3.00
29	Elston Howard (W/ bat.)	20.00	10.00	6.00
30	Brooks Robinson (Kneeling w/ glove.)	35.00	17.50	10.50
	Panel (11)	175.00	87.00	52.00
31	Frank Robinson (Uniform number shows.)	35.00	17.50	10.50
32	Sandy Koufax (Glove in front.)	75.00	37.50	22.50
33	Rocky Colavito (Kansas City)	25.00	12.50	7.50
	Panel (12)	90.00	45.00	27.00
34	Al Kaline (Holding two bats.)	40.00	20.00	12.00
35	Ken Boyer (Cap to waist.)	10.00	5.00	3.00
36	Tommy Davis (Batting)	10.00	5.00	3.00

1964 Bazooka Stamps

Occasionally mislabeled "Topps Stamps," the 1964 Bazooka stamps were produced by Topps, but found only in boxes of Bazooka bubble gum. Issued in sheets of 10, 100 color stamps make up the set. Each stamp measures 1" x 1-1/2" in size. While the stamps are not individually numbered, the sheets are numbered one through 10. The stamps are commonly found as complete sheets of 10 and are priced in that fashion in the checklist that follows.

		NM	EX	VG
	Complete Sheet Set (10x10):	750.00	375.00	225.00
	Common Sheet:	35.00	17.50	10.00
	Common Stamp:	4.00	2.00	1.25
1	Max Alvis, Ed Charles, Dick Ellsworth, Jimmie Hall, Frank Malzone, Milt Pappas, Vada Pinson, Tony Taylor, Pete Ward, Bill White	35.00	17.50	10.50
2	Bob Aspromonte, Larry Jackson, Willie Mays, Al McBean, Bill Monbouquette, Bobby Richardson, Floyd Robinson, Frank Robinson, Norm Siebern, Don Zimmer	80.00	40.00	25.00

		NM	EX	VG
3	Ernie Banks, Roberto Clemente, Curt Flood, Jesse Gonder, Woody Held, Don Lock, Dave Nicholson, Joe Pepitone, Brooks Robinson, Carl Yastrzemski	120.00	60.00	35.00
4	Hank Aguirre, Jim Grant, Harmon Killebrew, Jim Maloney, Juan Marichal, Bill Mazeroski, Juan Pizarro, Boog Powell, Ed Roebuck, Ron Santo	85.00	45.00	25.00
5	Jim Bouton, Norm Cash, Orlando Cepeda, Tommy Harper, Chuck Hinton, Albie Pearson, Ron Perranoski, Dick Radatz, Johnny Romano, Carl Willey	45.00	25.00	15.00
6	Steve Barber, Jim Fregosi, Tony Gonzalez, Mickey Mantle, Jim O'Toole, Gary Peters, Rich Rollins, Warren Spahn, Dick Stuart, Joe Torre	165.00	80.00	50.00
7	Felipe Alou, George Altman, Ken Boyer, Rocky Colavito, Jim Davenport, Tommy Davis, Bill Freehan, Bob Friend, Ken Johnson, Billy Moran	40.00	20.00	12.00
8	Earl Battey, Ernie Broglio, Johnny Callison, Donn Clendenon, Don Drysdale, Jim Gentile, Elston Howard, Claude Osteen, Billy Williams, Hal Woodeshick	55.00	27.50	16.50
9	Hank Aaron, Jack Baldschun, Wayne Causey, Moe Drabowsky, Dick Groat, Frank Howard, Al Jackson, Jerry Lumpe, Ken McBride, Rusty Staub	65.00	32.50	19.50
10	Vic Davalillo, Dick Farrell, Ron Hunt, Al Kaline, Sandy Koufax, Eddie Mathews, Willie McCovey, Camilo Pascual, Lee Thomas	85.00	45.00	25.00

1965 Bazooka

The 1965 Bazooka set is identical to the 1963 and 1964 sets. Different players were added each year and different photographs were used for those players being included again. Individual cards cut from the boxes measure 1-9/16" x 2-1/2". Complete three-card panels measure 2-1/2" x 4-11/16". Cards are again blank-backed.

		NM	EX	VG
	Complete Set, Panels (12):	1,300	650.00	400.00
	Complete Set, Singles (36):	900.00	450.00	275.00
	Common Player:	10.00	5.00	3.00
	Panel (1)	275.00	135.00	85.00
1	Mickey Mantle (Batting lefty.)	200.00	100.00	60.00
2	Larry Jackson	10.00	5.00	3.00
3	Chuck Hinton	10.00	5.00	3.00
	Panel (2)	40.00	20.00	12.00
4	Tony Oliva	12.50	6.25	3.75
5	Dean Chance	10.00	5.00	3.00
6	Jim O'Toole	10.00	5.00	3.00
	Panel (3)	125.00	65.00	35.00
7	Harmon Killebrew (Bat on shoulder.)	35.00	17.50	10.50
8	Pete Ward	10.00	5.00	3.00
9	Hank Aaron (Batting)	75.00	37.50	22.50
	Panel (4)	125.00	62.00	37.00
10	Dick Radatz	10.00	5.00	3.00
11	Boog Powell	12.50	6.25	3.75
12	Willie Mays (Looking down.)	75.00	37.50	22.50
	Panel (5)	250.00	125.00	75.00
13	Bob Veale	10.00	5.00	3.00
14	Roberto Clemente (Batting)	100.00	50.00	30.00
15	Johnny Callison (Batting, no screen in background.)	10.00	5.00	3.00
	Panel (6)	60.00	30.00	18.00
16	Joe Torre	15.00	7.50	4.50
17	Billy Williams (Batting)	25.00	12.50	7.50
18	Bob Chance	10.00	5.00	3.00
	Panel (7)	50.00	25.00	15.00
19	Bob Aspromonte	10.00	5.00	3.00
20	Joe Christopher	10.00	5.00	3.00
21	Jim Bunning	25.00	12.50	7.50
	Panel (8)	75.00	37.50	22.50
22	Jim Fregosi	10.00	5.00	3.00
23	Bob Gibson	30.00	15.00	9.00

	NM	EX	VG
24 Juan Marichal	25.00	12.50	7.50
Panel (9)	40.00	20.00	12.00
25 Dave Wickersham	10.00	5.00	3.00
26 Ron Hunt (Throwing)	10.00	5.00	3.00
27 Gary Peters (Portrait)	10.00	5.00	3.00
Panel (10)	85.00	42.50	25.00
28 Ron Santo	15.00	7.50	4.50
29 Elston Howard (W/ glove.)	12.50	6.25	3.75
30 Brooks Robinson (Portrait)	35.00	17.50	10.50
Panel (11)	200.00	100.00	60.00
31 Frank Robinson (Portrait)	35.00	17.50	10.50
32 Sandy Koufax (Hands over head.)	100.00	50.00	30.00
33 Rocky Colavito (Cleveland)	20.00	10.00	6.00
Panel (12)	75.00	37.00	22.00
34 Al Kaline (Portrait)	35.00	17.50	10.50
35 Ken Boyer (Portrait)	10.00	5.00	3.00
36 Tommy Davis (Fielding)	10.00	5.00	3.00

1966 Bazooka

The 1966 Bazooka set was increased to 48 cards. Printed in panels of three on the bottoms of boxes of bubble gum, the full-color cards are blank-backed and numbered. Individual cards measure 1-9/16" x 2-1/2"; panels measure 2-1/2" x 4-11/16". Most of those 1966 Bazooka cards which have the same player/number combination as 1967 share the same photo and are indistinguishable as singles or panels; year of issue for complete boxes can be distinguished by the small photo on front of Koufax (1966) or Mantle (1967).

	NM	EX	VG
Complete Set, Panels (16):	2,200	1,100	650.00
Complete Set, Singles (48):	1,500	750.00	450.00
Common Player:	10.00	5.00	3.00
Panel (1)	175.00	85.00	50.00
1 Sandy Koufax	100.00	50.00	30.00
2 Willie Horton	13.50	6.75	4.00
3 Frank Howard	13.50	6.75	4.00
Panel (2)	60.00	30.00	18.00
4 Richie Allen	16.50	8.25	5.00
5 Mel Stottlemyre	10.00	5.00	3.00
6 Tony Conigliaro	20.00	10.00	6.00
Panel (3)	400.00	200.00	120.00
7 Mickey Mantle	300.00	150.00	90.00
8 Leon Wagner	10.00	5.00	3.00
9 Ed Kranepool	10.00	5.00	3.00
Panel (4)	120.00	60.00	36.00
10 Juan Marichal	35.00	17.50	10.00
11 Harmon Killebrew	50.00	25.00	15.00
12 Johnny Callison	10.00	5.00	3.00
Panel (5)	100.00	50.00	30.00
13 Roy McMillan	10.00	5.00	3.00
14 Willie McCovey	40.00	20.00	12.00
15 Rocky Colavito	30.00	15.00	9.00
Panel (6)	150.00	75.00	45.00
16 Willie Mays	80.00	40.00	24.00
17 Sam McDowell	10.00	5.00	3.00
18 Vern Law	10.00	5.00	3.00
Panel (7)	80.00	40.00	24.00
19 Jim Fregosi	10.00	5.00	3.00
20 Ron Fairly	10.00	5.00	3.00
21 Bob Gibson	40.00	20.00	12.00
Panel (8)	110.00	55.00	35.00
22 Carl Yastrzemski	60.00	30.00	18.00
23 Bill White	10.00	5.00	3.00
24 Bob Aspromonte	10.00	5.00	3.00
Panel (9)	150.00	75.00	45.00
25 Dean Chance (California)	10.00	5.00	3.00
26 Roberto Clemente	100.00	50.00	30.00
27 Tony Cloninger	10.00	5.00	3.00
Panel (10)	135.00	65.00	40.00
28 Curt Blefary	10.00	5.00	3.00
29 Milt Pappas	10.00	5.00	3.00
30 Hank Aaron	80.00	40.00	24.00
Panel (11)	130.00	65.00	40.00
31 Jim Bunning	40.00	20.00	12.00
32 Frank Robinson (Portrait)	50.00	25.00	15.00
33 Bill Skowron	13.50	6.75	4.00
Panel (12)	100.00	50.00	30.00
34 Brooks Robinson	50.00	25.00	15.00
35 Jim Wynn	10.00	5.00	3.00
36 Joe Torre	17.50	8.75	5.25
Panel (13)	225.00	110.00	65.00
37 Jim Grant	10.00	5.00	3.00
38 Pete Rose	135.00	65.00	40.00
39 Ron Santo	20.00	10.00	6.00
Panel (14)	90.00	45.00	27.50
40 Tom Tresh	13.50	6.75	4.00
41 Tony Oliva	13.50	6.75	4.00
42 Don Drysdale	40.00	20.00	12.00

	NM	EX	VG
Panel (15)	40.00	20.00	12.00
43 Pete Richert	10.00	5.00	3.00
44 Bert Campaneris	10.00	5.00	3.00
45 Jim Maloney	10.00	5.00	3.00
Panel (16)	130.00	65.00	40.00
46 Al Kaline	50.00	25.00	15.00
47 Eddie Fisher	10.00	5.00	3.00
48 Billy Williams	40.00	20.00	12.00

1967 Bazooka

The 1967 Bazooka set is identical in design to the sets of 1964-1966. Printed in panels of three on the bottoms of bubble gum boxes, the set is made up of 48 full-color, blank-backed, numbered cards. Individual cards measure 1-9/16" x 2-1/2"; complete panels measure 2-1/2" x 4-11/16". Most of those 1967 Bazooka cards which have the same player/number combination as 1966 share the same photo and are indistinguishable as singles or panels; complete boxes can be distinguished by the small photo on front of Koufax (1966) or Mantle (1967).

	NM	EX	VG
Complete Set, Panels (18):	2,400	1,200	700.00
Complete Set, Singles (48):	1,500	750.00	450.00
Common Player:	10.00	5.00	3.00
Panel (1)	40.00	20.00	12.00
1 Rick Reichardt	10.00	5.00	3.00
2 Tommie Agee	10.00	5.00	3.00
3 Frank Howard	12.50	6.25	3.75
Panel (2)	55.00	27.50	16.50
4 Richie Allen	17.50	8.75	5.25
5 Mel Stottlemyre	12.50	6.25	3.75
6 Tony Conigliaro	12.50	6.25	3.75
Panel (3)	600.00	300.00	180.00
7 Mickey Mantle	400.00	200.00	120.00
8 Leon Wagner	10.00	5.00	3.00
9 Gary Peters	10.00	5.00	3.00
Panel (4)	150.00	75.00	45.00
10 Juan Marichal	50.00	25.00	15.00
11 Harmon Killebrew	60.00	30.00	18.00
12 Johnny Callison	10.00	5.00	3.00
Panel (5)	135.00	65.00	40.00
13 Denny McLain	20.00	10.00	6.00
14 Willie McCovey	50.00	25.00	15.00
15 Rocky Colavito	30.00	15.00	9.00
Panel (6)	150.00	75.00	45.00
16 Willie Mays	90.00	45.00	27.00
17 Sam McDowell	10.00	5.00	3.00
18 Jim Kaat	13.50	6.75	4.00
Panel (7)	100.00	50.00	30.00
19 Jim Fregosi	10.00	5.00	3.00
20 Ron Fairly	10.00	5.00	3.00
21 Bob Gibson	50.00	25.00	15.00
Panel (8)	120.00	60.00	36.00
22 Carl Yastrzemski	65.00	32.50	20.00
23 Bill White	10.00	5.00	3.00
24 Bob Aspromonte	10.00	5.00	3.00
Panel (9)	175.00	85.00	50.00
25 Dean Chance (Minnesota)	10.00	5.00	3.00
26 Roberto Clemente	100.00	50.00	30.00
27 Tony Cloninger	10.00	5.00	3.00
Panel (10)	150.00	75.00	45.00
28 Curt Blefary	10.00	5.00	3.00
29 Phil Regan	10.00	5.00	3.00
30 Hank Aaron	90.00	45.00	27.00
Panel (11)	175.00	85.00	50.00
31 Jim Bunning	50.00	25.00	15.00
32 Frank Robinson (Batting)	60.00	30.00	18.00
33 Ken Boyer	10.00	5.00	3.00
Panel (12)	120.00	60.00	36.00
34 Brooks Robinson	60.00	30.00	18.00
35 Jim Wynn	10.00	5.00	3.00
36 Joe Torre	17.50	8.75	5.25
Panel (13)	275.00	135.00	80.00
37 Tommy Davis	10.00	5.00	3.00
38 Pete Rose	150.00	75.00	45.00
39 Ron Santo	20.00	10.00	6.00
Panel (14)	100.00	50.00	30.00
40 Tom Tresh	12.00	6.00	3.50
41 Tony Oliva	12.50	6.25	3.75
42 Don Drysdale	50.00	25.00	15.00
Panel (15)	40.00	20.00	12.00
43 Pete Richert	10.00	5.00	3.00
44 Bert Campaneris	10.00	5.00	3.00
45 Jim Maloney	10.00	5.00	3.00
Panel (16)	175.00	85.00	50.00
46 Al Kaline	60.00	30.00	18.00
47 Matty Alou	10.00	5.00	3.00
48 Billy Williams	50.00	25.00	15.00

1968 Bazooka

The design of the 1968 Bazooka set is radically different from previous years. The player cards are situated on the sides of the boxes with the box back containing "Tipps From The Topps." Four unnumbered player cards, measuring 1-1/4" x 3-1/8", are featured on each box. The box back includes a small player photo plus illustrated tips on various aspects of the game of baseball. Boxes are numbered 1-15 on the top

panels. There are 56 different player cards in the set, with four of the cards (Agee, Drysdale, Rose, Santo) being used twice to round out the set of 15 boxes.

	NM	EX	VG
Complete Box Set (15):	4,250	2,125	1,250
Complete Singles Set (60):	3,000	1,500	900.00
Common Player:	10.00	5.00	3.00
Box 1 - Bunting	275.00	135.00	80.00
1 Maury Wills	15.00	7.50	4.50
(1) Clete Boyer	15.00	7.50	4.50
(2) Paul Casanova	10.00	5.00	3.00
(3) Al Kaline	65.00	32.50	20.00
(4) Tom Seaver	80.00	40.00	25.00
Box 2 - Batting	250.00	125.00	75.00
2 Carl Yastrzemski	80.00	40.00	25.00
(5) Matty Alou	10.00	5.00	3.00
(6) Bill Freehan	10.00	5.00	3.00
(7) Jim Hunter	45.00	22.50	13.50
(8) Jim Lefebvre	10.00	5.00	3.00
Box 3 - Stealing Bases	175.00	85.00	50.00
3 Bert Campaneris	10.00	5.00	3.00
(9) Bobby Knoop	10.00	5.00	3.00
(10) Tim McCarver	15.00	7.50	4.50
(11) Frank Robinson	65.00	32.50	20.00
(12) Bob Veale	10.00	5.00	3.00
Box 4 - Sliding	100.00	50.00	30.00
4 Maury Wills	15.00	7.50	4.50
(13) Joe Azcue	10.00	5.00	3.00
(14) Tony Conigliaro	15.00	7.50	4.50
(15) Ken Holtzman	10.00	5.00	3.00
(16) Bill White	10.00	5.00	3.00
Box 5 - The Double Play	315.00	155.00	95.00
5 Julian Javier	10.00	5.00	3.00
(17) Hank Aaron	175.00	87.00	52.00
(18) Juan Marichal	45.00	22.50	13.50
(19) Joe Pepitone	17.50	9.00	5.00
(20) Rico Petrocelli	15.00	7.50	4.50
Box 6 - Playing 1st Base	375.00	185.00	110.00
6 Orlando Cepeda	50.00	25.00	15.00
(21) Tommie Agee	10.00	5.00	3.00
(22a) Don Drysdale (No period after "A" in team name.)	40.00	20.00	12.00
(22b) Don Drysdale (Period after "A.")	40.00	20.00	12.00
(23) Pete Rose	175.00	87.00	52.00
(24) Ron Santo	17.50	9.00	5.00
Box 7 - Playing 2nd Base	225.00	110.00	65.00
7 Bill Mazeroski	50.00	25.00	15.00
(25) Jim Bunning	45.00	22.50	13.50
(26) Frank Howard	15.00	7.50	4.50
(27) John Roseboro	10.00	5.00	3.00
(28) George Scott	10.00	5.00	3.00
Box 8 - Playing 3rd Base	275.00	135.00	80.00
8 Brooks Robinson	65.00	32.50	20.00
(29) Tony Gonzalez	10.00	5.00	3.00
(30) Willie Horton	15.00	7.50	4.50
(31) Harmon Killebrew	65.00	32.50	20.00
(32) Jim McGlothlin	10.00	5.00	3.00
Box 9 - Playing Shortstop	150.00	75.00	45.00
9 Jim Fregosi	10.00	5.00	3.00
(33) Max Alvis	10.00	5.00	3.00
(34) Bob Gibson	45.00	22.50	13.50
(35) Tony Oliva	15.00	7.50	4.50
(36) Vada Pinson	15.00	7.50	4.50
Box 10 - Catching	160.00	80.00	45.00
10 Joe Torre	17.50	9.00	5.00
(37) Dean Chance	10.00	5.00	3.00
(38) Tommy Davis	10.00	5.00	3.00
(39) Ferguson Jenkins	45.00	22.50	13.50
(40) Rick Monday	10.00	5.00	3.00
Box 11 - Pitching	850.00	425.00	255.00
11 Jim Lonborg	15.00	7.50	4.50
(41) Curt Flood	15.00	7.50	4.50
(42) Joel Horlen	10.00	5.00	3.00
(43) Mickey Mantle	650.00	325.00	195.00
(44) Jim Wynn	10.00	5.00	3.00
Box 12 - Fielding the Pitcher's Position	375.00	185.00	110.00
12 Mike McCormick	10.00	5.00	3.00
(45) Roberto Clemente	200.00	100.00	60.00
(46) Al Downing	10.00	5.00	3.00
(47) Don Mincher	10.00	5.00	3.00
(48) Tony Perez	45.00	22.00	13.50
Box 13 - Coaching	225.00	110.00	65.00
13 Frank Crosetti	15.00	7.50	4.50
(49) Rod Carew	55.00	27.50	16.50
(50) Willie McCovey	55.00	27.50	16.50
(51) Ron Swoboda	10.00	5.00	3.00
(52) Earl Wilson	10.00	5.00	3.00
Box 14 - Playing the Outfield	250.00	125.00	75.00
14 Willie Mays	175.00	87.00	52.00

		NM	EX	VG
(53)	Richie Allen	15.00	7.50	4.50
(54)	Gary Peters	10.00	5.00	3.00
(55)	Rusty Staub	17.50	9.00	5.00
(56)	Billy Williams	50.00	25.00	15.00
Box 15 - Base Running		375.00	185.00	110.00
15	Lou Brock	55.00	27.50	16.50
(57)	Tommie Agee	10.00	5.00	3.00
(58)	Don Drysdale	40.00	20.00	12.00
(59)	Pete Rose	175.00	87.00	52.00
(60)	Ron Santo	17.50	9.00	5.00

1969-70 Bazooka

Issued over a two-year span, the 1969-70 Bazooka set utilized the box bottom and sides. The bottom, entitled "Baseball Extra," features an historic event in baseball; the 3" x 6-1/4" panels are numbered 1-12. Two "All-Time Great" cards were located on each side of the box. These cards are not numbered and have no distinct borders; individual cards measure 1-1/4" x 3-1/8". The prices in the checklist that follows are for complete boxes only. Cards/panels cut from the boxes have a greatly reduced value - 25 percent of the complete box prices for all cut pieces.

		NM	EX	VG
Complete Set (12):		325.00	160.00	100.00
Common Box:		20.00	10.00	6.00
1	No-Hit Duel By Toney & Vaughn (Mordecai Brown, Ty Cobb, Willie Keeler, Eddie Plank)	30.00	15.00	9.00
2	Alexander Conquers Yanks (Rogers Hornsby, Ban Johnson, Walter Johnson, Al Simmons)	20.00	10.00	6.00
3	Yanks' Lazzeri Sets AL Record (Grover Alexander, Chief Bender, Christy Mathewson, Cy Young)	25.00	12.50	7.50
4	HR Almost Hit Out Of Stadium (Hugh Duffy, Lou Gehrig, Tris Speaker, Joe Tinker)	20.00	10.00	6.00
5	4 Consecutive Homers By Lou (Frank Chance, Mickey Cochrane, John McGraw, Babe Ruth)	35.00	17.50	10.00
6	No-Hit Game By Walter Johnson (Johnny Evers, Walter Johnson, John McGraw, Cy Young)	20.00	10.00	6.00
7	Twelve RBIs By Bottomley (Ty Cobb, Eddie Collins, Johnny Evers, Lou Gehrig)	35.00	17.50	10.00
8	Ty Ties Record (Mickey Cochrane, Eddie Collins, Mel Ott, Honus Wagner)	20.00	10.00	6.00
9	Babe Ruth Hits 3 HRs In Game (Cap Anson, Jack Chesbro, Al Simmons, Tris Speaker)	35.00	17.50	10.00
10	Calls Shot In Series Game (Nap Lajoie, Connie Mack, Rabbit Maranville, Ed Walsh)	35.00	17.50	10.00
11	Ruth's 60th HR Sets New Record (Frank Chance, Nap Lajoie, Mel Ott, Joe Tinker)	35.00	17.50	10.00
12	Double Shutout By Ed Reulbach (Rogers Hornsby, Rabbit Maranville, Christy Mathewson, Honus Wagner)	20.00	10.00	6.00

1971 Bazooka Numbered Set

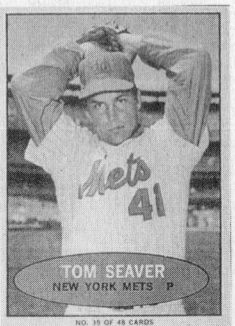

The 1971 Bazooka numbered set is a proof set produced by the company after the unnumbered set was released. The set is comprised of 48 cards as opposed to the 36 cards which make up the unnumbered set. Issued in panels of three, the 12 cards not found in the unnumbered set are #1-3, 13-15, 34-36 and 43-45. All other cards are identical to those found in the unnumbered set. The cards, which measure 2" x 2-5/8", contain full-color photos and are blank-backed.

		NM	EX	VG
Complete Panel Set (16):		1,300	655.00	400.00
Complete Singles Set (48):		950.00	475.00	275.00
Common Player:		7.50	3.75	2.25
Panel (1)		100.00	50.00	30.00
1	Tim McCarver	12.50	6.25	3.75
2	Frank Robinson	35.00	17.50	10.00
3	Bill Mazeroski	30.00	15.00	9.00
Panel (2)		100.00	50.00	30.00
4	Willie McCovey	30.00	15.00	9.00
5	Carl Yastrzemski	40.00	20.00	12.00
6	Clyde Wright	7.50	3.75	2.25
Panel (3)		60.00	30.00	18.00
7	Jim Merritt	7.50	3.75	2.25
8	Luis Aparicio	25.00	12.50	7.50
9	Bobby Murcer	12.50	6.25	3.75
Panel (4)		30.00	15.00	9.00
10	Rico Petrocelli	7.50	3.75	2.25
11	Sam McDowell	7.50	3.75	2.25
12	Cito Gaston	7.50	3.75	2.25
Panel (5)		85.00	42.50	25.00
13	Ferguson Jenkins	25.00	12.50	7.50
14	Al Kaline	35.00	17.50	10.00
15	Ken Harrelson	7.50	3.75	2.25
Panel (6)		115.00	55.00	35.00
16	Tommie Agee	7.50	3.75	2.25
17	Harmon Killebrew	35.00	17.50	10.00
18	Reggie Jackson	45.00	22.50	13.50
Panel (7)		60.00	30.00	18.00
19	Juan Marichal	25.00	12.50	7.50
20	Frank Howard	10.00	5.00	3.00
21	Bill Melton	7.50	3.75	2.25
Panel (8)		125.00	65.00	35.00
22	Brooks Robinson	35.00	17.50	10.00
23	Hank Aaron	60.00	30.00	18.00
24	Larry Dierker	7.50	3.75	2.25
Panel (9)		60.00	30.00	18.00
25	Jim Fregosi	7.50	3.75	2.25
26	Billy Williams	30.00	15.00	9.00
27	Dave McNally	7.50	3.75	2.25
Panel (10)		65.00	32.50	20.00
28	Rico Carty	7.50	3.75	2.25
29	Johnny Bench	35.00	17.50	10.00
30	Tommy Harper	7.50	3.75	2.25
Panel (11)		110.00	55.00	30.00
31	Bert Campaneris	7.50	3.75	2.25
32	Pete Rose	50.00	25.00	15.00
33	Orlando Cepeda	25.00	12.50	7.50
Panel (12)		65.00	32.50	20.00
34	Maury Wills	7.50	3.75	2.25
35	Tom Seaver	35.00	17.50	10.00
36	Tony Oliva	10.00	5.00	3.00
Panel (13)		120.00	60.00	35.00
37	Bill Freehan	7.50	3.75	2.25
38	Roberto Clemente	75.00	37.50	22.50
39	Claude Osteen	7.50	3.75	2.25
Panel (14)		65.00	32.50	20.00
40	Rusty Staub	12.50	6.25	3.75
41	Bob Gibson	30.00	15.00	9.00
42	Amos Otis	7.50	3.75	2.25
Panel (15)		55.00	27.50	16.50
43	Jim Wynn	7.50	3.75	2.25
44	Richie Allen	20.00	10.00	6.00
45	Tony Conigliaro	15.00	7.50	4.50
Panel (16)		110.00	55.00	35.00
46	Randy Hundley	7.50	3.75	2.25
47	Willie Mays	60.00	30.00	18.00
48	Jim Hunter	25.00	12.50	7.50

1971 Bazooka Unnumbered Set

FRANK HOWARD
WASHINGTON SENATORS OF

This Bazooka set was issued in 1971, consisting of 36 full-color, blank-backed, unnumbered cards. Printed in panels of three on the bottoms of bubble gum boxes, individual cards measure 2" x 2-5/8"; complete panels measure 2-5/8" x 5-5/16". In the checklist that follows, the cards have been numbered by panel using the name of the player who appears on the left end of the panel.

		NM	EX	VG
Complete Panel Set (12):		700.00	350.00	210.00
Complete Singles Set (36):		600.00	300.00	180.00
Common Player:		5.00	2.50	1.50
Panel (1)		110.00	55.00	30.00
(1)	Tommie Agee	5.00	2.50	1.50
(2)	Harmon Killebrew	35.00	17.50	10.00
(3)	Reggie Jackson	45.00	22.50	13.50
Panel (2)		110.00	55.00	30.00
(4)	Bert Campaneris	5.00	2.50	1.50
(5)	Pete Rose	50.00	25.00	15.00
(6)	Orlando Cepeda	25.00	12.50	7.50
Panel (3)		65.00	32.50	20.00
(7)	Rico Carty	5.00	2.50	1.50
(8)	Johnny Bench	40.00	20.00	12.00
(9)	Tommy Harper	5.00	2.50	1.50
Panel (4)		90.00	45.00	27.50
(10)	Bill Freehan	5.00	2.50	1.50
(11)	Roberto Clemente	60.00	30.00	18.00
(12)	Claude Osteen	5.00	2.50	1.50
Panel (5)		55.00	27.50	16.50
(13)	Jim Fregosi	5.00	2.50	1.50
(14)	Billy Williams	30.00	15.00	9.00
(15)	Dave McNally	5.00	2.50	1.50
Panel (6)		110.00	55.00	30.00
(16)	Randy Hundley	5.00	2.50	1.50
(17)	Willie Mays	50.00	25.00	15.00
(18)	Jim Hunter	25.00	12.50	7.50
Panel (7)		55.00	27.50	16.50
(19)	Juan Marichal	25.00	12.50	7.50
(20)	Frank Howard	7.50	3.75	2.25
(21)	Bill Melton	5.00	2.50	1.50
Panel (8)		100.00	50.00	30.00
(22)	Willie McCovey	30.00	15.00	9.00
(23)	Carl Yastrzemski	40.00	20.00	12.00
(24)	Clyde Wright	5.00	2.50	1.50
Panel (9)		55.00	27.50	16.50
(25)	Jim Merritt	5.00	2.50	1.50
(26)	Luis Aparicio	25.00	12.50	7.50
(27)	Bobby Murcer	9.00	4.50	2.75
Panel (10)		25.00	12.50	7.50
(28)	Rico Petrocelli	5.00	2.50	1.50
(29)	Sam McDowell	5.00	2.50	1.50
(30)	Cito Gaston	5.00	2.50	1.50
Panel (11)		115.00	55.00	35.00
(31)	Brooks Robinson	35.00	17.50	10.50
(32)	Hank Aaron	50.00	25.00	15.00
(33)	Larry Dierker	5.00	2.50	1.50
Panel (12)		60.00	30.00	18.00
(34)	Rusty Staub	7.50	3.75	2.25
(35)	Bob Gibson	30.00	15.00	9.00
(36)	Amos Otis	7.50	3.75	2.25

1930 Becker Bros. Theatre

Only recently brought to light, the issue date attributed here is uncertain and may be clarified if and when additions to the checklist are made. About postcard size, the cards have sepia portraits of Philadelphia A's players on front, identified in the white border at bottom. Backs have advertising for the theatre, including a list of upcoming features.

		NM	EX	VG
Common Player:		150.00	75.00	45.00
(1)	Max Bishop	150.00	75.00	45.00
(2)	Mickey Cochrane	250.00	125.00	75.00
(3)	Sammy Hale	150.00	75.00	45.00
(4)	Jimmie Foxx	300.00	150.00	90.00
(5)	Al Simmons	250.00	125.00	75.00

1958 Bell Brand Dodgers

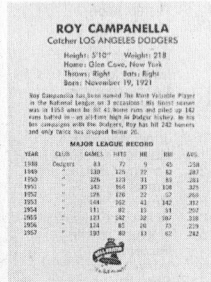

Celebrating the Dodgers first year of play in Los Angeles, Bell Brand inserted 10 different unnum- bered cards in their bags of potato chips and corn chips. The cards, which measure 3" x 4", have a sepia-colored photo inside a 1/4" green woodgrain border. The card backs feature statistical and biographical information and include the Bell Brand logo. Roy Campanella is included in the set despite a career-ending car wreck that prevented him from ever playing in Los Angeles.

		NM	EX	VG
Complete Set (10):		5,500	2,750	1,650
Common Player:		125.00	65.00	35.00
1	Roy Campanella	400.00	200.00	120.00
2	Gino Cimoli (SP)	1,200	600.00	360.00
3	Don Drysdale	350.00	175.00	100.00
4	Junior Gilliam	125.00	65.00	35.00
5	Gil Hodges	350.00	175.00	105.00
6	Sandy Koufax	1,350	675.00	410.00
7	Johnny Podres (SP)	600.00	300.00	180.00
8	Pee Wee Reese	400.00	200.00	120.00
9	Duke Snider	900.00	450.00	270.00
10	Don Zimmer	135.00	65.00	40.00

1958 Bell Brand Dodgers Ad Poster

Evidently a point-of-purchase in-store display to draw attention to its premiere offering of baseball cards, this 22" x 36" blank-back poster is, like the cards themselves, printed in green and sepia on white. The top pictures a super-size picture of Don Drysdale's card from the set.

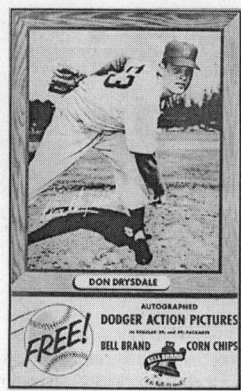

	NM	EX	VG
Bell Brand Dodgers Ad Poster (Don Drysdale)	4,250	2,100	1,250

1960 Bell Brand Dodgers

Bell Brand returned with a baseball card set in 1960 that was entirely different in style to their previous effort. The cards, which measure 2-1/2" x 3-1/2", feature beautiful, full-color photos. The backs carry a short player biography, the 1960 Dodgers home schedule, and the Bell Brand logo. Twenty different numbered cards were inserted in various size bags of potato chips and corn chips. Although sealed in cellophane, the cards were still subject to grease stains. Cards #'s 6, 12 and 18 are the scarcest in the set.

		NM	EX	VG
Complete Set (20):		1,500	750.00	450.00
Common Player:		45.00	22.50	13.50
1	Norm Larker	45.00	22.50	13.50
2	Duke Snider	150.00	75.00	45.00
3	Danny McDevitt	45.00	22.50	13.50
4	Jim Gilliam	50.00	25.00	15.00
5	Rip Repulski	45.00	22.50	13.50
6	Clem Labine (SP)	90.00	45.00	27.50
7	John Roseboro	45.00	22.50	13.50
8	Carl Furillo	60.00	30.00	18.00
9	Sandy Koufax	300.00	150.00	90.00
10	Joe Pignatano	45.00	22.50	13.50
11	Chuck Essegian	45.00	22.50	13.50
12	John Klippstein (SP)	150.00	75.00	45.00
13	Ed Roebuck	45.00	22.50	13.50
14	Don Demeter	45.00	22.50	13.50
15	Roger Craig	45.00	22.50	13.50
16	Stan Williams	45.00	22.50	13.50
17	Don Zimmer	60.00	30.00	18.00
18	Walter Alston (SP)	100.00	50.00	30.00
19	Johnny Podres	60.00	30.00	18.00
20	Maury Wills	75.00	37.50	22.50

1961 Bell Brand Dodgers

The 1961 Bell Brand set is identical in format to the previous year, although printed on thinner stock. Cards can be distinguished from the 1960 set by the 1961 schedule on the backs. The cards, which measure 2-7/16" x 3-1/2", are numbered by the player's uniform number. Twenty different cards were inserted into various size potato chip and corn chip packages, each card being sealed in a cellophane wrapper.

	NM	EX	VG
Complete Set (20):	1,500	750.00	450.00
Common Player:	50.00	25.00	15.00

3	Willie Davis	60.00	30.00	18.00
4	Duke Snider	175.00	85.00	50.00
5	Norm Larker	50.00	25.00	15.00
8	John Roseboro	50.00	25.00	15.00
9	Wally Moon	50.00	25.00	15.00
11	Bob Lillis	50.00	25.00	15.00
12	Tom Davis	60.00	30.00	18.00
14	Gil Hodges	150.00	75.00	45.00
16	Don Demeter	50.00	25.00	15.00
19	Jim Gilliam	60.00	30.00	18.00
22	John Podres	60.00	30.00	18.00
24	Walter Alston	75.00	37.50	22.50
30	Maury Wills	110.00	55.00	30.00
32	Sandy Koufax	250.00	125.00	75.00
34	Norm Sherry	60.00	30.00	18.00
37	Ed Roebuck	50.00	25.00	15.00
38	Roger Craig	50.00	25.00	15.00
40	Stan Williams	50.00	25.00	15.00
43	Charlie Neal	50.00	25.00	15.00
51	Larry Sherry	60.00	30.00	18.00

1962 Bell Brand Dodgers

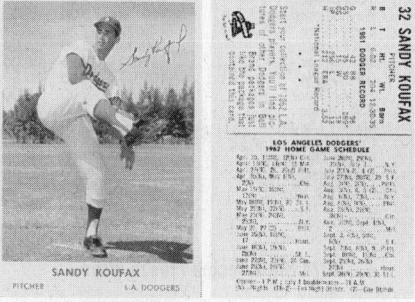

The 1962 Bell Brand set is identical in style to the previous two years and cards can be distinguished by the 1962 Dodgers schedule on the back. Each card measures 2-7/16" x 3-1/2" and is numbered by the player's uniform number. Printed on glossy stock, the 1962 set was less susceptible to grease stains.

		NM	EX	VG
Complete Set (20):		1,700	850.00	500.00
Common Player:		50.00	25.00	15.00
3	Willie Davis	50.00	25.00	15.00
4	Duke Snider	200.00	100.00	60.00
6	Ron Fairly	50.00	25.00	15.00
8	John Roseboro	50.00	25.00	15.00
9	Wally Moon	50.00	25.00	15.00
12	Tom Davis	50.00	25.00	15.00
16	Ron Perranoski	50.00	25.00	15.00
19	Jim Gilliam	55.00	27.50	16.50
20	Daryl Spencer	50.00	25.00	15.00
22	John Podres	55.00	27.50	16.50
24	Walter Alston	75.00	37.50	22.50
25	Frank Howard	55.00	27.50	16.50
30	Maury Wills	90.00	45.00	27.50
32	Sandy Koufax	250.00	125.00	75.00
34	Norm Sherry	60.00	30.00	18.00
37	Ed Roebuck	50.00	25.00	15.00
40	Stan Williams	50.00	25.00	15.00
51	Larry Sherry	60.00	30.00	18.00
53	Don Drysdale	125.00	65.00	35.00
56	Lee Walls	50.00	25.00	15.00

1962 Bell Brand Dodgers Ad Poster

This 8-1/2" x 11-1/2" color poster was distributed to retailers to solicit sales of Bell Brand items. The sheet has actual size pictures of six of the cards from the set. On back is retailer information.

	NM	EX	VG
1962 Bell Brand Ad Poster (Koufax, Roseboro, Wills, Moon, Snider, Sherry)	900.00	450.00	275.00

1951 Berk Ross

Entitled "Hit Parade of Champions," the 1951 Berk Ross set features 72 stars of various sports. The cards, which measure 2-1/16" x 2-1/2" and have tinted color photographs, were issued in four boxes containing two-card panels. The issue is divided into four subsets with the first ten players of each series being baseball players. Only the baseball players are listed in the checklist that follows. Complete panels are valued 50 percent higher than the sum of the individual cards.

		NM	EX	VG
Complete Boxed Set (72):		2,100	1,100	650.00
Complete Baseball Set (40):		1,325	660.00	395.00
Common Player:		13.50	6.75	4.00
1-1	Al Rosen	16.00	8.00	5.00
1-2	Bob Lemon	20.00	10.00	6.00
1-3	Phil Rizzuto	50.00	25.00	15.00
1-4	Hank Bauer	16.00	8.00	5.00
1-5	Billy Johnson	13.50	6.75	4.00
1-6	Jerry Coleman	13.50	6.75	4.00
1-7	Johnny Mize	25.00	12.50	7.50
1-8	Dom DiMaggio	20.00	10.00	6.00
1-9	Richie Ashburn	30.00	15.00	9.00
1-10	Del Ennis	13.50	6.75	4.00
2-1	Stan Musial	150.00	75.00	45.00
2-2	Warren Spahn	25.00	12.50	7.50
2-3	Tommy Henrich	16.00	8.00	5.00
2-4	Larry "Yogi" Berra	100.00	50.00	30.00
2-5	Joe DiMaggio	300.00	150.00	90.00
2-6	Bobby Brown	13.50	6.75	4.00
2-7	Granville Hamner	13.50	6.75	4.00
2-8	Willie Jones	13.50	6.75	4.00
2-9	Stanley Lopata	13.50	6.75	4.00
2-10	Mike Goliat	13.50	6.75	4.00
3-1	Ralph Kiner	20.00	10.00	6.00
3-2	Billy Goodman	13.50	6.75	4.00
3-3	Allie Reynolds	16.00	8.00	5.00
3-4	Vic Raschi	16.00	8.00	5.00
3-5	Joe Page	13.50	6.75	4.00
3-6	Eddie Lopat	13.50	6.75	4.00
3-7	Andy Seminick	13.50	6.75	4.00
3-8	Dick Sisler	13.50	6.75	4.00
3-9	Eddie Waitkus	13.50	6.75	4.00
3-10	Ken Heintzelman	13.50	6.75	4.00
4-1	Gene Woodling	16.00	8.00	5.00
4-2	Cliff Mapes	13.50	6.75	4.00
4-3	Fred Sanford	13.50	6.75	4.00
4-4	Tommy Bryne	13.50	6.75	4.00
4-5	Eddie (Whitey) Ford	180.00	90.00	55.00
4-6	Jim Konstanty	13.50	6.75	4.00
4-7	Russ Meyer	13.50	6.75	4.00
4-8	Robin Roberts	20.00	10.00	6.00
4-9	Curt Simmons	13.50	6.75	4.00
4-10	Sam Jethroe	13.50	6.75	4.00

1952 Berk Ross

Although the card size is different (2" x 3"), the style of the fronts and backs of the 1952 Berk Ross set is similar to the previous year's effort. Seventy-two unnumbered cards make up the set. Rizzuto is included twice in the set and the Blackwell and Fox cards have transposed backs. The cards were issued individually rather than as two-card panels like in 1951.

		NM	EX	VG
Complete Set (72):		5,000	2,500	1,500
Common Player:		25.00	12.50	7.50
(1)	Richie Ashburn	50.00	25.00	15.00
(2)	Hank Bauer	30.00	15.00	9.00
(3)	Larry "Yogi" Berra	175.00	85.00	50.00
(4)	Ewell Blackwell (Photo actually Nelson Fox.)	75.00	37.50	22.50
(5)	Bobby Brown	25.00	12.50	7.50
(6)	Jim Busby	25.00	12.50	7.50
(7)	Roy Campanella	140.00	70.00	40.00
(8)	Chico Carrasquel	25.00	12.50	7.50
(9)	Jerry Coleman	25.00	12.50	7.50
(10)	Joe Collins	25.00	12.50	7.50
(11)	Alvin Dark	25.00	12.50	7.50
(12)	Dom DiMaggio	35.00	17.50	10.00
(13)	Joe DiMaggio	425.00	210.00	125.00
(14)	Larry Doby	40.00	20.00	12.00
(15)	Bobby Doerr	40.00	20.00	12.00
(16)	Bob Elliot (Elliott)	25.00	12.50	7.50
(17)	Del Ennis	25.00	12.50	7.50
(18)	Ferris Fain	25.00	12.50	7.50
(19)	Bob Feller	100.00	50.00	30.00
(20)	Nelson Fox (Photo actually Ewell Blackwell.)	125.00	60.00	35.00

(21)	Ned Garver	25.00	12.50	7.50
(22)	Clint Hartung	25.00	12.50	7.50
(23)	Jim Hearn	25.00	12.50	7.50
(24)	Gil Hodges	75.00	37.50	22.50
(25)	Monte Irvin	40.00	20.00	12.00
(26)	Larry Jansen	25.00	12.50	7.50
(27)	George Kell	40.00	20.00	12.00
(28)	Sheldon Jones	25.00	12.50	7.50
(29)	Monte Kennedy	25.00	12.50	7.50
(30)	Ralph Kiner	40.00	20.00	12.00
(31)	Dave Koslo	25.00	12.50	7.50
(32)	Bob Kuzava	25.00	12.50	7.50
(33)	Bob Lemon	40.00	20.00	12.00
(34)	Whitey Lockman	25.00	12.50	7.50
(35)	Eddie Lopat	25.00	12.50	7.50
(36)	Sal Maglie	25.00	12.50	7.50
(37)	Mickey Mantle	2,000	1,000	600.00
(38)	Billy Martin	90.00	45.00	27.50
(39)	Willie Mays	500.00	250.00	150.00
(40)	Gil McDougal (McDougald)	30.00	15.00	9.00
(41)	Orestes Minoso	30.00	15.00	9.00
(42)	Johnny Mize	50.00	25.00	15.00
(43)	Tom Morgan	25.00	12.50	7.50
(44)	Don Mueller	25.00	12.50	7.50
(45)	Stan Musial	250.00	125.00	75.00
(46)	Don Newcombe	35.00	17.50	10.00
(47)	Ray Noble	25.00	12.50	7.50
(48)	Joe Ostrowski	25.00	12.50	7.50
(49)	Mel Parnell	25.00	12.50	7.50
(50)	Vic Raschi	25.00	12.50	7.50
(51)	Pee Wee Reese	125.00	65.00	35.00
(52)	Allie Reynolds	30.00	15.00	9.00
(53)	Bill Rigney	25.00	12.50	7.50
(54)	Phil Rizzuto (Bunting)	90.00	45.00	27.00
(55)	Phil Rizzuto (Swinging)	200.00	100.00	60.00
(56)	Robin Roberts	40.00	20.00	12.00
(57)	Eddie Robinson	25.00	12.50	7.50
(58)	Jackie Robinson	325.00	160.00	100.00
(59)	Elwin "Preacher" Roe	25.00	12.50	7.50
(60)	Johnny Sain	30.00	15.00	9.00
(61)	Albert "Red" Schoendienst	40.00	20.00	12.00
(62)	Duke Snider	140.00	70.00	40.00
(63)	George Spencer	25.00	12.50	7.50
(64)	Eddie Stanky	25.00	12.50	7.50
(65)	Henry Thompson	25.00	12.50	7.50
(66)	Bobby Thomson	30.00	15.00	9.00
(67)	Vic Wertz	25.00	12.50	7.50
(68)	Waldon Westlake	25.00	12.50	7.50
(69)	Wes Westrum	25.00	12.50	7.50
(70)	Ted Williams	450.00	225.00	135.00
(71)	Gene Woodling	30.00	15.00	9.00
(72)	Gus Zernial	25.00	12.50	7.50

1956 Big League Stars Statues

While the plastic statues in this set are virtually identical to the set issued in 1955 by Dairy Queen, the packaging of the Big League Stars statues on a card with all the usual elements of a baseball card makes them more collectible. The DQ versions of the statues are white, while the Big League versions are bronze colored. The statues measure about 3" tall and were sold in a 4" x 5" cardboard and plastic blister pack for about 19 cents. Complete league sets were also sold in a large package. The singles package features the player's name in a large banner near the top with his team printed below and line drawings of ballplayers in action around the statue. Backs have a player portrait photo with facsimile autograph, position, team, previous year and career stats and a career summary. A perforated tab at bottom can be pulled out to make a stand for the display. Most packages are found with the hole at top punched out to allow for hanging on a hook. Besides singles, larger packages of nine National or American league statues were also sold in a window-box. The set is checklisted alphabetically.

		NM	EX	VG
Complete Set (18):		4,000	2,000	1,200
Common Player:		60.00	30.00	18.00
UNOPENED PACKAGED				
STATUES				
(1)	John Antonelli	125.00	65.00	35.00
(2)	Bob Avila	125.00	65.00	35.00
(3)	Yogi Berra	400.00	200.00	120.00
(4)	Roy Campanella	400.00	200.00	120.00
(5)	Larry Doby	175.00	85.00	50.00
(6)	Del Ennis	125.00	65.00	35.00
(7)	Jim Gilliam	150.00	75.00	45.00
(8)	Gil Hodges	400.00	200.00	120.00
(9)	Harvey Kuenn	125.00	65.00	35.00
(10)	Bob Lemon	150.00	75.00	45.00
(11)	Mickey Mantle	2,000	1,000	600.00
(12)	Ed Mathews	300.00	150.00	90.00
(13)	Minnie Minoso	125.00	65.00	35.00
(14)	Stan Musial	600.00	300.00	180.00
(15)	Pee Wee Reese	400.00	200.00	120.00
(16)	Al Rosen	125.00	65.00	35.00
(17)	Duke Snider	400.00	200.00	120.00

(18)	Mickey Vernon	125.00	65.00	35.00
	STATUES			
(1)	John Antonelli	40.00	20.00	12.00
(2)	Bob Avila	40.00	20.00	12.00
(3)	Yogi Berra	150.00	75.00	45.00
(4)	Roy Campanella	150.00	75.00	45.00
(5)	Larry Doby	60.00	30.00	18.00
(6)	Del Ennis	40.00	20.00	12.00
(7)	Jim Gilliam	50.00	25.00	15.00
(8)	Gil Hodges	125.00	62.00	37.00
(9)	Harvey Kuenn	40.00	20.00	12.00
(10)	Bob Lemon	60.00	30.00	18.00
(11)	Mickey Mantle	300.00	150.00	90.00
(12)	Ed Mathews	100.00	50.00	30.00
(13)	Minnie Minoso	50.00	25.00	15.00
(14)	Stan Musial	200.00	100.00	60.00
(15)	Pee Wee Reese	150.00	75.00	45.00
(16)	Al Rosen	45.00	22.00	13.50
(17)	Duke Snider	150.00	75.00	45.00
(18)	Mickey Vernon	40.00	20.00	12.00
	PACKAGE/CARD ONLY			
(1)	John Antonelli	50.00	25.00	15.00
(2)	Bob Avila	50.00	25.00	15.00
(3)	Yogi Berra	150.00	75.00	45.00
(4)	Roy Campanella	150.00	75.00	45.00
(5)	Larry Doby	75.00	37.50	22.00
(6)	Del Ennis	50.00	25.00	15.00
(7)	Jim Gilliam	65.00	32.50	20.00
(8)	Gil Hodges	100.00	50.00	30.00
(9)	Harvey Kuenn	50.00	25.00	15.00
(10)	Bob Lemon	75.00	37.50	22.00
(11)	Mickey Mantle	1,200	600.00	360.00
(12)	Ed Mathews	125.00	62.50	37.50
(13)	Minnie Minoso	75.00	37.50	22.00
(14)	Stan Musial	175.00	85.00	50.00
(15)	Pee Wee Reese	150.00	75.00	45.00
(16)	Al Rosen	50.00	25.00	15.00
(17)	Duke Snider	150.00	75.00	45.00
(18)	Mickey Vernon	50.00	25.00	15.00

1978 Big T/Tastee Freeze discs

One player from each major league team was selected for inclusion in this discs set distributed by Big T family restaurants and Tastee Freeze stands in North Carolina, and possibly other parts of the country. The 3-3/8" diameter discs have a sepia-toned player portrait photo at center within a white diamond and surrounded by a brightly colored border with four colored stars at top. Licensed by the Players Association through Michael Schecter Associates, the photos have had uniform logos removed. Backs are printed in red, white and blue and have the sponsor's logos and a line of 1977 stats, along with a card number.

		NM	EX	VG
Complete Set (26):		30.00	15.00	9.00
Common Player:		2.00	1.00	.60
1	Buddy Bell	2.00	1.00	.60
2	Jim Palmer	8.00	4.00	2.50
3	Steve Garvey	5.00	2.50	1.50
4	Jeff Burroughs	2.00	1.00	.60
5	Greg Luzinski	2.00	1.00	.60
6	Lou Brock	8.00	4.00	2.50
7	Thurman Munson	5.00	2.50	1.50
8	Rod Carew	8.00	4.00	2.50
9	George Brett	20.00	10.00	6.00
10	Tom Seaver	15.00	7.50	4.50
11	Willie Stargell	8.00	4.00	2.50
12	Jerry Koosman	2.00	1.00	.60
13	Bill North	2.00	1.00	.60
14	Richie Zisk	2.00	1.00	.60
15	Bill Madlock	2.00	1.00	.60
16	Carl Yastrzemski	15.00	7.50	4.50
17	Dave Cash	2.00	1.00	.60
18	Bob Watson	2.00	1.00	.60
19	Dave Kingman	2.00	1.00	.60
20	Gene Tenace	2.00	1.00	.60
21	Ralph Garr	2.00	1.00	.60
22	Mark Fidrych	4.00	2.00	1.25
23	Frank Tanana	2.00	1.00	.60
24	Larry Hisle	2.00	1.00	.60
25	Bruce Bochte	2.00	1.00	.60
26	Bob Bailor	2.00	1.00	.60

1955-60 Bill and Bob Braves Postcards

One of the most popular and scarce of the 1950s color postcard series is the run of Milwaukee Braves known as "Bill and Bobs." While some of the cards do carry a photo credit acknowledging the pair, and a few add a Bradenton, Fla., (spring training home of the Braves) address, little else is known about the issuer. The cards themselves appear to have been purchased by the players to honor photo and autograph requests. Several of the cards carry facsimile autographs pre-printed on the front. The cards feature crisp full-color photos on their borderless fronts. Postcard backs have a variety of printing including card numbers, photo credits, a Kodachrome logo and player name. Some cards are found with some of those elements, some with none. There is some question whether Frank Torre's card is actually a Bill and Bob product, because it is 1/16" narrower than the standard 3-1/2" x 5-1/2"

format of the other cards, features the player with a Pepsi bottle in his hand and is rubber-stamped on back with a Pepsi bottler's address. The Torre card is usually collected along with the rest of the set.

		NM	EX	VG
Complete Set (20):		4,600	2,300	1,350
Common Player:		100.00	50.00	30.00
(1)	Hank Aaron	1,200	600.00	360.00
(2)	Joe Adcock (Fielding)	185.00	90.00	55.00
(3)	Joe Adcock (Bat on shoulder.)	185.00	90.00	55.00
(4)	Joe Adcock (Kneeling with two bats.)	145.00	75.00	45.00
(5)	Billy Bruton (Kneeling)	185.00	90.00	55.00
(6)	Billy Bruton (Throwing)	250.00	125.00	75.00
(7)	Bob Buhl	100.00	50.00	30.00
(8)	Lou Burdette	100.00	50.00	30.00
(9)	Gene Conley	100.00	50.00	30.00
(10)	Wes Covington (Kneeling, one bat.)	145.00	75.00	45.00
(11)	Wes Covington (Kneeling, seven bats.)	145.00	75.00	45.00
(12)	Del Crandall (Kneeling, one bat.)	135.00	65.00	40.00
(13)	Del Crandall (Kneeling, two bats.)	135.00	65.00	40.00
(14)	Chuck Dressen	145.00	75.00	45.00
(15)	Charlie Grimm	245.00	120.00	75.00
(16)	Fred Haney	235.00	115.00	70.00
(17)	Bob Keely	185.00	90.00	55.00
(18)	Eddie Mathews	400.00	200.00	120.00
(19)	Warren Spahn	500.00	250.00	150.00
(20)	Frank Torre	245.00	120.00	75.00

1923-24 Billiken

Apparently issued as a premium with its Billiken brand cigars, these cards were issued by Villaamil, Santalla y Ca. About 2" x 2-5/8", the cards have black-and-white posed photos surrounded with a white border. Below the picture the player's last name and team are presented in typewriter style. Among the scarcest and most popular of the pre-war Cuban issues, the set features many players from the Negro Leagues. Counterfeits are known.

		NM	EX	VG
Common Player:		800.00	325.00	160.00
	ALMENDARES			
(1)	Bernardo Baro	1,200	480.00	240.00
(2)	Manuel Cueto	900.00	360.00	180.00
(3)	Valentin Dreke	1,200	480.00	240.00
(4)	Isidro Fabre	900.00	360.00	180.00
(5)	Jose Maria Fernandez	900.00	360.00	180.00
(6)	Oscar Fuhr	800.00	325.00	160.00
(7)	Bienvenido "Hooks" Gimenez (Jimenez)	1,200	480.00	240.00
(8)	"Snake" Henry (Henry)	1,000	400.00	200.00
(9)	Ramon "Mike" Herrera	800.00	325.00	160.00
(10)	Jesse Hubbard	1,500	600.00	300.00
(11)	Armando Marsans	1,800	720.00	360.00
(12)	Jackie May (Jakie)	900.00	360.00	180.00
(13)	Eugenio Morin	800.00	325.00	160.00
(14)	Joseito Rodriguez	800.00	325.00	160.00
(15)	Nip Winters	2,000	800.00	400.00
	HABANA			
(16)	Eufemio Abreu	900.00	360.00	180.00
(17)	John Bischoff	800.00	325.00	160.00
(18)	Clark	800.00	325.00	160.00
(19)	Andy Cooper	5,000	2,000	1,000
(20)	Mack Eglefton (Eggleston)	1,300	520.00	260.00
(21)	Bienvenido "Hooks" Gimenez (Jimenez)	1,200	480.00	240.00
(22)	Marcelino Guerra	800.00	325.00	160.00
(23)	Oscar Levis	900.00	360.00	180.00
(24)	John Henry "Pop" Lloid (Lloyd)	19,500	7,800	3,900
(25)	Juanelo Mirabal	900.00	360.00	180.00

(26)	Bartolo Portuando (Portuondo)	1,200	480.00	240.00
(27)	Raphael "Busta" Quintana	800.00	325.00	160.00
(28)	Buster Ross	800.00	325.00	160.00
(29)	Clint Thomas	1,500	600.00	300.00
(30)	Edgar Westley (Wesley)	1,500	600.00	300.00

MARIANAO

(31)	Merito Acosta	800.00	325.00	160.00
(32)	Jose Acostica	800.00	325.00	160.00
(33)	D. Brown	800.00	325.00	160.00
(34)	E. Brown	800.00	325.00	160.00
(35)	Rogelio Crespo	800.00	325.00	160.00
(36)	Harry Deberry	800.00	325.00	160.00
(37)	Charlie Dressen	900.00	360.00	180.00
(38)	Freddie Fitzmann (Fitzsimmons)	800.00	325.00	160.00
(39)	Griffin	800.00	325.00	160.00
(40)	Ernie Krueger	800.00	325.00	160.00
(41)	Slim Love	800.00	325.00	160.00
(42)	Jose "Pepin" Perez	800.00	325.00	160.00
(43)	Rgal (Rigal)	800.00	325.00	160.00
(44)	Hank Sceiber (Schreiber)	800.00	325.00	160.00
(45)	Cristobal Torriente	19,500	7,800	3,900

SANTA CLARA

(46)	Oscar Charleston	19,500	7,800	3,900
(47)	Rube Currie	1,500	600.00	300.00
(48)	Pedro Dibut	900.00	360.00	180.00
(49)	Eddie Douglas (Douglass)	1,500	600.00	300.00
(50)	Frank Duncan	1,500	600.00	300.00
(51)	Oliver Marcell (Marcelle)	5,000	2,000	1,000
(52)	Mayari (Esteban Montalvo)	900.00	360.00	180.00
(53)	Jose Mendez	6,000	2,400	1,200
(54)	Augustin "Tinti" Molina	800.00	325.00	160.00
(55)	Dobie Moore	1,500	600.00	300.00
(56)	Alejandro Oms	2,000	800.00	400.00
(57)	Herman Rios	900.00	360.00	180.00
(58)	Julio Rojo	900.00	360.00	180.00
(59)	Red Ryan	1,200	480.00	240.00
(60)	Frank Wardfield (Warfield)	1,500	600.00	300.00

1916 Block and Kuhl Co.

TOM SEATON
P.—Chicago Cubs
161

Best known for its use as a promotional medium for The Sporting News, this 200-card set can be found with ads on the back for several local and regional businesses. Among them is the Block and Kuhl department store, Peoria, Ill. Type card and superstar collectors can expect to pay a significant premium for individual cards with Block and Kuhl's advertising. The checklist is believed to generally parallel the 1916 M101-4 Blank Backs. Cards measure 1-5/8" x 3" and are printed in black-and-white.

(See 1916 M101-4 Blank Backs for checklist.)

1911 Blome's Chocolates (E94)

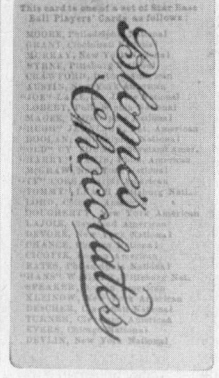

Advertising for Blome's Chocolates overprinted in purple on the back of these cards is one of several brands produced by George Close Candy Co. Type collectors will pay a premium of up to 5-7X for a Blome's version as opposed to the generic Close Candy version of the same player.

(See 1911 George Close Candy Co. for checklist and base card values.)

1933 Blue Bird Babe Ruth

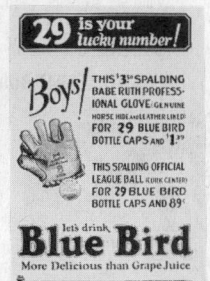

A small hoard of the (a) cards appeared in the market in early 1994 making available a card which had previously been virtually unknown. Printed in black-and-white on thin card stock, the piece measures 3-7/8" x 5-7/8". The photo on front was used in modified form on several other early-1930s issues. The back offers balls and gloves available for redemption with soft drink bottle caps and cash. The discovery of the (b) version came in 1999.

		NM	EX	VG
(1a)	Babe Ruth (Batting follow-through, front view.)	2,000	1,000	600.00
(1b)	Babe Ruth (Batting follow-through, side view.)	3,500	1,750	1,000

1930 Blue Ribbon Malt Chicago Cubs

These player pictures were originally printed as part of a 40" x 12" advertising piece by Blue Ribbon Malt. However, if cut from the piece, there is no identification of the issuer. Individual black-and-white pictures have facsimile autographs on front and measure 3-1/2" high by 1-7/16" to 3" wide. The backs are blank. The unnumbered pictures are checklisted here in alphabetical order, with names as they appear on the photos.

		NM	EX	VG
Complete Uncut Sheet:		500.00	250.00	150.00
Complete Set, Singles (28):		335.00	165.00	100.00
Common Player:		20.00	10.00	6.00
(1)	Clyde Beck	20.00	10.00	6.00
(2)	Lester Bell	20.00	10.00	6.00
(3)	Clarence Blair	20.00	10.00	6.00
(4)	Fred Blake	20.00	10.00	6.00
(5)	Jimmie Burke	20.00	10.00	6.00
(6)	Guy Bush	20.00	10.00	6.00
(7)	Hazen "Kiki" Cuyler	40.00	20.00	12.00
(8)	Woody English	20.00	10.00	6.00
(9)	Eddie Farrell	20.00	10.00	6.00
(10)	Charlie Grimm	20.00	10.00	6.00
(11)	Leo "Gabby" Hartnett	40.00	20.00	12.00
(12)	Clift Heathcote	20.00	10.00	6.00
(13)	Rogers Hornsby	65.00	32.00	19.50
(14)	George L. Kelly	40.00	20.00	12.00
(15)	Pierce "Pat" Malone	20.00	10.00	6.00
(16)	Joe McCarthy	20.00	10.00	6.00
(17)	Lynn Nelson	20.00	10.00	6.00
(18)	Bob Osborn	20.00	10.00	6.00
(19)	Jess Petty	20.00	10.00	6.00
(20)	Charlie Root	20.00	10.00	6.00
(21)	Ray Schalk	40.00	20.00	12.00
(22)	John Schulte	20.00	10.00	6.00
(23)	Al Shealy	20.00	10.00	6.00
(24)	Riggs Stephenson	20.00	10.00	6.00
(25)	Dan Taylor	20.00	10.00	6.00
(26)	Zack Taylor	20.00	10.00	6.00
(27)	Bud Teachout	20.00	10.00	6.00
(28)	Lewis "Hack" Wilson	60.00	30.00	18.00

1930 Blue Ribbon Malt Chicago White Sox

These player pictures were originally printed as part of a 40" x 12" advertising piece by Blue Ribbon Malt. However, if cut from the piece, there is no identification of the issuer. Individual black-and-white pictures have facsimile autographs on front and measure 3-1/2" high by 1-7/16" to 2-7/8" wide. The backs are blank. The unnumbered pictures are checklisted here in alphabetical order, with names as they appear on the photos.

		NM	EX	VG
Complete Uncut Sheet:		1,000	500.00	300.00
Complete Set (27):		400.00	200.00	120.00
Common Player:		20.00	10.00	6.00
(1)	"Chick" Autry	20.00	10.00	6.00
(2)	"Red" Barnes	20.00	10.00	6.00
(3)	Moe Berg	60.00	30.00	18.00
(4)	Garland Braxton	20.00	10.00	6.00
(5)	Donie Bush	20.00	10.00	6.00
(6)	Pat Caraway	20.00	10.00	6.00
(7)	Bill Cissell	20.00	10.00	6.00
(8)	"Bud" Clancy	20.00	10.00	6.00
(9)	Clyde Crouse	20.00	10.00	6.00
(10)	U.C. Faber	50.00	25.00	15.00
(11)	Bob Fothergill	20.00	10.00	6.00
(12)	Frank J. "Dutch" Henry	20.00	10.00	6.00
(13)	Smead Jolley	20.00	10.00	6.00
(14)	Bill "Willie" Kamm	20.00	10.00	6.00
(15)	Bernard "Mike" Kelly	20.00	10.00	6.00
(16)	Johnny Kerr	20.00	10.00	6.00
(17)	Ted Lyons	50.00	25.00	15.00
(18)	Harold McKain	20.00	10.00	6.00
(19)	"Jim" Moore	20.00	10.00	6.00
(20)	"Greg" Mulleavy	20.00	10.00	6.00
(21)	Carl N. Reynolds	20.00	10.00	6.00
(22)	Blondy Ryan	20.00	10.00	6.00
(23)	"Benny" Tate	20.00	10.00	6.00
(24)	Tommy Thomas	20.00	10.00	6.00
(25)	Ed Walsh, Jr.	20.00	10.00	6.00
(26)	Johnny Watwood	20.00	10.00	6.00
(27)	Bob Weiland	20.00	10.00	6.00

1930 Blue Ribbon Malt Premiums

The manner of distribution for this series is unknown. And, while the name of the sponsor does not appear, the similarity to other Blue Ribbon Malt issues pinpoints their source. The premiums are a 5" x 7" black-and-white photo (sometimes, but not always, mounted on a heavy gray cardboard 6-1/4" x 8-3/4" backing). A facsimile autograph is on the photo. This incomplete checklist is presented alphabetically by team.

		NM	EX	VG
Common Player:		225.00	110.00	65.00

CHICAGO CUBS

(1)	Clyde Beck	225.00	110.00	65.00
(2)	Lester Bell	225.00	110.00	65.00
(3)	Clarence Blair	225.00	110.00	65.00
(4)	Fred Blake	225.00	110.00	65.00
(5)	Jimmy Burke	225.00	110.00	65.00
(6)	Guy Bush	225.00	110.00	65.00
(7)	Hal Carlson	225.00	110.00	65.00
(8)	Hazen "Kiki" Cuyler	300.00	150.00	90.00
(9)	Woody English	225.00	110.00	65.00
(10)	Charlie Grimm	225.00	110.00	65.00
(11)	Leo "Gabby" Hartnett	300.00	150.00	90.00
(12)	Cliff Heathcote	225.00	110.00	65.00
(13)	Rogers Hornsby	400.00	200.00	120.00
(14)	Perce "Pat" Malone	225.00	110.00	65.00
(15)	Joe McCarthy	275.00	135.00	80.00
(16)	Malcolm Moss	225.00	110.00	65.00
(17)	Lynn Nelson	225.00	110.00	65.00
(18)	Bob Osborn	225.00	110.00	65.00
(19)	Charles Root	225.00	110.00	65.00
(20)	Ray Schalk	275.00	135.00	80.00
(21)	John Schulte	225.00	110.00	65.00
(22)	Al Shealy	225.00	110.00	65.00
(23)	Riggs Stephenson	225.00	110.00	65.00
(24)	Dan Taylor	225.00	110.00	65.00
(25)	Zack Taylor	225.00	110.00	65.00
(26)	Chas. J. Tolson	225.00	110.00	65.00
(27)	Hal Totten (Announcer)	225.00	110.00	65.00
(28)	Lewis "Hack" Wilson	350.00	175.00	105.00

CHICAGO WHITE SOX

(1)	Donie Bush	225.00	110.00	65.00
(2)	Bill Cissell	225.00	110.00	65.00
(4)	Red Faber	275.00	135.00	85.00
(5)	Smead Jolley	225.00	110.00	65.00
(7)	Willie Kamm	225.00	110.00	65.00
(9)	Ted Lyons	275.00	135.00	85.00
(11)	Carl Reynolds	225.00	110.00	65.00
(13)	Art Shires	225.00	110.00	65.00
(15)	Tommy Thomas	225.00	110.00	65.00
(16)	Johnny Watwood	225.00	110.00	65.00

1931 Blue Ribbon Malt

Players of the Chicago Cubs and White Sox are featured in this series of 4-7/8" x 6-7/8" black-and-white photos. Each blank-backed photo is bordered in white with "Compliments of BLUE RIBBON MALT-America's Biggest Seller" printed in the bottom border and a facsimile autograph across the photo. It is likely players other than those listed here were also issued.

		NM	EX	VG
	Common Player:	90.00	45.00	27.00
(1)	Lu Blue	90.00	45.00	27.00
(2)	Lew Fonseca	90.00	45.00	27.00
(3)	Vic Frazier	90.00	45.00	27.00
(4)	John Kerr	90.00	45.00	27.00
(5)	Bob Smith	90.00	45.00	27.00
(6)	Billy Sullivan	90.00	45.00	27.00
(7)	Lewis "Hack" Wilson	125.00	62.00	37.00

1931 Blum's Baseball Bulletin Premiums

The year of issue presented is speculative, based on biographical information on the relatively few examples studied. This series of 9-1/2" x 13-5/8" (Small) or 11-1/2" x 13-3/4" (Large) black-and-white blank-back pictures was, according to a credit line beneath the bottom frame of baseballs, "Compiled by Fred J. Blum, Publisher, Blum's Baseball Bulletin." The checklist here is incomplete.

		NM	EX	VG
	Common Player:	200.00	100.00	60.00
(1)	Edward T. Collins (S)	300.00	150.00	90.00
(2)	Jacob E. Daubert (S)	200.00	100.00	60.00
(3)	William E. Donovan (L)	200.00	100.00	60.00
(4)	John J. Evers (S)	300.00	150.00	90.00
(5)	Lou Gehrig (L)	350.00	175.00	105.00
(6)	Henry K. Groh (L)	200.00	100.00	60.00
(7)	Lefty Grove (L)	400.00	200.00	120.00
(8)	Walter Johnson (S)	500.00	250.00	150.00
(9)	Napoleon Lajoie (S)	350.00	175.00	105.00
(10)	Walter J.V. Maranville (S)	300.00	150.00	90.00
(11)	James (Wicky) McAvoy (L)	200.00	100.00	60.00
(12)	Rochester 1911 (Team composite.) (L)	200.00	100.00	60.00
(13)	Billy Southworth (L)	200.00	100.00	60.00
(14)	Tristam Speaker (S)	400.00	200.00	120.00
(15)	George Toporcer (L)	200.00	100.00	60.00
(16)	Arthur C (Dazzy) Vance	200.00	100.00	60.00

1961-1963 Bobbin' Head Dolls

Some of the top stars of the day were caricatured in the first generation of bobbin' head dolls. Additionally, Mantle and Maris were depicted in a pair of color 5" x 7" advertising photos depicting the home run heroes of 1961 holding their dolls. The players are pictured in belt-to-cap photos wearing road uniforms and posed in a stadium setting. Backs are blank.

	NM	EX	VG
Roberto Clemente (6-1/2" doll)	4,500	2,250	1,350
Roberto Clemente (Picture box.)	1,000	500.00	300.00
Mickey Mantle (Ad photo.)	325.00	160.00	95.00
Mickey Mantle (6-1/2" doll, round or square base)	1,100	550.00	330.00
Mickey Mantle (Mini (4-1/2") doll.)	1,500	750.00	450.00
Mickey Mantle (Large or small picture box.)	750.00	375.00	225.00
Roger Maris (Ad photo.)	175.00	87.00	52.00
Roger Maris (6-1/2" doll)	450.00	225.00	135.00
Roger Maris (Mini (5-1/2") doll.)	650.00	325.00	195.00
Roger Maris (Large or small picture box.)	900.00	450.00	275.00

	NM	EX	VG
Willie Mays (White base, dark face, 6-1/2" doll.)	750.00	375.00	225.00
Willie Mays (White base, light face, 6-1/2" doll.)	475.00	235.00	140.00
Willie Mays (Gold base, 6-1/2" doll.)	2,250	1,125	675.00

1947 Bond Bread

Tommy Holmes

Issued by "Homogenized" Bond Bread in 1947, this set consists of 48 unnumbered black-and-white cards, each measuring about 2-1/4" x 3-1/2" with rounded or square corners. Of the 48 cards, 44 are baseball players; four picture boxers. Borderless fronts have either portraits or posed action photos and the player's facsimile autograph or name in script. In the 1980s a large quantity of half the cards in the set (all with square corners) was uncovered in a New York warehouse. Sometime after 2000, the square-cornered cards were illegally reprinted, often sold in high-graded slabs from unknown grading companies. Those cards that were not known to be affected by the find/reprinting are indicated in the checklist here with an "SP." The issue was designated in the American Card Catalog as W571 / D305.

		NM	EX	VG
	Complete Set (48):	1,600	800.00	475.00
	Common Player:	15.00	7.50	4.50
(1)	Rex Barney (SP)	20.00	10.00	6.00
(2)	Yogi Berra (SP)	75.00	37.50	22.50
(3)	Ewell Blackwell	15.00	7.50	4.50
(4)	Lou Boudreau	20.00	10.00	6.00
(5)	Ralph Branca (SP)	20.00	10.00	6.00
(6)	Harry Brecheen	15.00	7.50	4.50
(7)	Dom DiMaggio (SP)	50.00	25.00	15.00
(8)	Joe DiMaggio (SP)	275.00	135.00	85.00
(9)	Bobbie Doerr (Bobby)	20.00	10.00	6.00
(10)	Bruce Edwards (SP)	20.00	10.00	6.00
(11)	Bob Elliott	15.00	7.50	4.50
(12)	Del Ennis	15.00	7.50	4.50
(13)	Bob Feller	25.00	12.50	7.50
(14)	Carl Furillo (SP)	35.00	17.50	10.00
(15)	Cid Gordon (Sid)(SP)	20.00	10.00	6.00
(16)	Joe Gordon	15.00	7.50	4.50
(17)	Joe Hatten (SP)	20.00	10.00	6.00
(18)	Gil Hodges (SP)	75.00	37.50	22.50
(19)	Tommy Holmes	15.00	7.50	4.50
(20)	Larry Janson (Jansen) (SP)	20.00	10.00	6.00
(21)	Sheldon Jones (SP)	20.00	10.00	6.00
(22)	Edwin Joost (SP)	20.00	10.00	6.00
(23)	Charlie Keller (SP)	20.00	10.00	6.00
(24)	Ken Keltner	15.00	7.50	4.50
(25)	Buddy Kerr (SP)	20.00	10.00	6.00
(26)	Ralph Kiner	20.00	10.00	6.00
(27)	John Lindell (SP)	20.00	10.00	6.00
(28)	Whitey Lockman (SP)	20.00	10.00	6.00
(29)	Willard Marshall (SP)	20.00	10.00	6.00
(30)	Johnny Mize	20.00	10.00	6.00
(31)	Stan Musial	60.00	30.00	18.00
(32)	Andy Pafko	15.00	7.50	4.50
(33)	Johnny Pesky	15.00	7.50	4.50
(34)	Pee Wee Reese (SP)	125.00	65.00	35.00
(35)	Phil Rizzuto	30.00	15.00	9.00
(36)	Aaron Robinson	15.00	7.50	4.50
(37)	Jackie Robinson	90.00	45.00	27.50
(38)	John Sain	15.00	7.50	4.50
(39)	Enos Slaughter	20.00	10.00	6.00
(40)	Vern Stephens	15.00	7.50	4.50
(41)	George Tebbetts (SP)	20.00	10.00	6.00
(42)	Bob Thomson (SP)	25.00	12.50	7.50
(43)	Johnny Vandermeer (VanderMeer) (SP)	20.00	10.00	6.00
(44)	Ted Williams	90.00	45.00	27.00
	BOXERS			
(45)	Primo Carnera	15.00	7.50	4.50
(46)	Marcel Cerdan (SP)	40.00	20.00	12.00
(47)	Jake LaMotta (SP)	60.00	30.00	18.00
(48)	Joe Louis	30.00	15.00	9.00

1947 Bond Bread Exhibits

The manner of distribution of these variants of the "Bond Bread" (W571 / D305) baseball cards is believed to have been via penny arcade dispensers. About the same size as contemporary Exhibit Supply Co. cards (3-3/8" x 5-3/8"), these are printed in black-and-white and blank-backed. Over 75 percent of the baseball players known in the base Bond Bread set have been reported in this format, plus one player, Walker Cooper, not in the base set. The four W571/D305 boxers have not yet been reported in this format.

		NM	EX	VG
	Complete Set (33):	1,250	625.00	375.00
	Common Player:	25.00	12.50	7.50
(1)	Rex Barney			
(2)	Yogi Berra			

		NM	EX	VG
(3)	Ewell Blackwell	25.00	12.50	7.50
(4)	Lou Boudreau	30.00	15.00	9.00
(5)	Ralph Branca			
(6)	Harry Brecheen	25.00	12.50	7.50
(--)	Walker Cooper	50.00	25.00	15.00
(7)	Dom DiMaggio	30.00	15.00	9.00
(8)	Joe DiMaggio	200.00	100.00	60.00
(9)	Bobbie Doerr (Bobby)	35.00	17.50	10.00
(10)	Bruce Edwards			
(11)	Bob Elliott	25.00	12.50	7.50
(12)	Del Ennis	25.00	12.50	7.50
(13)	Bob Feller	40.00	20.00	12.00
(14)	Carl Furillo	100.00	50.00	30.00
(15)	Cid Gordon (Sid)			
(16)	Joe Gordon	25.00	12.50	7.50
(17)	Joe Hatten			
(18)	Gil Hodges	90.00	45.00	27.50
(19)	Tommy Holmes	25.00	12.50	7.50
(20)	Larry Janson (Jansen)	25.00	12.50	7.50
(21)	Sheldon Jones	25.00	12.50	7.50
(22)	Edwin Joost	25.00	12.50	7.50
(23)	Charlie Keller			
(24)	Ken Keltner	25.00	12.50	7.50
(25)	Buddy Kerr	25.00	12.50	7.50
(26)	Ralph Kiner	30.00	15.00	9.00
(27)	John Lindell	25.00	12.50	7.50
(28)	Whitey Lockman	25.00	12.50	7.50
(29)	Willard Marshall			
(30)	Johnny Mize	30.00	15.00	9.00
(31)	Stan Musial	75.00	37.50	22.50
(32)	Andy Pafko	25.00	12.50	7.50
(33)	Johnny Pesky	25.00	12.50	7.50
(34)	Pee Wee Reese	100.00	50.00	30.00
(35)	Phil Rizzuto	50.00	25.00	15.00
(36)	Aaron Robinson	25.00	12.50	7.50
(37)	Jackie Robinson	175.00	90.00	55.00
(38)	John Sain	25.00	12.50	7.50
(39)	Enos Slaughter	30.00	15.00	9.00
(40)	Vern Stephens	25.00	12.50	7.50
(41)	George Tebbetts	25.00	12.50	7.50
(42)	Bob Thomson			
(43)	Johnny Vandermeer (VanderMeer)	25.00	12.50	7.50
(44)	Ted Williams	175.00	85.00	55.00

1947 Bond Bread Premiums

While there is no empirical evidence, it is believed these 6-5/8" x 9" black-and-white, blank-back player pictures are associated with the Bond Bread card issue, since they share the same photos and script names, right down to the misspellings. They were likely made available to bread buyers as some sort of premium. The checklist presented here is the same as that of the card issue. Though not all of the premium pictures have been confirmed, it is reasonable to presume their existence.

		NM	EX	VG
	Common Player:	40.00	20.00	12.00
(1)	Rex Barney	40.00	20.00	12.00
(2)	Yogi Berra	150.00	75.00	45.00
(3)	Ewell Blackwell	40.00	20.00	12.00
(4)	Lou Boudreau	75.00	37.50	22.50
(5)	Ralph Branca	60.00	30.00	18.00
(6)	Harry Brecheen	40.00	20.00	12.00
(7)	Dom DiMaggio	60.00	30.00	18.00
(8)	Joe DiMaggio	600.00	300.00	180.00
(9)	Bobbie Doerr (Bobby)	60.00	30.00	18.00
(10)	Bruce Edwards	40.00	20.00	12.00
(11)	Bob Elliott	40.00	20.00	12.00
(12)	Del Ennis	50.00	25.00	15.00
(13)	Bob Feller	150.00	75.00	45.00
(14)	Carl Furillo	60.00	30.00	18.00
(15)	Cid Gordon (Sid)	40.00	20.00	12.00
(16)	Joe Gordon	40.00	20.00	12.00
(17)	Joe Hatten	40.00	20.00	12.00
(18)	Gil Hodges	100.00	50.00	30.00
(19)	Tommy Holmes	40.00	20.00	12.00
(20)	Larry Janson (Jansen)	40.00	20.00	12.00
(21)	Sheldon Jones	40.00	20.00	12.00
(22)	Edwin Joost	40.00	20.00	12.00
(23)	Charlie Keller	45.00	22.50	13.50
(24)	Ken Keltner	40.00	20.00	12.00
(25)	Buddy Kerr	40.00	20.00	12.00
(26)	Ralph Kiner	75.00	37.50	22.50
(27)	John Lindell	40.00	20.00	12.00
(28)	Whitey Lockman	40.00	20.00	12.00
(29)	Willard Marshall	40.00	20.00	12.00
(30)	Johnny Mize	75.00	37.50	22.50
(31)	Stan Musial	300.00	150.00	90.00
(32)	Andy Pafko	40.00	20.00	12.00
(33)	Johnny Pesky	40.00	20.00	12.00
(34)	Pee Wee Reese	150.00	75.00	45.00
(35)	Phil Rizzuto	150.00	75.00	45.00
(36)	Aaron Robinson	40.00	20.00	12.00
(37)	Jackie Robinson	1,000	500.00	300.00

		NM	EX	VG
(38)	John Sain	50.00	25.00	15.00
(39)	Enos Slaughter	75.00	37.50	22.50
(40)	Vern Stephens	40.00	20.00	12.00
(41)	George Tebbetts	40.00	20.00	12.00
(42)	Bob Thomson	60.00	30.00	18.00
(43)	Johnny Van Der Meer (VanderMeer)	40.00	20.00	12.00
(44)	Ted Williams	350.00	175.00	100.00
BOXERS				
(45)	Primo Carnera	45.00	22.50	13.50
(46)	Marcel Cerdan	40.00	20.00	12.00
(47)	Jake LaMotta	60.00	30.00	18.00
(48)	Joe Louis	75.00	37.50	22.50

1947 Bond Bread Perforated, Dual-Sided

The manner of distribtion for this variant of the "Bond Bread" (W571/D305) cards is unknown, although anecdotal evidence suggests a connection with Bar Nunn show stores. About the size of the commonly seen blank-backed baseball cards (2-1/4" x 3-1/2"), these differ in that they have two, three or four sides perforated, indicating they were issued in sheet form. Also, this group has, instead of a blank back, another picture. All but one of the pictures seen thus far are of Western movie stars. None are named on the cards, but they include John Wayne, Hopalong Cassidy, Gene Autry and Noah Berry. The only non-Western back seen is Michigan quarterback Bob Chappius, paired with Tommy Holmes. Thus far, none of the short-printed Bond Bread cards have been seen in this format. Assigned numbers correspond to the Bond Bread set.

		NM	EX	VG
Complete Set (24):		550.00	275.00	165.00
Common Card:				
(3)	Ewell Blackwell	15.00	7.50	4.50
(4)	Lou Boudreau	22.50	11.00	6.75
(6)	Harry Brecheen	15.00	7.50	4.50
(9)	Bobbie Doerr (Bobby)	22.50	11.00	6.75
(11)	Bob Elliott	15.00	7.50	4.50
(12)	Del Ennis	15.00	7.50	4.50
(13)	Bob Feller	25.00	12.50	7.50
(16)	Joe Gordon	15.00	7.50	4.50
(19)	Tommy Holmes	15.00	7.50	4.50
(24)	Ken Keltner	15.00	7.50	4.50
(26)	Ralph Kiner	22.50	11.00	6.75
(30)	Johnny Mize	22.50	11.00	6.75
(31)	Stan Musial	60.00	30.00	18.00
(32)	Andy Pafko	15.00	7.50	4.50
(33)	Johnny Pesky	15.00	7.50	4.50
(35)	Phil Rizzuto	30.00	15.00	9.00
(36)	Aaron Robinson	15.00	7.50	4.50
(37)	Jackie Robinson	110.00	55.00	35.00
(38)	John Sain	15.00	7.50	4.50
(39)	Enos Slaughter	22.50	11.00	6.75
(40)	Vern Stephens	15.00	7.50	4.50
(44)	Ted Williams	110.00	55.00	35.00
BOXERS				
(45)	Primo Carnera	15.00	7.50	4.50
(48)	Joe Louis	30.00	15.00	9.00

1947 Bond Bread Jackie Robinson

The modern major leagues' first black player is featured in this set issued by Bond Bread in 1947. The cards, measuring 2-1/4" x 3-1/2", are black-and-white photos of Robinson in various action and portrait poses. The cards are unnumbered and bear three different backs advertising Bond Bread. Four cards use a horizontal format. Card #6 was issued in greater quantities and perhaps was a promotional card; its back is the only one containing a short biography of Robinson.

		NM	EX	VG
Complete Set (13):		28,500	14,250	8,000
Common Card:		2,250	1,125	650.00
(1)	Jackie Robinson (Awaiting pitch.)	2,250	1,125	650.00
(2)	Jackie Robinson (Batting, white shirt sleeves.)	2,250	1,125	650.00
(3)	Jackie Robinson (Batting, no shirt sleeves.)	2,250	1,125	650.00
(4)	Jackie Robinson (Leaping, scoreboard in background.)	2,250	1,125	650.00
(5)	Jackie Robinson (Leaping, no scoreboard.)	2,250	1,125	650.00
(6)	Jackie Robinson (Portrait, facsimile autograph.)	2,250	1,125	650.00
(7)	Jackie Robinson (Portrait, holding glove in air.)	2,250	1,125	650.00
(8)	Jackie Robinson (Running down baseline.)	2,250	1,125	650.00
(9)	Jackie Robinson (Running to catch ball.)	2,250	1,125	650.00
(10)	Jackie Robinson (Sliding)	2,250	1,125	650.00
(11)	Jackie Robinson (Stretching for throw, ball in glove.)	2,250	1,125	650.00
(12)	Jackie Robinson (Stretching for throw, no ball visible.)	2,250	1,125	650.00
(13)	Jackie Robinson (Throwing)	2,250	1,125	650.00

1912 Boston American Series Red Sox Postcards

Star players from the World Champion Red Sox are featured in two sets of postcards issued by one of the city's daily newspapers. This set carries the notation "Boston American Series" at bottom right and is approximately 3-1/2" x 5-1/2". The cards are printed in sepia tones with a cream border. At bottom is the player name and position on two lines. Backs have typical postcard markings and a three-line notation, "PHOTOS OF / NOTED BALL PLAYERS / BOSTON SUNDAY AMERICAN SERIES."

		NM	EX	VG
Complete Set (6):		2,400	1,200	725.00
Common Player:		400.00	200.00	120.00
(1)	Forrest Cady	400.00	200.00	120.00
(2)	Hub Perdue	400.00	200.00	120.00
(3)	Tris Speaker	550.00	275.00	165.00
(4)	Jake Stahl	400.00	200.00	120.00
(5)	Heinie Wagner	400.00	200.00	120.00
(6)	Joe Wood	400.00	200.00	120.00

1936 Boston American Sport Stamps

Similar to several contemporary issues, the Sport Stamps were printed on the pages of the daily newspaper over the course of the season. About 2" x 3-1/2", depending on the length of the biography and how well they were cut off the paper, they are printed in black-and-white. A tightly cropped player portrait is centered on a 2" x 2-5/8" stamp design with the paper's name above and the player's name, position and team below. The checklist may not be complete. Two of the players (Castleman, R. Johnson) have the paper at top listed as "SUNDAY ADVERTISER." Many of the stamps were issued in pairs, and at least a couple of football players are known, as well as the listed baseball players.

		NM	EX	VG
Common Player:		12.00	6.00	3.50
(1)	J. (John) Allen	12.00	6.00	3.50
(2)	I. (Ivy) Andrews	12.00	6.00	3.50
(3)	E. (Elden)(Eldon) Auker	12.00	6.00	3.50
(4)	E. (Earl) Averill	20.00	10.00	6.00
(5)	R. (Richard) Bartell	12.00	6.00	3.50
(6)	R. (Roy) Bell	12.00	6.00	3.50
(7)	R. (Raymond) Benge	12.00	6.00	3.50
(8)	M. (Morris) Berg	30.00	15.00	9.00
(9)	Walter Berger	12.00	6.00	3.50
(10)	C. (Charles) Berry	12.00	6.00	3.50
(11)	(George) Blaeholder	12.00	6.00	3.50
(12)	A. (Albert) Blanche	12.00	6.00	3.50
(13)	D. (Darrell) Blanton	12.00	6.00	3.50
(14)	O. (Oswald) Bleuge (Bluege)	12.00	6.00	3.50
(15)	W. (William) Bolton	12.00	6.00	3.50
(16)	H. (Henry) Bonura	12.00	6.00	3.50
(17)	J. (James) Bottomley	20.00	10.00	6.00
(18)	J. (Joseph) Bowman	12.00	6.00	3.50
(19)	E. (Edward) Brandt	12.00	6.00	3.50
(20)	C. (Clinton) Brown	12.00	6.00	3.50
(21)	J. (John) Burnett	12.00	6.00	3.50
(22)	G. (Guy) Bush	12.00	6.00	3.50
(23)	A. (Albert) Butcher	12.00	6.00	3.50
(24)	E. (Earl) Caldwell	12.00	6.00	3.50
(25)	D. (Dolph) Camilli	12.00	6.00	3.50
(26)	B. (Bruce) Campbell	12.00	6.00	3.50
(27)	J. (Joseph) Cascarella	12.00	6.00	3.50
(28)	C. (Clyde) Castleman	12.00	6.00	3.50
(29)	P. (Philip) Cavarretta	12.00	6.00	3.50
(30)	W. (William) Chapman	12.00	6.00	3.50
(31)	L. (Louis) Chiozza	12.00	6.00	3.50
(32)	H. (Harland)(Harlond) Clift	12.00	6.00	3.50
(33)	G. (Gordon) Cochrane	25.00	12.50	7.50
(34)	J. (James) Collins	12.00	6.00	3.50
(35)	A. (Allen) Cooke	12.00	6.00	3.50
(36)	J. (Joseph) Coscarart	12.00	6.00	3.50
(37)	Roger Cramer	12.00	6.00	3.50
(38)	J. (Joseph) Cronin	20.00	10.00	6.00
(39)	F. (Frank) Crosetti	15.00	7.50	4.50
(40)	A. (Alvin) Crowder	12.00	6.00	3.50
(41)	A. (Anthony) Cuccinello	12.00	6.00	3.50
(42)	H. (Hazen) Cuyler	20.00	10.00	6.00
(43)	H. (Harry) Danning	12.00	6.00	3.50
(44)	V. (Virgil) Davis	12.00	6.00	3.50
(45)	J. (Jerome) Dean	35.00	17.50	10.50
(46)	P. (Paul) Dean	16.00	8.00	4.75
(47)	J. (Joseph) Demaree	12.00	6.00	3.50
(48)	Paul Derringer	12.00	6.00	3.50
(49)	G. (George) Dickey	12.00	6.00	3.50
(50)	W. (William) Dickey	25.00	12.50	7.50
(51)	L. (Leo) Durocher	20.00	10.00	6.00
(52)	J. (James) Dykes	12.00	6.00	3.50
(53)	G. (George) Earnshaw	12.00	6.00	3.50
(54)	E. (Elmwood)(Elwood) English	12.00	6.00	3.50
(55)	R. (Robert) Feller	25.00	12.50	7.50
(56)	R. (Richard) Ferrell	20.00	10.00	6.00
(57)	Wes Ferrell	12.00	6.00	3.50
(58)	(Louis) Finney	12.00	6.00	3.50
(59)	F. (Fred) Fitzsimmons	12.00	6.00	3.50
(60)	Jimmy Foxx	30.00	15.00	9.00
(61)	(Fred) Frankhouse	12.00	6.00	3.50
(62)	L. (Lawrence) French	12.00	6.00	3.50
(63)	(Frank) Frisch	20.00	10.00	6.00
(64)	A. (August) Galan	12.00	6.00	3.50
(65)	H. (Heny)(Henry) Gehrig	60.00	30.00	18.00
(66)	C. (Charles) Gehringer	20.00	10.00	6.00
(67)	(Charles) Gelbert	12.00	6.00	3.50
(68)	A. (Angelo) Giuliani	12.00	6.00	3.50
(69)	V. (Vernon) Gomez	20.00	10.00	6.00
(70)	L. (Leon) Goslin	20.00	10.00	6.00
(71)	R. (Robert) Grace	12.00	6.00	3.50
(72)	C. (Charles) Grimm	12.00	6.00	3.50
(73)	Robert Grove	25.00	12.50	7.50
(74)	G. (George) Haas	12.00	6.00	3.50
(75)	I. (Irving) Hadley	12.00	6.00	3.50
(76)	M. (Melvin) Harder	12.00	6.00	3.50
(77)	C. (Charles) Hartnett	20.00	10.00	6.00
(78)	M. (Minter) Hayes	12.00	6.00	3.50
(79)	R. (Ralston) Hemsley	12.00	6.00	3.50
(80)	F. (Floyd) Herman	12.00	6.00	3.50
(81)	(Michael) Higgins	12.00	6.00	3.50
(82)	M. (Myril) Hoag	12.00	6.00	3.50
(83)	E. (Elon) Hogsett	12.00	6.00	3.50
(84)	R. (Rogers) Hornsby	25.00	12.50	7.50
(85)	W. (Waite) Hoyt	20.00	10.00	6.00
(86)	W. (Willis) Hudlin	12.00	6.00	3.50
(87)	T. (Travis) Jackson	20.00	10.00	6.00
(88)	R. (Robert) Johnson	12.00	6.00	3.50
(89)	R. (Roy) Johnson	12.00	6.00	3.50
(90)	B. (Baxter) Jordan	12.00	6.00	3.50
(91)	W. (William) Jurgess (Jurges)	12.00	6.00	3.50
(92)	(Lloyd) Kennedy	12.00	6.00	3.50
(93)	C. (Charles) Klein	20.00	10.00	6.00
(94)	(William) Knickerbocker	12.00	6.00	3.50
(95)	J. (John) Knott	12.00	6.00	3.50
(96)	M. (Mark) Koenig	12.00	6.00	3.50
(97)	J. (Joseph) Kuhel	12.00	6.00	3.50
(98)	L. (Lynford) Lary	12.00	6.00	3.50
(99)	H. (Harry) Lavagetto	12.00	6.00	3.50
(100)	A. (Anthony) Lazzeri	20.00	10.00	6.00
(101)	W. (William) Lee	12.00	6.00	3.50
(102)	H. (Henry) Leiber	12.00	6.00	3.50
(103)	Wm. (William) Lewis	12.00	6.00	3.50
(104)	E. (Edward) Linke	12.00	6.00	3.50
(105)	E. (Ernest) Lombardi	20.00	10.00	6.00
(106)	Al Lopez	20.00	10.00	6.00
(107)	C. (Charles) Lucas	12.00	6.00	3.50
(108)	T. (Theodore) Lyons	20.00	10.00	6.00
(109)	Dan MacFayden	12.00	6.00	3.50
(110)	P. (Percy)(Perce) Malone	12.00	6.00	3.50
(111)	A. (Augustus) Mancuso	12.00	6.00	3.50
(112)	(John) Martin	15.00	7.50	4.50
(113)	J. (Joseph) Medwick	20.00	10.00	6.00
(114)	E. (Edmund) Miller	12.00	6.00	3.50
(115)	J. (John) Mize	20.00	10.00	6.00
(116)	Gene Moore	12.00	6.00	3.50
(117)	R. (Randolph) Moore	12.00	6.00	3.50
(118)	V. (Van Lingle) Mungo	12.00	6.00	3.50
(119)	C. (Charles) Myer	12.00	6.00	3.50
(120)	A. (Alfred) Niemiec	12.00	6.00	3.50
(121)	(Fred) Ostermueller	12.00	6.00	3.50
(122)	M. (Melvin) Ott	25.00	12.50	7.50
(123)	L. (LeRoy) Parmelee	12.00	6.00	3.50
(124)	A. (Anthony) Piet	12.00	6.00	3.50
(125)	A. (Alvin) Powell	12.00	6.00	3.50
(126)	F. (Frank) Pytlak	12.00	6.00	3.50
(127)	R. (Ray) Radcliff	12.00	6.00	3.50
(128)	R. (Robert) Reis	12.00	6.00	3.50
(129)	(Carl) Reynolds	12.00	6.00	3.50
(130)	J. (John) Rhodes	12.00	6.00	3.50
(131)	R. (Robert) Roth	12.00	6.00	3.50
(132)	C. (Charles) Root	12.00	6.00	3.50
(133)	L. (Lynwood) Rowe	12.00	6.00	3.50
(134)	C. (Charles) Ruffing	20.00	10.00	6.00
(135)	F. (Fred) Schulte	12.00	6.00	3.50
(136)	H. (Harold) Schumacher	12.00	6.00	3.50
(137)	J. (James) Sewell	12.00	6.00	3.50
(138)	A. (Aloysius) Simmons	20.00	10.00	6.00

		NM	EX	VG
(139)	J. (Julius) Soulters (Solters)	12.00	6.00	3.50
(140)	G. (George) Stainback	12.00	6.00	3.50
(141)	J. (Johnathan)(John) Stone	12.00	6.00	3.50
(142)	J. (Joseph) Stripp	12.00	6.00	3.50
(143)	W. (William) Terry	20.00	10.00	6.00
(144)	T. (Thomas) Thevenow	12.00	6.00	3.50
(145)	A. (Alphonse) Thomas	12.00	6.00	3.50
(146)	C. (Cecil) Travis	12.00	6.00	3.50
(147)	H. (Harold) Traynor	20.00	10.00	6.00
(148)	H. (Harold) Trosky	12.00	6.00	3.50
(149)	R. (Russell) Van Atta	12.00	6.00	3.50
(150)	F. (Floyd) Vaughan	20.00	10.00	6.00
(151)	J. (Joseph) Vosmik	12.00	6.00	3.50
(152)	G. (Gerald) Walker	12.00	6.00	3.50
(153)	W. (William) Walter	12.00	6.00	3.50
(154)	L. (Lloyd) Waner	20.00	10.00	6.00
(155)	P. (Paul) Waner	20.00	10.00	6.00
(156)	L. (Lonnie) Warneke	12.00	6.00	3.50
(157)	G. (George) Watkins	12.00	6.00	3.50
(158)	J. (Joyner) White	12.00	6.00	3.50
(159)	(Burgess) Whitehead	12.00	6.00	3.50
(160)	(Earl) Whitehill	12.00	6.00	3.50
(161)	A. (Arthur) Whitney	12.00	6.00	3.50
(162)	J. (Jack) Wilson	12.00	6.00	3.50
(163)	J. (James) Wilson	12.00	6.00	3.50

1912 Boston Daily American Souvenir Postcards

A second style of postcard issued by a local newspaper to honor the World Champions is labeled at bottom-left "Boston American Souvenir." The 3-1/2" x 5-1/2" cards are printed in black on a cream-colored stock. The player name and position are printed inside the photo frame. In the bottom-right border is a union logo and the number "96." The back has standard postcard markings.

		NM	EX	VG
Common Player:		450.00	225.00	135.00
(1)	Forrest Cady	450.00	225.00	135.00
(2)	Ray Collins	450.00	225.00	135.00
(3)	Rabbit Maranville	600.00	300.00	180.00
(4)	Heinie Wagner	450.00	225.00	135.00
(5)	Joe Wood	500.00	250.00	150.00

1912 Boston Garter

If it weren't for the checklist printed on the back of the few known specimens, the extent of this extremely rare issue would be unknown. Many of the cards mentioned on the back have yet to be seen. Issued by the George Frost Co. of Boston, and packed one card per box of a dozen garters, the approximately 4" x 8-1/4" cards are printed in color lithography on the front, and black-and-white on the back. Fronts have a picture of the player standing near his locker or sitting in a chair, dressing in his uniform. The issuer's Boston-brand garter is prominently shown below the player's boxer shorts. A window in the background displays a cityscape or ballpark scene. There was a card issued for one player on each of the 16 major league teams of the day. Large-format (21-1/2" x 11-1/4") cardboard window display posters which reproduce pairs of the cards are sometimes seen in the hobby.

		NM	EX	VG
Common Player:		30,000	12,000	7,250
(1)	Bob Bescher	30,000	12,000	7,250
(2)	Roger Bresnahan	40,000	15,000	8,250
(3)	Frank Chance	40,000	15,000	9,000
(4)	Hal Chase	30,000	12,500	7,500
(5)	Fred Clarke	40,000	13,750	8,250
(6)	Eddie Collins	40,000	13,750	8,250
(7)	Charles Dooin	30,000	12,000	7,250
(8)	Hugh Jennings	40,000	13,750	8,250
(9)	Walter Johnson	60,000	17,500	10,500
(10)	Johnny Kling	30,000	12,000	7,250
(11)	Larry Lajoie	45,000	15,000	9,000
(12)	Frank LaPorte	30,000	12,000	7,250
(13)	Christy Mathewson	75,000	37,500	22,500
(14)	Nap Rucker	30,000	12,000	7,250
(15)	Tris Speaker	45,000	15,000	9,000
(16)	Ed Walsh	40,000	13,750	8,250

1914 Boston Garter - Color

 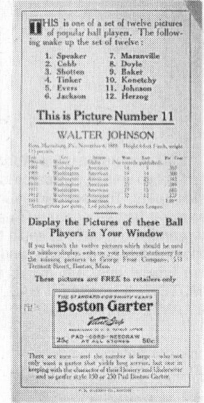

The second of what are presumed to have been three annual issue by the George Frost Co., Boston, contains 12 cards. The colorful lithograph fronts have a player picture in front of a ballpark diagram. A large Boston-brand garter appears at the bottom. Baseballs with the Boston Garter name appear in each upper corner. Black-and-white backs have a checklist for the set, career statistics for the player pictured and details on the cards' availability. Retailers received one card per box of dozen garters and could write to the company to complete the set. About 4" x 8-1/4", they were intended to be displayed in shop windows.

		NM	EX	VG
Common Player:		7,500	3,000	1,800
1	Tris Speaker	30,000	10,000	6,000
2	Ty Cobb	60,000	17,500	10,500
3	Burt Shotten (Shotton)	7,500	3,000	1,800
4	Joe Tinker	15,000	6,250	3,750
5	Johnny Evers	15,500	6,250	3,750
6	Joe Jackson	100,000	30,000	18,000
7	Rabbit Maranville	15,000	6,250	3,750
8	Larry Doyle	7,500	3,000	1,800
9	Frank Baker	15,000	6,250	3,750
10	Ed Konetchy	7,500	3,000	1,800
11	Walter Johnson	35,000	10,000	6,000
12	Buck Herzog	7,500	3,000	1,800

1914 Boston Garter - Sepia

The 1914 date attributed to this 10-card set may or may not be accurate. Since the company's other two known issues can be reliably dated and were produced using the color lithographic process, it is presumed that the use of photographs would have come later. Fronts of the approximately 3-3/4" x 6-1/4" cards feature a green duo-tone photo of the player. His last name appears in white script at the bottom, along with a baseball with the Boston Garter name. Backs have a checklist of the set and information on how retail store owners can send for additional cards to supplement those which were packaged one per box of a dozen garters.

	NM	EX	VG
Complete Set (10):	140,000	70,000	42,500

		NM	EX	VG
Common Player:		15,000	7,500	4,500
1	Christy Mathewson	35,000	20,000	12,500
2	Red Murray	7,500	3,750	2,250
3	Eddie Collins	15,000	7,500	4,500
4	Hugh Jennings	15,000	7,500	4,500
5	Hal Chase	12,000	6,000	3,600
6	Bob Bescher	7,500	3,750	2,250
7	Red Dooin	7,500	3,750	2,250
8	Larry Lajoie	15,000	7,500	4,500
9	Tris Speaker	20,000	10,000	6,000
10	Heinie Zimmerman	7,500	3,750	2,250

1909 Boston Herald Supplements

Members of the Red Sox and Braves were featured in this series of supplements in the Boston Sunday Herald. About 7-1/4" x 9-3/4", the blank-back, posed-action pictures are sepia toned. A black box at bottom has player identification, an issue date and a note to "See Story on Sporting Page." While the pictures themselves are numbered, this checklist, almost certainly incomplete, is arranged alphabetically. Some of the pictures show cross-town rivals on the same piece.

		NM	EX	VG
BOSTON BRAVES				
(1)	Chick Autry	200.00	100.00	60.00
(2)	Johnny Bates	200.00	100.00	60.00
(3)	Ginger Beaumont	200.00	100.00	60.00
(4)	Beals Becker	200.00	100.00	60.00
(5)	Frank Bowerman	200.00	100.00	60.00
(6)	Jack Coffey	200.00	100.00	60.00
(7)	Peaches Graham	200.00	100.00	60.00
(8)	Al Mattern	200.00	100.00	60.00
(9)	Harry Smith	200.00	100.00	60.00
(10)	Bill Sweeney	200.00	100.00	60.00
(11)	("Tom") Thomas H. Tuckey	200.00	100.00	60.00
BOSTON RED SOX				
(1)	Charlie Chech	200.00	100.00	60.00
(2)	Bill Carrigan	200.00	100.00	60.00
(3)	Pat Donahue	200.00	100.00	60.00
(4)	"Doc" (Harry H.) Gessler	200.00	100.00	60.00
(5)	Harry Hooper	300.00	150.00	90.00
(5)	Harry Lord	200.00	100.00	60.00
(6)	Amby McConnell	200.00	100.00	60.00
(7)	Harry Niles	200.00	100.00	60.00
(8)	Tris Speaker	400.00	200.00	120.00
BOSTON BRAVES/RED SOX				
(1)	Johnny Bates, Harry Hooper	150.00	75.00	45.00
(2)	Ginger Beaumont, Tris Speaker	150.00	75.00	45.00
(3)	Ed Cicotte, Tommy Tuckey	250.00	125.00	75.00
(4)	Bill Dahlen, Heinie Wagner	150.00	75.00	45.00
(5)	Doc Gessler, Frank Bowerman	150.00	75.00	45.00
(6)	Harry Lord, Unknown Brave	150.00	75.00	45.00
(7)	Amby McConnell, Jack Coffey	150.00	75.00	45.00
(8)	Harry Smith, Pat Donahue	150.00	75.00	45.00
(9)	Jake Stahl, Chick Autrey (Autry)	150.00	75.00	45.00

1908 Boston Oyster House Chicago Cubs

Located in Chicago, not Boston, this restaurant featured, according to its advertising, "The 'Cubs' Dining Room." In keeping with that theme, the business adopted as a promotion the set of Cubs/Teddy Bear postcards issued the previous year by Grignon, a local publisher. The restaurant version has on its back a 1908 Cubs home schedule and rudimentary scorecard, along with standard postcard markings.

	NM	EX	VG
Common Player:	500.00	250.00	150.00

Stars: 1X
(See 1907 Grignon Chicago Cubs postcards for checklist and base values.)

1908 Boston Red Sox Foldout Postcard

At first glance this standard-size (about 5-1/2" x 3-1/2") postcard reveals on its front only portrait photos of the the owners and grounds of the Boston Red Sox, with a cotter-pinned baseball at left printed in red. Hidden behind the ball, however, is an accordian-folded strip of black-and-white player photos, printed front-to-back, in a size of about 1-1/8" x 1-3/4".

	NM	EX	VG
1908 Boston Red Sox	4,500	2,250	1,350

1910 Boston Red Sox Cabinets

Details are lacking on this high-quality photographic issue depicting the 1910 Red Sox. The sepia photos picture the players in full-length poses and are glued to cardboard mattes. There is no identification on the pieces, nor on the decorative paper folders in which they were apparently originally sold.

		NM	EX	VG
Common Player:		350.00	175.00	100.00
(1)	Hugh Bradley	350.00	175.00	100.00
(2)	Bill Carrigan	350.00	175.00	100.00
(3)	Ed Cicotte	1,000	500.00	300.00
(4)	Ray Collins	350.00	175.00	100.00
(5)	Clyde Engle	350.00	175.00	100.00
(6)	Larry Gardner	350.00	175.00	100.00
(7)	Charley Hall	350.00	175.00	100.00
(8)	Harry Hooper	750.00	375.00	225.00
(9)	Ben Hunt	350.00	175.00	100.00
(10)	Duffy Lewis	500.00	250.00	150.00
(11)	Tom Madden	350.00	175.00	100.00
(12)	Doc Moskiman	350.00	175.00	100.00
(13)	Harry Smith	350.00	175.00	100.00
(14)	Tris Speaker	1,000	500.00	300.00
(15)	Jake Stahl	350.00	175.00	100.00
(16)	Heinie Wagner	350.00	175.00	100.00

1912 Boston Red Sox Tattoos

This set of tattoos is similar to a number of other issues of the era, most of which were made in Germany. This issue features members of the World Champion Boston Red Sox. Approximately 1-3/8" x 1-3/4", the tattoos are printed in mirror-image in bright colors. Images are crude line art with no resemblance to the actual players. Players are identified at bottom by at least a last name. A position is designated in the background of the picture. These items were issued on a perforated sheet. "Collins" may represent retired Red Sox Jimmy Collins or 1912 pitcher Ray Collins. The unnumbered tattoos are listed here alphabetically, though the listing may not be complete.

		NM	EX	VG
Complete Set (13):		475.00	235.00	140.00
Common Player:		35.00	17.50	10.00
(1)	Hugh Bedient	35.00	17.50	10.00
(2)	Hick Cady	35.00	17.50	10.00
(3)	Collins	35.00	17.50	10.00
(4)	Clyde Engle	35.00	17.50	10.00
(5)	Charley Hall	35.00	17.50	10.00
(6)	Martin Krug	35.00	17.50	10.00
(7)	Jerry McCarthy (Mascot)	35.00	17.50	10.00
(8)	Les Nunamaker	35.00	17.50	10.00
(9)	Larry Pape	35.00	17.50	10.00
(10)	Tris Speaker	125.00	65.00	35.00
(11)	Jake Stahl	35.00	17.50	10.00
(12)	Heinie Wagner	35.00	17.50	10.00
(13)	Joe Wood	50.00	25.00	15.00

1940 Boston Red Sox Photo Pack

Approximately 6" x 9", these blank-back, black-and-white pictures depict the BoSox in (usually) neck-to-cap poses. The pictures are bordered in white and there is a facsimile autograph on each photo.

		NM	EX	VG
Complete Set (25):		300.00	150.00	75.00
Common Player:		8.00	4.00	2.50
(1)	Jim Bagby	8.00	4.00	2.50
(2)	Bill Butland	8.00	4.00	2.50

(3)	Tom Carey	8.00	4.00	2.50
(4)	Doc Cramer	8.00	4.00	2.50
(5)	Joe Cronin	15.00	7.50	4.50
(6)	Gene Desautels	8.00	4.00	2.50
(7)	Emerson Dickman	8.00	4.00	2.50
(8)	Dom DiMaggio	15.00	7.50	4.50
(9)	Bobby Doerr	15.00	7.50	4.50
(10)	Lou Finney	8.00	4.00	2.50
(11)	Jimmie Foxx	35.00	17.50	10.00
(12)	Denny Galehouse	8.00	4.00	2.50
(13)	Joe Glenn	8.00	4.00	2.50
(14)	Lefty Grove	30.00	15.00	9.00
(15)	Mickey Harris	8.00	4.00	2.50
(16)	Herbie Hash	8.00	4.00	2.50
(17)	Joe Heving	8.00	4.00	2.50
(18)	Leo Nonnenkamp	8.00	4.00	2.50
(19)	Fritz Ostermueller	8.00	4.00	2.50
(20)	Mickey Owen	8.00	4.00	2.50
(21)	John Peacock	8.00	4.00	2.50
(22)	Jim Tabor	8.00	4.00	2.50
(23)	Charles Wagner	8.00	4.00	2.50
(24)	Ted Williams	60.00	30.00	18.00
(25)	Jack Wilson	8.00	4.00	2.50

1941 Boston Red Sox Photo Pack

Approximately 6" x 9", these blank-back, black-and-white pictures depict the BoSox in informal poses, most leaning on the dugout top step. The pictures are bordered in white and there is a facsimile autograph on each photo. It is possible this checklist (arranged alphabetically) is incomplete as other players may have been added to or deleted from the set to conform to roster changes during the season.

		NM	EX	VG
Complete Set (25):		200.00	100.00	60.00
Common Player:		8.00	4.00	2.50
(1)	Paul Campbell	8.00	4.00	2.50
(2)	Tom Carey	8.00	4.00	2.50
(3)	Joe Cronin	20.00	10.00	6.00
(4)	Emerson Dickman	8.00	4.00	2.50
(5)	Dom DiMaggio	15.00	7.50	4.50
(6)	Joe Dobson	8.00	4.00	2.50
(7)	Bobby Doerr	12.00	6.00	3.50
(8)	Lou Finney	8.00	4.00	2.50
(9)	Bill Fleming	8.00	4.00	2.50
(10)	Pete Fox	8.00	4.00	2.50
(11)	Jimmie Foxx	30.00	15.00	9.00
(12)	Lefty Grove	25.00	12.50	7.50
(13)	Mickey Harris	8.00	4.00	2.50
(14)	Tex Hughson	8.00	4.00	2.50
(15)	Earl Johnson	8.00	4.00	2.50
(16)	Lefty Judd	8.00	4.00	2.50
(17)	Dick Newsome	8.00	4.00	2.50
(18)	Skeeter Newsome	8.00	4.00	2.50
(19)	John Peacock	8.00	4.00	2.50
(20)	Frank Pytlak	8.00	4.00	2.50
(21)	Mike Ryba	8.00	4.00	2.50
(22)	Stan Spence	8.00	4.00	2.50
(23)	Jim Tabor	8.00	4.00	2.50
(24)	Charlie Wagner	8.00	4.00	2.50
(25)	Ted Williams	50.00	25.00	15.00
(26)	Jack Wilson	8.00	4.00	2.50

1942 Boston Red Sox Photo Pack

In a format of approximately 6-1/2" x 9", these team-issued player portraits are blank-backed, black-and-white with a white border. Most photos are chest-to-cap presentations and all have a facsimile autograph. Some of the players in the issue can be seen wearing the "HEALTH" patch which MLB adopted during World War II. This checklist may not be complete as it is possible some players were added or deleted from the set to reflect mid-season roster moves.

		NM	EX	VG
Complete Set (25):		275.00	135.00	85.00
Common Player:		10.00	5.00	3.00
(1)	Mace Brown	10.00	5.00	3.00
(2)	Bill Butland	10.00	5.00	3.00
(3)	Paul Campbell	10.00	5.00	3.00
(4)	Tom Carey	10.00	5.00	3.00
(5)	Ken Chase	10.00	5.00	3.00
(6)	Bill Conroy	10.00	5.00	3.00
(7)	Joe Cronin	20.00	10.00	6.00
(8)	Dom DiMaggio	20.00	10.00	6.00
(9)	Joe Dobson	10.00	5.00	3.00
(10)	Bobby Doerr	20.00	10.00	6.00
(11)	Lou Finney	10.00	5.00	3.00
(12)	Pete Fox	10.00	5.00	3.00
(13)	Jimmie Foxx	40.00	20.00	12.00
(14)	Tex Hughson	10.00	5.00	3.00

(15)	Oscar Judd	10.00	5.00	3.00
(16)	Tony Lupien	10.00	5.00	3.00
(17)	Dick Newsome	10.00	5.00	3.00
(18)	Skeeter Newsome	10.00	5.00	3.00
(19)	John Peacock	10.00	5.00	3.00
(20)	Johnny Pesky	10.00	5.00	3.00
(21)	Mike Ryba	10.00	5.00	3.00
(22)	Jim Tabor	10.00	5.00	3.00
(23)	Yank Terry	10.00	5.00	3.00
(24)	Charlie Wagner	10.00	5.00	3.00
(25)	Ted Williams	60.00	30.00	18.00

1943 Boston Red Sox Photo Pack

In a format of approximately 6-1/2" x 9", these team-issued player portraits are blank-backed, black-and-white with a white border. Most photos are chest-to-cap presentations and all have a facsimile autograph. Some of the players in the issue can be seen wearing the "HEALTH" patch which MLB adopted during World War II. This checklist may not be complete as it is possible some players were added or deleted from the set to reflect mid-season roster moves.

		NM	EX	VG
Complete Set (24):		125.00	65.00	40.00
Common Player:		8.00	4.00	2.50
(1)	Mace Brown	8.00	4.00	2.50
(2)	Ken Chase	8.00	4.00	2.50
(3)	Bill Conroy	8.00	4.00	2.50
(4)	Joe Cronin	15.00	7.50	4.50
(5)	Joe Dobson	8.00	4.00	2.50
(6)	Bobby Doerr	15.00	7.50	4.50
(7)	Pete Fox	8.00	4.00	2.50
(8)	Ford Garrison	8.00	4.00	2.50
(9)	Tex Hughson	8.00	4.00	2.50
(10)	Oscar Judd	8.00	4.00	2.50
(11)	Andy Karl	8.00	4.00	2.50
(12)	Eddie Lake	8.00	4.00	2.50
(13)	John Lazor	8.00	4.00	2.50
(14)	Lou Lucier	10.00	5.00	3.00
(15)	Tony Lupien	8.00	4.00	2.50
(16)	Dee Miles	8.00	4.00	2.50
(17)	Dick Newsome	8.00	4.00	2.50
(18)	Skeeter Newsome	8.00	4.00	2.50
(19)	Roy Partee	8.00	4.00	2.50
(20)	John Peacock	8.00	4.00	2.50
(21)	Mike Ryba	8.00	4.00	2.50
(22)	Al Simmons	15.00	7.50	4.50
(23)	Jim Tabor	8.00	4.00	2.50
(24)	Yank Terry	8.00	4.00	2.50

1946 Boston Red Sox Photo Pack

The American League champion Red Sox are featured in this team-issue photo pack. The player portraits are printed in black-and-white on heavy paper in 6-1/2" x 9" format. The photos have a white border and a facsimile autograph on front. Backs are blank. The unnumbered pictures are listed here in alphabetical order.

		NM	EX	VG
Complete Set (25):		225.00	110.00	65.00
Common Player:		6.00	3.00	1.75
(1)	Ernie Andres	6.00	3.00	1.75
(2)	Jim Bagby	6.00	3.00	1.75
(3)	Mace Brown	6.00	3.00	1.75
(4)	Joe Cronin	12.00	6.00	3.50
(5)	Leon Culbertston	6.00	3.00	1.75
(6)	Mel Deutsch	6.00	3.00	1.75
(7)	Dom DiMaggio	10.00	5.00	3.00
(8)	Joe Dobson	6.00	3.00	1.75
(9)	Bobby Doerr	12.00	6.00	3.50
(10)	Boo Ferriss	6.00	3.00	1.75
(11)	Mickey Harris	6.00	3.00	1.75

(12)	Randy Heflin	6.00	3.00	1.75
(13)	Tex Hughson	6.00	3.00	1.75
(14)	Earl Johnson	6.00	3.00	1.75
(15)	Ed McGah	6.00	3.00	1.75
(16)	George Metkovich	6.00	3.00	1.75
(17)	Roy Partee	6.00	3.00	1.75
(18)	Eddie Pellagrini	6.00	3.00	1.75
(19)	Johnny Pesky	7.50	3.75	2.25
(20)	Rip Russell	6.00	3.00	1.75
(21)	Mike Ryba	6.00	3.00	1.75
(22)	Charlie Wagner	6.00	3.00	1.75
(23)	Hal Wagner	6.00	3.00	1.75
(24)	Ted Williams	60.00	30.00	18.00
(25)	Rudy York	6.00	3.00	1.75

1947 Boston Red Sox Photo Pack

In the same 6-1/2" x 9" format which the team had used for its photo packs since 1942, this set of black-and-white, blank-back pictures features (usually) chest-to-cap portraits with white borders, a dark background and a facsimile autograph in the picture. Some of the photos were re-used from previous years' issues, or were re-issued in subsequent years. The unnumbered pictures are checklisted here in alphabetical order. This list may or may not be complete; it is possible other players' photos were added or deleted to reflect seasonal roster changes.

		NM	EX	VG
Complete Set (25):		200.00	100.00	60.00
Common Player:		6.00	3.00	1.75
(1)	Joe Cronin	15.00	7.50	4.50
(2)	Leon Culberson	6.00	3.00	1.75
(3)	Dom DiMaggio	12.50	6.25	3.75
(4)	Joseph Dobson	6.00	3.00	1.75
(5)	Bobby Doerr	15.00	7.50	4.50
(6)	Harry Dorish	6.00	3.00	1.75
(7)	Dave "Boo" Ferriss	6.00	3.00	1.75
(8)	Tommy Fine	6.00	3.00	1.75
(9)	Don Gutteridge	6.00	3.00	1.75
(10)	Mickey Harris	6.00	3.00	1.75
(11)	Tex Hughson	6.00	3.00	1.75
(12)	Earl Johnson	6.00	3.00	1.75
(13)	Bob Klinger	6.00	3.00	1.75
(14)	Sam Mele	6.00	3.00	1.75
(15)	Wally Moses	6.00	3.00	1.75
(16)	Johnny Murphy	6.00	3.00	1.75
(17)	Mel Parnell	6.00	3.00	1.75
(18)	Roy Partee	6.00	3.00	1.75
(19)	Eddie Pellagrini	6.00	3.00	1.75
(20)	Johnny Pesky	7.50	3.75	2.25
(21)	Rip Russell	6.00	3.00	1.75
(22)	Birdie Tebbetts	6.00	3.00	1.75
(23)	Ted Williams	60.00	30.00	18.00
(24)	Rudy York	6.00	3.00	1.75
(25)	Bill Zuber	6.00	3.00	1.75

1948 Boston Red Sox Photo Pack

In the same 6-1/2" x 9" format which the team had used for its photo packs since 1942, this set of black-and-white, blank-back pictures features (usually) chest-to-cap portraits with white borders, a dark background and a facsimile autograph in the picture. Some of the photos were re-used from previous years' issues, or were re-issued in subsequent years. The unnumbered pictures are checklisted here in alphabetical order. This list may or may not be complete; it is possible other players' photos were added or deleted to reflect seasonal roster changes.

	NM	EX	VG
Complete Set (25):	200.00	100.00	60.00

Common Player:		6.00	3.00	1.75
(1)	Matt Batts	6.00	3.00	1.75
(2)	Dom DiMaggio	15.00	7.50	4.50
(3)	Joseph Dobson	6.00	3.00	1.75
(4)	Bobby Doerr	15.00	7.50	4.50
(5)	Harry Dorish	6.00	3.00	1.75
(6)	Dave "Boo" Ferriss	6.00	3.00	1.75
(7)	Dennis Galehouse	6.00	3.00	1.75
(8)	Billy Goodman	6.00	3.00	1.75
(9)	Mickey Harris	6.00	3.00	1.75
(10)	Bill Hitchcock	6.00	3.00	1.75
(11)	Earl Johnson	6.00	3.00	1.75
(12)	Jake Jones	6.00	3.00	1.75
(13)	Ellis Kinder	6.00	3.00	1.75
(14)	Jack Kramer	6.00	3.00	1.75
(15)	Joe McCarthy	15.00	7.50	4.50
(16)	Maurice McDermott	6.00	3.00	1.75
(17)	Sam Mele	6.00	3.00	1.75
(18)	Wally Moses	6.00	3.00	1.75
(19)	Mel Parnell	6.00	3.00	1.75
(20)	Johnny Pesky	7.50	3.75	2.25
(21)	Stan Spence	6.00	3.00	1.75
(22)	Vern Stephens	6.00	3.00	1.75
(23)	Chuck Stobbs	6.00	3.00	1.75
(24)	Birdie Tebbetts	6.00	3.00	1.75
(25)	Ted Williams	60.00	30.00	18.00

1949 Boston Red Sox Photo Pack

In the same 6-1/2" x 9" format the team used for its photo packs since 1942, this set of black-and-white, blank-back pictures features (usually) chest-to-cap portraits with white borders, a dark background and a facsimile autograph within the picture. Some of the photos were re-used from previous years' issues, or were re-issued in subsequent years. The unnumbered pictures are checklisted here in alphabetical order.

		NM	EX	VG
Complete Set (25):		200.00	100.00	60.00
Common Player:		6.00	3.00	1.80
(1)	Matt Batts	6.00	3.00	1.80
(2)	Merrill Combs	6.00	3.00	1.80
(3)	Dom DiMaggio	15.00	7.50	4.50
(4)	Joe Dobson	6.00	3.00	1.80
(5)	Bobby Doerr	15.00	7.50	4.50
(6)	David "Boo" Ferris	6.00	3.00	1.80
(7)	Bill Goodman	6.00	3.00	1.80
(8)	Mickey Harris	6.00	3.00	1.80
(9)	Billy Hitchcock	6.00	3.00	1.80
(10)	Tex Hughson	6.00	3.00	1.80
(11)	Earl Johnson	6.00	3.00	1.80
(12)	Ellis Kinder	6.00	3.00	1.80
(13)	Jack Kramer	6.00	3.00	1.80
(14)	Joe McCarthy	15.00	7.50	4.50
(15)	Sam Mele	6.00	3.00	1.80
(16)	Tommy O'Brien	6.00	3.00	1.80
(17)	Mel Parnell	6.00	3.00	1.80
(18)	Johnny Pesky	6.00	3.00	1.80
(19)	Frank Quinn	6.00	3.00	1.80
(20)	Vern Stephens	6.00	3.00	1.80
(21)	Chuck Stobbs	6.00	3.00	1.80
(22)	Lou Stringer	6.00	3.00	1.80
(23)	Birdie Tebbetts	6.00	3.00	1.80
(24)	Ted Williams	60.00	30.00	18.00
(25)	Al Zarilla	6.00	3.00	1.80

1950 Boston Red Sox Photo Pack

In the same approximately 6-1/2" x 9" format which the team had used for its photo packs since the 1940s, this set of black-and-white, blank-back pictures features (usually) chest-to-cap portraits with white borders, a dark background and a facsimile autograph within the photo. Some of the photos were re-used from previous years' issues. The unnumbered pictures are checklisted here in alphabetical order. This list may or may not be complete; it is possible other players' photos were added or deleted to reflect seasonal roster changes.

		NM	EX	VG
Complete Set (25):		150.00	75.00	40.00
Common Player:		4.00	2.00	1.25
(1)	Matt Batts	4.00	2.00	1.25
(2)	Earle Combs	7.50	3.75	2.25
(3)	Dom DiMaggio	9.00	4.50	2.75
(4)	Joe Dobson	4.00	2.00	1.25
(5)	Bobby Doerr	9.00	4.50	2.75
(6)	Walt Dropo	12.00	6.00	3.50
(7)	Bill Goodman	4.00	2.00	1.25
(8)	Earl Johnson	4.00	2.00	1.25
(9)	Ken Keltner	4.00	2.00	1.25
(10)	Ellis Kinder	4.00	2.00	1.25
(11)	Walt Masterson	4.00	2.00	1.25
(12)	Joe McCarthy	9.00	4.50	2.75
(13)	Maurice McDermott	4.00	2.00	1.25
(14)	Al Papai	4.00	2.00	1.25
(15)	Mel Parnell	4.00	2.00	1.25
(16)	Johnny Pesky	4.00	2.00	1.25
(17)	Buddy Rosar	4.00	2.00	1.25
(18)	Charley Schanz	4.00	2.00	1.25
(19)	Vern Stephens	4.00	2.00	1.25
(20)	Chuck Stobbs	4.00	2.00	1.25
(21)	Lou Stringer	4.00	2.00	1.25
(22)	Birdie Tebbetts	4.00	2.00	1.25
(23)	Ted Williams	30.00	15.00	9.00
(24)	Tom Wright	4.00	2.00	1.25
(25)	Al Zarilla	4.00	2.00	1.25

1953 Boston Red Sox Photo Pack

In the same approximately 6-1/2" x 9" format which the team had used for its photo packs since the 1940s, this set of black-and-white, blank-back pictures features (usually) chest-to-cap portraits with white borders, a dark background and a facsimile autograph within the photo. Some of the photos were re-used from previous years' issues. The unnumbered pictures are checklisted here in alphabetical order. This list may or may not be complete; it is possible other players' photos were added or deleted to reflect seasonal roster changes.

		NM	EX	VG
Complete Set (30):		120.00	60.00	35.00
Common Player:		4.00	2.00	1.25
(1)	Milt Bolling	4.00	2.00	1.25
(2)	Lou Boudreau	9.00	4.50	2.75
(3)	Harold Brown	4.00	2.00	1.25
(4)	Bill Consolo	4.00	2.00	1.25
(5)	Dom DiMaggio	15.00	7.50	4.50
(6)	Hoot Evers	4.00	2.00	1.25
(7)	Ben Flowers	4.00	2.00	1.25
(8)	Hershell Freeman	4.00	2.00	1.25
(9)	Dick Gernert	4.00	2.00	1.25
(10)	Bill Goodman	4.00	2.00	1.25
(11)	Marv Grissom	4.00	2.00	1.25
(12)	Ken Holcombe	4.00	2.00	1.25
(13)	Sid Hudson	4.00	2.00	1.25
(14)	George Kell	9.00	4.50	2.75
(15)	Bill Kennedy	4.00	2.00	1.25
(16)	Ellis Kinder	4.00	2.00	1.25
(17)	Ted Lepcio	4.00	2.00	1.25
(18)	Johnny Lipon	4.00	2.00	1.25
(19)	Maurice McDermott	4.00	2.00	1.25
(20)	John Merson	4.00	2.00	1.25
(21)	Gus Niarhos	4.00	2.00	1.25
(22)	Willard Nixon	4.00	2.00	1.25
(23)	Mel Parnell	4.00	2.00	1.25
(24)	Jim Piersall	6.00	3.00	1.75
(25)	Gene Stephens	4.00	2.00	1.25
(26)	Tommy Umphlett	4.00	2.00	1.25
(27)	Bill Werle	4.00	2.00	1.25
(28)	Sam White	4.00	2.00	1.25
(29)	Del Wilber	4.00	2.00	1.25
(30)	Al Zarilla	4.00	2.00	1.25

1954 Boston Red Sox Photo Pack

In the same approximately 6-1/2" x 9" format which the team had used for its photo packs since the 1940s, this set of black-and-white, blank-back pictures features (usually) chest-to-cap portraits with white borders and a facsimile autograph within the photo. Some of the photos were re-used from previous years' issues. The unnumbered pictures are checklisted here in alphabetical order. This list may or may not be complete; it is possible other players' photos were added or deleted to reflect seasonal roster changes. The set was sold in a red and white paper envelope.

		NM	EX	VG
Complete Set (30):		125.00	62.50	37.50
Common Player:		4.00	2.00	1.25
(1)	Harry Agganis	15.00	7.50	4.50
(2)	Milt Bolling	4.00	2.00	1.25
(3)	Lou Boudreau	9.00	4.50	2.75
(4)	Tom Brewer	4.00	2.00	1.25
(5)	Harold Brown	4.00	2.00	1.25
(6)	Truman Clevenger	4.00	2.00	1.25
(7)	Bill Consolo	4.00	2.00	1.25
(8)	Joe Dobson	4.00	2.00	1.25
(9)	Hoot Evers	4.00	2.00	1.25
(10)	Dick Gernert	4.00	2.00	1.25
(11)	Bill Goodman	4.00	2.00	1.25
(12)	Bill Henry	4.00	2.00	1.25
(13)	Tom Herrin	4.00	2.00	1.25
(14)	Sid Hudson	4.00	2.00	1.25
(15)	Jackie Jensen	6.00	3.00	1.75
(16)	George Kell	9.00	4.50	2.75
(17)	Leo Kiely	4.00	2.00	1.25
(18)	Ellis Kinder	4.00	2.00	1.25
(19)	Ted Lepcio	4.00	2.00	1.25
(20)	Charlie Maxwell	4.00	2.00	1.25
(21)	Willard Nixon	4.00	2.00	1.25
(22)	Karl Olsen	4.00	2.00	1.25
(23)	Mickey Owen	4.00	2.00	1.25
(24)	Mel Parnell	4.00	2.00	1.25
(25)	Jim Piersall	6.00	3.00	1.75
(26)	Frank Sullivan	4.00	2.00	1.25
(27)	Bill Werle	4.00	2.00	1.25
(28)	Sammy White	4.00	2.00	1.25
(29)	Ted Williams	30.00	15.00	9.00
(30)	Del Wilber	4.00	2.00	1.25

1957 Boston Red Sox Photo Pack

JIMMY PIERSALL

In approximately the same 5" x 7" black-and-white, blank-back format as the later Jay Publishing issues, this team issue is distinguished by the lack of a team name in the bottom border. Some of the photos were re-used in the following year's issue. Sets were originally sold in a manila envelope for 25 cents.

		NM	EX	VG
Complete Set (12):		45.00	22.00	13.50
Common Player:		3.00	1.50	.90
(1)	Tom Brewer	3.00	1.50	.90
(2)	Dick Gernert	3.00	1.50	.90
(3)	Mike Higgins	3.00	1.50	.90
(4)	Jackie Jensen	4.50	2.25	1.25
(5)	Frank Malzone	3.00	1.50	.90
(6)	Gene Mauch	4.50	2.25	1.25
(7)	Jimmy Piersall	4.50	2.25	1.25
(8)	Dave Sisler	3.00	1.50	.90
(9)	Frank Sullivan	3.00	1.50	.90
(10)	Mickey Vernon	3.00	1.50	.90
(11)	Sammy White	3.00	1.50	.90
(12)	Ted Williams	20.00	10.00	6.00

1958 Boston Red Sox Photo Pack

In approximately the same 5" x 7" black-and-white, blank-back format as the contemporary Jay Publishing issues, this team issue is distinguished by the lack of a team name in the

bottom border. Some of the photos were re-used from the previous year's issue. Sets were originally sold in a manila envelope for 25 cents.

		NM	EX	VG
Complete Set (12):		45.00	22.00	13.50
Common Player:		3.00	1.50	.90
(1)	Ken Aspromonte	3.00	1.50	.90
(2)	Tom Brewer	3.00	1.50	.90
(3)	Mike Higgins	3.00	1.50	.90
(4)	Jack Jensen	4.50	2.25	1.25
(5)	Frank Malzone	3.00	1.50	.90
(6)	Will Nixon	3.00	1.50	.90
(7)	Jim Piersall	4.50	2.25	1.25
(8)	Pete Runnels	3.00	1.50	.90
(9)	Gene Stephens	3.00	1.50	.90
(10)	Frank Sullivan	3.00	1.50	.90
(11)	Sam White	3.00	1.50	.90
(12)	Ted Williams	20.00	10.00	6.00

1959 Boston Red Sox Photo Pack

In approximately the same 5" x 7" black-and-white, blank-back format as the contemporary Jay Publishing issues, this team issue is distinguished by the lack of a team name in the bottom border. Some of the photos were re-used from the previous years' issues. Sets were originally sold in a manila envelope for 25 cents.

		NM	EX	VG
Complete Set (12):		45.00	22.00	13.50
Common Player:		3.00	1.50	.90
(1)	Tom Brewer	3.00	1.50	.90
(2)	Don Buddin	3.00	1.50	.90
(3)	Dick Gernert	3.00	1.50	.90
(4)	Mike Higgins	3.00	1.50	.90
(5)	Jack Jensen	4.50	2.25	1.25
(6)	Frank Malzone	3.00	1.50	.90
(7)	Jim Piersall	4.50	2.25	1.25
(8)	Pete Runnels	3.00	1.50	.90
(9)	Gene Stephens	3.00	1.50	.90
(10)	Frank Sullivan	3.00	1.50	.90
(11)	Sam White	3.00	1.50	.90
(12)	Ted Williams	20.00	10.00	6.00

1960 Boston Red Sox Photo Pack

In approximately the same 5" x 7" black-and-white, blank-back format as the contemporary Jay Publishing issues, this team issue is distinguished by the lack of a team name in the bottom border. Some of the photos were re-used from the previous years' issues. Sets were originally sold in a manila envelope for 25 cents. The fact that more than 12 players are known indicates there were some changes in specific contents over the course of the season to reflect roster changes.

		NM	EX	VG
Complete Set (14):		50.00	25.00	15.00
Common Player:		3.00	1.50	.90
(1)	Tom Brewer	3.00	1.50	.90
(2)	Don Buddin	3.00	1.50	.90
(3)	Jerry Casale	3.00	1.50	.90
(4)	Ike Delock	3.00	1.50	.90
(5)	Pumpsie Green	3.00	1.50	.90
(6)	Bill Jurges	3.00	1.50	.90
(7)	Frank Malzone	3.00	1.50	.90
(8)	Pete Runnels	3.00	1.50	.90
(9)	Ed Sadowski	3.00	1.50	.90
(10)	Gene Stephens	3.00	1.50	.90
(11)	Willie Tasby	3.00	1.50	.90
(12)	Bobby Thomson	3.00	1.50	.90
(13)	Vic Wertz	3.00	1.50	.90
(14)	Ted Williams	20.00	10.00	6.00

1968 Boston Red Sox Team Issue

About 5-1/2" x 7-1/2", these black-and-white player pictures have posed photos, bordered in white, with a facsimile autograph. Backs are blank. The alphabetized checklist here is likely incomplete.

		NM	EX	VG
Complete Set (8):		15.00	7.50	4.50
Common Player:		2.00	1.00	.60
(1a)	Mike Andrews ("B" on cap.)	2.00	1.00	.60
(1b)	Mike Andrews (No "B.")	2.00	1.00	.60
(2)	Darrell Brandon	2.00	1.00	.60
(3)	Bobby Doerr	3.00	1.50	.90
(4)	Ken Harrelson	2.50	1.25	.70
(5)	Jim Lonborg	2.50	1.25	.70
(6)	Rico Petrocelli	3.00	1.50	.90
(7)	Reggie Smith	2.50	1.25	.70
(8)	Dick Williams	2.00	1.00	.60

1969 Boston Red Sox Team Issue

This team-issue photo pack features black-and-white portrait photos on a 4-1/4" x 7" blank-back format, similar to the team's 1971 issue. The player's name and team nickname are designated in the white border at top. The unnumbered cards are checklisted here in alphabetical order.

		NM	EX	VG
Complete Set (12):		60.00	30.00	15.00
Common Player:		4.00	2.00	1.25
(1)	Mike Andrews	4.00	2.00	1.25
(2)	Tony Conigliaro	9.00	4.50	2.75
(3)	Russ Gibson	4.00	2.00	1.25
(4)	Dalton Jones	4.00	2.00	1.25
(5)	Bill Landis	4.00	2.00	1.25
(6)	Jim Lonborg	5.00	2.50	1.50
(7)	Sparky Lyle	4.00	2.00	1.25
(8)	Rico Petrocelli	5.00	2.50	1.50
(9)	George Scott	5.00	2.50	1.50
(10)	Reggie Smith	4.00	2.00	1.25
(11)	Dick Williams	4.00	2.00	1.25
(12)	Carl Yastrzemski	15.00	7.50	4.50

1978 Boston Red Sox of the 1950s-1960s

The date of actual issue, the name of the issuer and even the "official" title of this collectors' edition card set is currently unknown. The 2-1/2" x 3-1/2" cards are printed in black-and-white on front and backs. Fronts have the style of the 1953 Bowmans, with only a player photo and a white border. Backs are reminiscent of the 1955 Bowman, with player identification, career highlights, stats and a Red Sox trivia question. Cards #1-64 concentrate on the 1950s, cards #65-128 feature 1960s players.

		NM	EX	VG
Complete Set (128):		100.00	50.00	30.00
Common Player:		4.00	2.00	1.25
1	Harry Agganis	12.00	6.00	3.50
2	Ken Aspromonte	4.00	2.00	1.25
3	Bobby Avila	4.00	2.00	1.25
4	Frank Baumann	4.00	2.00	1.25
5	Lou Berberet	4.00	2.00	1.25
6	Milt Bolling	4.00	2.00	1.25
7	Lou Boudreau	6.00	3.00	1.75
8	Ted Bowsfield	4.00	2.00	1.25
9	Tom Brewer	4.00	2.00	1.25
10	Don Buddin	4.00	2.00	1.25
11	Jerry Casale	4.00	2.00	1.25
12	Billy Consolo	4.00	2.00	1.25
13	Pete Daley	4.00	2.00	1.25
14	Ike Delock	4.00	2.00	1.25
15	Dom DiMaggio	9.00	4.50	2.75
16	Bobby Doerr	6.00	3.00	1.75
17	Walt Dropo	5.00	2.50	1.50
18	Arnie Earley	4.00	2.00	1.25
19	Hoot Evers	4.00	2.00	1.25
20	Mike Fornieles	4.00	2.00	1.25
21	Gary Geiger	4.00	2.00	1.25
22	Don Gile	4.00	2.00	1.25
23	Joe Ginsberg	4.00	2.00	1.25
24	Billy Goodman	4.00	2.00	1.25
25	Pumpsie Green	4.00	2.00	1.25
26	Grady Hatton	4.00	2.00	1.25
27	Billy Herman	5.00	2.50	1.50
28	Jackie Jensen	5.00	2.50	1.50
29	George Kell	6.00	3.00	1.75
30	Marty Keough	4.00	2.00	1.25
31	Leo Kiely	4.00	2.00	1.25
32	Ellis Kinder	4.00	2.00	1.25
33	Billy Klaus	4.00	2.00	1.25
34	Don Lenhardt	4.00	2.00	1.25
35	Ted Lepcio	4.00	2.00	1.25
36	Frank Malzone	4.00	2.00	1.25
37	Gene Mauch	4.00	2.00	1.25
38	Maury McDermott	4.00	2.00	1.25
39	Bill Monbouquette	4.00	2.00	1.25
40	Chet Nichols	4.00	2.00	1.25
41	Willard Nixon	4.00	2.00	1.25
42	Jim Pagliaroni	4.00	2.00	1.25
43	Mel Parnell	4.00	2.00	1.25
44	Johnny Pesky	4.00	2.00	1.25
45	Jimmy Piersall	5.00	2.50	1.50
46	Bob Porterfield	4.00	2.00	1.25
47	Pete Runnels	4.00	2.00	1.25
48	Dave Sisler	4.00	2.00	1.25
49	Riverboat Smith	4.00	2.00	1.25
50	Gene Stephens	4.00	2.00	1.25
51	Vern Stephens	4.00	2.00	1.25
52	Chuck Stobbs	4.00	2.00	1.25
53	Dean Stone	4.00	2.00	1.25
54	Frank Sullivan	4.00	2.00	1.25
55	Haywood Sullivan	4.00	2.00	1.25
56	Birdie Tebbetts	4.00	2.00	1.25
57	Mickey Vernon	4.00	2.00	1.25
58	Vic Wertz	4.00	2.00	1.25

#	Player	NM	EX	VG
59	Sammy White	4.00	2.00	1.25
60	Ted Williams	20.00	10.00	6.00
61	Ted Wills	4.00	2.00	1.25
62	Earl Wilson	4.00	2.00	1.25
63	Al Zarilla	4.00	2.00	1.25
64	Norm Zauchin	4.00	2.00	1.25
65	Ted Williams, Carl Yastrzemski	12.00	6.00	3.50
66	Dick Williams, Carl Yastrzemski, Jim Lonborg, George Scott	10.00	5.00	3.00
67	Tony Conigliaro, Billy Conigliaro	9.00	4.50	2.75
68	Jerry Adair	4.00	2.00	1.25
69	Mike Andrews	4.00	2.00	1.25
70	Gary Bell	4.00	2.00	1.25
71	Dennis Bennett	4.00	2.00	1.25
72	Ed Bressoud	4.00	2.00	1.25
73	Ken Brett	4.00	2.00	1.25
74	Lu Clinton	4.00	2.00	1.25
75	Billy Conigliaro	5.00	2.50	1.50
76	Tony Conigliaro	6.00	3.00	1.75
77	Gene Conley	4.00	2.00	1.25
78	Ray Culp	4.00	2.00	1.25
79	Dick Ellsworth	4.00	2.00	1.25
80	Joe Foy	4.00	2.00	1.25
81	Russ Gibson	4.00	2.00	1.25
82	Jim Gosger	4.00	2.00	1.25
83	Lennie Green	4.00	2.00	1.25
84	Ken Harrelson	4.00	2.00	1.25
85	Tony Horton	4.00	2.00	1.25
86	Elston Howard	5.00	2.50	1.50
87	Dalton Jones	4.00	2.00	1.25
88	Eddie Kasko	4.00	2.00	1.25
89	Joe Lahoud	4.00	2.00	1.25
90	Jack Lamabe	4.00	2.00	1.25
91	Jim Lonborg	5.00	2.50	1.50
92	Sparky Lyle	5.00	2.50	1.50
93	Felix Mantilla	4.00	2.00	1.25
94	Roman Mejias	4.00	2.00	1.25
95	Don McMahon	4.00	2.00	1.25
96	Dave Morehead	4.00	2.00	1.25
97	Gerry Moses	4.00	2.00	1.25
98	Mike Nagy	4.00	2.00	1.25
99	Russ Nixon	4.00	2.00	1.25
100	Gene Oliver	4.00	2.00	1.25
101	Dan Osinski	4.00	2.00	1.25
102	Rico Petrocelli	5.00	2.50	1.50
103	Juan Pizarro	4.00	2.00	1.25
104	Dick Radatz	4.00	2.00	1.25
105	Vicente Romo	4.00	2.00	1.25
106	Mike Ryan	4.00	2.00	1.25
107	Jose Santiago	4.00	2.00	1.25
108	Chuck Schilling	4.00	2.00	1.25
109	Dick Schofield	4.00	2.00	1.25
110	Don Schwall	4.00	2.00	1.25
111	George Scott	4.00	2.00	1.25
112	Norm Siebern	4.00	2.00	1.25
113	Sonny Seibert	4.00	2.00	1.25
114	Reggie Smith	4.00	2.00	1.25
115	Bill Spanswick	4.00	2.00	1.25
116	Tracy Stallard	4.00	2.00	1.25
117	Lee Stange	4.00	2.00	1.25
118	Jerry Stephenson	4.00	2.00	1.25
119	Dick Stuart	4.00	2.00	1.25
120	Tom Sturdivant	4.00	2.00	1.25
121	Jose Tartabull	4.00	2.00	1.25
122	George Thomas	4.00	2.00	1.25
123	Lee Thomas	4.00	2.00	1.25
124	Bob Tillman	4.00	2.00	1.25
125	Gary Waslewski	4.00	2.00	1.25
126	Dick Williams	4.00	2.00	1.25
127	John Wyatt	4.00	2.00	1.25
128	Carl Yastrzemski	12.00	6.00	3.50

1979 Boston Red Sox Team Issue

The origins of this Boston Red Sox card set are unclear. It may have been a team issue. The wide white bottom border beneath the black-and-white photo on the 2-1/2" x 3-1/2" cards may have been intended for autographing. Backs have player personal data and complete major and minor league stats. The checklist here, listed alphabetically, may not be complete.

#	Player	NM	EX	VG
	Complete Set (24):	50.00	25.00	15.00
	Common Player:	3.00	1.50	.90
(1)	Gary Allenson	3.00	1.50	.90
(2)	Jack Brohamer	3.00	1.50	.90
(3)	Tom Burgmeier	3.00	1.50	.90
(4)	Rick Burleson	3.00	1.50	.90
(5)	Bill Campbell	3.00	1.50	.90
(6)	Dick Drago	3.00	1.50	.90
(7)	Dennis Eckersley	12.00	6.00	3.50
(8)	Dwight Evans	4.50	2.25	1.25
(9)	Carlton Fisk	15.00	7.50	4.50
(10)	Andy Hassler	3.00	1.50	.90
(11)	Butch Hobson	3.00	1.50	.90
(12)	Fred Lynn	7.50	3.75	2.25
(13)	Bob Montgomery	3.00	1.50	.90
(14)	Mike O'Berry	3.00	1.50	.90
(15)	Jerry Remy	3.00	1.50	.90
(16)	Steve Renko	3.00	1.50	.90
(17)	Jim Rice	7.50	3.75	2.25
(18)	George Scott	4.50	2.25	1.25
(19)	Bob Stanley	3.00	1.50	.90
(20)	Mike Torrez	3.00	1.50	.90
(21)	Larry Wolfe	3.00	1.50	.90
(22)	Jim Wright	3.00	1.50	.90
(23)	Carl Yastrzemski	20.00	10.00	6.00
(24)	Gary Hancock, Stan Papi (Two-sided.)	3.00	1.50	.90

1917 Boston Store

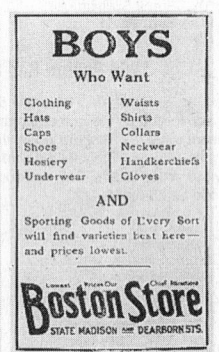

One of several regional advertisers to use this 200-card set as a promotional medium was this Chicago department store. While variations are known of cards #76, 90, 121, 146, and 190 in the Collins-McCarthy ad-back version of this set, it is unclear whether those variations also exist in the Boston Store issue. The American Card Catalog listed these 2" x 3-1/4" black-and-white cards as H801-8.

#	Player	NM	EX	VG
	Complete Set (200):	80,000	40,000	24,000
	Common Player:	150.00	75.00	45.00
1	Sam Agnew	150.00	75.00	45.00
2	Grover Alexander	800.00	400.00	240.00
3	W.S. Alexander (W.E.)	150.00	75.00	45.00
4	Leon Ames	150.00	75.00	45.00
5	Fred Anderson	150.00	75.00	45.00
6	Ed Appleton	150.00	75.00	45.00
7	Jimmy Archer	150.00	75.00	45.00
8	Jimmy Austin	150.00	75.00	45.00
9	Jim Bagby	150.00	75.00	45.00
10	H.D. Baird	150.00	75.00	45.00
11	J. Franklin Baker	500.00	250.00	150.00
12	Dave Bancroft	500.00	250.00	150.00
13	Jack Barry	150.00	75.00	45.00
14	Joe Benz	150.00	75.00	45.00
15	Al Betzel	150.00	75.00	45.00
16	Ping Bodie	150.00	75.00	45.00
17	Joe Boehling	150.00	75.00	45.00
18	Eddie Burns	150.00	75.00	45.00
19	George Burns	150.00	75.00	45.00
20	Geo. J. Burns	150.00	75.00	45.00
21	Joe Bush	150.00	75.00	45.00
22	Owen Bush	150.00	75.00	45.00
23	Bobby Byrne	150.00	75.00	45.00
24	Forrest Cady	150.00	75.00	45.00
25	Max Carey	500.00	250.00	150.00
26	Ray Chapman	200.00	100.00	60.00
27	Larry Cheney	150.00	75.00	45.00
28	Eddie Cicotte	900.00	450.00	275.00
29	Tom Clarke	150.00	75.00	45.00
30	Ty Cobb	4,250	2,125	1,275
31	Eddie Collins	500.00	250.00	150.00
32	"Shauno" Collins (Shano)	150.00	75.00	45.00
33	Fred Coumbe	150.00	75.00	45.00
34	Harry Coveleskie (Coveleski)	150.00	75.00	45.00
35	Gavvy Cravath	500.00	250.00	150.00
36	Sam Crawford	500.00	250.00	150.00
37	Geo. Cutshaw	150.00	75.00	45.00
38	Jake Daubert	150.00	75.00	45.00
39	Geo. Dauss	150.00	75.00	45.00
40	Charles Deal	150.00	75.00	45.00
41	"Wheezer" Dell	150.00	75.00	45.00
42	William Doak	150.00	75.00	45.00
43	Bill Donovan	150.00	75.00	45.00
44	Larry Doyle	150.00	75.00	45.00
45	Johnny Evers	500.00	250.00	150.00
46	Urban Faber	500.00	250.00	150.00
47	"Hap" Felsch	1,500	750.00	450.00
48	Bill Fischer	150.00	75.00	45.00
49	Ray Fisher	150.00	75.00	45.00
50	Art Fletcher	150.00	75.00	45.00
51	Eddie Foster	150.00	75.00	45.00
52	Jacques Fournier	150.00	75.00	45.00
53	Del Gainer (Gainor)	150.00	75.00	45.00
54	Bert Gallia	150.00	75.00	45.00
55	"Chic" Gandil (Chick)	450.00	225.00	135.00
56	Larry Gardner	150.00	75.00	45.00
57	Joe Gedeon	150.00	75.00	45.00
58	Gus Getz	150.00	75.00	45.00
59	Frank Gilhooley	150.00	75.00	45.00
60	Wm. Gleason	150.00	75.00	45.00
61	M.A. Gonzales (Gonzalez)	200.00	100.00	60.00
62	Hank Gowdy	150.00	75.00	45.00
63	John Graney	150.00	75.00	45.00
64	Tom Griffith	150.00	75.00	45.00
65	Heinie Groh	150.00	75.00	45.00
66	Bob Groom	150.00	75.00	45.00
67	Louis Guisto	150.00	75.00	45.00
68	Earl Hamilton	150.00	75.00	45.00
69	Harry Harper	150.00	75.00	45.00
70	Grover Hartley	150.00	75.00	45.00
71	Harry Heilmann	500.00	250.00	150.00
72	Claude Hendrix	150.00	75.00	45.00
73	Olaf Henriksen	150.00	75.00	45.00
74	John Henry	150.00	75.00	45.00
75	"Buck" Herzog	150.00	75.00	45.00
76a	Hugh High (White stockings, photo actually Claude Williams.)	400.00	200.00	120.00
76b	Hugh High (Black stockings, correct photo.)	200.00	100.00	60.00
77	Dick Hoblitzell	150.00	75.00	45.00
78	Walter Holke	150.00	75.00	45.00
79	Harry Hooper	500.00	250.00	150.00
80	Rogers Hornsby	750.00	375.00	225.00
81	Ivan Howard	150.00	75.00	45.00
82	Joe Jackson	12,500	6,250	3,750
83	Harold Janvrin	150.00	75.00	45.00
84	William James	150.00	75.00	45.00
85	C. Jamieson	150.00	75.00	45.00
86	Hugh Jennings	500.00	250.00	150.00
87	Walter Johnson	1,100	550.00	330.00
88	James Johnston	150.00	75.00	45.00
89	Fielder Jones	150.00	75.00	45.00
90a	Joe Judge (Bat on right shoulder, photo actually Ray Morgan.)	400.00	200.00	120.00
90b	Joe Judge (Bat on left shoulder, correct photo.)	200.00	100.00	60.00
91	Hans Lobert	150.00	75.00	45.00
92	Benny Kauff	150.00	75.00	45.00
93	Wm. Killefer Jr.	150.00	75.00	45.00
94	Ed. Konetchy	150.00	75.00	45.00
95	John Lavan	150.00	75.00	45.00
96	Jimmy Lavender	150.00	75.00	45.00
97	"Nemo" Leibold	150.00	75.00	45.00
98	H.B. Leonard	150.00	75.00	45.00
99	Duffy Lewis	150.00	75.00	45.00
100	Tom Long	150.00	75.00	45.00
101	Wm. Louden	150.00	75.00	45.00
102	Fred Luderus	150.00	75.00	45.00
103	Lee Magee	150.00	75.00	45.00
104	Sherwood Magee	150.00	75.00	45.00
105	Al Mamaux	150.00	75.00	45.00
106	Leslie Mann	150.00	75.00	45.00
107	"Rabbit" Maranville	500.00	250.00	150.00
108	Rube Marquard	500.00	250.00	150.00
109	Armando Marsans	240.00	120.00	72.00
110	J. Erskine Mayer	150.00	75.00	45.00
111	George McBride	150.00	75.00	45.00
112	Lew McCarty	150.00	75.00	45.00
113	John J. McGraw	500.00	250.00	150.00
114	Jack McInnis	150.00	75.00	45.00
115	Lee Meadows	150.00	75.00	45.00
116	Fred Merkle	150.00	75.00	45.00
117	"Chief" Meyers	150.00	75.00	45.00
118	Clyde Milan	150.00	75.00	45.00
119	Otto Miller	150.00	75.00	45.00
120	Clarence Mitchell	150.00	75.00	45.00
121a	Ray Morgan (Bat on left shoulder, photo actually Joe Judge.)	400.00	200.00	120.00
121b	Ray Morgan (Bat on right shoulder, correct photo.)	200.00	100.00	60.00
122	Guy Morton	150.00	75.00	45.00
123	"Mike" Mowrey	150.00	75.00	45.00
124	Elmer Myers	150.00	75.00	45.00
125	"Hy" Myers	150.00	75.00	45.00
126	A.E. Neale	300.00	150.00	90.00
127	Arthur Nehf	150.00	75.00	45.00
128	J.A. Niehoff	150.00	75.00	45.00
129	Steve O'Neill	150.00	75.00	45.00
130	"Dode" Paskert	150.00	75.00	45.00
131	Roger Peckinpaugh	200.00	100.00	60.00
132	"Pol" Perritt	150.00	75.00	45.00
133	"Jeff" Pfeffer	150.00	75.00	45.00
134	Walter Pipp	150.00	75.00	45.00
135	Derril Pratt (Derrill)	150.00	75.00	45.00
136	Bill Rariden	150.00	75.00	45.00
137	E.C. Rice	500.00	250.00	150.00
138	Wm. A. Ritter (Wm. H.)	150.00	75.00	45.00
139	Eppa Rixey	500.00	250.00	150.00
140	Davey Robertson	150.00	75.00	45.00
141	"Bob" Roth	150.00	75.00	45.00
142	Ed. Roush	500.00	250.00	150.00
143	Clarence Rowland	150.00	75.00	45.00
144	Dick Rudolph	150.00	75.00	45.00
145	William Rumler	150.00	75.00	45.00
146a	Reb Russell (Pitching follow-thru, photo actually Mellie Wolfgang.)	400.00	200.00	120.00
146b	Reb Russell (Hands at side, correct photo.)	200.00	100.00	60.00
147	"Babe" Ruth	25,000	12,500	7,500
148	Vic Saier	150.00	75.00	45.00
149	"Slim" Sallee	150.00	75.00	45.00
150	Ray Schalk	500.00	250.00	150.00
151	Walter Schang	150.00	75.00	45.00
152	Frank Schulte	150.00	75.00	45.00
153	Ferd Schupp	150.00	75.00	45.00
154	Everett Scott	150.00	75.00	45.00
155	Hank Severeid	150.00	75.00	45.00
156	Howard Shanks	150.00	75.00	45.00
157	Bob Shawkey	150.00	75.00	45.00
158	Jas. Sheckard	150.00	75.00	45.00
159	Ernie Shore	150.00	75.00	45.00
160	C.H. Shorten	150.00	75.00	45.00
161	Burt Shotton	150.00	75.00	45.00
162	Geo. Sisler	800.00	400.00	240.00
163	Elmer Smith	150.00	75.00	45.00
164	J. Carlisle Smith	150.00	75.00	45.00
165	Fred Snodgrass	150.00	75.00	45.00
166	Tris Speaker	750.00	375.00	225.00
167	Oscar Stanage	150.00	75.00	45.00
168	Charles Stengel	500.00	250.00	150.00
169	Milton Stock	150.00	75.00	45.00

		NM	EX	VG
170	Amos Strunk	150.00	75.00	45.00
171	"Zeb" Terry	150.00	75.00	45.00
172	"Jeff" Tesreau	150.00	75.00	45.00
173	Chester Thomas	150.00	75.00	45.00
174	Fred Toney	150.00	75.00	45.00
175	Terry Turner	150.00	75.00	45.00
176	George Tyler	150.00	75.00	45.00
177	Jim Vaughn	150.00	75.00	45.00
178	Bob Veach	150.00	75.00	45.00
179	Oscar Vitt	150.00	75.00	45.00
180	Hans Wagner	3,000	1,500	900.00
181	Clarence Walker	150.00	75.00	45.00
182	Jim Walsh	150.00	75.00	45.00
183	Al Walters	150.00	75.00	45.00
184	W. Wambsganss	150.00	75.00	45.00
185	Buck Weaver	1,200	600.00	350.00
186	Carl Weilman	150.00	75.00	45.00
187	Zack Wheat	500.00	250.00	150.00
188	Geo. Whitted	150.00	75.00	45.00
189	Joe Wilhoit	150.00	75.00	45.00
190a	Claude Williams (Black stockings, photo actually Hugh High.)	800.00	400.00	240.00
190b	Claude Williams (White stockings, correct photo.)	1,500	750.00	450.00
191	Fred Williams	150.00	75.00	45.00
192	Art Wilson	150.00	75.00	45.00
193	Lawton Witt	150.00	75.00	45.00
194	Joe Wood	200.00	100.00	60.00
195	William Wortman	150.00	75.00	45.00
196	Steve Yerkes	150.00	75.00	45.00
197	Earl Yingling	150.00	75.00	45.00
198	"Pep" Young (Photo actually Ralph Young.)	150.00	75.00	45.00
199	Rollie Zeider	150.00	75.00	45.00
200	Henry Zimmerman	150.00	75.00	45.00

1909 Boston Sunday Post Red Sox Stars

Members of the Boston American League team are presented in this series of Sunday supplements from one of the city's daily newspapers. Measuring about 8" x 10", and possibly having been issued in two-page spreads, the blank-back pieces combine artist's renderings of action photos with circular portraits about 2-3/8" in diameter, printed in sepia tones. At bottom is printed the player name, team, position and a caption for the picture, along with the newspaper's credit line. It is possible this checklist is incomplete since a few of the team's stars have yet to be reported.

		NM	EX	VG
Common Player:		150.00	75.00	45.00
(1)	Frank Arellanes	150.00	75.00	45.00
(2)	William Carrigan	150.00	75.00	45.00
(3)	Charles Chech	150.00	75.00	45.00
(4)	Edward Cicotte	250.00	125.00	75.00
(5)	Harry Hooper	250.00	125.00	75.00
(6)	Harry Lord	150.00	75.00	45.00
(7)	Ambrose McConnell	150.00	75.00	45.00
(8)	Harry Niles	150.00	75.00	45.00
(9)	Tris Speaker	300.00	150.00	90.00
(10)	Edward Spencer	150.00	75.00	45.00
(11)	Garland Stahl	150.00	75.00	45.00
(12)	Harry Wolter	150.00	75.00	45.00

1972 Bowery Bank Joe DiMaggio

These cards were issued to promote the New York City bank's relationship with spokesman Joe DiMaggio. The 2-1/2" x 3-1/2" cards have a posed color photo on front. The back has a black-and-white portrait, biographical data, career highlights and stats on a pink background.

	NM	EX	VG
Joe DiMaggio	17.50	9.00	5.00

1948 Bowman

Bowman Gum Co.'s premiere set of 1948 was one of the first major issues of the post-war period. Forty-eight black-and-white cards comprise the set, with each card measuring 2-1/16" x 2-1/2". The card backs, printed in black ink on gray stock, include the card number and the player's name, team, position, and a short biography. Twelve cards (marked with an "SP") were printed in short supply when they were removed from the 36-card printing sheet to make room for the set's high numbers (#37-48).

		NM	EX	VG
Complete Set (48):		5,000	2,500	1,500
Common Player (1-36):		60.00	30.00	18.00
Common Player (37-48):		60.00	30.00	18.00
1	Bob Elliott	150.00	60.00	18.00
2	Ewell Blackwell	140.00	70.00	40.00
3	Ralph Kiner	300.00	150.00	90.00
4	Johnny Mize	170.00	84.50	50.00
5	Bob Feller	450.00	220.00	130.00
6	Yogi Berra	700.00	350.00	210.00
7	Pete Reiser (SP)	300.00	150.00	90.00
8	Phil Rizzuto (SP)	550.00	270.00	160.00
9	Walker Cooper	60.00	30.00	18.00
10	Buddy Rosar	60.00	30.00	18.00
11	Johnny Lindell	60.00	30.00	18.00
12	Johnny Sain	140.00	70.00	40.00
13	Willard Marshall (SP)	120.00	60.00	36.00
14	Allie Reynolds	130.00	64.50	40.00
15	Eddie Joost	60.00	30.00	18.00
16	Jack Lohrke (SP)	120.00	60.00	36.00
17	Enos Slaughter	210.00	100.00	60.00
18	Warren Spahn	500.00	250.00	150.00
19	Tommy Henrich	120.00	60.00	36.00
20	Buddy Kerr (SP)	120.00	60.00	36.00
21	Ferris Fain	80.00	40.00	24.00
22	Floyd (Bill) Bevens (SP)	120.00	60.00	36.00
23	Larry Jansen	60.00	30.00	18.00
24	Emil (Dutch) Leonard (SP)	120.00	60.00	36.00
25	Barney McCoskey (McCosky)	60.00	30.00	18.00
26	Frank Shea (SP)	120.00	60.00	36.00
27	Sid Gordon	60.00	30.00	18.00
28	Emil Verban (SP)	120.00	60.00	36.00
29	Joe Page (SP)	250.00	130.00	70.00
30	Whitey Lockman (SP)	150.00	75.00	45.00
31	Bill McCahan	60.00	30.00	18.00
32	Bill Rigney	60.00	30.00	18.00
33	Billy Johnson	60.00	30.00	18.00
34	Sheldon Jones (SP)	120.00	60.00	36.00
35	Snuffy Stirnweiss	60.00	30.00	18.00
36	Stan Musial	1,500	750.00	450.00
37	Clint Hartung	120.00	60.00	36.00
38	Red Schoendienst	400.00	200.00	120.00
39	Augie Galan	120.00	60.00	36.00
40	Marty Marion	200.00	100.00	60.00
41	Rex Barney	170.00	85.00	50.00
42	Ray Poat	120.00	60.00	36.00
43	Bruce Edwards	160.00	80.00	48.00
44	Johnny Wyrostek	120.00	60.00	36.00
45	Hank Sauer	120.00	60.00	36.00
46	Herman Wehmeier	120.00	60.00	36.00
47	Bobby Thomson	280.00	140.00	80.00
48	Dave Koslo	320.00	80.00	45.00

1949 Bowman

In 1949, Bowman increased the size of its issue to 240 numbered cards. The 2-1/16" x 2-1/2" cards are black-and-white photos overprinted with team uniform colors on a background of various solid pastel colors. Beginning with card #109 in the set, Bowman added the players' names on the card fronts. Twelve cards (#4, 78, 83, 85, 88, 98, 109, 124, 127, 132 and 143), which were produced in the first four series of printings, were reprinted in the seventh series with either a card front or back modification. These variations are noted in the checklist. Cards #1-3 and 5-73 can be found with either white or gray backs. The complete set value shown here does not include the higher priced variation cards.

	NM	EX	VG
Complete Set (240):	15,000	7,500	4,500

		NM	EX	VG
Common Player (1-144):		20.00	10.00	6.00
Common Player (145-240):		50.00	25.00	15.00
1	Vernon Bickford	200.00	15.00	9.00
2	"Whitey" Lockman	20.00	10.00	6.00
3	Bob Porterfield	20.00	10.00	6.00
4a	Jerry Priddy (No name on front.)	20.00	10.00	6.00
4b	Jerry Priddy (Name on front.)	60.00	30.00	18.00
5	Hank Sauer	20.00	10.00	6.00
6	Phil Cavarretta	20.00	10.00	6.00
7	Joe Dobson	20.00	10.00	6.00
8	Murry Dickson	20.00	10.00	6.00
9	Ferris Fain	20.00	10.00	6.00
10	Ted Gray	20.00	10.00	6.00
11	Lou Boudreau	60.00	30.00	18.00
12	Cass Michaels	20.00	10.00	6.00
13	Bob Chesnes	20.00	10.00	6.00
14	Curt Simmons	50.00	25.00	15.00
15	Ned Garver	30.00	15.00	9.00
16	Al Kozar	20.00	10.00	6.00
17	Earl Torgeson	20.00	10.00	6.00
18	Bobby Thomson	65.00	32.50	20.00
19	Bobby Brown	75.00	37.50	22.50
20	Gene Hermanski	20.00	10.00	6.00
21	Frank Baumholtz	20.00	10.00	6.00
22	Harry "P-Nuts" Lowrey	20.00	10.00	6.00
23	Bobby Doerr	60.00	30.00	18.00
24	Stan Musial	425.00	180.00	100.00
25	Carl Scheib	20.00	10.00	6.00
26	George Kell	65.00	32.50	20.00
27	Bob Feller	300.00	150.00	75.00
28	Don Kolloway	20.00	10.00	6.00
29	Ralph Kiner	95.00	47.50	27.50
30	Andy Seminick	20.00	10.00	6.00
31	Dick Kokos	20.00	10.00	6.00
32	Eddie Yost	20.00	10.00	6.00
33	Warren Spahn	250.00	125.00	62.50
34	Dave Koslo	20.00	10.00	6.00
35	Vic Raschi	100.00	50.00	30.00
36	Pee Wee Reese	225.00	112.50	56.75
37	John Wyrostek	20.00	10.00	6.00
38	Emil Verban	20.00	10.00	6.00
39	Bill Goodman	20.00	10.00	6.00
40	"Red" Munger	20.00	10.00	6.00
41	Lou Brissie	20.00	10.00	6.00
42	"Hoot" Evers	20.00	10.00	6.00
43	Dale Mitchell	20.00	10.00	6.00
44	Dave Philley	20.00	10.00	6.00
45	Wally Westlake	20.00	10.00	6.00
46	Robin Roberts	250.00	125.00	62.50
47	Johnny Sain	50.00	25.00	15.00
48	Willard Marshall	20.00	10.00	6.00
49	Frank Shea	30.00	15.00	9.00
50	Jackie Robinson	1,250	625.00	375.00
51	Herman Wehmeier	20.00	10.00	6.00
52	Johnny Schmitz	20.00	10.00	6.00
53	Jack Kramer	20.00	10.00	6.00
54	Marty Marion	35.00	17.50	10.00
55	Eddie Joost	20.00	10.00	6.00
56	Pat Mullin	20.00	10.00	6.00
57	Gene Bearden	20.00	10.00	6.00
58	Bob Elliott	20.00	10.00	6.00
59	Jack Lohrke	20.00	10.00	6.00
60	Yogi Berra	350.00	175.00	87.50
61	Rex Barney	25.00	12.50	7.50
62	Grady Hatton	20.00	10.00	6.00
63	Andy Pafko	20.00	10.00	6.00
64	Dom DiMaggio	75.00	37.50	22.50
65	Enos Slaughter	80.00	40.00	24.00
66	Elmer Valo	20.00	10.00	6.00
67	Alvin Dark	50.00	25.00	15.00
68	Sheldon Jones	20.00	10.00	6.00
69	Tommy Henrich	55.00	27.50	16.50
70	Carl Furillo	150.00	75.00	37.50
71	Vern Stephens	20.00	10.00	6.00
72	Tommy Holmes	20.00	10.00	6.00
73	Billy Cox	45.00	22.50	13.50
74	Tom McBride	20.00	10.00	6.00
75	Eddie Mayo	20.00	10.00	6.00
76	Bill Nicholson	20.00	10.00	6.00
77	Ernie Bonham	20.00	10.00	6.00
78a	Sam Zoldak (No name on front.)	20.00	10.00	6.00
78b	Sam Zoldak (Name on front.)	60.00	30.00	18.00
79	Ron Northey	20.00	10.00	6.00
80	Bill McCahan	20.00	10.00	6.00
81	Virgil "Red" Stallcup	20.00	10.00	6.00
82	Joe Page	35.00	17.50	10.00
83a	Bob Scheffing (No name on front.)	20.00	10.00	6.00
83b	Bob Scheffing (Name on front.)	60.00	30.00	18.00
84	Roy Campanella	800.00	400.00	200.00
85a	Johnny Mize (No name on front.)	85.00	42.50	25.00
85b	Johnny Mize (Name on front.)	120.00	60.00	36.00
86	Johnny Pesky	20.00	10.00	6.00
87	Randy Gumpert	20.00	10.00	6.00
88a	Bill Salkeld (No name on front.)	20.00	10.00	6.00
88b	Bill Salkeld (Name on front.)	60.00	30.00	18.00
89	Mizell Platt	20.00	10.00	6.00
90	Gil Coan	20.00	10.00	6.00
91	Dick Wakefield	20.00	10.00	6.00
92	Willie Jones	20.00	10.00	6.00
93	Ed Stevens	20.00	10.00	6.00
94	Mickey Vernon	30.00	15.00	9.00
95	Howie Pollett	20.00	10.00	6.00
96	Taft Wright	20.00	10.00	6.00
97	Danny Litwhiler	20.00	10.00	6.00
98a	Phil Rizzuto (No name on front.)	275.00	137.50	68.75
98b	Phil Rizzuto (Name on front.)	280.00	190.00	85.00
99	Frank Gustine	20.00	10.00	6.00
100	Gil Hodges	300.00	150.00	75.00
101	Sid Gordon	25.00	12.50	7.50
102	Stan Spence	20.00	10.00	6.00
103	Joe Tipton	20.00	10.00	6.00

		NM	EX	VG
104	*Ed Stanky*	35.00	17.50	10.00
105	Bill Kennedy	20.00	10.00	6.00
106	Jake Early	20.00	10.00	6.00
107	Eddie Lake	20.00	10.00	6.00
108	Ken Heintzelman	20.00	10.00	6.00
109a	Ed Fitz Gerald (Script name on back.)	20.00	10.00	6.00
109b	Ed Fitz Gerald (Printed name on back.)	60.00	30.00	18.00
110	*Early Wynn*	150.00	75.00	37.50
111	Red Schoendienst	80.00	40.00	24.00
112	Sam Chapman	20.00	10.00	6.00
113	Ray Lamanno	20.00	10.00	6.00
114	Allie Reynolds	65.00	32.50	20.00
115	Emil "Dutch" Leonard	20.00	10.00	6.00
116	Joe Hatten	20.00	10.00	6.00
117	Walker Cooper	20.00	10.00	6.00
118	Sam Mele	20.00	10.00	6.00
119	Floyd Baker	20.00	10.00	6.00
120	Cliff Fannin	20.00	10.00	6.00
121	Mark Christman	20.00	10.00	6.00
122	George Vico	20.00	10.00	6.00
123	Johnny Blatnick	20.00	10.00	6.00
124a	Danny Murtaugh (Script name on back.)	20.00	10.00	6.00
124b	Danny Murtaugh (Printed name on back.)	60.00	30.00	18.00
125	Ken Keltner	20.00	10.00	6.00
126a	Al Brazle (Script name on back.)	20.00	10.00	6.00
126b	Al Brazle (Printed name on back.)	60.00	30.00	18.00
127a	Henry Majeski	20.00	10.00	6.00
127b	Henry Majeski (Printed name on back.)	60.00	30.00	18.00
128	Johnny Vander Meer	35.00	17.50	10.00
129	Billy Johnson	30.00	15.00	9.00
130	Harry "The Hat" Walker	25.00	12.50	7.50
131	Paul Lehner	20.00	10.00	6.00
132a	Al Evans (Script name on back.)	20.00	10.00	6.00
132b	Al Evans (Printed name on back.)	60.00	30.00	18.00
133	Aaron Robinson	20.00	10.00	6.00
134	Hank Borowy	20.00	10.00	6.00
135	Stan Rojek	20.00	10.00	6.00
136	Hank Edwards	20.00	10.00	6.00
137	Ted Wilks	20.00	10.00	6.00
138	"Buddy" Rosar	20.00	10.00	6.00
139	Hank "Bow-Wow" Arft	20.00	10.00	6.00
140	Ray Scarborough	20.00	10.00	6.00
141	"Tony" Lupien	20.00	10.00	6.00
142	Eddie Waitkus	20.00	10.00	6.00
143a	Bob Dillinger (Script name on back.)	20.00	10.00	6.00
143b	Bob Dillinger (Printed name on back.)	60.00	30.00	18.00
144	Mickey Haefner	20.00	10.00	6.00
145	"Blix" Donnelly	50.00	25.00	15.00
146	Mike McCormick	55.00	27.50	16.50
147	Elmer Singleton	50.00	25.00	15.00
148	Bob Swift	50.00	25.00	15.00
149	Roy Partee	60.00	30.00	18.00
150	Allie Clark	50.00	25.00	15.00
151	Mickey Harris	50.00	25.00	15.00
152	Clarence Maddern	50.00	25.00	15.00
153	Phil Masi	50.00	25.00	15.00
154	Clint Hartung	50.00	25.00	15.00
155	Mickey Guerra	50.00	25.00	15.00
156	Al Zarilla	50.00	25.00	15.00
157	Walt Masterson	50.00	25.00	15.00
158	Harry Brecheen	50.00	25.00	15.00
159	Glen Moulder	50.00	25.00	15.00
160	Jim Blackburn	50.00	25.00	15.00
161	"Jocko" Thompson	50.00	25.00	15.00
162	*Preacher Roe*	120.00	60.00	30.00
163	Clyde McCullough	50.00	25.00	15.00
164	*Vic Wertz*	70.00	35.00	20.00
165	"Snuffy" Stirnweiss	60.00	30.00	18.00
166	Mike Tresh	50.00	25.00	15.00
167	Boris "Babe" Martin	50.00	25.00	15.00
168	Doyle Lade	50.00	25.00	15.00
169	Jeff Heath	50.00	25.00	15.00
170	Bill Rigney	50.00	25.00	15.00
171	Dick Fowler	50.00	25.00	15.00
172	Eddie Pellagrini	50.00	25.00	15.00
173	Eddie Stewart	50.00	25.00	15.00
174	*Terry Moore*	125.00	65.00	35.00
175	Luke Appling	140.00	70.00	35.00
176	Ken Raffensberger	50.00	25.00	15.00
177	Stan Lopata	50.00	25.00	15.00
178	Tommy Brown	55.00	27.50	16.50
179	Hugh Casey	55.00	27.50	16.50
180	Connie Berry	50.00	25.00	15.00
181	Gus Niarhos	50.00	25.00	15.00
182	Hal Peck	50.00	25.00	15.00
183	Lou Stringer	50.00	25.00	15.00
184	Bob Chipman	50.00	25.00	15.00
185	Pete Reiser	70.00	35.00	20.00
186	"Buddy" Kerr	50.00	25.00	15.00
187	Phil Marchildon	50.00	25.00	15.00
188	Karl Drews	50.00	25.00	15.00
189	Earl Wooten	50.00	25.00	15.00
190	*Jim Hearn*	60.00	30.00	18.00
191	Joe Haynes	50.00	25.00	15.00
192	Harry Gumbert	50.00	25.00	15.00
193	Ken Trinkle	50.00	25.00	15.00
194	Ralph Branca	95.00	47.50	27.50
195	Eddie Bockman	50.00	25.00	15.00
196	Fred Hutchinson	50.00	25.00	15.00
197	Johnny Lindell	60.00	30.00	18.00
198	Steve Gromek	50.00	25.00	15.00
199	"Tex" Hughson	50.00	25.00	15.00
200	Jess Dobernic	50.00	25.00	15.00
201	Sibby Sisti	50.00	25.00	15.00
202	Larry Jansen	50.00	25.00	15.00
203	Barney McCosky	50.00	25.00	15.00
204	Bob Savage	50.00	25.00	15.00
205	Dick Sisler	50.00	25.00	15.00
206	Bruce Edwards	55.00	27.50	16.50
207	Johnny Hopp	50.00	25.00	15.00
208	"Dizzy" Trout	50.00	25.00	15.00
209	Charlie Keller	85.00	42.50	25.00
210	Joe Gordon	50.00	25.00	15.00
211	Dave "Boo" Ferris	50.00	25.00	15.00
212	Ralph Hamner	50.00	25.00	15.00
213	Charles "Red" Barrett	50.00	25.00	15.00
214	*Richie Ashburn*	600.00	300.00	150.00
215	Kirby Higbe	50.00	25.00	15.00
216	"Schoolboy" Rowe	50.00	25.00	15.00
217	Marino Pieretti	50.00	25.00	15.00
218	Dick Kryhoski	50.00	25.00	15.00
219	*Virgil "Fire" Trucks*	60.00	30.00	18.00
220	Johnny McCarthy	50.00	25.00	15.00
221	Bob Muncrief	50.00	25.00	15.00
222	Alex Kellner	50.00	25.00	15.00
223	Bob Hofman	50.00	25.00	15.00
224	*Satchel Paige*	1,450	725.00	435.00
225	Gerry Coleman	100.00	50.00	30.00
226	*Duke Snider*	1,000	500.00	300.00
227	Fritz Ostermueller	50.00	25.00	15.00
228	Jackie Mayo	50.00	25.00	15.00
229	*Ed Lopat*	100.00	50.00	30.00
230	Augie Galan	50.00	25.00	15.00
231	Earl Johnson	50.00	25.00	15.00
232	George McQuinn	50.00	25.00	15.00
233	*Larry Doby*	300.00	150.00	75.00
234	"Rip" Sewell	50.00	25.00	15.00
235	Jim Russell	50.00	25.00	15.00
236	Fred Sanford	60.00	30.00	18.00
237	Monte Kennedy	50.00	25.00	15.00
238	*Bob Lemon*	200.00	100.00	50.00
239	Frank McCormick	50.00	25.00	15.00
240	Norm "Babe" Young (Photo actually Bobby Young.)	125.00	30.00	15.00

1950 Bowman

The quality of the 1950 Bowman issue showed a marked improvement over the company's previous efforts. The cards are color art reproductions of actual photographs and measure 2-1/16" x 2-1/2". Backs include the same type of information found in the previous year's issue but are designed in a horizontal format. Cards found in the first two series (#1-72) are the scarcer of the issue. The backs of the final 72 cards (#181-252) can be found with or without the copyright line at the bottom of the card, the "without" version being the less common.

		NM	EX	VG
	Complete Set (252):	12,500	6,000	3,500
	Common Player (1-72):	50.00	25.00	15.00
	Common Player (73-252):	20.00	10.00	6.00
1	Mel Parnell	175.00	87.50	43.75
2	Vern Stephens	50.00	25.00	15.00
3	Dom DiMaggio	130.00	65.00	40.00
4	*Gus Zernial*	90.00	45.00	27.50
5	Bob Kuzava	50.00	25.00	15.00
6	Bob Feller	300.00	150.00	90.00
7	Jim Hegan	50.00	25.00	15.00
8	George Kell	125.00	65.00	35.00
9	Vic Wertz	50.00	25.00	15.00
10	Tommy Henrich	75.00	37.50	22.50
11	Phil Rizzuto	325.00	162.50	81.25
12	Joe Page	65.00	32.50	15.00
13	Ferris Fain	50.00	25.00	15.00
14	Alex Kellner	50.00	25.00	15.00
15	Al Kozar	50.00	25.00	15.00
16	*Roy Sievers*	90.00	45.00	27.50
17	Sid Hudson	50.00	25.00	15.00
18	Eddie Robinson	50.00	25.00	15.00
19	Warren Spahn	300.00	150.00	75.00
20	Bob Elliott	50.00	25.00	15.00
21	Pee Wee Reese	300.00	150.00	75.00
22	Jackie Robinson	1,200	600.00	300.00
23	*Don Newcombe*	140.00	70.00	35.00
24	Johnny Schmitz	50.00	25.00	15.00
25	Hank Sauer	50.00	25.00	15.00
26	Grady Hatton	50.00	25.00	15.00
27	Herman Wehmeier	50.00	25.00	15.00
28	Bobby Thomson	100.00	50.00	30.00
29	Ed Stanky	60.00	30.00	18.00
30	Eddie Waitkus	50.00	25.00	15.00
31	*Del Ennis*	80.00	40.00	24.00
32	Robin Roberts	150.00	75.00	37.50
33	Ralph Kiner	125.00	60.00	35.00
34	Murry Dickson	50.00	25.00	15.00
35	Enos Slaughter	125.00	60.00	35.00
36	Eddie Kazak	50.00	25.00	15.00
37	Luke Appling	100.00	50.00	30.00
38	Bill Wight	50.00	25.00	15.00
39	Larry Doby	125.00	62.50	31.25
40	Bob Lemon	125.00	60.00	35.00
41	"Hoot" Evers	50.00	25.00	15.00
42	Art Houtteman	50.00	25.00	15.00
43	Bobby Doerr	100.00	50.00	30.00
44	Joe Dobson	50.00	25.00	15.00
45	Al Zarilla	50.00	25.00	15.00
46	Yogi Berra	400.00	200.00	100.00
47	Jerry Coleman	60.00	30.00	18.00
48	Lou Brissie	50.00	25.00	15.00
49	Elmer Valo	50.00	25.00	15.00
50	Dick Kokos	50.00	25.00	15.00
51	Ned Garver	50.00	25.00	15.00
52	Sam Mele	50.00	25.00	15.00
53	Clyde Vollmer	50.00	25.00	15.00
54	Gil Coan	50.00	25.00	15.00
55	"Buddy" Kerr	50.00	25.00	15.00
56	*Del Crandell* (Crandall)	55.00	27.50	16.50
57	Vernon Bickford	50.00	25.00	15.00
58	Carl Furillo	65.00	32.50	20.00
59	Ralph Branca	60.00	30.00	18.00
60	Andy Pafko	50.00	25.00	15.00
61	Bob Rush	50.00	25.00	15.00
62	Ted Kluszewski	150.00	75.00	45.00
63	Ewell Blackwell	50.00	25.00	15.00
64	Alvin Dark	50.00	25.00	15.00
65	Dave Koslo	50.00	25.00	15.00
66	Larry Jansen	50.00	25.00	15.00
67	Willie Jones	50.00	25.00	15.00
68	Curt Simmons	50.00	25.00	15.00
69	Wally Westlake	50.00	25.00	15.00
70	Bob Chesnes	50.00	25.00	15.00
71	Red Schoendienst	85.00	42.50	25.00
72	Howie Pollet	50.00	25.00	15.00
73	Willard Marshall	20.00	10.00	6.00
74	*Johnny Antonelli*	40.00	20.00	12.00
75	Roy Campanella	300.00	150.00	75.00
76	Rex Barney	25.00	12.50	7.50
77	Duke Snider	300.00	150.00	75.00
78	Mickey Owen	20.00	10.00	6.00
79	Johnny Vander Meer	25.00	12.50	7.50
80	Howard Fox	20.00	10.00	6.00
81	Ron Northey	20.00	10.00	6.00
82	"Whitey" Lockman	20.00	10.00	6.00
83	Sheldon Jones	20.00	10.00	6.00
84	Richie Ashburn	125.00	62.50	31.25
85	Ken Heintzelman	20.00	10.00	6.00
86	Stan Rojek	20.00	10.00	6.00
87	Bill Werle	20.00	10.00	6.00
88	Marty Marion	30.00	15.00	9.00
89	George Munger	20.00	10.00	6.00
90	Harry Brecheen	20.00	10.00	6.00
91	Cass Michaels	20.00	10.00	6.00
92	Hank Majeski	20.00	10.00	6.00
93	Gene Bearden	20.00	10.00	6.00
94	Lou Boudreau	70.00	35.00	20.00
95	Aaron Robinson	20.00	10.00	6.00
96	Virgil "Fire" Trucks	20.00	10.00	6.00
97	Maurice McDermott	20.00	10.00	6.00
98	Ted Williams	1,100	550.00	275.00
99	Billy Goodman	20.00	10.00	6.00
100	Vic Raschi	50.00	25.00	15.00
101	Bobby Brown	55.00	27.50	16.50
102	Billy Johnson	30.00	15.00	9.00
103	Eddie Joost	20.00	10.00	6.00
104	Sam Chapman	20.00	10.00	6.00
105	Bob Dillinger	20.00	10.00	6.00
106	Cliff Fannin	20.00	10.00	6.00
107	Sam Dente	20.00	10.00	6.00
108	Ray Scarborough	20.00	10.00	6.00
109	Sid Gordon	20.00	10.00	6.00
110	Tommy Holmes	20.00	10.00	6.00
111	Walker Cooper	20.00	10.00	6.00
112	Gil Hodges	125.00	60.00	35.00
113	Gene Hermanski	20.00	10.00	6.00
114	*Wayne Terwilliger*	25.00	12.50	7.50
115	Roy Smalley	20.00	10.00	6.00
116	Virgil "Red" Stallcup	20.00	10.00	6.00
117	Bill Rigney	20.00	10.00	6.00
118	Clint Hartung	20.00	10.00	6.00
119	Dick Sisler	20.00	10.00	6.00
120	Jocko Thompson	20.00	10.00	6.00
121	Andy Seminick	20.00	10.00	6.00
122	Johnny Hopp	20.00	10.00	6.00
123	Dino Restelli	20.00	10.00	6.00
124	Clyde McCullough	20.00	10.00	6.00
125	Del Rice	20.00	10.00	6.00
126	Al Brazle	20.00	10.00	6.00
127	Dave Philley	20.00	10.00	6.00
128	Phil Masi	20.00	10.00	6.00
129	Joe Gordon	20.00	10.00	6.00
130	Dale Mitchell	20.00	10.00	6.00
131	Steve Gromek	20.00	10.00	6.00
132	Mickey Vernon	20.00	10.00	6.00
133	Don Kolloway	20.00	10.00	6.00
134	"Dizzy" Trout	20.00	10.00	6.00
135	Pat Mullin	20.00	10.00	6.00
136	"Buddy" Rosar	20.00	10.00	6.00
137	Johnny Pesky	20.00	10.00	6.00
138	Allie Reynolds	60.00	30.00	18.00
139	Johnny Mize	65.00	32.50	20.00
140	Pete Suder	20.00	10.00	6.00
141	Joe Coleman	20.00	10.00	6.00
142	*Sherman Lollar*	25.00	12.50	7.50
143	Eddie Stewart	20.00	10.00	6.00
144	Al Evans	20.00	10.00	6.00
145	Jack Graham	20.00	10.00	6.00
146	Floyd Baker	20.00	10.00	6.00
147	*Mike Garcia*	30.00	15.00	9.00
148	Early Wynn	70.00	35.00	20.00
149	Bob Swift	20.00	10.00	6.00
150	George Vico	20.00	10.00	6.00
151	Fred Hutchinson	20.00	10.00	6.00
152	Ellis Kinder	20.00	10.00	6.00
153	Walt Masterson	20.00	10.00	6.00
154	Gus Niarhos	30.00	15.00	9.00
155	Frank "Spec" Shea	30.00	15.00	9.00
156	Fred Sanford	30.00	15.00	9.00
157	Mike Guerra	20.00	10.00	6.00
158	Paul Lehner	20.00	10.00	6.00
159	Joe Tipton	20.00	10.00	6.00
160	Mickey Harris	20.00	10.00	6.00
161	Sherry Robertson	20.00	10.00	6.00
162	Eddie Yost	20.00	10.00	6.00

163	Earl Torgeson	20.00	10.00	6.00
164	Sibby Sisti	20.00	10.00	6.00
165	Bruce Edwards	25.00	12.50	7.50
166	Joe Hatten	25.00	12.50	7.50
167	Preacher Roe	50.00	25.00	15.00
168	Bob Scheffing	20.00	10.00	6.00
169	Hank Edwards	20.00	10.00	6.00
170	Emil Leonard	20.00	10.00	6.00
171	Harry Gumbert	20.00	10.00	6.00
172	Harry Lowrey	20.00	10.00	6.00
173	Lloyd Merriman	20.00	10.00	6.00
174	*Henry Thompson*	30.00	15.00	9.00
175	Monte Kennedy	20.00	10.00	6.00
176	"Blix" Donnelly	20.00	10.00	6.00
177	Hank Borowy	20.00	10.00	6.00
178	Eddy Fitz Gerald	20.00	10.00	6.00
179	Charles Diering	20.00	10.00	6.00
180	Harry "The Hat" Walker	20.00	10.00	6.00
181	Marino Pieretti	20.00	10.00	6.00
182	Sam Zoldak	20.00	10.00	6.00
183	Mickey Haefner	20.00	10.00	6.00
184	Randy Gumpert	20.00	10.00	6.00
185	Howie Judson	20.00	10.00	6.00
186	Ken Keltner	20.00	10.00	6.00
187	Lou Stringer	20.00	10.00	6.00
188	Earl Johnson	20.00	10.00	6.00
189	Owen Friend	20.00	10.00	6.00
190	Ken Wood	20.00	10.00	6.00
191	Dick Starr	20.00	10.00	6.00
192	Bob Chipman	20.00	10.00	6.00
193	Pete Reiser	30.00	15.00	9.00
194	Billy Cox	35.00	17.50	10.00
195	Phil Cavarretta	20.00	10.00	6.00
196	Doyle Lade	20.00	10.00	6.00
197	Johnny Wyrostek	20.00	10.00	6.00
198	Danny Litwhiler	20.00	10.00	6.00
199	Jack Kramer	20.00	10.00	6.00
200	Kirby Higbe	20.00	10.00	6.00
201	Pete Castiglione	20.00	10.00	6.00
202	Cliff Chambers	20.00	10.00	6.00
203	Danny Murtaugh	20.00	10.00	6.00
204	Granny Hamner	20.00	10.00	6.00
205	Mike Goliat	20.00	10.00	6.00
206	Stan Lopata	20.00	10.00	6.00
207	Max Lanier	20.00	10.00	6.00
208	Jim Hearn	20.00	10.00	6.00
209	Johnny Lindell	20.00	10.00	6.00
210	Ted Gray	20.00	10.00	6.00
211	Charlie Keller	30.00	15.00	9.00
212	Gerry Priddy	20.00	10.00	6.00
213	Carl Scheib	20.00	10.00	6.00
214	Dick Fowler	20.00	10.00	6.00
215	Ed Lopat	50.00	25.00	15.00
216	Bob Porterfield	30.00	15.00	9.00
217	Casey Stengel	70.00	35.00	20.00
218	Cliff Mapes	30.00	15.00	9.00
219	*Hank Bauer*	70.00	35.00	20.00
220	Leo Durocher	60.00	30.00	18.00
221	Don Mueller	20.00	10.00	6.00
222	Bobby Morgan	25.00	12.50	7.50
223	Jimmy Russell	25.00	12.50	7.50
224	Jack Banta	25.00	12.50	7.50
225	Eddie Sawyer	20.00	10.00	6.00
226	*Jim Konstanty*	30.00	15.00	9.00
227	Bob Miller	20.00	10.00	6.00
228	Bill Nicholson	20.00	10.00	6.00
229	Frank Frisch	40.00	20.00	12.00
230	Bill Serena	20.00	10.00	6.00
231	Preston Ward	20.00	10.00	6.00
232	*Al Rosen*	55.00	27.50	16.50
233	Allie Clark	20.00	10.00	6.00
234	*Bobby Shantz*	45.00	22.50	13.50
235	Harold Gilbert	20.00	10.00	6.00
236	Bob Cain	20.00	10.00	6.00
237	Bill Salkeld	20.00	10.00	6.00
238	Nippy Jones	20.00	10.00	6.00
239	Bill Howerton	20.00	10.00	6.00
240	Eddie Lake	20.00	10.00	6.00
241	Neil Berry	20.00	10.00	6.00
242	Dick Kryhoski	20.00	10.00	6.00
243	Johnny Groth	20.00	10.00	6.00
244	Dale Coogan	20.00	10.00	6.00
245	Al Papai	20.00	10.00	6.00
246	*Walt Dropo*	35.00	17.50	10.00
247	*Irv Noren*	30.00	15.00	9.00
248	*Sam Jethroe*	40.00	20.00	12.00
249	"Snuffy" Stirnweiss	20.00	10.00	6.00
250	Ray Coleman	20.00	10.00	6.00
251	Les Moss	20.00	10.00	6.00
252	Billy DeMars	65.00	20.00	7.50

1951 Bowman

MICKEY VERNON

JAMES VERNON
First Base—Washington Senators
Born: Marcus Hook, Pa., April 22, 1918
Height: 6-2   Weight: 180
Bats: Left   Throws: Left

James "Mickey" Vernon batted .281 in 118 games in 1950. Drove in 75 runs. Tied for top fielding percentage in the League with a .991 mark. Began the season with Cleveland, but after 28 games was switched back to Washington where all of major-league career has been spent except 1949 which was with Cleveland. First full season in the majors: 1941. Top AL batter, 1946. In service 2 years.

No. 65 in the 1951 SERIES
BASEBALL PICTURE CARDS
©1951 Bowman Gum, Inc., Phila., Pa., U.S.A.

In 1951, Bowman increased the number of cards in its set for the third consecutive year when it issued 324 cards. The cards are, like 1950, color art reproductions of actual photographs but now measure 2-1/16" x 3-1/8" in size. The player's name is in a black strip on front. Several of the pictures are enlargements of the 1950 version. The high-numbered series (#253-324), which includes the rookie cards of Mantle and Mays, are the scarcest of the issue.

		NM	EX	VG
	Complete Set (324):	20,000	9,500	5,500
	Common Player (1-252):	17.50	9.00	5.00
	Common Player (253-324):	40.00	20.00	12.00
1	*Whitey Ford*	1,500	550.00	225.00
2	Yogi Berra	400.00	200.00	100.00
3	Robin Roberts	100.00	50.00	25.00
4	Del Ennis	17.50	9.00	5.00
5	Dale Mitchell	17.50	9.00	5.00
6	Don Newcombe	50.00	25.00	12.50
7	Gil Hodges	125.00	62.50	31.25
8	Paul Lehner	17.50	9.00	5.00
9	Sam Chapman	17.50	9.00	5.00
10	Red Schoendienst	75.00	37.50	22.50
11	"Red" Munger	17.50	9.00	5.00
12	Hank Majeski	17.50	9.00	5.00
13	Ed Stanky	20.00	10.00	6.00
14	Alvin Dark	17.50	9.00	5.00
15	Johnny Pesky	17.50	9.00	5.00
16	Maurice McDermott	17.50	9.00	5.00
17	Pete Castiglione	17.50	9.00	5.00
18	Gil Coan	17.50	9.00	5.00
19	Sid Gordon	17.50	9.00	5.00
20	Del Crandall	17.50	9.00	5.00
21	"Snuffy" Stirnweiss	17.50	9.00	5.00
22	Hank Sauer	17.50	9.00	5.00
23	"Hoot" Evers	17.50	9.00	5.00
24	Ewell Blackwell	17.50	9.00	5.00
25	Vic Raschi	40.00	20.00	12.00
26	Phil Rizzuto	175.00	87.50	43.75
27	Jim Konstanty	17.50	9.00	5.00
28	Eddie Waitkus	17.50	9.00	5.00
29	Allie Clark	17.50	9.00	5.00
30	Bob Feller	125.00	62.50	31.25
31	Roy Campanella	300.00	150.00	75.00
32	Duke Snider	300.00	150.00	75.00
33	Bob Hooper	17.50	9.00	5.00
34	Marty Marion	25.00	12.50	7.50
35	Al Zarilla	17.50	9.00	5.00
36	Joe Dobson	17.50	9.00	5.00
37	Whitey Lockman	17.50	9.00	5.00
38	Al Evans	17.50	9.00	5.00
39	Ray Scarborough	17.50	9.00	5.00
40	*Gus Bell*	30.00	15.00	9.00
41	Eddie Yost	17.50	9.00	5.00
42	Vern Bickford	17.50	9.00	5.00
43	Billy DeMars	17.50	9.00	5.00
44	Roy Smalley	17.50	9.00	5.00
45	Art Houtteman	17.50	9.00	5.00
46	George Kell	50.00	25.00	15.00
47	Grady Hatton	17.50	9.00	5.00
48	Ken Raffensberger	17.50	9.00	5.00
49	Jerry Coleman	20.00	10.00	6.00
50	Johnny Mize	50.00	25.00	15.00
51	Andy Seminick	17.50	9.00	5.00
52	Dick Sisler	17.50	9.00	5.00
53	Bob Lemon	50.00	25.00	15.00
54	*Ray Boone*	35.00	17.50	10.00
55	Gene Hermanski	20.00	10.00	6.00
56	Ralph Branca	50.00	25.00	15.00
57	Alex Kellner	17.50	9.00	5.00
58	Enos Slaughter	50.00	25.00	15.00
59	Randy Gumpert	17.50	9.00	5.00
60	"Chico" Carrasquel	20.00	10.00	6.00
61	Jim Hearn	17.50	9.00	5.00
62	Lou Boudreau	45.00	22.50	13.50
63	Bob Dillinger	17.50	9.00	5.00
64	Bill Werle	17.50	9.00	5.00
65	Mickey Vernon	17.50	9.00	5.00
66	Bob Elliott	17.50	9.00	5.00
67	Roy Sievers	17.50	9.00	5.00
68	Dick Kokos	17.50	9.00	5.00
69	Johnny Schmitz	17.50	9.00	5.00
70	Ron Northey	17.50	9.00	5.00
71	Jerry Priddy	17.50	9.00	5.00
72	Lloyd Merriman	17.50	9.00	5.00
73	Tommy Byrne	20.00	10.00	6.00
74	Billy Johnson	20.00	10.00	6.00
75	Russ Meyer	17.50	9.00	5.00
76	Stan Lopata	17.50	9.00	5.00
77	Mike Goliat	17.50	9.00	5.00
78	Early Wynn	60.00	30.00	18.00
79	Jim Hegan	17.50	9.00	5.00
80	Pee Wee Reese	200.00	100.00	50.00
81	Carl Furillo	55.00	27.50	16.50
82	Joe Tipton	17.50	9.00	5.00
83	Carl Scheib	17.50	9.00	5.00
84	Barney McCosky	17.50	9.00	5.00
85	Eddie Kazak	17.50	9.00	5.00
86	Harry Brecheen	17.50	9.00	5.00
87	Floyd Baker	17.50	9.00	5.00
88	Eddie Robinson	17.50	9.00	5.00
89	Henry Thompson	17.50	9.00	5.00
90	Dave Koslo	17.50	9.00	5.00
91	Clyde Vollmer	17.50	9.00	5.00
92	Vern Stephens	17.50	9.00	5.00
93	Danny O'Connell	17.50	9.00	5.00
94	Clyde McCullough	17.50	9.00	5.00
95	Sherry Robertson	17.50	9.00	5.00
96	Sandy Consuegra	17.50	9.00	5.00
97	Bob Kuzava	17.50	9.00	5.00
98	Willard Marshall	17.50	9.00	5.00
99	Earl Torgeson	17.50	9.00	5.00
100	Sherman Lollar	17.50	9.00	5.00
101	Owen Friend	17.50	9.00	5.00
102	Emil "Dutch" Leonard	17.50	9.00	5.00
103	Andy Pafko	17.50	9.00	5.00
104	Virgil "Fire" Trucks	17.50	9.00	5.00
105	Don Kolloway	17.50	9.00	5.00
106	Pat Mullin	17.50	9.00	5.00
107	Johnny Wyrostek	17.50	9.00	5.00
108	Virgil Stallcup	17.50	9.00	5.00

109	Allie Reynolds	45.00	22.50	13.50
110	Bobby Brown	30.00	15.00	9.00
111	Curt Simmons	17.50	9.00	5.00
112	Willie Jones	17.50	9.00	5.00
113	Bill "Swish" Nicholson	17.50	9.00	5.00
114	Sam Zoldak	17.50	9.00	5.00
115	Steve Gromek	17.50	9.00	5.00
116	Bruce Edwards	20.00	10.00	6.00
117	Eddie Miksis	20.00	10.00	6.00
118	Preacher Roe	50.00	25.00	12.50
119	Eddie Joost	17.50	9.00	5.00
120	Joe Coleman	17.50	9.00	5.00
121	Gerry Staley	17.50	9.00	5.00
122	*Joe Garagiola*	100.00	50.00	25.00
123	Howie Judson	17.50	9.00	5.00
124	Gus Niarhos	17.50	9.00	5.00
125	Bill Rigney	17.50	9.00	5.00
126	Bobby Thomson	50.00	25.00	15.00
127	*Sal Maglie*	75.00	37.50	22.50
128	Ellis Kinder	17.50	9.00	5.00
129	Matt Batts	17.50	9.00	5.00
130	Tom Saffell	17.50	9.00	5.00
131	Cliff Chambers	17.50	9.00	5.00
132	Cass Michaels	17.50	9.00	5.00
133	Sam Dente	17.50	9.00	5.00
134	Warren Spahn	150.00	75.00	37.50
135	Walker Cooper	17.50	9.00	5.00
136	Ray Coleman	17.50	9.00	5.00
137	Dick Starr	17.50	9.00	5.00
138	Phil Cavarretta	17.50	9.00	5.00
139	Doyle Lade	17.50	9.00	5.00
140	Eddie Lake	17.50	9.00	5.00
141	Fred Hutchinson	17.50	9.00	5.00
142	Aaron Robinson	17.50	9.00	5.00
143	Ted Kluszewski	60.00	30.00	18.00
144	Herman Wehmeier	17.50	9.00	5.00
145	Fred Sanford	17.50	9.00	5.00
146	Johnny Hopp	17.50	9.00	5.00
147	Ken Heintzelman	17.50	9.00	5.00
148	Granny Hamner	17.50	9.00	5.00
149	"Bubba" Church	17.50	9.00	5.00
150	Mike Garcia	17.50	9.00	5.00
151	Larry Doby	70.00	35.00	20.00
152	Cal Abrams	20.00	10.00	6.00
153	Rex Barney	20.00	10.00	6.00
154	Pete Suder	17.50	9.00	5.00
155	Lou Brissie	17.50	9.00	5.00
156	Del Rice	17.50	9.00	5.00
157	Al Brazle	17.50	9.00	5.00
158	Chuck Diering	17.50	9.00	5.00
159	Eddie Stewart	17.50	9.00	5.00
160	Phil Masi	17.50	9.00	5.00
161	Wes Westrum	17.50	9.00	5.00
162	Larry Jansen	17.50	9.00	5.00
163	Monte Kennedy	17.50	9.00	5.00
164	Bill Wight	17.50	9.00	5.00
165	Ted Williams	800.00	400.00	200.00
166	Stan Rojek	17.50	9.00	5.00
167	Murry Dickson	17.50	9.00	5.00
168	Sam Mele	17.50	9.00	5.00
169	Sid Hudson	17.50	9.00	5.00
170	Sibby Sisti	17.50	9.00	5.00
171	Buddy Kerr	17.50	9.00	5.00
172	Ned Garver	17.50	9.00	5.00
173	Hank Arft	17.50	9.00	5.00
174	Mickey Owen	17.50	9.00	5.00
175	Wayne Terwilliger	17.50	9.00	5.00
176	Vic Wertz	17.50	9.00	5.00
177	Charlie Keller	17.50	9.00	5.00
178	Ted Gray	17.50	9.00	5.00
179	Danny Litwhiler	17.50	9.00	5.00
180	Howie Fox	17.50	9.00	5.00
181	Casey Stengel	100.00	50.00	25.00
182	Tom Ferrick	20.00	10.00	6.00
183	Hank Bauer	35.00	17.50	10.00
184	Eddie Sawyer	17.50	9.00	5.00
185	Jimmy Bloodworth	17.50	9.00	5.00
186	Richie Ashburn	100.00	50.00	30.00
187	Al Rosen	35.00	17.50	10.00
188	*Roberto Avila*	25.00	12.50	7.50
189	Erv Palica	20.00	10.00	6.00
190	Joe Hatten	20.00	10.00	6.00
191	Billy Hitchcock	17.50	9.00	5.00
192	Hank Wyse	17.50	9.00	5.00
193	Ted Wilks	17.50	9.00	5.00
194	Harry "Peanuts" Lowrey	17.50	9.00	5.00
195	Paul Richards	20.00	10.00	6.00
196	*Bill Pierce*	32.50	16.00	10.00
197	Bob Cain	17.50	9.00	5.00
198	*Monte Irvin*	120.00	60.00	30.00
199	Sheldon Jones	17.50	9.00	5.00
200	Jack Kramer	17.50	9.00	5.00
201	Steve O'Neill	17.50	9.00	5.00
202	Mike Guerra	17.50	9.00	5.00
203	*Vernon Law*	40.00	20.00	12.00
204	Vic Lombardi	17.50	9.00	5.00
205	Mickey Grasso	17.50	9.00	5.00
206	Connie Marrero	17.50	9.00	5.00
207	Billy Southworth	35.00	17.50	10.50
208	"Blix" Donnelly	17.50	9.00	5.00
209	Ken Wood	17.50	9.00	5.00
210	Les Moss	17.50	9.00	5.00
211	Hal Jeffcoat	17.50	9.00	5.00
212	Bob Rush	17.50	9.00	5.00
213	Neil Berry	17.50	9.00	5.00
214	Bob Swift	17.50	9.00	5.00
215	Kent Peterson	17.50	9.00	5.00
216	Connie Ryan	17.50	9.00	5.00
217	Joe Page	27.50	13.50	8.00
218	Ed Lopat	32.50	16.00	10.00
219	*Gene Woodling*	40.00	20.00	12.00
220	Bob Miller	17.50	9.00	5.00
221	Dick Whitman	17.50	9.00	5.00
222	Thurman Tucker	17.50	9.00	5.00
223	Johnny Vander Meer	25.00	12.50	7.50
224	Billy Cox	27.50	13.50	8.00
225	*Dan Bankhead*	30.00	15.00	9.00
226	Jimmy Dykes	17.50	9.00	5.00

		NM	EX	VG
227	Bobby Shantz	20.00	10.00	6.00
228	*Cloyd Boyer*	17.50	9.00	5.00
229	Bill Howerton	17.50	9.00	5.00
230	Max Lanier	17.50	9.00	5.00
231	Luis Aloma	17.50	9.00	5.00
232	*Nellie Fox*	250.00	125.00	62.50
233	Leo Durocher	40.00	20.00	12.00
234	Clint Hartung	17.50	9.00	5.00
235	Jack Lohrke	17.50	9.00	5.00
236	"Buddy" Rosar	17.50	9.00	5.00
237	Billy Goodman	17.50	9.00	5.00
238	Pete Reiser	20.00	10.00	6.00
239	Bill MacDonald	17.50	9.00	5.00
240	Joe Haynes	17.50	9.00	5.00
241	Irv Noren	17.50	9.00	5.00
242	Sam Jethroe	17.50	9.00	5.00
243	Johnny Antonelli	17.50	9.00	5.00
244	Cliff Fannin	17.50	9.00	5.00
245	John Berardino	25.00	12.50	7.50
246	Bill Serena	17.50	9.00	5.00
247	Bob Ramazotti	17.50	9.00	5.00
248	*Johnny Klippstein*	17.50	9.00	5.00
249	Johnny Groth	17.50	9.00	5.00
250	Hank Borowy	17.50	9.00	5.00
251	Willard Ramsdell	17.50	9.00	5.00
252	"Dixie" Howell	17.50	9.00	5.00
253	*Mickey Mantle*	9,500	3,100	2,000
254	*Jackie Jensen*	100.00	50.00	25.00
255	Milo Candini	40.00	20.00	12.00
256	Ken Silvestri	40.00	20.00	12.00
257	Birdie Tebbetts	40.00	20.00	12.00
258	*Luke Easter*	45.00	22.50	13.50
259	Charlie Dressen	40.00	20.00	12.00
260	*Carl Erskine*	100.00	50.00	25.00
261	Wally Moses	40.00	20.00	12.00
262	Gus Zernial	40.00	20.00	12.00
263	Howie Pollet	40.00	20.00	12.00
264	Don Richmond	40.00	20.00	12.00
265	*Steve Bilko*	40.00	20.00	12.00
266	Harry Dorish	40.00	20.00	12.00
267	Ken Holcombe	40.00	20.00	12.00
268	Don Mueller	40.00	20.00	12.00
269	Ray Noble	40.00	20.00	12.00
270	Willard Nixon	40.00	20.00	12.00
271	Tommy Wright	40.00	20.00	12.00
272	Billy Meyer	40.00	20.00	12.00
273	Danny Murtaugh	40.00	20.00	12.00
274	George Metkovich	40.00	20.00	12.00
275	Bucky Harris	50.00	25.00	15.00
276	Frank Quinn	40.00	20.00	12.00
277	Roy Hartsfield	40.00	20.00	12.00
278	Norman Roy	40.00	20.00	12.00
279	Jim Delsing	40.00	20.00	12.00
280	Frank Overmire	40.00	20.00	12.00
281	Al Widmar	40.00	20.00	12.00
282	Frank Frisch	55.00	27.50	16.50
283	Walt Dubiel	40.00	20.00	12.00
284	Gene Bearden	40.00	20.00	12.00
285	Johnny Lipon	40.00	20.00	12.00
286	Bob Usher	40.00	20.00	12.00
287	Jim Blackburn	40.00	20.00	12.00
288	Bobby Adams	40.00	20.00	12.00
289	Cliff Mapes	50.00	25.00	15.00
290	Bill Dickey	150.00	75.00	37.50
291	Tommy Henrich	55.00	27.50	16.50
292	Eddie Pellagrini	40.00	20.00	12.00
293	Ken Johnson	40.00	20.00	12.00
294	Jocko Thompson	40.00	20.00	12.00
295	Al Lopez	100.00	50.00	25.00
296	Bob Kennedy	40.00	20.00	12.00
297	Dave Philley	40.00	20.00	12.00
298	Joe Astroth	40.00	20.00	12.00
299	Clyde King	50.00	25.00	15.00
300	Hal Rice	40.00	20.00	12.00
301	Tommy Glaviano	40.00	20.00	12.00
302	Jim Busby	40.00	20.00	12.00
303	Marv Rotblatt	40.00	20.00	12.00
304	Allen Gettel	40.00	20.00	12.00
305	*Willie Mays*	3,600	1,100	575.00
306	*Jim Piersall*	120.00	60.00	30.00
307	Walt Masterson	40.00	20.00	12.00
308	Ted Beard	40.00	20.00	12.00
309	Mel Queen	40.00	20.00	12.00
310	Erv Dusak	40.00	20.00	12.00
311	Mickey Harris	40.00	20.00	12.00
312	*Gene Mauch*	50.00	25.00	15.00
313	Ray Mueller	40.00	20.00	12.00
314	Johnny Sain	45.00	22.50	13.50
315	Zack Taylor	40.00	20.00	12.00
316	Duane Pillette	40.00	20.00	12.00
317	*Smoky Burgess*	60.00	30.00	18.00
318	Warren Hacker	40.00	20.00	12.00
319	Red Rolfe	40.00	20.00	12.00
320	Hal White	40.00	20.00	12.00
321	Earl Johnson	40.00	20.00	12.00
322	Luke Sewell	40.00	20.00	12.00
323	*Joe Adcock*	100.00	50.00	25.00
324	Johnny Pramesa	125.00	62.50	31.25

1952 Bowman

Bowman reverted to a 252-card set in 1952, but retained the card size (2-1/16" x 3-1/8") employed the preceding year. The cards, which are color art reproductions of actual photographs, feature a facsimile autograph on front.

		NM	EX	VG
	Complete Set (252):	10,000	5,000	3,000
	Common Player (1-216):	20.00	10.00	6.00
	Common Player (217-252):	40.00	20.00	12.00
1	Yogi Berra	600.00	300.00	150.00
2	Bobby Thomson	60.00	30.00	15.00
3	Fred Hutchinson	20.00	10.00	6.00
4	Robin Roberts	80.00	40.00	20.00
5	*Minnie Minoso*	120.00	60.00	30.00
6	Virgil "Red" Stallcup	20.00	10.00	6.00
7	Mike Garcia	20.00	10.00	6.00
8	Pee Wee Reese	150.00	75.00	37.50
9	Vern Stephens	20.00	10.00	6.00
10	Bob Hooper	20.00	10.00	6.00
11	Ralph Kiner	50.00	25.00	12.50
12	Max Surkont	20.00	10.00	6.00
13	Cliff Mapes	20.00	10.00	6.00
14	Cliff Chambers	20.00	10.00	6.00
15	Sam Mele	20.00	10.00	6.00
16	Omar Lown	20.00	10.00	6.00
17	Ed Lopat	55.00	27.50	16.50
18	Don Mueller	20.00	10.00	6.00
19	Bob Cain	20.00	10.00	6.00
20	Willie Jones	20.00	10.00	6.00
21	Nellie Fox	100.00	50.00	25.00
22	Willard Ramsdell	20.00	10.00	6.00
23	Bob Lemon	60.00	30.00	18.00
24	Carl Furillo	50.00	25.00	15.00
25	Maurice McDermott	20.00	10.00	6.00
26	Eddie Joost	20.00	10.00	6.00
27	Joe Garagiola	30.00	15.00	9.00
28	Roy Hartsfield	20.00	10.00	6.00
29	Ned Garver	20.00	10.00	6.00
30	Red Schoendienst	45.00	22.50	13.50
31	Eddie Yost	20.00	10.00	6.00
32	Eddie Miksis	20.00	10.00	6.00
33	*Gil McDougald*	60.00	30.00	18.00
34	Al Dark	20.00	10.00	6.00
35	Granny Hamner	20.00	10.00	6.00
36	Cass Michaels	20.00	10.00	6.00
37	Vic Raschi	30.00	15.00	9.00
38	Whitey Lockman	20.00	10.00	6.00
39	Vic Wertz	20.00	10.00	6.00
40	"Bubba" Church	20.00	10.00	6.00
41	"Chico" Carrasquel	20.00	10.00	6.00
42	Johnny Wyrostek	20.00	10.00	6.00
43	Bob Feller	150.00	75.00	37.50
44	Roy Campanella	250.00	125.00	62.50
45	Johnny Pesky	20.00	10.00	6.00
46	Carl Scheib	20.00	10.00	6.00
47	Pete Castiglione	20.00	10.00	6.00
48	Vernon Bickford	20.00	10.00	6.00
49	Jim Hearn	20.00	10.00	6.00
50	Gerry Staley	20.00	10.00	6.00
51	Gil Coan	20.00	10.00	6.00
52	Phil Rizzuto	150.00	75.00	37.50
53	Richie Ashburn	120.00	60.00	30.00
54	Billy Pierce	25.00	12.50	7.50
55	Ken Raffensberger	20.00	10.00	6.00
56	Clyde King	25.00	12.50	7.50
57	Clyde Vollmer	20.00	10.00	6.00
58	Hank Majeski	20.00	10.00	6.00
59	Murry Dickson	20.00	10.00	6.00
60	Sid Gordon	20.00	10.00	6.00
61	Tommy Byrne	20.00	10.00	6.00
62	Joe Presko	20.00	10.00	6.00
63	Irv Noren	20.00	10.00	6.00
64	Roy Smalley	20.00	10.00	6.00
65	Hank Bauer	50.00	25.00	15.00
66	Sal Maglie	25.00	12.50	7.50
67	Johnny Groth	20.00	10.00	6.00
68	Jim Busby	20.00	10.00	6.00
69	Joe Adcock	20.00	10.00	6.00
70	Carl Erskine	40.00	20.00	12.00
71	Vernon Law	20.00	10.00	6.00
72	Earl Torgeson	20.00	10.00	6.00
73	Jerry Coleman	30.00	15.00	9.00
74	Wes Westrum	20.00	10.00	6.00
75	George Kell	45.00	22.50	13.50
76	Del Ennis	20.00	10.00	6.00
77	Eddie Robinson	20.00	10.00	6.00
78	Lloyd Merriman	20.00	10.00	6.00
79	Lou Brissie	20.00	10.00	6.00
80	Gil Hodges	100.00	50.00	30.00
81	Billy Goodman	20.00	10.00	6.00
82	Gus Zernial	20.00	10.00	6.00
83	Howie Pollet	20.00	10.00	6.00
84	Sam Jethroe	20.00	10.00	6.00
85	Marty Marion	25.00	12.50	7.50
86	Cal Abrams	25.00	12.50	7.50
87	Mickey Vernon	20.00	10.00	6.00
88	Bruce Edwards	20.00	10.00	6.00
89	Billy Hitchcock	20.00	10.00	6.00
90	Larry Jansen	20.00	10.00	6.00
91	Don Kolloway	20.00	10.00	6.00
92	Eddie Waitkus	20.00	10.00	6.00
93	Paul Richards	20.00	10.00	6.00
94	Luke Sewell	20.00	10.00	6.00
95	Luke Easter	20.00	10.00	6.00
96	Ralph Branca	40.00	20.00	12.00
97	Willard Marshall	20.00	10.00	6.00
98	Jimmy Dykes	20.00	10.00	6.00
99	Clyde McCullough	20.00	10.00	6.00
100	Sibby Sisti	20.00	10.00	6.00
101	Mickey Mantle	2,500	1,250	625.00
102	Peanuts Lowrey	20.00	10.00	6.00
103	Joe Haynes	20.00	10.00	6.00
104	Hal Jeffcoat	20.00	10.00	6.00
105	Bobby Brown	35.00	17.50	10.00
106	Randy Gumpert	20.00	10.00	6.00
107	Del Rice	20.00	10.00	6.00
108	George Metkovich	20.00	10.00	6.00

		NM	EX	VG
109	Tom Morgan	30.00	15.00	9.00
110	Max Lanier	20.00	10.00	6.00
111	"Hoot" Evers	20.00	10.00	6.00
112	"Smoky" Burgess	20.00	10.00	6.00
113	Al Zarilla	20.00	10.00	6.00
114	Frank Hiller	20.00	10.00	6.00
115	Larry Doby	60.00	30.00	18.00
116	Duke Snider	200.00	100.00	60.00
117	Bill Wight	20.00	10.00	6.00
118	Ray Murray	20.00	10.00	6.00
119	Bill Howerton	20.00	10.00	6.00
120	Chet Nichols	20.00	10.00	6.00
121	Al Corwin	20.00	10.00	6.00
122	Billy Johnson	20.00	10.00	6.00
123	Sid Hudson	20.00	10.00	6.00
124	Birdie Tebbetts	20.00	10.00	6.00
125	Howie Fox	20.00	10.00	6.00
126	Phil Cavarretta	20.00	10.00	6.00
127	Dick Sisler	20.00	10.00	6.00
128	Don Newcombe	45.00	22.50	13.50
129	Gus Niarhos	20.00	10.00	6.00
130	Allie Clark	20.00	10.00	6.00
131	Bob Swift	20.00	10.00	6.00
132	Dave Cole	20.00	10.00	6.00
133	Dick Kryhoski	20.00	10.00	6.00
134	Al Brazle	20.00	10.00	6.00
135	Mickey Harris	20.00	10.00	6.00
136	Gene Hermanski	20.00	10.00	6.00
137	Stan Rojek	20.00	10.00	6.00
138	Ted Wilks	20.00	10.00	6.00
139	Jerry Priddy	20.00	10.00	6.00
140	Ray Scarborough	20.00	10.00	6.00
141	Hank Edwards	20.00	10.00	6.00
142	Early Wynn	45.00	22.50	13.50
143	Sandy Consuegra	20.00	10.00	6.00
144	Joe Hatten	20.00	10.00	6.00
145	Johnny Mize	80.00	40.00	24.00
146	Leo Durocher	45.00	22.50	13.50
147	Marlin Stuart	20.00	10.00	6.00
148	Ken Heintzelman	20.00	10.00	6.00
149	Howie Judson	20.00	10.00	6.00
150	Herman Wehmeier	20.00	10.00	6.00
151	Al Rosen	30.00	15.00	9.00
152	Billy Cox	40.00	20.00	12.00
153	Fred Hatfield	20.00	10.00	6.00
154	Ferris Fain	20.00	10.00	6.00
155	Billy Meyer	20.00	10.00	6.00
156	Warren Spahn	120.00	60.00	30.00
157	Jim Delsing	20.00	10.00	6.00
158	Bucky Harris	30.00	15.00	9.00
159	Dutch Leonard	20.00	10.00	6.00
160	Eddie Stanky	20.00	10.00	6.00
161	Jackie Jensen	45.00	22.50	13.50
162	Monte Irvin	55.00	27.50	16.50
163	Johnny Lipon	20.00	10.00	6.00
164	Connie Ryan	20.00	10.00	6.00
165	Saul Rogovin	20.00	10.00	6.00
166	Bobby Adams	20.00	10.00	6.00
167	Bob Avila	20.00	10.00	6.00
168	Preacher Roe	35.00	17.50	10.00
169	Walt Dropo	20.00	10.00	6.00
170	Joe Astroth	20.00	10.00	6.00
171	Mel Queen	20.00	10.00	6.00
172	Ebba St. Claire	20.00	10.00	6.00
173	Gene Bearden	20.00	10.00	6.00
174	Mickey Grasso	20.00	10.00	6.00
175	Ransom Jackson	20.00	10.00	6.00
176	Harry Brecheen	20.00	10.00	6.00
177	Gene Woodling	35.00	17.50	10.00
178	Dave Williams	20.00	10.00	6.00
179	Pete Suder	20.00	10.00	6.00
180	Eddie Fitz Gerald	20.00	10.00	6.00
181	Joe Collins	30.00	15.00	9.00
182	Dave Koslo	20.00	10.00	6.00
183	Pat Mullin	20.00	10.00	6.00
184	Curt Simmons	20.00	10.00	6.00
185	Eddie Stewart	20.00	10.00	6.00
186	Frank Smith	20.00	10.00	6.00
187	Jim Hegan	20.00	10.00	6.00
188	Charlie Dressen	30.00	15.00	9.00
189	Jim Piersall	30.00	15.00	9.00
190	Dick Fowler	20.00	10.00	6.00
191	*Bob Friend*	25.00	12.50	7.50
192	John Cusick	20.00	10.00	6.00
193	Bobby Young	20.00	10.00	6.00
194	Bob Porterfield	20.00	10.00	6.00
195	Frank Baumholtz	20.00	10.00	6.00
196	Stan Musial	600.00	300.00	150.00
197	*Charlie Silvera*	35.00	17.50	10.00
198	Chuck Diering	20.00	10.00	6.00
199	Ted Gray	20.00	10.00	6.00
200	Ken Silvestri	20.00	10.00	6.00
201	Ray Coleman	20.00	10.00	6.00
202	Harry Perkowski	20.00	10.00	6.00
203	Steve Gromek	20.00	10.00	6.00
204	Andy Pafko	20.00	10.00	6.00
205	Walt Masterson	20.00	10.00	6.00
206	Elmer Valo	20.00	10.00	6.00
207	George Strickland	20.00	10.00	6.00
208	Walker Cooper	20.00	10.00	6.00
209	Dick Littlefield	20.00	10.00	6.00
210	Archie Wilson	20.00	10.00	6.00
211	Paul Minner	20.00	10.00	6.00
212	Solly Hemus	20.00	10.00	6.00
213	Monte Kennedy	20.00	10.00	6.00
214	Ray Boone	20.00	10.00	6.00
215	Sheldon Jones	20.00	10.00	6.00
216	Matt Batts	20.00	10.00	6.00
217	Casey Stengel	125.00	60.00	35.00
218	Willie Mays	1,500	750.00	375.00
219	Neil Berry	40.00	20.00	12.00
220	Russ Meyer	40.00	20.00	12.00
221	Lou Kretlow	40.00	20.00	12.00
222	"Dixie" Howell	40.00	20.00	12.00
223	*Harry Simpson*	45.00	22.50	13.50
224	Johnny Schmitz	40.00	20.00	12.00
225	Del Wilber	40.00	20.00	12.00
226	Alex Kellner	40.00	20.00	12.00

		NM	EX	VG
227	Clyde Sukeforth	40.00	20.00	12.00
228	Bob Chipman	40.00	20.00	12.00
229	Hank Arft	40.00	20.00	12.00
230	Frank Shea	40.00	20.00	12.00
231	*Dee Fondy*	40.00	20.00	12.00
232	Enos Slaughter	100.00	50.00	25.00
233	Bob Kuzava	50.00	25.00	15.00
234	Fred Fitzsimmons	40.00	20.00	12.00
235	Steve Souchock	40.00	20.00	12.00
236	Tommy Brown	40.00	20.00	12.00
237	Sherman Lollar	40.00	20.00	12.00
238	*Roy McMillan*	40.00	20.00	12.00
239	Dale Mitchell	40.00	20.00	12.00
240	*Billy Loes*	45.00	22.50	13.50
241	Mel Parnell	40.00	20.00	12.00
242	Everett Kell	40.00	20.00	12.00
243	"Red" Munger	40.00	20.00	12.00
244	*Lew Burdette*	60.00	30.00	18.00
245	George Schmees	40.00	20.00	12.00
246	Jerry Snyder	40.00	20.00	12.00
247	John Pramesa	40.00	20.00	12.00
248a	Bill Werle (. after G and most of W missing)	40.00	20.00	12.00
248b	Bill Werle (Full signature.)			
249	Henry Thompson	40.00	20.00	12.00
250	Ike Delock	40.00	20.00	12.00
251	Jack Lohrke	40.00	20.00	12.00
252	Frank Crosetti	125.00	62.50	31.25

1952 Bowman Proofs

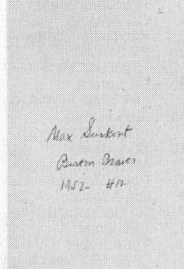

Coincident to Topps issue of its "Giant Size" baseball cards in 1952, Bowman began experimenting with up-sizing its card issues from the then-current 2-1/16" x 3-1/8". A group of proof cards was produced using 12 players from the '52 Bowman set. The proofs are 2-1/2" x 3-3/4", overall about 45% larger than the issued '52s. Each proof is found in two types, black-and-white and color. Both have blank-backs except for hand-written notes with the player's name, team and card number in the '52 set. Many of the proofs feature slight differences from the issued versions, such as uniform changes, elimination of background elements or picture cropping. The color proofs include a facsimile autograph. A small group of these proof cards entered the hobby early in the 1980s when a former Bowman executive disposed of his hobby card files. The proofs are numbered according to their number within the 1952 Bowman set.

		NM	EX	VG
	Common Player, B/W:	600.00	300.00	180.00
	Common Player, Color:	900.00	450.00	270.00
1	Yogi Berra (B/W)	2,000	1,000	600.00
1	Yogi Berra (Color)	3,200	1,600	960.00
2	Bobby Thomson (B/W)	600.00	300.00	180.00
2	Bobby Thomson (Color)	2,000	1,000	600.00
3	Fred Hutchinson (B/W)	800.00	400.00	240.00
3	Fred Hutchinson (Color)	900.00	450.00	270.00
4	Robin Roberts (B/W)	1,450	725.00	435.00
4	Robin Roberts (Color)	2,400	1,200	720.00
10	Bob Hooper (B/W)	800.00	400.00	240.00
10	Bob Hooper (Color)	900.00	450.00	270.00
11	Ralph Kiner (B/W)	1,450	725.00	435.00
11	Ralph Kiner (Color)	2,400	1,200	720.00
12	Max Surkont (B/W)	800.00	400.00	240.00
12	Max Surkont (Color)	900.00	450.00	270.00
13	Cliff Mapes (B/W)	800.00	400.00	240.00
13	Cliff Mapes (Color)	900.00	450.00	270.00
14	Cliff Chambers (B/W)	800.00	400.00	240.00
14	Cliff Chambers (Color)	900.00	450.00	270.00
34	Alvin Dark (B/W)	800.00	400.00	240.00
34	Alvin Dark (Color)	900.00	450.00	270.00
39	Vic Wertz (B/W)	800.00	400.00	240.00
39	Vic Wertz (Color)	900.00	450.00	270.00
142	Early Wynn (B/W)	1,300	650.00	390.00
142	Early Wynn (Color)	2,400	1,200	720.00
176	Harry Brecheen (B/W)	800.00	400.00	240.00
176	Harry Brecheen (Color)	900.00	450.00	270.00

1953 Bowman

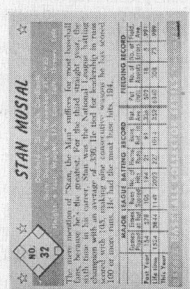

The first set of contemporary major league players featuring actual color photographs, the 160-card 1953 Bowman color set remains one of the most popular issues of the postwar era. The set is greatly appreciated for its uncluttered look; card fronts that contain no names, teams or facsimile autographs. Bowman increased the size of the cards to 2-1/2" x 3-3/4" to better compete with Topps' larger format. Bowman copied an idea from the 1952 Topps set and developed card backs that gave player career and previous-year statistics. The high-numbered cards (#113-160) are the scarcest of the set, with #113-128 being especially scarce.

		NM	EX	VG
	Complete Set (160):	16,000	7,500	4,250
	Common Player (1-112):	35.00	17.50	10.00
	Common Player (113-160):	90.00	45.00	25.00
1	Davey Williams	175.00	87.50	43.75
2	Vic Wertz	45.00	17.50	10.00
3	Sam Jethroe	35.00	17.50	10.00
4	Art Houtteman	35.00	17.50	10.00
5	Sid Gordon	35.00	17.50	10.00
6	Joe Ginsberg	35.00	17.50	10.00
7	Harry Chiti	35.00	17.50	10.00
8	Al Rosen	55.00	27.50	16.50
9	Phil Rizzuto	250.00	125.00	62.50
10	Richie Ashburn	150.00	75.00	37.50
11	Bobby Shantz	35.00	17.50	10.00
12	Carl Erskine	50.00	25.00	15.00
13	Gus Zernial	35.00	17.50	10.00
14	Billy Loes	55.00	27.50	16.50
15	Jim Busby	35.00	17.50	10.00
16	Bob Friend	35.00	17.50	10.00
17	Gerry Staley	35.00	17.50	10.00
18	Nellie Fox	150.00	75.00	37.50
19	Al Dark	35.00	17.50	10.00
20	Don Lenhardt	35.00	17.50	10.00
21	Joe Garagiola	50.00	25.00	15.00
22	Bob Porterfield	35.00	17.50	10.00
23	Herman Wehmeier	35.00	17.50	10.00
24	Jackie Jensen	45.00	22.50	13.50
25	"Hoot" Evers	35.00	17.50	10.00
26	Roy McMillan	35.00	17.50	10.00
27	Vic Raschi	70.00	35.00	20.00
28	"Smoky" Burgess	45.00	22.50	13.50
29	Roberto Avila	35.00	17.50	10.00
30	Phil Cavarretta	35.00	17.50	10.00
31	Jimmy Dykes	35.00	17.50	10.00
32	Stan Musial	600.00	300.00	150.00
33	Pee Wee Reese	1,000	500.00	250.00
34	Gil Coan	35.00	17.50	10.00
35	Maury McDermott	35.00	17.50	10.00
36	Minnie Minoso	85.00	42.50	25.00
37	Jim Wilson	35.00	17.50	10.00
38	Harry Byrd	35.00	17.50	10.00
39	Paul Richards	35.00	17.50	10.00
40	Larry Doby	100.00	50.00	25.00
41	Sammy White	35.00	17.50	10.00
42	Tommy Brown	35.00	17.50	10.00
43	Mike Garcia	35.00	17.50	10.00
44	Hank Bauer, Yogi Berra, Mickey Mantle	800.00	400.00	200.00
45	Walt Dropo	35.00	17.50	10.00
46	Roy Campanella	350.00	175.00	87.50
47	Ned Garver	35.00	17.50	10.00
48	Hank Sauer	35.00	17.50	10.00
49	Eddie Stanky	35.00	17.50	10.00
50	Lou Kretlow	35.00	17.50	10.00
51	Monte Irvin	55.00	27.50	16.50
52	Marty Marion	45.00	22.50	13.50
53	Del Rice	35.00	17.50	10.00
54	"Chico" Carrasquel	35.00	17.50	10.00
55	Leo Durocher	70.00	35.00	20.00
56	Bob Cain	35.00	17.50	10.00
57	Lou Boudreau	75.00	37.50	22.50
58	Willard Marshall	35.00	17.50	10.00
59	Mickey Mantle	2,200	1,100	550.00
60	Granny Hamner	35.00	17.50	10.00
61	George Kell	60.00	30.00	18.00
62	Ted Kluszewski	90.00	45.00	27.50
63	Gil McDougald	100.00	50.00	25.00
64	Curt Simmons	35.00	17.50	10.50
65	Robin Roberts	125.00	62.50	31.25
66	Mel Parnell	35.00	17.50	10.00
67	Mel Clark	35.00	17.50	10.00
68	Allie Reynolds	80.00	40.00	20.00
69	Charlie Grimm	35.00	17.50	10.00
70	Clint Courtney	35.00	17.50	10.00
71	Paul Minner	35.00	17.50	10.00
72	Ted Gray	35.00	17.50	10.00
73	Billy Pierce	40.00	20.00	12.00
74	Don Mueller	35.00	17.50	10.00
75	Saul Rogovin	35.00	17.50	10.00
76	Jim Hearn	35.00	17.50	10.00
77	Mickey Grasso	35.00	17.50	10.00
78	Carl Furillo	80.00	40.00	25.00
79	Ray Boone	35.00	17.50	10.00
80	Ralph Kiner	115.00	55.00	35.00
81	Enos Slaughter	100.00	50.00	25.00
82	Joe Astroth	35.00	17.50	10.00
83	Jack Daniels	35.00	17.50	10.00
84	Hank Bauer	80.00	40.00	25.00
85	Solly Hemus	35.00	17.50	10.00
86	Harry Simpson	35.00	17.50	10.00
87	Harry Perkowski	35.00	17.50	10.00
88	Joe Dobson	35.00	17.50	10.00
89	Sandalio Consuegra	35.00	17.50	10.00
90	Joe Nuxhall	35.00	17.50	10.00
91	Steve Souchock	35.00	17.50	10.00
92	Gil Hodges	300.00	150.00	75.00
93	Billy Martin, Phil Rizzuto	300.00	150.00	75.00
94	Bob Addis	35.00	17.50	10.00
95	Wally Moses	35.00	17.50	10.00
96	Sal Maglie	65.00	32.50	20.00
97	Eddie Mathews	350.00	175.00	87.50
98	Hector Rodriguez	35.00	17.50	10.00
99	Warren Spahn	350.00	175.00	87.50
100	Bill Wight	35.00	17.50	10.00
101	Red Schoendienst	100.00	50.00	25.00
102	Jim Hegan	35.00	17.50	10.00
103	Del Ennis	35.00	17.50	10.00
104	Luke Easter	35.00	17.50	10.00
105	Eddie Joost	35.00	17.50	10.00
106	Ken Raffensberger	35.00	17.50	10.00
107	Alex Kellner	35.00	17.50	10.00
108	Bobby Adams	35.00	17.50	10.00
109	Ken Wood	35.00	17.50	10.00
110	Bob Rush	35.00	17.50	10.00
111	Jim Dyck	35.00	17.50	10.00
112	Toby Atwell	35.00	17.50	10.00
113	Karl Drews	90.00	45.00	25.00
114	Bob Feller	500.00	250.00	125.00
115	Cloyd Boyer	90.00	45.00	25.00
116	Eddie Yost	90.00	45.00	25.00
117	Duke Snider	600.00	300.00	150.00
118	Billy Martin	400.00	200.00	100.00
119	Dale Mitchell	90.00	45.00	25.00
120	Marlin Stuart	90.00	45.00	25.00
121	Yogi Berra	800.00	400.00	200.00
122	Bill Serena	90.00	45.00	25.00
123	Johnny Lipon	90.00	45.00	25.00
124	Charlie Dressen	100.00	50.00	25.00
125	Fred Hatfield	90.00	45.00	25.00
126	Al Corwin	90.00	45.00	25.00
127	Dick Kryhoski	90.00	45.00	25.00
128	"Whitey" Lockman	90.00	45.00	25.00
129	Russ Meyer	95.00	47.50	27.50
130	Cass Michaels	90.00	45.00	25.00
131	Connie Ryan	90.00	45.00	25.00
132	Fred Hutchinson	90.00	45.00	25.00
133	Willie Jones	90.00	45.00	25.00
134	Johnny Pesky	90.00	45.00	25.00
135	Bobby Morgan	95.00	47.50	27.50
136	Jim Brideweser	100.00	50.00	30.00
137	Sam Dente	90.00	45.00	25.00
138	"Bubba" Church	90.00	45.00	25.00
139	Pete Runnels	90.00	45.00	25.00
140	Alpha Brazle	90.00	45.00	25.00
141	Frank "Spec" Shea	90.00	45.00	25.00
142	Larry Miggins	90.00	45.00	25.00
143	Al Lopez	100.00	50.00	25.00
144	Warren Hacker	90.00	45.00	25.00
145	George Shuba	125.00	60.00	35.00
146	Early Wynn	200.00	100.00	50.00
147	Clem Koshorek	90.00	45.00	25.00
148	Billy Goodman	90.00	45.00	25.00
149	Al Corwin	90.00	45.00	25.00
150	Carl Scheib	90.00	45.00	25.00
151	Joe Adcock	90.00	45.00	25.00
152	Clyde Vollmer	90.00	45.00	25.00
153	Whitey Ford	825.00	410.00	245.00
154	Omar "Turk" Lown	90.00	45.00	25.00
155	Allie Clark	90.00	45.00	25.00
156	Max Surkont	90.00	45.00	25.00
157	Sherman Lollar	90.00	45.00	25.00
158	Howard Fox	90.00	45.00	25.00
159	Mickey Vernon (Photo actually Floyd Baker.)	95.00	47.50	27.50
160	Cal Abrams	500.00	250.00	125.00

1953 Bowman Black & White

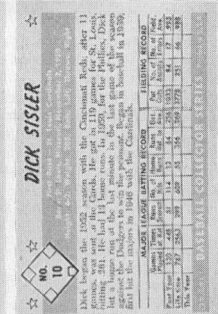

The 1953 Bowman black-and-white set is similar in all respects to the 1953 Bowman color cards, except that it lacks color. Sixty-four cards, which measure 2-1/2" x 3-3/4", comprise the set.

		NM	EX	VG
	Complete Set (64):	4,500	2,125	1,275
	Common Player:	55.00	25.00	15.00
1	Gus Bell	150.00	75.00	37.50
2	Willard Nixon	65.00	30.00	15.00
3	Bill Rigney	55.00	25.00	15.00
4	Pat Mullin	55.00	25.00	15.00
5	Dee Fondy	55.00	25.00	15.00
6	Ray Murray	55.00	25.00	15.00
7	Andy Seminick	55.00	25.00	15.00
8	Pete Suder	55.00	25.00	15.00
9	Walt Masterson	55.00	25.00	15.00
10	Dick Sisler	55.00	25.00	15.00
11	Dick Gernert	55.00	25.00	15.00
12	Randy Jackson	55.00	25.00	15.00
13	Joe Tipton	55.00	25.00	15.00
14	Bill Nicholson	55.00	25.00	15.00
15	Johnny Mize	125.00	62.50	31.25
16	Stu Miller	55.00	25.00	15.00
17	Virgil Trucks	55.00	25.00	15.00
18	Billy Hoeft	55.00	25.00	15.00
19	Paul LaPalme	55.00	25.00	15.00
20	Eddie Robinson	55.00	25.00	15.00
21	Clarence "Bud" Podbielan	55.00	25.00	15.00
22	Matt Batts	55.00	25.00	15.00
23	Wilmer Mizell	55.00	25.00	15.00
24	Del Wilber	55.00	25.00	15.00

#	Player			
25	Johnny Sain	100.00	50.00	30.00
26	Preacher Roe	90.00	45.00	25.00
27	Bob Lemon	175.00	87.50	43.75
28	Hoyt Wilhelm	125.00	62.50	31.25
29	Sid Hudson	55.00	25.00	15.00
30	Walker Cooper	55.00	25.00	15.00
31	Gene Woodling	100.00	50.00	30.00
32	Rocky Bridges	55.00	25.00	15.00
33	Bob Kuzava	55.00	25.00	15.00
34	Ebba St. Clair (St. Claire)	55.00	25.00	15.00
35	Johnny Wyrostek	55.00	25.00	15.00
36	Jim Piersall	90.00	45.00	25.00
37	Hal Jeffcoat	55.00	25.00	15.00
38	Dave Cole	55.00	25.00	15.00
39	Casey Stengel	350.00	175.00	87.50
40	Larry Jansen	55.00	25.00	15.00
41	Bob Ramazotti	55.00	25.00	15.00
42	Howie Judson	55.00	25.00	15.00
43a	Hal Bevan (Birth year 1950.)	55.00	25.00	15.00
43b	Hal Bevan (Birth year 1930.)	120.00	60.00	35.00
44	Jim Delsing	55.00	25.00	15.00
45	Irv Noren	100.00	50.00	30.00
46	Bucky Harris	100.00	50.00	35.00
47	Jack Lohrke	55.00	25.00	15.00
48	Steve Ridzik	55.00	25.00	15.00
49	Floyd Baker	55.00	25.00	15.00
50	Emil "Dutch" Leonard	55.00	25.00	15.00
51	Lew Burdette	75.00	35.00	20.00
52	Ralph Branca	100.00	50.00	30.00
53	Morris Martin	55.00	25.00	15.00
54	Bill Miller	55.00	25.00	15.00
55	Don Johnson	55.00	25.00	15.00
56	Roy Smalley	55.00	25.00	15.00
57	Andy Pafko	55.00	25.00	15.00
58	Jim Konstanty	55.00	25.00	15.00
59	Duane Pillette	55.00	25.00	15.00
60	Billy Cox	80.00	40.00	20.00
61	Tom Gorman	80.00	40.00	25.00
62	Keith Thomas	55.00	25.00	15.00
63	Steve Gromek	55.00	25.00	15.00
64	Andy Hansen	75.00	25.00	15.00

1953 Bowman Color Proofs

Four subjects are known to have survived in proof form created prior to the production of Bowman's landmark 1953 color card set. In the same 2-1/2" x 3-3/4" size as the issued cards, the proofs are blank-backed and lack the black frame line separating the picture from the white border. The Enos Slaughter card is otherwise identical to the issued version. The Spahn was changed to a different, more close-up picture for the issued card. The "Dodgers In Action" card was never issued, nor was the Ferris Fain card, probably due to Fain's trade from the A's to the White Sox prior to the 1953 season.

	NM	EX	VG
Complete Set (4):	7,200	3,600	2,150
Common Player:	1,125	560.00	325.00
(1) Dodgers In Action	3,300	1,650	990.00
(2) Ferris Fain	2,450	1,225	735.00
(3) Enos Slaughter	1,125	560.00	325.00
(4) Warren Spahn	2,700	1,350	810.00

1954 Bowman

Bowman's 1954 set consists of 224 full-color cards that measure 2-1/2" x 3-3/4". It is believed that contractual problems caused the withdrawal of card #66 (Ted Williams) from the set, creating one of the most sought-after scarcities of the postwar era. The Williams card was replaced by Jim Piersall (who is also #210) in subsequent print runs. The set contains over 40 variations, most involving statistical errors on the card

backs that were corrected. On most cards neither variation carries a premium value as both varieties appear to have been printed in equal amounts. The complete set price that follows does not include all variations or #66 Williams.

#	Player	NM	EX	VG
	Complete Set (224):	5,000	2,400	1,400
	Common Player (1-128):	10.00	5.00	3.00
	Common Player (129-224):	12.00	6.00	3.50
1	Phil Rizzuto	200.00	100.00	50.00
2	Jack Jensen	50.00	25.00	12.50
3	Marion Fricano	10.00	5.00	3.00
4	Bob Hooper	10.00	5.00	3.00
5	Billy Hunter	10.00	5.00	3.00
6	Nellie Fox	80.00	40.00	20.00
7	Walter Dropo	10.00	5.00	3.00
8	Jim Busby	10.00	5.00	3.00
9	Dave Williams	10.00	5.00	3.00
10	Carl Erskine	25.00	12.50	7.50
11	Sid Gordon	10.00	5.00	3.00
12a	Roy McMillan (551/1290 At Bat)	12.00	6.00	3.50
12b	Roy McMillan (557/1296 At Bat)	15.00	7.50	4.50
13	Paul Minner	10.00	5.00	3.00
14	Gerald Staley	10.00	5.00	3.00
15	Richie Ashburn	75.00	37.50	18.75
16	Jim Wilson	10.00	5.00	3.00
17	Tom Gorman	12.50	6.25	3.75
18	"Hoot" Evers	10.00	5.00	3.00
19	Bobby Shantz	10.00	5.00	3.00
20	Artie Houtteman	10.00	5.00	3.00
21	Vic Wertz	10.00	5.00	3.00
22a	Sam Mele (213/1661 Putouts)	12.00	6.00	3.50
22b	Sam Mele (217/1665 Putouts)	15.00	7.50	4.50
23	*Harvey Kuenn*	20.00	10.00	6.00
24	Bob Porterfield	10.00	5.00	3.00
25a	Wes Westrum (1.000/.987 Field Avg.)	12.00	6.00	3.50
25b	Wes Westrum (.982/.986 Field Avg.)	15.00	7.50	4.50
26a	Billy Cox (1.000/.960 Field Avg.)	15.00	7.50	4.50
26b	Billy Cox (.972/.960 Field Avg.)	20.00	10.00	6.00
27	Dick Cole	10.00	5.00	3.00
28a	Jim Greengrass (Birthplace Addison, N.J.)	20.00	10.00	6.00
28b	Jim Greengrass (Birthplace Addison, N.Y.)	12.00	6.00	3.50
29	Johnny Klippstein	10.00	5.00	3.00
30	Del Rice	10.00	5.00	3.00
31	"Smoky" Burgess	10.00	5.00	3.00
32	Del Crandall	10.00	5.00	3.00
33a	Vic Raschi (No trade line.)	27.50	13.50	8.25
33b	Vic Raschi (Traded line.)	50.00	25.00	15.00
34	Sammy White	10.00	5.00	3.00
35a	Eddie Joost (Quiz answer is 8.)	12.00	6.00	3.50
35b	Eddie Joost (Quiz answer is 33.)	15.00	7.50	4.50
36	George Strickland	10.00	5.00	3.00
37	Dick Kokos	10.00	5.00	3.00
38a	Minnie Minoso (.895/.961 Field Avg.)	25.00	12.50	7.50
38b	Minnie Minoso (.963/.963 Field Avg.)	30.00	15.00	9.00
39	Ned Garver	10.00	5.00	3.00
40	Gil Coan	10.00	5.00	3.00
41a	Alvin Dark (.986/.960 Field Avg.)	12.00	6.00	3.50
41b	Alvin Dark (.968/.960 Field Avg.)	15.00	7.50	4.50
42	Billy Loes	15.00	7.50	4.50
43a	Bob Friend (20 shutouts in quiz question)	12.00	6.00	3.50
43b	Bob Friend (16 shutouts in quiz question)	15.00	7.50	4.50
44	Harry Perkowski	10.00	5.00	3.00
45	Ralph Kiner	35.00	17.50	10.00
46	"Rip" Repulski	10.00	5.00	3.00
47a	Granny Hamner (.970/.953 Field Avg.)	12.00	6.00	3.50
47b	Granny Hamner (.953/.951 Field Avg.)	15.00	7.50	4.50
48	Jack Dittmer	10.00	5.00	3.00
49	Harry Byrd	12.50	6.25	3.75
50	George Kell	30.00	15.00	9.00
51	Alex Kellner	10.00	5.00	3.00
52	Joe Ginsberg	10.00	5.00	3.00
53a	Don Lenhardt (.969/.984 Field Avg.)	12.00	6.00	3.50
53b	Don Lenhardt (.966/.983 Field Avg.)	15.00	7.50	4.50
54	"Chico" Carrasquel	10.00	5.00	3.00
55	Jim Delsing	10.00	5.00	3.00
56	Maurice McDermott	10.00	5.00	3.00
57	Hoyt Wilhelm	27.50	13.50	8.25
58	Pee Wee Reese	100.00	50.00	25.00
59	Bob Schultz	10.00	5.00	3.00
60	Fred Baczewski	10.00	5.00	3.00
61a	Eddie Miksis (.954/.962 Field Avg.)	12.00	6.00	3.50
61b	Eddie Miksis (.954/.961 Field Avg.)	15.00	7.50	4.50
62	Enos Slaughter	35.00	17.50	10.00
63	Earl Torgeson	10.00	5.00	3.00
64	Eddie Mathews	80.00	40.00	20.00
65	Mickey Mantle	1,900	950.00	570.00
66a	Ted Williams	3,000	1,500	750.00
66b	Jimmy Piersall	75.00	37.50	18.75
67a	Carl Scheib (.306 Pct. with two lines under bio)	25.00	12.50	7.50
67b	Carl Scheib (.306 Pct. with one line under bio)	12.00	6.00	3.50
67c	Carl Scheib (.300 Pct.)	15.00	7.50	4.50
68	Bob Avila	10.00	5.00	3.00
69	Clinton Courtney	10.00	5.00	3.00
70	Willard Marshall	10.00	5.00	3.00

#	Player	NM	EX	VG
71	Ted Gray	10.00	5.00	3.00
72	Ed Yost	10.00	5.00	3.00
73	Don Mueller	10.00	5.00	3.00
74	Jim Gilliam	35.00	17.50	10.00
75	Max Surkont	10.00	5.00	3.00
76	Joe Nuxhall	10.00	5.00	3.00
77	Bob Rush	10.00	5.00	3.00
78	Sal Yvars	10.00	5.00	3.00
79	Curt Simmons	10.00	5.00	3.00
80a	Johnny Logan (106 Runs)	12.00	6.00	3.50
80b	Johnny Logan (100 Runs)	15.00	7.50	4.50
81a	Jerry Coleman (1.000/.975 Field Avg.)	15.00	7.50	4.50
81b	Jerry Coleman (.952/.975 Field Avg.)	20.00	10.00	6.00
82a	Bill Goodman (.965/.986 Field Avg.)	12.00	6.00	3.50
82b	Bill Goodman (.972/.985 Field Avg.)	15.00	7.50	4.50
83	Ray Murray	10.00	5.00	3.00
84	Larry Doby	45.00	22.50	13.50
85a	Jim Dyck (.926/.956 Field Avg.)	12.00	6.00	3.50
85b	Jim Dyck (.947/.960 Field Avg.)	15.00	7.50	4.50
86	Harry Dorish	10.00	5.00	3.00
87	Don Lund	10.00	5.00	3.00
88	Tommy Umphlett	10.00	5.00	3.00
89	Willie Mays	500.00	250.00	125.00
90	Roy Campanella	150.00	75.00	37.50
91	Cal Abrams	10.00	5.00	3.00
92	Ken Raffensberger	10.00	5.00	3.00
93a	Bill Serena (.983/.966 Field Avg.)	12.00	6.00	3.50
93b	Bill Serena (.977/.966 Field Avg.)	15.00	7.50	4.50
94a	Solly Hemus (476/1343 Assists)	12.00	6.00	3.50
94b	Solly Hemus (477/1343 Assists)	15.00	7.50	4.50
95	Robin Roberts	40.00	20.00	12.00
96	Joe Adcock	10.00	5.00	3.00
97	Gil McDougald	20.00	10.00	6.00
98	Ellis Kinder	10.00	5.00	3.00
99a	Peter Suder (.985/.974 Field Avg.)	12.00	6.00	3.50
99b	Peter Suder (.978/.974 Field Avg.)	15.00	7.50	4.50
100	Mike Garcia	10.00	5.00	3.00
101	*Don Larsen*	40.00	20.00	12.00
102	Bill Pierce	10.00	5.00	3.00
103a	Stephen Souchock (144/1192 Putouts)	12.00	6.00	3.50
103b	Stephen Souchock (147/1195 Putouts)	15.00	7.50	4.50
104	Frank Spec Shea	10.00	5.00	3.00
105a	Sal Maglie (Quiz answer is 8.)	20.00	10.00	6.00
105b	Sal Maglie (Quiz answer is 1904.)	30.00	15.00	9.00
106	Clem Labine	20.00	10.00	6.00
107	Paul LaPalme	10.00	5.00	3.00
108	Bobby Adams	10.00	5.00	3.00
109	Roy Smalley	10.00	5.00	3.00
110	Red Schoendienst	30.00	15.00	9.00
111	Murry Dickson	10.00	5.00	3.00
112	Andy Pafko	10.00	5.00	3.00
113	Allie Reynolds	20.00	10.00	6.00
114	Willard Nixon	10.00	5.00	3.00
115	Don Bollweg	10.00	5.00	3.00
116	Luke Easter	10.00	5.00	3.00
117	Dick Kryhoski	10.00	5.00	3.00
118	Bob Boyd	10.00	5.00	3.00
119	Fred Hatfield	10.00	5.00	3.00
120	Mel Hoderlein	10.00	5.00	3.00
121	Ray Katt	10.00	5.00	3.00
122	Carl Furillo	30.00	15.00	9.00
123	Toby Atwell	10.00	5.00	3.00
124a	Gus Bell (15/27 Errors)	12.00	6.00	3.50
124b	Gus Bell (11/26 Errors)	15.00	7.50	4.50
125	Warren Hacker	10.00	5.00	3.00
126	Cliff Chambers	10.00	5.00	3.00
127	Del Ennis	10.00	5.00	3.00
128	Ebba St. Claire	10.00	5.00	3.00
129	Hank Bauer	35.00	17.50	10.00
130	Milt Bolling	12.00	6.00	3.50
131	Joe Astroth	12.00	6.00	3.50
132	Bob Feller	75.00	37.50	18.75
133	Duane Pillette	12.00	6.00	3.50
134	Luis Aloma	12.00	6.00	3.50
135	Johnny Pesky	12.00	6.00	3.50
136	Clyde Vollmer	12.00	6.00	3.50
137	Al Corwin	12.00	6.00	3.50
138a	Gil Hodges (.993/.991 Field Avg.)	80.00	40.00	20.00
138b	Gil Hodges (.992/.991 Field Avg.)	100.00	50.00	30.00
139a	Preston Ward (.961/.992 Field Avg.)	15.00	7.50	4.50
139b	Preston Ward (.990/.992 Field Avg.)	17.50	8.75	5.25
140a	Saul Rogovin (7-12 Won/Lost with 2 Strikeouts)	15.00	7.50	4.50
140b	Saul Rogovin (7-12 Won/Lost with 62 Strikeouts)	17.50	8.75	5.25
140c	Saul Rogovin (8-12 Won/Lost)	40.00	20.00	12.00
141	Joe Garagiola	30.00	15.00	9.00
142	Al Brazle	12.00	6.00	3.50
143	Willie Jones	12.00	6.00	3.50
144	*Ernie Johnson*	30.00	15.00	9.00
145a	Billy Martin (.985/.983 Field Avg.)	80.00	40.00	20.00
145b	Billy Martin (.983/.982 Field Avg.)	90.00	45.00	25.00

#	Player	NM	EX	VG
146	Dick Gernert	12.00	6.00	3.50
147	Joe DeMaestri	12.00	6.00	3.50
148	Dale Mitchell	12.00	6.00	3.50
149	Bob Young	12.00	6.00	3.50
150	Cass Michaels	12.00	6.00	3.50
151	Pat Mullin	12.00	6.00	3.50
152	Mickey Vernon	12.00	6.00	3.50
153a	"Whitey" Lockman (100/331 Assists)	15.00	7.50	4.50
153b	"Whitey" Lockman (102/333 Assists)	17.50	8.75	5.25
154	Don Newcombe	50.00	25.00	12.50
155	*Frank Thomas*	25.00	12.50	7.50
156a	Rocky Bridges (320/467 Assists)	15.00	7.50	4.50
156b	Rocky Bridges (328/475 Assists)	17.50	8.75	5.25
157	Omar Lown	12.00	6.00	3.50
158	Stu Miller	12.00	6.00	3.50
159	John Lindell	12.00	6.00	3.50
160	Danny O'Connell	12.00	6.00	3.50
161	Yogi Berra	175.00	87.50	43.75
162	Ted Lepcio	12.00	6.00	3.50
163a	Dave Philley (152 Games, no traded line)	50.00	25.00	15.00
163b	Dave Philley (152 Games, traded line)	22.50	11.00	6.75
163c	Dave Philley (157 Games, traded line)	27.50	13.50	8.25
164	Early Wynn	45.00	22.50	13.50
165	Johnny Groth	12.00	6.00	3.50
166	Sandy Consuegra	12.00	6.00	3.50
167	Bill Hoeft	12.00	6.00	3.50
168	Edward Fitz Gerald	12.00	6.00	3.50
169	Larry Jansen	12.00	6.00	3.50
170	Duke Snider	240.00	120.00	60.00
171	Carlos Bernier	12.00	6.00	3.50
172	Andy Seminick	12.00	6.00	3.50
173	Dee Fondy	12.00	6.00	3.50
174a	Pete Castiglione (.966/.959 Field Avg.)	15.00	7.50	4.50
174b	Pete Castiglione (.970/.959 Field Avg.)	17.50	8.75	5.25
175	Mel Clark	12.00	6.00	3.50
176	Vernon Bickford	12.00	6.00	3.50
177	Whitey Ford	125.00	62.50	31.25
178	Del Wilber	12.00	6.00	3.50
179a	Morris Martin (44 ERA)	15.00	7.50	4.50
179b	Morris Martin (4.44 ERA)	17.50	8.75	5.25
180	Joe Tipton	12.00	6.00	3.50
181	Les Moss	12.00	6.00	3.50
182	Sherman Lollar	12.00	6.00	3.50
183	Matt Batts	12.00	6.00	3.50
184	Mickey Grasso	12.00	6.00	3.50
185a	*Daryl Spencer* (.941/.944 Field Avg.)	15.00	7.50	4.50
185b	*Daryl Spencer* (.933/.936 Field Avg.)	17.50	8.75	5.25
186	Russ Meyer	15.00	7.50	4.50
187	Vern Law	12.00	6.00	3.50
188	Frank Smith	12.00	6.00	3.50
189	Ransom Jackson	12.00	6.00	3.50
190	Joe Presko	12.00	6.00	3.50
191	Karl Drews	12.00	6.00	3.50
192	Lew Burdette	15.00	7.50	4.50
193	Eddie Robinson	12.00	6.00	3.50
194	Sid Hudson	12.00	6.00	3.50
195	Bob Cain	12.00	6.00	3.50
196	Bob Lemon	30.00	15.00	9.00
197	Lou Kretlow	12.00	6.00	3.50
198	Virgil Trucks	12.00	6.00	3.50
199	Steve Gromek	12.00	6.00	3.50
200	Connie Marrero	12.00	6.00	3.50
201	Bob Thomson	20.00	10.00	6.00
202	George Shuba	15.00	7.50	4.50
203	Vic Janowicz	25.00	12.50	7.50
204	Jack Collum	12.00	6.00	3.50
205	Hal Jeffcoat	12.00	6.00	3.50
206	Steve Bilko	12.00	6.00	3.50
207	Stan Lopata	12.00	6.00	3.50
208	Johnny Antonelli	12.00	6.00	3.50
209	Gene Woodling (Photo reversed.)	35.00	17.50	10.00
210	Jimmy Piersall	35.00	17.50	10.00
211	Jim Robertson	12.00	6.00	3.50
212a	Owen Friend (.964/.957 Field Avg.)	15.00	7.50	4.50
212b	Owen Friend (.967/.958 Field Avg.)	17.50	8.75	5.25
213	Dick Littlefield	12.00	6.00	3.50
214	Ferris Fain	12.00	6.00	3.50
215	Johnny Bucha	12.00	6.00	3.50
216a	Jerry Snyder (.988/.988 Field Avg.)	15.00	7.50	4.50
216b	Jerry Snyder (.968/.958 Field Avg.)	17.50	8.75	5.25
217a	Henry Thompson (.956/.951 Field Avg.)	15.00	7.50	4.50
217b	Henry Thompson (.958/.952 Field Avg.)	17.50	8.75	5.25
218	Preacher Roe	35.00	17.50	10.00
219	Hal Rice	12.00	6.00	3.50
220	Hobie Landrith	12.00	6.00	3.50
221	Frank Baumholtz	12.00	6.00	3.50
222	Memo Luna	15.00	7.50	4.50
223	Steve Ridzik	12.00	6.00	3.50
224	Billy Bruton	45.00	12.00	5.00

1955 Bowman

Bowman produced its final baseball card set as an independent card maker in 1955, a popular issue that has color player photographs placed inside a television set design. The set consists of 320 cards measuring 2-1/2" x 3-3/4". High-numbered cards (#225-320) appear to have replaced certain low-numbered cards on the press sheets and are scarcer. The high series includes 31 umpire cards.

#	Player	NM	EX	VG
	Complete Set (320):	7,000	3,500	2,000
	Common Player (1-224):	12.50	6.25	3.75
	Common Player (225-320):	25.00	12.50	7.50
1	Hoyt Wilhelm	100.00	50.00	25.00
2	Al Dark	15.00	7.50	4.50
3	Joe Coleman	12.50	6.25	3.75
4	Eddie Waitkus	12.50	6.25	3.75
5	Jim Robertson	12.50	6.25	3.75
6	Pete Suder	12.50	6.25	3.75
7	Gene Baker	12.50	6.25	3.75
8	Warren Hacker	12.50	6.25	3.75
9	Gil McDougald	25.00	12.50	7.50
10	Phil Rizzuto	125.00	62.50	31.25
11	Billy Bruton	12.50	6.25	3.75
12	Andy Pafko	12.50	6.25	3.75
13	Clyde Vollmer	12.50	6.25	3.75
14	Gus Keriazakos	12.50	6.25	3.75
15	*Frank Sullivan*	12.50	6.25	3.75
16	Jim Piersall	12.50	6.25	3.75
17	Del Ennis	12.50	6.25	3.75
18	Stan Lopata	12.50	6.25	3.75
19	Bobby Avila	12.50	6.25	3.75
20	Al Smith	12.50	6.25	3.75
21	Don Hoak	15.00	7.50	4.50
22	Roy Campanella	125.00	62.50	31.25
23	Al Kaline	150.00	75.00	37.50
24	Al Aber	12.50	6.25	3.75
25	Minnie Minoso	30.00	15.00	9.00
26	Virgil Trucks	12.50	6.25	3.75
27	Preston Ward	12.50	6.25	3.75
28	Dick Cole	12.50	6.25	3.75
29	Red Schoendienst	25.00	12.50	7.50
30	Bill Sarni	12.50	6.25	3.75
31	Johnny Temple	12.50	6.25	3.75
32	Wally Post	12.50	6.25	3.75
33	Nellie Fox	60.00	30.00	15.00
34	Clint Courtney	12.50	6.25	3.75
35	Bill Tuttle	12.50	6.25	3.75
36	Wayne Belardi	12.50	6.25	3.75
37	Pee Wee Reese	120.00	60.00	30.00
38	Early Wynn	25.00	12.50	7.50
39	Bob Darnell	15.00	7.50	4.50
40	Vic Wertz	12.50	6.25	3.75
41	Mel Clark	12.50	6.25	3.75
42	Bob Greenwood	12.50	6.25	3.75
43	Bob Buhl	12.50	6.25	3.75
44	Danny O'Connell	12.50	6.25	3.75
45	Tom Umphlett	12.50	6.25	3.75
46	Mickey Vernon	12.50	6.25	3.75
47	Sammy White	12.50	6.25	3.75
48a	Milt Bolling (Frank Bolling back.)	20.00	10.00	6.00
48b	Milt Bolling (Milt Bolling back.)	20.00	10.00	6.00
49	Jim Greengrass	12.50	6.25	3.75
50	Hobie Landrith	12.50	6.25	3.75
51	Elvin Tappe	12.50	6.25	3.75
52	Hal Rice	12.50	6.25	3.75
53	Alex Kellner	12.50	6.25	3.75
54	Don Bollweg	12.50	6.25	3.75
55	Cal Abrams	12.50	6.25	3.75
56	Billy Cox	12.50	6.25	3.75
57	Bob Friend	12.50	6.25	3.75
58	Frank Thomas	12.50	6.25	3.75
59	Whitey Ford	100.00	50.00	25.00
60	Enos Slaughter	30.00	15.00	9.00
61	Paul LaPalme	12.50	6.25	3.75
62	Royce Lint	12.50	6.25	3.75
63	Irv Noren	15.00	7.50	4.50
64	Curt Simmons	12.50	6.25	3.75
65	*Don Zimmer*	30.00	15.00	9.00
66	George Shuba	15.00	7.50	4.50
67	Don Larsen	30.00	15.00	9.00
68	*Elston Howard*	80.00	40.00	24.00
69	Bill Hunter	15.00	7.50	4.50
70	Lew Burdette	12.50	6.25	3.75
71	Dave Jolly	12.50	6.25	3.75
72	Chet Nichols	12.50	6.25	3.75
73	Eddie Yost	12.50	6.25	3.75
74	Jerry Snyder	12.50	6.25	3.75
75	Brooks Lawrence	12.50	6.25	3.75
76	Tom Poholsky	12.50	6.25	3.75
77	Jim McDonald	12.50	6.25	3.75
78	Gil Coan	12.50	6.25	3.75
79	Willie Miranda	12.50	6.25	3.75
80	Lou Limmer	12.50	6.25	3.75
81	Bob Morgan	12.50	6.25	3.75
82	Lee Walls	12.50	6.25	3.75
83	Max Surkont	12.50	6.25	3.75
84	George Freese	12.50	6.25	3.75
85	Cass Michaels	12.50	6.25	3.75
86	Ted Gray	12.50	6.25	3.75
87	Randy Jackson	12.50	6.25	3.75
88	Steve Bilko	12.50	6.25	3.75
89	Lou Boudreau	25.00	12.50	7.50
90	Art Ditmar	12.50	6.25	3.75
91	Dick Marlowe	12.50	6.25	3.75

#	Player	NM	EX	VG
92	George Zuverink	12.50	6.25	3.75
93	Andy Seminick	12.50	6.25	3.75
94	Hank Thompson	12.50	6.25	3.75
95	Sal Maglie	12.50	6.25	3.75
96	Ray Narleski	12.50	6.25	3.75
97	John Podres	30.00	15.00	8.25
98	Jim Gilliam	27.50	13.50	8.25
99	Jerry Coleman	15.00	7.50	4.50
100	Tom Morgan	15.00	7.50	4.50
101a	Don Johnson (Ernie Johnson (Braves) on front.)	60.00	30.00	18.00
101b	Don Johnson (Don Johnson (Orioles) on front.)	27.50	13.50	8.25
102	Bobby Thomson	17.50	8.75	5.25
103	Eddie Mathews	80.00	40.00	20.00
104	Bob Porterfield	12.50	6.25	3.75
105	Johnny Schmitz	12.50	6.25	3.75
106	Del Rice	12.50	6.25	3.75
107	Solly Hemus	12.50	6.25	3.75
108	Lou Kretlow	12.50	6.25	3.75
109	Vern Stephens	12.50	6.25	3.75
110	Bob Miller	12.50	6.25	3.75
111	Steve Ridzik	12.50	6.25	3.75
112	Granny Hamner	12.50	6.25	3.75
113	Bob Hall	12.50	6.25	3.75
114	Vic Janowicz	12.50	6.25	3.75
115	Roger Bowman	12.50	6.25	3.75
116	Sandy Consuegra	12.50	6.25	3.75
117	Johnny Groth	12.50	6.25	3.75
118	Bobby Adams	12.50	6.25	3.75
119	Joe Astroth	12.50	6.25	3.75
120	Ed Burtschy	12.50	6.25	3.75
121	Rufus Crawford	12.50	6.25	3.75
122	Al Corwin	12.50	6.25	3.75
123	Marv Grissom	12.50	6.25	3.75
124	Johnny Antonelli	12.50	6.25	3.75
125	Paul Giel	12.50	6.25	3.75
126	Billy Goodman	12.50	6.25	3.75
127	Hank Majeski	12.50	6.25	3.75
128	Mike Garcia	12.50	6.25	3.75
129	Hal Naragon	12.50	6.25	3.75
130	Richie Ashburn	50.00	25.00	15.00
131	Willard Marshall	12.50	6.25	3.75
132a	Harvey Kueen (Misspelled last name.)	25.00	12.50	7.50
132b	Harvey Kuenn (Corrected)	35.00	17.50	10.00
133	Charles King	12.50	6.25	3.75
134	Bob Feller	80.00	40.00	20.00
135	Lloyd Merriman	12.50	6.25	3.75
136	Rocky Bridges	12.50	6.25	3.75
137	Bob Talbot	12.50	6.25	3.75
138	Davey Williams	12.50	6.25	3.75
139	Billy & Bobby Shantz	15.00	7.50	4.50
140	Bobby Shantz	12.50	6.25	3.75
141	Wes Westrum	12.50	6.25	3.75
142	Rudy Regalado	12.50	6.25	3.75
143	Don Newcombe	25.00	12.50	7.50
144	Art Houtteman	12.50	6.25	3.75
145	Bob Nieman	12.50	6.25	3.75
146	Don Liddle	12.50	6.25	3.75
147	Sam Mele	12.50	6.25	3.75
148	Bob Chakales	12.50	6.25	3.75
149	Cloyd Boyer	12.50	6.25	3.75
150	Bill Klaus	12.50	6.25	3.75
151	Jim Brideweser	12.50	6.25	3.75
152	Johnny Klippstein	12.50	6.25	3.75
153	Eddie Robinson	15.00	7.50	4.50
154	*Frank Lary*	12.50	6.25	3.75
155	Gerry Staley	12.50	6.25	3.75
156	Jim Hughes	15.00	7.50	4.50
157a	Ernie Johnson (Don Johnson (Orioles) picture on front.)	15.00	7.50	4.50
157b	Ernie Johnson (Ernie Johnson (Braves) picture on front.)	30.00	15.00	9.00
158	Gil Hodges	40.00	20.00	12.00
159	Harry Byrd	12.50	6.25	3.75
160	Bill Skowron	40.00	20.00	12.00
161	Matt Batts	12.50	6.25	3.75
162	Charlie Maxwell	12.50	6.25	3.75
163	Sid Gordon	12.50	6.25	3.75
164	Toby Atwell	12.50	6.25	3.75
165	Maurice McDermott	12.50	6.25	3.75
166	Jim Busby	12.50	6.25	3.75
167	Bob Grim	15.00	7.50	4.50
168	Yogi Berra	125.00	62.50	31.25
169	Carl Furillo	27.50	13.50	8.25
170	Carl Erskine	25.00	12.50	7.50
171	Robin Roberts	32.50	16.00	10.00
172	Willie Jones	12.50	6.25	3.75
173	"Chico" Carrasquel	12.50	6.25	3.75
174	Sherman Lollar	12.50	6.25	3.75
175	Wilmer Shantz	12.50	6.25	3.75
176	Joe DeMaestri	12.50	6.25	3.75
177	Willard Nixon	12.50	6.25	3.75
178	Tom Brewer	12.50	6.25	3.75
179	Hank Aaron	300.00	150.00	75.00
180	Johnny Logan	12.50	6.25	3.75
181	Eddie Miksis	12.50	6.25	3.75
182	Bob Rush	12.50	6.25	3.75
183	Ray Katt	12.50	6.25	3.75
184	Willie Mays	275.00	137.50	68.75
185	Vic Raschi	12.50	6.25	3.75
186	Alex Grammas	12.50	6.25	3.75
187	Fred Hatfield	12.50	6.25	3.75
188	Ned Garver	12.50	6.25	3.75
189	Jack Collum	12.50	6.25	3.75
190	Fred Baczewski	12.50	6.25	3.75
191	Bob Lemon	30.00	15.00	9.00
192	George Strickland	12.50	6.25	3.75
193	Howie Judson	12.50	6.25	3.75
194	Joe Nuxhall	12.50	6.25	3.75
195a	Erv Palica (No traded line.)	30.00	15.00	9.00
195b	Erv Palica (Traded line.)	125.00	60.00	35.00
196	Russ Meyer	15.00	7.50	4.50
197	Ralph Kiner	35.00	17.50	10.00
198	Dave Pope	12.50	6.25	3.75
199	Vernon Law	12.50	6.25	3.75

200	Dick Littlefield	12.50	6.25	3.75
201	Allie Reynolds	25.00	12.50	7.50
202	Mickey Mantle	675.00	335.00	200.00
203	Steve Gromek	12.50	6.25	3.75
204a	Frank Bolling	45.00	22.50	13.50
	(Milt Bolling back.)			
204b	Frank Bolling	30.00	15.00	9.00
	(Frank Bolling back.)			
205	"Rip" Repulski	12.50	6.25	3.75
206	Ralph Beard	12.50	6.25	3.75
207	Frank Shea	12.50	6.25	3.75
208	Ed Fitz Gerald	12.50	6.25	3.75
209	"Smoky" Burgess	12.50	6.25	3.75
210	Earl Torgeson	12.50	6.25	3.75
211	John "Sonny" Dixon	12.50	6.25	3.75
212	Jack Dittmer	12.50	6.25	3.75
213	George Kell	30.00	15.00	9.00
214	Billy Pierce	12.50	6.25	3.75
215	Bob Kuzava	12.50	6.25	3.75
216	Preacher Roe	15.00	7.50	4.50
217	Del Crandall	12.50	6.25	3.75
218	Joe Adcock	12.50	6.25	3.75
219	"Whitey" Lockman	12.50	6.25	3.75
220	Jim Hearn	12.50	6.25	3.75
221	Hector "Skinny" Brown	12.50	6.25	3.75
222	Russ Kemmerer	12.50	6.25	3.75
223	Hal Jeffcoat	12.50	6.25	3.75
224	Dee Fondy	12.50	6.25	3.75
225	Paul Richards	25.00	12.50	7.50
226	W.F. McKinley (Umpire)	30.00	15.00	9.00
227	Frank Baumholtz	25.00	12.50	7.50
228	John M. Phillips	25.00	12.50	7.50
229	Jim Brosnan	25.00	12.50	7.50
230	Al Brazle	25.00	12.50	7.50
231	Jim Konstanty	25.00	12.50	7.50
232	Birdie Tebbetts	25.00	12.50	7.50
233	Bill Serena	25.00	12.50	7.50
234	Dick Bartell	25.00	12.50	7.50
235	J.A. Paparella (Umpire)	30.00	15.00	9.00
236	Murry Dickson	25.00	12.50	7.50
237	Johnny Wyrostek	25.00	12.50	7.50
238	Eddie Stanky	25.00	12.50	7.50
239	Edwin A. Rommel (Umpire)	30.00	15.00	9.00
240	Billy Loes	25.00	12.50	7.50
241	John Pesky	25.00	12.50	7.50
242	Ernie Banks	350.00	175.00	87.50
243	Gus Bell	25.00	12.50	7.50
244	Duane Pillette	25.00	12.50	7.50
245	Bill Miller	25.00	12.50	7.50
246	Hank Bauer	45.00	22.50	13.50
247	Dutch Leonard	25.00	12.50	7.50
248	Harry Dorish	25.00	12.50	7.50
249	Billy Gardner	25.00	12.50	7.50
250	Larry Napp (Umpire)	30.00	15.00	9.00
251	Stan Jok	25.00	12.50	7.50
252	Roy Smalley	25.00	12.50	7.50
253	Jim Wilson	25.00	12.50	7.50
254	Bennett Flowers	25.00	12.50	7.50
255	Pete Runnels	25.00	12.50	7.50
256	Owen Friend	25.00	12.50	7.50
257	Tom Alston	25.00	12.50	7.50
258	John W. Stevens (Umpire)	30.00	15.00	9.00
259	*Don Mossi*	35.00	17.50	10.00
260	Edwin H. Hurley (Umpire)	30.00	15.00	9.00
261	Walt Moryn	25.00	12.50	7.50
262	Jim Lemon	25.00	12.50	7.50
263	Eddie Joost	25.00	12.50	7.50
264	Bill Henry	25.00	12.50	7.50
265	Al Barlick (Umpire)	60.00	30.00	15.00
266	Mike Fornieles	25.00	12.50	7.50
267	George Honochick (Umpire)	50.00	25.00	15.00
268	Roy Lee Hawes	25.00	12.50	7.50
269	Joe Amalfitano	25.00	12.50	7.50
270	Chico Fernandez	25.00	12.50	7.50
271	Bob Hooper	25.00	12.50	7.50
272	John Flaherty (Umpire)	30.00	15.00	9.00
273	"Bubba" Church	25.00	12.50	7.50
274	Jim Delsing	25.00	12.50	7.50
275	William T. Grieve (Umpire)	30.00	15.00	9.00
276	Ike Delock	25.00	12.50	7.50
277	Ed Runge (Umpire)	30.00	15.00	9.00
278	*Charles Neal*	35.00	17.50	10.00
279	Hank Soar (Umpire)	30.00	15.00	9.00
280	Clyde McCullough	25.00	12.50	7.50
281	Charles Berry (Umpire)	30.00	15.00	9.00
282	Phil Cavarretta	25.00	12.50	7.50
283	Nestor Chylak (Umpire)	60.00	30.00	15.00
284	William A. Jackowski (Umpire)	30.00	15.00	9.00
285	Walt Dropo	25.00	12.50	7.50
286	Frank Secory (Umpire)	30.00	15.00	9.00
287	Ron Mrozinski	25.00	12.50	7.50
288	Dick Smith	25.00	12.50	7.50
289	Art Gore (Umpire)	30.00	15.00	9.00
290	Hershell Freeman	25.00	12.50	7.50
291	Frank Dascoli (Umpire)	30.00	15.00	9.00
292	Marv Blaylock	25.00	12.50	7.50
293	Thomas D. Gorman (Umpire)	30.00	15.00	9.00
294	Wally Moses	25.00	12.50	7.50
295	Lee Ballanfant (Umpire)	30.00	15.00	9.00
296	*Bill Virdon*	30.00	15.00	9.00
297	"Dusty" Boggess (Umpire)	30.00	15.00	9.00
298	Charlie Grimm	25.00	12.50	7.50
299	Lonnie Warneke (Umpire)	30.00	15.00	9.00
300	Tommy Byrne	30.00	15.00	9.00
301	William Engeln (Umpire)	30.00	15.00	9.00
302	*Frank Malzone*	30.00	15.00	9.00
303	Jocko Conlan (Umpire)	60.00	30.00	15.00
304	Harry Chiti	25.00	12.50	7.50
305	Frank Umont (Umpire)	30.00	15.00	9.00
306	Bob Cerv	30.00	15.00	9.00
307	"Babe" Pinelli (Umpire)	25.00	12.50	7.50
308	Al Lopez	35.00	17.50	10.00
309	Hal Dixon (Umpire)	30.00	15.00	9.00
310	Ken Lehman	30.00	15.00	9.00
311	Larry Goetz (Umpire)	30.00	15.00	9.00
312	Bill Wight	25.00	12.50	7.50
313	Augie Donatelli (Umpire)	30.00	15.00	9.00
314	Dale Mitchell	25.00	12.50	7.50

315	Cal Hubbard (Umpire)	60.00	30.00	18.00
316	Marion Fricano	25.00	12.50	7.50
317	Bill Summers (Umpire)	30.00	15.00	9.00
318	Sid Hudson	25.00	12.50	7.50
319	Al Schroll	25.00	12.50	7.50
320	George Susce, Jr.	60.00	30.00	15.00

1956 Bowman Prototypes

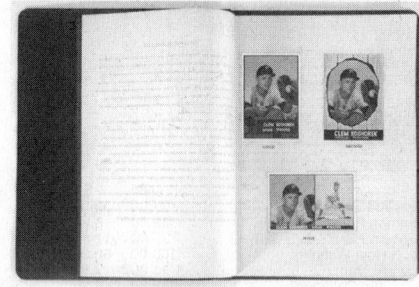

To gauge consumer demand for a 1956 baseball card set that it never issued, Bowman produced a "Baseball Card Preference Study" report. The report survives today in the form of a 24-page notebook that includes samples of the three designs apparently preferred by the pre-teen boys surveyed. All three cards are glued to one page of the report and all feature the photo of Pirates catcher Clem Koshorek used in the 1953 Bowman set. It is believed only two of the reports survive.

(Sold for $10,440 in 5/05 auction.)

1963 George Brace All Time Chicago Cubs

The year of issue attributed here is only theoretical. The set consists of a window envelope which contains 18 5-1/4" x 7" black-and-white photos of former Cubs greats by famed Chicago baseball photographer George Brace. The blank-backed unnumbered pictures have player identification in the white border at bottom. They are checklisted here alphabetically.

		NM	EX	VG
Complete Set (18):		50.00	25.00	15.00
Common Player:		7.50	3.75	2.25
(1)	Grover Cleveland Alexander	10.00	5.00	3.00
(2)	Cap Anson	10.00	5.00	3.00
(3)	Three Finger Brown	9.00	4.50	2.75
(4)	Frank Chance	9.00	4.50	2.75
(5)	Johnny Evers	9.00	4.50	2.75
(6)	Charlie Grimm	7.50	3.75	2.25
(7)	Stan Hack	7.50	3.75	2.25
(8)	Gabby Hartnett	7.50	3.75	2.25
(9)	Billy Herman	7.50	3.75	2.25
(10)	Charlie Hollocher	7.50	3.75	2.25
(11)	Billy Jurges	7.50	3.75	2.25
(12)	Johnny Kling	7.50	3.75	2.25
(13)	Joe McCarthy	7.50	3.75	2.25
(14)	Ed Reulbach	7.50	3.75	2.25
(15)	Albert Spalding	7.50	3.75	2.25
(16)	Joe Tinker	9.00	4.50	2.75
(17)	Hippo Vaughn	7.50	3.75	2.25
(18)	Hack Wilson	9.00	4.50	2.75

1974 Bramac 1933 National League All-Stars

This early collectors issue features black-and-white photos of the premiere N.L. All-Star team in their distinctive game uniforms. Cards are in a 2-1/2" x 3-1/4" format.

	NM	EX	VG
Complete Set (18):	30.00	15.00	9.00
Common Player:	6.00	3.00	1.75

1	Paul Waner	6.00	3.00	1.75
2	Woody English	6.00	3.00	1.75
3	Dick Bartell	6.00	3.00	1.75
4	Chuck Klein	6.00	3.00	1.75
5	Tony Cuccinello	6.00	3.00	1.75
6	Lefty O'Doul	6.00	3.00	1.75
7	Gabby Hartnett	6.00	3.00	1.75
8	Lon Warneke	6.00	3.00	1.75
9	Wally Berger	6.00	3.00	1.75
10	Chick Hafey	6.00	3.00	1.75
11	Frank Frisch	6.00	3.00	1.75
12	Carl Hubbell	6.00	3.00	1.75
13	Bill Hallahan	6.00	3.00	1.75
14	Hal Schumacher	6.00	3.00	1.75
15	Pie Traynor	6.00	3.00	1.75
16	Bill Terry	6.00	3.00	1.75
17	Pepper Martin	6.00	3.00	1.75
18	Jimmy Wilson	6.00	3.00	1.75

1908-11 H.H. Bregstone Browns/Cardinals Post Cards (PC743)

Among the rarest of the early 20th Century baseball player postcards are those of the the St. Louis Browns and Cardinals from H.H. Bregstone, also of St. Louis. The 3-1/2" x 5-1/2" cards feature sepia player photos that are borderless at top and sides. At bottom is a box with the player's name, team, position, league and the issuer's address. Backs are standard postcard format. The unnumbered cards are checklisted here alphabetically within team. With a single exception (Gregory), all of the Browns players are from 1909, while the range of Cardinals spans the era 1908-1911.

		NM	EX	VG
Complete Set, Browns (22):		9,500	4,750	2,750
Complete Set, Cardinals (34):		18,000	9,000	5,500
Common Player:		500.00	250.00	150.00
ST. LOUIS BROWNS				
(1)	Bill Bailey	500.00	250.00	150.00
(2)	Lou Criger	500.00	250.00	150.00
(3)	Dode Criss	500.00	250.00	150.00
(4)	Bill Dineen	500.00	250.00	150.00
(5)	Hobe Ferris	500.00	250.00	150.00
(6)	Bill Graham	500.00	250.00	150.00
(7)	B Gregory	500.00	250.00	150.00
(8)	Art Griggs	500.00	250.00	150.00
(9)	Roy Hartzell	500.00	250.00	150.00
(10)	Danny Hoffman	500.00	250.00	150.00
(11)	Harry Howell	500.00	250.00	150.00
(12)	Tom Jones	500.00	250.00	150.00
(13)	Jimmy McAleer	500.00	250.00	150.00
(14)	Ham Patterson	500.00	250.00	150.00
(15)	Barney Pelty	500.00	250.00	150.00
(16)	Al Schweitzer	500.00	250.00	150.00
(17)	Wib Smith	500.00	250.00	150.00
(18)	Jim Stephens	500.00	250.00	150.00
(19)	George Stone	500.00	250.00	150.00
(20)	Rube Waddell	750.00	375.00	225.00
(21)	Bobby Wallace	750.00	375.00	225.00
(22)	Jimmy Williams	500.00	250.00	150.00
ST. LOUIS CARDINALS				
(1)	Jap Barbeau	500.00	250.00	150.00
(2)	Shad Barry	500.00	250.00	150.00
(3)	Fred Beebe	500.00	250.00	150.00
(4)	Frank Betcher	500.00	250.00	150.00
(5)	Jack Bliss	500.00	250.00	150.00
(6)	Roger Bresnahan	800.00	400.00	240.00
(7)	Bobby Byrne	500.00	250.00	150.00
(8)	Chappie Charles	500.00	250.00	150.00
(9)	Frank Corridon	500.00	250.00	150.00
(10)	Joe Delahanty	700.00	350.00	210.00
(11)	Rube Ellis	500.00	250.00	150.00
(12)	Steve Evans	500.00	250.00	150.00
(13)	Art Fromme	500.00	250.00	150.00
(14)	Rube Geyer	500.00	250.00	150.00
(15)	Billy Gilbert	500.00	250.00	150.00
(16)	Bob Harmon	500.00	250.00	150.00
(17)	Irv Higginbotham	500.00	250.00	150.00
(18)	Tom Higgins	500.00	250.00	150.00
(19)	Art Hoelskoetter	500.00	250.00	150.00
(20)	Miller Huggins	750.00	375.00	225.00
(21)	Rudy Hulswitt	500.00	250.00	150.00
(22)	Adam Johnson	500.00	250.00	150.00
(23)	Ed Konetchy	500.00	250.00	150.00
(24)	Johnny Lush	500.00	250.00	150.00
(25)	Lee Magee	500.00	250.00	150.00
(26)	Stoney McGlynn	500.00	250.00	150.00
(27)	Rebel Oakes	500.00	250.00	150.00
(28)	Bill O'Hara	500.00	250.00	150.00
(29)	Patsy O'Rourke	500.00	250.00	150.00
(30)	Ed Phelps	500.00	250.00	150.00

		NM	EX	VG
(31)	Charlie Rhodes	500.00	250.00	150.00
(32)	Elmer Rieger	500.00	250.00	150.00
(33)	Slim Sallee	500.00	250.00	150.00
(34)	Vic Willis	750.00	375.00	225.00

1903-1904 Breisch-Williams

Many veteran collectors now believe that Breisch Williams Confectionary Co. of Oxford, Pa., was just one of several firms that used the black-and-white card issue cataloged as E107 as a premium. A relatively small percentage of E107s are found with a purple rubber-stamped "THE BREISCH- WILLIAMS CO" message diagonally on back. It is speculated the stamp may have been used to "cancel" cards there were returned in a prize redemption program. The overprinted cards currently carry a premium of 2-3X the value of blank-backed or "One of a ..." E107s. With only a single known exception, all Breisch-Williams stamped cards are of Type 1.

(See E107 Type 1 and Type 2 for checklist and base value information.)

1909-10 C.A. Briggs Co. (E97)

CY. YOUNG, BOSTON, NAT'L.

This card is one of a set of 30 BALL PLAYERS Cards, as follows :
AUSTIN, New York American
BRADLEY, Cleveland American
BIRMINGHAM, Cleveland American
BRANSFIELD, Philadelphia National
CARRIGAN, Boston American
CAMNITZ, Pittsburg National
DURHAM, New York American
DYGERT, Philadelphia American
DOOLAN, Philadelphia National
DEVORE, New York National
DAVIS, Philadelphia American
HEMPHILL, New York American
HEINCHMAN, Cleveland American
HARTSEL, Philadelphia American
KROH, Chicago National
KLEINOW, New York American
KELLY, Boston National
KEELER, New York National
McINTYRE, Detroit American
McCONNELL, Boston American
MOORE, Philadelphia National
MULLIN, Detroit American
MURRAY, New York National
MEYERS, New York National
NICHOLS, Cleveland American
ROSSMAN, Detroit American
SULLIVAN, Chicago American
STEINFELDT, Chicago National
SCHLEI, New York National
CY. YOUNG, Cleveland American
C.A. BRIGGS CO., Lozenge Makers
Boston, Mass.

Measuring approximately 1-1/2" x 2-3/4", this set is nearly identical to several other candy issues of the same period. Designated as E97 in the American Card Catalog, the set was issued in 1909-1910 by "C.A. Briggs Co., Lozenge Makers of Boston, Mass." The front of the card shows a tinted player photo, with the player's last name, position and team printed below. Backs are printed in brown and checklist the 30 players in the set alphabetically. The C.A. Briggs Co. name appears at the bottom. Black-and-white examples of this set have also been found on a thin paper stock with blank backs and are believed to be "proof cards." They are valued about 2-3X the figures shown here. Five variations are also found in the set. The more expensive variations are not included in the complete set price.

		NM	EX	VG
Complete Set (30):		60,000	24,000	12,000
Common Player:		2,500	1,000	500.00
Proofs: 2-3X				
(1)	Jimmy Austin	2,500	1,000	500.00
(2)	Joe Birmingham	2,500	1,000	500.00
(3)	Bill Bradley	2,500	1,000	500.00
(4)	Kitty Bransfield	2,500	1,000	500.00
(5)	Howie Camnitz	2,500	1,000	500.00
(6)	Bill Carrigan	2,500	1,000	500.00
(7)	Harry Davis	750.00	1,000	500.00
(8)	Josh Devore	2,500	1,000	500.00
(9a)	Mickey Dolan (Doolan)	2,500	1,000	500.00
(9b)	Mickey Doolan	2,500	1,000	500.00
(10)	Bull Durham	2,500	1,000	500.00
(11)	Jimmy Dygert	2,500	1,000	500.00
(12a)	Topsy Hartsell (Hartsel)	4,000	1,500	750.00
(12b)	Topsy Hartsel	2,500	1,000	500.00
(13)	Bill Heinchman (Hinchman)	2,500	1,000	500.00
(14)	Charlie Hemphill	2,500	1,000	500.00
(15)	Wee Willie Keeler	8,000	3,200	1,600
(16)	Joe Kelly (Kelley)	8,000	3,200	1,600
(17)	Red Kleinow	2,500	1,000	500.00
(18)	Rube Kroh	2,500	1,000	500.00
(19)	Matty McIntyre	2,500	1,000	500.00
(20)	Amby McConnell	2,500	1,000	500.00
(21)	Chief Meyers	2,500	1,000	500.00
(22)	Earl Moore	2,500	1,000	500.00
(23)	George Mullin	2,500	1,000	500.00
(24)	Red Murray	2,500	1,000	500.00
(25a)	Simon Nichols (Nicholls) (Philadelphia)	10,000	5,000	2,000
(25b)	Simon Nichols (Nicholls) (Cleveland)	4,000	1,500	750.00
(26)	Claude Rossman	4,000	1,500	750.00
(27)	Admiral Schlei	2,500	1,000	500.00
(28a)	Harry Steinfeld (Name incorrect.)	4,400	1,800	900.00
(28b)	Harry Steinfeldt (Name correct.)	4,400	1,800	900.00
(29a)	Dennis Sullivan (Chicago)	2,500	1,000	500.00
(29b)	Dennis Sullivan (Boston)	20,000	12,000	6,000
(30a)	Cy. Young (Cleveland) (Picture actually Irv Young.)	15,000	6,000	3,000
(30b)	Cy. Young (Boston) (Picture actually Irv Young.)	20,000	12,000	6,000

1933 C.A. Briggs Co. Babe Ruth

Stars in a variety of sports are featured in this series of candy issues. Card #24 has a drawing on front against a red background. The player bears more than a passing resemblance to Babe Ruth and on the back of the 2-3/8" x 2-7/8"

card, along with a short history of baseball, Babe Ruth and his $52,000 contract for 1933 are mentioned. At bottom are details for redeeming a set of the 31 cards for baseball equipment or a pound of chocolates.

		NM	EX	VG
24	Baseball (Babe Ruth)	1,000	500.00	300.00

1953-54 Briggs Meats

The Briggs Meat set was issued over a two-year span (1953-54) and features 28 players from the Washington Senators and 12 from the New York teams. The set was issued in two-card panels on hot dog packages sold in the Washington, D.C. vicinity. The color cards, which are blank-backed and measure 2-1/4" x 3-1/2", are printed on waxed cardboard. Pictures of the New York players can also be found on cards in the 1954 Dan-Dee Potato Chips and 1953-1955 Stahl-Meyer Franks sets. There is a slight difference in style between the Senators cards and those of the New York players. The white panel beneath the photo of the Washington players includes a facsimile autograph plus a few biographical details about the player. The New York players' cards have only the player's name and facsimile signature in that panel. Several of the Senators cards command a premium for scarcity.

		NM	EX	VG
Complete Set (40):		35,000	17,500	7,000
Common Player:		900.00	450.00	180.00
(1)	Hank Bauer	1,000	500.00	200.00
(2)	James Busby	900.00	450.00	180.00
(3)	Tommy Byrne	900.00	450.00	180.00
(4)	Gil Coan	900.00	450.00	180.00
(5)	John Dixon	900.00	450.00	180.00
(6)	Carl Erskine	1,000	500.00	200.00
(7)	Edward Fitzgerald (Fitz Gerald)	900.00	450.00	180.00
(8)	Newton Grasso	900.00	450.00	180.00
(9)	Melvin Hoderlein	900.00	450.00	180.00
(10)	Gil Hodges	1,500	750.00	300.00
(11)	Monte Irvin	1,000	500.00	200.00
(12)	Jackie Jensen	950.00	475.00	190.00
(13)	Whitey Lockman	900.00	450.00	180.00
(14)	Mickey Mantle	7,500	3,750	1,500
(15)	Conrado Marrero	900.00	450.00	180.00
(16)	Walter Masterson	900.00	450.00	180.00
(17)	Carmen Mauro	900.00	450.00	180.00
(18)	Willie Mays	4,500	2,250	900.00
(19)	Mickey McDermott	900.00	450.00	180.00
(20)	Gil McDougald	1,000	500.00	200.00
(21)	Julio Moreno	900.00	450.00	180.00
(22)	Don Mueller	900.00	450.00	180.00
(23)	Don Newcombe	1,000	500.00	200.00
(24)	Robert Oldis	900.00	450.00	180.00
(25)	Erwin Porterfield	900.00	450.00	180.00
(26)	Phil Rizzuto	1,200	600.00	240.00
(27)	James Runnels	900.00	450.00	180.00
(28)	John Schmitz	900.00	450.00	180.00
(29)	Angel Scull	900.00	450.00	180.00
(30)	Frank Shea	900.00	450.00	180.00
(31)	Albert Sima	900.00	450.00	180.00
(32)	Duke Snider	1,800	900.00	360.00
(33)	Charles Stobbs	900.00	450.00	180.00
(34)	Willard Terwilliger	900.00	450.00	180.00
(35)	Joe Tipton	900.00	450.00	180.00
(36)	Thomas Umphlett	900.00	450.00	180.00
(37)	Gene Verble	900.00	450.00	180.00
(38)	James Vernon	900.00	450.00	180.00
(39)	Clyde Vollmer	900.00	450.00	180.00
(40)	Edward Yost	900.00	450.00	180.00

1947 Brillantina Sol de Oro Managers

The approximately 6" x 8" black-and-white pictures were issued in conjunction with a contest run by an Havana shampoo company. Fronts have photos of the managers of Cuba's four professional teams, bordered in white, with a facsimile

autograph and message. A sponsor's credit line is in the bottom margin. Backs have further promotional copy for the shampoo and rules of the contest.

		NM	EX	VG
Complete Set (4):		600.00	300.00	180.00
Common Player:		150.00	75.00	45.00
(1)	Salvador Hernandez	150.00	75.00	45.00
(2)	Adolfo Luque	250.00	125.00	75.00
(3)	Napoleon Reyes	200.00	100.00	60.00
(4)	Lazaro Salazar	150.00	75.00	45.00

1909-12 Broad Leaf Cigarettes

Cards with the Broad Leaf brand advertising on back can be found among the three most popular cigarette card issues circa 1910: T205 Gold Border, T206 White Border and T207 Brown Background. Two types are seen in T206, one that mentions "350 Subjects" and another, much rarer, that mentions "460 Subjects." Because some of the scarcer cards in T207 are often found with Broadleaf (as it was then spelled) backs, it is not practical to quote a value multiplier; premiums for such cards have already been factored into the prices under T207. In T205, Broad Leaf backs can be found printed in either black or brown-olive green.

PREMIUMS:
T205: 5X
T206 350 Subjects: 9-12X
T206 460 Subjects, Common: 50-60X
T206 460 Subjects, HoF: 15-25X
(See T205, T206, T207 for checklists.)

1974 Broder N.Y. Mets Tour of Japan

Veteran collector Ed Broder who was stationed with the U.S. Army in Japan, produced this collectors' issue chronicling the goodwill tour undertaken by the National League Champion N.Y. Mets. Nominally measuring about 1-7/8" x 3", cards have borderless black-and-white photos on front with no player identification or other graphics. Backs have player name, team and "1974 New York Mets Tour of Japan" in typewriter font along with a team logo. The unnumbered cards are checklisted here alphabetically.

		NM	EX	VG
Complete Set (20):		60.00	30.00	18.00
Common Player:		4.00	2.00	1.25
(1)	Yogi Berra	20.00	10.00	6.00
(2)	Wayne Garrett	8.00	4.00	2.50

		NM	EX	VG
(3)	Ron Hodges	8.00	4.00	2.50
(4)	Tsuneo Horiuchi	8.00	4.00	2.50
(5)	Kazumasa Kono	4.00	2.00	1.25
(6)	Jerry Koosman	8.00	4.00	2.50
(7)	Ed Kranepool, John Milner, unidentified Japanese player, Joe Torre	4.00	2.00	1.25
(8)	Jon Matlack	8.00	4.00	2.50
(9)	Felix Millan	8.00	4.00	2.50
(10)	John Milner	8.00	4.00	2.50
(11)	Shigeo Nagashima	10.00	5.00	3.00
(12)	Sadaharu Oh	15.00	7.50	4.50
(13)	Tom Seaver	40.00	20.00	12.00
(14)	Yososhi Sekimoto	4.00	2.00	1.25
(15)	Tamio Suetsugu	4.00	2.00	1.25
(16)	Kazumi Takahashi	4.00	2.00	1.25
(17)	Yoshima Takahashi	4.00	2.00	1.25
(18)	George Theodore	8.00	4.00	2.50
(19)	Joe Torre, Kazuyoshi Yamamoto	15.00	7.50	4.50
(20)	Kazuyoshi Yamamoto, Tetsuhara Kawakami	10.00	5.00	3.00

1975 Broder All-Time N.Y. Mets

Nolan Ryan 1966-71

Veteran collector Ed Broder produced this collectors' issue. Nominally measuring about 1-7/8" x 3-1/8", cards have borderless black-and-white photos on front. Some cards have the dates of their tenure with the team on front. The unnumbered cards are checklisted here alphabetically.

		NM	EX	VG
Complete Set (12):		45.00	22.50	13.50
Common Player:		4.00	2.00	1.25
(1)	Yogi Berra	7.50	3.75	2.25
(2)	Bud Harrelson	4.00	2.00	1.25
(3)	Jim Hickman	4.00	2.00	1.25
(4)	Al Jackson	4.00	2.00	1.25
(5)	Cleon Jones	4.00	2.00	1.25
(6)	Jerry Koosman	4.00	2.00	1.25
(7)	Ed Kranepool	4.00	2.00	1.25
(8)	Tug McGraw	4.00	2.00	1.25
(9)	Nolan Ryan	15.00	7.50	4.50
(10)	Tom Seaver	9.00	4.50	2.75
(11)	Warren Spahn	6.00	3.00	1.75
(12)	Casey Stengal (Stengel)	6.00	3.00	1.75

1975 Broder 1962 "Original" N.Y. Mets

Sherman Jones

Veteran collector Ed Broder produced this collectors' issue. Nominally measuring about 2" x 3", cards have borderless black-and-white photos on front with only the player name for identification. Backs are blank. The unnumbered cards are checklisted alphabetically.

		NM	EX	VG
Complete Set (15):		50.00	25.00	15.00
Common Player:		5.00	2.50	1.50
(1)	Richie Ashburn	10.00	5.00	3.00
(2)	Gus Bell	5.00	2.50	1.50
(3)	Roger Craig	5.00	2.50	1.50
(4)	Gil Hodges	10.00	5.00	3.00
(5)	Rogers Hornsby	7.50	3.75	2.25
(6)	Sherman Jones	5.00	2.50	1.50
(7)	Rod Kanehl	5.00	2.50	1.50
(8)	Clem Labine	5.00	2.50	1.50
(9)	Hobie Landrith	5.00	2.50	1.50
(10)	R.G. Miller	5.00	2.50	1.50

		NM	EX	VG
(11)	Wilmer Mizell	5.00	2.50	1.50
(12)	Charley Neal	5.00	2.50	1.50
(13)	Casey Stengal (Stengel)	7.50	3.75	2.25
(14)	Frank Thomas	5.00	2.50	1.50
(15)	Marv Throneberry	5.00	2.50	1.50

1975 Broder Major Leagues - The 1950's

Veteran collector Ed Broder produced this collectors' issue. Nominally measuring about 2" x 3", cards have borderless black-and-white photos on front with only the player name for identification. Backs are blank. The unnumbered cards are checklisted here alphabetically. The set is notable in that a number of familiar players are pictured with teams not seen on their Topps and Bowman cards. The set sold originally for $2.20.

		NM	EX	VG
Complete Set (28):		100.00	50.00	30.00
Common Player:		4.00	2.00	1.25
(1)	Bobby Adams	4.00	2.00	1.25
(2)	Richie Ashburn	6.50	3.25	2.00
(3)	Ken Aspromonte	4.00	2.00	1.25
(4)	Ray Boone	5.00	2.50	1.50
(5)	Lou Boudreau	6.50	3.25	2.00
(6)	Smoky Burgess	4.00	2.00	1.25
(7)	Phil Cavaretta (Cavarretta)	4.00	2.00	1.25
(8)	Gene Conley	4.00	2.00	1.25
(9)	Del Crandell (Crandall)	4.00	2.00	1.25
(10)	Bob Friend	4.00	2.00	1.25
(11)	Harvey Haddix	4.00	2.00	1.25
(12)	Fred Haney	4.00	2.00	1.25
(13)	Ted Kluszewski	5.00	2.50	1.50
(14)	Jim Konstanty	4.00	2.00	1.25
(15)	Sandy Koufax	7.50	3.75	2.25
(16)	Harvey Kuenn	4.00	2.00	1.25
(17)	Bob Lemon	6.00	3.00	1.75
(18)	Marty Marion	4.00	2.00	1.25
(19)	Minnie Minoso	5.00	2.50	1.50
(20)	Stan Musial	7.00	3.50	2.00
(21)	Albie Pearson	4.00	2.00	1.25
(22)	Paul Richards	4.00	2.00	1.25
(23)	Hank Sauer	4.00	2.00	1.25
(24)	Herb Score	4.00	2.00	1.25
(25)	Bob Skinner	4.00	2.00	1.25
(26)	Enos Slaughter	6.00	3.00	1.75
(27)	Gus Triandos	4.00	2.00	1.25
(28)	Gus Zernial	4.00	2.00	1.25

1975 Broder Major League Postcards

This series of 3-1/8" x 5-1/8", borderless, blank-back pictures was advertised as the first in a proposed series designed to accommodate player autographs. Only California Angels and Montreal Expos players are included. The cards are printed on thin cardboard and feature close-up portraits with the player name in black type.

		NM	EX	VG
Complete Set (9):		25.00	12.50	7.50
Common Player:		3.00	1.50	.90
(1)	Tim Foli	3.00	1.50	.90
(2)	Barry Foote	3.00	1.50	.90
(3)	Mike Jorgensen	3.00	1.50	.90
(4)	Larry Lintz	3.00	1.50	.90
(5)	Dave McNally	3.00	1.50	.90
(6)	Steve Rodgers (Rogers)	3.00	1.50	.90
(7)	Nolan Ryan	10.00	5.00	3.00
(8)	Bill Singer	3.00	1.50	.90
(9)	Dick Williams	3.00	1.50	.90

1978 Broder Photocards

lloyd waner

This collectors' issue features late 1970s photos of some of the game's stars from the 1920s-1960s. Cards are printed in 3-1/2" x 5-1/2", blank-back, black-and-white format on thick grayback card stock. Cards were printed four to a sheet and often found on uncut sheets.

		NM	EX	VG
Complete Set (20):		40.00	20.00	12.00
Common Player:		3.00	1.50	.90
(1)	Walt Alston	3.00	1.50	.90
(2)	Luke Appling	3.00	1.50	.90
(3)	Ernie Banks	4.50	2.25	1.25
(4)	Yogi Berra	4.50	2.25	1.25
(5)	Bill Dickey	4.00	2.00	1.25
(6)	Bob Feller (Pitching)	4.00	2.00	1.25
(7)	Bob Feller (Portrait)	4.00	2.00	1.25
(8)	Billy Herman	3.00	1.50	.90
(9)	Bob Lemon	3.00	1.50	.90
(10)	Mickey Mantle	6.00	3.00	1.75
(11)	Willie Mays (Batting)	5.00	2.50	1.50
(12)	Willie Mays (Portrait)	5.00	2.50	1.50

		NM	EX	VG
(13)	Johnny Mize	3.00	1.50	.90
(14)	Pee Wee Reese	4.00	2.00	1.25
(15)	Allie Reynolds	3.00	1.50	.90
(16)	Brooks Robinson	4.00	2.00	1.25
(17)	Enos Slaughter	3.00	1.50	.90
(18)	Warren Spahn	3.00	1.50	.90
(19)	Lloyd Waner	3.00	1.50	.90
(20)	Ted Williams	5.00	2.50	1.50

1940 Brooklyn Dodgers Picture Pack

Rookie Pee Wee Reese appears in this team-issued set of black-and-white pictures. The 6" x 9" pictures have player portraits surrounded by a white border. A facsimile autograph appears on front. Backs are blank. The unnumbered pictures are checklisted here in alphabetical order. Because of roster changes, it is possible the specific makeup of the packs may have changed once or more over the course of the season. Some of the pictures were reused in subsequent years' offerings.

		NM	EX	VG
Complete Set (25):		150.00	75.00	45.00
Common Player:		8.00	4.00	2.50
(1)	Dolf Camilli	8.00	4.00	2.50
(2)	Tex Carleton	8.00	4.00	2.50
(3)	Hugh Casey	8.00	4.00	2.50
(4)	Pete Coscarart	8.00	4.00	2.50
(5)	Curt Davis	8.00	4.00	2.50
(6)	Leo Durocher	12.00	6.00	3.50
(7)	Fred Fitzsimmons	8.00	4.00	2.50
(8)	Herman Franks	8.00	4.00	2.50
(9)	Joe Gallagher	8.00	4.00	2.50
(10)	Charlie Gilbert	8.00	4.00	2.50
(11)	Luke Hamlin	8.00	4.00	2.50
(12)	Johnny Hudson	8.00	4.00	2.50
(13)	Newt Kimball	8.00	4.00	2.50
(14)	Cookie Lavagetto	8.00	4.00	2.50
(15)	Gus Mancuso	8.00	4.00	2.50
(16)	Joe Medwick	12.00	6.00	3.50
(17)	Van Lingle Mungo	10.00	5.00	3.00
(18)	Babe Phelps	8.00	4.00	2.50
(19)	Tot Pressnell	8.00	4.00	2.50
(20)	Pee Wee Reese	24.00	12.00	7.25
(21)	Vito Tamulis	8.00	4.00	2.50
(22)	Joe Vosmik	8.00	4.00	2.50
(23)	Dixie Walker	8.00	4.00	2.50
(24)	Jimmy Wasdell	8.00	4.00	2.50
(25)	Whitlow Wyatt	8.00	4.00	2.50

1941 Brooklyn Dodgers Picture Pack

Mace Brown

This team-issued set of 6" x 9" black-and-white pictures has player portraits surrounded by a white border. A facsimile autograph appears on front. Backs are blank. The unnumbered pictures are checklisted here in alphabetical order. Because of roster changes, it is possible the specific makeup of the packs may have changed once or more over the course of the season and that there may have been players issued other than those listed here. Some of the pictures were reused the 1940 offering. Team-issued pictures of 1940-41 can be differentiated from later years by their ballpark backgrounds.

		NM	EX	VG
Complete Set (25):		185.00	95.00	55.00
Common Player:		10.00	5.00	3.00
(1)	Mace Brown	10.00	5.00	3.00
(2)	Dolph Camilli	10.00	5.00	3.00
(3)	Hugh Casey	10.00	5.00	3.00
(4)	Pete Coscarart	10.00	5.00	3.00
(5)	Curt Davis	10.00	5.00	3.00
(6)	Leo Durocher	15.00	7.50	4.50
(7)	Fred Fitzsimmons	10.00	5.00	3.00
(8)	Luke Hamlin	10.00	5.00	3.00

		NM	EX	VG
(9)	Billy Herman	15.00	7.50	4.50
(10)	Kirby Higbe	10.00	5.00	3.00
(11)	Newt Kimball	10.00	5.00	3.00
(12)	Harry "Cookie" Lavagetto	10.00	5.00	3.00
(13)	Joe Medwick	15.00	7.50	4.50
(14)	Mickey Owen	10.00	5.00	3.00
(15)	Babe Phelps	10.00	5.00	3.00
(16)	Pee Wee Reese	25.00	12.50	7.50
(17)	Pete Reiser	10.00	5.00	3.00
(18)	Lew Riggs	10.00	5.00	3.00
(19)	Bill Swift	10.00	5.00	3.00
(20)	Vito Tamulis	10.00	5.00	3.00
(21)	Joe Vosmik	10.00	5.00	3.00
(22)	Dixie Walker	10.00	5.00	3.00
(23)	Jimmy Wasdell	10.00	5.00	3.00
(24)	Kemp Wicker	10.00	5.00	3.00
(25)	Whit Wyatt	10.00	5.00	3.00

1942 Brooklyn Dodgers Picture Pack

This set of 6" x 9" black-and-white team-issued pictures features player portrait photos in a studio setting. The pictures have a white border all around, and there is a facsimile autograph on front. Backs are blank. The unnumbered pictures are checklisted here alphabetically. Pictures from the 1942 and 1943 photo packs are indistinguishable except for player selection.

		NM	EX	VG
Complete Set (25):		150.00	75.00	45.00
Common Player:		8.00	4.00	2.50
(1)	Johnny Allen	8.00	4.00	2.50
(2)	Frenchy Bordagaray	8.00	4.00	2.50
(3)	Dolf Camilli	8.00	4.00	2.50
(4)	Hugh Casey	8.00	4.00	2.50
(5)	Curt Davis	8.00	4.00	2.50
(6)	Leo Durocher	12.00	6.00	3.50
(7)	Larry French	8.00	4.00	2.50
(8)	Augie Galan	8.00	4.00	2.50
(9)	Ed Head	8.00	4.00	2.50
(10)	Billy Herman	12.00	6.00	3.50
(11)	Kirby Higbe	8.00	4.00	2.50
(12)	Alex Kampouris	8.00	4.00	2.50
(13)	Newt Kimball	8.00	4.00	2.50
(14)	Joe Medwick	12.00	6.00	3.50
(15)	Mickey Owen	8.00	4.00	2.50
(16)	Pee Wee Reese	16.00	8.00	4.75
(17)	Pete Reiser	10.00	5.00	3.00
(18)	Lew Riggs	8.00	4.00	2.50
(19)	Johnny Rizzo	8.00	4.00	2.50
(20)	Schoolboy Rowe	10.00	5.00	3.00
(21)	Billy Sullivan	8.00	4.00	2.50
(22)	Arky Vaughan	12.00	6.00	3.50
(23)	Dixie Walker	8.00	4.00	2.50
(24)	Les Webber	8.00	4.00	2.50
(25)	Whitlow Wyatt	8.00	4.00	2.50

1943 Brooklyn Dodgers Picture Pack

This set of 6" x 9" black-and-white team-issued pictures features player portrait photos in a studio setting. The pictures have a white border all around, and there is a facsimile autograph on front. Backs are blank. The unnumbered pictures are checklisted here alphabetically. Pictures from the 1942 and 1943 photo packs are indistinguishable except for player selection.

		NM	EX	VG
Complete Set (25):		150.00	75.00	45.00
Common Player:		8.00	4.00	2.50
(1)	Johnny Allen	8.00	4.00	2.50
(2)	Frenchy Bordagaray	8.00	4.00	2.50
(3)	Bob Bragan	10.00	5.00	3.00
(4)	Dolf Camilli	8.00	4.00	2.50
(5)	Johnny Cooney	8.00	4.00	2.50

		NM	EX	VG
(6)	John Corriden	8.00	4.00	2.50
(7)	Curt Davis	8.00	4.00	2.50
(8)	Leo Durocher	12.00	6.00	3.50
(9)	Fred Fitzsimmons	8.00	4.00	2.50
(10)	Augie Galan	8.00	4.00	2.50
(11)	Al Glossop	8.00	4.00	2.50
(12)	Ed Head	8.00	4.00	2.50
(13)	Billy Herman	12.00	6.00	3.50
(14)	Kirby Higbe	8.00	4.00	2.50
(15)	Max Macon	8.00	4.00	2.50
(16)	Joe Medwick	12.00	6.00	3.50
(17)	Rube Melton	8.00	4.00	2.50
(18)	Dee Moore	8.00	4.00	2.50
(19)	"Buck" Newsom	10.00	5.00	3.00
(20)	Mickey Owen	8.00	4.00	2.50
(21)	Arky Vaughan	12.00	6.00	3.50
(22)	Dixie Walker	8.00	4.00	2.50
(23)	Paul Waner	12.00	6.00	3.50
(24)	Les Webber	8.00	4.00	2.50
(25)	Whitlow Wyatt	8.00	4.00	2.50

1946 Brooklyn Dodgers Picture Pack

This team-issued set of player portrait pictures is in a blank-back 6-1/2" x 9" format. A facsimile autograph appears on front. Like many souvenir-stand photo packs of the era, it is possible the specific contents of this product may have changed during the course of the season as players joined and left the team.

		NM	EX	VG
Complete Set (25):		125.00	65.00	40.00
Common Player:		6.00	3.00	1.80
(1)	Andy Anderson	6.00	3.00	1.80
(2)	Henry Behrman	6.00	3.00	1.80
(3)	Ralph Branca	6.00	3.00	1.80
(4)	Hugh Casey	6.00	3.00	1.80
(5)	Leo Durocher	9.00	4.50	2.75
(6)	Carl Furillo	12.00	6.00	3.50
(7)	Augie Galan	6.00	3.00	1.80
(8)	Hal Gregg	6.00	3.00	1.80
(9)	Joe Hatten	6.00	3.00	1.80
(10)	Al Head	6.00	3.00	1.80
(11)	Art Herring	6.00	3.00	1.80
(12)	Billy Herman	9.00	4.50	2.75
(13)	Gene Hermanski	6.00	3.00	1.80
(14)	Kirby Higbe	6.00	3.00	1.80
(15)	Harry "Cookie" Lavagetto	6.00	3.00	1.80
(16)	Vic Lombardi	6.00	3.00	1.80
(17)	Pee Wee Reese	12.00	6.00	3.50
(18)	Pete Reiser	6.00	3.00	1.80
(19)	Stan Rojek	6.00	3.00	1.80
(20)	Mike Sandlock	6.00	3.00	1.80
(21)	Eddie Stanky	7.50	3.75	2.25
(22)	Ed Stevens	6.00	3.00	1.80
(23)	Dixie Walker	6.00	3.00	1.80
(24)	Les Webber	6.00	3.00	1.80
(25)	Dick Whitman	6.00	3.00	1.80

1947 Brooklyn Dodgers Picture Pack

This team-issued set of player portrait pictures is in a blank-back 6-1/2" x 9" format. A facsimile autograph appears on front. Like many souvenir-stand photo packs of the era, it is possible the specific contents of this product may have changed during the course of the season as players joined and left the team.

		NM	EX	VG
Complete Set (25):		350.00	175.00	105.00
Common Player:		9.00	4.50	2.75
(1)	Ray Blades	9.00	4.50	2.75
(2)	Bobby Bragan	9.00	4.50	2.75
(3)	Ralph Branca	9.00	4.50	2.75

		NM	EX	VG
(4)	Tommy Brown	9.00	4.50	2.75
(5)	Hugh Casey	9.00	4.50	2.75
(6)	Ed Chandler	9.00	4.50	2.75
(7)	Carl Furillo	20.00	10.00	6.00
(8)	Hal Gregg	9.00	4.50	2.75
(9)	Joe Hatten	9.00	4.50	2.75
(10)	Gene Hermanski	9.00	4.50	2.75
(11)	Gil Hodges	40.00	20.00	12.00
(12)	Spider Jorgensen	9.00	4.50	2.75
(13)	Clyde King	9.00	4.50	2.75
(14)	Vic Lombardi	9.00	4.50	2.75
(15)	Rube Melton	9.00	4.50	2.75
(16)	Eddie Miksis	9.00	4.50	2.75
(17)	Pee Wee Reese	30.00	15.00	9.00
(18)	Pete Reiser	9.00	4.50	2.75
(19)	Jackie Robinson	80.00	40.00	24.00
(20)	Stan Rojek	9.00	4.50	2.75
(21)	Burt Shotton	9.00	4.50	2.75
(22)	Duke Snider	40.00	20.00	12.00
(23)	Eddie Stanky	12.50	6.25	3.75
(24)	Harry Taylor	9.00	4.50	2.75
(25)	Dixie Walker	9.00	4.50	2.75

1948 Brooklyn Dodgers Picture Pack

This team-issued set of player portrait pictures is in a blank-back 6-1/2" x 9" format. A facsimile autograph appears on front. Like many souvenir-stand photo packs of the era, it is possible the specific contents of this product may have changed during the course of the season as players joined and left the team, and that pictures were re-used from year-to-year.

		NM	EX	VG
Complete Set (26):		300.00	150.00	95.00
Common Player:		8.00	4.00	2.50
(1)	Rex Barney	8.00	4.00	2.50
(2)	Ray Blades	8.00	4.00	2.50
(3)	Bobby Bragan	8.00	4.00	2.50
(4)	Ralph Branca	8.00	4.00	2.50
(5)	Tommy Brown	8.00	4.00	2.50
(6)	Hugh Casey	8.00	4.00	2.50
(7)	Billy Cox	8.00	4.00	2.50
(8)	Leo Durocher	15.00	7.50	4.50
(9)	Bruce Edwards	8.00	4.00	2.50
(10)	Carl Furillo	20.00	10.00	6.00
(11)	Joe Hatten	8.00	4.00	2.50
(12)	Gene Hermanski	8.00	4.00	2.50
(13)	Gil Hodges	30.00	15.00	9.00
(14)	Spider Jorgensen	8.00	4.00	2.50
(15)	Don Lund	8.00	4.00	2.50
(16)	Eddie Miksis	8.00	4.00	2.50
(17)	Jake Pitler	8.00	4.00	2.50
(18)	Pee Wee Reese	25.00	12.50	7.50
(19)	Pete Reiser	8.00	4.00	2.50
(20)	Jackie Robinson	65.00	32.00	19.50
(21)	Preacher Roe	12.00	6.00	3.50
(22)	Burt Shotton	8.00	4.00	2.50
(23)	Clyde Sukeforth	8.00	4.00	2.50
(24)	Harry Taylor	8.00	4.00	2.50
(25)	Arky Vaughan	15.00	7.50	4.50
(26)	Preston Ward	8.00	4.00	2.50

1949 Brooklyn Dodgers Picture Pack

This team-issued set of player portrait pictures is in a blank-back 6-1/2" x 9" format. A facsimile autograph appears on front. Like many souvenir-stand photo packs of the era, it is possible the specific contents of this product may have changed during the course of the season as players joined and left the team, and that pictures were re-used from year-to-year.

		NM	EX	VG
Complete Set (25):		575.00	300.00	160.00
Common Player:		8.00	5.00	3.00
(1)	Jack Banta	8.00	5.00	3.00
(2)	Rex Barney	8.00	5.00	3.00
(3)	Ralph Branca	12.50	6.25	3.75
(4)	Tommy Brown	8.00	5.00	3.00
(5)	Roy Campanella	200.00	100.00	60.00
(6)	Billy Cox	8.00	5.00	3.00
(7)	Bruce Edwards	8.00	5.00	3.00
(8)	Carl Furillo	20.00	10.00	6.00
(9)	Joe Hatten	8.00	5.00	3.00
(10)	Gene Hermanski	8.00	5.00	3.00
(11)	Gil Hodges	40.00	20.00	12.00
(12)	Johnny Hopp	8.00	5.00	3.00
(13)	Spider Jorgensen	8.00	5.00	3.00
(14)	Mike McCormick	8.00	5.00	3.00
(15)	Eddie Miksis	8.00	5.00	3.00
(16)	Don Newcombe	100.00	50.00	30.00
(17)	Erv Palica	8.00	5.00	3.00
(18)	Jake Pitler	8.00	5.00	3.00
(19)	Pee Wee Reese	50.00	25.00	15.00
(20)	Jackie Robinson	75.00	37.00	22.00
(21)	Preacher Roe	12.50	6.25	3.75
(22)	Burt Shotton	8.00	5.00	3.00
(23)	Duke Snider	50.00	25.00	15.00
(24)	Milt Stock	8.00	5.00	3.00
(25)	Clyde Sukeforth	8.00	5.00	3.00

1952 Brooklyn Dodgers Schedule Cards

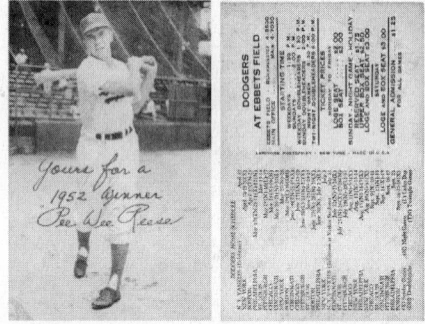

These postcard-size black-and-white cards have popular Dodgers players on front and the 1952 season's schedule printed on back. Some cards have a postcard-style back on which the right side has space for an address. Others cards have ticket price information in that space. How many different cards were issued is not known. Credit on the back is given to Lumitone Photoprint of New York.

	NM	EX	VG
Common Card:	400.00	110.00	67.00
Gil Hodges	400.00	200.00	120.00
Pee Wee Reese	400.00	200.00	120.00
Jackie Robinson	600.00	300.00	180.00
Duke Snider	400.00	200.00	120.00

1955 Brooklyn Dodgers Picture Pack

This set of approximately 5" x 7" blank-back, black-and-white pictures was a souvenir stand item at Ebbets Field. Player photos are chest-to-cap portraits surrounded by a white border with the player name at bottom in all-caps, followed by the team nickname in upper- and lower-case type. The unnumbered pictures are listed here alphabetically. The set was sold for 25 cents in a white paper envelope with "WORLD CHAMPION Dodgers" printed in blue.

		NM	EX	VG
Complete Set (12):		100.00	50.00	30.00
Common Player:		8.00	4.00	2.50
(1)	Walter Alston	8.00	4.00	2.50
(2)	Roy Campanella	20.00	10.00	6.00
(3)	Carl Erskine	8.00	4.00	2.50
(4)	Carl Furillo	10.00	5.00	3.00
(5)	Gil Hodges	16.00	8.00	4.75
(6)	Randy Jackson	8.00	4.00	2.50
(7)	Clem Labine	8.00	4.00	2.50
(8)	Don Newcombe	8.00	4.00	2.50
(9)	Johnny Podres	8.00	4.00	2.50
(10)	Peewee Reese	13.50	6.75	4.00
(11)	Jackie Robinson	24.00	12.00	7.25
(12)	Duke Snider	16.00	8.00	4.75

1956 Brooklyn Dodgers Picture Pack

DON DRYSDALE, Dodgers

This set of 5" x 7" blank-back, black-and-white pictures was a souvenir stand item at Ebbets Field. Player photos are surrounded by a white border at bottom in all-caps, followed by the team nickname in upper- and lower-case type. The unnumbered pictures are listed here alphabetically. The same photos were offered in a 50-piece Yankees-Dodgers "World Series Picture Portfolio."

		NM	EX	VG
Complete Set (25):		250.00	125.00	75.00
Common Player:		10.00	5.00	3.00
(1)	Walter Alston	12.50	6.25	3.75
(2)	Sandy Amoros	12.50	6.25	3.75
(3)	Joe Becker	10.00	5.00	3.00
(4)	Don Bessent	10.00	5.00	3.00
(5)	Roy Campanella	30.00	15.00	9.00
(6)	Roger Craig	10.00	5.00	3.00
(7)	Don Drysdale	25.00	12.50	7.50
(8)	Carl Erskine	12.50	6.25	3.75
(9)	Chico Fernandez	10.00	5.00	3.00
(10)	Carl Furillo	15.00	7.50	4.50
(11)	Jim Gilliam	15.00	7.50	4.50
(12)	Billy Herman	12.50	6.25	3.75
(13)	Gil Hodges	25.00	12.50	7.50
(14)	Randy Jackson	10.00	5.00	3.00
(15)	Sandy Koufax	35.00	17.50	10.50
(16)	Clem Labine	12.50	6.25	3.75
(17)	Sal Maglie	10.00	5.00	3.00
(18)	Charlie Neal	10.00	5.00	3.00
(19)	Don Newcombe	12.50	6.25	3.75
(20)	Jake Pitler	10.00	5.00	3.00
(21)	Peewee Reese	20.00	10.00	6.00
(22)	Jackie Robinson	35.00	17.50	10.50
(23)	Ed Roebuck	10.00	5.00	3.00
(24)	Duke Snider	25.00	12.50	7.50
(25)	Al Walker	10.00	5.00	3.00

1957 Brooklyn Dodgers Picture Pack

In their final year in Brooklyn, the Dodgers issued this souvenir-stand picture pack, offered for 25 cents. The pictures are 5" x 7", blank-back, black-and-white. Player portraits are surrounded by a white border with the player name at bottom in all-caps and "Dodgers" in upper- and lower-case type. The unnumbered pictures are listed here alphabetically.

		NM	EX	VG
Complete Set (12):		125.00	65.00	40.00
Common Player:		10.00	5.00	3.00
(1)	Walter Alston	15.00	7.50	4.50
(2)	Roy Campanella	25.00	12.50	7.50
(3)	Carl Furillo	15.00	7.50	4.50
(4)	Jim Gilliam	15.00	7.50	4.50
(5)	Gil Hodges	20.00	10.00	6.00
(6)	Randy Jackson	10.00	5.00	3.00
(7)	Clem Labine	10.00	5.00	3.00
(8)	Sal Maglie	10.00	5.00	3.00
(9)	Don Newcombe	12.50	6.25	3.75
(10)	Johnny Podres	15.00	7.50	4.50
(11)	Peewee Reese	20.00	10.00	6.00
(12)	Duke Snider	20.00	10.00	6.00

1953-55 Brown & Bigelow

Some of baseball's biggest stars, either as they appeared in the mid-1950s or as spirit images, instruct All-American boys in the skills of baseball on this series of cards. Produced by the St. Paul firm of Brown & Bigelow, the 2-1/4" x 3-1/2", round-cornered cards can be found either as playing cards or with schedules printed on the back. The cards could be customized by local sponsors in a panel at the bottom of the artwork. The Medcalf artwork is also seen on contemporary wall and desk calendars and other printed items.

		NM	EX	VG
	UNOPENED DECKS			
(1)	Ty Cobb	45.00	22.50	13.50
(2)	Lou Gehrig	50.00	25.00	15.00
(3)	Connie Mack	30.00	15.00	9.00
(4)	John McGraw	30.00	15.00	9.00
(5)	Babe Ruth	65.00	32.50	20.00
(6)	Honus Wagner	40.00	20.00	12.00
	SINGLE CARDS			
(1)	Ty Cobb	6.00	3.00	1.75
(2)	Lou Gehrig	8.00	4.00	2.50
(3)	Connie Mack	4.00	2.00	1.25
(4)	John McGraw	4.00	2.00	1.25
(5)	Babe Ruth	10.00	5.00	3.00
(6)	Honus Wagner	5.00	2.50	1.50

1911-14 Brunners Bread (D304)

 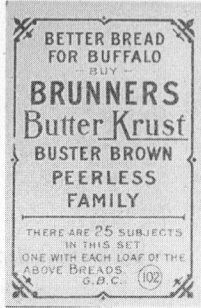

(See 1911-1914 General Baking Co. for checklist and values.)

1908-1910 Brush Detroit Tigers Postcards

The makers of this short-lived (1907-11) automobile evidently engaged members of the hometown team to endorse their product. The 3-1/2" x 5-3/8" black-and-white postcards have a bordered photo on front showing a Tigers player (in uniform or suit) with the auto. A few lines of petry about the player complete the design. Backs have typical postcard format. It is likely the checklist here is incomplete.

		NM	EX	VG
(1)	Ty Cobb	4,000	2,000	1,200
(2)	William Coughlin	750.00	375.00	225.00
(3)	Bill Donovan	750.00	375.00	225.00
			750.00	
(4)	Hughie Jennings (Hands on steering wheel.)	1,500	750.00	450.00
(5)	Hughie Jennings (Hands in air.)	1,500	750.00	450.00
(6)	Matty McIntyre	750.00	375.00	225.00
(7)	George Mullin	750.00	375.00	225.00
(8)	Germany Schaefer, Charley O'Leary	750.00	375.00	225.00
(9)	Charlie Schmidt	750.00	375.00	225.00
(10)	Ira Thomas	750.00	375.00	225.00

1979 Bubble Yum Toronto Blue Jays

 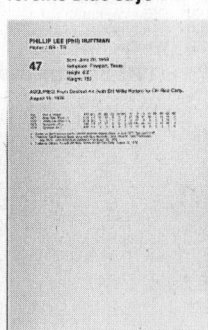

Members of the Toronto Blue Jays in the team's third season are featured in this set of 5-1/2" x 8-1/2" black-and-white player pictures. Fronts feature player portraits identified by their full name and position. In the wide bottom border are team and sponsor logos. Backs have player biographical data, major and minor league stats, acquisition information and career highlights. Cards are numbered by uniform number.

		NM	EX	VG
Complete Set (20):		65.00	32.50	20.00
Common Player:		4.00	2.00	1.25
1	Bob Bailor	4.00	2.00	1.25
4	Alfredo Griffin	4.00	2.00	1.25
7	Roy Hartsfield	4.00	2.00	1.25
9	Rick Cerone	4.00	2.00	1.25
10	John Mayberry	4.00	2.00	1.25
11	Luis Gomez	4.00	2.00	1.25
13	Roy Howell	4.00	2.00	1.25
18	Jim Clancy	4.00	2.00	1.25
19	Otto Velez	4.00	2.00	1.25
20	Al Woods	4.00	2.00	1.25

		NM	EX	VG
21	Rico Carty	4.00	2.00	1.25
22	Rick Bosetti	4.00	2.00	1.25
23	Dave Lemanczyk	4.00	2.00	1.25
24	Tom Underwood	4.00	2.00	1.25
31	Bobby Doerr	6.00	3.00	1.75
34	Jesse Jefferson	4.00	2.00	1.25
38	Balor Moore	4.00	2.00	1.25
44	Tom Buskey	4.00	2.00	1.25
46	Dave Freisleben	4.00	2.00	1.25
47	Phil Huffman	4.00	2.00	1.25

1976 Buckmans Discs

One of several regional sponsors of player disc sets in 1976 was Buckmans Ice Cream Village in Rochester, N.Y. The discs are 3-3/8" diameter with a black-and-white player portrait photo in the center of the baseball design. A line of red stars is above, while the left and right panels feature one of several bright colors. Produced by Michael Schecter Associates under license from the Major League Baseball Players Association, the player photos have had uniform and cap logos removed. Backs are printed in red and purple. The unnumbered checklist here is presented in alphabetical order.

		NM	EX	VG
Complete Set (70):		60.00	30.00	18.00
Common Player:		.75	.40	.25
(1)	Henry Aaron	6.00	3.00	1.75
(2)	Johnny Bench	3.50	1.75	1.00
(3)	Vida Blue	.75	.40	.25
(4)	Larry Bowa	.75	.40	.25
(5)	Lou Brock	2.50	1.25	.70
(6)	Jeff Burroughs	.75	.40	.25
(7)	John Candelaria	.75	.40	.25
(8)	Jose Cardenal	.75	.40	.25
(9)	Rod Carew	2.50	1.25	.70
(10)	Steve Carlton	2.50	1.25	.70
(11)	Dave Cash	.75	.40	.25
(12)	Cesar Cedeno	.75	.40	.25
(13)	Ron Cey	.75	.40	.25
(14)	Carlton Fisk	2.50	1.25	.70
(15)	Tito Fuentes	.75	.40	.25
(16)	Steve Garvey	2.00	1.00	.60
(17)	Ken Griffey	.75	.40	.25
(18)	Don Gullett	.75	.40	.25
(19)	Willie Horton	.75	.40	.25
(20)	Al Hrabosky	.75	.40	.25
(21)	Catfish Hunter	2.50	1.25	.70
(22)	Reggie Jackson (A's)	5.00	2.50	1.50
(23)	Randy Jones	.75	.40	.25
(24)	Jim Kaat	.75	.40	.25
(25)	Don Kessinger	.75	.40	.25
(26)	Dave Kingman	.75	.40	.25
(27)	Jerry Koosman	.75	.40	.25
(28)	Mickey Lolich	.75	.40	.25
(29)	Greg Luzinski	.75	.40	.25
(30)	Fred Lynn	.75	.40	.25
(31)	Bill Madlock	.75	.40	.25
(32)	Carlos May (White Sox)	.75	.40	.25
(33)	John Mayberry	.75	.40	.25
(34)	Bake McBride	.75	.40	.25
(35)	Doc Medich	.75	.40	.25
(36)	Andy Messersmith (Dodgers)	.75	.40	.25
(37)	Rick Monday	.75	.40	.25
(38)	John Montefusco	.75	.40	.25
(39)	Jerry Morales	.75	.40	.25
(40)	Joe Morgan	2.50	1.25	.70
(41)	Thurman Munson	2.50	1.25	.70
(42)	Bobby Murcer	.75	.40	.25
(43)	Al Oliver	.75	.40	.25
(44)	Jim Palmer	2.50	1.25	.70
(45)	Dave Parker	.75	.40	.25
(46)	Tony Perez	2.50	1.25	.70
(47)	Jerry Reuss	.75	.40	.25
(48)	Brooks Robinson	3.00	1.50	.90
(49)	Frank Robinson	3.00	1.50	.90
(50)	Steve Rogers	.75	.40	.25
(51)	Pete Rose	6.00	3.00	1.75
(52)	Nolan Ryan	20.00	10.00	6.00
(53)	Manny Sanguillen	.75	.40	.25
(54)	Mike Schmidt	5.00	2.50	1.50
(55)	Tom Seaver	3.00	1.50	.90
(56)	Ted Simmons	.75	.40	.25
(57)	Reggie Smith	.75	.40	.25
(58)	Willie Stargell	2.50	1.25	.70
(59)	Rusty Staub	.75	.40	.25
(60)	Rennie Stennett	.75	.40	.25
(61)	Don Sutton	2.50	1.25	.70
(62)	Andy Thornton (Cubs)	.75	.40	.25
(63)	Luis Tiant	.75	.40	.25
(64)	Joe Torre	1.50	.70	.45
(65)	Mike Tyson	.75	.40	.25
(66)	Bob Watson	.75	.40	.25
(67)	Wilbur Wood	.75	.40	.25
(68)	Jimmy Wynn	.75	.40	.25
(69)	Carl Yastrzemski	3.50	1.75	1.00
(70)	Richie Zisk	.75	.40	.25

1916 Bucyrus Brewing Co. (M101-4)

One of a dozen or so firms that utilized Felix Mendelsohn's baseball card issue as an advertising medium was this Ohio brewery. Unlike the other companies, however, Bucyrus did not issue individual cards, but only a 42" x 28" uncut sheet containing all 200 cards and labeled "1916 - BASEBALL'S HALL OF FAME - 1916." If cut from the sheet, the single cards would be indistinguishable from the blank-back version of M101-4.

	NM	EX	VG
Complete Uncut Sheet:	35,000	25,000	15,000

(See 1916 M101-4 Blank Backs for checklist.)

1950 Buitoni Macaroni Joe DiMaggio Pins

At least two styles of 1-1/2" diameter pinback buttons are known from the Yankee Clipper's association with a New York pasta company. One style has a black-and-white portrait photo at the center of a red-stiched baseball design. Printed in red at top is "JOE DiMAGGIO / TV CLUB." At bottom is the program sponsor's name. Another style has a photo of the player with a bat over his shoulder on a yellow background. "JOE DiMAGGIO CLUB" is at top, "BUITONI/FOODS CORP." at bottom, both in red. Each style was reproduced in 2-1/4" size early in the 21st Century; those replicas have no collectible value.

	NM	EX	VG
Joe DiMaggio (Portrait)	500.00	250.00	150.00
Joe DiMaggio (W/ bat.)	1,200	600.00	360.00

1932 Bulgaria Sport Tobacco

Despite the name of the sponsoring issuer, this set of cards is a product of Germany. Only a single major league ballplayer is pictured among the 272 cards in the set: Babe Ruth, who shares a card with boxing great Max Schmeling in a photo taken in the U.S. The black-and-white cards in the set measure 1-5/8" x 2-3/8" and have backs printed in German, including a card number.

		NM	EX	VG
256	Babe Ruth, Max Schmeling	300.00	150.00	90.00

1952-1953 Burger Beer Cincinnati Reds

Whether or not they were a promotional issue of Burger Beer (they are not marked as to issuer), advanced collectors of 1950s Reds memorabilia ascribe these 8" x 10-1/2" black-and-white photos to the long-time Reds sponsor because of their similarity to later Burger editions. The blank-back photos have portraits or posed action shots surrounded with white borders. In the wide bottom border is a C Reds logo, with the player name and (usually) position at right in all-capitals. The Clyde King picture, which can be reliably dated to 1953, his only season with the Reds, is a portrait drawing, rather than a

photo, and has no position listed. The unnumbered pictures are listed here alphabetically and the checklist presented is likely incomplete.

		NM	EX	VG
Common Player:		30.00	15.00	9.00
(1)	Joe Adcock (Fielding)	40.00	20.00	12.00
(2)	Bob Borkowski (Batting follow-through.)	30.00	15.00	9.00
(3)	Jim Greengrass	30.00	15.00	9.00
(4)	Grady Hatton (Portrait)	30.00	15.00	9.00
(5)	Niles Jordan (Portrait)	30.00	15.00	9.00
(6)	Clyde King (Portrait art.)	30.00	15.00	9.00
(7)	Willard Marshall (Batting follow-through.)	30.00	15.00	9.00
(8)	Ed Pellagrini (Portrait)	30.00	15.00	9.00
(9)	Bud Podbielan (Portrait)	30.00	15.00	9.00
(10)	Frank Smith	30.00	15.00	9.00
(11)	John Temple (Batting follow-through.)	30.00	15.00	9.00
(12)	Herm Wehmeier	30.00	15.00	9.00

1955 Burger Beer Cincinnati Reds

The evidence attributing these 8-1/2" x 11" black-and-white player pictures to one of the team's radio sponsors, Burger Beer, is apocryphal, based largely on the format, which is similar to the company's 1956-64 promotional issues. This series has player portraits or poses bordered in white. In the bottom border, flanked by team logos are three lines of capital-letter typography with the player's name, position and team. Backs are blank. This checklist is likely not complete.

		NM	EX	VG
Common Player:		30.00	15.00	9.00
(1)	Gus Bell	30.00	15.00	9.00
(2)	Rocky Bridges	30.00	15.00	9.00
(3)	Jackie Collum	30.00	15.00	9.00
(4)	Art Fowler	30.00	15.00	9.00
(5)	Ray Jablonski	30.00	15.00	9.00
(6)	Johnny Klippstein	30.00	15.00	9.00
(7)	Ted Kluszewski	45.00	22.00	13.50
(8)	Roy McMillan	30.00	15.00	9.00
(9)	Rudy Minarcin	30.00	15.00	9.00
(10)	Joe Nuxhall	45.00	22.00	13.50
(11)	Wally Post	30.00	15.00	9.00
(12)	Gerry Staley	30.00	15.00	9.00
(13)	Birdie Tebbetts	30.00	15.00	9.00

1956-1957 Burger Beer Cincinnati Reds

The 1956 and 1957 series of 8-1/2" x 11" black-and-white player photos from one of the Reds' broadcast sponsors can be distinguished from later issues by the presence of an advertising slogan at the bottom of the otherwise blank black, "COURTESY OF BURGER - A FINER BEER YEAR AFTER YEAR." Players are identified on the bottom front border in large capital letters. Because at least one player is known in both portrait and posed action photos, poses other than portraits are indicated in parentheses.

		NM	EX	VG
Common Player:		30.00	15.00	9.00
(1)	Ed Bailey (Portrait to top button.)	30.00	15.00	9.00
(2)	Ed Bailey (Portrait to chest showing number.)	30.00	15.00	9.00
(3)	Gus Bell (Portrait to chest showing number.)	30.00	15.00	9.00
(4)	Joe Black	30.00	15.00	9.00
(5)	Smoky Burgess (Batting)	35.00	17.50	10.50
(6)	George Crowe (Batting)	30.00	15.00	9.00
(7)	Don Hoak	30.00	15.00	9.00
(8)	Waite Hoyt (Broadcaster)	30.00	15.00	9.00
(9)	Ray Jablonski (Throwing)	30.00	15.00	9.00
(10)	Hal Jeffcoat (Follow-through.)	30.00	15.00	9.00
(11)	Ted Kluszewski (Batting)	50.00	25.00	15.00

		NM	EX	VG
(12)	Ted Kluszewski (Portrait to top button.)	50.00	25.00	15.00
(13)	Brooks Lawrence (Follow-through.)	30.00	15.00	9.00
(14)	Roy McMillan (Batting)	30.00	15.00	9.00
(15)	Roy McMillan (Fielding)	30.00	15.00	9.00
(16)	Roy McMillan (Portrait to second button.)	30.00	15.00	9.00
(17)	Jackie Moran (Broadcaster)	30.00	15.00	9.00
(18)	Joe Nuxhall	30.00	15.00	9.00
(19)	Wally Post	30.00	15.00	9.00
(20)	Frank Robinson (Fielding)	150.00	75.00	45.00
(21)	Frank Robinson (Portrait, white cap.)	125.00	62.00	37.00
(22)	Birdie Tebbetts	30.00	15.00	9.00
(23)	Johnny Temple (Portrait to second button.)	30.00	15.00	9.00
(24)	Johnny Temple (Portrait to chest showing number.)	30.00	15.00	9.00
(25)	Johnny Temple (Ready to throw.)	30.00	15.00	9.00
(26)	Bob Thurman (Batting)	30.00	15.00	9.00

1958-1959 Burger Beer Cincinnati Reds

THOMAS

The 1958-1959 series of 8-1/2" x 11" black-and-white player photos can be distinguished by the presence of an advertising slogan at the bottom of the otherwise blank black, "COURTESY OF SPARKLE * BREWED BURGER BEER / HAVE FUN - HAVE A BURGER." Players are identified by first and last name, or by last name only on the bottom front border in large capital letters. The team name may or may not appear, as well.

		NM	EX	VG
Common Player:		30.00	15.00	9.00
(1)	Ed. Bailey (Portrait)	30.00	15.00	9.00
(2)	Gus Bell (Portrait, dark cap.)	30.00	15.00	9.00
(4)	Waite Hoyt (At microphone.)	30.00	15.00	9.00
(6)	Jerry Lynch (Portrait)	30.00	15.00	9.00
(7)	Roy McMillan (Portrait)	30.00	15.00	9.00
(8)	(Don) Newcombe (Portrait)	30.00	15.00	9.00
(9)	Joe Nuxhall (Follow-through.)	30.00	15.00	9.00
(11)	Vada Pinson (Portrait)	45.00	22.00	13.50
(12)	Bob Purkey (Portrait)	30.00	15.00	9.00
(13)	Frank Robinson (Batting, dark cap.)	125.00	62.00	37.00
(14)	Frank Robinson (Fielding)	125.00	62.00	37.00
(15)	Frank Robinson (Portrait, white cap.)	125.00	62.00	37.00
(16)	Manager Mayo Smith (Adjusting cap.)	30.00	15.00	9.00
(17)	John Temple (Portrait)	30.00	15.00	9.00
(18)	Frank Thomas (Batting)	30.00	15.00	9.00
(19)	(Frank) Thomas (Portrait)	30.00	15.00	9.00

1960-64 Burger Beer Cincinnati Reds

VADA PINSON

The sponsor is not identified (except on 1959 issues which are marked on back, "COURTESY OF SPARKLE * BREWED BURGER BEER / HAVE FUN - HAVE A BURGER)," nor the year of issue published on these 8-1/2" x 11" player photos. Uniform and cap styles can give some idea of when the photos were taken. Photos are black-and-white portraits or action poses surrounded by white borders with the player and team names at bottom. Backs are blank. The unnumbered photos are listed here in alphabetical order. Some photos were re-issued year after year with only minor changes in cropping; these are not listed separately. This checklist will likely remain incomplete for some time. Gaps have been in the assigned numbering to accommodate future additions.

	NM	EX	VG
Common Player:	15.00	7.50	4.50

		NM	EX	VG
(1)	Ed Bailey (Portrait)	15.00	7.50	4.50
(2)	Ed. Bailey (Portrait)	15.00	7.50	4.50
(3)	Don Blasingame (Fielding)	15.00	7.50	4.50
(4)	Gus Bell (Batting)	15.00	7.50	4.50
(5)	Gus Bell (Fielding fly ball.)	15.00	7.50	4.50
(6)	Gus Bell (Portrait)	15.00	7.50	4.50
(7)	Gordon Coleman (Bat behind cap.)	15.00	7.50	4.50
(8)	Gordon Coleman (Bat behind shoulder.)	15.00	7.50	4.50
(9)	Gordon Coleman (Fielding)	15.00	7.50	4.50
(11)	John Edwards (Portrait, light tower in background.)	15.00	7.50	4.50
(12)	John Edwards (Portrait, no tower.)	15.00	7.50	4.50
(13)	Gene Freese (Fielding)	15.00	7.50	4.50
(14)	Jay Hook (Follow-through.)	15.00	7.50	4.50
(15)	Waite Hoyt (Portrait at microphone.) (Announcer)	15.00	7.50	4.50
(16)	Waite Hoyt (Portrait w/ folder.) (Announcer)	15.00	7.50	4.50
(17)	Fred Hutchinson (Portrait, C on vest.)	15.00	7.50	4.50
(18)	Fred Hutchinson (Portrait, half of "1" and "C.")	15.00	7.50	4.50
(19)	Fred Hutchinson (Portrait, C Reds on vest.)	15.00	7.50	4.50
(20)	Fred. Hutchinson (Only top of chest emblem shows.)	15.00	7.50	4.50
(22)	Joey Jay (Follow-through.)	15.00	7.50	4.50
(23)	Joey Jay (Portrait)	15.00	7.50	4.50
(24)	Eddie Kasko (Batting)	15.00	7.50	4.50
(25)	Eddie Kasko (Fielding)	15.00	7.50	4.50
(26)	Gene Kelly (Announcer)	15.00	7.50	4.50
(27)	Jerry Lynch (Batting)	15.00	7.50	4.50
(28)	Jim Maloney (Portrait)	15.00	7.50	4.50
(29)	Roy McMillan (Fielding)	15.00	7.50	4.50
(31)	Don Newcombe (Wind-up.)	20.00	10.00	6.00
(32)	Joe Nuxhall (Follow-through, long-sleeve undershirt.)	15.00	7.50	4.50
(33)	Joe Nuxhall (Follow-through, short-sleeve undershirt.)	15.00	7.50	4.50
(34)	Jim O'Toole (Portrait)	15.00	7.50	4.50
(35)	Jim O'Toole (Wind-up.)	15.00	7.50	4.50
(36)	Jim O'Toole (Follow-through.)	15.00	7.50	4.50
(37)	Don Pavletich (Portrait)	15.00	7.50	4.50
(38)	Vada Pinson (Batting, no players in background.)	20.00	10.00	6.00
(39)	Vada Pinson (Batting, players in background.)	20.00	10.00	6.00
(40)	Vada Pinson (Catching fly ball.)	20.00	10.00	6.00
(41)	Vada Pinson (Hands on knees.)	20.00	10.00	6.00
(43)	Wally Post (Batting)	15.00	7.50	4.50
(44)	Wally Post (Portrait)	15.00	7.50	4.50
(45)	Bob Purkey (Pitching, right foot visible.)	15.00	7.50	4.50
(46)	Bob Purkey (Pitching, right foot not visible.)	15.00	7.50	4.50
(47)	Bob Purkey (Portrait, teeth don't show.)	15.00	7.50	4.50
(48)	Bob Purkey (Portrait, teeth show.)	15.00	7.50	4.50
(50)	Frank Robinson (Batting, dark cap.)	45.00	22.00	13.50
(51)	Frank Robinson (Batting, white cap.)	45.00	22.00	13.50
(52)	Frank Robinson (Fielding fly ball.)	45.00	22.00	13.50
(53)	Frank Robinson (Portrait, pinstripes, black background.)	45.00	22.00	13.50
(54)	Frank Robinson (Portrait, pinstripes, natural sky background.)	45.00	22.00	13.50
(55)	Frankie Robinson (Head turned back to camera.)	45.00	22.00	13.50
(56)	Pete Rose (Portrait to chest.)	200.00	100.00	60.00

1977 Burger Chef Funmeal Discs

The largest of the disc sets produced by Michael Schechter Associates is the 216-piece issue for the Burger Chef fast food restaurant chain. The discs were issued nine-per-team on a cardboard tray accompanying a 69-cent Funmeal for kids. The 2-3/8" discs could be punched out of the tray. They share the basic design of other MSA discs of the era. A black-and-white player photo is in the center of a baseball design. Because the discs were licensed only by the Players Association, the player photos have had cap logos airbrushed away. The left and right side panels are one of several bright colors. Backs feature a Burger Chef cartoon character in color. The individual discs are unnumbered.

		NM	EX	VG
Complete Set, Trays (24):		100.00	50.00	30.00
Complete Set, Singles (216):		90.00	45.00	27.00
Common Player:		.75	.35	.20
1A	Cincinnati Reds (Full tray.)	20.00	10.00	6.00
(1A1)	Johnny Bench	4.50	2.25	1.25
(1A2)	Dave Concepcion	.75	.35	.20
(1A3)	Dan Driessen	.75	.35	.20
(1A4)	George Foster	.75	.35	.20
(1A5)	Cesar Geronimo	.75	.35	.20
(1A6)	Ken Griffey	1.25	.60	.40
(1A7)	Joe Morgan	3.50	1.75	1.00
(1A8)	Gary Nolan	.75	.35	.20
(1A9)	Pete Rose	7.50	3.75	2.25
2A	St. Louis Cardinals (Full tray.)	10.00	5.00	3.00
(2A1)	Lou Brock	3.50	1.75	1.00
(2A2)	John Denny	.75	.35	.20
(2A3)	Pete Falcone	.75	.35	.20
(2A4)	Keith Hernandez	.75	.40	.25
(2A5)	Al Hrabosky	.75	.35	.20
(2A6)	Bake McBride	.75	.35	.20
(2A7)	Ken Reitz	.75	.35	.20
(2A8)	Ted Simmons	.75	.35	.20
(2A9)	Mike Tyson	.75	.35	.20
3A	Detroit Tigers (Full tray.)	8.00	4.00	2.50
(3A1)	Mark Fidrych	1.50	.70	.45
(3A2)	Bill Freehan	.75	.35	.20
(3A3)	John Hiller	.75	.35	.20
(3A4)	Willie Horton	.75	.35	.20
(3A5)	Ron LeFlore	.75	.35	.20
(3A6)	Ben Oglivie	.75	.35	.20
(3A7)	Aurelio Rodriguez	.75	.35	.20
(3A8)	Rusty Staub	1.25	.60	.40
(3A9)	Jason Thompson	.75	.35	.20
4A	Cleveland Indians (Full tray.)	8.00	4.00	2.50
(4A1)	Buddy Bell	.75	.35	.20
(4A2)	Frank Duffy	.75	.35	.20
(4A3)	Dennis Eckersley	2.75	1.50	.80
(4A4)	Ray Fosse	.75	.35	.20
(4A5)	Wayne Garland	.75	.35	.20
(4A6)	Duane Kuiper	.75	.35	.20
(4A7)	Dave LaRoche	.75	.35	.20
(4A8)	Rick Manning	.75	.35	.20
(4A9)	Rick Waits	.75	.35	.20
5A	Chicago White Sox (Full tray.)	8.00	4.00	2.50
(5A1)	Jack Brohamer	.75	.35	.20
(5A2)	Bucky Dent	1.00	.50	.30
(5A3)	Ralph Garr	.75	.35	.20
(5A4)	Bart Johnson	.75	.35	.20
(5A5)	Lamar Johnson	.75	.35	.20
(5A6)	Chet Lemon	.75	.35	.20
(5A7)	Jorge Orta	.75	.35	.20
(5A8)	Jim Spencer	.75	.35	.20
(5A9)	Richie Zisk	.75	.35	.20
6A	Chicago Cubs (Full tray.)	8.00	4.00	2.50
(6A1)	Bill Bonham	.75	.35	.20
(6A2)	Bill Buckner	1.25	.60	.40
(6A3)	Ray Burris	.75	.35	.20
(6A4)	Jose Cardenal	.75	.35	.20
(6A5)	Bill Madlock	.75	.35	.20
(6A6)	Jerry Morales	.75	.35	.20
(6A7)	Rick Reuschel	.75	.35	.20
(6A8)	Manny Trillo	.75	.35	.20
(6A9)	Joe Wallis	.75	.35	.20
7A	Minnesota Twins (Full tray.)	10.00	5.00	3.00
(7A1)	Lyman Bostock	.75	.35	.20
(7A2)	Rod Carew	3.50	1.75	1.00
(7A3)	Mike Cubbage	.75	.35	.20
(7A4)	Dan Ford	.75	.35	.20
(7A5)	Dave Goltz	.75	.35	.20
(7A6)	Larry Hisle	.75	.35	.20
(7A7)	Tom Johnson	.75	.35	.20
(7A8)	Bobby Randall	.75	.35	.20
(7A9)	Butch Wynegar	.75	.35	.20
8A	Houston Astros (Full tray.)	8.00	4.00	2.50
(8A1)	Enos Cabell	.75	.35	.20
(8A2)	Cesar Cedeno	.75	.35	.20
(8A3)	Jose Cruz	.75	.35	.20
(8A4)	Joe Ferguson	.75	.35	.20
(8A5)	Ken Forsch	.75	.35	.20
(8A6)	Roger Metzger	.75	.35	.20
(8A7)	J.R. Richard	.75	.35	.20
(8A8)	Leon Roberts	.75	.35	.20
(8A9)	Bob Watson	.75	.35	.20
1B	Baltimore Orioles (Full tray.)	15.00	7.50	4.50
(1B1)	Mark Belanger	.75	.35	.20
(1B2)	Paul Blair	.75	.35	.20
(1B3)	Al Bumbry	.75	.35	.20
(1B4)	Doug DeCinces	.75	.35	.20
(1B5)	Ross Grimsley	.75	.35	.20
(1B6)	Lee May	.75	.35	.20
(1B7)	Jim Palmer	3.50	1.75	1.00
(1B8)	Brooks Robinson	4.50	2.25	1.25
(1B9)	Ken Singleton	.75	.35	.20
2B	Boston Red Sox (Full tray.)	15.00	7.50	4.50
(2B1)	Rick Burleson	.75	.35	.20
(2B2)	Dwight Evans	.75	.40	.25
(2B3)	Carlton Fisk	3.50	1.75	1.00
(2B4)	Fergie Jenkins	2.75	1.50	.80
(2B5)	Bill Lee	.75	.35	.20
(2B6)	Fred Lynn	.75	.40	.25
(2B7)	Jim Rice	1.50	.70	.45
(2B8)	Luis Tiant	.75	.35	.20
(2B9)	Carl Yastrzemski	4.50	2.25	1.25
3B	Kansas City Royals (Full tray.)	13.50	6.75	4.00
(3B1)	Doug Bird	.75	.35	.20
(3B2)	George Brett	6.00	3.00	1.75
(3B3)	Dennis Leonard	.75	.35	.20
(3B4)	John Mayberry	.75	.35	.20
(3B5)	Hal McRae	.75	.35	.20
(3B6)	Amos Otis	.75	.35	.20
(3B7)	Fred Patek	.75	.35	.20
(3B8)	Tom Poquette	.75	.35	.20
(3B9)	Paul Splittorff	.75	.35	.20
4B	Milwaukee Brewers (Full tray.)	10.00	5.00	3.00
(4B1)	Jerry Augustine	.75	.35	.20
(4B2)	Sal Bando	.75	.35	.20
(4B3)	Von Joshua	.75	.35	.20
(4B4)	Sixto Lezcano	.75	.35	.20
(4B5)	Charlie Moore	.75	.35	.20
(4B6)	Ed Rodriguez	.75	.35	.20
(4B7)	Jim Slaton	.75	.35	.20
(4B8)	Bill Travers	.75	.35	.20
(4B9)	Robin Yount	3.50	1.75	1.00
5B	Texas Rangers (Full tray.)	10.00	5.00	3.00

(5B1)	Juan Beniquez	.75	.35	.20
(5B2)	Bert Blyleven	.75	.35	.20
(5B3)	Bert Campaneris	.75	.35	.20
(5B4)	Tom Grieve	.75	.35	.20
(5B5)	Mike Hargrove	.75	.35	.20
(5B6)	Toby Harrah	.75	.35	.20
(5B7)	Gaylord Perry	2.75	1.50	.80
(5B8)	Lenny Randle	.75	.35	.20
(5B9)	Jim Sundberg	.75	.35	.20
6B	Atlanta Braves (Full tray.)	8.00	4.00	2.50
(6B1)	Jeff Burroughs	.75	.35	.20
(6B2)	Darrel Chaney	.75	.35	.20
(6B3)	Gary Matthews	.75	.35	.20
(6B4)	Andy Messersmith	.75	.35	.20
(6B5)	Willie Montanez	.75	.35	.20
(6B6)	Phil Niekro	2.75	1.50	.80
(6B7)	Tom Paciorek	.75	.35	.20
(6B8)	Jerry Royster	.75	.35	.20
(6B9)	Dick Ruthven	.75	.35	.20
7B	Pittsburgh Pirates (Full tray.)	10.00	5.00	3.00
(7B1)	John Candelaria	.75	.35	.20
(7B2)	Duffy Dyer	.75	.35	.20
(7B3)	Al Oliver	1.25	.60	.40
(7B4)	Dave Parker	.75	.40	.25
(7B5)	Jerry Reuss	.75	.35	.20
(7B6)	Bill Robinson	.75	.35	.20
(7B7)	Willie Stargell	3.50	1.75	1.00
(7B8)	Rennie Stennett	.75	.35	.20
(7B9)	Frank Taveras	.75	.35	.20
8B	New York Yankees (Full tray.)	20.00	10.00	6.00
(8B1)	Chris Chambliss	.75	.35	.20
(8B2)	Don Gullett	.75	.35	.20
(8B3)	Catfish Hunter	2.75	1.50	.80
(8B4)	Reggie Jackson	5.00	2.50	1.50
(8B5)	Thurman Munson	4.50	2.25	1.25
(8B6)	Graig Nettles	.75	.35	.20
(8B7)	Willie Randolph	.75	.35	.20
(8B8)	Mickey Rivers	.75	.35	.20
(8B9)	Roy White	.75	.35	.20
1C	California Angels (Full tray.)	25.00	12.50	7.50
(1C1)	Bobby Bonds	.75	.35	.20
(1C2)	Dave Chalk	.75	.35	.20
(1C3)	Bobby Grich	.75	.35	.20
(1C4)	Paul Hartzell	.75	.35	.20
(1C5)	Ron Jackson	.75	.35	.20
(1C6)	Jerry Remy	.75	.35	.20
(1C7)	Joe Rudi	.75	.35	.20
(1C8)	Nolan Ryan	16.00	8.00	4.75
(1C9)	Frank Tanana	.75	.35	.20
2C	Oakland A's (Full tray.)	8.00	4.00	2.50
(2C1)	Stan Bahnsen	.75	.35	.20
(2C2)	Vida Blue	.75	.35	.20
(2C3)	Phil Garner	.75	.35	.20
(2C4)	Paul Lindblad	.75	.35	.20
(2C5)	Mike Norris	.75	.35	.20
(2C6)	Bill North	.75	.35	.20
(2C7)	Manny Sanguillen	.75	.35	.20
(2C8)	Mike Torrez	.75	.35	.20
(2C9)	Claudell Washington	.75	.35	.20
3C	Los Angeles Dodgers (Full tray.)	10.00	5.00	3.00
(3C1)	Ron Cey	.75	.35	.20
(3C2)	Steve Garvey	2.00	1.00	.60
(3C3)	Davey Lopes	.75	.35	.20
(3C4)	Rick Monday	.75	.35	.20
(3C5)	Doug Rau	.75	.35	.20
(3C6)	Rick Rhoden	.75	.35	.20
(3C7)	Reggie Smith	.75	.35	.20
(3C8)	Don Sutton	2.75	1.50	.80
(3C9)	Steve Yeager	.75	.35	.20
4C	Montreal Expos (Full tray.)	10.00	5.00	3.00
(4C1)	Gary Carter	3.00	1.50	.90
(4C2)	Dave Cash	.75	.35	.20
(4C3)	Tim Foli	.75	.35	.20
(4C4)	Barry Foote	.75	.35	.20
(4C5)	Larry Parrish	.75	.35	.20
(4C6)	Tony Perez	3.00	1.50	.90
(4C7)	Steve Rogers	.75	.35	.20
(4C8)	Del Unser	.75	.35	.20
(4C9)	Ellis Valentine	.75	.35	.20
5C	New York Mets (Full tray.)	13.50	6.75	4.00
(5C1)	Bud Harrelson	.75	.35	.20
(5C2)	Dave Kingman	1.00	.50	.30
(5C3)	Jerry Koosman	.75	.35	.20
(5C4)	Ed Kranepool	.75	.35	.20
(5C5)	Skip Lockwood	.75	.35	.20
(5C6)	Jon Matlack	.75	.35	.20
(5C7)	Felix Millan	.75	.35	.20
(5C8)	Tom Seaver	4.50	2.25	1.25
(5C9)	John Stearns	.75	.35	.20
6C	Philadelphia Phillies (Full tray.)	15.00	7.50	4.50
(6C1)	Bob Boone	1.00	.50	.30
(6C2)	Larry Bowa	.75	.35	.20
(6C3)	Steve Carlton	3.50	1.75	1.00
(6C4)	Jay Johnstone	.75	.35	.20
(6C5)	Jim Kaat	1.25	.60	.40
(6C6)	Greg Luzinski	.75	.40	.25
(6C7)	Garry Maddox	.75	.35	.20
(6C8)	Tug McGraw	1.25	.60	.40
(6C9)	Mike Schmidt	6.00	3.00	1.75
7C	San Diego Padres (Full tray.)	10.00	5.00	3.00
(7C1)	Rollie Fingers	2.75	1.50	.80
(7C2)	George Hendrick	.75	.35	.20
(7C3)	Enzo Hernandez	.75	.35	.20
(7C4)	Mike Ivie	.75	.35	.20
(7C5)	Randy Jones	.75	.35	.20
(7C6)	Butch Metzger	.75	.35	.20
(7C7)	Dave Rader	.75	.35	.20
(7C8)	Gene Tenace	.75	.35	.20
(7C9)	Dave Winfield	3.50	1.75	1.00
8C	San Francisco Giants (Full tray.)	8.00	4.00	2.50
(8C1)	Jim Barr	.75	.35	.20
(8C2)	Willie Crawford	.75	.35	.20
(8C3)	Larry Herndon	.75	.35	.20
(8C4)	Randy Moffitt	.75	.35	.20
(8C5)	John Montefusco	.75	.35	.20
(8C6)	Bobby Murcer	.75	.35	.20
(8C7)	Marty Perez	.75	.35	.20
(8C8)	Chris Speier	.75	.35	.20
(8C9)	Gary Thomasson	.75	.35	.20

1977 Burger King Tigers

This series of color 8" x 10" player portraits was given away one per week at Detroit area Burger Kings. Backs are blank and there is no player identification on the front. The photos are checklisted here alphabetically.

		NM	EX	VG
Complete Set (4):		40.00	20.00	12.00
Common Player:		10.00	5.00	3.00
(1)	Mark Fidrych (Holding glove.)	15.00	7.50	4.50
(2)	Ron LeFlore (Black guy w/bat.)	10.00	5.00	3.00
(3)	Dave Rozema (Winding up.)	10.00	5.00	3.00
(4)	Mickey Stanley (White guy w/bat.)	10.00	5.00	3.00

1977 Burger King Yankees

The first Topps-produced set for Burger King restaurants was issued in the New York area, featuring the A.L. champion Yankees. Twenty-two players plus an unnumbered checklist were issued at the beginning of the promotion with card #23 (Lou Piniella) being added to the set later. The "New York Post" reported production of the first 22 player cards at about 170,000 of each. The Piniella card was issued in limited quantities. Cards are 2-1/2" x 3-1/2" and have fronts identical to the regular 1977 Topps set except for numbers 2, 6, 7, 13, 14, 15, 17, 20 and 21. These cards feature different poses or major picture-cropping variations. It should be noted that very minor cropping variations between the regular Topps sets and the Burger King issues exist throughout the years the sets were produced.

		NM	EX	VG
Complete Set w/Piniella (24):		20.00	10.00	6.00
Complete Set no Piniella (23):		13.50	6.75	4.00
Common Player:		.25	.13	.08
1	Yankees Team (Billy Martin)	.75	.40	.25
2	Thurman Munson	5.00	2.50	1.50
3	Fran Healy	.25	.13	.08
4	Catfish Hunter	1.50	.70	.45
5	Ed Figueroa	.25	.13	.08
6	Don Gullett	.25	.13	.08
7	Mike Torrez	.25	.13	.08
8	Ken Holtzman	.25	.13	.08
9	Dick Tidrow	.25	.13	.08
10	Sparky Lyle	.40	.20	.12
11	Ron Guidry	.45	.25	.14
12	Chris Chambliss	.25	.13	.08
13	Willie Randolph	.45	.25	.14
14	Bucky Dent	.25	.13	.08
15	Graig Nettles	.60	.30	.20
16	Fred Stanley	.25	.13	.08
17	Reggie Jackson	5.00	2.50	1.50
18	Mickey Rivers	.25	.13	.08
19	Roy White	.40	.20	.12
20	Jim Wynn	.40	.20	.12
21	Paul Blair	.25	.13	.08
22	Carlos May	.25	.13	.08
23	Lou Piniella	15.00	7.50	4.50
---	Checklist	.05	.03	.02

1978 Burger King Astros

Burger King restaurants in the Houston area distributed a Topps-produced set showcasing the Astros. Cards are standard 2-1/2" x 3-1/2" and are numbered 1-22, plus and unnumbered checklist. Fronts are identical to the regular 1978 Topps set with the exception of card numbers 21, Dave Bergman, who appeared on a Rookie Outfielders cards in the '78 Topps set; and 22, Jesus Alou, who did not have a card in the regular issue. Although not noted in the following checklist, it should

be remembered that very minor picture-cropping variations between the regular Topps issues and the 1977-1980 Burger King sets do exist.

		NM	EX	VG
Complete Set (23):		15.00	7.50	4.50
Common Player:		.75	.40	.25
1	Bill Virdon	.90	.45	.25
2	Joe Ferguson	.75	.40	.25
3	Ed Herrmann	.75	.40	.25
4	J.R. Richard	1.50	.70	.45
5	Joe Niekro	1.25	.60	.40
6	Floyd Bannister	.75	.40	.25
7	Joaquin Andujar	.75	.40	.25
8	Ken Forsch	.75	.40	.25
9	Mark Lemongello	.75	.40	.25
10	Joe Sambito	.75	.40	.25
11	Gene Pentz	.75	.40	.25
12	Bob Watson	.90	.45	.25
13	Julio Gonzalez	.75	.40	.25
14	Enos Cabell	.75	.40	.25
15	Roger Metzger	.75	.40	.25
16	Art Howe	.90	.45	.25
17	Jose Cruz	1.00	.50	.30
18	Cesar Cedeno	1.00	.50	.30
19	Terry Puhl	.75	.40	.25
20	Wilbur Howard	.75	.40	.25
21	Dave Bergman	.75	.40	.25
22	Jesus Alou	1.00	.50	.30
---	Checklist	.10	.05	.03

1978 Burger King Rangers

Issued by Burger King restaurants in the Dallas-Fort Worth area, this Topps-produced set features the Texas Rangers. Cards are standard 2-1/2" x 3-1/2" and identical in style to the regular 1978 Topps set with the following exceptions: #'s 5, 8, 10, 12, 17, 21 and 22. An unnumbered checklist card was included with the set.

		NM	EX	VG
Complete Set (23):		15.00	7.50	4.50
Common Player:		.75	.40	.25
1	Billy Hunter	.75	.40	.25
2	Jim Sundberg	.75	.40	.25
3	John Ellis	.75	.40	.25
4	Doyle Alexander	.75	.40	.25
5	Jon Matlack	.75	.40	.25
6	Dock Ellis	.75	.40	.25
7	George Medich	.75	.40	.25
8	Fergie Jenkins	6.00	3.00	1.75
9	Len Barker	.75	.40	.25
10	Reggie Cleveland	.75	.40	.25
11	Mike Hargrove	1.00	.50	.30
12	Bump Wills	1.00	.50	.30
13	Toby Harrah	1.00	.50	.30
14	Bert Campaneris	1.00	.50	.30
15	Sandy Alomar	1.00	.50	.30
16	Kurt Bevacqua	.75	.40	.25
17	Al Oliver	1.50	.70	.45
18	Juan Beniquez	.75	.40	.25
19	Claudell Washington	.75	.40	.25
20	Richie Zisk	.75	.40	.25
21	John Lowenstein	.75	.40	.25
22	Bobby Thompson	.75	.40	.25
---	Checklist	.10	.05	.03

1978 Burger King Tigers

Rookie cards of Morris, Trammell and Whitaker make the Topps-produced 1978 Burger King Detroit Tigers issue the most popular of the BK sets. Twenty-two player cards and an unnumbered checklist make up the set which was issued in the Detroit area. Cards measure 2-1/2" x 3-1/2", and are identical to the regular 1978 Topps issue with the following exceptions: #'s 6, 7, 8, 13, 15 and 16. Numerous minor picture-cropping variations between the regular Topps issues and the Burger King sets appear from 1977-1980; these minor variations are not noted in the following checklist.

	NM	EX	VG
Complete Set (23):	25.00	12.50	7.50
Common Player:	.75	.40	.25
1 Ralph Houk	.90	.45	.25
2 Milt May	.75	.40	.25
3 John Wockenfuss	.75	.40	.25
4 Mark Fidrych	2.50	1.25	.70
5 Dave Rozema	.75	.40	.25
6 Jack Billingham	.75	.40	.25
7 Jim Slaton	.75	.40	.25
8 Jack Morris	3.00	1.50	.90
9 John Hiller	.75	.40	.25
10 Steve Foucault	.75	.40	.25
11 Milt Wilcox	.75	.40	.25
12 Jason Thompson	.75	.40	.25
13 Lou Whitaker	6.00	3.00	1.75
14 Aurelio Rodriguez	.75	.40	.25
15 Alan Trammell	10.00	5.00	3.00
16 Steve Dillard	.75	.40	.25
17 Phil Mankowski	.75	.40	.25
18 Steve Kemp	.75	.40	.25
19 Ron LeFlore	.90	.45	.25
20 Tim Corcoran	.75	.40	.25
21 Mickey Stanley	.75	.40	.25
22 Rusty Staub	.90	.45	.25
--- Checklist	.10	.05	.03

1978 Burger King Yankees

 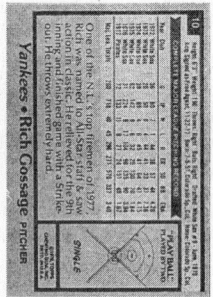

Produced by Topps for Burger King outlets in the New York area for the second year in a row, the 1978 Yankees set contains 22 cards plus an unnumbered checklist. The cards are numbered 1 through 22 and are the standard size of 2-1/2" x 3-1/2". The cards feature the same pictures found in the regular 1978 Topps set except for numbers 10, 11 and 16. Only those variations containing different poses or major picture-cropping differences are noted. Numerous minor picture-cropping variations, that are very insignificant in nature, exist between the regular Topps sets and the Burger King issues of 1977-1980.

	NM	EX	VG
Complete Set (23):	15.00	7.50	4.50
Common Player:	.50	.25	.15
1 Billy Martin	1.50	.70	.45
2 Thurman Munson	5.00	2.50	1.50
3 Cliff Johnson	.50	.25	.15
4 Ron Guidry	1.00	.50	.30
5 Ed Figueroa	.50	.25	.15
6 Dick Tidrow	.50	.25	.15
7 Catfish Hunter	2.00	1.00	.60
8 Don Gullett	.50	.25	.15
9 Sparky Lyle	1.00	.50	.30
10 Rich Gossage	1.50	.70	.45
11 Rawly Eastwick	.50	.25	.15
12 Chris Chambliss	.50	.25	.15
13 Willie Randolph	1.00	.50	.30
14 Graig Nettles	1.00	.50	.30
15 Bucky Dent	1.00	.50	.30
16 Jim Spencer	.50	.25	.15
17 Fred Stanley	.50	.25	.15
18 Lou Piniella	1.25	.60	.40
19 Roy White	1.00	.50	.30
20 Mickey Rivers	.50	.25	.15
21 Reggie Jackson	6.00	3.00	1.75
22 Paul Blair	.50	.25	.15
--- Checklist	.10	.05	.03

1979 Burger King Phillies

Twenty-two Phillies players are featured in the 1979 Burger King issue given out in the Philadelphia area. The Topps-produced set, measuring 2-1/2" x 3-1/2", also includes an unnumbered checklist. Cards are identical to the regular 1979 Topps set except #1, 11, 12, 13, 14, 17 and 22, which

have different poses. Very minor picture-cropping variations between the regular Topps issues and the Burger King sets can be found throughout the four years the cards were produced, but only those variations featuring major changes are noted in the checklists.

	NM	EX	VG
Complete Set (23):	7.50	3.75	2.25
Common Player:	.25	.13	.08
1 Danny Ozark	.25	.13	.08
2 Bob Boone	.45	.25	.14
3 Tim McCarver	.50	.25	.15
4 Steve Carlton	1.50	.70	.45
5 Larry Christenson	.25	.13	.08
6 Dick Ruthven	.25	.13	.08
7 Ron Reed	.25	.13	.08
8 Randy Lerch	.25	.13	.08
9 Warren Brusstar	.25	.13	.08
10 Tug McGraw	.40	.20	.12
11 Nino Espinosa	.25	.13	.08
12 Doug Bird	.25	.13	.08
13 Pete Rose	3.00	1.50	.90
14 Manny Trillo	.25	.13	.08
15 Larry Bowa	.40	.20	.12
16 Mike Schmidt	3.00	1.50	.90
17 Pete Mackanin	.25	.13	.08
18 Jose Cardenal	.25	.13	.08
19 Greg Luzinski	.25	.13	.08
20 Garry Maddox	.25	.13	.08
21 Bake McBride	.25	.13	.08
22 Greg Gross	.25	.13	.08
--- Checklist	.08	.04	.02

1979 Burger King Yankees

The New York Yankees were featured in a Topps-produced Burger King set for the third consecutive year in 1979. Once again, 22 numbered player cards and an unnumbered checklist made up the set. Cards measure 2-1/2" x 3-1/2", and are identical to the 1979 Topps regular set except for #4, 8, 9 and 22 which included new poses. Numerous minor picture cropping variations between the regular Topps issue and the Burger King sets of 1977-1980 exist.

	NM	EX	VG
Complete Set (23):	7.50	3.75	2.25
Common Player:	.25	.13	.08
1 Yankees Team (Bob Lemon)	.75	.40	.25
2 Thurman Munson	2.50	1.25	.70
3 Cliff Johnson	.25	.13	.08
4 Ron Guidry	.60	.30	.20
5 Jay Johnstone	.40	.20	.12
6 Catfish Hunter	1.25	.60	.40
7 Jim Beattie	.25	.13	.08
8 Luis Tiant	.40	.20	.12
9 Tommy John	.75	.40	.25
10 Rich Gossage	.60	.30	.20
11 Ed Figueroa	.25	.13	.08
12 Chris Chambliss	.25	.13	.08
13 Willie Randolph	.40	.20	.12
14 Bucky Dent	.40	.20	.12
15 Graig Nettles	.40	.20	.12
16 Fred Stanley	.25	.13	.08
17 Jim Spencer	.25	.13	.08
18 Lou Piniella	.60	.30	.20
19 Roy White	.40	.20	.12
20 Mickey Rivers	.25	.13	.08
21 Reggie Jackson	4.00	2.00	1.25
22 Juan Beniquez	.25	.13	.08
--- Checklist	.06	.03	.02

1980 Burger King Phillies

Philadelphia-area Burger King outlets issued a 23-card set featuring the Phillies for the second in a row in 1980. The Topps-produced set, measuring 2-1/2" x 3-1/2", contains 22 player cards and an unnumbered checklist. Fronts are identical in design to the regular 1980 Topps sets with the following excep-

tions: #1, 3, 8, 14 and 22 feature new poses. Very minor picture-cropping variations between the regular Topps issues and the Burger King sets exist in all years. Those minor differences are not noted in the checklists. The 1980 Burger King sets were the first to include the Burger King logo on the card backs.

	NM	EX	VG
Complete Set (23):	6.00	3.00	1.75
Common Player:	.10	.05	.03
1 Dallas Green	.15	.08	.05
2 Bob Boone	.50	.25	.15
3 Keith Moreland	.25	.13	.08
4 Pete Rose	2.50	1.25	.70
5 Manny Trillo	.10	.05	.03
6 Mike Schmidt	2.50	1.25	.70
7 Larry Bowa	.20	.10	.06
8 John Vukovich	.10	.05	.03
9 Bake McBride	.10	.05	.03
10 Garry Maddox	.10	.05	.03
11 Greg Luzinski	.25	.13	.08
12 Greg Gross	.10	.05	.03
13 Del Unser	.10	.05	.03
14 Lonnie Smith	.40	.20	.12
15 Steve Carlton	1.00	.50	.30
16 Larry Christenson	.10	.05	.03
17 Nino Espinosa	.10	.05	.03
18 Randy Lerch	.10	.05	.03
19 Dick Ruthven	.10	.05	.03
20 Tug McGraw	.15	.08	.05
21 Ron Reed	.10	.05	.03
22 Kevin Saucier	.10	.05	.03
--- Checklist	.05	.03	.02

1980 Burger King Pitch, Hit & Run

In 1980, Burger King issued, in conjunction with its "Pitch, Hit & Run" promotion, a Topps-produced set featuring pitchers (card #s 1-11), hitters (#s 12-22), and base stealers (#s 23-33). Fronts, which carry the Burger King logo, are identical in design to the regular 1980 Topps set except for numbers 1, 4, 5, 7, 9, 10, 16, 17, 18, 22, 23, 27, 28, 29 and 30, which feature different poses. Cards measure 2-1/2" x 3-1/2" in size. An unnumbered checklist was included with the set.

	NM	EX	VG
Complete Set (34):	10.00	5.00	3.00
Common Player:	.10	.05	.03
1 Vida Blue	.10	.05	.03
2 Steve Carlton	1.00	.50	.30
3 Rollie Fingers	.65	.35	.20
4 Ron Guidry	.25	.13	.08
5 Jerry Koosman	.10	.05	.03
6 Phil Niekro	.65	.35	.20
7 Jim Palmer	1.00	.50	.30
8 J.R. Richard	.10	.05	.03
9 Nolan Ryan	4.00	2.00	1.25
10 Tom Seaver	1.00	.50	.30
11 Bruce Sutter	1.00	.50	.30
12 Don Baylor	.10	.05	.03
13 George Brett	2.00	1.00	.60
14 Rod Carew	1.00	.50	.30
15 George Foster	.10	.05	.03
16 Keith Hernandez	.10	.05	.03
17 Reggie Jackson	1.50	.70	.45
18 Fred Lynn	.10	.05	.03
19 Dave Parker	.10	.05	.03
20 Jim Rice	.30	.15	.09
21 Pete Rose	3.00	1.50	.90
22 Dave Winfield	1.00	.50	.30
23 Bobby Bonds	.10	.05	.03
24 Enos Cabell	.10	.05	.03
25 Cesar Cedeno	.10	.05	.03
26 Julio Cruz	.10	.05	.03
27 Ron LeFlore	.10	.05	.03
28 Dave Lopes	.10	.05	.03
29 Omar Moreno	.10	.05	.03
30 Joe Morgan	1.00	.50	.30
31 Bill North	.10	.05	.03
32 Frank Taveras	.10	.05	.03

| 33 | Willie Wilson | .10 | .05 | .03 |
| --- | Checklist | .05 | .03 | .02 |

1916 Burgess-Nash Clothiers

This 200-card set can be found with ads on the back for several local and regional businesses. Among them is Burgess-Nash clothiers, from Omaha, Neb. Type card and superstar collectors can expect to pay a significant premium for cards with the Burgess-Nash advertising, compared to the generic M101-4 Blank Backs values. Cards measure about 1-5/8" x 3" and are printed in black-and-white.

PREMIUM: 6-12X
(See 1916 M101-4 Blank Backs for checklist.)

1935 George Burke Detroit Tigers Photo Stamps

This team set of black-and-white, 1-1/16" x 1-1/4" photo stamps was produced by baseball photographer George Burke. The set was printed on two sheets of 12 players each. Each stamp has the player's name, position abbreviation and city in black or white typography. The blank-backed ungummed stamps of the 1935 World's Champs are checklisted here in alphabetical order.

		NM	EX	VG
	Complete Set (24):	325.00	160.00	95.00
	Common Player:	10.00	5.00	3.00
(1)	Elden Auker	10.00	5.00	3.00
(2)	Del Baker	10.00	5.00	3.00
(3)	Tom Bridges	10.00	5.00	3.00
(4)	Herman Clifton	10.00	5.00	3.00
(5)	Mickey Cochrane	30.00	15.00	9.00
(6)	Alvin Crowder	10.00	5.00	3.00
(7)	Ervin Fox	10.00	5.00	3.00
(8)	Charles Gehringer	30.00	15.00	9.00
(9)	Leon Goslin	30.00	15.00	9.00
(10)	Henry Greenberg	45.00	22.50	13.50
(11)	Raymond Hayworth	10.00	5.00	3.00
(12)	Elon Hogsett	10.00	5.00	3.00
(13)	Roxie Lawson	10.00	5.00	3.00
(14)	Marvin Owen	10.00	5.00	3.00
(15)	Ralph Perkins	10.00	5.00	3.00
(16)	Frank Reiber	10.00	5.00	3.00
(17)	Wm. Rogell	10.00	5.00	3.00
(18)	Lynwood Rowe	12.50	6.25	3.75
(19)	Henry Schuble	10.00	5.00	3.00
(20)	Hugh Shelley	10.00	5.00	3.00
(21)	Victor Sorrell	10.00	5.00	3.00
(22)	Joseph Sullivan	10.00	5.00	3.00
(23)	Gerald Walker	10.00	5.00	3.00
(24)	Joyner White	10.00	5.00	3.00

1935-37 George Burke Postage Stamp Photos

These small (3/4" x 1") black-and-white stamps were produced by Chicago baseball portraitist George Burke for sale to individual players for use in answering fan mail. The stamps were not a big seller, though the checklist presented alphabetically here is surely incomplete. The unnumbered stamps, which are blank-backed, were not self-adhesive and were printed in sheets of at least six of the same player. Some of the photo-stamps have facsimile autographs, others do not.

	NM	EX	VG
Common Player:	10.00	5.00	3.00
Luke Appling	20.00	10.00	6.00
Jimmy Austin	10.00	5.00	3.00
Dick Bartell	10.00	5.00	3.00
Huck Betts	10.00	5.00	3.00
George Blaeholder	10.00	5.00	3.00
Jim Bottomley	20.00	10.00	6.00
Earl Browne	10.00	5.00	3.00
Irving Burns	10.00	5.00	3.00
Sam Byrd	10.00	5.00	3.00
Gilly Campbell	10.00	5.00	3.00
James (Tex) Carleton	10.00	5.00	3.00
Hugh Casey	10.00	5.00	3.00
James "Rip" Collins	10.00	5.00	3.00
Earle Combs	20.00	10.00	6.00
Adam Comorosky	10.00	5.00	3.00
Jocko Conlan	20.00	10.00	6.00
Kiki Cuyler	20.00	10.00	6.00
Paul Derringer	10.00	5.00	3.00
Jim DeShong	10.00	5.00	3.00
Bill Dickey	20.00	10.00	6.00
Bill Dietrich	10.00	5.00	3.00
Carl Doyle	10.00	5.00	3.00
Chuck Dressen	10.00	5.00	3.00
Jimmy Dykes	10.00	5.00	3.00
Hank Erickson	10.00	5.00	3.00
Wes Ferrell	10.00	5.00	3.00
Arthur Fletcher	10.00	5.00	3.00
Jimmie Foxx	40.00	20.00	12.00
(Facsimile autograph.)			
Jimmie Foxx (No autograph.)	40.00	20.00	12.00
Larry French	10.00	5.00	3.00
Benny Frey	10.00	5.00	3.00
Tony Freitas	10.00	5.00	3.00
Frankie Frisch	20.00	10.00	6.00
Ed Gharrity	10.00	5.00	3.00
Lefty Gomez	20.00	10.00	6.00
Charlie Grimm	10.00	5.00	3.00
Stan Hack	10.00	5.00	3.00
Chick Hafey	20.00	10.00	6.00
Mel Harder	10.00	5.00	3.00
Bucky Harris	20.00	10.00	6.00
Gabby Hartnett	20.00	10.00	6.00
Roy Henshaw	10.00	5.00	3.00
Babe Herman	15.00	7.50	4.50
Billy Herman	20.00	10.00	6.00
Leroy Herrmann	10.00	5.00	3.00
Myril Hoag	10.00	5.00	3.00
Al Hollingsworth	10.00	5.00	3.00
Carl Hubbell	30.00	15.00	9.00
Bob Johnson	10.00	5.00	3.00
Douglas Johnson	10.00	5.00	3.00
Si Johnson	10.00	5.00	3.00
George L. Kelly	20.00	10.00	6.00
Chuck Klein	20.00	10.00	6.00
Mark Koenig	10.00	5.00	3.00
Tony Lazzeri	30.00	15.00	9.00
Bill Lee	10.00	5.00	3.00
Dutch Leonard	10.00	5.00	3.00
Ernie Lombardi	20.00	10.00	6.00
Al Lopez	20.00	10.00	6.00
Adolfo Luque	15.00	7.50	4.50
Earle Mack	10.00	5.00	3.00
Roy Mahaffey	10.00	5.00	3.00
Gus Mancuso	10.00	5.00	3.00
Rabbit Maranville	20.00	10.00	6.00
Johnny Marcum	10.00	5.00	3.00
Joe McCarthy	20.00	10.00	6.00
Eric McNair	10.00	5.00	3.00
Van Lingle Mungo	10.00	5.00	3.00
Skeeter Newsome	10.00	5.00	3.00
Mel Ott	40.00	20.00	12.00
Claude Passeau	10.00	5.00	3.00
Monte Pearson	10.00	5.00	3.00
Raymond Pepper	10.00	5.00	3.00
Charlie Root	10.00	6.00	3.00
Red Ruffing	20.00	10.00	6.00
George Selkirk	10.00	5.00	3.00
Joe Sewell	20.00	10.00	6.00
Luke Sewell	10.00	5.00	3.00
Al Simmons	20.00	10.00	6.00
Casey Stengel	20.00	10.00	6.00
Riggs Stephenson	10.00	5.00	3.00
Alan Strange	10.00	5.00	3.00
Gus Suhr	10.00	5.00	3.00
Billy Sullivan	10.00	5.00	3.00
Dan Taylor	10.00	5.00	3.00
Fay Thomas	10.00	5.00	3.00
Hal Trosky	10.00	5.00	3.00
Honus Wagner	40.00	20.00	12.00
Rube Walberg	10.00	5.00	3.00
Paul Waner	20.00	10.00	6.00
Lon Warneke	10.00	5.00	3.00
Harold Warstler	10.00	5.00	3.00
Billy Webb	10.00	5.00	3.00
Whitlow Wyatt	10.00	5.00	3.00

1933 Butter Cream (R306)

The 1933 Butter Cream set consists of unnumbered, black-and-white cards which measure 1-1/4" x 3-1/2". Backs feature a contest in which the collector was to estimate players' statistics by a specific date. Two different backs are known: 1) Estimate through Sept. 1 and no company address, and 2) Estimate through Oct. 1 with the Butter Cream address. The ACC designation for the set is R306.

 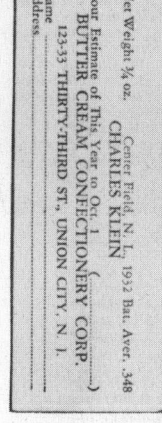

		NM	EX	VG
	Complete Set w/o Ruth:	25,000	12,500	6,000
	Common Player:	750.00	375.00	165.00
(1)	Earl Averill	1,000	500.00	225.00
(2)	Ed. Brandt	750.00	375.00	165.00
(3)	Guy T. Bush	750.00	375.00	165.00
(4)	Gordon Cochrane	1,000	500.00	225.00
(5)	Joe Cronin	1,000	500.00	225.00
(6)	George Earnshaw	750.00	375.00	165.00
(7)	Wesley Ferrell	750.00	375.00	165.00
(8)	"Jimmy" E. Foxx	2,000	1,000	440.00
(9)	Frank C. Frisch	1,000	500.00	225.00
(10)	Charles M. Gelbert	750.00	375.00	165.00
(11)	"Lefty" Robert M. Grove	1,200	600.00	265.00
(12)	Leo Charles Hartnett	1,000	500.00	225.00
(13)	"Babe" Herman	750.00	375.00	165.00
(14)	Charles Klein	1,000	500.00	220.00
(15)	Ray Kremer	750.00	375.00	165.00
(16)	Fred C. Linstrom (Lindstrom)	1,000	500.00	225.00
(17)	Ted A. Lyons	1,000	500.00	225.00
(18)	"Pepper" John L. Martin	900.00	450.00	200.00
(19)	Robert O'Farrell	750.00	375.00	165.00
(20)	Ed. A. Rommel	750.00	375.00	165.00
(21)	Charles Root	750.00	375.00	165.00
(22)	Harold "Muddy" Ruel (Herold)	750.00	375.00	165.00
(23)	Babe Ruth	30,000	15,000	6,600
(24)	"Al" Simmons	1,000	500.00	225.00
(25)	"Bill" Terry	1,000	500.00	225.00
(26)	George E. Uhle	750.00	375.00	165.00
(27)	Lloyd J. Waner	1,000	500.00	225.00
(28)	Paul G. Waner	1,000	500.00	225.00
(29)	Hack Wilson	1,000	500.00	225.00
(30)	Glen. Wright	750.00	375.00	165.00

1934 Butterfinger (R310)

Cards in this set were available as a premium with Butterfinger and other candy products. The unnumbered cards measure approximately 7-3/4" x 9-1/2" and can be found printed either on paper or heavy cardboard. The cardboard variety carry red advertising for Butterfinger and are valued about 4X the paper version. The black-and-white cards feature a player photo with facsimile autograph. Similar cards in a 6-1/2" x 8-1/2" format are a companion Canadian issue.

		NM	EX	VG
	Complete Set (65):	6,500	3,250	2,000
	Common Player:	60.00	30.00	18.00
	Cardboard Ad Variety: 4X	.00	.00	.00
(1)	Earl Averill	110.00	55.00	35.00
(2)	Richard Bartell	60.00	30.00	18.00
(3)	Larry Benton	60.00	30.00	18.00
(4)	Walter Berger	60.00	30.00	18.00
(5)	Jim Bottomly (Bottomley)	110.00	55.00	35.00
(6)	Ralph Boyle	60.00	30.00	18.00
(7)	Tex Carleton	60.00	30.00	18.00
(8)	Owen T. Carroll	60.00	30.00	18.00
(9)	Ben Chapman	60.00	30.00	18.00
(10)	Gordon (Mickey) Cochrane	110.00	55.00	35.00
(11)	James Collins	60.00	30.00	18.00
(12)	Joe Cronin	110.00	55.00	35.00
(13)	Alvin Crowder	60.00	30.00	18.00
(14)	"Dizzy" Dean	240.00	120.00	75.00
(15)	Paul Derringer	60.00	30.00	18.00
(16)	William Dickey	125.00	62.00	37.00
(17)	Leo Durocher	110.00	55.00	35.00
(18)	George Earnshaw	60.00	30.00	18.00
(19)	Richard Ferrell	110.00	55.00	35.00
(20)	Lew Fonseca	60.00	30.00	18.00
(21a)	Jimmy Fox (Name incorrect.)	225.00	110.00	70.00
(21b)	Jimmy Foxx (Name correct.)	185.00	95.00	55.00

		NM	EX	VG
(22)	Benny Frey	60.00	30.00	18.00
(23)	Frankie Frisch	110.00	55.00	35.00
(24)	Lou Gehrig	750.00	375.00	225.00
(25)	Charles Gehringer	110.00	55.00	35.00
(26)	Vernon Gomez	110.00	55.00	35.00
(27)	Ray Grabowski	60.00	30.00	18.00
(28)	Robert (Lefty) Grove	150.00	75.00	45.00
(29)	George (Mule) Haas	60.00	30.00	18.00
(30)	"Chick" Hafey	110.00	55.00	35.00
(31)	Stanley Harris	110.00	55.00	35.00
(32)	J. Francis Hogan	60.00	30.00	18.00
(33)	Ed Holley	60.00	30.00	18.00
(34)	Rogers Hornsby	150.00	75.00	45.00
(35)	Waite Hoyt	110.00	55.00	35.00
(36)	Walter Johnson	250.00	125.00	75.00
(37)	Jim Jordan	60.00	30.00	18.00
(38)	Joe Kuhel	60.00	30.00	18.00
(39)	Hal Lee	60.00	30.00	18.00
(40)	Gus Mancuso	60.00	30.00	18.00
(41)	Henry Manush	110.00	55.00	35.00
(42)	Fred Marberry	60.00	30.00	18.00
(43)	Pepper Martin	85.00	45.00	25.00
(44)	Oscar Melillo	60.00	30.00	18.00
(45)	Johnny Moore	60.00	30.00	18.00
(46)	Joe Morrissey	60.00	30.00	18.00
(47)	Joe Mowrey	60.00	30.00	18.00
(48)	Bob O'Farrell	60.00	30.00	18.00
(49)	Melvin Ott	125.00	65.00	35.00
(50)	Monte Pearson	60.00	30.00	18.00
(51)	Carl Reynolds	60.00	30.00	18.00
(52)	Charles Ruffing	110.00	55.00	35.00
(53)	Babe Ruth	750.00	375.00	225.00
(54)	John "Blondy" Ryan	60.00	30.00	18.00
(55)	Al Simmons	110.00	55.00	35.00
(56)	Al Spohrer	60.00	30.00	18.00
(57)	Gus Suhr	60.00	30.00	18.00
(58)	Steve Swetonic	60.00	30.00	18.00
(59)	Dazzy Vance	110.00	55.00	35.00
(60)	Joe Vosmik	60.00	30.00	18.00
(61)	Lloyd Waner	110.00	55.00	35.00
(62)	Paul Waner	110.00	55.00	35.00
(63)	Sam West	60.00	30.00	18.00
(64)	Earl Whitehill	60.00	30.00	18.00
(65)	Jimmy Wilson	60.00	30.00	18.00

1934 Butterfinger - Canadian (V94)

Similar to the U.S. issue, though smaller in size at 6-1/2" x 8-1/2", these black-and-white paper cards include a number of players not found in the U.S. issue. Like the "regular" Butterfinger cards, each of the Canadian pieces includes a facsimile autograph on the front; backs are blank. The existence of Canadian versions of Lou Gehrig and Babe Ruth are now questionable.

		NM	EX	VG
Complete Set (58):		3,500	1,750	1,100
Common Player:		50.00	25.00	15.00
(1)	Earl Averill	100.00	50.00	30.00
(2)	Larry Benton	50.00	25.00	15.00
(3)	Jim Bottomly (Bottomley)	100.00	50.00	30.00
(4)	Tom Bridges	50.00	25.00	15.00
(5)	Bob Brown	50.00	25.00	15.00
(6)	Owen T. Carroll	50.00	25.00	15.00
(7)	Gordon (Mickey) Cochrane	100.00	50.00	30.00
(8)	Roger Cramer	50.00	25.00	15.00
(9)	Joe Cronin	100.00	50.00	30.00
(10)	Alvin Crowder	50.00	25.00	15.00
(11)	"Dizzy" Dean	185.00	95.00	55.00
(12)	Edward Delker	50.00	25.00	15.00
(13)	William Dickey	125.00	62.00	37.00
(14)	Richard Ferrell	100.00	50.00	30.00
(15)	Lew Fonseca	50.00	25.00	15.00
(16a)	Jimmy Fox (Name incorrect.)	145.00	75.00	45.00
(16b)	Jimmy Foxx (Name correct.)	145.00	75.00	45.00
(17)	Chick Fullis	50.00	25.00	15.00
(19)	Charles Gehringer	100.00	50.00	30.00
(20)	Vernon Gomez	100.00	50.00	30.00
(21)	Robert (Lefty) Grove	125.00	62.00	37.00
(22)	George (Mule) Haas	50.00	25.00	15.00
(23)	"Chick" Hafey	100.00	50.00	30.00
(24)	Stanley Harris	100.00	50.00	30.00
(25)	Frank Higgins	50.00	25.00	15.00
(26)	J. Francis Hogan	50.00	25.00	15.00
(27)	Ed Holley	50.00	25.00	15.00
(28)	Waite Hoyt	100.00	50.00	30.00
(29)	Jim Jordan	50.00	25.00	15.00
(30)	Hal Lee	50.00	25.00	15.00
(31)	Gus Mancuso	50.00	25.00	15.00
(32)	Oscar Melillo	50.00	25.00	15.00
(33)	Austin Moore	50.00	25.00	15.00
(34)	Randy Moore	50.00	25.00	15.00
(35)	Joe Morrissey	50.00	25.00	15.00
(36)	Joe Mowrey	50.00	25.00	15.00
(37)	Bobo Newsom	50.00	25.00	15.00
(38)	Ernie Orsatti	50.00	25.00	15.00
(39)	Carl Reynolds	50.00	25.00	15.00
(40)	Walter Roettger	50.00	25.00	15.00
(42)	John "Blondy" Ryan	50.00	25.00	15.00
(43)	John Salveson	50.00	25.00	15.00
(44)	Al Simmons	100.00	50.00	30.00
(45)	Al Smith	50.00	25.00	15.00
(46)	Harold Smith	50.00	25.00	15.00
(47)	Allyn Stout	50.00	25.00	15.00
(48)	Fresco Thompson	50.00	25.00	15.00
(49)	Art Veltman	50.00	25.00	15.00
(50)	Johnny Vergez	50.00	25.00	15.00
(51)	Gerald Walker	50.00	25.00	15.00
(52)	Paul Waner	100.00	50.00	30.00
(53)	Burgess Whitehead	50.00	25.00	15.00
(54)	Earl Whitehill	50.00	25.00	15.00
(55)	Robert Weiland	50.00	25.00	15.00
(56)	Jimmy Wilson	50.00	25.00	15.00
(57)	Bob Worthington	50.00	25.00	15.00
(58)	Tom Zachary	50.00	25.00	15.00

1911-14 Butter Krust Bread (D304)

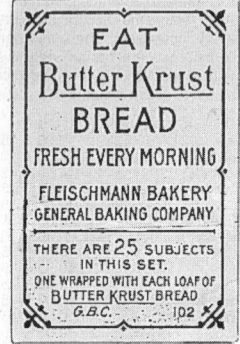

EAT
Butter Krust
BREAD
FRESH EVERY MORNING
FLEISCHMANN BAKERY
GENERAL BAKING COMPANY
THERE ARE 25 SUBJECTS IN THIS SET. ONE WRAPPED WITH EACH LOAF OF BUTTER KRUST BREAD
G.B.C. 102

(See 1911-14 General Baking Co. for checklist and values.)

1933 Button Gum

(See 1933 Cracker Jack.)

1914 B18 Blankets

These 5-1/4"-square flannels were issued in 1914 wrapped around several popular brands of tobacco. The flannels, whose American Card Catalog designation is B18, picked up the nickname blankets because many of them were sewn together to form bed covers or throws. Different color combinations on the flannels exist for all 10 teams included in the set. The complete set price includes only the lowest-priced variation for each of the 90 players.

		NM	EX	VG
Complete Set (90):		7,000	3,500	2,000
Complete Set W/Variations (202):		55,000	27,500	16,500
Common Player:		40.00	20.00	12.00
(1a)	Babe Adams (Purple pennants.)	80.00	40.00	25.00
(1b)	Babe Adams (Red pennants.)	130.00	65.00	40.00
(2a)	Sam Agnew (Purple basepaths.)	80.00	40.00	25.00
(2b)	Sam Agnew (Red basepaths.)	125.00	65.00	35.00
(3a)	Eddie Ainsmith (Green pennants.)	40.00	20.00	12.00
(3b)	Eddie Ainsmith (Brown pennants.)	40.00	20.00	12.00
(4a)	Jimmy Austin (Purple basepaths.)	80.00	40.00	25.00
(4b)	Jimmy Austin (Red basepaths.)	90.00	45.00	27.00
(5a)	Del Baker (White infield.)	40.00	20.00	12.00
(5b)	Del Baker (Brown infield.)	150.00	75.00	45.00
(5c)	Del Baker (Red infield.)	1,650	825.00	495.00
(6a)	Johnny Bassler (Purple pennants.)	90.00	45.00	27.00
(6b)	Johnny Bassler (Yellow pennants.)	125.00	65.00	35.00
(7a)	Paddy Bauman (Baumann) (White infield.)	40.00	20.00	12.00
(7b)	Paddy Bauman (Baumann) (Brown infield.)	150.00	75.00	45.00
(7c)	Paddy Bauman (Baumann) (Red infield.)	1,650	825.00	495.00
(8a)	Luke Boone (Blue infield.)	40.00	20.00	12.00
(8b)	Luke Boone (Green infield.)	40.00	20.00	12.00
(9a)	George Burns (Brown basepaths.)	40.00	20.00	12.00
(9b)	George Burns (Green basepaths.)	40.00	20.00	12.00
(10a)	Tioga George Burns (White infield.)	40.00	20.00	12.00
(10b)	Tioga George Burns (Brown infield.)	150.00	75.00	45.00
(10c)	Tioga George Burns (Red infield.)	1,650	825.00	495.00
(11a)	Max Carey (Purple pennants.)	150.00	75.00	45.00
(11b)	Max Carey (Red pennants.)	175.00	85.00	55.00
(12a)	Marty Cavanaugh (Kavanagh) (White infield.)	40.00	20.00	12.00
(12b)	Marty Cavanaugh (Kavanagh) (Brown infield.)	150.00	75.00	45.00
(12c)	Marty Cavanaugh (Kavanagh) (Red infield.)	1,650	825.00	495.00
(12d)	Marty Cavanaugh (Kavanagh)	200.00	100.00	60.00
(13a)	Frank Chance (Green infield.)	100.00	50.00	30.00
(13b)	Frank Chance (Brown pennants, blue infield.)	100.00	50.00	30.00
(13c)	Frank Chance (Yellow pennants, blue infield.)	450.00	225.00	135.00
(14a)	Ray Chapman (Purple pennants.)	125.00	65.00	35.00
(14b)	Ray Chapman (Yellow pennants.)	200.00	100.00	60.00
(15a)	Ty Cobb (White infield.)	500.00	250.00	150.00
(15b)	Ty Cobb (Brown infield.)	700.00	350.00	210.00
(15c)	Ty Cobb (Red infield.)	15,000	7,500	4,500
(16a)	King Cole (Blue infield.)	40.00	20.00	12.00
(16b)	King Cole (Green infield.)	40.00	20.00	12.00
(17a)	Joe Connolly (White infield.)	40.00	20.00	12.00
(17b)	Joe Connolly (Brown infield.)	150.00	75.00	45.00
(17c)	Joe Connolly (Red infield.)	1,650	825.00	495.00
(18a)	Harry Coveleski (White infield.)	40.00	20.00	12.00
(18b)	Harry Coveleski (Brown infield.)	150.00	75.00	45.00
(18c)	Harry Coveleski (Red infield.)	1,650	825.00	495.00
(19a)	George Cutshaw (Blue infield.)	40.00	20.00	12.00
(19b)	George Cutshaw (Green infield.)	40.00	20.00	12.00
(20a)	Jake Daubert (Blue infield.)	45.00	22.50	13.50
(20b)	Jake Daubert (Green infield.)	45.00	22.50	13.50
(21a)	Ray Demmitt (White infield.)	40.00	20.00	12.00
(21b)	Ray Demmitt (Brown infield.)	150.00	75.00	45.00
(21c)	Ray Demmitt (Red infield.)	1,650	825.00	495.00
(22a)	Bill Doak (Purple pennants.)	80.00	40.00	24.00
(22b)	Bill Doak (Yellow pennants.)	125.00	65.00	35.00
(23a)	Cozy Dolan (Purple pennants.)	80.00	40.00	25.00
(23b)	Cozy Dolan (Yellow pennants.)	150.00	75.00	45.00
(24a)	Larry Doyle (Brown basepaths.)	45.00	22.50	13.50
(24b)	Larry Doyle (Green basepaths.)	45.00	22.50	13.50
(25a)	Art Fletcher (Brown basepaths.)	40.00	20.00	12.00
(25b)	Art Fletcher (Green basepaths.)	40.00	20.00	12.00
(26a)	Eddie Foster (Brown pennants.)	40.00	20.00	12.00
(26b)	Eddie Foster (Green pennants.)	40.00	20.00	12.00
(27a)	Del Gainor (White infield.)	50.00	25.00	15.00
(27b)	Del Gainor (Brown infield.)	150.00	75.00	45.00
(28a)	Chick Gandil (Brown pennants.)	100.00	50.00	30.00
(28b)	Chick Gandil (Green pennants.)	125.00	65.00	35.00
(29a)	George Gibson (Purple pennants.)	80.00	40.00	25.00
(29b)	George Gibson (Red pennants.)	90.00	45.00	27.00
(30a)	Hank Gowdy (White infield.)	40.00	20.00	12.00
(30b)	Hank Gowdy (Brown infield.)	150.00	75.00	45.00
(30c)	Hank Gowdy (Red infield.)	1,650	825.00	495.00
(31a)	Jack Graney (Purple pennants.)	90.00	45.00	27.00
(31b)	Jack Graney (Yellow pennants.)	125.00	65.00	35.00
(32a)	Eddie Grant (Brown basepaths.)	40.00	20.00	12.00
(32b)	Eddie Grant (Green basepaths.)	40.00	20.00	12.00
(33a)	Tommy Griffith (White infield, green pennants.)	40.00	20.00	12.00
(33b)	Tommy Griffith (White infield, red pennants.)	1,500	750.00	450.00
(33c)	Tommy Griffith (Brown infield.)	125.00	65.00	35.00
(33d)	Tommy Griffith (Red infield.)	1,650	825.00	495.00
(34a)	Earl Hamilton (Purple basepaths.)	80.00	40.00	25.00
(34b)	Earl Hamilton (Red basepaths.)	90.00	45.00	27.00
(35a)	Roy Hartzell (Blue infield.)	40.00	20.00	12.00
(35b)	Roy Hartzell (Green infield.)	40.00	20.00	12.00
(36a)	Miller Huggins (Purple pennants.)	160.00	80.00	45.00
(36b)	Miller Huggins (Yellow pennants.)	245.00	120.00	75.00
(37a)	John Hummel (Blue infield.)	40.00	20.00	12.00
(37b)	John Hummel (Green infield.)	40.00	20.00	12.00
(38a)	Ham Hyatt (Purple pennants.)	80.00	40.00	24.00
(38b)	Ham Hyatt (Red pennants.)	90.00	45.00	27.00
(39a)	Joe Jackson (Purple pennants.)	1,350	675.00	400.00
(39b)	Joe Jackson (Yellow pennants.)	1,100	550.00	330.00
(40a)	Bill James (White infield.)	40.00	20.00	12.00
(40b)	Bill James (Brown infield.)	160.00	80.00	50.00
(40c)	Bill James (Red infield.)	1,650	825.00	495.00
(41a)	Walter Johnson (Brown pennants.)	300.00	150.00	90.00
(41b)	Walter Johnson (Green pennants.)	275.00	135.00	80.00
(42a)	Ray Keating (Blue infield.)	40.00	20.00	12.00
(42b)	Ray Keating (Green infield.)	40.00	20.00	12.00
(43a)	Joe Kelley (Kelly) (Purple pennants.)	90.00	45.00	27.00
(43b)	Joe Kelley (Kelly) (Red pennants.)	90.00	45.00	27.00
(44a)	Ed Konetchy (Purple pennants.)	60.00	30.00	18.00
(44b)	Ed Konetchy (Red pennants.)	90.00	45.00	27.00

		NM	EX	VG
(45a)	Nemo Leibold (Purple pennants.)	75.00	37.50	22.00
(45b)	Nemo Leibold (Yellow pennants.)	150.00	75.00	45.00
(46a)	Fritz Maisel (Blue infield.)	40.00	20.00	12.00
(46b)	Fritz Maisel (Green infield.)	40.00	20.00	12.00
(47a)	Les Mann (White infield.)	40.00	20.00	12.00
(47b)	Les Mann (Brown infield.)	150.00	75.00	45.00
(47c)	Les Mann (Red infield.)	1,650	825.00	495.00
(48a)	Rabbit Maranville (White infield.)	130.00	65.00	39.00
(48b)	Rabbit Maranville (Brown infield.)	250.00	125.00	75.00
(48c)	Rabbit Maranville (Red infield.)	3,000	1,500	900.00
(49a)	Bill McAllister (McAllester) (Purple basepaths.)	80.00	40.00	25.00
(49b)	Bill McAllister (McAllester) (Red basepaths.)	100.00	50.00	30.00
(50a)	George McBride (Brown pennants.)	40.00	20.00	12.00
(50b)	George McBride (Green pennants.)	40.00	20.00	12.00
(51a)	Chief Meyers (Brown basepaths.)	40.00	20.00	12.00
(51b)	Chief Meyers (Green basepaths.)	40.00	20.00	12.00
(52a)	Clyde Milan (Brown pennants.)	40.00	20.00	12.00
(52b)	Clyde Milan (Green pennants.)	40.00	20.00	12.00
(53a)	J. Miller (Purple pennants.)	80.00	40.00	25.00
(53b)	J. Miller (Yellow pennants.)	125.00	65.00	35.00
(54a)	Otto Miller (Blue infield.)	40.00	20.00	12.00
(54b)	Otto Miller (Green infield.)	40.00	20.00	12.00
(55a)	Willie Mitchell (Purple pennants.)	80.00	40.00	25.00
(55b)	Willie Mitchell (Yellow pennants.)	150.00	75.00	45.00
(56a)	Danny Moeller (Brown pennants.)	40.00	20.00	12.00
(56b)	Danny Moeller (Green pennants.)	40.00	20.00	12.00
(57a)	Ray Morgan (Brown pennants.)	40.00	20.00	12.00
(57b)	Ray Morgan (Green pennants.)	40.00	20.00	12.00
(58a)	George Moriarty (White infield.)	40.00	20.00	12.00
(58b)	George Moriarty (Brown infield.)	150.00	75.00	45.00
(58c)	George Moriarty (Red infield.)	1,650	825.00	495.00
(59a)	Mike Mowrey (Purple pennants.)	80.00	40.00	25.00
(59b)	Mike Mowrey (Red pennants.)	90.00	45.00	27.00
(60a)	Red Murray (Brown basepaths.)	40.00	20.00	12.00
(60b)	Red Murray (Green basepaths.)	40.00	20.00	12.00
(61a)	Ivy Olson (Purple pennants.)	80.00	40.00	25.00
(61b)	Ivy Olson (Yellow pennants.)	160.00	80.00	50.00
(62a)	Steve O'Neill (Purple pennants.)	75.00	37.50	22.00
(62b)	Steve O'Neill (Red pennants.)	150.00	75.00	45.00
(62c)	Steve O'Neill (Yellow pennants.)	150.00	75.00	45.00
(63a)	Marty O'Toole (Purple pennants.)	80.00	40.00	25.00
(63b)	Marty O'Toole (Red pennants.)	90.00	45.00	27.00
(64a)	Roger Peckinpaugh (Blue infield.)	45.00	22.50	13.50
(64b)	Roger Peckinpaugh (Green infield.)	45.00	22.50	13.50
(65a)	Hub Perdue (White infield.)	40.00	20.00	12.00
(65b)	Hub Perdue (Brown infield.)	150.00	75.00	45.00
(65c)	Hub Purdue (Red infield.)	1,650	825.00	495.00
(66a)	Del Pratt (Purple basepaths.)	80.00	40.00	25.00
(66b)	Del Pratt (Red basepaths.)	90.00	45.00	27.00
(67a)	Hank Robinson (Purple pennants.)	80.00	40.00	25.00
(67b)	Hank Robinson (Yellow pennants.)	130.00	65.00	40.00
(68a)	Nap Rucker (Blue infield.)	40.00	20.00	12.00
(68b)	Nap Rucker (Green infield.)	40.00	20.00	12.00
(69a)	Slim Sallee (Purple pennants.)	100.00	50.00	30.00
(69b)	Slim Sallee (Yellow pennants.)	150.00	75.00	45.00
(70a)	Howard Shanks (Brown pennants.)	40.00	20.00	12.00
(70b)	Howard Shanks (Green pennants.)	40.00	20.00	12.00
(70c)	Howard Shanks (White infield.)	80.00	40.00	25.00
(71a)	Burt Shotton (Purple basepaths.)	75.00	37.50	22.00
(71b)	Burt Shotton (Red basepaths.)	40.00	20.00	12.00
(72a)	Red Smith (Blue infield.)	40.00	20.00	12.00
(72b)	Red Smith (Green infield.)	40.00	20.00	12.00
(73a)	Fred Snodgrass (Brown basepaths.)	40.00	20.00	12.00
(73b)	Fred Snodgrass (Green basepaths.)	80.00	40.00	24.00
(74a)	Bill Steele (Purple pennants.)	150.00	75.00	45.00
(74b)	Bill Steele (Yellow pennants.)	100.00	50.00	30.00
(75a)	Casey Stengel (Blue infield.)	100.00	50.00	30.00
(75b)	Casey Stengel (Green infield.)	40.00	20.00	12.00
(76a)	Jeff Sweeney (Blue infield.)	40.00	20.00	12.00
(76b)	Jeff Sweeney (Green infield.)	40.00	20.00	12.00
(77a)	Jeff Tesreau (Brown basepaths.)	40.00	20.00	12.00
(77b)	Jeff Tesreau (Green basepaths.)	80.00	40.00	25.00
(78a)	Terry Turner (Purple pennants.)	150.00	75.00	45.00
(78b)	Terry Turner (Yellow pennants.)	40.00	20.00	12.00
(79a)	Lefty Tyler (White infield.)	150.00	75.00	45.00
(79b)	Lefty Tyler (Brown infield.)			

		NM	EX	VG
(79c)	Lefty Tyler (Red infield.)	1,650	825.00	495.00
(80a)	Jim Viox (Purple pennants.)	80.00	40.00	25.00
(80b)	Jim Viox (Red pennants.)	90.00	45.00	27.00
(81a)	Bull Wagner (Blue infield.)	40.00	20.00	12.00
(81b)	Bull Wagner (Green infield.)	40.00	20.00	12.00
(82a)	Bobby Wallace (Purple basepaths.)	150.00	75.00	45.00
(82b)	Bobby Wallace (Red basepaths.)	150.00	75.00	45.00
(83a)	Dee Walsh (Purple basepaths.)	80.00	40.00	25.00
(83b)	Dee Walsh (Red basepaths.)	90.00	45.00	27.00
(84a)	Jimmy Walsh (Blue infield.)	40.00	20.00	12.00
(84b)	Jimmy Walsh (Green infield.)	40.00	20.00	12.00
(85a)	Bert Whaling (White infield.)	40.00	20.00	12.00
(85b)	Bert Whaling (Brown infield.)	150.00	75.00	45.00
(85c)	Bert Whaling (Red infield.)	1,650	825.00	495.00
(86a)	Zach Wheat (Blue infield.)	125.00	65.00	35.00
(86b)	Zach Wheat (Green infield.)	100.00	50.00	30.00
(87a)	Possum Whitted (Purple pennants.)	80.00	40.00	25.00
(87b)	Possum Whitted (Yellow pennants.)	125.00	65.00	35.00
(88a)	Gus Williams (Purple basepaths.)	80.00	40.00	25.00
(88b)	Gus Williams (Red basepaths.)	90.00	45.00	27.00
(89a)	Owen Wilson (Purple pennants.)	80.00	40.00	25.00
(89b)	Owen Wilson (Yellow pennants.)	150.00	75.00	45.00
(90a)	Hooks Wiltse (Brown basepaths.)	40.00	20.00	12.00
(90b)	Hooks Wiltse (Green basepaths.)	40.00	20.00	12.00

1937 BF-UNC Felt Pennants

Based on the known player-team combinations in this probably incomplete checklist, 1937 seems the most likely date of issue. The pennants measure about 2-1/4" across the top and taper to a point at the end of their 5" length. About halfway down is a blue-and-white trapezoid with a player photo within a circle on a pinstriped background. The team name is printed in two lines at top. It is believed each player can be found with more than one base pennant color and team-name printing.

		NM	EX	VG
Common Player:		150.00	75.00	45.00
(1)	Dizzy Dean	650.00	325.00	195.00
(2)	Bobby Feller	500.00	250.00	150.00
(3)	Hank Greenberg	500.00	250.00	150.00
(4)	Lefty Grove	450.00	225.00	135.00
(5)	Joe Moore	150.00	75.00	45.00
(6)	Wallace Moses	150.00	75.00	45.00
(7)	Lynwood Rowe	150.00	75.00	45.00
(7)	Joe Stripp	150.00	75.00	45.00
(8)	Floyd Vaughan	400.00	200.00	120.00

1916 BF2 Felt Pennants

Issued circa 1916, this unnumbered set consists of 97 felt pennants with a small black-and-white player photo glued to each. The triangular pennants measure approximately 2-7/8" across the top and taper to a length of about 5-3/4" long, while the photos are 1-3/4" x 1-1/4" and appear to be identical to photos used for M101-4/M101-5 issues of the same period. The pennants list the player's name and team. The pennants were given away as premiums with the purchase of five-cent loaves of Ferguson Bakery bread in the Roxbury, Mass., area.

(See 1916 Ferguson Bakery Felt Pennants for checklist and values.)

1936-37 BF3 Felt Player/Team Pennants

The checklists for these series of felt pennants issued circa 1936-1938 are not complete, and new examples are still being reported. The pennants do not carry any manufacturer's name although packages found with various pieces attribute the issues to Red Ball Sales, a gum company in Chicago, and Grandpa Brands Co., Cincinnati, another gum company. One pennant was given away with the purchase of a stick of gum, and at least one wrapper indicates large format (28" x 12") versions of the Red Ball pennants could be had in a redemption program. The pennants vary in size slightly but generally measure approximately 2-1/2" x 4-1/2" and were issued in various styles and colors. Most of the printing is white, although some pennants have been found with other colors of printing, and the same pennant is often found in more than one color combination. The pennants feature both individual players and teams, including some minor league clubs. The pennants were grouped together in the American Card Catalog under the designation of BF3. Advanced collectors have categorized the pennants into a number of basic design types, depending on what elements are included on the pennant. The unnumbered felts are listed alphabetically within type. Gaps have been left in the assigned numbers to accommodate future discoveries.

	NM	EX	VG
Common Pennant:	25.00	12.50	7.50

1936-37 Type 1 - Player Name and Silhouette

Generic silhouette figures in action poses are featured at the left end of this series of pennants. Player names at right can be found in a number of different typographic styles. Gaps have been left in the assigned numbering for future additions.

		NM	EX	VG
Common Pennant:		60.00	30.00	18.00
(1)	Luke Appling (Batting)	80.00	40.00	25.00
(2)	Earl Averill (Batting)	80.00	40.00	25.00
(3)	Wally Berger (Fielding)	60.00	30.00	18.00
(4)	Zeke Bonura (Fielding)	60.00	30.00	18.00
(5)	Dolph Camilli (Fielding)	60.00	30.00	18.00
(6)	Ben Chapman (Batting)	60.00	30.00	18.00
(7)	Mickey Cochrane (Catching)	90.00	45.00	27.00
(8)	Rip Collins (Batting)	60.00	30.00	18.00
(9)	Joe Cronin (Batting)	80.00	40.00	25.00
(10)	Kiki Cuyler (Running)	80.00	40.00	25.00
(11)	Dizzy Dean (Pitching)	135.00	65.00	40.00
(12)	Frank Demaree (Batting)	60.00	30.00	18.00
(13)	Paul Derringer (Pitching)	60.00	30.00	18.00
(14)	Bill Dickey (Catching)	90.00	45.00	27.00
(15)	Jimmy Dykes (Fielding)	60.00	30.00	18.00
(16)	Bob Feller (Pitching)	110.00	55.00	35.00
(17)	Wes Ferrell (Batting)	60.00	30.00	18.00
(19)	Jimmy Foxx	100.00	50.00	30.00
(20)	Larry French (Pitching)	60.00	30.00	18.00
(21)	Franky Frisch (Running)	90.00	45.00	27.00
(23)	Lou Gehrig (Throwing)	300.00	150.00	90.00
(24)	Charlie Gehringer (Running)	90.00	45.00	27.00
(25)	Lefty Gomez (Pitching)	80.00	40.00	25.00
(26)	Goose Goslin (Batting)	80.00	40.00	25.00
(30)	Hank Greenberg (Fielding)	110.00	55.00	35.00
(31)	Charley Grimm (Fielding)	60.00	30.00	18.00
(33)	Lefty Grove (Pitching)	90.00	45.00	27.00
(34)	Gabby Hartnett (Catching)	80.00	40.00	25.00
(35)	Rollie Hemsley (Catching)	60.00	30.00	18.00
(36)	Billy Herman (Fielding)	80.00	40.00	25.00
(37)	Frank Higgins (Fielding)	60.00	30.00	18.00
(38)	Rogers Hornsby (Batting)	100.00	50.00	30.00
(39)	Carl Hubbell (Pitching)	90.00	45.00	27.00
(40)	Chuck Klein (Throwing)	80.00	40.00	25.00
(41)	Tony Lazzeri (Batting)	80.00	40.00	25.00
(42)	Hank Leiber (Batting)	60.00	30.00	18.00
(43)	Ernie Lombardi (Catching)	80.00	40.00	25.00
(44)	Al Lopez (Throwing)	80.00	40.00	25.00
(45)	Gus Mancuso (Running)	60.00	30.00	18.00
(46)	Heinie Manush (Batting)	80.00	40.00	25.00
(47)	Pepper Martin (Batting)	70.00	35.00	20.00
(48)	Joe McCarthy (Kneeling)	80.00	40.00	25.00
(49)	Wally Moses (Running)	60.00	30.00	18.00
(50)	Van Mungo (Standing)	60.00	30.00	18.00
(52)	Mel Ott (Throwing)	90.00	45.00	27.00
(53)	Schoolboy Rowe (Pitching)	60.00	30.00	18.00
(54)	Babe Ruth (Batting)	450.00	225.00	135.00
(55)	George Selkirk (Batting)	60.00	30.00	18.00

(56)	Luke Sewell (Sliding)	60.00	30.00	18.00
(57)	Joe Stripp (Batting)	60.00	30.00	18.00
(58)	Pie Traynor (Batting)	80.00	40.00	25.00
(59)	Hal Trosky (Fielding)	60.00	30.00	18.00
(60)	Floyd Vaughan	80.00	40.00	25.00
	(Running, script name.)			
(61)	Floyd Vaughan	80.00	40.00	25.00
	(Running, block name.)			
(62)	Joe Vosmik (Running)	60.00	30.00	18.00
(64)	Paul Waner (Batting)	80.00	40.00	25.00
(65)	Lon Warneke (Pitching)	60.00	30.00	18.00
(66)	Jimmy Wilson (Fielding)	60.00	30.00	18.00

1936-37 Type 2 - Player's Name, Team Nickname, Figure

Team nicknames have been added at the spine of this style of pennant. As with Type 1, some players can be found in more than one pose and/or typography. Gaps have been left in the assigned numbering to accomodate future additions.

		NM	EX	VG
Common Pennant:		60.00	30.00	18.00
(1)	Luke Appling	80.00	40.00	25.00
	(Batting, block name.)			
(2)	Luke Appling	80.00	40.00	25.00
	(Batting, script name.)			
(3)	Earl Averill (Fielding)	80.00	40.00	25.00
(4)	Earl Averill (Running)	80.00	40.00	24.00
(5)	Wally Berger (Throwing)	60.00	30.00	18.00
(6)	Zeke Bonura (Batting)	60.00	30.00	18.00
(7)	Dolph Camilli (Batting)	60.00	30.00	18.00
(8)	Ben Chapman (Throwing)	60.00	30.00	18.00
(9)	Mickey Cochrane (Throwing)	90.00	45.00	27.00
(10)	Rip Collins (Batting)	60.00	30.00	18.00
(11)	Joe Cronin (Throwing)	80.00	40.00	25.00
(12)	Kiki Cuyler (Throwing)	80.00	40.00	25.00
(13)	Dizzy Dean (Batting)	110.00	55.00	35.00
(14)	Dizzy Dean (Throwing)	110.00	55.00	35.00
(15)	Frank Demaree (Batting)	60.00	30.00	18.00
(16)	Paul Derringer (Throwing)	60.00	30.00	18.00
(17)	Bill Dickey (Throwing)	110.00	55.00	35.00
(18)	Joe DiMaggio	260.00	130.00	80.00
	(Block letters through figure.)			
(19)	Joe DiMaggio (Script)	260.00	130.00	80.00
(20)	Jimmy Dykes (Throwing)	60.00	30.00	18.00
(21)	Bob Feller (Block letters.)	110.00	55.00	35.00
(22)	Bob Feller (Script)	110.00	55.00	35.00
(23)	Wes Ferrell (Throwing)	60.00	30.00	18.00
(24)	Larry French (Batting)	60.00	30.00	18.00
(25)	Frank Frisch (Fielding)	90.00	45.00	27.00
(27)	Lou Gehrig	300.00	150.00	90.00
	(Batting, block letters.)			
(28)	Lou Gehrig (Batting, script.)	300.00	150.00	90.00
(29)	Lou Gehrig (Fielding)	300.00	150.00	90.00
(31)	Lefty Gomez (Pitching)	90.00	45.00	27.00
(32)	Goose Goslin (Throwing)	90.00	45.00	27.00
(33)	Hank Greenberg (Batting)	110.00	55.00	35.00
(34)	Hank Greenberg (Throwing)	110.00	55.00	35.00
(35)	Charlie Grimm (Fielding)	60.00	30.00	18.00
(36)	Lefty Grove (Batting)	90.00	45.00	27.00
(37)	Lefty Grove (Pitching)	90.00	45.00	27.00
(38)	Gabby Hartnett (Batting)	80.00	40.00	25.00
(39)	Gabby Hartnett (Catching)	80.00	40.00	25.00
(40)	Billy Herman (Batting, facing right, name over figure.)	80.00	40.00	25.00
(41)	Billy Herman (Batting, facing right, name through body.)	80.00	40.00	25.00
(42)	Billy Herman (Batting, facing left.)	80.00	40.00	25.00
(44)	Roger (Rogers) Hornsby (Batting)	100.00	50.00	30.00
(45)	Carl Hubbell (Pitching)	90.00	45.00	27.00
(49)	Tony Lazzeri (Throwing)	80.00	40.00	25.00
(50)	Hank Leiber (Batting)	60.00	30.00	18.00
(52)	Ernie Lombardi (Batting)	80.00	40.00	25.00
(54)	Gus Mancuso (Batting)	60.00	30.00	18.00
(55)	Heinie Manush (Batting)	80.00	40.00	25.00
(56)	Pepper Martin (Batting)	75.00	37.50	22.00
(57)	Joe McCarthy (Batting)	80.00	40.00	25.00
(58)	Joe Medwick (Batting)	80.00	40.00	25.00
(59)	Van Lingle Mungo (Batting)	80.00	40.00	25.00
(60)	Van Lingo Mungo (Lingle) (Batting)	60.00	30.00	18.00
(64)	Schoolboy Rowe (Batting)	60.00	30.00	18.00
(65)	Babe Ruth (Batting)	450.00	225.00	135.00
(67)	George Selkirk (Batting)	60.00	30.00	18.00
(68)	Luke Sewell (Batting)	60.00	30.00	18.00
(69)	Joe Stripp (Batting)	60.00	30.00	18.00
(70)	Bill Terry (Batting)	80.00	40.00	25.00
(71)	Bill Terry (Fielding)	80.00	40.00	25.00
(73)	Pie Traynor (Throwing)	80.00	40.00	25.00
(74)	Hal Trosky (Batting)	60.00	30.00	18.00
(75)	Floyd Vaughan (Batting)	60.00	30.00	18.00
(76)	Joe Vosmik (Throwing)	60.00	30.00	18.00
(77)	Paul Waner (Batting)	80.00	40.00	25.00
(80)	Lon Warneke (Batting)	60.00	30.00	18.00
(81)	Lon Warneke (Wind-up.)	60.00	30.00	18.00
(83)	Jimmy Wilson (Pitching)	60.00	30.00	18.00

1936-37 Type 3 - Player's Name, Team Nickname

No player silhouettes are found on this series of pennants. The player name is at right, with his team's nickname at the spine. Despite the fact he left the team in 1934, Babe Ruth's pennant shows him with the Yankees. Gaps have been left in the assigned numbering to accomodate future additions.

		NM	EX	VG
Common Pennant:		60.00	30.00	18.00
(1)	Luke Appling (Block letters.)	80.00	40.00	25.00
(2)	Luke Appling (Script)	80.00	40.00	25.00
(4)	Wally Berger	60.00	30.00	18.00
(6)	Zeke Bonura	60.00	30.00	18.00
(7)	Dolph Camilli	60.00	30.00	18.00
(9)	Ben Chapman	60.00	30.00	18.00
(10)	Mickey Cochrane	80.00	40.00	25.00
(11)	Rip Collins	60.00	30.00	18.00
(12)	Joe Cronin	80.00	40.00	25.00
(13)	Kiki Cuyler	80.00	40.00	25.00
(14)	Dizzy Dean	135.00	65.00	40.00
(15)	Frank Demaree	60.00	30.00	18.00
(16)	Paul Derringer	60.00	30.00	18.00
(17)	Bill Dickey	110.00	55.00	35.00
(18)	Joe DiMaggio (Script name.)	300.00	150.00	90.00
(19)	Jimmy Dykes	60.00	30.00	18.00
(20)	Bob Feller (Script name.)	110.00	55.00	35.00
(21)	Wes Ferrell	60.00	30.00	18.00
(22)	Jimmie Foxx	90.00	45.00	27.00
(23)	Larry French	60.00	30.00	18.00
(24)	Franky Frisch	80.00	40.00	25.00
(25)	Lou Gehrig (Script name.)	300.00	150.00	90.00
(26)	Charlie Gehringer	80.00	40.00	25.00
(28)	Lefty Gomez	80.00	40.00	25.00
(29)	Goose Goslin	80.00	40.00	24.00
(30)	Hank Greenberg	90.00	45.00	27.00
(31)	Charley Grimm	60.00	30.00	18.00
(32)	Lefty Grove	90.00	45.00	27.00
(33)	Gabby Hartnett	80.00	40.00	25.00
(35)	Rollie Hemsley	60.00	30.00	18.00
(36)	Billy Herman (Block letters.)	80.00	40.00	25.00
(37)	Billy Herman (Script)	80.00	40.00	25.00
(38)	Frank Higgins	60.00	30.00	18.00
(39)	Roger Hornsby (Rogers)	90.00	45.00	27.00
(40)	Carl Hubbell	80.00	40.00	25.00
(41)	Chuck Klein	80.00	40.00	25.00
(42)	Tony Lazzeri	80.00	40.00	25.00
(44)	Hank Leiber	60.00	30.00	18.00
(45)	Ernie Lombardi	80.00	40.00	25.00
(46)	Al Lopez	80.00	40.00	25.00
(48)	Gus Mancuso	60.00	30.00	18.00
(49)	Heinie Manush	80.00	40.00	25.00
(50)	Pepper Martin	70.00	35.00	20.00
(51)	Joe McCarthy	80.00	40.00	25.00
(52)	Joe Medwick	80.00	40.00	25.00
(53)	Wally Moses	60.00	30.00	18.00
(54)	Van Mungo	60.00	30.00	18.00
(55)	Mel Ott	80.00	40.00	25.00
(56)	Schoolboy Rowe	60.00	30.00	18.00
(57)	Babe Ruth	400.00	200.00	120.00
(58)	George Selkirk	60.00	30.00	18.00
(59)	Luke Sewell	60.00	30.00	18.00
(60)	Al Simmons	80.00	40.00	25.00
(61)	Joe Stripp	60.00	30.00	18.00
(62)	Bill Terry	80.00	40.00	25.00
(63)	Pie Traynor	80.00	40.00	25.00
(64)	Hal Trosky	60.00	30.00	18.00
(65)	Joe Vosmik	60.00	30.00	18.00
(66)	Floyd Vaughan	80.00	40.00	25.00
(67)	Paul Waner	80.00	40.00	25.00
(68)	Lon Warneke	60.00	30.00	18.00
(71)	Jimmy Wilson	60.00	30.00	18.00

1936-37 Type 4 - Team Nickname and Silhouette Player

One of two closely related series of these collectible pennants, this type has a team nickname in combination with a silhouette figure of one or more baseball figures. Collectors should be aware that similar pennants, perhaps even sharing the same designs, were issued circa 1950 in boxes of candy from American Nut & Chocolate of Boston. The AN&C pen-

nants should be distinguishable by their smaller size of approximately 4" x 1-7/8". Gaps in the assigned numbering have been left to accomodate future additions.

		NM	EX	VG
Common Pennant:		40.00	20.00	12.00
(1)	Athletics (Fielder)	40.00	20.00	12.00
(2)	Browns (Catcher)	40.00	20.00	12.00
(3)	Cubs (Batter)	40.00	20.00	12.00
(4)	Dodgers (Batter)	40.00	20.00	12.00
(5)	Dodgers (Fielder)	40.00	20.00	12.00
(7)	Giants (Sliding into base.)	40.00	20.00	12.00
(8)	Giants (Standing at base.)	40.00	20.00	12.00
(9)	Giants (Two players.)	40.00	20.00	12.00
(10)	Phillies (Pitcher)	40.00	20.00	12.00
(12)	Reds (Batter)	40.00	20.00	12.00
(13)	Reds (catcher)	40.00	20.00	12.00
(14)	Reds (Pitcher)	40.00	20.00	12.00
(15)	Red Sox (Batter and catcher.)	40.00	20.00	12.00
(16)	White Sox (Batter left of team name.)	40.00	20.00	12.00
(17)	White Sox (Batter inside "W.")	40.00	20.00	12.00
(18)	White Sox (Catcher)	40.00	20.00	12.00
(19)	White Sox (Profile)	40.00	20.00	12.00
(20)	White Sox (Pitcher)	40.00	20.00	12.00
(21)	Yankees (Batter)	40.00	20.00	12.00
(22)	Yankees (Fielder)	40.00	20.00	12.00

1936-37 Type 5 - Team Nickname with Emblem

Closely related to the Type 4 style, these pennants combine a team nickname with a symbolic figure or depictions of baseball equipment. Collectors should be aware that similar pennants, perhaps even sharing the same designs, were issued circa 1950 in boxes of candy from American Nut & Chocolate of Boston. The AN&C pennants should be distinguishable by their smaller size of approximately 4" x 1-7/8". Gaps have been left in the numbering to accomodate future additions.

		NM	EX	VG
Common Pennant:		40.00	20.00	12.00
(1)	Athletics (Elephant, no tusks.)	40.00	20.00	12.00
(2)	Athletics (Elephant, w/tusks.)	40.00	20.00	12.00
(3)	Athletics (Gothic script, w/bat, ball.)	40.00	20.00	12.00
(5)	Bees (Bee is crossbar of "B.")	40.00	20.00	12.00
(6)	Bees (Bee is loops of "B.")	40.00	20.00	12.00
(7)	Brooklyn (Crossed bats over "B.")	40.00	20.00	12.00
(9)	Browns (Ball)	40.00	20.00	12.00
(10)	Browns (Bat)	40.00	20.00	12.00
(11)	Browns (Bat is spine of "B," balls in loops.	40.00	20.00	12.00
(12)	Cardinals (Bat)	40.00	20.00	12.00
(13)	Cardinals (Cardinal inside "C," profile.)	40.00	20.00	12.00
(14)	Cardinals (Cardinal inside "C" front view.)	40.00	20.00	12.00
(15)	Cardinals (Four birds on "C.")	40.00	20.00	12.00
(16)	Cubs (Cub w/bat.)	40.00	20.00	12.00
(17)	Cubs (Cub's head.)	40.00	20.00	12.00
(18)	Cubs (Cub sitting in "C.")	40.00	20.00	12.00
19	Cubs (Full-body profile.)	40.00	20.00	12.00
(20)	Dodgers (Ball)	40.00	20.00	12.00
(21)	Dodgers (Ball, bat and glove.)	40.00	20.00	12.00
(22)	Dodgers (Trolley car.)	40.00	20.00	12.00
(23)	Giants (Crossed bats and ball.)	40.00	20.00	12.00
(25)	Indians (Indians)	40.00	20.00	12.00
(26)	Indians (Indian profile, nine feathers.)	40.00	20.00	12.00
(27)	Indians (Indian profile, headdress.)	40.00	20.00	12.00
(30)	Phillies (Liberty Bell)	40.00	20.00	12.00
(32)	Pirates (Pirate, no knife.)	40.00	20.00	12.00
(33)	Pirates (Pirate w/knife.)	40.00	20.00	12.00
(34)	Pirates (Peg-legged pirate w/sword.)	40.00	20.00	12.00
(35)	Pirates (Skull and crossed bones.)	40.00	20.00	12.00
(36)	Reds (Man with stein.)	40.00	20.00	12.00
(37)	Reds (W/ball.)	40.00	20.00	12.00
(39)	Red Sox (Ball)	40.00	20.00	12.00
(40)	Red Sox (Bat)	40.00	20.00	12.00
(41)	Red Sox (Ball and bat.)	40.00	20.00	12.00
(42)	Red Sox (Stocking)	40.00	20.00	12.00
(44)	Senators (Bat)	40.00	20.00	12.00
(45)	Senators (Cap. Dome, "S" superimposed.)	40.00	20.00	12.00
(46)	Senators (Capital Dome, "S" to right.)	40.00	20.00	12.00
(47)	Senators (Man's profile in top hat.)	40.00	20.00	12.00
(48)	Sox (W/bat and ball.)	40.00	20.00	12.00
(49)	Tigers (Bat left, ball right.)	40.00	20.00	12.00
(50)	Tigers (Cap)	40.00	20.00	12.00
(51)	Tigers (Prowling tiger.)	40.00	20.00	12.00
(52)	Tigers (Tiger head in circle.)	40.00	20.00	12.00
(53)	Tigers (Tiger head, no circle.)	40.00	20.00	12.00

1936-37 Type 6 - Team Name Only

		NM	EX	VG
Common Pennant:		40.00	20.00	12.00
(1)	ATHLETICS	40.00	20.00	12.00
(2)	ATHLETICS	40.00	20.00	12.00
	(PHILA. on spine.)			
(3)	BEES	40.00	20.00	12.00
(4)	BEES (BOSTON on spine.)	40.00	20.00	12.00
(5)	CARDINALS	40.00	20.00	12.00
(6)	CUBS	40.00	20.00	12.00
(7)	CUBS (CHICAGO on spine.)	40.00	20.00	12.00
(8)	DODGERS	40.00	20.00	12.00
(9)	DODGERS	40.00	20.00	12.00
	(BROOKLYN on spine.)			
(10)	GIANTS	40.00	20.00	12.00
(11)	GIANTS	40.00	20.00	12.00
	(NEW YORK on spine.)			
(12)	INDIANS	40.00	20.00	12.00
(13)	PHILLIES	40.00	20.00	12.00
(14)	PHILLIES	40.00	20.00	12.00
	(PHILLIES on spine.)			
(15)	PIRATES	40.00	20.00	12.00
(16)	PIRATES	40.00	20.00	12.00
	(PITTSBURGH on spine.)			
(17)	REDS	40.00	20.00	12.00
(18)	REDS	40.00	20.00	12.00
	(CINCINNATI on spine.)			
(19)	SENATORS	40.00	20.00	12.00
(20)	WASH. SENATORS	40.00	20.00	12.00
(21)	SOX	40.00	20.00	12.00
(22)	TIGERS	40.00	20.00	12.00
(23)	WHITE SOX	40.00	20.00	12.00
(24)	YANKEES	40.00	20.00	12.00
(25)	YANKEES	40.00	20.00	12.00
	(NEW YORK on spine.)			

1936 Type 7 - Player, Team W/pennant, Cap, Ball, etc.

This group of pennants is slightly longer, at about 5-1/4", than the majority of BF 3 pennants. It is believed that two players from each team will eventually be accounted for.

		NM	EX	VG
Common Pennant:		40.00	20.00	12.00
(1)	Luke Appling	55.00	27.00	16.50
(2)	Wally Berger	40.00	20.00	12.00
(3)	Dolph Camilli	40.00	20.00	12.00
(4)	Dizzy Dean	90.00	45.00	27.00
(5)	Frank Demaree	40.00	20.00	12.00
(6)	Joe DiMaggio	200.00	100.00	60.00
(7)	Jimmie Foxx	75.00	37.00	22.00
(8)	Lou Gehrig	200.00	100.00	60.00
(9)	Earl Grace	40.00	20.00	12.00
(10)	Hank Greenberg	75.00	37.00	22.00
(11)	Gabby Hartnett	55.00	27.00	16.50
(12)	Rollie Hemsley	40.00	20.00	12.00
(13)	Carl Hubbell	55.00	27.00	16.50
(14)	Bob Johnson	40.00	20.00	12.00
(15)	Ernie Lombardi	55.00	27.00	16.50
(16)	Al Lopez	55.00	27.00	16.50
(17)	Joe Medwick	55.00	27.00	16.50
(18)	Van Lingle Mungo	45.00	22.00	13.50
(19)	Billy Myers	40.00	20.00	12.00
(20)	Mel Ott	55.00	27.00	16.50
(21)	Frank Pytlak	40.00	20.00	12.00
(23)	Schoolboy Rowe	40.00	20.00	12.00
(25)	Hal Trosky	40.00	20.00	12.00
(28)	Arky Vaughan	55.00	27.00	16.50
(29)	Paul Waner	55.00	27.00	16.50
(30)	Earl Whitehill	40.00	20.00	12.00

1936-37 Type 8 - Misc. Designs

Pennants in this series are generally unique in their style and do not fit into any of the other categories.

		NM	EX	VG
Common Pennant:		60.00	30.00	18.00
(1)	Wes Ferrell ("RED SOX" reversed out of bat on spine.)	60.00	30.00	18.00
(2)	Larry French (Name, team, year on ball.)	60.00	30.00	18.00
(3)	Goose Goslin (Name above and below bat, "TIGERS" on bat.)	75.00	37.50	22.00
(4)	Charley Root (Name above and below bat, "CUBS" on bat.)	60.00	30.00	18.00
(5)	Billy Sullivan ("INDIANS" reversed out of bat on spine.)	60.00	30.00	18.00
(6)	CHAMPIONS/YANKEES/1936 (Team name in red triangle at center.)	100.00	50.00	30.00

1937 Type 9 - Player Name, 1937 on Ball, Team Name

Players from only four teams - Bees, Cardinals, Cubs and White Sox - are known in this style. The pennants have a large baseball at left with three panels containing the player's first name, last name and "1937." At right is the team nickname.

		NM	EX	VG
Common Pennant:		60.00	30.00	18.00
(1)	Luke Appling	80.00	40.00	25.00
(2)	Wally Berger	60.00	30.00	18.00
(3)	Zeke Bonura	60.00	30.00	18.00
(4)	Frenchy Bordagaray	60.00	30.00	18.00
(5)	Clint Brown	60.00	30.00	18.00
(6)	Clay Bryant	60.00	30.00	18.00
(7)	Guy Bush	60.00	30.00	18.00
(8)	Sugar Cain	60.00	30.00	18.00
(9)	Tex Carleton	60.00	30.00	18.00
(10)	Phil Cavaretta (Cavarretta)	60.00	30.00	18.00
(11)	Phil Cavarretta	60.00	30.00	18.00
(12)	Irving Cherry	60.00	30.00	18.00
(13)	Ripper Collins	60.00	30.00	18.00
(14)	Tony Cuccinello	60.00	30.00	18.00
(15)	Curt Davis	60.00	30.00	18.00
(16)	Dizzy Dean	135.00	65.00	40.00
(17)	Paul Dean	75.00	37.50	22.00
(18)	Frank Demaree	60.00	30.00	18.00
(19)	Bill Dietrich	60.00	30.00	18.00
(20)	Vinc DiMaggio (Vince)	75.00	37.50	22.00
(21)	Leo Durocher	80.00	40.00	25.00
(22)	Jimmy Dykes	60.00	30.00	18.00
(23)	Burt Fletcher	60.00	30.00	18.00
(24)	Wes Flowers	60.00	30.00	18.00
(25)	Vic Frasier	60.00	30.00	18.00
(26)	Larry French	60.00	30.00	18.00
(27)	Linus Frey	60.00	30.00	18.00
(28)	Frank Frisch	80.00	40.00	25.00
(29)	Augie Galan	60.00	30.00	18.00
(30)	Charlie Grimm	60.00	30.00	18.00
(31)	Geo. Haas	60.00	30.00	18.00
(32)	Stan Hack	70.00	35.00	21.00
(33)	Jessie Haines	80.00	40.00	25.00
(34)	Gabby Hartnett	80.00	40.00	25.00
(35)	Minter Hayes	60.00	30.00	18.00
(36)	Billy Herman	80.00	40.00	25.00
(37)	Walter Highbee (Kirby Higbe)	60.00	30.00	18.00
(38)	Roy Johnson	60.00	30.00	18.00
(39)	Baxter Jordan	60.00	30.00	18.00
(40)	Billy Jurges	60.00	30.00	18.00
(41)	Vernon Kennedy	60.00	30.00	18.00
(42)	Mike Kreevich	60.00	30.00	18.00
(43)	Bill Lee	60.00	30.00	18.00
(44)	Thorn Lee	60.00	30.00	18.00
(45)	Al Lopez	80.00	40.00	25.00
(46)	Andy Lotshaw	60.00	30.00	18.00
(47)	Ted Lyons	80.00	40.00	25.00
(48)	Dan MacFayden	60.00	30.00	18.00
(49)	Henry Majeski	60.00	30.00	18.00
(50)	Pepper Martin	70.00	35.00	20.00
(51)	Stuart Martin	60.00	30.00	18.00
(52)	Joe Marty	60.00	30.00	18.00
(53)	Tommy McBride	60.00	30.00	18.00
(54)	Bill McKechnie	80.00	40.00	25.00
(55)	Joe Medwick	80.00	40.00	25.00
(56)	Steve Mesner	60.00	30.00	18.00
(57)	Hank Meyer	60.00	30.00	18.00
(58)	Johnny Mize	80.00	40.00	25.00
(59)	Gene Moore	60.00	30.00	18.00
(60)	Terry Moore	60.00	30.00	18.00
(61)	Ken O'Dea	60.00	30.00	18.00
(62)	Brusie Ogrodowski	60.00	30.00	18.00
(63)	Tony Piet	60.00	30.00	18.00
(64)	Ray Radcliff	60.00	30.00	18.00
(65)	Bob Reis	60.00	30.00	18.00
(66)	Dunc Rigney	60.00	30.00	18.00
(67)	Les Rock	60.00	30.00	18.00
(68)	Chas. Root	60.00	30.00	18.00
(69)	Larry Rosenthal	60.00	30.00	18.00

		NM	EX	VG
(73)	Luke Sewell	60.00	30.00	18.00
(74)	Merv Shea	60.00	30.00	18.00
(75)	Tuck Stainback	60.00	30.00	18.00
(76)	Hank Steinbacher	60.00	30.00	18.00
(77)	Monty Stratton	70.00	35.00	20.00
(78)	Ken Sylvestri	60.00	30.00	18.00
(79)	Billie Urbanski	60.00	30.00	18.00
(81)	Fred Walker	60.00	30.00	18.00
(82)	Lon Warneke	60.00	30.00	18.00
(83)	Johnnie Whitehead	60.00	30.00	18.00

1938 Type 10 - Player Name, 1938 on Ball, Team Name

Identical in format to the 1937 version, these pennants feature only members of the Detroit Tigers. The player's first name, last name and "1938" are stacked on the panels of a large baseball design at left, while "TIGERS" is at right.

		NM	EX	VG
Common Pennant:		60.00	30.00	18.00
(1)	Harry Eisenstat	60.00	30.00	18.00
(2)	Pete Fox	60.00	30.00	18.00
(3)	Vern Kennedy	60.00	30.00	18.00
(4)	Roxie Lawson	60.00	30.00	18.00
(5)	Tony Piet	60.00	30.00	18.00
(6)	Rudy York	60.00	30.00	18.00

1936-37 Type 11 - Minor League and Team

Minor league team nicknames and a league designation are combined with a player figure or symbol in this series. The checklist is believed complete with eight teams each from the Southern Association, International League and American Association.

		NM	EX	VG
Complete Set (24):		950.00	475.00	275.00
Common Pennant:		40.00	20.00	12.00
(1)	Barons - Southern	40.00	20.00	12.00
(2)	Bears - International	40.00	20.00	12.00
(3)	Bisons - International	40.00	20.00	12.00
(4)	Blues - Amer. Assn.	40.00	20.00	12.00
(5)	Brewers - Amer. Assn.	40.00	20.00	12.00
(6)	Chicks - Southern	40.00	20.00	12.00
(7)	Chiefs - International	40.00	20.00	12.00
(8)	Colonels - Amer. Assn.	40.00	20.00	12.00
(9)	Crackers - Sou'n. Ass'n.	40.00	20.00	12.00
(10)	Giants - International	40.00	20.00	12.00
(11)	Indians - Amer. Assn.	40.00	20.00	12.00
(12)	Lookouts - Sou'n. Ass'n.	40.00	20.00	12.00
(13)	Maple Leafs - International	40.00	20.00	12.00
(14)	Millers - Amer. Assn.	40.00	20.00	12.00
(15)	Mud Hens - Amer. Assn.	40.00	20.00	12.00
(16)	Orioles - International	40.00	20.00	12.00
(17)	Pelicans - Sou'n. Ass'n.	40.00	20.00	12.00
(18)	Red Birds - Amer. Assn.	40.00	20.00	12.00
(19)	Red Wings - Int'l	40.00	20.00	12.00
(20)	Royals - Int'l	40.00	20.00	12.00
(21)	Saints - Amer. Assn.	40.00	20.00	12.00
(22)	Smokies - Southern	40.00	20.00	12.00
(23)	Travelers - Sou'n. Ass'n.	40.00	20.00	12.00
(24)	Vols - Sou'n Ass'n.	40.00	20.00	12.00

1936-37 Type 12 - Jumbo Teams

According to advertising on the Red Ball Gum packaging with which most types of the Bf3 felt pennants were sold, jumbo size - about 28-1/2" x 11" - versions of 16 team pennants could be had by redeeming 25 wrappers and 15 cents for each desired pennant. The large-format pennants are identical in design to some of the smaller pieces from Types 4, 5 and 8.

	NM	EX	VG
Complete Set (16):			

Common Pennant:			
		300.00	150.00	90.00

		NM	EX	VG
Common Pennant:		300.00	150.00	90.00
(1)	Boston Bees	300.00	150.00	90.00
(2)	Boston Red Sox	300.00	150.00	90.00
(3)	Brooklyn Dodgers	300.00	150.00	90.00
(4)	Chicago Cubs	300.00	150.00	90.00
(5)	Chicago White Sox	300.00	150.00	90.00
(6)	Cincinnati Reds	300.00	150.00	90.00
(7)	Cleveland Indians	300.00	150.00	90.00
(8)	Detroit Tigers	300.00	150.00	90.00
(9)	New York Giants	300.00	150.00	90.00
(10)	New York Yankees	400.00	200.00	120.00
(11)	Philadelphia Athletics	300.00	150.00	90.00
(12)	Philadelphia Phillies	300.00	150.00	90.00
(13)	Pittsburgh Pirates	300.00	150.00	90.00
(14)	St. Louis Browns	300.00	150.00	90.00
(15)	St. Louis Cardinals	300.00	150.00	90.00
(16)	Washington Senators	300.00	150.00	90.00

1937 BF104 Blankets

A throwback to the 1914 B18 blankets, little is known about these 3-1/2"-square felts. They were designated as BF104 in the American Card Catalog. The issuer and manner of distribution remain a mystery. Subjects are depicted in either portrait or action artwork. This checklist likely is not complete.

		NM	EX	VG
Common Player:		300.00	150.00	90.00
(1)	Moe Berg	500.00	250.00	150.00
(2)	Cy Blanton	300.00	150.00	90.00
(3)	Earle Brucker	300.00	150.00	90.00
(4)	Mickey Cochrane	600.00	300.00	180.00
(5)	Joe Cronin	600.00	300.00	180.00
(6)	Tony Cuccinello	300.00	150.00	90.00
(7)	Dizzy Dean	1,200	600.00	360.00
(8)	Frank Demaree	300.00	150.00	90.00
(9)	Jimmie Foxx	900.00	450.00	275.00
(10)	Larry French	300.00	150.00	90.00
(11)	Frankie Frisch	600.00	300.00	180.00
(12)	Hank Greenberg	1,000	500.00	300.00
(13)	Gabby Hartnett	600.00	300.00	180.00
(14)	Billy Herman	600.00	300.00	180.00
(15)	Woody Jensen	300.00	150.00	90.00
(16)	Billy Jurges	300.00	150.00	90.00
(17)	Harry Kelly (Kelley)	300.00	150.00	90.00
(18)	Thornton Lee	300.00	150.00	90.00
(19)	Danny MacFayden	300.00	150.00	90.00
(20)	Connie Mack	600.00	300.00	180.00
(21)	Stu Martin	300.00	150.00	90.00
(22)	Joe Medwick	600.00	300.00	180.00
(23)	Ray Mueller	300.00	150.00	90.00
(24)	L. Newsome	300.00	150.00	90.00
(25)	Monty Stratton	405.00	200.00	120.00
(26)	Pie Traynor	600.00	300.00	180.00
(27)	Jim Turner	300.00	150.00	90.00
(28)	Bill Werber	300.00	150.00	90.00
(29)	Jack Wilson	300.00	150.00	90.00
(30)	Rudy York	300.00	150.00	90.00

C

1909 Cabanas

In conjunction with a post-season visit by the A.L. Champion Detroit Tigers (who without Hall of Famer Ty Cobb and Sam Crawford won only four of 12 games from the locals), Cabanas brand cigarettes issued this set. About 1-1/2" x 2-1/4" the cards feature black-and-white portrait photos. Players from the Almendares team have a blue frame and some colorized blue details on their uniforms, Havana players are in red, the Tigers are in gray. Printed on backs of the cards is (roughly translated) "The best way to form a valuable collection of baseball players of the Cuban clubs and the foreign visitors is to smoke Cabanas." It is unknown whether the checklists presented here alphabetically are complete.

		NM	EX	VG
Common Cuban Player:		600.00	300.00	175.00
Common Tigers Player:		900.00	450.00	275.00
ALMENDARES B.B.C.				
(1)	Rafael Almeida	700.00	350.00	210.00
(2)	Armando Cabanas	700.00	350.00	210.00
(3)	Alfredo Cabrera	600.00	300.00	175.00
(4)	Regino "Mamelo" Garcia	1,150	575.00	345.00
(5a)	Heliodoro Hidalgo (C.F.)	1,150	575.00	345.00
(5b)	Heliodoro Hidalgo (C.F. Jabuco)	1,150	575.00	345.00
(6)	Armando Marsans	700.00	350.00	210.00
(7)	Esteban Prats	600.00	300.00	175.00
(8)	Carlos "Bebe" Royer	700.00	350.00	210.00
HABANA B.B.C.				
(1)	Luis Bustamante	2,250	1,125	675.00
(2)	Luis "Chico" Gonzalez	600.00	300.00	175.00
(3)	Valentin "Sirique" Gonzalez	600.00	300.00	175.00
(4)	Ricardo Hernandez	600.00	300.00	175.00
(5)	Preston "Pete" Hill (Value Undetermined)			
(6)	Angel D. Mesa	600.00	300.00	175.00
(7)	Augustin "Tinti" Molina	700.00	350.00	210.00
(8)	Carlos "Chino" Moran	600.00	300.00	175.00
(9)	Luis "Mulo" Padron	3,500	1,750	1,050
(10)	Elilio Palomino	600.00	300.00	175.00
(11)	Pastor H. Pareda	600.00	300.00	180.00
(12)	Agustin Parpetti	2,000	1,000	600.00
(13)	Inocencio Perez	600.00	300.00	175.00
(14)	Bruce Petway	7,500	3,750	2,250
(15)	Gonzalo Sanchez	600.00	300.00	175.00
DETROIT TIGERS				
(1)	C. Beckendorff (Beckendorf)	900.00	450.00	275.00
(2)	Owen (Donie) Bush	900.00	450.00	275.00
(3)	Hopke	900.00	450.00	275.00
(4)	David Jones	900.00	450.00	275.00
(5)	William Lelivelt	900.00	450.00	275.00
(6)	Matty Mc. Intyre	900.00	450.00	275.00
(7)	George Moriarty	900.00	450.00	275.00
(8)	George Mullin	900.00	450.00	275.00
(9)	Frank O'Laughlin (O'Loughlin) (Umpire)	1,200	600.00	360.00
(10)	Charles O'Leary	900.00	450.00	275.00
(11)	Charles Schmidt	900.00	450.00	275.00
(12)	Edgar Willetts (Willett)	900.00	450.00	275.00

1955 Cain's Jimmy Piersall

The date of issue is speculative for these promotional postcards. The borderless black-and-white photo on the front of the 3-1/2" x 5-1/2" cards shows the popular BoSox star in a fielding pose. A blue facsimile autograph is printed at top. The postcard-format back has a drawing of the product beneath an advertising message bearing Piersall's signature. Similar cards advertising Colonial Meats are also known.

	NM	EX	VG
Autographed:	125.00	65.00	35.00
Jimmy Piersall (Mayonnaise)	80.00	40.00	24.00
Jimmy Piersall (Potato chips.)	80.00	40.00	24.00
Jimmy Piersall (Riviera dressing.)	80.00	40.00	24.00

1965 California Angels Matchbook Covers

These 1-1/2" x 4-1/2" matchbooks can be found with the advertising of two different banks printed on them; both are products of the local Universal Match Corp., and are printed in black and gold on white on front, with the inside surface in black-and-white. The County National Bank version has the player portrait photo within a plain black frame. Inside, the CNB matchbooks have player identification and personal data and 1964 stats. There is also an offer to redeem 15 different players' matchbooks for two free game tickets. The Santa Ana Savings matchbooks have the same player information and ads for the bank and the Angels' radio station. The player photos on front of the Santa Ana matchbooks have a gold frame.

Values shown are for complete but empty covers, with the striker surface intact. Complete matchbooks with matches bring about 2X the values quoted.

		NM	EX	VG
Complete Set (15):		120.00	60.00	35.00
Common Player:		10.00	5.00	3.00
(1)	Dean Chance	12.50	6.25	3.75
(2)	Lu Clinton	10.00	5.00	3.00
(3)	Jim Fregosi	10.00	5.00	3.00
(4)	Ed Kirkpatrick	10.00	5.00	3.00
(5)	Bobby Knoop	10.00	5.00	3.00
(6)	Barry Latman	10.00	5.00	3.00
(7)	Bob Lee	10.00	5.00	3.00
(8)	Ken McBride	10.00	5.00	3.00
(9)	Fred Newman	10.00	5.00	3.00
(10)	Jimmy Piersall	20.00	10.00	6.00
(11)	Rick Reichardt	10.00	5.00	3.00
(12)	Bill Rigney	10.00	5.00	3.00
(13)	Bob Rodgers	10.00	5.00	3.00
(14)	Tom Satriano	10.00	5.00	3.00
(15)	Willie Smith	10.00	5.00	3.00

1976 California Pacific Bank

Whether these are a legitimate promotional issue or a made-for-collectors set is unknown. The cards may have been created for use at autograph appearances at a Fullerton, Calif., bank. About 3-5/8" x 5", though the size varies, the black-and-white blank-back cards have player photos on front (some of which are reproductions of team-issued photos) and a promotional message describing the bank's "Big League Service." Two poses of Steve Carlton are known.

		NM	EX	VG
Complete Set (7):		60.00	30.00	18.00
Common Player:		5.00	2.50	1.50
(1)	Steve Busby	5.00	2.50	1.50
(2)	Steve Carlton	15.00	7.50	4.50
(3)	Steve Carlton	15.00	7.50	4.50
(4)	Bill Russell	5.00	2.50	1.50
(5)	Mike Schmidt	20.00	10.00	6.00
(6)	Ted Simmons	5.00	2.50	1.50
(7)	Don Sutton	10.00	5.00	3.00

1950 Callahan Hall of Fame

These cards, which feature artist Mario DeMarco's drawings of Hall of Famers, were produced from 1950 through 1956 and sold by the Baseball Hall of Fame in Cooperstown and at major league ballparks. The cards measure 1-3/4" x 2-1/2" and include a detailed player biography on the back. When introduced in 1950 the set included all members of the Hall of Fame up to that time, and then new cards were added each year as more players were elected. Therefore, cards of players appearing in all previous editions are more common than those players who appeared in just one or two years. When the set was discontinued in 1956 it consisted of 82 cards, which is now considered a complete set. The cards are not numbered and are listed here alphabetically. B.E. Callahan of Chicago, the publisher of "Who's Who in Baseball," produced the card set.

		NM	EX	VG
	Original 1950 Boxed Set (62):	500.00	250.00	150.00
	Complete Set (82):	1,900	950.00	575.00
	Common Player:	6.00	3.00	1.75
(1)	Grover Alexander	25.00	12.50	7.50
(2)	"Cap" Anson	15.00	7.50	4.50
(3)	J. Franklin "Home Run" Baker	150.00	75.00	45.00
(4)	Edward G. Barrow	35.00	17.50	10.00
(5a)	Charles "Chief" Bender (Bio ends ". . . immortal name for him.")	25.00	12.50	7.50
(5b)	Charles "Chief" Bender (Bio ends ". . . died in 1954.")	35.00	17.50	10.00
(6)	Roger Bresnahan	10.00	5.00	3.00
(7)	Dan Brouthers	15.00	7.50	4.50
(8)	Mordecai Brown	10.00	5.00	3.00
(9)	Morgan G. Bulkeley	10.00	5.00	3.00
(10)	Jesse Burkett	16.00	8.00	4.75
(11)	Alexander Cartwright	12.50	6.25	3.75
(12)	Henry Chadwick	12.00	6.00	3.50
(13)	Frank Chance	16.00	8.00	4.75
(14)	Albert B. Chandler	350.00	175.00	100.00
(15)	Jack Chesbro	7.50	3.75	2.25
(16)	Fred Clarke	10.00	5.00	3.00
(17)	Ty Cobb	50.00	25.00	15.00
(18a)	Mickey Cochran (Name incorrect.)	10.00	5.00	3.00
(18b)	Mickey Cochrane (Name correct.)	12.00	6.00	3.50
(19a)	Eddie Collins (Second paragraph of bio begins "Eddie had every . . .")	9.00	4.50	2.75
(19b)	Eddie Collins (Second paragraph of bio begins "He was brilliant . . .")	13.50	6.75	4.00
(20)	Jimmie Collins	12.50	6.25	3.75
(21)	Charles A. Comiskey	12.50	6.25	3.75
(22)	Tom Connolly	50.00	25.00	15.00
(23)	Candy Cummings	9.00	4.50	2.75
(24)	Dizzy Dean	45.00	22.50	13.50
(25)	Ed Delahanty	6.00	3.00	1.75
(26a)	Bill Dickey (First paragraph of bio ends ". . . He was right-handed all the way.")	30.00	15.00	9.00
(26b)	Bill Dickey (First paragraph of bio ends ". . . during his final year.")	35.00	17.50	10.50
(27)	Joe DiMaggio	180.00	90.00	54.00
(28)	Hugh Duffy	7.50	3.75	2.25
(29)	Johnny Evers	13.50	6.75	4.00
(30)	Buck Ewing	10.00	5.00	3.00
(31)	Jimmie Foxx	20.00	10.00	6.00
(32)	Frank Frisch	6.00	3.00	1.75
(33)	Lou Gehrig	85.00	42.50	25.00
(34a)	Charles Gehringer (White cap.)	9.00	4.50	2.75
(34b)	Charlie Gehringer (Dark cap.)	11.00	5.50	3.25
(35)	Clark Griffith	6.00	3.00	1.75
(36)	Lefty Grove	10.00	5.00	3.00
(37)	Leo "Gabby" Hartnett	40.00	20.00	12.00
(38)	Harry Heilmann	25.00	12.50	7.50
(39)	Rogers Hornsby	16.00	8.00	4.75
(40)	Carl Hubbell	12.00	6.00	3.50
(41)	Hughey Jennings	6.00	3.00	1.75
(42)	Ban Johnson	7.50	3.75	2.25
(43)	Walter Johnson	10.00	5.00	3.00
(44)	Willie Keeler	7.50	3.75	2.25
(45)	Mike Kelly	10.00	5.00	3.00
(46)	Bill Klem	65.00	32.50	20.00
(47)	Napoleon Lajoie	11.00	5.50	3.25
(48)	Kenesaw M. Landis	6.00	3.00	1.75
(49)	Ted Lyons	100.00	50.00	30.00
(50)	Connie Mack	12.00	6.00	3.50
(51)	Walter Maranville	20.00	10.00	6.00
(52)	Christy Mathewson	10.00	5.00	3.00
(53)	Tommy McCarthy	12.50	6.25	3.75
(54)	Joe McGinnity	6.00	3.00	1.75
(55)	John McGraw	10.00	5.00	3.00
(56)	Charles Nichols	16.00	8.00	4.75
(57)	Jim O'Rourke	9.00	4.50	2.75
(58)	Mel Ott	16.00	8.00	4.75
(59)	Herb Pennock	9.00	4.50	2.75
(60)	Eddie Plank	10.00	5.00	3.00
(61)	Charles Radbourne	10.00	5.00	3.00
(62)	Wilbert Robinson	6.00	3.00	1.75
(63)	Babe Ruth	90.00	45.00	27.50
(64)	Ray "Cracker" Schalk	30.00	15.00	9.00
(65)	Al Simmons	60.00	30.00	18.00
(66a)	George Sisler (Bio ends "Sisler today is . . .")	13.50	6.75	4.00
(66b)	George Sisler (Bio ends "Sisler was chosen as . . .")	9.00	4.50	2.75
(67)	A. G. Spalding	10.00	5.00	3.00
(68)	Tris Speaker	16.00	8.00	4.75
(69)	Bill Terry	30.00	15.00	9.00
(70)	Joe Tinker	10.00	5.00	3.00
(71)	"Pie" Traynor	10.00	5.00	3.00
(72)	Clarence A. "Dazzy" Vance	30.00	15.00	9.00
(73)	Rube Waddell	9.00	4.50	2.75
(74)	Hans Wagner	30.00	15.00	9.00
(75)	Bobby Wallace	13.50	6.75	4.00
(76)	Ed Walsh	10.00	5.00	3.00
(77a)	Paul Waner (Complete black frame line around picture.)	9.00	4.50	2.75
(77b)	Paul Waner (Bottom missing on black frame line around picture.)	40.00	20.00	12.00
(78)	George Wright	7.50	3.75	2.25

		NM	EX	VG
(79)	Harry Wright	20.00	10.00	6.00
(80)	Cy Young	12.50	6.25	3.75
(---)	Museum Exterior View (No date at top of list on back.)	35.00	17.50	10.00
(---)	Museum Exterior View (Date "1954" on top of list on back.)	60.00	30.00	18.00
(---)	Museum Interior View (Back copy ends, ". . . to all baseball men.")	30.00	15.00	9.00
(---)	Museum Interior View (Back copy ends ". . . playing days are concluded.")	13.50	6.75	4.00

1898 Cameo Pepsin Gum Pins

The first large set of baseball player pins is this issue from Whitehead & Hoag, advertising Cameo Pepsin Gum. The 1-1/4" pins have a sepia player portrait photo at center, with name and team at top left and right. It is very difficult to find pins with clear pictures as they tend to darken or fade with time. Pins were issued with a paper inset in back advertising the gum, but are often found there with the paper missing. It is likely that there will be future additions to this checklist. The unnumbered pins are presented here in alphabetical order.

		NM	EX	VG
	Common Player:	1,050	525.00	325.00
(1)	John Anderson	1,050	525.00	325.00
(2)	Cap Anson	3,300	1,300	800.00
(3)	Jimmy Bannon	1,050	525.00	325.00
(4)	Billy Barnie	1,050	525.00	325.00
(5)	Marty Bergen	1,050	525.00	325.00
(6)	Beville (Indianapolis)	1,050	525.00	325.00
(7)	Louis Bierbauer	1,050	525.00	325.00
(8)	Frank Bowerman	1,050	525.00	325.00
(9)	Ted Breitenstein	1,050	525.00	325.00
(10)	Herbert "Buttons" Briggs	1,050	525.00	325.00
(11)	Richard Brown	1,050	525.00	325.00
(12)	Eddie Burk (Burke)	1,050	525.00	325.00
(13)	Jesse Burkett	3,300	1,300	800.00
(14)	Frank "Buster" Burrell	1,050	525.00	325.00
(15)	Jimmy Canavan	1,050	525.00	325.00
	Cupid Childs	1,050	525.00	325.00
(16)	William (Dad) Clark (Clarke)	1,050	525.00	325.00
	Boileryard Clark (Clarke) (Balt.)	1,050	525.00	325.00
(17)	Jack Clements	1,050	525.00	325.00
	Archibald B. Cole (Cedar Rapids)	1,050	525.00	325.00
(18)	Jimmy Collins	2,850	1,300	800.00
(19)	Tommy Corcoran	1,050	525.00	325.00
(20)	James Corkman (Cockman) (Indianapolis)	1,050	525.00	325.00
(21)	Lave Cross	1,050	525.00	325.00
(22)	Nig Cuppy	1,050	525.00	325.00
(23)	Bill Dahlen	1,050	525.00	325.00
(24)	Bill Dammon (Dammann)	1,050	525.00	325.00
(25)	Dan Daub	1,050	525.00	325.00
(26)	George Decker	1,050	525.00	325.00
(27)	Ed Delahanty	3,300	1,300	800.00
(28)	Cozy Dolan	1,050	525.00	325.00
(29)	Tim Donahue	1,050	525.00	325.00
(30)	Patsy Donovan	1,050	525.00	325.00
(31)	Frank Donnelly (Cedar Rapids) (Cedar Rapids)	1,050	525.00	325.00
(32)	Hugh Duffy	2,850	1,300	800.00
(33)	Jack Dunn	1,050	525.00	325.00
(34)	Frank Dwyer	1,050	525.00	325.00
(35)	Bones Ely	1,050	525.00	325.00
(36)	Bill Everett (Everitt)	1,050	525.00	325.00
(37)	Buck Ewing	3,300	1,650	1,000
(38)	James Fields (Buffalo)	1,050	525.00	325.00
	Al Fisher (Cedar Rapids)	1,050	525.00	325.00
	Chauncey Fisher (Brooklyn)	1,050	525.00	325.00
(39)	Tim Flood	1,050	525.00	325.00
(40)	Frank Foreman (Indianapolis)	1,050	525.00	325.00
	James Franklin (Owner - Buffalo)	1,050	525.00	325.00
	William Fuller (Cedar Rapids)	1,050	525.00	325.00
(41)	Charlie Ganzel	1,050	525.00	325.00
(42)	Jot Goar (Pittsburgh)	1,050	525.00	325.00
(43)	Jot Goar (Indianapolis)	1,050	525.00	325.00
(44)	Bill Gray (Indianapolis)	1,050	525.00	325.00
(45)	Mike Griffin	1,050	525.00	325.00
(46)	Clark Griffith	2,650	1,300	800.00
(47)	John Grim	1,050	525.00	325.00
(48)	Billy Hamilton	2,750	1,375	825.00
(49)	Bill Hart	1,050	525.00	325.00
(50)	Charles Hastings	1,050	525.00	325.00
(51)	Pink Hawley	1,050	525.00	325.00
(52)	Belden Hill (Cedar Rapids)	1,050	525.00	325.00
(53)	Bill Hoffer	1,050	525.00	325.00
(54)	George Hogriever (Indianapolis)	1,050	525.00	325.00
(55)	Bug Holliday	1,050	525.00	325.00
(56)	Elmer Horton (Baltimore)	1,050	525.00	325.00
(57)	Dummy Hoy	2,450	1,550	900.00
(58)	Jim Hughey	1,050	525.00	325.00
	Edwin Hutchinson (Cedar Rapids)	1,050	525.00	325.00
(59)	Charlie Irwin	1,050	525.00	325.00

		NM	EX	VG
(60)	Hughie Jennings	2,650	1,300	800.00
(61)	Willie Keeler	2,650	1,300	800.00
(62)	A.F. Kennedy (Cedar Rapids)	1,050	525.00	325.00
(63)	Frank Killen	1,050	525.00	325.00
(64)	Malachi Kittredge	1,050	525.00	325.00
(65)	Candy LaChance	1,050	525.00	325.00
(66)	Bill Lange	1,050	525.00	325.00
(67)	Herman Long	1,050	525.00	325.00
(68)	Bobby Lowe	1,050	525.00	325.00
(69)	Denny Lyons	1,050	525.00	325.00
(70)	Connie Mack	3,300	1,300	800.00
	Louis Mahaffy (Mahaffey) (Cedar Rapids)	1,050	525.00	325.00
(71)	Willard Mains	1,050	525.00	325.00
	Jimmy McAleer (Cleveland)	1,050	525.00	325.00
(72)	Barry McCormick	1,050	525.00	325.00
	McDougal (Cedar Rapids)	1,050	525.00	325.00
(73)	Chippy McGarr	1,050	525.00	325.00
(74)	John McGraw	1,750	1,100	650.00
	Ed McKean (Cleveland)	1,050	525.00	325.00
(75)	Sadie McMann (McMahon)	1,050	525.00	325.00
(76)	Bid McPhee	4,200	2,450	1,100
(77)	Bill Merritt	1,050	525.00	325.00
(78)	Dusty Miller	1,050	525.00	325.00
(79)	Frank Motz (Indianapolis)	1,050	525.00	325.00
(80)	Kid Nichols	2,750	1,375	825.00
	Tom O'Brien (Balt.)	1,050	525.00	325.00
(81)	Jack O'Connor	1,050	525.00	325.00
(82)	John Pappaulan (Pappalau) (Pitcher, not R.F.)	1,050	525.00	325.00
(83)	Harley Payne	1,050	525.00	325.00
(84)	Heinie Peitz	1,050	525.00	325.00
(85)	Silver Bill Phillips (Indianapolis)	1,050	525.00	325.00
(86)	Arlie Pond	1,050	525.00	325.00
(87)	Jack Powell	1,050	525.00	325.00
	Joe Quinn (Balt.)	1,050	525.00	325.00
(88)	Bill Reidy	1,050	525.00	325.00
(89)	Heinie Reitz	1,050	525.00	325.00
(90)	Billy Rhines	1,050	525.00	325.00
(91)	Claude Richie (Ritchey)	1,050	525.00	325.00
(92)	Jack Rowe (Buffalo)	1,050	525.00	325.00
(93)	Jimmy Ryan (Chicago)	1,050	525.00	325.00
	Jack (John) Ryan (Boston)	1,050	525.00	325.00
(94)	Pop Schreiver (Schriver)	1,050	525.00	325.00
	Cy Seymour	1,050	525.00	325.00
(95)	Billy Shindle	1,050	525.00	325.00
(96)	"Broadway" Aleck Smith	1,050	525.00	325.00
(97)	Elmer Smith (Pittsburg)	1,050	525.00	325.00
(98)	Germany Smith	1,050	525.00	325.00
	Harry T. Smith (Buffalo)	1,050	525.00	325.00
(99)	Louis Sockalexis	2,000	1,300	650.00
(100)	George Speer (Milwaukee)	1,050	525.00	325.00
(101)	Jake Stentzel (Stenzel)	1,050	525.00	325.00
	Jack Stivetts	1,050	525.00	325.00
(102)	Joe Sugden	1,050	525.00	325.00
(103)	Jim "Suter" Sullivan	1,050	525.00	325.00
(104)	Patsy Tebeau	1,050	525.00	325.00
(105)	Fred Tenney	1,050	525.00	325.00
(106)	Adonis Terry	1,050	525.00	325.00
(107)	Tommy Tucker (Boston)	1,050	525.00	325.00
(108)	William Urquhart (Buffalo)	1,050	525.00	325.00
	Edward Van Buren (Cedar Rapids)	1,050	525.00	325.00
(109)	Farmer Vaughn	1,050	525.00	325.00
(110)	Bobby Wallace	2,650	1,300	800.00
(111)	Bill Watkins (Indianapolis)	1,050	525.00	325.00
(112)	William Weaver (Milwaukee)	1,050	525.00	325.00
(113)	Robert Wood (Indianapolis)	1,050	525.00	325.00
(114)	Cy Young	4,400	2,200	1,300
(115)	Chief Zimmer	1,300	625.00	400.00
(116)	1897 Brooklyn Team	1,400	700.00	400.00
(117)	1897 Buffalo Team	1,400	700.00	400.00
(118)	1897 Indianapolis Team	1,400	700.00	400.00
(119)	1897 Pittsburgh Team	1,400	700.00	400.00
(120)	1897 Toronto Team	1,400	700.00	400.00
	1897 New Castle Baseball Club 1897	1,400	700.00	400.00

1958 Roy Campanella Career Summary Card

This card was probably produced to allow Campy to respond to fan mail following his career-ending auto wreck in 1957. The 3-1/8" x 5" card is printed in black-and-white on thin semi-gloss cardboard. Front has a portrait photo and facsimile autograph, with a white stripe at top and bottom. The back has a career statistical summary, apparently taken from a contemporary Baseball Register.

	NM	EX	VG
Roy Campanella	20.00	10.00	6.00

1974 Capital Publishing Co.

This ambitious collectors issue offered more than 100 cards of "old-timers" in an attractive 4-1/8" x 5-1/4" format.

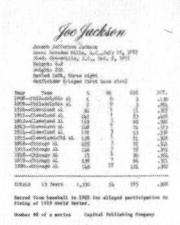

Card fronts have black-and-white photos with white borders all-around. Backs have player identification, biographical data and major league stats.

		NM	EX	VG
Complete Set (104):		200.00	100.00	60.00
Common Player:		6.00	3.00	1.75
1	Babe Ruth	15.00	7.50	4.50
2	Lou Gehrig	10.00	5.00	3.00
3	Ty Cobb	9.00	4.50	2.75
4	Jackie Robinson	7.50	3.75	2.25
5	Roger Connor	6.00	3.00	1.75
6	Harry Heilmann	6.00	3.00	1.75
7	Clark Griffith	6.00	3.00	1.75
8	Ed Walsh	6.00	3.00	1.75
9	Hugh Duffy	6.00	3.00	1.75
10	Russ Christopher	6.00	3.00	1.75
11	Snuffy Stirnweiss	6.00	3.00	1.75
12	Willie Keeler	6.00	3.00	1.75
13	Buck Ewing	6.00	3.00	1.75
14	Tony Lazzeri	6.00	3.00	1.75
15	King Kelly	6.00	3.00	1.75
16	Jimmy McAleer	6.00	3.00	1.75
17	Frank Chance	6.00	3.00	1.75
18	Sam Zoldak	6.00	3.00	1.75
19	Christy Mathewson	7.50	3.75	2.25
20	Eddie Collins	6.00	3.00	1.75
21	Cap Anson	6.00	3.00	1.75
22	Steve Evans	6.00	3.00	1.75
23	Mordecai Brown	6.00	3.00	1.75
24	Don Black	6.00	3.00	1.75
25	Home Run Baker	6.00	3.00	1.75
26	Jack Chesbro	6.00	3.00	1.75
27	Gil Hodges	6.00	3.00	1.75
28	Dan Brouthers	6.00	3.00	1.75
29	Don Hoak	6.00	3.00	1.75
30	Herb Pennock	6.00	3.00	1.75
31	Vern Stephens	6.00	3.00	1.75
32	Cy Young	7.50	3.75	2.25
33	Ed Cicotte	7.50	3.75	2.25
34	Sam Jones	6.00	3.00	1.75
35	Ed Waitkus	6.00	3.00	1.75
36	Roger Bresnahan	6.00	3.00	1.75
37	Fred Merkle	6.00	3.00	1.75
38	Ed Delehanty (Delahanty)	6.00	3.00	1.75
39	Tris Speaker	6.00	3.00	1.75
40	Fred Clarke	6.00	3.00	1.75
41	Johnny Evers	6.00	3.00	1.75
42	Mickey Cochrane	6.00	3.00	1.75
43	Nap Lajoie	6.00	3.00	1.75
44	Charles Comiskey	6.00	3.00	1.75
45	Sam Crawford	6.00	3.00	1.75
46	Ban Johnson	6.00	3.00	1.75
47	Ray Schalk	6.00	3.00	1.75
48	Pat Moran	6.00	3.00	1.75
49	Walt Judnich	6.00	3.00	1.75
50	Bill Killefer	6.00	3.00	1.75
51	Jimmie Foxx	6.00	3.00	1.75
52	Red Rolfe	6.00	3.00	1.75
53	Howie Pollett	6.00	3.00	1.75
54	Wally Pipp	6.00	3.00	1.75
55	Chief Bender	6.00	3.00	1.75
56	Connie Mack	6.00	3.00	1.75
57	Bump Hadley	6.00	3.00	1.75
58	Al Simmons	6.00	3.00	1.75
59	Hughie Jennings	6.00	3.00	1.75
60	Johnny Allen	6.00	3.00	1.75
61	Fred Snodgrass	6.00	3.00	1.75
62	Heinie Manush	6.00	3.00	1.75
63	Dazzy Vance	6.00	3.00	1.75
64	George Sisler	6.00	3.00	1.75
65	Jim Bottomley	6.00	3.00	1.75
66	Ray Chapman	6.00	3.00	1.75
67	Hal Chase	6.00	3.00	1.75
68	Jack Barry	6.00	3.00	1.75
69	George Burns	6.00	3.00	1.75
70	Jim Barrett	6.00	3.00	1.75
71	Grover Alexander	6.00	3.00	1.75
72	Elmer Flick	6.00	3.00	1.75
73	Jake Flowers	6.00	3.00	1.75
74	Al Orth	6.00	3.00	1.75
75	Cliff Aberson	6.00	3.00	1.75
76	Moe Berg	7.50	3.75	2.25
77	Bill Bradley	6.00	3.00	1.75
78	Max Bishop	6.00	3.00	1.75
79	Jimmy Austin	6.00	3.00	1.75
80	Beals Becker	6.00	3.00	1.75
81	Jack Clements	6.00	3.00	1.75
82	Cy Blanton	6.00	3.00	1.75
83	Garland Braxton	6.00	3.00	1.75
84	Red Ames	6.00	3.00	1.75
85	Hippo Vaughn	6.00	3.00	1.75
86	Ray Caldwell	6.00	3.00	1.75
87	Clint Brown	6.00	3.00	1.75
88	Joe Jackson	15.00	7.50	4.50
89	Pete Appleton	6.00	3.00	1.75
90	Ed Brandt	6.00	3.00	1.75
91	Walter Johnson	7.50	3.75	2.25
92	Dizzy Dean	6.00	3.00	1.75
93	Nick Altrock	6.00	3.00	1.75
94	Buck Weaver	7.50	3.75	2.25
95	George Blaeholder	6.00	3.00	1.75
96	Jim Bagby	6.00	3.00	1.75
97	Ted Blankenship	6.00	3.00	1.75
98	Babe Adams	6.00	3.00	1.75
99	Lefty Williams	7.50	3.75	2.25
100	Tommy Bridges	6.00	3.00	1.75
101	Rube Benton	6.00	3.00	1.75
102	Unknown	6.00	3.00	1.75
103	Max Butcher	6.00	3.00	1.75
104	Chick Gandil	7.50	3.75	2.25

1945-46 Caramelo Deportivo Cuban League

One of the better-known of Cuba's baseball card issues is the 100-card set issued by Caramelo Deportivo (Sporting Caramels) covering the 1945-46 Cuban winter league season. Printed in black-and-white on very thin 1-7/8" x 2-5/8" paper, the cards were intended to be pasted into an album issued for the purpose. Fronts have a card number, but no player identification; backs have the player's name, a few biographical and career details and an ad for the issuer, in as many as three different configurations. Many former and future Major Leaguers and stars of the U.S. Negro Leagues will be found on this checklist; sometimes providing the only cards issued contemporary with their playing careers.

		NM	EX	VG
Complete Set, No Reyes (99):		6,500	3,250	1,950
Common Player:		25.00	12.50	7.50
Album:		200.00	100.00	60.00
1	Caramelo Deportivo Title Card	7.50	3.75	2.25
2	Action Scene	12.50	6.25	3.75
3	Amado Maestri (Umpire)	25.00	12.50	7.50
4	Bernardino Rodriguez (Umpire)	25.00	12.50	7.50
5	Quico Magrinat (Umpire)	25.00	12.50	7.50
6	Cuco Conder (Announcer)	25.00	12.50	7.50
7	Marianao Team Banner	10.00	5.00	3.00
8	Armando Marsans	75.00	37.50	22.00
9	Jose Fernandez	25.00	12.50	7.50
10	Jose Luis Colas	25.00	12.50	7.50
11	"Charlotio" Orta (Charolito)	25.00	12.50	7.50
12	Barney Serrell	50.00	25.00	15.00
13	Claro Duany	30.00	15.00	9.00
14	Antonio Castanos	25.00	12.50	7.50
15	Virgilio Arteaga	25.00	12.50	7.50
16	Gilberto Valdivia	25.00	12.50	7.50
17	Jugo Cabrera	25.00	12.50	7.50
18	Lazaro Salazar	75.00	37.50	22.00
19	Julio Moreno	25.00	12.50	7.50
20	Oliverio Ortiz	25.00	12.50	7.50
21	Lou Knerr	25.00	12.50	7.50
22	Francisco Campos	25.00	12.50	7.50
23	Red Adams	25.00	12.50	7.50
24	Sandalio Consuegra	25.00	12.50	7.50
25	Ray Dandridge	800.00	400.00	240.00
26	Booker McDaniels	40.00	20.00	12.00
27	Orestes Minoso	675.00	335.00	200.00
28	Daniel Parra	25.00	12.50	7.50
29	Roberto Estalella	25.00	12.50	7.50
30	Raymond Brown	2,150	1,100	650.00
31	Havana Team Banner	10.00	5.00	3.00
32	Miguel Gonzalez	40.00	20.00	12.00
33	Julio Rojo	25.00	12.50	7.50
34	Herberto Blanco	25.00	12.50	7.50
35	Pedro Formenthal	30.00	15.00	9.00
36	Rene Monteagudo	25.00	12.50	7.50
37	Carlos Blanco	25.00	12.50	7.50
38	Salvador Hernandez	25.00	12.50	7.50
39	Rogelio Linares	25.00	12.50	7.50
40	Antonio Ordenana	25.00	12.50	7.50
41	Pedro Jiminez	25.00	12.50	7.50
42	Charley Kaiser	25.00	12.50	7.50
43	Manuel "Cocaina" Garcia	80.00	40.00	24.00
44	Sagua Hernandez	25.00	12.50	7.50
45	Lou Klein	25.00	12.50	7.50
46	Manuel Hidalgo	25.00	12.50	7.50
47	Dick Sisler	35.00	17.50	10.00
48	Jim Rebel	25.00	12.50	7.50
49	Raul Navarro	25.00	12.50	7.50
50	Pedero Medina	25.00	12.50	7.50
51	Charlie (Terries) McDuffie	75.00	37.50	22.00
52	Fred Martin	25.00	12.50	7.50
53	Julian Acosta	25.00	12.50	7.50
54	Cienfuegos Team Banner	10.00	5.00	3.00
55	Adolfo Luque	125.00	62.00	37.00
56	Jose Ramos	25.00	12.50	7.50
57	Conrado Perez	25.00	12.50	7.50
58	Antonio Rodriguez	25.00	12.50	7.50
59	Alejandro Crespo	30.00	15.00	9.00
60	Roland Gladu	25.00	12.50	7.50
61	Pedro Pages	25.00	12.50	7.50
62	Silvio Garcia	80.00	40.00	24.00
63	Carlos Colas	25.00	12.50	7.50
64	Salvatore Maglie	125.00	60.00	35.00
65	Martin Dihigo	1,250	625.00	375.00
66	Luis Tiant Sr.	185.00	90.00	55.00
67	Jim Roy	25.00	12.50	7.50
68	Ramon Roger	25.00	12.50	7.50
69	Adrian Zabala	25.00	12.50	7.50
70	Armando Gallart	25.00	12.50	7.50
71	Jose Zardon	25.00	12.50	7.50
72	Ray Berres	25.00	12.50	7.50
73	Napoleon Reyes (SP)	1,500	750.00	450.00
74	Jose Gomez	25.00	12.50	7.50
75	Loevigildo Xiques	25.00	12.50	7.50
76	Almendares Team Banner	10.00	5.00	3.00
77	Reinaldo Coreiro	25.00	12.50	7.50
78	Bartalo Portaundo (Bartolo Portuondo)	25.00	12.50	7.50
79	Jacinto Roque	25.00	12.50	7.50
80	Hector Arago	25.00	12.50	7.50
81	Gilberto Torres	30.00	15.00	9.00
82	Roberto Ortiz	30.00	15.00	9.00
83	Hector Rodriguez	25.00	12.50	7.50
84	Chifian Clark	40.00	20.00	12.00
85	Fermin Guerra	30.00	15.00	9.00
86	Jorge Comellas	25.00	12.50	7.50
87	Regino Otero	25.00	12.50	7.50
88	Tomas de la Cruz	30.00	15.00	9.00
89	Mario Diaz	25.00	12.50	7.50
90	Luis Aloma	25.00	12.50	7.50
91	Lloyd Davenport	40.00	20.00	12.00
92	Agapito Mayor	25.00	12.50	7.50
93	Ramon Bragana	100.00	50.00	30.00
94	Avelino Canizares	25.00	12.50	7.50
95	Santiago Ulrich	25.00	12.50	7.50
96	Beto Avila	50.00	25.00	15.00
97	Santos Amaro	30.00	15.00	9.00
98	Andres Fleitas	25.00	12.50	7.50
99	Limonar Martinez	25.00	12.50	7.50
100	Juan Montero	25.00	12.50	7.50

1946-47 Caramelo Deportivo Cuban League

Following its 100-card issue of the previous Cuban winter league season, this candy company issued a 185-card set for 1946-47. Besides more players, extra cards included banners, stadiums, managers, umpires and sportscasters. Printed on paper stock and intended to be pasted into an accompanying album, the cards measure about 1-7/8" x 2-1/2", though inconsistent cutting creates both over- and under-sized cards. Fronts have black-and-white player photos and a card number. Photos are often fuzzy or dark, indicative of their having been picked up from another source, such as a newspaper. Backs repeat the card number and have the player name at top, along with his Cuban League and, frequently, U.S. professional affiliation. Some 60 of the players in the set played in the segregated Negro Leagues of the era. A large ad for the candy and its sellers appear at bottom of the back. Because of the thin stock and placement in albums, these cards are usually found creased and/or with back damage.

		NM	EX	VG
Complete Set (185):		12,000	6,000	3,600
Common Player:		50.00	25.00	15.00
Album:		250.00	125.00	75.00
1	Introduction Card	25.00	12.50	7.50
2	New El Cerro Stadium	25.00	12.50	7.50
3	Stadium La Tropical	25.00	12.50	7.50
4	Maestri, Bernardino and Magrinat (El Cerro umpires.)	50.00	25.00	15.00
5	La Tropical umpires (Atan, Lopez, Vidal and Morales)	50.00	25.00	15.00
6	Cuco Conde (Announcer)	25.00	12.50	7.50
7	Cienfuegos Team Banner	25.00	12.50	7.50
8	Martin Dihigo	750.00	375.00	225.00
9a	Napoleon Reyes	60.00	30.00	18.00
9b	Napoleon Reyes	60.00	30.00	18.00
10	Adrian Zabala	50.00	25.00	15.00
11	Roland Gladu	50.00	25.00	15.00
12	Alejandro Crespo	100.00	50.00	30.00
13	Alejandro Carrasquel	50.00	25.00	15.00
14	Napoleon Heredia	50.00	25.00	15.00
15	Andres Mesa	50.00	25.00	15.00
16	Pedro Pages	50.00	25.00	15.00
17	Danny Gardella	50.00	25.00	15.00
18	Conrado Perez	50.00	25.00	15.00
19	Myron Hayworth	50.00	25.00	15.00
20	Pedro Miro	50.00	25.00	15.00
21	Guillermo Vargas	50.00	25.00	15.00
22	Hoot Gibson	50.00	25.00	15.00
23	Rafael Noble	55.00	27.50	16.50
24	Ramon Roger	50.00	25.00	15.00
25	Luis Arango	50.00	25.00	15.00
26	Roy Zimmerman	50.00	25.00	15.00
27	Luis Tiant Sr.	125.00	65.00	35.00
28	Jean Roy	55.00	27.50	16.50
29	Stanislov Bread	50.00	25.00	15.00
30	Walter Nothe	50.00	25.00	15.00
31	Vinicio Garcia	50.00	25.00	15.00
32	Dan (Max) Manning	200.00	100.00	60.00
33	Habana Lions Team Banner	25.00	12.50	7.50
34	Miguel A. Gonzalez	80.00	40.00	24.00
35	Pedro Formental	100.00	50.00	30.00

36	Ray Navarro	50.00	25.00	15.00
37	Pedro Jiminez	50.00	25.00	15.00
38	Rene Monteagudo	50.00	25.00	15.00
39	Salvador Hernandez	50.00	25.00	15.00
40	Hugh ('Terris) Mc. Duffie	70.00	35.00	20.00
41	Herberto Blanco	50.00	25.00	15.00
42	Harry (Henry) Kimbro	130.00	65.00	40.00
43	Lloyd (Lennie) Pearson	180.00	90.00	55.00
44	W. Bell	55.00	27.50	16.50
45	Carlos Blanco	50.00	25.00	15.00
46	Hank Thompson	70.00	35.00	20.00
47	Manuel ("Cocaina") Garcia	150.00	75.00	45.00
48	Alberto Hernandez	50.00	25.00	15.00
49	Tony Ordenana	50.00	25.00	15.00
50	Lazaro Medina	50.00	25.00	15.00
51	Fred Martin	50.00	25.00	15.00
52	Eddie (Jim) Lamarque	150.00	75.00	45.00
53	Juan Montero	50.00	25.00	15.00
54	Lou Klein	50.00	25.00	15.00
55	Pablo Garcia	50.00	25.00	15.00
56	Julio Rojo	50.00	25.00	15.00
57	Almendares Team Banner	25.00	12.50	7.50
58	Adolfo Luque	90.00	45.00	27.50
59	Cheo Ramos	50.00	25.00	15.00
60	Avelino Canizares	50.00	25.00	15.00
61	George Hausmann	50.00	25.00	15.00
62	Homero Ariosa	50.00	25.00	15.00
63	Santos Amaro	50.00	25.00	15.00
64	Hank Robinson	60.00	30.00	18.00
65	Lazaro Salazar	200.00	100.00	60.00
66	Andres Fleitas	50.00	25.00	15.00
67	Hector Rodriguez	80.00	40.00	24.00
68	Jorge Comellas	50.00	25.00	15.00
69	Lloyd Davenport	130.00	65.00	40.00
70	Tomas de la Cruz	50.00	25.00	15.00
71a	Roberto Ortiz	80.00	40.00	24.00
71b	Roberto Ortiz	50.00	25.00	15.00
72	Jess (Gentry) Jessup	130.00	65.00	40.00
73	Agapito Mayor	50.00	25.00	15.00
74	William	50.00	25.00	15.00
75	Santiago Ullrich	50.00	25.00	15.00
76	Coty Leal	50.00	25.00	15.00
77	Max Lanier	55.00	27.50	16.50
78	Buck O'Neill	800.00	400.00	240.00
79	Mario Ariosa	50.00	25.00	15.00
80	Lefty Gaines	130.00	65.00	40.00
81	Marianao Team Banner	25.00	12.50	7.50
82	Armando Marsans	80.00	40.00	24.00
83	Antonio Castanos	50.00	25.00	15.00
84	Orestes Minoso	200.00	100.00	60.00
85	Murray Franklin	50.00	25.00	15.00
86	Roberto Estalella	50.00	25.00	15.00
87	A. Castro	50.00	25.00	15.00
88	Gilberto Valdivia	50.00	25.00	15.00
89	Baffeth (Lloyd "Pepper" Bassett)	130.00	65.00	40.00
90	Oliverio Ortiz	50.00	25.00	15.00
91	Francisco Campos	50.00	25.00	15.00
92	Sandalio Consuegra	65.00	32.50	20.00
93	Lorenzo Cabrera	50.00	25.00	15.00
94	Roberto Avila	80.00	40.00	24.00
95	Chanquilon Diaz	50.00	25.00	15.00
96	Pedro Diaz	50.00	25.00	15.00
97	Cochihuila Valenzuela	50.00	25.00	15.00
98	Ramon Carneado	50.00	25.00	15.00
99	Aristonico Correoso	50.00	25.00	15.00
100	Daniel Doy	50.00	25.00	15.00
101	Joe Lindsay	50.00	25.00	15.00
102	Habana Reds Team Banner	25.00	12.50	7.50
103	Gilberto Torres	50.00	25.00	15.00
104	Oscar Rodriguez	50.00	25.00	15.00
105	Isidoro Leon	50.00	25.00	15.00
106	Julio Moreno	50.00	25.00	15.00
107	Chulungo del Monte	50.00	25.00	15.00
108	Len Hooker	100.00	50.00	30.00
109	Antonio Napoles	50.00	25.00	15.00
110	Orlando Suarez	50.00	25.00	15.00
111	Guillermo Monje	50.00	25.00	15.00
112	Isasio Gonzalez	50.00	25.00	15.00
113	Regino Otero	50.00	25.00	15.00
114	Angel Fleitas	50.00	25.00	15.00
115	Jorge Torres	50.00	25.00	15.00
116	Claro Duany	100.00	50.00	30.00
117	Charles Perez	50.00	25.00	15.00
118	Francisco Quicutis	50.00	25.00	15.00
119	Lazaro Bernal	50.00	25.00	15.00
120	Tommy Warren	50.00	25.00	15.00
121	Clarence Iott	55.00	27.00	16.50
122	P. Newcomb (Don Newcombe)	600.00	300.00	180.00
123	Gilberto Castillo	50.00	25.00	15.00
124	Matanzas Team Banner	25.00	12.50	7.50
125	Silvio Garcia	200.00	100.00	60.00
126	Bartolo Portuondo	50.00	25.00	15.00
127	Pedro Arango	50.00	25.00	15.00
128	Yuyo Acosta	50.00	25.00	15.00
129	Jose Cendan	50.00	25.00	15.00
130	Eddie Chandler	50.00	25.00	15.00
131	Rogelio Martinez	50.00	25.00	15.00
132	Atares Garcia	50.00	25.00	15.00
133	Manuel Godinez	50.00	25.00	15.00
134	John Williams	130.00	65.00	40.00
135	Emilio Cabrera	50.00	25.00	15.00
136	Barney Serrell	130.00	65.00	40.00
137	Armando Gallart	50.00	25.00	15.00
138	Ruben Garcia	50.00	25.00	15.00
139	Loevigildo Xiques	50.00	25.00	15.00
140	Chifian (Chiflan) Clark	130.00	65.00	40.00
141	Jacinto Roque	50.00	25.00	15.00
142	John (Johnny) Davis	150.00	75.00	45.00
143	Norman Wilson	50.00	25.00	15.00
144	Camaguey Team Banner	25.00	12.50	7.50
145	Antonio Rodriguez	50.00	25.00	15.00
146	Manuel Parrado	50.00	25.00	15.00
147	Leon Treadway	50.00	25.00	15.00
148	Amado Ibanez	50.00	25.00	15.00
149	Teodoro Oxamendi	50.00	25.00	15.00
150	Adolfo Cabrera	50.00	25.00	15.00

151	Oscar Garmendia	50.00	25.00	15.00
152	Hector Arago	50.00	25.00	15.00
153	Evelio Martinez	50.00	25.00	15.00
154	Raquel Antunez	50.00	25.00	15.00
155	Lino Donoso	50.00	25.00	15.00
156	Eliecer Alvarez	50.00	25.00	15.00
157	George Brown	50.00	25.00	15.00
158	Roberto Johnson	50.00	25.00	15.00
159	Rafael Franco	50.00	25.00	15.00
160	Miguel A. Carmona	50.00	25.00	15.00
161	Lilo Fano	50.00	25.00	15.00
162	Orestes Pereda	50.00	25.00	15.00
163	Pedro Diaz	50.00	25.00	15.00
164	Oriente Team Banner	25.00	12.50	7.50
165	Fermin Guerra	50.00	25.00	15.00
166	Jose M. Fernandez	50.00	25.00	15.00
167	Cando Lopez	50.00	25.00	15.00
168	Conrado Marrero	60.00	30.00	18.00
169	Oscar del Calvo	50.00	25.00	15.00
170	Booker McDaniels	150.00	75.00	45.00
171	Rafael Rivas	50.00	25.00	15.00
172	Daniel Parra	50.00	25.00	15.00
173	L. Holleman	50.00	25.00	15.00
174	Rogelio Valdes	50.00	25.00	15.00
175	Raymond Dandridge	950.00	475.00	285.00
176	Manuel Hidalgo	50.00	25.00	15.00
177	Miguel Lastra	50.00	25.00	15.00
178	Luis Minsal	50.00	25.00	15.00
179	Andres Vazquez	50.00	25.00	15.00
180	Jose A. Zardon	50.00	25.00	15.00
181	Jose Luis Colas	50.00	25.00	15.00
182	Rogelio Linares	50.00	25.00	15.00
183	Mario Diaz	50.00	25.00	15.00
184	R. Verdes	50.00	25.00	15.00
185	Indio Jiminez	50.00	25.00	15.00

1948-1949 Caramelos El Indio

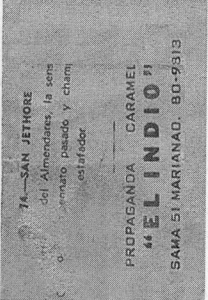

Perhaps the rarest of the late-1940s Cuban caramel cards is this issue picturing members of the island's four-team professional winter league. Measuring 1-5/8" x 2-7/16", the cards are printed in black-and-white on thick paper stock. Front photos are bordered in black with no player identification. On back at top is a card number and player name, along with a few words about the player. At bottom is an ad for the sponsor. Many American players, including Negro Leaguers, are included in the issue. The set is arranged alphabetically by team. An album was available in which to mount the cards. As with most contemporary Cuban issues, low-grade survivors are the norm, with Good condition being about the best seen, making the pricing here somewhat hypothetical.

		NM	EX	VG
Common Player:		200.00	100.00	60.00
Album:		300.00	150.00	90.00
1	Fermin Guerra	275.00	135.00	80.00
2	Rodolfo Fernandez	200.00	100.00	60.00
3	Reinaldo Cordeiro	200.00	100.00	60.00
4	Andres Fleitas	200.00	100.00	60.00
5	Tango Suarez	200.00	100.00	60.00
6	Ken Connors (Kevin "Chuck")	600.00	300.00	180.00
7	Rene Gonzalez	200.00	100.00	60.00
8	Jinny Bloodwrth (Jimmy Bloodworth)	275.00	135.00	80.00
9	Sojito Gallardo	200.00	100.00	60.00
10	Hector Rodriguez	275.00	135.00	80.00
11	Avelino Canizares	200.00	100.00	60.00
12	Gilberto Torres	200.00	100.00	60.00
13	Monte Yrving (Monte Irvin)	1,600.00	800.00	475.00
14	San Jethore (Sam Jethroe)	325.00	160.00	100.00
15	Al Gionfrido (Gionfriddo)	275.00	135.00	80.00
16	Santos Amaro	275.00	135.00	80.00
17	Hiram Gonzalez	200.00	100.00	60.00
18	Conrado Marrero	275.00	135.00	80.00
19	Jorge Comellas	200.00	100.00	60.00
20	Agapito Mayor	200.00	100.00	60.00
21	Octavio Rubert	200.00	100.00	60.00
22	Tata Solis	200.00	100.00	60.00
23	Morris Martin	275.00	135.00	80.00
24	Cyde (Clyde) King	275.00	135.00	80.00
25	Miguel Angel Gonzalez	325.00	160.00	100.00
26	Joseito Rodriguez	200.00	100.00	60.00
27	Sungo Carreras	200.00	100.00	60.00
28	Hank Anderson	275.00	135.00	80.00
29	Emilio Cabrera	200.00	100.00	60.00
30	Lennox Pearson	325.00	160.00	100.00
31	Herberto Blanco	200.00	100.00	60.00
32	Pablo Garcia	200.00	100.00	60.00
33	Chino Hidalgo	200.00	100.00	60.00
34	Amado Ibanez	200.00	100.00	60.00
35	Carlos Blanco	200.00	100.00	60.00
36	Henry Thompson	275.00	135.00	80.00
37	Henry Kimbro	275.00	135.00	80.00
38	Pedro Formental	275.00	135.00	80.00
39	Saguita Hernandez	200.00	100.00	60.00
40	Francisco Quicutis	200.00	100.00	60.00

41	George Stancer (Stanceu)	275.00	135.00	80.00
42	Jim Yockin (Yochim)	275.00	135.00	80.00
43	Tony Lorenzo	200.00	100.00	60.00
44	Rafael Rivas	200.00	100.00	60.00
45	Jose Cerdan	200.00	100.00	60.00
46	Cocaina Garcia	325.00	160.00	100.00
47	Bill Schuster	275.00	135.00	80.00
48	Oliverio Ortiz	200.00	100.00	60.00
49	Salvador Hernandez	200.00	100.00	60.00
50	Oscar Rodriguez	200.00	100.00	60.00
51	Julio Rojo	200.00	100.00	60.00
52	Ray Noble	250.00	125.00	75.00
53	Regino Otero	200.00	100.00	60.00
54	Peter Coscarat (Coscarart)	275.00	135.00	80.00
55	Jimmy Redmond	275.00	135.00	80.00
56	Mc. Quillan (Glenn McQuillen)	275.00	135.00	80.00
57	Stan Bread	275.00	135.00	80.00
58	Armando Gallart	200.00	100.00	60.00
59	Angel Fleitas	200.00	100.00	60.00
60	Pedro Pages	200.00	100.00	60.00
61	Alejandro Crespo	275.00	135.00	80.00
62	Jose Luis Colas	200.00	100.00	60.00
63	Conrado Perez	200.00	100.00	60.00
64	Coaker Tripletl (Triplett)	275.00	135.00	80.00
65	Pedro Dunabeitia	200.00	100.00	60.00
66	Maik Sukont (Max Surkont)	275.00	135.00	80.00
67	Max Mamming (Manning)	525.00	260.00	150.00
68	Jom Mikan	275.00	135.00	80.00
69	Herman Bess (Besse)	275.00	135.00	80.00
70	Wito (Luis) Aloma	275.00	135.00	80.00
71	Raul Lopez	200.00	100.00	60.00
72	Silvio Garcia	300.00	150.00	90.00
73	Gilberto Torres	200.00	100.00	60.00
74	Pipo de la Noval	200.00	100.00	60.00
75	Jose Maria Fernandez	200.00	100.00	60.00
76	Vitico Munoz	200.00	100.00	60.00
77	Luis Suarez	200.00	100.00	60.00
78	Wilfredo Salas	200.00	100.00	60.00
79	Julio Moreno	200.00	100.00	60.00
80	Bill Harrington	275.00	135.00	80.00
81	Oreste (Minnie) Minoso	525.00	260.00	150.00
82	Clarence Hicks	275.00	135.00	80.00
83	Pedro Ballester	200.00	100.00	60.00
84	Jose Hawerton	200.00	100.00	60.00
85	Ramon Roger	200.00	100.00	60.00
86	M Arenciba	200.00	100.00	60.00
87	Louis Kahn	275.00	135.00	80.00
88	Mario Diaz	200.00	100.00	60.00
89	Chiquitin Cabrera	200.00	100.00	60.00
90	Beto Avila	200.00	100.00	60.00
91	Cisco Campos	200.00	100.00	60.00
92	Johnny Simmons	275.00	135.00	80.00
93	Claro Duany	275.00	135.00	80.00
94	Clyde (Dave) Barnhill	800.00	400.00	240.00
95	Clarence Beer	275.00	135.00	80.00
96	Joaquin Gutierrez	200.00	100.00	60.00

1955 Carling Beer Cleveland Indians

Apparently the first of a line of premium photos which extended into the early 1960s. Measuring 8-1/2" x 12" and printed in black-and-white on semi-gloss thin card stock, these photocards are blank-backed. The 1955 Carling photos are identifiable from the 1956 issue, with which they share a "DBL" prefix to the card number in the lower-right corner, by the phrase "Great Champions" appearing just under the player photo.

	NM	EX	VG
Complete Set (11):	750.00	375.00	225.00
Common Player:	60.00	30.00	18.00
96A Ralph Kiner	110.00	55.00	35.00
96Ba Larry Doby	100.00	50.00	30.00
96Bb Herb Score	75.00	37.50	22.50
96C Al Rosen	75.00	37.50	22.50
96D Mike Garcia	60.00	30.00	18.00
96E Early Wynn	90.00	45.00	27.50
96F Bob Feller	150.00	75.00	45.00
96G Jim Hegan	60.00	30.00	18.00
96H George Strickland	60.00	30.00	18.00
96K Bob Lemon	90.00	45.00	27.50
96L Art Houtteman	60.00	30.00	18.00

1956 Carling Beer Cleveland Indians

This set was sponsored by Carling Black Label Beer. The oversized (8-1/2" x 12") cards feature black-and-white posed photos with the player's name in a white strip and a Carling ad at the bottom of the card front. Backs are blank. Like the cards issued in 1955, the 1956 set carries a DBL 96 series indication in the lower-right corner and lists brewery locations as Cleveland, St. Louis and Belleville, Ill. Unlike the '55 photocards, however, the first line under the player photo on the 1956 issue is "Premium Quality." Cards numbered DBL 96I and DBL 96J are unknown.

	NM	EX	VG
Complete Set (10):	900.00	450.00	275.00
Common Player:	60.00	30.00	18.00
96A Al Smith	60.00	30.00	18.00
96B Herb Score	120.00	60.00	35.00
96C Al Rosen	90.00	45.00	27.50
96D Mike Garcia	60.00	30.00	18.00
96E Early Wynn	120.00	60.00	35.00
96F Bob Feller	200.00	100.00	60.00
96G Jim Hegan	60.00	30.00	18.00
96H George Strickland	60.00	30.00	18.00
96K Bob Lemon	120.00	60.00	35.00
96L Art Houtteman	60.00	30.00	18.00

1957 Carling Beer Cleveland Indians

The fact that Kerby Farrell managed the Indians only in 1957 pinpoints the year of issue for those Carling Beer photocards which carry a DBL 179 series number in the lower-right corner. Following the black-and-white, blank-backed 8-1/2" x 12" format of earlier issues, the 1957 Carlings list on the bottom line breweries at Cleveland; Frankenmuth, Mich.; Natick, Mass., and, Belleville, Ill. Cards numbered DBL 179I and DBL 179J are are currently unknown.

	NM	EX	VG
Complete Set (10):	900.00	450.00	275.00
Common Player:	60.00	30.00	18.00
179A Vic Wertz	60.00	30.00	18.00
179B Early Wynn	100.00	50.00	30.00
179C Herb Score	90.00	45.00	27.50
179D Bob Lemon	100.00	50.00	30.00
179E Ray Narleski	60.00	30.00	18.00
179F Jim Hegan	60.00	30.00	18.00
179G Bob Avila	60.00	30.00	18.00
179H Al Smith	60.00	30.00	18.00
179K Kerby Farrell	60.00	30.00	18.00
179L Rocky Colavito	300.00	150.00	90.00

1958 Carling Beer Cleveland Indians

Identical in format to earlier issues, the 1958 premium photos can be distinguished by the card number printed in the lower-right corner. Cards in the 1958 series have numbers which begin with a DBL 2 or DBL 217 prefix.

	NM	EX	VG
Complete Set (10):	725.00	360.00	215.00
Common Player:	60.00	30.00	18.00
2 Vic Wertz	60.00	30.00	18.00
217 Minnie Minoso	100.00	50.00	30.00
217B Gene Woodling	60.00	30.00	18.00
217C Russ Nixon	60.00	30.00	18.00
217D Bob Lemon	120.00	60.00	35.00
217E Bobby Bragan	60.00	30.00	18.00
217F Cal McLish	60.00	30.00	18.00
217G Rocky Colavito	150.00	75.00	45.00
217H Herb Score	100.00	50.00	30.00
217J Chico Carrasquel	60.00	30.00	18.00

1959 Carling Beer Cleveland Indians

The appearance of Billy Martin among Carling photocards labeled with a DBL 266 prefix fixes the year of issue to 1959, the fiery second baseman's only year with the Tribe. Once again the 8-1/2" x 12" black-and-white, blank-backed cards follow the format of previous issues. Breweries listed on the bottom of the 1959 Carlings are Cleveland; Atlanta; Frankenmuth, Mich.; Natick, Mass.; Belleville, Ill., and, Tacoma, Wash.

	NM	EX	VG
Complete Set (6):	600.00	300.00	180.00
Common Player:	75.00	37.50	22.50
266A Vic Power	75.00	37.50	22.50
266B Minnie Minoso	100.00	50.00	30.00
266C Herb Score	100.00	50.00	30.00
266D Rocky Colavito	150.00	75.00	45.00
266E Jimmy Piersall	100.00	50.00	30.00
266F Billy Martin	150.00	75.00	45.00

1960 Carling Beer

Because of the numbering and the fact that manager Joe Gordon was at the helm in 1960, these are believed to be from that year. Like the others, these are 8-1/2" x 12-1/2", black and white, and blank-backed.

	NM	EX	VG
Checklist is likely incomplete			
DBL347D Joe Gordon	100.00	50.00	30.00
DBL347E Bubba Phillips	60.00	30.00	18.00
DBL347K Tito Francona	60.00	30.00	18.00

1961 Carling Beer Cleveland Indians

Totally different player selection and the use of an LB prefix to the number in the lower-right corner define the 1961 issue from Carling Beer. Otherwise the photocards share the same 8-1/2" x 12" black-and-white format with earlier issues. The blank-backed cards of the 1961 issue list only a single brewery, Cleveland, at the bottom of the ad portion of the issues. The checklist here is arranged alphabetically. Cards numbered LB 420I and LB420J are unknown.

	NM	EX	VG
Complete Set (10):	600.00	300.00	180.00
Common Player:	60.00	30.00	18.00
420A Jimmy Piersall	100.00	50.00	30.00
420B Willie Kirkland	60.00	30.00	18.00
420C Johnny Antonelli	60.00	30.00	18.00
420D John Romano	60.00	30.00	18.00
420E Woodie Held	60.00	30.00	18.00
420F Tito Francona	60.00	30.00	18.00
420G Jim Perry	90.00	45.00	27.50
420H Bubba Phillips	60.00	30.00	18.00
420K John Temple	60.00	30.00	18.00
420L Vic Power	60.00	30.00	18.00

1909-11 Carolina Brights

Among the last of the T206 cards printed, those with Carolina Brights advertising on back are scarce and command a significant premium. The advertising on back is printed in black.

PREMIUMS:
Common Player: 5-6X
Typical Hall of Famer: 3-4X
(See T206 for checklist and base card values.)

1976 Carousel Discs

One of several regional sponsors of player disc sets in 1976 was the Michigan snack bar chain, Carousel. The sponsor's discs are unique in that they do not have pre-printed backs, but rather have a black rubber-stamp on the otherwise blank back. To date more than 20 such stamps have been seen, reportedly from New Jersey to Alaska. The discs are 3-3/8" diameter with a black-and-white player portrait photo in the center of the baseball design. A line of red stars is above, while the left and right panels feature one of several bright colors. Produced by Michael Schecter Associates under license from the Major League Baseball Players Association, the player photos have had uniform and cap logos removed. The unnumbered checklist here is presented in alphabetical order.

	NM	EX	VG
Complete Set (70):	35.00	17.50	10.00
Common Player:	2.00	1.00	.60
(1) Henry Aaron	12.50	6.25	3.75
(2) Johnny Bench	7.50	3.75	2.25
(3) Vida Blue	2.00	1.00	.60
(4) Larry Bowa	2.00	1.00	.60
(5) Lou Brock	5.00	2.50	1.50
(6) Jeff Burroughs	2.00	1.00	.60
(7) John Candelaria	2.00	1.00	.60
(8) Jose Cardenal	2.00	1.00	.60
(9) Rod Carew	5.00	2.50	1.50
(10) Steve Carlton	5.00	2.50	1.50
(11) Dave Cash	2.00	1.00	.60
(12) Cesar Cedeno	2.00	1.00	.60
(13) Ron Cey	2.00	1.00	.60
(14) Carlton Fisk	5.00	2.50	1.50
(15) Tito Fuentes	2.00	1.00	.60
(16) Steve Garvey	3.50	1.75	1.00
(17) Ken Griffey	2.00	1.00	.60
(18) Don Gullett	2.00	1.00	.60
(19) Willie Horton	2.00	1.00	.60
(20) Al Hrabosky	2.00	1.00	.60
(21) Catfish Hunter	5.00	2.50	1.50
(22a) Reggie Jackson (A's)	7.50	3.75	2.25
(22b) Reggie Jackson (Orioles)	10.00	5.00	3.00
(23) Randy Jones	2.00	1.00	.60
(24) Jim Kaat	2.00	1.00	.60
(25) Don Kessinger	2.00	1.00	.60
(26) Dave Kingman	1.75	.90	.50
(27) Jerry Koosman	2.00	1.00	.60
(28) Mickey Lolich	2.00	1.00	.60
(29) Greg Luzinski	2.00	1.00	.60
(30) Fred Lynn	2.00	1.00	.60
(31) Bill Madlock	2.00	1.00	.60
(32a) Carlos May (White Sox)	3.00	1.50	.90
(32b) Carlos May (Yankees)	2.00	1.00	.60
(33) John Mayberry	2.00	1.00	.60
(34) Bake McBride	2.00	1.00	.60
(35) Doc Medich	2.00	1.00	.60
(36a) Andy Messersmith (Dodgers)	3.00	1.50	.90
(36b) Andy Messersmith (Braves)	2.00	1.00	.60
(37) Rick Monday	2.00	1.00	.60
(38) John Montefusco	2.00	1.00	.60
(39) Jerry Morales	2.00	1.00	.60
(40) Joe Morgan	5.00	2.50	1.50
(41) Thurman Munson	4.50	2.25	1.25
(42) Bobby Murcer	2.00	1.00	.60
(43) Al Oliver	2.00	1.00	.60
(44) Jim Palmer	5.00	2.50	1.50
(45) Dave Parker	2.00	1.00	.60
(46) Tony Perez	5.00	2.50	1.50
(47) Jerry Reuss	2.00	1.00	.60
(48) Brooks Robinson	6.00	3.00	1.75
(49) Frank Robinson	6.00	3.00	1.75
(50) Steve Rogers	2.00	1.00	.60
(51) Pete Rose	12.50	6.25	3.75
(52) Nolan Ryan	15.00	7.50	4.50
(53) Manny Sanguillen	2.00	1.00	.60
(54) Mike Schmidt	12.00	6.00	3.50
(55) Tom Seaver	5.00	2.50	1.50
(56) Ted Simmons	2.00	1.00	.60
(57) Reggie Smith	2.00	1.00	.60
(58) Willie Stargell	5.00	2.50	1.50
(59) Rusty Staub	1.75	.90	.50
(60) Rennie Stennett	2.00	1.00	.60
(61) Don Sutton	5.00	2.50	1.50
(62a) Andy Thornton (Cubs)	3.00	1.50	.90
(62b) Andy Thornton (Expos)	2.00	1.00	.60
(63) Luis Tiant	2.00	1.00	.60
(64) Joe Torre	3.00	1.50	.90
(65) Mike Tyson	2.00	1.00	.60
(66) Bob Watson	2.00	1.00	.60
(67) Wilbur Wood	2.00	1.00	.60
(68) Jimmy Wynn	2.00	1.00	.60
(69) Carl Yastrzemski	6.00	3.00	1.75
(70) Richie Zisk	2.00	1.00	.60

1973 Norm Cash Day Card

As part of the Tiger Stadium festivities on August 12, this 7" x 5" color card was given to fans. Besides an action photo of the feared slugger, his facsimile autograph appears.

	NM	EX	VG
Norm Cash	12.50	6.25	3.75

1939 Centennial of Baseball Stamps

Part of the pagentry surrounding the 1939 centennial of the fabled beginnings of baseball was this set of player and history stamps and an accompanying 36-page album. The single stamps measure about 1-5/8" x 2-1/8" and are blank-backed. Stamps #1-13 deal with the game's history; most feature artwork by famed baseball artist and former major league pitcher Al Demaree. Stamps #14-25 feature photos of the game's greats in tombstone frames surrounded by colorful borders.

		NM	EX	VG
Complete Set, w/Album (25):		1,000	500.00	300.00
Common Player:		50.00	25.00	15.00
Common Historical:		20.00	10.00	6.00
Uncut Stamp Sheet (25):		1,000	500.00	300.00
Album:		80.00	40.00	25.00
1	Abner Doubleday	50.00	25.00	15.00
2	1849 Knickerbockers	50.00	25.00	15.00
3	Ball/bat Standards	20.00	10.00	6.00
4	1858 Brooklyn vs. New York Series	50.00	25.00	15.00
5	1859 Amherst vs. Williams Series	20.00	10.00	6.00
6	Curve Ball (Arthur Cummings)	50.00	25.00	15.00
7	First Admission Fee	20.00	10.00	6.00
8	First Professional Players	50.00	25.00	15.00
9	First No-Hitter (George Bradley)	50.00	25.00	15.00
10	Morgan G. Bulkeley	50.00	25.00	15.00
11	First World's Champions	50.00	25.00	15.00
12	Byron Bancroft (Ban) Johnson	50.00	25.00	15.00
13	First Night Game	20.00	10.00	6.00
14	Grover Cleveland Alexander	60.00	30.00	18.00
15	Tyrus Raymond Cobb	150.00	75.00	45.00
16	Eddie Collins	50.00	25.00	15.00
17	Wee Willie Keeler	50.00	25.00	15.00
18	Walter Perry Johnson	75.00	37.50	22.50
19	Napoleon (Larry) Lajoie	50.00	25.00	15.00
20	Christy Mathewson	75.00	37.50	22.50
21	George Herman (Babe) Ruth	300.00	150.00	90.00
22	George Sisler	50.00	25.00	15.00
23	Tristam E. (Tris) Speaker	60.00	30.00	18.00
24	Honus Wagner	100.00	50.00	30.00
25	Denton T. (Cy) Young	75.00	37.50	22.50

1952 Central National Bank of Cleveland

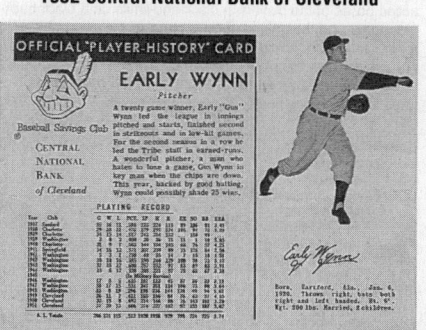

The scope of this issue is undetermined. It is possible a player card was given as a premium for deposits in the bank's "Baseball Savings Club." The cards are about 6-3/4" x 4-3/4", printed in dark blue on cream-colored stock with a blank back. Titled "OFFICIAL "PLAYER-HISTORY" CARD", it features an action pose, facsimile signature, personal data, career summary and complete stats.

	NM	EX	VG
Common Player:	100.00	50.00	30.00
Early Wynn	200.00	100.00	60.00

1929 Certified's Ice Cream Pins

Unless or until further players are seen in this series, the date of issue will have to remain uncertain. Apparently given away by Wrigley Field's ice cream concessionaire, these 1" diameter pin-backs feature player portraits and typography in sepia tones lithographed on a white background.

		NM	EX	VG
Complete Set (5):		2,600	1,300	775.00
Common Player:		450.00	225.00	135.00
(1)	Joe Bush	450.00	225.00	135.00
(2)	Kiki Cuyler	600.00	300.00	180.00
(3)	Rogers Hornsby	725.00	360.00	215.00
(4)	Riggs Stephenson	450.00	225.00	135.00
(5)	Hack Wilson	600.00	300.00	180.00

1964 Challenge the Yankees Game

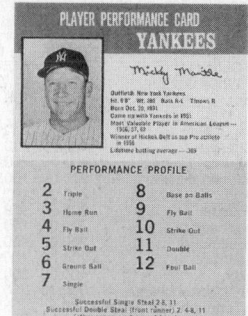

The 50 player cards in this set were part of a boxed dice baseball game produced by Hassenfeld Bros. of Pawtucket, R.I. Cards are approximately 4" x 5-1/2" and blank-backed, featuring a small black-and-white photo, a facsimile autograph and a few biographical details and stats. Player selection is virtually the same for the games issued in 1964 and 1965, and the only way to distinguish cards from each year is to study the stats. Cards are unnumbered and are checklisted below in alphabetical order.

		NM	EX	VG
Complete Boxed Set:		1,200	600.00	350.00
Complete Card Set (50):		850.00	425.00	250.00
Common Player:		9.00	4.50	2.75
(1)	Hank Aaron	150.00	75.00	45.00
(2)	Yogi Berra	45.00	22.50	13.50
(3)	Johnny Blanchard	9.00	4.50	2.75
(4)	Jim Bouton	20.00	10.00	6.00
(5)	Clete Boyer	15.00	7.50	4.50
(6)	Marshall Bridges	9.00	4.50	2.75
(7)	Harry Bright	9.00	4.50	2.75
(8)	Tom Cheney	9.00	4.50	2.75
(9)	Del Crandall	9.00	4.50	2.75
(10)	Al Downing	9.00	4.50	2.75
(11)	Whitey Ford	40.00	20.00	12.00
(12)	Tito Francona	9.00	4.50	2.75
(13)	Jake Gibbs	9.00	4.50	2.75
(14)	Pedro Gonzalez	9.00	4.50	2.75
(15)	Dick Groat	9.00	4.50	2.75
(16)	Steve Hamilton	9.00	4.50	2.75
(17)	Elston Howard	20.00	10.00	6.00
(18)	Al Kaline	45.00	22.50	13.50
(19)	Tony Kubek	30.00	15.00	9.00
(20)	Phil Linz	9.00	4.50	2.75
(21)	Hector Lopez	9.00	4.50	2.75
(22)	Art Mahaffey	9.00	4.50	2.75
(23)	Frank Malzone	9.00	4.50	2.75
(24)	Mickey Mantle	250.00	125.00	75.00
(25)	Juan Marichal	30.00	15.00	9.00
(26)	Roger Maris	75.00	37.50	22.50
(27)	Eddie Mathews	30.00	15.00	9.00
(28)	Bill Mazeroski	30.00	15.00	9.00
(29)	Ken McBride	9.00	4.50	2.75
(30)	Willie McCovey	30.00	15.00	9.00
(31)	Tom Metcalf	9.00	4.50	2.75
(32)	Jim O'Toole	9.00	4.50	2.75
(33)	Milt Pappas	9.00	4.50	2.75
(34)	Joe Pepitone	15.00	7.50	4.50
(35)	Ron Perranoski	9.00	4.50	2.75
(36)	Johnny Podres	9.00	4.50	2.75
(37)	Dick Radatz	9.00	4.50	2.75
(38)	Hal Reniff	9.00	4.50	2.75
(39)	Bobby Richardson	30.00	15.00	9.00
(40)	Rich Rollins	9.00	4.50	2.75
(41)	Ron Santo	20.00	10.00	6.00
(42)	Moose Skowron	20.00	10.00	6.00
(43)	Duke Snider	30.00	15.00	9.00
(44)	Bill Stafford	9.00	4.50	2.75
(45)	Ralph Terry	9.00	4.50	2.75
(46)	Tom Tresh	15.00	7.50	4.50
(47)	Pete Ward	9.00	4.50	2.75
(48)	Carl Warwick	9.00	4.50	2.75
(49)	Stan Williams	9.00	4.50	2.75
(50)	Carl Yastrzemski	75.00	37.50	22.50

1965 Challenge the Yankees Game

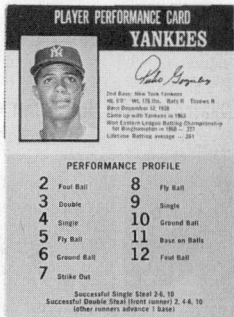

The player cards in this set were part of a boxed dice baseball game produced by Hassenfeld Bros. of Pawtucket, R.I. Cards are approximately 4" x 5-1/2" and blank-backed, featuring a small black-and-white photo, a facsimile autograph and a few biographical details and stats. Player selection is virtually the same for the games issued in 1964 and 1965, and the only way to distinguish cards from each year is to study the stats. Cards are unnumbered and are checklisted below in alphabetical order. The card of Yankee pitcher Rollie Sheldon was apparently withdrawn following his May 3 trade to Kansas City and is scarcer than the rest of the set.

		NM	EX	VG
Complete Boxed Set:		1,500	750.00	450.00
Complete Card Set (50):		1,000	500.00	300.00
Common Player:		10.00	5.00	3.00
(1)	Henry Aaron	125.00	62.00	37.00
(2)	Johnny Blanchard	10.00	5.00	3.00
(3)	Jim Bouton	12.50	6.25	3.75
(4)	Clete Boyer	12.50	6.25	3.75
(5)	Leon Carmel	10.00	5.00	3.00
(6)	Joe Christopher	10.00	5.00	3.00
(7)	Vic Davalillo	10.00	5.00	3.00
(8)	Al Downing	10.00	5.00	3.00
(9)	Whitey Ford	50.00	25.00	15.00
(10)	Bill Freehan	10.00	5.00	3.00
(11)	Jim Gentile	10.00	5.00	3.00
(12)	Jake Gibbs	10.00	5.00	3.00
(13)	Pedro Gonzalez	10.00	5.00	3.00
(14)	Dick Groat	10.00	5.00	3.00
(15)	Steve Hamilton	10.00	5.00	3.00
(16)	Elston Howard	20.00	10.00	6.00
(17)	Al Kaline	50.00	25.00	15.00
(18)	Tony Kubek	25.00	12.50	7.50
(19)	Phil Linz	10.00	5.00	3.00
(20)	Don Lock	10.00	5.00	3.00
(21)	Hector Lopez	10.00	5.00	3.00
(22)	Art Mahaffey	10.00	5.00	3.00
(23)	Frank Malzone	10.00	5.00	3.00
(24)	Mickey Mantle	350.00	175.00	100.00
(25)	Juan Marichal	40.00	20.00	12.00
(26)	Roger Maris	90.00	45.00	27.00
(27)	Eddie Mathews	50.00	25.00	15.00
(28)	Bill Mazeroski	40.00	20.00	12.00
(29)	Ken McBride	10.00	5.00	3.00
(30)	Tim McCarver	15.00	7.50	4.50
(31)	Willie McCovey	40.00	20.00	12.00
(32)	Tom Metcalf	10.00	5.00	3.00
(33)	Pete Mikkelsen	10.00	5.00	3.00
(34)	Jim O'Toole	10.00	5.00	3.00
(35)	Milt Pappas	10.00	5.00	3.00
(36)	Joe Pepitone	12.50	6.25	3.75
(37)	Ron Perranoski	10.00	5.00	3.00
(38)	Johnny Podres	12.50	6.25	3.75
(39)	Dick Radatz	10.00	5.00	3.00
(40)	Pedro Ramos	10.00	5.00	3.00
(41)	Hal Reniff	10.00	5.00	3.00
(42)	Bobby Richardson	25.00	12.50	7.50
(43)	Rich Rollins	10.00	5.00	3.00
(44)	Ron Santo	20.00	10.00	6.00
(45)	Rollie Sheldon (SP)	75.00	37.00	22.00
(46)	Bill Stafford	10.00	5.00	3.00
(47)	Mel Stottlemyre	12.50	6.25	3.75
(48)	Tom Tresh	12.50	6.25	3.75
(49)	Pete Ward	10.00	5.00	3.00
(50)	Carl Yaztrzemski	75.00	37.00	22.00

1947 Champ Hats Premiums

The attributed date is speculative, based on the limited known player selection. These 8" x 10" sepia photo cards have player pictures in uniform. In the wide bottom border is: "(Player Name) says:" and an ad message. Backs are blank.

DixieWalker says: "CHAMP HATS are sure winners in style and quality"

	NM	EX	VG
Common Player:	250.00	125.00	75.00
(1) Mickey Vernon	250.00	125.00	75.00
(2) Dixie Walker	250.00	125.00	75.00

1957-1962 Charcoal Steak House Ted Kluszewski

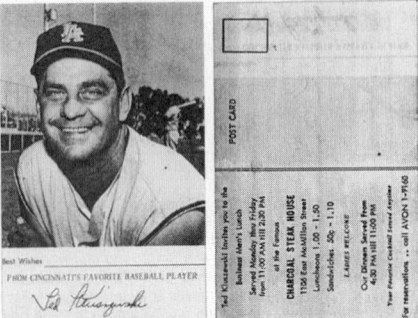

The true scope of this issue combined with the related Ted Kluszewski Steak House cards (see also) is not known. Based on cards showing Klu in Reds and Angels uniforms, it is possible examples may yet be seen in Pirates and White Sox uniforms. About 4" x 6", the black-and-white cards have a facsimile signature of Kluszewski on front. The back is in postcard style and advertises the Cincinnati restaurant he operated with Jack Stayin.

	NM	EX	VG
Ted Kluszewski (Angels)	75.00	40.00	25.00

1961 Chemstrand Iron-On Patches

 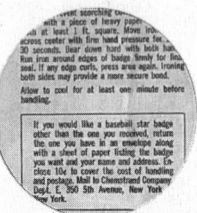

These colorful 2-1/2" diameter cloth patches were included with the purchase of a boy's sport shirt for a short period in 1961. The patches were issued in a cello package with instructions for ironing it onto the shirt. The package also offered the opportunity to trade the player patch for a different star.

	NM	EX	VG
Complete Set (9):	550.00	275.00	165.00
Common Player:	40.00	20.00	12.00
(1) Ernie Banks	75.00	37.50	22.00
(2) Yogi Berra	75.00	37.50	22.00
(3) Nellie Fox	60.00	30.00	18.00
(4) Dick Groat	40.00	20.00	12.00
(5) Al Kaline	60.00	30.00	18.00
(6) Harmon Killebrew	60.00	30.00	18.00
(7) Frank Malzone	40.00	20.00	12.00
(8) Willie Mays	115.00	55.00	35.00
(9) Warren Spahn	60.00	30.00	18.00

1976 Chevrolet Baseball Centennial Prints

In conjunction with the centennial of organized baseball, Chevrolet commissioned a set of paintings by artist Robert Thom which were reproduced in an 8-1/2" x 11" format and distributed by local auto dealers. Fronts carry the picture's title in the white border at bottom. Backs have a description of the picture on front.

	NM	EX	VG
Complete Set (4):	40.00	20.00	12.00
Common Print:	8.00	4.00	2.50
(1) The First Game (1876)	8.00	4.00	2.50
(2) The Gashouse Gang (Pepper Martin, Bill Werber)	8.00	4.00	2.50
(3) The Mighty Babe (Babe Ruth)	15.00	7.50	4.50
(4) The Record Breaker (Hank Aaron)	12.50	6.25	3.75

1908 Chicago Cubs/White Sox Postcards

The issuer of this postcard set is unknown. The only identification on the card is a dollar sign within a shield which appears near the center on back, along with standard postcard indicia. Fronts of the 3-7/16" x 5-3/8" cards have black-and-white player photos on a gray background. A plain strip at bottom has the player's name on a top line; his position and team on a second line. The checklist presented here is probably not complete.

	NM	EX	VG
Complete Set, Cubs (11):	3,000	1,500	900.00
Complete Set, White Sox (9):	3,500	1,750	1,000
Common Player:	200.00	100.00	60.00
CUBS			
(1) Mordecai Brown	400.00	200.00	120.00
(2) Frank Chance	400.00	200.00	120.00
(3) Johnny Evers	400.00	200.00	120.00
(4) Solly Hoffman (Hofman)	200.00	100.00	60.00
(5) John Kling	200.00	100.00	60.00
(6) "Jack" Pfiester	200.00	100.00	60.00
(7) Edw. Reulbach	200.00	100.00	60.00
(8) James Sheckard	200.00	100.00	60.00
(9) Harry Steinfeldt	200.00	100.00	60.00
(10) Joe Tinker	400.00	200.00	120.00
(11) Chicago National League, Cubs. (Team photo.)	500.00	250.00	150.00
WHITE SOX			
(1) "Nic" Altrock	400.00	200.00	120.00
(2) "Jakey" Atz	500.00	250.00	150.00
(3) Geo. Davis	600.00	300.00	180.00
(4) "Jiggs" Donahue	300.00	150.00	90.00
(5) "Pat" Dougherty	300.00	150.00	90.00
(6) "Eddie" Hahn	300.00	150.00	90.00
(7) Frank Isbell	300.00	150.00	90.00
(8) Fielder Jones	300.00	150.00	90.00
(9) "Ed" Walsh	650.00	325.00	195.00

1972 Chicago Cubs & Chicago White Sox Color Caricatures

Produced by Chi-Foursome, Inc., these color caricatures were intended for sale at gas stations and supermarkets, but were never released at these locations. Apparently, only a small quantity was sold at Wrigley Field, and it is believed only about 3,000 of each player was produced. The caricatures were produced on 11" x 14" textured cardboard stock, with a facsimile autograph next to each player on front. Backs are blank.

	NM	EX	VG
CUBS	10.00	5.00	3.00
Complete Set (15):	100.00	50.00	30.00
Common Player:	10.00	5.00	3.00
Ernie Banks	20.00	10.00	6.00
Glenn Beckert	10.00	5.00	3.00
Fergie Jenkins	14.00	7.00	4.50
Don Kessinger	10.00	5.00	3.00
Milt Pappas	10.00	5.00	3.00
Joe Pepitone	10.00	5.00	3.00
Ron Santo	20.00	10.00	6.00
Billy Williams	10.00	5.00	3.00
WHITE SOX	10.00	5.00	3.00
Mike Andrews	10.00	5.00	3.00
Ed Herrmann	10.00	5.00	3.00
Pat Kelly	10.00	5.00	3.00
Carlos May	10.00	5.00	3.00
Bill Melton	14.00	7.00	4.50
Chuck Tanner	10.00	5.00	3.00
Wilbur Wood	14.00	7.00	4.50

1931 Chicago Cubs Picture Pack

In the second-year of team-issued photo packs during the 1930s-1940s was this set of 1931 Cubs. The 6-1/8" x 9-1/2" sepia-toned pictures have facsimile autographs across the front and a white border around. Backs are blank. Like all the team's other photo packs, it is possible the specific make-up

of the 30 pictures in each set changed as personnel came and went during the season. A number of non-playing team personnel are also in the set.

	NM	EX	VG
Complete Set (35):	450.00	225.00	135.00
Common Player:	12.50	6.25	3.75
(1) Ed Baecht	12.50	6.25	3.75
(2) Clyde Beck	12.50	6.25	3.75
(3) Les Bell	12.50	6.25	3.75
(4) Clarence Blair	12.50	6.25	3.75
(5) John F. Blake	12.50	6.25	3.75
(6) Guy Bush	12.50	6.25	3.75
(7) Kiki Cuyler	30.00	15.00	9.00
(8) Woody English	12.50	6.25	3.75
(9) Earl Grace	12.50	6.25	3.75
(10) Charlie Grimm	15.00	7.50	4.50
(11) Gabby Hartnett	30.00	15.00	9.00
(12) Rollie Hemsley	12.50	6.25	3.75
(13) Rogers Hornsby	60.00	30.00	18.00
(14) Bill Jurges	12.50	6.25	3.75
(15) Pat Malone	12.50	6.25	3.75
(16) Jakie May	12.50	6.25	3.75
(17) John Moore	12.50	6.25	3.75
(18) Charley O'Leary	12.50	6.25	3.75
(19) Charlie Root	15.00	7.50	4.50
(20) Ray Schalk	30.00	15.00	9.00
(21) Bob Smith	12.50	6.25	3.75
(22) Riggs Stephenson	15.00	7.50	4.50
(23) Les Sweetland	12.50	6.25	3.75
(24) Dan Taylor	12.50	6.25	3.75
(25) Zack Taylor	12.50	6.25	3.75
(26) Bud Teachout	12.50	6.25	3.75
(27) Lon Warneke	12.50	6.25	3.75
(28) Hack Wilson	45.00	22.00	13.50
Non-Playing Personnel			
(29) Margaret Donahue	12.50	6.25	3.75
(30) Bob Lewis (Traveling secretary.)	12.50	6.25	3.75
(31) Andy Lotshaw (Trainer)	12.50	6.25	3.75
(32) John Seys	12.50	6.25	3.75
(33) William Veeck (President)	45.00	22.00	13.50
(34) W.M. Walker (VP)	12.50	6.25	3.75
(35) P.K. Wrigley	12.50	6.25	3.75
(36) William Wrigley (Owner)	17.50	8.75	5.25

1932 Chicago Cubs Picture Pack

This is one of many Cubs team issues of player pictures in the 1930s-1940s. The large format (6-1/8" x 9-1/4") set features action poses of the players in black-and-white on a black background. A bit of the ground at the players' feet is also included in the photo portion. A white facsimile autograph in the black background identifies the player. Backs are blank. The unnumbered pictures are checklisted here in alphabetical order. Some pictures of non-playing personnel were also issued.

	NM	EX	VG
Complete Set (35):	325.00	165.00	100.00
Common Player:	12.50	6.25	3.75
(1) Guy Bush	12.50	6.25	3.75
(2) Gilly Campbell	12.50	6.25	3.75
(3) Red Corriden	12.50	6.25	3.75
(4) Kiki Cuyler	25.00	12.50	7.50
(5) Frank Demaree	12.50	6.25	3.75
(6) Woody English	12.50	6.25	3.75
(7) Burleigh Grimes	25.00	12.50	7.50
(8) Charlie Grimm	12.50	6.25	3.75
(9) Marv Gudat	12.50	6.25	3.75
(10) Stan Hack	15.00	7.50	4.50

		NM	EX	VG
(11)	Gabby Hartnett	25.00	12.50	7.50
(12)	Rollie Hemsley	12.50	6.25	3.75
(13)	Billy Herman	25.00	12.50	7.50
(14)	LeRoy Herrmann	12.50	6.25	3.75
(15)	Billy Jurges	12.50	6.25	3.75
(16)	Mark Koenig	12.50	6.25	3.75
(17)	Pat Malone	12.50	6.25	3.75
(18)	Jake May	12.50	6.25	3.75
(19)	Johnny Moore	12.50	6.25	3.75
(20)	Charley O'Leary	12.50	6.25	3.75
(21)	Lance Richbourg	12.50	6.25	3.75
(22)	Charlie Root	15.00	7.50	4.50
(23)	Bob Smith	12.50	6.25	3.75
(24)	Riggs Stephenson	15.00	7.50	4.50
(25)	Harry Taylor	12.50	6.25	3.75
(26)	Zack Taylor	12.50	6.25	3.75
(27)	Bud Tinning	12.50	6.25	3.75
(28)	Lon Warneke	12.50	6.25	3.75
Non-Playing Personnel				
(29)	Marge Donahue	12.50	6.25	3.75
(30)	Bob Lewis (Traveling secretary.)	12.50	6.25	3.75
(31)	John Seys	12.50	6.25	3.75
(32)	Bill Veeck (President)	25.00	12.50	7.50
(33)	W.M. Walker	12.50	6.25	3.75
(34)	Phil Wrigley	12.50	6.25	3.75
(35)	William Wrigley	12.50	6.25	3.75

1932 Chicago Cubs Team Issue

Because of its similarity in format to the team's picture pack issue of 1932, it is presumed this card set was also a team production. The blank-back cards are about 2-1/4" x 2-1/2" with player poses and a bit of ground underfoot set against a white background which has a facsimile autograph. This checklist is incomplete and arranged alphabetically.

	NM	EX	VG
Common Player:			
Charlie Grimm	300.00	150.00	90.00
Marv Gudat	300.00	150.00	90.00
Stanley C. Hack	350.00	175.00	100.00
Rolly Hemsley	300.00	150.00	90.00
Jakie May	300.00	150.00	90.00
Bud Tinning	300.00	150.00	90.00

1933 Chicago Cubs Picture Pack

Likely a concession stand souvenir item, this large format (5-7/8" x 8-7/8"), set features action poses of the players in black-and-white on a black background. A bit of the ground at the players' feet is also included in the photo portion. A white facsimile autograph in the black background identifies the player. Backs are blank. The unnumbered pictures are checklisted here in alphabetical order. Some pictures of non-playing personnel were included.

		NM	EX	VG
Complete Set (30):		275.00	135.00	85.00
Common Player:		12.50	6.25	3.75
(1)	Guy Bush	12.50	6.25	3.75
(2)	Gilly Campbell	12.50	6.25	3.75
(3)	John M. Corriden	12.50	6.25	3.75
(4)	Kiki Cuyler	25.00	12.50	7.50
(5)	J. Frank Demaree	12.50	6.25	3.75
(6)	Woody English	12.50	6.25	3.75
(7)	Burleigh A. Grimes	25.00	12.50	7.50
(8)	Charlie Grimm	12.50	6.25	3.75
(9)	Leo "Gabby" Hartnett	25.00	12.50	7.50
(10)	Harvey Hendrick	12.50	6.25	3.75
(11)	Roy Henshaw	12.50	6.25	3.75
(12)	Babe Herman	15.00	7.50	4.50
(13)	William Herman	25.00	12.50	7.50
(14)	William Jurges	12.50	6.25	3.75
(15)	Mark Koenig	12.50	6.25	3.75
(16)	Perce "Pat" Malone	12.50	6.25	3.75
(17)	Lynn Nelson	12.50	6.25	3.75
(18)	Charlie Root	15.00	7.50	4.50
(19)	John Schulte	12.50	6.25	3.75
(20)	Riggs Stephenson	15.00	7.50	4.50
(21)	Zack Taylor	12.50	6.25	3.75
(22)	Bud Tinning	12.50	6.25	3.75
(23)	L. Warneke	12.50	6.25	3.75
Non-Playing Personnel				
(24)	Margaret Donahue	12.50	6.25	3.75
(25)	Robert C. Lewis (Traveling secretary.)	12.50	6.25	3.75
(26)	John O. Seys	12.50	6.25	3.75
(27)	William L. Veeck (President)	25.00	12.50	7.50
(28)	W.M. Walker	12.50	6.25	3.75
(29)	Philip K. Wrigley	12.50	6.25	3.75
(30)	Wm. Wrigley	12.50	6.25	3.75

1936 Chicago Cubs Picture Pack

Nearly identical in format to the 1933 issue, these 5-7/8" x 8-7/8" pictures are printed in black-and-white on a black background with (usually) a white facsimile autograph. Backs are blank. The specific make-up of photo packs sold at Wrigley Field may have changed over the course of the season as players came and went. The unnumbered pictures are checklisted here in alphabetical order.

		NM	EX	VG
Complete Set (34):		240.00	120.00	72.00
Common Player:		9.00	4.50	2.75
(1)	Ethan Allen	9.00	4.50	2.75
(2)	Clay Bryant	9.00	4.50	2.75
(3)	Tex Carleton	9.00	4.50	2.75
(4)	Phil Cavarretta	12.00	6.00	3.50
(5)	John Corriden	9.00	4.50	2.75
(6)	Frank Demaree	9.00	4.50	2.75
(7)	Curt Davis	9.00	4.50	2.75
(8)	Woody English	9.00	4.50	2.75
(9)	Larry French	9.00	4.50	2.75
(10)	Augie Galan	9.00	4.50	2.75
(11)	Johnny Gill	9.00	4.50	2.75
(12)	Charlie Grimm	12.00	6.00	3.50
(13)	Stan Hack	12.00	6.00	3.50
(14)	Gabby Hartnett	18.00	9.00	5.50
(15)	Roy Henshaw	9.00	4.50	2.75
(16)	Billy Herman	18.00	9.00	5.50
(17)	Roy Johnson	9.00	4.50	2.75
(18)	Bill Jurges	9.00	4.50	2.75
(19)	Chuck Klein	18.00	9.00	5.50
(20)	Fabian Kowalik	9.00	4.50	2.75
(21)	Bill Lee	9.00	4.50	2.75
(22)	Gene Lillard	9.00	4.50	2.75
(23)	Ken O'Dea	9.00	4.50	2.75
(24)	Charlie Root	12.00	6.00	3.50
(25)	Clyde Shoun	9.00	4.50	2.75
(26)	Tuck Stainback	9.00	4.50	2.75
(27)	Walter Stephenson	9.00	4.50	2.75
(28)	Lon Warneke	9.00	4.50	2.75
Non-Playing personnel				
(29)	Margaret Donahue	9.00	4.50	2.75
(30)	Bob Lewis (Traveling secretary.)	9.00	4.50	2.75
(31)	Andy Lotshaw (Trainer)	9.00	4.50	2.75
(32)	John O. Seys	9.00	4.50	2.75
(33)	Charles Weber	9.00	4.50	2.75
(34)	Wrigley Field	18.00	9.00	5.50

1939 Chicago Cubs Picture Pack

The use of a textured paper stock for these 6-1/2" x 9" pictures helps identify the 1939 team issue. The pictures once again feature sepia portrait photos with a white border. A facsimile autograph is at bottom. Backs are blank. The specific make-up of photo packs sold at Wrigley Field may have changed over the course of the season as players came and went. The unnumbered pictures are checklisted here in alphabetical order.

		NM	EX	VG
Complete Set (25):		225.00	115.00	65.00
Common Player:		9.00	4.50	2.75
(1)	Dick Bartell	9.00	4.50	2.75
(2)	Clay Bryant	9.00	4.50	2.75
(3)	Phil Cavarretta	12.00	6.00	3.50
(4)	John Corriden	9.00	4.50	2.75
(5)	Dizzy Dean	40.00	20.00	12.00
(6)	Larry French	9.00	4.50	2.75
(7)	Augie Galan	9.00	4.50	2.75
(8)	Bob Garbark	9.00	4.50	2.75
(9)	Jim Gleeson	9.00	4.50	2.75
(10)	Stan Hack	12.00	6.00	3.50
(11)	Gabby Hartnett	20.00	10.00	6.00
(12)	Billy Herman	20.00	10.00	6.00
(13)	Roy Johnson	9.00	4.50	2.75
(14)	Bill Lee	9.00	4.50	2.75
(15)	Hank Leiber	9.00	4.50	2.75
(16)	Gene Lillard	9.00	4.50	2.75
(17)	Gus Mancuso	9.00	4.50	2.75
(18)	Bobby Mattick	9.00	4.50	2.75
(19)	Vance Page	9.00	4.50	2.75
(20)	Claude Passeau	9.00	4.50	2.75
(21)	Carl Reynolds	9.00	4.50	2.75
(22)	Charlie Root	12.00	6.00	3.50
(23)	Glenn "Rip" Russell	9.00	4.50	2.75
(24)	Jack Russell	9.00	4.50	2.75
(25)	Earl Whitehill	9.00	4.50	2.75

1940 Chicago Cubs Picture Pack

The 1940 team-issue is identical in format to the 1939s: 6-1/2" x 9", printed on rough-surfaced paper stock with black-and-white portraits surrounded by a wide border and a facsimile autograph on front. Study of the uniforms, however, may help differentiate the issue from 1939, as the 1940 uniforms have no stripe on the shoulders. It is possible that 1939 pictures continued to be issued in the 1940 photo packs and that specific make-up of the packs changed with the team's roster. The blank-back pictures are unnumbered and checklisted here in alphabetical order.

		NM	EX	VG
Complete Set (25):		80.00	40.00	24.00
Common Player:		9.00	4.50	2.75
(1)	Dick Bartell	9.00	4.50	2.75
(2)	Clay Bryant	9.00	4.50	2.75
(3)	Phil Cavarretta	12.00	6.00	3.50
(4)	John Corriden	9.00	4.50	2.75
(5)	Bob Collins	9.00	4.50	2.75
(6)	"Del" Dallessandro	9.00	4.50	2.75
(7)	Larry French	9.00	4.50	2.75
(8)	Augie Galan	9.00	4.50	2.75
(9)	Jim Gleeson	9.00	4.50	2.75
(10)	Stan Hack	12.00	6.00	3.50
(11)	Gabby Hartnett	20.00	10.00	6.00
(12)	Billy Herman	20.00	10.00	6.00
(13)	Roy Johnson	9.00	4.50	2.75
(14)	Bill Lee	9.00	4.50	2.75
(15)	Hank Leiber	9.00	4.50	2.75
(16)	Bobby Mattick	9.00	4.50	2.75
(17)	Jake Mooty	9.00	4.50	2.75
(18)	Bill Nicholson	9.00	4.50	2.75
(19)	Vance Page	9.00	4.50	2.75
(20)	Claude Passeau	9.00	4.50	2.75
(21)	Ken Raffensberger	9.00	4.50	2.75
(22)	Bill Rogell	9.00	4.50	2.75
(23)	Charlie Root	9.00	4.50	2.75
(24)	Rip Russell	9.00	4.50	2.75
(25)	Al Todd	9.00	4.50	2.75

1941 Chicago Cubs Picture Pack

A change of paper stock to a smooth finish helps differentiate the 1941 team-issue from previous years' offerings. Size remains at 6-1/2" x 9" with sepia player portraits surrounded by a white border and overprinted with a facsimile autograph. Backs are blank on these unnumbered photos. The pictures are listed here in alphabetical order.

		NM	EX	VG
Complete Set (25):		190.00	95.00	57.00
Common Player:		9.00	4.50	2.75
(1)	Phil Cavarretta	12.00	6.00	3.50
(2)	Dom Dallessandro	9.00	4.50	2.75
(3)	Paul Erickson	9.00	4.50	2.75
(4)	Larry French	9.00	4.50	2.75
(5)	Augie Galan	9.00	4.50	2.75
(6)	Greek George	9.00	4.50	2.75
(7)	Charlie Gilbert	9.00	4.50	2.75
(8)	Stan Hack	12.00	6.00	3.50
(9)	Johnny Hudson	9.00	4.50	2.75
(10)	Bill Lee	9.00	4.50	2.75
(11)	Hank Leiber	9.00	4.50	2.75
(12)	Clyde McCullough	9.00	4.50	2.75
(13)	Jake Mooty	9.00	4.50	2.75
(14)	Bill Myers	9.00	4.50	2.75
(15)	Bill Nicholson	9.00	4.50	2.75
(16)	Lou Novikoff	9.00	4.50	2.75
(17)	Vern Olsen	9.00	4.50	2.75
(18)	Vance Page	9.00	4.50	2.75
(19)	Claude Passeau	9.00	4.50	2.75
(20)	Tot Pressnell	9.00	4.50	2.75
(21)	Charlie Root	12.00	6.00	3.50
(22)	Bob Scheffing	9.00	4.50	2.75
(23)	Lou Stringer	9.00	4.50	2.75
(24)	Bob Sturgeon	9.00	4.50	2.75
(25)	Cubs Staff (Dizzy Dean, Charlie Grimm, Dick Spalding, Jimmie Wilson)	12.00	6.00	3.50

1942 Chicago Cubs Picture Pack

The relatively small number of photos in this team-issued set indicates it may have been issued as a supplement to update earlier photo packs with players who were new to the Cubs. In the same 6-1/2" x 9" format as previous issues, the 1942s are printed in sepia on a smooth-surfaced paper. A facsimile autograph graces the front and the portrait photo is surrounced by a border. Backs are blank and the pictures are not numbered. The checklist here is in alphabetical order.

		NM	EX	VG
Complete Set (26):		175.00	90.00	55.00
Common Player:		9.00	4.50	2.75
(1)	Hiram Bithorn	12.00	6.00	3.50
(2)	Phil Cavarretta	9.00	4.50	2.75
(3)	"Del" Dallasandro	9.00	4.50	2.75
(4)	Paul Erickson	9.00	4.50	2.75
(5)	Bill Fleming	9.00	4.50	2.75
(6)	Charlie Gilbert	9.00	4.50	2.75
(7)	Stan Hack	15.00	7.50	4.50
(8)	Ed Hanyzewski	9.00	4.50	2.75
(9)	Chico Hernandez	9.00	4.50	2.75
(10)	Bill Lee	9.00	4.50	2.75
(11)	Harry Lowrey	9.00	4.50	2.75
(12)	Clyde McCullough	9.00	4.50	2.75
(13)	Lennie Merullo	9.00	4.50	2.75
(14)	Jake Mooty	9.00	4.50	2.75
(15)	Bill Nicholson	9.00	4.50	2.75
(16)	Lou Novikoff	9.00	4.50	2.75
(17)	Vern Olsen	9.00	4.50	2.75
(18)	Claude Passeau	9.00	4.50	2.75
(19)	Tot Pressnell	9.00	4.50	2.75
(20)	Glen "Rip" Russell	9.00	4.50	2.75
(21)	Bob Scheffing	9.00	4.50	2.75
(22)	Johnny Schmitz	9.00	4.50	2.75
(23)	Lou Stringer	9.00	4.50	2.75
(24)	Bob Sturgeon	9.00	4.50	2.75
(25)	Kiki Cuyler, Dick Spalding, Jimmie Wilson	9.00	4.50	2.75
(26)	Jimmie Wilson, Dick Spalding, Charlie Grimm, Dizzy Dean	15.00	7.50	4.50

1943 Chicago Cubs Picture Pack

It is impossible to differentiate pictures from the 1943 issue from those of early years and of 1944, since many pictures were reused and the format is identical: 6-1/2" x 9", black-and-white portrait photos with facsimile autograph and white borders. Backs are blank and the photos are not numbered. They are checklisted here alphabetically.

		NM	EX	VG
Complete Set (25):		215.00	105.00	65.00
Common Player:		9.00	4.50	2.75
(1)	Dick Barrett	9.00	4.50	2.75
(2)	Heinz Becker	9.00	4.50	2.75
(3)	Hiram Bithorn	12.00	6.00	3.50
(4)	Phil Cavarretta	9.00	4.50	2.75
(5)	"Del" Dallasandro	9.00	4.50	2.75
(6)	Paul Derringer	9.00	4.50	2.75
(7)	Paul Erickson	9.00	4.50	2.75
(8)	Bill Fleming	9.00	4.50	2.75
(9)	Stan Hack	12.00	6.00	3.50
(10)	Ed Hanyzewski	9.00	4.50	2.75
(11)	Chico Hernandez	9.00	4.50	2.75
(12)	Bill Lee	9.00	4.50	2.75
(13)	Peanuts Lowrey	9.00	4.50	2.75
(14)	Stu Martin	9.00	4.50	2.75
(15)	Clyde McCullough	9.00	4.50	2.75
(16)	Len Merullo	9.00	4.50	2.75
(17)	Bill Nicholson	9.00	4.50	2.75

(18)	Lou Novikoff	9.00	4.50	2.75
(19)	Claude Passeau	9.00	4.50	2.75
(20)	Ray Prim	9.00	4.50	2.75
(21)	Eddie Stanky	12.00	6.00	3.50
(22)	Al Todd	9.00	4.50	2.75
(23)	Lon Warneke	9.00	4.50	2.75
(24)	Hank Wyse	9.00	4.50	2.75
(25)	Cubs Coaches (Kiki Cuyler, Dick Spalding, Jimmie Wilson)			

1944 Chicago Cubs Picture Pack

A slight size reduction, to 6" x 8-1/2", helps identify the team's 1944 photo pack. The pictures feature black-and-white portrait photos with a white border. A facsimile autograph is at bottom. Backs are blank. The specific make-up of photo packs sold at Wrigley Field may have changed over the course of the season as players came and went. The unnumbered pictures are checklisted here in alphabetical order.

		NM	EX	VG
Complete Set (25):		215.00	105.00	65.00
Common Player:		9.00	4.50	2.75
(1)	Heinz Becker	9.00	4.50	2.75
(2)	John Burrows	9.00	4.50	2.75
(3)	Phil Cavarretta	12.00	6.00	3.50
(4)	"Del" Dallessandro	9.00	4.50	2.75
(5)	Paul Derringer	9.00	4.50	2.75
(6)	Roy Easterwood	9.00	4.50	2.75
(7)	Paul Erickson	9.00	4.50	2.75
(8)	Bill Fleming	9.00	4.50	2.75
(9)	Jimmie Foxx	30.00	15.00	9.00
(10)	Ival Goodman	9.00	4.50	2.75
(11)	Ed Hanyzewski	9.00	4.50	2.75
(12)	Billy Holm	9.00	4.50	2.75
(13)	Don Johnson	9.00	4.50	2.75
(14)	Garth Mann	9.00	4.50	2.75
(15)	Len Merullo	9.00	4.50	2.75
(16)	John Miklos	9.00	4.50	2.75
(17)	Bill Nicholson	9.00	4.50	2.75
(18)	Lou Novikoff	9.00	4.50	2.75
(19)	Andy Pafko	12.00	6.00	3.50
(20)	Ed Sauer	9.00	4.50	2.75
(21)	Bill Schuster	9.00	4.50	2.75
(22)	Eddie Stanky	12.00	6.00	3.50
(23)	Hy Vandenberg	9.00	4.50	2.75
(24)	Hank Wyse	9.00	4.50	2.75
(25)	Tony York	9.00	4.50	2.75

1924 Chicago Evening American Cubs/White Sox Pins

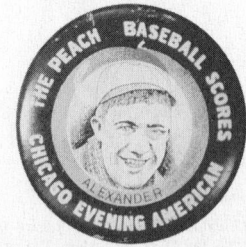

These 1-3/8" diameter pins were issued by the Chicago Evening American newspaper to promote its peach-colored sports section. Rather crude blue-and-white line drawings of the players are at center, within an orange peach with the player's name at bottom. Borders are either white or dark blue. The pins were produced by Greenduck Metal Stamping of Chicago.

		NM	EX	VG
Complete Set (12):		3,500	1,750	1,000
Common Player:		200.00	100.00	65.00
(1)	Grover Alexander	750.00	375.00	225.00
(2)	Eddie Collins	450.00	225.00	135.00
(3)	"Red" Faber	350.00	175.00	105.00
(4)	Ray Grimes	200.00	100.00	65.00
(5)	Charlie Hollocher	200.00	100.00	65.00
(6)	Harry Hooper	350.00	175.00	105.00
(7)	Willie Kamm	200.00	100.00	65.00
(8)	Bill Killefer	200.00	100.00	65.00
(9)	Bob O'Farrell	200.00	100.00	65.00
(10)	Charlie Robertson	200.00	100.00	65.00
(11)	Ray Schalk	350.00	175.00	105.00
(12)	Jigger Statz	200.00	100.00	65.00

1930 Chicago Evening American Pins

Members of the Cubs and White Sox are featured on this series of pins issued by one of the local daily newspapers. Player portraits are featured in black-and-white on a white background on these 1-1/4" celluloid pins. Above the picture are the player's position, last name and team; below is the sponsor's name. The unnumbered pins are listed here in alphabetical order within team.

		NM	EX	VG
Complete Set (20):		6,500	3,250	1,950
Common Player:		250.00	125.00	75.00
Chicago Cubs Team Set (11):		3,500	1,750	1,000
(1)	Les Bell	250.00	125.00	75.00
(2)	Guy Bush	250.00	125.00	75.00
(3)	Kiki Cuyler	350.00	175.00	100.00
(4)	Woody English	250.00	125.00	75.00
(5)	Charlie Grimm	250.00	125.00	75.00
(6)	Gabby Hartnett	350.00	175.00	100.00
(7)	Rogers Hornsby	750.00	375.00	225.00
(8)	Joe McCarthy	350.00	175.00	100.00
(9)	Charlie Root	250.00	125.00	75.00
(10)	Riggs Stephenson	250.00	125.00	75.00
(11)	Hack Wilson	400.00	200.00	120.00
Chicago White Sox Team Set (9):		3,000	1,500	900.00
(1)	Moe Berg	1,000	500.00	300.00
(2)	Bill Cissel (Cissell)	250.00	125.00	75.00
(3)	Red Faber	350.00	175.00	105.00
(4)	Bill Hunnefield	250.00	125.00	75.00
(5)	Smead Jolley	250.00	125.00	75.00
(6)	Willie Kamm	250.00	125.00	75.00
(7)	Jimmy Moore	250.00	125.00	75.00
(8)	Carl Reynolds	250.00	125.00	75.00
(9)	Art Shires	250.00	125.00	75.00

1930 Chicago Herald and Examiner Babe Ruth Premium

This premium picture with a black-and-white batting pose of Ruth was issued by a Chicago newspaper. Two sizes are known, approximately 8-1/2" x 11-1/2" and 5" x 7". The pictures are blank-back. The year attributed is speculative.

	NM	EX	VG
Babe Ruth (Large)	1,350	625.00	400.00
Babe Ruth (Small)	1,350	625.00	400.00

1976 Chicagoland Collectors Association Chicago Greats

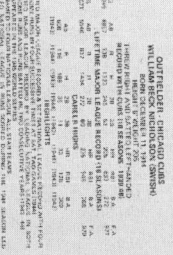

Former stars of the Cubs and White Sox are featured in this collectors issue produced in conjunction with an early sports card and memorabilia show in Chicago. The 2-1/2" x 3-1/2" cards feature black-and-white action photos at center of most cards, with a portrait photo inset at top. Graphics around the front are in red. Backs have detailed career summaries. A starting team, manager and president for each of the Chicago teams is represented in the issue. Complete sets were originally sold for about $2 with uncut sheets sold for $6.

		NM	EX	VG
Complete Set (25):		15.00	7.50	4.50
Common Player:		2.00	1.00	.60
(1)	Luke Appling	2.00	1.00	.60
(2)	Ernie Banks	6.00	3.00	1.75
(3)	Zeke Bonura	2.00	1.00	.60
(4)	Phil Cavarretta	2.00	1.00	.60
(5)	Jimmy Dykes	2.00	1.00	.60
(6)	Red Faber, Ted Lyons	2.00	1.00	.60
(7)	Nellie Fox	4.00	2.00	1.25
(8)	Larry French	2.00	1.00	.60
(9)	Charlie Grimm	2.00	1.00	.60
(10)	Gabby Hartnett	2.00	1.00	.60
(11)	Billy Herman	2.00	1.00	.60
(12)	Mike Kreevich	2.00	1.00	.60
(13)	Sherman Lollar	2.00	1.00	.60
(14)	Al Lopez	2.00	1.00	.60
(15)	Minnie Minoso	3.00	1.50	.90
(16)	Wally Moses	2.00	1.00	.60
(17)	Bill Nicholson	2.00	1.00	.60
(18)	Claude Passeau	2.00	1.00	.60
(19)	Billy Pierce	2.00	1.00	.60
(20)	Ron Santo	2.00	1.00	.60
(21)	Hank Sauer	2.00	1.00	.60
(22)	Riggs Stephenson	2.00	1.00	.60
(23)	Bill Veeck	2.00	1.00	.60
(24)	P.K. Wrigley	2.00	1.00	.60
(25)	Checklist	2.00	1.00	.60

1915 Chicago Tribune Supplements

As the 1915 baseball season opened, the Chicago Sunday Tribune ran supplements in its April 4 and April 11 editions featuring pictures of Chicago players. The black-and-white pictures are 8" x 11". Saier is pictured in uniform, the others are in street clothes. Printed in the white border beneath each photo is "Supplement to The Chicago Sunday Tribune, April 4 (or) 11, 1915." Each picture bears a facsimile autograph of the player and is blank-backed.

		NM	EX	VG
Complete Set (4):		400.00	200.00	120.00
Common Player:		50.00	25.00	15.00
(1)	Roger Bresnahan (April 11)	100.00	50.00	30.00
(2)	Eddie Collins (April 11)	100.00	50.00	30.00
(3)	Vic Saier (April 11)	50.00	25.00	15.00
(4)	Joe Tinker (April 4)	150.00	75.00	45.00

1917 Chicago White Sox Team Issue

This set of the World Champion White Sox (including several of the notorious Black Sox) was produced by Davis Printing Works in Chicago and apparently sold as a complete boxed set by the team. Individual cards measure about 1-11/16" x 2-3/4". Fronts feature full-length black-and-white photos of the players on a light background with a white border. Player name and position are in black beneath the picture. Backs are blank. To date, only one set is known to exist. It sold at auction in 1991 for $45,100, again in 1997 for $46,000 and in 2001 for $50,330. The unnumbered cards are checklisted here alphabetically.

Complete Set (25):
Value Undetermined
(1) Joe Benz
(2) Eddie Cicotte

(3) Eddie Collins
(4) Shano Collins
(5) Charles Comiskey
(6) Dave Danforth
(7) Red Faber
(8) Happy Felsch
(9) Chick Gandil
(10) Kid Gleason
(11) Joe Jackson
(12) Joe Jenkins
(13) Ted Jourdan
(14) Nemo Leibold
(15) Byrd Lynn
(16) Fred McMullin
(17) Eddie Murphy
(18) Swede Risberg
(19) Pants Rowland
(20) Reb Russell
(21) Ray Schalk
(22) James Scott
(23) Buck Weaver
(24) Lefty Williams
(25) Mellie Wolfgang

1940 Chicago White Sox Photo Pack

This set of souvenir photos was produced by Andy Lotshaw, who was a Cubs trainer. The 5-1/2" x 6-3/4" pictures have a sepia pose bordered in white, with a facsimile autograph. Backs are blank. The unnumbered pictures are checklisted here in alphabetical order.

		NM	EX	VG
Complete Set (25):		300.00	150.00	90.00
Common Player:		15.00	7.50	4.50
(1)	Pete Appleton	15.00	7.50	4.50
(2)	Luke Appling	30.00	15.00	9.00
(3)	Clint Brown	15.00	7.50	4.50
(4)	Bill Dietrich	15.00	7.50	4.50
(5)	Jimmy Dykes	15.00	7.50	4.50
(6)	Mule Haas	15.00	7.50	4.50
(7)	Jack Hayes	15.00	7.50	4.50
(8)	Bob Kennedy	15.00	7.50	4.50
(9)	Jack Knott	15.00	7.50	4.50
(10)	Mike Kreevich	15.00	7.50	4.50
(11)	Joe Kuhel	15.00	7.50	4.50
(12)	Thornton Lee	15.00	7.50	4.50
(13)	Ted Lyons	25.00	12.50	7.50
(14)	Eric McNair	15.00	7.50	4.50
(15)	John Rigney	15.00	7.50	4.50
(16)	Larry Rosenthal	15.00	7.50	4.50
(17)	Ken Silvestri	15.00	7.50	4.50
(18)	Eddie Smith	15.00	7.50	4.50
(19)	J. Solters	15.00	7.50	4.50
(20)	Monty Stratton	20.00	10.00	6.00
(21)	Mike Tresh	15.00	7.50	4.50
(22)	Tom Turner	15.00	7.50	4.50
(23)	Skeeter Webb	20.00	10.00	6.00
(24)	Ed Weiland	15.00	7.50	4.50
(25)	Taft Wright	15.00	7.50	4.50

1948 Chicago White Sox Photo Pack

The last-place White Sox of 1948 are immortalized in this team-issued set of player photos. Individual players are pictured in a 6-1/2" x 9" portrait photo with a thin white border around. A facsimile autograph also appears on front. Backs are blank. A team photo was also included in the set. The photo pack was sold in a large white envelope with a red and blue team logo. The unnumbered pictures are checklisted here in alphabetical order.

		NM	EX	VG
Complete Set (30):		180.00	90.00	54.00
Common Player:		7.50	3.75	2.25
(1)	Luke Appling	18.00	9.00	5.50
(2)	Floyd Baker	7.50	3.75	2.25
(3)	Fred Bradley	7.50	3.75	2.25
(4)	Earl Caldwell	7.50	3.75	2.25
(5)	Red Faber	15.00	7.50	4.50
(6)	Bob Gillespie	7.50	3.75	2.25
(7)	Jim Goodwin	12.00	6.00	3.50
(8)	Orval Grove	7.50	3.75	2.25
(9)	Earl Harrist	7.50	3.75	2.25
(10)	Joe Haynes	7.50	3.75	2.25
(11)	Ralph Hodgin	7.50	3.75	2.25
(12)	Howie Judson	7.50	3.75	2.25
(13)	Bob Kennedy	7.50	3.75	2.25
(14)	Don Kolloway	7.50	3.75	2.25
(15)	Tony Lupien	7.50	3.75	2.25
(16)	Ted Lyons	15.00	7.50	4.50
(17)	Cass Michaels	7.50	3.75	2.25
(18)	Bing Miller	7.50	3.75	2.25

(19)	Buster Mills	7.50	3.75	2.25
(20)	Glen Moulder	7.50	3.75	2.25
(21)	Frank Papish	7.50	3.75	2.25
(22)	Ike Pearson	7.50	3.75	2.25
(23)	Dave Philley	7.50	3.75	2.25
(24)	Aaron Robinson	7.50	3.75	2.25
(25)	Mike Tresh	7.50	3.75	2.25
(26)	Jack Wallaesa	7.50	3.75	2.25
(27)	Ralph Weigel	7.50	3.75	2.25
(28)	Bill Wight	7.50	3.75	2.25
(29)	Taft Wright	7.50	3.75	2.25
(30)	Team Picture	18.00	9.00	5.50

1960-64 Chicago White Sox Ticket Stubs

From 1960-64 tickets to White Sox home games at Comiskey Park were issued bearing player photos. Along with the photos on the backs of the 1-5/16" x 2-5/8" ticket stubs are career information and facsimile autographs. Photos were generally re-used from year to year and color variations, depending on the type of ticket, are known. Players from each year are listed here alphabetically.

		NM	EX	VG
Complete Set (113):		2,250	1,125	675.00
Common Player:		30.00	15.00	9.00
60-1	Luis Aparicio	75.00	37.00	22.00
60-2	Earl Battey	30.00	15.00	9.00
60-3	Frank Baumann	30.00	15.00	9.00
60-4	Dick Donovan	30.00	15.00	9.00
60-5	Nelson Fox	75.00	37.00	22.00
60-6	Gene Freese	30.00	15.00	9.00
60-7	Ted Kluszewski	60.00	30.00	18.00
60-8	Jim Landis	30.00	15.00	9.00
60-9	Barry Latman	30.00	15.00	9.00
60-10	Sherm Lollar	30.00	15.00	9.00
60-11	Al Lopez	45.00	22.00	13.50
60-12	Turk Lown	30.00	15.00	9.00
60-13	Orestes Minoso	50.00	25.00	15.00
60-14	Bill Pierce	30.00	15.00	9.00
60-15	Jim Rivera	30.00	15.00	9.00
60-16	Bob Shaw	30.00	15.00	9.00
60-17	Roy Sievers	30.00	15.00	9.00
60-18	Al Smith	30.00	15.00	9.00
60-19	Gerry Staley	30.00	15.00	9.00
60-20	Early Wynn	45.00	22.00	13.50
61-1	Luis Aparicio	75.00	37.00	22.00
61-2	Frank Baumann	30.00	15.00	9.00
61-3	Camilo Carreon	30.00	15.00	9.00
61-4	Sam Esposito	30.00	15.00	9.00
61-5	Nelson Fox	75.00	37.00	22.00
61-6	Billy Goodman	30.00	15.00	9.00
61-7	Jim Landis	30.00	15.00	9.00
61-8	Sherman Lollar	30.00	15.00	9.00
61-9	Al Lopez	45.00	22.00	13.50
61-10	J.C. Martin	30.00	15.00	9.00
61-11	Cal McLish	30.00	15.00	9.00
61-12	Orestes Minoso	50.00	25.00	15.00
61-13	Bill Pierce	30.00	15.00	9.00
61-14	Juan Pizarro	30.00	15.00	9.00
61-15	Bob Roselli	30.00	15.00	9.00
61-16	Herb Score	35.00	17.50	10.50
61-17	Bob Shaw	30.00	15.00	9.00
61-18	Roy Sievers	30.00	15.00	9.00
61-19	Al Smith	30.00	15.00	9.00
61-20	Gerry Staley	30.00	15.00	9.00
61-21	Early Wynn	45.00	22.00	13.50
62-1	Luis Aparicio	75.00	37.00	22.00
62-2	Frank Baumann	30.00	15.00	9.00
62-3	John Buzhardt	30.00	15.00	9.00
62-4	Camilo Carreon	30.00	15.00	9.00
62-5	Joe Cunningham	30.00	15.00	9.00
62-6	Bob Farley	30.00	15.00	9.00
62-7	Eddie Fisher	30.00	15.00	9.00
62-8	Nelson Fox	75.00	37.00	22.00
62-9	Jim Landis	30.00	15.00	9.00
62-10	Sherm Lollar	30.00	15.00	9.00
62-11	Al Lopez	45.00	22.00	13.50
62-12	Turk Lown	30.00	15.00	9.00
62-13	J.C. Martin	30.00	15.00	9.00
62-14	Cal McLish	30.00	15.00	9.00
62-15	Gary Peters	30.00	15.00	9.00
62-16	Juan Pizarro	30.00	15.00	9.00
62-17	Floyd Robinson	30.00	15.00	9.00
62-18	Bob Roselli	30.00	15.00	9.00
62-19	Herb Score	35.00	17.50	10.50
62-20	Al Smith	30.00	15.00	9.00
62-21	Charles Smith	30.00	15.00	9.00
62-22	Early Wynn	45.00	22.00	13.50
63-1	Frank Baumann	30.00	15.00	9.00

		NM	EX	VG
63-2	John Buzhardt	30.00	15.00	9.00
63-3	Camilo Carreon	30.00	15.00	9.00
63-4	Joe Cunningham	30.00	15.00	9.00
63-5	Dave DeBusschere	40.00	20.00	12.00
63-6	Eddie Fisher	30.00	15.00	9.00
63-7	Nelson Fox	75.00	37.00	22.00
63-8	Ron Hansen	30.00	15.00	9.00
63-9	Ray Herbert	30.00	15.00	9.00
63-10	Mike Hershberger	30.00	15.00	9.00
63-11	Joe Horlen	30.00	15.00	9.00
63-12	Grover Jones	30.00	15.00	9.00
63-13	Mike Joyce	30.00	15.00	9.00
63-14	Frank Kreutzer	30.00	15.00	9.00
63-15	Jim Landis	30.00	15.00	9.00
63-16	Sherman Lollar	30.00	15.00	9.00
63-17	Al Lopez	45.00	22.00	13.50
63-18	J.C. Martin	30.00	15.00	9.00
63-19	Charlie Maxwell	30.00	15.00	9.00
63-20	Dave Nicholson	30.00	15.00	9.00
63-21	Juan Pizarro	30.00	15.00	9.00
63-22	Floyd Robinson	30.00	15.00	9.00
63-23	Charley Smith	30.00	15.00	9.00
63-24	Pete Ward	30.00	15.00	9.00
63-25	Al Weis	30.00	15.00	9.00
63-26	Hoyt Wilhelm	45.00	22.00	13.50
63-27	Dom Zanni	30.00	15.00	9.00
64-1	Fritz Ackley	30.00	15.00	9.00
64-2	Frank Baumann	30.00	15.00	9.00
64-3	Don Buford	30.00	15.00	9.00
64-4	John Buzhardt	30.00	15.00	9.00
64-5	Camilo Carreon	30.00	15.00	9.00
64-6	Joe Cunningham	30.00	15.00	9.00
64-7	Dave DeBusschere	40.00	20.00	12.00
64-8	Eddie Fisher	30.00	15.00	9.00
64-9	Jim Golden	30.00	15.00	9.00
64-10	Ron Hansen	30.00	15.00	9.00
64-11	Ray Herbert	30.00	15.00	9.00
64-12	Mike Hershberger	30.00	15.00	9.00
64-13	Joe Horlen	30.00	15.00	9.00
64-14	Jim Landis	30.00	15.00	9.00
64-15	Al Lopez	45.00	22.00	13.50
64-16	J.C. Martin	30.00	15.00	9.00
64-17	Dave Nicholson	30.00	15.00	9.00
64-18	Gary Peters	30.00	15.00	9.00
64-19	Juan Pizarro	30.00	15.00	9.00
64-20	Floyd Robinson	30.00	15.00	9.00
64-21	Gene Stephens	30.00	15.00	9.00
64-22	Pete Ward	30.00	15.00	9.00
64-23	Al Weis	30.00	15.00	9.00
64-24	Hoyt Wilhelm	45.00	22.00	13.50

1899 Chickering Studio Boston Beaneaters Cabinets

These oversize (8-7/8" x 9-7/8") cabinet cards feature virtually every regular on the 1899 National League runners-up and this checklist may not be complete. The cards feature chest-up, capless sepia portraits of the players, glued to either black or gray cardboard mounts with the advertising of Boston's Elmer Chickering Studio in silver or gold leaf at bottom. Players are identified by first and last name in fancy black script at the bottom of the photo. Backs are blank.

		NM	EX	VG
Common Player:		3,000	650.00	425.00
(1)	Harvey Bailey	3,000	650.00	425.00
(2)	Martin Bergen	3,000	650.00	425.00
(3)	William Clarke	3,000	650.00	425.00
(4)	Jimmy Collins	7,500	2,700	1,725
(5)	Hugh Duffy	9,000	3,200	1,900
(6)	Billy Hamilton	7,500	3,000	1,800
(7)	Frank Killen	3,000	650.00	425.00
(8)	Ted Lewis	3,000	650.00	425.00
(9)	Herman Long	7,500	2,425	1,450
(10)	Bobby Lowe	3,000	1,125	675.00
(11)	Jouett Meekin	7,500	1,500	900.00
(12)	Charles Nichols	9,000	3,200	1,875
(13)	Fred Tenney	3,000	650.00	425.00

1956-1957 Chicle Peloteros

One of the few gumcard issues from Cuba, this set took a cue from American companies by skip-numbering the set to keep youngsters buying gum in search of cards that did not exist. The cards measure about 2" x 3". Fronts have color portrait photos bordered in white with the player name and card number in a colored strip below. Backs are in black-and-white with a few biographical notes and career highlights. The cards are printed on thick gray stock. A colorful album to house the cards was also produced.

		NM	EX	VG
Complete Set (40):		2,750	1,375	850.00
Common Player:		60.00	30.00	18.00
Album:		100.00	50.00	30.00
2	Emilio Cabrera	60.00	30.00	18.00
4	Conrado Marrero	100.00	50.00	30.00
5	Silvio Garcia	250.00	125.00	75.00
6	Russel (Russell) Nixon	75.00	37.50	22.50
7	Enrique Izquierdo	60.00	30.00	18.00
8	Lou Skinner	60.00	30.00	18.00
9	Robert Mc Kee	60.00	30.00	18.00
10	Gonzalo Naranjo	60.00	30.00	18.00
11	Trompoloco Rodriguez	60.00	30.00	18.00
12	Evelio Hernandez	60.00	30.00	18.00
26	Oscar Rodriguez	60.00	30.00	18.00
27	Jose (Cheo) Ramos	60.00	30.00	18.00
28	Napoleon Heredia	60.00	30.00	18.00
29	Camilo Pascual	150.00	75.00	45.00
30	Pedro Ramos	90.00	45.00	27.50
31	Rene Gutierrez	60.00	30.00	18.00
32	Julio (Jiqui) Moreno	65.00	32.50	20.00
33	Bud Daley	65.00	32.50	20.00
34	Dick Tomaneck (Tomanek)	60.00	30.00	18.00
35	Rafael Noble	65.00	32.50	20.00
50	Gilberto Torres	60.00	30.00	18.00
51	Salvador Hernandez	60.00	30.00	18.00
52	Pipo de la Noval	60.00	30.00	18.00
53	Juan Soler	60.00	30.00	18.00
54	Oscar Sierra	60.00	30.00	18.00
55	Billy Muffet (Muffett)	60.00	30.00	18.00
56	Robert Bluaylock (Blaylock)	60.00	30.00	18.00
57	Edwin Mayers	60.00	30.00	18.00
58	Vicente Amor	60.00	30.00	18.00
59	Raul Sanchez	60.00	30.00	18.00
75	Napoleon Reyes	90.00	45.00	27.50
76	Jose Maria Fernandez	90.00	45.00	27.50
77	Juan Izaguirre	60.00	30.00	18.00
79	Rene Friol	60.00	30.00	18.00
80	Asdrubal Baro	60.00	30.00	18.00
82	Juan Delis	60.00	30.00	18.00
83	Julio Becquer	60.00	30.00	18.00
84	Rodolfo Arias	60.00	30.00	18.00
86	Patricio Quintana	60.00	30.00	18.00
87	Aldo Salvent	60.00	30.00	18.00

1900 Chickering Studio Cabinets

The extent of this issue of standard-format (about 4-1/4" x 6-1/2") cabinets is unknown. Fronts have a studio pose with a decorative studio logo in the bottom border. Backs have a large ad for the renowned Boston photographer.

		NM	EX	VG
Common Player:				
(1)	Win Mercer	1,500	750.00	450.00
(2)	Kid Nichols	9,000	4,500	2,750

1977 Chilly Willee Discs

Virtually identical in format to the several locally sponsored disc sets of the previous year, these 3-3/8" diameter player discs were given away at participating frozen drink stands. Discs once again feature black-and-white player portrait photos in the center of a baseball design. The left and right panels are in one of several bright colors. Licensed by the Players Association through Mike Schechter Associates, the player photos carry no uniform logos. Backs are printed in blue and red. The unnumbered discs are checklisted here alphabetically.

		NM	EX	VG
Complete Set (70):		65.00	32.50	20.00
Common Player:		1.00	.50	.30
(1)	Sal Bando	1.00	.50	.30
(2)	Buddy Bell	1.00	.50	.30
(3)	Johnny Bench	5.00	2.50	1.50
(4)	Larry Bowa	1.00	.50	.30
(5)	Steve Braun	1.00	.50	.30
(6)	George Brett	12.00	6.00	3.50
(7)	Lou Brock	5.00	2.50	1.50
(8)	Jeff Burroughs	1.00	.50	.30
(9)	Bert Campaneris	1.00	.50	.30
(10)	John Candelaria	1.00	.50	.30
(11)	Jose Cardenal	1.00	.50	.30
(12)	Rod Carew	5.00	2.50	1.50
(13)	Steve Carlton	5.00	2.50	1.50
(14)	Dave Cash	1.00	.50	.30
(15)	Cesar Cedeno	1.00	.50	.30
(16)	Ron Cey	1.00	.50	.30
(17)	Dave Concepcion	1.00	.50	.30
(18)	Dennis Eckersley	5.00	2.50	1.50
(19)	Mark Fidrych	2.50	1.25	.70
(20)	Rollie Fingers	4.00	2.00	1.25
(21)	Carlton Fisk	5.00	2.50	1.50
(22)	George Foster	1.00	.50	.30
(23)	Wayne Garland	1.00	.50	.30
(24)	Ralph Garr	1.00	.50	.30
(25)	Steve Garvey	2.00	1.00	.60
(26)	Cesar Geronimo	1.00	.50	.30
(27)	Bobby Grich	1.00	.50	.30
(28)	Ken Griffey Sr.	1.00	.50	.30
(29)	Don Gullett	1.00	.50	.30
(30)	Mike Hargrove	1.00	.50	.30
(31)	Al Hrabosky	1.00	.50	.30
(32)	Catfish Hunter	4.00	2.00	1.25
(33)	Reggie Jackson	10.00	5.00	3.00
(34)	Randy Jones	1.00	.50	.30
(35)	Dave Kingman	1.00	.50	.30
(36)	Jerry Koosman	1.00	.50	.30
(37)	Dave LaRoche	1.00	.50	.30
(38)	Greg Luzinski	1.00	.50	.30
(39)	Fred Lynn	1.00	.50	.30
(40)	Bill Madlock	1.00	.50	.30
(41)	Rick Manning	1.00	.50	.30
(42)	Jon Matlock	1.00	.50	.30
(43)	John Mayberry	1.00	.50	.30
(44)	Hal McRae	1.00	.50	.30
(45)	Andy Messersmith	1.00	.50	.30
(46)	Rick Monday	1.00	.50	.30
(47)	John Montefusco	1.00	.50	.30
(48)	Joe Morgan	5.00	2.50	1.50
(49)	Thurman Munson	4.00	2.00	1.25
(50)	Bobby Murcer	1.00	.50	.30
(51)	Bill North	1.00	.50	.30
(52)	Jim Palmer	5.00	2.50	1.50
(53)	Tony Perez	5.00	2.50	1.50
(54)	Jerry Reuss	1.00	.50	.30
(55)	Brooks Robinson	5.00	2.50	1.50
(56)	Pete Rose	10.00	5.00	3.00
(57)	Joe Rudi	1.00	.50	.30
(58)	Nolan Ryan	20.00	10.00	6.00
(59)	Manny Sanguillen	1.00	.50	.30
(60)	Mike Schmidt	12.00	6.00	3.50
(61)	Tom Seaver	5.00	2.50	1.50
(62)	Bill Singer	1.00	.50	.30
(63)	Willie Stargell	5.00	2.50	1.50
(64)	Rusty Staub	1.50	.70	.45
(65)	Luis Tiant	1.00	.50	.30
(66)	Bob Watson	1.00	.50	.30
(67)	Butch Wynegar	1.00	.50	.30
(68)	Carl Yastrzemski	5.00	2.50	1.50
(69)	Robin Yount	5.00	2.50	1.50
(70)	Richie Zisk	1.00	.50	.30

1929 Churchman's Cigarettes

Though he is identified nowhere on this English cigarette card, the home run swing of Babe Ruth on the front is unmistakable. The last of a set of 25 "Sports & Games in Many Lands" series, the approximately 2-5/8" x 1-3/8" cards have color artwork on the front and green-and-white backs. The back of the baseball card provides a short history of "The great national sport of the U.S.A."

		NM	EX	VG
25	Baseball, U.S.A. (Babe Ruth)	350.00	175.00	100.00

1963 Cincinnati Enquirer Reds' Scrapbook

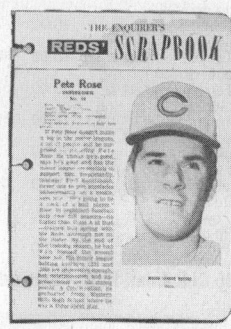

One of the city's newspapers carried this series that could be cut out of the newspaper and saved. The black-and-white clippings feature a player photo, stats, career notes and biographical data.

		NM	EX	VG
Complete Set (33):		150.00	75.00	45.00
Common Player:		3.00	1.50	.90
(1)	Don Blasingame	3.00	1.50	.90
(2)	Harry Bright	3.00	1.50	.90
(3)	Jim Brosnan	3.00	1.50	.90
(4)	Leo Cardenas	3.00	1.50	.90
(5)	Gerry Coleman	3.00	1.50	.90
(6)	John Edwards	3.00	1.50	.90
(7)	Sam Ellis	3.00	1.50	.90
(8)	Hank Foiles	3.00	1.50	.90
(9)	Gene Freese	3.00	1.50	.90
(10)	Jesse Gonder	3.00	1.50	.90
(11)	Tommy Harper	3.00	1.50	.90
(12)	Bill Henry	3.00	1.50	.90
(13)	Ken Hunt	3.00	1.50	.90
(14)	Fred Hutchinson	3.00	1.50	.90
(15)	Joey Jay	3.00	1.50	.90
(16)	Eddie Kasko	3.00	1.50	.90
(17)	Marty Keough	3.00	1.50	.90
(18)	Johnny Klippstein	3.00	1.50	.90
(19)	Jerry Lynch	3.00	1.50	.90
(20)	Jim Maloney	3.00	1.50	.90
(21)	Joe Nuxhall	4.50	2.25	1.25
(22)	Jim O'Toole	3.00	1.50	.90
(23)	Jim Owens	3.00	1.50	.90
(24)	Don Pavletich	3.00	1.50	.90
(25)	Vada Pinson	6.00	3.00	1.75
(26)	Wally Post	3.00	1.50	.90
(27)	Bob Purkey	3.00	1.50	.90
(28)	Frank Robinson	20.00	10.00	6.00
(29)	Pete Rose	90.00	45.00	27.00
(30)	Dave Sisler	3.00	1.50	.90
(31)	John Tsitouris	3.00	1.50	.90
(32)	Ken Walters	3.00	1.50	.90
(33)	Al Worthington	3.00	1.50	.90

1980 Cincinnati Enquirer Cincinnati Reds

This set of paper "cards" was printed within the pages of the Cincinnati Enquirer newspaper. The 2-1/4" x 3" cards are printed in black-and-white (both front and back) on newsprint. Dotted lines show where the cards were to be cut. Fronts have a player photo and a drawing of Riverfront Stadium. The team logo is in an upper corner and player identification in a black band towards the bottom. Backs have biographical and career details along with stats. Cards are checklisted here according to the uniform numbers printed on front.

		NM	EX	VG
Complete Set (32):		100.00	50.00	30.00
Common Player:		3.00	1.50	.90
2	Russ Nixon	3.00	1.50	.90
3	John McNamara	3.00	1.50	.90
4	Harry Dunlop	3.00	1.50	.90
5	Johnny Bench	9.00	4.50	2.75
6	Bill Fischer	3.00	1.50	.90
7	Hector Cruz	3.00	1.50	.90
9	Vic Correll	3.00	1.50	.90
11	Ron Plaza	3.00	1.50	.90
12	Harry Spilman	3.00	1.50	.90
13	Dave Concepcion	3.00	1.50	.90
15	George Foster	3.00	1.50	.90
16	Ron Oester	3.00	1.50	.90
19	Don Werner	3.00	1.50	.90
20	Cesar Geronimo	3.00	1.50	.90
22	Dan Driessen	3.00	1.50	.90
23	Rick Auerbach	3.00	1.50	.90
25	Ray Knight	3.00	1.50	.90
26	Junior Kennedy	3.00	1.50	.90

28	Sam Mejias	3.00	1.50	.90
29	Dave Collins	3.00	1.50	.90
30	Ken Griffey	3.00	1.50	.90
31	Paul Moskau	3.00	1.50	.90
34	Sheldon Burnside	3.00	1.50	.90
35	Frank Pastore	3.00	1.50	.90
36	Mario Soto	3.00	1.50	.90
37	Dave Tomlin	3.00	1.50	.90
40	Doug Bair	3.00	1.50	.90
41	Tom Seaver	7.50	3.75	2.25
42	Bill Bonham	3.00	1.50	.90
44	Charlie Leibrandt	3.00	1.50	.90
47	Tom Hume	3.00	1.50	.90
51	Mike LaCoss	3.00	1.50	.90

1938 Cincinnati Post Reds

Over the course of several weeks during the summer of 1938, daily editions of the Cincinnati Post sports section carried a set of player portraits designed to be cut out and saved. The pieces measure 6" x 11" and feature a large photo with facsimile autograph, topped by a headline and carrying a short biography below. Everything is in black-and-white. The unnumbered series is checklisted here in alphabetical order.

		NM	EX	VG
Complete Set (25):		450.00	225.00	135.00
Common Player:		20.00	10.00	6.00
(1)	Wally Berger	30.00	15.00	9.00
(2)	Joe Cascarella	20.00	10.00	6.00
(3)	Harry Craft	20.00	10.00	6.00
(4)	Dusty Cooke	20.00	10.00	6.00
(5)	Peaches Davis	20.00	10.00	6.00
(6)	Paul Derringer	25.00	12.50	7.50
(7)	Linus (Junior) Frey	20.00	10.00	6.00
(8)	Lee Gamble	20.00	10.00	6.00
(9)	Ival Goodman	20.00	10.00	6.00
(10)	Hank Gowdy	20.00	10.00	6.00
(11)	Lee Grissom	20.00	10.00	6.00
(12)	Willard Hershberger	25.00	12.50	7.50
(13)	Don Lang	20.00	10.00	6.00
(14)	Ernie Lombardi	35.00	17.50	10.50
(15)	Buck McCormick	20.00	10.00	6.00
(16)	Bill McKechnie	35.00	17.50	10.50
(17)	Whitey Moore	20.00	10.00	6.00
(18)	Billy Myers	20.00	10.00	6.00
(19)	Clifford Richardson	20.00	10.00	6.00
(20)	Lewis Riggs	20.00	10.00	6.00
(21)	Edd Roush	35.00	17.50	10.50
(22)	Gene Schott	20.00	10.00	6.00
(23)	Johnny Vander Meer	30.00	15.00	9.00
(24)	Bucky Walter	20.00	10.00	6.00
(25)	James Weaver	20.00	10.00	6.00

1919-20 Cincinnati Reds Postcards

Two versions of each of the cards in this issue are known. Picturing members of the 1919 World Champions, the foils of the Black Sox scandal, these 3-1/2" x 5-1/2" cards have black-and-white player poses on front. In the white border at bottom (or occasionally, at top) are two lines of type. The top line has the player name and position. The second line can be found in two versions. One reads, "Cincinnati 'Reds' - Champions of National League 1919," the other, presumably a second printing following the World Series, reads, "Cincinnati 'Reds' World's Champions 1919." Backs are printed with standard postcard indicia. Some cards have been found with the advertising of Mt. Union Dairy on the back. The unnumbered cards are checklisted here in alphabetical order.

		NM	EX	VG
Complete Set (24):		3,000	1,500	900.00
Common Player:		150.00	75.00	45.00
(1)	Nick Allen	150.00	75.00	45.00
(2)	Rube Bressler	150.00	75.00	45.00
(3)	Jake Daubert	150.00	75.00	45.00
(4)	Pat Duncan	150.00	75.00	45.00
(5)	Hod Eller	150.00	75.00	45.00
(6)	Ray Fisher	150.00	75.00	45.00
(7)	Eddie Gerner	150.00	75.00	45.00
(8)	Heinie Groh	150.00	75.00	45.00
(9)	Larry Kopf	150.00	75.00	45.00
(10)	Adolfo Luque	175.00	85.00	50.00
(11)	Sherwood Magee	150.00	75.00	45.00
(12)	Roy Mitchell	150.00	75.00	45.00
(13)	Pat Moran	150.00	75.00	45.00
(14)	Greasy Neale	200.00	100.00	60.00
(15)	Bill Rariden	150.00	75.00	45.00
(16)	Morris Rath	150.00	75.00	45.00
(17)	Walter Reuther (Ruether)	150.00	75.00	45.00
(18)	Jimmy Ring	150.00	75.00	45.00
(19)	Eddie Roush	400.00	200.00	120.00
(20)	Harry Sallee	150.00	75.00	45.00
(21)	Hank Schreiber	150.00	75.00	45.00
(22)	Charles See	150.00	75.00	45.00

(23)	Jimmy Smith	150.00	75.00	45.00
(24)	Ivy Wingo	150.00	75.00	45.00

1938 Cincinnati Reds team issue

This set of 2" x 3" cards were sold as a boxed set at the ballpark. Fronts feature a black-and-white photo of the player with his name and position in a red strip beneath the picture. Backs have the player's name, position and a generally flattering description of the player's talents. The cards are not numbered. In the American Card Catalog, this issue was designated W711-1.

		NM	EX	VG
Complete Set (23):		1,000	500.00	300.00
Common Player:		40.00	20.00	12.00
(1)	Wally Berger ("... in a trade with the Giants in June.")	40.00	20.00	12.00
(2)	Joe Cascarella	40.00	20.00	12.00
(3)	Allen "Dusty" Cooke	40.00	20.00	12.00
(4)	Harry Craft	40.00	20.00	12.00
(5)	Ray "Peaches" Davis	40.00	20.00	12.00
(6)	Paul Derringer ("Won 22 games...this season.")	40.00	20.00	12.00
(7)	Linus Frey ("... only 25 now.")	40.00	20.00	12.00
(8)	Lee Gamble ("... Syracuse last year.")	40.00	20.00	12.00
(9)	Ival Goodman (No mention of 30 homers.)	40.00	20.00	12.00
(10)	Harry "Hank" Gowdy	40.00	20.00	12.00
(11)	Lee Grissom (No mention of 1938.)	40.00	20.00	12.00
(12)	Willard Hershberger	100.00	50.00	30.00
(13)	Ernie Lombardi (No mention of 1938 MVP.)	225.00	110.00	67.00
(14)	Frank McCormick	40.00	20.00	12.00
(15)	Bill McKechnie ("Last year he led ...")	200.00	100.00	60.00
(16)	Lloyd "Whitey" Moore ("... last year with Syracuse.")	40.00	20.00	12.00
(17)	Billy Myers ("... in his fourth year.")	40.00	20.00	12.00
(18)	Lee Riggs ("... in his fourth season ...")	40.00	20.00	12.00
(19)	Eddie Roush	200.00	100.00	60.00
(20)	Gene Schott	40.00	20.00	12.00
(21)	Johnny Vander Meer (Portrait)	75.00	37.00	22.00
(22)	Wm. "Bucky" Walter ("... won 14 games ...")	40.00	20.00	12.00
(23)	Jim Weaver	40.00	20.00	12.00

1939 Cincinnati Reds Team Issue

An updating by one season of the team-issued 1938 W711-1 set, most of the players and poses on the 2" x 3" cards remained the same. A close study of the career summary on the card's back is necessary to determine which year of issue is at hand. The Livengood card is believed to have been withdrawn from distribution early and is scarce.

		NM	EX	VG
Complete Set (27):		1,250	625.00	375.00
Common Player:		40.00	20.00	12.00
(1)	Wally Berger ("... in a trade with the Giants in June, 1938.")	40.00	20.00	12.00
(2)	Nino Bongiovanni	40.00	20.00	12.00
(3)	Stanley "Frenchy" Bordagaray	40.00	20.00	12.00
(4)	Harry Craft	40.00	20.00	12.00
(5)	Ray "Peaches" Davis	40.00	20.00	12.00
(6)	Paul Derringer ("Won 21 games ... last year.")	45.00	22.00	13.50
(7)	Linus Frey ("... only 26 now.")	40.00	20.00	12.00
(8)	Lee Gamble ("... Syracuse in 1937.")	40.00	20.00	12.00
(9)	Ival Goodman (Mentions hitting 30 homers.)	40.00	20.00	12.00
(10)	Harry "Hank" Gowdy	40.00	20.00	12.00
(11)	Lee Grissom (Mentions 1938.)	40.00	20.00	12.00
(12)	Willard Hershberger	100.00	50.00	30.00
(13)	Eddie Joost	40.00	20.00	12.00
(14)	Wes Livengood	250.00	125.00	75.00
(15)	Ernie Lombardi (Mentions MVP of 1938.)	225.00	110.00	67.00
(16)	Frank McCormick	40.00	20.00	12.00
(17)	Bill McKechnie ("In 1937 he led ...")	200.00	100.00	60.00
(18)	Lloyd "Whitey" Moore ("... in 1937 with Syracuse.")	40.00	20.00	12.00
(19)	Billy Myers ("... in his fifth year ...")	40.00	20.00	12.00
(20)	Lee Riggs ("... in his fifth season...")	40.00	20.00	12.00
(21)	Les Scarsella	40.00	20.00	12.00
(22)	Eugene "Junior" Thompson	40.00	20.00	12.00
(23)	Johnny Vander Meer (Pitching)	50.00	25.00	15.00

		NM	EX	VG
(24)	Wm. "Bucky" Walters ("Won 15 games ...")	40.00	20.00	12.00
(25)	Jim Weaver	40.00	20.00	12.00
(26)	Bill Werber	40.00	20.00	12.00
(27)	Jimmy Wilson	40.00	20.00	12.00

1940 Cincinnati Reds Team Issue

Another early Reds team issue, this set of black-and-white 2-1/8" x 2-5/8" cards is unnumbered and features player portrait photos on the front. Name, position, biographical information, and five years' worth of stats are on the back. The Reds were World Champions in 1940 (defeating Detroit), and the set features several special World Series cards, making it one of the first to feature events as well as individuals. The set was listed in the American Card Catalog as W711-2.

		NM	EX	VG
Complete Set (35):		900.00	450.00	275.00
Common Player:		25.00	12.50	7.50
(1)	Morris Arnovich	25.00	12.50	7.50
(2)	William (Bill) Baker	25.00	12.50	7.50
(3)	Joseph Beggs	25.00	12.50	7.50
(4)	Harry Craft	25.00	12.50	7.50
(5)	Paul Derringer	25.00	12.50	7.50
(6)	Linus Frey	25.00	12.50	7.50
(7)	Ival Goodman	25.00	12.50	7.50
(8)	Harry (Hank) Gowdy	25.00	12.50	7.50
(9)	Witt Guise	25.00	12.50	7.50
(10)	Harry (Socko) Hartman	25.00	12.50	7.50
(11)	Willard Hershberger	35.00	17.50	10.50
(12)	John Hutchings	25.00	12.50	7.50
(13)	Edwin Joost	25.00	12.50	7.50
(14)	Ernie Lombardi	60.00	30.00	18.00
(15)	Frank McCormick	25.00	12.50	7.50
(16)	Myron McCormick	25.00	12.50	7.50
(17)	William Boyd McKechnie	60.00	30.00	18.00
(18)	Lloyd (Whitey) Moore	25.00	12.50	7.50
(19)	William (Bill) Myers	25.00	12.50	7.50
(20)	Lewis Riggs	25.00	12.50	7.50
(21)	Elmer Riddle	25.00	12.50	7.50
(22)	James A. Ripple	25.00	12.50	7.50
(23)	Milburn Shoffner	25.00	12.50	7.50
(24)	Eugene Thompson	25.00	12.50	7.50
(25)	James Turner	25.00	12.50	7.50
(26)	John Vander Meer	30.00	15.00	9.00
(27)	Wm. (Bucky) Walters	25.00	12.50	7.50
(28)	William (Bill) Werber	25.00	12.50	7.50
(29)	James Wilson	25.00	12.50	7.50
(30)	The Cincinnati Reds	25.00	12.50	7.50
(31)	The Cincinnati Reds World Champions	25.00	12.50	7.50
(32)	Tell the World About the Cincinnati Reds	25.00	12.50	7.50
(33)	Tell the World About the Cincinnati Reds Champions	25.00	12.50	7.50
(34)	Results 1940 World's Series	25.00	12.50	7.50
(35)	Debt. of Gratitude to Wm. Koeh Co.	25.00	12.50	7.50

1954-1955 Cincinnati Reds Postcards

The first team-issued Redlegs postcards of the modern era were produced during the 1954 and 1955 seasons for use by players in answering fan requests for pictures and autographs. The cards are 3-1/2" x 5-5/8", printed in black-and-white on non-glossy cardboard stock. Fronts have poses which are borderless at top and sides. At bottom is a 3/4" white strip which is either blank or which has the player and team name printed. Many cards are found with stamped facsimile autographs, and/or authentically signed. Backs have a vertical line at center. At top-left is: "Cincinnati Baseball Club / Crosley Field / Cincinnati, Ohio." While there is no stamp box on the back, many of the cards have been postally used. The issue was listed in the "American Card Catalog" as PC746.

		NM	EX	VG
Common Player:		15.00	7.50	4.50
(1)	Bobby Adams (Fielding)	15.00	7.50	4.50
(2)	Bobby Adams (Portrait to neck.)	15.00	7.50	4.50
(3)	Dr. Wayne Anderson (Trainer) (Chest-up.)	30.00	15.00	9.00
(4)	Fred Baczewski (Ready to pitch.)	15.00	7.50	4.50
(5)	Ed Bailey (Batting to waist.)	15.00	7.50	4.50
(6)	Dick Bartell (Portrait to neck.)	15.00	7.50	4.50
(7)	Dick Bartell (Portrait to shoulders.)	15.00	7.50	4.50
(8)	Matt Batts (Batting follow-through.)	15.00	7.50	4.50
(9)	Gus Bell (Portrait to neck.)	15.00	7.50	4.50
(10)	Gus Bell (Waist up, ready to hit.)	15.00	7.50	4.50
(11)	Joe Black (Standing in dugout.)	15.00	7.50	4.50
(12)	Bob Borkowski (Batting follow-through.)	15.00	7.50	4.50
(13)	Buzz Boyle (Scout) (Chest-up in suit.)	40.00	20.00	12.00
(14)	Rocky Bridges (Portrait to neck.)	15.00	7.50	4.50
(15)	Smoky Burgess (Portrait to neck.)	15.00	7.50	4.50
(16)	Jackie Collum (Pitching follow-through.)	15.00	7.50	4.50
(17)	Jackie Collum (Portrait to neck.)	15.00	7.50	4.50
(18)	Powell Crosley, Jr. (Portrait)(President)	15.00	7.50	4.50
(19)	Jimmy Dykes (Standing in dugout.)	15.00	7.50	4.50
(20)	Nino Escalera (Portrait to neck.)	15.00	7.50	4.50
(21)	Tom Ferrick (Portrait to neck.)	15.00	7.50	4.50
(22)	Art Fowler (Hands over head.)	15.00	7.50	4.50
(23)	Art Fowler (Portrait to neck.)	15.00	7.50	4.50
(24)	Hershell Freeman (Portrait to shoulders.)	15.00	7.50	4.50
(26)	Jim Greengrass (Waist-up, batting.)	15.00	7.50	4.50
(27)	Don Gross (Portrait to neck.)	15.00	7.50	4.50
(28)	Charley Harmon (Batting to belt.)	15.00	7.50	4.50
(29)	Ray Jablonski (Batting to belt.)	15.00	7.50	4.50
(30)	Howie Judson (Portrait to neck.)	15.00	7.50	4.50
(31)	Johnny Klippstein (Pitching follow-through.)	15.00	7.50	4.50
(32)	Ted Kluszewski (Batting, cut out sleeves.)	30.00	15.00	9.00
(33)	Ted Kluszewski (Batting to belt.)	30.00	15.00	9.00
(34)	Ted Kluszewski (Batting follow-through, full length.)	30.00	15.00	9.00
(35)	Ted Kluszewski (Batting follow-through to waist.)	30.00	15.00	9.00
(36)	Ted Kluszewski (Batting follow-through, #18 on back.)	30.00	15.00	9.00
(37)	Ted Kluszewski (Stretching at 1B.)	30.00	15.00	9.00
(38)	Ted Kluszewski (Standing w/ four bats.)	30.00	15.00	9.00
(39)	Ted Kluszewski (Portrait to neck, looking right.)	30.00	15.00	9.00
(40)	Ted Kluszewski (Portrait to shoulders, leaning right.)	30.00	15.00	9.00
(41)	Hobie Landrith (Catching)	15.00	7.50	4.50
(42)	Hobie Landrith (Pose to neck.)	15.00	7.50	4.50
(43)	William McKechnie, Jr. (Portrait)(Farm club supervisor.)	15.00	7.50	4.50
(44)	Roy McMillan (Portrait to neck.)	15.00	7.50	4.50
(45)	Roy McMillan (Ready to hit.)	15.00	7.50	4.50
(46)	Lloyd Merriman (Ready to hit.)	15.00	7.50	4.50
(47)	Rudy Minarcin (Portrait to neck.)	15.00	7.50	4.50
(48)	Rudy Minarcin (Portrait to shoulders, chain.)	15.00	7.50	4.50
(49)	Joe Nuxhall (Portrait to neck.)	15.00	7.50	4.50
(51)	Joe Nuxhall (Pitching follow-through.)	15.00	7.50	4.50
(52)	Stan Palys (Batting follow-through.)	15.00	7.50	4.50
(53)	Harry Perkowski (Portrait to neck.)	15.00	7.50	4.50
(54)	Bud Podbielan (Ready to pitch, belt visible.)	15.00	7.50	4.50
(55)	Bud Podbielan (Ready to pitch, no belt.)	15.00	7.50	4.50
(56)	Wally Post (Ready to hit to belt, fans in back.)	22.50	11.00	6.75
(57)	Wally Post (Ready to hit to hips.)	22.50	11.00	6.75
(58)	Wally Post (Batting follow-through, pole on left.)	22.50	11.00	6.75
(59)	Wally Post (Batting follow-through, no pole.)	22.50	11.00	6.75
(60)	Wally Post (Portrait to neck.)	22.50	11.00	6.75
(61)	Ken Raffensberger (Pitching wind-up.)	15.00	7.50	4.50
(62)	Steve Ridzik (Portrait to neck.)	15.00	7.50	4.50
(63)	Connie Ryan (Portrait to neck.)	15.00	7.50	4.50
(64)	Moe Savransky (Portrait to neck.)	15.00	7.50	4.50
(65)	Andy Seminick (Batting follow-through.)	15.00	7.50	4.50
(66)	Al Silvera (Portrait to shoulders.)	15.00	7.50	4.50
(67)	Frank Smith (Ready to pitch.)	15.00	7.50	4.50
(68)	Milt Smith (Portrait to shoulders.)	15.00	7.50	4.50
(69)	Gerry Staley (Ready to pitch.)	15.00	7.50	4.50
(70)	Birdie Tebbetts (Portrait to neck.)	15.00	7.50	4.50
(71)	Birdie Tebbetts (Portrait to shoulders.)	15.00	7.50	4.50
(72)	Johnny Temple (Portrait to neck, mouth closed.)	15.00	7.50	4.50
(73)	Johnny Temple (Portrait to neck, mouth open.)	15.00	7.50	4.50
(74)	Bob Thurman (Batting follow-through.)	15.00	7.50	4.50
(76)	Corky Valentine (Pitching follow-through.)	15.00	7.50	4.50
(77)	Herm Wehmeier (Portrait to neck.)	15.00	7.50	4.50
(78)	George Zuverink (Portrait to neck.)	15.00	7.50	4.50
(79)	Crosley Field	15.00	7.50	4.50

1956 Cincinnati Reds Postcards

TOM ACKER
Cincinnati Redlegs

After a number of years issuing printed postcards for players to answer fan mail, the team began a three-year run of glossy black-and-white photographic sets in 1956. About 3-1/2" x 5-3/4", the cards usually feature portrait photos, though some action poses are also seen. The pictures are bordered in white with a 1" or so border at bottom with the player and team names. Differentiating the 1956s from similarly formatted issues in 1957-1958 is best done on back. The 1956 cards are divided-back with "Post Card" at top. At right, in the stamp box, is "Place Postage Stamp Here" and, at bottom, "This space for address." Cards are numbered here alphabetically, with gaps left in the assigned numbering for future additions.

		NM	EX	VG
Complete Set (31):		350.00	175.00	105.00
Common Player:		10.00	5.00	3.00
(1)	Tom Acker	10.00	5.00	3.00
(2)	Ed Bailey	10.00	5.00	3.00
(3)	Gus Bell	10.00	5.00	3.00
(4)	Joe Black	10.00	5.00	3.00
(5)	"Rocky" Bridges	10.00	5.00	3.00
(6)	"Smoky" Burgess	12.50	6.25	3.75
(7)	George Crowe	10.00	5.00	3.00
(8)	Jim Dyck	10.00	5.00	3.00
(9)	Jimmy Dykes	10.00	5.00	3.00
(11)	Bruce Edwards (Non-'56 back.)	10.00	5.00	3.00
(12)	Tom Ferrick	10.00	5.00	3.00
(13)	Joe Frazier	10.00	5.00	3.00
(14)	Hersh Freeman	10.00	5.00	3.00
(15)	Alex Grammas	10.00	5.00	3.00
(16)	Don Gross	10.00	5.00	3.00
(17)	Ray Jablonski	10.00	5.00	3.00
(18)	Larry Jansen	10.00	5.00	3.00
(19)	Hal Jeffcoat	10.00	5.00	3.00
(21)	Johnny Klippstein	10.00	5.00	3.00
(22)	Ted Kluszewski	20.00	10.00	6.00
(23)	Brooks Lawrence	10.00	5.00	3.00
(24)	Frank McCormick	10.00	5.00	3.00
(25)	Roy McMillan	10.00	5.00	3.00
(26)	Joe Nuxhall	12.50	6.25	3.75
(27)	Stan Palys ('56 back.)	10.00	5.00	3.00
(28)	Stan Palys (Non-'56 back.)	10.00	5.00	3.00
(29)	Wally Post	10.00	5.00	3.00
(31)	Frank Robinson	75.00	37.00	22.00
(32)	"Birdie" Tebbetts	10.00	5.00	3.00
(33)	Johnny Temple	10.00	5.00	3.00
(34)	Bob Thurman	10.00	5.00	3.00

1957 Cincinnati Reds Picture Pack

FRANK ROBINSON, Redlegs

Similar in format to the Jay Publishing photo packs, this appears to be a team-issued souvenir item, with many of the pictures having been seen in other team-related contexts. The black-and-white, blank-backed pictures measure 5" x 7". They can be differentiated from contemporary Jay photos by the fact that only the team nickname, "Redlegs," appears, rather than city and team. Player names are in all-caps.

	NM	EX	VG
Complete Set (12):	45.00	22.50	13.50
Common Player:	4.00	2.00	1.25
(1) Ed Bailey	4.00	2.00	1.25
(2) Gus Bell	4.00	2.00	1.25
(3) Smoky Burgess	4.00	2.00	1.25
(4) Hersh Freeman	4.00	2.00	1.25
(5) Ted Kluszewski	7.50	3.75	2.25
(6) Brooks Lawrence	4.00	2.00	1.25
(7) Roy McMillan	4.00	2.00	1.25
(8) Joe Nuxhall	4.00	2.00	1.25
(9) Wally Post	4.00	2.00	1.25
(10) Frank Robinson	15.00	7.50	4.50
(11) Birdie Tebbetts	4.00	2.00	1.25
(12) Johnny Temple	4.00	2.00	1.25

1957 Cincinnati Reds Postcards

The second in a long run of glossy-front, black-and-white annual postcard issues, the 1957 can often be distinguished from the 1956 and 1958 cards by the appearance of players in sleeveless uniforms with dark undershirts. Even more distinguishing is that the 1957s, on back, have "PHOTO POST CARD" across the top, and lack the notice "This Space for Address" which appeared on the 1956 cards. The '57s can also be identified by "Divolite Peerless" which appears in the postage-stamp box. The 3-1/2" x 5-3/4" cards have white borders. At bottom is 1" white space with the player name and "Cincinnati Redlegs" and space for an autograph. The unnumbered cards are checklisted here in alphabetical order.

	NM	EX	VG
Complete Set (34):	300.00	150.00	90.00
Common Player:	9.00	4.50	2.75
(1) Tom Acker	9.00	4.50	2.75
(2) Ed Bailey	9.00	4.50	2.75
(3) Gus Bell	9.00	4.50	2.75
(4) "Rocky" Bridges	9.00	4.50	2.75
(5) "Smoky" Burgess	11.00	5.50	3.25
(6) George Crowe	9.00	4.50	2.75
(7) Bobby Durnbaugh	9.00	4.50	2.75
(8) Jimmy Dykes	9.00	4.50	2.75
(9) Tom Ferrick	9.00	4.50	2.75
(10) Art Fowler	9.00	4.50	2.75
(11) Hersh Freeman	9.00	4.50	2.75
(12) Alex Grammas	9.00	4.50	2.75
(13) Don Gross	9.00	4.50	2.75
(14) Warren Hacker	9.00	4.50	2.75
(15) Bobby Henrich	9.00	4.50	2.75
(16) Don Hoak	11.00	5.50	3.25
(17) Hal Jeffcoat	9.00	4.50	2.75
(18) Johnny Klippstein	9.00	4.50	2.75
(19) Ted Kluszewski (Batting)	18.00	9.00	5.50
(20) Ted Kluszewski (Portrait)	18.00	9.00	5.50
(21) Brooks Lawrence	9.00	4.50	2.75
(22) Jerry Lynch	9.00	4.50	2.75
(23) Frank McCormick	9.00	4.50	2.75
(24) Roy McMillan	9.00	4.50	2.75
(25) Joe Nuxhall	9.00	4.50	2.75
(26) Wally Post	9.00	4.50	2.75
(27) Frank Robinson	45.00	22.00	13.50
(28) Raul Sanchez	9.00	4.50	2.75
(29) Art Schult	9.00	4.50	2.75
(30) "Birdie" Tebbetts	9.00	4.50	2.75
(31) Johnny Temple	9.00	4.50	2.75
(32) Bob Thurman	9.00	4.50	2.75
(33) Pete Whisenant (Batting)	9.00	4.50	2.75
(34) Pete Whisenant (Portrait)	9.00	4.50	2.75

1958 Cincinnati Reds Postcards

Cards from the third of a long run of glossy-front, black-and-white annual postcard issues can be most often distinguished from similarly formatted 1956-57 cards by the appearance of players in white uniforms with white caps. Two back styles are known. One, like the 1957 issue, has a postage box with "Divolite Peerless" inside and one without the box, but with "Post Card" and "Actual Photograph." Both have a vertical dividing line. The 3-1/2" x 5-3/4" cards have white borders. At bottom is 1" white space with the player name and "Cincinnati Redlegs" and space for an autograph. The unnumbered cards are checklisted here in alphabetical order, though this list may not be complete as several stars are unknown in this style.

WALT DROPO
Cincinnati Redlegs

	NM	EX	VG
Complete Set (30):	300.00	150.00	90.00
Common Player:	9.00	4.50	2.75
(1) Tom Acker	9.00	4.50	2.75
(2) Dr. Wayne Anderson (Trainer)	9.00	4.50	2.75
(3) Ed Bailey	9.00	4.50	2.75
(4) Steve Bilko	9.00	4.50	2.75
(5) "Smoky" Burgess	11.00	5.50	3.25
(6) George Crowe	9.00	4.50	2.75
(7) Walt Dropo	9.00	4.50	2.75
(8) Jimmie Dykes	9.00	4.50	2.75
(9) Tom Ferrick	9.00	4.50	2.75
(10) Dee Fondy	9.00	4.50	2.75
(11) Alex Grammas	9.00	4.50	2.75
(12) Harvey Haddix	9.00	4.50	2.75
(13) Hal Jeffcoat	9.00	4.50	2.75
(14) Alex Kellner	9.00	4.50	2.75
(15) Johnny Klippstein	9.00	4.50	2.75
(16) Turk Lown	9.00	4.50	2.75
(17) Jerry Lynch	9.00	4.50	2.75
(18) Roy McMillan	9.00	4.50	2.75
(19) Ed Miksis (Pinstripes)	9.00	4.50	2.75
(20) Joe Nuxhall	10.00	5.00	3.00
(21) Vada Pinson	15.00	7.50	4.50
(22) Bob Purkey	9.00	4.50	2.75
(23) Charley Rabe	9.00	4.50	2.75
(24) John Riddle	9.00	4.50	2.75
(25) Willard Schmidt	9.00	4.50	2.75
(26) Manager "Birdie" Tebbetts (Portrait to neck.)	9.00	4.50	2.75
(27) Manager "Birdie" Tebbetts (Portrait, white background, #1 shows.)	9.00	4.50	2.75
(28) Johnny Temple	9.00	4.50	2.75
(29) Bob Thurman	9.00	4.50	2.75
(30) Pete Whisenant	9.00	4.50	2.75

1969 Citgo Coins

This 20-player set of small (about 1" in diameter) metal coins was issued by Citgo in 1969 to commemorate professional baseball's 100th anniversary. The brass-coated coins, susceptible to oxidation, display the player in a crude portrait with his name across the top. The backs honor the 100th anniversary of pro ball. The coins are unnumbered but are generally checklisted according to numbers that appear on a red, white and blue paper display folder that was available from Citgo by mail.

	NM	EX	VG
Complete Set (20):	80.00	40.00	25.00
Common Player:	2.00	1.00	.60
Cardboard Display Folder:	30.00	15.00	9.00
Unopened Pack:	12.00	.00	.00
1 Denny McLain	2.50	1.25	.70
2 Dave McNally	2.00	1.00	.60
3 Jim Lonborg	2.00	1.00	.60
4 Harmon Killebrew	6.50	3.25	2.00
5 Mel Stottlemyre	2.00	1.00	.60
6 Willie Horton	2.00	1.00	.60
7 Jim Fregosi	2.00	1.00	.60
8 Rico Petrocelli	2.00	1.00	.60
9 Stan Bahnsen	2.00	1.00	.60
10 Frank Howard	2.50	1.25	.70
11 Joe Torre	2.50	1.25	.70
12 Jerry Koosman	2.00	1.00	.60
13 Ron Santo	3.50	1.75	1.00
14 Pete Rose	20.00	10.00	6.00
15 Rusty Staub	2.00	1.00	.60
16 Henry Aaron	20.00	10.00	6.00
17 Richie Allen	3.50	1.75	1.00
18 Ron Swoboda	2.00	1.00	.60
19 Willie McCovey	6.50	3.25	2.00
20 Jim Bunning	5.00	2.50	1.50

1969 Citgo New York Mets

One of several regional issues in the Mets World Championship season of 1969, this set of 8" x 10" player portraits was sponsored by Citgo, whose gas stations distributed the pictures with fuel purchases. Fronts feature large portraits and smaller action pictures of the player, done in pastels, set

against a bright pastel background. The paintings are the work of noted celebrity artist John Wheeldon. Beneath the pictures is a facsimile autograph. The player's name is printed in the bottom border. Backs are printed in black-and-white and include biography and career details, full major and minor league stats and a self-portrait and biography of the artist. Logos of the Mets, the Players Association and the sponsor complete the back design. The unnumbered player pictures are checklisted in alphabetical order.

	NM	EX	VG
Complete Set (8):	65.00	32.00	19.50
Common Player:	6.50	3.25	2.00
(1) Tommie Agee	8.00	4.00	2.50
(2) Ken Boswell	6.50	3.25	2.00
(3) Gary Gentry	6.50	3.25	2.00
(4) Jerry Grote	6.50	3.25	2.00
(5) Cleon Jones	6.50	3.25	2.00
(6) Jerry Koosman	8.00	4.00	2.50
(7) Ed Kranepool	6.50	3.25	2.00
(8) Tom Seaver	25.00	12.50	7.50

1975 Clark & Sons Baseball Favorites

To commemorate the firm's 10 years in business and the Boston Red Sox first pennant since 1967, Clark & Sons Locksmiths of Rhode Island issued this set of Red Sox greats. Two versions were issued. The first has a "324 Waterman Avenue, Providence" address on back. A second printing corrected the errors to "324A Waterman Avenue, East Providence" and added a wavy line around the photo and name on front. Cards measure 2-1/2" x 3-5/8" and are printed in black-and-white.

	NM	EX	VG
Complete Set (4):	12.50	6.25	3.75
Common Player:	1.25	.60	.40
1 Bobby Doerr	2.00	1.00	.60
2 Ted Williams	10.00	5.00	3.00
3 Dom DiMaggio	2.50	1.25	.70
4 Johnny Pesky	1.25	.60	.40

1921 Clark's Bread

It is not known to what extent this set's checklist of base cards and possible variations parallels the contemporary blank-back 1921-1922 W575-1 strip cards. The cards measure about 2" x 3-1/4" and are printed in black-and-white. It is unknown in which region the bread cards might have been issued. Collectors have been known to pay a premium of 10X for this version.

	NM	EX	VG
Common Player:	600.00	300.00	180.00

(See 1921 American Caramel Series of 80 or 1922 W575-1 for checklists and base card values.)

1972 Classic Cards

The set depicts players from 1900-1909 in sepiatone photos printed on thin, cream-colored card stock by the Flint, MI company not related to the 1990s card maker of the same name. The first series features sequentially numbered cards, the remainder marked only with a series number. Card size is 2-3/4" x 4-1/2" for the first series and 2-3/4" x 4-1/4" for the last three 30-card series.

		NM	EX	VG
	Complete Set (120):	50.00	25.00	10.00
	Common Player:	2.00	1.00	.60
1	Griffith, Cincinnati	2.00	1.00	.60
2	Johnson, Washington	2.00	1.00	.60
3	Ganley, Washington	2.00	1.00	.60
4	Tinker, Chicago	2.00	1.00	.60
5	Chance, Chicago	2.00	1.00	.60
6	Conroy, Washington	2.00	1.00	.60
7	Bresnahan, N.Y.	2.00	1.00	.60
8	Powell, Pittsburgh	2.00	1.00	.60
9	Pfeister, Chicago	2.00	1.00	.60
10	McCarthy, Boston	2.00	1.00	.60
11	McConnell, Boston	2.00	1.00	.60
12	Jennings, Detroit	2.00	1.00	.60
13	Lennox, Brooklyn	2.00	1.00	.60
14	McCormick, N.Y.	2.00	1.00	.60
15	Merkle, N.Y.	2.00	1.00	.60
16	Hoblitzell, Cincinnati	2.00	1.00	.60
17	Dahlen, Boston	2.00	1.00	.60
18	Chance, Chicago	2.00	1.00	.60
19	Ferguson, Boston	2.00	1.00	.60
20	Camnitz, Pittsburgh	2.00	1.00	.60
21	N.Y. (Neal Ball)	2.00	1.00	.60
22	Hemphill, N.Y.	2.00	1.00	.60
23	Baker, Philadelphia	2.00	1.00	.60
24	Mathewson, N.Y.	5.00	2.50	1.50
25	Burch, Brooklyn	2.00	1.00	.60
26	Grant, Philadelphia	2.00	1.00	.60
27	Ames, N.Y.	2.00	1.00	.60
28	Newton, N.Y.	2.00	1.00	.60
29	Moran, Chicago	2.00	1.00	.60
30	Lajoie, Cleveland	2.00	1.00	.60
(31)	Abstein, Pittsburgh	2.00	1.00	.60
(32)	Brown, Chicago	2.00	1.00	.60
(33)	Campbell, Cincinnati	2.00	1.00	.60
(34)	Cobb, Detroit	5.00	2.50	1.50
(35)	Crawford, Detroit	2.00	1.00	.60
(36)	Devlin, N.Y.	2.00	1.00	.60
(37)	Dooin, Philadelphia	2.00	1.00	.60
(38)	Dougherty, Chicago	2.00	1.00	.60
(39)	Downey, Cincinnati	2.00	1.00	.60
(40)	Doyle, New York	2.00	1.00	.60
(41)	Dunn, Brooklyn	2.00	1.00	.60
(42)	Durham, N.Y.	2.00	1.00	.60
(43)	Gibson, Pittsburgh	2.00	1.00	.60
(44)	Hartzel, Philadelphia	2.00	1.00	.60
(45)	Higginbotham, Chicago	2.00	1.00	.60
(46)	Hinchman	2.00	1.00	.60
(47)	Lajoie	2.00	1.00	.60
(48)	Mowery, Cincinnati	2.00	1.00	.60
(49)	Mullin, Detroit	2.00	1.00	.60
(50)	O'Hara, New York	2.00	1.00	.60
(51)	Overall, Chicago	2.00	1.00	.60
(52)	Perring, Cleveland	2.00	1.00	.60
(53)	Rossman, Detroit	2.00	1.00	.60
(54)	Schmidt, Detroit	2.00	1.00	.60
(55)	Steinfeldt, Chicago	2.00	1.00	.60
(56)	Stone, St. Louis	2.00	1.00	.60
(57)	Titus, Philadelphia	2.00	1.00	.60
(58)	Wagner, Pittsburgh	2.00	1.00	.60
(59)	Wamhow, N.Y.	2.00	1.00	.60
(60)	Wiltse, New York	2.00	1.00	.60
(61)	Barger, Brooklyn	2.00	1.00	.60
(62)	Bergen, Brooklyn	2.00	1.00	.60
(63)	Bowerman, Boston	2.00	1.00	.60
(64)	Bransfeld, Philadelphia	2.00	1.00	.60
(65)	Bresnahan, St. Louis	2.00	1.00	.60
(66)	Coakley, Chicago	2.00	1.00	.60
(67)	Donovan, Detroit	2.00	1.00	.60
(68)	Elberfeld, New York	2.00	1.00	.60
(69)	Evers, Chicago	2.00	1.00	.60
(70)	Fromme, Cincinnati	2.00	1.00	.60
(71)	Herzog, N.Y.	2.00	1.00	.60
(72)	Hummell, Cincinnati	2.00	1.00	.60
(73)	Jordan, Brooklyn	2.00	1.00	.60
(74)	Keeler, New York	2.00	1.00	.60
(75)	Lumley, Brooklyn	2.00	1.00	.60
(76)	Maddox, Pittsburgh	2.00	1.00	.60
(77)	McGinnity, New York	2.00	1.00	.60
(78)	McGraw, New York	2.00	1.00	.60
(79)	McIntyre, Brooklyn	2.00	1.00	.60
(80)	Moriarity, New York	2.00	1.00	.60
(81)	Pastorius, Brooklyn	2.00	1.00	.60
(82)	Purtell, Chicago	2.00	1.00	.60
(83)	Schulte, Chicago	2.00	1.00	.60
(84)	Sebring, Brooklyn	2.00	1.00	.60
(85)	Smith, Washington	2.00	1.00	.60
(86)	Speaker, Boston	5.00	2.50	1.50
(87)	Spencer, Boston	2.00	1.00	.60
(88)	Tuckey, Boston	2.00	1.00	.60
(89)	Vaughn, New York	2.00	1.00	.60
(90)	Wheat, Brooklyn	2.00	1.00	.60
(91)	Altzier, Chicago	2.00	1.00	.60
(92)	Bender, Philadelphia	2.00	1.00	.60
(93)	Cincinnati (Bob Ewing)	2.00	1.00	.60
(94)	Bresnahan, St. Louis	2.00	1.00	.60
(95)	Chappelle, Boston	2.00	1.00	.60
(96)	Chase, New York	2.00	1.00	.60
(97)	Daley, Cincinnati	2.00	1.00	.60
(98)	Davis, Philadelphia	2.00	1.00	.60
(99)	Delahanty, St. Louis	2.00	1.00	.60
(100)	Donohue, Washington	2.00	1.00	.60
(101)	Doyle, New York	2.00	1.00	.60
(102)	Ellis, St. Louis	2.00	1.00	.60
(103)	Graham, St. Louis	2.00	1.00	.60
(104)	Herzog, New York	2.00	1.00	.60
(105)	Hyatt, Pittsburgh	2.00	1.00	.60
(106)	Konetchy, St. Louis	2.00	1.00	.60
(107)	Lake, New York	2.00	1.00	.60
(108)	Lord, Boston	2.00	1.00	.60
(109)	New York (Luther Taylor)	2.00	1.00	.60
(110)	McLean, Cincinnati	2.00	1.00	.60
(111)	Needham, Chicago	2.00	1.00	.60
(112)	Pearce, Cincinnati	2.00	1.00	.60
(113)	Powell, Pittsburgh	2.00	1.00	.60
(114)	Purtell, Chicago	2.00	1.00	.60
(115)	Schreck, Philadelphia	2.00	1.00	.60
(116)	Storke, Pittsburgh	2.00	1.00	.60
(117)	Strunk, Philadelphia	2.00	1.00	.60
(118)	Summers, Detroit	2.00	1.00	.60
(119)	Thomas, Philadelphia	2.00	1.00	.60
(120)	Wagner, Boston	2.00	1.00	.60

1973 Roberto Clemente Memorial Postcard

This collectors' issue postcard was isusued as a memorial. In standard 3-1/2" x 5-1/2" format with a postcard-style back, the black-and-white card has printed in the wide bottom border, the player's name, dates of his birth and death and, "In Memory OF A COURAGEOUS HUMAN BEING." On back is a credit line to Allied Printing.

	NM	EX	VG
Roberto Clemente	25.00	12.50	7.50

1913 Cleveland Indians Schedule Postcards

The extent to which the team may have used this type of postcard to announce forthcoming home series is unknown. It can be assumed other cards with other players featured were used during the course of the season. About 7" x 3-1/2", the card has a portrait photo on the left end of its black-and-white front. On back, in red and black, are details of upcoming series and ticket outlet information.

	NM	EX	VG
Joe Birmingham	900.00	450.00	275.00
Ray Chapman	1,350	675.00	400.00
Jack Graney	900.00	450.00	275.00
Joe Jackson, Fred Clarke (Pirates exhibition game.)	2,500	1,250	750.00
Doc Johnston	900.00	450.00	275.00
Willie Mitchell	900.00	450.00	275.00

1947 Cleveland Indians Picture Pack

The first of several annual issues of player photo packs, the 1947 version offered "autographed photos" of all players on the team's roster as of July 1. All players were presented in studio quality portraits in 6" x 8-1/2" format, lithographed on heavy paper with a facsimile autograph. A thin white border surrounds the photo. Backs are blank. The photos were sold in sets for 50 cents. The unnumbered pictures are checklisted here alphabetically.

		NM	EX	VG
	Complete Set (25):	100.00	50.00	30.00
	Common Player:	3.00	1.50	.90
(1)	Don Black	4.00	2.00	1.25
(2)	Eddie Bockman	3.00	1.50	.90
(3)	Lou Boudreau	9.00	4.50	2.75
(4)	Jack Conway	3.00	1.50	.90
(5)	Larry Doby	25.00	12.50	7.50
(6)	Hank Edwards	3.00	1.50	.90
(7)	"Red" Embree	3.00	1.50	.90
(8)	Bob Feller	25.00	12.50	7.50
(9)	Les Fleming	3.00	1.50	.90
(10)	Allen Gettel	3.00	1.50	.90
(11)	Joe Gordon	3.00	1.50	.90
(12)	Steve Gromek	3.00	1.50	.90
(13)	Mel Harder	4.50	2.25	1.25
(14)	Jim Hegan	3.00	1.50	.90
(15)	Ken Keltner	4.50	2.25	1.25
(16)	Ed Klieman	3.00	1.50	.90
(17)	Bob Lemon	9.00	4.50	2.75
(18)	Al Lopez	9.00	4.50	2.75
(19)	George Metkovich	3.00	1.50	.90
(20)	Dale Mitchell	4.00	2.00	1.25
(21)	Hal Peck	3.00	1.50	.90
(22)	Eddie Robinson	3.00	1.50	.90
(23)	Hank Ruszkowski	3.00	1.50	.90
(24)	Pat Seerey	3.00	1.50	.90
(25)	Bryan Stephens	3.00	1.50	.90
(26)	Les Willis	3.00	1.50	.90

1947 Van Patrick Cleveland Indians Postcards

Fans could obtain these black-and-white postcard-size (3-1/2" x 5-1/2") photos of their favorite Indians players by writing to radio broadcaster Van Patrick. Backs do not have postcard markings, and carry a message from Patrick. The unnumbered cards are checklisted here alphabetically, though the listing may not be complete.

		NM	EX	VG
	Common Player:	100.00	50.00	30.00
(1)	Don Black	100.00	50.00	30.00
(2)	Eddie Bockman	100.00	50.00	30.00
(3)	Lou Boudreau	200.00	100.00	60.00
(4)	Jack Conway	100.00	50.00	30.00
(5)	Hank Edwards	100.00	50.00	30.00
(6)	Red Embree	100.00	50.00	30.00
(7)	Bob Feller (Pitching)	300.00	150.00	90.00
(8)	Bob Feller (Pitching, leg in air.)	300.00	150.00	90.00
(9)	Les Fleming	100.00	50.00	30.00
(10)	Allen Gettel	100.00	50.00	30.00
(11)	Joe Gordon	125.00	62.00	37.00
(12)	Steve Gromek	100.00	50.00	30.00
(13)	Mel Harder	125.00	62.00	37.00
(14)	Jim Hegan	110.00	55.00	33.00
(15)	Ken Keltner	110.00	55.00	33.00
(16)	Ed Klieman	100.00	50.00	30.00
(17)	Bob Lemon	200.00	100.00	60.00
(18)	Al Lopez	200.00	100.00	60.00
(19)	George Metkovich	100.00	50.00	30.00
(20)	Dale Mitchell	100.00	50.00	30.00
(21)	Hal Peck	100.00	50.00	30.00
(22)	Eddie Robinson	100.00	50.00	30.00
(23)	Hank Ruszkowski	100.00	50.00	30.00
(24)	Pat Seerey	100.00	50.00	30.00
(25)	Bryan Stephens	100.00	50.00	30.00
(26)	Les Willis	100.00	50.00	30.00

1948-52 Cleveland Indians Pencil Clips

These celluloid and steel pencil clips were sold at the ballpark to be used on pencils given away with scorecards. The round button portion of the clip is about 3/4" in diameter, while the clip itself is a little over 1-1/2". Black-and-white player por-traits are centered in a colored border with the team name at top and player name at bottom. While many of the same players and photos were used year after year, issue date of the clips can be determined by the border color. In 1951-1952, when blue borders were used, the year is distinguished by the pres-ence (1951) or absence (1952) of a white union logo on back.

		NM	EX	VG
Common Player:		35.00	17.50	10.50
1948 (Black)				
(1)	Gene Bearden	35.00	17.50	10.50
(2)	John Berardino	40.00	20.00	12.00
(3)	Don Black	35.00	17.50	10.50
(4)	Lou Boudreau	45.00	22.00	13.50
(5)	Russ Christopher	35.00	17.50	10.50
(6)	Allie Clark	35.00	17.50	10.50
(7)	Larry Doby	60.00	30.00	18.00
(8)	Hank Edwards	35.00	17.50	10.50
(9)	Bob Feller	50.00	25.00	15.00
(10)	Al Gettel	35.00	17.50	10.50
(11)	Joe Gordon	35.00	17.50	10.50
(12)	Walt Judnich	35.00	17.50	10.50
(13)	Ken Keltner	35.00	17.50	10.50
(14)	Bob Lemon	45.00	22.00	13.50
(15)	Dale Mitchell	35.00	17.50	10.50
(16)	Bob Muncrief	35.00	17.50	10.50
(17)	Eddie Robinson	35.00	17.50	10.50
(18)	Pat Seerey	35.00	17.50	10.50
(19)	Joe Tipton	35.00	17.50	10.50
(20)	Thurman Tucker	35.00	17.50	10.50
1949 (Brown)				
(1)	Gene Bearden	35.00	17.50	10.50
(2)	Ray Boone	35.00	17.50	10.50
(3)	Lou Boudreau	45.00	22.00	13.50
(4)	Allie Clark	35.00	17.50	10.50
(5)	Larry Doby	55.00	27.00	16.50
(6)	Bob Feller	50.00	25.00	15.00
(7)	Mike Garcia	35.00	17.50	10.50
(8)	Joe Gordon	35.00	17.50	10.50
(9)	Steve Gromek	35.00	17.50	10.50
(10)	Jim Hegan	35.00	17.50	10.50
(11)	Ken Keltner	35.00	17.50	10.50
(12)	Bob Kennedy	35.00	17.50	10.50
(13)	Bob Lemon	45.00	22.00	13.50
(14)	Dale Mitchell	35.00	17.50	10.50
(15)	Satchel Paige	125.00	62.00	37.00
(16)	Mike Tresh	35.00	17.50	10.50
(17)	Bill Veeck	45.00	22.00	13.50
(18)	Mickey Vernon	35.00	17.50	10.50
(19)	Early Wynn	45.00	22.00	13.50
(20)	Sam Zoldak	35.00	17.50	10.50
1950 (White)				
(1)	Bobby Avila	35.00	17.50	10.50
(2)	Al Benton	35.00	17.50	10.50
(3)	Ray Boone	35.00	17.50	10.50
(4)	Lou Boudreau	45.00	22.00	13.50
(5)	Larry Doby	55.00	27.00	16.50
(6)	Luke Easter	40.00	20.00	12.00
(7)	Bob Feller	50.00	25.00	15.00
(8)	Mike Garcia	40.00	20.00	12.00
(9)	Steve Gromek	35.00	17.50	10.50
(10)	Jim Hegan	35.00	17.50	10.50
(11)	Bob Kennedy	35.00	17.50	10.50
(12)	Bob Lemon	45.00	22.00	13.50
(13)	Dale Mitchell	35.00	17.50	10.50
(14)	Ray Murray	35.00	17.50	10.50
(15)	Al Rosen	40.00	20.00	12.00
(16)	Thurman Tucker	35.00	17.50	10.50
(17)	Dick Weik	35.00	17.50	10.50
(18)	Early Wynn	45.00	22.00	13.50
1950 (Blue w/union logo.)				
(1)	Bobby Avila	35.00	17.50	10.50
(2)	Ray Boone	35.00	17.50	10.50
(3)	Larry Doby	55.00	27.00	16.50
(4)	Luke Easter	40.00	20.00	12.00
(5)	Bob Feller	50.00	25.00	15.00
(6)	Jim Hegan	35.00	17.50	10.50
(7)	Bob Kennedy	35.00	17.50	10.50
(8)	Bob Lemon	45.00	22.00	13.50
(9)	Al Lopez	45.00	22.00	13.50
(10)	Dale Mitchell	35.00	17.50	10.50
(11)	Al Rosen	40.00	20.00	12.00
(12)	Early Wynn	45.00	22.00	13.50
1952 (Blue, no logo.)				
(1)	Bobby Avila	35.00	17.50	10.50
(2)	Lou Brissie	35.00	17.50	10.50
(3)	Bob Chakales	35.00	17.50	10.50
(4)	Merrill Combs	35.00	17.50	10.50
(5)	Larry Doby	55.00	27.00	16.50
(6)	Luke Easter	40.00	20.00	12.00

(7)	Bob Feller	50.00	25.00	15.00
(8)	Mike Garcia	40.00	20.00	12.00
(9)	Steve Gromek	35.00	17.50	10.50
(10)	Jim Hegan	35.00	17.50	10.50
(11)	Sam Jones	35.00	17.50	10.50
(12)	Bob Lemon	45.00	22.00	13.50
(13)	Barney McCosky	35.00	17.50	10.50
(14)	Dale Mitchell	35.00	17.50	10.50
(15)	Pete Reiser	35.00	17.50	10.50
(16)	Al Rosen	45.00	22.50	13.50
(17)	Harry Simpson	35.00	17.50	10.50
(18)	Birdie Tebbetts	35.00	17.50	10.50
(19)	Early Wynn	45.00	22.00	13.50

1948 Cleveland Indians Picture Pack

For its second year of production as a souvenir sales item, the Indians picture pack utilized the basic format of the previous year: black-and-white photos with a white border and facsimile autograph. Backs were again blank. The 1948 set can be differentiated from the 1947 issue by its size; at 6-1/2" x 9", the '48s are larger by a half-inch horizontally and verti-cally. The unnumbered pictures are checklisted here in alpha-betical order. The specific content of the packs may have changed over the course of the season with roster moves.

		NM	EX	VG
Complete Set (33):		300.00	150.00	90.00
Common Player:		6.00	3.00	1.75
(1)	Gene Bearden	6.00	3.00	1.75
(2)	Johnny Berardino	12.00	6.00	3.50
(3)	Don Black	7.50	3.75	2.25
(4)	Lou Boudreau	20.00	10.00	6.00
(5)	Russ Christopher	6.00	3.00	1.75
(6)	Allie Clark	6.00	3.00	1.75
(7)	Larry Doby	25.00	12.50	7.50
(8)	Hank Edwards	6.00	3.00	1.75
(9)	Bob Feller	25.00	12.50	7.50
(10)	Joe Gordon	6.00	3.00	1.75
(11)	Hank Greenberg (GM, in uniform.)	40.00	20.00	12.00
(12)	Hank Greenberg (GM, in civies.)	20.00	10.00	6.00
(13)	Steve Gromek	6.00	3.00	1.75
(14)	Mel Harder	6.00	3.00	1.75
(15)	Jim Hegan	6.00	3.00	1.75
(16)	Walt Judnich	6.00	3.00	1.75
(17)	Ken Keltner	6.00	3.00	1.75
(18)	Bob Kennedy	6.00	3.00	1.75
(19)	Ed Klieman	6.00	3.00	1.75
(20)	Bob Lemon	20.00	10.00	6.00
(21)	Al Lopez	20.00	10.00	6.00
(22)	Bill McKechnie	20.00	10.00	6.00
(23)	Dale Mitchell	6.00	3.00	1.75
(24)	Bob Muncrief	6.00	3.00	1.75
(25)	Satchel Paige	60.00	30.00	18.00
(26)	Hal Peck	6.00	3.00	1.75
(27)	Eddie Robinson	6.00	3.00	1.75
(28)	Muddy Ruel	6.00	3.00	1.75
(29)	Joe Tipton	6.00	3.00	1.75
(30)	Thurman Tucker	6.00	3.00	1.75
(31)	Bill Veeck (Owner)	20.00	10.00	6.00
(32)	Sam Zoldak	6.00	3.00	1.75
(33)	Cleveland Municipal Stadium	9.00	4.50	2.75

1949 Cleveland Indians Display Photos

BOB FELLER - P, CLEVELAND INDIANS

Members of the Tribe are pictured (in the same poses found on their photo-pack issues) on these large-format (11" x 14") display photos, said to have been used for in-stadium promotions. It is possible there are others besides those checklisted here.

		NM	EX	VG
Complete Set (11):		650.00	325.00	200.00
Common Player:		40.00	20.00	12.00
(1)	Ray Boone	45.00	22.00	13.50
(2)	Larry Doby	100.00	50.00	30.00
(3)	Luke Easter	50.00	25.00	15.00
(4)	Bob Feller	125.00	62.00	37.00
(5)	Jim Hegan	40.00	20.00	12.00
(6)	Bob Kennedy	40.00	20.00	12.00
(7)	Bob Lemon	75.00	37.00	22.00
(8)	Al Lopez	75.00	37.00	22.00
(9)	Dale Mitchell	40.00	20.00	12.00
(10)	Al Rosen	50.00	25.00	15.00
(11)	Early Wynn	75.00	37.00	22.00

1949 Cleveland Indians Picture Pack - Action

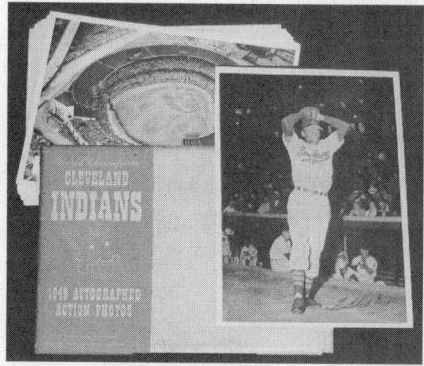

Posed action photos are the focus of this team-issued picture pack. The black-and-white 6-1/2" x 9" photos feature white borders all around and a facsimile autograph on front. Backs are blank. The set was sold in a red and white paper envelope labeled "World Champion Cleveland Indians Auto-graphed Action Photos." Backs are blank. The unnumbered pictures are checklisted here alphabetically. Unmarked reprints of this team-issue, complete with mailing envelope, were made in the late 1980s.

		NM	EX	VG
Complete Set (30):		175.00	90.00	55.00
Common Player:		4.00	2.00	1.25
(1)	Bob Avila	6.00	3.00	1.75
(2)	Gene Bearden	4.00	2.00	1.25
(3)	Al Benton	4.00	2.00	1.25
(4)	John Berardino	12.00	6.00	3.50
(5)	Ray Boone	6.00	3.00	1.75
(6)	Lou Boudreau	16.00	8.00	4.75
(7)	Allie Clark	4.00	2.00	1.25
(8)	Larry Doby	17.50	8.75	5.25
(9)	Bob Feller	20.00	10.00	6.00
(10)	Mike Garcia	6.00	3.00	1.75
(11)	Joe Gordon	4.00	2.00	1.25
(12)	Hank Greenberg (GM)	12.00	6.00	3.50
(13)	Steve Gromek	4.00	2.00	1.25
(14)	Jim Hegan	4.00	2.00	1.25
(15)	Ken Keltner	4.00	2.00	1.25
(16)	Bob Kennedy	4.00	2.00	1.25
(17)	Bob Lemon	12.00	6.00	3.50
(18)	Dale Mitchell	4.00	2.00	1.25
(19)	Satchel Paige	40.00	20.00	12.00
(20)	Frank Papish	4.00	2.00	1.25
(21)	Hal Peck	4.00	2.00	1.25
(22)	Al Rosen	8.00	4.00	2.50
(23)	Mike Tresh	4.00	2.00	1.25
(24)	Thurman Tucker	4.00	2.00	1.25
(25)	Bill Veeck (Owner)	12.00	6.00	3.50
(26)	Mickey Vernon	6.00	3.00	1.75
(27)	Early Wynn	12.00	6.00	3.50
(28)	Sam Zoldak	4.00	2.00	1.25
(29)	Indians coaches (Mel Harder, Steve O'Neill, Bill McKechnie, Muddy Ruel, George Susce)			
(30)	Municipal Stadium	6.00	3.00	1.75

1949 Cleveland Indians Picture Pack - Portraits

This set of player photos was produced by Big League Novelty Co., Cleveland, as credited on the paper envelope in which they were sold. The envelope has a crowned, big-nosed Indian caricature and mini-pictures of three of the players. The pictures are in a 6-1/2" x 9" blank-back format. They are black-and-white and virtually all depict the players in chest-to-cap portraits (many the same as previous and later years' issues) with a facsimile autograph. The unnumbered pictures are checklisted here alphabetically.

		NM	EX	VG
	Complete Set (20):	75.00	40.00	25.00
	Common Player:	3.00	1.50	.90
(1)	Bob Avila	4.50	2.25	1.25
(2)	Gene Bearden	3.00	1.50	.90
(3)	John Berardino	4.50	2.25	1.25
(4)	Lou Boudreau	7.50	3.75	2.25
(5)	Larry Doby	10.00	5.00	3.00
(6)	Bob Feller	12.50	6.25	3.75
(7)	Mike Garcia	4.50	2.25	1.25
(8)	Joe Gordon	3.00	1.50	.90
(9)	Steve Gromek	3.00	1.50	.90
(10)	Jim Hegan	3.00	1.50	.90
(11)	Ken Keltner	3.00	1.50	.90
(12)	Bob Kennedy	3.00	1.50	.90
(13)	Bob Lemon	5.00	2.50	1.50
(14)	Dale Mitchell	3.00	1.50	.90
(15)	Satchel Paige	30.00	15.00	9.00
(16)	Hal Peck	3.00	1.50	.90
(17)	Thurman Tucker	3.00	1.50	.90
(18)	Mickey Vernon	4.00	2.00	1.25
(19)	Early Wynn	5.00	2.50	1.50
(20)	Sam Zoldak	3.00	1.50	.90

1949 Cleveland Indians Sun Picture Camera

Lou Boudreau

These novelty cards are self-developing photoprints sold by the team in packages of four that included negatives and pieces of photo-sensative paper which were used to make the 1-7/8" x 2" black-and-white blank-back pictures. Because existing negatives could be used to make many new prints, values for the prints themselves are low. Prices quoted here are for negative/print combinations.

		NM	EX	VG
	Complete Set Negatives/Prints (20):	3,000	1,500	900.00
	Common Negative/Print:	125.00	65.00	35.00
(1)	Gene Bearden	125.00	65.00	35.00
(2)	Al Benton	125.00	65.00	35.00
(3)	Ray Boone	125.00	65.00	35.00
(4)	Lou Boudreau	200.00	100.00	60.00
(5)	Allie Clark	125.00	65.00	35.50
(6)	Larry Doby	250.00	125.00	75.00
(7)	Bob Feller	250.00	125.00	75.00
(8)	Mike Garcia	135.00	70.00	40.00
(9)	Joe Gordon	125.00	65.00	35.00
(10)	Steve Gromek	125.00	65.00	35.00
(11)	Jim Hegan	125.00	65.00	35.00
(12)	Ken Keltner	135.00	70.00	40.00
(13)	Bob Kennedy	125.00	65.00	35.00
(14)	Bob Lemon	200.00	100.00	60.00
(15)	Dale Mitchell	125.00	65.00	35.00
(16)	Hal Peck	125.00	65.00	35.00
(17)	Satchel Paige	400.00	200.00	120.00
(18)	Thurman Tucker	125.00	65.00	35.00
(19)	Mickey Vernon	125.00	65.00	35.00
(20)	Early Wynn	200.00	100.00	60.00

1950 Cleveland Indians Picture Pack

Similar in format to previous years' issues, these 6-1/2" x 9" black-and-white player poses have a white border and facsimile autograph on front. Backs are blank. The unnumbered photos are checklisted here alphabetically. It is possible the contents of specific picture packs changed over the course of the season to reflect roster moves.

	NM	EX	VG
Complete Set (27):	160.00	80.00	50.00
Common Player:	4.00	2.00	1.20

(1)	Bobby Avila	5.00	2.50	1.50
(2)	Gene Bearden	4.00	2.00	1.20
(3)	Al Benton	4.00	2.00	1.20
(4)	Ray Boone	5.00	2.50	1.50
(5)	Lou Boudreau	12.00	6.00	3.50
(6)	Allie Clark	4.00	2.00	1.20
(7)	Larry Doby	17.50	8.75	5.25
(8)	Luke Easter	6.00	3.00	1.75
(9)	Bob Feller	20.00	10.00	6.00
(10)	Jess Flores	4.00	2.00	1.20
(11)	Mike Garcia	5.00	2.50	1.50
(12)	Joe Gordon	4.00	2.00	1.20
(13)	Hank Greenberg (GM)	12.00	6.00	3.50
(14)	Steve Gromek	4.00	2.00	1.20
(15)	Jim Hegan	4.00	2.00	1.20
(16)	Bob Kennedy	4.00	2.00	1.20
(17)	Bob Lemon	12.00	6.00	3.50
(18)	Dale Mitchell	4.00	2.00	1.20
(19)	Ray Murray	4.00	2.00	1.20
(20)	Chick Pieretti	4.00	2.00	1.20
(21)	Al Rosen	6.00	3.00	1.75
(22)	Dick Rozek	4.00	2.00	1.20
(23)	Ellis Ryan (Owner)	4.00	2.00	1.20
(24)	Thurman Tucker	4.00	2.00	1.20
(25)	Early Wynn	12.00	6.00	3.50
(26)	Sam Zoldak	4.00	2.00	1.20
(27)	Cleveland Municipal Stadium	8.00	4.00	2.50

1951 Cleveland Indians Picture Pack

While this set of Indians pictures shares the 6-1/2" x 9" format of the Tribe's other team issues of the era, it is unique in its use of a much glossier front surface. Pictures are, with the exception of the manager, game-action or posed-action in black-and-white, bordered in white and with a facsimile autograph. Backs are blank. It is unknown whether this checklist is complete or whether players were added or removed to reflect in-season roster changes.

		NM	EX	VG
	Complete Set (26):	150.00	75.00	45.00
	Common Player:	4.00	2.00	1.25
(1)	Bob Avila	4.00	2.00	1.25
(2)	Gene Bearden	4.00	2.00	1.25
(3)	Ray Boone	6.00	3.00	1.75
(4)	Lou Brissie	4.00	2.00	1.25
(5)	Bob Chakales	4.00	2.00	1.25
(6)	Sam Chapman	4.00	2.00	1.25
(7)	Merrill Combs	4.00	2.00	1.25
(8)	Larry Doby	15.00	7.50	4.50
(9)	Luke Easter	6.00	3.00	1.75
(10)	Red Fahr	4.00	2.00	1.25
(11)	Bob Feller	20.00	10.00	6.00
(12)	Mike Garcia	6.00	3.00	1.75
(13)	Steve Gromek	4.00	2.00	1.25
(14)	Jim Hegan	4.00	2.00	1.25
(15)	Bob Kennedy	4.00	2.00	1.25
(16)	Bob Lemon	12.50	6.25	3.75
(17)	Al Lopez	12.50	6.25	3.75
(18)	Milt Neilsen	4.00	2.00	1.25
(19)	Al Rosen	8.00	4.00	2.50
(20)	Dick Rozek	4.00	2.00	1.25
(21)	Harry Simpson	4.00	2.00	1.25
(22)	Snuffy Stirnweiss	4.00	2.00	1.25
(23)	Birdie Tebbetts	4.00	2.00	1.25
(24)	Johnny Vander Meer	6.00	3.00	1.75
(25)	Early Wynn	12.50	6.25	3.75
(26)	George Zuverink	4.00	2.00	1.25

1952 Cleveland Indians Picture Pack

Like the 1951 Picture Pack, these pictures contain action poses, but are slightly smaller at 6" x 8-3/4". Unnumbered prints here are checklisted alphabetically.

		NM	EX	VG
	Complete Set (25):	150.00	75.00	45.00
	Common Player:	6.00	3.00	2.00
(1)	Bobby Avila	6.00	3.00	2.00
(2)	Johnny Bernardino	6.00	3.00	2.00
(3)	Ray Boone	6.00	3.00	2.00
(4)	Lou Brissie	6.00	3.00	2.00
(5)	Merrill Combs	6.00	3.00	2.00
(6)	Larry Doby	12.00	6.00	4.00
(7)	Luke Easter	6.00	3.00	2.00
(8)	Bob Feller	20.00	10.00	6.00
(9)	Jim Fridley	6.00	3.00	2.00
(10)	Mike Garcia	6.00	3.00	2.00
(11)	Steve Gromek	6.00	3.00	2.00
(12)	Mickey Harris	6.00	3.00	2.00
(13)	Jim Hegan	6.00	3.00	2.00
(14)	Sam Jones	6.00	3.00	2.00

(15)	Bob Lemon	12.00	6.00	4.00
(16)	Al Lopez	12.00	6.00	4.00
(17)	Dale Mitchell	6.00	3.00	2.00
(18)	Barney McCosky	6.00	3.00	2.00
(19)	Pete Reiser	6.00	3.00	2.00
(20)	Al Rosen	6.00	3.00	2.00
(21)	Dick Rozek	6.00	3.00	2.00
(22)	Harry Simpson	6.00	3.00	2.00
(23)	Birdie Tebbetts	6.00	3.00	2.00
(24)	Joe Tipton	6.00	3.00	2.00
(25)	Early Wynn	12.00	6.00	4.00

1954 Cleveland Indians Picture Pack

Because many of the pictures found in the championship season picture pack are the same poses found in earlier issues, size can be used to differentiate the years of issue. For 1954, the pictures were down-sized slightly in height, to a 6" x 8-3/4" format, and printed on heavier paper than in previous years. Each of the portraits, poses and action photos are bordered in white and include a facsimile autograph. The unnumbered pictures are checklisted here alphabetically.

		NM	EX	VG
	Complete Set (27):	125.00	65.00	40.00
	Common Player:	4.00	2.00	1.25
(1)	Bobby Avila	4.00	2.00	1.25
(2)	Sam Dente	4.00	2.00	1.25
(3)	Larry Doby	10.00	5.00	3.00
(4)	Bob Feller	15.00	7.50	4.50
(5)	Mike Garcia	4.00	2.00	1.25
(6)	Bill Glynn	4.00	2.00	1.25
(7)	Mike Hegan	4.00	2.00	1.25
(8)	Bob Hooper	4.00	2.00	1.25
(9)	Dave Hoskins	4.00	2.00	1.25
(10)	Art Houtteman	4.00	2.00	1.25
(11)	Bob Lemon	7.50	3.75	2.25
(12)	Al Lopez	7.50	3.75	2.25
(13)	Hank Majeski	4.00	2.00	1.25
(14)	Dale Mitchell	4.00	2.00	1.25
(15)	Don Mossi	6.00	3.00	1.75
(16)	Hal Naragon	4.00	2.00	1.25
(17)	Ray Narleski	4.00	2.00	1.25
(18)	Hal Newhouser	7.50	3.75	2.25
(19)	Dave Philley	4.00	2.00	1.25
(20)	Dave Pope	4.00	2.00	1.25
(21)	Rudy Regaldo	4.00	2.00	1.25
(22)	Al Rosen	6.00	3.00	1.75
(23)	Al Smith	4.00	2.00	1.25
(24)	George Strickland	4.00	2.00	1.25
(25)	Vic Wertz	4.00	2.00	1.25
(26)	Wally Westlake	4.00	2.00	1.25
(27)	Early Wynn	7.50	3.75	2.25

1955 Cleveland Indians Postcards

These team-issued black-and-white player postcards can be distinguished from earlier and later issues by the uniformity of the photos. All pictures are head-and-shoulder portraits against a white background. Players are wearing caps with Chief Wahoo inside a "C." Some cards are found with a notation on back, "Pub. by Ed Wood, Forestville, Calif." Cards were sent out to fans by the team and/or player and are usually found with an autograph on front.

		NM	EX	VG
	Complete Set (29):	400.00	200.00	120.00
	Common Player:	12.00	6.00	3.50
(1)	Bob Avila	15.00	7.50	4.50
(2)	Tony Cuccinello	12.00	6.00	3.50
(3)	Bud Daley	12.00	6.00	3.50
(4)	Sam Dente	12.00	6.00	3.50
(5)	Larry Doby	18.00	9.00	5.50
(6)	Bob Feller	30.00	15.00	9.00
(7)	Hank Foiles	12.00	6.00	3.50
(8)	Mike Garcia	12.00	6.00	3.50
(9)	Mel Harder	12.00	6.00	3.50
(10)	Jim Hegan	12.00	6.00	3.50
(11)	Art Houtteman	12.00	6.00	3.50
(12)	Ralph Kiner	20.00	10.00	6.00
(13)	Red Kress	12.00	6.00	3.50
(14)	Ken Kuhn	12.00	6.00	3.50
(15)	Bob Lemon	18.00	9.00	5.50
(16)	Bill Lobe	12.00	6.00	3.50
(17)	Dale Mitchell	12.00	6.00	3.50
(18)	Don Mossi	12.00	6.00	3.50
(19)	Hal Naragon	12.00	6.00	3.50
(20)	Ray Narleski	12.00	6.00	3.50
(21)	Dave Philley	12.00	6.00	3.50
(22)	Al Rosen	15.00	7.50	4.50
(23)	Herb Score	24.00	12.00	7.25
(24)	Al Smith	12.00	6.00	3.50
(25)	George Strickland	12.00	6.00	3.50

(26)	Vic Wertz	12.00	6.00	3.50
(27)	Wally Westlake	12.00	6.00	3.50
(28)	Bill Wright	12.00	6.00	3.50
(29)	Early Wynn	18.00	9.00	5.50

1956 Cleveland Indians Picture Pack

The Indians used a mix of styles in its souvenir picture pack for 1956. About 6-1/8" x 8-7/8", with white borders and blank backs, the pictures have a mix of portraits and posed action photos. Some pictures have a facsimile autograph while others have the players name in a white strip.

		NM	EX	VG
Complete Set (22):		90.00	45.00	27.50
Common Player:		4.00	2.00	1.25
(1)	Earl Averill	4.00	2.00	1.25
(2)	Bob Avila	4.00	2.00	1.25
(3)	Jim Busby	4.00	2.00	1.25
(4)	Chico Carrasquel	4.00	2.00	1.25
(5)	Rocky Colavito	20.00	10.00	6.00
(6)	Bob Feller	15.00	7.50	4.50
(7)	Mike Garcia	4.00	2.00	1.25
(8)	Jim Hegan	4.00	2.00	1.25
(9)	Art Houtteman	4.00	2.00	1.25
(10)	Bob Lemon	7.50	3.75	2.25
(11)	Al Lopez	7.50	3.75	2.25
(12)	Sam Mele	4.00	2.00	1.25
(13)	Dale Mitchell	4.00	2.00	1.25
(14)	Don Mossi	4.00	2.00	1.25
(15)	Hal Naragon	4.00	2.00	1.25
(16)	Ray Narleski	4.00	2.00	1.25
(17)	Al Rosen	5.00	2.50	1.50
(18)	Herb Score	7.50	3.75	2.25
(19)	Al Smith	4.00	2.00	1.25
(20)	George Strickland	4.00	2.00	1.25
(21)	Gene Woodling	4.00	2.00	1.25
(22)	Early Wynn	7.50	3.75	2.25

1937 Cleveland Press Indians Album

These newspaper cut-outs from the 1937 Cleveland Press depict Cleveland Indians players and coaches staff. Published at the start of their new season. Each cut-out has a paragraph at the bottom highlighting the player's performance in the 1936 season. The cut-outs measure 3-1/2 wide but measure between 7-9 inches long depending on the length of text and photo.

		NM	EX	VG
Complete Set (29):		300.00	150.00	75.00
Common player:		10.00	5.00	2.50
1	Frank Pytlak	10.00	5.00	2.50
2	Roy Weatherly	10.00	5.00	2.50
3	Roy Hughes	10.00	5.00	2.50
4	Bruce Campbell	10.00	5.00	2.50
5	Lyn Lary	10.00	5.00	2.50
6	Julius Solters	15.00	7.50	4.50
7	Earl Averill	15.00	7.50	4.50
8	Mel Harder	10.00	5.00	2.50
9	Tom Drake	10.00	5.00	2.50
10	Billy Sullivan	10.00	5.00	2.50
11	Whitlow Wyatt	10.00	5.00	2.50
12	Denny Galehouse	10.00	5.00	2.50
13	Earl Whitehill	10.00	5.00	2.50
14	Willis Hudlin	10.00	5.00	2.50
15	Odell Hale	10.00	5.00	2.50
16	Carl Fischer	10.00	5.00	2.50
17	Joe Becker	10.00	5.00	2.50
18	Bob Feller	30.00	15.00	9.00
19	Hal Trosky	15.00	7.50	4.50
20	Jeff Heath	10.00	5.00	2.50
21	Ivy Paul Andrews	10.00	5.00	2.50
22	Lloyd Brown	10.00	5.00	2.50
23	Johnny Allen	10.00	5.00	2.50
24	Joe Heving	10.00	5.00	2.50
25	John Kroner	10.00	5.00	2.50
26	George Uhle	10.00	5.00	2.50
27	Wally Schang	10.00	5.00	2.50
28	Max Weisman	10.00	5.00	2.50
29	Steve O'Neill	10.00	5.00	2.50

1884 Climax Poster

"Representatives of Professional Baseball in America" is the title of this sepia-toned lithograph produced by Lorillard tobacco as a premium for its Climax Red Tin Tag Plug chew. About 26" x 20", the poster depicts 16 top stars, managers and executives in street-clothed portraits on a background of ballplayers, equipment and ballparks.

	NM	EX	VG
1884 Climax	25,000	12,500	7,500
Representatives of Baseball			

1911 George Close Candy Co. (E94)

This 1911 issue is nearly identical to several contemporary candy and caramel sets. Issued by The George Close Co. of Cambridge, Mass., the approximately 1-1/2" x 2-3/4" cards feature color-tinted black-and-white player photos. Each card can be found with any of seven different background colors (blue, gold, green, olive, red, violet and yellow). Backs carry a set checklist. Eleven different back variations are known to exist. One variation contains just the checklist without any advertising, while 10 other variations include overprinted backs advertising various candy products manufactured by Close. The set carries the ACC designation E94.

		NM	EX	VG
Complete Set (30):		103,500	52,000	31,000
Common Player:		1,800	900.00	350.00
Advertising Backs: 4-6X				
(1)	Jimmy Austin	1,800	900.00	350.00
(2)	Johnny Bates	1,800	900.00	350.00
(3)	Bob Bescher	1,800	900.00	350.00
(4)	Bobby Byrne	1,800	900.00	350.00
(5)	Frank Chance	2,500	1,250	550.00
(6)	Ed Cicotte	3,000	1,500	650.00
(7)	Ty Cobb	20,000	10,000	3,600
(8)	Sam Crawford	2,100	1,050	630.00
(9)	Harry Davis	1,800	900.00	350.00
(10)	Art Devlin	1,800	900.00	350.00
(11)	Josh Devore	1,800	900.00	350.00
(12)	Mickey Doolan	1,800	900.00	350.00
(13)	Patsy Dougherty	1,800	900.00	350.00
(14)	Johnny Evers	2,500	1,250	550.00
(15)	Eddie Grant	1,800	900.00	350.00
(16)	Hugh Jennings	2,500	1,250	550.00
(17)	Red Kleinow	1,800	900.00	350.00
(18)	Joe Lake	1,800	900.00	350.00
(19)	Nap Lajoie	3,000	1,500	750.00
(20)	Tommy Leach	1,800	900.00	350.00
(21)	Hans Lobert	1,800	900.00	350.00
(22)	Harry Lord	1,800	900.00	350.00
(23)	Sherry Magee	1,800	900.00	350.00
(24)	John McGraw	2,500	1,250	600.00
(25)	Earl Moore	1,800	900.00	350.00
(26)	Red Murray	1,800	900.00	350.00
(27)	Tris Speaker	4,000	2,000	1,000
(28)	Terry Turner	1,800	900.00	350.00
(29)	Honus Wagner	20,000	10,000	3,600
(30)	"Old" Cy Young	15,000	7,500	2,500

1961 Cloverleaf Dairy Minnesota Twins

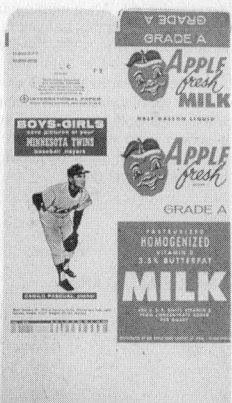

These unnumbered cards picture members of the debut Minnesota Twins team. Measuring approximately 3-3/4" x 7-3/4", the cards were actually side panels from Cloverleaf (and Apple Fresh brand) Milk cartons. Complete cartons are valued at about twice the prices listed. The card includes a black-and-white player photo with name, position, personal data and year-by-year statistics appearing below. Green graphics highlight the panels. Some pictures were reissued in 1962 but can be differentiated from the 1961 set by the stats at bottom.

		NM	EX	VG
Complete Set (17):		1,125	550.00	335.00
Common Player:		75.00	37.00	22.00
(1)	Earl Battey	75.00	37.00	22.00
(2)	Reno Bertoia	75.00	37.00	22.00
(3)	Billy Gardner	75.00	37.00	22.00
(4)	Paul Giel	75.00	37.00	22.00
(5)	Lenny Green	75.00	37.00	22.00
(6)	Jim Kaat	80.00	40.00	24.00
(7)	Jack Kralick	75.00	37.00	22.00
(8)	Don Lee	75.00	37.00	22.00
(9)	Jim Lemon	75.00	37.00	22.00
(10)	Billy Martin	90.00	45.00	27.00
(11)	Don Mincher	75.00	37.00	22.00
(12)	Camilo Pascual	80.00	40.00	24.00
(13)	Pedro Ramos	75.00	37.00	22.00
(14)	Chuck Stobbs	75.00	37.00	22.00
(15)	Bill Tuttle	75.00	37.00	22.00
(16)	Jose Valdivielso	75.00	37.00	22.00
(17)	Zoilo Versalles	80.00	40.00	24.00

1962 Cloverleaf Dairy Minnesota Twins

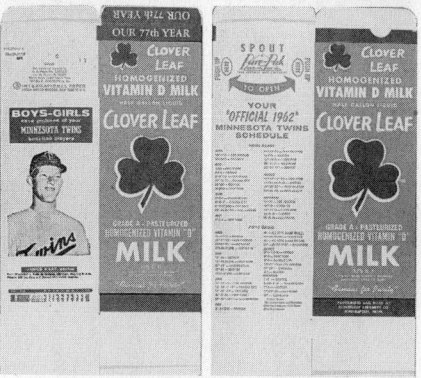

These unnumbered cards picture members of the Minnesota Twins. Measuring approximately 3-3/4" x 7-3/4", the cards were actually side panels from Cloverleaf (and Apple Fresh brand) Milk cartons. Complete cartons are valued at about twice the prices listed. The card includes a black-and-white player photo with name, position, personal data and year-by-year statistics appearing below. Green graphics highlight the panels. Some pictures were reissued in 1962 but can be differentiated from the 1961 set by the stats at bottom.

		NM	EX	VG
Complete Set (24):		1,400	700.00	425.00
Common Player:		75.00	37.00	22.00
(1)	Bernie Allen	75.00	37.00	22.00
(2)	George Banks	75.00	37.00	22.00
(3)	Earl Battey	75.00	37.00	22.00
(4)	Joe Bonikowski	75.00	37.00	22.00
(5)	John Goryl	75.00	37.00	22.00
(6)	Lenny Green	75.00	37.00	22.00
(7)	Jim Kaat	80.00	40.00	24.00
(8)	Jack Kralick	75.00	37.00	22.00
(9)	Jim Lemon	75.00	37.00	22.00
(10)	Georges Maranda	75.00	37.00	22.00
(11)	Orlando Martinez	75.00	37.00	22.00
(12)	Don Mincher	75.00	37.00	22.00
(13)	Ray Moore	75.00	37.00	22.00
(14)	Hal Naragon	75.00	37.00	22.00
(15)	Camilo Pascual	80.00	40.00	24.00
(16)	Vic Power	80.00	40.00	24.00
(17)	Rich Rollins	75.00	37.00	22.00
(18)	Theodore Sadowski	75.00	37.00	22.00
(19)	Albert Stange	75.00	37.00	22.00
(20)	Dick Stigman	75.00	37.00	22.00
(21)	Bill Tuttle	75.00	37.00	22.00
(22)	Zoilo Versalles	80.00	40.00	24.00
(23)	Gerald Zimmerman	75.00	37.00	22.00
(24)	Manager and Coaches (Floyd Baker, Edward Fitz Gerald, Gordon Maltzberger, Sam Mele, George Strickland)	75.00	37.00	22.00

1912 Ty Cobb Postcard

There is no indication of a publisher on this card, nor that it is part of a multi-player series. In standard postcard format of 5-1/2" x 3-1/2", the card has a black-and-white photograph of a smiling Cobb and a caption in the bottom border, "TY COBB WORLD'S GREATEST BALL PLAYER AND HIS FAVORITE BAT." The divided back has standard postcard markings.

	NM	EX	VG
Ty Cobb	3,500	1,750	1,000

1947 Coca-Cola All Time Sports Favorite

In 1947 Coke produced a series of 10 All Time Sports Favorite cardboard signs. On heavy cardboard with a framed look, the 13" x 15" signs have color artwork at center. In the bottom border are a few words about the athlete, along with a Coke bottle and round red logo. Only one baseball player appears in the series.

	NM	EX	VG
Ty Cobb	2,000	1,000	600.00

1952 Coca-Cola Playing Tips Test Cards

Apparently a regional issue to test the concept of baseball playing tips cards inserted into cartons of soda bottles, these test cards have a number of differences to the version which was more widely issued. The test cards feature a colorful drawing of the player with a bottle of Coke, along with his name in script and his team. Backs are printed in red on gray cardboard. Rizzuto's card has been seen with three different playing tips. Mays' card has a biography instead of a playing tip. The cards are irregularly shaped, measuring about 3-1/2" at their widest point, and about 7-1/2" in length.

	NM	EX	VG
Complete Set (4):	9,000	4,500	2,700
(1) Willie Mays	5,000	2,500	1,500
(2) Phil Rizzuto (Bunting tips.)	2,500	1,250	750.00
(3) Phil Rizzuto (Pitching tips.)	2,500	1,250	750.00
(4) Phil Rizzuto (SS fielding tips.)	2,500	1,250	750.00

1952 Coca-Cola Playing Tips

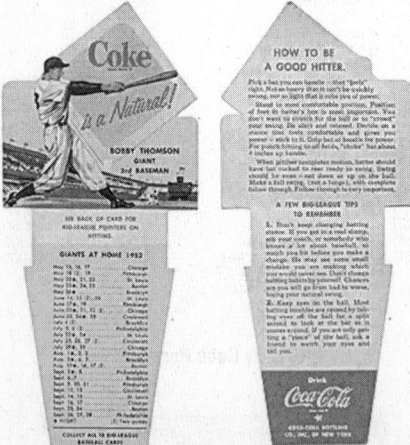

While more widely distributed than the three test cards, the 10-card set of playing tips cards is still scarce today. Issued in the metropolitan New York region, the cards include only players from the Yankees, Giants and Dodgers. Fronts feature color paintings of players in action, though the artwork bears little actual resemblance to the players named. The phrase "Coke is a natural" is in the background on pennants, panels, etc. The player's name, team and position are included in the picture. In the portion of the card meant to be inserted into the soda-bottle carton, the home schedule of the player's team for 1952 is presented. Printed in red on back are tips for playing the position of the pictured player. Cards are irregularly shaped, measuring about 3-1/2" at their widest point, and 7-1/2" in length. The unnumbered cards are checklisted here in alphabetical order.

	NM	EX	VG
Complete Set (10):	2,100	1,050	625.00
Common Player:	160.00	80.00	50.00
(1) Hank Bauer	275.00	135.00	82.00
(2) Carl Furillo	350.00	175.00	105.00
(3) Gil Hodges	450.00	225.00	135.00

(4) Ed Lopat	190.00	95.00	57.00
(5) Gil McDougald	250.00	125.00	75.00
(6) Don Mueller	150.00	75.00	45.00
(7) Pee Wee Reese	450.00	225.00	135.00
(8) Bobby Thomson (3B)	250.00	125.00	75.00
(9) Bobby Thomson (Hitting)	350.00	175.00	105.00
(10) Wes Westrum	150.00	75.00	45.00

1953 Coca-Cola Signs

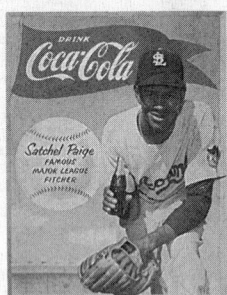

The attributed date is approximate, based on the uniforms in which the players are pictured. It is possible the series was issued over more than one year. The signs vary in size from about 10" x 12" to 12" x 15" and are made of cardboard. Some are die-cut to produce an irregular shape. Players are pictured in color artwork holding a bottle of Coke with one of several styles of Coca-Cola logo in the background.

	NM	EX	VG
Common Player:	750.00	375.00	225.00
(1) Bill Bruton	800.00	400.00	240.00
(2) Roy Campanella	2,500	1,250	750.00
(3) Larry Doby	1,500	750.00	450.00
(4) Monte Irvin	1,500	750.00	450.00
(5) Satchel Paige	4,000	2,000	1,200
(6) Phil Rizzuto	2,500	1,250	750.00

1967-68 Coca-Cola Bottle Caps

Over two seasons, bottles of Coke products (Coca-Cola, Fresca, Tab and Fanta) were sealed with caps bearing the pictures of major league ballplayers. The 1" diameter caps have a small baseball symbol on the top of the cap. Inside, protected by a clear plastic liner, is a black-and-white portrait photo of a player. (Most photos have cap insignia blacked out.) His team nickname is printed at top, his name at bottom and his position at right. To the left of the picture is an identification number, usually with a letter prefix. In areas with major league baseball teams, regional issues of the caps featured local players with a letter prefix to the number. Also released in those areas were American League or National League All-Star sets, with cap number preceded by an "A" or "N." In areas not served by major league teams, a 35-cap All-Star series with no prefix letter was issued. While most caps were identical in both years of issue, some player team changes, etc., were reflected in updated caps in 1968. Severe bending by bottle openers and rust are specific detriments to condition often found on these caps. Collectors usually save these caps without regard to which specific brand of soda appears on top, though obviously the Coca-Cola pieces are much more common. Cap-saver sheets were available which, when filled, could be exchanged for a team set of photocards (see 1967 Dexter Press Premiums) or other prizes.

	NM	EX	VG
Complete Set (580):	4,000	2,000	1,200
Common Player:	5.00	2.50	1.50
Playing Tips (16):	3.00	1.50	.90
Sprite, Fresca, Tab + 10 Percent			

MAJOR LEAGUE ALL-STARS

1	Richie Allen	7.50	3.75	2.25
2	Pete Rose	32.50	16.00	9.75
3	Brooks Robinson	25.00	12.50	7.50
4	Marcelino Lopez	5.00	2.50	1.50
5	Rusty Staub	5.00	2.50	1.50
6	Ron Santo	7.50	3.75	2.25
7	Jim Nash	5.00	2.50	1.50
8	Jim Fregosi	5.00	2.50	1.50
9	Paul Casanova	5.00	2.50	1.50
10	Willie Mays	45.00	22.50	13.50
11	Willie Stargell	15.00	7.50	4.50
12	Tony Oliva	7.50	3.75	2.25
13	Joe Pepitone	7.50	3.75	2.25
14	Juan Marichal	12.00	6.00	3.50
15	Jim Bunning	12.00	6.00	3.50
16	Claude Osteen	5.00	2.50	1.50
17	Carl Yastrzemski	25.00	12.50	7.50
18	Harmon Killebrew	25.00	12.50	7.50
19	Hank Aaron	45.00	22.50	13.50
20	Joe Torre	7.50	3.75	2.25
21	Ernie Banks	25.00	12.50	7.50
22	Al Kaline	25.00	12.50	7.50
23	Frank Robinson	25.00	12.50	7.50
24	Max Alvis	5.00	2.50	1.50
25	Elston Howard	7.50	3.75	

26	Gaylord Perry	12.00	6.00	3.50
27	Bill Mazeroski	12.00	6.00	3.50
28	Ron Swoboda	5.00	2.50	1.50
29	Vada Pinson	7.50	3.75	2.25
30	Joe Morgan	25.00	12.50	7.50
31	Cleon Jones	5.00	2.50	1.50
32	Willie Horton	5.00	2.50	1.50
33	Leon Wagner	5.00	2.50	1.50
34	George Scott	5.00	2.50	1.50
35	Ed Charles	5.00	2.50	1.50

NATIONAL LEAGUE ALL-STARS

N7	Tom Seaver	15.00	7.00	4.50
N19	Hank Aaron	40.00	20.00	12.00
N20	Jim Bunning	10.00	5.00	3.00
N21	Joe Torre	6.00	3.00	1.75
N22	Claude Osteen	5.00	2.50	1.50
N23	Ron Santo	6.00	3.00	1.75
N24	Joe Morgan	20.00	10.00	6.00
N25	Richie Allen	6.00	3.00	1.75
N26	Ron Swoboda	5.00	2.50	1.50
N27	Ernie Banks	20.00	10.00	6.00
N28	Bill Mazeroski	12.00	6.00	3.50
N29	Willie Stargell	12.00	6.00	3.50
N30	Pete Rose	25.00	12.50	7.50
N31	Gaylord Perry	10.00	5.00	3.00
N32	Rusty Staub	5.00	2.50	1.50
N33	Vada Pinson	6.00	3.00	1.75
N34	Juan Marichal	10.00	5.00	3.00
N35	Cleon Jones	5.00	2.50	1.50

AMERICAN LEAGUE ALL-STARS

A19	Al Kaline	20.00	10.00	6.00
A20	Frank Howard	5.00	2.50	1.50
A21	Brooks Robinson	20.00	10.00	6.00
A22	George Scott	5.00	2.50	1.50
A23	Willie Horton	5.00	2.50	1.50
A24	Jim Fregosi	5.00	2.50	1.50
A25	Ed Charles	5.00	2.50	1.50
A26	Harmon Killebrew	20.00	10.00	6.00
A27	Tony Oliva	6.00	3.00	1.75
A28	Joe Pepitone	6.00	3.00	1.75
A29	Elston Howard	6.00	3.00	1.75
A30	Jim Nash	5.00	2.50	1.50
A31	Marcelino Lopez	5.00	2.50	1.50
A32	Frank Robinson	20.00	10.00	6.00
A33	Leon Wagner	5.00	2.50	1.50
A34	Max Alvis	5.00	2.50	1.50
A35	Paul Casanova	5.00	2.50	1.50

PLAYING TIPS

19	SS fields ball . . .	3.00	1.50	.90
20	2b relays . . .	3.00	1.50	.90
21	1b completes DP	3.00	1.50	.90
22	Pitcher fields bunt . . .	3.00	1.50	.90
23	2b relays . . .	3.00	1.50	.90
24	1b complete DP	3.00	1.50	.90
25	CF makes catch . . .	3.00	1.50	.90
26	Catcher tags runner	3.00	1.50	.90

1967 ATLANTA BRAVES

B1	Gary Geiger	5.00	2.50	1.50
B2	Ty Cline	5.00	2.50	1.50
B3	Hank Aaron	45.00	22.50	13.50
B4	Gene Oliver	5.00	2.50	1.50
B5	Tony Cloninger	5.00	2.50	1.50
B6	Denis Menke	5.00	2.50	1.50
B7	Denny Lemaster	5.00	2.50	1.50
B8	Woody Woodward	5.00	2.50	1.50
B9	Joe Torre	7.50	3.75	2.25
B10	Ken Johnson	5.00	2.50	1.50
B11	Bob Bruce	5.00	2.50	1.50
B12	Felipe Alou	7.50	3.75	2.25
B13	Clete Boyer	5.00	2.50	1.50
B14	Wade Blasingame	5.00	2.50	1.50
B15	Don Schwall	5.00	2.50	1.50
B16	Dick Kelley	5.00	2.50	1.50
B17	Rico Carty	6.00	3.00	1.75
B18	Mack Jones	5.00	2.50	1.50

1968 ATLANTA BRAVES

B1	Cecil Upshaw	5.00	2.50	1.50
B2	Tito Francona	5.00	2.50	1.50
B3	Hank Aaron	40.00	20.00	12.00
B4	Pat Jarvis	5.00	2.50	1.50
B5	Tony Cloninger	5.00	2.50	1.50
B6	Phil Niekro	15.00	7.50	4.50
B7	Felix Millan	5.00	2.50	1.50
B8	Woody Woodward	5.00	2.50	1.50
B9	Joe Torre	7.50	3.75	2.25
B10	Ken Johnson	5.00	2.50	1.50
B11	Marty Martinez	5.00	2.50	1.50
B12	Felipe Alou	7.50	3.75	2.25
B13	Clete Boyer	5.00	2.50	1.50
B14	Sonny Jackson	5.00	2.50	1.50
B15	Deron Johnson	5.00	2.50	1.50
B16	Claude Raymond	5.00	2.50	1.50
B17	Rico Carty	6.00	3.00	1.75
B18	Mack Jones	5.00	2.50	1.50

1967 BALTIMORE ORIOLES

O1	Dave McNally	5.00	2.50	1.50
O2	Luis Aparicio	20.00	10.00	6.00
O3	Paul Blair	5.00	2.50	1.50
O4	Frank Robinson	25.00	12.50	7.50
O5	Jim Palmer	30.00	15.00	9.00
O6	Russ Snyder	5.00	2.50	1.50
O7	Stu Miller	5.00	2.50	1.50
O8	Dave Johnson	5.00	2.50	1.50
O9	Andy Etchebarren	5.00	2.50	1.50
O10	Brooks Robinson	25.00	12.50	7.50
O11	John Powell	12.00	6.00	3.50
O12	Sam Bowens	5.00	2.50	1.50
O13	Curt Blefary	5.00	2.50	1.50
O14	Ed Fisher	5.00	2.50	1.50
O15	Wally Bunker	5.00	2.50	1.50
O16	Moe Drabowsky	5.00	2.50	1.50
O17	Larry Haney	5.00	2.50	1.50
O18	Tom Phoebus	5.00	2.50	1.50

1968 BALTIMORE ORIOLES

O1	Dave McNally	5.00	2.50	1.50
O2	Jim Hardin	5.00	2.50	1.50
O3	Paul Blair	5.00	2.50	1.50
O4	Frank Robinson	25.00	12.50	7.50

O5	Bruce Howard	5.00	2.50	1.50
O6	John O'Donoghue	5.00	2.50	1.50
O7	Dave May	5.00	2.50	1.50
O8	Dave Johnson	5.00	2.50	1.50
O9	Andy Etchebarren	5.00	2.50	1.50
O10	Brooks Robinson	25.00	12.50	7.50
O11	John Powell	8.00	4.00	2.50
O12	Pete Richert	5.00	2.50	1.50
O13	Curt Blefary	5.00	2.50	1.50
O14	Mark Belanger	6.00	3.00	1.75
O15	Wally Bunker	5.00	2.50	1.50
O16	Don Buford	5.00	2.50	1.50
O17	Larry Haney	5.00	2.50	1.50
O18	Tom Phoebus	5.00	2.50	1.50

1967 BOSTON RED SOX

R1	Lee Stange	5.00	2.50	1.50
R2	Carl Yastrzemski	30.00	15.00	9.00
R3	Don Demeter	5.00	2.50	1.50
R4	Jose Santiago	5.00	2.50	1.50
R5	Darrell Brandon	5.00	2.50	1.50
R6	Joe Foy	5.00	2.50	1.50
R7	Don McMahon	5.00	2.50	1.50
R8	Dalton Jones	5.00	2.50	1.50
R9	Mike Ryan	5.00	2.50	1.50
R10	Bob Tillman	5.00	2.50	1.50
R11	Rico Petrocelli	6.00	3.00	1.75
R12	George Scott	5.00	2.50	1.50
R13	George Smith	5.00	2.50	1.50
R14	Dennis Bennett	5.00	2.50	1.50
R15	Hank Fischer	5.00	2.50	1.50
R16	Jim Lonborg	6.00	3.00	1.75
R17	Jose Tartabull	5.00	2.50	1.50
R18	George Thomas	5.00	2.50	1.50

1968 BOSTON RED SOX

R1	Lee Stange	5.00	2.50	1.50
R2	Gary Waslewski	5.00	2.50	1.50
R3	Gary Bell	5.00	2.50	1.50
R4	John Wyatt	5.00	2.50	1.50
R5	Darrell Brandon	5.00	2.50	1.50
R6	Joe Foy	5.00	2.50	1.50
R7	Ray Culp	5.00	2.50	1.50
R8	Dalton Jones	5.00	2.50	1.50
R9	Gene Oliver	5.00	2.50	1.50
R10	Jose Santiago	5.00	2.50	1.50
R11	Rico Petrocelli	6.00	3.00	1.75
R12	George Scott	5.00	2.50	1.50
R13	Mike Andrews	5.00	2.50	1.50
R14	Dick Ellsworth	5.00	2.50	1.50
R15	Norm Siebern	5.00	2.50	1.50
R16	Jim Lonborg	6.00	3.00	1.75
R17	Jerry Adair	5.00	2.50	1.50
R18	Elston Howard	5.00	2.50	1.50

1967 CALIFORNIA ANGELS

L19	Len Gabrielson	5.00	2.50	1.50
L20	Jackie Hernandez	5.00	2.50	1.50
L21	Paul Schaal	5.00	2.50	1.50
L22	Lew Burdette	5.00	2.50	1.50
L23	Jimmie Hall	5.00	2.50	1.50
L24	Fred Newman	5.00	2.50	1.50
L25	Don Mincher	5.00	2.50	1.50
L26	Bob Rodgers	5.00	2.50	1.50
L27	Jack Sanford	5.00	2.50	1.50
L28	Bobby Knoop	5.00	2.50	1.50
L29	Jose Cardenal	5.00	2.50	1.50
L30	Jim Fregosi	5.00	2.50	1.50
L31	George Brunet	5.00	2.50	1.50
L32	Marcelino Lopez	5.00	2.50	1.50
L33	Minnie Rojas	5.00	2.50	1.50
L34	Jay Johnstone	5.00	2.50	1.50
L35	Ed Kirkpatrick	5.00	2.50	1.50

1967 CHICAGO CUBS

C1	Ferguson Jenkins	15.00	7.50	4.50
C2	Ernie Banks	30.00	15.00	9.00
C3	Glenn Beckert	5.00	2.50	1.50
C4	Bob Hendley	5.00	2.50	1.50
C5	John Boccabella	5.00	2.50	1.50
C6	Ron Campbell	5.00	2.50	1.50
C7	Ray Culp	5.00	2.50	1.50
C8	Adolfo Phillips	5.00	2.50	1.50
C9	Don Bryant	5.00	2.50	1.50
C10	Randy Hundley	5.00	2.50	1.50
C11	Ron Santo	6.00	3.00	1.75
C12	Lee Thomas	5.00	2.50	1.50
C13	Billy Williams	25.00	12.50	7.50
C14	Ken Holtzman	5.00	2.50	1.50
C15	Cal Koonce	5.00	2.50	1.50
C16	Curt Simmons	5.00	2.50	1.50
C17	George Altman	5.00	2.50	1.50
C18	Bryon Browne	5.00	2.50	1.50

CHICAGO WHITE SOX

L1	Gary Peters	5.00	2.50	1.50
L2	Jerry Adair	5.00	2.50	1.50
L3	Al Weis	5.00	2.50	1.50
L4	Pete Ward	5.00	2.50	1.50
L5	Hoyt Wilhelm	15.00	7.50	4.50
L6	Don Buford	5.00	2.50	1.50
L7	John Buzhardt	5.00	2.50	1.50
L8	Wayne Causey	5.00	2.50	1.50
L9	Jerry McNertney	5.00	2.50	1.50
L10	Ron Hansen	5.00	2.50	1.50
L11	Tom McCraw	5.00	2.50	1.50
L12	Jim O'Toole	5.00	2.50	1.50
L13	Bill Skowron	6.00	3.00	1.75
L14	Joel Horlen	5.00	2.50	1.50
L15	Tommy John	12.00	6.00	3.50
L16	Bob Locker	5.00	2.50	1.50
L17	Ken Berry	5.00	2.50	1.50
L18	Tommie Agee	5.00	2.50	1.50

1967 CINCINNATI REDS

F1	Floyd Robinson	5.00	2.50	1.50
F2	Leo Cardenas	5.00	2.50	1.50
F3	Gordy Coleman	5.00	2.50	1.50
F4	Tommy Harper	5.00	2.50	1.50
F5	Tommy Helms	5.00	2.50	1.50
F6	Deron Johnson	5.00	2.50	1.50
F7	Jim Maloney	5.00	2.50	1.50
F8	Tony Perez	25.00	12.50	7.50
F9	Don Pavletich	5.00	2.50	1.50
F10	John Edwards	5.00	2.50	1.50
F11	Vada Pinson	7.50	3.75	2.25
F12	Chico Ruiz	5.00	2.50	1.50
F13	Pete Rose	40.00	20.00	12.00
F14	Bill McCool	5.00	2.50	1.50
F15	Joe Nuxhall	5.00	2.50	1.50
F16	Milt Pappas	5.00	2.50	1.50
F17	Art Shamsky	5.00	2.50	1.50
F18	Dick Simpson	5.00	2.50	1.50

1967 CLEVELAND INDIANS

I1	Luis Tiant	6.00	3.00	1.75
I2	Max Alvis	5.00	2.50	1.50
I3	Larry Brown	5.00	2.50	1.50
I4	Rocky Colavito	10.00	5.00	3.00
I5	John O'Donoghue	5.00	2.50	1.50
I6	Pedro Gonzalez	5.00	2.50	1.50
I7	Gary Bell	5.00	2.50	1.50
I8	Sonny Siebert	5.00	2.50	1.50
I9	Joe Azcue	5.00	2.50	1.50
I10	Lee Maye	5.00	2.50	1.50
I11	Chico Salmon	5.00	2.50	1.50
I12	Leon Wagner	5.00	2.50	1.50
I13	Fred Whitfield	5.00	2.50	1.50
I14	Jack Kralick	5.00	2.50	1.50
I15	Sam McDowell	6.00	3.00	1.75
I16	Dick Radatz	5.00	2.50	1.50
I17	Vic Davalillo	5.00	2.50	1.50
I18	Chuck Hinton	5.00	2.50	1.50

1968 CLEVELAND INDIANS

I1	Luis Tiant	6.00	3.00	1.75
I2	Max Alvis	5.00	2.50	1.50
I3	Larry Brown	5.00	2.50	1.50
I4	Tommy Harper	5.00	2.50	1.50
I5	Vern Fuller	5.00	2.50	1.50
I6	Jose Cardenal	5.00	2.50	1.50
I7	Dave Nelson	5.00	2.50	1.50
I8	Sonny Siebert	5.00	2.50	1.50
I9	Joe Azcue	5.00	2.50	1.50
I10	Lee Maye	5.00	2.50	1.50
I11	Chico Salmon	5.00	2.50	1.50
I12	Leon Wagner	5.00	2.50	1.50
I13	Eddie Fisher	5.00	2.50	1.50
I14	Stan Williams	5.00	2.50	1.50
I15	Sam McDowell	6.00	3.00	1.75
I16	Steve Hargan	5.00	2.50	1.50
I17	Vic Davalillo	5.00	2.50	1.50
I18	Duke Sims	5.00	2.50	1.50

1967 DETROIT TIGERS

T1	Larry Sherry	5.00	2.50	1.50
T2	Norm Cash	7.50	3.75	2.25
T3	Jerry Lumpe	5.00	2.50	1.50
T4	Dave Wickersham	5.00	2.50	1.50
T5	Joe Sparma	5.00	2.50	1.50
T6	Dick McAuliffe	5.00	2.50	1.50
T7	Fred Gladding	5.00	2.50	1.50
T8	Jim Northrup	5.00	2.50	1.50
T9	Bill Freehan	5.00	2.50	1.50
T10	Earl Wilson	5.00	2.50	1.50
T11	Dick Tracewski	5.00	2.50	1.50
T12	Don Wert	5.00	2.50	1.50
T13	Jake Wood	5.00	2.50	1.50
T14	Mickey Lolich	6.00	3.00	1.75
T15	Johnny Podres	5.00	2.50	1.50
T16	Bill Monbouquette	5.00	2.50	1.50
T17	Al Kaline	30.00	15.00	9.00
T18	Willie Horton	5.00	2.50	1.50

1968 DETROIT TIGERS

T1	Ray Oyler	5.00	2.50	1.50
T2	Norm Cash	7.50	3.75	2.25
T3	Mike Marshall	5.00	2.50	1.50
T4	Mickey Stanley	5.00	2.50	1.50
T5	Joe Sparma	5.00	2.50	1.50
T6	Dick McAuliffe	5.00	2.50	1.50
T7	Gates Brown	5.00	2.50	1.50
T8	Jim Northrup	5.00	2.50	1.50
T9	Bill Freehan	5.00	2.50	1.50
T10	Earl Wilson	5.00	2.50	1.50
T11	Dick Tracewski	5.00	2.50	1.50
T12	Don Wert	5.00	2.50	1.50
T13	Dennis Ribant	5.00	2.50	1.50
T14	Mickey Lolich	6.00	3.00	1.75
T15	Denny McLain	12.00	6.00	3.50
T16	Ed Mathews	25.00	12.50	7.50
T17	Al Kaline	30.00	15.00	9.00
T18	Willie Horton	5.00	2.50	1.50

1967 HOUSTON ASTROS

H1	Dave Giusti	5.00	2.50	1.50
H2	Bob Aspromonte	5.00	2.50	1.50
H3	Ron Davis	5.00	2.50	1.50
H4	Claude Raymond	5.00	2.50	1.50
H5	Barry Latman	5.00	2.50	1.50
H6	Chuck Harrison	5.00	2.50	1.50
H7	Bill Heath	5.00	2.50	1.50
H8	Sonny Jackson	5.00	2.50	1.50
H9	John Bateman	5.00	2.50	1.50
H10	Ron Brand	5.00	2.50	1.50
H11	Aaron Pointer	5.00	2.50	1.50
H12	Joe Morgan	25.00	12.50	7.50
H13	Rusty Staub	6.00	3.00	1.75
H14	Mike Cuellar	5.00	2.50	1.50
H15	Larry Dierker	5.00	2.50	1.50
H16	Dick Farrell	5.00	2.50	1.50
H17	Jim Landis	5.00	2.50	1.50
H18	Ed Mathews	25.00	12.50	7.50

1968 HOUSTON ASTROS

H1	Dave Giusti	5.00	2.50	1.50
H2	Bob Aspromonte	5.00	2.50	1.50
H3	Ron Davis	5.00	2.50	1.50
H4	Julio Gotay	5.00	2.50	1.50
H5	Fred Gladding	5.00	2.50	1.50
H6	Lee Thomas	5.00	2.50	1.50
H7	Wade Blasingame	5.00	2.50	1.50
H8	Denis Menke	5.00	2.50	1.50
H9	John Bateman	5.00	2.50	1.50
H10	Ron Brand	5.00	2.50	1.50
H11	Doug Rader	5.00	2.50	1.50
H12	Joe Morgan	25.00	12.50	7.50
H13	Rusty Staub	6.00	3.00	1.75
H14	Mike Cuellar	5.00	2.50	1.50
H15	Larry Dierker	5.00	2.50	1.50
H16	Denny Lemaster	5.00	2.50	1.50
H17	Jim Wynn	5.00	2.50	1.50
H18	Don Wilson	5.00	2.50	1.50

1967 KANSAS CTIY ATHLETICS

K1	Jim Nash	5.00	2.50	1.50
K2	Bert Campaneris	5.00	2.50	1.50
K3	Ed Charles	5.00	2.50	1.50
K4	Wes Stock	5.00	2.50	1.50
K5	John Odom	5.00	2.50	1.50
K6	Ossie Chavarria	5.00	2.50	1.50
K7	Jack Aker	5.00	2.50	1.50
K8	Dick Green	5.00	2.50	1.50
K9	Phil Roof	5.00	2.50	1.50
K10	Rene Lacheman	5.00	2.50	1.50
K11	Mike Hershberger	5.00	2.50	1.50
K12	Joe Nossek	5.00	2.50	1.50
K13	Roger Repoz	5.00	2.50	1.50
K14	Chuck Dobson	5.00	2.50	1.50
K15	Jim Hunter	15.00	7.50	4.50
K16	Lew Krausse	5.00	2.50	1.50
K17	Danny Cater	5.00	2.50	1.50
K18	Jim Gosger	5.00	2.50	1.50

1967 LOS ANGELES DODGERS

L1	Phil Regan	5.00	2.50	1.50
L2	Bob Bailey	5.00	2.50	1.50
L3	Ron Fairly	5.00	2.50	1.50
L4	Joe Moeller	5.00	2.50	1.50
L5	Don Sutton	15.00	7.50	4.50
L6	Ron Hunt	5.00	2.50	1.50
L7	Jim Brewer	5.00	2.50	1.50
L8	Lou Johnson	5.00	2.50	1.50
L9	John Roseboro	5.00	2.50	1.50
L10	Jeff Torborg	5.00	2.50	1.50
L11	John Kennedy	5.00	2.50	1.50
L12	Jim Lefebvre	5.00	2.50	1.50
L13	Wes Parker	5.00	2.50	1.50
L14	Bob Miller	5.00	2.50	1.50
L15	Claude Osteen	5.00	2.50	1.50
L16	Ron Perranoski	5.00	2.50	1.50
L17	Willie Davis	5.00	2.50	1.50
L18	Al Ferrera	5.00	2.50	1.50

1968 LOS ANGELES DODGERS

L1	Phil Regan	5.00	2.50	1.50
L2	Bob Bailey	5.00	2.50	1.50
L3	Ron Fairly	5.00	2.50	1.50
L4	Jim Brewer	5.00	2.50	1.50
L5	Don Sutton	15.00	7.50	4.50
L6	Tom Haller	5.00	2.50	1.50
L7	Rocky Colavito	12.00	6.00	3.50
L8	Jim Grant	5.00	2.50	1.50
L9	Jim Campanis	5.00	2.50	1.50
L10	Jeff Torborg	5.00	2.50	1.50
L11	Zoilo Versalles	6.00	3.00	1.75
L12	Jim Lefebvre	5.00	2.50	1.50
L13	Wes Parker	5.00	2.50	1.50
L14	Bill Singer	5.00	2.50	1.50
L15	Claude Osteen	5.00	2.50	1.50
L16	Len Gabrielson	5.00	2.50	1.50
L17	Willie Davis	5.00	2.50	1.50
L18	Al Ferrera	5.00	2.50	1.50

1967 MINNESOTA TWINS

M1	Ron Kline	5.00	2.50	1.50
M2	Bob Allison	6.00	3.00	1.75
M3	Earl Battey	5.00	2.50	1.50
M4	Jim Merritt	5.00	2.50	1.50
M5	Jim Perry	6.00	3.00	1.75
M6	Harmon Killebrew	25.00	12.50	7.50
M7	Dave Boswell	5.00	2.50	1.50
M8	Rich Rollins	5.00	2.50	1.50
M9	Jerry Zimmerman	5.00	2.50	1.50
M10	Al Worthington	5.00	2.50	1.50
M11	Cesar Tovar	5.00	2.50	1.50
M12	Sandy Valdespino	5.00	2.50	1.50
M13	Zoilo Versalles	6.00	3.00	1.75
M14	Dean Chance	6.00	3.00	1.75
M15	Jim Grant	5.00	2.50	1.50
M16	Jim Kaat	9.00	4.50	2.75
M17	Tony Oliva	10.00	5.00	3.00
M18	Andy Kosco	5.00	2.50	1.50

1968 MINNESOTA TWINS

M1	Rich Reese	5.00	2.50	1.50
M2	Bob Allison	6.00	3.00	1.75
M3	Ron Perranoski	5.00	2.50	1.50
M4	John Roseboro	5.00	2.50	1.50
M5	Jim Perry	6.00	3.00	1.75
M6	Harmon Killebrew	25.00	12.50	7.50
M7	Dave Boswell	5.00	2.50	1.50
M8	Rich Rollins	5.00	2.50	1.50
M9	Jerry Zimmerman	5.00	2.50	1.50
M10	Al Worthington	5.00	2.50	1.50
M11	Cesar Tovar	5.00	2.50	1.50
M12	Jim Merritt	5.00	2.50	1.50
M13	Bob Miller	5.00	2.50	1.50
M14	Dean Chance	6.00	3.00	1.75
M15	Ted Uhlaender	5.00	2.50	1.50
M16	Jim Kaat	9.00	4.50	2.75
M17	Tony Oliva	10.00	5.00	3.00
M18	Rod Carew	40.00	20.00	12.00

1967 NEW YORK METS

V19	Chuck Hiller	5.00	2.50	1.50
V20	Johnny Lewis	5.00	2.50	1.50
V21	Ed Kranepool	5.00	2.50	1.50
V22	Al Luplow	5.00	2.50	1.50
V23	Don Cardwell	5.00	2.50	1.50
V24	Cleon Jones	5.00	2.50	1.50
V25	Bob Shaw	5.00	2.50	1.50
V26	John Stephenson	5.00	2.50	1.50
V27	Ron Swoboda	5.00	2.50	1.50
V28	Ken Boyer	6.00	3.00	1.75
V29	Ed Bressoud	5.00	2.50	1.50
V30	Tommy Davis	5.00	2.50	1.50
V31	Roy McMillan	5.00	2.50	1.50
V32	Jack Fisher	5.00	2.50	1.50
V33	Tug McGraw	6.00	3.00	1.75
V34	Jerry Grote	5.00	2.50	1.50
V35	Jack Hamilton	5.00	2.50	1.50

1967 NEW YORK YANKEES

V1	Mel Stottlemyre	5.00	2.50	1.50
V2	Ruben Amaro	5.00	2.50	1.50
V3	Jake Gibbs	5.00	2.50	1.50
V4	Dooley Womack	5.00	2.50	1.50
V5	Fred Talbot	5.00	2.50	1.50
V6	Horace Clarke	5.00	2.50	1.50
V7	Jim Bouton	6.00	3.00	1.75
V8	Mickey Mantle	125.00	60.00	35.00
V9	Elston Howard	7.50	3.75	2.25
V10	Hal Reniff	5.00	2.50	1.50
V11	Charley Smith	5.00	2.50	1.50
V12	Bobby Murcer	6.00	3.00	1.75
V13	Joe Pepitone	6.00	3.00	1.75
V14	Al Downing	5.00	2.50	1.50
V15	Steve Hamilton	5.00	2.50	1.50
V16	Fritz Peterson	5.00	2.50	1.50
V17	Tom Tresh	6.00	3.00	1.75
V18	Roy White	6.00	3.00	1.75

1967 PHILADELPHIA PHILLIES

P1	Richie Allen	7.50	3.75	2.25
P2	Bob Wine	5.00	2.50	1.50
P3	Johnny Briggs	5.00	2.50	1.50
P4	John Callison	5.00	2.50	1.50
P5	Doug Clemens	5.00	2.50	1.50
P6	Dick Groat	5.00	2.50	1.50
P7	Dick Ellsworth	5.00	2.50	1.50
P8	Phil Linz	5.00	2.50	1.50
P9	Clay Dalrymple	5.00	2.50	1.50
P10	Bob Uecker	10.00	5.00	3.00
P11	Cookie Rojas	5.00	2.50	1.50
P12	Tony Taylor	5.00	2.50	1.50
P13	Bill White	5.00	2.50	1.50
P14	Larry Jackson	5.00	2.50	1.50
P15	Chris Short	5.00	2.50	1.50
P16	Jim Bunning	15.00	7.50	4.50
P17	Tony Gonzalez	5.00	2.50	1.50
P18	Don Lock	5.00	2.50	1.50

1967 PITTSBURGH PIRATES

E1	Al McBean	5.00	2.50	1.50
E2	Gene Alley	5.00	2.50	1.50
E3	Donn Clendenon	5.00	2.50	1.50
E4	Bob Veale	5.00	2.50	1.50
E5	Pete Mikkelsen	5.00	2.50	1.50
E6	Bill Mazeroski	20.00	10.00	6.00
E7	Steve Blass	5.00	2.50	1.50
E8	Manny Mota	5.00	2.50	1.50
E9	Jim Pagliaroni	5.00	2.50	1.50
E10	Jesse Gonder	5.00	2.50	1.50
E11	Jose Pagan	5.00	2.50	1.50
E12	Willie Stargell	25.00	12.50	7.50
E13	Maury Wills	9.00	4.50	2.75
E14	Elroy Face	5.00	2.50	1.50
E15	Woodie Fryman	5.00	2.50	1.50
E16	Vern Law	5.00	2.50	1.50
E17	Matty Alou	5.00	2.50	1.50
E18	Roberto Clemente	60.00	30.00	18.00

1967 SAN FRANCISCO GIANTS

G1	Bob Bolin	5.00	2.50	1.50
G2	Ollie Brown	5.00	2.50	1.50
G3	Jim Davenport	5.00	2.50	1.50
G4	Tito Fuentes	5.00	2.50	1.50
G5	Norm Siebern	5.00	2.50	1.50
G6	Jim Hart	5.00	2.50	1.50
G7	Juan Marichal	15.00	7.50	4.50
G8	Hal Lanier	5.00	2.50	1.50
G9	Tom Haller	5.00	2.50	1.50
G10	Bob Barton	5.00	2.50	1.50
G11	Willie McCovey	20.00	10.00	6.00
G12	Mike McCormick	5.00	2.50	1.50
G13	Frank Linzy	5.00	2.50	1.50
G14	Ray Sadecki	5.00	2.50	1.50
G15	Gaylord Perry	15.00	7.50	4.50
G16	Lindy McDaniel	5.00	2.50	1.50
G17	Willie Mays	60.00	30.00	18.00
G18	Jesus Alou	5.00	2.50	1.50

1968 SAN FRANCISCO GIANTS

G1	Bob Bolin	5.00	2.50	1.50
G2	Ollie Brown	5.00	2.50	1.50
G3	Jim Davenport	5.00	2.50	1.50
G4	Bob Barton	5.00	2.50	1.50
G5	Jack Hiatt	5.00	2.50	1.50
G6	Jim Hart.	5.00	2.50	1.50
G7	Juan Marichal	15.00	7.50	4.50
G8	Hal Lanier	5.00	2.50	1.50
G9	Ron Hunt	5.00	2.50	1.50
G10	Ron Herbel	5.00	2.50	1.50
G11	Willie McCovey	20.00	10.00	6.00
G12	Mike McCormick	5.00	2.50	1.50
G13	Frank Linzy	5.00	2.50	1.50
G14	Ray Sadecki	5.00	2.50	1.50
G15	Gaylord Perry	15.00	7.50	4.50
G16	Lindy McDaniel	5.00	2.50	1.50
G17	Willie Mays	60.00	30.00	18.00
G18	Jesus Alou	5.00	2.50	1.50

1967 WASHINGTON SENATORS

S1	Bob Humphreys	5.00	2.50	1.50
S2	Bernie Allen	5.00	2.50	1.50
S3	Ed Brinkman	5.00	2.50	1.50
S4	Pete Richert	5.00	2.50	1.50
S5	Camilo Pascual	5.00	2.50	1.50
S6	Frank Howard	7.50	3.75	2.25
S7	Casey Cox	5.00	2.50	1.50
S8	Jim King	5.00	2.50	1.50
S9	Paul Casanova	5.00	2.50	1.50
S10	Dick Lines	5.00	2.50	1.50
S11	Dick Nen	5.00	2.50	1.50
S12	Ken McMullen	5.00	2.50	1.50
S13	Bob Saverine	5.00	2.50	1.50
S14	Jim Hannan	5.00	2.50	1.50
S15	Darold Knowles	5.00	2.50	1.50
S16	Phil Ortega	5.00	2.50	1.50
S17	Ken Harrelson	5.00	2.50	1.50
S18	Fred Valentine	5.00	2.50	1.50

1971 Coca-Cola Houston Astros

The constitution and distribution of these Coke premium pictures is unknown. Players are pictured in pastel drawings on the semi-gloss fronts of these 8" x 11" sheets. (The punch holes on the photographed card are not original.) A black facsimile autograph appears in the lower portion of the drawing and the player's name is printed in black in the white bottom border. Backs are printed in blue and red with a background photo of the Astrodome. Data on back includes biographical information, complete pro record and career summary. The unnumbered cards are checklisted here in alphabetical order; but this list is probably not complete.

		NM	EX	VG
Complete Set (12):		50.00	25.00	15.00
Common Player:		5.00	2.50	1.50
(1)	Jesus Alou	5.00	2.50	1.50
(2)	Wade Blasingame (SP)	9.00	4.50	2.75
(3)	Cesar Cedeno	7.50	3.75	2.25
(4)	Larry Dierker	7.50	3.75	2.25
(5)	John Edwards	5.00	2.50	1.50
(6)	Denis Menke	5.00	2.50	1.50
(7)	Roger Metzger	5.00	2.50	1.50
(8)	Joe Morgan	15.00	7.50	4.50
(9)	Doug Rader	5.00	2.50	1.50
(10)	Bob Watson	5.00	2.50	1.50
(11)	Don Wilson	5.00	2.50	1.50
(12)	Jim Wynn (SP)	12.00	6.00	3.50

1978 Coca-Cola/WPLO Atlanta Braves

Co-sponsored by Coke and a local radio station, this set of Braves cards is rendered in blue-and-white line art portraits in a 3" x 4-1/4" format. A soda discount coupon was distributed with the set.

		NM	EX	VG
Complete Set (14):		30.00	15.00	9.00
Common Player:		3.00	1.50	.90
(1)	Barry Bonnell	3.00	1.50	.90
(2)	Jeff Burroughs	3.00	1.50	.90
(3)	Rick Camp	3.00	1.50	.90
(4)	Gene Garber	3.00	1.50	.90
(5)	Rod Gilbreath	3.00	1.50	.90
(6)	Bob Horner	4.50	2.25	1.25
(7)	Glenn Hubbard	3.00	1.50	.90
(8)	Gary Matthews	3.00	1.50	.90
(9)	Larry McWilliams	3.00	1.50	.90
(10)	Dale Murphy	9.00	4.50	2.75
(11)	Phil Niekro	5.00	2.50	1.50
(12)	Rowland Office	3.00	1.50	.90
(13)	Biff Pocoroba	3.00	1.50	.90
(14)	Jerry Royster	3.00	1.50	.90

1979 Coca-Cola/7-Eleven MVPs

The co-MVPs of the National League for 1979 are pictured on this 5" x 7" blank-back photo card. A red band at top identifies the player and the award. At bottom are Coke and 7-Eleven logos.

	NM	EX	VG
Keith Hernandez, Willie Stargell	6.00	3.00	1.80

1955 Coffee-Time Syrup Jimmy Piersall

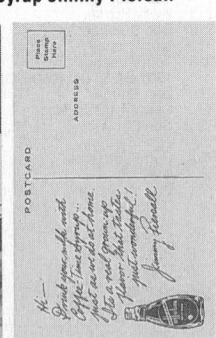

The date of issue is speculative for this promotional postcard. The borderless black-and-white photo on the front on this 3-1/2" x 5-1/2" card shows the popular BoSox star in a relaxed pose with right arm on knee. A blue facsimile autograph is printed at center. The postcard-format back has at left a product picture and an advertising message bearing Piersall's signature. Similar cards advertising Colonial Meats, Cain's and other products are also known, valued similarly.

	NM	EX	VG
Autographed: 2-3X	125.00	65.00	35.00
Jimmy Piersall	80.00	40.00	24.00

1909-1911 Colgan's Chips Stars of the Diamond (E254)

This unusual set of 1-7/16"-diameter round cards was issued over a three-year period by the Colgan Gum Co., Louisville, Ky. The cards were inserted in five-cent tins of Colgan's Mint Chips and Violet Chips brands of gum. The borderless cards feature a black-and-white player portrait on the front along with the player's last name, team and league. On more than a dozen cards, variations are known in the size of the photo and/or lettering on front. Since they cannot be identified without another card to compare with, they are noted here only with an asterisk. The card back identifies the set as "Stars of the Diamond" and carries advertising for Colgan's Gum. Some backs are seen with a line of type at the bottom stating, "208 IN PRESENT SERIES." Over 225 different players were pictured over the three-year period, but because of team changes and other notable variations, at least 289 different cards exist. This issue was catalogued as E254 in the American Card Catalog. A number of cards and variations which had been listed in earlier editions of this catalog have been eliminated for lack of proof of their existence. Gaps have been left in the assigned numbering to accommodate future additions. Persons with "Stars of the Diamond" players or variations that do no appear on this list should contact the editor. Recent hobby finds suggest a rare variation with violet- printed backs exist, perhaps packaged with "Violet Chips." Further confirmation is required before pricing data will be established.

		NM	EX	VG
Common Player:		75.00	35.00	20.00
Round Tin Package:		30.00	15.00	9.00
(1)	Ed Abbaticchio	75.00	35.00	20.00
(2)	Fred Abbott	75.00	35.00	20.00
(3a)	Bill Abstein (Pittsburg)	75.00	35.00	20.00
(3b)	Bill Abstein (Jersey City)	75.00	35.00	20.00
(4)	Babe Adams	75.00	35.00	20.00
(5)	Doc Adkins	75.00	35.00	20.00
(6a)	Dave Altizer (Cincinnati)	75.00	35.00	20.00
(6b)	Dave Altizer (Minneapolis)	75.00	35.00	20.00
(7)	Nick Altrock	95.00	50.00	30.00
(8)	Red Ames	75.00	35.00	20.00
(9a)	Jimmy Austin (New York)	75.00	35.00	20.00
(9b)	Jimmy Austin (St. Louis)	75.00	35.00	20.00
(10a)	Charlie Babb (Memphis)	75.00	35.00	20.00
(10b)	Charlie Babb (Norfolk)	75.00	35.00	20.00
(11)	Baerwald	75.00	35.00	20.00
(12)	Bill Bailey	75.00	35.00	20.00
(13)	Home Run Baker (*)	215.00	110.00	65.00
(14)	Jack Barry (*)	75.00	35.00	20.00
(15a)	Bill Bartley (Curved letters.)	75.00	35.00	20.00
(15b)	Bill Bartley (Horizontal letters.)	75.00	35.00	20.00
(16a)	Johnny Bates (Cincinnati)	75.00	35.00	20.00

(16b)	Johnny Bates (Philadelphia, black letters.)	75.00	35.00	20.00
(16c)	Johnny Bates (Philadelphia, white letters.)	75.00	35.00	20.00
(17)	Dick Bayless	75.00	35.00	20.00
(18a)	Ginger Beaumont (Boston)	75.00	35.00	20.00
(18b)	Ginger Beaumont (Chicago)	75.00	35.00	20.00
(18c)	Ginger Beaumont (St. Paul)	75.00	35.00	20.00
(19)	Beals Becker	75.00	35.00	20.00
(20)	George Bell	75.00	35.00	20.00
(21a)	Harry Bemis (Cleveland)	75.00	35.00	20.00
(21b)	Harry Bemis (Columbus)	75.00	35.00	20.00
(22a)	Heinie Berger (Cleveland)	75.00	35.00	20.00
(22b)	Heinie Berger (Columbus)	75.00	35.00	20.00
(23)	Beumiller	75.00	35.00	20.00
(24)	Joe Birmingham	75.00	35.00	20.00
(25)	Kitty Bransfield	75.00	35.00	20.00
(26)	Roger Bresnahan	215.00	110.00	65.00
(27)	Al Bridwell	75.00	35.00	20.00
(28)	Lew Brockett	75.00	35.00	20.00
(29)	Al Burch (*)	75.00	35.00	20.00
(30)	Burke	75.00	35.00	20.00
(31)	Donie Bush	75.00	35.00	20.00
(32)	Bill Byers	75.00	35.00	20.00
(33)	Howie Cammitz (Camnitz)	75.00	35.00	20.00
(34a)	Charlie Carr (Indianapolis)	75.00	35.00	20.00
(34b)	Charlie Carr (Utica)	75.00	35.00	20.00
(35)	Frank Chance	215.00	110.00	65.00
(36)	Hal Chase	150.00	80.00	40.00
(37)	Bill Clancy (Clancey)	75.00	35.00	20.00
(38a)	Fred Clarke (Pittsburg)	215.00	110.00	65.00
(38b)	Fred Clarke (Pittsburgh)	215.00	110.00	65.00
(39)	Tommy Clarke (Cincinnati)	75.00	35.00	20.00
(40)	Bill Clymer	75.00	35.00	20.00
(41)	Ty Cobb (*)	1,140	570.00	340.00
(42)	Eddie Collins	215.00	110.00	65.00
(43)	Bunk Congalton	75.00	35.00	20.00
(44)	Wid Conroy	75.00	35.00	20.00
(45)	Ernie Courtney	75.00	35.00	20.00
(46a)	Harry Coveleski (Cincinnati)	75.00	35.00	20.00
(46b)	Harry Coveleski (Chattanooga)	75.00	35.00	20.00
(47)	Doc Crandall	75.00	35.00	20.00
(48)	Gavvy Cravath	75.00	35.00	20.00
(49)	Dode Criss	75.00	35.00	20.00
(50a)	Jake Daubert (Memphis)	75.00	35.00	20.00
(50b)	Jake Daubert (Brooklyn)	75.00	35.00	20.00
(51)	Harry Davis (Philadelphia)	75.00	35.00	20.00
(52)	Davis (St. Paul)	75.00	35.00	20.00
(53)	Frank Delahanty	75.00	35.00	20.00
(54a)	Ray Demmett (Demmitt) (New York)	75.00	35.00	20.00
(54b)	Ray Demmett (Demmitt) (Montreal)	75.00	35.00	20.00
(55)	Art Devlin	75.00	35.00	20.00
(56)	Wild Bill Donovan	75.00	35.00	20.00
(57)	Mickey Doolin (Doolan)	75.00	35.00	20.00
(58)	Patsy Dougherty	75.00	35.00	20.00
(59)	Tom Downey	75.00	35.00	20.00
(60)	Larry Doyle	75.00	35.00	20.00
(61)	Jack Dunn	95.00	50.00	30.00
(62)	Dick Eagan (Egan)	75.00	35.00	20.00
(63a)	Kid Elberfield (Elberfeld) (Washington)	75.00	35.00	20.00
(63b)	Kid Elberfield (Elberfeld) (New York)	75.00	35.00	20.00
(64)	Rube Ellis	75.00	35.00	20.00
(65)	Clyde Engle (Boston)	75.00	35.00	20.00
(66)	Steve Evans (Horizontal letters.)	75.00	35.00	20.00
(67)	Johnny Evers	215.00	110.00	65.00
(68)	Cecil Ferguson	75.00	35.00	20.00
(69)	Hobe Ferris	75.00	35.00	20.00
(70)	Field (*)	75.00	35.00	20.00
(71)	Fitzgerald	75.00	35.00	20.00
(72a)	Patsy Flaherty (Kansas City)	75.00	35.00	20.00
(72b)	Patsy Flaherty (Atlanta)	75.00	35.00	20.00
(73)	Jack Flater	75.00	35.00	20.00
(74a)	Elmer Flick (Cleveland)	215.00	110.00	65.00
(74b)	Elmer Flick (Toledo)	215.00	110.00	65.00
(75a)	James Freck (Frick, Baltimore)	90.00	45.00	30.00
(75b)	James Freck (Frick, Toronto)	75.00	35.00	20.00
(76)	Jerry Freeman (Photo actually Buck Freeman.)	75.00	35.00	20.00
(77)	Art Fromme (*)	75.00	35.00	20.00
(78a)	Larry Gardner (Boston)	75.00	35.00	20.00
(78b)	Larry Gardner (New York)	75.00	35.00	20.00
(79)	Harry Gaspar	75.00	35.00	20.00
(80a)	Gus Getz (Boston)	75.00	35.00	20.00
(80b)	Gus Getz (Indianapolis)	75.00	35.00	20.00
(81)	George Gibson	75.00	35.00	20.00
(82a)	Moose Grimshaw (Toronto)	75.00	35.00	20.00
(82b)	Moose Grimshaw (Louisville)	75.00	35.00	20.00
(83)	Ed Hahn	75.00	35.00	20.00
(84)	John Halla (*)	75.00	35.00	20.00
(85)	Ed Hally (Holly)	75.00	35.00	20.00
(86)	Charlie Hanford	75.00	35.00	20.00
(87)	Topsy Hartsel	75.00	35.00	20.00
(88a)	Roy Hartzell (St. Louis)	75.00	35.00	20.00
(88b)	Roy Hartzell (New York)	75.00	35.00	20.00
(89)	Weldon Henley	75.00	35.00	20.00
(91)	Harry Hinchman	75.00	35.00	20.00
(92)	Solly Hofman	75.00	35.00	20.00
(93a)	Harry Hooper (Boston Na'l)	215.00	110.00	65.00
(93b)	Harry Hooper (Boston Am. L.)	240.00	120.00	75.00
(94)	Howard (*)	75.00	35.00	20.00
(95a)	Hughes (No name in uniform.)	75.00	35.00	20.00
(95b)	Hughes (Name and team name in uniform.)	75.00	35.00	20.00
(96b)	Rudy Hulswitt (St. Louis)	75.00	35.00	20.00
(96c)	Rudy Hulswitt (Chattanooga)	75.00	35.00	20.00
(97)	John Hummel	75.00	35.00	20.00
(98)	George Hunter	75.00	35.00	20.00
(99)	Hugh Jennings	215.00	110.00	65.00
(100)	Davy Jones	75.00	35.00	20.00
(101)	Tom Jones	75.00	35.00	20.00
(102a)	Tim Jordon (Jordan, Brooklyn)	75.00	35.00	20.00
(102b)	Tim Jordon (Jordan, Atlanta)	75.00	35.00	20.00

(102c)	Tim Jordon (Jordan, Louisville)	75.00	35.00	20.00
(103)	Addie Joss	240.00	120.00	75.00
(104)	Al Kaiser	75.00	35.00	20.00
(105)	Joe Kelly (Kelley)	215.00	110.00	65.00
(106)	Bill Killefer (*)	75.00	35.00	20.00
(107a)	Ed Killian (Detroit)	75.00	35.00	20.00
(107b)	Ed Killian (Toronto)	75.00	35.00	20.00
(108)	Otto Knabe	75.00	35.00	20.00
(109)	Jack Knight	75.00	35.00	20.00
(111)	Ed Konetchy	75.00	35.00	20.00
(112)	Rube Kroh	75.00	35.00	20.00
(113)	James Lafitte	75.00	35.00	20.00
(114)	Lakoff	75.00	35.00	20.00
(115)	Frank Lange	75.00	35.00	20.00
(116a)	Frank LaPorte (St. Louis)	75.00	35.00	20.00
(116b)	Frank LaPorte (New York)	75.00	35.00	20.00
(117)	Tommy Leach	75.00	35.00	20.00
(118)	Bill Lelivelt	75.00	35.00	20.00
(119a)	Jack Lewis (Milwaukee)	75.00	35.00	20.00
(119b)	Jack Lewis (Indianapolis)	75.00	35.00	20.00
(120a)	Vive Lindaman (Boston)	75.00	35.00	20.00
(120b)	Vive Lindaman (Louisville)	75.00	35.00	20.00
(120c)	Vive Lindaman (Indianapolis)	75.00	35.00	20.00
(121)	Bris Lord	75.00	35.00	20.00
(122a)	Harry Lord (Boston)	75.00	35.00	20.00
(122b)	Harry Lord (Chicago)	75.00	35.00	20.00
(123)	Bill Ludwig (Milwaukee)	75.00	35.00	20.00
(124)	Nick Maddox	75.00	35.00	20.00
(125a)	Manser (Jersey City)	75.00	35.00	20.00
(125b)	Manser (Rochester)	75.00	35.00	20.00
(126)	Al Mattern	75.00	35.00	20.00
(127)	Bill Matthews	75.00	35.00	20.00
(128)	George McBride	75.00	35.00	20.00
(129)	Joe McCarthy (Toledo)	215.00	110.00	65.00
(130)	McConnell	75.00	35.00	20.00
(131)	Moose McCormick	75.00	35.00	20.00
(132)	Dan McGann	75.00	35.00	20.00
(133)	Jim McGinley	75.00	35.00	20.00
(134)	Iron Man McGinnity	215.00	110.00	65.00
(135a)	Matty McIntyre (Detroit)	75.00	35.00	20.00
(135b)	Matty McIntyre (Chicago)	75.00	35.00	20.00
(136)	Larry McLean (*)(Three photo size variations known.)	75.00	35.00	20.00
(137)	Fred Merkle	75.00	35.00	20.00
(138a)	Merritt (Buffalo)	75.00	35.00	20.00
(138b)	Merritt (Jersey City)	75.00	35.00	20.00
(139)	Meyer (Newark)	75.00	35.00	20.00
(140)	Chief Meyers (New York)	75.00	35.00	20.00
(141)	Clyde Milan	75.00	35.00	20.00
(142)	Dots Miller	75.00	35.00	20.00
(143)	Mike Mitchell	75.00	35.00	20.00
(144)	Moran	75.00	35.00	20.00
(145a)	Bill Moriarty (Louisville)	75.00	35.00	20.00
(145b)	Bill Moriarty (Omaha)	75.00	35.00	20.00
(146)	George Moriarty	75.00	35.00	20.00
(147a)	George Mullen (Name incorrect.)	75.00	35.00	20.00
(147b)	George Mullin (Name correct.)	75.00	35.00	20.00
(148a)	Simmy Murch (Chattanooga)	75.00	35.00	20.00
(148b)	Simmy Murch (Indianapolis)	75.00	35.00	20.00
(149)	Danny Murphy	75.00	35.00	20.00
(150a)	Red Murray (New York, white letters.)	75.00	35.00	12.00
(150b)	Red Murray (St. Paul)	75.00	35.00	20.00
(151)	Billy Nattress (*)	75.00	35.00	20.00
(152a)	Red Nelson (St. Louis)	75.00	35.00	20.00
(152b)	Red Nelson (Toledo)	75.00	35.00	20.00
(153)	Rebel Oakes	75.00	35.00	20.00
(154)	Fred Odwell	75.00	35.00	20.00
(155a)	Al Orth (New York)	75.00	35.00	20.00
(155b)	Al Orth (Indianapolis)	75.00	35.00	20.00
(156)	Fred Osborn	75.00	35.00	20.00
(157)	Orval Overall	75.00	35.00	20.00
(158)	Owens	75.00	35.00	20.00
(159)	Fred Parent	75.00	35.00	20.00
(161a)	Dode Paskert (Cincinnati)	75.00	35.00	20.00
(161b)	Dode Paskert (Philadelphia)	75.00	35.00	20.00
(162)	Heinie Peitz	75.00	35.00	20.00
(163)	Bob Peterson	75.00	35.00	20.00
(164)	Jake Pfeister	75.00	35.00	20.00
(165)	Deacon Phillipe (Phillippe)	75.00	35.00	20.00
(166a)	Ollie Pickering (Louisville)	75.00	35.00	20.00
(166b)	Ollie Pickering (Minneapolis)	75.00	35.00	20.00
(166c)	Ollie Pickering (Omaha)	75.00	35.00	20.00
(167a)	Billy Purtell (Chicago)	75.00	35.00	20.00
(167b)	Billy Purtell (Boston)	75.00	35.00	20.00
(168)	Bugs Raymond	75.00	35.00	20.00
(169)	Pat Regan (Ragan)	75.00	35.00	20.00
(170)	Barney Reilly	75.00	35.00	20.00
(171)	Duke Reilly (Reilley)	75.00	35.00	20.00
(172)	Ed Reulbach	75.00	35.00	20.00
(173)	Claude Ritchey	75.00	35.00	20.00
(174)	Lou Ritter	75.00	35.00	20.00
(175)	William "Rabbit" Robinson (Louisville)	75.00	35.00	20.00
(176)	Rock	75.00	35.00	20.00
(177a)	Jack Rowan (Cincinnati)	75.00	35.00	20.00
(177b)	Jack Rowan (Philadelphia)	75.00	35.00	20.00
(178)	Nap Rucker	75.00	35.00	20.00
(179a)	Dick Rudolph (New York)	75.00	35.00	20.00
(179b)	Dick Rudolph (Toronto)	75.00	35.00	20.00
(180)	Jack Ryan (St. Paul)(Photo actually Jimmy Ryan.)	75.00	35.00	20.00
(181)	Slim Sallee	75.00	35.00	20.00
(182a)	Bill Schardt (Birmingham)	75.00	35.00	20.00
(182b)	Bill Schardt (Milwaukee)	75.00	35.00	20.00
(183)	Jimmy Scheckard (Sheckard)	75.00	35.00	20.00
(184a)	George Schirm (Birmingham)	75.00	35.00	20.00
(184b)	George Schirm (Buffalo)	75.00	35.00	20.00
(185)	Larry Schlafly	75.00	35.00	20.00
(186)	Wildfire Schulte	75.00	35.00	20.00
(187a)	James Seabaugh (Looking to left, photo actually Julius Weisman.)	75.00	35.00	20.00
(187b)	James Seabaugh (Looking straight ahead, correct photo.)	75.00	35.00	20.00
(188)	Selby (*)	75.00	35.00	20.00

(189a)	Cy Seymour (New York)	75.00	35.00	20.00
(189b)	Cy Seymour (Baltimore)	75.00	35.00	20.00
(190)	Hosea Siner	75.00	35.00	20.00
(191)	G. Smith	75.00	35.00	20.00
(192a)	Sid Smith (Atlanta)	75.00	35.00	20.00
(192b)	Sid Smith (Buffalo)	75.00	35.00	20.00
(193)	Fred Snodgrass	75.00	35.00	20.00
(194a)	Bob Spade (Cincinnati)	75.00	35.00	20.00
(194b)	Bob Spade (Newark)	75.00	35.00	20.00
(195a)	Tully Sparks (Philadelphia)	75.00	35.00	20.00
(195b)	Tully Sparks (Richmond)	75.00	35.00	20.00
(196)	Tris Speaker (Boston Am.)	260.00	120.00	80.00
(197)	Tubby Spencer	75.00	35.00	20.00
(198)	Jake Stahl	75.00	35.00	20.00
(199)	John Stansberry (Stansbury)	75.00	35.00	20.00
(200)	Harry Steinfeldt (*)	75.00	35.00	20.00
(201)	George Stone	75.00	35.00	20.00
(202)	George Stovall	75.00	35.00	20.00
(203)	Gabby Street	75.00	35.00	20.00
(204a)	Sullivan (Louisville)	75.00	35.00	20.00
(204b)	Sullivan (Omaha)	75.00	35.00	20.00
(205a)	Ed Summers (No white in uniform.)	75.00	35.00	20.00
(205b)	Ed Summers (White in uniform.)	75.00	35.00	20.00
(206)	Suter	75.00	35.00	20.00
(207)	Lee Tannehill	75.00	35.00	20.00
(208)	Taylor	75.00	35.00	20.00
(209)	Joe Tinker	215.00	110.00	65.00
(210)	John Titus	75.00	35.00	20.00
(211)	Terry Turner	75.00	35.00	20.00
(212a)	Bob Unglaub (Washington)	75.00	35.00	20.00
(212b)	Bob Unglaub (Lincoln)	75.00	35.00	20.00
(213a)	Rube Waddell (St. Louis)	215.00	110.00	65.00
(213b)	Rube Waddell (Minneapolis)	215.00	110.00	65.00
(213c)	Rube Waddell (Newark)	215.00	110.00	65.00
(214)	Honus Wagner (*)	1,140	570.00	340.00
(215)	Walker	75.00	35.00	20.00
(216)	Waller	75.00	35.00	20.00
(217)	Clarence Wauner (Wanner)	75.00	35.00	20.00
(218)	Julius Weisman (Name correct.)	75.00	35.00	20.00
(219)	Jack White (Buffalo)	75.00	35.00	20.00
(220)	Kirby White (Boston)	75.00	35.00	20.00
(221)	Julius Wiesman (Weisman)	75.00	35.00	20.00
(222)	Ed Willett	75.00	35.00	20.00
(223)	Otto Williams	75.00	35.00	20.00
(224)	Owen Wilson	75.00	35.00	20.00
(225)	Hooks Wiltse	75.00	35.00	20.00
(226a)	Orville Woodruff (Indianapolis)	75.00	35.00	20.00
(226b)	Orville Woodruff (Louisville)	75.00	35.00	20.00
(227)	Woods	75.00	35.00	20.00
(228)	Cy Young	570.00	280.00	170.00
(229)	Bill Zimmerman	75.00	35.00	20.00
(230)	Heinie Zimmerman	75.00	35.00	20.00

1912 Colgan's Chips Red Borders (E270)

This set, issued in 1912 by Colgan Gum Co., Louisville, Ky., is very similar to the 1909-11 Colgan's release. Measuring about 1-3/8" in diameter, the black-and-white player pictures were inserted in tins of Colgan's Mint and Violet Chips gum. They are differentiated from the earlier issues by their distinctive red borders and by the back of the cards, which advises collectors to "Send 25 Box Tops" for a photo of the "World's Pennant Winning Team." The issue is designated as the E270 Red Border set in the American Card Catalog. A Red Border card of Gavvy Cravath previous cataloged is now believed not to exist.

		NM	EX	VG
Complete Set (181):		50,000	25,000	14,400
Common Player:		250.00	125.00	75.00
(1)	Ed Abbaticchio	250.00	125.00	75.00
(2)	Fred Abbott	250.00	125.00	75.00
(3)	Babe Adams	250.00	125.00	75.00
(4)	Doc Adkins	250.00	125.00	75.00
(5)	Red Ames	250.00	125.00	75.00
(6)	Charlie Babb	250.00	125.00	75.00
(7)	Bill Bailey	250.00	125.00	75.00
(8)	Home Run Baker	400.00	250.00	150.00
(9)	Jack Barry	250.00	125.00	75.00
(10)	Johnny Bates	250.00	125.00	75.00
(11)	Dick Bayless	250.00	125.00	75.00
(12)	Ginger Beaumont	250.00	125.00	75.00
(13)	Beals Becker	250.00	125.00	75.00
(14)	George Bell	250.00	125.00	75.00
(15)	Harry Bemis	250.00	125.00	75.00
(16)	Heinie Berger	250.00	125.00	75.00
(17)	Beumiller	250.00	125.00	75.00
(18)	Joe Birmingham	250.00	125.00	75.00
(19)	Kitty Bransfield	250.00	125.00	75.00
(20)	Roger Bresnahan	500.00	250.00	150.00
(21)	Lew Brockett	250.00	125.00	75.00
(22)	Al Burch	250.00	125.00	75.00
(23)	Donie Bush	250.00	125.00	75.00
(24)	Bill Byers	250.00	125.00	75.00
(25)	Howie Cammitz (Camnitz)	250.00	125.00	75.00
(26)	Charlie Carr	250.00	125.00	75.00
(27)	Frank Chance	500.00	250.00	150.00
(28)	Hal Chase	305.00	150.00	91.00
(29)	Fred Clarke (Pittsburg)	500.00	250.00	150.00

(30)	Tommy Clarke (Cincinnati)	250.00	125.00	75.00
(31)	Bill Clymer	250.00	125.00	75.00
(32)	Ty Cobb	3,750	1,875	1,125
(33)	Eddie Collins	500.00	250.00	150.00
(34)	Wid Conroy	250.00	125.00	75.00
(35)	Harry Coveleski	250.00	125.00	75.00
(37)	Dode Criss	250.00	125.00	75.00
(38)	Jake Daubert	250.00	125.00	75.00
(39)	Harry Davis (Philadelphia)	250.00	125.00	75.00
(40)	Davis (St. Paul)	250.00	125.00	75.00
(41)	Frank Delahanty	250.00	125.00	75.00
(42)	Ray Demmett (Demmitt)	250.00	125.00	75.00
(43)	Art Devlin	250.00	125.00	75.00
(44)	Wild Bill Donovan	250.00	125.00	75.00
(45)	Mickey Doolin (Doolan)	250.00	125.00	75.00
(46)	Patsy Dougherty	250.00	125.00	75.00
(47)	Tom Downey	250.00	125.00	75.00
(48)	Larry Doyle	250.00	125.00	75.00
(49)	Jack Dunn	250.00	125.00	75.00
(50)	Dick Eagan (Egan)	250.00	125.00	75.00
(51)	Kid Elberfield (Elberfeld)	250.00	125.00	75.00
(52)	Rube Ellis	250.00	125.00	75.00
(53)	Steve Evans	250.00	125.00	75.00
(54)	Johnny Evers	500.00	250.00	150.00
(55)	Cecil Ferguson	250.00	125.00	75.00
(56)	Hobe Ferris	250.00	125.00	75.00
(57)	Fisher	250.00	125.00	75.00
(58)	Fitzgerald	250.00	125.00	75.00
(59)	Elmer Flick	500.00	250.00	150.00
(60)	James Freck (Frick)	250.00	125.00	75.00
(61)	Art Fromme	250.00	125.00	75.00
(62)	Harry Gaspar	250.00	125.00	75.00
(63)	George Gibson	250.00	125.00	75.00
(64)	Moose Grimshaw	250.00	125.00	75.00
(65)	John Halla	250.00	125.00	75.00
(66)	Ed Hally (Holly)	250.00	125.00	75.00
(67)	Charlie Hanford	250.00	125.00	75.00
(68)	Topsy Hartsel	250.00	125.00	75.00
(69)	Roy Hartzell	250.00	125.00	75.00
(70)	Weldon Henley (Two sizes photo variations noted.)	250.00	125.00	75.00
(71)	Harry Hinchman	250.00	125.00	75.00
(72)	Solly Hofman	250.00	125.00	75.00
(73)	Harry Hooper	500.00	250.00	150.00
(74)	Howard	250.00	125.00	75.00
(75)	Hughes	250.00	125.00	75.00
(76)	Rudy Hulswitt	250.00	125.00	75.00
(77)	John Hummel	250.00	125.00	75.00
(78)	George Hunter	250.00	125.00	75.00
(79)	Hugh Jennings	500.00	250.00	150.00
(80)	Davy Jones	250.00	125.00	75.00
(81)	Tom Jones	250.00	125.00	75.00
(82)	Tim Jordon (Jordan)	250.00	125.00	75.00
(83)	Joe Kelly (Kelley)	500.00	250.00	150.00
(84)	Bill Killefer	250.00	125.00	75.00
(85)	Ed Killian	250.00	125.00	75.00
(86)	Otto Knabe	250.00	125.00	75.00
(87)	Jack Knight	250.00	125.00	75.00
(88)	Ed Konetchy	250.00	125.00	75.00
(89)	Rube Kroh	250.00	125.00	75.00
(90)	LaCrosse (Photo actually Bill Schardt.)	250.00	125.00	75.00
(91)	Frank LaPorte	250.00	125.00	75.00
(92)	Tommy Leach	250.00	125.00	75.00
(93)	Jack Lelivelt	250.00	125.00	75.00
(94)	Jack Lewis	250.00	125.00	75.00
(95)	Vive Lindaman	250.00	125.00	75.00
(96)	Bris Lord	250.00	125.00	75.00
(97)	Harry Lord	250.00	125.00	75.00
(98)	Bill Ludwig	250.00	125.00	75.00
(99)	Nick Maddox	250.00	125.00	75.00
(100)	Manser	250.00	125.00	75.00
(101)	Al Mattern	250.00	125.00	75.00
(102)	George McBride	250.00	125.00	75.00
(103)	Joe McCarthy (Toledo)	500.00	250.00	150.00
(104)	McConnell	250.00	125.00	75.00
(105)	Moose McCormick	250.00	125.00	75.00
(106)	Dan McGann	250.00	125.00	75.00
(107)	Jim McGinley	250.00	125.00	75.00
(108)	Iron Man McGinnity	500.00	250.00	150.00
(109)	Matty McIntyre	250.00	125.00	75.00
(110)	Larry McLean	250.00	125.00	75.00
(111)	Fred Merkle	250.00	125.00	75.00
(112)	Merritt	250.00	125.00	75.00
(113)	Meyer (Newark)	250.00	125.00	75.00
(114)	Chief Meyers	250.00	125.00	75.00
(115)	Clyde Milan	250.00	125.00	75.00
(116)	Dots Miller	250.00	125.00	75.00
(117)	Mike Mitchell	250.00	125.00	75.00
(118)	Bill Moriarty (Omaha)	250.00	125.00	75.00
(119)	George Moriarty (Detroit)	250.00	125.00	75.00
(120)	George Mullen (Mullin)	250.00	125.00	75.00
(121)	Simmy Murch (Chattanooga)	250.00	125.00	75.00
(122)	Simmy Murch (Indianapolis)	250.00	125.00	75.00
(123)	Danny Murphy	250.00	125.00	75.00
(124)	Red Murray	250.00	125.00	75.00
(125)	Red Nelson	250.00	125.00	75.00
(126)	Rebel Oakes	250.00	125.00	75.00
(127)	Orval Overall	250.00	125.00	75.00
(128)	Owens	250.00	125.00	75.00
(129)	Fred Parent	250.00	125.00	75.00
(130)	Dode Paskert	250.00	125.00	75.00
(131)	Bob Peterson	250.00	125.00	75.00
(132)	Jake Pfeister (Pfiester)	250.00	125.00	75.00
(133)	Deacon Phillipe (Phillippe)	250.00	125.00	75.00
(134)	Ollie Pickering	250.00	125.00	75.00
(135)	Heinie Pietz (Peitz)	250.00	125.00	75.00
(136)	Bugs Raymond	250.00	125.00	75.00
(137)	Pat Regan (Ragan)	250.00	125.00	75.00
(138)	Ed Reulbach	250.00	125.00	75.00
(139)	Robinson	250.00	125.00	75.00
(140)	Rock	250.00	125.00	75.00
(141)	Jack Rowan	250.00	125.00	75.00
(142)	Nap Rucker	250.00	125.00	75.00
(143)	Dick Rudolph	250.00	125.00	75.00
(144)	Slim Sallee	250.00	125.00	75.00
(145)	Jimmy Scheckard (Sheckard)	250.00	125.00	75.00
(146)	George Schirm	250.00	125.00	75.00
(147)	Wildfire Schulte	250.00	125.00	75.00
(148)	James Seabaugh	250.00	125.00	75.00
(149)	Selby	250.00	125.00	75.00
(150)	Cy Seymour	250.00	125.00	75.00
(151)	Hosea Siner	250.00	125.00	75.00
(152)	Sid Smith	250.00	125.00	75.00
(153)	Fred Snodgrass	250.00	125.00	75.00
(154)	Bob Spade	250.00	125.00	75.00
(155)	Tully Sparks	250.00	125.00	75.00
(156)	Tris Speaker	750.00	375.00	225.00
(157)	Tubby Spencer	250.00	125.00	75.00
(158)	John Stausberry (Stansbury)	250.00	125.00	75.00
(159)	Harry Steinfeldt	250.00	125.00	75.00
(160)	George Stone	250.00	125.00	75.00
(161)	George Stovall	250.00	125.00	75.00
(162)	Gabby Street	250.00	125.00	75.00
(163)	Sullivan (Omaha)	250.00	125.00	75.00
(164)	John Sullivan (Louisville)	250.00	125.00	75.00
(165)	Ed Summers	250.00	125.00	75.00
(166)	Joe Tinker	500.00	250.00	150.00
(167)	John Titus	250.00	125.00	75.00
(168)	Terry Turner	250.00	125.00	75.00
(169)	Bob Unglaub	250.00	125.00	75.00
(170)	Rube Waddell	500.00	250.00	150.00
(171)	Walker	250.00	125.00	75.00
(172)	Waller	250.00	125.00	75.00
(173)	Kirby White (Boston)	250.00	125.00	75.00
(174)	Jack White (Buffalo)	250.00	125.00	75.00
(175)	Julius Wiesman (Weisman)	250.00	125.00	75.00
(176)	Otto Williams	250.00	125.00	75.00
(177)	Hooks Wiltse	250.00	125.00	75.00
(178)	Orville Woodruff	250.00	125.00	75.00
(179)	Woods	250.00	125.00	75.00
(180)	Cy Young	1,560	780.00	470.00
(181)	Bill Zimmerman	250.00	125.00	75.00
(182)	Heinie Zimmerman	250.00	125.00	75.00

1913 Colgan's Chips Tin Tops

Except for the backs, these round black-and-white cards (about 1-7/16" in diameter) are identical to the 1909-11 Colgan's Chips issue, and were inserted in tin cannisters of Colgan's Mint Chips and Violet Chips. The front features a portrait photo along with the player's last name, team and, where necessary, league. The back advises collectors to "Send 25 Tin Tops" and a two-cent stamp to receive a photo of the "World's Pennant Winning Team." The set carries the designation E270 in the American Card Catalog.

		NM	EX	VG
	Complete Set (222):	60,000	30,000	18,000
	Common Player:	180.00	90.00	54.00
(1)	Ed Abbaticchio	180.00	90.00	54.00
(2)	Doc Adkins	180.00	90.00	54.00
(3)	Joe Agler	180.00	90.00	54.00*
(4)	Eddie Ainsmith	180.00	90.00	54.00
(5)	Whitey Alperman	180.00	90.00	54.00
(6)	Red Ames (New York)	180.00	90.00	54.00
(7)	Red Ames (Cincinnati)	180.00	90.00	54.00
(8)	Jimmy Archer	180.00	90.00	54.00
(9)	Tommy Atkins (Atlanta)	180.00	90.00	54.00
(10)	Tommy Atkins (Ft. Wayne)	180.00	90.00	54.00
(11)	Jake Atz (New Orleans)	180.00	90.00	54.00
(12)	Jake Atz (Providence)	180.00	90.00	54.00
(13)	Jimmy Austin	180.00	90.00	54.00
(14)	Home Run Baker	360.00	180.00	110.00
(15)	Johnny Bates	180.00	90.00	54.00
(16)	Beck (Buffalo)	180.00	90.00	54.00
(17)	Beebe	180.00	90.00	54.00
(18)	Harry Bemis	180.00	90.00	54.00
(19)	Bob Bescher	180.00	90.00	54.00
(20)	Beumiller (Louisville)	180.00	90.00	54.00
(21)	Joe Birmingham	180.00	90.00	54.00
(22)	Bliss	180.00	90.00	54.00
(23)	Roger Bresnahan	360.00	180.00	110.00
(24)	Al Bridwell	180.00	90.00	54.00
(25)	George Brown (Browne)	180.00	90.00	54.00
(26)	Al Burch	180.00	90.00	54.00
(27)	Burns	180.00	90.00	54.00
(28)	Donie Bush	180.00	90.00	54.00
(29)	Bobby Byrne	180.00	90.00	54.00
(30)	Nixey Callahan	180.00	90.00	54.00
(31)	Howie Camnitz	180.00	90.00	54.00
(32)	Billy Campbell	180.00	90.00	54.00
(33)	Charlie Carr	180.00	90.00	54.00
(34)	Jay Cashion	180.00	90.00	54.00
(35)	Frank Chance	360.00	180.00	110.00
(36)	Hal Chase	220.00	110.00	65.00
(37)	Ed Cicotte	270.00	135.00	80.00
(38)	Clarke (Indianapolis)	180.00	90.00	54.00
(39)	Fred Clarke (Pittsburg)	360.00	180.00	110.00
(40)	Tommy Clarke (Cincinnati)	180.00	90.00	54.00
(41)	Clemons	180.00	90.00	54.00
(42)	Bill Clymer	180.00	90.00	54.00
(43)	Ty Cobb	2,400	1,200	720.00
(44)	Eddie Collins	360.00	180.00	110.00
(45)	Bunk Congalton (Omaha)	180.00	90.00	54.00
(46)	Bunk Congalton (Toledo)	180.00	90.00	54.00
(47)	Cook	180.00	90.00	54.00
(48)	Jack Coombs	180.00	90.00	54.00
(49)	Corcoran	180.00	90.00	54.00
(50)	Gavvy Cravath	180.00	90.00	54.00
(51)	Sam Crawford	360.00	180.00	110.00
(52)	Bill Dahlen	180.00	90.00	54.00
(53)	Bert Daniels	180.00	90.00	54.00
(54a)	Jake Daubert	180.00	90.00	54.00
(54b)	Jake Daubert (White cap.)	180.00	90.00	54.00
(55)	Josh Devore (Cincinnati)	180.00	90.00	54.00
(56)	Josh Devore (New York)	180.00	90.00	54.00
(57)	Mike Donlin	180.00	90.00	54.00
(58)	Wild Bill Donovan	180.00	90.00	54.00
(59)	Red Dooin	180.00	90.00	54.00
(60)	Mickey Doolan	180.00	90.00	54.00
(61)	Larry Doyle	180.00	90.00	54.00
(62)	Delos Drake	180.00	90.00	54.00
(63)	Dick Egan	180.00	90.00	54.00
(64)	Kid Elberfield (Elberfeld)	180.00	90.00	54.00
(65)	Roy Ellam	180.00	90.00	54.00
(66)	Elliott	180.00	90.00	54.00
(67)	Rube Ellis	180.00	90.00	54.00
(68)	Elwert	180.00	90.00	54.00
(69)	Clyde Engle	180.00	90.00	54.00
(70)	Jimmy Esmond	180.00	90.00	54.00
(71)	Steve Evans	180.00	90.00	54.00
(72)	Johnny Evers	360.00	180.00	110.00
(73)	Hobe Ferris	180.00	90.00	54.00
(74)	Russ Ford	180.00	90.00	54.00
(75)	Ed Foster	180.00	90.00	54.00
(76)	Friel	180.00	90.00	54.00
(77)	John Frill	180.00	90.00	54.00
(78)	Art Fromme	180.00	90.00	54.00
(79)	Gus Getz (Newark)	180.00	90.00	54.00
(80)	George Gibson	180.00	90.00	54.00
(81)	Graham	180.00	90.00	54.00
(82)	Eddie Grant (Cincinnati)	180.00	90.00	54.00
(83)	Eddie Grant (New York)	180.00	90.00	54.00
(84)	Gravath	180.00	90.00	54.00
(85)	Grief	180.00	90.00	54.00
(86)	Bob Groom	180.00	90.00	54.00
(87)	Topsy Hartsel	180.00	90.00	54.00
(88)	Roy Hartzell	180.00	90.00	54.00
(89)	Harry Hinchman	180.00	90.00	54.00
(90)	Dick Hoblitzell	180.00	90.00	54.00
(91)	Happy Hogan (St. Louis)	180.00	90.00	54.00
(92)	Happy Hogan (San Francisco)	180.00	90.00	54.00
(93)	Harry Hooper	360.00	180.00	110.00
(94)	Miller Huggins	360.00	180.00	110.00
(95)	Hughes (Milwaukee)	180.00	90.00	54.00
(96)	Hughes (Rochester)	180.00	90.00	54.00
(97)	Rudy Hulswitt	180.00	90.00	54.00
(98)	John Hummel	180.00	90.00	54.00
(99)	George Hunter	180.00	90.00	54.00
(100)	Shoeless Joe Jackson	20,000	4,800	2,880
(101)	Jameson (Buffalo)	180.00	90.00	54.00
(102)	Hugh Jennings	360.00	180.00	110.00
(103)	Pete Johns	180.00	90.00	54.00
(104)	Walter Johnson	780.00	390.00	235.00
(105)	Davy Jones (Toledo)	180.00	90.00	54.00
(106)	Tim Jordan	180.00	90.00	54.00
(107)	Bob Keefe	180.00	90.00	54.00
(108)	Wee Willie Keeler	360.00	180.00	110.00
(109)	Joe Kelly (Kelley)	360.00	180.00	110.00
(110)	Ed Killian	180.00	90.00	54.00
(111)	Bill Killifer (Killefer)	180.00	90.00	54.00
(112)	Johnny Kling (Boston)	180.00	90.00	54.00
(113)	Klipfer	180.00	90.00	54.00
(114)	Otto Knabe	180.00	90.00	54.00
(115)	Jack Knight	180.00	90.00	54.00
(116)	Ed Konetchy	180.00	90.00	54.00
(117)	Paul Krichell	180.00	90.00	54.00
(118)	James Lafitte	180.00	90.00	54.00
(119)	Nap Lajoie	360.00	180.00	110.00
(120)	Frank Lange	180.00	90.00	54.00
(121)	Lee	180.00	90.00	54.00
(122)	Jack Lewis	180.00	90.00	54.00
(123)	Harry Lord	180.00	90.00	54.00
(124)	Johnny Lush	180.00	90.00	54.00
(125)	Madden	180.00	90.00	54.00
(126)	Nick Maddox	180.00	90.00	54.00
(127)	Sherry Magee	180.00	90.00	54.00
(128)	Manser	180.00	90.00	54.00
(129)	Frank Manusch (Manush) (New Orleans)	180.00	90.00	54.00
(130)	Frank Manush (Toledo)	180.00	90.00	54.00
(131)	Rube Marquard	360.00	180.00	110.00
(132)	McAllister	180.00	90.00	54.00
(133)	George McBride	180.00	90.00	54.00
(134)	McCarthy (Newark)	180.00	90.00	54.00
(135)	Joe McCarthy (Toledo)	360.00	180.00	110.00
(136)	McConnell	180.00	90.00	54.00
(137)	Moose McCormick	180.00	90.00	54.00
(138)	Larry McLean	180.00	90.00	54.00
(139)	Fred Merkle	180.00	90.00	54.00
(140)	Chief Meyers	180.00	90.00	54.00
(141)	Clyde Milan	180.00	90.00	54.00
(142)	Miller (Columbus)	180.00	90.00	54.00
(143)	Dots Miller (Pittsburg)	180.00	90.00	54.00
(144)	Clarence Mitchell	180.00	90.00	54.00
(145)	Mike Mitchell	180.00	90.00	54.00
(146)	Roy Mitchell	180.00	90.00	54.00
(147)	Carlton Molesworth	180.00	90.00	54.00
(148)	Herbie Moran	180.00	90.00	54.00
(149)	George Moriarty	180.00	90.00	54.00
(150)	George Mullen (Mullin)	180.00	90.00	54.00
(151)	Danny Murphy	180.00	90.00	54.00
(152)	Murray (Buffalo)	180.00	90.00	54.00
(153)	Jim Murray	180.00	90.00	54.00
(154)	Niles (Indianapolis)	180.00	90.00	54.00
(155)	Jake Northrop	180.00	90.00	54.00
(156)	Rebel Oakes	180.00	90.00	54.00
(157)	Rube Oldring	180.00	90.00	54.00
(158)	Steve O'Neil (O'Neill)	180.00	90.00	54.00
(159)	O'Rourke	180.00	90.00	54.00
(160)	Owens (Minneapolis)	180.00	90.00	54.00
(161)	Larry Pape	180.00	90.00	54.00
(162)	Fred Parent	180.00	90.00	54.00
(163)	Dode Paskert	180.00	90.00	54.00
(164)	Heinie Peitz	180.00	90.00	54.00
(165)	Perry	180.00	90.00	54.00
(166)	Billy Purtell	180.00	90.00	54.00

		NM	EX	VG
(167)	Bill Rariden	180.00	90.00	54.00
(168)	Morrie Rath	180.00	90.00	54.00
(169)	Bugs Raymond	180.00	90.00	54.00
(170)	Ed Reulbach	180.00	90.00	54.00
(171)	Nap Rucker	180.00	90.00	54.00
(172)	Dick Rudolph	180.00	90.00	54.00
(173)	Bud Ryan	180.00	90.00	54.00
(174)	Slim Sallee	180.00	90.00	54.00
(176)	Ray Schalk	180.00	90.00	54.00
(177)	Schardt (Indianapolis)	180.00	90.00	54.00
(178)	Jimmy Scheckard (Sheckard)	180.00	90.00	54.00
(179)	Wildfire Schulte	180.00	90.00	54.00
(180)	Bob Shawkey	180.00	90.00	54.00
(181)	Skeeter Shelton	180.00	90.00	54.00
(182)	Burt Shotten (Shotton)	180.00	90.00	54.00
(183)	Sisson (Atlanta)	180.00	90.00	54.00
(184)	Smith (Montreal)	180.00	90.00	54.00
(185)	Sid Smith (Atlanta)	180.00	90.00	54.00
(186)	Sid Smith (Newark)	180.00	90.00	54.00
(187)	Fred Snodgrass	180.00	90.00	54.00
(188)	Tris Speaker	540.00	270.00	160.00
(189)	Jake Stahl	180.00	90.00	54.00
(190)	John Stansberry (Stansbury)	180.00	90.00	54.00
(191)	Amos Strunk	180.00	90.00	54.00
(192)	Sullivan	180.00	90.00	54.00
(193)	Suter	180.00	90.00	54.00
(194)	Harry Swacina	180.00	90.00	54.00
(195)	Bill Sweeney	180.00	90.00	54.00
(196)	Jeff Sweeney	180.00	90.00	54.00
(197)	Lee Tannehill	180.00	90.00	54.00
(198)	Dummy Taylor (Topeka)	300.00	150.00	90.00
(199)	Jim Thorpe	12,000	3,900	2,340
(200)	Joe Tinker	360.00	180.00	110.00
(201)	John Titus (Boston)	180.00	90.00	54.00
(202)	John Titus (Philadelphia)	180.00	90.00	54.00
(203)	Terry Turner	180.00	90.00	54.00
(204)	Bob Unglaub	180.00	90.00	54.00
(205)	Viebahn	180.00	90.00	54.00
(206)	Rube Waddell	360.00	180.00	110.00
(207)	Honus Wagner	2,500	750.00	450.00
(208)	Bobby Wallace	360.00	180.00	110.00
(209)	Ed Walsh	360.00	180.00	110.00
(210)	Jack Warhop	180.00	90.00	54.00
(211)	Harry Welchouce (Welchonce)	180.00	90.00	54.00
(212)	Zach Wheat	360.00	180.00	110.00
(213)	Kirb. White	180.00	90.00	54.00
(214)	Kaiser Wilhelm	180.00	90.00	54.00
(215a)	Ed Willett	180.00	90.00	54.00
(215b)	Ed Willett (White cap.)	180.00	90.00	54.00
(216)	Otto Williams	180.00	90.00	54.00
(217)	Owen Wilson	180.00	90.00	54.00
(218)	Hooks Wiltse	180.00	90.00	54.00
(219)	Joe Wood	180.00	90.00	54.00
(220)	Orville Woodruff	180.00	90.00	54.00
(221)	Joe Yeager	180.00	90.00	54.00
(222)	Bill Zimmerman	180.00	90.00	54.00
(223)	Heinie Zimmerman	180.00	90.00	54.00

1909 "Colgan's Chips" Square Proofs

COLLINS
Phila. Am. L.

Though widely identified as being connected to the Colgan's Chips disc issues of 1909-1912, there is nothing to tie these square cards to the gum company except for the shared use of player photos. The squares measure about 1-3/8" x 1-3/4" and are blank-backed. Black-and-white player portrait photos have a last name and team identification beneath. Many, but not all, of the surviving specimens have paper and/or glue residue on back, leading to speculation they may have been part of an advertising piece. The extent of the checklist is unknown, with verified examples listed here.

		NM	EX	VG
Common Player:		250.00	120.00	80.00
(9)	Red Ames	250.00	120.00	80.00
(12)	Charlie Babb (Memphis)	250.00	120.00	80.00
(13)	Baerwald (Memphis)	250.00	124.00	74.00
(15)	Home Run Baker	600.00	300.00	180.00
(18)	Johnny Bates	250.00	120.00	80.00
(20)	Ginger Beaumont (Boston)	250.00	120.00	80.00
(21)	Beals Becker	250.00	120.00	80.00
(29)	Roger Bresnahan	600.00	300.00	180.00
(30)	Al Bridwell	250.00	120.00	80.00
(31)	Lew Brockett	250.00	124.00	74.00
(32)	Al Burch	250.00	120.00	80.00
(34)	Donie Bush	250.00	120.00	80.00
(36)	Howie Camnitz	250.00	120.00	80.00
(38)	Frank Chance	600.00	300.00	180.00
(41)	Fred Clarke (Pittsburg)	600.00	300.00	180.00
(44)	Ty Cobb	4,000	2,000	1,200
(45)	Eddie Collins	600.00	300.00	180.00
(52)	Dode Criss	250.00	120.00	80.00
(54)	Jake Daubert (Memphis)	250.00	120.00	80.00
(55)	Harry Davis (Philadelphia)	250.00	120.00	80.00
(58)	Ray Demmett (Demmitt) (New York)	250.00	120.00	80.00
(69)	Clyde Engle (New York)	250.00	120.00	80.00

(70)	Steve Evans	250.00	120.00	80.00
(71)	Johnny Evers	600.00	300.00	180.00
(83)	Harry Gaspar	250.00	120.00	80.00
(84)	Gus Getz (Boston)	250.00	120.00	80.00
(85)	George Gibson	250.00	120.00	80.00
(96)	Harry Hooper (Boston A.L.)	600.00	300.00	180.00
(103)	Hugh Jennings	600.00	300.00	180.00
(107)	Addie Joss	600.00	300.00	180.00
(114)	Otto Knabe	250.00	120.00	80.00
(118)	James Lafitte	250.00	120.00	80.00
(124)	Bill Lelivelt	250.00	120.00	80.00
(129)	Bill Ludwig (Milwaukee)	250.00	120.00	80.00
(131)	Nick Maddox	250.00	120.00	80.00
(150)	Dots Miller	250.00	120.00	80.00
(151)	Mike Mitchell	250.00	120.00	80.00
(157)	Danny Murphy	250.00	120.00	80.00
(170)	Heinie Peitz	250.00	120.00	80.00
(190)	Bill Schardt (Milwaukee)	250.00	120.00	80.00
(197)	Cy Seymour (New York)	250.00	124.00	74.00
(201)	Fred Snodgrass	250.00	120.00	80.00
(209)	Bob Spade (Cincinnati)	250.00	120.00	80.00
(215)	Bob Unglaub	250.00	120.00	80.00
(220)	Rube Waddell (St. Louis)	600.00	300.00	180.00
(221)	Honus Wagner (Pittsburg)	1,500	750.00	450.00
(231)	Owen Wilson	250.00	120.00	80.00
(232)	Hooks Wiltse	250.00	120.00	80.00
(234)	Woods (Buffalo)	250.00	120.00	80.00

1917 Collins-McCarthy (E135)

This is one of the 200 pictures comprising BASEBALL'S HALL of FAME There are 199 others Distributed by Collins-McCarthy Candy Co. SAN FRANCISCO : CAL. "Just a little better" Zee Nut and Candy Makers

Collins

Produced by the Collins-McCarthy Candy Co. of San Francisco, the 200-card, black-and-white set represents the company's only venture into issuing non-Pacific Coast League players. The cards, numbered alphabetically, measure 2" x 3-1/4" and are printed on thin stock. Though the set is entitled "Baseball's Hall of Fame," many nondescript players appear in the issue. The complete set price does not include the more expensive variations. The same cards can be found with the advertising of other regional issuers on back, or blank-backed. Blank backs are much more scarce.

		NM	EX	VG
Complete Set (200):		70,000	35,000	21,000
Common Player:		150.00	75.00	45.00
1	Sam Agnew	150.00	75.00	45.00
2	Grover Alexander	1,000	700.00	300.00
3	W.S. Alexander (W.E.)	150.00	75.00	45.00
4	Leon Ames	150.00	75.00	45.00
5	Fred Anderson	150.00	75.00	45.00
6	Ed Appleton	150.00	75.00	45.00
7	Jimmy Archer	150.00	75.00	45.00
8	Jimmy Austin	150.00	75.00	45.00
9	Jim Bagby	150.00	75.00	45.00
10	H.D. Baird	150.00	75.00	45.00
11	J. Franklin Baker	350.00	175.00	100.00
12	Dave Bancroft	350.00	175.00	100.00
13	Jack Barry	150.00	75.00	45.00
14	Joe Benz	150.00	75.00	45.00
15	Al Betzel	150.00	75.00	45.00
16	Ping Bodie	150.00	75.00	45.00
17	Joe Boehling	150.00	75.00	45.00
18	Eddie Burns	150.00	75.00	45.00
19	George Burns	150.00	75.00	45.00
20	Geo. J. Burns	150.00	75.00	45.00
21	Joe Bush	150.00	75.00	45.00
22	Owen Bush	150.00	75.00	45.00
23	Bobby Byrne	150.00	75.00	45.00
24	Forrest Cady	150.00	75.00	45.00
25	Max Carey	1,000	700.00	300.00
26	Ray Chapman	175.00	85.00	50.00
27	Larry Cheney	150.00	75.00	45.00
28	Eddie Cicotte	1,000	700.00	300.00
29	Tom Clarke	150.00	75.00	45.00
30	Ty Cobb	5,000	3,000	2,000
31	Eddie Collins	1,000	700.00	300.00
32	"Shauno" Collins (Shano)	150.00	75.00	45.00
33	Fred Coumbe	150.00	75.00	45.00
34	Harry Coveleskie (Coveleski)	150.00	75.00	45.00
35	Gavvy Cravath	150.00	75.00	45.00
36	Sam Crawford	1,000	700.00	300.00
37	Geo. Cutshaw	150.00	75.00	45.00
38	Jake Daubert	150.00	75.00	45.00
39	Geo. Dauss	150.00	75.00	45.00
40	Charles Deal	150.00	75.00	45.00
41	"Wheezer" Dell	150.00	75.00	45.00
42	William Doak	150.00	75.00	45.00
43	Bill Donovan	150.00	75.00	45.00
44	Larry Doyle	150.00	75.00	45.00
45	Johnny Evers	1,000	700.00	300.00
46	Urban Faber	1,000	700.00	300.00
47	"Hap" Felsch	1,000	700.00	300.00
48	Bill Fischer	150.00	75.00	45.00
49	Ray Fisher	150.00	75.00	45.00
50	Art Fletcher	150.00	75.00	45.00
51	Eddie Foster	150.00	75.00	45.00

52	Jacques Fournier	150.00	75.00	45.00
53	Del Gainer (Gainor)	150.00	75.00	45.00
54	Bert Gallia	150.00	75.00	45.00
55	"Chic" Gandil (Chick)	1,000	700.00	300.00
56	Larry Gardner	150.00	75.00	45.00
57	Joe Gedeon	150.00	75.00	45.00
58	Gus Getz	150.00	75.00	45.00
59	Frank Gilhooley	150.00	75.00	45.00
60	Wm. Gleason	150.00	75.00	45.00
61	M.A. Gonzales (Gonzalez)	165.00	80.00	50.00
62	Hank Gowdy	150.00	75.00	45.00
63	John Graney	150.00	75.00	45.00
64	Tom Griffith	150.00	75.00	45.00
65	Heinie Groh	150.00	75.00	45.00
66	Bob Groom	150.00	75.00	45.00
67	Louis Guisto	150.00	75.00	45.00
68	Earl Hamilton	150.00	75.00	45.00
69	Harry Harper	150.00	75.00	45.00
70	Grover Hartley	150.00	75.00	45.00
71	Harry Heilmann	5,000	4,000	2,000
72	Claude Hendrix	150.00	75.00	45.00
73	Olaf Henriksen	150.00	75.00	45.00
74	John Henry	150.00	75.00	45.00
75	"Buck" Herzog	150.00	75.00	45.00
76a	Hugh High (White stockings, photo actually Claude Williams.)	200.00	100.00	60.00
76b	Hugh High (Black stockings, correct photo.)	175.00	85.00	50.00
77	Dick Hoblitzell	150.00	75.00	45.00
78	Walter Holke	150.00	75.00	45.00
79	Harry Hooper	1,000	700.00	300.00
80	Rogers Hornsby	20,000	12,500	7,000
81	Ivan Howard	150.00	75.00	45.00
82	Joe Jackson	16,500	8,500	5,000
83	Harold Janvrin	150.00	75.00	45.00
84	William James	150.00	75.00	45.00
85	C. Jamieson	150.00	75.00	45.00
86	Hugh Jennings	1,000	700.00	300.00
87	Walter Johnson	3,000	2,000	1,000
88	James Johnston	150.00	75.00	45.00
89	Fielder Jones	150.00	75.00	45.00
90a	Joe Judge (Bat on right shoulder, photo actually Ray Morgan.)	200.00	100.00	60.00
90b	Joe Judge (Bat on left shoulder, correct photo.)	175.00	85.00	50.00
91	Hans Lobert	150.00	75.00	45.00
92	Benny Kauff	150.00	75.00	45.00
93	Wm. Killefer Jr.	150.00	75.00	45.00
94	Ed. Konetchy	150.00	75.00	45.00
95	John Lavan	150.00	75.00	45.00
96	Jimmy Lavender	150.00	75.00	45.00
97	"Nemo" Leibold	150.00	75.00	45.00
98	H.B. Leonard	150.00	75.00	45.00
99	Duffy Lewis	150.00	75.00	45.00
100	Tom Long	150.00	75.00	45.00
101	Wm. Louden	150.00	75.00	45.00
102	Fred Luderus	150.00	75.00	45.00
103	Lee Magee	150.00	75.00	45.00
104	Sherwood Magee	150.00	75.00	45.00
105	Al Mamaux	150.00	75.00	45.00
106	Leslie Mann	150.00	75.00	45.00
107	"Rabbit" Maranville	1,000	700.00	300.00
108	Rube Marquard	1,000	700.00	300.00
109	Armando Marsans	165.00	80.00	50.00
110	J. Erskine Mayer	150.00	75.00	45.00
111	George McBride	150.00	75.00	45.00
112	Lew McCarty	150.00	75.00	45.00
113	John J. McGraw	1,000	700.00	300.00
114	Jack McInnis	150.00	75.00	45.00
115	Lee Meadows	150.00	75.00	45.00
116	Fred Merkle	150.00	75.00	45.00
117	"Chief" Meyers	150.00	75.00	45.00
118	Clyde Milan	150.00	75.00	45.00
119	Otto Miller	150.00	75.00	45.00
120	Clarence Mitchell	150.00	75.00	45.00
121a	Ray Morgan (Bat on left shoulder, photo actually Joe Judge.)	200.00	100.00	60.00
121b	Ray Morgan (Bat on right shoulder, correct photo.)	175.00	85.00	50.00
122	Guy Morton	150.00	75.00	45.00
123	"Mike" Mowrey	150.00	75.00	45.00
124	Elmer Myers	150.00	75.00	45.00
125	"Hy" Myers	150.00	75.00	45.00
126	A.E. Neale	165.00	80.00	50.00
127	Arthur Nehf	150.00	75.00	45.00
128	J.A. Niehoff	150.00	75.00	45.00
129	Steve O'Neill	150.00	75.00	45.00
130	"Dode" Paskert	150.00	75.00	45.00
131	Roger Peckinpaugh	150.00	75.00	45.00
132	"Pol" Perritt	150.00	75.00	45.00
133	"Jeff" Pfeffer	150.00	75.00	45.00
134	Walter Pipp	150.00	75.00	45.00
135	Derril Pratt (Derrill)	150.00	75.00	45.00
136	Bill Rariden	150.00	75.00	45.00
137	E.C. Rice	350.00	175.00	100.00
138	Wm. A. Ritter (Wm. H.)	150.00	75.00	45.00
139	Eppa Rixey	1,000	700.00	300.00
140	Davey Robertson	150.00	75.00	45.00
141	"Bob" Roth	150.00	75.00	45.00
142	Ed. Roush	1,000	700.00	300.00
143	Clarence Rowland	150.00	75.00	45.00
144	Dick Rudolph	150.00	75.00	45.00
145	William Rumler	150.00	75.00	45.00
146a	Reb Russell (Pitching follow-thru, photo actually Mellie Wolfgang.)	200.00	100.00	60.00
146b	Reb Russell (Hands at side, correct photo.)	175.00	85.00	50.00
147	"Babe" Ruth	12,500	6,250	3,750
148	Vic Saier	150.00	75.00	45.00
149	"Slim" Sallee	150.00	75.00	45.00
150	Ray Schalk	1,000	700.00	300.00
151	Walter Schang	150.00	75.00	45.00
152	Frank Schulte	150.00	75.00	45.00
153	Ferd Schupp	150.00	75.00	45.00

		NM	EX	VG
154	Everett Scott	150.00	75.00	45.00
155	Hank Severeid	150.00	75.00	45.00
156	Howard Shanks	150.00	75.00	45.00
157	Bob Shawkey	150.00	75.00	45.00
158	Jas. Sheckard	150.00	75.00	45.00
159	Ernie Shore	150.00	75.00	45.00
160	C.H. Shorten	150.00	75.00	45.00
161	Burt Shotton	150.00	75.00	45.00
162	Geo. Sisler	1,000	700.00	300.00
163	Elmer Smith	150.00	75.00	45.00
164	J. Carlisle Smith	150.00	75.00	45.00
165	Fred Snodgrass	150.00	75.00	45.00
166	Tris Speaker	2,000	1,500	1,000
167	Oscar Stanage	150.00	75.00	45.00
168	Charles Stengel	1,000	700.00	500.00
169	Milton Stock	150.00	75.00	45.00
170	Amos Strunk	150.00	75.00	45.00
171	"Zeb" Terry	150.00	75.00	45.00
172	"Jeff" Tesreau	150.00	75.00	45.00
173	Chester Thomas	150.00	75.00	45.00
174	Fred Toney	150.00	75.00	45.00
175	Terry Turner	150.00	75.00	45.00
176	George Tyler	150.00	75.00	45.00
177	Jim Vaughn	150.00	75.00	45.00
178	Bob Veach	150.00	75.00	45.00
179	Oscar Vitt	150.00	75.00	45.00
180	Hans Wagner	3,500	1,750	1,000
181	Clarence Walker	150.00	75.00	45.00
182	Jim Walsh	150.00	75.00	45.00
183	Al Walters	150.00	75.00	45.00
184	W. Wambsganss	150.00	75.00	45.00
185	Buck Weaver	1,000	500.00	300.00
186	Carl Weilman	150.00	75.00	45.00
187	Zack Wheat	1,000	700.00	300.00
188	Geo. Whitted	150.00	75.00	45.00
189	Joe Wilhoit	150.00	75.00	45.00
190a	Claude Williams (Black stockings, photo actually Hugh High.)	600.00	300.00	180.00
190b	Claude Williams (White stockings, correct photo.)	750.00	375.00	225.00
191	Fred Williams	150.00	75.00	45.00
192	Art Wilson	150.00	75.00	45.00
193	Lawton Witt	150.00	75.00	45.00
194	Joe Wood	150.00	75.00	45.00
195	William Wortman	150.00	75.00	45.00
196	Steve Yerkes	150.00	75.00	45.00
197	Earl Yingling	150.00	75.00	45.00
198	"Pep" (Ralph) Young	150.00	75.00	45.00
199	Rollie Zeider	150.00	75.00	45.00
200	Henry Zimmerman	150.00	75.00	45.00

1954 Colonial Meats Jimmy Piersall

These promotional postcards are known in at least two varieties. Each of the 3-1/2" x 5-1/2" cards shows the popular BoSox star in a portrait pose with facsimile autograph. The postcard-format back has at left a cartoon butcher and an advertising message bearing Piersall's signature. Similar cards advertising Cain's grocery products are also known.

		NM	EX	VG
	Autographed: 2-3X	125.00	65.00	35.00
(1)	Jimmy Piersall (Chest-to-cap, back printed in black.)	80.00	40.00	24.00
(2)	Jimmy Piersall (Waist-to-cap, back printed in black and blue.)	80.00	40.00	24.00

1888 Conly Cabinets

Contemporary, but much less numerous than, the Old Judge cabinet cards is this issue from a Boston photo studio. Carrying an April, 1888, copyright date, the 4-1/4" x 6-1/2" have sepia photos of the players in action poses. Backs have decorative advertising for the studio. The extent of the checklist is unknown.

	NM	EX	VG
John Clarkson (Ball in hands at chest.)	3,000	1,200	725.00
John Clarkson (Ball in hands at chest.)	3,000	1,200	725.00
John Clarkson (Right arm at back.)	3,000	1,200	725.00
John Clarkson (Right arm extended.)	3,000	1,200	725.00

1891 Conly Studio Cabinets

The extent of this issue from a Boston photo studio is unknown. The checklist begins here with three players from the Boston Reds American Associations champions. The 4-1/4" x 6-1/2" cards have a sepia portrait photo of the player in street clothes. Back has decorative advertising for the studio.

		NM	EX	VG
	Common Player:	1,000	500.00	300.00
(1)	Duke Farrell	1,200	500.00	300.00
(2)	George Haddock	1,200	500.00	300.00
(3)	Cub Stricker	1,200	500.00	300.00

1950s-70s L.L. Cook Milwaukee Braves/Brewers Postcards

From a period of (roughly) 1956 through 1972 the L.L. Cook Co. of Milwaukee undertook the production of black-and-white photo postcards for various members of the local teams. Apparently printed to order to allow players and staff to respond to fan requests for pictures and autographs, the 3-1/2" x 5-1/2" cards have (usually) borderless poses on front. Postcard-style divided backs may or may not have a credit line vertically at center, and various versions of the standard postcard markings are seen. This checklist is likely incomplete.

		NM	EX	VG
	Common Player:	30.00	15.00	9.00
(1)	Hank Aaron	150.00	75.00	45.00
(2)	Tommie Aaron	30.00	15.00	9.00
(3)	Joe Adcock	40.00	20.00	12.00
(4)	Ed Bailey	30.00	15.00	9.00
(5)	Frank Bolling	30.00	15.00	9.00
(6)	Bobby Bragan	30.00	15.00	9.00
(7)	Ty Cline	30.00	15.00	9.00
(8)	Wes Covington	30.00	15.00	9.00
(9)	Ray Crone (White name on front.)	30.00	15.00	9.00
(10)	Ray Crone (No name.)	30.00	15.00	9.00
(11)	Fred Haney	30.00	15.00	9.00
(12)	Ernie Johnson	30.00	15.00	9.00
(13)	Ernie Johnson (Part of light tower shows.)	30.00	15.00	9.00
(14)	Charlie Lau	30.00	15.00	9.00
(15)	Mike Krsnich	30.00	15.00	9.00
(16)	Roy McMillan	30.00	15.00	9.00
(17)	Jerry McNertney (Brewers)	30.00	15.00	9.00
(18)	Don Nottebart	30.00	15.00	9.00
(19)	Phil Paine	30.00	15.00	9.00
(20)	Ron Piche	30.00	15.00	9.00
(21)	Juan Pizarro	30.00	15.00	9.00
(22)	Bob Sadowski	30.00	15.00	9.00

		NM	EX	VG
(13)	Red Schoendienst	50.00	25.00	15.00
(14)	George Scott (Brewers)	30.00	15.00	9.00
(15)	Bob Shaw	30.00	15.00	9.00
(16)	Warren Spahn (Artwork portrait, white background.)	40.00	20.00	12.00
(17)	Warren Spahn (Artwork portrait, yellow in background.)	40.00	20.00	12.00
(18)	Warren Spahn (Eating with son.)	30.00	15.00	9.00
(19)	Warren Spahn (Showing son new car.)	30.00	15.00	9.00
(20)	Warren Spahn (In car, waving to family.)	30.00	15.00	9.00
(21)	Al Spangler	30.00	15.00	9.00
(22)	Frank Torre (Holding Pepsi.)	30.00	15.00	9.00
(23)	Frank Torre (Holding Pepsi, facsimile autograph.)	30.00	15.00	9.00
(24)	Frank Torre (Holding Pepsi, Brave patch shows.)	30.00	15.00	9.00
(25)	Joe Torre (Kneeling)	40.00	20.00	12.00
(26)	Joe Torre (Portrait)	40.00	20.00	12.00

1910 Coupon Cigarettes Type 1 (T213)

Though they feature the same pictures used in the contemporary T206 tobacco issue, Coupon Cigarette cards make up three distinct sets, produced between 1910 and 1919. Type 1 Coupon cards feature a mix of players from the National and American Leagues, and the Southern League. Nominally the traditional 1-7/16" x 2-1/8" cigarette-card size, fronts of the Coupons are identical to the more popular T206 series. Backs, however, clearly identify the cards as being a product of Coupon Cigarettes and allow the collector to easily differentiate among the three types. Type 1 cards, produced in 1910, carry a general advertisement for Coupon "Mild" Cigarettes, with no mention of price. Distribution of the Coupons was limited to the Louisiana area, making the set very difficult to checklist and even moreso to collect. Numerous variations further complicate the situation. It is quite possible the checklists here are incomplete and additions will surface in the future. Type 1 cards are considered the rarest of the Coupon issues, and, because they were printed on a thinner stock, they are especially difficult to find in top condition.

		NM	EX	VG
	Complete Set (68):	30,000	15,000	8,500
	Common Player:	450.00	170.00	85.00
(1)	Harry Bay	450.00	170.00	85.00
(2)	Beals Becker	450.00	170.00	85.00
(3)	Chief Bender	1,275	500.00	250.00
(4)	Bernhard	450.00	170.00	85.00
(5)	Ted Breitenstein	450.00	170.00	85.00
(6)	Bobby Byrne	450.00	170.00	85.00
(7)	Billy Campbell	450.00	170.00	85.00
(8)	Scoops Carey	1,275	500.00	250.00
(9)	Frank Chance	1,275	500.00	250.00
(10)	Chappy Charles	450.00	170.00	85.00
(11)	Hal Chase (Portrait)	625.00	250.00	125.00
(12)	Hal Chase (Throwing)	625.00	250.00	125.00
(13)	Ty Cobb	11,625	4,650	2,325
(14)	Bill Cranston	450.00	170.00	85.00
(15)	Birdie Cree	450.00	170.00	85.00
(16)	Wild Bill Donovan	450.00	170.00	85.00
(17)	Mickey Doolan	450.00	170.00	85.00
(18)	Jean Dubuc	450.00	170.00	85.00
(19)	Joe Dunn	450.00	170.00	85.00
(20)	Roy Ellam	450.00	170.00	85.00
(21)	Clyde Engle	450.00	170.00	85.00
(22)	Johnny Evers	1,275	500.00	250.00
(23)	Art Fletcher	450.00	170.00	85.00
(24)	Charlie Fritz	450.00	170.00	85.00
(25)	Ed Greminger	450.00	170.00	85.00
(26)	Bill Hart (Little Rock)	450.00	170.00	85.00
(27)	Jimmy Hart (Montgomery)	450.00	170.00	85.00
(28)	Topsy Hartsel	450.00	170.00	85.00
(29)	Gordon Hickman	450.00	170.00	85.00
(30)	Danny Hoffman	450.00	170.00	85.00
(31)	Harry Howell	450.00	170.00	85.00
(32)	Miller Huggins (Hands at mouth.)	1,275	500.00	250.00
(33)	Miller Huggins (Portrait)	1,275	500.00	250.00
(34)	George Hunter	450.00	170.00	85.00
(35)	A.O. "Dutch" Jordan	450.00	170.00	85.00
(36)	Ed Killian	450.00	170.00	85.00
(37)	Otto Knabe	450.00	170.00	85.00
(38)	Frank LaPorte	450.00	170.00	85.00
(39)	Ed Lennox	450.00	170.00	85.00
(40)	Harry Lentz (Sentz)	450.00	170.00	85.00
(41)	Rube Marquard	1,275	500.00	250.00
(42)	Doc Marshall	450.00	170.00	85.00

		NM	EX	VG
(43)	Christy Mathewson	3,225	1,300	650.00
(44)	George McBride	450.00	170.00	85.00
(45)	Pryor McElveen	450.00	170.00	85.00
(46)	Matty McIntyre	450.00	170.00	85.00
(47)	Mike Mitchell	450.00	170.00	85.00
(48)	Carlton Molesworth	450.00	170.00	85.00
(49)	Mike Mowrey	450.00	170.00	85.00
(50)	Chief Myers (Meyers) (Batting)	450.00	170.00	85.00
(51)	Chief Myers (Meyers) (Fielding)	450.00	170.00	85.00
(52)	Dode Paskert	450.00	170.00	85.00
(53)	Hub Perdue	450.00	170.00	85.00
(54)	Arch Persons	450.00	170.00	85.00
(55)	Ed Reagan	450.00	170.00	85.00
(56)	Bob Rhoades (Rhoads)	450.00	170.00	85.00
(57)	Ike Rockenfeld	450.00	170.00	85.00
(58)	Claude Rossman	450.00	170.00	85.00
(59)	Boss Schmidt	450.00	170.00	85.00
(60)	Sid Smith	450.00	170.00	85.00
(61)	Charlie Starr	450.00	170.00	85.00
(62)	Gabby Street	450.00	170.00	85.00
(63)	Ed Summers	450.00	170.00	85.00
(64)	Jeff Sweeney	450.00	170.00	85.00
(65)	Ira Thomas	450.00	170.00	85.00
(66)	Woodie Thornton	450.00	170.00	85.00
(67)	Ed Willett	450.00	170.00	85.00
(68)	Owen Wilson	450.00	170.00	85.00

1914-16 Coupon Cigarettes Type 2 (T213)

Though they feature the same photos used in the contemporary T206 tobacco issue, Coupon Cigarette cards make up three distinct sets, produced between 1910 and 1919. Type 2 Coupons feature a mix of players from the three major leagues (National, American and Federal), and several minor leagues. The 1-7/16" x 2-5/8" Coupon fronts are virtually identical, except for the use of blue typography, to the more popular T206 series. Backs, however, clearly identify the cards as being a product of Coupon Cigarettes and allow the collector to easily differentiate among the three types. Type 2 cards, issued from 1914 to 1916, contain the words "MILD and SWEET" and "20 for 5 cents." Distribution of the Coupon cards was limited to the Louisiana area, making the set difficult to checklist and even moreso to collect. Numerous variations further complicate the situation. It is quite possible the checklists here are incomplete and additions will surface in the future. Although Type 2 cards are the most common, they were printed with a "glossy" coating, making them susceptible to cracking and creasing.

		NM	EX	VG
	Complete Set (188):	80,000	36,000	17,500
	Common Player:	275.00	125.00	60.00
(1)	Red Ames (Cincinnati)	275.00	125.00	60.00
(2)	Red Ames (St. Louis)	275.00	125.00	60.00
(3)	Home Run Baker (Phila. Amer.)	550.00	245.00	120.00
(4)	Home Run Baker (Philadelphia Amer.)	600.00	275.00	130.00
(5)	Home Run Baker (New York)	550.00	245.00	120.00
(6)	Cy Barger	275.00	125.00	60.00
(7)	Chief Bender (Trees in background, Philadelphia Amer.)	550.00	245.00	120.00
(8)	Chief Bender (Trees in background, Baltimore.)	550.00	245.00	120.00
(9)	Chief Bender (Trees in background, Philadelphia Nat.)	550.00	245.00	120.00
(10)	Chief Bender (No trees, Philadelphia Amer.)	550.00	245.00	120.00
(11)	Chief Bender (No trees, Baltimore.)	550.00	245.00	120.00
(12)	Chief Bender (No trees, Philadelphia Natl.)	550.00	240.00	120.00
(13)	Bill Bradley	275.00	125.00	60.00
(14)	Roger Bresnahan (Chicago)	550.00	245.00	120.00
(15)	Roger Bresnahan (Toledo)	550.00	245.00	120.00
(16)	Al Bridwell (St. Louis)	275.00	125.00	60.00
(17)	Al Bridwell (Nashville)	275.00	125.00	60.00
(18)	Mordecai Brown (Chicago)	550.00	245.00	120.00
(19)	Mordecai Brown (St. Louis)	550.00	245.00	120.00
(20)	Bobby Byrne	275.00	125.00	60.00
(21)	Howie Camnitz (Arm at side.)	275.00	125.00	60.00
(22)	Howie Camnitz (Pittsburgh, hands above head.)	275.00	125.00	60.00
(23)	Howie Camnitz (Savannah, hands above head.)	275.00	125.00	60.00
(24)	Billy Campbell	275.00	125.00	60.00
(25)	Frank Chance (Batting, New York.)	550.00	245.00	120.00
(26)	Frank Chance (Los Angeles, batting.)	600.00	270.00	130.00
(27)	Frank Chance (New York, portrait.)	550.00	245.00	120.00
(28)	Frank Chance (Los Angeles, portrait.)	600.00	270.00	130.00
(29)	Bill Chapelle (Brooklyn, "R" on shirt.)	275.00	125.00	60.00
(30)	Larry Chapelle (Chappel) (Cleveland, no "R" on shirt, photo actually Bill Chapelle.)	275.00	125.00	60.00
(31)	Hal Chase (Chicago, holding trophy.)	365.00	165.00	80.00
(32)	Hal Chase (Buffalo, holding trophy.)	365.00	165.00	80.00
(33)	Hal Chase (Chicago, portrait, blue background.)	365.00	165.00	80.00
(34)	Hal Chase (Buffalo, portrait, blue background.)	365.00	165.00	80.00
(35)	Hal Chase (Chicago, throwing.)	365.00	165.00	80.00
(36)	Hal Chase (Buffalo, throwing.)	365.00	165.00	80.00
(37)	Ty Cobb (Portrait)	7,250	3,250	1,600
(38)	Ty Cobb (Bat off shoulder.)	6,000	2,700	1,325
(39)	Eddie Collins (Philadelphia, "A" on shirt.)	600.00	270.00	130.00
(40)	Eddie Collins (Chicago, "A" on shirt.)	600.00	270.00	130.00
(41)	Eddie Collins (Chicago, no "A" on shirt.)	600.00	270.00	130.00
(42)	Doc Crandall (St. Louis Fed.)	275.00	125.00	60.00
(43)	Doc Crandall (St. Louis Amer.)	275.00	125.00	60.00
(44)	Sam Crawford	550.00	245.00	120.00
(45)	Birdie Cree	275.00	125.00	60.00
(46)	Harry Davis (Phila. Amer.)	275.00	125.00	60.00
(47)	Harry Davis (Philadelphia Amer.)	275.00	125.00	60.00
(48)	Ray Demmitt (Chicago Amer. (New York uniform.))	275.00	125.00	60.00
(49)	Ray Demmitt (Chicago Amer. (St. Louis uniform.))	275.00	125.00	60.00
(50)	Josh Devore (Philadelphia)	275.00	125.00	60.00
(51)	Josh Devore (Chillicothe)	275.00	125.00	60.00
(52)	Mike Donlin (New York)	275.00	125.00	60.00
(53)	Mike Donlin (.300 batter 7 years)	275.00	125.00	60.00
(54)	Wild Bill Donovan	275.00	125.00	60.00
(55)	Mickey Doolan (Baltimore, batting.)	275.00	125.00	60.00
(56)	Mickey Doolan (Chicago, batting.)	275.00	125.00	60.00
(57)	Mickey Doolan (Baltimore, fielding.)	275.00	125.00	60.00
(58)	Mickey Doolan (Chicago, fielding.)	275.00	125.00	60.00
(59)	Tom Downey	275.00	125.00	60.00
(60)	Larry Doyle (Batting)	275.00	125.00	60.00
(61)	Larry Doyle (Portrait)	275.00	125.00	60.00
(62)	Jean Dubuc	275.00	125.00	60.00
(63)	Jack Dunn (Picture is Joe Dunn.)	275.00	125.00	60.00
(64)	Kid Elberfield (Elberfeld) (Brooklyn)	275.00	125.00	60.00
(65)	Kid Elberfield (Elberfeld) (Chatanooga)	275.00	125.00	60.00
(66)	Steve Evans	275.00	125.00	60.00
(67)	Johnny Evers	550.00	245.00	120.00
(68)	Russ Ford	275.00	125.00	60.00
(69)	Art Fromme	275.00	125.00	60.00
(70)	Chick Gandil (Washington)	1,000	450.00	220.00
(71)	Chick Gandil (Cleveland)	550.00	245.00	120.00
(72)	Rube Geyer	275.00	125.00	60.00
(73)	Clark Griffith	550.00	245.00	120.00
(74)	Bob Groom	275.00	125.00	60.00
(75)	Buck Herzog ("B" on shirt.)	300.00	135.00	66.00
(76)	Buck Herzog (No "B" on shirt.)	400.00	180.00	88.00
(77)	Dick Hoblitzell (Cincinnati)	275.00	125.00	60.00
(78)	Dick Hoblitzell (Boston Nat.)	275.00	125.00	60.00
(79)	Dick Hoblitzell (Boston Amer.)	275.00	125.00	60.00
(80)	Solly Hofman	275.00	125.00	60.00
(81)	Solly Hofman (Hofman)	275.00	125.00	60.00
(82)	Miller Huggins (Hands at mouth.)	550.00	245.00	120.00
(83)	Miller Huggins (Portrait)	550.00	245.00	120.00
(84)	John Hummel (Brooklyn Nat.)	275.00	125.00	60.00
(85)	John Hummel (Brooklyn)	275.00	125.00	60.00
(86)	Hughie Jennings (Both hands showing.)	550.00	245.00	120.00
(87)	Hughie Jennings (One hand showing.)	550.00	245.00	120.00
(88)	Walter Johnson	2,500	1,125	550.00
(89)	Tim Jordan (Toronto)	275.00	125.00	60.00
(90)	Tim Jordan (Ft. Worth)	275.00	125.00	60.00
(91)	Joe Kelley (New York)	550.00	245.00	120.00
(92)	Joe Kelley (Toronto)	550.00	245.00	120.00
(93)	Otto Knabe	275.00	125.00	60.00
(94)	Ed Konetchy (Pittsburgh Nat.)	275.00	125.00	60.00
(95)	Ed Konetchy (Pittsburgh Fed.)	275.00	125.00	60.00
(96)	Ed Konetchy (Boston)	275.00	125.00	60.00
(97)	Harry Krause	275.00	125.00	60.00
(98)	Nap Lajoie (Phila. Amer.)	550.00	245.00	120.00
(99)	Nap Lajoie (Philadelphia Amer.)	550.00	245.00	120.00
(100)	Nap Lajoie (Cleveland)	550.00	245.00	120.00
(101)	Tommy Leach (Chicago)	275.00	125.00	60.00
(102)	Tommy Leach (Cincinnati)	275.00	125.00	60.00
(103)	Tommy Leach (Rochester)	275.00	125.00	60.00
(104)	Ed Lennox	275.00	125.00	60.00
(105)	Sherry Magee (Phila. Nat.)	275.00	125.00	60.00
(106)	Sherry Magee (Philadelphia Nat.)	275.00	125.00	60.00
(107)	Sherry Magee (Boston)	275.00	125.00	60.00
(108)	Rube Marquard (New York, pitching, "NY" on shirt.)	600.00	270.00	130.00
(109)	Rube Marquard (Brooklyn, pitching, no "NY" on shirt.)	550.00	245.00	120.00
(110)	Rube Marquard (New York, portrait, "NY" on shirt.)	550.00	245.00	120.00
(111)	Rube Marquard (Brooklyn, portrait, no "NY" on shirt.)	550.00	245.00	120.00
(112)	Christy Mathewson	3,000	1,350	660.00
(113)	John McGraw (Glove at side.)	550.00	245.00	120.00
(114)	John McGraw (Portrait)	550.00	245.00	120.00
(115)	Larry McLean	275.00	125.00	60.00
(116)	George McQuillan (Pittsburgh)	275.00	125.00	60.00
(117)	George McQuillan (Phila. Nat.)	275.00	125.00	60.00
(118)	George McQuillan (Philadelphia Nat.)	275.00	125.00	60.00
(119)	Fred Merkle	275.00	125.00	60.00
(120)	Chief Meyers (New York, fielding.)	275.00	125.00	60.00
(121)	Chief Meyers (Brooklyn, fielding.)	275.00	125.00	60.00
(122)	Chief Meyers (New York, portrait.)	275.00	125.00	60.00
(123)	Chief Meyers (Brooklyn, portrait.)	275.00	125.00	60.00
(124)	Dots Miller	275.00	125.00	60.00
(125)	Mike Mitchell	275.00	125.00	60.00
(126)	Mike Mowrey (Pittsburgh Nat.)	275.00	125.00	60.00
(127)	Mike Mowrey (Pittsburgh Fed.)	275.00	125.00	60.00
(128)	Mike Mowrey (Brooklyn)	275.00	125.00	60.00
(129)	George Mullin (Indianapolis)	275.00	125.00	60.00
(130)	George Mullin (Newark)	275.00	125.00	60.00
(131)	Danny Murphy	275.00	125.00	60.00
(132)	Red Murray (New York)	275.00	125.00	60.00
(133)	Red Murray (Chicago)	275.00	125.00	60.00
(134)	Red Murray (Kansas City)	275.00	125.00	60.00
(135)	Tom Needham	275.00	125.00	60.00
(136)	Rebel Oakes	275.00	125.00	60.00
(137)	Rube Oldring (Phila. Amer.)	275.00	125.00	60.00
(138)	Rube Oldring (Philadelphia Amer.)	275.00	125.00	60.00
(139)	Dode Paskert (Phila. Nat.)	275.00	125.00	60.00
(140)	Dode Paskert (Philadelphia Nat.)	275.00	125.00	60.00
(141)	Billy Purtell	275.00	125.00	60.00
(142)	Jack Quinn (Baltimore)	275.00	125.00	60.00
(143)	Jack Quinn (Vernon)	275.00	125.00	60.00
(144)	Ed Reulbach (Brooklyn Nat.)	275.00	125.00	60.00
(145)	Ed Reulbach (Brooklyn Fed.)	275.00	125.00	60.00
(146)	Ed Reulbach (Pittsburgh)	275.00	125.00	60.00
(147)	Nap Rucker (Brooklyn)	275.00	125.00	60.00
(148)	Nap Rucker (Brooklyn Nat.)	275.00	125.00	60.00
(149)	Dick Rudolph	275.00	125.00	60.00
(150)	Germany Schaefer (Washington, "W" on shirt.)	275.00	125.00	60.00
(151)	Germany Schaefer (K.C. Fed., "W" on shirt.)	275.00	125.00	60.00
(152)	Germany Schaefer (New York, no "W" on shirt.)	275.00	125.00	60.00
(153)	Admiral Schlei (Batting)	275.00	125.00	60.00
(154)	Admiral Schlei (Portrait)	275.00	125.00	60.00
(155)	Boss Schmidt	275.00	125.00	60.00
(156)	Wildfire Schulte	275.00	125.00	60.00
(157)	Frank Smith	275.00	125.00	60.00
(158)	Tris Speaker	1,200	540.00	265.00
(159)	George Stovall	275.00	125.00	60.00
(160)	Gabby Street (Catching)	275.00	125.00	60.00
(161)	Gabby Street (Portrait)	275.00	125.00	60.00
(162)	Ed Summers	275.00	125.00	60.00
(163)	Bill Sweeney (Boston)	275.00	125.00	60.00
(164)	Bill Sweeney (Chicago)	275.00	125.00	60.00
(165)	Jeff Sweeney (New York)	275.00	125.00	60.00
(166)	Jeff Sweeney (Richmond)	275.00	125.00	60.00
(167)	Ira Thomas (Phila. Amer.)	275.00	125.00	60.00
(168)	Ira Thomas (Philadelphia Amer.)	275.00	125.00	60.00
(169)	Joe Tinker (Chicago Fed., bat off shoulder.)	550.00	245.00	120.00
(170)	Joe Tinker (Chicago Nat., bat off shoulder.)	550.00	245.00	120.00
(171)	Joe Tinker (Chicago Fed., bat off shoulder.)	550.00	245.00	120.00
(172)	Joe Tinker (Chicago Nat., bat off shoulder.)	550.00	245.00	120.00
(173)	Heinie Wagner	275.00	125.00	60.00
(174)	Jack Warhop (New York, "NY" on shirt.)	275.00	125.00	60.00
(175)	Jack Warhop (St. Louis, no "NY" on shirt.)	275.00	125.00	60.00
(176)	Zach Wheat (Brooklyn)	550.00	245.00	120.00
(177)	Zach Wheat (Brooklyn Nat.)	550.00	245.00	120.00
(178)	Kaiser Wilhelm	275.00	125.00	60.00
(179)	Ed Willett (St. Louis)	275.00	125.00	60.00
(180)	Ed Willett (Memphis)	275.00	125.00	60.00
(181)	Owen Wilson	275.00	125.00	60.00
(182)	Hooks Wiltse (New York, pitching.)	275.00	125.00	60.00
(183)	Hooks Wiltse (Brooklyn, pitching.)	275.00	125.00	60.00
(184)	Hooks Wiltse (Jersey City, pitching.)	275.00	125.00	60.00
(185)	Hooks Wiltse (New York, portrait.)	275.00	125.00	60.00
(186)	Hooks Wiltse (Brooklyn, portrait.)	275.00	125.00	60.00
(187)	Hooks Wiltse (Jersey City, portrait.)	275.00	125.00	60.00
(188)	Heinie Zimmerman	275.00	125.00	60.00

1919 Coupon Cigarettes Type 3 (T213)

Though using the same photos seen in the contemporary T206 tobacco issue, Coupon Cigarette cards comprise three distinct sets produced between 1910 and 1919. Coupon cards feature a mix of players from the National and American Leagues, and several minor leagues. Slightly smaller than the usual cigarette-card format, Type 3 Coupons nominally measure 1-3/8" x 2-9/16", but are more prone to original size deviations than Type 1 or Type 2 Coupons. Except for the blue ink used in the player identification line, the fronts of the Coupon

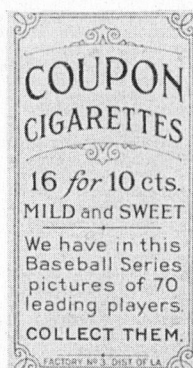

cards are virtually identical to the more popular T206 series. Backs, however, clearly identify the cards as being a product of Coupon Cigarettes and allow the collector to easily differentiate among the three types. Type 3 cards, issued in 1919, advertise "16 for 10 cts." and mention "70 leading players." Distribution of the Coupon cards was limited to the Louisiana area, making the set difficult to checklist and even more difficult to collect. Numerous variations further complicate the situation. It is quite possible the checklists here are incomplete and additions will surface in the future. While most Type 3 Coupons mention on their backs, "FACTORY No. 3, DIST OF LA," some have been seen with that designation blacked out and an overprint applied citing "FACTORY No. 8, DIST OF LA."

		NM	EX	VG
Complete Set (70):		30,000	13,500	6,750
Common Player:		300.00	135.00	65.00
(1)	Red Ames	300.00	135.00	65.00
(2)	Home Run Baker	600.00	275.00	130.00
(3)	Chief Bender	600.00	275.00	130.00
	(No trees in background.)			
(4)	Chief Bender	600.00	275.00	130.00
	(Trees in background.)			
(5)	Roger Bresnahan	600.00	275.00	130.00
(6)	Al Bridwell	300.00	135.00	65.00
(7)	Miner Brown	600.00	275.00	130.00
(8)	Bobby Byrne	300.00	135.00	65.00
(9)	Frank Chance (Batting)	600.00	275.00	130.00
(10)	Frank Chance (Portrait)	600.00	275.00	130.00
(11)	Hal Chase (Holding trophy.)	450.00	200.00	100.00
(12)	Hal Chase (Portrait)	450.00	200.00	100.00
(13)	Hal Chase (Throwing)	450.00	200.00	100.00
(14)	Ty Cobb (Batting)	3,750	1,675	825.00
(15)	Ty Cobb (Portrait)	3,750	1,675	825.00
(16)	Eddie Collins	600.00	275.00	130.00
(17)	Sam Crawford	600.00	275.00	130.00
(18)	Harry Davis	300.00	135.00	65.00
(19)	Mike Donlin	300.00	135.00	65.00
(20)	Wild Bill Donovan	300.00	135.00	65.00
(21)	Mickey Doolan (Batting)	300.00	135.00	65.00
(22)	Mickey Doolan (Fielding)	300.00	135.00	65.00
(23)	Larry Doyle (Batting)	300.00	135.00	65.00
(24)	Larry Doyle (Portrait)	300.00	135.00	65.00
(25)	Jean Dubuc	300.00	135.00	65.00
(26)	Jack Dunn	300.00	135.00	65.00
(27)	Kid Elberfeld	300.00	135.00	65.00
(28)	Johnny Evers	600.00	275.00	130.00
(29)	Chick Gandil	550.00	250.00	125.00
(30)	Clark Griffith	600.00	275.00	130.00
(31)	Buck Herzog	300.00	135.00	65.00
(32)	Dick Hoblitzell	300.00	135.00	65.00
(33)	Miller Huggins	600.00	275.00	130.00
	(Hands at mouth.)			
(34)	Miller Huggins (Portrait)	600.00	275.00	130.00
(35)	John Hummel	300.00	135.00	65.00
(36)	Hughie Jennings	600.00	275.00	130.00
	(Both hands showing.)			
(37)	Hughie Jennings	600.00	275.00	130.00
	(One hand showing.)			
(38)	Walter Johnson	900.00	400.00	200.00
(39)	Tim Jordan	300.00	135.00	65.00
(40)	Joe Kelley	600.00	275.00	130.00
(41)	Ed Konetchy	300.00	135.00	65.00
(42)	Larry Lajoie	600.00	275.00	130.00
(43)	Sherry Magee	300.00	135.00	65.00
(44)	Rube Marquard	600.00	275.00	130.00
(45)	Christy Mathewson	1,200	540.00	265.00
(47)	John McGraw (Glove at side.)	600.00	275.00	130.00
(48)	John McGraw (Portrait)	600.00	275.00	130.00
(49)	George McQuillan	300.00	135.00	65.00
(50)	Fred Merkle	300.00	135.00	65.00
(51)	Dots Miller	300.00	135.00	65.00
(52)	Mike Mowrey	300.00	135.00	65.00
(53)	Chief Myers (Meyers)	300.00	135.00	65.00
	(Brooklyn)			
(54)	Chief Myers (Meyers)	300.00	135.00	65.00
	(New Haven)			
(55)	Dode Paskert	300.00	135.00	65.00
(56)	Jack Quinn	300.00	135.00	65.00
(57)	Ed Reulbach	300.00	135.00	65.00
(58)	Nap Rucker	300.00	135.00	65.00
(59)	Dick Rudolph	300.00	135.00	65.00
(60)	Herman Schaeffer (Schaefer)	300.00	135.00	65.00
(61)	Wildfire Schulte	300.00	135.00	65.00
(62)	Tris Speaker	750.00	335.00	165.00
(63)	Gabby Street (Catching)	300.00	135.00	65.00
(64)	Gabby Street (Portrait)	300.00	135.00	65.00
(65)	Jeff Sweeney	300.00	135.00	65.00
(66)	Ira Thomas	300.00	135.00	65.00
(67)	Joe Tinker	600.00	275.00	130.00
(68)	Zach Wheat	600.00	275.00	130.00
(69)	Geo. Wiltse	300.00	135.00	65.00
(70)	Heinie Zimmerman	300.00	135.00	65.00

1919 Coupon Cigarettes Type 3, Factory 8 Overprint

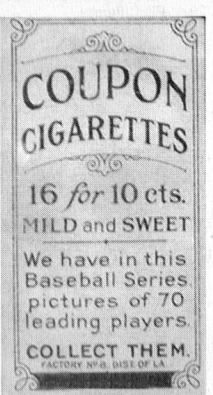

Of interest to specialty collectors is a variation of Type 3 Coupon cards on which the normal "FACTORY No. 3 . . ." line at bottom back has been blacked out and a "FACTORY No. 8 . . ." designation overprinted. The extent of the overprint checklist is unknown and at least one card (Cobb, bat off shoulder) is found as a Factory 8, but not yet verified to exist as a Factory 3 version.

	NM	EX	VG
Common Player:	600.00	300.00	180.00
Hall of Famers: 4-6X			
Chief Bender (No trees.)			
Ty Cobb (Bat off shoulder.)			
Eddie Collins			
Jean Dubuc			
Hughie Jennings			
(Both hands showing.)			
Rube Marquard			
John McGraw (Portrait)			

1914 Cracker Jack (E145)

The 1914 Cracker Jack set, whose ACC designation is E145-1, is one of the most popular of the "E" card sets and features baseball stars from the American, National and Federal leagues. The 2-1/4" x 3" cards, are printed on thin stock and were inserted in boxes of Cracker Jack. The 1914 issue consists of 144 cards with tinted color photographs on a red background. Numbered backs feature a short biography plus an advertisement. The advertising on the low-numbered cards in the set indicates that 10 million cards were issued, while the high-numbered cards boast that 15 million were printed.

		NM	EX	VG
Complete Set (144):		375,000	115,000	45,000
Common Player:		850.00	260.00	100.00
1	Otto Knabe	2,000	325.00	125.00
2	Home Run Baker	2,350	775.00	350.00
3	Joe Tinker	2,350	775.00	350.00
4	Larry Doyle	850.00	260.00	100.00
5	Ward Miller	850.00	260.00	100.00
6	Eddie Plank	2,500	825.00	375.00
7	Eddie Collins	2,300	760.00	345.00
8	Rube Oldring	850.00	260.00	100.00
9	Artie Hoffman (Hofman)	850.00	260.00	100.00
10	Stuffy McInnis	850.00	260.00	100.00
11	George Stovall	850.00	260.00	100.00
12	Connie Mack	3,600	1,200	540.00
13	Art Wilson	850.00	260.00	100.00
14	Sam Crawford	2,300	760.00	345.00
15	Reb Russell	850.00	260.00	100.00
16	Howie Camnitz	850.00	260.00	100.00
17a	Roger Bresnahan	7,500	2,475	1,125
	(No number on back.)			
17b	Roger Bresnahan	2,300	760.00	345.00
	(Number on back.)			
18	Johnny Evers	2,300	760.00	345.00
19	Chief Bender	2,300	760.00	345.00
20	Cy Falkenberg	850.00	260.00	100.00
21	Heinie Zimmerman	850.00	260.00	100.00
22	Smokey Joe Wood	1,500	495.00	225.00
23	Charles Comiskey	2,300	760.00	345.00
24	George Mullen (Mullin)	850.00	260.00	100.00
25	Mike Simon	850.00	260.00	100.00
26	Jim Scott	850.00	260.00	100.00
27	Bill Carrigan	850.00	260.00	100.00
28	Jack Barry	850.00	260.00	100.00
29	Vean Gregg	850.00	260.00	100.00
30	Ty Cobb	30,000	10,000	4,500
31	Heinie Wagner	850.00	260.00	100.00
32	Mordecai Brown	2,300	760.00	345.00
33	Amos Strunk	850.00	260.00	100.00
34	Ira Thomas	850.00	260.00	100.00
35	Harry Hooper	2,300	760.00	345.00
36	Ed Walsh	2,300	760.00	345.00
37	Grover C. Alexander	9,000	2,975	1,350
38	Red Dooin	850.00	260.00	100.00
39	Chick Gandil	1,625	535.00	245.00
40	Jimmy Austin	850.00	260.00	100.00
41	Tommy Leach	850.00	260.00	100.00
42	Al Bridwell	850.00	260.00	100.00
43	Rube Marquard	3,900	1,300	585.00
44	Jeff Tesreau	850.00	260.00	100.00
45	Fred Luderus	850.00	260.00	100.00
46	Bob Groom	850.00	260.00	100.00
47	Josh Devore	850.00	260.00	100.00
48	Harry Lord	850.00	260.00	100.00
49	Dots Miller	850.00	260.00	100.00
50	John Hummell (Hummel)	850.00	260.00	100.00
51	Nap Rucker	850.00	260.00	100.00
52	Zach Wheat	2,300	760.00	345.00
53	Otto Miller	850.00	260.00	100.00
54	Marty O'Toole	850.00	260.00	100.00
55	Dick Hoblitzel (Hoblitzell)	850.00	260.00	100.00
56	Clyde Milan	850.00	260.00	100.00
57	Walter Johnson	8,500	2,800	1,275
58	Wally Schang	850.00	260.00	100.00
59	Doc Gessler	850.00	260.00	100.00
60	Rollie Zeider	850.00	260.00	100.00
61	Ray Schalk	2,300	760.00	345.00
62	Jay Cashion	850.00	260.00	100.00
63	Babe Adams	850.00	260.00	100.00
64	Jimmy Archer	850.00	260.00	100.00
65	Tris Speaker	7,200	2,400	1,080
66	Nap Lajoie	7,200	2,400	1,080
67	Doc Crandall	850.00	260.00	100.00
68	Honus Wagner	16,500	5,450	2,475
69	John McGraw	2,300	760.00	345.00
70	Fred Clarke	2,300	760.00	345.00
71	Chief Meyers	850.00	260.00	100.00
72	Joe Boehling	850.00	260.00	100.00
73	Max Carey	2,300	760.00	345.00
74	Frank Owens	850.00	260.00	100.00
75	Miller Huggins	2,300	760.00	345.00
76	Claude Hendrix	850.00	260.00	100.00
77	Hughie Jennings	2,300	760.00	345.00
78	Fred Merkle	850.00	260.00	100.00
79	Ping Bodie	850.00	260.00	100.00
80	Ed Reulbach	850.00	260.00	100.00
81	Jim Delehanty (Delahanty)	850.00	260.00	100.00
82	Gavvy Cravath	850.00	260.00	100.00
83	Russ Ford	850.00	260.00	100.00
84	Elmer Knetzer	850.00	260.00	100.00
85	Buck Herzog	850.00	260.00	100.00
86	Burt Shotten	850.00	260.00	100.00
87	Hick Cady	850.00	260.00	100.00
88	Christy Mathewson	120,000	40,000	18,000
89	Larry Cheney	850.00	260.00	100.00
90	Frank Smith	850.00	260.00	100.00
91	Roger Peckinpaugh	900.00	295.00	135.00
92	Al Demaree	850.00	260.00	100.00
93	Del Pratt	850.00	260.00	100.00
94	Eddie Cicotte	2,200	725.00	330.00
95	Ray Keating	850.00	260.00	100.00
96	Beals Becker	850.00	260.00	100.00
97	Rube Benton	850.00	260.00	100.00
98	Frank Laporte (LaPorte)	850.00	260.00	100.00
99	Frank Chance	9,000	3,000	1,350
100	Tom Seaton	850.00	260.00	100.00
101	Wildfire Schulte	850.00	260.00	100.00
102	Ray Fisher	850.00	260.00	100.00
103	Joe Jackson	65,000	21,450	9,750
104	Vic Saier	850.00	260.00	100.00
105	Jimmy Lavender	850.00	260.00	100.00
106	Joe Birmingham	850.00	260.00	100.00
107	Tom Downey	850.00	260.00	100.00
108	Sherry Magee	850.00	260.00	100.00
109	Fred Blanding	850.00	260.00	100.00
110	Bob Bescher	850.00	260.00	100.00
111	Nixey Callahan	850.00	260.00	100.00
112	Jeff Sweeney	850.00	260.00	100.00
113	George Suggs	850.00	260.00	100.00
114	George Moriarity (Moriarty)	850.00	260.00	100.00
115	Ad Brennan	850.00	260.00	100.00
116	Rollie Zeider	850.00	260.00	100.00
117	Ted Easterly	850.00	260.00	100.00
118	Ed Konetchy	850.00	260.00	100.00
119	George Perring	850.00	260.00	100.00
120	Mickey Doolan	850.00	260.00	100.00
121	Hub Perdue	850.00	260.00	100.00
122	Donie Bush	850.00	260.00	100.00
123	Slim Sallee	850.00	260.00	100.00
124	Earle Moore (Earl)	850.00	260.00	100.00
125	Bert Niehoff	850.00	260.00	100.00
126	Walter Blair	850.00	260.00	100.00
127	Butch Schmidt	850.00	260.00	100.00
128	Steve Evans	850.00	260.00	100.00
129	Ray Caldwell	850.00	260.00	100.00
130	Ivy Wingo	850.00	260.00	100.00
131	George Baumgardner	850.00	260.00	100.00
132	Les Nunamaker	850.00	260.00	100.00
133	Branch Rickey	8,000	2,650	1,200
134	Armando Marsans	900.00	295.00	135.00
135	Bill Killifer (Killefer)	850.00	260.00	100.00
136	Rabbit Maranville	2,750	900.00	410.00
137	Bill Rariden	850.00	260.00	100.00
138	Hank Gowdy	850.00	260.00	100.00
139	Rebel Oakes	850.00	260.00	100.00
140	Danny Murphy	850.00	260.00	100.00
141	Cy Barger	850.00	260.00	100.00
142	Gene Packard	850.00	260.00	100.00
143	Jake Daubert	850.00	260.00	100.00
144	Jimmy Walsh	2,000	350.00	110.00

1915 Cracker Jack (E145)

The 1915 Cracker Jack set (E145-2) is a reissue of the 1914 edition with some card additions and deletions, team designation changes, and new poses. A total of 176 cards comprise the set. Cards can be distinguished as either 1914 or 1915 by the advertising on the backs. The 1914 cards call the set complete at 144 pictures; the 1915 version notes 176 pictures. Backs of 1915 Cracker Jack cards are printed upside-down in relation to the front. A complete set and an album were available from the company.

		NM	EX	VG
Complete Set (176):		150,000	60,000	30,000
Common Player (1-144):		300.00	110.00	65.00
Common Player (145-176):		325.00	130.00	65.00
Album:		750.00	375.00	225.00
1	Otto Knabe	1,400	475.00	125.00
2	Home Run Baker	1,100	450.00	225.00
3	Joe Tinker	1,100	450.00	225.00
4	Larry Doyle	300.00	110.00	65.00
5	Ward Miller	300.00	110.00	65.00
6	Eddie Plank	1,350	550.00	275.00
7	Eddie Collins	1,200	480.00	240.00
8	Rube Oldring	300.00	110.00	65.00
9	Artie Hoffman (Hofman)	300.00	110.00	65.00
10	Stuffy McInnis	300.00	110.00	65.00
11	George Stovall	300.00	110.00	65.00
12	Connie Mack	1,100	450.00	225.00
13	Art Wilson	300.00	110.00	65.00
14	Sam Crawford	1,100	450.00	225.00
15	Reb Russell	300.00	110.00	65.00
16	Howie Camnitz	300.00	110.00	65.00
17	Roger Bresnahan	1,100	450.00	225.00
18	Johnny Evers	1,100	450.00	225.00
19	Chief Bender	1,100	450.00	225.00
20	Cy Falkenberg	300.00	110.00	65.00
21	Heinie Zimmerman	300.00	110.00	65.00
22	Smokey Joe Wood	800.00	325.00	160.00
23	Charles Comiskey	1,100	450.00	225.00
24	George Mullen (Mullin)	300.00	110.00	65.00
25	Mike Simon	300.00	110.00	65.00
26	Jim Scott	300.00	110.00	65.00
27	Bill Carrigan	300.00	110.00	65.00
28	Jack Barry	300.00	110.00	65.00
29	Vean Gregg	300.00	110.00	65.00
30	Ty Cobb	11,500	4,600	2,300
31	Heinie Wagner	300.00	110.00	65.00
32	Mordecai Brown	1,250	500.00	250.00
33	Amos Strunk	300.00	110.00	65.00
34	Ira Thomas	300.00	110.00	65.00
35	Harry Hooper	1,100	450.00	225.00
36	Ed Walsh	1,100	450.00	225.00
37	Grover C. Alexander	3,250	1,300	650.00
38	Red Dooin	300.00	110.00	65.00
39	Chick Gandil	800.00	325.00	160.00
40	Jimmy Austin	300.00	110.00	65.00
41	Tommy Leach	300.00	110.00	65.00
42	Al Bridwell	300.00	110.00	65.00
43	Rube Marquard	1,100	450.00	225.00
44	Jeff Tesreau	300.00	110.00	65.00
45	Fred Luderus	300.00	110.00	65.00
46	Bob Groom	300.00	110.00	65.00
47	Josh Devore	300.00	110.00	65.00
48	Steve O'Neill	300.00	110.00	65.00
49	Dots Miller	300.00	110.00	65.00
50	John Hummell (Hummel)	300.00	110.00	65.00
51	Nap Rucker	300.00	110.00	65.00
52	Zach Wheat	1,100	450.00	225.00
53	Otto Miller	300.00	110.00	65.00
54	Marty O'Toole	300.00	110.00	65.00
55	Dick Hoblitzel (Hoblitzell)	300.00	110.00	65.00
56	Clyde Milan	300.00	110.00	65.00
57	Walter Johnson	6,000	2,400	1,200
58	Wally Schang	300.00	110.00	65.00
59	Doc Gessler	300.00	110.00	65.00
60	Oscar Dugey	300.00	110.00	65.00
61	Ray Schalk	1,100	450.00	225.00
62	Willie Mitchell	300.00	110.00	65.00
63	Babe Adams	300.00	110.00	65.00
64	Jimmy Archer	300.00	110.00	65.00
65	Tris Speaker	1,700	680.00	340.00
66	Nap Lajoie	1,550	625.00	310.00
67	Doc Crandall	300.00	110.00	65.00
68	Honus Wagner	9,000	3,600	1,800
69	John McGraw	1,100	450.00	225.00
70	Fred Clarke	1,100	450.00	225.00
71	Chief Meyers	300.00	110.00	65.00
72	Joe Boehling	300.00	110.00	65.00
73	Max Carey	1,100	450.00	225.00
74	Frank Owens	300.00	110.00	65.00
75	Miller Huggins	1,100	450.00	225.00
76	Claude Hendrix	300.00	110.00	65.00
77	Hughie Jennings	1,100	450.00	225.00
78	Fred Merkle	300.00	110.00	65.00
79	Ping Bodie	300.00	110.00	65.00
80	Ed Reulbach	300.00	110.00	65.00
81	Jim Delehanty (Delahanty)	300.00	110.00	65.00
82	Gavvy Cravath	300.00	110.00	65.00
83	Russ Ford	300.00	110.00	65.00
84	Elmer Knetzer	300.00	110.00	65.00
85	Buck Herzog	300.00	110.00	65.00
86	Burt Shotten	300.00	110.00	65.00
87	Hick Cady	300.00	110.00	65.00
88	Christy Mathewson	6,600	2,650	1,325
89	Larry Cheney	300.00	110.00	65.00
90	Frank Smith	300.00	110.00	65.00
91	Roger Peckinpaugh	350.00	140.00	70.00
92	Al Demaree	300.00	110.00	65.00
93	Del Pratt	300.00	110.00	65.00
94	Eddie Cicotte	1,000	400.00	200.00
95	Ray Keating	300.00	110.00	65.00
96	Beals Becker	300.00	110.00	65.00
97	Rube Benton	300.00	110.00	65.00
98	Frank Laporte (LaPorte)	300.00	110.00	65.00
99	Hal Chase	600.00	240.00	120.00
100	Tom Seaton	300.00	110.00	65.00
101	Wildfire Schulte	300.00	110.00	65.00
102	Ray Fisher	300.00	110.00	65.00
103	Joe Jackson	27,500	11,000	5,500
104	Vic Saier	300.00	110.00	65.00
105	Jimmy Lavender	300.00	110.00	65.00
106	Joe Birmingham	300.00	110.00	65.00
107	Tom Downey	300.00	110.00	65.00
108	Sherry Magee	300.00	110.00	65.00
109	Fred Blanding	300.00	110.00	65.00
110	Bob Bescher	300.00	110.00	65.00
111	Herbie Moran	300.00	110.00	65.00
112	Ed Sweeney	300.00	110.00	65.00
113	George Suggs	300.00	110.00	65.00
114	George Moriarity (Moriarty)	300.00	110.00	65.00
115	Ad Brennan	300.00	110.00	65.00
116	Rollie Zeider	300.00	110.00	65.00
117	Ted Easterly	300.00	110.00	65.00
118	Ed Konetchy	300.00	110.00	65.00
119	George Perring	300.00	110.00	65.00
120	Mickey Doolan	300.00	110.00	65.00
121	Hub Perdue	300.00	110.00	65.00
122	Donie Bush	300.00	110.00	65.00
123	Slim Sallee	300.00	110.00	65.00
124	Earle Moore (Earl)	300.00	110.00	65.00
125	Bert Niehoff	300.00	110.00	65.00
126	Walter Blair	300.00	110.00	65.00
127	Butch Schmidt	300.00	110.00	65.00
128	Steve Evans	300.00	110.00	65.00
129	Ray Caldwell	300.00	110.00	65.00
130	Ivy Wingo	300.00	110.00	65.00
131	George Baumgardner	300.00	110.00	65.00
132	Les Nunamaker	300.00	110.00	65.00
133	Branch Rickey	1,100	450.00	225.00
134	Armando Marsans	425.00	175.00	85.00
135	Bill Killifer (Killefer)	300.00	110.00	65.00
136	Rabbit Maranville	1,100	450.00	225.00
137	Bill Rariden	300.00	110.00	65.00
138	Hank Gowdy	300.00	110.00	65.00
139	Rebel Oakes	300.00	110.00	65.00
140	Danny Murphy	300.00	110.00	65.00
141	Cy Barger	300.00	110.00	65.00
142	Gene Packard	300.00	110.00	65.00
143	Jake Daubert	300.00	110.00	65.00
144	Jimmy Walsh	300.00	110.00	65.00
145	Ted Cather	325.00	130.00	65.00
146	Lefty Tyler	325.00	130.00	65.00
147	Lee Magee	325.00	130.00	65.00
148	Owen Wilson	325.00	130.00	65.00
149	Hal Janvrin	325.00	130.00	65.00
150	Doc Johnston	325.00	130.00	65.00
151	Possum Whitted	325.00	130.00	65.00
152	George McQuillen (McQuillan)	325.00	130.00	65.00
153	Bill James	325.00	130.00	65.00
154	Dick Rudolph	325.00	130.00	65.00
155	Joe Connolly	325.00	130.00	65.00
156	Jean Dubuc	325.00	130.00	65.00
157	George Kaiserling	325.00	130.00	65.00
158	Fritz Maisel	325.00	130.00	65.00
159	Heinie Groh	325.00	130.00	65.00
160	Benny Kauff	325.00	130.00	65.00
161	Edd Rousch (Roush)	1,250	500.00	250.00
162	George Stallings	325.00	130.00	65.00
163	Bert Whaling	325.00	130.00	65.00
164	Bob Shawkey	325.00	130.00	65.00
165	Eddie Murphy	325.00	130.00	65.00
166	Bullet Joe Bush	325.00	130.00	65.00
167	Clark Griffith	1,250	500.00	250.00
168	Vin Campbell	325.00	130.00	65.00
169	Ray Collins	325.00	130.00	65.00
170	Hans Lobert	325.00	130.00	65.00
171	Earl Hamilton	325.00	130.00	65.00
172	Erskine Mayer	450.00	180.00	90.00
173	Tilly Walker	325.00	130.00	65.00
174	Bobby Veach	325.00	130.00	65.00
175	Joe Benz	325.00	130.00	65.00
176	Hippo Vaughn	1,300	200.00	75.00

1933 Cracker Jack Pins (PR4)

Although no manufacturer is indicated on the pins themselves, the manufacturer has been identified as Button Gum, but there is still some indication that Cracker Jack inserted this 25-player set in their products circa 1933. Each pin measures 13/16" in diameter and features a line drawing of a player portrait. The unnumbered pins are printed in blue and gray with backgrounds found in either yellow or gray.

		NM	EX	VG
Complete Set (25):		1,600	800.00	475.00
Common Player:		35.00	17.50	10.00
(1)	Charles Berry	35.00	17.50	10.00
(2)	Bill Cissell	35.00	17.50	10.00
(3)	KiKi Cuyler	60.00	30.00	18.00
(4)	Dizzy Dean	100.00	50.00	30.00
(5)	Wesley Ferrell	35.00	17.50	10.00
(6)	Frank Frisch	60.00	30.00	18.00
(7)	Lou Gehrig	250.00	125.00	75.00
(8)	Vernon Gomez	60.00	30.00	18.00
(9)	Goose Goslin	60.00	30.00	18.00
(10)	George Grantham	35.00	17.50	10.00
(11)	Charley Grimm	35.00	17.50	10.00
(12)	Lefty Grove	75.00	37.00	22.00
(13)	Gabby Hartnett	60.00	30.00	18.00
(14)	Travis Jackson	60.00	30.00	18.00
(15)	Tony Lazzeri	60.00	30.00	18.00
(16)	Ted Lyons	60.00	30.00	18.00
(17)	Rabbit Maranville	60.00	30.00	18.00
(18)	Carl Reynolds	35.00	17.50	10.00
(19)	Charles Ruffing	60.00	30.00	18.00
(20)	Al Simmons	60.00	30.00	18.00
(21)	Gus Suhr	35.00	17.50	10.00
(22)	Bill Terry	60.00	30.00	18.00
(23)	Dazzy Vance	60.00	30.00	18.00
(24)	Paul Waner	60.00	30.00	18.00
(25)	Lon Warneke	35.00	17.50	10.00

1979 Larry Crain Prints

"Baseball's Greatest Team," as voted during baseball's centennial, was featured on a set of 8-1/2" x 11" black-and-white prints by artist Larry Crain. Each print is signed and numbered by the artist. The set of 11 was originally sold for $25.

		NM	EX	VG
Complete Set (11):		25.00	12.50	7.50
Common Player:		3.00	1.50	.90
(1)	Yogi Berra	3.00	1.50	.90
(2)	Joe DiMaggio	5.00	2.50	1.50
(3)	Lou Gehrig	4.00	2.00	1.25
(4)	Rogers Hornsby	3.00	1.50	.90
(5)	Walter Johnson	3.00	1.50	.90
(6)	Willie Mays	4.00	2.00	1.25
(7)	Brooks Robinson	3.00	1.50	.90
(8)	Babe Ruth	5.00	2.50	1.50
(9)	Warren Spahn	3.00	1.50	.90
(10)	Casey Stengel	3.00	1.50	.90
(11)	Honus Wagner	3.00	1.50	.90

1976 Crane Potato Chips Discs

This unnumbered 70-card set of player discs was issued with Crane Potato Chips in 1976. The front of the discs are designed to look like a baseball with the player's black-and-white portrait in the center and vital data in side panels containing one of several bright colors. Discs measure 3-3/8" in diameter. This is the most common among several regionally issued sets sharing the same card fronts with different ads on back. The discs were produced by Michael Schechter Associates under license from the players' union. All uniform and cap logos have been deleted from the discs' photos. The unnumbered discs are checklisted here in alphabetical order. Several of the discs have team variations reflecting player moves. These are known only among the Crane discs and have not been verified in the issues of other advertisers.

		NM	EX	VG
Complete Set (70):		25.00	12.50	7.50
Common Player:		1.00	.50	.30
(1)	Henry Aaron	9.00	4.50	2.75
(2)	Johnny Bench	4.00	2.00	1.25
(3)	Vida Blue	1.00	.50	.30
(4)	Larry Bowa	1.00	.50	.30
(5)	Lou Brock	3.00	1.50	.90
(6)	Jeff Burroughs	1.00	.50	.30
(7)	John Candelaria	1.00	.50	.30
(8)	Jose Cardenal	1.00	.50	.30
(9)	Rod Carew	3.00	1.50	.90
(10)	Steve Carlton	3.00	1.50	.90
(11)	Dave Cash	1.00	.50	.30
(12)	Cesar Cedeno	1.00	.50	.30
(13)	Ron Cey	1.00	.50	.30
(14)	Carlton Fisk	3.00	1.50	.90
(15)	Tito Fuentes	1.00	.50	.30
(16)	Steve Garvey	2.00	1.00	.60
(17)	Ken Griffey	1.00	.50	.30
(18)	Don Gullett	1.00	.50	.30
(19)	Willie Horton	1.00	.50	.30
(20)	Al Hrabosky	1.00	.50	.30
(21)	Catfish Hunter	3.00	1.50	.90
(22a)	Reggie Jackson (A's)	6.00	3.00	1.75
(22b)	Reggie Jackson (Orioles)	15.00	7.50	4.50
(23)	Randy Jones	1.00	.50	.30
(24)	Jim Kaat	1.00	.50	.30
(25)	Don Kessinger	1.00	.50	.30
(26)	Dave Kingman	1.00	.50	.30
(27)	Jerry Koosman	1.00	.50	.30
(28)	Mickey Lolich	1.00	.50	.30
(29)	Greg Luzinski	1.00	.50	.30
(30)	Fred Lynn	1.00	.50	.30
(31)	Bill Madlock	1.00	.50	.30
(32a)	Carlos May (White Sox)	1.00	.50	.30
(32b)	Carlos May (Yankees)	1.00	.50	.30
(33)	John Mayberry	1.00	.50	.30
(34)	Bake McBride	1.00	.50	.30
(35)	Doc Medich	1.00	.50	.30
(36a)	Andy Messersmith (Dodgers)	1.00	.50	.30
(36b)	Andy Messersmith (Braves)	1.00	.50	.30
(37)	Rick Monday	1.00	.50	.30
(38)	John Montefusco	1.00	.50	.30
(39)	Jerry Morales	1.00	.50	.30

		NM	EX	VG
(40)	Joe Morgan	3.00	1.50	.90
(41)	Thurman Munson	3.00	1.50	.90
(42)	Bobby Murcer	1.00	.50	.30
(43)	Al Oliver	1.00	.50	.30
(44)	Jim Palmer	3.00	1.50	.90
(45)	Dave Parker	1.00	.50	.30
(46)	Tony Perez	3.00	1.50	.90
(47)	Jerry Reuss	1.00	.50	.30
(48)	Brooks Robinson	3.50	1.75	1.00
(49)	Frank Robinson	3.50	1.75	1.00
(50)	Steve Rogers	1.00	.50	.30
(51)	Pete Rose	8.00	4.00	2.50
(52)	Nolan Ryan	15.00	7.50	4.50
(53)	Manny Sanguillen	1.00	.50	.30
(54)	Mike Schmidt	6.00	3.00	1.75
(55)	Tom Seaver	4.00	2.00	1.25
(56)	Ted Simmons	1.00	.50	.30
(57)	Reggie Smith	1.00	.50	.30
(58)	Willie Stargell	3.00	1.50	.90
(59)	Rusty Staub	1.00	.50	.30
(60)	Rennie Stennett	1.00	.50	.30
(61)	Don Sutton	3.00	1.50	.90
(62a)	Andy Thornton (Cubs)	1.00	.50	.30
(62b)	Andy Thornton (Expos)	1.00	.50	.30
(63)	Luis Tiant	1.00	.50	.30
(64)	Joe Torre	2.00	1.00	.60
(65)	Mike Tyson	1.00	.50	.30
(66)	Bob Watson	1.00	.50	.30
(67)	Wilbur Wood	1.00	.50	.30
(68)	Jimmy Wynn	1.00	.50	.30
(69)	Carl Yastrzemski	4.00	2.00	1.25
(70)	Richie Zisk	1.00	.50	.30

1913 Cravats Felt Pennants

Little is known about this felt pennant issue, including the complete checklist. The name "Cravats" in the baseball above the player picture may represent the issuer, or describe the issue; the word "cravat" is an arcane term for a triangular piece of cloth. The pennants measure 4-1/8" across the top and are 9" long. Background colors are dark, with all printing in white. At center is a line art represntation of the player, with his name horizontally beneath and his team nickname vertically at bottom. At top is a bat and ball logo with the "Cravats" name. Most specimens are seen with a metal ring reinforcing the hole punched at top center. The known checklist points to 1913 as the most probable year of issue.

		NM	EX	VG
Common Player:		250.00	125.00	75.00
(1)	Eddie Ainsmith	250.00	125.00	75.00
(2)	"Home Run" Baker	450.00	225.00	135.00
(3)	Hugh Bedient	250.00	125.00	75.00
(4)	Ray Caldwell	250.00	125.00	75.00
(5)	Jack Coombs	250.00	125.00	75.00
(6)	C.S. Dooin	250.00	125.00	75.00
(7)	Lawrence Doyle	250.00	125.00	75.00
(8)	Ed Konethy (Konetchy)	250.00	125.00	75.00
(9)	James Lavender	250.00	125.00	75.00
(10)	John J. McGraw	450.00	225.00	135.00
(11)	Stuffy McInnes (McInnis)	250.00	125.00	75.00
(12)	Christy Mathewson	1,150	575.00	345.00
(13)	J.T. (Chief) Meyer (Meyers)	250.00	125.00	75.00
(14)	Nap Rucker	250.00	125.00	75.00
(15)	Tris Speaker	600.00	300.00	180.00
(16)	Ed Sweeney	250.00	125.00	75.00
(17)	Jeff Tesreau	250.00	125.00	75.00
(18)	Ira Thomas	250.00	125.00	75.00
(19)	Joe Tinker	450.00	225.00	135.00
(20)	Ed Walsh	450.00	225.00	135.00

1922 Cream Nut/Goodie Bread

According to the advertising on back this set should comprise half of the known players from the generic W573 strip card issue. The black-and-white cards, about 2-1/16" x 3-3/8", share their format and player selection not only with W573, but also E120 American Caramel. Printed horizontally on the backs is: "Ask Your Dealer for / CREAM NUT or GOODIE BREAD / and get / A BASE BALL STAR / 120 Different Subjects." The location of the issuing entity, the specific manner of distribution and

the checklist are unknown as only a handful of this particular ad-back series have survived. Collectors will pay a premium for this version above the normal W573 blank-back.

(See 1922 W573.)

1909 Croft's Candy (E92)

Because they share the format and pictures with several related issues (Croft's Cocoa, Dockman Gum, Nadja Caramels, etc.) this set shared the E92 designation in the American Card Catalog. It is more logical to present these sets as separate issues, based on the advertising which appears on back. Fronts of the 1-1/2" x 2-3/4" cards feature a color lithograph of the player. His last name, position and team are printed in black in the border below. Backs have a shield-shaped logo for Croft's Candy, a product of Croft & Allen Co., Philadelphia. Backs can be found printed in black, in blue (scarcer) or in red (extremely rare). Cards are unnumbered and the checklist is presented here alphabetically.

		NM	EX	VG
Complete Set (50):		125,000	50,000	25,000
Common Player:		1,065	425.00	220.00
Blue Back: 2-3X				
Red Back: Value Undeterminted				
(1)	Jack Barry	1,565	625.00	315.00
(2)	Harry Bemis	1,065	425.00	220.00
(3)	Chief Bender (Striped cap.)	4,065	1,625	815.00
(4)	Chief Bender (White cap.)	3,440	1,375	690.00
(5)	Bill Bergen	1,065	425.00	220.00
(6)	Bob Bescher	1,065	425.00	220.00
(7)	Al Bridwell	1,065	425.00	220.00
(8)	Doc Casey	1,065	425.00	220.00
(9)	Frank Chance	3,440	1,375	690.00
(10)	Hal Chase	2,000	815.00	405.00
(11)	Ty Cobb	18,750	7,500	3,750
(12)	Eddie Collins	3,750	1,500	750.00
(13)	Sam Crawford	2,815	1,125	565.00
(14)	Harry Davis	1,065	425.00	220.00
(15)	Art Devlin	1,065	425.00	220.00
(16)	Wild Bill Donovan	1,065	425.00	220.00
(17)	Red Dooin	1,500	600.00	300.00
(18)	Mickey Doolan	1,065	425.00	220.00
(19)	Patsy Dougherty	1,065	425.00	220.00
(20)	Larry Doyle (Throwing)	1,065	425.00	220.00
(21)	Larry Doyle (With bat.)	1,065	425.00	220.00
(22)	Johnny Evers	3,440	1,375	690.00
(23)	George Gibson	1,065	425.00	220.00
(24)	Topsy Hartsel	1,065	425.00	220.00
(25)	Fred Jacklitsch	1,500	600.00	300.00
(26)	Hugh Jennings	2,815	1,125	565.00
(27)	Red Kleinow	1,065	425.00	220.00
(28)	Otto Knabe	1,250	500.00	250.00
(29)	Jack Knight	1,500	600.00	300.00
(30)	Nap Lajoie	4,065	1,625	815.00
(31)	Hans Lobert	1,065	425.00	220.00
(32)	Sherry Magee	1,065	425.00	220.00
(33)	Christy Matthewson (Mathewson)	9,690	3,875	1,940
(34)	John McGraw	2,815	1,125	565.00
(35)	Larry McLean	1,065	425.00	220.00
(36)	Dots Miller (Batting)	1,065	425.00	220.00
(37)	Dots Miller (Fielding)	1,500	600.00	300.00
(38)	Danny Murphy	1,065	425.00	220.00
(39)	Bill O'Hara	4,065	425.00	220.00
(40)	Germany Schaefer	1,065	425.00	220.00
(41)	Admiral Schlei	1,065	425.00	220.00
(42)	Boss Schmidt	1,065	425.00	220.00
(43)	Johnny Seigle (Siegle)	1,065	425.00	220.00
(44)	Dave Shean	1,065	425.00	220.00
(45)	Boss Smith (Schmidt)	1,065	425.00	220.00
(46)	Joe Tinker	2,815	1,125	565.00
(47)	Honus Wagner (Batting)	15,000	6,000	3,000
(48)	Honus Wagner (Throwing)	15,000	6,000	3,000
(49)	Cy Young	8,125	3,250	1,625
(50)	Heinie Zimmerman	1,065	425.00	220.00

1909 Croft's Cocoa (E92)

Like related issues once cataloged together as E92 (Croft's Candy, Dockman Gum, Nadja Caramels, etc.), these 1-1/2" x 2-3/4" cards feature a color player lithograph on front, which his name, position and team printed in the white border below. Backs have an ad for Crofts Swiss Milk Cocoa of Philadelphia. The checklist, presented here alphabetically, is identical to that of Croft's Candy.

		NM	EX	VG
Complete Set (50):		97,500	37,500	18,750
Common Player:		790.00	315.00	150.00
(1)	Jack Barry	1,200	490.00	240.00
(2)	Harry Bemis	790.00	315.00	150.00
(3)	Chief Bender (Striped hat.)	3,000	1,200	600.00
(4)	Chief Bender (White hat.)	1,800	720.00	360.00
(5)	Bill Bergen	790.00	315.00	150.00
(6)	Bob Bescher	790.00	315.00	150.00
(7)	Al Bridwell	790.00	315.00	150.00
(8)	Doc Casey	790.00	315.00	150.00
(9)	Frank Chance	1,650	660.00	330.00
(10)	Hal Chase	1,240	495.00	250.00
(11)	Ty Cobb	22,500	9,000	5,000
(12)	Eddie Collins	1,650	675.00	340.00
(13)	Sam Crawford	1,650	675.00	340.00
(14)	Harry Davis	790.00	315.00	150.00
(15)	Art Devlin	790.00	315.00	150.00
(16)	Wild Bill Donovan	790.00	315.00	150.00
(17)	Red Dooin	1,240	495.00	250.00
(18)	Mickey Doolan	790.00	315.00	150.00
(19)	Patsy Dougherty	790.00	315.00	150.00
(20)	Larry Doyle (Throwing)	790.00	315.00	150.00
(21)	Larry Doyle (With bat.)	790.00	315.00	150.00
(22)	Johnny Evers	3,150	1,260	640.00
(23)	George Gibson	790.00	315.00	150.00
(24)	Topsy Hartsel	790.00	315.00	150.00
(25)	Fred Jacklitsch	1,240	495.00	250.00
(26)	Hugh Jennings	1,650	675.00	340.00
(27)	Red Kleinow	790.00	315.00	150.00
(28)	Otto Knabe	1,240	495.00	250.00
(29)	Jack Knight	1,240	495.00	250.00
(30)	Nap Lajoie	2,025	825.00	415.00
(31)	Hans Lobert	790.00	315.00	150.00
(32)	Sherry Magee	790.00	315.00	150.00
(33)	Christy Matthewson (Mathewson)	10,125	4,050	2,500
(34)	John McGraw	1,650	675.00	340.00
(35)	Larry McLean	790.00	315.00	150.00
(36)	Dots Miller (Batting)	790.00	315.00	150.00
(37)	Dots Miller (Fielding)	1,240	495.00	250.00
(38)	Danny Murphy	790.00	315.00	150.00
(39)	Bill O'Hara	790.00	315.00	150.00
(40)	Germany Schaefer	790.00	315.00	150.00
(41)	Admiral Schlei	790.00	315.00	150.00
(42)	Boss Schmidt	790.00	315.00	150.00
(43)	Johnny Seigle (Siegle)	1,015	405.00	205.00
(44)	Dave Shean	790.00	315.00	150.00
(45)	Boss Smith (Schmidt)	790.00	315.00	150.00
(46)	Joe Tinker	1,650	675.00	340.00
(47)	Honus Wagner (Batting)	5,625	2,250	1,125
(48)	Honus Wagner (Throwing)	5,625	2,250	1,125
(49)	Cy Young	5,250	2,100	1,050
(50)	Heinie Zimmerman	790.00	315.00	150.00

1969 Crown Brooks Robinson

The attributed date is speculative. This 3-9/16" x 5-11/16" card feaures a black-and-white portrait photo on front with the player name in blue scrip. A blue panel at bottom has the gas company's logo and an ad slogan. On back is a black, red and white coupon offering a discount on a baseball. A blank panel at bottom was intended for use by individual service stations to print their name and address.

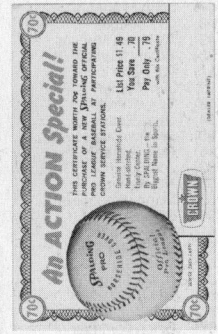

BROOKS ROBINSON CHOOSES CROWN for ACTION!

	NM	EX	VG
Brooks Robinson	150.00	75.00	45.00

1977-78 Cubic Corp. Sports Deck Playing Cards

Playing cards featuring pencil drawings of stars in various sports were produced on a limited basis in the late 1970s by Cubic Corp. of San Diego. The cards are standard bridge size (2-1/4" x 3-1/2") with rounded corners and feature the artwork of Al Landsman along with a facsimile autograph within a colored frame. Each deck has the same athlete on the back and sold for $1.60. There is no indication of the manufacturer on individual cards, it is only found on the box. It is believed most of the decks were only produced in limited sample quantities. Similar cards were produced for Pepsi and are listed thereunder. Only the baseball players are checklisted here, in alphabetical order.

		NM	EX	VG
(1)	Johnny Bench (Boxed deck.)	17.50	8.75	5.25
(1)	Johnny Bench (Single card.)	.50	.25	.15
(2)	Lou Gehrig (Boxed deck.)	25.00	12.50	7.50
(2)	Lou Gehrig (Single card.)	1.50	.70	.45
(3)	Catfish Hunter (Boxed deck.)	15.00	7.50	4.50
(3)	Catfish Hunter (Single card.)	.50	.25	.15
(4)	Randy Jones (Boxed deck.)	10.00	5.00	3.00
(4)	Randy Jones (Single card.)	.50	.25	.15
(5)	Mickey Mantle (Boxed deck.)	40.00	20.00	12.00
(5)	Mickey Mantle (Single card.)	4.00	2.00	1.25
(6)	Butch Metzger (Boxed deck.)	10.00	5.00	3.00
(6)	Butch Metzger (Single card.)	.50	.25	.15
(7)	Joe Morgan (Boxed deck.)	12.50	6.25	3.75
(7)	Joe Morgan (Single card.)	.50	.25	.15
(8)	Stan Musial (Boxed deck.)	25.00	12.50	7.50
(8)	Stan Musial (Single card.)	1.50	.70	.45
(9)	Jackie Robinson (Boxed deck.)	25.00	12.50	7.50
(9)	Jackie Robinson (Single card.)	1.50	.70	.45
(10)	Pete Rose (Boxed deck.)	35.00	17.50	10.00
(10)	Pete Rose (Single card.)	1.00	.50	.30
(11)	Babe Ruth (Boxed deck.)	30.00	15.00	9.00
(11)	Babe Ruth (Single card.)	3.00	1.50	.90
(12)	Tom Seaver (Boxed deck.)	30.00	15.00	9.00
(12)	Tom Seaver (Single card.)	1.00	.50	.30
(13)	Frank Tanana (Boxed deck.)	10.00	5.00	3.00
(13)	Frank Tanana (Single card.)	.50	.25	.15
(14)	Phillies logo/autographs (Boxed deck.)	10.00	5.00	3.00
(14)	Phillies logo/autographs (Single card.)	1.00	.50	.30

1911 Cullivan's Fireside Philadelphia A's (T208)

The 1911 T208 Firesides, an 18-card Philadelphia Athletics set issued by the Thomas Cullivan Tobacco Company of Syracuse, N.Y., is among the rarest of all 20th Century tobacco issues. Cullivan issued the set to commemorate the Athletics' 1910 Championship season, and, except for pitcher Jack Coombs, the checklist includes nearly all key members of the club, including manager Connie Mack. The cards are the standard size for tobacco issues, about 1-1/2" x 2-5/8". The front of each card features a player portrait set against a colored background. The player's name and the word "Athletics" appear at the bottom, while "World's Champions 1910" is printed along the top. Backs advertise the set as the "Athletics Series" and advise that one card is included in each package of "Cullivan's Fireside Plain Scrap" tobacco. The same checklist was used for a similar Athletics set issued by Rochester Baking/Williams Baking (D359). Blank-backed versions are also known to exist.

		NM	EX	VG
Common Player:		11,250	5,625	3,375
(1)	Home Run Baker	25,000	12,500	7,500
(2)	Jack Barry	11,250	5,625	3,375
(3)	Chief Bender	25,000	12,500	7,500
(4)	Eddie Collins	25,000	12,500	7,500
(5)	Harry Davis	11,250	5,625	3,375
(6)	Jimmy Dygert	11,250	5,625	3,375
(7)	Topsy Hartsel	11,250	5,625	3,375
(8)	Harry Krause	11,250	5,625	3,375
(9)	Jack Lapp	11,250	5,625	3,375
(10)	Paddy Livingston	11,250	5,625	3,375
(11)	Bris Lord	11,250	5,625	3,375
(12)	Connie Mack	25,000	12,500	7,500
(13)	Cy Morgan	11,250	5,625	3,375
(14)	Danny Murphy	11,250	5,625	3,375
(15)	Rube Oldring	12,500	5,625	3,375
(16)	Eddie Plank	28,125	14,065	8,440
(17)	Amos Strunk	11,250	5,625	3,375
(18)	Ira Thomas	11,250	5,625	3,375

1964+ Curteichcolor Hall of Fame Plaque Postcards

(See Hall of Fame Yellow Plaque Postcards for checklist, price data.)

1909-12 Cycle Cigarettes

Cycle brand advertising found on the backs of T205, T206 and T207 cards generally indicates a slightly greater degree of scarcity than the most common back variations from those sets. While a value multiplier can generate a ballpark approximation of value for most cards from T205 and T206, it is not practical for T207s because all Cycle cards from that set are scarce and much of that scarcity has already been factored into the individual player prices quoted in the base T207 listings.

PREMIUMS:
T205: 1-1.5X
T206 350 Series: 1-1.5X
T206 460 Series: 2-3X
(See T205, T206, T207 for checklists and base card values.)

D

1959 Dad's Cookies Exhibits

A Vancouver bakery that issued several type of hockey cards in later years created this set of baseball cards by over-printing the usually blank backs of the 64 cards in Exhibit Supply Co.'s 1959 issue. Cards measure 3-3/8" x 5-3/8" and are printed in reddish-gray-brown. The back indicates an album was available to house the set.

 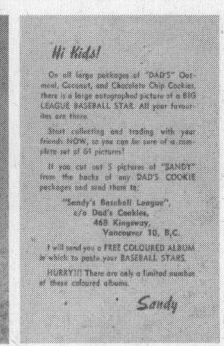

		NM	EX	VG
Complete Set (64):		3,000	1,500	900.00
Common Player:		35.00	17.50	10.00
(1)	Hank Aaron	200.00	100.00	60.00
(2)	Joe Adcock (Script name.)	35.00	17.50	10.00
(3)	Johnny Antonelli (Giants)	35.00	17.50	10.00
(4)	Luis Aparicio (Portrait)	80.00	40.00	24.00
(5)	Richie Ashburn (Phillies)	100.00	50.00	30.00
(6)	Ed Bailey (With cap.)	35.00	17.50	10.00
(7)	Ernie Banks (Bat on shoulder, script name.)	150.00	75.00	45.00
(8)	Hank Bauer (N.Y. cap.)	50.00	25.00	15.00
(9)	Yogi Berra	150.00	75.00	45.00
(10)	Don Blasingame	35.00	17.50	10.00
(11)	Bill Bruton	35.00	17.50	10.00
(12)	Lew Burdette (Pitching, side view.)	35.00	17.50	10.00
(13)	Chico Carrasquel (Portrait)	35.00	17.50	10.00
(14)	Orlando Cepeda (To chest.)	80.00	40.00	24.00
(15)	Bob Cerv (A's cap.)	35.00	17.50	10.00
(16)	Delmar Crandall	35.00	17.50	10.00
(17)	Alvin Dark (Cubs)	35.00	17.50	10.00
(18)	Larry Doby	80.00	40.00	24.00
(19)	Dick Donovan (Sox cap.)	35.00	17.50	10.00
(20)	Don Drysdale (Portrait)	90.00	45.00	27.00
(21)	Del Ennis	35.00	17.50	10.00
(22)	Whitey Ford (Pitching)	125.00	62.00	37.00
(23)	Nelson Fox	80.00	40.00	24.00
(24)	Bob Friend	35.00	17.50	10.00
(25)	Billy Goodman (Batting)	35.00	17.50	10.00
(26)	Whitey Herzog	35.00	17.50	10.00
(27)	Gil Hodges (LA on cap.)	75.00	37.50	22.00
(28)	Elston Howard	50.00	25.00	15.00
(29)	Jackie Jensen	50.00	25.00	15.00
(30)	Al Kaline (Portrait w/ two bats.)	100.00	50.00	30.00
(31)	Harmon Killebrew (Batting)	100.00	50.00	30.00
(32)	Billy Klaus	35.00	17.50	10.00
(33)	Ted Kluzewski (Kluszewski) (Pirates uniform.)	60.00	30.00	18.00
(34)	Tony Kubek (Light background.)	60.00	30.00	18.00
(35)	Harvey Kuenn (D on cap.)	35.00	17.50	10.00
(36)	Don Larsen	35.00	17.50	10.00
(37)	Johnny Logan	35.00	17.50	10.00
(38)	Dale Long (C on cap.)	35.00	17.50	10.00
(39)	Mickey Mantle (Batting, no pinstripes, "c k" of "Mickey" separated.)	350.00	175.00	100.00
(40)	Eddie Mathews	100.00	50.00	30.00
(41)	Willie Mays (Portrait)	200.00	100.00	60.00
(42)	Bill Mazeroski (Portrait)	80.00	40.00	24.00
(43)	Lindy McDaniel	35.00	17.50	10.00
(44)	Gil McDougald	45.00	22.50	13.50
(45)	Orestes Minoso (C on cap.)	45.00	22.50	13.50
(46)	Stan Musial	175.00	87.00	52.00
(47)	Don Newcombe (Plain jacket.)	45.00	22.50	13.50
(48)	Andy Pafko (Yours truly.) (Plain uniform.)	35.00	17.50	10.00
(49)	Billy Pierce	35.00	17.50	10.00
(50)	Robin Roberts (Script name.)	80.00	40.00	24.00
(51)	Carl Sawatski (P on cap.)	35.00	17.50	10.00
(52)	Herb Score (C on cap.)	35.00	17.50	10.00
(53)	Roy Sievers (Portrait, W on cap, light background.)	35.00	17.50	10.00
(54)	Curt Simmons	35.00	17.50	10.00
(55)	Bill Skowron	50.00	25.00	15.00
(56)	Duke Snider (LA on cap.)	100.00	50.00	30.00
(57)	Warren Spahn (M on cap.)	100.00	50.00	30.00
(58)	Frankie Thomas (Photo actually Bob Skinner.)	50.00	25.00	15.00
(59)	Earl Torgeson (Plain uniform.)	35.00	17.50	10.00
(60)	Gus Triandos	35.00	17.50	10.00
(61)	Vic Wertz (Portrait)	35.00	17.50	10.00
(62)	Ted Williams (Sincerely yours.) (#9 not showing)	200.00	100.00	60.00
(63)	Gene Woodling (Script name.)	35.00	17.50	10.00
(64)	Gus Zernial (Script name.)	35.00	17.50	10.00

1972 Daily Juice Co.

This one-card "set" was regionally issued to Roberto Clemente Fan Club members. Large numbers of the cards found their way into the hobby, including in uncut sheet form. The cards feature a full-color front black-and-white back. The card measures the standard 2-1/2" in width but is somewhat longer, at 3-3/4". This unnumbered card remains about the least expensive baseball card that was issued during Clemente's lifetime.

ROBERTO CLEMENTE FAN CLUB

MEMBERSHIP CARD

Name _____

Send for latest FREE 8 x 10 Full Color Picture of Roberto Clemente available for framing. Send to Roberto Clemente Fan Club, P.O. Box 2100, Pittsburgh, Pa. 15230. Enclose 25c for postage and handling.

Sponsored by DAILY JUICE CO., Oakmont, Pa.

	NM	EX	VG
Uncut Sheet (30):	200.00	100.00	60.00
1 Roberto Clemente	15.00	7.50	4.50

1950s Dairy Council Curt Simmons Postcard

Issued by "The Dairy Council," probably locally, this black-and-white postcard features an action-pose photo of the star Phillies pitcher. There is a white facsimile autograph on front. Back of the 3-3/4" x 5-3/4" card has another facsimile autograph and the legend, "Dairy Council and the Philadelphia Phillies join me in wishing you good luck and good health."

	NM	EX	VG
Curt Simmons	60.00	30.00	18.00

1976 Dairy Isle Discs

One of several regional sponsors of player disc sets in 1976 was the upstate New York area outlet, Dairy Isle. The discs are 3-3/8" diameter with a black-and-white player portrait photo in the center of the baseball design. A line of red stars is above, while the left and right panels feature one of several bright colors. Produced by Michael Schecter Associates under license from the Major League Baseball Players Association, the player photos have had uniform and cap logos removed. Backs are printed in red and purple. The unnumbered checklist here is presented in alphabetical order.

		NM	EX	VG
Complete Set (70):		45.00	22.50	13.50
Common Player:		1.00	.50	.30
(1)	Henry Aaron	10.00	5.00	3.00
(2)	Johnny Bench	4.50	2.25	1.25
(3)	Vida Blue	1.00	.50	.30
(4)	Larry Bowa	1.00	.50	.30
(5)	Lou Brock	4.00	2.00	1.25
(6)	Jeff Burroughs	1.00	.50	.30
(7)	John Candelaria	1.00	.50	.30
(8)	Jose Cardenal	1.00	.50	.30
(9)	Rod Carew	4.00	2.00	1.25
(10)	Steve Carlton	4.00	2.00	1.25
(11)	Dave Cash	1.00	.50	.30
(12)	Cesar Cedeno	1.00	.50	.30
(13)	Ron Cey	1.00	.50	.30
(14)	Carlton Fisk	4.00	2.00	1.25
(15)	Tito Fuentes	1.00	.50	.30
(16)	Steve Garvey	3.00	1.50	.90
(17)	Ken Griffey	1.00	.50	.30
(18)	Don Gullett	1.00	.50	.30
(19)	Willie Horton	1.00	.50	.30
(20)	Al Hrabosky	1.00	.50	.30
(21)	Catfish Hunter	4.00	2.00	1.25
(22)	Reggie Jackson (A's)	6.00	3.00	1.75
(23)	Randy Jones	1.00	.50	.30
(24)	Jim Kaat	1.00	.50	.30
(25)	Don Kessinger	1.00	.50	.30
(26)	Dave Kingman	1.00	.50	.30
(27)	Jerry Koosman	1.00	.50	.30
(28)	Mickey Lolich	1.00	.50	.30
(29)	Greg Luzinski	1.00	.50	.30
(30)	Fred Lynn	1.00	.50	.30
(31)	Bill Madlock	1.00	.50	.30
(32)	Carlos May (White Sox)	1.00	.50	.30
(33)	John Mayberry	1.00	.50	.30
(34)	Bake McBride	1.00	.50	.30
(35)	Doc Medich	1.00	.50	.30
(36)	Andy Messersmith	1.00	.50	.30
(37)	Rick Monday	1.00	.50	.30
(38)	John Montefusco	1.00	.50	.30
(39)	Jerry Morales	1.00	.50	.30
(40)	Joe Morgan	4.00	2.00	1.25
(41)	Thurman Munson	3.00	1.50	.90
(42)	Bobby Murcer	1.00	.50	.30
(43)	Al Oliver	1.00	.50	.30
(44)	Jim Palmer	4.00	2.00	1.25
(45)	Dave Parker	1.00	.50	.30
(46)	Tony Perez	4.00	2.00	1.25
(47)	Jerry Reuss	1.00	.50	.30
(48)	Brooks Robinson	4.50	2.25	1.25
(49)	Frank Robinson	4.50	2.25	1.25
(50)	Steve Rogers	1.00	.50	.30
(51)	Pete Rose	10.00	5.00	3.00
(52)	Nolan Ryan	20.00	10.00	6.00
(53)	Manny Sanguillen	1.00	.50	.30
(54)	Mike Schmidt	6.00	3.00	1.75
(55)	Tom Seaver	4.50	2.25	1.25
(56)	Ted Simmons	1.00	.50	.30
(57)	Reggie Smith	1.00	.50	.30
(58)	Willie Stargell	4.00	2.00	1.25
(59)	Rusty Staub	1.25	.60	.40
(60)	Rennie Stennett	1.00	.50	.30
(61)	Don Sutton	4.00	2.00	1.25
(62)	Andy Thornton (Cubs)	1.00	.50	.30
(63)	Luis Tiant	1.00	.50	.30
(64)	Joe Torre	3.00	1.50	.90
(65)	Mike Tyson	1.00	.50	.30
(66)	Bob Watson	1.00	.50	.30
(67)	Wilbur Wood	1.00	.50	.30
(68)	Jimmy Wynn	1.00	.50	.30
(69)	Carl Yastrzemski	4.50	2.25	1.25
(70)	Richie Zisk	1.00	.50	.30

1977 Dairy Isle Discs

Virtually identical in format to the 1976 issue (substituting red and blue for the back ad in 1977, instead of the previous year's red and purple), these 3-3/8" diameter player discs were given away at Dairy Isle outlets. Discs once again feature black-and-white player portrait photos in the center of a baseball design. The left and right panels are in one of several bright colors. Licensed by the players' association through Mike Schechter Associates, the player photos carry no uniform logos. The unnumbered discs are checklisted here alphabetically.

		NM	EX	VG
Complete Set (70):		30.00	15.00	9.00
Common Player:		1.00	.50	.30
(1)	Sal Bando	1.00	.50	.30
(2)	Buddy Bell	1.00	.50	.30
(3)	Johnny Bench	4.50	2.25	1.25
(4)	Larry Bowa	1.00	.50	.30
(5)	Steve Braun	1.00	.50	.30
(6)	George Brett	10.00	5.00	3.00
(7)	Lou Brock	3.50	1.75	1.00
(8)	Jeff Burroughs	1.00	.50	.30
(9)	Bert Campaneris	1.00	.50	.30
(10)	John Candelaria	1.00	.50	.30
(11)	Jose Cardenal	1.00	.50	.30
(12)	Rod Carew	3.50	1.75	1.00
(13)	Steve Carlton	3.50	1.75	1.00
(14)	Dave Cash	1.00	.50	.30
(15)	Cesar Cedeno	1.00	.50	.30
(16)	Ron Cey	1.00	.50	.30
(17)	Dave Concepcion	1.00	.50	.30
(18)	Dennis Eckersley	3.50	1.75	1.00
(19)	Mark Fidrych	2.00	1.00	.60
(20)	Rollie Fingers	3.50	1.75	1.00
(21)	Carlton Fisk	3.50	1.75	1.00
(22)	George Foster	1.00	.50	.30
(23)	Wayne Garland	1.00	.50	.30
(24)	Ralph Garr	1.00	.50	.30
(25)	Steve Garvey	3.50	1.75	1.00
(26)	Cesar Geronimo	1.00	.50	.30
(27)	Bobby Grich	1.00	.50	.30
(28)	Ken Griffey	1.00	.50	.30
(29)	Don Gullett	1.00	.50	.30
(30)	Mike Hargrove	1.00	.50	.30
(31)	Al Hrabosky	1.00	.50	.30
(32)	Jim Hunter	3.50	1.75	1.00
(33)	Reggie Jackson	6.00	3.00	1.75
(34)	Randy Jones	1.00	.50	.30
(35)	Dave Kingman	1.00	.50	.30
(36)	Jerry Koosman	1.00	.50	.30
(37)	Dave LaRoche	1.00	.50	.30
(38)	Greg Luzinski	1.00	.50	.30
(39)	Fred Lynn	1.00	.50	.30
(40)	Bill Madlock	1.00	.50	.30
(41)	Rick Manning	1.00	.50	.30
(42)	Jon Matlack	1.00	.50	.30
(43)	John Mayberry	1.00	.50	.30
(44)	Hal McRae	1.00	.50	.30
(45)	Andy Messersmith	1.00	.50	.30
(46)	Rick Monday	1.00	.50	.30
(47)	John Montefusco	1.00	.50	.30
(48)	Joe Morgan	3.50	1.75	1.00
(49)	Thurman Munson	2.50	1.25	.70
(50)	Bobby Murcer	1.00	.50	.30
(51)	Bill North	1.00	.50	.30
(52)	Jim Palmer	3.50	1.75	1.00
(53)	Tony Perez	3.50	1.75	1.00
(54)	Jerry Reuss	1.00	.50	.30
(55)	Brooks Robinson	4.50	2.25	1.25
(56)	Pete Rose	10.00	5.00	3.00
(57)	Joe Rudi	1.00	.50	.30
(58)	Nolan Ryan	15.00	7.50	4.50
(59)	Manny Sanguillen	1.00	.50	.30
(60)	Mike Schmidt	6.00	3.00	1.75
(61)	Tom Seaver	4.50	2.25	1.25
(62)	Bill Singer	1.00	.50	.30
(63)	Willie Stargell	3.50	1.75	1.00
(64)	Rusty Staub	1.25	.60	.40
(65)	Luis Tiant	1.00	.50	.30
(66)	Bob Watson	1.00	.50	.30
(67)	Butch Wynegar	1.00	.50	.30
(68)	Carl Yastrzemski	4.50	2.25	1.25
(69)	Robin Yount	3.50	1.75	1.00
(70)	Richie Zisk	1.00	.50	.30

1956 Dairy Queen Stars Statues

This set is identical in composition and manufacture to the carded figures sold as Big League Stars (see listing). The DQ versions of the statues are white, while the Big League versions are bronze colored. The statues measure about 3" tall and were evidently sold or given away with a purchase at the chain of ice cream shops.

		NM	EX	VG
Complete Set (18):		1,100	550.00	350.00
Common Player:		40.00	20.00	12.00
(1)	John Antonelli	40.00	20.00	12.00
(2)	Bob Avila	40.00	20.00	12.00
(3)	Yogi Berra	100.00	50.00	30.00
(4)	Roy Campanella	100.00	50.00	30.00
(5)	Larry Doby	65.00	32.50	20.00
(6)	Del Ennis	40.00	20.00	12.00
(7)	Jim Gilliam	40.00	20.00	12.00
(8)	Gil Hodges	75.00	37.50	22.50
(9)	Harvey Kuenn	40.00	20.00	12.00
(10)	Bob Lemon	50.00	25.00	15.00
(11)	Mickey Mantle	325.00	160.00	100.00
(12)	Ed Mathews	75.00	37.50	22.50
(13)	Minnie Minoso	40.00	20.00	12.00
(14)	Stan Musial	160.00	80.00	50.00
(15)	Pee Wee Reese	100.00	50.00	30.00
(16)	Al Rosen	40.00	20.00	12.00
(17)	Duke Snider	100.00	50.00	30.00
(18)	Mickey Vernon	40.00	20.00	12.00

1954 Dan-Dee Potato Chips

 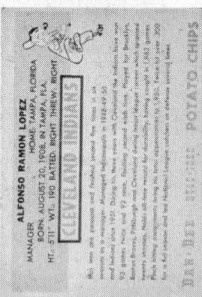

Issued in bags of potato chips, the cards in this 29-card set are commonly found with grease stains despite their waxed surface. The unnumbered cards, which measure 2-1/2" x 3-5/8", feature color pictures. Backs have player statistical and biographical information. The set consists mostly of players from the Indians and Pirates. Photos of the Yankees players were also used for the Briggs Meats and Stahl-Meyer Franks sets.

		NM	EX	VG
Complete Set (29):		7,000	2,750	1,350
Common Player:		110.00	45.00	20.00
(1)	Bob Avila	110.00	45.00	20.00
(2)	Hank Bauer	135.00	55.00	25.00
(3)	Walker Cooper (SP)	375.00	150.00	75.00
(4)	Larry Doby	140.00	55.00	25.00
(5)	Luke Easter	125.00	50.00	25.00
(6)	Bob Feller	350.00	140.00	70.00
(7)	Bob Friend	110.00	45.00	20.00
(8)	Mike Garcia	110.00	45.00	20.00

		NM	EX	VG
(9)	Sid Gordon	110.00	45.00	20.00
(10)	Jim Hegan	110.00	45.00	20.00
(11)	Gil Hodges	450.00	180.00	90.00
(12)	Art Houtteman	110.00	45.00	20.00
(13)	Monte Irvin	140.00	55.00	25.00
(14)	Paul LaPalm (LaPalme)	110.00	45.00	20.00
(15)	Bob Lemon	140.00	55.00	25.00
(16)	Al Lopez	140.00	55.00	25.00
(17)	Mickey Mantle	2,400	960.00	460.00
(18)	Dale Mitchell	110.00	45.00	20.00
(19)	Phil Rizzuto	250.00	100.00	50.00
(20)	Curtis Roberts	110.00	45.00	20.00
(21)	Al Rosen	125.00	50.00	25.00
(22)	Red Schoendienst	140.00	55.00	25.00
(23)	Paul Smith (SP)	390.00	150.00	75.00
(24)	Duke Snider	300.00	120.00	60.00
(25)	George Strickland	110.00	45.00	20.00
(26)	Max Surkont	110.00	45.00	20.00
(27)	Frank Thomas (SP)	200.00	80.00	40.00
(28)	Wally Westlake	110.00	45.00	20.00
(29)	Early Wynn	140.00	55.00	25.00

1977 Tom Daniels Burleigh Grimes

The career of Hall of Fame spitballer Burleigh Grimes is traced in this collectors' issue. The 2-1/2" x 3-1/2" cards have black-and-white photos from Grimes' collection, bordered in bright blue. A card title is in black in the bottom border. Backs are printed in black and blue on white and have a description of the front photo. One card in each set is authentically auto-graphed by Grimes. Price at issue was $3.50; uncut sheets were also available.

		NM	EX	VG
	Complete Set (16):	10.00	5.00	3.00
	Common Card:	1.00	.50	.30
1	Dodger Manager 1937-38	1.00	.50	.30
2	"Lord Burleigh"	1.00	.50	.30
3	Last Spitballers	1.00	.50	.30
4	Grimes, Hornsby, McGraw, Roush	1.00	.50	.30
5	Winning Combination	1.00	.50	.30
6	World Champion	1.00	.50	.30
7	"Old Stubblebeard"	1.00	.50	.30
8	Grimes Meets McCarthy	1.00	.50	.30
9	Dodger Greats	1.00	.50	.30
10	"The Babe"	2.00	1.00	.60
11	Dodger Strategists	1.00	.50	.30
12	Bender and Grimes	1.00	.50	.30
13	Number '270'	1.00	.50	.30
14	The Origin	1.00	.50	.30
15	1964 HoF Inductees	1.00	.50	.30
16	"Lord Burleigh" 1977	1.00	.50	.30

1910 Darby Chocolates (E271)

The 1910 Darby Chocolates cards are among the rarest of all candy cards. The cards were printed on boxes of "Pennant" Chocolates, two players per box - one each on front and back. The cards feature black-and-white player action photos outlined with a thick dark shadow. The boxes are accented with orange or green graphics. Most of the known examples of this set were not found until 1982 when a group in fire-damaged condition was inadvisedly subjected to restoration. Values shown here are for cards in untampered-with state of preservation. Values for restored cards must be adjusted significantly downward. This checklist may or may not be complete.

		NM	EX	VG
	Common Player:	12,000	6,000	3,500
(1)	Jimmy Archer	12,000	6,000	3,600
(2)	Chief Bender	16,000	8,000	4,800
(3)	Bob Bescher	12,000	6,000	3,600
(4)	Roger Bresnahan	16,000	8,000	4,800
(5)	Al Bridwell	12,000	6,000	3,600
(6)	Mordicai Brown (Mordecai)	16,000	8,000	4,800
(7)	"Eddie" Cicotte	13,500	6,750	4,000
(8)	Fred Clark (Clarke)	12,000	6,000	3,600
(9)	Ty. Cobb (Batting)	30,000	15,000	9,000
(10)	"Ty" Cobb (Fielding)	30,000	15,000	9,000
(11)	King Cole	12,000	6,000	3,600
(12)	E. Collins	16,000	8,000	4,800
(13)	Wid Conroy	12,000	6,000	3,600
(14)	"Sam" Crawford	16,000	8,000	4,800
(15)	Bill Dahlin (Dahlen)	12,000	6,000	3,600
(16)	Bill Donovan	12,000	6,000	3,600
(17)	"Pat" Dougherty	12,000	6,000	3,600
(18)	Kid Elberfeld	12,000	6,000	3,600
(19)	"Johnny" Evers	16,000	8,000	4,800
(20)	Charlie Herzog	12,000	6,000	3,600
(21)	Hughie Jennings	16,000	8,000	4,800
(22)	Walter Johnson	20,000	10,000	6,000
(23)	Ed Konetchy	12,000	6,000	3,600
(24)	Tommy Leach	12,000	6,000	3,600
(25)	Fred Luderous (Luderus)	12,000	6,000	3,600
(26)	"Mugsy" McGraw	16,000	8,000	4,800
(27)	"Mike" Mowery (Mowrey)	12,000	6,000	3,600
(28)	Jack Powell	12,000	6,000	3,600
(29)	Slim Sallee	12,000	6,000	3,600
(30)	James Scheckard (Sheckard)	12,000	6,000	3,600
(31)	Walter Snodgrass	12,000	6,000	3,600
(32)	"Tris" Speaker	17,500	8,750	5,250
(33)	Charlie Suggs	12,000	6,000	3,600
(34)	Fred Tenney	12,000	6,000	3,600
(35)	"Jim" Vaughn	12,000	6,000	3,600
(36)	"Hans" Wagner	40,000	13,750	8,250

1911 Harry Davis Day Postcard

In his final season with the Philadelphia Athletics, the star first baseman of the famed $100,000 Infield was honored with a "day" at Shibe Park. This standard-size black-and-white postcard was created to remind fans to attend the event. A pre-printed message on back over the facsimile signature of Connie Mack urges fans to "show our appreciation of what Captain Davis has done for baseball and the city of his birth."

	NM	EX	VG
Harry Davis	750.00	375.00	225.00

1970 Dayton Daily News Bubble-Gumless Cards

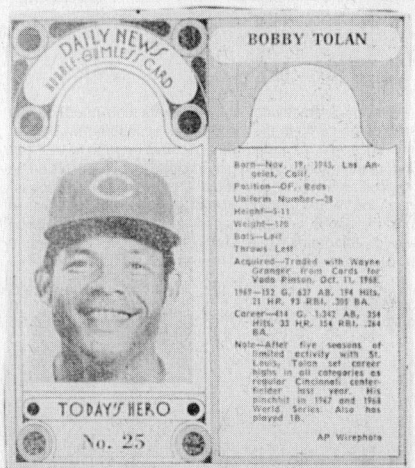

These "cards" are actually newspaper clippings which were issued on a daily basis during the baseball season by the Ohio newspaper. Labeled "Today's Hero," the clippings measure approximately 3-1/2" x 4" and are printed in black-and-white. At left is a portrait photo of the player, at right are personal data, stats and career highlights.

		NM	EX	VG
	Complete Set (160):	2,000	1,000	600.00
	Common Player:	9.00	4.50	2.75
1	Pete Rose	40.00	20.00	12.00
2	Johnny Bench	20.00	10.00	6.00
3	Maury Wills	12.00	6.00	3.50
4	Harmon Killebrew	20.00	10.00	6.00
5	Frank Robinson	20.00	10.00	6.00
6	Willie Mays	60.00	30.00	18.00
7	Hank Aaron	60.00	30.00	18.00
8	Tom Seaver	20.00	10.00	6.00
9	Sam McDowell	9.00	4.50	2.75
10	Rico Petrocelli	9.00	4.50	2.75
11a	Tony Perez (Dark cap.)	20.00	10.00	6.00
11b	Tony Perez (Light cap.)	20.00	10.00	6.00
12	Hoyt Wilhelm	15.00	7.50	4.50
13	Alex Johnson	9.00	4.50	2.75
14	Gary Nolan	9.00	4.50	2.75
15	Al Kaline	25.00	12.50	7.50
16	Bob Gibson	15.00	7.50	4.50
17	Larry Dierker	9.00	4.50	2.75
18	Ernie Banks	30.00	15.00	9.00
19	Lee May	9.00	4.50	2.75
20	Claude Osteen	9.00	4.50	2.75
21	Tony Horton	9.00	4.50	2.75
22	Mack Jones	9.00	4.50	2.75
23	Wally Bunker	9.00	4.50	2.75
24	Bill Hands	9.00	4.50	2.75
25	Bobby Tolan	9.00	4.50	2.75
26	Jim Wynn	9.00	4.50	2.75
27	Tom Haller	9.00	4.50	2.75
28	Carl Yastrzemski	25.00	12.50	7.50
29	Jim Merritt	9.00	4.50	2.75
30	Tony Oliva	12.00	6.00	3.50
31	Reggie Jackson	40.00	20.00	12.00
32	Bob Clemente	90.00	45.00	27.00
33	Tommy Helms	9.00	4.50	2.75
34	Boog Powell	12.00	6.00	3.50
35	Mickey Lolich	9.00	4.50	2.75
36	Frank Howard	12.00	6.00	3.50
37	Jim McGlothlin	9.00	4.50	2.75
38	Rusty Staub	12.00	6.00	3.50
39	Mel Stottlemyre	9.00	4.50	2.75
40	Rico Carty	9.00	4.50	2.75
41	Nate Colbert	9.00	4.50	2.75
42	Wayne Granger	9.00	4.50	2.75
43	Mike Hegan	9.00	4.50	2.75
44	Jerry Koosman	9.00	4.50	2.75
45	Jim Perry	9.00	4.50	2.75
46	Pat Corrales	9.00	4.50	2.75
47	Dick Bosman	9.00	4.50	2.75
48	Bert Campaneris	9.00	4.50	2.75
49	Larry Hisle	9.00	4.50	2.75
50	Bernie Carbo	9.00	4.50	2.75
51	Wilbur Wood	9.00	4.50	2.75
52	Dave McNally	9.00	4.50	2.75
53	Andy Messersmith	9.00	4.50	2.75
54	Jimmy Stewart	9.00	4.50	2.75
55	Luis Aparicio	15.00	7.50	4.50
56	Mike Cuellar	9.00	4.50	2.75
57	Bill Grabarkewitz	9.00	4.50	2.75
58	Dick Dietz	9.00	4.50	2.75
59	Dave Concepcion	9.00	4.50	2.75
60	Gary Gentry	9.00	4.50	2.75
61	Don Money	9.00	4.50	2.75
62	Rod Carew	20.00	10.00	6.00
63	Denis Menke	9.00	4.50	2.75
64	Hal McRae	9.00	4.50	2.75
65	Felipe Alou	9.00	4.50	2.75
66	Richie Hebner	9.00	4.50	2.75
67	Don Sutton	15.00	7.50	4.50
68	Wayne Simpson	9.00	4.50	2.75
69	Art Shamsky	9.00	4.50	2.75
70	Luis Tiant	9.00	4.50	2.75
71	Clay Carroll	9.00	4.50	2.75
72	Jim Hickman	9.00	4.50	2.75
73	Clarence Gaston	9.00	4.50	2.75
74	Angel Bravo	9.00	4.50	2.75
75	Jim Hunter	15.00	7.50	4.50
76	Lou Piniella	10.00	5.00	3.00
77	Jim Bunning	15.00	7.50	4.50
78	Don Gullett	9.00	4.50	2.75
79	Dan Cater	9.00	4.50	2.75
80	Richie Allen	13.50	6.75	4.00
81	Jim Bouton	10.00	5.00	3.00
82	Jim Palmer	15.00	7.50	4.50
83	Woody Woodward	9.00	4.50	2.75
84	Tom Agee	9.00	4.50	2.75
85	Carlos May	9.00	4.50	2.75
86	Ray Washburn	9.00	4.50	2.75
87	Denny McLain	10.00	5.00	3.00
88	Lou Brock	15.00	7.50	4.50
89	Ken Henderson	9.00	4.50	2.75
90	Roy White	9.00	4.50	2.75
91	Chris Cannizzaro	9.00	4.50	2.75
92	Willie Horton	9.00	4.50	2.75
93	Jose Cardenal	9.00	4.50	2.75
94	Jim Fregosi	9.00	4.50	2.75
95	Richie Hebner	9.00	4.50	2.75
96	Tony Conigliaro	10.00	5.00	3.00
97	Tony Cloninger	9.00	4.50	2.75
98	Mike Epstein	9.00	4.50	2.75
99	Ty Cline	9.00	4.50	2.75
100	Tommy Harper	9.00	4.50	2.75
101	Jose Azcue	9.00	4.50	2.75
102a	Glenn Beckert	9.00	4.50	2.75
102b	Ray Fosse	9.00	4.50	2.75
103	Not Issued			
104	Gerry Moses	9.00	4.50	2.75
105	Bud Harrelson	9.00	4.50	2.75
106	Joe Torre	13.50	6.75	4.00
107	Dave Johnson	9.00	4.50	2.75
108	Don Kessinger	9.00	4.50	2.75
109	Bill Freehan	9.00	4.50	2.75
110	Sandy Alomar	9.00	4.50	2.75
111	Matty Alou	9.00	4.50	2.75
112	Joe Morgan	15.00	7.50	4.50
113	John Odom	9.00	4.50	2.75
114	Amos Otis	9.00	4.50	2.75
115	Jay Johnstone	9.00	4.50	2.75
116	Ron Perranoski	9.00	4.50	2.75
117	Manny Mota	9.00	4.50	2.75
118	Billy Conigliaro	9.00	4.50	2.75
119	Leo Cardenas	9.00	4.50	2.75
120	Rich Reese	9.00	4.50	2.75
121	Ron Santo	12.00	6.00	3.50
122	Gene Michael	9.00	4.50	2.75
123	Milt Pappas	9.00	4.50	2.75
124	Joe Pepitone	10.00	5.00	3.00
125	Jose Cardenal	9.00	4.50	2.75
126	Jim Northrup	9.00	4.50	2.75
127	Wes Parker	9.00	4.50	2.75
128	Fritz Peterson	9.00	4.50	2.75
129	Phil Regan	9.00	4.50	2.75
130	John Callison	9.00	4.50	2.75
131	Cookie Rojas	9.00	4.50	2.75
132	Claude Raymond	9.00	4.50	2.75

133	Darrel Chaney	9.00	4.50	2.75
134	Gary Peters	9.00	4.50	2.75
135	Del Unser	9.00	4.50	2.75
136	Joey Foy	9.00	4.50	2.75
137	Luke Walker	9.00	4.50	2.75
138	Bill Mazeroski	15.00	7.50	4.50
139	Tony Taylor	9.00	4.50	2.75
140	Leron Lee	9.00	4.50	2.75
141	Jesus Alou	9.00	4.50	2.75
142	Donn Clendenon	9.00	4.50	2.75
143	Merv Rettenmund	9.00	4.50	2.75
144	Bob Moose	9.00	4.50	2.75
145	Jim Kaat	10.00	5.00	3.00
146	Randy Hundley	9.00	4.50	2.75
147	Jim McAndrew	9.00	4.50	2.75
148	Manny Sanguillen	9.00	4.50	2.75
149	Bob Allison	9.00	4.50	2.75
150	Jim Maloney	9.00	4.50	2.75
151	Don Buford	9.00	4.50	2.75
152	Gene Alley	9.00	4.50	2.75
153	Cesar Tovar	9.00	4.50	2.75
154	Brooks Robinson	20.00	10.00	6.00
155	Milt Wilcox	9.00	4.50	2.75
156	Willie Stargell	20.00	10.00	6.00
157	Paul Blair	9.00	4.50	2.75
158	Andy Etchebarren	9.00	4.50	2.75
159	Mark Belanger	9.00	4.50	2.75
160	Elrod Hendricks	9.00	4.50	2.75

1973 Dean's Photo Service San Diego Padres

A true rookie-year issue for Dave Winfield is included in this set of 5-1/2" x 8-1/2" black-and-white, blank-backed player photos sponsored by Dean's Photo Service and given away by the team in five six-card series at various home games. Pictures have posed player portraits surrounded by a white border. Beneath are the name and position, with team and sponsor logos at bottom. The set is checklisted here alphabetically.

		NM	EX	VG
Complete Set (31):		80.00	40.00	24.00
Common Player:		4.00	2.00	1.25
(1)	Steve Arlin	4.00	2.00	1.25
(2)	Mike Caldwell	4.00	2.00	1.25
(3)	Dave Campbell	4.00	2.00	1.25
(4)	Nate Colbert	4.00	2.00	1.25
(5)	Mike Corkins	4.00	2.00	1.25
(6)	Pat Corrales	4.00	2.00	1.25
(7)	Jim Davenport	4.00	2.00	1.25
(8)	Dave Garcia	4.00	2.00	1.25
(9)	Clarence Gaston	4.00	2.00	1.25
(10)	Bill Greif	4.00	2.00	1.25
(11)	John Grubb	4.00	2.00	1.25
(12)	Enzo Hernandez	4.00	2.00	1.25
(13)	Randy Jones	4.00	2.00	1.25
(14)	Fred Kendall	4.00	2.00	1.25
(15)	Clay Kirby	4.00	2.00	1.25
(16)	Leron Lee	4.00	2.00	1.25
(17)	Dave Marshall	4.00	2.00	1.25
(18)	Don Mason	4.00	2.00	1.25
(19)	Jerry Morales	4.00	2.00	1.25
(20)	Ivan Murrell	4.00	2.00	1.25
(21)	Fred Norman	4.00	2.00	1.25
(22)	Johnny Podres	4.00	2.00	1.25
(23)	Dave Roberts	4.00	2.00	1.25
(24)	Vicente Romo	4.00	2.00	1.25
(25)	Gary Ross	4.00	2.00	1.25
(26)	Bob Skinner	4.00	2.00	1.25
(27)	Derrel Thomas	4.00	2.00	1.25
(28)	Rich Troedson	4.00	2.00	1.25
(29)	Whitey Wietelmann	4.00	2.00	1.25
(30)	Dave Winfield	25.00	12.50	7.50
(31)	Don Zimmer	5.00	2.50	1.50

1974 Dean's Photo Service San Diego Padres

This issue shares the same basic format as the years which preceded it and succeeded it. Fronts of the 5-1/2" x 8-1/2" cards have a large player portrait or pose at top, with the player's name and position below. In the wide white border at bottom are the team and sponsor's logos. Backs, for the first time, have a lengthy career summary, personal data and full professional stats. All printing is in black-and-white. The unnumbered cards are checklisted here alphabetically.

		NM	EX	VG
Complete Set (30)		70.00	35.00	21.00
Common Player:		4.00	2.00	1.25
(1)	Matty Alou	4.00	2.00	1.25
(2)	Bob Barton	4.00	2.00	1.25
(3)	Glenn Beckert	4.00	2.00	1.25
(4)	Jack Bloomfield	4.00	2.00	1.25
(5)	Nate Colbert	4.00	2.00	1.25
(6)	Mike Corkins	4.00	2.00	1.25
(7)	Jim Davenport	4.00	2.00	1.25
(8)	Dave Freisleben	4.00	2.00	1.25
(9)	Cito Gaston	4.00	2.00	1.25
(10)	Bill Greif	4.00	2.00	1.25
(11)	Johnny Grubb	4.00	2.00	1.25
(12)	Larry Hardy	4.00	2.00	1.25
(13)	Enzo Hernandez	4.00	2.00	1.25
(14)	Dave Hilton	4.00	2.00	1.25
(15)	Randy Jones	4.00	2.00	1.25
(16)	Fred Kendall	4.00	2.00	1.25
(17)	Gene Locklear	4.00	2.00	1.25
(18)	Willie McCovey	10.00	5.00	3.00
(19)	John McNamara	4.00	2.00	1.25
(20)	Rich Morales	4.00	2.00	1.25
(21)	Bill Posedel	4.00	2.00	1.25
(22)	Dave Roberts	4.00	2.00	1.25
(23)	Vicente Romo	4.00	2.00	1.25
(24)	Dan Spillner	4.00	2.00	1.25
(25)	Bob Tolan	4.00	2.00	1.25
(26)	Derrel Thomas	4.00	2.00	1.25
(27)	Rich Troedson	4.00	2.00	1.25
(28)	Whitey Wietelmann	4.00	2.00	1.25
(29)	Bernie Williams	4.00	2.00	1.25
(30)	Dave Winfield	15.00	7.50	4.50

1975 Dean's Photo Service San Diego Padres

Player biographical data and stats continued on the backs of the cards in the 1975 series sponsored by Dean's. Once again the black-and-white pictures were in 5-1/2" x 8-1/2" format. Fronts have the player photo at top, with his name and position beneath. At bottom are the team and sponsor logos. The Padres logo consists of a cartoon character robed monk in various baseball poses. The pictures were given away at autograph nights during the season. The unnumbered photos are checklisted here in alphabetical order.

		NM	EX	VG
Complete Set (30):		60.00	30.00	18.00
Common Player:		4.00	2.00	1.25
(1)	Jim Davenport	4.00	2.00	1.25
(2)	Bob Davis	4.00	2.00	1.25
(3)	Rich Folkers	4.00	2.00	1.25
(4)	Alan Foster	4.00	2.00	1.25
(5)	Dave Freisleben	4.00	2.00	1.25
(6)	Danny Frisella	4.00	2.00	1.25
(7)	Tito Fuentes	4.00	2.00	1.25
(8)	Bill Greif	4.00	2.00	1.25
(9)	Johnny Grubb	4.00	2.00	1.25
(10)	Enzo Hernandez	4.00	2.00	1.25
(11)	Randy Hundley (Blank back.)	4.00	2.00	1.25
(12)	Mike Ivie	4.00	2.00	1.25
(13)	Jerry Johnson	4.00	2.00	1.25
(14)	Randy Jones	4.00	2.00	1.25
(15)	Fred Kendall	4.00	2.00	1.25
(16)	Ted Kubiak	4.00	2.00	1.25
(17)	Gene Locklear	4.00	2.00	1.25
(18)	Willie McCovey	10.00	5.00	3.00
(19)	Joe McIntosh	4.00	2.00	1.25
(20)	John McNamara	4.00	2.00	1.25
(21)	Tom Morgan	4.00	2.00	1.25
(22)	Dick Sharon	4.00	2.00	1.25
(23)	Dick Sisler	4.00	2.00	1.25
(24)	Dan Spillner	4.00	2.00	1.25
(25)	Brent Strom	4.00	2.00	1.25
(26)	Bobby Tolan	4.00	2.00	1.25
(27)	Dave Tomlin	4.00	2.00	1.25
(28)	Hector Torres (Blank back.)	4.00	2.00	1.25
(29)	Whitey Wietelmann	4.00	2.00	1.25
(30)	Dave Winfield	15.00	7.50	4.50

1976 Dean's Photo Service San Diego Padres

The last of four black-and-white team sets which were sponsored by Dean's was issued in 1976. The format was little different than previous years. Cards are 5-1/2" x 8-1/2" black-and-white. Fronts have a player portrait or pose surrounded

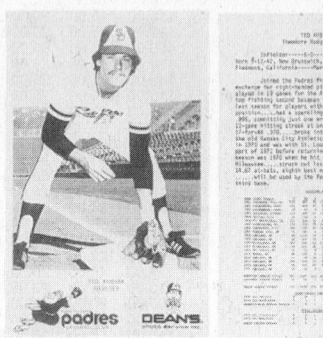

by a white border. At bottom front are team and sponsor logos. Backs have personal data, a career summary and complete professional stats. The unnumbered cards are checklisted here in alphabetical order.

		NM	EX	VG
Complete Set (30):		60.00	30.00	18.00
Common Player:		4.00	2.00	1.25
(1)	Joe Amalfitano	4.00	2.00	1.25
(2)	Roger Craig	4.00	2.00	1.25
(3)	Bob Davis	4.00	2.00	1.25
(4)	Willie Davis	4.00	2.00	1.25
(5)	Rich Folkers	4.00	2.00	1.25
(6)	Alan Foster	4.00	2.00	1.25
(7)	Dave Freisleben	4.00	2.00	1.25
(8)	Tito Fuentes	4.00	2.00	1.25
(9)	John Grubb	4.00	2.00	1.25
(10)	Enzo Hernandez	4.00	2.00	1.25
(11)	Mike Ivie	4.00	2.00	1.25
(12)	Jerry Johnson	4.00	2.00	1.25
(13)	Randy Jones	4.00	2.00	1.25
(14)	Fred Kendall	4.00	2.00	1.25
(15)	Ted Kubiak	4.00	2.00	1.25
(16)	Willie McCovey	10.00	5.00	3.00
(17)	John McNamara	4.00	2.00	1.25
(18)	Luis Melendez	4.00	2.00	1.25
(19)	Butch Metzger	4.00	2.00	1.25
(20)	Doug Rader	4.00	2.00	1.25
(21)	Merv Rettenmund	4.00	2.00	1.25
(22)	Ken Reynolds	4.00	2.00	1.25
(23)	Dick Sisler	4.00	2.00	1.25
(24)	Dan Spillner	4.00	2.00	1.25
(25)	Brent Strom	4.00	2.00	1.25
(26)	Dave Tomlin	4.00	2.00	1.25
(27)	Hector Torres	4.00	2.00	1.25
(28)	Jerry Turner	4.00	2.00	1.25
(29)	Whitey Wietelmann	4.00	2.00	1.25
(30)	Dave Winfield	15.00	7.50	4.50

1938 Dizzy Dean's Service Station

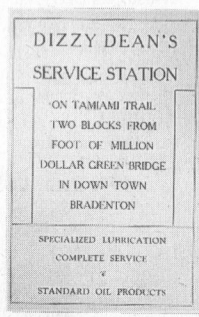

The date of issue of this one-card set is only a guess. The 4" x 6" black-and-white card advertises Dean's service station in Florida.

	NM	EX	VG
Dizzy Dean	350.00	175.00	100.00

1978 Dearborn Show

#13 NORM CASH

Former members of the Detroit Tigers, some of whom were scheduled to appear as autograph guests, are featured in this collectors' issue produced in conjunction with the 1978 Dearborn Baseball Card & Sports Memorabilia Show. The 2-5/8" x 3-5/8" cards have black-and-white player photos on front with the player name and card number in the white border at bottom. Backs, also in black-and-white, advertise the fall, 1978, and spring, 1979 shows.

		NM	EX	VG
	Complete Set (18):	60.00	30.00	18.00
	Common Player:	4.00	2.00	1.25
1	Rocky Colavito	15.00	7.50	4.50
2	Ervin Fox	4.00	2.00	1.25
3	Lynwood Rowe	4.00	2.00	1.25
4	Gerald Walker	4.00	2.00	1.25
5	Leon Goslin	4.00	2.00	1.25
6	Harvey Kuenn	6.00	3.00	1.75
7	Frank Howard	6.00	3.00	1.75
8	Woodie Fryman	4.00	2.00	1.25
9	Don Wert	4.00	2.00	1.25
10	Jim Perry	4.00	2.00	1.25
11	Mayo Smith	4.00	2.00	1.25
12	Al Kaline	20.00	10.00	6.00
13	Norm Cash	12.00	6.00	3.50
14	Mickey Cochrane	9.00	4.50	2.75
15	Fred Marberry	4.00	2.00	1.25
16	Bill Freehan	6.00	3.00	1.75
17	Charlie Gehringer	9.00	4.50	2.75
18	Jim Northrup	4.00	2.00	1.25

1980 Delacorte Press

As a promotion for its book, "Number 1," written by Billy Martin, Delacorte Press issued this card picturing Martin somewhat in the style of a 1978 Topps manager card. The 3-1/2" x 2-1/2" card has a black-and-white photo of Martin as a Yankees manager, and a color photo as the A's manager. The front is bordered in red. Backs are printed in black, white and red with biographical details and promotional copy for the book.

		NM	EX	VG
1	Billy Martin	6.00	3.00	1.75

1971 Dell Today's Team Stamps

This issue was produced as a series of individual team (plus one All-Star) albums. The 8-1/2" x 10-7/8" booklets offer team and league histories and stats, photos of all-time team stars and two pages of 12 player stamps each. Each stamp is 1-7/8" x 2-15/16" and has a posed color photo and black facsimile autograph on front. Backs have the player name, biographical details and a few career highlights, along with an underprint of the team logo. The stamps are perforated for easy seperation, though there are no spaces in the 12-page album for their housing once removed from the sheet. The team albums were sold individually (39 cents) as well as in six-team divisional sets ($2). The checklist is arranged alphabetically by team within league; individual stamps are unnumbered.

		NM	EX	VG
	Complete Set, Albums (25):	225.00	110.00	65.00
	Complete Set, Stamps (600):	175.00	90.00	50.00
	Common Player:	1.00	.50	.30
	Complete All-Star Album:	20.00	10.00	6.00
(1)	Hank Aaron	7.50	3.75	2.25
(2)	Luis Aparicio	2.50	1.25	.70
(3)	Ernie Banks	5.00	2.50	1.50
(4)	Johnny Bench	3.00	1.50	.90
(5)	Rico Carty	1.00	.50	.30
(6)	Roberto Clemente	10.00	5.00	3.00
(7)	Bob Gibson	2.50	1.25	.70
(8)	Willie Horton	1.00	.50	.30
(9)	Frank Howard	1.50	.70	.45
(10)	Reggie Jackson	6.00	3.00	1.75
(11)	Fergie Jenkins	1.50	.70	.45
(12)	Alex Johnson	1.00	.50	.30
(13)	Al Kaline	3.00	1.50	.90
(14)	Harmon Killebrew	3.00	1.50	.90
(15)	Willie Mays	7.50	3.75	2.25

(16)	Sam McDowell	1.00	.50	.30
(17)	Denny McLain	1.50	.70	.45
(18)	Boog Powell	1.50	.70	.45
(19)	Brooks Robinson	3.00	1.50	.90
(20)	Frank Robinson	3.00	1.50	.90
(21)	Pete Rose	7.50	3.75	2.25
(22)	Tom Seaver	3.00	1.50	.90
(23)	Rusty Staub	1.50	.70	.45
(24)	Carl Yastrzemski	3.00	1.50	.90
	Complete Atlanta Braves Album:	15.00	7.50	4.50
(1)	Hank Aaron	7.50	3.75	2.25
(2)	Tommie Aaron	1.00	.50	.30
(3)	Hank Allen	1.00	.50	.30
(4)	Clete Boyer	1.50	.70	.45
(5)	Oscar Brown	1.00	.50	.30
(6)	Rico Carty	1.00	.50	.30
(7)	Orlando Cepeda	2.50	1.25	.70
(8)	Bob Didier	1.00	.50	.30
(9)	Ralph Garr	1.00	.50	.30
(10)	Gil Garrido	1.00	.50	.30
(11)	Ron Herbel	1.00	.50	.30
(12)	Sonny Jackson	1.00	.50	.30
(13)	Pat Jarvis	1.00	.50	.30
(14)	Larry Jaster	1.00	.50	.30
(15)	Hal King	1.00	.50	.30
(16)	Mike Lum	1.00	.50	.30
(17)	Felix Millan	1.00	.50	.30
(18)	Jim Nash	1.00	.50	.30
(19)	Phil Niekro	2.00	1.00	.60
(20)	Bob Priddy	1.00	.50	.30
(21)	Ron Reed	1.00	.50	.30
(22)	George Stone	1.00	.50	.30
(23)	Cecil Upshaw	1.00	.50	.30
(24)	Hoyt Wilhelm	2.00	1.00	.60
	Complete Chicago Cubs Album:	15.00	7.50	4.50
(1)	Ernie Banks	5.00	2.50	1.50
(2)	Glenn Beckert	1.00	.50	.30
(3)	Danny Breeden	1.00	.50	.30
(4)	Johnny Callison	1.00	.50	.30
(5)	Jim Colborn	1.00	.50	.30
(6)	Joe Decker	1.00	.50	.30
(7)	Bill Hands	1.00	.50	.30
(8)	Jim Hickman	1.00	.50	.30
(9)	Ken Holtzman	1.00	.50	.30
(10)	Randy Hundley	1.00	.50	.30
(11)	Fergie Jenkins	2.00	1.00	.60
(12)	Don Kessinger	1.00	.50	.30
(13)	J.C. Martin	1.00	.50	.30
(14)	Bob Miller	1.00	.50	.30
(15)	Milt Pappas	1.00	.50	.30
(16)	Joe Pepitone	1.00	.50	.30
(17)	Juan Pizarro	1.00	.50	.30
(18)	Paul Popovich	1.00	.50	.30
(19)	Phil Regan	1.00	.50	.30
(20)	Roberto Rodriguez	1.00	.50	.30
(21)	Ken Rudolph	1.00	.50	.30
(22)	Ron Santo	1.50	.70	.45
(23)	Hector Torres	1.00	.50	.30
(24)	Billy Williams	2.50	1.25	.70
	Complete Cincinnati Reds Album:	20.00	10.00	6.00
(1)	Johnny Bench	3.00	1.50	.90
(2)	Angel Bravo	1.00	.50	.30
(3)	Bernie Carbo	1.00	.50	.30
(4)	Clay Carroll	1.00	.50	.30
(5)	Darrel Chaney	1.00	.50	.30
(6)	Ty Cline	1.00	.50	.30
(7)	Tony Cloninger	1.00	.50	.30
(8)	Dave Concepcion	1.00	.50	.30
(9)	Pat Corrales	1.00	.50	.30
(10)	Greg Garrett	1.00	.50	.30
(11)	Wayne Granger	1.00	.50	.30
(12)	Don Gullett	1.00	.50	.30
(13)	Tommy Helms	1.00	.50	.30
(14)	Lee May	1.00	.50	.30
(15)	Jim McGlothlin	1.00	.50	.30
(16)	Hal McRae	1.00	.50	.30
(17)	Jim Merritt	1.00	.50	.30
(18)	Gary Nolan	1.00	.50	.30
(19)	Tony Perez	2.50	1.25	.70
(20)	Pete Rose	7.50	3.75	2.25
(21)	Wayne Simpson	1.00	.50	.30
(22)	Jimmy Stewart	1.00	.50	.30
(23)	Bobby Tolan	1.00	.50	.30
(24)	Woody Woodward	1.00	.50	.30
	Complete Houston Astros Album:	10.00	5.00	3.00
(1)	Jesus Alou	1.00	.50	.30
(2)	Jack Billingham	1.00	.50	.30
(3)	Ron Cook	1.00	.50	.30
(4)	George Culver	1.00	.50	.30
(5)	Larry Dierker	1.00	.50	.30
(6)	Jack DiLauro	1.00	.50	.30
(7)	Johnny Edwards	1.00	.50	.30
(8)	Fred Gladding	1.00	.50	.30
(9)	Tom Griffin	1.00	.50	.30
(10)	Skip Guinn	1.00	.50	.30
(11)	Jack Hiatt	1.00	.50	.30
(12)	Denny Lemaster	1.00	.50	.30
(13)	Marty Martinez	1.00	.50	.30
(14)	John Mayberry	1.00	.50	.30
(15)	Denis Menke	1.00	.50	.30
(16)	Norm Miller	1.00	.50	.30
(17)	Joe Morgan	2.50	1.25	.70
(18)	Doug Rader	1.00	.50	.30
(19)	Jim Ray	1.00	.50	.30
(20)	Scipio Spinks	1.00	.50	.30
(21)	Bob Watkins	1.00	.50	.30
(22)	Bob Watson	1.00	.50	.30
(23)	Don Wilson	1.00	.50	.30
(24)	Jim Wynn	1.00	.50	.30
	Complete Los Angeles Dodgers Album:	12.50	6.25	3.75
(1)	Rich Allen	1.50	.70	.45
(2)	Jim Brewer	1.00	.50	.30
(3)	Bill Buckner	1.00	.50	.30

(4)	Willie Crawford	1.00	.50	.30
(5)	Willie Davis	1.00	.50	.30
(6)	Al Downing	1.00	.50	.30
(7)	Steve Garvey	6.00	3.00	1.75
(8)	Billy Grabarkewitz	1.00	.50	.30
(9)	Tom Haller	1.00	.50	.30
(10)	Jim Lefebvre	1.00	.50	.30
(11)	Pete Mikkelsen	1.00	.50	.30
(12)	Joe Moeller	1.00	.50	.30
(13)	Manny Mota	1.00	.50	.30
(14)	Claude Osteen	1.00	.50	.30
(15)	Wes Parker	1.00	.50	.30
(16)	Jose Pena	1.00	.50	.30
(17)	Bill Russell	1.00	.50	.30
(18)	Duke Sims	1.00	.50	.30
(19)	Bill Singer	1.00	.50	.30
(20)	Mike Strahler	1.00	.50	.30
(21)	Bill Sudakis	1.00	.50	.30
(22)	Don Sutton	2.00	1.00	.60
(23)	Jeff Torborg	1.00	.50	.30
(24)	Maury Wills	1.00	.50	.30
	Complete Montreal Expos Album:	10.00	5.00	3.00
(1)	Bob Bailey	1.00	.50	.30
(2)	John Bateman	1.00	.50	.30
(3)	John Boccabella	1.00	.50	.30
(4)	Ron Brand	1.00	.50	.30
(5)	Boots Day	1.00	.50	.30
(6)	Jim Fairey	1.00	.50	.30
(7)	Ron Fairly	1.00	.50	.30
(8)	Jim Gosger	1.00	.50	.30
(9)	Don Hahn	1.00	.50	.30
(10)	Ron Hunt	1.00	.50	.30
(11)	Mack Jones	1.00	.50	.30
(12)	Jose Laboy	1.00	.50	.30
(13)	Mike Marshall	1.00	.50	.30
(14)	Dan McGinn	1.00	.50	.30
(15)	Carl Morton	1.00	.50	.30
(16)	John O'Donoghue	1.00	.50	.30
(17)	Adolfo Phillips	1.00	.50	.30
(18)	Claude Raymond	1.00	.50	.30
(19)	Steve Renko	1.00	.50	.30
(20)	Marv Staehle	1.00	.50	.30
(21)	Rusty Staub	1.25	.60	.40
(22)	Bill Stoneman	1.00	.50	.30
(23)	Gary Sutherland	1.00	.50	.30
(24)	Bobby Wine	1.00	.50	.30
	Complete New York Mets Album:	25.00	12.50	7.50
(1)	Tommie Agee	1.00	.50	.30
(2)	Bob Aspromonte	1.00	.50	.30
(3)	Ken Boswell	1.00	.50	.30
(4)	Dean Chance	1.00	.50	.30
(5)	Donn Clendenon	1.00	.50	.30
(6)	Duffy Dyer	1.00	.50	.30
(7)	Dan Frisella	1.00	.50	.30
(8)	Wayne Garrett	1.00	.50	.30
(9)	Gary Gentry	1.00	.50	.30
(10)	Jerry Grote	1.00	.50	.30
(11)	Bud Harrelson	1.00	.50	.30
(12)	Cleon Jones	1.00	.50	.30
(13)	Jerry Koosman	1.00	.50	.30
(14)	Ed Kranepool	1.00	.50	.30
(15)	Dave Marshall	1.00	.50	.30
(16)	Jim McAndrew	1.00	.50	.30
(17)	Tug McGraw	1.00	.50	.30
(18)	Nolan Ryan	20.00	10.00	6.00
(19)	Ray Sadecki	1.00	.50	.30
(20)	Tom Seaver	3.00	1.50	.90
(21)	Art Shamsky	1.00	.50	.30
(22)	Ron Swoboda	1.00	.50	.30
(23)	Ron Taylor	1.00	.50	.30
(24)	Al Weis	1.00	.50	.30
	Complete Philadelphia Phillies Album:	10.00	5.00	3.00
(1)	Larry Bowa	1.00	.50	.30
(2)	Johnny Briggs	1.00	.50	.30
(3)	Bryon Browne	1.00	.50	.30
(4)	Jim Bunning	2.00	1.00	.60
(5)	Billy Champion	1.00	.50	.30
(6)	Mike Compton	1.00	.50	.30
(7)	Denny Doyle	1.00	.50	.30
(8)	Roger Freed	1.00	.50	.30
(9)	Woody Fryman	1.00	.50	.30
(10)	Oscar Gamble	1.00	.50	.30
(11)	Terry Harmon	1.00	.50	.30
(12)	Larry Hisle	1.00	.50	.30
(13)	Joe Hoerner	1.00	.50	.30
(14)	Deron Johnson	1.00	.50	.30
(15)	Barry Lersch	1.00	.50	.30
(16)	Tim McCarver	1.50	.70	.45
(17)	Don Money	1.00	.50	.30
(18)	Mike Ryan	1.00	.50	.30
(19)	Dick Selma	1.00	.50	.30
(20)	Chris Short	1.00	.50	.30
(21)	Ron Stone	1.00	.50	.30
(22)	Tony Taylor	1.00	.50	.30
(23)	Rick Wise	1.00	.50	.30
(24)	Billy Wilson	1.00	.50	.30
	Complete Pittsburgh Pirates Album:	30.00	15.00	9.00
(1)	Gene Alley	1.00	.50	.30
(2)	Steve Blass	1.00	.50	.30
(3)	Nelson Briles	1.00	.50	.30
(4)	Jim Campanis	1.00	.50	.30
(5)	Dave Cash	1.00	.50	.30
(6)	Roberto Clemente	10.00	5.00	3.00
(7)	Vic Davalillo	1.00	.50	.30
(8)	Dock Ellis	1.00	.50	.30
(9)	Jim Grant	1.00	.50	.30
(10)	Dave Giusti	1.00	.50	.30
(11)	Richie Hebner	1.00	.50	.30
(12)	Jackie Hernandez	1.00	.50	.30
(13)	Johnny Jeter	1.00	.50	.30
(14)	Lou Marone	1.00	.50	.30
(15)	Jose Martinez	1.00	.50	.30
(16)	Bill Mazeroski	2.50	1.25	.70
(17)	Bob Moose	1.00	.50	.30

No.	Name			
(18)	Al Oliver	1.25	.60	.40
(19)	Jose Pagan	1.00	.50	.30
(20)	Bob Robertson	1.00	.50	.30
(21)	Manny Sanguillen	1.00	.50	.30
(22)	Willie Stargell	2.50	1.25	.70
(23)	Bob Veale	1.00	.50	.30
(24)	Luke Walker	1.00	.50	.30
	Complete San Diego Padres Album:	10.00	5.00	3.00
(1)	Jose Arcia	1.00	.50	.30
(2)	Bob Barton	1.00	.50	.30
(3)	Fred Beene	1.00	.50	.30
(4)	Ollie Brown	1.00	.50	.30
(5)	Dave Campbell	1.00	.50	.30
(6)	Chris Cannizzaro	1.00	.50	.30
(7)	Nate Colbert	1.00	.50	.30
(8)	Mike Corkins	1.00	.50	.30
(9)	Tommy Dean	1.00	.50	.30
(10)	Al Ferrara	1.00	.50	.30
(11)	Rod Gaspar	1.00	.50	.30
(12)	Cito Gaston	1.00	.50	.30
(13)	Enzo Hernandez	1.00	.50	.30
(14)	Clay Kirby	1.00	.50	.30
(15)	Don Mason	1.00	.50	.30
(16)	Ivan Murrell	1.00	.50	.30
(17)	Gerry Nyman	1.00	.50	.30
(18)	Tom Phoebus	1.00	.50	.30
(19)	Dave Roberts	1.00	.50	.30
(20)	Gary Ross	1.00	.50	.30
(21)	Al Santorini	1.00	.50	.30
(22)	Al Severinsen	1.00	.50	.30
(23)	Ron Slocum	1.00	.50	.30
(24)	Ed Spiezio	1.00	.50	.30
	Complete San Francisco Giants Album:	12.50	6.25	3.75
(1)	Bobby Bonds	1.25	.60	.40
(2)	Ron Bryant	1.00	.50	.30
(3)	Don Carrithers	1.00	.50	.30
(4)	John Cumberland	1.00	.50	.30
(5)	Mike Davison	1.00	.50	.30
(6)	Dick Dietz	1.00	.50	.30
(7)	Tito Fuentes	1.00	.50	.30
(8)	Russ Gibson	1.00	.50	.30
(9)	Jim Ray Hart	1.00	.50	.30
(10)	Bob Heise	1.00	.50	.30
(11)	Ken Henderson	1.00	.50	.30
(12)	Steve Huntz	1.00	.50	.30
(13)	Frank Johnson	1.00	.50	.30
(14)	Jerry Johnson	1.00	.50	.30
(15)	Hal Lanier	1.00	.50	.30
(16)	Juan Marichal	2.00	1.00	.60
(17)	Willie Mays	7.50	3.75	2.25
(18)	Willie McCovey	2.50	1.25	.70
(19)	Don McMahon	1.00	.50	.30
(20)	Jim Moyer	1.00	.50	.30
(21)	Gaylord Perry	2.00	1.00	.60
(22)	Frank Reberger	1.00	.50	.30
(23)	Rich Robertson	1.00	.50	.30
(24)	Bernie Williams	1.00	.50	.30
	Complete St. Louis Cardinals Album:	10.00	5.00	3.00
(1)	Matty Alou	1.00	.50	.30
(2)	Jim Beauchamp	1.00	.50	.30
(3)	Frank Bertaina	1.00	.50	.30
(4)	Lou Brock	2.50	1.25	.70
(5)	George Brunet	1.00	.50	.30
(6)	Jose Cardenal	1.00	.50	.30
(7)	Steve Carlton	2.50	1.25	.70
(8)	Moe Drabowsky	1.00	.50	.30
(9)	Bob Gibson	2.50	1.25	.70
(10)	Joe Hague	1.00	.50	.30
(11)	Julian Javier	1.00	.50	.30
(12)	Leron Lee	1.00	.50	.30
(13)	Frank Linzy	1.00	.50	.30
(14)	Dal Maxvill	1.00	.50	.30
(15)	Jerry McNertney	1.00	.50	.30
(16)	Fred Norman	1.00	.50	.30
(17)	Milt Ramirez	1.00	.50	.30
(18)	Dick Schofield	1.00	.50	.30
(19)	Mike Shannon	1.00	.50	.30
(20)	Ted Sizemore	1.00	.50	.30
(21)	Bob Stinson	1.00	.50	.30
(22)	Carl Taylor	1.00	.50	.30
(23)	Joe Torre	1.50	.70	.45
(24)	Mike Torrez	1.00	.50	.30
	Complete Baltimore Orioles Album:	15.00	7.50	4.50
(1)	Mark Belanger	1.00	.50	.30
(2)	Paul Blair	1.00	.50	.30
(3)	Don Buford	1.00	.50	.30
(4)	Terry Crowley	1.00	.50	.30
(5)	Mike Cuellar	1.00	.50	.30
(6)	Clay Dalrymple	1.00	.50	.30
(7)	Pat Dobson	1.00	.50	.30
(8)	Andy Etchebarren	1.00	.50	.30
(9)	Dick Hall	1.00	.50	.30
(10)	Jim Hardin	1.00	.50	.30
(11)	Elrod Hendricks	1.00	.50	.30
(12)	Grant Jackson	1.00	.50	.30
(13)	Dave Johnson	1.00	.50	.30
(14)	Dave Leonhard	1.00	.50	.30
(15)	Marcelino Lopez	1.00	.50	.30
(16)	Dave McNally	1.00	.50	.30
(17)	Curt Motton	1.00	.50	.30
(18)	Jim Palmer	2.00	1.00	.60
(19)	Boog Powell	1.00	.50	.30
(20)	Merv Rettenmund	1.00	.50	.30
(21)	Brooks Robinson	3.00	1.50	.90
(22)	Frank Robinson	3.00	1.50	.90
(23)	Pete Richert	1.00	.50	.30
(24)	Chico Salmon	1.00	.50	.30
	Complete Boston Red Sox Album:	15.00	7.50	4.50
(1)	Luis Aparicio	2.50	1.25	.70
(2)	Bobby Bolin	1.00	.50	.30
(3)	Ken Brett	1.00	.50	.30
(4)	Billy Conigliaro	1.00	.50	.30
(5)	Ray Culp	1.00	.50	.30
(6)	Mike Flore	1.00	.50	.30
(7)	John Kennedy	1.00	.50	.30
(8)	Cal Koonce	1.00	.50	.30
(9)	Joe Lahoud	1.00	.50	.30
(10)	Bill Lee	1.00	.50	.30
(11)	Jim Lonborg	1.00	.50	.30
(12)	Sparky Lyle	1.00	.50	.30
(13)	Mike Nagy	1.00	.50	.30
(14)	Don Pavletich	1.00	.50	.30
(15)	Gary Peters	1.00	.50	.30
(16)	Rico Petrocelli	1.00	.50	.30
(17)	Vicente Romo	1.00	.50	.30
(18)	Tom Satriano	1.00	.50	.30
(19)	George Scott	1.00	.50	.30
(20)	Sonny Siebert	1.00	.50	.30
(21)	Reggie Smith	1.00	.50	.30
(22)	Jarvis Tatum	1.00	.50	.30
(23)	Ken Tatum	1.00	.50	.30
(24)	Carl Yastrzemski	3.00	1.50	.90
	Complete California Angels Album:	10.00	5.00	3.00
(1)	Sandy Alomar	1.00	.50	.30
(2)	Joe Azcue	1.00	.50	.30
(3)	Ken Berry	1.00	.50	.30
(4)	Gene Brabender	1.00	.50	.30
(5)	Billy Cowan	1.00	.50	.30
(6)	Tony Conigliaro	1.50	.70	.45
(7)	Eddie Fisher	1.00	.50	.30
(8)	Jim Fregosi	1.00	.50	.30
(9)	Tony Gonzales (Gonzalez)	1.00	.50	.30
(10)	Alex Johnson	1.00	.50	.30
(11)	Fred Lasher	1.00	.50	.30
(12)	Jim Maloney	1.00	.50	.30
(13)	Rudy May	1.00	.50	.30
(14)	Ken McMullen	1.00	.50	.30
(15)	Andy Messersmith	1.00	.50	.30
(16)	Gerry Moses	1.00	.50	.30
(17)	Syd O'Brien	1.00	.50	.30
(18)	Mel Queen	1.00	.50	.30
(19)	Roger Repoz	1.00	.50	.30
(20)	Archie Reynolds	1.00	.50	.30
(21)	Chico Ruiz	1.00	.50	.30
(22)	Jim Spencer	1.00	.50	.30
(23)	Clyde Wright	1.00	.50	.30
(24)	Billy Wynne	1.00	.50	.30
	Complete Chicago White Sox Album:	10.00	5.00	3.00
(1)	Luis Alvarado	1.00	.50	.30
(2)	Mike Andrews	1.00	.50	.30
(3)	Tom Egan	1.00	.50	.30
(4)	Steve Hamilton	1.00	.50	.30
(5)	Ed Hermann	1.00	.50	.30
(6)	Joel Horlen	1.00	.50	.30
(7)	Tommy John	1.25	.60	.40
(8)	Bart Johnson	1.00	.50	.30
(9)	Jay Johnstone	1.00	.50	.30
(10)	Duane Josephson	1.00	.50	.30
(11)	Pat Kelly	1.00	.50	.30
(12)	Bobby Knoop	1.00	.50	.30
(13)	Carlos May	1.00	.50	.30
(14)	Lee Maye	1.00	.50	.30
(15)	Tom McGraw	1.00	.50	.30
(16)	Bill Melton	1.00	.50	.30
(17)	Rich Morales	1.00	.50	.30
(18)	Tom Murphy	1.00	.50	.30
(19)	Don O'Riley	1.00	.50	.30
(20)	Rick Reichardt	1.00	.50	.30
(21)	Bill Robinson	1.00	.50	.30
(22)	Bob Spence	1.00	.50	.30
(23)	Walt Williams	1.00	.50	.30
(24)	Wilbur Wood	1.00	.50	.30
	Complete Cleveland Indians Album:	10.00	5.00	3.00
(1)	Rick Austin	1.00	.50	.30
(2)	Buddy Bradford	1.00	.50	.30
(3)	Larry Brown	1.00	.50	.30
(4)	Lou Camilli	1.00	.50	.30
(5)	Vince Colbert	1.00	.50	.30
(6)	Ray Fosse	1.00	.50	.30
(7)	Alan Foster	1.00	.50	.30
(8)	Roy Foster	1.00	.50	.30
(9)	Rich Hand	1.00	.50	.30
(10)	Steve Hargan	1.00	.50	.30
(11)	Ken Harrelson	1.00	.50	.30
(12)	Jack Heidemann	1.00	.50	.30
(13)	Phil Hennigan	1.00	.50	.30
(14)	Dennis Higgins	1.00	.50	.30
(15)	Chuck Hinton	1.00	.50	.30
(16)	Tony Horton	1.00	.50	.30
(17)	Ray Lamb	1.00	.50	.30
(18)	Eddie Leon	1.00	.50	.30
(19)	Sam McDowell	1.00	.50	.30
(20)	Graig Nettles	1.25	.60	.40
(21)	Mike Paul	1.00	.50	.30
(22)	Vada Pinson	1.25	.60	.40
(23)	Ken Suarez	1.00	.50	.30
(24)	Ted Uhlaender	1.00	.50	.30
	Complete Detroit Tigers Album:	10.00	5.00	3.00
(1)	Ed Brinkman	1.00	.50	.30
(2)	Gates Brown	1.00	.50	.30
(3)	Ike Brown	1.00	.50	.30
(4)	Les Cain	1.00	.50	.30
(5)	Norm Cash	1.50	.70	.45
(6)	Joe Coleman	1.00	.50	.30
(7)	Bill Freehan	1.00	.50	.30
(8)	Cesar Gutierrez	1.00	.50	.30
(9)	John Hiller	1.00	.50	.30
(10)	Willie Horton	1.00	.50	.30
(11)	Dalton Jones	1.00	.50	.30
(12)	Al Kaline	3.00	1.50	.90
(13)	Mike Kilkenny	1.00	.50	.30
(14)	Mickey Lolich	1.00	.50	.30
(15)	Dick McAuliffe	1.00	.50	.30
(16)	Joe Niekro	1.00	.50	.30
(17)	Jim Northrup	1.00	.50	.30
(18)	Daryl Patterson	1.00	.50	.30
(19)	Jimmie Price	1.00	.50	.30
(20)	Bob Reed	1.00	.50	.30
(21)	Aurelio Rodriguez	1.00	.50	.30
(22)	Fred Scherman	1.00	.50	.30
(23)	Mickey Stanley	1.00	.50	.30
(24)	Tom Timmermann	1.00	.50	.30
	Complete Kansas City Royals Album:	10.00	5.00	3.00
(1)	Ted Abernathy	1.00	.50	.30
(2)	Wally Bunker	1.00	.50	.30
(3)	Tom Burgmeier	1.00	.50	.30
(4)	Bill Butler	1.00	.50	.30
(5)	Bruce Dal Canton	1.00	.50	.30
(6)	Dick Drago	1.00	.50	.30
(7)	Bobby Floyd	1.00	.50	.30
(8)	Gail Hopkins	1.00	.50	.30
(9)	Joe Keough	1.00	.50	.30
(10)	Ed Kirkpatrick	1.00	.50	.30
(11)	Tom Matchick	1.00	.50	.30
(12)	Jerry May	1.00	.50	.30
(13)	Aurelio Monteagudo	1.00	.50	.30
(14)	Dave Morehead	1.00	.50	.30
(15)	Bob Oliver	1.00	.50	.30
(16)	Amos Otis	1.00	.50	.30
(17)	Fred Patek	1.00	.50	.30
(18)	Lou Piniella	1.25	.60	.40
(19)	Cookie Rojas	1.00	.50	.30
(20)	Jim Rooker	1.00	.50	.30
(21)	Paul Schaal	1.00	.50	.30
(22)	Rich Severson	1.00	.50	.30
(23)	George Spriggs	1.00	.50	.30
(24)	Carl Taylor	1.00	.50	.30
	Complete Milwaukee Brewers Album:	10.00	5.00	3.00
(1)	Dave Baldwin	1.00	.50	.30
(2)	Dick Ellsworth	1.00	.50	.30
(3)	John Gelnar	1.00	.50	.30
(4)	Tommy Harper	1.00	.50	.30
(5)	Mike Hegan	1.00	.50	.30
(6)	Bob Humphreys	1.00	.50	.30
(7)	Andy Kosco	1.00	.50	.30
(8)	Lew Krausse	1.00	.50	.30
(9)	Ted Kubiak	1.00	.50	.30
(10)	Skip Lockwood	1.00	.50	.30
(11)	Dave May	1.00	.50	.30
(12)	Bob Meyer	1.00	.50	.30
(13)	John Morris	1.00	.50	.30
(14)	Marty Pattin	1.00	.50	.30
(15)	Roberto Pena	1.00	.50	.30
(16)	Eduardo Rodriguez	1.00	.50	.30
(17)	Phil Roof	1.00	.50	.30
(18)	Ken Sanders	1.00	.50	.30
(19)	Ted Savage	1.00	.50	.30
(20)	Russ Snyder	1.00	.50	.30
(21)	Bob Tillman	1.00	.50	.30
(22)	Bill Voss	1.00	.50	.30
(23)	Danny Walton	1.00	.50	.30
(24)	Floyd Wicker	1.00	.50	.30
	Complete Minnesota Twins Album:	15.00	7.50	4.50
(1)	Brant Alyea	1.00	.50	.30
(2)	Bert Blyleven	1.00	.50	.30
(3)	Dave Boswell	1.00	.50	.30
(4)	Leo Cardenas	1.00	.50	.30
(5)	Rod Carew	2.50	1.25	.70
(6)	Tom Hall	1.00	.50	.30
(7)	Jim Holt	1.00	.50	.30
(8)	Jim Kaat	1.00	.50	.30
(9)	Harmon Killebrew	2.50	1.25	.70
(10)	Charlie Manuel	1.00	.50	.30
(11)	George Mitterwald	1.00	.50	.30
(12)	Tony Oliva	1.25	.60	.40
(13)	Ron Perranoski	1.00	.50	.30
(14)	Jim Perry	1.00	.50	.30
(15)	Frank Quilici	1.00	.50	.30
(16)	Rich Reese	1.00	.50	.30
(17)	Rick Renick	1.00	.50	.30
(18)	Danny Thompson	1.00	.50	.30
(19)	Luis Tiant	1.00	.50	.30
(20)	Tom Tischinski	1.00	.50	.30
(21)	Cesar Tovar	1.00	.50	.30
(22)	Stan Williams	1.00	.50	.30
(23)	Dick Woodson	1.00	.50	.30
(24)	Bill Zepp	1.00	.50	.30
	Complete New York Yankees Album:	15.00	7.50	4.50
(1)	Jack Aker	1.00	.50	.30
(2)	Stan Bahnsen	1.00	.50	.30
(3)	Curt Blefary	1.00	.50	.30
(4)	Bill Burbach	1.00	.50	.30
(5)	Danny Cater	1.00	.50	.30
(6)	Horace Clarke	1.00	.50	.30
(7)	John Ellis	1.00	.50	.30
(8)	Jake Gibbs	1.00	.50	.30
(9)	Ron Hansen	1.00	.50	.30
(10)	Mike Kekich	1.00	.50	.30
(11)	Jerry Kenney	1.00	.50	.30
(12)	Ron Klimkowski	1.00	.50	.30
(13)	Steve Kline	1.00	.50	.30
(14)	Mike McCormick	1.00	.50	.30
(15)	Lindy McDaniel	1.00	.50	.30
(16)	Gene Michael	1.00	.50	.30
(17)	Thurman Munson	1.50	.70	.45
(18)	Bobby Murcer	1.25	.60	.40
(19)	Fritz Peterson	1.00	.50	.30
(20)	Mel Stottlemyre	1.00	.50	.30
(21)	Pete Ward	1.00	.50	.30
(22)	Gary Waslewski	1.00	.50	.30
(23)	Roy White	1.00	.50	.30
(24)	Ron Woods	1.00	.50	.30
	Complete Oakland A's Album:	15.00	7.50	4.50
(1)	Felipe Alou	1.00	.50	.30
(2)	Sal Bando	1.00	.50	.30
(3)	Vida Blue	1.00	.50	.30
(4)	Bert Campaneris	1.00	.50	.30
(5)	Ron Clark	1.00	.50	.30
(6)	Chuck Dobson	1.00	.50	.30
(7)	Dave Duncan	1.00	.50	.30

		NM	EX	VG
(8)	Frank Fernandez	1.00	.50	.30
(9)	Rollie Fingers	2.00	1.00	.60
(10)	Dick Green	1.00	.50	.30
(11)	Steve Hovley	1.00	.50	.30
(12)	Catfish Hunter	2.00	1.00	.60
(13)	Reggie Jackson	6.00	3.00	1.75
(14)	Marcel Lacheman	1.00	.50	.30
(15)	Paul Lindblad	1.00	.50	.30
(16)	Bob Locker	1.00	.50	.30
(17)	Don Mincher	1.00	.50	.30
(18)	Rick Monday	1.00	.50	.30
(19)	John Odom	1.00	.50	.30
(20)	Jim Roland	1.00	.50	.30
(21)	Joe Rudi	1.00	.50	.30
(22)	Diego Segui	1.00	.50	.30
(23)	Bob Stickels	1.00	.50	.30
(24)	Gene Tenace	1.00	.50	.30
	Complete Washington	12.50	6.25	3.75
	Senators Album:			
(1)	Bernie Allen	1.00	.50	.30
(2)	Dick Bosman	1.00	.50	.30
(3)	Jackie Brown	1.00	.50	.30
(4)	Paul Casanova	1.00	.50	.30
(5)	Casey Cox	1.00	.50	.30
(6)	Tim Cullen	1.00	.50	.30
(7)	Mike Epstein	1.00	.50	.30
(8)	Curt Flood	1.25	.60	.40
(9)	Joe Foy	1.00	.50	.30
(10)	Jim French	1.00	.50	.30
(11)	Bill Gogolewski	1.00	.50	.30
(12)	Tom Grieve	1.00	.50	.30
(13)	Joe Grzenda	1.00	.50	.30
(14)	Frank Howard	1.25	.60	.40
(15)	Joe Janeski	1.00	.50	.30
(16)	Darold Knowles	1.00	.50	.30
(17)	Elliott Maddox	1.00	.50	.30
(18)	Denny McLain	1.25	.60	.40
(19)	Dave Nelson	1.00	.50	.30
(20)	Horacio Pina	1.00	.50	.30
(21)	Jim Shellenback	1.00	.50	.30
(22)	Ed Stroud	1.00	.50	.30
(23)	Del Unser	1.00	.50	.30
(24)	Don Wert	1.00	.50	.30

1933 DeLong (R333)

The DeLong Co. of Boston was among the first to sell baseball cards with gum, issuing a set of 24 cards in 1933. DeLong cards measure about 1-15/16" x 2-15/16", with black-and-white player photos on a color background. The photos show the players in various action poses and positions them in the middle of a miniature stadium setting so that they appear to be giants. Most of the cards are vertically designed, but a few are horizontal. Backs were by Austen Lake, editor of the Boston Transcript, and contain tips to help youngsters become better ballplayers. The ACC designation for this set is R333.

		NM	EX	VG
	Complete Set (24):	30,000	8,000	4,000
	Common Player:	700.00	280.00	140.00
1	"Marty" McManus	1,260	280.00	140.00
2	Al Simmons	945.00	385.00	190.00
3	Oscar Melillo	700.00	280.00	140.00
4	William (Bill) Terry	945.00	385.00	190.00
5	Charlie Gehringer	945.00	385.00	190.00
6	Gordon (Mickey) Cochrane	945.00	385.00	190.00
7	Lou Gehrig	7,700	3,080	1,260
8	Hazen S. (Kiki) Cuyler	945.00	385.00	190.00
9	Bill Urbanski	700.00	280.00	140.00
10	Frank J. (Lefty) O'Doul	980.00	395.00	195.00
11	Freddie Lindstrom	945.00	385.00	190.00
12	Harold (Pie) Traynor	945.00	385.00	190.00
13	"Rabbit" Maranville	945.00	385.00	190.00
14	Vernon "Lefty" Gomez	945.00	385.00	190.00
15	Riggs Stephenson	700.00	280.00	140.00
16	Lon Warneke	700.00	280.00	140.00
17	Pepper Martin	700.00	280.00	140.00
18	Jimmy Dykes	700.00	280.00	140.00
19	Chick Hafey	945.00	385.00	190.00
20	Joe Vosmik	700.00	280.00	140.00
21	Jimmy Foxx (Jimmie)	1,260	505.00	250.00
22	Charles (Chuck) Klein	945.00	385.00	190.00
23	Robert (Lefty) Grove	1,540	595.00	300.00
24	"Goose" Goslin	945.00	385.00	190.00

1934 Al Demaree Die-Cuts (R304)

Among the rarest 1930s gum cards are those issued by Dietz Gum Co., a Chicago confectioner, in packages of "Ball Players in Action Chewing Gum." The cards are so rare that the complete checklist may never be known. The set was cataloged as R304 in the American Card Catalog. The cards feature photographic portraits of players set upon cartoon bodies drawn by former major league pitcher Demaree. The photo and artwork are generally in black-and-white, while the players on

some teams have blue or red uniform details printed on. The cards can be folded to create a stand-up figure, but did not have a background to be cut or torn away, as is common with most die-cut baseball cards. Unfolded, the cards measure 6-1/2" long and from 1-5/8" to 1-3/4" wide, depending on pose.

		NM	EX	VG
	Common Player:	500.00	250.00	150.00
3	Earle Combs	825.00	410.00	245.00
4	Babe Ruth	12,500	6,250	3,750
5	Sam Byrd	600.00	300.00	180.00
6	Tony Lazzeri	825.00	410.00	245.00
7	Frank Crosetti	750.00	375.00	225.00
9	Lou Gehrig	12,000	6,000	3,600
10	Lefty Gomez	825.00	410.00	245.00
11	Mule Haas	500.00	250.00	150.00
12	Evar Swenson	500.00	250.00	150.00
13	Marv Shea	500.00	250.00	150.00
14	Al Simmons (Throwing)	825.00	410.00	245.00
15	Jack Hayes	500.00	250.00	150.00
16	Al Simmons (Batting)	825.00	410.00	245.00
17	Jimmy Dykes	500.00	250.00	150.00
18	Luke Appling	825.00	410.00	245.00
19	Ted Lyons	825.00	410.00	245.00
20	Red Kress	500.00	250.00	150.00
21	Gee Walker	500.00	250.00	150.00
22	Charlie Gehringer	825.00	410.00	245.00
23	Mickey Cochrane (Catching)	825.00	410.00	245.00
24	Mickey Cochrane (Batting)	825.00	410.00	245.00
25	Pete Fox	500.00	250.00	150.00
26	Firpo Marberry	500.00	250.00	150.00
28	Mickey Owen	500.00	250.00	150.00
35	Joe Vosmik	500.00	250.00	150.00
38	Harley Boss	500.00	250.00	150.00
41	Jack Burns	500.00	250.00	150.00
45	Ray Pepper	500.00	250.00	150.00
46	Bruce Campbell	500.00	250.00	150.00
48	Art Scharein	500.00	250.00	150.00
49	George Blaeholder	500.00	250.00	150.00
50	Rogers Hornsby	1,100	550.00	330.00
51	Eric McNair	500.00	250.00	150.00
54	Jimmie Foxx	1,250	625.00	375.00
56	Dib Williams	500.00	250.00	150.00
57	Lou Finney	500.00	250.00	150.00
61	Ossie Bluege	500.00	250.00	150.00
63	John Stone	500.00	250.00	150.00
64	Joe Cronin	825.00	410.00	245.00
66	Buddy Myer	500.00	250.00	150.00
67	Earl Whitehill	500.00	250.00	150.00
68	Fred Schulte	500.00	250.00	150.00
71	Ed Morgan	500.00	250.00	150.00
74	Carl Reynolds	500.00	250.00	150.00
76	Bill Cissell	500.00	250.00	150.00
77	Johnny Hodapp	500.00	250.00	150.00
78	Dusty Cooke	500.00	250.00	150.00
79	Lefty Grove	825.00	410.00	245.00
80	Max Bishop	500.00	250.00	150.00
81	Hughie Critz	500.00	250.00	150.00
82	Gus Mancuso	500.00	250.00	150.00
83	Kiddo Davis	500.00	250.00	150.00
84	Blondy Ryan	500.00	250.00	150.00
86	Travis Jackson	825.00	410.00	245.00
87	Mel Ott	1,100	550.00	330.00
89	Bill Terry	825.00	410.00	245.00
90	Carl Hubbell	1,100	550.00	330.00
91	Tony Cuccinello	500.00	250.00	150.00
92	Al Lopez	825.00	410.00	245.00
94	Johnny Frederick	500.00	250.00	150.00
96	Hack Wilson	850.00	425.00	255.00
97	Danny Taylor	500.00	250.00	150.00
98	Van Mungo	500.00	250.00	150.00
99	John Frederick	500.00	250.00	150.00
100	Sam Leslie	500.00	250.00	150.00
101	Sparky Adams	500.00	250.00	150.00
102a	Mark Koenig	500.00	250.00	150.00
102b	Ernie Lombardi	825.00	410.00	245.00
107	Syl Johnson	500.00	250.00	150.00
108	Jim Bottomley	825.00	410.00	245.00
110	Adam Comorosky	500.00	250.00	150.00
111	Dick Bartell	500.00	250.00	150.00
112	Harvey Hendrick	500.00	250.00	150.00
115	Don Hurst (Batting)	500.00	250.00	150.00
117	Prince Oana	900.00	450.00	270.00
118	Ed Holley	500.00	250.00	150.00
120	Don Hurst (Throwing)	500.00	250.00	150.00

		NM	EX	VG
121	Spud Davis	500.00	250.00	150.00
122	George Watkins	500.00	250.00	150.00
123	Frankie Frisch	825.00	410.00	245.00
124	Pepper Martin (Batting)	500.00	250.00	150.00
125	Ripper Collins	500.00	250.00	150.00
126	Dizzy Dean	1,250	625.00	375.00
127	Pepper Martin (Fielding)	500.00	250.00	150.00
128	Joe Medwick	825.00	410.00	245.00
129	Leo Durocher	825.00	410.00	245.00
130	Ernie Orsatti	500.00	250.00	150.00
132	Shanty Hogan	500.00	250.00	150.00
133a	Wes Shulmerich (Schulmerich)	500.00	250.00	150.00
133b	Randy Moore	500.00	250.00	150.00
135	Wally Berger	500.00	250.00	150.00
136	Pinky Whitney	500.00	250.00	150.00
137	Wally Berger	500.00	250.00	150.00
139	Rabbit Maranville	825.00	410.00	245.00
140	Ben Cantwell	500.00	250.00	150.00
141	Gus Suhr	500.00	250.00	150.00
142	Earl Grace	500.00	250.00	150.00
144	Arky Vaughan	825.00	410.00	245.00
145	Pie Traynor (Hitting)	825.00	410.00	245.00
146	Tommy Thevenow	500.00	250.00	150.00
147	Lloyd Waner	825.00	410.00	245.00
148	Paul Waner	825.00	410.00	245.00
149	Pie Traynor (Throwing)	825.00	410.00	245.00
151	Kiki Cuyler	825.00	410.00	245.00
152	Gabby Hartnett	825.00	410.00	245.00
153	Chuck Klein (Throwing)	825.00	410.00	245.00
154	Chuck Klein	825.00	410.00	245.00
155	Bill Jurges	500.00	250.00	150.00
156	Woody English	500.00	250.00	150.00
158	Billy Herman	825.00	410.00	245.00
160	Charlie Grimm	500.00	250.00	150.00
161	Cy Rigler (Umpire)	900.00	450.00	275.00
162	Bill Klem (Umpire)	1,250	625.00	375.00
167	George Hildebrand (Umpire)	500.00	250.00	150.00
	(Observed specimens of cards below have had the tabs removed making it impossible to identify card numbers.)			
----	Willie Kamm	500.00	250.00	150.00
----	Pinky Higgins	500.00	250.00	150.00
----	Bob Johnson	500.00	250.00	150.00
----	Roy Mahaffey	500.00	250.00	150.00
----	Buck Jordan	500.00	250.00	150.00

1950-51 Denia Puerto Rican League

JIM DAVIS

This issue was produced in conjunction with the 1950-51 Puerto Rican League winter season. Measurements vary slightly from a norm of about 1-3/4" x 2-1/8". Cards have colorized portrait photos with blank backs, probably intended to be glued into an album. Cards are unnumbered. This checklist is alphabetized, with gaps left for what is believed to be 57 uncataloged cards. Some of the players are veterans of the Negro Leagues and American major and minor leagues. Black-and-white reprints of the cards are known. A few cards have been found with a prize-redemption stamp on back.

		NM	EX	VG
	Common Player:	125.00	65.00	40.00
(1)	Alberto Alberdeston	125.00	65.00	40.00
(2)	Jaime Almendro	125.00	65.00	40.00
(3)	Yiyo Alonso	125.00	65.00	40.00
(4)	Luis (Tite) Arroyo	150.00	75.00	45.00
(5)	Pedro J. Arroyo	125.00	65.00	40.00
(6)	Joe Atkins	150.00	75.00	45.00
(7)	Eugene Baker	200.00	100.00	60.00
(8)	Dan Bankhead	200.00	100.00	60.00
(9)	Sammy Bankhead	1,200	600.00	360.00
(10)	Ramon Bayron	125.00	65.00	40.00
(11)	Hiram Bithorn	200.00	100.00	60.00
(12)	Rafael Blasini	125.00	65.00	40.00
(13)	Bob Boyd	150.00	75.00	45.00
(14)	Roger Breard	125.00	65.00	40.00
(15)	Stan Breard	125.00	65.00	40.00
(16)	Barney Brown	1,000	500.00	300.00
(17)	Raymond Brown	2,000	1,000	600.00
(18)	Willard Brown	2,000	1,000	600.00
(19)	Jose A. Burgos	125.00	65.00	40.00
(20)	Joe Buzas	125.00	65.00	40.00
(21)	Luis R. Cabrera	125.00	65.00	40.00
(22)	Rafael Casanovas	125.00	65.00	40.00
(23)	N. Zurdo Castro	125.00	65.00	40.00
(24)	Perucho Cepeda	800.00	400.00	240.00
(25)	T. Gomez Checo	125.00	65.00	40.00
(26)	Al Cihoki (Cihocki)	125.00	65.00	40.00
(27)	Buster Clarkson	250.00	125.00	75.00
(28)	Francisco Coimbre	800.00	400.00	240.00
(29)	Eugene Collins	350.00	175.00	105.00
(30)	Monchile Concepcion	150.00	75.00	45.00
(31)	Charlie Corin	125.00	65.00	40.00

(32)	Herminio Cortfu	125.00	65.00	40.00
(33)	Johnny Cox	125.00	65.00	40.00
(34)	George Crowe	200.00	100.00	60.00
(35)	Jim Davis	125.00	65.00	40.00
(36)	Johnny Davis	450.00	225.00	135.00
(37)	Piper Davis	450.00	225.00	135.00
(38)	Leon Day	6,000	3,000	1,800
(39)	Ellis "Cot" Deal	150.00	75.00	45.00
(40)	Jack Dittmer	125.00	65.00	40.00
(41)	Verdes Drake	150.00	75.00	45.00
(42)	Saturnino Escalera	125.00	65.00	40.00
(43)	C. Guillaro Estrella	125.00	65.00	40.00
(44)	S. Federico	125.00	65.00	40.00
(45)	Dumbo Fernandez	125.00	65.00	40.00
(46)	Elias Frias	125.00	65.00	40.00
(47)	Les Fusselmann (Fusselman)	125.00	65.00	40.00
(48)	Felipe Garcia	125.00	65.00	40.00
(49)	(Carden) Gillenwater	125.00	65.00	40.00
(50)	Jim Gilliam	250.00	125.00	75.00
(51)	Ruben Gomez	200.00	100.00	60.00
(52)	Faelo Gonzalez	125.00	65.00	40.00
(53)	Gely Goyco	125.00	65.00	40.00
(54)	Jack Harshmann (Harshman)	125.00	65.00	40.00
(55)	Rudy Hernandez	125.00	65.00	40.00
(56)	Roy Hughes	125.00	65.00	40.00
(57)	Pachy Irizarry	125.00	65.00	40.00
(58)	Indian (Indio) Jiminez	125.00	65.00	40.00
(59)	Sam Jones	125.00	65.00	40.00
(60)	Walt Judnich	125.00	65.00	40.00
(61)	Russ Kearns	125.00	65.00	40.00
(62)	Billy Klaus	150.00	75.00	45.00
(63)	Jim Lamarque	350.00	175.00	105.00
(64)	Red Lynn	125.00	65.00	40.00
(65)	Bob Malloy	125.00	65.00	40.00
(66)	Clifford Mapes	125.00	65.00	40.00
(67)	Canena Marquez	450.00	225.00	135.00
(68)	Achin Matos	125.00	65.00	40.00
(69)	Benny Meyers	125.00	65.00	40.00
(70)	Henry Miller	150.00	75.00	45.00
(71)	Oscar Mir Flores	125.00	65.00	40.00
(72)	Jose E. Montalvo	125.00	65.00	40.00
(73)	Willie Morales	125.00	65.00	40.00
(74)	Gallego Munoz	125.00	65.00	40.00
(75)	Earl Naylor	125.00	65.00	40.00
(76)	Ernest Nevel	125.00	65.00	40.00
(77)	Don Nicholas	125.00	65.00	40.00
(78)	John O'Donnell	125.00	65.00	40.00
(79)	Guayuvin Olivo	150.00	75.00	45.00
(80)	Miguel Payano	125.00	65.00	40.00
(81)	Les Peden	125.00	65.00	40.00
(82)	Juan Perez	125.00	65.00	40.00
(83)	Palomo Perez	125.00	65.00	40.00
(84)	German Pizarro	125.00	65.00	40.00
(85)	Dave Pope	150.00	75.00	45.00
(86)	Milton Ralat	125.00	65.00	40.00
(87)	Enrique Reinoso	125.00	65.00	40.00
(88)	Roberto Rivera	125.00	65.00	40.00
(89)	Julio Rodriguez	125.00	65.00	40.00
(90)	Pedro Rodriguez	125.00	65.00	40.00
(91)	Domingo Rosello	125.00	65.00	40.00
(92)	Joe Rossi	125.00	65.00	40.00
(93)	Miguel Rueda	125.00	65.00	40.00
(94)	Ramon Salgado	125.00	65.00	40.00
(95)	Juan Sanchez	125.00	65.00	40.00
(96)	Carlos M. Santiago	125.00	65.00	40.00
(97)	Jose G. Santiago	125.00	65.00	40.00
(98)	V. Scarpatte	125.00	65.00	40.00
(99)	Jose Seda	125.00	65.00	40.00
(100)	Barney Serrell	350.00	175.00	105.00
(101)	Al Smith	200.00	100.00	60.00
(102)	Jose St. Clair	125.00	65.00	40.00
(103)	Tetelo Sterling	125.00	65.00	40.00
(104)	Russ Sullivan	125.00	65.00	40.00
(105)	Lonnie Summers	150.00	75.00	45.00
(106)	Jim Tabor	125.00	65.00	40.00
(107)	Bert Thiel	125.00	65.00	40.00
(108)	Valmy Thomas	125.00	65.00	40.00
(109)	Bob Thurman	350.00	175.00	105.00
(110)	Tiant Tineo	125.00	65.00	40.00
(111)	Gilberto Torres	125.00	65.00	40.00
(112)	Manuel Traboux	125.00	65.00	40.00
(113)	Joe Tuminelli	125.00	65.00	40.00
(114)	Jose L. Velazquez	125.00	65.00	40.00
(115)	Ben Wade	150.00	75.00	45.00
(116)	Johnny Williams	250.00	125.00	75.00
(117)	Marvin Williams	150.00	75.00	45.00
(118)	Artie Wilson	450.00	225.00	135.00
(119)	Pedrin Zorrilla	125.00	65.00	40.00
(120)	Pito entrevista a Hornsby	300.00	150.00	90.00
(121)	El galardon del triunfo	125.00	65.00	40.00
(122)	Fanaticos de alta posicion	125.00	65.00	40.00
(123)	VOLO LA VERJA	125.00	65.00	40.00

1950-51 Denia Puerto Rican League - Action

115- Gilliam dió out a Casanovas

These 2-1/2" x 3-1/2" cards are part of a set of about 150 covering many different sports. The pictures are colorized photographs and the cards are blank-backed, intended to be glued into an album. The number of baseball subjects is not known. Confirmed subjects are listed here, with identified players listed parenthetically.

		NM	EX	VG
Common Card:		50.00	25.00	15.00
1	Tetelo tambien joronea. (Tetelo Vargas)	85.00	40.00	25.00
2	Taborn saca en home. (Earl Taborn)	50.00	25.00	15.00
3	Se la aguo la blanqueada.	50.00	25.00	15.00
4	R. Blasini se lesiona. (Rafael Blasini)	50.00	25.00	15.00
5	Atkins mofa, Polaco safe. (Joe Atkins)	50.00	25.00	15.00
6	CERCADO.	50.00	25.00	15.00
7	Pitcher se desliza - safe.	50.00	25.00	15.00
8	Fdo. Ramos tras homer (Fernando Ramos)	50.00	25.00	15.00
9	Wilson safe en terecera. (Artie Wilson)	65.00	30.00	20.00
10	Tiro malo - SAFE.	50.00	25.00	15.00
11	VILLODAS LO ESPERA - OUT. (Luis Villodas)	50.00	25.00	15.00
12	Perry da out a Gilliam - (Alonso Perry, Jim Gilliam)	85.00	40.00	25.00
13	Safe en primera -	50.00	25.00	15.00
14	Medina obsequia a Brown. (Medina Chapman, Willard Brown)	200.00	100.00	60.00
15	Tiro malo, Almendaro anota. (Jaime Almendro)	50.00	25.00	15.00
16	Ramos toco primero - OUT. (Fernando Ramos)	50.00	25.00	15.00
17	Brazo contra brazo -	50.00	25.00	15.00
18	Pedroso felicitado tras homer - (Fernando Pedroso)	50.00	25.00	15.00
19	QUE PASA, CEFO? (Cefo Conde)	50.00	25.00	15.00
20	Canena estafa home - (Canena Marquez)	65.00	30.00	20.00
21	Buen slide - SAFE.	50.00	25.00	15.00
22	Mucha vista, Powell. (Bill Powell)	50.00	25.00	15.00
23	OUT FORZADO.	50.00	25.00	15.00
24	Alomar out en home. (Guinea Alomar)	50.00	25.00	15.00
25	Regreso a base - SAFE.	50.00	25.00	15.00
26	Pitcher trata sorprender - SAFE.	50.00	25.00	15.00
27	LOS RECUERDA USTED?	50.00	25.00	15.00
28	Leo Thomas sale de juego. (Leo Thomas)	50.00	25.00	15.00
29	Atkins es felicitado por tribu. (Joe Atkins)	50.00	25.00	15.00
30	Trio campeonil cagueno (Manuel Hernandez, Quincy Trouppe, Chet Brewer)	135.00	65.00	40.00
31	Llegando y llegando -	50.00	25.00	15.00
32	El fotografoen accion -	50.00	25.00	15.00
33	El fotografo en accion	50.00	25.00	15.00
34	No me toques Arroyito - OUT. (Luis "Tite" Arroyo)	50.00	25.00	15.00
35	Taborn propina out. (Earl Taborn)	50.00	25.00	15.00
36	El Mucaro conecta homer - (Bob Thurman)	65.00	30.00	20.00
37	PANTALONES Y FALDAS. (Jose G. Santiago)	50.00	25.00	15.00
38	Buzas en la derrota. (Joe Buzas)	50.00	25.00	15.00
39	El Gran Jurado se reune. (Raymond Brown)	135.00	65.00	40.00
40	Canena se desliza - (Canena Marquez)	65.00	30.00	20.00
41	Que dijo el umpire?	50.00	25.00	15.00
42	Bernier sabe escurrirse - (Carlos Bernier)	50.00	25.00	15.00
43	Se la escapo, la bola - SAFE.	50.00	25.00	15.00
44	Squeeze play perfecto.	50.00	25.00	15.00
45	Cuidado, que la lleva!	50.00	25.00	15.00
46	Que el umpire diga -	50.00	25.00	15.00
47	Pepe Lucas boto la bola. (Pepe Lucas)	50.00	25.00	15.00
48	Gachito se apunta hit.	50.00	25.00	15.00
49	Peloteros o Luchadores?	50.00	25.00	15.00
50	Otoniel lo toca - OUT. (Otoniel Ortiz)	50.00	25.00	15.00
51	Premian a Jorge Rosas. (Jorge Rosas)	50.00	25.00	15.00
52	Markland dio homerun - (Jim Markland)	50.00	25.00	15.00
53	Blasini safe en primera. (Rafael Blasini)	50.00	25.00	15.00
54	Graham conecto homer - (Jack Graham)	50.00	25.00	15.00
55	Penalver se prepara - SAFE.	50.00	25.00	15.00
56	No quiere riesgos	50.00	25.00	15.00
57	Bin Torres esquiva - SAFE. (Bin Torres)	50.00	25.00	15.00
58	Mutua embestida- SAFE.	50.00	25.00	15.00
59	Lo sacaron a media base.	50.00	25.00	15.00
60	Llego transqueando.	50.00	25.00	15.00
61	Quedate quieto - dice el coach.	50.00	25.00	15.00
62	Buscando en vano su presa -	50.00	25.00	15.00
63	Besando la base?	50.00	25.00	15.00
64	Pescaron al Jueyito. (Jueyito Andrade)	50.00	25.00	15.00
65	Greco da tremendo toletazo.	50.00	25.00	15.00
66	Thomas catcher, Wallaesa al bate. (Valmy Thomas, Jack Wallaesa)	50.00	25.00	15.00
67	Trofeos de TRIPLE CAMPEON.	50.00	25.00	15.00
74	H. Reyes lanza, Sanchez Batea. (Herminio Reyes, Juan Sanchez)	50.00	25.00	15.00
77	Wilson apacigua a Bernier . . . (Artie Wilson, Carlos Bernier)	85.00	40.00	25.00
78	Cogida de cuatro estrellas . . .	50.00	25.00	15.00
80	Davis out de Gachito - Wallaesa . . . (Johnny Davis, Jack Wallaesa)	50.00	25.00	15.00
81	Arroyo busca double-play. (Pedro J. Arroyo)	50.00	25.00	15.00
82	Ruben sale por lesion. (Ruben Gomez)	50.00	25.00	15.00
83	SAFE EN EL PLATO.	50.00	25.00	15.00
84	Buen esfuerzo, pero en vano	50.00	25.00	15.00
85	ESTAS TRISTE, JONES? (Sam Jones)	50.00	25.00	15.00
87	Equipo ESTRELLAS NATIVAS	50.00	25.00	15.00
88	Arroyo batea, Scarpatte recibe (Pedro J. Arroyo, V. Scarpatte)	50.00	25.00	15.00
93	Cihoki recoge . . . out (Al Cihocki)	50.00	25.00	15.00
95	El arbitro pensativo . . . out.	50.00	25.00	15.00
97	Buena atrapada . . . del fotografo.	50.00	25.00	15.00
103	Villodas da hit. . . (Luis Villodas)	50.00	25.00	15.00
106	HIT EL BATAZO . . .	50.00	25.00	15.00
110	LO COGIERON LLEGANDO	50.00	25.00	15.00
115	Gilliam dio out a Casanovas (Jim Gilliam, Rafael Casanovas)	85.00	40.00	25.00
124	Canena pone fuera a Bernier . . . (Canena Marquez, Carlos Bernier)	50.00	25.00	15.00
137	Terminado el swing . . .	50.00	25.00	15.00

1932 Charles Denby Cigars Cubs

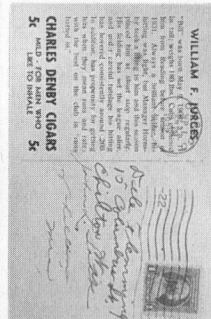

This series of Chicago Cubs postcards was issued by the Fendrich Cigar Co., Evansville, Ind., to promote its Charles Denby brand in 1932. It is the last major tobacco-card issue produced before World War II. The cards are a standard post-card size (5-1/4" x 3-3/8") and feature a glossy black-and-white player photo with a facsimile autograph. In typical post-card style, the back of the card is divided in half, with a printed player profile on the left and room for the mailing address on the right. The back also includes an advertisement for Charles Denby Cigars, the mild five-cent cigar "for men who like to inhale." Eight players are known but more may exist.

		NM	EX	VG
Complete Set (8):		3,750	1,850	1,100
Common Player:		500.00	200.00	100.00
(1)	Hazen Cuyler	625.00	250.00	125.00
(2)	Elwood English	500.00	200.00	100.00
(3)	Charles J. Grimm	500.00	200.00	100.00
(4)	William Herman	750.00	300.00	150.00
(5)	Rogers Hornsby	1,000	400.00	200.00
(6)	William F. Jurges	500.00	200.00	100.00
(7)	Riggs Stephenson	500.00	200.00	100.00
(8)	Lonnie Warneke	500.00	200.00	100.00

1909 Derby Cigars N.Y. Giants

Although there is no advertising on these cards to indicate their origin, it is believed that this set was issued by Derby Cigars, a product of American Tobacco Co. A dozen different subjects, all New York Giants, have been found. The cards, many of which appear to be hand-cut measure about 1-3/4" x

2-3/4". The cards feature an oval black-and-white player portrait on a red background. The player's name and position are in a white strip at bottom.

		NM	EX	VG
	Complete Set (12):	40,000	16,000	8,000
	Common Player:	3,250	1,300	650.00
(1)	Josh Devore	3,250	1,300	650.00
(2)	Larry Doyle	3,250	1,300	650.00
(3)	Art Fletcher	3,250	1,300	650.00
(4)	Buck Herzog	3,250	1,300	650.00
(5)	Rube Marquard	3,750	1,500	750.00
(6)	Christy Mathewson	7,500	3,000	1,500
(7)	Fred Merkle	3,250	1,300	650.00
(8)	Chief Meyers	3,250	1,300	650.00
(9)	Red Murray	3,250	1,300	650.00
(10)	John McGraw	3,500	1,400	700.00
(11)	Fred Snodgrass	3,250	1,300	650.00
(12)	Hooks Wiltse	3,250	1,300	650.00

1977 Detroit Caesars Discs

Virtually identical in format to the several locally sponsored disc sets of the previous year, these 3-3/8" diameter player discs were sponsored by a professional slow-pitch softball team. Discs once again feature black-and-white player portrait photos in the center of a baseball design. The left and right panels are in one of several bright colors. Licensed by the Players Association through Mike Schechter Associates, the player photos carry no uniform logos. Backs are printed in green. The unnumbered discs are checklisted here alphabetically.

		NM	EX	VG
	Complete Set (70):	125.00	65.00	35.00
	Common Player:	2.50	1.25	.75
(1)	Sal Bando	2.50	1.25	.75
(2)	Buddy Bell	2.50	1.25	.75
(3)	Johnny Bench	6.00	3.00	1.75
(4)	Larry Bowa	2.50	1.25	.75
(5)	Steve Braun	2.50	1.25	.75
(6)	George Brett	15.00	7.50	4.50
(7)	Lou Brock	6.00	3.00	1.75
(8)	Jeff Burroughs	2.50	1.25	.75
(9)	Bert Campaneris	2.50	1.25	.75
(10)	John Candelaria	2.50	1.25	.75
(11)	Jose Cardenal	2.50	1.25	.75
(12)	Rod Carew	4.50	2.25	1.25
(13)	Steve Carlton	4.50	2.25	1.25
(14)	Dave Cash	2.50	1.25	.75
(15)	Cesar Cedeno	2.50	1.25	.75
(16)	Ron Cey	2.50	1.25	.75
(17)	Dave Concepcion	2.50	1.25	.75
(18)	Dennis Eckersley	3.00	1.50	.90
(19)	Mark Fidrych	5.00	2.50	1.50
(20)	Rollie Fingers	5.00	2.50	1.50
(21)	Carlton Fisk	6.00	3.00	1.75
(22)	George Foster	2.50	1.25	.75
(23)	Wayne Garland	2.50	1.25	.75
(24)	Ralph Garr	2.50	1.25	.75
(25)	Steve Garvey	4.00	2.00	1.25
(26)	Cesar Geronimo	2.50	1.25	.75
(27)	Bobby Grich	2.50	1.25	.75
(28)	Ken Griffey Sr.	2.50	1.25	.75
(29)	Don Gullett	2.50	1.25	.75
(30)	Mike Hargrove	2.50	1.25	.75
(31)	Al Hrabosky	2.50	1.25	.75
(32)	Jim Hunter	5.00	2.50	1.50
(33)	Reggie Jackson	9.00	4.50	2.75
(34)	Randy Jones	2.50	1.25	.75
(35)	Dave Kingman	3.50	1.75	1.00
(36)	Jerry Koosman	2.50	1.25	.75
(37)	Dave LaRoche	2.50	1.25	.75
(38)	Greg Luzinski	2.50	1.25	.75
(39)	Fred Lynn	2.50	1.25	.75
(40)	Bill Madlock	2.50	1.25	.75
(41)	Rick Manning	2.50	1.25	.75
(42)	Jon Matlock	2.50	1.25	.75
(43)	John Mayberry	2.50	1.25	.75
(44)	Hal McRae	2.50	1.25	.75
(45)	Andy Messersmith	2.50	1.25	.75
(46)	Rick Monday	2.50	1.25	.75
(47)	John Montefusco	2.50	1.25	.75
(48)	Joe Morgan	6.00	3.00	1.75
(49)	Thurman Munson	5.00	2.50	1.50
(50)	Bobby Murcer	2.50	1.25	.75
(51)	Bill North	2.50	1.25	.75
(52)	Jim Palmer	6.00	3.00	1.75
(53)	Tony Perez	5.00	2.50	1.50
(54)	Jerry Reuss	2.50	1.25	.75
(55)	Brooks Robinson	5.00	2.50	1.50
(56)	Pete Rose	15.00	7.50	4.50
(57)	Joe Rudi	2.50	1.25	.75
(58)	Nolan Ryan	30.00	15.00	9.00
(59)	Manny Sanguillen	2.50	1.25	.75
(60)	Mike Schmidt	15.00	7.50	4.50
(61)	Tom Seaver	7.50	3.75	2.25
(62)	Bill Singer	2.50	1.25	.75
(63)	Willie Stargell	6.00	3.00	1.75
(64)	Rusty Staub	3.50	1.75	1.00
(65)	Luis Tiant	2.50	1.25	.75
(66)	Bob Watson	2.50	1.25	.75
(67)	Butch Wynegar	2.50	1.25	.75
(68)	Carl Yastrzemski	7.50	3.75	2.25
(69)	Robin Yount	6.00	3.00	1.75
(70)	Richie Zisk	2.50	1.25	.75

1908 Detroit Free Press Tigers Postcards

Most of the stars of the 1907-09 American League Champion Detroit Tigers are found in this set of postcards issued by a local newspaper and reportedly sold at the stadium for $1 a set. The cards are 3-1/2" x 5-1/4", printed in black-and-white. Fronts have a border around the photo with the line, "Copyright by the Detroit Free Press, 1908" beneath the photo. At bottom is the player's last name in capital letters with his position in parentheses. Backs have standard postcard indicia. The unnumbered cards are checklisted here alphabetically. It is possible this list is not complete.

		NM	EX	VG
	Complete Set (11):	4,000	2,000	1,200
	Common Player:	400.00	200.00	120.00
(1)	Ty Cobb	950.00	475.00	285.00
(2)	Sam Crawford	400.00	200.00	120.00
(3)	Wild Bill Donovan	400.00	200.00	120.00
(4)	Hughie Jennings	400.00	200.00	120.00
(5)	Ed Killian	400.00	200.00	120.00
(6)	Matty McIntyre	400.00	200.00	120.00
(7)	George Mullen (Mullin)	400.00	200.00	120.00
(8)	Charley O'Leary	400.00	200.00	120.00
(9)	Boss Schmidt	400.00	200.00	120.00
(10)	Ed Summer (Summers)	400.00	200.00	120.00
(11)	Ed Willett	400.00	200.00	120.00

1934 Detroit Tigers Team Issue

This set of blank-back, postcard-sized black-and-white player photo cards is presumed to have been a team issue. A recently-discovered poster associates them with Detroit retailer Newton Annis Furs. Photos have white borders with the wider top border having three stipes. Player name and position are printed within the picture. The unnumbered cards are checklisted here alphabetically.

		NM	EX	VG
	Complete Set (23):	1,200	600.00	350.00
	Common Player:	60.00	30.00	18.00
(1)	Eldon Auker	60.00	30.00	18.00
(2)	Del Baker	60.00	30.00	18.00
(3)	Tommy Bridges	60.00	30.00	18.00
(4)	Mickey Cochrane	150.00	75.00	45.00
(5)	General Crowder	60.00	30.00	18.00
(6)	Frank Doljack	60.00	30.00	18.00
(7)	Carl Fischer	60.00	30.00	18.00
(8)	Pete Fox	60.00	30.00	18.00
(9)	Charlie Gehringer	150.00	75.00	45.00
(10)	Goose Goslin	150.00	75.00	45.00
(11)	"Hank" Greenberg	250.00	125.00	75.00
(12)	Luke Hamlin	60.00	30.00	18.00
(13)	Ray Hayworth	60.00	30.00	18.00
(14)	Elon Hogsett	60.00	30.00	18.00
(15)	Firpo Marberry	60.00	30.00	18.00
(16)	Marvin Owen	60.00	30.00	18.00
(17)	Cy Perkins	60.00	30.00	18.00
(18)	Billy Rogell	60.00	30.00	18.00
(19)	Schoolboy Rowe	60.00	30.00	18.00
(20)	Heinie Schuble	60.00	30.00	18.00
(21)	Vic Sorrell	60.00	30.00	18.00
(22)	Gee Walker	60.00	30.00	18.00
(23)	Jo-Jo White	60.00	30.00	18.00

1935 Detroit Free Press Tigers

Colorized photos with brightly colored backgrounds and borders are featured in this series of newspaper pictures featuring the World Champion Detroit Tigers. About 9" x 11", the pictures are blank-backed. It is unclear whether these pictures were included with newspaper purchases or were sold as sets. The unnumbered pictures are checklisted here in alphabetical order. In the American Card Catalog, the set carried the designation M120.

		NM	EX	VG
	Complete Set (26):	1,000	500.00	300.00
	Common Player:	40.00	20.00	12.00
(1)	Eldon Auker	40.00	20.00	12.00
(2)	Del Baker	40.00	20.00	12.00
(3)	Tommy Bridges	40.00	20.00	12.00
(4)	Flea Clifton	40.00	20.00	12.00
(5)	Gordon Stanley (Mickey) Cochrane	100.00	50.00	30.00
(6)	Alvin Crowder	40.00	20.00	12.00
(7)	Frank Doljack	40.00	20.00	12.00
(8)	Carl Fischer	40.00	20.00	12.00
(9)	Pete Fox	40.00	20.00	12.00
(10)	Charles Gehringer	75.00	37.50	22.50
(11)	Goose Goslin	75.00	37.50	22.50
(12)	Henry Greenberg	125.00	65.00	35.00
(13)	Luke Hamlin	40.00	20.00	12.00
(14)	Ray Hayworth	40.00	20.00	12.00
(15)	Elon Hogsett	40.00	20.00	12.00
(16)	Joe Louis (boxer)	100.00	50.00	30.00
(17)	Firpo Marberry	40.00	20.00	12.00
(18)	Marvin Owen	40.00	20.00	12.00
(19)	Cy Perkins	40.00	20.00	12.00
(20)	Billy Rogell	40.00	20.00	12.00
(21)	Lynwood (Schoolboy) Rowe	45.00	22.50	13.50
(22)	Heinie Schuble	40.00	20.00	12.00
(23)	Vic Sorrell	40.00	20.00	12.00
(24)	Joe Sullivan	40.00	20.00	12.00
(25)	Jerry Walker	40.00	20.00	12.00
(26)	Jo-Jo White	40.00	20.00	12.00

1968 Detroit Free Press Bubblegumless Tiger Cards

The World Champion Tigers are featured in this series of newspaper inserts published in August, 1968, by the "Detroit Magazine" rotogravure section of the Sunday "Detroit Free Press." The full-color fronts and the backs were printed on separate pages to allow them to be cut out and pasted on cardboard to make a baseball card. Backs are horizontally formatted and include a drawing of the player at left; biographical data and recent stats at right. Card elements measure 2-1/2" x 3-1/2". Values quoted are for front/back pairs. Unmatched fronts are priced at 45 percent of the prices shown; backs should be priced at 30 percent.

		NM	EX	VG
	Complete Set, Uncut Pages:	250.00	125.00	75.00
	Complete Set, Singles (28):	200.00	100.00	60.00
	Common Player:	10.00	5.00	3.00
(1)	Gates Brown	10.00	5.00	3.00
(2)	Norm Cash	15.00	7.50	4.50
(3)	Tony Cuccinello	10.00	5.00	3.00
(4)	Pat Dobson	10.00	5.00	3.00
(5)	Bill Freehan	12.50	6.25	3.75
(6)	John Hiller	10.00	5.00	3.00
(7)	Willie Horton	10.00	5.00	3.00
(8)	Al Kaline	35.00	17.50	10.50
(9)	Fred Lasher	10.00	5.00	3.00
(10)	Mickey Lolich	15.00	7.50	4.50
(11)	Tom Matchick	10.00	5.00	3.00
(12)	Dick McAuliffe	10.00	5.00	3.00

		NM	EX	VG
(13)	Denny McLain	12.50	6.25	3.75
(14)	Don McMahon	10.00	5.00	3.00
(15)	Wally Moses	10.00	5.00	3.00
(16)	Jim Northrup	10.00	5.00	3.00
(17)	Ray Oyler	10.00	5.00	3.00
(18)	Daryl Patterson	10.00	5.00	3.00
(19)	Jim Price	10.00	5.00	3.00
(20)	Johnny Sain	10.00	5.00	3.00
(21)	Mayo Smith	10.00	5.00	3.00
(22)	Joe Sparma	10.00	5.00	3.00
(23)	Mickey Stanley	10.00	5.00	3.00
(24)	Dick Tracewski	10.00	5.00	3.00
(25)	Jon Warden	10.00	5.00	3.00
(26)	Don Wert	10.00	5.00	3.00
(27)	Earl Wilson	10.00	5.00	3.00
(28)	Jon Wyatt (John)	10.00	5.00	3.00

1978 Detroit Free Press Tigers

In its Sunday color magazine of April 16, 1978, the newspaper printed presumably authorized reproductions of all 1978 Topps cards which featured members of the Detroit Tigers. The magazine has a cover photo of Mark Fidrych. In the centerspread, reproduced in color, are pictures of the fronts of 20 Tigers cards. Two pages later the cards of three departed Tigers, five multi-player rookie cards and the team card are printed, also in full color. Three more pages have the backs of the cards, printed in black-and-white, rather than the orange-and-blue of genuine Topps cards. Instructions with the article invited readers to cut out the fronts and backs and paste them onto pieces of cardboard to make their own cards. Values shown are for complete front/back pairs.

		NM	EX	VG
Complete Magazine:		60.00	30.00	20.00
Complete Set, Singles (28):		30.00	15.00	9.00
Common Player:		3.00	1.50	.90
21	Steve Kemp	3.00	1.50	.90
45	Mark Fidrych	6.00	3.00	1.75
68	Steve Foucault	3.00	1.50	.90
94	Chuck Scrivener	3.00	1.50	.90
124	Dave Rozema	3.00	1.50	.90
151	Milt Wilcox	3.00	1.50	.90
176	Milt May	3.00	1.50	.90
232	Mickey Stanley	3.00	1.50	.90
258	John Hiller	3.00	1.50	.90
286	Ben Oglivie	3.00	1.50	.90
342	Aurelio Rodriguez	3.00	1.50	.90
370	Rusty Staub	6.00	3.00	1.75
385	Tito Fuentes	3.00	1.50	.90
404	Tigers team card (Color checklist back.)	6.00	3.00	1.75
456	Vern Ruhle	3.00	1.50	.90
480	Ron LeFlore	3.50	1.75	1.00
515	Tim Corcoran	3.00	1.50	.90
536	Roric Harrison	3.00	1.50	.90
559	Phil Mankowski	3.00	1.50	.90
607	Fernando Arroyo	3.00	1.50	.90
633	Tom Veryzer	3.00	1.50	.90
660	Jason Thompson	3.00	1.50	.90
684	Ralph Houk	3.50	1.75	1.00
701	Tom Hume, Larry Landreth, Steve McCatty, Bruce Taylor (Rookie Pitchers)	3.00	1.50	.90
703	Larry Andersen, Tim Jones, Mickey Mahler, Jack Morris (Rookie Pitchers)	7.50	3.75	2.25
704	Garth Iorg, Dave Oliver, Sam Perlozzo, Lou Whitaker (Rookie 2nd Basemen)	9.00	4.50	2.75
707	Mickey Klutts, Paul Molitor, Alan Trammell, U.L. Washington (Rookie Shortstops)	20.00	10.00	6.00
708	Bo Diaz, Dale Murphy, Lance Parrish, Ernie Whitt (Rookie Catchers)	10.00	5.00	3.00
723	Johnny Wockenfuss	3.00	1.50	.90

1964 Detroit Tigers Milk Bottle Caps

These small (1-5/16" diameter) cardboard milk bottle caps feature line drawings of the 1964 Tigers. The caps are printed in dark blue and orange on front and blank on back.

The unnumbered caps are checklisted here in alphabetical order. A wire staple is found in most caps. The caps were reportedly produced for Twin Pines Dairy for use on bottles of chocolate milk.

		NM	EX	VG
Complete Set (14):		400.00	200.00	120.00
Common Player:		25.00	12.50	7.50
(1)	Hank Aguirre	25.00	12.50	7.50
(2)	Billy Bruton	25.00	12.50	7.50
(3)	Norman Cash	50.00	25.00	15.00
(4)	Don Demeter	25.00	12.50	7.50
(5)	Chuck Dressen	25.00	12.50	7.50
(6)	Bill Freehan	35.00	17.50	10.50
(7)	Al Kaline	150.00	75.00	45.00
(8)	Frank Lary	25.00	12.50	7.50
(9)	Jerry Lumpe	25.00	12.50	7.50
(10)	Dick McAuliffe	25.00	12.50	7.50
(11)	Bubba Phillips	25.00	12.50	7.50
(12)	Ed Rakow	25.00	12.50	7.50
(13)	Phil Regan	25.00	12.50	7.50
(14)	Dave Wickersham	25.00	12.50	7.50

1936 Detroit Times Sports Stamps

The date of issue listed is approximate and the actual period of issue may have spanned more than one year. Printed as part of the regular newspaper page, these feature items have a stamp-design photo element of about 2" x 2-1/2" atop a biographical and career summary.

		NM	EX	VG
Common Player:		15.00	7.50	4.50
(1)	Eldon Auker	15.00	7.50	4.50
(2)	Del Baker	15.00	7.50	4.50
(3)	Tommy Bridges	15.00	7.50	4.50
(4)	Jack Burns	15.00	7.50	4.50
(5)	Ty Cobb	40.00	20.00	12.00
(6)	Mickey Cochrane (Dark cap.)	20.00	10.00	6.00
(7)	Mickey Cochrane (White cap.)	20.00	10.00	6.00
(8)	Joe Cronin	20.00	10.00	6.00
(9)	Alvin Crowder	15.00	7.50	4.50
(10a)	Dizzy Dean (Bio first line "Star pitcher of.")	30.00	15.00	9.00
(10b)	Dizzy Dean (Bio "of" on second line.)	30.00	15.00	9.00
(11)	Paul Dean	15.00	7.50	4.50
(12)	Wes Ferrell	15.00	7.50	4.50
(13)	Pete Fox	15.00	7.50	4.50
(14)	Jimmy Foxx	30.00	15.00	9.00
(15)	Frank Frisch	20.00	10.00	6.00
(16a)	Lou Gehrig (Bio first line "...slugging first.")	40.00	20.00	12.00
(16b)	Lou Gehrig (Bio first line "slugging.")	40.00	20.00	12.00
(17)	Charles Gehringer	20.00	10.00	6.00
(18)	Chas. Gehringer	20.00	10.00	6.00
(19)	Lefty Gomez	20.00	10.00	6.00
(20a)	Goose Goslin (White cap.)	20.00	10.00	6.00
(20b)	Goose Goslin (Dark cap.)	20.00	10.00	6.00
(21)	Hank Greenberg	20.00	10.00	6.00
(22)	Charley Grimm	15.00	7.50	4.50
(23)	Ray Hayworth	15.00	7.50	4.50
(24)	Elon Hogsett	15.00	7.50	4.50
(25)	Walter Johnson	30.00	15.00	9.00
(26)	Chuck Klein	20.00	10.00	6.00
(27)	Connie Mack	20.00	10.00	6.00
(28)	Heinie Manush	20.00	10.00	6.00
(29)	Van Lingle Mungo	15.00	7.50	4.50
(30)	Glenn Myatt	15.00	7.50	4.50
(31)	Steve O'Neill	15.00	7.50	4.50
(32)	Billy Rogell	15.00	7.50	4.50
(33a)	Schoolboy Rowe (White cap.)	15.00	7.50	4.50
(33b)	Schoolboy Rowe (Dark cap.)	15.00	7.50	4.50
(34)	Babe Ruth	40.00	20.00	12.00
(35)	Al Simmons	30.00	15.00	9.00
(36)	Vic Sorrell	15.00	7.50	4.50
(37)	Tris Speaker	30.00	15.00	9.00
(38)	Casey Stengel	20.00	10.00	6.00
(39)	Joe Sullivan	15.00	7.50	4.50
(40)	Bill Terry	15.00	7.50	4.50
(41)	Joe Vosmik	15.00	7.50	4.50
(42)	Gerry Walker	15.00	7.50	4.50
(43)	Lon Warneke	15.00	7.50	4.50
(44)	Jo Jo White	15.00	7.50	4.50
(45)	Earl Whitehill	15.00	7.50	4.50
(46)	Jimmy Wilson	15.00	7.50	4.50

1966 Dexter Press California Angels

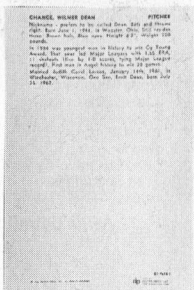

Less well-known than the New York firm's premium issues for Coca-Cola are Dexter Press' team issues. Sold for 50 cents in a cellophane bag with a colorful cardboard header the team issues are in the same basic design as the premium cards of 1967, but measure only 4" x 5-7/8". Though they were sold in sets of eight, more individual cards exist for the known teams, so it is evident there was some exchange of cards within the sets over the course of the sales period. Cards have color player poses with a black facsimile autograph at top and with or without a white border around. Backs are printed in blue with personal data and career highlights at top and copyright information at bottom. The cards are checklisted here alphabetically.

		NM	EX	VG
Complete Set (17):		100.00	50.00	30.00
Common Player:		10.00	5.00	3.00
(1)	Jose Cardenal	10.00	5.00	3.00
(2)	George Brunet	10.00	5.00	3.00
(3)	Dean Chance	12.00	6.00	3.50
(4)	Jim Fregosi	10.00	5.00	3.00
(5)	Ed Kirkpatrick	10.00	5.00	3.00
(6)	Bob Knoop	10.00	5.00	3.00
(7)	Bob Lee	10.00	5.00	3.00
(8)	Marcelino Lopez	10.00	5.00	3.00
(9)	Fred Newman	10.00	5.00	3.00
(10)	Albie Pearson	10.00	5.00	3.00
(11)	Jim Piersall	13.50	6.75	4.00
(12)	Rick Reichardt	10.00	5.00	3.00
(13)	Bob Rodgers	10.00	5.00	3.00
(14)	Paul Schaal	10.00	5.00	3.00
(15)	Norm Siebern	10.00	5.00	3.00
(16)	Willie Smith	10.00	5.00	3.00
(17)	Anaheim Stadium	10.00	5.00	3.00

1966 Dexter Press California Angels 8x10

The extent to which this larger format premium parallels the smaller set is currently unknown.

		NM	EX	VG
Common Player:		10.00	5.00	3.00
(1)	Dean Chance	15.00	7.50	4.50
(2)	Willie Smith	10.00	5.00	3.00

1966 Dexter Press California Angels Booklet

This souvenir-stand bound booklet offered pictures of the 1966 California Angels in two different sizes. Each 8-1/8" x 3-1/2" page features a pair of identical color photo cards. A post-card-size (3-1/2" x 5-1/2") portrait has a facsimile autograph of the player at top, attached by perforations to a 2-1/4" x 3-1/2" card, which in turn is perforated into the bound end of the book. Booklets originally sold for 50 cents. The unnumbered cards are checklisted here in alphabetical order.

		NM	EX	VG
Complete Booket:		150.00	75.00	45.00
Complete Set, Large (10):		60.00	30.00	18.00
Complete Set, Small (10):		40.00	20.00	12.00
Common Player, Large:		8.00	4.00	2.40
Common Player, Small:		6.00	3.00	1.80
Large Format (3-1/2" x 5-1/2")				
(1)	Jose Cardenal	8.00	4.00	2.50
(2)	Dean Chance	8.00	4.00	2.50
(3)	Jim Fregosi	8.00	4.00	2.50
(4)	Bob Knoop	8.00	4.00	2.50
(5)	Albie Pearson	8.00	4.00	2.50
(6)	Rick Reichardt	8.00	4.00	2.50
(7)	Bob Rodgers	8.00	4.00	2.50
(8)	Paul Schaal	8.00	4.00	2.50
(9)	Willie Smith	8.00	4.00	2.50
(10)	Anaheim Stadium	8.00	4.00	2.50
Small Format (2-1/4" x 3-1/2")				
(1)	Jose Cardenal	6.00	3.00	1.80
(2)	Dean Chance	6.00	3.00	1.80
(3)	Jim Fregosi	6.00	3.00	1.80
(4)	Bob Knoop	6.00	3.00	1.80
(5)	Albie Pearson	6.00	3.00	1.80

		NM	EX	VG
(6)	Rick Reichardt	6.00	3.00	1.80
(7)	Bob Rodgers	6.00	3.00	1.80
(8)	Paul Schaal	6.00	3.00	1.80
(9)	Willie Smith	6.00	3.00	1.80
(10)	Anaheim Stadium	6.00	3.00	1.80

1966-67 Dexter Press N.Y. Yankees

Less commonly encountered than the later Dexter Press/Coca-Cola premium issues are the team-set photocards produced by the New York firm. Cards were sold in bagged sets with a colorful cardboard header. Virtually identical in design to the 5-1/2" x 7" premium cards of 1967, the team-set pictures measure 4" x 5-7/8" with a white border around, and a black facsimile autograph at the top of, color player poses. Backs are printed in blue with a few biographical details at top and copyright information at bottom. The unnumbered cards are checklisted here in alphabetical order.

		NM	EX	VG
Complete Set (12):		200.00	100.00	60.00
Common Player:		15.00	7.50	4.50
(1)	Jim Bouton	17.50	8.75	5.25
(2)	Horace Clarke	15.00	7.50	4.50
(3)	Al Downing	15.00	7.50	4.50
(4)	Whitey Ford	20.00	10.00	6.00
(5)	Steve Hamilton	15.00	7.50	4.50
(6)	Elston Howard	17.50	8.75	5.25
(7)	Mickey Mantle	60.00	30.00	18.00
(8)	Joe Pepitone	17.50	8.75	5.25
(9)	Bill Robinson	15.00	7.50	4.50
(10)	Mel Stottlemyre	15.00	7.50	4.50
(11)	Tom Tresh	17.50	8.75	5.25
(12)	Steve Whitaker	15.00	7.50	4.50

1967 Dexter Press Premiums

Among the most attractive baseball collectibles issued during the 1960s were the cards produced by Dexter Press and issued in team sets as a premium by Coca-Cola. Eighteen of the 20 Major League teams participated in the promotion (only one California Angels player and no St. Louis Cardinals). The cards are in 5-1/2" x 7" glossy format. All of the color photos are waist-to-cap poses shot during spring training, and all cards feature a black facsimile autograph at the top of the photo. The cards have a 1/4" white border around the picture. Backs are printed in blue on white and include a few biographical details and career highlights. Nine of the 12 players in the All-Star issue can be differentiated from the same players' cards in the team sets by the lengthier biographies on back. The bios on the cards of Bunning, Mays and Santo are the same in both versions. While each of the cards has a number printed on back in the lower-right, they are checklisted alphabetically within team. Sixteen of the Dexter Press premiums were issued in a smaller, borderless sticker set in 1983; it is an unauthorized collector issue.

		NM	EX	VG
Complete Set (229):		1,500	750.00	450.00
Common Player:		5.00	2.50	1.50
ALL-STARS				
(1)	Jim Bunning	7.50	3.75	2.25
(2)	Roberto Clemente	15.00	7.50	4.50
(3)	Willie Davis	5.00	2.50	1.50
(4)	Al Kaline	10.00	5.00	3.00
(5)	Harmon Killebrew	10.00	5.00	3.00
(6)	Willie Mays	12.50	6.25	3.75
(7)	Joe Pepitone	6.00	3.00	1.75
(8)	Brooks Robinson	10.00	5.00	3.00
(9)	Frank Robinson	10.00	5.00	3.00
(10)	Ron Santo	6.00	3.00	1.75
(11)	Joe Torre	6.00	3.00	1.75
(12)	Carl Yastrzemski	12.00	6.00	3.50
CALIFORNIA ANGELS				
(13)	Paul Schall	125.00	62.00	37.00

HOUSTON ASTROS				
(14)	Bob Aspromonte	5.00	2.50	1.50
(15)	John Bateman	5.00	2.50	1.50
(16)	Ron Davis	5.00	2.50	1.50
(17)	Larry Dierker	5.00	2.50	1.50
(18)	Dick Farrell	5.00	2.50	1.50
(19)	Dave Giusti	5.00	2.50	1.50
(20)	Chuck Harrison	5.00	2.50	1.50
(21)	Sonny Jackson	5.00	2.50	1.50
(22)	Jim Landis	5.00	2.50	1.50
(23)	Eddie Mathews	10.00	5.00	3.00
(24)	Joe Morgan	12.00	6.00	3.50
(25)	Rusty Staub	7.50	3.75	2.25
KANSAS CITY ATHLETICS				
(26)	Jack Aker	5.00	2.50	1.50
(27)	Campy Campaneris	5.00	2.50	1.50
(28)	Danny Cater	5.00	2.50	1.50
(29)	Ed Charles	5.00	2.50	1.50
(30)	Ossie Chavarria	5.00	2.50	1.50
(31)	Dick Green	5.00	2.50	1.50
(32)	Mike Hershberger	5.00	2.50	1.50
(33)	Lew Krausse	5.00	2.50	1.50
(34)	Jim Nash	5.00	2.50	1.50
(35)	Joe Nossek	5.00	2.50	1.50
(36)	Roger Repoz	5.00	2.50	1.50
(37)	Phil Roof	5.00	2.50	1.50
ATLANTA BRAVES				
(38)	Hank Aaron	25.00	12.50	7.50
(39)	Felipe Alou	6.00	3.00	1.75
(40)	Wade Blasingame	5.00	2.50	1.50
(41)	Clete Boyer	5.00	2.50	1.50
(42)	Bob Bruce	5.00	2.50	1.50
(43)	Ty Cline	5.00	2.50	1.50
(44)	Tony Cloninger	5.00	2.50	1.50
(45)	Ken Johnson	5.00	2.50	1.50
(46)	Dennis Menke	5.00	2.50	1.50
(47)	Gene Oliver	5.00	2.50	1.50
(48)	Joe Torre	7.50	3.75	2.25
(49)	Woody Woodward	5.00	2.50	1.50
CHICAGO CUBS				
(50)	George Altman	5.00	2.50	1.50
(51)	Ernie Banks	18.00	9.00	5.50
(52)	Glen Beckert (Glenn)	5.00	2.50	1.50
(53)	John Boccabella	5.00	2.50	1.50
(54)	Ray Culp	5.00	2.50	1.50
(55)	Ken Holtzman	5.00	2.50	1.50
(56)	Randy Hundley	5.00	2.50	1.50
(57)	Cal Koonce	5.00	2.50	1.50
(58)	Adolfo Phillips	5.00	2.50	1.50
(59)	Ron Santo	6.00	3.00	1.75
(60)	Lee Thomas	5.00	2.50	1.50
(61)	Billy Williams	10.00	5.00	3.00
LOS ANGELES DODGERS				
(62)	Bob Bailey	5.00	2.50	1.50
(63)	Willie Davis	5.00	2.50	1.50
(64)	Ron Fairly	5.00	2.50	1.50
(65)	Ron Hunt	5.00	2.50	1.50
(66)	Lou Johnson	5.00	2.50	1.50
(67)	John Kennedy	5.00	2.50	1.50
(68)	Jim Lefebvre	5.00	2.50	1.50
(69)	Claude Osteen	5.00	2.50	1.50
(70)	Wes Parker	5.00	2.50	1.50
(71)	Ron Perranoski	5.00	2.50	1.50
(72)	Phil Regan	5.00	2.50	1.50
(73)	Don Sutton	7.50	3.75	2.25
SAN FRANCISCO GIANTS				
(74)	Jesus Alou	5.00	2.50	1.50
(75)	Ollie Brown	5.00	2.50	1.50
(76)	Jim Davenport	5.00	2.50	1.50
(77)	Tito Fuentes	5.00	2.50	1.50
(78)	Tom Haller	5.00	2.50	1.50
(79)	Jim Hart	5.00	2.50	1.50
(80)	Hal Lanier	5.00	2.50	1.50
(81)	Willie Mays	15.00	7.50	4.50
(82)	Mike McCormick	5.00	2.50	1.50
(83)	Willie McCovey	12.00	6.00	3.50
(84)	Gaylord Perry	8.00	4.00	2.50
(85)	Norman Siebern	5.00	2.50	1.50
CLEVELAND INDIANS				
(86)	Max Alvis	5.00	2.50	1.50
(87)	Joe Azcue	5.00	2.50	1.50
(88)	Gary Bell	5.00	2.50	1.50
(89)	Larry Brown	5.00	2.50	1.50
(90)	Rocky Colavito	7.50	3.75	2.25
(91)	Vic Davalillo	5.00	2.50	1.50
(92)	Pedro Gonzalez	5.00	2.50	1.50
(93)	Chuck Hinton	5.00	2.50	1.50
(94)	Sam McDowell	6.00	3.00	1.75
(95)	Luis Tiant	6.00	3.00	1.75
(96)	Leon Wagner	5.00	2.50	1.50
(97)	Fred Whitfield	5.00	2.50	1.50
NEW YORK METS				
(98)	Ed Bressoud	5.00	2.50	1.50
(99)	Ken Boyer	7.00	3.50	2.00
(100)	Tommy Davis	6.00	3.00	1.75
(101)	Jack Fisher	5.00	2.50	1.50
(102)	Jerry Grote	5.00	2.50	1.50
(103)	Jack Hamilton	5.00	2.50	1.50
(104)	Cleon Jones	6.00	3.00	1.75
(105)	Ed Kranepool	5.00	2.50	1.50
(106)	Johnny Lewis	5.00	2.50	1.50
(107)	Bob Shaw	5.00	2.50	1.50
(108)	John Stephenson	5.00	2.50	1.50
(109)	Ron Swoboda	5.00	2.50	1.50
BALTIMORE ORIOLES				
(110)	Luis Aparicio	10.00	5.00	3.00
(111)	Curt Blefary	5.00	2.50	1.50
(112)	Wally Bunker	5.00	2.50	1.50
(113)	Andy Etchebarren	5.00	2.50	1.50
(114)	Eddie Fisher	5.00	2.50	1.50
(115)	Dave Johnson	5.00	2.50	1.50
(116)	Dave McNally	5.00	2.50	1.50
(117)	Jim Palmer	10.00	5.00	3.00
(118)	John "Boog" Powell	8.00	4.00	2.50
(119)	Brooks Robinson	15.00	7.50	4.50
(120)	Frank Robinson	15.00	7.50	4.50
(121)	Russ Snyder	5.00	2.50	1.50

PHILADELPHIA PHILLIES				
(122)	Rich Allen	7.50	3.75	2.25
(123)	John Briggs	5.00	2.50	1.50
(124)	Jim Bunning	7.50	3.75	2.25
(125)	Johnny Callison	5.00	2.50	1.50
(126)	Clay Dalrymple	5.00	2.50	1.50
(127)	Dick Groat	5.00	2.50	1.50
(128)	Larry Jackson	5.00	2.50	1.50
(129)	Don Lock	5.00	2.50	1.50
(130)	Cookie Rojas	5.00	2.50	1.50
(131)	Chris Short	5.00	2.50	1.50
(132)	Tony Taylor	5.00	2.50	1.50
(133)	Bill White	5.00	2.50	1.50
PITTSBURGH PIRATES				
(134)	Gene Alley	5.00	2.50	1.50
(135)	Matty Alou	5.00	2.50	1.50
(136)	Roberto Clemente	45.00	22.00	13.50
(137)	Donn Clendenon	5.00	2.50	1.50
(138)	Woodie Fryman	5.00	2.50	1.50
(139)	Vern Law	5.00	2.50	1.50
(140)	Bill Mazeroski	10.00	5.00	3.00
(141)	Manny Mota	5.00	2.50	1.50
(142)	Jim Pagliaroni	5.00	2.50	1.50
(143)	Wilver Stargell	12.00	6.00	3.50
(144)	Bob Veale	5.00	2.50	1.50
(145)	Maury Wills	6.00	3.00	1.75
CINCINNATI REDS				
(146)	Leo Cardenas	5.00	2.50	1.50
(147)	Gordy Coleman	5.00	2.50	1.50
(148)	Johnny Edwards	5.00	2.50	1.50
(149)	Tommy Harper	5.00	2.50	1.50
(150)	Tommy Helms	5.00	2.50	1.50
(151)	Deron Johnson	5.00	2.50	1.50
(152)	Jim Maloney	5.00	2.50	1.50
(153)	Bill McCool	5.00	2.50	1.50
(154)	Milt Pappas	5.00	2.50	1.50
(155)	Vada Pinson	6.00	3.00	1.75
(156)	Pete Rose	30.00	15.00	9.00
(157)	Art Shamsky	5.00	2.50	1.50
BOSTON RED SOX				
(158)	Don Demeter	5.00	2.50	1.50
(159)	Bill Fischer	5.00	2.50	1.50
(160)	Joe Foy	5.00	2.50	1.50
(161)	Dalton Jones	5.00	2.50	1.50
(162)	Jim Lonborg	5.00	2.50	1.50
(163)	Rico Petrocelli	5.00	2.50	1.50
(164)	Jose Santiago	5.00	2.50	1.50
(165)	George Scott	5.00	2.50	1.50
(166)	George Smith	5.00	2.50	1.50
(167)	Jose Tartabull	5.00	2.50	1.50
(168)	Bob Tillman	5.00	2.50	1.50
(169)	Carl Yastrzemski	15.00	7.50	4.50
WASHINGTON SENATORS				
(170)	Bernie Allen	5.00	2.50	1.50
(171)	Ed Brinkman	5.00	2.50	1.50
(172)	Paul Casanova	5.00	2.50	1.50
(173)	Ken Harrelson	5.00	2.50	1.50
(174)	Frank Howard	6.00	3.00	1.75
(175)	Jim King	5.00	2.50	1.50
(176)	Ken McMullen	5.00	2.50	1.50
(177)	Dick Nen	5.00	2.50	1.50
(178)	Phil Ortega	5.00	2.50	1.50
(179)	Pete Richert	5.00	2.50	1.50
(180)	Bob Saverine	5.00	2.50	1.50
(181)	Fred Valentine	5.00	2.50	1.50
DETROIT TIGERS				
(182)	Norm Cash	6.00	3.00	1.75
(183)	Bill Freehan	5.00	2.50	1.50
(184)	Willie Horton	5.00	2.50	1.50
(185)	Al Kaline	12.00	6.00	3.50
(186)	Mickey Lolich	5.00	2.50	1.50
(187)	Jerry Lumpe	5.00	2.50	1.50
(188)	Dick McAuliffe	5.00	2.50	1.50
(189)	Johnny Podres	5.00	2.50	1.50
(190)	Joe Sparma	5.00	2.50	1.50
(191)	Dave Wickersham	5.00	2.50	1.50
(192)	Earl Wilson	5.00	2.50	1.50
(193)	Don Wert	5.00	2.50	1.50
MINNESOTA TWINS				
(194)	Bob Allison	5.00	2.50	1.50
(195)	Earl Battey	5.00	2.50	1.50
(196)	Dave Boswell	5.00	2.50	1.50
(197)	Dean Chance	5.00	2.50	1.50
(198)	Mudcat Grant	5.00	2.50	1.50
(199)	Harmon Killebrew	12.00	6.00	3.50
(200)	Jim Merritt	5.00	2.50	1.50
(201)	Tony Oliva	8.00	4.00	2.50
(202)	Rich Rollins	5.00	2.50	1.50
(203)	Ted Uhlaender	5.00	2.50	1.50
(204)	Sandy Valdespino	5.00	2.50	1.50
(205)	Zoilo Versalles	5.00	2.50	1.50
CHICAGO WHITE SOX				
(206)	Tommie Agee	5.00	2.50	1.50
(207)	Ken Berry	5.00	2.50	1.50
(208)	Don Buford	5.00	2.50	1.50
(209)	Ron Hansen	5.00	2.50	1.50
(210)	Joel Horlen	5.00	2.50	1.50
(211)	Tommy John	6.00	3.00	1.75
(212)	Bob Locker	5.00	2.50	1.50
(213)	Tommy McCraw	5.00	2.50	1.50
(214)	Jerry McNertney	5.00	2.50	1.50
(215)	Jim O'Toole	5.00	2.50	1.50
(216)	Bill "Moose" Skowron	7.00	3.50	2.00
(217)	Pete Ward	5.00	2.50	1.50
NEW YORK YANKEES				
(218)	Jim Bouton	6.00	3.00	1.75
(219)	Horace Clarke	5.00	2.50	1.50
(220)	Al Downing	5.00	2.50	1.50
(221)	Steve Hamilton	5.00	2.50	1.50
(222)	Elston Howard	7.50	3.75	2.25
(223)	Mickey Mantle	40.00	20.00	12.00
(224)	Joe Pepitone	6.00	3.00	1.75
(225)	Fritz Peterson	5.00	2.50	1.50
(226)	Charley Smith	5.00	2.50	1.50
(227)	Mel Stottlemyre	6.00	3.00	1.75
(228)	Tom Tresh	6.00	3.00	1.75
(229)	Roy White	6.00	3.00	1.75

1967 Dexter Press Team Posters

These 17" x 11" color posters reproduce the 12 cards (or on the Cubs sheet, three additional players) found in the 1967 Dexter Press premium team sets, in images about 2" x 3". The cards are pictured on a solid color background with color team logos. Printed on back are player identification and biographical information. Dexter Press copyright and credit lines are at bottom. It is not known whether other teams involved in the premium program can also be found in poster format.

	NM	EX	VG
California Angels	135.00	65.00	40.00
Chicago Cubs	180.00	90.00	55.00
Chicago White Sox	135.00	65.00	40.00
N.Y. Mets	180.00	90.00	55.00
N.Y. Yankees	300.00	150.00	90.00
Washington Senators	180.00	90.00	55.00

1968 Dexter Press Postcards

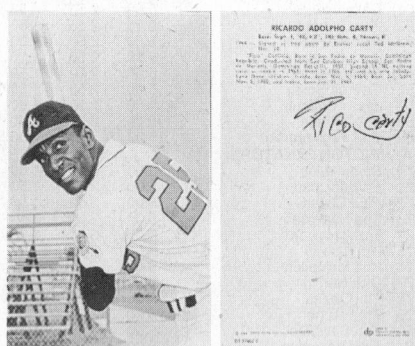

In its second year of printing premium cards for Coca-Cola, Dexter Press changed format and greatly reduced the number of participating teams and players. Only six teams were represented by 12-card sets, while an additional four teams had one or two players included. For 1968, Dexter Press produced its premiums in postcard (3-1/2" x 5-1/2") size. The cards featured borderless color player poses on front. Backs were printed in blue on white and included a facsimile autograph, biographical details and career highlights. Cards carry a Dexter Press serial number on back, but are checklisted here alphabetically within team.

	NM	EX	VG
Complete Set (77):	400.00	200.00	120.00
Common Player:	4.00	2.00	1.25
CALIFORNIA ANGELS			
(1) Jim Fregosi	6.00	3.00	1.75
HOUSTON ASTROS			
(2) Bob Aspromonte	4.00	2.00	1.25
(3) John Bateman	4.00	2.00	1.25
(4) Ron Brand	4.00	2.00	1.25
(5) Mike Cuellar	4.00	2.00	1.25
(6) Ron Davis	4.00	2.00	1.25
(7) Dave Giusti	4.00	2.00	1.25
(8) Julio Gotay	4.00	2.00	1.25
(9) Denny Lemaster	4.00	2.00	1.25
(10) Denis Menke	4.00	2.00	1.25
(11) Joe Morgan	10.00	5.00	3.00
(12) Rusty Staub	5.00	2.50	1.50
(13) Jim Wynn	4.00	2.00	1.25
ATLANTA BRAVES			
(14) Hank Aaron	15.00	7.50	4.50
(15) Felipe Alou	5.00	2.50	1.50
(16) Clete Boyer	4.00	2.00	1.25
(17) Clay Carroll	4.00	2.00	1.25
(18) Rico Carty	4.00	2.00	1.25
(19) Tony Cloninger	4.00	2.00	1.25
(20) Sonny Jackson	4.00	2.00	1.25
(21) Ray Jarvis	4.00	2.00	1.25
(22) Ken Johnson	4.00	2.00	1.25
(23) Phil Niekro	8.00	4.00	2.50
(24) Joe Torre	7.50	3.75	2.25
(25) Woody Woodward	4.00	2.00	1.25
SAN FRANCISCO GIANTS			
(26) Jesus Alou	4.00	2.00	1.25
(27) Bob Bolin	4.00	2.00	1.25
(28) Jim Davenport	4.00	2.00	1.25
(29) Jim Hart	4.00	2.00	1.25
(30) Jack Hiatt	4.00	2.00	1.25
(31) Ron Hunt	4.00	2.00	1.25
(32) Frank Linzy	4.00	2.00	1.25
(33) Juan Marichal	9.00	4.50	2.75
(34) Willie Mays	15.00	7.50	4.50
(35) Mike McCormick	4.00	2.00	1.25
(36) Gaylord Perry	8.00	4.00	2.50
(37) Ray Sadecki	4.00	2.00	1.25
BALTIMORE ORIOLES			
(38) Mark Belanger	4.00	2.00	1.25
(39) Paul Blair	4.00	2.00	1.25
(40) Curt Blefary	4.00	2.00	1.25
(41) Don Buford	4.00	2.00	1.25
(42) Moe Drabowsky	4.00	2.00	1.25
(43) Andy Etchebarren	4.00	2.00	1.25
(44) Dave Johnson	4.00	2.00	1.25
(45) Dave McNally	4.00	2.00	1.25
(46) Tom Phoebus	4.00	2.00	1.25
(47) Boog Powell	5.00	2.50	1.50
(48) Brooks Robinson	12.00	6.00	3.50
(49) Frank Robinson	12.00	6.00	3.50
PHILADELPHIA PHILLIES			
(50) Dick Allen	9.00	4.50	2.75
PITTSBURGH PIRATES	.00	.00	.00
(51) Roberto Clemente	25.00	12.50	7.50
(52) Bill Mazeroski	10.00	5.00	3.00
BOSTON RED SOX			
(53) Jerry Adair	4.00	2.00	1.25
(54) Mike Andrews	4.00	2.00	1.25
(55) Gary Bell	4.00	2.00	1.25
(56) Darrell Brandon	4.00	2.00	1.25
(57) Dick Ellsworth	4.00	2.00	1.25
(58) Joe Foy	4.00	2.00	1.25
(59) Dalton Jones	4.00	2.00	1.25
(60) Jim Lonborg	5.00	2.50	1.50
(61) Dave Morehead	4.00	2.00	1.25
(62) Rico Petrocelli	4.00	2.00	1.25
(63) George Scott	4.00	2.00	1.25
(64) John Wyatt	4.00	2.00	1.25
DETROIT TIGERS			
(65) Bill Freehan	6.00	3.00	1.75
MINNESOTA TWINS			
(66) Bob Allison	4.00	2.00	1.25
(67) Dave Boswell	4.00	2.00	1.25
(68) Rod Carew	10.00	5.00	3.00
(69) Dean Chance	4.00	2.00	1.25
(70) Jim Kaat	4.00	2.00	1.25
(71) Harmon Killebrew	10.00	5.00	3.00
(72) Russ Nixon	4.00	2.00	1.25
(73) Tony Oliva	6.00	3.00	1.75
(74) Rich Rollins	4.00	2.00	1.25
(75) John Roseboro	4.00	2.00	1.25
(76) Cesar Tovar	4.00	2.00	1.25
(77) Ted Uhlaender	4.00	2.00	1.25

1979 Dexter Press Hall of Fame Plaque Postcards

(See Hall of Fame (Dexter Press) for checklist, value data.)

1960 Diamond Associates Postcards

 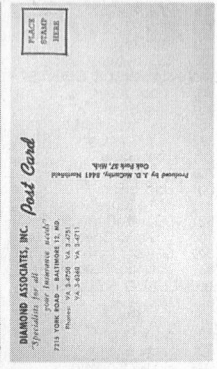

Based on the uniform style depicted on front, the actual year of issue for this card could be anywhere between 1958-1962. Produced by photographer J.D. McCarthy, apparently for the star catcher's off-season business, the 3-1/4" x 5-1/2" black-and-white card has a facsimile autograph on front. The postcard-style back has the address and phone numbers of the insurance company.

	NM	EX	VG
Gus Triandos	30.00	15.00	9.00

1940 Diamond Dust Punchboard Cards

These paper cards are the consolation prizes from a popular gambling device of the Depression era, the punchboard. For five cents a customer could choose one of 624 holes on the punchboard and push a wood or metal punch through the paper on front, driving out the back a 1" x about 1-3/4" picture of a baseball player. Fifteen of the players were $1 winners and were produced in much shorter supply than the others; any which were redeemed would probably have been destroyed. The pictures are printed on ribbed paper to assist in fitting them into the board. They are pictures taken from the photos on contemporary "Salutation" Exhibit cards, though without uniform logos. They are printed in bright colors with the player name in a color bar at bottom. Backs are blank. The unnumbered cards are listed here in alphabetical order, with an asterisk indicating winners. The punchboard itself is highly collectible, with colorful baseball graphics and player pictures and names. Earlier and later versions of Diamond Dust punchboards are also known, but have not been checklisted.

		NM	EX	VG
Complete Set (33):		850.00	425.00	250.00
Common Player:		15.00	7.50	4.50
Complete Unused Punchboard:		1,200	600.00	350.00
(1)	Luke Appling (*)	45.00	22.00	13.50
(2)	Earl Averill (*)	45.00	22.00	13.50
(3)	Adolf Camilli	15.00	7.50	4.50
(4)	Harland Clift (Harland)	15.00	7.50	4.50
(5)	Joe Cronin (*)(Unconfirmed)	45.00	22.00	13.50
(6)	Tony Cuccinello	15.00	7.50	4.50
(7)	Dizzy Dean	35.00	17.50	10.50
(8)	Bill Dickey (*)	50.00	25.00	15.00
(9)	Joe DiMaggio (*)	125.00	62.00	37.00
(10)	Bob Feller	30.00	15.00	9.00
(11)	Jimmie Foxx (*)	45.00	22.00	13.50
(12)	Charlie Gehringer (*)	45.00	22.00	13.50
(13)	Lefty Gomez	25.00	12.50	7.50
(14)	Hank Greenberg	30.00	15.00	9.00
(15)	Lefty Grove	25.00	12.50	7.50
(16)	Gabby Hartnett	15.00	7.50	4.50
(17)	Carl Hubbell	25.00	12.50	7.50
(18)	Bob Johnson	15.00	7.50	4.50
(19)	Chuck Klein	25.00	12.50	7.50
(20)	Bill Lee	15.00	7.50	4.50
(21)	Ernie Lombardi (*)	45.00	22.00	13.50
(22)	Frank McCormick (*)	25.00	12.50	7.50
(23)	Joe Medwick	25.00	12.50	7.50
(24)	Johnny Mize (*)	45.00	22.00	13.50
(25)	Buck Newson (Newsom)	15.00	7.50	4.50
(26)	Mel Ott (*)	45.00	22.00	13.50
(27)	Johnny Rizzo (*)	25.00	12.50	7.50
(28)	Red Ruffing (*)(Unconfirmed)	45.00	22.00	13.50
(29)	Cecil Travis	15.00	7.50	4.50
(30)	Johnny Vander Meer	15.00	7.50	4.50
(31)	Arky Vaughan (*)	45.00	22.00	13.50
(32)	Lon Warneke	15.00	7.50	4.50
(33)	Rudy York (*)(Unconfirmed)	25.00	12.50	7.50

1979 Diamond Greats

Card collector, dealer and later Donruss photographer Jack Wallin produced this collectors' issue. Cards are in the 2-1/2" x 3-1/2" format, printed in black-and-white and blank-backed. Besides the player photo on front, there is identification and a line of career stats. Four 100-card series were issued. Series 1 concentrates on Yankees, Giants, Senators and Dodgers. Series 2 comprises the Cubs, White Sox, Cardinals and Browns. The third series features Braves, Red Sox, Reds and Indians. Series 4 concentrates on the Phillies, A's, Pirates and Tigers.

		NM	EX	VG
Complete Set (400):		275.00	135.00	85.00
Series 1 (1-100):		60.00	30.00	18.00
Series 2 (101-200):		50.00	25.00	15.00
Series 3 (201-300):		50.00	25.00	15.00
Series 4 (301-400):		50.00	25.00	15.00
Common Player:		2.00	1.00	.60
1	Joe DiMaggio	12.00	6.00	3.50
2	Ben Chapman	2.00	1.00	.60
3	Joe Dugan	2.00	1.00	.60
4	Bobby Shawkey	2.00	1.00	.60
5	Joe Sewell	2.00	1.00	.60
6	George Pipgras	2.00	1.00	.60
7	George Selkirk	2.00	1.00	.60
8	Babe Dahlgren	2.00	1.00	.60
9	Spud Chandler	2.00	1.00	.60
10	Duffy Lewis	2.00	1.00	.60
11	Lefty Gomez	3.00	1.50	.90
12	Atley Donald	2.00	1.00	.60
13	Whitey Witt	2.00	1.00	.60
14	Marius Russo	2.00	1.00	.60

#	Name			
15	Buddy Rosar	2.00	1.00	.60
16	Russ Van Atta	2.00	1.00	.60
17	Johnny Lindell	2.00	1.00	.60
18	Bobby Brown	2.00	1.00	.60
19	Tony Kubek	2.50	1.25	.70
20	Joe Beggs	2.00	1.00	.60
21	Don Larsen	2.50	1.25	.70
22	Andy Carey	2.00	1.00	.60
23	Johnny Kucks	2.00	1.00	.60
24	Elston Howard	2.50	1.25	.70
25	Roger Maris	4.00	2.00	1.25
26	Rube Marquard	2.50	1.25	.70
27	Sam Leslie	2.00	1.00	.60
28	Freddy Leach	2.00	1.00	.60
29	Fred Fitzsimmons	2.00	1.00	.60
30	Bill Terry	2.50	1.25	.70
31	Joe Moore	2.00	1.00	.60
32	Waite Hoyt	2.00	1.00	.60
33	Travis Jackson	2.00	1.00	.60
34	Gus Mancuso	2.00	1.00	.60
35	Carl Hubbell	3.00	1.50	.90
36	Bill Voiselle	2.00	1.00	.60
37	Hank Leiber	2.00	1.00	.60
38	Burgess Whitehead	2.00	1.00	.60
39	Johnny Mize	3.00	1.50	.90
40	Bill Lohrman	2.00	1.00	.60
41	Bill Rigney	2.00	1.00	.60
42	Cliff Melton	2.00	1.00	.60
43	Willard Marshall	2.00	1.00	.60
44	Wes Westrum	2.00	1.00	.60
45	Monte Irvin	3.00	1.50	.90
46	Marv Grissom	2.00	1.00	.60
47	Clyde Castleman	2.00	1.00	.60
48	Harry Gumbert	2.00	1.00	.60
49	Daryl Spencer	2.00	1.00	.60
50	Willie Mays	9.00	4.50	2.75
51	Sam West	2.00	1.00	.60
52	Fred Schulte	2.00	1.00	.60
53	Cecil Travis	2.00	1.00	.60
54	Tommy Thomas	2.00	1.00	.60
55	Dutch Leonard	2.00	1.00	.60
56	Jimmy Wasdell	2.00	1.00	.60
57	Doc Cramer	2.00	1.00	.60
58	Harland Clift (Harlond)	2.00	1.00	.60
59	Ken Chase	2.00	1.00	.60
60	Buddy Lewis	2.00	1.00	.60
61	Ossie Bluege	2.00	1.00	.60
62	Chuck Stobbs	2.00	1.00	.60
63	Jimmy DeShong	2.00	1.00	.60
64	Roger Wolff	2.00	1.00	.60
65	Luke Sewell	2.00	1.00	.60
66	Sid Hudson	2.00	1.00	.60
67	Jack Russell	2.00	1.00	.60
68	Walt Masterson	2.00	1.00	.60
69	George Myatt	2.00	1.00	.60
70	Monte Weaver	2.00	1.00	.60
71	Cliff Bolton	2.00	1.00	.60
72	Ray Scarborough	2.00	1.00	.60
73	Albie Pearson	2.00	1.00	.60
74	Gil Coan	2.00	1.00	.60
75	Roy Sievers	2.00	1.00	.60
76	Burleigh Grimes	2.00	1.00	.60
77	Charlie Hargreaves	2.00	1.00	.60
78	Babe Herman	2.00	1.00	.60
79	Fred Frankhouse	2.00	1.00	.60
80	Al Lopez	2.00	1.00	.60
81	Lonny Frey	2.00	1.00	.60
82	Dixie Walker	2.00	1.00	.60
83	Kirby Higbe	2.00	1.00	.60
84	Bobby Bragan	2.00	1.00	.60
85	Leo Durocher	2.00	1.00	.60
86	Woody English	2.00	1.00	.60
87	Preacher Roe	2.00	1.00	.60
88	Vic Lombardi	2.00	1.00	.60
89	Clyde Sukeforth	2.00	1.00	.60
90	Pee Wee Reese	5.00	2.50	1.50
91	Joe Hatten	2.00	1.00	.60
92	Gene Hermanski	2.00	1.00	.60
93	Ray Benge	2.00	1.00	.60
94	Duke Snider	5.00	2.50	1.50
95	Walter Alston	2.00	1.00	.60
96	Don Drysdale	3.00	1.50	.90
97	Andy Pafko	2.00	1.00	.60
98	Don Zimmer	2.00	1.00	.60
99	Carl Erskine	2.00	1.00	.60
100	Dick Williams	2.00	1.00	.60
101	Charlie Grimm	2.00	1.00	.60
102	Clarence Blair	2.00	1.00	.60
103	Johnny Moore	2.00	1.00	.60
104	Clay Bryant	2.00	1.00	.60
105	Billy Herman	2.00	1.00	.60
106	Hy Vandenberg	2.00	1.00	.60
107	Lennie Merullo	2.00	1.00	.60
108	Hank Wyse	2.00	1.00	.60
109	Dom Dallessandro	2.00	1.00	.60
110	Al Epperly	2.00	1.00	.60
111	Bill Nicholson	2.00	1.00	.60
112	Vern Olsen	2.00	1.00	.60
113	Johnny Schmitz	2.00	1.00	.60
114	Bob Scheffing	2.00	1.00	.60
115	Bob Rush	2.00	1.00	.60
116	Roy Smalley	2.00	1.00	.60
117	Ransom Jackson	2.00	1.00	.60
118	Cliff Chambers	2.00	1.00	.60
119	Harry Chiti	2.00	1.00	.60
120	Johnny Klippstein	2.00	1.00	.60
121	Gene Baker	2.00	1.00	.60
122	Walt Moryn	2.00	1.00	.60
123	Dick Littlefield	2.00	1.00	.60
124	Bob Speake	2.00	1.00	.60
125	Hank Sauer	2.00	1.00	.60
126	Monty Stratton	2.50	1.25	.70
127	Johnny Kerr	2.00	1.00	.60
128	Milt Gaston	2.00	1.00	.60
129	Eddie Smith	2.00	1.00	.60
130	Larry Rosenthal	2.00	1.00	.60
131	Orval Grove	2.00	1.00	.60
132	Johnny Hodapp	2.00	1.00	.60
133	Johnny Rigney	2.00	1.00	.60
134	Willie Kamm	2.00	1.00	.60
135	Ed Lopat	2.00	1.00	.60
136	Smead Jolley	2.00	1.00	.60
137	Ralph Hodgin	2.00	1.00	.60
138	Ollie Bejma	2.00	1.00	.60
139	Zeke Bonura	2.00	1.00	.60
140	Al Hollingsworth	2.00	1.00	.60
141	Thurman Tucker	2.00	1.00	.60
142	Cass Michaels	2.00	1.00	.60
143	Bill Wight	2.00	1.00	.60
144	Don Lenhardt	2.00	1.00	.60
145	Sammy Esposito	2.00	1.00	.60
146	Jack Harshman	2.00	1.00	.60
147	Turk Lown	2.00	1.00	.60
148	Jim Landis	2.00	1.00	.60
149	Bob Shaw	2.00	1.00	.60
150	Minnie Minoso	2.50	1.25	.70
151	Les Bell	2.00	1.00	.60
152	Taylor Douthit	2.00	1.00	.60
153	Jack Rothrock	2.00	1.00	.60
154	Terry Moore	2.00	1.00	.60
155	Max Lanier	2.00	1.00	.60
156	Don Gutteridge	2.00	1.00	.60
157	Stu Martin	2.00	1.00	.60
158	Stan Musial	5.00	2.50	1.50
159	Frank Crespi	2.00	1.00	.60
160	Johnny Hopp	2.00	1.00	.60
161	Ernie Koy	2.00	1.00	.60
162	Joe Garagiola	3.00	1.50	.90
163	Ed Kazak	2.00	1.00	.60
164	Joe Orengo	2.00	1.00	.60
165	Howie Krist	2.00	1.00	.60
166	Enos Slaughter	3.00	1.50	.90
167	Ray Sanders	2.00	1.00	.60
168	Walker Cooper	2.00	1.00	.60
169	Nippy Jones	2.00	1.00	.60
170	Dick Sisler	2.00	1.00	.60
171	Harvey Haddix	2.00	1.00	.60
172	Solly Hemus	2.00	1.00	.60
173	Ray Jablonski	2.00	1.00	.60
174	Alex Grammas	2.00	1.00	.60
175	Joe Cunningham	2.00	1.00	.60
176	Debs Garms	2.00	1.00	.60
177	Chief Hogsett	2.00	1.00	.60
178	Alan Strange	2.00	1.00	.60
179	Rick Ferrell	2.00	1.00	.60
180	Jack Kramer	2.00	1.00	.60
181	Jack Knott	2.00	1.00	.60
182	Bob Harris	2.00	1.00	.60
183	Billy Hitchcock	2.00	1.00	.60
184	Jim Walkup	2.00	1.00	.60
185	Roy Cullenbine	2.00	1.00	.60
186	Bob Muncrief	2.00	1.00	.60
187	Chet Laabs	2.00	1.00	.60
188	Vern Kennedy	2.00	1.00	.60
189	Bill Trotter	2.00	1.00	.60
190	Denny Galehouse	2.00	1.00	.60
191	Al Zarilla	2.00	1.00	.60
192	Hank Arft	2.00	1.00	.60
193	Nelson Potter	2.00	1.00	.60
194	Ray Coleman	2.00	1.00	.60
195	Bob Dillinger	2.00	1.00	.60
196	Dick Kokos	2.00	1.00	.60
197	Bob Cain	2.00	1.00	.60
198	Virgil Trucks	2.00	1.00	.60
199	Duane Pillette	2.00	1.00	.60
200	Bob Turley	2.00	1.00	.60
201	Wally Berger	2.00	1.00	.60
202	John Lanning	2.00	1.00	.60
203	Buck Jordan	2.00	1.00	.60
204	Jim Turner	2.00	1.00	.60
205	Johnny Cooney	2.00	1.00	.60
206	Hank Majeski	2.00	1.00	.60
207	Phil Masi	2.00	1.00	.60
208	Tony Cuccinello	2.00	1.00	.60
209	Whitey Wietelmann	2.00	1.00	.60
210	Lou Fette	2.00	1.00	.60
211	Vince DiMaggio	2.50	1.25	.70
212	Huck Betts	2.00	1.00	.60
213	Red Barrett	2.00	1.00	.60
214	Pinkey Whitney	2.00	1.00	.60
215	Tommy Holmes	2.00	1.00	.60
216	Ray Berres	2.00	1.00	.60
217	Mike Sandlock	2.00	1.00	.60
218	Max Macon	2.00	1.00	.60
219	Sibby Sisti	2.00	1.00	.60
220	Johnny Beazley	2.00	1.00	.60
221	Bill Posedel	2.00	1.00	.60
222	Connie Ryan	2.00	1.00	.60
223	Del Crandall	2.00	1.00	.60
224	Bob Addis	2.00	1.00	.60
225	Warren Spahn	3.00	1.50	.90
226	Johnny Pesky	2.00	1.00	.60
227	Dom DiMaggio	2.50	1.25	.70
228	Emerson Dickman	2.00	1.00	.60
229	Bobby Doerr	2.00	1.00	.60
230	Tony Lupien	2.00	1.00	.60
231	Roy Partee	2.00	1.00	.60
232	Stan Spence	2.00	1.00	.60
233	Jim Bagby	2.00	1.00	.60
234	Buster Mills	2.00	1.00	.60
235	Fabian Gaffke	2.00	1.00	.60
236	George Metkovich	2.00	1.00	.60
237	Tom McBride	2.00	1.00	.60
238	Charlie Wagner	2.00	1.00	.60
239	Eddie Pellagrini	2.00	1.00	.60
240	Harry Dorish	2.00	1.00	.60
241	Ike Delock	2.00	1.00	.60
242	Mel Parnell	2.00	1.00	.60
243	Matt Batts	2.00	1.00	.60
244	Gene Stephens	2.00	1.00	.60
245	Milt Bolling	2.00	1.00	.60
246	Charlie Maxwell	2.00	1.00	.60
247	Willard Nixon	2.00	1.00	.60
248	Sammy White	2.00	1.00	.60
249	Dick Gernert	2.00	1.00	.60
250	Rico Petrocelli	2.00	1.00	.60
251	Edd Roush	2.00	1.00	.60
252	Mark Koenig	2.00	1.00	.60
253	Jimmy Outlaw	2.00	1.00	.60
254	Ethan Allen	2.00	1.00	.60
255	Tony Freitas	2.00	1.00	.60
256	Frank McCormick	2.00	1.00	.60
257	Bucky Walters	2.00	1.00	.60
258	Harry Craft	2.00	1.00	.60
259	Nate Andrews	2.00	1.00	.60
260	Ed Lukon	2.00	1.00	.60
261	Elmer Riddle	2.00	1.00	.60
262	Lee Grissom	2.00	1.00	.60
263	Johnny Vander Meer	2.00	1.00	.60
264	Eddie Joost	2.00	1.00	.60
265	Kermit Wahl	2.00	1.00	.60
266	Ival Goodman	2.00	1.00	.60
267	Clyde Vollmer	2.00	1.00	.60
268	Grady Hatton	2.00	1.00	.60
269	Ted Kluszewski	3.00	1.50	.90
270	Johnny Pramesa	2.00	1.00	.60
271	Joe Black	2.50	1.25	.70
272	Roy McMillan	2.00	1.00	.60
273	Wally Post	2.00	1.00	.60
274	Joe Nuxhall	2.00	1.00	.60
275	Jerry Lynch	2.00	1.00	.60
276	Stan Coveleski	2.00	1.00	.60
277	Bill Wambsganss	2.00	1.00	.60
278	Bruce Campbell	2.00	1.00	.60
279	George Uhle	2.00	1.00	.60
280	Earl Averill	2.00	1.00	.60
281	Whit Wyatt	2.00	1.00	.60
282	Oscar Grimes	2.00	1.00	.60
283	Roy Weatherly	2.00	1.00	.60
284	Joe Dobson	2.00	1.00	.60
285	Bob Feller	3.00	1.50	.90
286	Jim Hegan	2.00	1.00	.60
287	Mel Harder	2.00	1.00	.60
288	Ken Keltner	2.00	1.00	.60
289	Red Embree	2.00	1.00	.60
290	Al Milnar	2.00	1.00	.60
291	Lou Boudreau	2.00	1.00	.60
292	Ed Klieman	2.00	1.00	.60
293	Steve Gromek	2.00	1.00	.60
294	George Strickland	2.00	1.00	.60
295	Gene Woodling	2.00	1.00	.60
296	Hank Edwards	2.00	1.00	.60
297	Don Mossi	2.00	1.00	.60
298	Eddie Robinson	2.00	1.00	.60
299	Sam Dente	2.00	1.00	.60
300	Herb Score	2.00	1.00	.60
301	Dolf Camilli	2.00	1.00	.60
302	Jack Warner	2.00	1.00	.60
303	Ike Pearson	2.00	1.00	.60
304	Johnny Peacock	2.00	1.00	.60
305	Gene Corbett	2.00	1.00	.60
306	Walt Millies	2.00	1.00	.60
307	Vance Dinges	2.00	1.00	.60
308	Joe Marty	2.00	1.00	.60
309	Hugh Mulcahey	2.00	1.00	.60
310	Boom Boom Beck	2.00	1.00	.60
311	Charley Schanz	2.00	1.00	.60
312	John Bolling	2.00	1.00	.60
313	Danny Litwhiler	2.00	1.00	.60
314	Emil Verban	2.00	1.00	.60
315	Andy Semenick	2.00	1.00	.60
316	John Antonelli	2.00	1.00	.60
317	Robin Roberts	3.00	1.50	.90
318	Richie Ashburn	3.00	1.50	.90
319	Curt Simmons	2.00	1.00	.60
320	Murry Dickson	2.00	1.00	.60
321	Jim Greengrass	2.00	1.00	.60
322	Gene Freese	2.00	1.00	.60
323	Bobby Morgan	2.00	1.00	.60
324	Don Demeter	2.00	1.00	.60
325	Eddie Sawyer	2.00	1.00	.60
326	Bob Johnson	2.00	1.00	.60
327	Ace Parker	3.00	1.50	.90
328	Joe Hauser	2.00	1.00	.60
329	Walt French	2.00	1.00	.60
330	Tom Ferrick	2.00	1.00	.60
331	Bill Werber	2.00	1.00	.60
332	Walt Masters	2.00	1.00	.60
333	Les McCrabb	2.00	1.00	.60
334	Ben McCoy	2.00	1.00	.60
335	Eric Tipton	2.00	1.00	.60
336	Al Rubeling	2.00	1.00	.60
337	Nick Etten	2.00	1.00	.60
338	Carl Scheib	2.00	1.00	.60
339	Dario Lodigiani	2.00	1.00	.60
340	Earle Brucker	2.00	1.00	.60
341	Al Brancato	2.00	1.00	.60
342	Lou Limmer	2.00	1.00	.60
343	Elmer Valo	2.00	1.00	.60
344	Bob Hooper	2.00	1.00	.60
345	Joe Astroth	2.00	1.00	.60
346	Pete Suder	2.00	1.00	.60
347	Dave Philley	2.00	1.00	.60
348	Gus Zernial	2.00	1.00	.60
349	Bobby Shantz	2.00	1.00	.60
350	Joe DeMaestri	2.00	1.00	.60
351	Fred Lindstrom	2.00	1.00	.60
352	Red Lucas	2.00	1.00	.60
353	Clyde Barnhart	2.00	1.00	.60
354	Nick Strincevich	2.00	1.00	.60
355	Lloyd Waner	2.00	1.00	.60
356	Guy Bush	2.00	1.00	.60
357	Joe Bowman	2.00	1.00	.60
358	Al Todd	2.00	1.00	.60
359	Mace Brown	2.00	1.00	.60
360	Larry French	2.00	1.00	.60
361	Elbie Fletcher	2.00	1.00	.60
362	Woody Jensen	2.00	1.00	.60
363	Rip Sewell	2.00	1.00	.60
364	Johnny Dickshot	2.00	1.00	.60
365	Pete Coscarart	2.00	1.00	.60
366	Bud Hafey	2.00	1.00	.60
367	Ken Heintzelman	2.00	1.00	.60
368	Wally Westlake	2.00	1.00	.60

369	Frank Gustine	2.00	1.00	.60
370	Smoky Burgess	2.00	1.00	.60
371	Dick Groat	2.00	1.00	.60
372	Vern Law	2.00	1.00	.60
373	Bob Skinner	2.00	1.00	.60
374	Don Cardwell	2.00	1.00	.60
375	Bob Friend	2.00	1.00	.60
376	Frank O'Rourke	2.00	1.00	.60
377	Birdie Tebbetts	2.00	1.00	.60
378	Charlie Gehringer	3.00	1.50	.90
379	Eldon Auker	2.00	1.00	.60
380	Tuck Stainback	2.00	1.00	.60
381	Chet Morgan	2.00	1.00	.60
382	Johnny Lipon	2.00	1.00	.60
383	Paul Richards	2.00	1.00	.60
384	Johnny Gorsica	2.00	1.00	.60
385	Ray Hayworth	2.00	1.00	.60
386	Jimmy Bloodworth	2.00	1.00	.60
387	Gene Desautels	2.00	1.00	.60
388	Jo Jo White	2.00	1.00	.60
389	Boots Poffenberger	2.00	1.00	.60
390	Barney McCosky	2.00	1.00	.60
391	Dick Wakefield	2.00	1.00	.60
392	Johnny Groth	2.00	1.00	.60
393	Steve Souchock	2.00	1.00	.60
394	George Vico	2.00	1.00	.60
395	Hal Newhouser	2.00	1.00	.60
396	Ray Herbert	2.00	1.00	.60
397	Jim Bunning	2.00	1.00	.60
398	Frank Lary	2.00	1.00	.60
399	Harvey Kuenn	2.00	1.00	.60
400	Eddie Mathews	3.00	1.50	.90

1911 Diamond Gum Pins (PE2)

The World's Champion Philadelphia A's are well represented and specially marked in this series of small 1" diameter pins. The sepia-toned center portion of the pin has a player portrait photo with his last name, team and league in white at left and right. Around that is a metallic blue border with a white inscription; either "World's Champions" on the A's players, or "Free with Diamond Gum" on the other players.

		NM	EX	VG
Complete Set (31):		30,000	15,000	9,000
Common Player:		500.00	250.00	150.00
(1)	Babe Adams	500.00	250.00	150.00
(2)	Home Run Baker	1,200	600.00	360.00
(3)	Chief Bender	1,200	600.00	360.00
(4)	Mordecai Brown	1,200	600.00	360.00
(5)	Donie Bush	500.00	250.00	150.00
(6)	Bill Carrigan	500.00	250.00	150.00
(7)	Frank Chance	1,200	600.00	360.00
(8)	Hal Chase	800.00	400.00	240.00
(9)	Ty Cobb	3,000	1,500	900.00
(10)	Eddie Collins	1,200	600.00	360.00
(11)	George Davis	500.00	250.00	150.00
(12)	Red Dooin	500.00	250.00	150.00
(13)	Larry Doyle	500.00	250.00	150.00
(14)	Johnny Evers	1,200	600.00	360.00
(15)	Miller Huggins	1,200	600.00	360.00
(16)	Hughie Jennings	1,200	600.00	360.00
(17)	Nap Lajoie	1,200	600.00	360.00
(18)	Harry Lord	500.00	250.00	150.00
(19)	Christy Mathewson	2,000	1,000	600.00
(20)	Dots Miller	500.00	250.00	150.00
(21)	George Mullen (Mullin)	500.00	250.00	150.00
(22)	Danny Murphy	500.00	250.00	150.00
(23)	Orval Overall	500.00	250.00	150.00
(24)	Eddie Plank	1,250	625.00	375.00
(25)	Ryan (Rochester)	500.00	250.00	150.00
(26)	Jimmie Savage (Rochester)	500.00	250.00	150.00
(27)	Hack Simmons	500.00	250.00	150.00
(28)	Ira Thomas	500.00	250.00	150.00
(29)	Joe Tinker	1,200	600.00	360.00
(30)	Honus Wagner	2,500	1,250	750.00
(31)	Cy Young	2,000	1,000	600.00

1934 Diamond Matchbooks - Silver Border

During much of the Great Depression, the hobby of matchbook collecting swept the country. Generally selling at two for a penny, the matchbooks began to feature photos and artwork to attract buyers. In the late 1930s, several series of sports subjects were issued by Diamond Match Co., of New York City. The first issue was a set of 200 baseball players known to collectors as "silver border" for the color of the photo frame on of the approximately 1-1/2" x 4-1/8" (open) matchbooks. Player portrait or posed photos are printed in sepia on front, and can be found bordered in either red, green, blue or orange (though it is unclear whether all players can actually be found in the red version), theoretically creating an 800-piece color variation set. The player's name and team are printed on the "saddle" and there is a career summary on back, along with a design of glove, ball and bats. Matchbooks are commonly collected with the matches removed and the striker at back-bottom intact. Pieces without the striker are valued at 50 percent of these listed prices. Complete covers with matches bring a premium of 2-3X. The players are listed here alphabetically.

		NM	EX	VG
Complete Set (200):		4,500	2,250	1,350
Common Player:		20.00	10.00	6.00
(1)	Earl Adams	20.00	10.00	6.00
(2)	Ethan Allen	20.00	10.00	6.00
(3)	Eldon L. Auker	20.00	10.00	6.00
(4)	Delmar David Baker	20.00	10.00	6.00
(5)	Richard "Dick" Bartell	20.00	10.00	6.00
(6)	Walter Beck	20.00	10.00	6.00
(7)	Herman Bell	20.00	10.00	6.00
(8)	Ray Benge	20.00	10.00	6.00
(9)	Larry J. Benton	20.00	10.00	6.00
(10)	Louis W. Berger	20.00	10.00	6.00
(11)	Walter "Wally" Berger	20.00	10.00	6.00
(12)	Ray Berres	20.00	10.00	6.00
(13)	Charlie Berry	20.00	10.00	6.00
(14)	Walter M. "Huck" Betts	20.00	10.00	6.00
(15)	Ralph Birkofer	20.00	10.00	6.00
(16)	George F. Blaeholder	20.00	10.00	6.00
(17)	Jim Bottomley	40.00	20.00	12.00
(18a)	Ralph Boyle (Photo actually Virgil Davis, white cap.)	20.00	10.00	6.00
(18b)	Ralph Boyle (Correct photo, cark cap.)	20.00	10.00	6.00
(19)	Ed Brandt	20.00	10.00	6.00
(20)	Don Brennan	20.00	10.00	6.00
(21)	Irving (Jack) Burns	20.00	10.00	6.00
(22)	Guy "Joe" Bush	20.00	10.00	6.00
(23)	Adolph Camilli	20.00	10.00	6.00
(24)	Ben Cantwell	20.00	10.00	6.00
(25)	Tex Carleton	20.00	10.00	6.00
(26)	Owen Carroll	20.00	10.00	6.00
(27)	Louis Chiozza	20.00	10.00	6.00
(28)	Watson Clark	20.00	10.00	6.00
(29)	James A. Collins	20.00	10.00	6.00
(30)	Phil Collins	20.00	10.00	6.00
(31)	Edward J. Connolly	20.00	10.00	6.00
(32)	Raymond F. Coombs	20.00	10.00	6.00
(33)	Roger Cramer	20.00	10.00	6.00
(34)	Clifford Crawford	20.00	10.00	6.00
(35)	Hugh M. Critz	20.00	10.00	6.00
(36)	Alvin Crowder	20.00	10.00	6.00
(37)	Tony Cuccinello	20.00	10.00	6.00
(38)	Hazen "Kiki" Cuyler	40.00	20.00	12.00
(39)	Virgil Davis	20.00	10.00	6.00
(40)	Jerome "Dizzy" Dean	80.00	40.00	24.00
(41)	Paul Dean	35.00	17.50	10.50
(42)	Edward Delker	20.00	10.00	6.00
(43)	Paul Derringer	20.00	10.00	6.00
(44)	Eugene DeSautel	20.00	10.00	6.00
(45)	William J. Dietrich	20.00	10.00	6.00
(46)	Frank F. Doljack	20.00	10.00	6.00
(47)	Edward F. Durham	20.00	10.00	6.00
(48)	Leo Durocher	40.00	20.00	12.00
(49)	Jim Elliott	20.00	10.00	6.00
(50)	Charles D. English	20.00	10.00	6.00
(51)	Elwood G. English	20.00	10.00	6.00
(52)	Richard Ferrell	40.00	20.00	12.00
(53)	Wesley Ferrell (EXISTENCE DOUBTED)			
(54)	Charles W. Fischer	20.00	10.00	6.00
(55)	Freddy Fitzsimmons	20.00	10.00	6.00
(56)	Lew Fonseca	20.00	10.00	6.00
(57)	Fred Frankhouse	20.00	10.00	6.00
(58)	John Frederick	20.00	10.00	6.00
(59)	Benny Frey (Reds)	20.00	10.00	6.00
(60)	Linus Frey (Dodgers)	20.00	10.00	6.00
(61)	Frankie Frisch	45.00	22.00	13.50
(62)	Chick Fullis	20.00	10.00	6.00
(63)	August Galan	20.00	10.00	6.00
(64)	Milton Galatzer	120.00	60.00	36.00
(65)	Dennis W. Galehouse	20.00	10.00	6.00
(66)	Milton Gaston	20.00	10.00	6.00
(67)	Chas. Gehringer	45.00	22.00	13.50
(68)	Edward P. Gharrity	20.00	10.00	6.00
(69)	George Gibson	20.00	10.00	6.00
(70)	Isidore Goldstein	250.00	125.00	75.00
(71)	"Hank" Gowdy	20.00	10.00	6.00
(72)	Earl Grace	20.00	10.00	6.00
(73)	Chas. Grimm (Fielding)	20.00	10.00	6.00
(74)	Chas. Grimm (Portrait)	20.00	10.00	6.00
(75)	Frank T. Grube	20.00	10.00	6.00
(76)	Richard Gyselman	20.00	10.00	6.00
(77)	Stanley C. Hack	25.00	12.50	7.50
(78)	Irving Hadley	20.00	10.00	6.00
(79)	Charles "Chick" Hafey	40.00	20.00	12.00
(80)	Harold A. Haid	20.00	10.00	6.00
(81)	Jesse Haines	40.00	20.00	12.00
(82)	Odell A. Hale	20.00	10.00	6.00
(83)	Bill Hallahan	20.00	10.00	6.00
(84)	Luke D. Hamlin	20.00	10.00	6.00
(85)	Roy Hansen	20.00	10.00	6.00
(86)	Melvin Harder	20.00	10.00	6.00
(87)	William M. Harris	20.00	10.00	6.00
(88)	Gabby Hartnett	40.00	20.00	12.00

(89)	Harvey Hendrick	20.00	10.00	6.00
(90)	Floyd "Babe" Herman	25.00	12.50	7.50
(91)	William Herman	40.00	20.00	12.00
(92)	J. Francis Hogan	20.00	10.00	6.00
(93)	Elon Hogsett	20.00	10.00	6.00
(94)	Waite Hoyt	40.00	20.00	12.00
(95)	Carl Hubbell	50.00	25.00	15.00
(96)	Silas K. Johnson	20.00	10.00	6.00
(97)	Sylvester Johnson	20.00	10.00	6.00
(98)	Roy M. Joiner	20.00	10.00	6.00
(99)	Baxter Jordan	20.00	10.00	6.00
(100)	Arndt Jorgens	20.00	10.00	6.00
(101)	William F. Jurges	20.00	10.00	6.00
(102)	Vernon Kennedy	20.00	10.00	6.00
(103)	John F. Kerr	20.00	10.00	6.00
(104)	Charles "Chuck" Klein	40.00	20.00	12.00
(105)	Theodore Kleinhans	20.00	10.00	6.00
(106)	Bill Klem (Umpire)	125.00	65.00	35.00
(107)	Robert G. Kline	20.00	10.00	6.00
(108)	William Knickerbocker	20.00	10.00	6.00
(109)	Jack H. Knott	20.00	10.00	6.00
(110)	Mark Koenig	20.00	10.00	6.00
(111)	William Lawrence	20.00	10.00	6.00
(112)	Thornton S. Lee	20.00	10.00	6.00
(113)	Wm. C. "Bill" Lee	20.00	10.00	6.00
(114)	Emil Leonard	20.00	10.00	6.00
(115)	Ernest Lombardi	40.00	20.00	12.00
(116)	Alfonso Lopez	40.00	20.00	12.00
(117)	Red Lucas	20.00	10.00	6.00
(118)	Ted Lyons	40.00	20.00	12.00
(119)	Daniel MacFayden	20.00	10.00	6.00
(120)	Ed. Majeski	20.00	10.00	6.00
(121)	Leroy Mahaffey	20.00	10.00	6.00
(122)	Pat Malone	20.00	10.00	6.00
(123)	Leo Mangum	20.00	10.00	6.00
(124)	Rabbit Maranville	40.00	20.00	12.00
(125)	Charles K. Marrow	20.00	10.00	6.00
(126)	William McKechnie	40.00	20.00	12.00
(127)	Justin McLaughlin	20.00	10.00	6.00
(128)	Marty McManus	20.00	10.00	6.00
(129)	Eric McNair	20.00	10.00	6.00
(130)	Joe Medwick	40.00	20.00	12.00
(131)	Jim Mooney	20.00	10.00	6.00
(132)	Joe Moore	20.00	10.00	6.00
(133)	John Moore	20.00	10.00	6.00
(134)	Randy Moore	20.00	10.00	6.00
(135)	Joe Morrissey	20.00	10.00	6.00
(136)	Joseph Mowrey	20.00	10.00	6.00
(137)	Fred W. Muller	20.00	10.00	6.00
(138)	Van Mungo	25.00	12.50	7.50
(139)	Glenn Myatt	20.00	10.00	6.00
(140a)	Lynn Nelson (Photo actually Eugene DeSautel, no "C" on cap.)	20.00	10.00	6.00
(140b)	Lynn Nelson (Correct photo, "C" on cap.)	20.00	10.00	6.00
(141)	Henry Oana	60.00	30.00	18.00
(142)	Lefty O'Doul	35.00	17.50	10.50
(143)	Robert O'Farrell	20.00	10.00	6.00
(144)	Ernest Orsatti	20.00	10.00	6.00
(145)	Fritz R. Ostermueller	20.00	10.00	6.00
(146)	Melvin Ott	45.00	22.00	13.50
(147)	Roy Parmelee	20.00	10.00	6.00
(148)	Ralph Perkins	20.00	10.00	6.00
(149)	Frank Pytlak	20.00	10.00	6.00
(150)	Ernest C. Quigley (Umpire)	45.00	22.00	13.50
(151)	George Rensa	20.00	10.00	6.00
(152)	Harry Rice	20.00	10.00	6.00
(153)	Walter Roettger	20.00	10.00	6.00
(154)	William G. Rogell	20.00	10.00	6.00
(155)	Edwin A. Rommel	20.00	10.00	6.00
(156)	Charlie Root	20.00	10.00	6.00
(157)	John Rothrock	20.00	10.00	6.00
(158)	Jack Russell	20.00	10.00	6.00
(159)	Blondy Ryan	20.00	10.00	6.00
(160)	Alexander (Al) Schacht	35.00	17.50	10.50
(161)	Wesley Schultmerick	20.00	10.00	6.00
(162)	Truett B. Sewell	20.00	10.00	6.00
(163)	Gordon Slade	20.00	10.00	6.00
(164)	Bob Smith	20.00	10.00	6.00
(165)	Julius J. Solters	20.00	10.00	6.00
(166)	Glenn Spencer	20.00	10.00	6.00
(167)	Al Spohrer	20.00	10.00	6.00
(168)	George Stainback	20.00	10.00	6.00
(169)	Albert "Dolly" Stark (Umpire)	40.00	20.00	12.00
(170)	Casey Stengel	50.00	25.00	15.00
(171)	Riggs Stephenson	20.00	10.00	6.00
(172)	Walter C. Stewart	20.00	10.00	6.00
(173)	Lin Storti	20.00	10.00	6.00
(174)	Allyn (Fish Hook) Stout	20.00	10.00	6.00
(175)	Joe Stripp	20.00	10.00	6.00
(176)	Gus Suhr	20.00	10.00	6.00
(177)	Billy Sullivan, Jr.	20.00	10.00	6.00
(178)	Benny Tate	20.00	10.00	6.00
(179)	Danny Taylor	20.00	10.00	6.00
(180)	Tommy Thevenow	20.00	10.00	6.00
(181)	Bud Tinning	20.00	10.00	6.00
(182)	Cecil Travis	20.00	10.00	6.00
(183)	Forest F. Twogood	20.00	10.00	6.00
(184)	Bill Urbanski	20.00	10.00	6.00
(185)	Dazzy Vance	40.00	20.00	12.00
(186)	Arthur Veltman (SP)	100.00	50.00	30.00
(187)	John L. Vergez	20.00	10.00	6.00
(188)	Gerald (Jerry) Walker	20.00	10.00	6.00
(189)	William H. Walker	20.00	10.00	6.00
(190)	Lloyd Waner	40.00	20.00	12.00
(191)	Paul Waner	40.00	20.00	12.00
(192)	Lon Warnecke	20.00	10.00	6.00
(193)	Harold B. Warstler	20.00	10.00	6.00
(194)	Bill Werber	20.00	10.00	6.00
(195)	Joyner White	20.00	10.00	6.00
(196)	Arthur Whitney	20.00	10.00	6.00
(197)	James Wilson	20.00	10.00	6.00
(198)	Lewis (Hack) Wilson	40.00	20.00	12.00
(199)	Ralph L. Winegarner	20.00	10.00	6.00
(200)	Thomas Zachary	20.00	10.00	6.00

1935 Diamond Matchbooks - Black Border

Only 24 players were issued in the 1935 Diamond Match-book baseball series. Similar in design to the 1934 issue, these 1-1/2" x 4-1/8" matchbooks have sepia player portrait photos on front, framed in either red, green or blue. The overall borders of the cover are black. Backs of the 1935 issue feature a career summary overprinted on a silhouetted batting figure. The "sad-dle" has the player name and team superimposed on a base-ball. These matchbooks are commonly collected with the matches removed and the striker at back-bottom intact. Pieces without the striker are valued at 50 percent of these listed prices. Complete covers with matches bring a premium of 2-3X. The players are listed here alphabetically.

		NM	EX	VG
Complete Set (24):		850.00	425.00	250.00
Common Player:		25.00	12.50	7.50
(1)	Ethan Allen (Red)	25.00	12.50	7.50
(2)	Walter Berger (Red)	25.00	12.50	7.50
(3)	Tommy Carey (Blue)	25.00	12.50	7.50
(4)	Louis Chiozza (Blue)	25.00	12.50	7.50
(5)	Jerome (Dizzy) Dean (Green)	65.00	32.50	20.00
(6)	Frankie Frisch (Red)	50.00	25.00	15.00
(7)	Charles Grimm (Blue)	25.00	12.50	7.50
(8)	Charles Hafey (Red)	40.00	20.00	12.00
(9)	J. Francis Hogan (Red)	25.00	12.50	7.50
(10)	Carl Hubbell (Green)	50.00	25.00	15.00
(11)	Charles Klein (Green)	40.00	20.00	12.00
(12)	Ernest Lombardi (Blue)	40.00	20.00	12.00
(13)	Alfonso Lopez (Blue)	40.00	20.00	12.00
(14)	Rabbit Maranville (Green)	40.00	20.00	12.00
(15)	Joe Moore (Red)	25.00	12.50	7.50
(16)	Van Mungo (Green)	25.00	12.50	7.50
(17)	Melvin (Mel) Ott (Blue)	50.00	25.00	15.00
(18)	Gordon Slade (Green)	25.00	12.50	7.50
(19)	Casey Stengel (Green)	50.00	25.00	15.00
(20)	Tommy Thevenow (Red)	25.00	12.50	7.50
(21)	Lloyd Waner (Red)	40.00	20.00	12.00
(22)	Paul Waner (Green)	50.00	25.00	15.00
(23)	Lon Warnecke (Blue)	25.00	12.50	7.50
(24)	James Wilson (Blue)	25.00	12.50	7.50

1935-36 Diamond Matchbooks

By the career summaries on back of these covers it is evi-dent this series was issued over a two-year period. Measuring about 1-1/2" x 4-1/8", the fronts have posed player photos printed in sepia. Borders can be found in red, green or blue, and it is believed that most, if not all, players can be found in those three color varieties. Matchbooks in this series do not have the team name on back beneath the player name, as is the case on later series. Collectors generally prefer match-books to be complete with striker surface on bottom-back, though with matches removed. Values shown should be halved for covers without strikers. Complete with matches, covers will sell for a 2-3X premium over the values shown.

		NM	EX	VG
Complete Set (156):		3,500	1,750	1,000
Common Player:		20.00	10.00	6.00
(1)	Ethan Allen	20.00	10.00	6.00
(2)	Melo Almada	30.00	15.00	9.00
(3)	Eldon Auker	20.00	10.00	6.00
(4)	Dick Bartell	20.00	10.00	6.00
(5)	Aloysius Bejma	20.00	10.00	6.00
(6)	Ollie Bejma	20.00	10.00	6.00
(7)	Roy Chester Bell	20.00	10.00	6.00
(8)	Louis Berger	20.00	10.00	6.00
(9)	Walter Berger	20.00	10.00	6.00
(10)	Ralph Birkofer	20.00	10.00	6.00
(11)	Max Bishop	20.00	10.00	6.00
(12)	George Blaeholder	20.00	10.00	6.00
(13)	Henry (Zeke) Bonura	20.00	10.00	6.00
(14)	Jim Bottomley	35.00	17.50	10.50
(15)	Ed Brandt	20.00	10.00	6.00
(16)	Don Brennan	20.00	10.00	6.00
(17)	Lloyd Brown	20.00	10.00	6.00
(18)	Walter G. Brown	20.00	10.00	6.00
(19)	Claiborne Bryant	20.00	10.00	6.00
(20)	Jim Bucher	20.00	10.00	6.00
(21)	John Burnett	20.00	10.00	6.00
(22)	Irving Burns	20.00	10.00	6.00
(23)	Merritt Cain	20.00	10.00	6.00
(24)	Ben Cantwell	20.00	10.00	6.00
(25)	Tommy Carey	20.00	10.00	6.00
(26)	Tex Carleton	20.00	10.00	6.00
(27)	Joseph Cascarella	20.00	10.00	6.00
(28)	Thomas H. Casey	20.00	10.00	6.00
(29)	George Caster	20.00	10.00	6.00
(30)	Phil Cavarretta	20.00	10.00	6.00
(31)	Louis Chiozza	20.00	10.00	6.00
(32)	Edward Cihocki	20.00	10.00	6.00
(33)	Herman E. Clifton	20.00	10.00	6.00
(34)	Richard Coffman	20.00	10.00	6.00
(35)	Edward P. Coleman	20.00	10.00	6.00
(36)	James A. Collins	20.00	10.00	6.00
(37)	John Conlan	40.00	20.00	12.00
(38)	Roger Cramer	20.00	10.00	6.00
(39)	Hugh M. Critz	20.00	10.00	6.00
(40)	Alvin Crowder	20.00	10.00	6.00
(41)	Tony Cuccinello	20.00	10.00	6.00
(42)	Hazen "Kiki" Cuyler	35.00	17.50	10.50
(43)	Virgil Davis	20.00	10.00	6.00
(44)	Jerome Dean	75.00	37.00	22.00
(45)	Paul Derringer	20.00	10.00	6.00
(46)	James DeShong	20.00	10.00	6.00
(47)	William Dietrich	20.00	10.00	6.00
(48)	Leo Durocher	35.00	17.50	10.50
(49)	George Earnshaw	20.00	10.00	6.00
(50)	Elwood English	20.00	10.00	6.00
(51)	Louis Finney	20.00	10.00	6.00
(52)	Charles Fischer	20.00	10.00	6.00
(53)	Freddy Fitzsimmons	20.00	10.00	6.00
(54)	Benny Frey	20.00	10.00	6.00
(55)	Linus B. Frey	20.00	10.00	6.00
(56)	Frankie Frisch	40.00	20.00	12.00
(57)	August Galan	20.00	10.00	6.00
(58)	Milton Galatzer	20.00	10.00	6.00
(59)	Dennis Galehouse	20.00	10.00	6.00
(60)	Debs Garms	20.00	10.00	6.00
(61)	Angelo J. Giuliani	20.00	10.00	6.00
(62)	Earl Grace	20.00	10.00	6.00
(63)	Charles Grimm	20.00	10.00	6.00
(64)	Frank Grube	20.00	10.00	6.00
(65)	Stanley Hack	25.00	12.50	7.50
(66)	Irving "Bump" Hadley	20.00	10.00	6.00
(67)	Odell Hale	20.00	10.00	6.00
(68)	Bill Hallahan	20.00	10.00	6.00
(69)	Roy Hansen	20.00	10.00	6.00
(70)	Melvin Harder	20.00	10.00	6.00
(71)	Charles Hartnett	35.00	17.50	10.50
(72)	"Gabby" Hartnett	35.00	17.50	10.50
(73)	Clyde Hatter	20.00	10.00	6.00
(74)	Raymond Hayworth	20.00	10.00	6.00
(75)	Raymond Hayworth (W/chest protector.)	20.00	10.00	6.00
(76)	William Herman	35.00	17.50	10.50
(77)	Gordon Hinkle	20.00	10.00	6.00
(78)	George Hockette	20.00	10.00	6.00
(79)	James Holbrook	20.00	10.00	6.00
(80)	Alex Hooks	20.00	10.00	6.00
(81)	Waite Hoyt	35.00	17.50	10.50
(82)	Carl Hubbell	40.00	20.00	12.00
(83)	Roy M. Joiner	20.00	10.00	6.00
(84)	Sam Jones	20.00	10.00	6.00
(85)	Baxter Jordan	20.00	10.00	6.00
(86)	Arndt Jorgens	20.00	10.00	6.00
(87)	William F. Jurges	20.00	10.00	6.00
(88)	William Kamm	20.00	10.00	6.00
(89)	Vernon Kennedy	20.00	10.00	6.00
(90)	John Kerr	20.00	10.00	6.00
(91)	Charles Klein	40.00	20.00	12.00
(92)	Ted Kleinhans	20.00	10.00	6.00
(93)	Wm. Knickerbocker (Thighs-up.)	20.00	10.00	6.00
(94)	Wm. Knickerbocker (Waist-up.)	20.00	10.00	6.00
(95)	Jack Knott	20.00	10.00	6.00
(96)	Mark Koenig	20.00	10.00	6.00
(97)	Fabian L. Kowalik	20.00	10.00	6.00
(98)	Ralph Kress	20.00	10.00	6.00
(99)	Wm. C. "Bill" Lee	20.00	10.00	6.00
(100)	Louis Legett	20.00	10.00	6.00
(101)	Emil "Dutch" Leonard	20.00	10.00	6.00
(102)	Fred Lindstrom	35.00	17.50	10.50
(103)	Edward Linke (Pole in background.)	20.00	10.00	6.00
(104)	Edward Linke (No pole.)	20.00	10.00	6.00
(105)	Ernest Lombardi	35.00	17.50	10.50
(106)	Al Lopez	35.00	17.50	10.50
(107)	John Marcum	20.00	10.00	6.00
(108)	William McKechnie	35.00	17.50	10.50
(109)	Eric McNair	20.00	10.00	6.00
(110)	Joe Medwick	35.00	17.50	10.50
(111)	Oscar Melillo	20.00	10.00	6.00
(112)	John Michaels	20.00	10.00	6.00
(113)	Joe Moore	20.00	10.00	6.00
(114)	John Moore	20.00	10.00	6.00
(115)	Wallace Moses	20.00	10.00	6.00
(116)	Joseph Milligan	20.00	10.00	6.00
(117)	Van Mungo	25.00	12.50	7.50
(118)	Glenn Myatt	20.00	10.00	6.00
(119)	James O'Dea	20.00	10.00	6.00
(120)	Ernest Orsatti	20.00	10.00	6.00
(121)	Fred Ostermueller	20.00	10.00	6.00
(122)	Melvin "Mel" Ott	40.00	20.00	12.00
(123)	LeRoy Parmelee	20.00	10.00	6.00
(124)	Monte Pearson	20.00	10.00	6.00
(125)	Raymond Pepper	20.00	10.00	6.00
(126)	Raymond Phelps	20.00	10.00	6.00
(127)	George Pipgras	20.00	10.00	6.00
(128)	Frank Pytlak	20.00	10.00	6.00
(129)	Gordon Rhodes	20.00	10.00	6.00
(130)	Charlie Root	20.00	10.00	6.00
(131)	John Rothrock	20.00	10.00	6.00
(132)	Herold "Muddy" Ruel	20.00	10.00	6.00
(133)	Jack Saltzgaver	20.00	10.00	6.00
(134)	Fred Schulte	20.00	10.00	6.00
(135)	George Selkirk	20.00	10.00	6.00
(136)	Mervyn Shea	20.00	10.00	6.00
(137)	Al Spohrer	20.00	10.00	6.00
(138)	George Stainback	20.00	10.00	6.00
(139)	Casey Stengel	40.00	20.00	12.00
(140)	Walter Stephenson	20.00	10.00	6.00
(141)	Lee Stine	20.00	10.00	6.00
(142)	John Stone	20.00	10.00	6.00
(143)	Gus Suhr	20.00	10.00	6.00
(144)	Tommy Thevenow	20.00	10.00	6.00
(145)	Fay Thomas	20.00	10.00	6.00
(146)	Leslie Tietje	20.00	10.00	6.00
(147)	Bill Urbanski	20.00	10.00	6.00
(148)	William H. Walker	20.00	10.00	6.00
(149)	Lloyd Waner	40.00	20.00	12.00
(150)	Paul Waner	40.00	20.00	12.00
(151)	Lon Warnecke	20.00	10.00	6.00
(152)	Harold Warstler	20.00	10.00	6.00
(153)	Bill Werber	20.00	10.00	6.00
(154)	Vernon Wiltshere	20.00	10.00	6.00
(155)	James Wilson	20.00	10.00	6.00
(156)	Ralph Winegarner	20.00	10.00	6.00

1936 Diamond Matchbooks - Team on Back

This is the smallest series of baseball player matchbooks, with only 13 subjects, each found with borders of red, green or blue. Player poses on front are printed in sepia (except one variation of Grimm that is in black-and-white). This series can be differentiated from contemporary series by the appearance of the player's team name on back, beneath his name. Backs have a career summary. About 1-1/2" x 4-1/8", these match-books are commonly collected with the matches removed and the striker at back bottom intact. Pieces without the striker are valued at 50 percent of these listed prices. Complete covers with matches bring a premium of 2-3X. The players are listed here alphabetically.

		NM	EX	VG
Complete Set (13):		350.00	175.00	100.00
Common Player:				
(1)	Tommy Carey	20.00	10.00	6.00
(2)	Tony Cuccinello	20.00	10.00	6.00
(3)	Freddy Fitzsimmons	20.00	10.00	6.00
(4)	Frank Frisch	45.00	22.00	13.50
(5a)	Charles Grimm (Home uniform, b/w.)	20.00	10.00	6.00
(5b)	Charlie Grimm (Home uniform, sepia.)	20.00	10.00	6.00
(6)	Charlie Grimm (Road uniform.)	20.00	10.00	6.00
(7)	Carl Hubbell	45.00	22.00	13.50
(8)	Baxter Jordan	20.00	10.00	6.00
(9)	Chuck Klein	45.00	22.00	13.50
(10)	Al Lopez	35.00	17.50	10.50
(11)	Joe Medwick	35.00	17.50	10.50
(12)	Van Lingle Mungo	25.00	12.50	7.50
(13)	Mel Ott	45.00	22.00	13.50

1936 Diamond Matchbooks - Chicago Cubs

This short series of baseball player matchbooks can each be found with borders of red, green or blue. Except for Dean, all photos are portraits, printed in sepia or black-and-white.

Dean and Paul Waner are the only subjects in the set who were not members of the Chicago Cubs. This series can be differentiated from 1935-36 Diamond Matchbooks only by studying the career summary and stats on back. About 1-1/2" x 4-1/8", these matchbooks are commonly collected with the matches removed and the striker at back-bottom intact. Pieces without the striker are valued at 50 percent of these listed prices. Complete covers with matches bring a premium of 2-3X. The players are listed here alphabetically.

		NM	EX	VG
Complete Set (23):		350.00	175.00	100.00
Common Player:		12.50	6.25	3.75
(1)	Claiborne Bryant	12.50	6.25	3.75
(2)	Tex Carleton	12.50	6.25	3.75
(3)	Phil Cavarretta	12.50	6.25	3.75
(4)	James A. Collins	12.50	6.25	3.75
(5)	Curt Davis	12.50	6.25	3.75
(6)	Jerome "Dizzy" Dean	50.00	25.00	15.00
(7)	Frank Demaree	12.50	6.25	3.75
(8)	Larry French	12.50	6.25	3.75
(9)	Linus R. Frey	12.50	6.25	3.75
(10)	August Galan	12.50	6.25	3.75
(11)	Bob Garbark	12.50	6.25	3.75
(12)	Stanley Hack	15.00	7.50	4.50
(13)	Charles Hartnett	30.00	15.00	9.00
(14)	William Herman	30.00	15.00	9.00
(15)	William F. Jurges	12.50	6.25	3.75
(16)	William C. "Bill" Lee	12.50	6.25	3.75
(17)	Joe Marty	12.50	6.25	3.75
(18)	James K. O'Dea	12.50	6.25	3.75
(19)	LeRoy Parmelee	12.50	6.25	3.75
(20)	Charlie Root	12.50	6.25	3.75
(21)	Clyde Shoun	12.50	6.25	3.75
(22)	George Stainback	12.50	6.25	3.75
(23)	Paul Waner	40.00	20.00	12.00

1889 Diamond S Cigars Boston N.L.

(See 1889 Number 7 Cigars for checklist and value information.)

1934-36 Diamond Stars (R327)

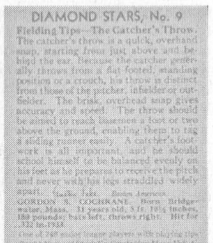

Issued from 1934-36, the Diamond Stars set (ACC designation R327) consists of 108 cards. Produced by National Chicle, the cards measure 2-3/8" x 2-7/8" and are color art renderings of actual photographs on art deco backgrounds. The year of issue can usually be determined by the player's statistics found on the reverse of the card. Backs also feature either a player biography or a playing tip. Some cards can be found with either green or blue printing on the backs. The complete set price does not include the higher priced variations which make up the 170-card "master" set.

		NM	EX	VG
Complete Set (108):		22,500	9,000	4,000
Complete Set (170):		35,000	14,000	6,250
Common Player (1-84):		100.00	35.00	20.00
Common Player (85-96):		200.00	85.00	45.00
Common Player (97-108):		500.00	245.00	120.00
1a	"Lefty" Grove (1934 green back)	5,040	770.00	245.00
1b	"Lefty" Grove (1935 green back)	5,040	770.00	245.00
2a	Al Simmons (1934 green back)	840.00	225.00	155.00
2b	Al Simmons (1935 green back)	840.00	225.00	155.00
2c	Al Simmons (1936 blue back)	910.00	365.00	180.00
3a	"Rabbit" Maranville (1934 green back)	455.00	180.00	90.00
3b	"Rabbit" Maranville (1935 green back)	455.00	180.00	90.00
4a	"Buddy" Myer (1934 green back)	100.00	35.00	20.00
4b	"Buddy" Myer (1935 green back)	100.00	35.00	20.00
4c	"Buddy" Myer (1936 blue back)	105.00	45.00	20.00
5a	Tom Bridges (1934 green back)	100.00	35.00	20.00
5b	Tom Bridges (1935 green back)	100.00	35.00	20.00
5c	Tom Bridges (1936 blue back)	105.00	45.00	20.00
6a	Max Bishop (1934 green back)	100.00	35.00	20.00
6b	Max Bishop (1935 green back)	100.00	35.00	20.00
7a	Lew Fonseca (1934 green back)	100.00	35.00	20.00
7b	Lew Fonseca (1935 green back)	100.00	35.00	20.00
8a	Joe Vosmik (1934 green back)	100.00	35.00	20.00
8b	Joe Vosmik (1935 green back)	100.00	35.00	20.00
8c	Joe Vosmik (1936 blue back)	105.00	45.00	20.00
9a	"Mickey" Cochrane (1934 green back)	455.00	180.00	90.00
9b	"Mickey" Cochrane (1935 green back)	455.00	180.00	90.00
9c	"Mickey" Cochrane (1936 blue back)	525.00	210.00	105.00
10a	Roy Mahaffey (1934 green back)	100.00	35.00	20.00
10b	Roy Mahaffey (1935 green back)	100.00	35.00	20.00
10c	Roy Mahaffey (1936 blue back)	105.00	45.00	20.00
11a	Bill Dickey (1934 green back)	525.00	210.00	105.00
11b	Bill Dickey (1935 green back)	525.00	210.00	105.00
12a	Dixie Walker (1934 green back)	100.00	35.00	20.00
12b	Dixie Walker (1935 green back)	100.00	35.00	20.00
12c	Dixie Walker (1936 blue back)	105.00	45.00	20.00
13a	George Blaeholder (1934 green back)	100.00	35.00	20.00
13b	George Blaeholder (1935 green back)	100.00	35.00	20.00
14a	Bill Terry (1934 green back)	455.00	180.00	90.00
14b	Bill Terry (1935 green back)	455.00	180.00	90.00
15a	Dick Bartell (1934 green back)	100.00	35.00	20.00
15b	Dick Bartell (1935 green back)	100.00	35.00	20.00
16a	Lloyd Waner (1934 green back)	455.00	180.00	90.00
16b	Lloyd Waner (1935 green back)	455.00	180.00	90.00
16c	Lloyd Waner (1936 blue back)	560.00	225.00	115.00
17a	Frankie Frisch (1934 green back)	455.00	180.00	90.00
17b	Frankie Frisch (1935 green back)	455.00	180.00	90.00
18a	"Chick" Hafey (1934 green back)	455.00	180.00	90.00
18b	"Chick" Hafey (1935 green back)	455.00	180.00	90.00
19a	Van Mungo (1934 green back)	315.00	125.00	65.00
19b	Van Mungo (1935 green back)	315.00	125.00	65.00
20a	"Shanty" Hogan (1934 green back)	100.00	35.00	20.00
20b	"Shanty" Hogan (1935 green back)	100.00	35.00	20.00
21a	Johnny Vergez (1934 green back)	100.00	35.00	20.00
21b	Johnny Vergez (1935 green back)	100.00	35.00	20.00
22a	Jimmy Wilson (1934 green back)	100.00	35.00	20.00
22b	Jimmy Wilson (1935 green back)	100.00	35.00	20.00
22c	Jimmy Wilson (1936 blue back)	105.00	45.00	20.00
23a	Bill Hallahan (1934 green back)	100.00	35.00	20.00
23b	Bill Hallahan (1935 green back)	100.00	35.00	20.00
24a	"Sparky" Adams (1934 green back)	100.00	35.00	20.00
24b	"Sparky" Adams (1935 green back)	100.00	35.00	20.00
25	Walter Berger	100.00	35.00	20.00
26a	"Pepper" Martin (1935 green back)	160.00	65.00	30.00
26b	"Pepper" Martin (1936 blue back)	175.00	70.00	35.00
27	"Pie" Traynor	200.00	85.00	45.00
28	"Al" Lopez	200.00	85.00	45.00
29	Robert Rolfe	100.00	35.00	20.00
30a	"Heinie" Manush (1935 green back)	200.00	85.00	45.00
30b	"Heinie" Manush (1936 blue back)	245.00	100.00	50.00
31a	"Kiki" Cuyler (1935 green back)	200.00	85.00	45.00
31b	"Kiki" Cuyler (1936 blue back)	245.00	100.00	50.00
32	Sam Rice	200.00	85.00	45.00
33	"Schoolboy" Rowe	125.00	50.00	20.00
34	Stanley Hack	125.00	50.00	20.00
35	Earle Averill	200.00	85.00	45.00
36a	Earnie Lombardi	560.00	225.00	115.00
36b	Ernie Lombardi	245.00	100.00	50.00
37	"Billie" Urbanski	100.00	35.00	20.00
38	Ben Chapman	100.00	35.00	20.00
39	Carl Hubbell	295.00	120.00	55.00
40	"Blondy" Ryan	100.00	35.00	20.00
41	Harvey Hendrick	100.00	35.00	20.00
42	Jimmy Dykes	100.00	35.00	20.00
43	Ted Lyons	200.00	85.00	45.00
44	Rogers Hornsby	525.00	210.00	105.00
45	"Jo Jo" White	100.00	35.00	20.00
46	"Red" Lucas	100.00	35.00	20.00
47	Cliff Bolton	100.00	35.00	20.00
48	"Rick" Ferrell	200.00	85.00	45.00
49	"Buck" Jordan	100.00	35.00	20.00
50	"Mel" Ott	310.00	120.00	55.00
51	John Whitehead	100.00	35.00	20.00
52	George Stainback	100.00	35.00	20.00
53	Oscar Melillo	100.00	35.00	20.00
54a	"Hank" Greenburg (Greenberg)	1,260	505.00	250.00
54b	"Hank" Greenberg	805.00	325.00	160.00
55	Tony Cuccinello	100.00	35.00	20.00
56	"Gus" Suhr	100.00	35.00	20.00
57	Cy Blanton	100.00	35.00	20.00
58	Glenn Myatt	100.00	35.00	20.00
59	Jim Bottomley	200.00	85.00	45.00
60	Charley "Red" Ruffing	200.00	85.00	45.00
61	"Billie" Werber	100.00	35.00	20.00
62	Fred M. Frankhouse	100.00	35.00	20.00
63	"Stonewall" Jackson	200.00	85.00	45.00
64	Jimmie Foxx	560.00	225.00	115.00
65	"Zeke" Bonura	100.00	35.00	20.00
66	"Ducky" Medwick	200.00	85.00	45.00
67	Marvin Owen	100.00	35.00	20.00
68	"Sam" Leslie	100.00	35.00	20.00
69	Earl Grace	100.00	35.00	20.00
70	"Hal" Trosky	100.00	35.00	20.00
71	"Ossie" Bluege	100.00	35.00	20.00
72	"Tony" Piet	100.00	35.00	20.00
73a	"Fritz" Ostermueller (1935 green back)	100.00	35.00	20.00
73b	"Fritz" Ostermueller (1935 blue back)	100.00	35.00	20.00
73c	"Fritz" Ostermueller (1936 blue back)	105.00	45.00	20.00
74a	Tony Lazzeri (1935 green back)	365.00	140.00	70.00
74b	Tony Lazzeri (1935 blue back)	365.00	140.00	70.00
74c	Tony Lazzeri (1936 blue back)	385.00	155.00	77.00
75a	Irving Burns (1935 green back)	100.00	35.00	20.00
75b	Irving Burns (1935 blue back)	100.00	35.00	20.00
75c	Irving Burns (1936 blue back)	105.00	45.00	20.00
76a	Bill Rogell (1935 green back)	100.00	35.00	20.00
76b	Bill Rogell (1935 blue back)	105.00	45.00	20.00
76c	Bill Rogell (1936 blue back)	105.00	45.00	20.00
77a	Charlie Gehringer (1935 green back)	350.00	140.00	70.00
77b	Charlie Gehringer (1935 blue back)	350.00	140.00	70.00
77c	Charlie Gehringer (1936 blue back)	370.00	140.00	70.00
78a	Joe Kuhel (1935 green back)	100.00	35.00	20.00
78b	Joe Kuhel (1935 blue back)	100.00	35.00	20.00
78c	Joe Kuhel (1936 blue back)	105.00	45.00	20.00
79a	Willis Hudlin (1935 green back)	100.00	35.00	20.00
79b	Willis Hudlin (1935 blue back)	100.00	35.00	20.00
79c	Willis Hudlin (1936 blue back)	105.00	45.00	20.00
80a	Louis Chiozza (1935 green back)	100.00	35.00	20.00
80b	Louis Chiozza (1935 green back)	100.00	35.00	20.00
80c	Louis Chiozza (1936 blue back)	105.00	45.00	20.00
81a	Bill DeLancey (1935 green back)	100.00	35.00	20.00
81b	Bill DeLancey (1935 green back)	100.00	35.00	20.00
81c	Bill DeLancey (1936 blue back)	105.00	45.00	20.00
82a	John Babich (1935 green back)	100.00	35.00	20.00
82b	John Babich (1935 blue back)	100.00	35.00	20.00
q2c	John Babich (1936 blue back)	105.00	45.00	20.00
83a	Paul Waner (1935 green back)	200.00	85.00	45.00
83b	Paul Waner (1935 blue back)	200.00	85.00	45.00
83c	Paul Waner (1936 blue back)	225.00	85.00	45.00
84a	Sam Byrd (1935 green back)	100.00	35.00	20.00
84b	Sam Byrd (1935 blue back)	100.00	35.00	20.00
84c	Sam Byrd (1936 blue back)	105.00	45.00	20.00
85	Julius Solters	200.00	85.00	45.00
86	Frank Crosetti	350.00	140.00	70.00
87	Steve O'Neil (O'Neill)	200.00	85.00	45.00
88	Geo. Selkirk	200.00	85.00	45.00
89	Joe Stripp	200.00	85.00	45.00
90	Ray Hayworth	200.00	85.00	45.00
91	Bucky Harris	455.00	185.00	90.00
92	Ethan Allen	200.00	85.00	45.00
93	Alvin Crowder	200.00	85.00	45.00
94	Wes Ferrell	200.00	85.00	45.00
95	Luke Appling	455.00	185.00	90.00
96	Lew Riggs	200.00	85.00	45.00
97	"Al" Lopez	840.00	335.00	170.00
98	"Schoolboy" Rowe	500.00	245.00	120.00
99	"Pie" Traynor	805.00	325.00	160.00
100	Earle Averill (Earl)	805.00	325.00	160.00
101	Dick Bartell	500.00	245.00	120.00
102	Van Mungo	665.00	265.00	135.00
103	Bill Dickey	1,085	435.00	215.00
104	Robert Rolfe	500.00	245.00	120.00
105	"Ernie" Lombardi	840.00	335.00	170.00
106	"Red" Lucas	500.00	245.00	120.00
107	Stanley Hack	630.00	250.00	125.00
108	Walter Berger	1,120	280.00	135.00

1924 Diaz Cigarettes

NEW YORK AMERICAN B. B. C.

No. 2.

Fume Cigarros
TOMAS GUTIERREZ

La persona que nos entregue la colección completa de Pitchers consistente en 136 Postalitas Nos. 1 al 136, será gratificada con un lujoso Album que contiene los jugadores todos de las Ligas Nacional y Americana con las Postalitas ya impresas.
Cia. Cigarrera Diaz, S. A. Finlay 66 (antes Zanja). Habana.

WAITE C. HOYT
Pitcher

Because they were printed in Cuba and feature only pitchers, the 1924 Diaz Cigarette cards are among the rarest and most intriguing of all tobacco issues. Produced in Havana for the Diaz brand, the black-and-white cards measure 1-3/4" x 2-1/2" and were printed on a semi-gloss stock. The player's name and position are listed at the bottom of the card, while his team and league appear at the top. According to the card backs, printed in Spanish, the set consists of 136 cards - all major league pitchers. But to date only the cards checklisted here have been discovered, and several of them never played in the major leagues.

		NM	EX	VG
Common Player:		900.00	360.00	180.00
1	Walter P. Johnson	5,250	2,200	1,100
2	Waite C. Hoyt	1,500	600.00	300.00
3	Grover C. Alexander	2,250	900.00	450.00
4	Thomas Sheehan	900.00	360.00	180.00
5	Pete Donohue	900.00	360.00	180.00
6	Herbert J. Pennock	1,350	550.00	275.00
7				
8	Carl Mays	1,100	450.00	225.00
9				
10	Allan S. Sothoron (Allen)	900.00	360.00	180.00
11	Wm. Piercy	900.00	360.00	180.00
12	Curtis Fullerton	900.00	360.00	180.00
13	Hollis Thurston	900.00	360.00	180.00
14	George Walberg	900.00	360.00	180.00
15	Fred Heimach	900.00	360.00	180.00
16	Sherrod M. Smith	900.00	360.00	180.00
17	Warren H. Ogden	900.00	360.00	180.00
18	Ernest P. Osborne (Earnest)	900.00	360.00	180.00
19	Walter H. Ruether	900.00	360.00	180.00
20	Burleigh A. Grimes	1,350	550.00	275.00
21	Joseph Genewich	900.00	360.00	180.00
22	Victor Aldridge	900.00	360.00	180.00
23	Arnold E. Stone	900.00	360.00	180.00
24	Lester C. Howe	900.00	360.00	180.00
25	George K. Murry (Murray)	900.00	360.00	180.00
26	Herman Pillette	900.00	360.00	180.00
27	John D. Couch	900.00	360.00	180.00
28	Tony C. Kaufmann	900.00	360.00	180.00
29	Frank (Jake) May	900.00	360.00	180.00
30	Howard J. Ehmke	900.00	360.00	180.00
31				
32				
33	Gorham V. Leverett	900.00	360.00	180.00
34	Bryan Harris	900.00	360.00	180.00
35	Paul F. Schreiber	900.00	360.00	180.00
36	Dewey Hinkle	900.00	360.00	180.00
37	Arthur C. Vance	1,350	550.00	275.00
38	Jesse J. Haines	1,350	550.00	275.00
39	Earl Hamilton	900.00	360.00	180.00
40	A. Wilbur Cooper	900.00	360.00	180.00
41	Thomas F. Long	900.00	360.00	180.00
42	Alex Ferguson	900.00	360.00	180.00
43	Chester Ross	900.00	360.00	180.00
44	John J. Quinn (Middle initual actually P.)	900.00	360.00	180.00
45	Ray C. Kolp	900.00	360.00	180.00
46	Arthur N. Nehf	900.00	360.00	180.00
47				
48				
49	Edwin A. Rommel	900.00	360.00	180.00
50	Theodore A. Lyons	1,350	550.00	275.00
51	Roy Meeker	900.00	360.00	180.00
52	John D. Stuart	900.00	360.00	180.00
53	Joseph Oeschger	900.00	360.00	180.00
54	Wayland Dean	900.00	360.00	180.00
55	Guy Morton	900.00	360.00	180.00
56	William L. Doak	900.00	360.00	180.00
57	Edward J. Pfeffer	900.00	360.00	180.00
58	Sam Gray	900.00	360.00	180.00
59				
60	Godfrey Brogan	900.00	360.00	180.00
61				
62	Howard E. Baldwin	900.00	360.00	180.00
63	Bert Lewis	900.00	360.00	180.00
64				
65	Dennis Burns	900.00	360.00	180.00
66	Roline C. Naylor (Roleine)	900.00	360.00	180.00
67	Walter H. Huntzinger	900.00	360.00	180.00
68	S. F. Baumgartner	900.00	360.00	180.00
69				
70	Clarence E. Mitchell	900.00	360.00	180.00
71				
72	Charles F. Clazner (Glazner)	900.00	360.00	180.00
73				
74				
75	Dennis J. Gearin	900.00	360.00	180.00
76	Jonathan T. Zachary	900.00	360.00	180.00
77				
78	Jess F. Winter (Jesse Winters)	900.00	360.00	180.00
79	Charles Ruffing	1,350	550.00	275.00
80	John W. Cooney	900.00	360.00	180.00
81	Leslie J. Bush (Middle initial A.)	900.00	360.00	180.00
82	William Harris	900.00	360.00	180.00
83	Joseph B. Shaute	900.00	360.00	180.00
84				
85	Eppa J. Rixey	1,350	550.00	275.00
86	William L. Sherdel	900.00	360.00	180.00
87	John C. Benton	900.00	360.00	180.00
88	Arthur R. Decatur	900.00	360.00	180.00
89	Harry G. Shriver	900.00	360.00	180.00
90	John D. Morrison	900.00	360.00	180.00
91	Walter M. Betts	900.00	360.00	180.00
92	Oscar Roettger	900.00	360.00	180.00
93				
94	Mike Cvengros	900.00	360.00	180.00
95	Leo L. Dickerman	900.00	360.00	180.00
96	Philip B. Weinart	2,400	960.00	480.00
97	Nicholas Dumovich	900.00	360.00	180.00
98				
99	Timothy A. McNamara	900.00	360.00	180.00
100	Allan Russell	900.00	360.00	180.00
101	Ted Blankenship	900.00	360.00	180.00

		NM	EX	VG
102	Howard E. Baldwin	900.00	360.00	180.00
103	Frank T. Davis	900.00	360.00	180.00
104	James C. Edwards	900.00	360.00	180.00
105	Hubert F. Pruett	900.00	360.00	180.00
106	Richard Rudolph	900.00	360.00	180.00
107				
108	Claude Jonnard	900.00	360.00	180.00
109				
110				
111	John M. Bentley (Initial actually N.)			
112	Wilfred D. Ryan	900.00	360.00	180.00
113	George D. Metivier	900.00	360.00	180.00
114				
115	Sylvester Johnson	900.00	360.00	180.00
116	O.L. Fuhr	900.00	360.00	180.00
117				
118	Stanley Coveleski	1,350	550.00	275.00
119	Dave C. Danforth	900.00	360.00	180.00
120	Elam Van Gilder	900.00	360.00	180.00
121	Bert Cole	900.00	360.00	180.00
122	Kenneth E. Holoway (Holloway)	900.00	360.00	180.00
123	Charles Robertson	900.00	360.00	180.00
124				
125	George Dauss	900.00	360.00	180.00
126				
127				
128				
129	Phillip Bedgood	900.00	360.00	180.00
130	Fred Wingfield	900.00	360.00	180.00
131	George Mogridge	900.00	360.00	180.00
132	J. Martina	900.00	360.00	180.00
133	B.F. Speece	900.00	360.00	180.00
134	Harold Carlson	900.00	360.00	180.00
135	Wilbert W. Hubbell	900.00	360.00	180.00
136	Milton Gaston	900.00	360.00	180.00

(The following pitchers are known to have been included in the set, though their card numbers are unknown. They are listed here alphabetically, though the names may be different on the cards.)

		NM	EX	VG
---	Jess L. Barnes	900.00	360.00	180.00
---	Virgil E. Barnes	900.00	360.00	180.00
---	William Bayne	900.00	360.00	180.00
---	Lawrence J. Benton	900.00	360.00	180.00
---	Warren Collins (Rip)	900.00	360.00	180.00
---	Joubert Davenport (Lum)	900.00	360.00	180.00
---	Urban C. Faber	900.00	360.00	180.00
---	Robert K. Hasty	900.00	360.00	180.00
---	Frank J. Henry	900.00	360.00	180.00
---	Samuel P. Jones	900.00	360.00	180.00
---	Adolfo Luque	900.00	360.00	180.00
---	Fred Marberry	900.00	360.00	180.00
---	Richard W. Marquard	900.00	360.00	180.00
---	Walter H. McGrew (Slim)	900.00	360.00	180.00
---	Herbert McQuaid	900.00	360.00	180.00
---	Hugh A. McQuillan	900.00	360.00	180.00
---	Lee Meadows	900.00	360.00	180.00
---	Louis A. North	900.00	360.00	180.00
---	George W. Pipgras	900.00	360.00	180.00
---	James J. Ring	900.00	360.00	180.00
---	Robert Shawkey	900.00	360.00	180.00
---	Urban J. Shocker	900.00	360.00	180.00
---	George Uhle	900.00	360.00	180.00
---	John R. Watson	900.00	360.00	180.00
---	Ed L. Wells	900.00	360.00	180.00
---	Byron W. Yarrison	900.00	360.00	180.00
---	Paul V. Zahniser	900.00	360.00	180.00

1962 Dickson Orde & Co.

One of several English tobacco cards to include baseball among a series of world's sports, this card is of marginal interest to U.S. collectors because its color front pictures (from the back) a batter who could be Babe Ruth as part of a baseball scene on the front of the 2-5/8" x 1-3/8" card. The short description of baseball on the card's black-and-white back does mention Ruth. The "Sports of the Countries" series comprises 25 cards.

		NM	EX	VG
11	America (Babe Ruth)	25.00	12.50	7.50

1980 Did You Know . . . ?

This collectors' edition was produced by artist Mel (?) Anderson. The blank-backed 3-1/4" x 6-3/8" cards have black-and-white drawings of ballplayers and a "Did You Know" trivia fact. The unnumbered cards are checklisted here alphabetically.

		NM	EX	VG
Complete Set (30):		25.00	12.50	7.50
Common Player:		2.00	1.00	.60
(1)	Richie Ashburn	4.00	2.00	1.25
(2)	Hank Bauer	2.50	1.25	.70
(3)	Ewell "The Whip" Blackwell	2.50	1.25	.70
(4)	Johnny Callison	2.00	1.00	.60
(5)	Roger "Doc" Cramer	2.00	1.00	.60
(6)	Harry Danning	2.00	1.00	.60
(7)	Ferris Fain	2.00	1.00	.60
(8)	Ned Garver	2.00	1.00	.60
(9)	Harvey Haddix	2.00	1.00	.60
(10)	Clint Hartung	2.00	1.00	.60
(11)	"Bobo" Holloman	2.00	1.00	.60
(12)	Ron Hunt	2.00	1.00	.60
(13)	Howard "Spud" Krist	2.00	1.00	.60
(14)	Emil "Dutch" Leonard	2.00	1.00	.60
(15)	Buddy Lewis	2.00	1.00	.60
(16)	Jerry Lynch	2.00	1.00	.60
(17)	Roy McMillan	2.00	1.00	.60
(18)	Johnny Mize	3.00	1.50	.90
(19)	Hugh Mulcahy	2.00	1.00	.60
(20)	Hal Newhouser	2.00	1.00	.60
(21)	Jim Perry	2.00	1.00	.60
(22)	Phil Rizzuto	4.00	2.00	1.25
(23)	Bobby Shantz	2.00	1.00	.60
(24)	Roy Sievers	2.00	1.00	.60
(25)	Nick Testa	3.00	1.50	.90
(26)	Cecil Travis	2.00	1.00	.60
(27)	Elmer "Valiant" Valo	2.00	1.00	.60
(28)	Bill Werber	2.00	1.00	.60
(29)	Mickey Witek	2.00	1.00	.60
(30)	Hal Woodeshick	2.00	1.00	.60

1907-09 Dietsche Detroit Tigers Postcards (PC765-1)

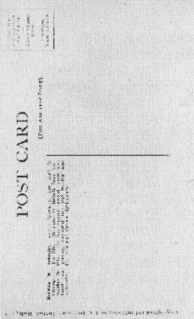

Three apparent annual issues (1907-09) of the home team by Detroit postcard publisher A.C. Dietsche, these 3-1/2" x 5-1/2" black-and-white postcards have most of the photographic background on front blackened out. The player's last name usually appears on the front. On back, along with the postcard legalities are a short player biography and a dated copyright line. The postcards were sold in sets of 15 cards for 25 cents.

		NM	EX	VG
Common Player:		150.00	60.00	30.00
Series 1 - 1907				
	Complete Set (16):	7,000	2,800	1,400
(1)	Tyrus R. Cobb (Batting)	2,000	800.00	400.00
(2)	Tyrus R. Cobb (Fielding)	3,000	1,200	600.00
(3)	William Coughlin	150.00	60.00	30.00
(4)	Samuel S. Crawford	325.00	130.00	65.00
(5)	William E. Donovan	150.00	60.00	30.00
(6)	Jerome W. Downs	150.00	60.00	30.00
(7)	Hughie A. Jennings	325.00	130.00	65.00
(8)	David Jones	150.00	60.00	30.00
(9)	Edward H. Killian	150.00	60.00	30.00
(10)	George J. Mullin	150.00	60.00	30.00
(11)	Charles O'Leary	150.00	60.00	30.00
(12)	Fred T. Payne	150.00	60.00	30.00
(13)	Claude Rossman	150.00	60.00	30.00
(14)	Herman W. Schaefer	150.00	60.00	30.00
(15)	Charles Schmidt	150.00	60.00	30.00
(16)	Edward Siever	150.00	60.00	30.00
Series 2 - 1908				
	Complete Set (22):	6,000	2,400	1,200
(1)	Henry Beckendorf	180.00	70.00	35.00
(2)	Owen Bush	180.00	70.00	35.00
(3)	Tyrus R. Cobb	2,500	1,000	500.00

		NM	EX	VG
(4)	William Coughlin	180.00	70.00	35.00
(5)	Sam Crawford	350.00	140.00	70.00
(6)	William E. Donovan	180.00	70.00	35.00
(7)	Jerome W. Downs	180.00	70.00	35.00
(8)	Hughie A. Jennings	350.00	140.00	70.00
(9)	Tom Jones	180.00	70.00	35.00
(10)	Edward H. Killian	180.00	70.00	35.00
(11)	Matthew McIntyre	180.00	70.00	35.00
(12)	George J. Moriarty	180.00	70.00	35.00
(13)	George J. Mullin	180.00	70.00	35.00
(14)	Charles O'Leary	180.00	70.00	35.00
(15)	Fred T. Payne	180.00	70.00	35.00
(16)	Germany Schaefer	180.00	70.00	35.00
(17)	Charles Schmidt	180.00	70.00	35.00
(18)	Oscar Stanage	180.00	70.00	35.00
(19)	Oren Edgar Summers	180.00	70.00	35.00
(20)	Ira Thomas	180.00	70.00	35.00
(21)	Edgar Willett	180.00	70.00	35.00
(22)	George Winter	180.00	70.00	35.00

Series 3 - 1909

		NM	EX	VG
	Complete Set (4):	750.00	300.00	150.00
(1)	James Delehanty	200.00	80.00	40.00
(2)	Tom Jones	180.00	70.00	35.00
(3)	Ralph Works	180.00	70.00	35.00
(4)	Detroit Tigers Team	300.00	125.00	60.00

1907 Dietsche Chicago Cubs Postcards (PC765-2)

This series of early Cubs postcards was published by the same Detroit printer who issued Tigers postcard series from 1907-09. The Dietsche Cubs postcards are scarcer than the Tigers issues because they were only offered for sale in Detroit in conjunction with the 1907 World Series between the Tigers and Cubs, and few people bought the visiting team's cards. The 3-1/2" x 5-1/2" black-and-white cards have most of the photographic background blacked out on front. The player's last name may or may not appear on the front. Postcard style backs include a short career summary and a dated copyright line. The 15-card sets originally sold for 25 cents.

		NM	EX	VG
	Complete Set (15):	5,500	2,200	1,100
	Common Player:	340.00	135.00	65.00
(1)	Mordecai Brown	500.00	200.00	100.00
(2)	Frank L. Chance	500.00	200.00	100.00
(3)	John Evers	500.00	200.00	100.00
(4)	Arthur F. Hoffman (Hofman)	340.00	135.00	65.00
(5)	John Kling	340.00	135.00	65.00
(6)	Carl Lundgren	340.00	135.00	65.00
(7)	Patrick J. Moran	340.00	135.00	65.00
(8)	Orval Overall	340.00	135.00	65.00
(9)	John A. Pfeister	340.00	135.00	65.00
(10)	Edw. M. Ruelbach	340.00	135.00	65.00
(11)	Frank M. Schulte	340.00	135.00	65.00
(12)	James T. Sheckard	340.00	135.00	65.00
(13)	James Slagle	340.00	135.00	65.00
(14)	Harry Steinfeldt	340.00	135.00	65.00
(15)	Joseph B. Tinker	500.00	200.00	100.00

1907 Dietsche Posters

The images found on the Dietsche postcards were conglomerated on a pair of black-and-white cardboard posters. About 22" square, the posters are headlined: "FRANK CHANCE AND HIS 1907 PENNANT WINNERS" and "HUGHIE JENNINGS AND HIS GREA 1970 TIGERS."

	NM	EX	VG
1907 Chicago Cubs	1,000	500.00	300.00
1907 Detroit Tigers	1,000	500.00	300.00

1934 Dietz Gum Ball Players in Action

See 1934 Al Demaree Die-cuts (R304).

1942 Joe DiMaggio Candy Box Card

With no maker's name visible, this crudely executed war-era card is believed to have been printed on a candy box. In a format of 2-7/16" x 3-3/16" it is printed in blue and orange on white, is perforated on the sides and blank-backed.

	NM	EX	VG
Joe DiMaggio	150.00	75.00	45.00

1950 Joe DiMaggio Oriental Tour Postcard

In the post-season of 1950, during the Korean War, Joe DiMaggio led a goodwill tour of the Orient, including stops to visit the troops and to baseball-related destinations in Japan. This Italian postcard shows DiMaggio and Lefty O'Doul in a colorized photo surrounded by Japanese schoolboy ballplayers. The postcard-style back describes the scene. The card measures about 6" x 4".

	NM	EX	VG
Joe DiMaggio	125.00	65.00	40.00

1951 Joe DiMaggio Baseball Shoes

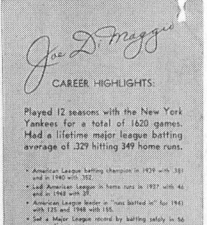

This 2-1/2" x 3-1/2" card was included with DiMaggio brand baseball shoes. A hole punched in the upper-left corner allowed the card to be attached to the shoe strings. Front has an action pose of DiMaggio printed in black-and-white on a dark green background. A facsimile autograph is at center. At bottom is printed: "THE YANKEE CLIPPER." The back has another facsimile signature and the player's career highlights through the 1950 season.

	NM	EX	VG
Joe DiMaggio (Hang-tag card.)	140.00	70.00	40.00
Joe DiMaggio (Complete box, shoes, tag.)	650.00	325.00	200.00

1972-83 Dimanche/Derniere Heure Photos

From 1972-74, and 1977-83, the Montreal magazine Dimanche / Derniere Heure (loosely translated, "Sunday / Latest Hour," issued color photos of Expos (and a few other) players. The 8-1/2" x 11" photos are printed on semi-gloss paper stock that is punched for a three-ring binder. Fronts have a large color photo with player data, stats and career highlights printed in black beneath - all in French. At left or top is usually the issue date in which the photo was included in the magazine. Backs are blank.

	NM	EX	VG
Common Player:	5.00	2.50	1.50
(Stars are valued up to $50.)			

1972 Dimanche/Derniere Heure Expos

		NM	EX	VG
	Complete Set (27):	155.00	78.00	47.00
	Common Player:	5.00	2.50	1.50
(1)	Bill Stoneman (April 9)	5.00	2.50	1.50
(2)	John Boccabella (April 16)	5.00	2.50	1.50
(3)	Gene Mauch (April 23)	5.00	2.50	1.50
(4)	Ron Hunt (April 30)	5.00	2.50	1.50
(5)	Steve Renko (May 7)	5.00	2.50	1.50
(6)	Boots Day (May 14)	5.00	2.50	1.50
(7)	Bob Bailey (May 21)	5.00	2.50	1.50
(8)	Ernie McAnally (May 28)	5.00	2.50	1.50
(9)	Ken Singleton (June 4)	5.00	2.50	1.50
(10)	Ron Fairly (June 11)	5.00	2.50	1.50
(11)	Ron Woods (June 18)	5.00	2.50	1.50
(12)	Mike Jorgensen (June 25)	5.00	2.50	1.50
(13)	Bobby Wine (July 2)	5.00	2.50	1.50
(14)	Mike Torrez (July 9)	5.00	2.50	1.50
(15)	Terry Humphrey (July 16)	5.00	2.50	1.50
(16)	Jim Fairey (July 23)	5.00	2.50	1.50
(17)	Tim Foli (July 30)	5.00	2.50	1.50
(18)	Clyde Mashore (Aug. 6)	5.00	2.50	1.50
(19)	Tim McCarver (Aug. 13)	9.00	4.50	2.75
(20)	Hector Torres (Aug. 20)	5.00	2.50	1.50
(21)	Tom Walker (Aug. 27)	5.00	2.50	1.50
(22)	Cal McLish (Sept. 3)	5.00	2.50	1.50
(23)	Balor Moore (Sept. 10)	5.00	2.50	1.50
(24)	John Strohmayer (Sept. 17)	5.00	2.50	1.50
(25)	Larry Doby (Sept. 24)	12.00	6.00	3.50
(26)	Hal Breeden (Oct. 1)	5.00	2.50	1.50
(27)	Mike Marshall (Oct. 8)	5.00	2.50	1.50

1973 Dimanche/Derniere Heure National Leaguers

		NM	EX	VG
	Complete Set (16):	185.00	90.00	55.00
	Common Player:	6.00	3.00	1.75
(1)	Roberto Clemente (April 15)	25.00	12.50	7.50
(2)	Coco Laboy (April 22)	6.00	3.00	1.75
(3)	Rusty Staub (April 29)	8.00	4.00	2.50
(4)	Johnny Bench (May 6)	12.50	6.25	3.75
(5)	Ferguson Jenkins (May 13)	9.00	4.50	2.75
(6)	Bob Gibson (May 20)	10.00	5.00	3.00
(7)	Hank Aaron (May 27)	20.00	10.00	6.00
(8)	Willie Montanez (June 3)	6.00	3.00	1.75
(9)	Willie McCovey (June 10)	10.00	5.00	3.00

		NM	EX	VG
(10)	Willie Davis (June 17)	6.00	3.00	1.75
(11)	Steve Carlton (June 24)	10.00	5.00	3.00
(12)	Willie Stargell (July 1)	10.00	5.00	3.00
(13)	Dave Bristol (July 8)	6.00	3.00	1.75
(14)	Larry Bowa (July 15)	6.00	3.00	1.75
(15)	Pete Rose (July 22)	20.00	10.00	6.00
(16)	Pepe Frias (July 29)	6.00	3.00	1.75

1974 Dimanche/Derniere Heure Expos

		NM	EX	VG
Complete Set (10):		40.00	20.00	12.00
Common Player:		5.00	2.50	1.50
(1)	Dennis Blair	5.00	2.50	1.50
(2)	Don Carrithers	5.00	2.50	1.50
(3)	Jim Cox	5.00	2.50	1.50
(4)	Willie Davis	5.00	2.50	1.50
(5)	Don Demola	5.00	2.50	1.50
(6)	Barry Foote	5.00	2.50	1.50
(7)	Larry Lintz	5.00	2.50	1.50
(8)	John Montague	5.00	2.50	1.50
(9)	Steve Rogers	5.00	2.50	1.50
(10)	Chuck Taylor	5.00	2.50	1.50

1977 Dimanche/Derniere Heure Expos

		NM	EX	VG
Complete Set (26):		125.00	62.00	37.00
Common Player:		5.00	2.50	1.50
(1)	Steve Rogers (April 24)	5.00	2.50	1.50
(2)	Tim Foli (May 1)	5.00	2.50	1.50
(3)	Dick Williams (May 8)	5.00	2.50	1.50
(4)	Larry Parrish (May 15)	5.00	2.50	1.50
(5)	Jose Morales (May 22)	5.00	2.50	1.50
(6)	Don Stanhouse (May 29)	5.00	2.50	1.50
(7)	Gary Carter (June 5)	10.00	5.00	3.00
(8)	Ellis Valentine (June 12)	5.00	2.50	1.50
(9)	Dave Cash (June 19)	5.00	2.50	1.50
(10)	Jackie Brown (June 26)	5.00	2.50	1.50
(11)	Barry Foote (July 3)	5.00	2.50	1.50
(12)	Dan Warthen (July 10)	5.00	2.50	1.50
(13)	Tony Perez (July 17)	10.00	5.00	3.00
(14)	Wayne Garrett (July 24)	5.00	2.50	1.50
(15)	Bill Atkinson (July 31)	5.00	2.50	1.50
(16)	Joe Kerrigan (Aug. 7)	5.00	2.50	1.50
(17)	Mickey Vernon (Aug. 14)	5.00	2.50	1.50
(18)	Jeff Terpko (Aug. 21)	5.00	2.50	1.50
(19)	Andre Dawson (Aug. 28)	10.00	5.00	3.00
(20)	Del Unser (Sept. 4)	5.00	2.50	1.50
(21)	Stan Brewer (Sept. 11)	5.00	2.50	1.50
(22)	Warren Cromartie (Sept. 18)	5.00	2.50	1.50
(23)	Santo Alcala (Sept. 25)	5.00	2.50	1.50
(24)	Wayne Twitchell (Oct. 2)	5.00	2.50	1.50
(25)	Pepe Frias (Oct. 9)	5.00	2.50	1.50
(26)	Sam Mejias (Oct. 16)	5.00	2.50	1.50

1978 Dimanche/Derniere Heure Expos

		NM	EX	VG
Complete Set (13):		62.00	31.00	18.50
Common Player:		5.00	2.50	1.50
(1)	Ross Grimsley (May 7)	5.00	2.50	1.50
(2)	Chris Speier (May 14)	5.00	2.50	1.50
(3)	Norm Sherry (May 21)	5.00	2.50	1.50
(4)	Hal Dues (May 28)	5.00	2.50	1.50
(5)	Rudy May (June 4)	5.00	2.50	1.50
(6)	Stan Papi (June 11)	5.00	2.50	1.50
(7)	Darold Knowles (June 18)	5.00	2.50	1.50
(8)	Bob Reece (June 25)	5.00	2.50	1.50
(9)	Dan Schatzeder (July 2)	5.00	2.50	1.50
(10)	Jim Brewer (July 9)	5.00	2.50	1.50
(11)	Mike Garman (July 16)	5.00	2.50	1.50
(12)	Woodie Fryman (July 23)	5.00	2.50	1.50
(13)	Ed Hermann	5.00	2.50	1.50

1979 Dimanche/Derniere Heure Expos

		NM	EX	VG
Complete Set (8):		35.00	17.50	10.50
Common Player:		5.00	2.50	1.50
(1)	Bill Lee (May 6)	5.00	2.50	1.50
(2)	Elias Sosa (May 13)	5.00	2.50	1.50
(3)	Tommy Hutton (May 20)	5.00	2.50	1.50
(4)	Tony Solaita (May 27)	5.00	2.50	1.50
(5)	Rodney Scott (June 3)	5.00	2.50	1.50
(6)	Duffy Dyer (June 10)	5.00	2.50	1.50
(7)	Jim Mason (June 17)	5.00	2.50	1.50
(8)	Ken Macha (June 24)	5.00	2.50	1.50

1980 Dimanche/Derniere Heure Expos

		NM	EX	VG
Complete Set (23):		125.00	62.00	37.00
Common Player:		5.00	2.50	1.50
(1)	Steve Rogers (April 20)	5.00	2.50	1.50
(2)	Dick Williams (April 27)	5.00	2.50	1.50
(3)	Bill Lee (May 4)	5.00	2.50	1.50
(4)	Jerry White (May 11)	5.00	2.50	1.50
(5)	Scott Sanderson (May 18)	5.00	2.50	1.50
(6)	Ron LeFlore (May 25)	5.00	2.50	1.50
(7)	Elias Sosa (June 1)	5.00	2.50	1.50
(8)	Ellis Valentine (June 8)	5.00	2.50	1.50
(9)	Rodney Scott (June 22)	5.00	2.50	1.50
(10)	Woodie Fryman (June 29)	5.00	2.50	1.50
(11)	Chris Speier (July 6)	5.00	2.50	1.50
(12)	Warren Cromartie (July 13)	5.00	2.50	1.50
(13)	Stan Bahnsen (July 20)	5.00	2.50	1.50
(14)	Tommy Hutton (July 27)	5.00	2.50	1.50
(15)	Bill Almon (Aug. 3)	5.00	2.50	1.50
(16)	Fred Norman (Aug. 10)	5.00	2.50	1.50
(17)	Andre Dawson (Aug. 17)	10.00	5.00	3.00
(18)	John Tamargo (Aug. 24)	5.00	2.50	1.50
(19)	Larry Parrish (Aug. 31)	5.00	2.50	1.50
(20)	David Palmer (Sept. 7)	5.00	2.50	1.50
(21)	Tony Bernazard (Sept. 14)	5.00	2.50	1.50
(22)	Gary Carter (Sept. 21)	10.00	5.00	3.00
(23)	Ken Macha (Sept. 28)	5.00	2.50	1.50

1888 Dixie Cigarettes Girl Baseball Players (N48)

(See 1888 Allen & Ginter Girl Baseball Players.)

1937 Dixie Lids

This unnumbered set of Dixie cup ice cream tops was issued in 1937 and consists of 24 different lids, although only six picture sports stars; four of whom are baseball players. The lids are found in two different sizes, either 2-11/16" in diameter or 2-5/16" in diameter. The 1937 Dixie lids have their "picture" side printed in black or dark red. The reverse carries the advertising of one of many local dairies which packaged the ice cream treats. The lids must have the small tab still intact to command top value.

	NM	EX	VG
Complete Set (4):	700.00	350.00	210.00
Common Player:	180.00	90.00	55.00

		NM	EX	VG
(1)	Charles Gehringer	180.00	90.00	55.00
(2)	Charles ("Gabby") Hartnett	180.00	90.00	55.00
(3)	Carl Hubbell (Mouth closed.)	195.00	95.00	55.00
(4)	Joe Medwick	180.00	90.00	55.00

1937 Dixie Lids Premiums

Issued as a premium offer in conjunction with the 1937 Dixie lids, this unnumbered set of color 8" x 10" pictures was printed on heavy paper and features the same subjects as the Dixie lids set. The 1937 Dixie premiums have a distinctive dark green band along the left margin containing the player's name. The back has smaller photos of the player in action with a large star at the top and a player write-up. The 1937 premiums are easily distinguished from the 1938 issue by the use of yellow ink for the names in the left border. A "My Scrapbook of Stars" album was issued in which to house the 24 sports and movie stars issued in the series.

		NM	EX	VG
Complete Set (4):		500.00	250.00	150.00
Common Player:		150.00	75.00	45.00
Album:		300.00	150.00	90.00
(2)	Charles Gehringer	150.00	75.00	45.00
(3)	Charles (Gabby) Hartnett	150.00	75.00	45.00
(4)	Carl Hubbell	175.00	87.00	52.00
(5)	Joe (Ducky) Medwick	150.00	75.00	45.00

1938 Dixie Lids

Similar to its set of the previous year, the 1938 Dixie lids set is a 24-subject set that includes six sports stars - four of whom are baseball players. The lids are found in two sizes, either 2-11/16" in diameter or 2-5/16" in diameter. The 1938 Dixie Lids have their "picture" side printed in blue ink. The reverse carries advertising from one of many local dairies which packaged the ice cream cups. Dixie lids must have the small tab still intact to command top value.

		NM	EX	VG
Complete Set (4):		600.00	300.00	180.00
Common Player:		80.00	40.00	25.00
(1)	Bob Feller	200.00	100.00	60.00
(2)	Jimmie Foxx	200.00	100.00	60.00
(3)	Carl Hubbell (Mouth open.)	175.00	85.00	50.00
(4)	Wally Moses	80.00	40.00	25.00

1938 Dixie Lids Premiums

Issued in conjunction with the 1938 Dixie cup lids, this unnumbered set of 8" x 10" pictures contains the same subjects. A colored border surrounds the entire picture with the player's name in black at left. The back contains smaller photos of the player in action with his name in script at the top and a short write-up. A "My Scrapbook of Stars" album was issued in which to house the 24 sports and movie stars that comprise the complete series.

		NM	EX	VG
Complete Set (4):		425.00	210.00	125.00
Common Player:		62.00	31.00	18.50
Album:		300.00	150.00	90.00
(1)	Bob Feller	125.00	62.00	37.00
(2)	Jimmy Foxx	125.00	62.00	37.00
(3)	Carl Hubbell	125.00	62.00	37.00
(4)	Wally Moses	60.00	30.00	18.00

1952 Dixie Lids

After a 14-year break, another Dixie lid set, featuring 24 baseball players, appeared in 1952. The unnumbered lids are found in three sizes, the most common being 2-11/16" in diameter. Somewhat scarcer, and carrying a modest premium over the values listed, are lids in sizes of 2-1/4" or 3-3/16". All are printed with a blue tint on their "picture" side. The backs carry advertising from one of the many local or regional dairies which packaged the ice cream treats. The Dixie lids of the 1950s can be distinguished from earlier issues because the bottom of the photo is squared off to accomodate the player's name. Dixie lids must contain the small tab to command top value.

		NM	EX	VG
Complete Set (24):		5,500	2,750	1,650
Common Player:		200.00	100.00	60.00
(1)	Richie Ashburn	325.00	160.00	95.00
(2)	Tommy Byrne	200.00	100.00	60.00
(3)	Chico Carrasquel	200.00	100.00	60.00
(4)	Pete Castiglione	200.00	100.00	60.00
(5)	Walker Cooper	200.00	100.00	60.00
(6)	Billy Cox	225.00	110.00	65.00
(7)	Ferris Fain	200.00	100.00	60.00
(8)	Bobby Feller	350.00	175.00	100.00
(9)	Nelson Fox	325.00	160.00	95.00
(10)	Monte Irvin	275.00	135.00	80.00
(11)	Ralph Kiner	275.00	135.00	80.00
(12)	Cass Michaels	200.00	100.00	60.00
(13)	Don Mueller	200.00	100.00	60.00
(14)	Mel Parnell	200.00	100.00	60.00
(15)	Allie Reynolds	225.00	110.00	65.00
(16)	Preacher Roe	225.00	110.00	65.00
(17)	Connie Ryan	200.00	100.00	60.00
(18)	Hank Sauer	200.00	100.00	60.00
(19)	Al Schoendienst	275.00	135.00	80.00
(20)	Andy Seminick	200.00	100.00	60.00
(21)	Bobby Shantz	200.00	100.00	60.00
(22)	Enos Slaughter	275.00	135.00	80.00
(23)	Virgil Trucks	200.00	100.00	60.00
(24)	Gene Woodling	250.00	125.00	75.00

1952 Dixie Lids Premiums

This unnumbered set of 24 player photos was issued as a premium in conjunction with the 1952 Dixie cup lids and features the same subjects. The player's team and facsimile autograph appear along the bottom of the 8" x 10" blank-backed photo, which was printed on heavy paper. The 1952 Dixie premiums show the player's 1951 season statistics in the lower right corner.

		NM	EX	VG
Complete Set (24):		2,250	1,125	675.00
Common Player:		90.00	45.00	25.00
(1)	Richie Ashburn	225.00	110.00	65.00
(2)	Tommy Byrne	90.00	45.00	25.00
(3)	Chico Carrasquel	90.00	45.00	25.00
(4)	Pete Castiglione	90.00	45.00	25.00
(5)	Walker Cooper	90.00	45.00	25.00
(6)	Billy Cox	100.00	50.00	30.00
(7)	Ferris Fain	90.00	45.00	25.00
(8)	Bob Feller	225.00	110.00	65.00
(9)	Nelson Fox	200.00	100.00	60.00
(10)	Monte Irvin	125.00	60.00	35.00
(11)	Ralph Kiner	125.00	60.00	35.00
(12)	Cass Michaels	90.00	45.00	25.00
(13)	Don Mueller	90.00	45.00	25.00
(14)	Mel Parnell	90.00	45.00	25.00
(15)	Allie Reynolds	100.00	50.00	30.00
(16)	Preacher Roe	100.00	50.00	30.00
(17)	Connie Ryan	90.00	45.00	25.00
(18)	Hank Sauer	90.00	45.00	25.00
(19)	Al Schoendienst	125.00	60.00	35.00
(20)	Andy Seminick	90.00	45.00	25.00
(21)	Bobby Shantz	90.00	45.00	25.00
(22)	Enos Slaughter	125.00	60.00	35.00
(23)	Virgil Trucks	90.00	45.00	25.00
(24)	Gene Woodling	100.00	50.00	30.00

1953 Dixie Lids

The 1953 Dixie lids set again consists of 24 unnumbered players and is identical in design to the 1952 set. Lids are either 2-1/4" or 2-11/16"in diameter and must include the small tab to command top value. Backs of the lids may be found with advertising of many local or regional dairies which packaged the ice cream cups.

		NM	EX	VG
Complete Set (24):		4,000	2,000	1,200
Common Player:		120.00	60.00	35.00
(1)	Richie Ashburn	250.00	125.00	75.00
(2)	Chico Carrasquel	120.00	60.00	35.00
(3)	Billy Cox	130.00	65.00	40.00
(4)	Ferris Fain	120.00	60.00	35.00
(5)	Nelson Fox	200.00	100.00	60.00
(6a)	Sid Gordon (Boston)	240.00	120.00	70.00
(6b)	Sid Gordon (Milwaukee)	120.00	60.00	35.00
(7)	Warren Hacker	120.00	60.00	35.00
(8)	Monte Irvin	200.00	100.00	60.00
(9)	Jackie Jensen	180.00	90.00	55.00
(10a)	Ralph Kiner (Pittsburgh)	350.00	175.00	100.00
(10b)	Ralph Kiner (Chicago)	200.00	100.00	60.00
(11)	Ted Kluszewski	200.00	100.00	60.00
(12)	Bob Lemon	200.00	100.00	60.00
(13)	Don Mueller	120.00	60.00	35.00
(14)	Mel Parnell	120.00	60.00	35.00
(15)	Jerry Priddy	120.00	60.00	35.00
(16)	Allie Reynolds	130.00	65.00	40.00
(17)	Preacher Roe	130.00	65.00	40.00
(18)	Hank Sauer	120.00	60.00	35.00
(19)	Al Schoendienst	200.00	100.00	60.00
(20)	Bobby Shantz	120.00	60.00	35.00
(21)	Enos Slaughter	200.00	100.00	60.00
(22a)	Warren Spahn (Boston)	550.00	275.00	165.00
(22b)	Warren Spahn (Milwaukee)	500.00	250.00	150.00
(23a)	Virgil Trucks (Chicago)	250.00	125.00	75.00
(23b)	Virgil Trucks (St. Louis)	150.00	75.00	45.00
(24)	Gene Woodling	130.00	65.00	40.00

1953 Dixie Lids Premiums

This set of 8" x 10" photos was issued as a premium in conjunction with the 1953 Dixie lids set and includes the same subjects. A premium picture could be obtained in exchange for 12 lids. The player's team and facsimile autograph are at the bottom of the unnumbered, blank-backed photos. His 1952 season stats are shown in the lower right corner.

		NM	EX	VG
Complete Set (24):		3,000	1,500	900.00
Common Player:		100.00	50.00	30.00
(1)	Richie Ashburn	250.00	125.00	75.00
(2)	Chico Carrasquel	100.00	50.00	30.00
(3)	Billy Cox	120.00	60.00	35.00
(4)	Ferris Fain	100.00	50.00	30.00
(5)	Nelson Fox	200.00	100.00	60.00
(6)	Sid Gordon	100.00	50.00	30.00
(7)	Warren Hacker	100.00	50.00	30.00
(8)	Monte Irvin	180.00	90.00	55.00
(9)	Jack Jensen	120.00	60.00	35.00
(10)	Ralph Kiner	180.00	90.00	55.00
(11)	Ted Kluszewski	180.00	90.00	55.00
(12)	Bob Lemon	180.00	90.00	55.00
(13)	Don Mueller	100.00	50.00	30.00
(14)	Mel Parnell	100.00	50.00	30.00
(15)	Jerry Priddy	100.00	50.00	30.00
(16)	Allie Reynolds	120.00	60.00	35.00
(17)	Preacher Roe	120.00	60.00	35.00
(18)	Hank Sauer	100.00	50.00	30.00
(19)	Al Schoendienst	180.00	90.00	55.00
(20)	Bobby Shantz	120.00	60.00	35.00
(21)	Enos Slaughter	180.00	90.00	55.00
(22)	Warren Spahn	260.00	130.00	75.00
(23)	Virgil Trucks	100.00	50.00	30.00
(24)	Gene Woodling	120.00	60.00	35.00

1954 Dixie Lids

The 1954 Dixie lids set consists of 18 players. Each player is foind in both a "left" and "right" version. The picture side features a black-and-white photo. The lids usually measure 2-11/16" in diameter, although two other sizes (2-1/4"

and 3-3/16") also exist and are valued at a significant premium above the prices listed. The 1954 Dixie lids are similar to earlier issues, except they carry an offer for a "3-D Starviewer" around the outside edge. The small tabs must be attached to command top value. The lids are unnumbered. Backs can be found with advertising from many local or regional dairies which packaged the ice cream cups.

		NM	EX	VG
Complete Set (18):		2,000	1,000	600.00
Common Player:		120.00	60.00	35.00
2-1/4" or 3-3/16": 2-3X				
(1)	Richie Ashburn	250.00	125.00	75.00
(2)	Clint Courtney	120.00	60.00	35.00
(3)	Sid Gordon	120.00	60.00	35.00
(4)	Billy Hoeft	120.00	60.00	35.00
(5)	Monte Irvin	200.00	100.00	60.00
(6)	Jackie Jensen	130.00	65.00	40.00
(7)	Ralph Kiner	200.00	100.00	60.00
(8)	Ted Kluszewski	200.00	100.00	60.00
(9)	Gil McDougald	130.00	65.00	40.00
(10)	Minny Minoso	130.00	65.00	40.00
(11)	Danny O'Connell	120.00	60.00	35.00
(12)	Mel Parnell	120.00	60.00	35.00
(13)	Preacher Roe	130.00	65.00	40.00
(14)	Al Rosen	130.00	65.00	40.00
(15)	Al Schoendienst	200.00	100.00	60.00
(16)	Enos Slaughter	200.00	100.00	60.00
(17)	Gene Woodling	130.00	65.00	40.00
(18)	Gus Zernial	120.00	60.00	35.00

1909 Dockman & Sons Gum (E92)

Once cataloged as a part of the E92 compendium, the John Dockman & Sons Gum card issue differs from the Croft's Candy/Cocoa sets in that it has 10 fewer cards. Otherwise the format (1-1/2" x 2-3/4") and color litho player pictures are identical. Beneath the player picture on front is his last name, position and team. Backs, which describe the set as having 50 cards, are an ad for the gum company. Cards are checklisted here alphabetically.

		NM	EX	VG
Complete Set (40):		50,000	20,000	10,000
Common Player:		910.00	365.00	180.00
(1)	Harry Bemis	910.00	365.00	180.00
(2)	Chief Bender	1,620	660.00	330.00
(3)	Bill Bergen	910.00	365.00	180.00
(4)	Bob Bescher	910.00	365.00	180.00
(5)	Al Bridwell	910.00	365.00	180.00
(6)	Doc Casey	910.00	365.00	180.00
(7)	Frank Chance	1,800	720.00	360.00
(8)	Hal Chase	1,110	450.00	220.00
(9)	Sam Crawford	1,620	660.00	330.00
(10)	Harry Davis	910.00	365.00	180.00
(11)	Art Devlin	910.00	365.00	180.00
(12)	Wild Bill Donovan	910.00	365.00	180.00
(13)	Mickey Doolan	910.00	365.00	180.00
(14)	Patsy Dougherty	910.00	365.00	180.00
(15)	Larry Doyle (Throwing)	910.00	365.00	180.00
(16)	Larry Doyle (With bat.)	910.00	365.00	180.00
(17)	George Gibson	910.00	365.00	180.00
(18)	Topsy Hartsel	910.00	365.00	180.00
(19)	Hugh Jennings	1,620	660.00	330.00
(20)	Red Kleinow	910.00	365.00	180.00
(21)	Nap Lajoie	1,800	720.00	360.00
(22)	Hans Lobert	910.00	365.00	180.00
(23)	Sherry Magee	910.00	365.00	180.00
(24)	Christy Matthewson (Mathewson)	5,400	2,160	1,080
(25)	John McGraw	1,620	660.00	330.00
(26)	Larry McLean	910.00	365.00	180.00
(27)	Dots Miller	910.00	365.00	180.00
(28)	Danny Murphy	910.00	365.00	180.00
(29)	Bill O'Hara	910.00	365.00	180.00
(30)	Germany Schaefer	910.00	365.00	180.00
(31)	Admiral Schlei	910.00	365.00	180.00
(32)	Boss Schmidt	910.00	365.00	180.00
(33)	Johnny Seigle	910.00	365.00	180.00

		NM	EX	VG
(34)	Dave Shean	910.00	365.00	180.00
(35)	Boss Smith (Schmidt)	910.00	365.00	180.00
(36)	Joe Tinker	1,620	660.00	330.00
(37)	Honus Wagner (Batting)	10,000	2,880	1,440
(38)	Honus Wagner (Throwing)	10,000	2,880	1,440
(39)	Cy Young	4,200	1,680	840.00
(40)	Heinie Zimmerman	910.00	365.00	180.00

1969-1972 Dodge Postcards

1969 Dodge Polara 500

Bill's Best Catch of the Year...
Dodge Fever

Bill Freehan
Detroit All-Star Catcher

Between 1969-1972 Dodge issued a series of black-and-white promotional postcards featuring sports figures endorsing the car company's line-up. Player portrait photos on front are combined with a photo of one of the cars and some extraneous sales copy. Divided backs of the 5-1/2" x 3-1/2" cards have a couple sentences of career summary or highlights and a sales pitch. Only the baseball players are listed here, though stars from football, basketball, golf, hockey and racing were also included in the series.

		NM	EX	VG
Common Player:		15.00	7.50	4.50
(1)	Lou Brock (1970)	40.00	20.00	12.00
(2)	Lou Brock (1971)	40.00	20.00	12.00
(3)	Bill Freehan (1969)	30.00	15.00	9.00
(4)	Bill Freehan (1971)	15.00	7.50	4.50
(5)	Bill Freehan (1972)	15.00	7.50	4.50
(6)	Joe Garagiola (1970)	20.00	10.00	6.00
(7)	Mickey Lolich (1969)	15.00	7.50	4.50

1888-1889 Dogs Head Cabinets (N173)

DOGS HEAD &
OLD JUDGE CIGARETTES

(See 1888-1889 Old Judge Cabinets.)

1950 Dominican Republic

151 Phill Rizzuto

Selection of known Major League players makes 1950 the best guess for year of issue of this Caribbean card set. Like many contemporary Latin issues, these were probably produced to be collected in an accompanying album. Printed on fragile paper in blue, red or green duo-tones, the cards measure about 1-5/8" x 2-3/8" and are blank-backed. The set may or may not be complete at 292, the highest number currently known. Players featured in the issue are drawn from the Dominican and Cuban winter leagues (including Negro Leagues and minor league players) as well as the majors. In the bottom border beneath the player photo is a card number and name. Names are frequently misspelled and this list may not have succeeded in correcting all of them, particularly the Latino players. It is hoped that gaps in the checklist will eventually be filled with confirmed specimens. Many of the photos on these cards appear to have been lifted - some even with the typography intact - from Bowman baseball cards of the era. Some, perhaps all, of the cards were printed in more than one color.

		NM	EX	VG
Common Player:				10.00
1	Guillermo Estrella			10.00
2	Benitez Redondo			10.00
3	Vidal Lopez			10.00
4	R. del Monte y C.			10.00
5				
6				
7	Juan Delfin Garcia			10.00
8	J. Raf. Carretero			10.00
9	J. Benjamin (Papo)			10.00
10				
11	Rufo E. Felix			10.00
12	Gallego Munoz			10.00
13	Julio A. Lara			10.00
14				
15				
16	Rafael Espada			10.00
17	Aladino Paez			10.00
18				
19	Pepe Lucas			10.00
20	Manolete Caceres			10.00
21	E.A. Lantigua			10.00
22	Olmedo Suarez			10.00
23	Chucho Ramos			10.00
24	Gullabin Olivo			10.00
25	Jose Luis Velazquez			10.00
26				
27	Felle Delgado			10.00
28				
29				
30	Alcibades Colon			10.00
31	Horacio Martinez			10.00
32	Ramon Burgos			10.00
33	Carlos A. Piallo			10.00
34	W.E. Springfield			10.00
35	Fiquito Suarez			10.00
36				
37				
38	Rafael Ortiz			10.00
39				
40				
41	Tetelo Vargas			10.00
42	Miguel Rueda			10.00
43	Hector Salazar			10.00
44				
45	Rafael Vargas			10.00
46				
47				
48				
49				
50	Gerard Thorne			10.00
51	Bienvenido Arias			10.00
52	Son Howell			15.00
53				
54				
55				
56				
57	P. Mateo (Richard)			10.00
58				
59				
60	Martin Dihigo			150.00
61				
62				
63				
64				
65	Octavio Blanco			10.00
66	Daniel Rodriguez			10.00
67				
68	Luis Villodas			10.00
69	Miguel Aracena			10.00
70	Amor Diaz			10.00
71	Juan B. Perdomo			10.00
72	Julio Martinez			10.00
73	Fernando Bueno			10.00
74	Rene Gutierrez			10.00
75	Israel Hernandez			10.00
76	Tomas Gomez Checo			10.00
77				
78	Miguel Tian Tineo			10.00
79	Rafael Valdez			10.00
80	Calampio Leon			10.00
81	Leonardo Coicochea			10.00
82	Herberto Blanco			10.00
83				
84	Rogelio Martinez			10.00
85				
86				
87	Silvio Garcia			10.00
88				
89	Napoleon Reyes			15.00
90				
91				
92				
93	Claro Duane (Duany)			10.00
94				
95				
96	Regino Otero			10.00
97	Avelino Canizares			10.00
98	Sandalio Consuegra			25.00
99	Roberto R. Topane			10.00
100	Jaok Cassin (Jack Cassini)			20.00
101	Jaime B. Prendesgart (Jim Prendergast)			20.00
102	Pablo Garcia			10.00
103				
104				
105				
106	Alejandro Crespo			20.00
107	Hiran Gonzalez			10.00
108	Rafael Noble			20.00
109				
110	Jose R. Lopez			10.00
111				
112				
113	Gilberto Torres			10.00
114				
115	Patato Pascual			10.00
116				
117				
118				
119	Gilberto Valdivia			10.00
120	Svdor. Hernandez			10.00
121				
122				
123				
124	Pedro Formental (Formenthal)			10.00
125				
126				
127				
128				
129				
130				
131				
132				
133				
134				
135	H. Wilson			25.00
136				
137				
138				
139	Carl Hubbell			35.00
140				
141				
142	Cocaina Garcia			10.00
143				
144				
145				
146				
147				
148				
149				
150				
151	Phill Rizzuto (Phil)			75.00
152	Bill Mc Cahan			20.00
153				
154	Allie Reynolds			55.00
155	Gill Coan (Gil)			20.00
156				
157	Mizell Platt			20.00
158				
159	Al S. "Red" (Schoendienst)			50.00
160	Jack Lorke (Lohrke)			20.00
161				
162				
163	Bill Nicholson			20.00
164	Sam Mele			20.00
165	Bob Schiffino (Scheffing)			20.00
166				
167				
168				
169	Harri Gumbert (Harry)			20.00
170				
171	Johnny Wyrostek			20.00
172				
173				
174				
175				
176				
177	Ken Keltner			25.00
178				
179	Harry Walker			25.00
180				
181				
182				
183				
184				
185	Sibby Sisti			20.00
186				
187	Eddie Waiticus (Waitkus)			25.00
188	Eddie Lake			20.00
189				
190	Hank Arft			20.00
191				
192				
193				
194	Walker Cooper			20.00
195	Al Brazle			20.00
196	Sam Champmann (Chapman)			20.00
197				
198	Doyle Lade			20.00
199				
200	Henry Eduards (Edwards)			20.00
201				
202				
203	N.Y. "Baby" (Norman "Babe" Young)			20.00
204				
205				
206	Bob Feller			75.00
207	Ralph Branca			35.00
208				
209				
210				
211	Larry (Yogi) Berra			75.00
212	Eddie Joost			20.00
213				
214				
215				
216				
217				
218				
219	Gil Hodges			55.00
220				
221				
222				
223	James, Vernon (Mickey)			25.00
224				
225				
226				

227		
228		
229		
230		
231		
232		
233		
234	Pete Raiser (Reiser)	30.00
235		
236	Bob Elliot	20.00
237		
238	Lou Boudreau	45.00
239	Danny Murtany	25.00
	(Photo is Joe Gordon.)	
240	Jakie Robinson (Jackie)	125.00
241		
242		
243	Tommy Henrick (Henrich)	25.00
244	Pee Wee Reese	55.00
245	Bobby Brower (Brown)	25.00
246		
247		
248	Enos Slaughter	35.00
249		
250		
251	Tommy Henrich	25.00
252	George Koslo (Dave)	20.00
253	Frank Gustino (Gustine)	20.00
254		
255		
256		
257	Bill Rigney	20.00
258		
259	Rex Barney	25.00
260		
261	Mark Christman	20.00
262	Whetey Lockman (Whitey)	20.00
263		
264	Ralph Kiner	55.00
265		
266	Cliff Fannin	20.00
267	Joe Page	25.00
268		
269		
270		
271	Johnny Sain	30.00
272		
273		
274		
275		
276		
277		
278		
279	Joe Dobson	20.00
280		
281	Carrol Lockman (Whitey)	20.00
282		
283	Monte Kennedy	20.00
284		
285		
286	Carlos Bernier	20.00
287		
288		
289	Buster Clarkson	20.00
290	Williard Brown (Willard)	25.00
291	Jim Rivera	25.00
292	Saturnino Escalera	20.00

1958 Dominican Republic

The date of issue is speculative, based on the known winter ball career of the sole card known. The identity of the issuer and manner of distribution is unknown, though from their wide borders it is possible these were printed on some type of box or package and intended to be cut out and possibly placed into an album, as is customary with many Latin American baseball card issues. The cards are nominally about 2" x 2-1/2" and are printed in sepia on thin, blank-back cardboard. As with many issues of the era and area, when these cards are found they are usually in wretched condition.

	NM	EX	VG
Felipe R. Alou			35.00

1959 Dominican Republic

The date of issue is speculative. The identity of the issuer and manner of distribution is unknown, though they appear to have been sold in strips or panels and intended to be separated and possibly placed into an album, as is customary with many Latin American baseball cards. The cards are nominally about 2-1/8" x 3-1/4" and printed in black or blue on thin, blank-back cardboard. As with many issues of the era and area, when these cards are found they are usually in wretched condition. These players certainly represent only a portion of the checklist.

	NM	EX	VG
Walter James			15.00
Osvaldo Virgil			25.00

1966 Dominican Republic

The date of issue is speculative, based on the fact these cards "borrowed" their images from 1965 Topps cards. The identity of the issuer and manner of distribution is unknown, though from their wide borders it is possible these were printed on some type of box or package and intended to be cut out and possibly placed into an album, as is customary with many Latin American baseball card issues. The cards are nominally about 1-3/4" x 2-1/2" and are printed in red on thin, blank-back cardboard. As with many issues of the era and area, when these cards are found they are usually in wretched condition. These players probably represent only a portion of the checklist which may or may not comprise only Major League players.

		NM	EX	VG
(1)	Sandy Koufax			200.00
(2)	Juan Marichal			100.00
(3)	Willy Mays (Willie)			200.00
(4)	Willy McCovy (Willie McCovey)			45.00

1937 Donut Co. of American Thrilling Moments

The official title of this multi-subject card set is "Thrilling Moments in the Lives of Famous Americans." The cards, about 1-7/8" x 2-7/8", were printed in groups of 18 on donut boxes. Each card is printed in black-and-white on a single background color. The cards themselves do not name the famous American depicted, but his biography is found in the album which was issued to house the set. Cards are blank-backed. There is only a single baseball playered in the 72-card set.

	NM	EX	VG
Beloved Baseball Idol of All Boys (Babe Ruth)	4,000	1,600	800.00

1952-55 Dormand Postcards

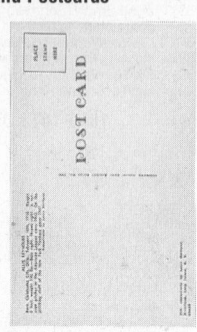

This mid-1950s issue features only selected players from the Yankees, Brooklyn Dodgers, White Sox and Philadelphia A's. Apparently produced on order by the players by Louis Dormand, a Long Island, N.Y., photographer, the cards were used to honor fan requests for photos and autographs. All cards have a facsimile autograph printed in front. Otherwise the fronts of these 3-1/2" x 5-1/2" postcards feature only sharp color photos with no border. Backs, printed in blue or green, feature a few player biographical and career details, one or two lines identifying the producer and usually product and series numbers. Most have a Kodachrome logo. Some cards do not have all of these elements and several are found blank-backed. The Gil Hodges card is considerably scarcer than the others in the set, with those of Jim Konstanty, Elston Howard, and Casey Stengel also seldom seen. Besides the standard-sized cards listed below, there are oversize versions of Rizzuto's and Mantle's cards. A variation of Johnny Sain's card shows his Arkansas Chevrolet dealership in a photo above the player's picture. The complete set price includes only the standard-size cards.

		NM	EX	VG
Common Player:		25.00	12.50	7.50
101a	Phil Rizzuto (Large autograph parallel to top.)	40.00	20.00	12.00
101b	Phil Rizzuto (Small autograph parallel to top.)	45.00	22.50	13.50
101c	Phil Rizzuto (Autograph angles downward.)	50.00	25.00	15.00
101d	Phil Rizzuto (9" x 12")	55.00	27.50	16.50
102	Yogi Berra	65.00	32.50	20.00
103	Ed Lopat	30.00	15.00	9.00
104	Hank Bauer (Small autograph.)	30.00	15.00	9.00
104	Hank Bauer (Large autograph.)	35.00	17.50	10.50
105	Joe Collins (Patch on sleeve, autograph at top.)	60.00	30.00	18.00
105	Joe Collins (Patch on sleeve, autograph at bottom.)	60.00	30.00	18.00
105	Joe Collins (No patch on sleeve.)	40.00	20.00	12.00
106	Ralph Houk	30.00	15.00	9.00
107	Bill Miller	27.50	13.50	8.25
108	Ray Scarborough	35.00	17.50	10.00
109	Allie Reynolds	25.00	12.50	7.50
110	Gil McDougald (Small autograph.)	25.00	12.50	7.50
110	Gil McDougald (Large autograph.)	25.00	12.50	7.50
111	Mickey Mantle (Bat on shoulder.)	100.00	50.00	30.00
111	Mickey Mantle (Batting stance, 3-1/2" x 5-1/2".)	75.00	37.50	22.50
111	Mickey Mantle (Bat on shoulder, 6" x 9".)	550.00	275.00	165.00
111	Mickey Mantle (Bat on shoulder, 9" x 12".)	1,200	600.00	360.00
112	Johnny Mize	90.00	45.00	27.50
113	Casey Stengel (Autograph at top.)	165.00	80.00	50.00
113	Casey Stengel (Autograph at bottom.)	165.00	80.00	50.00
114	Bobby Shantz (Autograph parallel to top.)	40.00	20.00	12.00
114	Bobby Shantz (Autograph angles downward.)	40.00	20.00	12.00
115	Whitey Ford	60.00	30.00	18.00
116	Johnny Sain (Beginning windup.)	35.00	17.50	10.00
116	Johnny Sain (Leg kick.)	25.00	12.50	7.50
116	Johnny Sain (With auto dealership ad.)	150.00	75.00	45.00
117	Jim McDonald	25.00	12.50	7.50
118	Gene Woodling	25.00	12.50	7.50
119	Charlie Silvera	30.00	15.00	9.00
120	Don Bollweg	25.00	12.50	7.50
121	Billy Pierce	30.00	15.00	9.00
122	Chico Carrasquel	25.00	12.50	7.50
123	Willie Miranda	25.00	12.50	7.50
124	Carl Erskine	65.00	32.50	20.00
125	Roy Campanella	150.00	75.00	45.00
126	Jerry Coleman	25.00	12.50	7.50
127	Pee Wee Reese	50.00	25.00	15.00
128	Carl Furillo	50.00	25.00	15.00
129	Gil Hodges	75.00	37.50	22.50
130	Billy Martin	30.00	15.00	9.00
131	Not Issued			
132	Irv Noren	35.00	17.50	10.50
133	Enos Slaughter	65.00	32.50	20.00
134	Tom Gorman	25.00	12.50	7.50
135	Ed Robinson	35.00	17.50	10.00
136	Frank Crosetti	35.00	17.50	10.00

		NM	EX	VG
137	Not Issued			
138	Jim Konstanty	150.00	75.00	45.00
139	Elston Howard	150.00	75.00	45.00
140	Bill Skowron	150.00	75.00	45.00

1941 Double Play (R330)

JOE DI MAGGIO
NEW YORK YANKEES. Center fielder. Born Nov. 25, 1914. Bats right. Throws right. Height 6 ft. Weight 195 lbs. Batted .352.
No. 63 Double Play

CHARLEY KELLER
NEW YORK YANKEES. Left fielder. Born Sept. 12, 1916. Bats left. Throws right. Height 5 ft. 10 in. Wt. 190 lbs. Batted .286.
No. 64 Double Play

Issued by Gum Products Inc., Cambridge, Mass., this set comprises 75 numbered cards with two consecutive numbers per card featuring 150 (130 different) players. The blank-backed cards measure about 3-1/8" x 2-1/2". Most feature sepia-toned portrait photos. Cards 81-82 through 99-100 have vertical "in action" photos of 40 of the players who also appear in portraits. The last 50 cards in the series are scarcer than the early numbers. Cards which have been cut in half to form single cards have little collector value.

		NM	EX	VG
Complete Set (75):		10,000	4,000	2,000
Common Player (1/2-99/100):		70.00	25.00	12.50
Common Player (101/102-149/150):		90.00	35.00	15.00
1-2	Larry French, Vance Page	90.00	30.00	15.00
3-4	Billy Herman, Stanley Hack	125.00	50.00	25.00
5-6	Linus Frey, John Vander Meer	75.00	30.00	15.00
7-8	Paul Derringer, Bucky Walters	70.00	25.00	12.50
9-10	Frank McCormick, Bill Werber	70.00	25.00	12.50
11-12	Jimmy Ripple, Ernie Lombardi	85.00	35.00	15.00
13-14	Alex Kampouris, John Wyatt	70.00	25.00	12.50
15-16	Mickey Owen, Paul Waner	110.00	45.00	20.00
17-18	Cookie Lavagetto, Harold Reiser	75.00	30.00	15.00
19-20	Jimmy Wasdell, Dolph Camilli	70.00	25.00	12.50
21-22	Dixie Walker, Ducky Medwick	110.00	45.00	20.00
23-24	Harold Reese, Kirby Higbe	600.00	240.00	120.00
25-26	Harry Danning, Cliff Melton	70.00	25.00	12.50
27-28	Harry Gumbert, Burgess Whitehead	70.00	25.00	12.50
29-30	Joe Orengo, Joe Moore	70.00	25.00	12.50
31-32	Mel Ott, Babe Young	200.00	80.00	40.00
33-34	Lee Handley, Arky Vaughan	110.00	45.00	20.00
35-36	Bob Klinger, Stanley Brown	70.00	25.00	12.50
37-38	Terry Moore, Gus Mancuso	70.00	25.00	12.50
39-40	Johnny Mize, Enos Slaughter	700.00	280.00	140.00
41-42	John Cooney, Sibby Sisti	70.00	25.00	12.50
43-44	Max West, Carvel Rowell	70.00	25.00	12.50
45-46	Danny Litwhiler, Merrill May	70.00	25.00	12.50
47-48	Frank Hayes, Al Brancato	70.00	25.00	12.50
49-50	Bob Johnson, Bill Nagel	70.00	25.00	12.50
51-52	Buck Newsom, Hank Greenberg	200.00	80.00	40.00
53-54	Barney McCosky, Charley Gehringer	140.00	55.00	25.00
55-56	Pinky Higgins, Dick Bartell	70.00	25.00	12.50
57-58	Ted Williams, Jim Tabor	650.00	260.00	130.00
59-60	Joe Cronin, Jimmy Foxx	275.00	110.00	55.00
61-62	Lefty Gomez, Phil Rizzuto	675.00	275.00	135.00
63-64	Joe DiMaggio, Charley Keller	750.00	300.00	150.00
65-66	Red Rolfe, Bill Dickey	125.00	50.00	25.00
67-68	Joe Gordon, Red Ruffing	120.00	45.00	25.00
69-70	Mike Tresh, Luke Appling	110.00	45.00	20.00
71-72	Moose Solters, John Rigney	70.00	25.00	12.50
73-74	Buddy Meyer, Ben Chapman (Myer)	70.00	25.00	12.50
75-76	Cecil Travis, George Case	70.00	25.00	12.50
77-78	Joe Krakauskas, Bob Feller	200.00	80.00	40.00
79-80	Ken Keltner, Hal Trosky	70.00	25.00	12.50
81-82	Ted Williams, Joe Cronin/IA	550.00	220.00	110.00
83-84	Joe Gordon, Charley Keller/IA	90.00	35.00	15.00
85-86	Hank Greenberg, Red Ruffing/IA	225.00	90.00	45.00
87-88	Hal Trosky, George Case/IA	70.00	25.00	12.50
89-90	Mel Ott, Burgess Whitehead/IA	210.00	85.00	40.00
91-92	Harry Danning, Harry Gumbert/IA	70.00	25.00	12.50
93-94	Babe Young, Cliff Melton/IA	70.00	25.00	12.50
95-96	Jimmy Ripple, Bucky Walters/IA	70.00	25.00	12.50
97-98	Stanley Hack, Bob Klinger/IA	70.00	25.00	12.50
99-100	Johnny Mize, Dan Litwhiler/IA	135.00	55.00	25.00
101-102	Dom Dallessandro, Augie Galan	70.00	25.00	12.50
103-104	Bill Lee, Phil Cavarretta	90.00	35.00	15.00
105-106	Lefty Grove, Bobby Doerr	210.00	85.00	40.00
107-108	Frank Pytlak, Dom DiMaggio	115.00	45.00	20.00
109-110	Gerald Priddy, John Murphy	90.00	35.00	15.00
111-112	Tommy Henrich, Marius Russo	100.00	40.00	20.00
113-114	Frank Crosetti, John Sturm	100.00	40.00	20.00
115-116	Johnny Johnson, Myron McCormick	90.00	35.00	15.00
117-118	Eddie Joost, Ernie Koy	90.00	35.00	15.00
119-120	Lloyd Waner, Hank Majeski	125.00	50.00	25.00
121-122	Buddy Hassett, Eugene Moore	90.00	35.00	15.00

		NM	EX	VG
123-124	Nick Etten, John Rizzo	90.00	35.00	15.00
125-126	Sam Chapman, Wally Moses	90.00	35.00	15.00
127-128	John Babich, Richard Siebert	90.00	35.00	15.00
129-130	Nelson Potter, Benny McCoy	90.00	25.00	15.00
131-132	Clarence Campbell, Louis Boudreau	125.00	50.00	25.00
133-134	Rolly Hemsley, Mel Harder	90.00	35.00	15.00
135-136	Gerald Walker, Joe Heving	90.00	35.00	15.00
137-138	John Rucker, Ace Adams	90.00	35.00	15.00
139-140	Morris Arnovich, Carl Hubbell	225.00	90.00	45.00
141-142	Lew Riggs, Leo Durocher	135.00	55.00	25.00
143-144	Fred Fitzsimmons, Joe Vosmik	90.00	35.00	15.00
145-146	Frank Crespi, Jim Brown	90.00	35.00	15.00
147-148	Don Heffner, Harland Clift (Harland)	90.00	35.00	15.00
149-150	Debs Garms, Elbie Fletcher	90.00	35.00	15.00

1976 Douglas Cool Papa Bell

This collectors' issue was produced following the 1974 induction of James "Cool Papa" Bell into the Hall of Fame. Collector John Douglas collaborated with Bell to produce the set chronicling Bell's career (1922-46) in the Negro and Latin American pro leagues. Fronts have vintage sepia-toned photos of Bell surrounded by a yellow, green or orange woodgrain frame with a title plaque at bottom. Backs are in brown-and-white with a drawing of Bell at top and autobiographical material at center. A description of the photo and copyright data are at bottom. The unnumbered cards are checklisted here alphabetically by their titles.

		NM	EX	VG
Complete Set (13):		10.00	5.00	3.00
Common Card:		1.00	.50	.30
(1)	Amazing Speed	1.00	.50	.30
(2)	Brock Sets SB Record	1.00	.50	.30
(3)	Cool Papa	1.00	.50	.30
(4)	Cuba, 1928	1.00	.50	.30
(5)	Great Fielder, Too	1.00	.50	.30
(6)	HOF, Cooperstown	1.00	.50	.30
(7)	HOF Favorite	1.00	.50	.30
(8)	Induction Day, 1974	1.00	.50	.30
(9)	Monarchs' Manager	1.00	.50	.30
(10)	On Deck in Cuba	1.00	.50	.30
(11)	The Mexican Leagues	1.00	.50	.30
(12)	Touring Havana	1.00	.50	.30
(13)	With Josh Gibson	1.00	.50	.30

1977 Douglas Johnny Mize

In an effort to promote Johnny Mize for induction to the Hall of Fame, John Douglas created this collectors' issue. The Big Cat's career is traced on a series of 3-1/4" x 3-7/8" cards with black-and-white photos on a greenish-brown background. Black-and-white backs have a drawing of Mize at top with lengthy narrative below. The unnumbered cards are checklisted here by the title which appears on the front. Mize was selected for the Hall of Fame in 1981.

		NM	EX	VG
Complete Set (20):		9.00	4.50	2.75
Common Card:		1.00	.50	.30
(1)	Blattner, Gordon, Lombardi, Mize, Marshall	1.00	.50	.30
(2)	Call for Phillip Morris	1.00	.50	.30
(3)	Cardinal Slugger	1.00	.50	.30
(4)	Card's Big Stick	1.00	.50	.30
(5)	Early Photo - 1913	1.00	.50	.30
(6)	51 Homers, 1947	1.00	.50	.30
(7)	Home Run, 1952 Series	1.00	.50	.30
(8)	June 16, 1953	1.00	.50	.30
(9)	Louisville Poster - 1947	1.00	.50	.30
(10)	Mize, Happy Chandler, Bucky Harris	1.00	.50	.30
(11)	Mize, Reynolds, Johnson	1.00	.50	.30
(12)	N.L. Homer Champ 1948	1.00	.50	.30
(13)	Series MVP - 1952	1.00	.50	.30
(14)	St. Louis Star	1.00	.50	.30
(15)	The Navy - 1943	1.00	.50	.30

		NM	EX	VG
(16)	Vu-Master Slide	1.00	.50	.30
(17)	With Enos Slaughter	1.00	.50	.30
(18)	With Roy Rogers	1.00	.50	.30
(19)	With Terry Moore	1.00	.50	.30
(20)	Woodling, Raschi, Mize - 1952	1.00	.50	.30

1978 Dover Publications Great Players Postcards

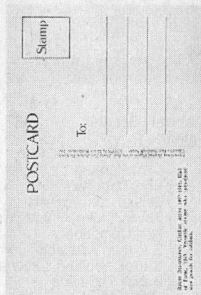

This set of 32 collectors' issue postcards was originally issued in the form of an 8" x 11" booklet from which individual cards could be separated. The 3-7/8" x 5-1/2" cards are perforated on two sides, depending on their placement on a four-card page. Fronts have borderless sepia photos. Black-and-white backs have standard postcard indicia, copyright data, player identification and a brief career summary. The unnumbered cards are checklisted here alphabetically.

		NM	EX	VG
Complete Set, Booklet:		7.50	3.75	2.25
Complete Set, Singles (32):		7.50	3.75	2.25
Common Player:		.50	.25	.15
(1)	Grover Cleveland Alexander	.60	.30	.20
(2)	Chief Bender	.50	.25	.15
(3)	Roger Bresnahan	.50	.25	.15
(4)	Bullet Joe Bush	.50	.25	.15
(5)	Frank Chance	.50	.25	.15
(6)	Ty Cobb	1.25	.60	.40
(7)	Eddie Collins	.50	.25	.15
(8)	Stan Coveleski	.50	.25	.15
(9)	Sam Crawford	.50	.25	.15
(10)	Frankie Frisch	.50	.25	.15
(11)	Goose Goslin	.50	.25	.15
(12)	Harry Heilmann	.50	.25	.15
(13)	Rogers Hornsby	.75	.40	.25
(14)	Joe Jackson	4.00	2.00	1.25
(15)	Hughie Jennings	.50	.25	.15
(16)	Walter Johnson	1.00	.50	.30
(17)	Sad Sam Jones	.50	.25	.15
(18)	Rabbit Maranville	.50	.25	.15
(19)	Rube Marquard	.50	.25	.15
(20)	Christy Mathewson	1.00	.50	.30
(21)	John McGraw	.50	.25	.15
(22)	Herb Pennock	.50	.25	.15
(23)	Eddie Plank	.50	.25	.15
(24)	Edd Roush	.50	.25	.15
(25)	Babe Ruth	4.00	2.00	1.25
(26)	George Sisler	.50	.25	.15
(27)	Tris Speaker	.75	.40	.25
(28)	Casey Stengel	.50	.25	.15
(29)	Joe Tinker	.50	.25	.15
(30)	Pie Traynor	.50	.25	.15
(31)	Dazzy Vance	.50	.25	.15
(32)	Cy Young	.75	.40	.25

1925 Drake's

DRAKE'S CAKE

Made from the finest ingredients obtainable. Best butter, eggs, sugar, milk, fruits, spices etc. — and plenty of them. Old fashioned home methods are then applied in our spotless kitchens to give you this result. Always open for inspection.

This is one of a series of 64 pictures of prominent film stars. They will be found in most packages of DRAKE'S CAKE. Get the others, too.

Among a series of 64 movie stars packaged with Drake's Cake in the mid-1920s was a card of Babe Ruth, who did some movie work for Universal Pictures at the time. The 2-7/16" x 4-3/16" black-and-white card has a portrait of Ruth on front, with his name, studio and card number in the bottom border. Backs have been seen with at least two styles of advertising, one for Drake's Cake and one for Yankee Cake.

		NM	EX	VG
61	Babe Ruth	3,750	1,875	1,125

1950 Drake's

Entitled "TV Baseball Series," the 1950 Drake's Bakeries set pictures 36 different players on a television screen format. The cards, 2-1/2" x 2-1/2", contain black-and-white photos surrounded by a black border. Backs carry a player biography plus an advertisement advising collectors to look for the cards in packages of Oatmeal or Jumble cookies.

		NM	EX	VG
Complete Set (36):		7,500	3,000	1,500
Common Player:		150.00	60.00	30.00
1	Elwin "Preacher" Roe	250.00	100.00	50.00
2	Clint Hartung	150.00	60.00	30.00
3	Earl Torgeson	150.00	60.00	30.00
4	Leland "Lou" Brissie	150.00	60.00	30.00
5	Edwin "Duke" Snider	500.00	200.00	100.00
6	Roy Campanella	500.00	200.00	100.00
7	Sheldon "Available" Jones	150.00	60.00	30.00
8	Carroll "Whitey" Lockman	150.00	60.00	30.00
9	Bobby Thomson	175.00	70.00	35.00
10	Dick Sisler	150.00	60.00	30.00
11	Gil Hodges	300.00	120.00	60.00
12	Eddie Waitkus	150.00	60.00	30.00
13	Bobby Doerr	250.00	100.00	50.00
14	Warren Spahn	300.00	120.00	60.00
15	John "Buddy" Kerr	150.00	60.00	30.00
16	Sid Gordon	150.00	60.00	30.00
17	Willard Marshall	150.00	60.00	30.00
18	Carl Furillo	300.00	120.00	60.00
19	Harold "Pee Wee" Reese	400.00	160.00	80.00
20	Alvin Dark	150.00	60.00	30.00
21	Del Ennis	150.00	60.00	30.00
22	Ed Stanky	150.00	60.00	30.00
23	Tommy "Old Reliable" Henrich	175.00	70.00	35.00
24	Larry "Yogi" Berra	500.00	200.00	100.00
25	Phil "Scooter" Rizzuto	500.00	200.00	100.00
26	Jerry Coleman	150.00	60.00	30.00
27	Joe Page	150.00	60.00	30.00
28	Allie Reynolds	175.00	70.00	35.00
29	Ray Scarborough	150.00	60.00	30.00
30	George "Birdie" Tebbetts	150.00	60.00	30.00
31	Maurice "Lefty" McDermott	150.00	60.00	30.00
32	Johnny Pesky	150.00	60.00	30.00
33	Dom "Little Professor" DiMaggio	190.00	75.00	35.00
34	Vern "Junior" Stephens	150.00	60.00	30.00
35	Bob Elliott	150.00	60.00	30.00
36	Enos "Country" Slaughter	325.00	130.00	65.00

1909-11 Drum Cigarettes

Other than Ty Cobb brand, Drum is the rarest of the various cigarette advertisements to be found on the backs of T206. Typography on the back is printed in a plum color. Multipliers shown are for "common" players; Hall of Fame players and other high-demand cards command a lesser premium relative to common-brand backs. Among T205 backs, Drum, printed in brown, ranks as the scarcest of the brands.

PREMIUMS
T205: 25X
T206: 40X
(See T205, T206 for checklists and base card values.)

1972 Don Drysdale's Restaurant Postcards

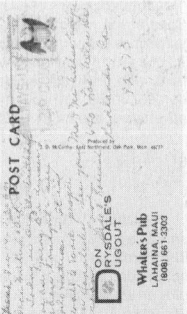

The date cited is taken from the postmark of an observed example. The actual span during which the cards were current is unknown. These versions of J.D. McCarthy postcards have on their 3-1/4" x 5-1/2" fronts a borderless black-and-white pose. The salutation and facsimile autograph are incuse printed in blue ink. Postcard style backs are known in three styles. One advertises Don Drysdale's Dugout in Santa Ana, Calif., another advertises his Club 53 in Kona, Hawaii, while a third advertizes Don Drysdale's Dugout and the Whaler's Pub on Maui.

	NM	EX	VG
Don Drysdale	16.00	8.00	4.75

1965 Dugan Bros. Casey Stengel

In celebration of the Ol' Perfesser's 75th birthday, the N.Y. Mets held a birthday party for him at Shea Stadium on July 25. This approximately 2-1/2" x 3-1/2" card was given to each of the 40,000+ fans in attendance, sponsored by Dugan Bros., a local bakery which also provided a birthday cake for the occasion. Unfortunately, Stengel was unable to attend the fete; early that morning he broke his hip leaving a nightclub, ending his managerial career. The card is printed in blue on white. The back provides career highlights.

	NM	EX	VG
Casey Stengel	25.00	12.50	7.50

1888 Duke Talk of the Diamond (N135)

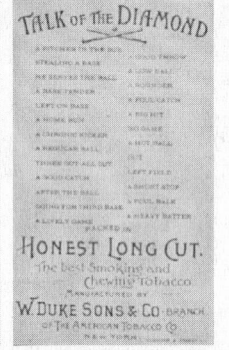

One of the more obscure 19th Century tobacco issues is a 25-card set issued by Honest Long Cut Tobacco in the late 1880's. Titled "Talk of the Diamond," the set features full-color cards measuring 4-1/8" x 2-1/2". Each card features a cartoon-like drawing illustrating a popular baseball term or expression. The left portion of the card pictures an unspecified player in a fielding position, and some of the artwork for that part of the set was borrowed from the more popular Buchner Gold Coin set (N284) issued about the same time. Because the "Talk of the Diamond" set does not feature individual players, it has never really captured the attention of baseball card collectors. It does, however, hold interest as a novelty item of the period. It carries an N135 American Card Catalog designation.

		NM	EX	VG
Complete Set (25):		9,350	3,850	1,925
Common Card:		385.00	155.00	75.00
(1)	A Base Tender	400.00	155.00	75.00
(2)	A Big Hit	400.00	155.00	75.00
(3)	A Chronic Kicker	400.00	155.00	75.00
(4)	A Foul Balk	400.00	155.00	75.00
(5)	A Foul Catch	400.00	155.00	75.00
(6)	A Good Catch	400.00	155.00	75.00
(7)	A Good Throw	400.00	155.00	75.00
(8)	A Heavy Batter	400.00	155.00	75.00
(9)	A Home Run	400.00	155.00	75.00
(10)	A Hot Ball	400.00	155.00	75.00
(11)	A Low Ball	400.00	155.00	75.00
(12)	A Pitcher in the Box	400.00	155.00	75.00
(13)	A Regular Ball	400.00	155.00	75.00
(14)	A Rounder	400.00	155.00	75.00
(15)	A Short Stop	400.00	155.00	75.00
(16)	After the Ball	400.00	155.00	75.00
(17)	Going for Third Base	400.00	155.00	75.00
(18)	He Serves the Ball	400.00	155.00	75.00
(19)	Left Field	400.00	155.00	75.00
(20)	Left on Base	400.00	155.00	75.00
(21)	Lively Game	400.00	155.00	75.00
(22)	No Game	400.00	155.00	75.00
(23)	Out	400.00	155.00	75.00
(24)	Stealing a Base	400.00	155.00	75.00
(25)	Three out-All out	400.00	155.00	75.00

1889 Duke's Terrors of America

Officially titled "The Terrors of America and their Doings," this set of tobacco inserts features color artwork of boys in all manners of activities, some mischievous. Several of the cards picture the lads playing sports, including baseball. The cards were issued in three sizes. The smallest measure 1-7/16" x 2-3/4" and have an ad on the checklist back for Duke's Cigarettes. A slightly larger 1-3/4" x 3-1/8" version advertises Duke's Mixture. The largest features the card design on an ornate background and measures 2-1/2" x 4-3/16", advertising Honest Long Cut on back.

	NM	EX	VG
Duke's Cigarettes	80.00	40.00	24.00
Duke's Mixture	100.00	50.00	30.00
Honest Long Cut	200.00	100.00	60.00

1969 Dunkin' Donuts Chicago Cubs Bumper Stickers

This series of Cubs novelty collectibles was the first of two annual presentations. The stickers measure about 8" x 4" and have at their left end a photographic portrait of a player at one end of an artwork bat on a black background. At right is a baseball design with the sponsor's logo. A second version exists with "Cub Power" in place of the DD advertising. The unnumbered stickers are checklisted here alphabetically.

		NM	EX	VG
Complete Set (6):		350.00	175.00	100.00
Common Player:		30.00	15.00	9.00
(1)	Ernie Banks	125.00	65.00	35.00
(2)	Glenn Beckert	30.00	15.00	9.00
(3)	Randy Hundley	30.00	15.00	9.00
(4)	Don Kessinger	30.00	15.00	9.00
(5)	Ron Santo	60.00	30.00	18.00
(6)	Billy Williams	75.00	37.00	22.00

1970 Dunkin' Donuts Chicago Cubs Bumper Stickers

This series of Cubs novelty collectibles was the second of two annual presentations. The stickers measure about 8" x 4" and have at their left end a photographic portrait (without cap) of a player in a vaguely baseball-like design. In upper-left is a blue facsimile autograph. At right is "Cubs are no. 1," at bottom is a DD credit line. Basic color scheme of the graphics is red, white and blue. The unnumbered stickers are checklisted here alphabetically.

		NM	EX	VG
Complete Set (6):		350.00	175.00	100.00
Common Player:		30.00	15.00	9.00
(1)	Ernie Banks	125.00	62.00	37.00
(2)	Glenn Beckert	30.00	15.00	9.00
(3)	Randy Hundley	30.00	15.00	9.00
(4)	Don Kessinger	30.00	15.00	9.00
(5)	Ron Santo	60.00	30.00	18.00
(6)	Billy Williams	75.00	37.00	22.00

1947 DuPont Cavalcade of America Premium

This 6" x 9" black-and-white card was distributed by NBC radio in conjunction with one of its weekly programs, which featured Babe Ruth on Sept. 29, 1947. The front has a bordered photo of Ruth in his classic batting follow-through. The back has information about the broadcast and details "The Babe's 54 Major League Records."

	NM	EX	VG
Babe Ruth	500.00	250.00	150.00

1972 Durochrome Chicago White Sox Decals

While they are technically stickers rather than decals, this set of six White Sox was given away during the course of half a dozen "Decal Days" at Comiskey Park, as listed on the peel-off back. The stickers measure 3-9/16" x 4-9/16" and feature posed action photos of the players in their vintage red-trimmed uniforms. Fronts have a facsimile autograph and, in the bottom border, the team name. Backs are printed in green and have a few vital statistics, an ad by the manufacturer and an enigmatic row of numbers at the bottom. The unnumbered stickers are checklisted here in alphabetical order.

		NM	EX	VG
Complete Set (6):		60.00	30.00	18.00
Common Player:		9.00	4.50	2.75
(1)	Richard Allen	25.00	12.50	7.50
(2)	Ed Hermann	9.00	4.50	2.75
(3)	Bart Johnson	9.00	4.50	2.75
(4)	Carlos May	9.00	4.50	2.75
(5)	Bill Melton	9.00	4.50	2.75
(6)	Wilbur Wood	9.00	4.50	2.75

E

1914 E. & S. Publishing Co.

Currently, a dozen players have been reported from this issue. Front of the 5-1/2" x 3-3/4" postcards has a large portrait or action picture of the player at center, with a number of cartoons around. The printing is in blue ink. The back is done in ornate typography with copyright line, stamp box, etc. Other players may yet be discovered.

		NM	EX	VG
(1)	"Jimmie" Archer	300.00	150.00	90.00
(2)	Joe Benz	300.00	150.00	90.00
(3)	Frank Chance	300.00	150.00	90.00
(4)	Ty Cobb	4,500	2,250	1,350
(5)	Miller Huggins	600.00	300.00	180.00
(6)	Joe Jackson	6,000	3,000	1,800
(7)	James Lavender	300.00	150.00	90.00
(8)	Christy Mathewson	2,500	1,250	750.00
(9)	"Tex" Russell	300.00	150.00	90.00
(10)	Frank Schulte	300.00	150.00	90.00
(11)	Jim Scott	300.00	150.00	90.00
(12)	Art Wilson	300.00	150.00	90.00

1940s Eagle Hall of Fame

The date of this issue can only be approximated, probably in the late 1940s. The 9-1/4" x 11-1/4" cards have high-gloss sepia photos on thick cardboard. A wood-look frame and identification plaques are pictured around the central photo. Backs are blank. The pictures were issued by the Carnegie (Pa.) Aerie of the Eagles, lodge #1134, according to the bottom "plaque." At top is "Eagle Hall of Fame." Presumably the four ballplayers and two boxers known were all members of that fraternal order. The unnumbered pieces are checklisted alphabetically.

		NM	EX	VG
Complete Set (6):		700.00	350.00	210.00
Common Player:		40.00	20.00	12.00
(1)	Bob Fitzsimmons (Boxer)	40.00	20.00	12.00
(2)	Lefty Grove	150.00	75.00	45.00
(3)	Stan Musial	200.00	100.00	60.00
(4)	John Sullivan (Boxer)	75.00	37.00	22.00
(5)	Honus Wagner	175.00	87.00	52.00
(6)	Cy Young	175.00	87.00	52.00

1979 Early Red Sox Favorites

This collectors' issue from Maine features players of the 1920s-1930s Red Sox. Cards are printed in black-and-white in a 2-5/8" x 3-3/4" format. Front photos are bordered in white and have identification of the players overprinted in black. Backs have a few stats, highlights or an explanation of the photo on front. Many cards feature more than one player.

		NM	EX	VG
Complete Set (24):		40.00	20.00	12.00
Common Player:		4.00	2.00	1.25
1	New Fenway Park	4.00	2.00	1.25
2	Mrs. Tom Yawkey and Mrs. Eddie Collins	4.00	2.00	1.25
3	Red Sox Outfielders - 1932 (Tom Oliver, Earl Webb, Jack Rothrock)	4.00	2.00	1.25
4	Red Sox Ace Pitchers (John Marcum, Wes Ferrell, Lefty Grove, Fritz Ostermueller)	4.00	2.00	1.25
5	John Gooch	4.00	2.00	1.25
6	Red Sox Recruits at Sarasota, Fla. (Joe Cronin)	4.00	2.00	1.25
7	Danny MacFayden	4.00	2.00	1.25
8	Dale Alexander	4.00	2.00	1.25
9	Robert (Fatsy) Fothergill	4.00	2.00	1.25
10	Red Sox Sunday Morning Workout	4.00	2.00	1.25
11	Jimmie Foxx (Signing ball for Mrs. Yawkey.)	6.00	3.00	1.75
12	Lefty Grove (Presented keys to new car.)	6.00	3.00	1.75

13	"Fireball" Lefty Grove	6.00	3.00	1.75
14	Praciticing Base Stealing (Jack Rothrock, Urban Pickering)	4.00	2.00	1.25
15	Tom Daly, Al Schacht, Herb Pennock	4.00	2.00	1.25
16	Eddie Collins, Heinie Manush	6.00	3.00	1.75
17	Tris Speaker	6.00	3.00	1.75
18	Home Run Star (Jimmie Foxx)	6.00	3.00	1.75
19	Smead Jolley	4.00	2.00	1.25
20	Hal Trosky, Jimmie Foxx	4.00	2.00	1.25
21	Herold "Muddy" Ruel, Wilcy "Fireman" Moore	4.00	2.00	1.25
22	Bob Quinn, Shano Collins	4.00	2.00	1.25
23	Tom Oliver	4.00	2.00	1.25
24	Joe Cronin, Herb Pennock, Buetter	4.00	2.00	1.25

1966 East Hills Pirates

Stores in the East Hills Shopping Center, a large mall located in suburban Pittsburgh, distributed cards from this 25-card full-color set in 1966. The cards, which measure 3-1/4" x 4-1/4", are blank-backed and are numbered by the players' uniform numbers. The numbers appear in the lower right corners of the cards.

		NM	EX	VG
Complete Set (25):		50.00	25.00	15.00
Common Player:		2.50	1.25	.70
3	Harry Walker	2.50	1.25	.70
7	Bob Bailey	2.50	1.25	.70
8	Willie Stargell	10.00	5.00	3.00
9	Bill Mazeroski	10.00	5.00	3.00
10	Jim Pagliaroni	2.50	1.25	.70
11	Jose Pagan	2.50	1.25	.70
12	Jerry May	2.50	1.25	.70
14	Gene Alley	2.50	1.25	.70
15	Manny Mota	2.50	1.25	.70
16	Andy Rodgers	2.50	1.25	.70
17	Donn Clendenon	2.50	1.25	.70
18	Matty Alou	2.50	1.25	.70
19	Pete Mikkelsen	2.50	1.25	.70
20	Jesse Gonder	2.50	1.25	.70
21	Bob Clemente	30.00	15.00	9.00
22	Woody Fryman	2.50	1.25	.70
24	Jerry Lynch	2.50	1.25	.70
25	Tommie Sisk	2.50	1.25	.70
26	Roy Face	2.50	1.25	.70
28	Steve Blass	2.50	1.25	.70
32	Vernon Law	3.50	1.75	1.00
34	Al McBean	2.50	1.25	.70
39	Bob Veale	2.50	1.25	.70
43	Don Cardwell	2.50	1.25	.70
45	Gene Michael	2.50	1.25	.70

1933 Eclipse Import

Issued in 1933, this set was sold in eight-card strips. Numbered from 401 through 424, the cards measure 2-7/16" x 2-7/8". The design features a crude colored drawing of the player on the front. The back of the card displays the card number at the top followed by the player's name, team and a brief write-up. Card numbers 403, 413, and 414 are missing and probably correspond to the three unnumbered cards in the set. The set carries an American Card Catalog designation of R337.

		NM	EX	VG
Complete Set (24):		7,500	3,000	1,500
Common Player:		165.00	65.00	30.00
401	Johnny Vergez	165.00	65.00	30.00
402	Babe Ruth	1,200	480.00	240.00
403	Not Issued			
404	George Pipgras	165.00	65.00	30.00
405	Bill Terry	425.00	170.00	85.00
406	George Connally	165.00	65.00	30.00
407	Watson Clark	165.00	65.00	30.00
408	"Lefty" Grove	500.00	200.00	100.00
409	Henry Johnson	165.00	65.00	30.00
410	Jimmy Dykes	165.00	65.00	30.00

411	Henry Hine Schuble	165.00	65.00	30.00
412	Bucky Harris	425.00	170.00	85.00
413	Not Issued			
414	Not Issued			
415	Al Simmons	425.00	170.00	85.00
416	Henry "Heinie" Manush	425.00	170.00	85.00
417	Glen Myatt (Glenn)	165.00	65.00	30.00
418	Babe Herman	175.00	70.00	35.00
419	Frank Frisch	425.00	170.00	85.00
420	Tony Lazzeri	425.00	170.00	85.00
421	Paul Waner	425.00	170.00	85.00
422	Jimmy Wilson	165.00	65.00	30.00
423	Charles Grimm	165.00	65.00	30.00
424	Dick Bartell	165.00	65.00	30.00
----	Jimmy Fox (Jimmie Foxx)	600.00	240.00	120.00
----	Roy Johnson	165.00	65.00	30.00
----	Pie Traynor	425.00	170.00	85.00

1942 Editorial Bruguera Babe Ruth

The Babe is the only baseball player appearing is this 12-card series of "Figuras deportivas de fama mundial" (World famous sports figures) issued in Spain. The cards are blank-backed, about 4-3/4" x 3-1/2", with color artwork on front.

	NM	EX	VG
Babe Ruth	175.00	90.00	50.00

1930s Edwards, Ringer & Bigg Cigarettes

Though he is identified nowhere on this English cigarette card, the home run swing of Babe Ruth on the front is unmistakable. The last card in a set of 25 "Sports & Games in Many Lands" series, the approximately 2-5/8" x 1-3/8" cards have color artwork on the front and green-and-white backs. The back of the baseball card provides a short history of "The great national sport of the U.S.A." The card is nearly identical to the much more common 1929 Churchman's brand, except for the ads on back and the lack on the later card of the Churchman's name on top-right front.

		NM	EX	VG
25	Baseball, U.S.A. (Babe Ruth)	400.00	200.00	120.00

1909-11 El Principe de Gales Cigarettes

PREMIUMS:
Commons: 1-2X
Hall of Famers: 1-2X
(See T206 for checklist and base card values.)

1976 English's Chicken Baltimore Orioles Lids

It is uncertain whether the checklist presented here is complete. These 8-3/8" diameter fried chicken bucket lids are printed on heavy waxed cardboard in black-and-white. Cap logos have been airbrushed off. A few previous seasons' stats are printed to the left and right of the player photo.

		NM	EX	VG
Complete Set (4):		45.00	22.50	13.50
Common Player:		9.00	4.50	2.75
(1)	Mike Cuellar	9.00	4.50	1.75
(2)	Ken Holtzman	9.00	4.50	1.75
(3)	Lee May	9.00	4.50	1.75
(4)	Jim Palmer	20.00	10.00	6.00

1963-1973 Equitable Sports Hall of Fame

This series of black-and-white art prints was produced over more than a decade. About 8" x 11", the prints feature the artwork of Robert Riger or George Loh, reproduced from ads for the life insurance company. Nearly 95 pieces honoring athletes from many sports were produced. Only the baseball players are listed here.

		NM	EX	VG
Common Player:		6.00	3.00	1.80
(1)	Ernie Banks	7.50	3.75	2.25
(2)	Roy Campanella	7.50	3.75	2.25
(3)	Johnny Evers	6.00	3.00	1.80
(4)	Bob Feller	6.00	3.00	1.80
(5)	Lou Gehrig	10.00	5.00	3.00
(6)	Lefty Grove	6.00	3.00	1.80
(7)	Tommy Henrich	6.00	3.00	1.80
(8)	Carl Hubbell	6.00	3.00	1.80
(9)	Al Kaline	6.00	3.00	1.80
(10)	Jerry Koosman	6.00	3.00	1.80
(11)	Mickey Mantle	15.00	7.50	4.50
(12)	Eddie Mathews	6.00	3.00	1.80
(13)	Willie Mays	9.00	4.50	2.75
(14)	Stan Musial	9.00	4.50	2.75
(15)	Pee Wee Reese	6.00	3.00	1.80
(16)	Allie Reynolds	6.00	3.00	1.80
(17)	Robin Roberts	6.00	3.00	1.80
(18)	Brooks Robinson	6.00	3.00	1.80
(19)	Red Ruffing	6.00	3.00	1.80
(20)	Babe Ruth	12.50	6.25	3.75
(21)	Warren Spahn	6.00	3.00	1.80

1954 Esskay Hot Dogs Orioles

Measuring 2-1/4" x 3-1/2", the 1954 Esskay Hot Dogs set features the Baltimore Orioles. The unnumbered color cards were issued in panels of two on packages of hot dogs and are usually found with grease stains. The cards have waxed fronts with blank backs on a white stock. Complete boxes of Esskay Hot Dogs are scarce and command a price of 2-3 times greater than the single card values.

		NM	EX	VG
Complete Set (34):		45,000	18,000	9,000
Common Player:		1,500	600.00	300.00
(1)	Neil Berry	1,500	600.00	300.00
(2)	Michael Blyzka	1,500	600.00	300.00
(3)	Harry Brecheen	1,500	600.00	300.00
(4)	Gil Coan	1,500	600.00	300.00
(5)	Joe Coleman	1,500	600.00	300.00
(6)	Clinton Courtney	1,500	600.00	300.00
(7)	Charles E. Diering	1,500	600.00	300.00
(8)	Jimmie Dykes	1,500	600.00	300.00
(9)	Frank J. Fanovich	1,500	600.00	300.00
(10)	Howard Fox	1,500	600.00	300.00
(11)	Jim Fridley	1,500	600.00	300.00
(12)	Vinicio "Chico" Garcia	1,500	600.00	300.00
(13)	Jehosie Heard	2,000	800.00	400.00
(14)	Darrell Johnson	1,500	600.00	300.00
(15)	Bob Kennedy	1,500	600.00	300.00
(16)	Dick Kokos	1,500	600.00	300.00
(17)	Dave Koslo	1,500	600.00	300.00
(18)	Lou Kretlow	1,500	600.00	300.00
(19)	Richard D. Kryhoski	1,500	600.00	300.00
(20)	Don Larsen	2,500	1,000	500.00
(21)	Donald E. Lenhardt	1,500	600.00	300.00
(22)	Richard Littlefield	1,500	600.00	300.00
(23)	Sam Mele	1,500	600.00	300.00
(24)	Les Moss	1,500	600.00	300.00
(25)	Ray L. Murray	1,500	600.00	300.00
(26a)	"Bobo" Newsom (No stadium lights in background.)	1,750	700.00	350.00
(26b)	"Bobo" Newson (Stadium lights in background.)	1,750	700.00	350.00
(27)	Tom Oliver	1,500	600.00	300.00
(28)	Duane Pillette	1,500	600.00	300.00
(29)	Francis M. Skaff	1,500	600.00	300.00
(30)	Marlin Stuart	1,500	600.00	300.00
(31)	Robert L. Turley	2,250	900.00	450.00
(32)	Eddie Waitkus	1,500	600.00	300.00
(33)	Vic Wertz	1,500	600.00	300.00
(34)	Robert G. Young	1,500	600.00	300.00

1955 Esskay Hot Dogs Orioles

For the second consecutive year, Esskay Meats placed baseball cards of Orioles players on their boxes of hot dogs. The unnumbered, color cards measure 2-1/4" x 3-1/2" and can be distinguished from the previous year by their unwaxed fronts and blank gray backs. Many of the same photos from 1954 were used with only minor picture-cropping differences. For 1955, only one player card per box was printed. The space which was occupied by the second player card in 1954 carried a prize redemption coupon on 1955 boxes.

		NM	EX	VG
Complete Set (26):		37,500	15,000	7,500
Common Player:		1,500	600.00	300.00
(1)	Cal Abrams	1,500	600.00	300.00
(2)	Robert S. Alexander	1,500	600.00	300.00
(3)	Harry Byrd	1,500	600.00	300.00
(4)	Gil Coan	1,500	600.00	300.00
(5)	Joseph P. Coleman	1,500	600.00	300.00
(6)	William R. Cox	1,500	600.00	300.00
(7)	Charles E. Diering	1,500	600.00	300.00
(8)	Walter A. Evers	1,500	600.00	300.00
(9)	Don Johnson	1,500	600.00	300.00
(10)	Robert D. Kennedy	1,500	600.00	300.00
(11)	Lou Kretlow	1,500	600.00	300.00
(12)	Robert L. Kuzava	1,500	600.00	300.00
(13)	Fred Marsh	1,500	600.00	300.00
(14)	Charles Maxwell	1,500	600.00	300.00
(15)	Jimmie McDonald	1,500	600.00	300.00
(16)	Bill Miller	1,500	600.00	300.00
(17)	Willy Miranda	1,500	600.00	300.00
(18)	Raymond L. Moore	1,500	600.00	300.00
(19)	John Lester Moss	1,500	600.00	300.00
(20)	"Bobo" Newsom	1,500	600.00	300.00
(21)	Duane Pillette	1,500	600.00	300.00
(22)	Edward S. Waitkus	1,500	600.00	300.00
(23)	Harold W. Smith	1,500	600.00	300.00
(24)	Gus Triandos	1,500	600.00	300.00
(25)	Eugene R. Woodling	1,750	700.00	350.00
(26)	Robert G. Young	1,500	600.00	300.00

1972 Esso Hispanic Coins

Little is known of these coins, except that they were distributed in Puerto Rico. Even the sponsor, Esso Oil Co., is not mentioned anywhere on the pieces. Made of aluminum and 1-1/4" in diameter, coin fronts have a portrait of the player with his name above. Backs are in Spanish and have the player's position, team, height, weight, date and place of birth. The coins of Tony Perez and, to a lesser extent, Rod Carew are scarcer than the others. A person receiving a Perez coin was able to exchange it for a full tank of gas. In 2006, a brass-finish Roberto Clemente coin was first reported, probably also a short-printed exchange coin.

		NM	EX	VG
Complete Set (13):		325.00	160.00	95.00
Common Player:		9.00	4.50	2.75
(1)	Luis Aparicio	15.00	7.50	4.50
(2)	Rod Carew	50.00	25.00	15.00
(3)	Rico Carty	9.00	4.50	2.75
(4)	Cesar Cedeno	9.00	4.50	2.75
(5)	Orlando Cepeda	15.00	7.50	4.50
(6)	Roberto Clemente	110.00	55.00	35.00
(7)	Mike Cuellar	9.00	4.50	2.75
(8)	Juan Marichal	15.00	7.50	4.50
(9)	Felix Millan	9.00	4.50	2.75
(10)	Guillermo Montanez	9.00	4.50	2.75
(11)	Tony Oliva	12.00	6.00	3.50
(12a)	Tany Perez (Tony)	75.00	37.50	22.50
(12b)	Tony Perez	75.00	37.50	22.50
(13)	Manny Sanguillen	9.00	4.50	2.75

1949 Eureka Sportstamps

The commissioner of baseball, president of the National League and 198 N.L. players are included in this issue. The stamps were issued on team sheets measuring 7-1/2" x 10", with individual stamps measuring 1-1/2" x 2". An album issued with the set provided short player biographies. The stamps feature colorized posed player action photos. At bottom is a yellow strip with the player's name, stamp number and copyright line. Stamps are numbered alphabetically within teams.

		NM	EX	VG
Complete Set (200):		900.00	450.00	275.00
Common Player:		5.00	2.50	1.50
Album w/mounted stamps:		400.00	200.00	120.00
Album:		75.00	37.50	22.00
1	Albert B. (Happy) Chandler	15.00	7.50	4.50
2	Ford Frick	5.00	2.50	1.50
3	Billy Southworth	5.00	2.50	1.50
4	Johnny Antonelli	5.00	2.50	1.50
5	Red Barrett	5.00	2.50	1.50
6	Clint Conatser	5.00	2.50	1.50
7	Alvin Dark	5.00	2.50	1.50
8	Bob Elliott	5.00	2.50	1.50
9	Glenn Elliott	5.00	2.50	1.50
10	Elbie Fletcher	5.00	2.50	1.50
11	Bob Hall	5.00	2.50	1.50
12	Jeff Heath	5.00	2.50	1.50
13	Bobby Hogue	5.00	2.50	1.50
14	Tommy Holmes	5.00	2.50	1.50
15	Al Lakeman	5.00	2.50	1.50
16	Phil Masi	5.00	2.50	1.50
17	Nelson Potter	5.00	2.50	1.50
18	Pete Reiser	10.00	5.00	3.00
19	Rick Rickert	5.00	2.50	1.50
20	Connie Ryan	5.00	2.50	1.50
21	Jim Russell	5.00	2.50	1.50
22	Johnny Sain	10.00	5.00	3.00
23	Bill Salkeld	5.00	2.50	1.50
24	Sibby Sisti	5.00	2.50	1.50
25	Warren Spahn	25.00	12.50	7.50
26	Eddie Stanky	5.00	2.50	1.50
27	Bill Voiselle	5.00	2.50	1.50
28	Bert Shotton	5.00	2.50	1.50
29	Jack Banta	5.00	2.50	1.50
30	Rex Barney	7.50	3.75	2.25
31	Ralph Branca	15.00	7.50	4.50
32	Tommy Brown	5.00	2.50	1.50
33	Roy Campanella	40.00	20.00	12.00

34	Billy Cox	7.50	3.75	2.25
35	Bruce Edwards	5.00	2.50	1.50
36	Carl Furillo	20.00	10.00	6.00
37	Joe Hatten	5.00	2.50	1.50
38	Gene Hermanski	5.00	2.50	1.50
39	Gil Hodges	25.00	12.50	7.50
40	Johnny Jorgensen	5.00	2.50	1.50
41	Lefty Martin	5.00	2.50	1.50
42	Mike McCormick	5.00	2.50	1.50
43	Eddie Miksis	5.00	2.50	1.50
44	Paul Minner	5.00	2.50	1.50
45	Sam Narron	10.00	5.00	3.00
46	Don Newcombe	20.00	10.00	6.00
47	Jake Pitler	5.00	2.50	1.50
48	Pee Wee Reese	35.00	17.50	10.50
49	Jackie Robinson	50.00	25.00	15.00
50	Duke Snider	40.00	20.00	12.00
51	Dick Whitman	5.00	2.50	1.50
52	Forrest Burgess	10.00	5.00	3.00
53	Phil Cavaretta	5.00	2.50	1.50
54	Bob Chipman	5.00	2.50	1.50
55	Walter Dubiel	5.00	2.50	1.50
56	Hank Edwards	5.00	2.50	1.50
57	Frankie Gustine	5.00	2.50	1.50
58	Hal Jeffcoat	5.00	2.50	1.50
59	Emil Kush	5.00	2.50	1.50
60	Doyle Lade	5.00	2.50	1.50
61	Dutch Leonard	5.00	2.50	1.50
62	Peanuts Lowrey	5.00	2.50	1.50
63	Gene Mauch	7.50	3.75	2.25
64	Cal McLish	5.00	2.50	1.50
65	Rube Novotney	5.00	2.50	1.50
66	Andy Pafko	5.00	2.50	1.50
67	Bob Ramozzotti	5.00	2.50	1.50
68	Herman Reich	5.00	2.50	1.50
69	Bob Rush	5.00	2.50	1.50
70	Johnny Schmitz	5.00	2.50	1.50
71	Bob Scheffing	5.00	2.50	1.50
72	Roy Smalley	5.00	2.50	1.50
73	Emil Verban	5.00	2.50	1.50
74	Al Walker	5.00	2.50	1.50
75	Harry Walker	5.00	2.50	1.50
76	Bucky Walters	5.00	2.50	1.50
77	Bob Adams	5.00	2.50	1.50
78	Ewell Blackwell	5.00	2.50	1.50
79	Jimmy Bloodworth	5.00	2.50	1.50
80	Walker Cooper	5.00	2.50	1.50
81	Tony Cuccinello	5.00	2.50	1.50
82	Jess Dobernic	5.00	2.50	1.50
83	Eddie Erautt	5.00	2.50	1.50
84	Frank Fanovich	5.00	2.50	1.50
85	Howie Fox	5.00	2.50	1.50
86	Grady Hatton	5.00	2.50	1.50
87	Homer Howell	5.00	2.50	1.50
88	Ted Kluszewski	20.00	10.00	6.00
89	Danny Litwhiler	5.00	2.50	1.50
90	Everett Lively	5.00	2.50	1.50
91	Lloyd Merriman	5.00	2.50	1.50
92	Phil Page	5.00	2.50	1.50
93	Kent Peterson	5.00	2.50	1.50
94	Ken Raffensberger	5.00	2.50	1.50
95	Luke Sewell	5.00	2.50	1.50
96	Virgil Stallcup	5.00	2.50	1.50
97	Johnny Vander Meer	10.00	5.00	3.00
98	Herman Wehmeier	5.00	2.50	1.50
99	Johnny Wyrostek	5.00	2.50	1.50
100	Benny Zientara	5.00	2.50	1.50
101	Leo Durocher	12.50	6.25	3.75
102	Hank Behrman	5.00	2.50	1.50
103	Augie Galan	5.00	2.50	1.50
104	Sid Gordon	5.00	2.50	1.50
105	Bert Haas	5.00	2.50	1.50
106	Andy Hansen	5.00	2.50	1.50
107	Clint Hartung	5.00	2.50	1.50
108	Kirby Higbe	5.00	2.50	1.50
109	George Hausman	5.00	2.50	1.50
110	Larry Jansen	5.00	2.50	1.50
111	Sheldon Jones	5.00	2.50	1.50
112	Monte Kennedy	5.00	2.50	1.50
113	Buddy Kerr	5.00	2.50	1.50
114	Dave Koslo	5.00	2.50	1.50
115	Joe Lafata	5.00	2.50	1.50
116	Whitey Lockman	5.00	2.50	1.50
117	Jack Lohrke	5.00	2.50	1.50
118	Willard Marshall	5.00	2.50	1.50
119	Bill Milne	5.00	2.50	1.50
120	Johnny Mize	15.00	7.50	4.50
121	Don Mueller	5.00	2.50	1.50
122	Ray Mueller	5.00	2.50	1.50
123	Bill Rigney	5.00	2.50	1.50
124	Bobby Thomson	7.50	3.75	2.25
125	Sam Webb	5.00	2.50	1.50
126	Wesley Westrum	5.00	2.50	1.50
127	Eddie Sawyer	5.00	2.50	1.50
128	Richie Ashburn	30.00	15.00	9.00
129	Benny Bengough	5.00	2.50	1.50
130	Charlie Bicknell	5.00	2.50	1.50
131	Buddy Blattner	5.00	2.50	1.50
132	Hank Borowy	5.00	2.50	1.50
133	Ralph Caballero	5.00	2.50	1.50
134	Blix Donnelly	5.00	2.50	1.50
135	Del Ennis	5.00	2.50	1.50
136	Granville Hamner	5.00	2.50	1.50
137	Ken Heintzelman	5.00	2.50	1.50
138	Stan Hollmig	5.00	2.50	1.50
139	Willie Jones	5.00	2.50	1.50
140	Jim Konstanty	5.00	2.50	1.50
141	Stan Lopata	5.00	2.50	1.50
142	Jackie Mayo	5.00	2.50	1.50
143	Bill Nicholson	5.00	2.50	1.50
144	Robin Roberts	60.00	30.00	18.00
145	Schoolboy Rowe	5.00	2.50	1.50
146	Andy Seminick	5.00	2.50	1.50
147	Ken Silvestri	5.00	2.50	1.50
148	Curt Simmons	5.00	2.50	1.50
149	Dick Sisler	5.00	2.50	1.50
150	Ken Trinkle	5.00	2.50	1.50
151	Eddie Waitkus	5.00	2.50	1.50

152	Bill Meyer	5.00	2.50	1.50
153	Monte Basgall	5.00	2.50	1.50
154	Eddie Bockman	5.00	2.50	1.50
155	Ernie Bonham	5.00	2.50	1.50
156	Hugh Casey	5.00	2.50	1.50
157	Pete Castiglione	5.00	2.50	1.50
158	Cliff Chambers	5.00	2.50	1.50
159	Murry Dickson	5.00	2.50	1.50
160	Ed Fitz Gerald	5.00	2.50	1.50
161	Les Fleming	5.00	2.50	1.50
162	Hal Gregg	5.00	2.50	1.50
163	Goldie Holt	5.00	2.50	1.50
164	Johnny Hopp	5.00	2.50	1.50
165	Ralph Kiner	20.00	10.00	6.00
166	Vic Lombardi	5.00	2.50	1.50
167	Clyde McCullough	5.00	2.50	1.50
168	Danny Murtaugh	5.00	2.50	1.50
169	Bill Posedel	5.00	2.50	1.50
170	Elmer Riddle	5.00	2.50	1.50
171	Stan Rojek	5.00	2.50	1.50
172	Rip Sewell	5.00	2.50	1.50
173	Eddie Stevens	5.00	2.50	1.50
174	Dixie Walker	5.00	2.50	1.50
175	Bill Werle	5.00	2.50	1.50
176	Wally Westlake	5.00	2.50	1.50
177	Eddie Dyer	5.00	2.50	1.50
178	Bill Baker	5.00	2.50	1.50
179	Al Brazle	5.00	2.50	1.50
180	Harry Brecheen	5.00	2.50	1.50
181	Chuck Diering	5.00	2.50	1.50
182	Joe Garagiola	13.50	6.75	4.00
183	Tom Galviano	5.00	2.50	1.50
184	Jim Hearn	5.00	2.50	1.50
185	Ken Johnson	5.00	2.50	1.50
186	Nippy Jones	5.00	2.50	1.50
187	Ed Kazak	5.00	2.50	1.50
188	Lou Klein	5.00	2.50	1.50
189	Marty Marion	5.00	2.50	1.50
190	George Munger	5.00	2.50	1.50
191	Stan Musial	45.00	22.00	13.50
192	Spike Nelson	5.00	2.50	1.50
193	Howie Pollet	5.00	2.50	1.50
194	Bill Reeder	5.00	2.50	1.50
195	Del Rice	5.00	2.50	1.50
196	Ed Sauer	5.00	2.50	1.50
197	Red Schoendienst	20.00	10.00	6.00
198	Enos Slaughter	20.00	10.00	6.00
199	Ted Wilks	5.00	2.50	1.50
200	Ray Yochim	5.00	2.50	1.50

1914 Evening Sun N.Y. Giants

The World's Champion 1913 N.Y. Giants are featured in this set of newspaper supplements titled, "Evening Sun's Gallery of Famous Baseball Players." It is believed the paper was published in Norwich, N.Y. Slightly larger than 9" x 12", the supplements feature black-and-white portraits by Lawrence Semon, who also produced a contemporary series of baseball postcards.

		NM	EX	VG
Complete Set (21):		7,000	3,500	2,100
Common Player:		200.00	100.00	60.00
(1)	George Burns	200.00	100.00	60.00
(2)	Doc Crandall	200.00	100.00	60.00
(3)	Al Demaree	200.00	100.00	60.00
(4)	Art Fletcher	200.00	100.00	60.00
(5)	Art Fromme	200.00	100.00	60.00
(6)	Grover Hartley	200.00	100.00	60.00
(7)	Buck Herzog	200.00	100.00	60.00
(8)	Rube Marquard	400.00	200.00	120.00
(9)	Christy Mathewson	1,200	600.00	360.00
(10)	Moose McCormick	200.00	100.00	60.00
(11)	John McGraw	400.00	200.00	120.00
(12)	Fred Merkle	200.00	100.00	60.00
(13)	Chief Meyers	200.00	100.00	60.00
(14)	Red Murray	200.00	100.00	60.00
(15)	Wilbert Robinson	400.00	200.00	120.00
(16)	Arthur Shafer	200.00	100.00	60.00
(17)	Fred Snodgrass	200.00	100.00	60.00
(18)	Jeff Tesreau	200.00	100.00	60.00
(19)	Jim Thorpe	1,750	875.00	525.00
(20)	Art Wilson	200.00	100.00	60.00
(21)	Hooks Wiltse	200.00	100.00	60.00

1916 Everybody's

Where "Everybody's" department store was located is unknown, but in 1916 they chose to use baseball cards to promote their boy's wear department. The approximately 1-5/8" x 3" black-and-white cards share the format and checklist with the much more common M101-4 blank-back version and several other regional advertisers. Everybody's is one of the scarcest advertising backs to be found in this issue and the cards command a premium from type-card and superstar collectors. There are four styles of typography on back.

DICK RUDOLPH
P.—Boston Braves
149

EVERYBODY'S
BOYS' CLOTHING DEPARTMENT
Fourth Floor

Premium: 6-9X
  (See 1916 M101-4 Blank Backs for checklist and base card values.)

1921 Exhibits

Geo H "Babe" Ruth
OUTFIELDER, NEW YORK, AM L.

Ty R Cobb
OUTFIELDER, DETROIT AM. L.

The Exhibit Supply Company of Chicago issued the first in a long series of postcard-size (3-3/8" x 5-3/8") baseball cards in 1921. The Exhibit cards were commonly sold in "penny arcade" vending machines. The 1921 series consists of 64 cards and includes four players from each of the 16 major league teams. The cards feature black-and-white photos with the player's name printed in a fancy script. The player's position and team appear below the name in small, hand-lettered capital letters. American League is designated as "AM.L.," which can help differentiate the 1921 series from future years. Some of the cards contain white borders while others do not. All have blank backs. There are various spelling errors in the picture legends.

		NM	EX	VG
Complete Set (64):		11,000	5,500	3,250
Common Player:		75.00	35.00	20.00
(1)	Chas. B. Adams	75.00	35.00	20.00
(2)	Grover C. Alexander	275.00	135.00	80.00
(3)	David Bancroft	175.00	85.00	50.00
(4)	Geo. J. Burns	75.00	35.00	20.00
(5)	Owen Bush	75.00	35.00	20.00
(6)	Max J. Carey	175.00	85.00	50.00
(7)	Ty R. Cobb	1,000	500.00	300.00
(8)	Eddie T. Collins	175.00	85.00	50.00
(9)	John Collins	75.00	35.00	20.00
(10)	Stanley Coveleskie (Coveleski)	200.00	100.00	60.00
(11)	Walton E. Cruise	75.00	35.00	20.00
(12)	Jacob E. Daubert	75.00	35.00	20.00
(13)	George Dauss	75.00	35.00	20.00
(14)	Charles A. Deal	75.00	35.00	20.00
(15)	Joe A. Dugan	75.00	35.00	20.00
(16)	James Dykes	75.00	35.00	20.00
(17)	U.C. "Red" Faber	175.00	85.00	50.00
(18)	J.F. Fournier	75.00	35.00	20.00
(19)	Frank F. Frisch	175.00	85.00	50.00
(20)	W.L. Gardner	75.00	35.00	20.00
(21)	H.M. "Hank" Gowdy	75.00	35.00	20.00
(22)	Burleigh A. Grimes	200.00	100.00	60.00
(23)	Heinie Groh	75.00	35.00	20.00
(24)	Jesse Haines	200.00	100.00	60.00
(25)	Sam Harris (Stanley)	200.00	100.00	60.00
(26)	Walter L. Holke	75.00	35.00	20.00
(27)	Charles J. Hollicher (Hollocher)	75.00	35.00	20.00
(28)	Rogers Hornsby	325.00	160.00	95.00
(29)	James H. Johnson (Johnston)	75.00	35.00	20.00
(30)	Walter P. Johnson	750.00	375.00	225.00
(31)	Sam P. Jones	75.00	35.00	20.00
(32)	Geo. L. Kelly	200.00	100.00	60.00
(33)	Dick Kerr	75.00	35.00	20.00
(34)	William L. Killifer (Killefer)	75.00	35.00	20.00
(35)	Ed Konetchy	75.00	35.00	20.00
(36)	John "Doc" Lavan	75.00	35.00	20.00
(37)	Walter J. Maranville	175.00	85.00	50.00
(38)	Carl W. Mays	75.00	35.00	20.00
(39)	J. "Stuffy" McInnis	75.00	35.00	20.00
(40)	Rollie C. Naylor (Earle)	75.00	35.00	20.00
(41)	A. Earl Neale (Earle)	125.00	60.00	35.00
(42)	Ivan M. Olsen	75.00	35.00	20.00
(43)	S.F. "Steve" O'Neil (O'Neill)	75.00	35.00	20.00
(44)	Robert (Roger) Peckinpaugh	75.00	35.00	20.00

(45)	Ralph "Cy" Perkins	75.00	35.00	20.00
(46)	Raymond R. Powell	75.00	35.00	20.00
(47)	Joe "Goldie" Rapp	75.00	35.00	20.00
(48)	Edgar S. Rice	175.00	85.00	50.00
(49)	Jimmy Ring	75.00	35.00	20.00
(50)	Geo. H. "Babe" Ruth	2,750	1,375	825.00
(51)	Ray W. Schalk	175.00	85.00	50.00
(52)	Wallie Schang	75.00	35.00	20.00
(53)	Everett Scott	75.00	35.00	20.00
(54)	H.S. Shanks (Photo actually Wally Schang.)	75.00	35.00	20.00
(55)	Urban Shocker	75.00	35.00	20.00
(56)	Geo. H. Sisler	175.00	85.00	50.00
(57)	Tris Speaker	325.00	160.00	95.00
(58)	John Tobin	75.00	35.00	20.00
(59)	Robt. Veach	75.00	35.00	20.00
(60)	Zack D. Wheat	175.00	85.00	50.00
(61)	Geo. B. Whitted	75.00	35.00	20.00
(62)	Cy Williams	75.00	35.00	20.00
(63)	Kenneth R. Williams	75.00	35.00	20.00
(64)	Ivy B. Wingo	75.00	35.00	20.00

1922 Exhibits

Moses Yellowhorse
PITTSBURGH, N.L.

The Exhibit Supply Co. continued the 3-3/8" x 5-3/8" format in 1922 but doubled the number of cards in the series to 128, including eight players from each team. All but nine of the players who appeared in the 1921 series are pictured in the 1922 set, along with 74 new players. The cards again display black-and-white photos with blank backs. Some photos have white borders. The player's name appears in script with the postition and team below in small block capital letters. American League is designated as "A.L." Again, there are several spelling errors and incorrect player identifications. Only the 74 new additions are included in this checklist.

		NM	EX	VG
Complete Set (74):		7,500	3,750	2,250
Common Player:		85.00	40.00	25.00
(1)	Jim Bagby	85.00	40.00	25.00
(2)	J. Frank Baker	150.00	75.00	45.00
(3)	Walter Barbare	85.00	40.00	25.00
(4)	Turner Barber	85.00	40.00	25.00
(5)	John Bassler	85.00	40.00	25.00
(6)	Carlson L. Bigbee (Carson)	85.00	40.00	25.00
(7)	Sam Bohne	85.00	42.00	25.00
(8)	Geo. Burns	85.00	40.00	25.00
(9)	George Burns	85.00	40.00	25.00
(10)	Jeo Bush (Joe)	85.00	40.00	25.00
(11)	Leon Cadore	85.00	40.00	25.00
(12)	Jim Caveney	85.00	40.00	25.00
(13)	Wilbur Cooper	85.00	40.00	25.00
(14)	George Cutshaw	85.00	40.00	25.00
(15)	Dave Danforth	85.00	40.00	25.00
(16)	Bill Doak	85.00	40.00	25.00
(17)	Joe Dugan	85.00	40.00	25.00
(18)	Pat Duncan	85.00	40.00	25.00
(19)	Howard Emke (Ehmke)	85.00	40.00	25.00
(20)	Wm. Evans (Umpire)	375.00	185.00	110.00
(21)	Bib Falk (Bibb)	85.00	40.00	25.00
(22)	Dana Fillingin (Fillingim)	85.00	40.00	25.00
(23)	Ira Flagstead	85.00	40.00	25.00
(24)	(Art) Fletcher	85.00	40.00	25.00
(25)	(Wally) Gerber	85.00	40.00	25.00
(26)	Ray Grimes	85.00	40.00	25.00
(27)	Harry Heilman (Heilmann)	150.00	75.00	45.00
(28)	George Hildebrand (Umpire)	200.00	100.00	60.00
(29)	Wibur Hubbell (Wilbert)	85.00	40.00	25.00
(30)	Bill Jacobson	85.00	40.00	25.00
(31)	E.R. Johnson	85.00	40.00	25.00
(32)	Joe Judge	85.00	40.00	25.00
(33)	Bill Klem (Umpire)	375.00	185.00	110.00
(34)	Harry Liebold (Leibold)	85.00	40.00	25.00
(35)	Walter Mails	85.00	40.00	25.00
(36)	Geo. Maisel	85.00	40.00	25.00
(37)	Lee Meadows	85.00	40.00	25.00
(38)	Clyde Milam (Milan)	85.00	40.00	25.00
(39)	Ed (Bing) Miller	85.00	40.00	25.00
(40)	Hack Miller	85.00	40.00	25.00
(41)	George Moriarty (Umpire)	200.00	100.00	60.00
(42)	Robert Muesel (Meusel)	85.00	40.00	25.00
(43)	Harry Myers	85.00	40.00	25.00
(44)	Arthur Nehf	85.00	40.00	25.00
(45)	Joe Oeschger	85.00	40.00	25.00
(46)	Geo. O'Neil	85.00	40.00	25.00
(47)	Roger Peckinpaugh	85.00	40.00	25.00
(48)	Val Picinich	85.00	40.00	25.00
(49)	Bill Piercy	85.00	40.00	25.00
(50)	Derrill Pratt	85.00	40.00	25.00
(51)	Jack Quinn	85.00	40.00	25.00
(52)	Walter Reuther (Ruether)	85.00	40.00	25.00

(53)	Charles Rigler (Umpire)	200.00	100.00	60.00
(54)	Eppa Rixey	150.00	75.00	45.00
(55)	Chas. Robertson	85.00	40.00	25.00
(56)	Everett Scott	85.00	40.00	25.00
(57)	Earl Sheely	85.00	40.00	25.00
(58)	Earl Smith (portrait)	85.00	40.00	25.00
(59)	Earl Smith (Standing) (Photo actually Brad Kocher.)	85.00	40.00	25.00
(60)	Elmer Smith	85.00	40.00	25.00
(61)	Jack Smith (Photo actually Jimmy Smith.)	85.00	40.00	25.00
(62)	Sherrod Smith	85.00	40.00	25.00
(63)	Frank Snyder	85.00	40.00	25.00
(64)	Allan Sothoron (Allen)	85.00	40.00	25.00
(65)	Arnold Statz	85.00	40.00	25.00
(66)	Milton Stock	85.00	40.00	25.00
(67)	James Tierney	85.00	40.00	25.00
(68)	George Toporcer	85.00	40.00	25.00
(69)	Clarence (Tilly) Walker	85.00	40.00	25.00
(70)	Curtis Walker	85.00	40.00	25.00
(71)	Aaron Ward	85.00	40.00	25.00
(72)	Joe Wood	100.00	50.00	30.00
(73)	Moses Yellowhorse	400.00	300.00	200.00
(74)	Ross Young (Youngs)	150.00	75.00	45.00

1922 Eastern Exhibit Supply Co.

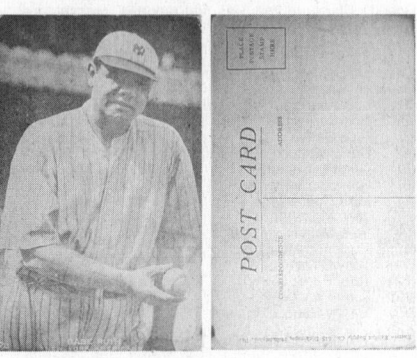

POST CARD

Postcard-style backs differentiate these cards from the more common Exhibit Supply Co., cards from Chicago. This 20-card series was produced by a Philadelphia company, although on some cards, the Eastern Exhibit copyright line on back has been blacked out and that of the Chicago company printed beneath it. The black-and-white cards measure 3-3/8" x 5-5/8".

		NM	EX	VG
Complete Set (20):		4,200	2,100	1,250
Common Player:		80.00	40.00	20.00
(1)	Grover Alexander	200.00	100.00	60.00
(2)	Dave Bancroft	125.00	65.00	35.00
(3)	Jesse Barnes	80.00	40.00	20.00
(4)	Joe Bush	80.00	40.00	20.00
(5)	Ty Cobb	750.00	375.00	225.00
(6)	Eddie Collins	125.00	65.00	35.00
(7)	Urban Faber	125.00	65.00	35.00
(8)	Clarence Galloway	80.00	40.00	20.00
(9)	Heinie Groh	80.00	40.00	20.00
(10)	Harry Heilmann	125.00	65.00	35.00
(11)	Charlie Hollocher	80.00	40.00	20.00
(12)	Rogers Hornsby	200.00	100.00	60.00
(13)	Walter Johnson	375.00	185.00	110.00
(14)	Eddie Rommel	80.00	40.00	20.00
(15)	Babe Ruth	1,550	775.00	465.00
(16)	Ray Schalk	125.00	65.00	35.00
(17)	Wallie Schang	80.00	40.00	20.00
(18)	Tris Speaker	200.00	100.00	60.00
(19)	Zach Wheat	125.00	65.00	35.00
(20)	Kenneth Williams	80.00	40.00	20.00

1923-24 Exhibits

Raymond R Powell

John J. McGraw
MANAGER, NEW YORK, N.L.

The Exhibit cards for 1923 and 1924 are generally collected as a single 128-card series. The format remained basically the same as the previous year, 3-3/8" x 5-3/8", with black-and-white photos (some surrounded by a white border) and blank backs. The player's name is again shown in script with the position and team printed below in a small, square block-type style. Many of the same photos were used from previous years, although some are cropped differently, and some players have new team designations, background changes, team emblems removed, borders added or taken away, and other minor changes. Fifty-eight new cards are featured, including 38 players pictured for the first time in an Exhibit set. Only the 58 new cards are included in this checklist.

		NM	EX	VG
	Complete Set (59):	20,000	10,000	6,000
	Common Player:	225.00	110.00	65.00
(1)	Clyde Barnhart	225.00	110.00	65.00
(2)	Ray Blades	225.00	110.00	65.00
(3)	James Bottomley	400.00	200.00	120.00
(4)	George Burns	225.00	110.00	65.00
(5)	Dan Clark	225.00	110.00	65.00
(6)	Bill Doak	225.00	110.00	65.00
(7)	Joe Dugan	225.00	110.00	65.00
(8)	Howard J. Ehmke	225.00	110.00	65.00
(9)	Ira Flagstead	225.00	110.00	65.00
(10)	J.F. Fournier	225.00	110.00	65.00
(11)	Howard Freigan (Freigau)	225.00	110.00	65.00
(12)	C.E. Galloway	225.00	110.00	65.00
(13)	Joe Genewich	225.00	110.00	65.00
(14)	Mike Gonzales (Gonzalez)	275.00	135.00	82.00
(15)	H.M. "Hank" Gowdy	225.00	110.00	65.00
(16)	Charles Grimm	225.00	110.00	65.00
(17)	Heinie Groh	225.00	110.00	65.00
(18)	Chas. L. Harnett (Hartnett)	400.00	200.00	120.00
(19)	George Harper	225.00	110.00	65.00
(20)	Slim Harris (Harriss)	225.00	110.00	65.00
(21)	Clifton Heathcote	225.00	110.00	65.00
(22)	Andy High	225.00	110.00	65.00
(23)	Walter L. Holke	225.00	110.00	65.00
(24)	Charles D. Jamieson	225.00	110.00	65.00
(25)	Willie Kamm	225.00	110.00	65.00
(26)	Tony Kaufmann	225.00	110.00	65.00
(27)	Dudley Lee	225.00	110.00	65.00
(28)	Harry Liebold (Leibold)	225.00	110.00	65.00
(29)	Aldofo Luque	225.00	110.00	65.00
(30)	W.C. (Wid) Matthews	225.00	110.00	65.00
(31)	John J. McGraw	400.00	200.00	120.00
(32)	J. "Stuffy" McInnis	225.00	110.00	65.00
(33)	Johnny Morrison	225.00	110.00	65.00
(34)	John A. Mostil	225.00	110.00	65.00
(35)	J.F. O'Neill (Should be S.F.)	225.00	110.00	65.00
(36)	Ernest Padgett	225.00	110.00	65.00
(37)	Val Picinich	225.00	110.00	65.00
(38)	Bill Piercy	225.00	110.00	65.00
(39)	Herman Pillette	225.00	110.00	65.00
(40)	Wallie Pipp	275.00	135.00	82.00
(41)	Raymond R. Powell (Black background.)	225.00	110.00	65.00
(43)	Del. Pratt	225.00	110.00	65.00
(44)	E.E. Rigney	225.00	110.00	65.00
(45)	Eddie Rommel	225.00	110.00	65.00
(46)	Geo. H. "Babe" Ruth	12,000	6,500	5,000
(47)	Muddy Ruel	225.00	110.00	65.00
(48)	J.H. Sand	225.00	110.00	65.00
(49)	Henry Severeid	225.00	110.00	65.00
(50)	Joseph Sewell	400.00	200.00	120.00
(51)	Al. Simmons	1,000	500.00	300.00
(52)	R.E. Smith	225.00	110.00	65.00
(53)	Sherrod Smith	225.00	110.00	65.00
(54)	Casey Stengel	500.00	400.00	300.00
(55)	J.R. Stevenson (Stephenson)	225.00	110.00	65.00
(56)	James Tierney	225.00	110.00	65.00
(57)	Robt. Veach	225.00	110.00	65.00
(58)	L. Woodall	225.00	110.00	65.00
(59)	Russell G. Wrighstone	225.00	110.00	65.00

1925 Exhibits

The 1925 series of Exhibits contains 128 unnumbered cards, each measuring 3-3/8" x 5-3/8". The player's name (in all capital letters), position and team (along with a line reading "Made in U.S.A.") are printed in a small white box in a lower corner of the card. Most of the photos are vertical, however a few are horizontal. There are several misspellings in the set. Lou Gehrig's first baseball card appears in this issue. The cards are listed here in alphabetical order.

		NM	EX	VG
	Complete Set (128):	32,500	16,000	9,750
	Common Player:	125.00	65.00	35.00
(1)	Sparky Adams	125.00	65.00	35.00
(2)	Grover C. Alexander	300.00	150.00	90.00
(3)	David Bancroft	200.00	100.00	60.00
(4)	Jesse Barnes	125.00	65.00	35.00
(5)	John Bassler	125.00	65.00	35.00
(6)	Lester Bell	125.00	65.00	35.00
(7)	Lawrence Benton	125.00	65.00	35.00
(8)	Carson Bigbee	125.00	65.00	35.00
(9)	Max Bishop	125.00	65.00	35.00
(10)	Raymond Blates (Blades)	125.00	65.00	35.00

(11)	Oswald Bluege	125.00	65.00	35.00
(12)	James Bottomly (Bottomley)	200.00	100.00	60.00
(13)	Raymond Bressler	125.00	65.00	35.00
(14)	John Brooks	125.00	65.00	35.00
(15)	Maurice Burrus	125.00	65.00	35.00
(16)	Max Carey	200.00	100.00	60.00
(17)	Tyrus Cobb	1,100	550.00	330.00
(18)	Eddie Collins	200.00	100.00	60.00
(19)	Stanley Coveleski	200.00	100.00	60.00
(20)	Hugh M. Critz	125.00	65.00	35.00
(21)	Hazen Cuyler	225.00	110.00	65.00
(22)	George Dauss	125.00	65.00	35.00
(23)	I.M. Davis	125.00	65.00	35.00
(24)	John H. DeBerry	125.00	65.00	35.00
(25)	Art Decatur	125.00	65.00	35.00
(26)	Peter Donohue	125.00	65.00	35.00
(27)	Charles Dressen	125.00	65.00	35.00
(28)	James J. Dykes	125.00	65.00	35.00
(29)	Howard Ehmke	125.00	65.00	35.00
(30)	Bib Falk (Bibb)	125.00	65.00	35.00
(31)	Wilson Fewster	125.00	65.00	35.00
(32)	Max Flack	125.00	65.00	35.00
(33)	Ira Flagstead	125.00	65.00	35.00
(34)	Jacques F. Fournier	125.00	65.00	35.00
(35)	Howard Freigau	125.00	65.00	35.00
(36)	Frank Frisch	200.00	100.00	60.00
(37)	Henry L. Gehrig	12,000	6,000	3,600
(38)	Joseph Genewich	125.00	65.00	35.00
(39)	Walter Gerber	125.00	65.00	35.00
(40)	Frank Gibson	125.00	65.00	35.00
(41)	Leon Goslin	200.00	100.00	60.00
(42)	George Grantham	125.00	65.00	35.00
(43)	Samuel Gray	125.00	65.00	35.00
(44)	Burleigh A. Grimes	200.00	100.00	60.00
(45)	Charles Grimm	125.00	65.00	35.00
(46)	Heine Groh (Heinie)	125.00	65.00	35.00
(47)	Samuel Hale	125.00	65.00	35.00
(48)	George Harper	125.00	65.00	35.00
(49)	David Harris	125.00	65.00	35.00
(50)	Stanley Harris	200.00	100.00	60.00
(51)	Leo Hartnett	200.00	100.00	60.00
(52)	Nelson Hawks	125.00	65.00	35.00
(53)	Harry Heilmann	200.00	100.00	60.00
(54)	Walter Henline	125.00	65.00	35.00
(55)	Walter Holke	125.00	65.00	35.00
(56)	Harry Hooper	200.00	100.00	60.00
(57)	Rogers Hornsby	300.00	150.00	90.00
(58)	Wilbur Hubbell	125.00	65.00	35.00
(59)	Travis C. Jackson	200.00	100.00	60.00
(60)	William Jacobson	125.00	65.00	35.00
(61)	Charles Jamieson	125.00	65.00	35.00
(62)	James H. Johnson (Johnston)	125.00	65.00	35.00
(63)	Walter Johnson	400.00	200.00	120.00
(64)	Joseph Judge	125.00	65.00	35.00
(65)	Willie Kamm	125.00	65.00	35.00
(66)	Ray Kremer	125.00	65.00	35.00
(67)	Walter Lutzke	125.00	65.00	35.00
(68)	Walter Maranville	200.00	100.00	60.00
(69)	John ("Stuffy") McInnes (McInnis)	125.00	65.00	35.00
(70)	Martin McManus	125.00	65.00	35.00
(71)	Earl McNeely	125.00	65.00	35.00
(72)	Emil Meusel	125.00	65.00	35.00
(73)	Edmund (Bing) Miller	125.00	65.00	35.00
(74)	John Mokan	125.00	65.00	35.00
(75)	Clarence Mueller	125.00	65.00	35.00
(76)	Robert W. Muesel (Meusel)	125.00	65.00	35.00
(77)	Glenn Myatt	125.00	65.00	35.00
(78)	Arthur Nehf	125.00	65.00	35.00
(79)	George O'Neil	125.00	65.00	35.00
(80)	Frank O'Rourke	125.00	65.00	35.00
(81)	Ralph Perkins	125.00	65.00	35.00
(82)	Valentine Picinich	125.00	65.00	35.00
(83)	Walter C. Pipp	125.00	65.00	35.00
(84)	John Quinn	125.00	65.00	35.00
(85)	Emory Rigney	125.00	65.00	35.00
(86)	Eppa Rixey	200.00	100.00	60.00
(87)	Edwin Rommel	125.00	65.00	35.00
(88)	Ed (Edd) Roush	200.00	100.00	60.00
(89)	Harold Ruel (Herold)	125.00	65.00	35.00
(90)	Charles Ruffing	200.00	100.00	60.00
(91)	George H. "Babe" Ruth	1,700	850.00	510.00
(92)	John Sand	125.00	65.00	35.00
(93)	Henry Severid (Severeid)	125.00	65.00	35.00
(94)	Joseph Sewell	200.00	100.00	60.00
(95)	Ray Shalk (Schalk)	200.00	100.00	60.00
(96)	Walter H. Shang (Schang)	125.00	65.00	35.00
(97)	J.R. Shawkey	125.00	65.00	35.00
(98)	Earl Sheely	125.00	65.00	35.00
(99)	William Sherdell (Sherdel)	125.00	65.00	35.00
(100)	Urban J. Shocker	125.00	65.00	35.00
(101)	George Sissler (Sisler)	200.00	100.00	60.00
(102)	Earl Smith	125.00	65.00	35.00
(103)	Sherrod Smith	125.00	65.00	35.00
(104)	Frank Snyder	125.00	65.00	35.00
(105)	Wm. H. Southworth	125.00	65.00	35.00
(106)	Tristram Speaker	300.00	150.00	90.00
(107)	Milton J. Stock	125.00	65.00	35.00
(108)	Homer Summa	125.00	65.00	35.00
(109)	William Terry	225.00	110.00	65.00
(110)	Hollis Thurston	125.00	65.00	35.00
(111)	John Tobin	125.00	65.00	35.00
(112)	Philip Todt	125.00	65.00	35.00
(113)	George Torporcer (Toporcer)	125.00	65.00	35.00
(114)	Harold Traynor	200.00	100.00	60.00
(115)	A.C. "Dazzy" Vance	200.00	100.00	60.00
(116)	Robert Veach (Photo actually Ernest Vache.)	125.00	65.00	35.00
(117)	William Wambsganss	125.00	65.00	35.00
(118)	Aaron Ward	125.00	65.00	35.00
(119)	A.J. Weis	125.00	65.00	35.00
(120)	Frank Welch	125.00	65.00	35.00
(121)	Zack Wheat	200.00	100.00	60.00
(122)	Fred Williams	125.00	65.00	35.00
(123)	Kenneth Williams	125.00	65.00	35.00
(124)	Ernest Wingard	125.00	65.00	35.00

(125)	Ivy Wingo	125.00	65.00	35.00
(126)	Al Wings (Wingo)	125.00	65.00	35.00
(127)	Larry Woodall	125.00	65.00	35.00
(128)	Glen Wright (Glenn)	125.00	65.00	35.00

1925-31 Postcard-Back Four-on-One Exhibits

The Exhibit Supply Company experimented with a four-on-one format in the late 1920s, ultimately adopting the format for several years from 1929-1938 for its main issues. This group of cards contains seven known cards in two distinct formats; a mixed subjects group containing two baseball players and two boxers or two entertainers; and a group containing four baseball players. The mixed subjects group was issued first, very likely circa 1926-1928 and is the rarer of the two. The all-baseball group certainly was issued as late as 1931 based on the team designations of certain players. Examples have been found with blank backs, postcard backs, and a postcard back with coupon (1 known), and in a variety of colors. Some cards have been found with two contrasting colors used, primarily blue and orange.

		NM	EX	VG
(1)	Lou Gehrig, Lefty Grove, Pete Donahue, Gordon Cochrane	2,200	1,100	650.00
(2)	Lefty O'Doul, Dazzy Vance, Hughey Critz, Art Shires	650.00	325.00	195.00
(3)	Eugene Criqui (Boxer), Dave Shade (Boxer), Joe Judge, Ty Cobb	3,000	1,500	900.00
(4)	Joe Judge, Ty Cobb, Charlie Chaplin (Actor), Marie Prevost (Actress)	2,500	1,250	750.00
(5)	Joe Judge, Paul Waner, Willie Kamm, Travis Jackson	750.00	375.00	225.00
(6)	Bucky Harris, Heinie Groh, Jack Dempsey (Boxer), Rocky Kansas (Boxer)	750.00	375.00	225.00
(7)	Walter Johnson, Al Simmons, Gene Tunney (Boxer), Benny Leonard (Boxer)	2,500	1,250	750.00
(8)	Babe Ruth, Rogers Hornsby, Mickey Walker (Boxer), Georges Carpentier (Boxer)	3,500	1,750	1,000

1925-31 Postcard-Back Exhibits

These cards can be found with plain backs; postcard backs including the legend: "This Side for Correspondence"; and postcard backs including the legend "Not to be used in Exhibit machines." Some printings also have the legend "Made in U.S.A." added to the backs. Cards will rarely be found with a coupon on the back corner. The fronts are borderless photos that generally have the player's name, team, and league designation handwritten across the fronts. Over the years of issue, players were added to and removed from the set and corrections were made to account for team changes, resulting in significant short-prints and variations. Cards can be found in a variety of colors. The "plain background" cards designated below are "cut-outs" of previous images reused against plain backgrounds.

		NM	EX	VG
	Common Player:	90.00	45.00	25.00
(1)	Virgie Barnes	90.00	45.00	25.00
(2)	Johnny Bassler	90.00	45.00	25.00
(3)	Sammy Bohne	200.00	100.00	60.00
(4)	Jim Bottomley	250.00	125.00	75.00
(5)	Ty Cobb (Detroit)	900.00	450.00	270.00
(6)	Ty Cobb (Athletics)	900.00	450.00	270.00
(7)	Mickey Cochrane	250.00	125.00	75.00
(8)	Urban Faber (Photo background.)	250.00	125.00	75.00
(9)	Urban Faber (Plain background.)	500.00	250.00	150.00
(10)	Jack Fournier	90.00	45.00	25.00
(11)	Jimmy Foxx	600.00	300.00	180.00
(12)	Frank Frisch (New York)	250.00	125.00	75.00
(13)	Frank Frisch (St. Louis)	450.00	225.00	135.00
(14)	Lou Gehrig (Batting, photo background.)	2,000	1,000	600.00
(15)	Lou Gehrig (Batting, plain background.)	4,000	2,000	1,200
(16)	Lou Gehrig (Portrait)	2,000	1,000	600.00
(17)	Tom Griffith	90.00	45.00	25.00
(18)	Heinie Groh	90.00	45.00	25.00
(19)	Lefty Grove	500.00	250.00	150.00
(20)	George Haas	90.00	45.00	25.00
(21)	Stanley Harris	250.00	125.00	75.00
(22)	Charlie Hartnett (Photo background.)	250.00	125.00	75.00
(23)	Charlie Hartnett (Plain background.)	500.00	250.00	150.00
(24)	Harry Heilmann	250.00	125.00	75.00
(25)	Rogers Hornsby (St. Louis)	600.00	300.00	180.00
(26)	Rogers Hornsby (Boston)	600.00	300.00	180.00
(27)	Rogers Hornsby (Chicago)	600.00	300.00	180.00
(28)	Walter Johnson	600.00	300.00	180.00
(29)	Jimmy Johnston	90.00	45.00	25.00
(30)	Joe Judge	90.00	45.00	25.00
(31)	George Kelly	250.00	125.00	75.00
(32)	Chuck Klein	250.00	125.00	75.00
(33)	Hugh McQuillan	180.00	90.00	54.00
(34)	"Bob" Meusel	90.00	45.00	25.00
(35)	Bing Miller	90.00	45.00	25.00
(36)	Lefty O'Doul	150.00	75.00	45.00
(37)	Roger Peckinpaugh (Washington)	200.00	100.00	60.00
(38)	Roger Peckinpaugh (Cleveland)	500.00	300.00	200.00
(39)	Ralph Pinelli	90.00	45.00	25.00
(40)	Walter Pipp	125.00	60.00	35.00
(41)	Jimmy Ring	90.00	45.00	25.00
(42)	Eppa Rixey	250.00	125.00	75.00

		NM	EX	VG
(43)	Ed Rouch (Edd Roush) (Cincinnati)	250.00	125.00	75.00
(44)	Ed Rouch (Edd Roush) (New York)	375.00	185.00	110.00
(45)	Babe Ruth (Pose)	2,200	1,100	660.00
(46)	Babe Ruth (Batting follow-through.)	2,200	1,100	660.00
(47)	John Sand	90.00	45.00	25.00
(48)	Everett Scott	180.00	90.00	54.00
(49)	Al Simmons (View from side, "AM.L.")	500.00	250.00	150.00
(50)	Al Simmons (View from front, "A.L.")	250.00	125.00	75.00
(51)	George Sisler (Photo background.)	250.00	125.00	75.00
(52)	George Sisler (Plain background.)	500.00	250.00	150.00
(53)	Jack Smith	90.00	45.00	25.00
(54)	Tris Speaker (Photo background.)	350.00	175.00	100.00
(55)	Tris Speaker (Plain background.)	700.00	350.00	210.00
(56)	Phil Todt (Photo background.)	90.00	45.00	25.00
(57)	Phil Todt (Plain background.)	180.00	90.00	54.00
(58)	Specs Toporcer	180.00	90.00	54.00
(59)	Pie Traynor	250.00	125.00	75.00
(60)	Dazzy Vance	250.00	125.00	75.00
(61)	Rube Walberg	90.00	45.00	25.00
(62)	Paul Waner (Batting, photo background)	250.00	125.00	75.00
(63)	Paul Waner (Batting, plain background)	500.00	250.00	150.00
(64)	Paul Waner (Portrait)	250.00	125.00	75.00
(65)	Zack Wheat	250.00	125.00	75.00
(66)	Cy Williams	90.00	45.00	25.00
(67)	Hack Wilson	250.00	125.00	75.00
(68)	Jimmy Wilson (Photo background.)	90.00	45.00	25.00
(69)	Jimmy Wilson (Plain background.)	180.00	90.00	54.00

1925 Champions Babe Ruth Exhibit

This is part of a (presumably) 32-card multi-sport "World's Champions" issue and the only baseball player in the set. The 3-3/8" x 5-3/8" card is printed in black-and-white and has a blank back.

	NM	EX	VG
Babe Ruth	3,500	2,500	1,000

1926 Exhibits

The 1926 Exhibit cards are the same size (3-3/8" x 5-3/8") as previous Exhibit issues but are easily distinguished because of their blue-gray color. The set consists of 128 cards, 91 of which are identical to the photos in the 1925 series. The 37 new photos do not include the boxed caption used in 1925. The cards are unnumbered and are listed alphabetically.

		NM	EX	VG
Complete Set (128):		22,500	11,250	6,750
Common Player:		125.00	60.00	35.00
(1)	Sparky Adams	125.00	60.00	35.00
(2)	David Bancroft	400.00	200.00	120.00
(3)	John Bassler	125.00	60.00	35.00
(4)	Lester Bell	125.00	60.00	35.00
(5)	John M. Bentley	125.00	60.00	35.00
(6)	Lawrence Benton	125.00	60.00	35.00
(7)	Carson Bigbee	125.00	60.00	35.00
(8)	George Bischoff (Team actually Boston A.L.)	125.00	60.00	35.00
(9)	Max Bishop	125.00	60.00	35.00
(10)	J. Fred Blake	125.00	60.00	35.00
(11)	Ted Blankenship	125.00	60.00	35.00
(12)	Raymond Blates (Blades)	125.00	60.00	35.00
(13)	Lucerne A. Blue (Luzerne)	125.00	60.00	35.00
(14)	Oswald Bluege	125.00	60.00	35.00
(15)	James Bottomly (Bottomley)	400.00	200.00	120.00
(16)	Raymond Bressler	125.00	60.00	35.00
(17)	Geo. H. Burns	125.00	60.00	35.00
(18)	Maurice Burrus	125.00	60.00	35.00
(19)	John Butler	125.00	60.00	35.00
(20)	Max Carey	400.00	200.00	120.00
(21)	Tyrus Cobb	1,400	700.00	425.00
(22)	Eddie Collins	400.00	200.00	120.00
(23)	Patrick T. Collins	125.00	60.00	35.00
(24)	Earl B. Combs (Earle)	225.00	110.00	65.00
(25)	James E. Cooney	125.00	60.00	35.00
(26)	Stanley Coveleski	400.00	200.00	120.00
(27)	Hugh M. Critz	125.00	60.00	35.00
(28)	Hazen Cuyler	400.00	200.00	120.00
(29)	George Dauss	125.00	60.00	35.00
(30)	Peter Donohue	125.00	60.00	35.00
(31)	Charles Dressen	125.00	60.00	35.00
(32)	James J. Dykes	125.00	60.00	35.00
(33)	Bib Falk (Bibb)	125.00	60.00	35.00
(34)	Edward S. Farrell	125.00	60.00	35.00
(35)	Wilson Fewster	125.00	60.00	35.00
(36)	Ira Flagstead	125.00	60.00	35.00
(37)	Howard Freigau	125.00	60.00	35.00
(38)	Bernard Friberg	125.00	60.00	35.00
(39)	Frank Frisch	400.00	200.00	120.00
(40)	Jacques F. Fumier (Fournier)	125.00	60.00	35.00
(41)	Joseph Galloway (Clarence)(Photo reversed.)	125.00	60.00	35.00
(42)	Henry L. Gehrig	2,350	1,175	725.00
(43)	Charles Gehringer	500.00	250.00	150.00
(44)	Joseph Genewich	125.00	60.00	35.00
(45)	Walter Gerber	125.00	60.00	35.00
(46)	Leon Goslin	400.00	200.00	120.00
(47)	George Grantham	125.00	60.00	35.00
(48)	Burleigh A. Grimes	200.00	100.00	60.00
(49)	Charles Grimm	125.00	60.00	35.00
(50)	Fred Haney	125.00	60.00	35.00
(51)	Wm. Hargrave	125.00	60.00	35.00
(52)	George Harper	125.00	60.00	35.00
(53)	Stanley Harris	200.00	100.00	60.00
(54)	Leo Hartnett	200.00	100.00	60.00
(55)	Joseph Hauser	125.00	60.00	35.00
(56)	C.E. Heathcote	125.00	60.00	35.00
(57)	Harry Heilmann	400.00	200.00	120.00
(58)	Walter Henline	125.00	60.00	35.00
(59)	Ramon Herrera	125.00	60.00	35.00
(60)	Andrew A. High	125.00	60.00	35.00
(61)	Rogers Hornsby	450.00	225.00	135.00
(62)	Clarence Huber	125.00	60.00	35.00
(63)	Wm. Hunnefield (Photo actually Tommy Thomas.)	125.00	60.00	35.00
(64)	William Jacobson	125.00	60.00	35.00
(65)	Walter Johnson	600.00	300.00	180.00
(66)	Joseph Judge	125.00	60.00	35.00
(67)	Willie Kamm	125.00	60.00	35.00
(68)	Ray Kremer	125.00	60.00	35.00
(69)	Anthony Lazzeri	500.00	250.00	150.00
(70)	Frederick Lindstrom	450.00	225.00	125.00
(71)	Walter Lutzke	125.00	60.00	35.00
(72)	John Makan (Mokan)	125.00	60.00	35.00
(73)	Walter Maranville	400.00	200.00	125.00
(74)	Martin McManus	125.00	60.00	35.00
(75)	Earl McNeely	125.00	60.00	35.00
(76)	Hugh A. McQuillan	125.00	60.00	35.00
(77)	Douglas McWeeny	125.00	60.00	35.00
(78)	Oscar Melillo	125.00	60.00	35.00
(79)	Edmund (Bind)(Bing) Miller	125.00	60.00	35.00
(80)	Clarence Mueller	125.00	60.00	35.00
(81)	Robert W. Muesel (Meusel)	125.00	60.00	35.00
(82)	Joseph W. Munson	125.00	60.00	35.00
(83)	Emil Musel (Meusel)	125.00	60.00	35.00
(84)	Glenn Myatt	125.00	60.00	35.00
(85)	Bernie F. Neis	125.00	60.00	35.00
(86)	Robert O'Farrell	125.00	60.00	35.00
(87)	George O'Neil	125.00	60.00	35.00
(88)	Frank O'Rourke	125.00	60.00	35.00
(89)	Ralph Perkins	125.00	60.00	35.00
(90)	Walter C. Pipp	135.00	65.00	40.00
(91)	Emory Rigney	125.00	60.00	35.00
(92)	James J. Ring	125.00	60.00	35.00
(93)	Eppa Rixey	200.00	100.00	60.00
(94)	Edwin Rommel	125.00	60.00	35.00
(95)	Ed. Roush	200.00	100.00	60.00
(96)	Harold Ruel (Herold)	125.00	60.00	35.00
(97)	Charles Ruffing	400.00	200.00	125.00
(98)	Geo. H. "Babe" Ruth	1,875	935.00	560.00
(99)	John Sand	125.00	60.00	35.00
(100)	Joseph Sewell	200.00	100.00	60.00
(101)	Ray Shalk (Schalk)	400.00	200.00	125.00
(102)	J.R. Shawkey	125.00	60.00	35.00
(103)	Earl Sheely	125.00	60.00	35.00
(104)	William Sherdell (Sherdel)	125.00	60.00	35.00
(105)	Urban J. Shocker	125.00	60.00	35.00
(106)	George Sissler (Sisler)	400.00	200.00	125.00
(107)	Earl Smith	125.00	60.00	35.00
(108)	Sherrod Smith	125.00	60.00	35.00
(109)	Frank Snyder	125.00	60.00	35.00
(110)	Tristram Speaker	425.00	210.00	125.00
(111)	Fred Spurgeon	125.00	60.00	35.00
(112)	Homer Summa	125.00	60.00	35.00
(113)	Edward Taylor	125.00	60.00	35.00
(114)	J. Taylor	125.00	60.00	35.00
(115)	William Terry	400.00	200.00	120.00
(116)	Hollis Thurston	125.00	60.00	35.00
(117)	Philip Todt	125.00	60.00	35.00
(118)	George Torporcer (Toporcer)	125.00	60.00	35.00
(119)	Harold Traynor	400.00	200.00	120.00
(120)	Wm. Wambsganss	125.00	60.00	35.00
(121)	John Warner	125.00	60.00	35.00
(122)	Zach Wheat	400.00	200.00	120.00
(123)	Kenneth Williams	125.00	60.00	35.00
(124)	Ernest Wingard	125.00	60.00	35.00
(125)	Fred Wingfield	125.00	60.00	35.00
(126)	Ivy Wingo	125.00	60.00	35.00
(127)	Glen Wright (Glenn)	125.00	60.00	35.00
(128)	Russell Wrightstone	125.00	60.00	35.00

1927 Exhibits

The Exhibit Supply Co. issued a set of 64 cards in 1927, each measuring 3-3/8" x 5-3/8". The set can be identified from earlier issues by its light green tint. The player's name and team appear in capital letters in one lower corner, while "Ex. Sup. Co., Chgo." and "Made in U.S.A." appear in the other. All 64 photos used in the 1927 set were borrowed from previous issues, but 13 players are listed with new teams. There are several misspellings and other labeling errors in the set. The unnumbered cards are listed here in alphabetical order. Cards will rarely be found with a corner coupon in purple printed or stamped on the back of the card.

		NM	EX	VG
Complete Set (64):		11,000	5,500	3,250
Common Player:		75.00	35.00	20.00
(1)	Sparky Adams	75.00	35.00	20.00
(2)	Grover C. Alexander	250.00	125.00	75.00
(3)	David Bancroft	150.00	75.00	45.00
(4)	John Bassler	75.00	35.00	20.00
(5)	John M. Bentley (Middle initial actually N.)	75.00	35.00	20.00
(6)	Fred Blankenship (Ted)	75.00	35.00	20.00
(7)	James Bottomly (Bottomley)	150.00	75.00	45.00
(8)	Raymond Bressler	75.00	35.00	20.00
(9)	Geo. H. Burns	75.00	35.00	20.00
(10)	John Buttler (Butler)	75.00	35.00	20.00
(11)	Tyrus Cobb	1,100	550.00	330.00
(12)	Eddie Collins	150.00	75.00	45.00
(13)	Hazen Cuyler	150.00	75.00	45.00
(14)	George Daus (Dauss)	75.00	35.00	20.00
(15)	A.R. Decatur	75.00	35.00	20.00
(16)	Wilson Fewster	75.00	35.00	20.00
(17)	Ira Flagstead	75.00	35.00	20.00
(18)	Henry L. Gehrig	1,200	600.00	360.00
(19)	Charles Gehringer	150.00	75.00	45.00
(20)	Joseph Genewich	75.00	35.00	20.00
(21)	Leon Goslin	150.00	75.00	45.00
(22)	Burleigh A. Grimes	150.00	75.00	45.00
(23)	Charles Grimm	75.00	35.00	20.00
(24)	Fred Haney	75.00	35.00	20.00
(25)	Wm. Hargrave	75.00	35.00	20.00
(26)	George Harper	75.00	35.00	20.00
(27)	Leo Hartnett	150.00	75.00	45.00
(28)	Clifton Heathcote	75.00	35.00	20.00
(29)	Harry Heilman (Heillmann)	150.00	75.00	45.00
(30)	Walter Henline	75.00	35.00	20.00
(31)	Andrew High	75.00	35.00	20.00
(32)	Rogers Hornsby	250.00	125.00	75.00
(33)	Wm. Hunnefield (Photo actually Tommy Thomas.)	75.00	35.00	20.00
(34)	Walter Johnson	650.00	325.00	195.00
(35)	Willie Kamm	75.00	35.00	20.00
(36)	Ray Kremer	75.00	35.00	20.00
(37)	Anthony Lazzeri	150.00	75.00	45.00
(38)	Frederick Lindstrom (Frederick)	150.00	75.00	45.00
(39)	Walter Lutzke	75.00	35.00	20.00
(40)	John "Stuffy" McInnes (McInnis)	75.00	35.00	20.00
(41)	John Mokan	75.00	35.00	20.00
(42)	Robert W. Muesel (Meusel)	75.00	35.00	20.00
(43)	Glenn Myatt	75.00	35.00	20.00
(44)	Bernie Neis	75.00	35.00	20.00
(45)	Robert O'Farrell	75.00	35.00	20.00
(46)	Walter C. Pipp	100.00	50.00	30.00
(47)	Eppa Rixey	150.00	75.00	45.00
(48)	Harold Ruel (Herold)	75.00	35.00	20.00
(49)	Geo. H. "Babe" Ruth	2,100	1,100	630.00
(50)	Ray Schalk	150.00	75.00	45.00
(51)	George Sissler (Sisler)	150.00	75.00	45.00
(52)	Earl Smith	75.00	35.00	20.00
(53)	Wm. H. Southworth	75.00	35.00	20.00
(54)	Tristam Speaker (Tristram)	250.00	125.00	75.00
(55)	J. Taylor	75.00	35.00	20.00
(56)	Philip Todt	75.00	35.00	20.00
(57)	Harold Traynor	150.00	75.00	45.00
(58)	William Wambsganns (Wambsganss)	75.00	35.00	20.00
(59)	Zach Wheat	150.00	75.00	45.00

		NM	EX	VG
(60)	Kenneth Williams	75.00	35.00	20.00
(61)	Ernest Wingard	75.00	35.00	20.00
(62)	Fred Wingfield	75.00	35.00	20.00
(63)	Ivy Wingo	75.00	35.00	20.00
(64)	Russell Wrightstone	75.00	35.00	20.00

1928 Exhibits

The Exhibit Supply Co. switched to a blue tint for the photos in its 64-card set in 1928. There are 36 new photos in the set, including 24 new players. Four players from the previous year are shown with new teams and 24 of the cards are identical to the 1927 series, except for the color of the card. They are blank backed, or found with a purple printed or stamped corner coupon on the back. The photos are captioned in the same style as the 1927 set. The set again includes some misspelling and incorrect labels. The cards are unnumbered and are listed here in alphabetical order.

		NM	EX	VG
Complete Set (64):		9,500	4,750	2,750
Common Player:		80.00	40.00	20.00
(1)	Grover C. Alexander	400.00	200.00	120.00
(2)	David Bancroft	200.00	100.00	60.00
(3)	Virgil Barnes	80.00	40.00	20.00
(4)	Francis R. Blades	80.00	40.00	20.00
(5)	L.A. Blue	80.00	40.00	20.00
(6)	Edward W. Brown	80.00	40.00	20.00
(7)	Max G. Carey	200.00	100.00	60.00
(8)	Chalmer W. Cissell	80.00	40.00	20.00
(9)	Gordon S. Cochrane	200.00	100.00	60.00
(10)	Pat Collins	80.00	40.00	20.00
(11)	Hugh M. Critz	80.00	40.00	20.00
(12)	Howard Ehmke	80.00	40.00	20.00
(13)	E. English	80.00	40.00	20.00
(14)	Bib Falk (Bibb)	80.00	40.00	20.00
(15)	Ira Flagstead	80.00	40.00	20.00
(16)	Robert Fothergill	80.00	40.00	20.00
(17)	Frank Frisch	200.00	100.00	60.00
(18)	Lou Gehrig	1,200	600.00	360.00
(19)	Leon Goslin	200.00	100.00	60.00
(20)	Eugene Hargrave	80.00	40.00	20.00
(21)	Charles R. Hargraves (Hargreaves)	80.00	40.00	20.00
(22)	Stanley Harris	200.00	100.00	60.00
(23)	Bryan "Slim" Harriss	80.00	40.00	20.00
(24)	Leo Hartnett	200.00	100.00	60.00
(25)	Joseph Hauser	80.00	40.00	20.00
(26)	Fred Hoffman (Hofmann)	80.00	40.00	20.00
(27)	J. Francis Hogan	80.00	40.00	20.00
(28)	Rogers Hornsby	300.00	150.00	90.00
(29)	Chas. Jamieson	80.00	40.00	20.00
(30)	Sam Jones	80.00	40.00	20.00
(31)	Ray Kremer	80.00	40.00	20.00
(32)	Fred Leach	80.00	40.00	20.00
(33)	Fredrick Lindstrom (Frederick)	200.00	100.00	60.00
(34)	Adolph Luque (Adolfo)	100.00	50.00	30.00
(35)	Theodore Lyons	200.00	100.00	60.00
(36)	Harry McCurdy	80.00	40.00	20.00
(37)	Glenn Myatt	80.00	40.00	20.00
(38)	John Ogden (Photo actually Warren Ogden.)	80.00	40.00	20.00
(39)	James Ring	80.00	40.00	20.00
(40)	A.C. Root (Should be C.H.)	80.00	40.00	20.00
(41)	Edd. Roush	200.00	100.00	60.00
(42)	Harold Ruel (Herold)	80.00	40.00	20.00
(43)	Geo. H. "Babe" Ruth	1,350	675.00	400.00
(44)	Henry Sand	80.00	40.00	20.00
(45)	Fred Schulte	80.00	40.00	20.00
(46)	Joseph Sewell	200.00	100.00	60.00
(47)	Walter Shang (Schang)	80.00	40.00	20.00
(48)	Urban J. Shocker	80.00	40.00	20.00
(49)	Al. Simmons	200.00	100.00	60.00
(50)	Earl Smith	80.00	40.00	20.00
(51)	Robert Smith	80.00	40.00	20.00
(52)	Jack Tavener	80.00	40.00	20.00
(53)	J. Taylor	80.00	40.00	20.00
(54)	Philip Todt	80.00	40.00	20.00
(55)	Geo. Uhle	80.00	40.00	20.00
(56)	Arthur "Dazzy" Vance	200.00	100.00	60.00
(57)	Paul Waner	200.00	100.00	60.00
(58)	Earl G. Whitehill (Middle initial actually O.)	80.00	40.00	20.00
(59)	Fred Williams	80.00	40.00	20.00
(60)	James Wilson	80.00	40.00	20.00
(61)	L.R. (Hack) Wilson	200.00	100.00	60.00
(62)	Lawrence Woodall	80.00	40.00	20.00
(63)	Glen Wright (Glenn)	80.00	40.00	20.00
(64)	William A. Zitzman (Zitzmann)	80.00	40.00	20.00

1929-30 Four-on-One Exhibits

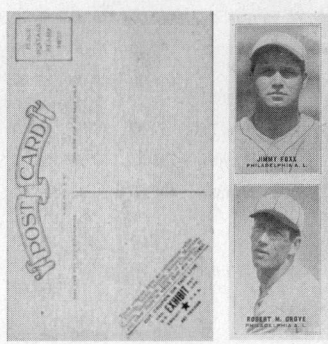

Although the size of the card remained the same, the Exhibit Supply Co. of Chicago began putting four players' pictures on each card in 1929 - a practice that would continue for the next decade. Known as "four-on-one" cards, the players are identified by name and team at the bottom of the photos, which are separated by borders. The 32 cards in the 1929-30 series have postcard backs and were printed in a wide range of color combinations of black, brown and blue ink on blue, orange, green, red, white, and yellow backgrounds. Most of the backs are uncolored, however, cards with a black on red front have been seen with red backs, and cards with blue on yellow fronts have been seen with yellow backs. There are numerous spelling and caption errors in the set, and the player identified as Babe Herman is actually Jesse Petty.

		NM	EX	VG
Complete Set (32):		5,500	2,750	1,600
Common Card:		65.00	32.00	20.00
(1)	Earl J. Adams, R. Bartell, Earl Sheely, Harold Traynor	150.00	75.00	45.00
(2)	Dale Alexander, C. Gehringer, G.F. McManus (Should be M.J.), H.F. Rice	150.00	75.00	45.00
(3)	Grover C. Alexander, James Bottomly (Bottomley), Frank Frisch, James Wilson	250.00	125.00	75.00
(4)	Martin G. Autrey (Autry), Alex Metzler, Carl Reynolds, Alphonse Thomas	65.00	32.50	20.00
(5)	Earl Averill, B.A. Falk, K. Holloway, L. Sewell	150.00	75.00	45.00
(6)	David Bancroft, Del L. Bisonette (Bissonette), John H. DeBerry, Floyd C. Herman (Photo actually Jesse Petty.)	150.00	75.00	45.00
(7)	C.E. Beck, Leo Hartnett, Rogers Hornsby, L.R. (Hack) Wilson	200.00	100.00	60.00
(8)	Ray Benge, Lester L. Sweetland, A.C. Whitney, Cy. Williams	65.00	32.50	20.00
(9)	Benny Bengough, Earl B. Coombs (Combs), Waite Hoyt, Anthony Lazzeri	200.00	100.00	60.00
(10)	L. Benton, Melvin Ott, Andrew Reese, William Terry	150.00	75.00	45.00
(11)	Max Bishop, James Dykes, Samuel Hale, Homer Summa	65.00	32.50	20.00
(12)	L.A. Blue, O. Melillo, F.O. Rourke (Frank O'Rourke), F. Schulte	65.00	32.50	20.00
(13)	Oswald Bluege, Leon Goslin, Joseph Judge, Harold Ruel (Herold)	150.00	75.00	45.00
(14)	Chalmer W. Cissell, John W. Clancy, Willie Kamm, John L. Kerr (Kerr's middle initial actually "F.")	65.00	32.50	20.00
(15)	Gordon S. Cochrane, Jimmy Foxx, Robert M. Grove, George Haas	250.00	125.00	75.00
(16)	Pat Collins, Joe Dugan, Edward Farrel (Farrell), George Sisler	150.00	75.00	45.00
(17)	H.M. Critz, G.L. Kelly, V.J. Picinich, W.C. Walker	150.00	75.00	45.00
(18)	Nick Cullop, D'Arcy Flowers, Harvey Hendrick, Arthur "Dazzy" Vance	150.00	75.00	45.00
(19)	Hazen Cuyler, E. English, C.J. Grimm, C.H. Root	150.00	75.00	45.00
(20)	Taylor Douthit, Chas. M. Gilbert (Gelbert), Chas. J. Hafey, Fred G. Haney	150.00	75.00	45.00
(21)	Leo Durocher, Henry L. Gehrig, Mark Koenig, Geo. H. "Babe" Ruth	1,400	700.00	400.00
(22)	L.A. Fonseca, Carl Lind, J. Sewell, J. Tavener	150.00	75.00	45.00
(23)	H.E. Ford, C.F. Lucas, C.A. Pittenger, E.V. Purdy	65.00	32.50	20.00
(24)	Bernard Friberg, Donald Hurst, Frank O'Doul, Fresco Thompson	65.00	32.50	20.00
(25)	S. Gray, R. Kress, H. Manush, W.H. Shang (Schang)	150.00	75.00	45.00
(26)	Charles R. Hargreaves, Ray Kremer, Lloyd Waner, Paul Waner	150.00	75.00	45.00
(27)	George Harper, Fred Maguire, Lance Richbourg, Robert Smith	65.00	32.50	20.00
(28)	Jack Hayes, Sam P. Jones, Chas. M. Myer, Sam Rice	150.00	75.00	45.00
(29)	Harry E. Heilman (Heilman), C.N. Richardson, M.J. Shea, G.E. Uhle	150.00	75.00	45.00
(30)	J.A. Heving, R.R. Reeves (Should be R.E.), J. Rothrock, C.H. Ruffing	150.00	75.00	45.00
(31)	J.F. Hogan, T.C. Jackson, Fred Lindstrom, J.D. Welsh	150.00	75.00	45.00
(32)	W.W. Regan, H. Rhyne, D. Taitt, P.J. Todt	65.00	32.50	20.00

1929 Exhibit "Star Picture Stamps"

This series of movie star Exhibit cards includes pictures of other celebrities who were featured in contemporary movies. Produced by Exhibit Supply Co. of Chicago, whose advertising appears on the postcard-style back, this 5-3/8" x 3-3/8" card has a variety of colors on the front which pictures the stars in the format of eight "Star Pictures Stamps". On this card, Ruth is pictured in the uniform he wore in the 1927 film "The Babe Comes Home."

	NM	EX	VG
Babe Ruth (W/Tom Mix, Charles Lindbergh, Charlie Chaplin, Jack Dempsey, Harold Lloyd, Douglas Fairbanks and Al Jolson.)	750.00	375.00	225.00

1931-32 Four-on-One Exhibits

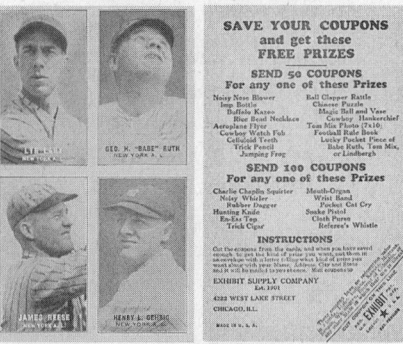

The 1931-1932 series issued by the Exhibit Co. again consisted of 32 cards, each picturing four players. The series can be differentiated from the previous year by the coupon backs, which list various premiums available (including kazoos, toy pistols and other prizes). The cards again were printed in various color combinations, including; black on green, blue on green, black on orange, black on red, blue on white and black on yellow. There are numerous spelling and caption errors in the series. The Babe Herman/Jesse Petty error of the previous year was still not corrected, and the card of Rick Ferell not only misspells his name ("Farrel"), but also pictures the wrong player (Edward Farrell).

		NM	EX	VG
Complete Set (32):		5,500	2,750	1,600
Common Card:		90.00	45.00	27.00
(1)	Earl J. Adams, James Bottomly (Bottomley), Frank Frisch, James Wilson	150.00	75.00	45.00
(2)	Dale Alexander, C. Gehringer, G.F. McManus (Should be M.J.), G.E. Uhle	150.00	75.00	45.00
(3)	L.L. Appling (Should be L.B.), Chalmer W. Cissell, Willie Kamm, Ted Lyons	150.00	75.00	45.00
(4)	Buzz Arlett, Ray Benge, Chuck Klein, A.C. Whitney	150.00	75.00	45.00
(5)	Earl Averill, B.A. Falk, L.A. Fonseca, L. Sewell	150.00	75.00	45.00
(6)	Richard Bartell, Bernard Friberg, Donald Hurst, Harry McCurdy	90.00	45.00	27.00
(7)	Walter Berger, Fred Maguire, Lance Richbourg, Earl Sheely	90.00	45.00	27.00
(8)	Chas. Berry, Robt. Reeves, R.R. Reeves (Should be R.E.), J. Rothrock	90.00	45.00	27.00

		NM	EX	VG
(9)	Del L. Bisonette (Bissonette), Floyd C. Herman (Photo - J. Petty, Jack Quinn, Glenn Wright)	90.00	45.00	27.00
(10)	L.A. Blue, Smead Jolley, Carl Reynolds, Henry Tate	90.00	45.00	27.00
(11)	O. Bluege, Joe Judge, Chas. M. Myer, Sam Rice	150.00	75.00	45.00
(12)	John Boley, James Dykes, E.J. Miller, Al. Simmons	150.00	75.00	45.00
(13)	Gordon S. Cochrane, Jimmy Foxx, Robert M. Grove, George Haas	325.00	160.00	95.00
(14)	Adam Comorosky, Gus Suhr, T.J. Thevenow, Harold Traynor	150.00	75.00	45.00
(15)	Earl B. Coombs (Combs), W. Dickey, Anthony Lazzeri, H. Pennock	225.00	110.00	65.00
(16)	H.M. Critz, J.F. Hogan, T.C. Jackson, Fred Lindstrom	150.00	75.00	45.00
(17)	Joe Cronin, H. Manush, F. Marberry, Roy Spencer	150.00	75.00	45.00
(18)	Nick Cullop, Les Durocher (Leo), Harry Heilmann, W.C. Walker	150.00	75.00	45.00
(19)	Hazen Cuyler, E. English, C.J. Grimm, C.H. Root	150.00	75.00	45.00
(20)	Taylor Douthit, Chas. M. Gilbert (Gelbert), Chas. J. Hafey, Bill Hallahan	90.00	45.00	27.00
(21)	Richard Farrel (Ferrell), S. Gray, R. Kress, W. Stewart (Photo actually Ed Farrell.)	90.00	45.00	27.00
(22)	W. Ferrell, J. Goldman, Hunnefield, Ed Morgan	90.00	45.00	27.00
(23)	Fred Fitzsimmons, Robert O'Farrell, Melvin Ott, William Terry	150.00	75.00	45.00
(24)	D'Arcy Flowers, Frank O'Doul, Fresco Thompson, Arthur "Dazzy" Vance	150.00	75.00	45.00
(25)	H.E. Ford (Should be H.H.), Gooch, C.F. Lucas, W. Roettger	90.00	45.00	27.00
(26)	E. Funk, W. Hoyt, Mark Koenig, Wallie Schang	90.00	45.00	27.00
(27)	Henry L. Gehrig, Lyn Lary, James Reese (Photo actually Andy Reese.), Geo. H. "Babe" Ruth	1,150	575.00	345.00
(28)	George Grantham, Ray Kremer, Lloyd Waner, Paul Waner	150.00	75.00	45.00
(29)	Leon Goslin, O. Melillo, F.O. Rourke (Frank O'Rourke), F. Schulte	150.00	75.00	45.00
(30)	Leo Hartnett, Rogers Hornsby, J.R. Stevenson (Stephenson), L.R. (Hack) Wilson	200.00	100.00	60.00
(31)	D. MacFayden, H. Rhyne, Bill Sweeney, E.W. Webb	90.00	45.00	27.00
(32)	Walter Maranville, Randolph Moore, Alfred Spohrer, J.T. Zachary	150.00	75.00	45.00

1931-32 Babe Ruth Exhibit

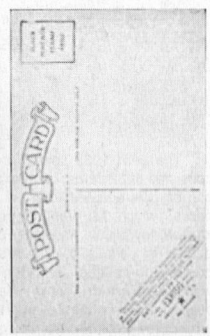

The rarest Exhibit card to feature Babe Ruth, this circa 1931 issue has a photographic portrait of him in dress clothes, and is part of a 32-card movie stars series. Found in black-and-white or various color tints, this approximately 3-1/2" x 5-1/2" card has a facsimile autograph in white on front. It can be found with either a postcard-style back or a back offering premium merchandise.

	NM	EX	VG
Babe Ruth	900.00	450.00	270.00

1933 Four-on-One Exhibits

The 1933 series of four-on-one Exhibits consists of 16 cards with blank backs. Color combinations include: blue on green, black on orange, black on red, blue on white and black on yellow. Most have a plain, white back, although the black on yellow cards are also found with a yellow back. Most of the pictures used are reprinted from previous series, and there are some spelling and caption errors, including the Richard Ferrell/Edward Farrel mixup from the previous year. Al Lopez is shown as "Vincent" Lopez.

	NM	EX	VG
Complete Set (16):	4,000	2,000	1,200
Common Card:	85.00	40.00	25.00

		NM	EX	VG
(1)	Earl J. Adams, Frank Frisch, Chas. Gilbert (Gelbert), Bill Hallahan	150.00	75.00	45.00
(2)	Earl Averill, W. Ferrell, Ed Morgan, L. Sewell	150.00	75.00	45.00
(3)	Richard Bartell, Ray Benge, Donald Hurst, Chuck Klein	150.00	75.00	45.00
(4)	Walter Berger, Walter Maranville, Alfred Spohrer, J.T. Zachary	150.00	75.00	45.00
(5)	Charles Berry, L.A. Blue, Ted Lyons, Bob Seeds	150.00	75.00	45.00
(6)	Chas. Berry, D. MacFayden, H. Rhyne, E.W. Webb	85.00	40.00	25.00
(7)	Mickey Cochrane, Jimmy Foxx, Robert M. Grove, Al. Simmons	450.00	225.00	135.00
(8)	H.M. Critz, Fred Fitzsimmons, Fred Lindstrom, Robert O'Farrell	150.00	75.00	45.00
(9)	W. Dickey, Anthony Lazzeri, H. Pennock, George H. "Babe" Ruth	2,000	1,000	600.00
(10)	Taylor Douthit, George Grantham, Chas. J. Hafey, C.F. Lucas	150.00	75.00	45.00
(11)	E. English, C.J. Grimm, C.H. Root, J.R. Stevenson (Stephenson)	85.00	40.00	25.00
(12)	Richard Farrel (Farrell), Leon Goslin, S. Gray, O. Melillo (photo actually Ed Farrell)	150.00	75.00	45.00
(13)	C. Gehringer, "Muddy" Ruel, Jonathan Stone (first name - John, G.E. Uhle	150.00	75.00	45.00
(14)	Joseph Judge, H. Manush, F. Marberry, Roy Spencer	150.00	75.00	45.00
(15)	Vincent Lopez (Al), Frank O'Doul, Arthur "Dazzy" Vance, Glenn Wright	150.00	75.00	45.00
(16)	Gus Suhr, Tom J. Thevenow, Lloyd Waner, Paul Waner	150.00	75.00	45.00

1934 Four-on-One Exhibits

This 16-card series issued by the Exhibit Co. in 1934 is again blank-backed and continues the four-on-one format in a 3-3/8" x 5-3/8" size. The 1934 series can be differentiated from previous years by the more subdued colors of the cards, which include lighter shades of blue, brown, green and violet - all printed on white card stock. Many new photos were also used in the 1934 series. Of the 64 players included, 25 appear for the first time and another 16 were given new poses. Spelling was improved, but Al Lopez is still identified as "Vincent."

	NM	EX	VG
Complete Set (16):	2,750	1,350	825.00
Common Card:	75.00	35.00	20.00

		NM	EX	VG
(1)	Luke Appling, George Earnshaw, Al Simmons, Evar Swanson	125.00	60.00	35.00
(2)	Earl Averill, W. Ferrell, Willie Kamm, Frank Pytlak	125.00	60.00	35.00
(3)	Richard Bartell, Donald Hurst, Wesley Schulmerich, Jimmy Wilson	75.00	35.00	20.00
(4)	Walter Berger, Ed Brandt, Frank Hogan, Bill Urbanski	75.00	35.00	20.00
(5)	Jim Bottomley, Chas. J. Hafey, Botchi Lombardi, Tony Piet	125.00	60.00	35.00
(6)	Irving Burns, Irving Hadley, Rollie Hemsley, O. Melillo	75.00	35.00	20.00
(7)	Bill Cissell, Rick Ferrell, Lefty Grove, Roy Johnson	125.00	60.00	35.00
(8)	Mickey Cochrane, C. Gehringer, Goose Goslin, Fred Marberry	125.00	60.00	35.00
(9)	George Cramer (Roger), Jimmy Foxx, Frank Higgins, Slug Mahaffey	150.00	75.00	45.00
(10)	Joe Cronin, Alvin Crowder, Joe Kuhel, H. Manush	125.00	60.00	35.00
(11)	W. Dickey, Lou Gehrig, Vernon Gomez, Geo. H. "Babe" Ruth	1,400	700.00	425.00
(12)	E. English, C.J. Grimm, Chas. Klein, Lon Warneke	125.00	60.00	35.00
(13)	Frank Frisch, Bill Hallahan, Pepper Martin, John Rothrock	125.00	60.00	35.00
(14)	Carl Hubbell, Mel Ott, Blondy Ryan, Bill Terry	150.00	75.00	45.00
(15)	Leonard Koenecke, Sam Leslie, Vincent Lopez (Al), Glenn Wright	125.00	60.00	35.00
(16)	T.J. Thevenow, Pie Traynor, Lloyd Waner, Paul Waner	125.00	60.00	35.00

1935 Four-on-One Exhibits

Continuing with the same four-on-one format, the Exhibit Supply Co. issued another 16-card series in 1935. All cards were printed in a slate-blue color with a blank back. Seventeen of the players included in the 1935 series appear for the first time. While another 11 are shown with new poses. There are several spelling and caption errors. Babe Ruth appears in a regular Exhibit issue for the last time.

	NM	EX	VG
Complete Set (16):	4,000	2,000	1,200
Common Card:	75.00	35.00	20.00

		NM	EX	VG
(1)	Earl Averill, Mel Harder, Willie Kamm, Hal Trosky	125.00	60.00	35.00
(2)	Walter Berger, Ed Brandt, Frank Hogan, "Babe" Ruth	1,300	650.00	350.00
(3)	Henry Bonura, Jimmy Dykes, Ted Lyons, Al Simmons	125.00	60.00	35.00
(4)	Jimmy Bottomley, Paul Derringer, Chas. J. Hafey, Botchi Lombardi	125.00	60.00	35.00
(5)	Irving Burns, Rollie Hemsley, O. Melillo, L.N. Newson	75.00	35.00	20.00
(6)	Guy Bush, Pie Traynor, Floyd Vaughn (Vaughan), Paul Waner	125.00	60.00	35.00
(7)	Mickey Cochrane, C. Gehringer, Goose Goslin, Linwood Rowe (Lynwood)	125.00	60.00	35.00
(8)	Phil Collins, John "Blondy" Ryan, Geo. Watkins, Jimmy Wilson	75.00	35.00	20.00
(9)	George Cramer (Roger), Jimmy Foxx, Bob Johnson, Slug Mahaffey	150.00	75.00	45.00
(10)	Hughie Critz, Carl Hubbell, Mel Ott, Bill Terry	150.00	75.00	45.00
(11)	Joe Cronin, Rick Ferrell, Lefty Grove, Billy Werber	145.00	70.00	40.00
(12)	Tony Cuccinello, Vincent Lopez (Al), Van Mungo, Dan Taylor (photo actually George Puccinelli)	125.00	60.00	35.00
(13)	Jerome "Dizzy" Dean, Paul Dean, Frank Frisch, Pepper Martin	325.00	160.00	95.00
(14)	W. Dickey, Lou Gehrig, Vernon Gomez, Tony Lazzeri	900.00	450.00	275.00
(15)	C.J. Grimm, Gabby Hartnett, Chas. Klein, Lon Warneke	125.00	60.00	35.00
(16)	H. Manush, Buddy Meyer (Myer), Fred Schulte, Earl Whitehill	125.00	60.00	35.00

1936 Four-on-One Exhibits

The 1936 series of four-on-one cards again consisted of 16 cards in either green or slate blue with plain, blank backs. The series can be differentiated from the previous year's

Exhibit cards by the line "PTD. IN U.S.A." at the bottom. Of the 64 players pictured, 16 appear for the first time and another nine are shown in new poses. The series is again marred by several spelling and caption errors.

		NM	EX	VG
Complete Set (16):		3,000	1,500	900.00
Common Card:		80.00	40.00	25.00
(1)	Paul Andrews, Harland Clift (Harland), Rollie Hemsley, Sammy West	80.00	40.00	25.00
(2)	Luke Appling, Henry Bonura, Jimmy Dykes, Ted Lyons	100.00	50.00	30.00
(3)	Earl Averill, Mel Harder, Hal Trosky, Joe Vosmik	100.00	50.00	30.00
(4)	Walter Berger, Danny MacFayden, Bill Urbanski, Pinky Whitney	80.00	40.00	25.00
(5)	Charles Berry, Frank Higgins, Bob Johnson, Puccinelli	80.00	40.00	25.00
(6)	Ossie Bluege, Buddy Meyer (Myer), L.N. Newsom, Earl Whitehill	80.00	40.00	25.00
(7)	Stan. Bordagaray, Dutch Brandt, Fred Lindstrom, Van Mungo	100.00	50.00	30.00
(8)	Guy Bush, Pie Traynor, Floyd Vaughn (Vaughan), Paul Waner	100.00	50.00	30.00
(9)	Dolph Camilli, Curt Davis, Johnny Moore, Jimmy Wilson	80.00	40.00	25.00
(10)	Mickey Cochrane, C. Gehringer, Goose Goslin, Linwood Rowe (Lynwood)	100.00	50.00	30.00
(11)	Joe Cronin, Rick Ferrell, Jimmy Foxx, Lefty Grove	175.00	85.00	50.00
(12)	Jerome "Dizzy" Dean, Paul Dean, Frank Frisch, Joe "Ducky" Medwick	300.00	150.00	90.00
(13)	Paul Derringer, Babe Herman, Alex Kampouris, Botchi Lombardi	100.00	50.00	30.00
(14)	Augie Galan, Gabby Hartnett, Billy Herman, Lon Warneke	100.00	50.00	30.00
(15)	Lou Gehrig, Vernon Gomez, Tony Lazzeri, Red Ruffing	1,300	650.00	390.00
(16)	Carl Hubbell, Gus Mancuso, Mel Ott, Bill Terry	125.00	60.00	35.00

1937 Four-on-One Exhibits

The 1937 four-on-one Exhibit cards were printed in either green or bright blue. The backs are again blank. The 1937 cards are difficult to distinguish from the 1936 series, because both contain the "PTD. IN U.S.A." line along the bottom. Of the 64 photos, 47 are re-issues from previous series.

		NM	EX	VG
Complete Set (16):		2,750	1,350	825.00
Common Card:		60.00	30.00	18.00
(1)	Earl Averill, Bob Feller, Frank Pytlak, Hal Trosky	150.00	75.00	45.00
(2)	Luke Appling, Henry Bonura, Jimmy Dykes, Vernon Kennedy	125.00	60.00	35.00
(3)	Walter Berger, Alfonso Lopez, Danny MacFayden, Bill Urbanski	125.00	60.00	35.00
(4)	Cy Blanton, Gus Suhr, Floyd Vaughn (Vaughan), Paul Waner	125.00	60.00	35.00
(5)	Dolph Camilli, Johnny Moore, Wm. Walters, Pinky Whitney	60.00	30.00	18.00
(6)	Harland Clift (Harland), Rollie Hemsley, Orval Hildebrand (Oral), Sammy West	60.00	30.00	18.00
(7)	Mickey Cochrane, C. Gehringer, Goose Goslin, Linwood Rowe (Lynwood)	125.00	60.00	35.00
(8)	Joe Cronin, Rick Ferrell, Jimmy Foxx, Lefty Grove	150.00	75.00	45.00
(9)	Jerome "Dizzy" Dean, Stuart Martin, Joe "Ducky" Medwick, Lon Warneke	175.00	85.00	50.00
(10)	Paul Derringer, Botchi Lombardi, Lew Riggs, Phil Weintraub	125.00	60.00	35.00
(11)	Joe DiMaggio, Lou Gehrig, Vernon Gomez, Tony Lazzeri	1,325	660.00	375.00
(12)	E. English, Johnny Moore, Van Mungo, Gordon Phelps	60.00	30.00	18.00

		NM	EX	VG
(13)	Augie Galan, Gabby Hartnett, Billy Herman, Bill Lee	125.00	60.00	35.00
(14)	Carl Hubbell, Sam Leslie, Gus. Mancuso, Mel Ott	125.00	60.00	35.00
(15)	Bob Johnson, Harry Kelly (Kelley), Wallace Moses, Billy Weber (Werber)	60.00	30.00	18.00
(16)	Joe Kuhel, Buddy Meyer (Myer), L.N. Newsom, Jonathan Stone (First name actually John.)	60.00	30.00	18.00

1938 Four-on-One Exhibits

The Exhibit Co. used its four-on-one format for the final time in 1938, issuing another 16-card series. The cards feature brown printing on white stock with the line "MADE IN U.S.A." appearing along the bottom. The backs are blank. Twelve players appeared for the first time and three others are shown in new poses. Again, there are several spelling and caption mistakes.

		NM	EX	VG
Complete Set (16):		3,250	1,600	975.00
Common Card:		83.00	41.00	25.00
(1)	Luke Appling, Mike Kreevich, Ted Lyons, L. Sewell	125.00	60.00	35.00
(2)	Morris Arnovich, Chas. Klein, Wm. Walters, Pinky Whitney	125.00	60.00	35.00
(3)	Earl Averill, Bob Feller, Odell Hale, Hal Trosky	165.00	80.00	50.00
(4)	Beau Bell, Harland Clift (Harland), L.N. Newsom, Sammy West	80.00	40.00	25.00
(5)	Cy Blanton, Gus Suhr, Floyd Vaughn (Vaughan), Paul Waner	125.00	60.00	35.00
(6)	Tom Bridges, C. Gehringer, Hank Greenberg, Rudy York	125.00	60.00	35.00
(7)	Dolph Camilli, Leo Durocher, Van Mungo, Gordon Phelps	125.00	60.00	35.00
(8)	Joe Cronin, Jimmy Foxx, Lefty Grove, Joe Vosmik	165.00	80.00	50.00
(9)	Tony Cuccinello, Vince DiMaggio, Roy Johnson, Danny MacFayden (Photo actually George Puccinelli.)	90.00	45.00	25.00
(10)	Jerome "Dizzy" Dean, Augie Galan, Gabby Hartnett, Billy Herman	200.00	100.00	60.00
(11)	Paul Derringer, Ival Goodman, Botchi Lombardi, Lew Riggs	125.00	60.00	35.00
(12)	W. Dickey, Joe DiMaggio, Lou Gehrig, Vernon Gomez	1,375	685.00	400.00
(13)	Rick Ferrell, W. Ferrell, Buddy Meyer (Myer), Jonathan Stone (First name actually John.)	125.00	60.00	35.00
(14)	Carl Hubbell, Hank Leiber, Mel Ott, Jim Ripple	130.00	65.00	40.00
(15)	Bob Johnson, Harry Kelly (Kelley), Wallace Moses, Billy Weber (Werber)	80.00	40.00	25.00
(16)	Stuart Martin, Joe "Ducky" Medwick, Johnny Mize, Lon Warneke	125.00	60.00	35.00

1939-46 Salutation Exhibits

Referred to as "Exhibits" because they were issued by the Exhibit Supply Co. of Chicago, Ill., the bulk of this group was produced over an eight-year span, though production and sale of some players' cards continued well into the period of the 1947-66 Exhibits. These cards are frequently called "Salutations" because of the personalized greeting found on the card. The black-and-white cards, which measure 3-3/8" x 5-3/8", are unnumbered and blank-backed. Most Exhibits were sold through vending machines for a penny. The complete set price includes all variations.

		NM	EX	VG
Complete Set (83):		6,500	3,250	1,950
Common Player:		15.00	7.50	4.50
(1)	Luke Appling ("Made In U.S.A." in left corner.)	20.00	10.00	6.00
(2)	Luke Appling ("Made In U.S.A." in right corner.)	45.00	22.50	13.50
(3)	Earl Averill	400.00	200.00	120.00
(4)	Charles "Red" Barrett	20.00	10.00	6.00
(5)	Henry "Hank" Borowy	15.00	7.50	4.50
(6)	Lou Boudreau (Large projection, small projection. Look at the feet and bat top.)	25.00	12.50	7.50
(7)	Adolf Camilli	30.00	15.00	9.00
(8)	Phil Cavarretta	15.00	7.50	4.50
(9)	Harland Clift (Harland)	20.00	10.00	6.00
(10)	Tony Cuccinello	50.00	30.00	20.00
(11)	Dizzy Dean	140.00	70.00	45.00
(12)	Paul Derringer	20.00	10.00	6.00
(13)	Bill Dickey ("Made In U.S.A." in left corner.)	35.00	17.50	10.00
(14)	Bill Dickey ("Made In U.S.A." in right corner.)	55.00	27.50	16.50
(15)	Joe DiMaggio (Issued into the 1950s.)	150.00	75.00	45.00
(16)	Bob Elliott	15.00	7.50	4.50
(17)	Bob Feller (Portrait)	120.00	60.00	35.00
(18)	Bob Feller (Pitching)	50.00	25.00	15.00
(19)	Dave Ferriss	45.00	22.50	13.50
(20)	Jimmy Foxx	75.00	37.50	22.50
(21)	Lou Gehrig	1,750	875.00	525.00
(22)	Charlie Gehringer	150.00	100.00	50.00
(23)	Vernon Gomez	300.00	150.00	100.00
(24)	Joe Gordon (Cleveland)	30.00	15.00	10.00
(25)	Joe Gordon (New York)	30.00	15.00	10.00
(26)	Hank Greenberg (Truly yours.)	35.00	17.50	10.00
(27)	Hank Greenberg (Very truly yours.)	160.00	80.00	50.00
(28)	Robert Grove	50.00	25.00	15.00
(29)	Gabby Hartnett	350.00	225.00	150.00
(30)	Buddy Hassett	20.00	10.00	6.00
(31)	Jeff Heath (Large projection.)	25.00	12.50	7.50
(32)	Jeff Heath (Small projection.)	25.00	12.50	7.50
(33)	Kirby Higbe	20.00	10.00	6.00
(34)	Tommy Holmes (Yours truly: with and without "An Exhibit Card.")	15.00	7.50	4.50
(35)	Tommy Holmes (Sincerely yours.)	130.00	65.00	40.00
(36)	Carl Hubbell	40.00	20.00	12.00
(37)	Bob Johnson	40.00	20.00	12.00
(38)	Charles Keller ("MADE IN U.S.A." left corner.)	25.00	12.50	7.50
(39)	Charles Keller ("MADE IN U.S.A." right corner.)	15.00	7.50	4.50
(40)	Ken Keltner	25.00	12.50	7.50
(41)	Chuck Klein	350.00	225.00	150.00
(42)	Mike Kreevich	300.00	200.00	100.00
(43)	Joe Kuhel	20.00	10.00	6.00
(44)	Bill Lee	20.00	10.00	6.00
(45)	Ernie Lombardi (Cordially)	325.00	160.00	95.00
(46)	Ernie Lombardi (Cordially yours: Large projection, small projection. Look at the cropping on the lead foot.)	20.00	10.00	6.00
(47)	Martin Marion ("An Exhibit Card" in lower-left.)	20.00	10.00	6.00
(48)	Marty Marion (No "An Exhibit Card.")	20.00	10.00	6.00
(49)	Merrill May	25.00	12.50	7.50
(50)	Frank McCormick ("Made In U.S.A." in left corner.)	30.00	15.00	9.00
(51)	Frank McCormick ("Made In U.S.A." in right corner.)	15.00	7.50	4.50
(52)	George McQuinn ("Made In U.S.A." in left corner.)	20.00	10.00	6.00
(53)	George McQuinn ("Made In U.S.A." in right corner.)	15.00	7.50	4.50
(54)	Joe Medwick	55.00	27.50	16.50
(55)	Johnny Mize ("Made In U.S.A." in left corner.)	35.00	17.50	10.00
(56)	Johnny Mize ("Made In U.S.A." in right corner.)	20.00	10.00	6.00
(57)	Hugh Mulcahy	150.00	75.00	45.00
(58)	Hal Newhouser	30.00	15.00	9.00
(59)	Buck Newson (Newsom)	275.00	135.00	80.00
(60)	Louis (Buck) Newsom	15.00	7.50	4.50
(61)	Mel Ott ("Made In U.S.A." in left corner.)	40.00	20.00	12.00
(62)	Mel Ott ("Made In U.S.A." in right corner.)	25.00	12.50	7.50
(63)	Andy Pafko ("C" on cap.)	20.00	10.00	6.00
(64)	Andy Pafko (Plain cap.)	15.00	7.50	4.50
(65)	Claude Passeau	15.00	7.50	4.50
(66)	Howard Pollet ("Made In U.S.A." in left corner.)	20.00	10.00	6.00
(67)	Howard Pollet ("Made In U.S.A." in right corner.)	15.00	7.50	4.50
(68)	Pete Reiser ("Made In U.S.A." in left corner.)	45.00	22.50	13.50
(69)	Pete Reiser ("Made In U.S.A." in right corner.)	20.00	10.00	6.00
(70)	Johnny Rizzo	300.00	200.00	100.00
(71)	Glenn Russell	75.00	37.50	22.00

		NM	EX	VG
(72)	George Stirnweiss	20.00	10.00	6.00
(73)	Cecil Travis	45.00	20.00	12.50
(74)	Paul Trout	15.00	7.50	4.50
(75)	Johnny Vander Meer	65.00	32.50	20.00
(76)	Arky Vaughn (Vaughan)	22.50	11.00	6.75
(77)	Fred "Dixie" Walker ("D" on cap.)	20.00	10.00	6.00
(78)	Fred "Dixie" Walker ("D" blanked out.)	60.00	30.00	18.00
(79)	"Bucky" Walters	15.00	7.50	4.50
(80)	Lon Warneke	20.00	10.00	6.00
(81)	Ted Williams (#9 shows)	375.00	185.00	110.00
(82)	Ted Williams (#9 not showing: large projection, small projection. Look at the space from the bottom of the foot at the right side to the card bottom.)	45.00	22.50	13.50
(83)	Rudy York (large projection, small projection.)	20.00	10.00	6.00

1947-66 Exhibits

Produced by the Exhibit Supply Co. of Chicago, these issues cover a span of 20 years. Each unnumbered, black-and-white card is printed on heavy cardboard measuring 3-3/8" x 5-3/8" and is blank-backed. The company issued new sets each year, with many players being repeated year after year. Other players appeared in only one or two years, thereby creating levels of scarcity. Many cards can be found with minor variations in the wording and placement of the credit line at bottom. Some pieces have been found printed on a semi-gloss paper stock, perhaps as proofs. Their value is 50 percent or less than the issued version.

		NM	EX	VG
	Common Player:	9.00	4.50	2.75
(1)	Hank Aaron	30.00	15.00	9.00
(2)	Joe Adcock (White signature.)	9.00	4.50	2.75
(3)	Joe Adcock (Black signature.)	10.00	5.00	3.00
(4)	Max Alvis	30.00	15.00	9.00
(5)	Johnny Antonelli (Braves)	9.00	4.50	2.75
(6)	Johnny Antonelli (Giants)	10.00	5.00	3.00
(7)	Luis Aparicio (Portrait)	12.00	6.00	3.50
(8)	Luis Aparicio (Batting)	17.50	8.75	5.25
(9)	Luke Appling (With and without "An Exhibit Card.")	20.00	10.00	6.00
(10)	Ritchie Ashburn (Phillies, first name incorrect. With and without "An Exhibit Card.")	12.00	6.00	3.50
(11)	Richie Ashburn (Phillies, first name correct.)	12.00	6.00	3.50
(12)	Richie Ashburn (Cubs)	17.50	8.75	5.25
(13)	Bob Aspromonte	9.00	4.50	2.75
(14)	Toby Atwell	9.00	4.50	2.75
(15)	Ed Bailey (With cap.)	10.00	5.00	3.00
(16)	Ed Bailey (No cap.)	9.00	4.50	2.75
(17)	Gene Baker	9.00	4.50	2.75
(18)	Ernie Banks (Bat on shoulder, script signature.)	55.00	27.50	16.50
(19)	Ernie Banks (Bat on shoulder, plain signature.)	17.50	8.75	5.25
(20)	Ernie Banks (Portrait)	30.00	15.00	9.00
(21)	Steve Barber	9.00	4.50	2.75
(22)	Earl Battey	10.00	5.00	3.00
(23)	Matt Batts	9.00	4.50	2.75
(24)	Hank Bauer (N.Y. cap.)	10.00	5.00	3.00
(25)	Hank Bauer (Plain cap.)	12.00	6.00	3.50
(26)	Frank Baumholtz	9.00	4.50	2.75
(27)	Gene Bearden (With and without "An Exhibit Card.")	9.00	4.50	2.75
(28)	Joe Beggs	15.00	7.50	4.50
(29)	Larry "Yogi" Berra	60.00	30.00	18.00
(30a)	Yogi Berra ("MADE IN U.S.A." lower-right.)	35.00	17.50	10.00
(30b)	Yogi Berra ("PRINTED IN U.S.A." lower-right. With and without "An Exhibit Card.")	35.00	17.50	10.00
(31)	Steve Bilko	10.00	5.00	3.00
(32)	Ewell Blackwell (Pitching)	10.00	5.00	3.00
(33)	Ewell Blackwell (Portrait)	9.00	4.50	2.75
(34)	Don Blasingame (St. Louis cap.)	9.00	4.50	2.75
(35)	Don Blasingame (Plain cap.)	17.50	8.75	5.25
(36)	Ken Boyer	12.00	6.00	3.50
(37)	Ralph Branca (With and without "An Exhibit Card.")	12.00	6.00	3.50
(38)	Jackie Brandt	40.00	20.00	12.00
(39)	Harry Brecheen	9.00	4.50	2.75
(40)	Tom Brewer	13.50	6.75	4.00
(41)	Lou Brissie	10.00	5.00	3.00
(42)	Bill Bruton	9.00	4.50	2.75
(43)	Lew Burdette (Pitching, side view.)	9.00	4.50	2.75
(44)	Lew Burdette (Pitching, front view.)	10.00	5.00	3.00
(45)	Johnny Callison	12.50	6.25	3.75
(46)	Roy Campanella	25.00	12.50	7.50
(47)	Chico Carrasquel (Portrait)	15.00	7.50	4.50
(48)	Chico Carrasquel (Leaping)	9.00	4.50	2.75
(49)	George Case	13.50	6.75	4.00
(50)	Hugh Casey	40.00	30.00	20.00
(51)	Norm Cash	12.00	6.00	3.50
(52)	Orlando Cepeda (Portrait)	15.00	7.50	4.50
(53)	Orlando Cepeda (Batting)	15.00	7.50	4.50
(54)	Bob Cerv (A's cap.)	12.00	6.00	3.50
(55)	Bob Cerv (Plain cap.)	20.00	10.00	6.00
(56)	Dean Chance	9.00	4.50	2.75
(57)	Spud Chandler	40.00	30.00	20.00
(58)	Tom Cheney	9.00	4.50	2.75
(59)	Bubba Church	10.00	5.00	3.00
(60)	Roberto Clemente	40.00	20.00	12.00
(61)	Rocky Colavito (Portrait)	35.00	17.50	10.00
(62)	Rocky Colavito (Batting)	25.00	12.50	7.50
(63)	Choo Choo Coleman	12.00	6.00	3.50
(64)	Gordy Coleman	30.00	15.00	9.00
(65)	Jerry Coleman	10.00	5.00	3.00
(66)	Mort Cooper	35.00	17.50	10.00
(67)	Walker Cooper (With and without "Made in USA")	9.00	4.50	2.75
(68)	Roger Craig	12.00	6.00	3.50
(69)	Delmar Crandall	9.00	4.50	2.75
(70)	Joe Cunningham (Batting)	40.00	20.00	12.00
(71)	Joe Cunningham (Portrait)	65.00	32.00	19.50
(72)	Guy Curtwright (Curtright)	10.00	5.00	3.00
(73)	Bud Daley	35.00	17.50	10.00
(74)	Alvin Dark (Braves)	12.00	6.00	3.50
(75)	Alvin Dark (Giants)	10.00	5.00	3.00
(76)	Alvin Dark (Cubs)	12.00	6.00	3.50
(77)	Murray Dickson (Murry)	25.00	12.50	7.50
(78)	Bob Dillinger (With and without "An Exhibit Card.")	12.00	6.00	3.50
(79)	Dom DiMaggio	25.00	12.50	7.50
(80)	Joe Dobson	25.00	15.00	10.00
(81a)	Larry Doby (Three forms: Without "An Exhibit Card," with "An Exhibit Card," and with "An Exhibit Card" scratched out.)	40.00	20.00	12.00
(81b)	Larry Doby (Bat well off right border.)	25.00	12.50	7.50
(82a)	Bobby Doerr ("AN EXHIBIT CARD" lower-left.)	15.00	7.50	4.50
(82b)	Bobby Doerr (No "AN EXHIBIT CARD.")	15.00	7.50	4.50
(83)	Dick Donovan (Plain cap.)	12.00	6.00	3.50
(84)	Dick Donovan (Sox cap.)	9.00	4.50	2.75
(85)	Walter Dropo	9.00	4.50	2.75
(86)	Don Drysdale (Glove at waist.)	20.00	10.00	6.00
(87)	Don Drysdale (Portrait)	35.00	17.50	10.00
(88)	Luke Easter	15.00	7.50	4.50
(89)	Bruce Edwards	15.00	7.50	4.50
(90)	Del Ennis	15.00	7.50	4.50
(91)	Al Evans	10.00	5.00	3.00
(92)	Walter Evers	9.00	4.50	2.75
(93)	Ferris Fain (Fielding)	12.00	6.00	3.50
(94)	Ferris Fain (Portrait)	15.00	7.50	4.50
(95)	Dick Farrell	9.00	4.50	2.75
(96)	Ed "Whitey" Ford	30.00	15.00	9.00
(97)	Whitey Ford (Pitching)	30.00	15.00	9.00
(98)	Whitey Ford (Portrait)	175.00	85.00	50.00
(99)	Dick Fowler	12.50	6.25	3.75
(100)	Nelson Fox	25.00	12.50	7.50
(101)	Tito Francona	9.00	4.50	2.75
(102)	Bob Friend	9.00	4.50	2.75
(103)	Carl Furillo	25.00	12.50	7.50
(104)	Augie Galan	30.00	15.00	9.00
(105)	Jim Gentile	9.00	4.50	2.75
(106)	Tony Gonzalez	9.00	4.50	2.75
(107)	Billy Goodman (Leaping)	17.50	8.75	5.25
(108)	Billy Goodman (Batting)	12.00	6.00	3.50
(109)	Ted Greengrass (Jim)	9.00	4.50	2.75
(110)	Dick Groat	10.00	5.00	3.00
(111)	Steve Gromek	9.00	4.50	2.75
(112)	Johnny Groth	9.00	4.50	2.75
(113)	Orval Grove	15.00	7.50	4.50
(114)	Frank Gustine (Pirates uniform.)	20.00	10.00	6.00
(115)	Frank Gustine (Plain uniform.)	10.00	5.00	3.00
(116)	Berthold Haas	20.00	10.00	6.00
(117)	Grady Hatton	10.00	5.00	3.00
(118)	Jim Hegan	9.00	4.50	2.75
(119)	Tom Henrich	12.00	6.00	3.50
(120)	Ray Herbert	15.00	7.50	4.50
(121)	Gene Hermanski	10.00	5.00	3.00
(122)	Whitey Herzog	12.00	6.00	3.50
(123)	Kirby Higbe	30.00	15.00	9.00
(124)	Chuck Hinton	9.00	4.50	2.75
(125)	Don Hoak	15.00	7.50	4.50
(126)	Gil Hodges ("B" on cap.)	12.50	6.25	3.75
(127)	Gil Hodges ("LA" on cap.)	25.00	12.50	7.50
(128)	Johnny Hopp	25.00	15.00	8.00
(129)	Elston Howard	12.00	6.00	3.50
(130)	Frank Howard	15.00	7.50	4.50
(131)	Ken Hubbs	30.00	15.00	9.00
(132)	Tex Hughson	25.00	15.00	8.00
(133)	Fred Hutchinson	60.00	30.00	18.00
(134)	Monty Irvin (Monte)	12.00	6.00	3.50
(135)	Joey Jay	9.00	4.50	2.75
(136)	Jackie Jensen	45.00	22.50	13.50
(137)	Sam Jethroe	10.00	5.00	3.00
(138)	Bill Johnson	30.00	15.00	9.00
(139)	Walter Judnich	13.50	6.75	4.00
(140)	Al Kaline (Kneeling)	25.00	12.50	7.50
(141)	Al Kaline (Portrait w/ two bats.)	17.50	8.75	5.25
(142)	George Kell	20.00	10.00	6.00
(143)	Charley Keller (With and without "An Exhibit Card.")	12.50	6.25	3.75
(144)	Alex Kellner	9.00	4.50	2.75
(145)	Kenn (Ken) Keltner	10.00	5.00	3.00
(146)	Harmon Killebrew (With bat.)	50.00	25.00	15.00
(147)	Harmon Killebrew (Throwing)	40.00	20.00	12.00
(148)	Harmon Killebrew (Killebrew) (Portrait)	50.00	25.00	15.00
(149)	Ellis Kinder	9.00	4.50	2.75
(150)	Ralph Kiner	25.00	12.50	7.50
(151)	Billy Klaus	30.00	15.00	9.00
(152)	Ted Kluzewski (Kluszewski) (Batting)	17.50	8.75	5.25
(153)	Ted Kluzewski (Kluszewski) (Pirates uniform.)	12.00	6.00	3.50
(154)	Ted Kluzewski (Kluszewski) (Plain uniform.)	17.50	8.75	5.25
(155)	Don Kolloway	20.00	10.00	6.00
(156)	Jim Konstanty	10.00	5.00	3.00
(157)	Sandy Koufax	40.00	20.00	12.00
(158)	Ed Kranepool	55.00	27.50	16.50
(159)	Tony Kubek (Light background.)	16.00	8.00	4.75
(160)	Tony Kubek (Dark background.)	45.00	22.50	13.50
(161)	Harvey Kuenn ("D" on cap.)	30.00	15.00	9.00
(162)	Harvey Kuenn (Plain cap.)	16.00	8.00	4.75
(163)	Harvey Kuenn ("SF" on cap.)	15.00	7.50	4.50
(164)	Whitey Kurowski	30.00	15.00	9.00
(165)	Eddie Lake	25.00	15.00	8.00
(166)	Jim Landis	9.00	4.50	2.75
(167)	Don Larsen	10.00	5.00	3.00
(168)	Bob Lemon (Glove not visible.)	15.00	7.50	4.50
(169)	Bob Lemon (Glove partially visible.)	25.00	12.50	7.50
(170)	Buddy Lewis	25.00	12.50	7.50
(171)	Johnny Lindell	35.00	17.50	10.00
(172)	Phil Linz	25.00	12.50	7.50
(173)	Don Lock	25.00	12.50	7.50
(174)	Whitey Lockman	9.00	4.50	2.75
(175)	Johnny Logan	9.00	4.50	2.75
(176)	Dale Long ("P" on cap.)	9.00	4.50	2.75
(177)	Dale Long ("C" on cap.)	20.00	10.00	6.00
(178)	Ed Lopat	10.00	5.00	3.00
(179)	Harry Lowery (Name misspelled.)	10.00	5.00	3.00
(180)	Harry Lowrey (Name correct.)	10.00	5.00	3.00
(181)	Sal Maglie	9.00	4.50	2.75
(182)	Art Mahaffey	10.00	5.00	3.00
(183)	Hank Majeski	9.00	4.50	2.75
(184)	Frank Malzone	16.00	8.00	4.75
(185)	Mickey Mantle (Batting, full-length.)	140.00	70.00	40.00
(186)	Mickey Mantle (Batting, waist-up, "ck" in "Mickey" connected.)	120.00	60.00	35.00
(187)	Mickey Mantle (Batting, waist-up, "c k" in "Mickey" connected.)	175.00	85.00	50.00
(188)	Mickey Mantle (Portrait)	600.00	300.00	180.00
(189)	Martin Marion	20.00	10.00	6.00
(190)	Roger Maris	25.00	12.50	7.50
(191)	Willard Marshall (With and without "An Exhibit Card.")	10.00	5.00	3.00
(192)	Eddie Matthews (Name incorrect.)	16.00	8.00	4.75
(193)	Eddie Mathews (Name correct.)	30.00	15.00	9.00
(194)	Ed Mayo	10.00	5.00	3.00
(195)	Willie Mays (Batting)	45.00	22.50	13.50
(196)	Willie Mays (Portrait)	60.00	30.00	18.00
(197)	Bill Mazeroski (Portrait)	16.00	8.00	4.75
(198)	Bill Mazeroski (Batting)	16.00	8.00	4.75
(199)	Ken McBride	15.00	7.50	4.50
(200)	Barney McCaskey (McCosky)	13.50	6.75	4.00
(201)	Barney McCoskey (McCosky)	200.00	100.00	50.00
(202)	Lindy McDaniel	9.00	4.50	2.75
(203a)	Gil McDougald ("MADE IN U.S.A." lower-right.)	15.00	7.50	4.50
(203b)	Gil McDougald ("PRINTED IN U.S.A." lower-right.)	15.00	7.50	4.50
(204)	Albert Mele	30.00	15.00	9.00
(205)	Sam Mele	20.00	10.00	6.00
(206)	Orestes Minoso ("C" on cap.)	12.50	6.25	3.75
(207)	Orestes Minoso (Sox on cap.)	9.00	4.50	2.75
(208)	Dale Mitchell	9.00	4.50	2.75
(209)	Wally Moon	12.00	6.00	3.50
(210)	Don Mueller	10.00	5.00	3.00
(211)	Stan Musial ("Made in USA" and "Printed in USA")	60.00	30.00	18.00
(212)	Stan Musial (Batting)	70.00	35.00	20.00
(213)	Charley Neal	15.00	7.50	4.50
(214)	Don Newcombe (Shaking hands.)	25.00	12.50	7.50
(215)	Don Newcombe (Dodgers on jacket.)	9.00	4.50	2.75
(216)	Don Newcombe (Plain jacket.)	10.00	5.00	3.00
(217)	Hal Newhouser	35.00	17.50	10.00
(218)	Ron Northey	20.00	10.00	6.00
(219)	Bill O'Dell	9.00	4.50	2.75
(220)	Joe Page	20.00	10.00	6.00
(221)	Satchel Paige	90.00	45.00	25.00
(222)	Milt Pappas	9.00	4.50	2.75
(223)	Camilo Pascual	9.00	4.50	2.75
(224)	Albie Pearson	25.00	12.50	7.50
(225)	Johnny Pesky	9.00	4.50	2.75
(226)	Gary Peters	25.00	12.50	7.50
(227)	Dave Philley	9.00	4.50	2.75
(228)	Billy Pierce	9.00	4.50	2.75
(229)	Jimmy Piersall	15.00	7.50	4.50
(230)	Vada Pinson	12.50	6.25	3.75
(231)	Bob Porterfield	9.00	4.50	2.75
(232)	John "Boog" Powell	45.00	22.50	13.50
(233)	Vic Raschi	15.00	7.50	4.50
(234)	Harold "Peewee" Reese (Fielding, ball partially visible.)	35.00	17.50	10.00
(235)	Harold "Peewee" Reese (Fielding, ball not visible.)	25.00	12.50	7.50
(236)	Del Rice	12.50	6.25	3.75
(237)	Bobby Richardson	125.00	60.00	35.00

(238)	Phil Rizzuto (Has a small and large projection. The large projection is known in two forms: with "An Exhibit Card," and with "An Exhibit Card" scratched out.)	25.00	12.50	7.50
(239)	Robin Roberts (White signature.)	14.50	7.25	4.25
(240)	Robin Roberts (Black signature.)	25.00	12.50	7.50
(241)	Brooks Robinson	17.50	8.75	5.25
(242)	Eddie Robinson	9.00	4.50	2.75
(243)	Floyd Robinson	17.50	8.75	5.25
(244)	Frankie Robinson	60.00	30.00	18.00
(245)	Jackie Robinson	50.00	25.00	15.00
(246)	Preacher Roe	35.00	17.50	10.00
(247)	Bob Rogers (Rodgers)	30.00	15.00	9.00
(248)	Richard Rollins	25.00	12.50	7.50
(249)	Pete Runnels	13.50	6.75	4.00
(250)	John Sain	12.50	6.25	3.75
(251)	Ron Santo	25.00	12.50	7.50
(252)	Henry Sauer	10.00	5.00	3.00
(253)	Carl Sawatski ("M" on cap.)	9.00	4.50	2.75
(254)	Carl Sawatski ("P" on cap.)	9.00	4.50	2.75
(255)	Carl Sawatski (Plain cap.)	17.50	8.75	5.25
(256)	Johnny Schmitz	10.00	5.00	3.00
(257)	Red Schoendeinst (Schoendienst) (Fielding, name in white.)	25.00	12.50	7.50
(258)	Red Schoendeinst (Schoendienst) (Fielding, name in red-brown.)	30.00	15.00	9.00
(259)	Red Schoendinst (Schoendienst) (Batting)	12.50	6.25	3.75
(260)	Herb Score ("C" on cap.)	15.00	7.50	4.50
(261)	Herb Score (Plain cap.)	17.50	8.75	5.25
(262)	Andy Seminick	9.00	4.50	2.75
(263)	Rip Sewell	20.00	10.00	6.00
(264)	Norm Siebern	9.00	4.50	2.75
(265)	Roy Sievers (Batting)	15.00	7.50	4.50
(266)	Roy Sievers (Portrait, "W" on cap, light background.)	12.00	6.00	3.50
(267)	Roy Sievers (Portrait, "W" on cap, dark background.)	10.00	5.00	3.00
(268)	Roy Sievers (Portrait, plain cap.)	20.00	10.00	6.00
(269)	Curt Simmons	10.00	5.00	3.00
(270)	Dick Sisler	10.00	5.00	3.00
(271)	Bill Skowron	12.50	6.25	3.75
(272)	Bill "Moose" Skowron	65.00	32.50	20.00
(273)	Enos Slaughter	20.00	10.00	6.00
(274)	Duke Snider ("B" on cap.)	22.50	11.00	6.75
(275)	Duke Snider ("LA" on cap.)	20.00	10.00	6.00
(276)	Warren Spahn ("B" on cap.)	20.00	10.00	6.00
(277)	Warren Spahn ("M" on cap.)	20.00	10.00	6.00
(278)	Stanley Spence	16.00	8.00	4.75
(279)	Ed Stanky (Plain uniform. With and without "An Exhibit Card")	17.50	8.75	5.25
(280)	Ed Stanky (Giants uniform.)	10.00	5.00	3.00
(281)	Vern Stephens (Batting)	10.00	5.00	3.00
(282)	Vern Stephens (Portrait)	10.00	5.00	3.00
(283)	Ed Stewart	10.00	5.00	3.00
(284)	Snuffy Stirnweiss	12.50	6.25	3.75
(285)	George "Birdie" Tebbetts	17.50	8.75	5.25
(286)	Frankie Thomas (Photo actually Bob Skinner.)	35.00	17.50	10.00
(287)	Frank Thomas (Portrait, "Best Wishes.")	16.00	8.00	4.75
(288)	Lee Thomas	9.00	4.50	2.75
(289)	Bobby Thomson (With and without "An Exhibit Card")	25.00	12.50	7.50
(290)	Earl Torgeson (Braves uniform.)	9.00	4.50	2.75
(291)	Earl Torgeson (Plain uniform.)	10.00	5.00	3.00
(292)	Gus Triandos	12.00	6.00	3.50
(293)	Virgil Trucks	9.00	4.50	2.75
(294)	Johnny Vandermeer (VanderMeer)	25.00	12.50	7.50
(295)	Emil Verban	12.00	6.00	3.50
(296)	Mickey Vernon (Throwing)	15.00	7.50	4.50
(297)	Mickey Vernon (Batting)	9.00	4.50	2.75
(298)	Bill Voiselle	30.00	15.00	9.00
(299)	Leon Wagner	6.50	3.25	1.75
(300)	Eddie Waitkus x(Throwing, Chicago uniform.)	40.00	20.00	12.00
(301)	Eddie Waitkus (Throwing, plain uniform.)	10.00	5.00	3.00
(302)	Eddie Waitkus (Portrait)	15.00	7.50	4.50
(303)	Dick Wakefield	10.00	5.00	3.00
(304)	Harry Walker	40.00	20.00	12.00
(305)	Bucky Walters	20.00	10.00	6.00
(306)	Pete Ward	75.00	37.50	22.50
(307)	Herman Wehmeier	10.00	5.00	3.00
(308)	Vic Wertz (Batting)	9.00	4.50	2.75
(309)	Vic Wertz (Portrait)	9.00	4.50	2.75
(310)	Wally Westlake	10.00	5.00	3.00
(311)	Wes Westrum	17.50	8.75	5.25
(312)	Billy Williams	20.00	10.00	6.00
(313)	Maurice Wills	15.00	7.50	4.50
(314)	Gene Woodling (White signature.)	9.00	4.50	2.75
(315)	Gene Woodling (Black signature.)	12.00	6.00	3.50
(316)	Taffy Wright	10.00	5.00	3.00
(317)	Carl Yastrazemski (Yastrzemski)	200.00	100.00	60.00
(318)	Al Zarilla	12.50	6.25	3.75
(319)	Gus Zernial (White signature.)	9.00	4.50	2.75
(320)	Gus Zernial (Black signature.)	12.00	6.00	3.50
(321)	Braves Team - 1948	50.00	25.00	15.00
(322)	Dodgers Team - 1949	75.00	37.50	22.50
(323)	Dodgers Team - 1952	65.00	32.50	20.00
(324)	Dodgers Team - 1955	125.00	60.00	35.00
(325)	Dodgers Team - 1956	60.00	30.00	18.00
(326)	Giants Team - 1951	60.00	30.00	18.00
(327a)	Giants Team - 1954 (Plain back.)	50.00	25.00	15.00

(328)	Indians Team - 1948	55.00	27.50	16.50
(329)	Indians Team - 1954	50.00	25.00	15.00
(330)	Phillies Team - 1950	40.00	20.00	12.00
(331)	Yankees Team - 1949	60.00	30.00	18.00
(332)	Yankees Team - 1950	65.00	32.50	20.00
(333)	Yankees Team - 1951	65.00	32.50	20.00
(334)	Yankees Team - 1952	70.00	35.00	20.00
(335)	Yankees Team - 1955	70.00	35.00	20.00
(336)	Yankees Team - 1956	70.00	35.00	20.00

1948 Baseball's Great Hall of Fame Exhibits

Titled "Baseball's Great Hall of Fame," this 32-player set features black and white player photos against a gray background. The photos are accented by Greek columns on either side with brief player information printed at the bottom. The blank-backed cards are unnumbered and are listed here alphabetically. The cards measure 3-3/8" x 5-3/8". Collectors should be aware that 24 cards from this set were reprinted on whiter stock in 1974.

		NM	EX	VG
	Complete Set (33):	500.00	250.00	150.00
	Common Player:	7.50	3.75	2.25
(1)	Grover Cleveland Alexander	15.00	7.50	4.50
(2)	Roger Bresnahan	7.50	3.75	2.25
(3)	Frank Chance	7.50	3.75	2.25
(4)	Jack Chesbro	7.50	3.75	2.25
(5)	Fred Clarke	7.50	3.75	2.25
(6)	Ty Cobb	55.00	27.50	16.50
(7)	Mickey Cochrane	7.50	3.75	2.25
(8)	Eddie Collins	7.50	3.75	2.25
(9)	Hugh Duffy	7.50	3.75	2.25
(10)	Johnny Evers	7.50	3.75	2.25
(11)	Frankie Frisch	7.50	3.75	2.25
(12)	Lou Gehrig	35.00	17.50	10.00
(13)	Clark Griffith	7.50	3.75	2.25
(14)	Robert "Lefty" Grove	7.50	3.75	2.25
(15)	Rogers Hornsby	10.00	5.00	3.00
(16)	Carl Hubbell	7.50	3.75	2.25
(17)	Hughie Jennings	7.50	3.75	2.25
(18)	Walter Johnson	15.00	7.50	4.50
(19)	Willie Keeler	7.50	3.75	2.25
(20)	Napolean Lajoie	7.50	3.75	2.25
(21)	Connie Mack	7.50	3.75	2.25
(22)	Christy Matthewson (Mathewson)	20.00	10.00	6.00
(23)	John J. McGraw	7.50	3.75	2.25
(24)	Eddie Plank	7.50	3.75	2.25
(25)	Babe Ruth (Batting)	60.00	30.00	18.00
(26)	Babe Ruth (Standing with bats.)	250.00	125.00	75.00
(27)	George Sisler	7.50	3.75	2.25
(28)	Tris Speaker	10.00	5.00	3.00
(29)	Joe Tinker	7.50	3.75	2.25
(30)	Rube Waddell	7.50	3.75	2.25
(31)	Honus Wagner	25.00	12.50	7.50
(32)	Ed Walsh	7.50	3.75	2.25
(33)	Cy Young	15.00	7.50	4.50

1953 Canadian Exhibits

This Canadian-issued set consists of 64 cards and includes both major leaguers and players from the Montreal Royals of the International League. The cards are slightly smaller than the U.S. exhibit cards, measuring 3-1/4" x 5-1/4",

and are numbered. The blank-backed cards were printed on gray stock. Card numbers 1-32 have a green or red tint, while card numbers 33-64 have a blue or reddish-brown tint.

		NM	EX	VG
	Complete Set (64):	1,750	875.00	525.00
	Common Player (1-32):	15.00	7.50	4.50
	Common Player (33-64):	9.00	4.50	2.75
1	Preacher Roe	20.00	10.00	6.00
2	Luke Easter	20.00	10.00	6.00
3	Gene Bearden	15.00	7.50	4.50
4	Chico Carrasquel	20.00	10.00	6.00
5	Vic Raschi	20.00	10.00	6.00
6	Monty (Monte) Irvin	30.00	15.00	9.00
7	Henry Sauer	15.00	7.50	4.50
8	Ralph Branca	20.00	10.00	6.00
9	Ed Stanky	20.00	10.00	6.00
10	Sam Jethroe	15.00	7.50	4.50
11	Larry Doby	30.00	15.00	9.00
12	Hal Newhouser	30.00	15.00	9.00
13	Gil Hodges	50.00	25.00	15.00
14	Harry Brecheen	15.00	7.50	4.50
15	Ed Lopat	20.00	10.00	6.00
16	Don Newcombe	25.00	12.50	7.50
17	Bob Feller	60.00	30.00	18.00
18	Tommy Holmes	15.00	7.50	4.50
19	Jackie Robinson	65.00	35.00	20.00
20	Roy Campanella	55.00	25.00	15.00
21	Harold "Peewee" Reese	50.00	25.00	15.00
22	Ralph Kiner	40.00	20.00	12.00
23	Dom DiMaggio	25.00	12.50	7.50
24	Bobby Doerr	30.00	15.00	9.00
25	Phil Rizzuto	50.00	25.00	15.00
26	Bob Elliott	15.00	7.50	4.50
27	Tom Henrich	20.00	10.00	6.00
28	Joe DiMaggio	200.00	100.00	60.00
29	Harry Lowery (Lowrey)	15.00	7.50	4.50
30	Ted Williams	75.00	37.50	22.50
31	Bob Lemon	40.00	20.00	12.00
32	Warren Spahn	50.00	25.00	15.00
33	Don Hoak	25.00	12.50	7.50
34	Bob Alexander	15.00	7.50	4.50
35	John Simmons	15.00	7.50	4.50
36	Steve Lembo	15.00	7.50	4.50
37	Norman Larker	20.00	10.00	6.00
38	Bob Ludwick	15.00	7.50	4.50
39	Walter Moryn	20.00	10.00	6.00
40	Charlie Thompson	15.00	7.50	4.50
41	Ed Roebuck	20.00	10.00	6.00
42	Russell Rose	15.00	7.50	4.50
43	Edmundo (Sandy) Amoros	25.00	12.50	7.50
44	Bob Milliken	15.00	7.50	4.50
45	Art Fabbro	15.00	7.50	4.50
46	Spook Jacobs	15.00	7.50	4.50
47	Carmen Mauro	15.00	7.50	4.50
48	Walter Fiala	15.00	7.50	4.50
49	Rocky Nelson	15.00	7.50	4.50
50	Tom La Sorda (Lasorda)	60.00	30.00	18.00
51	Ronnie Lee	15.00	7.50	4.50
52	Hampton Coleman	15.00	7.50	4.50
53	Frank Marchio	15.00	7.50	4.50
54	William Sampson	15.00	7.50	4.50
55	Gil Mills	15.00	7.50	4.50
56	Al Ronning	15.00	7.50	4.50
57	Stan Musial	75.00	37.50	22.50
58	Walker Cooper	9.00	4.50	2.75
59	Mickey Vernon	9.00	4.50	2.75
60	Del Ennis	9.00	4.50	2.75
61	Walter Alston	40.00	20.00	12.00
62	Dick Sisler	9.00	4.50	2.75
63	Billy Goodman	9.00	4.50	2.75
64	Alex Kellner	9.00	4.50	2.75

1955 Exhibits - Post Card Backs

For an unknkown purpose, the 64 Exhibit cards issued in 1955 (including many re-issued from earlier years) were produced in a very limited edition with a post card back, as opposed to the blank-back format usually found on the 3-3/8" x 5-3/8" cards. The postcard back can be found with or without the words "A Mutoscope Card."

		NM	EX	VG
	Complete Set (64):	6,000	3,000	1,800
	Common Player:	50.00	30.00	20.00
(1)	Joe Adcock	50.00	25.00	15.00
(2)	Ritchie (Richie) Ashburn	90.00	45.00	27.00
(3)	Toby Atwell	50.00	25.00	15.00
(4)	Gene Baker	50.00	25.00	15.00
(5)	Ernie Banks (Bat on shoulder, printed name.)	150.00	75.00	45.00
(6)	Matt Batts	50.00	25.00	15.00
(7)	Frank Baumholtz	50.00	25.00	15.00
(8)	Yogi Berra	150.00	75.00	45.00
(9)	Steve Bilko	50.00	25.00	15.00
(10)	Roy Campanella	125.00	62.00	37.00

		NM	EX	VG
(11)	Chico Carrasquel (Leaping)	50.00	25.00	15.00
(12)	Alvin Dark (Giants)	50.00	25.00	15.00
(13)	Larry Doby	90.00	45.00	27.00
(14)	Walter Dropo	50.00	25.00	15.00
(15)	Del Ennis	50.00	25.00	15.00
(16)	Ferris Fain (Portrait)	90.00	45.00	27.00
(17)	Bob Feller (Yours truly.)	200.00	100.00	60.00
(18)	Billy Goodman (Leaping)	90.00	45.00	27.00
(19)	Ted (Jim) Greengrass	50.00	25.00	15.00
(20)	Steve Gromek	50.00	25.00	15.00
(21)	Johnny Groth	50.00	25.00	15.00
(22)	Jim Hegan	50.00	25.00	15.00
(23)	Gene Hermanski	50.00	25.00	15.00
(24)	Gil Hodges (B on cap.)	100.00	50.00	30.00
(25)	Monty (Monte) Irvin	90.00	45.00	27.00
(26)	Al Kaline (Kneeling)	150.00	75.00	45.00
(27)	George Kell	90.00	45.00	27.00
(28)	Alex Kellner	50.00	25.00	15.00
(29)	Ted Kluszewski (Kluszewski) (Batting)	125.00	62.00	37.00
(30)	Bob Lemon (Glove not showing.)	90.00	45.00	27.00
(31)	Whitey Lockman	50.00	25.00	15.00
(32)	Ed Lopat	60.00	30.00	18.00
(33)	Sal Maglie	50.00	25.00	15.00
(34)	Mickey Mantle (Batting, waist-up.)	800.00	400.00	240.00
(35)	Ed Matthews (Mathews)	125.00	62.00	37.00
(36)	Willie Mays (Batting)	400.00	200.00	120.00
(37)	Gil McDougald	60.00	30.00	18.00
(38)	Sam Mele	50.00	25.00	15.00
(39)	Orestes Minoso (C on cap.)	90.00	45.00	27.00
(40)	Dale Mitchell	50.00	25.00	15.00
(41)	Stan Musial (Kneeling)	200.00	100.00	60.00
(42)	Andy Pafko (Yours truly.) (C on cap.)	50.00	25.00	15.00
(43)	Bob Porterfield	50.00	25.00	15.00
(44)	Vic Raschi	50.00	25.00	15.00
(45)	Harold "Peewee" Reese	125.00	62.00	37.00
(46)	Phil Rizzuto	125.00	62.00	37.00
(47)	Robin Roberts	90.00	45.00	27.00
(48)	Jackie Robinson	300.00	150.00	90.00
(49)	Henry Sauer	50.00	25.00	15.00
(50)	Johnny Schmitz	50.00	25.00	15.00
(51)	Red Schoendinst (Schoendienst)	90.00	45.00	27.00
(52)	Andy Seminick	50.00	25.00	15.00
(53)	Duke Snider (B on cap.)	125.00	62.00	37.00
(54)	Warren Spahn (B on cap.)	125.00	62.00	37.00
(55)	Vern Stephens (Portrait)	50.00	25.00	15.00
(56)	Earl Torgeson (Braves uniform.)	50.00	25.00	15.00
(57)	Virgil Trucks	50.00	25.00	15.00
(58)	Mickey Vernon (Batting)	50.00	25.00	15.00
(59)	Eddie Waitkus	50.00	25.00	15.00
(60)	Vic Wertz (Batting)	50.00	25.00	15.00
(61)	Gene Woodling	50.00	25.00	15.00
(62)	Gus Zernial	50.00	25.00	15.00
(63)	Cleveland Indians 1954 American League Champions	300.00	150.00	90.00
(64)	New York Giants 1954 National League Champions	300.00	150.00	90.00

1959 Exhibits - Dad's Cookies

(See 1959 Dad's Cookies.)

1961 Exhibits - Wrigley Field

JOHN JOSEPH EVERS

Distributed at Chicago's Wrigley Field circa 1961, this 24-card set features members of the Baseball Hall of Fame. The cards measure 3-3/8" x 5-3/8" and include the player's full name along the bottom. They were printed on gray stock and have a postcard back or blank back. The set is unnumbered.

		NM	EX	VG
Complete Set (24):		750.00	375.00	225.00
Common Player:		10.00	5.00	3.00
(1)	Grover Cleveland Alexander	15.00	7.50	4.50
(2)	Adrian Constantine Anson	12.50	6.25	3.75
(3)	John Franklin Baker	10.00	5.00	3.00
(4)	Roger Phillip Bresnahan	10.00	5.00	3.00
(5)	Mordecai Peter Brown	10.00	5.00	3.00
(6)	Frank Leroy Chance	10.00	5.00	3.00
(7)	Tyrus Raymond Cobb	145.00	75.00	45.00
(8)	Edward Trowbridge Collins	10.00	5.00	3.00
(9)	James J. Collins	10.00	5.00	3.00
(10)	John Joseph Evers	10.00	5.00	3.00
(11)	Henry Louis Gehrig	145.00	75.00	45.00
(12)	Clark C. Griffith	10.00	5.00	3.00
(13)	Walter Perry Johnson	25.00	12.50	7.50
(14)	Anthony Michael Lazzeri	10.00	5.00	3.00
(15)	James Walter Vincent Maranville	10.00	5.00	3.00
(16)	Christopher Mathewson	30.00	15.00	9.00
(17)	John Joseph McGraw	10.00	5.00	3.00
(18)	Melvin Thomas Ott	10.00	5.00	3.00
(19)	Herbert Jeffries Pennock	10.00	5.00	3.00
(20)	George Herman Ruth	180.00	90.00	55.00
(21)	Aloysius Harry Simmons	10.00	5.00	3.00
(22)	Tristram Speaker	25.00	12.50	7.50
(23)	Joseph B. Tinker	10.00	5.00	3.00
(24)	John Peter Wagner	40.00	20.00	12.00

1962 Pittsburgh Exhibits

The attributed date is approximate since none is shown on the cards; nor is a credit line to the manufacturer. Player content suggests Pittsburgh was the center of distribution and veteran collectors report having received the cards in penny arcade vending machines at Kennywood Amusement Park near there. It has also been reported that the cards were given over the counter as prizes for getting a winning gumball from a machine. The 3-1/4" x 5-1/4" cards are printed in black-and-white, or red, black and white. They are usually blank-backed, but examples have been seen with apparrent prize references printed on back. Most of the card "denominations" can be found with more than one subject. Besides the ballplayers listed here, the set contained TV and movie cowboys, rock-and-roll stars, boxers, wrestlers and cartoon characters.

		NM	EX	VG
Complete Set (81):		2,500	1,250	750.00
Common Player:		5.00	2.50	1.50
AC	Bill Mazeroski	25.00	12.50	7.50
2C	Whitey Ford	30.00	15.00	9.00
2C	Al Kaline	20.00	10.00	6.00
2C	Pirates logo cartoon	5.00	2.50	1.50
4C	Frank Robinson	20.00	10.00	6.00
4C	Babe Ruth	125.00	65.00	35.00
5C	Wilmer Mizell	5.00	2.50	1.50
5C	Mickey Mantle	175.00	85.00	50.00
5C	Honus Wagner	35.00	17.50	10.00
6C	Eddie Mathews	20.00	10.00	6.00
6C	Willie Mays	90.00	45.00	27.00
7C	Dodgers' "Bum" cartoon logo	5.00	2.50	1.50
7C	Eddie Mathews	20.00	10.00	6.00
7C	Willie Mays	90.00	45.00	27.00
8C	Walter Johnson	20.00	10.00	6.00
8C	Mickey Mantle	175.00	85.00	50.00
8C	Wilmer Mizell	5.00	2.50	1.50
9C	Hank Aaron	90.00	45.00	27.00
9C	Frank Robinson	20.00	10.00	6.00
10C	Lew Burdette	5.00	2.50	1.50
JC	Harvey Haddix	5.00	2.50	1.50
JC	Bill Mazeroski	25.00	12.50	7.50
JC	Al McBean	5.00	2.50	1.50
QC	Ty Cobb	60.00	30.00	18.00
QC	Whitey Ford	30.00	15.00	9.00
QC	Don Leppert	5.00	2.50	1.50
KC	Al Kaline	20.00	10.00	6.00
KC	Honus Wagner	35.00	17.50	10.00
AS	Lew Burdette	5.00	2.50	1.50
AS	Ty Cobb	60.00	30.00	18.00
2S	Smoky Burgess	5.00	2.50	1.50
3S	Don Hoak	5.00	2.50	1.50
4S	Roy Face	5.00	2.50	1.50
5S	Roberto Clemente	125.00	65.00	35.00
5S	Danny Murtaugh	5.00	2.50	1.50
6S	Christy Mathewson	25.00	12.50	7.50
6S	Dick Stuart	5.00	2.50	1.50
7S	Christy Mathewson	25.00	12.50	7.50
7S	Dick Stuart	5.00	2.50	1.50
8S	Danny Murtaugh	5.00	2.50	1.50
9S	Roy Face	5.00	2.50	1.50
10S	Don Hoak	5.00	2.50	1.50
JS	Smoky Burgess	5.00	2.50	1.50
QS	Walter Johnson	20.00	10.00	6.00
QS	Babe Ruth	125.00	65.00	35.00
KS	Hank Aaron	90.00	45.00	27.00
KS	Harvey Haddix	5.00	2.50	1.50
AH	Don Drysdale	20.00	10.00	6.00
AH	Ken Boyer	5.00	2.50	1.50
2H	Satchel Paige	60.00	30.00	18.00
3H	Rocky Colavito	20.00	10.00	6.00
4H	Stan Musial	50.00	25.00	15.00
4H	Bobby Richardson	15.00	7.50	4.50
5H	Ken Boyer	5.00	2.50	1.50
5H	Harmon Killebrew	20.00	10.00	6.00
6H	Luis Aparicio	20.00	10.00	6.00
6H	Ralph Kiner	20.00	10.00	6.00
7H	Sandy Koufax	75.00	37.50	22.00
8H	Warren Spahn	20.00	10.00	6.00
9H	Jimmy Piersall	5.00	2.50	1.50
10H	Yogi Berra	30.00	15.00	9.00
10H	Ralph Kiner	20.00	10.00	6.00
JH	Orlando Cepeda	20.00	10.00	6.00
JH	Ken Boyer	5.00	2.50	1.50
QH	Roger Maris	75.00	37.50	22.00
QH	Stan Musial	50.00	25.00	15.00
KH	Bob Purkey	5.00	2.50	1.50
AD	Don Drysdale	20.00	10.00	6.00
AD	Don Hoak	5.00	2.50	1.50
2D	Satchel Paige	60.00	30.00	18.00
6D	Luis Aparicio	20.00	10.00	6.00
6D	Ernie Banks	25.00	12.50	7.50
7D	Bill Virdon	5.00	2.50	1.50
7D	Sandy Koufax	75.00	37.50	22.00
8D	Bob Skinner	5.00	2.50	1.50
9D	Dick Groat	5.00	2.50	1.50
10D	Vernon Law	5.00	2.50	1.50
JD	Joe Adcock	5.00	2.50	1.50
JD	Orlando Cepeda	20.00	10.00	6.00
QD	Roger Maris	75.00	37.50	22.00
KD	Bob Friend	5.00	2.50	1.50

1962 Statistic Back Exhibits

In 1962, the Exhibit Supply Co. added career statistics to the yearly set they produced. The black-and-white, unnumbered cards measure 3-3/8" x 5-3/8". The statistics found on the back are printed in black or red.

		NM	EX	VG
Complete Set (32):		500.00	250.00	150.00
Common Player:		6.00	3.00	1.75
Red Backs: 1.5X				
(1)	Hank Aaron	35.00	17.50	10.00
(2)	Luis Aparicio	15.00	7.50	4.50
(3)	Ernie Banks	25.00	12.50	7.50
(4)	Larry "Yogi" Berra	25.00	12.50	7.50
(5)	Ken Boyer	7.50	3.75	2.25
(6)	Lew Burdette	6.00	3.00	1.75
(7)	Norm Cash	7.50	3.75	2.25
(8)	Orlando Cepeda	15.00	7.50	4.50
(9)	Roberto Clemente	50.00	25.00	15.00
(10)	Rocky Colavito	15.00	7.50	4.50
(11)	Ed "Whitey" Ford	17.50	8.75	5.25
(12)	Nelson Fox	15.00	7.50	4.50
(13)	Tito Francona	6.00	3.00	1.75
(14)	Jim Gentile	6.00	3.00	1.75
(15)	Dick Groat	6.00	3.00	1.75
(16)	Don Hoak	6.00	3.00	1.75
(17)	Al Kaline	17.50	8.75	5.25
(18)	Harmon Killebrew	17.50	8.75	5.25
(19)	Sandy Koufax	30.00	15.00	9.00
(20)	Jim Landis	6.00	3.00	1.75
(21)	Art Mahaffey	6.00	3.00	1.75
(22)	Frank Malzone	6.00	3.00	1.75
(23)	Mickey Mantle	100.00	50.00	30.00
(24)	Roger Maris	17.50	8.75	5.25
(25)	Eddie Mathews	17.50	8.75	5.25
(26)	Willie Mays	35.00	17.50	10.00
(27)	Wally Moon	6.00	3.00	1.75
(28)	Stan Musial	30.00	15.00	9.00
(29)	Milt Pappas	6.00	3.00	1.75
(30)	Vada Pinson	7.50	3.75	2.25
(31)	Norm Siebern	6.00	3.00	1.75
(32)	Warren Spahn	17.50	8.75	5.25

1963 Statistic Back Exhibits

The Exhibit Supply Co. issued a 64-card set with career statistics on the backs of the cards in 1963. The unnumbered, black-and-white cards are printed on thick cardboard and measure 3-3/8" x 5-3/8" in size. The statistics on the back are only found printed in red.

	NM	EX	VG
Complete Set (64):	900.00	450.00	275.00
Common Player:	7.50	3.75	2.25
(1) Hank Aaron	35.00	17.50	10.00
(2) Luis Aparicio	15.00	7.50	4.50
(3) Bob Aspromonte	7.50	3.75	2.25
(4) Ernie Banks	25.00	12.50	7.50
(5) Steve Barber	7.50	3.75	2.25
(6) Earl Battey	7.50	3.75	2.25
(7) Larry "Yogi" Berra	25.00	12.50	7.50
(8) Ken Boyer	9.00	4.50	2.75
(9) Lew Burdette	7.50	3.75	2.25
(10) Johnny Callison	7.50	3.75	2.25
(11) Norm Cash	9.00	4.50	2.75
(12) Orlando Cepeda	15.00	7.50	4.50
(13) Dean Chance	7.50	3.75	2.25
(14) Tom Cheney	7.50	3.75	2.25
(15) Roberto Clemente	40.00	20.00	12.00
(16) Rocky Colavito	15.00	7.50	4.50
(17) Choo Choo Coleman	7.50	3.75	2.25
(18) Roger Craig	7.50	3.75	2.25
(19) Joe Cunningham	7.50	3.75	2.25
(20) Don Drysdale	15.00	7.50	4.50
(21) Dick Farrell	7.50	3.75	2.25
(22) Ed "Whitey" Ford	20.00	10.00	6.00
(23) Nelson Fox	15.00	7.50	4.50
(24) Tito Francona	7.50	3.75	2.25
(25) Jim Gentile	7.50	3.75	2.25
(26) Tony Gonzalez	7.50	3.75	2.25
(27) Dick Groat	7.50	3.75	2.25
(28) Ray Herbert	7.50	3.75	2.25
(29) Chuck Hinton	7.50	3.75	2.25
(30) Don Hoak	7.50	3.75	2.25
(31) Frank Howard	9.00	4.50	2.75
(32) Ken Hubbs	12.00	6.00	3.50
(33) Joey Jay	7.50	3.75	2.25
(34) Al Kaline	15.00	7.50	4.50
(35) Harmon Killebrew	15.00	7.50	4.50
(36) Sandy Koufax	30.00	15.00	9.00
(37) Harvey Kuenn	7.50	3.75	2.25
(38) Jim Landis	7.50	3.75	2.25
(39) Art Mahaffey	7.50	3.75	2.25
(40) Frank Malzone	7.50	3.75	2.25
(41) Mickey Mantle	150.00	75.00	45.00
(42) Roger Maris	15.00	7.50	4.50
(43) Eddie Mathews	15.00	7.50	4.50
(44) Willie Mays	35.00	17.50	10.00
(45) Bill Mazeroski	15.00	7.50	4.50
(46) Ken McBride	7.50	3.75	2.25
(47) Wally Moon	7.50	3.75	2.25
(48) Stan Musial	30.00	15.00	9.00
(49) Charlie Neal	7.50	3.75	2.25
(50) Bill O'Dell	7.50	3.75	2.25
(51) Milt Pappas	7.50	3.75	2.25
(52) Camilo Pascual	7.50	3.75	2.25
(53) Jimmy Piersall	9.00	4.50	2.75
(54) Vada Pinson	9.00	4.50	2.75
(55) Brooks Robinson	20.00	10.00	6.00
(56) Frankie Robinson	20.00	10.00	6.00
(57) Pete Runnels	7.50	3.75	2.25
(58) Ron Santo	9.00	4.50	2.75
(59) Norm Siebern	7.50	3.75	2.25
(60) Warren Spahn	20.00	10.00	6.00
(61) Lee Thomas	7.50	3.75	2.25
(62) Leon Wagner	7.50	3.75	2.25
(63) Billy Williams	15.00	7.50	4.50
(64) Maurice Wills	13.50	6.75	4.00

1974 Baseball's Great Hall of Fame Exhibits

Two dozen of the cards from the 1948 issue were reprinted in 1974 by the original publisher, Exhibit Supply Co., Chicago. The 1974 reissues are in the same 3-3/8" x 5-3/8" format as the originals, and in the same design. They are blank-backed and printed on a thinner, slicker cardboard stock than the 1948 cards. The reprints can be found printed in black, blue or brown. The unnumbered cards are checklisted here alphabetically.

	NM	EX	VG
Complete Set (24):	20.00	10.00	6.00
Common Player:	3.00	1.50	.90
(1) Grover Cleveland Alexander	3.50	1.75	1.00
(2) Roger Bresnahan	3.00	1.50	.90
(3) Frank Chance	3.00	1.50	.90
(4) Jack Chesbro	3.00	1.50	.90
(5) Fred Clarke	3.00	1.50	.90
(6) Ty Cobb	10.00	5.00	3.00
(7) Mickey Cochrane	3.00	1.50	.90
(8) Eddie Collins	3.00	1.50	.90
(9) Johnny Evers	3.00	1.50	.90
(10) Frankie Frisch	3.00	1.50	.90
(11) Clark Griffith	3.00	1.50	.90
(12) Robert "Lefty" Grove	3.00	1.50	.90
(13) Rogers Hornsby	4.00	2.00	1.25
(14) Hughie Jennings	3.00	1.50	.90
(15) Walter Johnson	5.00	2.50	1.50
(16) Connie Mack	3.00	1.50	.90
(17) Christy Mathewson	5.00	2.50	1.50
(18) John McGraw	3.00	1.50	.90
(19) George Sisler	3.00	1.50	.90
(20) Joe Tinker	3.00	1.50	.90
(21) Rube Waddell	3.00	1.50	.90
(22) Honus Wagner	6.00	3.00	1.75
(23) Ed Walsh	3.00	1.50	.90
(24) Cy Young	5.00	2.50	1.50

1977 Baseball's Great Hall of Fame Exhibits

A second set of "Baseball's Great Hall of Fame" exhibit cards was produced in 1977, most cards featuring more recent players than the 1948 issue. The cards were produced in the same 3-3/8" x 5-3/8" blank-back, black-and-white design as the 1948 cards, and are a genuine product of Exhibit Supply Co., Chicago. The new cards were printed on an extremely high grade of semi-gloss cardboard, in contrast to the earlier versions. Production was announced at 500,000 cards. The unnumbered cards are checklisted here alphabetically.

	NM	EX	VG
Complete Set (32):	35.00	17.50	10.00
Common Player:	2.00	1.00	.60
(1) Luke Appling	2.00	1.00	.60
(2) Ernie Banks	3.00	1.50	.90
(3) Yogi Berra	3.00	1.50	.90
(4) Roy Campanella	3.00	1.50	.90
(5) Roberto Clemente	9.00	4.50	2.75
(6) Alvin Dark	2.00	1.00	.60
(7) Joe DiMaggio	9.00	4.50	2.75
(8) Bob Feller	2.00	1.00	.60
(9) Whitey Ford	2.00	1.00	.60
(10) Jimmie Foxx	2.00	1.00	.60
(11) Lou Gehrig	9.00	4.50	2.75
(12) Charlie Gehringer	2.00	1.00	.60
(13) Hank Greenberg	2.50	1.25	.70
(14) Gabby Hartnett	2.00	1.00	.60
(15) Carl Hubbell	2.00	1.00	.60
(16) Al Kaline	2.00	1.00	.60
(17) Mickey Mantle	15.00	7.50	4.50
(18) Willie Mays	6.00	3.00	1.75
(19) Johnny Mize	2.00	1.00	.60
(20) Stan Musial	4.00	2.00	1.25
(21) Mel Ott	2.00	1.00	.60
(22) Satchel Paige	2.50	1.25	.70
(23) Robin Roberts	2.00	1.00	.60
(24) Jackie Robinson	6.00	3.00	1.75
(25) Babe Ruth	12.00	6.00	3.50
(26) Duke Snider	2.00	1.00	.60
(27) Warren Spahn	2.00	1.00	.60
(28) Tris Speaker	2.00	1.00	.60
(29) Honus Wagner	3.00	1.50	.90
(30) Ted Williams	6.00	3.00	1.75
(31) Rudy York	2.00	1.00	.60
(32) Cy Young	2.00	1.00	.60

1980 Exhibits

Following the purchase of the "remains" of the Exhibit Supply Co., by a collector in the late 1970s, this set of Exhibits was issued in 1980. The set utilized photos from earlier issues in the same 3-3/8" x 5-3/8" size. Each card carries a notation in white at the bottom, "An Exhibit Card 1980," to distinguish them from the older version. Sets could be purchased printed in sepia, red or blue, at $4.50 per set. A total of 5,000 sets were reported printed. The unnumbered cards are checklisted here alphabetically.

	NM	EX	VG
Complete Set (32):	40.00	20.00	12.00
Common Player:	2.00	1.00	.60
(1) Johnny Antonelli	2.00	1.00	.60
(2) Richie Ashburn	2.00	1.00	.60
(3) Earl Averill	2.00	1.00	.60
(4) Ernie Banks	4.00	2.00	1.25
(5) Ewell Blackwell	2.00	1.00	.60
(6) Lou Brock	2.00	1.00	.60
(7) Dean Chance	2.00	1.00	.60
(8) Roger Craig	2.00	1.00	.60
(9) Lou Gehrig	20.00	10.00	6.00
(10) Gil Hodges	2.00	1.00	.60
(11) Jack Jensen	2.00	1.00	.60
(12) Willie Keeler	2.00	1.00	.60
(13) George Kell	2.00	1.00	.60
(14) Alex Kellner	2.00	1.00	.60
(15) Harmon Killebrew	2.00	1.00	.60
(16) Dale Long	2.00	1.00	.60
(17) Sal Maglie	2.00	1.00	.60
(18) Roger Maris	4.00	2.00	1.25
(19) Willie Mays	13.50	6.75	4.00
(20) Minnie Minoso	2.00	1.00	.60
(21) Stan Musial	10.00	5.00	3.00
(22) Billy Pierce	2.00	1.00	.60
(23) Jimmy Piersall	2.00	1.00	.60
(24) Eddie Plank	2.00	1.00	.60
(25) Pete Reiser	2.00	1.00	.60
(26) Brooks Robinson	2.00	1.00	.60
(27) Pete Runnels	2.00	1.00	.60
(28) Herb Score	2.00	1.00	.60
(29) Warren Spahn	2.00	1.00	.60
(30) Billy Williams	2.00	1.00	.60
(31) 1948 Boston Braves Team	3.00	1.50	.90
(32) 1948 Cleveland Indians Team	3.00	1.50	.90

1980 Hall of Fame Exhibits

Following the purchase of the "remains" of the Exhibit Supply Co., by a collector in the late 1970s, this set of Exhibits was issued in 1980. The set utilizies photos from earlier issues in the same 3-3/8" x 5-3/8" size. Each card has a notation in white at the bottom, "An Exhibit Card 1980 Hall Of Fame," to distinguish them from the older version. Sets could be purchased printed in sepia, red or blue for $5. The unnumbered cards are checklisted here alphabetically.

	NM	EX	VG
Complete Set (32):	25.00	12.50	7.50
Common Player:	2.00	1.00	.60
(1) Grover Cleveland Alexander	2.50	1.25	.70
(2) Lou Boudreau	2.00	1.00	.60
(3) Roger Bresnahan	2.00	1.00	.60
(4) Roy Campanella	2.00	1.00	.60

(5)	Frank Chance	2.00	1.00	.60
(6)	Ty Cobb	5.00	2.50	1.50
(7)	Mickey Cochrane	2.00	1.00	.60
(8)	Dizzy Dean	2.50	1.25	.70
(9)	Joe DiMaggio	6.00	3.00	1.75
(10)	Bill Dickey	2.00	1.00	.60
(11)	Johnny Evers	2.00	1.00	.60
(12)	Jimmy Foxx	2.50	1.25	.70
(13)	Vernon Gomez	2.00	1.00	.60
(14)	Robert "Lefty" Grove	2.00	1.00	.60
(15)	Hank Greenberg	2.50	1.25	.70
(16)	Rogers Hornsby	2.00	1.00	.60
(17)	Carl Hubbell	2.00	1.00	.60
(18)	Hughie Jennings	2.00	1.00	.60
(19)	Walter Johnson	2.50	1.25	.70
(20)	Napoleon Lajoie	2.00	1.00	.60
(21)	Bob Lemon	2.00	1.00	.60
(22)	Mickey Mantle	12.00	6.00	3.50
(23)	Christy Mathewson	2.00	1.00	.60
(24)	Mel Ott	2.00	1.00	.60
(25)	Satchel Paige	2.50	1.25	.70
(26)	Jackie Robinson	4.00	2.00	1.25
(27)	Babe Ruth	9.00	4.50	2.75
(28)	Tris Speaker	2.00	1.00	.60
(29)	Joe Tinker	2.00	1.00	.60
(30)	Honus Wagner	3.00	1.50	.90
(31)	Ted Williams	4.00	2.00	1.25
(32)	Cy Young	2.50	1.25	.70

1990s Exhibit Card Unauthorized Reprints

Sometime during the 1990s (and possibly continuing today), unauthorized reprints of 16 popular Exhibit cards from the 1940s and 1950s were made. Besides printing anomalies on front resulting from re-screening genuine cards, the reprints are on the wrong weight (too thin) and color (too white on back) of cardboard. Collectors should use caution when purchasing any of the cards found in this group. Because the reprints are unauthorized, they have no collector value.

Complete Set (16):		
(1)	Hank Aaron	
(2)	Yogi Berra	
(3)	Roy Campanella	
(4)	Whitey Ford (Pitching)	
(5)	Nelson Fox	
(6)	Gil Hodges ("B"on cap.)	
(7)	Mickey Mantle (Batting, waist-up, "ck" in "Mickey" connected.)	
(8)	Willie Mays (Batting)	
(9)	Stan Musial (Kneeling)	
(10)	Don Newcombe ("Dodgers" on jacket.)	
(11)	Harold "Peewee" Reese (Ball partially visible.)	
(12)	Duke Snider ("B" on cap.)	
(13)	Warren Spahn ("B" on cap.)	
(14)	Ted Williams (#9 not showing)	
(15)	1956 Brooklyn Dodgers	
(16)	1956 N.Y. Yankees	

1910 E-UNC Candy

Little is known about these 1910-era cards except that they appear to have been cut from a candy box. Printed in blue or red duo-tone and blank-backed, the cards measure about 2-3/4" per side. A 1-3/8" x 2-1/2" central image has a player photo with a diamond design around. Player identification is in a white strip at bottom.

	NM	EX	VG
Common Player:	715.00	360.00	210.00
(1) "Ty" Cobb	3,000	1,500	900.00
(2) Eddie Collins	715.00	360.00	210.00
(3) Johnny Evers	715.00	360.00	210.00
(4) "Christy" Mathewson	1,425	715.00	430.00
(5) "Honus" Wagner	1,800	900.00	540.00
(6) "Cy" Young	1,425	715.00	430.00

1936 E-UNC Candy

These cards appear to be a secondary use of the center portions of the 1936 S and S Game cards, having the same player photos and data in a size which varies from about 1-3/4" to 1-7/8" wide and between 2-3/8" and 2-1/2" tall. These differ in that instead of the green backs found on most of the game cards, these have plain backs which are sometimes found with a rubber-stamped message to present the card for a free gift or candy bar. These stamps indicate the cards were used as a prize premium in an as yet unidentified candy company's promotion. With more than half of the S and S players known in this candy company version, it is not unreasonable to assume the checklists for both sets are the same.

		NM	EX	VG
Complete Set (52):		3,000	1,500	900.00
Common Player:		45.00	22.50	13.50
(1)	Luke Appling	90.00	45.00	25.00
(2)	Earl Averill	90.00	45.00	25.00
(3)	Zeke Bonura	45.00	22.50	13.50
(4)	Dolph Camilli	45.00	22.50	13.50
(5)	Ben Cantwell	45.00	22.50	13.50
(6)	Phil Cavaretta (Cavarretta)	45.00	22.50	13.50
(7)	Rip Collins	45.00	22.50	13.50
(8)	Joe Cronin	90.00	45.00	25.00
(9)	Frank Crosetti	60.00	30.00	18.00
(10)	Kiki Cuyler	90.00	45.00	25.00
(11)	Virgil Davis	45.00	22.50	13.50
(12)	Frank Demaree	45.00	22.50	13.50
(13)	Paul Derringer	45.00	22.50	13.50
(14)	Bill Dickey	120.00	60.00	35.00
(15)	Woody English	45.00	22.50	13.50
(16)	Fred Fitzsimmons	45.00	22.50	13.50
(17)	Richard Ferrell	90.00	45.00	25.00
(18)	Pete Fox	45.00	22.50	13.50
(19)	Jimmy Foxx	150.00	75.00	45.00
(20)	Larry French	45.00	22.50	13.50
(21)	Frank Frisch	100.00	50.00	30.00
(22)	August Galan	45.00	22.50	13.50
(23)	Chas. Gehringer	100.00	50.00	30.00
(24)	John Gill	45.00	22.50	13.50
(25)	Charles Grimm	45.00	22.50	13.50
(26)	Mule Haas	45.00	22.50	13.50
(27)	Stanley Hack	45.00	22.50	13.50
(28)	Bill Hallahan	45.00	22.50	13.50
(29)	Melvin Harder	45.00	22.50	13.50
(30)	Gabby Hartnett	90.00	45.00	25.00
(31)	Ray Hayworth	45.00	22.50	13.50
(32)	Ralston Hemsley	45.00	22.50	13.50
(33)	Bill Herman	90.00	45.00	25.00
(34)	Frank Higgins	45.00	22.50	13.50
(35)	Carl Hubbell	120.00	60.00	35.00
(36)	Bill Jurges	45.00	22.50	13.50
(37)	Vernon Kennedy	45.00	22.50	13.50
(38)	Chuck Klein	90.00	45.00	25.00
(39)	Mike Kreevich	45.00	22.50	13.50
(40)	Bill Lee	45.00	22.50	13.50
(41)	Jos. Medwick	90.00	45.00	25.00
(42)	Van Mungo	45.00	22.50	13.50
(43)	James O'Dea	45.00	22.50	13.50
(44)	Mel Ott	120.00	60.00	35.00
(45)	Rip Radcliff	45.00	22.50	13.50
(46)	Pie Traynor	90.00	45.00	25.00
(47)	Arky Vaughan (Vaughn)	90.00	45.00	25.00
(48)	Joe Vosmik	45.00	22.50	13.50
(49)	Lloyd Waner	90.00	45.00	25.00
(50)	Paul Waner	90.00	45.00	25.00
(51)	Lon Warneke	45.00	22.50	13.50
(52)	Floyd Young	45.00	22.50	13.50

1909-11 E90-1, E90-2, E90-3 American Caramel

(See 1909-11 American Caramel Co. for checklists, values.)

1908-09 E91 American Caramel Co.

(See 1908-09 American Caramel Co. for checklists, values.)

1909 E92 Nadja Caramels

(See 1909 Nadja Caramels.)

1910 E93 Standard Caramel Co.

(See 1910 Standard Caramel Co. for checklist, values.)

1911 E94

(See 1911 George Close Candy Co. for checklist and value data.)

1909 E95 Philadelphia Caramel

(See 1909 Philadelphia Caramel for checklist, price guide.)

1910 E96 Philadelphia Caramel

(See 1910 Philadelphia Caramel for checklist, values.)

1910 E98 "Set of 30"

This set of 30 subjects was issued in 1910 and is closely related to several other early candy issues that are nearly identical. The cards measure 1-1/2" x 2-3/4" and feature color lithograph player pictures. The backs, printed in brown, contain a checklist of the set but no advertising or other information indicating the manufacturer. The set was designated E98 by the "American Card Catalog." While the cards are unnumbered, they are listed here according to the numbers on the back checklist. Some or all of the cards may be found with different colored backgrounds.

		NM	EX	VG
Complete Set (30):		75,000	30,000	15,000
Common Player:		1,500	480.00	180.00
(1)	Christy Matthewson (Mathewson)	15,000	7,500	2,800
(2)	John McGraw	2,500	860.00	350.00
(3)	Johnny Kling	1,500	480.00	200.00
(4)	Frank Chance	2,150	860.00	350.00
(5)	"Hans" Wagner	15,000	3,400	2,000
(6)	Fred Clarke	2,150	860.00	350.00
(7)	Roger Bresnahan	2,150	860.00	350.00
(8)	Hal Chase	2,000	800.00	350.00
(9)	Russ Ford	1,200	480.00	180.00
(10)	"Ty" Cobb	9,000	3,600	2,000
(11)	Hughey Jennings	2,150	860.00	350.00
(12)	Chief Bender	2,150	860.00	350.00
(13)	Ed Walsh	2,750	1,500	400.00
(14)	"Cy" Young (Picture actually Irv Young.)	9,000	3,000	1,500
(15)	Al Bridwell	1,500	480.00	180.00
(16)	Miner Brown	2,150	860.00	350.00
(17)	George Mullin	1,500	480.00	180.00
(18)	Chief Meyers	1,500	480.00	180.00
(19)	Hippo Vaughn	3,500	1,750	400.00
(20)	Red Dooin	3,000	1,500	400.00
(21)	Fred Tenny (Tenney)	1,500	480.00	180.00
(22)	Larry McLean	1,500	480.00	180.00
(23)	Nap Lajoie	5,000	2,500	1,000
(24)	Joe Tinker	2,150	860.00	350.00
(25)	Johnny Evers	2,150	860.00	350.00
(26)	Harry Davis	1,500	480.00	180.00
(27)	Eddie Collins	2,150	860.00	350.00
(28)	Bill Dahlen	3,000	1,500	500.00
(29)	"Connie" Mack	5,000	2,500	1,000
(30)	Jack Coombs	3,500	1,750	400.00

1909 E101 "Set of 50"

This 50-card set is closely related to the E92 issues by Nadja, Croft's, Dockman, etc. The fronts of the E101 cards are identical to the E92 set, but the back is "anonymous," containing no advertising or other information regarding the set's sponsor. The backs read simply "This card is one of a set of 50 Base Ball Players Prominent Members of National and American Leagues."

	NM	EX	VG
Complete Set (50):	75,000	30,000	15,000

Common Player:	950.00	400.00	200.00
(1) Jack Barry	950.00	400.00	200.00
(2) Harry Bemis	950.00	400.00	200.00
(3) Chief Bender (White hat.)	3,700	1,500	750.00
(4) Chief Bender (Striped hat.)	4,200	1,700	850.00
(5) Bill Bergen	950.00	400.00	200.00
(6) Bob Bescher	950.00	400.00	200.00
(7) Al Bridwell	1,500	600.00	300.00
(8) Doc Casey	950.00	400.00	200.00
(9) Frank Chance	3,700	1,500	750.00
(10) Hal Chase	3,200	1,300	650.00
(11) Ty Cobb	20,000	8,000	4,000
(12) Eddie Collins	3,700	1,500	750.00
(13) Sam Crawford	3,700	1,500	750.00
(14) Harry Davis	1,500	600.00	300.00
(15) Art Devlin	950.00	400.00	200.00
(16) Wild Bill Donovan	950.00	400.00	200.00
(17) Red Dooin	950.00	400.00	200.00
(18) Mickey Doolan	950.00	400.00	200.00
(19) Patsy Dougherty	950.00	400.00	200.00
(20) Larry Doyle (With bat.)	950.00	400.00	200.00
(21) Larry Doyle (Throwing)	950.00	400.00	200.00
(22) Johnny Evers	3,700	1,500	750.00
(23) George Gibson	950.00	400.00	200.00
(24) Topsy Hartsel	950.00	400.00	200.00
(25) Fred Jacklitsch	950.00	400.00	200.00
(26) Hugh Jennings	3,700	1,500	750.00
(27) Red Kleinow	950.00	400.00	200.00
(28) Otto Knabe	950.00	400.00	200.00
(29) Jack Knight	950.00	400.00	200.00
(30) Nap Lajoie	3,700	1,500	750.00
(31) Hans Lobert	950.00	400.00	200.00
(32) Sherry Magee	950.00	400.00	200.00
(33) Christy Matthewson (Mathewson)	13,500	5,400	2,700
(34) John McGraw	3,700	1,500	750.00
(35) Larry McLean	950.00	400.00	200.00
(36) Dots Miller (Batting)	950.00	400.00	200.00
(37) Dots Miller (Fielding)	950.00	400.00	200.00
(38) Danny Murphy	950.00	400.00	200.00
(39) Bill O'Hara	950.00	400.00	200.00
(40) Germany Schaefer	1,500	600.00	300.00
(41) Admiral Schlei	950.00	400.00	200.00
(42) Boss Schmidt	950.00	400.00	200.00
(43) Johnny Seigle	1,500	600.00	300.00
(44) Dave Shean	950.00	400.00	200.00
(45) Boss Smith (Schmidt)	950.00	400.00	200.00
(46) Joe Tinker	3,700	1,500	750.00
(47) Honus Wagner (Batting)	17,500	7,000	3,500
(48) Honus Wagner (Throwing)	17,500	7,000	3,500
(49) Cy Young	12,500	5,000	2,500
(50) Heinie Zimmerman	950.00	400.00	200.00

1909 E102 "Set of 25"

Wagner, s.s. Pittsburg Nat'l

One of many similar early candy card sets, this set - designated as E102 in the American Card Catalog - was published no earlier than mid-1909. The producer of the set is unknown. Measuring approximately 1-1/2" x 2-3/4", the set is almost identical in design to the E101 set and other closely related issues. The set consists of 25 players, which are checklisted on the back of the card. Four of the players have been found in two variations, resulting in 29 different cards. Because there is no advertising on the cards, the set can best be identified by the words - "This Picture is one of a Set of Twenty-five Base Ball Players, as follows" - which appears on the back of each card.

	NM	EX	VG
Complete Set (29):	55,000	22,000	11,000
Common Player:	850.00	350.00	175.00
(1) Chief Bender	1,450	575.00	290.00
(2) Bob Bescher	850.00	350.00	175.00
(3) Hal Chase	900.00	360.00	180.00
(4) Ty Cobb	15,000	6,000	3,000
(5) Eddie Collins	1,450	575.00	290.00
(6) Sam Crawford	1,450	575.00	290.00
(7) Wild Bill Donovan	850.00	350.00	175.00
(8) Red Dooin	850.00	350.00	175.00
(9) Patsy Dougherty	850.00	350.00	175.00
(10) Larry Doyle (Batting)	850.00	350.00	175.00
(11) Larry Doyle (Throwing)	850.00	350.00	175.00
(12) Johnny Evers	1,450	575.00	290.00
(13) Red Kleinow	850.00	350.00	175.00
(14) Otto Knabe	850.00	350.00	175.00
(15) Nap Lajoie	1,825	725.00	365.00
(16) Hans Lobert	850.00	350.00	175.00
(17) Sherry Magee	850.00	350.00	175.00
(18) Christy Matthewson (Mathewson)	5,000	2,000	1,000
(19) Dots Miller (Batting)	850.00	350.00	175.00
(20) Dots Miller (Fielding)	1,650	650.00	325.00
(21) Danny Murphy	850.00	350.00	175.00
(22) Germany Schaefer	850.00	350.00	175.00
(23) Boss Schmidt	850.00	350.00	175.00
(24) Dave Shean	850.00	350.00	175.00
(25) Boss Smith (Schmidt)	850.00	350.00	175.00
(26) Joe Tinker	1,450	575.00	290.00
(27) Honus Wagner (Batting)	10,000	2,600	1,300
(28) Honus Wagner (Throwing)	10,000	2,600	1,300
(29) Heinie Zimmerman	850.00	350.00	175.00

1910 E104 Nadja Caramels

(See 1910 Nadja Caramels.)

1915 E106 American Caramel Co.

(See 1915 American Caramel Co.)

1903-1904 E107 Type 1

 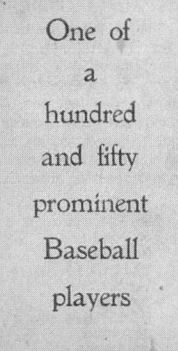

W. GLEASON, 2 B, Phila., N

One of
a
hundred
and fifty
prominent
Baseball
players

Identified by the American Card Catalog as E107, this set is significant because it was one of the first major baseball card sets since the 1880s. It established the pattern for most of the tobacco and candy cards that followed over the next two decades. Measuring approximately 1-3/8" x 2-5/8", cards feature black-and-white player photos with the name, position and team in the bottom border. Most are found either with black back printing reading, "One of a hundred and fifty prominent Baseball players," or blank-backed, in about equal numbers. Also found are cards with a purple diagonal overprint stating "THE BREISCH-WILLIAMS CO." Type 1 consists of 147 known different players, plus 11 additional variations. The Type 2 cards are thicker than those of Type 1 and some (Keeler and Delehanty) cards have captions different from those found in Type 1. Values shown for EX and NM grades are mostly theoretical, as few cards are known in better than VG condition.

	NM	EX	VG
Common Player:	10,200	4,080	2,040
Breisch-Williams Overprint: 2-3X			
(1a) John Anderson (St. Louis)	10,200	4,080	2,040
(1b) John Anderson (New York)	10,200	4,080	2,040
(2) Jimmy Barret (Barrett)	10,200	4,080	2,040
(3) Ginger Beaumont	10,200	4,080	2,040
(4) Fred Beck	10,200	4,080	2,040
(5) Jake Beckley	30,000	15,000	9,000
(6) Harry Bemis	10,200	4,080	2,040
(7) Chief Bender	30,000	15,000	9,000
(8) Bill Bernhard	10,200	4,080	2,040
(9) Harry Bey (Bay)	10,200	4,080	2,040
(10) Bill Bradley	10,200	4,080	2,040
(11) Fritz Buelow	10,200	4,080	2,040
(12) Nixey Callahan	10,200	4,080	2,040
(13) Scoops Carey	10,200	4,080	2,040
(14) Charley Carr	10,200	4,080	2,040
(15) Bill Carrick	10,200	4,080	2,040
(16) Doc Casey	10,500	4,080	2,040
(17) Frank Chance	30,000	15,000	9,000
(18) Jack Chesbro	30,000	15,000	9,000
(19) Boileryard Clark (Clarke)	10,200	4,080	2,040
(20) Fred Clarke	30,000	15,000	9,000
(21) Jimmy Collins	30,000	15,000	9,000
(22) Duff Cooley	10,200	4,080	2,040
(23) Tommy Corcoran	10,200	4,080	2,040
(24) Bill Coughlan (Coughlin)	10,200	4,080	2,040
(25) Lou Criger	10,200	4,080	2,040
(26) Lave Cross	10,200	4,080	2,040
(27) Monte Cross	10,200	4,080	2,040
(28a) Bill Dahlen (Brooklyn)	10,200	4,080	2,040
(28b) Bill Dahlen (New York)	17,000	4,080	2,040
(29) Tom Daly	10,200	4,080	2,040
(30) George Davis	30,000	15,000	9,000
(31) Harry Davis	10,200	4,080	2,040
(32) Ed Delehanty (Delahanty)	30,000	15,000	9,000
(33) Gene DeMont (DeMontreville)	10,200	4,080	2,040
(34a) Pop Dillon (Detroit)	10,200	4,080	2,040
(34b) Pop Dillon (Brooklyn)	16,200	8,100	4,800
(35) Bill Dineen (Dinneen)	10,200	4,080	2,040
(36) Red Donahue	10,200	4,080	2,040
(37) Mike Donlin	10,200	4,080	2,040
(38) Patsy Donovan	10,200	4,080	2,040
(39) Patsy Dougherty (Photo actually Tom Hughes.)	10,200	4,080	2,040
(40) Klondike Douglass	10,200	4,080	2,040
(41a) Jack Doyle (Brooklyn)	10,200	4,080	2,040
(41b) Jack Doyle (Philadelphia)	10,200	4,080	2,040
(42) Lew Drill	10,200	4,080	2,040
(43) Jack Dunn	10,200	4,080	2,040
(44a) Kid Elberfield (Elberfeld) (Detroit)	10,200	4,080	2,040
(44b) Kid Elberfield (Elberfeld) (No team designation.)	10,200	4,080	2,040
(45) Duke Farrell	10,200	4,080	2,040
(46) Hobe Ferris	10,200	4,080	2,040
(47) Elmer Flick	30,000	15,000	9,000
(48) Buck Freeman	10,200	4,080	2,040
(49) Bill Freil (Friel)	10,200	4,080	2,040
(50) Dave Fultz	10,200	4,080	2,040
(51) Ned Garvin	10,200	4,080	2,040
(52) Billy Gilbert	10,200	4,080	2,040
(53) Harry Gleason	10,200	4,080	2,040
(54a) Kid Gleason (New York)	10,200	4,080	2,040
(54b) Kid Gleason (Philadelphia)	10,200	4,080	2,040
(55) John Gochnauer (Gochnaur)	10,200	4,080	2,040
(56) Danny Green	10,200	4,080	2,040
(57) Noodles Hahn	10,200	4,080	2,040
(58) Bill Hallman	10,200	4,080	2,040
(59) Ned Hanlon	30,000	15,000	9,000
(60) Dick Harley	10,200	4,080	2,040
(61) Jack Harper	10,200	4,080	2,040
(62) Topsy Hartsell (Hartsel)	10,200	4,080	2,040
(63) Emmet Heidrick	10,200	4,080	2,040
(64) Charlie Hemphill	10,200	4,080	2,040
(65) Weldon Henley	10,200	4,080	2,040
(66) Piano Legs Hickman	10,200	4,080	2,040
(67) Harry Howell	10,200	4,080	2,040
(68) Frank Iasbel (Isbell)	10,200	4,080	2,040
(69) Fred Jacklitzch (Jacklitsch)	10,200	4,080	2,040
(70) Fielder Jones (Chicago)	10,200	4,080	2,040
(71) Charlie Jones (Boston)	10,200	4,080	2,040
(72) Addie Joss	30,000	15,000	9,000
(73) Mike Kahoe	10,200	4,080	2,040
(74) Wee Willie Keeler	30,000	15,000	9,000
(75) Joe Kelley	30,000	15,000	9,000
(76) Brickyard Kennedy	10,200	4,080	2,040
(77) Frank Kitson	10,200	4,080	2,040
(78a) Malachi Kittredge (Boston)	10,200	4,080	2,040
(78b) Malachi Kittredge (Washington)	10,200	4,080	2,040
(79) Candy LaChance	10,200	4,080	2,040
(80) Nap Lajoie	30,000	15,000	9,000
(81) Tommy Leach	10,200	4,080	2,040
(82a) Watty Lee (Washington)	10,200	4,080	2,040
(82b) Watty Lee (Pittsburg)	10,200	4,080	2,040
(83) Sam Leever	10,200	4,080	2,040
(84) Herman Long	10,200	4,080	2,040
(85a) Billy Lush (Detroit)	10,200	4,080	2,040
(85b) Billy Lush (Cleveland)	10,200	4,080	2,040
(86) Christy Mathewson	78,000	39,000	24,000
(87) Sport McAllister	10,200	4,080	2,040
(88) Jack McCarthy	10,200	4,080	2,040
(89) Barry McCormick	10,200	4,080	2,040
(90) Ed McFarland (Chicago)	10,200	4,080	2,040
(91) Herm McFarland (New York)	10,200	4,080	2,040
(92) Joe McGinnity	30,000	15,000	9,000
(93) John McGraw	30,000	15,000	9,000
(94a) Deacon McGuire (Brooklyn)	10,200	4,080	2,040
(94b) Deacon McGuire (New York)	17,000	4,080	2,040
(95) Jock Menefee	10,200	4,080	2,040
(96) Sam Mertes	10,200	4,080	2,040
(97) Roscoe Miller (Picture actually George Mullin.)	10,200	4,080	2,040
(98) Fred Mitchell	10,200	4,080	2,040
(99) Earl Moore	10,200	4,080	2,040
(100) Danny Murphy	10,200	4,080	2,040
(101) Jack O'Connor	10,200	4,080	2,040
(102) Al Orth	10,200	4,080	2,040
(103) Dick Padden	10,200	4,080	2,040
(104) Freddy Parent	10,200	4,080	2,040
(105) Roy Patterson	10,200	4,080	2,040
(106) Heinie Peitz	10,200	4,080	2,040
(107) Deacon Phillipi (Phillippe)	10,200	4,080	2,040
(108) Wiley Piatt	10,200	4,080	2,040
(109) Ollie Pickering	10,200	4,080	2,040
(110) Eddie Plank	78,000	39,000	24,000
(111a) Ed Poole (Cincinnati)	10,200	4,080	2,040
(111b) Ed Poole (Brooklyn)	10,200	4,080	2,040
(112a) Jack Powell (St. Louis)	10,200	4,080	2,040
(112b) Jack Powell (New York)	10,200	4,080	2,040
(113) Mike Powers	10,200	4,080	2,040
(114) Claude Ritchie (Ritchey)	10,200	4,080	2,040
(115) Jimmy Ryan	10,200	4,080	2,040
(116) Ossee Schreckengost	10,200	4,080	2,040
(117) Kip Selbach	10,200	4,080	2,040
(118) Socks Seybold	10,200	4,080	2,040
(119) Jimmy Sheckard	10,200	4,080	2,040
(120) Ed Siever	10,200	4,080	2,040
(121) Harry Smith	10,200	4,080	2,040
(122) Tully Sparks	10,200	4,080	2,040
(123) Jake Stahl	10,200	4,080	2,040
(124) Harry Steinfeldt	10,200	4,080	2,040
(125) Sammy Strang	10,200	4,080	2,040
(126) Willie Sudhoff	10,200	4,080	2,040
(127) Joe Sugden	10,200	4,080	2,040
(128) Billy Sullivan	10,200	4,080	2,040
(129) Jack Taylor	10,200	4,080	2,040
(130) Fred Tenney	10,200	4,080	2,040
(131) Roy Thomas	10,200	4,080	2,040
(132a) Jack Thoney (Cleveland)	10,200	4,080	2,040
(132b) Jack Thoney (New York)	10,200	4,080	2,040
(133) Jack Townsend	10,200	4,080	2,040
(134) George Van Haltren	10,200	4,080	2,040
(135) Rube Waddell	30,000	15,000	9,000
(136) Honus Wagner	360,000	180,000	108,000
(137) Bobby Wallace	30,000	15,000	9,000
(138) Jack Warner	10,200	4,080	2,040
(139) Jimmy Wiggs	10,200	4,080	2,040
(140) Jimmy Williams	10,200	4,080	2,040
(141) Vic Willis	30,000	15,000	9,000
(142) Hooks Wiltse	10,200	4,080	2,040
(143) George Winters (Winter)	10,200	4,080	2,040
(144) Bob Wood	10,200	4,080	2,040
(145) Joe Yeager	9,600	4,800	2,880
(146) Cy Young	90,000	45,000	27,000
(147) Chief Zimmer	10,200	4,080	2,040

1903-1904 E107 Type 2

DELAHANTY, Fielder, Wash.

Many of the Type 2 E107 cards seen to date do not measure the nominal 1-3/8" x 2-5/8" of the Type 1 cards, often having been cut more narrowly. Once thought to have been cut from an advertising piece, it now appears these were a regular production issue, as at least one specimen has been found with the purple diagonal overprint stating "THE BREISCH-WILLIAMS CO." Type 2 cards are printed on a thicker and more gray card stock than Type 1 and at least a few (Keeler and Delahanty) cards have captions different from those found in Type 1. NM values are principally theoretical as few cards in known in conditions better than EX.

		NM	EX	VG
Common Player:		9,000	3,600	1,800
(1)	Ed Delahanty (Delahanty)	50,000	20,000	10,000
(2)	Jack Doyle	9,000	3,600	1,800
(3)	Wee Willie Keeler	50,000	20,000	10,000
(4)	Nap Lajoie	50,000	20,000	10,000
(5)	Tommy Leach	9,000	3,600	1,800
(6)	Socks Seybold	9,000	3,600	1,800
(7)	Fred Tenney	9,000	3,600	1,800
(8)	Rube Waddell	50,000	20,000	10,000

1922 E120 American Caramel Series of 240

(See 1922 American Caramel Series of 240.)

1921-22 E121 American Caramel Series of 80/120

(See 1921 American Caramel Series of 80, Series of 120.)

1922 E122 American Caramel Series of 80

(See 1922 American Caramel Series of 80 for checklist, values.)

1910 E125 American Caramel Die-Cuts

(See 1910 American Caramel Die-Cuts for checklist, values.)

1927 E126 American Caramel Series of 60

(See 1927 American Caramel Series of 60.)

1927 E210 York Caramels

(See York Caramels.)

1921 E253 Oxford Confectionery

(See 1921 Oxford Confectionery.)

F

1961 F & M Bank Minnesota Twins Matchbook Covers

The star players on the inaugural Twins team are featured in this series of matchbook covers. The 1-1/2" x 4-7/16" matchbooks are printed in black, red and blue on white, and

include a player portrait (players are shown wearing Washington Senators caps) and team logo on front. The sponsoring bank's picture and logo are on back. Inside the front cover are a few details about the player. Values shown are for complete but empty covers, with the striker surface intact. Complete matchbooks with matches bring about 2X the values quoted.

		NM	EX	VG
Complete Set (10):		70.00	35.00	20.00
Common Player:		7.50	3.75	2.25
(1)	Bob Allison	12.00	6.00	3.50
(2)	Earl Battey	9.00	4.50	2.75
(3)	Reno Bertoia	7.50	3.75	2.25
(4)	Billy Gardner	7.50	3.75	2.25
(5)	Lenny Green	7.50	3.75	2.25
(6)	Harmon Killebrew	20.00	10.00	6.00
(7)	Cookie Lavagetto	7.50	3.75	2.25
(8)	Jim Lemon	12.00	6.00	3.50
(9)	Camilo Pascual	12.00	6.00	3.50
(10)	Pedro Ramos	7.50	3.75	2.25

1962 F & M Bank Minnesota Twins Matchbook Covers

The '62 Twins are featured in this series of matchbook covers. The 1-1/2" x 4-7/16" matchbooks are printed in black, red and blue on white, and include a player portrait (new players who did not appear in the 1961 set are shown in Twins caps) and team logo on front. The sponsoring bank's picture and logo are on back. Inside the front cover are a few details about the player. Values shown are for complete but empty covers, with the striker surface intact. Complete matchbooks with matches bring about 2X the values quoted.

		NM	EX	VG
Complete Set (10):		75.00	37.00	22.00
Common Player:		7.50	3.75	2.25
(1)	Bob Allison	12.00	6.00	3.50
(2)	Earl Battey	9.00	4.50	2.75
(3)	Lenny Green	7.50	3.75	2.25
(4)	Jim Kaat	12.00	6.00	3.50
(5)	Harmon Killebrew	20.00	10.00	6.00
(6)	Jack Kralick	7.50	3.75	2.25
(7)	Jim Lemon	12.00	6.00	3.50
(8)	Camilo Pascual	12.00	6.00	3.50
(9)	Pedro Ramos	7.50	3.75	2.25
(10)	Zoilo Versalles	12.00	6.00	3.50

1966 Fairway Minnesota Twins

Color portraits of Twins favorites comprise this regional issue from a local grocery chain. The 8" x 10" glossy pictures have blue facsimile autographs on front and a white border. Black-and-white backs have a lengthy career summary, biographical data and full major and minor league stats. The unnumbered pictures are checklisted here in alphabetical order. There are no markings on the picture to identify the Fairway store.

		NM	EX	VG
Complete Set (17):		175.00	85.00	55.00
Common Player:		7.50	3.75	2.25
(1)	Bernie Allen	7.50	3.75	2.25
(2)	Bob Allison	13.50	6.75	4.00
(3)	Earl Battey	10.00	5.00	3.00
(4)	Jim Grant	7.50	3.75	2.25
(5)	Jimmie Hall	7.50	3.75	2.25
(6)	Jim Kaat	15.00	7.50	4.50
(7)	Harmon Killebrew	30.00	15.00	9.00
(8)	Jim Merritt	7.50	3.75	2.25
(9)	Don Mincher	7.50	3.75	2.25
(10)	Tony Oliva	15.00	7.50	4.50
(11)	Camilo Pascual	10.00	5.00	3.00
(12)	Jim Perry	10.00	5.00	3.00
(13)	Frank Quilici	7.50	3.75	2.25
(14)	Rich Rollins	7.50	3.75	2.25
(15)	Sandy Valdespino	7.50	3.75	2.25
(16)	Zoilo Versalles	13.50	6.75	4.00
(17)	Al Worthington	7.50	3.75	2.25

1964 Falstaff Beer

This 6" x 4" black-and-white postcard pictures the principal radio announcers for the CBS "Game of the Week" sponsored by the brewing company and was probably used to respond to fan requests for autographs. Facsimile signatures of the Hall of Famers are featured on front.

	NM	EX	VG
"Dizzy" Dean, "Pee Wee Reese"	20.00	10.00	6.00

1977 Family Fun Centers Padres

For 1977, Family Fun Centers, a chain of mini theme parks, took over sponsorship of the Padres annual issue of black-and-white player photos. The 5-1/2" x 8-1/2" photos have a large player pose at top-center, with his name and position below. In the bottom corners are team and sponsor logos. Backs have biographical data, complete stats and career highlights. Players are checklisted here alphabetically.

		NM	EX	VG
Complete Set (33):		90.00	45.00	27.50
Common Player:		4.50	2.25	1.25
(1)	Billy Almon	4.50	2.25	1.25
(2)	Joey Amalfitano	4.50	2.25	1.25
(3)	Tucker Ashford	4.50	2.25	1.25
(4)	Mike Champion	4.50	2.25	1.25
(5)	Roger Craig	4.50	2.25	1.25
(6)	Alvin Dark	4.50	2.25	1.25
(7)	Bob Davis	4.50	2.25	1.25
(8)	Rollie Fingers	12.50	6.25	3.75
(9)	Dave Freisleben	4.50	2.25	1.25
(10)	Tom Griffin	4.50	2.25	1.25
(11)	George Hendrick	4.50	2.25	1.25
(12)	Mike Ivie	4.50	2.25	1.25
(13)	Randy Jones	4.50	2.25	1.25
(14)	John McNamara	4.50	2.25	1.25
(15)	Bob Owchinko	4.50	2.25	1.25
(16)	Merv Rettenmund	4.50	2.25	1.25
(17)	Gene Richards	4.50	2.25	1.25
(18)	Dave Roberts	4.50	2.25	1.25
(19)	Jackie Robinson (Blank back.)	25.00	12.50	7.50
(20)	Rick Sawyer	4.50	2.25	1.25
(21)	Pat Scanlon	4.50	2.25	1.25
(22)	Bob Shirley	4.50	2.25	1.25
(23)	Bob Skinner	4.50	2.25	1.25
(24)	Dan Spillner	4.50	2.25	1.25
(25)	Gary Sutherland	4.50	2.25	1.25
(26)	Gene Tenace	4.50	2.25	1.25
(27)	Dave Tomlin	4.50	2.25	1.25
(28)	Jerry Turner	4.50	2.25	1.25
(29)	Bobby Valentine	4.50	2.25	1.25
(30)	Dave Wehrmeister	4.50	2.25	1.25
(31)	Whitey Wietelmann	4.50	2.25	1.25
(32)	Don Williams	4.50	2.25	1.25
(33)	Dave Winfield	15.00	7.50	4.50

1978 Family Fun Centers Angels

NOLAN RYAN

The players, manager and coaches of the '78 Angels are featured in this set of 3-1/2" x 5-1/2" sepia-tone cards. The unnumbered cards are checklisted here alphabetically.

		NM	EX	VG
Complete Set (38):		90.00	45.00	25.00
Common Player:		2.50	1.25	.70
(1)	Don Aase	2.50	1.25	.70
(2)	Mike Barlow	2.50	1.25	.70
(3)	Don Baylor	3.50	1.75	1.00

		NM	EX	VG
(4)	Lyman Bostock	2.50	1.25	.70
(5)	Ken Brett	2.50	1.25	.70
(6)	Dave Chalk	2.50	1.25	.70
(7)	Bob Clear	2.50	1.25	.70
(8)	Brian Downing	2.50	1.25	.70
(9)	Ron Fairly	2.50	1.25	.70
(10)	Gil Flores	2.50	1.25	.70
(11)	Dave Frost	2.50	1.25	.70
(12)	Dave Garcia	2.50	1.25	.70
(13)	Bobby Grich	2.50	1.25	.70
(14)	Tom Griffin	2.50	1.25	.70
(15)	Marv Grissom	2.50	1.25	.70
(16)	Ike Hampton	2.50	1.25	.70
(17)	Paul Hartzell	2.50	1.25	.70
(18)	Terry Humphrey	2.50	1.25	.70
(19)	Ron Jackson	2.50	1.25	.70
(20)	Chris Knapp	2.50	1.25	.70
(21)	Ken Landreaux	2.50	1.25	.70
(22)	Carney Lansford	2.50	1.25	.70
(23)	Dave LaRoche	2.50	1.25	.70
(24)	John McNamara	2.50	1.25	.70
(25)	Dyar Miller	2.50	1.25	.70
(26)	Rick Miller	2.50	1.25	.70
(27)	Balor Moore	2.50	1.25	.70
(28)	Rance Mulliniks	2.50	1.25	.70
(29)	Floyd Rayford	2.50	1.25	.70
(30)	Jimmie Reese	4.00	2.00	1.25
(31)	Merv Rettenmund	2.50	1.25	.70
(32)	Joe Rudi	2.50	1.25	.70
(33)	Nolan Ryan	45.00	22.50	13.50
(34)	Bob Skinner	2.50	1.25	.70
(35)	Tony Solaita	2.50	1.25	.70
(36)	Frank Tanana	2.50	1.25	.70
(37)	Dickie Thon	2.50	1.25	.70
---	Header Card	.70	.35	.20

1978 Family Fun Centers Padres

In conjunction with the Padres' hosting of the 1978 All-Star Game, Family Fun Centers issued this set of cards covering the players, coaches, announcers and even the owner. The 3-1/2" x 5-1/2" cards have a plaque look with a 3" x 3-1/4" posed color photo set on a wood background. The player's name is in a gold box at bottom, with the team and sponsor's logos in between. Backs are in black-and-white with a player portrait photo and facsimile autograph at bottom, a few biographical details and career stats at top and an essay in the middle titled, "My Greatest Thrill in Baseball." A uniform number appears at top-left. The set is checklisted here in alphabetical order.

		NM	EX	VG
	Complete Set (39):	75.00	37.50	22.50
	Common Player:	3.00	1.50	.90
(1)	Bill Almon	3.00	1.50	.90
(2)	Tucker Ashford	3.00	1.50	.90
(3)	Chuck Baker	3.00	1.50	.90
(4)	Dave Campbell (Announcer)	3.00	1.50	.90
(5)	Mike Champion	3.00	1.50	.90
(6)	Jerry Coleman (Announcer)	3.00	1.50	.90
(7)	Roger Craig	3.00	1.50	.90
(8)	John D'Acquisto	3.00	1.50	.90
(9)	Bob Davis	3.00	1.50	.90
(10)	Chuck Estrada	3.00	1.50	.90
(11)	Rollie Fingers	9.00	4.50	2.75
(12)	Dave Freisleben	3.00	1.50	.90
(13)	Oscar Gamble	3.00	1.50	.90
(14)	Fernando Gonzalez	3.00	1.50	.90
(15)	Billy Herman	4.00	2.00	1.25
(16)	Randy Jones	3.00	1.50	.90
(17)	Ray Kroc (owner)	5.00	2.50	1.50
(18)	Mark Lee	3.00	1.50	.90
(19)	Mickey Lolich	3.00	1.50	.90
(20)	Bob Owchinko	3.00	1.50	.90
(21)	Broderick Perkins	3.00	1.50	.90
(22)	Gaylord Perry	9.00	4.50	2.75
(23)	Eric Rasmussen	3.00	1.50	.90
(24)	Don Reynolds	3.00	1.50	.90
(25)	Gene Richards	3.00	1.50	.90
(26)	Dave Roberts	3.00	1.50	.90
(27)	Phil Roof	3.00	1.50	.90
(28)	Bob Shirley	3.00	1.50	.90
(29)	Ozzie Smith	60.00	30.00	18.00
(30)	Dan Spillner	3.00	1.50	.90
(31)	Rick Sweet	3.00	1.50	.90
(32)	Gene Tenace	3.00	1.50	.90
(33)	Derrel Thomas	3.00	1.50	.90
(34)	Jerry Turner	3.00	1.50	.90
(35)	Dave Wehrmeister	3.00	1.50	.90
(36)	Whitey Wietelmann	3.00	1.50	.90
(37)	Don Williams	3.00	1.50	.90
(38)	Dave Winfield	15.00	7.50	4.50
(39)	All-Star Game	3.00	1.50	.90

1979 Family Fun Centers Padres

Each card features a posed color photo against a woodgrain border. Fronts have player identification, the Padres mascot and the logo of one of the sponsors - Family Fun Centers or Dean's Photo Service. Black-and-white backs have player personal data, major and minor league stats, a notation to "COLLECT ALL 36 CARDS" and a list of distribution dates. The 3-1/4" x 4-3/4" cards were issued in 12-1/2" x 9-1/2" perforated panels of six cards plus a coupon from each sponsor. Panels were given out one per month May through September at promotional games, making the set difficult to complete. Cards #25-30 have not been confirmed as issued.

		NM	EX	VG
	Complete Set (30):	60.00	30.00	18.00
	Common Player:	3.00	1.50	.90
1	Roger Craig	3.00	1.50	.90
2	John D'Acquisto	3.00	1.50	.90
3	Ozzie Smith	25.00	12.50	7.50
4	KGB Chicken	4.00	2.00	1.25
5	Gene Richards	3.00	1.50	.90
6	Jerry Turner	3.00	1.50	.90
7	Bob Owchinko	3.00	1.50	.90
8	Gene Tenace	3.00	1.50	.90
9	Whitey Wietelmann	3.00	1.50	.90
10	Bill Almon	3.00	1.50	.90
11	Dave Winfield	15.00	7.50	4.50
12	Mike Hargrove	3.00	1.50	.90
13	Fernando Gonzalez	3.00	1.50	.90
14	Barry Evans	3.00	1.50	.90
15	Steve Mura	3.00	1.50	.90
16	Chuck Estrada	3.00	1.50	.90
17	Bill Fahey	3.00	1.50	.90
18	Gaylord Perry	6.00	3.00	1.75
19	Dan Briggs	3.00	1.50	.90
20	Billy Herman	4.00	2.00	1.25
21	Mickey Lolich	3.00	1.50	.90
22	Broderick Perkins	3.00	1.50	.90
23	Fred Kendall	3.00	1.50	.90
24	Rollie Fingers	6.00	3.00	1.75
31	Bobby Tolan	3.00	1.50	.90
32	Doug Rader	3.00	1.50	.90
33	Dave Campbell	3.00	1.50	.90
34	Jay Johnstone	3.00	1.50	.90
35	Mark Lee	3.00	1.50	.90
36	Bob Shirley	3.00	1.50	.90

1980 Family Fun Centers Padres

Six Padres players or staff are featured on these 13" x 10" or 12-1/2" x 9-1/2" coupon sheets. At the right end of each glossy paper sheet is a group of coupons and advertising for the recreation centers, printed in black, yellow and green. At left are six photos. Each of the 3" x 4" photos has a color player pose. At either top or bottom, depending on placement on the sheet, is the player name in black, "FAMILY FUN CENTER" in green and a red building logo. Backs are blank and the sheets are not perforated.

		NM	EX	VG
	Complete Set (7):	80.00	40.00	24.00
	Common Sheet:	7.00	3.50	2.00
(1)	Kurt Bevacqua, Dave Cash, Paul Dade, Rollie Fingers, Don Williams, Dave Winfield	20.00	10.00	6.00
(2)	Ed Brinkman, Dave Edwards, Jack Krol, Luis Salazar, Craig Stimac, John Urrea	7.00	3.50	2.00
(3)	Jerry Coleman, John D'Acquisto, Bill Fahey, Randy Jones, Gene Richards, Ozzie Smith	30.00	15.00	9.00
(4)	Dave Campbell, Juan Eichelberger, Barry Evans, Bobby Tolan, Jerry Turner, Rick Wise	7.00	3.50	2.00
(5)	John Curtis, Al Heist, Gary Lucas, Willie Montanez, Aurelio Rodriguez, Gene Tenace	7.00	3.50	2.00
(6)	Eddie Doucette, Chuck Estrada, Tim Flannery, Eric Rasmussen, Bob Shirley, San Diego Chicken	10.00	5.00	3.00
(7)	Von Joshua, Fred Kendall, Dennis Kinney, Jerry Mumphrey, Steve Mura, Dick Phillips	7.00	3.50	2.00

1916 Famous and Barr Clothiers

The advertisement for this St. Louis clothier is among the most commonly found on the backs of this 200-player set that parallels the more common M101-5 Blank Backs issue. Famous and Barr was one of many regional advertisers to use the cards for local promotions. Premiums over the same cards in M101-5 Blank Backs are modest for most players, but can be substantial for the top stars. The cards are printed in black-and-white and measure 1-5/8" x 3".

		NM	EX	VG
	Complete Set (200):	143,750	57,500	28,750
	Common Player:	125.00	50.00	25.00
1	Babe Adams	190.00	65.00	25.00
2	Sam Agnew	125.00	50.00	25.00
3	Eddie Ainsmith	125.00	50.00	25.00
4	Grover Alexander	2,065	825.00	415.00
5	Leon Ames	125.00	50.00	25.00
6	Jimmy Archer	125.00	50.00	25.00
7	Jimmy Austin	125.00	50.00	25.00
8	J. Franklin Baker	720.00	290.00	145.00
9	Dave Bancroft	720.00	290.00	145.00
10	Jack Barry	125.00	50.00	25.00
11	Zinn Beck	125.00	50.00	25.00
12	Lute Boone	125.00	50.00	25.00
13	Joe Benz	125.00	50.00	25.00
14	Bob Bescher	125.00	50.00	25.00
15	Al Betzel	125.00	50.00	25.00
16	Roger Bresnahan	720.00	290.00	145.00
17	Eddie Burns	125.00	50.00	25.00
18	Geo. J. Burns	125.00	50.00	25.00
19	Joe Bush	125.00	50.00	25.00
20	Owen Bush	125.00	50.00	25.00
21	Art Butler	125.00	50.00	25.00
22	Bobbie Byrne	125.00	50.00	25.00
23a	Forrest Cady (MAY NOT EXIST)			
23b	Mordecai Brown	720.00	290.00	145.00
24	Jimmy Callahan	125.00	50.00	25.00
25	Ray Caldwell	125.00	50.00	25.00
26	Max Carey	720.00	290.00	145.00
27	George Chalmers	125.00	50.00	25.00
28	Frank Chance	720.00	290.00	145.00
29	Ray Chapman	155.00	65.00	30.00
30	Larry Cheney	125.00	50.00	25.00
31	Eddie Cicotte	720.00	290.00	145.00
32	Tom Clarke	125.00	50.00	25.00
33	Eddie Collins	720.00	290.00	145.00
34	"Shauno" Collins	125.00	50.00	25.00
35	Charles Comisky (Comiskey)	720.00	290.00	145.00
36	Joe Connolly	125.00	50.00	25.00
37	Luther Cook	125.00	50.00	25.00
38	Jack Coombs	125.00	50.00	25.00
39	Dan Costello	125.00	50.00	25.00
40	Harry Coveleskie (Coveleski)	125.00	50.00	25.00
41	Gavvy Cravath	125.00	50.00	25.00
42	Sam Crawford	720.00	290.00	145.00
43	Jean Dale	125.00	50.00	25.00
44	Jake Daubert	125.00	50.00	25.00
45	Geo. A. Davis Jr.	125.00	50.00	25.00
46	Charles Deal	125.00	50.00	25.00
47	Al Demaree	125.00	50.00	25.00
48	William Doak	125.00	50.00	25.00
49	Bill Donovan	125.00	50.00	25.00
50	Charles Dooin	125.00	50.00	25.00
51	Mike Doolan	125.00	50.00	25.00
52	Larry Doyle	125.00	50.00	25.00
53	Jean Dubuc	125.00	50.00	25.00
54	Oscar Dugey	125.00	50.00	25.00
55	Johnny Evers	720.00	290.00	145.00
56	Urban Faber	720.00	290.00	145.00
57	"Hap" Felsch	1,000	400.00	200.00
58	Bill Fischer	125.00	50.00	25.00

59	Ray Fisher	125.00	50.00	25.00
60	Max Flack	125.00	50.00	25.00
61	Art Fletcher	125.00	50.00	25.00
62	Eddie Foster	125.00	50.00	25.00
63	Jacques Fournier	125.00	50.00	25.00
64	Del Gainer (Gainor)	125.00	50.00	25.00
65	Larry Gardner	125.00	50.00	25.00
66	Joe Gedeon	125.00	50.00	25.00
67	Gus Getz	125.00	50.00	25.00
68	Geo. Gibson	125.00	50.00	25.00
69	Wilbur Good	125.00	50.00	25.00
70	Hank Gowdy	125.00	50.00	25.00
71	John Graney	125.00	50.00	25.00
72	Tom Griffith	125.00	50.00	25.00
73	Heinie Groh	125.00	50.00	25.00
74	Earl Hamilton	125.00	50.00	25.00
75	Bob Harmon	125.00	50.00	25.00
76	Roy Hartzell	125.00	50.00	25.00
77	Claude Hendrix	125.00	50.00	25.00
78	Olaf Henriksen	125.00	50.00	25.00
79	John Henry	125.00	50.00	25.00
80	"Buck" Herzog	125.00	50.00	25.00
81	Hugh High	125.00	50.00	25.00
82	Dick Hoblitzell	125.00	50.00	25.00
83	Harry Hooper	720.00	290.00	145.00
84	Ivan Howard	125.00	50.00	25.00
85	Miller Huggins	720.00	290.00	145.00
86	Joe Jackson	25,000	10,000	5,000
87	William James	125.00	50.00	25.00
88	Harold Janvrin	125.00	50.00	25.00
89	Hugh Jennings	720.00	290.00	145.00
90	Walter Johnson	2,190	875.00	440.00
91	Fielder Jones	125.00	50.00	25.00
92	Bennie Kauff	125.00	50.00	25.00
93	Wm. Killefer Jr.	125.00	50.00	25.00
94	Ed. Konetchy	125.00	50.00	25.00
95	Napoleon Lajoie	720.00	290.00	145.00
96	Jack Lapp	125.00	50.00	25.00
97a	John Lavan (Correct spelling.)	125.00	50.00	25.00
97b	John Lavin (Incorret spelling.) (MAY NOT EXIST)			
98	Jimmy Lavender	125.00	50.00	25.00
99	"Nemo" Leibold	125.00	50.00	25.00
100	H.B. Leonard	125.00	50.00	25.00
101	Duffy Lewis	125.00	50.00	25.00
102	Hans Lobert	125.00	50.00	25.00
103	Tom Long	125.00	50.00	25.00
104	Fred Luderus	125.00	50.00	25.00
105	Connie Mack	720.00	290.00	145.00
106	Lee Magee	125.00	50.00	25.00
107	Al. Mamaux	125.00	50.00	25.00
108	Leslie Mann	125.00	50.00	25.00
109	"Rabbit" Maranville	720.00	290.00	145.00
110	Rube Marquard	720.00	290.00	145.00
111	Armando Marsans	155.00	65.00	30.00
112	J. Erskine Mayer	155.00	65.00	30.00
113	George McBride	125.00	50.00	25.00
114	John J. McGraw	720.00	290.00	145.00
115	Jack McInnis	125.00	50.00	25.00
116	Fred Merkle	125.00	50.00	25.00
117	Chief Meyers	125.00	50.00	25.00
118	Clyde Milan	125.00	50.00	25.00
119	Otto Miller	125.00	50.00	25.00
120	Willie Mitchel (Mitchell)	125.00	50.00	25.00
121	Fred Mollwitz	125.00	50.00	25.00
122	J. Herbert Moran	125.00	50.00	25.00
123	Pat Moran	125.00	50.00	25.00
124	Ray Morgan	125.00	50.00	25.00
125	Geo. Moriarty	125.00	50.00	25.00
126	Guy Morton	125.00	50.00	25.00
127	Ed. Murphy (Photo actually Danny Murphy.)	125.00	50.00	25.00
128	John Murray	125.00	50.00	25.00
129	"Hy" Myers	125.00	50.00	25.00
130	J.A. Niehoff	125.00	50.00	25.00
131	Leslie Nunamaker	125.00	50.00	25.00
132	Rube Oldring	125.00	50.00	25.00
133	Oliver O'Mara	125.00	50.00	25.00
134	Steve O'Neill	125.00	50.00	25.00
135	"Dode" Paskert	125.00	50.00	25.00
136	Roger Peckinpaugh (Photo actually Gavvy Cravath.)	125.00	50.00	25.00
137	E.J. Pfeffer (Photo actually Jeff Pfeffer.)	125.00	50.00	25.00
138	Geo. Pierce (Pearce)	125.00	50.00	25.00
139	Walter Pipp	125.00	50.00	25.00
140	Derril Pratt (Derrill)	125.00	50.00	25.00
141	Bill Rariden	125.00	50.00	25.00
142	Eppa Rixey	720.00	290.00	145.00
143	Davey Robertson	125.00	50.00	25.00
144	Wilbert Robinson	720.00	290.00	145.00
145	Bob Roth	125.00	50.00	25.00
146	Ed. Roush	720.00	290.00	145.00
147	Clarence Rowland	125.00	50.00	25.00
148	"Nap" Rucker	125.00	50.00	25.00
149	Dick Rudolph	125.00	50.00	25.00
150	Reb Russell	125.00	50.00	25.00
151	Babe Ruth	68,750	27,500	13,750
152	Vic Saier	125.00	50.00	25.00
153	"Slim" Sallee	125.00	50.00	25.00
154	"Germany" Schaefer	125.00	50.00	25.00
155	Ray Schalk	720.00	290.00	145.00
156	Walter Schang	125.00	50.00	25.00
157	Chas. Schmidt	125.00	50.00	25.00
158	Frank Schulte	125.00	50.00	25.00
159	Jim Scott	125.00	50.00	25.00
160	Everett Scott	125.00	50.00	25.00
161	Tom Seaton	125.00	50.00	25.00
162	Howard Shanks	125.00	50.00	25.00
163	Bob Shawkey (Photo actually Jack McInnis.)	125.00	50.00	25.00
164	Ernie Shore	125.00	50.00	25.00
165	Burt Shotton	125.00	50.00	25.00
166	George Sisler	720.00	290.00	145.00
167	J. Carlisle Smith	125.00	50.00	25.00
168	Fred Snodgrass	125.00	50.00	25.00
169	Geo. Stallings	125.00	50.00	25.00

170	Oscar Stanage (Photo actually Chas. Schmidt.)	125.00	50.00	25.00
171	Charles Stengel	815.00	325.00	165.00
172	Milton Stock	125.00	50.00	25.00
173	Amos Strunk (Photo actually Olaf Henriksen.)	125.00	50.00	25.00
174	Billy Sullivan	125.00	50.00	25.00
175	Chas. Tesreau	125.00	50.00	25.00
176	Jim Thorpe	13,750	5,500	2,750
177	Joe Tinker	720.00	290.00	145.00
178	Fred Toney	125.00	50.00	25.00
179	Terry Turner	125.00	50.00	25.00
180	Jim Vaughn	125.00	50.00	25.00
181	Bob Veach	125.00	50.00	25.00
182	James Voix	125.00	50.00	25.00
183	Oscar Vitt	125.00	50.00	25.00
184	Hans Wagner	5,000	1,065	530.00
185	Clarence Walker (Photo not Walker.)	125.00	50.00	25.00
186	Zach Wheat	720.00	290.00	145.00
187	Ed. Walsh	720.00	290.00	145.00
188	Buck Weaver	720.00	290.00	145.00
189	Carl Weilman	125.00	50.00	25.00
190	Geo. Whitted	125.00	50.00	25.00
191	Fred Williams	125.00	50.00	25.00
192	Art Wilson	125.00	50.00	25.00
193	J. Owen Wilson	125.00	50.00	25.00
194	Ivy Wingo	125.00	50.00	25.00
195	"Mel" Wolfgang	125.00	50.00	25.00
196	Joe Wood	220.00	90.00	45.00
197	Steve Yerkes	125.00	50.00	25.00
198	Rollie Zeider	125.00	50.00	25.00
199	Heiny Zimmerman	125.00	50.00	25.00
200	Ed. Zwilling	125.00	50.00	25.00

1906 Fan Craze - American League

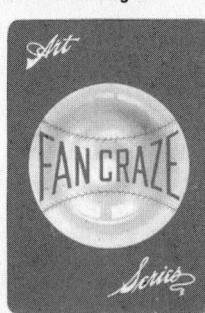

One of the earliest 20th Century baseball card sets, this issue from the Fan Craze Co. of Cincinnati was designed as a deck of playing cards and was intended to be used as a baseball table game. Separate sets were issued for the National League, with backs printed in red, and the American League, which are blue-backed. Both sets feature black-and-white player portraits in an oval vignette with the player's name and team below. The top of the card indicates one of many various baseball plays, such as "Single," "Out at First," "Strike," "Stolen Base," etc. The unnumbered cards measure 2-1/2" x 3-1/2". An ad card identifies the set as "An Artistic Constellation of Great Stars." Sears sold the set for 48 cents, postpaid.

		NM	EX	VG
Complete Set (51):		8,250	4,125	2,475
Complete Boxed Set:		9,350	4,675	2,750
Common Player:		90.00	45.00	25.00
(1)	Nick Altrock	110.00	55.00	35.00
(2)	Jim Barrett	90.00	45.00	25.00
(3)	Harry Bay	90.00	45.00	25.00
(4)	Albert Bender	330.00	165.00	100.00
(5)	Bill Bernhardt	90.00	45.00	25.00
(6)	W. Bradley	90.00	45.00	25.00
(7)	Jack Chesbro	330.00	165.00	100.00
(8)	Jimmy Collins	330.00	165.00	100.00
(9)	Sam Crawford	330.00	165.00	100.00
(10)	Lou Criger	90.00	45.00	25.00
(11)	Lave Cross	90.00	45.00	25.00
(12)	Monte Cross	90.00	45.00	25.00
(13)	Harry Davis	90.00	45.00	25.00
(14)	Bill Dinneen	90.00	45.00	25.00
(15)	Pat (Bill) Donovan	90.00	45.00	25.00
(16)	Pat Dougherty	90.00	45.00	25.00
(17)	Norman Elberfield (Elberfeld)	90.00	45.00	25.00
(18)	Hoke Ferris (Hobe)	90.00	45.00	25.00
(19)	Elmer Flick	330.00	165.00	100.00
(20)	Buck Freeman	90.00	45.00	25.00
(21)	Fred Glade	90.00	45.00	25.00
(22)	Clark Griffith	330.00	165.00	100.00
(23)	Charley Hickman	90.00	45.00	25.00
(24)	Wm. Holmes	90.00	45.00	25.00
(25)	Harry Howell	90.00	45.00	25.00
(26)	Frank Isbel (Isbell)	90.00	45.00	25.00
(27)	Albert Jacobson	90.00	45.00	25.00
(28)	Ban Johnson	330.00	165.00	100.00
(29)	Fielder Jones	90.00	45.00	25.00
(30)	Adrian Joss	330.00	165.00	100.00
(31)	Billy Keeler	330.00	165.00	100.00
(32)	Napolean Lajoie	330.00	165.00	100.00
(33)	Connie Mack	330.00	165.00	100.00
(34)	Jimmy McAleer	90.00	45.00	25.00
(35)	Jim McGuire	90.00	45.00	25.00
(36)	Earl Moore	90.00	45.00	25.00
(37)	George Mullen (Mullin)	90.00	45.00	25.00
(38)	Billy Owen (Frank Owens)	90.00	45.00	25.00
(39)	Fred Parent	90.00	45.00	25.00
(40)	Case Patten	90.00	45.00	25.00
(41)	Ed Plank	550.00	275.00	165.00
(42)	Ossie Schreckengost	90.00	45.00	25.00
(43)	Jake Stahl	90.00	45.00	25.00
(44)	Fred (George) Stone	90.00	45.00	25.00
(45)	Wm. Sudhoff	90.00	45.00	25.00
(46)	Roy (Terry) Turner	90.00	45.00	25.00
(47)	G.E. Waddell	330.00	165.00	100.00
(48)	Bob Wallace	330.00	165.00	100.00
(49)	G. Harris White	90.00	45.00	25.00
(50)	Geo. Winters (Winter)	90.00	45.00	25.00
(51)	Cy Young	1,320	660.00	395.00

1906 Fan Craze - National League

Identical in size and format to the American League set of two years previous, this set of unnumbered cards was issued by the Fan Craze Co. of Cincinnati in 1906 and was designed like a deck of playing cards. The cards were intended to be used in playing a baseball table game. The National League cards are printed with red backs and black-and-white player photos on front. Sears sold the set for 48 cents postpaid.

		NM	EX	VG
Complete Set (54):		11,000	5,500	3,300
Complete Boxed Set:		17,600	8,800	5,225
Common Player:		65.00	35.00	20.00
(1)	Leon Ames	65.00	35.00	20.00
(2)	Clarence Beaumont	65.00	35.00	20.00
(3)	Jake Beckley	330.00	165.00	100.00
(4)	Billy Bergen	65.00	35.00	20.00
(5)	Roger Bresnahan	330.00	165.00	100.00
(6)	George Brown (Browne)	65.00	35.00	20.00
(7)	Mordacai Brown	330.00	165.00	100.00
(8)	Jas. Casey	65.00	35.00	20.00
(9)	Frank Chance	330.00	165.00	100.00
(10)	Fred Clarke	330.00	165.00	100.00
(11)	Thos. Corcoran	65.00	35.00	20.00
(12)	Bill Dahlen	65.00	35.00	20.00
(13)	Mike Donlin	65.00	35.00	20.00
(14)	Charley Dooin	65.00	35.00	20.00
(15)	Mickey Doolin (Doolan)	65.00	35.00	20.00
(16)	Hugh Duffy	330.00	165.00	100.00
(17)	John E. Dunleavy	65.00	35.00	20.00
(18)	Bob Ewing	65.00	35.00	20.00
(19)	"Chick" Fraser	65.00	35.00	20.00
(20)	J. Edward (Edward H.) Hanlon	330.00	165.00	100.00
(21)	G.E. Howard	65.00	35.00	20.00
(22)	Miller Huggins	330.00	165.00	100.00
(23)	Joseph Kelley	330.00	165.00	100.00
(24)	John Kling	65.00	35.00	20.00
(25)	Tommy Leach	65.00	35.00	20.00
(26)	Harry Lumley	65.00	35.00	20.00
(27)	Carl Lundgren	65.00	35.00	20.00
(28)	Bill Maloney	65.00	35.00	20.00
(29)	Dan McGann	65.00	35.00	20.00
(30)	Joe McGinnity	330.00	165.00	100.00
(31)	John J. McGraw	330.00	165.00	100.00
(32)	Harry McIntire (McIntyre)	65.00	35.00	20.00
(33)	Charley Nichols	550.00	275.00	165.00
(34)	Mike O'Neil (O'Neill)	65.00	35.00	20.00
(35)	Orville (Orval) Overall	65.00	35.00	20.00
(36)	Frank Pfeffer	65.00	35.00	20.00
(37)	Deacon Phillippe	65.00	35.00	20.00
(38)	Charley Pittinger	65.00	35.00	20.00
(39)	Harry C. Pulliam	65.00	35.00	20.00
(40)	Claude Ritchey	65.00	35.00	20.00
(41)	Ed Ruelbach (Reulbach)	65.00	35.00	20.00
(42)	J. Bentley Seymour	65.00	35.00	20.00
(43)	Jim Sheckard	65.00	35.00	20.00
(44)	Jack Taylor	65.00	35.00	20.00
(45)	Luther H. Taylor	220.00	110.00	65.00
(46)	Fred Tenny (Tenney)	65.00	35.00	20.00
(47)	Harry Theilman (Jake Thielman)	65.00	35.00	20.00
(48)	Roy Thomas	65.00	35.00	20.00
(49)	Hans Wagner	5,000	2,065	1,240
(50)	Jake Weimer	65.00	35.00	20.00
(51)	Bob Wicker	65.00	35.00	20.00
(52)	Victor Willis	330.00	165.00	100.00
(53)	Lew (George "Hooks") Wiltsie	65.00	35.00	20.00
(54)	Irving Young	65.00	35.00	20.00

1922 Fans Cigarettes (T231)

FRANK BAKER   61

More mystery surrounds this obscure set than any other tobacco issue. In fact, the only evidence of its existence until 1992 was a photocopy of a single card of Pittsburgh Pirates outfielder Carson Bigbee. Even the owner of the card is unknown. Cards measure approximately 2-1/2" x 1-1/2" and are black-and-white. Adding to the mystery is the number "85" which appears in the lower right corner on the front of the card, apparently indicating there were at least that many cards in the set. In 1992 card "61" was reported. Card backs displays the player's batting averages for each season from 1918 through 1921 and includes the line: "I select (name) leading batter of all (position), packed with FANS cigarettes." The statement is followed by blanks for a person to fill in their name and address, as if the card were some sort of "ballot." With only one specimen known of each, these are among the rarest baseball cards in the hobby. Their American Card Catalog designation is T231.

Values Undetermined
61   Frank Baker
85   Carson Bigbee

1939 Father & Son Shoes

Chuck Klein, outfielder, Phillies
Compliments Father & Son Shoes

This set features Phillies and A's players and was distributed in the Philadelphia area in 1939 by Father & Son Shoes stores. The unnumbered black and white cards measure 3" x 4". The player's name, position and team appear below the photo, along with the line "Compliments of Fathers & Son Shoes." The backs are blank. The checklist, arranged here alphabetically, may be incomplete.

		NM	EX	VG
Complete Set (17):		5,000	2,500	1,500
Common Player:		300.00	150.00	90.00
(1)	Morrie Arnovich	300.00	150.00	90.00
(2)	Earl Brucker	300.00	150.00	90.00
(3)	George Caster	300.00	150.00	90.00
(4)	Sam Chapman	300.00	150.00	90.00
(5)	Spud Davis	300.00	150.00	90.00
(6)	Joe Gantenbein	300.00	150.00	90.00
(7)	Bob Johnson	300.00	150.00	90.00
(8)	Chuck Klein	750.00	375.00	225.00
(9)	Herschel Martin	300.00	150.00	90.00
(10)	Merrill May	300.00	150.00	90.00
(11)	Wally Moses	300.00	150.00	90.00
(12)	Emmett Mueller	300.00	150.00	90.00
(13)	Hugh Mulcahy	300.00	150.00	90.00
(14)	Skeeter Newsome	300.00	150.00	90.00
(15)	Claude Passeau	300.00	150.00	90.00
(16)	George Scharien (Scharein)	300.00	150.00	90.00
(17)	Dick Siebert	300.00	150.00	90.00

1913 Fatima Team Cards (T200)

 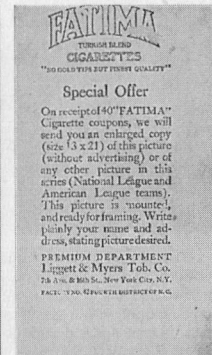

Issued by the Ligget & Myers Tobacco Co. in 1913 with Fatima brand cigarettes, the T200 set consists of eight National and eight American League team cards. The cards measure 2-5/8" x 4-3/4" and are glossy photographs on paper stock. Although it is unknown why, several of the cards are more difficult to obtain than others. The team cards feature 369 different players, managers and mascots. The card backs contain an offer for an enlarged copy (13" x 21") of a team card, minus the advertising on front, in exchange for 40 Fatima cigarette coupons.

	NM	EX	VG
Complete Set (16):	20,000	10,000	6,000
Common Card:	575.00	285.00	175.00

(1)	Boston Nationals	2,000	500.00	300.00
(2)	Brooklyn Nationals	950.00	475.00	285.00
(3)	Chicago Nationals	575.00	285.00	175.00
(4)	Cincinnati Nationals	700.00	350.00	210.00
(5)	New York Nationals	1,100	550.00	330.00
(6)	Philadelphia Nationals	575.00	285.00	175.00
(7)	Pittsburgh Nationals	750.00	375.00	225.00
(8)	St. Louis Nationals	1,750	875.00	525.00
(9)	Boston Americans	1,650	825.00	500.00
(10)	Chicago Americans	1,000	500.00	300.00
(11)	Cleveland Americans	1,900	950.00	575.00
(12)	Detroit Americans	3,750	1,875	1,125
(13)	New York Americans	2,250	1,125	675.00
(14)	Philadelphia Americans	650.00	325.00	200.00
(15)	St. Louis Americans	1,600	800.00	480.00
(16)	Washington Americans	2,100	1,050	625.00

1913 Fatima Premiums

DETROIT AMERICANS

Among the rarest of the tobacco cards are the large-format (21" x 13") versions of the T200 Fatima team photos which could be obtained by redeeming 40 coupons from cigarette packs. The premium-size team photos are virtually identical to the smaller cards, except they do not carry the Fatima advertising on the front. Because of their large size, the premiums are seldom seen in top grade. The complete set price is quoted as a hypothetical proposition only; none is known.

		NM	EX	VG
Common Card:		7,500	3,500	2,000
(1)	Boston Nationals	8,000	4,000	2,400
(2)	Brooklyn Nationals	8,000	4,000	2,400
(3)	Chicago Nationals	9,500	4,750	2,850
(4)	Cincinnati Nationals	7,500	3,500	2,000
(5)	New York Nationals	8,000	4,000	2,400
(6)	Philadelphia Nationals	7,500	3,500	2,000
(7)	Pittsburg Nationals	10,000	5,000	3,000
(8)	St. Louis Nationals	7,500	3,750	2,250
(9)	Boston Americans	12,500	6,250	3,750
(10)	Chicago Americans	8,000	4,000	2,400
(11)	Cleveland Americans	15,000	7,500	4,500
(12)	Detroit Americans	15,000	7,500	4,500
(13)	New York Americans	12,500	6,250	3,750
(14)	Philadelphia Americans	9,250	4,625	2,775
(15)	St. Louis Americans	9,000	4,500	2,700
(16)	Washington Americans	7,500	3,500	2,000

1913-1915 Fatima Posters

FAMOUS PITCHER OF "SENATORS"

These blank-back, black-and-white (1913) or b/w with a color picture of a cigarette pack (1914-15) window posters were produced by Pictorial News Co. of New York for distribution by Fatima Cigarettes, whose advertising appears in the lower-right corner of the 12-1/2" x 19" pictures. To the left of the advertising are a couple of sentences about the player(s) pictured (usually in an action pose). The pictures are numbered, but there is currently no idea as to the extent of the issue.

		NM	EX	VG
6	Frank Chance's New York Americans in Bermuda	1,200	600.00	360.00
15	Christy Mathewson	6,000	3,000	2,000
22	Ty Cobb	7,500	3,500	2,500
31	Pittsburgh Pirates Only Hope of West in National Race	1,000	500.00	300.00
33	Joe Jackson	4,500	2,250	1,350
35	Athletics' Star Pitchers the Giants Will Have to Beat (Chief Bender, Jack Coombs, Eddie Plank)	450.00	225.00	135.00
36	Cleveland Strong Second in the American League Race	650.00	325.00	200.00
43	Chicago Cubs team	1,200	600.00	360.00

45	Plays that Made Baseball History (Various action photos.)	250.00	125.00	75.00
51	Walter Johnson	5,500	2,750	1,650
56	Opposing Pitchers in the Coming World's Series Battles (Christy Mathewson, Rube Marquard, Jeff Tesreau, Al Demaree, Chief Bender, Boardwalk Brown, Byron Houck, Eddie Plank)	650.00	325.00	195.00
105	Giants 'Clearing the Deck for Action' Down in Marlin (Mathewson, Snodgrass, Fletcher, etc.)	325.00	160.00	95.00
153	American League Pennant Winners Ready For the World's Series (1914 Philadelphia A's)	1,500	750.00	450.00
226	Ty Cobb, The Most Talked About Man in Big League Baseball	7,500	3,750	2,250
259	(1915 Philadelphia Phillies)	2,500	1,250	750.00
260	Red Sox Ready to do Battle for World's Championship (1915 Red Sox)	3,500	1,750	1,050

1914 Fatima (T222)

Alexander-Phila. Nationals

FATIMA
TURKISH BLEND
CIGARETTES
"NO GOLD TIPS BUT FINEST QUALITY"

Collection of 100 photographs of famous Baseball players, American Athletic champions and Photoplay stars.

"FATIMA" Cigarette Coupons have a value of at out 1½c each in procuring premiums described in our illustrated catalogue—an assortment of about 800 useful and valuable premiums.

Liggett & Myers Tob. Co.
FACTORY NO. 25 SECOND DISTRICT OF VA.

Unlike the typical 20th Century tobacco card issues, the T222 Fatima cards are glossy photographs on a thin paper stock and measure a larger 2-1/2" x 4-1/2". According to the back of the card, the set includes "100 photographs of famous Baseball Players, American Athletic Champions and Photoplay stars." The baseball portion of the set appears to be complete at 52. The set includes players from 13 of the 16 major league teams (no Red Sox, White Sox or Pirates). Most cards are seen with a small black number from 2-9 or 12-15 beneath the player's name. The same number can be found on up to seven cards. Cards with numbers 12-15 are considered short-prints and so designated in this alphabetical checklist.

		NM	EX	VG
Complete Set (52):		137,500	56,250	28,125
Common Player:		1,440	565.00	280.00
(1)	Grover Alexander	20,000	4,500	2,250
(2)	Jimmy Archer	1,440	565.00	280.00
(3)	Jimmy Austin (SP)	3,440	1,375	690.00
(4)	Jack Barry	1,440	565.00	280.00
(5)	George Baumgardner (SP)	3,440	1,375	690.00
(6)	Rube Benton	1,440	565.00	280.00
(7)	Roger Bresnahan	4,500	1,815	905.00
(8)	Boardwalk Brown	1,440	565.00	280.00
(9)	George Burns	1,440	565.00	280.00
(10)	Bullet Joe Bush	1,440	565.00	280.00
(11)	George Chalmers	1,440	565.00	280.00
(12)	Frank Chance	4,500	1,815	905.00
(13)	Al Demaree	1,440	565.00	280.00
(14)	Art Fletcher	1,440	565.00	280.00
(15)	Earl Hamilton (SP)	3,440	1,375	690.00
(16)	John Henry (SP)	3,440	1,375	690.00
(17)	Byron Houck	1,440	565.00	280.00
(18)	Miller Huggins	4,500	1,815	905.00
(19)	Hughie Jennings	4,500	1,815	905.00
(20)	Walter Johnson (SP)	15,625	6,250	3,125
(21)	Ray Keating (SP)	3,440	1,375	690.00
(22)	Jack Lapp	1,440	565.00	280.00
(23)	Tommy Leach	1,440	565.00	280.00
(24)	Nemo Leibold (SP)	3,440	1,375	690.00
(25)	Jack Lelivelt (SP)	3,440	1,375	690.00
(26)	Hans Lobert (SP)	3,440	1,375	690.00
(27)	Lee Magee (SP)	3,440	1,375	690.00
(28)	Sherry Magee (SP)	3,440	1,375	690.00
(29)	Fritz Maisel	1,440	565.00	280.00
(30)	Rube Marquard	4,500	1,815	905.00
(31)	George McBride (SP)	3,440	1,375	690.00
(32)	Stuffy McInnis	1,440	565.00	280.00
(33)	Larry McLean	1,440	565.00	280.00
(34)	Ray Morgan (SP)	3,440	1,375	690.00
(35)	Eddie Murphy	1,440	565.00	280.00
(36)	Red Murray	1,440	565.00	280.00
(37)	Rube Oldring	1,440	565.00	280.00
(38)	Bill Orr	1,440	565.00	280.00
(39)	Hub Perdue	1,440	565.00	280.00
(40)	Art Phelan	1,440	565.00	280.00
(41)	Ed Reulbach	1,440	565.00	280.00
(42)	Vic Saier	1,140	565.00	280.00
(43)	Slim Sallee	1,440	565.00	280.00
(44)	Wally Schang	1,440	565.00	280.00
(45)	Wildfire Schulte (SP)	3,440	1,375	690.00
(46)	J.C. "Red" Smith (SP)	3,440	1,375	690.00

		NM	EX	VG
(47)	Amos Strunk	1,440	565.00	280.00
(48)	Bill Sweeney	1,440	565.00	280.00
(49)	Lefty Tyler	1,440	565.00	280.00
(50)	Ossie Vitt	1,440	565.00	280.00
(51)	Ivy Wingo	1,440	565.00	280.00
(52)	Heinie Zimmerman	1,440	565.00	280.00

1955 Felin's Franks

Because of the relatively few specimens in collectors' hands, it is believed this hot dog issue was never actually released. The 4" x 3-5/8" round-cornered panels have a red border front and back with a color player photo on the left side of the front. At right-front are the 1954 stats of a player different than that pictured. Each half of the front shares a large black number. According to the card back, hot dog buyers were supposed to match the pictures and stats of 30 different players to have a chance to win prizes.

		NM	EX	VG
Common Player:		1,250	625.00	375.00
1	Mayo Smith	1,250	625.00	375.00
2	Unknown (Probably coach Benny Bengough.)			
3	Wally Moses	1,250	625.00	375.00
4	Whit Wyatt	1,250	625.00	375.00
5	Maje McDonnell	1,250	625.00	375.00
6	Wiechec (Trainer)	750.00	375.00	225.00
7	Murry Dickson	1,250	625.00	375.00
8	Earl Torgeson	1,250	625.00	375.00
9	Bobby Morgan	1,250	625.00	375.00
10	John Meyer	1,250	625.00	375.00
11	Bob Miller	1,250	625.00	375.00
12	Jim Owens	1,250	625.00	375.00
13	Steve Ridzik	1,250	625.00	375.00
14	Robin Roberts	2,000	1,000	600.00
15	Unknown (Probably Curt Simmons.)			
16	Herm Wehmeier	1,250	625.00	375.00
17	Smoky Burgess	1,250	625.00	375.00
18	Stan Lopata	1,250	625.00	375.00
19	Gus Niarhos	1,250	625.00	375.00
20	Floyd Baker	1,250	625.00	375.00
21	Marv Blaylock	1,250	625.00	375.00
22	Granny Hamner	1,250	625.00	375.00
23	Willie Jones	1,250	625.00	375.00
24	Unknown			
25	Unknown			
26	Richie Ashburn	2,250	1,125	675.00
27	Joe Lonnett	1,250	625.00	375.00
28	Mel Clark	1,250	625.00	375.00
29	Bob Greenwood	1,250	625.00	375.00
30	Unknown			

1913 Fenway Breweries/Tom Barker Game

Presumably distributed as a promotion for its Fenway brand of beer, a specially labeled boxed set of the Tom Barker baseball game cards was issued. Only the box, the Score Card and the card of Frank "Home Run" Baker are found bearing the red advertising overprint.

	NM	EX	VG
Complete Set (54):	6,000	3,000	1,800
Frank Baker	175.00	90.00	55.00
Score Card	40.00	20.00	12.00

1916 Ferguson Bakery Felt Pennants (BF2)

Issued circa 1916, this unnumbered set consists of 97 felt pennants with a small black-and-white player photo glued to each. The triangular pennants measure approximately 2-7/8" across the wide top and taper to a length of about 6". The photos are about 1-1/4" x 1-3/4" and appear to be identical to photos used for The Sporting News issues of the same period. The pennants list the player's name and team. The pennants were given away as premiums with the purchase of five-cent

loaves of Ferguson Bakery Bread in the Roxbury, Mass. area. It is believed that each player can be found on several different-ent colors of background felt.

		NM	EX	VG
Complete Set (97):		27,500	13,500	8,250
Common Player:		175.00	85.00	50.00
(1)	Grover Alexander	600.00	300.00	180.00
(2)	Jimmy Archer	175.00	85.00	50.00
(3)	J. Franklin Baker	450.00	225.00	135.00
(4)	Dave Bancroft	450.00	225.00	135.00
(5)	Jack Barry	175.00	85.00	50.00
(6)	"Chief" Bender	450.00	225.00	135.00
(7)	Joe Benz	175.00	85.00	50.00
(8)	Mordecai Brown	450.00	225.00	135.00
(9)	Geo. J. Burns	175.00	85.00	50.00
(10)	"Donie" Bush	175.00	85.00	50.00
(11)	Forrest Cady	175.00	85.00	50.00
(12)	Max Carey	450.00	225.00	135.00
(13)	Ray Chapman	300.00	150.00	90.00
(14)	Ty Cobb	1,800	900.00	550.00
(15)	Eddie Collins	450.00	225.00	135.00
(16)	"Shauno" Collins	175.00	85.00	50.00
(17)	Charles Comiskey	450.00	225.00	135.00
(18)	Harry Coveleskie (Coveleski)	175.00	85.00	50.00
(19)	Gavvy Cravath	175.00	85.00	50.00
(20)	Sam Crawford	450.00	225.00	135.00
(21)	Jake Daubert	175.00	85.00	50.00
(22)	Josh Devore	175.00	85.00	50.00
(23)	Charles Dooin	175.00	85.00	50.00
(24)	Larry Doyle	175.00	85.00	50.00
(25)	Jean Dubuc	175.00	85.00	50.00
(26)	Johnny Evers	450.00	225.00	135.00
(27)	Urban Faber	450.00	225.00	135.00
(28)	Eddie Foster	175.00	85.00	50.00
(29)	Del Gainer (Gainor)	175.00	85.00	50.00
(30)	"Chic" Gandil	375.00	185.00	110.00
(31)	Joe Gedeon	175.00	85.00	50.00
(32)	Hank Gowdy	175.00	85.00	50.00
(33)	Earl Hamilton	175.00	85.00	50.00
(34)	Claude Hendrix	175.00	85.00	50.00
(35)	Buck Herzog	175.00	85.00	50.00
(36)	Harry Hooper	450.00	225.00	135.00
(37)	Miller Huggins	450.00	225.00	135.00
(38)	Joe Jackson	3,500	1,750	1,000
(39)	William James	175.00	85.00	50.00
(40)	Hugh Jennings	450.00	225.00	135.00
(41)	Walter Johnson	900.00	450.00	275.00
(42)	Fielder Jones	175.00	85.00	50.00
(43)	Joe Judge	175.00	85.00	50.00
(44)	Benny Kauff	175.00	85.00	50.00
(45)	Wm. Killefer	175.00	85.00	50.00
(46)	Napoleon Lajoie	450.00	225.00	135.00
(47)	Jack Lapp	175.00	85.00	50.00
(48)	John Lavan	175.00	85.00	50.00
(49)	Jimmy Lavender	175.00	85.00	50.00
(50)	"Dutch" Leonard	175.00	85.00	50.00
(51)	Duffy Lewis	175.00	85.00	50.00
(52)	Hans Lobert	175.00	85.00	50.00
(53)	Fred Luderus	175.00	85.00	50.00
(54)	Connie Mack	450.00	225.00	135.00
(55)	Sherwood Magee	175.00	85.00	50.00
(56)	Al Mamaux	175.00	85.00	50.00
(57)	"Rabbit" Maranville	450.00	225.00	135.00
(58)	Rube Marquard	450.00	225.00	135.00
(59)	George McBride	175.00	85.00	50.00
(60)	John J. McGraw	450.00	225.00	135.00
(61)	Jack McInnis	175.00	85.00	50.00
(62)	Fred Merkle	175.00	85.00	50.00
(63)	Chief Meyers	175.00	85.00	50.00
(64)	Clyde Milan	175.00	85.00	50.00
(65)	Otto Miller	175.00	85.00	50.00
(66)	Pat Moran	175.00	85.00	50.00
(67)	Ray Morgan	175.00	85.00	50.00
(68)	Guy Morton	175.00	85.00	50.00
(69)	Ed. Murphy	175.00	85.00	50.00
(70)	Rube Oldring	175.00	85.00	50.00
(71)	"Dode" Paskert	175.00	85.00	50.00
(72)	Walter Pipp	175.00	85.00	50.00
(73)	Clarence Rowland	175.00	85.00	50.00
(74)	"Nap" Rucker	175.00	85.00	50.00
(75)	Dick Rudolph	175.00	85.00	50.00
(76)	Reb Russell	175.00	85.00	50.00
(77)	Vic Saier	175.00	85.00	50.00
(78)	"Slim" Sallee	175.00	85.00	50.00
(79)	Ray Schalk	450.00	225.00	135.00
(80)	Walter Schang	175.00	85.00	50.00
(81)	Frank Schulte	175.00	85.00	50.00
(82)	Jim Scott	175.00	85.00	50.00
(83)	George Sisler	450.00	225.00	135.00
(84)	Geo. Stallings	175.00	85.00	50.00
(85)	Oscar Stanage	175.00	85.00	50.00
(86)	"Jeff" Tesreau	175.00	85.00	50.00
(87)	Joe Tinker	450.00	225.00	135.00
(88)	Geo. Tyler	175.00	85.00	50.00
(89)	Jim Vaughn	175.00	85.00	50.00
(90)	Bobby Veach	175.00	85.00	50.00
(91)	Hans Wagner	1,350	675.00	400.00
(92)	Ed. Walsh	450.00	225.00	135.00
(93)	Buck Weaver	750.00	375.00	225.00
(94)	Ivy Wingo	175.00	85.00	50.00
(95)	Joe Wood	350.00	175.00	100.00
(96)	"Pep" Young	175.00	85.00	50.00
(97)	Heiny Zimmerman	175.00	85.00	50.00

1916 Ferguson Bakery Photo Prize Pennants

As part of its baseball insert and premium program, the Roxbury, Mass., bakery issued this series of large (9" x 24") felt pennants bearing a black-and-white player photo (3" x 5"). The colorful pennants are decorated with baseball graphics and have player and team identification. The pennants were a premium for redeeming 50 tickets from five-cent loaves of bread. Examples of the large-format pennants are so scarce only a handful of players are checklisted thus far.

		NM	EX	VG
Common Player:		9,000	4,500	2,750
(1)	Grover Alexander	15,000	7,500	4,500
(2)	Jack Barry	9,000	4,500	2,750
(3)	Ty Cobb	20,000	10,000	6,000
(4)	Bill Donovan	9,000	4,500	2,750
(5)	Miller Huggins	12,500	6,250	3,750
(6)	John McGraw	12,500	6,250	3,750

1957 Fine Arts Studio

 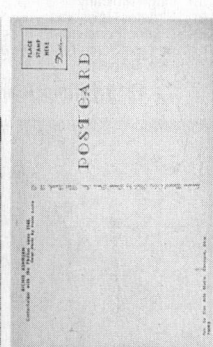

The date of issue on this card is theoretical with no real evidence present on the piece. Published by Fine Arts Studio of Cleveland, the 3-1/2" x 5-1/2" card has a borderless color photo on front. Player identification is on back with standard postcard markings and credit lines to the publisher and printer (Dexter Press of New York).

	NM	EX	VG
75062 Richie Ashburn	100.00	50.00	30.00

1959 First Federal Savings Famous Senators Matchbooks

Star Senators of the 20th Century are featured in this series of matchbook covers. The 1-1/2" x 4-1/2" matchbooks include a black-and-white player portrait photo and team logo on front. The sponsoring bank's advertising is on back. Player identification and information are printed inside. Values shown are for complete but empty covers, with the striker surface intact. Complete matchbooks with matches bring about 2X the values quoted.

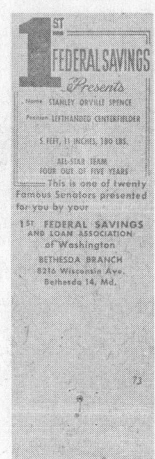

	NM	EX	VG
Complete Set (20):	325.00	160.00	95.00
Common Player:	15.00	7.50	4.50
(1) Nick Altrock	15.00	7.50	4.50
(2) Ossie Bluege	15.00	7.50	4.50
(3) Joe Cronin	20.00	10.00	6.00
(4) Alvin Crowder	15.00	7.50	4.50
(5) Goose Goslin	20.00	10.00	6.00
(6) Clark Griffith	20.00	10.00	6.00
(7) Bucky Harris	20.00	10.00	6.00
(8) Walter Johnson	45.00	22.00	13.50
(9) Joe Judge	15.00	7.50	4.50
(10) Harmon Killebrew	25.00	12.50	7.50
(11) Joe Kuhel	15.00	7.50	4.50
(12) Buddy Lewis	15.00	7.50	4.50
(13) Clyde Milan	15.00	7.50	4.50
(14) Buddy Myer	15.00	7.50	4.50
(15) Roger Peckinpaugh	15.00	7.50	4.50
(16) Sam Rice	20.00	10.00	6.00
(17) Roy Sievers	15.00	7.50	4.50
(18) Stanley Spence	15.00	7.50	4.50
(19) Mickey Vernon	15.00	7.50	4.50
(20) Samuel West	15.00	7.50	4.50

1953 First National Super Market Boston Red Sox

Four of the early 1950s Red Sox appear in this series issued by a Boston grocery chain. The cards may have been distributed in conjunction with players' in-store appearances. The cards measure 3-3/4" x 5" and are printed in black-and-white. A facsimile autograph appears on the front. Backs have the sponsor's advertising. The unnumbered cards are checklisted here alphabetically. See also 1953 Stop & Shop Boston Red Sox.

	NM	EX	VG
Complete Set (4):	2,500	1,250	750.00
Common Player:	750.00	375.00	225.00
(1) Billy Goodman	750.00	375.00	225.00
(2) Ellis Kinder	750.00	375.00	225.00
(3) Mel Parnell	750.00	375.00	225.00
(4) Sammy White	750.00	375.00	225.00

1951 Fischer's Bread Labels

This set of end-labels from loaves of bread consists of 32 player photos, each measuring approximately 2-3/4" square. The labels include the player's name, team and position, along with a few words about him. The bakery's slogan "Bread For Energy" appears in a dark band along the bottom. The set, which is unnumbered, was distributed in the Northeast.

	NM	EX	VG
Complete Set (32):	25,000	10,000	5,000
Common Player:	750.00	375.00	225.00
(1) Vern Bickford	750.00	300.00	150.00
(2) Ralph Branca	825.00	325.00	175.00
(3) Harry Brecheen	750.00	300.00	150.00
(4) "Chico" Carrasquel	750.00	300.00	150.00
(5) Cliff Chambers	750.00	300.00	150.00
(6) "Hoot" Evers	750.00	300.00	150.00
(7) Ned Garver	750.00	300.00	150.00
(8) Billy Goodman	750.00	300.00	150.00
(9) Gil Hodges	1,350	550.00	275.00
(10) Larry Jansen	750.00	300.00	150.00
(11) Willie Jones	750.00	300.00	150.00
(12) Eddie Joost	750.00	300.00	150.00
(13) George Kell	1,250	500.00	250.00
(14) Alex Kellner	750.00	300.00	150.00
(15) Ted Kluszewski	1,200	480.00	240.00
(16) Jim Konstanty	750.00	300.00	150.00
(17) Bob Lemon	1,250	500.00	250.00
(18) Cass Michaels	750.00	300.00	150.00
(19) Johnny Mize	1,250	500.00	250.00
(20) Irv Noren	750.00	300.00	150.00
(21) Andy Pafko	750.00	300.00	150.00
(22) Joe Page	750.00	300.00	150.00
(23) Mel Parnell	750.00	300.00	150.00
(24) Johnny Sain	825.00	330.00	165.00
(25) "Red" Schoendienst	1,250	500.00	250.00
(26) Roy Sievers	750.00	300.00	150.00
(27) Roy Smalley	750.00	300.00	150.00
(28) Herman Wehmeier	750.00	300.00	150.00
(29) Bill Werle	750.00	300.00	150.00
(30) Wes Westrum	750.00	300.00	150.00
(31) Early Wynn	1,250	500.00	250.00
(32) Gus Zernial	750.00	300.00	150.00

1970 Flavor-est Milk Milwaukee Brewers

Mike Hershberger

While purporting to be a dairy issue, this is actually a collectors' set produced by Illinois hobbyist Bob Solon. The cards picture members of the 1970 Brewers in their first year in Milwaukee. Posed action photos and portraits are printed in blue-and-white on a 2-3/8" x 4-1/4" format. The pictures are borderless at top and sides. At bottom is a white strip with the player name. Backs have a dairy ad. The unnumbered cards are checklisted here alphabetically. Ironically, this set was later reissued in a marked reprint.

	NM	EX	VG
Complete Set (24):	25.00	12.50	7.50
Common Player:	2.50	1.25	.70
(1) Gene Brabender	2.50	1.25	.70
(2) Dave Bristol	2.50	1.25	.70
(3) Wayne Comer	2.50	1.25	.70
(4) Cal Ermer	2.50	1.25	.70
(5) Greg Goossen	2.50	1.25	.70
(6) Tom Harper	3.50	1.75	1.00
(7) Mike Hegan	3.50	1.75	1.00
(8) Mike Hershberger	2.50	1.25	.70
(9) Steve Hovley	2.50	1.25	.70
(10) John Kennedy	2.50	1.25	.70
(11) Lew Krausse	2.50	1.25	.70
(12) Ted Kubiak	2.50	1.25	.70
(13) Bob Locker	2.50	1.25	.70
(14) Roy McMillan	2.50	1.25	.70
(15) Jerry McNertney	2.50	1.25	.70
(16) Bob Meyer	2.50	1.25	.70
(17) John Morris	2.50	1.25	.70
(18) John O'Donoghue	2.50	1.25	.70
(19) Marty Pattin	2.50	1.25	.70
(20) Rich Rollins	2.50	1.25	.70
(21) Phil Roof	2.50	1.25	.70
(22) Ted Savage	2.50	1.25	.70
(23) Russ Snyder	2.50	1.25	.70
(24) Dan Walton	3.50	1.75	1.00

1923 Fleer

While only a few specimens are known to date, from the print on the back it can be presumed that all 60 of the baseball players from the blank-back strip card set cataloged as W515 were also issued with Fleer advertising on the verso. Several cards are also known with boxers, indicating another 60 cards of non-baseball athletes and other famous people were also

produced. The 1-5/8" x 2-3/8" cards feature crude color line art of the player on front, with a black-and-white ad on back. The cards pre-date by more than a decade Fleer's "Cops and Robbers" set of 1935, and are some 35 years in advance of Fleer's first modern baseball issue.

	NM	EX	VG
Complete Set (60):	15,000	7,500	4,500
Common Player:	175.00	85.00	50.00
1 Bill Cunningham	175.00	85.00	50.00
2 Al Mamaux	175.00	85.00	50.00
3 "Babe" Ruth	1,325	660.00	400.00
4 Dave Bancroft	350.00	175.00	105.00
5 Ed Rommel	175.00	85.00	50.00
6 "Babe" Adams	175.00	85.00	50.00
7 Clarence Walker	175.00	85.00	50.00
8 Waite Hoyt	350.00	175.00	105.00
9 Bob Shawkey	175.00	85.00	50.00
10 "Ty" Cobb	1,000	500.00	300.00
11 George Sisler	350.00	175.00	105.00
12 Jack Bentley	175.00	85.00	50.00
13 Jim O'Connell	175.00	85.00	50.00
14 Frank Frisch	350.00	175.00	105.00
15 Frank Baker	350.00	175.00	105.00
16 Burleigh Grimes	350.00	175.00	105.00
17 Wally Schang	175.00	85.00	50.00
18 Harry Heilman (Heilmann)	350.00	175.00	105.00
19 Aaron Ward	175.00	85.00	50.00
20 Carl Mays	200.00	100.00	60.00
21 The Meusel Bros. (Bob Meusel, Irish Meusel)	225.00	110.00	67.00
22 Arthur Nehf	175.00	85.00	50.00
23 Lee Meadows	175.00	85.00	50.00
24 "Casey" Stengel	375.00	185.00	110.00
25 Jack Scott	175.00	85.00	50.00
26 Kenneth Williams	175.00	85.00	50.00
27 Joe Bush	175.00	85.00	50.00
28 Tris Speaker	400.00	200.00	120.00
29 Ross Young (Youngs)	350.00	175.00	105.00
30 Joe Dugan	175.00	85.00	50.00
31 The Barnes Bros. (Jesse Barnes, Virgil Barnes)	200.00	100.00	60.00
32 George Kelly	350.00	175.00	105.00
33 Hugh McQuillen (McQuillan)	175.00	85.00	50.00
34 Hugh Jennings	350.00	175.00	105.00
35 Tom Griffith	175.00	85.00	50.00
36 Miller Huggins	350.00	175.00	105.00
37 "Whitey" Witt	175.00	85.00	50.00
38 Walter Johnson	500.00	250.00	150.00
39 "Wally" Pipp	200.00	100.00	60.00
40 "Dutch" Reuther (Ruether)	175.00	85.00	50.00
41 Jim Johnston	175.00	85.00	50.00
42 Willie Kamm	175.00	85.00	50.00
43 Sam Jones	175.00	85.00	50.00
44 Frank Snyder	175.00	85.00	50.00
45 John McGraw	350.00	175.00	105.00
46 Everett Scott	175.00	85.00	50.00
47 "Babe" Ruth	1,325	660.00	400.00
48 Urban Shocker	175.00	85.00	50.00
49 Grover Alexander	400.00	200.00	120.00
50 "Rabbit" Maranville	350.00	175.00	105.00
51 Ray Schalk	350.00	175.00	105.00
52 "Heinie" Groh	175.00	85.00	50.00
53 Wilbert Robinson	350.00	175.00	105.00
54 George Burns	175.00	85.00	50.00
55 Rogers Hornsby	400.00	200.00	120.00
56 Zack Wheat	350.00	175.00	105.00
57 Eddie Roush	350.00	175.00	105.00
58 Eddie Collins	350.00	175.00	105.00
59 Charlie Hollocher	175.00	85.00	50.00
60 Red Faber	350.00	175.00	105.00

1959 Fleer Ted Williams

This 80-card 1959 Fleer set tells the life of baseball great Ted Williams, from his childhood years up to 1958. The full-color cards measure 2-1/2" x 3-1/2" in size and make use of both horizontal and vertical formats. The card backs, all designed horizontally, contain a continuing biography of Williams. Card #68 was withdrawn from the set early in production and is scarce. Counterfeit cards of #68 have been produced and can be distinguished by a cross-hatch pattern which appears over the photo on the card fronts.

		NM	EX	VG
	Complete Set (80):	1,250	625.00	312.50
	Common Card:	15.00	7.50	3.75
	Wax Pack (6):	400.00	.00	.00
1	The Early Years	100.00	50.00	25.00
2	Ted's Idol (Babe Ruth)	120.00	60.00	30.00
3	Practice Makes Perfect	15.00	7.50	3.75
4	1934 - Ted Learns The Fine Points	15.00	7.50	3.75
5	Ted's Fame Spreads - 1935-36	15.00	7.50	3.75
6	Ted Turns Professional	20.00	10.00	6.00
7	1936 - From Mound To Plate	15.00	7.50	3.75
8	1937 - First Full Season	15.00	7.50	3.75
9	1937 - First Step To The Majors (With Eddie Collins.)	15.00	7.50	3.75
10	1938 - Gunning As A Pastime	15.00	7.50	3.75
11	1938 - First Spring Training (With Jimmie Foxx.)	30.00	15.00	9.00
12	1939 - Burning Up The Minors	20.00	10.00	6.00
13	1939 - Ted Shows He Will Stay	15.00	7.50	3.75
14	Outstanding Rookie of 1939	20.00	10.00	6.00
15	1940 - Williams Licks Sophomore Jinx	20.00	10.00	6.00
16	1941 - Williams' Greatest Year	15.00	7.50	3.75
17	1941 - How Ted Hit .400	30.00	15.00	9.00
18	1941 - All-Star Hero	15.00	7.50	3.75
19	1942 - Ted Wins Triple Crown	15.00	7.50	3.75
20	1942 - On To Naval Training	15.00	7.50	3.75
21	1943 - Honors For Williams	15.00	7.50	3.75
22	1944 - Ted Solos	15.00	7.50	3.75
23	1944 - Williams Wins His Wings	15.00	7.50	3.75
24	1945 - Sharpshooter	15.00	7.50	3.75
25	1945 - Ted Is Discharged	15.00	7.50	3.75
26	1946 - Off To A Flying Start	15.00	7.50	3.75
27	July 9, 1946 - One Man Show	15.00	7.50	3.75
28	July 14, 1946 - The Williams Shift	15.00	7.50	3.75
29	July 21, 1946, Ted Hits For The Cycle	20.00	10.00	6.00
30	1946 - Beating The Williams Shift	15.00	7.50	3.75
31	Oct. 1946 - Sox Lose The Series	15.00	7.50	3.75
32	1946 - Most Valuable Player	15.00	7.50	3.75
33	1947 - Another Triple Crown For Ted	15.00	7.50	3.75
34	1947 - Ted Sets Runs-Scored Record	15.00	7.50	3.75
35	1948 - The Sox Miss The Pennant	15.00	7.50	3.75
36	1948 - Banner Year For Ted	15.00	7.50	3.75
37	1949 - Sox Miss Out Again	15.00	7.50	3.75
38	1949 - Power Rampage	15.00	7.50	3.75
39	1950 - Great Start (With Joe Cronin and Eddie Collins.)	15.00	7.50	3.75
40	July 11, 1950 - Ted Crashes Into Wall	15.00	7.50	3.75
41	1950 - Ted Recovers	15.00	7.50	3.75
42	1951 - Williams Slowed By Injury	15.00	7.50	3.75
43	1951 - Leads Outfielders In Double Play	15.00	7.50	3.75
44	1952 - Back To The Marines	15.00	7.50	3.75
45	1952 - Farewell To Baseball?	15.00	7.50	3.75
46	1952 - Ready For Combat	15.00	7.50	3.75
47	1953 - Ted Crash Lands Jet	15.00	7.50	3.75
48	July 14, 1953 - Ted Returns	15.00	7.50	3.75
49	1953 - Smash Return	15.00	7.50	3.75
50	March 1954 - Spring Injury	15.00	7.50	3.75
51	May 16, 1954 - Ted Is Patched Up	15.00	7.50	3.75
52	1954 - Ted's Comeback	15.00	7.50	3.75
53	1954 - Ted's Comeback Is A Sucess	15.00	7.50	3.75
54	Dec. 1954, Fisherman Ted Hooks a Big On	15.00	7.50	3.75
55	1955 - Ted Decides Retirement Is "No Go (With Joe Cronin.)	15.00	7.50	3.75
56	1955 - 2,000th Major League Hit	15.00	7.50	3.75
57	1956 - Ted Reaches 400th Homer	15.00	7.50	3.75
58	1957 - Williams Hits .388	15.00	7.50	3.75
59	1957 - Hot September For Ted	15.00	7.50	3.75
60	1957 - More Records For Ted	15.00	7.50	3.75
61	1957 - Outfielder Ted	15.00	7.50	3.75
62	1958 - 6th Batting Title For Ted	15.00	7.50	3.75
63	Ted's All-Star Record	35.00	17.50	10.00
64	1958 - Daughter And Famous Daddy	15.00	7.50	3.75
65	August 30, 1958	15.00	7.50	3.75
66	1958 - Powerhouse	15.00	7.50	3.75
67	Two Famous Fishermen (With Sam Snead.)	20.00	10.00	6.00
68	Jan. 23, 1959 - Ted Signs For 1959	650.00	325.00	162.50
69	A Future Ted Williams?	15.00	7.50	3.75
70	Ted Williams & Jim Thorpe	30.00	15.00	9.00
71	Ted's Hitting Fundamentals #1	15.00	7.50	3.75
72	Ted's Hitting Fundamentals #2	15.00	7.50	3.75
73	Ted's Hitting Fundamentals #3	15.00	7.50	3.75
74	Here's How!	15.00	7.50	3.75
75	Williams' Value To Red Sox (With Babe Ruth, Eddie Collins.)	30.00	15.00	9.00
76	Ted's Remarkable "On Base" Record	15.00	7.50	3.75
77	Ted Relaxes	15.00	7.50	3.75
78	Honors For Williams	15.00	7.50	3.75
79	Where Ted Stands	25.00	12.50	7.50
80	Ted's Goals For 1959	40.00	15.00	9.00

1960 Fleer Baseball Greats

The 1960 Fleer Baseball Greats set consists of 78 cards of the game's top players from the past, plus a card of Ted Williams, who was in his final major league season. The cards are standard size (2-1/2" x 3-1/2") and feature color photos inside blue, green, red or yellow borders. The card backs carry a short player biography plus career hitting or pitching statistics. Unissued cards with a Pepper Martin back (#80), but with another player pictured on the front, exist. All have been either cancelled with a slit cut out of the bottom, or show evidence of having been hand-cut from a sheet.

		NM	EX	VG
	Complete Set (79):	500.00	250.00	125.00
	Common Player:	6.00	3.00	1.50
	Wax Pack:	300.00	.00	.00
1	Nap Lajoie	22.50	7.50	4.00
2	Christy Mathewson	16.00	8.00	5.00
3	Babe Ruth	100.00	50.00	25.00
4	Carl Hubbell	6.00	3.00	1.50
5	Grover Cleveland Alexander	15.00	7.50	4.50
6	Walter Johnson	20.00	10.00	6.00
7	Chief Bender	6.00	3.00	1.50
8	Roger Bresnahan	6.00	3.00	1.50
9	Mordecai Brown	6.00	3.00	1.50
10	Tris Speaker	6.00	3.00	1.50
11	Arky Vaughan	6.00	3.00	1.50
12	Zack Wheat	6.00	3.00	1.50
13	George Sisler	6.00	3.00	1.50
14	Connie Mack	6.00	3.00	1.50
15	Clark Griffith	6.00	3.00	1.50
16	Lou Boudreau	6.00	3.00	1.50
17	Ernie Lombardi	6.00	3.00	1.50
18	Heinie Manush	6.00	3.00	1.50
19	Marty Marion	6.00	3.00	1.50
20	Eddie Collins	6.00	3.00	1.50
21	Rabbit Maranville	6.00	3.00	1.50
22	Joe Medwick	6.00	3.00	1.50
23	Ed Barrow	6.00	3.00	1.50
24	Mickey Cochrane	6.00	3.00	1.50
25	Jimmy Collins	6.00	3.00	1.50
26	Bob Feller	13.50	6.75	4.00
27	Luke Appling	6.00	3.00	1.50
28	Lou Gehrig	100.00	50.00	25.00
29	Gabby Hartnett	6.00	3.00	1.50
30	Chuck Klein	6.00	3.00	1.50
31	Tony Lazzeri	6.00	3.00	1.50
32	Al Simmons	6.00	3.00	1.50
33	Wilbert Robinson	6.00	3.00	1.50
34	Sam Rice	6.00	3.00	1.50
35	Herb Pennock	6.00	3.00	1.50
36	Mel Ott	6.00	3.00	1.50
37	Lefty O'Doul	6.00	3.00	1.50
38	Johnny Mize	6.00	3.00	1.50
39	Bing Miller	6.00	3.00	1.50
40	Joe Tinker	6.00	3.00	1.50
41	Frank Baker	6.00	3.00	1.50
42	Ty Cobb	50.00	25.00	12.50
43	Paul Derringer	6.00	3.00	1.50
44	Cap Anson	6.00	3.00	1.50
45	Jim Bottomley	6.00	3.00	1.50
46	Eddie Plank	6.00	3.00	1.50
47	Cy Young	16.00	8.00	5.00
48	Hack Wilson	6.00	3.00	1.50
49	Ed Walsh	6.00	3.00	1.50
50	Frank Chance	6.00	3.00	1.50
51	Dazzy Vance	6.00	3.00	1.50
52	Bill Terry	6.00	3.00	1.50
53	Jimmy Foxx	15.00	7.50	4.50
54	Lefty Gomez	6.00	3.00	1.50
55	Branch Rickey	6.00	3.00	1.50
56	Ray Schalk	6.00	3.00	1.50
57	Johnny Evers	6.00	3.00	1.50
58	Charlie Gehringer	6.00	3.00	1.50
59	Burleigh Grimes	6.00	3.00	1.50
60	Lefty Grove	6.00	3.00	1.50
61	Rube Waddell	6.00	3.00	1.50
62	Honus Wagner	15.00	7.50	4.50
63	Red Ruffing	6.00	3.00	1.50
64	Judge Landis	6.00	3.00	1.50
65	Harry Heilmann	6.00	3.00	1.50
66	John McGraw	6.00	3.00	1.50
67	Hughie Jennings	6.00	3.00	1.50
68	Hal Newhouser	6.00	3.00	1.50
69	Waite Hoyt	6.00	3.00	1.50
70	Bobo Newsom	6.00	3.00	1.50
71	Earl Averill	6.00	3.00	1.50
72	Ted Williams	80.00	40.00	20.00
73	Warren Giles	6.00	3.00	1.50
74	Ford Frick	6.00	3.00	1.50
75	Ki Ki Cuyler	6.00	3.00	1.50
76	Paul Waner	6.00	3.00	1.50
77	Pie Traynor	6.00	3.00	1.50
78	Lloyd Waner	6.00	3.00	1.50
79	Ralph Kiner	6.00	3.00	1.50
80	Pepper Martin (Unissued, slit-cancelled proof, Lefty Grove, Joe Tinker or Eddie Collins on front.)	2,000	800.00	400.00
80	Pepper Martin (Unissued hand-cut proof. Lefty Grove, Eddie Collins or Joe Tinker on front.)	2,750	1,350	825.00

1960-62 Fleer Team Logo Decals

These colorful team logo decals were pack inserts in Fleer's 1960-62 baseball card issues. The decals measure 2-1/4" x 3". Those issued in 1960 have a blue background on front. The 1961-62 decals have a white background on front. Backs have advertising for Fleer bubblegum and instructions on applying the decals. The 1961 decals have back printing in blue; the 1962s are in red.

	NM	EX	VG
Complete Set, 1960 (16):	100.00	50.00	30.00
Complete Set, 1961 (18):	100.00	50.00	30.00
Complete Set, 1962 (20):	250.00	125.00	75.00
1960 team decal, blue background	9.00	4.50	2.75
1961 decal, white background, blue back	4.50	2.25	1.25
1962 decal, white background, red back	9.00	4.50	2.75

1961 Fleer Baseball Greats

In 1961, Fleer issued another set utilizing the Baseball Greats theme. The 154-card set was issued in two series and features a color (or colorized) player portrait against a colored background. The player's name is located in a pennant at bottom. Card backs feature orange and black on white stock and contain player biographical and statistical information. The cards measure 2-1/2" x 3-1/2" in size. Five-cent wax packs included five cards plus a team logo decal and sticker.

		NM	EX	VG
	Complete Set (154):	1,100	550.00	275.00
	Common Player:	8.00	4.00	2.00
	Wax Pack (5+1+1):	265.00		
1	Checklist (Frank Baker, Ty Cobb, Zach Wheat)	50.00	25.00	12.50
2	G.C. Alexander	9.00	4.50	2.25
3	Nick Altrock	8.00	4.00	2.00
4	Cap Anson	8.00	4.00	2.00
5	Earl Averill	8.00	4.00	2.00
6	Home Run Baker	8.00	4.00	2.00
7	Dave Bancroft	8.00	4.00	2.00
8	Chief Bender	8.00	4.00	2.00
9	Jim Bottomley	8.00	4.00	2.00
10	Roger Bresnahan	8.00	4.00	2.00
11	Mordecai Brown	8.00	4.00	2.00
12	Max Carey	8.00	4.00	2.00
13	Jack Chesbro	8.00	4.00	2.00
14	Ty Cobb	50.00	25.00	12.50
15	Mickey Cochrane	8.00	4.00	2.00
16	Eddie Collins	8.00	4.00	2.00
17	Earle Combs	8.00	4.00	2.00
18	Charles Comiskey	8.00	4.00	2.00
19	Ki Ki Cuyler	8.00	4.00	2.00
20	Paul Derringer	8.00	4.00	2.00
21	Howard Ehmke	8.00	4.00	2.00
22	Billy Evans	8.00	4.00	2.00
23	Johnny Evers	8.00	4.00	2.00
24	Red Faber	8.00	4.00	2.00
25	Bob Feller	10.00	5.00	3.00
26	Wes Ferrell	8.00	4.00	2.00

27	Lew Fonseca	8.00	4.00	2.00
28	Jimmy Foxx	9.00	4.50	2.25
29	Ford Frick	8.00	4.00	2.00
30	Frankie Frisch	8.00	4.00	2.00
31	Lou Gehrig	100.00	50.00	25.00
32	Charlie Gehringer	8.00	4.00	2.00
33	Warren Giles	8.00	4.00	2.00
34	Lefty Gomez	8.00	4.00	2.00
35	Goose Goslin	8.00	4.00	2.00
36	Clark Griffith	8.00	4.00	2.00
37	Burleigh Grimes	8.00	4.00	2.00
38	Lefty Grove	8.00	4.00	2.00
39	Chick Hafey	8.00	4.00	2.00
40	Jesse Haines	8.00	4.00	2.00
41	Gabby Hartnett	8.00	4.00	2.00
42	Harry Heilmann	8.00	4.00	2.00
43	Rogers Hornsby	8.00	4.00	2.00
44	Waite Hoyt	8.00	4.00	2.00
45	Carl Hubbell	8.00	4.00	2.00
46	Miller Huggins	8.00	4.00	2.00
47	Hughie Jennings	8.00	4.00	2.00
48	Ban Johnson	8.00	4.00	2.00
49	Walter Johnson	12.00	6.00	3.50
50	Ralph Kiner	8.00	4.00	2.00
51	Chuck Klein	8.00	4.00	2.00
52	Johnny Kling	8.00	4.00	2.00
53	Judge Landis	8.00	4.00	2.00
54	Tony Lazzeri	8.00	4.00	2.00
55	Ernie Lombardi	8.00	4.00	2.00
56	Dolf Luque	8.00	4.00	2.00
57	Heinie Manush	8.00	4.00	2.00
58	Marty Marion	8.00	4.00	2.00
59	Christy Mathewson	12.00	6.00	3.50
60	John McGraw	8.00	4.00	2.00
61	Joe Medwick	8.00	4.00	2.00
62	Bing Miller	8.00	4.00	2.00
63	Johnny Mize	8.00	4.00	2.00
64	Johnny Mostil	8.00	4.00	2.00
65	Art Nehf	8.00	4.00	2.00
66	Hal Newhouser	8.00	4.00	2.00
67	Bobo Newsom	8.00	4.00	2.00
68	Mel Ott	8.00	4.00	2.00
69	Allie Reynolds	8.00	4.00	2.00
70	Sam Rice	8.00	4.00	2.00
71	Eppa Rixey	8.00	4.00	2.00
72	Edd Roush	8.00	4.00	2.00
73	Schoolboy Rowe	8.00	4.00	2.00
74	Red Ruffing	8.00	4.00	2.00
75	Babe Ruth	120.00	60.00	30.00
76	Joe Sewell	8.00	4.00	2.00
77	Al Simmons	8.00	4.00	2.00
78	George Sisler	8.00	4.00	2.00
79	Tris Speaker	8.00	4.00	2.00
80	Fred Toney	8.00	4.00	2.00
81	Dazzy Vance	8.00	4.00	2.00
82	Jim Vaughn	8.00	4.00	2.00
83	Big Ed Walsh	8.00	4.00	2.00
84	Lloyd Waner	8.00	4.00	2.00
85	Paul Waner	8.00	4.00	2.00
86	Zach Wheat	8.00	4.00	2.00
87	Hack Wilson	8.00	4.00	2.00
88	Jimmy Wilson	8.00	4.00	2.00
89	Checklist	60.00	30.00	15.00
	(George Sisler, Pie Traynor)			
90	Babe Adams	8.00	4.00	2.00
91	Dale Alexander	8.00	4.00	2.00
92	Jim Bagby	8.00	4.00	2.00
93	Ossie Bluege	8.00	4.00	2.00
94	Lou Boudreau	8.00	4.00	2.00
95	Tommy Bridges	8.00	4.00	2.00
96	Donnie Bush (Donie)	8.00	4.00	2.00
97	Dolph Camilli	8.00	4.00	2.00
98	Frank Chance	8.00	4.00	2.00
99	Jimmy Collins	8.00	4.00	2.00
100	Stanley Coveleskie	8.00	4.00	2.00
	(Coveleski)			
101	Hughie Critz	8.00	4.00	2.00
102	General Crowder	8.00	4.00	2.00
103	Joe Dugan	8.00	4.00	2.00
104	Bibb Falk	8.00	4.00	2.00
105	Rick Ferrell	8.00	4.00	2.00
106	Art Fletcher	8.00	4.00	2.00
107	Dennis Galehouse	8.00	4.00	2.00
108	Chick Galloway	8.00	4.00	2.00
109	Mule Haas	8.00	4.00	2.00
110	Stan Hack	8.00	4.00	2.00
111	Bump Hadley	8.00	4.00	2.00
112	Billy Hamilton	8.00	4.00	2.00
113	Joe Hauser	8.00	4.00	2.00
114	Babe Herman	8.00	4.00	2.00
115	Travis Jackson	8.00	4.00	2.00
116	Eddie Joost	8.00	4.00	2.00
117	Addie Joss	8.00	4.00	2.00
118	Joe Judge	8.00	4.00	2.00
119	Joe Kuhel	8.00	4.00	2.00
120	Nap Lajoie	8.00	4.00	2.00
121	Dutch Leonard	8.00	4.00	2.00
122	Ted Lyons	8.00	4.00	2.00
123	Connie Mack	8.00	4.00	2.00
124	Rabbit Maranville	8.00	4.00	2.00
125	Fred Marberry	8.00	4.00	2.00
126	Iron Man McGinnity	8.00	4.00	2.00
127	Oscar Melillo	8.00	4.00	2.00
128	Ray Mueller	8.00	4.00	2.00
129	Kid Nichols	8.00	4.00	2.00
130	Lefty O'Doul	8.00	4.00	2.00
131	Bob O'Farrell	8.00	4.00	2.00
132	Roger Peckinpaugh	8.00	4.00	2.00
133	Herb Pennock	8.00	4.00	2.00
134	George Pipgras	8.00	4.00	2.00
135	Eddie Plank	8.00	4.00	2.00
136	Ray Schalk	8.00	4.00	2.00
137	Hal Schumacher	8.00	4.00	2.00
138	Luke Sewell	8.00	4.00	2.00
139	Bob Shawkey	8.00	4.00	2.00
140	Riggs Stephenson	8.00	4.00	2.00
141	Billy Sullivan	8.00	4.00	2.00
142	Bill Terry	8.00	4.00	2.00

143	Joe Tinker	8.00	4.00	2.00
144	Pie Traynor	8.00	4.00	2.00
145	George Uhle	8.00	4.00	2.00
146	Hal Troskey (Trosky)	8.00	4.00	2.00
147	Arky Vaughan	8.00	4.00	2.00
148	Johnny Vander Meer	8.00	4.00	2.00
149	Rube Waddell	8.00	4.00	2.00
150	Honus Wagner	50.00	25.00	12.50
151	Dixie Walker	8.00	4.00	2.00
152	Ted Williams	120.00	60.00	30.00
153	Cy Young	12.00	6.00	3.50
154	Ross Young (Youngs)	8.00	4.00	2.00

1961 Fleer World Champions Pennant Decals

The winner of each World Series from 1913-1960 is honored in this pack insert. The 3" x 1-1/4" decals have a large red or blue pennant at center, with a team name or logo and the "WORLD CHAMPIONS" notation. The year of the Series win is at left on the pennant. The number of games won by each team is at top and botom on right. Backs offer instructions for applying the decals.

		NM	EX	VG
	Complete Set (48):	300.00	150.00	90.00
	Common Decal:	6.00	3.00	1.75
(1)	1913 - A's	6.00	3.00	1.75
(2)	1914 - Braves	6.00	3.00	1.75
(3)	1915 - Red Sox	6.00	3.00	1.75
(4)	1916 - Red Sox	6.00	3.00	1.75
(5)	1917 - White Sox	6.00	3.00	1.75
(6)	1918 - Red Sox	6.00	3.00	1.75
(7)	1919 - Reds	9.00	4.50	2.75
(8)	1920 - Indians	6.00	3.00	1.75
(9)	1921 - Giants	6.00	3.00	1.75
(10)	1922 - Giants	6.00	3.00	1.75
(11)	1923 - Yankees	7.50	3.75	2.25
(12)	1924 - Senators	6.00	3.00	1.75
(13)	1925 - Yankees	7.50	3.75	2.25
(14)	1926 - Cardinals	6.00	3.00	1.75
(15)	1927 - Yankees	7.50	3.75	2.25
(14)	1928 - Yankees	7.50	3.75	2.25
(15)	1929 - A's	6.00	3.00	1.75
(16)	1930 - A's	6.00	3.00	1.75
(17)	1931 - Cardinals	6.00	3.00	1.75
(18)	1932 - Yankees	7.50	3.75	2.25
(19)	1933 - Giants	6.00	3.00	1.75
(20)	1934 - Cardinals	6.00	3.00	1.75
(21)	1935 - Tigers	6.00	3.00	1.75
(22)	1936 - Yankees	7.50	3.75	2.25
(23)	1937 - Yankees	7.50	3.75	2.25
(24)	1938 - Yankees	7.50	3.75	2.25
(25)	1939 - Yankees	7.50	3.75	2.25
(26)	1940 - Reds	6.00	3.00	1.75
(27)	1941 - Yankees	7.50	3.75	2.25
(28)	1942 - Cardinals	6.00	3.00	1.75
(29)	1943 - Yankees	7.50	3.75	2.25
(30)	1944 - Cardinals	6.00	3.00	1.75
(31)	1945 - Tigers	6.00	3.00	1.75
(32)	1946 - Cardinals	6.00	3.00	1.75
(33)	1947 - Yankees	7.50	3.75	2.25
(34)	1948 - Indians	6.00	3.00	1.75
(35)	1949 - Yankees	7.50	3.75	2.25
(36)	1950 - Yankees	7.50	3.75	2.25
(37)	1951 - Yankees	7.50	3.75	2.25
(38)	1952 - Yankees	7.50	3.75	2.25
(41)	1953 - Yankees	7.50	3.75	2.25
(42)	1954 - Giants	6.00	3.00	1.75
(43)	1955 - Dodgers	9.00	4.50	2.75
(44)	1956 - Yankees	7.50	3.75	2.25
(45)	1957 - Braves	7.50	3.75	2.25
(46)	1958 - Yankees	7.50	3.75	2.25
(47)	1959 - Dodgers	9.00	4.50	2.75
(48)	1960 - Pirates	9.00	4.50	2.75

1963 Fleer

A lawsuit by Topps stopped Fleer's 1963 set at one series of 66 cards. Issued with a cookie rather than gum, the set features color photos of current players. The card backs include statistical information for 1962 and career plus a brief player biography. The cards, which measure 2-1/2" x 3-1/2", are numbered 1-66. An unnumbered checklist was issued with the set and is included in the complete set price in the checklist that follows. The checklist and #46 Adcock are scarce.

		NM	EX	VG
	Complete Set (67):	1,500	750.00	450.00
	Common Player:	10.00	5.00	3.00
	Wax Pack:	1,000		
1	Steve Barber	40.00	10.00	5.00
2	Ron Hansen	10.00	5.00	3.00
3	Milt Pappas	10.00	5.00	3.00
4	Brooks Robinson	100.00	50.00	25.00
5	Willie Mays	175.00	87.50	43.75
6	Lou Clinton	10.00	5.00	3.00
7	Bill Monbouquette	10.00	5.00	3.00
8	Carl Yastrzemski	100.00	50.00	25.00
9	Ray Herbert	10.00	5.00	3.00
10	Jim Landis	10.00	5.00	3.00
11	Dick Donovan	10.00	5.00	3.00
12	Tito Francona	10.00	5.00	3.00
13	Jerry Kindall	10.00	5.00	3.00
14	Frank Lary	10.00	5.00	3.00
15	Dick Howser	10.00	5.00	3.00
16	Jerry Lumpe	10.00	5.00	3.00
17	Norm Siebern	10.00	5.00	3.00
18	Don Lee	10.00	5.00	3.00
19	Albie Pearson	10.00	5.00	3.00
20	Bob Rodgers	10.00	5.00	3.00
21	Leon Wagner	10.00	5.00	3.00
22	Jim Kaat	15.00	7.50	4.50
23	Vic Power	10.00	5.00	3.00
24	Rich Rollins	10.00	5.00	3.00
25	Bobby Richardson	17.50	9.00	5.00
26	Ralph Terry	10.00	5.00	3.00
27	Tom Cheney	10.00	5.00	3.00
28	Chuck Cottier	10.00	5.00	3.00
29	Jimmy Piersall	12.50	6.25	3.75
30	Dave Stenhouse	10.00	5.00	3.00
31	Glen Hobbie	10.00	5.00	3.00
32	Ron Santo	25.00	12.50	7.50
33	Gene Freese	10.00	5.00	3.00
34	Vada Pinson	12.50	6.25	3.75
35	Bob Purkey	10.00	5.00	3.00
36	Joe Amalfitano	10.00	5.00	3.00
37	Bob Aspromonte	10.00	5.00	3.00
38	Dick Farrell	10.00	5.00	3.00
39	Al Spangler	10.00	5.00	3.00
40	Tommy Davis	10.00	5.00	3.00
41	Don Drysdale	75.00	37.50	18.75
42	Sandy Koufax	200.00	100.00	50.00
43	*Maury Wills*	100.00	50.00	25.00
44	Frank Bolling	10.00	5.00	3.00
45	Warren Spahn	75.00	37.50	18.75
46	Joe Adcock (SP)	150.00	75.00	37.50
47	Roger Craig	10.00	5.00	3.00
48	Al Jackson	10.00	5.00	3.00
49	Rod Kanehl	10.00	5.00	3.00
50	Ruben Amaro	10.00	5.00	3.00
51	John Callison	10.00	5.00	3.00
52	Clay Dalrymple	10.00	5.00	3.00
53	Don Demeter	10.00	5.00	3.00
54	Art Mahaffey	10.00	5.00	3.00
55	"Smoky" Burgess	10.00	5.00	3.00
56	Roberto Clemente	175.00	87.50	43.75
57	Elroy Face	10.00	5.00	3.00
58	Vernon Law	10.00	5.00	3.00
59	Bill Mazeroski	20.00	10.00	6.00
60	Ken Boyer	12.50	6.25	3.75
61	Bob Gibson	75.00	37.50	18.75
62	Gene Oliver	10.00	5.00	3.00
63	Bill White	13.50	6.75	4.00
64	Orlando Cepeda	22.50	11.00	6.75
65	Jimmy Davenport	10.00	5.00	3.00
66	Billy O'Dell	20.00	10.00	5.00
---	Checklist (SP)	450.00	225.00	112.50

1966 Fleer All Star Match Baseball

This seldom-seen issue was produced in the years when Fleer was locked out of the "regular" baseball card market. Standard 2-1/2" x 3-1/2" format cards are designed for playing a baseball match game. Backs have a portion of a black-and-white photo of Dodger pitcher Don Drysdale, which can be assembled in jigsaw puzzle fashion. Fronts are printed in red, blue, yellow and black, and numbered F1-F66. Because single cards have little collector appeal, the value of a set is considerably higher than the sum of the parts.

	NM	EX	VG
Complete Set (66):	400.00	200.00	120.00
Common Card:	6.00	3.00	1.75

Wax Pack: 200.00
  Don Drysdale

1968-70 Fleer Major League Baseball Patches

 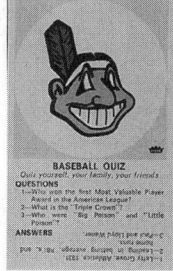

From 1968-70, Fleer sold bubblegum in wax packs which also included four team logo/quiz cards and half a dozen cloth patches, all for a dime. The 2-9/16" x 4-1/16" cards are blank-back and have on front a color team logo at top and three baseball trivia questions at bottom. The cloth patches are about 2-1/2" x 3-5/16" and are die-cut to allow the team logos and nameplates to be removed from the paper backing and stuck on jackets, etc.

		NM	EX	VG
Complete Set Logo Cards (24):		18.00	9.00	5.50
Common Logo Card:		1.50	.70	.45
Complete Set Cloth Patches (29):		35.00	17.50	10.00
Common Cloth Patch:		1.50	.75	.45
Wax Pack:		2.00		
Wax Box (24):		30.00		

LOGO/QUIZ CARDS

		NM	EX	VG
(1)	Atlanta Braves	1.50	.70	.45
(2)	Baltimore Orioles	1.50	.70	.45
(3)	Boston Red Sox	1.50	.70	.45
(4)	California Angels	1.50	.70	.45
(5)	Chicago Cubs	1.50	.70	.45
(6)	Chicago White Sox	1.50	.70	.45
(7)	Cincinnati Reds	1.50	.70	.45
(8)	Cleveland Indians	1.50	.70	.45
(9)	Detroit Tigers	1.50	.70	.45
(10)	Houston Astros	1.50	.70	.45
(11)	Kansas City Royals	1.50	.70	.45
(12)	Los Angeles Dodgers	1.50	.70	.45
(13)	Minnesota Twins	1.50	.70	.45
(14)	Montreal Expos	2.50	1.25	.70
(15)	New York Mets	3.00	1.50	.90
(16)	New York Yankees	4.00	2.00	1.25
(17)	Oakland A's	2.50	1.25	.70
(18)	Philadelphia Phillies	1.50	.70	.45
(19)	Pittsburgh Pirates	1.50	.70	.45
(20)	San Diego Padres	2.50	1.25	.70
(21)	San Francisco Giants	1.50	.70	.45
(22)	Seattle Pilots	6.00	3.00	1.75
(23)	St. Louis Cardinals	1.50	.70	.45
(24)	Washington Senators	1.50	.70	.45

TEAM LOGO CLOTH PATCHES

		NM	EX	VG
(1)	Atlanta Braves	1.50	.70	.45
(2)	Baltimore Orioles	1.50	.70	.45
(3)	Boston Red Sox	1.50	.70	.45
(4)	California Angels	1.50	.70	.45
(5)	Chicago Cubs	1.50	.70	.45
(6)	Chicago White Sox	1.50	.70	.45
(7)	Cincinnati Reds	1.50	.70	.45
(8)	Cleveland Indians (Indian head)	1.50	.70	.45
(9)	Cleveland Indians (Btg Indian.)	1.50	.70	.45
(10)	Detroit Tigers	1.50	.70	.45
(11)	Houston Astros	1.50	.70	.45
(12)	Kansas City Royals	1.50	.70	.45
(13)	Los Angeles Dodgers	1.50	.70	.45
(14)	Milwaukee Brewers (M)	1.50	.70	.45
(15)	Milwaukee Brewers (Batting keg.)	1.50	.70	.45
(16)	Minnesota Twins	1.50	.70	.45
(17)	Montreal Expos	2.00	1.00	.60
(18)	New York Mets	2.00	1.00	.60
(19)	New York Yankees	3.00	1.50	.90
(20)	Oakland A's (Plain ball.)	2.00	1.00	.60
(21)	Oakland A's ("The SWINGIN,'" white shoes, on ball.)	1.50	.70	.45
(22)	Philadelphia Phillies	1.50	.70	.45
(23)	Pittsburgh Pirates	1.50	.70	.45
(24)	San Diego Padres	2.00	1.00	.60
(25)	San Francisco Giants	1.50	.70	.45
(26)	Seattle Pilots	3.00	1.50	.90
(27)	St. Louis Cardinals	1.50	.70	.45
(28)	Washington Senators	1.50	.70	.45
(29)	Major League Baseball	1.50	.70	.45

1969 Fleer Cap Plaques

This set of novelty plaques features 3D impressions of each team's cap on thin plastic stock in a 3" x 4" format. Each cap plaque was sold in a wrapper with an easel backing board, surviving specimens of which are quite scarce.

		NM	EX	VG
Complete Set (24):		1,200	600.00	350.00
Common Plaque:		45.00	22.50	13.50
Easel Backing Board:		22.00	11.00	6.50
Unopened Pack:		45.00		
(1)	Atlanta Braves	50.00	25.00	15.00
(2)	Baltimore Orioles	60.00	30.00	18.00
(3)	Boston Red Sox	50.00	25.00	15.00
(4)	California Angels	45.00	22.50	13.50
(5)	Chicago Cubs	60.00	30.00	18.00
(6)	Chicago White Sox	45.00	22.50	13.50
(7)	Cincinnati Reds	45.00	22.50	13.50
(8)	Cleveland Indians	45.00	22.50	13.50
(9)	Detroit Tigers	45.00	22.50	13.50
(10)	Houston Astros	45.00	22.50	13.50
(11)	Kansas City Royals	45.00	22.50	13.50
(12)	Los Angeles Dodgers	50.00	25.00	15.00
(13)	Minnesota Twins	45.00	22.50	13.50
(14)	Montreal Expos	45.00	22.50	13.50
(15)	New York Mets	75.00	37.50	22.50
(16)	New York Yankees	115.00	55.00	35.00
(17)	Oakland A's	60.00	30.00	18.00
(18)	Philadelphia Phillies	45.00	22.50	13.50
(19)	Pittsburgh Pirates	50.00	25.00	15.00
(20)	San Diego Padres	45.00	22.50	13.50
(21)	San Francisco Giants	45.00	22.50	13.50
(22)	Seattle Pilots	125.00	62.50	37.00
(23)	St. Louis Cardinals	50.00	25.00	15.00
(24)	Washington Senators	50.00	25.00	15.00

1970 Fleer Team Logo Decals

These colorful team logo decals were pack inserts in Fleer's 1970 World Series issue. The decals measure 2-7/16" x 2-3/4". Backs have instructions for applying the decals.

		NM	EX	VG
Complete Set (24):		90.00	45.00	27.50
Common Team:		7.50	3.75	2.25
(1)	Atlanta Braves	7.50	3.75	2.25
(2)	Baltimore Orioles	9.00	4.50	2.75
(3)	Boston Red Sox	7.50	3.75	2.25
(4)	California Angels	7.50	3.75	2.25
(5)	Chicago Cubs	7.50	3.75	2.25
(6)	Chicago White Sox	7.50	3.75	2.25
(7)	Cincinnati Reds	7.50	3.75	2.25
(8)	Cleveland Indians	7.50	3.75	2.25
(9)	Detroit Tigers	7.50	3.75	2.25
(10)	Houston Astros	7.50	3.75	2.25
(11)	Kansas City Royals	7.50	3.75	2.25
(12)	Los Angeles Dodgers	7.50	3.75	2.25
(13)	Milwaukee Brewers	7.50	3.75	2.25
(14)	Minnesota Twins	7.50	3.75	2.25
(15)	Montreal Expos	7.50	3.75	2.25
(16)	New York Mets	7.50	3.75	2.25
(17)	New York Yankees	9.00	4.50	2.75
(18)	Oakland A's	7.50	3.75	2.25
(19)	Philadelphia Phillies	7.50	3.75	2.25
(20)	Pittsburgh Pirates	9.00	4.50	2.75
(21)	San Diego Padres	7.50	3.75	2.25
(22)	San Francisco Giants	7.50	3.75	2.25
(23)	St. Louis Cardinals	7.50	3.75	2.25
(24)	Washington Senators	10.00	5.00	3.00

1970 Fleer World Series

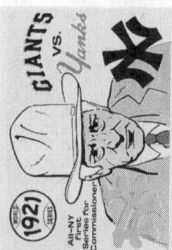

Utilizing the artwork done by Robert Laughlin a few years earlier for a privately marketed set, Fleer offered the first of two World Series highlights sets in 1970. Cards have color front with light blue backs. No card was issued for the 1904 World Series because no Series was played. Cards are checklisted in chronological order.

		NM	EX	VG
Complete Set (66):		150.00	75.00	45.00
Common Card:		1.50	.70	.45
Wax Pack:		35.00		
1	1903 Red Sox/Pirates	2.50	1.25	.70
2	1905 Giants/A's (Christy Mathewson)	2.50	1.25	.70
3	1906 White Sox/Cubs	1.50	.70	.45
4	1907 Cubs/Tigers	1.50	.70	.45
5	1908 Cubs/Tigers (Tinker/Evers/Chance)	3.00	1.50	.90
6	1909 Pirates/Tigers (Honus Wagner/Ty Cobb)	7.50	3.75	2.25
7	1910 A's/Cubs (Chief Bender/Jack Coombs)	2.00	1.00	.60
8	1911 A's/Giants (John McGraw)	2.00	1.00	.60
9	1912 Red Sox/Giants	2.00	1.00	.60
10	1913 A's/Giants	1.50	.70	.45
11	1914 Braves/A's	2.00	1.00	.60
12	1915 Red Sox/Phillies (Babe Ruth)	5.00	2.50	1.50
13	1916 Red Sox/Dodgers (Babe Ruth)	5.00	2.50	1.50
14	1917 White Sox/Giants	1.50	.70	.45
15	1918 Red Sox/Cubs	1.50	.70	.45
16	1919 Reds/White Sox	3.00	1.50	.90
17	1920 Indians/Dodgers (Stan Coveleski)	2.00	1.00	.60
18	1921 Giants/Yankees (Kenesaw Landis)	2.00	1.00	.60
19	1922 Giants/Yankees (Heinie Groh)	2.00	1.00	.60
20	1923 Yankees/Giants (Babe Ruth)	7.50	3.75	2.25
21	1924 Senators/Giants (John McGraw)	2.50	1.25	.70
22	1925 Pirates/Senators (Walter Johnson)	3.00	1.50	.90
23	1926 Cardinals/Yankees (Grover Cleveland Alexander/Tony Lazzeri)	3.00	1.50	.90
24	1927 Yankees/Pirates	2.50	1.25	.70
25	1928 Yankees/Cardinals (Babe Ruth/Lou Gehrig)	7.50	3.75	2.25
26	1929 A's/Cubs	1.50	.70	.45
27	1930 A's/Cardinals	1.50	.70	.45
28	1931 Cardinals/A's (Pepper Martin)	2.00	1.00	.60
29	1932 Yankees/Cubs (Babe Ruth/Lou Gehrig)	7.50	3.75	2.25
30	1933 Giants/Senators (Mel Ott)	2.50	1.25	.70
31	1934 Cardinals/Tigers	1.50	.70	.45
32	1935 Tigers/Cubs (Charlie Gehringer/Tommy Bridges)	2.00	1.00	.60
33	1936 Yankees/Giants	2.00	1.00	.60
34	1937 Yankees/Giants (Carl Hubbell)	2.50	1.25	.70
35	1938 Yankees/Cubs (Lou Gehrig)	4.00	2.00	1.25
36	1939 Yankees/Reds	1.50	.70	.45
37	1940 Reds/Tigers (Mike McCormick)	1.50	.70	.45
38	1941 Yankees/Dodgers	2.00	1.00	.60
39	1942 Cardinals/Yankees	1.50	.70	.45
40	1943 Cardinals/Yankees	1.50	.70	.45
41	1944 Cardinals/Browns	2.00	1.00	.60
42	1945 Tigers/Cubs (Hank Greenberg)	2.50	1.25	.70
43	1946 Cardinals/Red Sox (Enos Slaughter)	2.00	1.00	.60
44	1947 Yankees/Dodgers (Al Gionfriddo)	2.00	1.00	.60
45	1948 Indians/Braves	1.50	.70	.45
46	1949 Yankees/Dodgers (Allie Reynolds/Preacher Roe)	2.00	1.00	.60
47	1950 Yankees/Phillies	2.00	1.00	.60
48	1951 Yankees/Giants	1.50	.70	.45
49	1952 Yankees/Dodgers (Johnny Mize/Duke Snider)	2.50	1.25	.70
50	1953 Yankees/Dodgers (Carl Erskine)	2.00	1.00	.60
51	1954 Giants/Indians (Johnny Antonelli)	1.50	.70	.45
52	1955 Dodgers/Yankees	2.00	1.00	.60
53	1956 Yankees/Dodgers	2.00	1.00	.60
54	1957 Braves/Yankees (Lew Burdette)	3.00	1.50	.90
55	1958 Yankees/Braves (Bob Turley)	1.50	.70	.45
56	1959 Dodgers/White Sox (Chuck Essegian)	2.00	1.00	.60
57	1960 Pirates/Yankees	2.00	1.00	.60
58	1961 Reds/Yankees (Whitey Ford)	2.00	1.00	.60
59	1962 Yankees/Giants	1.50	.70	.45
60	1963 Dodgers/Yankees (Bill Skowron)	1.50	.70	.45
61	1964 Cardinals/Yankees (Bobby Richardson)	2.00	1.00	.60
62	1965 Dodgers/Twins	2.00	1.00	.60
63	1966 Orioles/Dodgers	1.50	.70	.45
64	1967 Cardinals/Red Sox	1.50	.70	.45
65	1968 Tigers/Cardinals	2.00	1.00	.60
66	1969 Mets/Orioles	4.50	2.25	1.25

1971-80 Fleer World Series

New artwork by Robert Laughlin is featured in the second of Fleer's World Series highlights sets. Fronts feature color art with backs printed in black. It appears as if the original set issued in 1971 was updated intermittently.

	NM	EX	VG
Complete Set (68):	135.00	65.00	40.00
Complete Set (75):	350.00	175.00	100.00
Common Card:	2.00	1.00	.60
Wax Pack:	30.00		
1 1903 Red Sox/Pirates (Cy Young)	6.00	3.00	1.75
2 1904 No World Series (John McGraw)	5.00	2.50	1.50
3 1905 Giants/A's (Christy Mathewson/Chief Bender)	5.00	2.50	1.50
4 1906 White Sox/Cubs	2.00	1.00	.60
5 1907 Cubs/Tigers	2.00	1.00	.60
6 1908 Cubs/Tigers (Ty Cobb)	5.00	2.50	1.50
7 1909 Pirates/Tigers	2.50	1.25	.70
8 1910 A's/Cubs (Eddie Collins)	2.50	1.25	.70
9 1911 A's/Giants (Home Run Baker)	2.50	1.25	.70
10 1912 Red Sox/Giants	2.00	1.00	.60
11 1913 A's/Giants (Christy Mathewson)	3.00	1.50	.90
12 1914 Braves/A's	2.00	1.00	.60
13 1915 Red Sox/Phillies (Grover Cleveland Alexander)	3.00	1.50	.90
14 1916 Red Sox/Dodgers (Jack Coombs)	2.00	1.00	.60
15 1917 White Sox/Giants (Red Faber)	2.50	1.25	.70
16 1918 Red Sox/Cubs (Babe Ruth)	6.00	3.00	1.75
17 1919 Reds/White Sox	4.00	2.00	1.25
18 1920 Indians/Dodgers (Elmer Smith)	2.50	1.25	.70
19 1921 Giants/Yankees (Waite Hoyt)	4.00	2.00	1.25
20 1922 Giants/Yankees (Art Nehf)	2.50	1.25	.70
21 1923 Yankees/Giants (Herb Pennock)	2.50	1.25	.70
22 1924 Senators/Giants (Walter Johnson)	4.00	2.00	1.25
23 1925 Pirates/Senators (Walter Johnson/Ki Ki Cuyler)	4.00	2.00	1.25
24 1926 Cardinals/Yankees (Rogers Hornsby)	4.00	2.00	1.25
25 1927 Yankees/Pirates	2.50	1.25	.70
26 1928 Yankees/Cardinals (Lou Gehrig)	5.00	2.50	1.50
27 1929 A's/Cubs (Howard Ehmke)	2.00	1.00	.60
28 1930 A's/Cardinals (Jimmie Foxx)	3.00	1.50	.90
29 1931 Cardinals/A's (Pepper Martin)	2.50	1.25	.70
30 1932 Yankees/Cubs (Babe Ruth)	6.00	3.00	1.75
31 1933 Giants/Senators (Carl Hubbell)	3.00	1.50	.90
32 1934 Cardinals/Tigers	2.00	1.00	.60
33 1935 Tigers/Cubs (Mickey Cochrane)	2.50	1.25	.70
34 1936 Yankees/Giants (Red Rolfe)	2.50	1.25	.70
35 1937 Yankees/Giants (Tony Lazerri)	4.00	2.00	1.25
36 1938 Yankees/Cubs	3.00	1.50	.90
37 1939 Yankees/Reds	3.00	1.50	.90
38 1940 Reds/Tigers (Mike McCormick)	2.00	1.00	.60
39 1941 Yankees/Dodgers (Charlie Keller)	2.50	1.25	.70
40 1942 Cardinals/Yankees (Whitey Kurowski/Johnny Beazley)	2.00	1.00	.60
41 1943 Yankees/Cardinals (Spud Chandler)	2.00	1.00	.60
42 1944 Cardinals/Browns (Mort Cooper)	2.50	1.25	.70
43 1945 Tigers/Cubs (Hank Greenberg)	3.00	1.50	.90
44 1946 Cardinals/Red Sox (Enos Slaughter)	2.50	1.25	.70
45 1947 Yankees/Dodgers (Johnny Lindell/Hugh Casey)	2.50	1.25	.70
46 1948 Indians/Braves	2.00	1.00	.60
47 1949 Yankees/Dodgers (Preacher Roe)	2.00	1.00	.60
48 1950 Yankees/Phillies (Allie Reynolds)	2.50	1.25	.70
49 1951 Yankees/Giants (Ed Lopat)	2.50	1.25	.70
50 1952 Yankees/Dodgers (Johnny Mize)	2.50	1.25	.70
51 1953 Yankees/Dodgers	2.50	1.25	.70
52 1954 Giants/Indians	2.00	1.00	.60
53 1955 Dodgers/Yankees (Duke Snider)	4.00	2.00	1.25
54 1956 Yankees/Dodgers	2.50	1.25	.70
55 1957 Braves/Yankees	2.50	1.25	.70
56 1958 Yankees/Braves (Hank Bauer)	2.50	1.25	.70
57 1959 Dodgers/White Sox (Duke Snider)	3.00	1.50	.90
58 1960 Pirates/Yankees (Bill Skowron/Bobby Richardson)	2.50	1.25	.70
59 1961 Yankees/Reds (Whitey Ford)	2.00	1.00	.60
60 1962 Yankees/Giants	2.00	1.00	.60
61 1963 Dodgers/Yankees	2.00	1.00	.60
62 1964 Cardinals/Yankees	2.50	1.25	.70
63 1965 Dodgers/Twins	2.50	1.25	.70

64 1966 Orioles/Dodgers	2.00	1.00	.60
65 1967 Cardinals/Red Sox	2.00	1.00	.60
66 1968 Tigers/Cardinals	2.50	1.25	.70
67 1969 Mets/Orioles	6.00	3.00	1.75
68 1970 Orioles/Reds	5.00	2.50	1.50
69 1971 Pirates/Orioles (Roberto Clemente)	35.00	17.50	10.00
70 1972 A's/Reds	15.00	7.50	4.50
71 1973 A's/Mets	15.00	7.50	4.50
(72) 1974 A's/Dodgers	50.00	25.00	15.00
(73) 1975 Reds/Red Sox	50.00	25.00	15.00
(74) 1976 Reds/Yankees	50.00	25.00	15.00
(75) 1977 Yankees/Dodgers	50.00	25.00	15.00

1972 Fleer Famous Feats

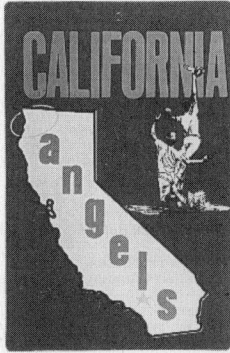

This 40-card set by sports artist R.G. Laughlin is oversized, 2-1/2" x 4". It features the pen and ink work of the artist, with several colors added to the front. The backs are printed in blue on white card stock. The Major League Baseball logo appears on the front of the card, one of the few Laughlin issues to do so. Selling price at issue was about $3.

	NM	EX	VG
Complete Set (40):	40.00	20.00	12.00
Common Player:	1.50	.75	.45
1 Joe McGinnity	2.00	1.00	.60
2 Rogers Hornsby	3.50	1.75	1.00
3 Christy Mathewson	4.00	2.00	1.25
4 Dazzy Vance	2.00	1.00	.60
5 Lou Gehrig	7.50	3.75	2.25
6 Jim Bottomley	2.00	1.00	.60
7 Johnny Evers	2.00	1.00	.60
8 Walter Johnson	4.00	2.00	1.25
9 Hack Wilson	2.00	1.00	.60
10 Wilbert Robinson	2.00	1.00	.60
11 Cy Young	3.50	1.75	1.00
12 Rudy York	1.50	.75	.45
13 Grover C. Alexander	2.00	1.00	.60
14 Fred Toney, Hippo Vaughn	1.50	.75	.45
15 Ty Cobb	7.50	3.75	2.25
16 Jimmie Foxx	3.50	1.75	1.00
17 Hub Leonard	1.50	.75	.45
18 Eddie Collins	2.00	1.00	.60
19 Joe Oeschger, Leon Cadore	1.50	.75	.45
20 Babe Ruth	9.00	4.50	2.75
21 Honus Wagner	4.00	2.00	1.25
22 Red Rolfe	1.50	.75	.45
23 Ed Walsh	2.00	1.00	.60
24 Paul Waner	2.00	1.00	.60
25 Mel Ott	2.50	1.25	.70
26 Eddie Plank	2.00	1.00	.60
27 Sam Crawford	2.00	1.00	.60
28 Napoleon Lajoie	2.00	1.00	.60
29 Ed Reulbach	1.50	.75	.45
30 Pinky Higgins	1.50	.75	.45
31 Bill Klem	2.00	1.00	.60
32 Tris Speaker	3.00	1.50	.90
33 Hank Gowdy	1.50	.75	.45
34 Lefty O'Doul	1.50	.75	.45
35 Lloyd Waner	2.00	1.00	.60
36 Chuck Klein	2.00	1.00	.60
37 Deacon Phillippe	1.50	.75	.45
38 Ed Delahanty	2.00	1.00	.60
39 Jack Chesbro	2.00	1.00	.60
40 Willie Keeler	2.00	1.00	.60

1973 Fleer Team Logo Decals

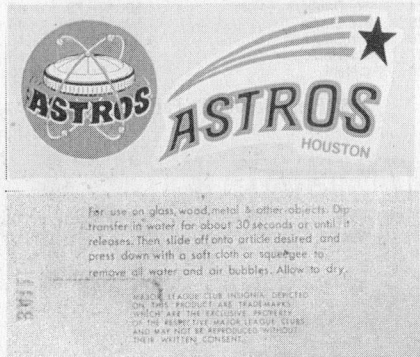

These colorful team logo decals were pack inserts in Fleer's "Wildest Days and Plays." The decals measure 4" x 2-11/16". Backs have instructions for applying the decals.

	NM	EX	VG
Complete Set (24):	110.00	55.00	33.00
Common Team:	9.00	4.50	2.75
(1) Atlanta Braves	9.00	4.50	2.75
(2) Baltimore Orioles	9.00	4.50	2.75
(3) Boston Red Sox	9.00	4.50	2.75
(4) California Angels	9.00	4.50	2.75
(5) Chicago Cubs	9.00	4.50	2.75
(6) Chicago White Sox	9.00	4.50	2.75
(7) Cincinnati Reds	9.00	4.50	2.75
(8) Cleveland Indians	9.00	4.50	2.75
(9) Detroit Tigers	9.00	4.50	2.75
(10) Houston Astros	9.00	4.50	2.75
(11) Kansas City Royals	9.00	4.50	2.75
(12) Los Angeles Dodgers	9.00	4.50	2.75
(13) Milwaukee Brewers	9.00	4.50	2.75
(14) Minnesota Twins	9.00	4.50	2.75
(15) Montreal Expos	9.00	4.50	2.75
(16) New York Mets	12.00	6.00	3.50
(17) New York Yankees	10.00	5.00	3.00
(18) Oakland A's	10.00	5.00	3.00
(19) Philadelphia Phillies	9.00	4.50	2.75
(20) Pittsburgh Pirates	11.00	5.50	3.25
(21) San Diego Padres	9.00	4.50	2.75
(22) San Francisco Giants	9.00	4.50	2.75
(23) St. Louis Cardinals	9.00	4.50	2.75
(24) Texas Rangers	12.00	6.00	3.50

1973 Fleer Team Signs

Each of the major league teams was represented in this issue of thick oversized (7-3/4" x 11-1/2") team logo signs. The blank-back signs have rounded corners and a grommeted hole at top-center for hanging. The unnumbered signs are checklisted here alphabetically.

	NM	EX	VG
Complete Set (24):	35.00	17.50	10.00
Common Team:	4.00	2.00	1.25
(1) Atlanta Braves	4.00	2.00	1.25
(2) Baltimore Orioles	4.00	2.00	1.25
(3) Boston Red Sox	4.00	2.00	1.25
(4) California Angels	4.00	2.00	1.25
(5) Chicago Cubs	4.00	2.00	1.25
(6) Chicago White Sox	4.00	2.00	1.25
(7) Cincinnati Reds	5.00	2.50	1.50
(8) Cleveland Indians	4.00	2.00	1.25
(9) Detroit Tigers	4.00	2.00	1.25
(10) Houston Astros	4.00	2.00	1.25
(11) Kansas City Royals	4.00	2.00	1.25
(12) Los Angeles Dodgers	4.00	2.00	1.25
(13) Milwaukee Brewers	4.00	2.00	1.25
(14) Minnesota Twins	4.00	2.00	1.25
(15) Montreal Expos	4.00	2.00	1.25
(16) New York Mets	5.00	2.50	1.50
(17) New York Yankees	5.00	2.50	1.50
(18) Oakland A's	5.00	2.50	1.50
(19) Philadelphia Phillies	4.00	2.00	1.25
(20) Pittsburgh Pirates	4.00	2.00	1.25
(21) St. Louis Cardinals	4.00	2.00	1.25
(22) San Francisco Giants	4.00	2.00	1.25
(23) San Diego Padres	4.00	2.00	1.25
(24) Texas Rangers	4.00	2.00	1.25

1973 Fleer Wildest Days and Plays

This 42-card set highlights unusual plays and happenings in baseball history, with the fronts featuring artwork by R.G. Laughlin. The cards are 2-1/2" x 4" and printed with color on the front and in red on the back. Original retail price was about $3.25.

		NM	EX	VG
	Complete Set (42):	35.00	17.50	10.00
	Common Player:	1.50	.70	.45
1	Cubs and Phillies Score 49 Runs in Game	1.50	.70	.45
2	Frank Chance Five HBP's in One Day	2.00	1.00	.60
3	Jim Thorpe Homered Into Three States	2.00	1.00	.60
4	Eddie Gaedel Midget in Majors	2.00	1.00	.60
5	Most Tied Game Ever	1.50	.70	.45
6	Seven Errors in One Inning	1.50	.70	.45
7	Four 20-Game Winners But No Pennant	1.50	.70	.45
8	Dummy Hoy Umpire Signals Strikes	2.00	1.00	.60
9	Fourteen Hits in One Inning	1.50	.70	.45
10	Yankees Not Shut Out for Two Years	1.50	.70	.45
11	Buck Weaver 17 Straight Fouls	2.00	1.00	.60
12	George Sisler Greatest Thrill	1.50	.70	.45
13	Wrong-Way Baserunner	1.50	.70	.45
14	Kiki Cuyler Sits Out Series	1.50	.70	.45
15	Grounder Climbed Wall	1.50	.70	.45
16	Gabby Street Washington Monument	1.50	.70	.45
17	Mel Ott Ejected Twice	2.00	1.00	.60
18	Shortest Pitching Career	1.50	.70	.45
19	Three Homers in One Inning	1.50	.70	.45
20	Bill Byron Singing Umpire	1.50	.70	.45
21	Fred Clarke Walking Steal of Home	1.50	.70	.45
22	Christy Mathewson 373rd Win Discovered	2.00	1.00	.60
23	Hitting Through the Unglaub Arc	1.50	.70	.45
24	Jim O'Rourke Catching at 52	1.50	.70	.45
25	Fired for Striking Out in Series	1.50	.70	.45
26	Eleven Run Inning on One Hit	1.50	.70	.45
27	58 Innings in 3 Days	1.50	.70	.45
28	Homer on Warm-up Pitch	1.50	.70	.45
29	Giants Win 26 Straight But Finish Fourth	1.50	.70	.45
30	Player Who Stole First Base	1.50	.70	.45
31	Ernie Shore Perfect Game in Relief	1.50	.70	.45
32	Greatest Comeback	1.50	.70	.45
33	All-Time Flash-in-the-Pan	1.50	.70	.45
34	Pruett Fanned Ruth 19 Out of 31	2.00	1.00	.60
35	Fixed Batting Race (Ty Cobb, Nap Lajoie)	2.00	1.00	.60
36	Wild Pitch Rebound Play	1.50	.70	.45
37	17 Straight Scoring Innings	1.50	.70	.45
38	Wildest Opening Day	1.50	.70	.45
39	Baseball's Strike One	1.50	.70	.45
40	Opening Day No-Hitter That Didn't Count	1.50	.70	.45
41	Jimmie Foxx 6 Straight Walks in One Game	2.00	1.00	.60
42	Entire Team Hit and Scored in Inning	1.50	.70	.45

1974 Fleer Baseball Firsts

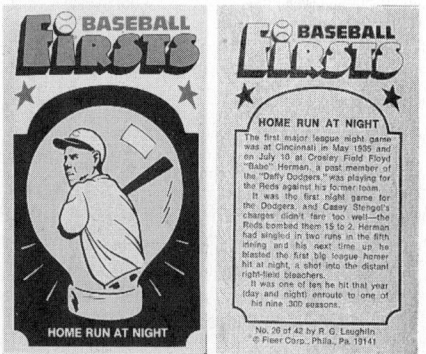

HOME RUN AT NIGHT

This 42-card set from Fleer is titled "Baseball Firsts" and features several historical moments in baseball, as captured through the artwork of sports artist R.G. Laughlin. The cards are 2-1/2" x 4" and are numbered on the back, which is gray card stock with black printing. The set is not licensed by Major League Baseball.

		NM	EX	VG
	Complete Set (42):	80.00	40.00	25.00
	Common Player:	2.00	1.00	.60
1	Slide	2.00	1.00	.60
2	Spring Training	2.00	1.00	.60
3	Bunt	2.00	1.00	.60
4	Catcher's Mask	2.00	1.00	.60
5	Four Straight Homers (Lou Gehrig)	10.00	5.00	3.00
6	Radio Broadcast	2.00	1.00	.60
7	Numbered Uniforms	2.00	1.00	.60
8	Shin Guards	2.00	1.00	.60
9	Players Association	2.00	1.00	.60
10	Knuckleball	2.00	1.00	.60
11	Player With Glasses	2.00	1.00	.60
12	Baseball Cards	12.00	6.00	3.50
13	Standardized Rules	2.00	1.00	.60
14	Grand Slam	2.00	1.00	.60
15	Player Fined	2.00	1.00	.60

		NM	EX	VG
16	Presidential Opener	2.00	1.00	.60
17	Player Transaction	2.00	1.00	.60
18	All-Star Game	2.00	1.00	.60
19	Scoreboard	2.00	1.00	.60
20	Cork-center Ball	2.00	1.00	.60
21	Scorekeeping	2.00	1.00	.60
22	Domed Stadium	2.00	1.00	.60
23	Batting Helmet	2.00	1.00	.60
24	Fatality	4.00	2.00	1.25
25	Unassisted Triple Play	2.00	1.00	.60
26	Home Run at Night	2.00	1.00	.60
27	Black Major Leaguer	4.00	2.00	1.25
28	Pinch Hitter	2.00	1.00	.60
29	Million Dollar World Series	2.00	1.00	.60
30	Tarpaulin	2.00	1.00	.60
31	Team Initials	2.00	1.00	.60
32	Pennant Playoff	2.00	1.00	.60
33	Glove	2.00	1.00	.60
34	Curve Ball	2.00	1.00	.60
35	Night Game	2.00	1.00	.60
36	Admission Charge	2.00	1.00	.60
37	Farm System	2.00	1.00	.60
38	Telecast	2.00	1.00	.60
39	Commissioner	2.00	1.00	.60
40	.400 Hitter	2.00	1.00	.60
41	World Series	2.00	1.00	.60
42	Player Into Service	2.00	1.00	.60

1975 Fleer Pioneers of Baseball

This 28-card set did not draw a great deal of interest in the hobby. The cards are slightly oversized (2-1/2" x 4") and feature sepia-toned photographs of old baseball players. The backs feature information about the player and the card number. A "Pioneers of Baseball" banner appears at the top of the card back. Each 10-cent pack included one card and one each cloth team pennant and patch, plus a stick of gum.

		NM	EX	VG
	Complete Set (28):	20.00	10.00	6.00
	Common Player:	1.50	.75	.45
	Wax Pack:	6.00		
	Wax Box (24):	65.00		
1	Cap Anson	1.50	.75	.45
2	Harry Wright	1.50	.75	.45
3	Buck Ewing	1.50	.75	.45
4	A.G. Spalding	1.50	.75	.45
5	Old Hoss Radbourn	1.50	.75	.45
6	Dan Brouthers	1.50	.75	.45
7	Roger Bresnahan	1.50	.75	.45
8	Mike Kelly	1.50	.75	.45
9	Ned Hanton	1.50	.75	.45
10	Ed Delahanty	1.50	.75	.45
11	Pud Galvin	1.50	.75	.45
12	Amos Rusie	1.50	.75	.45
13	Tommy McCarthy	1.50	.75	.45
14	Ty Cobb	6.00	3.00	1.75
15	John McGraw	1.50	.75	.45
16	Home Run Baker	1.50	.75	.45
17	Johnny Evers	1.50	.75	.45
18	Nap Lajoie	1.50	.75	.45
19	Cy Young	2.50	1.25	.70
20	Eddie Collins	1.50	.75	.45
21	John Glasscock	1.50	.75	.45
22	Hal Chase	1.50	.75	.45
23	Mordecai Brown	1.50	.75	.45
24	Jake Daubert	1.50	.75	.45
25	Mike Donlin	1.50	.75	.45
26	John Clarkson	1.50	.75	.45
27	Buck Herzog	1.50	.75	.45
28	Art Nehf	1.50	.75	.45

1980 Fleer Baseball's Famous Feats

Yet another incarnation of Robert Laughlin's "Baseball's Famous Feats" cartoon artwork is this 22-card issue, in standard 2-1/2" x 3-1/2" format. The player art is backed with team logo and pennant stickers, creating a huge variety of possible front/back combinations. The cards are licensed by Major League Baseball and numbered on the front.

		NM	EX	VG
	Complete Set (22):	6.00	3.00	1.75
	Common Player:	.75	.40	.25
1	Grover Cleveland Alexander	.75	.40	.25
2	Jimmy (Jimmie) Foxx	1.00	.50	.30
3	Ty Cobb	1.50	.70	.45
4	Walter Johnson	1.00	.50	.30
5	Hack Wilson	.75	.40	.25
6	Tris Speaker	1.00	.50	.30
7	Hank Gowdy	.75	.40	.25
8	Bill Klem	.75	.40	.25
9	Ed Reulbach	.75	.40	.25
10	Fred Toney, Hippo Vaughn	.75	.40	.25
11	Joe Oeschger, Leon Cadore	.75	.40	.25
12	Lloyd Waner	.75	.40	.25
13	Eddie Plank	.75	.40	.25
14	Deacon Phillippe	.75	.40	.25
15	Ed Dalahanty (Delahanty)	.75	.40	.25
16	Eddie Collins	.75	.40	.25
17	Jack Chesbro	.75	.40	.25
18	Red Rolfe	.75	.40	.25
19	Ed Walsh	.75	.40	.25
20	Honus Wagner	1.25	.60	.40
21	Nap Lajoie	.75	.40	.25
22	Cy Young	1.00	.50	.30

1980 Fleer World Series/Team Logo Stickers

World Series cards similar to previous Fleer issues of the 1970s were issued in a new version in 1980. Wax packs containing five stickercards and a piece of bubblegum were offered for a nickel. Each card/sticker combination carried a World Series cartoon card from one of the Autumn Classics from 1940-1979. Unlike the earlier Fleer-Laughlin W.S. cards, these are backed with a team-logo sticker, some of which bear the team's 1979 record, and some of which do not.

		NM	EX	VG
	Complete Set (40):	50.00	25.00	15.00
	Common Card:	1.50	.75	.45
	Wax Pack (5):	4.00		
	Wax Box (36):	80.00		
(1)	1940 Reds/Tigers (Mike McCormick)	1.50	.75	.45
(2)	1941 Yankees/Dodgers (Charlie Keller)	2.25	1.25	.75
(3)	1942 Cardinals/Yankees (Whitey Kurowski/Johnny Beazley)	2.25	1.25	.75
(4)	1943 Yankees/Cardinals (Spud Chandler)	2.25	1.25	.75
(5)	1944 Cardinals/Browns (Mort Cooper)	2.25	1.25	.75
(6)	1945 Tigers/Cubs (Hank Greenberg)	3.00	1.50	.90
(7)	1946 Cardinals/Red Sox (Enos Slaughter)	1.50	.75	.45
(8)	1947 Yankees/Dodgers (Johnny Lindell/Hugh Casey)	3.00	1.50	.90
(9)	1948 Indians/Braves	1.50	.75	.45
(10)	1949 Yankees/Dodgers (Preacher Roe)	3.00	1.50	.90
(11)	1950 Yankees/Phillies (Allie Reynolds)	3.00	1.50	.90
(12)	1951 Yankees/Giants (Ed Lopat)	3.00	1.50	.90
(13)	1952 Yankees/Dodgers (Johnny Mize)	4.00	2.00	1.25
(14)	1953 Yankees/Dodgers	4.00	2.00	1.25
(15)	1954 Giants/Indians	3.00	1.50	.90
(16)	1955 Dodgers/Yankees (Duke Snider)	4.50	2.25	1.25
(17)	1956 Yankees/Dodgers	4.00	2.00	1.25
(18)	1957 Braves/Yankees	4.00	2.00	1.25
(19)	1958 Yankees/Braves (Hank Bauer)	3.00	1.50	.90
(20)	1959 Dodgers/White Sox (Duke Snider)	3.00	1.50	.90
(21)	1960 Pirates/Yankees (Bill Skowron/Bobby Richardson)	4.50	2.25	1.25
(22)	1961 Yankees/Reds (Whitey Ford)	3.00	1.50	.90
(23)	1962 Yankees/Giants	3.00	1.50	.90
(24)	1963 Dodgers/Yankees	3.00	1.50	.90
(25)	1964 Cardinals/Yankees	3.00	1.50	.90
(26)	1965 Dodgers/Twins	1.50	.75	.45
(27)	1966 Orioles/Dodgers	1.50	.75	.45
(28)	1967 Cardinals/Red Sox	1.50	.75	.45
(29)	1968 Tigers/Cardinals	1.50	.75	.45

		NM	EX	VG
(30)	1969 Mets/Orioles	4.00	2.00	1.25
(31)	1970 Orioles/Reds	1.50	.75	.45
(32)	1971 Pirates/Orioles	1.50	.75	.45
(33)	1972 A's/Reds	1.50	.75	.45
(34)	1973 A's/Mets	1.50	.75	.45
(35)	1974 A's/Dodgers	1.50	.75	.45
(36)	1975 Reds/Red Sox	2.25	1.25	.75
(37)	1976 Reds/Yankees	1.50	.75	.45
(38)	1977 Yankees/Dodgers	2.25	1.25	.75
(39)	1978 Yankees/Dodgers	2.25	1.25	.75
(40)	1979 Pirates/Orioles	2.25	1.25	.75

1916 Fleischmann Bakery (D381)

B.W. KOCHER, Catcher
New York National

Send or bring 20 of these coupons with 50 cents to
FLEISCHMANN BAKERY, 440 East 61st Street,
New York City, and receive a beautiful leather Kodak
Album, in which you can mount your pictures of base
ball players. Will hold 100 photos.

These cards were issued by a New York City bakery, pre-sumably given away with the purchase of bread or other goods. The blank-back cards are printed in black-and-white in a 2-3/4" x 5-3/8" format. Fronts have player photos with the name, team and position in two lines beneath. Most cards have an Underwood & Underwood copyright notice on the pic-ture. At bottom is a coupon that could be redeemed for an album to house the cards. Prices shown here are for cards without the coupon. Cards with coupon are valued at about the premium shown below. Cards are checklisted here in alphabetical order. Some cards can be found with differing sizes of the player's photo and/or with wrong and corrected photos. A nearly identical issue was produced contemporarily by Ferguson Bread. The two can be distinguished by the two-line identification on front of the Fleischmann cards, and one-line identification on Fergusons.

		NM	EX	VG
Common Player:		400.00	200.00	100.00
With Coupon: 4-6X				
(1)	Babe Adams	400.00	200.00	100.00
(2)	Grover Alexander	700.00	300.00	150.00
(3)	Walt E. Alexander	400.00	200.00	100.00
(4)	Frank Allen	400.00	200.00	100.00
(5)	Fred Anderson	400.00	200.00	100.00
(6)	Dave Bancroft	550.00	225.00	110.00
(7)	Jack Barry	400.00	200.00	100.00
(8a)	Beals Becker (No uniform logo.)	400.00	200.00	100.00
(8b)	Beals Becker (Partial uniform logo.)	400.00	200.00	100.00
(9)	Eddie Burns	400.00	200.00	100.00
(10)	George J. Burns	400.00	200.00	100.00
(11)	Bobby Byrne	400.00	200.00	100.00
(12)	Ray Caldwell	400.00	200.00	100.00
(13)	James Callahan	400.00	200.00	100.00
(14)	William Carrigan	400.00	200.00	100.00
(15)	Larry Cheney	400.00	200.00	100.00
(16a)	Tom Clark (No hand/glove.)	400.00	200.00	100.00
(16b)	Tom Clark (Hand and glove show.)	400.00	200.00	100.00
(17)	Ty Cobb	2,900	1,450	725.00
(18a)	Ray W. Collins (Partial top button.)	400.00	200.00	100.00
(18b)	Ray W. Collins (Full top button.)	400.00	200.00	100.00
(19)	Jack Coombs	400.00	200.00	100.00
(20)	A. Wilbur Cooper	400.00	200.00	100.00
(21)	George Cutshaw	400.00	200.00	100.00
(22)	Jake Daubert	400.00	200.00	100.00
(23)	Wheezer Dell	400.00	200.00	100.00
(24)	Bill Donovan	400.00	200.00	100.00
(25)	Larry Doyle	400.00	200.00	100.00
(26)	R.J. Egan	400.00	200.00	100.00
(27)	Johnny Evers	550.00	225.00	110.00
(28)	Ray Fisher	400.00	200.00	100.00
(29)	Harry Gardner (Larry)	400.00	200.00	100.00
(30)	Joe Gedeon	400.00	200.00	100.00
(31)	Larry Gilbert	400.00	200.00	100.00
(32)	Frank Gilhooley	400.00	200.00	100.00
(33)	Hank Gowdy	400.00	200.00	100.00
(34)	Sylvanus Gregg	400.00	200.00	100.00
(35)	Tom Griffith	400.00	200.00	100.00
(36)	Heinie Groh	400.00	200.00	100.00
(37)	Bob Harmon	400.00	200.00	100.00
(38)	Roy A. Hartzell	400.00	200.00	100.00
(39)	Claude Hendrix	400.00	200.00	100.00
(40)	Olaf Henriksen	400.00	200.00	100.00
(41)	Buck Herzog	400.00	200.00	100.00
(42)	Hugh High	400.00	200.00	100.00
(43)	Dick Hoblitzell	400.00	200.00	100.00
(44)	Herb Hunter	400.00	200.00	100.00
(45)	Harold Janvrin	400.00	200.00	100.00
(46)	Hugh Jennings	550.00	225.00	110.00
(47)	John Johnston	400.00	200.00	100.00
(48)	Erving Kantlehner	400.00	200.00	100.00
(49)	Benny Kauff	400.00	200.00	100.00
(50a)	Ray Keating (Error, striped cap, photo is Kocher.)	400.00	200.00	100.00
(50b)	Ray Keating (Correct, "NY" on cap.)	400.00	200.00	100.00
(51)	Wade Killefer	400.00	200.00	100.00
(52a)	Elmer Knetzer (Error, no "B" on cap, photo is Konetchy.)	400.00	200.00	100.00
(52b)	Elmer Knetzer (Correct, "B" on cap.)	400.00	200.00	100.00
(53a)	B.W. Kocher (Error, "NY" on cap, photo is Keating.)	400.00	200.00	100.00
(53b)	B.W. Kocher (Correct, striped cap.)	400.00	200.00	100.00
(54a)	Ed. Konetchy (Error, "B" on cap, photo is Knetzer.)	400.00	200.00	100.00
(54b)	Ed. Konetchy (Correct, no "B" on cap.)	400.00	200.00	100.00
(55)	Fred Lauderous (Luderous)	400.00	200.00	100.00
(56)	Dutch Leonard	400.00	200.00	100.00
(57)	Duffy Lewis	400.00	200.00	100.00
(58)	Slim Love	400.00	200.00	100.00
(59)	Albert L. Mamaux	400.00	200.00	100.00
(60)	Rabbit Maranville	550.00	225.00	110.00
(61)	Rube Marquard	540.00	215.00	110.00
(62)	Christy Mathewson	1,900	950.00	475.00
(63)	Bill McKechnie	550.00	225.00	110.00
(64)	Chief Meyer (Meyers)	400.00	200.00	100.00
(65)	Otto Miller	400.00	200.00	100.00
(66)	Fred Mollwitz	400.00	200.00	100.00
(67)	Herbie Moran	400.00	200.00	100.00
(68)	Mike Mowrey	400.00	200.00	100.00
(69)	Dan Murphy	400.00	200.00	100.00
(70)	Art Nehf	400.00	200.00	100.00
(71)	Rube Oldring	400.00	200.00	100.00
(72)	Oliver O'Mara	400.00	200.00	100.00
(73)	Dode Paskert	400.00	200.00	100.00
(74)	D.C. Pat Ragan	400.00	200.00	100.00
(75)	William A. Rariden	400.00	200.00	100.00
(76)	Davis Robertson	400.00	200.00	100.00
(77)	Wm. Rodgers	400.00	200.00	100.00
(78)	Edw. F. Rousch (Roush)	550.00	225.00	110.00
(79)	Nap Rucker	400.00	200.00	100.00
(80)	Dick Rudolph	400.00	200.00	100.00
(81)	Wally Schang	400.00	200.00	100.00
(82)	Rube Schauer	400.00	200.00	100.00
(83)	Pete Schneider	400.00	200.00	100.00
(84)	Ferd Schupp	400.00	200.00	100.00
(85)	Ernie Shore	400.00	200.00	100.00
(86)	Red Smith	400.00	200.00	100.00
(87)	Fred Snodgrass	400.00	200.00	100.00
(88)	Tris Speaker	700.00	350.00	175.00
(89)	George Stallings	400.00	200.00	100.00
(90)	Casey Stengel	600.00	300.00	150.00
(91)	Sailor Stroud	400.00	200.00	100.00
(92)	Amos Strunk	400.00	200.00	100.00
(93)	Chas. (Jeff) Tesreau	400.00	200.00	100.00
(94a)	Chester D. Thomas (One button shows.)	400.00	200.00	100.00
(94b)	Chester D. Thomas (Two buttons.)	400.00	200.00	100.00
(95)	Fred Toney	400.00	200.00	100.00
(96)	Walt Tragesser	400.00	200.00	100.00
(97)	Honus Wagner	5,000	1,000	500.00
(98)	Carl Weilman	400.00	200.00	100.00
(99)	Zack Wheat	550.00	225.00	110.00
(100)	George Whitted	400.00	200.00	100.00
(101)	Arthur Wilson	400.00	200.00	100.00
(102)	Ivy Wingo	400.00	200.00	100.00
(103)	Joe Wood	500.00	250.00	125.00

1940s Ford Babe Ruth Premium

CONSULTANT
FORD MOTOR COMPANY
AMERICAN LEGION JUNIOR BASEBALL

The exact date of this premium photo's issue is unknown. The approximately 5" x 6-1/2" blank-back, black-and-white photo features Ruth in an oft-seen batting pose. In the wide white bor-der at bottom is printed, "CONSULTANT / FORD MOTOR COM-PANY / AMERICAN LEGION JUNIOR BASEBALL."

	NM	EX	VG
Babe Ruth	300.00	150.00	90.00

1961 Ford Pittsburgh Pirates Prints

The year after the team's dramatic World Series win over the Yankees, Pittsburgh area Ford dealers distributed a set of six player prints. The blank-back, 11-7/8" x 14-3/4" prints fea-ture action drawings of the players by artist Robert Riger. Some of the prints are horizontal in format, some are vertical. A Ford Motor Co. copyright line appears in the lower-left cor-ner and a line at bottom center identifies the player in the form

CLEMENTE LINES ONE OVER SECOND

of a title for the picture. The unnumbered prints are listed here in alphabetical order. The pictures were reprinted by an unau-thorized party circa 1998.

		NM	EX	VG
Complete Set (6):		125.00	65.00	35.00
Common Player:		15.00	7.50	4.50
(1)	BOB FRIEND COMES IN WITH THE FAST ONE (Bob Friend)	15.00	7.50	4.50
(2)	CLEMENTE LINES ONE OVER SECOND (Roberto Clemente)	75.00	37.50	22.00
(3)	GROAT CUTS DOWN A BRAVE STEAL (Dick Groat)	15.00	7.50	4.50
(4)	HOAK HANDLES A HOT SHOT AT THIRD (Don Hoak)	15.00	7.50	4.50
(5)	MAZ GETS THE BIG HIT (Bill Mazeroski)	30.00	15.00	9.00
(6)	THE LAW (Vern Law)	15.00	7.50	4.50

1962 Ford Detroit Tigers Postcards

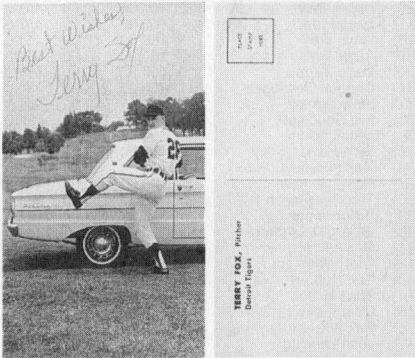

TERRY FOX, Pitcher
Detroit Tigers

Because baseball card collectors have to compete with auto memorabilia hobbyists for these scarce cards, they are among the most valuable postcard issues of the early 1960s. In 3-1/4" x 5-1/2" postcard format, the full-color cards feature photos taken on a golf course of players posed in front of var-ious new Fords. White backs have a name, position and team, with a box for a stamp. Probably given out in conjunction with autograph appearances at car dealers (they are frequently found autographed), the set lacks some of the team's biggest stars (Al Kaline, Norm Cash), and includes coaches and even trainer Jack Homel. Probably because of lack of demand, the coaches' and trainer's cards are the scarcest to find today. The unnumbered cards are checklisted here alphabetically.

		NM	EX	VG
Complete Set (16):		1,425	710.00	425.00
Common Player:		60.00	30.00	18.00
(1)	Hank Aguirre	90.00	45.00	27.50
(2)	Steve Boros	120.00	60.00	35.00
(3)	Dick Brown	90.00	45.00	27.50
(4)	Jim Bunning	150.00	75.00	45.00
(5)	Phil Cavaretta	135.00	65.00	40.00
(6)	Rocky Colavito	185.00	90.00	55.00
(7)	Terry Fox	60.00	30.00	18.00
(8)	Purn Goldy	75.00	37.50	22.50
(9)	Jack Homel	135.00	65.00	40.00
(10)	Ron Kline	90.00	45.00	27.50
(11)	Don Mossi	60.00	30.00	18.00
(12)	George Myatt	120.00	60.00	35.00
(13)	Ron Nischwitz	90.00	45.00	27.50
(14)	Larry Osborne	60.00	30.00	18.00
(15)	Phil Regan	90.00	45.00	27.50
(16)	Mike Roarke	135.00	65.00	40.00

1938 Foto Fun

An early attempt at a self-developing player photocard (a technology that Topps used in the 1940s-50s) used a black-and-white negative and a piece of photo paper to create a blue-tint photo that could be placed in a gold cardboard frame. The back of the 2-3/4" x 3-5/8" frame is printed in brown and gives instructions for developing the photo. The checklist of the unnumbered cards, presented here alphabetically, may or may not be complete at 93.

		NM	EX	VG
	Common Player:	160.00	80.00	45.00
(1)	Luke Appling	375.00	185.00	110.00
(2)	Morris Arnovich	160.00	80.00	45.00
(3)	Eldon Auker	160.00	80.00	45.00
(4)	Jim Bagby	160.00	80.00	45.00
(5)	Red Barrett	160.00	80.00	45.00
(6)	Roy Bell	160.00	80.00	45.00
(7)	Wally Berger	160.00	80.00	45.00
(8)	Oswald Bluege	160.00	80.00	45.00
(9)	Frenchy Bordagaray	160.00	80.00	45.00
(10)	Tom Bridges	160.00	80.00	45.00
(11)	Dolf Camilli	160.00	80.00	45.00
(12)	Ben Chapman	160.00	80.00	45.00
(13)	Harland Clift (Harlond)	160.00	80.00	45.00
(14)	Harry Craft	160.00	80.00	45.00
(15)	Roger Cramer	160.00	80.00	45.00
(16)	Joe Cronin	375.00	185.00	110.00
(17)	Tony Cuccinello	160.00	80.00	45.00
(18)	Kiki Cuyler	375.00	185.00	110.00
(19)	Ellsworth Dahlgren	160.00	80.00	45.00
(20)	Harry Danning	160.00	80.00	45.00
(21)	Frank Demaree	160.00	80.00	45.00
(22)	Gene Desautels	160.00	80.00	45.00
(23)	Jim Deshong	160.00	80.00	45.00
(24)	Bill Dickey	450.00	225.00	135.00
(25)	Lou Fette	160.00	80.00	45.00
(26)	Lou Finney	160.00	80.00	45.00
(27)	Larry French	160.00	80.00	45.00
(28)	Linus Frey	160.00	80.00	45.00
(29)	Augie Galan	160.00	80.00	45.00
(30)	Debs Garms	160.00	80.00	45.00
(31)	Charles Gehringer	450.00	225.00	135.00
(32)	Lefty Gomez	450.00	225.00	135.00
(33)	Ival Goodman	160.00	80.00	45.00
(34)	Lee Grissom	160.00	80.00	45.00
(35)	Stan Hack	180.00	90.00	55.00
(36)	Irving Hadley	160.00	80.00	45.00
(37)	Rollie Hemsley	160.00	80.00	45.00
(38)	Tommy Henrich	160.00	80.00	45.00
(39)	Billy Herman	375.00	185.00	110.00
(40)	Willard Hershberger	160.00	80.00	45.00
(41)	Michael Higgins	160.00	80.00	45.00
(42)	Oral Hildebrand	160.00	80.00	45.00
(43)	Carl Hubbell	450.00	225.00	135.00
(44)	Willis Hudlin	160.00	80.00	45.00
(45)	Mike Kreevich	160.00	80.00	45.00
(46)	Ralph Kress	160.00	80.00	45.00
(47)	John Lanning	160.00	80.00	45.00
(48)	Lyn Lary	160.00	80.00	45.00
(49)	Cookie Lavagetto	160.00	80.00	45.00
(50)	Thornton Lee	160.00	80.00	45.00
(51)	Ernie Lombardi	375.00	185.00	110.00
(52)	Al Lopez	375.00	185.00	110.00
(53)	Ted Lyons	375.00	185.00	110.00
(54)	Danny MacFayden	160.00	80.00	45.00
(55)	Max Macon	160.00	80.00	45.00
(56)	Pepper Martin	250.00	125.00	75.00
(57)	Joe Marty	160.00	80.00	45.00
(58)	Frank McCormick	160.00	80.00	45.00
(59)	Bill McKechnie	375.00	185.00	110.00
(60)	Joe Medwick	375.00	185.00	110.00
(61)	Cliff Melton	160.00	80.00	45.00
(62)	Charley Meyer (Myer)	160.00	80.00	45.00
(63)	John Mize	450.00	225.00	135.00
(64)	Terry Moore	180.00	90.00	55.00
(65)	Whitey Moore	160.00	80.00	45.00
(66)	Emmett Mueller	160.00	80.00	45.00
(67)	Hugh Mulcahy	160.00	80.00	45.00
(68)	Van L. Mungo	160.00	80.00	45.00
(69)	Johnny Murphy	160.00	80.00	45.00
(70)	Lynn Nelson	160.00	80.00	45.00
(71)	Mel Ott	450.00	225.00	135.00
(72)	Monte Pearson	160.00	80.00	45.00
(73)	Bill Rogell	160.00	80.00	45.00
(74)	George Selkirk	160.00	80.00	45.00
(75)	Milt Shofner	160.00	80.00	45.00
(76)	Al Simmons	375.00	185.00	110.00
(77)	Clyde Shoun	160.00	80.00	45.00
(78)	Gus Suhr	160.00	80.00	45.00
(79)	Billy Sullivan	160.00	80.00	45.00
(80)	Cecil Travis	160.00	80.00	45.00
(81)	Pie Traynor	375.00	185.00	110.00
(82)	Hal Trosky	160.00	80.00	45.00
(83)	Jim Turner	160.00	80.00	45.00
(84)	Johnny Vander Meer	160.00	80.00	45.00
(85)	Oscar Vitt	160.00	80.00	45.00
(86)	Gerald Walker	160.00	80.00	45.00
(87)	Paul Waner	375.00	185.00	110.00
(88)	Rabbit Warstler	160.00	80.00	45.00
(89)	Bob Weiland	160.00	80.00	45.00
(90)	Burgess Whitehead	160.00	80.00	45.00
(91)	Earl Whitehill	160.00	80.00	45.00
(92)	Rudy York	160.00	80.00	45.00
(93)	Del Young	160.00	80.00	45.00

1887 Four Base Hits

Although the exact origin of this set is still in doubt, the Four Base Hits cards are among the rarest and most sought after of all 19th century tobacco issues. There is some speculation that the cards, measuring 2-1/4" x 3-7/8", were produced by Charles Gross & Co. because of their similarity to the Kalamazoo Bats issues, but there is also some evidence to support the theory that they were issued by August Beck & Co., producer of the Yum Yum set. The Four Base Hits cards feature sepia-toned photos with the player's name and position below the picture, and the words "Smoke Four Base Hits. Four For 10 Cents." along the bottom. The card labeled "Daily" is a double error. The name should have been spelled "Daly," but the card actually pictures Billy Sunday. Many of the cards on this surely incomplete checklist are known to survive in only a single example; few in grades above VG.

		NM	EX	VG
	Common Player:	35,000	15,000	
(1)	John Clarkson	150,000	80,000	
(2)	Tido Daily (Daly) (Photo is Billy Sunday.)	60,000	24,000	
(3)	Pat Deasley	35,000	15,000	
(4)	Mike Dorgan	35,000	15,000	
(5)	Buck Ewing	175,000	80,000	
(6)	Pete Gillespie	35,000	15,000	
(7)	Frank Hankinson	35,000	15,000	
(8)	King Kelly	250,000	120,000	
(9)	Al Mays	35,000	15,000	
(10)	Jim Mutrie	35,000	15,000	
(11)	Chief Roseman	35,000	15,000	
(12)	Marty Sullivan	35,000	15,000	
(13)	Rip Van Haltren	35,000	15,000	
(14)	John Ward	150,000	80,000	
(15)	Mickey Welch	150,000	80,000	

1960s Nellie Fox Bowl Postcard

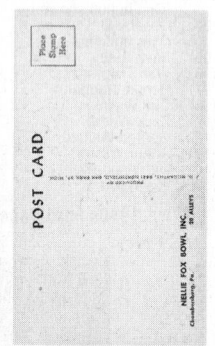

This specially marked version of a typical J.D. McCarthy postcard advertises on back the White Sox second baseman's bowling enterprise in Chambersburg, Pa. The card is black-and-white with a facsimile autograph on front.

	NM	EX	VG
Nellie Fox	35.00	17.50	10.50

1980 Franchise Babe Ruth

The first in a series of collectors' issues relative to Maryland baseball, this 80-card set chronicles the life - on and off the field - of Babe Ruth. Fronts of the 2-1/2" x 3-1/2" cards

have black-and-white photos surrounded by wide white borders. Backs are printed in red and black and include a caption and description of the front photo. At the time of issue, the set sold for about $8.

	NM	EX	VG
Complete Set (80):	35.00	17.50	10.00
Common Card:	1.00	.50	.30
1-80	Babe Ruth		

1961 Franklin Milk

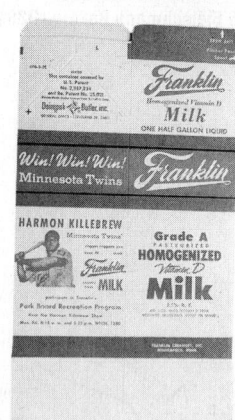

While it is not part of the contemporary Cloverleaf Dairy milk carton Minnesota Twins issues, this carton is often collected alongside the others. Printed in red and blue, the portion of the milk carton advertising Harmon Killebrew's radio show measures about 4" x 4-1/2".

		NM	EX	VG
(1)	Harmon Killebrew (Complete carton.)	1,600	800.00	480.00
(1)	Harmon Killebrew (Cut panel).	250.00	125.00	75.00

1964 Freihofer's Philadelphia Phillies

The attributed date is speculative, based on the players checklisted from this issue. These 8" x 10" pictures feature studio poses and are printed on heavy, non-glossy paper. A white border surrounds the photo, with the player name in typewriter-style all-caps at bottom. Backs are blank. Two styles of advertising have been seen imprinted on the pictures. Type 1 pictures have a bakery logo as part of the legend "ANOTHER FAVORITE / FROM FREIHOFER'S / that's who!" Type 2 pictures have a script inscription: "Best WISHES to a / Fellow Freihofer's Booster."

	NM	EX	VG
TYPE 1 (Logo)			
Ruben Amaro	50.00	25.00	15.00
Wes Covington	50.00	25.00	15.00
TYPE 2 (No logo.)			
Wes Covington	30.00	15.00	9.00

1963 French Bauer Reds Milk Caps

This regional set of cardboard milk bottle caps was issued in the Cincinnati area in 1963 and features 30 members of the Cincinnati Reds. The unnumbered, blank-backed discs are approximately 1-1/4" in diameter and feature rather crude drawings of the players with their names in script alongside the artwork and the words "Visit Beautiful Crosley Field/See The Reds in Action" along the outside. An album was issued to house the set. Some caps have been seen with incorrect picture/name combinations.

		NM	EX	VG
Complete Set (30):		1,300	650.00	400.00
Common Player:		25.00	12.50	7.50
Album:		100.00	50.00	30.00
(1)	Don Blasingame	25.00	12.50	7.50
(2)	Leo Cardenas	25.00	12.50	7.50
(3)	Gordon Coleman	25.00	12.50	7.50
(4)	Wm. O. DeWitt	25.00	12.50	7.50
(5)	John Edwards	25.00	12.50	7.50
(6)	Jesse Gonder	25.00	12.50	7.50
(7)	Tommy Harper	25.00	12.50	7.50
(8)	Bill Henry	25.00	12.50	7.50
(9)	Fred Hutchinson	25.00	12.50	7.50
(10)	Joey Jay	25.00	12.50	7.50
(11)	Eddie Kasko	25.00	12.50	7.50
(12)	Marty Keough	25.00	12.50	7.50
(13)	Jim Maloney	25.00	12.50	7.50
(14)	Joe Nuxhall	30.00	15.00	9.00
(15)	Reggie Otero	25.00	12.50	7.50
(16)	Jim O'Toole	25.00	12.50	7.50
(17)	Jim Owens	25.00	12.50	7.50
(18)	Vada Pinson	30.00	15.00	9.00
(19)	Bob Purkey	25.00	12.50	7.50
(20)	Frank Robinson	125.00	60.00	35.00
(21)	Dr. Richard Rohde	25.00	12.50	7.50
(22)	Pete Rose	500.00	250.00	150.00
(23)	Ray Shore	25.00	12.50	7.50
(24)	Dick Sisler	25.00	12.50	7.50
(25)	Bob Skinner	25.00	12.50	7.50
(26)	John Tsitorius	25.00	12.50	7.50
(27)	Jim Turner	25.00	12.50	7.50
(28)	Ken Walters	25.00	12.50	7.50
(29)	Al Worthington	25.00	12.50	7.50
(30)	Dom Zanni	25.00	12.50	7.50

1946 Friedman's Dodger Aces Postcard

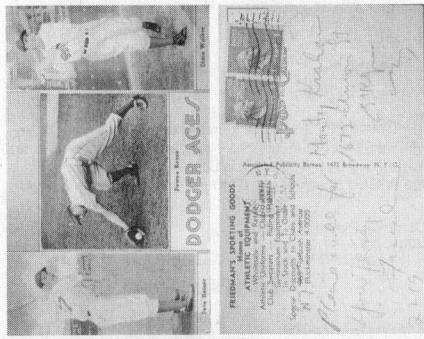

The date of issue is conjectural and could actually have been anytime in the 1940s until 1947, though the cards continued to be used at least into 1953 according to postally used examples. The 5-1/2" x 3-1/2" postcard has a linen finish on front and features color posed action photos of three Dodgers stars. Backs have information about the sporting goods store, a postage stamp box and a credit line to Associated Publicity Bureau.

	NM	EX	VG
Dodger Aces (Pete Reiser, Pewee (Pee Wee) Reese, Dixie Walker)	35.00	17.50	10.50

1960-61 Fritos Ticket Folders

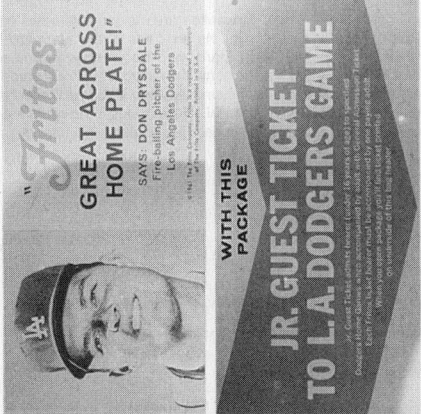

Only a few players are known in this issue of folders which includes a "Jr. Guest Ticket" to selected Dodgers games. About 5-5/8" x 3", the folder has a black-and-white player portrait on front and is highlighted in red and yellow. When opened, the folder has advertising for Fritos corn chips (or other Firtos-Lay brands) and a Dodgers home schedule. Others may exist.

		NM	EX	VG
Common Player:		90.00	45.00	25.00
(1)	Don Drysdale (1960) (Crispies advertising.)	250.00	125.00	75.00
(1)	Don Drysdale (1961)	200.00	100.00	60.00
(2)	Gil Hodges (1960)	200.00	100.00	60.00
(3)	Frank Howard (1961)	90.00	45.00	25.00
(4)	Wally Moon (1960)	150.00	75.00	45.00

		NM	EX	VG
(5)	Charley Neal (1960)	150.00	75.00	45.00

1977 Fritsch One-Year Winners

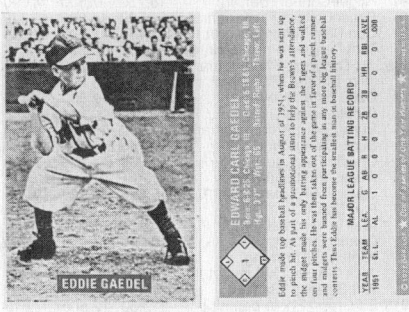

First printed in 1977, this collector's issue features players with brief, but often well-known, major league baseball careers. Because of the timing or duration of their playing days, few ever appeared on a major baseball card issue. The 2-1/2" x 3-1/2" cards have black-and-white photos on front, bordered in green, with the player name in white within a green strip at bottom. Backs are printed in black, red and white in similitude of the 1953 Bowman backs and contain personal data, stats and career highlights.

		NM	EX	VG
Complete Set (18):		12.00	6.00	3.50
Common Player:		1.00	.50	.30
1	Eddie Gaedel	5.00	2.50	1.50
2	Chuck Connors	3.00	1.50	.90
3	Joe Brovia	1.00	.50	.30
4	Ross Grimsley	1.00	.50	.30
5	Bob Thorpe	1.00	.50	.30
6	Pete Gray	5.00	2.50	1.50
7	Cy Buker	1.00	.50	.30
8	Ted Fritsch	2.00	1.00	.60
9	Ron Necciai	1.00	.50	.30
10	Nino Escalera	1.00	.50	.30
11	Bobo Holloman	1.00	.50	.30
12	Tony Roig	1.00	.50	.30
13	Paul Pettit	1.00	.50	.30
14	Paul Schramka	1.00	.50	.30
15	Hal Trosky	1.00	.50	.30
16	Floyd Wooldridge	1.00	.50	.30
17	Jim Westlake	1.00	.50	.30
18	Leon Brinkopf	1.00	.50	.30

1979 Fritsch One-Year Winners

Players with short major-league careers, few of whom appeared on contemporary baseball cards, are featured in the second collectors' series of "One-Year Winners." The cards are numbered contiguously from the end of the 1977 issue and share a back format printed in red, white and black. Fronts of the 1979 issue have a white border and feature color player photos with a shadow box beneath carrying the name.

		NM	EX	VG
Complete Set (36):		40.00	20.00	12.00
Common Player:		3.00	1.50	.90
19	Daryl Robertson	3.00	1.50	.90
20	Gerry Schoen	3.00	1.50	.90
21	Jim Brenneman	3.00	1.50	.90
22	Pat House	3.00	1.50	.90
23	Ken Poulsen	3.00	1.50	.90
24	Arlo Brunsberg	3.00	1.50	.90
25	Jay Hankins	3.00	1.50	.90
26	Chuck Nieson	3.00	1.50	.90
27	Dick Joyce	3.00	1.50	.90
28	Jim Ellis	3.00	1.50	.90
29	John Duffie	3.00	1.50	.90
30	Vern Holtgrave	3.00	1.50	.90
31	Bill Bethea	3.00	1.50	.90
32	Joe Moock	3.00	1.50	.90
33	John Hoffman	3.00	1.50	.90
34	Jorge Rubio	3.00	1.50	.90
35	Fred Rath	3.00	1.50	.90
36	Jess Hickman	3.00	1.50	.90
37	Tom Fisher	3.00	1.50	.90
38	Dick Scott	3.00	1.50	.90
39	Jim Hibbs	3.00	1.50	.90
40	Paul Gilliford	3.00	1.50	.90
41	Bob Botz	3.00	1.50	.90
42	Jack Kubiszyn	3.00	1.50	.90
43	Rich Rusteck	3.00	1.50	.90
44	Roy Gleason	3.00	1.50	.90
45	Glenn Vaughn	3.00	1.50	.90
46	Bill Graham	3.00	1.50	.90
47	Dennis Musgraves	3.00	1.50	.90
48	Ron Henry	3.00	1.50	.90
49	Mike Jurewicz	3.00	1.50	.90
50	Pidge Browne	3.00	1.50	.90
51	Ron Keller	3.00	1.50	.90
52	Doug Gallagher	3.00	1.50	.90
53	Dave Thies	3.00	1.50	.90
54	Don Eaddy	3.00	1.50	.90

1928 Fro-joy (F52)

Boys—Girls:

Fro-joy Ice Cream, in Fro-joy Cones, builds bone and strength. Eat one every day.

Chock-full of "YOUTH UNITS"

PICTURE NO. 1

This is the first in a series of six pictures of "Babe" Ruth being given free with Fro-joy Cones during Fro-joy Cone Week, August 6th-11th, 1928. The complete set can be exchanged for a large reproduction of "Babe" Ruth's autographed photo. Ask your dealer for a FREE circular giving full details.

George Herman ("Babe") Ruth

"The Sultan of Swat," who holds the world's record for home-run hits in a single season with 60 circuit clouts during the regular playing season of 1927, eclipsed by 2 more against Pittsburgh during the World's Series games last year.

Capitalizing on the extreme popularity of Babe Ruth, these cards were given away with ice cream cones during the Aug. 6-11, 1928, "Fro-joy Cone Week." The 2-1/16" x 4" cards have black-and-white photos on front with a title and a few sentences explaining the photo. Backs contain advertising for Fro-joy Ice Cream and Cones. An uncut sheet along with a large-format action photo of Ruth was available in a mail-in redemption offer. Virtually all uncut sheets offered in the market today, and all color Fro-joy cards are modern counterfeits. Purchase of an uncut sheet without the original mailing envelope and/or premium picture is not advised. Cards graded by a major authentication firm carry a significant premium due to the prevalence of single-card counterfeits in the market.

		NM	EX	VG
Complete Set (6):		3,250	1,625	975.00
Uncut Sheet:		2,575	1,275	775.00
1	George Herman ("Babe") Ruth	750.00	375.00	225.00
2	Look Out, Mr. Pitcher!	500.00	250.00	150.00
3	Bang! The Babe Lines One Out!	500.00	250.00	150.00
4	When the "Babe" Comes Home	500.00	250.00	150.00
5	"Babe" Ruth's Grip!	200.00	100.00	60.00
6	Ruth is a Crack Fielder	500.00	250.00	150.00

1928 Fro-Joy Premium Photo

This 8-1/2" x 10" photo of Babe Ruth was given away when a complete set of individual Fro-joy Babe Ruth cards was sent in for redemption. It is extremely scarce in its own right and is vital for verification of the authenticity of uncut Fro-joy card sheets. The premium photo is printed in blue in the debossed center area of a cream-colored card. A facsimile autograph of Ruth adorns the image.

	NM	EX	VG
Babe Ruth	1,200	600.00	360.00

1969 Fud's Photography Montreal Expos

This collectors' issue was produced by Bob Solon sometime after 1969. The 3-1/2" x 3" black-and-white horizontal cards have action photos of the players with a white strip in the lower-right corner bearing the name. In the white border at top is "Compliments of," while the purported photo studio name is centered at bottom. Backs are blank. The unnumbered cards are checklisted here alphabetically.

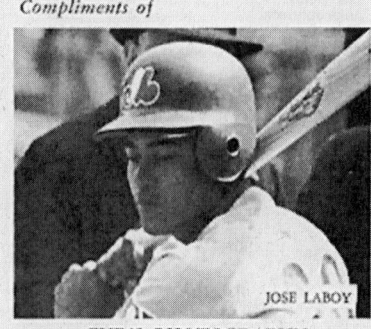

Compliments of

FUD'S PHOTOGRAPHY

JOSE LABOY

		NM	EX	VG
Complete Set (14):		40.00	20.00	12.00
Common Player:		4.00	2.00	1.25
(1)	Bob Bailey	4.00	2.00	1.25
(2)	John Bateman	4.00	2.00	1.25
(3)	Don Bosch	4.00	2.00	1.25
(4)	Jim Grant	4.00	2.00	1.25
(5)	Mack Jones	4.00	2.00	1.25
(6)	Jose Laboy	4.00	2.00	1.25
(7)	Dan McGinn	4.00	2.00	1.25
(8)	Cal McLish	4.00	2.00	1.25
(9)	Carl Morton	4.00	2.00	1.25
(10)	Manny Mota	6.00	3.00	1.75
(11)	Rusty Staub	9.00	4.50	2.75
(12)	Gary Sutherland	4.00	2.00	1.25
(13)	Mike Wegener	4.00	2.00	1.25
(14)	Floyd Wicker	4.00	2.00	1.25

1888 G & B Chewing Gum (E223)

NEW YORK'S

NATIONAL LEAGUE
CHEWING GUM.
G.&B. N.Y.

This set, issued with G&B Chewing Gum, is the first baseball card issued with candy or gum and the only 19th Century candy issue. The cards in the G&B set are small, measuring approximately 1-1/16" x 2-1/8", and nearly identical in format to the August Beck Yum Yum tobacco issue (N403). Many of the photos and pictures were shared between the sets. The player's name and position appear in thin capital letters below the photo, followed by either "National League" or "American League" (actually referring to the American Association). At the very bottom of the card, the manufacturer, "G & B N.Y." is indicated. Some of the "National League" cards also include the words "Chewing Gum" under the league designation. The set was assigned the ACC number E223. All of the action poses and some of the portraits are line drawings rather than photographs. Gaps have been left in the assigned numbering to accommodate future additions.

		NM	EX	VG
Common Player:		10,000	4,000	2,500
(3)	Cap Anson (Batting)	25,000	10,000	6,250
(4)	Cap Anson (Photo portrait.)	37,500	15,000	9,375
(7)	Lady Baldwin (Detroit) (Left arm extended.)	10,000	4,000	2,500
(9)	Mark Baldwin (Chicago) (Bat at side.)	10,000	4,000	2,500
(10)	Mark Baldwin (Chicago)(Photo portrait.)	31,250	12,500	7,815
(13)	Sam Barkley (Line portrait.)	10,000	4,000	2,500
(15)	Steve Brady (Photo portrait.)	31,250	12,500	7,815
(17)	Dan Brouthers (Pose unrecorded.)	31,250	12,500	7,815
(19)	Willard (California) Brown (Photo portrait.)	31,250	12,500	7,815
(20)	Willard (California) Brown (Line art.)	10,000	4,000	2,500
(23)	Charles Buffington (Buffinton)(Photo portrait.)	31,250	12,500	7,815
(25)	Tom Burns (Photo portrait.)	31,250	12,500	7,815
(27)	Doc Bushong (Line portrait.)	10,000	4,000	2,500
(29)	Bob Caruthers (Line portrait.)	10,000	4,000	2,500
(33)	John Clarkson (Photo portrait.)	37,500	15,000	9,375

(35)	John Coleman (Photo portrait.)	31,250	12,500	7,815
(37)	Charlie Comiskey (Line portrait.)	18,750	7,500	4,690
(39)	Roger Connor (Batting)	18,750	7,500	4,690
(40)	Roger Connor (Photo portrait.)	37,500	15,000	9,375
(43)	Con Daily (Photo portrait.)	31,250	12,500	7,815
(45)	Tom Deasley (Photo portrait.)	31,250	12,500	7,815
(47)	Jim Donahue (Photo portrait.)	31,250	12,500	7,815
(49)	Mike Dorgan (Photo portrait.)	31,250	12,500	7,815
(51)	Dude Esterbrook (Photo portrait.)	31,250	12,500	7,815
(53)	Buck Ewing (Photo portrait.)	37,500	15,000	9,375
(54)	Buck Ewing (With bat.)	18,750	7,500	4,690
(57)	Charlie Ferguson (Right arm head-high.)	10,000	4,000	2,500
(59)	Silver Flint (Line portrait.)	15,625	6,250	3,905
(61)	Pud Galvin (Ball in hands at front.)	18,750	7,500	4,690
(63)	Charlie Getzein (Getzien)(Throwing)	10,000	4,000	2,500
(65)	Jack Glasscock (Line art.)	10,000	4,000	2,500
(67)	Will Gleason (Batting)	10,000	4,000	2,500
(69)	Ed Greer (Photo portrait.)	31,250	12,500	7,815
(71)	Frank Hankinson (Photo portrait.)	31,250	12,500	7,815
(73)	Ned Hanlon (Batting)	18,750	7,500	4,690
(75)	Pete Hotaling (Batting)	15,625	6,250	3,905
(77)	Spud Johnson (Batting)	10,000	4,000	2,500
(79)	Tim Keefe (Ball in hands above waist.)	18,750	7,500	4,690
(80)	Tim Keefe (Batting)	18,750	7,500	4,690
(81)	Tim Keefe (Photo portrait.)	37,500	15,000	9,375
(83)	King Kelly (Batting)	25,000	10,000	6,250
(84)	King Kelly (Photo, standing by urn.)	100,000	20,000	12,500
(87)	Gus Krock (Photo portrait.)	31,250	12,500	7,815
(89)	Arlie Latham (Line portrait.)	10,000	4,000	2,500
(91)	Connie Mack (Throwing)	37,500	15,000	9,375
(93)	Kid Madden (Pitching)	10,000	4,000	2,500
(95)	Al Mays (Photo portrait.)	31,250	12,500	7,815
(97)	Jumbo McGinnis (Line portrait.)	10,000	4,000	2,500
(99)	Doggie Miller (Leaning on bat.)	10,000	4,000	2,500
(101)	John Morrill (Bat at side.)	10,000	4,000	2,500
(103)	James Mutrie (Photo portrait.)	31,250	12,500	7,815
(105)	Hugh Nicoll (Nicol) (Line portrait.)	10,000	4,000	2,500
(107)	Tip O'Neill (Line portrait.)	10,000	4,000	2,500
(109)	Jim O'Rourke (Photo portrait.)	37,500	15,000	9,375
(111)	Dave Orr (Batting)	10,000	4,000	2,500
(112)	Dave Orr (Photo portrait.)	31,250	12,500	7,815
(115)	Fred Pfeffer (Bat on shoulder.)	10,000	4,000	2,500
(117)	Henry Porter (Pitching)	10,000	4,000	2,500
(119)	Al Reache (Reach) (Line portrait.) (Possibly unique; value undetermined.)	.00	.00	.00
(121)	Danny Richardson (Batting)	10,000	4,000	2,500
(122)	Danny Richardson (Photo portrait.)	31,250	12,500	7,815
(125)	Yank Robinson (Line portrait.)	10,000	4,000	2,500
(127)	Chief Roseman (Photo portrait.)	31,250	12,500	7,815
(129)	Jimmy Ryan (Photo portrait.)	31,250	12,500	7,815
(130)	Jimmy Ryan (Throwing)	10,000	4,000	2,500
(133)	Pop Smith (Photo portrait.)	31,250	12,500	7,815
(137)	Bill Sowders (Ball in hands at chest.)	10,000	4,000	2,500
(138)	Bill Sowders (Throwing)	10,000	4,000	2,500
(139)	Albert Spaulding (Spalding) (Line portrait.) (Possibly unique; value undetermined.)	.00	.00	.00
(141)	Marty Sullivan (Line portrait.)	10,000	4,000	2,500
(143)	Billy Sunday (Fielding)	15,620	6,250	3,905
(144)	Billy Sunday (Photo portrait.)	34,375	13,750	8,595
(145)	Ezra Sutton (Batting)	10,000	4,000	2,500
(149)	Sam Thompson (Batting)	18,750	7,500	4,690
(153)	Mike Tiernan (Batting)	10,000	4,000	2,500
(154)	Mike Tiernan (Photo portrait.)	31,250	12,500	7,815
(157)	Larry Twitchell (Photo portrait.)	31,250	12,500	7,815
(159)	Rip Van Haltren (Photo portrait.)	31,250	12,500	7,815
(161)	Chris Von Der Ahe (Line portrait.)	10,000	4,000	2,500
(165)	John Ward (Photo portrait.)	37,500	15,000	9,375
(169)	Mickey Welch (Ball in hands above waist.)	18,750	7,500	4,690
(170)	Mickey Welch (Right arm extended forward.)	18,750	7,500	4,690
(171)	Mickey Welch (Photo portrait.)	37,500	15,000	9,375
(173)	Curt Welsh (Welch)	10,000	4,000	2,500
(177)	Jim Whitney	10,000	4,000	2,500
(181)	Pete Wood (Throwing)	10,000	4,000	2,500

1966 H.F. Gardner Postcards

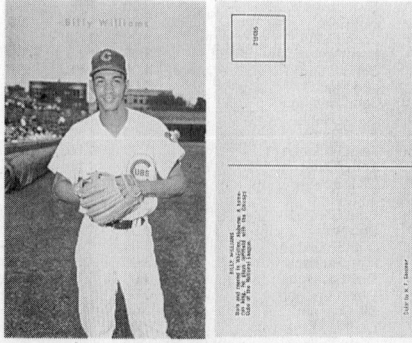

Billy Williams

Baseball players (and track legend Jesse Owens) who were born in Alabama are featured in this issue credited on some of the cards' backs to a Bessemer, Ala., firm, Scenic South Card Co. Fronts feature borderless color photos attributed to H.F. Gardner. The date given is somewhat arbitrary based on the mention of the Atlanta Braves on the back of a card. Cards are in standard 3-1/2" x 5-1/2" postcard size and format. A brief biography of the athletes appears on the back, along with the credits. A quantity of the Aarons and Williams cards were found in a warehouse in 1999, driving down their prices.

		NM	EX	VG
Complete Set (5):		15.00	7.50	4.50
Common Player:		3.00	1.50	.90
(1)	Hank Aaron, Tommie Aaron	6.00	3.00	1.75
(2)	Bill Bruton	3.50	1.75	1.00
(3)	Lee Maye	3.50	1.75	1.00
(4)	Jesse Owens	4.50	2.25	1.25
(5)	Billy Williams	3.00	1.50	.90

1922 Gassler's American Maid Bread

Gassler's American Maid Bread

JOE JUDGE
1st B.—Washington Americans

These 2" x 3-1/4" black-and-white cards are one of several versions of the W575-1 strip cards with custom-printed advertising on the backs. It is unknown whether each card in the W575-1 checklist can be found with the Gassler's back.

	NM	EX	VG
Common Player:	150.00	75.00	45.00
Stars: 4-6X			

(See W575-1 for checklist; Gassler values 3X-4X.)

1962 Gehl's Ice Cream

Issued only in the Milwaukee area to promote sales of Gold-Mine brand ice cream, the six cards in this black-and-white set all feature Roger Maris, who the previous year had broken Babe Ruth's season home run record. The 4" x 5" cards are blank backed and each has a facsimile autograph on front reading "To My / Gold Mine Pal / Roger Maris." The cards are unnumbered; a description of each is provided in the checklist.

		NM	EX	VG
Complete Set (6):		1,600	800.00	480.00
Common Card:		400.00	200.00	120.00
(1)	Roger Maris (Bat on shoulder, close-up.)	400.00	200.00	120.00
(2)	Roger Maris (Bat on shoulder, photo to waist.)	400.00	200.00	120.00
(3)	Roger Maris (Batting stance.)	400.00	200.00	120.00
(4)	Roger Maris ("Hitting My 61st," ballpark photo.)	325.00	160.00	100.00
(5)	Roger Maris (Holding bat in hands.)	400.00	200.00	120.00
(6)	Roger Maris (Portrait in warm-up jacket.)	400.00	200.00	120.00

1941 Lou Gehrig Memorial Ticket

On July 4, 1941, just a month after his death, the N.Y. Yankees scheduled special memorial ceremonies for the Iron Horse. Tickets for the event picture Gehrig and were issued in several colors and price ranges based on seat location. Most often found in stub form of about 3-3/8" x 2-1/2", full tickets are also occasionally seen, probably because a rainout on July 4 forced the ceremonies to the following Sunday.

	NM	EX	VG
Lou Gehrig (Ticket stub.)	1,300	650.00	390.00
Lou Gehrig (Full ticket.)	3,250	1,625	975.00

1911-14 General Baking Co. (D304)

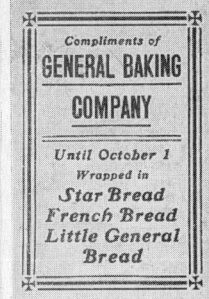

This issue by a bakery based in Buffalo, N.Y., is similar in design to contemporary tobacco and candy cards, but is larger in size, at 1-3/4" x 2-1/2". Fronts feature a color lithograph with the player's name and team below in capital letters. Some players who changed teams in 1913-14 are found with the team name obliterated at bottom by a black line. Five different back styles are known, listed here by the principal brand name: 1) Brunners, 2) Butter Krust, 3) General Baking Co., 4) Weber Bakery, 5) Martens Bakery. The complete set price does not include "no-team" variations. Modern counterfeits of the issue are widely seen in the hobby market.

		NM	EX	VG
Complete Set (25):		270,000	108,000	54,000
Common Player:		3,200	1,300	650.00
(1)	J. Frank Baker	11,000	4,000	2,000
(2)	Jack Barry	3,000	1,300	650.00
(3)	George Bell	3,200	1,250	650.00
(4)	Charles Bender	10,500	4,000	2,000
(5a)	Frank Chance (Chicago)	10,500	4,000	2,000
(5b)	Frank Chance (No team.)	14,000	5,500	2,600
(6a)	Hal Chase (N.Y.)	4,000	2,000	800.00
(6b)	Hal Chase (No team.)	5,000	2,200	1,000
(7)	Ty Cobb	125,000	75,000	20,000
(8)	Eddie Collins	10,500	4,000	2,000
(9a)	Otis Crandall (N.Y.)	3,200	1,350	650.00
(9b)	Otis Crandall (No team.)	4,800	2,000	900.00
(10)	Sam Crawford	10,500	4,000	2,000
(11a)	John Evers (Chicago)	10,500	4,000	2,000
(11b)	John Evers (No team.)	14,000	5,200	2,600
(12)	Arthur Fletcher	3,200	1,300	650.00
(13a)	Charles Herzog (N.Y.)	3,200	1,300	650.00
(13b)	Charles Herzog (No team.)	4,800	2,000	900.00
(14)	M. (Billy) Kelly	3,200	1,300	650.00
(15)	Napoleon Lajoie	14,000	6,200	3,400
(16)	Rube Marquard	10,500	4,000	2,000
(17)	Christy Mathewson	40,000	19,000	5,800
(18)	Fred Merkle	3,200	1,300	650.00
(19)	"Chief" Meyers	3,200	1,300	650.00
(20)	Marty O'Toole	3,200	1,300	650.00
(21)	Nap. Rucker	3,200	1,300	650.00
(22)	Arthur Shafer	3,200	1,300	650.00
(23)	Fred Tenny (Tenney)	8,000	5,800	3,000
(24)	Honus Wagner	60,000	30,000	8,000
(25)	Cy Young	35,000	16,000	5,000

1915 General Baking Co. (D303)

Issued in 1915 by the General Baking Co., these unnumbered cards measure 1-1/2" x 2-3/4". The player pictures and format of the cards are identical to the E106 set, but the D303 cards are easily identified by the advertisement for General Baking on the back.

		NM	EX	VG
Complete Set (51):		80,000	32,000	16,000
Common Player:		1,600	800.00	300.00
(1)	Jack Barry	1,600	800.00	300.00
(2)	Chief Bender (Blue background.)	3,000	1,700	800.00
(3)	Chief Bender (Green background.)	3,000	1,750	800.00

		NM	EX	VG
(4)	Bob Bescher (New York)	1,600	800.00	300.00
(5)	Bob Bescher (St. Louis)	1,600	800.00	300.00
(6)	Roger Bresnahan	3,000	1,750	800.00
(7)	Al Bridwell	1,600	800.00	300.00
(8)	Donie Bush	1,600	800.00	300.00
(9)	Hal Chase (Catching)	1,800	800.00	360.00
(10)	Hal Chase (Portrait)	1,800	900.00	360.00
(11)	Ty Cobb (Batting)	20,000	10,000	4,000
(12)	Ty Cobb (Leaning on bat.)	30,000	15,000	6,000
(13)	Eddie Collins	3,000	1,700	800.00
(14)	Sam Crawford	3,000	1,700	800.00
(15)	Ray Demmitt	1,600	800.00	300.00
(16)	Wild Bill Donovan	1,600	800.00	300.00
(17)	Red Dooin	1,600	800.00	300.00
(18)	Mickey Doolan	1,600	800.00	300.00
(19)	Larry Doyle	1,600	800.00	300.00
(20)	Clyde Engle	1,600	800.00	300.00
(21)	Johnny Evers	3,000	1,700	800.00
(22)	Art Fromme	1,600	800.00	300.00
(23)	George Gibson (Catching, back view.)	1,600	800.00	300.00
(24)	George Gibson (Catching, front view.)	1,600	800.00	300.00
(25)	Roy Hartzell	1,600	800.00	300.00
(26)	Fred Jacklitsch	1,600	800.00	300.00
(27)	Hugh Jennings	3,000	1,750	800.00
(28)	Otto Knabe	1,600	800.00	300.00
(29)	Nap Lajoie	4,000	2,000	1,000
(30)	Hans Lobert	1,600	800.00	300.00
(31)	Rube Marquard	1,500	850.00	400.00
(32)	Christy Mathewson	10,000	7,000	3,000
(33)	John McGraw	1,500	850.00	400.00
(34)	George McQuillan	1,600	800.00	300.00
(35)	Dots Miller	1,600	800.00	300.00
(36)	Danny Murphy	1,600	800.00	300.00
(37)	Rebel Oakes	1,600	800.00	300.00
(38)	Eddie Plank (No position on front.)	3,000	1,700	750.00
(39)	Eddie Plank (Position on front.)	6,000	3,000	1,500
(40)	Germany Schaefer	1,600	800.00	300.00
(41)	Boss Smith (Schmidt)	1,600	800.00	300.00
(42)	Tris Speaker	8,000	3,500	1,500
(43)	Oscar Stanage	1,600	800.00	300.00
(44)	George Stovall	1,600	800.00	300.00
(45)	Jeff Sweeney	1,600	800.00	300.00
(46)	Joe Tinker (Batting)	2,000	1,200	600.00
(47)	Joe Tinker (Portrait)	2,000	1,200	600.00
(48)	Honus Wagner (Batting)	20,000	10,000	4,000
(49)	Honus Wagner (Throwing)	30,000	15,000	6,000
(50)	Hooks Wiltse	1,600	800.00	300.00
(51)	Heinie Zimmerman	1,600	800.00	300.00

1908 General Photo Co. St. Louis Browns Postcards

The extent of this postcard issue by a hometown printer is unknown. It is likely other single-player postcards were issued. Approximately 3-1/2" x 5-1/2", the cards are black-and-white with a credit line on bottom: "Photo by General Photo Co., 610 Granite Bldg., St. Louis." On the team photo card, players are identified below the group photo.

		NM	EX	VG
(1)	"Rube" Waddell	500.00	250.00	150.00
(2)	St. Louis Browns - 1908	750.00	375.00	225.00

1948 Gentle's Bread Boston Braves

These 3" x 9" waxed-paper end labels were found on loaves of Gentle's bread. Printed in blue and red, the labels depict action poses of the National League Champion '48 Braves. A facsimile autograph appears with the photo. Backs are blank. The unnumbered labels are checklisted here alphabetically.

		NM	EX	VG
Complete Set (9):		3,000	1,500	900.00
Common Player:		400.00	200.00	120.00
(1)	Alvin Dark	450.00	225.00	135.00
(2)	Bob Elliott	400.00	200.00	120.00
(3)	Tommy Heath	400.00	200.00	120.00
(4)	Tommy Holmes	400.00	200.00	120.00
(5)	Phil Masi	400.00	200.00	120.00
(6)	John Sain	450.00	225.00	135.00
(7)	Warren Spahn	600.00	300.00	180.00
(8)	Eddie Stanky	450.00	225.00	135.00
(9)	Earl Torgeson	400.00	200.00	120.00

1956 Gentry Magazine Ty Cobb

In issue #20 of Gentry magazine, dated Fall, 1956, a feature article on card collecting was enhanced with the inclusion of an original Ty Cobb card tipped onto an interior page. Measuring about 4" x 2-1/4" and blank-backed, the color card is similar in design to the T205 tobacco card issue.

	NM	EX	VG
Complete Magazine:	125.00	65.00	40.00
Ty Cobb	90.00	45.00	27.00

1909-10 German Baseball Stamps

A marginal notation "Made in Germany" on one of the stamps in this series identifies its origins. Little else in known of them. The stamps measure about 1-3/8" to 1-1/2" by 1-3/4" to 1-7/8". They are printed in bright colors on a pink background with name and team in blue. Because of their European origins, there are many mistakes in player and team names. The crude pictures are not representative of the player named. Unnumbered stamps are listed here in alphabetical order. It is evident several different configurations of 35-stamp sheets must have been issued.

		NM	EX	VG
Complete Sheet (35):		1,150	575.00	345.00
Complete Set (41):		1,300	650.00	400.00
Common Player:		65.00	32.50	20.00
(1)	Ginger Beaumont	65.00	32.50	20.00
(2)	Frank Bowerman	65.00	32.50	20.00
(3)	Kitty Bransfield	65.00	32.50	20.00
(4)	Al Bridwell	65.00	32.50	20.00
(5a)	Roger Bresnahan (Light shirt.)	100.00	50.00	30.00
(5b)	Roger Bresnahan (Dark shirt.)	100.00	50.00	30.00
(6)	Bill Carrigan	65.00	32.50	20.00
(7)	Hal Chase	80.00	40.00	24.00
(8)	Eddie Collins	100.00	50.00	30.00
(9)	Harry Davis	65.00	32.50	20.00
(10)	Wild Bill Donovan	65.00	32.50	20.00
(11)	Larry Doyle	65.00	32.50	20.00
(12)	Jean Dubuc	65.00	32.50	20.00
(13)	Kid Elberfield (Elberfeld)	65.00	32.50	20.00
(14)	Dick Hoblitzell	65.00	32.50	20.00
(15)	Solly Hoffman (Hofman)	65.00	32.50	20.00
(16)	Tim Jordan	65.00	32.50	20.00
(17)	Willie Keeler	100.00	50.00	30.00
(18)	Nap Lajoie	100.00	50.00	30.00
(19)	Tommy Leach	65.00	32.50	20.00
(20)	Christy Mathewson	325.00	160.00	100.00
(21)	Dots Miller	65.00	32.50	20.00
(22)	John McGraw	100.00	50.00	30.00

		NM	EX	VG
(23)	Eddie Plank	100.00	50.00	30.00
(24)	Jack Rowan	65.00	32.50	20.00
(25)	Nap Rucker	65.00	32.50	20.00
(26)	Shannon (Boston)	65.00	32.50	20.00
(27)	Frank Smith	65.00	32.50	20.00
(28)	Tris Speaker	120.00	60.00	35.00
(29)	Jake Stahl	65.00	32.50	20.00
(30)	Lee Tannehill	65.00	32.50	20.00
(31)	Fred Tenney	65.00	32.50	20.00
(32)	Ira Thomas	65.00	32.50	20.00
(33)	Joe Tinker	100.00	50.00	30.00
(34)	Honus Wagner	285.00	140.00	85.00
(35)	Jimmy Williams	65.00	32.50	20.00
(36)	Cy Young	165.00	85.00	50.00
(37)	Baseball	15.00	7.50	4.50
(38)	Bat	15.00	7.50	4.50
(39)	Body Protector	15.00	7.50	4.50
(40)	Catcher's Mask	15.00	7.50	4.50
(41)	Crossed Bats	15.00	7.50	4.50
(42)	Glove	15.00	7.50	4.50

1923 German Baseball Transfers

With crude artwork lifted from the W515 strip card set, this issue of baseball player (and boxer) transfers was produced in Germany. Approximately 1-3/16" x 1-1/2", the stamps are printed in red on a green background. All of the design, except for the "MADE IN GERMANY" notation in the white bottom margin, is in mirror-image, befitting their use as tattoos or transfers. Two of the baseball players are double-prints. The unnumbered stamps (baseball only) are checklisted here alphabetically.

		NM	EX	VG
Complete Baseball Set (13):		350.00	175.00	105.00
Complete Sheet (25):		400.00	200.00	120.00
Common Player:		40.00	20.00	12.00
(1)	Grover Alexander	45.00	22.00	13.50
(2)	Dave Bancroft	40.00	20.00	12.00
(3)	George (J.) Burns	30.00	15.00	9.00
(4)	"Ty" Cobb	100.00	50.00	30.00
(5)	Red Faber (DP)	25.00	12.50	7.50
(6)	Arthur Nehf	30.00	15.00	9.00
(7)	"Babe" Ruth	200.00	100.00	60.00
(8)	Ray Schalk	40.00	20.00	12.00
(9)	Everett Scott	30.00	15.00	9.00
(10)	Bob Shawkey	30.00	15.00	9.00
(11)	Tris Speaker	45.00	22.00	13.50
(12)	"Casey" Stengel	45.00	22.00	13.50
(13)	Zack Wheat (DP)	30.00	15.00	9.00

1922 Lou Gertenrich

One of the most attractive advertising backs of the 1920s is found on this version of the 1922 issue which is most often found with American Caramel ads on back. Gertenrich had a three-game major league career between 1901-1903, supporting his advertising claim of "The Baseball Player Candy Manufacturer." Probably originating in Chicago, these cards are 2" x 3-1/2" black-and-white. The set shares the checklist with the American Caramel Co. (E121) set of 120. Because of the scarcity and appeal of this regional issue, the Gertenrich versions carry a substantial premium for type-card and superstar collectors.

	NM	EX	VG
Common Player:	600.00	300.00	175.00
Stars: 3-4X			

(See 1922 American Caramel Series of 120 for checklist.)

1888 Gilbert & Bacon Cabinets

The known range of this cabinet card issue comprises mostly members of the 1888 Philadelphia Athletics and Phillies. The posed action photos on the approximately 4-1/4" x 6-1/2" cards are the same pictures seen on many of the players' Old Judge and Old Judge cabinet cards. The G&B cabinets have an embossed

Goodwin & Co. copyright seal. An elaborate typescript Gilbert & Bacon studio logo is found in the bottom-left border, with the city named at right. Backs have an ornate studio logo.

		NM	EX	VG
Common Player:		3,000	1,200	700.00
(1)	Louis Bierbauer	3,000	1,200	700.00
(2)	Bill Blair	3,000	1,200	700.00
(3)	Charlie Ferguson (Ball in hands at chest.)	3,000	1,200	700.00
(4)	Charlie Ferguson (Batting)	3,000	1,200	700.00
(5)	Charlie Ferguson (Throwing)	3,000	1,200	700.00
(6)	Kid Gleason	3,000	1,200	700.00
(7)	John Henry	3,000	1,200	700.00
(8)	Henry Larkin	3,000	1,200	700.00
(9)	Denny Lyons	3,000	1,200	700.00
(10)	Deacon McGuire (Bat behind head.)	3,000	1,200	700.00
(11)	Deacon McGuire (Bat on shoulder.)	3,000	1,200	700.00
(12)	Deacon McGuire (Fielding, hands at waist.)	3,000	1,200	700.00
(13)	Deacon McGuire (Fielding, hands head-high.)	3,000	1,200	700.00
(14)	Deacon McGuire (Throwing)	3,000	1,200	700.00
(15)	George Pinkney (Bat at 45-degree angle.)	3,000	1,200	700.00
(16)	George Pinkney (Bat at 60-degree angle.)	3,000	1,200	700.00
(17)	George Pinkney (Bat nearly horizontal.)	3,000	1,200	700.00
(18)	George Pinkney (Fielding fly ball.)	3,000	1,200	700.00
(19)	George Pinkney (Fielding line drive.)	3,000	1,200	700.00
(20)	George Pinkney (Throwing)	3,000	1,200	700.00
(21)	Ben Sanders (Ball in hands at chest.)	3,000	1,200	700.00
(22)	Ben Sanders (Batting)	3,000	1,200	700.00
(23)	Ben Sanders (Fielding fly ball.)	3,000	1,200	700.00
(24)	Ben Sanders (Throwing)	3,000	1,200	700.00
(25)	Harry Stovey	3,000	1,200	700.00
(26)	Michael Sullivan	3,000	1,200	700.00
(27)	Gus Weyhing	3,000	1,200	700.00
(28)	John Weyhing	3,000	1,200	700.00

1916 Gimbels

This version of the 1916 M101-5 and M101-4 Blank Backs can be found with three slightly different styles of typography on back.

	NM	EX	VG
Common Player:	130.00	65.00	40.00
Stars: 1-2X			

(See 1916 M101-5 and M101-4 Blank Backs for checklists and base pricing.)

1953 Glendale Hot Dogs Tigers

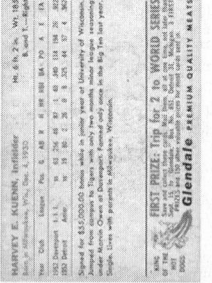

Glendale Meats issued these unnumbered, full-color cards (2-5/8" x 3-3/4") in packages of hot dogs Featuring only Detroit Tigers players, the card fronts contain a player picture with his name, a facsimile autograph, and the Tigers logo. Backs carry player statistical and biographical information plus an offer for a trip for two to the World Series. Collectors were advised to mail all the cards they had saved to Glendale Meats. The World Series trip plus 150 other prizes were to be given to the individuals sending in the most cards. As with most cards issued with food products, high-grade cards are tough to find because of the cards' susceptibility to stains. The Houtteman card is extremely scarce.

	NM	EX	VG
Complete Set (28):	27,500	11,000	5,500

		NM	EX	VG
Common Player:		900.00	365.00	180.00
(1)	Matt Batts	900.00	365.00	180.00
(2)	Johnny Bucha	900.00	365.00	180.00
(3)	Frank Carswell	900.00	365.00	180.00
(4)	Jim Delsing	900.00	365.00	180.00
(5)	Walt Dropo	900.00	365.00	180.00
(6)	Hal Erickson	900.00	365.00	180.00
(7)	Paul Foytack	900.00	365.00	180.00
(8)	Owen Friend	900.00	365.00	180.00
(9)	Ned Garver	900.00	365.00	180.00
(10)	Joe Ginsberg	900.00	365.00	180.00
(11)	Ted Gray	900.00	365.00	180.00
(12)	Fred Hatfield	900.00	365.00	180.00
(13)	Ray Herbert	900.00	365.00	180.00
(14)	Bill Hitchcock	900.00	365.00	180.00
(15)	Bill Hoeft	900.00	365.00	180.00
(16)	Art Houtteman	5,000	2,000	1,000
(17)	Milt Jordan	900.00	365.00	180.00
(18)	Harvey Kuenn	1,200	480.00	240.00
(19)	Don Lund	900.00	365.00	180.00
(20)	Dave Madison	900.00	365.00	180.00
(21)	Dick Marlowe	900.00	365.00	180.00
(22)	Pat Mullin	900.00	365.00	180.00
(23)	Bob Nieman	900.00	365.00	180.00
(24)	Johnny Pesky	900.00	365.00	180.00
(25)	Jerry Priddy	900.00	365.00	180.00
(26)	Steve Souchock	900.00	365.00	180.00
(27)	Russ Sullivan	900.00	365.00	180.00
(28)	Bill Wight	1,100	450.00	225.00

1916 Globe Clothing Store (H801-9)

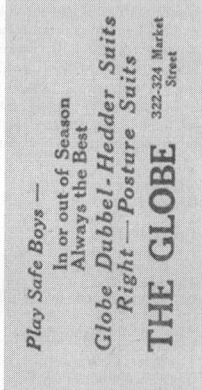

This 200-card set can be found with ads on the back for several local and regional businesses. Among them is the Globe clothing store in St. Louis. Type card, team- and single-player collectors may pay a modest premium for individual cards with the Globe store's advertising over the parallel 1916 M101-4 Blank Backs values. This version carries an "American Card Catalog" designation of H801-9. Cards measure 1-5/8" x 3" and are printed in black-and-white.

	NM	EX	VG
Common Player:	225.00	110.00	65.00
Stars: 2-3X			

(See 1916 M101-4 Blank Backs for checklist and base values.)

1969 Globe Imports Playing Cards

Largely ignored by collectors for more than 35 years, this issue has little to offer any but the most avid superstar collector. Printed in black-and-white on very thin white cardboard, either with blank backs, or with red-and-white checkerboard patterned backs, the cards measure 1-5/8" x 2-1/4". Muddy player action photos are at center of each card, with the player's name reversed out of a black strip at the bottom. It is likely this set was issued over a period of more than one year. The plain-back version was probably issued first, and has photos which include cap and jersey logos. The checked-back version seems to have been a later issue with many of the cards showing uniform logos airbrushed away. The photo quality of the checked-back cards is also much poorer than the plain-backs. A few players were substituted between the issues, and there may be more yet to be reported. The Babe Ruth AD card listed here is actually part of a multi-topic deck in similar format issued contemprarily with the baseball decks.

	NM	EX	VG
Complete Set (52+Joker):	20.00	10.00	6.00
Common Player:	.25	.15	.10

PLAIN BACK HEARTS

2	Chris Short	.25	.15	.10
3	Tony Conigliaro	.75	.40	.25
4	Bill Freehan	.25	.15	.10
5	Willie McCovey	2.00	1.00	.60
6	Joel Horlen	.25	.15	.10
7	Ernie Banks	2.00	1.00	.60
8	Jim Wynn	.25	.15	.10
9	Brooks Robinson	2.00	1.00	.60
10	Orlando Cepeda	1.00	.50	.30
J	Al Kaline	2.00	1.00	.60
Q	Gene Alley	.25	.15	.10
K	Rusty Staub	.75	.40	.25
A	Willie Mays	4.00	2.00	1.25

CLUBS

2	Reggie Smith	.25	.15	.10
3	Mike McCormick	.25	.15	.10
4	Tony Oliva	.50	.25	.15
5	Bud Harrelson	.25	.15	.10
6	Rick Reichardt	.25	.15	.10
7	Billy Williams	1.00	.50	.30
8	Pete Rose	6.00	3.00	1.75
9	Jim Maloney	.25	.15	.10
10	Tim McCarver	.75	.40	.25
J	Max Alvis	.25	.15	.10
Q	Ron Swoboda	.25	.15	.10
K	Johnny Callison	.25	.15	.10
A	Richie Allen	.75	.40	.25

DIAMONDS

2	Paul Casanova	.25	.15	.10
3	Juan Marichal	1.00	.50	.30
4	Jim Fregosi	.25	.15	.10
5	Earl Wilson	.25	.15	.10
6	Tony Horton	.25	.15	.10
7	Harmon Killebrew	2.00	1.00	.60
8	Tom Seaver	3.00	1.50	.90
9	Curt Flood	.75	.40	.25
10	Frank Robinson	2.00	1.00	.60
J	Bob Aspromonte	.25	.15	.10
Q	Lou Brock	2.00	1.00	.60
K	Jim Lonborg	.25	.15	.10
A(a)	Bob Gibson	2.00	1.00	.60
A(b)	Babe Ruth	12.00	6.00	3.60

SPADES .00 .00 .00

2	Cesar Tovar	.25	.15	.10
3	Rick Monday	.25	.15	.10
4	Richie Allen	.75	.40	.25
5	Mel Stottlemyre	.50	.25	.15
6	Tommy John	.75	.40	.25
7	Don Mincher	.25	.15	.10
8	Chico Cardenas	.25	.15	.10
9	Willie Davis	.25	.15	.10
10	Bert Campaneris	.25	.15	.10
J	Ron Santo	.75	.40	.25
Q	Al Ferrera	.25	.15	.10
K	Clete Boyer	.50	.25	.15
A(a)	Don Drysdale	3.00	1.50	.90
A(b)	Mickey Mantle	40.00	20.00	12.00

CHECKERBOARD BACK HEARTS

2	Chris Short	.25	.15	.10
3	Tony Conigliaro	.75	.40	.25
4	Bill Freehan	.25	.15	.10
5	Willie McCovey	2.00	1.00	.60
6	Joel Horlen	.25	.15	.10
7	Ernie Banks	2.00	1.00	.60
8	Jim Wynn	.25	.15	.10
9	Brooks Robinson	2.00	1.00	.60
10	Orlando Cepeda	1.00	.50	.30
J	Al Kaline	2.00	1.00	.60
Q	Gene Alley	.25	.15	.10
K	Rusty Staub	.75	.40	.25
A	Willie Mays	6.00	3.00	1.75

CLUBS

2	Reggie Smith	.25	.15	.10
3	Jerry Koosman	.25	.15	.10
4	Tony Oliva	.50	.25	.15
5	Bud Harrelson	.25	.15	.10
6	Rick Reichardt	.25	.15	.10
7	Billy Williams	1.00	.50	.30
8	Pete Rose	6.00	3.00	1.75
9	Jim Maloney	.25	.15	.10
10	Tim McCarver	.75	.40	.25
J	Max Alvis	.25	.15	.10
Q	Ron Swoboda	.25	.15	.10
K	Johnny Callison	.25	.15	.10
A	Richie Allen	.75	.40	.25

DIAMONDS

2	Paul Casanova	.25	.15	.10
3	Juan Marichal	1.00	.50	.30
4	Jim Fregosi	.25	.15	.10
5	Earl Wilson	.25	.15	.10
6	Tony Horton	.25	.15	.10
7	Harmon Killebrew	2.00	1.00	.60
8	Tom Seaver	3.00	1.50	.90
9	Curt Flood	.75	.40	.25
10	Frank Robinson	2.00	1.00	.60
J	Bob Aspromonte	.25	.15	.10
Q	Lou Brock	2.00	1.00	.60
K	Jim Lonborg	.25	.15	.10
A	Bob Gibson	2.00	1.00	.60

SPADES

2	Denny McLain	.50	.25	.15
3	Rick Monday	.25	.15	.10
4	Richie Allen	.75	.40	.25
5	Mel Stottlemyre	.50	.25	.15
6	Tommy John	.75	.40	.25
7	Don Mincher	.25	.15	.10
8	Chico Cardenas	.25	.15	.10
9	Willie Davis	.25	.15	.10
10	Bert Campaneris	.25	.15	.10
J	Ron Santo	.75	.40	.25
Q	Al Ferrera	.25	.15	.10
K	Clete Boyer	.50	.25	.15
A	Ken Harrelson	.25	.15	.10

1887 Gold Coin (Buchner) (N284)

KENNEDY, PITCHER, LACROSSE

Issued circa 1887, the N284 issue was produced by D. Buchner & Co.for its Gold Coin brand of chewing tobacco. Actually, the series was not comprised only of baseball players - actors, jockeys, firemen and policemen were also included. The cards, which measure 1-3/4" x 3", are color drawings. The set is not a popular one among collectors as the drawings do not in all cases represent the players designated on the cards. In most instances, players at a given position share the same drawing depicted on the card front. Three different card backs are found, all advising collectors to save the valuable chewing tobacco wrappers. Wrappers could be redeemed for various prizes.

		NM	EX	VG
	Complete Set (143):	135,000	60,000	27,500
	Common Player:	815.00	365.00	165.00
(1)	Ed Andrews (Hands at neck.)	815.00	365.00	165.00
(2)	Ed Andrews (Hands waist high.)	815.00	365.00	165.00
(3)	Cap Anson (Hands outstretched.)	4,065	1,815	815.00
(4)	Cap Anson (Left hand on hip.)	5,315	2,375	1,065
(5)	Tug Arundel	815.00	365.00	165.00
(6)	Sam Barkley (Pittsburg)	815.00	365.00	165.00
(7)	Sam Barkley (St. Louis)	815.00	365.00	165.00
(8)	Charley Bassett	815.00	365.00	165.00
(9)	Charlie Bastian	815.00	365.00	165.00
(10)	Ed Beecher	815.00	365.00	165.00
(11)	Charlie Bennett	815.00	365.00	165.00
(12)	Henry Boyle	815.00	365.00	165.00
(13)	Dan Brouthers (Hands outstretched.)	3,125	1,405	625.00
(14)	Dan Brouthers (With bat.)	3,125	1,405	625.00
(15)	Tom Brown	815.00	365.00	165.00
(16)	Jack Burdock	815.00	365.00	165.00
(17)	Oyster Burns (Baltimore)	815.00	365.00	165.00
(18)	Tom Burns (Chicago)	815.00	365.00	165.00
(19)	Doc Bushong	815.00	365.00	165.00
(20)	John Cahill	815.00	365.00	165.00
(21)	Cliff Carroll (Washington)	815.00	365.00	165.00
(22)	Fred Carroll (Pittsburg)	815.00	365.00	165.00
(23)	Bob Carruthers (Caruthers)	815.00	365.00	165.00
(24)	Dan Casey	815.00	365.00	165.00
(25)	John Clarkson (Ball at chest.)	2,815	1,250	565.00
(26)	John Clarkson (Arm oustretched.)	3,125	1,405	625.00
(27)	Jack Clements	815.00	365.00	165.00
(28)	John Coleman	815.00	365.00	165.00
(29)	Charles Comiskey	3,440	1,530	690.00
(30)	Roger Connor (Hands outstretched chest-level, "New York.")	2,815	1,250	565.00
(31)	Roger Connor (Hands oustreteched face-level, "N.Y.")	3,125	1,405	625.00
(32)	John Corbett	815.00	365.00	165.00
(33)	Sam Craig (Crane)	815.00	365.00	165.00
(34)	Sam Crane	815.00	365.00	165.00
(35)	John Crowley	815.00	365.00	165.00
(36)	Ed Cushmann (Cushman)	815.00	365.00	165.00
(37)	Ed Dailey (Daily)	815.00	365.00	165.00
(38)	Con Daley (Daily)	815.00	365.00	165.00
(39)	Pat Deasley	815.00	365.00	165.00
(40)	Jerry Denny (Hands on knees.)	815.00	365.00	165.00
(41)	Jerry Denny (Hands on thighs.)	815.00	365.00	165.00
(42)	Jim Donnelly	815.00	365.00	165.00
(43)	Jim Donohue (Donahue)	815.00	365.00	165.00
(44)	Mike Dorgan (Right field.)	815.00	365.00	165.00
(45)	Mike Dorgan (Batter.)	815.00	365.00	165.00
(46)	Fred Dunlap	815.00	365.00	165.00
(47)	Dude Esterbrook	815.00	365.00	165.00
(48)	Buck Ewing (Ready to tag.)	2,815	1,250	565.00
(49)	Buck Ewing (Hands at neck.)	3,125	1,405	625.00
(50)	Sid Farrar	815.00	365.00	165.00
(51)	Jack Farrell (Ready to tag.)	815.00	365.00	165.00
(52)	Jack Farrell (Hands at knees.)	815.00	365.00	165.00
(53)	Charlie Ferguson	815.00	365.00	165.00
(54)	Silver Flint	815.00	365.00	165.00
(55)	Jim Fogerty (Fogarty)	815.00	365.00	165.00
(56)	Tom Forster	815.00	365.00	165.00
(57)	Dave Foutz	815.00	365.00	165.00
(58)	Chris Fulmer	815.00	365.00	165.00
(59)	Joe Gerhardt	815.00	365.00	165.00
(60)	Charlie Getzein (Getzien)	815.00	365.00	165.00
(61)	Pete Gillespie (Left field.)	815.00	365.00	165.00
(62)	Pete Gillespie (Batter.)	815.00	365.00	165.00
(63)	Barney Gilligan	815.00	365.00	165.00
(64)	Jack Glasscock (Fielding grounder.)	815.00	365.00	165.00
(65)	Jack Glasscock (Hands on knees.)	815.00	365.00	165.00
(66)	Will Gleason	815.00	365.00	165.00
(67)	George Gore	815.00	365.00	165.00
(68)	Frank Hankinson	815.00	365.00	165.00
(69)	Ned Hanlon	2,815	1,250	565.00
(70)	Jim Hart	815.00	365.00	165.00
(71)	Egyptian Healy	815.00	365.00	165.00
(72)	Paul Hines (Centre field.)	815.00	365.00	165.00
(73)	Paul Hines (Batter.)	815.00	365.00	165.00
(74)	Joe Hornung	815.00	365.00	165.00
(75)	Arthur Irwin	815.00	365.00	165.00
(76)	Dick Johnston	815.00	365.00	165.00
(77)	Tim Keefe (Ball in hand.)	2,815	1,250	565.00
(78)	Tim Keefe (Ball out of hand.)	3,125	1,405	625.00
(79)	King Kelly (Right field.)	3,440	1,530	690.00
(80)	King Kelly (Catcher.)	3,440	1,530	690.00
(81)	Ted Kennedy	815.00	365.00	165.00
(82)	Matt Kilroy	815.00	365.00	165.00
(83)	Arlie Latham	815.00	365.00	165.00
(84)	Jimmy Manning	815.00	365.00	165.00
(85)	Bill McClellan	815.00	365.00	165.00
(86)	Jim McCormick	815.00	365.00	165.00
(87)	Jack McGeachy	815.00	365.00	165.00
(88)	Jumbo McGinnis	815.00	365.00	165.00
(89)	George Meyers (Myers)	815.00	365.00	165.00
(90)	Doggie Miller	815.00	365.00	165.00
(91)	John Morrill (Hands outstretched.)	815.00	365.00	165.00
(92)	John Morrill (Hands at neck.)	815.00	365.00	165.00
(93)	Tom Morrissy (Morrissey)	815.00	365.00	165.00
(94)	Joe Mulvey (Hands on knees.)	815.00	365.00	165.00
(95)	Joe Mulvey (Hands above head.)	815.00	365.00	165.00
(96)	Al Myers	815.00	365.00	165.00
(97)	Candy Nelson	815.00	365.00	165.00
(98)	Hugh Nichol	815.00	365.00	165.00
(99)	Billy O'Brien	815.00	365.00	165.00
(100)	Tip O'Neil (O'Neill)	815.00	365.00	165.00
(101)	Orator Jim O'Rourke (Hands cupped.)	3,125	1,405	625.00
(102)	Orator Jim O'Rourke (Hands on thighs.)	3,125	1,405	625.00
(103)	Dave Orr	815.00	365.00	165.00
(104)	Jimmy Peoples	815.00	365.00	165.00
(105)	Fred Pfeffer	815.00	365.00	165.00
(106)	Bill Phillips	815.00	365.00	165.00
(107)	Mark Polhemus	815.00	365.00	165.00
(108)	Henry Porter	815.00	365.00	165.00
(109)	Blondie Purcell	815.00	365.00	165.00
(110)	Old Hoss Radbourn (Hands at chest.)	2,815	1,250	565.00
(111)	Old Hoss Radbourn (Hands above waist.)	3,125	1,405	625.00
(112)	Danny Richardson (New York, hands at knees.)	815.00	365.00	165.00
(113)	Danny Richardson (New York, foot on base.)	815.00	365.00	165.00
(114)	Hardy Richardson (Detroit, hands at right shoulder.)	815.00	365.00	165.00
(115)	Hardy Richardson (Detroit, right hand above head.)	815.00	365.00	165.00
(116)	Yank Robinson	815.00	365.00	165.00
(117)	George Rooks	815.00	365.00	165.00
(118)	Chief Rosemann (Roseman)	815.00	365.00	165.00
(119)	Jimmy Ryan	815.00	365.00	165.00
(120)	Emmett Seery (Hands at right shoulder.)	815.00	365.00	165.00
(121)	Emmett Seery (Hands outstretched.)	815.00	365.00	165.00
(122)	Otto Shomberg (Schomberg)	815.00	365.00	165.00
(123)	Pap Smith	815.00	365.00	165.00
(124)	Joe Strauss	815.00	365.00	165.00
(125)	Danny Sullivan (St. Louis)	815.00	365.00	165.00
(126)	Marty Sullivan (Chicago)	815.00	365.00	165.00
(127)	Billy Sunday	1,565	700.00	315.00
(128)	Ezra Sutton	815.00	365.00	165.00
(129)	Sam Thompson (Hand at belt.)	2,815	1,250	565.00
(130)	Sam Thompson (Hands chest high.)	3,125	1,405	625.00
(131)	Chris Von Der Ahe	2,815	1,250	565.00
(132)	John Ward (Fielding grounder.)	2,815	1,250	565.00
(133)	John Ward (Hands by knee.)	3,125	1,405	625.00
(134)	John Ward (Hands on knees.)	3,125	1,405	625.00
(135)	Curt Welch	815.00	365.00	165.00
(136)	Deacon White	815.00	365.00	165.00
(137)	Art Whitney (Pittsburgh)	815.00	365.00	165.00
(138)	Jim Whitney (Washington)	815.00	365.00	165.00
(139)	Ned Williamson (Fielding grounder.)	815.00	365.00	165.00
(140)	Ned Williamson (Hands at chest.)	815.00	365.00	165.00
(141)	Medoc Wise	815.00	365.00	165.00
(142)	George Wood (Hands at right shoulder.)	815.00	365.00	165.00
(143)	George Wood (Stealing base.)	815.00	365.00	165.00

1961 Golden Press

8 Jerome Hanna Dean "Dizzy"

1900-1941 St. Louis, Chicago NL

During his first full five years in the major leagues, Dean won 120 games, for an average of 24 per year. In 1934 he reached his peak when he won 30 games, and lost only 7. That year Dizzy and his brother Paul each beat the Detroit Tigers twice to bring the World Series championship to St. Louis' Gas House Gang. Dean was the last major league pitcher to win 30 games. In the 1937 all-star game, a line drive hit Dean's toe and curtailed his brilliant pitching career.

Lifetime Record 12 yrs.

G	IP	W	L	PCT	SHO	SO
317	1966	150	83	.644	26	1155

Elected to Hall of Fame 1953

DIZZY DEAN pitcher

The 1961 Golden Press set features 33 players, all enshrined in the Baseball Hall of Fame. The full color cards measure 2-1/2" x 3-1/2" and came in a booklet with perforations so that they could be easily removed. Full books with the cards intact would command 50 percent over the set price in the checklist that follows. Card numbers 1-3 and 28-33 are slightly higher in price as they were located on the book's front and back covers, making them more susceptible to scuffing and wear. Cards in a larger (2-3/4" x 3-5/8") apparently unperforated format are also known, though their method of distribution is unclear.

		NM	EX	VG
	Complete Set (33):	100.00	50.00	30.00
	Complete Set in Book:	175.00	85.00	50.00
	Common Player:	3.00	1.50	.90
1	Mel Ott	3.00	1.50	.90
2	Grover Cleveland Alexander	5.00	2.50	1.50
3	Babe Ruth	40.00	20.00	12.00
4	Hank Greenberg	5.00	2.50	1.50
5	Bill Terry	3.00	1.50	.90
6	Carl Hubbell	3.00	1.50	.90
7	Rogers Hornsby	4.00	2.00	1.25
8	Dizzy Dean	5.00	2.50	1.50
9	Joe DiMaggio	20.00	10.00	6.00
10	Charlie Gehringer	3.00	1.50	.90
11	Gabby Hartnett	3.00	1.50	.90
12	Mickey Cochrane	3.00	1.50	.90
13	George Sisler	3.00	1.50	.90
14	Joe Cronin	3.00	1.50	.90
15	Pie Traynor	3.00	1.50	.90
16	Lou Gehrig	20.00	10.00	6.00
17	Lefty Grove	3.00	1.50	.90
18	Chief Bender	3.00	1.50	.90
19	Frankie Frisch	3.00	1.50	.90
20	Al Simmons	3.00	1.50	.90
21	Home Run Baker	3.00	1.50	.90
22	Jimmy Foxx	4.00	2.00	1.25
23	John McGraw	3.00	1.50	.90
24	Christy Mathewson	10.00	5.00	3.00
25	Ty Cobb	20.00	10.00	6.00
26	Dazzy Vance	3.00	1.50	.90
27	Bill Dickey	3.00	1.50	.90
28	Eddie Collins	3.00	1.50	.90
29	Walter Johnson	9.00	4.50	2.75
30	Tris Speaker	4.00	2.00	1.25
31	Nap Lajoie	3.00	1.50	.90
32	Honus Wagner	12.00	6.00	3.50
33	Cy Young	9.00	4.50	2.75

1955 Golden Stamp Books

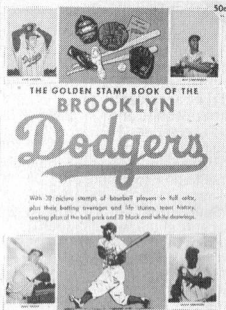

The 1954 World Series contestants, Cleveland and the Giants, along with the popular Dodgers and Braves are featured in this set of stamp books. The 32-page albums measure about 8-1/2" x 11" and include drawings and write-ups for each of the 32 players and managers featured. Other pages of the album include team histories, stats, etc. Sheets of 16 color stamps each are bound into the front and back of the album. Individual stamps measure about 2" x 2-5/8" and are unnumbered. Values shown are for complete albums with the stamps not pasted in; albums with stamps affixed to the pages are worth about 50 percent. The players for each team are listed in the order in which they appear in the album.

		NM	EX	VG
	Complete Set (4):	500.00	250.00	150.00
	Common Stamp:	5.00	2.50	1.50
S-1	**NEW YORK GIANTS ALBUM**	125.00	65.00	35.00
(1)	1954 Team Photo	5.00	2.50	1.50
(2)	Leo Durocher	6.00	3.00	1.75
(3)	Johnny Antonelli	5.00	2.50	1.50
(4)	Sal Maglie	5.00	2.50	1.50
(5)	Ruben Gomez	5.00	2.50	1.50
(6)	Hoyt Wilhelm	6.00	3.00	1.75
(7)	Marv Grissom	5.00	2.50	1.50
(8)	Jim Hearn	5.00	2.50	1.50
(9)	Paul Giel	5.00	2.50	1.50
(10)	Al Corwin	5.00	2.50	1.50
(11)	George Spencer	5.00	2.50	1.50
(12)	Don Liddle	5.00	2.50	1.50
(13)	Windy McCall	5.00	2.50	1.50
(14)	Al Worthington	5.00	2.50	1.50
(15)	Wes Westrum	5.00	2.50	1.50
(16)	Whitey Lockman	5.00	2.50	1.50
(17)	Dave Williams	5.00	2.50	1.50
(18)	Hank Thompson	5.00	2.50	1.50
(19)	Alvin Dark	5.00	2.50	1.50
(20)	Monte Irvin	7.50	3.75	2.25
(21)	Willie Mays	50.00	25.00	15.00
(22)	Don Mueller	5.00	2.50	1.50
(23)	Dusty Rhodes	5.00	2.50	1.50
(24)	Ray Katt	5.00	2.50	1.50
(25)	Joe Amalfitano	5.00	2.50	1.50
(26)	Bill Gardner	5.00	2.50	1.50
(27)	Foster Castleman	5.00	2.50	1.50
(28)	Bobby Hofman	5.00	2.50	1.50
(29)	Bill Taylor	5.00	2.50	1.50
(30)	Manager and Coaches	5.00	2.50	1.50
(31)	Bobby Weinstein (Batboy)	5.00	2.50	1.50
(32)	Polo Grounds	5.00	2.50	1.50
S-2	**MILWAUKEE BRAVES ALBUM**	125.00	65.00	35.00
(1)	1954 Team Photo	5.00	2.50	1.50
(2)	Charlie Grimm	5.00	2.50	1.50
(3)	Warren Spahn	7.50	3.75	2.25
(4)	Lew Burdette	5.00	2.50	1.50
(5)	Chet Nichols	5.00	2.50	1.50
(6)	Gene Conley	5.00	2.50	1.50
(7)	Bob Buhl	5.00	2.50	1.50
(8)	Jim Wilson	5.00	2.50	1.50
(9)	Dave Jolly	5.00	2.50	1.50
(10)	Ernie Johnson	5.00	2.50	1.50
(11)	Joey Jay	5.00	2.50	1.50
(12)	Dave Koslo	5.00	2.50	1.50
(13)	Charlie Gorin	5.00	2.50	1.50
(14)	Ray Crone	5.00	2.50	1.50
(15)	Del Crandall	5.00	2.50	1.50
(16)	Joe Adcock	5.00	2.50	1.50
(17)	Jack Dittmer	5.00	2.50	1.50
(18)	Eddie Mathews	15.00	7.50	4.50
(19)	Johnny Logan	5.00	2.50	1.50
(20)	Andy Pafko	5.00	2.50	1.50
(21)	Bill Bruton	5.00	2.50	1.50
(22)	Bobby Thomson	5.00	2.50	1.50
(23)	Charlie White	5.00	2.50	1.50
(24)	Danny O'Connell	5.00	2.50	1.50
(25)	Hank Aaron	50.00	25.00	15.00
(26)	Jim Pendleton	5.00	2.50	1.50
(27)	George Metkovich	5.00	2.50	1.50
(28)	Mel Roach	5.00	2.50	1.50
(29)	John Cooney	5.00	2.50	1.50
(30)	Bucky Walters	5.00	2.50	1.50
(31)	Charles Lacks (Trainer)	5.00	2.50	1.50
(32)	Milwaukee County Stadium	5.00	2.50	1.50
S-3	**BROOKLYN DODGERS ALBUM**	200.00	100.00	60.00
(1)	Walter Alston	6.00	3.00	1.75
(2)	Don Newcombe	6.00	3.00	1.75
(3)	Carl Erskine	5.00	2.50	1.50
(4)	Johnny Podres	5.00	2.50	1.50
(5)	Billy Loes	5.00	2.50	1.50
(6)	Russ Meyer	5.00	2.50	1.50
(7)	Jim Hughes	5.00	2.50	1.50
(8)	Sandy Koufax	100.00	50.00	30.00
(9)	Joe Black	5.00	2.50	1.50
(10)	Karl Spooner	5.00	2.50	1.50
(11)	Clem Labine	5.00	2.50	1.50
(12)	Roy Campanella	15.00	7.50	4.50
(13)	Gil Hodges	12.00	6.00	3.50
(14)	Jim Gilliam	6.00	3.00	1.75
(15)	Jackie Robinson	50.00	25.00	15.00
(16)	Pee Wee Reese	15.00	7.50	4.50
(17)	Duke Snider	15.00	7.50	4.50
(18)	Carl Furillo	6.00	3.00	1.75
(19)	Sandy Amoros	5.00	2.50	1.50
(20)	Frank Kellert	5.00	2.50	1.50
(21)	Don Zimmer	6.00	3.00	1.75
(22)	Al Walker	5.00	2.50	1.50
(23)	Tommy Lasorda	7.50	3.75	2.25
(24)	Ed Roebuck	5.00	2.50	1.50
(25)	Don Hoak	5.00	2.50	1.50
(26)	George Shuba	5.00	2.50	1.50
(27)	Billy Herman	6.00	3.00	1.75
(28)	Jake Pitler	5.00	2.50	1.50
(29)	Joe Becker	5.00	2.50	1.50
(30)	Doc Wendler (Trainer), Carl Furillo	5.00	2.50	1.50
(31)	Charlie Di Giovanna (Batboy)	5.00	2.50	1.50
(32)	Ebbets Field	5.00	2.50	1.50
S-4	**CLEVELAND INDIANS ALBUM**	100.00	50.00	30.00
(1)	Al Lopez	6.00	3.00	1.75
(2)	Bob Lemon	6.00	3.00	1.75
(3)	Early Wynn	6.00	3.00	1.75
(4)	Mike Garcia	5.00	2.50	1.50
(5)	Bob Feller	12.00	6.00	3.50
(6)	Art Houtteman	5.00	2.50	1.50
(7)	Herb Score	7.50	3.75	2.25
(8)	Don Mossi	7.50	3.75	2.25
(9)	Ray Narleski	5.00	2.50	1.50
(10)	Jim Hegan	5.00	2.50	1.50
(11)	Vic Wertz	5.00	2.50	1.50
(12)	Bobby Avila	5.00	2.50	1.50
(13)	George Strickland	5.00	2.50	1.50
(14)	Al Rosen	5.00	2.50	1.50
(15)	Larry Doby	6.00	3.00	1.75
(16)	Ralph Kiner	7.50	3.75	2.25
(17)	Al Smith	5.00	2.50	1.50
(18)	Wally Westlake	5.00	2.50	1.50
(19)	Hal Naragon	5.00	2.50	1.50
(20)	Hank Foiles	5.00	2.50	1.50
(21)	Hank Majeski	5.00	2.50	1.50
(22)	Bill Wight	5.00	2.50	1.50
(23)	Sam Dente	5.00	2.50	1.50
(24)	Dave Pope	5.00	2.50	1.50
(25)	Dave Philley	5.00	2.50	1.50
(26)	Dale Mitchell	5.00	2.50	1.50
(27)	Hank Greenberg (GM)	10.00	5.00	3.00
(28)	Mel Harder	5.00	2.50	1.50
(29)	Ralph Kress	5.00	2.50	1.50
(30)	Tony Cuccinello	5.00	2.50	1.50
(31)	Bill Lobe	5.00	2.50	1.50
(32)	Cleveland Municipal Stadium	5.00	2.50	1.50

1934 Gold Medal Foods (R313A)

This set of unnumbered, blank-backed cards was issued by Gold Medal Foods (the Minneapolis parent company of Wheaties) to commemorate the 1934 World Series. The black-and-white cards measure 3-1/4" x 5-3/8". The checklist comprises six members each of the Detroit Tigers and St. Louis Cardinals, who were participants in the '34 World Series.

		NM	EX	VG
	Complete Set (12):	1,000	500.00	300.00
	Common Player:	60.00	30.00	18.00
(1)	Tommy Bridges	60.00	30.00	18.00
(2)	Mickey Cochrane	90.00	45.00	27.50
(3)	Dizzy Dean	350.00	175.00	100.00
(4)	Paul Dean	75.00	37.50	22.50
(5)	Frank Frisch	90.00	45.00	27.50
(6)	"Goose" Goslin	90.00	45.00	27.50
(7)	William Hallahan	60.00	30.00	18.00
(8)	Fred Marberry	60.00	30.00	18.00
(9)	Johnny "Pepper" Martin	90.00	45.00	27.50
(10)	Joe Medwick	90.00	45.00	27.50
(11)	William Rogell	60.00	30.00	18.00
(12)	"Jo Jo" White	60.00	30.00	18.00

1930s Goodrich Tire Mickey Cochrane

Without postmarked examples for verification, the issue date of this promotional postcard can only be estimated. Front of the 5-1/4" x 3-1/4" postcard has line art of Cochrane and his endorsement for the company's tires. The card is printed in yellow, orange and black. The lower-right quadrant was likely left blank to allow local tire retailers to place their advertisement. Back of the card has a pre-printed one-cent stamp.

	NM	EX	VG
Mickey Cochrane	100.00	50.00	30.00

1888 Goodwin Champions (N162)

Issued in 1888 by New York's Goodwin & Co., the 50-card "Champions" set includes eight baseball players - seven from the National League and one from the American Association. The full-color cards, which measure 1-1/2" x 2-5/8", were inserted in packages of Old Judge and Gypsy Queen Cigarettes. A small ad for the cards lists all 50 subjects of the "Champions" set, which also included popular billiards players, bicyclists, marksmen, pugilists, runners, wrestlers, college football stars, weightlifters, and Wild West star Buffalo Bill Cody. Four of the eight baseball players in the set (Anson, Kelly, Keefe and Brouthers) are Hall of Famers. The cards feature very attractive player portraits, making the "Champions" set among the most beautiful of all the 19th Century tobacco inserts. All cards can be found with or without a tiny line of type at the bottom of the back which reads, "Geo. S. Harris & Sons, Lith, Phila."

	NM	EX	VG
Complete Set (8):	44,000	17,000	7,700
Common Player:	3,850	1,600	725.00
Album:	7,500	3,750	2,250
(1) Ed Andrews	3,850	1,600	725.00
(2) Cap Anson	14,000	4,950	2,200
(3) Dan Brouthers	5,500	3,325	1,050
(4) Bob Caruthers	3,850	1,600	725.00
(5) Fred Dunlap	3,850	1,600	725.00
(6) Jack Glasscock	3,850	1,600	725.00
(7) Tim Keefe	5,775	3,325	1,050
(8) King Kelly	8,525	3,300	1,600

1889 Goodwin & Co. Baseball Album (A35)

As a mail-in redemption premium for 75 coupons from its Old Judge and Dog's Head cigarette brands, Goodwin offered this 12-page lithographed album. In an unusual 8-1/4" diameter format, the pages have a single hole punched at the side and are attached by a fancy tasseled cord allowing them to be fanned out for viewing. Front and back covers of the album depict a baseball, with the inside covers advertising the cigarettes, as does the sixth page of the album. The nine other pages depict in vivid color either single stars of the game or groups of four players, with an emphasis on the N.Y. Giants champions of 1888. Backs of the pages offer player stats for the previous season and schedules for various leagues for 1889. Because these albums are sometimes offered as single pages, they are priced as such here.

	NM	EX	VG
Complete Album:	20,000	10,000	6,000
(1) Front Cover	225.00	110.00	65.00
(2) Mickey Welch, John Ward, Buck Ewing, Tim Keefe	1,100	550.00	330.00
(3) Cap Anson	4,000	1,500	900.00
(4) Jim O'Rourke, Danny Richardson, Roger Connor, George Gore	1,200	460.00	275.00
(5) Mike "King" Kelly	3,000	1,500	900.00
(6) Advertising	350.00	100.00	60.00
(7) John Ward	2,125	1,050	635.00
(8) Mike Slattery, Pat Murphy, Gil Hatfield, Ed Crane	750.00	375.00	225.00
(9) Charles Comiskey	2,125	1,050	635.00
(10) Willard Brown, Bill George, Elmer Foster, Michael Tiernan	850.00	425.00	255.00
(11) Jim Mutrie, Lidell Titcomb, Art Whitney, Willie Breslin - Mascot	875.00	435.00	260.00
(12) Back Cover	200.00	100.00	60.00

1933 Goudey (R319)

Goudey Gum Co.'s first baseball card issue was a 239-card effort in 1933. The cards are color art reproductions of either portrait or action photos. The numbered cards measure 2-3/8" x 2-7/8" and carry a short player biography on the reverse. Card #106 (Napoleon Lajoie) is listed in the set though it was not actually issued until 1934. The card is very scarce and is unique in that it carries a 1934 design front and a 1933 back. The Lajoie card is not included in the complete set prices quoted here. The ACC designation for the set is R319. Grading companies and auction houses have found a few examples of these cards with blue printing on the backs instead of the customary green.

	NM	EX	VG
Complete Set (239):	110,000	37,500	19,500
Common Player (1-40):	250.00	85.00	45.00
Common Player (41-44):	165.00	55.00	30.00
Common Player (45-52):	200.00	70.00	35.00
Common Player (53-240):	165.00	55.00	30.00
1 Benny Bengough	5,500	900.00	200.00
2 Arthur (Dazzy) Vance	1,100	385.00	190.00
3 Hugh Critz	350.00	120.00	60.00
4 Henry "Heinie" Schuble	350.00	120.00	60.00
5 Floyd (Babe) Herman	500.00	175.00	90.00
6a Jimmy Dykes (Age is 26 in bio.)	350.00	120.00	60.00
6b Jimmy Dykes (Age is 36 in bio.)	350.00	120.00	60.00
7 Ted Lyons	1,250	435.00	225.00
8 Roy Johnson	250.00	85.00	45.00
9 Dave Harris	250.00	85.00	45.00
10 Glenn Myatt	250.00	85.00	45.00
11 Billy Rogell	250.00	85.00	45.00
12 George Pipgras	250.00	87.00	45.00
13 Lafayette Thompson	250.00	85.00	45.00
14 Henry Johnson	250.00	85.00	45.00
15 Victor Sorrell	250.00	85.00	45.00
16 George Blaeholder	250.00	85.00	45.00
17 Watson Clark	250.00	85.00	45.00
18 Herold (Muddy) Ruel	250.00	85.00	45.00
19 Bill Dickey	900.00	315.00	160.00
20 Bill Terry	1,250	435.00	225.00
21 Phil Collins	250.00	85.00	45.00
22 Harold (Pie) Traynor	1,250	435.00	225.00
23 Hazen (Ki-Ki) Cuyler	1,250	435.00	225.00
24 Horace Ford	250.00	85.00	45.00
25 Paul Waner	1,750	610.00	315.00
26 Chalmer Cissell	250.00	85.00	45.00
27 George Connally	250.00	85.00	45.00
28 Dick Bartell	250.00	85.00	45.00
29 Jimmy Foxx	2,250	785.00	405.00
30 Frank Hogan	250.00	85.00	45.00
31 Tony Lazzeri	1,250	435.00	225.00
32 John (Bud) Clancy	250.00	85.00	45.00
33 Ralph Kress	250.00	85.00	45.00
34 Bob O'Farrell	250.00	85.00	45.00
35 Al Simmons	1,250	435.00	225.00
36 Tommy Thevenow	250.00	85.00	45.00
37 Jimmy Wilson	250.00	85.00	45.00
38 Fred Brickell	250.00	85.00	45.00
39 Mark Koenig	250.00	87.00	45.00
40 Taylor Douthit	250.00	85.00	45.00
41 Gus Mancuso	165.00	55.00	30.00
42 Eddie Collins	475.00	165.00	85.00
43 Lew Fonseca	165.00	55.00	30.00
44 Jim Bottomley	425.00	150.00	75.00
45 Larry Benton	200.00	70.00	35.00
46 Ethan Allen	200.00	70.00	35.00
47a Henry "Heinie" Manush (Chain-link fence at top left.)	600.00	210.00	110.00
47b Henry "Heinie" Manush (No fence.)	600.00	210.00	110.00
48 Marty McManus	200.00	70.00	35.00
49 Frank Frisch	800.00	280.00	145.00
50 Ed Brandt	200.00	70.00	35.00
51 Charlie Grimm	200.00	70.00	35.00
52 Andy Cohen	225.00	80.00	40.00
53 George Herman (Babe) Ruth	13,500	4,900	2,100
54 Ray Kremer	165.00	55.00	30.00
55 Perce (Pat) Malone	165.00	55.00	30.00
56 Charlie Ruffing	425.00	150.00	80.00
57 Earl Clark	165.00	55.00	30.00
58 Frank (Lefty) O'Doul	350.00	120.00	65.00
59 Edmund (Bing) Miller	165.00	55.00	30.00
60 Waite Hoyt	425.00	150.00	75.00
61 Max Bishop	165.00	55.00	30.00
62 "Pepper" Martin	275.00	90.00	50.00
63 Joe Cronin	425.00	150.00	75.00
64 Burleigh Grimes	425.00	150.00	75.00
65 Milton Gaston	165.00	55.00	30.00
66 George Grantham	165.00	55.00	30.00
67 Guy Bush	165.00	55.00	30.00
68 Horace Lisenbee	165.00	55.00	30.00
69 Randy Moore	165.00	55.00	30.00
70 Floyd (Pete) Scott	165.00	55.00	30.00
71 Robert J. Burke	165.00	55.00	30.00
72 Owen Carroll	165.00	55.00	30.00
73 Jesse Haines	425.00	150.00	75.00
74 Eppa Rixey	425.00	150.00	75.00
75 Willie Kamm	165.00	55.00	30.00
76 Gordon (Mickey) Cochrane	475.00	165.00	85.00
77 Adam Comorosky	165.00	55.00	30.00
78 Jack Quinn	165.00	55.00	30.00
79 Urban (Red) Faber	425.00	150.00	75.00
80 Clyde Manion	165.00	55.00	30.00
81 Sam Jones	165.00	55.00	30.00
82 Dibrell Williams	165.00	55.00	30.00
83 Pete Jablonowski	165.00	55.00	30.00
84 Glenn Spencer	165.00	55.00	30.00
85 John Henry "Heinie" Sand	165.00	55.00	30.00
86 Phil Todt	165.00	55.00	30.00
87 Frank O'Rourke	165.00	55.00	30.00
88 Russell Rollings	165.00	55.00	30.00
89 Tris Speaker	550.00	190.00	95.00
90 Jess Petty	165.00	55.00	30.00
91 Tom Zachary	165.00	55.00	30.00
92 Lou Gehrig	3,750	1,750	800.00
93 John Welch	165.00	55.00	30.00
94 Bill Walker	165.00	55.00	30.00
95 Alvin Crowder	165.00	55.00	30.00
96 Willis Hudlin	165.00	55.00	30.00
97 Joe Morrissey	165.00	55.00	30.00
98 Walter Berger	165.00	55.00	30.00
99 Tony Cuccinello	165.00	55.00	30.00
100 George Uhle	165.00	55.00	30.00
101 Richard Coffman	165.00	55.00	30.00
102 Travis C. Jackson	425.00	150.00	75.00
103 Earl Combs (Earle)	425.00	150.00	75.00
104 Fred Marberry	165.00	55.00	30.00
105 Bernie Friberg	165.00	55.00	30.00
106 Napoleon (Larry) Lajoie	37,500	24,000	8,500
106p Leo Durocher (Unique proof card.)		4,000	
107 Henry (Heinie) Manush	425.00	150.00	75.00
108 Joe Kuhel	165.00	55.00	30.00
109 Joe Cronin	425.00	150.00	75.00
110 Leon (Goose) Goslin (Portrait)	425.00	150.00	75.00
110p Leon (Goose) Goslin (Proof card, batting - same as #168 - name in two lines on front.)	1,200	420.00	215.00
111 Monte Weaver	165.00	55.00	30.00
112 Fred Schulte	165.00	55.00	30.00
113 Oswald Bluege	165.00	55.00	30.00
114 Luke Sewell	165.00	55.00	30.00
115 Cliff Heathcote	165.00	55.00	30.00
116 Eddie Morgan	165.00	55.00	30.00
117 Walter (Rabbit) Maranville	425.00	150.00	75.00
118 Valentine J. (Val) Picinich	165.00	55.00	30.00
119 Rogers Hornsby	1,250	435.00	225.00
120 Carl Reynolds	165.00	55.00	30.00
121 Walter Stewart	165.00	55.00	30.00
122 Alvin Crowder	165.00	55.00	30.00
123 Jack Russell (Orange background, white cap.)	165.00	55.00	30.00
123(p a) Jack Russell (Proof card, red background, dark cap - same as #167 - name in one line in front.)	600.00	210.00	110.00
123(p b) Luke Sewell (Proof card, otherwise identical to #163.)	8,000	2,800	1,450
124 Earl Whitehill	165.00	55.00	30.00
125 Bill Terry	425.00	150.00	75.00
126 Joe Moore	165.00	55.00	30.00
127 Melvin Ott	725.00	250.00	125.00
128 Charles (Chuck) Klein	450.00	155.00	80.00
129 Harold Schumacher	165.00	55.00	30.00
130 Fred Fitzsimmons	165.00	55.00	30.00
131 Fred Frankhouse	165.00	55.00	30.00
132 Jim Elliott	165.00	55.00	30.00
133 Fred Lindstrom	425.00	150.00	75.00
134 Edgar (Sam) Rice	425.00	150.00	75.00
135 Elwood (Woody) English	165.00	55.00	30.00
136 Flint Rhem	165.00	55.00	30.00
137 Fred (Red) Lucas	165.00	55.00	30.00
138 Herb Pennock	415.00	145.00	75.00
139 Ben Cantwell	165.00	55.00	30.00
140 Irving (Bump) Hadley	165.00	55.00	30.00
141 Ray Benge	165.00	55.00	30.00
142 Paul Richards	165.00	55.00	30.00
143 Glenn Wright	165.00	55.00	30.00
144 George Herman (Babe) Ruth (Double-print; replaced card #106 on press sheet.)	8,000	2,900	1,350
145 George Walberg	165.00	55.00	30.00
146 Walter Stewart	165.00	55.00	30.00
147 Leo Durocher	425.00	150.00	75.00
148 Eddie Farrell	165.00	55.00	30.00
149 George Herman (Babe) Ruth	9,500	3,600	2,000
150 Ray Kolp	165.00	55.00	30.00
151 D'Arcy (Jake) Flowers	165.00	55.00	30.00
152 James (Zack) Taylor	165.00	55.00	30.00
153 Charles (Buddy) Myer	165.00	55.00	30.00
154 Jimmy Foxx	1,600	500.00	200.00
155 Joe Judge	165.00	55.00	30.00
156 Danny Macfayden (MacFayden)	165.00	55.00	30.00
157 Sam Byrd	165.00	55.00	30.00
158 Morris (Moe) Berg	700.00	250.00	150.00
159 Oswald Bluege	165.00	55.00	30.00
160 Lou Gehrig	4,000	1,775	750.00
161 Al Spohrer	165.00	55.00	30.00
162 Leo Mangum	165.00	55.00	30.00
163 Luke Sewell	165.00	55.00	30.00
164 Lloyd Waner	450.00	155.00	75.00
165 Joe Sewell	450.00	155.00	75.00
166 Sam West	165.00	55.00	30.00
167 Jack Russell (Name on two lines, see also #123p.)	165.00	55.00	30.00
168 Leon (Goose) Goslin (Name on one line, see also #110p.)	600.00	210.00	110.00
169 Al Thomas	165.00	55.00	30.00
170 Harry McCurdy	165.00	55.00	30.00
171 Charley Jamieson	165.00	55.00	30.00
172 Billy Hargrave	165.00	55.00	30.00
173 Roscoe Holm	165.00	55.00	30.00
174 Warren (Curley) Ogden	165.00	55.00	30.00
175 Dan Howley	165.00	55.00	30.00
176 John Ogden	165.00	55.00	30.00
177 Walter French	165.00	55.00	30.00
178 Jackie Warner	165.00	55.00	30.00
179 Fred Leach	165.00	55.00	30.00
180 Eddie Moore	165.00	55.00	30.00
181 George Herman (Babe) Ruth	7,250	3,400	1,600
182 Andy High	165.00	55.00	30.00
183 George Walberg	165.00	55.00	30.00
184 Charley Berry	165.00	55.00	30.00
185 Bob Smith	165.00	55.00	30.00
186 John Schulte	165.00	55.00	30.00
187 Henry (Heinie) Manush	425.00	150.00	75.00
188 Rogers Hornsby	1,200	425.00	215.00
189 Joe Cronin	425.00	150.00	75.00
190 Fred Schulte	165.00	55.00	30.00
191 Ben Chapman	165.00	55.00	30.00
192 Walter Brown	165.00	55.00	30.00
193 Lynford Lary	165.00	55.00	30.00
194 Earl Averill	425.00	150.00	75.00
195 Evar Swanson	165.00	55.00	30.00
196 Leroy Mahaffey	165.00	55.00	30.00
197 Richard (Rick) Ferrell	425.00	150.00	75.00
198 Irving (Jack) Burns	165.00	55.00	30.00
199 Tom Bridges	165.00	55.00	30.00
200 Bill Hallahan	165.00	55.00	30.00
201 Ernie Orsatti	165.00	55.00	30.00
202 Charles Leo (Gabby) Hartnett	425.00	150.00	75.00
203 Lonnie Warneke	165.00	55.00	30.00
204 Jackson Riggs Stephenson	165.00	55.00	30.00
205 Henry (Heinie) Meine	165.00	55.00	30.00
206 Gus Suhr	165.00	55.00	30.00
207 Melvin Ott	1,300	400.00	200.00
208 Byrne (Bernie) James	165.00	44.00	22.00
209 Adolfo Luque	200.00	70.00	36.00
210 Virgil Davis	165.00	55.00	30.00
211 Lewis (Hack) Wilson	700.00	250.00	140.00
212 Billy Urbanski	165.00	55.00	30.00
213 Earl Adams	165.00	55.00	30.00
214 John Kerr	165.00	55.00	30.00
215 Russell Van Atta	165.00	55.00	30.00
216 Vernon Gomez	425.00	150.00	75.00
217 Frank Crosetti	275.00	96.00	49.00
218 Wesley Ferrell	165.00	55.00	30.00
219 George (Mule) Haas	165.00	55.00	30.00
220 Robert (Lefty) Grove	775.00	275.00	140.00

221	Dale Alexander	165.00	55.00	30.00
222	Charley Gehringer	600.00	210.00	110.00
223	Jerome (Dizzy) Dean	1,500	500.00	275.00
224	Frank Demaree	165.00	55.00	30.00
225	Bill Jurges	165.00	55.00	30.00
226	Charley Root	165.00	55.00	30.00
227	Bill Herman	425.00	150.00	75.00
228	Tony Piet	165.00	55.00	30.00
229	Floyd Vaughan	425.00	150.00	75.00
230	Carl Hubbell	725.00	255.00	130.00
231	Joe Moore	165.00	55.00	30.00
232	Frank (Lefty) O'Doul	250.00	85.00	45.00
233	Johnny Vergez	165.00	55.00	30.00
234	Carl Hubbell	725.00	255.00	130.00
235	Fred Fitzsimmons	165.00	55.00	30.00
236	George Davis	165.00	55.00	30.00
237	Gus Mancuso	165.00	55.00	30.00
238	Hugh Critz	165.00	55.00	30.00
239	Leroy Parmelee	165.00	55.00	30.00
240	Harold Schumacher	350.00	75.00	35.00

1934 Goudey (R320)

The 1934 Goudey set contains 96 cards (2-3/8" x 2-7/8") that feature color art reproductions of player photographs. Card fronts have two different designs; one featuring a small portrait photo of Lou Gehrig with the the words "Lou Gehrig says..." inside a blue strip at the bottom, while the other design carries a red "Chuck Klein says..." strip and also has his photo. The card backs contain a short player biography that purports to have been written by Gehrig or Klein. The ACC designation for the set is R320. Albums, blue for N.L., and magenta for A.L., were given away to the person who bought the last penny pack in each box of high-numbers or who mailed 50 wrappers to the gum company.

		NM	EX	VG
Complete Set (96):		30,000	11,000	5,250
Common Player (1-48):		120.00	45.00	20.00
Common Player (49-72):		160.00	55.00	25.00
Common Player (73-96):		250.00	100.00	50.00
Album:		500.00	250.00	150.00
1	Jimmy Foxx	4,500	600.00	210.00
2	Gordon (Mickey) Cochrane	550.00	220.00	110.00
3	Charlie Grimm	120.00	45.00	20.00
4	Elwood (Woody) English	120.00	45.00	20.00
5	Ed Brandt	120.00	45.00	20.00
6	Jerome (Dizzy) Dean	1,700	400.00	190.00
7	Leo Durocher	350.00	140.00	70.00
8	Tony Piet	120.00	45.00	20.00
9	Ben Chapman	120.00	45.00	20.00
10	Charles (Chuck) Klein	350.00	140.00	70.00
11	Paul Waner	350.00	140.00	70.00
12	Carl Hubbell	350.00	140.00	70.00
13	Frank Frisch	350.00	140.00	70.00
14	Willie Kamm	120.00	45.00	20.00
15	Alvin Crowder	120.00	45.00	20.00
16	Joe Kuhel	120.00	45.00	20.00
17	Hugh Critz	120.00	45.00	20.00
18	Henry (Heinie) Manush	350.00	140.00	70.00
19	Robert (Lefty) Grove	675.00	225.00	110.00
20	Frank Hogan	120.00	45.00	20.00
21	Bill Terry	350.00	140.00	70.00
22	Floyd Vaughan	350.00	140.00	70.00
23	Charley Gehringer	475.00	190.00	95.00
24	Ray Benge	120.00	45.00	20.00
25	Roger Cramer	120.00	45.00	20.00
26	Gerald Walker	120.00	45.00	20.00
27	Luke Appling	350.00	140.00	70.00
28	Ed. Coleman	120.00	45.00	20.00
29	Larry French	120.00	45.00	20.00
30	Julius Solters	120.00	45.00	20.00
31	Baxter Jordan	120.00	45.00	20.00
32	John (Blondy) Ryan	120.00	45.00	20.00
33	Frank (Don) Hurst	120.00	45.00	20.00
34	Charles (Chick) Hafey	350.00	140.00	70.00
35	Ernie Lombardi	350.00	140.00	70.00
36	Walter (Huck) Betts	120.00	45.00	20.00
37	Lou Gehrig	4,750	1,800	850.00
38	Oral Hildebrand	120.00	45.00	20.00
39	Fred Walker	120.00	45.00	20.00
40	John Stone	120.00	45.00	20.00
41	George Earnshaw	120.00	45.00	20.00
42	John Allen	120.00	45.00	20.00
43	Dick Porter	120.00	45.00	20.00
44	Tom Bridges	120.00	45.00	20.00
45	Oscar Melillo	120.00	45.00	20.00
46	Joe Stripp	120.00	45.00	20.00
47	John Frederick	120.00	45.00	20.00
48	James (Tex) Carleton	120.00	45.00	20.00
49	Sam Leslie	160.00	55.00	25.00
50	Walter Beck	160.00	55.00	25.00
51	Jim (Rip) Collins	160.00	55.00	25.00
52	Herman Bell	160.00	55.00	25.00
53	George Watkins	160.00	55.00	25.00
54	Wesley Schulmerich	160.00	55.00	25.00
55	Ed Holley	160.00	55.00	25.00
56	Mark Koenig	160.00	55.00	25.00
57	Bill Swift	160.00	55.00	25.00

58	Earl Grace	160.00	55.00	25.00
59	Joe Mowry	160.00	55.00	25.00
60	Lynn Nelson	160.00	55.00	25.00
61	Lou Gehrig	3,800	1,625	800.00
62	Henry Greenberg	1,350	550.00	275.00
63	Minter Hayes	160.00	55.00	25.00
64	Frank Grube	160.00	55.00	25.00
65	Cliff Bolton	160.00	55.00	25.00
66	Mel Harder	160.00	55.00	25.00
67	Bob Weiland	160.00	55.00	25.00
68	Bob Johnson	160.00	55.00	25.00
69	John Marcum	160.00	55.00	25.00
70	Ervin (Pete) Fox	160.00	55.00	25.00
71	Lyle Tinning	160.00	55.00	25.00
72	Arndt Jorgens	160.00	55.00	25.00
73	Ed Wells	250.00	100.00	50.00
74	Bob Boken	250.00	100.00	50.00
75	Bill Werber	250.00	100.00	50.00
76	Hal Trosky	250.00	100.00	50.00
77	Joe Vosmik	250.00	100.00	50.00
78	Frank (Pinkey) Higgins	250.00	100.00	50.00
79	Eddie Durham	250.00	100.00	50.00
80	Marty McManus	250.00	100.00	50.00
81	Bob Brown	250.00	100.00	50.00
82	Bill Hallahan	250.00	100.00	50.00
83	Jim Mooney	250.00	100.00	50.00
84	Paul Derringer	250.00	100.00	50.00
85	Adam Comorosky	250.00	100.00	50.00
86	Lloyd Johnson	250.00	100.00	50.00
87	George Darrow	250.00	100.00	50.00
88	Homer Peel	250.00	100.00	50.00
89	Linus Frey	250.00	100.00	50.00
90	Hazen (Ki-Ki) Cuyler	250.00	100.00	50.00
91	Dolph Camilli	250.00	100.00	50.00
92	Steve Larkin	250.00	100.00	50.00
93	Fred Ostermueller	250.00	100.00	50.00
94	Robert A. (Red) Rolfe	400.00	160.00	80.00
95	Myril Hoag	250.00	100.00	50.00
96	Jim DeShong	525.00	160.00	60.00

1933-34 Goudey Premiums (R309-1)

Consisting of just four unnumbered cards, this set of black-and-white photos was printed on heavy cardboard and issued as a premium by the Goudey Gum Co. in 1933. Cards (1), (2), and (4) were issued in 1933 and card (3) was issued in 1934. The cards measure 5-1/2" x 8-13/16" and are accented with a gold, picture-frame border and an easel on the back. Besides the game's greatest player, the set has team photos of the 1933 All-Star squads from each league and the World's Champion 1933 N.Y. Giants.

		NM	EX	VG
Complete Set (4):		3,250	1,625	975.00
Common Card:		600.00	300.00	180.00
(1)	American League All Stars	650.00	325.00	195.00
(2)	National League All Stars	600.00	300.00	180.00
(3)	"Worlds Champions 1933" (New York Giants)	750.00	375.00	225.00
(4)	George Herman (Babe) Ruth	1,350	675.00	405.00

1935 Goudey 4-in-1 (R321)

The 1935 Goudey set features color portraits of four players (usually) from the same team on each card. Thirty-six card fronts make up the set with 114 front/back combinations existing. The card backs form nine different puzzles: 1) Tigers Team, 2) Chuck Klein, 3) Frankie Frisch, 4) Mickey Cochrane, 5) Joe Cronin, 6) Jimmy Foxx, 7) Al Simmons, 8) Indians Team, and 9) Senators Team. The cards, which measure 2-3/8" x 2-7/8", have an ACC designation of R321. The numbering has been assigned for this checklist on the basis of alphabetical order of the players found on each card front.

		NM	EX	VG
Complete Set (36):		11,000	4,400	2,200
Complete Set (114):		62,500	25,000	12,500
Common Card:		125.00	50.00	25.00
(1)	Sparky Adams, Jim Bottomley, Adam Comorosky, Tony Piet	300.00	120.00	60.00
(2)	Ethan Allen, Fred Brickell, Bubber Jonnard, Jimmie Wilson	125.00	50.00	15.00
(3)	Johnny Allen, Jimmie Deshong, Red Rolfe, Dixie Walker (DeShong)	125.00	50.00	15.00
(4)	Luke Appling, Jimmie Dykes, George Earnshaw, Luke Sewell	300.00	120.00	60.00
(5)	Earl Averill, Oral Hildebrand, Willie Kamm, Hal Trosky	300.00	120.00	60.00
(6)	Dick Bartell, Hughie Critz, Gus Mancuso, Mel Ott	300.00	120.00	60.00
(7)	Ray Benge, Fred Fitzsimmons, Mark Koenig, Tom Zachary	125.00	30.00	15.00
(8)	Larry Benton, Ben Cantwell, Flint Rhem, Al Spohrer	125.00	30.00	15.00

(9)	Charlie Berry, Bobby Burke, Red Kress, Dazzy Vance	300.00	120.00	60.00
(10)	Max Bishop, Bill Cissell, Joe Cronin, Carl Reynolds	300.00	120.00	60.00
(11)	George Blaeholder, Dick Coffman, Oscar Melillo, Sammy West	125.00	30.00	15.00
(12)	Cy Blanton, Babe Herman, Tom Padden, Gus Suhr	125.00	30.00	15.00
(13)	Zeke Bonura, Mule Haas, Jackie Hayes, Ted Lyons	300.00	120.00	60.00
(14)	Jim Bottomley, Adam Comorosky, Willis Hudlin, Glenn Myatt	300.00	120.00	60.00
(15)	Ed Brandt, Fred Frankhouse, Shanty Hogan, Gene Moore	125.00	50.00	25.00
(16)	Ed Brandt, Rabbit Maranville, Marty McManus, Babe Ruth	3,250	1,000	450.00
(17)	Tommy Bridges, Mickey Cochrane, Charlie Gehringer, Billy Rogell	350.00	140.00	70.00
(18)	Jack Burns, Frank Grube, Rollie Hemsley, Bob Weiland	125.00	30.00	15.00
(19)	Guy Bush, Waite Hoyt, Lloyd Waner, Paul Waner	350.00	140.00	70.00
(20)	Sammy Byrd, Danny MacFayden, Pepper Martin, Bob O'Farrell	125.00	30.00	15.00
(21a)	Gilly Campbell, Ival Goodman, Alex Kampouris, Billy Meyers (Myers) (no "Meyers")	200.00	80.00	40.00
(21b)	Gilly Campbell, Ival Goodman, Alex Kampouris, Billy Meyers (Myers)	150.00	60.00	30.00
(22)	Tex Carleton, Dizzy Dean, Frankie Frisch, Ernie Orsatti	650.00	260.00	130.00
(23)	Watty Clark, Lonny Frey, Sam Leslie, Joe Stripp	125.00	30.00	15.00
(24)	Mickey Cochrane, Willie Kamm, Muddy Ruel, Al Simmons	350.00	140.00	70.00
(25)	Ed Coleman, Doc Cramer, Bob Johnson, Johnny Marcum	125.00	30.00	15.00
(26)	General Crowder, Goose Goslin, Firpo Marberry, Heinie Schuble	300.00	120.00	60.00
(27)	Kiki Cuyler, Woody English, Burleigh Grimes, Chuck Klein	350.00	140.00	70.00
(28)	Bill Dickey, Tony Lazzeri, Pat Malone, Red Ruffing	400.00	160.00	80.00
(29)	Rick Ferrell, Wes Ferrell, Fritz Ostermueller, Bill Werber	300.00	120.00	60.00
(30)	Pete Fox, Hank Greenberg, Schoolboy Rowe, Gee Walker	350.00	140.00	70.00
(31)	Jimmie Foxx, Pinky Higgins, Roy Mahaffey, Dib Williams	400.00	160.00	80.00
(32)	Bump Hadley, Lyn Lary, Heinie Manush, Monte Weaver	300.00	120.00	60.00
(33)	Mel Harder, Bill Knickerbocker, Lefty Stewart, Joe Vosmik	125.00	30.00	15.00
(34)	Travis Jackson, Gus Mancuso, Hal Schumacher, Bill Terry	300.00	120.00	60.00
(35)	Joe Kuhel, Buddy Meyer, John Stone, Earl Whitehill (Myer)	125.00	30.00	15.00
(36)	Red Lucas, Tommy Thevenow, Pie Traynor, Glenn Wright	300.00	120.00	60.00

1935 Goudey Puzzle-Backs

Each of the 36 card fronts in 1935 Goudey can be found with from two to four different backs that could be used to assemble a six-piece (single player) or 12-piece (team photo or composite) puzzle. This listing checklists the different backs found with each front as well as the cards that comprise each of the nine puzzles. The numbers given for each puzzle piece correspond to the assigned numbers of the card fronts.

Sparky Adams, Jim Bottomley, Adam Comorosky, Tony Piet
1H   Tigers, H
3F   Frisch, F
4F   Cochrane, F
5F   Cronin, F
Ethan Allen, Fred Brickell, Bubber Jonnard, Jimmie Wilson
1E   Tigers, E
3C   Frisch, C
5C   Cronin, C
6C   Foxx, C
Johnny Allen, Jimmie Deshong, Red Rolfe, Dixie Walker (DeShong)
8E   Indians, E

9E Senators, E
Luke Appling, Jimmie Dykes, George Earnshaw, Luke Sewell
1I Tigers, I
2F Klein, F
6F Foxx, F
7F Simmons, F
Earl Averill, Oral Hildebrand, Willie Kamm, Hal Trosky
1L Tigers, L
2E Klein, E
6E Foxx, E
7E Simmons, E
Dick Bartell, Hughie Critz, Gus Mancuso, Mel Ott
2A Klein, A
4A Cochrane, A
7A Simmons, A
Ray Benge, Fred Fitzsimmons, Mark Koenig, Tom Zachary
8A Indians, A
9A Senators, A
Larry Benton, Ben Cantwell, Flint Rhem, Al Spohrer
8L Indians, L
9L Senators, L
Charlie Berry, Bobby Burke, Red Kress, Dazzy Vance
2C Klein, C
4C Cochrane, C
7C Simmons, C
Max Bishop, Bill Cissell, Joe Cronin, Carl Reynolds
1G Tigers, G
3E Frisch, E
5E Cronin, E
6E Foxx, E
George Blaeholder, Dick Coffman, Oscar Melillo, Sammy West
1F Tigers, F
3D Frisch, D
5D Cronin, D
6D Foxx, D
Cy Blanton, Babe Herman, Tom Padden, Gus Suhr
8K Indians, K
9K Senators, K
Zeke Bonura, Mule Haas, Jackie Hayes, Ted Lyons
8B Indians, B
9B Senators, B
Jim Bottomley, Adam Comorosky, Willis Hudlin, Glenn Myatt
1K Tigers, K
3B Frisch, B
5B Cronin, B
6B Foxx, B
Ed Brandt, Fred Frankhouse, Shanty Hogan, Gene Moore
2E Klein, E
4E Cochrane, E
7E Simmons, E
Ed Brandt, Rabbit Maranville, Marty McManus, Babe Ruth
1J Tigers, J
3A Frisch, A
4A Cochrane, A
5A Cronin, A
Tommy Bridges, Mickey Cochrane, Charlie Gehringer, Billy Rogell
1D Tigers, D
2D Klein, D
6D Foxx, D
7D Simmons, D
Jack Burns, Frank Grube, Rollie Hemsley, Bob Weiland
8C Indians, C
9C Senators, C
Guy Bush, Waite Hoyt, Lloyd Waner, Paul Waner
1E Tigers, E
3C Frisch, C
4C Cochrane, C
5C Cronin, C
Sammy Byrd, Danny MacFayden, Pepper Martin, Bob O'Farrell
2F Klein, F
4F Cochrane, F
7F Simmons, F
Gilly Campbell, Ival Goodman, Alex Kampouris, Billy Meyers (Myers)
8D Indians, D
9D Senators, D
Tex Carleton, Dizzy Dean, Frankie Frisch, Ernie Orsatti
1A Tigers, A
2A Klein, A
6A Foxx, A
7A Simmons, A
Watty Clark, Lonny Frey, Sam Leslie, Joe Stripp
1G Tigers, G
3E Frisch, E
4E Cochrane, E
5E Cronin, E
Mickey Cochrane, Willie Kamm, Muddy Ruel, Al Simmons
1J Tigers, J
3A Frisch, A
5A Cronin, A
6A Foxx, A
Ed Coleman, Doc Cramer, Bob Johnson, Johnny Marcum
8J Indians, J
9J Senators, J
General Crowder, Goose Goslin, Firpo Marberry, Heinie Schuble
1H Tigers, H
3F Frisch, F
5F Cronin, F
6F Foxx, F
Kiki Cuyler, Woody English, Burleigh Grimes, Chuck Klein
1F Tigers, F
3D Frisch, D
4D Cochrane, D
5D Cronin, D
Bill Dickey, Tony Lazzeri, Pat Malone, Red Ruffing
2D Klein, D
4D Cochrane, D
7D Simmons, D
Rick Ferrell, Wes Ferrell, Fritz Ostermueller, Bill Werber
8G Indians, G
9G Senators, G

Pete Fox, Hank Greenberg, Schoolboy Rowe, Gee Walker
8F Indians, F
9F Senators, F
Jimmie Foxx, Pinky Higgins, Roy Mahaffey, Dib Williams
1B Tigers, B
2B Klein, B
6B Foxx, B
7B Simmons, B
Bump Hadley, Lyn Lary, Heinie Manush, Monte Weaver
1C Tigers, C
2C Klein, C
6C Foxx, C
7C Simmons, C
Mel Harder, Bill Knickerbocker, Lefty Stewart, Joe Vosmik
8I Indians, I
9I Senators, I
Travis Jackson, Gus Mancuso, Hal Schumacher, Bill Terry
1K Tigers, K
3B Frisch, B
4B Cochrane, B
5B Cronin, B
Joe Kuhel, Buddy Meyer, John Stone, Earl Whitehill (Myer)
8H Indians, H
9H Senators, H
Red Lucas, Tommy Thevenow, Pie Traynor, Glenn Wright
2B Klein, B
4B Cochrane, B
7B Simmons, B

Picture 1, Detroit Tigers Team Photo

A (22)
B (31)
C (32)
D (17)
E (2)
E (19)
F (11)
F (27)
G (10)
G (23)
H (1)
H (26)
I (4)
J (16)
J (24)
K (14)
K (34)
L (5)

Picture 2, Chuck Klein

A (6)
A (22)
B (31)
B (36)
C (9)
C (32)
D (17)
D (28)
E (5)
E (15)
F (4)
F (20)

Picture 3, Frankie Frisch

A (16)
A (24)
B (14))
B (34)
C (2)
C (19)
D (11)
D (27)
D (10)
E (23)
F (1)
F (26)

Picture 4, Gordon (Mickey) Cochrane

A (6)
A (16)
B (34)
B (36)
C (9)
C (19)
D (27)
D (28)
E (15)
E (23)
F (1)
F (20)

Picture 5, Joe Cronin

A (16)
A (24)
B (14)
B (34)
C (2)
C (19)
D (11)
D (27)
E (10)
E (23)
F (1)
F (26)

Picture 6, Jimmy (Jimmie) Foxx

A (22)
A (24)
B (14)
B (31)
C (2)
C (32)
D (11)
D (17)
E (5)
E (10)
F (4)
F (26)

Picture 7, Al Simmons

A (6)
A (22)
B (31)
B (36)
C (9)
C (32)
D (17)
D (28)
E (5)
E (15)
F (4)
F (20)

Picture 8, Cleve. Indians Composite

A (7)
B (13)
C (18)
D (21)
E (3)
F (30)
G (34)
H (35)
I (32)
J (25)
K (12)
L (8)

Picture 9, Wash. Senators Composite

A (7)
B (13)
C (18)
D (21)
E (3)
F (30)
G (29)
H (35)
I (33)
J (25)
K (12)
L (8)

1935 Goudey Premiums (R309-2)

The black-and-white photos in this set were issued as a premium by retailers in exchange for coupons from 10 Goudey wrappers in 1935. The pictures measure 5-1/2" x 9" (or a bit longer), and are printed on thin, glossy paper. The unnumbered set includes three team collages and players, whose names are written in script in the "wide pen" style.

	NM	EX	VG
Complete Set (16):	5,000	2,500	1,500
Common Player:	275.00	135.00	82.00
(1) Elden Auker	275.00	135.00	82.00
(2) Johnny Babich	275.00	135.00	82.00
(3) Dick Bartell	275.00	135.00	82.00
(4) Lester R. Bell	275.00	135.00	82.00
(5) Wally Berger	275.00	135.00	82.00
(6) Mickey Cochrane	400.00	200.00	120.00
(7) Ervin Fox, Leon "Goose" Goslin, Gerald Walker	325.00	160.00	97.00
(8) Vernon Gomez	400.00	200.00	120.00
(9) Hank Greenberg	500.00	250.00	150.00
(10) Oscar Melillo	275.00	135.00	82.00
(11) Mel Ott	400.00	200.00	120.00
(12) Schoolboy Rowe	275.00	135.00	82.00
(13) Vito Tamulis	275.00	135.00	82.00
(14) Boston Red Sox	300.00	150.00	90.00
(15) Cleveland Indians	300.00	150.00	90.00
(16) Washington Senators	300.00	150.00	90.00

1936 Goudey (R322)

The 1936 Goudey set consists of black-and-white cards measuring 2-3/8" x 2-7/8". A facsimile autograph is positioned on the card fronts. Backs contain a brief player biography and were designed to play a baseball game. Different game situations (out, single, double, etc.) are given on each card. Numerous front/back combinations exist in the set. The ACC designation for the set is R322.

	NM	EX	VG
Complete Set (25):	2,625	1,300	785.00
Common Player:	80.00	40.00	25.00
(1) Walter Berger	80.00	40.00	25.00
(2) Henry Bonura	80.00	40.00	25.00
(3) Stan Bordagaray	80.00	40.00	25.00
(4) Bill Brubaker	80.00	40.00	25.00
(5) Dolf Camilli	80.00	40.00	25.00
(6) Clydell Castleman	80.00	40.00	25.00
(7) "Mickey" Cochrane	175.00	85.00	50.00
(8) Joe Coscarart	80.00	40.00	25.00
(9) Frank Crosetti	110.00	55.00	30.00
(10) "Kiki" Cuyler	140.00	70.00	40.00
(11) Paul Derringer	80.00	40.00	25.00
(12) Jimmy Dykes	80.00	40.00	25.00
(13) "Rick" Ferrell	140.00	70.00	40.00
(14) "Lefty" Gomez	175.00	85.00	50.00
(15) Hank Greenberg	275.00	135.00	80.00
(16) "Bucky" Harris	140.00	70.00	40.00
(17) "Rolly" Hemsley	80.00	40.00	25.00
(18) Frank Higgins	80.00	40.00	25.00
(19) Oral Hildebrand	80.00	40.00	25.00
(20) "Chuck" Klein	140.00	70.00	40.00
(21) "Pepper" Martin	110.00	55.00	30.00
(22) "Buck" Newsom	80.00	40.00	25.00
(23) Joe Vosmik	80.00	40.00	25.00
(24) Paul Waner	140.00	70.00	40.00
(25) Bill Werber	80.00	40.00	25.00

1936 Goudey "Wide Pen" Premiums (R314)

The premium cards originally listed in the American Card Catalog as R314 are known to generations of collectors as "Wide Pens" because of the distinctive, thick style of cursive printing used for the facsimile autographs. Current thinking is that the issue is actually comprised of several distinct types issued over the course of at least two years and sharing a basic 3-1/4" x 5-1/2" black-and-white unnumbered format. Dates attributed are speculative.

1936 Goudey "Wide Pen" Premiums - Type 1

Al Simmons

These in-store premiums are known to collectors as "Wide Pens" because of the distinctive, thick style of cursive printing used for the facsimile autographs. Cards have a 3-1/4" x 5-1/2" black-and-white, unnumbered format. Type 1 cards have bordered photos with "LITHO IN U.S.A." in the bottom border.

	NM	EX	VG
Complete Set (120):	9,000	3,750	1,250
Common Player:	60.00	25.00	15.00
(1) Ethan Allen (Kneeling)	60.00	25.00	15.00
(2) Earl Averill (Portrait)	90.00	38.00	23.00
(3) Dick Bartell (Portrait)	60.00	25.00	15.00
(4) Dick Bartell (Sliding)	60.00	25.00	15.00
(5) Walter Berger (Portrait)	60.00	25.00	15.00
(6) Geo. Blaeholder (Portrait)	60.00	25.00	15.00
(7) "Cy" Blanton (Portrait)	60.00	25.00	15.00
(8) "Cliff" Bolton (Portrait)	60.00	25.00	15.00
(9) Stan Bordagaray (Portrait)	60.00	25.00	15.00
(10) Tommy Bridges (Portrait)	60.00	25.00	15.00
(11) Bill Brubaker (Portrait)	60.00	25.00	15.00
(12) Sam Byrd (Portrait)	60.00	25.00	15.00
(13) Dolph Camilli (Portrait)	60.00	25.00	15.00
(14) Clydell Castleman (Pitching)	60.00	25.00	15.00
(15) Clydell Castleman (Portrait)	60.00	25.00	15.00
(16) "Phil" Cavaretta (Cavarretta) (Fielding)	60.00	25.00	15.00
(17) Ben Chapman, Bill Werber	75.00	31.00	19.50
(18) "Mickey" Cochrane (Portrait)	100.00	42.00	26.00
(19) Earl Coombs (Earle Combs) (Batting)	90.00	38.00	23.00
(20) Joe Coscarart (Portrait)	60.00	25.00	15.00
(21) Joe Cronin (Kneeling)	90.00	38.00	23.00
(22) Frank Crosetti (Batting)	65.00	27.00	17.00
(23) Tony Cuccinello (Portrait)	60.00	25.00	15.00
(24) "Kiki" Cuyler (Portrait)	90.00	38.00	23.00
(25) Curt Davis (Pitching)	60.00	25.00	15.00
(26) Virgil Davis (Catching)	60.00	25.00	15.00
(27) Paul Derringer (Portrait)	60.00	25.00	15.00
(28) "Bill" Dickey (Catching)	100.00	42.00	26.00
(29) Joe DiMaggio, Joe McCarthy	850.00	355.00	220.00

	NM	EX	VG
(30) Jimmy Dykes (Kneeling)	60.00	25.00	15.00
(31) "Rick" Ferrell (Catching)	90.00	38.00	23.00
(32) "Wes" Ferrell (Portrait)	60.00	25.00	15.00
(33) Rick Ferrell, Wes Ferrell	100.00	42.00	26.00
(34) Lou Finney (Portrait)	60.00	25.00	15.00
(35) Ervin "Pete" Fox (Portrait)	60.00	25.00	15.00
(36) Tony Freitas (Portrait)	60.00	25.00	15.00
(37) Lonnie Frey (Batting)	60.00	25.00	15.00
(38) Frankie Frisch (Portrait)	90.00	38.00	23.00
(39) "Augie" Galan (Portrait)	60.00	25.00	15.00
(40) Charles Gehringer (Portrait)	100.00	42.00	26.00
(41) Charlie Gelbert (Portrait)	60.00	25.00	15.00
(42) "Lefty" Gomez (Portrait)	100.00	42.00	26.00
(43) "Goose" Goslin (Portrait)	90.00	38.00	23.00
(44) Earl Grace (Catching)	60.00	25.00	15.00
(45) Hank Greenberg (Portrait)	260.00	110.00	68.00
(46) "Mule" Haas (Batting)	60.00	25.00	15.00
(47) Odell Hale (Portrait)	60.00	25.00	15.00
(48) Bill Hallahan (Portrait)	60.00	25.00	15.00
(49) "Mel" Harder (Portrait)	60.00	25.00	15.00
(50) "Bucky" Harris (Portrait)	90.00	38.00	23.00
(51) "Gabby" Hartnett (Catching)	90.00	38.00	23.00
(52) Ray Hayworth (Catching)	60.00	25.00	15.00
(53) "Rolly" Hemsley (Catching)	60.00	25.00	15.00
(54) Babe Herman (Portrait)	75.00	31.00	19.50
(55) Frank Higgins (Portrait)	60.00	25.00	15.00
(56) Oral Hildebrand (Portrait)	60.00	25.00	15.00
(57) Myril Hoag (Portrait)	60.00	25.00	15.00
(58) Waite Hoyt (Pitching)	90.00	38.00	23.00
(59) Woody Jensen (Batting)	60.00	25.00	15.00
(60) Bob Johnson (Batting)	60.00	25.00	15.00
(61) "Buck" Jordan (Portrait)	60.00	25.00	15.00
(62) Alex Kampouris (Portrait)	60.00	25.00	15.00
(63) "Chuck" Klein (Portrait)	90.00	38.00	23.00
(64) Joe Kuhel (Portrait)	60.00	25.00	15.00
(65) Lyn Lary (Portrait)	60.00	25.00	15.00
(66) Harry Lavagetto (Portrait)	60.00	25.00	15.00
(67) Sam Leslie (Portrait)	60.00	25.00	15.00
(68) Freddie Lindstrom (Portrait)	90.00	38.00	23.00
(69) Ernie Lombardi (Throwing)	90.00	38.00	23.00
(70) "Al" Lopez (Throwing)	90.00	38.00	23.00
(71) Dan MacFayden (Portrait)	60.00	25.00	15.00
(72) John Marcum (Pitching)	60.00	25.00	15.00
(73) "Pepper" Martin (Portrait)	75.00	31.00	19.50
(74) Eric McNair (Portrait)	60.00	25.00	15.50
(75) "Ducky" Medwick (Kneeling)	90.00	38.00	23.00
(76) Gene Moore (Portrait)	60.00	25.00	15.00
(77) Randy Moore (Portrait)	60.00	25.00	15.00
(78) Terry Moore (Portrait)	60.00	25.00	15.00
(79) Edw. Moriarty (Portrait)	60.00	25.00	15.00
(80) "Wally" Moses (Portrait)	60.00	25.00	15.00
(81) "Buddy" Myer (Batting)	60.00	25.00	15.00
(82) "Buck" Newsom (Portrait)	60.00	25.00	15.00
(83) Steve O'Neill, Frank Pytlak	60.00	25.00	15.00
(84) Fred Ostermueller (Portrait)	60.00	25.00	15.00
(85) Marvin Owen (Portrait)	60.00	25.00	15.00
(86) Tommy Padden (Portrait)	60.00	25.00	15.00
(87) Ray Pepper (Batting)	60.00	25.00	15.00
(88) Tony Piet (Portrait)	60.00	25.00	15.00
(89) "Rabbit" Pytlak (Throwing)	60.00	25.00	15.00
(90) "Rip" Radcliff (Portrait)	60.00	25.00	15.00
(91) Bobby Reis (Portrait)	60.00	25.00	15.00
(92) "Lew" Riggs (Fielding)	60.00	25.00	15.00
(93) Bill Rogell (Portrait)	60.00	25.00	15.00
(94) "Red" Rolfe (Portrait)	60.00	25.00	15.00
(95) "Schoolboy" Rowe (Portrait)	65.00	27.00	17.00
(96) Al Schacht (Portrait)	75.00	31.00	19.50
(97) "Luke" Sewell (Catching)	60.00	25.00	15.00
(98) Al Simmons (Portrait)	90.00	38.00	23.00
(99) John Stone (Portrait)	60.00	25.00	15.00
(100) Gus Suhr (Fielding)	60.00	25.00	15.00
(101) Joe Sullivan (Portrait)	60.00	25.00	15.00
(102) Bill Swift (Portrait)	60.00	25.00	15.00
(103) Vito Tamulis (Portrait)	60.00	25.00	15.00
(104) Dan Taylor (Portrait)	60.00	25.00	15.00
(105) Cecil Travis (Portrait)	60.00	25.00	15.00
(106) Hal Trosky (Portrait)	60.00	25.00	15.00
(107) "Bill" Urbanski (Portrait)	60.00	25.00	15.00
(108) Russ Van Atta (Portrait)	60.00	25.00	15.00
(109) "Arky" Vaughan (Portrait)	90.00	38.00	23.00
(110) Gerald Walker (Portrait)	60.00	25.00	15.00
(111) "Buck" Walter (Walters) (Portrait)	60.00	25.00	15.00
(112a) Lloyd Waner (Portrait) (No "LITHO IN U.S.A.")	90.00	38.00	23.00
(112b) Lloyd Waner (Portrait) ("LITHO IN U.S.A.)	90.00	38.00	23.00
(113) Paul Waner (Portrait)	90.00	38.00	23.00
(114) "Lon" Warneke (Portrait)	60.00	25.00	15.00
(115) "Rabbit" Warstler (Batting)	60.00	25.00	15.00
(116) Bill Werber (Portrait)	60.00	25.00	15.00
(117) Jo Jo" White (Portrait)	60.00	25.00	15.00
(118) Burgess Whitehead (Portrait)	60.00	25.00	15.00
(119) John Whitehead (Portrait)	60.00	25.00	15.00
(120) Whitlow Wyatt (Portrait)	60.00	25.00	15.00

1936 Goudey "Wide Pen" Premiums - Type 2

These 3-1/4" x 5-1/2" black-and-white, unnumbered cards are known as "Wide Pens" because of the distinctive cursive printing of the facsimile autographs. Type 2 and Type 3 cards share their photos. Type 2 cards have borders, but no "LITHO IN U.S.A." line. Some Type 2 cards also share their photos with Type 1, but have a different projection (size). Those are indicated parenthetically with an asterisk.

	NM	EX	VG
Complete Set (24):	2,700	1,250	750.00
Common Player:	90.00	40.00	25.00
(1) Mel Almada (Kneeling)	110.00	49.00	27.00
(2) Lucius Appling (Portrait)	135.00	61.00	34.00
(3) Henry Bonura (Portrait)	90.00	40.00	25.00
(4) Ben Chapman, Bill Werber	120.00	54.00	30.00
(5) Herman Clifton (Batting)	90.00	40.00	25.00
(6) Roger "Doc" Cramer (Portrait)	90.00	40.00	25.00
(7) Joe Cronin (Kneeling*)	135.00	61.00	34.00
(8) Jimmy Dykes (Kneeling*)	90.00	40.00	25.00

	NM	EX	VG
(9) Erwin "Pete" Fox (Ervin) (Portrait*)	90.00	40.00	25.00
(10) Jimmy Foxx (Portrait)	260.00	115.00	65.00
(11) Hank Greenberg (Portrait*)	350.00	155.00	87.00
(12) Oral Hildebrand (Portrait*)	90.00	40.00	25.00
(13) Alex Hooks (Fielding)	90.00	40.00	25.00
(14) Willis Hudlin (Throwing)	90.00	40.00	25.00
(15) Bill Knickerbocker (Portrait)	90.00	40.00	25.00
(16) Heine (Heinie) Manush (Portrait)	135.00	61.00	34.00
(17) Steve O'Neill (Portrait)	90.00	40.00	25.00
(18) Marvin Owen (Portrait*)	90.00	40.00	25.00
(19) Al Simmons (Bats on shoulder.)	135.00	61.00	34.00
(20) Lem "Moose" Solters (Batting) (First name actually Julius.)	90.00	40.00	25.00
(21) Hal Trosky (Batting)	90.00	40.00	25.00
(22) Joe Vosmik (Batting)	90.00	40.00	25.00
(23) Joe Vosmik (Portrait)	90.00	40.00	25.00
(24) Earl Whitehill (Throwing)	90.00	40.00	25.00

1936 Goudey "Wide Pen" Premiums - Type 3

Al Simmons

These 3-1/4" x 5-1/2" black-and-white, unnumbered cards are known as "Wide Pens" because of the distinctive cursive printing of the facsimile autographs. Type 2 and Type 3 cards share their photos. Type 3 cards are borderless and some also share their photos with Type 1, but have a different projection (size). Those are indicated parenthetically with an asterisk.

	NM	EX	VG
Complete Set (24):	2,700	1,250	750.00
Common Player:	90.00	40.00	25.00
(1) Mel Almada (Kneeling)	120.00	54.00	30.00
(2) Lucius Appling (Portrait)	135.00	61.00	34.00
(3) Henry Bonura (Portrait)	90.00	40.00	25.00
(4) Ben Chapman, Bill Werber	120.00	54.00	30.00
(5) Herman Clifton (Batting)	90.00	40.00	25.00
(6) Roger "Doc" Cramer (Portrait)	90.00	40.00	25.00
(7) Joe Cronin (Kneeling*)	135.00	61.00	34.00
(8) Jimmy Dykes (Kneeling*)	90.00	40.00	25.00
(9) Erwin "Pete" Fox (Ervin) (Portrait*)	90.00	40.00	25.00
(10) Jimmy Foxx (Portrait)	260.00	115.00	65.00
(11) Hank Greenberg (Portrait*)	350.00	155.00	87.00
(12) Oral Hildebrand (Portrait*)	90.00	40.00	25.00
(13) Alex Hooks (Fielding)	90.00	40.00	25.00
(14) Willis Hudlin (Throwing)	90.00	40.00	25.00
(15) Bill Knickerbocker (Portrait)	90.00	40.00	25.00
(16) Heine (Heinie) Manush (Portrait)	135.00	61.00	34.00
(17) Steve O'Neill (Portrait)	90.00	40.00	25.00
(18) Marvin Owen (Portrait*)	90.00	40.00	25.00
(19) Al Simmons (Bats on shoulder.)	135.00	61.00	34.00
(20) Lem "Moose" Solters (Batting) (First name actually Julius.)	90.00	40.00	25.00
(21) Hal Trosky (Batting)	90.00	40.00	25.00
(22) Joe Vosmik (Batting)	90.00	40.00	25.00
(23) Joe Vosmik (Portrait)	90.00	40.00	25.00
(24) Earl Whitehill (Throwing)	90.00	40.00	25.00

1937 Goudey "Wide Pen" Premiums - Type 4

These premium cards are known to generations of collectors as "Wide Pens" because of the distinctive, thick style of cursive typography used for the facsimile autographs. They have a 3-1/4" x 5-1/2" black-and-white, unnumbered format. Type 4 cards are printed on a paper stock usually described as "creamy." They are bordered, but do not have a "LITHO IN U.S.A." line. Type 5 cards share the creamy paper stock of Type 4, and may have been part of the same issue, which would indicate Canadian origins. An asterisk after the pose indicates a photo shared with Type 1, though possibly of a larger or smaller projection.

		NM	EX	VG
Complete Set (36):		6,750	3,000	1,800
Common Player:		90.00	40.00	25.00
(1)	"Luke" Appling (Batting)	135.00	61.00	34.00
(2)	Earl Averill (Portrait*)	135.00	61.00	34.00
(3)	"Cy" Blanton (Pitching)	90.00	40.00	25.00
(4)	"Zeke" Bonura (Batting)	90.00	40.00	25.00
(5)	Tom Bridges (Throwing)	90.00	40.00	25.00
(6)	Tommy Bridges (Portrait*)	90.00	40.00	25.00
(7)	Mickey Cochrane (Portrait*)	135.00	61.00	34.00
(8)	Joe Cronin (Kneeling)	135.00	61.00	34.00
(9)	"Joe" DiMaggio (Portrait)	3,000	1,350	750.00
(10)	"Bobby" Doerr (Doerr) (Batting)	135.00	61.00	34.00
(11)	Jimmy Dykes (Fielding)	90.00	40.00	25.00
(12)	"Bob" Feller (Pitching)	300.00	135.00	75.00
(13)	"Elbie" Fletcher (Fielding)	90.00	40.00	25.00
(14)	Erwin "Pete" Fox (Ervin) (Portrait*)	90.00	40.00	25.00
(15)	Pete Fox (Batting)	90.00	40.00	25.00
(16)	"Gus" Galan (Batting)	90.00	40.00	25.00
(17)	Charles Gehringer (Portrait*)	135.00	61.00	34.00
(18)	Hank Greenberg (Portrait*)	225.00	100.00	56.00
(19)	"Goose" Goslin (Portrait)	135.00	61.00	34.00
(20)	Mel Harder (Portrait)	90.00	40.00	25.00
(21)	"Gabby" Hartnett (Catching*)	135.00	61.00	34.00
(22)	Ray Hayworth (Catching*)	90.00	40.00	25.00
(23)	"Pinky" Higgins (Batting)	90.00	40.00	25.00
(24)	Carl Hubbell (Pitching)	135.00	61.00	34.00
(25)	"Wally" Moses (Batting)	90.00	40.00	25.00
(26)	Lou Newsom (Portrait)	90.00	40.00	25.00
(27)	Marvin Owen (Portrait*)	90.00	40.00	25.00
(28)	Bill Rogell (Portrait*)	90.00	40.00	25.00
(29)	"Schoolboy" Rowe (Pitching)	90.00	40.00	25.00
(30)	"Schoolboy" Rowe (Portrait*)	90.00	40.00	25.00
(31)	Al Simmons (Portrait*)	135.00	61.00	34.00
(32)	Julius Solters (Batting)	90.00	40.00	25.00
(33)	"Hal" Trosky (Batting)	90.00	40.00	25.00
(34)	Joe Vosmik (Kneeling)	90.00	40.00	25.00
(35)	"Jo Jo" White (Portrait*)	135.00	61.00	34.00
(36)	Johnnie Whitehead (Pitching)	90.00	40.00	25.00

1937 Goudey "Wide Pen" Premiums - Type 5

These premium cards are known as "Wide Pens" because of the distinctive, thick style of cursive printing used for the facsimile autographs. they have a 3-1/4" x 5-1/2" black-and-white, unnumbered format. The photos are bordered, but do not have a "LITHO IN U.S.A." line. Type 5 cards are printed on a paper stock usually described as "creamy" and may have been part of the same issue as Type 4. Type 5 is comprised only of Toronto and Montreal (International League) players.

		NM	EX	VG
Complete Set (39):		4,750	2,400	1,350
Common Player:		135.00	65.00	35.00
(1)	Buddy Bates	135.00	65.00	35.00
(2)	Del Bisonette (Portrait)	135.00	65.00	35.00
(3)	Lincoln Blakely	135.00	65.00	35.00
(4)	Isaac J. Boone	135.00	65.00	35.00
(5)	John H. Burnett (Batting)	135.00	65.00	35.00
(6)	Leon Chagon	135.00	65.00	35.00
(7)	Gus Dugas (Portrait)	135.00	65.00	35.00
(8)	Henry N. Erickson (Catching)	135.00	65.00	35.00
(9)	Art Funk (Portrait)	135.00	65.00	35.00
(10)	George Granger (Portrait)	135.00	65.00	35.00
(11)	Thomas G. Heath	135.00	65.00	35.00
(12)	Phil Hensiek (Portrait)	135.00	65.00	35.00
(13)	Leroy Herrmann (Throwing)	135.00	65.00	35.00
(14)	Henry Johnson	135.00	65.00	35.00
(15)	Hal King (Portrait)	135.00	65.00	35.00
(16)	Charles F. Lucas (Portrait)	135.00	65.00	35.00
(17)	Edward S. Miller (Batting) (Middle initial actually R.)	135.00	65.00	35.00
(18)	Jake F. Mooty (Pitching)	135.00	65.00	35.00
(19)	Guy Moreau (Portrait, street clothes.)	135.00	65.00	35.00
(20)	George Murray (Portrait)	135.00	65.00	35.00
(21)	Glenn Myatt	135.00	65.00	35.00
(22)	Lauri Myllykangas	135.00	65.00	35.00
(23)	Francis J. Nicholas (Pitching)	135.00	65.00	35.00
(24)	Bill O'Brien (Montreal trainer)	135.00	65.00	35.00
(25)	Thomas Oliver (Batting)	135.00	65.00	35.00
(26)	James Pattison	135.00	65.00	35.00
(27)	Crip Polli (Portrait)	135.00	65.00	35.00
(28)	Harlan Pool (Bats)	135.00	65.00	35.00
(29)	Walter Purcey (Pitching)	135.00	65.00	35.00
(30)	Bill Rhiel	135.00	65.00	35.00
(31)	Ben Sankey	135.00	65.00	35.00
(32)	Les Scarcella (Scarsella) (Kneeling)	135.00	65.00	35.00
(33)	Bob Seeds (Portrait)	135.00	65.00	35.00
(34)	Frank Shaugnessy (Portrait)	135.00	65.00	35.00
(35)	Harry Smythe (Portrait)	135.00	65.00	35.00
(36)	Ben Tate (Portrait)	135.00	65.00	35.00
(37)	Fresco Thompson (Portrait)	135.00	65.00	35.00
(38)	Charles Wilson (Portrait)	135.00	65.00	35.00
(39)	Francis Wistert (Portrait)	135.00	65.00	35.00

1937 Goudey Knot Hole League

Though they do not picture or name any players, the fact these game cards were issued by Goudey makes them collectible for many hobbyists. While they carry a copyright date

of 1935, the cards were not issued until 1937. About 2-3/8" x 2-7/8", and printed in red, white and blue, the cards were intended to be used to play a baseball game using the situations printed on the fronts. Despite advertising a series of 100 cards, only 24 were actually issued. The cards were designated R325 in the American Card Catalog.

		NM	EX	VG
Complete Set (24):		450.00	180.00	90.00
Common Card:		25.00	10.00	5.00
1	Double / Foul	25.00	10.00	5.00
2	Steals Home!! / Strike	25.00	10.00	5.00
3	Ball / Out	25.00	10.00	5.00
4	Strike / Ball	25.00	10.00	5.00
5	Strike / Wild Pitch	25.00	10.00	5.00
6	Ball / Out	25.00	10.00	5.00
7	Bunt - Scratch Hit!! / Stolen Base !!	25.00	10.00	5.00
8	Hit by Pitched Ball / Out	25.00	10.00	5.00
9	Foul / Ball	25.00	10.00	5.00
10	Foul / Double!	25.00	10.00	5.00
11	Out / Ball	25.00	10.00	5.00
12	Foul / Force Out	25.00	10.00	5.00
13	Out / Single	25.00	10.00	5.00
14	Strike / Ball	25.00	10.00	5.00
15	Foul Tip / Strike!	25.00	10.00	5.00
16	Three Bagger / Out	25.00	10.00	5.00
17	Ball / Out	25.00	10.00	5.00
18	Out!! / Error!!!	25.00	10.00	5.00
19	Strike / Foul	25.00	10.00	5.00
20	Out / Double Play	25.00	10.00	5.00
21	!!Home Run!! / Ball	25.00	10.00	5.00
22	Out / Strike	25.00	10.00	5.00
23	Ball / Out	25.00	10.00	5.00
24	Lout!! / Error!!!	25.00	10.00	5.00

1937 Goudey Thum Movies

These 2" x 3" baseball novelty booklets create the illusion of baseball action in motion when the pages are rapidly flipped. The booklets are numbered on the top of the back page. Thum Movies were listed in the American Card Catalog as R342.

		NM	EX	VG
Complete Set (13):		1,750	875.00	525.00
Common Player:		70.00	35.00	20.00
1	John Irving Burns	70.00	35.00	20.00
2	Joe Vosmik	70.00	35.00	20.00
3	Mel Ott	225.00	110.00	65.00
4	Joe DiMaggio	525.00	260.00	155.00
5	Wally Moses	70.00	35.00	20.00
6	Van Lingle Mungo	70.00	35.00	20.00
7	Luke Appling	100.00	50.00	30.00
8	Bob Feller	225.00	110.00	65.00
9	Paul Derringer	70.00	35.00	20.00
10	Paul Waner	100.00	50.00	30.00
11	Joe Medwick	100.00	50.00	30.00
12	James Emory Foxx	225.00	110.00	65.00
13	Wally Berger	70.00	35.00	20.00

1938 Goudey (R323)

Sometimes referred to as the Goudey Heads-Up set, this issue begins numbering (#241) where the 1933 Goudey set left off. On the card fronts, a photo is used for the player's head with the body being a cartoon drawing. Twenty-four different players are pictured twice in the set. Cards #241-264 feature plain backgrounds on the fronts. Cards #265-288 contain the same basic design and photo but include small drawings and comments within the background. Backs have player statistical and biographical information. The ACC designation for the issue is R323.

		NM	EX	VG
Complete Set (48):		29,000	11,500	5,750
Common Player (241-264):		200.00	85.00	30.00
Common Player (265-288):		225.00	100.00	35.00
241	Charlie Gehringer	600.00	250.00	100.00
242	Ervin Fox	300.00	100.00	40.00
243	Joe Kuhel	200.00	85.00	30.00
244	Frank DeMaree	200.00	85.00	30.00
245	Frank Pytlak	200.00	85.00	30.00
246a	Ernie Lombardi (Red Sox)	800.00	320.00	160.00
246b	Ernie Lombardi (Reds followed by black drawing.)	450.00	180.00	90.00
246c	Ernie Lombardi (Reds)	350.00	140.00	70.00
247	Joe Vosmik	200.00	85.00	30.00
248	Dick Bartell	200.00	85.00	30.00
249	Jimmy Foxx	900.00	350.00	150.00
250	Joe DiMaggio	5,000	2,000	1,100
251	Bump Hadley	200.00	85.00	30.00
252	Zeke Bonura	200.00	85.00	30.00
253	Hank Greenberg	1,100	450.00	225.00
254	Van Lingle Mungo	300.00	120.00	60.00
255	Julius Solters	200.00	85.00	30.00
256	Vernon Kennedy	200.00	85.00	30.00
257	Al Lopez	425.00	200.00	85.00
258	Bobby Doerr	500.00	200.00	85.00
259	Bill Werber	200.00	85.00	30.00
260	Rudy York	200.00	85.00	30.00
261	Rip Radcliff	200.00	85.00	30.00
262	Joe Ducky Medwick	425.00	200.00	85.00
263	Marvin Owen	200.00	85.00	30.00
264	Bob Feller	2,000	700.00	300.00
265	Charlie Gehringer	600.00	200.00	100.00
266	Ervin Fox	225.00	100.00	35.00
267	Joe Kuhel	225.00	100.00	35.00
268	Frank DeMaree	225.00	100.00	35.00
269	Frank Pytlak	225.00	100.00	35.00
270	Ernie Lombardi	500.00	225.00	100.00
271	Joe Vosmik	225.00	100.00	35.00
272	Dick Bartell	225.00	100.00	35.00
273	Jimmy Foxx	1,200	500.00	200.00
274	Joe DiMaggio	5,250	2,000	1,100
275	Bump Hadley	225.00	100.00	35.00
276	Zeke Bonura	225.00	100.00	35.00
277	Hank Greenberg	1,300	600.00	300.00
278	Van Lingle Mungo	225.00	100.00	35.00
279	Julius Solters	225.00	100.00	35.00
280	Vernon Kennedy	225.00	100.00	35.00
281	Al Lopez	500.00	225.00	90.00
282	Bobby Doerr	550.00	250.00	100.00
283	Bill Werber	225.00	100.00	35.00
284	Rudy York	225.00	100.00	35.00
285	Rip Radcliff	225.00	100.00	35.00
286	Joe Ducky Medwick	600.00	250.00	100.00
287	Marvin Owen	225.00	100.00	35.00
288	Bob Feller	2,250	900.00	450.00

1938 Goudey Big League Baseball Movies

Probably issued in both 1937-38, according to the biographies on back, this set of "flip movies" was comprised of small (2" x 3") booklets whose pages produced a movie effect when flipped rapidly, similar to a penny arcade novelty popular at the time. There are 13 players in the set; each movie having two clearly labeled parts. The cover of the booklets identify the set as "Big League Baseball Movies." They carry the American Card Catalog designation R326.

		NM	EX	VG
Complete Set (26):		3,750	1,875	1,125
Common Player:		75.00	37.50	22.50
1a	John Irving Burns (Part 1)	75.00	37.50	22.50
1b	John Irving Burns (Part 2)	75.00	37.50	22.50
2a	Joe Vosmik (Part 1)	75.00	37.50	22.50
2b	Joe Vosmik (Part 2)	75.00	37.50	22.50
3a	Mel Ott (Part 1)	185.00	95.00	55.00
3b	Mel Ott (Part 2)	185.00	95.00	55.00
4a	Joe DiMaggio (Part 1, Joe DiMaggio cover photo.)	475.00	235.00	140.00
4aa	Joe DiMaggio (Part 1, Vince DiMaggio cover photo.)	375.00	185.00	110.00
4b	Joe DiMaggio (Part 2, Joe DiMaggio cover photo.)	475.00	235.00	140.00
4ba	Joe DiMaggio (Part 2, Vince DiMaggio cover photo.)	375.00	185.00	110.00

5a	Wally Moses (Part 1)	75.00	37.50	22.50
5b	Wally Moses (Part 2)	75.00	37.50	22.50
6a	Van Lingle Mungo (Part 1)	75.00	37.50	22.50
6b	Van Lingle Mungo (Part 2)	75.00	37.50	22.50
7a	Luke Appling (Part 1)	110.00	55.00	35.00
7b	Luke Appling (Part 2)	110.00	55.00	35.00
8a	Bob Feller (Part 1)	225.00	110.00	65.00
8b	Bob Feller (Part 2)	225.00	110.00	65.00
9a	Paul Derringer (Part 1)	75.00	37.50	22.50
9b	Paul Derringer (Part 2)	75.00	37.50	22.50
10a	Paul Waner (Part 1)	110.00	55.00	35.00
10b	Paul Waner (Part 2)	110.00	55.00	35.00
11a	Joe Medwick (Part 1)	110.00	55.00	35.00
11b	Joe Medwick (Part 2)	110.00	55.00	35.00
12a	James Emory Foxx (Part 1)	260.00	130.00	75.00
12b	James Emory Foxx (Part 2)	260.00	130.00	75.00
13a	Wally Berger (Part 1)	75.00	37.50	22.50
13b	Wally Berger (Part 2)	75.00	37.50	22.50

1939 Goudey Premiums (R303-A)

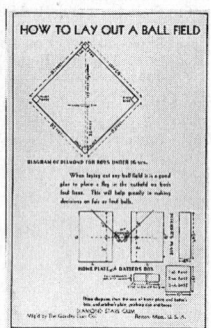

Although this unnumbered set of paper premiums has the name "Diamond Stars Gum" on the back, it is not related to National Chicle's Diamond Stars card sets. Rather, this 48-player set was a premium issued by the Goudey Gum Co. Each premium photo measures 4" x 6-3/16" and is printed in a brown-toned sepia. The front of the photo includes a facsimile autograph, while the back contains drawings that illustrate various baseball tips. These pictures are soemtimes found with top and bottom border trimmed to a depth of 5-3/4" for distribution in Canada.

		NM	EX	VG
Complete Set (48):		6,000	2,400	1,200
Common Player:		75.00	30.00	15.00
(1)	Luke Appling	135.00	55.00	25.00
(2)	Earl Averill	135.00	55.00	25.00
(3)	Wally Berger	75.00	30.00	15.00
(4)	Darrell Blanton	75.00	30.00	15.00
(5)	Zeke Bonura	75.00	30.00	15.00
(6)	Mace Brown	75.00	30.00	15.00
(7)	George Case	75.00	30.00	15.00
(8)	Ben Chapman	75.00	30.00	15.00
(9)	Joe Cronin	135.00	55.00	25.00
(10)	Frank Crosetti	90.00	36.00	18.00
(11)	Paul Derringer	75.00	30.00	15.00
(12)	Bill Dickey	150.00	60.00	30.00
(13)	Joe DiMaggio	650.00	260.00	130.00
(14)	Bob Feller	225.00	90.00	45.00
(15)	Jimmy (Jimmie) Foxx	235.00	95.00	45.00
(16)	Charles Gehringer	135.00	55.00	25.00
(17)	Lefty Gomez	135.00	55.00	25.00
(18)	Ival Goodman	75.00	30.00	15.00
(19)	Joe Gordon	75.00	30.00	15.00
(20)	Hank Greenberg	175.00	70.00	35.00
(21)	Buddy Hassett	75.00	30.00	15.00
(22)	Jeff Heath	75.00	30.00	15.00
(23)	Tom Henrich	75.00	30.00	15.00
(24)	Billy Herman	135.00	54.00	27.00
(25)	Frank Higgins	75.00	30.00	15.00
(26)	Fred Hutchinson	75.00	30.00	15.00
(27)	Bob Johnson	75.00	30.00	15.00
(28)	Ken Keltner	75.00	30.00	15.00
(29)	Mike Kreevich	75.00	30.00	15.00
(30)	Ernie Lombardi	135.00	55.00	25.00
(31)	Gus Mancuso	75.00	30.00	15.00
(32)	Eric McNair	75.00	30.00	15.00
(33)	Van Mungo	75.00	30.00	15.00
(34)	Buck Newsom	75.00	30.00	15.00
(35)	Mel Ott	150.00	55.00	25.00
(36)	Marvin Owen	75.00	30.00	15.00
(37)	Frank Pytlak	75.00	30.00	15.00
(38)	Woodrow Rich	75.00	30.00	15.00
(39)	Charley Root	75.00	30.00	15.00
(40)	Al Simmons	135.00	55.00	25.00
(41)	James Tabor	75.00	30.00	15.00
(42)	Cecil Travis	75.00	30.00	15.00
(43)	Hal Trosky	75.00	30.00	15.00
(44)	Arky Vaughan	135.00	55.00	25.00
(45)	Joe Vosmik	75.00	30.00	15.00
(46)	Lon Warneke	75.00	30.00	15.00
(47)	Ted Williams	1,050	420.00	210.00
(48)	Rudy York	75.00	30.00	15.00

1939 Goudey Premiums (R303-B)

Although larger (4-3/4" x 7-1/4" to 7-3/8"), the photos in this 24-player set are identical to those in the R303-A issue of the same year, and the format of the set is unchanged. The set, designated as R303-B in the American Card Catalog, can be found in both black-and-white and sepia-toned, with backs printed in brown.

		NM	EX	VG
Complete Set (24):		2,500	1,000	500.00
Common Player:		60.00	24.00	12.00
(1)	Luke Appling	90.00	35.00	15.00
(2)	George Case	60.00	25.00	12.00
(3)	Ben Chapman	60.00	25.00	12.00
(4)	Joe Cronin	90.00	35.00	15.00
(5)	Bill Dickey	110.00	45.00	20.00
(6)	Joe DiMaggio	600.00	240.00	120.00
(7)	Bob Feller	150.00	60.00	30.00
(8)	Jimmy (Jimmie) Foxx	175.00	70.00	35.00
(9)	Lefty Gomez	90.00	35.00	15.00
(10)	Ival Goodman	60.00	25.00	12.00
(11)	Joe Gordon	60.00	25.00	12.00
(12)	Hank Greenberg	125.00	50.00	25.00
(13)	Jeff Heath	60.00	25.00	12.00
(14)	Billy Herman	90.00	35.00	15.00
(15)	Frank Higgins	60.00	25.00	12.00
(16)	Ken Keltner	60.00	25.00	12.00
(17)	Mike Kreevich	60.00	25.00	12.00
(18)	Ernie Lombardi	90.00	35.00	15.00
(19)	Gus Mancuso	60.00	25.00	12.00
(20)	Mel Ott	110.00	45.00	20.00
(21)	Al Simmons	90.00	35.00	15.00
(22)	Arky Vaughan	90.00	35.00	15.00
(23)	Joe Vosmik	60.00	25.00	12.00
(24)	Rudy York	60.00	25.00	12.00

1941 Goudey (R324)

Goudey Gum's last set was issued in 1941. The 2-3/8" x 2-7/8" (size approximate due to imprecise cutting) cards feature black-and-white photos set against blue, green, red or yellow backgrounds. The player's name, team and position plus the card number are supposed to be situated in a box at the bottom of the card. However, due to vagaries of cutting, some or all of the bottom printing might appear at the top of the card, greatly reducing its value. The card backs are blank. The ACC designation for the set is R324.

		NM	EX	VG
Complete Set (33):		8,500	3,400	1,700
Common Player:		250.00	100.00	50.00
1	Hugh Mulcahy	250.00	100.00	50.00
2	Harland Clift	250.00	100.00	50.00
3	Louis Chiozza	250.00	100.00	50.00
4	Warren (Buddy) Rosar	250.00	100.00	50.00
5	George McQuinn	250.00	100.00	50.00
6	Emerson Dickman	250.00	100.00	50.00
7	Wayne Ambler	250.00	100.00	50.00
8	Bob Muncrief	250.00	100.00	50.00
9	Bill Dietrich	250.00	100.00	50.00
10	Taft Wright	250.00	100.00	50.00
11	Don Heffner	250.00	100.00	50.00
12	Fritz Ostermueller	250.00	100.00	50.00
13	Frank Hayes	250.00	100.00	50.00
14	John (Jack) Kramer	250.00	100.00	50.00
15	Dario Lodigiani	275.00	110.00	55.00
16	George Case	250.00	100.00	50.00
17	Vito Tamulis	250.00	100.00	50.00
18	Whitlow Wyatt	250.00	100.00	50.00
19	Bill Posedel	250.00	100.00	50.00
20	Carl Hubbell	675.00	275.00	125.00
21	Harold Warstler (SP)	400.00	175.00	85.00
22	Joe Sullivan (SP)	400.00	175.00	85.00
23	Norman (Babe) Young (SP)	400.00	175.00	85.00
24	Stanley Andrews (SP)	400.00	175.00	85.00
25	Morris Arnovich (SP)	700.00	260.00	90.00
26	Elburt Fletcher	250.00	100.00	50.00
27	Bill Crouch	275.00	110.00	55.00
28	Al Todd	250.00	100.00	50.00
29	Debs Garms	250.00	100.00	50.00
30	Jim Tobin	250.00	100.00	50.00
31	Chester Ross	250.00	100.00	50.00
32	George Coffman	250.00	100.00	50.00
33	Mel Ott	600.00	240.00	120.00

1955 Robert Gould All Stars Cards

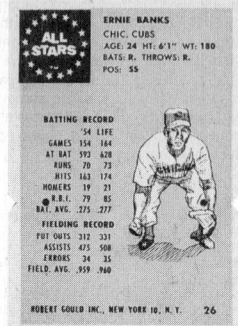

One of three issues of miniature plastic player statues issued in the mid-Fifties was the All Stars series by Robert Gould Inc. of New York. The white plastic statues, which sold for about a quarter, came rubber-banded to a baseball card. The card measures 2-1/2" x 3-1/2" with a white border. A rather crude black-and-white line drawing of the player is set against a green background. There are a few biographical details and 1954 and lifetime stats. An "All Stars" logo is in an upper corner, while the card number is at lower-right. The cards are blank-backed. All cards have a pair of notches at the sides and two punch holes to hold the rubber band. Prices shown here are for the cards alone. A 2-5/8" x 3-5/8" album reproducing all 28 player cards was also issued.

		NM	EX	VG
Complete Set, Cards (28):		8,500	4,250	2,500
Common Player:		250.00	125.00	75.00
Album:		200.00	100.00	50.00
1	Willie Mays	1,100	550.00	325.00
2	Gus Zernial	250.00	125.00	75.00
3	Red Schoendienst	325.00	160.00	95.00
4	Chico Carrasquel	250.00	125.00	75.00
5	Jim Hegan	250.00	125.00	75.00
6	Curt Simmons	250.00	125.00	75.00
7	Bob Porterfield	250.00	125.00	75.00
8	Jim Busby	250.00	125.00	75.00
9	Don Mueller	250.00	125.00	75.00
10	Ted Kluszewski	275.00	135.00	80.00
11	Ray Boone	250.00	125.00	75.00
12	Smoky Burgess	250.00	125.00	75.00
13	Bob Rush	250.00	125.00	75.00
14	Early Wynn	300.00	150.00	90.00
15	Bill Bruton	250.00	125.00	75.00
16	Gus Bell	250.00	125.00	75.00
17	Jim Finigan	250.00	125.00	75.00
18	Granny Hamner	250.00	125.00	75.00
19	Hank Thompson	250.00	125.00	75.00
20	Joe Coleman	250.00	125.00	75.00
21	Don Newcombe	275.00	135.00	80.00
22	Richie Ashburn	325.00	160.00	95.00
23	Bobby Thomson	250.00	125.00	75.00
24	Sid Gordon	250.00	125.00	75.00
25	Gerry Coleman	250.00	125.00	75.00
26	Ernie Banks	850.00	425.00	255.00
27	Billy Pierce	250.00	125.00	75.00
28	Mel Parnell	250.00	125.00	75.00

1955 Robert Gould All Stars Statues

One of three issues of miniature plastic player statues issued in the mid-Fifties was the All Stars series by Robert Gould Inc. of New York. The white plastic statues, which sold for about a quarter, came rubber-banded to a baseball card. Depending on pose, they vary in size from around 2" to 2-1/2". The figures have a round base with the player's name. Prices shown here are for the statues alone. The statues were also sold in seven-player boxed sets labeled "A" through "D."

		NM	EX	VG
Complete Set, Statues (28):		1,500	750.00	450.00
Common Player:		40.00	20.00	12.00
1	Willie Mays	300.00	150.00	90.00
2	Gus Zernial	40.00	20.00	12.00
3	Red Schoendienst	75.00	37.00	22.00
4	Chico Carrasquel	40.00	20.00	12.00
5	Jim Hegan	40.00	20.00	12.00
6	Curt Simmons	40.00	20.00	12.00
7	Bob Porterfield	40.00	20.00	12.00
8	Jim Busby	40.00	20.00	12.00

		NM	EX	VG
9	Don Mueller	40.00	20.00	12.00
10	Ted Kluszewski	50.00	25.00	15.00
11	Ray Boone	40.00	20.00	12.00
12	Smoky Burgess	40.00	20.00	12.00
13	Bob Rush	40.00	20.00	12.00
14	Early Wynn	60.00	30.00	18.00
15	Bill Bruton	40.00	20.00	12.00
16	Gus Bell	40.00	20.00	12.00
17	Jim Finigan	40.00	20.00	12.00
18	Granny Hamner	40.00	20.00	12.00
19	Hank Thompson	40.00	20.00	12.00
20	Joe Coleman	40.00	20.00	12.00
21	Don Newcombe	45.00	22.00	13.50
22	Richie Ashburn	75.00	37.00	22.00
23	Bobby Thomson	45.00	22.00	13.50
24	Sid Gordon	40.00	20.00	12.00
25	Gerry Coleman	40.00	20.00	12.00
26	Ernie Banks	240.00	120.00	72.00
27	Billy Pierce	40.00	20.00	12.00
28	Mel Parnell	40.00	20.00	12.00

1978 Grand Slam

26 Bill Terry
1st Base

Was the National League's last .400 hitter. Played all 14 years with the Giants, collecting 2193 hits and a lifetime batting average of .341. From 1927 through 1935 Bill's average never dipped below .320 with a high of .401 in 1930 with 254 hits. Was player-manager from 1932 through 1936. Collected over 200 hits in a season six times. Played in three World Series, Batting .295 in 16 games. Managed the Giants from 1937 through 1941. A member of the Baseball Hall of Fame, being inducted in 1954.

GRAND SLAM 1978

Bill Terry

This collectors' edition card set was produced by Jack Wallin. The black-and-white 2-1/4" x 3-1/4" cards have player poses or action photos on front, with the name in the white border at bottom. Backs have a career summary.

		NM	EX	VG
	Complete Set (200):	120.00	60.00	35.00
	Common Player:	2.00	1.00	.60
1	Leo Durocher	2.00	1.00	.60
2	Bob Lemon	2.00	1.00	.60
3	Earl Averill	2.00	1.00	.60
4	Dale Alexander	2.00	1.00	.60
5	Hank Greenberg	12.00	6.00	3.50
6	Waite Hoyt	2.00	1.00	.60
7	Al Lopez	2.00	1.00	.60
8	Lloyd Waner	2.00	1.00	.60
9	Bob Feller	2.00	1.00	.60
10	Guy Bush	2.00	1.00	.60
11	Stan Hack	2.00	1.00	.60
12	Zeke Bonura	2.00	1.00	.60
13	Wally Moses	2.00	1.00	.60
14	Fred Fitzsimmons	2.00	1.00	.60
15	Johnny Vander Meer	2.00	1.00	.60
16	Riggs Stephenson	2.00	1.00	.60
17	Bucky Walters	2.00	1.00	.60
18	Charlie Grimm	2.00	1.00	.60
19	Phil Cavarretta	2.00	1.00	.60
20	Wally Berger	2.00	1.00	.60
21	Joe Sewell	2.00	1.00	.60
22	Edd Roush	2.00	1.00	.60
23	Johnny Mize	2.00	1.00	.60
24	Bill Dickey	2.00	1.00	.60
25	Lou Boudreau	2.00	1.00	.60
26	Bill Terry	2.00	1.00	.60
27	Willie Kamm	2.00	1.00	.60
28	Charlie Gehringer	2.00	1.00	.60
29	Stan Coveleski	2.00	1.00	.60
30	Larry French	2.00	1.00	.60
31	George Kelly	2.00	1.00	.60
32	Terry Moore	2.00	1.00	.60
33	Billy Herman	2.00	1.00	.60
34	Babe Herman	2.00	1.00	.60
35	Carl Hubbell	2.00	1.00	.60
36	Buck Leonard	2.00	1.00	.60
37	Gus Suhr	2.00	1.00	.60
38	Burleigh Grimes	2.00	1.00	.60
39	Al Fonseca	2.00	1.00	.60
40	Travis Jackson	2.00	1.00	.60
41	Enos Slaughter	2.00	1.00	.60
42	Fred Lindstrom	2.00	1.00	.60
43	Rick Ferrell	2.00	1.00	.60
44	Cookie Lavagetto	2.00	1.00	.60
45	Stan Musial	12.00	6.00	3.50
46	Hal Trosky	2.00	1.00	.60
47	Hal Newhouser	2.00	1.00	.60
48	Paul Dean	2.00	1.00	.60
49	George Halas	6.00	3.00	1.75
50	Jocko Conlan	2.00	1.00	.60
51	Joe DiMaggio	30.00	15.00	9.00
52	Bobby Doerr	2.00	1.00	.60
53	Carl Reynolds	2.00	1.00	.60
54	Pete Reiser	2.00	1.00	.60
55	Frank McCormick	2.00	1.00	.60
56	Mel Harder	2.00	1.00	.60
57	George Uhle	2.00	1.00	.60
58	Doc Cramer	2.00	1.00	.60
59	Taylor Douthit	2.00	1.00	.60
60	Cecil Travis	2.00	1.00	.60
61	James Bell	2.00	1.00	.60
62	Charlie Keller	2.00	1.00	.60
63	Bill Hallahan	2.00	1.00	.60
64	Debs Garms	2.00	1.00	.60
65	Rube Marquard	2.00	1.00	.60
66	Rube Walberg	2.00	1.00	.60
67	Augie Galan	2.00	1.00	.60

68	George Pipgras	2.00	1.00	.60
69	Hal Schumacher	2.00	1.00	.60
70	Dolf Camilli	2.00	1.00	.60
71	Paul Richards	2.00	1.00	.60
72	Judy Johnson	2.00	1.00	.60
73	Frank Crosetti	2.00	1.00	.60
74	Harry Lowery	2.00	1.00	.60
75	Walter Alston	2.00	1.00	.60
76	Dutch Leonard	2.00	1.00	.60
77	Barney McCosky	2.00	1.00	.60
78	Joe Dobson	2.00	1.00	.60
79	George Kell	2.00	1.00	.60
80	Ted Lyons	2.00	1.00	.60
81	Johnny Pesky	2.00	1.00	.60
82	Hank Borowy	2.00	1.00	.60
83	Ewell Blackwell	2.00	1.00	.60
84	Pee Wee Reese	12.00	6.00	3.50
85	Monte Irvin	2.00	1.00	.60
86	Joe Moore	2.00	1.00	.60
87	Joe Wood	2.00	1.00	.60
88	Babe Dahlgren	2.00	1.00	.60
89	Bibb Falk	2.00	1.00	.60
90	Ed Lopat	2.00	1.00	.60
91	Rip Sewell	2.00	1.00	.60
92	Marty Marion	2.00	1.00	.60
93	Taft Wright	2.00	1.00	.60
94	Allie Reynolds	2.00	1.00	.60
95	Harry Walker	2.00	1.00	.60
96	Tex Hughson	2.00	1.00	.60
97	George Selkirk	2.00	1.00	.60
98	Dom DiMaggio	10.00	5.00	3.00
99	Walker Cooper	2.00	1.00	.60
100	Phil Rizzuto	10.00	5.00	3.00
101	Robin Roberts	2.00	1.00	.60
102	Joe Adcock	2.00	1.00	.60
103	Hank Bauer	2.00	1.00	.60
104	Frank Baumholtz	2.00	1.00	.60
105	Ray Boone	2.00	1.00	.60
106	Smoky Burgess	2.00	1.00	.60
107	Walt Dropo	2.00	1.00	.60
108	Alvin Dark	2.00	1.00	.60
109	Carl Erskine	2.00	1.00	.60
110	Dick Donovan	2.00	1.00	.60
111	Dee Fondy	2.00	1.00	.60
112	Mike Garcia	2.00	1.00	.60
113	Bob Friend	2.00	1.00	.60
114	Ned Garver	2.00	1.00	.60
115	Billy Goodman	2.00	1.00	.60
116	Larry Jansen	2.00	1.00	.60
117	Jackie Jensen	2.00	1.00	.60
118	John Antonelli	2.00	1.00	.60
119	Ted Kluszewski	2.00	1.00	.60
120	Harvey Kuenn	2.00	1.00	.60
121	Clem Labine	2.00	1.00	.60
122	Red Schoendienst	2.00	1.00	.60
123	Don Larsen	2.00	1.00	.60
124	Vern Law	2.00	1.00	.60
125	Charlie Maxwell	2.00	1.00	.60
126	Wally Moon	2.00	1.00	.60
127	Bob Nieman	2.00	1.00	.60
128	Don Newcombe	2.00	1.00	.60
129	Wally Post	2.00	1.00	.60
130	Johnny Podres	2.00	1.00	.60
131	Vic Raschi	2.00	1.00	.60
132	Dusty Rhodes	2.00	1.00	.60
133	Jim Rivera	2.00	1.00	.60
134	Pete Runnels	2.00	1.00	.60
135	Hank Sauer	2.00	1.00	.60
136	Roy Sievers	2.00	1.00	.60
137	Bobby Shantz	2.00	1.00	.60
138	Curt Simmons	2.00	1.00	.60
139	Bob Skinner	2.00	1.00	.60
140	Bill Skowron	2.00	1.00	.60
141	Warren Spahn	2.00	1.00	.60
142	Gerry Staley	2.00	1.00	.60
143	Frank Thomas	2.00	1.00	.60
144	Bobby Thomson	2.00	1.00	.60
145	Bob Turley	2.00	1.00	.60
146	Vic Wertz	2.00	1.00	.60
147	Bill Virdon	2.00	1.00	.60
148	Gene Woodling	2.00	1.00	.60
149	Eddie Yost	2.00	1.00	.60
150	Sandy Koufax	25.00	12.50	7.50
151	Lefty Gomez	2.00	1.00	.60
152	Al Rosen	2.00	1.00	.60
153	Vince DiMaggio	2.00	1.00	.60
154	Bill Nicholson	2.00	1.00	.60
155	Mark Koenig	2.00	1.00	.60
156	Max Lanier	2.00	1.00	.60
157	Ken Keltner	2.00	1.00	.60
158	Whit Wyatt	2.00	1.00	.60
159	Marv Owen	2.00	1.00	.60
160	Red Lucas	2.00	1.00	.60
161	Babe Phelps	2.00	1.00	.60
162	Pete Donohue	2.00	1.00	.60
163	Johnny Cooney	2.00	1.00	.60
164	Glenn Wright	2.00	1.00	.60
165	Willis Hudlin	2.00	1.00	.60
166	Tony Cuccinello	2.00	1.00	.60
167	Bill Bevens	2.00	1.00	.60
168	Dave Ferris	2.00	1.00	.60
169	Whitey Kurowski	2.00	1.00	.60
170	Buddy Hassett	2.00	1.00	.60
171	Ossie Bluege	2.00	1.00	.60
172	Hoot Evers	2.00	1.00	.60
173	Thornton Lee	2.00	1.00	.60
174	Virgil Davis	2.00	1.00	.60
175	Bob Shawkey	2.00	1.00	.60
176	Smead Jolley	2.00	1.00	.60
177	Andy High	2.00	1.00	.60
178	George McQuinn	2.00	1.00	.60
179	Mickey Vernon	2.00	1.00	.60
180	Birdie Tebbetts	2.00	1.00	.60
181	Jack Kramer	2.00	1.00	.60
182	Don Kolloway	2.00	1.00	.60
183	Claude Passeau	2.00	1.00	.60
184	Frank Shea	2.00	1.00	.60
185	Bob O'Farrell	2.00	1.00	.60

186	Bob Johnson	2.00	1.00	.60
187	Ival Goodman	2.00	1.00	.60
188	Mike Kreevich	2.00	1.00	.60
189	Joe Stripp	2.00	1.00	.60
190	Mickey Owen	2.00	1.00	.60
191	Hughie Critz	2.00	1.00	.60
192	Ethan Allen	2.00	1.00	.60
193	Billy Rogell	2.00	1.00	.60
194	Joe Kuhel	2.00	1.00	.60
195	Dale Mitchell	2.00	1.00	.60
196	Eldon Auker	2.00	1.00	.60
197	Johnny Beazley	2.00	1.00	.60
198	Spud Chandler	2.00	1.00	.60
199	Ralph Branca	2.00	1.00	.60
200	Joe Cronin	2.00	1.00	.60

1957-58 Graphics Arts Service Detroit Tigers Postcards

This series of Tigers postcards was issued over a two-year span by a Cincinnati printer. The 3-3/16" x 5-7/16" cards have a black-and-white borderless player photo on front with or without a facsimile autograph. Backs have standard postcard indicia, including the producer's name and address.

		NM	EX	VG
	Complete Set (22):	1,500	750.00	450.00
	Common Player:	60.00	30.00	18.00
(1)	Al Aber	60.00	30.00	18.00
(2)	Hank Aguirre	60.00	30.00	18.00
(3)	Reno Bertoia (Fielding)	60.00	30.00	18.00
(4)	Reno Bertoia (Portrait)	60.00	30.00	18.00
(5)	Frank Bolling	60.00	30.00	18.00
(6)	Jim Bunning	120.00	60.00	35.00
(7)	Jack Dittmer	60.00	30.00	18.00
(8)	Paul Foytack	60.00	30.00	18.00
(9)	Jim Hegan	60.00	30.00	18.00
(10)	Tommy Henrich	80.00	40.00	24.00
(11)	Billy Hoeft	60.00	30.00	18.00
(12)	Frank House	60.00	30.00	18.00
(13)	Al Kaline	180.00	90.00	55.00
(14)	Harvey Kuenn	80.00	40.00	24.00
(15)	Don Lee	60.00	30.00	18.00
(16)	Billy Martin	90.00	45.00	25.00
(17)	Tom Morgan	60.00	30.00	18.00
(18)	J.W. Porter	60.00	30.00	18.00
(19)	Ron Samford	60.00	30.00	18.00
(20)	Bob Shaw	60.00	30.00	18.00
(21)	Lou Sleater	60.00	30.00	18.00
(22)	Tim Thompson	60.00	30.00	18.00

1888 Gray Studio Cabinets

The posed action photos on the approximately 4-1/4" x 6-1/2" cards are the same pictures seen on many of the players' Old Judge and Old Judge cabinet cards. Gray cabinets are found with two fancy logotypes at lower-left. On one, the tail of the "y" underscores the "Gra," while on the other, fancy decorations bookend the studio name. The Boston address of the studio is at lower-right. Players are not identified on the cards, and the backs are blank.

		NM	EX	VG
	Common Player:	1,500	700.00	450.00
(1)	Charlie Buffinton (Batting)	1,500	700.00	450.00
(2)	Charlie Buffinton (Right arm forward.)	1,500	700.00	450.00
(3)	Dan Casey (Arms at sides.)	1,500	700.00	450.00

(4)	Dan Casey (Ball in hands at chest.)	1,500	700.00	450.00
(5)	Dan Casey (Left arm outstretched.)	1,500	700.00	450.00
(6)	Jack Clements (Batting)	1,500	700.00	450.00
(7)	Jack Clements (Fielding, hands chest-high.)	1,500	700.00	450.00
(8)	Jack Clements (Hands on knees.)	1,500	700.00	450.00
(12)	Ed Daily (Batting)	1,500	700.00	450.00
(13)	Ed Daily (Holding ball in front of face.)	1,500	700.00	450.00
(14)	Ed Daily (Throwing)	1,500	700.00	450.00
(16)	Sid Farrar (Arms crossed.)	1,500	700.00	450.00
(17)	Sid Farrar (Fielding grounder.)	1,500	700.00	450.00
(18)	Sid Farrar (Fielding fly ball.)	1,500	700.00	450.00
(19)	Sid Farrar (Right hand on belt buckle.)	1,500	700.00	450.00
(21)	Charlie Ferguson (Ball in hands at chest.)	1,500	700.00	450.00
(22)	Charlie Ferguson (Batting)	1,500	700.00	450.00
(23)	Charlie Ferguson (Tagging Tommy McCarthy.)	1,800	900.00	550.00
(24)	Charlie Ferguson (Throwing, right arm back.)	1,500	700.00	450.00
(26)	Jim Fogarty (Batting)	1,500	700.00	450.00
(27)	Jim Fogarty (Fielding grounder.)	1,500	700.00	450.00
(28)	Jim Fogarty (Fielding, hands at neck.)	1,500	700.00	450.00
(29)	Jim Fogarty (Fielding on the run.)	1,500	700.00	450.00
(32)	Tom Gunning (Fielding, hands at knees.)	1,500	700.00	450.00
(33)	Arthur Irwin (Batting)	1,500	700.00	450.00
(34)	Arthur Irwin (Fielding, hands chest-high.)	1,500	700.00	450.00
(35)	Arthur Irwin (Throwing)	1,500	700.00	450.00
(39)	Tommy McCarthy (Batting)	3,000	1,500	900.00
(40)	Tommy McCarthy (Fielding, hands chest-high.)	3,000	1,500	900.00
(41)	Tommy McCarthy (Tagging baserunner.)	3,000	1,500	900.00
(42)	Tommy McCarthy (Throwing)	3,000	1,500	900.00
(44)	Deacon McGuire (Batting)	1,500	700.00	450.00
(45)	Deacon McGuire (Fielding, hands chest-high.)	1,500	700.00	450.00
(48)	Joe Mulvey (Batting)	1,500	700.00	450.00
(49)	Joe Mulvey (Fielding, hands at waist.)	1,500	700.00	450.00
(50)	Joe Mulvey (Watching ball.)	1,500	700.00	450.00
(60)	George Wood (Batting)	1,500	700.00	450.00
(61)	George Wood (Fielding fly ball.)	1,500	700.00	450.00
(62)	George Wood (Fielding grounder.)	1,500	700.00	450.00
(63)	George Wood (Throwing)	1,500	700.00	450.00

1975-76 Great Plains Greats

This collectors' issue was issued in two series in conjunction with shows conducted by the Great Plains Sports Collectors Association. Cards are about 2-5/8" x 3-3/4". Fronts have black-and-white photos with heavy colored frames and white borders. Player name is overprinted on a diamond at bottom. Backs have a career summary and stats, and a sponsor's ad. The 1975 issue (#1-24) was sponsored by Sheraton Inns; the 1976 cards (#25-42) were sponsored by Nu-Sash Corp.

		NM	EX	VG
	Complete Set (43):	20.00	10.00	6.00
	Common Player:	1.00	.50	.30
1	Bob Feller	2.00	1.00	.60
2	Carl Hubbell	1.00	.50	.30
3	Jocko Conlan	1.00	.50	.30
4	Hal Trosky	1.00	.50	.30
5	Allie Reynolds	1.00	.50	.30
6	Burleigh Grimes	1.00	.50	.30
7	Jake Beckley	1.00	.50	.30
8	Al Simmons	1.00	.50	.30
9	Paul Waner	1.00	.50	.30
10	Chief Bender	1.00	.50	.30
11	Fred Clarke	1.00	.50	.30
12	Jim Bottomley	1.00	.50	.30
13	Dave Bancroft	1.00	.50	.30
14	Bing Miller	1.00	.50	.30
15	Walter Johnson	2.50	1.25	.70
16	Grover Alexander	2.50	1.25	.70
17	Bob Johnson	1.00	.50	.30
18	Roger Maris	2.50	1.25	.70
19	Ken Keltner	1.00	.50	.30
20	Red Faber	1.00	.50	.30
21	"Cool Papa" Bell	1.00	.50	.30
22	Yogi Berra	2.50	1.25	.70
23	Fred Lindstrom	1.00	.50	.30
24	Ray Schalk	1.00	.50	.30
---	Checklist	.10	.05	.03

25	Lloyd Waner	1.00	.50	.30
26	Johnny Hopp	1.00	.50	.30
27	Mel Harder	1.00	.50	.30
28	Dutch Leonard	1.00	.50	.30
29	Bob O'Farrell	1.00	.50	.30
30	Cap Anson	1.00	.50	.30
31	Dazzy Vance	1.00	.50	.30
32	Red Schoendienst	1.00	.50	.30
33	George Pipgras	1.00	.50	.30
34	Harvey Kuenn	1.00	.50	.30
35	Red Ruffing	1.00	.50	.30
36	Roy Sievers	1.00	.50	.30
37	Ken Boyer	1.00	.50	.30
38	Al Smith	1.00	.50	.30
39	Casey Stengel	1.00	.50	.30
40	Bob Gibson	1.50	.70	.45
41	Mickey Mantle	10.00	5.00	3.00
42	Denny McLain	1.00	.50	.30

1908-1909 Greenfield's Chocolates Postcards

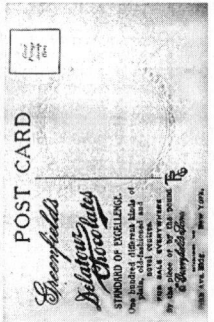

These special advertising versions of the Rose Co. postcards were produced circa 1908-09. The 3-1/2" x 5-1/2" cards feature a black-and-white player portrait photo at center, surrounded by an embossed round gold frame. The player's surname and (usually) team are in a white panel under the photo. The background is green and includes crossed bats and a baseball, a diamond diagram and pictures of a fielder and batter. The postcard-format back is printed in black-and-white with a TRC logo at bottom-center. Printed at left in ornate typography is advertising for the New York confectioner. Two back styles are known apparently the result of the candy company's move from Fifth Ave. to Barclay St. (or vice versa) during the issuing period. It is unknown how many of the player postcards in the Rose Co. series can be found with this advertising on back. While much rarer than Rose Co. cards without the advertising, the Greenfield's version currently carries only modest premium value, perhaps 10-20 percent higher than the regular version.

(See 1908-1909 Rose Company Postcards for checklist and base values.)

1916 Green-Joyce

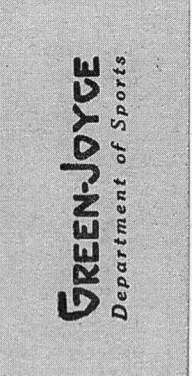

Best known for its use as a promotional medium for The Sporting News, this 200-card set can be found with blank backs or with ads on the back for several local and regional businesses. Among them is Green-Joyce "Department of Sports," location Columbus, OH. Type-card and superstar collectors can expect to pay a premiu, for individual cards with Green- Joyce advertising as opposed to the more common M101-4 blank-back values. Cards measure 1-5/8" x 3" and are printed in black-and-white.

PREMIUM: 3-4X
(See 1916 M101-4 Blank Backs for checklist and base values.)

1969 Greiner Tires Pittsburgh Pirates

One of the scarcer of the many Pirates regionals of the late 1960s is this eight-card issue. Printed on heavy paper in black-and-white, the 5-1/2" x 8-1/2" cards are blank-backed and unnumbered. They are checklisted here alphabetically. Some sources say the Matty Alou card is scarcer than the rest of the set.

		NM	EX	VG
	Complete Set (8):	80.00	40.00	24.00
	Common Player:	4.50	2.25	1.25
(1)	Gene Alley	4.50	2.25	1.25
(2)	Matty Alou	30.00	15.00	9.00
(3)	Steve Blass	4.50	2.25	1.25
(4)	Roberto Clemente	30.00	15.00	9.00
(5)	Jerry May	4.50	2.25	1.25
(6)	Bill Mazeroski	12.50	6.25	3.75
(7)	Larry Shepard	4.50	2.25	1.25
(8)	Willie Stargell	12.50	6.25	3.75

1928 Greiners Bread

This set of about 1-3/8" x 2-1/2" black-and-white cards is believed to parallel the W502 strip card set. Only a few examples are known, and they are too scarce to price.

		NM	EX	VG
	Complete Set (60):	8,500	3,500	1,750
	Common Player:	75.00	30.00	15.00
1	Burleigh Grimes			
2	Walter Reuther (Ruether)			
3	Joe Dugan			
4	Red Faber			
5	Gabby Hartnett			
6	Babe Ruth			
7	Bob Meusel			
8	Herb Pennock			
9	George Burns			
10	Joe Sewell			
11	George Uhle			
12	Bob O'Farrell			
13	Rogers Hornsby			
14	"Pie" Traynor			
15	Clarence Mitchell			
16	Eppa Jepha Rixey			
17	Carl Mays			
18	Adolfo Luque			
19	Dave Bancroft			
20	George Kelly			
21	Earl (Earle) Combs			
22	Harry Heilmann			
23	Ray W. Schalk			
24	Johnny Mostil			
25	Hack Wilson			
26	Lou Gehrig			
27	Ty Cobb			
28	Tris Speaker			
29	Tony Lazzeri			
30	Waite Hoyt			
31	Sherwood Smith			
32	Max Carey			
33	Eugene Hargrave			
34	Miguel L. Gonzales (Miguel A. Gonzalez)			
35	Joe Judge			
36	E.C. (Sam) Rice			
37	Earl Sheely			
38	Sam Jones			
39	Bib (Bibb) A. Falk			
40	Willie Kamm			
41	Stanley Harris			
42	John J. McGraw			
43	Artie Nehf			
44	Grover Alexander			
45	Paul Waner			
46	William H. Terry			
47	Glenn Wright			
48	Earl Smith			
49	Leon (Goose) Goslin			
50	Frank Frisch			
51	Joe Harris			
52	Fred (Cy) Williams			
53	Eddie Roush			
54	George Sisler			
55	Ed. Rommel			
56	Rogers Peckinpaugh (Roger)			
57	Stanley Coveleskie (Coveleski)			
58	Lester Bell			
59	L. Waner			
60	John P. McInnis			

1974 Greyhound Heroes on the Base Paths

The first of three annual baseball card folders honoring the stolen base leaders and runners-up in each league, this 20" x 9" five-panel sheet features six 4" x 3" cards printed in black-and-white with sepia graphics. Backs are printed in black, brown and white. Besides the cards, the folder contains information about the bus company's award, as well as major league stolen base records and base-stealing tips. Besides individual cards of the 1974 winner and runner-up in each league, the folder has cards picturing all winners and runners-up since 1965.

		NM	EX	VG
Complete Set, Folder:		10.00	5.00	3.00
Complete Set, Singles:		8.00	4.00	2.50
Common Player:		2.00	1.00	.60
(1)	Lou Brock	4.00	2.00	1.25
(2)	Rod Carew	4.00	2.00	1.25
(3)	Davey Lopes	2.00	1.00	.60
(4)	Bill North	2.00	1.00	.60
(5)	A.L. Winners/Runners-Up (Don Buford, Bert Campaneris, Rod Carew, Tommy Harper, Dave Nelson, Bill North, Amos Otis, Fred Patek)	2.00	1.00	.60
(6)	N.L. Winners/Runners-Up (Lou Brock, Jose Cardenal, Sonny Jackson, Davey Lopes, Joe Morgan, Bobby Tolan, Maury Wills)	2.00	1.00	.60

1975 Greyhound Heroes on the Base Paths

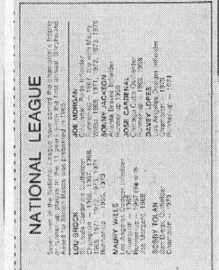

Six perforated 3-7/8" x 3" cards are featured on this folded five-panel 20" x 9" sheet honoring top base stealers in both leagues for the 1975 season. Four of the cards have each league's SB leader and runner-up in a black-and-white portrait photo with blue background. Backs are printed in black, blue and white and include major league stats. There are also two action photo cards with lists on the back of each year's winner and runner-up for the Greyhound Stolen Base Awards since 1965.

		NM	EX	VG
Complete Set, Folder:		7.00	3.50	2.00
Complete Set, Singles:		4.00	2.00	1.25
Common Player:		1.50	.70	.45
(1)	Davey Lopes	1.50	.70	.45
(2)	Davey Lopes (Action)	1.50	.70	.45
(3)	Joe Morgan	2.50	1.25	.70
(4)	Bill North (Action)	1.50	.70	.45
(5)	Mickey Rivers	1.50	.70	.45
(6)	Claudell Washington	1.50	.70	.45

1976 Greyhound Heroes on the Base Paths

The last of three annual baseball card folders honoring the stolen base leaders and runners-up in each league, this 20" x 9" five-panel sheet features six 4" x 3" cards printed in black-and-white with sepia graphics. Backs are printed in

black, brown and white. Besides the cards, the folder contains information about the bus company's award, as well as major league stolen base records and base-stealing tips. Besides individual cards of the 1974 winner and runner-up in each league, the folder includes two action-photo cards listing all winners and runners-up since 1965.

		NM	EX	VG
Complete Set, Folder:		6.00	3.00	1.75
Complete Set, Singles:		5.00	2.50	1.50
Common Player:		1.50	.70	.45
(1)	Ronald Le Flore	1.50	.70	.45
(2)	Davey Lopes	1.50	.70	.45
(3)	Davey Lopes (Action)	1.50	.70	.45
(4)	Joe Morgan	3.00	1.50	.90
(5)	Bill North	1.50	.70	.45
(6)	Bill North (Action)	1.50	.70	.45

1907 Grignon Chicago Cubs Postcards

The eventual 1907 World Champion Cubs are featured in this set of novelty postcards. Fronts of the 3-1/2" x 5-1/2" horizontal cards have a green background with white border. The central figure on each is a teddy bear in a baseball pose. In an upper corner is a black-and-white circular portrait of one of the Cubs, with identification below. A line of infield chatter - i.e., "This is a Cinch" - completes the design. Backs have standard postcard markings and some have been seen with advertising for local businesses. The unnumbered cards are checklisted here alphabetically.

		NM	EX	VG
Complete Set (16):		12,000	6,000	3,500
Common Player:		475.00	235.00	140.00
(1)	Mordecai Brown	1,600	800.00	480.00
(2)	Frank Chance	1,600	800.00	480.00
(3)	John Evers	1,600	800.00	480.00
(4)	Arthur Hofman	475.00	235.00	140.00
(5)	John Kling	475.00	235.00	140.00
(6)	Carl Lundgren	475.00	235.00	140.00
(7)	Pat Moran	475.00	235.00	140.00
(8)	Orvie Overall	475.00	235.00	140.00
(9)	Jack Pfeister	475.00	235.00	140.00
(10)	Ed Reulbach	475.00	235.00	140.00
(11)	Frank Schulte	475.00	235.00	140.00
(12)	James Sheckard	475.00	235.00	140.00
(13)	James Slagle	475.00	235.00	140.00
(14)	Harry Steinfeldt	475.00	235.00	140.00
(15)	Jack Taylor	475.00	235.00	140.00
(16)	Joe Tinker	1,600	800.00	480.00

"1959-60" Gulf Oil Corporation

These fantasy/fraud cards were first reported in the hobby in 1999, though the copyright line on back purports to date them from 1959-1960. Two types of cards were produced, one series of eight featuring line-art portraits, the other featuring re-screened photos taken from team photo packs and similar sources. Cards are 2-1/2" x 3-1/2" printed in black-and-white. The unnumbered cards are checklisted here alphabetically within series. Because the cards were illegally produced in violation of player rights and team copyrights, no collector value is attributed.

Complete Set (16):
Artwork Series
(1) Ty Cobb
(2) Bill Dickey
(3) Joe DiMaggio
(4) Lou Gehrig
(5) Rogers Hornsby
(6) Walter Johnson
(7) Babe Ruth
(8) Pie Traynor
Photo Series
(1) Don Drysdale
(2) Bob Gibson
(3) Sandy Koufax
(4) Mickey Mantle
(5) Roger Maris

(6) Willie Mays
(7) Willie McCovey
(8) Stan Musial

1956 Gum Products Adventure

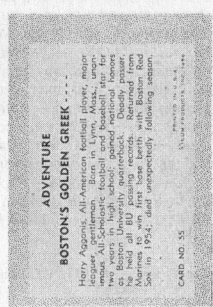

This series of 100 cards depicts all manner of action and adventure scenes, including several sports subjects, one of which is a baseball player. The card depicts Boston U. quarterback and Boston Red Sox prospect Harry Agganis, who died unexpectedly in 1955. The 3-1/2" x 2-1/2" horizontal card has a central portrait artwork of Agganis as a Red Sox, surrounded by other scenes from his personal and sporting life. The black-and-white back has a short biography.

		NM	EX	VG
55	Harry Agganis (Boston's Golden Greek)	25.00	12.50	7.50

1948 Gunther Beer Washington Senators Postcards

These postcards were apparently made available by writing to the radio voice of the Senators, Arch McDonald. A pre-printed message on the left side of the back urges the fan to keep listening to McDonald's program, sponsored by "Gunther's, the dry, beery beer." The black-and-white cards measure 3-1/2" x 5-1/2" and feature portrait photos of the Washington players. Most cards have two players side-by-side while manager Joe Kuhel has his own card. Player names are in heavy black letters across their chests. The cards are unnumbered and it is possible others will surface.

		NM	EX	VG
Complete Set (11):		3,000	1,500	900.00
Common Card:		285.00	140.00	85.00
(1)	Joe Kuhel	285.00	140.00	85.00
(2)	Gil Coan, Mickey Vernon	285.00	140.00	85.00
(3)	Al Evans, Scott Cary	285.00	140.00	85.00
(4)	Tom Ferrick, Harold Keller	285.00	140.00	85.00
(5)	Mickey Haefner, Forrest Thompson	285.00	140.00	85.00
(6)	Sid Hudson, Al Kozar	285.00	140.00	85.00
(7)	Walter Masterson, Rick Ferrell	325.00	160.00	95.00
(8)	Marino Pieretti, Leon Culberson	285.00	140.00	85.00
(9)	Sherrard Robertson, Eddie Lyons	285.00	140.00	85.00
(10)	Ray Scarborough, Kenneth McCreight	285.00	140.00	85.00
(11)	Early Wynn, Eddie Yost	400.00	200.00	120.00

1923-1924 Tomas Gutierrez

The largest of the Cuban baseball card issues of the 1920s, this is also one of the scarcest and most popular. Printed in dark brown (some backs are in black) on sepia paper, the 1-5/8" x 2-3/8" cards were inserted into packs of Diaz cigarettes. Cards have portrait photos on front with team name at top and the player name (sometimes misspelled and sometimes a nickname) and position below. Backs, which can be found in three styles, have the card number and an offer for an album. It is the album offer which accounts for much of this issue's scarcity. The album was a hardcover, ornate book with pictures of each card pre-printed. It is believed that the album was available by turning in a complete set of the cards, which were not returned. Adding to the set's popularity is its inclusion of many Negro Leagues players including future Hall of Famers Oscar Charleston and Pop Lloyd. Following the checklist are the names of cards known to exist from their presence in the album, but whose number is unknkown.

		NM	EX	VG
Complete Set (85): Value Undetermined				
Common Player:		350.00	140.00	70.00
Album:		4,500	2,250	1,350
SANTA CLARA				
1	Agustin "Tinti" Molina	350.00	140.00	70.00
2	Julio Rojo	450.00	180.00	90.00
3	Frank Duncan	1,750	700.00	350.00
4	Eustaquio "Bombin" Pedroso	2,250	900.00	450.00
5	Dave Brown	2,250	900.00	450.00
6	Pedro Dibut	450.00	180.00	90.00
7	Rube Currie	1,750	700.00	350.00
8	Jose Mendez	6,000	2,400	1,200
9	Esteban "Mayari" Montalvo	850.00	340.00	170.00
10	Frank Warfield	1,750	700.00	350.00
11	Oliver Marcelle	2,250	900.00	450.00
12	Dobie Moore	1,750	700.00	350.00
13	Herman Matias Rios	350.00	140.00	70.00
14	Oscar Charleston	20,000	8,000	4,000
15	Alejandro Oms	2,250	900.00	450.00
16	Pablo "Champion" Mesa	850.00	340.00	170.00
17	Bill Holland	2,250	900.00	450.00
18	Oscar "Heavy" Johnson	2,250	900.00	450.00
ALMENDARES				
19	Eugenio Morin	350.00	140.00	70.00
20	Snake Henry	350.00	140.00	70.00
21	Manuel Cueto	350.00	140.00	70.00
22	Jesse Hubbard	850.00	340.00	170.00
23	Kakin Gonzalez	350.00	140.00	70.00
24	Jose Maria Fernandez	350.00	140.00	70.00
25	Oscar Rodriguez	350.00	140.00	70.00
26	Lucas Boada	350.00	140.00	70.00
27	Eusebio "Papo" Gonzalez	350.00	140.00	70.00
28	Ramon "Paito" Herrera	350.00	140.00	70.00
29	Bernardo Baro	850.00	340.00	170.00
30	Armando Marsans	1,200	480.00	240.00
31	Isidro Fabre	850.00	340.00	170.00
32				
33	Valentin Dreke	850.00	340.00	170.00
34	Joseito Rodriguez	350.00	140.00	70.00
35	Jose "Cheo" Ramos	350.00	140.00	70.00
36	Willis "Pud" Flournoy	1,200	480.00	240.00
37	Oscar Tuero	350.00	140.00	70.00
38	Rafael Almeida	850.00	340.00	170.00
39	Almendares Pennant	350.00	140.00	70.00
---	Oscar Fuhr	350.00	140.00	70.00
MARIANAO				
40				
41	Don Brown	350.00	140.00	70.00
42		.00	.00	.00
43	(Ed) Morris	350.00	140.00	70.00
44	Ernie Krueger	350.00	140.00	70.00
45				
46	(Harry) McCurdy	350.00	140.00	70.00
47	Jose "Acostica" Acosta	350.00	140.00	70.00
48	Jacinto Calvo	350.00	140.00	70.00
49	(Eddie) Brown	350.00	140.00	70.00
50	(Rosy) Ryan	350.00	140.00	70.00
51	Rogelio Crespo	350.00	140.00	70.00
52	Hank Deberry	350.00	140.00	70.00
53	(Art) Phelan	350.00	140.00	70.00
54				
55	(Jimmy) Cooney	350.00	140.00	70.00
56a	H. Scheiber (Hank Schreiber) (Infielder)	350.00	140.00	70.00
56b	H. Scheiber (Hank Schreiber) (Infielder)	350.00	140.00	70.00
57				
58				
59				
---	Marianao Pennant	350.00	140.00	70.00
---	Merito Acosta	350.00	140.00	70.00
---	Otis Brannan	350.00	140.00	70.00
---	Charlie Dressen	450.00	180.00	90.00
---	Emilio Palmero	350.00	140.00	70.00
---	Jose "Pepin" Perez	350.00	140.00	70.00
---	Jess Petty	450.00	180.00	90.00
HAVANA				
60	Buster Ross	350.00	140.00	70.00
61	Juanelo Mirabal	350.00	140.00	70.00
62	Cristobal Torriente	17,500	7,000	3,500
63	John Henry "Pop" Lloyd	20,000	8,000	4,000
64	Oscar Levis	700.00	280.00	140.00
65	Pelayo Chacon	850.00	340.00	170.00
66	Eufemio Abreu	350.00	140.00	70.00
67	Mack Eggleston	850.00	340.00	170.00
68	(Tauca "Manzanillo") Campos	350.00	140.00	70.00
69	Raphael "Busta" Quintana	350.00	140.00	70.00
70	Merven "Red" Ryan	850.00	340.00	170.00
71	(Danny) Clark	350.00	140.00	70.00
72	Clint Thomas	1,000	400.00	200.00
73	Adolfo Luque	1,200	480.00	240.00
74	Marcelino Guerra	350.00	140.00	70.00
75	Bartolo Portuondo	850.00	340.00	170.00
76	Andy Cooper	6,000	2,400	1,200
77	(John) Bischoff	350.00	140.00	70.00
78	Edgar Wesley	1,750	700.00	350.00
79	Havana Pennant	350.00	140.00	70.00
---	Jacinto Calvo	300.00	120.00	60.00
---	Bienvenido "Hooks" Jimenez	250.00	100.00	50.00
MISCELLANEOUS				
80	Hector Magrinat (Umpire)	350.00	140.00	70.00
81	Valentin "Sirique" Gonzalez (Umpire)	350.00	140.00	70.00
82	Slim Love (Marianao)	350.00	140.00	70.00
83	Cristobal Torriente (Marianao)	17,500	7,000	3,500
84				
85	Jakie May (Almendares)	450.00	180.00	90.00

1887 Gypsy Queen (N175)

The 1887 Gypsy Queen set is very closely related to the N172 Old Judge set and employs the same photos. Gypsy Queens are easily identified by the advertising along the top. A line near the bottom lists the player's name, position and team, followed by an 1887 copyright line and words "Cigarettes" and "Goodwin & Co. N.Y." Although the checklist is still considered incomplete, some 140 different poses have been discovered so far. Gypsy Queens were issued in two distinct sizes, the more common version measuring 1-1/2" x 2-1/2" (same as Old Judge) and a larger size measuring 2" x 3-1/2" which are considered extremely rare. The large Gypsy Queens are identical in format to the smaller size; the nine known examples are designated here.

		NM	EX	VG
Common Player:		3,300	1,650	1,200
(13)	J. (Tug) Arundel (Fielding)	3,300	1,650	1,200
(17)	Mark Baldwin	3,300	1,650	1,200
(19 1)	Sam Barkley (Fielding)	3,300	1,650	1,200
(19 2)	Sam Barkley (Tagging player.)	3,300	1,650	1,200
(19 3)	Sam Barkley (Throwing)	3,300	1,650	1,200
(35)	Henry Boyle (Right arm outstretched.)	3,300	1,650	1,200
(43 1)	Dan Brouthers (Looking at ball.)	8,250	4,125	2,475
(43 2)	Dan Brouthers (Looking to right.)	8,250	4,125	2,475
(44 1)	Tom Brown (Pittsburgh, bat at side.)	3,300	1,650	1,200
(44 2)	Tom Brown (Pittsburgh, catching.)	3,300	1,650	1,200
(45L)	Willard (California) Brown (N.Y., large, throwing.)	20,625	10,300	6,200
(45 1)	Willard (California) Brown (N.Y., throwing.)	3,300	1,650	1,200
(45 2)	Willard (California) Brown (N.Y., wearing mask.)	3,800	1,900	1,125
(50)	Charlie Buffington (Buffinton) (Bat at 45 degrees.)	3,300	1,650	1,200
(51)	Ernie Burch (Fielding, hands above head, outdoors.)	4,000	1,650	1,200
(53)	Jack Burdock (Fielding grounder.)	4,000	1,650	1,200
(55)	Watch Burnham	3,300	1,650	1,200
(59)	Tom Burns	3,300	1,650	1,200
(60)	Doc Bushong (Brown's Champions)	5,850	2,925	1,750
(61)	John (Patsy) Cahill	3,300	1,650	1,200
(68)	Fred Carroll (Bat at side.)	3,300	1,650	1,200
(71)	Bob Caruthers	3,300	1,650	1,200
(72 1)	Dan Casey (Hands at chest.)	3,800	1,900	1,125
(72 2)	Dan Casey (Left arm extended.)	3,300	1,650	1,200
(79 1)	Jack Clements (Hands on knees.)	3,300	1,650	1,200
(79 2)	Jack Clements (With bat.)	3,300	1,650	1,200
(83)	John Coleman (Bat at side.)	3,300	1,650	1,200
(86)	Charlie Comiskey	8,250	4,125	2,475
(88 1)	Roger Connor (Hands on knees.)	29,150	15,450	9,300
(88 2)	Roger Connor (Bat at 45 degrees.)	8,250	4,125	2,475
(89)	Dick Conway	3,300	1,650	1,200
(94)	Larry Corcoran	3,300	1,650	1,200
(97 1)	Sam Crane (Fielding grounder.)	3,300	1,650	1,200
(97 2)	Sam Crane (With bat.)	3,300	1,650	1,200
(109)	Ed Dailey	3,300	1,650	1,200
(113)	Abner Dalrymple (Right arm cap-high.)	3,300	1,650	1,200

		NM	EX	VG
(117)	Dell Darling	3,300	1,650	1,200
(121 1)	Pat Dealey (Bat at side.)	3,300	1,650	1,200
(121 2)	Pat Dealey (Bat on shoulder.)	3,300	1,650	1,200
(125L)	Jerry Denny (Large, with bat.)	20,625	10,300	6,200
(125 1)	Jerry Denny (Catching)	3,300	1,650	1,200
(125 2)	Jerry Denny (With bat.)	3,300	1,650	1,200
(130)	Jim Donnelly (Bat at 45 degrees.)	3,300	1,650	1,200
(133)	Mike Dorgan (Arms crossed.)	3,300	1,650	1,200
(149L)	Buck Ewing (Large, catching fly ball.)	32,000	15,450	9,300
(149 1)	Buck Ewing (Bat at 45 degrees.)	8,250	4,125	2,475
(149 2)	Buck Ewing (Fielding fly ball.)	8,250	4,125	2,475
(149 3)	Buck Ewing (Fielding ground ball.)	8,250	4,125	2,475
(156 1)	Jack Farrell (Bat at side.)	3,300	1,650	1,200
(156 2)	Jack Farrell (Bat in air.)	3,300	1,650	1,200
(156 3)	Jack Farrell (Fielding)	3,300	1,650	1,200
(156 4)	Jack Farrell (Hands on thighs.)	3,300	1,650	1,200
(158 1)	Charlie Ferguson (Hands at chest.)	4,000	1,650	1,200
(158 2)	Charlie Ferguson (Right arm extended back.)	4,000	1,650	1,200
(158 3)	Charlie Ferguson (Tagging player.)	3,300	1,650	1,200
(158 4)	Charlie Ferguson (With bat.)	3,300	1,650	1,200
(161 1)	Jocko Fields (Catching)	3,300	1,650	1,200
(161 2)	Jocko Fields (Tagging player.)	3,800	1,900	1,125
(161 3)	Jocko Fields (Throwing)	3,300	1,650	1,200
(167 1)	Jim Fogarty (Bat on shoulder.)	3,300	1,650	1,200
(167 2)	Jim Fogarty (Fielding fly ball.)	3,300	1,650	1,200
(171)	Dave Foutz (Brown's Champions)	5,850	2,925	1,750
(178)	John Gaffney (Bending to right.)	3,300	1,650	1,200
(171 1)	Pud Galvin (Leaning on bat.)	8,250	4,125	2,475
(171 2)	Pud Galvin (Without bat.)	8,250	4,125	2,475
(184 1)	Emil Geiss (Hands above waist.)	3,300	1,650	1,200
(184 2)	Emil Geiss (Right hand extended.)	3,300	1,650	1,200
(191 1)	Pete Gillespie (Fielding)	3,300	1,650	1,200
(191 2)	Pete Gillespie (With bat.)	3,300	1,650	1,200
(192)	Barney Gilligan	3,300	1,650	1,200
(194 1)	Jack Glasscock (Hands on knees.)	3,300	1,650	1,200
(194 2)	Jack Glasscock (Throwing)	3,300	1,650	1,200
(194 3)	Jack Glasscock (With bat.)	3,300	1,650	1,200
(195)	Bill Gleason (Brown's Champions)	5,850	2,925	1,700
(199 1)	George Gore (Fielding)	3,300	1,650	1,200
(199 2)	George Gore (Hand at head level.)	3,300	1,650	1,200
(202)	Ed Greer (Batting, outdoors.)	5,150	2,600	1,550
(207 1)	Tom Gunning (Stooping to catch low ball on left.)	3,300	1,650	1,200
(207 2)	Tom Gunning (Bending, hands by right knee.)	3,300	1,650	1,200
(215 1)	Ned Hanlon (Catching)	8,250	4,125	2,475
(215 2)	Ned Hanlon (Bat at 45 degrees.)	8,250	4,125	2,475
(218 1)	John Harkins (Hands above waist, outdoors.)	4,000	1,650	1,200
(218 2)	John Harkins (Throwing, outdoors.)	5,150	2,600	1,550
(223)	Egyptian Healey (Healy) (Batting)	3,300	1,650	1,200
(232)	Paul Hines (Hands at sides.)	3,300	1,650	1,200
(241)	Joe Horning (Hornung) (Bat at 45 degrees.)	3,300	1,650	1,200
(244)	Nat Hudson (Brown's Champions)	5,850	2,925	1,700
(248 1)	Arthur Irwin (Batting)	3,300	1,650	1,200
(248 2)	Arthur Irwin (Fielding, hands below knees.)	3,300	1,650	1,200
(253 1)	Dick Johnston (Catching)	3,300	1,650	1,200
(253 2)	Dick Johnston (With bat.)	3,300	1,650	1,200
(256L)	Tim Keefe (Large, ball in hands at chest.)	33,000	16,500	10,000
(256 1)	Tim Keefe (Ball in hands at chest.)	8,250	4,125	2,475
(256 2)	Tim Keefe (Hands above waist, facing front.)	8,250	4,125	2,475
(256 3)	Tim Keefe (Right hand extended at head level.)	8,250	4,125	2,475
(256 4)	Tim Keefe (With bat.)	8,250	4,125	2,475
(261L)	King Kelly (Large, bat horizontal.)	34,800	16,900	10,100
(261 1)	King Kelly (Fielding, hands chest-high.)	12,375	6,200	3,700
(261 2)	King Kelly (Portrait)	12,375	6,200	3,700
(261 4)	King Kelly (With bat.)	11,700	5,850	3,500
(262)	Rudy Kemmler	3,300	1,650	1,200
(273 1)	Bill Krieg (Fielding thigh-high ball.)	3,300	1,650	1,200
(273 2)	Bill Krieg (With bat.)	3,300	1,650	1,200
(278)	Arlie Latham	3,300	1,650	1,200
(302 1)	Mike Mattimore (Hands above head.)	3,300	1,650	1,200
(302 2)	Mike Mattimore (Hands at neck.)	3,300	1,650	1,200
(302 3)	Mike Mattimore (Sliding)	3,300	1,650	1,200
(307 1)	Tommy McCarthy (Catching)	8,250	4,125	2,475
(307 2)	Tommy McCarthy (Sliding)	8,250	4,125	2,475
(307 3)	Tommy McCarthy (With bat.)	8,250	4,125	2,475
(309)	Bill McClellan	3,300	1,650	1,200
(311 1)	Jim McCormick (Ball in hands at chest.)	3,300	1,650	1,200
(311 2)	Jim McCormick (Bat at 45 degrees.)	3,300	1,650	1,200
(316 1)	Jack McGeachy (Bat at 45 degrees.)	4,000	1,650	1,125
(316 2)	Jack McGeachy (Fielding ball over head.)	5,150	2,600	1,550
(318 1)	Deacon McGuire (Batting)	3,300	1,650	1,200
(318 2)	Deacon McGuire (Catching)	3,300	1,650	1,200

(321)	Alex McKinnon (Fielding, hands waist-high.)	3,300	1,650	1,200
(326 1)	Jim McTamany (Bat on shoulder, outdoors.)	4,000	1,650	1,125
(326 2)	Jim McTamany (Fielding, outdoors.)	4,000	1,650	1,125
(330)	Doggie Miller	3,300	1,650	1,200
(336)	John Morrell (Morrill) (Hands on hips.)	3,800	1,900	1,125
(339)	Joe Mulvey (Fiedling ball at waist.)	3,300	1,650	1,200
(344 1)	Al Myers (Washington, bat vertical.)	3,300	1,650	1,200
(344 2)	Al Myers (Washington, hands on knees.)	3,300	1,650	1,200
(344 3)	Al Myers (Portrait, with arms folded.)	3,300	1,650	1,200
(345 1)	George Myers (Indianapolis, stooping.)	3,300	1,650	1,200
(345 2)	George Myers (Indianapolis, with bat.)	3,300	1,650	1,200
(347)	Billy Nash (Portrait)	3,300	1,650	1,200
(353)	Hugh Nicol (Brown's Champions)	5,850	2,925	1,700
(358)	Jack O'Brien (Bat over shoulder, outdoors.)	3,300	1,650	1,200
(362 1)	Hank O'Day (Ball in hand.)	3,300	1,650	1,200
(362 2)	Hank O'Day (With bat.)	3,300	1,650	1,200
(365)	Tip O'Neill (Brown's Champions)	6,425	3,200	1,900
(366)	Orator Jim O'Rourke (Fielding)	6,200	3,100	1,850
(367)	Tom O'Rourke (Bat at 45 degrees.)	3,300	1,650	1,200
(371)	Jimmy Peeples (Catching, outdoors.)	3,300	1,650	1,200
(374)	Fred Pfeffer (Throwing)	3,300	1,650	1,200
(378)	George Pinkney (Pinckney)	3,300	1,650	1,200
(380)	Henry Porter (Throwing, right hand cap-high, outdoors.)	4,000	1,650	1,125
(386)	Old Hoss Radbourn (With bat.)	8,250	4,125	2,475
(393L)	Danny Richardson (N.Y., large, bat at 45 degrees.)	24,200	12,000	7,200
(393 1)	Danny Richardson (N.Y., bat at 45 degrees.)	3,300	1,650	1,200
(393 2)	Danny Richardson (N.Y., moving to left, arms at sides.)	3,300	1,650	1,200
(394)	Hardy Richardson (Detroit)	3,300	1,650	1,200
(396)	John Roach (Batting)	3,300	1,650	1,200
(399)	Yank Robinson (Brown's Champions)	5,850	2,925	1,700
(403)	Jack Rowe (Bat at side.)	3,300	1,650	1,200
(405)	Jimmy Ryan (Ball in hands at chest.)	3,300	1,650	1,200
(415 1)	Emmett Seery (Arms folded.)	3,300	1,650	1,200
(415 2)	Emmett Seery (Ball in hands.)	3,300	1,650	1,200
(415 3)	Emmett Seery (Catching)	3,300	1,650	1,200
(425 1)	George Shoch (Batting, w/umpire.)	3,300	1,650	1,200
(425 2)	George Schoch (Shoch) (Fielding, hands head high.)	3,300	1,650	1,200
(426)	Otto Shomberg (Schomberg) (Ball in hands at shoulder.)	3,300	1,650	1,200
(435)	Pop Smith	3,300	1,650	1,200
(446 1)	Bill Stemmyer (Stemmeyer) (Ball in hands at chest.)	3,300	1,650	1,200
(446 2)	Bill Stemmyer (Stemmeyer) (With bat.)	3,300	1,650	1,200
(459 1)	Ezra Sutton (Fielding)	3,300	1,650	1,200
(459 2)	Ezra Sutton (Throwing)	3,300	1,650	1,200
(459 3)	Ezra Sutton (With bat.)	3,300	1,650	1,200
(460)	Ed Swartwood (Kneeling to field, outdoors.)	5,150	2,600	1,550
(464)	Pop Tate (Fielding)	3,300	1,650	1,200
(467)	William "Adonis" Terry (Batting outdoors.)	3,300	1,650	1,200
(468 1)	Sam Thompson (Arms folded.)	8,250	4,125	2,475
(468 2)	Sam Thompson (Bat at side.)	8,250	4,125	2,475
(468 3)	Sam Thompson (Swinging at ball.)	8,250	4,125	2,475
(469L)	Mike Tiernan (Large, fielding fly ball.)	20,625	10,300	6,200
(469)	Mike Tiernan (Fielding grounder.)	3,300	1,650	1,200
(472)	Steve Toole (With bat, outdoors.)	5,150	2,600	1,550
(480 1)	Larry Twitchell (Hands by chest.)	3,300	1,650	1,200
(480 2)	Larry Twitchell (Right hand extended.)	3,300	1,650	1,200
(489)	Chris Von Der Ahe	4,800	2,400	1,375
(491L)	John Ward (Large, throwing.)	32,000	15,450	9,300
(491)	John Ward	8,250	4,125	2,475
(493)	Bill Watkins (Portrait)	3,300	1,650	1,200
(498)	Curt Welch	3,300	1,650	1,200
(511 1)	Art Whitney (Pittsburgh, bending.)	3,300	1,650	1,200
(511 2)	Art Whitney (Pittsburgh, with bat.)	3,300	1,650	1,200
(513)	Jim Whitney (Washington, throwing, r. hand waist-high.)	3,300	1,650	1,200
(515)	Ned Williamson (Throwing)	4,000	1,650	1,125
(519)	Sam Wise	3,300	1,650	1,200
(521 1)	George Wood (Batting)	3,300	1,650	1,200
(521 2)	George Wood (Throwing)	3,300	1,650	1,200

H

1953 H-O Instant Oatmeal Records

Baseball playing tips from several star New York players are featured in this set of box-top premium records. For 25 cents and two oatmeal box tops, a set of three of the four records could be ordered by mail. The records are 4-3/4" in

diameter and have a color player portrait with facsimile autograph on the back side, while the grooved recording side has an action pose in black-and-white.

	NM	EX	VG
Complete Set (4):	1,050	525.00	315.00
Common Player:	160.00	80.00	48.00
(1) Roy Campanella	350.00	175.00	105.00
(2) "Whitey" Lockman	175.00	87.00	52.00
(3) Allie Reynolds	225.00	110.00	67.00
(4) Duke Snider	350.00	175.00	105.00

1922 Haffner's Big-Tayto-Loaf Bread

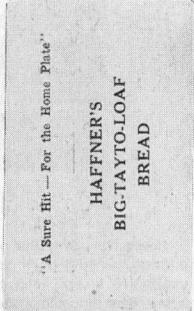

The bakery ad on the back is all that sets this issue apart from the blank-back W575-1 and several other versions with different sponsors named on back. The cards are 2" x 3-1/4" black-and-white. It is unknown whether each of the cards in the W575-1 checklist can be found in the Haffner's version.

PREMIUMS:
Common Players: 5-6X
Hall of Famers: 3-4X
(See W575-1 for checklist and card values.)

1951 Hage's Ice Cream Cleveland Indians

Similar in format to the Pacific Coast League cards produced by the dairy from 1949-51, these cards feature former members of the San Diego Padres, then a farm club of the Indians. Cards measure 2-5/8" x 3-1/8" and are printed in tones of sepia and green. Fronts have posed action photos similar to those found on contemporary Num Num and team photo pack pictures. A small white box on front has the player name and "CLEVELAND." There is a white border around the front photo. Backs are blank and unnumbered; the cards are presented here in alphabetical order.

	NM	EX	VG
Complete Set (6):	5,000	2,500	1,500
Common Player:	850.00	425.00	250.00
(1) Ray Boone	850.00	425.00	250.00
(2) Allie Clark	850.00	425.00	250.00
(3) Jesse Flores	850.00	425.00	250.00
(4) Johnny Gorsica	400.00	200.00	100.00
(5) Dennis Luby (fielding)	375.00	185.00	110.00
(6) Al Olsen	850.00	425.00	250.00
(7) Al Rosen	900.00	450.00	270.00
(8) Harry Simpson	300.00	150.00	90.00
(9) George Zuverink	850.00	425.00	250.00

1888 Joseph Hall Cabinets

These cabinet-sized (6-1/2" x 4-1/2") cards feature team photos taken by Joseph Hall, a well-known photographer of the day. Extremely rare, all have Hall's name beneath the photo and some include his Brooklyn address. The team is identified in large capital letters with the individual players

identified in smaller type on both sides. Fourteen teams are known to date, but others may also exist, and Hall may have produced similar team cabinets in other years as well.

		NM	EX	VG
Common Team:		6,000	3,000	1,800
(1)	Athletic Ball Club, 1888	12,000	6,000	3,600
(2)	Baltimore Ball Club, 1888	16,800	8,400	5,000
(3)	Boston Ball Club, 1888	18,000	9,000	5,400
(4)	Brooklyn Ball Club, 1888	21,000	10,500	6,300
(5)	Chicago Ball Club, 1888	42,000	21,000	12,000
(6)	Cincinnati Ball Club, 1888	18,000	9,000	5,400
(7)	Cleveland Ball Club, 1888	15,000	7,500	4,500
(8)	Detroit Ball Club, 1888	19,200	9,600	5,800
(9)	Indianapolis Ball Club, 1888	18,000	9,000	5,400
(10)	Kansas City Ball Club, 1888	21,000	10,500	6,300
(11)	Louisville Ball Club, 1888	15,000	7,500	4,500
(12)	New York Ball Club, League Champions - 1889 (Wearing baseball uniforms.)	27,000	13,500	8,100
(13)	New York Ball Club, 1888 (Wearing tuxedos.)	22,000	11,000	6,660
(14)	St. Louis Baseball Club, 1888	15,000	7,500	4,500
(15)	Washington Baseball Club, 1888	48,000	24,000	14,400

1888 Joseph Hall Imperial Cabinets

Besides the standard-sized team-photo cabinet cards, super-sized versions of some (possibly all) teams were also available in a format known to collectors as an imperial cabinet. The large pictures use the same photos as the regular cabinets, enlarged to sizes as diverse as approximately 13" x 10" and 24" x 19" and mounted on heavy black or white backing boards. Printed on the mount in gold are the team name, date, player names and the Joseph Hall studio identification. Only those teams which have actually been observed in this format are listed here, with values generally set by their infrequent appearances in hobby auctions.

	NM	EX	VG
Cincinnati Ball Club, 1888 (13" x 10")	13,750	6,350	3,750
New York Ball Club/1888 (13" x 10")	20,625	9,525	5,625
St. Louis Ball Club - 1888 (24" x 19")	13,750	6,350	3,750

1908 Hall's Studio N.Y. Giants Cabinets

Members of the N.Y. Giants are pictured in this series of approximately 4-1/2" x 6-1/2" cabinet photos from New York City photographer, Hall's Studio. The players are all identically posed bare-headed in white shirts buttoned at the collar. It is unknown whether this checklist is complete.

	NM	EX	VG
Common Player:	600.00	300.00	180.00
(1) Al Bridwell	600.00	300.00	180.00
(2) Doc Crandall	600.00	300.00	180.00
(3) Larry Doyle	600.00	300.00	180.00
(4) Buck Herzog	600.00	300.00	180.00
(5) Rube Marquard	800.00	400.00	240.00
(6) John McGraw	800.00	400.00	240.00
(7) Fred Merkle	600.00	300.00	180.00

1939-43 Hall of Fame Sepia Postcards

The first Hall of Fame postcards were issued in two types between 1939-1943. They share an identical format and are differentiated by the typography on back, one set having been issued prior to the Hall of Fame's opening in June, 1939, and a later version issued after the opening. The 3-1/2" x 5-1/2" cards are similar in format to the later series printed in black-and-white and various colors, but this initial effort is printed in sepia on a cream-colored background. Most fronts picture the plaque of one of the 25 first inductees, with a wide bottom border to accomodate an autograph. Designated Type 1, this issue has a back caption which ends with, "National interest centers in the Centennial Celebration in 1939 at Cooperstown." The later version, Type 2, ends its description, "The National Base Ball Museum and Hall of Fame and Doubleday Field are maintained here as a Shrine to the national game." On both types, vertically at centers is a credit line "Pub. by National Base Ball Museum." At right are a stamp box and line for the mailing address. The unnumbered cards are listed here in alphabetical order within type.

		NM	EX	VG
	Complete Set, Type 1 (35):	2,800	1,400	840.00
	Complete Set, Type 2 (37):	3,250	1,625	975.00
	Common Card:	60.00	30.00	18.00
	TYPE 1			
(1)	G.C. Alexander	100.00	50.00	30.00
(2)	Adrian Anson	100.00	50.00	30.00
(3)	Morgan Bulkeley	100.00	50.00	30.00
(4)	Alexander Cartwright	100.00	50.00	30.00
(5)	Henry Chadwick	100.00	50.00	30.00
(6)	Ty Cobb	225.00	110.00	65.00
(7)	Eddie Collins	100.00	50.00	30.00
(8)	Chas. Comiskey	100.00	50.00	30.00
(9)	Candy Cummings	100.00	50.00	30.00
(10)	Buck Ewing	100.00	50.00	30.00
(11)	Ban Johnson	100.00	50.00	30.00
(12)	Walter Johnson	175.00	85.00	50.00
(13)	Willie Keeler	100.00	50.00	30.00
(14)	Napoleon Lajoie	100.00	50.00	30.00
(15)	Connie Mack	100.00	50.00	30.00
(16)	Christy Mathewson	175.00	85.00	50.00
(17)	John McGraw	100.00	50.00	30.00
(18)	Chas. Radbourne	100.00	50.00	30.00
(19)	Babe Ruth	450.00	225.00	135.00
(20)	George Sisler	100.00	50.00	30.00
(21)	Al Spalding	100.00	50.00	30.00
(22)	Tris Speaker	100.00	50.00	30.00
(23)	Honus Wagner	200.00	100.00	60.00
(24)	George Wright	100.00	50.00	30.00
(25)	Cy Young	150.00	75.00	45.00
(26)	The Abner Doubleday Baseball	50.00	25.00	15.00
(27)	Abner Doubleday, Major Gen'l	50.00	25.00	15.00
(28)	Doubleday Field in its Original State	50.00	25.00	15.00
(29)	Doubleday Field in 1938	50.00	25.00	15.00
(30)	Exhibition Game on Doubleday Field	50.00	25.00	15.00
(31)	Exterior - Ntl. Baseball Hall of Fame (no title on front)	50.00	25.00	15.00
(32)	Interior - Ntl. Baseball Museum	50.00	25.00	15.00
(33)	The Bust of Christy Mathewson	50.00	25.00	15.00
(34)	Entrance of the Hall of Fame	50.00	25.00	15.00
(35)	Ntl. Baseball Museum "Immortals"	50.00	25.00	15.00
	TYPE 2			
(1)	G.C. Alexander	100.00	50.00	30.00
(2)	Adrian Anson	100.00	50.00	30.00
(3)	Morgan Bulkeley	100.00	50.00	30.00
(4)	Alexander Cartwright	100.00	50.00	30.00
(5)	Henry Chadwick	100.00	50.00	30.00
(6)	Ty Cobb	225.00	110.00	65.00
(7)	Eddie Collins	100.00	50.00	30.00
(8)	Charles Comiskey	100.00	50.00	30.00
(9)	Candy Cummings	100.00	50.00	30.00
(10)	Buck Ewing	100.00	50.00	30.00
(11)	Lou Gehrig	300.00	150.00	90.00
(12)	Rogers Hornsby	125.00	65.00	35.00
(13)	Ban Johnson	100.00	50.00	30.00
(14)	Walter Johnson	175.00	85.00	50.00
(15)	Willie Keeler	100.00	50.00	30.00
(16)	Napoleon Lajoie	100.00	50.00	30.00
(17)	Connie Mack	100.00	50.00	30.00
(18)	Christy Mathewson	175.00	85.00	50.00
(19)	John McGraw	100.00	50.00	30.00
(20)	Chas. Radbourne	100.00	50.00	30.00
(21)	Babe Ruth	450.00	225.00	135.00
(22)	George Sisler	100.00	50.00	30.00
(23)	Al Spalding	100.00	50.00	30.00
(24)	Tris Speaker	100.00	50.00	30.00
(25)	Honus Wagner	200.00	100.00	60.00
(26)	George Wright	100.00	50.00	30.00
(27)	Cy Young	150.00	75.00	45.00
(28)	The Abner Doubleday Baseball	50.00	25.00	15.00
(29)	Abner Doubleday, Major Gen'l	50.00	25.00	15.00
(30)	Doubleday Field in its Original State	50.00	25.00	15.00
(31)	Doubleday Field in 1938	50.00	25.00	15.00
(32)	Exhibition Game on Doubleday Field	50.00	25.00	15.00
(33)	Exterior - Ntl. Baseball Hall of Fame	50.00	25.00	15.00
(34)	Interior - Ntl. Baseball Hall of Fame	50.00	25.00	15.00
(35)	The Bust of Christy Mathewson	50.00	25.00	15.00
(36)	Entrance of the Hall of Fame	50.00	25.00	15.00
(37)	Ntl. Baseball Museum - "Immortals"	50.00	25.00	15.00

1944-63 Hall of Fame Black-and-White Plaque Postcards

(See listings cataloged under Albertype and Artvue.)

1939-63 Hall of Fame B/W Plaque Postcards - Autographed

Collecting Hall of Fame plaque postcards autographed by inductees has long been popular in the hobby. Obviously, completion of a set is impossible because many Hall of Famers have been inducted posthumously. Generally, the value of a genuinely autographed HoF plaque postcard is not so much dependent on star status of the player, but on the perception of how many such cards could have been autographed in his remaining lifetime. Players who died within months of their induction or who were un-cooperative with autograph requests have cards that are far more valuable than many players of greater renown. While the majority of the players checklisted here could have signed both Albertye and Artvue cards, some players are possible only on the latter brand because their induction or death happened after 1952. Values quoted are for cards signed on the front. Cards signed on back can be worth 50 percent less.

	NM	EX	VG
Complete Set (55): Value Undetermined			
G.C. Alexander	1,250	1,125	935.00
Frank Baker	1,600	1,450	1,200
Ed Barrow	1,500	1,350	1,125
Chief Bender	550.00	500.00	410.00
Jesse Burkett	1,100	990.00	825.00
Max Carey	100.00	90.00	75.00
Fred Clarke	1,700	1,525	1,275
Ty Cobb	2,500	2,250	1,875
Mickey Cochrane	1,500	1,350	1,125
Eddie Collins	8,000	7,200	6,000
Tom Connolly	3,000	2,700	2,250
Sam Crawford	550.00	500.00	410.00
Joe Cronin	200.00	180.00	150.00
Dizzy Dean	325.00	290.00	245.00
Bill Dickey	150.00	135.00	110.00
Joe DiMaggio	550.00	500.00	410.00
Hugh Duffy	1,500	1,350	1,125
Johnny Evers	450.00	400.00	335.00
Bob Feller	35.00	30.00	25.00
Elmer Flick	500.00	450.00	375.00
Jimmie Foxx	4,000	3,600	3,000
Frankie Frisch	400.00	360.00	300.00
Lou Gehrig (Sepia only.)	2,000	1,800	1,500
Charlie Gehringer	60.00	55.00	45.00
Hank Greenberg	325.00	290.00	245.00
Clark Griffith	2,750	2,475	2,050
Lefty Grove	250.00	225.00	185.00
Gabby Hartnett	475.00	425.00	355.00
Rogers Hornsby	1,600	1,450	1,200
Carl Hubbell	65.00	58.00	49.00
(Deduct 33 percent for post-stroke signature.)			
Walter Johnson	1,400	1,250	1,050
Nap Lajoie	2,500	2,250	1,875
Ted Lyons	300.00	275.00	225.00
Connie Mack	1,450	1,300	1,100
Joe McCarthy	200.00	180.00	150.00
Bill McKechnie	900.00	810.00	675.00
Kid Nichols	3,500	3,150	2,625
Mel Ott	1,600	1,450	1,200
Sam Rice	175.00	155.00	130.00
Eppa Rixey (Possible but unlikely.)			
Jackie Robinson	2,250	2,025	1,675
Edd Roush	75.00	65.00	55.00
Babe Ruth (Value Undetermined)			
Ray Schalk	500.00	450.00	375.00
Al Simmons	1,750	1,575	1,300
George Sisler	500.00	450.00	375.00
Tris Speaker	1,500	1,350	1,125

	NM	EX	VG
Bill Terry	60.00	55.00	45.00
Joe Tinker	550.00	500.00	410.00
Pie Traynor	850.00	765.00	635.00
Dazzy Vance	1,700	1,525	1,275
Honus Wagner	2,800	2,525	2,100
Bobby Wallace	2,000	1,800	1,500
Ed Walsh	1,250	1,125	935.00
Paul Waner	1,550	1,400	1,150
Zack Wheat	650.00	585.00	485.00
Cy Young	2,400	2,150	1,800

1963 Hall of Fame Picture Pack

The attributed date is only approximate for this set of 5" x 7" black-and-white, blank-back pictures sold by the Hall of Fame. In the wide border beneath the player photo are identification, teams and years played, a few stats and induction year along with an HoF logo. Some of the same pictures were repeated in the later version of the issue.

		NM	EX	VG
	Complete Set (24):	40.00	20.00	12.00
	Common Player:	3.00	1.50	.90
(1)	Grover Alexander	4.00	2.00	1.25
(2)	Ty Cobb	6.00	3.00	1.75
(3)	Mickey Cochrane	3.00	1.50	.90
(4)	Eddie Collins	3.00	1.50	.90
(5)	Joe Cronin	3.00	1.50	.90
(6)	Bill Dickey	3.00	1.50	.90
(7)	Joe DiMaggio	7.50	3.75	2.25
(8)	Bob Feller	4.00	2.00	1.25
(9)	Frank Frisch	3.00	1.50	.90
(10)	Lou Gehrig	7.50	3.75	2.25
(11)	Rogers Hornsby	3.00	1.50	.90
(12)	Walter Johnson	4.00	2.00	1.25
(13)	Connie Mack	3.00	1.50	.90
(14)	Christy Mathewson	4.00	2.00	1.25
(15)	John McGraw	3.00	1.50	.90
(16)	Jackie Robinson	5.00	2.50	1.50
(17)	Babe Ruth	10.00	5.00	3.00
(18)	George Sisler	3.00	1.50	.90
(19)	Tris Speaker	3.00	1.50	.90
(20)	Bill Terry	3.00	1.50	.90
(21)	Pie Traynor	3.00	1.50	.90
(22)	Honus Wagner	4.00	2.00	1.25
(23)	Paul Waner	3.00	1.50	.90
(24)	Cy Young	4.00	2.00	1.25

1973 Hall of Fame Picture Pack

This set of 5" x 6-3/4" black-and-white player photos picture "Baseball's Greats Enshrined at Cooperstown, N.Y." Player career data is printed in the wide white border at bottom and there is a Hall of Fame logo at lower-left. The unnumbered pictures are listed here in alphabetical order.

		NM	EX	VG
	Complete Set (20):	20.00	10.00	6.00
	Common Player:	2.00	1.00	.60
(1)	Yogi Berra	3.00	1.50	.90
(2)	Roy Campanella	3.00	1.50	.90
(3)	Ty Cobb	4.00	2.00	1.25
(4)	Joe Cronin	2.50	1.25	.70
(5)	Dizzy Dean	3.00	1.50	.90
(6)	Joe DiMaggio	7.50	3.75	2.25
(7)	Bob Feller	3.00	1.50	.90
(8)	Lou Gehrig	7.50	3.75	2.25
(9)	Rogers Hornsby	3.00	1.50	.90
(10)	Sandy Koufax	5.00	2.50	1.50
(11)	Christy Mathewson	3.00	1.50	.90
(12)	Stan Musial	3.00	1.50	.90
(13)	Satchel Paige	3.00	1.50	.90
(14)	Jackie Robinson	5.00	2.50	1.50
(15)	Babe Ruth	10.00	5.00	3.00
(16)	Warren Spahn	2.50	1.25	.70
(17)	Casey Stengel	3.00	1.50	.90
(18)	Honus Wagner	3.00	1.50	.90
(19)	Ted Williams	5.00	2.50	1.50
(20)	Cy Young	3.00	1.50	.90

1979 Hall of Fame (Dexter Press) Plaque Postcards

This short-lived series, begun no later than 1979, features the Hall of Fame inductees' plaques on bright backgrounds of red, orange, blue and green. Because of the cards' color and finish, they are difficult to autograph.

		NM	EX	VG
	Complete Set (53):	350.00	175.00	105.00
	Common Player:	6.00	3.00	1.75
(1)	Grover Alexander	6.00	3.00	1.75
(2)	Lou Boudreau	6.00	3.00	1.75
(3)	Roy Campanella	10.00	5.00	3.00
(4)	Roberto Clemente	20.00	10.00	6.00
(5)	Ty Cobb	15.00	7.50	4.50
(6)	Stan Coveleski	6.00	3.00	1.75
(7)	Sam Crawford	6.00	3.00	1.75
(8)	Martin Dihigo	6.00	3.00	1.75
(9)	Joe DiMaggio	22.50	11.00	6.75
(10)	Billy Evans	6.00	3.00	1.75
(11)	Johnny Evers	6.00	3.00	1.75
(12)	Red Faber	6.00	3.00	1.75
(13)	Elmer Flick	6.00	3.00	1.75
(14)	Ford Frick	6.00	3.00	1.75
(15)	Frank Frisch	6.00	3.00	1.75
(16)	Pud Galvin	6.00	3.00	1.75
(17)	Lou Gehrig	20.00	10.00	6.00
(18)	Warren Giles	6.00	3.00	1.75
(19)	Will Harridge	6.00	3.00	1.75
(20)	Harry Heilmann	6.00	3.00	1.75
(21)	Harry Hooper	6.00	3.00	1.75
(22)	Waite Hoyt	6.00	3.00	1.75
(23)	Miller Huggins	6.00	3.00	1.75
(24)	Judy Johnson	6.00	3.00	1.75
(25)	Addie Joss	6.00	3.00	1.75
(26)	Tim Keefe	6.00	3.00	1.75
(27)	Willie Keeler	6.00	3.00	1.75
(28)	George Kelly	6.00	3.00	1.75
(29)	Sandy Koufax	15.00	7.50	4.50
(30)	Nap Lajoie	6.00	3.00	1.75
(31)	Pop Lloyd	6.00	3.00	1.75
(32)	Connie Mack	6.00	3.00	1.75
(33)	Larry MacPhail	6.00	3.00	1.75
(34)	Mickey Mantle	25.00	12.50	7.50
(35)	Heinie Manush	6.00	3.00	1.75
(36)	Eddie Mathews	6.00	3.00	1.75
(37)	Willie Mays	15.00	7.50	4.50
(38)	Ducky Medwick	6.00	3.00	1.75
(39)	Stan Musial	12.00	6.00	3.50
(40)	Herb Pennock	6.00	3.00	1.75
(41)	Edd Roush	6.00	3.00	1.75
(42)	Babe Ruth	25.00	12.50	7.50
(43)	Amos Rusie	6.00	3.00	1.75
(44)	Ray Schalk	6.00	3.00	1.75
(45)	Al Simmons	6.00	3.00	1.75
(46)	Albert Spalding	6.00	3.00	1.75
(47)	Joe Tinker	6.00	3.00	1.75
(48)	Pie Traynor	6.00	3.00	1.75
(49)	Dazzy Vance	6.00	3.00	1.75
(50)	Lloyd Waner	6.00	3.00	1.75
(51)	Ted Williams	20.00	10.00	6.00
(52)	Hack Wilson	6.00	3.00	1.75
(53)	Ross Youngs	6.00	3.00	1.75

1979 HoF (Dexter Press) Plaque Postcards - Autographed

		NM	EX	VG
(2)	Lou Boudreau	30.00	27.00	22.00
(3)	Roy Campanella (Value Undetermined)			
(6)	Stan Coveleski	50.00	45.00	37.00
(9)	Joe DiMaggio	350.00	315.00	260.00
(22)	Waite Hoyt	100.00	90.00	75.00
(24)	Judy Johnson	65.00	60.00	50.00
(28)	George Kelly	75.00	65.00	55.00
(29)	Sandy Koufax	150.00	135.00	110.00
(34)	Mickey Mantle	400.00	360.00	300.00
(36)	Eddie Mathews	50.00	45.00	37.00
(37)	Willie Mays	50.00	45.00	37.00
(39)	Stan Musial	25.00	22.00	18.50
(41)	Edd Roush	50.00	45.00	37.00
(50)	Lloyd Waner	50.00	45.00	37.00
(51)	Ted Williams	300.00	270.00	225.00

1964-Date Hall of Fame Yellow Plaque Postcards

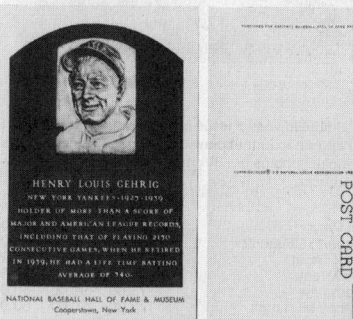

Since 1964 a number of related series of Hall of Fame Plaque Postcards have been produced by a pair of printers. The 3-1/2" x 5-1/2" postcards were first produced by Curteich-color and, later, by Mike Roberts Color Productions. Like earlier HoF postcards, these series feature a color photo of an inductee's plaque on a yellow background. Black-and-white backs have a variety of player information, postcard indicia, copyright data and credit lines. Few hobbyists attempt to collect these by issuer, rather trying to assemble a complete set of each player regardless of who did the printing and when.

Prior to 1977, single postcards sold for five cents at the HoF gift shop; in 1977 the price doubled to a dime, with complete sets (about 150) selling for $6. Today a complete set is available from the Hall of Fame for about $45, with singles at 25 cents apiece.

	NM	EX	VG
Complete Set (281)	45.00	22.00	13.50
Common Player:	.50	.25	.15
Hank Aaron	.50	.25	.15
Grover Alexander	.50	.25	.15
Walter Alston	.50	.25	.15
Sparky Anderson	.50	.25	.15
Cap Anson	.50	.25	.15
Luis Aparicio	.50	.25	.15
Luke Appling	.50	.25	.15
Richie Ashburn	.50	.25	.15
Earl Averill	.50	.25	.15
Frank Baker	.50	.25	.15
Dave Bancroft	.50	.25	.15
Ernie Banks	.50	.25	.15
Al Barlick	.50	.25	.15
Ed Barrow	.50	.25	.15
Jake Beckley	.50	.25	.15
Cool Papa Bell	.50	.25	.15
Johnny Bench	.50	.25	.15
Chief Bender	.50	.25	.15
Yogi Berra	.50	.25	.15
Wade Boggs	.50	.25	.15
Jim Bottomley	.50	.25	.15
Lou Boudreau	.50	.25	.15
Roger Bresnahan	.50	.25	.15
George Brett	.50	.25	.15
Lou Brock	.50	.25	.15
Dan Brouthers	.50	.25	.15
Mordecai Brown	.50	.25	.15
Ray Brown	.50	.25	.15
Willard Brown	.50	.25	.15
Morgan Bulkeley	.50	.25	.15
Jim Bunning	.50	.25	.15
Jesse Burkett	.50	.25	.15
Roy Campanella	.50	.25	.15
Rod Carew	.50	.25	.15
Max Carey	.50	.25	.15
Steve Carlton	.50	.25	.15
Gary Carter	.50	.25	.15
Alexander Cartwright	.50	.25	.15
Orlando Cepeda	.50	.25	.15
Henry Chadwick	.50	.25	.15
Frank Chance	.50	.25	.15
A.B. (Happy) Chandler	.50	.25	.15
Oscar Charleston	.50	.25	.15
Jack Chesbro	.50	.25	.15
Nestor Chylak	.50	.25	.15
Fred Clarke	.50	.25	.15
John Clarkson	.50	.25	.15
Roberto Clemente	.50	.25	.15
Ty Cobb	.50	.25	.15
Mickey Cochrane	.50	.25	.15
Eddie Collins	.50	.25	.15
Jimmy Collins	.50	.25	.15
Earle Combs	.50	.25	.15
Charles Comiskey	.50	.25	.15
Jocko Conlan	.50	.25	.15
Tom Connolly	.50	.25	.15
Roger Connor	.50	.25	.15
Andy Cooper	.50	.25	.15
Stan Coveleski	.50	.25	.15
Sam Crawford	.50	.25	.15
Joe Cronin	.50	.25	.15
Candy Cummings	.50	.25	.15
Kiki Cuyler	.50	.25	.15
Ray Dandridge	.50	.25	.15
George Davis	.50	.25	.15
Leon Day	.50	.25	.15
Dizzy Dean	.50	.25	.15
Ed Delahanty	.50	.25	.15
Bill Dickey	.50	.25	.15
Martin Dihigo	.50	.25	.15
Joe DiMaggio	.50	.25	.15
Larry Doby	.50	.25	.15
Bobby Doerr	.50	.25	.15
Barney Dreyfuss	.50	.25	.15
Don Drysdale	.50	.25	.15
Hugh Duffy	.50	.25	.15
Leo Durocher	.50	.25	.15
Dennis Eckersley	.50	.25	.15
Billy Evans	.50	.25	.15
Johnny Evers	.50	.25	.15
Buck Ewing	.50	.25	.15
Red Faber	.50	.25	.15
Bob Feller	.50	.25	.15
Rick Ferrell	.50	.25	.15
Rollie Fingers	.50	.25	.15
Carlton Fisk	.50	.25	.15
Elmer Flick	.50	.25	.15
Whitey Ford	.50	.25	.15
Bill Foster	.50	.25	.15
Rube Foster	.50	.25	.15
Nellie Fox	.50	.25	.15
Jimmie Foxx	.50	.25	.15
Ford Frick	.50	.25	.15
Frank Frisch	.50	.25	.15
Pud Galvin	.50	.25	.15
Lou Gehrig	.50	.25	.15
Charlie Gehringer	.50	.25	.15
Bob Gibson	.50	.25	.15
Josh Gibson	.50	.25	.15
Warren Giles	.50	.25	.15
Lefty Gomez	.50	.25	.15
Goose Goslin	.50	.25	.15
Rich "Goose" Gossage	.50	.25	.15
Frank Grant	.50	.25	.15
Hank Greenberg	.50	.25	.15
Clark Griffith	.50	.25	.15
Burleigh Grimes	.50	.25	.15
Lefty Grove	.50	.25	.15
Tony Gwynn	.50	.25	.15
Chick Hafey	.50	.25	.15
Jesse Haines	.50	.25	.15
Billy Hamilton	.50	.25	.15
Ned Hanlon	.50	.25	.15
Will Harridge	.50	.25	.15
Bucky Harris	.50	.25	.15
Gabby Hartnett	.50	.25	.15
Harry Heilmann	.50	.25	.15
Billy Herman	.50	.25	.15
Pete Hill	.50	.25	.15
Harry Hooper	.50	.25	.15
Rogers Hornsby	.50	.25	.15
Waite Hoyt	.50	.25	.15
Cal Hubbard	.50	.25	.15
Carl Hubbell	.50	.25	.15
Miller Huggins	.50	.25	.15
William Hulbert	.50	.25	.15
Catfish Hunter	.50	.25	.15
Monte Irvin	.50	.25	.15
Reggie Jackson	.50	.25	.15
Travis Jackson	.50	.25	.15
Fergie Jenkins	.50	.25	.15
Hughie Jennings	.50	.25	.15
Ban Johnson	.50	.25	.15
Judy Johnson	.50	.25	.15
Walter Johnson	.50	.25	.15
Addie Joss	.50	.25	.15
Al Kaline	.50	.25	.15
Tim Keefe	.50	.25	.15
Willie Keeler	.50	.25	.15
George Kell	.50	.25	.15
Joe Kelley	.50	.25	.15
George Kelly	.50	.25	.15
Mike "King" Kelly	.50	.25	.15
Harmon Killebrew	.50	.25	.15
Ralph Kiner	.50	.25	.15
Chuck Klein	.50	.25	.15
Bill Klem	.50	.25	.15
Sandy Koufax	.50	.25	.15
Bowie Kuhn	.50	.25	.15
Nap Lajoie	.50	.25	.15
Kenesaw M. Landis	.50	.25	.15
Tommy Lasorda	.50	.25	.15
Tony Lazzeri	.50	.25	.15
Bob Lemon	.50	.25	.15
Buck Leonard	.50	.25	.15
Freddie Lindstrom	.50	.25	.15
Pop Lloyd	.50	.25	.15
Ernie Lombardi	.50	.25	.15
Al Lopez	.50	.25	.15
Ted Lyons	.50	.25	.15
Connie Mack	.50	.25	.15
Biz Mackey	.50	.25	.15
Larry MacPhail	.50	.25	.15
Effa "Effie" Manley	.50	.25	.15
Mickey Mantle	.50	.25	.15
Heinie Manush	.50	.25	.15
Rabbit Maranville	.50	.25	.15
Juan Marichal	.50	.25	.15
Rube Marquard	.50	.25	.15
Eddie Mathews	.50	.25	.15
Christy Mathewson	.50	.25	.15
Willie Mays	.50	.25	.15
Bill Mazeroski	.50	.25	.15
Joe McCarthy	.50	.25	.15
Tommy McCarthy	.50	.25	.15
Willie McCovey	.50	.25	.15
Joe McGinnity	.50	.25	.15
Bill McGowan	.50	.25	.15
John McGraw	.50	.25	.15
Bill McKechnie	.50	.25	.15
Lee MacPhail	.50	.25	.15
Bid McPhee	.50	.25	.15
Ducky Medwick	.50	.25	.15
Jose Mendez	.50	.25	.15
Johnny Mize	.50	.25	.15
Paul Molitor	.50	.25	.15
Joe Morgan	.50	.25	.15
Eddie Murray	.50	.25	.15
Stan Musial	.50	.25	.15
Hal Newhouser	.50	.25	.15
Kid Nichols	.50	.25	.15
Phil Niekro	.50	.25	.15
Walter O'Malley	.50	.25	.15
Jim O'Rourke	.50	.25	.15
Mel Ott	.50	.25	.15
Satchel Paige	.50	.25	.15
Jim Palmer	.50	.25	.15
Herb Pennock	.50	.25	.15
Tony Perez	.50	.25	.15
Gaylord Perry	.50	.25	.15
Ed Plank	.50	.25	.15
Alex Pompez	.50	.25	.15
Cum Posey	.50	.25	.15
Kirby Puckett	.50	.25	.15
Charles Radbourne	.50	.25	.15
Pee Wee Reese	.50	.25	.15
Sam Rice	.50	.25	.15
Cal Ripken Jr.	.50	.25	.15
Branch Rickey	.50	.25	.15
Eppa Rixey	.50	.25	.15
Phil Rizzuto	.50	.25	.15
Robin Roberts	.50	.25	.15
Brooks Robinson	.50	.25	.15
Frank Robinson	.50	.25	.15
Jackie Robinson	.50	.25	.15
Wilbert Robinson	.50	.25	.15
Bullet Rogan	.50	.25	.15
Edd Roush	.50	.25	.15
Red Ruffing	.50	.25	.15
Amos Rusie	.50	.25	.15
Babe Ruth	.50	.25	.15
Nolan Ryan	.50	.25	.15
Ryne Sandberg	.50	.25	.15
Louis Santop	.50	.25	.15
Ray Schalk	.50	.25	.15
Mike Schmidt	.50	.25	.15

Red Schoendienst	.50	.25	.15
Tom Seaver	.50	.25	.15
Frank Selee	.50	.25	.15
Joe Sewell	.50	.25	.15
Al Simmons	.50	.25	.15
George Sisler	.50	.25	.15
Enos Slaughter	.50	.25	.15
Hilton Smith	.50	.25	.15
Ozzie Smith	.50	.25	.15
Duke Snider	.50	.25	.15
Billy Southworth	.50	.25	.15
Warren Spahn	.50	.25	.15
Albert Spalding	.50	.25	.15
Tris Speaker	.50	.25	.15
Willie Stargell	.50	.25	.15
Turkey Stearnes	.50	.25	.15
Casey Stengel	.50	.25	.15
Mule Suttles	.50	.25	.15
Don Sutton	.50	.25	.15
Ben Taylor	.50	.25	.15
Bill Terry	.50	.25	.15
Sam Thompson	.50	.25	.15
Joe Tinker	.50	.25	.15
Cristobal Torriente	.50	.25	.15
Paul Traynor	.50	.25	.15
Dazzy Vance	.50	.25	.15
Arky Vaughan	.50	.25	.15
Bill Veeck	.50	.25	.15
Rube Waddell	.50	.25	.15
Honus Wagner	.50	.25	.15
Bobby Wallace	.50	.25	.15
Ed Walsh	.50	.25	.15
Lloyd Waner	.50	.25	.15
Paul Waner	.50	.25	.15
Monte Ward	.50	.25	.15
Earl Weaver	.50	.25	.15
George Weiss	.50	.25	.15
Mickey Welch	.50	.25	.15
Willie Wells	.50	.25	.15
Zack Wheat	.50	.25	.15
Sol White	.50	.25	.15
Hoyt Wilhelm	.50	.25	.15
J.L. Wilkinson	.50	.25	.15
Billy Williams	.50	.25	.15
Dick Williams	.50	.25	.15
Joe Williams	.50	.25	.15
Ted Williams	.50	.25	.15
	.50		
Vic Willis	.50	.25	.15
Hack Wilson	.50	.25	.15
Jud Wilson	.50	.25	.15
Dave Winfield	.50	.25	.15
George Wright	.50	.25	.15
Harry Wright	.50	.25	.15
Early Wynn	.50	.25	.15
Carl Yastrzemski	.50	.25	.15
Tom Yawkey	.50	.25	.15
Cy Young	.50	.25	.15
Ross Youngs	.50	.25	.15
Robin Yount	.50	.25	.15

1964-Date Hall of Fame Yellow Plaque Postcards - Autographed

This listing represents the Curteichcolor and Mike Roberts yellow Hall of Fame plaque postcards which are known to exist, or in a few cases are theoretically possible. Value of genuinely autographed HoF plaque postcards is not so much dependent on star status of the player, but on perception of how many such cards could exist given the time the player remained alive and in good health following his selection at Cooperstown. Players who died or were incapacitated shortly after induction may have more valuable autographed cards than currently living players of greater renown. Values quoted are for cards autographed on front; cards signed on the back can be worth 50 percent less.

	NM	EX	VG
Hank Aaron	55.00	45.00	35.00
Walter Alston	150.00	120.00	90.00
Sparky Anderson	55.00	45.00	35.00
Luis Aparicio	15.00	12.00	9.00
Luke Appling	20.00	16.00	12.00
Richie Ashburn	55.00	45.00	35.00
Earl Averill	50.00	40.00	30.00
Dave Bancroft	2,250	1,800	1,350
Ernie Banks	45.00	35.00	25.00
Al Barlick	15.00	12.00	9.00
Cool Papa Bell	50.00	40.00	30.00
Johnny Bench	45.00	36.00	27.00
Yogi Berra	25.00	20.00	15.00

Wade Boggs	50.00	40.00	30.00
Lou Boudreau	15.00	12.00	9.00
George Brett	125.00	100.00	75.00
Lou Brock	30.00	24.00	18.00
Jim Bunning	40.00	32.00	24.00
Roy Campanella (Value Undetermined)			
Rod Carew	50.00	40.00	30.00
Max Carey	60.00	50.00	35.00
Steve Carlton	35.00	30.00	20.00
Gary Carter	100.00	80.00	60.00
Orlando Cepeda	35.00	30.00	20.00
A.B. (Happy) Chandler	20.00	16.00	12.00
Earle Combs	300.00	240.00	180.00
Jocko Conlan	25.00	20.00	15.00
Stan Coveleski	30.00	24.00	18.00
"Stanislaus Kowalewski"	150.00	120.00	90.00
Sam Crawford	600.00	480.00	360.00
Joe Cronin	50.00	40.00	30.00
Ray Dandridge	15.00	12.00	9.00
Dizzy Dean	300.00	240.00	180.00
Bill Dickey	50.00	40.00	30.00
Joe DiMaggio	225.00	180.00	135.00
Larry Doby	90.00	70.00	50.00
Bobby Doerr	7.50	6.00	4.50
Don Drysdale	45.00	35.00	25.00
Dennis Eckersley	75.00	60.00	45.00
Red Faber	165.00	130.00	100.00
Bob Feller	7.50	6.00	4.50
Rick Ferrell	15.00	12.00	9.00
Rollie Fingers	20.00	16.00	12.00
Carlton Fisk	80.00	65.00	45.00
Elmer Flick	600.00	480.00	360.00
Whitey Ford	35.00	30.00	20.00
Jimmie Foxx (Usually signed on back.)	1,750	1,400	1,050
Ford Frick	225.00	180.00	135.00
Frank Frisch	300.00	240.00	180.00
Charlie Gehringer	30.00	24.00	18.00
Bob Gibson	30.00	24.00	18.00
Lefty Gomez	35.00	30.00	20.00
Goose Goslin (Usually signed on back; value of such $750-1,000.)	2,250	1,800	1,350
Hank Greenberg	175.00	140.00	100.00
Burleigh Grimes	35.00	30.00	20.00
Lefty Grove	160.00	130.00	95.00
Tony Gwynn	150.00	120.00	90.00
Chick Hafey	725.00	580.00	435.00
Jesse Haines	125.00	100.00	75.00
Bucky Harris	325.00	260.00	195.00
Gabby Hartnett	725.00	580.00	435.00
Billy Herman	12.00	9.50	7.25
Harry Hooper	235.00	190.00	140.00
Waite Hoyt	40.00	32.00	24.00
Cal Hubbard	1,250	1,000	750.00
Carl Hubbell (Pre-stroke.)	40.00	32.00	24.00
Carl Hubbell (Post-stroke.)	25.00	20.00	15.00
Catfish Hunter	30.00	24.00	18.00
Monte Irvin	10.00	8.00	6.00
Reggie Jackson	75.00	60.00	45.00
Travis Jackson	30.00	24.00	18.00
Fergie Jenkins	15.00	12.00	9.00
Judy Johnson	30.00	24.00	18.00
Al Kaline	20.00	16.00	12.00
George Kell	7.50	6.00	4.50
George Kelly	40.00	32.00	24.00
Harmon Killebrew	25.00	20.00	15.00
Ralph Kiner	15.00	12.00	9.00
Sandy Koufax	125.00	100.00	75.00
Tommy Lasorda	100.00	80.00	60.00
Bob Lemon	12.00	9.50	7.25
Buck Leonard (Post-stroke autographed cards worth 50 percent.)	15.00	12.00	9.00
Freddie Lindstrom	75.00	60.00	45.00
Al Lopez	40.00	32.00	24.00
Ted Lyons	45.00	35.00	25.00
Lee MacPhail	35.00	28.00	21.00
Mickey Mantle	235.00	190.00	140.00
Heinie Manush	325.00	260.00	195.00
Juan Marichal	15.00	12.00	9.00
Rube Marquard	40.00	32.00	24.00
Eddie Mathews	25.00	20.00	15.00
Willie Mays	50.00	40.00	30.00
Bill Mazeroski	50.00	40.00	30.00
Joe McCarthy	80.00	65.00	45.00
Willie McCovey	35.00	28.00	21.00
Bill McKechnie (Possible, not likely.)			
Ducky Medwick	185.00	150.00	110.00
Johnny Mize	15.00	12.00	9.00
Paul Molitor	90.00	75.00	55.00
Joe Morgan	30.00	24.00	18.00
Eddie Murray	125.00	100.00	75.00
Stan Musial	25.00	20.00	15.00
Hal Newhouser	15.00	12.00	9.00
Phil Niekro	35.00	30.00	20.00
Satchel Paige	235.00	190.00	140.00
Jim Palmer	20.00	16.00	12.00
Tony Perez	50.00	40.00	30.00
Gaylord Perry	25.00	20.00	15.00
Kirby Puckett	125.00	100.00	75.00
Pee Wee Reese	45.00	35.00	25.00
Sam Rice	185.00	150.00	110.00
Cal Ripken Jr.	100.00	80.00	60.00
Phil Rizzuto	30.00	24.00	18.00
Robin Roberts	12.50	10.00	7.50
Brooks Robinson	12.50	10.00	7.50
Frank Robinson	25.00	20.00	15.00
Jackie Robinson (Often signed on back; value of such $550.)	1,600	1,275	960.00
Edd Roush	30.00	24.00	18.00
Red Ruffing	200.00	160.00	120.00
Nolan Ryan	65.00	50.00	40.00
Ryne Sandberg	60.00	45.00	35.00
Ray Schalk	450.00	360.00	270.00

Mike Schmidt	80.00	65.00	50.00
Red Schoendienst	30.00	24.00	18.00
Tom Seaver	40.00	32.00	24.00
Joe Sewell	15.00	12.00	9.00
George Sisler	200.00	160.00	120.00
Enos Slaughter	10.00	8.00	6.00
Ozzie Smith	95.00	75.00	55.00
Duke Snider	20.00	16.00	12.00
Warren Spahn	20.00	16.00	12.00
Willie Stargell	50.00	40.00	30.00
Casey Stengel	225.00	180.00	135.00
Bruce Sutter	60.00	45.00	35.00
Don Sutton	40.00	32.00	24.00
Bill Terry	25.00	20.00	15.00
Pie Traynor	850.00	680.00	510.00
Lloyd Waner	30.00	24.00	18.00
Paul Waner (Possible, not likely.)			
Earl Weaver	35.00	30.00	20.00
George Weiss (Possible, not likely.)			
Zack Wheat	450.00	360.00	270.00
Hoyt Wilhelm	15.00	12.00	9.00
Billy Williams	15.00	12.00	9.00
Ted Williams	200.00	160.00	120.00
Dave Winfield	100.00	80.00	60.00
Early Wynn	25.00	20.00	15.00
Carl Yastrzemski	55.00	45.00	35.00
Robin Yount	150.00	120.00	90.00

1973 Jack Hamilton's "The Pzazz" Postcard

 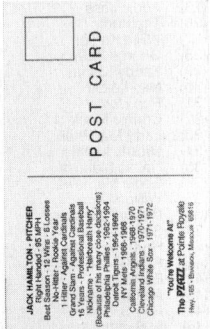

The date attributed is speculative, based on the not totally honest major league career summary printed on the back of this standard-size, black-and-white postcard. The front reproduces a J.D. McCarthy postcard of the pitcher in a New York Mets uniform. There is a white border all around and a facsimile autograph in blue. The back has a few career highlights and advertisement for Hamilton's "The Pzazz" restaurant in Branson, Mo.

	NM	EX	VG
Jack Hamilton	6.00	3.00	1.75

1961 Harmony Milk Pittsburgh Pirates

The attributed year of issue is approximate and subject to change if and when further players are added to the checklist. These premium photos are 8" x 10" in format, round-cornered with blank backs.

	NM	EX	VG
Common Player:	175.00	90.00	50.00
(1) Roberto Clemente	600.00	300.00	180.00
(2) Dick Groat	175.00	90.00	50.00
(3) Don Hoak	175.00	90.00	50.00
(4) Vern Law	175.00	90.00	50.00
(5) Danny Murtaugh	175.00	90.00	50.00

1928 Harrington's Ice Cream

Sharing the same format and checklist with several other (Tharp's, Yeungling's, Sweetman, etc.) contemporary ice cream sets this 60-card set includes all of the top stars of the day. Cards are printed in black-and-white on a 1-3/8" x 2-1/2" format. The player's name and a card number appear either in a strip within the frame of the photo, or printed in the border beneath the photo. Card backs have a redemption offer that includes an ice cream bar in exchange for a Babe Ruth card, or a gallon of ice cream for a complete set of 60.

		NM	EX	VG
	Complete Set (60):	20,000	8,000	4,000
	Common Player:	90.00	35.00	20.00
1	Burleigh Grimes	350.00	140.00	70.00
2	Walter Reuther (Ruether)	90.00	35.00	20.00
3	Joe Dugan	90.00	35.00	20.00
4	Red Faber	350.00	140.00	70.00
5	Gabby Hartnett	350.00	140.00	70.00
6	Babe Ruth	5,000	2,000	1,000
7	Bob Meusel	90.00	35.00	20.00
8	Herb Pennock	350.00	140.00	70.00
9	George Burns	90.00	35.00	20.00
10	Joe Sewell	350.00	140.00	70.00
11	George Uhle	90.00	35.00	20.00
12	Bob O'Farrell	90.00	35.00	20.00
13	Rogers Hornsby	450.00	180.00	90.00
14	"Pie" Traynor	350.00	140.00	70.00
15	Clarence Mitchell	90.00	35.00	20.00
16	Eppa Jepha Rixey	350.00	140.00	70.00
17	Carl Mays	125.00	50.00	25.00
18	Adolfo Luque	100.00	40.00	20.00
19	Dave Bancroft	350.00	140.00	70.00
20	George Kelly	350.00	140.00	70.00
21	Earl (Earle) Combs	350.00	140.00	70.00
22	Harry Heilmann	350.00	140.00	70.00
23	Ray W. Schalk	350.00	140.00	70.00
24	Johnny Mostil	90.00	35.00	20.00
25	Hack Wilson	350.00	140.00	70.00
26	Lou Gehrig	6,000	1,400	700.00
27	Ty Cobb	1,500	600.00	300.00
28	Tris Speaker	450.00	180.00	90.00
29	Tony Lazzeri	350.00	140.00	70.00
30	Waite Hoyt	350.00	140.00	70.00
31	Sherwood Smith	90.00	35.00	20.00
32	Max Carey	350.00	140.00	70.00
33	Eugene Hargrave	90.00	35.00	20.00
34	Miguel L. Gonzalez (Middle initial A.)	100.00	40.00	20.00
35	Joe Judge	90.00	35.00	20.00
36	E.C. (Sam) Rice	350.00	140.00	70.00
37	Earl Sheely	90.00	35.00	20.00
38	Sam Jones	90.00	35.00	20.00
39	Bib (Bibb) A. Falk	90.00	35.00	20.00
40	Willie Kamm	90.00	35.00	20.00
41	Stanley Harris	350.00	140.00	70.00
42	John J. McGraw	350.00	140.00	70.00
43	Artie Nehf	90.00	35.00	20.00
44	Grover Alexander	450.00	180.00	90.00
45	Paul Waner	350.00	140.00	70.00
46	William H. Terry	350.00	140.00	70.00
47	Glenn Wright	90.00	35.00	20.00
48	Earl Smith	90.00	35.00	20.00
49	Leon (Goose) Goslin	350.00	140.00	70.00
50	Frank Frisch	350.00	140.00	70.00
51	Joe Harris	90.00	35.00	20.00
52	Fred (Cy) Williams	90.00	35.00	20.00
53	Eddie Roush	350.00	140.00	70.00
54	George Sisler	350.00	140.00	70.00
55	Ed. Rommel	90.00	35.00	20.00
56	Rogers Peckinpaugh (Roger)	90.00	35.00	20.00
57	Stanley Coveleskie (Coveleski)	350.00	140.00	70.00
58	Lester Bell	90.00	35.00	20.00
59	L. Waner	350.00	140.00	70.00
60	John P. McInnis	90.00	35.00	20.00

1930-1931 Harrison Studio Homestead Grays Postcards

Whether the famed Negro League powerhouse team, the Homestead Grays, were in Little Rock, Ark., for spring training or on a barnstorming tour, they became the subjects of a series of postcards from the local photographer, Harrison Stu-

dio. The cards are in standard postcard format, featuring borderless black-and-white photographic poses. It is likely the checklist here is incomplete.

(1) Josh Gibson (Front/back autographed card sold at auction 4/06 for $81,200.)
(2) Ted Page
(3) Ambrose Reed
(4) Homestead Grays 1930 Team Photo
(5) Homestead Grays 1931 Team Photo

1911-12 Hassan Cigarettes

Prior to its sole sponsorship of the T202 Triplefolders set of 1912, Hassan was one of 10 American Tobacco Co. brands advertising on the backs of 1911 T205 Gold Borders. Two different factories are noted on these backs, No. 30 and No. 649, the former being slightly scarcer, though currently no more valuable. Hassan backs in T205 are printed in green and do not command any significant premium in the market.

(See T202, T205.)

1887 Hastings Cabinets

From the Boston studio of G.H. Hastings, this standard-format (about 3-3/4" x 5-3/4") cabinet card depicts the 19th Century's most popular star in stylish street clothers. Printed beneath the portrait is a copyright line, player and team identification and the logo and address of the studio. Back is blank. It is unknown whether other ballplayers' portraits were produced, though it is likely.

	NM	EX	VG
M.J. Kelly	12,500	5,000	2,500

1952 Hawthorn-Mellody Chicago White Sox Pins

This issue was sponsored by a local dairy. The 1-3/8" diameter pins have sepia lithographs of the players with "Club of Champs" printed above. A non-pictorial membership button is also part of the set. The unnumbered pins are listed here in alphabetical order.

		NM	EX	VG
	Complete Set (11):	400.00	200.00	120.00
	Common Player:	35.00	17.50	10.50
(1)	Ray Coleman	35.00	17.50	10.50
(2)	Sam Dente	35.00	17.50	10.50
(3)	Joe Dobson	35.00	17.50	10.50
(4)	Nelson Fox	80.00	40.00	24.00
(5)	Sherman Lollar	45.00	22.00	13.50
(6)	Bill Pierce	45.00	22.00	13.50

		NM	EX	VG
(7)	Eddie Robinson	35.00	17.50	10.50
(8)	Hector Rodriguez	35.00	17.50	10.50
(9)	Eddie Stewart	35.00	17.50	10.50
(10)	Al Zarilla	35.00	17.50	10.50
(11)	Member's pin	15.00	7.50	4.50

1959 R.H. Hayes Postcards

Whether there are any other player postcards distributed by R.H. Hayes of Kansas is unknown. Produced for Hayes by Dexter Press, which issued cards for Coke in later years, the 3-1/2" x 5-1/2" postcard has a borderless color photo on front with a facsimile autograph at bottom. The postcard back has credit lines for Hayes and Dexter and a short biography of the player.

		NM	EX	VG
(1)	Hank Bauer	45.00	22.50	13.50

1911 Helmar Stamps (T332)

A collectible departure from the traditional tobacco cards of the period, Helmar Cigarettes in 1911 issued a series of small major league baseball player "stamps." The stamps, each measuring approximately 1-1/8" x 1-3/8", feature a black and white player portrait surrounded by a colorful, ornate frame. The stamps were originally issued in a 2" x 2-1/2" glassine envelope which advertised the Helmar brand and promoted "Philately - the Popular European Rage." To date, 181 different player stamps have been found. The set includes as many as 50 different frame designs. The Helmar stamp set has been assigned a T332 designation by the American Card Catalog.

		NM	EX	VG
	Complete Set (180):	8,000	4,000	2,400
	Common Player:	50.00	25.00	15.00
(1)	Babe Adams	50.00	25.00	15.00
(2)	Red Ames	50.00	25.00	15.00
(3)	Jimmy Archer	50.00	25.00	15.00
(4)	Jimmy Austin	50.00	25.00	15.00
(5)	Home Run Baker	100.00	50.00	30.00
(6)	Neal Ball	50.00	25.00	15.00
(7)	Cy Barger	50.00	25.00	15.00
(8)	Jack Barry	50.00	25.00	15.00
(9)	Johnny Bates	50.00	25.00	15.00
(10)	Fred Beck	50.00	25.00	15.00
(11)	Beals Becker	50.00	25.00	15.00
(12)	George Bell	50.00	25.00	15.00
(13)	Chief Bender	100.00	50.00	30.00
(14)	Bob Bescher	50.00	25.00	15.00
(15)	Joe Birmingham	50.00	25.00	15.00
(16)	John Bliss	50.00	25.00	15.00
(17)	Bruno Block	50.00	25.00	15.00
(18)	Ping Bodie	50.00	25.00	15.00
(19)	Roger Bresnahan	100.00	50.00	30.00
(20)	Al Bridwell	50.00	25.00	15.00
(21)	Lew Brockett	50.00	25.00	15.00
(22)	Mordecai Brown	100.00	50.00	30.00
(23)	Bill Burns	50.00	25.00	15.00
(24)	Donie Bush	50.00	25.00	15.00
(25)	Bobby Byrne	50.00	25.00	15.00
(26)	Nixey Callahan	50.00	25.00	15.00
(27)	Howie Camnitz	50.00	25.00	15.00
(28)	Max Carey	100.00	50.00	30.00
(29)	Bill Carrigan	50.00	25.00	15.00
(30)	Frank Chance	100.00	50.00	30.00
(31)	Hal Chase	50.00	25.00	15.00
(32)	Ed Cicotte	80.00	40.00	24.00
(33)	Fred Clarke	100.00	50.00	30.00
(34)	Tommy Clarke	50.00	25.00	15.00
(35)	Ty Cobb	750.00	375.00	225.00
(36)	King Cole	50.00	25.00	15.00
(37)	Eddie Collins (Philadelphia)	100.00	50.00	30.00
(38)	Shano Collins (Chicago)	50.00	25.00	15.00

(39)	Wid Conroy	50.00	25.00	15.00
(40)	Doc Crandall	50.00	25.00	15.00
(41)	Sam Crawford	100.00	50.00	30.00
(42)	Birdie Cree	50.00	25.00	15.00
(43)	Bill Dahlen	50.00	25.00	15.00
(44)	Jake Daubert	50.00	25.00	15.00
(45)	Harry Davis	50.00	25.00	15.00
(46)	Jim Delahanty	50.00	25.00	15.00
(47)	Art Devlin	50.00	25.00	15.00
(48)	Josh Devore	50.00	25.00	15.00
(49)	Mike Donlin	50.00	25.00	15.00
(50)	Wild Bill Donovan	50.00	25.00	15.00
(51)	Red Dooin	50.00	25.00	15.00
(52)	Mickey Doolan	50.00	25.00	15.00
(53)	Patsy Dougherty	50.00	25.00	15.00
(54)	Tom Downey	50.00	25.00	15.00
(55)	Larry Doyle	50.00	25.00	15.00
(56)	Louis Drucke	50.00	25.00	15.00
(57)	Clyde Engle	50.00	25.00	15.00
(58)	Tex Erwin	50.00	25.00	15.00
(59)	Steve Evans	50.00	25.00	15.00
(60)	Johnny Evers	100.00	50.00	30.00
(61)	Jack Ferry	50.00	25.00	15.00
(62)	Ray Fisher	50.00	25.00	15.00
(63)	Art Fletcher	50.00	25.00	15.00
(64)	Russ Ford	50.00	25.00	15.00
(65)	Art Fromme	50.00	25.00	15.00
(66)	Earl Gardner	50.00	25.00	15.00
(67)	Harry Gaspar	50.00	25.00	15.00
(68)	George Gibson	50.00	25.00	15.00
(69)	Roy Golden	50.00	25.00	15.00
(70)	Hank Gowdy	50.00	25.00	15.00
(71)	Peaches Graham	50.00	25.00	15.00
(72)	Eddie Grant	50.00	25.00	15.00
(73)	Dolly Gray	50.00	25.00	15.00
(74)	Clark Griffith	100.00	50.00	30.00
(75)	Bob Groom	50.00	25.00	15.00
(76)	Bob Harmon	50.00	25.00	15.00
(77)	Grover Hartley	50.00	25.00	15.00
(78)	Arnold Hauser	50.00	25.00	15.00
(79)	Buck Herzog	50.00	25.00	15.00
(80)	Dick Hoblitzell	50.00	25.00	15.00
(81)	Solly Hoffman (Hofman)	50.00	25.00	15.00
(82)	Miller Huggins	100.00	50.00	30.00
(83)	Long Tom Hughes	50.00	25.00	15.00
(84)	John Hummel	50.00	25.00	15.00
(85)	Hughie Jennings	100.00	50.00	30.00
(86)	Walter Johnson	275.00	135.00	82.00
(87)	Davy Jones	50.00	25.00	15.00
(88)	Johnny Kling	50.00	25.00	15.00
(89)	Otto Knabe	50.00	25.00	15.00
(90)	Jack Knight	50.00	25.00	15.00
(91)	Ed Konetchy	50.00	25.00	15.00
(92)	Harry Krause	50.00	25.00	15.00
(93)	Nap Lajoie	100.00	50.00	30.00
(94)	Joe Lake	50.00	25.00	15.00
(95)	Frank LaPorte	50.00	25.00	15.00
(96)	Tommy Leach	50.00	25.00	15.00
(97)	Lefty Leifield	50.00	25.00	15.00
(98)	Ed Lennox	50.00	25.00	15.00
(99)	Paddy Livingston	50.00	25.00	15.00
(100)	Hans Lobert	50.00	25.00	15.00
(101)	Harry Lord	50.00	25.00	15.00
(102)	Fred Luderus	50.00	25.00	15.00
(103)	Sherry Magee	50.00	25.00	15.00
(104)	Rube Marquard	100.00	50.00	30.00
(105)	Christy Mathewson	300.00	150.00	90.00
(106)	Al Mattern	50.00	25.00	15.00
(107)	George McBride	50.00	25.00	15.00
(108)	Amby McConnell	50.00	25.00	15.00
(109)	John McGraw	100.00	50.00	30.00
(110)	Harry McIntire (McIntyre)	50.00	25.00	15.00
(111)	Matty McIntyre	50.00	25.00	15.00
(112)	Larry McLean	50.00	25.00	15.00
(113)	Fred Merkle	50.00	25.00	15.00
(114)	Chief Meyers	50.00	25.00	15.00
(115)	Clyde Milan	50.00	25.00	15.00
(116)	Dots Miller	50.00	25.00	15.00
(117)	Mike Mitchell	50.00	25.00	15.00
(118)	Earl Moore	50.00	25.00	15.00
(119)	Pat Moran	50.00	25.00	15.00
(120)	George Moriarty	50.00	25.00	15.00
(121)	Mike Mowrey	50.00	25.00	15.00
(122)	George Mullin	50.00	25.00	15.00
(123)	Danny Murphy	50.00	25.00	15.00
(124)	Red Murray	50.00	25.00	15.00
(125)	Tom Needham	50.00	25.00	15.00
(126)	Rebel Oakes	50.00	25.00	15.00
(127)	Rube Oldring	50.00	25.00	15.00
(128)	Marty O'Toole	50.00	25.00	15.00
(129)	Fred Parent	50.00	25.00	15.00
(130)	Dode Paskert	50.00	25.00	15.00
(131)	Barney Pelty	50.00	25.00	15.00
(132)	Eddie Phelps	50.00	25.00	15.00
(133)	Jack Powell	50.00	25.00	15.00
(134)	Jack Quinn	50.00	25.00	15.00
(135)	Ed Reulbach	50.00	25.00	15.00
(136)	Lew Richie	50.00	25.00	15.00
(137)	Reggie Richter	50.00	25.00	15.00
(138)	Jack Rowan	50.00	25.00	15.00
(139)	Nap Rucker	50.00	25.00	15.00
(140)	Slim Sallee	50.00	25.00	15.00
(141)	Doc Scanlan	50.00	25.00	15.00
(142)	Germany Schaefer	50.00	25.00	15.00
(143)	Boss Schmidt	50.00	25.00	15.00
(144)	Wildfire Schulte	50.00	25.00	15.00
(145)	Jim Scott	50.00	25.00	15.00
(146)	Tillie Shafer	50.00	25.00	15.00
(147)	Dave Shean	50.00	25.00	15.00
(148)	Jimmy Sheckard	50.00	25.00	15.00
(149)	Mike Simon	50.00	25.00	15.00
(150)	Fred Snodgrass	50.00	25.00	15.00
(151)	Tris Speaker	125.00	62.00	37.00
(152)	Oscar Stanage	50.00	25.00	15.00
(153)	Bill Steele	50.00	25.00	15.00
(154)	Harry Stovall	50.00	25.00	15.00
(155)	Gabby Street	50.00	25.00	15.00
(156)	George Suggs	50.00	25.00	15.00

(157)	Billy Sullivan	50.00	25.00	15.00
(158)	Bill Sweeney	50.00	25.00	15.00
(159)	Jeff Sweeney	50.00	25.00	15.00
(160)	Lee Tannehill	50.00	25.00	15.00
(161)	Ira Thomas	50.00	25.00	15.00
(162)	Joe Tinker	100.00	50.00	30.00
(163)	John Titus	50.00	25.00	15.00
(164)	Fred Toney	50.00	25.00	15.00
(165)	Terry Turner	50.00	25.00	15.00
(166)	Hippo Vaughn	50.00	25.00	15.00
(167)	Heinie Wagner	50.00	25.00	15.00
(168)	Bobby Wallace	100.00	50.00	30.00
(169)	Ed Walsh	100.00	50.00	30.00
(170)	Jack Warhop	50.00	25.00	15.00
(171)	Zach Wheat	100.00	50.00	30.00
(172)	Doc White	50.00	25.00	15.00
(173)	Ed Willett	50.00	25.00	15.00
(174)	Art Wilson (New York)	50.00	25.00	15.00
(175)	Owen Wilson (Pittsburgh)	50.00	25.00	15.00
(176)	Hooks Wiltse	50.00	25.00	15.00
(177)	Harry Wolter	50.00	25.00	15.00
(178)	Harry Wolverton	50.00	25.00	15.00
(179)	Cy Young	400.00	200.00	120.00
(180)	Irv Young	50.00	25.00	15.00

1910 Hermes Ice Cream Pirates Pins

The World's Champion Pittsburgh Pirates are featured on this colorful set of 1-1/4" pins. Sepia player portraits at center have a yellow border around with a blue banner at bottom and a skull and crossbones. The players are not identified on the buttons, making them difficult to collect.

		NM	EX	VG
Complete Set (12):		11,000	5,500	3,250
Common Player:		450.00	225.00	135.00
(1)	Bill Abstein	450.00	225.00	135.00
(2)	Red Adams	450.00	225.00	135.00
(3)	Bobby Byrne	450.00	225.00	135.00
(4)	Howie Camnitz	450.00	225.00	135.00
(5)	Fred Clarke	450.00	225.00	135.00
(6)	George Gibson	450.00	225.00	135.00
(7)	Tommy Leach	450.00	225.00	135.00
(8)	Sam Leever	450.00	225.00	135.00
(9)	Dots Miller	450.00	225.00	135.00
(10)	Mike Simon	450.00	225.00	135.00
(11)	Honus Wagner	6,500	3,250	2,000
(12)	Owen Wilson	450.00	225.00	135.00

1916 Herpolsheimer Co.

HOWARD SHANKS
L. F.—Washington Am.
·160·

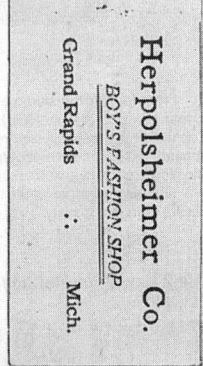

Grand Rapids :: Mich.

Herpolsheimer Co.

BOY'S FASHION SHOP

Advertising for a Michigan clothier is all that differentiates these cards from the more common Sporting News or blank-back M101-4 versions and those of other regional advertisers. The cards are black-and-white in 1-5/8" x 3" format. The Herpolsheimer cards command a significant premium from type-card and superstar collectors.

PREMIUMS:
Common Players: 3-4X
Hall of Famers: 2-3X
(See 1916 M101-4 Blank Backs for checklist and price guide.)

1921 Herpolsheimer's

Issued by a Grand Rapids, Mich., department store that also produced a card set in 1916, this issue shares a basic format with the blank-backed strip-card set designated W575-1, though the known checklist of the Herpolsheimers includes cards that have not yet been verified in W575-1. It is also not known to what extent the variations listed among W575-1 are found among the Michigan store's version. The Herpolsheimer's cards differ from the strip cards in the inclusion of the advertising on the back and sometimes in photo and/or caption details. The 2-1/16" x 3-3/8" black-and-white cards are much scarcer than the strip-card version. The checklist pre-

CHARLES STENGEL
R. F.—Philadelphia Nationals

HERPOLSHEIMER'S
Boys Fashion Shop
THE HOME OF
BOY'S FASHIONABLE CLOTHING
SECOND FLOOR

sented here is incomplete. Gaps have been left in the assgned numbering to accomodate future additions. This set only game to the hobby's attention late in 2004 through a series of eBay auctions. Currently only a single example is known of each card. All known examples have a pencilled figure and dollar sign on back.

		NM	EX	VG
Common Player:				450.00
(3)	Grover Alexander			1,100
(5)	J. Franklin Baker			750.00
(11)	Jim Bagby			450.00
(13)	Ping Bodie			450.00
(15)	George Burns			450.00
(16)	Geo. J. Burns			450.00
(18)	Owen Bush			450.00
(21)	Ty Cobb			4,000
(22)	Eddie Collins			750.00
(28)	George Dauss			450.00
(29)	Dave Davenport			450.00
(30)	Charles Deal			450.00
(33)	William Doak			450.00
(34)	Bill Donovan (Pitching)			450.00
(39)	Urban Faber (Dark uniform.)			750.00
(45)	Art Fletcher			450.00
(47)	Jacques Fournier			450.00
(49)	W.L. Gardner			450.00
(52)	"Kid" Gleason			450.00
(54)	Hank Gowdy			450.00
(55)	John Graney (L.F.)			450.00
(57)	Tom Griffith			450.00
(67)	John Henry			450.00
(74)	Rogers Hornsby (2nd B.)			2,000
(79)	Hugh Jennings			450.00
(80)	Walter Johnson			4,500
(82)	James Johnston			450.00
(84)	Joe Judge (Batting)			450.00
(89)	P.J. Kilduff			450.00
(93)	"Nemo" Leibold			450.00
(94)	Duffy Lewis			450.00
(95)	Al Mamaux			450.00
(96)	"Rabbit" Maranville			750.00
(101)	John McGraw (Manager)			750.00
(102)	Jack McInnis			450.00
(107)	Clyde Milan			450.00
(109)	Otto Miller			450.00
(112)	Guy Morton			450.00
(115)	Eddie Murphy			450.00
(116)	"Hy" Myers (C.F.)			450.00
(123)	Steve O'Neill			450.00
(124)	Roger Peckinbaugh (Peckinpaugh)			450.00
(125)	Jeff Pfeffer (Brooklyn)			450.00
(133)	E.C. Rice			750.00
(134)	Eppa Rixey, Jr.			750.00
(145)	Babe Ruth (R.F.)			10,000
(149)	"Slim" Sallee (Glove showing.)			450.00
(151)	Ray Schalk (Bunting)			750.00
(153)	Walter Schang			450.00
(155)	Everett Scott (Boston)			450.00
(173)	Tris Speaker (Manager)			1,250
(175)	Charles Stengel (Batting)			750.00
(177)	Milton Stock			450.00
(178)	Amos Strunk (R.F.)			450.00
(181)	Zeb Terry (White uniform.)			450.00
(182)	Chester Thomas			450.00
(183)	Fred Toney (Both feet on ground.)			450.00
(186)	George Tyler			450.00
(187)	Jim Vaughn (Dark cap.)			450.00
(190)	Bob Veach (Arms folded.)			450.00
(191)	Oscar Vitt (3rd B.)			450.00
(193)	W. Wambsganss			450.00
(194)	Carl Weilman			450.00
(195)	Zach Wheat			750.00
(196)	George Whitted			450.00
(198)	Ivy B. Wingo			450.00
(200)	Joe Wood			675.00
(202)	"Pep" (Ralph) Young			450.00

1888 S.F. Hess (N338-2)

The most popular of the S.F. Hess & Co. issues, this 21-card set was issued in 1889 and pictures 16 players from the New York Giants, two New York Mets players, two from St. Louis and one from Detroit. The cards measure 2-3/4" x 1-1/2" and feature sepia-toned photographs, most of which are enclosed in ovals with a dark background. The player's name is printed in capital letters just beneath the photo, and the S.F. Hess & Co. logo appears at the bottom (without using the Creole Cigarette brand name).

		NM	EX	VG
	Common Player:	7,900	3,950	2,500
(1)	Bill Brown	7,900	3,950	2,500
(2)	Roger Conner (Connor)	20,000	10,000	6,000
(3)	Ed Crane	7,900	3,950	2,500
(4)	Buck Ewing	21,000	10,500	6,200
(5)	Elmer Foster	7,900	3,950	2,500
(6)	Wm. George	7,900	3,950	2,500
(7)	Joe Gerhardt	7,900	3,950	2,500
(8)	Chas. Getzein (Getzien)	7,900	3,950	2,500
(9)	Geo. Gore	7,900	3,950	2,500
(10)	Gil Hatfield	7,900	3,950	2,500
(11)	Tim Keefe	20,000	10,000	6,000
(12)	Arlie Latham	7,900	3,950	2,500
(13)	Pat Murphy	7,900	3,950	2,500
(14)	Jim Mutrie	7,900	3,950	2,500
(15)	Dave Orr	7,900	3,950	2,500
(16)	Danny Richardson	7,900	3,950	2,500
(17)	Mike Slattery	7,900	3,950	2,500
(18)	Silent Mike Tiernan	7,900	3,950	2,500
(19)	Lidell Titcomb	7,900	3,950	2,500
(20)	Johnny Ward	20,000	10,000	6,000
(21)	Curt Welch	7,900	3,950	2,500
(22)	Mickey Welch	20,000	10,000	6,000
(23)	Arthur Whitney	7,900	3,950	2,500

1909-11 Hindu Cigarettes

Hindu backs are among the more difficult to find among the various cigarette-brand ads seen on T205 and T206 cards. T206s are usually found with the ad printed in brown ink. Much scarcer are those with the ad in red. Fewer than 50 T205s have ever been seen with the Hindu ad on back, printed in brown. Multipliers shown are for "common" player cards. Cards of Hall of Famers or other high-demand cards are usually figured by using a multiplier of about one-half those shown here.

PREMIUMS
T205: 15-20X
T206 Brown Commons: 8-10X
T206 Brown Hall of Famers: 5-7X
T206 Brown Southern Leaguers: 3-4X
T206 Red Commons: 15X
T206 Red Hall of Famers: 10X
    (See T205, T206 for checklists and base card values.)

1958 Hires Root Beer Test Set

PITCHER—SAN FRANCISCO GIANTS

Among the scarcest of the regional issues of the late 1950s is the eight-card test issue which preceded the Hires Root Beer set of 66 cards. The test cards differ from the regular issue in that they have sepia-toned, rather than color pictures, which are set against plain yellow or orange backgrounds (much like the 1958 Topps), instead of viewed through a knothole. Like the regular Hires cards, the 2-5/16" x 3-1/2" cards were issued with an attached wedge-shaped tab of like size. The tab offered membership in Hires' baseball fan club, and served to hold the card into the carton of bottled root beer with which it was given away.

		NM	EX	VG
	Complete Set, W/Tab (8):	10,000	4,000	2,000
	Common Player, W/Tab:	725.00	290.00	145.00
	Complete Set, No Tab (8):	3,000	1,200	600.00
	Common Player, No Tab:	250.00	100.00	50.00
	WITH TAB			
(1)	Johnny Antonelli	725.00	290.00	145.00
(2)	Jim Busby	725.00	290.00	145.00
(3)	Chico Fernandez	725.00	290.00	145.00
(4)	Bob Friend	725.00	290.00	145.00
(5)	Vern Law	725.00	290.00	145.00
(6)	Stan Lopata	725.00	290.00	145.00
(7)	Willie Mays	5,000	2,000	1,000
(8)	Al Pilarcik	725.00	290.00	145.00
	NO TAB			
(1)	Johnny Antonelli	250.00	100.00	50.00
(2)	Jim Busby	250.00	100.00	50.00
(3)	Chico Fernandez	250.00	100.00	50.00
(4)	Bob Friend	250.00	100.00	50.00
(5)	Vern Law	250.00	100.00	50.00
(6)	Stan Lopata	250.00	100.00	50.00
(7)	Willie Mays	1,300	525.00	250.00
(8)	Al Pilarcik	250.00	100.00	50.00

1958 Hires Root Beer

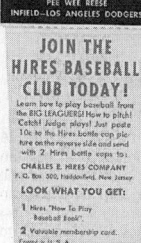

PEE WEE REESE
INFIELD—LOS ANGELES DODGERS

Like most baseball cards issued with a tab in the 1950s, the Hires cards are extremely scarce today in their original form. The basic card was attached to a wedge-shaped tab that served the dual purpose of offering a fan club membership and of holding the card into the cardboard carton of soda bottles with which it was distributed. Measurements of the card vary somewhat, from about 2-3/8" to 2-5/8" wide and 3-3/8" to 3-5/8" tall (without tab). The tab extends for another 3-1/2". Numbering of the Hires set begins at 10 and goes through 76, with card #69 never issued, making a set complete at 66 cards.

		NM	EX	VG
	Complete Set, W/Tab (66):	5,250	2,650	1,550
	Common Player, W/Tab:	60.00	30.00	18.00
	Complete Set, No Tab (66):	3,250	1,600	975.00
	Common Player, No Tab:	35.00	17.50	10.00
	WITH TAB			
10	Richie Ashburn	165.00	80.00	50.00
11	Chico Carrasquel	60.00	30.00	18.00
12	Dave Philley	60.00	30.00	18.00
13	Don Newcombe	110.00	55.00	35.00
14	Wally Post	60.00	30.00	18.00
15	Rip Repulski	60.00	30.00	18.00
16	Chico Fernandez	60.00	30.00	18.00
17	Larry Doby	95.00	50.00	25.00
18	Hector Brown	60.00	30.00	18.00
19	Danny O'Connell	60.00	30.00	18.00
20	Granny Hamner	60.00	30.00	18.00
21	Dick Groat	60.00	30.00	18.00
22	Ray Narleski	60.00	30.00	18.00
23	Pee Wee Reese	165.00	85.00	50.00
24	Bob Friend	60.00	30.00	18.00
25	Willie Mays	500.00	250.00	150.00
26	Bob Nieman	60.00	30.00	18.00
27	Frank Thomas	60.00	30.00	18.00
28	Curt Simmons	60.00	30.00	18.00
29	Stan Lopata	60.00	30.00	18.00
30	Bob Skinner	60.00	30.00	18.00
31	Ron Kline	60.00	30.00	18.00
32	Willie Miranda	60.00	30.00	18.00
33	Bob Avila	60.00	30.00	18.00
34	Clem Labine	90.00	45.00	27.50
35	Ray Jablonski	60.00	30.00	18.00
36	Bill Mazeroski	110.00	55.00	35.00
37	Billy Gardner	60.00	30.00	18.00
38	Pete Runnels	60.00	30.00	18.00
39	Jack Sanford	60.00	30.00	18.00

		NM	EX	VG
40	Dave Sisler	60.00	30.00	18.00
41	Don Zimmer	90.00	45.00	27.00
42	Johnny Podres	90.00	45.00	27.50
43	Dick Farrell	60.00	30.00	18.00
44	Hank Aaron	425.00	210.00	125.00
45	Bill Virdon	60.00	30.00	18.00
46	Bobby Thomson	75.00	37.50	22.50
47	Willard Nixon	60.00	30.00	18.00
48	Billy Loes	60.00	30.00	18.00
49	Hank Sauer	60.00	30.00	18.00
50	Johnny Antonelli	60.00	30.00	18.00
51	Daryl Spencer	60.00	30.00	18.00
52	Ken Lehman	75.00	37.50	22.50
53	Sammy White	60.00	30.00	18.00
54	Charley Neal	75.00	37.50	22.50
55	Don Drysdale	165.00	80.00	50.00
56	Jack Jensen	65.00	32.50	20.00
57	Ray Katt	60.00	30.00	18.00
58	Franklin Sullivan	60.00	30.00	18.00
59	Roy Face	60.00	30.00	18.00
60	Willie Jones	60.00	30.00	18.00
61	Duke Snider (SP)	250.00	125.00	75.00
62	Whitey Lockman	60.00	30.00	18.00
63	Gino Cimoli	75.00	37.00	22.50
64	Marv Grissom	60.00	30.00	18.00
65	Gene Baker	60.00	30.00	18.00
66	George Zuverink	60.00	30.00	18.00
67	Ted Kluszewski	135.00	70.00	40.00
68	Jim Busby	60.00	30.00	18.00
69	Not Issued			
70	Curt Barclay	60.00	30.00	18.00
71	Hank Foiles	60.00	30.00	18.00
72	Gene Stephens	60.00	30.00	18.00
73	Al Worthington	60.00	30.00	18.00
74	Al Walker	60.00	30.00	18.00
75	Bob Boyd	60.00	30.00	18.00
76	Al Pilarcik	60.00	30.00	18.00
	NO TAB			
10	Richie Ashburn	110.00	55.00	35.00
11	Chico Carrasquel	35.00	17.50	10.00
12	Dave Philley	35.00	17.50	10.00
13	Don Newcombe	65.00	32.50	20.00
14	Wally Post	35.00	17.50	10.00
15	Rip Repulski	35.00	17.50	10.00
16	Chico Fernandez	35.00	17.50	10.00
17	Larry Doby	75.00	37.50	22.50
18	Hector Brown	35.00	17.50	10.00
19	Danny O'Connell	35.00	17.50	10.00
20	Granny Hamner	35.00	17.50	10.00
21	Dick Groat	35.00	17.50	10.00
22	Ray Narleski	35.00	17.50	10.00
23	Pee Wee Reese	100.00	50.00	30.00
24	Bob Friend	35.00	17.50	10.00
25	Willie Mays	200.00	100.00	60.00
26	Bob Nieman	35.00	17.50	10.00
27	Frank Thomas	35.00	17.50	10.00
28	Curt Simmons	35.00	17.50	10.00
29	Stan Lopata	35.00	17.50	10.00
30	Bob Skinner	35.00	17.50	10.00
31	Ron Kline	35.00	17.50	10.00
32	Willie Miranda	35.00	17.50	10.00
33	Bob Avila	35.00	17.50	10.00
34	Clem Labine	45.00	22.50	13.50
35	Ray Jablonski	35.00	17.50	10.00
36	Bill Mazeroski	75.00	37.50	22.50
37	Billy Gardner	35.00	17.50	10.00
38	Pete Runnels	35.00	17.50	10.00
39	Jack Sanford	35.00	17.50	10.00
40	Dave Sisler	35.00	17.50	10.00
41	Don Zimmer	45.00	22.50	13.50
42	Johnny Podres	45.00	22.50	13.50
43	Dick Farrell	35.00	17.50	10.00
44	Hank Aaron	200.00	100.00	60.00
45	Bill Virdon	35.00	17.50	10.00
46	Bobby Thomson	45.00	22.50	13.50
47	Willard Nixon	35.00	17.50	10.00
48	Billy Loes	35.00	17.50	10.00
49	Hank Sauer	35.00	17.50	10.00
50	Johnny Antonelli	35.00	17.50	10.00
51	Daryl Spencer	35.00	17.50	10.00
52	Ken Lehman	40.00	20.00	12.00
53	Sammy White	35.00	17.50	10.00
54	Charley Neal	40.00	20.00	12.00
55	Don Drysdale	75.00	37.50	22.50
56	Jack Jensen	40.00	20.00	12.00
57	Ray Katt	35.00	17.50	10.00
58	Franklin Sullivan	35.00	17.50	10.00
59	Roy Face	35.00	17.50	10.00
60	Willie Jones	35.00	17.50	10.00
61	Duke Snider (SP)	180.00	90.00	55.00
62	Whitey Lockman	35.00	17.50	10.00
63	Gino Cimoli	40.00	20.00	10.00
64	Marv Grissom	35.00	17.50	10.00
65	Gene Baker	35.00	17.50	10.00
66	George Zuverink	35.00	17.50	10.00
67	Ted Kluszewski	75.00	37.50	22.50
68	Jim Busby	35.00	17.50	10.00
69	Not Issued			
70	Curt Barclay	35.00	17.50	10.00
71	Hank Foiles	35.00	17.50	10.00
72	Gene Stephens	35.00	17.50	10.00
73	Al Worthington	35.00	17.50	10.00
74	Al Walker	35.00	17.50	10.00
75	Bob Boyd	35.00	17.50	10.00
76	Al Pilarcik	35.00	17.50	10.00

1951-52 Hit Parade of Champions

(See 1951-52 Berk Ross.)

1977 Holiday Inn Discs

Virtually identical in format to the several locally sponsored disc sets of the previous year, these 3-3/8" diameter player discs were given away five at a time with the purchase of a children's dinner at some 72 participating Holiday Inns in the Midwest. Discs once again feature black-and-white player portrait photos in the center of a baseball design. The left and right panels are in one of several bright colors. Licensed by the Players Association through Mike Schechter Associates, the player photos carry no uniform logos. Backs are printed in green. The unnumbered discs are checklisted here alphabetically.

		NM	EX	VG
Complete Set (70):		160.00	80.00	45.00
Common Player:		2.00	1.00	.60
(1)	Sal Bando	2.00	1.00	.60
(2)	Buddy Bell	2.00	1.00	.60
(3)	Johnny Bench	6.00	3.00	1.75
(4)	Larry Bowa	2.00	1.00	.60
(5)	Steve Braun	2.00	1.00	.60
(6)	George Brett	20.00	10.00	6.00
(7)	Lou Brock	6.00	3.00	1.75
(8)	Jeff Burroughs	2.00	1.00	.60
(9)	Bert Campaneris	2.00	1.00	.60
(10)	John Candelaria	2.00	1.00	.60
(11)	Jose Cardenal	2.00	1.00	.60
(12)	Rod Carew	6.00	3.00	1.75
(13)	Steve Carlton	6.00	3.00	1.75
(14)	Dave Cash	2.00	1.00	.60
(15)	Cesar Cedeno	2.00	1.00	.60
(16)	Ron Cey	2.00	1.00	.60
(17)	Dave Concepcion	2.00	1.00	.60
(18)	Dennis Eckersley	5.00	2.50	1.50
(19)	Mark Fidrych	3.00	1.50	.90
(20)	Rollie Fingers	5.00	2.50	1.50
(21)	Carlton Fisk	6.00	3.00	1.75
(22)	George Foster	2.00	1.00	.60
(23)	Wayne Garland	2.00	1.00	.60
(24)	Ralph Garr	2.00	1.00	.60
(25)	Steve Garvey	4.00	2.00	1.25
(26)	Cesar Geronimo	2.00	1.00	.60
(27)	Bobby Grich	2.00	1.00	.60
(28)	Ken Griffey Sr.	2.50	1.25	.70
(29)	Don Gullett	2.00	1.00	.60
(30)	Mike Hargrove	2.00	1.00	.60
(31)	Al Hrabosky	2.00	1.00	.60
(32)	Jim Hunter	5.00	2.50	1.50
(33)	Reggie Jackson	10.00	5.00	3.00
(34)	Randy Jones	2.00	1.00	.60
(35a)	Dave Kingman (Mets)	2.50	1.25	.70
(35b)	Dave Kingman (Padres)	4.00	2.00	1.25
(36)	Jerry Koosman	2.00	1.00	.60
(37)	Dave LaRoche	2.00	1.00	.60
(38)	Greg Luzinski	2.00	1.00	.60
(39)	Fred Lynn	2.00	1.00	.60
(40)	Bill Madlock	2.00	1.00	.60
(41)	Rick Manning	2.00	1.00	.60
(42)	Jon Matlock	2.00	1.00	.60
(43)	John Mayberry	2.00	1.00	.60
(44)	Hal McRae	2.00	1.00	.60
(45)	Andy Messersmith	2.00	1.00	.60
(46)	Rick Monday	2.00	1.00	.60
(47)	John Montefusco	2.00	1.00	.60
(48)	Joe Morgan	6.00	3.00	1.75
(49)	Thurman Munson	4.00	2.00	1.25
(50)	Bobby Murcer	2.00	1.00	.60
(51)	Bill North	2.00	1.00	.60
(52)	Jim Palmer	6.00	3.00	1.75
(53)	Tony Perez	5.00	2.50	1.50
(54)	Jerry Reuss	2.00	1.00	.60
(55)	Brooks Robinson	6.00	3.00	1.75
(56)	Pete Rose	15.00	7.50	4.50
(57)	Joe Rudi	2.00	1.00	.60
(58)	Nolan Ryan	40.00	20.00	12.00
(59)	Manny Sanguillen	2.00	1.00	.60
(60)	Mike Schmidt	15.00	7.50	4.50
(61)	Tom Seaver	6.00	3.00	1.75
(62)	Bill Singer	2.00	1.00	.60
(63)	Willie Stargell	6.00	3.00	1.75
(64)	Rusty Staub	3.00	1.50	.90
(65)	Luis Tiant	2.00	1.00	.60
(66)	Bob Watson	2.00	1.00	.60
(67)	Butch Wynegar	2.00	1.00	.60
(68)	Carl Yastrzemski	7.50	3.75	2.25
(69)	Robin Yount	6.00	3.00	1.75
(70)	Richie Zisk	2.00	1.00	.60

1925 Holland World's Champions Washington Senators

The World's Champion Washington Senators were featured on a set issued in Winnipeg, Manitoba, of all places. The 1-1/2" x 3" cards have player portrait photos printed in blue on front. The black-printed back has a redemption offer of cards for ice cream. Like many such offers it appears as if card #16 was intentionally withheld or minimally distributed, making it very scarce today.

		NM	EX	VG
Complete Set, No #16 (17):		17,500	8,750	5,250
Common Player:		800.00	400.00	240.00
1	Ralph Miller	800.00	400.00	240.00
2	Earl McNeely	800.00	400.00	240.00
3	Allan Russell	800.00	400.00	240.00
4	Ernest Shirley	800.00	400.00	240.00
5	Sam Rice	1,200	600.00	360.00
6	Muddy Ruel	800.00	400.00	240.00
7	Ossie Bluege	800.00	400.00	240.00
8	Nemo Leibold	800.00	400.00	240.00
9	Paul Zahniser	800.00	400.00	240.00
10	Firpo Marberry	800.00	400.00	240.00
11	Warren Ogden	800.00	400.00	240.00
12	George Mogridge	800.00	400.00	240.00
13	Tom Zachary	800.00	400.00	240.00
14	Goose Goslin	1,200	600.00	360.00
15	Joe Judge	800.00	400.00	240.00
16	Roger Peckinpaugh	2,500	1,250	750.00
17	Bucky Harris	1,200	600.00	360.00
18	Walter Johnson	3,500	1,750	1,000

1916 Holmes to Homes Bread

Most often found with blank backs, this 200-card set can also be found with ads on the back for several local and regional businesses. Among them is Holmes to Homes Milk-Made Bread, location unknown. Type card collectors and superstar collectors can expect to pay a significant premium for individual cards with Holmes to Homes advertising. Cards measure 1-5/8" x 3" and are printed in black-and-white.

(See 1916 M101-5 Blank Backs for checklist and base value information.)

1921 Holsum Bread

Issued by the Weil Baking Co., New Orleans, which produced several sets in the 1910s, this issue shares a format, but not the checklist of the 1921 American Caramel Co. set known as E121, Series of 80, and the contemporary W575-1 blank-back strip cards. To what extent the base cards and known variations in those set are found among the Holsum version is unknown. The Holsum cards differ from E121 primarily in the advertising on the back and sometimes in photo and/or caption details. The approximately 2" x 3-1/4" black-and-white cards are much scarcer than the caramel version. The trial checklist presented here is incomplete.

		NM	EX	VG
Common Player:		350.00	175.00	100.00
(4)	Jimmy Austin	350.00	175.00	100.00
(7)	Dave Bancroft	600.00	300.00	180.00
(13)	Jack Barry	350.00	175.00	100.00
(16)	Ping Bodie	350.00	175.00	100.00
(19)	George Burns	350.00	175.00	100.00
(26)	Ray Chapman	425.00	210.00	125.00
(28)	Eddie Cicotte	600.00	300.00	180.00

(37)	Geo. Cutshaw	350.00	175.00	100.00
(39)	Charles Deal (Dark uniform.)	350.00	175.00	100.00
(42)	Johnny Evers	600.00	300.00	180.00
(46)	Urban Faber (Dark uniform.)	600.00	300.00	180.00
(50)	Art Fletcher	350.00	175.00	100.00
(51)	Eddie Foster	350.00	175.00	100.00
(52)	Jacques Fournier	350.00	175.00	100.00
(53)	Hank Gowdy	350.00	175.00	100.00
(54)	Tom Griffith	350.00	175.00	100.00
(80)	Rogers Hornsby	1,250	625.00	375.00
(85)	Joe Jackson (Value Undetermined)			
(88)	Walter Johnson (Hands at chest.)	2,000	1,000	600.00
(93)	Wm. Killefer Jr.	350.00	175.00	100.00
(95)	John Lavan	350.00	175.00	100.00
(97)	H.B. Leonard	350.00	175.00	100.00
(99)	Duffy Lewis	350.00	175.00	100.00
(105)	Al Mamaux	350.00	175.00	100.00
(107)	"Rabbit" Maranville	600.00	300.00	180.00
(116)	Otto Miller	350.00	175.00	100.00
(122)	Guy Morton	350.00	175.00	100.00
(124)	"Hy" Myers	350.00	175.00	100.00
(127)	Arthur Nehf	350.00	175.00	100.00
(129)	Steve O'Neill	350.00	175.00	100.00
(133)	Jeff Pfeffer	350.00	175.00	100.00
(136)	Bill Rariden	350.00	175.00	100.00
(137)	Bob Roth	350.00	175.00	100.00
(153)	Walter Schang	350.00	175.00	100.00
(155)	Scott Everett	350.00	175.00	100.00
(162)	Geo. Sisler	600.00	300.00	180.00
(164)	J. Carlisle Smith	350.00	175.00	100.00
(168)	Charles Stengel	600.00	300.00	180.00
(170)	Amos Strunk (Batting, Chicago Americans.)	350.00	175.00	100.00
(171)	Amos Strunk (Arms at side, Chicago White Sox.)	350.00	175.00	100.00
(173)	Chester Thomas	350.00	175.00	100.00
(174)	Fred Toney	350.00	175.00	100.00
(175)	Jim Vaughn	350.00	175.00	100.00
(178)	Bob Veach	350.00	175.00	100.00
(184)	W. Wambsganss	350.00	175.00	100.00
(186)	Carl Weilman	350.00	175.00	100.00
(187)	Zack Wheat	600.00	300.00	180.00
(190)	Claude Williams (White stockings, correct photo.)	2,500	1,250	750.00
(202)	Pep Young	350.00	175.00	100.00

1959 Home Run Derby

GIL HODGES
LOS ANGELES DODGERS

This 20-card unnumbered set was produced by American Motors to publicize the Home Run Derby television program. The cards measure approximately 3-1/4" x 5-1/4" and feature black-and-white player photos on blank-backed white stock. The player name and team are printed beneath the photo. This set was reprinted (marked as such) in 1988 by Card Collectors' Co. of New York. An advertising poster is sometimes seen which is essentially an uncut sheet of the cards with a promotional message at bottom.

		NM	EX	VG
Complete Set (20):		10,000	5,000	3,000
Common Player:		175.00	85.00	50.00
Advertising Poster:		3,500	1,750	1,000
(1)	Hank Aaron	900.00	450.00	275.00
(2)	Bob Allison	175.00	85.00	50.00
(3)	Ernie Banks	700.00	350.00	210.00
(4)	Ken Boyer	200.00	100.00	60.00
(5)	Bob Cerv	175.00	85.00	50.00
(6)	Rocky Colavito	325.00	160.00	100.00
(7)	Gil Hodges	325.00	160.00	100.00
(8)	Jackie Jensen	175.00	85.00	50.00
(9)	Al Kaline	600.00	300.00	180.00
(10)	Harmon Killebrew	600.00	300.00	180.00
(11)	Jim Lemon	175.00	85.00	50.00
(12)	Mickey Mantle	2,250	1,125	675.00
(13)	Ed Mathews	550.00	275.00	165.00
(14)	Willie Mays	900.00	450.00	270.00
(15)	Wally Post	175.00	85.00	50.00
(16)	Frank Robinson	550.00	275.00	165.00
(17)	Mark Scott (host)	350.00	175.00	100.00
(18)	Duke Snider	600.00	300.00	180.00
(19)	Dick Stuart	175.00	85.00	50.00
(20)	Gus Triandos	175.00	85.00	50.00

1894 Honest (Duke) Cabinets (N142)

These color cabinet cards, which measure 6" x 9-1/2", were produced by W.H. Duke for its Honest tobacco brand. The player name is centered at the bottom of the card front.

The brand name "Honest" is located in the lower-left corner with the words "New York" in the lower-right corner. Three bicyclists are also part of the set.

	NM	EX	VG
Complete Set (4):	49,500	24,750	14,850
Common Player:	9,350	4,675	2,750
(1) G.S. Davis	12,100	6,050	4,600
(2) E.J. Delahanty	17,600	8,800	7,000
(3) W.M. Nash	9,350	4,675	4,000
(4) W. Robinson	18,425	9,215	6,000

1911-12 Honest Long Cut Tobacco

Advertising, printed in black, for Honest Long Cut tobacco is among the more commonly found on the backs of T205 Gold Border cards of 1911. The brand also advertised on the multi-sport T227 Series of Champions in 1912.

(See T205, T227 for checklists and values.)

1927 Honey Boy

The date of issue for this rare Canadian issue is conjectural. These black-and-white 1-5/8" x 2-3/8" cards were issued by the Purity Ice Cream Company in Winnipeg, Canada, and were redeemable as a set of 21 for a brick of "Delicious Honey Boy Ice Cream." Besides the major leaguers in the set, there are also cards of local amateurs and semi-pros, including hockey Hall of Famer Steamer Maxwell and Chicago Blackhawks star Cecil Browne. The major leaguers are not identified by team, nor do their photos have team insignias present. When redeemed, cards were punch-cancelled. Values shown are for uncancelled cards; cards exhibiting the punch-holes would be worth about 50 percent of the indicated figures.

	NM	EX	VG
Complete Set (21):	24,000	12,000	7,500
Common (Major League) Player:	900.00	450.00	275.00
1 "Steamer" Maxwell (Arenas)	2,000	1,000	600.00
2 Cecil Browne (Dominion Express)	400.00	200.00	120.00
3 Carson McVey (Transcona)	400.00	200.00	120.00
4 Sam Perlman (Tigers)	400.00	200.00	120.00
5 "Snake" Siddle (Arenas)	400.00	200.00	120.00
6 Eddie Cass (Columbus)	400.00	200.00	120.00
7 Jimmy Bradley (Columbus)	400.00	200.00	120.00
8 Gordon Caslake (Dominion Express)	400.00	200.00	120.00
9 Ward McVey (Tigers)	400.00	200.00	120.00
10 "Tris" Speaker	1,800	900.00	540.00

11 George Sisler	1,500	750.00	450.00
12 E. Meusel	900.00	450.00	275.00
13 Ed. Roush	1,500	750.00	450.00
14 "Babe" Ruth	8,500	4,250	2,550
15 Harry Heilmann	1,500	750.00	450.00
16 Heinie Groh	900.00	450.00	275.00
17 Eddie Collins	1,500	750.00	450.00
18 Grover Alexander	1,650	825.00	495.00
19 Dave Bancroft	1,500	750.00	450.00
20 Frank Frisch	1,500	750.00	450.00
21 George Burns	900.00	450.00	275.00

1905-1909 Carl Horner Cabinets

Carl Horner was the premier baseball portraitist of the early 20th Century. From his Boston studio came the images of the day's stars and journeymen which live on today on some of the most popular baseball cards of the era - including the famed T206 Honus Wagner. Highly collectible in their own right are the cabinet photos produced by the studio. Because of rarity, values can be determined only on those rare occasions when an example comes onto the market. Because the body of his work was accomplished over a number of years, mounting style and other technical details of the generally 5-1/2" x 7" cabinets may vary. Because the players are not identified on the cabinet, identification can be a problem, though quite often a contemporary notation of the player's name can be found written on back.

	NM	EX	VG
Common Player:	1,000	500.00	300.00
Nick Altrock	2,500	1,250	750.00
Frank Arrelanes (Arellanes)	2,000	1,000	600.00
Frank Baker	3,500	1,750	1,050
Harry Barton	2,000	1,000	600.00
Jake Beckley	3,500	1,750	1,050
Frank Chance	3,500	1,750	1,050
Eddie Collins	3,500	1,750	1,050
Bill Dahlen	2,000	1,000	600.00
Frank Delahanty	2,250	1,125	675.00
Kid Elberfeld	2,000	1,000	600.00
Billy Gilbert	2,000	1,000	600.00
Danny Green	2,000	1,000	600.00
Walter Johnson	15,000	3,250	1,950
Addie Joss	4,000	2,000	1,200
Harry Krause	2,000	1,000	600.00
Rube Kroh	2,000	1,000	600.00
Bris Lord	2,000	1,000	600.00
Charlie Lush	2,000	1,000	600.00
Earl Moore	2,000	1,000	600.00
Harry Niles	2,000	1,000	600.00
Billy Sullivan	2,000	1,000	600.00
Joe Tinker	3,500	1,750	1,050
Honus Wagner	20,000	4,500	2,700
Victor Willis	3,500	1,750	1,050

1959 Hostess Bob Turley

The date attributed to this card is speculative. The 3-1/2" x 4-3/8" black-and-white card has an action pose of the Yankees pitcher on front surrounded by a white border. On back is a list of Hostess Cakes products.

	NM	EX	VG
Bob Turley	125.00	60.00	40.00

1975 Hostess

The first of what would become five annual issues, the 1975 Hostess set consists of 50 three-card panels which formed the bottom of boxes of family-size snack cake products. Unlike many similar issues, the Hostess cards do not share common borders, so it was possible to cut them neatly and evenly from the box. Well-cut single cards measure 2-1/4" x 3-1/4", while a three-card panel measures 7-1/4" x 3-1/4". Because some of the panels were issued on packages of less popular snack cakes, they are somewhat scarcer today. Since

the hobby was quite well-developed when the Hostess cards were first issued, there is no lack of complete panels. Even unused complete boxes are available today. Some of the photos in this issue also appear on Topps cards of the era.

	NM	EX	VG
Complete Panel Set (50):	350.00	175.00	100.00
Complete Set, Singles (150):	165.00	80.00	50.00
Common Panel:	5.00	2.50	1.50
Common Player:	1.00	.50	.30
Panel (1)	5.00	2.50	1.50
1 Bobby Tolan	1.00	.50	.30
2 Cookie Rojas	1.00	.50	.30
3 Darrell Evans	1.25	.60	.40
Panel (2)	10.00	5.00	3.00
4 Sal Bando	1.00	.50	.30
5 Joe Morgan	5.00	2.50	1.50
6 Mickey Lolich	1.25	.60	.40
Panel (3)	10.00	5.00	3.00
7 Don Sutton	4.50	2.25	1.25
8 Bill Melton	1.00	.50	.30
9 Tim Foli	1.00	.50	.30
Panel (4)	5.00	2.50	1.50
10 Joe Lahoud	1.00	.50	.30
11a Bert Hooten (Incorrect spelling.)	1.50	.70	.45
11b Burt Hooton (Corrected)	1.00	.50	.30
12 Paul Blair	1.00	.50	.30
Panel (5)	5.00	2.50	1.50
13 Jim Barr	1.00	.50	.30
14 Toby Harrah	1.00	.50	.30
15 John Milner	1.00	.50	.30
Panel (6)	5.00	2.50	1.50
16 Ken Holtzman	1.00	.50	.30
17 Cesar Cedeno	1.00	.50	.30
18 Dwight Evans	1.00	.50	.30
Panel (7)	10.00	5.00	3.00
19 Willie McCovey	5.00	2.50	1.50
20 Tony Oliva	1.25	.60	.40
21 Manny Sanguillen	1.00	.50	.30
Panel (8)	10.00	5.00	3.00
22 Mickey Rivers	1.00	.50	.30
23 Lou Brock	5.00	2.50	1.50
24 Graig Nettles	1.50	.70	.45
Panel (9)	5.00	2.50	1.50
25 Jim Wynn	1.00	.50	.30
26 George Scott	1.00	.50	.30
27 Greg Luzinski	1.00	.50	.30
Panel (10)	15.00	7.50	4.50
28 Bert Campaneris	1.00	.50	.30
29 Pete Rose	12.50	6.25	3.75
30 Buddy Bell	1.00	.50	.30
Panel (11)	5.00	2.50	1.50
31 Gary Matthews	1.00	.50	.30
32 Fred Patek	1.00	.50	.30
33 Mike Lum	1.00	.50	.30
Panel (12)	5.00	2.50	1.50
34 Ellie Rodriguez	1.00	.50	.30
35 Milt May	1.00	.50	.30
36 Willie Horton	1.00	.50	.30
Panel (13)	10.00	5.00	3.00
37 Dave Winfield	5.00	2.50	1.50
38 Tom Grieve	1.00	.50	.30
39 Barry Foote	1.00	.50	.30
Panel (14)	5.00	2.50	1.50
40 Joe Rudi	1.00	.50	.30
41 Bake McBride	1.00	.50	.30
42 Mike Cuellar	1.00	.50	.30
Panel (15)	5.00	2.50	1.50
43 Garry Maddox	1.00	.50	.30
44 Carlos May	1.00	.50	.30
45 Bud Harrelson	1.00	.50	.30
Panel (16)	10.00	5.00	3.00
46 Dave Chalk	1.00	.50	.30
47 Dave Concepcion	1.00	.50	.30
48 Carl Yastrzemski	7.50	3.75	2.25
Panel (17)	10.00	5.00	3.00
49 Steve Garvey	3.00	1.50	.90
50 Amos Otis	1.00	.50	.30
51 Ricky Reuschel	1.00	.50	.30
Panel (18)	10.00	5.00	3.00
52 Rollie Fingers	4.50	2.25	1.25
53 Bob Watson	1.00	.50	.30
54 John Ellis	1.00	.50	.30
Panel (19)	10.00	5.00	3.00
55 Bob Bailey	1.00	.50	.30
56 Rod Carew	6.00	3.00	1.75
57 Richie Hebner	1.00	.50	.30
Panel (20)	20.00	10.00	6.00
58 Nolan Ryan	15.00	7.50	4.50
59 Reggie Smith	1.00	.50	.30

60	Joe Coleman	1.00	.50	.30
Panel (21)		10.00	5.00	3.00
61	Ron Cey	1.00	.50	.30
62	Darrell Porter	1.00	.50	.30
63	Steve Carlton	5.00	2.50	1.50
Panel (22)		5.00	2.50	1.50
64	Gene Tenace	1.00	.50	.30
65	Jose Cardenal	1.00	.50	.30
66	Bill Lee	1.00	.50	.30
Panel (23)		5.00	2.50	1.50
67	Davey Lopes	1.00	.50	.30
68	Wilbur Wood	1.00	.50	.30
69	Steve Renko	1.00	.50	.30
Panel (24)		10.00	5.00	3.00
70	Joe Torre	3.00	1.50	.90
71	Ted Sizemore	1.00	.50	.30
72	Bobby Grich	1.00	.50	.30
Panel (25)		12.50	6.25	3.75
73	Chris Speier	1.00	.50	.30
74	Bert Blyleven	1.25	.60	.40
75	Tom Seaver	6.00	3.00	1.75
Panel (26)		5.00	2.50	1.50
76	Nate Colbert	1.00	.50	.30
77	Don Kessinger	1.00	.50	.30
78	George Medich	1.00	.50	.30
Panel (27)		20.00	10.00	6.00
79	Andy Messersmith	1.00	.50	.30
80	Robin Yount	12.50	6.25	3.75
81	Al Oliver	1.25	.60	.40
Panel (28)		15.00	7.50	4.50
82	Bill Singer	1.00	.50	.30
83	Johnny Bench	6.00	3.00	1.75
84	Gaylord Perry	4.50	2.25	1.25
Panel (29)		5.00	2.50	1.50
85	Dave Kingman	1.00	.50	.30
86	Ed Herrmann	1.00	.50	.30
87	Ralph Garr	1.00	.50	.30
Panel (30)		12.50	6.25	3.75
88	Reggie Jackson	7.50	3.75	2.25
89a	Doug Radar (Incorrect spelling.)	1.50	.70	.45
89b	Doug Rader (Corrected)	1.00	.50	.30
90	Elliott Maddox	1.00	.50	.30
Panel (31)		5.00	2.50	1.50
91	Bill Russell	1.00	.50	.30
92	John Mayberry	1.00	.50	.30
93	Dave Cash	1.00	.50	.30
Panel (32)		5.00	2.50	1.50
94	Jeff Burroughs	1.00	.50	.30
95	Ted Simmons	1.00	.50	.30
96	Joe Decker	1.00	.50	.30
Panel (33)		10.00	5.00	3.00
97	Bill Buckner	1.25	.60	.40
98	Bobby Darwin	1.00	.50	.30
99	Phil Niekro	4.50	2.25	1.25
Panel (34)		5.00	2.50	1.50
100	Mike Sundberg (Jim)	1.00	.50	.30
101	Greg Gross	1.00	.50	.30
102	Luis Tiant	1.00	.50	.30
Panel (35)		5.00	2.50	1.50
103	Glenn Beckert	1.00	.50	.30
104	Hal McRae	1.00	.50	.30
105	Mike Jorgensen	1.00	.50	.30
Panel (36)		5.00	2.50	1.50
106	Mike Hargrove	1.00	.50	.30
107	Don Gullett	1.00	.50	.30
108	Tito Fuentes	1.00	.50	.30
Panel (37)		5.00	2.50	1.50
109	Johnny Grubb	1.00	.50	.30
110	Jim Kaat	1.25	.60	.40
111	Felix Millan	1.00	.50	.30
Panel (38)		5.00	2.50	1.50
112	Don Money	1.00	.50	.30
113	Rick Monday	1.00	.50	.30
114	Dick Bosman	1.00	.50	.30
Panel (39)		10.00	5.00	3.00
115	Roger Metzger	1.00	.50	.30
116	Fergie Jenkins	4.50	2.25	1.25
117	Dusty Baker	1.25	.60	.40
Panel (40)		10.00	5.00	3.00
118	Billy Champion	1.00	.50	.30
119	Bob Gibson	5.00	2.50	1.50
120	Bill Freehan	1.00	.50	.30
Panel (41)		5.00	2.50	1.50
121	Cesar Geronimo	1.00	.50	.30
122	Jorge Orta	1.00	.50	.30
123	Cleon Jones	1.00	.50	.30
Panel (42)		10.00	5.00	3.00
124	Steve Busby	1.00	.50	.30
125a	Bill Madlock (Pitcher)	1.50	.70	.45
125b	Bill Madlock (Infield)	1.00	.50	.30
126	Jim Palmer	5.00	2.50	1.50
Panel (43)		10.00	5.00	3.00
127	Tony Perez	5.00	2.50	1.50
128	Larry Hisle	1.00	.50	.30
129	Rusty Staub	1.25	.60	.40
Panel (44)		20.00	10.00	6.00
130	Hank Aaron	13.50	6.75	4.00
131	Rennie Stennett	1.00	.50	.30
132	Rico Petrocelli	1.00	.50	.30
Panel (45)		15.00	7.50	4.50
133	Mike Schmidt	12.50	6.25	3.75
134	Sparky Lyle	1.00	.50	.30
135	Willie Stargell	5.00	2.50	1.50
Panel (46)		10.00	5.00	3.00
136	Ken Henderson	1.00	.50	.30
137	Willie Montanez	1.00	.50	.30
138	Thurman Munson	5.00	2.50	1.50
Panel (47)		5.00	2.50	1.50
139	Richie Zisk	1.00	.50	.30
140	George Hendricks (Hendrick)	1.00	.50	.30
141	Bobby Murcer	1.50	.70	.45
Panel (48)		15.00	7.50	4.50
142	Lee May	1.00	.50	.30
143	Carlton Fisk	5.00	2.50	1.50
144	Brooks Robinson	6.00	3.00	1.75

Panel (49)		5.00	2.50	1.50
145	Bobby Bonds	1.25	.60	.40
146	Gary Sutherland	1.00	.50	.30
147	Oscar Gamble	1.00	.50	.30
Panel (50)		10.00	5.00	3.00
148	Jim Hunter	4.50	2.25	1.25
149	Tug McGraw	1.25	.60	.40
150	Dave McNally	1.00	.50	.30

1975 Hostess Twinkies

 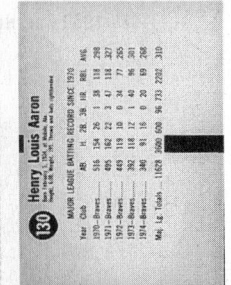

HANK AARON
DESIGNATED HITTER
Milwaukee BREWERS

Believed to have been issued only in selected markets, and on a limited basis at that, the 1975 Hostess Twinkie set features 60 of the cards from the "regular" Hostess set of that year. The cards were issued one per pack with the popular snack cake. Cards #1-36 are a direct pick-up from the Hostess set, while the remaining 24 cards in the set were selected from the more popular names in the remainder of the Hostess issue - with an emphasis on West Coast players. Thus, after card #36, the '75 Twinkie cards are skip-numbered from 40-136. In identical 2-1/4" x 3-1/4" size, the Twinkie cards differ from the Hostess issue only in the presence of small black bars at top and bottom center of the back of the card. While cards actually issued with snack cakes are virtually always found with brown stains, enough unissued cards were leaked into the hobby to provide clean examples for those willing to search them out and pay the price.

		NM	EX	VG
Complete Set (60):		800.00	325.00	80.00
Common Player:		4.00	1.50	.40
1	Bobby Tolan	4.00	1.50	.40
2	Cookie Rojas	4.00	1.50	.40
3	Darrell Evans	4.00	1.50	.40
4	Sal Bando	4.00	1.50	.40
5	Joe Morgan	24.00	9.50	2.50
6	Mickey Lolich	6.00	2.50	.60
7	Don Sutton	20.00	8.00	2.00
8	Bill Melton	4.00	1.50	.40
9	Tim Foli	4.00	1.50	.40
10	Joe Lahoud	4.00	1.50	.40
11	Bert Hooten (Burt Hooton)	4.00	1.50	.40
12	Paul Blair	4.00	1.50	.40
13	Jim Barr	4.00	1.50	.40
14	Toby Harrah	4.00	1.50	.40
15	John Milner	4.00	1.50	.40
16	Ken Holtzman	4.00	1.50	.40
17	Cesar Cedeno	4.00	1.50	.40
18	Dwight Evans	4.00	1.50	.40
19	Willie McCovey	24.00	9.50	2.50
20	Tony Oliva	8.00	3.25	.80
21	Manny Sanguillen	4.00	1.50	.40
22	Mickey Rivers	4.00	1.50	.40
23	Lou Brock	24.00	9.50	2.50
24	Graig Nettles	6.00	2.50	.60
25	Jim Wynn	4.00	1.50	.40
26	George Scott	4.00	1.50	.40
27	Greg Luzinski	4.00	1.50	.40
28	Bert Campaneris	4.00	1.50	.40
29	Pete Rose	80.00	32.00	8.00
30	Buddy Bell	4.00	1.50	.40
31	Gary Matthews	4.00	1.50	.40
32	Fred Patek	4.00	1.50	.40
33	Mike Lum	4.00	1.50	.40
34	Ellie Rodriguez	4.00	1.50	.40
35	Milt May (Photo actually Lee May.)	4.00	1.50	.40
36	Willie Horton	4.00	1.50	.40
40	Joe Rudi	4.00	1.50	.40
43	Garry Maddox	4.00	1.50	.40
46	Dave Chalk	4.00	1.50	.40
49	Steve Garvey	15.00	6.00	1.50
52	Rollie Fingers	20.00	8.00	2.00
58	Nolan Ryan	100.00	40.00	10.00
61	Ron Cey	4.00	1.50	.40
64	Gene Tenace	4.00	1.50	.40
65	Jose Cardenal	4.00	1.50	.40
67	Dave Lopes	4.00	1.50	.40
68	Wilbur Wood	4.00	1.50	.40
73	Chris Speier	4.00	1.50	.40
77	Don Kessinger	4.00	1.50	.40
79	Andy Messersmith	4.00	1.50	.40
80	Robin Yount	40.00	16.00	4.00
82	Bill Singer	4.00	1.50	.40
103	Glenn Beckert	4.00	1.50	.40
110	Jim Kaat	6.00	2.50	.60
112	Don Money	4.00	1.50	.40
113	Rick Monday	4.00	1.50	.40
122	Jorge Orta	4.00	1.50	.40
125	Bill Madlock	4.00	1.50	.40
130	Hank Aaron	75.00	30.00	7.50
136	Ken Henderson	4.00	1.50	.40

1976 Hostess

The second of five annual Hostess issues, the 1976 cards carried a "Bicentennial" color theme, with red, white and blue stripes at the bottom of the 2-1/4" x 3-1/4" cards. Like other

GEORGE BRETT
Kansas City ROYALS
THIRD BASE

George Howard Brett

Hostess issues, the cards were printed in panels of three as the bottom of family-size boxes of snack cake products. This leads to a degree of scarcity for some of the 150 cards in the set; those which were found on less-popular brands. A welltrimmed three-card panel measures 7-1/4" x 3-1/4". Some of the photos used in the 1976 Hostess set can also be found on Topps issues of the era. A "Hostess All-Star Team" album with spaces for 18 cards was available.

		NM	EX	VG
Complete Panel Set (50):		300.00	150.00	90.00
Complete Set, Singles (150):		250.00	125.00	75.00
Common Panel:		5.00	2.50	1.50
Common Player:		.75	.40	.25
Album:		20.00	10.00	6.00
Panel (1)		20.00	10.00	6.00
1	Fred Lynn	1.00	.50	.30
2	Joe Morgan	5.00	2.50	1.50
3	Phil Niekro	4.00	2.00	1.25
Panel (2)		10.00	5.00	3.00
4	Gaylord Perry	4.00	2.00	1.25
5	Bob Watson	.75	.40	.25
6	Bill Freehan	.75	.40	.25
Panel (3)		10.00	5.00	3.00
7	Lou Brock	5.00	2.50	1.50
8	Al Fitzmorris	.75	.40	.25
9	Rennie Stennett	.75	.40	.25
Panel (4)		10.00	5.00	3.00
10	Tony Oliva	1.00	.50	.30
11	Robin Yount	5.00	2.50	1.50
12	Rick Manning	.75	.40	.25
Panel (5)		7.00	3.50	2.00
13	Bobby Grich	.75	.40	.25
14	Terry Forster	.75	.40	.25
15	Dave Kingman	1.00	.50	.30
Panel (6)		10.00	5.00	3.00
16	Thurman Munson	4.50	2.25	1.25
17	Rick Reuschel	.75	.40	.25
18	Bobby Bonds	1.00	.50	.30
Panel (7)		10.00	5.00	3.00
19	Steve Garvey	3.50	1.75	1.00
20	Vida Blue	.75	.40	.25
21	Dave Rader	.75	.40	.25
Panel (8)		10.00	5.00	3.00
22	Johnny Bench	5.00	2.50	1.50
23	Luis Tiant	.75	.40	.25
24	Darrell Evans	.75	.40	.25
Panel (9)		7.00	3.50	2.00
25	Larry Dierker	.75	.40	.25
26	Willie Horton	.75	.40	.25
27	John Ellis	.75	.40	.25
Panel (10)		7.00	3.50	2.00
28	Al Cowens	.75	.40	.25
29	Jerry Reuss	.75	.40	.25
30	Reggie Smith	.75	.40	.25
Panel (11)		10.00	5.00	3.00
31	Bobby Darwin	.75	.40	.25
32	Fritz Peterson	.75	.40	.25
33	Rod Carew	5.00	2.50	1.50
Panel (12)		20.00	10.00	6.00
34	Carlos May	.75	.40	.25
35	Tom Seaver	6.00	3.00	1.75
36	Brooks Robinson	6.00	3.00	1.75
Panel (13)		7.00	3.50	2.00
37	Jose Cardenal	.75	.40	.25
38	Ron Blomberg	.75	.40	.25
39	Lee Stanton	.75	.40	.25
Panel (14)		7.00	3.50	2.00
40	Dave Cash	.75	.40	.25
41	John Montefusco	.75	.40	.25
42	Bob Tolan	.75	.40	.25
Panel (15)		7.00	3.50	2.00
43	Carl Morton	.75	.40	.25
44	Rick Burleson	.75	.40	.25
45	Don Gullett	.75	.40	.25
Panel (16)		7.00	3.50	2.00
46	Vern Ruhle	.75	.40	.25
47	Cesar Cedeno	.75	.40	.25
48	Toby Harrah	.75	.40	.25
Panel (17)		10.00	5.00	3.00
49	Willie Stargell	5.00	2.50	1.50
50	Al Hrabosky	.75	.40	.25
51	Amos Otis	.75	.40	.25
Panel (18)		7.00	3.50	2.00
52	Bud Harrelson	.75	.40	.25
53	Jim Hughes	.75	.40	.25
54	George Scott	.75	.40	.25
Panel (19)		10.00	5.00	3.00
55	Mike Vail	.75	.40	.25
56	Jim Palmer	5.00	2.50	1.50
57	Jorge Orta	.75	.40	.25
Panel (20)		7.00	3.50	2.00
58	Chris Chambliss	.75	.40	.25
59	Dave Chalk	.75	.40	.25
60	Ray Burris	.75	.40	.25
Panel (21)		10.00	5.00	3.00
61	Bert Campaneris	.75	.40	.25

62	Gary Carter	5.00	2.50	1.50
63a	Ron Cey	.75	.40	.25
63b	Ron Cey (Reversed negatives, unissued proof.)	35.00	17.50	10.50
	Panel (22)	27.50	13.50	8.25
64	Carlton Fisk	5.00	2.50	1.50
65	Marty Perez	.75	.40	.25
66	Pete Rose	12.00	6.00	3.50
	Panel (23)	7.00	3.50	2.00
67	Roger Metzger	.75	.40	.25
68	Jim Sundberg	.75	.40	.25
69	Ron LeFlore	.75	.40	.25
	Panel (24)	7.00	3.50	2.00
70	Ted Sizemore	.75	.40	.25
71	Steve Busby	.75	.40	.25
72	Manny Sanguillen	.75	.40	.25
	Panel (25)	10.00	5.00	3.00
73	Larry Hisle	.75	.40	.25
74	Pete Broberg	.75	.40	.25
75	Boog Powell	3.00	1.50	.90
	Panel (26)	8.00	4.00	2.50
76	Ken Singleton	.75	.40	.25
77	Rich Gossage	1.25	.60	.40
78	Jerry Grote	.75	.40	.25
	Panel (27)	35.00	17.50	10.50
79	Nolan Ryan	16.00	8.00	4.75
80	Rick Monday	.75	.40	.25
81	Graig Nettles	1.25	.60	.40
	Panel (28)	27.50	13.50	8.25
82	Chris Speier	.75	.40	.25
83	Dave Winfield	5.00	2.50	1.50
84	Mike Schmidt	7.50	3.75	2.25
	Panel (29)	10.00	5.00	3.00
85	Buzz Capra	.75	.40	.25
86	Tony Perez	5.00	2.50	1.50
87	Dwight Evans	.75	.40	.25
	Panel (30)	7.00	3.50	2.00
88	Mike Hargrove	.75	.40	.25
89	Joe Coleman	.75	.40	.25
90	Greg Gross	.75	.40	.25
	Panel (31)	7.00	3.50	2.00
91	John Mayberry	.75	.40	.25
92	John Candelaria	.75	.40	.25
93	Bake McBride	.75	.40	.25
	Panel (32)	20.00	10.00	6.00
94	Hank Aaron	12.00	6.00	3.50
95	Buddy Bell	.75	.40	.25
96	Steve Braun	.75	.40	.25
	Panel (33)	7.00	3.50	2.00
97	Jon Matlack	.75	.40	.25
98	Lee May	.75	.40	.25
99	Wilbur Wood	.75	.40	.25
	Panel (34)	7.00	3.50	2.00
100	Bill Madlock	.75	.40	.25
101	Frank Tanana	.75	.40	.25
102	Mickey Rivers	.75	.40	.25
	Panel (35)	10.00	5.00	3.00
103	Mike Ivie	.75	.40	.25
104	Rollie Fingers	4.00	2.00	1.25
105	Davey Lopes	.75	.40	.25
	Panel (36)	7.00	3.50	2.00
106	George Foster	.75	.40	.25
107	Denny Doyle	.75	.40	.25
108	Earl Williams	.75	.40	.25
	Panel (37)	7.00	3.50	2.00
109	Tom Veryzer	.75	.40	.25
110	J.R. Richard	.75	.40	.25
111	Jeff Burroughs	.75	.40	.25
	Panel (38)	17.50	8.75	5.25
112	Al Oliver	1.00	.50	.30
113	Ted Simmons	.75	.40	.25
114	George Brett	7.50	3.75	2.25
	Panel (39)	7.00	3.50	2.00
115	Frank Duffy	.75	.40	.25
116	Bert Blyleven	.75	.40	.25
117	Darrell Porter	.75	.40	.25
	Panel (40)	8.00	4.00	2.50
118	Don Baylor	1.00	.50	.30
119	Bucky Dent	.75	.40	.25
120	Felix Millan	.75	.40	.25
	Panel (41)	8.00	4.00	2.50
121a	Mike Cuellar	.75	.40	.25
121b	Andy Messersmith (Unissued proof.)	25.00	12.50	7.50
122	Gene Tenace	.75	.40	.25
123	Bobby Murcer	1.25	.60	.40
	Panel (42)	10.00	5.00	3.00
124	Willie McCovey	5.00	2.50	1.50
125	Greg Luzinski	.75	.40	.25
126	Larry Parrish	.75	.40	.25
	Panel (43)	8.00	4.00	2.50
127	Jim Rice	2.00	1.00	.60
128	Dave Concepcion	.75	.40	.25
129	Jim Wynn	.75	.40	.25
	Panel (44)	7.00	3.50	2.00
130	Tom Grieve	.75	.40	.25
131	Mike Cosgrove	.75	.40	.25
132	Dan Meyer	.75	.40	.25
	Panel(45)	7.00	3.50	2.00
133	Dave Parker	1.00	.50	.30
134	Don Kessinger	.75	.40	.25
135	Hal McRae	.75	.40	.25
	Panel (46)	13.50	6.75	4.00
136	Don Money	.75	.40	.25
137	Dennis Eckersley	5.00	2.50	1.50
138a	Fergie Jenkins	4.00	2.00	1.25
138b	Johnny Briggs (Unissued proof.)	25.00	12.50	7.50
	Panel (47)	10.00	5.00	3.00
139	Mike Torrez	.75	.40	.25
140	Jerry Morales	.75	.40	.25
141	Jim Hunter	4.00	2.00	1.25
	Panel (48)	7.00	3.50	2.00
142	Gary Matthews	.75	.40	.25
143	Randy Jones	.75	.40	.25
144	Mike Jorgensen	.75	.40	.25
	Panel (49)	17.50	8.75	5.25
145	Larry Bowa	.75	.40	.25

146	Reggie Jackson	7.50	3.75	2.25
147	Steve Yeager	.75	.40	.25
	Panel (50)	13.50	6.75	4.00
148	Dave May	.75	.40	.25
149	Carl Yastrzemski	6.00	3.00	1.75
150	Cesar Geronimo	.75	.40	.25

1976 Hostess Twinkies

The 60 cards in this regionally issued (test markets only) set closely parallel the first 60 cards in the numerical sequence of the "regular" 1976 Hostess issue. The singular difference is the appearance on the back of a black band toward the center of the card at top and bottom. Also unlike the three-card panels of the regular Hostess issue, the 2-1/4" x 3-1/4" Twinkie cards were issued singly, as the cardboard stiffener for the cellophane-wrapped snack cakes. While cards actually issued with snack cakes are virtually always found with brown stains, enough unissued cards were leaked into the hobby to provide clean examples for those willing to search them out and pay the price.

		NM	EX	VG
	Complete Set (60):	500.00	200.00	50.00
	Common Player:	4.00	1.50	.40
1	Fred Lynn	4.00	1.50	.40
2	Joe Morgan	24.00	9.50	2.50
3	Phil Niekro	20.00	8.00	2.00
4	Gaylord Perry	20.00	8.00	2.00
5	Bob Watson	4.00	1.50	.40
6	Bill Freehan	4.00	1.50	.40
7	Lou Brock	24.00	9.50	2.50
8	Al Fitzmorris	4.00	1.50	.40
9	Rennie Stennett	4.00	1.50	.40
10	Tony Oliva	6.00	2.50	.60
11	Robin Yount	24.00	9.50	2.50
12	Rick Manning	4.00	1.50	.40
13	Bobby Grich	4.00	1.50	.40
14	Terry Forster	4.00	1.50	.40
15	Dave Kingman	5.00	2.00	.50
16	Thurman Munson	15.00	6.00	1.50
17	Rick Reuschel	4.00	1.50	.40
18	Bobby Bonds	4.00	1.50	.40
19	Steve Garvey	12.00	4.75	1.25
20	Vida Blue	4.00	1.50	.40
21	Dave Rader	4.00	1.50	.40
22	Johnny Bench	24.00	9.50	2.50
23	Luis Tiant	4.00	1.50	.40
24	Darrell Evans	4.00	1.50	.40
25	Larry Dierker	4.00	1.50	.40
26	Willie Horton	4.00	1.50	.40
27	John Ellis	4.00	1.50	.40
28	Al Cowens	4.00	1.50	.40
29	Jerry Reuss	4.00	1.50	.40
30	Reggie Smith	4.00	1.50	.40
31	Bobby Darwin	4.00	1.50	.40
32	Fritz Peterson	4.00	1.50	.40
33	Rod Carew	24.00	9.50	2.50
34	Carlos May	4.00	1.50	.40
35	Tom Seaver	30.00	12.00	3.00
36	Brooks Robinson	24.00	9.50	2.50
37	Jose Cardenal	4.00	1.50	.40
38	Ron Blomberg	4.00	1.50	.40
39	Lee Stanton	4.00	1.50	.40
40	Dave Cash	4.00	1.50	.40
41	John Montefusco	4.00	1.50	.40
42	Bob Tolan	4.00	1.50	.40
43	Carl Morton	4.00	1.50	.40
44	Rick Burleson	4.00	1.50	.40
45	Don Gullett	4.00	1.50	.40
46	Vern Ruhle	4.00	1.50	.40
47	Cesar Cedeno	4.00	1.50	.40
48	Toby Harrah	4.00	1.50	.40
49	Willie Stargell	24.00	9.50	2.50
50	Al Hrabosky	4.00	1.50	.40
51	Amos Otis	4.00	1.50	.40
52	Bud Harrelson	4.00	1.50	.40
53	Jim Hughes	4.00	1.50	.40
54	George Scott	4.00	1.50	.40
55	Mike Vail	4.00	1.50	.40
56	Jim Palmer	20.00	8.00	2.00
57	Jorge Orta	4.00	1.50	.40
58	Chris Chambliss	4.00	1.50	.40
59	Dave Chalk	4.00	1.50	.40
60	Ray Burris	4.00	1.50	.40

1976 Hostess Unissued Proofs

To help prevent a recurrence of the errors which plagued Hostess' debut set in 1975, the company prepared proof sheets of the cards before they were printed onto the bottoms of snack cake boxes. Probably to have ready substitutes in case problems were found, or a card had to be withdrawn at the last minute, there were seven players printed in proof version that were never issued on boxes. In addition, changes to cards #61, 121 and 138 were made between the proof stage

and issued versions (they are detailed in the 1976 Hostess listings). The proofs share the format and 2-1/4" x 3-1/4" size of the issued cards.

		NM	EX	VG
	Complete Set (9):	400.00	200.00	120.00
	Common Player:	40.00	20.00	12.00
151	Fergie Jenkins (Issued as #138.)	75.00	37.50	22.50
152	Mike Cuellar (Issued as #121.)	40.00	20.00	12.00
153	Tom Murphy	40.00	20.00	12.00
154	Dusty Baker	40.00	20.00	12.00
155	Barry Foote	40.00	20.00	12.00
156	Steve Carlton	100.00	50.00	30.00
157	Richie Zisk	40.00	20.00	12.00
158	Ken Holtzman	40.00	20.00	12.00
159	Cliff Johnson	40.00	20.00	12.00

1977 Hostess

The third of five consecutive annual issues, the 1977 Hostess cards retained the same card size - 2-1/4" x 3-1/4", set size - 150 cards, and mode of issue - three cards on a 7-1/4" x 3-1/4" panel, as the previous two efforts. Because they were issued as the bottom panel of snack cake boxes, and because some brands of Hostess products were more popular than others, certain cards in the set are scarcer than others. A fold-out (to 8-1/2" x 22") All-Star Team album was available.

		NM	EX	VG
	Complete Panel Set (50):	250.00	125.00	75.00
	Complete Set, Singles (150):	200.00	100.00	60.00
	Common Panel:	4.00	2.00	1.25
	Common Player:	.75	.40	.25
	Album:	20.00	10.00	6.00
	Panel (1)	20.00	10.00	6.00
1	Jim Palmer	3.00	1.50	.90
2	Joe Morgan	3.00	1.50	.90
3a	Reggie Jackson	5.00	2.50	1.50
3b	Rod Carew (Unissued proof.)	20.00	10.00	6.00
	Panel (2)	25.00	12.50	7.50
4	Carl Yastrzemski	3.50	1.75	1.00
5	Thurman Munson	2.50	1.25	.70
6	Johnny Bench	3.50	1.75	1.00
	Panel (3)	30.00	15.00	9.00
7	Tom Seaver	3.00	1.50	.90
8	Pete Rose	7.50	3.75	2.25
9a	Rod Carew	3.00	1.50	.90
9b	Reggie Jackson (Unissued proof.)	75.00	37.00	22.00
	Panel (4)	4.00	2.00	1.25
10	Luis Tiant	.75	.40	.25
11	Phil Garner	.75	.40	.25
12	Sixto Lezcano	.75	.40	.25
	Panel (5)	4.00	2.00	1.25
13	Mike Torrez	.75	.40	.25
14	Davey Lopes	.75	.40	.25
15	Doug DeCinces	.75	.40	.25
	Panel (6)	4.00	2.00	1.25
16	Jim Spencer	.75	.40	.25
17	Hal McRae	.75	.40	.25
18	Mike Hargrove	.75	.40	.25
	Panel (7)	4.00	2.00	1.25
19	Willie Montanez	.75	.40	.25
20	Roger Metzger	.75	.40	.25
21	Dwight Evans	.75	.40	.25

#	Player	NM	EX	VG
	Panel (8)	5.00	2.50	1.50
22	Steve Rogers	.75	.40	.25
23	Jim Rice	1.25	.60	.40
24	Pete Falcone	.75	.40	.25
	Panel (9)	6.00	3.00	1.75
25	Greg Luzinski	.75	.40	.25
26	Randy Jones	.75	.40	.25
27	Willie Stargell	3.00	1.50	.90
	Panel (10)	5.00	2.50	1.50
28	John Hiller	.75	.40	.25
29	Bobby Murcer	.75	.40	.25
30	Rick Monday	.75	.40	.25
	Panel (11)	6.00	3.00	1.75
31	John Montefusco	.75	.40	.25
32	Lou Brock	3.00	1.50	.90
33	Bill North	.75	.40	.25
	Panel (12)	15.00	7.50	4.50
34	Robin Yount	3.00	1.50	.90
35	Steve Garvey	1.00	.50	.30
36	George Brett	5.00	2.50	1.50
	Panel (13)	4.00	2.00	1.25
37	Toby Harrah	.75	.40	.25
38	Jerry Royster	.75	.40	.25
39	Bob Watson	.75	.40	.25
	Panel (14)	5.00	2.50	1.50
40	George Foster	.75	.40	.25
41	Gary Carter	3.00	1.50	.90
42	John Denny	.75	.40	.25
	Panel (15)	20.00	10.00	6.00
43	Mike Schmidt	5.00	2.50	1.50
44	Dave Winfield	3.00	1.50	.90
45	Al Oliver	.90	.45	.25
	Panel (16)	4.00	2.00	1.25
46	Mark Fidrych	.75	.40	.25
47	Larry Herndon	.75	.40	.25
48	Dave Goltz	.75	.40	.25
	Panel (17)	4.00	2.00	1.25
49	Jerry Morales	.75	.40	.25
50	Ron LeFlore	.75	.40	.25
51	Fred Lynn	.75	.40	.25
	Panel (18)	4.00	2.00	1.25
52	Vida Blue	.75	.40	.25
53	Rick Manning	.75	.40	.25
54	Bill Buckner	.75	.40	.25
	Panel (19)	4.00	2.00	1.25
55	Lee May	.75	.40	.25
56	John Mayberry	.75	.40	.25
57	Darrel Chaney	.75	.40	.25
	Panel (20)	4.00	2.00	1.25
58	Cesar Cedeno	.75	.40	.25
59	Ken Griffey	.75	.40	.25
60	Dave Kingman	.75	.40	.25
	Panel (21)	4.00	2.00	1.25
61	Ted Simmons	.75	.40	.25
62	Larry Bowa	.75	.40	.25
63	Frank Tanana	.75	.40	.25
	Panel (22)	4.00	2.00	1.25
64	Jason Thompson	.75	.40	.25
65	Ken Brett	.75	.40	.25
66	Roy Smalley	.75	.40	.25
	Panel (23)	4.00	2.00	1.25
67	Ray Burris	.75	.40	.25
68	Rick Burleson	.75	.40	.25
69	Buddy Bell	.75	.40	.25
	Panel (24)	5.00	2.50	1.50
70	Don Sutton	2.50	1.25	.70
71	Mark Belanger	.75	.40	.25
72	Dennis Leonard	.75	.40	.25
	Panel (25)	5.00	2.50	1.50
73	Gaylord Perry	2.50	1.25	.70
74	Dick Ruthven	.75	.40	.25
75	Jose Cruz	.75	.40	.25
	Panel (26)	4.00	2.00	1.25
76	Cesar Geronimo	.75	.40	.25
77	Jerry Koosman	.75	.40	.25
78	Garry Templeton	.75	.40	.25
	Panel (27)	25.00	12.50	7.50
79	Jim Hunter	2.50	1.25	.70
80	John Candelaria	.75	.40	.25
81	Nolan Ryan	10.00	5.00	3.00
	Panel (28)	4.00	2.00	1.25
82	Rusty Staub	.90	.45	.25
83	Jim Barr	.75	.40	.25
84	Butch Wynegar	.75	.40	.25
	Panel (29)	4.00	2.00	1.25
85	Jose Cardenal	.75	.40	.25
86	Claudell Washington	.75	.40	.25
87	Bill Travers	.75	.40	.25
	Panel (30)	4.00	2.00	1.25
88	Rick Waits	.75	.40	.25
89	Ron Cey	.75	.40	.25
90	Al Bumbry	.75	.40	.25
	Panel (31)	4.00	2.00	1.25
91	Bucky Dent	.90	.45	.25
92	Amos Otis	.75	.40	.25
93	Tom Grieve	.75	.40	.25
	Panel (32)	4.00	2.00	1.25
94	Enos Cabell	.75	.40	.25
95	Dave Concepcion	.75	.40	.25
96	Felix Millan	.75	.40	.25
	Panel (33)	4.00	2.00	1.25
97	Bake McBride	.75	.40	.25
98	Chris Chambliss	.75	.40	.25
99	Butch Metzger	.75	.40	.25
	Panel (34)	4.00	2.00	1.25
100	Rennie Stennett	.75	.40	.25
101	Dave Roberts	.75	.40	.25
102	Lyman Bostock	.75	.40	.25
	Panel (35)	6.00	3.00	1.75
103	Rick Reuschel	.75	.40	.25
104	Carlton Fisk	3.00	1.50	.90
105	Jim Slaton	.75	.40	.25
	Panel (36)	5.00	2.50	1.50
106	Dennis Eckersley	2.50	1.25	.70
107	Ken Singleton	.75	.40	.25
108	Ralph Garr	.75	.40	.25
	Panel (37)	5.00	2.50	1.50
109	Freddie Patek	.75	.40	.25

#	Player	NM	EX	VG
110	Jim Sundberg	.75	.40	.25
111	Phil Niekro	2.50	1.25	.70
	Panel (38)	4.00	2.00	1.25
112	J.R. Richard	.75	.40	.25
113	Gary Nolan	.75	.40	.25
114	Jon Matlack	.75	.40	.25
	Panel (39)	7.50	3.75	2.25
115	Keith Hernandez	.75	.40	.25
116	Graig Nettles	.90	.45	.25
117	Steve Carlton	3.00	1.50	.90
	Panel (40)	4.00	2.00	1.25
118	Bill Madlock	.75	.40	.25
119	Jerry Reuss	.75	.40	.25
120	Aurelio Rodriguez	.75	.40	.25
	Panel (41)	4.00	2.00	1.25
121	Dan Ford	.75	.40	.25
122	Ray Fosse	.75	.40	.25
123	George Hendrick	.75	.40	.25
	Panel (42)	4.00	2.00	1.25
124	Alan Ashby	.75	.40	.25
125	Joe Lis	.75	.40	.25
126	Sal Bando	.75	.40	.25
	Panel (43)	5.00	2.50	1.50
127	Richie Zisk	.75	.40	.25
128	Rich Gossage	.75	.40	.25
129	Don Baylor	.75	.40	.25
	Panel (44)	4.00	2.00	1.25
130	Dave McKay	.75	.40	.25
131	Bobby Grich	.75	.40	.25
132	Dave Pagan	.75	.40	.25
	Panel (45)	4.00	2.00	1.25
133	Dave Cash	.75	.40	.25
134	Steve Braun	.75	.40	.25
135	Dan Meyer	.75	.40	.25
	Panel (46)	5.00	2.50	1.50
136	Bill Stein	.75	.40	.25
137	Rollie Fingers	2.50	1.25	.70
138	Brian Downing	.75	.40	.25
	Panel (47)	4.00	2.00	1.25
139	Bill Singer	.75	.40	.25
140	Doyle Alexander	.75	.40	.25
141	Gene Tenace	.75	.40	.25
	Panel (48)	4.00	2.00	1.25
142	Gary Matthews	.75	.40	.25
143	Don Gullett	.75	.40	.25
144	Wayne Garland	.75	.40	.25
	Panel (49)	4.00	2.00	1.25
145	Pete Broberg	.75	.40	.25
146	Joe Rudi	.75	.40	.25
147	Glenn Abbott	.75	.40	.25
	Panel (50)	4.00	2.00	1.25
148	George Scott	.75	.40	.25
149	Bert Campaneris	.75	.40	.25
150	Andy Messersmith	.75	.40	.25

1977 Hostess Twinkies

The 1977 Hostess Twinkie issue, at 150 different cards, is the largest of the single-panel Twinkie sets. It is also the most obscure. The cards, which measure 2-1/4" x 3-1/4" but are part of a larger panel, were found not only with Twinkies, but with Hostess Cupcakes as well. Cards #1-30 and 111-150 are Twinkies panels and #31-135 are Cupcakes panels. Complete Cupcakes panels are approximately 2-1/4" x 4-1/2" in size, while complete Twinkies panels measure 3-1/8" x 4-1/4". The photos used in the set are identical to those in the 1977 Hostess three-card panel set. The main difference is the appearance of a black band at the center of the card back. While cards actually issued with snack cakes are virtually always found with brown stains, enough unissued cards were leaked into the hobby to provide clean examples for those willing to search them out and pay the price.

		NM	EX	VG
	Complete Set (150):	725.00	300.00	75.00
	Common Player:	4.00	1.50	.40
1	Jim Palmer	25.00	10.00	2.50
2	Joe Morgan	25.00	10.00	2.50
3	Reggie Jackson	40.00	16.00	4.00
4	Carl Yastrzemski	32.50	13.00	3.25
5	Thurman Munson	15.00	6.00	1.50
6	Johnny Bench	25.00	10.00	2.50
7	Tom Seaver	25.00	10.00	2.50
8	Pete Rose	65.00	26.00	6.50
9	Rod Carew	25.00	10.00	2.50
10	Luis Tiant	4.00	1.50	.40
11	Phil Garner	4.00	1.50	.40
12	Sixto Lezcano	4.00	1.50	.40
13	Mike Torrez	4.00	1.50	.40
14	Dave Lopes	4.00	1.50	.40
15	Doug DeCinces	4.00	1.50	.40
16	Jim Spencer	4.00	1.50	.40
17	Hal McRae	4.00	1.50	.40
18	Mike Hargrove	4.00	1.50	.40
19	Willie Montanez	4.00	1.50	.40
20	Roger Metzger	4.00	1.50	.40
21	Dwight Evans	4.00	1.50	.40

#	Player	NM	EX	VG
22	Steve Rogers	4.00	1.50	.40
23	Jim Rice	12.50	5.00	1.25
24	Pete Falcone	4.00	1.50	.40
25	Greg Luzinski	4.00	1.50	.40
26	Randy Jones	4.00	1.50	.40
27	Willie Stargell	25.00	10.00	2.50
28	John Hiller	4.00	1.50	.40
29	Bobby Murcer	4.00	1.50	.40
30	Rick Monday	4.00	1.50	.40
31	John Montefusco	4.00	1.50	.40
32	Lou Brock	25.00	10.00	2.50
33	Bill North	4.00	1.50	.40
34	Robin Yount	25.00	10.00	2.50
35	Steve Garvey	12.50	5.00	1.25
36	George Brett	40.00	16.00	4.00
37	Toby Harrah	4.00	1.50	.40
38	Jerry Royster	4.00	1.50	.40
39	Bob Watson	4.00	1.50	.40
40	George Foster	4.00	1.50	.40
41	Gary Carter	25.00	10.00	2.50
42	John Denny	4.00	1.50	.40
43	Mike Schmidt	40.00	16.00	4.00
44	Dave Winfield	25.00	10.00	2.50
45	Al Oliver	4.00	1.50	.40
46	Mark Fidrych	6.50	2.50	.60
47	Larry Herndon	4.00	1.50	.40
48	Dave Goltz	4.00	1.50	.40
49	Jerry Morales	4.00	1.50	.40
50	Ron LeFlore	4.00	1.50	.40
51	Fred Lynn	4.00	1.50	.40
52	Vida Blue	4.00	1.50	.40
53	Rick Manning	4.00	1.50	.40
54	Bill Buckner	4.00	1.50	.40
55	Lee May	4.00	1.50	.40
56	John Mayberry	4.00	1.50	.40
57	Darrel Chaney	4.00	1.50	.40
58	Cesar Cedeno	4.00	1.50	.40
59	Ken Griffey	4.00	1.50	.40
60	Dave Kingman	6.50	2.50	.60
61	Ted Simmons	4.00	1.50	.40
62	Larry Bowa	4.00	1.50	.40
63	Frank Tanana	4.00	1.50	.40
64	Jason Thompson	4.00	1.50	.40
65	Ken Brett	4.00	1.50	.40
66	Roy Smalley	4.00	1.50	.40
67	Ray Burris	4.00	1.50	.40
68	Rick Burleson	4.00	1.50	.40
69	Buddy Bell	4.00	1.50	.40
70	Don Sutton	20.00	8.00	2.00
71	Mark Belanger	4.00	1.50	.40
72	Dennis Leonard	4.00	1.50	.40
73	Gaylord Perry	20.00	8.00	2.00
74	Dick Ruthven	4.00	1.50	.40
75	Jose Cruz	4.00	1.50	.40
76	Cesar Geronimo	4.00	1.50	.40
77	Jerry Koosman	4.00	1.50	.40
78	Garry Templeton	4.00	1.50	.40
79	Catfish Hunter	20.00	8.00	2.00
80	John Candelaria	4.00	1.50	.40
81	Nolan Ryan	100.00	40.00	10.00
82	Rusty Staub	6.50	2.50	.60
83	Jim Barr	4.00	1.50	.40
84	Butch Wynegar	4.00	1.50	.40
85	Jose Cardenal	4.00	1.50	.40
86	Claudell Washington	4.00	1.50	.40
87	Bill Travers	4.00	1.50	.40
88	Rick Waits	4.00	1.50	.40
89	Ron Cey	4.00	1.50	.40
90	Al Bumbry	4.00	1.50	.40
91	Bucky Dent	4.00	1.50	.40
92	Amos Otis	4.00	1.50	.40
93	Tom Grieve	4.00	1.50	.40
94	Enos Cabell	4.00	1.50	.40
95	Dave Concepcion	4.00	1.50	.40
96	Felix Millan	4.00	1.50	.40
97	Bake McBride	4.00	1.50	.40
98	Chris Chambliss	4.00	1.50	.40
99	Butch Metzger	4.00	1.50	.40
100	Rennie Stennett	4.00	1.50	.40
101	Dave Roberts	4.00	1.50	.40
102	Lyman Bostock	4.00	1.50	.40
103	Rick Reuschel	4.00	1.50	.40
104	Carlton Fisk	25.00	10.00	2.50
105	Jim Slaton	4.00	1.50	.40
106	Dennis Eckersley	20.00	8.00	2.00
107	Ken Singleton	4.00	1.50	.40
108	Ralph Garr	4.00	1.50	.40
109	Freddie Patek	4.00	1.50	.40
110	Jim Sundberg	4.00	1.50	.40
111	Phil Niekro	20.00	8.00	2.00
112	J. R. Richard	4.00	1.50	.40
113	Gary Nolan	4.00	1.50	.40
114	Jon Matlack	4.00	1.50	.40
115	Keith Hernandez	4.00	1.50	.40
116	Graig Nettles	4.00	1.50	.40
117	Steve Carlton	25.00	10.00	2.50
118	Bill Madlock	4.00	1.50	.40
119	Jerry Reuss	4.00	1.50	.40
120	Aurelio Rodriguez	4.00	1.50	.40
121	Dan Ford	4.00	1.50	.40
122	Ray Fosse	4.00	1.50	.40
123	George Hendrick	4.00	1.50	.40
124	Alan Ashby	4.00	1.50	.40
125	Joe Lis	4.00	1.50	.40
126	Sal Bando	4.00	1.50	.40
127	Richie Zisk	4.00	1.50	.40
128	Rich Gossage	4.00	1.50	.40
129	Don Baylor	6.50	2.50	.60
130	Dave McKay	4.00	1.50	.40
131	Bob Grich	4.00	1.50	.40
132	Dave Pagan	4.00	1.50	.40
133	Dave Cash	4.00	1.50	.40
134	Steve Braun	4.00	1.50	.40
135	Dan Meyer	4.00	1.50	.40
136	Bill Stein	4.00	1.50	.40
137	Rollie Fingers	20.00	8.00	2.00
138	Brian Downing	4.00	1.50	.40
139	Bill Singer	4.00	1.50	.40

Steve Garvey — Los Angeles DODGERS — FIRST BASE
Steven Patrick Garvey · 35

140	Doyle Alexander	4.00	1.50	.40
141	Gene Tenace	4.00	1.50	.40
142	Gary Matthews	4.00	1.50	.40
143	Don Gullett	4.00	1.50	.40
144	Wayne Garland	4.00	1.50	.40
145	Pete Broberg	4.00	1.50	.40
146	Joe Rudi	4.00	1.50	.40
147	Glenn Abbott	4.00	1.50	.40
148	George Scott	4.00	1.50	.40
149	Bert Campaneris	4.00	1.50	.40
150	Andy Messersmith	4.00	1.50	.40

1977 Hostess Unissued Proofs

KEN FORSCH — Houston ASTROS PITCHER
JERRY REUSS — Pittsburgh PIRATES PITCHER

The reason for the existence of these rare Hostess proofs is unknown, but there seems little doubt that they were never actually circulated; perhaps being held in reserve in case the cards actually printed on product boxes had to be replaced. The 10 cards were printed on a sheet in three-card panels, like the issued Hostess cards, plus a single of Briles. The proofs share the format of the issued cards, and the 2-1/4" x 3-1/4" size. Besides these "high number" proofs, there also exist numbering-variation proofs of cards #3, 9, 65 and 119 (see 1977 Hostess listings).

		NM	EX	VG
	Complete Set (10):	400.00	200.00	120.00
	Common Single:	40.00	20.00	12.00
151	Ed Kranepool	40.00	20.00	12.00
152	Ross Grimsley	40.00	20.00	12.00
153	Ken Brett	40.00	20.00	12.00
	(#65 in regular-issue set)			
154	Rowland Office	40.00	20.00	12.00
155	Rick Wise	40.00	20.00	12.00
156	Paul Splittorff	40.00	20.00	12.00
157	Jerry Augustine	40.00	20.00	12.00
158	Ken Forsch	40.00	20.00	12.00
159	Jerry Reuss	40.00	20.00	12.00
160	Nelson Briles	40.00	20.00	12.00

1978 Hostess

JOE FERGUSON — HOUSTON ASTROS
MICKEY RIVERS — NEW YORK YANKEES
PAUL SPLITTORFF — KANSAS CITY ROYALS

Other than the design on the front of the card, there was little different about the 1978 Hostess cards from the three years' issues which had preceded it, or the one which followed. The 2-1/4" x 3-1/4" cards were printed in panels of three (7-1/4" x 3-1/4") as the bottom of family-sized boxes of snack cakes. The 1978 set was again complete at 150 cards. Like other years of Hostess issues, there are scarcities within the 1978 set that are the result of those panels having been issued with less-popular brands of snack cakes.

		NM	EX	VG
	Complete Panel Set (50):	275.00	135.00	80.00
	Complete Set, Singles (150):	225.00	110.00	65.00
	Common Panel:	6.00	3.00	1.75
	Common Player:	.75	.40	.25
	Album:	25.00	12.50	7.50
	Panel (1)	6.00	3.00	1.75
1	Butch Hobson	.75	.40	.25
2	George Foster	.75	.40	.25
3	Bob Forsch	.75	.40	.25
	Panel (2)	13.50	6.75	4.00
4	Tony Perez	4.00	2.00	1.25
5	Bruce Sutter	4.00	2.00	1.25
6	Hal McRae	.75	.40	.25
	Panel (3)	7.50	3.75	2.25
7	Tommy John	1.25	.60	.40
8	Greg Luzinski	.75	.40	.25
9	Enos Cabell	.75	.40	.25

	Panel (4)	10.00	5.00	3.00
10	Doug DeCinces	.75	.40	.25
11	Willie Stargell	4.50	2.25	1.25
12	Ed Halicki	.75	.40	.25
	Panel (5)	6.00	3.00	1.75
13	Larry Hisle	.75	.40	.25
14	Jim Slaton	.75	.40	.25
15	Buddy Bell	.75	.40	.25
	Panel (6)	6.00	3.00	1.75
16	Earl Williams	.75	.40	.25
17	Glenn Abbott	.75	.40	.25
18	Dan Ford	.75	.40	.25
	Panel (7)	6.00	3.00	1.75
19	Gary Matthews	.75	.40	.25
20	Eric Soderholm	.75	.40	.25
21	Bump Wills	.75	.40	.25
	Panel (8)	6.00	3.00	1.75
22	Keith Hernandez	.75	.40	.25
23	Dave Cash	.75	.40	.25
24	George Scott	.75	.40	.25
	Panel (9)	20.00	10.00	6.00
25	Ron Guidry	1.25	.60	.40
26	Dave Kingman	.75	.40	.25
27	George Brett	9.00	4.50	2.75
	Panel (10)	6.00	3.00	1.75
28	Bob Watson	.75	.40	.25
29	Bob Boone	.90	.45	.25
30	Reggie Smith	.75	.40	.25
	Panel (11)	45.00	22.00	13.50
31	Eddie Murray	18.50	9.25	5.50
32	Gary Lavelle	.75	.40	.25
33	Rennie Stennett	.75	.40	.25
	Panel (12)	6.00	3.00	1.75
34	Duane Kuiper	.75	.40	.25
35	Sixto Lezcano	.75	.40	.25
36	Dave Rozema	.75	.40	.25
	Panel (13)	6.00	3.00	1.75
37	Butch Wynegar	.75	.40	.25
38	Mitchell Page	.75	.40	.25
39	Bill Stein	.75	.40	.25
	Panel (14)	6.00	3.00	1.75
40	Elliott Maddox	.75	.40	.25
41	Mike Hargrove	.75	.40	.25
42	Bobby Bonds	.75	.40	.25
	Panel (15)	20.00	10.00	6.00
43	Garry Templeton	.75	.40	.25
44	Johnny Bench	4.50	2.25	1.25
45	Jim Rice	1.50	.70	.45
	Panel (16)	17.50	8.75	5.25
46	Bill Buckner	.75	.40	.25
47	Reggie Jackson	9.00	4.50	2.75
48	Freddie Patek	.75	.40	.25
	Panel (17)	10.00	5.00	3.00
49	Steve Carlton	4.50	2.25	1.25
50	Cesar Cedeno	.75	.40	.25
51	Steve Yeager	.75	.40	.25
	Panel (18)	6.00	3.00	1.75
52	Phil Garner	.75	.40	.25
53	Lee May	.75	.40	.25
54	Darrell Evans	.75	.40	.25
	Panel (19)	6.00	3.00	1.75
55	Steve Kemp	.75	.40	.25
56a	Dusty Baker	.90	.45	.25
56b	Andre Thornton (Unissued proof.)	18.00	9.00	5.50
57	Ray Fosse	.75	.40	.25
	Panel (20)	6.00	3.00	1.75
58	Manny Sanguillen	.75	.40	.25
59	Tom Johnson	.75	.40	.25
60	Lee Stanton	.75	.40	.25
	Panel (21)	10.00	5.00	3.00
61	Jeff Burroughs	.75	.40	.25
62	Bobby Grich	.75	.40	.25
63	Dave Winfield	4.50	2.25	1.25
	Panel (22)	6.00	3.00	1.75
64	Dan Driessen	.75	.40	.25
65	Ted Simmons	.75	.40	.25
66	Jerry Remy	.75	.40	.25
	Panel (23)	6.00	3.00	1.75
67	Al Cowens	.75	.40	.25
68	Sparky Lyle	.75	.40	.25
69	Manny Trillo	.75	.40	.25
	Panel (24)	9.00	4.50	2.75
70	Don Sutton	4.00	2.00	1.25
71	Larry Bowa	.75	.40	.25
72	Jose Cruz	.75	.40	.25
	Panel (25)	10.00	5.00	3.00
73	Willie McCovey	4.50	2.25	1.25
74	Bert Blyleven	.75	.40	.25
75	Ken Singleton	.75	.40	.25
	Panel (26)	6.00	3.00	1.75
76	Bill North	.75	.40	.25
77	Jason Thompson	.75	.40	.25
78	Dennis Eckersley	4.00	2.00	1.25
	Panel (27)	6.00	3.00	1.75
79	Jim Sundberg	.75	.40	.25
80	Jerry Koosman	.75	.40	.25
81	Bruce Bochte	.75	.40	.25
	Panel (28)	45.00	22.00	13.50
82	George Hendrick	.75	.40	.25
83	Nolan Ryan	20.00	10.00	6.00
84	Roy Howell	.75	.40	.25
	Panel (29)	10.00	5.00	3.00
85	Butch Metzger	.75	.40	.25
86	George Medich	.75	.40	.25
87	Joe Morgan	4.50	2.25	1.25
	Panel (30)	6.00	3.00	1.75
88	Dennis Leonard	.75	.40	.25
89	Willie Randolph	.90	.45	.25
90	Bobby Murcer	.90	.45	.25
	Panel (31)	6.00	3.00	1.75
91	Rick Manning	.75	.40	.25
92	J.R. Richard	.75	.40	.25
93	Ron Cey	.75	.40	.25
	Panel (32)	6.00	3.00	1.75
94	Sal Bando	.75	.40	.25
95	Ron LeFlore	.75	.40	.25
96	Dave Goltz	.75	.40	.25

	Panel (33)	6.00	3.00	1.75
97	Dan Meyer	.75	.40	.25
98	Chris Chambliss	.75	.40	.25
99	Biff Pocoroba	.75	.40	.25
	Panel (34)	6.00	3.00	1.75
100	Oscar Gamble	.75	.40	.25
101	Frank Tanana	.75	.40	.25
102	Lenny Randle	.75	.40	.25
	Panel (35)	6.00	3.00	1.75
103	Tommy Hutton	.75	.40	.25
104	John Candelaria	.75	.40	.25
105	Jorge Orta	.75	.40	.25
	Panel (36)	6.00	3.00	1.75
106	Ken Reitz	.75	.40	.25
107	Bill Campbell	.75	.40	.25
108	Dave Concepcion	.75	.40	.25
	Panel (37)	6.00	3.00	1.75
109	Joe Ferguson	.75	.40	.25
110	Mickey Rivers	.75	.40	.25
111	Paul Splittorff	.75	.40	.25
	Panel (38)	20.00	10.00	6.00
112	Davey Lopes	.75	.40	.25
113	Mike Schmidt	9.00	4.50	2.75
114	Joe Rudi	.75	.40	.25
	Panel (39)	10.00	5.00	3.00
115	Milt May	.75	.40	.25
116	Jim Palmer	4.50	2.25	1.25
117	Bill Madlock	.75	.40	.25
	Panel (40)	6.00	3.00	1.75
118	Roy Smalley	.75	.40	.25
119	Cecil Cooper	.75	.40	.25
120	Rick Langford	.75	.40	.25
	Panel (41)	9.00	4.50	2.75
121	Ruppert Jones	.75	.40	.25
122	Phil Niekro	4.00	2.00	1.25
123	Toby Harrah	.75	.40	.25
	Panel (42)	6.00	3.00	1.75
124	Chet Lemon	.75	.40	.25
125	Gene Tenace	.75	.40	.25
126	Steve Henderson	.75	.40	.25
	Panel (43)	35.00	17.50	10.50
127	Mike Torrez	.75	.40	.25
128	Pete Rose	10.00	5.00	3.00
129	John Denny	.75	.40	.25
	Panel (44)	6.00	3.00	1.75
130	Darrell Porter	.75	.40	.25
131	Rick Reuschel	.75	.40	.25
132	Graig Nettles	.90	.45	.25
	Panel (45)	6.00	3.00	1.75
133	Garry Maddox	.75	.40	.25
134	Mike Flanagan	.75	.40	.25
135	Dave Parker	.75	.40	.25
	Panel (46)	10.00	5.00	3.00
136	Terry Whitfield	.75	.40	.25
137	Wayne Garland	.75	.40	.25
138	Robin Yount	4.50	2.25	1.25
	Panel (47)	20.00	10.00	6.00
139a	Gaylord Perry (San Diego)	4.00	2.00	1.25
139b	Gaylord Perry (Texas, unissued proof.)	30.00	15.00	9.00
140	Rod Carew	4.50	2.25	1.25
141	Wayne Gross	.75	.40	.25
	Panel (48)	9.00	4.50	2.75
142	Barry Bonnell	.75	.40	.25
143	Willie Montanez	.75	.40	.25
144	Rollie Fingers	4.00	2.00	1.25
	Panel (49)	35.00	17.50	10.50
145	Lyman Bostock	.75	.40	.25
146	Gary Carter	4.50	2.25	1.25
147	Ron Blomberg	.75	.40	.25
	Panel (50)	30.00	15.00	9.00
148	Bob Bailor	.75	.40	.25
149	Tom Seaver	5.00	2.50	1.50
150	Thurman Munson	4.00	2.00	1.25

1978 Hostess Unissued Proofs

Different versions of two of the issued cards (see 1978 Hostess #56, 139) plus 10 players who do not appear on the snack cake boxes constitute the proof set for '78 Hostess. The unissued proofs are identical in format to the cards actually issued and measure 2-1/4" x 3-1/4" at the dotted lines.

		NM	EX	VG
	Complete Set (10):	450.00	225.00	135.00
	Common Player:	50.00	25.00	15.00
151	Bill Robinson	50.00	25.00	15.00
152	Lou Piniella	75.00	37.50	22.50
153	Lamar Johnson	50.00	25.00	15.00
154	Mark Belanger	50.00	25.00	15.00
155	Ken Griffey	75.00	37.50	22.50
156	Ken Forsch	50.00	25.00	15.00
157	Ted Sizemore	50.00	25.00	15.00
158	Don Baylor	50.00	25.00	15.00
159	Dusty Baker	60.00	30.00	18.00
160	Al Oliver	75.00	37.50	22.50

1979 Hostess

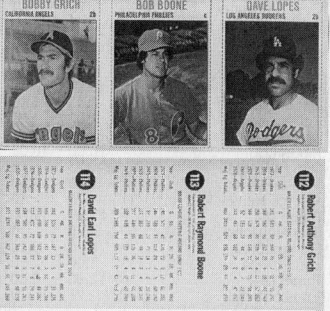

BOBBY GRICH — CALIFORNIA ANGELS 2b
BOB BOONE — PHILADELPHIA PHILLIES c
DAVE LOPES — LOS ANGELES DODGERS 2b

The last of five consecutive annual issues, the 1979 Hostess set retained the 150-card set size, 2-1/4" x 3-1/4" single-card size and 7-1/4" x 3-1/4" three-card panel format from the previous years. The cards were printed as the bottom panel on family-size boxes of Hostess snack cakes. Some panels, which were printed on less-popular brands, are somewhat scarcer today than the rest of the set. Like all Hostess issues, because the hobby was in a well-developed state at the time of issue, the 1979s survive today in complete panels and complete unused boxes for collectors who like original packaging.

		NM	EX	VG
	Complete Panel Set (50):	250.00	125.00	75.00
	Complete Singles Set (150):	175.00	85.00	50.00
	Common Panel:	4.50	2.25	1.25
	Common Single Player:	.75	.40	.25
	Panel (1)	7.50	3.75	2.25
1	John Denny	.75	.40	.25
2a	Jim Rice ("d-of", unissued proof)	15.00	7.50	4.50
2b	Jim Rice ("dh-of")	1.50	.70	.45
3	Doug Bair	.75	.40	.25
	Panel (2)	6.00	3.00	1.75
4	Darrell Porter	.75	.40	.25
5	Ross Grimsley	.75	.40	.25
6	Bobby Murcer	1.00	.50	.30
	Panel (3)	25.00	12.50	7.50
7	Lee Mazzilli	.75	.40	.25
8	Steve Garvey	1.50	.70	.45
9	Mike Schmidt	6.00	3.00	1.75
	Panel (4)	12.00	6.00	3.50
10	Terry Whitfield	.75	.40	.25
11	Jim Palmer	2.50	1.25	.70
12	Omar Moreno	.75	.40	.25
	Panel (5)	5.00	2.50	1.50
13	Duane Kuiper	.75	.40	.25
14	Mike Caldwell	.75	.40	.25
15	Steve Kemp	.75	.40	.25
	Panel (6)	5.00	2.50	1.50
16	Dave Goltz	.75	.40	.25
17	Mitchell Page	.75	.40	.25
18	Bill Stein	.75	.40	.25
	Panel (7)	5.00	2.50	1.50
19	Gene Tenace	.75	.40	.25
20	Jeff Burroughs	.75	.40	.25
21	Francisco Barrios	.75	.40	.25
	Panel (8)	7.50	3.75	2.25
22	Mike Torrez	.75	.40	.25
23	Ken Reitz	.75	.40	.25
24	Gary Carter	2.50	1.25	.70
	Panel (9)	9.00	4.50	2.75
25	Al Hrabosky	.75	.40	.25
26	Thurman Munson	1.50	.70	.45
27	Bill Buckner	.75	.40	.25
	Panel (10)	6.00	3.00	1.75
28	Ron Cey	.75	.40	.25
29	J.R. Richard	.75	.40	.25
30	Greg Luzinski	.75	.40	.25
	Panel (11)	5.00	2.50	1.50
31	Ed Ott	.75	.40	.25
32	Denny Martinez	.75	.40	.25
33	Darrell Evans	.75	.40	.25
	Panel (12)	5.00	2.50	1.50
34	Ron LeFlore	.75	.40	.25
35	Rick Waits	.75	.40	.25
36	Cecil Cooper	.75	.40	.25
	Panel (13)	15.00	7.50	4.50
37	Leon Roberts	.75	.40	.25
38a	Rod Carew (Large head.) (Botton of collar trim does not show.)	3.00	1.50	.90
38b	Rod Carew (Small head.) (Bottom of collar trim shows.)	3.00	1.50	.90
39	John Henry Johnson	.75	.40	.25
	Panel (14)	5.00	2.50	1.50
40	Chet Lemon	.75	.40	.25
41	Craig Swan	.75	.40	.25
42	Gary Matthews	.75	.40	.25
	Panel (15)	5.00	2.50	1.50
43	Lamar Johnson	.75	.40	.25
44	Ted Simmons	.75	.40	.25
45	Ken Griffey	.75	.40	.25
	Panel (16)	6.00	3.00	1.75
46	Freddie Patek	.75	.40	.25
47	Frank Tanana	.75	.40	.25
48	Rich Gossage	1.00	.50	.30
	Panel (17)	5.00	2.50	1.50
49	Burt Hooton	.75	.40	.25
50	Ellis Valentine	.75	.40	.25
51	Ken Forsch	.75	.40	.25
	Panel (18)	6.00	3.00	1.75
52	Bob Knepper	.75	.40	.25
53	Dave Parker	.75	.40	.25
54	Doug DeCinces	.75	.40	.25
	Panel (19)	20.00	10.00	6.00
55	Robin Yount	3.00	1.50	.90
56	Rusty Staub	1.00	.50	.30
57	Gary Alexander	.75	.40	.25
	Panel (20)	5.00	2.50	1.50
58	Julio Cruz	.75	.40	.25
59	Matt Keough	.75	.40	.25
60	Roy Smalley	.75	.40	.25
	Panel (21)	15.00	7.50	4.50
61	Joe Morgan	3.00	1.50	.90
62	Phil Niekro	2.00	1.00	.60
63	Don Baylor	.75	.40	.25
	Panel (22)	20.00	10.00	6.00
64	Dwight Evans	.75	.40	.25
65	Tom Seaver	3.00	1.50	.90
66	George Hendrick	.75	.40	.25
	Panel (23)	25.00	12.50	7.50
67	Rick Reuschel	.75	.40	.25
68	George Brett	6.00	3.00	1.75
69	Lou Piniella	1.00	.50	.30
	Panel (24)	12.00	6.00	3.50
70	Enos Cabell	.75	.40	.25
71	Steve Carlton	2.50	1.25	.70
72	Reggie Smith	.75	.40	.25
	Panel (25)	5.00	2.50	1.50
73	Rick Dempsey	.75	.40	.25
74	Vida Blue	.75	.40	.25
75	Phil Garner	.75	.40	.25
	Panel (26)	5.00	2.50	1.50
76	Rick Manning	.75	.40	.25
77	Mark Fidrych	1.00	.50	.30
78	Mario Guerrero	.75	.40	.25
	Panel (27)	5.00	2.50	1.50
79	Bob Stinson	.75	.40	.25
80	Al Oliver	.75	.40	.25
81	Doug Flynn	.75	.40	.25
	Panel (28)	7.50	3.75	2.25
82	John Mayberry	.75	.40	.25
83	Gaylord Perry	2.00	1.00	.60
84	Joe Rudi	.75	.40	.25
	Panel (29)	5.00	2.50	1.50
85	Dave Concepcion	.75	.40	.25
86	John Candelaria	.75	.40	.25
87	Pete Vuckovich	.75	.40	.25
	Panel (30)	5.00	2.50	1.50
88	Ivan DeJesus	.75	.40	.25
89	Ron Guidry	.75	.40	.25
90	Hal McRae	.75	.40	.25
	Panel (31)	6.00	3.00	1.75
91	Cesar Cedeno	.75	.40	.25
92	Don Sutton	2.00	1.00	.60
93	Andre Thornton	.75	.40	.25
	Panel (32)	5.00	2.50	1.50
94	Roger Erickson	.75	.40	.25
95	Larry Hisle	.75	.40	.25
96	Jason Thompson	.75	.40	.25
	Panel (33)	5.00	2.50	1.50
97	Jim Sundberg	.75	.40	.25
98	Bob Horner	.75	.40	.25
99	Ruppert Jones	.75	.40	.25
	Panel (34)	60.00	30.00	18.00
100	Willie Montanez	.75	.40	.25
101	Nolan Ryan	12.00	6.00	3.50
102	Ozzie Smith	15.00	7.50	4.50
	Panel (35)	12.00	6.00	3.50
103	Eric Soderholm	.75	.40	.25
104	Willie Stargell	2.50	1.25	.70
105a	Bob Bailor (Photo reversed, unissued proof.)	.75	.40	.25
105b	Bob Bailor (Photo corrected.)	.75	.40	.25
	Panel (36)	12.50	6.25	3.75
106	Carlton Fisk	2.50	1.25	.70
107	George Foster	.75	.40	.25
108	Keith Hernandez	.75	.40	.25
	Panel (37)	5.00	2.50	1.50
109	Dennis Leonard	.75	.40	.25
110	Graig Nettles	1.00	.50	.30
111	Jose Cruz	.75	.40	.25
	Panel (38)	5.00	2.50	1.50
112	Bobby Grich	.75	.40	.25
113	Bob Boone	.75	.40	.25
114	Davey Lopes	.75	.40	.25
	Panel (39)	15.00	7.50	4.50
115	Eddie Murray	3.00	1.50	.90
116	Jack Clark	.75	.40	.25
117	Lou Whitaker	.75	.40	.25
	Panel (40)	20.00	10.00	6.00
118	Miguel Dilone	.75	.40	.25
119	Sal Bando	.75	.40	.25
120	Reggie Jackson	6.00	3.00	1.75
	Panel (41)	15.00	7.50	4.50
121	Dale Murphy	2.00	1.00	.60
122	Jon Matlack	.75	.40	.25
123	Bruce Bochte	.75	.40	.25
	Panel (42)	12.50	6.25	3.75
124	John Stearns	.75	.40	.25
125	Dave Winfield	3.00	1.50	.90
126	Jorge Orta	.75	.40	.25
	Panel (43)	25.00	12.50	7.50
127	Garry Templeton	.75	.40	.25
128	Johnny Bench	3.00	1.50	.90
129	Butch Hobson	.75	.40	.25
	Panel (44)	6.00	3.00	1.75
130	Bruce Sutter	2.50	1.25	.70
131	Bucky Dent	.75	.40	.25
132	Amos Otis	.75	.40	.25
	Panel (45)	5.00	2.50	1.50
133	Bert Blyleven	.75	.40	.25
134	Larry Bowa	.75	.40	.25
135	Ken Singleton	.75	.40	.25
	Panel (46)	5.00	2.50	1.50
136	Sixto Lezcano	.75	.40	.25
137	Roy Howell	.75	.40	.25
138	Bill Madlock	.75	.40	.25
	Panel (47)	5.00	2.50	1.50
139	Dave Revering	.75	.40	.25
140	Richie Zisk	.75	.40	.25
141	Butch Wynegar	.75	.40	.25
	Panel (48)	25.00	12.50	7.50
142	Alan Ashby	.75	.40	.25
143	Sparky Lyle	.75	.40	.25
144	Pete Rose	7.50	3.75	2.25
	Panel (49)	6.00	3.00	1.75
145	Dennis Eckersley	2.50	1.25	.70
146	Dave Kingman	.75	.40	.25
147	Buddy Bell	.75	.40	.25
	Panel (50)	5.00	2.50	1.50
148	Mike Hargrove	.75	.40	.25
149	Jerry Koosman	.75	.40	.25
150	Toby Harrah	.75	.40	.25

1979 Hostess Unissued Proofs

Identical in format to the 150 cards which were issued on boxes of Hostess snack cakes, these cards were possibly prepared in the event trades of players in the issued set required quick replacement. The reason these cards were never released is unknown. Cards measure 2-1/4" x 3-1/4" at the dotted-line borders. While some of the proofs are numbered on back, others have no card number.

		NM	EX	VG
	Complete Set (17):	1,100	550.00	330.00
	Common Player:	50.00	25.00	15.00
151	Dusty Baker	60.00	30.00	18.00
152	Mark Belanger	60.00	30.00	18.00
154	Al Cowens	50.00	25.00	15.00
155	Dan Driessen	50.00	25.00	15.00
157	Steve Henderson	50.00	25.00	15.00
159	Tommy John	75.00	37.50	22.50
160	Garry Maddox	50.00	25.00	15.00
(161)	Willie McCovey	250.00	125.00	75.00
(162)	Scott McGregor	50.00	25.00	15.00
(163)	Bill Nahorodny	50.00	25.00	15.00
(164)	Terry Puhl	50.00	25.00	15.00
(165)	Willie Randolph	50.00	25.00	15.00
(166)	Jim Slaton	50.00	25.00	15.00
(167)	Paul Splittorff	50.00	25.00	15.00
(168)	Frank Taveras	50.00	25.00	15.00
(169)	Alan Trammell	125.00	65.00	35.00
(170)	Bump Wills	50.00	25.00	15.00

1971 House of Jazz

Controversy has dogged this card set since the first reports of its existence in the early 1970s. The legitimacy of the issue has been questioned though certain hobby journalists traced the cards to a record store which supposedly gave them away with music purchases, along with similar cards depicting musicians. The 2-3/8" x 3-1/2" cards are printed in black-and-white with round corners. Backs of some, but not all, cards have a blue-and-white address sticker for "HOUSE OF JAZZ, LTD." The unnumbered cards are checklisted here in alphabetical order.

		NM	EX	VG
	Complete Set (35):	200.00	100.00	60.00
	Common Player:	5.00	2.50	1.50
(1)	John Antonelli	5.00	2.50	1.50
(2)	Richie Ashburn	6.00	3.00	1.75
(3)	Ernie Banks	6.50	3.25	2.00
(4)	Hank Bauer	5.00	2.50	1.50
(5)	Joe DiMaggio	15.00	7.50	4.50
(6)	Bobby Doerr	5.00	2.50	1.50
(7)	Herman Franks	5.00	2.50	1.50
(8)	Lou Gehrig	15.00	7.50	4.50
(9)	Granny Hamner	5.00	2.50	1.50
(10)	Al Kaline	6.50	3.25	2.00
(11)	Harmon Killebrew	6.00	3.00	1.75
(12)	Jim Konstanty	5.00	2.50	1.50
(13)	Bob Lemon	5.00	2.50	1.50
(14)	Ed Lopat	5.00	2.50	1.50
(15)	Stan Lopata	5.00	2.50	1.50
(16)	Peanuts Lowrey	5.00	2.50	1.50
(17)	Mickey Mantle	35.00	17.50	10.00
(18)	Phil Marchildon	5.00	2.50	1.50
(19)	Walt Masterson	5.00	2.50	1.50
(20)	Ed Mathews	6.00	3.00	1.75
(21)	Willie Mays	10.00	5.00	3.00
(22)	Don Newcombe	5.00	2.50	1.50
(23)	Joe Nuxhall	5.00	2.50	1.50
(24)	Satchel Paige	7.50	3.75	2.25
(25)	Roy Partee	5.00	2.50	1.50
(26)	Jackie Robinson	7.50	3.75	2.25
(27)	Babe Ruth	20.00	10.00	6.00
(28)	Carl Scheib	5.00	2.50	1.50
(29)	Bobby Shantz	5.00	2.50	1.50
(30)	Burt Shotton	5.00	2.50	1.50
(31)	Duke Snider	6.50	3.25	1.75
(32)	Warren Spahn	6.00	3.00	1.75
(33)	Johnny Temple	5.00	2.50	1.50
(34)	Ted Williams	10.00	5.00	3.00
(35)	Early Wynn	5.00	2.50	1.50

1962 Houston Colt .45s Booklets

To introduce the members of the new Houston National League team, Phillips 66 gasoline sponsored (along with the team's cigarette and beer broadcast sponsors) this set of 24 player profile booklets given away one per week during the season. Fronts of the 16-page 5-3/8" x 7-7/16" booklets feature a blue and white action photo of the player on a bright orange background. Black and white graphics complete the design. The player's name appears in a Texas map outline. Backs have the 1962 Houston Colt .45s home-game schedule and details of the team's statewide radio network. Inside the booklet are a complete biography, stats and both posed and action photos of the players, along with families, teammates, etc. Because of player trades during the season, and lessened demand for some of the non-player booklets, some of the series are quite scarce. Each of the booklets can be found with different sponsors logos on front.

		NM	EX	VG
Complete Set (24):		240.00	120.00	72.00
Common Booklet:		15.00	7.50	4.50
(1)	Joe Amalfitano	15.00	7.50	4.50
(2)	Bob Aspromonte	15.00	7.50	4.50
(3)	Bob Bruce	15.00	7.50	4.50
(4)	Jim Campbell	18.00	9.00	5.50
(5)	Harry Craft	15.00	7.50	4.50
(6)	Dick Farrell	15.00	7.50	4.50
(7)	Dave Giusti	15.00	7.50	4.50
(8)	Jim Golden	15.00	7.50	4.50
(9)	J.C. Hartman	18.00	9.00	5.50
(10)	Ken Johnson	15.00	7.50	4.50
(11)	Norm Larker	15.00	7.50	4.50
(12)	Bob Lillis	15.00	7.50	4.50
(13)	Don McMahon	15.00	7.50	4.50
(14)	Roman Mejias	15.00	7.50	4.50
(15)	Jim Pendleton	18.00	9.00	5.50
(16)	Paul Richards (GM)	15.00	7.50	4.50
(17)	Bobby Shantz	30.00	15.00	9.00
(18)	Hal Smith	15.00	7.50	4.50
(19)	Al Spangler	15.00	7.50	4.50
(20)	Jim Umbricht	15.00	7.50	4.50
(21)	Carl Warwick	15.00	7.50	4.50
(22)	Hal Woodeshick	15.00	7.50	4.50
(23)	Coaches (James Adair, Bobby Bragan, Cot Deal, Luman Harris)	25.00	12.50	7.50
(24)	Announcers (Rene Cardenas, Orlando Diego, Gene Elston, Al Helfer, Lowell Passe, Guy Savage)	19.00	9.50	5.75

1967 Houston Astros Team Issue

This set of 12 player cards was issued by the Houston Astros, though the exact nature of the promotion is not known. Individual cards of 2-5/8" x 3-1/8" were printed on a perforated sheet about 9" x 10-1/2". Fronts have a posed color photo with a black facsimile autograph. Backs are printed in black on white with a yellow color block behind the player data and career notes. Full major and minor league stats are at bottom. The unnumbered cards are checklisted here in alphabetical order.

		NM	EX	VG
Complete Set, Sheet:		65.00	32.50	20.00
Complete Set, Singles (12):		65.00	32.50	20.00
Common Player:		8.00	4.00	2.50
(1)	Bob Aspromonte	8.00	4.00	2.50
(2)	John Bateman	8.00	4.00	2.50
(3)	Mike Cuellar	8.00	4.00	2.50
(4)	Larry Dierker	8.00	4.00	2.50
(5)	Dave Giusti	8.00	4.00	2.50
(6)	Grady Hatton	8.00	4.00	2.50
(7)	Bill Heath	8.00	4.00	2.50
(8)	Sonny Jackson	8.00	4.00	2.50
(9)	Ed Mathews	20.00	10.00	6.00
(10)	Joe Morgan	20.00	10.00	6.00
(11)	Rusty Staub	12.50	6.25	3.75
(12)	Jim Wynn	8.00	4.00	2.50

1953-1955 Howard Photo Service Postcards

Little is known about these postcards. Player and team combinations on the known pieces suggest a range of issue dates between 1953 and 1955. The 3-1/2" x 5-5/8" cards have

 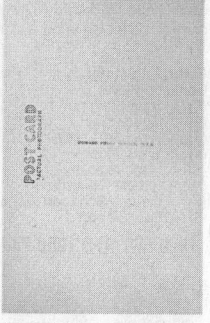

a glossy black-and-white front photo. A rubber-stamp on the back attributes the card to "Howard Photo Service, N.Y.C." The specific pose on the second Turley card is not known. It is possible other cards may yet be discovered.

		NM	EX	VG
Common Player:		20.00	10.00	6.00
(1)	Ned Garver	20.00	10.00	6.00
(2)	Billy Hitchcock	20.00	10.00	6.00
(3)	Dave Madison	20.00	10.00	6.00
(4)	Willie Mays	165.00	85.00	50.00
(5)	Willie Mays (Seven-Up ad on back.)	200.00	100.00	60.00
(6)	Bob Turley (Follow-through.)	30.00	15.00	9.00
(7)	Bob Turley (Wind-up.)	30.00	15.00	9.00

1976 HRT/RES 1942 Play Ball

 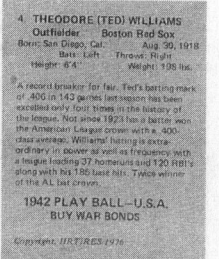

This "phantom" continuation of the Play Ball series of 1939-41 was the creation of Ted Taylor and Bob Schmierer, whose initials appear in the copyright line on back. The 2-1/2" x 3-1/8" cards feature black-and-white photos on front and were printed on gray clay-content cardboard in a near replication of the stock found on the vintage Play Ball series. Backs were also done in style reminiscent of 1940s issues. Besides player data and career summaries, backs have a "1942 PLAY BALL - U.S.A." title line and either a "Buy War Bonds" or "'Keep Baseball Going' - FDR" slogan above the 1976 copyright line. The pair produced a number of other original and reprint issues in the 1970s. All of the others carry advertisements for their "Philly" card shows.

		NM	EX	VG
Complete Set (36):		30.00	15.00	9.00
Common Card:		1.00	.50	.30
1	Lou Gehrig	7.50	3.75	2.25
2	Joe DiMaggio	7.50	3.75	2.25
3	Phil Rizzuto	3.00	1.50	.90
4	Ted Williams	6.00	3.00	1.75
5	Charles Wagner	1.00	.50	.30
6	Thornton Lee	1.00	.50	.30
7	Taft Wright	1.00	.50	.30
8	Jeff Heath	1.00	.50	.30
9	Roy Mack	1.00	.50	.30
10	Pat Mullin	1.00	.50	.30
11	Al Benton	1.00	.50	.30
12	Bob Harris	1.00	.50	.30
13	Roy Cullenbine	1.00	.50	.30
14	Cecil Travis	1.00	.50	.30
15	Buck Newsom	1.00	.50	.30
16	Eddie Collins Jr.	1.00	.50	.30
17	Dick Siebert	1.00	.50	.30
18	Dee Miles	1.00	.50	.30
19	Pete Reiser	1.00	.50	.30
20	Dolph Camilli	1.00	.50	.30
21	Curt Davis	1.00	.50	.30
22	Spud Krist	1.00	.50	.30
23	Frank Crespi	1.00	.50	.30
24	Elmer Riddle	1.00	.50	.30
25	Bucky Walters	1.00	.50	.30
26	Vince DiMaggio	1.50	.70	.45
27	Max Butcher	1.00	.50	.30
28	Mel Ott	3.00	1.50	.90
29	Bob Carpenter	1.00	.50	.30
30	Claude Passeau	1.00	.50	.30
31	Dom Dallessandro	1.00	.50	.30
32	Casey Stengel	3.00	1.50	.90
33	Alva Javery	1.00	.50	.30
34	Hans Lobert	1.00	.50	.30
35	Nick Etten	1.00	.50	.30
36	John Podgajny	1.00	.50	.30

1976-77 HRT/RES 1947 Bowman

Advertised as "The Set That Never Was," this collectors' issue from Ted Taylor and Bob Schmierer used a 2-1/8" x 2-1/2" black-and-white format and gray cardboard stock to replicate the feel of the first post-WWII baseball cards. The set was issued in

three series with advertising on back promoting the second (1976) and third (1977) annual EPSCC "Philly" shows. Series one (#1-49) was issued in 1976; series two (#50-81) and series three (#82-113) were 1977 issues.

		NM	EX	VG
Complete Set (113):		90.00	45.00	27.50
Common Player:		1.00	.50	.30
1	Bobby Doerr	1.00	.50	.30
2	Stan Musial	3.00	1.50	.90
3	Babe Ruth	7.50	3.75	2.25
4	Joe DiMaggio	6.00	3.00	1.75
5	Andy Pafko	1.00	.50	.30
6	Johnny Pesky	1.00	.50	.30
7	Gil Hodges	1.50	.70	.45
8	Tommy Holmes	1.00	.50	.30
9	Ralph Kiner	1.00	.50	.30
10	Yogi Berra	2.00	1.00	.60
11	Bob Feller	1.50	.70	.45
12	Joe Gordon	1.00	.50	.30
13	Eddie Joost	1.00	.50	.30
14	Del Ennis	1.00	.50	.30
15	Johnny Mize	1.00	.50	.30
16	Pee Wee Reese	1.25	.60	.40
17	Jackie Robinson	4.00	2.00	1.25
18	Enos Slaughter	1.00	.50	.30
19	Vern Stephens	1.00	.50	.30
20	Bobby Thomson	1.00	.50	.30
21	Ted Williams	6.00	3.00	1.75
22	Bob Elliott	1.00	.50	.30
23	Mickey Vernon	1.00	.50	.30
24	Ewell Blackwell	1.00	.50	.30
25	Lou Boudreau	1.00	.50	.30
26	Ralph Branca	1.00	.50	.30
27	Harry Breechen (Brecheen)	1.00	.50	.30
28	Dom DiMaggio	1.00	.50	.30
29	Bruce Edwards	1.00	.50	.30
30	Sam Chapman	1.00	.50	.30
31	George Kell	1.00	.50	.30
32	Jack Kramer	1.00	.50	.30
33	Hal Newhouser	1.00	.50	.30
34	Charlie Keller	1.00	.50	.30
35	Ken Keltner	1.00	.50	.30
36	Hank Greenberg	1.25	.60	.40
37	Howie Pollet	1.00	.50	.30
38	Luke Appling	1.00	.50	.30
39	Pete Suder	1.00	.50	.30
40	Johnny Sain	1.00	.50	.30
41	Phil Cavaretta (Cavarretta)	1.00	.50	.30
42	Johnny Vander Meer	1.00	.50	.30
43	Mel Ott	1.00	.50	.30
44	Walker Cooper	1.00	.50	.30
45	Birdie Tebbetts	1.00	.50	.30
46	George Stirnweiss	1.00	.50	.30
47	Connie Mack	1.00	.50	.30
48	Jimmie Foxx	1.00	.50	.30
49	Checklist (Joe DiMaggio, Babe Ruth)	1.50	.70	.45
(50)	Honus Wagner T206 Card (First series.)	1.00	.50	.30
51	Ted Taylor (First series.)	1.00	.50	.30
52	Bob Schmierer (First series.)	1.00	.50	.30
50	Schoolboy Rowe (Second series.)	1.00	.50	.30
51	Andy Seminick (Second series.)	1.00	.50	.30
52	Fred Walker (Second series.)	1.00	.50	.30
53	Virgil Trucks	1.00	.50	.30
54	Dizzy Trout	1.00	.50	.30
55	Walter Evers	1.00	.50	.30
56	Thurman Tucker	1.00	.50	.30
57	Fritz Ostermueller	1.00	.50	.30
58	Augie Galan	1.00	.50	.30
59	Norman Young	1.00	.50	.30
60	Skeeter Newsome	1.00	.50	.30
61	Jack Lohrke	1.00	.50	.30
62	Rudy York	1.00	.50	.30
63	Tex Hughson	1.00	.50	.30
64	Sam Mele	1.00	.50	.30
65	Fred Hutchinson	1.00	.50	.30
66	Don Black	1.00	.50	.30
67	Les Fleming	1.00	.50	.30
68	George McQuinn	1.00	.50	.30
69	Mike McCormick	1.00	.50	.30
70	Mickey Witek	1.00	.50	.30
71	Blix Donnelly	1.00	.50	.30
72	Elbie Fletcher	1.00	.50	.30
73	Hal Gregg	1.00	.50	.30
74	Dick Whitman	1.00	.50	.30
75	Johnny Neun	1.00	.50	.30
76	Doyle Lade	1.00	.50	.30
77	Ron Northey	1.00	.50	.30
78	Walker Cooper	1.00	.50	.30
79	Warren Spahn	1.00	.50	.30
80	Happy Chandler	1.00	.50	.30
81	Checklist (Connie Mack, Roy Mack, Connie Mack III)	1.00	.50	.30
82	Earle Mack	1.00	.50	.30
83	Buddy Rosar	1.00	.50	.30
84	Walt Judnich	1.00	.50	.30

		NM	EX	VG
85	Bob Kennedy	1.00	.50	.30
86	Mike Tresh	1.00	.50	.30
87	Sid Hudson	1.00	.50	.30
88	Eugene Thompson	1.00	.50	.30
89	Bill Nicholson	1.00	.50	.30
90	Stan Hack	1.00	.50	.30
91	Terry Moore	1.00	.50	.30
92	Ted Lyons	1.00	.50	.30
93	Barney McCosky	1.00	.50	.30
94	Stan Spence	1.00	.50	.30
95	Larry Jansen	1.00	.50	.30
96	Whitey Kurowski	1.00	.50	.30
97	Honus Wagner	1.50	.70	.45
98	Billy Herman	1.00	.50	.30
99	Jim Tabor	1.00	.50	.30
100	Phil Marchildon	1.00	.50	.30
101	Dave Ferriss	1.00	.50	.30
102	Al Zarilla	1.00	.50	.30
103	Bob Dillinger	1.00	.50	.30
104	Bob Lemon	1.00	.50	.30
105	Jim Hegan	1.00	.50	.30
106	Johnny Lindell	1.00	.50	.30
107	Willard Marshall	1.00	.50	.30
108	Walt Masterson	1.00	.50	.30
109	Carl Scheib	1.00	.50	.30
110	Bobby Brown	1.00	.50	.30
111	Cy Block	1.00	.50	.30
112	Sid Gordon	1.00	.50	.30
113	Checklist (Ty Cobb, Babe Ruth, Tris Speaker)	1.50	.70	.45

1977 HRT/RES Philadelphia 'Favorites'

This collectors' issue was produced by promoters Ted Taylor and Bob Schmierer to promote their third annual "Philly Show" in 1977. Printed in black-and-white on front and back, the 2-3/8" x 3-5/8" cards feature former Philadelphia A's and Phillies player photos on front, and an ad for the show on back. Cards were given away at area malls and sporting events to promote the show. Complete sets were originally sold for $2.75.

		NM	EX	VG
Complete Set (25):		30.00	15.00	9.00
Common Player:		2.00	1.00	.60
1	Connie Mack	2.00	1.00	.60
2	Larry Lajoie	2.50	1.25	.70
3	Eddie Collins	2.00	1.00	.60
4	Lefty Grove	2.50	1.25	.70
5	Al Simmons	2.00	1.00	.60
6	Jimmie Foxx	3.00	1.50	.90
7	Frank Baker	2.00	1.00	.60
8	Ferris Fain	2.00	1.00	.60
9	Jimmy Dykes	2.00	1.00	.60
10	Willie Jones	2.00	1.00	.60
11	Del Ennis	2.00	1.00	.60
12	Granny Hamner	2.00	1.00	.60
13	Andy Seminick	2.00	1.00	.60
14	Robin Roberts	4.00	2.00	1.25
15	Ed Delahanty	2.00	1.00	.60
16	Gavvy Cravath	2.00	1.00	.60
17	Cy Williams	2.00	1.00	.60
18	Chuck Klein	2.00	1.00	.60
19	Rich Ashburn	4.00	2.00	1.25
20	Bobby Shantz	2.00	1.00	.60
21	Gus Zernial	2.00	1.00	.60
22	Eddie Sawyer	2.00	1.00	.60
23	Grover Alexander	2.00	1.00	.60
24	Wally Moses	2.00	1.00	.60
25	Connie Mack Stadium	2.00	1.00	.60

1978 HRT/RES 1939 Father and Son Reprints

Reprints of scarce 1939 Father and Son Shoes cards of local ballplayers (minus the original advertising on front) were created by Ted Taylor and Bob Schmierer to pro-

mote their fourth "Philly Show" in March, 1978. The 3" x 4" cards have black-and-white player photos on front. Backs carry an ad for the show and information about the reprints.

		NM	EX	VG
Complete Set (8):		7.50	3.75	2.25
Common Player:		1.00	.50	.30
(1)	Sam Chapman	1.00	.50	.30
(2)	Chuck Klein	1.50	.70	.45
(3)	Herschel Martin	1.00	.50	.30
(4)	Wally Moses	1.00	.50	.30
(5)	Hugh Mulcahy	1.00	.50	.30
(6)	Skeeter Newsome	1.00	.50	.30
(7)	George Scharien (Scharein)	1.00	.50	.30
(8)	Dick Siebert	1.00	.50	.30

1979 HRT/RES 1950 Phillies/A's "Doubleheaders"

Though their names or initials do not appear on the cards, this collectors' set was issued by Ted Taylor and Bob Schmierer to promote the March and September 1979, "Philly Shows," the sixth and seventh in the show's history. Borrowing from the format of the 1941 "Doubleheaders" bubblegum card issue, these 2-1/2" x 2-1/8" cards depict members of the 1950 Phillies "Whiz Kids" and the 1950 A's, the last team managed by Connie Mack. Fronts are printed in blue and white, backs in maroon and white. The dual-player cards feature various ads on back, while the managers' cards have a team narrative. The unnumbered cards are checklisted here alphabetically within team, by the last name of the player on the left.

		NM	EX	VG
Complete Set (30):		25.00	12.50	7.50
Common Card:		1.50	.70	.45
(1)	Joe Astroth, Dick Fowler	1.50	.70	.45
(2)	Sam Chapman, Lou Brissie	1.50	.70	.45
(3)	Bob Dillinger, Billy Hitchcock	1.50	.70	.45
(4)	Ben Guintini, Joe Tipton	1.50	.70	.45
(5)	Bob Hooper, Barney McCosky	1.50	.70	.45
(6)	Eddie Joost, Kermit Wahl	1.50	.70	.45
(7)	Ed Klieman, Mike Guerra	1.50	.70	.45
(8)	Paul Lehner, Ferris Fain	1.50	.70	.45
(9)	Connie Mack	1.50	.70	.45
(10)	Earle Mack, Mickey Cochrane	1.50	.70	.45
(11)	Wally Moses, Carl Scheib	1.50	.70	.45
(12)	Pete Suder, Alex Kellner	1.50	.70	.45
(13)	Elmer Valo, Bobby Shantz	1.50	.70	.45
(14)	Bob Wellman, Joe Coleman	1.50	.70	.45
(15)	Hank Wyse, Gene Markland	1.50	.70	.45
(16)	Johnny Blatnik, Ed Wright	1.50	.70	.45
(17)	Ralph Caballero, Bubba Church	1.50	.70	.45
(18)	Milo Candini, Hank Borowy	1.50	.70	.45
(19)	Blix Donnelly, Bill Nicholson	1.50	.70	.45
(20)	Del Ennis, Ken Heintzelman	1.50	.70	.45
(21)	Mike Goliat, Dick Whitman	1.50	.70	.45
(22)	Granny Hamner, Rich Ashburn	3.50	1.75	1.00
(23)	Willie Jones, Russ Meyer	1.50	.70	.45
(24)	Jim Konstanty, Ken Silvestri	1.50	.70	.45
(25)	Stan Lopata, Eddie Waitkus	1.50	.70	.45
(26)	Ed Sanicki, Robin Roberts	3.50	1.75	1.00
(27)	Eddie Sawyer	1.50	.70	.45
(28)	Andy Seminick, Ken Trinkle	1.50	.70	.45
(29)	Dick Sisler, Stan Hollmig (DP)	1.50	.70	.45
(30)	Jocko Thompson, Curt Simmons	1.50	.70	.45

1957-1959 Hudepohl Beer Cincinnati Reds

These 8" x 10" black-and-white photos were distributed by Hudepohl Beer, although the brewery or brand is not mentioned on the pictures. They are identical in format to the team-issued publicity photos. The Hudepohl pictures differ from the team-issue in that the beer pictures have a semigloss finish and no printing on the back, while the team pictures have a glossy surface and a four-line warning on back not to use them for advertising purposes. The pictures have portrait or posed action photos, sometimes with the background removed. They are bordered in white with the player and team name at bottom. The type style is sans-serif for 1957 pictures, and serifed in 1959. Years of issue have been attributed according to corresponding team-issue photos and uni-

forms pictured. Because so many of the Hudepohl pictures are found autographed, it is possible they were distributed in conjunction with player promotional appearances. This checklist may well not be complete.

		NM	EX	VG
Common Player:		20.00	10.00	6.00
1957 (Redlegs, sans-serif.)				
	Ed. Bailey (Batting)	20.00	10.00	6.00
	George Crowe (Batting)	20.00	10.00	6.00
	Ted Kluszewski (Batting)	35.00	17.50	10.50
	Brooks Lawrence (Follow-through.)	20.00	10.00	6.00
	Roy McMillan (Batting)	20.00	10.00	6.00
	Joe Nuxhall (Follow-through.)	25.00	12.50	7.50
	Manager "Birdie" Tebbetts (Portrait)	20.00	10.00	6.00
1959 (Reds, serif.)				
	Brooks Lawrence (Portrait)	20.00	10.00	6.00

1960 Hudepohl Beer Cincinnati Reds

These 8" x 10" black-and-white photos were distributed by Hudepohl Beer, although the brewery or brand is not mentioned on the pictures. Similar in format to the team-issued publicity photos, the Hudepohl pictures differ in that they have a semi-gloss finish and no printing on the back, while the team pictures have a glossy surface and a four-line warning on back not to use them for advertising purposes. The pictures have portrait or posed action photos, sometimes with the background removed. They are bordered in white with the player and team name at bottom in a light sans-serif type. Years of issue have been attributed according to corresponding team-issue photos and uniforms pictured. Because so many of the Hudepohl pictures are found autographed, it is possible they were distributed in conjunction with player promotional appearances. This checklist may not be complete.

		NM	EX	VG
Common Player:		20.00	10.00	6.00
(1)	Ed. Bailey	20.00	10.00	6.00
(2)	Gus Bell	20.00	10.00	6.00
(3)	Jerry Lynch	20.00	10.00	6.00
(4)	Roy McMillan	20.00	10.00	6.00
(5)	Don Newcombe	20.00	10.00	6.00
(6)	Joe Nuxhall	25.00	12.50	7.50
(7)	Vada Pinson	30.00	15.00	9.00
(8)	Frank Robinson	85.00	42.00	25.00

1907 Geo. W. Hull Chicago White Sox Postcards

 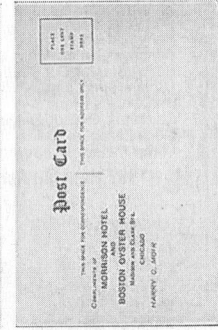

Members of the World Champion White Sox are featured on this single-team issue. Horizontal in format, the black-and-white cards measure about 5-1/2" x 3-1/2". All of the cards share a basic design of a player action posed photo at right, with his name, position, and "White Sox, World's Champions" in a white box beneath. The main part of the card pictures a clothesline full of white socks, each of which has a small round portrait photo of one of the players - 15 in all. In a larger portrait at lower-left is team owner Charles Comiskey. In the white border at top, each card has a witty statement such as "String of World-Beaters" and "Not Worn By Ladies, But Admired By Them." In the bottom border is, "Copyright 1907, Geo. W. Hull." Backs have been seen with a schedule of home games and with an ad from the Morrison Hotel and Boston Oyster House of Chicago.

		NM	EX	VG
Complete Set (16):		10,000	5,000	3,000
Common Player:		600.00	300.00	180.00
(1)	Nick Altrock	600.00	300.00	180.00
(2)	George Davis	950.00	475.00	285.00
(3)	Jiggs Donahue	600.00	300.00	180.00
(4)	Pat Dougherty	600.00	300.00	180.00
(5)	Eddie Hahn	600.00	300.00	180.00
(6)	Frank Isbell	600.00	300.00	180.00
(7)	Fielder Jones	600.00	300.00	180.00
(8)	Ed McFarland	600.00	300.00	180.00
(9)	Frank Owens	600.00	300.00	180.00
(10)	Roy Patterson	600.00	300.00	180.00
(11)	George Rohe	600.00	300.00	180.00
(12)	Frank Smith	600.00	300.00	180.00
(13)	Billy Sullivan	600.00	300.00	180.00
(14)	Lee Tannehill	600.00	300.00	180.00
(15)	Eddie Walsh	950.00	475.00	285.00
(16)	Doc White	600.00	300.00	180.00

1953 Hunter Wieners Cardinals

From the great era of the regionally issued hot dog cards in the mid-1950s, the 1953 Hunter wieners set of St. Louis Cardinals is among the rarest today. Originally issued in two-card panels, the cards are most often found as 2-1/4" x 3-1/4" singles today when they can be found at all. The cards feature a light blue facsimile autograph printed over the stat box at the bottom. They are blank-backed.

		NM	EX	VG
Complete Set (26):		10,000	5,000	3,000
Common Player:		300.00	150.00	90.00
(1)	Steve Bilko	300.00	150.00	90.00
(2)	Cloyd Boyer	300.00	150.00	90.00
(3)	Al Brazle	300.00	150.00	90.00
(4)	Cliff Chambers	300.00	150.00	90.00
(5)	Michael Clark	300.00	150.00	90.00
(6)	Jack Crimian	300.00	150.00	90.00
(7)	Lester Fusselman	300.00	150.00	90.00
(8)	Harvey Haddix	325.00	160.00	100.00
(9)	Solly Hemus	300.00	150.00	90.00
(10)	Ray Jablonski	300.00	150.00	90.00
(11)	William Johnson	300.00	150.00	90.00
(12)	Harry Lowrey	300.00	150.00	90.00
(13)	Lawrence Miggins	300.00	150.00	90.00
(14)	Stuart Miller	300.00	150.00	90.00
(15)	Wilmer Mizell	300.00	150.00	90.00
(16)	Stanley Musial	3,000	1,500	900.00
(17)	Joseph Presko	300.00	150.00	90.00
(18)	Delbert Rice	300.00	150.00	90.00
(19)	Harold Rice	300.00	150.00	90.00
(20)	Willard Schmidt	300.00	150.00	90.00
(21)	Albert Schoendienst	650.00	325.00	195.00
(22)	Richard Sisler	300.00	150.00	90.00
(23)	Enos Slaughter	650.00	325.00	195.00
(24)	Gerald Staley	300.00	150.00	90.00
(25)	Edward Stanky	325.00	160.00	97.00
(26)	John Yuhas	300.00	150.00	90.00

1954 Hunter Wieners Cardinals

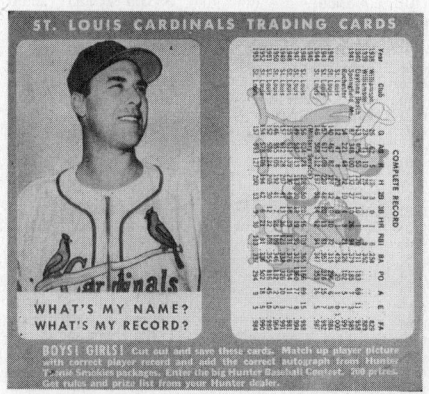

A nearly impossible set to complete today by virtue of the method of its issue, the 1954 Hunter hot dog set features what would traditionally be the front and back of a normal baseball card on two different cards. The "front," has a color photo with a box at bottom challenging the collector to name the player and quote his stats. The "back" features cartoon Cardinals in action, and contains the answers. However, because both parts were printed on a single panel. Because most of the back (non-picture) portions of the panels were thrown away years ago, it is a formidable challenge to complete a '54 Hunter set today. There is no back printing on the 2-1/4" x 3-1/2" cards.

		NM	EX	VG
Complete Set (30):		9,000	4,500	2,700
Common Player:		250.00	125.00	75.00
(1)	Tom Alston	250.00	125.00	75.00
(2)	Steve Bilko	250.00	125.00	75.00
(3)	Al Brazle	250.00	125.00	75.00
(4)	Tom Burgess	250.00	125.00	75.00
(5)	Cot Deal	250.00	125.00	75.00
(6)	Alex Grammas	250.00	125.00	75.00
(7)	Harvey Haddix	250.00	125.00	75.00

(8)	Solly Hemus	250.00	125.00	75.00
(9)	Ray Jablonski	250.00	125.00	75.00
(10)	Royce Lint	250.00	125.00	75.00
(11)	Peanuts Lowrey	250.00	125.00	75.00
(12)	Memo Luna	250.00	125.00	75.00
(13)	Stu Miller	250.00	125.00	75.00
(14)	Stan Musial	2,000	1,000	600.00
(15)	Tom Poholsky	250.00	125.00	75.00
(16)	Bill Posedel	250.00	125.00	75.00
(17)	Joe Presko	250.00	125.00	75.00
(18)	Dick Rand	250.00	125.00	75.00
(19)	Vic Raschi	250.00	125.00	75.00
(20)	Rip Repulski	250.00	125.00	75.00
(21)	Del Rice	250.00	125.00	75.00
(22)	John Riddle	250.00	125.00	75.00
(23)	Mike Ryba	250.00	125.00	75.00
(24)	Red Schoendienst	500.00	250.00	150.00
(25)	Dick Schofield	275.00	135.00	82.00
(26)	Enos Slaughter	500.00	250.00	150.00
(27)	Gerry Staley	250.00	125.00	75.00
(28)	Ed Stanky	250.00	125.00	75.00
(29)	Ed Yuhas	250.00	125.00	75.00
(30)	Sal Yvars	250.00	125.00	75.00

1955 Hunter Wieners Cardinals

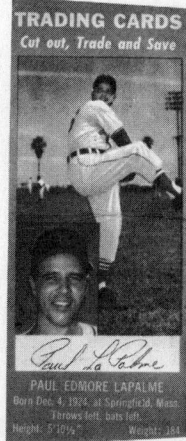

The 1955 team set of St. Louis Cardinals, included with packages of Hunter hot dogs, features the third format change in three years of issue. For 1955, the cards were printed in a tall, narrow (2" wide with the height tapering from 4-3/4" at left to 4-1/2" at right) format, two to a panel. The cards feature both a posed action photo and a portrait photo, along with a facsimile autograph and brief biographical data on the front. There is no back printing, as the cards were part of the wrapping for packages of hot dogs.

		NM	EX	VG
Complete Set (30):		11,000	5,500	3,250
Common Player:		250.00	125.00	75.00
(1)	Thomas Edison Alston	250.00	125.00	75.00
(2)	Kenton Lloyd Boyer	675.00	335.00	200.00
(3)	Harry Lewis Elliott	250.00	125.00	75.00
(4)	John Edward Faszholz	250.00	125.00	75.00
(5)	Joseph Filmore Frazier	250.00	125.00	75.00
(6)	Alexander Pete Grammas	250.00	125.00	75.00
(7)	Harvey Haddix	250.00	125.00	75.00
(8)	Solly Joseph Hemus	250.00	125.00	75.00
(9)	Lawrence Curtis Jackson	250.00	125.00	75.00
(10)	Tony R. Jacobs	250.00	125.00	75.00
(11)	Gordon Bassett Jones	250.00	125.00	75.00
(12)	Paul Edmore LaPalme	250.00	125.00	75.00
(13)	Brooks Ulysses Lawrence	250.00	125.00	75.00
(14)	Wallace Wade Moon	400.00	200.00	120.00
(15)	Stanley Frank Musial	2,700	1,350	810.00
(16)	Thomas George Poholsky	250.00	125.00	75.00
(17)	William John Posedel	250.00	125.00	75.00
(18)	Victor Angelo John Raschi	250.00	125.00	75.00
(19)	Eldon John Repulski	250.00	125.00	75.00
(20)	Delbert Rice	250.00	125.00	75.00
(21)	John Ludy Riddle	250.00	125.00	75.00
(22)	William F. Sarni	250.00	125.00	75.00
(23)	Albert Fred Schoendienst	550.00	275.00	165.00
(24)	Richard John Schofield (Actually John Richard.)	250.00	125.00	75.00
(25)	Frank Thomas Smith	250.00	125.00	75.00
(26)	Edward R. Stanky	275.00	135.00	82.00
(27)	Bobby Gene Tiefenauer	250.00	125.00	75.00
(28)	William Charles Virdon	400.00	200.00	120.00
(29)	Frederick E. Walker	250.00	125.00	75.00
(30)	Floyd Lewis Woolridge	250.00	125.00	75.00

1941 Huskies

This advertising card was issued by Huskies Whole Wheat Flakes cereal. In black-and-white, the card measures about 5-1/2" x 3-1/2". Facsimile autographs appear on the borderless front photo.

	NM	EX	VG
John Vander Meer, Frank McCormick	125.00	65.00	40.00

1976 Icee Drinks Reds

Issued in 1976 in the Cincinnati area by Icee Drinks, this 12-card set of semi-circular cards features members of the Reds. The cards measure approximately 2" in diameter with the bottom of the disc squared off. The cards were originally issued as soft drink lids. Fronts have a portrait photo in black-and-white, with uniform logos removed. Backs are blank. The cards are unnumbered. A 7" x 12" cap saver sheet was also available; it does not picture the players.

		NM	EX	VG
Complete Set (12):		60.00	30.00	18.00
Common Player:		2.00	1.00	.60
Saver Sheet:		27.00	13.50	8.00
(1)	Johnny Bench	10.00	5.00	3.00
(2)	Dave Concepcion	2.25	1.25	.70
(3)	Rawly Eastwick	2.00	1.00	.60
(4)	George Foster	2.25	1.25	.70
(5)	Cesar Geronimo	2.00	1.00	.60
(6)	Ken Griffey	2.50	1.25	.70
(7)	Don Gullett	2.00	1.00	.60
(8)	Will McEnaney	2.00	1.00	.60
(9)	Joe Morgan	6.00	3.00	1.75
(10)	Gary Nolan	2.00	1.00	.60
(11)	Tony Perez	4.00	2.00	1.25
(12)	Pete Rose	27.50	13.50	8.25

1963 I.D.L. Drug Store Pittsburgh Pirates

This set of 26 black-and-white cards was regionally distributed. The 4" x 5" semi-gloss cards are blank-backed and unnumbered. The checklist is arranged alphabetically. Johnny Logan's card is considered scarce and may have been pulled from distribution early.

		NM	EX	VG
Complete Set (27):		225.00	115.00	65.00
Common Player:		7.50	3.75	2.25
(1)	Bob Bailey	7.50	3.75	2.25
(2)	Forrest "Smoky" Burgess	7.50	3.75	2.25
(3)	Don Cardwell	7.50	3.75	2.25
(4)	Roberto Clemente	75.00	37.00	22.00
(5)	Donn Clendenon	10.00	5.00	3.00
(6)	Roy Face	7.50	3.75	2.25
(7)	Earl Francis	7.50	3.75	2.25
(8)	Bob Friend	7.50	3.75	2.25
(9)	Joe Gibbon	7.50	3.75	2.25
(10)	Julio Gotay	7.50	3.75	2.25
(11)	Harvey Haddix	7.50	3.75	2.25
(12)	Johnny Logan (SP)	15.00	7.50	4.50
(13)	Bill Mazeroski	25.00	12.50	7.50
(14)	Al McBean	7.50	3.75	2.25
(15)	Danny Murtaugh	7.50	3.75	2.25
(16)	Sam Narron	7.50	3.75	2.25

		NM	EX	VG
(17)	Ron Northey	7.50	3.75	2.25
(18)	Frank Oceak	7.50	3.75	2.25
(19)	Jim Pagliaroni	7.50	3.75	2.25
(20)	Ted Savage	7.50	3.75	2.25
(21)	Dick Schofield	7.50	3.75	2.25
(22)	Bob Skinner (SP)	15.00	7.50	4.50
(23)	Willie Stargell	25.00	12.50	7.50
(24)	Tom Sturdivant	7.50	3.75	2.25
(25)	Virgil "Fire" Trucks	7.50	3.75	2.25
(26)	Bob Veale	7.50	3.75	2.25
(27)	Bill Virdon	7.50	3.75	2.25

1916 Indianapolis Brewing Co.

THIS is one of a series of 200 pictures of Major League Baseball Players — all action pictures.

Complete set will be sent to you upon receipt of 25 cents

INDIANAPOLIS BREWING CO.
INDIANAPOLIS, INDIANA

LIEBER'S GOLD MEDAL
PROGRESS BEER
LIEBER'S SPECIAL BREW

World's Standard of Perfection

HOWARD SHANKS
L. F.—Washington Am.
160

Best known in blank-back form or with ads on back for The Sporting News, this 200-card set can be found with the imprint of several other local and regional businesses. Among them is the Indianapolis Brewing Co. Type-card and superstar collectors can expect to pay a significant premium for individual cards with Indianapolis Brewing advertising. The checklist parallels that of the 1916 M101-4 Blank Backs. Cards measure 1-5/8" x 3" and are printed in black-and-white. The brewery originally advertised the set on its "Facts for Fans" booklet, at a cost of 25 cents.

		NM	EX	VG
	Complete Set (200):	96,000	48,000	28,800
	Common Player:	240.00	120.00	75.00
1	Babe Adams	360.00	120.00	75.00
2	Sam Agnew	240.00	120.00	75.00
3	Eddie Ainsmith	240.00	120.00	75.00
4	Grover Alexander	720.00	360.00	215.00
5	Leon Ames	240.00	120.00	75.00
6	Jimmy Archer	240.00	120.00	75.00
7	Jimmy Austin	240.00	120.00	75.00
8	H.D. Baird	240.00	120.00	75.00
9	J. Franklin Baker	540.00	270.00	160.00
10	Dave Bancroft	540.00	270.00	160.00
11	Jack Barry	240.00	120.00	75.00
12	Zinn Beck	240.00	120.00	75.00
13	"Chief" Bender	540.00	270.00	160.00
14	Joe Benz	240.00	120.00	75.00
15	Bob Bescher	240.00	120.00	75.00
16	Al Betzel	240.00	120.00	75.00
17	Mordecai Brown	540.00	270.00	160.00
18	Eddie Burns	240.00	120.00	75.00
19	George Burns	240.00	120.00	75.00
20	Geo. J. Burns	240.00	120.00	70.00
21	Joe Bush	240.00	120.00	75.00
22	"Donie" Bush	240.00	120.00	75.00
23	Art Butler	240.00	120.00	75.00
24	Bobbie Byrne	240.00	120.00	75.00
25	Forrest Cady	240.00	120.00	75.00
26	Jimmy Callahan	240.00	120.00	75.00
27	Ray Caldwell	240.00	120.00	75.00
28	Max Carey	540.00	270.00	160.00
29	George Chalmers	240.00	120.00	75.00
30	Ray Chapman	270.00	135.00	80.00
31	Larry Cheney	240.00	120.00	75.00
32	Eddie Cicotte	540.00	270.00	160.00
33	Tom Clarke	240.00	120.00	75.00
34	Eddie Collins	540.00	270.00	160.00
35	"Shauno" Collins	240.00	120.00	75.00
36	Charles Comiskey	540.00	270.00	160.00
37	Joe Connolly	240.00	120.00	75.00
38	Ty Cobb	3,600	1,800	1,080
39	Harry Coveleskie (Coveleski)	240.00	120.00	75.00
40	Gavvy Cravath	240.00	120.00	75.00
41	Sam Crawford	540.00	270.00	160.00
42	Jean Dale	240.00	120.00	75.00
43	Jake Daubert	240.00	120.00	75.00
44	Charles Deal	240.00	120.00	75.00
45	Al Demaree	240.00	120.00	75.00
46	Josh Devore	240.00	120.00	75.00
47	William Doak	240.00	120.00	75.00
48	Bill Donovan	240.00	120.00	75.00
49	Charles Dooin	240.00	120.00	75.00
50	Mike Doolan	240.00	120.00	75.00
51	Larry Doyle	240.00	120.00	75.00
52	Jean Dubuc	240.00	120.00	75.00
53	Oscar Dugey	240.00	120.00	75.00
54	Johnny Evers	540.00	270.00	160.00
55	Urban Faber	540.00	270.00	160.00
56	"Hap" Felsch	720.00	360.00	215.00
57	Bill Fischer	240.00	120.00	75.00
58	Ray Fisher	240.00	120.00	75.00
59	Max Flack	240.00	120.00	75.00
60	Art Fletcher	240.00	120.00	75.00
61	Eddie Foster	240.00	100.00	75.00
62	Jacques Fournier	240.00	120.00	75.00
63	Del Gainer (Gainor)	240.00	120.00	75.00
64	"Chic" Gandil	540.00	270.00	160.00
65	Larry Gardner	240.00	120.00	75.00
66	Joe Gedeon	240.00	120.00	75.00
67	Gus Getz	240.00	120.00	75.00
68	Geo. Gibson	240.00	120.00	75.00
69	Wilbur Good	240.00	120.00	75.00
70	Hank Gowdy	240.00	120.00	75.00
71	John Graney	240.00	120.00	75.00
72	Clark Griffith	540.00	270.00	160.00
73	Tom Griffith	240.00	120.00	75.00
74	Heinie Groh	240.00	120.00	75.00
75	Earl Hamilton	240.00	120.00	75.00
76	Bob Harmon	240.00	120.00	75.00
77	Roy Hartzell	240.00	120.00	75.00
78	Claude Hendrix	240.00	120.00	75.00
79	Olaf Henriksen	240.00	120.00	75.00
80	John Henry	240.00	120.00	75.00
81	"Buck" Herzog	240.00	120.00	75.00
82	Hugh High	240.00	120.00	75.00
83	Dick Hoblitzell	240.00	120.00	75.00
84	Harry Hooper	540.00	270.00	160.00
85	Ivan Howard	240.00	120.00	75.00
86	Miller Huggins	540.00	270.00	160.00
87	Joe Jackson	20,000	7,500	4,500
88	William James	240.00	120.00	75.00
89	Harold Janvrin	240.00	120.00	75.00
90	Hugh Jennings	540.00	270.00	160.00
91	Walter Johnson	1,800	900.00	540.00
92	Fielder Jones	240.00	120.00	75.00
93	Joe Judge	240.00	120.00	75.00
94	Bennie Kauff	240.00	120.00	75.00
95	Wm. Killefer Jr.	240.00	120.00	75.00
96	Ed. Konetchy	240.00	120.00	75.00
97	Napoleon Lajoie	600.00	300.00	180.00
98	Jack Lapp	240.00	120.00	75.00
99	John Lavan	240.00	120.00	75.00
100	Jimmy Lavender	240.00	120.00	75.00
101	"Nemo" Leibold	240.00	120.00	75.00
102	H.B. Leonard	240.00	120.00	75.00
103	Duffy Lewis	240.00	120.00	75.00
104	Hans Lobert	240.00	120.00	75.00
105	Tom Long	240.00	120.00	75.00
106	Fred Luderus	240.00	120.00	75.00
107	Connie Mack	540.00	270.00	160.00
108	Lee Magee	240.00	120.00	75.00
109	Sherwood Magee	240.00	120.00	75.00
110	Al. Mamaux	240.00	120.00	75.00
111	Leslie Mann	240.00	120.00	75.00
112	"Rabbit" Maranville	540.00	270.00	160.00
113	Rube Marquard	540.00	270.00	160.00
114	J. Erskine Mayer	360.00	180.00	110.00
115	George McBride	240.00	120.00	75.00
116	John J. McGraw	540.00	270.00	160.00
117	Jack McInnis	240.00	120.00	75.00
118	Fred Merkle	240.00	120.00	75.00
119	Chief Meyers	240.00	120.00	75.00
120	Clyde Milan	240.00	120.00	75.00
121	John Miller	240.00	120.00	75.00
122	Otto Miller	240.00	120.00	75.00
123	Willie Mitchell	240.00	120.00	75.00
124	Fred Mollwitz	240.00	120.00	75.00
125	Pat Moran	240.00	120.00	75.00
126	Ray Morgan	240.00	120.00	75.00
127	Geo. Moriarty	240.00	120.00	75.00
128	Guy Morton	240.00	120.00	75.00
129	Mike Mowrey	240.00	120.00	75.00
130	Ed. Murphy	240.00	120.00	75.00
131	"Hy" Myers	240.00	120.00	75.00
132	J.A. Niehoff	240.00	120.00	75.00
133	Rube Oldring	240.00	120.00	75.00
134	Oliver O'Mara	240.00	120.00	75.00
135	Steve O'Neill	240.00	120.00	75.00
136	"Dode" Paskert	240.00	120.00	75.00
137	Roger Peckinpaugh	240.00	120.00	75.00
138	Walter Pipp	240.00	120.00	75.00
139	Derril Pratt (Derrill)	240.00	120.00	75.00
140	Pat Ragan	240.00	120.00	75.00
141	Bill Rariden	240.00	120.00	75.00
142	Eppa Rixey	540.00	270.00	160.00
143	Davey Robertson	240.00	120.00	75.00
144	Wilbert Robinson	540.00	270.00	160.00
145	Bob Roth	240.00	120.00	75.00
146	Ed. Roush	540.00	270.00	160.00
147	Clarence Rowland	240.00	120.00	75.00
148	"Nap" Rucker	240.00	120.00	75.00
149	Dick Rudolph	240.00	120.00	75.00
150	Reb Russell	240.00	120.00	75.00
151	Babe Ruth	24,000	12,000	7,200
152	Vic Saier	240.00	120.00	75.00
153	"Slim" Sallee	240.00	120.00	75.00
154	Ray Schalk	540.00	270.00	160.00
155	Walter Schang	240.00	120.00	75.00
156	Frank Schulte	240.00	120.00	75.00
157	Everett Scott	240.00	120.00	75.00
158	Jim Scott	240.00	120.00	75.00
159	Tom Seaton	240.00	120.00	75.00
160	Howard Shanks	240.00	120.00	75.00
161	Bob Shawkey	240.00	120.00	75.00
162	Ernie Shore	240.00	120.00	75.00
163	Burt Shotton	240.00	120.00	75.00
164	Geo. Sisler	540.00	270.00	160.00
165	J. Carlisle Smith	240.00	120.00	75.00
166	Fred Snodgrass	240.00	120.00	75.00
167	Geo. Stallings	240.00	120.00	75.00
168	Oscar Stanage	240.00	120.00	75.00
169	Charles Stengel	540.00	270.00	160.00
170	Milton Stock	240.00	120.00	75.00
171	Amos Strunk	240.00	120.00	75.00
172	Billy Sullivan	240.00	120.00	75.00
173	"Jeff" Tesreau	240.00	120.00	75.00
174	Joe Tinker	540.00	270.00	160.00
175	Fred Toney	240.00	120.00	75.00
176	Terry Turner	240.00	120.00	75.00
177	George Tyler	240.00	120.00	75.00
178	Jim Vaughn	240.00	120.00	75.00
179	Bob Veach	240.00	120.00	75.00
180	James Viox	240.00	120.00	75.00
181	Oscar Vitt	240.00	120.00	75.00
182	Hans Wagner	5,000	1,200	720.00
183	Clarence Walker	240.00	120.00	75.00
184	Ed. Walsh	540.00	270.00	160.00
185	W. Wambsganss (Photo actually Fritz Coumbe.)	240.00	120.00	75.00
186	Buck Weaver	2,000	450.00	270.00
187	Carl Weilman	240.00	120.00	75.00
188	Zach Wheat	540.00	270.00	160.00
189	Geo. Whitted	240.00	120.00	75.00
190	Fred Williams	240.00	120.00	75.00
191	Art Wilson	240.00	120.00	75.00
192	J. Owen Wilson	240.00	120.00	75.00
193	Ivy Wingo	240.00	120.00	75.00
194	"Mel" Wolfgang	240.00	120.00	75.00
195	Joe Wood	360.00	180.00	110.00
196	Steve Yerkes	240.00	120.00	75.00
197	"Pep" Young	240.00	120.00	75.00
198	Rollie Zeider	240.00	120.00	75.00
199	Heiny Zimmerman	240.00	120.00	75.00
200	Ed. Zwilling	240.00	120.00	75.00

1923 Curtis Ireland Candy (E123)

 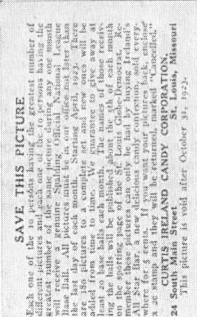

SAVE THIS PICTURE

This set, identified in the ACC as E123, was issued in 1923 by the Curtis Ireland Candy Corp. of St. Louis and was distributed with Ireland's "All Star Bars." Except for the backs, the Ireland set is identical to the Willard Chocolate V100 set of the same year. Measuring 3-1/4" x 2-1/16", the cards feature sepia-toned photos with the player's name in script on the front. The backs advertise a contest which required the collector to mail in the cards in exchange for prizes, which probably explains their relative scarcity today.

		NM	EX	VG
	Complete Set (180):	125,000	50,000	30,000
	Common Player:	600.00	240.00	150.00
(1)	Chas. B Adams	600.00	240.00	150.00
(2)	Grover C. Alexander	1,000	400.00	250.00
(3)	J.P. Austin	600.00	240.00	150.00
(4)	J.C. Bagby	600.00	240.00	150.00
(5)	J. Franklin Baker	900.00	360.00	225.00
(6)	David J. Bancroft	900.00	360.00	225.00
(7)	Turner Barber	600.00	240.00	150.00
(8)	Jesse L. Barnes	600.00	240.00	150.00
(9)	J.C. Bassler	600.00	240.00	150.00
(10)	L.A. Blue	600.00	240.00	150.00
(11)	Norman D. Boeckel	600.00	240.00	150.00
(12)	F.L. Brazil (Brazill)	600.00	240.00	150.00
(13)	G.H. Burns	600.00	240.00	150.00
(14)	Geo. J. Burns	600.00	240.00	150.00
(15)	Leon Cadore	600.00	240.00	150.00
(16)	Max G. Carey	900.00	360.00	225.00
(17)	Harold G. Carlson	600.00	240.00	150.00
(18)	Lloyd R. Christenberry (Christenbury)	600.00	240.00	150.00
(19)	Vernon J. Clemons	600.00	240.00	150.00
(20)	T.R. Cobb	8,500	3,400	2,125
(21)	Bert Cole	600.00	240.00	150.00
(22)	John F. Collins	600.00	240.00	150.00
(23)	S. Coveleskie (Coveleski)	900.00	360.00	225.00
(24)	Walton E. Cruise	600.00	240.00	150.00
(25)	G.W. Cutshaw	600.00	240.00	150.00
(26)	Jacob E. Daubert	600.00	240.00	150.00
(27)	Geo. Dauss	600.00	240.00	150.00
(28)	F.T. Davis	600.00	240.00	150.00
(29)	Chas. A. Deal	600.00	240.00	150.00
(30)	William L. Doak	600.00	240.00	150.00
(31)	William E. Donovan	600.00	240.00	150.00
(32)	Hugh Duffy	900.00	360.00	225.00
(33)	J.A. Dugan	600.00	240.00	150.00
(34)	Louis B. Duncan	600.00	240.00	150.00
(35)	James Dykes	600.00	240.00	150.00
(36)	H.J. Ehmke	600.00	240.00	150.00
(37)	F.R. Ellerbe	600.00	240.00	150.00
(38)	E.G. Erickson	600.00	240.00	150.00
(39)	John J. Evers	900.00	360.00	225.00
(40)	U.C. Faber	900.00	360.00	225.00
(41)	B.A. Falk	600.00	240.00	150.00
(42)	Max Flack	600.00	240.00	150.00
(43)	Lee Fohl	600.00	240.00	150.00
(44)	Jacques F. Fournier	600.00	240.00	150.00
(45)	Frank F. Frisch	900.00	360.00	225.00
(46)	C.E. Galloway	600.00	240.00	150.00
(47)	W.C. Gardner	600.00	240.00	150.00
(48)	E.P. Gharrity	600.00	240.00	150.00
(49)	Geo. Gibson	600.00	240.00	150.00
(50)	Wm. Gleason	600.00	240.00	150.00
(51)	William Gleason	600.00	240.00	150.00
(52)	Henry M. Gowdy	600.00	240.00	150.00
(53)	I.M. Griffin	600.00	240.00	150.00
(54)	Thomas Griffith	600.00	240.00	150.00
(55)	Burleigh A. Grimes	900.00	360.00	225.00
(56)	Charles J. Grimm	600.00	240.00	150.00
(57)	Jesse J. Haines	900.00	360.00	225.00

		NM	EX	VG
(58)	S.R. Harris	900.00	360.00	225.00
(59)	W.B. Harris	600.00	240.00	150.00
(60)	R.K. Hasty	600.00	240.00	150.00
(61)	H.E. Heilman (Heilmann)	900.00	360.00	225.00
(62)	Walter J. Henline	600.00	240.00	150.00
(63)	Walter L. Holke	600.00	240.00	150.00
(64)	Charles J. Hollocher	600.00	240.00	150.00
(65)	H.B. Hooper	900.00	360.00	225.00
(66)	Rogers Hornsby	1,250	500.00	310.00
(67)	W.C. Hoyt	900.00	360.00	225.00
(68)	Miller Huggins	900.00	360.00	225.00
(69)	W.C. Jacobsen (Jacobson)	600.00	240.00	150.00
(70)	C.D. Jamieson	600.00	240.00	150.00
(71)	Ernest Johnson	600.00	240.00	150.00
(72)	W.P. Johnson	2,250	900.00	560.00
(73)	James H. Johnston	600.00	240.00	150.00
(74)	R.W. Jones	600.00	240.00	150.00
(75)	Samuel Pond Jones	600.00	240.00	150.00
(76)	J.I. Judge	600.00	240.00	150.00
(77)	James W. Keenan	600.00	240.00	150.00
(78)	Geo. L. Kelly	900.00	360.00	225.00
(79)	Peter J. Kilduff	600.00	240.00	150.00
(80)	William Killefer	600.00	240.00	150.00
(81)	Lee King	600.00	240.00	150.00
(82)	Ray Kolp	600.00	240.00	150.00
(83)	John Lavan	600.00	240.00	150.00
(84)	H.L. Leibold	600.00	240.00	150.00
(85)	Connie Mack	900.00	360.00	225.00
(86)	J.W. Mails	600.00	240.00	150.00
(87)	Walter J. Maranville	900.00	360.00	225.00
(88)	Richard W. Marquard	900.00	360.00	225.00
(89)	C.W. Mays	650.00	260.00	160.00
(90)	Geo. F. McBride	600.00	240.00	150.00
(91)	H.M. McClellan	600.00	240.00	150.00
(92)	John J. McGraw	900.00	360.00	225.00
(93)	Austin B. McHenry	600.00	240.00	150.00
(94)	J. McInnis	600.00	240.00	150.00
(95)	Douglas McWeeney (McWeeny)	600.00	240.00	150.00
(96)	M. Menosky	600.00	240.00	150.00
(97)	Emil F. Meusel	600.00	240.00	150.00
(98)	R. Meusel	600.00	240.00	150.00
(99)	Henry W. Meyers	600.00	240.00	150.00
(100)	J.C. Milan	600.00	240.00	150.00
(101)	John K. Miljus	600.00	240.00	150.00
(102)	Edmund J. Miller	600.00	240.00	150.00
(103)	Elmer Miller	600.00	240.00	150.00
(104)	Otto L. Miller	600.00	240.00	150.00
(105)	Fred Mitchell	600.00	240.00	150.00
(106)	Geo. Mogridge	600.00	240.00	150.00
(107)	Patrick J. Moran	600.00	240.00	150.00
(108)	John D. Morrison	600.00	240.00	150.00
(109)	J.A. Mostil	600.00	240.00	150.00
(110)	Clarence F. Mueller	600.00	240.00	150.00
(111)	A. Earle Neale	650.00	260.00	160.00
(112)	Joseph Oeschger	600.00	240.00	150.00
(113)	Robert J. O'Farrell	600.00	240.00	150.00
(114)	J.C. Oldham	600.00	240.00	150.00
(115)	I.M. Olson	600.00	240.00	150.00
(116)	Geo. M. O'Neil	600.00	240.00	150.00
(117)	S.F. O'Neill	600.00	240.00	150.00
(118)	Frank J. Parkinson	600.00	240.00	150.00
(119)	Geo. H. Paskert	600.00	240.00	150.00
(120)	R.T. Peckinpaugh	600.00	240.00	150.00
(121)	H.J. Pennock	900.00	360.00	225.00
(122)	Ralph Perkins	600.00	240.00	150.00
(123)	Edw. J. Pfeffer	600.00	240.00	150.00
(124)	W.C. Pipp	600.00	240.00	150.00
(125)	Charles Elmer Ponder	600.00	240.00	150.00
(126)	Raymond R. Powell	600.00	240.00	150.00
(127)	D.B. Pratt	600.00	240.00	150.00
(128)	Joseph Rapp	600.00	240.00	150.00
(129)	John H. Rawlings	600.00	240.00	150.00
(130)	E.S. Rice (Should be E.C.)	900.00	360.00	225.00
(131)	Branch Rickey	1,000	400.00	250.00
(132)	James J. Ring	600.00	240.00	150.00
(133)	Eppa J. Rixey	900.00	360.00	225.00
(134)	Davis A. Robertson	600.00	240.00	150.00
(135)	Edwin Rommel	600.00	240.00	150.00
(136)	Edd J. Roush	900.00	360.00	225.00
(137)	Harold Ruel (Herold)	600.00	240.00	150.00
(138)	Allen Russell	600.00	240.00	150.00
(139)	G.H. Ruth	12,500	5,000	3,125
(140)	Wilfred D. Ryan	600.00	240.00	150.00
(141)	Henry F. Sallee	600.00	240.00	150.00
(142)	W.H. Schang	600.00	240.00	150.00
(143)	Raymond H. Schmandt	600.00	240.00	150.00
(144)	Everett Scott	600.00	240.00	150.00
(145)	Henry Severeid	600.00	240.00	150.00
(146)	Jos. W. Sewell	900.00	360.00	225.00
(147)	Howard S. Shanks	600.00	240.00	150.00
(148)	E.H. Sheely	600.00	240.00	150.00
(149)	Ralph Shinners	600.00	240.00	150.00
(150)	U.J. Shocker	600.00	240.00	150.00
(151)	G.H. Sisler	900.00	360.00	225.00
(152)	Earl L. Smith	600.00	240.00	150.00
(153)	Earl S. Smith	600.00	240.00	150.00
(154)	Geo. A. Smith	600.00	240.00	150.00
(155)	J.W. Smith	600.00	240.00	150.00
(156)	Tris E. Speaker	1,350	540.00	335.00
(157)	Arnold Staatz	600.00	240.00	150.00
(158)	J.R. Stephenson	600.00	240.00	150.00
(159)	Milton J. Stock	600.00	240.00	150.00
(160)	John L. Sullivan	600.00	240.00	150.00
(161)	H.F. Tormahlen	600.00	240.00	150.00
(162)	Jas. A. Tierney	600.00	240.00	150.00
(163)	J.T. Tobin	600.00	240.00	150.00
(164)	Jas. L. Vaughn	600.00	240.00	150.00
(165)	R.H. Veach	600.00	240.00	150.00
(166)	C.W. Walker	600.00	240.00	150.00
(167)	A.L. Ward	600.00	240.00	150.00
(168)	Zack D. Wheat	900.00	360.00	225.00
(169)	George B. Whitted	600.00	240.00	150.00
(170)	Irvin K. Wilhelm	600.00	240.00	150.00
(171)	Roy H. Wilkinson	600.00	240.00	150.00
(172)	Fred C. Williams	600.00	240.00	150.00
(173)	K.R. Williams	600.00	240.00	150.00
(174)	Sam'l W. Wilson	600.00	240.00	150.00
(175)	Ivy B. Wingo	600.00	240.00	150.00
(176)	L.W. Witt	600.00	240.00	150.00
(177)	Joseph Wood	650.00	260.00	160.00
(178)	E. Yaryan	600.00	240.00	150.00
(179)	R.S. Young	600.00	240.00	150.00
(180)	Ross Young (Youngs)	900.00	360.00	225.00

1967 Irvindale Dairy Atlana Braves

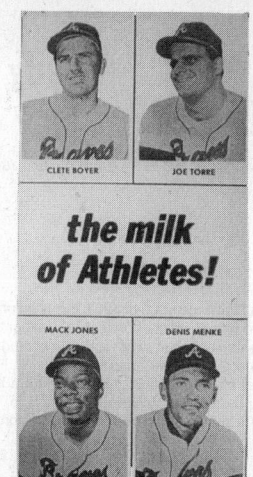

This quartet of Braves was printed in shades of deep red on the white background of a milk carton panel. Well-cut individual pieces measure 1-3/4" x 2-5/8" and are blank-backed.

		NM	EX	VG
Complete Set, Panel:		250.00	125.00	75.00
Complete Set, Singles:		175.00	85.00	45.00
Common Player:		40.00	20.00	12.00
(1)	Clete Boyer	40.00	20.00	12.00
(2)	Mack Jones	40.00	20.00	12.00
(3)	Denis Menke	40.00	20.00	12.00
(4)	Joe Torre	60.00	30.00	18.00

1976 Isaly's/Sweet William discs

One of several regional sponsors of player disc sets in 1976 was the Pittsburgh area dairy store chain, Isaly's, and the Sweet William restaurants. The discs are 3-3/8" diameter with a black-and-white player portrait photo in the center of the baseball design. A line of red stars is above, while the left and right panels feature one of several bright colors. Produced by Michael Schecter Associates under license from the Major League Baseball Players Association, the player photos have had uniform and cap logos removed. Backs are printed in red and purple. The unnumbered checklist here is presented in alphabetical order.

		NM	EX	VG
Complete Set (70):		15.00	7.50	4.50
Common Player:		.50	.25	.15
(1)	Henry Aaron	4.00	2.00	1.25
(2)	Johnny Bench	2.00	1.00	.60
(3)	Vida Blue	.50	.25	.15
(4)	Larry Bowa	.50	.25	.15
(5)	Lou Brock	2.00	1.00	.60
(6)	Jeff Burroughs	.50	.25	.15
(7)	John Candelaria	.50	.25	.15
(8)	Jose Cardenal	.50	.25	.15
(9)	Rod Carew	2.00	1.00	.60
(10)	Steve Carlton	2.00	1.00	.60
(11)	Dave Cash	.50	.25	.15
(12)	Cesar Cedeno	.50	.25	.15
(13)	Ron Cey	.50	.25	.15
(14)	Carlton Fisk	2.00	1.00	.60
(15)	Tito Fuentes	.50	.25	.15
(16)	Steve Garvey	1.50	.70	.45
(17)	Ken Griffey	.50	.25	.15
(18)	Don Gullett	.50	.25	.15
(19)	Willie Horton	.50	.25	.15
(20)	Al Hrabosky	.50	.25	.15
(21)	Catfish Hunter	2.00	1.00	.60
(22)	Reggie Jackson (A's)	3.00	1.50	.90
(23)	Randy Jones	.50	.25	.15
(24)	Jim Kaat	.50	.25	.15
(25)	Don Kessinger	.50	.25	.15
(26)	Dave Kingman	.50	.25	.15
(27)	Jerry Koosman	.50	.25	.15
(28)	Mickey Lolich	.50	.25	.15
(29)	Greg Luzinski	.50	.25	.15
(30)	Fred Lynn	.50	.25	.15
(31)	Bill Madlock	.50	.25	.15
(32)	Carlos May (White Sox)	.50	.25	.15
(33)	John Mayberry	.50	.25	.15
(34)	Bake McBride	.50	.25	.15
(35)	Doc Medich	.50	.25	.15
(36)	Andy Messersmith (Dodgers)	.50	.25	.15
(37)	Rick Monday	.50	.25	.15
(38)	John Montefusco	.50	.25	.15
(39)	Jerry Morales	.50	.25	.15
(40)	Joe Morgan	2.00	1.00	.60
(41)	Thurman Munson	2.00	1.00	.60
(42)	Bobby Murcer	.50	.25	.15
(43)	Al Oliver	.50	.25	.15
(44)	Jim Palmer	2.00	1.00	.60
(45)	Dave Parker	.50	.25	.15
(46)	Tony Perez	2.00	1.00	.60
(47)	Jerry Reuss	.50	.25	.15
(48)	Brooks Robinson	2.00	1.00	.60
(49)	Frank Robinson	2.00	1.00	.60
(50)	Steve Rogers	.50	.25	.15
(51)	Pete Rose	6.00	3.00	1.75
(52)	Nolan Ryan	12.00	6.00	3.50
(53)	Manny Sanguillen	.50	.25	.15
(54)	Mike Schmidt	3.00	1.50	.90
(55)	Tom Seaver	2.00	1.00	.60
(56)	Ted Simmons	.50	.25	.15
(57)	Reggie Smith	.50	.25	.15
(58)	Willie Stargell	2.00	1.00	.60
(59)	Rusty Staub	.75	.40	.25
(60)	Rennie Stennett	.50	.25	.15
(61)	Don Sutton	2.00	1.00	.60
(62)	Andy Thornton (Cubs)	.50	.25	.15
(63)	Luis Tiant	.50	.25	.15
(64)	Joe Torre	1.50	.70	.45
(65)	Mike Tyson	.50	.25	.15
(66)	Bob Watson	.50	.25	.15
(67)	Wilbur Wood	.50	.25	.15
(68)	Jimmy Wynn	.50	.25	.15
(69)	Carl Yastrzemski	2.50	1.25	.70
(70)	Richie Zisk	.50	.25	.15

1976 ISCA Hoosier Hot-Stove All-Stars

Famous native Hoosier ballplayers are featured in this collectors' issue from the Indiana Sports Collectors Assn. The 2-5/8" x 3-5/8" cards have black-and-white player photos on front framed in the state's outline. Red and blue graphics on a white background complete the design. Backs are in black and blue on white and include a career summary. A star on the state map at bottom indicates where the player was born.

		NM	EX	VG
Complete Set (26):		15.00	7.50	4.50
Common Player:		2.00	1.00	.60
1	Edd Roush	2.00	1.00	.60
2	Sam Thompson	2.00	1.00	.60
3	Chuck Klein	2.00	1.00	.60
4	Lou Criger	2.00	1.00	.60
5	Amos Rusie	2.00	1.00	.60
6	Billy Herman	2.00	1.00	.60
7	George Dauss	2.00	1.00	.60
8	Tom Thevenow	2.00	1.00	.60
9	Mordecai Brown	2.00	1.00	.60
10	Freddie Fitzsimmons	2.00	1.00	.60
11	Art Nehf	2.00	1.00	.60
12	Carl Erskine	3.00	1.50	.90
13	Don Larsen	3.00	1.50	.90
14	Gil Hodges	6.00	3.00	1.75
15	Pete Fox	2.00	1.00	.60
16	Butch Henline	2.00	1.00	.60
17	Doc Crandall	2.00	1.00	.60
18	Dizzy Trout	2.00	1.00	.60
19	Donie Bush	2.00	1.00	.60
20	Max Carey	2.00	1.00	.60
21	Eugene Hargrave, William Hargrave	2.00	1.00	.60
22	Sam Rice	2.00	1.00	.60
23	Babe Adams	2.00	1.00	.60
24	Cy Williams	2.00	1.00	.60
25	1913 Indianapolis Federal League Team	2.00	1.00	.60
26	Paul Frisz	2.00	1.00	.60

J

1912 J=K Candy

Originally printed on the front and back of candy boxes which advertised "100 Principal League Players," the extent of this series is currently unknown and the checklist presented here is almost certainly incomplete. The blank-back, black-and-white cards can be found in two sizes, 1-7/8" x 3-1/2" if printed on the box front, or 1-7/8" x 2-7/8" if printed on back. Player photos are framed with an ornate-cornered border. In a plaque at bottom, all in capital letters, are the player's name, position, team and league; the latter three designations are abbreviated. Gaps have been left in the assigned numbering to accommodate future discoveries.

	NM	EX	VG
Type I Common:	2,000	1,200	750.00
Type II Common:	3,000	1,500	1,000
(1) Hugh Bedient	2,000	1,200	750.00
(2) Hick Cady	2,000	1,200	750.00
(3) Bill Carrigan (Type II)	3,000	1,500	1,000
(4) Hal Chase	2,500	1,250	800.00
(5) Eddie Collins	3,000	1,500	900.00
(6) Doc Crandall	2,000	1,200	750.00
(7) Lou Criger	2,000	1,200	750.00
(8) Harry Davis	2,000	1,200	750.00
(9) Jim Delahanty	2,000	1,200	750.00
(10) Art Devlin	2,000	1,200	750.00
(11) Josh Devore (Type II)	3,000	1,500	1,000
(12) Larry Doyle	2,000	1,200	750.00
(13) Larry Gardner	2,000	1,200	750.00
(14) George Gibson	2,000	1,200	750.00
(15) Charley Hall	2,000	1,200	750.00
(16) Topsy Hartsel	2,000	1,200	750.00
(17) Buck Herzog (Type II)	3,000	1,500	1,000
(18) Solly Hofman	2,000	1,200	750.00
(19) Marty Krug	2,000	1,200	750.00
(20) Napoleon Lajoie	6,000	3,000	1,800
(21) Duffy Lewis	2,000	1,200	750.00
(22) Rube Marquard	3,000	1,500	1,000
(23) Christy Mathewson	6,000	3,000	1,800
(24) John McGraw	3,000	1,500	900.00
(25) Red Murray	2,000	1,200	750.00
(26) Harry Niles	2,000	1,200	750.00
(27) Orval Overall	2,000	1,200	750.00
(28) Larry Pape	2,000	1,200	750.00
(29) Ed Reulbach	2,000	1,200	750.00
(30) Cy Seymour	2,000	1,200	750.00
(31) Jimmy Sheckard	2,000	1,200	750.00
(32) Hack Simmons	2,000	1,200	750.00
(33) Tris Speaker (Type II)	5,000	2,500	1,500
(34) Jake Stahl	2,000	1,200	750.00
(35) Oscar Stanage	2,000	1,200	750.00
(36) Harry Steinfeldt	2,000	1,200	750.00
(37) Jeff Tesreau (Type II)	3,000	1,500	1,000
(38) Ira Thomas	2,000	1,200	750.00
(39) Joe Tinker	3,000	1,500	1,000
(40) Honus Wagner (Type II)	12,000	6,000	3,600
(41) Ed Walsh	3,000	1,500	1,000
(43) Owen Wilson	2,000	1,200	750.00

1969 Jack In The Box California Angels

HOYT WILHELM
Pitcher
Career Record, 2.47 ERA

This regional issue was distributed a few cards per week at the chain's fast food restaurants. Blank-back cards are printed in black-and-white on thin white stock in a 1-15/16" x 3-1/2" format. The checklist for the unnumbered cards is presented here alphabetically.

	NM	EX	VG
Complete Set (13):	30.00	15.00	9.00
Common Player:	3.00	1.50	.90
(1) Sandy Alomar	3.00	1.50	.90
(2) Joe Azcue	3.00	1.50	.90
(3) Jim Fregosi	3.50	1.75	1.00
(4) Lou Johnson	3.00	1.50	.90
(5) Jay Johnstone	6.00	3.00	1.75
(6) Rudy May	3.00	1.50	.90
(7) Jim McGlothlin	3.00	1.50	.90

(8) Andy Messersmith	3.00	1.50	.90
(9) Tom Murphy	3.00	1.50	.90
(10) Rick Reichardt	3.00	1.50	.90
(11) Aurelio Rodriguez	3.00	1.50	.90
(12) Jim Spencer	3.00	1.50	.90
(13) Hoyt Wilhelm	10.00	5.00	3.00

1971 Jack In The Box California Angels

Unlike the legitimate issue of 1969, this is an unauthorized collectors issue with no official connection to either the team of the fast food restaurant chain. The cards are printed in horizontal format on 4" x 2-1/2" manila paper in black ink. Fronts have a player portrait photo at left. Stacked at right are the player's name, team, position and Jack in the Box logo. Backs are blank. The set is checklisted here in alphabetical order.

	NM	EX	VG
Complete Set (10):	25.00	12.50	7.50
Common Player:	3.00	1.50	.90
(1) Sandy Alomar	3.00	1.50	.90
(2) Ken Berry	3.00	1.50	.90
(3) Tony Conigliaro	15.00	7.50	4.50
(4) Jim Fregosi	3.00	1.50	.90
(5) Alex Johnson	3.00	1.50	.90
(6) Rudy May	3.00	1.50	.90
(7) Andy Messersmith	3.00	1.50	.90
(8) "Lefty" Phillips	3.00	1.50	.90
(9) Jim Spencer	3.00	1.50	.90
(10) Clyde Wright	3.00	1.50	.90

1970 Jack in the Box Pittsburgh Pirates

DAVE GIUSTI
Pittsburgh Pirates P
1969: 22q. 3-7 3.60

Though this set is known within the hobby as the "Jack in the Box" Pirates, it bears no such advertising and has no actual connection to the restaurant chain; they are a collector's issue. The black-and-white cards measure 2" x 3-1/2" and are blank-backed. Beneath the photo on front is the player identification and a few stats from the 1969 season.

	NM	EX	VG
Complete Set (12):	35.00	17.50	10.00
Common Player:	3.00	1.50	.90
(1) Gene Alley	3.00	1.50	.90
(2) Dave Cash	3.00	1.50	.90
(3) Dock Ellis	3.00	1.50	.90
(4) Dave Giusti	3.00	1.50	.90
(5) Jerry May	3.00	1.50	.90
(6) Bill Mazeroski	12.50	6.25	3.75
(7) Al Oliver	6.00	3.00	1.75
(8) Jose Pagan	3.00	1.50	.90
(9) Fred Patek	3.00	1.50	.90
(10) Bob Robertson	3.00	1.50	.90
(11) Manny Sanguillen	4.50	2.25	1.25
(12) Willie Stargell	12.50	6.25	3.75

1954 Bill Jacobellis N.Y. Giants

In the Giants' championship season, New York photographer Bill Jacobellis produced this set of player/team pictures, probably to be sold at the Polo Grounds souvenir stands. The black-and-white pictures are blank-backed and measure about 8-1/4" x 10-1/2", printed on semi-gloss paper. The player name is centered in bold type in the white bottom border; at right is "Bill Jacobellis Photo." The unnumbered pictures are listed here in alphabetical order.

James (Dusty) Rhodes

	NM	EX	VG
Complete Set (8):	110.00	55.00	32.50
Common Player:	12.50	6.25	3.75
(1) John Antonelli	12.50	6.25	3.75
(2) Alvin Dark	12.50	6.25	3.75
(3) Ruben Gomez	12.50	6.25	3.75
(4) Whitey Lockman	12.50	6.25	3.75
(5) Willie Mays	60.00	30.00	18.00
(6) Don Mueller	12.50	6.25	3.75
(7) James (Dusty) Rhodes	12.50	6.25	3.75
(8) N.Y. Giants of 1954	20.00	10.00	6.00

1968 Jamesway Trucking Co.

PETE ROSE
CINCINNATI REDS

Although it doesn't say so in the red logo which decorates this black-and-white card, Jamesway was a Southern Ohio trucking company. The 4" x 5-1/4" card is blank-backed. The purpose for which the card was created and its manner of distribution is unknown.

	NM	EX	VG
Pete Rose	275.00	135.00	85.00

1958-1965 Jay Publishing Picture Packs

JOHN CALLISON, Philadelphia Phillies

JOHN CALLISON, Philadelphia Phillies

The name "Picture Packs" has been used to describe this massive series of 5" x 7" black-and-white player photos issued by Jay Publishing's Big League Books division over the eight-year period from 1958-1965. The company also produced yearbooks for various major league teams during that period; many of the photos used in the yearbooks also appear in the Picture Packs. Picture Pack sets consist of 12 player/manager photos with name, city and team nickname in the bottom border. They were available by mail, at the ballparks and in stores. They were sold in either plain brown or white envelopes, or in clear plastic. Most were printed on a glossy, slick paper stock, although the quality of the paper may vary from team to team and year to year. The photos were issued anonymously, with no indication of the producer or year of issue. Two different types were issued, differentiated by the typeface used in the captions. Type 1 photos, issued from 1958 through 1961, were printed with a sans-serif style typeface, while Type 2 photos, issued from 1962 through 1965, used a serif typeface. Besides team sets there were a few special picture packs such as All-Stars, old-timers and World Series participants. Some years' team-set packs were updated (sometimes more than once) to reflect roster changes. Many pictures were reused from year to year.

	NM	EX	VG
Typical Team Set:	40.00	20.00	12.00
Common Player:	3.00	1.50	.90
Typical Hall of Famer:	10.00	5.00	3.00
Superstars:	20.00	10.00	6.00

1962 Jell-O

Virtually identical in content to the 1962 Post cereal cards, the '62 Jell-O set of 197 was only issued in the Midwest. Players and card numbers are identical in the two sets, except Brooks Robinson (#29), Ted Kluszewski (#82) and Smoky Burgess (#176) were not issued in the Jell-O version. The Jell-O cards are easy to distinguish from the Post of that year by the absence of the red oval Post logo and red or blue border around the stat box. Cards which have been neatly trimmed from the box on which they were printed will measure 3-1/2" x 2-1/2". Cards of some non-star players can be very scarce because 'they originally appeared on a limited number of boxes, or unpopular flavors or sizes.

		NM	EX	VG
	Complete Set (197):	4,250	2,125	1,065
	Common Player:	5.00	2.50	1.25
1	Bill Skowron	30.00	12.00	7.50
2	Bobby Richardson	500.00	200.00	125.00
3	Cletis Boyer	30.00	12.00	7.50
4	Tony Kubek	35.00	14.00	9.00
5	Mickey Mantle	300.00	150.00	75.00
6	Roger Maris	125.00	50.00	30.00
7	Yogi Berra	60.00	30.00	15.00
8	Elston Howard	30.00	12.00	7.50
9	Whitey Ford	60.00	25.00	15.00
10	Ralph Terry	25.00	10.00	6.25
11	John Blanchard	30.00	12.00	7.50
12	Luis Arroyo	15.00	6.00	3.75
13	Bill Stafford	30.00	12.00	7.50
14	Norm Cash	20.00	8.00	5.00
15	Jake Wood	5.00	2.50	1.25
16	Steve Boros	5.00	2.50	1.25
17	Chico Fernandez	5.00	2.50	1.25
18	Billy Bruton	5.00	2.50	1.25
19	Ken Aspromonte	5.00	2.50	1.25
20	Al Kaline	75.00	30.00	17.50
21	Dick Brown	5.00	2.50	1.25
22	Frank Lary	5.00	2.50	1.25
23	Don Mossi	5.00	2.50	1.25
24	Phil Regan	5.00	2.50	1.25
25	Charley Maxwell	5.00	2.50	1.25
26	Jim Bunning	30.00	12.00	7.50
27	Jim Gentile	5.00	2.50	1.25
28	Marv Breeding	5.00	2.50	1.25
29	Not Issued			
30	Ron Hansen	5.00	2.50	1.25
31	Jackie Brandt	50.00	20.00	12.50
32	Dick Williams	5.00	2.50	1.25
33	Gus Triandos	5.00	2.50	1.25
34	Milt Pappas	5.00	2.50	1.25
35	Hoyt Wilhelm	30.00	12.00	7.50
36	Chuck Estrada	5.00	2.50	1.25
37	Vic Power	5.00	2.50	1.25
38	Johnny Temple	5.00	2.50	1.25
39	Bubba Phillips	30.00	12.00	7.50
40	Tito Francona	5.00	2.50	1.25
41	Willie Kirkland	5.00	2.50	1.25
42	John Romano	5.00	2.50	1.25
43	Jim Perry	15.00	6.00	3.75
44	Woodie Held	5.00	2.50	1.25
45	Chuck Essegian	5.00	2.50	1.25
46	Roy Sievers	15.00	6.00	3.75
47	Nellie Fox	40.00	16.00	10.00
48	Al Smith	15.00	6.00	3.75
49	Luis Aparicio	40.00	16.00	10.00
50	Jim Landis	5.00	2.50	1.25
51	Minnie Minoso	25.00	10.00	6.25
52	Andy Carey	30.00	12.00	7.50
53	Sherman Lollar	5.00	2.50	1.25
54	Bill Pierce	5.00	2.50	1.25
55	Early Wynn	50.00	20.00	12.50
56	Chuck Schilling	60.00	30.00	15.00
57	Pete Runnels	5.00	2.50	1.25
58	Frank Malzone	20.00	8.00	5.00
59	Don Buddin	15.00	6.00	3.75
60	Gary Geiger	5.00	2.50	1.25
61	Carl Yastrzemski	200.00	100.00	50.00
62	Jackie Jensen	60.00	24.00	15.00
63	Jim Pagliaroni	30.00	12.00	7.50
64	Don Schwall	5.00	2.50	1.25
65	Dale Long	5.00	2.50	1.25
66	Chuck Cottier	20.00	8.00	5.00
67	Billy Klaus	30.00	12.00	7.50
68	Coot Veal	5.00	2.50	1.25
69	Marty Keough	60.00	25.00	15.00
70	Willie Tasby	60.00	25.00	15.00
71	Gene Woodling	5.00	2.50	1.25
72	Gene Green	60.00	25.00	15.00
73	Dick Donovan	15.00	6.00	3.75
74	Steve Bilko	25.00	10.00	6.25
75	Rocky Bridges	30.00	12.00	7.50
76	Eddie Yost	15.00	6.00	3.75
77	Leon Wagner	15.00	6.00	3.75
78	Albie Pearson	15.00	6.00	3.75
79	Ken Hunt	20.00	8.00	5.00
80	Earl Averill	75.00	30.00	17.50
81	Ryne Duren	15.00	6.00	3.75
82	Not Issued			
83	Bob Allison	15.00	6.00	3.75
84	Billy Martin	20.00	8.00	5.00
85	Harmon Killebrew	75.00	30.00	17.50
86	Zoilo Versalles	15.00	6.00	3.75
87	Lennie Green	50.00	25.00	12.50
88	Bill Tuttle	60.00	25.00	15.00
89	Jim Lemon	90.00	45.00	22.50
90	Earl Battey	30.00	12.00	7.50
91	Camilo Pascual	25.00	10.00	6.25
92	Norm Siebern	5.00	2.50	1.25
93	Jerry Lumpe	5.00	2.50	1.25
94	Dick Howser	15.00	6.00	3.75
95	Gene Stephens	60.00	25.00	15.00
96	Leo Posada	15.00	6.00	3.75
97	Joe Pignatano	15.00	6.00	3.75
98	Jim Archer	15.00	6.00	3.75
99	Haywood Sullivan	30.00	12.00	7.50
100	Art Ditmar	5.00	2.50	1.25
101	Gil Hodges	80.00	40.00	20.00
102	Charlie Neal	15.00	6.00	3.75
103	Daryl Spencer	15.00	6.00	3.75
104	Maury Wills	30.00	12.00	7.50
105	Tommy Davis	30.00	12.00	7.50
106	Willie Davis	15.00	6.00	3.75
107	John Roseboro	60.00	25.00	15.00
108	John Podres	30.00	12.00	7.50
109	Sandy Koufax	80.00	40.00	20.00
110	Don Drysdale	25.00	12.50	7.50
111	Larry Sherry	75.00	37.50	18.75
112	Jim Gilliam	30.00	12.00	7.50
113	Norm Larker	60.00	25.00	15.00
114	Duke Snider	70.00	35.00	17.50
115	Stan Williams	60.00	25.00	15.00
116	Gordon Coleman	70.00	35.00	17.50
117	Don Blasingame	30.00	12.00	7.50
118	Gene Freese	50.00	20.00	12.50
119	Ed Kasko	60.00	25.00	15.00
120	Gus Bell	30.00	12.00	7.50
121	Vada Pinson	15.00	6.00	3.75
122	Frank Robinson	40.00	16.00	10.00
123	Bob Purkey	15.00	6.00	3.75
124	Joey Jay	15.00	6.00	3.75
125	Jim Brosnan	15.00	6.00	3.75
126	Jim O'Toole	15.00	6.00	3.75
127	Jerry Lynch	15.00	6.00	3.75
128	Wally Post	15.00	6.00	3.75
129	Ken Hunt	15.00	6.00	3.75
130	Jerry Zimmerman	15.00	6.00	3.75
131	Willie McCovey	60.00	25.00	15.00
132	Jose Pagan	30.00	12.00	7.50
133	Felipe Alou	15.00	6.00	3.75
134	Jim Davenport	15.00	6.00	3.75
135	Harvey Kuenn	15.00	6.00	3.75
136	Orlando Cepeda	50.00	20.00	12.50
137	Ed Bailey	15.00	6.00	3.75
138	Sam Jones	15.00	6.00	3.75
139	Mike McCormick	15.00	6.00	3.75
140	Juan Marichal	60.00	25.00	15.00
141	Jack Sanford	15.00	6.00	3.75
142	Willie Mays	80.00	40.00	20.00
143	Stu Miller	70.00	35.00	17.50
144	Joe Amalfitano	15.00	6.00	3.75
145	Joe Adcock	15.00	6.00	3.75
146	Frank Bolling	30.00	12.00	7.50
147	Ed Mathews	75.00	37.50	18.75
148	Roy McMillan	5.00	2.50	1.25
149	Hank Aaron	75.00	37.50	18.75
150	Gino Cimoli	30.00	12.00	7.50
151	Frank J. Thomas	5.00	2.50	1.25
152	Joe Torre	60.00	25.00	15.00
153	Lou Burdette	15.00	6.00	3.75
154	Bob Buhl	5.00	2.50	1.25
155	Carlton Willey	5.00	2.50	1.25
156	Lee Maye	50.00	20.00	12.50
157	Al Spangler	60.00	25.00	15.00
158	Bill White	80.00	40.00	20.00
159	Ken Boyer	55.00	27.50	13.75
160	Joe Cunningham	15.00	6.00	3.75
161	Carl Warwick	15.00	6.00	3.75
162	Carl Sawatski	65.00	32.50	16.25
163	Lindy McDaniel	5.00	2.50	1.25
164	Ernie Broglio	15.00	6.00	3.75
165	Larry Jackson	5.00	2.50	1.25
166	Curt Flood	25.00	10.00	6.25
167	Curt Simmons	60.00	25.00	15.00
168	Alex Grammas	30.00	12.00	7.50
169	Dick Stuart	15.00	6.00	3.75
170	Bill Mazeroski	60.00	25.00	15.00
171	Don Hoak	15.00	6.00	3.75
172	Dick Groat	15.00	6.00	3.75
173	Roberto Clemente	180.00	90.00	45.00
174	Bob Skinner	30.00	12.00	7.50
175	Bill Virdon	60.00	25.00	15.00
176	Not Issued			
177	Elroy Face	15.00	6.00	3.75
178	Bob Friend	15.00	6.00	3.75
179	Vernon Law	30.00	12.00	7.50
180	Harvey Haddix	60.00	25.00	15.00
181	Hal Smith	30.00	12.00	7.50
182	Ed Bouchee	50.00	20.00	12.50
183	Don Zimmer	60.00	25.00	15.00
184	Ron Santo	35.00	15.00	9.00
185	Andre Rodgers	5.00	2.50	1.25
186	Richie Ashburn	50.00	20.00	12.50
187	George Altman	5.00	2.50	1.25
188	Ernie Banks	50.00	20.00	12.50
189	Sam Taylor	5.00	2.50	1.25
190	Don Elston	5.00	2.50	1.25
191	Jerry Kindall	50.00	20.00	12.50
192	Pancho Herrera	5.00	2.50	1.25
193	Tony Taylor	5.00	2.50	1.25
194	Ruben Amaro	30.00	12.00	7.50
195	Don Demeter	5.00	2.50	1.25
196	Bobby Gene Smith	60.00	25.00	15.00
197	Clay Dalrymple	5.00	2.50	1.25
198	Robin Roberts	60.00	25.00	15.00
199	Art Mahaffey	5.00	2.50	1.25
200	John Buzhardt	5.00	2.50	1.25

1963 Jell-O

Like the other Post and Jell-O issues of the era, the '63 Jell-O set includes many scarce cards; primarily those which were printed as the backs of less popular brands and sizes of the gelatin dessert. Slightly smaller than the virtually identical Post cereal cards of the same year, the 200 cards in the Jell-O issue measure 3-3/8" x 2-1/2". The easiest way to distinguish 1963 Jell-O cards from Post cards is by the red line that separates the 1962 stats from the lifetime stats. On Post cards, the line extends almost all the way to the side borders, on the Jell-O cards, the line begins and ends much closer to the stats. The high value of some non-star players' cards can be attributed to scarcity caused by the cards having originally been printed on unpopular flavors or sizes.

		NM	EX	VG
	Complete Set (200):	5,500	2,200	1,325
	Common Player:	7.50	3.00	2.00
1	Vic Power	15.00	6.00	3.50
2	Bernie Allen	65.00	25.00	15.00
3	Zoilo Versalles	65.00	25.00	15.00
4	Rich Rollins	7.50	3.00	2.00
5	Harmon Killebrew	50.00	20.00	12.50
6	Lenny Green	35.00	15.00	10.00
7	Bob Allison	15.00	6.00	3.50
8	Earl Battey	55.00	22.50	13.50
9	Camilo Pascual	10.00	4.00	2.50
10	Jim Kaat	60.00	25.00	15.00
11	Jack Kralick	7.50	3.00	2.00
12	Bill Skowron	65.00	25.00	15.00
13	Bobby Richardson	10.00	4.00	2.50
14	Cletis Boyer	7.50	3.00	2.00
15	Mickey Mantle	125.00	62.50	31.25
16	Roger Maris	40.00	15.00	10.00
17	Yogi Berra	30.00	12.00	7.50
18	Elston Howard	35.00	15.00	10.00
19	Whitey Ford	20.00	8.00	5.00
20	Ralph Terry	7.50	3.00	2.00
21	John Blanchard	30.00	12.00	7.50
22	Bill Stafford	25.00	10.00	6.00
23	Tom Tresh	7.50	3.00	2.00
24	Steve Bilko	7.50	3.00	2.00
25	Bill Moran	7.50	3.00	2.00
26	Joe Koppe	7.50	3.00	2.00
27	Felix Torres	7.50	3.00	2.00
28	Leon Wagner	10.00	4.00	2.50
29	Albie Pearson	7.50	3.00	2.00
30	Lee Thomas	7.50	3.00	2.00
31	Bob Rodgers	65.00	25.00	15.00
32	Dean Chance	7.50	3.00	2.00
33	Ken McBride	35.00	15.00	10.00
34	George Thomas	35.00	15.00	10.00
35	Joe Cunningham	60.00	25.00	15.00
36	Nelson Fox	12.50	5.00	3.00
37	Luis Aparicio	12.50	5.00	3.00
38	Al Smith	7.50	3.00	2.00
39	Floyd Robinson	7.50	3.00	2.00
40	Jim Landis	7.50	3.00	2.00
41	Charlie Maxwell	7.50	3.00	2.00
42	Sherman Lollar	15.00	6.00	3.50
43	Early Wynn	20.00	8.00	5.00
44	Juan Pizarro	75.00	30.00	17.50
45	Ray Herbert	50.00	20.00	12.50
46	Norm Cash	17.50	7.00	4.50
47	Steve Boros	35.00	15.00	10.00
48	Dick McAuliffe	7.50	3.00	2.00
49	Bill Bruton	15.00	6.00	3.75
50	Rocky Colavito	25.00	10.00	6.00
51	Al Kaline	30.00	12.00	7.50
52	Dick Brown	35.00	15.00	10.00
53	Jim Bunning	15.00	6.00	3.50
54	Hank Aguirre	7.50	3.00	2.00
55	Frank Lary	40.00	15.00	10.00
56	Don Mossi	40.00	15.00	10.00
57	Jim Gentile	7.50	3.00	2.00
58	Jackie Brandt	7.50	3.00	2.00
59	Brooks Robinson	30.00	12.00	7.50
60	Ron Hansen	7.50	3.00	2.00
61	Jerry Adair	100.00	50.00	25.00
62	John Powell	9.00	3.50	2.25
63	Russ Snyder	35.00	15.00	10.00
64	Steve Barber	7.50	3.00	2.00
65	Milt Pappas	40.00	15.00	10.00
66	Robin Roberts	10.00	4.00	2.50
67	Tito Francona	7.50	3.00	2.00

68	Jerry Kindall	35.00	15.00	10.00
69	Woodie Held	7.50	3.00	2.00
70	Bubba Phillips	7.50	3.00	2.00
71	Chuck Essegian	7.50	3.00	2.00
72	Willie Kirkland	35.00	15.00	10.00
73	Al Luplow	35.00	15.00	10.00
74	Ty Cline	55.00	27.50	13.75
75	Dick Donovan	7.50	3.00	2.00
76	John Romano	7.50	3.00	2.00
77	Pete Runnels	12.50	5.00	3.00
78	Ed Bressoud	100.00	40.00	25.00
79	Frank Malzone	7.50	3.00	2.00
80	Carl Yastrzemski	100.00	40.00	25.00
81	Gary Geiger	7.50	3.00	2.00
82	Lou Clinton	40.00	15.00	10.00
83	Earl Wilson	7.50	3.00	2.00
84	Bill Monbouquette	7.50	3.00	2.00
85	Norm Siebern	7.50	3.00	2.00
86	Jerry Lumpe	9.00	3.50	2.00
87	Manny Jimenez	9.00	3.50	2.25
88	Gino Cimoli	12.50	5.00	3.00
89	Ed Charles	70.00	35.00	17.50
90	Ed Rakow	7.50	3.00	2.00
91	Bob Del Greco	125.00	62.50	31.25
92	Haywood Sullivan	40.00	15.00	10.00
93	Chuck Hinton	7.50	3.00	2.00
94	Ken Retzer	35.00	15.00	10.00
95	Harry Bright	30.00	12.00	7.50
96	Bob Johnson	10.00	4.00	2.50
97	Dave Stenhouse	35.00	15.00	10.00
98	Chuck Cottier	7.50	3.00	2.00
99	Tom Cheney	9.00	3.50	2.00
100	Claude Osteen	75.00	30.00	17.50
101	Orlando Cepeda	15.00	6.00	3.50
102	Charley Hiller	35.00	15.00	10.00
103	Jose Pagan	35.00	15.00	10.00
104	Jim Davenport	7.50	3.00	2.00
105	Harvey Kuenn	7.50	3.00	2.00
106	Willie Mays	60.00	30.00	15.00
107	Felipe Alou	7.50	3.00	2.00
108	Tom Haller	35.00	15.00	10.00
109	Juan Marichal	25.00	10.00	6.00
110	Jack Sanford	12.50	5.00	3.00
111	Bill O'Dell	7.50	3.00	2.00
112	Willie McCovey	100.00	40.00	25.00
113	Lee Walls	35.00	15.00	10.00
114	Jim Gilliam	60.00	25.00	15.00
115	Maury Wills	10.00	4.00	2.50
116	Ron Fairly	7.50	3.00	2.00
117	Tommy Davis	7.50	3.00	2.00
118	Duke Snider	20.00	8.00	5.00
119	Willie Davis	20.00	8.00	5.00
120	John Roseboro	7.50	3.00	2.00
121	Sandy Koufax	50.00	20.00	12.50
122	Stan Williams	50.00	25.00	12.50
123	Don Drysdale	12.50	5.00	3.00
124	Daryl Spencer	7.50	3.00	2.00
125	Gordy Coleman	7.50	3.00	2.00
126	Don Blasingame	50.00	20.00	12.50
127	Leo Cardenas	7.50	3.00	2.00
128	Eddie Kasko	80.00	35.00	20.00
129	Jerry Lynch	7.50	3.00	2.00
130	Vada Pinson	7.50	3.00	2.00
131	Frank Robinson	20.00	8.00	5.00
132	John Edwards	40.00	15.00	10.00
133	Joey Jay	7.50	3.00	2.00
134	Bob Purkey	7.50	3.00	2.00
135	Marty Keough	95.00	47.50	23.75
136	Jim O'Toole	40.00	15.00	10.00
137	Dick Stuart	7.50	3.00	2.00
138	Bill Mazeroski	12.50	5.00	3.00
139	Dick Groat	7.50	3.00	2.00
140	Don Hoak	7.50	3.00	2.00
141	Bob Skinner	12.50	5.00	3.00
142	Bill Virdon	7.50	3.00	2.00
143	Roberto Clemente	100.00	40.00	25.00
144	Smoky Burgess	7.50	3.00	2.00
145	Bob Friend	7.50	3.00	2.00
146	Al McBean	50.00	20.00	12.50
147	ElRoy Face	7.50	3.00	2.00
148	Joe Adcock	7.50	3.00	2.00
149	Frank Bolling	7.50	3.00	2.00
150	Roy McMillan	7.50	3.00	2.00
151	Eddie Mathews	12.50	5.00	3.00
152	Hank Aaron	50.00	20.00	12.50
153	Del Crandall	35.00	15.00	10.00
154	Bob Shaw	7.50	3.00	2.00
155	Lew Burdette	7.50	3.00	2.00
156	Joe Torre	50.00	20.00	12.50
157	Tony Cloninger	100.00	50.00	25.00
158	Bill White	7.50	3.00	2.00
159	Julian Javier	60.00	25.00	15.00
160	Ken Boyer	9.00	3.50	2.00
161	Julio Gotay	75.00	30.00	17.50
162	Curt Flood	25.00	10.00	6.00
163	Charlie James	65.00	25.00	15.00
164	Gene Oliver	50.00	20.00	12.50
165	Ernie Broglio	15.00	6.00	3.50
166	Bob Gibson	135.00	67.50	33.75
167	Lindy McDaniel	35.00	15.00	10.00
168	Ray Washburn	7.50	3.00	2.00
169	Ernie Banks	40.00	15.00	10.00
170	Ron Santo	15.00	6.00	3.50
171	George Altman	7.50	3.00	2.00
172	Billy Williams	100.00	40.00	25.00
173	Andre Rodgers	75.00	30.00	17.50
174	Ken Hubbs	15.00	6.00	3.75
175	Don Landrum	60.00	25.00	15.00
176	Dick Bertell	65.00	25.00	15.00
177	Roy Sievers	7.50	3.00	2.00
178	Tony Taylor	35.00	15.00	10.00
179	John Callison	7.50	3.00	2.00
180	Don Demeter	7.50	3.00	2.00
181	Tony Gonzalez	80.00	40.00	20.00
182	Wes Covington	50.00	20.00	12.50
183	Art Mahaffey	7.50	3.00	2.00
184	Clay Dalrymple	7.50	3.00	2.00
185	Al Spangler	7.50	3.00	2.00

186	Roman Mejias	7.50	3.00	2.00
187	Bob Aspromonte	200.00	100.00	50.00
188	Norm Larker	7.50	3.00	2.00
189	Johnny Temple	7.50	3.00	2.00
190	Carl Warwick	35.00	15.00	10.00
191	Bob Lillis	35.00	15.00	10.00
192	Dick Farrell	90.00	45.00	22.50
193	Gil Hodges	15.00	6.00	3.50
194	Marv Throneberry	7.50	3.00	2.00
195	Charlie Neal	75.00	30.00	17.50
196	Frank Thomas	25.00	10.00	6.00
197	Richie Ashburn	15.00	6.00	3.50
198	Felix Mantilla	60.00	25.00	15.00
199	Rod Kanehl	35.00	15.00	10.00
200	Roger Craig	75.00	30.00	17.50

1969 Jewel Food Chicago Cubs

This set of premium pictures was issued by the midwest regional home-delivery food service. The pictures are 6" x 9" color poses with white borders and blank backs. A facsimile autograph appears on front.

		NM	EX	VG
	Complete Set (20):	125.00	65.00	35.00
	Common Player:	6.00	3.00	1.80
(1)	Ted Abernathy	6.00	3.00	1.80
(2)	Hank Aguirre	6.00	3.00	1.80
(3)	Ernie Banks	30.00	15.00	9.00
(4)	Glenn Beckert	7.50	3.75	2.25
(5)	Bill Hands	6.00	3.00	1.80
(6)	Jim Hickman	6.00	3.00	1.80
(7)	Kenny Holtzman	6.00	3.00	1.75
(8)	Randy Hundley	7.50	3.75	2.25
(9)	Fergie Jenkins	12.50	6.25	3.75
(10)	Don Kessinger	7.50	3.75	2.25
(11)	Rich Nye	6.00	3.00	1.80
(12)	Paul Popovich	6.00	3.00	1.80
(13)	Jim Qualls	6.00	3.00	1.80
(14)	Phil Regan	6.00	3.00	1.80
(15)	Ron Santo	15.00	7.50	4.50
(16)	Dick Selma	6.00	3.00	1.80
(17)	Willie Smith	6.00	3.00	1.80
(18)	Al Spangler	6.00	3.00	1.80
(19)	Billy Williams	15.00	7.50	4.50
(20)	Don Young	6.00	3.00	1.80

1973 Jewel Food Baseball Photos

Jewel Food Stores, a midwestern grocery chain, issued three team sets of large-format baseball player photos in 1973. The 5-7/8" x 9" blank-back photos are full color and feature a facsimile autograph. Photos were sold in groups of four or five per week at five or ten cents per picture. There are 24 Milwaukee Brewers in the issue, and 16 each Chicago Cubs and Chicago White Sox. The unnumbered cards are alphabetized by team in the checklist below.

		NM	EX	VG
CHICAGO CUBS				
	Complete Set (16):	40.00	20.00	12.00
	Common Player:	4.00	2.00	1.25
(1)	Jack Aker	4.00	2.00	1.25
(2)	Glenn Beckert	5.00	2.50	1.50
(3)	Jose Cardenal	4.00	2.00	1.25
(4)	Carmen Fanzone	4.00	2.00	1.25
(5)	Burt Hooton	4.00	2.00	1.25
(6)	Fergie Jenkins	10.00	5.00	3.00
(7)	Don Kessinger	5.00	2.50	1.50
(8)	Jim Hickman	4.00	2.00	1.25

(9)	Randy Hundley	5.00	2.50	1.50
(10)	Bob Locker	4.00	2.00	1.25
(11)	Rick Monday	4.00	2.00	1.25
(12)	Milt Pappas	4.00	2.00	1.25
(13)	Rick Reuschel	4.00	2.00	1.25
(14)	Ken Rudolph	4.00	2.00	1.25
(15)	Ron Santo	10.00	5.00	3.00
(16)	Billy Williams	15.00	7.50	4.50
CHICAGO WHITE SOX				
	Complete Set (16):	30.00	15.00	9.00
	Common Player:	4.00	2.00	1.25
(17)	Dick Allen	7.50	3.75	2.25
(18)	Mike Andrews	4.00	2.00	1.25
(19)	Stan Bahnsen	4.00	2.00	1.25
(20)	Eddie Fisher	4.00	2.00	1.25
(21)	Terry Forster	4.00	2.00	1.25
(22)	Ken Henderson	4.00	2.00	1.25
(23)	Ed Herman	4.00	2.00	1.25
(24)	John Jeter	4.00	2.00	1.25
(25)	Pat Kelly	4.00	2.00	1.25
(26)	Eddie Leon	4.00	2.00	1.25
(27)	Carlos May	4.00	2.00	1.25
(28)	Bill Melton	4.00	2.00	1.25
(29)	Tony Muser	4.00	2.00	1.25
(30)	Jorge Orta	4.00	2.00	1.25
(31)	Rick Reichardt	4.00	2.00	1.25
(32)	Wilbur Wood	4.00	2.00	1.25
MILWAUKEE BREWERS				
	Complete Set (25):	35.00	17.50	10.00
	Common Player:	4.00	2.00	1.25
(33)	Jerry Bell	4.00	2.00	1.25
(34)	John Briggs	4.00	2.00	1.25
(35)	Ollie Brown	4.00	2.00	1.25
(36)	Billy Champion	4.00	2.00	1.25
(37)	Jim Colborn	4.00	2.00	1.25
(38)	Bob Coluccio	4.00	2.00	1.25
(39)	John Felske	4.00	2.00	1.25
(40)	Pedro Garcia	4.00	2.00	1.25
(41)	Rob Gardner	4.00	2.00	1.25
(42)	Bob Heise	4.00	2.00	1.25
(43)	Tim Johnson	4.00	2.00	1.25
(44)	Joe Lahoud	4.00	2.00	1.25
(45)	Frank Linzy	4.00	2.00	1.25
(46)	Skip Lockwood	4.00	2.00	1.25
(47)	Dave May	4.00	2.00	1.25
(48)	Bob Mitchell	4.00	2.00	1.25
(49)	Don Money	4.00	2.00	1.25
(50)	Bill Parsons	4.00	2.00	1.25
(51)	Darrell Porter	4.00	2.00	1.25
(52)	Eduardo Rodriguez	4.00	2.00	1.25
(53)	Ellie Rodriguez	4.00	2.00	1.25
(54)	George Scott	5.00	2.50	1.50
(55)	Chris Short	4.00	2.00	1.25
(56)	Jim Slaton	4.00	2.00	1.25
(57)	John Vukovich	4.00	2.00	1.25

1977 Jewel Food Chicago Cubs/White Sox

Once again in 1977, Jewel grocery stores in the Chicago area offered photos of local players with specific product purchases over a four-week period. The 5-7/8" x 9" color photos are printed on heavy paper. Fronts have player poses, a facsimile signature and the MLB Players Association logo in the upper-left corner. Backs are blank. The pictures are not numbered and are checklisted here alphabetically within team. It was reported 12,000 of each picture were produced.

		NM	EX	VG
	Complete Set, Cubs (16):	12.00	6.00	3.50
	Complete Set, White Sox (16):	12.00	6.00	3.50
	Common Player:	1.50	.70	.45
CHICAGO CUBS				
(1)	Larry Biittner	1.50	.70	.45
(2)	Bill Bonham	1.50	.70	.45
(3)	Bill Buckner	2.50	1.25	.70
(4)	Ray Burris	1.50	.70	.45
(5)	Jose Cardenal	1.50	.70	.45
(6)	Gene Clines	1.50	.70	.45
(7)	Ivan DeJesus	1.50	.70	.45
(8)	Willie Hernandez	1.50	.70	.45
(9)	Mike Krukow	1.50	.70	.45
(10)	George Mitterwald	1.50	.70	.45
(11)	Jerry Morales	1.50	.70	.45
(12)	Bobby Murcer	2.50	1.25	.70
(13)	Steve Ontiveros	1.50	.70	.45
(14)	Rick Reuschel	1.50	.70	.45
(15)	Bruce Sutter	3.50	1.75	1.00
(16)	Manny Trillo	1.50	.70	.45
CHICAGO WHITE SOX				
(1)	Alan Bannister	1.50	.70	.45
(2)	Francisco Barrios	1.50	.70	.45
(3)	Jim Essian	1.50	.70	.45
(4)	Oscar Gamble	1.50	.70	.45

(5)	Ralph Garr	1.50	.70	.45
(6)	Lamar Johnson	1.50	.70	.45
(7)	Chris Knapp	1.50	.70	.45
(8)	Ken Kravec	1.50	.70	.45
(9)	Lerrin LaGrow	1.50	.70	.45
(10)	Chet Lemon	1.50	.70	.45
(11)	Jorge Orta	1.50	.70	.45
(12)	Eric Soderholm	1.50	.70	.45
(13)	Jim Spencer	1.50	.70	.45
(14)	Steve Stone	2.50	1.25	.70
(15)	Wilbur Wood	1.50	.70	.45
(16)	Richie Zisk	1.50	.70	.45

1949 Jimmy Fund Boston Braves Die-cuts

The reigning National League champions undertook the support of the Jimmy Fund, a Boston charity for children's cancer research, with a set of die-cut counter cards accompanying contributions boxes. Between about 6" and 8" at the base, and up to a foot tall, these heavy cardboard pieces feature sepia-toned player action photos in front of a large baseball on which is written, "THANK YOU! in behalf of 'JIMMY.'" with a facsimile signature below. Backs have a fold-out easel to stand the card up, and a notation that following the fund drive, the card should be given to the largest contributor at that location.

		NM	EX	VG
	Complete Set (20):	15,000	7,500	4,500
	Common Player:	750.00	375.00	225.00
(1)	Johnny Antonelli	750.00	375.00	225.00
(2)	Red Barrett	750.00	375.00	225.00
(3)	Vern Bickford	750.00	375.00	225.00
(4)	Clint Conatser	750.00	375.00	225.00
(5)	Al Dark	750.00	375.00	225.00
(6)	Bob Elliott	750.00	375.00	225.00
(7)	Glenn Elliott	750.00	375.00	225.00
(8)	Bobby Hogue	750.00	375.00	225.00
(9)	Tommy Holmes	750.00	375.00	225.00
(10)	Pete Reiser	750.00	375.00	225.00
(11)	Marv Rickert	750.00	375.00	225.00
(12)	Jim Russell	750.00	375.00	225.00
(13)	Connie Ryan	750.00	375.00	225.00
(14)	Johnny Sain	850.00	425.00	255.00
(15)	Bill Salkeld	750.00	375.00	225.00
(16)	Sibby Sisti	750.00	375.00	225.00
(17)	Warren Spahn	1,200	600.00	360.00
(18)	Don Thompson	750.00	375.00	225.00
(19)	Earl Torgeson	750.00	375.00	225.00
(20)	Bill Voiselle	750.00	375.00	225.00

1978 JJH Reading Remembers

This collectors' issue was created to honor baseball players (and a few others) who were born, lived in or played in Berks County, Pa., particularly in Reading. The cards are 3" x 4" featuring borderless sepia photos on front. Most of the photos picture players in big league uniforms. Backs are in black-and-white and have career stats and summaries. A number of major leaguers who did not have cards contemporary with their careers are found in this set. Cards are numbered by uniform number. Production was reported as 1,000 sets.

		NM	EX	VG
	Complete Set (23):	25.00	12.50	7.50
	Common Player:	2.00	1.00	.60
1	Whitey Kurowski	2.00	1.00	.60
6	Carl Furillo	5.00	2.50	1.50
9	Roger Maris	10.00	5.00	3.00
12	Stan Wetzel	2.00	1.00	.60
17	Doug Clemens	2.00	1.00	.60
18	Randy Gumpert	2.00	1.00	.60
18	Ty Stofflet (Softball)	2.00	1.00	.60

21	George Eyrich	2.00	1.00	.60
23	Vic Wertz	2.00	1.00	.60
24	Lenny Moore (Football)	2.00	1.00	.60
25	Dick Gernert	2.00	1.00	.60
27	Herb Score	2.00	1.00	.60
27	Charlie Wagner	2.00	1.00	.60
28	Carl Mathias	2.00	1.00	.60
32	Jesse Levan	2.00	1.00	.60
34	Betz Klopp	2.00	1.00	.60
36	Robin Roberts	9.00	4.50	2.75
39	Bob Katz	2.00	1.00	.60
39	Harry Schaeffer	2.00	1.00	.60
40	Tommy Brown (Baseball/Football)	1.50	.70	.45
46	Dom Dallessandro	2.00	1.00	.60
---	Lauer's Park	2.00	1.00	.60
---	John Updike (Author)	2.00	1.00	.60

1950s J.J.K. Copyart Postcards

Issued from about 1950 through at least 1956, this series of glossy black-and-white player postcards appears to have been produced on order of the individual players to respond to fan requests for pictures and/or autographs. Fronts have player poses bordered in white in about 3-1/2" x 5-1/2" format; most have facsimile autographs. Backs have typical postcard layout with a credit line to J.J.K. Copyart Photographers of New York City. Some players are known in more than one pose.

		NM	EX	VG
	Common Player:	15.00	7.50	4.50
	BOSTON/MILWAUKEE BRAVES			
(1)	Del Crandall	15.00	7.50	4.50
(2)	Tommy Holmes	15.00	7.50	4.50
(3)	Willard Marshall	15.00	7.50	4.50
(4)	Eddie Mathews	60.00	30.00	18.00
(5)	Eddie Mathews	60.00	30.00	18.00
(6)	Danny O'Connell	15.00	7.50	4.50
(7)	Sibby Sisti	15.00	7.50	4.50
(8)	Eddie Stanky	25.00	12.50	7.50
	BROOKLYN DODGERS			
(1)	Jackie Robinson	200.00	100.00	60.00
	NEW YORK GIANTS			
(1)	Johnny Antonelli	15.00	7.50	4.50
(2)	Johnny Antonelli	15.00	7.50	4.50
(3)	Sam Calderone	15.00	7.50	4.50
(4)	Jim Hearn	15.00	7.50	4.50
(5)	Jim Hearn	15.00	7.50	4.50
(6)	Larry Jansen	15.00	7.50	4.50
(7)	Whitey Lockman	15.00	7.50	4.50
(8)	Whitey Lockman	15.00	7.50	4.50
(9)	Don Mueller	15.00	7.50	4.50
(10)	Bill Rigney	15.00	7.50	4.50
(11)	Bill Rigney	15.00	7.50	4.50
(12)	Hank Sauer	15.00	7.50	4.50
(13)	Red Schoendienst	30.00	15.00	9.00
(14)	Daryl Spencer	15.00	7.50	4.50
(15)	Eddie Stanky	25.00	12.50	7.50
(16)	Wes Westrum	15.00	7.50	4.50
(17)	Wes Westrum	15.00	7.50	4.50
(18)	Hoyt Wilhelm	30.00	15.00	9.00
(19)	Al Worthington	15.00	7.50	4.50
	PHILADELPHIA PHILLIES			
(1)	Del Ennis	15.00	7.50	4.50
(2)	Robin Roberts	30.00	15.00	9.00
(3)	Curt Simmons	15.00	7.50	4.50

1973 Johnny Pro Orioles

This regional set of large (4-1/4" x 7-1/4") die-cut cards was issued by Johnny Pro Enterprises Inc. of Baltimore and features only Orioles. The cards were designed to be punched out and folded to make baseball player figures that can stand up. The full-color die-cut figures appear against a green background. The cards are numbered according to the player's uniform number, which appears in a white box along with his name and position. The backs are blank. Three players (Robinson, Grich, and Palmer) appear in two poses each, and cards of Orlando Pena were not die-cut. Values listed are for complete cards not punched out. Cards originally sold for 15 cents apiece.

		NM	EX	VG
	Complete Set (28):	135.00	65.00	40.00
	Common Player:	3.00	1.50	.90
1	Al Bumbry	3.00	1.50	.90
2	Rich Coggins	3.00	1.50	.90
3a	Bobby Grich (Batting)	5.00	2.50	1.50
3b	Bobby Grich (Fielding)	5.00	2.50	1.50
4	Earl Weaver	6.00	3.00	1.75
5a	Brooks Robinson (Batting)	25.00	12.50	7.50
5b	Brooks Robinson (Fielding)	25.00	12.50	7.50
6	Paul Blair	4.00	2.00	1.25
7	Mark Belanger	4.00	2.00	1.25
8	Andy Etchebarren	3.00	1.50	.90
10	Elrod Hendricks	3.00	1.50	.90
11	Terry Crowley	3.00	1.50	.90
12	Tommy Davis	4.00	2.00	1.25
13	Doyle Alexander	3.00	1.50	.90
14	Merv Rettenmund	3.00	1.50	.90
15	Frank Baker	3.00	1.50	.90
19	Dave McNally	4.00	2.00	1.25
21	Larry Brown	3.00	1.50	.90
22a	Jim Palmer (Follow-through.)	15.00	7.50	4.50
22b	Jim Palmer (Wind-up)	15.00	7.50	4.50
23	Grant Jackson	3.00	1.50	.90
25	Don Baylor	6.00	3.00	1.75
26	Boog Powell	7.00	3.50	2.00
27	Orlando Pena	8.00	4.00	2.50
32	Earl Williams	3.00	1.50	.90
34	Bob Reynolds	3.00	1.50	.90
35	Mike Cuellar	5.00	2.50	1.50
39	Eddie Watt	3.00	1.50	.90

1974 Johnny Pro Phillies

Although slightly smaller (3-3/4" x 7-1/8") and featuring members of the Phillies, this set is very similar to the 1973 Johnny Pro Orioles set. The full-color die-cut player figures are set against a white background. Again, the set is numbered according to the player's uniform number. The values listed are for complete cards.

		NM	EX	VG
	Complete Set (12):	150.00	75.00	45.00
	Common Player:	3.00	1.50	.90
8	Bob Boone	7.50	3.75	2.25
10	Larry Bowa	7.50	3.75	2.25
16	Dave Cash	3.00	1.50	.90
19	Greg Luzinski	5.00	2.50	1.50
20	Mike Schmidt	100.00	50.00	30.00
22	Mike Anderson	3.00	1.50	.90
24	Bill Robinson	3.00	1.50	.90
25	Del Unser	3.00	1.50	.90
27	Willie Montanez	3.00	1.50	.90
32	Steve Carlton	25.00	12.50	7.50
37	Ron Schueler	3.00	1.50	.90
41	Jim Lonborg	3.00	1.50	.90

1922 Henry A. Johnson Wholesale Confectioner

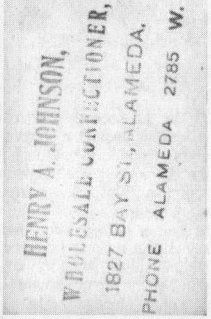

To compete with other candy issues featuring baseball cards as premiums, Alameda, Calif., confectioner Henry A. Johnson purchased uncut sheets of the blank-back strip cards known as W575-1, overprinted their backs and packaged them with his Likem brand candy bars. The advertising on back gives the firm's name, address and telephone number. Collectors can expect to pay a premium of about 3X for this version. Only the type style shown here can definitely be traced to the 1920s. Other styles of typography are known to have been applied in the 1980s and later.

	NM	EX	VG
Common Player:	85.00	42.50	25.00
Stars: 2-3X			

(See W575-1 for checklist and base card values.)

1953 Johnston Cookies Braves

The first and most common of three annual issues, the '53 Johnstons were inserted into boxes of cookies on a regional basis. Complete sets were also available via a mail-in offer from the company, whose factory sits in the shadow of Milwaukee County Stadium. While at first glance appearing to be color photos; the pictures on the 25 cards in the set are actually well-done colorizations of black-and-white photos. Cards measure 2-9/16" x 3-5/8". Write-ups on the backs were "borrowed" from the Braves' 1953 yearbook.

	NM	EX	VG
Complete Set (25):	500.00	250.00	150.00
Common Player:	15.00	7.50	4.50
1 Charlie Grimm	15.00	7.50	4.50
2 John Antonelli	15.00	7.50	4.50
3 Vern Bickford	15.00	7.50	4.50
4 Bob Buhl	15.00	7.50	4.50
5 Lew Burdette	15.00	7.50	4.50
6 Dave Cole	15.00	7.50	4.50
7 Ernie Johnson	15.00	7.50	4.50
8 Dave Jolly	15.00	7.50	4.50
9 Don Liddle	15.00	7.50	4.50
10 Warren Spahn	150.00	75.00	45.00
11 Max Surkont	15.00	7.50	4.50
12 Jim Wilson	15.00	7.50	4.50
13 Sibby Sisti	15.00	7.50	4.50
14 Walker Cooper	15.00	7.50	4.50
15 Del Crandall	15.00	7.50	4.50
16 Ebba St. Claire	15.00	7.50	4.50
17 Joe Adcock	15.00	7.50	4.50
18 George Crowe	15.00	7.50	4.50
19 Jack Dittmer	15.00	7.50	4.50
20 Johnny Logan	15.00	7.50	4.50
21 Ed Mathews	150.00	75.00	45.00
22 Bill Bruton	15.00	7.50	4.50
23 Sid Gordon	15.00	7.50	4.50
24 Andy Pafko	15.00	7.50	4.50
25 Jim Pendleton	15.00	7.50	4.50

1954 Johnston Cookies Braves

In its second of three annual issues, Johnston's increased the number of cards in its 1954 Braves issue to 35, and switched to an unusual size, a narrow format, 2" x 3-7/8". Cards are listed here by uniform number. After his early-season injury (which gave Hank Aaron a chance to play regularly), Bobby Thomson's card was withdrawn, accounting for its scarcity and high value. Uncut sheets of 42 cards (including seven double-prints) in a size of about 12-1/2" x 27-3/4" are not uncommon. A 21-1/2" x 31" wall-hanging display poster with die-cuts into which cards could be inserted was available as a premium offer.

	NM	EX	VG
Complete Set (35):	1,500	750.00	450.00
Common Player:	20.00	10.00	6.00
Uncut Sheet:	4,750	2,400	1,400
Display Poster:	500.00	250.00	150.00
1 Del Crandall	20.00	10.00	6.00
3 Jim Pendleton	20.00	10.00	6.00
4 Danny O'Connell	20.00	10.00	6.00
5 Henry Aaron	750.00	375.00	225.00
6 Jack Dittmer	20.00	10.00	6.00
9 Joe Adcock	20.00	10.00	6.00
10 Robert Buhl	20.00	10.00	6.00
11 Phillip Paine (Phillips)(DP)	20.00	10.00	6.00
12 Ben Johnson	20.00	10.00	6.00
13 Sibby Sisti	20.00	10.00	6.00
15 Charles Gorin	20.00	10.00	6.00
16 Chet Nichols	20.00	10.00	6.00
17 Dave Jolly (DP)	20.00	10.00	6.00
19 Jim Wilson (DP)	20.00	10.00	6.00
20 Ray Crone	20.00	10.00	6.00
21 Warren Spahn (DP)	100.00	50.00	30.00
22 Gene Conley	20.00	10.00	6.00
23 Johnny Logan (DP)	20.00	10.00	6.00
24 Charlie White	20.00	10.00	6.00
27 George Metkovich	20.00	10.00	6.00
28 John Cooney	20.00	10.00	6.00
29 Paul Burris	20.00	10.00	6.00
31 Wm. Walters (DP)	20.00	10.00	6.00
32 Ernest T. Johnson	20.00	10.00	6.00
33 Lew Burdette	20.00	10.00	6.00
34 Bob Thomson (SP)	165.00	80.00	50.00
35 Robert Keely	20.00	10.00	6.00
38 Billy Bruton	20.00	10.00	6.00
40 Charles Grimm	20.00	10.00	6.00
41 Ed Mathews	100.00	50.00	30.00
42 Sam Calderone (DP)	20.00	10.00	6.00
47 Joey Jay	20.00	10.00	6.00
48 Andy Pafko	20.00	10.00	6.00
--- Dr. Charles Lacks (Asst. trainer.)	20.00	10.00	6.00
--- Joseph F. Taylor (Asst. trainer.)	20.00	10.00	6.00

1955 Johnston Cookies Braves

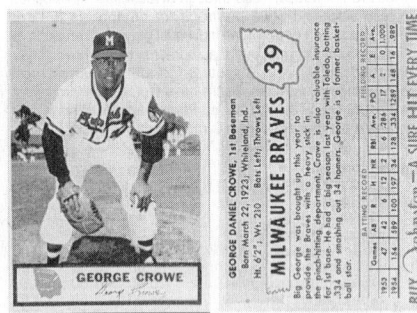

A third change in size and format was undertaken in the final year of Braves sets produced by Johnston's. The 35 cards in the 1955 set were issued in six fold-out panels of six cards each (Andy Pafko was double-printed). As in 1954, cards are numbered by uniform number, except those of the team equipment manager, trainer and road secretary (former Boston star Duffy Lewis). Single cards measure 2-7/8" x 4". Besides including panels in boxes of cookies, the '55 Johnstons could be ordered for five cents per panel by mail. The scarcest of the Johnston's issues, the 1955 set can be found today still in complete panels, or as single cards.

	NM	EX	VG
Complete Folder Set (6):	1,250	625.00	375.00
Complete Singles Set (35):	1,500	750.00	450.00
Common Player:	30.00	20.00	12.00
Common Folder:	200.00	100.00	60.00
1 Del Crandall	30.00	20.00	12.00
3 Jim Pendleton	30.00	20.00	12.00
4 Danny O'Connell	30.00	20.00	12.00
6 Jack Dittmer	30.00	20.00	12.00
9 Joe Adcock	30.00	20.00	12.00
10 Bob Buhl	30.00	20.00	12.00
11 Phil Paine	30.00	20.00	12.00
12 Ray Crone	30.00	20.00	12.00
15 Charlie Gorin	30.00	20.00	12.00
16 Dave Jolly	30.00	20.00	12.00
17 Chet Nichols	30.00	20.00	12.00
18 Chuck Tanner	30.00	20.00	12.00
19 Jim Wilson	30.00	20.00	12.00
20 Dave Koslo	30.00	20.00	12.00
21 Warren Spahn	100.00	50.00	30.00
22 Gene Conley	30.00	20.00	12.00
23 John Logan	30.00	20.00	12.00
24 Charlie White	30.00	20.00	12.00
28 Johnny Cooney	30.00	20.00	12.00
30 Roy Smalley	30.00	20.00	12.00
31 Bucky Walters	30.00	20.00	12.00
32 Ernie Johnson	30.00	20.00	12.00
33 Lew Burdette	30.00	20.00	12.00
34 Bobby Thomson	35.00	17.50	10.50
35 Bob Keely	30.00	20.00	12.00
38 Billy Bruton	30.00	20.00	12.00
39 George Crowe	30.00	20.00	12.00
40 Charlie Grimm	30.00	20.00	12.00
41 Eddie Mathews	100.00	50.00	30.00
44 Hank Aaron	450.00	225.00	135.00
47 Joe Jay	30.00	20.00	12.00
48 Andy Pafko	30.00	20.00	12.00
---- Dr. Charles K. Lacks	30.00	20.00	12.00
--- Duffy Lewis	30.00	20.00	12.00

		NM	EX	VG
---	Joe Taylor	30.00	20.00	12.00
Series 1 Folder		475.00	240.00	140.00
	Hank Aaron, Lew Burdette, Del Crandall, Charlie Gorin, Bob Keely, Danny O'Connell			
Series 2 Folder		160.00	80.00	45.00
	Joe Adcock, Joe Jay, Dr. Charles K. Lacks, Chet Nichols, Andy Pafko, Charlie White			
Series 3 Folder		175.00	90.00	50.00
	Gene Conley, George Crowe, Jim Pendleton, Roy Smalley, Warren Spahn, Joe Taylor			
Series 4 Folder		160.00	80.00	45.00
	Billy Bruton, John Cooney, Dave Jolly, Dave Koslo, Johnny Logan, Andy Pafko			
Series 5 Folder		190.00	95.00	55.00
	Ray Crone, Ernie Johnson, Duffy Lewis, Eddie Mathews, Phil Paine, Chuck Tanner			
Series 6 Folder		160.00	80.00	45.00
	Bob Buhl, Jack Dittmer, Charlie Grimm, Bobby Thomson, Bucky Walters, Jim Wilson			

1976 Jerry Jonas Productions All Time Greats

This card set was produced only in prototype form with an estimated 50 of each printed. The cards were designed to introduce a baseball card promotion to team executives at their annual World Series meeting. The 2-3/4" x 3-3/4" cards have black-and-white player photos at center with colored borders reminiscent of the 1975 Topps cards. Backs are printed in black on blue and feature biographical data, career highlights and stats along with a credit line to Jerry Jones Productions. The proposed promotion was never adopted. The unnumbered cards are checklisted here in alphabetical order.

		NM	EX	VG
Complete Set, Uncut Sheet:		450.00	225.00	135.00
Complete Set, Singles (8):		450.00	225.00	135.00
Common Player:		30.00	15.00	9.00
(1)	Grover Alexander	30.00	15.00	9.00
(2)	Rogers Hornsby	30.00	15.00	9.00
(3)	Sandy Koufax	150.00	75.00	45.00
(4)	Willie Mays	100.00	50.00	30.00
(5)	Stan Musial	50.00	25.00	15.00
(6)	Mel Ott	30.00	15.00	9.00
(7)	Robin Roberts	30.00	15.00	9.00
(8)	Honus Wagner	30.00	15.00	9.00

1911 Jones, Keyser & Arras Cabinets

Contemporary with the better-known Sporting Life, Turkey Red and Pinkerton cabinet photos, this series of baseball player cabinets was issued by the New York City studio of Jones, Keyser & Arras, whose address appears on the back of the card. The 4-1/2" x 7-1/4" cabinets have photos glued to stiff gray cardboard mounts. Both photo and mount are numbered within the known range of 301-349, making it likely there are 50 baseball players in the series. Most known subjects are from the three New York teams of the era. Photos carry at bottom a stylized J, K & A logo, a 1911 copyright and a number. That number is repeated in the bottom border of the mount, along with the player's last name and the team/league. Several photos are known which have been removed from the mount, making identification difficult.

		NM	EX	VG
	Common Player:	2,400	1,200	720.00
301	Russ Ford	2,400	1,200	720.00
303	John Warhop	2,400	1,200	720.00
304	Bill Dahlen	2,400	1,200	720.00
306	Zack Wheat	4,000	2,000	1,200
307	Al Bridwell	2,400	1,200	720.00
308	Red Murray	2,400	1,200	720.00
310	Fred Snodgrass	2,400	1,200	720.00
311	Red Ames	2,400	1,200	720.00
312	Fred Merkle	2,400	1,200	720.00
313	Art Devlin	2,400	1,200	720.00
314	Hooks Wiltse	2,400	1,200	720.00
315	Josh Devore	2,400	120.00	720.00
316	Eddie Collins	4,000	2,000	1,200
317	Ed Reulbach	2,400	1,200	720.00
318	Jimmy Scheckard (Sheckard)	2,400	120.00	720.00
320	Frank Schulte	2,400	1,200	720.00
321	Solly Hofman	2,400	1,200	720.00
322	Bill Bergen	2,400	1,200	720.00
323	George Bell	2,400	1,200	720.00
324	Nap Rucker	2,400	120.00	720.00
325	Fred Clarke	4,000	2,000	1,200
326	Clark Griffith, Mgr.	4,000	2,000	1,200
327	Roger Bresnahan	4,000	2,000	1,200
328	Fred Tenney	2,400	1,200	720.00
329	Harry Lord	2,400	1,200	720.00
331	Walter Johnson	12,000	6,000	3,600
332	Nap Lajoie	4,000	2,000	1,200
333	Joe Tinker	4,000	2,000	1,200
334	Mordecai Brown	4,000	2,000	1,200
336	Jimmy Archer	2,400	1,200	720.00
338	Nixey Callahan	2,400	1,200	720.00
340	Hal Chase	3,500	1,750	1,050
341	Larry Doyle	2,400	1,200	720.00
342	Chief Meyers	2,400	1,200	720.00
343	Christy Mathewson	12,000	6,000	3,600
344	Bugs Raymond	2,400	1,200	720.00
345	John J. McGraw, Mgr.	4,000	2,000	1,200
346	Honus Wagner	15,000	7,500	4,500
347	Ty Cobb	25,000	12,500	7,500
348	Johnny Evers	4,000	2,000	1,200
349	Frank Chance	4,000	2,000	1,200

1863 Jordan & Co.

Because this card pictures a ballplayer on front with advertising on back, it has been described as the world's first baseball card. The 2-7/16" x 4-1/16" card doubled as a ticket to a benefit (to the players!) series of matches between New York and Brooklyn teams and all-stars at Hoboken, N.J., in Sept., 1863. The ticket cards were sold for 50 cents apiece, twice the cost of regular admission. According to surviving records, photos of four different players were used on the tickets.

(1) William Crossley (1/08 auction, $7,100)
(2) William Hammond (12/04 auction, $19,364)
(3) Sam Wright (Unknown)
(4) Harry Wright (Clipped-corners, 7/00 auction, $83,545.)

1931 Josetti Tobacco

This is one of several early 1930s German cigarette cards to picture Babe Ruth. In this case he is pictured on the 1-5/8" x 2-3/8" black-and-white card with American comedic actor Harold Lloyd. The card is part of a numbered set of 272 movie star cards. Backs are printed in German. The card can be found with Ruth's first name printed as George or as Babe.

	NM	EX	VG
151a George Ruth, Harold Lloyd	450.00	225.00	135.00
151b Babe Ruth, Harold Lloyd	450.00	225.00	135.00

1910 Ju-Ju Drums (E286)

Issued in 1910 with Ju Ju Drum Candy, this extremely rare set of circular baseball cards is very similar in design to the more common Colgan's Chips cards. About the size of a silver dollar (1-7/16" in diameter) the cards display a player photo on the front with the player's name and team printed below in a semi-circle design. The backs carry advertising for Ju-Ju Drums. The checklist contains 45 different players to date, but the issue - known as E286 in the American Card Catalog - is so rare that others are likely to exist.

		NM	EX	VG
	Complete Set (45):	40,000	16,000	8,000
	Common Player:	750.00	300.00	175.00
(1)	Eddie Ainsmith	750.00	300.00	175.00
(2)	Jimmy Austin	750.00	300.00	175.00
(3)	Chief Bender	1,500	600.00	360.00
(4)	Bob Bescher	750.00	300.00	175.00
(5)	Bruno Bloch (Block)	750.00	300.00	175.00
(6)	Frank Burke	750.00	300.00	175.00
(7)	Donie Bush	750.00	300.00	175.00
(8)	Frank Chance	1,500	600.00	360.00
(9)	Harry Cheek	750.00	300.00	175.00
(10)	Ed Cicotte	1,500	600.00	360.00
(11)	Ty Cobb	6,500	2,600	1,550
(12)	King Cole	750.00	300.00	175.00
(13)	Jack Coombs	750.00	300.00	175.00
(14)	Bill Dahlen	750.00	300.00	175.00
(15)	Bert Daniels	750.00	300.00	175.00
(16)	Harry Davis	750.00	300.00	175.00
(17)	Larry Doyle	750.00	300.00	175.00
(18)	Rube Ellis	750.00	300.00	175.00
(19)	Cecil Ferguson	750.00	300.00	175.00
(20)	Russ Ford	750.00	300.00	175.00
(21)	Bob Harnion (Harmon)	750.00	300.00	175.00
(22)	Ham Hyatt	750.00	300.00	175.00
(23)	Red Kellifer (Killifer)	750.00	300.00	175.00
(24)	Art Kruger (Krueger)	750.00	300.00	175.00
(25)	Tommy Leach	750.00	300.00	175.00
(26)	Harry Lumley	750.00	300.00	175.00
(27)	Christy Mathewson	3,500	1,400	840.00
(28)	John McGraw	1,500	600.00	360.00
(29)	Deacon McGuire	750.00	300.00	175.00
(30)	Chief Meyers	750.00	300.00	175.00
(31)	Otto Miller	750.00	300.00	175.00
(32)	Charlie Mullen	750.00	300.00	175.00
(33)	Tom Needham	750.00	300.00	175.00
(34)	Rube Oldring	750.00	300.00	175.00
(35)	Barney Pelty	750.00	300.00	175.00
(36)	Ed Reulbach	750.00	300.00	175.00
(37)	Jack Rowan	750.00	300.00	175.00
(38)	Dave Shean	750.00	300.00	175.00
(39)	Tris Speaker	2,000	800.00	480.00
(40)	Ed Sweeney	750.00	300.00	175.00
(41)	Honus Wagner	4,500	1,800	1,075
(42)	Jimmy Walsh	750.00	300.00	175.00
(43)	Kirby White	750.00	300.00	175.00
(44)	Ralph Works	750.00	300.00	175.00
(45)	Elmer Zacher	750.00	300.00	175.00

1893 Just So Tobacco

This set is so rare that only a dozen or so examples are known, although it is possible others remain to be reported. The set features only members of the Cleveland club, known then as the "Spiders." Measuring 2-1/2" x 3-7/8", these sepia-colored cards were printed on heavy paper. The player appears in a portrait photo with his name beneath and an ad for Just So Tobacco at bottom. The existence of this set wasn't even established until the 1960s, and for 15 years only two subjects were known. In 1981 and 1989 several more

cards were discovered. To date only one or two copies of each of the known cards have turned up in collectors' hands, making it among the rarest of all baseball card issues.

		NM	EX	VG
	Common Player:	30,000	19,000	
(1)	F.W. Boyd	30,000	19,000	
(2)	Burkette (Jesse Burkett) (Unique. Trimmed and restored. Value undetermined.)			
(3)	C.L. Childs ("Cupid")	30,000	19,000	
(4)	John Clarkson	100,000	18,000	
(5)	J.O. Connor (John O'Connor)	30,000	19,000	
(6)	G. Cuppy	30,000	19,000	
(7)	G.W. Davies	30,000	19,000	
(8)	C.M. Hastings	30,000	19,000	
(9)	E.J. McKean	30,000	19,000	
(10)	CAPt Tebeau ("Patsy")	30,000	19,000	
(11)	J.K. Virtue	30,000	19,000	
(12)	T.C. Williams	30,000	19,000	
(13)	D.T. Young (Cy)(Unique. Value undetermined.)			
(14)	C.L. Zimmer ("Chief")	30,000	19,000	

K

1950s Kabaya Caramel Babe Ruth

This card was part of a series produced by an Okayama, Japan candy company. The card measures about 1-1/2" x 2-1/8" with color artwork of Ruth on front. On back is Japanese script within the design of an open book.

	NM	EX	VG
Babe Ruth	1,200	600.00	350.00

1955 Kahn's Wieners Reds

The first of what would become 15 successive years of baseball card issues by the Kahn's meat company of Cincinnati is also the rarest. The set consists of six Cincinnati Redlegs player cards, 3-1/4" x 4". Printed in black and white, with blank backs, the '55 Kahn's cards were distributed at a one-day promotional event at a Cincinnati amusement park, where the featured players were on hand to sign autographs. Like the other Kahn's issues through 1963, the '55 cards have a 1/2" white panel containing an advertising message below the player photo. These cards are sometimes found with this portion cut off, greatly reducing the value of the card.

		NM	EX	VG
	Complete Set (6):	6,500	3,250	2,000
	Common Player:	1,000	500.00	300.00
(1)	Gus Bell	1,250	625.00	375.00
(2)	Ted Kluszewski	1,450	725.00	435.00
(3)	Roy McMillan	1,000	500.00	300.00
(4)	Joe Nuxhall	1,000	500.00	300.00
(5)	Wally Post	1,000	500.00	300.00
(6)	Johnny Temple	1,000	500.00	300.00

1956 Kahn's Wieners Reds

In 1956, Kahn's expanded its baseball card program to include 15 Redlegs players, and began issuing the cards one per pack in packages of hot dogs. Because the cards were packaged in direct contact with the meat, they are often found today in stained condition. In 3-1/4" x 4" format, black and white with blank backs, the '56 Kahn's cards can be distinguished from later issues by the presence of full stadium photographic backgrounds behind the player photos. Like all Kahn's issues, the 1956 set is unnumbered; the checklists are arranged alphabetically for convenience. The set features the first-ever baseball card of Hall of Famer Frank Robinson.

	NM	EX	VG
Complete Set (15):	3,250	1,625	1,000
Common Player:	150.00	75.00	45.00
(1) Ed Bailey	150.00	75.00	45.00
(2) Gus Bell	175.00	90.00	55.00
(3) Joe Black	225.00	110.00	65.00
(4) "Smoky" Burgess	200.00	100.00	60.00
(5) Art Fowler	150.00	75.00	45.00
(6) Hershell Freeman	150.00	75.00	45.00
(7) Ray Jablonski	150.00	75.00	45.00
(8) John Klippstein	150.00	75.00	45.00
(9) Ted Kluszewski	365.00	180.00	110.00
(10) Brooks Lawrence	150.00	75.00	45.00
(11) Roy McMillan	150.00	75.00	45.00
(12) Joe Nuxhall	150.00	75.00	45.00
(13) Wally Post	150.00	75.00	45.00
(14) Frank Robinson	1,000	500.00	300.00
(15) Johnny Temple	150.00	75.00	45.00

1957 Kahn's Wieners

In its third season of baseball card issue, Kahn's kept the basic 3-1/4" x 4" format, with black-and-white photos and blank backs. The issue was expanded to 28 players, all Pirates or Reds. The last of the blank-backed Kahn's sets until 1966, the 1957 Kahn's players can be distinguished from the 1956 issue by the general lack of background photo detail, in favor of a neutral light gray background. The Dick Groat card appears with two name variations, a facsimile autograph, "Richard Groat," and a printed "Dick Groat." Both Groat varieties are included in the complete set price.

	NM	EX	VG
Complete Set (29):	4,000	2,000	1,200
Common Player:	80.00	40.00	24.00
(1) Tom Acker	80.00	40.00	24.00
(2) Ed Bailey	80.00	40.00	24.00
(3) Gus Bell	100.00	50.00	30.00
(4) Smoky Burgess	100.00	50.00	30.00
(5) Roberto Clemente	1,250	625.00	375.00
(6) George Crowe	80.00	40.00	24.00
(7) Elroy Face	80.00	40.00	24.00
(8) Hershell Freeman	80.00	40.00	24.00
(9) Robert Friend	80.00	40.00	24.00
(10a) Dick Groat	190.00	95.00	55.00
(10b) Richard Groat	190.00	95.00	55.00
(11) Don Gross	80.00	40.00	24.00
(12) Warren Hacker	80.00	40.00	24.00
(13) Don Hoak	80.00	40.00	24.00
(14) Hal Jeffcoat	80.00	40.00	24.00
(15) Ron Kline	80.00	40.00	24.00
(16) John Klippstein	80.00	40.00	24.00
(17) Ted Kluszewski	225.00	110.00	65.00
(18) Brooks Lawrence	80.00	40.00	24.00
(19) Dale Long	80.00	40.00	24.00
(20) Bill Mazeroski	325.00	160.00	95.00
(21) Roy McMillan	80.00	40.00	24.00
(22) Joe Nuxhall	80.00	40.00	24.00
(23) Wally Post	80.00	40.00	24.00
(24) Frank Robinson	300.00	150.00	90.00
(25) Johnny Temple	80.00	40.00	24.00
(26) Frank Thomas	80.00	40.00	24.00
(27) Bob Thurman	80.00	40.00	24.00
(28) Lee Walls	80.00	40.00	24.00

1958 Kahn's Wieners

Long-time Cincinnati favorite Wally Post became the only Philadelphia Phillies ballplayer to appear in the 15-year run of Kahn's issues when he was traded in 1958, but included as part of the otherwise exclusively Pirates-Reds set. Like previous years, the '58 Kahn's were 3-1/4" x 4", with black and white player photos. Unlike previous years, however, the cards had printing on the back, a story by the pictured player, titled "My Greatest Thrill in Baseball." Quite similar to the 1959 issue, the '58 Kahn's can be distinguished by the fact that the top line of the advertising panel at bottom has the word "Wieners" in 1958, but not in 1959. Several of cards in the set appear to have been short-printed.

MY GREATEST THRILL IN BASEBALL
By GEORGE CROWE

	NM	EX	VG
Complete Set (29):	4,500	2,250	1,350
Common Player:	100.00	50.00	30.00
(1) Ed Bailey	100.00	50.00	30.00
(2) Gene Baker	100.00	50.00	30.00
(3) Gus Bell	110.00	55.00	35.00
(4) Smoky Burgess	110.00	55.00	35.00
(5) Roberto Clemente	900.00	450.00	275.00
(6) George Crowe	100.00	50.00	30.00
(7) Elroy Face	100.00	50.00	30.00
(8) Henry Foiles	100.00	50.00	30.00
(9) Dee Fondy	100.00	50.00	30.00
(10) Robert Friend	100.00	50.00	30.00
(11) Richard Groat	110.00	55.00	35.00
(12) Harvey Haddix	100.00	50.00	30.00
(13) Don Hoak	110.00	55.00	35.00
(14) Hal Jeffcoat	110.00	55.00	35.00
(15) Ronald L. Kline	110.00	55.00	35.00
(16) Ted Kluszewski	200.00	100.00	60.00
(17) Vernon Law	100.00	50.00	30.00
(18) Brooks Lawrence	100.00	50.00	30.00
(19) Bill Mazeroski	300.00	150.00	90.00
(20) Roy McMillan	100.00	50.00	30.00
(21) Joe Nuxhall	100.00	50.00	30.00
(22) Wally Post	300.00	150.00	90.00
(23) John Powers	100.00	50.00	30.00
(24) Robert T. Purkey	100.00	50.00	30.00
(25) Charles Rabe	300.00	150.00	90.00
(26) Frank Robinson	600.00	300.00	180.00
(27) Robert Skinner	100.00	50.00	30.00
(28) Johnny Temple	100.00	50.00	30.00
(29) Frank Thomas	300.00	150.00	90.00

1959 Kahn's Wieners

THE TOUGHEST PLAY I HAVE TO MAKE
by VADA PINSON

A third team was added to the Kahn's lineup in 1959, the Cleveland Indians joining the Pirates and Reds. Again printed in black-and-white in the 3-1/4" x 4" size, the 1959 Kahn's cards can be differentiated from the previous issue by the lack of the word "Wieners" on the top line of the advertising panel at bottom. Backs again featured a story written by the pictured player, such as "The Toughest Play I Had to Make," "My Most Difficult Moment in Baseball," etc. A number of the cards were short-printed.

	NM	EX	VG
Complete Set (38):	6,000	3,000	1,800
Common Player:	75.00	37.50	22.50
(1) Ed Bailey	75.00	37.50	22.50
(2) Gary Bell	75.00	37.50	22.50
(3) Gus Bell	75.00	37.50	22.50
(4) Richard Brodowski	500.00	250.00	150.00
(5) Forrest Burgess	75.00	37.50	22.50
(6) Roberto Clemente	850.00	425.00	255.00
(7) Rocky Colavito	325.00	160.00	100.00
(8) ElRoy Face	75.00	37.50	22.50
(9) Robert Friend	75.00	37.50	22.50
(10) Joe Gordon	75.00	37.50	22.50
(11) Jim Grant	75.00	37.50	22.50
(12) Richard M. Groat	90.00	45.00	27.00
(13) Harvey Haddix	450.00	225.00	135.00
(14) Woodie Held	450.00	225.00	135.00
(15) Don Hoak	75.00	37.50	22.50
(16) Ronald Kline	75.00	37.50	22.50
(17) Ted Kluszewski	200.00	100.00	60.00
(18) Vernon Law	75.00	37.50	22.50
(19) Jerry Lynch	75.00	37.50	22.50
(20) Billy Martin	115.00	55.00	35.00
(21) Bill Mazeroski	250.00	125.00	75.00
(22) Cal McLish	450.00	225.00	135.00
(23) Roy McMillan	75.00	37.50	22.50
(24) Minnie Minoso	80.00	40.00	24.00
(25) Russell Nixon	75.00	37.50	22.50
(26) Joe Nuxhall	75.00	37.50	22.50
(27) Jim Perry	75.00	37.50	22.50
(28) Vada Pinson	200.00	100.00	60.00
(29) Vic Power	75.00	37.50	22.50
(30) Robert Purkey	75.00	37.50	22.50
(31) Frank Robinson	235.00	120.00	75.00
(32) Herb Score	75.00	37.50	22.50
(33) Robert Skinner	75.00	37.50	22.50
(34) George Strickland	275.00	135.00	85.00
(35) Richard L. Stuart	75.00	37.50	22.50
(36) John Temple	75.00	37.50	22.50
(37) Frank Thomas	75.00	37.50	22.50
(38) George A. Witt	75.00	37.50	22.50

1960 Kahn's Wieners

Three more teams joined the Kahn's roster in 1960, the Chicago Cubs, Chicago White Sox and St. Louis Cardinals. Again 3-1/4" x 4" with black-and-white photos, the 1960 Kahn's cards featured for the first time player stats and personal data on the back, except Harvey Kuenn, which was issued with blank back, probably because of the lateness of his trade to the Indians.

	NM	EX	VG
Complete Set (42):	3,000	1,500	900.00
Common Player:	40.00	20.00	12.00
(1) Ed Bailey	40.00	20.00	12.00
(2) Gary Bell	40.00	20.00	12.00
(3) Gus Bell	45.00	22.50	13.50
(4) Forrest Burgess	45.00	22.50	13.50
(5) Gino N. Cimoli	40.00	20.00	12.00
(6) Roberto Clemente	725.00	360.00	215.00
(7) ElRoy Face	40.00	20.00	12.00
(8) Tito Francona	40.00	20.00	12.00
(9) Robert Friend	40.00	20.00	12.00
(10) Jim Grant	40.00	20.00	12.00
(11) Richard Groat	40.00	20.00	12.00
(12) Harvey Haddix	40.00	20.00	12.00
(13) Woodie Held	40.00	20.00	12.00
(14) Bill Henry	40.00	20.00	12.00
(15) Don Hoak	40.00	20.00	12.00
(16) Jay Hook	40.00	20.00	12.00
(17) Eddie Kasko	40.00	20.00	12.00
(18) Ronnie Kline	50.00	25.00	15.00
(19) Ted Kluszewski	300.00	150.00	90.00
(20) Harvey Kuenn	200.00	100.00	60.00
(21) Vernon S. Law	45.00	22.50	13.50
(22) Brooks Lawrence	40.00	20.00	12.00
(23) Jerry Lynch	40.00	20.00	12.00
(24) Billy Martin	90.00	45.00	27.00
(25) Bill Mazeroski	150.00	75.00	45.00
(26) Cal McLish	40.00	20.00	12.00
(27) Roy McMillan	40.00	20.00	12.00
(28) Don Newcombe	45.00	22.50	13.50
(29) Russ Nixon	40.00	20.00	12.00
(30) Joe Nuxhall	40.00	20.00	12.00
(31) James J. O'Toole	40.00	20.00	12.00
(32) Jim Perry	45.00	22.50	13.50
(33) Vada Pinson	65.00	32.50	20.00
(34) Vic Power	40.00	20.00	12.00
(35) Robert T. Purkey	40.00	20.00	12.00
(36) Frank Robinson	200.00	100.00	60.00
(37) Herb Score	45.00	22.50	13.50
(38) Robert R. Skinner	40.00	20.00	12.00
(39) Richard L. Stuart	40.00	20.00	12.00
(40) John Temple	40.00	20.00	12.00
(41) Frank Thomas	50.00	25.00	15.00
(42) Lee Walls	40.00	20.00	12.00

1961 Kahn's Wieners

After a single season, the Chicago and St. Louis teams dropped out of the Kahn's program, but the 1961 set was larger than ever, at 43 cards. The same basic format - 3-1/4" x 4" size, black-and-white photos and statistical information on the back - was retained. For the first time in '61, the meat company made complete sets of the Kahn's cards available to collectors via a mail-in offer. This makes the 1961 and later Kahn's cards considerably easier to obtain than the earlier issues.

	NM	EX	VG
Complete Set (43):	2,650	1,300	800.00
Common Player:	40.00	20.00	12.00
(1) John A. Antonelli	40.00	20.00	12.00
(2) Ed Bailey	40.00	20.00	12.00
(3) Gary Bell	40.00	20.00	12.00
(4) Gus Bell	45.00	22.00	13.50
(5) James P. Brosnan	40.00	20.00	12.00
(6) Forrest Burgess	45.00	22.00	13.50
(7) Gino Cimoli	40.00	20.00	12.00
(8) Roberto Clemente	825.00	410.00	245.00

At the top of the right column, continuing from the previous set:

	NM	EX	VG
(36) John Temple	75.00	37.50	22.50
(37) Frank Thomas	75.00	37.50	22.50
(38) George A. Witt	75.00	37.50	22.50

(9)	Gordon Coleman	40.00	20.00	12.00
(10)	Jimmie Dykes	40.00	20.00	12.00
(11)	ElRoy Face	40.00	20.00	12.00
(12)	Tito Francona	40.00	20.00	12.00
(13)	Gene L. Freese	40.00	20.00	12.00
(14)	Robert Friend	40.00	20.00	12.00
(15)	Jim Grant	40.00	20.00	12.00
(16)	Richard M. Groat	40.00	20.00	12.00
(17)	Harvey Haddix	40.00	20.00	12.00
(18)	Woodie Held	40.00	20.00	12.00
(19)	Don Hoak	40.00	20.00	12.00
(20)	Jay Hook	40.00	20.00	12.00
(21)	Joe Jay	40.00	20.00	12.00
(22)	Eddie Kasko	40.00	20.00	12.00
(23)	Willie Kirkland	40.00	20.00	12.00
(24)	Vernon S. Law	40.00	20.00	12.00
(25)	Jerry Lynch	40.00	20.00	12.00
(26)	Jim Maloney	40.00	20.00	12.00
(27)	Bill Mazeroski	150.00	75.00	45.00
(28)	Wilmer D. Mizell	40.00	20.00	12.00
(29)	Glenn R. Nelson	40.00	20.00	12.00
(30)	James J. O'Toole	40.00	20.00	12.00
(31)	Jim Perry	40.00	20.00	12.00
(32)	John M. Phillips	40.00	20.00	12.00
(33)	Vada E. Pinson Jr.	55.00	27.00	16.50
(34)	Wally Post	40.00	20.00	12.00
(35)	Vic Power	40.00	20.00	12.00
(36)	Robert T. Purkey	40.00	20.00	12.00
(37)	Frank Robinson	250.00	125.00	75.00
(38)	John A. Romano Jr.	40.00	20.00	12.00
(39)	Dick Schofield	40.00	20.00	12.00
(40)	Robert Skinner	40.00	20.00	12.00
(41)	Hal Smith	40.00	20.00	12.00
(42)	Richard Stuart	40.00	20.00	12.00
(43)	John E. Temple	40.00	20.00	12.00

1962 Kahn's Wieners

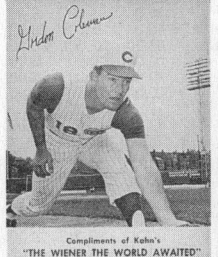

Gordon Coleman

Compliments of Kahn's
"THE WIENER THE WORLD AWAITED"

Besides the familiar Reds, Pirates and Indians players in the 1962 Kahn's set, a fourth team was added, the Minnesota Twins, though the overall size of the set was decreased from the previous year, to 38 players in 1962. The cards retained the 3-1/4" x 4" black-and-white format of previous years. The '62 Kahn's set is awash in variations. Besides the photo and front design variations on the Bell, Purkey and Power cards, each Cleveland player can be found with two back variations, listing the team either as "Cleveland" or "Cleveland Indians." The complete set values listed below include all variations.

		NM	EX	VG
Complete Set (51):		2,250	1,125	675.00
Common Player:		15.00	7.50	4.50
(1a)	Gary Bell (Cleveland Indians back.)	100.00	50.00	30.00
(1b)	Gary Bell (Cleveland back.)	35.00	17.50	10.00
(2)	James P. Brosnan	15.00	7.50	4.50
(3)	Forrest Burgess	30.00	15.00	9.00
(4)	Leonardo Cardenas	15.00	7.50	4.50
(5)	Roberto Clemente	250.00	125.00	75.00
(6a)	Ty Cline (Cleveland Indians back.)	70.00	35.00	20.00
(6b)	Ty Cline (Cleveland back.)	30.00	15.00	9.00
(7)	Gordon Coleman	15.00	7.50	4.50
(8)	Dick Donovan	30.00	15.00	9.00
(9)	John Edwards	15.00	7.50	4.50
(10a)	Tito Francona (Cleveland Indians back.)	70.00	35.00	20.00
(10b)	Tito Francona (Cleveland back.)	30.00	15.00	9.00
(11)	Gene Freese	15.00	7.50	4.50
(12)	Robert B. Friend	20.00	10.00	6.00
(13)	Joe Gibbon	75.00	37.50	22.50
(14a)	Jim Grant (Cleveland Indians back.)	70.00	35.00	20.00
(14b)	Jim Grant (Cleveland back.)	30.00	15.00	9.00
(15)	Richard M. Groat	40.00	20.00	12.00
(16)	Harvey Haddix	15.00	7.50	4.50
(17a)	Woodie Held (Cleveland Indians back.)	70.00	35.00	20.00
(17b)	Woodie Held (Cleveland back.)	30.00	15.00	9.00
(18)	Bill Henry	15.00	7.50	4.50
(19)	Don Hoak	15.00	7.50	4.50
(20)	Ken Hunt	15.00	7.50	4.50
(21)	Joseph R. Jay	15.00	7.50	4.50
(22)	Eddie Kasko	15.00	7.50	4.50
(23a)	Willie Kirkland (Cleveland Indians back.)	70.00	35.00	20.00
(23b)	Willie Kirkland (Cleveland back.)	30.00	15.00	9.00
(24a)	Barry Latman (Cleveland Indians back.)	70.00	35.00	20.00
(24b)	Barry Latman (Cleveland back.)	30.00	15.00	9.00
(25)	Jerry Lynch	15.00	7.50	4.50
(26)	Jim Maloney	20.00	10.00	6.00
(27)	Bill Mazeroski	100.00	50.00	30.00
(28)	Jim O'Toole	15.00	7.50	4.50

(29a)	Jim Perry (Cleveland Indians back.)	70.00	35.00	20.00
(29b)	Jim Perry (Cleveland back.)	30.00	15.00	9.00
(30a)	John M. Phillips (Cleveland Indians back.)	70.00	35.00	20.00
(30b)	John M. Phillips (Cleveland back.)	30.00	15.00	9.00
(31)	Vada E. Pinson	30.00	15.00	9.00
(32)	Wally Post	15.00	7.50	4.50
(33a)	Vic Power (Cleveland Indians back.)	70.00	35.00	20.00
(33b)	Vic Power (Cleveland back.)	30.00	15.00	9.00
(33c)	Vic Power (Minnesota Twins back.)	150.00	75.00	45.00
(34a)	Robert T. Purkey (No autograph.)	150.00	75.00	45.00
(34b)	Robert T. Purkey (With autograph.)	35.00	17.50	10.00
(35)	Frank Robinson	100.00	50.00	30.00
(36a)	John Romano (Cleveland Indians back.)	70.00	35.00	20.00
(36b)	John Romano (Cleveland back.)	30.00	15.00	9.00
(37)	Dick Stuart	15.00	7.50	4.50
(38)	Bill Virdon	15.00	7.50	4.50

1963 Kahn's Wieners

Compliments of Kahn's
"THE WIENER THE WORLD AWAITED"

In 1963, for the first time since Kahn's began issuing baseball cards in 1955, the design underwent a significant change, white borders were added to the top and sides of player photo. Also, the card size was changed to 3-3/16" x 4-1/4". Statistical and personal data continued to be printed on the card backs. Joining traditional Reds, Pirates and Indians personnel in the 1963 set were a handful of New York Yankees and Dick Groat, in his new identity as a St. Louis Cardinal.

		NM	EX	VG
Complete Set (30):		2,000	1,000	600.00
Common Player:		50.00	25.00	15.50
(1)	Robert Bailey	50.00	25.00	15.50
(2)	Don Blasingame	50.00	25.00	15.50
(3)	Clete Boyer	90.00	45.00	27.00
(4)	Forrest Burgess	60.00	30.00	18.00
(5)	Leonardo Cardenas	50.00	25.00	15.50
(6)	Roberto Clemente	350.00	175.00	105.00
(7)	Don Clendennon (Donn Clendenon)	50.00	25.00	15.50
(8)	Gordon Coleman	50.00	25.00	15.50
(9)	John A. Edwards	50.00	25.00	15.50
(10)	Gene Freese	50.00	25.00	15.50
(11)	Robert B. Friend	50.00	25.00	15.00
(12)	Joe Gibbon	50.00	25.00	15.50
(13)	Dick Groat	90.00	45.00	27.00
(14)	Harvey Haddix	50.00	25.00	15.00
(15)	Elston Howard	100.00	50.00	30.00
(16)	Joey Jay	50.00	25.00	15.50
(17)	Eddie Kasko	50.00	25.00	15.50
(18)	Tony Kubek	100.00	50.00	30.00
(19)	Jerry Lynch	50.00	25.00	15.50
(20)	Jim Maloney	60.00	30.00	18.00
(21)	Bill Mazeroski	150.00	75.00	45.00
(22)	Joe Nuxhall	60.00	30.00	18.00
(23)	Jim O'Toole	50.00	25.00	15.50
(24)	Vada E. Pinson	90.00	45.00	27.00
(25)	Robert T. Purkey	50.00	25.00	15.50
(26)	Bob Richardson	100.00	50.00	30.00
(27)	Frank Robinson	200.00	100.00	60.00
(28)	Bill Stafford	60.00	30.00	18.00
(29)	Ralph W. Terry	60.00	30.00	18.00
(30)	Bill Virdon	60.00	30.00	18.00

1964 Kahn's Wieners

Compliments of Kahn's
"THE WIENER THE WORLD AWAITED"

After nearly a decade of virtually identical card issues, the 1964 Kahn's issue was an abrupt change. In a new size, 3" x 3-1/2", the nearly square cards featured a borderless color photo. The only other design element on the front of the card was a facsimile autograph. The advertising slogan which had traditionally appeared on the front of the card was moved to

the back, where it joined the player's stats and personal data. The teams in the 1964 issue once again reverted to the Reds, Pirates and Indians.

		NM	EX	VG
Complete Set (31):		1,150	600.00	350.00
Common Player:		20.00	10.00	6.00
(1)	Max Alvis	20.00	10.00	6.00
(2)	Bob Bailey	20.00	10.00	6.00
(3)	Leonardo Cardenas	20.00	10.00	6.00
(4)	Roberto Clemente	300.00	150.00	90.00
(5)	Donn A. Clendenon	20.00	10.00	6.00
(6)	Victor Davalillo	20.00	10.00	6.00
(7)	Dick Donovan	20.00	10.00	6.00
(8)	John A. Edwards	20.00	10.00	6.00
(9)	Robert Friend	20.00	10.00	6.00
(10)	Jim Grant	20.00	10.00	6.00
(11)	Tommy Harper	20.00	10.00	6.00
(12)	Woodie Held	20.00	10.00	6.00
(13)	Joey Jay	20.00	10.00	6.00
(14)	Jack Kralick	20.00	10.00	6.00
(15)	Jerry Lynch	20.00	10.00	6.00
(16)	Jim Maloney	20.00	10.00	6.00
(17)	Bill Mazeroski	75.00	37.50	22.00
(18)	Alvin McBean	20.00	10.00	6.00
(19)	Joe Nuxhall	20.00	10.00	6.00
(20)	Jim Pagliaroni	20.00	10.00	6.00
(21)	Vada E. Pinson Jr.	35.00	17.50	10.00
(22)	Robert T. Purkey	20.00	10.00	6.00
(23)	Pedro Ramos	20.00	10.00	6.00
(24)	Frank Robinson	75.00	37.50	22.50
(25)	John Romano	20.00	10.00	6.00
(26)	Pete Rose	250.00	125.00	75.00
(27)	John Tsitouris	20.00	10.00	6.00
(28)	Robert A. Veale Jr.	20.00	10.00	6.00
(29)	Bill Virdon	20.00	10.00	6.00
(30)	Leon Wagner	20.00	10.00	6.00
(31)	Fred Whitfield	20.00	10.00	6.00

1965 Kahn's Wieners

Compliments of Kahn's
"THE WIENER THE WORLD AWAITED"

There was little change for the Kahn's issue in 1965 beyond the addition of Milwaukee Braves players to the Reds, Pirates and Indians traditionally included in the set. At 45 players, the 1965 issue was the largest of the Kahn's sets. Once again in 3" x 3-1/2" size, the 1965s retained the borderless color photo design of the previous season. A look at the stats on the back will confirm the year of issue, allowing differentiation between the 1964 and 1965 cards.

		NM	EX	VG
Complete Set (45):		1,250	625.00	400.00
Common Player:		15.00	7.50	4.50
(1)	Hank Aaron	125.00	65.00	35.00
(2)	Max Alvis	15.00	7.50	4.50
(3)	Jose Azcue	15.00	7.50	4.50
(4)	Bob Bailey	15.00	7.50	4.50
(5)	Frank Bolling	15.00	7.50	4.50
(6)	Leonardo Cardenas	15.00	7.50	4.50
(7)	Rico Ricardo Carty	15.00	7.50	4.50
(8)	Donn A. Clendenon	15.00	7.50	4.50
(9)	Tony Cloninger	15.00	7.50	4.50
(10)	Gordon Coleman	15.00	7.50	4.50
(11)	Victor Davalillo	15.00	7.50	4.50
(12)	John A. Edwards	15.00	7.50	4.50
(13)	Sam Ellis	15.00	7.50	4.50
(14)	Robert Friend	15.00	7.50	4.50
(15)	Tommy Harper	15.00	7.50	4.50
(16)	Chuck Hinton	15.00	7.50	4.50
(17)	Dick Howser	15.00	7.50	4.50
(18)	Joey Jay	15.00	7.50	4.50
(19)	Deron Johnson	15.00	7.50	4.50
(20)	Jack Kralick	15.00	7.50	4.50
(21)	Denny Lemaster	15.00	7.50	4.50
(22)	Jerry Lynch	15.00	7.50	4.50
(23)	Jim Maloney	15.00	7.50	4.50
(24)	Lee Maye	15.00	7.50	4.50
(25)	Bill Mazeroski	60.00	30.00	18.00
(26)	Alvin McBean	15.00	7.50	4.50
(27)	Bill McCool	15.00	7.50	4.50
(28)	Sam McDowell	20.00	10.00	6.00
(29)	Donald McMahon	15.00	7.50	4.50
(30)	Denis Menke	15.00	7.50	4.50
(31)	Joe Nuxhall	15.00	7.50	4.50
(32)	Gene Oliver	15.00	7.50	4.50
(33)	Jim O'Toole	15.00	7.50	4.50
(34)	Jim Pagliaroni	15.00	7.50	4.50
(35)	Vada E. Pinson Jr.	25.00	12.50	7.50
(36)	Frank Robinson	100.00	50.00	30.00
(37)	Pete Rose	300.00	150.00	90.00
(38)	Willie Stargell	60.00	30.00	18.00
(39)	Ralph W. Terry	15.00	7.50	4.50
(40)	Luis Tiant	20.00	10.00	6.00
(41)	Joe Torre	25.00	12.50	7.50
(42)	John Tsitouris	15.00	7.50	4.50
(43)	Robert A. Veale Jr.	15.00	7.50	4.50
(44)	Bill Virdon	15.00	7.50	4.50
(45)	Leon Wagner	15.00	7.50	4.50

1966 Kahn's Wieners

The fourth new format in five years greeted collectors with the introduction of Kahn's 1966 issue. The design consists of a color photo bordered by white and yellow vertical stripes. The player's name is printed above the photo, and a facsimile autograph appears across the photo. As printed, the cards are 2-13/16" x 4-9/16" in size. The player photo area is about 2-13/16" x x 2-11/16", separated at top by a dotted line from an advertising panel with a red rose logo and the word "Kahn's" and by a dotted line at bottom from an irregularly shaped piece marked "CUT ALONG DOTTED LINES." Naturally, many of the cards are found today with the top and/or bottom portion cut off. Values listed here are for complete uncut cards; those without the ad portion and bottom panel are valued at 50 percent or less. Players from the Cincinnati Reds, Pittsburgh Pirates, Cleveland Indians and Atlanta Braves were included in the set. Since the cards are blank-backed, collectors must learn to differentiate player poses to determine year of issue for some cards.

		NM	EX	VG
	Complete Set (32):	1,250	625.00	375.00
	Common Player:	15.00	7.50	4.50
(1)	Henry Aaron	200.00	100.00	60.00
(2)	Felipe Alou	20.00	10.00	6.00
(3)	Max Alvis	15.00	7.50	4.50
(4)	Robert Bailey	15.00	7.50	4.50
(5)	Wade Blasingame	15.00	7.50	4.50
(6)	Frank Bolling	15.00	7.50	4.50
(7)	Leo Cardenas	15.00	7.50	4.50
(8)	Roberto Clemente	400.00	200.00	120.00
(9)	Tony Cloninger	15.00	7.50	4.50
(10)	Vic Davalillo	15.00	7.50	4.50
(11)	John Edwards	15.00	7.50	4.50
(12)	Sam Ellis (White cap.)	15.00	7.50	4.50
(13)	Pedro Gonzalez	15.00	7.50	4.50
(14)	Tommy Harper	15.00	7.50	4.50
(15)	Deron Johnson	15.00	7.50	4.50
(16)	Mack Jones	15.00	7.50	4.50
(17)	Denny Lemaster	15.00	7.50	4.50
(18)	Jim Maloney (White cap.)	15.00	7.50	4.50
(19)	Bill Mazeroski	90.00	45.00	27.00
(20)	Bill McCool	15.00	7.50	4.50
(21)	Sam McDowell	25.00	12.50	7.50
(22)	Denis Menke	15.00	7.50	4.50
(23)	Joe Nuxhall	15.00	7.50	4.50
(24)	Jim Pagliaroni	15.00	7.50	4.50
(25)	Milt Pappas	15.00	7.50	4.50
(26)	Vada Pinson	25.00	12.50	7.50
(27)	Pete Rose (Right hand in glove.)	250.00	125.00	75.00
(28)	Sonny Siebert	15.00	7.50	4.50
(29)	Willie Stargell	90.00	45.00	27.00
(30)	Joe Torre	25.00	12.50	7.50
(31)	Bob Veale	15.00	7.50	4.50
(32)	Fred Whitfield	15.00	7.50	4.50

1967 Kahn's Wieners

Retaining the 1966 format, the '67 Kahn's set was expanded to 41 players by adding several New York Mets to the previous season's lineup of Reds, Pirates, Indians and Braves. Making this set especially challenging for collectors is the fact that some cards are found in a smaller size and/or with different colored stripes bordering the color player photo. On the majority of cards, the size remained about 2-13/16" x 4-9/16" (with ad at top and bottom panel; about 2-13/16" x 2-11/16" when cut on dotted lines). However, because of packing in different products, some cards can be found in 2-13/16" x 3-1/4" size (with ad; 2-13/16" x 2-1/8" without ad). The border stripe variations are listed below. Values quoted are for complete uncut cards;

values drop by 50 percent or more for cards without the ad and/or bottom panels. All variation cards are included in the valuations given for the complete set.

		NM	EX	VG
	Complete Set (51):	1,800	900.00	550.00
	Common Player:	20.00	10.00	6.00
(1a)	Henry Aaron (Large size.)	125.00	65.00	35.00
(1b)	Henry Aaron (Small size.)	125.00	65.00	35.00
(2)	Gene Alley	20.00	10.00	6.00
(3a)	Felipe Alou (Large size.)	25.00	12.50	7.50
(3b)	Felipe Alou (Small size.)	25.00	12.50	7.50
(4a)	Matty Alou (Yellow & white striped border.)	25.00	12.50	7.50
(4b)	Matty Alou (Red & white striped border.)	30.00	15.00	9.00
(5)	Max Alvis	20.00	10.00	6.00
(6a)	Ken Boyer (Yellow & white striped border.)	30.00	15.00	9.00
(6b)	Ken Boyer (Red, white & green striped border.)	35.00	17.50	10.00
(7)	Leo Cardenas	20.00	10.00	6.00
(8)	Rico Carty	20.00	10.00	6.00
(9)	Tony Cloninger	20.00	10.00	6.00
(10)	Tommy Davis	20.00	10.00	6.00
(11)	John Edwards	20.00	10.00	6.00
(12a)	Sam Ellis (Large size.) (Red cap.)	20.00	10.00	6.00
(12b)	Sam Ellis (Small size.) (Red cap.)	30.00	15.00	9.00
(13)	Jack Fisher	20.00	10.00	6.00
(14)	Steve Hargan	20.00	10.00	6.00
(15)	Tom Harper	20.00	10.00	6.00
(16a)	Tom Helms (Large size.)	20.00	10.00	6.00
(16b)	Tom Helms (Small size.)	35.00	17.50	10.00
(17)	Deron Johnson	20.00	10.00	6.00
(18)	Ken Johnson	20.00	10.00	6.00
(19)	Cleon Jones	20.00	10.00	6.00
(20a)	Ed Kranepool (Yellow & white striped border.)	20.00	10.00	6.00
(20b)	Ed Kranepool (Red & white striped border.)	30.00	15.00	9.00
(21a)	James Maloney (Yellow & white striped border.)	25.00	12.50	7.50
(21b)	James Maloney (Red & white striped border.)	30.00	15.00	9.00
(22)	Lee May	20.00	10.00	6.00
(23a)	Wm. Mazeroski (Large size.)	75.00	37.50	22.50
(23b)	Wm. Mazeroski (Small size.)	75.00	37.50	22.50
(24)	Wm. McCool	20.00	10.00	6.00
(25)	Sam McDowell (Blue sleeves.)	25.00	12.50	7.50
(26)	Dennis Menke (Denis)	20.00	10.00	6.00
(27)	Jim Pagliaroni	20.00	10.00	6.00
(28)	Don Pavletich	20.00	10.00	6.00
(29)	Tony Perez	60.00	30.00	18.00
(30)	Vada Pinson	30.00	15.00	9.00
(31)	Dennis Ribant	20.00	10.00	6.00
(32)	Pete Rose (Batting)	275.00	135.00	85.00
(33)	Art Shamsky	20.00	10.00	6.00
(34)	Bob Shaw	20.00	10.00	6.00
(35)	Sonny Siebert	20.00	10.00	6.00
(36)	Wm. Stargell (First name actually Wilver.)	80.00	40.00	24.00
(37a)	Joe Torre (Large size.)	35.00	17.50	10.00
(37b)	Joe Torre (Small size.)	35.00	17.50	10.00
(38)	Bob Veale	20.00	10.00	6.00
(39)	Leon Wagner	20.00	10.00	6.00
(40a)	Fred Whitfield (Large size.)	20.00	10.00	6.00
(40b)	Fred Whitfield (Small size.)	20.00	10.00	6.00
(41)	Woody Woodward	20.00	10.00	6.00

1968 Kahn's Wieners

The number of card size and stripe color variations increased with the 1968 Kahn's issue, though the basic card format was retained. Basic size is about 2-13/16" x 4-9/16" with top ad panel and bottom panel intact; 2-13/16" x 2-11/16" with ad and bottom panels cut off. Color photos are bordered by yellow and white vertical stripes. In addition to the basic issue, a number of the cards appear in a smaller, 2-13/16" x 3-1/4", size, while some appear with variations in the color of border stripes. One card, Maloney, can be found with a top portion advertising Blue Mountain brand meats, as well as Kahn's. The 1968 set features the largest number of teams represented in any Kahn's issue: Braves, Cubs, White Sox, Reds, Indians, Tigers, Mets and Pirates. Values quoted are for complete uncut cards, those without the ad and/or bottom panel are worth 50 percent or less. Complete set prices include all variations.

		NM	EX	VG
	Complete Set (56):	2,250	1,125	675.00
	Common Player:	20.00	10.00	6.00
(1a)	Hank Aaron (Large size.)	100.00	50.00	30.00
(1b)	Hank Aaron (Small size.)	125.00	62.00	37.00
(2)	Tommy Agee	20.00	10.00	6.00
(3a)	Gene Alley (Large size.)	20.00	10.00	6.00
(3b)	Gene Alley (Small size.)	30.00	15.00	9.00
(4)	Felipe Alou	25.00	12.50	7.50
(5a)	Matty Alou (Yellow striped border.)	25.00	12.50	7.50
(5b)	Matty Alou (Red striped border.)	25.00	12.50	7.50
(6a)	Max Alvis (Large size.)	20.00	10.00	6.00
(6b)	Max Alvis (Small size.)	30.00	15.00	9.00
(7)	Gerry Arrigo	20.00	10.00	6.00
(8)	John Bench	550.00	275.00	165.00
(9a)	Clete Boyer (Large size.)	20.00	10.00	6.00
(9b)	Clete Boyer (Small size.)	30.00	15.00	9.00
(10)	Larry Brown	20.00	10.00	6.00
(11a)	Leo Cardenas (Large size.)	20.00	10.00	6.00
(11b)	Leo Cardenas (Small size.)	30.00	15.00	9.00
(12a)	Bill Freehan (Large size.)	30.00	15.00	9.00
(12b)	Bill Freehan (Small size.)	30.00	15.00	9.00
(13)	Steve Hargan	20.00	10.00	6.00
(14)	Joel Horlen	20.00	10.00	6.00
(15)	Tony Horton	30.00	15.00	9.00
(16)	Willie Horton	25.00	12.50	7.50
(17)	Ferguson Jenkins	75.00	37.00	22.00
(18)	Deron Johnson	20.00	10.00	6.00
(19)	Mack Jones	20.00	10.00	6.00
(20)	Bob Lee	20.00	10.00	6.00
(21a)	Jim Maloney (Large size, rose logo.)	25.00	12.50	7.50
(21b)	Jim Maloney (Large size, Blue Mountain logo.)	60.00	30.00	18.00
(21c)	Jim Maloney (Small size, yellow & white striped border.)	30.00	15.00	9.00
(21d)	Jim Maloney (Small size, yellow, white & green striped border.)	30.00	15.00	9.00
(22a)	Lee May (Large size.)	25.00	12.50	7.50
(22b)	Lee May (Small size.)	30.00	15.00	9.00
(23a)	Wm. Mazeroski (Large size.)	50.00	25.00	15.00
(23b)	Wm. Mazeroski (Small size.)	65.00	32.50	20.00
(24)	Dick McAuliffe	20.00	10.00	6.00
(25)	Bill McCool	20.00	10.00	6.00
(26a)	Sam McDowell (Yellow striped border.)	25.00	12.50	7.50
(26b)	Sam McDowell (Red striped border.)	30.00	15.00	9.00
(27a)	Tony Perez (Yellow striped border.)	45.00	22.00	13.50
(27b)	Tony Perez (Red striped border.)	50.00	25.00	15.00
(28)	Gary Peters	20.00	10.00	6.00
(29a)	Vada Pinson (Large size.)	30.00	15.00	9.00
(29b)	Vada Pinson (Small size.)	30.00	15.00	9.00
(30)	Chico Ruiz	20.00	10.00	6.00
(31a)	Ron Santo (Yellow striped border.)	30.00	15.00	9.00
(31b)	Ron Santo (Red striped border.)	40.00	20.00	12.00
(32)	Art Shamsky	20.00	10.00	6.00
(33)	Luis Tiant (Arms above head.)	20.00	10.00	6.00
(34a)	Joe Torre (Large size.)	30.00	15.00	9.00
(34b)	Joe Torre (Small size.)	35.00	17.50	10.50
(35a)	Bob Veale (Large size.)	20.00	10.00	6.00
(35b)	Bob Veale (Small size.)	30.00	15.00	9.00
(36)	Leon Wagner	20.00	10.00	6.00
(37)	Billy Williams	75.00	37.00	22.00
(38)	Earl Wilson	20.00	10.00	6.00

1969 Kahn's Wieners

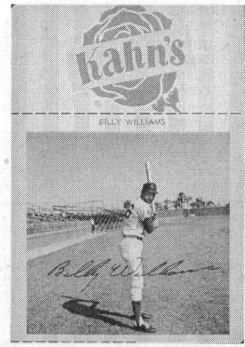

In its 15th consecutive year of baseball card issue, Kahn's continued the format adopted in 1966. The basic 22 players' cards were printed in about 2-13/16" x 4-9/16" size (with ad panel at top and bottom panel; 2-13/16" x 2-11/16" without panels) and are blanked-backed. Teams represented in the set are the Braves, Cubs, White Sox, Reds, Cardinals, Indians and Pirates. Cards feature a color photo and facsimile autograph bordered by yellow and white vertical stripes. At top is an ad panel consisting of the Kahn's red rose logo. However, because some cards were produced for inclusion in packages other than the standard hot dogs, a number of variations in card size and stripe color were created, as noted in the listings. The smaller size cards, 2-13/16" x 3-1/4" with top and bottom panels; 3/16" x 2-1/8" without panels, were created by more closely cropping the player photo at top and bottom. Values quoted are for complete uncut cards with both panels intact; deduct a minimum 50 percent for cards without the ad and/or bottom panel. Complete set values include all variations. For years an (18b) (red-striped border) Ron Santo had been documented. Recent evidence now suggests that such a variations does not exist.

		NM	EX	VG
Complete Set (29):		1,200	600.00	375.00
Common Player:		25.00	12.50	7.50
(1a)	Hank Aaron (Large size.)	125.00	62.00	37.00
(1b)	Hank Aaron (Small size.)	140.00	70.00	42.00
(2)	Matty Alou	25.00	12.50	7.50
(3)	Max Alvis	25.00	12.50	7.50
(4)	Gerry Arrigo	25.00	12.50	7.50
(5)	Steve Blass	25.00	12.50	7.50
(6)	Clay Carroll (Follow-through.)	25.00	12.50	7.50
(7)	Tony Cloninger	25.00	12.50	7.50
(8)	George Culver	25.00	12.50	7.50
(9)	Joel Horlen (Follow-through.)	25.00	12.50	7.50
(10)	Tony Horton (Batting)	35.00	17.50	10.50
(11)	Alex Johnson	25.00	12.50	7.50
(12a)	Jim Maloney (Large size.) (Arms at sides.)	30.00	15.00	9.00
(12b)	Jim Maloney (Small size.) (Arms at sides.)	35.00	17.50	10.50
(13a)	Lee May (Yellow striped border.) (Foot on bag.)	30.00	15.00	9.00
(13b)	Lee May (Red striped border.) (Foot on bag.)	35.00	17.50	10.50
(14a)	Bill Mazeroski (Yellow striped border.)	50.00	25.00	15.00
(14b)	Bill Mazeroski (Red striped border.)	55.00	27.00	16.50
(15a)	Sam McDowell (Yellow striped border.) (Right leg raised.)	30.00	15.00	9.00
(15b)	Sam McDowell (Red striped border.) (Right leg raised.)	35.00	17.50	10.50
(16a)	Tony Perez (Large size.) (Glove on base.)	60.00	30.00	18.00
(16b)	Tony Perez (Small size.) (Glove on base.)	75.00	37.50	22.50
(17)	Gary Peters (Follow-through.)	25.00	12.50	7.50
(18a)	Ron Santo (Yellow striped border.)	50.00	25.00	15.00
(18b)	Ron Santo (Red striped border. Now believed not to exist.)			
(19)	Luis Tiant (Arms at knees.)	25.00	12.50	7.50
(20)	Joe Torre	35.00	17.50	10.50
(21)	Bob Veale	25.00	12.50	7.50
(22)	Billy Williams (Bat behind head.)	80.00	40.00	24.00

1970s Kahn's Kielbasa Singles Carl Yastrzemski

The exact year or years of this label's issue are not known. The 4-7/8" x 3-1/8" cardboard package insert has a color portrait photo of baseball's most famous Polish player endorsing the polish sausage product.

	NM	EX	VG
Carl Yastrzemski	15.00	7.50	4.50

1887 Kalamazoo Bats (N690)

This set, issued circa 1887 by Charles Gross & Co. Phila., is one of the most difficult of all 19th Century tobacco issues. The cards measure a rather large 2-1/4" x 4" and feature a sepia-toned photograph on heavy cardboard. The player's name and team appear inside a white strip at the bottom of the photo, while a small ad for Kalamazoo Bats cigarettes is printed at the very bottom of the card. Some cards carry an 1887 copyright line, but there are indications that some of the cards date from 1886 or 1888. The unnumbered set pictures players from four teams - two from New York (Giants and Mets) and two from Philadelphia (Athletics and Phillies). A few of the cards picture

more than one player, and some Philadelphia cards have been found with an ad on the back offering various prizes in exchange for saving the cards. The set has been assigned the American Card Catalog number N690. This checklist is likely not complete. Players from the New York teams are significantly rarer than those of the Philadelphia teams.

		NM	EX	VG
Common Player:		6,250	3,750	2,500
Advertising-back: 1.5X				
(1)	Ed Andrews	6,250	3,750	2,500
(2)	Charles Bastian, Lyons	7,000	4,200	2,800
(3)	Lou Bierbauer	7,000	4,200	2,800
(4)	Lou Bierbauer, Gallagher	7,000	4,200	2,800
(5)	Charles Buffington (Buffinton)	6,250	3,750	2,500
(6)	Dan Casey	6,250	3,750	2,500
(7)	Jack Clements	7,000	4,200	2,800
(8)	Roger Connor (Three known.)	65,000	24,000	16,000
(9)	Larry Corcoran	7,500	4,500	3,000
(10)	Ed Cushman	17,500	10,500	7,000
(11)	Pat Deasley	17,500	10,500	7,000
(12)	Jim Devlin	6,250	3,750	2,500
(13)	Jim Donahue	17,500	10,500	7,000
(14)	Mike Dorgan	11,500	6,900	4,600
(15)	Dude Esterbrooke (Esterbrook)	17,500	10,500	7,000
(16)	Buck Ewing (Possibly unique.)	85,000	27,000	18,000
(17)	Sid Farrar	6,250	3,750	2,500
(18)	Charlie Ferguson	6,250	3,750	2,500
(19)	Jim Fogarty	6,250	3,750	2,500
(20)	Jim Fogarty, Deacon McGuire	7,000	4,200	2,800
(21)	Elmer Foster	17,500	10,500	7,000
(22)	Whitey Gibson	7,000	4,200	2,800
(23)	Pete Gillespie	17,500	10,500	7,000
(24)	Tom Gunning	6,250	3,750	2,500
(25)	Arthur Irwin	6,250	3,750	2,500
(26)	Arthur Irwin, Al Maul	7,000	4,200	2,800
(27)	Tim Keefe	65,000	21,000	14,000
(28)	Henry Larkin	7,000	4,200	2,800
(29)	Henry Larkins (Larkin), Jocko Milligan	7,000	4,200	2,800
(30)	Jack Lynch	17,500	10,500	7,000
(31)	Denny Lyons (Athletics)	35,000	21,000	14,000
(32)	Harry Lyons (Phila.)	7,000	4,200	2,800
(33)	Harry Lyons (Phila.), Billy Taylor	7,000	4,200	2,800
(34)	Fred Mann	7,000	4,200	2,800
(35)	Charlie Mason	7,000	4,200	2,800
(36)	Bobby Mathews	7,000	4,200	2,800
(37)	Al Maul	6,250	3,750	2,500
(38)	Al Mays	17,500	10,500	7,000
(39)	Chippy McGan (McGarr)	7,000	4,200	2,800
(40)	Deacon McGuire (Catching)	6,250	3,750	2,500
(41)	Deacon McGuire (Throwing)	6,250	3,750	2,500
(42)	Tom McLaughlin	17,500	10,500	7,000
(43)	Jocko Milligan, Harry Stowe (Stovey)	7,000	4,200	2,800
(44)	Joseph Mulvey	6,250	3,750	2,500
(45)	Candy Nelson	17,500	10,500	7,000
(46)	Orator Jim O'Rourke (Possibly unique.)	75,000	21,000	14,000
(47)	Dave Orr	17,500	10,500	7,000
(48)	Tom Poorman	6,250	3,750	2,500
(49)	Danny Richardson	17,500	10,500	7,000
(50)	Wilbert Robinson	10,500	6,300	4,200
(51)	Wilbert Robinson, Fred Mann	10,500	6,300	4,200
(52)	Chief Roseman	17,500	10,500	7,000
(53)	Ed Seward (Possibly unique.)	14,000	8,400	5,600
(54)	Harry Stowe (Stovey) (Hands on hips.)	75,000	21,000	14,000
(55)	Harry Stowe (Stovey) (Hands outstretched.)	7,000	4,200	2,800
(56)	George Townsend	7,000	4,200	2,800
(57)	Jocko Milligan, George Townsend	7,900	4,750	3,150
(58)	John Ward (Possibly unique.)	100,000	28,500	19,000
(59)	Gus Weyhing	24,000	14,500	9,500
(60)	George Wood	6,250	3,750	2,500
(61)	Harry Wright	40,000	25,000	15,000

1887 Kalamazoo Bats Cabinets (N690-1)

This extremely rare issue of cabinet cards was issued as a premium by Charles Gross & Co. of Philadelphia, makers of the Kalamazoo Bats brand of cigarettes. Two distinct types have been found, both measuring 4-1/4" x 6-1/2". One variety displays the photo on a black mount with the words "Smoke Kalamazoo Bats" embossed in gold to the left. The other contains no advertising, although there is an oval embossment on the card, along with the words "Chas. Gross & Co." and an 1887 copyright line.

These cards also have a distinctive pink color on the back of the cardboard mount. Because of the rarity of Kalamazoo Bats cabinets, and uncertainty as to completeness of this checklist, gaps have been left in the assigned numbering.

		NM	EX	VG
Common Player:		7,500	3,750	2,250
(1)	Ed Andrews	7,500	3,750	2,250
(2)	Charles Bastian, Daniel Casey, Billy Taylor	7,500	3,750	2,250
(3)	Charles Bastian, Denny Lyons	7,500	3,750	2,250
(4)	Louis Bierbauer, Gallagher	7,500	3,750	2,250
(5)	Charles Buffington (Buffinton)	7,500	3,750	2,250
(6)	Daniel Casey	7,500	3,750	2,250
(7)	Jack Clements	7,500	3,750	2,250
(8)	Jim Devlin	7,500	3,750	2,250
(9)	Sid Farrar	7,500	3,750	2,250
(10)	Charlie Ferguson	7,500	3,750	2,250
(11)	Jim Fogarty	7,500	3,750	2,250
(12)	Whitey Gibson	7,500	3,750	2,250
(13)	Tom Gunning	7,500	3,750	2,250
(14)	Arthur Irwin	7,500	3,750	2,250
(15)	Arthur Irwin, Al Maul	7,500	3,750	2,250
(16)	Henry Larkins (Larkin), Jocko Milligan	7,500	3,750	2,250
(17)	Harry Lyons	7,500	3,750	2,250
(18)	Harry Lyons, Billy Taylor	7,500	3,750	2,250
(19)	Fred Mann	7,500	3,750	2,250
(20)	Fred Mann, Wilbert Robinson	12,500	3,750	2,250
(21)	Bobby Mathews	7,500	3,750	2,250
(22)	Al Maul	7,500	3,750	2,250
(23)	Chippy McCan (McGarr)	7,500	3,750	2,250
(24)	Deacon McGuire (Fielding)	7,500	3,750	2,250
(25)	Deacon McGuire (Throwing)	7,500	3,750	2,250
(26)	Jocko Milligan, Harry Stowe (Stovey)	7,500	3,750	2,250
(27)	Joseph Mulvey	7,500	3,750	2,250
(28)	Tom Poorman	7,500	3,750	2,250
(29)	Ed Seward	7,500	3,750	2,250
(30)	Harry Stowe (Stovey)	7,500	3,750	2,250
(31)	George Townsend	7,500	3,750	2,250
(32)	George Wood	7,500	3,750	2,250
(33)	Harry Wright	31,250	5,625	3,425
(35)	Athletic Club (Three known, $9,031 paid in 12/04 auction for Good example.)			
(36)	Boston B.B.C. (Believed unique, mount restored, brought $14,434 in 5/05 auction.)			
(37)	Detroit B.B.C. (Believed unique.)			
(38)	Philadelphia B.B.C. (Believed unique, VG, brought $9,935 in 12/04 auction.)			
(39)	Pittsburg B.B.C. (Believed unique, sold for $62,299 in Excellent in 12/05 auction.)			

1887 Kalamazoo Bats Team Cards (N693)

The team photos in this set were issued by Charles Gross & Co. of Philadelphia as a promotion for its Kalamazoo Bats brand of cigarettes. The cards, which are similar in design and size (about 4" x 2-1/4") to the related N690 series, are extremely rare. They feature a team photo with the caption in a white box at the bottom of the photo and an ad for Kalamazoo Bats to the left.

		NM	EX	VG
Common Team:		10,000	3,575	2,175
(1)	Athletic Club	10,000	3,575	2,175
(2)	Baltimore B.B.C.	33,000	12,000	7,250
(3)	Boston B.B.C.	26,400	9,500	5,800
(4)	Detroit B.B.C.	27,500	10,000	6,000
(5)	Philadelphia B.B.C.	13,200	4,750	2,900
(6)	Pittsburg B.B.C.	33,000	3,575	2,275

1955 Kansas City Athletics Photo Pack

VIC POWER

In the first year following the team's move from Philadelphia to K.C., this set of player pictures was issued, probably sold as a souvenir stand item. The black-and-white photos are in an 8" x 10" format on heavy cardboard. Player poses or portraits are bordered in white with the player name in all-caps at bottom. Backs are blank. This checklist may be incomplete.

		NM	EX	VG
Complete Set (29):		200.00	100.00	60.00
Common Player:		9.00	4.50	2.75
(1)	Joe Astroth	9.00	4.50	2.75
(2)	Lou Boudreau	25.00	12.50	7.50
(3)	Cloyd Boyer	9.00	4.50	2.75
(4)	Art Ceccarelli	9.00	4.50	2.75
(5)	Harry Craft	9.00	4.50	2.75
(6)	Joe DeMaestri	9.00	4.50	2.75
(7)	Art Ditmar	9.00	4.50	2.75
(8)	Jim Finigan	9.00	4.50	2.75
(9)	Tom Gorman	9.00	4.50	2.75
(10)	Ray Herbert	9.00	4.50	2.75
(11)	Alex Kellner	9.00	4.50	2.75
(12)	Dick Kryhoski	9.00	4.50	2.75
(13)	Jack Littrell	9.00	4.50	2.75
(14)	Hector Lopez	9.00	4.50	2.75
(15)	Oscar Melillo	9.00	4.50	2.75
(16)	Arnie Portocarrero	9.00	4.50	2.75
(17)	Vic Power	15.00	7.50	4.50
(18)	Vic Raschi	12.00	6.00	3.50
(19)	Bill Renna	9.00	4.50	2.75
(20)	Johnny Sain	12.00	6.00	3.50
(21)	Bobby Shantz	12.00	6.00	3.50
(22)	Wilmer Shantz	9.00	4.50	2.75
(23)	Harry Simpson	15.00	7.50	4.50
(24)	Enos Slaughter	30.00	15.00	9.00
(25)	Lou Sleator	9.00	4.50	2.75
(26)	George Susce	9.00	4.50	2.75
(27)	Elmer Valo	9.00	4.50	2.75
(28)	Bill Wilson	9.00	4.50	2.75
(29)	Gus Zernial	15.00	7.50	4.50

1956-61 Kansas City Athletics Photocards

Issued over a period of several years these black-and-white photocards share an identical format. The cards are 3-1/4" x 5-1/2" with borderless poses and facsimile autographs on front. Backs are blank. The unnumbered cards are checklisted here in alphabetical order, though the list is surely not complete. Gaps have been left in the assigned numbering for future additions.

		NM	EX	VG
Common Player:		15.00	7.50	4.50
(1)	Jim Archer	15.00	7.50	4.50
(2)	Mike Baxes	15.00	7.50	4.50
(3)	Zeke Bella	15.00	7.50	4.50
(4)	Lou Boudreau	30.00	15.00	9.00
(5)	Cletis Boyer	20.00	10.00	6.00
(6)	Wally Burnette	15.00	7.50	4.50
(7)	Chico Carrasquel	17.50	8.75	5.25
(8)	Bob Cerv	15.00	7.50	4.50
(9)	Harry Chiti	15.00	7.50	4.50
(10)	Harry Craft	15.00	7.50	4.50
(11)	Jack Crimian	15.00	7.50	4.50
(12)	Bud Daley	15.00	7.50	4.50
(13)	Bob Davis	15.00	7.50	4.50
(14)	Joe DeMaestri	15.00	7.50	4.50
(15)	Art Ditmar	15.00	7.50	4.50
(16)	Jim Ewell (Trainer)	15.00	7.50	4.50
(17)	Jim Finigan	15.00	7.50	4.50
(18)	Hank Foiles	15.00	7.50	4.50
(19)	Ned Garver	17.50	8.75	5.25
(20)	Joe Ginsberg	15.00	7.50	4.50
(21)	Tom Gorman (Cap-to-knees.)	15.00	7.50	4.50
(22)	Tom Gorman (Pitching)	15.00	7.50	4.50
(23)	Bob Grim	15.00	7.50	4.50
(24)	Johnny Groth	15.00	7.50	4.50
(25)	Kent Hadley	15.00	7.50	4.50
(26)	Ray Herbert	15.00	7.50	4.50
(27)	Troy Herriage	15.00	7.50	4.50
(28)	Whitey Herzog	20.00	10.00	6.00
(29)	Frank House	15.00	7.50	4.50
(31)	Alex Kellner	15.00	7.50	4.50
(32)	Lou Kretlow	15.00	7.50	4.50
(33)	Hec Lopez	15.00	7.50	4.50
(34)	Roger Maris	125.00	62.00	37.00
(35)	Oscar Melillo	15.00	7.50	4.50
(36)	Rance Pless	15.00	7.50	4.50
(37)	Vic Power	20.00	10.00	6.00
(38)	Jose Santiago	15.00	7.50	4.50
(39)	Bobby Shantz	25.00	12.50	7.50

(41)	Harry Simpson	17.50	8.75	5.25
(42)	Lou Skizas	15.00	7.50	4.50
(43)	Enos Slaughter	45.00	22.00	13.50
(44)	Hal Smith	15.00	7.50	4.50
(45)	George Susce	15.00	7.50	4.50
(46)	Wayne Terwilliger	15.00	7.50	4.50
(47)	Charles Thompson	15.00	7.50	4.50
(48)	Dick Tomanek	15.00	7.50	4.50
(49)	Bill Tuttle	15.00	7.50	4.50
(52)	Jack Urban	15.00	7.50	4.50
(53)	Preston Ward	15.00	7.50	4.50
(54)	Dick Williams	17.50	8.75	5.25
(55)	Gus Zernial (Batting)	17.50	8.75	5.25
(56)	Gus Zernial (Fielding)	17.50	8.75	5.25

1929 Kashin Publications (R316)

This set of 101 unnumbered cards was issued in 25-card boxed series, with cards measuring 3-1/2" x 4-1/2". The cards feature black-and-white photos with the player's name printed in script near the bottom of the photo. Team and league are designated at bottom in printed letters. The backs of the cards are blank. Four of the cards (Hadley, Haines, Siebold and Todt) are considered to be scarcer than the rest of the set. Some cards have been seen with "MADE IN U.S.A." in one of the picture's lower corners; their significance and value are undetermined.

		NM	EX	VG
Complete Set (101):		9,500	4,750	2,750
Common Player:		40.00	20.00	12.00
(1)	Dale Alexander	40.00	20.00	12.00
(2)	Ethan N. Allen	40.00	20.00	12.00
(3)	Larry Benton	40.00	20.00	12.00
(4)	Moe Berg	250.00	125.00	75.00
(5)	Max Bishop	40.00	20.00	12.00
(6)	Del Bissonette	40.00	20.00	12.00
(7)	Lucerne A. Blue	40.00	20.00	12.00
(8)	James Bottomley	100.00	50.00	30.00
(9)	Guy T. Bush	40.00	20.00	12.00
(10)	Harold G. Carlson	40.00	20.00	12.00
(11)	Owen Carroll	40.00	20.00	12.00
(12)	Chalmers W. Cissell (Chalmer)	40.00	20.00	12.00
(13)	Earl Combs	100.00	50.00	30.00
(14)	Hugh M. Critz	40.00	20.00	12.00
(15)	H.J. DeBerry	40.00	20.00	12.00
(16)	Pete Donohue	40.00	20.00	12.00
(17)	Taylor Douthit	40.00	20.00	12.00
(18)	Chas. W. Dressen	40.00	20.00	12.00
(19)	Jimmy Dykes	40.00	20.00	12.00
(20)	Howard Ehmke	40.00	20.00	12.00
(21)	Elwood English	40.00	20.00	12.00
(22)	Urban Faber	100.00	50.00	30.00
(23)	Fred Fitzsimmons	40.00	20.00	12.00
(24)	Lewis A. Fonseca	40.00	20.00	12.00
(25)	Horace H. Ford	40.00	20.00	12.00
(26)	Jimmy Foxx	235.00	115.00	70.00
(27)	Frank Frisch	100.00	50.00	30.00
(28)	Lou Gehrig	1,125	560.00	335.00
(29)	Charles Gehringer	100.00	50.00	30.00
(30)	Leon Goslin	100.00	50.00	30.00
(31)	George Grantham	40.00	20.00	12.00
(32)	Burleigh Grimes	100.00	50.00	30.00
(33)	Robert Grove	200.00	100.00	60.00
(34)	Bump Hadley	150.00	75.00	45.00
(35)	Charlie Hafey	100.00	50.00	30.00
(36)	Jesse J. Haines	250.00	125.00	75.00
(37)	Harvey Hendrick	40.00	20.00	12.00
(38)	Floyd C. Herman	40.00	20.00	12.00
(39)	Andy High	40.00	20.00	12.00
(40)	Urban J. Hodapp	40.00	20.00	12.00
(41)	Frank Hogan	40.00	20.00	12.00
(42)	Rogers Hornsby	175.00	85.00	50.00
(43)	Waite Hoyt	100.00	50.00	30.00
(44)	Willis Hudlin	40.00	20.00	12.00
(45)	Frank O. Hurst	40.00	20.00	12.00
(46)	Charlie Jamieson	40.00	20.00	12.00
(47)	Roy C. Johnson	40.00	20.00	12.00
(48)	Percy Jones	40.00	20.00	12.00
(49)	Sam Jones	40.00	20.00	12.00
(50)	Joseph Judge	40.00	20.00	12.00
(51)	Willie Kamm	40.00	20.00	12.00
(52)	Charles Klein	100.00	50.00	30.00
(53)	Mark Koenig	40.00	20.00	12.00
(54)	Ralph Kress	40.00	20.00	12.00
(55)	Fred M. Leach	40.00	20.00	12.00
(56)	Fred Lindstrom	100.00	50.00	30.00
(57)	Ad Liska	40.00	20.00	12.00
(58)	Fred Lucas (Red)	40.00	20.00	12.00
(59)	Fred Maguire	40.00	20.00	12.00
(60)	Perce L. Malone	40.00	20.00	12.00
(61)	Harry Manush (Henry)	100.00	50.00	30.00
(62)	Walter Maranville	100.00	50.00	30.00

(63)	Douglas McWeeney (McWeeny)	40.00	20.00	12.00
(64)	Oscar Melillo	40.00	20.00	12.00
(65)	Ed "Bing" Miller	40.00	20.00	12.00
(66)	Frank O'Doul	80.00	40.00	24.00
(67)	Melvin Ott	200.00	100.00	60.00
(68)	Herbert Pennock	100.00	50.00	30.00
(69)	William W. Regan	40.00	20.00	12.00
(70)	Harry F. Rice	40.00	20.00	12.00
(71)	Sam Rice	100.00	50.00	30.00
(72)	Lance Richbourgh (Richbourg)	40.00	20.00	12.00
(73)	Eddie Rommel	40.00	20.00	12.00
(74)	Chas. H. Root	40.00	20.00	12.00
(75)	Ed (Edd) Roush	100.00	50.00	30.00
(76)	Harold Ruel (Herold)	40.00	20.00	12.00
(77)	Charles Ruffing	125.00	65.00	35.00
(78)	Jack Russell	40.00	20.00	12.00
(79)	Babe Ruth	1,650	825.00	500.00
(80)	Fred Schulte	40.00	20.00	12.00
(81)	Harry Seibold	150.00	75.00	45.00
(82)	Joe Sewell	100.00	50.00	30.00
(83)	Luke Sewell	40.00	20.00	12.00
(84)	Art Shires	40.00	20.00	12.00
(85)	Al Simmons	100.00	50.00	30.00
(86)	Bob Smith	40.00	20.00	12.00
(87)	Riggs Stephenson	40.00	20.00	12.00
(88)	Wm. H. Terry	100.00	50.00	30.00
(89)	Alphonse Thomas	40.00	20.00	12.00
(90)	Lafayette F. Thompson	40.00	20.00	12.00
(91)	Phil Todt	150.00	75.00	45.00
(92)	Harold J. Traynor	100.00	50.00	30.00
(93)	Dazzy Vance	100.00	50.00	30.00
(94)	Lloyd Waner	100.00	50.00	30.00
(95)	Paul Waner	100.00	50.00	30.00
(96)	Jimmy Welsh	40.00	20.00	12.00
(97)	Earl Whitehill	40.00	20.00	12.00
(98)	A.C. Whitney	40.00	20.00	12.00
(99)	Claude Willoughby	40.00	20.00	12.00
(100)	Hack Wilson	200.00	100.00	60.00
(101)	Tom Zachary	40.00	20.00	12.00

1964 KDKA Pittsburgh Pirates Portraits

Issued prior to the radio/TV stations' much more common color player cards of 1968, this seldom-seen regional issue presents the 1964 Pittsburgh Pirates in a set of 28 large-format (8" x 11-7/8") schedule cards. The cards are printed in sepia tones on blank-backed cardboard. Fronts present a player pose and a '64 Pirates schedule. A redemption offer states that a pair of Bucs' tickets will be given in exchange for a complete set of the portraits, and the pictures will be returned, presumably cancelled in some fashion. The unnumbered cards are checklisted here alphabetically. While the cards advertise the Pirates' broadcasting partners, they were actually issued by Sweet Clean laundry as stiffeners for men's shirts that had been washed. The laundry's name is not mentioned anywhere on the cards.

		NM	EX	VG
Complete Set (28):		3,500	1,750	1,000
Common Player:		100.00	50.00	30.00
(1)	Gene Alley	100.00	50.00	30.00
(2)	Bob Bailey	100.00	50.00	30.00
(3)	Frank Bork	100.00	50.00	30.00
(4)	Smoky Burgess	100.00	50.00	30.00
(5)	Tom Butters	100.00	50.00	30.00
(6)	Don Cardwell	100.00	50.00	30.00
(7)	Roberto Clemente	600.00	300.00	180.00
(8)	Donn Clendenon	100.00	50.00	30.00
(9)	Elroy Face	100.00	50.00	30.00
(10)	Gene Freese	100.00	50.00	30.00
(11)	Bob Friend	100.00	50.00	30.00
(12)	Joe Gibbon	100.00	50.00	30.00
(13)	Julio Gotay	100.00	50.00	30.00
(14)	Rex Johnston	100.00	50.00	30.00
(15)	Vernon Law	100.00	50.00	30.00
(16)	Jerry Lynch	100.00	50.00	30.00
(17)	Bill Mazeroski	250.00	125.00	75.00
(18)	Al McBean	100.00	50.00	30.00
(19)	Orlando McFarlane	100.00	50.00	30.00
(20)	Manny Mota	100.00	50.00	30.00
(21)	Danny Murtaugh	100.00	50.00	30.00
(22)	Jim Pagliaroni	100.00	50.00	30.00
(23)	Dick Schofield	100.00	50.00	30.00
(24)	Don Schwall	100.00	50.00	30.00
(25)	Tommie Sisk	100.00	50.00	30.00
(26)	Willie Stargell	250.00	125.00	75.00
(27)	Bob Veale	100.00	50.00	30.00
(28)	Bill Virdon	100.00	50.00	30.00

1968 KDKA Pittsburgh Pirates

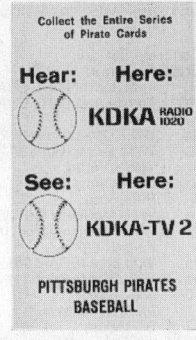

Collect the Entire Series
of Pirate Cards

Hear: Here:
KDKA RADIO 1020

See: Here:
KDKA-TV 2

PITTSBURGH PIRATES
BASEBALL

The most common of the many Pirates regional issues of the late 1960s, this 23-card set was sponsored by the Pirates' TV and radio flagship stations, KDKA in Pittsburgh. Cards measure 2-1/2" x 4" and feature at top front a color posed photo of the player, with no top or side borders. In the white panel beneath the photo are a facsimile autograph, the player's name, position and uniform number and the broadcasters' logo. Backs are printed in black on white and feature advertising for the radio and TV station. The checklist is presented here by uniform number.

	NM	EX	VG
Complete Set (23):	125.00	65.00	35.00
Common Player:	5.00	2.50	1.50
7 Larry Shepard	5.00	2.50	1.50
8 Willie Stargell	15.00	7.50	4.50
9 Bill Mazeroski	15.00	7.50	4.50
10 Gary Kolb	5.00	2.50	1.50
11 Jose Pagan	5.00	2.50	1.50
12 Gerry May (Jerry)	5.00	2.50	1.50
14 Jim Bunning	10.00	5.00	3.00
15 Manny Mota	5.00	2.50	1.50
17 Donn Clendenon	5.00	2.50	1.50
18 Matty Alou	5.00	2.50	1.50
21 Roberto Clemente	40.00	20.00	12.00
22 Gene Alley	5.00	2.50	1.50
25 Tommy Sisk	5.00	2.50	1.50
26 Roy Face	5.00	2.50	1.50
27 Ron Kline	5.00	2.50	1.50
28 Steve Blass	5.00	2.50	1.50
29 Juan Pizarro	5.00	2.50	1.50
30 Maury Wills	6.50	3.25	2.00
34 Al McBean	5.00	2.50	1.50
35 Manny Sanguillen	5.00	2.50	1.50
38 Bob Moose	5.00	2.50	1.50
39 Bob Veale	5.00	2.50	1.50
40 Dave Wickersham	5.00	2.50	1.50

1922 Keating Candy Co.

WALTER PIPP
1st B.—New York Americans

To compete with other candy issues featuring baseball cards as premiums, Sacramento, Calif., wholesale candy merchant James P. Keating appears to have purchased uncut sheets of the blank-back strip cards known as W575-1, overprinted their backs and packaged them with his product. The advertising on back is rubber-stamped. The fact that examples are known that have been cancelled with a hole punch probably indicates there was some sort of prize redemption program attached to the issue. Collectors can expect to pay a premium of about 3X for this version.

	NM	EX	VG
Common Player:	85.00	45.00	25.00
Stars: 3X			

(See 1922 W575-1 for checklist and base card values.)

1971 Keds Kedcards

BASEBALL

KEDKARD JOHNNY BENCH

These (usually) 2-1/4" x 2-1/8" cards were printed on the side of Keds athletic shoe boxes. The cards have colorful drawings of various athletes, with dotted lines for cutting. Backs are blank.

	NM	EX	VG
Complete Panel Set (3):	150.00	75.00	45.00
Complete Set (10):	120.00	60.00	35.00
Common Player:	8.00	4.00	2.50
PANEL 1	40.00	20.00	12.00
(1) Dave Bing (Basketball)	8.00	4.00	2.50
(2) Clark Graebner (Tennis)	8.00	4.00	2.50
(3) Jim Maloney	10.00	5.00	3.00
(4) Bubba Smith (Football)	10.00	5.00	3.00
PANEL 2	65.00	32.00	19.50
(5) Johnny Bench	30.00	15.00	9.00
(6) Willis Reed (Basketball)	10.00	5.00	3.00
(7) Bubba Smith (Football)	10.00	5.00	3.00
(8) Stan Smith (Tennis)	8.00	4.00	2.50
PANEL 3	50.00	25.00	15.00
(9) Willis Reed (Basketball) (5-1/4" x 3-1/2")	15.00	7.50	4.50
(10) Johnny Bench (5-1/4" x 3-1/2")	30.00	15.00	9.00

1937 Kellogg's Pep Sports Stamps

Kellogg's packaged a four-stamp panel of "Sports Stamps" in boxes of Pep cereal. While 24 panels comprise a complete set, six of the stamps were double-printed, creating a set of 90. Backs of the stamp panels gave details for ordering an album and game boards for playing with the stamps. The color-tinted stamps measure 1-1/8" x 2-3/4" individually, and 2-1/4" x 4-1/4" as a panel. Besides the ballplayers checklisted here, the Kellogg's/Pep stamps included football, tennis and golf players, swimmers, boxers, aviaitors and race horses. Baseball player stamps are listed here according to the number of the four-stamp panel on which they appeared. Prices for complete panels would be considerably higher, factoring in the other stamps on the sheet.

	NM	EX	VG
Complete Set (18):	900.00	450.00	275.00
Common Player:	60.00	30.00	18.00
Album:	300.00	150.00	100.00
1 Joe Medwick	60.00	30.00	18.00
3 Leo Durocher	60.00	30.00	18.00
5 Gabby Hartnett	60.00	30.00	18.00
6 Billy Herman	60.00	30.00	18.00
7 Luke Appling	60.00	30.00	18.00
8 Floyd Vaughan	60.00	30.00	18.00
9 Paul Waner	60.00	30.00	18.00
11 Bill Terry	60.00	30.00	18.00
12 George Selkirk	60.00	30.00	18.00
13 Walter Johnson	120.00	60.00	36.00
15 Lew Fonseca	60.00	30.00	18.00
16 Richard Ferrell	60.00	30.00	18.00
17 Johnny Evers	60.00	30.00	18.00
18 Sam West	60.00	30.00	18.00
19 Buddy Myer	60.00	30.00	18.00
20 Tris Speaker (Double print, also on Panel 23.)	60.00	30.00	18.00
21 Joe Tinker	60.00	30.00	18.00
22 Mordecai Brown	60.00	30.00	18.00
23 Tris Speaker (Double-print, also on Panel 20.)	60.00	30.00	18.00

1948 Kellogg's Corn Flakes Cuban Postcards

CORN FLAKES

These advertising postcards were issued in Cuba. The approximately 3-1/2" x 5-3/8" black-and-white cards have a portrait photo on front. A small logo for the cereal appears in the lower-left corner, while a facsimile autograph is at lower-right. The back is in traditional postcard format, printed in English. This checklist is likely incomplete.

	NM	EX	VG
(1) Tomas de la Cruz	400.00	200.00	120.00
(2) Salvador Hernandez	400.00	200.00	120.00
(3) Adolfo Luque	600.00	300.00	180.00
(4) Roberto Ortiz	400.00	200.00	120.00
(5) Napoleon Reyes	400.00	200.00	120.00
(6) Lazaro Salazar	400.00	200.00	120.00

1948 Kellogg's Pep Celebrities

PHIL CAVARETTA
First baseman and outfielder, Chicago Cubs. National league batting champion and most valuable player in 1945. Joined Cubs at age of 17 and has lifetime batting average of .292. Bats and throws left-handed.

Get Complete Series
with Kellogg's PEP

Five baseball players are included among the 18 athletes in this set of 1-3/8" x 1-5/8" cards. Fronts have player photos bordered in white. Backs have player name at top, a short career summary and a Kellogg's ad. The baseball players from the unnumbered set are listed here alphabetically.

	NM	EX	VG
Complete Set (5):	175.00	90.00	55.00
Common Player:	40.00	20.00	12.00
(1) Phil Cavaretta	40.00	20.00	12.00
(2) Orval Grove	40.00	20.00	12.00
(3) Mike Tresh	40.00	20.00	12.00
(4) Paul "Dizzy" Trout	40.00	20.00	12.00
(5) Dick Wakefield	40.00	20.00	12.00

1970 Kellogg's

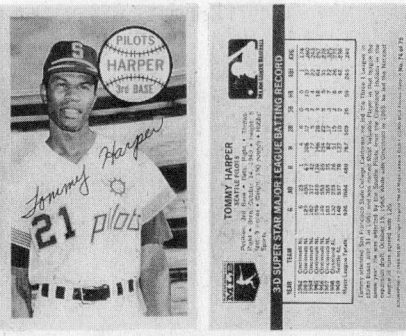

For 14 years in the 1970s and early 1980s, the Kellogg's cereal company provided Topps with virtually the only meaningful national competition in the baseball card market. Kellogg's kicked off its baseball card program in 1970 with a 75-player set of simulated 3-D cards. Single cards were available in selected brands of the company's cereal, while a mail-in program offered complete sets. The 3-D effect was achieved by the sandwiching of a clear color player photo between a purposely blurred stadium background scene and a layer of ribbed plastic. The relatively narrow dimension of the card, 2-1/4" x 3-1/2" and the nature of the plastic overlay seem to conspire to cause the cards to curl, often cracking the plastic layer, if not stored properly. Cards with major cracks in the plastic can be considered in Fair condition, at best.

	NM	EX	VG
Complete Set (75):	300.00	150.00	90.00
Common Player:	3.50	1.75	1.00
1 Ed Kranepool	3.50	1.75	1.00
2 Pete Rose	20.00	10.00	6.00
3 Cleon Jones	3.50	1.75	1.00
4 Willie McCovey	10.00	5.00	3.00
5 Mel Stottlemyre	3.50	1.75	1.00
6 Frank Howard	3.50	1.75	1.00
7 Tom Seaver	15.00	7.50	4.50
8 Don Sutton	10.00	5.00	3.00
9 Jim Wynn	3.50	1.75	1.00
10 Jim Maloney	3.50	1.75	1.00
11 Tommie Agee	3.50	1.75	1.00
12 Willie Mays	25.00	12.50	7.50
13 Juan Marichal	10.00	5.00	3.00
14 Dave McNally	3.50	1.75	1.00
15 Frank Robinson	15.00	7.50	4.50
16 Carlos May	3.50	1.75	1.00
17 Bill Singer	3.50	1.75	1.00
18 Rick Reichardt	3.50	1.75	1.00
19 Boog Powell	4.50	2.25	1.25
20 Gaylord Perry	10.00	5.00	3.00
21 Brooks Robinson	15.00	7.50	4.50
22 Luis Aparicio	10.00	5.00	3.00
23 Joel Horlen	3.50	1.75	1.00
24 Mike Epstein	3.50	1.75	1.00
25 Tom Haller	3.50	1.75	1.00

#	Player			
26	Willie Crawford	3.50	1.75	1.00
27	Roberto Clemente	35.00	17.50	10.00
28	Matty Alou	3.50	1.75	1.00
29	Willie Stargell	12.50	6.25	3.75
30	Tim Cullen	3.50	1.75	1.00
31	Randy Hundley	3.50	1.75	1.00
32	Reggie Jackson	20.00	10.00	6.00
33	Rich Allen	4.25	2.25	1.25
34	Tim McCarver	3.50	1.75	1.00
35	Ray Culp	3.50	1.75	1.00
36	Jim Fregosi	3.50	1.75	1.00
37	Billy Williams	12.50	6.25	3.75
38	Johnny Odom	3.50	1.75	1.00
39	Bert Campaneris	3.50	1.75	1.00
40	Ernie Banks	20.00	10.00	6.00
41	Chris Short	3.50	1.75	1.00
42	Ron Santo	6.00	3.00	1.75
43	Glenn Beckert	3.50	1.75	1.00
44	Lou Brock	12.50	6.25	3.75
45	Larry Hisle	3.50	1.75	1.00
46	Reggie Smith	3.50	1.75	1.00
47	Rod Carew	15.00	7.50	4.50
48	Curt Flood	3.50	1.75	1.00
49	Jim Lonborg	3.50	1.75	1.00
50	Sam McDowell	3.50	1.75	1.00
51	Sal Bando	3.50	1.75	1.00
52	Al Kaline	15.00	7.50	4.50
53	Gary Nolan	3.50	1.75	1.00
54	Rico Petrocelli	3.50	1.75	1.00
55	Ollie Brown	3.50	1.75	1.00
56	Luis Tiant	3.50	1.75	1.00
57	Bill Freehan	3.50	1.75	1.00
58	Johnny Bench	15.00	7.50	4.50
59	Joe Pepitone	3.50	1.75	1.00
60	Bobby Murcer	3.50	1.75	1.00
61	Harmon Killebrew	15.00	7.50	4.50
62	Don Wilson	3.50	1.75	1.00
63	Tony Oliva	3.50	1.75	1.00
64	Jim Perry	3.50	1.75	1.00
65	Mickey Lolich	3.50	1.75	1.00
66	Coco Laboy	3.50	1.75	1.00
67	Dean Chance	3.50	1.75	1.00
68	Ken Harrelson	3.50	1.75	1.00
69	Willie Horton	3.50	1.75	1.00
70	Wally Bunker	3.50	1.75	1.00
71a	Bob Gibson (1959 IP blank)	12.50	6.25	3.75
71b	Bob Gibson (1959 IP 76)	12.50	6.25	3.75
72	Joe Morgan	12.50	6.25	3.75
73	Denny McLain	3.50	1.75	1.00
74	Tommy Harper	3.50	1.75	1.00
75	Don Mincher	3.50	1.75	1.00

1971 Kellogg's

The scarcest and most valuable of the Kellogg's editions, the 75-card 1971 set was the only one not offered by the company on a mail-in basis. The only way to complete it was to buy ... and buy and buy ... boxes of cereal. Kellogg's again used the simulated 3-D effect in the cards' design, with the same result being many of the 2-1/4" x 3-1/2" cards are found today with cracks resulting from the cards' curling. A number of scarcer back variations are checklisted below. In addition, all 75 cards can be found with and without the 1970 date before the "Xograph" copyright line on the back; though there is no difference in value.

		NM	EX	VG
Complete Set (75):		1,000	500.00	300.00
Common Player:		13.50	6.75	4.00
1a	Wayne Simpson (SO 120)	13.50	6.75	4.00
1b	Wayne Simpson (SO 119)	20.00	10.00	6.00
2	Tom Seaver	30.00	15.00	9.00
3a	Jim Perry (IP 2238)	13.50	6.75	4.00
3b	Jim Perry (IP 2239)	20.00	10.00	6.00
4a	Bob Robertson (RBI 94)	13.50	6.75	4.00
4b	Bob Robertson (RBI 95)	20.00	10.00	6.00
5	Roberto Clemente	70.00	35.00	20.00
6a	Gaylord Perry (IP 2014)	25.00	12.50	7.50
6b	Gaylord Perry (IP 2015)	30.00	15.00	9.00
7a	Felipe Alou (1970 Oakland NL)	20.00	10.00	6.00
7b	Felipe Alou (1970 Oakland AL)	25.00	12.50	7.50
8	Denis Menke	13.50	6.75	4.00
9a	Don Kessinger (Hits 849)	13.50	6.75	4.00
9b	Don Kessinger (Hits 850)	20.00	10.00	6.00
10	Willie Mays	45.00	22.00	13.50
11	Jim Hickman	13.50	6.75	4.00
12	Tony Oliva	17.50	8.75	5.25
13	Manny Sanguillen	13.50	6.75	4.00
14a	Frank Howard (1968 Washington NL)	30.00	15.00	9.00
14b	Frank Howard (1968 Washington AL)	20.00	10.00	6.00
15	Frank Robinson	30.00	15.00	9.00

#	Player			
16	Willie Davis	13.50	6.75	4.00
17	Lou Brock	25.00	12.50	7.50
18	Cesar Tovar	13.50	6.75	4.00
19	Luis Aparicio	25.00	12.50	7.50
20	Boog Powell	17.50	8.75	5.25
21a	Dick Selma (SO 584)	13.50	6.75	4.00
21b	Dick Selma (SO 587)	20.00	10.00	6.00
22	Danny Walton	13.50	6.75	4.00
23	Carl Morton	13.50	6.75	4.00
24a	Sonny Siebert (SO 1054)	13.50	6.75	4.00
24b	Sonny Siebert (SO 1055)	20.00	10.00	6.00
25	Jim Merritt	13.50	6.75	4.00
26a	Jose Cardenal (Hits 828)	13.50	6.75	4.00
26b	Jose Cardenal (Hits 829)	20.00	10.00	6.00
27	Don Mincher	13.50	6.75	4.00
28a	Clyde Wright (California state logo.)	13.50	6.75	4.00
28b	Clyde Wright (Angels crest logo.)	20.00	10.00	6.00
29	Les Cain	13.50	6.75	4.00
30	Danny Cater	13.50	6.75	4.00
31	Don Sutton	25.00	12.50	7.50
32	Chuck Dobson	13.50	6.75	4.00
33	Willie McCovey	25.00	12.50	7.50
34	Mike Epstein	13.50	6.75	4.00
35a	Paul Blair (Runs 386)	13.50	6.75	4.00
35b	Paul Blair (Runs 385)	20.00	10.00	6.00
36a	Gary Nolan (SO 577)	13.50	6.75	4.00
36b	Gary Nolan (SO 581)	20.00	10.00	6.00
37	Sam McDowell	13.50	6.75	4.00
38	Amos Otis	13.50	6.75	4.00
39a	Ray Fosse (RBI 69)	13.50	6.75	4.00
39b	Ray Fosse (RBI 70)	20.00	10.00	6.00
40	Mel Stottlemyre	13.50	6.75	4.00
41	Cito Gaston	13.50	6.75	4.00
42	Dick Dietz	13.50	6.75	4.00
43	Roy White	13.50	6.75	4.00
44	Al Kaline	30.00	15.00	9.00
45	Carlos May	13.50	6.75	4.00
46a	Tommie Agee (RBI 313)	13.50	6.75	4.00
46b	Tommie Agee (RBI 314)	20.00	10.00	6.00
47	Tommy Harper	13.50	6.75	4.00
48	Larry Dierker	13.50	6.75	4.00
49	Mike Cuellar	13.50	6.75	4.00
50	Ernie Banks	30.00	15.00	9.00
51	Bob Gibson	25.00	12.50	7.50
52	Reggie Smith	13.50	6.75	4.00
53a	Matty Alou (RBI 273)	13.50	6.75	4.00
53b	Matty Alou (RBI 274)	20.00	10.00	6.00
54a	Alex Johnson (California state logo.)	13.50	6.75	4.00
54b	Alex Johnson (Angels crest logo.)	20.00	10.00	6.00
55	Harmon Killebrew	30.00	15.00	9.00
56	Billy Grabarkewitz	13.50	6.75	4.00
57	Rich Allen	17.50	8.75	5.25
58	Tony Perez	25.00	12.50	7.50
59a	Dave McNally (SO 1065)	13.50	6.75	4.00
59b	Dave McNally (SO 1067)	20.00	10.00	6.00
60a	Jim Palmer (SO 564)	25.00	12.50	7.50
60b	Jim Palmer (SO 567)	30.00	15.00	9.00
61	Billy Williams	25.00	12.50	7.50
62	Joe Torre	20.00	10.00	6.00
63a	Jim Northrup (AB 2773)	13.50	6.75	4.00
63b	Jim Northrup (AB 2772)	20.00	10.00	6.00
64a	Jim Fregosi (Calif. state logo - Hits 1326)	13.50	6.75	4.00
64b	Jim Fregosi (Calif. state logo - Hits 1327)	20.00	10.00	6.00
64c	Jim Fregosi (Angels crest logo.)	20.00	10.00	6.00
65	Pete Rose	60.00	30.00	18.00
66a	Bud Harrelson (RBI 112)	13.50	6.75	4.00
66b	Bud Harrelson (RBI 113)	20.00	10.00	6.00
67	Tony Taylor	13.50	6.75	4.00
68	Willie Stargell	25.00	12.50	7.50
69	Tony Horton	13.50	6.75	4.00
70a	Claude Osteen (No number.)	25.00	12.50	7.50
70b	Claude Osteen (#70 on back)	13.50	6.75	4.00
71	Glenn Beckert	13.50	6.75	4.00
72	Nate Colbert	13.50	6.75	4.00
73a	Rick Monday (AB 1705)	13.50	6.75	4.00
73b	Rick Monday (AB 1704)	20.00	10.00	6.00
74a	Tommy John (BB 444)	20.00	10.00	6.00
74b	Tommy John (BB 443)	25.00	12.50	7.50
75	Chris Short	13.50	6.75	4.00

1972 Kellogg's

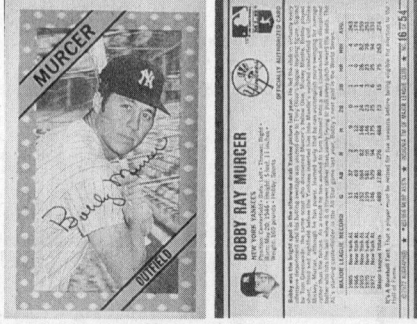

For 1972, Kellogg's reduced both the number of cards in its set and the dimensions of each card, moving to a 2-1/8" x 3-1/4" size and fixing the set at 54 cards. Once again, the cards were produced to simulate a 3-D effect (see description for 1970 Kellogg's). The set was available via a mail-in offer. The check-

list includes variations which resulted from the correction of erroneous statistics on the backs of some cards. The complete set values quoted do not include the scarcer variations.

		NM	EX	VG
Complete Set (54):		125.00	65.00	35.00
Common Player:		1.00	.50	.30
1a	Tom Seaver (1970 ERA 2.85)	10.00	5.00	3.00
1b	Tom Seaver (1970 ERA 2.81)	7.50	3.75	2.25
2	Amos Otis	1.00	.50	.30
3a	Willie Davis (Runs 842)	2.00	1.00	.60
3b	Willie Davis (Runs 841)	1.25	.60	.40
4	Wilbur Wood	1.00	.50	.30
5	Bill Parsons	1.00	.50	.30
6	Pete Rose	15.00	7.50	4.50
7a	Willie McCovey (HR 360)	6.00	3.00	1.75
7b	Willie McCovey (HR 370)	5.00	2.50	1.50
8	Fergie Jenkins	3.50	1.75	1.00
9a	Vida Blue (ERA 2.35)	2.00	1.00	.60
9b	Vida Blue (ERA 2.31)	1.25	.60	.40
10	Joe Torre	2.50	1.25	.70
11	Merv Rettenmund	1.00	.50	.30
12	Bill Melton	1.00	.50	.30
13a	Jim Palmer (Games 170)	6.00	3.00	1.75
13b	Jim Palmer (Games 168)	4.50	2.25	1.25
14	Doug Rader	1.00	.50	.30
15a	Dave Roberts (...Seaver, the NL leader...)	2.00	1.00	.60
15b	Dave Roberts (...Seaver, the league leader...)	1.25	.60	.40
16	Bobby Murcer	1.25	.60	.40
17	Wes Parker	1.00	.50	.30
18a	Joe Coleman (BB 394)	2.00	1.00	.60
18b	Joe Coleman (BB 393)	1.25	.60	.40
19	Manny Sanguillen	1.00	.50	.30
20	Reggie Jackson	10.00	5.00	3.00
21	Ralph Garr	1.00	.50	.30
22	Jim "Catfish" Hunter	3.50	1.75	1.00
23	Rick Wise	1.00	.50	.30
24	Glenn Beckert	1.00	.50	.30
25	Tony Oliva	1.00	.50	.30
26a	Bob Gibson (SO 2577)	6.00	3.00	1.75
26b	Bob Gibson (SO 2578)	4.50	2.25	1.25
27a	Mike Cuellar (1971 ERA 3.80)	2.00	1.00	.60
27b	Mike Cuellar (1971 ERA 3.08)	1.25	.60	.40
28	Chris Speier	1.00	.50	.30
29a	Dave McNally (ERA 3.18)	2.00	1.00	.60
29b	Dave McNally (ERA 3.15)	1.25	.60	.40
30	Chico Cardenas	1.00	.50	.30
31a	Bill Freehan (AVG. .263)	2.00	1.00	.60
31b	Bill Freehan (AVG. .262)	1.25	.60	.40
32a	Bud Harrelson (Hits 634)	2.00	1.00	.60
32b	Bud Harrelson (Hits 624)	1.25	.60	.40
33a	Sam McDowell (...less than 200 innings...)	2.00	1.00	.60
33b	Sam McDowell (...less than 225 innings...)	1.25	.60	.40
34a	Claude Osteen (1971 ERA 3.25)	2.00	1.00	.60
34b	Claude Osteen (1971 ERA 3.51)	1.25	.60	.40
35	Reggie Smith	1.00	.50	.30
36	Sonny Siebert	1.00	.50	.30
37	Lee May	1.00	.50	.30
38	Mickey Lolich	1.00	.50	.30
39a	Cookie Rojas (2B 149)	2.00	1.00	.60
39b	Cookie Rojas (2B 150)	1.25	.60	.40
40	Dick Drago	1.00	.50	.30
41	Nate Colbert	1.00	.50	.30
42	Andy Messersmith	1.00	.50	.30
43a	Dave Johnson (AVG. .262)	2.00	1.00	.60
43b	Dave Johnson (AVG. .264)	1.25	.60	.40
44	Steve Blass	1.00	.50	.30
45	Bob Robertson	1.00	.50	.30
46a	Billy Williams (...missed only one last season...)	6.00	3.00	1.75
46b	Billy Williams (Phrase omitted.)	4.50	2.25	1.25
47	Juan Marichal	4.00	2.00	1.25
48	Lou Brock	4.00	2.00	1.25
49	Roberto Clemente	17.50	8.75	5.25
50	Mel Stottlemyre	1.00	.50	.30
51	Don Wilson	1.00	.50	.30
52a	Sal Bando (RBI 355)	2.00	1.00	.60
52b	Sal Bando (RBI 356)	1.25	.60	.40
53a	Willie Stargell (2B 197)	6.00	3.00	1.75
53b	Willie Stargell (2B 196)	4.50	2.25	1.25
54a	Willie Mays (RBI 1855)	15.00	7.50	4.50
54b	Willie Mays (RBI 1856)	12.00	6.00	3.50

1972 Kellogg's All-Time Baseball Greats

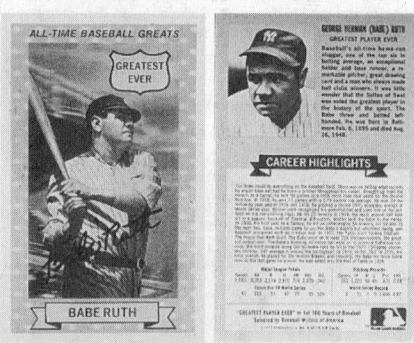

Kellogg's issued a second baseball card set in 1972, inserted into packages of breakfast rolls. The 2-1/4" x 3-1/2" cards also featured a simulated 3-D effect, but the 15 players in the set were "All-Time Baseball Greats," rather than current players. The set is virtually identical to a Rold Gold pretzel issue of 1970; the only difference being the 1972 copyright date on the back of the Kellog's cards, while the pretzel issue bears a 1970 date. The pretzel cards are considerably scarcer than the Kellogg's.

		NM	EX	VG
	Complete Set (15):	45.00	22.50	13.50
	Common Player:	2.50	1.25	.70
1	Walter Johnson	3.50	1.75	1.00
2	Rogers Hornsby	2.50	1.25	.70
3	John McGraw	2.50	1.25	.70
4	Mickey Cochrane	2.50	1.25	.70
5	George Sisler	2.50	1.25	.70
6	Babe Ruth	15.00	7.50	4.50
	(Portrait photo on back.)			
7	Robert "Lefty" Grove	2.50	1.25	.70
8	Harold "Pie" Traynor	2.50	1.25	.70
9	Honus Wagner	5.00	2.50	1.50
10	Eddie Collins	2.50	1.25	.70
11	Tris Speaker	2.50	1.25	.70
12	Cy Young	3.50	1.75	1.00
13	Lou Gehrig	10.00	5.00	3.00
14	Babe Ruth	15.00	7.50	4.50
	(Action photo on back.)			
15	Ty Cobb	10.00	5.00	3.00

1973 Kellogg's

The lone exception to Kellogg's long run of simulated 3-D effect cards came in 1973, when the cereal company's 54-card set was produced by "normal" printing methods. In 2-1/4" x 3-1/2" size, the design was otherwise quite compatible with the issues which preceded and succeeded it. Because it was available via a mail-in offer ($1.25 and two Raisin Bran boxtops), it is not as scarce as the earlier Kellogg's issues.

		NM	EX	VG
	Complete Set (54):	65.00	32.50	20.00
	Common Player:	.90	.45	.25
1	Amos Otis	.90	.45	.25
2	Ellie Rodriguez	.90	.45	.25
3	Mickey Lolich	.90	.45	.25
4	Tony Oliva	1.25	.60	.40
5	Don Sutton	3.50	1.75	1.00
6	Pete Rose	12.00	6.00	3.50
7	Steve Carlton	4.50	2.25	1.25
8	Bobby Bonds	.90	.45	.25
9	Wilbur Wood	.90	.45	.25
10	Billy Williams	4.50	2.25	1.25
11	Steve Blass	.90	.45	.25
12	Jon Matlack	.90	.45	.25
13	Cesar Cedeno	.90	.45	.25
14	Bob Gibson	4.50	2.25	1.25
15	Sparky Lyle	.90	.45	.25
16	Nolan Ryan	17.50	8.75	5.25
17	Jim Palmer	4.50	2.25	1.25
18	Ray Fosse	.90	.45	.25
19	Bobby Murcer	.90	.45	.25
20	Jim "Catfish" Hunter	3.50	1.75	1.00
21	Tug McGraw	.90	.45	.25
22	Reggie Jackson	9.00	4.50	2.75
23	Bill Stoneman	.90	.45	.25
24	Lou Piniella	.90	.45	.25
25	Willie Stargell	4.50	2.25	1.25
26	Dick Allen	2.50	1.25	.70
27	Carlton Fisk	4.50	2.25	1.25
28	Fergie Jenkins	3.50	1.75	1.00
29	Phil Niekro	3.50	1.75	1.00
30	Gary Nolan	.90	.45	.25
31	Joe Torre	2.50	1.25	.70
32	Bobby Tolan	.90	.45	.25
33	Nate Colbert	.90	.45	.25
34	Joe Morgan	4.50	2.25	1.25
35	Bert Blyleven	.90	.45	.25
36	Joe Rudi	.90	.45	.25
37	Ralph Garr	.90	.45	.25
38	Gaylord Perry	3.50	1.75	1.00
39	Bobby Grich	.90	.45	.25
40	Lou Brock	4.00	2.00	1.25
41	Pete Broberg	.90	.45	.25
42	Manny Sanguillen	.90	.45	.25
43	Willie Davis	.90	.45	.25
44	Dave Kingman	.90	.45	.25
45	Carlos May	.90	.45	.25
46	Tom Seaver	6.00	3.00	1.75
47	Mike Cuellar	.90	.45	.25
48	Joe Coleman	.90	.45	.25
49	Claude Osteen	.90	.45	.25
50	Steve Kline	.90	.45	.25
51	Rod Carew	4.50	2.25	1.25
52	Al Kaline	6.00	3.00	1.75
53	Larry Dierker	.90	.45	.25
54	Ron Santo	2.50	1.25	.70

1974 Kellogg's

For 1974, Kellogg's returned to the use of simulated 3-D for its 54-player baseball card issue (see 1970 Kellogg's listing for description). In 2-1/8" x 3-1/4" size, the cards were available as a complete set via a mail-in offer. The complete set price listed here does not include the more expensive variations.

		NM	EX	VG
	Complete Set (54):	65.00	32.50	20.00
	Common Player:	.90	.45	.25
1	Bob Gibson	3.50	1.75	1.00
2	Rick Monday	.90	.45	.25
3	Joe Coleman	.90	.45	.25
4	Bert Campaneris	.90	.45	.25
5	Carlton Fisk	4.00	2.00	1.25
6	Jim Palmer	3.50	1.75	1.00
7a	Ron Santo (Chicago Cubs)	2.25	1.25	.70
7b	Ron Santo (Chicago White Sox)	1.25	.60	.40
8	Nolan Ryan	16.00	8.00	4.75
9	Greg Luzinski	.90	.45	.25
10a	Buddy Bell (Runs 134)	2.25	1.25	.70
10b	Buddy Bell (Runs 135)	1.00	.50	.30
11	Bob Watson	.90	.45	.25
12	Bill Singer	.90	.45	.25
13	Dave May	.90	.45	.25
14	Jim Brewer	.90	.45	.25
15	Manny Sanguillen	.90	.45	.25
16	Jeff Burroughs	.90	.45	.25
17	Amos Otis	.90	.45	.25
18	Ed Goodson	.90	.45	.25
19	Nate Colbert	.90	.45	.25
20	Reggie Jackson	6.50	3.25	2.00
21	Ted Simmons	.90	.45	.25
22	Bobby Murcer	1.00	.50	.30
23	Willie Horton	1.00	.50	.30
24	Orlando Cepeda	3.50	1.75	1.00
25	Ron Hunt	.90	.45	.25
26	Wayne Twitchell	.90	.45	.25
27	Ron Fairly	.90	.45	.25
28	Johnny Bench	4.50	2.25	1.25
29	John Mayberry	.90	.45	.25
30	Rod Carew	4.00	2.00	1.25
31	Ken Holtzman	.90	.45	.25
32	Billy Williams	3.50	1.75	1.00
33	Dick Allen	1.50	.70	.45
34a	Wilbur Wood (SO 959)	1.50	.70	.45
34b	Wilbur Wood (SO 960)	1.00	.50	.30
35	Danny Thompson	.90	.45	.25
36	Joe Morgan	3.50	1.75	1.00
37	Willie Stargell	3.50	1.75	1.00
38	Pete Rose	10.00	5.00	3.00
39	Bobby Bonds	.90	.45	.25
40	Chris Speier	.90	.45	.25
41	Sparky Lyle	.90	.45	.25
42	Cookie Rojas	.90	.45	.25
43	Tommy Davis	.90	.45	.25
44	Jim "Catfish" Hunter	3.50	1.75	1.00
45	Willie Davis	.90	.45	.25
46	Bert Blyleven	.90	.45	.25
47	Pat Kelly	.90	.45	.25
48	Ken Singleton	.90	.45	.25
49	Manny Mota	.90	.45	.25
50	Dave Johnson	.90	.45	.25
51	Sal Bando	.90	.45	.25
52	Tom Seaver	4.50	2.25	1.25
53	Felix Millan	.90	.45	.25
54	Ron Blomberg	.90	.45	.25

1975 Kellogg's

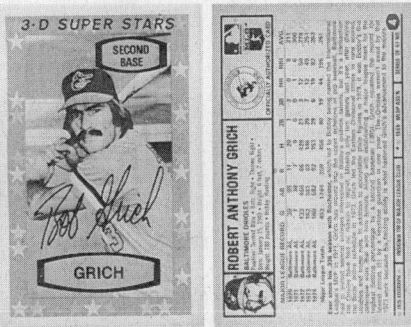

While the card size remained the same at 2-1/8" x 3-1/4", the size of the 1975 Kellogg's "3-D" set was increased by three, to 57 cards. Despite the fact cards could be obtained by

a mail-in offer, as well as in cereal boxes, the '75 Kellogg's are noticeably scarcer than the company's other issues, with the exception of the 1971 set. Also helping to raise the value of the cards is the presence of an unusually large number of current and future Hall of Famers.

		NM	EX	VG
	Complete Set (57):	175.00	90.00	55.00
	Common Player:	2.00	1.00	.60
1	Roy White	2.00	1.00	.60
2	Ross Grimsley	2.00	1.00	.60
3	Reggie Smith	2.00	1.00	.60
4a	Bob Grich ("...1973 work..." in last line)	3.00	1.50	.90
4b	Bob Grich (no "...1973 work...")	2.00	1.00	.60
5	Greg Gross	2.00	1.00	.60
6	Bob Watson	2.00	1.00	.60
7	Johnny Bench	10.00	5.00	3.00
8	Jeff Burroughs	2.00	1.00	.60
9	Elliott Maddox	2.00	1.00	.60
10	Jon Matlack	2.00	1.00	.60
11	Pete Rose	25.00	12.50	7.50
12	Leroy Stanton	2.00	1.00	.60
13	Bake McBride	2.00	1.00	.60
14	Jorge Orta	2.00	1.00	.60
15	Al Oliver	2.50	1.25	.70
16	John Briggs	2.00	1.00	.60
17	Steve Garvey	4.50	2.25	1.25
18	Brooks Robinson	10.00	5.00	3.00
19	John Hiller	2.00	1.00	.60
20	Lynn McGlothen	2.00	1.00	.60
21	Cleon Jones	2.00	1.00	.60
22	Fergie Jenkins	6.00	3.00	1.75
23	Bill North	2.00	1.00	.60
24	Steve Busby	2.00	1.00	.60
25	Richie Zisk	2.00	1.00	.60
26	Nolan Ryan	35.00	17.50	10.50
27	Joe Morgan	7.50	3.75	2.25
28	Joe Rudi	2.00	1.00	.60
29	Jose Cardenal	2.00	1.00	.60
30	Andy Messersmith	2.00	1.00	.60
31	Willie Montanez	2.00	1.00	.60
32	Bill Buckner	2.00	1.00	.60
33	Rod Carew	7.50	3.75	2.25
34	Lou Piniella	2.50	1.25	.70
35	Ralph Garr	2.00	1.00	.60
36	Mike Marshall	2.00	1.00	.60
37	Garry Maddox	2.00	1.00	.60
38	Dwight Evans	2.00	1.00	.60
39	Lou Brock	7.50	3.75	2.25
40	Ken Singleton	2.00	1.00	.60
41	Steve Braun	2.00	1.00	.60
42	Dick Allen	3.50	1.75	1.00
43	Johnny Grubb	2.00	1.00	.60
44a	Jim Hunter (Oakland)	9.00	4.50	2.75
44b	Jim Hunter (New York)	7.50	3.75	2.25
45	Gaylord Perry	6.00	3.00	1.75
46	George Hendrick	2.00	1.00	.60
47	Sparky Lyle	2.00	1.00	.60
48	Dave Cash	2.00	1.00	.60
49	Luis Tiant	2.00	1.00	.60
50	Cesar Geronimo	2.00	1.00	.60
51	Carl Yastrzemski	12.00	6.00	3.50
52	Ken Brett	2.00	1.00	.60
53	Hal McRae	2.00	1.00	.60
54	Reggie Jackson	15.00	7.50	4.50
55	Rollie Fingers	6.00	3.00	1.75
56	Mike Schmidt	15.00	7.50	4.50
57	Richie Hebner	2.00	1.00	.60

1976 Kellogg's

A sizeable list of corrected errors and other variation cards dots the checklist for the 57-card 1976 Kellogg's 3-D set. Again containing 57 cards, the first three cards in the set are found far less often than cards #4-57, indicating they were short-printed in relation to the rest of the set. The complete set values quoted below do not include the scarcer variation cards. Card size remained at 2-1/8" x 3-1/4". Cards #1-3 were significantly short-printed.

		NM	EX	VG
	Complete Set (57):	70.00	35.00	20.00
	Common Player:	1.25	.60	.40
1	Steve Hargan	10.00	5.00	3.00
2	Claudell Washington	10.00	5.00	3.00
3	Don Gullett	10.00	5.00	3.00
4	Randy Jones	1.25	.60	.40
5	Jim "Catfish" Hunter	3.50	1.75	1.00
6a	Clay Carroll (Cincinnati)	2.25	1.25	.70
6b	Clay Carroll (Chicago)	1.25	.60	.40
7	Joe Rudi	1.25	.60	.40
8	Reggie Jackson	9.00	4.50	2.75
9	Felix Millan	1.25	.60	.40
10	Jim Rice	2.00	1.00	.60
11	Bert Blyleven	1.25	.60	.40

		NM	EX	VG
12	Ken Singleton	1.25	.60	.40
13	Don Sutton	3.50	1.75	1.00
14	Joe Morgan	4.00	2.00	1.25
15	Dave Parker	1.50	.70	.45
16	Dave Cash	1.25	.60	.40
17	Ron LeFlore	1.25	.60	.40
18	Greg Luzinski	1.25	.60	.40
19	Dennis Eckersley	6.00	3.00	1.75
20	Bill Madlock	1.25	.60	.40
21	George Scott	1.25	.60	.40
22	Willie Stargell	4.00	2.00	1.25
23	Al Hrabosky	1.25	.60	.40
24	Carl Yastrzemski	7.50	3.75	2.25
25a	Jim Kaat (White Sox logo on back.)	3.00	1.50	.90
25b	Jim Kaat (Phillies logo on back.)	1.50	.70	.45
26	Marty Perez	1.25	.60	.40
27	Bob Watson	1.25	.60	.40
28	Eric Soderholm	1.25	.60	.40
29	Bill Lee	1.25	.60	.40
30a	Frank Tanana (1975 ERA 2.63)	2.00	1.00	.60
30b	Frank Tanana (1975 ERA 2.62)	1.25	.60	.40
31	Fred Lynn	1.50	.70	.45
32a	Tom Seaver (1967 PCT. 552)	7.50	3.75	2.25
32b	Tom Seaver (1967 Pct. .552)	6.00	3.00	1.75
33	Steve Busby	1.25	.60	.40
34	Gary Carter	4.00	2.00	1.25
35	Rick Wise	1.25	.60	.40
36	Johnny Bench	5.00	2.50	1.50
37	Jim Palmer	4.00	2.00	1.25
38	Bobby Murcer	1.50	.70	.40
39	Von Joshua	1.25	.60	.40
40	Lou Brock	4.00	2.00	1.25
41a	Mickey Rivers (last line begins "In three...")	2.00	1.00	.60
41b	Mickey Rivers (last line begins "The Yankees...")	1.25	.60	.40
42	Manny Sanguillen	1.25	.60	.40
43	Jerry Reuss	1.25	.60	.40
44	Ken Griffey	1.25	.60	.40
45a	Jorge Orta (AB 1616)	1.75	.90	.50
45b	Jorge Orta (AB 1615)	1.25	.60	.40
46	John Mayberry	1.25	.60	.40
47a	Vida Blue (2nd line reads "...pitched more innings ...")	2.25	1.25	.70
47b	Vida Blue (2nd line reads "...struck out more...")	1.25	.60	.40
48	Rod Carew	4.00	2.00	1.25
49a	Jon Matlack (1975 ER 87)	1.75	.90	.50
49b	Jon Matlack (1975 ER 86)	1.25	.60	.40
50	Boog Powell	2.25	1.25	.70
51a	Mike Hargrove (AB 935)	1.75	.90	.50
51b	Mike Hargrove (AB 934)	1.25	.60	.40
52a	Paul Lindblad (1975 ERA 2.72)	1.75	.90	.50
52b	Paul Lindblad (1975 ERA 2.73)	1.25	.60	.40
53	Thurman Munson	4.00	2.00	1.25
54	Steve Garvey	2.50	1.25	.70
55	Pete Rose	12.50	6.25	3.75
56a	Greg Gross (Games 302)	1.75	.90	.50
56b	Greg Gross (Games 334)	1.25	.60	.40
57	Ted Simmons	1.25	.60	.40

1977 Kellogg's

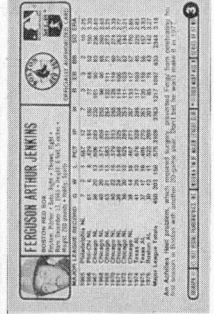

Other than another innovative card design to complement the simulated 3-D effect, there was little change in the 1977 Kellogg's issue. Set size remained at 57 cards, the set remained in the 2-1/8" x 3-1/4" format, and the cards were available either individually in boxes of cereal, or as a complete set via a mail-in box top offer. The 1977 set is the last in which Kellogg's used a player portrait photo on the back of the card.

		NM	EX	VG
Complete Set (57):		60.00	30.00	18.00
Common Player:		.75	.40	.25
1	George Foster	.75	.40	.25
2	Bert Campaneris	.75	.40	.25
3	Fergie Jenkins	2.50	1.25	.70
4	Dock Ellis	.75	.40	.25
5	John Montefusco	.75	.40	.25
6	George Brett	12.50	6.25	3.75
7	John Candelaria	.75	.40	.25
8	Fred Norman	.75	.40	.25
9	Bill Travers	.75	.40	.25
10	Hal McRae	.75	.40	.25
11	Doug Rau	.75	.40	.25
12	Greg Luzinski	.75	.40	.25
13	Ralph Garr	.75	.40	.25
14	Steve Garvey	1.50	.70	.45
15	Rick Manning	.75	.40	.25

		NM	EX	VG
16a	Lyman Bostock (Back photo is N.Y. Yankee Dock Ellis.)	7.50	3.75	2.25
16b	Lyman Bostock (Correct back photo.)	.75	.40	.25
17	Randy Jones	.75	.40	.25
18a	Ron Cey (58 homers in first sentence)	1.00	.50	.30
18b	Ron Cey (48 homers in first sentence)	.75	.40	.25
19	Dave Parker	.75	.40	.25
20	Pete Rose	15.00	7.50	4.50
21a	Wayne Garland (Last line begins "Prior to...")	1.00	.50	.30
21b	Wayne Garland (Last line begins "There he...")	.75	.40	.25
22	Bill North	.75	.40	.25
23	Thurman Munson	4.50	2.25	1.25
24	Tom Poquette	.75	.40	.25
25	Ron LeFlore	.75	.40	.25
26	Mark Fidrych	1.00	.50	.30
27	Sixto Lezcano	.75	.40	.25
28	Dave Winfield	7.50	3.75	2.25
29	Jerry Koosman	.75	.40	.25
30	Mike Hargrove	.75	.40	.25
31	Willie Montanez	.75	.40	.25
32	Don Stanhouse	.75	.40	.25
33	Jay Johnstone	.75	.40	.25
34	Bake McBride	.75	.40	.25
35	Dave Kingman	.75	.40	.25
36	Freddie Patek	.75	.40	.25
37	Garry Maddox	.75	.40	.25
38a	Ken Reitz (Last line begins "The previous...")	1.00	.50	.30
38b	Ken Reitz (Last line begins "In late...")	.75	.40	.25
39	Bobby Grich	.75	.40	.25
40	Cesar Geronimo	.75	.40	.25
41	Jim Lonborg	.75	.40	.25
42	Ed Figueroa	.75	.40	.25
43	Bill Madlock	.75	.40	.25
44	Jerry Remy	.75	.40	.25
45	Frank Tanana	.75	.40	.25
46	Al Oliver	1.00	.50	.30
47	Charlie Hough	.75	.40	.25
48	Lou Piniella	1.00	.50	.30
49	Ken Griffey	.75	.40	.25
50	Jose Cruz	.75	.40	.25
51	Rollie Fingers	2.50	1.25	.70
52	Chris Chambliss	.75	.40	.25
53	Rod Carew	4.50	2.25	1.25
54	Andy Messersmith	.75	.40	.25
55	Mickey Rivers	.75	.40	.25
56	Butch Wynegar	.75	.40	.25
57	Steve Carlton	3.50	1.75	1.00

1978 Kellogg's

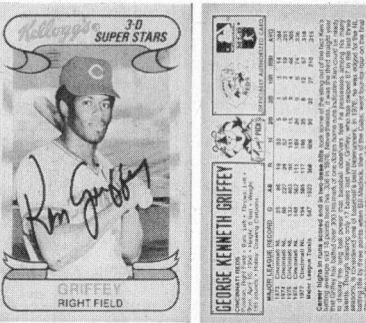

Besides the substitution of a Tony the Tiger drawing for a player portrait photo on the back of the card, the 1978 Kellogg's set offered no major changes from the previous few years issues. Cards were once again in the 2-1/8" x 3-1/4" format, with 57 cards comprising a complete set. Single cards were available in selected brands of the company's cereal, while complete sets could be obtained by a mail-in offer.

		NM	EX	VG
Complete Set (57):		60.00	30.00	18.00
Common Player:		.90	.45	.25
1	Steve Carlton	4.50	2.25	1.25
2	Bucky Dent	1.25	.60	.40
3	Mike Schmidt	13.50	6.75	4.00
4	Ken Griffey	.90	.45	.25
5	Al Cowens	.90	.45	.25
6	George Brett	13.50	6.75	4.00
7	Lou Brock	4.50	2.25	1.25
8	Rich Gossage	1.25	.60	.40
9	Tom Johnson	.90	.45	.25
10	George Foster	.90	.45	.25
11	Dave Winfield	4.50	2.25	1.25
12	Dan Meyer	.90	.45	.25
13	Chris Chambliss	.90	.45	.25
14	Paul Dade	.90	.45	.25
15	Jeff Burroughs	.90	.45	.25
16	Jose Cruz	.90	.45	.25
17	Mickey Rivers	.90	.45	.25
18	John Candelaria	.90	.45	.25
19	Ellis Valentine	.90	.45	.25
20	Hal McRae	.90	.45	.25
21	Dave Rozema	.90	.45	.25
22	Lenny Randle	.90	.45	.25
23	Willie McCovey	4.50	2.25	1.25
24	Ron Cey	.90	.45	.25
25	Eddie Murray	17.50	8.75	5.25
26	Larry Bowa	.90	.45	.25
27	Tom Seaver	5.00	2.50	1.50
28	Garry Maddox	.90	.45	.25

		NM	EX	VG
29	Rod Carew	4.50	2.25	1.25
30	Thurman Munson	4.50	2.25	1.25
31	Garry Templeton	.90	.45	.25
32	Eric Soderholm	.90	.45	.25
33	Greg Luzinski	.90	.45	.25
34	Reggie Smith	.90	.45	.25
35	Dave Goltz	.90	.45	.25
36	Tommy John	1.25	.60	.40
37	Ralph Garr	.90	.45	.25
38	Alan Bannister	.90	.45	.25
39	Bob Bailor	.90	.45	.25
40	Reggie Jackson	12.00	6.00	3.50
41	Cecil Cooper	.90	.45	.25
42	Burt Hooton	.90	.45	.25
43	Sparky Lyle	.90	.45	.25
44	Steve Ontiveros	.90	.45	.25
45	Rick Reuschel	.90	.45	.25
46	Lyman Bostock	.90	.45	.25
47	Mitchell Page	.90	.45	.25
48	Bruce Sutter	3.50	1.75	1.00
49	Jim Rice	2.50	1.25	.70
50	Bob Forsch	.90	.45	.25
51	Nolan Ryan	17.50	8.75	5.25
52	Dave Parker	.90	.45	.25
53	Bert Blyleven	.90	.45	.25
54	Frank Tanana	.90	.45	.25
55	Ken Singleton	.90	.45	.25
56	Mike Hargrove	.90	.45	.25
57	Don Sutton	3.50	1.75	1.00

1979 Kellogg's

For its 1979 3-D issue, Kellogg's increased the size of the set to 60 cards, but reduced the width of the cards to 1-15/16". Depth stayed the same as in previous years, 3-1/4". The narrower card format seems to have compounded the problem of curling and subsequent cracking of the ribbed plastic surface which helps give the card a 3-D effect. Cards with major cracks can be graded no higher than VG. The complete set price in the checklist that follows does not include the scarcer variations. Numerous minor variations featuring copyright and trademark logos can be found in the set.

		NM	EX	VG
Complete Set (60):		30.00	15.00	9.00
Common Player:		.60	.30	.20
1	Bruce Sutter	2.50	1.25	.70
2	Ted Simmons	.60	.30	.20
3	Ross Grimsley	.60	.30	.20
4	Wayne Nordhagen	.60	.30	.20
5a	Jim Palmer (PCT. .649)	3.00	1.50	.90
5b	Jim Palmer (PCT. .650)	3.00	1.50	.90
6	John Henry Johnson	.60	.30	.20
7	Jason Thompson	.60	.30	.20
8	Pat Zachry	.60	.30	.20
9	Dennis Eckersley	3.00	1.50	.90
10a	Paul Splittorff (IP 1665)	.60	.30	.20
10b	Paul Splittorff (IP 1666)	.60	.30	.20
11a	Ron Guidry (Hits 397)	.60	.30	.20
11b	Ron Guidry (Hits 396)	.60	.30	.20
12	Jeff Burroughs	.60	.30	.20
13	Rod Carew	3.00	1.50	.90
14a	Buddy Bell (No trade line in bio.)	1.00	.50	.30
14b	Buddy Bell (Trade line in bio.)	.60	.30	.20
15	Jim Rice	1.00	.50	.30
16	Garry Maddox	.60	.30	.20
17	Willie McCovey	3.00	1.50	.90
18	Steve Carlton	3.00	1.50	.90
19a	J. R. Richard (Stats begin with 1972.)	.60	.30	.20
19b	J. R. Richard (Stats begin with 1971.)	.60	.30	.20
20	Paul Molitor	3.00	1.50	.90
21a	Dave Parker (AVG. .281)	.60	.30	.20
21b	Dave Parker (AVG. .318)	.60	.30	.20
22a	Pete Rose (1978 3B 3)	7.50	3.75	2.25
22b	Pete Rose (1978 3B 33)	7.50	3.75	2.25
23a	Vida Blue (Runs 819)	.60	.30	.20
23b	Vida Blue (Runs 818)	.60	.30	.20
24	Richie Zisk	.60	.30	.20
25a	Darrell Porter (2B 101)	.60	.30	.20
25b	Darrell Porter (2B 111)	.60	.30	.20
26a	Dan Driessen (Games 642)	.60	.30	.20
26b	Dan Driessen (Games 742)	.60	.30	.20
27a	Geoff Zahn (1978 Minnesota)	.60	.30	.20
27b	Geoff Zahn (1978 Minnesota)	.60	.30	.20
28	Phil Niekro	2.50	1.25	.70
29	Tom Seaver	3.00	1.50	.90
30	Fred Lynn	.60	.30	.20
31	Bill Bonham	.60	.30	.20
32	George Foster	.60	.30	.20

		NM	EX	VG
33a	Terry Puhl (Last line of bio begins "Terry...")	.60	.30	.20
33b	Terry Puhl (Last line of bio begins "His...")	.60	.30	.20
34a	John Candelaria (Age is 24.)	.60	.30	.20
34b	John Candelaria (Age is 25.)	.60	.30	.20
35	Bob Knepper	.60	.30	.20
36	Freddie Patek	.60	.30	.20
37	Chris Chambliss	.60	.30	.20
38a	Bob Forsch (1977 Games 86)	.60	.30	.20
38b	Bob Forsch (1977 Games 35)	.60	.30	.20
39a	Ken Griffey (1978 AB 674)	.60	.30	.20
39b	Ken Griffey (1978 AB 614)	.60	.30	.20
40	Jack Clark	.60	.30	.20
41a	Dwight Evans (1978 Hits 13)	.60	.30	.20
41b	Dwight Evans (1978 Hits 123)	.60	.30	.20
42	Lee Mazzilli	.60	.30	.20
43	Mario Guerrero	.60	.30	.20
44	Larry Bowa	.60	.30	.20
45a	Carl Yastrzemski (Games 9930)	4.00	2.00	1.25
45b	Carl Yastrzemski (Games 9929)	4.00	2.00	1.25
46a	Reggie Jackson (1978 Games 162)	6.00	3.00	1.75
46b	Reggie Jackson (1978 Games 139)	6.00	3.00	1.75
47	Rick Reuschel	.60	.30	.20
48a	Mike Flanagan (1976 SO 57)	.60	.30	.20
48b	Mike Flanagan (1976 SO 56)	.60	.30	.20
49a	Gaylord Perry (1973 Hits 325)	2.50	1.25	.70
49b	Gaylord Perry (1973 Hits 315)	2.50	1.25	.70
50	George Brett	6.00	3.00	1.75
51a	Craig Reynolds (Last line of bio begins "He spent...")	.60	.30	.20
51b	Craig Reynolds (Last line of bio begins "In those...")	.60	.30	.20
52	Davey Lopes	.60	.30	.20
53a	Bill Almon (2B 31)	.60	.30	.20
53b	Bill Almon (2B 41)	.60	.30	.20
54	Roy Howell	.60	.30	.20
55	Frank Tanana	.60	.30	.20
56a	Doug Rau (1978 PCT. .577)	.60	.30	.20
56b	Doug Rau (1978 PCT. .625)	.60	.30	.20
57a	Rick Monday (1976 Runs 197)	.60	.30	.20
57b	Rick Monday (1976 Runs 107)	.60	.30	.20
58	Jon Matlack	.60	.30	.20
59a	Ron Jackson (Last line of bio begins "His best...")	.60	.30	.20
59b	Ron Jackson (Last line of bio begins "The Twins...")	.60	.30	.20
60	Jim Sundberg	.60	.30	.20

1980 Kellogg's

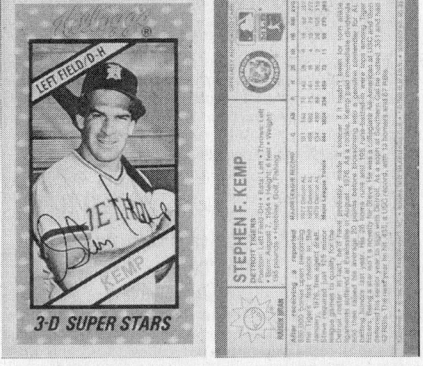

The 1980 cereal company issue featured the narrowest format of any Kellogg's card, 1-7/8" x 3-1/4". For the second straight year, set size remained at 60 cards, available either singly in boxes of cereal, or as complete sets by a mail-in offer.

		NM	EX	VG
	Complete Set (60):	25.00	12.50	7.50
	Common Player:	.60	.30	.20
1	Ross Grimsley	.60	.30	.20
2	Mike Schmidt	4.00	2.00	1.25
3	Mike Flanagan	.60	.30	.20
4	Ron Guidry	.60	.30	.20
5	Bert Blyleven	.60	.30	.20
6	Dave Kingman	.60	.30	.20
7	Jeff Newman	.60	.30	.20
8	Steve Rogers	.60	.30	.20
9	George Brett	4.00	2.00	1.25
10	Bruce Sutter	2.00	1.00	.60
11	Gorman Thomas	.60	.30	.20
12	Darrell Porter	.60	.30	.20
13	Roy Smalley	.60	.30	.20
14	Steve Carlton	2.00	1.00	.60
15	Jim Palmer	2.00	1.00	.60
16	Bob Bailor	.60	.30	.20
17	Jason Thompson	.60	.30	.20
18	Graig Nettles	.60	.30	.20
19	Ron Cey	.60	.30	.20
20	Nolan Ryan	7.50	3.75	2.25
21	Ellis Valentine	.60	.30	.20
22	Larry Hisle	.60	.30	.20
23	Dave Parker	.60	.30	.20
24	Eddie Murray	2.00	1.00	.60
25	Willie Stargell	2.00	1.00	.60
26	Reggie Jackson	4.00	2.00	1.25
27	Carl Yastrzemski	2.50	1.25	.70
28	Andre Thornton	.60	.30	.20
29	Davey Lopes	.60	.30	.20
30	Ken Singleton	.60	.30	.20
31	Steve Garvey	1.00	.50	.30

		NM	EX	VG
32	Dave Winfield	2.00	1.00	.60
33	Steve Kemp	.60	.30	.20
34	Claudell Washington	.60	.30	.20
35	Pete Rose	6.00	3.00	1.75
36	Cesar Cedeno	.60	.30	.20
37	John Stearns	.60	.30	.20
38	Lee Mazzilli	.60	.30	.20
39	Larry Bowa	.60	.30	.20
40	Fred Lynn	.60	.30	.20
41	Carlton Fisk	2.00	1.00	.60
42	Vida Blue	.60	.30	.20
43	Keith Hernandez	.60	.30	.20
44	Jim Rice	1.00	.50	.30
45	Ted Simmons	.60	.30	.20
46	Chet Lemon	.60	.30	.20
47	Fergie Jenkins	2.00	1.00	.60
48	Gary Matthews	.60	.30	.20
49	Tom Seaver	2.50	1.25	.70
50	George Foster	.60	.30	.20
51	Phil Niekro	2.00	1.00	.60
52	Johnny Bench	2.50	1.25	.70
53	Buddy Bell	.60	.30	.20
54	Lance Parrish	.60	.30	.20
55	Joaquin Andujar	.60	.30	.20
56	Don Baylor	.60	.30	.20
57	Jack Clark	.60	.30	.20
58	J.R. Richard	.60	.30	.20
59	Bruce Bochte	.60	.30	.20
60	Rod Carew	1.00	.50	.60

1969 Kelly's Potato Chips Pins

Consisting of 20 pins, each measuring approximately 1-3/16" in diameter, this set was issued by Kelly's Potato Chips in 1969 and has a heavy emphasis on St. Louis Cardinals. The pin has a black-and-white player photo in the center surrounded by either a red border (for A.L. players) or a blue border (for N.L. players) that displays the player's team and name at the top and bottom. "Kelly's" appears to the left while the word "Zip!" is printed to the right. The pins are unnumbered.

		NM	EX	VG
	Complete Set (20):	350.00	175.00	100.00
	Common Player:	5.00	2.50	1.50
(1)	Luis Aparicio	25.00	12.50	7.50
(2)	Ernie Banks	45.00	22.00	13.50
(3)	Glenn Beckert	5.00	2.50	1.50
(4)	Lou Brock	25.00	12.50	7.50
(5)	Curt Flood	5.00	2.50	1.50
(6)	Bob Gibson	25.00	12.50	7.50
(7)	Joel Horlen	5.00	2.50	1.50
(8)	Al Kaline	45.00	22.00	13.50
(9)	Don Kessinger	5.00	2.50	1.50
(10)	Mickey Lolich	5.00	2.50	1.50
(11)	Juan Marichal	25.00	12.50	7.50
(12)	Willie Mays	75.00	37.00	22.00
(13)	Tim McCarver	7.50	3.75	2.25
(14)	Denny McLain	6.00	3.00	1.75
(15)	Pete Rose	65.00	32.00	19.50
(16)	Ron Santo	7.50	3.75	2.25
(17)	Joe Torre	15.00	7.50	4.50
(18)	Pete Ward	5.00	2.50	1.50
(19)	Billy Williams	25.00	12.50	7.50
(20)	Carl Yastrzemski	60.00	30.00	18.00

1887 W.S. Kimball Champions (N184)

Similar to sets issued by Allen & Ginter and Goodwin, the Kimball tobacco company of Rochester, N.Y., issued its own 50-card set of "Champions of Games and Sport" in 1887, and included four baseball players among the "billiardists, girl riders, tight-rope walkers" and other popular celebrities featured in the series. Measuring 1-1/2" x 2-3/4", the color lithographed artwork on the card features a posed portrait, which occupies the top three-fourths, and a drawing of the player in action at the bottom. The back of the card contains an ad for Kimball Cigarettes along with a list of the various sports and activities depicted in the set. The Kimball promotion also included an album to house the card set.

		NM	EX	VG
	Complete Set (4):	5,500	2,200	1,650
	Common Player:	1,100	440.00	330.00
	Album:	4,125	1,650	1,000
(1)	E.A. Burch	1,650	550.00	425.00
(2)	Dell Darling	1,375	550.00	425.00
(3)	Hardie Henderson	1,375	550.00	425.00
(4)	James O'Neil (O'Neill)	1,375	550.00	450.00

1957-1959 Kiwanis Orioles Clinic

 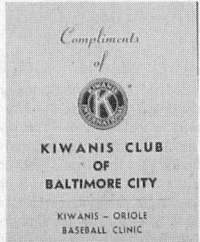

Details are lacking on this card which may or may not have been part of a series. Unless or until further players are checklisted, it is impossible to date the issue any more precisely. The front of the 2-7/8" x 3-1/4" card has a sepia photo that appears to have been copied from a team-issued postcard or picture. On back is the Kiwanis International logo with "Compliments / of" above and "KIWANIS CLUB / OF / BALTIMORE CITY / KIWANIS - ORIOLE / BASEBALL CLINIC" below.

	NM	EX	VG
Bob Nieman	40.00	20.00	12.00

1955-1957 Ted Kluszewski Steak House

 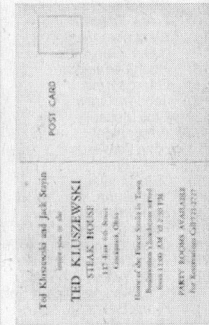

The true scope of this issue combined with the related Charcoal Steak House card (see also) is not known. Based on cards showing Klu in Reds and Angels uniforms, it is possible examples may yet be seen in Pirates and White Sox uniforms. Measuring about 3-1/2" x 5-1/2", the black-and-white cards have a facsimile signature of Kluszewski on front. The back is postcard style and advertises the Cincinnati restaurant he operated with Jack Stayin.

	NM	EX	VG
Ted Kluszewski (Reds, fielding, white cap.)	75.00	37.50	22.50
Ted Kluszewski (Reds, portrait, dark cap.)	100.00	50.00	30.00

1930s Knickerbocker Beer Yankees Premium

Jacob Ruppert, who owned both the Yankees and the Knickerbocker Brewing Co., is pictured on this 10" x 8" black-and-white, blank-backed premium photo with a trio of his Italian stars. Facsimile autographs of all are printed on front.

	NM	EX	VG
Tony Lazzeri, Jacob Ruppert, Joe DiMaggio, Frank Crosetti	150.00	75.00	45.00

1921 Koester Bread N.Y. Giants/Yankees

CHAS. STENGEL
Outf.—New York Nationals

The 1921 World Series was the first of many for the N.Y. Yankees, and it was the first "subway series," as their opponents were the Giants. This special card issue, a blank-backed version of the American Caramel Series of 120 (E121), featured the players, managers and coaches of each team. The 2" x about 3-1/4" cards feature black-and-white photos on front. They were distributed in October 1921, by E.H. Koester, a New York bakery. The unnumbered cards are checklisted here alphabetically within team. Several of the players in this issue do not appear in the contemporary American Caramel sets. A rarely seen album was issued to house the cards.

		NM	EX	VG
	Complete Set (52):	45,000	22,500	13,500
	Common Player:	500.00	250.00	150.00
	Album:	800.00	400.00	240.00
	N.Y. Giants Team Set:	19,000	9,500	5,700
(1)	Dave Bancroft	1,500	750.00	450.00
(2)	Jesse Barnes	500.00	250.00	150.00
(3)	Howard Berry	500.00	250.00	150.00
(4)	"Ed." Brown	500.00	250.00	150.00
(5)	Jesse Burkett	1,875	940.00	565.00
(6)	Geo. J. Burns	500.00	250.00	150.00
(7)	Cecil Causey	500.00	250.00	150.00
(8)	"Bill" Cunningham	500.00	250.00	150.00
(9)	"Phil" Douglas	500.00	250.00	150.00
(10)	Frank Frisch	1,500	750.00	450.00
(11)	Alexander Gaston	500.00	250.00	150.00
(12)	"Mike" Gonzalez	600.00	300.00	180.00
(13)	Hugh Jennings	1,500	750.00	450.00
(14)	George Kelly	1,500	750.00	450.00
(15)	John McGraw	1,500	750.00	450.00
(16)	Emil Meusel	500.00	250.00	150.00
(17)	Arthur Nehf	500.00	250.00	150.00
(18)	John Rawlings	500.00	250.00	150.00
(19)	"Bill" Ryan	500.00	250.00	150.00
(20)	"Slim" Sallee	500.00	250.00	150.00
(21)	"Pat" Shea	500.00	250.00	150.00
(22)	Earl Smith	500.00	250.00	150.00
(23)	Frank Snyder	500.00	250.00	150.00
(24)	Chas. Stengel	1,875	940.00	565.00
(25)	Fred Toney	500.00	250.00	150.00
(26)	Ross Young (Youngs)	1,875	940.00	565.00
	N.Y. Yankees Team Set:	26,000	13,000	7,800
(1)	Frank Baker	1,500	750.00	450.00
(2)	"Rip" Collins	500.00	250.00	150.00
(3)	Lou De Vormer	500.00	250.00	150.00
(4)	Alex Ferguson	500.00	250.00	150.00
(5)	William Fewster	500.00	250.00	150.00
(6)	Harry Harper	500.00	250.00	150.00
(7)	"Chicken" Hawks	500.00	250.00	150.00
(8)	Fred Hoffmann (Hofmann)	500.00	250.00	150.00
(9)	Waite Hoyt	1,500	750.00	450.00
(10)	Miller Huggins	1,500	750.00	450.00
(11)	Carl Mays	500.00	250.00	150.00
(12)	M.J. McNally	500.00	250.00	150.00
(13)	R. Meusel	500.00	250.00	150.00
(14)	Elmer Miller	500.00	250.00	150.00
(15)	John Mitchell	500.00	250.00	150.00
(16)	Chas. O'Leary	500.00	250.00	150.00
(17)	Roger Peckinpaugh	500.00	250.00	150.00
(18)	William Piercy	500.00	250.00	150.00
(19)	Walter Pipp	500.00	250.00	150.00
(20)	Jack Quinn	500.00	250.00	150.00
(21)	Tom Rogers	500.00	250.00	150.00
(22)	Robert Roth	500.00	250.00	150.00
(23)	George Ruth	15,000	7,500	4,500
(24)	Walter Schang	500.00	250.00	150.00
(25)	Robert Shawkey	500.00	250.00	150.00
(26)	Aaron Ward	500.00	250.00	150.00

1911-16 Kotton Tobacco

Cobb, c.f. Detroit Am.

KOTTON
CIGARETTES

NEVER GO OUT.

MADE BY

Peoples Tobacco Co. Ltd.

NEW ORLEANS, LA.

The T216 baseball card set, issued with several brands by the People's Tobacco Co., is the last of the Louisiana cigarette sets and the most confusing. Issued over a period of several years between 1911 and 1916, the set employs the same pictures as several contemporary caramel and bakery sets. Cards measure a nominal 1-1/2" x 2-5/8", though reasonable allowance must be made for original cutting variances. Positive identification can be made by the back of the cards. The Peoples Tobacco cards carry advertising for one of three brands of cigarettes: Kotton, Mino or Virginia Extra. The Kotton brand is the most common, with cards found in two types; one has a glossy front finish, while a second scarcer type is printed on a thin paper. The thin paper cards command an additional 15 percent premium. The glossy-front cards can be found with either of two ad styles on back: "KOTTON / TOBACCO" (Factory No. 11) or "KOTTON / CIGARETTES" (Factory No. 4). The cards include players from the American, National and Federal Leagues. The complete set price includes only the least expensive of each variation.

		NM	EX	VG
	Common Player:	990.00	495.00	300.00
(1)	Jack Barry (Batting)	990.00	495.00	300.00
(2)	Jack Barry (Fielding)	990.00	495.00	300.00
(3)	Harry Bemis	990.00	495.00	300.00
(4a)	Chief Bender (Philadelphia, striped cap.)	1,800	900.00	540.00
(4b)	Chief Bender (Baltimore, striped cap.)	1,800	900.00	540.00
(5a)	Chief Bender (Philadelphia, white cap.)	1,800	900.00	540.00
(5b)	Chief Bender (Baltimore, white cap.)	1,800	900.00	540.00
(6)	Bill Bergen	990.00	495.00	300.00
(7a)	Bob Bescher (Cincinnati)	990.00	495.00	300.00
(7b)	Bob Bescher (St. Louis)	990.00	495.00	300.00
(8)	Roger Bresnahan	1,800	900.00	540.00
(9)	Al Bridwell (Batting)	990.00	495.00	300.00
(10a)	Al Bridwell (New York, sliding.)	990.00	495.00	300.00
(10b)	Al Bridwell (St. Louis, sliding.)	990.00	495.00	300.00
(11)	Donie Bush	990.00	495.00	300.00
(12)	Doc Casey	990.00	495.00	300.00
(13)	Frank Chance	1,800	900.00	540.00
(14a)	Hal Chase (New York, fielding.)	990.00	495.00	300.00
(14b)	Hal Chase (Buffalo, fielding.)	1,800	900.00	540.00
(15)	Hal Chase (Portrait)	1,440	720.00	430.00
(16a)	Ty Cobb (Detroit Am., standing.)	24,000	12,000	7,200
(16b)	Ty Cobb (Detroit Americans, standing.)	21,000	10,500	6,300
(17)	Ty Cobb (Detroit Americans, batting.)	24,000	12,000	7,200
(18a)	Eddie Collins (Phila. Am.)	1,800	900.00	540.00
(18b)	Eddie Collins (Phila. Amer.)	1,800	900.00	540.00
(19)	Eddie Collins (Chicago)	1,800	900.00	540.00
(20a)	Sam Crawford (Small print.)	1,800	900.00	540.00
(20b)	Sam Crawford (Large print.)	1,800	900.00	540.00
(21)	Harry Davis	990.00	495.00	300.00
(22)	Ray Demmitt	990.00	495.00	300.00
(23)	Art Devlin	990.00	495.00	300.00
(24a)	Wild Bill Donovan (Detroit)	990.00	495.00	300.00
(24b)	Wild Bill Donovan (New York)	990.00	495.00	300.00
(25a)	Red Dooin (Philadelphia)	990.00	495.00	300.00
(25b)	Red Dooin (Cincinnati)	990.00	495.00	300.00
(26a)	Mickey Doolan (Philadelphia)	990.00	495.00	300.00
(26b)	Mickey Doolan (Baltimore)	990.00	495.00	300.00
(27)	Patsy Dougherty	990.00	495.00	300.00
(28a)	Larry Doyle, Larry Doyle (N.Y. Nat'l., batting.)	990.00	495.00	300.00
(28b)	Larry Doyle (New York Nat'l, batting.)	990.00	495.00	300.00
(29)	Larry Doyle (Throwing)	990.00	495.00	300.00
(30)	Clyde Engle	990.00	495.00	300.00
(31a)	Johnny Evers (Chicago)	1,800	900.00	540.00
(31b)	Johnny Evers (Boston)	1,800	900.00	540.00
(32)	Art Fromme	990.00	495.00	300.00
(33a)	George Gibson (Pittsburg Nat'l, back view.)	990.00	495.00	300.00
(33b)	George Gibson (Pittsburgh Nat'l., back view.)	990.00	495.00	300.00
(34a)	George Gibson (Pittsburg Nat'l., front view.)	990.00	495.00	300.00
(34b)	George Gibson (Pittsburgh Nat'l., front view.)	990.00	495.00	300.00
(35a)	Topsy Hartsel (Phila. Am.)	990.00	495.00	300.00
(35b)	Topsy Hartsel (Phila. Amer.)	990.00	495.00	300.00
(36)	Roy Hartzell (Batting)	990.00	495.00	300.00
(37)	Roy Hartzell (Catching)	990.00	495.00	300.00
(38a)	Fred Jacklitsch (Philadelphia)	990.00	495.00	300.00
(38b)	Fred Jacklitsch (Baltimore)	990.00	495.00	300.00
(39a)	Hughie Jennings (Orange background.)	1,800	900.00	540.00
(39b)	Hughie Jennings (Red background.)	1,800	900.00	540.00
(40)	Red Kleinow	990.00	495.00	300.00
(41a)	Otto Knabe (Philadelphia)	990.00	495.00	300.00
(41b)	Otto Knabe (Baltimore)	990.00	495.00	300.00
(42)	Jack Knight	990.00	495.00	300.00
(43a)	Nap Lajoie (Philadelphia, fielding.)	1,800	900.00	540.00
(43b)	Nap Lajoie (Cleveland, fielding.)	1,800	900.00	540.00
(44)	Nap Lajoie (Portrait)	1,800	900.00	540.00
(45a)	Hans Lobert (Cincinnati)	990.00	495.00	300.00
(45b)	Hans Lobert,(New York)	990.00	495.00	300.00
(46)	Sherry Magee	990.00	495.00	300.00
(47)	Rube Marquard	1,800	900.00	540.00
(48a)	Christy Matthewson (Mathewson) (Large print.)	5,400	2,700	1,620
(48b)	Christy Matthewson (Mathewson) (Small print.)	5,400	2,700	1,620
(49a)	John McGraw (Large print.)	1,800	900.00	540.00

		NM	EX	VG
(49b)	John McGraw (Small print.)	1,800	900.00	540.00
(50)	Larry McLean	990.00	495.00	300.00
(51)	George McQuillan	990.00	495.00	300.00
(52)	Dots Miller (Batting)	990.00	495.00	300.00
(53a)	Dots Miller (Pittsburg, fielding.)	990.00	495.00	300.00
(53b)	Dots Miller (St. Louis, fielding.)	990.00	495.00	300.00
(54a)	Danny Murphy (Philadelphia)	990.00	495.00	300.00
(54b)	Danny Murphy (Brooklyn)	990.00	495.00	300.00
(55)	Rebel Oakes	990.00	495.00	300.00
(56)	Bill O'Hara	990.00	495.00	300.00
(57)	Eddie Plank	2,400	1,200	720.00
(58a)	Germany Schaefer (Washington)	990.00	495.00	300.00
(58b)	Germany Schaefer (Newark)	990.00	495.00	300.00
(59)	Admiral Schlei	990.00	495.00	300.00
(60)	Boss Schmidt	990.00	495.00	300.00
(61)	Johnny Seigle	990.00	495.00	300.00
(62)	Dave Shean	990.00	495.00	300.00
(63)	Boss Smith (Schmidt)	990.00	495.00	300.00
(64)	Tris Speaker	2,400	1,200	720.00
(65)	Oscar Stanage	990.00	495.00	300.00
(66)	George Stovall	990.00	495.00	300.00
(67)	Jeff Sweeney	990.00	495.00	300.00
(68a)	Joe Tinker (Chicago Nat'l, batting.)	1,800	900.00	540.00
(68b)	Joe Tinker (Chicago Feds, batting.)	2,400	1,200	720.00
(69)	Joe Tinker (Portrait)	1,800	900.00	540.00
(70a)	Honus Wagner (Batting, S.S.)	18,000	9,000	5,400
(70b)	Honus Wagner (Batting, 2b.)	18,000	9,000	5,400
(71a)	Honus Wagner (Throwing, S.S.)	18,000	9,000	5,400
(71b)	Honus Wagner (Throwing, 2b.)	18,000	9,000	5,400
(72)	Hooks Wiltse	990.00	495.00	300.00
(73)	Cy Young	4,200	2,100	1,260
(74a)	Heinie Zimmerman (2b.)	990.00	495.00	300.00
(74b)	Heinie Zimmerman (3b.)	990.00	495.00	300.00

1964 Sandy Koufax's Tropicana Postcard

In the early 1960s, Dodgers pitcher Sandy Koufax owned the Tropicana Motor Hotel in Hollywood. Among the collectible souvenirs of that venture are a pair of color postcards picturing the player overlooking the pool. The original version pictures Koufax in civilian clothes. A later version uses the same photo, but has a Dodgers uniform crudely drawn on Koufax' photo.

	NM	EX	VG
Sandy Koufax (Civilian)	175.00	90.00	50.00
Sandy Koufax (Uniform)	150.00	75.00	45.00

1907 Krieg & Co. Chicago Cubs Base Ball Mail Card

Distributed by a shoe retailers' supply firm, this foldout black-and-white postcard features the World Champion Cubs. About 5-1/4" x 3-1/2" closed, the foldout opens to reveal portrait photos of 16 of the players, two per post-card size panel. Manager Frank Chance and the team president each have their own panel. The back cover of the mailer has a composite photo of the team, with a 1907 National League schedule on its flip side.

	NM	EX	VG
1907 Chicago Cubs Foldout	2,000	1,000	600.00

1976 Kroger Cincinnati Reds

Blank-backed and unnumbered, they are checklisted here alphabetically. Because the photos were licensed only by the players' union, and not Major League Baseball, photos do not show uniform logos. The grocery store chain gave away these 6 x 9 color photos, four per week, during a span in September and October.

	NM	EX	VG
Complete Set (16):	50.00	25.00	15.00
Common Player:	3.00	1.50	.90
Week 1			
(1) Dan Driessen	3.00	1.50	.90
(2) Ken Griffey Sr.	4.00	2.00	1.25
(3) Fred Norman	3.00	1.50	.90
(4) Pete Rose	25.00	12.50	7.50
Week 2			
(1) Ed Armbrister	3.00	1.50	.90
(2) Johnny Bench	15.00	7.50	4.50
(3) Jack Billingham	3.00	1.50	.90
(4) Tony Perez	8.00	4.00	2.50
Week 3			
(1) Rawly Eastwick	3.00	1.50	.90
(2) George Foster	4.00	2.00	1.25
(3) Cesar Geronimo	3.00	1.50	.90
(4) Don Gullett	3.00	1.50	.90
Week 4			
(1) Bob Bailey	3.00	1.50	.90
(2) Dave Concepcion	3.00	1.50	.90
(3) Joe Morgan	12.50	6.75	4.00
(4) Gary Nolan	3.00	1.50	.90

1977 Kurland Tom Seaver

These large-format (4-3/16" x 5-1/2") black-and-white cards appear to have been produced in conjunction with promotional appearances by Seaver for Kurland Cadillac-Oldsmobile, a metropolitan New York auto dealer. Most of the cards seen are autographed by Seaver. The back is blank.

	NM	EX	VG
Complete Set (2):	150.00	75.00	45.00
Common Card:	75.00	37.00	22.00
(1) Tom Seaver (N.Y. Mets)	75.00	37.00	22.00
(2) Tom Seaver (Cincinnati Reds)	75.00	37.00	22.00

1926 Kut Outs Giants/Yankees Die-Cuts

These black-and-white, blank-back, die-cut cards were sold as complete sets for 10 cents per team. The size varies with the pose depicted, but the cards are generally about 2" wide and 4-1/2" tall. The player's name is printed at the bottom of his photo. The unnumbered cards are checklisted here in alphabetical order by team. The issue is very similar to the Middy Bread Cardinals/Browns cards of 1927.

	NM	EX	VG
Complete Set (20):	14,500	5,800	2,900
Common Player:	350.00	140.00	70.00
N.Y. Giants Team Set:	4,500	1,800	900.00
(1) Ed Farrell	350.00	140.00	70.00
(2) Frank Frisch	600.00	240.00	120.00
(3) George Kelly	600.00	240.00	120.00
(4) Freddie Lindstrom	600.00	240.00	120.00
(5) John McGraw	600.00	240.00	120.00
(6) Emil Meusel	350.00	140.00	70.00
(7) John Scott	350.00	140.00	70.00
(8) Frank Snyder	350.00	140.00	70.00
(9) Billy Southworth	350.00	140.00	70.00
(10) Ross Young (Youngs)	600.00	240.00	120.00
N.Y. Yankees Team Set:	10,000	4,000	2,000
(11) Pat Collins	350.00	140.00	70.00
(12) Earle Combs	600.00	240.00	120.00
(13) Joe Dugan	350.00	140.00	70.00
(14) Lou Gehrig	2,500	1,000	500.00
(15) Miller Huggins	600.00	240.00	120.00
(16) Mark Koenig	350.00	140.00	70.00
(17) Tony Lazzeri	600.00	240.00	120.00
(18) Bob Meusel	350.00	140.00	70.00
(19) Herb Pennock	600.00	240.00	120.00
(20) Babe Ruth	5,000	2,000	1,000

L

1912 La Azora Cigars

These postcard-size (about 3-3/8" x 5-3/8") ad cards were issued by a Detroit cigar maker. Both cards feature of their front a borderless sepia photo of Ty Cobb, though he is not named. The backs differ somewhat in format and content, but basically provide the Tigers' home and road schedules for the season.

	NM	EX	VG
Complete Set (2):	5,000	2,500	1,500
(1) Ty Cobb (Fielding, home schedule.)	3,000	1,500	900.00
(2) Ty Cobb (Sliding, road schedule.)	3,000	1,500	900.00

1958-60 L.A. Dodgers Premium Pictures

Apparently issued over a period of years from 1958 through at least 1960, these black-and-white, 8-1/2" x 11" premium pictures were sold as a set through Dodgers souvenir outlets, though the make-up of a set changed with the comings and goings of players. The blank-backed pictures feature on front a pencil portrait of the player, with his name printed towards the bottom. The signature of sports artist Nicholas Volpe also appears on front. The unnumbered pictures are checklisted here alphabetically.

	NM	EX	VG
Complete Set (16):	300.00	150.00	90.00
Common Player:	15.00	7.50	4.50
(1) Walter Alston	17.50	8.75	5.25
(2) Roy Campanella	30.00	15.00	9.00
(3) Gino Cimoli	15.00	7.50	4.50
(4) Don Drysdale	30.00	15.00	9.00
(5) Carl Erskine	15.00	7.50	4.50
(6) Carl Furillo	20.00	10.00	6.00
(7) Jim Gilliam	17.50	8.75	5.25
(8) Gil Hodges	30.00	15.00	9.00
(9) Clem Labine	15.00	7.50	4.50
(10) Wally Moon	15.00	7.50	4.50
(11) Don Newcombe	17.50	8.75	5.25
(12) Johnny Podres	17.50	8.75	5.25
(13) Pee Wee Reese	30.00	15.00	9.00
(14) Rip Repulski	15.00	7.50	4.50
(15) Vin Scully, Jerry Doggett (Announcers)	15.00	7.50	4.50
(16) Duke Snider	30.00	15.00	9.00

1959 L.A. Dodgers Postcards

In the team's second year in California, the Dodgers began production of an on-going set of color player postcards. Cards were usually sold in 10-card packs in stadium souvenir stands. The makeup of the packs sold varied as players came and went and cards were issued or withdrawn. When supplies of any player's cards were exhausted, he would be included in the current printing. Various photographers and printers were responsible for the issue over the years, but all utilized a similar format of 3-1/2" x 5-1/2" glossy borderless fronts and postcard style backs. The initial effort in 1959 had no player identification on the front. Backs are printed in brown, including player ID, birthdate and place, copyright date and credits to Mirro Krome and Crocker Co. Cards are numbered as shown here, but with an "LA-D-" prefix. The set was also available in the form of an accordian-foldout.

	NM	EX	VG
Complete Set (12):	400.00	200.00	125.00
Common Player:	30.00	15.00	9.00
901 Duke Snider	40.00	20.00	12.00
902 Gil Hodges	35.00	17.50	10.00
903 Johnny Podres	30.00	15.00	9.00
904 Carl Furillo	30.00	15.00	9.00
905 Don Drysdale	40.00	20.00	12.00
906 Sandy Koufax	75.00	37.50	22.50
907 Jim Gilliam	30.00	15.00	9.00
908 Don Zimmer	30.00	15.00	9.00
909 Charlie Neal	30.00	15.00	9.00
910 Norm Larker (Photo actually Joe Pignatano.)	30.00	15.00	9.00
911 Clem Labine (Photo actually Stan Williams.)	30.00	15.00	9.00
912 John Roseboro	30.00	15.00	9.00

1960 L.A. Dodgers Postcards

Like many baseball souvenirs, this set of team-issued postcards was "Made in Japan." The 3-1/2" x 5-1/2" cards share the basic format of the 1959 premiere issue with borderless color poses on front and postcard-style back. Backs are printed in blue with player ID and copyright date, but the cards are unnumbered. They are checklisted here alphabetically. The Carl Furillo card is scarce because it was withdrawn when he retired after playing only eight games in 1960.

	NM	EX	VG
Complete Set (12):	250.00	125.00	75.00
Common Player:	12.50	6.25	3.75
(1) Walt Alston	12.50	6.25	3.75
(2) Roger Craig	12.50	6.25	3.75
(3) Don Drysdale	15.00	7.50	4.50
(4) Carl Furillo	75.00	37.00	22.00
(5) Gil Hodges	15.00	7.50	4.50
(6) Sandy Koufax	60.00	30.00	18.00
(7) Wally Moon	12.50	6.25	3.75
(8) Charlie Neal	12.50	6.25	3.75
(9) Johnny Podres	12.50	6.25	3.75
(10) John Roseboro	12.50	6.25	3.75
(11) Larry Sherry	12.50	6.25	3.75
(12) Duke Snider	15.00	7.50	4.50

1962 L.A. Dodgers Pins

The attributed date is speculative based on available checklist information. This series of, presumably, stadium souvenir pinback buttons is in an unusually large 3-1/2" format. The pins have black-and-white photos on a white or light blue background. Two styles of name presentation are known, those with names in a white strip at the bottom of the pin and those with the names overprinted on the photo and more towards the center.

	NM	EX	VG
Common Player:	75.00	37.50	22.00
NAME IN STRIP			
Don Drysdale	60.00	30.00	18.00
Duke Snider	125.00	62.00	37.00
NAME OVERPRINTED			
Gil Hodges	95.00	47.00	28.00
Sandy Koufax	500.00	250.00	150.00
Maury Wills	75.00	37.50	22.00

1963 L.A. Dodgers Pin-Ups

Borrowing on the concept of the 1938 Goudey Heads-up cards, this set was sold, probably at the stadium souvenir stands, in a white envelope labeled "Los Angeles Dodgers Pin-Ups." The cards feature large full-color head-and-cap photos set atop cartoon ballplayers' bodies. Cards are printed on 7-1/4" x 8-1/2" semi-gloss cardboard with blank backs. The player's name appears in black on the front, along with the instructions, "Push out character carefully. Take scissors and trim white around player's head." Each figure was die-cut to allow its easy removal from the background.

	NM	EX	VG
Complete Set (10):	75.00	35.00	25.00
Common Player:	6.00	3.00	1.75
(1) Tommy Davis	7.50	3.75	2.25
(2) Willie Davis	7.50	3.75	2.25
(3) Don Drysdale	10.00	5.00	3.00
(4) Ron Fairly	6.00	3.00	1.75
(5) Frank Howard	7.50	3.75	2.25
(6) Sandy Koufax	25.00	12.50	7.50
(7) Joe Moeller	6.00	3.00	1.75
(8) Ron Perranoski	6.00	3.00	1.75
(9) John Roseboro	6.00	3.00	1.75
(10) Maury Wills	7.50	3.75	2.25

1965 L.A. Dodgers Motion Pins

These "flasher" pins were issued in conjunction with the Dodgers' World Series appearance and ultimate victory in 1965. The 2-1/2" diameter pins feature player portraits on a seamed blue background resembling a baseball. When the angle of view is changed, the player's name and team logo and the starbursts pop in and out of sight.

	NM	EX	VG
Don Drysdale	15.00	7.50	4.50
Sandy Koufax	25.00	12.50	7.50
Dodgers Logo - "Our Champs"	15.00	7.50	4.50

1979 L.A. Dodgers

Presumed to be a collectors' issue due to lack of sponsors or licensors logos, this set features the top players of the '79 Dodgers. Fronts of the 2-1/2" x 3-3/8" cards are borderless color photos. Backs are printed in blue and white with career highlights and personal data. Cards are checklisted here in alphabetical order.

	NM	EX	VG
Complete Set (15):	15.00	7.50	4.50
Common Player:	2.00	1.00	.60
(1) Dusty Baker	3.00	1.50	.90
(2) Ron Cey	2.00	1.00	.60
(3) Terry Forster	2.00	1.00	.60
(4) Steve Garvey	4.00	2.00	1.25
(5) Burt Hooton	2.00	1.00	.60
(6) Charlie Hough	2.00	1.00	.60
(7) Tommy Lasorda	3.00	1.50	.90
(8) Dave Lopes	2.00	1.00	.60
(9) Rick Monday	2.00	1.00	.60
(10) Manny Mota	2.00	1.00	.60
(11) Doug Rau	2.00	1.00	.60
(12) Bill Russell	2.00	1.00	.60
(13) Reggie Smith	2.00	1.00	.60
(14) Don Sutton	4.00	2.00	1.25
(15) Steve Yeager	2.00	1.00	.60

1980 L.A. Dodgers Police

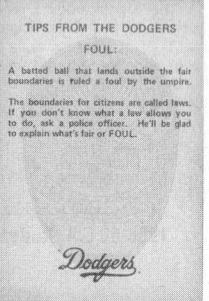

Producers of one of the most popular police and safety sets in the hobby, the Dodgers began this successful promotion in 1980. The 2-13/16" x 4-1/8" cards feature full-color photos on front, along with brief personal statistics. Backs include "Tips from the Dodgers" along with the team and LAPD logos. Cards are numbered by player uniform number, with an unnumbered team card also included in the set.

	NM	EX	VG
Complete Set (30):	6.00	3.00	1.75
Common Player:	.50	.25	.15
5 Johnny Oates	.50	.25	.15
6 Steve Garvey	2.00	1.00	.60
7 Steve Yeager	.50	.25	.15
8 Reggie Smith	.50	.25	.15
9 Gary Thomasson	.50	.25	.15
10 Ron Cey	.60	.30	.20
12 Dusty Baker	.60	.30	.20
13 Joe Ferguson	.50	.25	.15
15 Davey Lopes	.50	.25	.15
16 Rick Monday	.50	.25	.15
18 Bill Russell	.50	.25	.15
20 Don Sutton	2.00	1.00	.60
21 Jay Johnstone	.50	.25	.15
23 Teddy Martinez	.50	.25	.15
27 Joe Beckwith	.50	.25	.15
28 Pedro Guerrero	.50	.25	.15
29 Don Stanhouse	.50	.25	.15
30 Derrel Thomas	.50	.25	.15
31 Doug Rau	.50	.25	.15
34 Ken Brett	.50	.25	.15
35 Bob Welch	.50	.25	.15
37 Robert Castillo	.50	.25	.15
38 Dave Goltz	.50	.25	.15
41 Jerry Reuss	.50	.25	.15
43 Rick Sutcliffe	.60	.30	.20
44 Mickey Hatcher	.50	.25	.15
46 Burt Hooton	.50	.25	.15
49 Charlie Hough	.50	.25	.15
51 Terry Forster	.50	.25	.15
--- Team Photo	.50	.25	.15

1913 Napoleon Lajoie Game

Although individual cards are not marked, these cards were produced as part of a Parker Bros. baseball board game called "The National American Baseball Game." Each of the approximately 2-3/8" x 3-1/4", round-cornered cards has a

borderless photo on front picturing the Hall of Famer at bat. Backs have a chart of various baseball plays used in the game. Cards can be found with the Lajoie photo tinted either blue or red, the latter being somewhat scarcer.

	NM	EX	VG
Complete Game Set:	1,500	750.00	450.00
SINGLE CARD			
Napoleon Lajoie (Blue)	25.00	12.50	7.50
Napoleon Lajoie (Red)	45.00	22.50	13.50

1960 Lake To Lake Dairy Braves

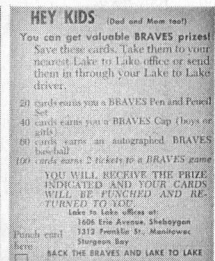

This 28-card set of unnumbered 2-1/2" x 3-1/4" cards offers a special challenge for the condition-conscious collector. Originally issued by being stapled to milk cartons, the cards were redeemable for prizes ranging from pen and pencil sets to Braves tickets. When sent in for redemption, the cards had a hole punched in the corner. Naturally, collectors most desire cards without the staple or punch holes. Cards are printed in blue ink on front, red ink on back. Because he was traded in May, and his card withdrawn, the Ray Boone card is scarce; the Billy Bruton card is unaccountably scarcer still.

	NM	EX	VG
Complete Set (28):	2,250	1,125	650.00
Common Player:	35.00	17.50	10.00
(1) Henry Aaron	500.00	250.00	150.00
(2) Joe Adcock	35.00	17.50	10.00
(3) Ray Boone	250.00	125.00	75.00
(4) Bill Bruton	500.00	250.00	150.00
(5) Bob Buhl	35.00	17.50	10.00
(6) Lou Burdette	35.00	17.50	10.00
(7) Chuck Cottier	35.00	17.50	10.00
(8) Wes Covington	35.00	17.50	10.00
(9) Del Crandall	35.00	17.50	10.00
(10) Charlie Dressen	35.00	17.50	10.00
(11) Bob Giggie	35.00	17.50	10.00
(12) Joey Jay	35.00	17.50	10.00
(13) Johnny Logan	35.00	17.50	10.00
(14) Felix Mantilla	35.00	17.50	10.00
(15) Lee Maye	35.00	17.50	10.00
(16) Don McMahon	35.00	17.50	10.00
(17) George Myatt	35.00	17.50	10.00
(18) Andy Pafko	35.00	17.50	10.00
(19) Juan Pizarro	35.00	17.50	10.00
(20) Mel Roach	35.00	17.50	10.00
(21) Bob Rush	35.00	17.50	10.00
(22) Bob Scheffing	35.00	17.50	10.00
(23) Red Schoendienst	75.00	37.50	22.50
(24) Warren Spahn	150.00	75.00	45.00
(25) Al Spangler	35.00	17.50	10.00
(26) Frank Torre	35.00	17.50	10.00
(27) Carl Willey	35.00	17.50	10.00
(28) Whitlow Wyatt	35.00	17.50	10.00

1923-24 La Moda

This is appears to be a parallel to the more frequently encountered Cuban cigar cards advertising the Billiken brand. Specialists feel that the La Moda ("The Fashion") branded cards survive at a rate about one per 10 Billikens, though demand is not such that prices follow such a ratio.

	NM	EX	VG
Common Player:	1,000	400.00	200.00
Stars: 2X			

(See 1923-24 Billiken for checklist and base card values.)

1970 La Pizza Royale Expos

This colorful collectors' issue features only Montreal Expos. Each of the 2-1/2" x 5" cards can be found printed in red, yellow, blue of green duo-tones. "La Pizza Royale" is printed in white above the player photo. Below the photo is the player's name and, in French, his position. Backs are blank and the cards are unnumbered. The checklist is presented here alphabetically. The La Pizza Royale cards are a fantasy issue produced by a collector for sale within the hobby.

La Pizza Royale

RUSTY STAUB
Voltigeur

	NM	EX	VG
Complete Set (14):	20.00	10.00	6.00
Common Player:	2.00	1.00	.60
(1) Bob Bailey	2.00	1.00	.60
(2) John Boccabella	2.00	1.00	.60
(3) Ron Fairly	3.00	1.50	.90
(4) Jim Gosger	2.00	1.00	.60
(5) Coco Laboy	2.00	1.00	.60
(6) Gene Mauch	3.00	1.50	.90
(7) Rich Nye	2.00	1.00	.60
(8) John O'Donoghue	2.00	1.00	.60
(9) Adolfo Phillips	2.00	1.00	.60
(10) Howie Reed	2.00	1.00	.60
(11) Marv Staehle	2.00	1.00	.60
(12) Rusty Staub	4.50	2.25	1.25
(13) Gary Sutherland	2.00	1.00	.60
(14) Bobby Wine	2.00	1.00	.60

1967 Laughlin World Series

Apparently a prototype set for subsequent offerings by the sports artist R.G. Laughlin that were produced by Fleer, this set of 64 cards was printed in black-and-white with the cartoon line drawings for which Laughlin was noted. The cards are an odd size, 2-3/4" x 3-1/2", like so many of the Laughlin/Fleer issues of the period. The text on the back is printed in red and offer details of the World Series from that year.

	NM	EX	VG
Complete Set (64):	450.00	225.00	135.00
Common Card:	9.00	4.50	2.75
1 1903 Red Sox/Pirates	9.00	4.50	2.75
2 1905 Giants/A's (Christy Mathewson)	20.00	10.00	6.00
3 1906 White Sox/Cubs	9.00	4.50	2.75
4 1907 Cubs/Tigers	9.00	4.50	2.75
5 1908 Cubs/Tigers (Joe Tinker, Evers, Frank Chance)	20.00	10.00	6.00
6 1909 Pirates/Tigers (Honus Wagner, Ty Cobb)	30.00	15.00	9.00
7 1910 A's/Cubs	9.00	4.50	2.75
8 1911 A's/Giants (John McGraw)	9.00	4.50	2.75
9 1912 Red Sox/Giants	9.00	4.50	2.75
10 1913 A's/Giants	9.00	4.50	2.75
11 1914 Braves/A's	9.00	4.50	2.75
12 1915 Red Sox/Phillies (Babe Ruth)	35.00	17.50	10.00
13 1916 White Sox/Dodgers (Babe Ruth)	35.00	17.50	10.00
14 1917 White Sox/Giants	9.00	4.50	2.75
15 1918 Red Sox/Cubs	9.00	4.50	2.75
16 1919 Reds/White Sox	35.00	17.50	10.00
17 1920 Indians/Dodgers (Bill Wambsganss)	9.00	4.50	2.75
18 1921 Giants/Yankees (Waite Hoyt)	9.00	4.50	2.75
19 1922 Giants/Yankees (Frank Frisch, Heinie Groh)	9.00	4.50	2.75
20 1923 Yankees/Giants (Babe Ruth)	35.00	17.50	10.00
21 1924 Senators/Giants (Walter Johnson)	15.00	7.50	4.50
22 1925 Pirates/Senators (Walter Johnson)	15.00	7.50	4.50
23 1926 Cardinals/Yankees (Grover Alexander, Anthony Lazzeri)	15.00	7.50	4.50
24 1927 Yankees/Pirates	9.00	4.50	2.75
25 1928 Yankees/Cardinals (Babe Ruth, Lou Gehrig)	35.00	17.50	10.00
26 1929 A's/Cubs	9.00	4.50	2.75
27 1930 A's/Cardinals	9.00	4.50	2.75

	NM	EX	VG
28 1931 Cardinals/A's (Pepper Martin)	9.00	4.50	2.75
29 1932 Yankees/Cubs (Babe Ruth)	35.00	17.50	10.00
30 1933 Giants/Senators (Mel Ott)	12.50	6.25	3.75
31 1934 Cardinals/Tigers (Dizzy Dean, Paul Dean)	20.00	10.00	6.00
32 1935 Tigers/Cubs	9.00	4.50	2.75
33 1936 Yankees/Giants	9.00	4.50	2.75
34a 1937 Yankees/Giants (Carl Hubbell) (#11 on uniform)	12.50	6.25	3.75
34b 1937 Yankees/Giants (Carl Hubbell) (#14 on uniform)	12.50	6.25	3.75
35 1938 Yankees/Cubs	9.00	4.50	2.75
36 1939 Yankees/Reds (Joe DiMaggio)	30.00	15.00	9.00
37 1940 Reds/Tigers	9.00	4.50	2.75
38 1941 Yankees/Dodgers (Mickey Owen)	9.00	4.50	2.75
39 1942 Cardinals/Yankees	9.00	4.50	2.75
40 1943 Yankees/Cardinals (Joe McCarthy)	9.00	4.50	2.75
41 1944 Cardinals/Browns	9.00	4.50	2.75
42 1945 Tigers/Cubs (Hank Greenberg)	15.00	7.50	4.50
43 1946 Cardinals/Red Sox (Enos Slaughter)	9.00	4.50	2.75
44 1947 Yankees/Dodgers (Al Gionfriddo)	9.00	4.50	2.75
45 1948 Indians/Braves (Bob Feller)	12.50	6.25	3.75
46 1949 Yankees/Dodgers (Allie Reynolds, Preacher Roe)	20.00	10.00	6.00
47 1950 Yankees/Phillies	9.00	4.50	2.75
48 1951 Yankees/Giants	9.00	4.50	2.75
49 1952 Yankees/Dodgers (Johnny Mize, Duke Snider)	20.00	10.00	6.00
50 1953 Yankees/Dodgers (Casey Stengel)	20.00	10.00	6.00
51 1954 Giants/Indians (Dusty Rhodes)	9.00	4.50	2.75
52 1955 Dodgers/Yankees (Johnny Podres)	20.00	10.00	6.00
53 1956 Yankees/Dodgers (Don Larsen)	25.00	12.50	7.50
54 1957 Braves/Yankees (Lew Burdette)	9.00	4.50	2.75
55 1958 Yankees/Braves (Hank Bauer)	9.00	4.50	2.75
56 1959 Dodgers/White Sox (Larry Sherry)	9.00	4.50	2.75
57 1960 Pirates/Yankees	25.00	12.50	7.50
58 1961 Yankees/Reds (Whitey Ford)	20.00	10.00	6.00
59 1962 Yankees/Giants	9.00	4.50	2.75
60 1963 Dodgers/Yankees (Sandy Koufax)	20.00	10.00	6.00
61 1964 Cardinals/Yankees (Mickey Mantle)	35.00	17.50	10.00
62 1965 Dodgers/Twins (Sandy Koufax)	9.00	4.50	2.75
63 1966 Orioles/Dodgers	9.00	4.50	2.75
64 1967 Cardinals/Red Sox (Bob Gibson)	9.00	4.50	2.75

1972 Laughlin Great Feats

Sports artist R.G. Laughlin created this set of 50 numbered cards and one unnumbered title card highlighting top performances by stars over the years. The cards depict the player in pen and ink, with one variation of the set adding flesh tones to the players. One variation of the set has red borders, the other (with the flesh tones) blue. The cards are blank backed and numbered on the front with a brief caption. Cards measure about 2-9/16" x 3-9/16". Sets originally sold for about $3.

	NM	EX	VG
Complete Set, Red (51):	45.00	22.50	13.50
Complete Set, Blue (51):	60.00	30.00	18.00
Common Player (Red):	1.50	.70	.45
Common Player (Blue): 1.5-2X			
1 Joe DiMaggio	12.00	6.00	3.50
2 Walter Johnson	4.50	2.25	1.25
3 Rudy York	1.50	.70	.45
4 Sandy Koufax	9.00	4.50	2.75
5 George Sisler	1.50	.70	.45
6 Iron Man McGinnity	1.50	.70	.45
7 Johnny VanderMeer	1.50	.70	.45
8 Lou Gehrig	12.00	6.00	3.50
9 Max Carey	1.50	.70	.45
10 Ed Delahanty	1.50	.70	.45
11 Pinky Higgins	1.50	.70	.45
12 Jack Chesbro	1.50	.70	.45
13 Jim Bottomley	1.50	.70	.45
14 Rube Marquard	1.50	.70	.45
15 Rogers Hornsby	1.50	.70	.45
16 Lefty Grove	1.50	.70	.45
17 Johnny Mize	1.50	.70	.45
18 Lefty Gomez	1.50	.70	.45
19 Jimmie Fox (Foxx)	1.50	.70	.45
20 Casey Stengel	1.50	.70	.45
21 Dazzy Vance	1.50	.70	.45
22 Jerry Lynch	1.50	.70	.45
23 Hughie Jennings	1.50	.70	.45
24 Stan Musial	4.50	2.25	1.25
25 Christy Mathewson	4.50	2.25	1.25
26 Elroy Face	1.50	.70	.45
27 Hack Wilson	1.50	.70	.45
28 Smoky Burgess	1.50	.70	.45
29 Cy Young	3.00	1.50	.90
30 Wilbert Robinson	1.50	.70	.45
31 Wee Willie Keeler	1.50	.70	.45
32 Babe Ruth	15.00	7.50	4.50
33 Mickey Mantle	15.00	7.50	4.50
34 Hub Leonard	1.50	.70	.45
35 Ty Cobb	7.50	3.75	2.25
36 Carl Hubbell	1.50	.70	.45
37 Joe Oeschger, Leon Cadore	1.50	.70	.45
38 Don Drysdale	1.50	.70	.45
39 Fred Toney, Hippo Vaughn	1.50	.70	.45
40 Joe Sewell	1.50	.70	.45
41 Grover Cleveland Alexander	1.50	.70	.45
42 Joe Adcock	1.50	.70	.45
43 Eddie Collins	1.50	.70	.45
44 Bob Feller	2.00	1.00	.60
45 Don Larsen	2.00	1.00	.60
46 Dave Philley	1.50	.70	.45
47 Bill Fischer	1.50	.70	.45
48 Dale Long	1.50	.70	.45
49 Bill Wambsganss	1.50	.70	.45
50 Roger Maris	4.50	2.25	1.25
--- Title Card	1.50	.70	.45

1973 Laughlin Super Stand-Ups

A dozen Hall of Famers are featured in this collectors' issue of stand-up figures. Printed in color on heavy cardboard, each is die-cut around the player action picture with typical measurements being 7" x 11". The stand-ups are much scarcer than most of the artist's other baseball issues. They are listed here alphabetically. The stand-ups originally retailed for $3.50 apiece.

	NM	EX	VG
Complete Set (13):	7,500	3,750	2,250
Common Player:	300.00	150.00	90.00
(1) Hank Aaron	650.00	325.00	195.00
(2) Johnny Bench	450.00	225.00	135.00
(3) Roberto Clemente	750.00	375.00	225.00
(4) Joe DiMaggio	750.00	375.00	225.00
(5) Lou Gehrig	750.00	375.00	225.00
(6) Gil Hodges	450.00	225.00	135.00
(7) Sandy Koufax	750.00	375.00	225.00
(8) Mickey Mantle	1,500	750.00	450.00
(9) Willie Mays	650.00	325.00	195.00
(10) Stan Musial	500.00	250.00	150.00
(11) Babe Ruth	1,200	600.00	360.00
(12) Tom Seaver	450.00	225.00	135.00
(13) Ted Williams	650.00	325.00	195.00

1974 Laughlin All-Star Games

With pen and ink drawings by R.G. Laughlin on the fronts, this set (40 cards) features one card from each year of the game from 1933 to 1973. The 2-3/4" x 3-3/8" cards show a player in black ink in front of a light blue background with a glossy finish, with red printing for the title of the set and the year. The backs are printed in blue, with the year of the All-Star Game serving as the card number. Issue price was $3.50.

		NM	EX	VG
Complete Set (40):		60.00	30.00	18.00
Common Player:		3.00	1.50	.90
33	Babe's Homer (Babe Ruth)	25.00	12.50	7.50
34a	Hub Fans Five (Carl Hubbell) (Uniform #11.)	4.50	2.25	1.25
34b	Hub Fans Five (Carl Hubbell) (Uniform #14.)	4.50	2.25	1.25
35	Foxx Smashes HR (Jimmie Foxx)	4.50	2.25	1.25
36	Ol' Diz Fogs 'Em (Dizzy Dean)	4.50	2.25	1.25
37	Four Hits for Ducky (Ducky Medwick)	3.00	1.50	.90
38	No-Hit Vandy (John VanderMeer)	3.00	1.50	.90
39	DiMaggio Homers (Joe DiMaggio)	20.00	10.00	6.00
40	West's 3-Run Shot (Max West)	3.00	1.50	.90
41	Vaughan Busts Two (Arky Vaughan)	3.00	1.50	.90
42	York's 2-Run Smash (Rudy York)	3.00	1.50	.90
43	Doerr's 3-Run Blast (Bobby Doerr)	3.00	1.50	.90
44	Cavarretta Reaches (Phil Cavarretta)	3.00	1.50	.90
46	Field Day for Ted (Ted Williams)	15.00	7.50	4.50
47	Big Cat Plants One (Johnny Mize)	3.00	1.50	.90
48	Raschi Pitches (Vic Raschi)	3.00	1.50	.90
49	Jackie Scores (Jackie Robinson)	12.00	6.00	3.50
50	Schoendienst Breaks (Red Schoendienst)	3.00	1.50	.90
51	Kiner Homers (Ralph Kiner)	3.00	1.50	.90
52	Sauer's Shot (Hank Sauer)	3.00	1.50	.90
53	Slaughter Hustles (Enos Slaughter)	3.00	1.50	.90
54	Rosen Hits (Al Rosen)	3.00	1.50	.90
55	Stan the Man's HR (Stan Musial)	7.50	3.75	2.25
56	Boyer Super (Ken Boyer)	3.00	1.50	.90
57	Kaline's Hits (Al Kaline)	4.50	2.25	1.25
58	Nellie Gets Two (Nellie Fox)	3.00	1.50	.90
59	Robbie Perfect (Frank Robinson)	4.50	2.25	1.25
60	Willie 3-for-4 (Willie Mays)	12.00	6.00	3.50
61	Bunning Hitless (Jim Bunning)	3.00	1.50	.90
62	Roberto Perfect (Roberto Clemente)	15.00	7.50	4.50
63	Monster Strikeouts (Dick Radatz)	3.00	1.50	.90
64	Callison's Homer (Johnny Callison)	3.00	1.50	.90
65	Stargell's Big Day (Willie Stargell)	3.00	1.50	.90
66	Brooks Gets Triple (Brooks Robinson)	4.50	2.25	1.25
67	Fergie Fans Six (Fergie Jenkins)	3.00	1.50	.90
68	Tom Terrific (Tom Seaver)	5.00	2.50	1.50
69	Stretch Belts Two (Willie McCovey)	3.00	1.50	.90
70	Yaz' Four Hits (Carl Yastrzemski)	4.50	2.25	1.25
71	Reggie Unloads (Reggie Jackson)	6.00	3.00	1.75
72	Henry Hammers (Hank Aaron)	12.00	6.00	3.50
73	Bonds Perfect (Bobby Bonds)	3.00	1.50	.90

1974 Laughlin Old-Time Black Stars

This set of slightly oversized cards (2-5/8" x 3-1/2") features drawings by R.G. Laughlin. The artwork is printed in brown and a light tan; backs are printed in brown on white stock. The set features many of the greatest players from the Negro Leagues. The cards carry no copyright date and no mention of the prolific Laughlin, but the simple line drawings are obviously his work, and a subsequent issue four years later by Laughlin removes any doubt. Original retail price at time of issue was about $3.25.

		NM	EX	VG
Complete Set (36):		60.00	30.00	18.00
Common Player:		2.00	1.00	.60
1	Smokey Joe Williams	5.00	2.50	1.50
2	Rap Dixon	2.00	1.00	.60
3	Oliver Marcelle	2.00	1.00	.60
4	Bingo DeMoss	4.00	2.00	1.25
5	Willie Foster	2.50	1.25	.70
6	John Beckwith	2.00	1.00	.60
7	Floyd (Jelly) Gardner	2.00	1.00	.60
8	Josh Gibson	10.00	5.00	3.00
9	Jose Mendez	5.00	2.50	1.50
10	Pete Hill	5.00	2.50	1.50
11	Buck Leonard	5.00	2.50	1.50
12	Jud Wilson	5.00	2.50	1.50
13	Willie Wells	5.00	2.50	1.50
14	Jimmie Lyons	2.00	1.00	.60
15	Satchel Paige	10.00	5.00	3.00
16	Louis Santop	5.00	2.50	1.50
17	Frank Grant	7.50	3.75	2.25
18	Christobel Torrienti	5.00	2.50	1.50
19	Bullet Rogan	4.00	2.00	1.25
20	Dave Malarcher	2.50	1.25	.70
21	Spot Poles	2.00	1.00	.60
22	Home Run Johnson	2.50	1.25	.70
23	Charlie Grant	4.00	2.00	1.25
24	Cool Papa Bell	5.00	2.50	1.50
25	Cannonball Dick Redding	2.00	1.00	.60
26	Ray Dandridge	5.00	2.50	1.50
27	Biz Mackey	7.50	3.75	2.25
28	Fats Jenkins	2.00	1.00	.60
29	Martin Dihigo	5.00	2.50	1.50
30	Mule Suttles	5.00	2.50	1.50
31	Bill Monroe	2.00	1.00	.60
32	Dan McClellan	2.00	1.00	.60
33	Pop Lloyd	5.00	2.50	1.50
34	Oscar Charleston	5.00	2.50	1.50
35	Andrew "Rube" Foster	5.00	2.50	1.50
36	William (Judy) Johnson	5.00	2.50	1.50

1974 Laughlin Sportslang

Featuring the cartoon artwork of R.G. Laughlin, this 41-card set features 40 cards (plus one unnumbered title card) detailing the history and derivation of slang terms from several sports. The cards are 2-3/4" x 3-1/4", with red and blue printing on the front and red on the back. The cards are numbered on the back.

		NM	EX	VG
Complete Set (41):		80.00	40.00	24.00
Common Card:		3.00	1.50	.80
1	Bull Pen	3.00	1.50	.80
2	Charley Horse	3.00	1.50	.80
3	Derby	3.00	1.50	.80
4	Anchor Man	3.00	1.50	.80
5	Mascot	3.00	1.50	.80
6	Annie Oakley	3.00	1.50	.80
7	Taxi Squad	3.00	1.50	.80
8	Dukes	3.00	1.50	.80
9	Rookie	3.00	1.50	.80
10	Jinx	3.00	1.50	.80
11	Dark Horse	3.00	1.50	.80
12	Hat Trick	3.00	1.50	.80
13	Bell Wether	3.00	1.50	.80
14	Love	3.00	1.50	.80
15	Red Dog	3.00	1.50	.80
16	Barnstorm	3.00	1.50	.80
17	Bull's Eye	3.00	1.50	.80
18	Rabbit Punch	3.00	1.50	.80
19	The Upper Hand	3.00	1.50	.80
20	Handi Cap	3.00	1.50	.80
21	Marathon	3.00	1.50	.80
22	Southpaw	3.00	1.50	.80
23	Boner	3.00	1.50	.80
24	Gridiron	3.00	1.50	.80
25	Fan	3.00	1.50	.80
26	Moxie	3.00	1.50	.80
27	Birdie	3.00	1.50	.80
28	Sulky	3.00	1.50	.80
29	Dribble	3.00	1.50	.80
30	Donnybrook	3.00	1.50	.80
31	The Real McCoy	3.00	1.50	.80
32	Even Stephen	3.00	1.50	.80
33	Chinese Homer	3.00	1.50	.80
34	English	3.00	1.50	.80
35	Garrison Finish	3.00	1.50	.80
36	Foot in the Bucket	3.00	1.50	.80
37	Steeple Chase	3.00	1.50	.80
38	Long Shot	3.00	1.50	.80
39	Nip and Tuck	3.00	1.50	.80
40	Battery	3.00	1.50	.80
----	Header Card	3.00	1.50	.80

1975 Laughlin Batty Baseball

This 25-card set depicts one humorous nickname for each of 24 Major League teams, plus one unnumbered title card. The cards are approximately standard size at 2-1/2" x 3-1/2", with simple black and white cartoon drawings on the front with orange back- grounds. The backs are blank and the cards are numbered on front.

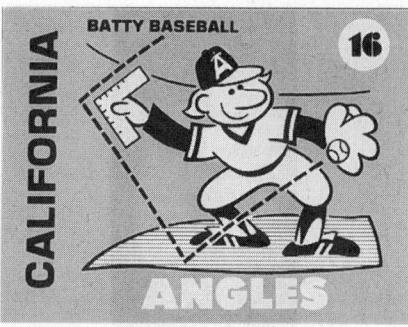

		NM	EX	VG
Complete Set (25):		60.00	30.00	18.00
Common Card:		3.00	1.50	.90
1	Oakland Daze	3.00	1.50	.90
2	Boston Wet Sox	3.00	1.50	.90
3	Cincinnati Dreads	3.00	1.50	.90
4	Chicago Wide Sox	3.00	1.50	.90
5	Milwaukee Boozers	3.00	1.50	.90
6	Philadelphia Fillies	3.00	1.50	.90
7	Cleveland Engines	3.00	1.50	.90
8	New York Mitts	3.00	1.50	.90
9	Texas Ranchers	3.00	1.50	.90
10	San Francisco Gents	3.00	1.50	.90
11	Houston Disastros	3.00	1.50	.90
12	Chicago Clubs	3.00	1.50	.90
13	Minnesota Wins	3.00	1.50	.90
14	St. Louis Gardeners	3.00	1.50	.90
15	New York Yankers	3.00	1.50	.90
16	California Angles	3.00	1.50	.90
17	Pittsburgh Irates	3.00	1.50	.90
18	Los Angeles Smoggers	3.00	1.50	.90
19	Baltimore Oreos	3.00	1.50	.90
20	Montreal Expose	3.00	1.50	.90
21	San Diego Parties	3.00	1.50	.90
22	Detroit Taggers	3.00	1.50	.90
23	Kansas City Broils	3.00	1.50	.90
24	Atlanta Briefs	3.00	1.50	.90
----	Header Card	3.00	1.50	.90

1976 Laughlin Diamond Jubilee

This set of 32 oversized cards (2-3/4" x 4") features Laughlin's drawings of baseball stars highlighting specific events or records. The fronts are printed in black and blue over a red background; the backs are numbered and printed in blue with information about the specific event. Sets originally sold for $3.50.

		NM	EX	VG
Complete Set (32):		90.00	45.00	25.00
Common Player:		2.00	1.00	.60
1	Nolan Ryan	30.00	15.00	9.00
2	Ernie Banks	4.50	2.25	1.25
3	Mickey Lolich	2.00	1.00	.60
4	Sandy Koufax	9.00	4.50	2.75
5	Frank Robinson	3.00	1.50	.90
6	Bill Mazeroski	3.00	1.50	.90
7	Catfish Hunter	2.00	1.00	.60
8	Hank Aaron	9.00	4.50	2.75
9	Carl Yastrzemski	3.00	1.50	.90
10	Jim Bunning	2.00	1.00	.60
11	Brooks Robinson	3.00	1.50	.90
12	John VanderMeer	2.00	1.00	.60
13	Harmon Killebrew	3.00	1.50	.90
14	Lou Brock	2.50	1.25	.70
15	Steve Busby	2.00	1.00	.60
16	Nate Colbert	2.00	1.00	.60
17	Don Larsen	2.50	1.25	.70
18	Willie Mays	9.00	4.50	2.75
19	David Clyde	2.00	1.00	.60
20	Mack Jones	2.00	1.00	.60
21	Mike Hegan	2.00	1.00	.60
22	Jerry Koosman	2.00	1.00	.60
23	Early Wynn	2.50	1.25	.70
24	Nellie Fox	2.50	1.25	.70
25	Joe DiMaggio	15.00	7.50	4.50
26	Jackie Robinson	12.00	6.00	3.50
27	Ted Williams	12.00	6.00	3.50
28	Lou Gehrig	12.00	6.00	3.50
29	Bobby Thomson	2.50	1.25	.70
30	Roger Maris	7.50	3.75	2.25
31	Harvey Haddix	2.00	1.00	.60
32	Babe Ruth	20.00	10.00	6.00

1976 Laughlin Indianapolis Clowns

In a departure from the style of most Laughlin issues, this 42-card set does not use his artwork but rather black and

Founder Syd Pollock

Syd Pollock organized the Miami Ethiopian Clowns in 1929. His concept was to create a black club that not only could play pro ball but add laughs and showmanship to the game. The Clowns preceded the Harlem Globetrotters by a year. The national semi-pro champions turned pro in 1942, becoming the Cincinnati Clowns and later the Indianapolis Clowns, as they won numerous Negro AL titles. Also a Braves scout, Pollock retired from traveling baseball in 1964, turning the team over to Ed Hamman. Syd passed away in 1968.

white photos framed by a light blue border. The cards are oversized at 2-5/8" x 4-1/4", with red printing on front and back. The cards are numberd on the front.

		NM	EX	VG
Complete Set (42):		30.00	15.00	9.00
Common Player:		.60	.30	.20
1	Ed Hamman (Ed the Clown)	1.00	.50	.30
2	Dero Austin	.60	.30	.20
3	James Williams (Natureboy)	.60	.30	.20
4	Sam Brison (Birmingham)	.60	.30	.20
5	Richard King (King Tut)	.60	.30	.20
6	Syd Pollock (Founder)	.60	.30	.20
7	Nataniel (Lefty) Small	.60	.30	.20
8	Grant Greene (Double Duty)	.60	.30	.20
9	Nancy Miller (Lady Umpire)	.60	.30	.20
10	Billy Vaughn	.60	.30	.20
11	Sam Brison (Putout for Sam)	.60	.30	.20
12	Ed Hamman	.60	.30	.20
13	Dero Austin (Home Delivery)	.60	.30	.20
14	Steve (Nub) Anderson	.60	.30	.20
15	Joe Cherry	.60	.30	.20
16	Reece (Goose) Tatum	3.00	1.50	.90
17	James Williams (Natureboy)	.60	.30	.20
18	Byron Purnell	.60	.30	.20
19	Bat Boy	.60	.30	.20
20	Spec BeBop	.60	.30	.20
21	Satchel Paige	5.00	2.50	1.50
22	Prince Jo Henry	.60	.30	.20
23	Ed Hamman, Syd Pollock	.60	.30	.20
24	Paul Casanova	.60	.30	.20
25	Steve (Nub) Anderson (Nub Singles)	.60	.30	.20
26	Comiskey Park	.60	.30	.20
27	Toni Stone (Second Basewoman)	1.50	.70	.45
28	Dero Austin (Small Target)	.60	.30	.20
29	Calling Dr. Kildare (Sam Brison, Natureboy Williams)	.60	.30	.20
30	Oscar Charleston	2.00	1.00	.60
31	Richard King (King Tut)	.60	.30	.20
32	Ed and Prospects (Ed Hamman, Joe Cherry, Hal King)	.60	.30	.20
33	Team Bus	.60	.30	.20
34	Hank Aaron	6.00	3.00	1.75
35	The Greta Yogi	1.50	.70	.45
36	W.H. (Chauff) Wilson	.60	.30	.20
37	Doin' Their Thing (Sam Brison, Sonny Jackson)	.60	.30	.20
38	Billy Vaughn (The Hard Way)	.60	.30	.20
39	James Williams (18 the easy way)	.60	.30	.20
40	Casey & Ed (Ed Hamman, Casey Stengel)	1.25	.60	.40
---	Header Card	.60	.30	.20
---	Baseball Laff Book	.60	.30	.20

1978 Laughlin Long Ago Black Stars

2. LARRY BROWN c

This sparkplug came from Birmingham to join the Pitt Keystones in 1921, and became one of the great defensive catchers of black baseball. He caught for the two Chicago teams of '26 and '27 that won the black World Series. After he threw out Ty Cobb three successive times in a '26 game in Havana, Ty asked the light-skinned Brown to join the Tigers—as a Cuban—but Larry declined. In '30 "Iron Man" Brown caught 234 games! He never pulled off his mask on a foul. A .300 hitter, Larry played longest for the Memphis Red Sox and also managed. He was voted catcher on many All-Star teams. Died in '72.
© 1978 R.G. Laughlin

In what appears very much like a second series save for slight title alteration, sports artist R.G. Laughlin produced this 36-card set in a format very similar to his 1974 issue highlighting Negro League stars. This set is printed in dark and light green on a non-glossy front, with printing on the back in black. Most of the more widely known Negro League stars appeared in the 1974 issue.

		NM	EX	VG
Complete Set (36):		60.00	30.00	18.00
Common Player:		1.50	.70	.45
1	Ted Trent	1.50	.70	.45
2	Larry Brown	1.50	.70	.45
3	Newt Allen	3.00	1.50	.90
4	Norman Stearns	4.50	2.25	1.25
5	Leon Day	6.00	3.00	1.75

6	Dick Lundy	1.50	.70	.45
7	Bruce Petway	1.50	.70	.45
8	Bill Drake	1.50	.70	.45
9	Chaney White	1.50	.70	.45
10	Webster McDonald	2.50	1.25	.70
11	Tommy Butts	1.50	.70	.45
12	Ben Taylor	4.50	2.25	1.25
13	James (Joe) Greene	1.50	.70	.45
14	Dick Seay	1.50	.70	.45
15	Sammy Hughes	1.50	.70	.45
16	Ted Page	3.00	1.50	.90
17	Willie Cornelius	1.50	.70	.45
18	Pat Patterson	1.50	.70	.45
19	Frank Wickware	1.50	.70	.45
20	Albert Haywood	1.50	.70	.45
21	Bill Holland	1.50	.70	.45
22	Sol White	4.50	2.25	1.25
23	Chet Brewer	3.00	1.50	.90
24	Crush Holloway	1.50	.70	.45
25	George Johnson	1.50	.70	.45
26	George Scales	1.50	.70	.45
27	Dave Brown	1.50	.70	.45
28	John Donaldson	1.50	.70	.45
29	William Johnson	3.00	1.50	.90
30	Bill Yancey	3.00	1.50	.90
31	Sam Bankhead	4.00	2.00	1.25
32	Leroy Matlock	1.50	.70	.45
33	Quincy Troupe	2.50	1.25	.70
34	Hilton Smith	3.00	1.50	.90
35	Jim Crutchfield	3.00	1.50	.90
36	Ted Radcliffe	4.00	2.00	1.25

1980 Laughlin Famous Feats

A set of 40 cards, this Famous Feats set by sports artist R.G. Laughlin carries a subtitle as the Second Series, apparently a reference to a 1972 issue of the same name by Laughlin that was produced by Fleer. Unlike many of the odd sized Laughlin issues, this one is the standard 2-1/2" x 3-1/2", with full color used with the artist's pen and ink drawings on the front. The cards are numbered on the front and the backs are blank.

		NM	EX	VG
Complete Set (40):		15.00	7.50	4.50
Common Player:		.75	.35	.20
1	Honus Wagner	2.50	1.25	.70
2	Herb Pennock	.75	.35	.20
3	Al Simmons	.75	.35	.20
4	Hack Wilson	.75	.35	.20
5	Dizzy Dean	1.50	.70	.45
6	Chuck Klein	.75	.35	.20
7	Nellie Fox	.75	.40	.25
8	Lefty Grove	.75	.35	.20
9	George Sisler	.75	.35	.20
10	Lou Gehrig	3.50	1.75	1.00
11	Rube Waddell	.75	.35	.20
12	Max Carey	.75	.35	.20
13	Thurman Munson	2.00	1.00	.60
14	Mel Ott	.75	.35	.20
15	Doc White	.75	.35	.20
16	Babe Ruth	6.00	3.00	1.75
17	Schoolboy Rowe	.75	.35	.20
18	Jackie Robinson	3.50	1.75	1.00
19	Joe Medwick	.75	.35	.20
20	Casey Stengel	.75	.35	.20
21	Roberto Clemente	4.50	2.25	1.25
22	Christy Mathewson	1.50	.70	.45
23	Jimmie Foxx	1.25	.60	.40
24	Joe Jackson	6.00	3.00	1.75
25	Walter Johnson	1.50	.70	.45
26	Tony Lazzeri	.75	.35	.20
27	Hugh Casey	.75	.35	.20
28	Ty Cobb	3.50	1.75	1.00
29	Stuffy McInnis	.75	.35	.20
30	Cy Young	1.25	.60	.40
31	Lefty O'Doul	.75	.35	.20
32	Eddie Collins	.75	.35	.20
33	Joe McCarty	.75	.35	.20
34	Ed Walsh	.75	.35	.20
35	George Burns	.75	.35	.20
36	Walt Dropo	.75	.35	.20
37	Connie Mack	.75	.35	.20
38	Babe Adams	.75	.35	.20
39	Rogers Hornsby	1.00	.50	.30
40	Grover C. Alexander	.75	.35	.20

1980 Laughlin 300/400/500

This unusual set features a combination of the line drawings of R.G. Laughlin and a photo head shot of the player depicted. The cards are actually square, 3-1/4" x 3-1/4", with a background in color depicting a baseball diamond. The set is based on 300 wins, batting .400 or better and 500 homers, with a total of 30 cards in the blank backed set. The cards are numbered on the front.

		NM	EX	VG
Complete Set (30):		25.00	12.50	7.50
Common Player:		1.50	.75	.45
1	Header Card	1.50	.75	.45
2	Babe Ruth	10.00	5.00	3.00
3	Walter Johnson	3.00	1.50	.90
4	Ty Cobb	6.00	3.00	1.75
5	Christy Mathewson	3.00	1.50	.90
6	Ted Williams	4.00	2.00	1.25
7	Bill Terry	1.50	.75	.45
8	Grover C. Alexander	1.50	.75	.45
9	Napoleon Lajoie	1.50	.75	.45
10	Willie Mays	4.00	2.00	1.25
11	Cy Young	3.00	1.50	.90
12	Mel Ott	1.50	.75	.45
13	Joe Jackson	10.00	5.00	3.00
14	Harmon Killebrew	1.50	.75	.45
15	Warren Spahn	1.50	.75	.45
16	Hank Aaron	4.00	2.00	1.25
17	Rogers Hornsby	1.50	.75	.45
18	Mickey Mantle	10.00	5.00	3.00
19	Lefty Grove	1.50	.75	.45
20	Ted Williams	4.00	2.00	1.25
21	Jimmie Fox	1.50	.75	.45
22	Eddie Plank	1.50	.75	.45
23	Frank Robinson	1.50	.75	.45
24	George Sisler	1.50	.75	.45
25	Eddie Mathews	1.50	.75	.45
26	Early Wynn	1.50	.75	.45
27	Ernie Banks	1.50	.75	.45
28	Harry Heilmann	1.50	.75	.45
29	Lou Gehrig	7.50	3.75	2.25
30	Willie McCovey	1.50	.75	.45

1929 Leader Novelty Candy Co.

Though unmarked as such, these cards are believed to have been an insert in boxes of Leader Novelty Candy, or at least were so advertised in the famous Copeland Collection auction of 1991. They are one of two "mini" versions of the R316 Kashin Publications cards (see also W553), though it is not known whether the entire 101-card Kashin set was so paralleled. While sizes seem to vary significantly, nominal measurements for this version are about 1-3/4" x 2-5/8". Cards have been seen in duotones of red, sepia, purple and green. They are unnumbered and blank-backed. This checklist is known to be incomplete. Gaps have been left in the assigned numbering to accommodate additions.

		NM	EX	VG
Common Player:		75.00	37.50	22.50
(7)	Lucerne A. Blue	75.00	37.00	22.00
(8)	James Bottomley	150.00	75.00	45.00
(13)	Earl (Earle) Combs	150.00	75.00	45.00
(26)	Jimmy Foxx	250.00	125.00	75.00
(27)	Frank Frisch	150.00	75.00	45.00
(33)	Robert Grove	175.00	87.00	52.00
(42)	Rogers Hornsby	200.00	100.00	60.00
(45)	Sam Jones	75.00	37.50	22.50
(50)	Joseph Judge	75.00	37.50	22.50
(52)	Charles Klein	150.00	75.00	45.00
(62)	Walter Maranville	150.00	75.00	45.00
(65)	Ed "Bing" Miller	75.00	37.00	22.00
(66)	Frank O'Doul	100.00	50.00	30.00
(67)	Melvin Ott	175.00	87.00	52.00
(74)	Eddie Rommel	75.00	37.00	22.00
(85)	Al Simmons	150.00	75.00	45.00
(92)	Harold J. Traynor	150.00	75.00	45.00
(93)	Dazzy Vance	150.00	75.00	45.00
(95)	Paul Waner	150.00	75.00	45.00
(100)	Hack Wilson	175.00	87.00	52.00

1922 Leader Theatre

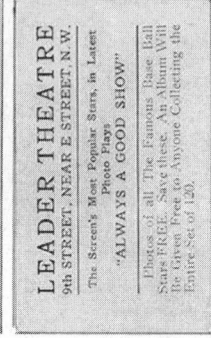

VAL PICINICH
CATCHER, WASHINGTON AMERICANS

This issue by a Washington, D.C. moviehouse is a version of the W573 and W575-1 strip card sets on which at least two forms of customized advertising were printed on the card backs. The ads state that 120 cards (paralleling W573 and/or W575-1) were originally issued in this version. An album was also offered.

	NM	EX	VG
Common Player:	500.00	225.00	150.00

(See 1922 W573 and W575-1 for checklists and base card values. Add 5X premium for non-commons.)

1949 Leaf

76---TED (The Kid) WILLIAMS

Right Fielder—Boston Red Sox
Age—31   Bats—left handed
Ht.—6'   Throws—right handed
Wgt.—190 lbs. Home—San Diego, Calif.

One of the greatest hitters of all time. Won 4th American league batting title in 1948 with .369 mark. Captured other swat crowns in 1941 (.406); 1942 (.356) and 1947 (.343). Hit 25 home runs last year. In 1946 won home run. championship with 38 round toppers. Has all-time batting average of .351.

ALL-STAR BASEBALL GUM

Collect this series of Diamond Greats

You'll be proud to show your gorgeous collection of baseball cards in beautiful, nautrally-colored. All-Star Album. Get it for only 3 Baseball Wrappers and 3c. Smashing color story. Learn all 3 big news black pages. You display 145 different Baseball cards.

Send Wrappers and Coin to
LEAF GUM CO., Box 5967 CHICAGO 80, ILL.

TED WILLIAMS

The first color baseball cards of the post-World War II era were the 98-card, 2-3/8" x 2-7/8", set produced by Chicago's Leaf Gum Co. for issue in 1949. One of the toughest postwar sets to complete, exactly half of the issue - 49 cards - are significantly harder to find than the others. Probably intended to confound bubblegum buyers of the day, the set is skip-numbered between 1-168. Card backs contain offers of felt pennants, an album for the cards or 5-1/2" x 7-1/2" premium photos of Hall of Famers. While some cards carry a 1948 copyright date on back, it is now believed the issue was not released until 1949. The complete set price does not include the higher value in the variation pairs.

		NM	EX	VG
Complete Set (98):		85,000	35,000	17,500
Common Player:		125.00	45.00	22.50
Common Short-print:		900.00	360.00	180.00
Album:		900.00	450.00	275.00
1	Joe DiMaggio	3,000	725.00	400.00
3	Babe Ruth	3,300	1,650	1,000
4	Stan Musial	1,700	850.00	510.00
5	Virgil Trucks (SP)	1,150	460.00	230.00
8	Satchel Paige (SP)	17,500	7,000	3,500
10	Paul Trout	125.00	45.00	22.50
11	Phil Rizzuto	325.00	130.00	65.00
13	Casimer Michaels (SP)	900.00	360.00	180.00
14	Billy Johnson	125.00	45.00	22.50
17	Frank Overmire	125.00	45.00	22.50
19	John Wyrostek (SP)	900.00	360.00	180.00
20	Hank Sauer (SP)	1,000	400.00	200.00
22	Al Evans	125.00	45.00	22.50
26	Sam Chapman	125.00	45.00	22.50
27	Mickey Harris	125.00	45.00	22.50
28	Jim Hegan	125.00	45.00	22.50
29	Elmer Valo	125.00	45.00	22.50
30	Bill Goodman (SP)	900.00	360.00	180.00
31	Lou Brissie	125.00	45.00	22.50
32	Warren Spahn	450.00	180.00	90.00
33	Harry Lowrey (SP)	900.00	360.00	180.00
36	Al Zarilla (SP)	900.00	360.00	180.00
38	Ted Kluszewski (SP)	300.00	120.00	60.00
39	Ewell Blackwell	130.00	50.00	25.00
42a	Kent Peterson (Red cap.)	1,100	440.00	220.00
42b	Kent Peterson (Black cap.)	125.00	45.00	22.50
43	Eddie Stevens (SP)	900.00	360.00	180.00
45	Ken Keltner (SP)	900.00	360.00	180.00
46	Johnny Mize	300.00	120.00	60.00
47	George Vico	125.00	45.00	22.50
48	Johnny Schmitz (SP)	900.00	360.00	180.00
49	Del Ennis	130.00	50.00	25.00
50	Dick Wakefield	125.00	45.00	22.50
51	Alvin Dark (SP)	1,750	700.00	350.00
53	John Vandermeer (Vander Meer)	225.00	90.00	45.00
54	Bobby Adams (SP)	900.00	360.00	180.00
55	Tommy Henrich (SP)	2,000	800.00	400.00
56	Larry Jensen	130.00	50.00	25.00
57	Bob McCall	125.00	45.00	22.50
59	Luke Appling	200.00	80.00	40.00
61	Jake Early	125.00	45.00	22.50
62	Eddie Joost (SP)	900.00	360.00	180.00
63	Barney McCosky (SP)	900.00	360.00	180.00

65	Bob Elliot (Elliott)	125.00	45.00	22.50
66	Orval Grove (SP)	900.00	360.00	180.00
68	Ed Miller (SP)	900.00	360.00	180.00
70	Honus Wagner	500.00	200.00	100.00
72	Hank Edwards	125.00	45.00	22.50
73	Pat Seerey	125.00	45.00	22.50
75	Dom DiMaggio (SP)	1,400	560.00	280.00
76	Ted Williams	2,600	1,300	780.00
77	Roy Smalley	125.00	45.00	22.50
78	Walter Evers (SP)	900.00	360.00	180.00
79	Jackie Robinson	1,800	550.00	325.00
81	George Kurowski (SP)	900.00	360.00	180.00
82	Johnny Lindell	125.00	45.00	22.50
83	Bobby Doerr	225.00	90.00	45.00
84	Sid Hudson	125.00	45.00	22.50
85	Dave Philley (SP)	900.00	360.00	180.00
86	Ralph Weigel	125.00	45.00	22.50
88	Frank Gustine (SP)	900.00	360.00	180.00
91	Ralph Kiner	175.00	70.00	35.00
93	Bob Feller (SP)	3,250	1,300	650.00
95	George Stirnweiss	125.00	45.00	22.50
97	Martin Marion	150.00	60.00	30.00
98	Hal Newhouser (SP)	1,800	725.00	360.00
102a	Gene Hermansk (Incorrect spelling.)	2,750	1,100	550.00
102b	Gene Hermanski (Correct spelling.)	135.00	55.00	25.00
104	Edward Stewart (SP)	900.00	360.00	180.00
106	Lou Boudreau	200.00	80.00	40.00
108	Matthew Batts (SP)	900.00	360.00	180.00
111	Gerald Priddy	125.00	45.00	22.50
113	Emil Leonard (SP)	900.00	360.00	180.00
117	Joe Gordon	125.00	45.00	22.50
120	George Kell (SP)	1,100	440.00	220.00
121	John Pesky (SP)	1,000	400.00	200.00
123	Clifford Fannin (SP)	900.00	360.00	180.00
125	Andy Pafko (SP)	160.00	65.00	30.00
127	Enos Slaughter (SP)	1,750	700.00	350.00
128	Warren Rosar	125.00	45.00	22.50
129	Kirby Higbe (SP)	900.00	360.00	180.00
131	Sid Gordon (SP)	900.00	360.00	180.00
133	Tommy Holmes (SP)	1,000	400.00	200.00
136a	Cliff Aberson (Full sleeve.)	125.00	50.00	25.00
136b	Cliff Aberson (Short sleeve.)	175.00	70.00	35.00
137	Harry Walker (SP)	900.00	360.00	180.00
138	Larry Doby (SP)	3,000	1,200	600.00
139	Johnny Hopp	125.00	45.00	22.50
142	Danny Murtaugh (SP)	1,000	400.00	200.00
143	Dick Sisler (SP)	900.00	360.00	180.00
144	Bob Dillinger (SP)	900.00	360.00	180.00
146	Harold Reiser (SP)	1,000	400.00	200.00
149	Henry Majeski (SP)	900.00	360.00	180.00
153	Floyd Baker (SP)	900.00	360.00	180.00
158	Harry Brecheen (SP)	900.00	360.00	180.00
159	Mizell Platt	125.00	45.00	22.50
160	Bob Scheffing (SP)	900.00	360.00	180.00
161	Vernon Stephens (SP)	1,000	400.00	200.00
163	Freddy Hutchinson (SP)	1,000	400.00	200.00
165	Dale Mitchell (SP)	1,000	400.00	200.00
168	Phil Cavaretta (SP)	900.00	360.00	180.00

1949 Leaf Premiums

These blank-back, sepia photos were available with the purchase of 1948 Leaf baseball cards. Measuring 5-5/8" x 7-1/4", the pictures have a facsimile autograph and a black box labeled "BASEBALL'S IMMORTALS" at bottom containing a short biography. The unnumbered pictures are checklisted alphabetically.

		NM	EX	VG
Complete Set (9):		6,000	3,000	1,800
Common Player:		400.00	200.00	120.00
(1)	Grover Alexander	450.00	225.00	135.00
(2)	Mickey Cochrane	400.00	200.00	120.00
(3)	Lou Gehrig	1,200	600.00	360.00
(4)	Walter Johnson	450.00	225.00	135.00
(5)	Christy Mathewson	525.00	260.00	155.00
(6)	John McGraw	400.00	200.00	120.00
(7)	Babe Ruth (Dark background, text boxes.)	1,200	600.00	360.00
(8)	Babe Ruth (Light background, no text.)	1,200	600.00	360.00
(9)	Ed Walsh	400.00	200.00	120.00

1960 Leaf Pre-Production

Evidently produced prior to final approval for the design of the 1960 Leaf set, these cards all feature much larger player photos than the issued versions. Generally the issued cards have cap-to-waist photos while the pre-production cards have to cap-to-chin shots. Backs of the pre-production cards are virtually identical to the regular cards. The pre-production cards were never publically issued and show evidence of having been hand-cut. The cards of Donovan and Jay appear to be more common than the others.

LUIS APARICIO
SHORTSTOP—CHICAGO WHITE SOX

	NM	EX	VG
Complete Set (8):	15,000	7,500	4,500
Common Player:	1,500	750.00	450.00
1 Luis Aparicio	4,500	2,250	1,350
12 Ken Boyer	2,150	1,075	645.00
17 Walt Moryn	1,250	625.00	375.00
23 Joey Jay	1,250	625.00	375.00
35 Jim Coates	2,250	1,125	675.00
58 Hal Smith	1,950	975.00	585.00
61 Vic Rehm	1,500	750.00	450.00
72 Dick Donovan	1,250	625.00	375.00

1960 Leaf

LUIS ERNESTO APARICIO, Jr.
SHORTSTOP—CHICAGO WHITE SOX

LUIS APARICIO
SHORTSTOP—CHICAGO WHITE SOX

While known to the hobby as "Leaf" cards, this set of 144 carries the copyright of Sports Novelties Inc., Chicago. The 2-1/2" x 3-1/2" cards feature black-and-white player portrait photos, with plain background. Cards were sold in nickel wax packs with a marble, rather than a piece of bubble gum. The second half of the set, #73-144, are quite scarce. Card #25, Jim Grant, is found in two versions, with his own picture (black cap) and with a photo of Brooks Lawrence (white cap). Three back variations of Hal Smith card #58 are also known. Complete set prices do not include variations. In the late 1990s, a large group of high-number (Series 2) boxes - in excess of 4,000 cards - was added to the surviving supply.

		NM	EX	VG
Complete Set (144):		2,000	1,000	500.00
Common Player (1-72):		9.00	4.50	2.75
Common Player (73-144):		12.00	6.00	3.50
Wax Pack, Series 1 (5):		120.00		
Wax Box, Series 1 (24):		2,400		
Wax Pack, Series 2 (5):		190.00		
Wax Box, Series 2 (24):		3,250		
1	Luis Aparicio	55.00	15.00	9.00
2	Woody Held	9.00	4.50	2.75
3	Frank Lary	9.00	4.50	2.75
4	Camilo Pascual	9.00	4.50	2.75
5	Frank Herrera	9.00	4.50	2.75
6	Felipe Alou	8.00	4.00	2.50
7	Bennie Daniels	9.00	4.50	2.75
8	Roger Craig	9.00	4.50	2.75
9	Eddie Kasko	9.00	4.50	2.75
10	Bob Grim	9.00	4.50	2.75
11	Jim Busby	9.00	4.50	2.75
12	Ken Boyer	17.50	8.75	5.25
13	Bob Boyd	9.00	4.50	2.75
14	Sam Jones	9.00	4.50	2.75
15	Larry Jackson	9.00	4.50	2.75
16	Roy Face	9.00	4.50	2.75
17	Walt Moryn	9.00	4.50	2.75
18	Jim Gilliam	8.00	4.00	2.50
19	Don Newcombe	8.00	4.00	2.50
20	Glen Hobbie	9.00	4.50	2.75
21	Pedro Ramos	9.00	4.50	2.75
22	Ryne Duren	8.00	4.00	2.50
23	Joe Jay	9.00	4.50	2.75
24	Lou Berberet	9.00	4.50	2.75
25a	Jim Grant (White cap, photo actually Brooks Lawrence.)	15.00	7.50	4.50
25b	Jim Grant (Dark cap, correct photo.)	22.50	11.00	6.75
26	Tom Borland	9.00	4.50	2.75
27	Brooks Robinson	25.00	12.50	7.50
28	Jerry Adair	9.00	4.50	2.75
29	Ron Jackson	9.00	4.50	2.75
30	George Strickland	9.00	4.50	2.75
31	Rocky Bridges	9.00	4.50	2.75
32	Bill Tuttle	9.00	4.50	2.75
33	Ken Hunt	9.00	4.50	2.75
34	Hal Griggs	9.00	4.50	2.75
35	Jim Coates	9.00	4.50	2.75
36	Brooks Lawrence	9.00	4.50	2.75
37	Duke Snider	30.00	15.00	9.00
38	Al Spangler	9.00	4.50	2.75
39	Jim Owens	9.00	4.50	2.75

		NM	EX	VG
40	Bill Virdon	9.00	4.50	2.75
41	Ernie Broglio	9.00	4.50	2.75
42	Andre Rodgers	9.00	4.50	2.75
43	Julio Becquer	9.00	4.50	2.75
44	Tony Taylor	9.00	4.50	2.75
45	Jerry Lynch	9.00	4.50	2.75
46	Clete Boyer	8.00	4.00	2.50
47	Jerry Lumpe	9.00	4.50	2.75
48	Charlie Maxwell	9.00	4.50	2.75
49	Jim Perry	9.00	4.50	2.75
50	Danny McDevitt	9.00	4.50	2.75
51	Juan Pizarro	9.00	4.50	2.75
52	*Dallas Green*	20.00	10.00	6.00
53	Bob Friend	9.00	4.50	2.75
54	Jack Sanford	9.00	4.50	2.75
55	Jim Rivera	9.00	4.50	2.75
56	Ted Wills	9.00	4.50	2.75
57	Milt Pappas	9.00	4.50	2.75
58a	Hal Smith (Team & position on back.)	9.00	4.50	2.75
58b	Hal Smith (Team blackened out on back.)	750.00	375.00	225.00
58c	Hal Smith (Team missing on back.)	75.00	37.50	22.50
59	Bob Avila	9.00	4.50	2.75
60	Clem Labine	9.00	4.50	2.75
61	Vic Rehm	9.00	4.50	2.75
62	John Gabler	9.00	4.50	2.75
63	John Tsitouris	9.00	4.50	2.75
64	Dave Sisler	9.00	4.50	2.75
65	Vic Power	9.00	4.50	2.75
66	Earl Battey	9.00	4.50	2.75
67	Bob Purkey	9.00	4.50	2.75
68	Moe Drabowsky	9.00	4.50	2.75
69	Hoyt Wilhelm	15.00	7.50	4.50
70	Humberto Robinson	9.00	4.50	2.75
71	Whitey Herzog	9.00	4.50	2.75
72	Dick Donovan	9.00	4.50	2.75
73	Gordon Jones	12.00	6.00	3.50
74	Joe Hicks	12.00	6.00	3.50
75	*Ray Culp*	12.00	6.00	3.50
76	Dick Drott	12.00	6.00	3.50
77	Bob Duliba	12.00	6.00	3.50
78	Art Ditmar	12.00	6.00	3.50
79	Steve Korcheck	12.00	6.00	3.50
80	Henry Mason	12.00	6.00	3.50
81	Harry Simpson	12.00	6.00	3.50
82	Gene Green	12.00	6.00	3.50
83	Bob Shaw	12.00	6.00	3.50
84	Howard Reed	12.00	6.00	3.50
85	Dick Stigman	12.00	6.00	3.50
86	Rip Repulski	12.00	6.00	3.50
87	Seth Morehead	12.00	6.00	3.50
88	Camilo Carreon	12.00	6.00	3.50
89	John Blanchard	17.50	8.75	5.25
90	Billy Hoeft	12.00	6.00	3.50
91	Fred Hopke	12.00	6.00	3.50
92	Joe Martin	12.00	6.00	3.50
93	Wally Shannon	12.00	6.00	3.50
94	Baseball's Two Hal Smiths	50.00	25.00	15.00
95	Al Schroll	12.00	6.00	3.50
96	John Kucks	12.00	6.00	3.50
97	Tom Morgan	12.00	6.00	3.50
98	Willie Jones	12.00	6.00	3.50
99	Marshall Renfroe	12.00	6.00	3.50
100	Willie Tasby	12.00	6.00	3.50
101	Irv Noren	12.00	6.00	3.50
102	Russ Snyder	12.00	6.00	3.50
103	Bob Turley	17.50	8.75	5.25
104	Jim Woods	12.00	6.00	3.50
105	Ronnie Kline	12.00	6.00	3.50
106	Steve Bilko	12.00	6.00	3.50
107	Elmer Valo	12.00	6.00	3.50
108	Tom McAvoy	12.00	6.00	3.50
109	Stan Williams	12.00	6.00	3.50
110	Earl Averill	12.00	6.00	3.50
111	Lee Walls	12.00	6.00	3.50
112	Paul Richards	12.00	6.00	3.50
113	Ed Sadowski	12.00	6.00	3.50
114	Stover McIlwain (Photo actually Jim McAnany.)	17.50	8.75	5.25
115	Chuck Tanner (Photo actually Ken Kuhn.)	17.50	8.75	5.25
116	Lou Klimchock	12.00	6.00	3.50
117	Neil Chrisley	12.00	6.00	3.50
118	Johnny Callison	12.00	6.00	3.50
119	Hal Smith	12.00	6.00	3.50
120	Carl Sawatski	12.00	6.00	3.50
121	Frank Leja	12.00	6.00	3.50
122	Earl Torgeson	12.00	6.00	3.50
123	Art Schult	12.00	6.00	3.50
124	Jim Brosnan	12.00	6.00	3.50
125	Sparky Anderson	60.00	30.00	18.00
126	Joe Pignatano	12.00	6.00	3.50
127	Rocky Nelson	12.00	6.00	3.50
128	Orlando Cepeda	45.00	22.50	13.50
129	Daryl Spencer	12.00	6.00	3.50
130	Ralph Lumenti	12.00	6.00	3.50
131	Sam Taylor	12.00	6.00	3.50
132	Harry Brecheen	12.00	6.00	3.50
133	Johnny Groth	12.00	6.00	3.50
134	Wayne Terwilliger	12.00	6.00	3.50
135	Kent Hadley	12.00	6.00	3.50
136	Faye Throneberry	12.00	6.00	3.50
137	Jack Meyer	12.00	6.00	3.50
138	*Chuck Cottier*	12.00	6.00	3.50
139	Joe DeMaestri	12.00	6.00	3.50
140	Gene Freese	12.00	6.00	3.50
141	Curt Flood	30.00	15.00	9.00
142	Gino Cimoli	12.00	6.00	3.50
143	Clay Dalrymple	12.00	6.00	3.50
144	Jim Bunning	50.00	25.00	15.00

1923 Lections

This series of cards was virtually unknown in the hobby until 1997 when 28 cards turned up in Albany, N.Y. The cards measure about 4" x 2-1/2" with rounded corners and are

EMIL MEUSEL
New York Giants

printed on very thick cardboard. At left front is an oval black-and-white player photo with name and team below. At right is green or orange art of a baseball game with the issuer's logo and trademark information. It is unknown with what, if any, product these cards were issued; a candy premium seems the most likely source. Most of the cards seen so far are in grades from Fair-Good, though a few are known in Ex-Mt.

		NM	EX	VG
Complete Set (10):		30,000	15,000	9,000
Common Player:		2,000	1,000	600.00
(1)	Frank Chance	3,500	1,750	1,050
(2)	Howard Ehmke	2,000	1,000	600.00
(3)	Frank Frisch	3,500	1,750	1,050
(4)	Roger (Rogers) Hornsby	5,000	2,500	1,500
(5)	Charles Jamieson	2,000	1,000	600.00
(6)	"Bob" Meusel	2,000	1,000	600.00
(7)	Emil Meusel	2,000	1,000	600.00
(8)	"Babe" Ruth	9,000	4,500	2,700
(9)	Charles Schmidt	2,000	1,000	600.00
(10)	"Bob" Shawkey	2,000	1,000	600.00

1975 Lee's Sweets

Professing to be an issue of 68 cards of "Baseball Greats," this collectors' issue first appeared about 1975. Only four players are known. Fronts of the 2-1/2" x 3-3/16" cards have crudely printed black-and-white player photos. Backs describe the series and give the Lee's Sweets address as Camp Hill, Ala.

		NM	EX	VG
Complete Set (4):		25.00	12.50	7.50
Common Player:		6.00	3.00	1.75
(1)	Ty Cobb	6.00	3.00	1.75
(2)	Joe DiMaggio	6.00	3.00	1.75
(3)	Lou Gehrig	6.00	3.00	1.75
(4)	Babe Ruth	12.00	6.00	3.50

1909-11 Lenox Cigarettes

Many collectors rank the Lenox back as the third rarest among T206, behind only Ty Cobb and Drum. Lenox cards can be found with the back printing in either black or brown.

PREMIUMS
Black, Common Players: 12-15X
Black, Hall of Famers: 8-10X
Brown, Common Players: 75-100X
Brown, Hall of Famers: 40-60X
    (See T206 for checklist and base card values.)

1969 Lincoln-Mercury Sports Panel Postcards

Various celebrity spokesmen on the Lincoln-Mercury Sports Panel can be found on a series of color postcards. In standard 5-1/2" x 3-1/2" format, cards have borderless color

photos on front of the spokesman standing with one of the company's new cars; a facsimile autograph also appears. Divided backs identify the player and the automobile.

	NM	EX	VG
Al Kaline	80.00	40.00	25.00

1906 Lincoln Publishing Philadelphia A's

Members of the American League Champions (says so right at the top) Philadelphia A's, decked out in their Sunday-best, are featured in this set of black-and-white postcards. The portraits are framed in fancy graphics which include a baseball, the dates 1905 and 1906 and the player's name in a banner beneath the photo. At bottom is a box with "ATHLETIC BASE BALL TEAM." Back of the approximately 3-1/2" x 5-1/2" cards has a box at upper-left enclosing "POST CARD." The unnumbered cards are listed here alphabetically.

		NM	EX	VG
Complete Set (20):		10,000	5,000	3,000
Common Player:		300.00	150.00	90.00
(1)	Chief Bender	1,500	750.00	450.00
(2)	Andy Coakley	300.00	150.00	90.00
(3)	Lave Cross	300.00	150.00	90.00
(4)	Monte Cross	300.00	150.00	90.00
(5)	Harry Davis	300.00	150.00	90.00
(6)	Jimmy Dygert	300.00	150.00	90.00
(7)	Topsy Hartsel	300.00	150.00	90.00
(8)	Weldon Henley	300.00	150.00	90.00
(9)	Danny Hoffman	300.00	150.00	90.00
(10)	John Knight	300.00	150.00	90.00
(11)	Bris Lord	300.00	150.00	90.00
(12)	Connie Mack	1,500	750.00	450.00
(13)	Danny Murphy	300.00	150.00	90.00
(14)	Joe Myers	300.00	150.00	90.00
(15)	Rube Oldring	300.00	150.00	90.00
(16)	Eddie Plank	2,000	1,000	600.00
(17)	Mike Powers	300.00	150.00	90.00
(18)	Ossee Schreckengost	300.00	150.00	90.00
(19)	Ralph Seybold	300.00	150.00	90.00
(20)	Rube Waddell	1,500	750.00	450.00

1975 Linnett MLB All-Stars

This series of pencil-portrait prints was done by sports artist Charles Linnett of Walpole, Mass. The black-and-white prints are on 8-1/2" x 11" textured paper, featuring a facsimile autograph of the player. Because the portraits are licensed only by the Players Association, the players are pictured capless with no uniform logos visible. Backs are blank. The 1975 pictures differ from the 1976 issue in that they include a printed player name, besides the facsimile autograph. At least some of the portraits were given away in a ballpark "Portrait Day" promotion at Fenway Park, sponsored by Grant City (W.T. Grant Co.) department stores. A coupon accompanying the SGA portraits offered a discount on a package of three pictures, apparently the standard retail offering that carried a $1.19 price tag. This rudimentary checklist is certainly incomplete.

		NM	EX	VG
Common Player:		6.00	3.00	1.75
(25)	Fred Lynn	9.00	4.50	2.75
(50)	Tom Seaver	9.00	4.50	2.75
(75)	Carl Yastrzemski	12.00	6.00	3.50

1976 Linnett Portraits

This series of pencil-portrait prints was done by sports artist Charles Linnett of Walpole, Mass., and includes baseball, football, hockey, NBA and Harlem Globetrotters players (only baseball listed here). The black-and-white prints are on 8-1/2" x 11" textured paper, featuring a facsimile autograph of the player. Because the portraits are licensed only by the Players Association, the players are pictured capless with no uniform logos visible. Backs are blank. The portraits originally sold for 50 cents apiece by mail.

		NM	EX	VG
Complete Baseball Set (176):		300.00	150.00	90.00
Common Player:		2.50	1.25	.75
(1)	Hank Aaron	10.00	5.00	3.00
(2)	Dick Allen	4.00	2.00	1.25
(3)	Matty Alou	2.50	1.25	.75
(4)	Mike Anderson	2.50	1.25	.75
(5)	Luis Aparicio	5.00	2.50	1.50
(6)	Sal Bando	2.50	1.25	.75
(7)	Mark Belanger	2.50	1.25	.70
(8)	Buddy Bell	2.50	1.25	.75
(9)	Johnny Bench	6.00	3.00	1.75
(10)	Jim Bibby	2.50	1.25	.75
(11)	Paul Blair	2.50	1.25	.75
(12)	Bert Blyleven	3.00	1.50	.90
(13)	Ron Blomberg	2.50	1.25	.75
(14)	Bob Bolin	2.50	1.25	.75
(15)	Bill Bonham	2.50	1.25	.75
(16)	Pedro Borbon	2.50	1.25	.75
(17)	Bob Boone	3.00	1.50	.90
(18)	Larry Bowa	2.50	1.25	.75
(19)	Steve Braun	2.50	1.25	.75
(20)	Ken Brett	2.50	1.25	.75
(21)	John Briggs	2.50	1.25	.75
(22)	Lou Brock	5.00	2.50	1.50
(23)	Jack Brohamer	2.50	1.25	.75
(24)	Steve Brye	2.50	1.25	.75
(25)	Bill Buckner	2.50	1.25	.70
(26)	Jeff Burroughs	2.50	1.25	.75
(27)	Steve Busby	2.50	1.25	.75
(28)	Bert Campaneris	2.50	1.25	.75
(29)	Bernie Carbo	2.50	1.25	.75
(30)	Jose Cardenal	2.50	1.25	.75
(31)	Steve Carlton	5.00	2.50	1.50
(32)	Rod Carew	5.00	2.50	1.50
(33)	Dave Cash	2.50	1.25	.75
(34)	Norm Cash	3.00	1.50	.90
(35)	Danny Cater	2.50	1.25	.75
(36)	Cesar Cedeno	2.50	1.25	.75
(37)	Orlando Cepeda	5.00	2.50	1.50
(38)	Ron Cey	2.50	1.25	.70
(39)	Chris Chambliss	2.50	1.25	.75
(40)	David Clyde	2.50	1.25	.75
(41)	Rich Coggins	2.50	1.25	.75
(42)	Jim Colborn	2.50	1.25	.75
(43)	Dave Concepcion	3.00	1.50	.90
(44)	Willie Crawford	2.50	1.25	.75
(45)	John Curtis	2.50	1.25	.75
(46)	Bobby Darwin	2.50	1.25	.75
(47)	Dan Driessen	2.50	1.25	.75
(48)	Duffy Dyer	2.50	1.25	.75
(49)	John Ellis	2.50	1.25	.75
(50)	Darrell Evans	2.50	1.25	.70
(51)	Dwight Evans	2.50	1.25	.75
(52)	Joe Ferguson	2.50	1.25	.75
(53)	Rollie Fingers	4.00	2.00	1.25
(54)	Carlton Fisk	5.00	2.50	1.50
(55)	Bill Freehan	2.50	1.25	.70
(56)	Jim Fregosi	2.50	1.25	.75
(57)	Oscar Gamble	2.50	1.25	.75
(58)	Pedro Garcia	2.50	1.25	.75
(59)	Ralph Garr	2.50	1.25	.75
(60)	Wayne Garrett	2.50	1.25	.75
(61)	Steve Garvey	2.50	1.25	.70
(62)	Cesar Geronimo	2.50	1.25	.75
(63)	Bob Gibson	5.00	2.50	1.50
(64)	Dave Giusti	2.50	1.25	.75
(65)	Bobby Grich	2.50	1.25	.75
(66)	Doug Griffin	2.50	1.25	.75
(67)	Mario Guerrero	2.50	1.25	.75
(68)	Don Gullett	2.50	1.25	.75
(69)	Tommy Harper	2.50	1.25	.75
(70)	Toby Harrah	2.50	1.25	.75
(71)	Bud Harrelson	2.50	1.25	.75
(72)	Vic Harris	2.50	1.25	.75
(73)	Richie Hebner	2.50	1.25	.75
(74)	George Hendrick	2.50	1.25	.75
(75)	Ed Hermann	2.50	1.25	.75
(76)	John Hiller	2.50	1.25	.75
(77)	Willie Horton	2.50	1.25	.75
(78)	Jim Hunter	4.00	2.00	1.25
(79)	Tommy Hutton	2.50	1.25	.75
(80)	Reggie Jackson	7.50	3.75	2.25
(81)	Fergie Jenkins	4.00	2.00	1.25
(82)	Dave Johnson	2.50	1.25	.75
(83)	Cleon Jones	2.50	1.25	.75
(84)	Al Kaline	6.00	3.00	1.75
(85)	John Kennedy	2.50	1.25	.75
(86)	Steve Kline	2.50	1.25	.75
(87)	Jerry Koosman	2.50	1.25	.75
(88)	Bill Lee	2.50	1.25	.75
(89)	Eddie Leon	2.50	1.25	.75
(90)	Bob Locker	2.50	1.25	.75
(91)	Mickey Lolich	3.00	1.50	.90
(92)	Jim Lonborg	2.50	1.25	.75
(93)	Davey Lopes	2.50	1.25	.75
(94)	Mike Lum	2.50	1.25	.75
(95)	Greg Luzinski	2.50	1.25	.75
(96)	Sparky Lyle	2.50	1.25	.75
(97)	Teddy Martinez	2.50	1.25	.75
(98)	Jon Matlack	2.50	1.25	.75
(99)	Dave May	2.50	1.25	.75
(100)	John Mayberry	2.50	1.25	.75
(101)	Willie Mays	10.00	5.00	3.00
(102)	Jim McAndrew	2.50	1.25	.75
(103)	Dick McAuliffe	2.50	1.25	.75
(104)	Sam McDowell	2.50	1.25	.70
(105)	Lynn McGlothen	2.50	1.25	.70
(106)	Tug McGraw	2.50	1.25	.75
(107)	Hal McRae	2.50	1.25	.75
(108)	Bill Melton	2.50	1.25	.75
(109)	Andy Messersmith	2.50	1.25	.75
(110)	Gene Michael	2.50	1.25	.75
(111)	Felix Millan	2.50	1.25	.75
(112)	Rick Miller	2.50	1.25	.75
(113)	John Milner	2.50	1.25	.75
(114)	Rick Monday	2.50	1.25	.75
(115)	Don Money	2.50	1.25	.75
(116)	Bob Montgomery	2.50	1.25	.75
(117)	Joe Morgan	5.00	2.50	1.50
(118)	Carl Morton	2.50	1.25	.75
(119)	Thurman Munson	4.00	2.00	1.25
(120)	Bobby Murcer	2.50	1.25	.75
(121)	Graig Nettles	3.00	1.50	.90
(122)	Jim Northrup	2.50	1.25	.75
(123)	Ben Oglivie	2.50	1.25	.75
(124)	Al Oliver	3.00	1.50	.90
(125)	Bob Oliver	2.50	1.25	.75
(126)	Jorge Orta	2.50	1.25	.75
(127)	Amos Otis	2.50	1.25	.75
(128)	Jim Palmer	5.00	2.50	1.50
(129)	Harry Parker	2.50	1.25	.75
(130)	Fred Patek	2.50	1.25	.75
(131)	Marty Pattin	2.50	1.25	.75
(132)	Tony Perez	4.00	2.00	1.25
(133)	Gaylord Perry	4.00	2.00	1.25
(134)	Jim Perry	2.50	1.25	.75
(135)	Rico Petrocelli	2.50	1.25	.75
(136)	Rick Reichardt	2.50	1.25	.75
(137)	Ken Reitz	2.50	1.25	.75
(138)	Jerry Reuss	2.50	1.25	.75
(139)	Bill Robinson	2.50	1.25	.75
(140)	Brooks Robinson	5.00	2.50	1.50
(141)	Frank Robinson	5.00	2.50	1.50
(142)	Cookie Rojas	2.50	1.25	.75
(143)	Pete Rose	9.00	4.50	2.75
(144)	Bill Russell	2.50	1.25	.75
(145)	Nolan Ryan	15.00	7.50	4.50
(146)	Manny Sanguillen	2.50	1.25	.75
(147)	George Scott	2.50	1.25	.75
(148)	Mike Schmidt	7.50	3.75	2.25
(149)	Tom Seaver	6.00	3.00	1.75
(150)	Sonny Siebert	2.50	1.25	.75
(151)	Ted Simmons	2.50	1.25	.75
(152)	Bill Singer	2.50	1.25	.75
(153)	Reggie Smith	2.50	1.25	.75
(154)	Chris Speier	2.50	1.25	.75
(155)	Charlie Spikes	2.50	1.25	.75
(156)	Paul Splittorff	2.50	1.25	.75
(157)	Mickey Stanley	2.50	1.25	.75
(158)	Lee Stanton	2.50	1.25	.75
(159)	Willie Stargell	5.00	2.50	1.50
(160)	Rusty Staub	3.00	1.50	.90
(161)	Rennie Stennett	2.50	1.25	.75
(162)	Steve Stone	3.00	1.50	.90
(163)	Mel Stottlemyre	2.50	1.25	.75
(164)	Don Sutton	4.00	2.00	1.25
(165)	George Theodore	2.50	1.25	.75
(166)	Danny Thompson	2.50	1.25	.75
(167)	Luis Tiant	3.00	1.50	.90
(168)	Joe Torre	3.50	1.75	1.00
(169)	Bobby Valentine	2.50	1.25	.75
(170)	Bob Veale	2.50	1.25	.75
(171)	Billy Williams	5.00	2.50	1.50
(172)	Wilbur Wood	2.50	1.25	.75
(173)	Jim Wynn	2.50	1.25	.75
(174)	Carl Yastrzemski	6.00	3.00	1.75
(175)	Robin Yount	5.00	2.50	1.50
(175)	Richie Zisk	2.50	1.25	.75

1976 Linnett Superstars

This infrequently encountered set of 36 cards has enjoyed little collector interest since its issue in 1976. Officially known as "Pee-Wee Superstars," the cards measure 4" x 5-5/8". Player

portraits by artist Charles Linnett are rendered in black-and-white pencil and set against a pale yellow background. Players are shown without caps or uniforms (most appear to be wearing white T-shirts). According to the logos at top the set was fully licensed by both the Players Association and Major League Baseball, and team logos do appear in the lower-left corner. A facsimile autograph in red or purple appears on each card. Front borders are bright purple, red, green, dark brown, or white. Card backs feature either a photo of an antique auto or a drawing of an historic sailing ship. Each of the 12 different back designs appears on one card from each team set. The Linnetts were sold in panels of six perforated cards. An offer on the back of each card makes 8" x 10" premium portraits of each player available for 95 cents. The premium pictures have about the same value as the cards. Inexplicably, the cards are numbered from 90-125. Only the World's Champion Cincinnati Reds, A.L. Champion Boston Red Sox and N.L. runner-up Dodgers are represented in the issue.

		NM	EX	VG
Complete Panel Set (6):		15.00	7.50	4.50
Complete Singles Set (36):		15.00	7.50	4.50
Common Player:		.60	.30	.20
Panel 1		7.50	3.75	2.25
90	Don Gullett	.60	.30	.20
91	Johnny Bench	2.50	1.25	.70
92	Tony Perez	1.25	.60	.40
93	Mike Lum	.60	.30	.20
94	Ken Griffey	.60	.30	.20
95	George Foster	.60	.30	.20
Panel 2		9.00	4.50	2.75
96	Joe Morgan	2.50	1.25	.70
97	Pete Rose	6.00	3.00	1.75
98	Dave Concepcion	.60	.30	.20
99	Cesar Geronimo	.60	.30	.20
100	Dan Driessen	.60	.30	.20
101	Pedro Borbon	.60	.30	.20
Panel 3		7.50	3.75	2.25
102	Carl Yastrzemski	2.50	1.25	.70
103	Fred Lynn	.60	.30	.20
104	Dwight Evans	.60	.30	.20
105	Ferguson Jenkins	1.25	.60	.40
106	Rico Petrocelli	.60	.30	.20
107	Denny Doyle	.60	.30	.20
Panel 4		6.00	3.00	1.75
108	Luis Tiant	.60	.30	.20
109	Carlton Fisk	2.50	1.25	.70
110	Rick Burleson	.60	.30	.20
111	Bill Lee	.60	.30	.20
112	Rick Wise	.60	.30	.20
113	Jim Rice	1.00	.50	.30
Panel 5		6.00	3.00	1.75
114	Davey Lopes	.60	.30	.20
115	Steve Garvey	1.25	.60	.40
116	Bill Russell	.60	.30	.20
117	Ron Cey	.60	.30	.20
118	Steve Yaeger	.60	.30	.20
119	Doug Rau	.60	.30	.20
Panel 6		6.00	3.00	1.75
120	Don Sutton	1.75	.90	.50
121	Joe Ferguson	.60	.30	.20
122	Mike Marshall	.60	.30	.20
123	Bill Buckner	.60	.30	.20
124	Rick Rhoden	.60	.30	.20
125	Ted Sizemore	.60	.30	.20

1923 Little Wonder Picture Series

Some versions of the W515-2 strip cards are found with part of a line of type in the top border that reads "THE LITTLE WONDER PICTURE SERIES" and includes a Underwood (U&U) logo.

(See W515-2.)

1887 Lone Jack St. Louis Browns (N370)

The Lone Jack set is among the rarest of all 19th Century tobacco issues. Issued by the Lone Jack Cigarette Co. of Lynchburg, Va., the set consists of 13 subjects, all members of the American Association champion St. Louis Browns. Photos for the set are enlarged versions of those used in the more popular N172 Old Judge series. Cards in the set measure 2-1/2" x 1-1/2" and carry an ad for Lone Jack Cigarettes along the bottom of the front. The set features the Browns' starting lineup for 1886 along with their two top pitchers, backup catcher and owner, Chris Von Der Ahe.

		NM	EX	VG
Common Player:		12,000	7,150	4,950
(1)	Doc Bushong	12,000	7,150	4,950
(2)	Parisian Bob Caruthers	12,000	7,150	4,950
(3)	Charles Commiskey (Comiskey)	75,000	12,000	8,000
(4)	Dave Foutz	12,000	7,150	4,950
(5)	Will Gleason	12,000	7,150	4,950
(6)	Nat Hudson	12,000	7,150	4,950
(7)	Rudy Kimler (Kemmler)	12,000	7,150	4,950
(8)	Arlie Latham	12,000	7,150	4,950
(9)	Little Nick Nicol	12,000	7,150	4,950
(10)	Tip O'Neil (O'Neill)	12,000	7,150	4,950
(11)	Yank Robinson	11,000	6,500	4,500
(12)	Chris Von Der Ahe	18,000	10,800	7,200
(13)	Curt Welsh (Welch)	12,000	7,150	4,950

1886 Lorillard Team Cards

 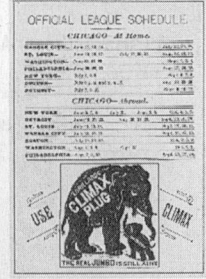

Issued in 1886 by Lorillard Tobacco Co., these 4" x 5-1/2" cards were issued for the Chicago, Detroit and New York baseball clubs. Each card carries the team's schedule (starting with June) on one side and features 11 player portraits enclosed in circles on the other. Each side has advertising for one of Lorillard's tobacco brands - Climax, Rebecca, etc.

		NM	EX	VG
Complete Set (4):		45,000	22,500	13,500
Common Team:		7,500	3,750	2,200
(1)	Chicago League Base Ball Club	13,500	7,200	6,000
(2)	Detroit League Base Ball Club	12,000	6,000	3,600
(3)	New York League Base Ball Club	10,000	5,000	3,250
(4)	Philadelphia League Base Ball Club	7,500	3,750	3,000

1949 Lummis Peanut Butter Phillies

This 12-card regional set featuring the Phillies was issued in the Philadelphia area by Lummis Peanut Butter in 1949. The cards measure 3-1/4" x 4-1/4" and are unnumbered. The fronts feature an action photo with a facsimile autograph, while the backs advertise a game ticket promotion by Lummis Peanut Butter. The same photos and checklist were also used for a regional sticker set issued by Sealtest Dairy the same year.

		NM	EX	VG
Complete Set (12):		22,500	11,250	6,750
Common Player:		1,350	675.00	400.00
(1)	Rich Ashburn	4,500	2,250	1,350
(2)	Hank Borowy	1,350	675.00	400.00
(3)	Del Ennis	1,500	750.00	450.00
(4)	Granny Hamner	1,350	675.00	400.00
(5)	Puddinhead Jones	1,350	675.00	400.00
(6)	Russ Meyer	1,350	675.00	400.00
(7)	Bill Nicholson	1,350	675.00	400.00
(8)	Robin Roberts	4,500	2,250	1,350
(9)	"Schoolboy" Rowe	1,350	675.00	400.00
(10)	Andy Seminick	1,350	675.00	400.00
(11)	Curt Simmons	1,500	750.00	450.00
(12)	Eddie Waitkus	1,350	675.00	400.00

1910 Luxello Cigars A's/Phillies Pins (P13)

Players from the two Philadelphia teams are pictured in this series of 7/8" black-and-white pins. The player's last name, team and position are printed below the photo; the Luxello Cigar name at top. On left and right are a horseshoe with monogram inside.

		NM	EX	VG
Complete Set (21):		17,500	8,750	5,250
Common Player:		750.00	375.00	225.00
	Philadelphia Athletics			
(1)	Franklin Baker	1,500	750.00	450.00
(2)	Jack Barry	750.00	375.00	225.00
(3)	Eddie Collins	1,500	750.00	450.00
(4)	John W. Coombs	750.00	375.00	225.00
(5)	Harry Davis	750.00	375.00	225.00
(6)	James Dygert	750.00	375.00	225.00
(7)	Heinie Heitmuller	750.00	375.00	225.00
(8)	Harry Krause	750.00	375.00	225.00
(9)	Paddy Livingston	750.00	375.00	225.00
(10)	Danny Murphy	750.00	375.00	225.00
(11)	Ed Plank	1,500	750.00	450.00
	Philadelphia Phillies			
(12)	John W. Bates	750.00	375.00	225.00
(13)	Chas. S. Dooin	750.00	375.00	225.00
(14)	Mike Doolan	750.00	375.00	225.00
(15)	Eddie Grant	750.00	375.00	225.00
(16)	Otto Knabe	750.00	375.00	225.00
(17)	Geo. McQuillan	750.00	375.00	225.00
(18)	Earl Moore	750.00	375.00	225.00
(19)	Lew Moren	750.00	375.00	225.00
(20)	Tully Sparks	750.00	375.00	225.00
(21)	John Titus	750.00	375.00	225.00

1912 L1 Leathers

One of the more unusual baseball collectibles of the tobacco era, the L1 "Leathers" were issued by Helmar Tobacco Co. in 1912 as a premium with its "Turkish Trophies" brand of cigarettes. The set featured 25 of the top baseball players and shared a checklist with the closely-related S81 "Silks," which were another part of the same promotion. The "Leathers," advertised as being 10" x 12", featured drawings of baseball players on horsehide-shaped pieces of leather. The drawings were based on the pictures used for the popular T3 Turkey Red series issued a year earlier. Twenty of the 25 players in the "Leathers" set are from the T3 set. Five pitchers (Rube Marquard, Rube Benton, Marty O'Toole, Grover Alexander and Russ Ford) not pictured in T3 were added to the "Leathers" set, and the Frank Baker error was corrected. According to the promotion, each "Leather" was available in exchange for 50 Helmar coupons. In addition to the 25 baseball stars, the "Leathers" set also included more than 100

other subjects, including female athletes and bathing beauties, famous generals, Indian chiefs, actresses, national flags, college mascots, and others.

		NM	EX	VG
Common Player:		3,000	1,500	900.00
86	Rube Marquard	7,500	3,750	2,250
87	Marty O'Toole	3,000	1,500	900.00
88	Rube Benton	3,000	1,500	900.00
89	Grover Alexander	8,500	4,250	2,550
90	Russ Ford	3,000	1,500	900.00
91	John McGraw	7,500	3,750	2,250
92	Nap Rucker	3,000	1,500	900.00
93	Mike Mitchell	3,000	1,500	900.00
94	Chief Bender	7,500	3,750	2,250
95	Home Run Baker	7,500	3,750	2,250
96	Nap Lajoie	7,500	3,750	2,250
97	Joe Tinker	7,500	3,750	2,250
98	Sherry Magee	3,000	1,500	900.00
99	Howie Camnitz	3,000	1,500	900.00
100	Eddie Collins	7,500	3,750	2,250
101	Red Dooin	3,000	1,500	900.00
102	Ty Cobb	45,000	22,500	13,500
103	Hugh Jennings	7,500	3,750	2,250
104	Roger Bresnahan	7,000	3,500	2,100
105	Jake Stahl	3,000	1,500	900.00
106	Tris Speaker	8,500	4,250	2,550
107	Ed Walsh	7,000	3,500	2,100
108	Christy Mathewson	15,000	7,500	4,500
109	Johnny Evers	7,000	3,500	2,100
110	Walter Johnson	15,000	7,500	4,500

M

1930s M-UNC Premiums

Recent auctions indicate these premiums are believed to either be related to R303 Goudey or Batter Up Photo Art Premiums. They are sized 5" x 8" and are dark red or maroon color.

Printed on glossy stock.
(1) Charles Gehringer
(2) Pepper Martin
(3) Joe Vosmik
(4) Lloyd Waner

1947 Mabley & Carew Cincinnati Reds

 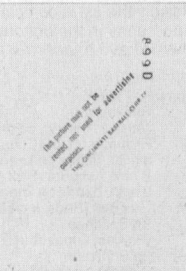

Pictures of Reds players and staff were given away and sold by the boys' shop of the Cincinnati department store. The black-and-white glossy photos measure 3-5/8" x 5-1/16" and have a white border. Backs have a rubber-stamped alphanumeric identifier and the notice: "This picture may not be rented nor used for advertising purposes. The Cincinnati Baseball Club." The players are not named on the pictures. Small groups of pictures were apparently given away in a tan-and-orange paper folder measuring about 3-7/8" x 5-1/4". The folder pictures the store, has a team roster and schedule and a coupon for purchasing addtional photos at a relatively hefty 10 cents apiece. The pictures are listed here alphabetically.

		NM	EX	VG
Complete Set (28):		850.00	425.00	250.00
Common Player:		30.00	15.00	9.00
Folder:		60.00	30.00	18.00
(1)	Bob Adams	30.00	15.00	9.00
(2)	Frank Baumholtz	30.00	15.00	9.00
(3)	Ewell Blackwell	40.00	20.00	12.00
(4)	Ed Erautt	30.00	15.00	9.00
(5)	Augie Galan	30.00	15.00	9.00
(6)	Harry Gumbert	30.00	15.00	9.00
(7)	Bert Haas	30.00	15.00	9.00
(8)	Grady Hatton	30.00	15.00	9.00
(9)	John Hetki	30.00	15.00	9.00
(10)	George Kelly	30.00	15.00	9.00
(11)	Ray Lamanno	30.00	15.00	9.00
(12)	Everett Lively	30.00	15.00	9.00
(13)	Ed Lukon	30.00	15.00	9.00
(14)	Eddie Miller	30.00	15.00	9.00
(15)	Ray Mueller	30.00	15.00	9.00
(16)	John Neun	30.00	15.00	9.00
(17)	Phil Page	30.00	15.00	9.00
(18)	Kent Peterson	30.00	15.00	9.00
(19)	Hugh Poland	30.00	15.00	9.00
(20)	Ken Raffensberger	30.00	15.00	9.00
(21)	Elmer Riddle	30.00	15.00	9.00
(22)	Tom Tatum	30.00	15.00	9.00
(23)	Johnny Vander Meer	40.00	20.00	12.00
(24)	Clyde Vollmer	30.00	15.00	9.00
(25)	Kermit Wahl	30.00	15.00	9.00
(26)	Bucky Walters	30.00	15.00	9.00
(27)	Babe Young	30.00	15.00	9.00
(28)	Ben Zientara	30.00	15.00	9.00

1951 Mabley & Carew Cincinnati Reds

This set is similar to the 1947 issue, with numbered player cards that were given away with a folder and schedule.

		NM	EX	VG
The checklist is incomplete.		.00	.00	.00
19	Lloyd Merriman	30.00	15.00	9.00
35	Ken Raffensberger	30.00	15.00	9.00

1950s-70s MacGregor Advisory Staff Photos

Advisory staff photos were a promotional item which debuted in the early 1950s, flourished in the Sixties and died in the early 1970s. Generally 8" x 10" (sometimes a little larger), these black-and-white (a few later were color) glossy photos picture players who had contracted with a major baseball equipment company to endorse and use their product. Usually the product - most often a glove - was prominently displayed in the photo. The pictures were often displayed in the windows of sporting goods stores or the walls of sports departments and were sometimes made available to customers. Because the companies tended to stick with players over the years, some photos were reissued, sometimes with and sometimes without a change of team, pose or typography. All MacGregor staff photos of the era are checklisted here in alphabetical order. Team designation and pose description is given for each known picture. The photos are checklisted here alphabetically. It is unlikely this list is complete. Several arrangements of typography in the bottom border are seen and some photos have a facsimile autograph.

	NM	EX	VG
Common Player:	15.00	7.50	4.50
Hank Aaron (Atlanta, batting, color.)	25.00	12.50	7.50
Richie Ashburn (Cubs, full-length, hands on knees.)	25.00	12.50	7.50
Richie Ashburn (Phillies, full-length, hands on knees.)	40.00	20.00	12.00
Gus Bell (Reds, kneeling.)	15.00	7.50	4.50
Ed Bouchee (Phillies, upper body.)	15.00	7.50	4.50
Ed Brinkman (Senators, upper body.)	15.00	7.50	4.50
Roberto Clemente (Full-length.)	125.00	65.00	35.00
Del Crandall (Braves, catching crouch in gear, large.)	15.00	7.50	4.50
Del Crandall (Braves, catching crouch in gear, small.)	15.00	7.50	4.50
Del Crandall (Braves, catching crouch, no gear.)	15.00	7.50	4.50
Del Crandall (Braves, kneeling, glove on knee.)	15.00	7.50	4.50
Al Downing (Dodgers, glove at waist.)	15.00	7.50	4.50
Al Downing (Yankees, upper body.)	15.00	7.50	4.50
Ron Hansen (White Sox, fielding.)	15.00	7.50	4.50
Tommy Helms (Reds, full-length.)	15.00	7.50	4.50
Randy Hundley (Cubs, upper body.)	15.00	7.50	4.50
Jackie Jensen (Red Sox, chest-up.)	15.00	7.50	4.50
Jack Jensen (Red Sox, full-length, batting.)	15.00	7.50	4.50
Jack Jensen (Red Sox, full-length, hands on knees.)	15.00	7.50	4.50
Ralph Kiner (Cubs, hands on knees.)	30.00	15.00	9.00
Ralph Kiner (Pirates, full-length.)	25.00	12.50	7.50
Ted Kluszewski (Reds, batting.)	25.00	12.50	7.50
Ted Kluszewski (White Sox, fielding.)	25.00	12.50	7.50
Ted Kluszewski (Reds, portrait.)	35.00	17.50	10.00
Johnny Kucks (Yankees, pitching.)	15.00	7.50	4.50
Willie Mays (Giants, full-length.)	90.00	45.00	27.00
Bill Mazeroski (Pirates, batting.)	30.00	15.00	9.00
Mike McCormick (Giants, follow-through.)	15.00	7.50	4.50
Gil McDougald (Yankees, throwing.)	15.00	7.50	4.50
Gil McDougald (Yankees, upper-body portrait.)	15.00	7.50	4.50
Tony Oliva (Twins, batting.)	15.00	7.50	4.50
Tony Oliva (Twins, upper body.)	15.00	7.50	4.50
Claude Osteen (Dodgers, pitching.)	15.00	7.50	4.50
Claude Osteen (Dodgers, portrait.)	15.00	7.50	4.50
Juan Pizzaro (White Sox, follow-through.)	15.00	7.50	4.50
Robin Roberts (Phillies, portrait.)	25.00	12.50	7.50
Robin Roberts (Phillies, follow-through.)	25.00	12.50	7.50
Frank Robinson (Orioles, portrait.)	25.00	12.50	7.50
Pete Rose (Reds, kneeling.)	35.00	17.50	10.00
Pete Rose (Reds, leading off, color.)	65.00	32.50	20.00
Pete Rose (Reds, chest-to-cap portrait.)	35.00	17.50	10.00
Al Schoendienst (Cardinals, kneeling.)	25.00	12.50	7.50
Warren Spahn (Boston Braves, follow-through.)	25.00	12.50	7.50
Daryl Spencer (Cardinals, fielding grounder.)	15.00	7.50	4.50
Don Sutton (Dodgers, color, ready to pitch.)	20.00	10.00	6.00
Frank Torre (Braves, ready to throw.)	15.00	7.50	4.50

1960 MacGregor

The MacGregor Sporting Goods Co. was one of the pioneers in celebrity marketing, creating an advisory staff in 1960 to promote its products. The 25-card set features black-and-white photography of several stars and lesser lights, and even a couple of managers. The cards are 3-3/4" x 5" with a thin white border and the words "MacGregor Baseball Advisory Staff of Champions" on the bottom panel. The cards are not numbered and are blank-backed, and include a facsimile autograph in white on the front photo. The checklist is arranged here alphabetically.

		NM	EX	VG
Complete Set (25):		700.00	350.00	210.00
Common Player:		15.00	7.50	4.50
1	Hank Aaron	110.00	55.00	35.00
2	Richie Ashburn	35.00	17.50	10.00
3	Gus Bell	15.00	7.50	4.50
4	Lou Berberet	15.00	7.50	4.50
5	Jerry Casale	15.00	7.50	4.50
6	Del Crandall	15.00	7.50	4.50
7	Art Ditmar	15.00	7.50	4.50
8	Gene Freese	15.00	7.50	4.50
9	James Gilliam	17.50	8.75	5.25
10	Ted Kluszewski	35.00	17.50	10.00
11	Jim Landis	15.00	7.50	4.50
12	Al Lopez	30.00	15.00	9.00
13	Willie Mays	110.00	55.00	35.00
14	Bill Mazeroski	35.00	17.50	10.00
15	Mike McCormick	15.00	7.50	4.50
16	Gil McDougald	15.00	7.50	4.50
17	Russ Nixon	15.00	7.50	4.50
18	Bill Rigney	15.00	7.50	4.50
19	Robin Roberts	35.00	17.50	10.00
20	Frank Robinson	45.00	22.50	13.50
21	John Roseboro	15.00	7.50	4.50
22	Red Schoendienst	35.00	17.50	10.00
23	Bill Skowron	20.00	10.00	6.00
24	Daryl Spencer	15.00	7.50	4.50
25	Johnny Temple	15.00	7.50	4.50

1960-70s MacGregor Pete Rose

Besides the several series of card issues and Advisory Staff photos issued over the years, MacGregor produced a number of special Pete Rose cards to promote its relationship with one of baseball's top stars of the 1960s and 1970s. All cards in this listing are in black-and-white with blank backs. The 1965-66 cards are 3-1/2" x 5". The later cards are 5" x 7-1/4" to 7-1/2".

		NM	EX	VG
1965	Pete Rose (Full-length photo, crouching w/glove.)	200.00	100.00	60.00
1966	Pete Rose (Half-length photo, crouching w/glove.)	200.00	100.00	60.00
1969	Pete Rose (Portrait to chest.)	100.00	50.00	30.00
1970	Pete Rose (Fielding, white background.)	75.00	37.50	22.00
1973	Pete Rose (Portrait)	75.00	37.50	22.00
1974	Pete Rose (Portrait to waist, w/glove.)	75.00	37.50	22.00

1965 MacGregor

The 1965 MacGregor set is similar to earlier issues, with only a slight change in dimension to 3-1/2" x 5-1/8" and reduced in size to only 10 players. All cards in this listing are blank-backed and unnumbered and have a glossy finish. They are checklisted here alphabetically.

		NM	EX	VG
Complete Set (10):		375.00	185.00	110.00
Common Player:		10.00	5.00	3.00
(1)	Roberto Clemente	150.00	75.00	45.00
(2)	Al Downing	10.00	5.00	3.00
(3)	Johnny Edwards	10.00	5.00	3.00
(4)	Ron Hansen	10.00	5.00	3.00
(5)	Deron Johnson	10.00	5.00	3.00
(6)	Willie Mays	135.00	65.00	40.00
(7)	Tony Oliva	15.00	7.50	4.50
(8)	Claude Osteen	10.00	5.00	3.00
(9)	Bobby Richardson	15.00	7.50	4.50
(10)	Zoilo Versalles	10.00	5.00	3.00

1970s MacGregor Advisory Staff Photos

This advisory staff photo series was among the last in a line of promotional items which debuted in the Sixties and died in the 1970s. While earlier advisory staff photos were generally 8" x 10", this later series of black-and-white glossy photos is in a 5" x 7" format. They picture players who had contracted with MacGregor to endorse and use its product. The pictures were often displayed in the windows of sporting goods stores or the walls of sports departments and were sometimes made available to customers. Because the companies tended to stick with players over the years, some photos were reissued, sometimes with a change of team, pose or typography. Known MacGregor staff photos of the era are checklisted here in alphabetical order. Team designation and pose description is given for each picture. It is unlikely this list is complete. Gaps have been left in the assigned numbering to accommodate future additions.

		NM	EX	VG
Common Player:		15.00	7.50	4.50
(1)	Hank Aaron (Braves, chest-to-cap.)	40.00	20.00	12.00
(2)	Rod Carew (Twins, chest-to-cap.)	25.00	12.50	7.50
(3)	Rod Carew (Twins, chin-to-cap.)	25.00	12.50	7.50
(5)	George Foster (Reds, chest-to-cap.)	15.00	7.50	4.50
(8)	Lee May (Orioles, chest-to-cap.)	15.00	7.50	4.50

		NM	EX	VG
(10)	Joe Morgan (Reds, neck-to-cap.)	25.00	12.50	7.50
(11)	Joe Morgan (Reds, waist-to-cap.)	25.00	12.50	7.50
(12)	Thurman Munson (Yankees, neck-to-cap.)	27.50	13.50	8.25
(15)	Tony Perez (Reds, neck-to-cap.)	25.00	12.50	7.50
(16)	Tony Perez (Expos, chest-to-cap.)	25.00	12.50	7.50
(20)	Don Sutton (Dodgers, chest-to-cap.)	20.00	10.00	6.00
(21)	Don Sutton (Dodgers, neck-to-cap.)	20.00	10.00	6.00

1975 MacGregor Advisory Staff Poster

This 19-1/2" x 26" color poster features Pete Rose in a game-action photo, leading off at first base. Two lines of type, "Winners Play MacGregor" and "The Greatest Name In Sports" are centered above the picture. Back is blank.

	NM	EX	VG
Pete Rose	50.00	25.00	15.00

1886 MacIntire Studio Cabinets

The number of baseball players who found themselves in front of the lens at the MacIntire photography studio in Philadelphia is unknown, but all those thus far seen were members of the 1886 Philadelphia National League team. In standard cabinet-card format of about 3-3/4" x 5-3/4", the pieces feature a cream-colored mount with a sepia photo.

		NM	EX	VG
	Common Player:	4,500	3,000	2,000
(1)	Tony Cusick	4,500	3,000	2,000
(2)	Edward Dailey	4,500	3,000	2,000
(3)	Jack Farrell	4,500	3,000	2,000
(4)	Charlie Ganzel	4,500	3,000	2,000
(5)	Deacon McGuire	4,500	3,000	2,000
(6)	Cannonball Titcomb	4,500	3,000	2,000
(7)	Harry Wright (Facing his right.)	10,000	4,500	2,800
(8)	Harry Wright (Pose unrecorded.)	10,000	4,500	2,800
(9)	Team Photo	6,500	4,500	2,800

1951 Connie Mack Book

CONNIE MACK

Washington, N. L., (Buffalo, P. L.), Pittsb'ch, N.L., (M'waukee, W.L.) Philadelphia, A. L. 1886-present

Connie Mack has perhaps had more personal friends than any living American. A star catcher, a model of clean sportsmanship, he made his fame as Manager of the Philadelphia A's. His teams have won 9 pennants and 5 World Series.

He did much to shape baseball rules, pioneered in developing the catching art, helped form the American League (the move which made big-league baseball big), and introduced modern overhand pitching.

His story is an American success saga: the small-town boy starting at 33c a day, building a business property worth millions. More than that, it's the living, breathing, history of America's national sport.

Read all about it in Connie Mack's "My 66 Years in the Big Leagues."

In conjunction with the publication of Connie Mack's book "My 66 Years in the Big Leagues," a folder of cards titled, "Four Mighty Heroes" was also issued. The folder contained a quartet of black-and-white player cards. Fronts feature a player photo against a white background. Backs have a bit of player career data and an ad for Mack's book. Cards measure 2-1/4" x 3-1/2".

		NM	EX	VG
	Complete Set (4):	1,900	950.00	575.00
	Common Player:	275.00	135.00	80.00
	Book:	60.00	30.00	18.00
(1)	Connie Mack	275.00	135.00	80.00
(2)	Christy Mathewson	400.00	200.00	120.00
(3)	Babe Ruth	1,000	500.00	300.00
(4)	Rube Waddell	275.00	135.00	80.00

1924 Walter Mails Card Game (WG7)

This set of playing cards features 56 subjects. Card backs are printed in either red or blue, featuring player and umpire figures in each corner. At center is the picture of a pitcher with the name of the game's creator beneath. Walter Mails was a major league pitcher between 1915-26. Fronts feature a black-and-white player photo with a facsimile autograph.

WALTER MAILS
Fan Out

Printed beneath are the player's name, position and team. At bottom is the designation of a play used in the card game. Both major and minor league players are included in the set. Cards are round-cornered and measure 2-5/16" x 3-1/2". The unnumbered cards are checklisted here alphabetically. It appears as if the blue-back set was issued first and in lesser quantities than those with red backs. Many variations of player personal data between the two colors of backs are reported.

		NM	EX	VG
	Complete Set (56):	12,000	6,000	3,500
	Common Player, Major Leaguer:	250.00	100.00	60.00
	Common Player, Minor Leaguer:	200.00	80.00	50.00
	Rules Card:	50.00	20.00	10.00
(1)	Russell "Buzz" Arlett	200.00	80.00	50.00
(2)	J.C. "Jim" Bagby	200.00	80.00	50.00
(3)	Dave "Beauty" Bancroft	500.00	200.00	125.00
(4)	Johnny Basseler (Bassler)	250.00	100.00	60.00
(5)	Jack Bentley	250.00	100.00	60.00
(6)	J.C. "Rube" Benton	250.00	100.00	60.00
(7)	Geo. Burns	250.00	100.00	60.00
(8)	"Bullet Joe" Bush	250.00	100.00	60.00
(9)	Harold P. Chavezo	200.00	80.00	50.00
(10)	Hugh Critz	200.00	80.00	50.00
(11)	"Jake" E. Daubert	250.00	100.00	60.00
(12)	Wheezer Dell	200.00	80.00	50.00
(13)	Joe Dugan	250.00	100.00	60.00
(14)	Pat Duncan	250.00	100.00	60.00
(15)	Howard J. Ehmke	250.00	100.00	60.00
(16)	Lewis Fonseca	250.00	100.00	60.00
(17)	Ray French	250.00	100.00	60.00
(18)	Ed Gharity (Gharrity)	250.00	100.00	60.00
(19)	Heinie Groh	250.00	100.00	60.00
(20)	George N. Groves	250.00	100.00	60.00
(21)	E.F. "Red" Hargrave	250.00	100.00	60.00
(22)	Elmer Jacobs	250.00	100.00	60.00
(23)	Walter Johnson	1,200	480.00	300.00
(24)	WM. "Duke" Kenworthy	250.00	100.00	60.00
(25)	Harry Krause	200.00	80.00	50.00
(26)	Ray Kremer	250.00	100.00	60.00
(27)	Walter Mails	250.00	100.00	60.00
(28)	Walter "Rabbitt" Maranville	500.00	200.00	125.00
(29)	John "Stuffy" McInnis	250.00	100.00	60.00
(30)	Marty McManus	250.00	100.00	60.00
(31)	Bob Meusel	250.00	100.00	60.00
(32)	Hack Miller	250.00	100.00	60.00
(33)	Pat J. Moran	250.00	100.00	60.00
(34)	Guy Morton	250.00	100.00	60.00
(35)	Johnny Mostil	250.00	100.00	60.00
(36)	Rod Murphy	200.00	80.00	50.00
(37)	Jimmy O'Connell	250.00	100.00	60.00
(38)	Steve O'Neil	250.00	100.00	60.00
(39)	Joe Oeschger	250.00	100.00	60.00
(40)	Roger Peckinpaugh	250.00	100.00	60.00
(41)	Ralph "Babe" Pinelli	250.00	100.00	60.00
(42)	Wally Pipp	250.00	100.00	60.00
(43)	Elmer Ponder	200.00	80.00	50.00
(44)	Sam Rice	500.00	200.00	125.00
(45)	Edwin Rommell (Rommel)	250.00	100.00	60.00
(46)	Walter Schmidt	250.00	100.00	60.00
(47)	Wilford Shupes	200.00	80.00	50.00
(48)	Joe Sewell	500.00	200.00	125.00
(49)	Pat Shea	200.00	80.00	50.00
(50)	W. "Paddy" Siglin	200.00	80.00	50.00
(51)	Geo. H. Sisler	500.00	200.00	125.00
(52)	William "Bill" Skiff	200.00	80.00	50.00
(53)	J. Smith	250.00	100.00	60.00
(54)	Harry "Suds" Sutherland	200.00	80.00	50.00
(55)	James A. Tierney	250.00	100.00	60.00
(56)	Geo. Uhle	250.00	100.00	60.00

1921-1930 Major League Ball Die-Cuts

COBB.
Center Field.
Batting Order 3

Detroit.
American League

These die-cut, blank-back player cards were issued over the period 1921-30 for use with a board game called, "Major League Ball - The Indoor Baseball Game Supreme," from The National Game Makers of Washington, D.C. Measuring about 2-1/2" to 2-3/4" tall x 1" to 1-1/4" wide, the cards were originally printed on a sheet of 14 from which they were punched out to play the game. The cards were issued in team sets with on-field roster changes reflected in the player cards over the years. Individual cards are generic, liberally sharing the same poses and portraits with identification possible only by changes to the uniform and the player ID printed in the box below the figure. That player data changed from year to year and the only way to determine exact year of issue is when the player card is found with a complete team set, often in a small pre-printed manila envelope. It is unknown whether all teams were issued in all years. According to information found with the game, stickers could be purchased each year to update the game's figures with new player identification. Beginning in at least 1925 player cards were numbered at bottom within team set.

	NM	EX	VG
Typical Team Set:	300.00	150.00	90.00
Common Player:	50.00	25.00	15.00
Typical Hall of Famer:	75.00	37.50	22.50
Ty Cobb	150.00	75.00	45.00
Lou Gehrig	200.00	100.00	60.00
Walter Johnson	125.00	65.00	40.00
Babe Ruth	350.00	175.00	100.00

1969 Major League Baseball Photostamps

This set of 216 player stamps, sponsored by the Major League Baseball Players Association (not authorized by MLB, thus the lack of team uniform insignia) was issued in professional baseball's centennial year of 1969 and was sold in 18 different uncut sheets, with 12 stamps on each sheet. Each individual stamp measured 2" x 3-1/4". There were nine sheets picturing National League players and nine picturing American Leaguers. The full-color stamps display facsimilie autographs on the fronts. The backs carry instructions to moisten the stamps and place them in a special album that was also available. Many sheets of these stamps were uncovered by a dealer in the early 1980s and they were available at inexpensive prices.

		NM	EX	VG
	Complete Sheet Set (18):	60.00	30.00	18.00
	Complete Singles Set (216):	60.00	30.00	18.00
	A.L. Album and Sheets:	25.00	12.50	7.50
	N.L. Album and Sheets:	35.00	17.50	10.00
	Common Sheet:	3.50	1.75	1.00
	Common Player:	.50	.25	.15
	Sheet A.L. 1	3.75	2.00	1.00
(1)	Don Buford	.50	.25	.15
(2)	Mike Andrews	.50	.25	.15
(3)	Max Alvis	.50	.25	.15
(4)	Bill Freehan	.50	.25	.15
(5)	Horace Clarke	.50	.25	.15
(6)	Bernie Allen	.50	.25	.15
(7)	Jim Fregosi	.50	.25	.15
(8)	Joe Horlen	.50	.25	.15
(9)	Jerry Adair	.50	.25	.15
(10)	Harmon Killebrew	3.00	1.50	.90
(11)	Johnny Odom	.50	.25	.15
(12)	Steve Barber	.50	.25	.15
	Sheet A.L. 2	2.50	1.25	.75
(13)	Tom Harper	.50	.25	.15
(14)	Boog Powell	1.00	.50	.30
(15)	Jose Santiago	.50	.25	.15
(16)	Sonny Siebert	.50	.25	.15
(17)	Mickey Lolich	.75	.40	.25
(18)	Tom Tresh	.75	.40	.25
(19)	Camilo Pascual	.50	.25	.15
(20)	Bob Rodgers	.50	.25	.15
(21)	Pete Ward	.50	.25	.15
(22)	Dave Morehead	.50	.25	.15
(23)	John Roseboro	.50	.25	.15
(24)	Bert Campaneris	.50	.25	.15
	Sheet A.L. 3	3.75	2.00	1.00
(25)	Danny Cater	.50	.25	.15
(26)	Rich Rollins	.50	.25	.15
(27)	Brooks Robinson	3.00	1.50	.90
(28)	Rico Petrocelli	.50	.25	.15
(29)	Larry Brown	.50	.25	.15
(30)	Norm Cash	.75	.40	.25
(31)	Jake Gibbs	.50	.25	.15
(32)	Mike Epstein	.50	.25	.15
(33)	George Brunet	.50	.25	.15
(34)	Tom McCraw	.50	.25	.15
(35)	Steve Whitaker	.50	.25	.15
(36)	Bob Allison	.50	.25	.15
	Sheet A.L. 4	2.50	1.25	.75
(37)	Jim Kaat	.65	.35	.20
(38)	Sal Bando	.50	.25	.15
(39)	Ray Oyler	.50	.25	.15
(40)	Dave McNally	.50	.25	.15

(41)	George Scott	.50	.25 .15
(42)	Joe Azcue	.50	.25 .15
(43)	Jim Northrup	.50	.25 .15
(44)	Fritz Peterson	.50	.25 .15
(45)	Paul Casanova	.50	.25 .15
(46)	Roger Repoz	.50	.25 .15
(47)	Tommy John	.75	.40 .25
(48)	Moe Drabowsky	.50	.25 .15
Sheet A.L. 5		2.50	1.25 .75
(49)	Ed Kirkpatrick	.50	.25 .15
(50)	Dean Chance	.50	.25 .15
(51)	Mike Hershberger	.50	.25 .15
(52)	Jack Aker	.50	.25 .15
(53)	Andy Etchebarren	.50	.25 .15
(54)	Ray Culp	.50	.25 .15
(55)	Luis Tiant	.65	.35 .20
(56)	Willie Horton	.50	.25 .15
(57)	Roy White	.50	.25 .15
(58)	Ken McMullen	.50	.25 .15
(59)	Rick Reichardt	.50	.25 .15
(60)	Luis Aparicio	3.00	1.50 .90
Sheet A.L. 6		2.50	1.25 .75
(61)	Ken Berry	.50	.25 .15
(62)	Wally Bunker	.50	.25 .15
(63)	Tony Oliva	1.00	.50 .30
(64)	Rick Monday	.50	.25 .15
(65)	Chico Salmon	.50	.25 .15
(66)	Paul Blair	.50	.25 .15
(67)	Jim Lonborg	.50	.25 .15
(68)	Zoilo Versalles	.50	.25 .15
(69)	Denny McLain	.75	.40 .25
(70)	Mel Stottlemyre	.50	.25 .15
(71)	Joe Coleman	.50	.25 .15
(72)	Bob Knoop	.50	.25 .15
Sheet A.L. 7		2.50	1.25 .75
(73)	Chuck Hinton	.50	.25 .15
(74)	Duane Josephson	.50	.25 .15
(75)	Roger Nelson	.50	.25 .15
(76)	Ted Uhlaender	.50	.25 .15
(77)	John Donaldson	.50	.25 .15
(78)	Tommy Davis	.50	.25 .15
(79)	Frank Robinson	3.00	1.50 .90
(80)	Dick Ellsworth	.50	.25 .15
(81)	Sam McDowell	.50	.25 .15
(82)	Dick McAuliffe	.50	.25 .15
(83)	Bill Robinson	.50	.25 .15
(84)	Frank Howard	.75	.40 .25
Sheet A.L. 8		5.00	2.50 1.50
(85)	Ed Brinkman	.50	.25 .15
(86)	Vic Davalillo	.50	.25 .15
(87)	Gary Peters	.50	.25 .15
(88)	Joe Foy	.50	.25 .15
(89)	Rod Carew	3.00	1.50 .90
(90)	Jim "Catfish" Hunter	2.00	1.00 .60
(91)	Gary Bell	.50	.25 .15
(92)	Dave Johnson	.50	.25 .15
(93)	Ken Harrelson	.50	.25 .15
(94)	Tony Horton	.50	.25 .15
(95)	Al Kaline	3.00	1.50 .90
(96)	Steve Hamilton	.50	.25 .15
Sheet A.L. 9		2.50	1.25 .75
(97)	Joseph Pepitone	.75	.40 .25
(98)	Ed Stroud	.50	.25 .15
(99)	Jim McGlothlin	.50	.25 .15
(100)	Wilbur Wood	.50	.25 .15
(101)	Paul Schaal	.50	.25 .15
(102)	Cesar Tovar	.50	.25 .15
(103)	Jim Nash	.50	.25 .15
(104)	Don Mincher	.50	.25 .15
(105)	Thomas Phoebus	.50	.25 .15
(106)	Reggie Smith	.50	.25 .15
(107)	Jose Cardenal	.50	.25 .15
(108)	Mickey Stanley	.50	.25 .15
Sheet N.L. 1		5.00	2.50 1.50
(109)	Billy Williams	2.00	1.00 .60
(110)	Mack Jones	.50	.25 .15
(111)	Tom Seaver	3.00	1.50 .90
(112)	Rich Allen	1.50	.70 .45
(113)	Bob Veale	.50	.25 .15
(114)	Curt Flood	.65	.35 .20
(115)	Pat Jarvis	.50	.25 .15
(116)	Jim Merritt	.50	.25 .15
(117)	Joe Morgan	2.50	1.25 .70
(118)	Tom Haller	.50	.25 .15
(119)	Larry Stahl	.50	.25 .15
(120)	Willie McCovey	2.50	1.25 .70
Sheet N.L. 2		6.00	3.00 1.75
(121)	Ron Hunt	.50	.25 .15
(122)	Ernie Banks	3.00	1.50 .90
(123)	Jim Fairey	.50	.25 .15
(124)	Tommy Agee	.50	.25 .15
(125)	Cookie Rojas	.50	.25 .15
(126)	Mateo Alou	.50	.25 .15
(127)	Mike Shannon	.50	.25 .15
(128)	Milt Pappas	.50	.25 .15
(129)	Johnny Bench	3.00	1.50 .90
(130)	Larry Dierker	.50	.25 .15
(131)	Willie Davis	.50	.25 .15
(132)	Tony Gonzalez	.50	.25 .15
Sheet N.L. 3		3.75	2.00 1.00
(133)	Dick Selma	.50	.25 .15
(134)	Jim Ray Hart	.50	.25 .15
(135)	Phil Regan	.50	.25 .15
(136)	Manny Mota	.50	.25 .15
(137)	Cleon Jones	.50	.25 .15
(138)	Rick Wise	.50	.25 .15
(139)	Willie Stargell	2.50	1.25 .70
(140)	Robert Gibson	2.50	1.25 .70
(141)	Rico Carty	.50	.25 .15
(142)	Gary Nolan	.50	.25 .15
(143)	Doug Rader	.50	.25 .15
(144)	Wes Parker	.50	.25 .15
Sheet N.L. 4		2.50	1.25 .75
(145)	Bill Singer	.50	.25 .15
(146)	Bill McCool	.50	.25 .15
(147)	Juan Marichal	2.00	1.00 .60
(148)	Randy Hundley	.50	.25 .15

(149)	"Mudcat" Grant	.50	.25 .15
(150)	Ed Kranepool	.50	.25 .15
(151)	Tony Taylor	.50	.25 .15
(152)	Gene Alley	.50	.25 .15
(153)	Dal Maxvill	.50	.25 .15
(154)	Felipe Alou	.65	.35 .20
(155)	Jim Maloney	.50	.25 .15
(156)	Jesus Alou	.50	.25 .15
Sheet N.L. 5		8.00	4.00 2.50
(157)	Curt Blefary	.50	.25 .15
(158)	Ron Fairly	.50	.25 .15
(159)	Dick Kelley	.50	.25 .15
(160)	Frank Linzy	.50	.25 .15
(161)	Fergie Jenkins	2.00	1.00 .60
(162)	Maury Wills	.75	.40 .25
(163)	Jerry Grote	.50	.25 .15
(164)	Chris Short	.50	.25 .15
(165)	Jim Bunning	2.00	1.00 .60
(166)	Nelson Briles	.50	.25 .15
(167)	Orlando Cepeda	2.50	1.25 .70
(168)	Pete Rose	8.00	4.00 2.50
Sheet N.L. 6		3.00	1.50 .90
(169)	Tony Cloninger	.50	.25 .15
(170)	Jim Wynn	.50	.25 .15
(171)	Jim Lefebvre	.50	.25 .15
(172)	Ron Davis	.50	.25 .15
(173)	Mike McCormick	.50	.25 .15
(174)	Ron Santo	.75	.40 .25
(175)	Ty Cline	.50	.25 .15
(176)	Jerry Koosman	.50	.25 .15
(177)	Mike Ryan	.50	.25 .15
(178)	Jerry May	.50	.25 .15
(179)	Tim McCarver	.75	.40 .25
(180)	Phil Niekro	2.00	1.00 .60
Sheet N.L. 7		15.00	7.50 4.50
(181)	Hank Aaron	5.00	2.50 1.50
(182)	Tommy Helms	.50	.25 .15
(183)	Denis Menke	.50	.25 .15
(184)	Don Sutton	2.00	1.00 .60
(185)	Al Ferrara	.50	.25 .15
(186)	Willie Mays	5.00	2.50 1.50
(187)	Bill Hands	.50	.25 .15
(188)	Rusty Staub	.70	.35 .20
(189)	Bud Harrelson	.50	.25 .15
(190)	Johnny Callison	.50	.25 .15
(191)	Roberto Clemente	8.00	4.00 2.50
(192)	Julian Javier	.50	.25 .15
Sheet N.L. 8		2.50	1.25 .75
(193)	Joe Torre	1.25	.60 .40
(194)	Bob Aspromonte	.50	.25 .15
(195)	Lee May	.50	.25 .15
(196)	Don Wilson	.50	.25 .15
(197)	Claude Osteen	.50	.25 .15
(198)	Ed Spiezio	.50	.25 .15
(199)	Hal Lanier	.50	.25 .15
(200)	Glenn Beckert	.50	.25 .15
(201)	Bob Bailey	.50	.25 .15
(202)	Ron Swoboda	.50	.25 .15
(203)	John Briggs	.50	.25 .15
(204)	Bill Mazeroski	2.50	1.25 .70
Sheet N.L. 9		3.75	2.00 1.00
(205)	Tommie Sisk	.50	.25 .15
(206)	Lou Brock	2.50	1.25 .70
(207)	Felix Millan	.50	.25 .15
(208)	Tony Perez	2.00	1.00 .60
(209)	John Edwards	.50	.25 .15
(210)	Len Gabrielson	.50	.25 .15
(211)	Ollie Brown	.50	.25 .15
(212)	Gaylord Perry	2.00	1.00 .60
(213)	Don Kessinger	.50	.25 .15
(214)	John Bateman	.50	.25 .15
(215)	Ed Charles	.50	.25 .15
(216)	Woodie Fryman	.50	.25 .15

1969 Major League Baseball Player Pins

ROBERTO CLEMENTE
PITTSBURGH PIRATES

Black-and-white or color player portraits (noted parenthetically) are featured in the center of a red, white and blue design on these 3-1/2" diameter pins. The existing checklist, which may be incomplete, shows a mix of contemporary and retired players. The celluloid pinback buttons were sold at concession stands around the Major Leagues. Production continued at least into 1970, based on some observed player/team combinations.

		NM	EX	VG
Common Player:		20.00	12.00	
(1)	Hank Aaron (B/W)	60.00	30.00	18.00
(2)	Tommie Agee (B/W)	20.00	10.00	6.00
(3)	Mike Andrews (B/W)	20.00	10.00	6.00
(4)	Mike Andrews (Color)	20.00	10.00	6.00
(5)	Luis Aparicio (B/W)	25.00	12.50	7.50
(6)	Ernie Banks (B/W)	60.00	30.00	18.00
(7)	Ernie Banks (B/W, 2-1/2")	60.00	30.00	18.00
(8)	Ernie Banks (Color)	60.00	30.00	18.00
(9)	Glenn Beckert (B/W)	20.00	10.00	6.00
(10)	Curt Blefary (B/W)	20.00	10.00	6.00

(11)	Ken Boswell (B/W)	20.00	10.00	6.00
(12)	Lou Brock (B/W)	30.00	15.00	9.00
(13)	John Callison (B/W)	20.00	10.00	6.00
(14)	Orlando Cepeda (B/W)	25.00	12.50	7.50
(15)	Ed Charles (B/W)	20.00	10.00	6.00
(16)	Horace Clarke (B/W)	20.00	10.00	6.00
(17)	Roberto Clemente (B/W)	75.00	37.00	22.00
(18)	Donn Clendenon (B/W)	20.00	10.00	6.00
(19)	Billy Conigliaro (B/W)	20.00	10.00	6.00
(20)	Tony Conigliaro (B/W)	25.00	12.50	7.50
(21)	Tony Conigliaro (Color)	25.00	12.50	7.50
(22)	Ray Culp (B/W)	20.00	10.00	6.00
(23)	Joe DiMaggio (B/W)	50.00	25.00	15.00
(24)	Don Drysdale (B/W)	30.00	15.00	9.00
(25)	Frank Fernandez (Color)	20.00	10.00	6.00
(26)	Curt Flood (B/W)	20.00	10.00	6.00
(27)	Lou Gehrig (B/W)	50.00	25.00	15.00
(28)	Bob Gibson (B/W)	30.00	15.00	9.00
(29)	Jerry Grote (B/W)	20.00	10.00	6.00
(30)	Jim Hickman (B/W)	20.00	10.00	6.00
(31)	Ken Holtzman (B/W)	20.00	10.00	6.00
(32)	Frank Howard (B/W)	22.50	11.00	6.75
(33)	Randy Hundley (B/W)	20.00	10.00	6.00
(34)	Reggie Jackson (Color)	60.00	30.00	18.00
(35)	Ferguson Jenkins (B/W)	30.00	15.00	9.00
(36)	Dalton Jones (B/W)	20.00	10.00	6.00
(37)	Al Kaline (B/W)	60.00	30.00	18.00
(38)	Don Kessinger (B/W)	20.00	10.00	6.00
(39)	Harmon Killebrew (B/W)	30.00	15.00	9.00
(40)	Jerry Koosman (Color)	20.00	10.00	6.00
(41)	Jim Lonborg (B/W)	20.00	10.00	6.00
(42)	Mickey Mantle (B/W)	100.00	50.00	30.00
(43)	Carlos May (B/W)	20.00	10.00	6.00
(44)	Willie Mays (B/W)	75.00	37.00	22.00
(45)	Willie McCovey (B/W)	25.00	12.50	7.50
(46)	Denny McLain (B/W)	22.50	11.00	6.75
(47)	Gene Michael (B/W)	20.00	10.00	6.00
(48)	Gene Michael (Color)	20.00	10.00	6.00
(49)	Bobby Murcer (Color)	22.50	11.00	6.75
(50)	Joe Pepitone (B/W)	25.00	12.50	7.50
(51)	Rico Petrocelli (B/W)	20.00	10.00	6.00
(52)	Rico Petrocelli (Color)	20.00	10.00	6.00
(53)	Pete Rose (B/W)	75.00	37.00	22.00
(54)	Babe Ruth (B/W)	50.00	25.00	15.00
(55)	Ron Santo (B/W)	22.50	11.00	6.75
(56)	Ron Santo (Color)	22.50	11.00	6.75
(57)	Ron Santo (B/W, 2-1/2")	60.00	30.00	18.00
(58)	George Scott (B/W)	20.00	10.00	6.00
(59)	Tom Seaver (B/W)	45.00	22.00	13.50
(60)	Tom Seaver (Color)	45.00	22.00	13.50
(61)	Reggie Smith (B/W)	20.00	10.00	6.00
(62)	Reggie Smith (Color)	20.00	10.00	6.00
(63)	Mel Stottlemyre (Color)	20.00	10.00	6.00
(64)	Tony Taylor (B/W, 2-1/2")	20.00	10.00	6.00
(65)	Joe Torre (B/W)	22.50	11.00	6.75
(66)	Tom Tresh (Color)	20.00	10.00	6.00
(67)	Pete Ward (B/W)	20.00	10.00	6.00
(68)	Roy White (B/W)	20.00	10.00	6.00
(69)	Billy Williams (B/W)	25.00	12.50	7.50
(70)	Carl Yastrzemski (B/W)	60.00	30.00	18.00
(71)	Carl Yastrzemski (Color)	60.00	30.00	18.00

1969 Major League Baseball Players Ass'n Pins

Issued by the Major League Baseball Players Association in 1969, this unnumbered set consists of 60 pins - 30 players from the N.L. and 30 from the A.L. Each pin measures approximately 7/8" in diameter and features a black-and-white player photo. A.L. players are surrounded by a red border, while N.L. players are framed in blue. The player's name and team appear at the top and bottom. Also along the bottom is a line reading "1969 MLBPA MFG. R.R. Winona, MINN."

		NM	EX	VG
Complete Set (60):		250.00	125.00	75.00
Common Player:		6.00	3.00	1.75
(1)	Hank Aaron	30.00	15.00	9.00
(2)	Richie Allen	10.00	5.00	3.00
(3)	Felipe Alou	7.50	3.75	2.25
(4)	Max Alvis	6.00	3.00	1.75
(5)	Luis Aparicio	12.50	6.25	3.75
(6)	Ernie Banks	15.00	7.50	4.50
(7)	Johnny Bench	15.00	7.50	4.50
(8)	Lou Brock	15.00	7.50	4.50
(9)	George Brunet	6.00	3.00	1.75
(10)	Johnny Callison	6.00	3.00	1.75
(11)	Rod Carew	15.00	7.50	4.50
(12)	Orlando Cepeda	12.50	6.25	3.75
(13)	Dean Chance	6.00	3.00	1.75
(14)	Roberto Clemente	40.00	20.00	12.00
(15)	Willie Davis	6.00	3.00	1.75
(16)	Don Drysdale	15.00	7.50	4.50
(17)	Ron Fairly	6.00	3.00	1.75
(18)	Curt Flood	6.00	3.00	1.75
(19)	Bill Freehan	6.00	3.00	1.75
(20)	Jim Fregosi	6.00	3.00	1.75
(21)	Bob Gibson	15.00	7.50	4.50

(22)	Ken Harrelson	6.00	3.00	1.75
(23)	Bud Harrelson	6.00	3.00	1.75
(24)	Jim Ray Hart	6.00	3.00	1.75
(25)	Tommy Helms	6.00	3.00	1.75
(26)	Joe Horlen	6.00	3.00	1.75
(27)	Tony Horton	7.50	3.75	2.25
(28)	Willie Horton	6.00	3.00	1.75
(29)	Frank Howard	7.50	3.75	2.25
(30)	Al Kaline	15.00	7.50	4.50
(31)	Don Kessinger	6.00	3.00	1.75
(32)	Harmon Killebrew	15.00	7.50	4.50
(33)	Jerry Koosman	6.00	3.00	1.75
(34)	Mickey Lolich	6.00	3.00	1.75
(35)	Jim Lonborg	6.00	3.00	1.75
(36)	Jim Maloney	6.00	3.00	1.75
(37)	Juan Marichal	12.50	6.25	3.75
(38)	Willie Mays	30.00	15.00	9.00
(39)	Tim McCarver	7.50	3.75	2.25
(40)	Willie McCovey	15.00	7.50	4.50
(41)	Sam McDowell	6.00	3.00	1.75
(42)	Denny McLain	7.50	3.75	2.25
(43)	Rick Monday	6.00	3.00	1.75
(44)	Tony Oliva	7.50	3.75	2.25
(45)	Joe Pepitone	7.50	3.75	2.25
(46)	Boog Powell	7.50	3.75	2.25
(47)	Rick Reichardt	6.00	3.00	1.75
(48)	Pete Richert	6.00	3.00	1.75
(49)	Brooks Robinson	15.00	7.50	4.50
(50)	Frank Robinson	15.00	7.50	4.50
(51)	Pete Rose	25.00	12.50	7.50
(52)	Ron Santo	9.00	4.50	2.75
(53)	Mel Stottlemyre	6.00	3.00	1.75
(54)	Ron Swoboda	6.00	3.00	1.75
(55)	Luis Tiant	6.00	3.00	1.75
(56)	Joe Torre	9.00	4.50	2.75
(57)	Pete Ward	6.00	3.00	1.75
(58)	Billy Williams	12.50	6.25	3.75
(59)	Jim Wynn	6.00	3.00	1.75
(60)	Carl Yastrzemski	15.00	7.50	4.50

1983 "1969" MLBPA Pins

Virtually identical in format to the 60-pin 1969 MLBPA issue, these pins were probably not issued prior to 1983 and despite what is printed thereon, are not a licensed issue of the Players Association. The 7/8" diameter pins have a black-and-white player portrait photo on a white background at center. The photo is bordered in red or blue with the player name at top and team at bottom in white. A copyright line on back reads, "1969 MLBPA MFG IN U.S.A." Latter-day pins can be distinguished from the 1969s by the absence of mention of Winona, Minn., on the replicas.

Complete Set (36):
(1) Hank Aaron
(2) Bob Allison
(3) Yogi Berra
(4) Roy Campanella
(5) Norm Cash
(6) Orlando Cepeda
(7) Roberto Clemente
(8) Joe DiMaggio
(9) Bobby Doerr
(10) Don Drysdale
(11) Bob Feller
(12) Whitey Ford
(13) Nellie Fox
(14) Frank Howard
(15) Jim "Catfish" Hunter
(16) Al Kaline
(17) Sandy Koufax
(18) Mickey Mantle
(19) Juan Marichal
(20) Eddie Mathews
(21) Willie Mays
(22) Willie McCovey
(23) Stan Musial
(24) Tony Oliva
(25) Satchel Paige
(26) Phil Rizzuto
(27) Robin Roberts
(28) Brooks Robinson
(29) Jackie Robinson
(30) Ron Santo
(31) Duke Snider
(32) Warren Spahn
(33) Bill Skowron
(34) Billy Williams
(35) Ted Williams
(36) Maury Wills

1970 Major League Baseball Photostamps

For a second year, ballplayer "stamps" were sold in conjunction with team albums. Approximately 1-7/8" x 3", the pieces are printed on glossy paper in full color with a white border and facsimile autograph. Backs, which are not

BILL MELTON

gummed, have gluing instructions and the players name at bottom. The 1970 issue can be differentiated from the 1969 issue in that they have uniform insignia present on the photos whereas the 1969 stamps do not. The unnumbered stamps are checklisted here alphabetically within team.

		NM	EX	VG
Complete Set (288):		200.00	100.00	60.00
Common Player:		1.00	.50	.30
ATLANTA BRAVES				
(1)	Hank Aaron	15.00	7.50	4.50
(2)	Bob Aspromonte	1.00	.50	.30
(3)	Rico Carty	1.00	.50	.30
(4)	Orlando Cepeda	6.00	3.00	1.75
(5)	Bob Didier	1.00	.50	.30
(6)	Tony Gonzalez	1.00	.50	.30
(7)	Pat Jarvis	1.00	.50	.30
(8)	Felix Millan	1.00	.50	.30
(9)	Jim Nash	1.00	.50	.30
(10)	Phil Niekro	4.00	2.00	1.25
(11)	Milt Pappas	1.00	.50	.30
(12)	Ron Reed	1.00	.50	.30
BALTIMORE ORIOLES				
(1)	Mark Belanger	1.00	.50	.30
(2)	Paul Blair	1.00	.50	.30
(3)	Don Buford	1.00	.50	.30
(4)	Mike Cuellar	1.00	.50	.30
(5)	Andy Etchebarren	1.00	.50	.30
(6)	Dave Johnson	1.00	.50	.30
(7)	Dave McNally	1.00	.50	.30
(8)	Tom Phoebus	1.00	.50	.30
(9)	Boog Powell	2.00	1.00	.60
(10)	Brooks Robinson	6.00	3.00	1.75
(11)	Frank Robinson	6.00	3.00	1.75
(12)	Chico Salmon	1.00	.50	.30
BOSTON RED SOX				
(1)	Mike Andrews	1.00	.50	.30
(2)	Ray Culp	1.00	.50	.30
(3)	Jim Lonborg	1.00	.50	.30
(4)	Sparky Lyle	1.00	.50	.30
(5)	Gary Peters	1.00	.50	.30
(6)	Rico Petrocelli	1.00	.50	.30
(7)	Vicente Romo	1.00	.50	.30
(8)	Tom Satriano	1.00	.50	.30
(9)	George Scott	1.00	.50	.30
(10)	Sonny Seibert	1.00	.50	.30
(11)	Reggie Smith	1.00	.50	.30
(12)	Carl Yastrzemski	6.00	3.00	1.75
CALIFORNIA ANGELS				
(1)	Sandy Alomar	1.00	.50	.30
(2)	Jose Azcue	1.00	.50	.30
(3)	Tom Egan	1.00	.50	.30
(4)	Jim Fregosi	1.00	.50	.30
(5)	Alex Johnson	1.00	.50	.30
(6)	Jay Johnstone	1.00	.50	.30
(7)	Rudy May	1.00	.50	.30
(8)	Andy Messersmith	1.00	.50	.30
(9)	Rick Reichardt	1.00	.50	.30
(10)	Roger Repoz	1.00	.50	.30
(11)	Aurelio Rodriguez	1.00	.50	.30
(12)	Ken Tatum	1.00	.50	.30
CHICAGO CUBS				
(1)	Ernie Banks	7.50	3.75	2.25
(2)	Glenn Beckert	1.00	.50	.30
(3)	Johnny Callison	1.00	.50	.30
(4)	Bill Hands	1.00	.50	.30
(5)	Randy Hundley	1.00	.50	.30
(6)	Ken Holtzman	1.00	.50	.30
(7)	Fergie Jenkins	4.00	2.00	1.25
(8)	Don Kessinger	1.00	.50	.30
(9)	Phil Regan	1.00	.50	.30
(10)	Ron Santo	2.00	1.00	.60
(11)	Dick Selma	1.00	.50	.30
(12)	Billy Williams	5.00	2.50	1.50
CHICAGO WHITE SOX				
(1)	Luis Aparicio	5.00	2.50	1.50
(2)	Ken Berry	1.00	.50	.30
(3)	Buddy Bradford	1.00	.50	.30
(4)	Ron Hansen	1.00	.50	.30
(5)	Joel Horlen	1.00	.50	.30
(6)	Tommy John	1.50	.70	.45
(7)	Duane Josephson	1.00	.50	.30
(8)	Bobby Knoop	1.00	.50	.30
(9)	Tom McCraw	1.00	.50	.30
(10)	Bill Melton	1.00	.50	.30
(11)	Walt Williams	1.00	.50	.30
(12)	Wilbur Wood	1.00	.50	.30
CINCINNATI REDS				
(1)	Johnny Bench	7.50	3.75	2.25
(2)	Tony Cloninger	1.00	.50	.30
(3)	Wayne Granger	1.00	.50	.30
(4)	Tommy Helms	1.00	.50	.30
(5)	Jim Maloney	1.00	.50	.30
(6)	Lee May	1.00	.50	.30
(7)	Jim McGlothlin	1.00	.50	.30

(8)	Jim Merritt	1.00	.50	.30
(9)	Gary Nolan	1.00	.50	.30
(10)	Tony Perez	5.00	2.50	1.50
(11)	Pete Rose	12.50	6.25	3.75
(12)	Bobby Tolan	1.00	.50	.30
CLEVELAND INDIANS				
(1)	Max Alvis	1.00	.50	.30
(2)	Larry Brown	1.00	.50	.30
(3)	Dean Chance	1.00	.50	.30
(4)	Dick Ellsworth	1.00	.50	.30
(5)	Vern Fuller	1.00	.50	.30
(6)	Ken Harrelson	1.00	.50	.30
(7)	Chuck Hinton	1.00	.50	.30
(8)	Tony Horton	1.00	.50	.30
(9)	Sam McDowell	1.00	.50	.30
(10)	Vada Pinson	1.50	.70	.45
(11)	Duke Sims	1.00	.50	.30
(12)	Ted Uhlaender	1.00	.50	.30
DETROIT TIGERS				
(1)	Norm Cash	1.50	.70	.45
(2)	Bill Freehan	1.00	.50	.30
(3)	Willie Horton	1.00	.50	.30
(4)	Al Kaline	7.50	3.75	2.25
(5)	Mike Kilkenny	1.00	.50	.30
(6)	Mickey Lolich	1.00	.50	.30
(7)	Dick McAuliffe	1.00	.50	.30
(8)	Denny McLain	1.50	.70	.45
(9)	Jim Northrup	1.00	.50	.30
(10)	Mickey Stanley	1.00	.50	.30
(11)	Tom Tresh	1.00	.50	.30
(12)	Earl Wilson	1.00	.50	.30
HOUSTON ASTROS				
(1)	Jesus Alou	1.00	.50	.30
(2)	Tommy Davis	1.00	.50	.30
(3)	Larry Dierker	1.00	.50	.30
(4)	Johnny Edwards	1.00	.50	.30
(5)	Fred Gladding	1.00	.50	.30
(6)	Denver Lemaster	1.00	.50	.30
(7)	Denis Menke	1.00	.50	.30
(8)	Joe Morgan	6.00	3.00	1.75
(9)	Joe Pepitone	1.50	.70	.45
(10)	Doug Rader	1.00	.50	.30
(11)	Don Wilson	1.00	.50	.30
(12)	Jim Wynn	1.00	.50	.30
KANSAS CITY ROYALS				
(1)	Jerry Adair	1.00	.50	.30
(2)	Wally Bunker	1.00	.50	.30
(3)	Bill Butler	1.00	.50	.30
(4)	Moe Drabowsky	1.00	.50	.30
(5)	Jackie Hernandez	1.00	.50	.30
(6)	Pat Kelly	1.00	.50	.30
(7)	Ed Kirkpatrick	1.00	.50	.30
(8)	Dave Morehead	1.00	.50	.30
(9)	Roger Nelson	1.00	.50	.30
(10)	Bob Oliver	1.00	.50	.30
(11)	Lou Piniella	1.50	.70	.45
(12)	Paul Schaal	1.00	.50	.30
LOS ANGELES DODGERS				
(1)	Willie Davis	1.00	.50	.30
(2)	Len Gabrielson	1.00	.50	.30
(3)	Tom Haller	1.00	.50	.30
(4)	Jim Lefebvre	1.00	.50	.30
(5)	Manny Mota	1.00	.50	.30
(6)	Claude Osteen	1.00	.50	.30
(7)	Wes Parker	1.00	.50	.30
(8)	Bill Russell	1.00	.50	.30
(9)	Bill Singer	1.00	.50	.30
(10)	Ted Sizemore	1.00	.50	.30
(11)	Don Sutton	4.00	2.00	1.25
(12)	Maury Wills	1.00	.50	.30
MINNESOTA TWINS				
(1)	Bob Allison	1.00	.50	.30
(2)	Dave Boswell	1.00	.50	.30
(3)	Leo Cardenas	1.00	.50	.30
(4)	Rod Carew	6.00	3.00	1.75
(5)	Jim Kaat	1.50	.70	.45
(6)	Harmon Killebrew	6.00	3.00	1.75
(7)	Tony Oliva	1.50	.70	.45
(8)	Jim Perry	1.00	.50	.30
(9)	Ron Perranoski	1.00	.50	.30
(10)	Rich Reese	1.00	.50	.30
(11)	Luis Tiant	1.00	.50	.30
(12)	Cesar Tovar	1.00	.50	.30
MONTREAL EXPOS				
(1)	John Bateman	1.00	.50	.30
(2)	Bob Bailey	1.00	.50	.30
(3)	Ron Brand	1.00	.50	.30
(4)	Ty Cline	1.00	.50	.30
(5)	Ron Fairly	1.00	.50	.30
(6)	Mack Jones	1.00	.50	.30
(7)	Jose Laboy	1.00	.50	.30
(8)	Claude Raymond	1.00	.50	.30
(9)	Joe Sparma	1.00	.50	.30
(10)	Rusty Staub	1.50	.70	.45
(11)	Bill Stoneman	1.00	.50	.30
(12)	Bobby Wine	1.00	.50	.30
NEW YORK METS				
(1)	Tommie Agee	1.00	.50	.30
(2)	Donn Clendenon	1.00	.50	.30
(3)	Joe Foy	1.00	.50	.30
(4)	Jerry Grote	1.00	.50	.30
(5)	Bud Harrelson	1.00	.50	.30
(6)	Cleon Jones	1.00	.50	.30
(7)	Jerry Koosman	1.00	.50	.30
(8)	Ed Kranepool	1.00	.50	.30
(9)	Nolan Ryan	25.00	12.50	7.50
(10)	Tom Seaver	6.00	3.00	1.75
(11)	Ron Swoboda	1.00	.50	.30
(12)	Al Weis	1.00	.50	.30
NEW YORK YANKEES				
(1)	Jack Aker	1.00	.50	.30
(2)	Curt Blefary	1.00	.50	.30
(3)	Danny Cater	1.00	.50	.30
(4)	Horace Clarke	1.00	.50	.30
(5)	Jake Gibbs	1.00	.50	.30
(6)	Steve Hamilton	1.00	.50	.30
(7)	Bobby Murcer	1.50	.70	.45
(8)	Fritz Peterson	1.00	.50	.30

(9)	Bill Robinson	1.00	.50	.30
(10)	Mel Stottlemyre	1.00	.50	.30
(11)	Pete Ward	1.00	.50	.30
(12)	Roy White	1.50	.70	.45

OAKLAND A's

(1)	Felipe Alou	1.50	.70	.45
(2)	Sal Bando	1.00	.50	.30
(3)	Bert Campaneris	1.00	.50	.30
(4)	Chuck Dobson	1.00	.50	.30
(5)	Tito Francona	1.00	.50	.30
(6)	Dick Green	1.00	.50	.30
(7)	Catfish Hunter	4.00	2.00	1.25
(8)	Reggie Jackson	10.00	5.00	3.00
(9)	Don Mincher	1.00	.50	.30
(10)	Rick Monday	1.00	.50	.30
(11)	John Odom	1.00	.50	.30
(12)	Ray Oyler	1.00	.50	.30

PHILADELPHIA PHILLIES

(1)	Johnny Briggs	1.00	.50	.30
(2)	Jim Bunning	4.00	2.00	1.25
(3)	Curt Flood	1.50	.70	.45
(4)	Woodie Fryman	1.00	.50	.30
(5)	Larry Hisle	1.00	.50	.30
(6)	Joe Hoerner	1.00	.50	.30
(7)	Grant Jackson	1.00	.50	.30
(8)	Tim McCarver	1.50	.70	.45
(9)	Mike Ryan	1.00	.50	.30
(10)	Chris Short	1.00	.50	.30
(11)	Tony Taylor	1.00	.50	.30
(12)	Rick Wise	1.00	.50	.30

PITTSBURGH PIRATES

(1)	Gene Alley	1.00	.50	.30
(2)	Matty Alou	1.00	.50	.30
(3)	Roberto Clemente	20.00	10.00	6.00
(4)	Ron Davis	1.00	.50	.30
(5)	Richie Hebner	1.00	.50	.30
(6)	Jerry May	1.00	.50	.30
(7)	Bill Mazeroski	6.00	3.00	1.75
(8)	Bob Moose	1.00	.50	.30
(9)	Al Oliver	1.50	.70	.45
(10)	Manny Sanguillen	1.00	.50	.30
(11)	Willie Stargell	5.00	2.50	1.50
(12)	Bob Veale	1.00	.50	.30

SAN DIEGO PADRES

(1)	Ollie Brown	1.00	.50	.30
(2)	Dave Campbell	1.00	.50	.30
(3)	Nate Colbert	1.00	.50	.30
(4)	Pat Dobson	1.00	.50	.30
(5)	Al Ferrera	1.00	.50	.30
(6)	Dick Kelley	1.00	.50	.30
(7)	Clay Kirby	1.00	.50	.30
(8)	Bill McCool	1.00	.50	.30
(9)	Frank Reberger	1.00	.50	.30
(10)	Tommie Sisk	1.00	.50	.30
(11)	Ed Spiezio	1.00	.50	.30
(12)	Larry Stahl	1.00	.50	.30

SAN FRANCISCO GIANTS

(1)	Bobby Bonds	1.50	.70	.45
(2)	Jim Davenport	1.00	.50	.30
(3)	Dick Dietz	1.00	.50	.30
(4)	Jim Ray Hart	1.00	.50	.30
(5)	Ron Hunt	1.00	.50	.30
(6)	Hal Lanier	1.00	.50	.30
(7)	Frank Linzy	1.00	.50	.30
(8)	Juan Marichal	5.00	2.50	1.50
(9)	Willie Mays	15.00	7.50	4.50
(10)	Mike McCormick	1.00	.50	.30
(11)	Willie McCovey	6.00	3.00	1.75
(12)	Gaylord Perry	4.00	2.00	1.25

SEATTLE PILOTS

(1)	Steve Barber	1.00	.50	.30
(2)	Bobby Bolin	1.00	.50	.30
(3)	George Brunet	1.00	.50	.30
(4)	Wayne Comer	1.00	.50	.30
(5)	John Donaldson	1.00	.50	.30
(6)	Tommy Harper	1.00	.50	.30
(7)	Mike Hegan	1.00	.50	.30
(8)	Mike Hershberger	1.00	.50	.30
(9)	Steve Hovley	1.00	.50	.30
(10)	Bob Locker	1.00	.50	.30
(11)	Gerry McNertney	1.00	.50	.30
(12)	Rich Rollins	1.00	.50	.30

ST. LOUIS CARDINALS

(1)	Richie Allen	2.50	1.25	.70
(2)	Nelson Briles	1.00	.50	.30
(3)	Lou Brock	6.00	3.00	1.75
(4)	Jose Cardenal	1.00	.50	.30
(5)	Steve Carlton	6.00	3.00	1.75
(6)	Vic Davalillo	1.00	.50	.30
(7)	Bob Gibson	6.00	3.00	1.75
(8)	Julian Javier	1.00	.50	.30
(9)	Dal Maxvill	1.00	.50	.30
(10)	Cookie Rojas	1.00	.50	.30
(11)	Mike Shannon	1.00	.50	.30
(12)	Joe Torre	3.00	1.50	.90

WASHINGTON SENATORS

(1)	Bernie Allen	1.00	.50	.30
(2)	Dick Bosman	1.00	.50	.30
(3)	Ed Brinkman	1.00	.50	.30
(4)	Paul Casanova	1.00	.50	.30
(5)	Joe Coleman	1.00	.50	.30
(6)	Mike Epstein	1.00	.50	.30
(7)	Frank Howard	1.50	.70	.45
(8)	Ken McMullen	1.00	.50	.30
(9)	John Roseboro	1.00	.50	.30
(10)	Ed Stroud	1.00	.50	.30
(11)	Del Unser	1.00	.50	.30
(12)	Zoilo Versalles	1.00	.50	.30

1910 Makaroff Cigarettes World Series Postcard

The text on this postcard indicates it may have been given out at World Series games in Philadelphia and Chicago. Two versions are known, one with Connie Mack's portrait at left and the Athletics score listed first, and one with Frank Chance's portrait at left and the Cubs score listed first. On the black-and-white address side are photographic portraits of the

A's and Cubs managers with appropriate team pennants. Below is scripted, "Saw the world's championship game to-day." Beneath that are lines to record the score. The front of the card is printed in black, white and red and has a picture of a smoking cigarette and a two-headed Russian eagle logo. At center is this "Dictum. / Think big, talk little, love much, laugh easily, / work hard, give freely, pay cash and be kind - / it is enough! Do these and you may smoke without / danger to your immortal soul."

	NM	EX	VG
Frank Chance, Connie Mack	350.00	175.00	100.00
Connie Mack, Frank Chance	350.00	175.00	100.00

1916 Mall Theatre

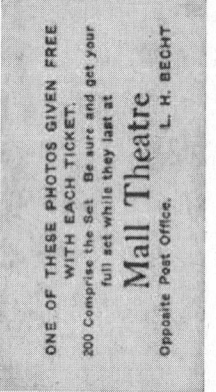

Best known for its use as a promotional medium for The Sporting News, this 200-card set can be found with ads on the back for several local and regional businesses. Among them is the Mall Theatre, location unknown. Type-card and super-star collectors can expect to pay a significant premium for individual cards with this advertising over generic 1916 M101-4 Blank Backs values. Cards measure 1-5/8" x 3" and are printed in black-and-white.

PREMIUM: 2-3X
(See 1916 M101-4 Blank Backs for checklist and base card values.)

1926-1927 Mallorquina Caramels

These tiny (about 3/4" x 1-1/8") cards were distributed with Mallorquina brand caramels in Cuba. The black-and-white images are printed on hard photographic paper stock. The bordered portrait photos on front have a box at bottom with player

identification and card number. Backs are printed in dark blue with the wording "LA MALLORQUINA / CARAMELOS / PELOTEROS" and a few graphic flourishes. The set's first 17 cards feature professional players, including a number of Negro Leagues stars. The last 83 cards in the set are Cuban amateurs. While there was probably some sort of album issued to house the set, none has been reported to date. Because the card of Hall of Famer Willie Foster is his only known career-contemporary issue, and that of Martin Dihigo is his earliest known, "book" values have not been assigned.

	Common Player	NM	EX	VG
		200.00	100.00	60.00
1	Adolfo Luque	750.00	375.00	225.00
2	Alfredo Cabrera	250.00	125.00	75.00
3	George Scales	350.00	175.00	105.00
4	Jose Maria Fernandez	250.00	125.00	75.00
5	Oliver Marcelle	3,000	1,500	900.00
6	Oscar Rodriguez	200.00	100.00	60.00
7	Martin Dihigo (Value Undetermined)			
8	Cheo Ramos	250.00	125.00	75.00
9	Pop Lloyd	4,500	2,250	1,350
10	Joe Olivares	200.00	100.00	60.00
11	Brujo Rosell	200.00	100.00	60.00
12	Willie Foster (Value Undetermined)			
13	Cho Cho Correa	250.00	125.00	75.00
14	Larry Brown	350.00	175.00	105.00
15	Oscar Levis	250.00	125.00	75.00
16	Raul Alvarez	250.00	125.00	75.00
17	Juan Eckelson	250.00	125.00	75.00
18	Quesada	200.00	100.00	60.00
19	J. Rosado	200.00	100.00	60.00
20	A. Unanuo	200.00	100.00	60.00
21	A. Echavarria	200.00	100.00	60.00
22	C. Beltran	200.00	100.00	60.00
23	J. Beltran	200.00	100.00	60.00
24	G. Orama	200.00	100.00	60.00
25	E. Carrillo	200.00	100.00	60.00
26	A. Casuso	200.00	100.00	60.00
27	A. Consuegra	200.00	100.00	60.00
28	R. Gallardo	200.00	100.00	60.00
29	M. Sotolongo	200.00	100.00	60.00
30	M. Llano	200.00	100.00	60.00
31	H. Rocamora	200.00	100.00	60.00
32	Calvo	200.00	100.00	60.00
33	R. Inclan	200.00	100.00	60.00
34	Mendizabal	200.00	100.00	60.00
35	H. Alonso	200.00	100.00	60.00
36	C. Leonard	200.00	100.00	60.00
37	Cap Cordova	200.00	100.00	60.00
38	Cordova	200.00	100.00	60.00
39	Sarasua	200.00	100.00	60.00
40	E. Cubillas	200.00	100.00	60.00
41	B. Wilryc	200.00	100.00	60.00
42	Morera	200.00	100.00	60.00
43	C. Fernandez	200.00	100.00	60.00
44	Milian	200.00	100.00	60.00
45	P. Espinosa	200.00	100.00	60.00
46	Macia	200.00	100.00	60.00
47	J. Lagueruela	200.00	100.00	60.00
48	Bernal	200.00	100.00	60.00
49	J.A. Ruiz	200.00	100.00	60.00
50	Unknown			
51	J. Gayoso	200.00	100.00	60.00
52	Castro	200.00	100.00	60.00
53	C. Hernandez	200.00	100.00	60.00
54	Reynolds	200.00	100.00	60.00
55	M. Rodriguez	200.00	100.00	60.00
56	P. Flores	200.00	100.00	60.00
57	A. Collazo	200.00	100.00	60.00
58	R. Gonzalez	200.00	100.00	60.00
59	A. Casas	200.00	100.00	60.00
60	Barcena	200.00	100.00	60.00
61	Quesada	200.00	100.00	60.00
62	Riquerin	200.00	100.00	60.00
63	Carbonere	200.00	100.00	60.00
64	Vega	200.00	100.00	60.00
65	Rodriguez	200.00	100.00	60.00
66	A. Castillo	200.00	100.00	60.00
67	Y. Balleste	200.00	100.00	60.00
68	Fernandez	200.00	100.00	60.00
69	Garros	200.00	100.00	60.00
70	Cabada	200.00	100.00	60.00
71	R.P. Fernandez	200.00	100.00	60.00
72	R. Cejas	200.00	100.00	60.00
73	Gros	200.00	100.00	60.00
74	Mendez	200.00	100.00	60.00
75	M. Sotolongo	200.00	100.00	60.00
76	E. Vela	200.00	100.00	60.00
77	A. Vela	200.00	100.00	60.00
78	F. Pinera	200.00	100.00	60.00
79	M. Valdes	200.00	100.00	60.00
80	L. Romero	200.00	100.00	60.00
81	A. Febles	200.00	100.00	60.00
82	Lugo	200.00	100.00	60.00
83	Polo Calvo	200.00	100.00	60.00
84	Silvio O. Farrill	200.00	100.00	60.00
85	Zalazar	200.00	100.00	60.00
86	Tapia	200.00	100.00	60.00
87	Hernandez	200.00	100.00	60.00
88	Manrrara	200.00	100.00	60.00
89	J. Deschapelle	200.00	100.00	60.00
90	Arguelles	200.00	100.00	60.00
91	E. Arechaede	200.00	100.00	60.00
92	E. Quintanal	200.00	100.00	60.00
93	M. Valdes	200.00	100.00	60.00
94	J. Martinez	200.00	100.00	60.00
95	R. Martinez	200.00	100.00	60.00
96	F. Gali	200.00	100.00	60.00
97	A. Martinez	200.00	100.00	60.00
98	G. Hernandez	200.00	100.00	60.00
99	A. Fernandez	200.00	100.00	60.00
100	Armando Figarola	200.00	100.00	60.00

1961 Manny's Baseball Land 8x10s

In 1961, Manny's Baseball Land issued 18 10-piece 8" x 10" printed black-and-white photo packs, arranged by team. Manny's was a next-door neighbor of Yankee Stadium and the nation's largest purveyor of baseball souvenirs. These photo sets were sold for $1.50 per team. The blank-back photos were printed on semi-gloss paper. Portraits or posed action photos were surrounded by a white border which contains the player's name in all caps at bottom. The unnumbered pictures are checklisted here alphabetically by and within team.

		NM	EX	VG
Complete Set (180):		2,500	1,250	750.00
Common Player:		10.00	5.00	3.00
BALTIMORE ORIOLES				
(1)	Jackie Brandt	10.00	5.00	3.00
(2)	Marv Breeding	10.00	5.00	3.00
(3)	Chuck Estrada	10.00	5.00	3.00
(4)	Jack Fisher	10.00	5.00	3.00
(5)	Jim Gentile	10.00	5.00	3.00
(6)	Ron Hansen	10.00	5.00	3.00
(7)	Milt Pappas	10.00	5.00	3.00
(8)	Brooks Robinson	30.00	15.00	9.00
(9)	Gus Triandos	10.00	5.00	3.00
(10)	Jerry Walker	10.00	5.00	3.00
BOSTON RED SOX				
(11)	Tom Brewer	10.00	5.00	3.00
(12)	Don Buddin	10.00	5.00	3.00
(13)	Gene Conley	10.00	5.00	3.00
(14)	Mike Fornieles	10.00	5.00	3.00
(15)	Gary Geiger	10.00	5.00	3.00
(16)	Pumpsie Green	10.00	5.00	3.00
(17)	Jackie Jensen	15.00	7.50	4.50
(18)	Frank Malzone	10.00	5.00	3.00
(19)	Pete Runnels	10.00	5.00	3.00
(20)	Vic Wertz	10.00	5.00	3.00
CHICAGO CUBS				
(21)	George Altman	10.00	5.00	3.00
(22)	Bob Anderson	10.00	5.00	3.00
(23)	Richie Ashburn	30.00	15.00	9.00
(24)	Ernie Banks	35.00	17.50	10.00
(25)	Don Cardwell	10.00	5.00	3.00
(26)	Moe Drabowsky	10.00	5.00	3.00
(27)	Don Elston	10.00	5.00	3.00
(28)	Jerry Kindall	10.00	5.00	3.00
(29)	Ron Santo	15.00	7.50	4.50
(30)	Bob Will	10.00	5.00	3.00
CHICAGO WHITE SOX				
(31)	Luis Aparicio	25.00	12.50	7.50
(32)	Frank Baumann	10.00	5.00	3.00
(33)	Sam Esposito	10.00	5.00	3.00
(34)	Nellie Fox	30.00	15.00	9.00
(35)	Jim Landis	10.00	5.00	3.00
(36)	Sherman Lollar	10.00	5.00	3.00
(37)	Minnie Minoso	20.00	10.00	6.00
(38)	Billy Pierce	10.00	5.00	3.00
(39)	Bob Shaw	10.00	5.00	3.00
(40)	Early Wynn	25.00	12.50	7.50
CINCINNATI REDLEGS				
(41)	Ed Bailey	10.00	5.00	3.00
(42)	Gus Bell	10.00	5.00	3.00
(43)	Gordon Coleman	10.00	5.00	3.00
(44)	Bill Henry	10.00	5.00	3.00
(45)	Jerry Lynch	10.00	5.00	3.00
(46)	Claude Osteen	10.00	5.00	3.00
(47)	Vada Pinson	12.50	6.25	3.75
(48)	Wally Post	10.00	5.00	3.00
(49)	Bob Purkey	10.00	5.00	3.00
(50)	Frank Robinson	35.00	17.50	10.00
CLEVELAND INDIANS				
(51)	Mike de la Hoz	10.00	5.00	3.00
(52)	Tito Francona	10.00	5.00	3.00
(53)	Woody Held	10.00	5.00	3.00
(54)	Barry Latman	10.00	5.00	3.00
(55)	Jim Perry	10.00	5.00	3.00
(56)	Bubba Phillips	10.00	5.00	3.00
(57)	Jim Piersall	12.50	6.25	3.75
(58)	Vic Power	10.00	5.00	3.00
(59)	John Romano	10.00	5.00	3.00
(60)	Johnny Temple	10.00	5.00	3.00
DETROIT TIGERS				
(61)	Hank Aguirre	10.00	5.00	3.00
(62)	Billy Bruton	10.00	5.00	3.00
(63)	Jim Bunning	25.00	12.50	7.50
(64)	Norm Cash	20.00	10.00	6.00
(65)	Rocky Colavito	25.00	12.50	7.50
(66)	Chico Fernandez	10.00	5.00	3.00
(67)	Paul Foytack	10.00	5.00	3.00
(68)	Al Kaline	35.00	17.50	10.00
(69)	Frank Lary	10.00	5.00	3.00
(70)	Don Mossi	10.00	5.00	3.00
KANSAS CITY ATHLETICS				
(71)	Hank Bauer	10.00	5.00	3.00
(72)	Andy Carey	10.00	5.00	3.00
(73)	Leo "Bud" Daley	10.00	5.00	3.00
(74)	Ray Herbert	10.00	5.00	3.00
(75)	John Kucks	10.00	5.00	3.00
(76)	Jerry Lumpe	10.00	5.00	3.00
(77)	Norm Siebern	10.00	5.00	3.00
(78)	Haywood Sullivan	10.00	5.00	3.00
(79)	Marv Throneberry	10.00	5.00	3.00
(80)	Dick Williams	10.00	5.00	3.00
LOS ANGELES ANGELS				
(81)	Ken Aspromonte	10.00	5.00	3.00
(82)	Steve Bilko	10.00	5.00	3.00
(83)	Bob Cerv	10.00	5.00	3.00
(84)	Ned Garver	10.00	5.00	3.00
(85)	Ken Hunt	10.00	5.00	3.00
(86)	Ted Kluszewski	25.00	12.50	7.50
(87)	Jim McAnany	10.00	5.00	3.00
(88)	Duke Maas	10.00	5.00	3.00
(89)	Albie Pearson	10.00	5.00	3.00
(90)	Eddie Yost	10.00	5.00	3.00
LOS ANGELES DODGERS				
(91)	Don Drysdale	30.00	15.00	9.00
(92)	Jim Gilliam	12.50	6.25	3.75
(93)	Frank Howard	12.50	6.25	3.75
(94)	Sandy Koufax	50.00	25.00	15.00
(95)	Norm Larker	10.00	5.00	3.00
(96)	Wally Moon	10.00	5.00	3.00
(97)	Charles Neal	10.00	5.00	3.00
(98)	Johnny Podres	12.50	6.25	3.75
(99)	Larry Sherry	10.00	5.00	3.00
(100)	Maury Wills	12.50	6.25	3.75
MILWAUKEE BRAVES				
(101)	Hank Aaron	50.00	25.00	15.00
(102)	Joe Adcock	10.00	5.00	3.00
(103)	Frank Bolling	10.00	5.00	3.00
(104)	Bob Buhl	10.00	5.00	3.00
(105)	Lew Burdette	10.00	5.00	3.00
(106)	Del Crandall	10.00	5.00	3.00
(107)	Ed Mathews	35.00	17.50	10.00
(108)	Roy McMillan	10.00	5.00	3.00
(109)	Warren Spahn	35.00	17.50	10.00
(110)	Al Spangler	10.00	5.00	3.00
MINNESOTA TWINS				
(111)	Bob Allison	10.00	5.00	3.00
(112)	Earl Battey	10.00	5.00	3.00
(113)	Reno Bertola (Bertoia)	10.00	5.00	3.00
(114)	Billy Consolo	10.00	5.00	3.00
(115)	Billy Gardner	10.00	5.00	3.00
(116)	Harmon Killebrew	35.00	17.50	10.00
(117)	Jim Lemon	10.00	5.00	3.00
(118)	Camilo Pascual	10.00	5.00	3.00
(119)	Pedro Ramos	10.00	5.00	3.00
(120)	Chuck Stobbs	10.00	5.00	3.00
NEW YORK YANKEES				
(121)	Larry "Yogi" Berra	35.00	17.50	10.00
(122)	John Blanchard	10.00	5.00	3.00
(123)	Ed "Whitey" Ford	35.00	17.50	10.00
(124)	Elston Howard	15.00	7.50	4.50
(125)	Tony Kubek	15.00	7.50	4.50
(126)	Mickey Mantle	65.00	32.50	20.00
(127)	Roger Maris	40.00	20.00	12.00
(128)	Bobby Richardson	15.00	7.50	4.50
(129)	Bill Skowron	15.00	7.50	4.50
(130)	Bob Turley	10.00	5.00	3.00
PHILADELPHIA PHILLIES				
(131)	John Callison	10.00	5.00	3.00
(132)	Dick Farrell	10.00	5.00	3.00
(133)	Pancho Herrera	10.00	5.00	3.00
(134)	Joe Koppe	10.00	5.00	3.00
(135)	Art Mahaffey	10.00	5.00	3.00
(136)	Gene Mauch	10.00	5.00	3.00
(137)	Jim Owens	10.00	5.00	3.00
(138)	Robin Roberts	30.00	15.00	9.00
(139)	Frank Sullivan	10.00	5.00	3.00
(140)	Tony Taylor	10.00	5.00	3.00
PITTSBURGH PIRATES				
(141)	Roberto Clemente	60.00	30.00	18.00
(142)	Roy Face	10.00	5.00	3.00
(143)	Bob Friend	10.00	5.00	3.00
(144)	Dick Groat	10.00	5.00	3.00
(145)	Harvey Haddix	10.00	5.00	3.00
(146)	Don Hoak	10.00	5.00	3.00
(147)	Vern Law	10.00	5.00	3.00
(148)	Bill Mazeroski	30.00	15.00	9.00
(149)	Wilmer Mizell	10.00	5.00	3.00
(150)	Bill Virdon	10.00	5.00	3.00
SAN FRANCISCO GIANTS				
(151)	Felipe Alou	12.50	6.25	3.75
(152)	Orlando Cepeda	30.00	15.00	9.00
(153)	Sam Jones	10.00	5.00	3.00
(154)	Harvey Kuenn	10.00	5.00	3.00
(155)	Willie Mays	50.00	25.00	15.00
(156)	Mike McCormick	10.00	5.00	3.00
(157)	Willie McCovey	30.00	15.00	9.00
(158)	Stu Miller	10.00	5.00	3.00
(159)	Billy O'Dell	10.00	5.00	3.00
(160)	Jack Sanford	10.00	5.00	3.00
ST. LOUIS CARDINALS				
(161)	Ernie Broglio	10.00	5.00	3.00
(162)	Ken Boyer	12.50	6.25	3.75
(163)	Joe Cunningham	10.00	5.00	3.00
(164)	Alex Grammas	10.00	5.00	3.00
(165)	Larry Jackson	10.00	5.00	3.00
(166)	Julian Javier	10.00	5.00	3.00
(167)	Lindy McDaniel	10.00	5.00	3.00
(168)	Stan Musial	45.00	22.50	13.50
(169)	Hal Smith	10.00	5.00	3.00
(170)	Daryl Spencer	10.00	5.00	3.00
WASHINGTON SENATORS				
(171)	Pete Daley	10.00	5.00	3.00
(172)	Dick Donovan	10.00	5.00	3.00
(173)	Bob Johnson	10.00	5.00	3.00
(174)	Marty Keough	10.00	5.00	3.00
(175)	Billy Klaus	10.00	5.00	3.00
(176)	Dale Long	10.00	5.00	3.00
(177)	Carl Mathias	10.00	5.00	3.00
(178)	Willie Tasby	10.00	5.00	3.00
(179)	Mickey Vernon	10.00	5.00	3.00
(180)	Gene Woodling	10.00	5.00	3.00

1959 Mickey Mantle's Holiday Inn Postcard

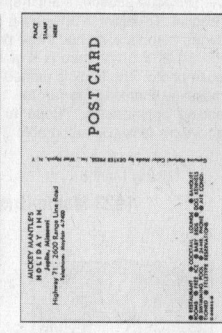

The attributed date is speculative. Much rarer than the more common pose of Mantle in civvies in his Joplin, Mo. motel's lounge, this approximately 3-1/2" x 5-1/2" card features two color poses of the Mick in Yankees uniform on its front. The postcard-style back is printed in blue and gives motel information and features.

	NM	EX	VG
Mickey Mantle	100.00	50.00	30.00

1962 Mickey Mantle's Holiday Inn Postcard

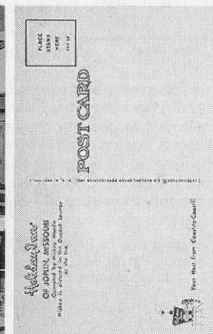

This color postcard pictures Mantle in civilian clothes. On the back of the standard-size (about 3-1/2" x 5-1/2") card it says the Mick is "pictured in the Dugout Lounge at the Inn." The "Inn" is the Joplin, Mo., Holiday Inn which Mantle owned. This was one of the more popular, and thus more common, of the souvenirs issued in conjunction with Mantle's motel.

	NM	EX	VG
Mickey Mantle	30.00	15.00	9.00

1962 Mickey Mantle's Holiday Inn Premium Photo

Probably issued in 1962, though not dated, this 8" x 10" photo pictures the M&M Boys in the lounge of Mantle's motel. Back is blank.

	NM	EX	VG
Mickey Mantle, Roger Maris	600.00	300.00	180.00

1963 Mickey Mantle Hospital Postcard

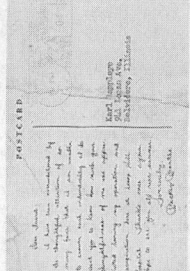

With a broken foot in 1963 following hard on a knee injury the previous season, Mantle spent considerable time in the hospital. To assist in answering a mountain of goodwill messages from fans, he had these postcards created. On front of the 3-1/2" x 5-1/2" card is a glossy black-and-white batting-pose photo. The back is printed in blue with a "Dear Friend" message thanking the fan for "the thoughtful attention" and ending optimistically, "Hope to see you all next season," above his facsimile autograph.

	NM	EX	VG
Mickey Mantle	450.00	225.00	135.00

1923 Maple Crispette (V117)

Issued by a Montreal candy company, these small (1-3/8" x 2-1/4") black-and-white cards were redeemable for baseball equipment, accounting for their scarcity today. Card #15, Stengel, was only discovered in 1992 and was obviously short-printed by the issuer to avoid giving away many bats, balls and gloves. Only a single specimen of the Stengel card is currently known; it is not included in the complete set prices.

		NM	EX	VG
	Complete Set, no Stengel (29):	27,000	10,800	6,720
	Common Player:	420.00	170.00	110.00
1	Jesse Barnes	420.00	170.00	110.00
2	Harold Traynor	720.00	290.00	180.00
3	Ray Schalk	720.00	290.00	180.00
4	Eddie Collins	720.00	290.00	180.00
5	Lee Fohl	420.00	170.00	110.00
6	Howard Summa	420.00	170.00	110.00
7	Waite Hoyt	720.00	290.00	180.00
8	Babe Ruth	8,700	3,600	1,920
9	Cozy Dolan	420.00	170.00	110.00
10	Johnny Bassler	420.00	170.00	110.00
11	George Dauss	420.00	170.00	110.00
12	Joe Sewell	720.00	290.00	180.00
13	Syl Johnson	420.00	170.00	110.00
14a	Wingo	420.00	170.00	110.00
14b	Ivy Wingo	420.00	170.00	110.00
15	Casey Stengel	18,000	9,000	4,500
16	Arnold Statz	420.00	170.00	110.00
17	Emil Meusel	420.00	170.00	110.00
18	Bill Jacobson	420.00	170.00	11.00
19	Jim Bottomley	2,000	290.00	180.00
20	Sam Bohne	540.00	215.00	130.00
21	Bucky Harris	720.00	290.00	180.00
22	Ty Cobb	3,000	1,200	750.00
23	Roger Peckinpaugh	420.00	170.00	110.00
24	Muddy Ruel	420.00	170.00	110.00
25	Bill McKechnie	720.00	290.00	180.00
26	Riggs Stephenson	420.00	170.00	110.00
27	Herb Pennock	720.00	290.00	180.00
28	Edd Roush	720.00	290.00	180.00
29	Bill Wambsganss	420.00	170.00	110.00
30	Walter Johnson	2,400	960.00	600.00

1962 Roger Maris Action Baseball Game

Baseball's new home run king was featured in this board game by Pressman Toy Co. Besides the colorful metal game board and other pieces, the set contains 88 playing cards. Each 2-1/4" x 3-1/2" card has a black-and-white photo on front of Maris in a batting pose, along with a white facsimile autograph. Backs have two possible game action plays printed, along with a copyright line.

	NM	EX	VG
Complete Game:	150.00	75.00	45.00

		NM	EX	VG
Single Card:		15.00	7.50	4.50
	Roger Maris			

1913-14 Martens Bakery

(See 1911-14 General Baking Co. (D304).)

1955 Mascot Dog Food

The date of issue shown is approximate. It is likely other players' cards exist, since the back mentions eight stars printed on the label, presumably of the dog food can. In black-and-white, the 3-1/2" x 5-1/2" card has on front a glossy action pose with a facsimile autograph personalized, "To My Mascot" and the player name and position printed in black in the bottom border. The back has an ad for a fan club offering an autographed 8" x 10" membership card and and set of eight postcards for a quarter and a label. label.

		NM	EX	VG
(1)	Robin Roberts	450.00	225.00	135.00

1971 Mattel Instant Replay Records

These 2-3/8" diameter plastic records were produced in conjunction with a hand-held, battery-operated record player. Paper inserts featured illustrations of players in baseball, football and basketball, as well as various racing vehicles and airplanes. The audio recounts career highlights of the depicted player. Additional records were sold in sets of four.

		NM	EX	VG
Complete Set (12):		250.00	125.00	75.00
Common Player:		10.00	5.00	3.00
(1)	Hank Aaron	30.00	15.00	9.00
(2)	Ernie Banks	15.00	7.50	4.50
(3)	Roberto Clemente	50.00	25.00	15.00
(4)	Al Kaline	15.00	7.50	4.50
(5)	Sandy Koufax	40.00	20.00	12.00
(6)	Roger Maris	15.00	7.50	4.50
(7)	Willie Mays (Plays one side only; came with record player purchase.)	12.00	6.00	3.50
(8)	Willie McCovey	12.00	6.00	3.50
(9)	Tony Oliva	10.00	5.00	3.00
(10)	Frank Robinson	13.50	6.75	4.00
(11)	Tom Seaver	15.00	7.50	4.50
(12)	Willie Stargell	12.00	6.00	3.50

1895 Mayo's Cut Plug (N300)

These 1-5/8" x 2-7/8" cards were issued by the Mayo Tobacco Works of Richmond, Va. There are 48 cards in the set, with 40 different players pictured. Twenty-eight of the players are pictured in uniform and 12 are shown in street clothes. Eight players appear both ways. Eight of the uniformed players also appear in two variations, creating the 48-card total. Card fronts are black-and-white or sepia portraits on black cardboard, with a Mayo's Cut Plug ad at the bottom of each card. Cards have a blank black back and are unnumbered.

		NM	EX	VG
Complete Set (48):		264,000	132,000	80,000
Common Player:		2,400	950.00	500.00
(1)	Charlie Abbey	2,400	950.00	500.00
(2)	Cap Anson	21,000	8,450	4,225
(3)	Jimmy Bannon	2,400	950.00	500.00
(4a)	Dan Brouthers (Baltimore on shirt.)	11,900	4,750	2,375
(4b)	Dan Brouthers (Louisville on shirt.)	13,200	5,300	2,650
(5)	Ed Cartwright	2,400	950.00	500.00
(6)	John Clarkson	7,900	3,150	1,600
(7)	Tommy Corcoran	2,400	950.00	500.00
(8)	Lave Cross	2,400	950.00	500.00
(9)	Bill Dahlen	3,000	1,200	600.00
(10)	Tom Daly	2,400	950.00	500.00
(11)	E.J. Delehanty (Delahanty)	15,800	6,325	3,150
(12)	Hugh Duffy	7,900	3,200	1,600
(13a)	Buck Ewing (Cleveland on shirt.)	13,200	5,300	2,650
(13b)	Buck Ewing (Cincinnati on shirt.)	10,000	4,000	2,000
(14)	Dave Foutz	2,400	950.00	500.00
(15)	Charlie Ganzel	2,400	950.00	500.00
(16a)	Jack Glasscock (Pittsburg on shirt.)	3,000	1,200	600.00
(16b)	Jack Glasscock (Louisville on shirt.)	2,400	950.00	500.00
(17)	Mike Griffin	2,400	950.00	500.00
(18a)	George Haddock (No team on shirt.)	3,300	1,300	650.00
(18b)	George Haddock (Philadelphia on shirt.)	2,400	950.00	500.00
(19)	Bill Hallman	2,400	950.00	500.00
(20)	Billy Hamilton	7,900	3,200	1,600
(21)	Bill Joyce	2,400	950.00	500.00
(22)	Brickyard Kennedy	2,400	950.00	500.00
(23a)	Tom Kinslow (No team on shirt.)	3,300	1,300	650.00
(23b)	Tom Kinslow (Pittsburg on shirt.)	2,400	950.00	500.00
(24)	Arlie Latham	2,400	950.00	500.00
(25)	Herman Long	2,400	950.00	500.00
(26)	Tom Lovett	2,400	950.00	500.00
(27)	Bobby Lowe	2,400	950.00	500.00
(28)	Tommy McCarthy	7,900	3,200	1,600
(29)	Yale Murphy	2,400	950.00	500.00
(30)	Billy Nash	2,400	950.00	500.00
(31)	Kid Nichols	13,200	5,300	2,650
(32a)	Fred Pfeffer (2nd Base)	2,400	950.00	500.00
(32b)	Fred Pfeffer (Retired)	2,400	950.00	500.00
(33)	Wilbert Robinson	7,900	3,200	1,600
(34a)	Amos Russie (Incorrect spelling.)	16,500	6,600	3,300
(34b)	Amos Rusie (Correct)	11,900	4,750	2,375
(35)	Jimmy Ryan	2,400	950.00	500.00
(36)	Bill Shindle	2,400	950.00	500.00
(37)	Germany Smith	2,400	950.00	500.00
(38)	Otis Stocksdale (Stockdale)	2,400	950.00	500.00
(39)	Tommy Tucker	2,400	950.00	500.00
(40a)	Monte Ward (2nd Base)	11,900	4,750	2,370
(40b)	Monte Ward (Retired)	10,000	4,000	2,000

1896 Mayo's Die-Cut Game Cards (N301)

Mayo Tobacco Works of Richmond, Va., issued an innovative, if not very popular, series of die-cut baseball player figures in 1896. These tiny (1-1/2" long by just 3/16" wide) cardboard figures were inserted in packages of Mayo's Cut Plug Tobacco and were designed to be used as part of a baseball board game. A "grandstand, base and teetotum" were available free by mail to complete the game pieces. Twenty-eight different die-cut figures were available, representing 26 unspecified New York and Boston players along with two umpires. The players are shown in various action poses - either running, batting, pitching or fielding. The backs carry an ad for Mayo's Tobacco. The players shown do not relate to any actual members of the New York or Boston clubs, diminishing the popularity of this issue, which has an American Card Catalog designation of N301.

		NM	EX	VG
	Complete Set (28):	4,000	1,600	800.00
	Common Player:	150.00	60.00	30.00
(1a)	Pitcher (Boston)	150.00	60.00	30.00
(1b)	Pitcher (New York)	150.00	60.00	30.00
(2a)	1st Baseman (Boston)	150.00	60.00	30.00
(2b)	1st Baseman (New York)	150.00	60.00	30.00
(3a)	2nd Baseman (Boston)	150.00	60.00	30.00
(3b)	2nd Baseman (New York)	150.00	60.00	30.00
(4a)	3rd Baseman (Boston)	150.00	60.00	30.00
(4b)	3rd Baseman (New York)	150.00	60.00	30.00
(5a)	Right Fielder (Boston)	150.00	60.00	30.00
(5b)	Right Fielder (New York)	150.00	60.00	30.00
(6a)	Center Fielder (Boston)	150.00	60.00	30.00
(6b)	Center Fielder (New York)	150.00	60.00	30.00
(7a)	Left Fielder (Boston)	150.00	60.00	30.00
(7b)	Left Fielder (New York)	150.00	60.00	30.00
(8a)	Short Stop (Boston)	150.00	60.00	30.00
(8b)	Short Stop (New York)	150.00	60.00	30.00
(9a)	Catcher (Boston)	150.00	60.00	30.00
(9b)	Catcher (New York)	150.00	60.00	30.00
(10a)	Batman (Boston)	150.00	60.00	30.00
(10b)	Batman (New York)	150.00	60.00	30.00
(11a)	Runner (Boston, standing upright.)	150.00	60.00	30.00
(11b)	Runner (New York, standing upright.)	150.00	60.00	30.00
(12a)	Runner (Boston, bent slightly forward)	150.00	60.00	30.00
(12b)	Runner (New York, bent slightly forward)	150.00	60.00	30.00
(13a)	Runner (Boston, bent well forward.)	150.00	60.00	30.00
(13b)	Runner (New York, bent well forward.)	150.00	60.00	30.00
(14)	Umpire (Facing front.)	150.00	60.00	30.00
(15)	Field Umpire (Rear view.)	150.00	60.00	30.00

1900 Mayo's Baseball Comics (T203)

"A Star Catcher"

UP TO DATE
BASE BALL COMICS
25 DIFFERENT DESIGNS
MAKE A COLLECTION
MAYO'S
CUT PLUG
IS ALWAYS GOOD
for
SMOKE and CHEW
5¢

As their name implies, the T203 Baseball Comics feature cartoon-like drawings that illustrate various baseball phrases and terminology. Issued with Winner Cut Plug and Mayo Cut Plug tobacco products, the complete set consists of 25 different comics, each measuring approximately 2-1/16" x 3-1/8". Because they do not picture individual players, these cards have never attracted much of a following among serious baseball card collectors. They do, however, hold some interest as a novelty item of the period.

		NM	EX	VG
	Complete Set (25):	3,000	1,500	650.00
	Common Card:	150.00	75.00	30.00
(1)	"A Crack Outfielder"	150.00	75.00	30.00
(2)	"A Fancy Twirler"	150.00	75.00	30.00
(3)	"A Fine Slide"	150.00	75.00	30.00
(4)	"A Fowl Bawl"	150.00	75.00	30.00
(5)	"A Great Game"	150.00	75.00	30.00
(6)	"A Home Run"	150.00	75.00	30.00
(7)	"An All Star Battery"	150.00	75.00	30.00
(8)	"A Short Stop"	150.00	75.00	30.00
(9)	"A Star Catcher"	150.00	75.00	30.00
(10)	"A White Wash"	150.00	75.00	30.00
(11)	"A Tie Game"	150.00	75.00	30.00
(12)	"A Two Bagger"	150.00	75.00	30.00
(13)	"A Wild Pitch"	150.00	75.00	30.00
(14)	"Caught Napping"	150.00	75.00	30.00
(15)	"On To The Curves"	150.00	75.00	30.00
(16)	"Out"	150.00	75.00	30.00
(17)	"Put Out On 1st"	150.00	75.00	30.00
(18)	"Right Over The Plate"	150.00	75.00	30.00
(19)	"Rooting For The Home Team"	150.00	75.00	30.00
(20)	"Stealing A Base"	150.00	75.00	30.00
(21)	"Stealing Home"	150.00	75.00	30.00
(22)	"Strike One"	150.00	75.00	30.00
(23)	"The Bleacher"	150.00	75.00	30.00
(24)	"The Naps"	150.00	75.00	30.00
(25)	"The Red Sox"	150.00	75.00	30.00

1948 Thom McAn Bob Feller Premium

This black-and-white 8" x 10" premium picture has on front a posed action photo and facsimile autograph. On back is a 25-question baseball quiz and advertising for the shoe store chain, along with a copyright for Melville Shoe Co.

What's Your Score on This Baseball Quiz?

Here are the Answers... Now Test Your Friends!

Thom McAn

	NM	EX	VG
Bob Feller	150.00	75.00	45.00

1950s-80s J.D. McCarthy Player Postcards

NORM LARKER

From the 1950s into the 1980s, Detroit area photographer J.D. McCarthy produced black-and-white postcards to order for hundreds of ballplayers to use in answering fan mail requests for pictures and autographs. Sizes and formats differed through the years, but most are about standard postcard size (3-1/2" x 5-1/2") with borderless poses on front. Some cards have a white strip with printed name on front, others have a facsimile autograph, while others have no identification at all. Some card fronts carry his stylized JcMD monogram. Backs, likewise, differ in the style and manner of their markings. Printing was generally done on thin, semi-gloss cardboard. Many players are found in more than one pose, or in cropping variations of a pose. Many players continued to re-order postcards long after their careers were over. Following McCarthy's death, archives of his negatives were sold into the hobby, making it theoretically possible for many cards to be reproduced in perpetuity. That mitigates against many of these cards attaining any great degree of collectible value, though they are popular with team and single-player collectors. Postally-used cards which carry a dated postmark are of the greatest value. Many cards, as the one pictured here, are autographed.

	NM	EX	VG
Common Player:	3.00	1.50	.90

1970 McDonald's Brewers

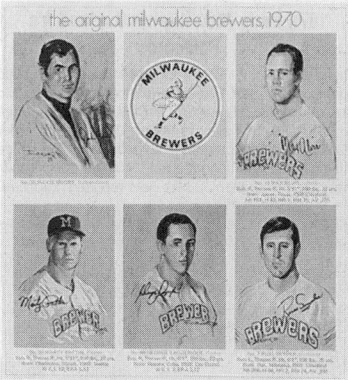

the original milwaukee brewers, 1970

MILWAUKEE BREWERS

BREWERS

McDonald's welcomed the American League Brewers to Milwaukee in 1970 by issuing a set of six baseball card panels. Five of the panels picture five players and a team logo, while the sixth panel contains six players, resulting in 31 different players. The panels measure 9" x 9-1/2" and feature full-color paintings of the players. Each sheet displays the heading, "the original milwaukee brewers, 1970." The cards are numbered by uniform number and the backs are blank. Although distributed by McDonald's, their name does not appear on the cards.

		NM	EX	VG
	Complete Sheet Set (6):	15.00	7.50	4.50
	Complete Singles Set (32):	15.00	7.50	4.50
	Common Player:	.50	.25	.15
1	Ted Kubiak	.50	.25	.15
2	Ted Savage	.50	.25	.15
4	Dave Bristol	.50	.25	.15
5	Phil Roof	.50	.25	.15

6	Mike Hershberger	.50	.25	.15
7	Russ Snyder	.50	.25	.15
8	Mike Hegan	.50	.25	.15
9	Rich Rollins	.50	.25	.15
10	Max Alvis	.50	.25	.15
11	John Kennedy	.50	.25	.15
12	Dan Walton	.50	.25	.15
15	Jerry McNertney	.50	.25	.15
18	Wes Stock	.50	.25	.15
20	Wayne Comer	.50	.25	.15
21	Tommy Harper	.50	.25	.15
23	Bob Locker	.50	.25	.15
24	Lew Krausse	.50	.25	.15
25	John Gelnar	.50	.25	.15
26	Roy McMillan	.50	.25	.15
27	Cal Ermer	.50	.25	.15
28	Sandy Valdespino	.50	.25	.15
30	Jackie Moore	.50	.25	.15
32	Gene Brabender	.50	.25	.15
33	Marty Pattin	.50	.25	.15
34	Greg Goossen	.50	.25	.15
35	John Morris	.50	.25	.15
36	Steve Hovley	.50	.25	.15
38	Bob Meyer	.50	.25	.15
39	Bob Bolin	.50	.25	.15
43	John O'Donoghue	.50	.25	.15
49	George Lauzerique	.50	.25	.15
---	Logo Card	.50	.25	.15

1974 McDonald's Gene Michael

GENE "THE STICK" MICHAEL

Gene "The Stick" Michael

Though there is no advertising or logo on this one-card "set," this black-and-white card of "The Stick" in his last year as a Yankee was distributed by a Staten Island McDonald's restaurant during an autograph appearance. The card measures 2-5/8" x 4-3/8" and is blank-backed.

	NM	EX	VG
Gene "The Stick" Michael	25.00	12.50	7.50

1974 McDonald's Padres Discs

SAN DIEGO PADRES
HOME GAME SCHEDULE
1974

Envisioned as part of a line of sports promotional sets, this concept died following the test with San Diego area McDonalds. At the July 30, 1974, game, Padres fans were given a hinged plastic baseball containing five Padres player photo discs plus a disc with the team's schedule and a Ronald McDonald disc which listed the dates on which the remaining eight player cards would be distributed at area McDonalds. Only 60,000 of the "starter set" discs were made, while 180,000 of each of the other player discs were printed. The 2-3/8" diameter discs feature a color photo on front and player stats on back. The promotion was the work of Photo Sports, Inc., of Los Angeles.

		NM	EX	VG
	Complete Set (15):	25.00	12.50	7.50
	Common Player:	1.00	.50	.30
(1)	Matty Alou	1.00	.50	.30
(2)	Glenn Beckert	3.00	1.50	.90
(3)	Nate Colbert	1.00	.50	.30
(4)	Bill Grief	1.00	.50	.30
(5)	John Grubb	1.00	.50	.30
(6)	Enzo Hernandez	3.00	1.50	.90
(7)	Randy Jones	3.00	1.50	.90

(8)	Fred Kendall	3.00	1.50	.90
(9)	Willie McCovey	6.00	3.00	1.75
(10)	John McNamara	3.00	1.50	.90
(11)	Dave Roberts	1.00	.50	.30
(12)	Bobby Tolan	1.00	.50	.30
(13)	Dave Winfield	15.00	7.50	4.50
(14)	Padres home game schedule	1.50	.70	.45
(15)	Ronald McDonald	1.50	.70	.45

1978 McDonald's Boston Red Sox

Reportedly because of a production problem, distribution of these cards was limited to a few Boston-area McDonald's restaurants for a very limited time. The blank-back, approximately 3-1/2" x 6" color cards have borderless portraits on front with the player's facsimile autograph. The cards were reportedly distributed in Treasure Chest meals for kids under 12.

		NM	EX	VG
Complete Set (6):		450.00	225.00	135.00
Common Player:		35.00	17.50	10.00
(1)	Rick Burleson	35.00	17.50	10.00
(2)	Carlton Fisk	125.00	60.00	35.00
(3)	Fred Lynn	75.00	37.50	22.50
(4)	Jim Rice	100.00	50.00	30.00
(5)	Luis Tiant	50.00	25.00	15.00
(6)	Carl Yastrzemski	150.00	75.00	45.00

1950-1952 Bill McGowan's School for Umpires

Over a period of at least three years in the early 1950s, Hall of Fame American League umpire Bill McGowan issued a series of black-and-white postcards to promote his umpires' school in Florida. The 3-1/2" x 5-1/2" cards have bordered or borderless photos on front, some of which bear the imprint of Grogan Photo, Danville, Ill.

		NM	EX	VG
(1)	Bill McGowan's Umpire School Cocoa - 1950 - Florida (Students on bleachers.)	60.00	30.00	20.00
(2)	Bill McGowman's Umpire School - 1950 - Florida (Students standing on field.)	60.00	30.00	20.00
(3)	Bill McGowan (1951)	500.00	250.00	150.00
(4)	Donatelli Instructs (Augie Donatelli) (1952)	65.00	32.50	20.00
(5)	Guglielmo Instructs (Augie Guglielmo) (1952)	65.00	32.50	20.00

1970s-80s Doug McWilliams Postcards

For more than two decades, California photographer Doug McWilliams (who also worked for Topps for 23 years) produced a series of black-and-white and color postcards for individual use by ballplayers, mostly members of the Oakland A's. Almost uniformly, the 3-1/2" x 5-1/2" cards have no graphics on front (a few have facsimile autographs), just a player pose or portrait. Backs have standard postcard markings, player identification, and McWilliams' credit lines. Backs carry a two-digit year of issue prefix to the card number. Postcards are printed in black-and-white unless noted.

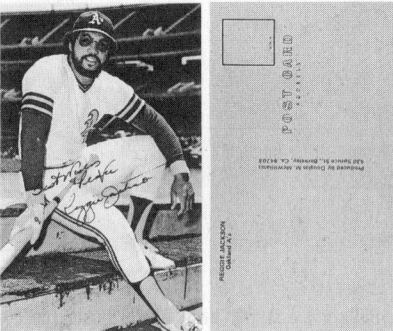

	NM	EX	VG
Common Player:	3.00	1.50	.90

(See individual years for checklists and values.)

1970 Doug McWilliams Postcards

		NM	EX	VG
1	Jim Roland	1.00	.50	.30
2a	Mudcat Grant, Mudcat Grant	1.50	.75	.45
2b	Mudcat Grant	1.50	.75	.45
3	Reggie Jackson (Color - only 50 produced.)	150.00	75.00	45.00
4	Darrell Osteen	1.00	.50	.30
5a	Tom Hafey (First printing.)	1.00	.50	.30
5b	Tom Hafey (Second printing.)	1.00	.50	.30
6	Chick Hafey	1.50	.75	.45

1970 Doug McWilliams Collectors' Issue Postcards

This set of black-and-white player postcards was produced by San Fransisco art photographer Doug McWilliams as a custom order for an Eastern collector. Fewer than 50 sets were reportedly produced. The 3-1/2" x 5-1/2" cards have glossy photographic fronts and standard postcard backs with player identification. The unnumbered cards are checklisted here in alphabetical order.

		NM	EX	VG
Complete Set (22):		400.00	200.00	125.00
Common Player:		20.00	10.00	6.00
(1)	Jerry Adair	20.00	10.00	6.00
(2)	Brant Alyea	20.00	10.00	6.00
(3)	Brant Alyea	20.00	10.00	6.00
(4)	Dwain Anderson	20.00	10.00	6.00
(5)	Curt Blefary	20.00	10.00	6.00
(6)	Bill Daniels	20.00	10.00	6.00
(7)	Mike Epstein	22.50	11.00	6.75
(8)	Adrian Garrett	20.00	10.00	6.00
(9)	Frank Fernandez	20.00	10.00	6.00
(10)	Mike Hegan	20.00	10.00	6.00
(11)	George Hendrick	20.00	10.00	6.00
(12)	Reggie Jackson	125.00	62.00	37.00
(13)	Reggie Jackson	125.00	62.00	37.00
(14)	Ron Klimkowski	20.00	10.00	6.00
(15)	Darold Knowles	20.00	10.00	6.00
(16)	Jerry Lumpe	20.00	10.00	6.00
(17)	Angel Mangual	20.00	10.00	6.00
(18)	Denny McLain	30.00	15.00	9.00
(19)	Denny McLain	30.00	15.00	9.00
(20)	Irv Noren	20.00	10.00	6.00
(21)	Ramon Webster	20.00	10.00	6.00
(22)	Dick Williams	20.00	10.00	6.00

1970 Doug McWilliams Oakland A's Postcards

These 3-1/2" x 5-1/2" black-and-white player postcards were produced by San Francisco photographer Doug McWilliams for sale by Sports Cards for Collectors, a forerunner of TCMA. Each card can be found either with or without borders on front, the latter having a slightly enlarged image. Player identification is on back. The unnumbered cards are checklisted here alphabetically. Fewer than 50 sets were reported produced.

		NM	EX	VG
Complete Set (42):		400.00	200.00	125.00
Common Player:		15.00	7.50	4.50
(1)	Felipe Alou	20.00	10.00	6.00
(2)	Sal Bando	20.00	10.00	6.00
(3)	Vida Blue	25.00	12.50	7.50
(4)	Bobby Brooks	15.00	7.50	4.50
(5)	Bert Campaneris	25.00	12.50	7.50
(6)	"Babe" Dahlgren	15.00	7.50	4.50
(7)	Tommy Davis	17.50	8.75	5.25
(8)	Chuck Dobson	15.00	7.50	4.50
(9)	John Donaldson	15.00	7.50	4.50
(10)	Al Downing	15.00	7.50	4.50
(11)	Jim Driscoll	15.00	7.50	4.50
(12)	Dave Duncan	15.00	7.50	4.50
(13)	Frank Fernandez	15.00	7.50	4.50
(14)	Rollie Fingers	45.00	22.00	13.50
(15)	Tito Francona	15.00	7.50	4.50
(16)	Jim Grant	20.00	10.00	6.00
(17)	Dick Green	15.00	7.50	4.50
(18)	Larry Haney	15.00	7.50	4.50
(19)	Bobby Hofman	15.00	7.50	4.50
(20)	Steve Hovley	15.00	7.50	4.50
(21)	Jim Hunter	45.00	22.00	13.50
(22)	Reggie Jackson	125.00	62.00	37.00
(23)	Dave Johnson	15.00	7.50	4.50
(24)	Marcel Lacheman	15.00	7.50	4.50
(25)	Tony LaRussa	40.00	20.00	12.00
(26)	Paul Lindblad	15.00	7.50	4.50
(27)	Bob Locker	15.00	7.50	4.50
(28)	John McNamara	15.00	7.50	4.50
(29)	Don Mincher	15.00	7.50	4.50

		NM	EX	VG
(30)	Rick Monday	15.00	7.50	4.50
(31)	"Blue Moon" Odom	17.50	8.75	5.25
(32)	Darrell Osteen	15.00	7.50	4.50
(33)	Ray Oyler	15.00	7.50	4.50
(34)	Roberto Pena	15.00	7.50	4.50
(35)	Bill Posedel	15.00	7.50	4.50
(36)	Roberto Rodriguez	15.00	7.50	4.50
(37)	Jim Roland	15.00	7.50	4.50
(38)	Joe Rudi	20.00	10.00	6.00
(39)	Diego Segui	15.00	7.50	4.50
(40)	Jose Tartabull	15.00	7.50	4.50
(41)	Gene Tenace	15.00	7.50	4.50
(42)	Dooley Womack	15.00	7.50	4.50

1971 Doug McWilliams Postcards

		NM	EX	VG
7	Larry Brown	3.00	1.50	.90
8a	Vida Blue (Color - first printing - KV3321.)	6.00	3.00	1.75
8b	Vida Blue (Color - second printing - KV3509.)	6.00	3.00	1.75
8c	Vida Blue (Color - third printing - KV4403.)	6.00	3.00	1.75
9	Dave Duncan	3.00	1.50	.90
10	George Hendrick (Color)	9.00	4.50	2.75
11	Mudcat Grant	3.00	1.50	.90
12	Mudcat Grant	3.00	1.50	.90

1972 Doug McWilliams Postcards

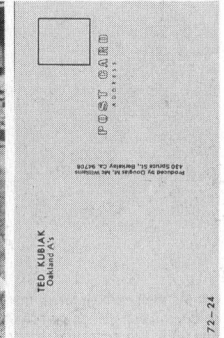

		NM	EX	VG
13	John Odom (Color)	6.00	3.00	1.75
14	Reggie Jackson (Color)	20.00	10.00	6.00
15	Sal Bando (Color)	6.00	3.00	1.75
16	Dan Cater	3.00	1.50	.90
17	Bob Locker	3.00	1.50	.90
18a	Joe Rudi (Equal edges to player.)	3.00	1.50	.90
18b	Joe Rudi (Bat close at bottom.)	3.00	1.50	.90
18c	Joe Rudi (Hand close to edge.)	3.00	1.50	.90
19	Larry Brown	3.00	1.50	.90
20a	Dick Green (First printing - glossy.)	3.00	1.50	.90
20b	Dick Green (Second printing - glossy, more contrast.)	3.00	1.50	.90
20c	Dick Green (Third printing - matte.)	3.00	1.50	.90
21	Vida Blue (Color)	6.00	3.00	1.75
22a	Joe Horlen (First printing - bright.)	3.00	1.50	.90
22b	Joe Horlen (Second printing - dark.)	3.00	1.50	.90
23	Gene Tenace (Color)	6.00	3.00	1.75
24a	Ted Kubiak (Glossy)	3.00	1.50	.90
24b	Ted Kubiak (Matte)	3.00	1.50	.90
A	Emeryville Ball Park	3.00	1.50	.90
B	Oakland Coliseum	3.00	1.50	.90

1973 Doug McWilliams Postcards

		NM	EX	VG
25	Rene Lachemann	3.00	1.50	.90
26	Tom Greive	3.00	1.50	.90
27	John Odom (Color)	6.00	3.00	1.75
28a	Rollie Fingers (First printing.)	9.00	4.50	2.75
28b	Rollie Fingers (Second printing - thinner stock.)	9.00	4.50	2.75
29	Jim Hunter (Color)	9.00	4.50	2.75
30	Ray Fosse (Color)	6.00	3.00	1.75
31	Charley Pride (Color)	15.00	7.50	4.50
32	Charley Pride (Color)	15.00	7.50	4.50
33	Bill North	3.00	1.50	.90
34	Damasco Blanco	3.00	1.50	.90

35	Paul Lindblad	3.00	1.50	.90
36	Rollie Fingers (Color)	9.00	4.50	2.75
37	Horacio Pina	3.00	1.50	.90
38	Bert Campaneris (Color)	7.50	3.75	2.25
39	Jim Holt (Color)	6.00	3.00	1.75
40	Sal Bando (Color)	6.00	3.00	1.75
41	Joe Rudi (Color)	6.00	3.00	1.75
42	Dick Williams (Color)	6.00	3.00	1.75
43	Jesus Alou	3.00	1.50	.90
44	Joe Niekro	3.75	2.00	1.25
45	Johnny Oates	3.00	1.50	.90

1974 Doug McWilliams Postcards

MANNY TRILLO Oakland A's

		NM	EX	VG
46a	Ray Fosse (Color - first printing - w/signature.)	6.00	3.00	1.75
46b	Ray Fosse (Color - second printing - no signature.)	6.00	3.00	1.75
46c	Ray Fosse (Color - third printing - no sig., very green grass.)	6.00	3.00	1.75
47	Jesus Alou	3.00	1.50	.90
48	John Summers	3.00	1.50	.90
49	Dal Maxvill	3.00	1.50	.90
50	Joe Rudi (Color)	6.00	3.00	1.75
51	Sal Bando (Color)	6.00	3.00	1.75
52	Reggie Jackson (Color)	20.00	10.00	6.00
53	Ted Kubiak (Color)	6.00	3.00	1.75
54	Dave Hamilton	3.00	1.50	.90
55	Gene Tenace (Color)	6.00	3.00	1.75
56a	Bob Locker (First printing - back foot near edge.)	3.00	1.50	.90
56b	Bob Locker (Second printing - foot 3/4" from edge.)	3.00	1.50	.90
57	Manny Trillo	3.00	1.50	.90

1975 Doug McWilliams Postcards

		NM	EX	VG
58a	Dan Godby (First printing.)	3.00	1.50	.90
58b	Dan Godby (Second printing - blank back.)	3.00	1.50	.90
58c	Dan Godby (Third printing - flat contrast.)	3.00	1.50	.90
59	Bob Locker	3.00	1.50	.90
60	Rollie Fingers (Color)	9.00	4.50	2.75
61	Glenn Abbott	3.00	1.50	.90
62	Jim Todd	3.00	1.50	.90
63	Phil Garner	3.00	1.50	.90
64	Paul Lindblad	3.00	1.50	.90
65	Bill North (Color)	6.00	3.00	1.75
66	Dick Sisler	3.00	1.50	.90
67	Angel Mangual	3.00	1.50	.90
68	Claudell Washington	3.00	1.50	.90

1976 Doug McWilliams Postcards

		NM	EX	VG
69	Oakland Coliseum (Color)	6.00	3.00	1.75
70	Sal Bando (Color)	6.00	3.00	1.75
71	Mike Torrez (Color)	6.00	3.00	1.75
72	Joe Lonnett	3.00	1.50	.90
73	Chuck Tanner	3.00	1.50	.90
74	Tommy Sandt	3.00	1.50	.90
75	Dick Bosman (Color)	6.00	3.00	1.75
76	Bert Campaneris (Color)	6.00	3.00	1.75
77	Ken Brett	6.00	3.00	1.75
78	Jim Todd (Color)	6.00	3.00	1.75
79	Jeff Newman	3.00	1.50	.90
80	John McCall	3.00	1.50	.90

1977 Doug McWilliams Postcards

		NM	EX	VG
81	Don Baylor (Color)	9.00	4.50	2.75
82	Lee Stange	3.00	1.50	.90
83	Rob Picciolo	3.00	1.50	.90
84	Jack Mc Keon (Color)	6.00	3.00	1.75
85	Rollie Fingers (Color)	9.00	4.50	2.75
86	Manny Sanguillen	3.00	1.50	.90
87	Tony Armas	3.00	1.50	.90
88	Jim Tyrone	3.00	1.50	.90
89	Wayne Gross	3.00	1.50	.90
90	Rick Langford	3.00	1.50	.90
91	Rich Gossage	3.00	1.50	.90
92	Phil Garner (Color)	6.00	3.00	1.75
93	Del Alston	3.00	1.50	.90
94	Bert Blyleven (Color)	7.50	3.75	2.25
95	Willie McCovey (Color)	9.00	4.50	2.75
96	Ken Brett (Color)	6.00	3.00	1.75
97	Doyle Alexander (Color)	6.00	3.00	1.75

1978 Doug McWilliams Postcards

		NM	EX	VG
98	Rene Lacheman	3.00	1.50	.90

99	Del Alston	3.00	1.50	.90
100	Lee Stange (Color)	6.00	3.00	1.75
101	Taylor Duncan	3.00	1.50	.90
102	Matt Keough	3.00	1.50	.90
103	Bruce Robinson	3.00	1.50	.90
104	Sal Bando (Color)	6.00	3.00	1.75

1979 Doug McWilliams Postcards

		NM	EX	VG
105	Alan Wirth	3.00	1.50	.90
106	Mike Edwards	3.00	1.50	.90
107	Craig Minetto	3.00	1.50	.90
108	Mike Morgan	3.00	1.50	.90
109	Brian Kingman	3.00	1.50	.90

1980 Doug McWilliams Postcards

		NM	EX	VG
110	Jim Essian	3.00	1.50	.90
111a	Willie McCovey (Color - first printing - no signature.)	9.00	4.50	2.75
111b	Willie McCovey (Color - second printing - w/signature, stamp at top.)	9.00	4.50	2.75
111c	Willie McCovey (Color - third printing - w/sig., stamp at bottom.)	9.00	4.50	2.75
112a	Willie McCovey (Color - first printing - no signature.)	9.00	4.50	2.75
112b	Willie McCovey (Color - second printing - w/signature.)	9.00	4.50	2.75

1964 Meadowgold Dairy

MICKEY MANTLE — SANDY KOUFAX — WILLIE MAYS — BILL MAZEROSKI

Four of the mid-60s' biggest stars appear as a panel on this milk carton issue. The four-player portion measures about 3-3/4" x 4-1/4" and is printed in shades of blue on the white background. Individual cards measure about 1-1/8" x 2-1/16" and are, of course, blank-backed. In 1998, a complete milk carton was sold at auction for $2,475.

		NM	EX	VG
Complete Set, Panel:		600.00	300.00	180.00
Complete Set, Singles (4):		475.00	250.00	150.00
Common Player:		60.00	30.00	18.00
(1)	Sandy Koufax	85.00	42.00	25.00
(2)	Mickey Mantle	260.00	130.00	78.00
(3)	Willie Mays	80.00	40.00	24.00
(4)	Bill Mazeroski	60.00	30.00	18.00

1911 Mecca Cigarettes

(See 1911 T201 Double Folders.)

1937 Joe "Ducky" Medwick

Little is known about these cards featuring the perennial All-Star of the Gashouse Gang. Both styles are in a round-cornered playing card format, about 2-1/4" x 3-1/2". Fronts have black-and-white artwork of Medwick swinging a bat against a large baseball. The background is black-and-orange with a facsimile autograph at bottom. Most cards are found with some sort of card-game baseball scenario on back, while another type has a black-and-white photo of Medwick signing autographs amid a gaggle of children. His name and the date appear at bottom. It is not known whether the two types of cards were distributed together.

	NM	EX	VG
Joe "Ducky" Medwick (Game card.)	45.00	22.50	13.50
Joe "Ducky" Medwick (Photo back.)	90.00	45.00	25.00

1910 Mello-Mint (E105)

Evers, 2b. Chicago Nat.

Issued circa 1910 by Smith's Mello-Mint, "The Texas Gum," this set of 50 cards shares the same checklist and artwork as the better known E101 set. Mello-Mint cards are slightly smaller, measuring approximately 1-3/8" x 2-5/8", and are printed on thin paper, making them difficult to find in top condition. Also contributing to condition problems is the fact that many cards were folded vertically to fit the packaging. The backs contain advertising, printed in green, for Mello-Mint Gum. The set carries an ACC designation of E105. Two finds of multiple examples of about eight cards in the 1980s can mislead collectors into thinking the rest of the cards in the set are more common than is actually the case. The cards most heavily over-represented in those finds are indicated with an asterisk.

		NM	EX	VG
Complete Set (50):		195,000	75,000	35,000
Common Player:		1,400	550.00	275.00
(1)	Jack Barry	3,200	1,300	650.00
(2)	Harry Bemis	3,200	1,300	650.00
(3)	Chief Bender (White hat.)	6,400	2,600	1,300
(4)	Chief Bender (Striped hat.)	6,400	2,600	1,300
(5)	Bill Bergen	3,200	1,300	650.00
(6)	Bob Bescher (*)	1,400	550.00	275.00
(7)	Al Bridwell	3,200	1,300	650.00
(8)	Doc Casey (*)	1,400	550.00	275.00
(9)	Frank Chance	7,200	2,900	1,450
(10)	Hal Chase	4,600	1,850	925.00
(11)	Ty Cobb	11,000	7,500	5,500
(12)	Eddie Collins	7,200	2,900	1,450
(13)	Sam Crawford	7,200	2,900	1,450
(14)	Harry Davis	3,200	1,300	650.00
(15)	Art Devlin	3,200	1,300	650.00
(16)	Wild Bill Donovan	3,200	1,300	650.00
(17)	Red Dooin	3,200	1,300	650.00
(18)	Mickey Doolan	3,200	1,300	650.00
(19)	Patsy Dougherty	3,200	1,300	650.00
(20)	Larry Doyle (With bat.)	3,200	1,300	650.00
(21)	Larry Doyle (Throwing)	3,200	1,300	650.00
(22)	Johnny Evers	7,200	2,900	1,450
(23)	George Gibson	3,200	1,300	650.00
(24)	Topsy Hartsel (*)	1,400	550.00	275.00
(25)	Fred Jacklitsch	3,200	1,300	650.00
(26)	Hugh Jennings	7,200	2,900	1,450
(27)	Red Kleinow	3,200	1,300	650.00
(28)	Otto Knabe	3,200	1,300	650.00
(29)	Jack Knight (*)	1,400	550.00	275.00
(30)	Nap Lajoie (*)	5,100	2,000	1,000
(31)	Hans Lobert	3,200	1,300	650.00
(32)	Sherry Magee	3,200	1,300	650.00
(33)	Christy Matthewson (Mathewson)	11,000	4,500	2,250
(34)	John McGraw	7,200	2,900	1,450
(35)	Larry McLean	3,200	1,300	650.00
(36)	Dots Miller (Batting)	3,200	1,300	650.00
(37)	Dots Miller (Fielding)	3,200	1,300	650.00
(38)	Danny Murphy (*)	1,400	550.00	275.00
(39)	Bill O'Hara	3,200	1,300	650.00
(40)	Germany Schaefer	3,200	1,300	650.00
(41)	Admiral Schlei	3,200	1,300	650.00
(42)	Boss Schmidt	3,200	1,300	650.00
(43)	Johnny Seigle	3,200	1,300	650.00
(44)	Dave Shean (*)	1,400	550.00	275.00
(45)	Boss Smith (Schmidt)	3,200	1,300	650.00
(46)	Joe Tinker	7,200	2,900	1,450
(47)	Honus Wagner (Batting)	10,500	4,200	2,100
(48)	Honus Wagner (Throwing)	11,000	7,500	5,500
(49)	Cy Young (*)	9,600	3,900	1,900
(50)	Heinie Zimmerman	3,200	1,300	650.00

1916 Felix Mendelsohn

JIM THORPE
R. F.—New York Giants
176

This Chicago printing and publishing firm was the originator of the card set often found bearing the advertising of The Sporting News on back, or less frequently with ads from other concerns. Mendelsohn is not mentioned on the cards, which are blank-backed. Fronts of the 1-5/8" x 3" black-and-white cards have a player photo, name, position abbreviation, team and card number. The first version of the set, designated M101-5 in the ACC, was prepared in advance of the 1916 season and offered in ads in The Sporting News for $1, or a framed uncut sheet for $2.50. An updated version, designated M101-4 in the American Card Catalog, was released later in the summer.

(See 1916 M101-4 and M101-5 Blank Backs and 1917 M-UNC.)

1917 Felix Mendelsohn (M101-UNC)

RAY SCHALK
CATCHER-CHICAGO WHITE SOX

These 2-1/4" x 4" blank-back, black-and-white cards may have been prototypes for a "Hall of Fame" card set advertised early in 1917 by Felix Mendelsohn in The Sporting News. A set of 200 was offered for $1, but may not have actually been produced. Each example of this set is believed to be unique.

(1) Walter Johnson (Value Undetermined)
(2) Christy Mathewson (Value Undetermined)
(3) Ray Schalk (Brought $1,464 in 4/05 auction, in Excellent condition.)

1917-1920 Felix Mendelsohn

Gandil
1st. B. Chicago White Sox.

This set of glossy black-and-white player photos was produced by Chicago publisher Felix Mendelsohn, whose initials appear beneath the copyright logo. The photos measure about 4-3/8" x 6-3/8" and feature action poses of the player whose name, position and team appear at the bottom of the borderless pictures. Four of the players in the checklist appear with two different teams, indicating the photos were issued over a period of several seasons. The set was offered in ads in The Sporting News at $5 for 100 pictures. This checklist may not be complete. Gaps have been left in the assigned numbering to accommodate future additions.

		NM	EX	VG
Complete Set (119):		40,000	20,000	12,000
Common Player:		125.00	60.00	35.00
(1)	Grover C. Alexander (Philadelphia)	600.00	300.00	180.00
(2)	Grover C. Alexander (Chicago)	600.00	300.00	180.00
(3)	Jim Bagby	125.00	60.00	35.00
(4)	Doug Baird	125.00	60.00	35.00
(5)	Franklin Baker	300.00	150.00	90.00
(6)	Dave Bancroft	300.00	150.00	90.00
(7)	Jack Barry	125.00	60.00	35.00
(8)	Johnny Bates	125.00	60.00	35.00
(9)	Carson Bigbee	125.00	60.00	35.00
(10)	"Ping" Bodie	125.00	60.00	35.00
(11)	George Burns	125.00	60.00	35.00
(12)	Joe Bush	125.00	60.00	35.00
(13)	Owen Bush	125.00	60.00	35.00
(14)	Ray Caldwell	125.00	60.00	35.00
(15)	Max Carey	300.00	150.00	90.00
(16)	Ray Chapman	150.00	75.00	45.00

(17)	Hal Chase	250.00	125.00	75.00
(18)	Eddie Cicotte	300.00	150.00	90.00
(19)	Ty Cobb	3,500	1,750	1,050
(20)	Eddie Collins	300.00	150.00	90.00
(21)	Harry Coveleskie (Coveleskie)	125.00	60.00	35.00
(22)	"Gavvy" Cravath	125.00	60.00	35.00
(23)	Sam Crawford	300.00	150.00	90.00
(24)	Walton Cruise	125.00	60.00	35.00
(26)	George Cutshaw	125.00	60.00	35.00
(27)	Jake Daubert	125.00	60.00	35.00
(28)	George Dauss	125.00	60.00	35.00
(29)	Dave Davenport	125.00	60.00	35.00
(30)	Bill Doak	125.00	60.00	35.00
(31)	Larry Doyle	125.00	60.00	35.00
(32)	George Dumont	125.00	60.00	35.00
(33)	Howard Ehmke	125.00	60.00	35.00
(34)	Urban Faber	300.00	150.00	90.00
(35)	Happy Felsch	600.00	300.00	180.00
(36)	Art Fletcher	125.00	60.00	35.00
(37)	Del Gainer (Gainor)	125.00	60.00	35.00
(38)	Chick Gandil	300.00	150.00	90.00
(39)	Larry Gardner	125.00	60.00	35.00
(40)	Mike Gonzales (Gonzalez)	125.00	60.00	35.00
(41)	Jack Graney	125.00	60.00	35.00
(42)	Heinie Groh	125.00	60.00	35.00
(43)	Earl Hamilton	125.00	60.00	35.00
(44)	Harry Heilmann	300.00	150.00	90.00
(45)	Buck Herzog	125.00	60.00	35.00
(46)	Hugh High (New York, photo actually Bob Shawkey.)	125.00	60.00	35.00
(47)	Hugh High (Detroit, correct photo.)	125.00	60.00	35.00
(48)	Bill Hinchman	125.00	60.00	35.00
(49)	Dick Hoblitzell	125.00	60.00	35.00
(51)	Walter Holke (New York)	125.00	60.00	35.00
(52)	Walter Holke (Boston)	125.00	60.00	35.00
(53)	Harry Hooper	300.00	150.00	90.00
(54)	Rogers Hornsby	400.00	200.00	120.00
(55)	Joe Jackson	5,000	2,500	1,500
(56)	Bill Jacobson	125.00	60.00	35.00
(57)	Walter Johnson	900.00	450.00	270.00
(58)	Sam Jones	125.00	60.00	35.00
(59)	Joe Judge	125.00	60.00	35.00
(60)	Benny Kauff	125.00	60.00	35.00
(61)	Bill Killefer	125.00	60.00	35.00
(62)	Ed Konetchy (Boston)	125.00	60.00	35.00
(63)	Ed Konetchy (Brooklyn)	125.00	60.00	35.00
(64)	Nemo Leibold	125.00	60.00	35.00
(65)	Duffy Lewis	125.00	60.00	35.00
(66)	Fred Luderas (Luderus)	125.00	60.00	35.00
(67)	Fred Luderus	125.00	60.00	35.00
(68)	Al Mamaux	125.00	60.00	35.00
(69)	Les Mann	125.00	60.00	35.00
(70)	"Rabbit" Maranville	300.00	150.00	90.00
(71)	Armando Marsans	125.00	60.00	35.00
(72)	John McGraw	300.00	150.00	90.00
(73)	Stuffy McInnis	125.00	60.00	35.00
(74)	Lee Meadows	125.00	60.00	35.00
(76)	Fred Merkle	125.00	60.00	35.00
(77)	Clyde Milan	125.00	60.00	35.00
(78)	Otto Miller	125.00	60.00	35.00
(79)	Guy Morton	125.00	60.00	35.00
(80)	Hy Myers	125.00	60.00	35.00
(81)	Greasy Neale	150.00	75.00	45.00
(82)	Dode Paskert	125.00	60.00	35.00
(83)	Roger Peckinpaugh	125.00	60.00	35.00
(84)	Jeff Pfeffer	125.00	60.00	35.00
(85)	Walter Pipp	125.00	60.00	35.00
(86)	Bill Rariden	125.00	60.00	35.00
(87)	Johnny Rawlings	125.00	60.00	35.00
(88)	Sam Rice	300.00	150.00	90.00
(89)	Dave Robertson	125.00	60.00	35.00
(90)	Bob Roth	125.00	60.00	35.00
(91)	Ed Roush	300.00	150.00	90.00
(92)	Dick Rudolph	125.00	60.00	35.00
(93)	Babe Ruth (Red Sox)	4,500	2,250	1,350
(94)	Babe Ruth (New York)	5,000	2,500	1,500
(95)	Vic Saier	125.00	60.00	35.00
(96)	Ray Schalk	300.00	150.00	90.00
(97)	Hank Severeid	125.00	60.00	35.00
(98)	Ernie Shore	125.00	60.00	35.00
(99)	Burt Shotton	125.00	60.00	35.00
(101)	George Sisler	300.00	150.00	90.00
(102)	Jack Smith	125.00	60.00	35.00
(103)	Frank Snyder	125.00	60.00	35.00
(104)	Tris Speaker	400.00	200.00	120.00
(105)	Oscar Stanage	125.00	60.00	35.00
(106)	Casey Stengel	300.00	150.00	90.00
(107)	Amos Strunk	125.00	60.00	35.00
(108)	Jeff Tesreau	125.00	60.00	35.00
(109)	Fred Toney	125.00	60.00	35.00
(110)	Terry Turner	125.00	60.00	35.00
(111)	Jim Vaughn	125.00	60.00	35.00
(112)	Bobby Veach	125.00	60.00	35.00
(113)	Oscar Vitt	125.00	60.00	35.00
(114)	"Honus" Wagner	3,000	1,500	900.00
(115)	Tilly Walker	125.00	60.00	35.00
(116)	Bill Wambsganss	125.00	60.00	35.00
(117)	"Buck" Weaver	600.00	300.00	180.00
(118)	Zack Wheat	300.00	150.00	90.00
(119)	George Whitted	125.00	60.00	35.00
(120)	Cy Williams	125.00	60.00	35.00
(121)	Ivy Wingo	125.00	60.00	35.00
(122)	Pep ("Pep") Young	125.00	60.00	35.00
(123)	Heinie Zimmerman	125.00	60.00	35.00

1975 Clarence Mengler Baseball's Best

This collectors' issue art set holds the distinction of being one of the first whose distribution was halted by the Major League Baseball Players Association for lack of a license to depict current players. Produced as an autograph medium by Illinois collector Clarence Mengler, the 5" x 3" blank-back cards have portraits drawn by Keith Peterson. Of the original production of 200 sets, fewer than half were sold before the union intervened with threatened legal action. Because of a

Hank Aaron

spelling error, the Ralph Garr card was withdrawn early. Hal McRae's card, also misspelled, was not withdrawn. Originally sold in five series, the unnumbered cards are checklisted alphabetically within series.

		NM	EX	VG
Complete Set (125):		150.00	75.00	45.00
Common Player:		1.00	.50	.30
SERIES A				
(1)	Sal Bando	1.00	.50	.30
(2)	Johnny Bench	4.00	2.00	1.25
(3)	Jack Billingham	1.00	.50	.30
(4)	Paul Blair	1.00	.50	.30
(5)	Bert Blyleven	1.50	.70	.45
(6)	Lou Brock	2.50	1.25	.70
(7)	Jeff Burroughs	1.00	.50	.30
(8)	Nate Colbert	1.00	.50	.30
(9)	Carlton Fisk	2.50	1.25	.70
(10)	Bob Gibson	2.50	1.25	.70
(11)	Ferguson Jenkins	2.00	1.00	.60
(12)	Bob Johnson	1.00	.50	.30
(13)	Dave McNally	1.00	.50	.30
(14)	Bobby Murcer	1.50	.70	.45
(15)	Tony Muser	1.00	.50	.30
(16)	Phil Niekro	2.00	1.00	.60
(17)	Brooks Robinson	3.00	1.50	.90
(18)	Frank Robinson	3.00	1.50	.90
(19)	Nolan Ryan	12.00	6.00	3.50
(20)	Mike Schmidt	6.00	3.00	1.75
(21)	Willie Stargell	2.50	1.25	.70
(22)	Andre Thornton	1.00	.50	.30
(23)	Bobby Tolan	1.00	.50	.30
(24)	Jim Wynn	1.00	.50	.30
(25)	Richie Zisk	1.00	.50	.30
SERIES B				
(26)	Hank Aaron	9.00	4.50	2.75
(27)	Larry Bowa	1.00	.50	.30
(28)	Steve Carlton	2.50	1.25	.70
(29)	Cesar Cedeno	1.00	.50	.30
(30)	Jim Colborn	1.00	.50	.30
(31)	Tim Foli	1.00	.50	.30
(32)	Steve Garvey	1.50	.70	.45
(33)	Bud Harrelson	1.00	.50	.30
(34)	Willie Horton	1.00	.50	.30
(35)	Jim Hunter	2.00	1.00	.60
(36)	Reggie Jackson	6.00	3.00	1.75
(37)	Billy Martin	1.50	.70	.45
(38)	Bake McBride	1.00	.50	.30
(39)	Andy Messersmith	1.00	.50	.30
(40)	Rick Monday	1.00	.50	.30
(41)	Joe Morgan	2.50	1.25	.70
(42)	Tony Oliva	1.50	.70	.45
(43)	Amos Otis	1.00	.50	.30
(44)	Gaylord Perry	2.00	1.00	.60
(45)	Tom Seaver	5.00	2.50	1.50
(46)	Ken Singleton	1.00	.50	.30
(47)	Chris Speier	1.00	.50	.30
(48)	Gene Tenace	1.00	.50	.30
(49)	Del Unser	1.00	.50	.30
(50)	Carl Yastrzemski	5.00	2.50	1.50
SERIES C				
(51)	Steve Busby	1.00	.50	.30
(52)	Jose Cardenal	1.00	.50	.30
(53)	Rod Carew	2.50	1.25	.70
(54)	Ron Cey	1.00	.50	.30
(55)	Willie Davis	1.00	.50	.30
(56)	Barry Foote	1.00	.50	.30
(57)	Ken Holtzman	1.00	.50	.30
(58)	Davey Lopes	1.00	.50	.30
(59)	Greg Luzinski	1.00	.50	.30
(60)	Sparky Lyle	1.00	.50	.30
(61)	Dave May	1.00	.50	.30
(62)	Lee May	1.00	.50	.30
(63)	Doc Medich	1.00	.50	.30
(64)	Bill Melton	1.00	.50	.30
(65)	Randy Moffitt	1.00	.50	.30
(66)	Don Money	1.00	.50	.30
(67)	Al Oliver	1.50	.70	.45
(68)	George Scott	1.00	.50	.30
(69)	Ted Simmons	1.00	.50	.30
(70)	Charlie Spikes	1.00	.50	.30
(71)	Rusty Staub	1.25	.60	.40
(72)	Jim Sundberg	1.00	.50	.30
(73)	Bob Watson	1.00	.50	.30
(74)	Dick Williams	1.00	.50	.30
(75)	Dave Winfield	2.50	1.25	.70
SERIES D				
(76)	Vida Blue	1.00	.50	.30
(77)	Bobby Bonds	1.00	.50	.30
(78)	Jerry Coleman	1.00	.50	.30
(79)	Bob Coluccio	1.00	.50	.30
(80)	Joe Decker	1.00	.50	.30
(81)	Darrell Evans	1.00	.50	.30
(82)	Ralph Gaar (Garr)(SP)	4.00	2.00	1.25
(83)	Richie Hebner	1.00	.50	.30
(84)	Ken Henderson	1.00	.50	.30
(85)	Bill Madlock	1.00	.50	.30
(86)	Jon Matlack	1.00	.50	.30
(87)	Carlos May	1.00	.50	.30
(88)	John Mayberry	1.00	.50	.30

		NM	EX	VG
(89)	Willie McCovey	2.50	1.25	.70
(90)	Lynn McGlothen	1.00	.50	.30
(91)	Tug McGraw	1.00	.50	.30
(92)	Roger Metzger	1.00	.50	.30
(93)	Jim Palmer	2.00	1.00	.60
(94)	Rico Petrocelli	1.00	.50	.30
(95)	Ellie Rodriguez	1.00	.50	.30
(96)	Steve Rogers	1.00	.50	.30
(97)	Pete Rose	9.00	4.50	2.75
(98)	Bill Singer	1.00	.50	.30
(99)	Don Sutton	2.00	1.00	.60
(100)	Billy Williams	2.50	1.25	.70
	SERIES E			
(101)	Mark Belanger	1.00	.50	.30
(102)	Buddy Bell	1.00	.50	.30
(103)	Jim Bibby	1.00	.50	.30
(104)	Bob Boone	1.00	.50	.30
(105)	Ken Brett	1.00	.50	.30
(106)	Ron Bryant	1.00	.50	.30
(107)	Bill Buckner	1.00	.50	.30
(108)	Buzz Capra	1.00	.50	.30
(109)	Dave Concepcion	1.00	.50	.30
(110)	Rollie Fingers	2.00	1.00	.60
(111)	Bill Freehan	1.00	.50	.30
(112)	Bobby Grich	1.00	.50	.30
(113)	Fred Kendall	1.00	.50	.30
(114)	Don Kessinger	1.00	.50	.30
(115)	Hal McCrae (McRae)	1.00	.50	.30
(116)	Thurman Munson	2.50	1.25	.70
(117)	Fred Patek	1.00	.50	.30
(118)	Doug Rader	1.00	.50	.30
(119)	A. (Aurelio) Rodriguez	1.00	.50	.30
(120)	Manny Sanguillen	1.00	.50	.30
(121)	Reggie Smith	1.00	.50	.30
(122)	Danny Thompson	1.00	.50	.30
(123)	Luis Tiant	1.00	.50	.30
(124)	Joe Torre	1.50	.70	.45
(125)	Wilbur Wood	1.00	.50	.30

1953-54 Marshall Merrell Milwaukee Braves Portfolio

One of several portfolios of Milwaukee Braves artwork produced during the team's first few years, this issue of 8" x 10" black-and-white lithographs was sold at County Stadium for 25 cents apiece. The player checklist here is believed to be complete, but it is possible other poses may yet be reported. The cards are blank-backed and unnumbered; the checklist here has been arranged alphabetically.

		NM	EX	VG
	Complete Set (25):	900.00	450.00	275.00
	Common Player:	25.00	12.50	7.50
(1)	Henry Aaron	200.00	100.00	60.00
(2)	Joe Adcock	25.00	12.50	7.50
(3)	Johnny Antonelli	25.00	12.50	7.50
(4)	Billy Bruton	25.00	12.50	7.50
(5)	Bob Buhl	25.00	12.50	7.50
(6)	Lou Burdette (Follow-through.)	25.00	12.50	7.50
(7)	Lew Burdette (Wind-up.)	25.00	12.50	7.50
(8)	Gene Conley	25.00	12.50	7.50
(9)	Del Crandall	25.00	12.50	7.50
(10)	Jack Dittmer	25.00	12.50	7.50
(11)	Sid Gordon (Batting)	25.00	12.50	7.50
(12)	Sid Gordon (Standing)	25.00	12.50	7.50
(13)	Charlie Grimm (Tomahawk on jersey.)	25.00	12.50	7.50
(14)	Charlie Grimm (No tomahawk.)	25.00	12.50	7.50
(15)	Don Liddle	25.00	12.50	7.50
(16)	Johnny Logan	25.00	12.50	7.50
(17)	Ed Mathews (Batting)	75.00	37.50	22.50
(18)	Ed Mathews (Standing)	75.00	37.50	22.50
(19)	Danny O'Connell	25.00	12.50	7.50
(20)	Andy Pafko	25.00	12.50	7.50
(21)	Jim Pendleton	25.00	12.50	7.50
(22)	Warren Spahn	75.00	37.50	22.50
(23)	Max Surkont	25.00	12.50	7.50
(24)	Bobby Thomson	45.00	22.50	13.50
(25)	Jim Wilson	25.00	12.50	7.50

1979 Metallic Creations Signature Miniatures

This collectors' issue was created by combining an approximately 3-1/2" tall pewter statue with a 3-5/8" x 5" baseball card. The statues were released in pewter at about $10 apiece and silver-plate at $20. The black-bordered cards feature color portraits in front of a pair of sepia action pictures. The artwork was by J. Payette. Fronts also feature a facsimile autograph. Backs have basic player personal data and career stats. It was reported that 5,000 of each card were printed, though most were never issued due to failure of the venture. The remaining cards and statues were sold into the hobby as remainders. It is unclear whether a Munson card exists, although the Munson statue and the Ryan card have been confirmed.

		NM	EX	VG
	Complete Set, Cards (20):	240.00	120.00	70.00
	Common Card:	7.50	3.75	2.25
	Complete Set, Pewter Statues (20):	200.00	100.00	60.00
	Common Statue:	7.50	3.75	2.25
	Silver-Plate Statues: 2X			
(1)	Hank Aaron (Card)	12.50	6.25	3.75
(1)	Hank Aaron (Statue)	12.50	6.25	3.75
(2)	Rod Carew (Card)	7.50	3.75	2.25
(2)	Rod Carew (Statue)	7.50	3.75	2.25
(3)	Cesar Cedeno (Card)	7.50	3.75	2.25
(4)	Ty Cobb (Card)	15.00	7.50	4.50
(4)	Ty Cobb (Statue)	12.50	6.25	3.75
(5)	Steve Garvey (Card)	15.00	7.50	4.50
(5)	Steve Garvey (Statue)	15.00	7.50	4.50
(6)	Lou Gehrig (Card)	15.00	7.50	4.50
(6)	Lou Gehrig (Statue)	15.00	7.50	4.50
(7)	Ron Guidry (Card)	7.50	3.75	2.25
(7)	Ron Guidry (Statue)	7.50	3.75	2.25
(8)	Rogers Hornsby (Card)	7.50	3.75	2.25
(8)	Rogers Hornsby (Statue)	7.50	3.75	2.25
(9)	Walter Johnson (Card)	10.00	5.00	3.00
(9)	Walter Johnson (Statue)	10.00	5.00	3.00
(10)	Ralph Kiner (Card)	7.50	3.75	2.25
(10)	Ralph Kiner (Statue)	7.50	3.75	2.25
(11)	Sandy Koufax (Card)	20.00	10.00	6.00
(11)	Sandy Koufax (Statue)	20.00	10.00	6.00
(12)	Davey Lopes (Card)	7.50	3.75	2.25
(12)	Davey Lopes (Statue)	7.50	3.75	2.25
(13)	Christy Mathewson (Card)	10.00	5.00	3.00
(13)	Christy Mathewson (Statue)	10.00	5.00	3.00
(14)	Willie Mays (Card)	15.00	7.50	4.50
(14)	Willie Mays (Statue)	15.00	7.50	4.50
(15)	Willie McCovey (Card)	10.00	5.00	3.00
(15)	Willie McCovey (Statue)	10.00	5.00	3.00
(16)	Thurman Munson (Statue)	10.00	5.00	3.00
(17)	Mel Ott (Card)	7.50	3.75	2.25
(17)	Mel Ott (Statue)	7.50	3.75	2.25
(18)	Babe Ruth (Card)	12.50	6.25	3.75
(18)	Babe Ruth (Statue)	12.50	6.25	3.75
(19)	Nolan Ryan (Card)	30.00	15.00	9.00
(20)	Tris Speaker (Card)	7.50	3.75	2.25
(20)	Tris Speaker (Statue)	7.50	3.75	2.25
(21)	Honus Wagner (Card)	10.00	5.00	3.00
(21)	Honus Wagner (Statue)	10.00	5.00	3.00

1938-39 Metropolitan Clothing Cincinnati Reds Postcards

(See 1937-39 Orcajo Cincinnati Reds postcards for checklist, values.)

1968 Metropolitan Museum of Art Burdick Collection

 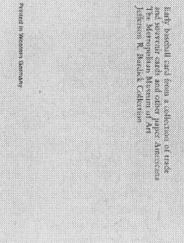

The date of issue is approximate for this set promoting New York's Metropolitan Museum of Art as the repository for the Jefferson Burdick collection, once the world's premier accumulation of trading cards. Burdick, author of the once-standard "American Card Catalog" donated his collection to the Met. The 2-3/4" x 3-5/8" black-and-white glossy card fronts reproduce 1928 R315 cards of major leaguers and earlier Zeenuts cards of minor leaguers. Backs have a few words about the museum and a "Printed in Western Germany" line. The unnumbered cards are checklisted here in alphabetical order.

		NM	EX	VG
	Complete Set (8):	125.00	65.00	35.00
	Common Player:	10.00	5.00	3.00
(1)	Max Bishop	10.00	5.00	3.00
(2)	Lou Gehrig	40.00	20.00	12.00
(3)	Carl Hubbell	15.00	7.50	4.50
(4)	Art Kores	10.00	5.00	3.00
(5)	Bill Leard	10.00	5.00	3.00
(6)	Babe Ruth	50.00	25.00	15.00
(7)	Dazzy Vance	10.00	5.00	3.00
(8)	Elmer Zacher	10.00	5.00	3.00

1931 Metropolitan Studio St. Louis Cardinals

Members of the St. Louis Cardinals are featured in this 30-card set. The cards were printed on heavy paper and feature sepia-toned photos. The player's name appears along the bottom white border below the photo. The cards measure 6-1/4" x 9-1/2" and are not numbered. Most cards feature the logo of Metropolitan Studio in a bottom corner, while others have "Sid Whiting St. Louis MO," and a few have no sponsor's credit.

		NM	EX	VG
	Complete Set (30):	1,800	810.00	450.00
	Common Player:	45.00	20.00	12.00
(1)	Earl "Sparky" Adams	45.00	20.00	12.00
(2)	Ray Blades	45.00	20.00	12.00
(3)	James Bottomley	95.00	45.00	25.00
(4)	Sam Breadon	45.00	20.00	12.00
(5)	James "Rip" Collins	45.00	20.00	12.00
(6)	Dizzy Dean	225.00	100.00	55.00
(7)	Paul Derringer	45.00	20.00	12.00
(8)	Jake Flowers	45.00	20.00	12.00
(9)	Frank Frisch	95.00	45.00	25.00
(10)	Charles Gelbert	45.00	20.00	12.00
(11)	Miguel Gonzales (Gonzalez)	80.00	35.00	20.00
(12)	Burleigh Grimes	95.00	45.00	25.00
(13)	Charles "Chick" Hafey	95.00	45.00	25.00
(14)	William Hallahan	45.00	20.00	12.00
(15)	Jesse Haines	95.00	45.00	25.00
(16)	Andrew High	45.00	20.00	12.00
(17)	Sylvester Johnson	45.00	20.00	12.00
(18)	Tony Kaufmann	45.00	20.00	12.00
(19)	James Lindsey	45.00	20.00	12.00
(20)	Gus Mancuso	45.00	20.00	12.00
(21)	John Leonard "Pepper" Martin	80.00	35.00	20.00
(22)	Ernest Orsatti	45.00	20.00	12.00
(23)	Charles Flint Rhem	45.00	20.00	12.00
(24)	Branch Rickey	125.00	55.00	35.00
(25)	Walter Roettger	45.00	20.00	12.00
(26)	Allyn Stout	45.00	20.00	12.00
(27)	"Gabby" Street	45.00	20.00	12.00
(28)	Clyde Wares	45.00	20.00	12.00
(29)	George Watkins	45.00	20.00	12.00
(30)	James Wilson	45.00	20.00	12.00

1979 Michigan Sports Collectors

Former Detroit Tigers, along with several baseball writers and announcers, including some who were appearing as autograph guests were featured in this collectors set issued in conjunction with the 1979 Troy, Mich. show. Cards are 3-1/2" x 5-1/16" black-and-white. Backs have personal data and a career summary of the pictured player, along with mention of the show. The unnumbered cards are checklisted alphabetically.

		NM	EX	VG
Complete Set (20):		20.00	10.00	6.00
Common Player:		3.00	1.50	.90
(1)	Gates Brown	3.00	1.50	.90
(2)	Norm Cash	5.00	2.50	1.50
(3)	Al Cicotte	3.00	1.50	.90
(4)	Roy Cullenbine	3.00	1.50	.90
(5)	Gene Desautels	3.00	1.50	.90
(6)	Hoot Evers	3.00	1.50	.90
(7)	Joe Falls	3.00	1.50	.90
(8)	Joe Ginsberg	3.00	1.50	.90
(9)	Ernie Harwell	3.00	1.50	.90
(10)	Ray Herbert	3.00	1.50	.90
(11)	John Hiller	3.00	1.50	.90
(12)	Billy Hoeft	3.00	1.50	.90
(13)	Ralph Houk	4.00	2.00	1.25
(14)	Cliff Kachline	3.00	1.50	.90
(15)	George Kell	5.00	2.50	1.50
(16)	Ron LeFlore	4.00	2.00	1.25
(17)	Barney McCosky	3.00	1.50	.90
(18)	Jim Northrup	3.00	1.50	.90
(19)	Dick Radatz	3.00	1.50	.90
(20)	Tom Timmermann	3.00	1.50	.90

1940 Michigan Sportservice Detroit Tigers

Apparently a team issue sent to persons who wrote the team or players for photos, these blank-back cards measure 4-1/8" x 6-1/4" and are printed in black-and-white. A facsimile autograph is printed over the central portrait, which is surrounded by a border of baseballs. A few career notes are printed under the photo. At bottom-left is a union printing label. At bottom-right is printed, "Copyrighted 1939, Michigan Sportservice, Inc. Unauthorized Reproduction Prohibited." The unnumbered cards are checklisted here alphabetically.

		NM	EX	VG
Complete Set (21):		5,400	2,700	1,650
Common Player:		300.00	150.00	90.00
(1)	Earl Averill	350.00	175.00	105.00
(2)	Dick Bartell	300.00	150.00	90.00
(3)	Roy "Beau" Bell	300.00	150.00	90.00
(4)	Al Benton	300.00	150.00	90.00
(5)	Tommy Bridges	300.00	150.00	90.00
(6)	Frank Croucher	300.00	150.00	90.00
(7)	Pete Fox	300.00	150.00	90.00
(8)	Charlie Gehringer	400.00	200.00	120.00
(9)	Hank Greenberg	550.00	275.00	165.00
(10)	John Gorsica	300.00	150.00	90.00
(11)	Pinky Higgins	300.00	150.00	90.00
(12)	Fred Hutchinson	300.00	150.00	90.00
(13)	Ralph "Red" Kress	300.00	150.00	90.00
(14)	Barney McCosky	300.00	150.00	90.00
(15)	Archie R. McKain	300.00	150.00	90.00
(16)	Hal Newhouser	350.00	175.00	105.00
(17)	Louis "Buck" Newsom	300.00	150.00	90.00
(18)	Schoolboy Rowe	300.00	150.00	90.00
(19)	Birdie Tebbetts	300.00	150.00	90.00
(20)	Dizzy Trout	300.00	150.00	90.00
(21)	Rudy York	300.00	150.00	90.00

1975 Mid-Atlantic Sports Collectors Assn.

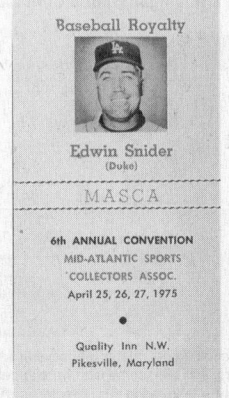

This "Baseball Royalty" collectors' set was issued in conjunction with the 1975 convention of the Mid-Atlantic Sports Collectors Association in Pikesville, Md. The blank-backed, 2-1/2" x 4-3/4" cards are printed in red and blue on white with player photos in blue. Each of the players in the set has a name or nickname pertaining to royalty. The unnumbered cards are checklisted here in alphabetical order.

		NM	EX	VG
Complete Set (8):		20.00	10.00	6.00
Common Player:		3.00	1.50	.90
(1)	Paul (Duke) Derringer	3.00	1.50	.90
(2)	Elroy (Baron of the Bullpen) Face	3.00	1.50	.90
(3)	Rogers (Rajah) Hornsby	5.00	2.50	1.50
(4)	(King) Carl Hubbell	4.00	2.00	1.25
(5)	Charley (King Kong) Keller	3.00	1.50	.90
(6)	Babe (Sultan of Swat) Ruth	10.00	5.00	3.00
(7)	(Prince) Hal Schumacher	3.00	1.50	.90
(8)	Edwin (Duke) Snider	7.50	3.75	2.25

1927 Middy Bread Browns/Cardinals Die-Cuts

St. Louis Cardinals and St. Louis Browns players comprise this set. Black-and-white, blank-backed and unnumbered, the cards are known only in die-cut form, and vary in size according to the player pose, with a typical card measuring 2-1/4" x 4" or so. The checklist, arranged here alphabetically, consists of 22 players from each team, but may be subject to future additions. Similar to the previous year's issue of Kut Outs Yankees and Giants die-cut cards, this issue features posed action photos with the backgrounds cut away and the player and team name printed at the bottom of the photo. Unlike the earlier New York issue, however, these cards carry an advertisement at bottom for Middy Bread and are presumably issued in the St. Louis area, though the exact method of their distribution is unknown. Cards are blank-backed and unnumbered. As with all die-cut cards, various appendages and bat ends were easily torn off and cards with such defects suffer severe loss of value.

		NM	EX	VG
Complete Set (44):		13,500	6,750	4,250
Common Player:		300.00	120.00	60.00
St. Louis Browns				
(1)	Spencer Adams	450.00	180.00	90.00
(2)	Win Ballou	300.00	120.00	60.00
(3)	Walter Beck	300.00	120.00	60.00
(4)	Herschel Bennett	300.00	120.00	60.00
(5)	Stewart Bolen	300.00	120.00	60.00
(6)	Leo Dixon	300.00	120.00	60.00
(7)	Chester Falk	300.00	120.00	60.00
(8)	Milton Gaston	300.00	120.00	60.00
(9)	Walter Gerber	300.00	120.00	60.00
(10)	Sam Jones	300.00	120.00	60.00
(11)	Oscar Melillo	300.00	120.00	60.00
(12)	Bing Miller	300.00	120.00	60.00
(13)	Otis Miller	300.00	120.00	60.00
(14)	Billie Mullen	300.00	120.00	60.00
(15)	Ernie Nevers	600.00	240.00	120.00
(16)	Steve O'Neill	300.00	120.00	60.00
(17)	Harry Rice	300.00	120.00	60.00
(18)	George Sisler	500.00	200.00	100.00
(19)	Walter Stewart	300.00	120.00	60.00
(20)	Elam VanGilder	300.00	120.00	60.00
(21)	Ken Williams	300.00	120.00	60.00
(22)	Ernie Wingard	300.00	120.00	60.00
St. Louis Cardinals				
(1)	Grover Alexander	600.00	240.00	120.00
(2)	Herman Bell	300.00	120.00	60.00
(3)	Lester Bell	300.00	120.00	60.00
(4)	Ray Blades	300.00	120.00	60.00
(5)	Jim Bottomley	500.00	200.00	100.00
(6)	Danny Clark	300.00	120.00	60.00
(7)	Taylor Douthit	300.00	120.00	60.00
(8)	Frank Frisch	500.00	200.00	100.00
(9)	Chick Hafey	500.00	200.00	100.00
(10)	Jesse Haines	500.00	200.00	100.00
(11)	Vic Keen	300.00	120.00	60.00
(12)	Carlise Littlejohn	300.00	120.00	60.00
(13)	Bob McGraw	300.00	120.00	60.00
(14)	Bob O'Farrell	300.00	120.00	60.00
(15)	Art Reinhardt	300.00	120.00	60.00
(16)	Jimmy Ring	300.00	120.00	60.00
(17)	Walter Roettger	300.00	120.00	60.00
(18)	Robert Schang	300.00	120.00	60.00
(19)	Willie Sherdel	300.00	120.00	60.00
(20)	Billy Southworth	300.00	120.00	60.00
(21)	Tommy Thevenow	300.00	120.00	60.00
(22)	George Toporcer	300.00	120.00	60.00

1976 Midwest Sports Collectors Convention

This collectors' issue was produced in conjunction with the 7th annual convention of the Midwest Sports Collectors in Troy, Mich. Former members of the Detroit Tigers, with an emphasis on the 1930s, are featured on the black-and-white, 2-3/8" x 2-7/8" cards. Players are depicted in portrait and action drawings, with personal data and career highlights added in either written or comic form. Backs advertise the show. The unnumbered cards are checklisted here in alphabetical order.

		NM	EX	VG
Complete Set (23):		15.00	7.50	4.50
Common Player:		3.00	1.50	.90
(1)	Eldon Auker	3.00	1.50	.90
(2)	Tommy Bridges	3.00	1.50	.90
(3)	Flea Clifton	3.00	1.50	.90
(4)	Mickey Cochrane	7.50	3.75	2.25
(5)	General Crowder	3.00	1.50	.90
(6)	Frank Doljack	3.00	1.50	.90
(7)	Carl Fischer	3.00	1.50	.90
(8)	Pete Fox	3.00	1.50	.90
(9)	Charlie Gehringer	6.00	3.00	1.75
(10)	Goose Goslin	4.50	2.25	1.25
(11)	Hank Greenberg	9.00	4.50	2.75
(12)	Luke Hamlin	3.00	1.50	.90
(13)	Ray Hayworth	3.00	1.50	.90
(14)	Chief Hogsett	3.00	1.50	.90
(15)	Firpo Marberry	3.00	1.50	.90
(16)	Marvin Owen	3.00	1.50	.90
(17)	Cy Perkins	3.00	1.50	.90
(18)	Bill Rogell	3.00	1.50	.90
(19)	Schoolboy Rowe	3.00	1.50	.90
(20)	Heinie Schuble	3.00	1.50	.90
(21)	Vic Sorrell	3.00	1.50	.90
(22)	Gee Walker	3.00	1.50	.90
(23)	Jo Jo White	3.00	1.50	.90

1980 Midwest Sports Collectors Convention

Reprints of a number of the player postcards of J.D. McCarthy were produced in conjunction with the 1980 Detroit show. The blank-backed, black-and-white postcards are 3-1/4" x 5-1/2" and all feature former Detroit Tigers. The unnumbered cards are checklisted here alphabetically.

		NM	EX	VG
Complete Set (11):		7.50	3.75	2.25
Common Player:		1.00	.50	.30
(1)	Bob Anderson	1.00	.50	.30
(2)	Babe Birrer	1.00	.50	.30
(3)	Frank Bolling	1.00	.50	.30
(4)	Jim Bunning	2.00	1.00	.60
(5)	Al Cicotte	1.00	.50	.30
(6)	Paul Foytack	1.00	.50	.30
(7)	Joe Ginsberg	1.00	.50	.30
(8)	Steve Gromek	1.00	.50	.30
(9)	Art Houtteman	1.00	.50	.30
(10)	Al Kaline	5.00	2.50	1.50
(11)	Harvey Kuenn	2.00	1.00	.60

1971 Milk Duds

These cards were issued on the backs of five-cent packages of Milk Duds candy. Most collectors prefer complete boxes, rather than cut-out cards, which measure approximately 1-13/16" x 2-5/8" when trimmed tightly. Values quoted below are for complete boxes. Cut cards will bring 50-75 percent of the quoted values. The set includes 37 National League and 32 American League players. Card numbers appear on the box flap, with each number from 1 through 24 being shared by three different players. A suffix (a, b and c) has been added for the collector's convenience. Harmon Killebrew, Brooks Robinson and Pete Rose were double-printed.

		NM	EX	VG
	Complete Set, Boxes:	1,000	500.00	300.00
	Complete Set, Singles (72):	500.00	250.00	150.00
	Common Player:	10.00	5.00	3.00
1a	Frank Howard	12.00	6.00	3.50
1b	Fritz Peterson	10.00	5.00	3.00
1c	Pete Rose	55.00	27.50	16.50
2a	Johnny Bench	15.00	7.50	4.50
2b	Rico Carty	10.00	5.00	3.00
2c	Pete Rose	55.00	27.50	16.50
3a	Ken Holtzman	10.00	5.00	3.00
3b	Willie Mays	50.00	25.00	15.00
3c	Cesar Tovar	10.00	5.00	3.00
4a	Willie Davis	10.00	5.00	3.00
4b	Harmon Killebrew	15.00	7.50	4.50
4c	Felix Millan	10.00	5.00	3.00
5a	Billy Grabarkewitz	10.00	5.00	3.00
5b	Andy Messersmith	10.00	5.00	3.00
5c	Thurman Munson	45.00	22.50	13.50
6a	Luis Aparicio	13.50	6.75	4.00
6b	Lou Brock	13.50	6.75	4.00
6c	Bill Melton	10.00	5.00	3.00
7a	Ray Culp	10.00	5.00	3.00
7b	Willie McCovey	20.00	10.00	6.00
7c	Luke Walker	10.00	5.00	3.00
8a	Roberto Clemente	115.00	55.00	35.00
8b	Jim Merritt	10.00	5.00	3.00
8c	Claud Osteen (Claude)	10.00	5.00	3.00
9a	Stan Bahnsen	10.00	5.00	3.00
9b	Sam McDowell	10.00	5.00	3.00
9c	Billy Williams	15.00	7.50	4.50
10a	Jim Hickman	10.00	5.00	3.00
10b	Dave McNally	10.00	5.00	3.00
10c	Tony Perez	20.00	10.00	6.00
11a	Hank Aaron	40.00	20.00	12.00
11b	Glen Beckert (Glenn)	10.00	5.00	3.00
11c	Ray Fosse	10.00	5.00	3.00
12a	Alex Johnson	10.00	5.00	3.00
12b	Gaylord Perry	13.50	6.75	4.00
12c	Wayne Simpson	10.00	5.00	3.00
13a	Dave Johnson	10.00	5.00	3.00
13b	George Scott	10.00	5.00	3.00
13c	Tom Seaver	25.00	12.50	7.50
14a	Bill Freehan	10.00	5.00	3.00
14b	Bud Harrelson	10.00	5.00	3.00
14c	Manny Sanguillen	10.00	5.00	3.00
15a	Bob Gibson	15.00	7.50	4.50
15b	Rusty Staub	12.00	6.00	3.50
15c	Roy White	10.00	5.00	3.00
16a	Jim Fregosi	10.00	5.00	3.00
16b	Catfish Hunter	13.50	6.75	4.00
16c	Mel Stottlemyer (Stottlemyre)	10.00	5.00	3.00
17a	Tommy Harper	10.00	5.00	3.00
17b	Frank Robinson	20.00	10.00	6.00
17c	Reggie Smith	10.00	5.00	3.00
18a	Orlando Cepeda	20.00	10.00	6.00
18b	Rico Petrocelli	10.00	5.00	3.00
18c	Brooks Robinson	20.00	10.00	6.00
19a	Tony Oliva	12.00	6.00	3.50
19b	Milt Pappas	10.00	5.00	3.00
19c	Bobby Tolan	10.00	5.00	3.00
20a	Ernie Banks	30.00	15.00	9.00
20b	Don Kessinger	10.00	5.00	3.00
20c	Joe Torre	12.00	6.00	3.50
21a	Fergie Jenkins	13.50	6.75	4.00
21b	Jim Palmer	15.00	7.50	4.50
21c	Ron Santo	12.00	6.00	3.50
22a	Randy Hundley	10.00	5.00	3.00
22b	Dennis Menke (Denis)	10.00	5.00	3.00
22c	Boog Powell	12.00	6.00	3.50
23a	Dick Dietz	10.00	5.00	3.00
23b	Tommy John	10.00	5.00	3.00
23c	Brooks Robinson	20.00	10.00	6.00
24a	Danny Cater	10.00	5.00	3.00
24b	Harmon Killebrew	15.00	7.50	4.50
24c	Jim Perry	12.00	6.00	3.50

1933 George C. Miller (R300)

George C. Miller & Co. of Boston, Mass., issued a 32-card set in one-cent packs of toffee in 1933. The set, which received limited distribution, consists of 16 National League and 16 American League players. The cards are color art reproductions of actual photographs and measure 2-3/8" x 2-7/8". Two distinct variations can be found for each card in the set. Type 1 cards have the names "Fox" and "Klien" misspelled on the back, while Type 2 cards have them correctly as "Foxx" and "Klein." Collectors were advised on the card backs to collect all 32 cards and return them for prizes. (Ivy Andrews' card was short-printed to avoid giving out too many prizes.) The cancelled cards were returned to the collector with the prize. Two forms of cancellation were used; one involved the complete trimming of the bottom one-quarter of the card, the other a diamond-shaped series of punch holes. Cancelled cards have a significantly decreased value.

		NM	EX	VG
	Complete Set (32):	65,000	30,000	16,000
	Common Player:	1,200	550.00	300.00
(1)	Dale Alexander	1,200	550.00	300.00
(2)	"Ivy" Paul Andrews	5,500	2,475	1,375
	Cut-cancelled: 1150.00			
	Punch-cancelled: 2,400			
(3)	Earl Averill	2,500	1,125	625.00
(4)	Dick Bartell	1,200	550.00	300.00
(5)	Walter Berger	1,200	550.00	300.00
(6)	Jim Bottomley	2,500	1,125	625.00
(7)	Joe Cronin	2,500	1,125	625.00
(8)	Jerome "Dizzy" Dean	3,000	1,350	750.00
(9)	William Dickey	2,500	1,125	625.00
(10)	Jimmy Dykes	1,200	550.00	300.00
(11)	Wesley Ferrell	1,200	550.00	300.00
(12)	Jimmy Foxx	3,500	1,575	875.00
(13)	Frank Frisch	2,500	1,125	625.00
(14)	Charlie Gehringer	2,500	1,125	625.00
(15)	Leon "Goose" Goslin	2,500	1,125	625.00
(16)	Charlie Grimm	1,200	550.00	300.00
(17)	Bob "Lefty" Grove	3,000	1,350	750.00
(18)	Charles "Chick" Hafey	2,500	1,125	625.00
(19)	Ray Hayworth	1,200	550.00	300.00
(20)	Charles "Chuck" Klein	2,500	1,125	625.00
(21)	Walter "Rabbit" Maranville	2,500	1,125	625.00
(22)	Oscar Melillo	1,200	550.00	300.00
(23)	Frank "Lefty" O'Doul	2,000	900.00	500.00
(24)	Melvin Ott	2,750	1,225	685.00
(25)	Carl Reynolds	1,200	550.00	300.00
(26)	Charles Ruffing	2,500	1,125	625.00
(27)	Al Simmons	2,500	1,125	625.00
(28)	Joe Stripp	1,200	550.00	300.00
(29)	Bill Terry	2,500	1,125	625.00
(30)	Lloyd Waner	2,500	1,125	625.00
(31)	Paul Waner	2,500	1,125	625.00
(32)	Lonnie Warneke	1,200	550.00	300.00

1969 Milton Bradley

The first of three sets issued by Milton Bradley over a four-year period, these cards were part of a baseball board game. The unnumbered cards measure 2" x 3" and have a white border surrounding the black-and-white player photo. The player's name appears above the photo in upper case letters. There are no team designations and the photos are airbrushed to eliminate team logos. Backs display biographical data along the top followed by a list of various game situations used in playing the board game. The cards have square corners. The 1969 and 1972 game cards are virtually identical in format. They can be differentiated by looking on the back at any numeral "1" in a line of red type. If the "1" does not have a base, it is a 1969 card; if there is a base, the card is a 1972. Besides individual player cards, there was a non-photographic team cards for each of the contemporary 24 Major League teams.

	NM	EX	VG
Complete Boxed Set:	400.00	200.00	120.00

		NM	EX	VG
	Complete Set (296):	150.00	75.00	45.00
	Common Player:	.50	.25	.15
	Team Card:	2.00	1.00	.60
(1)	Hank Aaron	30.00	15.00	9.00
(2)	Ted Abernathy	.50	.25	.15
(3)	Jerry Adair	.50	.25	.15
(4)	Tommy Agee	.50	.25	.15
(5)	Bernie Allen	.50	.25	.15
(6)	Hank Allen	.50	.25	.15
(7)	Richie Allen	5.00	2.50	1.50
(8)	Gene Alley	.50	.25	.15
(9)	Bob Allison	.50	.25	.15
(10)	Felipe Alou	1.00	.50	.30
(11)	Jesus Alou	.50	.25	.15
(12)	Matty Alou	.50	.25	.15
(13)	Max Alvis	.50	.25	.15
(14)	Mike Andrews	.50	.25	.15
(15)	Luis Aparicio	10.00	5.00	3.00
(16)	Jose Arcia	.50	.25	.15
(17)	Bob Asprómonte	.50	.25	.15
(18)	Joe Azcue	.50	.25	.15
(19)	Ernie Banks	20.00	10.00	6.00
(20)	Steve Barber	.50	.25	.15
(21)	John Bateman	.50	.25	.15
(22)	Glen Beckert (Glenn)	.50	.25	.15
(23)	Gary Bell	.50	.25	.15
(24)	John Bench	15.00	7.50	4.50
(25)	Ken Berry	.50	.25	.15
(26)	Frank Bertaina	.50	.25	.15
(27)	Paul Blair	.50	.25	.15
(28)	Wade Blasingame	.50	.25	.15
(29)	Curt Blefary	.50	.25	.15
(30)	John Boccabella	.50	.25	.15
(31)	Bobby Lee Bonds	1.00	.50	.30
(32)	Sam Bowens	.50	.25	.15
(33)	Ken Boyer	1.00	.50	.30
(34)	Charles Bradford	.50	.25	.15
(35)	Darrell Brandon	.50	.25	.15
(36)	Jim Brewer	.50	.25	.15
(37)	John Briggs	.50	.25	.15
(38)	Nelson Briles	.50	.25	.15
(39)	Ed Brinkman	.50	.25	.15
(40)	Lou Brock	10.00	5.00	3.00
(41)	Gates Brown	.50	.25	.15
(42)	Larry Brown	.50	.25	.15
(43)	George Brunet	.50	.25	.15
(44)	Jerry Buchek	.50	.25	.15
(45)	Don Buford	.50	.25	.15
(46)	Jim Bunning	7.50	3.75	2.25
(47)	Johnny Callison	.50	.25	.15
(48)	Campy Campaneris	.50	.25	.15
(49)	Jose Cardenal	.50	.25	.15
(50)	Leo Cardenas	.50	.25	.15
(51)	Don Cardwell	.50	.25	.15
(52)	Rod Carew	12.50	6.25	3.75
(53)	Paul Casanova	.50	.25	.15
(54)	Norm Cash	1.50	.70	.45
(55)	Danny Cater	.50	.25	.15
(56)	Orlando Cepeda	10.00	5.00	3.00
(57)	Dean Chance	.50	.25	.15
(58)	Ed Charles	.50	.25	.15
(59)	Horace Clarke	.50	.25	.15
(60)	Roberto Clemente	45.00	22.00	13.50
(61)	Donn Clendenon	.50	.25	.15
(62)	Ty Cline	.50	.25	.15
(63)	Nate Colbert	.50	.25	.15
(64)	Joe Coleman	.50	.25	.15
(65)	Bob Cox	.50	.25	.15
(66)	Mike Cuellar	.50	.25	.15
(67)	Ray Culp	.50	.25	.15
(68)	Clay Dalrymple	.50	.25	.15
(69)	Vic Davalillo	.50	.25	.15
(70)	Jim Davenport	.50	.25	.15
(71)	Ron Davis	.50	.25	.15
(72)	Tommy Davis	.50	.25	.15
(73)	Willie Davis	.50	.25	.15
(74)	Chuck Dobson	.50	.25	.15
(75)	John Donaldson	.50	.25	.15
(76)	Al Downing	.50	.25	.15
(77)	Moe Drabowsky	.50	.25	.15
(78)	Dick Ellsworth	.50	.25	.15
(79)	Mike Epstein	.50	.25	.15
(80)	Andy Etchebarren	.50	.25	.15
(81)	Ron Fairly	.50	.25	.15
(82)	Dick Farrell	.50	.25	.15
(83)	Curt Flood	1.00	.50	.30
(84)	Joe Foy	.50	.25	.15
(85)	Tito Francona	.50	.25	.15
(86)	Bill Freehan	.75	.40	.25
(87)	Jim Fregosi	.50	.25	.15
(88)	Woodie Fryman	.50	.25	.15
(89)	Len Gabrielson	.50	.25	.15
(90)	Cito Gaston	.50	.25	.15
(91)	Jake Gibbs	.50	.25	.15
(92)	Russ Gibson	.50	.25	.15
(93)	Dave Giusti	.50	.25	.15
(94)	Tony Gonzalez	.50	.25	.15
(95)	Jim Gosger	.50	.25	.15
(96)	Julio Gotay	.50	.25	.15
(97)	Dick Green	.50	.25	.15
(98)	Jerry Grote	.50	.25	.15
(99)	Jimmie Hall	.50	.25	.15
(100)	Tom Haller	.50	.25	.15
(101)	Steve Hamilton	.50	.25	.15
(102)	Ron Hansen	.50	.25	.15
(103)	Jim Hardin	.50	.25	.15
(104)	Tommy Harper	.50	.25	.15
(105)	Bud Harrelson	.50	.25	.15
(106)	Ken Harrelson	.50	.25	.15
(107)	Jim Hart	.50	.25	.15
(108)	Woodie Held	.50	.25	.15
(109)	Tommy Helms	.50	.25	.15
(110)	Elrod Hendricks	.50	.25	.15
(111)	Mike Hershberger	.50	.25	.15
(112)	Jack Hiatt	.50	.25	.15
(113)	Jim Hickman	.50	.25	.15
(114)	John Hiller	.50	.25	.15
(115)	Chuck Hinton	.50	.25	.15

(116)	Ken Holtzman	.50	.25	.15
(117)	Joel Horlen	.50	.25	.15
(118)	Tony Horton	.50	.25	.15
(119)	Willie Horton	.50	.25	.15
(120)	Frank Howard	1.00	.50	.30
(121)	Dick Howser	.50	.25	.15
(122)	Randy Hundley	.50	.25	.15
(123)	Ron Hunt	.50	.25	.15
(124)	Catfish Hunter	7.50	3.75	2.25
(125)	Al Jackson	.50	.25	.15
(126)	Larry Jackson	.50	.25	.15
(127)	Reggie Jackson	30.00	15.00	9.00
(128)	Sonny Jackson	.50	.25	.15
(129)	Pat Jarvis	.50	.25	.15
(130)	Julian Javier	.50	.25	.15
(131)	Ferguson Jenkins	7.50	3.75	2.25
(132)	Manny Jimenez	.50	.25	.15
(133)	Tommy John	1.00	.50	.30
(134)	Bob Johnson	.50	.25	.15
(135)	Dave Johnson	.50	.25	.15
(136)	Deron Johnson	.50	.25	.15
(137)	Lou Johnson	.50	.25	.15
(138)	Jay Johnstone	.50	.25	.15
(139)	Cleon Jones	.50	.25	.15
(140)	Dalton Jones	.50	.25	.15
(141)	Duane Josephson	.50	.25	.15
(142)	Jim Kaat	1.50	.70	.45
(143)	Al Kaline	15.00	7.50	4.50
(144)	Don Kessinger	.50	.25	.15
(145)	Harmon Killebrew	12.50	6.25	3.75
(146)	Harold King	.50	.25	.15
(147)	Ed Kirkpatrick	.50	.25	.15
(148)	Fred Klages	.50	.25	.15
(149)	Ron Kline	.50	.25	.15
(150)	Bobby Knoop	.50	.25	.15
(151)	Gary Kolb	.50	.25	.15
(152)	Andy Kosco	.50	.25	.15
(153)	Ed Kranepool	.50	.25	.15
(154)	Lew Krausse	.50	.25	.15
(155)	Harold Lanier	.50	.25	.15
(156)	Jim Lefebvre	.50	.25	.15
(157)	Denny Lemaster	.50	.25	.15
(158)	Dave Leonhard	.50	.25	.15
(159)	Don Lock	.50	.25	.15
(160)	Mickey Lolich	1.50	.70	.45
(161)	Jim Lonborg	.75	.40	.25
(162)	Mike Lum	.50	.25	.15
(163)	Al Lyle	.50	.25	.15
(164)	Jim Maloney	.50	.25	.15
(165)	Juan Marichal	8.00	4.00	2.50
(166)	J.C. Martin	.50	.25	.15
(167)	Marty Martinez	.50	.25	.15
(168)	Tom Matchick	.50	.25	.15
(169)	Ed Mathews	12.50	6.25	3.75
(170)	Dal Maxvill	.50	.25	.15
(171)	Jerry May	.50	.25	.15
(172)	Lee May	.50	.25	.15
(173)	Lee Maye	.50	.25	.15
(174)	Willie Mays	30.00	15.00	9.00
(175)	Bill Mazeroski	12.50	6.25	3.75
(176)	Richard McAuliffe	.50	.25	.15
(177)	Al McBean	.50	.25	.15
(178)	Tim McCarver	.75	.40	.25
(179)	Bill McCool	.50	.25	.15
(180)	Mike McCormick	.50	.25	.15
(181)	Willie McCovey	12.50	6.25	3.75
(182)	Tom McCraw	.50	.25	.15
(183)	Lindy McDaniel	.50	.25	.15
(184)	Sam McDowell	.75	.40	.25
(185)	Orlando McFarlane	.50	.25	.15
(186)	Jim McGlothlin	.50	.25	.15
(187)	Denny McLain	1.25	.60	.40
(188)	Ken McMullen	.50	.25	.15
(189)	Dave McNally	.50	.25	.15
(190)	Gerry McNertney	.50	.25	.15
(191)	Dennis Menke (Denis)	.50	.25	.15
(192)	Felix Millan	.50	.25	.15
(193)	Don Mincher	.50	.25	.15
(194)	Rick Monday	.50	.25	.15
(195)	Joe Morgan	10.00	5.00	3.00
(196)	Bubba Morton	.50	.25	.15
(197)	Manny Mota	.50	.25	.15
(198)	Jim Nash	.50	.25	.15
(199)	Dave Nelson	.50	.25	.15
(200)	Dick Nen	.50	.25	.15
(201)	Phil Niekro	7.50	3.75	2.25
(202)	Jim Northrup	.50	.25	.15
(203)	Richard Nye	.50	.25	.15
(204)	Johnny Odom	.50	.25	.15
(205)	Tony Oliva	1.00	.50	.30
(206)	Gene Oliver	.50	.25	.15
(207)	Phil Ortega	.50	.25	.15
(208)	Claude Osteen	.50	.25	.15
(209)	Ray Oyler	.50	.25	.15
(210)	Jose Pagan	.50	.25	.15
(211)	Jim Pagliaroni	.50	.25	.15
(212)	Milt Pappas	.50	.25	.15
(213)	Wes Parker	.50	.25	.15
(214)	Camilo Pascual	.50	.25	.15
(215)	Don Pavletich	.50	.25	.15
(216)	Joe Pepitone	.50	.25	.15
(217)	Tony Perez	10.00	5.00	3.00
(218)	Gaylord Perry	7.50	3.75	2.25
(219)	Jim Perry	.50	.25	.15
(220)	Gary Peters	.50	.25	.15
(221)	Rico Petrocelli	.50	.25	.15
(222)	Adolfo Phillips	.50	.25	.15
(223)	Tom Phoebus	.50	.25	.15
(224)	Vada Pinson	2.00	1.00	.60
(225)	Boog Powell	2.00	1.00	.60
(226)	Frank Quilici	.50	.25	.15
(227)	Doug Rader	.50	.25	.15
(228)	Rich Reese	.50	.25	.15
(229)	Phil Regan	.50	.25	.15
(230)	Rick Reichardt	.50	.25	.15
(231)	Rick Renick	.50	.25	.15
(232)	Roger Repoz	.50	.25	.15
(233)	Dave Ricketts	.50	.25	.15

(234)	Bill Robinson	.50	.25	.15
(235)	Brooks Robinson	15.00	7.50	4.50
(236)	Frank Robinson	15.00	7.50	4.50
(237)	Bob Rodgers	.50	.25	.15
(238)	Cookie Rojas	.50	.25	.15
(239)	Rich Rollins	.50	.25	.15
(240)	Phil Roof	.50	.25	.15
(241)	Pete Rose	30.00	15.00	9.00
(242)	John Roseboro	.50	.25	.15
(243)	Chico Ruiz	.50	.25	.15
(244)	Ray Sadecki	.50	.25	.15
(245)	Chico Salmon	.50	.25	.15
(246)	Jose Santiago	.50	.25	.15
(247)	Ron Santo	2.50	1.25	.70
(248)	Tom Satriano	.50	.25	.15
(249)	Paul Schaal	.50	.25	.15
(250)	Tom Seaver	15.00	7.50	4.50
(251)	Art Shamsky	.50	.25	.15
(252)	Mike Shannon	.50	.25	.15
(253)	Chris Short	.50	.25	.15
(254)	Dick Simpson	.50	.25	.15
(255)	Duke Sims	.50	.25	.15
(256)	Reggie Smith	.50	.25	.15
(257)	Willie Smith	.50	.25	.15
(258)	Russ Snyder	.50	.25	.15
(259)	Al Spangler	.50	.25	.15
(260)	Larry Stahl	.50	.25	.15
(261)	Lee Stange	.50	.25	.15
(262)	Mickey Stanley	.50	.25	.15
(263)	Willie Stargell	10.00	5.00	3.00
(264)	Rusty Staub	1.00	.50	.30
(265)	Mel Stottlemyre	.50	.25	.15
(266)	Ed Stroud	.50	.25	.15
(267)	Don Sutton	7.50	3.75	2.25
(268)	Ron Swoboda	.50	.25	.15
(269)	Jose Tartabull	.50	.25	.15
(270)	Tony Taylor	.50	.25	.15
(271)	Luis Tiant	1.00	.50	.30
(272)	Bob Tillman	.50	.25	.15
(273)	Bobby Tolan	.50	.25	.15
(274)	Jeff Torborg	.50	.25	.15
(275)	Joe Torre	2.50	1.25	.70
(276)	Cesar Tovar	.50	.25	.15
(277)	Dick Tracewski	.50	.25	.15
(278)	Tom Tresh	.75	.40	.25
(279)	Ted Uhlaender	.50	.25	.15
(280)	Del Unser	.50	.25	.15
(281)	Hilario Valdespino	.50	.25	.15
(282)	Fred Valentine	.50	.25	.15
(283)	Bob Veale	.50	.25	.15
(284)	Zoilo Versalles	.50	.25	.15
(285)	Pete Ward	.50	.25	.15
(286)	Al Weis	.50	.25	.15
(287)	Don Wert	.50	.25	.15
(288)	Bill White	.50	.25	.15
(289)	Roy White	.50	.25	.15
(290)	Fred Whitfield	.50	.25	.15
(291)	Hoyt Wilhelm	7.50	3.75	2.25
(292)	Billy Williams	10.00	5.00	3.00
(293)	Maury Wills	.75	.40	.25
(294)	Earl Wilson	.50	.25	.15
(295)	Wilbur Wood	.50	.25	.15
(296)	Jerry Zimmerman	.50	.25	.15

1970 Milton Bradley

TONY TAYLOR

3	CATCHER
4	1ST BASEMAN
5	LEFT FIELDER
6	2ND BASEMAN
8	3RD BASEMAN
9	SHORTSTOP
10	CENTER FIELDER
11	RIGHT FIELDER
12	PITCHER

TONY TAYLOR

IF 12/19/35 5-9 TR BR

Except for the slightly larger (2-3/8" x 3-1/2") size, the format of the 1970 Milton Bradley set is similar to the 1969 Milton Bradley issue. Again designed for use with a baseball board game, the unnumbered black-and-white cards have rounded corners and wide white borders. The player's name appears in capital letters beneath the photo with his position, birthdate, height and batting and throwing preference on a line below. The back of the card shows the player's name along the top followed by a list of possible game situations used in playing the board game. There are no team designations on the cards and all team insignias have been airbrushed from the photos.

		NM	EX	VG
	Complete Boxed Set:	175.00	85.00	45.00
	Complete Card Set (28):	120.00	55.00	30.00
	Common Player:	1.50	.70	.45
(1)	Hank Aaron	15.00	7.50	4.50
(2)	Ernie Banks	10.00	5.00	3.00
(3)	Lou Brock	7.50	3.75	2.25
(4)	Rod Carew	9.00	4.50	2.75
(5)	Roberto Clemente	15.00	7.50	4.50
(6)	Tommy Davis	1.50	.70	.45
(7)	Bill Freehan	1.50	.70	.45
(8)	Jim Fregosi	1.50	.70	.45
(9)	Tom Haller	1.50	.70	.45
(10)	Frank Howard	2.00	1.00	.60
(11)	Reggie Jackson	10.00	5.00	3.00
(12)	Harmon Killebrew	9.00	4.50	2.75

(13)	Mickey S. Lolich	1.50	.70	.45
(14)	Juan Marichal	6.00	3.00	1.75
(15)	Willie Mays	15.00	7.50	4.50
(16)	Willie McCovey	7.50	3.75	2.25
(17)	Sam McDowell	1.50	.70	.45
(18)	Dennis Menke (Denis)	1.50	.70	.45
(19)	Don Mincher	1.50	.70	.45
(20)	Phil Niekro	6.00	3.00	1.75
(21)	Rico Petrocelli	1.50	.70	.45
(22)	Boog Powell	2.00	1.00	.60
(23)	Frank Robinson	9.00	4.50	2.75
(24)	Pete Rose	15.00	7.50	4.50
(25)	Ron Santo	3.00	1.50	.90
(26)	Tom Seaver	9.00	4.50	2.75
(27)	Mel Stottlemyre	1.50	.70	.45
(28)	Tony Taylor	1.50	.70	.45

1972 Milton Bradley

ROBERTO CLEMENTE

The 1972 Milton Bradley set was again designed for use with a baseball table game. The 1972 cards are similar to the 1969 and 1970 issues. The unnumbered black-and-white cards measure 2" x 3" and display the player's name along the top of the card. Again, all team insignias have been eliminated by airbrushing, and there are no team designations indicated. Backs carry the player's name and personal data followed by a list of possible game situations used in playing the game. To differentiate a 1972 card from a 1969, look on back for a line of red type which contains the numeral "1." If the digit has a base, the card is a '72; if there is no base to the red "1," it is a 1969. Besides individual player cards, non-photographic team cards were issued for each of the contemporary 24 Major League teams.

		NM	EX	VG
	Complete Boxed Set:	400.00	200.00	120.00
	Complete Card Set (378):	350.00	175.00	110.00
	Common Player:	.50	.25	.15
	Team Card:	2.00	1.00	.60
(1)	Hank Aaron	25.00	12.50	7.50
(2)	Tommie Aaron	.50	.25	.15
(3)	Ted Abernathy	.50	.25	.15
(4)	Jerry Adair	.50	.25	.15
(5)	Tommy Agee	.50	.25	.15
(6)	Bernie Allen	.50	.25	.15
(7)	Hank Allen	.50	.25	.15
(8)	Richie Allen	1.50	.70	.45
(9)	Gene Alley	.50	.25	.15
(10)	Bob Allison	.50	.25	.15
(11)	Sandy Alomar	.50	.25	.15
(12)	Felipe Alou	.75	.40	.25
(13)	Jesus Alou	.50	.25	.15
(14)	Matty Alou	.50	.25	.15
(15)	Max Alvis	.50	.25	.15
(16)	Brant Alyea	.50	.25	.15
(17)	Mike Andrews	.50	.25	.15
(18)	Luis Aparicio	9.00	4.50	2.75
(19)	Jose Arcia	.50	.25	.15
(20)	Gerald Arrigo	.50	.25	.15
(21)	Bob Aspromonte	.50	.25	.15
(22)	Joe Azcue	.50	.25	.15
(23)	Robert Bailey	.50	.25	.15
(24)	Sal Bando	.50	.25	.15
(25)	Ernie Banks	17.50	8.75	5.25
(26)	Steve Barber	.50	.25	.15
(27)	Robert Barton	.50	.25	.15
(28)	John Bateman	.50	.25	.15
(29)	Glen Beckert (Glenn)	.50	.25	.15
(30)	John Bench	12.50	6.25	3.75
(31)	Ken Berry	.50	.25	.15
(32)	Frank Bertaina	.50	.25	.15
(33)	Paul Blair	.50	.25	.15
(34)	Stephen Blass	.50	.25	.15
(35)	Curt Blefary	.50	.25	.15
(36)	Bobby Bolin	.50	.25	.15
(37)	Bobby Lee Bonds	1.00	.50	.30
(38)	Donald Bosch	.50	.25	.15
(39)	Richard Bosman	.50	.25	.15
(40)	Dave Boswell	.50	.25	.15
(41)	Kenneth Boswell	.50	.25	.15
(42)	Cletis Boyer	.50	.25	.15
(43)	Ken Boyer	1.25	.60	.40
(44)	Charles Bradford	.50	.25	.15
(45)	Ronald Brand	.50	.25	.15
(46)	Ken Brett	.50	.25	.15
(47)	Jim Brewer	.50	.25	.15
(48)	John Briggs	.50	.25	.15
(49)	Nelson Briles	.50	.25	.15
(50)	Ed Brinkman	.50	.25	.15
(51)	James Britton	.50	.25	.15
(52)	Lou Brock	9.00	4.50	2.75
(53)	Gates Brown	.50	.25	.15
(54)	Larry Brown	.50	.25	.15
(55)	Ollie Brown	.50	.25	.15
(56)	George Brunet	.50	.25	.15

(57)	Don Buford	.50	.25	.15
(58)	Wallace Bunker	.50	.25	.15
(59)	Jim Bunning	6.00	3.00	1.75
(60)	William Butler	.50	.25	.15
(61)	Johnny Callison	.50	.25	.15
(62)	Campy Campaneris	.50	.25	.15
(63)	Jose Cardenal	.50	.25	.15
(64)	Leo Cardenas	.50	.25	.15
(65)	Don Cardwell	.50	.25	.15
(66)	Rod Carew	9.00	4.50	2.75
(67)	Cisco Carlos	.50	.25	.15
(68)	Steve Carlton	9.00	4.50	2.75
(69)	Clay Carroll	.50	.25	.15
(70)	Paul Casanova	.50	.25	.15
(71)	Norm Cash	1.50	.70	.45
(72)	Danny Cater	.50	.25	.15
(73)	Orlando Cepeda	9.00	4.50	2.75
(74)	Dean Chance	.50	.25	.15
(75)	Horace Clarke	.50	.25	.15
(76)	Roberto Clemente	30.00	15.00	9.00
(77)	Donn Clendenon	.50	.25	.15
(78)	Ty Cline	.50	.25	.15
(79)	Nate Colbert	.50	.25	.15
(80)	Joe Coleman	.50	.25	.15
(81)	William Conigliaro	.75	.40	.25
(82)	Casey Cox	.50	.25	.15
(83)	Mike Cuellar	.50	.25	.15
(84)	Ray Culp	.50	.25	.15
(85)	George Culver	.50	.25	.15
(86)	Vic Davalillo	.50	.25	.15
(87)	Jim Davenport	.50	.25	.15
(88)	Tommy Davis	.50	.25	.15
(89)	Willie Davis	.50	.25	.15
(90)	Larry Dierker	.50	.25	.15
(91)	Richard Dietz	.50	.25	.15
(92)	Chuck Dobson	.50	.25	.15
(93)	Pat Dobson	.50	.25	.15
(94)	John Donaldson	.50	.25	.15
(95)	Al Downing	.50	.25	.15
(96)	Moe Drabowsky	.50	.25	.15
(97)	John Edwards	.50	.25	.15
(98)	Thomas Egan	.50	.25	.15
(99)	Dick Ellsworth	.50	.25	.15
(100)	Mike Epstein	.50	.25	.15
(101)	Andy Etchebarren	.50	.25	.15
(102)	Ron Fairly	.50	.25	.15
(103)	Frank Fernandez	.50	.25	.15
(104)	Alfred Ferrara	.50	.25	.15
(105)	Michael Fiore	.50	.25	.15
(106)	Curt Flood	1.00	.50	.30
(107)	Vern Fuller	.50	.25	.15
(108)	Joe Foy	.50	.25	.15
(109)	Tito Francona	.50	.25	.15
(110)	Bill Freehan	.50	.25	.15
(111)	Jim Fregosi	.50	.25	.15
(112)	Woodie Fryman	.50	.25	.15
(113)	Len Gabrielson	.50	.25	.15
(114)	Philip Gagliano	.50	.25	.15
(115)	Cito Gaston	.50	.25	.15
(116)	Jake Gibbs	.50	.25	.15
(117)	Russ Gibson	.50	.25	.15
(118)	Dave Giusti	.50	.25	.15
(119)	Fred Gladding	.50	.25	.15
(120)	Tony Gonzalez	.50	.25	.15
(121)	Jim Gosger	.50	.25	.15
(122)	James Grant	.50	.25	.15
(123)	Thomas Griffin	.50	.25	.15
(124)	Dick Green	.50	.25	.15
(125)	Jerry Grote	.50	.25	.15
(126)	Tom Hall	.50	.25	.15
(127)	Tom Haller	.50	.25	.15
(128)	Steve Hamilton	.50	.25	.15
(129)	William Hands	.50	.25	.15
(130)	James Hannan	.50	.25	.15
(131)	Ron Hansen	.50	.25	.15
(132)	Jim Hardin	.50	.25	.15
(133)	Steve Hargan	.50	.25	.15
(134)	Tommy Harper	.50	.25	.15
(135)	Bud Harrelson	.50	.25	.15
(136)	Ken Harrelson	.50	.25	.15
(137)	Jim Hart	.50	.25	.15
(138)	Rich Hebner	.50	.25	.15
(139)	Michael Hedlund	.50	.25	.15
(140)	Tommy Helms	.50	.25	.15
(141)	Elrod Hendricks	.50	.25	.15
(142)	Ronald Herbel	.50	.25	.15
(143)	Jack Hernandez	.50	.25	.15
(144)	Mike Hershberger	.50	.25	.15
(145)	Jack Hiatt	.50	.25	.15
(146)	Jim Hickman	.50	.25	.15
(147)	Dennis Higgins	.50	.25	.15
(148)	John Hiller	.50	.25	.15
(149)	Chuck Hinton	.50	.25	.15
(150)	Larry Hisle	.50	.25	.15
(151)	Ken Holtzman	.50	.25	.15
(152)	Joel Horlen	.50	.25	.15
(153)	Tony Horton	.50	.25	.15
(154)	Willie Horton	.50	.25	.15
(155)	Frank Howard	.75	.40	.25
(156)	Robert Humphreys	.50	.25	.15
(157)	Randy Hundley	.50	.25	.15
(158)	Ron Hunt	.50	.25	.15
(159)	Catfish Hunter	6.00	3.00	1.75
(160)	Grant Jackson	.50	.25	.15
(161)	Reggie Jackson	15.00	7.50	4.50
(162)	Sonny Jackson	.50	.25	.15
(163)	Pat Jarvis	.50	.25	.15
(164)	Larry Jaster	.50	.25	.15
(165)	Julian Javier	.50	.25	.15
(166)	Ferguson Jenkins	6.00	3.00	1.75
(167)	Tommy John	1.00	.50	.30
(168)	Alexander Johnson	.50	.25	.15
(169)	Bob Johnson	.50	.25	.15
(170)	Dave Johnson	.50	.25	.15
(171)	Deron Johnson	.50	.25	.15
(172)	Jay Johnstone	.50	.25	.15
(173)	Cleon Jones	.50	.25	.15
(174)	Dalton Jones	.50	.25	.15

(175)	Mack Jones	.50	.25	.15
(176)	Richard Joseph	.50	.25	.15
(177)	Duane Josephson	.50	.25	.15
(178)	Jim Kaat	2.00	1.00	.60
(179)	Al Kaline	12.50	6.25	3.75
(180)	Richard Kelley	.50	.25	.15
(181)	Harold Kelly	.50	.25	.15
(182)	Gerald Kenney	.50	.25	.15
(183)	Don Kessinger	.50	.25	.15
(184)	Harmon Killebrew	9.00	4.50	2.75
(185)	Ed Kirkpatrick	.50	.25	.15
(186)	Bobby Knoop	.50	.25	.15
(187)	Calvin Koonce	.50	.25	.15
(188)	Jerry Koosman	.50	.25	.15
(189)	Andy Kosco	.50	.25	.15
(190)	Ed Kranepool	.50	.25	.15
(191)	Ted Kubiak	.50	.25	.15
(192)	Jose Laboy	.50	.25	.15
(193)	Joseph Lahoud	.50	.25	.15
(194)	William Landis	.50	.25	.15
(195)	Harold Lanier	.50	.25	.15
(196)	Fred Lasher	.50	.25	.15
(197)	John Lazar	.50	.25	.15
(198)	Jim Lefebvre	.50	.25	.15
(199)	Denny Lemaster	.50	.25	.15
(200)	Dave Leonhard	.50	.25	.15
(201)	Frank Linzy	.50	.25	.15
(202)	Mickey Lolich	.50	.25	.15
(203)	Jim Lonborg	.50	.25	.15
(204)	Mike Lum	.50	.25	.15
(205)	Al Lyle	.50	.25	.15
(206)	Jim Maloney	.50	.25	.15
(207)	Juan Marichal	7.50	3.75	2.25
(208)	David Marshall	.50	.25	.15
(209)	J.C. Martin	.50	.25	.15
(210)	Marty Martinez	.50	.25	.15
(211)	Tom Matchick	.50	.25	.15
(212)	Dal Maxvill	.50	.25	.15
(213)	Carlos May	.50	.25	.15
(214)	Jerry May	.50	.25	.15
(215)	Lee May	.50	.25	.15
(216)	Lee Maye	.50	.25	.15
(217)	Willie Mays	25.00	12.50	7.50
(218)	Bill Mazeroski	9.00	4.50	2.75
(219)	Richard McAuliffe	.50	.25	.15
(220)	Al McBean	.50	.25	.15
(221)	Tim McCarver	.75	.40	.25
(222)	Bill McCool	.50	.25	.15
(223)	Mike McCormick	.50	.25	.15
(224)	Willie McCovey	9.00	4.50	2.75
(225)	Tom McCraw	.50	.25	.15
(226)	Lindy McDaniel	.50	.25	.15
(227)	Sam McDowell	.50	.25	.15
(228)	Leon McFadden	.50	.25	.15
(229)	Daniel McGinn	.50	.25	.15
(230)	Jim McGlothlin	.50	.25	.15
(231)	Fred McGraw	.50	.25	.15
(232)	Denny McLain	.75	.40	.25
(233)	Ken McMullen	.50	.25	.15
(234)	Dave McNally	.50	.25	.15
(235)	Gerry McNertney	.50	.25	.15
(236)	William Melton	.50	.25	.15
(237)	Dennis Menke (Denis)	.50	.25	.15
(238)	John Messersmith	.50	.25	.15
(239)	Felix Millan	.50	.25	.15
(240)	Norman Miller	.50	.25	.15
(241)	Don Mincher	.50	.25	.15
(242)	Rick Monday	.50	.25	.15
(243)	Donald Money	.50	.25	.15
(244)	Barry Moore	.50	.25	.15
(245)	Bob Moose	.50	.25	.15
(246)	David Morehead	.50	.25	.15
(247)	Joe Morgan	9.00	4.50	2.75
(248)	Curt Motton	.50	.25	.15
(249)	Manny Mota	.50	.25	.15
(250)	Bob Murcer	.50	.25	.15
(251)	Thomas Murphy	.50	.25	.15
(252)	Ivan Murrell	.50	.25	.15
(253)	Jim Nash	.50	.25	.15
(254)	Joe Niekro	1.25	.60	.40
(255)	Phil Niekro	6.00	3.00	1.75
(256)	Gary Nolan	.50	.25	.15
(257)	Jim Northrup	.50	.25	.15
(258)	Richard Nye	.50	.25	.15
(259)	Johnny Odom	.50	.25	.15
(260)	John O'Donaghue	.50	.25	.15
(261)	Tony Oliva	1.00	.50	.30
(262)	Al Oliver	1.00	.50	.30
(263)	Robert Oliver	.50	.25	.15
(264)	Claude Osteen	.50	.25	.15
(265)	Ray Oyler	.50	.25	.15
(266)	Jose Pagan	.50	.25	.15
(267)	Jim Palmer	9.00	4.50	2.75
(268)	Milt Pappas	.50	.25	.15
(269)	Wes Parker	.50	.25	.15
(270)	Fred Patek	.50	.25	.15
(271)	Mike Paul	.50	.25	.15
(272)	Joe Pepitone	.50	.25	.15
(273)	Tony Perez	7.50	3.75	2.25
(274)	Gaylord Perry	6.00	3.00	1.75
(275)	Jim Perry	.50	.25	.15
(276)	Gary Peters	.50	.25	.15
(277)	Rico Petrocelli	.50	.25	.15
(278)	Tom Phoebus	.50	.25	.15
(279)	Lou Piniella	1.00	.50	.30
(280)	Vada Pinson	1.50	.70	.45
(281)	Boog Powell	1.50	.70	.45
(282)	Jim Price	.50	.25	.15
(283)	Frank Quilici	.50	.25	.15
(284)	Doug Rader	.50	.25	.15
(285)	Ron Reed	.50	.25	.15
(286)	Rich Reese	.50	.25	.15
(287)	Phil Regan	.50	.25	.15
(288)	Rick Reichardt	.50	.25	.15
(289)	Rick Renick	.50	.25	.15
(290)	Roger Repoz	.50	.25	.15
(291)	Mervin Rettenmund	.50	.25	.15
(292)	Dave Ricketts	.50	.25	.15

(293)	Juan Rios	.50	.25	.15
(294)	Bill Robinson	.50	.25	.15
(295)	Brooks Robinson	12.50	6.25	3.75
(296)	Frank Robinson	12.50	6.25	3.75
(297)	Aurelio Rodriguez	.50	.25	.15
(298)	Ellie Rodriguez	.50	.25	.15
(299)	Cookie Rojas	.50	.25	.15
(300)	Rich Rollins	.50	.25	.15
(301)	Vicente Romo	.50	.25	.15
(302)	Phil Roof	.50	.25	.15
(303)	Pete Rose	25.00	12.50	7.50
(304)	John Roseboro	.50	.25	.15
(305)	Chico Ruiz	.50	.25	.15
(306)	Mike Ryan	.50	.25	.15
(307)	Ray Sadecki	.50	.25	.15
(308)	Chico Salmon	.50	.25	.15
(309)	Manuel Sanguillen	.50	.25	.15
(310)	Ron Santo	3.00	1.50	.90
(311)	Tom Satriano	.50	.25	.15
(312)	Theodore Savage	.50	.25	.15
(313)	Paul Schaal	.50	.25	.15
(314)	Dick Schofield	.50	.25	.15
(315)	George Scott	.50	.25	.15
(316)	Tom Seaver	12.50	6.25	3.75
(317)	Art Shamsky	.50	.25	.15
(318)	Mike Shannon	.50	.25	.15
(319)	Chris Short	.50	.25	.15
(320)	Sonny Siebert	.50	.25	.15
(321)	Duke Sims	.50	.25	.15
(322)	William Singer	.50	.25	.15
(323)	Reggie Smith	.50	.25	.15
(324)	Willie Smith	.50	.25	.15
(325)	Russ Snyder	.50	.25	.15
(326)	Al Spangler	.50	.25	.15
(327)	James Spencer	.50	.25	.15
(328)	Ed Spiezio	.50	.25	.15
(329)	Larry Stahl	.50	.25	.15
(330)	Lee Stange	.50	.25	.15
(331)	Mickey Stanley	.50	.25	.15
(332)	Willie Stargell	9.00	4.50	2.75
(333)	Rusty Staub	2.00	1.00	.60
(334)	James Stewart	.50	.25	.15
(335)	George Stone	.50	.25	.15
(336)	William Stoneman	.50	.25	.15
(337)	Mel Stottlemyre	.50	.25	.15
(338)	Ed Stroud	.50	.25	.15
(339)	Ken Suarez	.50	.25	.15
(340)	Gary Sutherland	.50	.25	.15
(341)	Don Sutton	6.00	3.00	1.75
(342)	Ron Swoboda	.50	.25	.15
(343)	Fred Talbot	.50	.25	.15
(344)	Jose Tartabull	.50	.25	.15
(345)	Kenneth Tatum	.50	.25	.15
(346)	Tony Taylor	.50	.25	.15
(347)	Luis Tiant	.75	.40	.25
(348)	Bob Tillman	.50	.25	.15
(349)	Bobby Tolan	.50	.25	.15
(350)	Jeff Torborg	.50	.25	.15
(351)	Joe Torre	3.00	1.50	.90
(352)	Cesar Tovar	.50	.25	.15
(353)	Tom Tresh	.75	.40	.25
(354)	Ted Uhlaender	.50	.25	.15
(355)	Del Unser	.50	.25	.15
(356)	Bob Veale	.50	.25	.15
(357)	Zoilo Versalles	.50	.25	.15
(358)	Luke Walker	.50	.25	.15
(359)	Pete Ward	.50	.25	.15
(360)	Eddie Watt	.50	.25	.15
(361)	Ramon Webster	.50	.25	.15
(362)	Al Weis	.50	.25	.15
(363)	Don Wert	.50	.25	.15
(364)	Bill White	.50	.25	.15
(365)	Roy White	.50	.25	.15
(366)	Hoyt Wilhelm	6.00	3.00	1.75
(367)	Billy Williams	9.00	4.50	2.75
(368)	Walter Williams	.50	.25	.15
(369)	Maury Wills	.75	.40	.25
(370)	Don Wilson	.50	.25	.15
(371)	Earl Wilson	.50	.25	.15
(372)	Robert Wine	.50	.25	.15
(373)	Richard Wise	.50	.25	.15
(374)	Wilbur Wood	.50	.25	.15
(375)	William Woodward	.50	.25	.15
(376)	Clyde Wright	.50	.25	.15
(377)	James Wynn	.50	.25	.15
(378)	Jerry Zimmerman	.50	.25	.15

1957 Milwaukee Braves Picture Pack

HENRY AARON, Outfielder

Prior to the Jay Publishing Co. photo packs which dominated the market from 1958-62, the Braves issued this souvenir stand picture pack of 5" x 7" black-and-white, blank-back, player pictures. In the wide bottom border player names are printed in all-caps with the position indicated in upper- and lower-case letters. The unnumbered pictures are listed here in alphabetical order.

	NM	EX	VG
Complete Set (12):	100.00	50.00	30.00
Common Player:	7.50	3.75	2.25
(1) Hank Aaron	30.00	15.00	9.00
(2) Joe Adcock	7.50	3.75	2.25
(3) Lew Burdette	7.50	3.75	2.25
(4) Wes Covington	7.50	3.75	2.25
(5) Del Crandall	7.50	3.75	2.25
(6) Bob Hazle	7.50	3.75	2.25
(7) Johnny Logan	7.50	3.75	2.25
(8) Edwin Mathews	12.50	6.25	3.75
(9) Don McMahon	7.50	3.75	2.25
(10) Andy Pafko	7.50	3.75	2.25
(11) Red Schoendienst	10.00	5.00	3.00
(12) Warren Spahn	12.50	6.25	3.75

1965 Milwaukee Braves Picture Pack

HANK AARON, Braves

These 4-7/8" x 7-1/8" blank-back, black-and-white pictures were sold in groups of 12 in a white paper window envelope and possibly also as a complete set of 24. Besides the slight size difference, the team-issued pictures differ from the contemporary Jay Publishing pictures in that the city name is not included in the typography in the bottom border.

	NM	EX	VG
Complete Set (24):	75.00	37.50	22.50
Common Player:	3.00	1.50	.90
(1) Hank Aaron	15.00	7.50	4.50
(2) Sandy Alomar	3.00	1.50	.90
(3) Felipe Alou	3.00	1.50	.90
(4) Wade Blasingame	3.00	1.50	.90
(5) Frank Bolling	3.00	1.50	.90
(6) Bobby Bragan	3.00	1.50	.90
(7) Rico Carty	3.00	1.50	.90
(8) Ty Cline	3.00	1.50	.90
(9) Tony Cloninger	3.00	1.50	.90
(10) Mike de la Hoz	3.00	1.50	.90
(11) Hank Fischer	3.00	1.50	.90
(12) Mack Jones	3.00	1.50	.90
(13) Gary Kolb	3.00	1.50	.90
(14) Denny LeMaster	3.00	1.50	.90
(15) Eddie Mathews	6.00	3.00	1.75
(16) Lee Maye	3.00	1.50	.90
(17) Denis Menke	3.00	1.50	.90
(18) Billy O'Dell	3.00	1.50	.90
(19) Gene Oliver	3.00	1.50	.90
(20) Chi Chi Olivo	3.00	1.50	.90
(21) Dan Osinki (Osinski)	3.00	1.50	.90
(22) Bob Sadowski	3.00	1.50	.90
(23) Bobby Tiefenauer	3.00	1.50	.90
(24) Joe Torre	4.50	2.25	1.25

1980 Milwaukee Brewers/Pepsi Fan Club

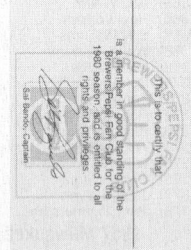

Star Milwaukee infielder Sal Bando is featured on this 2-1/2" x 3-1/2" membership card in a blue-bordered action pose. The back is printed in blue on white with both the team and soda logo.

	NM	EX	VG
Sal Bando	6.00	3.00	1.80

1912 Miner's Extra Series of Champions (T227)

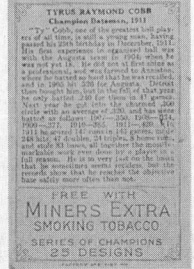

(See 1912 T227 Series of Champions for checklist, price guide.)

1977 Minneapolis Star Twins Scrapbook

Between July 4-August 12, the Star printed one player "Scrapbook" picture each day in the sports section. While sizes vary somewhat, most are about 4-3/16" x 10-3/16". Enclosed in a dotted-line border are a player portrait photo, facsimile autograph, position, uniform number, team logo, career highlights and full stats. Because they are printed on newsprint, the pictures are subject to rapid deterioration.

	NM	EX	VG
Complete Set (36):	100.00	50.00	30.00
Common Player:	4.00	2.00	1.25
7/4 Rod Carew	12.00	6.00	3.50
7/5 Geoff Zahn	4.00	2.00	1.25
7/6 Luis Gomez	4.00	2.00	1.25
7/7 Glenn Adams	4.00	2.00	1.25
7/8 Lyman Bostock	6.00	3.00	1.75
7/9 Bob Gorinski	4.00	2.00	1.25
7/11 Butch Wynegar	4.00	2.00	1.25
7/12 Rob Wilfong	4.00	2.00	1.25
7/13 Dave Goltz	4.00	2.00	1.25
7/14 Bill Butler	4.00	2.00	1.25
7/15 Bob Randall	4.00	2.00	1.25
7/16 Jeff Holly	4.00	2.00	1.25
7/18 Gene Mauch	4.00	2.00	1.25
7/19 Walt Terrell	4.00	2.00	1.25
7/20 Rich Chiles	4.00	2.00	1.25
7/21 Paul Thormodsgard	4.00	2.00	1.25
7/22 Dave Johnson	4.00	2.00	1.25
7/23 Mike Cubbage	4.00	2.00	1.25
7/25 Larry Hisle	4.00	2.00	1.25
7/26 Don McMahon	4.00	2.00	1.25
7/27 Glenn Borgmann	4.00	2.00	1.25
7/28 Craig Kusick	4.00	2.00	1.25
7/29 Ron Schueler	4.00	2.00	1.25
7/30 Karl Kuehl	4.00	2.00	1.25
8/1 Roy Smalley	4.00	2.00	1.25
8/2 Tony Oliva	7.50	3.75	2.25
8/3 Jerry Zimmerman	4.00	2.00	1.25
8/4 Dan Ford	4.00	2.00	1.25
8/5 Don Carrithers	4.00	2.00	1.25
8/6 Tom Johnson	4.00	2.00	1.25
8/8 Pete Redfern	4.00	2.00	1.25
8/9 Tom Burgmeier	4.00	2.00	1.25
8/10 Bud Bulling	4.00	2.00	1.25
8/11 Gary Serum	4.00	2.00	1.25
8/12 Calvin Griffith	4.00	2.00	1.25

1977-78 Minnesota Twins Team Issue

Produced by collector Barry Fritz, and sold by the team through its normal concession outlets, this set consists of two 25-card series. Cards 1-25 were issued in 1977; cards 26-50 in 1978. Measuring 2-5/8" x 3-3/4", card fronts feature quality color player poses with no other graphics. Backs are in black-and-white and have all player data, stats with the Twins and overall major league numbers, plus career highlights. Besides being sold as sets, the cards were also offered in uncut sheet form.

	NM	EX	VG
Complete Set (50):	35.00	17.50	10.00
Common Player:	1.00	.50	.30
1 Bob Allison	1.00	.50	.30
2 Earl Battey	1.00	.50	.30
3 Dave Boswell	1.00	.50	.30
4 Dean Chance	1.25	.60	.40
5 Jim Grant	1.25	.60	.40
6 Calvin Griffith	1.25	.60	.40
7 Jimmie Hall	1.00	.50	.30
8 Harmon Killebrew	6.00	3.00	1.75
9 Jim Lemon	1.00	.50	.30
10 Billy Martin	3.00	1.50	.90
11 Gene Mauch	1.00	.50	.30
12 Sam Mele	1.00	.50	.30
13 Metropolitan Stadium	1.50	.70	.45
14 Don Mincher	1.00	.50	.30
15 Tony Oliva	3.00	1.50	.90
16 Camilo Pascual	1.00	.50	.30
17 Jim Perry	1.25	.60	.40
18 Frank Quilici	1.00	.50	.30
19 Rich Reese	1.00	.50	.30
20 Bill Rigney	1.00	.50	.30
21 Cesar Tovar	1.00	.50	.30
22 Zoilo Versalles	1.00	.50	.30
23 Al Worthington	1.00	.50	.30
24 Jerry Zimmerman	1.00	.50	.30
25 Checklist / Souvenir List	1.00	.50	.30
26 Bernie Allen	1.00	.50	.30
27 Leo Cardenas	1.00	.50	.30
28 Ray Corbin	1.00	.50	.30
29 Joe Decker	1.00	.50	.30
30 Johnny Goryl	1.00	.50	.30
31 Tom Hall	1.00	.50	.30
32 Bill Hands	1.00	.50	.30
33 Jim Holt	1.00	.50	.30
34 Randy Hundley	1.00	.50	.30
35 Jerry Kindall	1.00	.50	.30
36 Johnny Klippstein	1.00	.50	.30
37 Jack Kralick	1.00	.50	.30
38 Jim Merritt	1.00	.50	.30
39 Joe Nossek	1.00	.50	.30
40 Ron Perranoski	1.00	.50	.30
41 Bill Pleis	1.00	.50	.30
42 Rick Renick	1.00	.50	.30
43 Jim Roland	1.00	.50	.30
44 Lee Stange	1.00	.50	.30
45 Dick Stigman	1.00	.50	.30
46 Danny Thompson	1.00	.50	.30
47 Ted Uhlaender	1.00	.50	.30
48 Sandy Valdespino	1.00	.50	.30
49 Dick Woodson	1.00	.50	.30
50 Checklist #26-50	1.00	.50	.30

1911-16 Mino Cigarettes (T216)

Wagner, 2b. Pittsburgh Nat'l

MINO CIGARETTES
MADE IN NEW ORLEANS
MILD AND SWEET
NOT IN THE TRUST
PEOPLES TOBACCO CO. Ltd.
Factory No. 4, District of La.
NEW ORLEANS, LA.

The T216 baseball card set, issued by several brands of the Peoples Tobacco Co., is the last of the Louisiana cigarette sets and the most confusing. Apparently issued over a period of several years between 1911 and 1916, the set employs the same pictures as several contemporary caramel and bakery sets. Positive identification can be made by the back of the cards. The Peoples Tobacco cards carry advertising for one of three brands of cigarettes: Kotton, Mino or Virginia Extra. The Kotton brand is the most common, while the Virginia Extra and Mino backs command a premium. T216 cards are found in two types; one has a glossy front finish, while a second scarcer type is printed on a thin paper. The thin paper cards command an additional 15% premium. The cards represent players from the American, National and Federal Leagues. Cards measure a nominal 1-1/2" x 2-5/8", though reasonable allowance for variance must be made on consideration of original standards for cutting.

	NM	EX	VG
Common Player:	1,920	870.00	480.00
(1) Jack Barry (Batting)	1,920	870.00	480.00
(2) Jack Barry (Fielding)	1,920	870.00	480.00
(3) Harry Bemis	1,920	870.00	480.00
(4a) Chief Bender (Philadelphia, striped cap.)	4,200	1,890	1,050
(4b) Chief Bender (Baltimore, striped cap.)	4,200	1,890	1,050
(5a) Chief Bender (Philadelphia, white cap.)	4,200	1,890	1,050
(5b) Chief Bender (Baltimore, white cap.)	4,200	1,890	1,050
(6) Bill Bergen	1,920	870.00	480.00
(7a) Bob Bescher (Cincinnati)	1,920	870.00	480.00
(7b) Bob Bescher (St. Louis)	1,920	870.00	480.00
(8) Roger Bresnahan	4,200	1,890	1,050
(9) Al Bridwell (Batting)	1,920	870.00	480.00
(10a) Al Bridwell (New York, sliding.)	1,920	870.00	480.00
(10b) Al Bridwell (St. Louis, sliding.)	1,920	870.00	480.00

(11)	Donie Bush	1,920	870.00	480.00
(12)	Doc Casey	1,920	870.00	480.00
(13)	Frank Chance	4,200	1,890	1,050
(14a)	Hal Chase (New York, fielding.)	1,920	870.00	480.00
(14b)	Hal Chase (Buffalo, fielding.)	1,920	870.00	480.00
(15)	Hal Chase (Portrait)	1,920	870.00	480.00
(16a)	Ty Cobb (Detroit Am., standing.)	36,000	16,200	9,000
(16b)	Ty Cobb (Detroit Americans, standing.)	36,000	16,200	9,000
(17)	Ty Cobb (Detroit Americans, batting.)	36,000	16,200	9,000
(18a)	Eddie Collins (Phila. Am.)	4,200	1,890	1,050
(18b)	Eddie Collins (Phila. Amer.)	4,200	1,890	1,050
(19)	Eddie Collins (Chicago)	4,200	1,890	1,050
(20a)	Sam Crawford (Small print.)	4,200	1,890	1,050
(20b)	Sam Crawford (Large print.)	4,200	1,890	1,050
(21)	Harry Davis	1,920	870.00	480.00
(22)	Ray Demmitt	1,920	870.00	480.00
(23)	Art Devlin	1,920	870.00	480.00
(24a)	Wild Bill Donovan (Detroit)	1,920	870.00	480.00
(24b)	Wild Bill Donovan (New York)	1,920	870.00	480.00
(25a)	Red Dooin (Philadelphia)	1,920	870.00	480.00
(25b)	Red Dooin (Cincinnati)	1,920	870.00	480.00
(26a)	Mickey Doolan (Philadelphia)	1,920	870.00	480.00
(26b)	Mickey Doolan (Baltimore)	1,920	870.00	480.00
(27)	Patsy Dougherty	1,920	870.00	480.00
(28a)	Larry Doyle (N.Y. Nat'l.),(W/bat.)	1,920	870.00	480.00
(28b)	Larry Doyle (New York Nat'l)(W/bat.)	1,920	870.00	480.00
(29)	Larry Doyle (Throwing)	1,920	870.00	480.00
(30)	Clyde Engle	1,920	870.00	480.00
(31a)	Johnny Evers (Chicago)	4,200	1,890	1,050
(31b)	Johnny Evers (Boston)	4,200	1,890	1,050
(32)	Art Fromme	1,920	870.00	480.00
(33a)	George Gibson (Pittsburg Nat'l., back view.)	1,920	870.00	480.00
(33b)	George Gibson (Pittsburgh Nat'l., back view.)	1,920	870.00	480.00
(34a)	George Gibson (Pittsburg Nat'l., front view.)	1,920	870.00	480.00
(34b)	George Gibson (Pittsburgh Nat'l., front view.)	1,920	870.00	480.00
(35a)	Topsy Hartsel (Phila. Am.)	1,920	870.00	480.00
(35b)	Topsy Hartsel (Phila. Amer.)	1,920	870.00	480.00
(36)	Roy Hartzell (Batting)	1,920	870.00	480.00
(37)	Roy Hartzell (Catching)	1,920	870.00	480.00
(38a)	Fred Jacklitsch (Philadelphia)	1,920	870.00	480.00
(38b)	Fred Jacklitsch (Baltimore)	1,920	870.00	480.00
(39a)	Hughie Jennings (Orange background.)	4,200	1,890	1,050
(39b)	Hughie Jennings (Red background.)	4,200	1,890	1,050
(40)	Red Kleinow	1,920	870.00	480.00
(41a)	Otto Knabe (Philadelphia)	1,920	870.00	480.00
(41b)	Otto Knabe (Baltimore)	1,920	870.00	480.00
(42)	Jack Knight	1,920	870.00	480.00
(43a)	Nap Lajoie (Philadelphia, fielding.)	4,800	2,160	1,200
(43b)	Nap Lajoie (Cleveland, fielding.)	4,800	2,160	1,200
(44)	Nap Lajoie (Portrait)	4,800	2,160	1,200
(45a)	Hans Lobert (Cincinnati)	1,920	870.00	480.00
(45b)	Hans Lobert (New York)	1,920	870.00	480.00
(46)	Sherry Magee	1,920	870.00	480.00
(47)	Rube Marquard	4,200	1,890	1,050
(48a)	Christy Matthewson (Mathewson) (Large print.)	18,000	8,100	4,500
(48b)	Christy Matthewson (Mathewson) (Small print.)	18,000	8,100	4,550
(49a)	John McGraw (Large print.)	4,200	1,890	1,050
(49b)	John McGraw (Small print.)	4,200	1,890	1,050
(50)	Larry McLean	1,920	870.00	480.00
(51)	George McQuillan	1,920	870.00	480.00
(52)	Dots Miller (Batting)	1,920	870.00	480.00
(53a)	Dots Miller (Pittsburg, fielding.)	1,920	870.00	480.00
(53b)	Dots Miller (St. Louis, fielding.)	1,920	870.00	480.00
(54a)	Danny Murphy (Philadelphia)	1,920	870.00	480.00
(54b)	Danny Murphy (Brooklyn)	1,920	870.00	480.00
(55)	Rebel Oakes	1,920	870.00	480.00
(56)	Bill O'Hara	1,920	870.00	480.00
(57)	Eddie Plank	5,400	2,430	1,350
(58a)	Germany Schaefer (Washington)	1,920	870.00	480.00
(58b)	Germany Schaefer (Newark)	1,920	870.00	480.00
(59)	Admiral Schlei	1,920	870.00	480.00
(60)	Boss Schmidt	1,920	870.00	480.00
(61)	Johnny Seigle	1,920	870.00	480.00
(62)	Dave Shean	1,920	870.00	480.00
(63)	Boss Smith (Schmidt)	1,920	870.00	480.00
(64)	Tris Speaker	7,800	3,510	1,950
(65)	Oscar Stanage	1,920	870.00	480.00
(66)	George Stovall	1,920	870.00	480.00
(67)	Jeff Sweeney	1,920	870.00	480.00
(68a)	Joe Tinker (Chicago Nat'l, batting.)	4,200	1,890	1,050
(68b)	Joe Tinker (Chicago Feds, batting.)	4,200	1,890	1,050
(69)	Joe Tinker (Portrait)	4,200	1,890	1,050
(70a)	Honus Wagner (Batting, S.S.)	30,000	13,500	7,500
(70b)	Honus Wagner (Batting, 2b.)	30,000	13,500	7,500
(71a)	Honus Wagner (Throwing, S.S.)	30,000	13,500	7,500
(71b)	Honus Wagner (Throwing, 2b.)	30,000	13,500	7,500
(72)	Hooks Wiltse	1,920	870.00	480.00
(73)	Cy Young	15,000	6,750	3,750
(74a)	Heinie Zimmerman (2b.)	1,920	870.00	480.00
(74b)	Heinie Zimmerman (3b.)	1,920	870.00	480.00

1962 Molinari's Restaurant Frank Malzone

This black-and-white J.D. McCarthy postcard of the former Red Sox infielder was given to patrons of an Oneonta, N.Y., restaurant in which Malzone was a partner with his brother-in-law. The card measures 3-1/4" x 5-1/2" and has a facsimile autograph on front. A similar promotional postcard is listed under Ticoa Tires.

	NM	EX	VG
Frank Malzone	15.00	7.50	4.50

1911 Monarch Typewriter Philadelphia A's

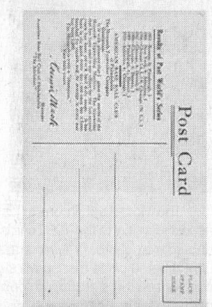

These black-and-white postcards (about 3-1/2" x 5") depict the World Champion 1910 Philadelphia A's. Fronts have posed player photos with a black pin stripe and white borders. The player's name and position are printed in the bottom border. "Compliments of THE MONARCH TYPEWRITER COMPANY" appears in the top border. Backs are rather standard postcard fare, but include data about the World Series between 1903-1910.

		NM	EX	VG
Complete Set (6):		8,000	4,000	2,400
Common Player:		1,150	575.00	350.00
(1)	John J. Barry	1,150	575.00	350.00
(2)	Chief Bender	1,650	825.00	500.00
(3)	Eddie Collins	1,650	825.00	500.00
(4)	Rube Oldring	1,150	575.00	350.00
(5)	Eddie Plank	1,650	825.00	500.00
(6)	Ira Thomas	1,150	575.00	350.00

1970 Montreal Expos Player Pins

Produced by "Best in Sports" for sale in the Montreal area for 35¢ apiece, these 1-3/4" diameter pinbacks feature action poses of the players set against a white background. The player's name at top is in black.

		NM	EX	VG
Complete Set (16):		350.00	175.00	100.00
Common Player:		25.00	12.50	7.50
(1)	John Bateman	25.00	12.50	7.50
(2)	Ron Brand	25.00	12.50	7.50
(3)	Ron Fairly	25.00	12.50	7.50
(4)	Mack Jones	25.00	12.50	7.50
(5)	Coco Laboy	25.00	12.50	7.50
(6)	Gene Mauch	25.00	12.50	7.50
(7)	Dan McGinn	25.00	12.50	7.50
(8)	Adolfo Phillips	25.00	12.50	7.50
(9)	Claude Raymond	25.00	12.50	7.50
(10)	Steve Renko	25.00	12.50	7.50
(11)	Marv Staehle	25.00	12.50	7.50
(12)	Rusty Staub	40.00	20.00	12.00
(13)	Bill Stoneman	25.00	12.50	7.50
(14)	Gary Sutherland	25.00	12.50	7.50
(15)	Bobby Wine	25.00	12.50	7.50
(16)	Expos team logo	10.00	5.00	3.00

1972-76 Montreal Expos Matchbook Covers

In 1972, 1973 and 1976, the Eddy Match Co., Montreal, issued series of seven matchbook covers featuring action photos. Fronts have a red, white and blue team logo on a white background. Backs have a bluetone action photo with the match-striking surface across the lower portion. The player in the photo is not identified on the matchbook. Inside of the 2-1/8" x 4-3/8" cover, printed in blue, is the team home schedule for that season. The unnumbered matchbook covers are checklisted here alphabetically by year. Values shown are for empty matchbooks; full matchbooks would be valued at 2-3X.

		NM	EX	VG
Complete Set (21):		40.00	20.00	12.00
Common Player:		4.00	2.00	1.25
1972				
(1)	Boots Day	4.00	2.00	1.25
(2)	Ron Fairly	4.00	2.00	1.25
(3)	Ron Hunt	4.00	2.00	1.25
(4)	Steve Renko	4.00	2.00	1.25
(5)	Rusty Staub	6.00	3.00	1.75
(6)	Bobby Wine	4.00	2.00	1.25
(7)	Hunt's 50th HBP (Scoreboard)	4.00	2.00	1.25
1973				
(1)	Tim Foli	4.00	2.00	1.25
(2)	Ron Hunt	4.00	2.00	1.25
(3)	Mike Jorgensen	4.00	2.00	1.25
(4)	Gene Mauch	4.00	2.00	1.25
(5)	Balor Moore	4.00	2.00	1.25
(6)	Ken Singleton	4.00	2.00	1.25
(7)	Bill Stoneman	4.00	2.00	1.25
1976				
(1)	Barry Foote	4.00	2.00	1.25
(2)	Mike Jorgensen	4.00	2.00	1.25
(3)	Pete Mackanin	4.00	2.00	1.25
(4)	Dale Murray	4.00	2.00	1.25
(5)	Larry Parrish	4.00	2.00	1.25
(6)	Steve Rogers	4.00	2.00	1.25
(7)	Dan Warthen	4.00	2.00	1.25

1916 Morehouse Baking Co.

TY COBB
C. F.—Detroit Americans
38

While this 200-card set is most often found with blank backs or with the advertising of "The Sporting News" on the back, a number of scarcer regional advertisers also can be found. This Massachusetts baker inserted the cards into bread loaves and offered a redemption program. Since cards are known that correspond to both versions of the parent M101 Blank Backs, it not known whether the bakery's version parallels M101-4 and M101-5 or is a hybrid of the two.

PREMIUM: 2X
(See 1916 M101-4 and M101-5 Blank Backs for checklist and price guide.)

1907 Morgan Stationery "Red Belt" Postcards

Only one player is individually identified in this series of postcards, though the identities of others have been discovered over the years. The 3-1/2" x 5-1/2" cards have colorized player and group photos on front with a title printed in white in the lower-left corner. Some photos were taken at the Reds ballpark, then known as the Palace of Fans. Cards include pictures of Reds and Pirates of the National League, and Toledo of the minors. Many of the players have bright red belts, thus the set's nickname. Postcard backs have a credit line: "The Morgan Stationery Co., Cincinnati, O., Publishers." The unnumbered cards are checklisted here alphabetically by title.

		NM	EX	VG
Complete Set (12):		3,250	1,625	950.00
Common Card:		275.00	135.00	80.00
(1)	After A High One	275.00	135.00	80.00
(2)	A Home Run	275.00	135.00	80.00
(3)	Hit & Run	275.00	135.00	80.00
(4)	In Consultation	275.00	135.00	80.00
(5)	It's All in the Game - "Noise" (Pat Moran)	275.00	135.00	80.00
(6)	Huggins Second Baseman Par Excellence (Miller Huggins) (Stadium background.)	325.00	160.00	95.00
(7)	Huggins Second Baseman Par Excellance (Miller Huggins) (Low buildings in background.)	325.00	160.00	95.00
(8)	Opening of the Season 1907	275.00	135.00	80.00
(9)	Out to the Long Green	275.00	135.00	80.00
(10)	Practise (Practice) Makes Perfect (Sam Leever)	275.00	135.00	80.00
(11)	Safe	275.00	135.00	80.00
(12)	Use Two If Necessary (Hans Lobert)	275.00	135.00	80.00

1959 Morrell Meats Dodgers

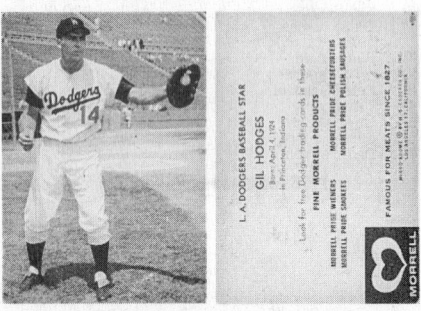

This set of Los Angeles Dodgers was the first issue of a three-year run for the Southern California meat company. The 12 cards in this 2-1/2" x 3-1/2" set are unnumbered and feature full-frame, unbordered color photos. Card backs feature a company ad and list only the player's name, birthdate and birthplace. Two errors exist in the set; the cards naming Clem Labine and Norm Larker show photos of Stan Williams and Joe Pignatano, respectively.

		NM	EX	VG
Complete Set (12):		3,500	1,750	1,000
Common Player:		100.00	50.00	30.00
(1)	Don Drysdale	200.00	100.00	60.00
(2)	Carl Furillo	150.00	75.00	45.00
(3)	Jim Gilliam	125.00	60.00	35.00
(4)	Gil Hodges	200.00	100.00	60.00
(5)	Sandy Koufax	2,000	1,000	600.00
(6)	Clem Labine (Photo actually Stan Williams.)	100.00	50.00	30.00
(7)	Norm Larker (Photo actually Joe Pignatano.)	100.00	50.00	30.00
(8)	Charlie Neal	100.00	50.00	30.00
(9)	Johnny Podres	125.00	60.00	35.00
(10)	John Roseboro	100.00	50.00	30.00
(11)	Duke Snider	200.00	100.00	60.00
(12)	Don Zimmer	125.00	60.00	35.00

1960 Morrell Meats Dodgers

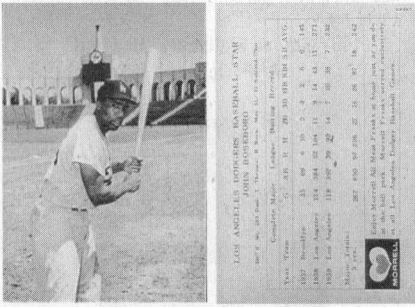

This 12-card set is the same 2-1/2" x 3-1/2" size as the 1959 set, and again features unbordered color card fronts. Five of the players included are new to the Morrell's sets. Card backs in 1960 list player statistics and brief personal data on each player. Cards of Gil Hodges, Carl Furillo and Duke Snider are apparently scarcer than others in the set.

		NM	EX	VG
Complete Set (12):		2,200	1,100	650.00
Common Player:		80.00	40.00	24.00
(1)	Walt Alston	90.00	45.00	27.50
(2)	Roger Craig	80.00	40.00	24.00
(3)	Don Drysdale	120.00	60.00	35.00
(4)	Carl Furillo	225.00	110.00	65.00
(5)	Gil Hodges	400.00	200.00	120.00
(6)	Sandy Koufax	500.00	250.00	150.00
(7)	Wally Moon	80.00	40.00	24.00
(8)	Charlie Neal	80.00	40.00	24.00

		NM	EX	VG
(9)	Johnny Podres	80.00	40.00	24.00
(10)	John Roseboro	80.00	40.00	24.00
(11)	Larry Sherry	80.00	40.00	24.00
(12)	Duke Snider	450.00	225.00	135.00

1961 Morrell Meats Dodgers

The Morrell set shrunk to just six cards in 1961, with a format almost identical to the 1960 cards. Card fronts are again full-color, unbordered photos. Player statistics appear on the backs. The unnumbered cards measure a slightly smaller 2-1/4" x 3-1/4", and comparison of statistical information can also distinguish the cards from the 1960 version.

		NM	EX	VG
Complete Set (6):		900.00	450.00	275.00
Common Player:		90.00	45.00	27.50
(1)	Tommy Davis	90.00	45.00	27.50
(2)	Don Drysdale	120.00	60.00	36.00
(3)	Frank Howard	90.00	45.00	27.50
(4)	Sandy Koufax	450.00	225.00	135.00
(5)	Norm Larker	90.00	45.00	27.50
(6)	Maury Wills	90.00	45.00	27.00

1910 Morton's Buster Brown Bread Tigers Pins (PD2)

Dating of these two issues is arbitrary, since there is no indication on the pins of vintage. Both sets feature members of the Detroit Tigers, American League champions of 1907-09. The Buster Brown Bread pins measure 1-1/4" in diameter and have a small black-and-white player portrait photo surrounded by a yellow border. Artwork to the left depicts Buster Brown with a tiger holding a blue banner with the Morton's name. The player photos carry no identification, which may make the checklist presented here somewhat tentative.

		NM	EX	VG
Complete Set (15):		10,000	5,000	3,000
Common Player:		450.00	225.00	135.00
(1)	Jimmy Archer	450.00	225.00	135.00
(2)	Heinie Beckendorf	450.00	225.00	135.00
(3)	Donie Bush	450.00	225.00	135.00
(4)	Ty Cobb	4,000	2,000	1,200
(5)	Sam Crawford	750.00	375.00	225.00
(6)	Wild Bill Donovan	450.00	225.00	135.00
(7)	Hughie Jennings	750.00	375.00	225.00
(8)	Tom Jones	450.00	225.00	135.00
(9)	Red Killefer	450.00	225.00	135.00
(10)	George Moriarty	450.00	225.00	135.00
(11)	George Mullin	450.00	225.00	135.00
(12)	Claude Rossman	450.00	225.00	135.00
(13)	"Germany" Schaefer	450.00	225.00	135.00
(14)	Ed Summers	450.00	225.00	135.00
(15)	Ed Willett	450.00	225.00	135.00

1910 Morton's Pennant Winner Bread Tigers Pins

The American League champion Detroit Tigers (1907-1909) are featured on this set of pins advertising -- appropriately -- Pennant Winner Bread. The 1-1/4" pins have black-

and-white player photos surrounded by a yellow border. A Detroit banner with tiger head superimposed is at bottom. The players are not identified anywhere on the pins, which may make this checklist somewhat arbitrary.

		NM	EX	VG
Complete Set (16):		12,000	6,000	3,500
Common Player:		500.00	250.00	150.00
(1)	Jimmy Archer	500.00	250.00	150.00
(2)	Heinie Beckendorf	500.00	250.00	150.00
(3)	Donie Bush	500.00	250.00	150.00
(4)	Ty Cobb	4,000	2,000	1,200
(5)	Sam Crawford	750.00	375.00	225.00
(6)	Wild Bill Donovan	500.00	250.00	150.00
(7)	Hughie Jennings	750.00	375.00	225.00
(8)	Davy Jones	500.00	250.00	150.00
(9)	Matty McIntyre	500.00	250.00	150.00
(10)	George Moriarty	500.00	250.00	150.00
(11)	George Mullin	500.00	250.00	150.00
(12)	Claude Rossman	500.00	250.00	150.00
(13)	Herman Schaeffer (Schaefer)	500.00	250.00	150.00
(14)	Charles Schmidt	500.00	250.00	150.00
(15)	Ed Summers	500.00	250.00	150.00
(16)	Ed Willett	500.00	250.00	150.00

1916 Mothers' Bread (D303)

Apparently issued in 1916 by the New Orleans branch of the General Baking Co., these unnumbered cards measure 1-1/2" x 2-3/4". The player pictures and format of the cards are identical to the 1915 American Caramel (E106) and 1914 General Baking Co. (D303) sets, but this issue carries an advertisement for Mothers' Bread on back. This version is much scarcer than the General Baking or American Caramel types. It is known that at least one player appears in this set who is not found in E106/D303 and many players are found with team, league and postion changes. The checklist here is incomplete and additions are welcome. Gaps have been left in the assigned numbering for future additions.

		NM	EX	VG
Common Player:		2,500	1,500	900.00
(1)	Chief Bender (Brooklyn Nat'l.)	6,000	2,700	1,500
(2)	Bob Bescher (St. Louis Nat'l)	2,500	1,500	900.00
(3)	Rube Bressler (Phila. Am.)	2,500	1,500	900.00
(4)	Donie Bush (Detroit American)	2,500	1,500	900.00
(5)	Hal Chase (Portrait, Cincinnati Nat'l.)	3,900	1,750	950.00
(6)	Bill Donovan (N.Y. Amer.)	2,500	1,500	900.00
(7)	Larry Doyle (N.Y. Nat'l)	2,500	1,500	900.00
(8)	Happy Felsch (Chicago Am.) (Picture actually Ray Demmitt.)	7,500	3,375	1,875
(9)	George Gibson	2,500	1,500	900.00
(11)	Roy Hartzell	2,500	1,500	900.00
(15)	Nap Lajoie (Phila. Americans)	6,000	2,700	1,500
(16)	Hans Lobert (New York Nat'l)	2,500	1,500	900.00
(17)	William Louden (Cincinnati Nat'l)(Picture is Otto Knabe.)	2,500	1,500	900.00
(20)	Rube Marquard (Brooklyn Nat'l)	6,000	2,700	1,500
(21)	Christy Matthewson (Mathewson)	15,000	8,000	5,000
(22)	Billy Meyer (Phila. Am.) (Picture is Fred Jacklitsch.)	2,500	1,500	900.00
(24)	Ray Morgan (Washington Am.) (Picture is Mike Doolan.)	2,500	1,500	900.00
(26)	Eddie Plank (St. Louis Am.)	10,000	4,500	2,500
(28)	Tris Speaker (Cleveland Am.)	8,000	4,000	2,000
(30)	Joe Tinker (Portrait, Mgr. Chicago Am.)	6,000	2,700	1,500
(33)	Honus Wagner (Batting)	30,000	15,000	8,000
(35)	Buck Weaver (Batting, picture is Joe Tinker.)	5,000	2,250	1,250

1919 Mother's Bread

Essentially a version of the W514 strip cards with an advertisement on the back, the Mother's Bread cards are much scarcer than the blank-backs with which they share a checklist. The cards are 1-1/2" x 2-1/2" with color drawings of the players on front, along with name, position, team, league and card number.

(See 1919 W514 for checklist; cards valued at 2.5X-3X W514 version.)

1955 Motorola Bob Feller Premium Photo

Dating of this promotional photo is approximate, based on the uniform details. The 8" x 10" glossy black-and-white photo features a facsimile autograph. Feller is described on the picture as "CONSULTANT ON YOUTH ACTIVITIES" for Motorola, Inc. The picture is blank-backed and its method of distribution is unknown.

	NM	EX	VG
Bob Feller	60.00	30.00	18.00

1976 Motorola

 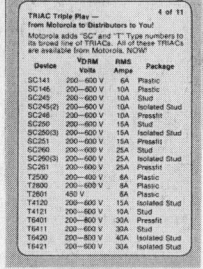

This set of (mostly) Hall of Famers was issued in conjunction with the annual convention of Motorola electronics dealers. Cards were issued singly in a wax wrapper with a piece of bubblegum. Sepia player photos are featured in an oval at center. Player identification and a career highlight are in the white frame around the photo. A sales message appears in a white box at bottom. Overall borders are rust colored. Backs have information about various Motorola products.

	NM	EX	VG
Complete Set (11):	25.00	12.50	7.50
Common Player:	2.50	1.25	.70
1 Honus Wagner	4.00	2.00	1.25
2 Nap Lajoie	2.50	1.25	.70
3 Ty Cobb	7.50	3.75	2.25
4 William Wambsganss	2.50	1.25	.70
5 Three Finger Brown	2.50	1.25	.70
6 Ray Schalk	2.50	1.25	.70
7 Frank Frisch	2.50	1.25	.70
8 Pud Galvin	2.50	1.25	.70
9 Babe Ruth	15.00	7.50	4.50
10 Grover Cleveland Alexander	3.00	1.50	.90
11 Frank L. Chance	2.50	1.25	.70

1943 M.P. & Co. (R302-1)

One of the few baseball card sets issued during World War II, this set of unnumbered cards, measuring approximately 2-5/8" x 2-1/4" was produced in two major types and at least five sub-types. The cards feature crude color drawings that have little resemblance to the player named. They were originally produced in strips and sold inexpensively in candy stores. The backs contain brief player write-ups. One major type has the player's full name, team and position on back. The second type has only the player's first and last name and position on back; no team. Variations in ink color and wording of the biographies on back are also seen. M.P. & Co. stands for Michael Pressner and Co., a New York City novelty and carnival supply firm.

	NM	EX	VG
Complete Set (24):	1,750	625.00	275.00
Common Player:	40.00	15.00	5.00
(1) Ernie Bonham	40.00	15.00	5.00
(2) Lou Boudreau	60.00	20.00	10.00
(3) Dolph Camilli	40.00	15.00	5.00
(4) Mort Cooper	40.00	15.00	5.00
(5) Walker Cooper	40.00	15.00	5.00
(6) Joe Cronin	60.00	20.00	10.00
(7) Hank Danning	40.00	15.00	5.00
(8) Bill Dickey	75.00	25.00	10.00
(9) Joe DiMaggio	300.00	100.00	45.00
(10) Bobby Feller	100.00	35.00	15.00
(11) Jimmy Foxx	75.00	25.00	10.00
(12) Hank Greenberg	100.00	35.00	15.00
(13) Stan Hack	40.00	15.00	5.00
(14) Tom Henrich	40.00	15.00	5.00
(15) Carl Hubbell	60.00	20.00	10.00
(16) Joe Medwick	60.00	20.00	10.00
(17) John Mize	60.00	20.00	10.00
(18) Lou Novikoff	40.00	15.00	5.00
(19) Mel Ott	60.00	20.00	10.00
(20) Pee Wee Reese	75.00	25.00	10.00
(21) Pete Reiser	40.00	15.00	5.00
(22) Charlie Ruffing	60.00	20.00	10.00
(23) Johnny VanderMeer	40.00	15.00	5.00
(24) Ted Williams	250.00	85.00	35.00

1949 M.P. & Co. (R302-2)

This set appears to be a re-issue of M.P. & Co.'s 1943 cards with several different players (although reusing the same pictures as the '43s). The cards, which measure about 2-11/16" x 2-1/4", feature crude drawings of generic baseball players which have little resemblance to the player named. Most backs include card number and player information. The numbering sequence begins with card 100. Numbers 104, 118, and 120 are unknown, while three of the cards are unnumbered. The set is assigned the American Card Catalog number R302-2.

	NM	EX	VG
Complete Set (25):	1,750	575.00	275.00
Common Player:	45.00	16.00	7.00
100 Lou Boudreau	60.00	20.00	9.00
101 Ted Williams	250.00	85.00	35.00
102 Buddy Kerr	45.00	16.00	7.00
103 Bobby Feller	75.00	25.00	10.00
104 Unknown			
105 Joe DiMaggio	325.00	115.00	50.00
106 Pee Wee Reese	75.00	25.00	10.00
107 Ferris Fain	45.00	16.00	7.00
108 Andy Pafko	45.00	16.00	7.00
109 Del Ennis	45.00	16.00	7.00
110 Ralph Kiner	60.00	20.00	9.00
111 Nippy Jones	45.00	16.00	7.00
112 Del Rice	45.00	16.00	7.00
113 Hank Sauer	45.00	16.00	7.00
114 Gil Coan	45.00	16.00	7.00
115 Eddie Joost	45.00	16.00	7.00
116 Alvin Dark	45.00	16.00	7.00
117 Larry Berra	75.00	25.00	10.00
118 Unknown			
119 Bob Lemon	60.00	20.00	9.00
120 Unknown			
121 Johnny Pesky	45.00	16.00	7.00
122 Johnny Sain	45.00	16.00	7.00
123 Hoot Evers	45.00	16.00	7.00
124 Larry Doby	60.00	20.00	9.00
---- Jimmy Foxx	100.00	35.00	15.00
---- Tom Henrich	45.00	16.00	7.00
---- Al Kozar	45.00	16.00	7.00

1948-49 M.P. & Co. Photoprints

One of several 1930s-1940s kits for do-it-yourself production of photos, this issue was produced in New York City by the novelty firm M.P. & Co. A complete outfit consists of a film negative and a piece of light-sensitive paper for producing the photo. The negative and resulting print measure about 2" x 2-1/4". The issue includes 13 subjects, mostly non-sport, but includes Babe Ruth.

	NM	EX	VG
Babe Ruth (Negative)	300.00	150.00	90.00
Babe Ruth (Print)	75.00	37.50	22.00

1976 Mr. Softee Iron-Ons

Anecdotal evidence connects these iron-on transfers with the Mr. Softee dairy chain. About 4-1/2" x 6" inches, the color transfers have a player portrait on a baseball background, very similar in format to the 1978 Royal Crown Cola iron-ons. Like the RC pieces, the pictures have team logos removed from caps. The Mr. Softees include the team nickname beneath the player picture, along with a Players Association logo and an undated Quaker copyright line. The extent of the checklist is unknown.

	NM	EX	VG
Common Player:	4.00	2.00	1.25
(1) George Brett	10.00	5.00	3.00
(2) Jim Hunter	6.00	3.00	1.75
(3) Randy Jones	4.00	2.00	1.25
(4) Dave Kingman	5.00	2.50	1.50
(5) Jerry Koosman	4.00	2.00	1.25
(6) Fred Lynn	5.00	2.50	1.50
(7) Joe Morgan	6.00	3.00	1.75
(8) Thurman Munson	10.00	5.00	3.00
(9) Amos Otis	4.00	2.00	1.25
(10) Bill Russell	4.00	2.00	1.25
(11) Nolan Ryan	12.00	6.00	3.60
(12) Mike Schmidt	10.00	5.00	3.00
(13) Tom Seaver	10.00	5.00	3.00

1977 Mrs. Carter's Bread Sports Illustrated Covers

This two-sport set was issued by Mrs. Carter's Bread. Fronts of the 3-1/2" x 4-3/4" cards reproduce SI covers in full color, surrounded by a white border. Backs have a special offer for SI subscriptions, and are printed in black and blue on white. Despite the higher card numbers, it does not appear any more than five were ever issued.

	NM	EX	VG
Complete Set (5):	35.00	17.50	10.00
Common Card:	3.00	1.50	.90
(1) George Brett	25.00	12.50	7.50
(2) George Foster	4.00	2.00	1.25
(3) Bump Wills	4.00	2.00	1.25
(4) Oakland Wins a Big One (Football)	4.00	2.00	1.25
(5) Michigan Is No. 1 (Football)	6.00	3.00	1.75

1921 Mrs. Sherlock's Bread Pins

The date of issue for these pins is uncertain. The 7/8" diameter pins feature black-and-white player photos with a red border. The player's last name and team are printed beneath the photo; above is "Mrs. Sherlock's Home Made Bread." The set is one of several sponsored by the Toledo bakery. The Babe Ruth pin was reproduced circa 1999 in 1-3/4" size; it has no collectible value.

	NM	EX	VG
Complete Set (10):	4,750	2,400	1,400
Common Player:	100.00	50.00	30.00
(1) Grover Alexander	350.00	175.00	100.00
(2) Ty Cobb	1,700	850.00	425.00
(3) Rogers Hornsby	375.00	185.00	110.00
(4) Walter Johnson	375.00	185.00	110.00
(5) Rabbit Maranville	300.00	150.00	90.00
(6) Pat Moran	100.00	50.00	30.00
(7) "Babe" Ruth	2,200	1,100	650.00
(8) George Sisler	300.00	150.00	90.00
(9) Tris Speaker	375.00	185.00	110.00
(10) Honus Wagner	700.00	350.00	210.00

1975-96 MSA

(See listings under Michael Schechter Associates.)

1916 M101-5 Blank Backs

JIM THORPE
R.F.—New York Giants
176

The Chicago printing and publishing firm of Felix Mendelsohn was the originator of this card set, which is often found bearing advertising on back of several businesses from around the country. Mendelsohn is not mentioned on the cards, which are blank-backed. Fronts of the 1-5/8" x 3" black-and-white cards have a player photo, name, position abbreviation, team and card number. The set was prepared in advance of the 1916 season and offered in ads in The Sporting News for $1, or a framed uncut sheet for $2.50. The blank-backs are the most common version of M101-5. There were at least two printings of the set, creating several variations to correct errors or replace players.

	NM	EX	VG
Complete Set (200):	82,500	41,250	24,200
Common Player:	90.00	45.00	30.00
1 Babe Adams	100.00	35.00	20.00
2 Sam Agnew	90.00	45.00	30.00
3 Eddie Ainsmith	90.00	45.00	30.00
4 Grover Alexander	550.00	275.00	165.00
5 Leon Ames	90.00	45.00	30.00
6 Jimmy Archer	90.00	45.00	30.00
7 Jimmy Austin	90.00	45.00	30.00
8 J. Franklin Baker	360.00	175.00	105.00
9 Dave Bancroft	360.00	175.00	105.00
10 Jack Barry	90.00	45.00	30.00
11 Zinn Beck	90.00	45.00	30.00
12a Beals Becker	275.00	135.00	80.00
12b Lute Boone	90.00	45.00	30.00
13 Joe Benz	90.00	45.00	30.00
14 Bob Bescher	90.00	45.00	30.00
15 Al Betzel	90.00	45.00	30.00
16 Roger Bresnahan	360.00	175.00	105.00
17 Eddie Burns	90.00	45.00	30.00
18 Geo. J. Burns	90.00	45.00	30.00
19 Joe Bush	90.00	45.00	30.00
20 Owen Bush	90.00	45.00	30.00
21 Art Butler	90.00	45.00	30.00
22 Bobbie Byrne	90.00	45.00	30.00
23a Forrest Cady	330.00	165.00	100.00
23b Mordecai Brown	360.00	175.00	105.00
24 Jimmy Callahan	90.00	45.00	30.00
25 Ray Caldwell	90.00	45.00	30.00
26 Max Carey	360.00	175.00	105.00
27 George Chalmers	90.00	45.00	30.00
28 Frank Chance	360.00	175.00	105.00
29 Ray Chapman	110.00	55.00	35.00
30 Larry Cheney	90.00	45.00	30.00
31 Eddie Cicotte	360.00	175.00	105.00
32 Tom Clarke	90.00	45.00	30.00
33 Eddie Collins	360.00	175.00	105.00
34 "Shauno" Collins	90.00	45.00	30.00
35 Charles Comisky (Comiskey)	360.00	175.00	105.00
36 Joe Connolly	90.00	45.00	30.00
37 Luther Cook	90.00	45.00	30.00
38 Jack Coombs	90.00	45.00	30.00
39 Dan Costello	90.00	45.00	30.00
40 Harry Coveleskie (Coveleski)	90.00	45.00	30.00
41 Gavvy Cravath	90.00	45.00	30.00
42 Sam Crawford	360.00	175.00	105.00
43 Jean Dale	90.00	45.00	30.00
44 Jake Daubert	90.00	45.00	30.00
45 Geo. A. Davis Jr.	90.00	45.00	30.00
46 Charles Deal	90.00	45.00	30.00
47 Al Demaree	90.00	45.00	30.00
48 William Doak	90.00	45.00	30.00
49 Bill Donovan	90.00	45.00	30.00

50 Charles Dooin	90.00	45.00	30.00
51 Mike Doolan	90.00	45.00	30.00
52 Larry Doyle	90.00	45.00	30.00
53 Jean Dubuc	90.00	45.00	30.00
54 Oscar Dugey	90.00	45.00	30.00
55 Johnny Evers	360.00	175.00	105.00
56 Urban Faber	360.00	175.00	105.00
57 "Hap" Felsch	2,000	415.00	250.00
58 Bill Fischer	90.00	45.00	30.00
59 Ray Fisher	90.00	45.00	30.00
60 Max Flack	90.00	45.00	30.00
61 Art Fletcher	90.00	45.00	30.00
62 Eddie Foster	90.00	45.00	30.00
63 Jacques Fournier	90.00	45.00	30.00
64 Del Gainer (Gainor)	90.00	45.00	30.00
65 Larry Gardner	90.00	45.00	30.00
66 Joe Gedeon	90.00	45.00	30.00
67 Gus Getz	90.00	45.00	30.00
68 Geo. Gibson	90.00	45.00	30.00
69 Wilbur Good	90.00	45.00	30.00
70 Hank Gowdy	90.00	45.00	30.00
71 John Graney	90.00	45.00	30.00
72 Tom Griffith	90.00	45.00	30.00
73 Heinie Groh	90.00	45.00	30.00
74 Earl Hamilton	90.00	45.00	30.00
75 Bob Harmon	90.00	45.00	30.00
76 Roy Hartzell	90.00	45.00	30.00
77 Claude Hendrix	90.00	45.00	30.00
78 Olaf Henriksen	90.00	45.00	30.00
79 John Henry	90.00	45.00	30.00
80 "Buck" Herzog	90.00	45.00	30.00
81 Hugh High	90.00	45.00	30.00
82 Dick Hoblitzell	90.00	45.00	30.00
83 Harry Hooper	360.00	175.00	105.00
84 Ivan Howard	90.00	45.00	30.00
85 Miller Huggins	360.00	175.00	105.00
86 Joe Jackson	15,000	4,950	2,970
87 William James	90.00	45.00	30.00
88 Harold Janvrin	90.00	45.00	30.00
89 Hugh Jennings	360.00	175.00	105.00
90 Walter Johnson	1,500	550.00	330.00
91 Fielder Jones	90.00	45.00	30.00
92 Bennie Kauff	90.00	45.00	30.00
93 Wm. Killefer Jr.	90.00	45.00	30.00
94 Ed. Konetchy	90.00	45.00	30.00
95 Napoleon Lajoie	360.00	175.00	105.00
96 Jack Lapp	90.00	45.00	30.00
97a John Lavan (Correct spelling.)	90.00	45.00	30.00
97b John Lavin (Incorrect spelling.)	90.00	45.00	30.00
98 Jimmy Lavender	90.00	45.00	30.00
99 "Nemo" Leibold	90.00	45.00	30.00
100 H.B. Leonard	90.00	45.00	30.00
101 Duffy Lewis	90.00	45.00	30.00
102 Hans Lobert	90.00	45.00	30.00
103 Tom Long	90.00	45.00	30.00
104 Fred Luderus	90.00	45.00	30.00
105 Connie Mack	360.00	175.00	105.00
106 Lee Magee	90.00	45.00	30.00
107 Al. Mamaux	90.00	45.00	30.00
108 Leslie Mann	90.00	45.00	30.00
109 "Rabbit" Maranville	360.00	175.00	105.00
110 Rube Marquard	360.00	175.00	105.00
111 Armando Marsans	100.00	50.00	30.00
112 J. Erskine Mayer	90.00	45.00	30.00
113 George McBride	90.00	45.00	30.00
114 John J. McGraw	360.00	175.00	105.00
115 Jack McInnis	90.00	45.00	30.00
116 Fred Merkle	90.00	45.00	30.00
117 Chief Meyers	90.00	45.00	30.00
118 Clyde Milan	90.00	45.00	30.00
119 Otto Miller	90.00	45.00	30.00
120 Willie Mitchel (Mitchell)	90.00	45.00	30.00
121 Fred Mollwitz	90.00	45.00	30.00
122 J. Herbert Moran	90.00	45.00	30.00
123 Pat Moran	90.00	45.00	30.00
124 Ray Morgan	90.00	45.00	30.00
125 Geo. Moriarty	90.00	45.00	30.00
126 Guy Morton	90.00	45.00	30.00
127 Ed. Murphy (Photo actually Danny Murphy.)	90.00	45.00	30.00
128 John Murray	90.00	45.00	30.00
129 "Hy" Myers	90.00	45.00	30.00
130 J.A. Niehoff	90.00	45.00	30.00
131 Leslie Nunamaker	90.00	45.00	30.00
132 Rube Oldring	90.00	45.00	30.00
133 Oliver O'Mara	90.00	45.00	30.00
134 Steve O'Neill	90.00	45.00	30.00
135 "Dode" Paskert	90.00	45.00	30.00
136 Roger Peckinpaugh (Photo actually Gavvy Cravath.)	90.00	45.00	30.00
137 E.J. Pfeffer (Photo actually Jeff Pfeffer.)	90.00	45.00	30.00
138 Geo. Pierce (Pearce)	90.00	45.00	30.00
139 Walter Pipp	90.00	45.00	30.00
140 Derril Pratt (Derrill)	90.00	45.00	30.00
141 Bill Rariden	90.00	45.00	30.00
142 Eppa Rixey	360.00	175.00	105.00
143 Davey Robertson	90.00	45.00	30.00
144 Wilbert Robinson	360.00	175.00	105.00
145 Bob Roth	90.00	45.00	30.00
146 Ed. Roush	360.00	175.00	105.00
147 Clarence Rowland	90.00	45.00	30.00
148 "Nap" Rucker	90.00	45.00	30.00
149 Dick Rudolph	90.00	45.00	30.00
150 Reb Russell	90.00	45.00	30.00
151 Babe Ruth	30,000	13,750	8,250
152 Vic Saier	90.00	45.00	30.00
153 "Slim" Sallee	90.00	45.00	30.00
154 "Germany" Schaefer	90.00	45.00	30.00
155 Ray Schalk	360.00	175.00	105.00
156 Walter Schang	90.00	45.00	30.00
157 Chas. Schmidt	90.00	45.00	30.00
158 Frank Schulte	90.00	45.00	30.00
159 Jim Scott	90.00	45.00	30.00
160 Everett Scott	90.00	45.00	30.00
161 Tom Seaton	90.00	45.00	30.00
162 Howard Shanks	90.00	45.00	30.00

163 Bob Shawkey (Photo actually Jack McInnis.)	90.00	45.00	30.00
164 Ernie Shore	90.00	45.00	30.00
165 Burt Shotton	90.00	45.00	30.00
166 George Sisler	360.00	175.00	105.00
167 J. Carlisle Smith	90.00	45.00	30.00
168 Fred Snodgrass	90.00	45.00	30.00
169 Geo. Stallings	90.00	45.00	30.00
170 Oscar Stanage (Photo actually Chas. Schmidt.)	90.00	45.00	30.00
171 Charles Stengel	360.00	175.00	105.00
172 Milton Stock	90.00	45.00	30.00
173 Amos Strunk (Photo actually Olaf Henriksen.)	90.00	45.00	30.00
174 Billy Sullivan	90.00	45.00	30.00
175 Chas. Tesreau	90.00	45.00	30.00
176 Jim Thorpe	19,250	9,625	5,775
177 Joe Tinker	360.00	175.00	105.00
178 Fred Toney	90.00	45.00	30.00
179 Terry Turner	90.00	45.00	30.00
180 Jim Vaughn	90.00	45.00	30.00
181 Bob Veach	90.00	45.00	30.00
182 James Viox	90.00	45.00	30.00
183 Oscar Vitt	90.00	45.00	30.00
184 Hans Wagner	3,000	660.00	395.00
185 Clarence Walker (Photo not Walker.)	90.00	45.00	30.00
186a Bobby Wallace	5,500	2,750	1,650
186b Zach Wheat	360.00	175.00	105.00
187 Ed. Walsh	360.00	175.00	105.00
188 Buck Weaver	2,000	360.00	215.00
189 Carl Weilman	90.00	45.00	30.00
190 Geo. Whitted	90.00	45.00	30.00
191 Fred Williams	90.00	45.00	30.00
192 Art Wilson	90.00	45.00	30.00
193 J. Owen Wilson	90.00	45.00	30.00
194 Ivy Wingo	90.00	45.00	30.00
195 "Mel" Wolfgang	90.00	45.00	30.00
196 Joe Wood	500.00	110.00	65.00
197 Steve Yerkes	90.00	45.00	30.00
198 Rollie Zeider	90.00	45.00	30.00
199 Heiny Zimmerman	90.00	45.00	30.00
200 Ed. Zwilling	90.00	45.00	30.00

1916 M101-4 Blank Backs

JOE JACKSON
L.F.—Chicago White Sox
87

The "update" version of this set is nearly identical to the earlier cards. The 200 black-and-white cards once again are printed with player photo, name, position, team and card number on front and blank backs. This version appears to have been sold directly to consumers by the manufacturer, Felix Mendelsohn of Chicago. The same cards can be found with advertising on back from several businesses around the country. Most of the players included on the 1-5/8" x 3" cards also appear in the prior edition. Despite being labeled in the American Card Catalog as M101-4, this version was issued after the M101-5 version, with the first advertising appearing in August 1916. The complete set price does not include variations.

	NM	EX	VG
Complete Set (200):	45,000	22,500	13,500
Common Player:	60.00	30.00	18.00
1 Babe Adams	75.00	30.00	18.00
2 Sam Agnew	60.00	30.00	18.00
3 Eddie Ainsmith	60.00	30.00	18.00
4 Grover Alexander	375.00	185.00	110.00
5 Leon Ames	60.00	30.00	18.00
6 Jimmy Archer	60.00	30.00	18.00
7 Jimmy Austin	60.00	30.00	18.00
8 H.D. Baird	60.00	30.00	18.00
9 J. Franklin Baker	300.00	150.00	90.00
10 Dave Bancroft	300.00	150.00	90.00
11 Jack Barry	60.00	30.00	18.00
12 Zinn Beck	60.00	30.00	18.00
13 "Chief" Bender	300.00	150.00	90.00
14 Joe Benz	60.00	30.00	18.00
15 Bob Bescher	60.00	30.00	18.00
16 Al Betzel	60.00	30.00	18.00
17 Mordecai Brown	300.00	150.00	90.00
18 Eddie Burns	60.00	30.00	18.00
19 George Burns	60.00	30.00	18.00
20 Geo. J. Burns	60.00	30.00	18.00
21 Joe Bush	60.00	30.00	18.00
22 "Donie" Bush	60.00	30.00	18.00
23 Art Butler	60.00	30.00	18.00
24 Bobbie Byrne	60.00	30.00	18.00
25 Forrest Cady	60.00	30.00	18.00

26	Jimmy Callahan	60.00	30.00	18.00
27	Ray Caldwell	60.00	30.00	18.00
28	Max Carey	300.00	150.00	90.00
29	George Chalmers	60.00	30.00	18.00
30	Ray Chapman	90.00	45.00	25.00
31	Larry Cheney	60.00	30.00	18.00
32	Eddie Cicotte	300.00	150.00	90.00
33	Tom Clarke	60.00	30.00	18.00
34	Eddie Collins	300.00	150.00	90.00
35	"Shauno" Collins	60.00	30.00	18.00
36	Charles Comiskey	300.00	150.00	90.00
37	Joe Connolly	60.00	30.00	18.00
38	Ty Cobb	2,500	1,250	750.00
39	Harry Coveleskie (Coveleski)	60.00	30.00	18.00
40	Gavvy Cravath	60.00	30.00	18.00
41	Sam Crawford	300.00	150.00	90.00
42	Jean Dale	60.00	30.00	18.00
43	Jake Daubert	60.00	30.00	18.00
44	Charles Deal	60.00	30.00	18.00
45	Al Demaree	60.00	30.00	18.00
46	Josh Devore	60.00	30.00	18.00
47	William Doak	60.00	30.00	18.00
48	Bill Donovan	60.00	30.00	18.00
49	Charles Dooin	60.00	30.00	18.00
50	Mike Doolan	60.00	30.00	18.00
51	Larry Doyle	60.00	30.00	18.00
52	Jean Dubuc	60.00	30.00	18.00
53	Oscar Dugey	60.00	30.00	18.00
54	Johnny Evers	300.00	150.00	90.00
55	Urban Faber	300.00	150.00	90.00
56	"Hap" Felsch	2,000	375.00	225.00
57	Bill Fischer	60.00	30.00	18.00
58	Ray Fisher	60.00	30.00	18.00
59	Max Flack	60.00	30.00	18.00
60	Art Fletcher	60.00	30.00	18.00
61	Eddie Foster	60.00	30.00	18.00
62	Jacques Fournier	60.00	30.00	18.00
63	Del Gainer (Gainor)	60.00	30.00	18.00
64	"Chic" Gandil	500.00	250.00	150.00
65	Larry Gardner	60.00	30.00	18.00
66	Joe Gedeon	60.00	30.00	18.00
67	Gus Getz	60.00	30.00	18.00
68	Geo. Gibson	60.00	30.00	18.00
69	Wilbur Good	60.00	30.00	18.00
70	Hank Gowdy	60.00	30.00	18.00
71	John Graney	60.00	30.00	18.00
72	Clark Griffith	300.00	150.00	90.00
73	Tom Griffith	60.00	30.00	18.00
74	Heinie Groh	60.00	30.00	18.00
75	Earl Hamilton	60.00	30.00	18.00
76	Bob Harmon	60.00	30.00	18.00
77	Roy Hartzell	60.00	30.00	18.00
78	Claude Hendrix	60.00	30.00	18.00
79	Olaf Henriksen	60.00	30.00	18.00
80	John Henry	60.00	30.00	18.00
81	"Buck" Herzog	60.00	30.00	18.00
82	Hugh High	60.00	30.00	18.00
83	Dick Hoblitzell	60.00	30.00	18.00
84	Harry Hooper	300.00	150.00	90.00
85	Ivan Howard	60.00	30.00	18.00
86	Miller Huggins	300.00	150.00	90.00
87	Joe Jackson	15,000	4,000	2,400
88	William James	60.00	30.00	18.00
89	Harold Janvrin	60.00	30.00	18.00
90	Hugh Jennings	300.00	150.00	90.00
91	Walter Johnson	800.00	400.00	240.00
92	Fielder Jones	60.00	30.00	18.00
93	Joe Judge	60.00	30.00	18.00
94	Bennie Kauff	60.00	30.00	18.00
95	Wm. Killefer Jr.	60.00	30.00	18.00
96	Ed. Konetchy	60.00	30.00	18.00
97	Napoleon Lajoie	375.00	185.00	110.00
98	Jack Lapp	60.00	30.00	18.00
99	John Lavan	60.00	30.00	18.00
100	Jimmy Lavender	60.00	30.00	18.00
101	"Nemo" Leibold	60.00	30.00	18.00
102	H.B. Leonard	60.00	30.00	18.00
103	Duffy Lewis	60.00	30.00	18.00
104	Hans Lobert	60.00	30.00	18.00
105	Tom Long	60.00	30.00	18.00
106	Fred Luderus	60.00	30.00	18.00
107	Connie Mack	300.00	150.00	90.00
108	Lee Magee	60.00	30.00	18.00
109	Sherwood Magee	60.00	30.00	18.00
110	Al. Mamaux	60.00	30.00	18.00
111	Leslie Mann	60.00	30.00	18.00
112	"Rabbit" Maranville	300.00	150.00	90.00
113	Rube Marquard	300.00	150.00	90.00
114	J. Erskine Mayer	125.00	65.00	35.00
115	George McBride	60.00	30.00	18.00
116	John J. McGraw	300.00	150.00	90.00
117	Jack McInnis	60.00	30.00	18.00
118	Fred Merkle	60.00	30.00	18.00
119	Chief Meyers	60.00	30.00	18.00
120	Clyde Milan	60.00	30.00	18.00
121	John Miller	60.00	30.00	18.00
122	Otto Miller	60.00	30.00	18.00
123	Willie Mitchell	60.00	30.00	18.00
124	Fred Mollwitz	60.00	30.00	18.00
125	Pat Moran	60.00	30.00	18.00
126	Ray Morgan	60.00	30.00	18.00
127	Geo. Moriarty	60.00	30.00	18.00
128	Guy Morton	60.00	30.00	18.00
129	Mike Mowrey	60.00	30.00	18.00
130	Ed. Murphy	60.00	30.00	18.00
131	"Hy" Myers	60.00	30.00	18.00
132	J.A. Niehoff	60.00	30.00	18.00
133	Rube Oldring	60.00	30.00	18.00
134	Oliver O'Mara	60.00	30.00	18.00
135	Steve O'Neill	60.00	30.00	18.00
136	"Dode" Paskert	60.00	30.00	18.00
137	Roger Peckinpaugh	60.00	30.00	18.00
138	Walter Pipp	75.00	37.50	22.50
139	Derril Pratt (Derrill)	60.00	30.00	18.00
140	Pat Ragan	60.00	30.00	18.00
141	Bill Rariden	60.00	30.00	18.00
142	Eppa Rixey	300.00	150.00	90.00
143	Davey Robertson	60.00	30.00	18.00

144	Wilbert Robinson	300.00	150.00	90.00
145	Bob Roth	60.00	30.00	18.00
146	Ed. Roush	300.00	150.00	90.00
147	Clarence Rowland	60.00	30.00	18.00
148	"Nap" Rucker	60.00	30.00	18.00
149	Dick Rudolph	60.00	30.00	18.00
150	Reb Russell	60.00	30.00	18.00
151	Babe Ruth	15,000	7,500	4,500
152	Vic Saier	60.00	30.00	18.00
153	"Slim" Sallee	60.00	30.00	18.00
154	Ray Schalk	300.00	150.00	90.00
155	Walter Schang	60.00	30.00	18.00
156	Frank Schulte	60.00	30.00	18.00
157	Everett Scott	60.00	30.00	18.00
158	Jim Scott	60.00	30.00	18.00
159	Tom Seaton	60.00	30.00	18.00
160	Howard Shanks	60.00	30.00	18.00
161	Bob Shawkey	60.00	30.00	18.00
162	Ernie Shore	60.00	30.00	18.00
163	Burt Shotton	60.00	30.00	18.00
164	Geo. Sisler	300.00	150.00	90.00
165	J. Carlisle Smith	60.00	30.00	18.00
166	Fred Snodgrass	60.00	30.00	18.00
167	Geo. Stallings	60.00	30.00	18.00
168a	Oscar Stanage (Catching)	60.00	30.00	24.00
168b	Oscar Stanage (Portrait to thighs.)	750.00	375.00	225.00
169	Charles Stengel	375.00	185.00	110.00
170	Milton Stock	60.00	30.00	18.00
171	Amos Strunk	60.00	30.00	18.00
172	Billy Sullivan	60.00	30.00	18.00
173	"Jeff" Tesreau	60.00	30.00	18.00
174	Joe Tinker	300.00	150.00	90.00
175	Fred Toney	60.00	30.00	18.00
176	Terry Turner	60.00	30.00	18.00
177	George Tyler	60.00	30.00	18.00
178	Jim Vaughn	60.00	30.00	18.00
179	Bob Veach	60.00	30.00	18.00
180	James Viox	60.00	30.00	18.00
181	Oscar Vitt	60.00	30.00	18.00
182	Hans Wagner	1,200	600.00	360.00
183	Clarence Walker	60.00	30.00	18.00
184	Ed. Walsh	300.00	150.00	90.00
185	W. Wambsganss (Photo actually Fritz Coumbe.)	60.00	30.00	18.00
186	Buck Weaver	600.00	300.00	180.00
187	Carl Weilman	60.00	30.00	18.00
188	Zach Wheat	300.00	150.00	90.00
189	Geo. Whitted	60.00	30.00	18.00
190	Fred Williams	60.00	30.00	18.00
191	Art Wilson	60.00	30.00	18.00
192	J. Owen Wilson	60.00	30.00	18.00
193	Ivy Wingo	60.00	30.00	18.00
194	"Mel" Wolfgang	60.00	30.00	18.00
195	Joe Wood	175.00	85.00	50.00
196	Steve Yerkes	60.00	30.00	18.00
197	"Pep" Young	60.00	30.00	18.00
198	Rollie Zeider	60.00	30.00	18.00
199	Heiny Zimmerman	60.00	30.00	18.00
200	Ed. Zwilling	60.00	30.00	18.00

N

1969 Nabisco Team Flakes

Frank Robinson—OF
Baltimore Orioles

This set of cards is seen in two different sizes: 1-15/16" x 3" and 1-3/4" x 2-15/16". This is explained by the varying widths of the card borders on the backs of Nabisco cereal packages. Cards are action color photos bordered in yellow. Twenty-four of the top players in the game are included in the set, which was issued in three series of eight cards each. No team insignias are visible on any of the cards. Packages described the cards as "Mini Posters."

		NM	EX	VG
	Complete Set (24):	475.00	240.00	140.00
	Common Player:	8.00	4.00	2.50
(1)	Hank Aaron	45.00	22.50	13.50
(2)	Richie Allen	12.50	6.25	3.75
(3)	Lou Brock	20.00	10.00	6.00
(4)	Paul Casanova	8.00	4.00	2.50
(5)	Roberto Clemente	95.00	47.50	28.00
(6)	Al Ferrara	8.00	4.00	2.50
(7)	Bill Freehan	8.00	4.00	2.50
(8)	Jim Fregosi	8.00	4.00	2.50
(9)	Bob Gibson	20.00	10.00	6.00

(10)	Tony Horton	8.00	4.00	2.50
(11)	Tommy John	8.00	4.00	2.50
(12)	Al Kaline	25.00	12.50	7.50
(13)	Jim Lonborg	8.00	4.00	2.50
(14)	Juan Marichal	20.00	10.00	6.00
(15)	Willie Mays	45.00	22.50	13.50
(16)	Rick Monday	8.00	4.00	2.50
(17)	Tony Oliva	8.00	4.00	2.50
(18)	Brooks Robinson	25.00	12.50	7.50
(19)	Frank Robinson	25.00	12.50	7.50
(20)	Pete Rose	35.00	17.50	10.00
(21)	Ron Santo	12.50	6.25	3.75
(22)	Tom Seaver	25.00	12.50	7.50
(23)	Rusty Staub	8.00	4.00	2.50
(24)	Mel Stottlemyre	8.00	4.00	2.50

1923-1924 Nacionales Cigarros

The baseball players in this mid-20s Cuban issue are part of a larger set which included boxers, actresses, actors, nudes, soccer players and others. The cards measure about 1-5/8" x 2-1/4" and have a distinctive wide black border on front. Backs identify the issue. An album was issued to house the set. The cards are printed on thin cardboard with a glossy finish.

		NM	EX	VG
	Complete Baseball Set (40):	60,000	24,000	12,000
	Common Player:	500.00	200.00	100.00
21	Rafael Almeida	1,500	600.00	300.00
22	Isidro Fabre	1,125	450.00	225.00
23	Eugenio Morin	500.00	200.00	100.00
24	Oscar Rodriguez	500.00	200.00	100.00
25	Joseito Rodriguez	500.00	200.00	100.00
26	Papo Gonzalez	500.00	200.00	100.00
27	Gutierrez	500.00	200.00	100.00
28	Valentin Dreke (Photo actually Lucas Boada.)	1,125	450.00	225.00
29	Jose Maria Fernandez	750.00	300.00	150.00
30	(Cheo) Ramos	500.00	200.00	100.00
31	Paito (Ramon Herrera)	500.00	200.00	100.00
32	Bernardo Baro	1,125	450.00	225.00
33	Manuel Cueto	750.00	300.00	150.00
34	(Oscar) Tuero	500.00	200.00	100.00
35	Kakin Gonzalez	500.00	200.00	100.00
36	Armando Marsans	1,500	600.00	300.00
37	Andy Cooper	9,000	3,600	1,800
38	Dolf Luque	2,500	1,000	500.00
39	Marcelino Guerra	500.00	200.00	100.00
40	Manzanillo (Tatic Campos)	500.00	200.00	100.00
41	Oscar Levis	750.00	300.00	150.00
42	Eufemio Abreu	500.00	200.00	100.00
43	Cristobal Torriente	12,000	4,800	2,400
44	Juanelo Mirabal	750.00	300.00	150.00
45	Merito Acosta	500.00	200.00	100.00
46	Jose Acostica (Acosta)	500.00	200.00	100.00
47	Rogelio Crespo	500.00	200.00	100.00
48	(Jacinto) Calvo	750.00	300.00	150.00
49	(Emilio) Palmero	750.00	300.00	150.00
50	Jose Mendez	9,000	3,600	1,800
51	Alejandro Oms	3,750	1,500	750.00
52	Pedro Dibut	750.00	300.00	150.00
53	Strike (Valentin "Sirique" Gonzalez)	500.00	200.00	100.00
54	Magrinat (Hector Magrinut)	500.00	200.00	100.00
55	Raphael Quintana	500.00	200.00	100.00
56	Bienvenido Jimenez	750.00	300.00	150.00
57	Bartolo Portuando (Portuondo)	1,500	600.00	300.00
58	(Pelayo) Chacon	1,500	600.00	300.00
59	Riant (Red Ryan)	1,500	600.00	300.00
60	Perico El Mano (Mascot)	500.00	200.00	100.00

1909 Nadja Caramels (E92)

Tinker, s.s. Chicago Nat'l

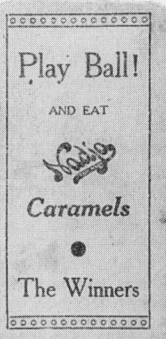

Play Ball!
AND EAT
Nadja
Caramels
The Winners

One of several 1909-10 issues produced for Nadja Caramels, this set can be distinguished by the players in the checklist (alphabetized here) and the type beneath the color player lithograph. In this set, the player's last name is in upper- and lower-case letters, and his position is given, along with the team. Backs of these 1-1/2" x 2-3/4" cards are identical to later Nadja issues, featuring an ad for the candy brand. Cataloged (along with the cards of Croft's Candy/Cocoa and Dockman Gum) as E92 in the "American Card Catalog," the Nadja set checklist differs from those in the other sets in that it is larger and contains a group of St. Louis players not found in the other sets. Nadja was a brand name of the Blake-Wenneker Candy Co. of St. Louis.

		NM	EX	VG
	Complete Set (62):	50,000	22,500	12,500
	Common Player:	550.00	220.00	110.00
(1)	Bill Bailey	550.00	220.00	110.00
(2)	Jack Barry	550.00	220.00	110.00
(3)	Harry Bemis	550.00	220.00	110.00
(4)	Chief Bender (Striped cap.)	1,020	455.00	305.00
(5)	Chief Bender (White cap.)	1,020	455.00	305.00
(6)	Bill Bergen	550.00	220.00	110.00
(7)	Bob Bescher	550.00	220.00	110.00
(8)	Roger Bresnahan	1,020	455.00	305.00
(9)	Al Bridwell	550.00	220.00	110.00
(10)	Doc Casey	550.00	220.00	110.00
(11)	Frank Chance	1,020	455.00	305.00
(12)	Hal Chase	780.00	350.00	235.00
(13)	Ty Cobb	7,500	3,360	2,250
(14)	Eddie Collins	1,020	455.00	305.00
(15)	Sam Crawford	1,020	455.00	305.00
(16)	Harry Davis	550.00	220.00	110.00
(17)	Art Devlin	550.00	220.00	110.00
(18)	Bill Donovan	550.00	220.00	110.00
(19)	Red Dooin	550.00	220.00	110.00
(20)	Mickey Doolan	550.00	220.00	110.00
(21)	Patsy Dougherty	550.00	220.00	110.00
(22)	Larry Doyle (Throwing)	550.00	220.00	110.00
(23)	Larry Doyle (With bat.)	550.00	220.00	110.00
(24)	Rube Ellis	550.00	220.00	110.00
(25)	Johnny Evers	1,020	455.00	305.00
(26)	George Gibson	550.00	220.00	110.00
(27)	Topsy Hartsel	550.00	220.00	110.00
(28)	Roy Hartzell (Batting)	550.00	220.00	110.00
(29)	Roy Hartzell (Fielding)	550.00	220.00	110.00
(30)	Harry Howell (Ready to pitch.)	550.00	220.00	110.00
(31)	Harry Howell (Follow-through.)	550.00	220.00	110.00
(32)	Fred Jacklitsch	550.00	220.00	110.00
(33)	Hugh Jennings	1,020	455.00	305.00
(34)	Red Kleinow	550.00	220.00	110.00
(35)	Otto Knabe	550.00	220.00	110.00
(36)	Jack Knight	550.00	220.00	110.00
(37)	Nap Lajoie	1,020	455.00	305.00
(38)	Hans Lobert	550.00	220.00	110.00
(39)	Sherry Magee	550.00	220.00	110.00
(40)	Christy Matthewson (Mathewson)	3,900	1,740	1,170
(41)	John McGraw	1,020	455.00	305.00
(42)	Larry McLean	550.00	220.00	110.00
(43)	Dots Miller (Batting)	550.00	220.00	110.00
(44)	Dots Miller (Fielding)	550.00	220.00	110.00
(45)	Danny Murphy	550.00	220.00	110.00
(46)	Rebel Oakes	550.00	220.00	110.00
(47)	Bill O'Hara	550.00	220.00	110.00
(48)	Eddie Phelps	550.00	220.00	110.00
(49)	Germany Schaefer	550.00	220.00	110.00
(50)	Admiral Schlei	550.00	220.00	110.00
(51)	Boss Schmidt	550.00	220.00	110.00
(52)	Johnny Seigle (Siegle)	550.00	220.00	110.00
(53)	Dave Shean	550.00	220.00	110.00
(54)	Boss Smith (Schmidt)	550.00	220.00	110.00
(55)	George Stone (Blue background.)	550.00	220.00	110.00
(56)	George Stone (Green background.)	550.00	220.00	110.00
(57)	Joe Tinker	1,020	455.00	305.00
(58)	Honus Wagner (Batting)	6,000	2,700	1,800
(59)	Honus Wagner (Throwing)	7,200	3,240	2,160
(60)	Bobby Wallace	1,020	455.00	305.00
(61)	Cy Young	2,520	1,140	750.00
(62)	Heinie Zimmerman	550.00	220.00	110.00

1910 Nadja Caramels Philadelphia Athletics (E104-1)

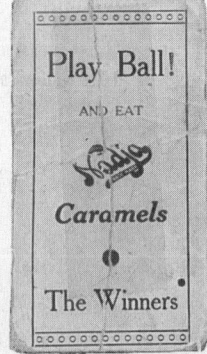

The 18 Philadelphia Athletics players in this set, can each be found in three different variations. Each of the approximately 1-1/2" x 2-3/4" cards can be found with a plain portrait lithograph on front, and either a blank back or a back containing a Nadja ad. Each player can also be found with a black

overprint on front, comprised of a white elephant figure on the uniform and the notation "World's Champions 1910" above. The overprinted cards are known only with blank backs, and are somewhat scarcer than the plain cards of either type. Nadja-back cards should be valued about the same as the overprinted type.

		NM	EX	VG
	Complete Set, No O/P, Blank Back (18):	20,000	9,000	6,000
	Complete Set, With O/P or Ad Back:	25,000	12,500	7,250
	Common Player:	1,000	450.00	300.00
(1a)	Home Run Baker	1,750	800.00	500.00
(1b)	Home Run Baker ("World's Champions")	3,600	1,800	900.00
(2a)	Jack Barry	1,000	450.00	300.00
(2b)	Jack Barry ("World's Champions")	3,600	1,800	900.00
(3a)	Chief Bender	1,750	800.00	500.00
(3b)	Chief Bender ("World's Champions")	3,600	1,800	900.00
(4a)	Eddie Collins	1,750	800.00	500.00
(4b)	Eddie Collins ("World's Champions")	3,600	1,800	900.00
(5a)	Harry Davis	1,000	450.00	300.00
(5b)	Harry Davis ("World's Champions")	3,600	1,800	900.00
(6a)	Jimmy Dygert (1910 above head)	1,000	450.00	300.00
(6b-1)	Jimmy Dygert ("World's Champions" 1910 above head)	3,600	1,800	900.00
(6b-2)	Jimmy Dygert (1910 at right)	3,600	1,800	900.00
(7a)	Topsy Hartsel	1,000	450.00	300.00
(7b)	Topsy Hartel ("World's Champions")	3,600	1,800	900.00
(8a)	Harry Krause	1,000	450.00	300.00
(8b)	Harry Krause ("World's Champions")	3,600	1,800	900.00
(9a)	Jack Lapp	1,000	450.00	300.00
(9b)	Jack Lapp ("World's Champions")	3,600	1,800	900.00
(10a)	Paddy Livingstone (Livingston)	1,000	450.00	300.00
(10b)	Paddy Livingstone (Livingston) ("World's Champions")	3,600	1,800	900.00
(11a)	Bris Lord	1,000	450.00	300.00
(11b)	Bris Lord ("World's Champions")	3,600	1,800	900.00
(12a)	Connie Mack	5,250	2,400	1,500
(12b)	Connie Mack	12,000	6,000	3,000
(13a)	Cy Morgan	1,000	450.00	300.00
(13b)	Cy Morgan ("World's Champions")	3,600	1,800	900.00
(14a)	Danny Murphy	1,000	450.00	300.00
(14b)	Danny Murphy ("World's Champions")	3,600	1,800	900.00
(15a)	Rube Oldring	1,000	450.00	300.00
(15b)	Rube Oldring ("World's Champions")	3,600	1,800	900.00
(16a)	Eddie Plank	8,100	3,600	2,400
(16b)	Eddie Plank ("World's Champions")	15,000	7,500	3,750
(17a)	Amos Strunk	1,000	450.00	300.00
(17b)	Amos Strunk ("World's Champions")	3,600	1,800	900.00
(18a)	Ira Thomas	1,000	450.00	300.00
(18b-1)	Ira Thomas ("World's Champions" 1910 above head)	3,600	1,800	900.00
(18b-2)	Ira Thomas (1910 at right)	3,600	1,800	900.00

1910 Nadja Caramels Pittsburgh Pirates (E104-2)

Similar to the contemporary American Caramel issue, this set of 1-1/2" x 2-3/4" cards features portrait color lithographs of the 1909 World's Champion Pittsburgh (spelled "Pittsburg") Pirates. Each card was issued with both blank back and with a back bearing a Nadja ad. The Nadja-backed cards are scarcer but command little premium.

		NM	EX	VG
	Complete Set (11):	17,500	7,900	5,250
	Common Player:	780.00	360.00	240.00
	Ad Back: 1.25X			
(1)	Babe Adams	780.00	360.00	240.00
(2)	Fred Clarke	1,800	810.00	540.00
(3)	George Gibson	780.00	360.00	240.00
(4)	Ham Hyatt	780.00	360.00	240.00
(5)	Tommy Leach	780.00	360.00	240.00
(6)	Sam Leever	780.00	360.00	240.00
(7)	Nick Maddox	780.00	360.00	240.00
(8)	Dots Miller	780.00	360.00	240.00
(9)	Deacon Phillippe	780.00	360.00	240.00
(10)	Honus Wagner	12,000	5,400	3,600
(11)	Owen Wilson	780.00	360.00	240.00

1910 Nadja Caramels (E104-3)

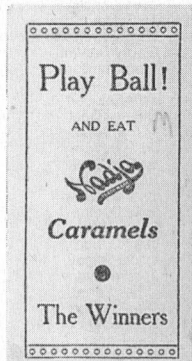

The cards in this issue can each be found with or without a Nadja ad on back; the latter being somewhat scarcer and carrying a premium over the values shown. These 1-1/2" x 2-3/4" cards can be distinguished from the 1909 issue by the line of type beneath the player portrait. On the 1910 cards, the player's last name is in all blue capital letters and there is no position designation given. This checklist is likely incomplete.

		NM	EX	VG
	Common Player:	1,440	660.00	420.00
	Ad Back: 1.25X			
(1)	Bill Abstein	1,440	660.00	420.00
(2)	Red Ames	1,440	660.00	420.00
(3)	Johnny Bates	1,440	660.00	420.00
(4)	Kitty Bransfield	1,440	660.00	420.00
(5)	Al Bridwell	1,440	660.00	420.00
(6)	Hal Chase	1,920	870.00	600.00
(7)	Doc Crandall	1,440	660.00	420.00
(8)	Sam Crawford	2,400	1,080	720.00
(9)	Jim Delehanty (Delahanty)	1,440	660.00	420.00
(10)	Art Devlin	1,440	660.00	420.00
(11)	Red Dooin	1,440	660.00	420.00
(12)	Mickey Doolan	1,440	660.00	420.00
(13)	Larry Doyle	1,440	660.00	420.00
(14)	Eddie Grant	1,440	660.00	420.00
(15)	Fred Jacklitsch	1,440	660.00	420.00
(16)	Hugh Jennings	2,400	1,080	720.00
(17)	Davy Jones	1,440	660.00	420.00
(18)	Tom Jones	1,440	660.00	420.00
(19)	Otto Knabe	1,440	660.00	420.00
(201)	Sherry Magee	1,440	660.00	420.00
(21)	John McGraw	2,400	1,080	720.00
(22)	Matty McIntyre	1,440	660.00	420.00
(23)	Earl Moore	1,440	660.00	420.00
(24)	Pat Moren (Moran)	1,440	660.00	420.00
(25)	George Moriarity	1,440	660.00	420.00
(26)	George Mullin	1,440	660.00	420.00
(27)	Red Murray	1,440	660.00	420.00
(28)	Simon Nicholls	1,440	660.00	420.00
(29)	Charley O'Leary	1,440	660.00	420.00
(30)	Admiral Schlei	1,440	660.00	420.00
(31)	Boss Schmidt	1,440	660.00	420.00
(32)	Cy Seymore (Seymour)	1,440	660.00	420.00
(33)	Tully Sparks	1,440	660.00	420.00
(34)	Ed Summers	1,440	660.00	420.00
(35)	Ed Willetts (Willett)	1,440	660.00	420.00
(36)	Vic Willis	2,400	1,080	720.00
(37)	Hooks Wiltse	1,440	660.00	420.00

1912 Napoleon Little Cigars

While this cigarette brand advertising on the backs of T207 cards is less commonly encountered than Recruit, collectors do not attach a commensurate premium to them, largely because each of the players can be found with more common back ads.

PREMIUM: 2X
(See T207 for checklist and base card values.)

1963 Nassau County Boy Scouts

According to the text on the back, six cards were issued in this set. The other subjects are unknown, and may not feature any additional baseball players. The standard-size cards are printed in blue-and-white, both front and back, including a duo-tone photo of Snider in his only season with the Mets.

	NM	EX	VG
(1) Duke Snider	150.00	75.00	45.00

1974 Nassau Tuberculosis and Respiratory Disease Assn.

TAKE THE ADVICE OF WHITEY FORD AND TURN THUMBS DOWN ON SMOKING

Smoking and sports don't mix. Don't handicap yourself with a bad habit. You'll lose the game before it begins.

Edward Charles "Whitey" Ford — Ht.: 5' 10". Wt.: 181. Bats and throws: Left. Born: Oct. 21, 1928. Home: Lake Success, N.Y. Signed by the Yankees in 1946 Whitey holds the World Series pitching record for the most consecutive scoreless innings (33.2) and the most wins (10). He pitched as a Yankee for 16 years and holds the highest percentage of wins in one (season) .862 with 25-4 in 1961.

Nassau Tuberculosis and Respiratory Disease Association

The date attributed to these cards is arbitrary. The black-and-white 2-1/2" x 3-1/2" cards have a photo of the Yankees pitcher on front and a career summary on back, along with an anti-smoking message.

	NM	EX	VG
Whitey Ford (Facing his right.)	45.00	22.50	13.50
Whitey Ford (Follow-through.)	45.00	22.50	13.50

1921-23 National Caramel (E220)

FRANKLIN "HOME RUN" BAKER
3rd B., N.Y. Yankees

This set consists of 120 of the leading BASE BALL STARS of the AMERICAN AND NATIONAL LEAGUES. Made only by — NATIONAL CARAMEL COMPANY LANCASTER, PENNA.

Issued circa 1921 to 1923, this 120-card set is sometimes confused with contemporary American Caramel issues, but is easy to identify because of the words "Made only by National Caramel Company" on the back. With due consideration to normal cutting variances on cards of this era and type, E220s measure about 2" x 3-1/4" and feature black-and-white photos with the player's name, position and team at the bottom. In addition to the line indicating the manufacturer, the backs read "This set consists of pictures of 120 of the leading Base Ball Stars of the American and National Leagues," There are 115 different players included in the set, with five players shown on two cards each. About half of the photos in the set are identical to those used in various American Caramel sets, leading to some confusion regarding the three sets.

	NM	EX	VG
Complete Set (120):	27,500	13,500	8,250
Common Player:	100.00	50.00	30.00
(1) Charles "Babe" Adams	100.00	50.00	30.00
(2) G.C. Alexander	400.00	200.00	120.00
(3) James Austin	100.00	50.00	30.00
(4) Jim Bagbyk (Bagby)	100.00	50.00	30.00
(5) Franklin "Home Run" Baker	300.00	150.00	90.00
(6) Dave Bancroft	300.00	150.00	90.00
(7) Turner Barber	100.00	50.00	30.00
(8) George Burns (Cincinnati)	100.00	50.00	30.00
(9) George Burns (Cleveland)	100.00	50.00	30.00
(10) Joe Bush	100.00	50.00	30.00
(11) Leon Cadore	100.00	50.00	30.00
(12) Max Carey	300.00	150.00	90.00
(13) Ty Cobb	1,750	875.00	525.00
(14) Eddie Collins	300.00	150.00	90.00
(15) John Collins	100.00	50.00	30.00
(16) Wilbur Cooper	100.00	50.00	30.00
(17) S. Coveleskie (Coveleski)	300.00	150.00	90.00
(18) Walton Cruise	100.00	50.00	30.00
(19) Wm. Cunningham	100.00	50.00	30.00
(20) George Cutshaw	100.00	50.00	30.00
(21) Jake Daubert	100.00	50.00	30.00
(22) Chas. A. Deal	100.00	50.00	30.00
(23) Bill Doak	100.00	50.00	30.00
(24) Joe Dugan	100.00	50.00	30.00
(25) Jimmy Dykes (Batting)	100.00	50.00	30.00
(26) Jimmy Dykes (Fielding)	100.00	50.00	30.00
(27) "Red" Faber	300.00	150.00	90.00
(28) "Chick" Fewster	100.00	50.00	30.00
(29) Wilson Fewster	100.00	50.00	30.00
(30) Ira Flagstead	100.00	50.00	30.00
(31) Arthur Fletcher	100.00	50.00	30.00
(32) Frank Frisch	300.00	150.00	90.00
(33) Larry Gardner	100.00	50.00	30.00
(34) Walter Gerber	100.00	50.00	30.00

		NM	EX	VG
(35)	Charles Glazner	100.00	50.00	30.00
(36)	Hank Gowdy	100.00	50.00	30.00
(37)	J.C. Graney (Should be J.G.)	100.00	50.00	30.00
(38)	Tommy Griffith	100.00	50.00	30.00
(39)	Charles Grimm	100.00	50.00	30.00
(40)	Heinie Groh	100.00	50.00	30.00
(41)	Byron Harris	100.00	50.00	30.00
(42)	Sam Harris (Bucky)	300.00	150.00	90.00
(43)	Harry Heilman (Heilmann)	300.00	150.00	90.00
(44)	Claude Hendrix	100.00	50.00	30.00
(45)	Walter Henline	100.00	50.00	30.00
(46)	Chas. Hollocher	100.00	50.00	30.00
(47)	Harry Hooper	300.00	150.00	90.00
(48)	Rogers Hornsby	400.00	200.00	120.00
(49)	Waite Hoyt	300.00	150.00	90.00
(50)	Wilbert Hubbell	100.00	50.00	30.00
(51)	Wm. Jacobson	100.00	50.00	30.00
(52)	Walter Johnson	850.00	425.00	255.00
(53)	Jimmy Johnston	100.00	50.00	30.00
(54)	Joe Judge	100.00	50.00	30.00
(55)	Geo. "Bingo" Kelly	300.00	150.00	90.00
(56)	Dick Kerr	100.00	50.00	30.00
(57)	Pete Kilduff (Bending)	100.00	50.00	30.00
(58)	Pete Kilduff (Leaping)	100.00	50.00	30.00
(59)	Larry Kopf	100.00	50.00	30.00
(60)	H.B. Leonard	100.00	50.00	30.00
(61)	Harry Liebold (Leibold)	100.00	50.00	30.00
(62)	Walter "Buster" Mails ("Duster")	100.00	50.00	30.00
(63)	Walter "Rabbit" Maranville	300.00	150.00	90.00
(64)	Carl Mays	100.00	50.00	30.00
(65)	Lee Meadows	100.00	50.00	30.00
(66)	Bob Meusel	100.00	50.00	30.00
(67)	Emil Meusel	100.00	50.00	30.00
(68)	J.C. Milan	100.00	50.00	30.00
(69)	Earl Neale	125.00	60.00	35.00
(70)	Robert Nehf (Arthur)	100.00	50.00	30.00
(71)	Bernie Neis	100.00	50.00	30.00
(72)	Joe Oeschger	100.00	50.00	30.00
(73)	Robert O'Farrell	100.00	50.00	30.00
(74)	Ivan Olson	100.00	50.00	30.00
(75)	Steve O'Neill	100.00	50.00	30.00
(76)	Geo. Paskert	100.00	50.00	30.00
(77)	Roger Peckinpaugh	100.00	50.00	30.00
(78)	Herb Pennock	300.00	150.00	90.00
(79)	Ralph "Cy" Perkins	100.00	50.00	30.00
(80)	Scott Perry (Photo actually Ed Rommel.)	100.00	50.00	30.00
(81)	Jeff Pfeffer	100.00	50.00	30.00
(82)	V.J. Picinich	100.00	50.00	30.00
(83)	Walter Pipp	115.00	55.00	35.00
(84)	Derrill Pratt	100.00	50.00	30.00
(85)	Goldie Rapp	100.00	50.00	30.00
(86)	Edgar Rice	300.00	150.00	90.00
(87)	Jimmy Ring	100.00	50.00	30.00
(88)	Eddie Rousch (Roush)	300.00	150.00	90.00
(89)	Babe Ruth	8,000	4,000	2,400
(90)	Raymond Schmandt	100.00	50.00	30.00
(91)	Everett Scott	100.00	50.00	30.00
(92)	Joe Sewell	300.00	150.00	90.00
(93)	Wally Shang (Schang)	100.00	50.00	30.00
(94)	Maurice Shannon	100.00	50.00	30.00
(95)	Bob Shawkey	100.00	50.00	30.00
(96)	Urban Shocker	100.00	50.00	30.00
(97)	George Sisler	300.00	150.00	90.00
(98)	Earl Smith	100.00	50.00	30.00
(99)	John Smith	100.00	50.00	30.00
(100)	Sherrod Smith	100.00	50.00	30.00
(101)	Frank Snyder (Crouching)	100.00	50.00	30.00
(102)	Frank Snyder (Standing)	100.00	50.00	30.00
(103)	Tris Speaker	400.00	200.00	120.00
(104)	Vernon Spencer	100.00	50.00	30.00
(105)	Chas. "Casey" Stengle (Stengel)	350.00	175.00	100.00
(106)	Milton Stock (Batting)	100.00	50.00	30.00
(107)	Milton Stock (Fielding)	100.00	50.00	30.00
(108)	James Vaughn	100.00	50.00	30.00
(109)	Robert Veach	100.00	50.00	30.00
(110)	Wm. Wambsgauss (Wambsganss)	100.00	50.00	30.00
(111)	Aaron Ward	100.00	50.00	30.00
(112)	Zach Wheat	300.00	150.00	90.00
(113)	George Whitted (Batting)	100.00	50.00	30.00
(114)	George Whitted (Fielding)	100.00	50.00	30.00
(115)	Fred C. Williams	100.00	50.00	30.00
(116)	Arthur Wilson	100.00	50.00	30.00
(117)	Ivy Wingo	100.00	50.00	30.00
(118)	Lawton Witt	100.00	50.00	30.00
(119)	"Pep" Young (Photo actually Ralph Young.)	100.00	50.00	30.00
(120)	Ross Young (Youngs)	300.00	150.00	90.00

1936 National Chicle "Fine Pens" (R313)

Issued in 1936 by the National Chicle Co., this set consists of 120 cards, measuring 3-1/4" x 5-3/8". The black-and-white cards are blank-backed and unnumbered. Although issued by National Chicle, the name of the company does not appear on the cards. The set includes individual player portraits with facsimilie autographs, multi-player cards and action photos. The cards, known in the hobby as "Fine Pen" because of the thin style of writing used for the facsimilie autographs, were originally available as an in-store premium.

		NM	EX	VG
Complete Set (120):		6,500	3,250	1,950
Common Player:		40.00	20.00	12.00
(1)	Melo Almada	45.00	22.50	13.50
(2)	Nick Altrock, Al Schacht	40.00	20.00	12.00
(3)	Paul Andrews	40.00	20.00	12.00
(4)	Elden Auker (Eldon)	40.00	20.00	12.00
(5)	Earl Averill	75.00	37.50	22.50
(6)	John Babich, James Bucher	40.00	20.00	12.00
(7)	Jim Becher (Bucher)	40.00	20.00	12.00
(8)	Moe Berg	150.00	75.00	45.00
(9)	Walter Berger	40.00	20.00	12.00
(10)	Charles Berry	40.00	20.00	12.00
(11)	Ralph Birkhofer (Birkofer)	40.00	20.00	12.00
(12)	Cy Blanton	40.00	20.00	12.00
(13)	O. Bluege	40.00	20.00	12.00
(14)	Cliff Bolton	40.00	20.00	12.00
(15)	Zeke Bonura	40.00	20.00	12.00
(16)	Stan Bordagaray, George Earnshaw	40.00	20.00	12.00
(17)	Jim Bottomley, Charley Gelbert	50.00	25.00	15.00
(18)	Thos. Bridges	40.00	20.00	12.00
(19)	Sam Byrd	40.00	20.00	12.00
(20)	Dolph Camilli	40.00	20.00	12.00
(21)	Dolph Camilli, Billy Jurges	40.00	20.00	12.00
(22)	Bruce Campbell	40.00	20.00	12.00
(23)	Walter "Kit" Carson	40.00	20.00	12.00
(24)	Ben Chapman	40.00	20.00	12.00
(25)	Harland Clift, Luke Sewell	40.00	20.00	12.00
(26)	Mickey Cochrane, Jimmy Fox (Foxx), Al Simmons	90.00	45.00	27.50
(27)	"Rip" Collins	40.00	20.00	12.00
(28)	Joe Cronin	75.00	37.50	22.50
(29)	Frank Crossetti (Crosetti)	40.00	20.00	12.00
(30)	Frank Crosetti, Jimmy Dykes	40.00	20.00	12.00
(31)	Kiki Cuyler, Gabby Hartnett	85.00	40.00	25.00
(32)	Paul Derringer	40.00	20.00	12.00
(33)	Bill Dickey, Hank Greenberg	90.00	45.00	27.50
(34)	Bill Dietrich	40.00	20.00	12.00
(35)	Joe DiMaggio, Hank Erickson	750.00	375.00	225.00
(36)	Carl Doyle	40.00	20.00	12.00
(37)	Charles Dressen, Bill Myers	40.00	20.00	12.00
(38)	Jimmie Dykes	40.00	20.00	12.00
(39)	Rick Ferrell, Wess Ferrell (Wes)	75.00	37.50	22.50
(40)	Pete Fox	40.00	20.00	12.00
(41)	Frankie Frisch	75.00	37.50	22.50
(42)	Milton Galatzer	40.00	20.00	12.00
(43)	Chas. Gehringer	75.00	37.50	22.50
(44)	Charley Gelbert	40.00	20.00	12.00
(45)	Joe Glenn	40.00	20.00	12.00
(46)	Jose Gomez	40.00	20.00	12.00
(47)	Lefty Gomez, Red Ruffing	90.00	45.00	27.50
(48)	Vernon Gomez	75.00	37.50	22.50
(49)	Leon Goslin	75.00	37.50	22.50
(50)	Hank Gowdy	40.00	20.00	12.00
(51)	"Hank" Greenberg	90.00	45.00	27.50
(52)	"Lefty" Grove	90.00	45.00	27.50
(53)	Stan Hack	40.00	20.00	12.00
(54)	Odell Hale	40.00	20.00	12.00
(55)	Wild Bill Hallahan	40.00	20.00	12.00
(56)	Mel Harder	40.00	20.00	12.00
(57)	Stanley Bucky Harriss (Harris)	75.00	37.50	22.50
(58)	Gabby Hartnett, Rip Radcliff	40.00	20.00	12.00
(59)	Gabby Hartnett, L. Waner	45.00	22.50	13.50
(60)	Gabby Hartnett, Lon Warnecke (Warneke)	40.00	20.00	12.00
(61)	Buddy Hassett	40.00	20.00	12.00
(62)	Babe Herman	40.00	20.00	12.00
(63)	Frank Higgins	40.00	20.00	12.00
(64)	Oral C. Hildebrand	40.00	20.00	12.00
(65)	Myril Hoag	40.00	20.00	12.00
(66)	Rogers Hornsby	90.00	45.00	27.50
(67)	Waite Hoyt	75.00	37.50	22.50
(68)	Willis G. Hudlin	40.00	20.00	12.00
(69)	"Woody" Jensen	40.00	20.00	12.00
(70)	Woody Jenson (Jensen)	40.00	20.00	12.00
(71)	William Knickerbocker	40.00	20.00	12.00
(72)	Joseph Kuhel	40.00	20.00	12.00
(73)	Cookie Lavagetto	40.00	20.00	12.00
(74)	Thornton Lee	40.00	20.00	12.00
(75)	Ernie Lombardi	75.00	37.50	22.50
(76)	Red Lucas	40.00	20.00	12.00
(77)	Connie Mack, John McGraw	75.00	37.50	22.50
(78)	Pepper Martin	40.00	20.00	12.00
(79)	George McQuinn	40.00	20.00	12.00
(80)	George McQuinn, Lee Stine	40.00	20.00	12.00
(81)	Joe Medwick	75.00	37.50	22.50
(82)	Oscar Melillo	40.00	20.00	12.00
(83)	"Buddy" Meyer (Myer)	40.00	20.00	12.00
(84)	Randy Moore	40.00	20.00	12.00
(85)	T. Moore, Jimmie Wilson	40.00	20.00	12.00
(86)	Wallace Moses	40.00	20.00	12.00
(87)	V. Mungo	40.00	20.00	12.00
(88)	Lamar Newsom (Newsome)	40.00	20.00	12.00
(89)	Lewis "Buck" Newsom (Louis)	40.00	20.00	12.00
(90)	Steve O'Neill	40.00	20.00	12.00
(91)	Tommie Padden	40.00	20.00	12.00
(92)	E. Babe Philips (Phelps)	40.00	20.00	12.00
(93)	Bill Rogel (Rogell)	40.00	20.00	12.00
(94)	Lynn "Schoolboy" Rowe	40.00	20.00	12.00
(95)	Luke Sewell	40.00	20.00	12.00
(96)	Al Simmons	75.00	37.50	22.50
(97)	Casey Stengel	80.00	40.00	24.00
(98)	Bill Swift	40.00	20.00	12.00
(99)	Cecil Travis	40.00	20.00	12.00

		NM	EX	VG
(100)	"Pie" Traynor	75.00	37.50	22.50
(101)	William Urbansky (Urbanski)	40.00	20.00	12.00
(102)	Arky Vaughn (Vaughan)	75.00	37.50	22.50
(103)	Joe Vosmik	40.00	20.00	12.00
(104)	Honus Wagner	135.00	65.00	40.00
(105)	Rube Walberg	40.00	20.00	12.00
(106)	Bill Walker	40.00	20.00	12.00
(107)	Gerald Walker	40.00	20.00	12.00
(108)	L. Waner, P. Waner, Big Jim Weaver	75.00	37.50	22.50
(109)	George Washington	40.00	20.00	12.00
(110)	Bill Werber	40.00	20.00	12.00
(111)	Sam West	40.00	20.00	12.00
(112)	Pinkey Whitney	40.00	20.00	12.00
(113)	Vernon Wiltshere (Wilshere)	40.00	20.00	12.00
(114)	"Pep" Young	40.00	20.00	12.00
(115)	Chicago White Sox 1936	40.00	20.00	12.00
(116)	Fence Busters	40.00	20.00	12.00
(117)	Talking It Over (Leo Durocher)	40.00	20.00	12.00
(118)	There She Goes! Chicago City Series	40.00	20.00	12.00
(119)	Ump Says No - Cleveland vs. Detroit	40.00	20.00	12.00
(120)	World Series 1935 (Phil Cavarretta, Goose Goslin, Lon Warneke)	40.00	20.00	12.00

1936 National Chicle Rabbit Maranville 'How To'

Issued by National Chicle in 1936, this 20-card set was a paper issue distributed with Batter-Up Gum. Unfolded, each paper measured 3-5/8" x 6". The numbered set featured a series of baseball tips from Rabbit Maranville and are illustrated with line drawings. American Card Catalog designation was R344.

		NM	EX	VG
Complete Set (20):		700.00	350.00	210.00
Common Card:		35.00	17.50	10.00
1	How to Pitch the Out Shoot	35.00	17.50	10.00
2	How to Throw the In Shoot	35.00	17.50	10.00
3	How to Pitch the Drop	35.00	17.50	10.00
4	How to Pitch the Floater	35.00	17.50	10.00
5	How to Run Bases	35.00	17.50	10.00
6	How to Slide	35.00	17.50	10.00
7	How to Catch Flies	35.00	17.50	10.00
8	How to Field Grounders	35.00	17.50	10.00
9	How to Tag A Man Out	35.00	17.50	10.00
10	How to Cover A Base	35.00	17.50	10.00
11	How to Bat	35.00	17.50	10.00
12	How to Steal Bases	35.00	17.50	10.00
13	How to Bunt	35.00	17.50	10.00
14	How to Coach Base Runner	35.00	17.50	10.00
15	How to Catch Behind the Bat	35.00	17.50	10.00
16	How to Throw to Bases	35.00	17.50	10.00
17	How to Signal	35.00	17.50	10.00
18	How to Umpire Balls and Strikes	35.00	17.50	10.00
19	How to Umpire Bases	35.00	17.50	10.00
20	How to Lay Out a Ball Field	35.00	17.50	10.00

1898-99 National Copper Plate Co. Portraits

Besides supplying The Sporting News with the player portrait supplements issued during 1899-1900, this Grand Rapids, Mich., firm also sold nearly identical pieces in portfolios of 50 in a hard-cover, string-bound book. Approximately 10" x 13", the pictures feature the players at the turn of the century in formal portrait poses; some are in uniform, some in civilian clothes. The pictures are vignetted on a white background with the player's full name, team and year of issue printed at bottom. At lower-left on most, but not all, of the pictures is National Copper Plate's credit line. Backs have a player biographies in elaborate scrollwork frames.

	NM	EX	VG
Complete Set (50):	60,000	30,000	18,000
Common Player:	1,100	425.00	200.00

		NM	EX	VG
(1)	M.F. Amole (M.G. "Doc")	1,100	425.00	200.00
(2)	A.C. Anson	2,400	950.00	480.00
(3)	Robert Becker	1,100	425.00	200.00
(4)	Martin Bergen	1,100	425.00	200.00
(5)	James J. Collins	2,100	850.00	425.00
(6)	Joe Corbett	1,100	425.00	200.00
(7)	Louis Criger	1,100	425.00	200.00
(8)	Lave Cross	1,100	425.00	200.00
(9)	Montford Cross	1,100	425.00	200.00
(10)	Eugene DeMontreville	1,100	425.00	200.00
(11)	Charlie Dexter	1,100	425.00	200.00
(12)	P.J. Donovan	1,100	425.00	200.00
(13)	Thomas Dowd	1,100	425.00	200.00
(14)	John J. Doyle	1,100	425.00	200.00
(15)	Hugh Duffy	1,800	700.00	350.00
(16)	Frank Dwyer	1,100	425.00	200.00
(17)	Fred Ely ("Bones")	1,100	425.00	200.00
(18)	A.F. Esterquest	1,100	425.00	200.00
(19)	Wm. Ewing	1,800	700.00	350.00
(20)	Elmer Harrison Flick	1,800	700.00	350.00
(21)	Daniel Friend	1,100	425.00	200.00
(22)	Geo. F. Gilpatrick (Gillpatrick)	1,100	425.00	200.00
(23)	J.M. Goar	1,100	425.00	200.00
(24)	Mike Griffin	1,100	425.00	200.00
(25)	Clark C. Griffith	1,800	700.00	350.00
(26)	Wm. Hill	1,100	425.00	200.00
(27)	Wm. E. Hoy (Dummy)	2,100	850.00	400.00
(28)	James Hughes	1,100	425.00	200.00
(29)	William Joyce	1,100	425.00	200.00
(30)	William Keeler	1,800	700.00	350.00
(31)	Joseph J. Kelley	1,800	700.00	350.00
(32)	William Kennedy	1,100	425.00	200.00
(33)	William Lange	1,100	425.00	200.00
(34)	John J. McGraw	1,800	700.00	350.00
(35)	W.B. Mercer (George B. "Win")	1,100	425.00	200.00
(36)	Charles A. Nichols	2,100	850.00	400.00
(37)	Jerry Nops	1,100	425.00	200.00
(38)	John O'Connor	1,100	425.00	200.00
(39)	Richard Padden	1,100	425.00	200.00
(40)	Wilber Robinson (Wilbert)	1,800	700.00	350.00
(41)	William Shindle	1,000	425.00	200.00
(42)	Charles Stahl	1,000	425.00	200.00
(43)	E.P. Stein	1,100	425.00	200.00
(44)	S.L. Thompson	2,100	850.00	400.00
(45)	John Wagner	2,900	1,150	575.00
(46)	R.J. Wallace	1,800	700.00	350.00
(47)	Victor L. Willis	1,800	700.00	350.00
(48)	Parke Wilson	1,100	425.00	200.00
(49)	George Yeager	1,100	425.00	200.00
(50)	C.L. Zimmer	1,100	425.00	200.00

1913 National Game (WG5)

The patent date on the ornate red-and-white backs identify this as a 1913 issue. Fronts of the 2-1/2" x 3-1/2" cards have a black-and-white photo and a pair of baseball play scenarios used to play the card game. Corners are rounded. The set contains 43 identified player cards, a group of nine action photos in which the players are not identified and two header cards. The unnumbered cards are checklisted in alphabetical order. This set carries the ACC designation of WG5.

		NM	EX	VG
Complete Set (54):		6,000	3,000	1,800
Common Player:		55.00	30.00	20.00
Action Photo Card:		16.50	8.25	5.00
(1)	Grover Alexander	800.00	100.00	60.00
(2)	Frank Baker	150.00	50.00	30.00
(3)	Chief Bender	150.00	50.00	30.00
(4)	Bob Bescher	55.00	30.00	20.00
(5)	Joe Birmingham	55.00	30.00	20.00
(6)	Roger Bresnahan	150.00	50.00	30.00
(7)	Nixey Callahan	55.00	30.00	20.00
(8)	Frank Chance	150.00	50.00	30.00
(9)	Hal Chase	75.00	37.50	22.50
(10)	Fred Clarke	150.00	50.00	30.00
(11)	Ty Cobb	1,000	300.00	180.00
(12)	Sam Crawford	150.00	50.00	30.00
(13)	Bill Dahlen	55.00	30.00	20.00
(14)	Jake Daubert	55.00	30.00	20.00
(15)	Red Dooin	55.00	30.00	20.00
(16)	Johnny Evers	150.00	50.00	30.00
(17)	Vean Gregg	55.00	30.00	20.00
(18)	Clark Griffith	150.00	50.00	30.00
(19)	Dick Hoblitzel	55.00	30.00	20.00
(20)	Miller Huggins	150.00	50.00	30.00
(21)	Joe Jackson	3,500	800.00	480.00
(22)	Hughie Jennings	150.00	50.00	30.00
(23)	Walter Johnson	500.00	125.00	75.00
(24)	Ed Konetchy	55.00	30.00	20.00
(25)	Nap Lajoie	150.00	50.00	30.00
(26)	Connie Mack	150.00	50.00	30.00
(27)	Rube Marquard	150.00	50.00	30.00
(28)	Christy Mathewson	500.00	125.00	75.00
(29)	John McGraw	150.00	50.00	30.00
(30)	Larry McLean	55.00	30.00	20.00
(31)	Clyde Milan	55.00	30.00	20.00
(32)	Marty O'Toole	55.00	30.00	20.00
(33)	Nap Rucker	55.00	30.00	20.00
(34)	Tris Speaker	200.00	75.00	45.00
(35)	Jake Stahl	55.00	30.00	20.00
(36)	George Stallings	55.00	30.00	20.00
(37)	George Stovall	55.00	30.00	20.00
(38)	Bill Sweeney	55.00	30.00	20.00
(39)	Joe Tinker	150.00	50.00	30.00
(40)	Honus Wagner	1,000	200.00	120.00
(41)	Ed Walsh	150.00	50.00	30.00
(42)	Joe Wood	55.00	30.00	20.00
(43)	Cy Young	500.00	125.00	75.00
(---)	Rules Card	55.00	30.00	20.00
(---)	Score Card	55.00	30.00	20.00
(1A)	Batter swinging, looking forward	15.00	7.50	4.50
(2A)	Batter swinging, looking back	15.00	7.50	4.50
(3A)	Runner sliding, fielder at bag	15.00	7.50	4.50
(4A)	Runner sliding, umpire behind (Some collectors believe the player in the picture is Ty Cobb and are willing to pay a premium for this card.)	75.00	37.50	22.50
(5A)	Runner sliding, hugging base	15.00	7.50	4.50
(6A)	Sliding play at plate, umpire at left	15.00	7.50	4.50
(7A)	Sliding play at plate, umpire at right	15.00	7.50	4.50
(8A)	Play at plate, runner standing	15.00	7.50	4.50
(9A)	Runner looking backwards	15.00	7.50	4.50

1952 National Tea Labels

Another set of bread end-labels, this checklist now comprises 44 players, although there is speculation that others remain to be cataloged. The unnumbered labels measure approximately 2-3/4" x 2-11/16" and are sometimes referred to as "Red Borders" because of their wide, red margins. The player's name and team are printed alongside his photo, and the slogan "Eat More Bread for Health" also appears on some labels.

		NM	EX	VG
Complete Set (44):		10,000	5,000	3,000
Common Player:		200.00	100.00	60.00
(1)	Gene Bearden	200.00	100.00	60.00
(2)	Yogi Berra	450.00	225.00	135.00
(3)	Lou Brissie	200.00	100.00	60.00
(4)	Sam Chapman	200.00	100.00	60.00
(5)	Chuck Diering	200.00	100.00	60.00
(6)	Dom DiMaggio	250.00	125.00	75.00
(7)	Bruce Edwards	200.00	100.00	60.00
(8)	Del Ennis	200.00	100.00	60.00
(9)	Ferris Fain	200.00	100.00	60.00
(10)	Bob Feller	375.00	185.00	110.00
(11)	Howie Fox	200.00	100.00	60.00
(12)	Sid Gordon	200.00	100.00	60.00
(13)	John Groth	200.00	100.00	60.00
(14)	Granny Hamner	200.00	100.00	60.00
(15)	Jim Hegan	200.00	100.00	60.00
(16)	Sheldon Jones	200.00	100.00	60.00
(17)	Howie Judson	200.00	100.00	60.00
(18)	Sherman Lollar	200.00	100.00	60.00
(19)	Clarence Marshall	200.00	100.00	60.00
(20)	Don Mueller	200.00	100.00	60.00
(21)	Danny Murtaugh	200.00	100.00	60.00
(22)	Dave Philley	200.00	100.00	60.00
(23)	Jerry Priddy	200.00	100.00	60.00
(24)	Bill Rigney	200.00	100.00	60.00
(25)	Robin Roberts	350.00	175.00	100.00
(26)	Eddie Robinson	200.00	100.00	60.00
(27)	Preacher Roe	225.00	110.00	65.00
(28)	Stan Rojek	200.00	100.00	60.00
(29)	Al Rosen	225.00	110.00	65.00
(30)	Bob Rush	200.00	100.00	60.00
(31)	Hank Sauer	200.00	100.00	60.00
(32)	Johnny Schmitz	200.00	100.00	60.00
(33)	Enos Slaughter	350.00	175.00	100.00
(34)	Duke Snider	400.00	200.00	120.00
(35)	Warren Spahn	375.00	185.00	110.00
(36)	Gerry Staley	200.00	100.00	60.00
(37)	Virgil Stallcup	200.00	100.00	60.00
(38)	George Stirnweiss	200.00	100.00	60.00
(39)	Earl Torgeson	200.00	100.00	60.00
(40)	Dizzy Trout	200.00	100.00	60.00
(41)	Mickey Vernon	200.00	100.00	60.00
(42)	Wally Westlake	200.00	100.00	60.00
(43)	Johnny Wyrostek	200.00	100.00	60.00
(44)	Eddie Yost	200.00	100.00	60.00

1922 Neilson's Chocolate Type 1 (V61)

J.T. ZACHARY
PITCHER, WASHINGTON AMERICANS

This set is closely related to the popular 1922 American Caramels (E120). The 120-card set was issued in Canada by Neilson's Chocolate Bars and carries the American Card Catalog designation V61. The front of the approximately 2" x 3-1/2" black-and-white cards has oval posed action photos with a decorative border. In the bottom border is the player name, position and team. Backs contain an ad for Neilson's Chocolates. Two types of cards exist. Type 1 is printed on heavy paper (similar to E120), has a card number in the lower-left corner and features Old English typography of the sponsor's name on back. Type 2 is printed on cardboard, has no card numbers and has no Old English typography on back.

		NM	EX	VG
	Complete Set (120):	27,500	11,000	5,500
	Common Player:	115.00	45.00	22.50
1	George Burns	115.00	45.00	22.50
2	John Tobin	115.00	45.00	22.50
3	J.T. Zachary	115.00	45.00	22.50
4	"Bullet" Joe Bush	115.00	45.00	22.50
5	Lu Blue	115.00	45.00	22.50
6	Clarence (Tillie) Walker	115.00	45.00	22.50
7	Carl Mays	115.00	45.00	22.50
8	Leon Goslin	300.00	120.00	60.00
9	Ed Rommel	115.00	45.00	22.50
10	Charles Robertson	115.00	45.00	22.50
11	Ralph (Cy) Perkins	115.00	45.00	22.50
12	Joe Sewell	300.00	120.00	60.00
13	Harry Hooper	300.00	120.00	60.00
14	Urban (Red) Faber	300.00	120.00	60.00
15	Bib Falk (Bibb)	115.00	45.00	22.50
16	George Uhle	115.00	45.00	22.50
17	Emory Rigney	115.00	45.00	22.50
18	George Dauss	115.00	45.00	22.50
19	Herman Pillette	115.00	45.00	22.50
20	Wallie Schang	115.00	45.00	22.50
21	Lawrence Woodall	115.00	45.00	22.50
22	Steve O'Neill	115.00	45.00	22.50
23	Edmund (Bing) Miller	115.00	45.00	22.50
24	Sylvester Johnson	115.00	45.00	22.50
25	Henry Severeid	115.00	45.00	22.50
26	Dave Danforth	115.00	45.00	22.50
27	Harry Heilmann	300.00	120.00	60.00
28	Bert Cole	115.00	45.00	22.50
29	Eddie Collins	300.00	120.00	60.00
30	Ty Cobb	3,500	1,400	700.00
31	Bill Wambsganss	115.00	45.00	22.50
32	George Sisler	300.00	120.00	60.00
33	Bob Veach	115.00	45.00	22.50
34	Earl Sheely	115.00	45.00	22.50
35	T.P. (Pat) Collins	115.00	45.00	22.50
36	Frank (Dixie) Davis	115.00	45.00	22.50
37	Babe Ruth	6,000	2,400	1,200
38	Bryan Harris	115.00	45.00	22.50
39	Bob Shawkey	115.00	45.00	22.50
40	Urban Shocker	115.00	45.00	22.50
41	Martin McManus	115.00	45.00	22.50
42	Clark Pittenger	115.00	45.00	22.50
43	"Deacon" Sam Jones	115.00	45.00	22.50
44	Waite Hoyt	300.00	120.00	60.00
45	Johnny Mostil	115.00	45.00	22.50
46	Mike Menosky	115.00	45.00	22.50
47	Walter Johnson	600.00	240.00	120.00
48	Wallie Pipp (Wally)	115.00	45.00	22.50
49	Walter Gerber	115.00	45.00	22.50
50	Ed Gharrity	115.00	45.00	22.50
51	Frank Ellerbe	115.00	45.00	22.50
52	Kenneth Williams	115.00	45.00	22.50
53	Joe Hauser	175.00	70.00	35.00
54	Carson Bigbee	115.00	45.00	22.50
55	Emil (Irish) Meusel	115.00	45.00	22.50
56	Milton Stock	115.00	45.00	22.50
57	Wilbur Cooper	115.00	45.00	22.50
58	Tom Griffith	115.00	45.00	22.50
59	Walter (Butch) Henline	115.00	45.00	22.50
60	Gene (Bubbles) Hargrave	115.00	45.00	22.50
61	Russell Wrightstone	115.00	45.00	22.50
62	Frank Frisch	300.00	120.00	60.00
63	Frank Parkinson	115.00	45.00	22.50
64	Walter (Dutch) Reuther (Ruether)	115.00	45.00	22.50
65	Bill Doak	115.00	45.00	22.50
66	Marty Callaghan	115.00	45.00	22.50
67	Sammy Bohne	175.00	70.00	35.00
68	Earl Hamilton	115.00	45.00	22.50
69	Grover C. Alexander	325.00	130.00	65.00
70	George Burns	115.00	45.00	22.50
71	Max Carey	300.00	120.00	60.00
72	Adolfo Luque	145.00	58.00	29.00
73	Dave (Beauty) Bancroft	300.00	120.00	60.00
74	Vic Aldridge	115.00	45.00	22.50
75	Jack Smith	115.00	45.00	22.50
76	Bob O'Farrell	115.00	45.00	22.50
77	Pete Donohue	115.00	45.00	22.50
78	Ralph Pinelli	115.00	45.00	22.50
79	Eddie Roush	300.00	120.00	60.00
80	Norman Boeckel	115.00	45.00	22.50
81	Rogers Hornsby	400.00	160.00	80.00
82	George Toporcer	115.00	45.00	22.50
83	Ivy Wingo	115.00	45.00	22.50
84	Virgil Cheeves	115.00	45.00	22.50
85	Vern Clemons	115.00	45.00	22.50
86	Lawrence (Hack) Miller	115.00	45.00	22.50
87	Johnny Kelleher	115.00	45.00	22.50
88	Heinie Groh	115.00	45.00	22.50
89	Burleigh Grimes	300.00	120.00	60.00
90	"Rabbit" Maranville	300.00	120.00	60.00
91	Charles (Babe) Adams	115.00	45.00	22.50
92	Lee King	115.00	45.00	22.50
93	Art Nehf	115.00	45.00	22.50
94	Frank Snyder	115.00	45.00	22.50
95	Raymond Powell	115.00	45.00	22.50
96	Wilbur Hubbell	115.00	45.00	22.50
97	Leon Cadore	115.00	45.00	22.50
98	Joe Oeschger	115.00	45.00	22.50
99	Jake Daubert	115.00	45.00	22.50
100	Will Sherdel	115.00	45.00	22.50
101	Hank DeBerry	115.00	45.00	22.50
102	Johnny Lavan	115.00	45.00	22.50
103	Jesse Haines	300.00	120.00	60.00
104	Joe (Goldie) Rapp	115.00	45.00	22.50
105	Oscar Ray Grimes	115.00	45.00	22.50
106	Ross Young (Youngs)	300.00	120.00	60.00
107	Art Fletcher	115.00	45.00	22.50
108	Clyde Barnhart	115.00	45.00	22.50
109	Louis (Pat) Duncan	115.00	45.00	22.50
110	Charlie Hollocher	115.00	45.00	22.50
111	Horace Ford	115.00	45.00	22.50
112	Bill Cunningham	115.00	45.00	22.50
113	Walter Schmidt	115.00	45.00	22.50
114	Joe Schultz	115.00	45.00	22.50
115	John Morrison	115.00	45.00	22.50
116	Jimmy Caveney	115.00	45.00	22.50
117	Zach Wheat	300.00	120.00	60.00
118	Fred (Cy) Williams	115.00	45.00	22.50
119	George Kelly	300.00	120.00	60.00
120	Jimmy Ring	115.00	45.00	22.50

1922 Neilson's Chocolate Type 2 (V61)

FRANK (DIXIE) DAVIS
PITCHER, ST. LOUIS AMERICANS

This set is closely related to the popular 1922 American Caramels (E120). The 120-card set was issued in Canada by Neilson's Chocolate Bars and carries the American Card Catalog designation V61. The front of the approximately 2" x 3-1/2" black-and-white cards has oval posed action photos with a decorative border. In the bottom border is the player name, position and team. Backs contain an ad for Neilson's Chocolates. Two types of cards exist. Type 1 is printed on heavy paper (similar to E120), has a card number in the lower-left corner and features Old English typography of the sponsor's name on back. Type 2 is printed on cardboard, has no card numbers and has no Old English typography on back.

		NM	EX	VG
	Complete Set (120):	42,500	17,000	8,500
	Common Player:	200.00	85.00	40.00
(1)	Charles (Babe) Adams	200.00	85.00	40.00
(2)	Vic Aldridge	200.00	85.00	40.00
(3)	Grover C. Alexander	750.00	300.00	150.00
(4)	Dave (Beauty) Bancroft	450.00	180.00	90.00
(5)	Clyde Barnhart	200.00	85.00	40.00
(6)	Carson Bigbee	200.00	85.00	40.00
(7)	Lu Blue	200.00	85.00	40.00
(8)	Norman Boeckel	200.00	85.00	40.00
(9)	Sammy Bohne	250.00	100.00	50.00
(10)	George Burns (Boston)	200.00	85.00	40.00
(11)	George Burns (Cincinnati)	200.00	85.00	40.00
(12)	""Bullet" Joe Bush	200.00	85.00	40.00
(13)	Leon Cadore	200.00	85.00	40.00
(14)	Marty Callaghan	200.00	85.00	40.00
(15)	Max Carey	450.00	180.00	90.00
(16)	Jimmy Caveney	200.00	85.00	40.00
(17)	Virgil Cheeves	200.00	85.00	40.00
(18)	Vern Clemons	200.00	85.00	40.00
(19)	Ty Cobb	5,500	2,200	1,100
(20)	Bert Cole	200.00	85.00	40.00
(21)	Eddie Collins	450.00	180.00	90.00
(22)	T.P. (Pat) Collins	200.00	85.00	40.00
(23)	Wilbur Cooper	200.00	85.00	40.00
(24)	Bill Cunningham	200.00	85.00	40.00
(25)	Dave Danforth	200.00	85.00	40.00
(26)	Jake Daubert	200.00	85.00	40.00
(27)	George Dauss	200.00	85.00	40.00
(28)	Frank (Dixie) Davis	200.00	85.00	40.00
(29)	Hank DeBerry	200.00	85.00	40.00
(30)	Bill Doak	200.00	85.00	40.00
(31)	Pete Donohue	200.00	85.00	40.00
(32)	Louis (Pat) Duncan	200.00	85.00	40.00
(33)	Frank Ellerbe	200.00	85.00	40.00
(34)	Urban (Red) Faber	450.00	180.00	90.00
(35)	Bib (Bibb) Falk	200.00	85.00	40.00
(36)	Art Fletcher	200.00	85.00	40.00
(37)	Horace Ford	200.00	85.00	40.00
(38)	Frank Frisch	450.00	180.00	90.00
(39)	Walter Gerber	200.00	85.00	40.00
(40)	Ed Gharrity	200.00	85.00	40.00
(41)	Leon Goslin	450.00	180.00	90.00
(42)	Tom Griffith	200.00	85.00	40.00
(43)	Burleigh Grimes	450.00	180.00	90.00
(44)	Oscar Ray Grimes	200.00	85.00	40.00
(45)	Heinie Groh	200.00	85.00	40.00
(46)	Jesse Haines	450.00	180.00	90.00
(47)	Earl Hamilton	200.00	85.00	40.00
(48)	Gene (Bubbles) Hargrave	200.00	85.00	40.00
(49)	Bryan Harris	200.00	85.00	40.00
(50)	Joe Hauser	350.00	140.00	70.00
(51)	Harry Heilmann	450.00	180.00	90.00
(52)	Walter (Butch) Henline	200.00	85.00	40.00
(53)	Charlie Hollocher	200.00	85.00	40.00
(54)	Harry Hooper	450.00	180.00	90.00
(55)	Rogers Hornsby	550.00	220.00	110.00
(56)	Waite Hoyt	450.00	180.00	90.00
(57)	Wilbert Hubbell	200.00	85.00	40.00
(58)	Sylvester Johnson	200.00	85.00	40.00
(59)	Walter Johnson	800.00	320.00	160.00
(60)	"Deacon" Sam Jones	200.00	85.00	40.00
(61)	Johnny Kelleher	200.00	85.00	40.00
(62)	George Kelly	450.00	180.00	90.00
(63)	Lee King	200.00	85.00	40.00
(64)	Johnny Lavan	200.00	85.00	40.00
(65)	Adolfo Luque	250.00	100.00	50.00
(66)	"Rabbit" Maranville	450.00	180.00	90.00
(67)	Carl Mays	200.00	85.00	40.00
(68)	Martin McManus	200.00	85.00	40.00
(69)	Mike Menosky	200.00	85.00	40.00
(70)	Emil (Irish) Meusel	200.00	85.00	40.00
(71)	Edmund (Bing) Miller	200.00	85.00	40.00
(72)	Lawrence (Hack) Miller	200.00	85.00	40.00
(73)	John Morrison	200.00	85.00	40.00
(74)	Johnny Mostil	200.00	85.00	40.00
(75)	Art Nehf	200.00	85.00	40.00
(76)	Joe Oeschger	200.00	85.00	40.00
(77)	Bob O'Farrell	200.00	85.00	40.00
(78)	Steve O'Neill	200.00	85.00	40.00
(79)	Frank Parkinson	200.00	85.00	40.00
(80)	Ralph (Cy) Perkins	200.00	85.00	40.00
(81)	Herman Pillette	200.00	85.00	40.00
(82)	Ralph Pinelli	200.00	85.00	40.00
(83)	Wallie (Wally) Pipp	200.00	85.00	40.00
(84)	Clark Pittinger	200.00	85.00	40.00
(85)	Raymond Powell	200.00	85.00	40.00
(86)	Joe (Goldie) Rapp	200.00	85.00	40.00
(87)	Walter (Dutch) Reuther	200.00	85.00	40.00
(88)	Emory Rigney	200.00	85.00	40.00
(89)	Jimmy Ring	200.00	85.00	40.00
(90)	Charles Robertson	200.00	85.00	40.00
(91)	Ed Rommel	200.00	85.00	40.00
(92)	Eddie Roush	450.00	180.00	90.00
(93)	Babe Ruth	7,500	3,000	1,500
(94)	Wallie (Wally) Schang	200.00	85.00	40.00
(95)	Walter Schmidt	200.00	85.00	40.00
(96)	Joe Schultz	200.00	85.00	40.00
(97)	Hank Severeid	200.00	85.00	40.00
(98)	Joe Sewell	450.00	180.00	90.00
(99)	Bob Shawkey	200.00	85.00	40.00
(100)	Earl Sheely	200.00	85.00	40.00
(101)	Will Sherdel	200.00	85.00	40.00
(102)	Urban Shocker	200.00	85.00	40.00
(103)	George Sisler	450.00	180.00	90.00
(104)	Jack Smith	200.00	85.00	40.00
(105)	Frank Snyder	200.00	85.00	40.00
(106)	Milton Stock	200.00	85.00	40.00
(107)	John Tobin	200.00	85.00	40.00
(108)	George Torporcer	200.00	85.00	40.00
(109)	George Uhle	200.00	85.00	40.00
(110)	Bob Veach	200.00	85.00	40.00
(111)	Clarence (Tillie) Walker	200.00	85.00	40.00
(112)	Bill Wambsganss	200.00	85.00	40.00
(113)	Zach Wheat	450.00	180.00	90.00
(114)	Fred (Cy) Williams	200.00	85.00	40.00
(115)	Kenneth Williams	200.00	85.00	40.00
(116)	Ivy Wingo	200.00	85.00	40.00
(117)	Lawrence Woodall	200.00	85.00	40.00
(118)	Russell Wrightstone	200.00	85.00	40.00
(119)	Ross Young (Youngs)	450.00	180.00	90.00
(120)	J.T. Zachary	200.00	85.00	40.00

1923 "Neilson's Chocolates"

This issue, purporting to come from the Canadian candy maker which had produced a 1922 set, was first reported in 1996. The cards appear to be genuine W572 strip cards which have had a Neilson's ad overprinted on the back many years later in an apparent effort to defraud collectors. These altered W572s would have to be significantly downgraded to adjust for the defacing. It can be expected that any card that appears in W572 can be found with the Neilson's back, but the "discovery" contained only 47 different players.

(See W572 for checklist.)

1959 Neptune Sardines Jimmy Piersall

Like the earlier advertising postcards he did for various Cain's food products, this 3-1/2" x 5-1/2" black-and-white postcard carries the endorsement of the popular Indians outfielder for Neptune brand sardines. The front has a borderless photo of the player in a batting pose with a facsimile autograph at top. The back has standard postcard indicia along with the ad message and a product picture.

	NM	EX	VG
Jimmy Piersall	50.00	25.00	15.00

1976-81 New England Sports Collectors

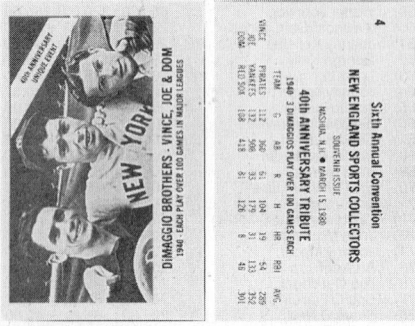

From the period 1976-81, the New England Sports Collectors club issued a series of postcard-size (3-1/2" x 5-1/4") black-and-white card promoting their annual shows in Nashua, N.H. No card was issued in 1978.

		NM	EX	VG
Complete Set (5):		30.00	15.00	9.00
Common Player:		6.00	3.00	1.75
1	Joe DiMaggio (1976)	8.00	4.00	2.50
2	Jackie Robinson (1977)	6.00	3.00	1.75
3	Ted Williams (1979)	7.00	3.50	2.00
4	Vince DiMaggio, Joe DiMaggio, Dom DiMaggio (1980)	6.00	3.00	1.75
5	Mickey Mantle (1981)	9.00	4.50	2.75

1895 Newsboy Cabinets (N566)

Issued in the 1890s by the National Tobacco Works, this massive cabinet card set was distributed as a premium with the Newsboy tobacco brand. Although the set contained over 500 popular actresses, athletes, politicians and other celebrities of the day, only about a dozen cards of baseball players have been found. The cards measure 4-1/4" x 6-1/2" and feature sepia-toned photographs mounted on a backing that usually has "Newsboy New York" printed at bottom. Each portrait photograph is numbered and a few of the photos are round. The ballplayers in the set are mostly members of the 1894 New York Giants with a couple of Brooklyn players. There are two known poses of John Ward. Cards have been seen with advertising on the back for Keystone cigars and Red Indian tobacco.

		NM	EX	VG
Common Player:		6,000	3,000	1,800
174	W.H. Murphy	6,000	3,000	1,800
175	Amos Rusie	15,000	4,500	2,750
176	Michael Tiernan	6,000	3,000	1,800
177	E.D. Burke	6,000	3,000	1,800
178	J.J. Doyle	6,000	3,000	1,800
179	W.B. Fuller	6,000	3,000	1,800
180	George Van Haltren	6,000	3,000	1,800
181	Dave Foutz	6,000	3,000	2,000
182	Jouett Meekin	6,000	3,000	1,800
183	Michael Griffin	6,000	3,000	1,800

201	W.H. (Dad) Clark (Clarke)	6,000	3,000	1,800
202	Parke Wilson	6,000	3,000	1,800
586	John Ward (Arms folded.)	9,250	4,625	2,775
587	John Ward (Bat at side.)	8,000	4,000	2,400

1886 New York Baseball Club (H812)

This rare 19th Century baseball issue can be classified under the general category of "trade" cards, a popular advertising vehicle of the period. The cards measure 3" x 4-3/4" and feature blue line-drawing portraits of members of the "New York Base Ball Club," which is printed along the top. As was common with this type of trade card, the bottom was left blank to accomodate various messages. The known examples of this set carry ads for local tobacco merchants and other businesses. The portraits are all based on the photographs used in the 1886 Old Judge set. The cards, which have been assigned an ACC designation of H812, are printed on thin paper rather than cardboard.

		NM	EX	VG
Complete Set (8):		84,000	37,200	20,400
Common Player:		7,200	3,200	1,450
(1)	T. Dealsey	7,200	3,200	1,450
(2)	M. Dorgan	7,200	3,200	1,450
(3)	T. Esterbrook	7,200	3,200	1,450
(4)	W. Ewing	16,200	8,100	4,800
(5)	J. Gerhardt	7,200	3,200	1,450
(6)	J. O'Rourke	16,200	8,100	4,800
(7)	D. Richardson	7,200	3,200	1,450
(8)	M. Welch	16,200	8,100	4,800

1969 N.Y. Boy Scouts

Cards featuring N.Y. Mets and Yankees players were used as a recruitment incentive in 1969. Cards are 2-1/2" x 3-1/2" and printed in black-and-white on thin cardboard. It is unknown, but likely, that players other than those checklisted here were also issued.

		NM	EX	VG
Common Player:		140.00	70.00	40.00
(1)	Tommy Agee	175.00	85.00	50.00
(2)	Bud Harrelson	175.00	85.00	50.00
(3)	Cleon Jones	175.00	85.00	50.00
(4)	Bobby Murcer	260.00	130.00	75.00
(5)	Art Shamsky	140.00	70.00	40.00
(6)	Tom Seaver	700.00	350.00	210.00
(7)	Mel Stottlemyre	260.00	130.00	75.00
(8)	Ron Swoboda	175.00	85.00	50.00

1879-80 N.Y. Clipper Woodcuts

The N.Y. Clipper was a weekly newspaper devoted to theater and sports (primarily baseball) coverage in New York City between 1853-1923. Like many contemporary papers, the Clipper featured woodcut engravings in its pages in a time before photographic reproduction of pictures was feasible. Between April 1879, and November 1880, the paper printed a series of baseball player portraits. The early pieces were titled "The Clipper Prize Winners." and numbered. All of the woodcuts are about 4-1/2" x 5-3/4" in size featuring portraits within ornate frames with identification and biographical details below. Collectors prefer the woodcuts to be neatly trimmed from the newspaper page, with the biography at bottom intact.

Because of the rarity of surviving examples, catalog values are undetermined. Many of these early stars of the game appear on no other contemprary cards or memorabilia issues.

1879
1	M.C. Dorgan (4/12)
2	H.F. McCormick (4/19)
3	Stephen A. Libby (4/26)
4	Roscoe C. Barnes (5/3)
5	David W. Force (5/10)
6	Herman Doescher (Dosher) (5/17)
7a	Joseph Hornung (5/24)
7b	William H. McGunnigle (5/31)
9	Harding Richardson (6/7)
(10)	James L. White (7/14)
(11)	Levi S. Meyerle (6/21)
(12)	Joe Start (6/28)
(13)	T.H. Mumam (Murnane) (7/5)
(14)	Thomas York (7/12)
(15)	Fred Dunlap (7/19)
(16)	A.J. Leonard (7/26)
(17)	J. Lee Richmond (8/2)
(18)	Charles N. Snyder (8/9)
(19)	John Cassidy (8/16)
(20)	Charles Fulmer (8/23)
(21)	Thomas Poorman (8/30)
(22)	John Ward (9/6)
(23)	Larry Corcoran (9/13)
(24)	Douglas Allison (9/20)
(25)	John J. Farrow (9/27)
(26)	E.N. Williamson (10/4)
(27)	George Wright (10/11)
(28)	John J. Burdock (10/18)
(29)	James O'Rourke (10/25)
(30)	Philip Baker (11/1)
(31)	Samuel W. Trott (11/8)
(32)	John Lynch (11/15)
(33)	A.G. Spalding (11/22)
(34)	John C. Chapman (11/29)
(35)	Paul A. Hines (12/6)
(36)	Frank C. Bancroft (12/13)
(37)	John T. O'Conner (12/20)
(38)	Andrew J. Piercy (12/27)

1880
(39)	Harold M. McClure (1/3)
(40)	J.H. Gifford (1/24)
(41)	Sam Wright (5/15)
(42)	T.J. Keefe (5/22)
(43)	M.J. Kelly (5/29)
(44)	John Troy (6/5)
(45)	Joe Quest (6/12)
(46)	Alonzo Knight (6/19)
(47)	Charles E. Mason (6/26)
(48)	F.E. Goldsmith (7/3)
(49)	R.E. McKelvy (7/10)
(50)	Wm. McLean (Umpire)(7/17)
(51)	C.A. McVey (7/24)
(52)	John Manning (7/31)
(53)	Harry D. Stovey (8/7)
(54)	George A. Wood (8/14)
(55)	Robert T. Mathews (8/21)
(56)	D. Brouthers (8/28)
(57)	C.M. Smith (9/4)
(58)	James L. Clinton (9/11)
(59)	A.J. Bushong (9/18)
(60)	William J. Sweeney (9/25)
(61)	Roger Connor (10/2)
(62)	William Hawes (10/9)
(63)	Frank S. Flint (10/16)
(64)	William L. Haug (10/23)
(65)	M. Welch (10/30)
(66)	Aaron B. Clapp (11/6)
(67)	John J. Smith (11/13)
(68)	George Creamer (11/20)

1905 N.Y. Giants Scorecard Postcard

Two versions, black-and-white and color, of this standard size (about 5-1/2" x 3-1/2") postcard were apparently available for several years as it is copyrighted 1905 but postally used examples from years later are often seen. The card has a black background with large cut-out letters "GIANTS" at center featuring action poses of six players. A grid at bottom allows by-inning scores of a game to be posted before mailing. The undivided back has an embellished double-ruled stamp box and a large ornate "Post Card" at top-center.

	NM	EX	VG
Black-and-White:	300.00	150.00	90.00
Color:	400.00	200.00	125.00

Frank Bowerman, Red Ames, Sam Mertes, Christy Mathewson, Iron Man McGinnity, Luther Taylor

1932 N.Y. Giants Schedule Postcards

These postcard-size (3-1/2" x 5-1/2") black-and-white cards have an action pose on front with the player's identification and previous season's stats. At bottom is information

CARL HUBBELL
28 years   Bats Right and Left   Throws Left
1931 Record Won 14 Lost 12 Earned Runs 2.65
Hubbell played in 36 games in 1931 season

about ladies' days, directions to the Polo Grounds and an offer to receive a free picture of a favorite player. The divided back has the team's 1932 schedule at left and space for addressing at right. There is also a credit line to Minden Press. The Carl Hubbell card is far more common than all others and can be found on either a thick or thin card stock that is unlike the stock on which the other players are found.

	NM	EX	VG
Common Player:	300.00	150.00	90.00
(1) Ethan Allen	300.00	150.00	90.00
(2) Herman Bell	300.00	150.00	90.00
(3) Hugh Critz	300.00	150.00	90.00
(4) Freddie Fitzsimmons	300.00	150.00	90.00
(5) Chick Fullis	300.00	150.00	90.00
(6) Sam Gibson	300.00	150.00	90.00
(7) Fran Healey (Healy)	300.00	150.00	90.00
(8) Frank Hogan	300.00	150.00	90.00
(9a) Carl Hubbell (Thin stock.)	100.00	50.00	30.00
(9b) Carl Hubbell (Thick stock.)	450.00	225.00	135.00
(10) Travis Jackson	450.00	225.00	135.00
(11) Len Koenecke	300.00	150.00	90.00
(12) Sam Leslie	300.00	150.00	90.00
(13) Freddy Lindstrom	450.00	225.00	135.00
(14) Dolf Luque	325.00	160.00	97.00
(15) Clarence Mitchell	300.00	150.00	90.00
(16) Jim Mooney	300.00	150.00	90.00
(17) Bob O'Farrell	300.00	150.00	90.00
(18) Mel Ott	600.00	300.00	180.00
(19) Roy Parmelee	300.00	150.00	90.00
(20) Bill Terry	450.00	225.00	135.00
(21) Johnny Vergez	300.00	150.00	90.00
(22) Bill Walker	300.00	150.00	90.00

1948 N.Y. Giants Photo Pack

This set of player photos was sold at Polo Grounds souvenir stands. Pictures have player portraits in a 6-1/2" x 9" format. The black-and-white photos are blank-backed and have facsimile autographs printed near the bottom on front. A white border surrounds the front. The unnumbered photos are checklisted here in alphabetical order. It is possible the specific lineup in the packs changed over the course of the season to reflect roster moves.

	NM	EX	VG
Complete Set (27):	200.00	100.00	60.00
Common Player:	5.00	2.50	1.50
(1) Jack Conway	5.00	2.50	1.50
(2) Walker Cooper	5.00	2.50	1.50
(3) Leo Durocher	9.00	4.50	2.75
(4) Sid Gordon	7.50	3.75	2.25
(5) Andy Hansen	5.00	2.50	1.50
(6) Clint Hartung	5.00	2.50	1.50
(7) Larry Jansen	5.00	2.50	1.50
(8) Sheldon Jones	5.00	2.50	1.50
(9) Monte Kennedy	5.00	2.50	1.50
(10) Buddy Kerr	5.00	2.50	1.50
(11) Dave Koslo	5.00	2.50	1.50
(12) Thornton Lee	5.00	2.50	1.50
(13) Mickey Livingston	5.00	2.50	1.50
(14) Whitey Lockman	5.00	2.50	1.50
(15) Jack Lohrke	5.00	2.50	1.50
(16) Willard Marshall	5.00	2.50	1.50
(17) Johnnie McCarthy	5.00	2.50	1.50
(18) Earl McGowan	7.50	3.75	2.25
(19) Johnny Mize	12.50	6.25	3.75
(20) Bobo Newsom	5.00	2.50	1.50
(21) Mel Ott	25.00	12.50	7.50
(22) Ray Poat	5.00	2.50	1.50
(23) Bobby Rhawn	5.00	2.50	1.50
(24) Bill Rigney	5.00	2.50	1.50
(25) Bobby Thomson	10.00	5.00	3.00

(26) Ken Trinkle	5.00	2.50	1.50
(27) Wesley N. Westrum	5.00	2.50	1.50

1949 N.Y. Giants Photo Pack

This set of player photos was sold at Polo Grounds souvenir stands. Pictures have player portraits in a 6-1/2" x 9" format. The black-and-white photos are blank-backed and have facsimile autographs printed near the bottom on front. A white border surrounds the front. The unnumbered photos are checklisted here in alphabetical order.

	NM	EX	VG
Complete Set (25):	200.00	100.00	60.00
Common Player:	5.00	2.50	1.50
(1) Hank Behrman	5.00	2.50	1.50
(2) Walker Cooper	5.00	2.50	1.50
(3) Leo Durocher	9.00	4.50	2.75
(4) Fred Fitzsimmons	5.00	2.50	1.50
(5) Frank Frisch	12.50	6.25	3.75
(6) Augie Galan	5.00	2.50	1.50
(7) Sid Gordon	7.50	3.75	2.25
(8) Bert Haas	5.00	2.50	1.50
(9) Andy Hansen	5.00	2.50	1.50
(10) Clint Hartung	5.00	2.50	1.50
(11) Bob Hofman	5.00	2.50	1.50
(12) Larry Jansen	5.00	2.50	1.50
(13) Sheldon Jones	5.00	2.50	1.50
(14) Monte Kennedy	5.00	2.50	1.50
(15) Buddy Kerr	5.00	2.50	1.50
(16) Dave Koslo	5.00	2.50	1.50
(17) Mickey Livingston	5.00	2.50	1.50
(18) Whitey Lockman	5.00	2.50	1.50
(19) Willard Marshall	5.00	2.50	1.50
(20) Johnny Mize	12.50	6.25	3.75
(21) Don Mueller	5.00	2.50	1.50
(22) Ray Poat	5.00	2.50	1.50
(23) Bobby Rhawn	5.00	2.50	1.50
(24) Bill Rigney	5.00	2.50	1.50
(25) Bobby Thomson	10.00	5.00	3.00

1954 N.Y. Journal-American

DODGERS AT HOME
1954

DUKE SNIDER
BROOKLYN DODGERS

SAVE THIS CARD!
It may be worth up to $200 cash
N.Y. JOURNAL-AMERICAN
OFFERS
$1,000.00 CASH DAILY FOR
LUCKY BASEBALL CARDS
Watch the Journal-American
Daily and Sunday for Winning
Players and Numbers
Copr. 1954, Hearst Con. Pub. Inc.

215340

Issued during the Golden Age of baseball in New York City, this 59-card set features only players from the Giants, Yankees and Dodgers. The 2" x 4" cards were issued at newsstands with the purchase of the now-extinct newspaper. Card fronts have promotional copy and a contest serial number in addition to the player's name. Cards are printed in black-and-white on colored stock and unnumbered. Backs feature team schedules. It has been theorized that a 60th card should exist, probably a Brooklyn Dodger. Each card can be found with the word "OFFERS" printed in either red or black, depending on the contest number at bottom. Numbers beginning with "0" have the word in black. Numbers 100000-150000 have the word in red or black, and numbers over 150000 have the word in red.

	NM	EX	VG
Complete Set (59):	4,750	2,400	1,400
Common Player:	20.00	10.00	6.00
(1) Johnny Antonelli	40.00	20.00	12.00
(2) Hank Bauer	45.00	22.50	13.50
(3) Yogi Berra	125.00	65.00	35.00
(4) Joe Black	65.00	32.50	20.00
(5) Harry Byrd	40.00	20.00	12.00
(6) Roy Campanella	200.00	100.00	60.00

(7) Andy Carey	40.00	20.00	12.00
(8) Jerry Coleman	40.00	20.00	12.00
(9) Joe Collins	40.00	20.00	12.00
(10) Billy Cox	65.00	32.50	20.00
(11) Al Dark	40.00	20.00	12.00
(12) Carl Erskine	65.00	32.50	20.00
(13) Whitey Ford	125.00	65.00	35.00
(14) Carl Furillo	90.00	45.00	27.50
(15) Junior Gilliam	90.00	45.00	27.50
(16) Ruben Gomez	40.00	20.00	12.00
(17) Marv Grissom	40.00	20.00	12.00
(18) Jim Hearn	40.00	20.00	12.00
(19) Gil Hodges	125.00	65.00	35.00
(20) Bobby Hofman	40.00	20.00	12.00
(21) Jim Hughes	65.00	32.50	20.00
(22) Monte Irvin	90.00	45.00	27.50
(23) Larry Jansen	40.00	20.00	12.00
(24) Ray Katt	40.00	20.00	12.00
(25) Steve Kraly	40.00	20.00	12.00
(26) Bob Kuzava	40.00	20.00	12.00
(27) Clem Labine	65.00	32.50	20.00
(28) Frank Leja	40.00	20.00	12.00
(29) Don Liddle	40.00	20.00	12.00
(30) Whitey Lockman	40.00	20.00	12.00
(31) Billy Loes	65.00	32.50	20.00
(32) Eddie Lopat	40.00	20.00	12.00
(33) Sal Maglie	40.00	20.00	12.00
(34) Mickey Mantle	650.00	325.00	200.00
(35) Willie Mays	375.00	185.00	110.00
(36) Gil McDougald	45.00	22.50	13.50
(37) Russ Meyer	65.00	32.50	20.00
(38) Bill Miller	40.00	20.00	12.00
(39) Tom Morgan	40.00	20.00	12.00
(40) Don Mueller	40.00	20.00	12.00
(41) Don Newcombe	75.00	37.50	22.50
(42) Irv Noren	40.00	20.00	12.00
(43) Erv Palica	65.00	32.50	20.00
(44) Pee Wee Reese	130.00	65.00	40.00
(45) Allie Reynolds	40.00	20.00	12.00
(46) Dusty Rhodes	40.00	20.00	12.00
(47) Phil Rizzuto	125.00	65.00	35.00
(48) Ed Robinson	40.00	20.00	12.00
(49) Jackie Robinson	235.00	115.00	70.00
(50) Preacher Roe	65.00	32.50	20.00
(51) George Shuba	65.00	32.50	20.00
(52) Duke Snider	200.00	100.00	60.00
(53) Hank Thompson	40.00	20.00	12.00
(54) Wes Westrum	40.00	20.00	12.00
(55) Hoyt Wilhelm	110.00	55.00	32.50
(56) Davey Williams	40.00	20.00	12.00
(57) Dick Williams	65.00	32.50	20.00
(58) Gene Woodling	45.00	22.50	13.50
(59) Al Worthington	40.00	20.00	12.00

1969 N.Y. News Mets Portfolio of Stars

To commemorate the N.Y. Mets miracle season of 1969, one of the city's daily newspapers, The News, issued a portfolio of player portraits done by editorial cartoonist Bruce Stark. The 9" x 12" pencil drawings are printed on heavy textured paper and were sold as a set in a folder labeled, "The 1969 Mets / A Portfolio of Stars." The black-and-white drawings are on a white background. A facsimile player autograph is printed at lower-left. At lower-right is the signature of the artist, Stark, along with the paper's logo and a union label. The blank-backed, unnumbered pieces are checklisted here alphabetically.

	NM	EX	VG
Complete Set (20):	225.00	110.00	70.00
Common Player:	7.50	3.75	2.25
(1) Tommie Agee	7.50	3.75	2.25
(2) Ken Boswell	7.50	3.75	2.25
(3) Don Cardwell	7.50	3.75	2.25
(4) Donn Clendenon	10.00	5.00	3.00
(5) Wayne Garrett	7.50	3.75	2.25
(6) Gary Gentry	7.50	3.75	2.25
(7) Jerry Grote	7.50	3.75	2.25
(8) Bud Harrelson	10.00	5.00	3.00
(9) Gil Hodges	20.00	10.00	6.00
(10) Cleon Jones	7.50	3.75	2.25
(11) Jerry Koosman	7.50	3.75	2.25
(12) Ed Kranepool	7.50	3.75	2.25
(13) Jim McAndrew	7.50	3.75	2.25
(14) Tug McGraw	10.00	5.00	3.00
(15) Nolan Ryan	150.00	75.00	45.00
(16) Tom Seaver	40.00	20.00	12.00
(17) Art Shamsky	7.50	3.75	2.25
(18) Ron Swoboda	7.50	3.75	2.25
(19) Ron Taylor	7.50	3.75	2.25
(20) Al Weis	7.50	3.75	2.25

1973 N.Y. News Mets/Yankees Caricatures

Between June 17 and August 26, the Sunday color comics section of the N.Y. News carried a centerspread picturing one Mets and one Yankees player as caricatured by artist

Bruce Stark. Each player picture is printed on newsprint in approximately 10-1/2" x 14-1/2", the pictures have a page of comics or other matter on their backs. Values shown are for single pages. Intact pairs or complete comics section would command a premium.

	NM	EX	VG
Complete Set (22):	200.00	100.00	60.00
Common Player:	6.00	3.00	1.75
METS			
(1) Yogi Berra (6/17)	17.50	8.75	5.25
(2) Tom Seaver (6/24)	15.00	7.50	4.50
(3) John Milner (7/1)	6.00	3.00	1.75
(4) Felix Millan (7/8)	6.00	3.00	1.75
(5) Bud Harrelson (7/15)	6.00	3.00	1.75
(6) Jim Fregosi (7/22)	6.00	3.00	1.75
(7) Jerry Grote (7/29)	6.00	3.00	1.75
(8) Cleon Jones (8/5)	6.00	3.00	1.75
(9) Willie Mays (8/12)	25.00	12.50	7.50
(10) Rusty Staub (8/19)	9.00	4.50	2.75
(11) Tug McGraw (8/26)	7.50	3.75	2.25
YANKEES			
(12) Ralph Houk (6/17)	7.50	3.75	2.25
(13) Mel Stottlemyre (6/24)	7.50	3.75	2.25
(14) Ron Blomberg (7/1)	6.00	3.00	1.75
(15) Horace Clarke (7/8)	6.00	3.00	1.75
(16) Gene Michael (7/15)	6.00	3.00	1.75
(17) Graig Nettles (7/22)	7.50	3.75	2.25
(18) Thurman Munson (7/29)	15.00	7.50	4.50
(19) Roy White (8/5)	9.00	4.50	2.75
(20) Bobby Murcer (8/12)	9.00	4.50	2.75
(21) Matty Alou (8/19)	6.00	3.00	1.75
(22) Sparky Lyle (8/26)	9.00	4.50	2.75

1916 N.Y. World Leaders in Baseball

This set of large-format (about 9" x 4") sepia-tone cards was issued to demonstrate the dominance of the World in New York City's newspaper wars. Each card has a portrait photo of a New York player. Most of the card is devoted to stats to boost the paper's claim as the "Pennant Winner in Advertising and Circulation." A note at left identifies the series as "'Leaders in Baseball' Series II.' It is not known whether this checklist is complete.

	NM	EX	VG
Common Player:	600.00	300.00	180.00
(1) Home Run Baker	750.00	375.00	225.00
(2) Jake Daubert	600.00	300.00	180.00
(3) Buck Herzog	600.00	300.00	180.00
(4) Dave Robertson	600.00	300.00	180.00

1944 N.Y. Yankees Stamps

One of the few paper collectibles issued during World War II, this set includes several players who do not appear on any other contemporary baseball card issue. The 1-3/4" x 2-3/8" stamps were issued on a single sheet with an album marking the Yankees 1943 World Series win. Stamps are in full color with the player's name in white on a red strip at bottom. The unnumbered stamps are checklisted here alphabetically. An album, about 6-1/2" x 3-1/2", was issued to display the stamps.

	NM	EX	VG
Complete Set (30):	100.00	50.00	30.00
Common Player:	12.00	6.00	3.50
Uncut Sheet:	145.00	75.00	45.00

	NM	EX	VG
Album:	40.00	20.00	12.00
(1) Ernie Bonham	12.00	6.00	3.50
(2) Hank Borowy	12.00	6.00	3.50
(3) Marvin Breuer	12.00	6.00	3.50
(4) Tommy Byrne	12.00	6.00	3.50
(5) Spud Chandler	15.00	7.50	4.50
(6) Earl Combs (Earle)	25.00	12.50	7.50
(7) Frank Crosetti	20.00	10.00	6.00
(8) Bill Dickey	35.00	17.50	10.50
(9) Atley Donald	12.00	6.00	3.50
(10) Nick Etten	12.00	6.00	3.50
(11) Art Fletcher	12.00	6.00	3.50
(12) Joe Gordon	15.00	7.50	4.50
(13) Oscar Grimes	12.00	6.00	3.50
(14) Rollie Hemsley	12.00	6.00	3.50
(15) Bill Johnson	12.00	6.00	3.50
(16) Charlie Keller	15.00	7.50	4.50
(17) John Lindell	15.00	7.50	4.50
(18) Joe McCarthy	25.00	12.50	7.50
(19) Bud Metheny	12.00	6.00	3.50
(20) Johnny Murphy	12.00	6.00	3.50
(21) Pat O'Daugherty	12.00	6.00	3.50
(22) Marius Russo	12.00	6.00	3.50
(23) John Schulte	12.00	6.00	3.50
(24) Ken Sears	12.00	6.00	3.50
(25) Tuck Stainbeck	12.00	6.00	3.50
(26) George Stirnweiss	12.00	6.00	3.50
(27) Jim Turner	12.00	6.00	3.50
(28) Roy Weatherly	12.00	6.00	3.50
(29) Charley Wensloff	12.00	6.00	3.50
(30) Bill Zuber	12.00	6.00	3.50

1947-50 N.Y. Yankees Picture Pack

These team-issued sets offered fans at the souvenir stand more than two dozen pictures of the players and staff. The 6-1/2" x 9" pictures are in black-and-white with a white border and a facsimile autograph. Backs are blank. Players repeated over the years were represented by the same picture. The unnumbered pictures are listed in alphabetical order by year of issue.

	NM	EX	VG
Common Player:	4.00	2.00	1.25
Complete 1947 Set (25):	100.00	50.00	30.00
(1) Yogi Berra	20.00	10.00	6.00
(2) Bill Bevens	4.00	2.00	1.25
(3) Bobby Brown	4.00	2.00	1.25
(4) Spud Chandler	4.00	2.00	1.25
(5) Frank Colman	4.00	2.00	1.25
(6) John Corriden	4.00	2.00	1.25
(7) Frank Crosetti	5.00	2.50	1.50
(8) Joe DiMaggio	40.00	20.00	12.00
(9) Chuck Dressen	4.00	2.00	1.25
(10) Randy Gumpert	4.00	2.00	1.25
(11) Bucky Harris	5.00	2.50	1.50
(12) Tommy Henrich	4.00	2.00	1.25
(13) Ralph Houk	5.00	2.50	1.50
(14) Don Johnson	4.00	2.00	1.25
(15) Bill Johnson	4.00	2.00	1.25
(16) Charlie Keller	5.00	2.50	1.50
(17) John Lindell	4.00	2.00	1.25
(18) George McQuinn	4.00	2.00	1.25
(19) Joe Page	4.00	2.00	1.25
(20) Allie Reynolds	5.00	2.50	1.50
(21) Phil Rizzuto	12.50	6.25	3.75
(22) Aaron Robinson	4.00	2.00	1.25
(23) Frank Shea	4.00	2.00	1.25
(24) Ken Silvestri	4.00	2.00	1.25
(25) George Stirnweiss	4.00	2.00	1.25
Complete 1948 Set (26):	100.00	50.00	30.00
(1) Yogi Berra	20.00	10.00	6.00
(2) Bobby Brown	4.00	2.00	1.25
(3) Red Corriden	4.00	2.00	1.25
(4) Frank Crosetti	5.00	2.50	1.50
(5) Joe DiMaggio	40.00	20.00	12.00
(6) Chuck Dressen	4.00	2.00	1.25
(7) Karl Drews	4.00	2.00	1.25
(8) Red Embree	4.00	2.00	1.25
(9) Randy Gumpert	4.00	2.00	1.25
(10) Bucky Harris	5.00	2.50	1.50
(11) Tommy Henrich	4.00	2.00	1.25
(12) Frank Hiller	4.00	2.00	1.25
(13) Bill Johnson	4.00	2.00	1.25
(14) Charlie Keller	5.00	2.50	1.50
(15) John Lindell	4.00	2.00	1.25
(16) Eddie Lopat	5.00	2.50	1.50
(17) Cliff Mapes	4.00	2.00	1.25
(18) George McQuinn	4.00	2.00	1.25
(19) Gus Niarhos	4.00	2.00	1.25
(20) George McQuinn	4.00	2.00	1.25
(21) Joe Page	4.00	2.00	1.25
(22) Vic Raschi	5.00	2.50	1.50
(23) Allie Reynolds	5.00	2.50	1.50
(24) Phil Rizzuto	12.50	6.25	3.75

	NM	EX	VG
(25) Frank Shea	4.00	2.00	1.25
(26) Snuffy Stirnweiss	4.00	2.00	1.25
Complete 1949 Set (25):	100.00	50.00	30.00
(1) Mel Allen	8.00	4.00	2.50
(2) Larry Berra	20.00	10.00	6.00
(3) Bobby Brown	4.00	2.00	1.25
(4) Tommy Byrne	4.00	2.00	1.25
(5) Jerry Coleman	4.00	2.00	1.25
(6) Frank Crosetti	5.00	2.50	1.50
(7) Bill Dickey	10.00	5.00	3.00
(8) Joe DiMaggio	40.00	20.00	12.00
(9) Tommy Henrich	4.00	2.00	1.25
(10) Bill Johnson	4.00	2.00	1.25
(11) Charlie Keller	5.00	2.50	1.50
(12) John Lindell	4.00	2.00	1.25
(13) Ed Lopat	5.00	2.50	1.50
(14) Gus Niarhos	4.00	2.00	1.25
(15) Joe Page	4.00	2.00	1.25
(16) Bob Porterfield	4.00	2.00	1.25
(17) Vic Raschi	4.00	2.00	1.25
(18) Allie Reynolds	5.00	2.50	1.50
(19) Phil Rizzuto	12.50	6.25	3.75
(20) Fred Sanford	4.00	2.00	1.25
(21) Frank Shea	4.00	2.00	1.25
(22) Casey Stengel	15.00	7.50	4.50
(23) George Stirnweiss	4.00	2.00	1.25
(24) Jim Turner	4.00	2.00	1.25
(25) Gene Woodling	5.00	2.50	1.50
Complete 1950 Set (25):	100.00	50.00	30.00
(1) Mel Allen	8.00	4.00	2.50
(2) Hank Bauer	5.00	2.50	1.50
(3) Larry Berra	20.00	10.00	6.00
(4) Bobby Brown	4.00	2.00	1.25
(5) Tommy Byrne	4.00	2.00	1.25
(6) Jerry Coleman	4.00	2.00	1.25
(7) Frank Crosetti	5.00	2.50	1.50
(8) Bill Dickey	10.00	5.00	3.00
(9) Joe DiMaggio	40.00	20.00	12.00
(10) Tommy Henrich	4.00	2.00	1.25
(11) Jack Jensen	7.50	3.75	2.25
(12) Bill Johnson	4.00	2.00	1.25
(13) Ed Lopat	5.00	2.50	1.50
(14) Cliff Mapes	4.00	2.00	1.25
(15) Joe Page	4.00	2.00	1.25
(16) Bob Porterfield	4.00	2.00	1.25
(17) Vic Raschi	5.00	2.50	1.50
(18) Allie Reynolds	5.00	2.50	1.50
(19) Phil Rizzuto	12.50	6.25	3.75
(20) Fred Sanford	4.00	2.00	1.25
(21) Charlie Silvera	5.00	2.50	1.50
(22) Casey Stengel	15.00	7.50	4.50
(23) George Stirnweiss	4.00	2.00	1.25
(24) Jim Turner	4.00	2.00	1.25
(25) Gene Woodling	5.00	2.50	1.50

1955-1957 N.Y. Yankees Picture Pack

The checklist for this set of 5" x 7" black-and-white, blank-back pictures does not allow pinpointing its year of issue more closely. Similar in format to the later Jay Publishing photo packs, this issue differs in that only the team name (in upper- and lower-case letters), and not the city, is presented along with the player name (all-caps) in the identification line in the bottom border. The set was sold for 25 cents in a manila envelope. The unnumbered pictures are listed here alphabetically.

	NM	EX	VG
Complete Set (12):	75.00	37.50	22.50
Common Player:	4.00	2.00	1.25
(1) Hank Bauer	5.00	2.50	1.50
(2) Yogi Berra	7.50	3.75	2.25
(3) Tommy Byrne	4.00	2.00	1.25
(4) Andy Carey	4.00	2.00	1.25
(5) Joe Collins	4.00	2.00	1.25
(6) Whitey Ford	7.50	3.75	2.25
(7) Elston Howard	5.00	2.50	1.50
(8) Mickey Mantle	35.00	17.50	10.00
(9) Billy Martin	5.00	2.50	1.50
(10) Gil McDougald	4.00	2.00	1.25
(11) Casey Stengel	7.50	3.75	2.25
(12) Bob Turley	4.00	2.00	1.25

1956 N.Y. Yankees "Action Pictures"

This set of 8" x 10" black-and-white pictures was sold for 75 cents in a paper envelope marked "12 ACTION / PICTURES." The white-bordered pictures have facsimile autographs or printed names on front and are blank-backed.

	NM	EX	VG
Complete Set (12):	125.00	65.00	49.00
Common Player:	6.00	3.00	1.75
(1) Hank Bauer	7.50	3.75	2.25
(2) Yogi Berra	15.00	7.50	4.50
(3) Andy Carey	6.00	3.00	1.75
(4) Joe Collins	6.00	3.00	1.75
(5) Whitey Ford	15.00	7.50	4.50
(6) Elston Howard	9.00	4.50	2.75
(7) Mickey Mantle	75.00	37.00	22.00
(8) Billy Martin	9.00	4.50	2.75

		NM	EX	VG
(9)	Gil McDougald	7.50	3.75	2.25
(10)	Phil Rizzuto	15.00	7.50	4.50
(11)	Bill Skowron	9.00	4.50	2.75
(12)	Bob Turley	7.50	3.75	2.25

1956 N.Y. Yankees Picture Pack

This set was issued, probably for sale at Yankee Stadium souvenir stands, in 1956, though some of the photos date as far back as 1951, and a few appear to have been taken during the 1955 World Series at Ebbets Field. Printed in black-and-white on semi-gloss paper, the pictures measure about 6" x 8-7/8". There is a 1/4" white border around the photo and a white strip at the bottom of each photo with the player's name. Backs are blank. The pictures are checklisted here in alphabetical order, but the list may not be complete. Some of the photos are familiar from their use on baseball cards, including the 1951 Bowman Mantle.

		NM	EX	VG
Complete Set (22):		275.00	135.00	80.00
Common Player:		8.00	4.00	2.50
(1)	Hank Bauer	10.00	5.00	3.00
(2)	Larry "Yogi" Berra	20.00	10.00	6.00
(3)	Tommy Byrne	8.00	4.00	2.50
(4)	Andy Carey	8.00	4.00	2.50
(5)	Bob Cerv	8.00	4.00	2.50
(6)	Gerry Coleman	8.00	4.00	2.50
(7)	Joe Collins	8.00	4.00	2.50
(8)	Ed "Whitey" Ford	20.00	10.00	6.00
(9)	Bob Grim	8.00	4.00	2.50
(10)	Elston Howard	10.00	5.00	3.00
(11)	Johnny Kucks	8.00	4.00	2.50
(12)	Don Larsen	12.50	6.25	3.75
(13)	Jerry Lumpe	8.00	4.00	2.50
(14)	Mickey Mantle	130.00	65.00	39.00
(15)	Billy Martin	15.00	7.50	4.50
(16)	Mickey McDermott	8.00	4.00	2.50
(17)	Gil McDougald	10.00	5.00	3.00
(18)	Tom Morgan	8.00	4.00	2.50
(19)	Irv Noren	8.00	4.00	2.50
(20)	Charlie Silvera	8.00	4.00	2.50
(21)	Bill Skowron	10.00	5.00	3.00
(22)	Bob Turley	10.00	5.00	3.00

1957 N.Y. Yankees Picture Pack

Nominally 8" x 10", the actual size on these blank-back, black-and-white pictures varies from about 7-1/2" to 8" wide by 9-7/8" x 10-1/8" tall. The player poses are surrounded with a white border. The player name is printed within the picture. Some of the photos used considerably pre-date the period of issue.

		NM	EX	VG
Complete Set (12):		125.00	65.00	40.00
Common Player:		10.00	5.00	3.00
(1)	Hank Bauer	12.50	6.25	3.75
(2)	Larry Berra	20.00	10.00	6.00
(3)	Andy Carey	10.00	5.00	3.00
(4)	Whitey Ford	20.00	10.00	6.00
(5)	Elston Howard	12.50	6.25	3.75
(6)	Tony Kubek	15.00	7.50	4.50
(7)	Don Larsen	12.50	6.25	3.75
(8)	Mickey Mantle	60.00	30.00	18.00
(9)	Gil McDougald	12.50	6.25	3.75
(10)	Bill Skowron	12.50	6.25	3.75
(11)	Bob Turley	12.50	6.25	3.75
(12)	Frank Crosetti, Bill Dickey, Casey Stengel, Jim Turner	10.00	5.00	3.00

1960 N.Y. Yankees "Action Pictures"

This set of 8" x 10" black-and-white pictures was sold for 75 cents in a paper envelope marked "12 ACTION / PICTURES." The white bordered pictures have facsimile autographs or printed names on front and are blank-backed.

		NM	EX	VG
Complete Set (12):		200.00	100.00	60.00
Common Player:		10.00	5.00	3.00
(1)	Larry Berra	20.00	10.00	6.00
(2)	Art Ditmar	10.00	5.00	3.00
(3)	Whitey Ford	20.00	10.00	6.00
(4)	Elston Howard	12.50	6.25	3.75
(5)	Tony Kubek	15.00	7.50	4.50
(6)	Hector Lopez	10.00	5.00	3.00
(7)	Mickey Mantle	60.00	30.00	18.00
(8)	Roger Maris	35.00	17.50	10.50
(9)	Bobby Richardson	12.50	6.25	3.75
(10)	Bill Skowron	12.50	6.25	3.75
(11)	Casey Stengel	15.00	7.50	4.50
(12)	Bob Turley	12.50	6.25	3.75

1970 N.Y. Yankees Clinic Schedule Postcards

This series of postcards was issued in conjunction with a series of baseball clinics which the Yankees put on for youngsters prior to selected home games. Fronts of the 3-1/2 x 5-1/2" glossy color cards have player portraits with a facsimile autograph in a white panel at bottom. Backs have player identification and career highlights, a schedule of the clinic days and credit line for Howard Photo Service. White and Murcer cards are scarce because of rainouts on their scheduled clinic appearance days. Cards are checklisted here in alphabetical order.

		NM	EX	VG
Complete Set (13):		130.00	65.00	40.00
Common Player:		3.00	1.50	.90
(1)	Stan Bahnsen	3.00	1.50	.90
(2)	Curt Blefary	3.00	1.50	.90
(3)	Danny Cater	3.00	1.50	.90
(4)	Horace Clarke	3.00	1.50	.90
(5)	Joe DiMaggio, Mickey Mantle	25.00	12.50	7.50
(6)	John Ellis	3.00	1.50	.90
(7)	Jerry Kenney	3.00	1.50	.90
(8)	Gene Michael	3.00	1.50	.90
(9)	Thurman Munson	30.00	15.00	9.00
(10)	Bobby Murcer	15.00	7.50	4.50
(11)	Fritz Peterson	3.00	1.50	.90
(12)	Mel Stottlemyre	4.50	2.25	1.25
(13)	Roy White	35.00	17.50	10.50

1971 N.Y. Yankees Clinic Schedule Postcards

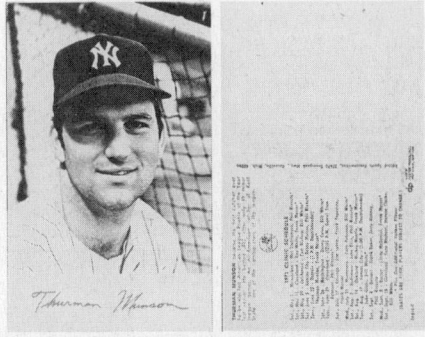

These postcards were issued in conjunction with a series of baseball clinics which the Yankees put on for youngsters prior to selected home games. Fronts of the 3-1/2" x 5-1/2" glossy color cards have player portraits with a facsimile autograph in a white panel at bottom. Backs are printed in blue, have player identification and career highlights and a schedule of the clinic days. Cards are checklisted here in alphabetical order.

		NM	EX	VG
Complete Set (16):		90.00	45.00	27.00
Common Player:		3.00	1.50	.90
(1)	Felipe Alou, Jim Lyttle	3.00	1.50	.90
(2)	Stan Bahnsen	3.00	1.50	.90
(3)	Frank Baker, Jerry Kenney	3.00	1.50	.90
(4)	Curt Blefary	3.00	1.50	.90
(5)	Danny Cater	3.00	1.50	.90
(6)	Horace Clarke, Gene Michael	3.00	1.50	.90
(7)	John Ellis	3.00	1.50	.90
(8)	Jake Gibbs	3.00	1.50	.90
(9)	Ralph Houk	3.00	1.50	.90
(10)	Mickey Mantle	30.00	15.00	9.00
(11)	Lindy McDaniel	3.00	1.50	.90
(12)	Thurman Munson	15.00	7.50	4.50
(13)	Bobby Murcer	4.50	2.25	1.25
(14)	Fritz Peterson	3.00	1.50	.90
(15)	Mel Stottlemyre	3.00	1.50	.90
(16)	Roy White	3.00	1.50	.90

1972 N.Y. Yankees Schedule Cards

The origins and distribution of these cards is unclear. They may have been a collector issue. The 2-1/4" x 3-1/2" cards are printed in blue and sepia. Fronts have player photos with a facsimile autograph in the white border at bottom, between a pair of team insignia. Backs have the team schedule. The unnumbered cards are listed here alphabetically.

		NM	EX	VG
Complete Set (8):		350.00	175.00	100.00
Common Player:		30.00	15.00	9.00
(1)	Felipe Alou	35.00	17.50	10.50
(2)	Ron Blomberg	30.00	15.00	9.00
(3)	Thurman Munson	225.00	110.00	67.00
(4)	Bobby Murcer	35.00	17.50	10.50
(5)	Mel Stottlemyre	30.00	15.00	9.00
(6)	Ron Swoboda	30.00	15.00	9.00
(7)	Roy White	35.00	17.50	10.50
(8)	Frank Messer, Phil Rizzuto, Bill White (Announcers)	30.00	15.00	9.00

1909 Niagara Baking Co.

This is a version of the set known as E101 "Set of 50" which has been rubber-stamped on back with an advertisement for Niagara Baking Co., of Lockport, N.Y. It is unclear whether all 50 cards in E101 can be found with the overprint. Because of the ease with which this regional variation could be faked, collectors must exercise extreme caution. Collectors can expect to pay a considerable premium over E101 prices for this version, especially for common players.

Values Undetermined
(See 1909 E101 for checklist.)

1953 Northland Bread Labels

This bread end-label set consists of 32 players - two from each major league team. The unnumbered black and white labels measure approximately 2-11/16" square and include the slogan "Bread for Energy" along the top. An album to house the labels was also part of the promotion.

		NM	EX	VG
Complete Set (32):		8,250	4,250	2,500
Common Player:		200.00	100.00	60.00
(1)	Cal Abrams	200.00	100.00	60.00
(2)	Richie Ashburn	400.00	200.00	120.00
(3)	Gus Bell	200.00	100.00	60.00
(4)	Jim Busby	200.00	100.00	60.00
(5)	Clint Courtney	200.00	100.00	60.00
(6)	Billy Cox	200.00	100.00	60.00
(7)	Jim Dyck	200.00	100.00	60.00
(8)	Nellie Fox	400.00	200.00	120.00
(9)	Sid Gordon	200.00	100.00	60.00
(10)	Warren Hacker	200.00	100.00	60.00
(11)	Jim Hearn	200.00	100.00	60.00
(12)	Fred Hutchinson	200.00	100.00	60.00
(13)	Monte Irvin	400.00	200.00	120.00
(14)	Jackie Jensen	225.00	110.00	65.00
(15)	Ted Kluszewski	350.00	175.00	100.00
(16)	Bob Lemon	400.00	200.00	120.00
(17)	Maury McDermott	200.00	100.00	60.00
(18)	Minny Minoso	350.00	175.00	105.00
(19)	Johnny Mize	400.00	200.00	120.00
(20)	Mel Parnell	200.00	100.00	60.00
(21)	Howie Pollet	200.00	100.00	60.00
(22)	Jerry Priddy	200.00	100.00	60.00
(23)	Allie Reynolds	200.00	100.00	60.00
(24)	Preacher Roe	250.00	125.00	75.00
(25)	Al Rosen	225.00	110.00	65.00
(26)	Connie Ryan	200.00	100.00	60.00
(27a)	Hank Sauer (Bread for Energy at top.)	200.00	100.00	60.00
(27b)	Hank Sauer (Top Taste at top.)	375.00	185.00	110.00
(28)	Red Schoendienst	400.00	200.00	120.00
(29)	Bobby Shantz	200.00	100.00	60.00
(30)	Enos Slaughter	400.00	200.00	120.00
(31)	Warren Spahn	400.00	200.00	120.00
(32)	Gus Zernial	200.00	100.00	60.00

1978 North Shore Dodge Cecil Cooper

As part of his work as promotional spokesman for a local auto dealership, popular Brewers first baseman Cecil Cooper appears on a one-card set which was given to fans and collectors during public appearances. The card is printed in black-and-white in standard 2-1/2" x 3-1/2" size and is often found with a genuine autograph on the front.

	NM	EX	VG
Cecil Cooper	6.00	3.00	1.75
Cecil Cooper (Autographed)	15.00	7.50	4.50

1980 Nostalgic Enterprises 1903 N.Y. Highlanders

New York City's first team in the American League, the 1903 Highlanders, are featured in this collectors' issue. Fronts of the 2-1/2" x 3-1/2" cards have black-and-white portrait photos with ornate graphics, highlighted in yellow, and a white border. Backs have season and lifetime stats, player data and an extensive career summary. The unnumbered cards are checklisted here in alphabetical order. Sets originally sold for about $2.50.

		NM	EX	VG
Complete Set (17):		15.00	7.50	4.50
Common Player:		2.00	1.00	.60
(1)	Monte Beville	2.50	1.25	.70
(2)	Jack Chesbro	2.00	1.00	.60
(3)	Wid Conroy	2.00	1.00	.60
(4)	Lefty Davis	2.00	1.00	.60

		NM	EX	VG
(5)	John Deering	2.50	1.25	.70
(6)	Kid Elberfeld	2.00	1.00	.60
(7)	Dave Fultz	2.00	1.00	.60
(8)	John Ganzel	2.00	1.00	.60
(9)	Clark Griffith	2.00	1.00	.60
(10)	Harry Howell	2.00	1.00	.60
(11)	Willie Keeler	2.00	1.00	.60
(12)	Herm McFarland	2.00	1.00	.60
(13)	Jack O'Connor	2.00	1.00	.60
(14)	Jesse Tannehill	2.00	1.00	.60
(15)	Jimmy Williams	2.00	1.00	.60
(16)	Jack Zalusky	2.50	1.25	.70
(17)	Header Card/Checklist	2.00	1.00	.60

1907-09 Novelty Cutlery Postcards (PC805)

An ornately bordered black-and-white or sepia portrait or action pose of the day's great players identifies these postcards from a Canton, Ohio, knife company. Cards measure the standard 3-1/2" x 5-1/2" size with postcard indicia on the back. The sponsor is identified in a tiny line of type beneath the lower-right corner of the player photo.

		NM	EX	VG
Complete Set (26):		60,000	30,000	18,000
Common Player:		1,400	560.00	280.00
(1)	Roger Bresnahan	1,800	720.00	360.00
(2)	Al Bridwell	1,400	560.00	280.00
(3)	Three Finger Brown	1,800	720.00	360.00
(4)	Frank Chance	1,800	720.00	360.00
(5)	Hal Chase	1,600	640.00	320.00
(6)	Ty Cobb	9,000	3,600	1,800
(7)	Eddie Collins	1,800	720.00	360.00
(8)	Sam Crawford	1,800	720.00	360.00
(9)	Art Devlin	1,400	560.00	280.00
(10)	Red Dooin	1,400	560.00	280.00
(11)	Elmer Flick	1,800	720.00	360.00
(12)	Sam Frock	1,400	560.00	280.00
(13)	George Gibson	1,400	560.00	280.00
(14)	Solly Hofman	1,400	560.00	280.00
(15)	Walter Johnston (Johnson)	3,000	1,200	600.00
(16)	Nap Lajoie	1,800	720.00	360.00
(17)	Bris Lord	1,400	560.00	280.00
(18)	Christy Mathewson	3,000	1,200	600.00
(19)	Orval Overall	1,400	560.00	280.00
(20)	Eddie Plank	1,800	720.00	360.00
(21)	Tris Speaker	2,500	1,000	500.00
(22)	Gabby Street	1,400	560.00	280.00
(23)	Honus Wagner	6,000	2,400	1,200
(24)	Ed Walsh	1,800	720.00	360.00
(25)	Ty Cobb, Honus Wagner	6,500	2,600	1,300
(26)	Johnny Evers, Germany Schaefer	1,600	640.00	320.00

1960 Nu-Card Baseball Hi-Lites

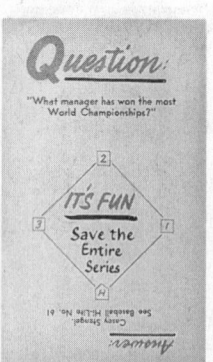

These large, 3-1/4" x 5-3/8" cards are printed in a mock newspaper format, with a headline, picture and story describing one of baseball's greatest moments. Cards #1-18 can be found either printed entirely in black, or in red-and-black, like the rest of the set. Each card is numbered in the upper-left corner. Backs offer a quiz question and answer.

		NM	EX	VG
Complete Set (72):		500.00	250.00	150.00
Common Player:		6.00	3.00	1.75
1	Babe Hits 3 Homers In A Series Game	40.00	20.00	12.00
2	Podres Pitching Wins Series	9.00	4.50	2.75
3	Bevans Pitches No Hitter, Almost	6.00	3.00	1.75

		NM	EX	VG
4	Box Score Devised By Reporter	6.00	3.00	1.75
5	VanderMeer Pitches 2 No Hitters	6.00	3.00	1.75
6	Indians Take Bums	6.00	3.00	1.75
7	DiMag Comes Thru	25.00	12.50	7.50
8	Mathewson Pitches 3 W.S. Shutouts	7.50	3.75	2.25
9	Haddix Pitches 12 Perfect Innings	6.00	3.00	1.75
10	Thomson's Homer Sinks Dodgers	9.00	4.50	2.75
11	Hubbell Strikes Out 5 A.L. Stars	6.00	3.00	1.75
12	Pickoff Ends Series (Marty Marion)	6.00	3.00	1.75
13	Cards Take Series From Yanks (Grover Cleveland Alexander)	6.00	3.00	1.75
14	Dizzy And Daffy Win Series	10.00	5.00	3.00
15	Owen Drops 3rd Strike	6.00	3.00	1.75
16	Ruth Calls His Shot	40.00	20.00	12.00
17	Merkle Pulls Boner	6.00	3.00	1.75
18	Larsen Hurls Perfect World Series Game	10.00	5.00	3.00
19	Bean Ball Ends Career of Mickey Cochrane	6.00	3.00	1.75
20	Banks Belts 47 Homers, Earns MVP Honors	6.00	3.00	1.75
21	Stan Musial Hits 5 Homers In 1 Day	12.50	6.25	3.75
22	Mickey Mantle Hits Longest Homer	60.00	30.00	18.00
23	Sievers Captures Home Run Title	6.00	3.00	1.75
24	Gehrig Consecutive Game Record Ends	25.00	12.50	7.50
25	Red Schoendienst Key Player In Victory	6.00	3.00	1.75
26	Midget Pinch-Hits For St. Louis Browns (Eddie Gaedel)	10.00	5.00	3.00
27	Willie Mays Makes Greatest Catch	25.00	12.50	7.50
28	Homer By Berra Puts Yanks In 1st Place	6.00	3.00	1.75
29	Campy National League's MVP	6.00	3.00	1.75
30	Bob Turley Hurls Yanks To Championship	6.00	3.00	1.75
31	Dodgers Take Series From Sox In Six	6.00	3.00	1.75
32	Furillo Hero As Dodgers Beat Chicago	6.00	3.00	1.75
33	Adcock Gets Four Homers And A Double	6.00	3.00	1.75
34	Dickey Chosen All Star Catcher	6.00	3.00	1.75
35	Burdette Beats Yanks In 3 Series Games	6.00	3.00	1.75
36	Umpires Clear White Sox Bench	6.00	3.00	1.75
37	Reese Honored As Greatest Dodger S.S.	7.50	3.75	2.25
38	Joe DiMaggio Hits In 56 Straight Games	30.00	15.00	9.00
39	Ted Williams Hits .406 For Season	25.00	12.50	7.50
40	Johnson Pitches 56 Scoreless Innings	6.00	3.00	1.75
41	Hodges Hits 4 Home Runs In Nite Game	6.00	3.00	1.75
42	Greenberg Returns To Tigers From Army	10.00	5.00	3.00
43	Ty Cobb Named Best Player Of All Time	15.00	7.50	4.50
44	Robin Roberts Wins 28 Games	6.00	3.00	1.75
45	Rizzuto's 2 Runs Save 1st Place	6.00	3.00	1.75
46	Tigers Beat Out Senators For Pennant (Hal Newhouser)	6.00	3.00	1.75
47	Babe Ruth Hits 60th Home Run	40.00	20.00	12.00
48	Cy Young Honored	6.00	3.00	1.75
49	Killebrew Starts Spring Training	6.00	3.00	1.75
50	Mantle Hits Longest Homer At Stadium	60.00	30.00	18.00
51	Braves Take Pennant (Hank Aaron)	6.00	3.00	1.75
52	Ted Williams Hero Of All Star Game	30.00	15.00	9.00
53	Robinson Saves Dodgers For Playoffs (Jackie Robinson)	12.50	6.25	3.75
54	Snodgrass Muffs A Fly Ball	6.00	3.00	1.75
55	Snider Belts 2 Homers	6.00	3.00	1.75
56	New York Giants Win 26 Straight Games (Christy Mathewson)	6.00	3.00	1.75
57	Ted Kluszewski Stars In 1st Game Win	6.00	3.00	1.75
58	Ott Walks 5 Times In A Single Game (Mel Ott)	6.00	3.00	1.75
59	Harvey Kuenn Takes Batting Title	6.00	3.00	1.75
60	Bob Feller Hurls 3rd No-Hitter Of Career	6.00	3.00	1.75
61	Yanks Champs Again! (Casey Stengel)	6.00	3.00	1.75
62	Aaron's Bat Beats Yankees In Series	10.00	5.00	3.00
63	Warren Spahn Beats Yanks in World Series	6.00	3.00	1.75
64	Ump's Wrong Call Helps Dodgers	6.00	3.00	1.75

65	Kaline Hits 3 Homers, 2 In Same Inning	6.00	3.00	1.75
66	Bob Allison Named A.L. Rookie of Year	6.00	3.00	1.75
67	McCovey Blasts Way Into Giant Lineup	6.00	3.00	1.75
68	Colavito Hits Four Homers In One Game	10.00	5.00	3.00
69	Erskine Sets Strike Out Record In W.S.	6.00	3.00	1.75
70	Sal Maglie Pitches No-Hit Game	6.00	3.00	1.75
71	Early Wynn Victory Crushes Yanks	6.00	3.00	1.75
72	Nellie Fox American League's M.V.P.	6.00	3.00	1.75

1961 Nu-Card Baseball Scoops

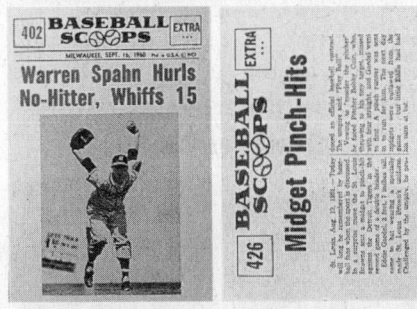

Very similar in style to their set of the year before, the Nu-Card Baseball Scoops were issued in a smaller 2-1/2" x 3-1/2" size, but still featured the mock newspaper card front. This 80-card set is numbered from 401 to 480, with numbers shown on both the card front and back. These cards, which commemorate great moments in individual players' careers, included only the headline and black and white photo on the fronts, with the descriptive story on the card backs. Cards are again printed in red and black. It appears the set may have been counterfeited, though when is not known. These cards can be determined by examining the card photo for unusual blurring and fuzziness.

		NM	EX	VG
	Complete Set (80):	400.00	200.00	120.00
	Common Player:	3.00	1.50	.90
	Wax Pack (7):	100.00	.00	.00
401	Gentile Powers Birds Into 1st	6.00	3.00	1.75
402	Warren Spahn Hurls No-Hitter, Whiffs 15	5.00	2.50	1.50
403	Mazeroski's Homer Wins Series For Bucs	10.00	5.00	3.00
404	Willie Mays' 3 Triples Paces Giants	15.00	7.50	4.50
405	Woodie Held Slugs 2 Homers, 6 RBIs	3.00	1.50	.90
406	Vern Law Winner Of Cy Young Award	3.00	1.50	.90
407	Runnels Makes 9 Hits in Twin-Bill	3.00	1.50	.90
408	Braves' Lew Burdette Wins No-Hitter	3.00	1.50	.90
409	Dick Stuart Hits 3 Homers, Single	3.00	1.50	.90
410	Don Cardwell Of Cubs Pitches No-Hit Game	3.00	1.50	.90
411	Camilo Pascual Strikes Out 15 Bosox	3.00	1.50	.90
412	Eddie Mathews Blasts 300th Big League HR	3.00	1.50	.90
413	Groat, NL Bat King, Named Loop's MVP	3.00	1.50	.90
414	AL Votes To Expand To 10 Teams (Gene Autry)	3.00	1.50	.90
415	Bobby Richardson Sets Series Mark	3.00	1.50	.90
416	Maris Nips Mantle For AL MVP Award	10.00	5.00	3.00
417	Merkle Pulls Boner	3.00	1.50	.90
418	Larsen Hurls Perfect World Series Game	5.00	2.50	1.50
419	Bean Ball Ends Career Of Mickey Cochrane	3.00	1.50	.90
420	Banks Belts 47 Homers, Earns MVP Award	6.00	3.00	1.75
421	Stan Musial Hits 5 Homers In 1 Day	9.00	4.50	2.75
422	Mickey Mantle Hits Longest Homer	35.00	17.50	10.50
423	Sievers Captures Home Run Title	3.00	1.50	.90
424	Gehrig Consecutive Game Record Ends	15.00	7.50	4.50
425	Red Schoendienst Key Player In Victory	3.00	1.50	.90
426	Midget Pinch-Hits For St. Louis Browns (Eddie Gaedel)	5.00	2.50	1.50
427	Willie Mays Makes Greatest Catch	20.00	10.00	6.00
428	Robinson Saves Dodgers For Playoffs	9.00	4.50	2.75
429	Campy Most Valuable Player	3.00	1.50	.90
430	Turley Hurls Yanks To Championship	3.00	1.50	.90
431	Dodgers Take Series From Sox In Six (Larry Sherry)	3.00	1.50	.90
432	Furillo Hero In 3rd World Series Game	3.00	1.50	.90

433	Adcock Gets Four Homers, Double	3.00	1.50	.90
434	Dickey Chosen All Star Catcher	3.00	1.50	.90
435	Burdette Beats Yanks In 3 Series Games	3.00	1.50	.90
436	Umpires Clear White Sox Bench	3.00	1.50	.90
437	Reese Honored As Greatest Dodgers S.S.	3.00	1.50	.90
438	Joe DiMaggio Hits In 56 Straight Games	20.00	10.00	6.00
439	Ted Williams Hits .406 For Season	20.00	10.00	6.00
440	Johnson Pitches 56 Scoreless Innings	3.00	1.50	.90
441	Hodges Hits 4 Home Runs In Nite Game	3.00	1.50	.90
442	Greenberg Returns To Tigers From Army	3.00	1.50	.90
443	Ty Cobb Named Best Player Of All Time	10.00	5.00	3.00
444	Robin Roberts Wins 28 Games	3.00	1.50	.90
445	Rizzuto's 2 Runs Save 1st Place	3.00	1.50	.90
446	Tigers Beat Out Senators For Pennant (Hal Newhouser)	3.00	1.50	.90
447	Babe Ruth Hits 60th Home Run	20.00	10.00	6.00
448	Cy Young Honored	4.50	2.25	1.25
449	Killebrew Starts Spring Training	3.00	1.50	.90
450	Mantle Hits Longest Homer At Stadium	35.00	17.50	10.50
451	Braves Take Pennant	3.00	1.50	.90
452	Ted Williams Hero Of All Star Game	20.00	10.00	6.00
453	Homer By Berra Puts Yanks In 1st Place	3.00	1.50	.90
454	Snodgrass Muffs A Fly Ball	3.00	1.50	.90
455	Babe Hits 3 Homers In A Series Game	25.00	12.50	7.50
456	New York Wins 26 Straight Games	3.00	1.50	.90
457	Ted Kluszewski Stars In 1st Series Win	3.00	1.50	.90
458	Ott Walks 5 Times In A Single Game	3.00	1.50	.90
459	Harvey Kuenn Takes Batting Title	3.00	1.50	.90
460	Bob Feller Hurls 3rd No-Hitter Of Career	3.00	1.50	.90
461	Yanks Champs Again! (Casey Stengel)	3.00	1.50	.90
462	Aaron's Bat Beats Yankees In Series	10.00	5.00	3.00
463	Warren Spahn Beats Yanks In World Series	3.00	1.50	.90
464	Ump's Wrong Call Helps Dodgers	3.00	1.50	.90
465	Kaline Hits 3 Homers, 2 In Same Inning	3.00	1.50	.90
466	Bob Allison Named A.L. Rookie Of Year	3.00	1.50	.90
467	DiMag Comes Thru	20.00	10.00	6.00
468	Colavito Hits Four Homers In One Game	3.50	1.75	1.00
469	Erskine Sets Strike Out Record In W.S.	3.00	1.50	.90
470	Sal Maglie Pitches No-Hit Game	3.00	1.50	.90
471	Early Wynn Victory Crushes Yanks	3.00	1.50	.90
472	Nellie Fox American League's MVP	3.00	1.50	.90
473	Pickoff Ends Series (Marty Marion)	3.00	1.50	.90
474	Podres Pitching Wins Series	3.00	1.50	.90
475	Owen Drops 3rd Strike	3.00	1.50	.90
476	Dizzy And Daffy Win Series	9.00	4.50	2.75
477	Mathewson Pitches 3 W.S. Shutouts	10.00	5.00	3.00
478	Haddix Pitches 12 Perfect Innings	3.00	1.50	.90
479	Hubbell Strike Out 5 A.L. Stars	3.00	1.50	.90
480	Homer Sinks Dodgers (Bobby Thomson)	6.00	3.00	1.75

1889 Number 7 Cigars (N526)

Three versions of this set picturing Boston Beaneaters (N.L.) players were issued in 1889. Number 7 and Diamond S brand cigars are the most commonly encountered advertising printed on the cards' backs. Cards with "C.S. White & Co." at top front are also known. The cards measure approximately 3-1/8" x 4-1/2" and feature black-and-white portrait drawings of the play-

ers with their name printed below in capital letters along with the team name. Backs carry ads for either Number 7 Cigars, a product of H.W.S. & Co. Howard W. Spurr & Co.), or Diamond S Cigars, advertised as the "Best 10 cent Cigar in America."

		NM	EX	VG
	Complete Set (15):	20,000	8,000	4,000
	Common Player:	1,100	450.00	400.00
(1)	C.W. Bennett	1,100	450.00	400.00
(2)	Dennis Brouthers	2,500	800.00	600.00
(3)	T.T. Brown	1,100	450.00	400.00
(4)	John G. Clarkson	2,500	800.00	600.00
(5)	C.W. Ganzel	1,100	450.00	400.00
(6)	James A. Hart	1,100	450.00	400.00
(7)	R.F. Johnston	1,100	450.00	400.00
(8)	M.J. Kelly	3,500	1,000	700.00
(9)	M.J. Madden	1,100	450.00	400.00
(10)	Wm. Nash	1,100	450.00	400.00
(11)	Jos. Quinn	1,100	450.00	400.00
(12)	Chas. Radbourn	2,500	800.00	600.00
(13)	J.B. Ray (Should be I.B.)	1,100	450.00	400.00
(14)	Hardie Richardson	1,100	450.00	400.00
(15)	Wm. Sowders	1,100	450.00	400.00

1949-1950 Num Num Cleveland Indians

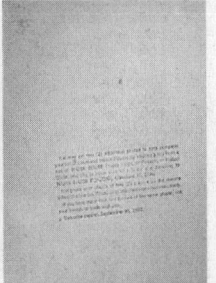

The 6-1/2" x 9" photopack pictures sold at Municipal Stadium in 1949 did double duty when they were also used as a premium for Num Num snack foods. A rubber-stamped notice on the back of the black-and-white photos offered two pictures for 10 cents and a box top, while encouraging trading. The pictures generally feature posed action shots with a facsimile autograph and white border. Backs are blank except for the rubber stamping. The unnumbered cards are checklisted here alphabetically.

		NM	EX	VG
	Complete Set (36):	1,850	925.00	550.00
	Common Player:	35.00	17.50	10.00
(1)	Bob Avila	35.00	17.50	10.00
(2)	Gene Bearden	35.00	17.50	10.00
(3)	Al Benton	35.00	17.50	10.00
(4)	John Berardino	45.00	22.50	13.50
(5)	Ray Boone	35.00	17.50	10.00
(6)	Lou Boudreau	65.00	30.00	15.00
(7)	Allie Clark	35.00	17.50	10.00
(8)	Larry Doby	65.00	30.00	15.00
(9)	Luke Easter	35.00	17.50	10.00
(10)	Bob Feller	125.00	60.00	30.00
(11)	Jess Flores	35.00	17.50	10.00
(12)	Mike Garcia	35.00	17.50	10.00
(13)	Joe Gordon	35.00	17.50	10.00
(14)	Hank Greenberg	125.00	65.00	35.00
(15)	Steve Gromek	35.00	17.50	10.00
(16)	Jim Hegan	35.00	17.50	10.00
(17)	Ken Keltner	35.00	17.50	10.00
(18)	Bob Kennedy	35.00	17.50	10.00
(19)	Bob Lemon	65.00	30.00	15.00
(20)	Dale Mitchell	35.00	17.50	10.00
(21)	Ray Murray	35.00	17.50	10.00
(22)	Satchell Paige	200.00	90.00	50.00
(23)	Frank Papish	35.00	17.50	10.00
(24)	Hal Peck	35.00	17.50	10.00
(25)	Chick Pieretti	35.00	17.50	10.00
(26)	Al Rosen	45.00	22.50	13.50
(27)	Dick Rozek (Glove out front.)	35.00	17.50	10.00
(28)	Dick Rozek (Glove under leg.)	35.00	17.50	10.00
(29)	Mike Tresh	35.00	17.50	10.00
(30)	Thurman Tucker	35.00	17.50	10.00
(31)	Bill Veeck	65.00	30.00	15.00
(32)	Mickey Vernon	35.00	17.50	10.00
(33)	Early Wynn	65.00	30.00	15.00
(34)	Sam Zoldak	35.00	17.50	10.00
(35)	Coaches (George Susce, Herold Ruel, Bill McKechnie, Steve O'Neill, Mel Harder)			
(36)	Municipal Stadium	35.00	17.50	10.00

1952 Num Num Cleveland Indians

Distributed with packages of Num Num potato chips, pretzels and other snack foods, this black-and-white set, like the 1950 issue, was also issued in a slightly different format directly by the team. The Num Num cards have a 1" tab at the bottom which could be redeemed, when a complete set was collected, for an autographed baseball. The team-issued version of the cards was printed without the tabs. Also like the 1950 Num Nums, Bob Kennedy's card is unaccountably scarce in the 1952 set. The '52 cards measure 3-1/2" x 5-1/2" including the tab, which has the card number on front, along with redemption details. Backs, also printed in black-and-white, repeat the card number in the upper-left corner. There is significant player biographical information and some 1951 season highlights. Cards with no tabs are worth about 1/3 less than the values quoted.

		NM	EX	VG
Complete Set, With Tabs (20):		5,750	2,300	1,150
Common Player, With Tab:		125.00	50.00	25.00
Complete Set, No Tabs (20):		3,250	1,300	650.00
Common Player, No Tab:		110.00	45.00	22.50
WITH TABS				
1	Lou Brissie	150.00	60.00	30.00
2	Jim Hegan	150.00	60.00	30.00
3	Birdie Tebbetts	150.00	60.00	30.00
4	Bob Lemon	300.00	120.00	60.00
5	Bob Feller	900.00	360.00	180.00
6	Early Wynn	300.00	120.00	60.00
7	Mike Garcia	150.00	60.00	30.00
8	Steve Gromek	150.00	60.00	30.00
9	Bob Chakales	150.00	60.00	30.00
10	Al Rosen	175.00	70.00	35.00
11	Dick Rozek	150.00	60.00	30.00
12	Luke Easter	175.00	70.00	35.00
13	Ray Boone	150.00	60.00	30.00
14	Bobby Avila	150.00	60.00	30.00
15	Dale Mitchell	150.00	60.00	30.00
16	Bob Kennedy (SP)	1,600	640.00	320.00
17	Harry Simpson	150.00	60.00	30.00
18	Larry Doby	300.00	120.00	60.00
19	Sam Jones	150.00	60.00	30.00
20	Al Lopez	300.00	120.00	60.00
NO TABS				
1	Lou Brissie	100.00	40.00	20.00
2	Jim Hegan	100.00	40.00	20.00
3	Birdie Tebbetts	100.00	40.00	20.00
4	Bob Lemon	200.00	80.00	40.00
5	Bob Feller	600.00	240.00	120.00
6	Early Wynn	200.00	80.00	40.00
7	Mike Garcia	100.00	40.00	20.00
8	Steve Gromek	100.00	40.00	20.00
9	Bob Chakales	100.00	40.00	20.00
10	Al Rosen	125.00	50.00	25.00
11	Dick Rozek	100.00	40.00	20.00
12	Luke Easter	125.00	50.00	25.00
13	Ray Boone	100.00	40.00	20.00
14	Bobby Avila	100.00	40.00	20.00
15	Dale Mitchell	100.00	40.00	20.00
16	Bob Kennedy (SP)	1,250	500.00	250.00
17	Harry Simpson	100.00	40.00	20.00
18	Larry Doby	200.00	80.00	40.00
19	Sam Jones	100.00	40.00	20.00
20	Al Lopez	200.00	80.00	40.00

O

1937 O-Pee-Chee

Kind of a combination of 1934 Goudeys and 1934-36 Batter Ups, the '37 OPC "Baseball Stars" set features black-and-white action photos against a stylized ballpark. About halfway up the 2-5/8" x 2-15/16" cards, the background was die-cut to allow it to be folded back to create a stand-up card. Backs are printed in English and French. The 40 cards in "Series A" are all American Leaguers, leading to speculation that a Series B of National League players was to have been issued at a later date. The set carries the American Card Catalog designation of V300.

		NM	EX	VG
Complete Set (40):		17,500	8,750	5,250
Common Player:		275.00	135.00	85.00
101	John Lewis	275.00	135.00	85.00
102	"Jack" Hayes	275.00	135.00	85.00
103	Earl Averill	400.00	200.00	120.00
104	Harland Clift (Harlond)	275.00	135.00	85.00
105	"Beau" Bell	275.00	135.00	85.00
106	Jimmy Foxx (Jimmie)	1,050	525.00	315.00
107	Hank Greenberg	1,325	660.00	400.00
108	George Selkirk	275.00	135.00	85.00
109	Wally Moses	275.00	135.00	85.00
110	"Gerry" Walker	275.00	135.00	85.00

111	"Goose" Goslin	400.00	200.00	120.00
112	Charlie Gehringer	425.00	210.00	125.00
113	Hal Trosky	275.00	135.00	85.00
114	"Buddy" Myer	275.00	135.00	85.00
115	Luke Appling	400.00	200.00	120.00
116	"Zeke" Bonura	275.00	135.00	85.00
117	Tony Lazzeri	425.00	210.00	125.00
118	Joe DiMaggio	4,100	2,050	1,225
119	Bill Dickey	600.00	300.00	180.00
120	Bob Feller	1,600	800.00	480.00
121	Harry Kelley	275.00	135.00	85.00
122	Johnny Allen	275.00	135.00	85.00
123	Bob Johnson	275.00	135.00	85.00
124	Joe Cronin	400.00	200.00	120.00
125	"Rip" Radcliff	275.00	135.00	85.00
126	Cecil Travis	275.00	135.00	85.00
127	Joe Kuhel	275.00	135.00	85.00
128	Odell Hale	275.00	135.00	85.00
129	Sam West	275.00	135.00	85.00
130	Ben Chapman	275.00	135.00	85.00
131	Monte Pearson	275.00	135.00	85.00
132	"Rick" Ferrell	400.00	200.00	120.00
133	Tommy Bridges	275.00	135.00	85.00
134	"Schoolboy" Rowe	275.00	135.00	85.00
135	Vernon Kennedy	275.00	135.00	85.00
136	"Red" Ruffing	400.00	200.00	120.00
137	"Lefty" Grove	500.00	250.00	150.00
138	Wes Farrell	275.00	135.00	85.00
139	"Buck" Newsom	275.00	135.00	85.00
140	Rogers Hornsby	750.00	375.00	225.00

1960 O-Pee-Chee Tattoos

Though much scarcer than the contemporary Topps version, this Canadian specialty bubblegum issue does not currently enjoy any price premium. The OPC type is identifiable by its imprint on the outside of the wrapper.

(See 1960 Topps Tattoos for description, checklist and price guide.)

1965 O-Pee-Chee

Identical in design to the 1965 Topps set, the Canadian-issued 1965 O-Pee-Chee set was printed on gray stock and consists of 283 cards, each measuring the standard 2-1/2" x 3-1/2". The words "Printed in Canada" appear along the bottom of the back of the cards. The checklist for '65 OPC parallels the first 283 cards in 1965 Topps.

	NM	EX	VG
Complete Set (283):	3,150	1,575	950.00
Common Player (1-196):	3.00	1.50	9.00
Common Player (197-283):	6.00	3.00	1.80
Stars: 2-3X Topps			

(See 1965 Topps #1-283 for checklist and star card values.)

1966 O-Pee-Chee

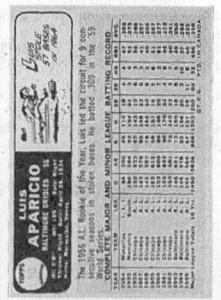

Utilizing the same design as the 1966 Topps set, the 1966 O-Pee-Chee set consists of 196 cards, measuring 2-1/2" x 3-1/2". The words "Ptd. in Canada" appear along the bottom on the back of the cards. The '66 OPC checklist parallels the first 196 cards in the Topps version.

	NM	EX	VG
Complete Set (196):	1,600	800.00	475.00
Common Player (1-196):	2.50	1.25	.75
Stars: 2-3X Topps			

(See 1966 Topps #1-196 for checklist and base star card values.)

1967 O-Pee-Chee

Cards in the 196-card Canadian set are nearly identical in design to the 1967 Topps set, except the words "Printed in Canada" are found on the back in the lower-right corner. Cards measure 2-1/2" x 3-1/2". The '67 OPC set parallels the first 196 cards on the Topps checklist, including "corrected" versions of the checklists and McCormick card.

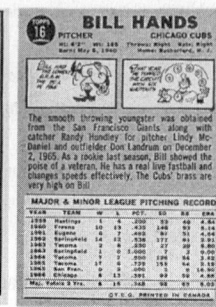

	NM	EX	VG
Complete Set (196):	1,100	550.00	330.00
Common Player (1-109):	2.00	1.00	.60
Common Player (110-196):	2.50	1.25	.75
Stars: 2-3X Topps			

(See 1967 Topps #1-196 for checklist and base star card values.)

1968 O-Pee-Chee

The O-Pee-Chee set for 1968 again consists of 196 cards, in the standard 2-1/2" x 3-1/2". The design is identical to the 1968 Topps set, except the color of the backs is slightly different and the words "Prd. in Canada" appear in the lower-right corner of the back. The checklist parallels the first 196 cards in '68 Topps, though only the "b" versions of the checklists and name-color variations are found in OPC.

	NM	EX	VG
Complete Set (196):	2,000	1,000	600.00
Common Player:	2.00	1.00	.60
Stars: 2-3X Topps			

(See 1968 Topps #1-196 for checklist and base star card values.)

177	Mets Rookies (Jerry Koosman, Nolan Ryan)	825.00	410.00	245.00

1968 O-Pee-Chee Posters

The 5" x 7" "All Star Pin-ups" were inserts to 1968 OPC wax packs, but are virtually identical to the Topps version issued in 1967. The OPC posters have a small "Ptd. in Canada" line at bottom. They feature a full-color picture with the player's name, position and team in a circle in the lower-right corner on front. The numbered set consists of 32 players (generally big names). Because the large paper pin-ups had to be folded several times to fit into the wax packs, they are almost never found in technical Mint or NM condition.

		NM	EX	VG
Complete Set (32):		300.00	150.00	90.00
Common Player:		3.00	1.50	.90
1	Brooks Robinson	12.00	6.00	3.50
2	Bert Campaneris	3.00	1.50	.90
3	Carl Yastrzemski	12.00	6.00	3.50
4	Roberto Clemente	25.00	12.50	7.50
5	Cleon Jones	3.00	1.50	.90
6	Don Drysdale	12.00	6.00	3.50
7	Orlando Cepeda	9.00	4.50	2.75
8	Hank Aaron	25.00	12.50	7.50
9	Tommie Agee	6.00	3.00	1.75
10	Boog Powell	4.50	2.25	1.25
11	Mickey Mantle	40.00	20.00	12.00
12	Chico Cardenas	3.00	1.50	.90
13	John Callison	3.00	1.50	.90
14	Frank Howard	3.75	2.00	1.25

15	Willie Mays	25.00	12.50	7.50
16	Sam McDowell	4.50	2.25	1.25
17	Al Kaline	12.00	6.00	3.50
18	Juan Marichal	9.00	4.50	2.75
19	Denny McLain	4.50	2.25	1.25
20	Matty Alou	3.00	1.50	.90
21	Felipe Alou	4.50	2.25	1.25
22	Joe Pepitone	4.50	2.25	1.25
23	Leon Wagner	3.00	1.50	.90
24	Bobby Knoop	3.00	1.50	.90
25	Tony Oliva	4.50	2.25	1.25
26	Joe Torre	4.50	2.25	1.25
27	Ron Santo	6.00	3.00	1.75
28	Willie McCovey	12.00	6.00	3.50
29	Frank Robinson	12.00	6.00	3.50
30	Ron Hunt	3.00	1.50	.90
31	Harmon Killebrew	12.00	6.00	3.50
32	Joe Morgan	12.00	6.00	3.50

1969 O-Pee-Chee

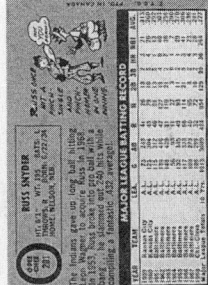

O-Pee-Chee increased the number of cards in its 1969 set to 218, maintaining the standard 2-1/2" x 3-1/2" size. The card design is identical to the 1969 Topps set, except for the appearance of an OPC logo on back, a slightly different color on the back and the words "Ptd. in Canada," which appear along the bottom. The checklist for '69 OPC parallels the Topps versions, but includes only the later-printed "b" versions of the variation cards. This was the first year for the N.L. expansion Montreal Expos, and the Canadian versions of their cards generally sell for a modest premium.

	NM	EX	VG
Complete Set (218):	775.00	375.00	225.00
Common Player:	2.50	1.25	.75
Stars: 1-2X Topps			
Expos: 1.5X Topps			

(See 1969 Topps #1-218 for checklist and base star card values.)

1969 O-Pee-Chee Deckle

Very similar in design to the Topps Deckle Edge set of the same year, the 1969 O-Pee-Chee set consists of 24 (rather than Topps' 33) unnumbered black-and-white cards. The Canadian version measures 2-1/8" x 3-1/8", slightly smaller than the Topps set, but features the same "deckle cut" borders. The OPC set is blank-backed and has the facsimile autographs in black ink, rather than blue.

		NM	EX	VG
Complete Set (24):		160.00	80.00	45.00
Common Player:		2.50	1.25	.75
(1)	Rich Allen	3.00	1.50	.90
(2)	Luis Aparicio	7.50	3.75	2.25
(3)	Rodney Carew	12.50	6.25	3.75
(4)	Roberto Clemente	30.00	15.00	9.00
(5)	Curt Flood	2.50	1.25	.75
(6)	Bill Freehan	2.50	1.25	.75
(7)	Robert Gibson	7.50	3.75	2.25
(8)	Ken Harrelson	2.50	1.25	.75
(9)	Tommy Helms	2.50	1.25	.75
(10)	Tom Haller	2.50	1.25	.75
(11)	Willie Horton	2.50	1.25	.70
(12)	Frank Howard	2.50	1.25	.75
(13)	Willie McCovey	10.00	5.00	3.00
(14)	Denny McLain	2.50	1.25	.75
(15)	Juan Marichal	7.50	3.75	2.25
(16)	Willie Mays	25.00	12.50	7.50
(17)	John "Boog" Powell	3.00	1.50	.90
(18)	Brooks Robinson	12.50	6.25	3.75
(19)	Ronald Santo	3.00	1.50	.90
(20)	Rusty Staub	3.00	1.50	.90

(21)	Mel Stottlemyre	2.50	1.25	.75
(22)	Luis Tiant	2.50	1.25	.75
(23)	Maurie Wills	2.50	1.25	.75
(24)	Carl Yastrzemski	12.50	6.25	3.75

1970 O-Pee-Chee

The 1970 O-Pee-Chee set, identical in design to the 1970 Topps set, expanded to 546 cards, measuring 2-1/2" x 3-1/2". The Canadian-issued O-Pee-Chee set is easy to distinguish because the backs are printed in both French and English and include the words "Printed in Canada." The '70 OPC checklist parallels the Topps versions. Besides the star cards generally bringing a premium over the Topps version due to scarcity, collectors pay a modest premium for OPC cards of Expos players.

	NM	EX	VG
Complete Set (546):	1,750	875.00	525.00
Common Player (1-459):	1.50	.75	.45
Common Player (460-546):	2.50	1.25	.75
Stars: 1-2X Topps			
Expos: 1.5X Topps			

(See 1970 Topps #1-546 for checklist and base card values.)

1971 O-Pee-Chee

For 1971 O-Pee-Chee increased the number of cards in its set to 752, the same as the 1971 Topps set, which shares the same black-bordered design. The backs of the OPC are printed in yellow, rather than green, in a slightly different format and (except card numbers 524-752) are printed in both French and English. The words "Printed in Canada" appear on the back. Fourteen of the OPC cards have different photos from their corresponding Topps' cards or list the player with a different team. The '71 OPC checklist parallels the Topps version. Because of relative scarcity, superstars in the OPC set command a premium, as do cards of the "local" Expos players.

	NM	EX	VG
Complete Set (752):	3,000	1,500	900.00
Common Player (1-523):	2.75	1.50	.80
Common Player (524-643):	4.50	2.25	1.25
Common Player (644-752):	6.50	3.25	2.00
Stars: 1-2X Topps			
Expos: 1.5X Topps			

(See 1971 Topps for checklist and base card values.)

1972 O-Pee-Chee

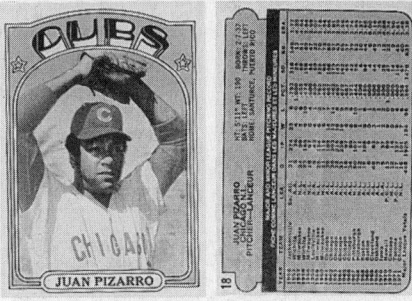

Identical in design to the Topps cards of the same year, the Canadian-issued 1972 O-Pee-Chee set numbers 525 cards, measuring 2-1/2" x 3-1/2". The backs state "Printed in Canada" and are written in both French and English. The O-Pee-Chee card of Gil Hodges notes the Mets' manager's death. The '72 OPC set parallels the first 525 cards on the '72 Topps checklist, though without any of the scarcer "a" varia-

tions. Because of relative scarcity, superstars in the OPC brand bring a premium over Topps cards, while increased demand for Expos players causes their cards to bring a similar modest premium.

	NM	EX	VG
Complete Set (525):	875.00	425.00	250.00
Common Player (1-263):	.60	.30	.20
Common Player (264-394):	.90	.45	.25
Common Player (395-525):	1.00	.50	.30
Stars: 1-2X Topps			
Expos: 1.5X Topps			

(See 1972 Topps #1-525 for checklist and base card values.)

1973 O-Pee-Chee

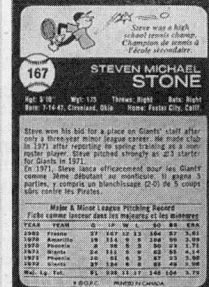

The 1973 Canadian-issued O-Pee-Chee set numbers 660 cards and is identical in design and checklist (including only the later-printed "b" variations) to the 1973 Topps set. The backs of the OPC cards are written in both French and English and contain the line "Printed in Canada" along the bottom. The cards measure 2-1/2" x 3-1/2". Unlike the '73 Topps set, which was issued in series of increasing scarcity throughout the summer, the '73 OPC cards were issued in a single series, with cards #529-660 being somewhat short-printed. OPC star cards generally sell for more than the Topps version due to relative scarcity, while Expos players in OPC rate a similar premium due to increased "local" demand.

	NM	EX	VG
Complete Set (660):	500.00	250.00	150.00
Common Player (1-528):	.75	.35	.20
Common Player (529-660):	1.25	.60	.40
Stars/Expos: 1.5X Topps			
Wax Pack (10):	55.00		
Wax Box (36):	1,900		

(See 1973 Topps for checklist and base card values.)

1973 O-Pee-Chee Team Checklists

Similar to the 1973 Topps team checklist cards, this set was produced in Canada. The set consists of 24 unnumbered cards (2-1/2" x 3-1/2") with blue borders. The card fronts contain facsimile autographs of players from the same team. The backs contain team checklists of players found in the 1973 O-Pee-Chee regular issue set. The card backs contain the French translation for Team Checklist plus a copyright line "O.P.C. Printed in Canada."

		NM	EX	VG
Complete Set (24):		40.00	20.00	12.00
Common Card:		3.00	1.50	.90
(1)	Atlanta Braves	3.00	1.50	.90
(2)	Baltimore Orioles	3.00	1.50	.90
(3)	Boston Red Sox	3.00	1.50	.90
(4)	California Angels	3.00	1.50	.90
(5)	Chicago Cubs	3.00	1.50	.90
(6)	Chicago White Sox	3.00	1.50	.90
(7)	Cincinnati Reds	4.00	2.00	1.25
(8)	Cleveland Indians	3.00	1.50	.90
(9)	Detroit Tigers	4.00	2.00	1.25
(10)	Houston Astros	3.00	1.50	.90
(11)	Kansas City Royals	3.00	1.50	.90
(12)	Los Angeles Dodgers	3.00	1.50	.90
(13)	Milwaukee Brewers	3.00	1.50	.90
(14)	Minnesota Twins	3.00	1.50	.90
(15)	Montreal Expos	6.00	3.00	1.75
(16)	New York Mets	4.00	2.00	1.25
(17)	New York Yankees	3.00	1.50	.90
(18)	Oakland A's	4.50	2.25	1.25
(19)	Philadelphia Phillies	3.00	1.50	.90
(20)	Pittsburgh Pirates	3.00	1.50	.90
(21)	St. Louis Cardinals	3.00	1.50	.90
(22)	San Diego Padres	3.00	1.50	.90
(23)	San Francisco Giants	3.00	1.50	.90
(24)	Texas Rangers	3.00	1.50	.90

1974 O-Pee-Chee

Again numbering 660 cards, the 1974 O-Pee-Chee set borrows its design and, except for 10 of the cards, shares its checklist with the Topps set of the same year. The cards measure the standard 2-1/2" x 3-1/2" and the backs are printed in both French and English and state "Printed in Canada." Because the OPC cards were printed later than Topps, there are no "Washington, Nat'l. League" variations in the Canadian set. Superstar cards and Expos players in OPC command a modest premium over the Topps version due to relative scarcity and increased local demand, respectively. Those OPC cards which differ from Topps are listed below, with the Topps version of each card number shown parenthetically.

		NM	EX	VG
Complete Set (660):		950.00	475.00	275.00
Common Player:		.50	.25	.15
Stars/Expos: 1.5X Topps				
Wax Pack (8):		65.00	.00	.00
Wax Box (36):		2,150.00	.00	.00
3	Aaron Special 1958-1959 (Aaron Special 1958-1961)	7.00	3.50	2.00
4	Aaron Special 1960-1961 (Aaron Special 1962-1965)	7.00	3.50	2.00
5	Aaron Special 1962-1963 (Aaron Special 1966-1969)	7.00	3.50	2.00
6	Aaron Special 1964-1965 (Aaron Special 1970-1973)	7.00	3.50	2.00
7	Aaron Special 1966-1967 (Jim Hunter)	7.00	3.50	2.00
8	Aaron Special 1968-1969 (George Theodore)	7.00	3.50	2.00
9	Aaron Special 1970-1973 (Mickey Lolich)	7.00	3.50	2.00
99	George Theodore (Brewers Mgr./Coaches)	1.50	.70	.45
166	Mickey Lolich (Royals Mgr./Coaches)	2.00	1.00	.60
196	Jim Hunter (Jim Fregosi)	7.50	3.75	2.25

(See 1974 Topps for checklist and base card values.)

1974 O-Pee-Chee Team Checklists

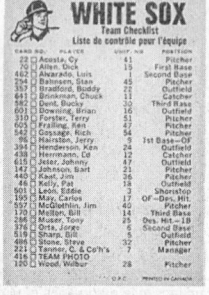

The 1974 O-Pee-Chee Team Checklists set is nearly identical to its Topps counterpart of the same year. Twenty-four unnumbered cards that measure 2-1/2" x 3-1/2" make up the set. The card fronts contain facsimile autographs while the backs carry a team checklist of player found in the regular issue O-Pee-Chee set of 1974. The cards have red borders and can be differentiated from the U.S. version by the "O.P.C. Printed in Canada" line on the back.

		NM	EX	VG
Complete Set (24):		25.00	12.50	7.50
Common Checklist:		1.50	.70	.40
(1)	Atlanta Braves	1.50	.70	.45
(2)	Baltimore Orioles	1.50	.70	.45
(3)	Boston Red Sox	1.50	.70	.45
(4)	California Angels	1.50	.70	.45
(5)	Chicago Cubs	1.50	.70	.45
(6)	Chicago White Sox	1.50	.70	.45
(7)	Cincinnati Reds	1.50	.70	.45
(8)	Cleveland Indians	1.50	.70	.45
(9)	Detroit Tigers	1.50	.70	.45
(10)	Houston Astros	1.50	.70	.45
(11)	Kansas City Royals	1.50	.70	.45
(12)	Los Angeles Dodgers	1.50	.70	.45
(13)	Milwaukee Brewers	1.50	.70	.45
(14)	Minnesota Twins	1.50	.70	.45
(15)	Montreal Expos	3.00	1.50	.90
(16)	New York Mets	1.50	.70	.45
(17)	New York Yankees	1.50	.70	.45
(18)	Oakland A's	1.50	.70	.45
(19)	Philadelphia Phillies	1.50	.70	.45
(20)	Pittsburgh Pirates	1.50	.70	.45
(21)	St. Louis Cardinals	1.50	.70	.45
(22)	San Diego Padres	1.50	.70	.45
(23)	San Francisco Giants	1.50	.70	.45
(24)	Texas Rangers	1.50	.70	.45

1975 O-Pee-Chee

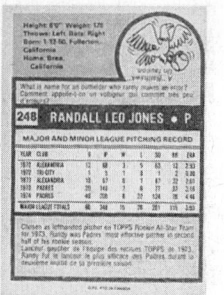

The 1975 O-Pee-Chee set was again complete at 660 cards, each measuring 2-1/2" x 3-1/2", and using the same design as the 1975 Topps set. The backs of the O-Pee-Chee cards are written in both French and English and state that the cards were printed in Canada. The checklist for OPC and Topps are identical in '75. Because they are relatively scarcer, OPC superstars sell for a premium over Topps. Expos players also enjoy a premium due to increased local demand.

	NM	EX	VG
Complete Set (660):	625.00	325.00	200.00
Common Player:	.45	.25	.15
Stars: 2X Topps			
Expos: 1.5X Topps			
Wax Pack (8):	30.00		
Wax Box (48):	1,200		

(See 1975 Topps for checklist and base card values.)

1976 O-Pee-Chee

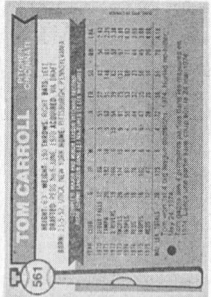

Identical in design to, and sharing a checklist with the 1976 Topps set, the Canadian-issued 1976 O-Pee-Chees comprise 660 cards, each 2-1/2" x 3-1/2". The backs are printed in both French and English and state "Ptd. in Canada." Stars and Expos players enjoy a modest premium over the Topps versions due to relative scarcity and increased local demand, respectively.

	NM	EX	VG
Complete Set (660):	700.00	350.00	210.00
Common Player:	.20	.10	.05
Stars/Expos 2X Topps			
Wax Pack (8):	30.00		
Wax Box (48):	750.00		

(See 1976 Topps for checklist and base card values.)

1977 O-Pee-Chee

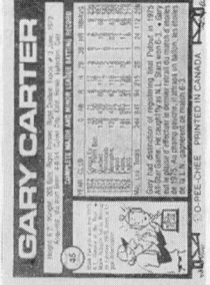

The 1977 O-Pee-Chee set represents a change in philosophy for the Canadian company. The design of the set is still identical to the Topps set of the same year, but the number of cards was reduced to 264 with more emphasis on players from the two Canadian teams. The backs are printed in both French and English and state "O-Pee-Chee Printed in Canada." About 1/3 of the photos in the OPC set differ from the corresponding Topps cards either with entirely different photos, airbrushed uniform changes, the removal of All-Star and Rookie Team designations, or significant photo cropping variations. Cards measure the standard 2-1/2" x 3-1/2".

		NM	EX	VG
Complete Set (264):		125.00	65.00	40.00
Common Player:		.25	.13	.08
Wax Pack (8):		12.00		
Wax Box (48):		285.00		
1	Batting Leaders (George Brett, Bill Madlock)	4.00	2.00	1.25
2	Home Run Leaders (Graig Nettles, Mike Schmidt)	2.75	1.50	.80
3	Runs Batted In Leaders (George Foster, Lee May)	.25	.13	.08
4	Stolen Base Leaders (Dave Lopes, Bill North)	.25	.13	.08
5	Victory Leaders (Randy Jones, Jim Palmer)	1.00	.50	.30
6	Strikeout Leaders (Nolan Ryan, Tom Seaver)	12.50	6.25	3.75
7	Earned Run Avg. Leaders (John Denny, Mark Fidrych)	.25	.13	.08
8	Leading Firemen (Bill Campbell, Rawly Eastwick)	.25	.13	.08
9	Mike Jorgensen	.25	.13	.08
10	Jim Hunter	4.00	2.00	1.25
11	Ken Griffey	.25	.13	.08
12	Bill Campbell	.25	.13	.08
13	Otto Velez	.25	.13	.08
14	Milt May	.25	.13	.08
15	Dennis Eckersley	4.00	2.00	1.25
16	John Mayberry	.25	.13	.08
17	Larry Bowa	.25	.13	.08
18	Don Carrithers	.25	.13	.08
19	Ken Singleton	.25	.13	.08
20	Bill Stein	.25	.13	.08
21	Ken Brett	.25	.13	.08
22	Gary Woods	.25	.13	.08
23	Steve Swisher	.25	.13	.08
24	Don Sutton	4.00	2.00	1.25
25	Willie Stargell	4.00	2.00	1.25
26	Jerry Koosman	.25	.13	.08
27	Del Unser	.25	.13	.08
28	Bob Grich	.25	.13	.08
29	Jim Slaton	.25	.13	.08
30	Thurman Munson	4.00	2.00	1.25
31	Dan Driessen	.25	.13	.08
32	Tom Bruno (Not in Topps.)	.25	.13	.08
33	Larry Hisle	.25	.13	.08
34	Phil Garner	.25	.13	.08
35	Mike Hargrove	.25	.13	.08
36	Jackie Brown	.25	.13	.08
37	Carl Yastrzemski	7.50	3.75	2.25
38	Dave Roberts	.25	.13	.08
39	Ray Fosse	.25	.13	.08
40	Dave McKay	.25	.13	.08
41	Paul Splittorff	.25	.13	.08
42	Garry Maddox	.25	.13	.08
43	Phil Niekro	4.00	2.00	1.25
44	Roger Metzger	.25	.13	.08
45	Gary Carter	7.50	3.75	2.25
46	Jim Spencer	.25	.13	.08
47	Ross Grimsley	.25	.13	.08
48	Bob Bailor	.25	.13	.08
49	Chris Chambliss	.25	.13	.08
50	Will McEnaney	.25	.13	.08
51	Lou Brock	4.50	2.25	1.25
52	Rollie Fingers	4.00	2.00	1.25
53	Chris Speier	.25	.13	.08
54	Bombo Rivera	.25	.13	.08
55	Pete Broberg	.25	.13	.08
56	Bill Madlock	.25	.13	.08
57	Rick Rhoden	.25	.13	.08
58	Blue Jay Coaches (Don Leppert, Bob Miller, Jackie Moore, Harry Warner)	.50	.25	.15
59	John Candelaria	.25	.13	.08
60	Ed Kranepool	.25	.13	.08
61	Dave LaRoche	.25	.13	.08
62	Jim Rice	.75	.40	.25
63	Don Stanhouse	.25	.13	.08
64	Jason Thompson	.25	.13	.08
65	Nolan Ryan	25.00	12.50	7.50
66	Tom Poquette	.25	.13	.08
67	Leon Hooten	.25	.13	.08
68	Bob Boone	.25	.13	.08
69	Mickey Rivers	.25	.13	.08
70	Gary Nolan	.25	.13	.08
71	Sixto Lezcano	.25	.13	.08
72	Larry Parrish	.25	.13	.08
73	Dave Goltz	.25	.13	.08
74	Bert Campaneris	.25	.13	.08
75	Vida Blue	.25	.13	.08
76	Rick Cerone	.25	.13	.08
77	Ralph Garr	.25	.13	.08
78	Ken Forsch	.25	.13	.08
79	Willie Montanez	.25	.13	.08
80	Jim Palmer	4.50	2.25	1.25
81	Jerry White	.25	.13	.08
82	Gene Tenace	.25	.13	.08
83	Bobby Murcer	.25	.13	.08
84	Garry Templeton	.25	.13	.08
85	Bill Singer	.25	.13	.08
86	Buddy Bell	.25	.13	.08
87	Luis Tiant	.25	.13	.08
88	Rusty Staub	.25	.13	.08
89	Sparky Lyle	.25	.13	.08
90	Jose Morales	.25	.13	.08
91	Dennis Leonard	.25	.13	.08
92	Tommy Smith	.25	.13	.08
93	Steve Carlton	5.50	2.75	1.75
94	John Scott	.25	.13	.08
95	Bill Bonham	.25	.13	.08
96	Dave Lopes	.25	.13	.08
97	Jerry Reuss	.25	.13	.08
98	Dave Kingman	.35	.20	.11
99	Dan Warthen	.25	.13	.08
100	Johnny Bench	7.50	3.75	2.25
101	Bert Blyleven	.25	.13	.08
102	Cecil Cooper	.25	.13	.08

#	Player	NM	EX	VG
103	Mike Willis	.25	.13	.08
104	Dan Ford	.25	.13	.08
105	Frank Tanana	.25	.13	.08
106	Bill North	.25	.13	.08
107	Joe Ferguson	.25	.13	.08
108	Dick Williams	.25	.13	.08
109	John Denny	.25	.13	.08
110	Willie Randolph	.25	.13	.08
111	Reggie Cleveland	.25	.13	.08
112	Doug Howard	.25	.13	.08
113	Randy Jones	.25	.13	.08
114	Rico Carty	.25	.13	.08
115	Mark Fidrych	2.75	1.50	.80
116	Darrell Porter	.25	.13	.08
117	Wayne Garrett	.25	.13	.08
118	Greg Luzinski	.25	.13	.08
119	Jim Barr	.25	.13	.08
120	George Foster	.25	.13	.08
121	Phil Roof	.25	.13	.08
122	Bucky Dent	.25	.13	.08
123	Steve Braun	.25	.13	.08
124	Checklist 1-132	.40	.20	.12
125	Lee May	.25	.13	.08
126	Woodie Fryman	.25	.13	.08
127	Jose Cardenal	.25	.13	.08
128	Doug Rau	.25	.13	.08
129	Rennie Stennett	.25	.13	.08
130	Pete Vuckovich	.25	.13	.08
131	Cesar Cedeno	.25	.13	.08
132	Jon Matlack	.25	.13	.08
133	Don Baylor	.30	.15	.09
134	Darrel Chaney	.25	.13	.08
135	Tony Perez	4.00	2.00	1.25
136	Aurelio Rodriguez	.25	.13	.08
137	Carlton Fisk	4.00	2.00	1.25
138	Wayne Garland	.25	.13	.08
139	Dave Hilton	.25	.13	.08
140	Rawly Eastwick	.25	.13	.08
141	Amos Otis	.25	.13	.08
142	Tug McGraw	.25	.13	.08
143	Rod Carew	5.50	2.75	1.75
144	Mike Torrez	.25	.13	.08
145	Sal Bando	.25	.13	.08
146	Dock Ellis	.25	.13	.08
147	Jose Cruz	.25	.13	.08
148	Alan Ashby	.25	.13	.08
149	Gaylord Perry	4.00	2.00	1.25
150	Keith Hernandez	.25	.13	.08
151	Dave Pagan	.25	.13	.08
152	Richie Zisk	.25	.13	.08
153	Steve Rogers	.25	.13	.08
154	Mark Belanger	.25	.13	.08
155	Andy Messersmith	.25	.13	.08
156	Dave Winfield	6.00	3.00	1.75
157	Chuck Hartenstein	.25	.13	.08
158	Manny Trillo	.25	.13	.08
159	Steve Yeager	.25	.13	.08
160	Cesar Geronimo	.25	.13	.08
161	Jim Rooker	.25	.13	.08
162	Tim Foli	.25	.13	.08
163	Fred Lynn	.25	.13	.08
164	Ed Figueroa	.25	.13	.08
165	Johnny Grubb	.25	.13	.08
166	Pedro Garcia	.25	.13	.08
167	Ron LeFlore	.25	.13	.08
168	Rich Hebner	.25	.13	.08
169	Larry Herndon	.25	.13	.08
170	George Brett	15.00	7.50	4.50
171	Joe Kerrigan	.25	.13	.08
172	Bud Harrelson	.25	.13	.08
173	Bobby Bonds	.25	.13	.08
174	Bill Travers	.25	.13	.08
175	John Lowenstein	.25	.13	.08
176	Butch Wynegar	.25	.13	.08
177	Pete Falcone	.25	.13	.08
178	Claudell Washington	.25	.13	.08
179	Checklist 133-264	.40	.20	.12
180	Dave Cash	.25	.13	.08
181	Fred Norman	.25	.13	.08
182	Roy White	.25	.13	.08
183	Marty Perez	.25	.13	.08
184	Jesse Jefferson	.25	.13	.08
185	Jim Sundberg	.25	.13	.08
186	Dan Meyer	.25	.13	.08
187	Fergie Jenkins	6.00	3.00	1.75
188	Tom Veryzer	.25	.13	.08
189	Dennis Blair	.25	.13	.08
190	Rick Manning	.25	.13	.08
191	Doug Bird	.25	.13	.08
192	Al Bumbry	.25	.13	.08
193	Dave Roberts	.25	.13	.08
194	Larry Christenson	.25	.13	.08
195	Chet Lemon	.25	.13	.08
196	Ted Simmons	.25	.13	.08
197	Ray Burris	.25	.13	.08
198	Expos Coaches (Jim Brewer, Billy Gardner, Mickey Vernon, Ozzie Virgil)	.25	.13	.08
199	Ron Cey	.25	.13	.08
200	Reggie Jackson	12.50	6.25	3.75
201	Pat Zachry	.25	.13	.08
202	Doug Ault	.25	.13	.08
203	Al Oliver	.25	.13	.08
204	Robin Yount	5.50	2.75	1.75
205	Tom Seaver	7.50	3.75	2.25
206	Joe Rudi	.25	.13	.08
207	Barry Foote	.25	.13	.08
208	Toby Harrah	.25	.13	.08
209	Jeff Burroughs	.25	.13	.08
210	George Scott	.25	.13	.08
211	Jim Mason	.25	.13	.08
212	Vern Ruhle	.25	.13	.08
213	Fred Kendall	.25	.13	.08
214	Rick Reuschel	.25	.13	.08
215	Hal McRae	.25	.13	.08
216	Chip Lang	.25	.13	.08
217	Graig Nettles	.30	.15	.09
218	George Hendrick	.25	.13	.08

#	Player	NM	EX	VG
219	Glenn Abbott	.25	.13	.08
220	Joe Morgan	4.50	2.25	1.25
221	Sam Ewing	.25	.13	.08
222	George Medich	.25	.13	.08
223	Reggie Smith	.25	.13	.08
224	Dave Hamilton	.25	.13	.08
225	Pepe Frias	.25	.13	.08
226	Jay Johnstone	.25	.13	.08
227	J.R. Richard	.25	.13	.08
228	Doug DeCinces	.25	.13	.08
229	Dave Lemanczyk	.25	.13	.08
230	Rick Monday	.25	.13	.08
231	Manny Sanguillen	.25	.13	.08
232	John Montefusco	.25	.13	.08
233	Duane Kuiper	.25	.13	.08
234	Ellis Valentine	.25	.13	.08
235	Dick Tidrow	.25	.13	.08
236	Ben Oglivie	.25	.13	.08
237	Rick Burleson	.25	.13	.08
238	Roy Hartsfield	.25	.13	.08
239	Lyman Bostock	.25	.13	.08
240	Pete Rose	13.50	6.75	4.00
241	Mike Ivie	.25	.13	.08
242	Dave Parker	.35	.20	.11
243	Bill Greif	.25	.13	.08
244	Freddie Patek	.25	.13	.08
245	Mike Schmidt	15.00	7.50	4.50
246	Brian Downing	.25	.13	.08
247	Steve Hargan	.25	.13	.08
248	Dave Collins	.25	.13	.08
249	Felix Millan	.25	.13	.08
250	Don Gullett	.25	.13	.08
251	Jerry Royster	.25	.13	.08
252	Earl Williams	.25	.13	.08
253	Frank Duffy	.25	.13	.08
254	Tippy Martinez	.25	.13	.08
255	Steve Garvey	2.75	1.50	.80
256	Alvis Woods	.25	.13	.08
257	John Hiller	.25	.13	.08
258	Dave Concepcion	.25	.13	.08
259	Dwight Evans	.25	.13	.08
260	Pete MacKanin	.25	.13	.08
261	George Brett (Record Breaker)	5.00	2.50	1.50
262	Minnie Minoso (Record Breaker)	.25	.13	.08
263	Jose Morales (Record Breaker)	.25	.13	.08
264	Nolan Ryan (Record Breaker)	12.50	6.25	3.75

1978 O-Pee-Chee

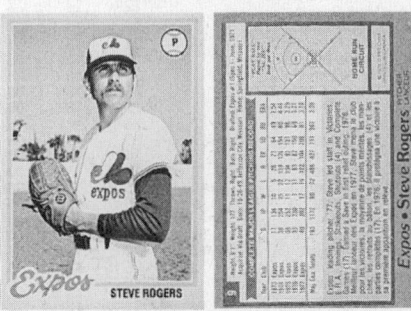

The 1978 O-Pee-Chee set was further reduced to 242 cards and again had heavy representation from the two Canadian teams. The cards measure the standard 2-1/2" x 3-1/2" and the backs are printed in both French and English. The cards use the same design as the 1978 Topps set. Some of the cards contain an extra line on the front indicating a team change.

		NM	EX	VG
	Complete Set (242):	120.00	60.00	35.00
	Common Player:	.25	.13	.08
	Wax Pack (10):	8.00		
	Wax Box (36):	200.00		
1	Batting Leaders (Rod Carew, Dave Parker)	.75	.40	.25
2	Home Run Leaders (George Foster, Jim Rice)	.25	.13	.08
3	Runs Batted In Leaders (George Foster, Larry Hisle)	.25	.13	.08
4	Stolen Base Leaders (Freddie Patek, Frank Taveras)	.25	.13	.08
5	Victory Leaders (Steve Carlton, Dave Goltz, Dennis Leonard, Jim Palmer)	.45	.25	.14
6	Strikeout Leaders (Phil Niekro, Nolan Ryan)	1.50	.70	.45
7	Earned Run Avg. Ldrs. (John Candelaria, Frank Tanana)	.25	.13	.08
8	Leading Firemen (Bill Campbell, Rollie Fingers)	.45	.25	.14
9	Steve Rogers	.25	.13	.08
10	Graig Nettles	.25	.13	.08
11	Doug Capilla	.25	.13	.08
12	George Scott	.25	.13	.08
13	Gary Woods	.25	.13	.08
14	Tom Veryzer	.25	.13	.08
15	Wayne Garland	.25	.13	.08
16	Amos Otis	.25	.13	.08
17	Larry Christenson	.25	.13	.08
18	Dave Cash	.25	.13	.08
19	Jim Barr	.25	.13	.08
20	Ruppert Jones	.25	.13	.08
21	Eric Soderholm	.25	.13	.08
22	Jesse Jefferson	.25	.13	.08
23	Jerry Morales	.25	.13	.08

#	Player	NM	EX	VG
24	Doug Rau	.25	.13	.08
25	Rennie Stennett	.25	.13	.08
26	Lee Mazzilli	.25	.13	.08
27	Dick Williams	.25	.13	.08
28	Joe Rudi	.25	.13	.08
29	Robin Yount	2.00	1.00	.60
30	Don Gullett	.25	.13	.08
31	Roy Howell	.25	.13	.08
32	Cesar Geronimo	.25	.13	.08
33	Rick Langford	.25	.13	.08
34	Dan Ford	.25	.13	.08
35	Gene Tenace	.25	.13	.08
36	Santo Alcala	.25	.13	.08
37	Rick Burleson	.25	.13	.08
38	Dave Rozema	.25	.13	.08
39	Duane Kuiper	.25	.13	.08
40	Ron Fairly	.25	.13	.08
41	Dennis Leonard	.25	.13	.08
42	Greg Luzinski	.25	.13	.08
43	Willie Montanez	.25	.13	.08
44	Enos Cabell	.25	.13	.08
45	Ellis Valentine	.25	.13	.08
46	Steve Stone	.25	.13	.08
47	Lee May	.25	.13	.08
48	Roy White	.25	.13	.08
49	Jerry Garvin	.25	.13	.08
50	Johnny Bench	2.00	1.00	.60
51	Garry Templeton	.25	.13	.08
52	Doyle Alexander	.25	.13	.08
53	Steve Henderson	.25	.13	.08
54	Stan Bahnsen	.25	.13	.08
55	Dan Meyer	.25	.13	.08
56	Rick Reuschel	.25	.13	.08
57	Reggie Smith	.25	.13	.08
58	Blue Jays Team	.50	.25	.15
59	John Montefusco	.25	.13	.08
60	Dave Parker	.25	.13	.08
61	Jim Bibby	.25	.13	.08
62	Fred Lynn	.25	.13	.08
63	Jose Morales	.25	.13	.08
64	Aurelio Rodriguez	.25	.13	.08
65	Frank Tanana	.25	.13	.08
66	Darrell Porter	.25	.13	.08
67	Otto Velez	.25	.13	.08
68	Larry Bowa	.25	.13	.08
69	Jim Hunter	1.50	.70	.45
70	George Foster	.25	.13	.08
71	Cecil Cooper	.25	.13	.08
72	Gary Alexander	.25	.13	.08
73	Paul Thormodsgard	.25	.13	.08
74	Toby Harrah	.25	.13	.08
75	Mitchell Page	.25	.13	.08
76	Alan Ashby	.25	.13	.08
77	Jorge Orta	.25	.13	.08
78	Dave Winfield	3.00	1.50	.90
79	Andy Messersmith	.25	.13	.08
80	Ken Singleton	.25	.13	.08
81	Will McEnaney	.25	.13	.08
82	Lou Piniella	.25	.13	.08
83	Bob Forsch	.25	.13	.08
84	Dan Driessen	.25	.13	.08
85	Dave Lemanczyk	.25	.13	.08
86	Paul Dade	.25	.13	.08
87	Bill Campbell	.25	.13	.08
88	Ron LeFlore	.25	.13	.08
89	Bill Madlock	.25	.13	.08
90	Tony Perez	.25	.13	.08
91	Freddie Patek	.25	.13	.08
92	Glenn Abbott	.25	.13	.08
93	Garry Maddox	.25	.13	.08
94	Steve Staggs	.25	.13	.08
95	Bobby Murcer	.25	.13	.08
96	Don Sutton	1.50	.70	.45
97	Al Oliver	.25	.13	.08
98	Jon Matlack	.25	.13	.08
99	Sam Mejias	.25	.13	.08
100	Pete Rose	6.00	3.00	1.75
101	Randy Jones	.25	.13	.08
102	Sixto Lezcano	.25	.13	.08
103	Jim Clancy	.25	.13	.08
104	Butch Wynegar	.25	.13	.08
105	Nolan Ryan	15.00	7.50	4.50
106	Wayne Gross	.25	.13	.08
107	Bob Watson	.25	.13	.08
108	Joe Kerrigan	.25	.13	.08
109	Keith Hernandez	.25	.13	.08
110	Reggie Jackson	5.00	2.50	1.50
111	Denny Doyle	.25	.13	.08
112	Sam Ewing	.25	.13	.08
113	Bert Blyleven	.25	.13	.08
114	Andre Thornton	.25	.13	.08
115	Milt May	.25	.13	.08
116	Jim Colborn	.25	.13	.08
117	Warren Cromartie	.25	.13	.08
118	Ted Sizemore	.25	.13	.08
119	Checklist 1-121	.35	.20	.11
120	Tom Seaver	2.50	1.25	.70
121	Luis Gomez	.25	.13	.08
122	Jim Spencer	.25	.13	.08
123	Leroy Stanton	.25	.13	.08
124	Luis Tiant	.25	.13	.08
125	Mark Belanger	.25	.13	.08
126	Jackie Brown	.25	.13	.08
127	Bill Buckner	.25	.13	.08
128	Bill Robinson	.25	.13	.08
129	Rick Cerone	.25	.13	.08
130	Ron Cey	.25	.13	.08
131	Jose Cruz	.25	.13	.08
132	Len Randle	.25	.13	.08
133	Bob Grich	.25	.13	.08
134	Jeff Burroughs	.25	.13	.08
135	Gary Carter	6.00	3.00	1.75
136	Milt Wilcox	.25	.13	.08
137	Carl Yastrzemski	2.50	1.25	.70
138	Dennis Eckersley	1.50	.70	.45
139	Tim Nordbrook	.25	.13	.08
140	Ken Griffey	.25	.13	.08
141	Bob Boone	.25	.13	.08

#	Player	NM	EX	VG
142	Dave Goltz	.25	.13	.08
143	Al Cowens	.25	.13	.08
144	Bill Atkinson	.25	.13	.08
145	Chris Chambliss	.25	.13	.08
146	Jim Slaton	.25	.13	.08
147	Bill Stein	.25	.13	.08
148	Bob Bailor	.25	.13	.08
149	J.R. Richard	.25	.13	.08
150	Ted Simmons	.25	.13	.08
151	Rick Manning	.25	.13	.08
152	Lerrin LaGrow	.25	.13	.08
153	Larry Parrish	.25	.13	.08
154	Eddie Murray	15.00	7.50	4.50
155	Phil Niekro	1.50	.70	.45
156	Bake McBride	.25	.13	.08
157	Pete Vuckovich	.25	.13	.08
158	Ivan DeJesus	.25	.13	.08
159	Rick Rhoden	.25	.13	.08
160	Joe Morgan	2.00	1.00	.60
161	Ed Ott	.25	.13	.08
162	Don Stanhouse	.25	.13	.08
163	Jim Rice	.50	.25	.15
164	Bucky Dent	.25	.13	.08
165	Jim Kern	.25	.13	.08
166	Doug Rader	.25	.13	.08
167	Steve Kemp	.25	.13	.08
168	John Mayberry	.25	.13	.08
169	Tim Foli	.25	.13	.08
170	Steve Carlton	2.00	1.00	.60
171	Pepe Frias	.25	.13	.08
172	Pat Zachry	.25	.13	.08
173	Don Baylor	.25	.13	.08
174	Sal Bando	.25	.13	.08
175	Alvis Woods	.25	.13	.08
176	Mike Hargrove	.25	.13	.08
177	Vida Blue	.25	.13	.08
178	George Hendrick	.25	.13	.08
179	Jim Palmer	2.00	1.00	.60
180	Andre Dawson	10.00	5.00	3.00
181	Paul Moskau	.25	.13	.08
182	Mickey Rivers	.25	.13	.08
183	Checklist 122-242	.35	.20	.11
184	Jerry Johnson	.25	.13	.08
185	Willie McCovey	2.00	1.00	.60
186	Enrique Romo	.25	.13	.08
187	Butch Hobson	.25	.13	.08
188	Rusty Staub	.45	.25	.14
189	Wayne Twitchell	.25	.13	.08
190	Steve Garvey	1.00	.50	.30
191	Rick Waits	.25	.13	.08
192	Doug DeCinces	.25	.13	.08
193	Tom Murphy	.25	.13	.08
194	Rich Hebner	.25	.13	.08
195	Ralph Garr	.25	.13	.08
196	Bruce Sutter	1.50	.70	.45
197	Tom Poquette	.25	.13	.08
198	Wayne Garrett	.25	.13	.08
199	Pedro Borbon	.25	.13	.08
200	Thurman Munson	2.00	1.00	.60
201	Rollie Fingers	1.50	.70	.45
202	Doug Ault	.25	.13	.08
203	Phil Garner	.25	.13	.08
204	Lou Brock	2.00	1.00	.60
205	Ed Kranepool	.25	.13	.08
206	Bobby Bonds	.25	.13	.08
207	Expos Team	.25	.13	.08
208	Bump Wills	.25	.13	.08
209	Gary Matthews	.25	.13	.08
210	Carlton Fisk	2.00	1.00	.60
211	Jeff Byrd	.25	.13	.08
212	Jason Thompson	.25	.13	.08
213	Larvell Blanks	.25	.13	.08
214	Sparky Lyle	.25	.13	.08
215	George Brett	6.00	3.00	1.75
216	Del Unser	.25	.13	.08
217	Manny Trillo	.25	.13	.08
218	Roy Hartsfield	.25	.13	.08
219	Carlos Lopez	.25	.13	.08
220	Dave Concepcion	.25	.13	.08
221	John Candelaria	.25	.13	.08
222	Dave Lopes	.25	.13	.08
223	Tim Blackwell	.25	.13	.08
224	Chet Lemon	.25	.13	.08
225	Mike Schmidt	6.00	3.00	1.75
226	Cesar Cedeno	.25	.13	.08
227	Mike Willis	.25	.13	.08
228	Willie Randolph	.25	.13	.08
229	Doug Bair	.25	.13	.08
230	Rod Carew	2.00	1.00	.60
231	Mike Flanagan	.25	.13	.08
232	Chris Speier	.25	.13	.08
233	Don Aase	.25	.13	.08
234	Buddy Bell	.25	.13	.08
235	Mark Fidrych	.30	.15	.09
236	Lou Brock (Record Breaker)	.75	.40	.25
237	Sparky Lyle (Record Breaker)	.25	.13	.08
238	Willie McCovey (Record Breaker)	.45	.25	.14
239	Brooks Robinson (Record Breaker)	.90	.45	.25
240	Pete Rose (Record Breaker)	2.00	1.00	.60
241	Nolan Ryan (Record Breaker)	10.00	5.00	3.00
242	Reggie Jackson (Record Breaker)	1.50	.70	.45

1979 O-Pee-Chee

The 1979 O-Pee-Chee cards are nearly identical in design to the Topps set of the same year, but display the O-Pee-Chee logo inside the baseball in the lower-left corner of the front. The number of cards in the set was increased to 374, each measuring 2-1/2" x 3-1/2".

 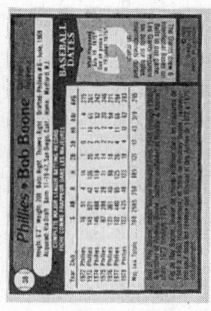

		NM	EX	VG
Complete Set (374):		80.00	40.00	24.00
Common Player:		.25	.13	.08
Wax Pack (10):		10.00		
Wax Box (36):		175.00		
1	Lee May	.25	.13	.08
2	Dick Drago	.25	.13	.08
3	Paul Dade	.25	.13	.08
4	Ross Grimsley	.25	.13	.08
5	Joe Morgan	2.00	1.00	.60
6	Kevin Kobel	.25	.13	.08
7	Terry Forster	.25	.13	.08
8	Paul Molitor	12.00	6.00	3.50
9	Steve Carlton	2.00	1.00	.60
10	Dave Goltz	.25	.13	.08
11	Dave Winfield	3.00	1.50	.90
12	Dave Rozema	.25	.13	.08
13	Ed Figueroa	.25	.13	.08
14	Alan Ashby	.25	.13	.08
15	Dale Murphy	2.50	1.25	.70
16	Dennis Eckersley	1.50	.70	.45
17	Ron Blomberg	.25	.13	.08
18	Wayne Twitchell	.25	.13	.08
19	Al Hrabosky	.25	.13	.08
20	Fred Norman	.25	.13	.08
21	Steve Garvey	1.00	.50	.30
22	Willie Stargell	2.00	1.00	.60
23	John Hale	.25	.13	.08
24	Mickey Rivers	.25	.13	.08
25	Jack Brohamer	.25	.13	.08
26	Tom Underwood	.25	.13	.08
27	Mark Belanger	.25	.13	.08
28	Elliott Maddox	.25	.13	.08
29	John Candelaria	.25	.13	.08
30	Shane Rawley	.25	.13	.08
31	Steve Yeager	.25	.13	.08
32	Warren Cromartie	.25	.13	.08
33	Jason Thompson	.25	.13	.08
34	Roger Erickson	.25	.13	.08
35	Gary Matthews	.25	.13	.08
36	Pete Falcone	.25	.13	.08
37	Dick Tidrow	.25	.13	.08
38	Bob Boone	.25	.13	.08
39	Jim Bibby	.25	.13	.08
40	Len Barker	.25	.13	.08
41	Robin Yount	2.00	1.00	.60
42	Sam Mejias	.25	.13	.08
43	Ray Burris	.25	.13	.08
44	Tom Seaver	2.50	1.25	.70
45	Roy Howell	.25	.13	.08
46	Jim Todd	.25	.13	.08
47	Frank Duffy	.25	.13	.08
48	Joel Youngblood	.25	.13	.08
49	Vida Blue	.25	.13	.08
50	Cliff Johnson	.25	.13	.08
51	Nolan Ryan	15.00	7.50	4.50
52	Ozzie Smith	20.00	10.00	6.00
53	Jim Sundberg	.25	.13	.08
54	Mike Paxton	.25	.13	.08
55	Lou Whitaker	1.00	.50	.30
56	Dan Schatzeder	.25	.13	.08
57	Rick Burleson	.25	.13	.08
58	Doug Bair	.25	.13	.08
59	Ted Martinez	.25	.13	.08
60	Bob Watson	.25	.13	.08
61	Jim Clancy	.25	.13	.08
62	Rowland Office	.25	.13	.08
63	Bobby Murcer	.25	.13	.08
64	Don Gullett	.25	.13	.08
65	Tom Paciorek	.25	.13	.08
66	Rick Rhoden	.25	.13	.08
67	Duane Kuiper	.25	.13	.08
68	Bruce Boisclair	.25	.13	.08
69	Manny Sarmiento	.25	.13	.08
70	Wayne Cage	.25	.13	.08
71	John Hiller	.25	.13	.08
72	Rick Cerone	.25	.13	.08
73	Dwight Evans	.25	.13	.08
74	Buddy Solomon	.25	.13	.08
75	Roy White	.25	.13	.08
76	Mike Flanagan	.25	.13	.08
77	Tom Johnson	.25	.13	.08
78	Glenn Burke	.25	.13	.08
79	Frank Taveras	.25	.13	.08
80	Don Sutton	1.50	.70	.45
81	Leon Roberts	.25	.13	.08
82	George Hendrick	.25	.13	.08
83	Aurelio Rodriguez	.25	.13	.08
84	Ron Reed	.25	.13	.08
85	Alvis Woods	.25	.13	.08
86	Jim Beattie	.25	.13	.08
87	Larry Hisle	.25	.13	.08
88	Mike Garman	.25	.13	.08
89	Tim Johnson	.25	.13	.08
90	Paul Splittorff	.25	.13	.08
91	Darrel Chaney	.25	.13	.08
92	Mike Torrez	.25	.13	.08
93	Eric Soderholm	.25	.13	.08

#	Player	NM	EX	VG
94	Ron Cey	.25	.13	.08
95	Randy Jones	.25	.13	.08
96	Bill Madlock	.25	.13	.08
97	Steve Kemp	.25	.13	.08
98	Bob Apodaca	.25	.13	.08
99	Johnny Grubb	.25	.13	.08
100	Larry Milbourne	.25	.13	.08
101	Johnny Bench	2.00	1.00	.60
102	Dave Lemanczyk	.25	.13	.08
103	Reggie Cleveland	.25	.13	.08
104	Larry Bowa	.25	.13	.08
105	Denny Martinez	1.00	.50	.30
106	Bill Travers	.25	.13	.08
107	Willie McCovey	2.00	1.00	.60
108	Wilbur Wood	.25	.13	.08
109	Dennis Leonard	.25	.13	.08
110	Roy Smalley	.25	.13	.08
111	Cesar Geronimo	.25	.13	.08
112	Jesse Jefferson	.25	.13	.08
113	Dave Revering	.25	.13	.08
114	Rich Gossage	.30	.15	.09
115	Steve Stone	.25	.13	.08
116	Doug Flynn	.25	.13	.08
117	Bob Forsch	.25	.13	.08
118	Paul Mitchell	.25	.13	.08
119	Toby Harrah	.25	.13	.08
120	Steve Rogers	.25	.13	.08
121	Checklist 1-125	.25	.13	.08
122	Balor Moore	.25	.13	.08
123	Rick Reuschel	.25	.13	.08
124	Jeff Burroughs	.25	.13	.08
125	Willie Randolph	.25	.13	.08
126	Bob Stinson	.25	.13	.08
127	Rick Wise	.25	.13	.08
128	Luis Gomez	.25	.13	.08
129	Tommy John	.25	.13	.08
130	Richie Zisk	.25	.13	.08
131	Mario Guerrero	.25	.13	.08
132	Oscar Gamble	.25	.13	.08
133	Don Money	.25	.13	.08
134	Joe Rudi	.25	.13	.08
135	Woodie Fryman	.25	.13	.08
136	Butch Hobson	.25	.13	.08
137	Jim Colborn	.25	.13	.08
138	Tom Grieve	.25	.13	.08
139	Andy Messersmith	.25	.13	.08
140	Andre Thornton	.25	.13	.08
141	Kevin Kravec	.25	.13	.08
142	Bobby Bonds	.25	.13	.08
143	Jose Cruz	.25	.13	.08
144	Dave Lopes	.25	.13	.08
145	Jerry Garvin	.25	.13	.08
146	Pepe Frias	.25	.13	.08
147	Mitchell Page	.25	.13	.08
148	Ted Sizemore	.25	.13	.08
149	Rich Gale	.25	.13	.08
150	Steve Ontiveros	.25	.13	.08
151	Rod Carew	2.00	1.00	.60
152	Lary Sorensen	.25	.13	.08
153	Willie Montanez	.25	.13	.08
154	Floyd Bannister	.25	.13	.08
155	Bert Blyleven	.25	.13	.08
156	Ralph Garr	.25	.13	.08
157	Thurman Munson	1.00	.50	.30
158	Bob Robertson	.25	.13	.08
159	Jon Matlack	.25	.13	.08
160	Carl Yastrzemski	2.50	1.25	.70
161	Gaylord Perry	1.50	.70	.45
162	Mike Tyson	.25	.13	.08
163	Cecil Cooper	.25	.13	.08
164	Pedro Borbon	.25	.13	.08
165	Art Howe	.25	.13	.08
166	Joe Coleman	.25	.13	.08
167	George Brett	6.00	3.00	1.75
168	Gary Alexander	.25	.13	.08
169	Chet Lemon	.25	.13	.08
170	Craig Swan	.25	.13	.08
171	Chris Chambliss	.25	.13	.08
172	John Montague	.25	.13	.08
173	Ron Jackson	.25	.13	.08
174	Jim Palmer	2.00	1.00	.60
175	Willie Upshaw	.75	.40	.25
176	Tug McGraw	.25	.13	.08
177	Bill Buckner	.25	.13	.08
178	Doug Rau	.25	.13	.08
179	Andre Dawson	3.50	1.75	1.00
180	Jim Wright	.25	.13	.08
181	Garry Templeton	.25	.13	.08
182	Bill Bonham	.25	.13	.08
183	Lee Mazzilli	.25	.13	.08
184	Alan Trammell	2.00	1.00	.60
185	Amos Otis	.25	.13	.08
186	Tom Dixon	.25	.13	.08
187	Mike Cubbage	.25	.13	.08
188	Sparky Lyle	.25	.13	.08
189	Juan Bernhardt	.25	.13	.08
190	Bump Wills	.25	.13	.08
191	Dave Kingman	.25	.13	.08
192	Lamar Johnson	.25	.13	.08
193	Lance Rautzhan	.25	.13	.08
194	Ed Herrmann	.25	.13	.08
195	Bill Campbell	.25	.13	.08
196	Gorman Thomas	.25	.13	.08
197	Paul Moskau	.25	.13	.08
198	Dale Murray	.25	.13	.08
199	John Mayberry	.25	.13	.08
200	Phil Garner	.25	.13	.08
201	Dan Ford	.25	.13	.08
202	Gary Thomasson	.25	.13	.08
203	Rollie Fingers	1.50	.70	.45
204	Al Oliver	.25	.13	.08
205	Doug Ault	.25	.13	.08
206	Scott McGregor	.25	.13	.08
207	Dave Cash	.25	.13	.08
208	Bill Plummer	.25	.13	.08
209	Ivan DeJesus	.25	.13	.08
210	Jim Rice	.75	.40	.25
211	Ray Knight	.25	.13	.08

		NM	EX	VG
212	Paul Hartzell	.25	.13	.08
213	Tim Foli	.25	.13	.08
214	Butch Wynegar	.25	.13	.08
215	Darrell Evans	.25	.13	.08
216	Ken Griffey	.25	.13	.08
217	Doug DeCinces	.25	.13	.08
218	Ruppert Jones	.25	.13	.08
219	Bob Montgomery	.25	.13	.08
220	Rick Manning	.25	.13	.08
221	Chris Speier	.25	.13	.08
222	Bobby Valentine	.25	.13	.08
223	Dave Parker	.25	.13	.08
224	Larry Biittner	.25	.13	.08
225	Ken Clay	.25	.13	.08
226	Gene Tenace	.25	.13	.08
227	Frank White	.25	.13	.08
228	Rusty Staub	.35	.20	.11
229	Lee Lacy	.25	.13	.08
230	Doyle Alexander	.25	.13	.08
231	Bruce Bochte	.25	.13	.08
232	Steve Henderson	.25	.13	.08
233	Jim Lonborg	.25	.13	.08
234	Dave Concepcion	.25	.13	.08
235	Jerry Morales	.25	.13	.08
236	Len Randle	.25	.13	.08
237	Bill Lee	.25	.13	.08
238	Bruce Sutter	1.50	.70	.45
239	Jim Essian	.25	.13	.08
240	Graig Nettles	.25	.13	.08
241	Otto Velez	.25	.13	.08
242	Checklist 126-250	.25	.13	.08
243	Reggie Smith	.25	.13	.08
244	Stan Bahnsen	.25	.13	.08
245	Garry Maddox	.25	.13	.08
246	Joaquin Andujar	.25	.13	.08
247	Dan Driessen	.25	.13	.08
248	Bob Grich	.25	.13	.08
249	Fred Lynn	.25	.13	.08
250	Skip Lockwood	.25	.13	.08
251	Craig Reynolds	.25	.13	.08
252	Willie Horton	.25	.13	.08
253	Rick Waits	.25	.13	.08
254	Bucky Dent	.25	.13	.08
255	Bob Knepper	.25	.13	.08
256	Miguel Dilone	.25	.13	.08
257	Bob Owchinko	.25	.13	.08
258	Al Cowens	.25	.13	.08
259	Bob Bailor	.25	.13	.08
260	Larry Christenson	.25	.13	.08
261	Tony Perez	1.50	.70	.45
262	Blue Jays Team	.25	.13	.08
263	Glenn Abbott	.25	.13	.08
264	Ron Guidry	.50	.25	.15
265	Ed Kranepool	.25	.13	.08
266	Charlie Hough	.25	.13	.08
267	Ted Simmons	.25	.13	.08
268	Jack Clark	.25	.13	.08
269	Enos Cabell	.25	.13	.08
270	Gary Carter	6.00	3.00	1.75
271	Sam Ewing	.25	.13	.08
272	Tom Burgmeier	.25	.13	.08
273	Freddie Patek	.25	.13	.08
274	Frank Tanana	.25	.13	.08
275	Leroy Stanton	.25	.13	.08
276	Ken Forsch	.25	.13	.08
277	Ellis Valentine	.25	.13	.08
278	Greg Luzinski	.25	.13	.08
279	Rick Bosetti	.25	.13	.08
280	John Stearns	.25	.13	.08
281	Enrique Romo	.25	.13	.08
282	Bob Bailey	.25	.13	.08
283	Sal Bando	.25	.13	.08
284	Matt Keough	.25	.13	.08
285	Biff Pocoroba	.25	.13	.08
286	Mike Lum	.25	.13	.08
287	Jay Johnstone	.25	.13	.08
288	John Montefusco	.25	.13	.08
289	Ed Ott	.25	.13	.08
290	Dusty Baker	.25	.13	.08
291	Rico Carty	.25	.13	.08
292	Nino Espinosa	.25	.13	.08
293	Rich Hebner	.25	.13	.08
294	Cesar Cedeno	.25	.13	.08
295	Darrell Porter	.25	.13	.08
296	Rod Gilbreath	.25	.13	.08
297	Jim Kern	.25	.13	.08
298	Claudell Washington	.25	.13	.08
299	Luis Tiant	.25	.13	.08
300	Mike Parrott	.25	.13	.08
301	Pete Broberg	.25	.13	.08
302	Greg Gross	.25	.13	.08
303	Darold Knowles	.25	.13	.08
304	Paul Blair	.25	.13	.08
305	Julio Cruz	.25	.13	.08
306	Hal McRae	.25	.13	.08
307	Ken Reitz	.25	.13	.08
308	Tom Murphy	.25	.13	.08
309	Terry Whitfield	.25	.13	.08
310	J.R. Richard	.25	.13	.08
311	Mike Hargrove	.25	.13	.08
312	Rick Dempsey	.25	.13	.08
313	Phil Niekro	1.50	.70	.45
314	Bob Stanley	.25	.13	.08
315	Jim Spencer	.25	.13	.08
316	George Foster	.25	.13	.08
317	Dave LaRoche	.25	.13	.08
318	Rudy May	.25	.13	.08
319	Jeff Newman	.25	.13	.08
320	Rick Monday	.25	.13	.08
321	Omar Moreno	.25	.13	.08
322	Dave McKay	.25	.13	.08
323	Mike Schmidt	6.00	3.00	1.75
324	Ken Singleton	.25	.13	.08
325	Jerry Remy	.25	.13	.08
326	Bert Campaneris	.25	.13	.08
327	Pat Zachry	.25	.13	.08
328	Larry Herndon	.25	.13	.08
329	Mark Fidrych	.25	.13	.08

		NM	EX	VG
330	Del Unser	.25	.13	.08
331	Gene Garber	.25	.13	.08
332	Bake McBride	.25	.13	.08
333	Jorge Orta	.25	.13	.08
334	Don Kirkwood	.25	.13	.08
335	Don Baylor	.25	.13	.08
336	Bill Robinson	.25	.13	.08
337	Manny Trillo	.25	.13	.08
338	Eddie Murray	3.00	1.50	.90
339	Tom Hausman	.25	.13	.08
340	George Scott	.25	.13	.08
341	Rick Sweet	.25	.13	.08
342	Lou Piniella	.25	.13	.08
343	Pete Rose	15.00	7.50	4.50
344	Stan Papi	.25	.13	.08
345	Jerry Koosman	.25	.13	.08
346	Hosken Powell	.25	.13	.08
347	George Medich	.25	.13	.08
348	Ron LeFlore	.25	.13	.08
349	Expos Team	.75	.40	.25
350	Lou Brock	2.00	1.00	.60
351	Bill North	.25	.13	.08
352	Jim Hunter	1.50	.70	.45
353	Checklist 251-374	.25	.13	.08
354	Ed Halicki	.25	.13	.08
355	Tom Hutton	.25	.13	.08
356	Mike Caldwell	.25	.13	.08
357	Larry Parrish	.25	.13	.08
358	Geoff Zahn	.25	.13	.08
359	Derrel Thomas	.25	.13	.08
360	Carlton Fisk	2.00	1.00	.60
361	John Henry Johnson	.25	.13	.08
362	Dave Chalk	.25	.13	.08
363	Dan Meyer	.25	.13	.08
364	Sixto Lezcano	.25	.13	.08
365	Rennie Stennett	.25	.13	.08
366	Mike Willis	.25	.13	.08
367	Buddy Bell	.25	.13	.08
368	Mickey Stanley	.25	.13	.08
369	Dave Rader	.25	.13	.08
370	Burt Hooton	.25	.13	.08
371	Keith Hernandez	.25	.13	.08
372	Bill Stein	.25	.13	.08
373	Hal Dues	.25	.13	.08
374	Reggie Jackson	3.00	1.50	.90

1980 O-Pee-Chee

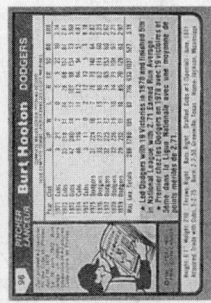

The 1980 Canadian-issued O-Pee-Chee set was again complete at 374 cards, which measure 2-1/2" x 3-1/2" and share the same design as the 1980 Topps set. The OPC cards are printed on a white stock, rather than the traditional gray stock used by Topps, and their backs are written in both French and English. Some of the cards include an extra line on the front indicating a new team designation.

		NM	EX	VG
Complete Set (374):		110.00	55.00	32.50
Common Player:		.15	.08	.05
Wax Pack (10):		10.00		
Wax Box (36):		290.00		
1	Craig Swan	.15	.08	.05
2	Denny Martinez	.15	.08	.05
3	Dave Cash	.15	.08	.05
4	Bruce Sutter	1.50	.70	.45
5	Ron Jackson	.15	.08	.05
6	Balor Moore	.15	.08	.05
7	Dan Ford	.15	.08	.05
8	Pat Putnam	.15	.08	.05
9	Derrel Thomas	.15	.08	.05
10	Jim Slaton	.15	.08	.05
11	Lee Mazzilli	.15	.08	.05
12	Del Unser	.15	.08	.05
13	Mark Wagner	.15	.08	.05
14	Vida Blue	.15	.08	.05
15	Jay Johnstone	.15	.08	.05
16	Julio Cruz	.15	.08	.05
17	Tony Scott	.15	.08	.05
18	Jeff Newman	.15	.08	.05
19	Luis Tiant	.15	.08	.05
20	Carlton Fisk	1.50	.70	.45
21	Dave Palmer	.15	.08	.05
22	Bombo Rivera	.15	.08	.05
23	Bill Fahey	.15	.08	.05
24	Frank White	.15	.08	.05
25	Rico Carty	.15	.08	.05
26	Bill Bonham	.15	.08	.05
27	Rick Miller	.15	.08	.05
28	J.R. Richard	.15	.08	.05
29	Joe Ferguson	.15	.08	.05
30	Bill Madlock	.15	.08	.05
31	Pete Vuckovich	.15	.08	.05
32	Doug Flynn	.15	.08	.05
33	Bucky Dent	.15	.08	.05
34	Mike Ivie	.15	.08	.05
35	Bob Stanley	.15	.08	.05
36	Al Bumbry	.15	.08	.05
37	Gary Carter	5.00	2.50	1.50

		NM	EX	VG
38	John Milner	.15	.08	.05
39	Sid Monge	.15	.08	.05
40	Bill Russell	.15	.08	.05
41	John Stearns	.15	.08	.05
42	Dave Stieb	1.25	.60	.40
43	Ruppert Jones	.15	.08	.05
44	Bob Owchinko	.15	.08	.05
45	Ron LeFlore	.15	.08	.05
46	Ted Sizemore	.15	.08	.05
47	Ted Simmons	.15	.08	.05
48	Pepe Frias	.15	.08	.05
49	Ken Landreaux	.15	.08	.05
50	Manny Trillo	.15	.08	.05
51	Rick Dempsey	.15	.08	.05
52	Cecil Cooper	.15	.08	.05
53	Bill Lee	.15	.08	.05
54	Victor Cruz	.15	.08	.05
55	Johnny Bench	1.50	.70	.45
56	Rich Dauer	.15	.08	.05
57	Frank Tanana	.15	.08	.05
58	Francisco Barrios	.15	.08	.05
59	Bob Horner	.30	.15	.09
60	Fred Lynn	.15	.08	.05
61	Bob Knepper	.15	.08	.05
62	Sparky Lyle	.15	.08	.05
63	Larry Cox	.15	.08	.05
64	Dock Ellis	.15	.08	.05
65	Phil Garner	.15	.08	.05
66	Greg Luzinski	.15	.08	.05
67	Checklist 1-125	.25	.13	.08
68	Dave Lemanczyk	.15	.08	.05
69	Tony Perez	1.50	.70	.45
70	Gary Thomasson	.15	.08	.05
71	Craig Reynolds	.15	.08	.05
72	Amos Otis	.15	.08	.05
73	Biff Pocoroba	.15	.08	.05
74	Matt Keough	.15	.08	.05
75	Bill Buckner	.15	.08	.05
76	John Castino	.15	.08	.05
77	Rich Gossage	.25	.13	.08
78	Gary Alexander	.15	.08	.05
79	Phil Huffman	.15	.08	.05
80	Bruce Bochte	.15	.08	.05
81	Darrell Evans	.15	.08	.05
82	Terry Puhl	.15	.08	.05
83	Jason Thompson	.15	.08	.05
84	Lary Sorenson	.15	.08	.05
85	Jerry Remy	.15	.08	.05
86	Tony Brizzolara	.15	.08	.05
87	Willie Wilson	.15	.08	.05
88	Eddie Murray	3.00	1.50	.90
89	Larry Christenson	.15	.08	.05
90	Bob Randall	.15	.08	.05
91	Greg Pryor	.15	.08	.05
92	Glenn Abbott	.15	.08	.05
93	Jack Clark	.15	.08	.05
94	Rick Waits	.15	.08	.05
95	Luis Gomez	.15	.08	.05
96	Burt Hooton	.15	.08	.05
97	John Henry Johnson	.15	.08	.05
98	Ray Knight	.15	.08	.05
99	Rick Reuschel	.15	.08	.05
100	Champ Summers	.15	.08	.05
101	Ron Davis	.15	.08	.05
102	Warren Cromartie	.15	.08	.05
103	Ken Reitz	.15	.08	.05
104	Hal McRae	.15	.08	.05
105	Alan Ashby	.15	.08	.05
106	Kevin Kobel	.15	.08	.05
107	Buddy Bell	.15	.08	.05
108	Dave Goltz	.15	.08	.05
109	John Montefusco	.15	.08	.05
110	Lance Parrish	.65	.35	.20
111	Mike LaCoss	.15	.08	.05
112	Jim Rice	.30	.15	.09
113	Steve Carlton	1.50	.70	.45
114	Sixto Lezcano	.15	.08	.05
115	Ed Halicki	.15	.08	.05
116	Jose Morales	.15	.08	.05
117	Dave Concepcion	.15	.08	.05
118	Joe Cannon	.15	.08	.05
119	Willie Montanez	.15	.08	.05
120	Lou Piniella	.15	.08	.05
121	Bill Stein	.15	.08	.05
122	Dave Winfield	3.00	1.50	.90
123	Alan Trammell	.30	.15	.09
124	Andre Dawson	4.00	2.00	1.25
125	Marc Hill	.15	.08	.05
126	Don Aase	.15	.08	.05
127	Dave Kingman	.15	.08	.05
128	Checklist 126-250	.25	.13	.08
129	Dennis Lamp	.15	.08	.05
130	Phil Niekro	1.00	.50	.30
131	Tim Foli	.15	.08	.05
132	Jim Clancy	.15	.08	.05
133	Bill Atkinson	.15	.08	.05
134	Paul Dade	.15	.08	.05
135	Dusty Baker	.15	.08	.05
136	Al Oliver	.15	.08	.05
137	Dave Chalk	.15	.08	.05
138	Bill Robinson	.15	.08	.05
139	Robin Yount	1.50	.70	.45
140	Dan Schatzeder	.15	.08	.05
141	Mike Schmidt	5.00	2.50	1.50
142	Ralph Garr	.15	.08	.05
143	Dale Murphy	1.00	.50	.30
144	Jerry Koosman	.15	.08	.05
145	Tom Veryzer	.15	.08	.05
146	Rick Bosetti	.15	.08	.05
147	Jim Spencer	.15	.08	.05
148	Gaylord Perry	1.00	.50	.30
149	Paul Blair	.15	.08	.05
150	Don Baylor	.15	.08	.05
151	Dave Rozema	.15	.08	.05
152	Steve Garvey	.50	.25	.15
153	Elias Sosa	.15	.08	.05
154	Larry Gura	.15	.08	.05
155	Tim Johnson	.15	.08	.05

#	Player	NM	EX	VG
156	Steve Henderson	.15	.08	.05
157	Ron Guidry	.20	.10	.06
158	Mike Edwards	.15	.08	.05
159	Butch Wynegar	.15	.08	.05
160	Randy Jones	.15	.08	.05
161	Denny Walling	.15	.08	.05
162	Mike Hargrove	.15	.08	.05
163	Dave Parker	.15	.08	.05
164	Roger Metzger	.15	.08	.05
165	Johnny Grubb	.15	.08	.05
166	Steve Kemp	.15	.08	.05
167	Bob Lacey	.15	.08	.05
168	Chris Speier	.15	.08	.05
169	Dennis Eckersley	1.00	.50	.30
170	Keith Hernandez	.15	.08	.05
171	Claudell Washington	.15	.08	.05
172	Tom Underwood	.15	.08	.05
173	Dan Driessen	.15	.08	.05
174	Al Cowens	.15	.08	.05
175	Rich Hebner	.15	.08	.05
176	Willie McCovey	1.50	.70	.45
177	Carney Lansford	.15	.08	.05
178	Ken Singleton	.15	.08	.05
179	Jim Essian	.15	.08	.05
180	Mike Vail	.15	.08	.05
181	Randy Lerch	.15	.08	.05
182	Larry Parrish	.15	.08	.05
183	Checklist 251-374	.25	.13	.08
184	George Hendrick	.15	.08	.05
185	Bob Davis	.15	.08	.05
186	Gary Matthews	.15	.08	.05
187	Lou Whitaker	.15	.08	.05
188	Darrell Porter	.15	.08	.05
189	Wayne Gross	.15	.08	.05
190	Bobby Murcer	.15	.08	.05
191	Willie Aikens	.15	.08	.05
192	Jim Kern	.15	.08	.05
193	Cesar Cedeno	.15	.08	.05
194	Joel Youngblood	.15	.08	.05
195	Ross Grimsley	.15	.08	.05
196	Jerry Mumphrey	.15	.08	.05
197	Kevin Bell	.15	.08	.05
198	Garry Maddox	.15	.08	.05
199	Dave Freisleben	.15	.08	.05
200	Ed Ott	.15	.08	.05
201	Enos Cabell	.15	.08	.05
202	Pete LaCock	.15	.08	.05
203	Fergie Jenkins	1.50	.70	.45
204	Milt Wilcox	.15	.08	.05
205	Ozzie Smith	5.00	2.50	1.50
206	Ellis Valentine	.15	.08	.05
207	Dan Meyer	.15	.08	.05
208	Barry Foote	.15	.08	.05
209	George Foster	.15	.08	.05
210	Dwight Evans	.15	.08	.05
211	Paul Molitor	5.00	2.50	1.50
212	Tony Solaita	.15	.08	.05
213	Bill North	.15	.08	.05
214	Paul Splittorff	.15	.08	.05
215	Bobby Bonds	.15	.08	.05
216	Butch Hobson	.15	.08	.05
217	Mark Belanger	.15	.08	.05
218	Grant Jackson	.15	.08	.05
219	Tom Hutton	.15	.08	.05
220	Pat Zachry	.15	.08	.05
221	Duane Kuiper	.15	.08	.05
222	Larry Hisle	.15	.08	.05
223	Mike Krukow	.15	.08	.05
224	Johnnie LeMaster	.15	.08	.05
225	Billy Almon	.15	.08	.05
226	Joe Niekro	.15	.08	.05
227	Dave Revering	.15	.08	.05
228	Don Sutton	1.00	.50	.30
229	John Hiller	.15	.08	.05
230	Alvis Woods	.15	.08	.05
231	Mark Fidrych	.15	.08	.05
232	Duffy Dyer	.15	.08	.05
233	Nino Espinosa	.15	.08	.05
234	Doug Bair	.15	.08	.05
235	George Brett	5.00	2.50	1.50
236	Mike Torrez	.15	.08	.05
237	Frank Taveras	.15	.08	.05
238	Bert Blyleven	.15	.08	.05
239	Willie Randolph	.15	.08	.05
240	Mike Sadek	.15	.08	.05
241	Jerry Royster	.15	.08	.05
242	John Denny	.15	.08	.05
243	Rick Monday	.15	.08	.05
244	Jesse Jefferson	.15	.08	.05
245	Aurelio Rodriguez	.15	.08	.05
246	Bob Boone	.15	.08	.05
247	Cesar Geronimo	.15	.08	.05
248	Bob Shirley	.15	.08	.05
249	Expos Team	.25	.13	.08
250	Bob Watson	.15	.08	.05
251	Mickey Rivers	.15	.08	.05
252	Mike Tyson	.15	.08	.05
253	Wayne Nordhagen	.15	.08	.05
254	Roy Howell	.15	.08	.05
255	Lee May	.15	.08	.05
256	Jerry Martin	.15	.08	.05
257	Bake McBride	.15	.08	.05
258	Silvio Martinez	.15	.08	.05
259	Jim Mason	.15	.08	.05
260	Tom Seaver	2.00	1.00	.60
261	Rick Wortham	.15	.08	.05
262	Mike Cubbage	.15	.08	.05
263	Gene Garber	.15	.08	.05
264	Bert Campaneris	.15	.08	.05
265	Tom Buskey	.15	.08	.05
266	Leon Roberts	.15	.08	.05
267	Ron Cey	.15	.08	.05
268	Steve Ontiveros	.15	.08	.05
269	Mike Caldwell	.15	.08	.05
270	Nelson Norman	.15	.08	.05
271	Steve Rogers	.15	.08	.05
272	Jim Morrison	.15	.08	.05
273	Clint Hurdle	.15	.08	.05

#	Player	NM	EX	VG
274	Dale Murray	.15	.08	.05
275	Jim Barr	.15	.08	.05
276	Jim Sundberg	.15	.08	.05
277	Willie Horton	.15	.08	.05
278	Andre Thornton	.15	.08	.05
279	Bob Forsch	.15	.08	.05
280	Joe Strain	.15	.08	.05
281	Rudy May	.15	.08	.05
282	Pete Rose	9.00	4.50	2.75
283	Jeff Burroughs	.15	.08	.05
284	Rick Langford	.15	.08	.05
285	Ken Griffey	.15	.08	.05
286	Bill Nahorodny	.15	.08	.05
287	Art Howe	.15	.08	.05
288	Ed Figueroa	.15	.08	.05
289	Joe Rudi	.15	.08	.05
290	Alfredo Griffin	.15	.08	.05
291	Dave Lopes	.15	.08	.05
292	Rick Manning	.15	.08	.05
293	Dennis Leonard	.15	.08	.05
294	Bud Harrelson	.15	.08	.05
295	Skip Lockwood	.15	.08	.05
296	Roy Smalley	.15	.08	.05
297	Kent Tekulve	.15	.08	.05
298	Scot Thompson	.15	.08	.05
299	Ken Kravec	.15	.08	.05
300	Blue Jays Team	.25	.13	.08
301	Scott Sanderson	.15	.08	.05
302	Charlie Moore	.15	.08	.05
303	Nolan Ryan	20.00	10.00	6.00
304	Bob Bailor	.15	.08	.05
305	Bob Stinson	.15	.08	.05
306	Al Hrabosky	.15	.08	.05
307	Mitchell Page	.15	.08	.05
308	Garry Templeton	.15	.08	.05
309	Chet Lemon	.15	.08	.05
310	Jim Palmer	1.50	.70	.45
311	Rick Cerone	.15	.08	.05
312	Jon Matlack	.15	.08	.05
313	Don Money	.15	.08	.05
314	Reggie Jackson	5.00	2.50	1.50
315	Brian Downing	.15	.08	.05
316	Woodie Fryman	.15	.08	.05
317	Alan Bannister	.15	.08	.05
318	Ron Reed	.15	.08	.05
319	Willie Stargell	1.50	.70	.45
320	Jerry Garvin	.15	.08	.05
321	Cliff Johnson	.15	.08	.05
322	Doug DeCinces	.15	.08	.05
323	Gene Richards	.15	.08	.05
324	Joaquin Andujar	.15	.08	.05
325	Richie Zisk	.15	.08	.05
326	Bob Grich	.15	.08	.05
327	Gorman Thomas	.15	.08	.05
328	Chris Chambliss	.15	.08	.05
329	Blue Jays Future Stars (Butch Edge, Pat Kelly, Ted Wilborn)	.25	.13	.08
330	Larry Bowa	.15	.08	.05
331	Barry Bonnell	.15	.08	.05
332	John Candelaria	.15	.08	.05
333	Toby Harrah	.15	.08	.05
334	Larry Biittner	.15	.08	.05
335	Mike Flanagan	.15	.08	.05
336	Ed Kranepool	.15	.08	.05
337	Ken Forsch	.15	.08	.05
338	John Mayberry	.15	.08	.05
339	Rick Burleson	.15	.08	.05
340	Milt May	.15	.08	.05
341	Roy White	.15	.08	.05
342	Joe Morgan	1.50	.70	.45
343	Rollie Fingers	1.00	.50	.30
344	Mario Mendoza	.15	.08	.05
345	Stan Bahnsen	.15	.08	.05
346	Tug McGraw	.15	.08	.05
347	Rusty Staub	.15	.08	.05
348	Tommy John	.15	.08	.05
349	Ivan DeJesus	.15	.08	.05
350	Reggie Smith	.15	.08	.05
351	Expos Future Stars (Tony Bernazard, Randy Miller, Jim Tamargo)	.40	.20	.12
352	Floyd Bannister	.15	.08	.05
353	Rod Carew	1.50	.70	.45
354	Otto Velez	.15	.08	.05
355	Gene Tenace	.15	.08	.05
356	Freddie Patek	.15	.08	.05
357	Elliott Maddox	.15	.08	.05
358	Pat Underwood	.15	.08	.05
359	Graig Nettles	.15	.08	.05
360	Rodney Scott	.15	.08	.05
361	Terry Whitfield	.15	.08	.05
362	Fred Norman	.15	.08	.05
363	Sal Bando	.15	.08	.05
364	Greg Gross	.15	.08	.05
365	Carl Yastrzemski	2.00	1.00	.60
366	Paul Hartzell	.15	.08	.05
367	Jose Cruz	.15	.08	.05
368	Shane Rawley	.15	.08	.05
369	Jerry White	.15	.08	.05
370	Rick Wise	.15	.08	.05
371	Steve Yeager	.15	.08	.05
372	Omar Moreno	.15	.08	.05
373	Bump Wills	.15	.08	.05
374	Craig Kusick	.15	.08	.05

1969 Oakland A's (Andersen)

Though they are sometimes identified as an issue of Jack in the Box restaurants, there is no identifier of that nature on these cards. In fact, they are a collectors' fantasy issue sold only within the hobby by Boston photographer Mike Andersen. The blank-back black-and-white cards measure 2-1/8" x 3-5/8". Beneath the portrait photo on front is the player's name, position and uniform number. The team name is in gothic script at bottom. Cards are checklisted here by uniform number.

5. Joe DiMaggio—coach
OAKLAND A's

		NM	EX	VG
Complete Set (21):		80.00	40.00	24.00
Common Player:		2.50	1.25	.75
1	Dick Green	2.50	1.25	.75
2	Danny Cater	2.50	1.25	.75
3	Mike Hershberger	2.50	1.25	.75
4	Phil Roof	2.50	1.25	.75
5	Joe DiMaggio (Coach)	30.00	15.00	9.00
6	Sal Bando	2.50	1.25	.75
7	Rick Monday	2.50	1.25	.75
9a	Bert Campaneris	5.00	2.50	1.50
9b	Reggie Jackson	45.00	22.00	13.50
13	Blue Moon Odom	3.50	1.75	1.00
17	Jim Pagliaroni	2.50	1.25	.75
19	Bert Campaneris	2.50	1.25	.75
20	Lew Krausse	2.50	1.25	.75
24	Joe Nossek	2.50	1.25	.75
25	Paul Lindblad	2.50	1.25	.75
27	Catfish Hunter	7.50	3.75	2.25
29	Chuck Dobson	2.50	1.25	.75
30	Jim Nash	2.50	1.25	.75
31	Ramon Webster	2.50	1.25	.75
35	Tom Reynolds	2.50	1.25	.75
42	Hank Bauer	2.50	1.25	.70

1969 Oakland A's (Broder)

Reggie Jackson
OAKLAND A's

A second issue of black-and-white collector cards featuring the 1969 A's was produced by West Coast collector/dealer Ed Broder. In larger (2-3/4" x 4") format the Broder issue is considerably scarcer than that produced by Mike Andersen. Availability of the Broders was advertised at 100 sets. The blank-back Broder cards have the player name in the wide white border beneath the photo. At bottom the city name is in gothic script with the A's logo on a baseball flying out of a stadium. The unnumbered cards are checklisted here alphabetically.

		NM	EX	VG
Complete Set (14):		65.00	32.50	20.00
Common Player:		2.00	1.00	.60
(1)	Sal Bando	2.00	1.00	.60
(2)	Hank Bauer	2.00	1.00	.60
(3)	Bert Campaneris	3.00	1.50	.90
(4)	Dan Cater	2.00	1.00	.60
(5)	Joe DiMaggio	15.00	7.50	4.50
(6)	Chuck Dobson	2.00	1.00	.60
(7)	Dick Green	2.00	1.00	.60
(8)	Mike Hershberger	2.00	1.00	.60
(9)	Jim Hunter	8.00	4.00	2.50
(10)	Reggie Jackson	25.00	12.50	7.50
(11)	Bob Johnson	2.00	1.00	.60
(12)	Rick Monday	2.00	1.00	.60
(13)	Johnny Moon Odom	4.00	2.00	1.25
(14)	Phil Roof	2.00	1.00	.60

1970 Oakland A's (Andersen)

Boston baseball photographer Mike Andersen produced a second collectors' issue of Oakland A's cards in 1970. Nearly identical in format to his 1969 issue, the '70 team set measures 2-1/4" x 3-5/8" with black-and-white player poses at center. Uniform number, name and team are in the bottom border. Backs are blank. Cards are checklisted here by uniform number.

45 - ROBERTO RODRIQUEZ
Oakland A's

	NM	EX	VG
Complete Set (24):	30.00	15.00	9.00
Common Player:	1.50	.75	.45
1 Dick Green	1.50	.75	.45
6 Sal Bando	1.50	.75	.45
7 Rick Monday	1.50	.75	.45
8 Felipe Alou	2.00	1.00	.60
9 Reggie Jackson	15.00	7.50	4.50
10 Dave Duncan	1.50	.75	.45
11 John McNamera (McNamara)	1.50	.75	.45
12 Larry Haney	1.50	.75	.45
13 Blue Moon Odom	2.00	1.00	.60
17 Roberto Pena	1.50	.75	.45
19 Bert Campaneris	2.00	1.00	.60
24 Diego Segui	1.50	.75	.45
25 Paul Lindblad	1.50	.75	.45
27 Catfish Hunter	4.00	2.00	1.25
28 Mudcat Grant	1.50	.75	.45
29 Chuck Dobson	1.50	.75	.45
30 Don Mincher	1.50	.75	.45
31 Jose Tartabull	1.50	.75	.45
33 Jim Roland	1.50	.75	.45
34 Rollie Fingers	4.00	2.00	1.25
36 Tito Francona	1.50	.75	.45
38 Al Downing	1.50	.75	.45
39 Frank Fernandez	1.50	.75	.45
45 Roberto Rodriguez	1.50	.75	.45

1968 Official Major League Players Baseball Marbles

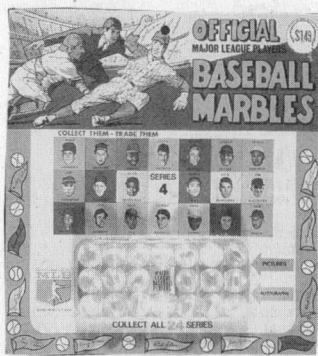

Produced by Creative Creations Inc., though not so identified on the marbles themselves, these approximately 3/4" hard plastic marbles have a player portrait photo (with cap logos removed) on one side and a facsimile autograph on the other, with "JAPAN" beneath. The marbles were issued in series of 20 on colorful cardboard packaging which pictures each player in the series. While the packaging says "Collect All 24 Series" only 120 marbles were actually issued. Suggested retail price at issue was $1.49 per series.

	NM	EX	VG
Complete Set (115):	675.00	325.00	200.00
Common Player:	4.00	2.00	1.25
(1) Hank Aaron	40.00	20.00	12.00
(2) Tommie Aaron	4.00	2.00	1.25
(3) Tommy Agee	4.00	2.00	1.25
(4) Richie Allen	7.00	3.50	2.00
(5) Gene Alley	4.00	2.00	1.25
(6) Bob Allison	4.00	2.00	1.25
(7) Felipe Alou	5.00	2.50	1.50
(8) Jesus Alou	4.00	2.00	1.25
(9) Matty Alou	4.00	2.00	1.25
(10) Max Alvis	4.00	2.00	1.25
(11) Mike Andrews	4.00	2.00	1.25
(12) Luis Aparicio	12.50	6.25	3.75
(13) Bob Aspromonte	4.00	2.00	1.25
(14) Stan Bahnsen	4.00	2.00	1.25
(15) Bob Bailey	4.00	2.00	1.25
(16) Ernie Banks	25.00	12.50	7.50
(17) Glenn Beckert	4.00	2.00	1.25
(18) Gary Bell	4.00	2.00	1.25
(19) Johnny Bench	30.00	15.00	9.00
(20) Ken Berry	4.00	2.00	1.25
(21) Paul Blair	4.00	2.00	1.25
(22) Bob Bolin	4.00	2.00	1.25
(23) Dave Boswell	4.00	2.00	1.25
(24) Nelson Briles	4.00	2.00	1.25
(25) Lou Brock	12.50	6.25	3.75
(26) Wally Bunker	4.00	2.00	1.25
(27) Johnny Callison	4.00	2.00	1.25
(28) Norm Cash	5.00	2.50	1.50
(29) Orlando Cepeda	12.50	6.25	3.75
(30) Dean Chance	4.00	2.00	1.25
(31) Roberto Clemente	50.00	25.00	15.00
(32) Donn Clendenon	4.00	2.00	1.25
(33) Tony Cloninger	4.00	2.00	1.25
(34) Tommy Davis	4.00	2.00	1.25
(35) Al Downing	4.00	2.00	1.25
(36) Curt Flood	4.00	2.00	1.25
(37) Bill Freehan	4.00	2.00	1.25
(38) Jim Fregosi	4.00	2.00	1.25
(39) Bob Gibson	12.50	6.25	3.75
(40) Jim "Mudcat" Grant	4.00	2.00	1.25
(41) Jerry Grote	4.00	2.00	1.25
(42) Jimmie Hall	4.00	2.00	1.25
(43) Tom Haller	4.00	2.00	1.25
(44) Ron Hansen	4.00	2.00	1.25
(45) Steve Hargan	4.00	2.00	1.25
(46) Ken Harrelson	4.00	2.00	1.25
(47) Jim Hart	4.00	2.00	1.25
(48) Jimmie Holt	4.00	2.00	1.25
(49) Joe Horlen	4.00	2.00	1.25
(50) Willie Horton	4.00	2.00	1.25
(51) Frank Howard	5.00	2.50	1.50
(52) Dick Hughes	4.00	2.00	1.25
(53) Randy Hundley	4.00	2.00	1.25
(54) Ron Hunt	4.00	2.00	1.25
(55) Jim "Catfish" Hunter	12.50	6.25	3.75
(56) Pat Jarvis	4.00	2.00	1.25
(57) Julian Javier	4.00	2.00	1.25
(58) Tommy John	6.00	3.00	1.75
(59) Deron Johnson	4.00	2.00	1.25
(60) Mack Jones	4.00	2.00	1.25
(61) Jim Kaat	5.00	2.50	1.50
(62) Al Kaline	20.00	10.00	6.00
(63) Don Kessinger	4.00	2.00	1.25
(64) Harmon Killebrew	20.00	10.00	6.00
(65) Jerry Koosman	4.00	2.00	1.25
(66) Jim Lefebvre	4.00	2.00	1.25
(67) Mickey Lolich	4.00	2.00	1.25
(68) Jim Lonborg	4.00	2.00	1.25
(69) Juan Marichal	12.50	6.25	3.75
(70) Roger Maris	30.00	15.00	9.00
(71) Ed Mathews	20.00	10.00	6.00
(72) Jerry May	4.00	2.00	1.25
(73) Willie Mays	40.00	20.00	12.00
(74) Dick McAuliffe	4.00	2.00	1.25
(75) Tim McCarver	5.00	2.50	1.50
(76) Willie McCovey	12.50	6.25	3.75
(77) Sam McDowell	4.00	2.00	1.25
(78) Denny McLain	5.00	2.50	1.50
(79) Dave McNally	4.00	2.00	1.25
(80) Denis Menke	4.00	2.00	1.25
(81) Jim Merritt	4.00	2.00	1.25
(82) Bob Miller	4.00	2.00	1.25
(83) Rick Monday	4.00	2.00	1.25
(84) Joe Morgan	12.50	6.25	3.75
(85) Gary Nolan	4.00	2.00	1.25
(86) Jim Northrup	4.00	2.00	1.25
(87) Rich Nye	4.00	2.00	1.25
(88) Tony Oliva	5.00	2.50	1.50
(89) Milt Pappas	4.00	2.00	1.25
(90) Camilo Pascual	4.00	2.00	1.25
(91) Joe Pepitone	5.00	2.50	1.50
(92) Tony Perez	12.50	6.25	3.75
(93) Jim Perry	4.00	2.00	1.25
(94) Gary Peters	4.00	2.00	1.25
(95) Fritz Peterson	4.00	2.00	1.25
(96) Rico Petrocelli	4.00	2.00	1.25
(97) Vada Pinson	5.00	2.50	1.50
(98) Boog Powell	5.00	2.50	1.50
(99) Rick Reichardt	4.00	2.00	1.25
(100) Brooks Robinson	15.00	7.50	4.50
(101) Frank Robinson	15.00	7.50	4.50
(102) Pete Rose	40.00	20.00	12.00
(103) Chico Salmon	4.00	2.00	1.25
(104) Ron Santo	5.00	2.50	1.50
(105) George Scott	4.00	2.00	1.25
(106) Tom Seaver	15.00	7.50	4.50
(107) Dick Selma	4.00	2.00	1.25
(108) Mike Shannon	4.00	2.00	1.25
(109) Joe Sparma	4.00	2.00	1.25
(110) Willie Stargell	12.50	6.25	3.75
(111) Mel Stottlemyre	4.00	2.00	1.25
(112) Luis Tiant	4.00	2.00	1.25
(114) Cesar Tovar	4.00	2.00	1.25
(115) Tom Tresh	4.50	2.25	1.25
(116) Pete Ward	4.00	2.00	1.25
(117) Billy Williams	12.50	6.25	3.75
(118) Maury Wills	4.00	2.00	1.25
(119) Earl Wilson	4.00	2.00	1.25
(120) Dooley Womack	4.00	2.00	1.25

1974 Oh Henry! Henry Aaron Premium Photo

This 8" x 10" black-and-white photo was prepared as a premium for Oh Henry! candy. It features a full-length pose of Aaron and has a facsimile inscribed autographed on front.

	NM	EX	VG
Henry Aaron	20.00	10.00	6.00

1959 Oklahoma Today Major Leaguers

 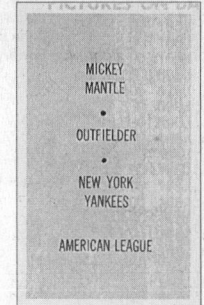

Contemporary and former ballplayers from the Sooner State were featured in this "card set" which was printed on the back cover of the Summer, 1959, issue of "Oklahoma Today" magazine. If cut from the cover, the cards measure about 1-11/16" x 2-3/4". Fronts have black-and-white photos on green, gold or aqua backgrounds. A white strip at bottom has the player name in red. Gray backs have the player name, position, team and league. The unnumbered cards are checklisted here in alphabetical order.

	NM	EX	VG
Complete Magazine:	1,350	675.00	400.00
Complete Set, Singles (20):	1,350	675.00	400.00
Common Player:	45.00	22.50	13.50
(1) Jerry Adair	45.00	22.50	13.50
(2) Harry Brecheen	45.00	22.00	13.50
(3) Johnny Callison	45.00	22.50	13.50
(4) Alvin Dark	45.00	22.50	13.50
(5) "Dizzy" Dean	60.00	30.00	18.00
(6) Paul Dean	45.00	22.50	13.50
(7) Don Demeter	45.00	22.50	13.50
(8) Carl Hubbell	50.00	25.00	15.00
(9) Mickey Mantle	500.00	250.00	150.00
(10) "Pepper" Martin	45.00	22.00	13.50
(11) Lindy McDaniel	45.00	22.50	13.50
(12) Von McDaniel	45.00	22.50	13.50
(13) Cal McLish	45.00	22.50	13.50
(14) Dale Mitchel (Mitchell)	45.00	22.50	13.50
(15) Allie Reynolds	45.00	22.50	13.50
(16) Warren Spahn	45.00	22.50	13.50
(17) Tom Sturdivant	45.00	22.00	13.50
(18) Jerry Walker	45.00	22.00	13.50
(19) Lloyd Waner	45.00	22.50	13.50
(20) Paul Waner	45.00	22.00	13.50

1948 Old Gold Jackie Robinson

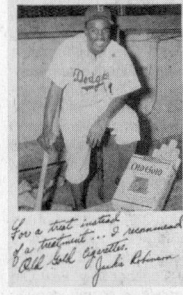

These postcard-size (3-1/2" x 5-1/2") advertising pieces picture Jackie Robinson and a pack of Old Gold cigarettes on their black-and-white fronts, along with an endorsement from the player and his facsimile autograph. Each back has a different presentation of biography and career summary.

	NM	EX	VG
Jackie Robinson (Fielding)	400.00	200.00	120.00
Jackie Robinson (In dugout.)	200.00	100.00	60.00

1886 Old Judge New York Giants (N167)

Produced in 1886, the rare N167 Old Judge tobacco cards were the first to be issued by New York's Goodwin & Co., the parent firm of Old Judge Cigarettes. The 1-1/2" x 2-1/2" sepia-toned cards were printed on thin paper and featured only members of the New York National League club. Twelve subjects are known to exist, six of whom are Hall of Famers. The front of each card lists the player's name, position and team and has the words "Old Judge" at the top. The backs contain another ad for the Old Judge brand and also include a line noting that the player poses were "copied from photo by J. Wood, 208 Bowery, N.Y."

	NM	EX	VG
Common Player:	50,000	25,000	15,000
(1) Roger Connor	112,500	56,250	33,750
(2) Larry Corcoran	50,000	25,000	15,000
(3) Mike Dorgan	50,000	25,000	15,000
(4) Dude Esterbrook	50,000	25,000	15,000
(5) Buck Ewing	120,000	60,000	30,000
(6) Joe Gerhardt	50,000	25,000	15,000
(7) Pete Gillespie	50,000	25,000	15,000
(8) Tim Keefe	112,500	56,250	33,750
(9) Orator Jim O'Rourke	112,500	56,250	33,750
(10) Danny Richardson	50,000	25,000	15,000
(11) John Ward	112,500	56,250	33,750
(12) Mickey Welsh (Welch)	112,500	56,250	33,750

1887-1890 Old Judge (N172)

This is one of the most fascinating of all card sets, being not only one of the first, but also the largest ever. The number of cards issued may never be finally determined. These cards were issued by the Goodwin & Co. tobacco firm in their Old Judge and, to a lesser extent, Gypsy Queen cigarettes. Players from more than 40 major and minor league teams are pictured on the nominally 1-7/16" x 2-1/2" cards (actual size varies), with some 500 different players known to exist. Up to 20 different pose, team and caption variations exist for some players. Cards were issued both with and without dates, numbered and unnumbered; and with both script and machine-printed identification. Known variations number over 3,500. The cards themselves are black-and-white (many now toned sepia or even pink) photographs pasted onto thick cardboard. They are blank-backed. Values shown here are for the most common examples of a specific player's cards, unless otherwise indicated. Demand for various photo, team, league, etc., variations can significantly affect value and, because of the relatively "thin" nature of the market for Old Judge cards, is subject to rapid fluctuations as collectors enter and leave the arena. These listings are presented alphabetically. Few Old Judge cards were issued with the player's first name, or even initial. Where verifiable, the first names have been added to these listings in the form most often encountered at the time of issue. Misspellings were common among the issue. Cases in which all of a player's cards were incorrectly spelled are listed by the misspelling, with the correct spelling in parentheses. In cases where the name was sometimes spelled correctly, and sometimes not, the incorrect spellings are provided thus: "(Also: ...)". For each player, the number of different photo/team combinations known is indicated. Minor changes in the player identification caption, such as addition of an initial, presence or absence of period or comma, abbreviation of position, or spelling of team name, are not included in the number of cards listed. Team designations for each player are listed, where known. Pose/designation variations which have historically attracted increased collector interest are specified. These include such subsets as the Brown's Champions and Mets "spotted tie" portrait cards of 1887, the Player's League designations of 1890 and some other popularly collected subsets, such as the dual-player cards. Cards which depict and name both players are listed here under each player's name and are numbered with a "DP" prefix. League designations found in the listings include: AA - American Association; NL - National League; PL - Player's League; WA - Western Association. Gaps have been left in the assigned numbering to accommodate future additions.

	NM	EX	VG
Common Card:	700.00	300.00	175.00

		NM	EX	VG
(1)	Gus Albert (Alberts) 7			
1 (a)	(Cleveland)	700.00	300.00	175.00
1 (b)	(Milwaukee)	700.00	300.00	175.00
(2)	Charles Alcott 6			
2 (a)	(Mansfield)	1,500	300.00	175.00
2 (b)	(St. Louis Whites WA)	975.00	425.00	250.00
(3)	Daniel Alexander 4			
3 (a)	(Des Moines)	920.00	400.00	230.00
(4)	Bob Allen 7			
4 (a)	(Philadelphia NL)	700.00	300.00	175.00
4 (a)	(Pittsburgh)	700.00	300.00	175.00
(5)	Myron Allen 6			
5 (a)	(Kansas City)	700.00	300.00	175.00
(6)	Billy Alvord 3			
6 (a)	(Des Moines)	700.00	300.00	175.00
6 (b)	(Toledo)	975.00	425.00	250.00
(7)	Varney Anderson 3			
7 (a)	(St. Paul)	11,500	300.00	175.00
(8)	Ed Andrews 6			
8 (a)	(Philadelphia NL)	700.00	300.00	175.00
DP 1	(Being tagged by Buster Hoover.)	920.00	400.00	230.00
(9)	Wally Andrews 3			
9 (a)	(Omaha)	850.00	375.00	200.00
(10)	Bill Annis 4			
10 (a)	(Omaha)	900.00	400.00	230.00
10 (b)	(Worcester)	700.00	300.00	175.00
(11)	Cap Anson			
	See Hall of Fame Section Following			
(12)	Joe Ardner 4			
12 (a)	(Kansas City)	700.00	300.00	175.00
12 (b)	(St. Joseph)	1,150	500.00	275.00
(13)	Tug Arundel 5			
13 (a)	(Indianapolis)	700.00	300.00	175.00
(14)	Jersey Bakley (Bakely) 5			
14 (a)	(Cleveland)	850.00	375.00	200.00
(15)	Kid Baldwin 5			
15 (a)	(Cincinnati)	700.00	300.00	175.00
(16)	Lady Baldwin 4			
16 (a)	(Detroit)	2,200	975.00	550.00
(17)	Mark Baldwin 10			
17 (a)	(Chicago NL)	850.00	375.00	200.00
17 (b)	(Chicago NL)(Portrait)	1,400	600.00	350.00
17 (c)	(Chicago PL)	2,250	1,000	550.00
17 (d)	(Columbus)	700.00	300.00	175.00
(18)	Jim Banning 5			
18 (a)	(Washington)	700.00	300.00	175.00
(19)	Sam Barkley 8			
19 (a)	(Kansas City)	975.00	425.00	250.00
19 (b)	(Pittsburgh)	920.00	400.00	230.00
DP 6	(Watching Jocko Fields field.)	1,250	575.00	300.00
DP 7	(Tagged by Jocko Fields.)	1,250	575.00	300.00
(20)	John Barnes (Also: Barns) 2			
20 (a)	(St. Paul)	1,400	600.00	350.00
(21)	Billy Barnie 1			
21 (a)	(Baltimore)	920.00	400.00	250.00
(22)	Charley Bassett 3			
22 (a)	(Indianapolis)	700.00	300.00	175.00
22 (b)	(New York NL)	700.00	300.00	175.00
(23)	Charlie Bastian 6			
23 (a)	(Chicago NL)	700.00	300.00	175.00
23 (b)	(Chicago PL)	2,700	1,200	600.00
23 (c)	(Philadelphia NL)	600.00	275.00	150.00
DP 2	(Being tagged by Pop Schriver.)	1,150	500.00	275.00
(24)	Ed Beatin (Also: Beattin) 3			
24 (a)	(Cleveland)	700.00	300.00	175.00
(25)	Jake Beckley			
	See Hall of Fame Section Following			
(26)	Stephen Behel 1			
26 (a)	(New York AA "dotted tie")	24,750	11,125	6,200
(27)	Charlie Bennett 1			
27 (a)	(Boston NL)	700.00	300.00	175.00
(28)	Lou Bierbauer (Also: Bierbaur) 5			
28 (a)	(Philadelphia AA)	1,025	450.00	250.00
DP 3	(Tagging Bob Gamble.)	1,600	725.00	400.00
(29)	Bill Bishop 4			
29 (a)	(Pittsburgh)	700.00	300.00	175.00
29 (b)	(Syracuse)	700.00	300.00	175.00
(30)	Bill Blair 5			
30 (a)	(Hamilton)	1,025	500.00	400.00
30 (b)	(Philadelphia AA)	700.00	300.00	175.00
(31)	Ned Bligh 6			
31 (a)	(Columbus)	700.00	300.00	175.00
(32)	Walter Bogart 5			
32 (a)	(Indianapolis)	700.00	300.00	175.00

		NM	EX	VG
(33)	Boyce 4			
33 (a)	(Washington) (Never played for Wash.)	920.00	400.00	230.00
(34)	Boyd 2			
34 (a)	(Chicago Maroons WA)	2,000	900.00	500.00
(35)	Henry Boyle 6			
35 (a)	(Indianapolis)	750.00	325.00	175.00
35 (b)	(New York NL) (Never played for N.Y.)	700.00	300.00	175.00
(36)	Jack Boyle 6			
36 (a)	(Chicago PL)	6,000	2,700	1,500
36 (b)	(St. Louis AA)	875.00	350.00	200.00
(37)	George Bradley 5			
37 (a)	(Sioux City)	700.00	300.00	175.00
(38)	Nick Bradley 4			
38 (a)	(Kansas City)	700.00	300.00	175.00
38 (b)	(Worcester)	700.00	300.00	175.00
(39)	Steve Brady 1			
39 (a)	(New York AA "dotted tie")	3,375	1,525	850.00
(40)	E.L. Breckenridge 1			
40 (a)	(Sacramento) (Value Undetermined)			
	Willie Breslin - See Mascot			
(41)	Timothy Brosnan (Also: Brosman) 8			
41 (a)	(Minneapolis)	700.00	300.00	175.00
41 (b)	(Sioux City)	700.00	300.00	175.00
(42)	Cal Broughton 5			
42 (a)	(St. Paul)	700.00	300.00	175.00
(43)	Dan Brouthers			
	See Hall of Fame Section Following			
(44)	Tom Brown 7			
44 (a)	(Boston NL)	700.00	300.00	175.00
44 (b)	(Boston PL)	2,700	1,200	700.00
44 (c)	(Pittsburgh)	600.00	275.00	150.00
(45)	Willard (California) Brown 6			
45 1	(New York NL)	700.00	300.00	175.00
45 1	(New York PL)	2,250	1,000	550.00
(46)	Pete Browning 5			
46 (a)	(Louisville)	5,450	2,425	1,350
(47)	Charlie Brynan (Also: Bryn) 6			
47 (a)	(Chicago NL)	750.00	325.00	200.00
47 (b)	(Des Moines)	800.00	350.00	200.00
(48)	Al Buckenberger 2			
48 (a)	(Columbus)	800.00	500.00	400.00
(49)	Dick Buckley 7			
49 (a)	(Indianapolis)	700.00	300.00	175.00
49 (b)	(New York NL)	700.00	300.00	175.00
(50)	Charlie Buffinton (Also: Buffington) 4			
50 (a)	(Philadelphia NL)	700.00	350.00	250.00
50 (b)	(Philadelphia PL)	2,700	1,200	600.00
(51)	Ernie Burch 8			
51 (a)	(Brooklyn)	2,300	1,025	575.00
51 (b)	(St. Louis Whites WA)	700.00	300.00	175.00
(52)	Bill Burdick 4			
52 (a)	(Indianapolis)	700.00	300.00	175.00
52 (b)	(Omaha)	850.00	375.00	200.00
(53)	Jack Burdock 5			
53 (a)	(Boston NL)	1,250	550.00	300.00
(54)	Bob Burks (Burk) 3			
54 (a)	(Sioux City)	920.00	400.00	230.00
(55)	Watch Burnham 1			
55 (a)	(Indianapolis)	800.00	400.00	300.00
(56)	Jim Burns 8			
56 (a)	(Kansas City)	850.00	375.00	200.00
56 (b)	(Omaha)	700.00	300.00	175.00
(58)	Oyster Burns 5			
58 (a)	(Baltimore)	700.00	300.00	175.00
58 (b)	(Brooklyn)	850.00	375.00	200.00
DP 22	(Being tagged by Sam Trott.)	1,150	500.00	275.00
(59)	Tom Burns (Also: "E. Burns") 4			
59 (a)	(Chicago NL)	700.00	300.00	175.00
(60)	Doc Bushong 6			
60 (a)	(Brooklyn)	850.00	375.00	200.00
60 2	(St. Louis AA "Brown's Champions")	1,000	450.00	300.00
(61)	John (Patsy) Cahill 2			
61 (a)	(Indianapolis)	700.00	300.00	175.00
(62)	Count Campau 7			
62 (a)	(Detroit)	700.00	300.00	175.00
62 (b)	(Kansas City)	700.00	300.00	175.00
(63)	Jimmy Canavan 3			
63 (a)	(Omaha)	700.00	300.00	175.00
(64)	Bart Cantz (Also: McCantz) 5			
64 (a)	(Baltimore)	700.00	300.00	175.00
64 (b)	(St. Louis Whites WA)	700.00	300.00	175.00

(65)	Jack Carney 5			
65 (a)	(Washington)	700.00	300.00	175.00
(66)	Hick Carpenter 5			
66 (a)	(Cincinnati)	700.00	300.00	175.00
66 (b)	(Tagging player.)	1,425	650.00	350.00
(67)	Cliff Carroll 2			
67 (a)	(Washington)	700.00	300.00	175.00
(68)	Fred Carroll 3			
68 (a)	(Pittsburgh)	700.00	300.00	175.00
(69)	Scrappy Carroll 8			
69 (a)	(Chicago NL)	700.00	300.00	175.00
69 (b)	(St. Paul)	700.00	300.00	175.00
(70)	Ed Cartwright 5			
70 (a)	(Kansas City)	700.00	300.00	175.00
70 (b)	(St. Joseph)	700.00	300.00	175.00
(71)	Bob Caruthers 7			
71 (a)	(Brooklyn)	750.00	325.00	200.00
71 (b)	(St. Louis AA "Brown's Champions")	1,875	850.00	450.00
(72)	Dan Casey 3			
72 (a)	(Philadelphia NL)	700.00	300.00	175.00
(73)	Elton Chamberlain 6			
73 (a)	(St. Louis)	700.00	300.00	175.00
(74)	Cupid Childs 5			
74 (a)	(Philadelphia NL)	1,150	500.00	275.00
74 (b)	(Syracuse)	920.00	400.00	230.00
	Chreve - See Shreve			
(75)	Bob Clark 6			
75 (a)	(Brooklyn)	700.00	300.00	175.00
DP 4	(Tagging Mickey Hughes.)	2,300	1,025	575.00
(76)	Spider Clark 4			
76 (a)	(Washington)	750.00	325.00	200.00
(77)	Dad Clarke (Also: Clark) 11			
77 (a)	(Chicago NL)	700.00	300.00	175.00
77 (b)	(Omaha)	850.00	375.00	200.00
(78)	John Clarkson			
	See Hall of Fame Section Following			
(79)	Jack Clements 3			
79 (a)	(Philadelphia NL)	700.00	300.00	175.00
(80)	Elmer Cleveland 6			
80 (a)	(New York NL)	700.00	300.00	175.00
(81)	Monk Cline 5			
81 (a)	(Sioux City)	700.00	300.00	175.00
(82)	Mike Cody 4			
82 (a)	(Des Moines)	920.00	400.00	230.00
(83)	John Coleman 5			
83 (a)	(Pittsburgh)	700.00	300.00	175.00
(84)	Bill Collins 13			
84 (a)	(Lowell)	700.00	300.00	175.00
84 (b)	(Newark)	825.00	375.00	200.00
84 (c)	(New York)	900.00	400.00	230.00
	(Never played for N.Y.)			
(85)	Hub Collins 6			
85 (a)	(Brooklyn)	700.00	300.00	175.00
85 (b)	(Louisville)	975.00	425.00	250.00
(86)	Charlie Comiskey			
	(Also: Commiskey)			
86 (a)	See Hall of Fame Section Following			
(87)	Pete Connell 2			
87 (a)	(Des Moines, 3B, dark uniform.)	700.00	325.00	175.00
87 (b)	(Des Moines, 1B, light uniform. Photo actually P.J. O'Connell.)	700.00	300.00	175.00
(88)	Roger Connor (Also: Conner)			
	See Hall of Fame Section Following			
(89)	Dick Conway 6			
89 (a)	(Boston NL)	1,025	450.00	250.00
89 (b)	(Worcester)	700.00	300.00	175.00
(90)	Jim Conway 5			
90 (a)	(Kansas City)	800.00	350.00	200.00
(91)	Pete Conway 10			
91 (a)	(Detroit)	800.00	350.00	200.00
91 (b)	(Pittsburgh)	700.00	300.00	175.00
91 (c)	(Indianapolis)	700.00	300.00	175.00
(92)	Paul Cook 4			
92 (a)	(Louisville)	700.00	300.00	175.00
(93)	Jimmy Cooney 5			
93 (a)	(Chicago NL)	700.00	300.00	175.00
93 (b)	(Omaha)	850.00	375.00	200.00
(94)	Larry Corcoran 4			
94 (a)	(Indianapolis)	850.00	375.00	200.00
94 (b)	(London)	850.00	375.00	200.00
(95)	Pop Corkhill 7			
95 (a)	(Brooklyn)	700.00	300.00	175.00
95 (b)	(Cincinnati)	800.00	350.00	200.00
(96)	Cannonball Crane 7			
96 (a)	(New York NL)	700.00	300.00	175.00
96 (b)	(New York PL)	2,700	1,200	600.00
(97)	Sam Crane 3			
97 (a)	(Washington)	700.00	300.00	175.00
(98)	Jack Crogan (Croghan) 5			
98 (a)	(Chicago Maroons WA)	2,000	900.00	500.00
(99)	John Crooks 7			
99 (a)	(Omaha)	850.00	375.00	200.00
99 (b)	(St. Louis Whites WA)	700.00	300.00	175.00
(100)	Lave Cross 6			
100 (a)	(Louisville)	700.00	300.00	175.00
100 (b)	(Philadelphia AA)	920.00	400.00	230.00
100 (c)	(Philadelphia PL)	2,700	1,200	600.00
(101)	William Crossley 5			
101 (a)	(Milwaukee)	750.00	325.00	200.00
(102)	Joe Crotty 5			
102 (a)	(New York AA "dotted tie")	2,800	1,250	700.00
102 (b)	(Sioux City)	700.00	300.00	175.00
(103)	Billy Crowell 9			
103 (a)	(Cleveland)	700.00	300.00	175.00
103 (b)	(St. Joseph)	700.00	300.00	175.00
(104)	Jim Cudworth 4			
104 (a)	(Worcester)	700.00	300.00	175.00
(105)	Bert Cunningham 6			
105 (a)	(Baltimore)	850.00	375.00	200.00
105 (b)	(Philadelphia PL)	2,700	1,200	600.00
(106)	Tacks Curtis 5			
106 (a)	(St. Joseph)	920.00	400.00	230.00
(107)	Ed Cushman 3			
107 (a)	(New York AA "dotted tie")	2,800	1,250	600.00
107 (b)	(New York AA)	2,300	300.00	175.00
107 (c)	(Toledo)	3,500	775.00	425.00
(108)	Tony Cusick 2			
108 (a)	(Milwaukee)	5,750	300.00	175.00
(109)	Edward Dailey (Also: Daley) 7			
109 (a)	(Columbus)	700.00	300.00	175.00
109 (b)	(Philadelphia NL)	700.00	300.00	175.00
109 (c)	(Washington)	700.00	300.00	175.00
(110)	Vincent Dailey 1			
110 (a)	(Oakland)(SGC-graded Poor auctioned for $101,100 12/05.)			
(111)	Bill Daley 2			
111 (a)	(Boston NL)	750.00	325.00	200.00
111 (b)	(Boston PL)	2,400	1,100	600.00
(112)	Con Daley (Daily) 9			
112 (a)	(Boston NL)	700.00	300.00	175.00
112 (b)	(No name, team, etc.)	2,600	1,150	650.00
112 (c)	(Indianapolis)	700.00	300.00	175.00
(113)	Abner Dalrymple 7			
113 (a)	(Denver)	1,050	475.00	250.00
113 (b)	(Pittsburgh)	800.00	350.00	200.00
(114)	Sun Daly 5			
114 (a)	(Minneapolis)	900.00	400.00	225.00
(115)	Tom Daly 7			
115 (a)	(Chicago NL)	800.00	350.00	200.00
115 (b)	(Chicago NL)(Portrait)	1,400	625.00	350.00
115 (c)	(Cleveland)	700.00	300.00	175.00
	(Never played with Cleveland.)			
(116)	Law Daniels 5			
116 (a)	(Kansas City)	700.00	300.00	175.00
(117)	Dell Darling 6			
117 (a)	(Chicago NL)	700.00	300.00	175.00
117 (b)	(Portrait)	1,400	625.00	350.00
117 (c)	(Chicago PL)	2,700	1,200	600.00
(118)	William Darnbrough 2			
118 (a)	(Denver)	850.00	375.00	200.00
(119)	D.J. Davin 2			
119 (a)	(Milwaukee)	5,750	300.00	175.00
(120)	Jumbo Davis 5			
120 (a)	(Kansas City)	700.00	300.00	175.00
(121)	Pat Dealey (Also: Dealy) 6			
121 (a)	(Washington)	775.00	350.00	200.00
(122)	Tom Deasley 20			
122 (a)	(New York NL)	700.00	300.00	175.00
122 (b)	(Washington)	700.00	300.00	175.00
(123)	Harry Decker 5			
123 (a)	(Philadelphia NL)	750.00	325.00	200.00
(124)	Ed Delahanty			
	See Hall of Fame Section Following			
(125)	Jerry Denny 4			
125 (a)	(Indianapolis)	700.00	300.00	175.00
125 (b)	(New York NL)	700.00	300.00	175.00
(126)	Jim Devlin (Also: Delvin) 5			
126 (a)	(St. Louis AA)	700.00	300.00	175.00
(127)	Tom Dolan 5			
127 (a)	(Denver)	700.00	300.00	175.00
127 (b)	(St. Louis AA)	700.00	300.00	175.00
(128)	Jack Donahue 1			
128 (a)	(San Francisco) (SGC-certified Poor, $52,240, 12/04 auction.)			
(129)	Jim Donahue (Also: Donohue) 7			
129 (a)	(New York AA "dotted tie")	3,375	1,525	850.00
129 (b)	(Kansas City)	700.00	300.00	175.00
(130)	Jim Donnelly 3			
130 (a)	(Washington)	850.00	375.00	200.00
(131)	Charlie Dooley 1			
131 (a)	(Oakland)(SGC-certified Poor, $52,240, 12/04 auction.)			
(132)	John Doran 2			
132 (a)	(Omaha)	920.00	400.00	230.00
(133)	Mike Dorgan 17			
133 (a)	(New York NL)	700.00	300.00	175.00
	(Sliding)	1,100	500.00	250.00
(134)	Con Doyle 1			
134 (a)	(San Francisco) (Value Undetermined)			
(135)	Charlie Duffe (Duffee) 5			
135 (a)	(St. Louis AA)	850.00	375.00	200.00
(136)	Hugh Duffy			
	See Hall of Fame Section Following			
(137)	Dan Dugdale 7			
137 (a)	(Chicago Maroons WA)	1,025	450.00	250.00
137 (b)	(Minneapolis)	750.00	335.00	185.00
(138)	Martin Duke 5			
138 (a)	(Minneapolis)	700.00	300.00	175.00
(139)	Fred Dunlap 9			
139 (b)	(Pittsburgh)	825.00	375.00	200.00
(140)	J.E. Dunn 5			
140 (a)	(Chicago Maroons WA)	2,300	1,100	600.00
(141)	Jesse Duryea 4			
141 (a)	(Cincinnati)	800.00	350.00	200.00
141 (b)	(St. Paul)	700.00	300.00	175.00
(142)	Frank Dwyer 5			
142 (a)	(Chicago NL)	700.00	300.00	175.00
142 (b)	(Chicago Maroons WA)	2,300	1,100	600.00
(143)	Billy Earle (Also: Earl) 4			
143 (a)	(Cincinnati)	700.00	300.00	175.00
143 (b)	(St. Paul)	700.00	300.00	175.00
(144)	Hi Ebright 2			
144 (a)	(Washington)	700.00	300.00	175.00
(145)	Red Ehret 4			
145 (a)	(Louisville)	700.00	300.00	175.00
	Eidner - See Weidner			
(146)	R. Emmerke 5			
146 (a)	(Des Moines)	800.00	350.00	200.00
(147)	Dude Esterbrook 11			
147 (a)	(Indianapolis)	700.00	300.00	175.00
147 (b)	(Louisville)	700.00	300.00	175.00
147 (c)	(New York AA)	1,300	575.00	325.00
147 (d)	(New York NL)	700.00	300.00	175.00
(148)	Henry Esterday (Easterday) 6			
148 (a)	(Columbus)	700.00	300.00	175.00
148 (b)	(Kansas City)	700.00	300.00	175.00
(149)	Buck Ewing			
	See Hall of Fame Section Following			
(150)	John Ewing 4			
150 (a)	(Louisville)	800.00	350.00	200.00
(151)	Jay Faatz 3			
151 (a)	(Cleveland)	800.00	350.00	200.00
(152)	Bill Fagan 5			
152 (a)	(Denver)	850.00	375.00	200.00
152 (b)	(Kansas City)	750.00	325.00	200.00
(153)	Bill Farmer 7			
153 (a)	(Pittsburgh)	700.00	300.00	175.00
153 (b)	(St. Paul)	850.00	375.00	200.00
(154)	Sid Farrar (Also: Farrer, Faraer) 8			
154 (a)	(Philadelphia NL)	700.00	300.00	175.00
154 (b)	(Philadelphia PL)	2,700	1,200	600.00
(155)	Duke Farrell (Also: Farrel) 5			
155 (a)	(Chicago NL)	700.00	300.00	175.00
155 (b)	(Chicago PL)	2,700	1,200	600.00
(156)	Jack Farrell 12			
156 (a)	(Baltimore)	700.00	300.00	175.00
156 (b)	(Washington)	700.00	300.00	175.00
156 (c)	(Washington)	875.00	400.00	230.00
	(Tagging Paul Hines.)			
(157)	Frank Fennelly 5			
157 (a)	(Cincinnati)	700.00	300.00	175.00
157 (b)	(Philadelphia AA)	700.00	300.00	175.00

(158) Charlie Ferguson 4
158 (a) (Philadelphia NL)   700.00 300.00 175.00

(159) Alex Ferson 5
159 (a) (Washington)   850.00 375.00 200.00

(160) Wallace Fessenden 4
160 1 (Umpire)   1,850   825.00 450.00

(161) Jocko Fields (Also: Field) 6
161 (a) (Pittsburgh)   700.00 300.00 175.00
DP 6   (Fielding, Sam Barkley   1,250   575.00 300.00
       looking on.)
DP 7   (Tagging Sam Barkley.)   1,250   575.00 300.00

(162) Fischer 3
162 (a) (Chicago Maroons WA)   25,875 11,500 6,475

(163) Thomas Flanigan
       (Flanagan) 4
163 (a) (Cleveland)   920.00 400.00 230.00
       (Never played for Cleveland.)
163 (b) (Sioux City)   700.00 300.00 175.00

(164) Silver Flint 5
164 (a) (Chicago NL)   1,025   450.00 250.00

(165) Thomas Flood 5
165 (a) (St. Joseph)   700.00 300.00 175.00

(166) Jocko Flynn 2
166 (a) (Omaha)(Two known.)   11,500

(167) Jim Fogarty (Also: Fogerty) 5
167 (a) (Philadelphia NL)   700.00 300.00 175.00

(168) Frank Foreman 6
168 (a) (Baltimore)   700.00 300.00 175.00
168 (b) (Cincinnati)   1,250   575.00 300.00

(169) Tom Forster
       (Also: "F.W. Foster") 3
169 (a) (Hartford)   700.00 300.00 175.00
169 (b) (Milwaukee, squatting.)   850.00 375.00 200.00
169 (c) (New York AA "dotted tie") 3,375   1,525   850.00
169 (d) Tom Forester   750.00 335.00 185.00
       (Milwaukee, standing.)

(170) Elmer Foster 7
170 (a) (New York AA "dotted tie") 6,200   2,750   1,550
170 (b) (New York NL)   700.00 300.00 175.00
170 (c) (Minneapolis)   700.00 300.00 175.00

(171) Dave Foutz 5
171 (a) (Brooklyn)   920.00 400.00 230.00
171 (b) (St. Louis AA "Brown's   1,700   750.00 400.00
       Champions")

(172) Julie Freeman 5
172 (a) (Milwaukee)   850.00 375.00 200.00

(173) Will Fry 4
173 (a) (St. Joseph)   850.00 375.00 250.00

(174) Frank Fudger 1
174 (a) (Oakland)
       (Value Undetermined)

(175) Shorty Fuller 5
175 (a) (St. Louis AA)   850.00 375.00 200.00

(176) William Fuller 5
176 (a) (Milwaukee)   920.00 400.00 230.00

(177) Chris Fulmer (Also: Fullmer) 6
177 (a) (Baltimore)   700.00 300.00 175.00
DP 8   (Tagging Tom Tucker.)   2,000   900.00 500.00

(178) John Gaffney 1
178 (a) (Washington)   875.00 400.00 225.00
DP 21 (Behind George Shoch.)   1,150   500.00 300.00

(179) Pud Galvin
       See Hall of Fame Section Following

(180) Bob Gamble 3
180 (a) (Philadelphia AA)   700.00 300.00 175.00
DP 3   (Being tagged by Lou   1,600   725.00 400.00
       Bierbaur.) (Bierbauer)

(181) Charlie Ganzel
       (Also: Gauzel) 5
181 (a) (Boston)   700.00 300.00 175.00
181 (b) (Detroit)   700.00 300.00 175.00

(182) Gid Gardner 5
182 (a) (Philadelphia NL)   700.00 300.00 175.00
182 (b) (Washington)   1,025   450.00 250.00
DP 9   (Tagging Miah Murray.)   2,875   1,300   700.00

(183) Hank Gastreich (Gastright) 5
183 (a) (Columbus)   700.00 300.00 175.00

(184) Emil Geiss 6
184 (a) (Chicago NL)   700.00 300.00 175.00

(185) Frank Genins (Also: Genius) 5
185 (a) (Sioux City)   750.00 325.00 200.00

(186) Bill George 5
186 (a) (New York NL)   800.00 350.00 200.00

(187) Joe Gerhardt 4
187 (a) (Jersey City)   800.00 325.00 200.00
187 (b) (New York NL)   1,400   625.00 350.00

(188) Charlie Getzein (Getzien) 6
188 (a) (Detroit)   700.00 300.00 175.00

188 (b) (Indianapolis)   700.00 300.00 175.00

(189) Whitey Gibson 1
189 (a) (Philadelphia AA, two known.) 11,500   3,800
       (2003 auction)

(190) Bob Gilks 6
190 (a) (Cleveland)   800.00 350.00 200.00

(191) Pete Gillespie 5
191 (a) (New York NL)   850.00 375.00 200.00

(192) Barney Gilligan 3
192 (a) (Detroit)   700.00 300.00 175.00
192 (b) (Washington)   725.00 325.00 200.00

(193) Frank Gilmore 5
193 (a) (Washington)   1,025   450.00 250.00

(194) Jack Glasscock (Also:
       Glassock, Glass, Cock) 5
194 (a) (Indianapolis)   775.00 350.00 200.00
194 (b) (New York NL)   700.00 300.00 175.00

(195) Bill Gleason 5
195 (a) (Louisville)   700.00 300.00 175.00
195 (b) (Philadelphia AA)   700.00 300.00 175.00
195 (c) (St. Louis AA "Brown's   2,200   1,000   550.00
       Champions")
DP 23 (W/ Curt Welch.)   2,300   1,100   600.00

(196) Kid Gleason 5
196 (a) (Philadelphia NL)   700.00 300.00 175.00

(197) Ed Glenn 5
197 (a) (Sioux City)   850.00 375.00 200.00

(198) Mike Goodfellow 9
198 (a) (Cleveland)   920.00 400.00 230.00
198 (b) (Detroit)   825.00 375.00 200.00

(199) George Gore 10
199 (a) (New York NL)   1,025   450.00 250.00
199 (b) (New York PL)   2,700   1,200   600.00

(200) Frank Graves 6
200 (a) (Minneapolis)   700.00 300.00 175.00

(201) Bill Greenwood 8
201 (a) (Baltimore)   1,250   575.00 300.00
201 (b) (Columbus)   800.00 350.00 200.00

(202) Ed Greer 3
202 (a) (Brooklyn)   850.00 375.00 200.00
DP 10 (Catching, Hardie   1,150   500.00 300.00
       Henderson batting.)

(203) Mike Griffin 6
203 (a) (Baltimore)   1,150   500.00 300.00
203 (b) (Philadelphia PL)   2,700   1,200   600.00

(204) Clark Griffith
       See Hall of Fame Section Following

(205) Henry Gruber 4
205 (a) (Cleveland)   700.00 300.00 175.00

(206) Ad Gumbert 5
206 (a) (Chicago NL)   700.00 300.00 175.00
206 (b) (Boston PL)   2,700   1,200   600.00

(207) Tom Gunning 4
207 (a) (Philadelphia AA)   700.00 300.00 175.00
207 (b) (Philadelphia NL)   700.00 300.00 175.00

(208) Joe Gunson 4
208 (a) (Kansas City)   750.00 325.00 200.00

(209) George Haddock 5
209 (a) (Washington)   700.00 300.00 175.00

(210) Frank Hafner 5
210 (a) (Kansas City)   750.00 325.00 200.00

(211) Willie Hahn (Mascot)
211 (a) (Chicago NL)   850.00 375.00 200.00
DP 24 (W/ Ned Williamson.)   4,000   1,800   1,000

       Halliday - See Holliday

(212) Bill Hallman 6
212 (a) (Philadelphia NL)   850.00 375.00 200.00
212 (b) (Philadelphia PL)   2,700   1,200   600.00

(213) Billy Hamilton
       See Hall of Fame Section Following

(214) Frank Hankinson 1
214 (a) (New York AA "dotted tie") 27,000 12,150 6,750

(215) Ned Hanlon 6
       See Hall of Fame Section Following

       Hannon - See Shannon

(216) Bill Hanrahan 9
216 (a) (Chicago Maroons WA)   1,025   450.00 250.00
216 (b) (Minneapolis)   700.00 300.00 175.00

(217) Al Hapeman 1
217 (a) (Sacramento)
       (Value Undetermined)

(218) John Harkins
       (Also: Harkens) 9
218 (a) (Baltimore)   800.00 350.00 200.00
218 (b) (Brooklyn)   700.00 300.00 175.00

(219) Bill Hart 5
219 (a) (Cincinnati)   700.00 300.00 175.00
       (Never played for Cincinnati.)
219 (b) (Des Moines)   850.00 375.00 200.00

(220) Bill Hasamdear
       (Hassamaer) 3
220 (a) (Kansas City)   800.00 350.00 200.00

(221) Gil Hatfield 5
221 (a) (New York NL)   800.00 350.00 200.00
221 (b) (New York PL)   2,700   1,200   600.00

(222) Bill Hawes (Also Howes) 5
222 (a) (Minneapolis)   800.00 350.00 200.00
222 (b) (St. Paul)   875.00 400.00 225.00

(223) John J. "Egyptian" Healey
       (Healy) 5
223 (a) (Indianapolis)   750.00 325.00 200.00
223 (b) (Washington)   920.00 400.00 230.00
223 (c) (Washington, portrait, w/ 34,500 15,525 8,625
       moustache, no cap, possibly
       unique.)

(224) John C. "Jack" Healy
       (Also: Healey) 8
224 (a) (Denver)   1,050   475.00 275.00
224 (b) (Omaha)   850.00 375.00 200.00

(225) Guy Hecker 5
225 (a) (Louisville)   2,200   975.00 550.00

(226) Tony Hellman 5
226 (a) (Sioux City)   800.00 375.00 200.00

(227) Hardie Henderson 13
227 (a) (Brooklyn)   700.00 300.00 175.00
227 (b) (Pittsburgh)   700.00 300.00 175.00
DP 10 (Batting, Ed Greer catching.) 1,150 500.00 300.00
DP 11 (Tagging Jimmy Peoples.)   1,600   725.00 400.00

(228) Moxie Hengle 10
228 (a) (Chicago Maroons WA)   1,425   650.00 350.00
228 (b) (Minneapolis)   920.00 400.00 230.00

(229) John Henry 5
229 (a) (Philadelphia)   700.00 300.00 175.00
       (Never actually played for
       Philadelphia.)

(230) Ed Herr 7
230 (a) (Milwaukee)   920.00 400.00 230.00
230 (b) (St. Louis Whites WA)   700.00 300.00 175.00

(231) Hunkey Hines 4
231 (a) (St. Louis Whites WA)   1,400   600.00 350.00

(232) Paul Hines 7
232 (a) (Indianapolis)   920.00 400.00 230.00
232 (b) (Washington)   850.00 375.00 200.00

(233) Frank Hoffman 4
233 (a) (Denver)   975.00 425.00 250.00

(234) Eddie Hogan 5
234 (a) (Cleveland)   775.00 350.00 200.00

(235) Bill Holbert 10
235 (a) (Brooklyn)   1,025   450.00 250.00
235 (b) (Jersey City)   1,025   450.00 250.00
235 (c) (New York AA "dotted tie") 10,700 4,800   2,650
235 (d) (New York AA)   700.00 300.00 175.00

(236) Bug Holliday (Also: Halliday) 7
236 (a) (Cincinnati)   700.00 300.00 175.00
236 (b) (Des Moines)   700.00 300.00 175.00

(238) Buster Hoover 3
238 (a) (Philadelphia)   700.00 300.00 175.00
238 (b) (Toronto)   775.00 350.00 200.00
       (Never played for Phila. in
       N172 era.)
DP 1   (Hoover tagging Ed Andrews.) 1,150 500.00 300.00

(239) Charlie Hoover 7
239 (a) (Chicago)   700.00 300.00 175.00
       (Never played for Chicago.)
239 (b) (Kansas City)   800.00 350.00 200.00

(240) Jack Horner (Also: Hodner) 6
240 (a) (Milwaukee)   700.00 300.00 175.00
240 (b) (New Haven)   700.00 300.00 175.00
240 (c) (Photo actually E.H. Warner.) 700.00 300.00 175.00
DP 5   (W/ Ed Warner.)   1,150   500.00 300.00

(241) Joe Hornung (Also: Horning) 6
241 (a) (Baltimore)   700.00 300.00 175.00
241 (b) (Boston)   850.00 375.00 200.00
241 (c) (New York NL)   700.00 300.00 175.00

(242) Pete Hotaling
       (Also: Hotoling) 4
242 (a) (Cleveland)   700.00 300.00 175.00

       Howes - See Hawes

(243) Dummy Hoy 5
243 (a) (Washington)   8,625   3,900   2,150

(244) Nat Hudson 6
244 (a) (St. Louis AA "Brown's   1,800   800.00 450.00
       Champions")
244 (b) (St. Louis AA)   700.00 300.00 175.00

(245) Mickey Hughes 7
245 (a) (Brooklyn)   700.00 300.00 175.00
DP 4   (Being tagged by Bob Clark.) 2,300 1,100   600.00

(246) Al Hungler 4			
246 (a) (Sioux City)	800.00	350.00	200.00
(247) Bill Hutchinson 4			
247 (a) (Chicago NL)	1,400	600.00	350.00
(248) Arthur Irwin 13			
248 (a) (Boston PL)	1,200	550.00	300.00
248 (b) (Philadelphia NL)	875.00	400.00	225.00
(Portrait, cap off.)	2,300	1,100	600.00
248 (c) (Washington)	700.00	300.00	175.00
(249) John Irwin 5			
249 (a) (Washington)	700.00	300.00	175.00
249 (b) (Wilkes-Barre)	875.00	400.00	225.00
(250) A.C. Jantzen 5			
250 (a) (Minneapolis)	800.00	350.00	200.00
(251) Frederick Jevne 5			
251 (a) (Minneapolis)	825.00	375.00	200.00
(252) Spud Johnson 6			
252 (a) (Columbus)	700.00	300.00	175.00
252 (b) (Kansas City)	920.00	400.00	230.00
(253) Dick Johnston 7			
253 (a) (Boston NL)	750.00	325.00	200.00
253 (b) (Boston PL)	2,700	1,200	600.00
(254) W.T. Jordan 5			
254 (a) (Minneapolis)	920.00	400.00	230.00
(255) Heinie Kappell (Kappel) 8			
255 (a) (Cincinnati)	700.00	300.00	175.00
255 (b) (Columbus)	700.00	300.00	175.00
(256) Tim (Also: Jim) Keefe,			
(Also: Keef, Keefep)			
See Hall of Fame Section Following			
(257) George Keefe 5			
257 (a) (Washington)	700.00	300.00	175.00
(258) Jim Keenan 5			
258 (a) (Cincinnati)	700.00	300.00	175.00
(259) Charlie Kelly 5			
259 (a) (Philadelphia AA)	1,850	825.00	450.00
(260) Honest John Kelly 4			
260 (a) (Louisville)	700.00	300.00	175.00
260 (b) (Umpire WA)	1,800	800.00	450.00
DP 14 (W/ Jim Powell.)	1,150	500.00	275.00
(261) King Kelly			
See Hall of Fame Section Following			
(262) Rudy Kemmler			
(Also: Kemler) 2			
262 (a) (St. Louis AA "Brown's	1,425	650.00	350.00
Champions")			
262 (b) (St. Paul)	700.00	300.00	175.00
(263) Ted Kennedy 9			
263 (a) (Des Moines)	850.00	375.00	200.00
263 (b) (Omaha)	1,150	500.00	275.00
(264) J.J. Kenyon 7			
264 (a) (Des Moines)	700.00	300.00	175.00
264 (b) (St. Louis Whites WA)	775.00	350.00	200.00
(265) John Kerins 6			
265 (a) (Louisville)	850.00	375.00	200.00
(266) Matt Kilroy 7			
266 (a) (Baltimore)	1,400	600.00	350.00
266 (b) (Boston PL)	2,700	1,200	600.00
(267) Silver King 3			
267 (a) (Chicago PL)	2,700	1,200	600.00
267 (b) (St. Louis AA)	700.00	300.00	175.00
(268) Gus Kloff (Klopf) 7			
268 (a) (Minneapolis)	700.00	300.00	175.00
268 (b) (St. Joseph)	700.00	300.00	175.00
DP 15 (W/ Bill Krieg.)	1,150	500.00	275.00
(269) Billy Klusman 7			
269 (a) (Denver)	1,100	500.00	250.00
269 (b) (Milwaukee)	700.00	300.00	175.00
(270) Phil Knell 5			
270 (a) (St. Joseph)	800.00	350.00	200.00
(271) Ed Knouff 5			
271 (a) (St. Louis AA)	800.00	350.00	200.00
(272) Charles Kremmeyer			
(Krehmeyer) 1			
272 (a) (Sacramento)(SGC-certified			
Fair, $50,233 12/04 auction.)			
(273) Bill Krieg (Also: Kreig) 14			
273 (a) (Minneapolis)	775.00	350.00	200.00
273 (b) (St. Joseph)	750.00	325.00	200.00
273 (c) (Washington)	700.00	300.00	175.00
DP 15 (W/ Gus Kloff.) (Klopf)	1,150	500.00	300.00
(274) Gus Krock 5			
274 (a) (Chicago NL)	700.00	300.00	175.00
(275) Willie Kuehne			
(Also: Kuchne) 5			
275 (a) (Pittsburgh)	700.00	300.00	175.00
(276) Fred Lange 5			
276 (a) (Chicago Maroons WA)	2,100	900.00	500.00

(277) Henry Larkin 4			
277 (a) (Philadelphia AA)	700.00	300.00	175.00
(278) Arlie Latham 7			
278 (a) (St. Louis AA "Brown's	1,625	725.00	400.00
Champions")			
278 (b) (St. Louis AA)	700.00	325.00	200.00
278 (c) (Chicago PL)	2,700	1,200	600.00
(279) Chuck Lauer 4			
279 (a) (Pittsburgh)	700.00	300.00	175.00
(280) John Leighton 5			
280 (a) (Omaha)	850.00	375.00	200.00
(281) Levy 1			
281 (a) (San Francisco)			
(Value Undetermined)			
(282) Tom Loftus 2			
282 (a) (Cleveland)	700.00	300.00	200.00
282 (b) (St. Louis Whites WA)	700.00	300.00	175.00
(283) Danny Long 1			
283 (a) (Oakland)			
(Value Undetermined)			
(284) Herman Long 7			
284 (a) (Chicago Maroons WA)	3,100	1,400	775.00
284 (b) (Kansas City)	900.00	400.00	250.00
(285) Tom Lovett 6			
285 (a) (Brooklyn)	900.00	400.00	250.00
285 (b) (Omaha)	850.00	375.00	200.00
(286) Bobby Lowe 6			
286 (a) (Milwaukee)	1,100	500.00	300.00
DP 18 (About to be tagged by Pat	1,400	600.00	350.00
Pettee.)			
(287) Jack Lynch 5			
287 (a) (New York AA "dotted tie")	3,375	1,500	850.00
287 (b) (New York AA)	700.00	300.00	175.00
(288) Denny Lyons 4			
288 (a) (Philadelphia AA)	700.00	300.00	175.00
(289) Harry Lyons 6			
289 (a) (St. Louis AA)	700.00	300.00	175.00
289 (b) (Jersey City)	700.00	300.00	175.00
(290) Connie Mack 3			
See Hall of Fame Section Following			
(291) Reddy Mack 6			
291 (a) (Baltimore)	800.00	350.00	200.00
291 (b) (Louisville)	700.00	300.00	175.00
(292) Jimmy Macullar 7			
292 (a) (Des Moines)	1,400	600.00	350.00
292 (b) (Milwaukee)	700.00	300.00	175.00
(293) Kid Madden 9			
293 (a) (Boston NL)	700.00	300.00	175.00
293 (b) (Boston NL)(Portrait)	2,875	1,300	700.00
293 (c) (Boston PL)	2,700	1,200	600.00
(294) Danny Mahoney 1			
294 (a) (St. Joseph)	2,525	1,125	600.00
(295) Willard Maines (Mains) 5			
295 (a) (St. Paul)	700.00	300.00	175.00
(296) Fred Mann 5			
296 (a) (Hartford)	700.00	300.00	175.00
296 (b) (St. Louis AA)	700.00	300.00	175.00
(Never played for St. Louis.)			
(297) Jimmy Manning 6			
297 (a) (Kansas City)	850.00	375.00	200.00
(298) Lefty Marr 7			
298 (a) (Cincinnati)	700.00	300.00	175.00
298 (b) (Columbus)	775.00	350.00	200.00
(299) Mascot (Willie Breslin 1)			
299 (a) New York NL (Caption reads	1,850	1,000	600.00
"New York Mascot.")			
(300) Leech Maskrey 5			
300 (a) (Des Moines)	700.00	300.00	175.00
300 (b) (Milwaukee)	700.00	300.00	175.00
300 (c) (Photo actually Jimmy	700.00	300.00	175.00
Macullar.)			
Massitt - See Messitt			
(301) Bobby Mathews 3			
301 (a) (Philadelphia AA)	900.00	400.00	250.00
(302) Mike Mattimore (Also:			
Mattemore) 19			
302 (a) (New York NL)	800.00	350.00	200.00
302 (b) (Philadelphia AA)	725.00	325.00	200.00
(303) Al Maul 7			
303 (a) (Pittsburgh)	700.00	300.00	175.00
(304) Al Mays 5			
304 (a) (New York AA "dotted tie")	3,375	1,525	850.00
304 (b) (Columbus)	700.00	300.00	175.00
(305) Jimmy McAleer 4			
305 (a) (Cleveland)	700.00	300.00	175.00
(306) John McCarthy (McCarty) 3			
306 (a) (Kansas City)	900.00	400.00	250.00

(307) Tommy McCarthy			
See Hall of Fame Section Following			
(308) Jim McCauley 3			
308 (a) (Chicago Maroons WA)	2,100	900.00	500.00
(309) Bill McClellan			
(Also: McClennan) 3			
309 (a) (Brooklyn)	700.00	300.00	175.00
309 (b) (Denver)	1,400	600.00	350.00
(310) Jim McCormack 4			
310 (a) (St. Louis Whites WA)	700.00	300.00	175.00
(311) Jim McCormick 10			
311 (a) (Chicago)	1,400	600.00	350.00
311 (b) (Portrait)	4,600	2,100	1,150
311 (c) (Pittsburgh)	850.00	375.00	200.00
(312) McCreachery 1			
312 (a) (Indianapolis)			
(Value Undetermined)			
(Nobody named McCreachery ever			
managed Indianapolis. Photo actually			
Deacon White.)			
(313) Tom McCullum (McCallum) 4			
313 (a) (Minneapolis)	700.00	300.00	175.00
(314) Jim McDonald 1			
314 (a) (Oakland)			
(Value Undetermined)			
(315) Chippy McGarr 5			
315 (a) (Kansas City)	700.00	300.00	175.00
315 (b) (St. Louis AA)	700.00	300.00	175.00
315 (c) (St. Louis AA, batting, umpire	875.00	400.00	225.00
behind.)			
(316) Jack McGeachy 4			
316 (a) (Indianapolis)	850.00	375.00	200.00
(317) John McGlone 7			
317 (a) (Cleveland)	700.00	300.00	175.00
317 (b) (Detroit)	700.00	300.00	175.00
(318) Deacon McGuire 5			
318 (a) (Philadelphia NL)	750.00	325.00	200.00
318 (b) (Toronto)	825.00	375.00	200.00
(319) Bill McGunnigle 1			
319 (a) (Brooklyn)	1,800	775.00	425.00
(320) Ed McKean 5			
320 (a) (Cleveland)	700.00	300.00	175.00
(321) Alex McKinnon 4			
321 (a) (Pittsburgh)	700.00	300.00	175.00
(322) Tom McLaughlin 1			
322 (a) (New York AA "dotted tie")	7,875	3,550	1,975
(323) Bid McPhee			
See Hall of Fame Section Following			
(324) Jack McQuaid 1			
324 (a) (Umpire)	2,300	1,025	575.00
(325) James McQuaid 3			
325 (a) (Denver)	1,800	775.00	425.00
(326) Jim McTamany			
(Also: McTammany) 6			
326 (a) (Brooklyn)	1,800	775.00	425.00
326 (b) (Columbus)	1,800	775.00	425.00
326 (c) (Kansas City)	1,800	775.00	425.00
(327) George McVey 9			
327 (a) (Denver)	700.00	300.00	175.00
327 (b) (Milwaukee)	700.00	300.00	175.00
327 (c) (St. Joseph)	750.00	325.00	200.00
(328) Pete Meegan 1			
328 (a) (San Francisco)			
(Value Undetermined)			
(329) John Messitt			
(Also: Massitt, Wassitt) 3			
329 (a) (Omaha)	1,325	600.00	325.00
Micholson - See Nicholson			
(330) Doggie Miller 5			
330 (a) (Pittsburgh)	700.00	300.00	175.00
(331) Joe Miller 3			
331 (a) (Minneapolis)	700.00	300.00	175.00
331 (b) (Omaha)	750.00	325.00	200.00
(332) Jocko Milligan 6			
332 (a) (Philadelphia PL)	2,700	1,200	600.00
332 (b) (St. Louis AA)	700.00	300.00	175.00
(333) E.L. Mills 5			
333 (a) (Milwaukee)	700.00	300.00	175.00
(334) Daniel Minnehan (Minahan) 4			
334 (a) (Minneapolis)	700.00	300.00	175.00
(335) Sam Moffet 3			
335 (a) (Indianapolis)	700.00	300.00	175.00
(336) John Morrill (Also: Morrell) 4			
336 (a) (Boston NL)	1,250	550.00	300.00
336 (b) (Boston NL)(Portrait)	2,100	900.00	500.00
336 (c) (Washington)	1,025	450.00	250.00
(337) Ed Morris 6			

337 (a) (Pittsburgh)	700.00	300.00	175.00
(338) Tony Mullane 7			
338 (a) (Cincinnati)	1,600	700.00	400.00
(339) Joe Mulvey 4			
339 (a) (Philadelphia NL)	700.00	300.00	175.00
339 (b) (Philadelphia PL)	2,700	1,200	600.00
(340) Pat Murphy 3			
340 (a) (New York NL)	700.00	300.00	175.00
(341) P.L. Murphy 5			
341 (a) (St. Paul)	700.00	300.00	175.00
(342) Miah Murray 5			
342 (a) (Washington)	700.00	300.00	175.00
DP 9 (Being tagged by Gid Gardner.)	2,875	1,300	700.00
(343) Jim Mutrie 3			
343 (a) (New York NL)	2,100	900.00	500.00
(344) Al Myers 6			
344 (a) (Philadelphia NL)	700.00	300.00	175.00
344 (b) (Washington)	775.00	350.00	200.00
(345) George Myers 3			
345 (a) (Indianapolis)	700.00	300.00	175.00
(346) Tom Nagle 6			
346 (a) (Chicago NL)	700.00	300.00	175.00
346 (b) (Omaha)	775.00	350.00	200.00
(347) Billy Nash 7			
347 (a) (Boston NL)	900.00	400.00	250.00
347 (b) (Tagging (unnamed) Old Hoss Radbourn.)	2,750	1,225	700.00
347 (c) (Boston PL)	2,700	1,200	600.00
(348) Jack Nelson 1			
348 (a) (New York AA "dotted tie")	7,875	3,550	1,975
(349) Kid Nichols SEE HALL OF FAME SECTION FOLLOWING			
(350) Samuel Nichols (Nichol) 4			
350 (a) (Pittsburgh)	700.00	300.00	175.00
(351) J.W. Nicholson 6			
351 (a) (Chicago Maroons WA)	2,100	900.00	500.00
(352) Parson Nicholson (Also: Micholson) 7			
352 (a) (Cleveland) (Never played for Cleveland.)	700.00	300.00	175.00
352 (b) (St. Louis Whites WA)	700.00	300.00	175.00
(353) Hugh Nicol (Also: Nicoll) 8			
353 (a) (St. Louis AA "Brown's Champions")	1,000	450.00	250.00
353 (b) (Cincinnati)	825.00	375.00	200.00
DP 16 (Side by side w/ John Reilly.)	2,300	1,025	575.00
DP 17 (Facing John Reilly.)	2,525	1,125	625.00
(354) Frederick Nyce 4			
354 (a) (Burlington)	700.00	300.00	175.00
354 (b) (St. Louis Whites WA)	700.00	300.00	175.00
(355) Doc Oberlander 8			
355 (a) (Cleveland)	700.00	300.00	175.00
355 (b) (Syracuse)	700.00	300.00	175.00
(356) Billy O'Brien 5			
356 (a) (Washington)	900.00	400.00	250.00
(357) Darby O'Brien 5			
357 (a) ("Brooklyns" or "Bk'ns")	700.00	300.00	175.00
(358) Jack O'Brien 8			
358 (a) (Baltimore)	700.00	300.00	175.00
358 (b) ("Brooklyn")	700.00	300.00	175.00
358 (c) ("Mini" photo.)	5,750	2,600	1,425
(359) John O'Brien 4			
359 (a) (Cleveland)	900.00	400.00	250.00
(360) P.J. O'Connell 5			
360 (a) (Des Moines)	750.00	325.00	200.00
360 (b) (Omaha)	800.00	350.00	200.00
(361) Jack O'Connor 8			
361 (a) (Cincinnati)	700.00	300.00	175.00
361 (b) (Columbus)	700.00	300.00	175.00
(362) Hank O'Day 3			
362 (a) (Washington)	800.00	350.00	200.00
(363) Harry O'Day 1			
363 (a) (Sacramento)(VALUE UNDETERMINED)			
(364) Norris O'Neill 1			
364 (a) (Oakland)(VALUE UNDETERMINED)			
(365) Tip O'Neill (Also: O'Neil) 11			
365 (a) (Chicago PL)	2,500	1,100	625.00
365 (b) (St. Louis AA "Brown's Champions")	1,875	850.00	475.00
365 (c) (St. Louis AA)	700.00	300.00	175.00
365 (d) (Photo actually Bill White.) (W/moustache, stooping to field grounder.)	975.00	425.00	250.00
(366) Orator Jim O'Rourke			

SEE HALL OF FAME SECTION FOLLOWING			
(367) Tom O'Rourke (Also: Rourke) 8			
367 (a) (Boston NL)	850.00	375.00	200.00
367 (b) (Jersey City)	700.00	300.00	175.00
(368) Dave Orr 10			
368 (a) (Brooklyn)	900.00	400.00	250.00
368 (b) (Columbus)	975.00	425.00	250.00
368 (c) (New York AA "dotted tie")	15,750	7,100	3,925
368 (d) (New York AA)	700.00	300.00	175.00
(369) Charlie Parsons 4			
369 (a) (Minneapolis)	700.00	300.00	175.00
(370) Owen Patton 8			
370 (a) (Des Moines)	700.00	300.00	175.00
370 (b) (Minneapolis)	850.00	375.00	200.00
(371) Jimmy Peeples (Peoples) 4			
371 (a) (Brooklyn)	700.00	300.00	175.00
371 (b) (Columbus)	800.00	350.00	200.00
DP 11 (Being tagged by Hardie Henderson.)	1,600	725.00	400.00
(372) Hip Perrier 1			
372 (a) (San Francisco)(VALUE UNDETERMINED)			
(373) Pat Pettee 4			
373 (a) (London)	700.00	300.00	175.00
373 (b) (Milwaukee)	700.00	300.00	175.00
DP 18 (About to tag Bobby Lowe.)	1,400	600.00	350.00
(374) Fred Pfeffer 5			
374 (a) (Chicago NL)	1,050	500.00	275.00
(375) Dick Phelan 5			
375 (a) (Des Moines)	700.00	300.00	175.00
(376) Bill Phillips 7			
376 (a) (Brooklyn, large photo.)	1,400	600.00	350.00
376 (b) (Brooklyn, mini photo.)	5,175	2,325	1,300
376 (c) (Kansas City)	800.00	350.00	200.00
(377) John Pickett 12			
377 (a) (Kansas City)	700.00	300.00	175.00
377 (b) (Philadelphia PL)	900.00	400.00	225.00
377 (c) (St. Paul)	700.00	300.00	175.00
(378) George Pinkney (Pinckney) 5			
378 (a) (Brooklyn)	700.00	300.00	175.00
(379) Tom Poorman (Also: Poor Man, Porrman) 7			
379 (a) (Milwaukee)	800.00	350.00	200.00
379 (b) (Philadelphia AA)	700.00	300.00	175.00
(380) Henry Porter 7			
380 (a) (Brooklyn)	1,500	675.00	375.00
380 (b) (Kansas City)	1,125	500.00	275.00
(381) Jim Powell 5			
381 (a) (Sioux City)	900.00	400.00	250.00
DP 14 (w/ Honest John Kelly.)	1,600	725.00	400.00
(382) Thomas Powers (Power) 1			
382 (a) (San Francisco)(VALUE UNDETERMINED)			
(383) Blondie Purcell 7			
383 (a) (Baltimore)	700.00	300.00	175.00
383 (b) (Philadelphia AA)	700.00	300.00	175.00
(384) Tom Quinn 5			
384 (a) (Baltimore)	875.00	400.00	250.00
(385) Joe Quinn 3			
385 (a) (Boston NL)	1,400	600.00	350.00
385 (b) (Des Moines)	700.00	300.00	175.00
(386) Old Hoss Radbourn SEE HALL OF FAME SECTION FOLLOWING			
(387) Paul Radford 8			
387 (a) (Brooklyn)	700.00	300.00	175.00
387 (b) (Cleveland)	700.00	300.00	175.00
(388) Tom Ramsey 3			
388 (a) (Louisville)	1,050	450.00	300.00
(389) Rehse 5			
389 (a) (Minneapolis)	800.00	350.00	200.00
(390) Charlie Reilly (Also: Riley) 4			
390 (a) (St. Paul)	700.00	300.00	175.00
(391) Long John Reilly 3			
391 (a) (Cincinnati)	1,050	450.00	250.00
DP 16 (Side by side w/ Hugh Nicol.)	2,300	1,125	575.00
DP 17 (Facing Hugh Nicol.)	2,600	1,150	625.00
(392) Charlie Reynolds 4			
392 (a) (Kansas City)	800.00	350.00	200.00
(393) Danny Richardson (Also: Richards) 5			
393 (a) (New York NL)	700.00	300.00	175.00
393 (b) (New York PL)	2,700	1,200	600.00
DP 12 (Being tagged by Tim Keefe.)	2,600	1,150	625.00
DP 13 (Sliding, Tim Keefe fielding ball.)	2,600	1,150	625.00
(394) Hardy Richardson 5			

394 (a) (Boston NL)	700.00	300.00	175.00
394 (b) (Detroit)	700.00	300.00	175.00
(395) Charlie Ripslager (Reipschlager) 1			
395 (a) (New York AA "dotted tie")	9,000	4,050	2,250
(396) John Roach 6			
396 (a) (New York NL)	775.00	350.00	200.00
(397) M.C. Robinson 6			
397 (a) (Minneapolis)	700.00	300.00	175.00
(398) Wilbert Robinson SEE HALL OF FAME SECTION FOLLOWING			
(399) Yank Robinson 6			
399 (a) (St. Louis AA "Brown's Champions")	1,500	675.00	375.00
399 (b) (St. Louis AA)	700.00	300.00	175.00
(400) George Rooks 6			
400 (a) (Chicago Maroons WA)	1,050	450.00	250.00
400 (b) (Detroit) (Never played for Detroit.)	700.00	300.00	175.00
(401) Chief Roseman 1			
401 (a) (New York AA "dotted tie")	7,850	3,525	1,950
Rourke - See Tom O'Rourke			
(402) Dave Rowe 8			
402 (a) (Denver)	1,600	725.00	400.00
402 (b) (Kansas City, portrait.)	6,325	2,850	1,600
402 (c) (Kansas City)	1,050	450.00	250.00
(403) Jack Rowe 3			
403 (a) (Detroit)	875.00	400.00	225.00
(404) Amos Rusie (Also: Russie) SEE HALL OF FAME SECTION FOLLOWING			
(405) Jimmy Ryan 8			
405 (a) (Chicago NL)	700.00	300.00	175.00
405 (b) (Chicago PL)	2,700	1,200	600.00
405 (c) (Philadelphia)(Never player for Phila.)	700.00	300.00	175.00
(406) Harry Sage 6			
406 (a) (Des Moines)	700.00	300.00	175.00
406 (b) (Toledo)	1,750	800.00	425.00
DP 19 (W/ Bill Van Dyke.) (Des Moines)	1,150	500.00	300.00
DP 20 (W/ Bill Van Dyke.) (Toledo)	1,150	500.00	300.00
(407) Ben Sanders 5			
407 (a) (Philadelphia NL)	700.00	300.00	175.00
407 (b) (Philadelphia PL)	2,700	1,200	600.00
(408) Frank Scheibeck 4			
408 (a) (Detroit)	850.00	375.00	200.00
(409) Al Schellhase 5			
409 (a) (St. Joseph)	900.00	400.00	250.00
(410) Bill Schenkel (Also: Schenkle) 4			
410 (a) (Milwaukee)	700.00	300.00	175.00
(411) L. Schildknecht 4			
411 (a) (Des Moines)	700.00	300.00	175.00
411 (b) (Milwaukee)	700.00	300.00	175.00
(412) Gus Schmelz 2			
412 (a) (Cincinnati)	1,800	775.00	425.00
Schoch - See Shoch			
(413) Jumbo Schoeneck 8			
413 (a) (Chicago Maroons WA)	2,325	1,125	600.00
413 (b) (Indianapolis)	700.00	300.00	175.00
(414) Pop Schriver 5			
414 (a) (Philadelphia NL)	700.00	300.00	175.00
DP 2 (Tagging Charlie Bastian.)	1,150	500.00	300.00
Schwartwood - See Swartwood			
(415) Emmett Seery 4			
415 (a) (Indianapolis)	700.00	300.00	175.00
(416) Billy Serad 5			
416 (a) (Cincinnati)	700.00	300.00	175.00
416 (b) (Toronto)	850.00	375.00	200.00
(417) Ed Seward 3			
417 (a) (Philadelphia AA)	700.00	300.00	175.00
(418) Orator Shafer (Shaffer) 4			
418 (a) (Des Moines)	700.00	300.00	175.00
(419) Taylor Shafer (Shaffer) 3			
419 (a) (St. Louis Whites WA)	700.00	300.00	175.00
419 (b) (St. Paul)	700.00	300.00	175.00
(420) Daniel Shannon (Also: Hannon) 6			
420 (a) (Louisville)	700.00	300.00	175.00
420 (b) (Omaha)	800.00	350.00	200.00
420 (c) (Philadelphia PL)	2,700	1,200	600.00
(421) Bill Sharsig 1			
421 (a) (Philadelphia AA)	700.00	300.00	175.00
(422) John Shaw 5			

422 (a) (Minneapolis) | 700.00 | 300.00 | 175.00

(423) Samuel Shaw 4
423 (a) (Baltimore) | 1,050 | 450.00 | 250.00
423 (b) (Newark) | 1,150 | 500.00 | 300.00

(424) Bill Shindle (Also: Shindel) 7
424 (a) (Baltimore) | 850.00 | 375.00 | 200.00
424 (b) (Philadelphia PL) | 3,300 | 1,500 | 825.00
("PL" not on card.)

(425) George Shoch
(Also: Schoch) 4
425 (a) (Washington) | 700.00 | 300.00 | 175.00
DP 21 (Batting, John Gaffney | 1,150 | 500.00 | 300.00
behind.)

(426) Otto Shomberg
(Schomberg) 3
426 (a) (Indianapolis) | 700.00 | 300.00 | 175.00

(427) Lev Shreve 7
427 (a) (Indianapolis) | 800.00 | 350.00 | 200.00

(428) Ed Silch 8
428 (a) (Brooklyn) | 700.00 | 300.00 | 175.00
428 (b) (Denver) | 825.00 | 375.00 | 225.00

(429) Mike Slattery 6
429 (a) (New York NL) | 700.00 | 300.00 | 175.00
429 (b) (New York PL) | 2,700 | 1,200 | 600.00

(430) Elmer Smith 5
430 (a) (Cincinnati) | 700.00 | 300.00 | 175.00

(431) Fred Smith 5
431 (a) (Des Moines) | 700.00 | 300.00 | 175.00

(432) Germany (Geo.) Smith 5
432 (a) (Brooklyn) | 700.00 | 300.00 | 175.00

(433) Nick Smith 5
433 (a) (St. Joseph) | 750.00 | 325.00 | 200.00

(434) Phenomenal Smith 10
434 (a) (Baltimore) | 775.00 | 350.00 | 200.00
434 (b) (Baltimore, portrait.) | 9,775 | 4,400 | 2,450
(No team designation.)
434 (c) (Philadelphia AA) | 1,250 | 550.00 | 300.00

(435) Pop Smith 5
435 (a) (Boston NL) | 775.00 | 350.00 | 200.00
435 (b) (Pittsburgh) | 700.00 | 300.00 | 175.00

(436) Skyrocket (Sam) Smith 4
436 (a) (Louisville) | 700.00 | 300.00 | 175.00

(437) Pete Somers 5
437 (a) (St. Louis AA) | 700.00 | 300.00 | 175.00
(Never played for St. Louis.)

(438) Joe Sommer (Also:
Sommers) 5
438 (a) (Baltimore) | 1,050 | 450.00 | 250.00

(439) Pete Sommers 7
439 (a) (Chicago NL) | 700.00 | 300.00 | 175.00
439 (b) (New York NL) | 700.00 | 300.00 | 175.00

(440) Bill Sowders 7
440 (a) (Boston NL) | 700.00 | 300.00 | 175.00

(441) John Sowders 4
441 (a) (Kansas City) | 750.00 | 325.00 | 200.00
441 (b) (St. Paul) | 700.00 | 300.00 | 175.00

(442) Charlie Sprague 9
442 (a) (Chicago NL) | 700.00 | 300.00 | 175.00
442 (b) (Chicago Maroons WA) | 1,050 | 450.00 | 250.00
442 (c) (Cleveland) | 775.00 | 350.00 | 200.00

(443) Ed Sproat 5
443 (a) (St. Louis Whites WA) | 975.00 | 425.00 | 250.00

(444) Harry Staley (Also: Stoley) 7
444 (a) (Pittsburgh) | 700.00 | 300.00 | 175.00
444 (b) (St. Louis Whites WA) | 775.00 | 350.00 | 200.00

(445) Dan Stearns (Also: Tearns) 4
445 (a) (Des Moines) | 700.00 | 300.00 | 175.00
445 (b) (Kansas City) | 850.00 | 375.00 | 225.00

(446) Bill Stemmeyer
(Also: Stemmyer) 6
446 (a) (Boston NL) | 700.00 | 300.00 | 175.00
446 (b) (Cleveland) | 1,050 | 450.00 | 250.00

(447) B.F. Stephens 3
447 (a) (Milwaukee) | 700.00 | 300.00 | 175.00

(448) John Sterling 4
448 (a) (Minneapolis) | 700.00 | 300.00 | 175.00

(449) Len Stockwell 1
449 (a) (San Francisco)
(Value Undetermined)

Stoley - See Staley

(450) Harry Stovey 9
450 (a) (Boston PL) | 2,700 | 1,200 | 600.00
450 (b) (Philadelphia AA) | 1,600 | 725.00 | 400.00

(451) Scott Stratton 5
451 (a) (Louisville) | 700.00 | 300.00 | 175.00

(452) Joe Strauss (Also: Straus) 8
452 (a) (Milwaukee) | 700.00 | 300.00 | 175.00

452 (b) (Omaha) | 825.00 | 375.00 | 225.00

(453) Cub Stricker 3
453 (a) (Cleveland) | 700.00 | 300.00 | 175.00

(454) Marty Sullivan 7
454 (a) (Chicago NL) | 700.00 | 300.00 | 175.00
454 (b) (Indianapolis) | 700.00 | 300.00 | 175.00

(455) Mike Sullivan 3
455 (a) (Philadelphia AA) | 700.00 | 300.00 | 175.00

(457) Billy Sunday 10
457 (a) (Chicago NL) | 2,100 | 900.00 | 500.00
457 (b) (Pittsburgh) | 1,800 | 775.00 | 425.00

(458) Sy Sutcliffe 5
458 (a) (Cleveland) | 900.00 | 400.00 | 250.00

(459) Ezra Sutton 8
459 (a) (Boston NL) | 700.00 | 300.00 | 175.00
459 (b) (Milwaukee) | 725.00 | 325.00 | 200.00

(460) Ed Swartwood
(Also: Schwartwood) 7
460 (a) (Brooklyn) | 700.00 | 300.00 | 175.00
460 (b) (Des Moines) | 700.00 | 300.00 | 175.00
460 (c) (Hamilton) | 825.00 | 375.00 | 225.00

(461) Park Swartzel 6
461 (a) (Kansas City) | 700.00 | 300.00 | 175.00

(462) Pete Sweeney
(Also: Sweeny) 5
462 (a) (Washington) | 1,050 | 450.00 | 250.00

(463) Louis Sylvester 1
463 (a) (Sacramento)
(Value Undetermined)

(464) Pop Tate 6
464 (a) (Baltimore) | 700.00 | 300.00 | 175.00
464 (b) (Boston NL) | 700.00 | 300.00 | 175.00

(465) Patsy (Oliver) Tebeau 8
465 (a) (Chicago NL) | 700.00 | 300.00 | 175.00
465 (b) (Cleveland) | 800.00 | 350.00 | 200.00

Tearns - See Stearns

(466) John Tener 5
466 (a) (Chicago NL) | 1,425 | 650.00 | 350.00

(467) Adonis Terry 5
467 (a) (Brooklyn) | 700.00 | 300.00 | 175.00

(468) Sam Thompson
See Hall of Fame Section Following

(469) Mike Tiernan 6
469 (a) (New York NL) | 700.00 | 300.00 | 175.00

(470) Cannonball Titcomb 5
470 (a) (New York NL) | 700.00 | 300.00 | 175.00

(471) Phil Tomney 4
471 (a) (Louisville) | 700.00 | 300.00 | 175.00

(472) Steve Toole 7
472 (a) (Brooklyn) | 850.00 | 375.00 | 225.00
472 (b) (Kansas City) | 700.00 | 300.00 | 175.00
472 (c) (Rochester) | 775.00 | 350.00 | 200.00

(473) George Townsend 3
473 (a) (Philadelphia AA) | 700.00 | 300.00 | 175.00

(474) Bill Traffley 4
474 (a) (Des Moines) | 700.00 | 300.00 | 175.00

(475) George Treadway
(Also: Tredway) 6
475 (a) (Denver) | 775.00 | 350.00 | 200.00
475 (b) (St. Paul) | 775.00 | 350.00 | 200.00

(476) Sam Trott 10
476 (a) (Baltimore) | 700.00 | 300.00 | 175.00
476 (b) (Newark) | 700.00 | 300.00 | 175.00
DP 22 (Tagging Oyster Burns.) | 1,150 | 500.00 | 300.00

(477) Tommy Tucker 5
477 (a) (Baltimore) | 1,400 | 600.00 | 350.00
DP 8 (Being tagged by Chris | 2,100 | 900.00 | 500.00
Fulmer.)

(478) A.M. Tuckerman 5
478 (a) (St. Paul) | 700.00 | 300.00 | 175.00

(479) George Turner 5
479 (a) (Minneapolis) | 700.00 | 300.00 | 175.00

(480) Larry Twitchell 6
480 (a) (Cleveland) | 700.00 | 300.00 | 175.00
480 (b) (Detroit) | 700.00 | 300.00 | 175.00

(481) Jim Tyng 3
481 (a) (Philadelphia NL) | 700.00 | 300.00 | 175.00

(482) Bill Van Dyke 3
482 (a) (Des Moines) | 700.00 | 300.00 | 175.00
482 (b) (Toledo) | 700.00 | 300.00 | 175.00
DP 19 (W/ Harry Sage.) | 1,150 | 500.00 | 300.00
(Des Moines)
DP 20 (W/ Harry Sage.) (Toledo) | 1,150 | 500.00 | 300.00

(483) George Van Haltren 4
483 (a) (Chicago NL) | 1,500 | 700.00 | 425.00

(484) Farmer Vaughn 7

484 (a) (Louisville) | 700.00 | 300.00 | 175.00
484 (b) (New York PL) | 2,700 | 1,200 | 600.00

(485) Peek-A-Boo Veach 4
485 (a) (Sacramento)
(Value Undetermined)
485 (b) (St. Paul) | 700.00 | 300.00 | 175.00

(486) Leon Viau 5
486 (a) (Cincinnati) | 775.00 | 350.00 | 200.00

(487) Bill Vinton 4
487 (a) (Minneapolis) | 800.00 | 350.00 | 200.00

(488) Joe Visner 5
488 (a) (Brooklyn) | 700.00 | 300.00 | 175.00

(489) Chris Von Der Ahe 1
489 (a) (St. Louis AA "Brown's | 4,050 | 1,800 | 1,000
Champions")

(490) Reddy Walsh 5
490 (a) (Omaha) | 850.00 | 375.00 | 225.00

(491) John Ward
See Hall of Fame Section Following

(492) Ed Warner 2
492 (a) (Milwaukee) | 700.00 | 300.00 | 175.00
DP 5 (W/ Jack Horner.) | 1,150 | 500.00 | 300.00

Wassitt - See Messitt

(493) Bill Watkins 2
493 (a) (Detroit) | 700.00 | 300.00 | 175.00
493 (b) (Kansas City) | 900.00 | 400.00 | 250.00

(494) Farmer Weaver 4
494 (a) (Louisville) | 1,800 | 900.00 | 450.00

(495) Charlie Weber 5
495 (a) (Sioux City) | 900.00 | 400.00 | 250.00

(496) Stump Weidman (Wiedman) 4
496 (a) (Detroit) | 700.00 | 300.00 | 175.00

(497) Wild Bill Weidner (Widner) 5
497 (a) (Columbus) | 900.00 | 400.00 | 250.00

(498) Curt Welch (Also: Welsh) 7
498 (a) (St. Louis AA "Brown's | 1,875 | 850.00 | 475.00
Champions")
498 (b) (Philadelphia AA) | 800.00 | 350.00 | 200.00
DP 23 (W/ Bill Gleason.) | 2,300 | 1,050 | 575.00

(499) Mickey Welch (Also: Welsh)
See Hall of Fame Section Following

(500) Jake Wells 2
500 (a) (Kansas City) | 1,325 | 600.00 | 325.00

(501) Frank Wells 1
501 (a) (Milwaukee) | 850.00 | 375.00 | 225.00

(502) Joe Werrick 5
502 (a) (Louisville) | 700.00 | 300.00 | 175.00
502 (b) (St. Paul) | 975.00 | 450.00 | 250.00

(503) Buck West 5
503 (a) (Minneapolis) | 850.00 | 375.00 | 225.00

(504) Gus Weyhing 3
504 (a) (Philadelphia AA) | 800.00 | 350.00 | 200.00

(505) John Weyhing 4
505 (a) (Columbus) | 700.00 | 300.00 | 175.00
505 (b) (Philadelphia AA) | 1,100 | 500.00 | 300.00
(Never played for Phila.)

(506) Bobby Wheelock 9
506 (a) (Boston NL) | 700.00 | 300.00 | 175.00
506 (b) (Detroit) | 700.00 | 300.00 | 175.00
(Never played for Detroit.)
506 (c) (Photo actually Con Daily.) | 700.00 | 300.00 | 175.00

(508) Pat Whitaker
(Also: Whitacre) 7
508 (a) (Baltimore) | 700.00 | 300.00 | 175.00
508 (b) (Philadelphia AA) | 700.00 | 300.00 | 175.00
(Never played for
Philadelphia.)

(509) Bill White 5
509 (a) (Louisville) | 700.00 | 300.00 | 175.00

(510) Deacon White 10
510 (a) (Detroit) | 1,550 | 700.00 | 375.00
510 (b) (Pittsburgh) | 700.00 | 300.00 | 175.00

(511) Art Whitney 7
511 (a) (New York NL) | 700.00 | 300.00 | 175.00
511 (b) (New York PL) | 2,700 | 1,200 | 600.00
511 (c) (Pittsburgh) | 700.00 | 300.00 | 175.00
511 (d) (W/dog.) | 4,800 | 2,150 | 1,200

(512) G. Whitney 5
512 (a) (St. Joseph) | 850.00 | 375.00 | 225.00

(513) Jim Whitney 4
513 (a) (Indianapolis) | 700.00 | 300.00 | 175.00
513 (b) (Washington) | 750.00 | 325.00 | 200.00

E. Williams, W. Williams -
See Ned Williamson

(514) Jimmy Williams 2
514 (a) (Cleveland) | 1,050 | 450.00 | 250.00

(515) Ned Williamson 8
515 (a) (Chicago NL) — 1,400 / 600.00 / 350.00
515 (c) (in dress clothes) — 5,175 / 2,325 / 1,300
515 (c) (Chicago PL) — 3,000 / 1,350 / 750.00
DP 24 (W/ Willie Hahn. (Mascot) — 4,000 / 1,800 / 1,200

(516) Tit Willis 5
516 (a) (Omaha) — 800.00 / 350.00 / 200.00

(517) Walt Wilmot 8
517 (a) (Chicago NL) — 700.00 / 300.00 / 175.00
517 (b) (Washington) — 750.00 / 325.00 / 200.00

(518) George Winkleman (Winkelman) 4
518 (a) (Hartford) — 2,500 / 400.00 / 225.00
518 (b) (Minneapolis) — 2,500 / 400.00 / 225.00

(519) Sam Wise 5
519 (a) (Boston NL) — 1,050 / 450.00 / 250.00
519 (b) (Washington) — 700.00 / 300.00 / 175.00

(520) Chicken Wolf 5
520 (a) (Louisville) — 750.00 / 325.00 / 200.00

(521) George Wood 5 (L.F.)
521 (a) (Philadelphia NL) — 700.00 / 300.00 / 175.00
521 (b) (Philadelphia PL) — 2,700 / 1,200 / 600.00

(522) Pete Wood 5 (P)
522 (a) (Philadelphia NL) — 875.00 / 400.00 / 225.00

(523) Harry Wright
See Hall of Fame Section Following

(524) Chief Zimmer 4
524 (a) (Cleveland) — 725.00 / 325.00 / 200.00

(525) Frank Zinn 3
525 (a) (Philadelphia AA) — 700.00 / 300.00 / 175.00

1887-1890 Old Judge Hall of Famers Pose Variations

Because of the popularity of collecting Old Judge cards of Hall of Famers, and the sometimes widely varying market values of different poses for those players, this appendix lists each known pose and/or caption variation. These listings disregard the presence, absence or placement of Old Judge advertising within the photo area. Caption variations consider only those machine-printed captions outside of the photo area.

	NM	EX	VG
(11) Cap Anson			
11 (a) Street Clothes			
(A.C. ANSON, Chicagoes)	10,200	4,600	2,550
(Chicago's)	10,200	4,600	2,550
(ANSON, CAPT., Chicagos (N L)	15,000	6,750	3,750
11 (b) In Uniform			
(Chicago N L)	250,000	75,000	40,000
(25) Jake Beckley			
25 (a) Pittsburgh			
(Batting, "O" just visible on jersey, Pittsburghs.)	5,400	2,430	1,350
(Batting, "O" just visible on jersey, Pittsburgs.)	5,400	2,425	1,350
(Fielding, ball knee-high, "BECKLEY, 1st B., Pittsburgs.")	5,400	2,430	1,350
(Fielding, hands neck-high, Pittsburgh.)	5,400	2,430	1,350
(Fielding, hands neck-high, "J. BECKLEY, 1st B., Pittsburghs.")	7,800	3,500	1,950
(Fielding, hands neck-high, Pittsburgs.)	5,400	2,430	1,350
25 (b) St. Louis Whites			
(Batting, "O" just visible on jersey.)	7,800	3,500	1,950
(Batting, "TLO" visible on jersey.)	7,800	3,500	1,950
(Fielding, ball knee-high, "J. BECKLEY, 1st B., St. Louis Whites.")	10,200	4,600	2,550
(Fielding, hands neck-high, "J. BECKLEY.")	6,000	2,700	1,500
(43) Dan Brouthers			

	NM	EX	VG
43 (a) Boston, N.L.			
(Bat at ready, looking to right, "1st B., Bostons.")	3,600	1,620	900.00
(Fielding, Brouthers on front, Bostons.)	3,120	1,400	780.00
43 (b) Boston, P.L.			
(Pose unrecorded.)	7,200	3,240	1,800
43 (c) Detroit			
(Bat at ready, looking down at ball.)	4,800	2,160	1,200
(Bat at ready, looking to right, "1st B., Detroits.")	4,500	2,000	1,125
(Fielding, "BROUTHERS, 1st B. Detroits.")	5,100	2,280	1,260
(Fielding, "D. BROUTHERS.")	4,800	2,160	1,200
(78) John Clarkson			
78 (a) Boston			
(Batting, Bostons.)	2,280	1,025	570.00
(Right arm forward, left hand on thigh, Bostons.)	2,280	1,025	570.00
(Right arm forward, left hand on thigh, "P., Bostons.")	2,280	1,025	570.00
(Right arm back, left hand clear of thigh, "P., Bostons.")	3,300	1,470	825.00
(Right hand hip-high, Bostons.)	1,620	725.00	400.00
78 (b) Chicago			
(Ball in hands at chest, "P. Chicago.")	3,000	1,350	750.00
(Batting, "P. Chicago.")	3,600	1,620	900.00
(Fielding, hands head-high, "P. Chicago.")	3,600	1,620	900.00
(Right arm forward, left hand on thigh, "P. Chicago.")	4,080	1,830	1,020
(Right arm back, left hand clear of thigh, "P. Chicago.")	3,000	1,350	750.00
(Right arm back, left hand on thigh, "P. Chicago.")	3,000	1,350	750.00
(Right hand hip-high, "P. Chicago.")	3,000	1,350	750.00
(86) Charlie Comiskey			
86 (a) St. Louis Browns			
("Brown's Champions")	7,620	3,420	1,890
86 (b) St. Louis Browns			
(Arms folded.)	.00	.00	.00
	5,100	2,300	1,275
(Batting, "COMISKEY, Capt. St. Louis Browns.")	6,720	3,030	1,680
(Fielding, hands head-high, "CHAS. COMISKEY, 1st B., Capt. St. Louis Browns.")	5,100	2,280	1,260
(Fielding, hands shoulder-high, "COMISKEY, Capt. St. Louis.")	5,100	2,280	1,260
(Fielding, hands shoulder-high, "C. COMMISKEY, 1st B., St. L. B's.")	4,800	2,160	1,200
(Sliding, "CHAS. COMISKEY, 1st B., Capt. St. Louis Brown.")	4,800	2,160	1,200
(Sliding, "COMISKEY, Capt., St. Louis.")	4,800	2,160	1,200
86 (c) Chicago, P.L.			
(Arms folded, "COMMISKEY, 1st B., Chicagos.")	24,000	10,800	6,000
(88) Roger Connor			
88 (a) New York, N.L.			
(Batter's box on floor, script name.)	6,900	3,100	1,700
(Bat on shoulder, name in script.)	6,900	3,100	1,700
(Bat on shoulder, N Y's.)	5,100	2,400	1,200
(Fielding, "B. CONNOR," New Yorks.)	5,100	2,400	1,200
(Fielding, hands at waist, "CONNER, 1st B., New Yorks.")	5,100	2,400	1,200
(Hands on knees, name in script.)	6,900	3,100	1,700
(Hands on knees, New York.)	4,800	2,160	1,200
(Hands on knees, New Yorks.)	4,800	2,160	1,200
(Hands on knees, N Y's.)	4,800	2,160	1,200
(124) Ed Delahanty			
124 (a) Philadelphia			
(Bat on right shoulder, "2d B., Phila.)	14,000	10,000	6,000
(Bat on right shoulder, "2d B., Phila's")	14,000	10,000	6,000
(Bat nearly horizontal, "2d B., Phila.")	14,000	10,000	6,000
(Fielding grounder, Phila.)	13,000	9,000	4,800
(Fielding, hands at waist, "2d B., Phila.")	12,000	7,600	4,200
(Fielding, hands at waist, Phila's.)	13,000	7,600	4,200
(Throwing, "2d B., Phila.")	15,000	10,500	5,900
(Throwing, Phila's.)	15,000	10,500	5,900
(136) Hugh Duffy			
136 (a) Chicago, N.L.			
(Batting, S.S. Chicago.)	3,600	1,620	900.00
(Batting, "H. DUFFY, S.S., Chicagos.)	3,600	1,625	900.00
(Batting, "DUFFY, S.S., Chicago's.")	3,600	1,620	900.00
(Fielding grounder, "H. DUFFY, S.S., Chicago.")	3,600	1,620	900.00
(Fielding grounder, Chicagos.)	3,600	1,620	900.00
(Fielding, hands chin-high, right heel behind left leg, Chicago.)	3,600	1,620	900.00
(Fielding, hands chin-high, right heel behind left leg, Chicagos.)	3,600	1,620	900.00

	NM	EX	VG
(Fielding, hands chin-high, right heel behind left leg, Chicago's.)	3,600	1,620	900.00
(Fielding, hands neck-high, feet apart, Chicago.)	3,600	1,620	900.00
(Throwing, right hand head-high, Chicago.)	3,600	1,620	900.00
(Throwing, right hand head-high, Chicago's.)	3,600	1,620	900.00
136 (b) Chicago, P.L.			
(Pose unrecorded.) (Value Undetermined)			
(149) Buck Ewing			
149 (a) New York, N.L.			
(Bat at 45 degrees, New Yorks.)	3,300	1,475	825.00
(Bat at 45 degrees, N Y's.)	3,300	1,470	825.00
(Bat in hand at side, New Yorks.)	3,300	1,470	825.00
(Bat nearly horizontal, Capt. New Yorks.)	3,300	1,470	825.00
(Bat nearly horizontal, Captain, New Yorks.)	3,300	1,470	825.00
(Fielding grounder, "BUCK EWING, Capt., New Yorks.)	3,300	1,470	825.00
(Fielding grounder, "EWING, C., New Yorks.)	3,300	1,470	825.00
(Fielding, hands head-high, New Yorks.)	3,300	1,470	825.00
(Fielding, hands head-high, N Y's.)	3,300	1,470	825.00
(Hands on knees, C. New Yorks.)	3,600	1,620	900.00
(Hands on knees, Captain, New Yorks.)	3,600	1,620	900.00
(Hands on knees, Capt. N Y's.)	3,600	1,620	900.00
(Running to left, C., New Yorks.)	3,600	1,620	900.00
(Running to left, Captain, New Yorks.)	3,600	1,620	900.00
(Sliding, C., New York.)	3,600	1,620	900.00
(Sliding, C., New Yorks.)	3,600	1,620	900.00
(Sliding, Capt., New York.)	3,600	1,620	900.00
(Throwing, right arm forward, C., New Yorks.)	4,200	1,900	1,050
(Throwing, right arm forward, Captain, New Yorks.)	4,200	1,900	1,050
(Throwing, right hand waist-high at side, "EWING, Captain, New Yorks.")	4,800	2,160	1,200
149 (b) New York, P.L.			
(Hands on knees, C. New York.(PL)	7,800	3,500	1,950
149 (c) With mascot Willie Breslin.	.00	.00	.00
("EWING & MASCOT, New Yorks")	9,000	4,050	2,250
(N. Y's)	9,000	4,050	2,250
149 (c) "EWING, MASCOT New York P L" (A Fair-Good example sold at auction 5/05 for $7,475.)			
(179) Pud Galvin			
179 (a) Pittsburgh			
(Arms at sides, P. Pittsburg.)	5,400	2,430	1,350
(Arms at sides, P. Pittsburgs.)	5,400	2,430	1,350
(Arms at sides, P. Pittsburgh.)	5,400	2,430	1,350
(Arms at sides, Pitcher.)	5,400	2,430	1,350
(Ball in hands above waist, P.)	4,500	2,000	1,125
(Ball in hands above waist, Pitcher.)	4,500	2,000	1,125
(Bat at ready, P.)	4,500	2,000	1,125
(Bat at ready, Pitcher.)	4,500	2,000	1,125
(Bat in hand at side, "GALVIN, P. Pittsburg.")	8,700	3,900	2,160
(Bat in hand at side, "GALVIN, Pitcher Pittsburg.")	8,750	3,900	2,160
(Bat in hand at side "GALVIN, P., Pittsburgs.")	8,700	3,900	2,160
(Bat in hand at side, "J. GALVIN, P., Pittsburghs.")	8,700	3,900	2,160
(Bat in hand at side, "JIM GALVIN.")	8,700	3,900	2,160
(204) Clark Griffith			
204 (a) Milwaukee			
(Ball in hands at chest.)	5,100	2,280	1,260
(Batting, looking at ball.)	5,100	2,300	1,275
(Batting, looking at camera, Milwaukee.)	5,100	2,280	1,260
(Batting, looking at camera, Milwaukees.)	6,000	2,700	1,500
(Pitching, hands at neck, Milwaukees.)	5,400	2,430	1,350
(Pitching, right hand head-high, Milwaukees.)	5,100	2,280	1,260
(213) Billy Hamilton			
213 (a) Kansas City			
(Batting, looking at camera, Kansas Citys.)	3,900	1,750	975.00
(Batting, looking up at ball, "L.F. KANSAS CITYS.")	3,900	1,740	975.00
(Batting, looking up at ball, K.C.s.)	3,900	1,740	975.00
(Fielding grounder.)	3,900	1,740	975.00
(Fielding, hands above waist, "L.F. Kansas Citys.")	3,900	1,740	975.00
(Fielding, hands neck-high, "L.F. Kansas Citys.")	3,900	1,740	975.00
213 (b) Philadelphia, N.L.			
(Fielding, hands above waist, Philadelphia N.L.)	2,880	1,300	720.00
(Fielding, hands neck-high, Philadelphia N.L.)	2,880	1,300	720.00
(215) Ned Hanlon			

215 (a)Boston
(Never played for Boston.)
(Bat in hand at sides, Bostons.)   3,600   1,620   900.00
215 (b)Detroit
(Bat in hand at side, C.F. Detroits.)   3,600   1,620   900.00
(Batting, Detroits.)   3,600   1,620   900.00
(Fielding, Detroits.)   3,600   1,620   900.00
215 (c)Pittsburgh
  .00   .00   .00
(Batting, Pittsburghs.)   3,900   1,620   975.00
(Fielding, C.F., Pittsburghs.)   3,900   1,620   975.00

(256)   Tim Keefe
256 (a)New York, N.L.
(Ball in hands, front view, "KEEFE, P., New Yorks.")   3,360   1,500   840.00
(Ball in hands, front view, TIM KEEFE, P. N.Y's.")   3,360   1,500   840.00
(Ball in hands, side view, "JIM KEEFE," New Yorks.)   3,360   1,500   840.00
(Ball in hands, side view, "TIM KEEFE," New Yorks.)   3,360   1,500   840.00
(Ball in hands, side view, "TIM KEEFE, P. N.Y's.")   3,360   1,500   840.00
(Bat nearly horizontal, "KEEFE, P., New Yorks.")   3,360   1,500   840.00
(Bat nearly horizontal, "TIM KEEF," New Yorks.)   3,360   1,500   840.00
(Bat nearly horizontal, "TIM KEEFE," New Yorks.)   3,360   1,500   840.00
(Bat nearly horizontal, "TIM KEEFE," N. Y's.)   3,360   1,500   840.00
(Bat nearly vertical, "TIM KEEFE, P. N.Y's.")   3,360   1,500   840.00
(Pitching, right hand at back, "JIM KEEFE," New Yorks.)   3,600   1,620   900.00
(Pitching, right hand at back, "TIM KEEF," New Yorks.)   3,600   1,620   900.00
(Pitching, right hand at back, "TIM KEEFE," New Yorks.)   3,600   1,620   900.00
(Pitching, right hand at back, "TIM KEEFE," N. Y's.)   3,600   1,620   900.00
(Pitching, right hand head-high, "KEEFE P., New Yorks.")   3,600   1,620   900.00
(Pitching, right hand head-high, "TIM KEEFE, P. N. Y's.")   3,600   1,620   900.00
(Pitching, right hand waist-high, "KEEFE, P., New Yorks.")   2,880   1,300   720.00
(Pitching, right hand waist-high, "TIM KEEFE, P. N.Y's.")   2,880   1,300   720.00
256 (b)New York, P.L.
(Pose unrecorded.) (VALUE UNDETERMINED)
DP 12 Tagging Danny Richardson.
("KEEFE, P., New Yorks")   2,700   1,225   675.00
("Keefe & Richardson")   2,700   1,200   675.00
("Keefe and Richardson Stealing 2d, N.Y's")   2,700   1,200   675.00
DP 13 Fielding Ball, Danny Richardson Sliding.
("Keefe and Richardson Stealing 2d, N.Y's")   3,600   1,620   900.00

(261)   King Kelly
261 (a)Chicago
(Bat at 45 degrees, left-handed, "$10,000 KELLY" Chicago on jersey.)   7,500   3,375   1,875
(Portrait, bare head, "$10,000 KELLY," Chicago on jersey.)   9,300   3,970   2,300
(Portrait in cap, "$10,000 KELLY," Chicago on jersey.)   7,800   3,500   1,950
261 (b)Boston, N.L.
(Bat at 45 degrees, "$10,000 KELLY.")   7,200   3,240   1,800
(Bat at 45 degrees, no position, Boston.)   6,000   2,700   1,500
(Bat at 45 degrees, "Kelly, C., Boston.")   4,800   2,160   1,200
(Bat at 45 degrees, "Kelly, C., Bostons.")   4,800   2,160   1,200
(Bat horizontal, "$10,000 KELLY.")   6,000   2,700   1,500
(Bat in left hand at side, "$10,000 KELLY.")   6,000   2,700   1,500
(Bat on right shoulder, "$10,000 KELLY.")   7,200   3,240   1,800
(Fielding, hands chest-high, "$10,000 KELLY.")   6,000   2,700   1,500
(Fielding, hands head-high, "$10,000 KELLY.")   6,000   2,700   1,500
(Portrait, bare head, "$10,000 KELLY," Boston on jersey.)   11,400   5,130   2,850
261 (c)Boston, P.L.
(Bat at 45 degrees, no position, Boston. (PL) (Value Undetermined)

(290)   Connie Mack
290 (a)Washington
(Batting, C.)   10,800   4,860   2,700
(Batting, Catcher.)   10,800   4,860   2,700
(Stooping, hands on knees, C. Washington.)   10,800   4,860   2,700
(Stooping, hands on knees, Catcher.)   10,800   4,860   2,700
(Throwing, C.)   10,800   4,860   2,700
(Throwing, Catcher, "C. MACK.")   10,800   4,860   2,700
(Throwing, Catcher, "MACK.")   10,800   4,860   2,700

(307)   Tommy McCarthy
307 (a)Philadelphia, N.L.
(Batting, indoor background, "2d B. Phila.")   4,200   1,900   1,050

(Batting, indoor background, "McCARTHY, Second Base, Philadelphia.")   4,200   1,900   1,050
(Fielding, hands chest-high, "McCARTHY, 2d B. Phila.")   5,400   2,430   1,350
(Fielding, hands chest-high, Philadelphia.)   5,400   2,430   1,350
(Sliding, indoor background, 2d B. Phila.)   4,800   2,160   1,200
(Sliding, Philadelphia.)   4,800   2,160   1,200
(Tagging player, Phila.)   4,200   1,900   1,050
(Tagging player, Philadelphia.)   4,200   1,900   1,050
(Throwing, 2d B. Phila.)   4,200   1,900   1,050
(Throwing, Philadelphia.)   4,200   1,900   1,050
307 (b)St. Louis Browns   .00   .00   .00
(Batting, indoor background, St. Louis Browns.)   3,300   1,470   825.00
(Batting, outdoor background, St. Louis.)   3,300   1,470   825.00
(Batting, outdoor background, St. Louis Browns.)   3,300   1,470   825.00
(Fielding, hands chest-high, 2d B. St. Louis.)   3,300   1,470   825.00
(Fielding, hands chest-high, C.F.)   3,300   1,470   825.00
(Fielding, hands head-high, "TOMMY CARTHY," St. Louis Brown.)   3,300   1,470   825.00
(Fielding, hands head-high, "TOMMY McCARTHY," St. Louis Brown.)   3,300   1,470   825.00
(Fielding, hands head-high, "cCARTHY, C. F. St. Louis Brown.")   3,300   1,470   825.00
(Fielding, hands head-high, "TOMMY McCARTHY" St. Louis Browns.)   3,300   1,470   825.00
(Fielding, hands head-high, "T. McCARTHY, C.F., St. Louis Browns.)   3,300   1,470   825.00
(Sliding, indoor background, "McCARTHY, 2d B. St. Louis.")   3,300   1,470   825.00
(Sliding, indoor background, C.F., St. Louis.)   3,300   1,470   825.00
(Sliding, outdoor background, St. Louis.)   3,300   1,470   825.00
(Sliding, outdoor background, C.F. St. Louis Browns.)   3,300   1,470   825.00
(Tagging player, 2d B.)   3,300   1,470   825.00
(Tagging player, C.F.)   3,300   1,470   825.00
(Throwing, "T. McCARTHY" St. Louis.)   3,600   1,620   900.00
(Throwing, "T. McCARTHY," St. Louis Browns.)   3,600   1,620   900.00
(Throwing, "McCARTHY," St. Louis Browns.)   3,600   1,620   900.00
(Throwing, "McCARTHY," C.F., St. Louis.)   3,600   1,620   900.00

(323)   Bid McPhee
323 (a)Cincinnati
(Batting, looking at ball, "McPHEE.")   22,500   10,125   5,625
(Batting, looking at ball, "JOHN McPHEE.")   22,500   10,125   5,625
(Batting, looking at camera, Cincinnati.)   22,500   10,125   5,625
(Batting, looking at camera, Cincinnati. (NL)   22,500   10,125   5,625
(Batting, looking at camera, Cincinnatti.)   22,500   10,125   5,625
(Fielding, hands ankle-high, "McPHEE, 2d B., Cincinnat.")   22,500   10,125   5,625
(Fielding, hands ankle-high, "JOHN McPHEE, 2d B., Cincinnatis.")   22,500   10,125   5,625
(Fielding, hands head-high, "McPHEE, 2d B., Cincinnati.")   22,500   10,125   5,625
(Fielding, hands head-high, "JOHN McPHEE, 2d B. Cincinnati.")   22,500   10,125   5,625
(Fielding, hands head-high, "McPHEE, 2d B., Cincinnatis.")   22,500   10,125   5,625
(Fielding, hands head-high, Cincinnatti.)   22,500   10,125   5,625
(Throwing, Cincinnati.)   22,500   10,125   5,625
(Throwing, Cincinnatti.)   22,500   10,125   5,625

(349)   Kid Nichols
349 (a)Omaha
(Batting, looking at ball, Omaha.)   9,000   4,050   2,250
(Batting, looking at camera, Omaha.)   9,000   4,050   2,250
(Batting, looking at camera, "NICHOLS, P., Omahas.")   9,000   4,050   2,250
(Pitching, hands at chest, Omaha.)   9,000   4,050   2,250
(Pitching, right hand behind back, Omaha.)   9,600   4,320   2,400
(Pitching, right hand behind back, "NICHOLS, P., Omahas.")   9,600   4,320   2,400
(Pitching, right hand forward, P., Omaha.)   9,600   4,320   2,400
(Pitching, right hand forward, P., Omahas.)   9,600   4,320   2,400

(366)   Orator Jim O'Rourke
366 (a)New York, N.L.
(Bat in hand at side, C., New Yorks.)   6,000   2,700   1,500
(Bat in hand at side, 3d B., New Yorks.)   6,000   2,700   1,500

(Bat in hand at side, 3d B. N.Y's.)   6,000   2,700   1,500
(Bat in hand at side, 3d B., N. Y's.)   6,000   2,700   1,500
(Batting, 3d B., New Yorks.)   6,000   2,700   1,500
(Batting, 3d B., N. Y's.)   6,000   2,700   1,500
(Fielding, "JIM O'ROURKE, 3d B. N. Y's.)   4,200   1,900   1,050
(Throwing, 3d B., N. Y's.)   4,800   2,160   1,200

(386)   Old Hoss Radbourn
386 (a)Boston, N.L.
(Bat on shoulder, P., Boston.)   3,900   1,740   975.00
(Bat on shoulder, P., Bostons.)   3,900   1,750   975.00
(Bat on shoulder, Pitcher, Boston.)   3,900   1,740   975.00
(Bat on shoulder, Pitcher, Bostons.)   3,900   1,740   975.00
(Hands at waist, no space visible between hands and belt, P.)   3,600   1,620   900.00
(Hands at waist, no space visible between hands and belt, Pitcher.)   3,600   1,620   900.00
(Hands at waist, white uniform visible between hands and belt, P.)   4,800   2,160   1,200
(Hands at waist, white uniform visible between hands and belt, Pitcher.)   4,800   2,160   1,200
(Hands on hips, P.)   10,800   4,860   2,700
(Hands on hips, Pitcher.)   10,800   4,860   2,700
(Portrait, P., Boston.)   9,600   4,320   2,400
(Portrait, Pitcher, Boston.)   9,900   4,440   2,430
(Tagging Billy Nash, P., Boston.)   5,400   2,430   1,350
(Tagging Billy Nash, Pitcher.)   5,400   2,430   1,350
386 (b)Boston, P.L.
(Hands on hips, Pitcher, Boston.(PL) (VALUE UNDETERMINED)

(398)   Wilbert Robinson
398 (a)Philadelphia Athletics
(Batting)   4,800   2,150   1,200
(Fielding, hands above head, C. Athletics.)   4,800   2,160   1,200
(Fielding, hands above head, C., Athletics.)   4,800   2,160   1,200
(Fielding, hands neck-high, C. Athletics.)   4,800   2,160   1,200
(Fielding, hands thigh-high.)   4,800   2,160   1,200
(Throwing)   4,800   2,160   1,200

(404)   Amos Rusie
404 (a)Indianapolis
(Batting, P., Indianapolis.)   4,200   1,900   1,050
(Pitching, hands at neck.)   4,200   1,900   1,050
(Pitching, right hand forward chin-high.)   4,200   1,900   1,050
(Pitching, right hand head-high to side, "RUSIE, P., Indianapolis.")   6,000   2,700   1,500
(Pitching, right hand head-high to side, "RUSSIE.")   6,000   2,700   1,500
(Ball in right hand, thigh-high "P., Indianapolis.")   6,300   2,820   1,560
404 (b)New York, N.L.
  .00   .00   .00
(Pitching, hands at neck, New Yorks.(NL)   24,000   10,800   6,000
(Pitching, right hand forward chin-high, New Yorks.(NL)   24,000   10,800   6,000

(468)   Sam Thompson
468 (a)Detroit
(Arms folded, R.F. Detroits.)   3,300   1,475   825.00
(Bat at 45 degrees, Detroits.)   3,900   1,740   975.00
(Bat in hand at side, Detroits.)   4,200   1,900   1,050
(Batting, ball above head, Detroits.)   3,000   1,350   750.00
(Batting, ball chest-high, R.F. Detroits.)   3,000   1,350   750.00
468 (b)Philadelphia, N.L.
  .00   .00   .00
(Arms folded, Phil'a.(NL)   2,640   1,190   660.00
(Bat in hand at side, Philadelphia.)   2,640   1,190   660.00
(Bat in hand at side, R.F., Philadelphias.)   2,640   1,190   660.00
(Bat in hand at side, Phila's.)   2,640   1,190   660.00

(491)   John Ward
491 (a)New York, N.L.
(Batting, New Yorks.)   2,880   1,300   720.00
(Batting, "Capt. JOHN WARD, S.S. N Y's.")   2,880   1,300   720.00
(Cap in hand at side, "Capt. JOHN WARD.")   4,200   1,900   1,050
(Cap in hand at side, "J. WARD, S.S., New Yorks.")   4,200   1,900   1,050
(Cap in hand at side, "JOHN WARD.")   4,200   1,900   1,050
(Hands behind back, New Yorks.)   3,000   1,350   750.00
(Hands behind back, "Capt. JOHN WARD, S.S. N Y's.")   3,000   1,350   750.00
(Hands on hips, "J.M. WARD, S.S. New Yorks.")   4,500   2,000   1,125
(Hands on hips, "Capt. JOHN WARD, S.S. N. Y's.")   6,600   2,970   1,650
(Portrait, "Capt. JOHN WARD.")   5,400   2,430   1,350
(Portrait, "J. WARD, S.S., New Yorks.")   5,400   2,430   1,350
(Portrait, "J.M. WARD, S.S., New Yorks.")   5,400   2,430   1,350

	NM	EX	VG
(Sliding, left hand raised, "Capt. JOHN WARD, S.S. N Y's.")	2,640	1,190	660.00
(Sliding, left hand raised, "J.M. WARD, S.S., New Yorks.")	2,640	1,190	660.00
(Sliding, left hand raised, "WARD.")	2,640	1,190	660.00
(Sliding, right hand raised, New Yorks.)	3,000	1,350	750.00
(Sliding, right hand raised, "Capt. JOHN WARD, S.S. N Y's.")	3,000	1,350	750.00
(Throwing, left profile, New Yorks.)	4,200	1,900	1,050
(Throwing, left profile, "Capt. JOHN WARD, S.S. N. Y's.")	4,200	1,900	1,050
(Throwing, right profile, "Capt. JOHN WARD, S.S. N. Y's.")	4,200	1,900	1,050
(Throwing, right profile, "JOHN WARD.")	4,200	1,900	1,050

(499) Mickey Welch
	NM	EX	VG
499 (a) New York, N.L.			
(Ball in hands above waist, "SMILING MICKEY.")	5,400	2,425	1,350
(Ball in hands above waist, "WELSH.")	5,400	2,430	1,350
(Right arm extended forward, "SMILING MICKEY.")	5,400	2,430	1,350
(Right hand at right thigh, "WELCH," New Yorks.)	5,400	2,430	1,350
(Right hand at right thigh, "WELCH," New Yorks.(NL))	5,400	2,430	1,350
(Right hand at right thigh, "WELSH," New Yorks.)	5,400	2,430	1,350
(Right hand head-high, "WELCH," New York.)	5,400	2,430	1,350
(Right hand head-high, "WELCH," N.Y's.)	5,400	2,430	1,350
(Right hand head-high, "WELSH," New York.)	5,400	2,430	1,350

(523) Harry Wright
	NM	EX	VG
523 (a) Philadelphia, N.L.			
(Portrait, looking to his right, beard clear of right side of collar, "HARRY WRIGHT, Man'g. Philas.")	18,000	8,100	4,500
(Portrait, looking to his right, beard just over right side of collar, "Mgr., Phila. N L.")	18,000	8,100	4,500
(Portrait, looking to his right, beard just over right side of collar, "Man'g. Phila.")	18,000	8,100	4,500
(Portrait, looking to his right, beard just over right side of collar, "Mgr. Phila's.")	18,000	8,100	4,500
(Portrait, looking to his left, "Man'g. Phila.")	18,000	8,100	4,500
(Portrait, looking to his left, "Man'g. Philas.")	18,000	8,100	4,500
(Portrait, looking to his left, Phila. (NL))	19,200	8,640	4,800
(Portrait, looking to his left, "Mgr. Phila's.")	18,000	8,100	5,400

1888-1889 Old Judge Cabinets (N173)

OLD JUDGE CIGARETTES Goodwin & Co. New York.

These cabinet cards were issued by Goodwin & Co. in 1888-89 as a premium available by exchanging coupons found in Old Judge or Dogs Head brand cigarettes. The cabinet cards consist of 3-3/4" x 5-3/4" photographs affixed to a cardboard backing that measures approximately 4-1/4" x 6-1/2". The mounting is usually pale yellow with gold-leaf trimmings, but backings have also been found in red, blue or black. An ad for Old Judge Cigarettes appears along the bottom of the cabinet. Cabinets obtained by exchanging coupons from Dogs Head cigarettes include an ad for both Old Judge and Dogs Head, and are scarcer. According to an advertising sheet, cabinets were available of "every prominent player in the National League, Western League and American Association." There will continue to be additions to this checklist. This list includes all confirmed photo and team variations; minor differences in spelling of team name, position abbreviations or punctuation are not recorded, except in the case of Hall of Famers. Several Old Judge cabinets are not known to exist in the standard N172 format.

	NM	EX	VG
Common Player:	2,200	1,300	975.00
Black or Colored Mount: 2X			

Unlisted Dogs Head: 2-3X
		NM	EX	VG
(4)	Bob Allen			
4 (a)	Pittsburgh, hands clasped at waist	2,200	1,300	975.00
4 (b)	Pittsburgh, batting, Dogs Head	5,250	3,150	2,250
(7)	Varney Anderson			
7 (a)	pitching, right hand head-high	2,200	1,300	975.00
(8)	Ed Andrews			
8 (a)	Philadelphia, both hands shoulder-high	2,200	1,300	975.00
8 (b)	Philadelphia, one hand above head	2,200	1,300	975.00
DP 1	being tagged by Buster Hoover	3,750	2,250	1,625
(9)	Wally Andrews			
9 (a)	Omaha, hands shoulder-high	2,200	1,300	975.00
(11)	Cap Anson	2,200	1,300	975.00
11 (a)	portrait	20,250	12,150	8,700
11 (b)	portrait, Dogs Head	45,000	27,000	18,750
(15)	Kid Baldwin	2,200	1,300	975.00
15 (a)	ball in right hand, head-high	2,200	1,300	975.00
(16)	Lady Baldwin	2,200	1,300	975.00
16 (a)	Detroit, pitching, left hand head-high	2,200	1,300	975.00
(17)	Mark Baldwin	2,200	1,300	975.00
17 (a)	Chicago, batting, heels together	2,200	1,300	975.00
17 (b)	Chicago, pitching, right hand above head	2,200	1,300	975.00
17 (c)	Chicago, pitching, right hand waist-high	2,200	1,300	975.00
(20)	John Barnes	2,200	1,300	975.00
20 (a)	portrait	2,200	1,300	975.00
		2,200	1,300	975.00
(21)	Billy Barnie	2,200	1,300	975.00
21 (a)	portrait	3,000	1,800	1,300
(22)	Charley Bassett	2,200	1,300	975.00
22 (a)	Indianapolis, bat at ready	2,200	1,300	975.00
		2,200	1,300	975.00
(23)	Charlie Bastian	2,200	1,300	975.00
23 (a)	Chicago, bat over shoulder	2,200	1,300	975.00
23 (b)	Chicago, fielding, hands chest-high	2,200	1,300	975.00
23 (c)	Philadelphia, stooping to field low ball	2,200	1,300	975.00
DP 2	Philadelphia, tagging Pop Schriver	3,750	2,250	1,625
(24)	Ed Beatin	2,200	1,300	975.00
24 (a)	pitching, right arm forward	2,200	1,300	975.00
		2,200	1,300	975.00
(27)	Charlie Bennett	2,200	1,300	975.00
27 (a)	batting	2,200	1,300	975.00
27 (b)	batting, Dogs Head	5,250	3,150	2,250
		2,200	1,300	975.00
(28)	Lou Bierbauer	2,200	1,300	975.00
28 (a)	fielding grounder	2,200	1,300	975.00
28 (b)	fielding, hands chest-high	3,375	2,000	1,450
28 (c)	throwing	3,750	2,250	1,650
(31)	Ned Bligh	2,200	1,300	975.00
31 (a)	fielding, hands head-high	2,200	1,300	975.00
		2,200	1,300	975.00
(32)	Bogart	2,200	1,300	975.00
32 (a)	fielding, hands chest-high	2,200	1,300	975.00
(35)	Henry Boyle	2,200	1,300	975.00
35 (a)	Indianapolis, pitch., right arm extended	2,200	1,300	975.00
(36)	Jack Boyle	2,200	1,300	975.00
36 (a)	St. Louis, bat at side	2,200	1,300	975.00
36 (b)	St. Louis, bat at ready	2,200	1,300	975.00
36 (c)	St. Louis, catching, hands knee-high	2,200	1,300	975.00
(37)	George Bradley	2,200	1,300	975.00
37 (a)	Sioux City, fielding, looking up at ball	2,200	1,300	975.00
(43)	Dan Brouthers	2,200	1,300	975.00
43 (a)	Boston, batting	5,625	3,375	2,400
43 (b)	Boston, batting, Dogs Head	9,750	5,850	4,200
43 (c)	Boston, fielding, hands at waist	5,625	3,375	2,400
43 (d)	Boston, throwing, horizontal format	6,000	3,600	2,600
43 (e)	Detroit, batting	5,625	3,375	2,400
(44)	Tom Brown	2,200	1,300	975.00
44 (a)	Boston, bat at ready	2,200	1,300	975.00
44 (b)	Boston, fielding	2,200	1,300	975.00
(45)	Willard (California) Brown	2,200	1,300	975.00
45 (a)	New York, bat at side	2,200	1,300	975.00
45 (b)	New York, throwing, mask in left hand	2,200	1,300	975.00
(46)	Pete Browning	2,200	1,300	975.00
46 (a)	batting, feet together	5,625	3,375	2,400
(47)	Charlie Brynan	2,200	1,300	975.00
47 (a)	Chicago, pitching, right arm neck-high	2,200	1,300	975.00
47 (b)	Des Moines, pitching, right arm forward	2,200	1,300	975.00
(48)	Al Buckenberger			
48 (a)	portrait, looking right	2,200	1,300	975.00

		NM	EX	VG
(49)	Dick Buckley			
49 (a)	Indianapolis, fielding, hands chest-high	2,200	1,300	975.00
(50)	Charlie Buffinton			
50 (a)	fielding, hands chest-high	2,200	1,300	975.00
50 (b)	pitch., right hand above head, Dogs Head	9,000	5,400	3,850
(52)	Jack Burdock			
52 (a)	fielding grounder	2,200	1,300	975.00
(56)	Jim Burns			
56 (a)	Kansas City, fielding grounder	2,200	1,300	975.00
(58)	Oyster Burns			
58 (a)	Brooklyn, bat at ready vertically	2,200	1,300	975.00
58 (b)	Brooklyn, throwing, right hand head-high	2,200	1,300	975.00
(59)	Tom Burns			
59 (a)	Chicago, bat at side	2,200	1,300	975.00
59 (b)	Chicago, bat at ready	2,200	1,300	975.00
59 (c)	Chicago, fielding	2,200	1,300	975.00
59 (c)	Chicago, tagging player	2,850	1,725	1,225
(60)	Doc Bushong			
60 (a)	stooping, hands waist-high	2,200	1,300	975.00
60 (b)	throwing	3,750	2,250	1,625
(63)	Jimmy Canavan			
63 (a)	batting	2,200	1,300	975.00
(66)	Hick Carpenter			
66 (a)	batting	2,200	1,300	975.00
(68)	Fred Carroll			
68 (a)	Pittsburgh, throwing	2,200	1,300	975.00
(69)	Scrappy Carroll			
69 (a)	St. Paul, fielding, hands chest-high	3,375	2,000	1,450
(70)	Ed Cartwright			
70 (a)	St. Joseph, throwing	2,200	1,300	975.00
(71)	Bob Caruthers			
71 (a)	batting, feet apart	2,200	1,300	975.00
71 (b)	holding ball in left hand, neck-high	7,125	4,275	3,000
(72)	Daniel Casey			
72 (a)	pitching, left hand shoulder-high	2,200	1,300	975.00
(73)	Elton Chamberlain			
73 (a)	batting, looking at camera	2,200	1,300	975.00
73 (b)	pitching, hands chest-high	2,200	1,300	975.00
73 (c)	pitching, right hand head-high	2,200	1,300	975.00
(74)	Cupid Childs			
74 (a)	fielding	2,200	1,300	975.00
(75)	Bob Clark			
75 (a)	Brooklyn, fielding, hands shoulder-high	2,200	1,300	975.00
75 (b)	Brooklyn, throwing	2,200	1,300	975.00
DP 4	Brooklyn, tagging Mickey Hughes	6,750	4,050	2,875
DP 4	Brooklyn, tagging M. Hughes, Dogs Head	8,250	4,950	3,550
	Clark, Chicago - See Dad Clarke	2,200	1,300	975.00
(76)	Spider Clark			
76 (a)	Washington, pose unrecorded	2,200	1,300	975.00
(77)	Dad Clark (Clarke)			
77 (a)	Chicago, right arm extended forward	2,200	1,300	975.00
77 (b)	Omaha, batting	2,200	1,300	975.00
(78)	John Clarkson			
78 (a)	Boston, batting	5,250	3,150	2,250
78 (b)	Boston, right arm forward, left on thigh	7,125	4,275	3,075
78 (c)	Boston, pitching, right arm back	5,250	3,150	2,250
78 (d)	Boston, pitching, arm back, Dogs Head	10,500	6,300	4,500
(79)	Jack Clements			
79 (a)	batting	2,200	1,300	975.00
79 (b)	fielding	3,225	1,950	1,375
79 (c)	hands on knees	2,200	1,300	975.00
(80)	Elmer Cleveland			
80 (a)	pose unrecorded	2,200	1,300	975.00
(81)	Monk Cline			
81 (a)	bat nearly vertical	2,200	1,300	975.00
(83)	John Coleman			
83 (a)	ball in hands at waist	2,200	1,300	975.00
83 (b)	bat in hands below waist	2,200	1,300	975.00
(85)	Hub Collins			
85 (a)	Brooklyn, batting	2,200	1,300	975.00
85 (b)	Brooklyn, fielding, hands chest-high	2,200	1,300	975.00
(86)	Charlie Comiskey			
86 (a)	arms folded	7,500	4,500	3,225
86 (b)	fielding, hands neck-high, ball visible	7,500	4,500	3,225

Item			
86 (c) fielding, hands shoulder-high, no ball	11,250	6,750	4,825
86 (d) sliding	14,250	8,550	6,100
(88) Roger Connor			
88 (a) batting, home plate, batter's boxes on floor	11,250	6,750	4,825
88 (b) batting, outdoors scene on backdrop	9,750	6,000	4,200
88 (c) fielding, hands at waist	7,500	4,500	3,225
88 (d) hands on knees	7,500	4,500	3,225
(89) Dick Conway			
90 (a) Boston, bat in hand at side	4,500	2,700	1,950
(90) Jim Conway			
90 (a) Kansas City, pitching, left ear visible	2,200	1,300	975.00
90 (b) K.C., pitching, left ear not visible	2,200	1,300	975.00
(91) Pete Conway			
91 (a) Detroit, pitching, right hand extended	2,200	1,300	975.00
(92) Paul Cook			
92 (a) fielding in mask	2,200	1,300	975.00
92 (b) tagging baserunner	2,200	1,300	975.00
(93) Jimmy Cooney			
93 (a) batting, Omaha, Dogs Head	5,250	3,150	2,250
(95) Pop Corkhill			
95 (a) Brooklyn, batting	2,200	1,300	975.00
95 (b) Brooklyn, fielding, hands neck-high	2,200	1,300	975.00
(96) Cannonball Crane			
96 (a) New York, pitching, right hand head-high	2,200	1,300	975.00
(99) John Crooks			
99 (a) Omaha, pose unrecorded	2,200	1,300	975.00
(100) Lave Cross			
100 (a) Louisville, hands on thighs	2,200	1,300	975.00
(105) Bert Cunningham			
105 (a) both arms waist level	2,200	1,300	975.00
(109) Edward Dailey			
109 (a) Columbus, pitching, right hand head-high	2,200	1,300	975.00
109 (b) Washington, pitch., right hand head-high	2,200	1,300	975.00
(111) Bill Daley			
111 (a) Boston, pitching, hands above waist	2,200	1,300	975.00
(112) Con Daley (Daily)			
112 (a) Indianapolis, right hand on hip	2,200	1,300	975.00
(113) Abner Dalrymple			
113 (a) Pittsburgh, hands on hips, feet apart	2,200	1,300	975.00
(114) Sun Daly			
114 (a) Minneapolis, fielding, hands chest-high	2,200	1,300	975.00
(115) Tom Daly			
115 (a) Chicago, fielding, hands chest-high	2,200	1,300	975.00
115 (b) Chicago, hands on knees	2,200	1,300	975.00
115 (c) Washington, fielding, hands chest-high	2,200	1,300	975.00
(117) Dell Darling			
117 (a) fielding, hands waist-high	2,200	1,300	975.00
(118) William Darnbrough			
118 (a) pitching	2,200	1,300	975.00
(123) Harry Decker			
123 (a) bat nearly horizontal	2,200	1,300	975.00
(124) Ed Delehanty			
124 (a) bat by shoulder	31,250	5,400	3,875
124 (b) bat horizontal	9,000	5,400	3,875
124 (c) fielding	22,500	13,500	9,675
(125) Jerry Denny			
125 (a) Indianapolis, batting	2,200	1,300	975.00
125 (b) Indianapolis, fielding	2,200	1,300	975.00
(126) Jim Devlin			
126 (a) pitching, left hand shoulder-high	2,200	1,300	975.00
126 (b) sliding	2,200	1,300	975.00
(130) Jim Donnelly			
130 (a) batting	2,200	1,300	975.00
(133) Mike Dorgan			
133 (a) sliding, horizontal format	3,375	2,000	1,450
(135) Charlie Duffe (Duffee)			
135 (a) batting	2,200	1,300	975.00
135 (b) fielding, bending to left	2,200	1,300	975.00
135 (c) fielding grounder	2,200	1,300	975.00
135 (d) fielding, standing upright	2,200	1,300	975.00
(136) Hugh Duffy			
136 (a) batting	4,875	2,925	2,100
136 (b) fielding, hands chin-high	4,875	2,925	2,100
136 (c) fielding grounder	6,000	3,600	2,600
(138) Martin Duke			
138 (a) ball in hands, chest-high	3,750	2,250	1,625
(139) Fred Dunlap			
139 (a) arms at side	2,200	1,300	975.00
139 (b) holding ball aloft	2,200	1,300	975.00
139 (c) holding ball aloft, Dogs Head	4,500	2,700	1,950
(141) Jesse Duryea			
141 (a) batting	2,200	1,300	975.00
(142) Frank Dwyer			
142 (a) bat at side	3,750	2,250	1,625
142 (b) bat in air	2,200	1,300	975.00
142 (c) fielding	2,200	1,300	975.00
(143) Billy Earle			
143 (a) Cincinnati, fielding, hands over head	2,200	1,300	975.00
(145) Red Ehret			
145 (a) batting	2,200	1,300	975.00
(147) Dude Esterbrook			
147 (a) Indianapolis, fielding grounder	2,200	1,300	975.00
147 (b) Indianapolis, fielding, hands chest-high	2,200	1,300	975.00
147 (c) Louisville, fielding, hands chest high	2,200	1,300	975.00
(149) Buck Ewing			
149 (a) New York, bat at side	6,000	3,600	2,600
149 (b) New York, bat in air	6,000	3,600	2,600
149 (c) New York, fielding, hands head-high	6,000	3,600	2,600
149 (d) New York, hands on knees	6,000	3,600	2,600
149 (e) New York, throwing, right arm extended forward	9,000	5,400	3,875
149 (f) New York, with mascot Willie Breslin	22,500	13,500	9,675
149 (g) New York, w/ mascot, Dogs Head	26,250	15,750	11,275
(150) John Ewing			
150 (a) Louisville, bat almost vertical	2,200	1,300	975.00
(151) Jay Faatz			
151 (a) throwing	2,200	1,300	975.00
151 (b) batting	2,200	1,300	975.00
(152) Bill Farmer			
152 (a) Pittsburgh, hands on knees	2,200	1,300	975.00
(154) Sid Farrar			
154 (a) fielding grounder	2,200	1,300	975.00
154 (b) fielding, hands head-high	2,200	1,300	975.00
(155) Duke Farrell			
155 (a) Chicago, fielding grounder	2,200	1,300	975.00
155 (b) Chicago, hands on knees	2,200	1,300	975.00
(157) Frank Fennelly			
157 (a) Cincinnati, fielding grounder	2,200	1,300	975.00
(158) Charlie Ferguson			
158 (a) pitching, hands at chest	2,200	1,300	975.00
(159) Alex Ferson			
159 (a) pitching, hands neck-high, looking front	2,200	1,300	975.00
(161) Jocko Fields			
161 (a) hands on thighs	2,200	1,300	975.00
(164) Silver Flint			
164 (a) batting	2,200	1,300	975.00
164 (b) catching, with mask, hands waist-high	3,000	1,800	1,300
(167) Jim Fogarty			
167 (a) batting	2,200	1,300	975.00
167 (b) fielding, hands neck-high	2,200	1,300	975.00
167 (c) running to left	2,200	1,300	975.00
167 (d) sliding	2,200	1,300	975.00
(168) Frank Foreman			
168 (a) Baltimore, ball in hands by right thigh	3,375	2,000	1,450
(170) Elmer Foster			
170 (a) Minneapolis, batting	2,200	1,300	975.00
170 (b) New York, fielding	2,200	1,300	975.00
(171) Dave Foutz			
171 (a) bat at 45 degrees	2,200	1,300	975.00
171 (b) throwing	2,200	1,300	975.00
(175) Shorty Fuller			
175 (a) St. Louis, fielding	2,200	1,300	975.00
175 (b) St. Louis, hands on knees	2,200	1,300	975.00
175 (c) St. Louis, swinging bat	2,200	1,300	975.00
(177) Chris Fulmer			
DP 8 tagging Tom Tucker, Dogs Head	6,750	4,050	2,875
(179) Pud Galvin			
179 (a) batting	5,625	3,375	2,400
(181) Charlie Ganzel			
181 (a) Boston, batting	2,200	1,300	975.00
181 (b) Boston, fielding, hands shoulder-high	3,750	2,250	1,625
181 (c) Boston, fielding, hands thigh-high	2,200	1,300	975.00
(182) Gid Gardner			
182 (a) Philadelphia, fielding low ball	2,200	1,300	975.00
(183) Hank Gastreich			
183 (a) pitching, left hand by thigh	2,200	1,300	975.00
(185) Frank Genins			
185 (a) batting, looking at ball	2,200	1,300	975.00
185 (b) batting, looking at camera	2,200	1,300	975.00
(186) Bill George			
186 (a) bat at side	2,200	1,300	975.00
(188) Charlie Getzein (Getzien)			
188 (a) pitching, hands above waist	2,200	1,300	975.00
(190) Bobby Gilks			
190 (a) batting	2,200	1,300	975.00
(192) Barney Gilligan			
192 (a) Washington, fielding	2,200	1,300	975.00
(193) Frank Gilmore			
193 (a) pitching, hands neck-high	2,200	1,300	975.00
(194) Jack Glasscock			
194 (a) Indianapolis, bat at side, Dogs Head	5,250	3,150	2,250
194 (b) Indianapolis, hands on knees	2,200	1,300	975.00
194 (c) Indianapolis, throwing	2,200	1,300	975.00
(195) Bill Gleason			
195 (a) Louisville, batting	2,200	1,300	975.00
195 (b) Louisville, stooping, hands clasped	2,200	1,300	975.00
DP 23 with Curt Welch	3,375	2,025	1,450
(196) Kid Gleason			
196 (a) Philadelphia, fielding grounder	3,375	2,025	1,450
196 (b) Philadelphia, ball in hands at chin	3,375	2,025	1,450
(197) Ed Glenn			
197 (a) fielding, hands neck-high	2,200	1,300	975.00
(199) George Gore			
199 (a) bat nearly horizontal	2,200	1,300	975.00
199 (b) bat at ready over left shoulder	2,200	1,300	975.00
199 (c) fielding grounder	2,200	1,300	975.00
(205) Henry Gruber			
205 (a) pitching, right hand chin-high	2,200	1,300	975.00
(206) Ad Gumbert			
206 (a) pitching, right hand eye-high	3,150	1,875	1,350
206 (b) pitching, right hand waist-high	2,200	1,300	975.00
(207) Tom Gunning			
207 (a) bending forward, hands by right knee	2,200	1,300	975.00
(208) Joe Gunson			
208 (a) wearing jacket	2,200	1,300	975.00
(212) Bill Hallman			
212 (a) leaning left to catch ball chest-high	2,200	1,300	975.00
(213) Billy Hamilton			
213 (a) Kansas City, batting: looking at camera	9,000	5,400	3,875
213 (b) Kansas City, fielding, hands neck-high	9,000	5,400	3,875
213 (c) Kansas City, fielding grounder	9,000	5,400	3,875
(215) Ned Hanlon			
215 (a) Detroit, batting	4,500	2,700	1,950
215 (b) Pittsburgh, fielding	4,875	2,925	2,100
(216) Bill Hanrahan			
216 (a) bat at side	2,200	1,300	975.00
(221) Gil Hatfield			
221 (a) bat at waist	2,200	1,300	975.00
221 (b) bat over shoulder	2,200	1,300	975.00
221 (c) fielding, hands chest-high	2,200	1,300	975.00
(223) Egyptian Healey (Healy)			
223 (a) Indianapolis, pitching, hands at chest	2,200	1,300	975.00
(227) Hardie Henderson			
227 (a) Brooklyn, outdoors, throwing, right hand head-high	3,000	1,800	1,300
(228) Moxie Hengle			
228 (a) Minneapolis, hands on knees	2,200	1,300	975.00
(229) John Henry			
229 (a) throwing, right hand neck-high	2,200	1,300	975.00
(231) Hunkey Hines			
231 (a) St. Louis Whites, fielding	2,200	1,300	975.00
(232) Paul Hines			
232 (a) Washington, arms at side	2,200	1,300	975.00
(233) Frank Hoffman			
233 (a) pitching, right hand head-high	2,200	1,300	975.00
(235) Bill Holbert			
235 (a) throwing	2,200	1,300	975.00
(236) Bug Holliday			
236 (a) Cincinnati, arms at side	2,200	1,300	975.00
236 (b) Cincinnati, ball in hands at shoulder	2,200	1,300	975.00

(238)	Buster Hoover			
238 (a)	Philadelphia, fielding, hands head-high	2,200	1,300	975.00
DP 1	being tagged by Ed Andrews	3,750	2,250	1,625

(239)	Charlie Hoover			
239 (a)	Chicago, fielding grounder (Never played for Chicago)	2,200	1,300	975.00
239 (b)	Kansas City, pose unrecorded	2,200	1,300	975.00

(241)	Joe Hornung			
241 (a)	Boston, batting	2,200	1,300	975.00

(243)	Dummy Hoy			
243 (a)	fielding grounder	6,750	4,050	2,875

(244)	Nat Hudson			
244 (a)	ball in hands waist-high	2,200	1,300	975.00
244 (b)	pitching, right hand head-high	2,200	1,300	975.00
244 (c)	pitching, right hand waist-high	2,200	1,300	975.00

(245)	Mickey Hughes			
245 (a)	holding ball at chest	2,200	1,300	975.00
245 (b)	holding ball at side	2,200	1,300	975.00
245 (c)	right hand extended	2,200	1,300	975.00
DP 4	being tagged by Bob Clark	5,625	3,375	2,400

(247)	Bill Hutchinson			
247 (a)	ball in hand, right heel hidden	2,200	1,300	975.00
247 (b)	ball in hand, right heel visible	2,200	1,300	975.00
247 (c)	batting	2,200	1,300	975.00

(248)	Arthur Irwin			
248 (a)	Philadelphia, fielding, hands chest-high	2,200	1,300	975.00
248 (b)	Phila., throwing, right hand head-high	2,200	1,300	975.00

(249)	John Irwin			
249 (a)	Washington, hands on knees	2,200	1,300	975.00
249 (b)	Washington, throwing	2,200	1,300	975.00

(250)	A.C. Jantzen			
250 (a)	batting, looking at camera	2,200	1,300	975.00

(252)	Spud Johnson			
252 (a)	Columbus, pose unrecorded	2,200	1,300	975.00

(253)	Dick Johnston			
253 (a)	batting, looking at ball	2,200	1,300	975.00
253 (b)	hands on hips	2,200	1,300	975.00
253 (c)	throwing right hand head high	2,200	1,300	975.00

(256)	Tim Keefe			
256 (a)	bat nearly horizontal, Old Judge	4,500	2,700	1,950
256 (b)	bat nearly horizontal, Dogs Head	18,750	11,250	8,100
256 (c)	ball in hands at chest	3,750	2,250	1,625
256 (d)	pitching, right hand head-high	4,500	2,700	1,950
256 (e)	pitching, right hand waist-high	4,500	2,700	1,950

(259)	Charlie Kelly			
259 (a)	Philadelphia, fielding, hands head-high	2,200	1,300	975.00

(261)	King Kelly			
261 (a)	"Kelly, Boston.", bat at 45-degree angle	9,000	5,400	3,875
261 (b)	"Kelly, Boston.", bat at 45-degree angle, Dogs Head	12,000	7,200	5,175
261 (c)	"Mike Kelly, C, Bostons", bat at 45-degree angle	9,000	5,400	3,875
261 (d)	"Kelly, Capt.", bat at 45-degree angle	9,000	5,400	3,875

(262)	Rudy Kemmler			
262 (a)	fielding, hands chest-high	2,200	1,300	975.00

(263)	Ted Kennedy			
263 (a)	Omaha, pose unrecorded	2,200	1,300	975.00

(264)	J.J. Kenyon			
264 (a)	Des Moines, right hand in glove, head-high	2,200	1,300	975.00

(265)	John Kerins			
265 (a)	hands on thighs	2,200	1,300	975.00

(266)	Matt Kilroy			
266 (a)	pitching, hands waist-high to left	2,200	1,300	975.00

(267)	Silver King			
267 (a)	St. Louis, pitching, hands chest-high	2,200	1,300	975.00
267 (b)	St. Louis, pitching, hands chin-high	2,200	1,300	975.00

(269)	Billy Klusman			
269 (a)	fielding grounder	2,200	1,300	975.00

(274)	Gus Krock			
274 (a)	ball in hands above waist	2,200	1,300	975.00
274 (b)	batting	2,200	1,300	975.00
274 (c)	pitching, right hand chin-high	2,200	1,300	975.00

(275)	Willie Kuehne			
275 (a)	fielding grounder	2,200	1,300	975.00

(277)	Henry Larkin			
277 (a)	fielding, hands thigh-high	2,200	1,300	975.00
277 (b)	right hand shoulder-high	2,200	1,300	975.00

(278)	Arlie Latham			
278 (a)	batting	2,200	1,300	975.00
278 (b)	throwing	4,125	2,475	1,750

(279)	Chuck Lauer			
279 (a)	fielding, hands chest-high	2,200	1,300	975.00

(280)	John Leighton			
280 (a)	batting	2,200	1,300	975.00
280 (b)	fielding	2,200	1,300	975.00

(284)	Herman Long			
284 (a)	Kansas City, bat at side	2,200	1,300	975.00
284 (b)	Kansas City, fielding, hands chest-high	2,200	1,300	975.00

(285)	Tom Lovett			
285 (a)	Brooklyn, bat on shoulder	2,200	1,300	975.00
285 (b)	Brooklyn, pitching, hands over head	2,200	1,300	975.00
285 (c)	Brooklyn, right hand extended	2,200	1,300	975.00

(288)	Denny Lyons			
288 (a)	Philadelphia AA, bat at ready	2,200	1,300	975.00
288 (b)	Phila. AA, fielding, left hand over head	2,200	1,300	975.00

(289)	Harry Lyons			
289 (a)	St. Louis, at first base	2,200	1,300	975.00

(290)	Connie Mack			
290 (a)	Washington, batting	31,250	11,250	8,100
290 (b)	Washington, squatting, hands on knees	31,250	13,500	9,675

(292)	Jimmy Macullar			
292 (a)	Des Moines, fielding, hands head-high	2,200	1,300	975.00

(293)	Kid Madden			
293 (a)	ball in hand over head	2,200	1,300	975.00
293 (b)	ball in hands, neck-high	2,200	1,300	975.00
293 (c)	ball in left hand, eye-high	2,200	1,300	975.00

(297)	Jimmy Manning			
297 (a)	bat at side	2,200	1,300	975.00
297 (b)	fielding grounder	2,200	1,300	975.00

(298)	Lefty Marr			
298 (a)	Columbus, left hand neck-high	2,200	1,300	975.00

(299)	Mascot (Willie Breslin)			
299 (a)	New York	4,125	2,475	1,750

(300)	Leech Maskrey			
300 (a)	Des Moines, ball in hands chin-high	2,200	1,300	975.00

(302)	Mike Mattimore			
302 (a)	Phila. AA, sliding, left hand raised	2,200	1,300	975.00

(303)	Al Maul			
303 (a)	pitching, hands at chest	2,200	1,300	975.00

(304)	Al Mays			
304 (a)	pitching, hands chest-high	2,200	1,300	975.00

(305)	Jimmy McAleer			
305 (a)	batting, looking at ball	2,200	1,300	975.00

(307)	Tommy McCarthy			
307 (a)	St. Louis, batting, indoors	5,250	3,150	2,250
307 (b)	St. Louis, right hand head-high, indoors	5,250	3,150	2,250
307 (c)	tagging player	6,900	4,125	2,950

(318)	Deacon McGuire			
318 (a)	Phila., fielding, hands shoulder-high	2,200	1,300	975.00

(319)	Bill McGunnigle			
319 (a)	looking to right	2,200	1,300	975.00

(320)	Ed McKean			
320 (a)	batting, looking at camera	2,200	1,300	975.00
320 (b)	fielding, hands over head	2,200	1,300	975.00

(325)	James McQuaid			
325 (a)	fielding, hands near chin	2,200	1,300	975.00

(330)	Doggie Miller			
330 (a)	Pittsburgh, ball in hands, Dogs Head	8,250	4,950	3,550
330 (b)	Pittsburgh, bat at side	2,200	1,300	975.00
330 (c)	fielding, hands chest-high	2,200	1,300	975.00

(331)	Joe Miller			
331 (a)	Minneapolis, bat at side	2,200	1,300	975.00
331 (b)	Minneapolis, fielding	2,200	1,300	975.00

(332)	Jocko Milligan			
332 (a)	bat at side	2,200	1,300	975.00
332 (b)	bat in air	2,200	1,300	975.00
332 (c)	fielding	2,200	1,300	975.00
332 (d)	throwing	2,200	1,300	975.00

(334)	Daniel Minnehan (Minahan)			
334 (a)	batting, looking at camera	2,200	1,300	975.00

(335)	Sam Moffet			
335 (a)	pose unrecorded	2,200	1,300	975.00

(336)	John Morrill			
336 (a)	Boston, batting	2,200	1,300	975.00

(338)	Tony Mullane			
338 (a)	ball in hands above waist	4,125	2,475	1,750

(339)	Joe Mulvey			
339 (a)	batting	2,200	1,300	975.00
339 (b)	fielding	2,200	1,300	975.00

(340)	Pat Murphy			
340 (a)	New York, fielding, hands chin-high	2,200	1,300	975.00

(341)	P.L. Murphy			
341 (a)	St. Paul, batting	3,000	1,800	1,300

(342)	Miah Murray			
342 (a)	on knee, hands at shoulder	2,200	1,300	975.00

(343)	Jim Mutrie			
343 (a)	seated	2,200	1,300	975.00
343 (b)	standing	2,200	1,300	975.00

(344)	Al Myers			
344 (a)	Wash., right hand at side, left at back	2,200	1,300	975.00

(345)	George Myers			
345 (a)	Indianapolis, batting	2,200	1,300	975.00

(346)	Tom Nagle			
346 (a)	batting	2,200	1,300	975.00
346 (b)	fielding, Dogs Head	9,000	5,400	3,875

(347)	Billy Nash			
347 (a)	hands on knees	3,375	2,025	1,450
347 (b)	throwing	2,200	1,300	975.00

(349)	Kid Nichols			
349 (a)	Omaha, batting, looking at ball	6,375	3,825	2,750
349 (b)	Omaha, pitching, right hand forward	6,375	3,825	2,750

(353)	Hugh Nicol			
DP 16	side by side with Reilly, "Long & Short"	3,375	2,025	1,450

(357)	Darby O'Brien			
357 (a)	Brooklyn, batting, looking at camera	2,200	1,300	975.00

(359)	John O'Brien			
359 (a)	Cleveland, batting	2,200	1,300	975.00
359 (b)	Cleveland, pose unrecorded, Dogs Head	7,125	4,275	3,075

(361)	Jack O'Connor			
361 (a)	Columbus, throwing	2,200	1,300	975.00

(362)	Hank O'Day			
362 (a)	ball in right hand, head-high	2,200	1,300	975.00

(365)	Tip O'Neill			
365 (a)	bat held horizontally	2,200	1,300	975.00
365 (b)	bat over shoulder	2,200	1,300	975.00
365 (c)	fielding grounder	2,200	1,300	975.00
365 (d)	throwing	4,350	2,625	1,875

(366)	Orator Jim O'Rourke			
366 (a)	New York, bat in hand at side	6,000	3,600	2,600
366 (b)	New York, batting	7,125	4,275	3,075
366 (c)	New York, throwing, hand head-high	5,250	3,150	2,250

(367)	Tom O'Rourke			
367 (a)	Boston, fielding, hands thigh-high	3,375	2,025	1,450

(368)	Dave Orr			
368 (a)	Columbus, bat at ready, nearly vertical	2,200	1,300	975.00

(370)	Owen Patton			
370 (a)	Des Moines, bat at head	2,200	1,300	975.00

(374)	Fred Pfeffer			
374 (a)	batting, looking at ball	2,200	1,300	975.00
374 (b)	tagging player	2,850	1,725	1,225
374 (c)	throwing, right-hand neck-high	2,200	1,300	975.00

(375)	Dick Phelan			
375 (a)	batting, looking at ball	2,200	1,300	975.00

(377)	Jack Pickett			
377 (a)	St. Paul, bat over shoulder	2,200	1,300	975.00
377 (b)	St. Paul, fielding grounder	2,200	1,300	975.00
377 (c)	St. Paul, throwing, right hand head-high	2,200	1,300	975.00

(378)	George Pinkney			
378 (a)	bat in air, nearly vertical	2,200	1,300	975.00
378 (b)	bat over shoulder	2,200	1,300	975.00
DP 25	(w/ Steve Toole)	6,750	4,050	2,875

(381)	Jim Powell			
381 (a)	batting, looking at camera	2,200	1,300	975.00

(383)	Blondie Purcell			
383 (a)	throwing	2,200	1,300	975.00

(385)	Joe Quinn			
385 (a)	ball in hands by chin	2,200	1,300	975.00
385 (b)	ready to run	2,200	1,300	975.00

(386)	Old Hoss Radbourn			
386 (a)	hands at waist, Dogs Head	9,750	5,850	4,200
386 (b)	hands on hips, bat on left	4,500	2,700	1,950
386 (c)	tagging player	5,250	3,150	2,250

(388)	Tom Ramsey			
388 (a)	bat at ready, nearly vertical	2,200	1,300	975.00
388 (b)	bat over right shoulder, Dogs Head	6,000	3,600	2,600

(390)	Charlie Reilly			
390 (a)	St. Paul, throwing	2,200	1,300	975.00

(391)	Long John Reilly			
391 (a)	Cincinnati, fielding	2,200	1,300	975.00
DP 16	side by side w/Nicol, "Long & Short"	3,375	2,025	1,450
(393)	Danny Richardson			
393 (a)	New York, moving left, arms at side	2,200	1,300	975.00
393 (b)	New York, throwing	2,200	1,300	975.00
(394)	Hardy Richardson			
394 (a)	Boston, bat over shoulder	2,200	1,300	975.00
394 (b)	Detroit, bat over shoulder	2,200	1,300	975.00
394 (c)	Boston, fielding, hands head-high	2,200	1,300	975.00
(398)	Wilbert Robinson			
398 (a)	Philadelphia AA, batting	5,625	3,375	2,475
398 (b)	Phila. AA, catching, hands neck-high	5,625	3,375	2,475
398 (c)	Philadelphia AA, throwing	5,625	3,375	2,475
(399)	Yank Robinson			
399 (a)	St. Louis, batting	3,150	1,875	1,350
399 (b)	St. Louis, fielding grounder	3,150	1,875	1,350
399 (c)	St. Louis, hands at chest	3,150	1,875	1,350
(402)	Dave Rowe			
402 (a)	Kansas City, fielding, Dogs Head	5,250	3,150	2,250
(403)	Jack Rowe			
403 (a)	Detroit, batting, looking at camera	2,200	1,300	975.00
403 (b)	Detroit, bat on shoulder, looking at ball	2,200	1,300	975.00
(404)	Amos Rusie			
404 (a)	Indianapolis, ball in right hand, thigh-high	11,250	6,750	4,875
(405)	Jimmy Ryan			
405 (a)	bat at side	3,150	1,875	1,350
405 (b)	batting	3,375	2,025	1,450
405 (c)	stooping for knee-high catch	3,150	1,875	1,350
405 (d)	throwing, left hand head-high	3,150	1,875	1,350
(407)	Ben Sanders			
407 (a)	batting	2,200	1,300	975.00
407 (b)	fielding	2,200	1,300	975.00
407 (c)	right hand head-high	2,200	1,300	975.00
(408)	Frank Scheibeck			
408 (a)	fielding, hand over head	2,200	1,300	975.00
(412)	Gus Schmelz			
412 (a)	portrait	2,200	1,300	975.00
(413)	Jumbo Schoeneck			
413 (a)	fielding, hands chin-high	2,200	1,300	975.00
(414)	Pop Schriver			
414 (a)	fielding, hands ankle-high	2,200	1,300	975.00
414 (b)	hands cupped chest-high	1,750	1,050	750.00
DP 2	being tagged by Charlie Bastian	3,750	2,250	1,750
(415)	Emmett Seery			
415 (a)	arms folded	2,200	1,300	975.00
(417)	Ed Seward			
417 (a)	ball in hands neck-high	2,200	1,300	975.00
(420)	Daniel Shannon			
420 (a)	Louisville, leaning to tag player	2,200	1,300	975.00
(421)	Bill Sharsig			
421 (a)	full length in bowler hat	2,200	1,300	975.00
(425)	George Shoch			
425 (a)	fielding grounder	2,200	1,300	975.00
(426)	Otto Shomberg (Schomberg)			
426 (a)	fielding, hands head-high	2,200	1,300	975.00
(427)	Lev Shreve			
427 (a)	right hand eye-high, looking at camera	2,200	1,300	975.00
(429)	Mike Slattery			
429 (a)	fielding, hands chest-high	2,200	1,300	975.00
(430)	Elmer Smith			
(431)	Germany Smith	2,200	1,300	975.00
431 (a)	Cincinnati, pitching, left hand head-high, looking at camera	2,200	1,300	975.00
431 (a)	Brooklyn, batting, looking at ball	2,200	1,300	975.00
431 (b)	Brooklyn, hands on knees	2,200	1,300	975.00
431 (c)	Brooklyn, right hand head-high	2,200	1,300	975.00
(435)	Pop Smith			
435 (a)	Boston, batting	2,200	1,300	975.00
435 (b)	Pittsburgh, batting	2,200	1,300	975.00
435 (c)	hands on knees	2,200	1,300	975.00
(439)	Pete Sommers			
439 (a)	portrait	3,375	2,025	1,450
(440)	Bill Sowders			
440 (a)	Boston, pitching, hands at throat	2,200	1,300	975.00
440 (b)	Boston, pitching, right hand cap-high, left hand waist-high	3,000	1,800	1,300
(442)	Charlie Sprague			

442 (a)	Chicago, left hand at back head-high	2,200	1,300	975.00
442 (b)	Cleveland, left hand at back head-high	2,200	1,300	975.00
(444)	Harry Staley			
444 (a)	pitching, right hand chest-high	2,200	1,300	975.00
(445)	Dan Stearns			
445 (a)	Kansas City, fielding, hands neck-high	3,750	2,250	1,750
(450)	Harry Stovey			
450 (a)	bat at ready by head	3,375	2,025	1,450
450 (b)	fielding, hands chest-high, Dogs Head	18,000	10,800	7,725
450 (c)	hands on knees	2,200	1,300	975.00
(451)	Scott Stratton			
451 (a)	batting	2,200	1,300	975.00
(452)	Joe Straus (Strauss)			
452 (a)	Milwaukee, kneeling, looking to right	2,200	1,300	975.00
452 (b)	Omaha, throwing	2,200	1,300	975.00
(453)	Cub Stricker			
453 (a)	fielding, hands over head	2,200	1,300	975.00
(454)	Marty Sullivan			
454 (a)	Chicago, batting, looking at ball	2,200	1,300	975.00
454 (b)	Indianapolis, hands chest-high	2,200	1,300	975.00
(457)	Billy Sunday			
457 (a)	Pittsburgh, bat at side	5,250	3,150	2,250
457 (b)	Pittsburgh, batting	7,500	4,500	3,225
457 (c)	Pittsburgh, fielding, hands thigh-high	5,250	3,150	2,250
(459)	Ezra Sutton			
459 (a)	batting, looking down at ball	2,200	1,300	975.00
459 (b)	fielding, hands shoulder-high	2,200	1,300	975.00
(461)	Park Swartzel			
461 (a)	arms at side	2,200	1,300	975.00
(464)	Pop Tate			
464 (a)	Boston, batting	2,200	1,300	975.00
(465)	Patsy Tebeau			
465 (a)	Chicago, fielding grounder	2,200	1,300	975.00
(466)	John Tener			
466 (a)	ball in right hand chin-high	3,750	2,250	1,750
466 (b)	batting	3,750	2,250	1,750
(467)	Adonis Terry			
467 (a)	arms extended horizontally	2,200	1,300	975.00
467 (b)	bat on shoulder	2,200	1,300	975.00
(468)	Sam Thompson			
468 (a)	Detroit, bat ready at 45 degree angle	9,750	5,850	4,200
468 (b)	Philadelphia, batting, ball above head	9,750	5,850	4,200
(469)	Mike Tiernan			
469 (a)	batting	2,200	1,300	975.00
469 (b)	sliding	3,375	2,025	1,450
469 (c)	throwing, left hand chin-high	2,200	1,300	975.00
(470)	Cannonball Titcomb			
470 (a)	pitching, hands chin-high	2,200	1,300	975.00
(471)	Phil Tomney			
471 (a)	fielding, hands over head	2,200	1,300	975.00
(472)	Steve Toole			
DP 25	(w/ George Pinkney (Pinckney))	6,750	4,050	2,875
(473)	George Townsend			
473 (a)	bat at ready by head	2,200	1,300	975.00
473 (b)	fielding. hands chest-high	2,200	1,300	975.00
(474)	Bill Traffley			
474 (a)	hands on thighs	2,200	1,300	975.00
(477)	Tommy Tucker			
477 (a)	ball in hands at chest	2,200	1,300	975.00
DP 8	being tagged by Chris Fulmer	6,750	4,050	2,875
(479)	George Turner			
479 (a)	fielding, hands head-high	2,200	1,300	975.00
(480)	Larry Twitchell			
480 (a)	Cleveland, pitching, hands at chest	2,200	1,300	975.00
480 (b)	Detroit, pitching, hands at chest	2,200	1,300	975.00
(481)	Jim Tyng			
481 (a)	pitching	2,200	1,300	975.00
(483)	George Van Haltren			
483 (a)	batting	4,500	2,700	1,950
483 (b)	ball in hands at waist	4,500	2,700	1,950
482 (c)	right hand at thigh	4,500	2,700	1,950
(484)	Farmer Vaughn			
484 (a)	bat at ready, looking at camera	2,200	1,300	975.00
(488)	Joe Visner			
488 (a)	arms at side	2,200	1,300	975.00
488 (b)	batting	2,200	1,300	975.00
488 (c)	throwing	2,200	1,300	975.00

(490)	Reddy Walsh			
490 (a)	batting	2,200	1,300	975.00
(491)	John Ward			
491 (a)	hands behind back	6,000	3,600	2,600
491 (b)	hands on hips	10,500	6,300	4,500
491 (c)	portrait in dress clothes) (Value Undetermine)	2,200	1,300	975.00
491 (d)	sliding, left arm in air	6,000	3,600	2,600
491 (e)	throwing, right profile	6,000	3,600	2,600
491 (f)	cap in right hand at side	6,000	3,600	2,600
491 (g)	cap in right hand at side, Dogs Head	9,000	5,400	3,875
(493)	Bill Watkins			
493 (a)	Detroit, portrait	2,200	1,300	975.00
493 (b)	Kansas City, portrait	2,200	1,300	975.00
(494)	Farmer Weaver			
494 (a)	fielding, left hand over head	2,200	1,300	975.00
(496)	Stump Weidman (Wiedman)			
496 (a)	New York, batting	2,200	1,300	975.00
(497)	Wild Bill Weidner (Widner)			
497 (a)	batting	2,200	1,300	975.00
(498)	Curt Welch			
498 (a)	Philadelphia AA, fielding grounder	2,200	1,300	975.00
DP 23	with Will Gleason	3,375	2,025	1,450
(499)	Mickey Welch			
499 (a)	N.Y., pitching, right arm extended forward, name incorrect (Welsh)	4,500	2,700	1,950
499 (b)	N.Y., pitching, right arm extended forward, name correct	4,500	2,700	1,950
499 (c)	N.Y., pitching, right arm behind head, Dogs Head	22,500	13,500	9,675
(504)	A.C. (Gus) Weyhing			
504 (a)	Philadelphia AA, right hand chest-high	2,200	1,300	975.00
(505)	John Weyhing			
505 (a)	Philadelphia AA, left hand chest-high (Never played for Philadelphia)	2,200	1,300	975.00
(510)	Deacon White			
510 (a)	Detroit, hands above head	2,200	1,300	975.00
510 (b)	looking down at ball	2,200	1,300	975.00
(511)	Art Whitney			
511 (a)	New York, with dog	18,750	11,250	8,100
511 (b)	New York, fielding, hands thigh-high	2,200	1,300	975.00
511 (c)	Pittsburgh, fielding, hands thigh-high	2,200	1,300	975.00
(512)	G. Whitney			
512 (a)	St. Joseph, batting, looking at ball	2,200	1,300	975.00
(513)	Jim Whitney			
513 (a)	Wash., pitching, right hand waist-high	2,200	1,300	975.00
(515)	Ned Williamson			
515 (a)	arms folded	2,200	1,300	975.00
515 (b)	batting, looking at ball	2,200	1,300	975.00
515 (c)	fielding	2,200	1,300	975.00
515 (d)	throwing	2,200	1,300	975.00
(516)	Tit Willis			
516 (a)	pitching, arms head-high	2,200	1,300	975.00
(517)	Walt Wilmot			
517 (a)	Washington, fielding, hands at chest	2,200	1,300	975.00
(519)	Sam Wise			
519 (a)	Boston, bat at side	2,200	1,300	975.00
519 (b)	Boston, hands on knees	3,000	1,800	1,300
(520)	Chicken Wolf			
520 (a)	bat at ready, team name visible on shirt	2,200	1,300	975.00
(521)	George Wood (L.F.)			
521 (a)	both hands neck-high	2,200	1,300	975.00
521 (b)	right hand head-high	2,200	1,300	975.00
(522)	Pete Wood (P.)			
522 (a)	bat on shoulder	2,200	1,300	975.00
(523)	Harry Wright			
523 (a)	portrait, looking to his left	30,000	18,000	13,000
(524)	Chief Zimmer			
524 (a)	fielding, hands at chest	2,200	1,300	975.00
524 (b)	throwing	2,200	1,300	975.00

1965 Old London Coins

These 1-1/2" diameter metal coins were included in Old London snack food packages. The 40 coins in this set feature two players from each of the major leagues' 20 teams, except St. Louis (3) and the New York Mets (1). Coin fronts have color photos and player names, while the silver-colored backs give a brief biography. An Old London logo is also displayed on each coin back. Space Magic Ltd. produced the coins. This is the same company which produced similar sets for Topps in 1964 and 1971.

	NM	EX	VG
Complete Set (40):	475.00	240.00	140.00
Common Player:	3.00	1.50	.90
(1) Henry Aaron	35.00	17.50	10.50
(2) Richie Allen	7.50	3.75	2.25
(3) Bob Allison	3.00	1.50	.90
(4) Ernie Banks	25.00	12.50	7.50
(5) Ken Boyer	4.50	2.25	1.25
(6) Jim Bunning	15.00	7.50	4.50
(7) Orlando Cepeda	12.50	6.25	3.75
(8) Dean Chance	3.00	1.50	.90
(9) Rocky Colavito	10.00	5.00	3.00
(10) Vic Davalillo	3.00	1.50	.90
(11) Tommy Davis	3.00	1.50	.90
(12) Ron Fairly	3.00	1.50	.90
(13) Dick Farrell	3.00	1.50	.90
(14) Jim Fregosi	3.00	1.50	.90
(15) Bob Friend	3.00	1.50	.90
(16) Dick Groat	3.00	1.50	.90
(17) Ron Hunt	3.00	1.50	.90
(18) Chuck Hinton	3.00	1.50	.90
(19) Ken Johnson	3.00	1.50	.90
(20) Al Kaline	20.00	10.00	6.00
(21) Harmon Killebrew	20.00	10.00	6.00
(22) Don Lock	3.00	1.50	.90
(23) Mickey Mantle	100.00	50.00	30.00
(24) Roger Maris	30.00	15.00	9.00
(25) Willie Mays	35.00	17.50	10.50
(26) Bill Mazeroski	12.50	6.25	3.75
(27) Gary Peters	3.00	1.50	.90
(28) Vada Pinson	3.50	1.75	1.00
(29) Boog Powell	4.50	2.25	1.25
(30) Dick Radatz	3.00	1.50	.90
(31) Brooks Robinson	20.00	10.00	6.00
(32) Frank Robinson	20.00	10.00	6.00
(33) Tracy Stallard	3.00	1.50	.90
(34) Joe Torre	7.50	3.75	2.25
(35) Leon Wagner	3.00	1.50	.90
(36) Pete Ward	3.00	1.50	.90
(37) Dave Wickersham	3.00	1.50	.90
(38) Billy Williams	15.00	7.50	4.50
(39) John Wyatt	3.00	1.50	.90
(40) Carl Yastrzemski	25.00	12.50	7.50

1909-11 Old Mill Cigarettes

T206 cards bearing the Old Mill advertising are, with a major exception, among the most common of the set's back variations. Two styles of Old Mill T206 backs are found. One, which appears on cards of major league players and minor leaguers other than those from the Southern leagues, mentions a "BASE BALL / SUBJECTS / LARGE ASSORTMENT." The other specifies the four Southern leagues from which the players depicted originate. In recent years advanced T206 specialists have become aware of a brown-ink version of the Southern leagues back, much rarer than the black-ink version usually found on both types of Old Mill backs. All of the confirmed brown-ink cards appear to have been hand-cut from a sheet, leading to speculation as to whether they represent an actual issued variation or were salvaged from a scrapped printing. Contemporary with the T206 issues, Old Mill also produced a lengthy series of red-bordered minor league player cards in 1910. Those are listed in the minor league section of this book.

PREMIUMS
Common: 1.25X
Stars/Mi. Leagues: 1X
Brown-ink So. Leagues: 10X
(See S74, T3, T206.)

1910 Old Put Cigar

This is a version of the anonymous E98 "Set of 30" on which an advertisement for "OLD PUT / 5 ct. CIGAR" has been rubber-stamped in purple. Because of the ease with which these could be faked, collectors must exercise extreme caution.

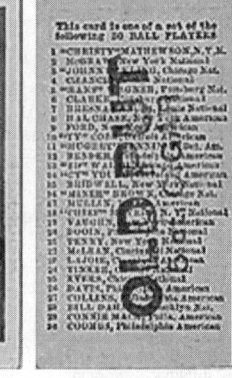

	NM	EX	VG
Common Player:	3,750	1,875	1,125
(1) Christy Matthewson (Mathewson)	12,000	6,000	3,600
(2) John McGraw	6,000	3,000	1,800
(3) Johnny Kling	3,750	1,875	1,025
(4) Frank Chance	6,000	3,000	1,800
(5) Hans Wagner	13,500	6,750	4,050
(6) Fred Clarke	3,750	1,875	1,025
(7) Roger Bresnahan	3,750	1,875	1,025
(8) Hal Chase	6,000	3,000	1,800
(9) Russ Ford	3,750	1,875	1,025
(10) "Ty" Cobb	16,500	8,250	4,950
(11) Hughey Jennings	3,750	1,875	1,025
(12) Chief Bender	6,000	3,000	1,800
(13) Ed Walsh	3,750	1,875	1,025
(14) Cy Young	12,000	6,000	3,600
(15) Al Bridwell	3,750	1,875	1,025
(16) Miner Brown	3,750	1,875	1,025
(17) George Mullin	3,750	1,875	1,025
(18) Chief Meyers	3,750	1,875	1,025
(19) Hippo Vaughn	3,750	1,875	1,025
(20) Red Dooin	3,750	1,875	1,025
(21) Fred Tenny (Tenney)	3,750	1,875	1,025
(22) Larry McLean	3,750	1,875	1,025
(23) Nap Lajoie	6,000	3,000	1,800
(24) Joe Tinker	6,000	3,000	1,800
(25) Johnny Evers	6,000	3,000	1,800
(26) Harry Davis	3,750	1,875	1,025
(27) Eddie Collins	6,000	3,000	1,800
(28) Bill Dahlen	3,750	1,875	1,025
(29) Connie Mack	6,000	3,000	1,800
(30) Jack Coombs	3,750	1,875	1,025

1951 Olmes Studio Postcards

This line of Philadelphia player postcards (all but one from the A's) was produced by a local photographer, probably for player use in satisfying fans' autograph requests. The 3-1/2" x 5-1/2" cards have a glossy black-and-white player photo on front. Backs have only standard postcard indicia and the Olmes credit line. Other players may remain to be checklisted. The unnumbered cards are listed here alphabetically.

	NM	EX	VG
Common Player:	75.00	37.50	22.50
(1) Sam Chapman	75.00	37.50	22.50
(2) Ferris Fain (Ready to hit, on grass.)	100.00	50.00	30.00
(3) Ferris Fain (Batting, choking up.)	100.00	50.00	30.00
(4) Ferris Fain (Batting, follow-through.)	100.00	50.00	30.00
(5) Ferris Fain (Kneeling)	100.00	50.00	30.00
(6) Dick Fowler	75.00	37.50	22.50
(7) Bob Hooper	75.00	37.50	22.50
(8) Skeeter Kell	75.00	37.00	22.50
(9) Paul Lehner	75.00	37.50	22.50
(10) Lou Limmer	75.00	37.50	22.50
(11) Barney McCosky	75.00	37.50	22.50
(12) Robin Roberts	275.00	135.00	80.00
(13) Carl Scheib	75.00	37.50	22.50
(14) Bobby Shantz	75.00	37.50	22.50
(15) Joe Tipton	75.00	37.50	22.50
(16) Gus Zernial (Batting)	100.00	50.00	30.00
(17) Gus Zernial (Kneeling)	100.00	50.00	30.00

1979 Open Pantry/Lake to Lake MACC

To benefit Milwaukee Athletes Against Childhood Cancer the Open Pantry convenience stores in Wisconsin teamed with Lake to Lake Dairy to produce this card set. Red, white

and black fronts of the 5" x 6" cards have a player photo, facsimile autograph and team logo. Backs are printed in red with a message from the player about the MACC fund. Besides members of the Milwaukee Brewers listed here, the set features Green Bay Packers and Milwaukee Bucks players. The unnumbered cards are checklisted here alphabetically.

	NM	EX	VG
Complete Set (12):	10.00	5.00	3.00
Common (Baseball) Player:	2.00	1.00	.60
(1) Jerry Augustine	3.00	1.50	.90
(2) Sal Bando	3.00	1.50	.90
(3) Cecil Cooper	4.00	2.00	1.25
(4) Larry Hisle	3.00	1.50	.90
(5) Lary Sorensen	3.00	1.50	.90

1910 "Orange Borders"

Known in the hobby as "Orange Borders," these 1-1/2" x 2-7/16" cards were issued in 1910 and were printed on candy boxes that displayed the words "American Sports and Candy and Jewelry." The end flaps indicate the producers as the "Geo. Davis Co., Inc." and the "P.R. Warren Co., Warrenville Lowell, Mass." According to the box, the complete set includes "144 leading ballplayers," but to date just over two dozen different subjects are known. When found today, these black and white photos are often surrounded by orange borders which, in reality, were part of the candy box. Similar in format to the "Baseball Bats" cards, Orange Borders have player names which are hand-lettered, rather than typeset. Gaps have been left in the assigned numbering to accomodate future additions to the checklist.

	NM	EX	VG
Common Player:	960.00	390.00	190.00
(1) Bill Bergen	960.00	390.00	190.00
(2) Bill Bradley	960.00	390.00	190.00
(3) Bill Carrigan	960.00	390.00	190.00
(4) Hal Chase	1,140	455.00	230.00
(5) Fred Clark (Clarke)	1,440	575.00	290.00
(6) Ty Cobb	12,000	4,800	2,400
(7) Sam Crawford	1,440	575.00	290.00
(8) Lou Criger	960.00	390.00	190.00
(9) Harry Davis	960.00	390.00	190.00
(11) Art Devlin	960.00	390.00	190.00
(12) Mickey Doolan	960.00	390.00	190.00
(13) George Gibson	960.00	390.00	190.00
(14) Addie Joss	1,560	625.00	315.00
(15) Nap Lajoie	1,440	575.00	290.00
(16) Frank LaPorte	960.00	390.00	190.00
(17) Harry Lord	960.00	390.00	190.00
(18) Christy Mathewson	5,400	2,160	1,080
(19) Amby McConnell	960.00	390.00	190.00
(21) John McGraw	1,440	575.00	290.00
(22) Dots Miller	960.00	390.00	190.00
(23) George Mullin	960.00	390.00	190.00
(24) Eddie Plank	1,440	575.00	290.00
(25) Tris Speaker	1,680	675.00	335.00
(26) Jake Stahl	960.00	390.00	190.00
(27) Honus Wagner (Batting)	9,000	3,600	1,800
(28) Honus Wagner (Portrait)	9,000	3,600	1,800
(29) Jack Warhop	960.00	390.00	190.00
(31) American League Champions, 1909 (Detroit)	2,400	960.00	480.00
(32) National League Champions, 1909 (Pittsburgh)	2,400	960.00	480.00

1976 Orbaker's Discs

One of several regional sponsors of player disc sets in 1976 was the Orbaker's restaurant chain. The discs are 3-3/8" diameter with a black-and-white player portrait photo in the center of the baseball design. A line of red stars is above, while the left and right panels feature one of several bright colors. Produced by Michael Schecter Associates under license from the Major League Baseball Players Association, the player photos have had uniform and cap logos removed. Backs are printed in red and purple. The unnumbered checklist here is presented in alphabetical order.

		NM	EX	VG
	Complete Set (70):	50.00	25.00	15.00
	Common Player:	1.00	.50	.30
(1)	Henry Aaron	20.00	10.00	6.00
(2)	Johnny Bench	6.00	3.00	1.75
(3)	Vida Blue	1.00	.50	.30
(4)	Larry Bowa	1.00	.50	.30
(5)	Lou Brock	4.00	2.00	1.25
(6)	Jeff Burroughs	1.00	.50	.30
(7)	John Candelaria	1.00	.50	.30
(8)	Jose Cardenal	1.00	.50	.30
(9)	Rod Carew	4.00	2.00	1.25
(10)	Steve Carlton	4.00	2.00	1.25
(11)	Dave Cash	1.00	.50	.30
(12)	Cesar Cedeno	1.00	.50	.30
(13)	Ron Cey	1.00	.50	.30
(14)	Carlton Fisk	4.00	2.00	1.25
(15)	Tito Fuentes	1.00	.50	.30
(16)	Steve Garvey	2.00	1.00	.60
(17)	Ken Griffey	1.00	.50	.30
(18)	Don Gullett	1.00	.50	.30
(19)	Willie Horton	1.00	.50	.30
(20)	Al Hrabosky	1.00	.50	.30
(21)	Catfish Hunter	3.00	1.50	.90
(22)	Reggie Jackson (A's)	12.00	6.00	3.50
(23)	Randy Jones	1.00	.50	.30
(24)	Jim Kaat	1.00	.50	.30
(25)	Don Kessinger	1.00	.50	.30
(26)	Dave Kingman	1.00	.50	.30
(27)	Jerry Koosman	1.00	.50	.30
(28)	Mickey Lolich	1.00	.50	.30
(29)	Greg Luzinski	1.00	.50	.30
(30)	Fred Lynn	1.00	.50	.30
(31)	Bill Madlock	1.00	.50	.30
(32)	Carlos May	1.00	.50	.30
(33)	John Mayberry	1.00	.50	.30
(34)	Bake McBride	1.00	.50	.30
(35)	Doc Medich	1.00	.50	.30
(36)	Andy Messersmith	1.00	.50	.30
(37)	Rick Monday	1.00	.50	.30
(38)	John Montefusco	1.00	.50	.30
(39)	Jerry Morales	1.00	.50	.30
(40)	Joe Morgan	4.00	2.00	1.25
(41)	Thurman Munson	3.00	1.50	.90
(42)	Bobby Murcer	1.00	.50	.30
(43)	Al Oliver	1.00	.50	.30
(44)	Jim Palmer	4.00	2.00	1.25
(45)	Dave Parker	1.00	.50	.30
(46)	Tony Perez	3.00	1.50	.90
(47)	Jerry Reuss	1.00	.50	.30
(48)	Brooks Robinson	6.00	3.00	1.75
(49)	Frank Robinson	6.00	3.00	1.75
(50)	Steve Rogers	1.00	.50	.30
(51)	Pete Rose	17.50	8.75	5.25
(52)	Nolan Ryan	25.00	12.50	7.50
(53)	Manny Sanguillen	1.00	.50	.30
(54)	Mike Schmidt	15.00	7.50	4.50
(55)	Tom Seaver	6.00	3.00	1.75
(56)	Ted Simmons	1.00	.50	.30
(57)	Reggie Smith	1.00	.50	.30
(58)	Willie Stargell	4.00	2.00	1.25
(59)	Rusty Staub	1.50	.70	.45
(60)	Rennie Stennett	1.00	.50	.30
(61)	Don Sutton	3.00	1.50	.90
(62)	Andy Thornton	1.00	.50	.30
(63)	Luis Tiant	1.00	.50	.30
(64)	Joe Torre	1.00	.50	.30
(65)	Mike Tyson	1.00	.50	.30
(66)	Bob Watson	1.00	.50	.30
(67)	Wilbur Wood	1.00	.50	.30
(68)	Jimmy Wynn	1.00	.50	.30
(69)	Carl Yastrzemski	6.00	3.00	1.75
(70)	Richie Zisk	1.00	.50	.30

1932 Orbit Gum Pins - Numbered (PR2)

Issued circa 1932, this skip-numbered set of small (13/16" diameter) pins was produced by Orbit Gum and carries the Amerian Card Catalog designation of PR2. A color player lithograph is set against a green background with the player's name and team printed on a strip of yellow below. The pin number is at the very bottom; pins after #40 are skip-numbered.

		NM	EX	VG
	Complete Set (53):	2,500	1,250	750.00
	Common Player:	30.00	15.00	9.00
1	Ivy Andrews	30.00	15.00	9.00
2	Carl Reynolds	30.00	15.00	9.00
3	Riggs Stephenson	30.00	15.00	9.00
4	Lon Warneke	30.00	15.00	9.00
5	Frank Grube	30.00	15.00	9.00
6	"Kiki" Cuyler	60.00	30.00	18.00
7	Marty McManus	30.00	15.00	9.00
8	Lefty Clark	30.00	15.00	9.00
9	George Blaeholder	30.00	15.00	9.00
10	Willie Kamm	30.00	15.00	9.00
11	Jimmy Dykes	30.00	15.00	9.00
12	Earl Averill	60.00	30.00	18.00
13	Pat Malone	30.00	15.00	9.00
14	Dizzy Dean	200.00	100.00	60.00
15	Dick Bartell	30.00	15.00	9.00
16	Guy Bush	30.00	15.00	9.00
17	Bud Tinning	30.00	15.00	9.00
18	Jimmy Foxx	150.00	75.00	45.00
19	Mule Haas	30.00	15.00	9.00
20	Lew Fonseca	30.00	15.00	9.00
21	Pepper Martin	40.00	20.00	12.00
22	Phil Collins	30.00	15.00	9.00
23	Bill Cissell	30.00	15.00	9.00
24	Bump Hadley	30.00	15.00	9.00
25	Smead Jolley	30.00	15.00	9.00
26	Burleigh Grimes	60.00	30.00	18.00
27	Dale Alexander	30.00	15.00	9.00
28	Mickey Cochrane	60.00	30.00	18.00
29	Mel Harder	30.00	15.00	9.00
30	Mark Koenig	30.00	15.00	9.00
31a	Lefty O'Doul (Dodgers)	50.00	25.00	15.00
31b	Lefty O'Doul (Giants)	90.00	45.00	27.00
32a	Woody English (With bat.)	30.00	15.00	9.00
32b	Woody English (Without bat.)	80.00	40.00	24.00
33a	Billy Jurges (With bat.)	30.00	15.00	9.00
33b	Billy Jurges (Without bat.)	80.00	40.00	24.00
34	Bruce Campbell	30.00	15.00	9.00
35	Joe Vosmik	30.00	15.00	9.00
36	Dick Porter	30.00	15.00	9.00
37	Charlie Grimm	30.00	15.00	9.00
38	George Earnshaw	30.00	15.00	9.00
39	Al Simmons	60.00	30.00	18.00
40	Red Lucas	30.00	15.00	9.00
51	Wally Berger	30.00	15.00	9.00
55	Jim Levey	30.00	15.00	9.00
58	Ernie Lombardi	60.00	30.00	18.00
64	Jack Burns	30.00	15.00	9.00
67	Billy Herman	60.00	30.00	18.00
72	Bill Hallahan	30.00	15.00	9.00
92	Don Brennan	30.00	15.00	9.00
96	Sam Byrd	30.00	15.00	9.00
99	Ben Chapman	30.00	15.00	9.00
103	John Allen	30.00	15.00	9.00
107	Tony Lazzeri	60.00	30.00	18.00
111	Earl Combs (Earle)	60.00	30.00	18.00
116	Joe Sewell	60.00	30.00	18.00
120	Vernon Gomez	60.00	30.00	18.00

1932 Orbit Gum Pins - Unnumbered (PR3)

This set, issued by Orbit Gum circa 1932, has the American Card Catalog designation PR3. The pins are identical to the PR2 set, except they are unnumbered.

		NM	EX	VG
	Complete Set (60):	3,750	1,850	1,100
	Common Player:	60.00	30.00	18.00
(1)	Dale Alexander	60.00	30.00	18.00
(2)	Ivy Andrews	60.00	30.00	18.00
(3)	Earl Averill	100.00	50.00	30.00
(4)	Dick Bartell	60.00	30.00	18.00
(5)	Wally Berger	60.00	30.00	18.00
(6)	George Blaeholder	60.00	30.00	18.00
(7)	Jack Burns	60.00	30.00	18.00
(8)	Guy Bush	60.00	30.00	18.00
(9)	Bruce Campbell	60.00	30.00	18.00
(10)	Bill Cissell	60.00	30.00	18.00
(11)	Lefty Clark	60.00	30.00	18.00
(12)	Mickey Cochrane	100.00	50.00	30.00
(13)	Phil Collins	60.00	30.00	18.00
(14)	"Kiki" Cuyler	100.00	50.00	30.00
(15)	Dizzy Dean	175.00	87.00	52.00
(16)	Jimmy Dykes	60.00	30.00	18.00
(17)	George Earnshaw	60.00	30.00	18.00
(18)	Woody English	60.00	30.00	18.00
(19)	Lew Fonseca	60.00	30.00	18.00
(20)	Jimmy (Jimmie) Foxx	175.00	87.00	52.00
(21)	Burleigh Grimes	100.00	50.00	30.00
(22)	Charlie Grimm	60.00	30.00	18.00
(23)	Lefty Grove	100.00	50.00	30.00
(24)	Frank Grube	60.00	30.00	18.00
(25)	Mule Haas	60.00	30.00	18.00
(26)	Bump Hadley	60.00	30.00	18.00
(27)	Chick Hafey	100.00	50.00	30.00
(28)	Jesse Haines	100.00	50.00	30.00
(29)	Bill Hallahan	60.00	30.00	18.00
(30)	Mel Harder	60.00	30.00	18.00
(31)	Gabby Hartnett	100.00	50.00	30.00
(32)	Babe Herman	65.00	32.00	19.50
(33)	Billy Herman	100.00	50.00	30.00
(34)	Rogers Hornsby	135.00	67.00	40.00
(35)	Roy Johnson	60.00	30.00	18.00
(36)	Smead Jolley	60.00	30.00	18.00
(37)	Billy Jurges	60.00	30.00	18.00
(38)	Willie Kamm	60.00	30.00	18.00
(39)	Mark Koenig	60.00	30.00	18.00
(40)	Jim Levey	60.00	30.00	18.00
(41)	Ernie Lombardi	100.00	50.00	30.00
(42)	Red Lucas	60.00	30.00	18.00
(43)	Ted Lyons	100.00	50.00	30.00
(44)	Connie Mack	100.00	50.00	30.00
(45)	Pat Malone	60.00	30.00	18.00
(46)	Pepper Martin	75.00	37.00	22.00
(47)	Marty McManus	60.00	30.00	18.00
(48)	Lefty O'Doul	80.00	40.00	24.00
(49)	Dick Porter	60.00	30.00	18.00
(50)	Carl Reynolds	60.00	30.00	18.00
(51)	Charlie Root	60.00	30.00	18.00
(52)	Bob Seeds	60.00	30.00	18.00
(53)	Al Simmons	100.00	50.00	30.00
(54)	Riggs Stephenson	60.00	30.00	18.00
(55)	Bud Tinning	60.00	30.00	18.00
(56)	Joe Vosmik	60.00	30.00	18.00
(57)	Rube Walberg	60.00	30.00	18.00
(58)	Paul Waner	100.00	50.00	30.00
(59)	Lon Warneke	60.00	30.00	18.00
(60)	Pinky Whitney	60.00	30.00	18.00

1937-39 Orcajo Cincinnati Reds Postcards (PC786)

Orcajo, a Dayton, Ohio, photo firm, issued a series of Reds player postcards (plus, inexplicably, Joe DiMaggio) from 1937-39. Besides those found with just the issuer's imprint on the back, some or all of the players' cards can be found with the advertising on front of the Val Decker Packing Co., a meat dealer, Metropolitan Clothing Co., and an inset photo of WHIO radio announcer Si Burick (the latter are the 1937 cards and have no Orcajo imprint on back, utilizing different photos than the 1938-39 cards). The 3-1/2" x 5-1/2" cards have glossy black-and-white player poses on front with the player's name overprinted. Backs have standard postcard indicia. A number of spelling errors and several variations exist. The unnumbered cards are checklisted here alphabetically; those with ads for the meat company, men's store or radio station are appropriately noted.

		NM	EX	VG
	Complete Set (37):	3,775	1,700	945.00
	Common Player:	100.00	45.00	25.00
(1)	Wally Berger	100.00	45.00	25.00
(2)	Bongiovanni (First name Nino.)	100.00	45.00	25.00
(3)	Frenchy Bordagaray	100.00	45.00	25.00
(4)	Joe Cascarella, Gene Schott (Val Decker only.)	100.00	45.00	25.00
(5)	Allan Cooke (Allen) (Val Decker only.)	100.00	45.00	25.00
(6)	Harry Craft (Also Val Decker.)	100.00	45.00	25.00
(7)	Kiki Cuyler (WHIO only.)	160.00	72.00	40.00
(8)	Ray Davis	100.00	45.00	25.00
(9)	Virgil Davis (Val Decker only.)	100.00	45.00	25.00
(10)	Paul Derringer (Also Val Decker.)	100.00	45.00	25.00
(11)	Joe DiMaggio	825.00	370.00	205.00
(12a)	Linus Frey (Also Val Decker.) (No right foot, large caption.)	100.00	45.00	25.00
(12b)	Linus Frey (Also Val Decker.) (Right foot shows, small caption.)	100.00	45.00	25.00
(13)	Lee Gamble	100.00	45.00	25.00
(14)	Ivan Goodman (Ival) (Also Val Decker.)	100.00	45.00	25.00
(15)	Hank Gowdy	100.00	45.00	25.00
(16)	Lee Grissom	100.00	45.00	25.00
(17a)	Willard Hershberger (Hershberger, name in white.) (Also Val Decker.)	100.00	45.00	25.00
(17b)	Willard Hershberger (Name in black.)	100.00	45.00	25.00

		NM	EX	VG
(18a)	Al Hollingsworth	100.00	45.00	25.00
(18b)	Al Hollingsworth (WHIO)	100.00	45.00	25.00
(18c)	Al Hollingsworth (Val Decker)	100.00	45.00	25.00
(19)	Hank Johnson	100.00	45.00	25.00
(20)	Edwin Joost	100.00	45.00	25.00
(21a)	Ernie Lombardi (Plain letters.) (Also Val Decker, Metro.)	160.00	72.00	40.00
(21b)	Ernie Lombardi (Fancy letters.) (Also Val Decker, Metro.)	160.00	72.00	40.00
(22)	Frank McCormick (Also Val Decker, Metro.)	100.00	45.00	25.00
(23)	Bill McKechnie (McKechnie)	145.00	65.00	36.00
(24)	Billy Meyers (Myers) (Also Val Decker.)	100.00	45.00	25.00
(25a)	Whitey Moore (Photo actually Bucky Walters.)	100.00	45.00	25.00
(25b)	Whitey Moore (Correct photo.)	100.00	45.00	25.00
(26)	Lew Riggs	100.00	45.00	25.00
(27)	Edd Roush (Val Decker only.)	145.00	65.00	36.00
(28a)	Leo Scarsella (Les)	160.00	72.00	40.00
(28b)	Les Scarcella (WHIO)	100.00	45.00	25.00
(29)	Gene Schott (WHIO)	100.00	45.00	25.00
(30)	Milburn Shoffner	100.00	45.00	25.00
(31)	Junior Thompson	100.00	45.00	25.00
(32a)	Johnny VanderMeer (Throwing) (Also Metro, Val Decker.)	175.00	79.00	44.00
(32b)	Johnny VanderMeer (Fielding)(Also Metro.)	175.00	79.00	44.00
(33)	Bucky Walters	100.00	45.00	25.00
(34)	Bill Werber	100.00	45.00	25.00
(35)	Dick West	100.00	45.00	25.00
(36)	Jimmie Wilson	100.00	45.00	25.00
(37)	Cincinnati Reds composite team card.	100.00	45.00	25.00

1933 Oriental Theatre

To advertise its movie schedule for the week of June 17-23, as well as a Father's Day prize drawing, the Oriental Theatre (location unknown) printed its message on the back of a 1929 Kashin Publications (R316) card or cards. The extent to which this overprinting was undertaken is unknown.

	NM	EX	VG
Ed "Bing" Miller	125.00	62.50	37.50

1912 A.F. Orr Louis Sockalexis Photocard

This 3-1/2" x 5-1/2" sepia photocard carries the copyright of A.F. Orr of Old Town, Maine, hometown of the original Cleveland Indian. At the time of the card's issue, the fallen diamond star was operating a ferry and probably commissioned this image for sale to tourists.

	NM	EX	VG
Louis Sockalexis	2,000	1,000	600.00

1963 Otto Milk

The attributed issue date of this commemorative milk carton is approximate. A 4" x 8" panel on the front of the milk carton has a picture and history of Honus Wagner printed in red and blue. Wagner is the only ballplayer in the milk carton series honoring Western Pennsylvania celebrities.

	NM	EX	VG
(1) Honus Wagner (Complete carton.)	250.00	125.00	75.00
(1) Honus Wagner (Cut panel.)	60.00	30.00	18.00

1938 Our National Game Pins

This unnumbered 30-pin set issued circa 1938 carries the American Card Catalog designation of PM8. The pins, which measure 7/8" in diameter, have a bendable "tab" rather than a pin back. The player photo is printed in blue-and-white. The player's name and team are printed at bottom. The pins were originally sold on a square of cardboard decorated with stars and stripes and imprinted "OUR NATIONAL GAME" above the pin, and "A BASEBALL HERO" below. A large number of the pins, complete with their cardboard backing, were found in a hoard in Oklahoma in the early 1990s.

		NM	EX	VG
Complete Set (30):		1,200	600.00	350.00
Common Player:		20.00	10.00	6.00
(1)	Wally Berger	20.00	10.00	6.00
(2)	Lou Chiozza	20.00	10.00	6.00
(3)	Joe Cronin	40.00	20.00	12.00
(4)	Frank Crosetti	25.00	12.50	7.50
(5)	Jerome (Dizzy) Dean	75.00	37.00	22.00
(6)	Frank DeMaree (Demaree)	20.00	10.00	6.00
(7)	Joe DiMaggio	100.00	50.00	30.00
(8)	Bob Feller	65.00	32.00	19.50
(9)	Jimmy Foxx (Jimmie)	75.00	37.00	22.00
(10)	Lou Gehrig	100.00	50.00	30.00
(11)	Charles Gehringer	50.00	25.00	15.00
(12)	Lefty Gomez	40.00	20.00	12.00
(13)	Hank Greenberg	65.00	32.00	19.50
(14)	Irving (Bump) Hadley	20.00	10.00	6.00
(15)	Leo Hartnett	40.00	20.00	12.00
(16)	Carl Hubbell	50.00	25.00	15.00
(17)	John (Buddy) Lewis	20.00	10.00	6.00
(18)	Gus Mancuso	20.00	10.00	6.00
(19)	Joe McCarthy	40.00	20.00	12.00
(20)	Joe Medwick	40.00	20.00	12.00
(21)	Joe Moore	20.00	10.00	6.00
(22)	Mel Ott	50.00	25.00	15.00
(23)	Jake Powell	20.00	10.00	6.00
(24)	Jimmy Ripple	20.00	10.00	6.00
(25)	Red Ruffing	40.00	20.00	12.00
(26)	Hal Schumacher	20.00	10.00	6.00
(27)	George Selkirk	20.00	10.00	6.00
(28)	"Al" Simmons	40.00	20.00	12.00
(29)	Bill Terry	40.00	20.00	12.00
(30)	Harold Trosky	20.00	10.00	6.00

1936 Overland Candy Co. (R301)

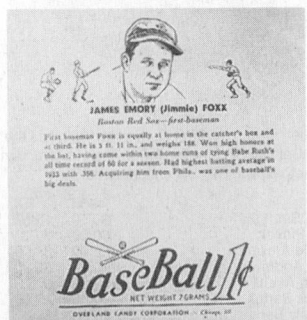

Used as wrappers for a piece of penny candy, these 5" x 5-1/4" waxed papers are usually found with resultant folds and creases, though unfolded examples are known. Printed in dark blue, the top of the wrapper features a line drawing portrait of the player, his formal name and nickname, team, position and career summary. The unnumbered wrappers are checklisted here alphabetically.

		NM	EX	VG
Complete Set (60):		45,000	20,000	9,000
Common Player:		650.00	300.00	130.00
(1)	Melo (Mel) Almada	650.00	300.00	130.00
(2)	Lucius B. (Luke) Appling	900.00	400.00	180.00

		NM	EX	VG
(3)	Howard Earl Averill	900.00	400.00	180.00
(4)	Walter Antone (Wally) Berger	650.00	300.00	130.00
(5)	Henry John (Zeke) Bonura	650.00	300.00	130.00
(6)	Dolph Camilli	650.00	300.00	130.00
(7)	Philip Joseph (Phil) Cavarretta	650.00	300.00	130.00
(8)	William Ben (Chappy) Chapman	650.00	300.00	130.00
(9)	Harland Clift (First name Harlond.)	650.00	300.00	130.00
(10a)	John Walter (Johnny) Cooney (Bees)	650.00	300.00	130.00
(10b)	John Walter (Johnny) Cooney (Dodgers)	650.00	300.00	130.00
(11)	Harry Danning	650.00	300.00	130.00
(12)	William N. (Bill) Dickey (Middle initial is N.)	950.00	425.00	190.00
(13a)	William J. (Bill) Dietrich (Athletics)	650.00	300.00	130.00
(13b)	William J. (Bill) Dietrich (White Sox)	650.00	300.00	130.00
(14)	Joseph (Deadpan Joe) DiMaggio	3,000	1,350	600.00
(15)	Wesley Cheek Ferrell	650.00	300.00	130.00
(16)	James Emory (Jimmie) Foxx	1,200	540.00	240.00
(17)	Henry Louis (Lou) Gehrig	3,150	1,425	630.00
(18)	Charles Leonard (Charley) Gehringer	900.00	400.00	180.00
(19)	Jose Luis (Chile) Gomez	650.00	300.00	130.00
(20)	Vernon (Lefty) Gomez	900.00	400.00	180.00
(21)	Joe Gordon	650.00	300.00	130.00
(22)	Henry (Hank) Greenberg	1,200	540.00	240.00
(23)	Robert Moses (Lefty) Grove	950.00	425.00	190.00
(24)	George W. (Mule) Haas	650.00	300.00	130.00
(25)	Ralston Burdett (Rollie) Hemsley	650.00	300.00	130.00
(26)	Michael Francis (Pinky) Higgins (Middle name Franklin.)	650.00	300.00	130.00
(27)	Oral Clyde (Hildy) Hildebrand	650.00	300.00	130.00
(28)	Robert Lee (Cherokee) Johnson	650.00	300.00	130.00
(29)	Baxter Byerly (Buck) Jordan	650.00	300.00	130.00
(30)	Ken Keltner	650.00	300.00	130.00
(31)	Fabian Kowalik	650.00	300.00	130.00
(32)	Harry A. Lavagetto	650.00	300.00	130.00
(33)	Anthony Michael (Poosh 'em Up) Lazzeri	900.00	400.00	180.00
(34)	Samuel A. Leslie	650.00	300.00	130.00
(35)	Dan (Slug) Lithwhiler (Last name Litwhiler.)	650.00	300.00	130.00
(36)	Theodore A. (Ted) Lyons	900.00	400.00	180.00
(37)	George McQuinn	650.00	300.00	130.00
(38)	John Robert (Skippy) Mize	900.00	400.00	180.00
(39)	Terry Moore	650.00	300.00	130.00
(40)	Charles Solomon (Buddy) Myer	650.00	300.00	130.00
(41)	Louis Norman (Buck) Newsom	650.00	300.00	130.00
(42)	Bill Nicholson	650.00	300.00	130.00
(43)	Raymond Pepper	650.00	300.00	130.00
(44)	Frank A. (Pity) Pytlak	650.00	300.00	130.00
(45)	Raymond Allen (Rip) Radcliff	650.00	300.00	130.00
(46)	Peter (Pete) Reiser (Correct name Harold Patrick.)	650.00	300.00	130.00
(47)	Carl Nettles (Sheeps) Reynolds	650.00	300.00	130.00
(48)	Robert Abial (Red) Rolfe	650.00	300.00	130.00
(49)	Lynwood Thomas (Schoolboy) Rowe	650.00	300.00	130.00
(50)	Aloysius Harry (Al) Simmons	900.00	400.00	180.00
(51)	Cecil Howard Travis (Middle name is Howell.)	650.00	300.00	130.00
(52)	Harold Arthus (Hal) Trosky	650.00	300.00	130.00
(53)	Joseph Franklin (Joe) Vosmik	650.00	300.00	130.00
(54)	Harold Burton (Rabbit) Warstler	650.00	300.00	130.00
(55)	William M. (Bill) Werber	650.00	300.00	130.00
(56)	Max West	650.00	300.00	130.00
(57)	Samuel F. (Sam) West	650.00	300.00	130.00
(58)	Whitlow (Whit) Wyatt	650.00	300.00	130.00

1921 Oxford Confectionery (E253)

Issued in 1921 by Oxford Confectionery of Oxford, Pa., this 20-card set was printed on thin paper and distributed with caramels. Each card measures 1-5/8" x 2-3/4" and features a black-and-white player photo with the player's name and team printed in a white band along the bottom. The back carries a checklist of the players in the set, 14 of whom are now in the Hall of Fame. The set is designated as E253 in the ACC.

		NM	EX	VG
Complete Set (20):		35,000	15,750	7,000
Common Player:		1,000	450.00	200.00
(1)	Grover Alexander	1,800	810.00	360.00

		NM	EX	VG
(2)	Dave Bancroft	1,200	540.00	240.00
(3)	Max Carey	1,200	540.00	240.00
(4)	Ty Cobb	6,000	2,700	1,200
(5)	Eddie Collins	1,200	540.00	240.00
(6)	Frankie Frisch	1,200	540.00	240.00
(7)	Burleigh Grimes	1,200	540.00	240.00
(8)	"Bill" Holke (Walter)	1,000	450.00	200.00
(9)	Rogers Hornsby	1,800	810.00	360.00
(10)	Walter Johnson	3,000	1,350	600.00
(11)	Lee Meadows	1,000	450.00	200.00
(12)	Cy Perkins	1,000	450.00	200.00
(13)	Derrill Pratt	1,000	450.00	200.00
(14)	Ed Rousch (Roush)	1,200	540.00	240.00
(15)	"Babe" Ruth	12,000	5,400	2,400
(16)	Ray Schalk	1,200	540.00	240.00
(17)	George Sisler	1,200	540.00	240.00
(18)	Tris Speaker	1,800	810.00	360.00
(19)	Cy Williams	1,000	450.00	200.00
(20)	Whitey Witt	1,000	450.00	200.00

P

1958 Packard-Bell

Issued by the "world's largest seller of TVs, radios and hi-fis," this set was distributed in California and features members of the newly arrived Los Angeles Dodgers and San Francisco Giants. The 3-1/2" x 5-1/2" black-and-white cards are unnumbered, checklisted here alphabetically.

		NM	EX	VG
Complete Set (7):		1,500	750.00	450.00
Common Player:		100.00	50.00	30.00
(1)	Walter Alston	125.00	65.00	35.00
(2)	John A. Antonelli	100.00	50.00	30.00
(3)	Jim Gilliam	125.00	65.00	35.00
(4)	Gil Hodges	200.00	100.00	60.00
(5)	Willie Mays	800.00	400.00	240.00
(6)	Bill Rigney	100.00	50.00	30.00
(7)	Hank Sauer	100.00	50.00	30.00

1978 Papa Gino's Discs

 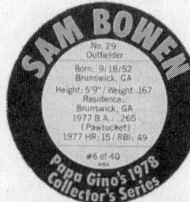

This promotion was largely confined to the Boston area, as 25 of the 40 players represented are Red Sox, the other 15 are all from American League teams. The 3-3/8" discs were given away with the purchase of soft drinks at the restaurant chain. Fronts have player portraits at center with name in the dark blue border at top and team below. Photos have the uniform logos airbrushed away because the discs were licensed only by the players' union, not MLB. Backs retain the color scheme with player data, previous season's stats, uniform and card numbers, sponsor's ad, etc.

		NM	EX	VG
Complete Set (40):		20.00	10.00	6.00
Common Player:		2.00	1.00	.60
1	Allen Ripley	2.00	1.00	.60
2	Jerry Remy	2.00	1.00	.60
3	Jack Brohamer	2.00	1.00	.60
4	Butch Hobson	2.00	1.00	.60
5	Dennis Eckersley	3.50	1.75	1.00
6	Sam Bowen	2.00	1.00	.60
7	Rick Burleson	2.00	1.00	.60
8	Carl Yastrzemski	5.00	2.50	1.50
9	Bill Lee	2.00	1.00	.60
10	Bob Montgomery	2.00	1.00	.60
11	Dick Drago	2.00	1.00	.60
12	Bob Stanley	2.00	1.00	.60
13	Fred Kendall	2.00	1.00	.60
14	Jim Rice	3.00	1.50	.90
15	George Scott	2.00	1.00	.60
16	Tom Burgmeier	2.00	1.00	.60
17	Frank Duffy	2.00	1.00	.60
18	Jim Wright	2.00	1.00	.60
19	Fred Lynn	2.00	1.00	.60

		NM	EX	VG
20	Bob Bailey	2.00	1.00	.60
21	Mike Torrez	2.00	1.00	.60
22	Bill Campbell	2.00	1.00	.60
23	Luis Tiant	2.00	1.00	.60
24	Dwight Evans	2.00	1.00	.60
25	Carlton Fisk	4.00	2.00	1.25
26	Reggie Jackson	5.00	2.50	1.50
27	Thurman Munson	3.50	1.75	1.00
28	Ron Guidry	2.00	1.00	.60
29	Bruce Bochte	2.00	1.00	.60
30	Richie Zisk	2.00	1.00	.60
31	Jim Palmer	4.00	2.00	1.25
32	Mark Fidrych	2.50	1.25	.70
33	Frank Tanana	2.00	1.00	.60
34	Buddy Bell	2.00	1.00	.60
35	Rod Carew	4.00	2.00	1.25
36	George Brett	7.50	3.75	2.25
37	Ralph Garr	2.00	1.00	.60
38	Larry Hisle	2.00	1.00	.60
39	Mitchell Page	2.00	1.00	.60
40	John Mayberry	2.00	1.00	.60

1974 Bob Parker 2nd Best

Star players who came in second, often to lesser-known players, in various statistical categories between 1899-1955 are featured in this collectors issue from Bob Parker. The blank-backed, black-and-white cards measure an unusual 3" x 8" and feature the story of the 1-2 finish in cartoon form. The unnumbered cards are listed here in chronological order.

		NM	EX	VG
Complete Set (25):		55.00	25.00	15.00
Common Player:		3.00	1.50	.90
(1)	Jesse Burkett, Ed Delahanty (1899)	3.00	1.50	.90
(2)	Hans Wagner, Cy Seymour (1905)	4.00	2.00	1.25
(3)	Gavvy Cravath, Jake Daubert (1913)	3.00	1.50	.90
(4)	Joe Jackson, Ty Cobb (1913)	10.00	5.00	3.00
(5)	Eddie Collins, Ty Cobb (1914)	4.00	2.00	1.25
(6)	Babe Ruth, Heinie Manush (1926)	7.50	3.75	2.25
(7)	Chick Hafey, Jim Bottomley, Hack Wilson (1928)	3.00	1.50	.90
(8)	Paul Waner, Rogers Hornsby (1928)	3.00	1.50	.90
(9)	Babe Herman, Lefty O'Doul (1929)	3.00	1.50	.90
(10)	Al Simmons, Lew Fonseca (1929)	3.00	1.50	.90
(11)	Lou Gehrig, Babe Ruth (1930)	10.00	5.00	3.00
(12)	Babe Herman, Bill Terry (1930)	3.00	1.50	.90
(13)	Chuck Klein, Hack Wilson (1930)	3.00	1.50	.90
(14)	Jim Bottomley, Bill Terry, Chick Hafey (1931)	3.00	1.50	.90
(15)	Jimmy (Jimmie) Foxx, Dale Alexander (1932)	3.00	1.50	.90
(16)	Spud Davis, Chuck Klein (1933)	3.00	1.50	.90
(17)	Heinie Manush, Jimmy Foxx (1933)	3.00	1.50	.90
(18)	Mel Ott, Wally Berger (1935)	3.00	1.50	.90
(19)	Joe Vosmik, Buddy Myer (1935)	3.00	1.50	.90
(20)	Blimp Phelps, Paul Waner (1936)	3.00	1.50	.90
(21)	Bobby Doerr, Lou Boudreau (1944)	3.00	1.50	.90
(22)	Stan Musial, Dixie Walker (1944)	4.00	2.00	1.25
(23)	George Kell, Billy Goodman (1950)	3.00	1.50	.90
(24)	Al Rosen, Mickey Vernon (1953)	3.00	1.50	.90
(25)	Vic Power, Al Kaline (1955)	3.00	1.50	.90

1976 Bob Parker More Baseball Cartoons

This collectors' issue showcased the pen and ink artwork of Ohio cartoonist Bob Parker on cards featuring current and former ballplayers from the great to the obscure. Cards are in 3-1/2" x 5" format with black-and-white fronts and blank backs.

		NM	EX	VG
Complete Set (24):		65.00	32.50	20.00
Common Card:		3.00	1.50	.90
1	Hank Aaron, Babe Ruth (All-Time HR Specialists)	7.50	3.75	2.25
2	Ernie Banks	4.00	2.00	1.25
3	Rod Carew	3.00	1.50	.90
4	Joe DiMaggio	15.00	7.50	4.50
5	Doug Flynn	3.00	1.50	.90
6	Mike Garcia	3.00	1.50	.90
7	Steve Garvey, Greg Luzinski (All-Stars)	3.00	1.50	.90
8	Lou Gehrig	15.00	7.50	4.50
9	Chuck Klein, Hack Wilson (Hall of Famers?)	3.00	1.50	.90
10	Don Larsen	3.00	1.50	.90
11	Fred Lynn	3.00	1.50	.90
12	Roy Majtyka	3.00	1.50	.90
13	Pepper Martin	3.00	1.50	.90
14	Christy Mathewson	5.00	2.50	1.50
15	Cal McVey	3.00	1.50	.90
16	Tony Perez	3.00	1.50	.90
17	Lou Gehrig, Babe Ruth (Great Moments)	15.00	7.50	4.50
18	Everett Scott	3.00	1.50	.90
19	Bobby Thomson	3.00	1.50	.90
20	Ted Williams (1939)	7.50	3.75	2.25
21	Ted Williams (Great Moments)	7.50	3.75	2.25
22	Bill Madlock	3.00	1.50	.90
23	Henry Chadwick, Buck Ewing, Albert Spalding, Honus Wagner (Hall of Famers)	3.00	1.50	.90
---	Checklist	3.00	1.50	.90

1977 Bob Parker Cincinnati Reds

In the late 1970s, Ohio cartoonist Bob Parker drew a series of Reds feature cartoons for the weekly "Reds Alert." Later, he assembled two groups of those cartoons into collectors' issue card sets. The cards are black-and-white with blank backs. Fronts have portraits and/or action main drawings, usually with some cartoon figures included to draw attention to the player's career highlights. Size is 3-1/2" x 5". The unnumbered series is listed in alphabetical order.

		NM	EX	VG
Complete Set (48):		110.00	55.00	32.50
Common Player:		3.00	1.50	.90
UNNUMBERED SERIES (24):		55.00	25.00	15.00
(1)	Sparky Anderson	4.00	2.00	1.25
(2)	Wally Berger	3.00	1.50	.90
(3)	Pedro Borbon	3.00	1.50	.90
(4)	Rube Bressler	3.00	1.50	.90
(5)	Gordy Coleman	3.00	1.50	.90
(6)	Dave Concepcion	3.00	1.50	.90
(7)	Harry Craft	3.00	1.50	.90
(8)	Hugh Critz	3.00	1.50	.90
(9)	Dan Driessen	3.00	1.50	.90
(10)	Pat Duncan	3.00	1.50	.90
(11)	Lonnie Frey	3.00	1.50	.90
(12)	Ival Goodman	3.00	1.50	.90
(13)	Heinie Groh	3.00	1.50	.90
(14)	Noodles Hahn	3.00	1.50	.90
(15)	Mike Lum	3.00	1.50	.90
(16)	Bill McKechnie	3.00	1.50	.90
(17)	Pat Moran	3.00	1.50	.90
(18)	Billy Myers	3.00	1.50	.90
(19)	Gary Nolan	3.00	1.50	.90
(20)	Fred Norman	3.00	1.50	.90
(21)	Jim O'Toole	3.00	1.50	.90
(22)	Vada Pinson	4.00	2.00	1.25
(23)	Bucky Walters	3.00	1.50	.90
(24)	Checklist	3.00	1.50	.90
NUMBERED SERIES (24):		60.00	30.00	18.00

1	Ted Kluszewski	6.00	3.00	1.75
2	Johnny Bench	10.00	5.00	3.00
3	Jim Maloney	3.00	1.50	.90
4	Bubbles Hargrave	3.00	1.50	.90
5	Don Gullett	3.00	1.50	.90
6	Joe Nuxhall	4.00	2.00	1.25
7	Edd Roush	3.00	1.50	.90
8	Wally Post	3.00	1.50	.90
9	George Wright	3.00	1.50	.90
10	George Foster	3.00	1.50	.90
11	Pete Rose	15.00	7.50	4.50
12	Red Lucas	3.00	1.50	.90
13	Joe Morgan	4.00	2.00	1.25
14	Eppa Rixey	3.00	1.50	.90
15	Bill Werber	3.00	1.50	.90
16	Frank Robinson	6.00	3.00	1.75
17	Dolf Luque	4.00	2.00	1.25
18	Paul Derringer	3.00	1.50	.90
19	Frank McCormick	3.00	1.50	.90
20	Ken Griffey	3.00	1.50	.90
21	Jack Billingham	3.00	1.50	.90
22	Larry Kopf	3.00	1.50	.90
23	Ernie Lombardi	3.00	1.50	.90
24	Johnny Vander Meer	3.00	1.50	.90

1977-81 Bob Parker Hall of Fame

This is one of many collectors issues produced in the mid to late 1970s by midwestern sports artist Bob Parker. The 3-3/8" x 5-1/2" cards are printed in sepia on tan cardboard; they are blank-backed. Fronts have a portrait drawing of the player, with career highlights in cartoon form. Three series were issued: #1-54 in 1977; #55-77 in 1980 and #78-100 in 1981. A header card was issued with each series.

		NM	EX	VG
Complete Set (103):		125.00	65.00	35.00
Common Player:		3.00	1.50	.90
First Series Set (55):		50.00	25.00	15.00
---	First Series Header	1.00	.50	.30
1	Grover Alexander	3.00	1.50	.90
2	Cap Anson	3.00	1.50	.90
3	Luke Appling	3.00	1.50	.90
4	Ernie Banks	4.00	2.00	1.25
5	Chief Bender	3.00	1.50	.90
6	Jim Bottomley	3.00	1.50	.90
7	Dan Brouthers	3.00	1.50	.90
8	Morgan Bulkeley	3.00	1.50	.90
9	Roy Campanella	7.50	3.75	2.25
10	Alexander Cartwright	3.00	1.50	.90
11	Henry Chadwick	3.00	1.50	.90
12	John Clarkson	3.00	1.50	.90
13	Ty Cobb	10.00	5.00	3.00
14	Eddie Collins	3.00	1.50	.90
16	Charles Comiskey	3.00	1.50	.90
17	Sam Crawford	3.00	1.50	.90
18	Dizzy Dean	4.00	2.00	1.25
19	Joe DiMaggio	16.00	8.00	4.75
20	Buck Ewing	3.00	1.50	.90
21	Bob Feller	4.00	2.00	1.25
22	Lou Gehrig	16.00	8.00	4.75
23	Goose Goslin	3.00	1.50	.90
24	Burleigh Grimes	3.00	1.50	.90
25	Chick Hafey	3.00	1.50	.90
26	Rogers Hornsby	3.00	1.50	.90
27	Carl Hubbell	3.00	1.50	.90
28	Miller Huggins	3.00	1.50	.90
29	Tim Keefe	3.00	1.50	.90
30	Mike Kelly	3.00	1.50	.90
31	Nap Lajoie	3.00	1.50	.90
32	Freddie Lindstrom	3.00	1.50	.90
33	Connie Mack	3.00	1.50	.90
34	Mickey Mantle	25.00	12.50	7.50
35	Heinie Manush	3.00	1.50	.90
36	Joe McGinnity	3.00	1.50	.90
37	John McGraw	3.00	1.50	.90
38	Ed Plank	3.00	1.50	.90
39	Eppa Rixey	3.00	1.50	.90
40	Jackie Robinson	12.00	6.00	3.50
41	Edd Roush	3.00	1.50	.90
42	Babe Ruth	20.00	10.00	6.00
43	Al Simmons	3.00	1.50	.90
44	Al Spalding	3.00	1.50	.90
45	Tris Speaker	3.00	1.50	.90
46	Casey Stengel	3.00	1.50	.90
47	Bill Terry	3.00	1.50	.90
48	Rube Waddell	3.00	1.50	.90
49	Honus Wagner	5.00	2.50	1.50
50	Paul Waner	3.00	1.50	.90
51	John Montgomery Ward	3.00	1.50	.90
52	Ted Williams	10.00	5.00	3.00
53	George Wright	3.00	1.50	.90
54	Harry Wright	3.00	1.50	.90
Second Series Set (24):		40.00	20.00	12.00
---	Second Series Header	1.00	.50	.30
55	Mordecai Brown	3.00	1.50	.90
56	Frank Chance	3.00	1.50	.90

57	Candy Cummings	3.00	1.50	.90
58	Frank Frisch	3.00	1.50	.90
59	Gabby Hartnett	3.00	1.50	.90
60	Billy Herman	3.00	1.50	.90
61	Waite Hoyt	3.00	1.50	.90
62	Walter Johnson	5.00	2.50	1.50
63	Kenesaw Landis	3.00	1.50	.90
64	Rube Marquard	3.00	1.50	.90
65	Christy Mathewson	6.00	3.00	1.75
66	Eddie Mathews	3.00	1.50	.90
67	Willie Mays	10.00	5.00	3.00
68	Bill McKechnie	3.00	1.50	.90
69	Stan Musial	7.50	3.75	2.25
70	Mel Ott	3.00	1.50	.90
71	Satchel Paige	7.50	3.75	2.25
72	Robin Roberts	3.00	1.50	.90
73	George Sisler	3.00	1.50	.90
74	Warren Spahn	3.00	1.50	.90
75	Joe Tinker	3.00	1.50	.90
76	Dazzy Vance	3.00	1.50	.90
77	Cy Young	6.00	3.00	1.75
Third Series Set (24):		40.00	20.00	12.00
---	Third Series Header	1.00	.50	.30
78	Home Run Baker	3.00	1.50	.90
79	Yogi Berra	4.00	2.00	1.25
80	Max Carey	3.00	1.50	.90
81	Roberto Clemente	16.00	8.00	4.75
82	Mickey Cochrane	3.00	1.50	.90
83	Roger Connor	3.00	1.50	.90
84	Joe Cronin	3.00	1.50	.90
85	Kiki Cuyler	3.00	1.50	.90
86	Johnny Evers	3.00	1.50	.90
87	Jimmie Foxx	3.00	1.50	.90
88	Charlie Gehringer	3.00	1.50	.90
89	Lefty Gomez	3.00	1.50	.90
90	Jesse Haines	3.00	1.50	.90
91	Will Harridge	3.00	1.50	.90
92	Monte Irvin	3.00	1.50	.90
93	Addie Joss	3.00	1.50	.90
94	Al Kaline	3.00	1.50	.90
95	Sandy Koufax	10.00	5.00	3.00
96	Rabbit Maranville	3.00	1.50	.90
97	Jim O'Rourke	3.00	1.50	.90
98	Wilbert Robinson	3.00	1.50	.90
99	Pie Traynor	3.00	1.50	.90
100	Zack Wheat	3.00	1.50	.90

1968-70 Partridge Meats Reds

These cards were produced in conjunction with Reds' autograph appearances at Kroger food stores in the Cincinnati area. Players' service with the Reds indicates this set was issued over a period of several years. Similar cards are known for other Cincinnati pro sports teams. The 1968 cards measure 4" x 5" and feature a black-and-white player photo set against a borderless white background. The player's name and team and the word "Likes" are printed in black, the ad for the issuing meat company at bottom is printed in red. Cards have a blank back. The 1969-70 cards are in the same format but in 3-3/4" x 5-1/2" format. The unnumbered cards are checklisted here in alphabetical order.

		NM	EX	VG
Complete Set (11):		500.00	250.00	150.00
Common Player:		20.00	10.00	6.00
(1)	Ted Abernathy	40.00	20.00	12.00
(2)	John Bench	50.00	25.00	15.00
(3)	Jimmy Bragan	20.00	10.00	6.00
(4)	Dave Bristol	40.00	20.00	12.00
(5)	Tommy Helms	40.00	20.00	12.00
(6)	Gary Nolan	20.00	10.00	6.00
(7)	Milt Pappas	40.00	20.00	12.00
(8)	Don Pavletich	40.00	20.00	12.00
(9)	Mel Queen	40.00	20.00	12.00
(10)	Pete Rose	150.00	75.00	45.00
(11)	Jim Stewart	40.00	20.00	12.00

1972 Partridge Meats Reds

Similar in format to the meat company's 1968-70 issue, these later cards are in a slightly different size - 3-3/4" x 5-1/2". The ad on the '72 cards reads "Photo courtesy of Partridge Meats."

	NM	EX	VG
Complete Set (7):	225.00	110.00	65.00
Common Player:	30.00	15.00	9.00
(1) Don Gullett	30.00	15.00	9.00
(2) Lee May	30.00	15.00	9.00
(3) Denis Menke	30.00	15.00	9.00
(4) Jim Merritt	30.00	15.00	9.00
(5) Gary Nolan	30.00	15.00	9.00
(6) Tony Perez	60.00	30.00	18.00
(7) Bob Tolan	30.00	15.00	9.00

1922 Wm. Paterson

Believed to have been a Canadian candy premium, this 50-card set of 2" x 3-1/4" cards features portrait or posed action photos with wide white borders. Beneath the photo is a card number, player name, team, and in two lines, "Wm. Paterson, Limited / Brantford, Canada." Backs are blank. Two distinct types are seen, black-and-white and sepia, though the reason for the variations is unknown.

		NM	EX	VG
Complete Set (50):		60,000	24,000	12,000
Common Player:		475.00	200.00	100.00
1	Eddie Roush	1,000	400.00	200.00
2	Rube Marquard	1,000	400.00	200.00
3	Del Gainor	475.00	200.00	100.00
4	George Sisler	1,000	400.00	200.00
5	Joe Bush	475.00	200.00	100.00
6	Joe Oeschger	475.00	200.00	100.00
7	Willie Kamm	475.00	200.00	100.00
8	John Watson	475.00	200.00	100.00
9	Dolf Luque	550.00	225.00	110.00
10	Miller Huggins	1,000	400.00	200.00
11	Wally Schang	475.00	200.00	100.00
12	Bob Shawkey	475.00	200.00	100.00
13	Tris Speaker	1,750	700.00	350.00
14	Hugh McQuillan	475.00	200.00	100.00
15	"Long George" Kelly	1,000	400.00	200.00
16	Ray Schalk	1,000	400.00	200.00
17	Sam Jones	475.00	200.00	100.00
18	Grover Alexander	1,750	700.00	350.00
19	Bob Meusel	475.00	200.00	100.00
20	"Irish" Emil Meusel	475.00	200.00	100.00
21	Rogers Hornsby	1,750	700.00	350.00
22	Harry Heilmann	1,000	400.00	200.00
23	Heinie Groh	1,000	400.00	200.00
24	Frank Frisch	1,000	400.00	200.00
25	Babe Ruth	15,000	6,000	3,000
26	Jack Bentley	475.00	200.00	100.00
27	Everett Scott	475.00	200.00	100.00
28	Max Carey	1,000	400.00	200.00
29	Chick Fewster	475.00	200.00	100.00
30	Cy Williams	475.00	200.00	100.00
31	Burleigh Grimes	1,000	400.00	200.00
32	Waite Hoyt	1,000	400.00	200.00
33	Frank Snyder	475.00	200.00	100.00
34	Clyde Milan	475.00	200.00	100.00
35	Eddie Collins	1,000	400.00	200.00
36	Travis Jackson	475.00	200.00	100.00
37	Ken Williams	475.00	200.00	100.00
38	Dave Bancroft	1,000	400.00	200.00
39	Mike McNally	475.00	200.00	100.00
40	John McGraw	1,000	400.00	200.00
41	Art Nehf	475.00	200.00	100.00
42	"Rabbit" Maranville	1,000	400.00	200.00
43	Charlie Grimm	475.00	200.00	100.00
44	Joe Judge	475.00	200.00	100.00
45	Wally Pipp	475.00	200.00	100.00
46	Ty Cobb	10,000	4,000	2,000
47	Walter Johnson	3,000	1,200	600.00
48	Jake Daubert	475.00	200.00	100.00
49	Zack Wheat	1,000	400.00	200.00
50	Herb Pennock	1,000	400.00	200.00

1921 Pathe Freres Phonograph Co.

One of the rarest early-1920s Babe Ruth items is this premium photo issued by Pathe Freres Phonograph Co. of Brooklyn. Ruth is pictured bare-headed in a pinstriped uniform on the front of this approximately 7" x 9-1/4" card, printed in green and gray tones with a white border. A photo credit to White Studios of New York is given on the front and there is a facsimile autograph at bottom front. The black-and-white back has a listing of Ruth's 1920 homers in a box at left, and a Pathe at bottom-right.

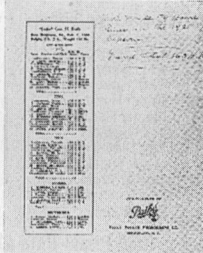

	NM	EX	VG
Babe Ruth	3,500	1,750	1,050

1910 PC796 Sepia Postcards

The manufacturer of these sepia-toned 3-1/2" x 5-1/2" postcards is unknown, but most of the photos utilized are familiar from other card issues of the era. Fronts have the player name at bottom in fancy capital letters. Backs have a standard divided postcard indicia. The set was given the PC796 designation in the "American Card Catalog." The unnumbered cards are checklisted here alphabetically.

		NM	EX	VG
Complete Set (25):		22,500	9,000	4,500
Common Player:		300.00	120.00	60.00
(1)	Roger Bresnahan	600.00	240.00	120.00
(2)	Al Bridwell	300.00	120.00	60.00
(3)	Mordecai Brown	600.00	240.00	120.00
(4)	Frank Chance	600.00	240.00	120.00
(5)	Hal Chase	450.00	180.00	90.00
(6)	Ty Cobb	4,250	1,700	850.00
(7)	Ty Cobb, Hanus Wagner	3,750	1,500	750.00
(8)	Eddie Collins	600.00	240.00	120.00
(9)	Sam Crawford	600.00	240.00	120.00
(10)	Art Devlin	300.00	120.00	60.00
(11)	Red Dooin	300.00	120.00	60.00
(12)	Johnny Evers, Germany Schaefer	400.00	160.00	80.00
(13)	Sam Frock	300.00	120.00	60.00
(14)	George Gibson	300.00	120.00	60.00
(15)	Artie Hoffman (Hofman)	300.00	120.00	60.00
(16)	Walter Johnson	1,200	480.00	240.00
(17)	Nap Lajoie	600.00	240.00	120.00
(18)	Harry Lord	300.00	120.00	60.00
(19)	Christy Mathewson	2,000	800.00	400.00
(20)	Orval Overall	300.00	120.00	60.00
(21)	Eddie Plank	600.00	240.00	120.00
(22)	Tris Speaker	750.00	300.00	150.00
(23)	Gabby Street	300.00	120.00	60.00
(24)	Honus Wagner	3,000	1,200	600.00
(25)	Ed Walsh	600.00	240.00	120.00

1869 Peck & Snyder Cincinnati Red Stockings - Small

Many consider this to be the first true baseball card in that it was produced in large quantities (relative to the cabinets and carte de visites of the era) and offered to firms wishing to place their advertising on the back. The 3-15/16" x 2-3/8" card features a sepia team photo on front of baseball's first real professional team, including Hall of Famers George and Harry

Wright. The Peck & Snyder ad back is the most commonly found, but others are known, including a back which lists only the team's line-up.

	NM	EX	VG
Cincinnati Red Stocking Team	25,000	15,000	10,000

1869 Peck & Snyder Cincinnati Red Stockings - Large

Many consider this to be the first true baseball card in that it was produced in large quantities (relative to the cabinets and carte de visites of the era) and offered to firms wishing to place their advertising on the back. The 4-3/16" x 3-5/16" card features a sepia team photo on front of baseball's first real professional team, including Hall of Famers George and Harry Wright. On this larger format, the players are identified on front with the team name in ornate black or red (slightly scarcer) type at bottom. Backs have been seen with ads for New York "Sportsman's "Emporium" along with a caricature of a bearded ballplayer, and for "The New York City Base Ball & Skate Emporium," with a large illsutration of an ice skate.

	NM	EX	VG
Cincinnati Red Stocking Team	35,000	25,000	18,000

1870 Peck & Snyder Chicago White Stockings

Using popular baseball teams of the day as an advertising medium, this apporoximately 4" x 2-3/4" black-and-white card pictures and identifies on front the 1870 Chicago White Stockings of pre-National Association days. On back is an ad for Peck & Snyder of New York City.

	NM	EX	VG
Chicago White Stockings	20,000	12,000	10,000

1870 Peck & Snyder New York Mutuals

Using popular baseball teams of the day as an advertising medium, this apporoximately 4" x 2-3/4" black-and-white card pictures and identifies on front the 1870 New York Mutuals of pre-National Association days. On back is a cartoon ad for Peck & Snyder of New York City.

	NM	EX	VG
New York Mutuals James Creighton	20,000	12,000	10,000

1870 Peck & Snyder Philadelphia Athletics

A composite photo of the players in street clothes is featured on this promotional card for the New York City sporting goods dealer whose advertising appears on back.

Philadelphia Athletics (Sold for $2,780 in 10/01 auction in Poor condition.)

1963 Pepsi-Cola Colt .45's

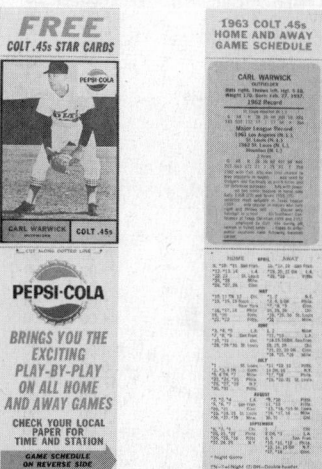

This issue was distributed regionally in Texas in bottled six-packs of Pepsi. The cards were issued on 2-3/8" x 9-1/8" panels. A 2-3/8" x 3-3/4" card was printed on each panel, which also included promos for Pepsi and the Colt .45's, as well as a team schedule. Card fronts are black-and-white posed action photos with blue and red trim. Backs offer player statistics and career highlights. The John Bateman card was apparently never distributed publicly and is among the rarest baseball cards of the 1960s. The unnumbered cards are checklisted here alphabetically. Values shown are for complete panels with top and bottom tabs; those without are valued about 25 percent.

		NM	EX	VG
Complete Set (16):		800.00	400.00	240.00
Common Player:		10.00	5.00	3.00
(1)	Bob Aspromonte	10.00	5.00	3.00
(2)	John Bateman (SP)	2,500	1,250	750.00
(3)	Bob Bruce	10.00	5.00	3.00
(4)	Jim Campbell	10.00	5.00	3.00
(5)	Dick Farrell	10.00	5.00	3.00
(6)	Ernie Fazio	10.00	5.00	3.00
(7)	Carroll Hardy	10.00	5.00	3.00
(8)	J.C. Hartman	10.00	5.00	3.00
(9)	Ken Johnson	10.00	5.00	3.00
(10)	Bob Lillis (SP)	375.00	185.00	110.00
(11)	Don McMahon	10.00	5.00	3.00
(12)	Pete Runnels	10.00	5.00	3.00
(13)	Al Spangler	10.00	5.00	3.00
(14)	Rusty Staub	35.00	17.50	10.00
(15)	Johnny Temple	10.00	5.00	3.00
(16)	Carl Warwick (SP)	300.00	150.00	90.00

1977 Pepsi-Cola Baseball Stars

An Ohio regional promotion (the checklist is extra heavy with Indians and Reds players), large numbers of these cards found their way into hobby dealers' hands. Designed to be inserted into cartons of soda, the cards have a 3-3/8" diameter central disc attached with perforations to a baseball glove design. A tab beneath the glove contains the checklist (the card discs themselves are unnumbered) and a coupon on back for ordering a player t-shirt, the offer for which is made on the back of the player disc. The Players Association logo appears on front, but the producer, Mike Schechter Associates, did not seek licensing by Major League Baseball, with the result that uniform logos have been removed from the black-and-white player photos. Prices shown are for complete glove/disc/tab cards. Values for unattached player discs would be no more than one-half of those shown. The discs of Reggie Jackson and Mike Schmidt can be found with either orange, green, purple, light blue or sky blue side panels; the other player discs are known in only one color each.

		NM	EX	VG
Complete Set (72):		35.00	17.50	10.00
W/Color Variations (80):		75.00	37.50	22.50
Common Player:		1.00	.50	.30
1	Robin Yount	4.00	2.00	1.25
2	Rod Carew	4.00	2.00	1.25
3	Butch Wynegar	1.00	.50	.30
4	Manny Sanguillen	1.00	.50	.30
5	Mike Hargrove	1.00	.50	.30
6	Larvel (Larvell) Blanks	1.00	.50	.30
7	Jim Kern	1.00	.50	.30
8	Pat Dobson	1.00	.50	.30
9	Rico Carty	1.00	.50	.30
10	John Grubb	1.00	.50	.30
11	Buddy Bell	1.00	.50	.30
12	Rick Manning	1.00	.50	.30
13	Dennis Eckersley	4.00	2.00	1.25
14	Wayne Garland	1.00	.50	.30
15	Dave LaRoche	1.00	.50	.30
16	Rick Waits	1.00	.50	.30
17	Ray Fosse	1.00	.50	.30
18	Frank Duffy	1.00	.50	.30
19	Duane Kuiper	1.00	.50	.30
20	Jim Palmer	4.00	2.00	1.25
21	Fred Lynn	1.00	.50	.30
22	Carlton Fisk	4.00	2.00	1.25
23	Carl Yastrzemski	6.00	3.00	1.75
24	Nolan Ryan	17.50	8.75	5.25
25	Bobby Grich	1.00	.50	.30
26	Ralph Garr	1.00	.50	.30
27	Richie Zisk	1.00	.50	.30
28	Ron LeFlore	1.00	.50	.30
29	Rusty Staub	1.00	.50	.30
30	Mark Fidrych	1.50	.70	.45
31	Willie Horton	1.00	.50	.30
32	George Brett	10.00	5.00	3.00
33	Amos Otis	1.00	.50	.30
34a	Reggie Jackson (Green)	7.50	3.75	2.25
34b	Reggie Jackson (Light blue.)	7.50	3.75	2.25
34c	Reggie Jackson (Orange)	7.50	3.75	2.25
34d	Reggie Jackson (Purple)	7.50	3.75	2.25
34e	Reggie Jackson (Sky blue.)	7.50	3.75	2.25
35	Don Gullett	1.00	.50	.30
36	Thurman Munson	3.00	1.50	.90
37	Al Hrabosky	1.00	.50	.30
38	Mike Tyson	1.00	.50	.30
39	Gene Tenace	1.00	.50	.30
40	George Hendrick	1.00	.50	.30
41	Chris Speier	1.00	.50	.30
42	John Montefusco	1.00	.50	.30
43	Pete Rose	10.00	5.00	3.00
44	Johnny Bench	5.00	2.50	1.50
45	Dan Driessen	1.00	.50	.30
46	Joe Morgan	4.00	2.00	1.25
47	Dave Concepcion	1.00	.50	.30
48	George Foster	1.00	.50	.30
49	Cesar Geronimo	1.00	.50	.30
50	Ken Griffey	1.00	.50	.30
51	Gary Nolan	1.00	.50	.30
52	Santo Alcala	1.00	.50	.30
53	Jack Billingham	1.00	.50	.30
54	Pedro Borbon	1.00	.50	.30
55	Rawly Eastwick	1.00	.50	.30
56	Fred Norman	1.00	.50	.30
57	Pat Zachary (Zachry)	1.00	.50	.30
58	Jeff Burroughs	1.00	.50	.30
59	Manny Trillo	1.00	.50	.30
60	Bob Watson	1.00	.50	.30
61	Steve Garvey	1.50	.70	.45
62	Don Sutton	4.00	2.00	1.25
63	John Candelaria	1.00	.50	.30
64	Willie Stargell	4.00	2.00	1.25
65	Jerry Reuss	1.00	.50	.30
66	Dave Cash	1.00	.50	.30
67	Tom Seaver	5.00	2.50	1.50
68	Jon Matlock	1.00	.50	.30
69	Dave Kingman	1.00	.50	.30
70a	Mike Schmidt (Green)	7.50	3.75	2.25
70b	Mike Schmidt (Light blue.)	7.50	3.75	2.25
70c	Mike Schmidt (Orange)	7.50	3.75	2.25
70d	Mike Schmidt (Purple)	7.50	3.75	2.25
70e	Mike Schmidt (Sky blue.)	7.50	3.75	2.25
71	Jay Johnstone	1.00	.50	.30
72	Greg Luzinski	1.00	.50	.30

1977 Pepsi-Cola Cincinnati Reds Playing Cards

Similar to a multi-sport series produced by Cubic Corp. (see also), these playing cards sets feature on the back the pencil drawings of Al Landsman. Each boxed deck featured one Reds star player within a red border. Also on each card back are a facsimile autograph and Pepsi logo. Cards are standard bridge size (2-1/4" x 3-1/2") with rounded corners. Decks were available by sending in 250 16-oz. Pepsi cap liners or a combination of cash and cap liners.

		NM	EX	VG
(1)	Johnny Bench (Boxed deck.)	35.00	17.50	10.00
(1)	Johnny Bench (Single card.)	1.50	.70	.45
(2)	Joe Morgan (Boxed deck.)	20.00	10.00	6.00
(2)	Joe Morgan (Single card.)	1.00	.50	.30
(3)	Pete Rose (Boxed deck.)	55.00	27.50	16.50
(3)	Pete Rose (Single card.)	4.00	2.00	1.25

1978 Pepsi-Cola Superstars

In its second year of producing carton-stuffer baseball cards, Cincinnati area Pepsi bottlers issued a 40-card set featuring 25 Reds players and 15 other major league stars. The entire carton insert measures 2-1/8" x 9-1/2". Besides the baseball card at top, there is a checklist and mail-in offer for playing cards featuring Johnny Bench, Joe Morgan and Pete Rose. The card element at the top measures 2-1/8" x 2-1/2". A player portrait, with uniform logos airbrushed off, is featured in black-and-white in a white star on a red background. The Major League Baseball Players Association logo appears in dark blue in the upper-left. Printed in black below are the player's name, team, position, birthdate and place and a few 1977 stats. In back, printed in red, white and blue, is part of the offer for the playing cards. Large quantities of this set found their way into hobby hands and they remain common today.

		NM	EX	VG
Complete Set (40):		30.00	15.00	9.00
Common Player:		.75	.35	.20
(1)	Sparky Anderson	2.00	1.00	.60
(2)	Rick Auerbach	.75	.35	.20
(3)	Doug Bair	.75	.35	.20
(4)	Buddy Bell	.75	.35	.20
(5)	Johnny Bench	4.00	2.00	1.25
(6)	Bill Bonham	.75	.35	.20
(7)	Pedro Borbon	.75	.35	.20
(8)	Larry Bowa	.75	.35	.20
(9)	George Brett	7.50	3.75	2.25
(10)	Jeff Burroughs	.75	.35	.20
(11)	Rod Carew	3.00	1.50	.90
(12)	Dave Collins	.75	.35	.20
(13)	Dave Concepcion	.75	.35	.20
(14)	Dan Driessen	.75	.35	.20
(15)	George Foster	.75	.35	.20
(16)	Steve Garvey	1.50	.70	.45
(17)	Cesar Geronimo	.75	.35	.20
(18)	Ken Griffey	.75	.35	.20
(19)	Ken Henderson	.75	.35	.20
(20)	Tom Hume	.75	.35	.20
(21)	Reggie Jackson	7.50	3.75	2.25
(22)	Junior Kennedy	.75	.35	.20
(23)	Dave Kingman	.75	.40	.25
(24)	Ray Knight	.75	.35	.20
(25)	Jerry Koosman	.75	.35	.20
(26)	Mike Lum	.75	.35	.20

(27)	Bill Madlock	.75	.35	.20
(28)	Joe Morgan	3.00	1.50	.90
(29)	Paul Moskau	.75	.35	.20
(30)	Fred Norman	.75	.35	.20
(31)	Jim Palmer	3.00	1.50	.90
(32)	Pete Rose	10.00	5.00	3.00
(33)	Nolan Ryan	12.50	6.25	3.75
(34)	Manny Sarmiento	.75	.35	.20
(35)	Tom Seaver	4.00	2.00	1.25
(36)	Ted Simmons	.75	.35	.20
(37)	Dave Tomlin	.75	.35	.20
(38)	Don Werner	.75	.35	.20
(39)	Carl Yastrzemski	4.00	2.00	1.25
(40)	Richie Zisk	.75	.35	.20

1980 Pepsi-Cola All-Stars Prototypes

These prototype cards were prepared by Topps and Mike Schechter Associates for a proposed Pepsi promotion. Three sets of the cards were given to Pepsi officials for consideration but only two were returned when the deal fell through. The third sheet was cut up and sold into the hobby. The Pepsi cards share the format of Topps' regular 1980 issue, although Pepsi logos have been added on front and back, name and banner colors changed on front and a position circle added. In 2005, a number of the individual cards were offered on eBay by Topps.

		NM	EX	VG
Common Player:		250.00	125.00	75.00
1	Rod Carew	1,000	500.00	300.00
2	Paul Molitor	1,000	500.00	300.00
3	George Brett	1,500	750.00	450.00
4	Robin Yount	1,000	500.00	300.00
5	Reggie Jackson	1,500	750.00	450.00
6	Fred Lynn	250.00	125.00	75.00
7	Ken Landreaux	250.00	125.00	75.00
8	Jim Sundberg	250.00	125.00	75.00
9	Ron Guidry (One known, other two cut from sheets and destroyed; negatives reversed.)	1,450	725.00	435.00
10	Jim Palmer	1,000	500.00	300.00
11	Goose Gossage	250.00	125.00	75.00
12	Keith Hernandez	250.00	125.00	75.00
13	Dave Lopes	250.00	125.00	75.00
14	Mike Schmidt	1,500	750.00	450.00
15	Garry Templeton	250.00	125.00	75.00
16	Dave Parker	250.00	125.00	75.00
17	George Foster	250.00	125.00	75.00
18	Dave Winfield	1,000	500.00	300.00
19	Ted Simmons	250.00	125.00	75.00
20	Steve Garvey	1,000	500.00	300.00
21	J.R. Richard	400.00	200.00	120.00
22	Bruce Sutter	1,000	500.00	300.00

1966 Gaylord Perry Insurance

The attributed date is arbitrary, near the middle of his stay with the S.F. Giants in whose uniform he is pictured on this approximately 3-1/2" x 5-1/2", blank-backed, black-and-white "business" card for his insurance agency.

	NM	EX	VG
Gaylord Perry	40.00	20.00	12.00

1971 Pete Rose & Johnny Bench Lincoln-Mercury Postcards

This series of promotional postcards was issued in 1970-71 in conjunction with a Dayton, Ohio, Lincoln-Mercury auto dealership owned by Reds teammates Rose and Bench. Fronts of the 5-1/2" x 3-1/2" postcards feature color photos of new cars. Black-and-white backs have portraits of the players, a description of the auto, the address of the dealership and a credit line for the postcard's printer. Besides those listed here, other auto fronts may exist.

		NM	EX	VG
Common Card:		25.00	12.50	7.50
(1)	Johnny Bench, Pete Rose (1971 Lincoln Continental Sedan)	25.00	12.50	7.50
(2)	Johnny Bench, Pete Rose (1971 Mercury Cougar Convertible)	25.00	12.50	7.50
(3)	Johnny Bench, Pete Rose (1971 Mercury Montego)	25.00	12.50	7.50

1972 Pete Rose & Johnny Bench Lincoln-Mercury Postcards

This series of promotional postcards was issued in 1971-72 in conjunction with a Dayton, Ohio, Lincoln-Mercury auto dealership owned by Reds teammates Rose and Bench. Fronts of the 5-1/2" x 3-1/2" postcards feature color photos of new cars. Black, white and backs have portraits of the players, a description of the auto, the address of the dealership and a credit line for the postcard's printer. Besides those listed here, other auto fronts may exist.

		NM	EX	VG
(1)	Pete Rose, Johnny Bench (1972 Mercury Marquis Brougham Colony Park Station Wagon)	25.00	12.50	7.50

1961 Peters Meats Twins

This set, featuring the first-year 1961 Minnesota Twins, is in a large, 4-5/8" x 3-1/2", format. Cards are on thick cardboard and heavily waxed, as they were used as partial packaging for the company's meat products. Card fronts feature full-color photos, team and Peters logos, and biographical information. The cards are blank-backed. Prices shown are for cards with the surrounding packaging panel. Cut cards are worth about 50-75 percent of the prices shown.

	NM	EX	VG
Complete Set, Panels (26):	1,600	800.00	475.00
Complete Set, Cards (26):	1,500	750.00	450.00
Common Player, Panel:	80.00	40.00	24.00
Common Player, Card:	50.00	25.00	15.00

		NM	EX	VG
1	Zoilo Versalles	160.00	80.00	48.00
2	Eddie Lopat	80.00	40.00	24.00
3	Pedro Ramos	160.00	80.00	48.00
4	Charles "Chuck" Stobbs	80.00	40.00	24.00
5	Don Mincher	80.00	40.00	24.00
6	Jack Kralick	80.00	40.00	24.00
7	Jim Kaat	125.00	65.00	35.00
8	Hal Naragon	80.00	40.00	24.00
9	Don Lee	80.00	40.00	24.00
10	Harry "Cookie" Lavagetto	80.00	40.00	24.00
11	Tom "Pete" Whisenant	80.00	40.00	24.00
12	Elmer Valo	80.00	40.00	24.00
13	Ray Moore	80.00	40.00	24.00
14	Billy Gardner	80.00	40.00	24.00
15	Lenny Green	80.00	40.00	24.00
16	Sam Mele	80.00	40.00	24.00
17	Jim Lemon	80.00	40.00	24.00
18	Harmon "Killer" Killebrew	400.00	200.00	120.00
19	Paul Giel	80.00	40.00	24.00
20	Reno Bertoia	80.00	40.00	24.00
21	Clyde McCullough	80.00	40.00	24.00
22	Earl Battey	80.00	40.00	24.00
23	Camilo Pascual	160.00	80.00	48.00
24	Dan Dobbek	80.00	40.00	24.00
25	Joe "Valvy" Valdivielso	80.00	40.00	24.00
26	Billy Consolo	80.00	40.00	24.00

1938-53 Philadelphia A's Team-Issue Photos

For a decade and a half the Philadelphia A's issued souvenir sets of black-and-white player photos. All are in a 7" x 10" format but the size of picture, the use of posed action and portrait photos and the type style of the name printed in the bottom border differ among the years. In many cases, pictures were re-issued year after year making it impossible 50 years later to reconstruct the composition of any particular year's issue. The unnumbered pictures are checklisted here alphabetically. Multiple player listings are the result of known pose variations. Gaps have been left in the assigned numbering for future additions.

		NM	EX	VG
Common Player:		12.00	6.00	3.50
(1)	Joe Astroth	12.00	6.00	3.50
(2)	Loren Babe	12.00	6.00	3.50
(3)	Johnny Babich	12.00	6.00	3.50
(4)	Bill Beckman	12.00	6.00	3.50
(5)	Joe Berry	12.00	6.00	3.50
(6)	Herman Besse	12.00	6.00	3.50
(7)	Hal Bevan	12.00	6.00	3.50
(8)	Henry Biasatti	12.00	6.00	3.50
(9)	Don Black	12.00	6.00	3.50
(10)	Lena Blackburne	12.00	6.00	3.50
(11)	Buddy Blair	12.00	6.00	3.50
(12)	Don Bollweg	12.00	6.00	3.50
(13)	Al Brancato	12.00	6.00	3.50
(14)	Lou Brissie	12.00	6.00	3.50
(15)	Earle Brucker	12.00	6.00	3.50
(16)	Earle Brucker	12.00	6.00	3.50
(17)	Earle Brucker	12.00	6.00	3.50
(18)	William Burgo	15.00	7.50	4.50
(19)	Joe Burns	12.00	6.00	3.50
(20)	Ed Burtschy	12.00	6.00	3.50
(21)	Edgar Busch	12.00	6.00	3.50
(22)	Harry Byrd	12.00	6.00	3.50
(23)	Fred Caligiuri	18.00	9.00	5.50
(24)	George Caster	12.00	6.00	3.50
(25)	Jim Castiglia	12.00	6.00	3.50
(27)	Sam Chapman	12.00	6.00	3.50
(28)	Sam Chapman	12.00	6.00	3.50
(29)	Sam Chapman	12.00	6.00	3.50
(30)	Russ Christopher	12.00	6.00	3.50
(31)	Joe Coleman	12.00	6.00	3.50
(32)	Eddie Collins Jr.	15.00	7.50	4.50
(33)	Lawrence Davis	12.00	6.00	3.50
(34)	Tom Davis	12.00	6.00	3.50
(35)	Chubby Dean	12.00	6.00	3.50
(36)	Joe DeMaestri	12.00	6.00	3.50
(37)	Russ Derry	12.00	6.00	3.50
(38)	Gene Desautels	12.00	6.00	3.50
(39)	Art Ditmar	12.00	6.00	3.50
(40)	Jimmy Dykes	12.00	6.00	3.50
(41)	Bob Estalella	12.00	6.00	3.50
(42)	Nick Etten	12.00	6.00	3.50
(43)	Ferris Fain	18.00	9.00	5.50
(44)	Tom Ferrick	12.00	6.00	3.50
(45)	Jim Finigan	12.00	6.00	3.50
(46)	Lewis Flick	12.00	6.00	3.50
(47)	Jesse Flores	12.00	6.00	3.50
(48)	Richard Fowler	12.00	6.00	3.50
(49)	Nelson Fox	30.00	15.00	9.00
(51)	Marion Fricano	12.00	6.00	3.50
(52)	Joe Gantenbein	12.00	6.00	3.50
(53)	Ford Garrison	12.00	6.00	3.50
(54)	Mike Guerra	12.00	6.00	3.50
(55)	Irv Hadley	12.00	6.00	3.50
(56)	Irv Hall	12.00	6.00	3.50
(57)	Luke Hamlin	12.00	6.00	3.50
(58)	Gene Handley	12.00	6.00	3.50
(59)	Bob Harris	12.00	6.00	3.50
(60)	Charlie Harris	12.00	6.00	3.50
(61)	Luman C. Harris (Full-length.)	12.00	6.00	3.50
(62)	Luman Harris	12.00	6.00	3.50
(63)	Frank Hayes	12.00	6.00	3.50
(64)	Bob Johnson	15.00	7.50	4.50
(65)	Bob Johnson	15.00	7.50	4.50
(66)	Eddie Joost	12.00	6.00	3.50
(67)	David Keefe	12.00	6.00	3.50
(68)	George Kell	20.00	10.00	6.00
(69)	Everett Kell	15.00	7.50	4.50
(70)	Alex Kellner	12.00	6.00	3.50
(71)	Alex Kellner	12.00	6.00	3.50
(72)	Lou Klein	12.00	6.00	3.50
(73)	Bill Knickerbocker	12.00	6.00	3.50
(74)	Jack Knott	12.00	6.00	3.50
(75)	Mike Kreevich	12.00	6.00	3.50
(76)	John Kucab	12.00	6.00	3.50
(77)	Paul Lehner	12.00	6.00	3.50
(78)	Bill Lillard	12.00	6.00	3.50
(79)	Lou Limmer	12.00	6.00	3.50
(80)	Lou Limmer	12.00	6.00	3.50
(81)	Dario Lodigiani	12.00	6.00	3.50
(82)	Connie Mack	20.00	10.00	6.00
(83)	Connie Mack	20.00	10.00	6.00
(84)	Connie Mack	20.00	10.00	6.00
(85)	Connie Mack	20.00	10.00	6.00
(86)	Earle Mack	15.00	7.50	4.50
(87)	Earle Mack	15.00	7.50	4.50
(88)	Felix Mackiewicz	12.00	6.00	3.50
(89)	Hank Majeski	12.00	6.00	3.50
(90)	Hank Majeski	12.00	6.00	3.50
(91)	Phil Marchildon	12.00	6.00	3.50
(92)	Phil Marchildon	12.00	6.00	3.50
(93)	Phil Marchildon	12.00	6.00	3.50
(94)	Morris Martin	12.00	6.00	3.50
(95)	Barney McCosky	12.00	6.00	3.50
(96)	Bennie McCoy	12.00	6.00	3.50
(97)	Les McCrabb	12.00	6.00	3.50
(98)	Bill McGhee	18.00	9.00	5.50
(99)	George McQuinn	12.00	6.00	3.50
(101)	Charlie Metro	12.00	6.00	3.50
(102)	Cass Michaels	12.00	6.00	3.50
(103)	Dee Miles	12.00	6.00	3.50
(104)	Wally Moses	12.00	6.00	3.50
(105)	Wally Moses	12.00	6.00	3.50
(106)	Ray Murray	12.00	6.00	3.50
(107)	Bill Nagel	12.00	6.00	3.50
(108)	Bobo Newsom	12.00	6.00	3.50
(109)	Skeeter Newsome	12.00	6.00	3.50
(110)	Hal Peck	12.00	6.00	3.50
(111)	Dave Philley	12.00	6.00	3.50
(112)	Cotton Pippen	12.00	6.00	3.50
(113)	Arnie Portocarrero	12.00	6.00	3.50
(114)	Nelson Potter	12.00	6.00	3.50
(115)	Vic Power	15.00	7.50	4.50
(116)	Jim Pruett	12.00	6.00	3.50
(117)	Bill Renna	12.00	6.00	3.50
(118)	Al Robertson	12.00	6.00	3.50
(119)	Ed Robinson	12.00	6.00	3.50
(120)	Buddy Rosar	12.00	6.00	3.50
(121)	Buddy Rosar	12.00	6.00	3.50
(122)	Al Rubeling	12.00	6.00	3.50
(123)	Joseph Rullo	18.00	9.00	5.50
(124)	Carl Scheib	12.00	6.00	3.50
(125)	Bill Shantz	15.00	7.50	4.50
(126)	Bob Shantz	18.00	9.00	5.50
(127)	Newman Shirley	12.00	6.00	3.50
(128)	Dick Siebert (Thigh-to-cap.)	12.00	6.00	3.50
(129)	Dick Siebert	12.00	6.00	3.50
(130)	Al Simmons	25.00	12.50	7.50
(131)	Al Simmons	25.00	12.50	7.50
(132)	Tuck Stainback	12.00	6.00	3.50
(133)	Pete Suder (Waist-to-cap.)	12.00	6.00	3.50
(134)	Pete Suder	12.00	6.00	3.50
(135)	Bob Swift	12.00	6.00	3.50
(136)	Keith Thomas	12.00	6.00	3.50
(137)	Eric Tipton	12.00	6.00	3.50
(138)	Bob Trice	12.00	6.00	3.50
(139)	Elmer Valo (Portrait to waist.)	12.00	6.00	3.50
(140)	Elmer Valo	12.00	6.00	3.50
(141)	Ozzie Van Brabant	18.00	9.00	5.50
(142)	Porter Vaughan	12.00	6.00	3.50
(143)	Harold Wagner	12.00	6.00	3.50
(144)	Harold Wagner	12.00	6.00	3.50
(145)	Jack Wallaesa	12.00	6.00	3.50
(146)	Johnny Welaj	12.00	6.00	3.50
(147)	Elwood Wheaton	15.00	7.50	4.50
(148)	Don White	12.00	6.00	3.50
(149)	Jo Jo White	12.00	6.00	3.50
(151)	Roger Wolff	12.00	6.00	3.50
(152)	Tom Wright	12.00	6.00	3.50
(153)	Gus Zernial	17.50	8.75	5.25
(154)	1938 A's Team	30.00	15.00	9.00
(155)	1939 A's Team	30.00	15.00	9.00
(156)	1940 A's Team	30.00	15.00	9.00
(157)	1941 A's Team	30.00	15.00	9.00
(158)	1942 A's Team	30.00	15.00	9.00
(159)	1943 A's Team	30.00	15.00	9.00
(160)	1944 A's Team	30.00	15.00	9.00
(161)	1945 A's Team	30.00	15.00	9.00
(162)	1946 A's Team	24.00	12.00	7.25
(163)	1948 A's Team	24.00	12.00	7.25
(164)	1949 A's Team	24.00	12.00	7.25
(165)	Shibe Park	30.00	15.00	9.00

1954 Philadelphia A's Stickers

The issuer of this novelty set and the exact scope of its checklist are currently unknown. The pieces are printed in black-and-white on 4-1/2" x 8-1/4" gummed-back paper. Instructions on front say, "(Moisten back. Paste on Cardboard and cut out.)" Only the player name is printed beneath the photo.

		NM	EX	VG
	Common Player:	25.00	12.50	7.50
(1)	Joe Astroth	25.00	12.50	7.50
(2)	Marion Fricano	25.00	12.50	7.50
(3)	Forrest Jacobs	25.00	12.50	7.50
(4)	Eddie Joost	25.00	12.50	7.50
(5)	Morrie Martin	25.00	12.50	7.50
(6)	Vic Power	35.00	17.50	10.50
(7)	Jim Robertson	25.00	12.50	7.50
(8)	Bob Shantz	35.00	17.50	10.50
(9)	Pete Suder	25.00	12.50	7.50
(10)	Bob Trice	25.00	12.50	7.50

1952 Philadelphia A's/Phillies Player Pins

Only players on the Philadelphia A's and Phillies are found in this series of player pinbacks. The 1-3/4" diameter celluloid pins have black-and-white player portraits on front. The player name is printed in block letters across his shoulders, while the team name is printed in script across the chest. It is possible other player pins may exist. The unnumbered pieces are checklisted here in alphabetical order.

		NM	EX	VG
	Common Player:	150.00	75.00	45.00
	Philadelphia Athletics			
(1)	Ferris Fain	200.00	100.00	60.00
(2)	Bobby Shantz	200.00	100.00	60.00
(3)	Gus Zernial	200.00	100.00	60.00
	Philadelphia Phillies			
(1)	Richie Ashburn	300.00	150.00	90.00
(2)	Del Ennis	150.00	75.00	45.00
(3)	Granny Hamner	150.00	75.00	45.00
(4)	Willie Jones	150.00	75.00	45.00
(5)	Jim Konstanty	150.00	75.00	45.00
(6)	Robin Roberts	300.00	150.00	90.00
(7)	Andy Seminick	150.00	75.00	45.00
(8)	Curt Simmons	150.00	75.00	45.00
(9)	Eddie Waitkus	150.00	75.00	45.00

1948 Philadelphia Bulletin Stand-Ups

These player pictures were printed in the "Fun Book" color section of the Sunday paper. The full-body pose cutouts carry facsimile autographs and were printed four per week on a page of about 9-1/2" x 14". While the individual pictures vary is size according to the pose, most are about 3" to 4" x 6-1/2" to 7". The player pictures are in black-and-white with a blue background and red base. They were intended to be cut out

around the heavy black line, pasted to cardboard and folded at their base to create a stand-up figure. Values shown here are for well trimmed pieces without evidence of mounting. Complete pages carry a premium somewhat greater than the sum of the players present.

		NM	EX	VG
	Common Player:	15.00	7.50	4.50
	PHILADELPHIA A's			
	June 13	75.00	37.00	22.00
(1)	Ferris Fain	15.00	7.50	4.50
(2)	Eddie Joost	15.00	7.50	4.50
(3)	Hank Majeski	15.00	7.50	4.50
(4)	Pete Suder	15.00	7.50	4.50
	June 20	75.00	37.00	22.00
(5)	Sam Chapman	15.00	7.50	4.50
(6)	Barney McCosky	15.00	7.50	4.50
(7)	Buddy Rosar	15.00	7.50	4.50
(8)	Elmer Valo	15.00	7.50	4.50
	June 27	75.00	37.00	22.00
(9)	Mike Guerra	15.00	7.50	4.50
(10)	Dick Fowler	15.00	7.50	4.50
(11)	Phil Marchildon	15.00	7.50	4.50
(12)	Carl Sheib	15.00	7.50	4.50
	July 4	75.00	37.00	22.00
(13)	Joe Coleman	15.00	7.50	4.50
(14)	Bob Savage	15.00	7.50	4.50
(15)	Don White	15.00	7.50	4.50
(16)	Rudy York	15.00	7.50	4.50
	July 11	75.00	37.00	22.00
(17)	Herman Franks	15.00	7.50	4.50
(18)	Charlie Harris	15.00	7.50	4.50
(19)	Bill McCahan	15.00	7.50	4.50
(20)	Skeeter Webb	15.00	7.50	4.50
	July 18	75.00	37.00	22.00
(21)	Lou Brissie	15.00	7.50	4.50
(22)	Ray Coleman	15.00	7.50	4.50
(23)	Billy DeMars	15.00	7.50	4.50
(24)	unknown	15.00	7.50	4.50
	PHILADELPHIA PHILLIES			
	July 25	90.00	45.00	27.00
(1)	Don Padgett	15.00	7.50	4.50
(2)	Schoolboy Rowe	15.00	7.50	4.50
(3)	Andy Seminick	15.00	7.50	4.50
(4)	Curt Simmons	20.00	10.00	6.00
	August 1	225.00	110.00	67.00
(5)	Richie Ashburn	150.00	75.00	45.00
(6)	Johnny Blatnik	15.00	7.50	4.50
(7)	Del Ennis	20.00	10.00	6.00
(8)	Harry Walker	15.00	7.50	4.50
	August 8	75.00	37.00	22.00
(9)	Bert Haas	15.00	7.50	4.50
(10)	Granny Hamner	15.00	7.50	4.50
(11)	Eddie Miller	15.00	7.50	4.50
(12)	Dick Sisler	15.00	7.50	4.50
	August 15	200.00	100.00	60.00
(13)	Ralph Caballero	15.00	7.50	4.50
(14)	Ed Heusser	15.00	7.50	4.50
(15)	Robin Roberts	125.00	62.00	37.00
(16)	Emil Verban	15.00	7.50	4.50
	August 22	75.00	37.00	22.00
(17)	Blix Donnelly	15.00	7.50	4.50
(18)	Walt Dubiel	15.00	7.50	4.50
(19)	Ken Heintzelman	15.00	7.50	4.50
(20)	Dutch Leonard	15.00	7.50	4.50
	August 29	75.00	37.00	22.00
(21)	Charlie Bicknell	15.00	7.50	4.50
(22)	Al Lakeman	15.00	7.50	4.50
(23)	Sam Nahem	15.00	7.50	4.50
(24)	Carvel "Bama" Rowell	15.00	7.50	4.50

1949 Philadelphia Bulletin A's/Phillies

Each Sunday between May 22 and July 24, 1949, the "Fun Book" rotogravure section of the Bulletin included a page of (usually) six baseball "cards" of the hometeam A's and Phillies which could be cut out and pasted to cardboard. The left side (front) of each card has a sepia portrait of the player, while a colored box at right (back) has biographical and career information. Uncut and unfolded, each card measures about 4-1/2" x 3-5/8". If cut out and pasted onto cardboard, the created cards would measure about 2-1/4" x 3-5/8". Complete pages measure about 9-1/2" x 13-3/8". Values shown are for single "cards" which have been cut off the page, but not pasted onto a backing.

		NM	EX	VG
	Complete Set (59):	1,600	800.00	480.00
	Common Player:	25.00	12.50	7.50
	MAY 22			
(1)	Richie Ashburn	265.00	130.00	79.00
(2)	Granny Hamner	25.00	12.50	7.50
(3)	Eddie Joost	25.00	12.50	7.50
(4)	Bill Nicholson	25.00	12.50	7.50
(5)	Buddy Rosar	25.00	12.50	7.50
(6)	Pete Suder	25.00	12.50	7.50
	MAY 29			
(7)	Hank Borowy	25.00	12.50	7.50
(8)	Del Ennis	35.00	17.50	10.50
(9)	Ferris Fain	35.00	17.50	10.50
(10)	Phil Marchildon	25.00	12.50	7.50
(11)	Wally Moses	25.00	12.50	7.50
(12)	Eddie Waitkus	25.00	12.50	7.50
	JUNE 5			
(13)	Dick Fowler	25.00	12.50	7.50
(14)	Willie Jones	25.00	12.50	7.50
(15)	Stan Lopata	25.00	12.50	7.50
(16)	Hank Majeski	25.00	12.50	7.50
(17)	Schoolboy Rowe	25.00	12.50	7.50
(18)	Elmer Valo	25.00	12.50	7.50
	JUNE 12			
(19)	Joe Coleman	25.00	12.50	7.50
(20)	Charley Harris	25.00	12.50	7.50
(21)	Russ Meyer	25.00	12.50	7.50
(22)	Eddie Miller	25.00	12.50	7.50
(23)	Robin Roberts	265.00	130.00	79.00
(24)	Taft Wright	25.00	12.50	7.50
	JUNE 19			
(25)	Lou Brissie	25.00	12.50	7.50
(26)	Ralph Caballero	25.00	12.50	7.50
(27)	Sam Chapman	25.00	12.50	7.50
(28)	Fermin (Mike) Guerra	25.00	12.50	7.50
(29)	Jim Konstanty	35.00	17.50	10.50
(30)	Curt Simmons	35.00	17.50	10.50
	JUNE 26			
(31)	Charles Bicknell	25.00	12.50	7.50
(32)	Ken Heintzelman	25.00	12.50	7.50
(33)	Alex Kellner	25.00	12.50	7.50
(34)	Barney McCosky	25.00	12.50	7.50
(35)	Bobby Shantz	35.00	17.50	10.50
(36)	Ken Trinkle	25.00	12.50	7.50
	JULY 3			
(37)	Blix Donnelly	25.00	12.50	7.50
(38)	Bill McCahan	25.00	12.50	7.50
(39)	Carl Scheib	25.00	12.50	7.50
(40)	Andy Seminick	25.00	12.50	7.50
(41)	Dick Sisler	25.00	12.50	7.50
(42)	Don White	25.00	12.50	7.50
	JULY 10			
(43)	Joe Astroth	25.00	12.50	7.50
(44)	Henry Biasetti	25.00	12.50	7.50
(45)	Buddy Blattner	25.00	12.50	7.50
(46)	Thomas O. Davis	25.00	12.50	7.50
(47)	Stan Hollmig	25.00	12.50	7.50
(48)	Jackie Mayo	25.00	12.50	7.50
	JULY 17			
(49)	Benny Bengough	25.00	12.50	7.50
(50)	Earle Brucker	25.00	12.50	7.50
(51)	Dusty Cooke	25.00	12.50	7.50
(52)	Jimmy Dykes	25.00	12.50	7.50
(53)	Cy Perkins	25.00	12.50	7.50
(54)	Al Simmons	40.00	20.00	12.00
	JULY 24			
(55)	Nellie Fox	265.00	130.00	79.00
(56)	Connie Mack	200.00	100.00	60.00
(57)	Earle Mack	25.00	12.50	7.50
(58)	Eddie Sawyer	25.00	12.50	7.50
(59)	Ken Silvestri	25.00	12.50	7.50

1950 Philadelphia Bulletin Pin-Ups

This series of 8" x 10" black-and-white portraits of Phillies players, coaches, and manager was produced in two versions. A (mostly) numbered newsprint version was issued one per day in the paper, between September 13-30. A premium version, printed on heavy paper with a semi-gloss finish and blank back, was made available to fans for a nickel at the newspaper's office or a dime by mail. Each of the pictures is a cap-less portrait with facsimile autograph on front. A number of players in the premium version were not issued in the newsprint style.

	NM	EX	VG
Complete Set (26):	900.00	450.00	275.00
Common Player:	40.00	20.00	12.00
(1) Rich Ashburn	75.00	37.00	22.00
(2) Jimmy Bloodworth	40.00	20.00	12.00
(3) Ralph Caballero	40.00	20.00	12.00
(4) Milo Candini	40.00	20.00	12.00
(5) Emory Church	40.00	20.00	12.00
(6) Sylvester (Blix) Donnelly	40.00	20.00	12.00
(7) Del Ennis	50.00	25.00	15.00
(8) Mike Goliat	40.00	20.00	12.00
(9) Gran Hamner	40.00	20.00	12.00
(10) Ken Heintzelman	40.00	20.00	12.00
(11) Stan Hollmig	40.00	20.00	12.00
(12) Ken Johnson	40.00	20.00	12.00
(13) Willie Jones	40.00	20.00	12.00
(14) Jim Konstanty	40.00	20.00	12.00
(15) Stan Lopata	40.00	20.00	12.00
(16) Russ Meyer	40.00	20.00	12.00
(17) Bob Miller	40.00	20.00	12.00
(18) Bill Nicholson	40.00	20.00	12.00
(19) Robin Roberts	65.00	32.00	19.50
(20) Eddie Sawyer	40.00	20.00	12.00
(21) Andy Seminick	40.00	20.00	12.00
(22) Ken Silvestri	40.00	20.00	12.00
(23) Curtis T. Simmons	50.00	25.00	15.00
(24) Dick Sisler	40.00	20.00	12.00
(25) Eddie Waitkus	40.00	20.00	12.00
(26) Dick Whitman	40.00	20.00	12.00

1964 Philadelphia Bulletin Phillies Album (Paper)

This series of newspaper features was the basis for the more often-encountered mail-in premiums. About 5-1/2" x 9", these pieces were printed in black-and-white in the sports section of the daily paper. The artwork is by staff artist Jim Porter. While the newspaper pieces are numbered, they are checklisted here in alphabetical order due to uncertainty about the original issue sequence.

	NM	EX	VG
Complete Set (27):	400.00	200.00	120.00
Common Player:	15.00	7.50	4.50
(1) Richie Allen	40.00	20.00	12.00
(2) Ruben Amaro	15.00	7.50	4.50
(3) Jack Baldschun	15.00	7.50	4.50
(4) Dennis Bennett	15.00	7.50	4.50
(5) John Boozer	15.00	7.50	4.50
(6) Johnny Briggs	15.00	7.50	4.50
(7) Jim Bunning	50.00	25.00	15.00
(8) Johnny Callison	15.00	7.50	4.50
(9) Danny Cater	15.00	7.50	4.50
(10) Wes Covington	15.00	7.50	4.50
(11) Ray Culp	15.00	7.50	4.50
(12) Clay Dalrymple	15.00	7.50	4.50
(13) Tony Gonzalez	15.00	7.50	4.50
(14) John Herrnstein	15.00	7.50	4.50
(15) Alex Johnson	15.00	7.50	4.50
(16) Art Mahaffey	15.00	7.50	4.50
(17) Gene Mauch	15.00	7.50	4.50
(18) Vic Power	15.00	7.50	4.50
(19) Ed Roebuck	15.00	7.50	4.50
(20) Cookie Rojas	15.00	7.50	4.50
(21) Bobby Shantz	15.00	7.50	4.50
(22) Chris Short	15.00	7.50	4.50
(23) Tony Taylor	15.00	7.50	4.50
(24) Frank Thomas	15.00	7.50	4.50
(25) Gus Triandos	15.00	7.50	4.50
(26) Bobby Wine	15.00	7.50	4.50
(27) Rick Wise	15.00	7.50	4.50

1964 Philadelphia Bulletin Phillies Album

Color artwork by Jim Ponter is featured in this series of newspaper inserts. Portrait and action figures are combined on a blank-backed 8" x 10" format, along with a facsimile autograph. The unnumbered pictures are checklisted here alphabetically, two varieties of Jim Bunning's picture have been reported.

	NM	EX	VG
Complete Set (28):	550.00	275.00	175.00
Common Player:	20.00	10.00	6.00
(1) Richie Allen	60.00	30.00	18.00
(2) Ruben Amaro	20.00	10.00	6.00
(3) Jack Baldschun	20.00	10.00	6.00
(4) Dennis Bennett	20.00	10.00	6.00
(5) John Boozer	20.00	10.00	6.00
(6) Johnny Briggs	20.00	10.00	6.00
(7) Jim Bunning (Pitching)	75.00	37.00	22.00
(8) Jim Bunning (Portrait)	60.00	30.00	18.00
(9) Johnny Callison	20.00	10.00	6.00
(10) Danny Cater	20.00	10.00	6.00
(11) Wes Covington	20.00	10.00	6.00
(12) Ray Culp	20.00	10.00	6.00
(13) Clay Dalrymple	20.00	10.00	6.00
(14) Tony Gonzalez	20.00	10.00	6.00
(15) John Herrnstein	20.00	10.00	6.00
(16) Alex Johnson	20.00	10.00	6.00
(17) Art Mahaffey	20.00	10.00	6.00
(18) Gene Mauch	20.00	10.00	6.00
(19) Vic Power	20.00	10.00	6.00
(20) Ed Roebuck	20.00	10.00	6.00
(21) Cookie Rojas	20.00	10.00	6.00
(22) Bobby Shantz	20.00	10.00	6.00
(23) Chris Short	20.00	10.00	6.00
(24) Tony Taylor	20.00	10.00	6.00
(25) Frank Thomas	20.00	10.00	6.00
(26) Gus Triandos	20.00	10.00	6.00
(27) Bobby Wine	20.00	10.00	6.00
(28) Rick Wise	20.00	10.00	6.00

1909 Philadelphia Caramel (E95)

Similar in style to several other early candy and caramel cards, the set designated as E95 by the American Card Catalog is a 25-card issue produced by the Philadelphia Caramel Co., Camden, N.J., in 1909. The cards measure approximately 1-1/2" x 2-5/8" and contain a full-color player drawing. The back, which differentiates the set from other similar issues, checklists the 25 players in black ink and displays the Philadelphia Caramel Co. name at the bottom. Blank-back cards printed on thinner stock exist; these are not proofs, but were cut off a "Base Ball Series" notebook cover, they are valued about 25-50 percent of a corresponding regular-issue card.

	NM	EX	VG
Complete Set (25):	50,000	20,000	10,000
Common Player:	850.00	350.00	125.00
1 Honus Wagner	13,000	5,200	2,600
2 Nick Maddox	850.00	350.00	125.00
3 Fred Merkle	850.00	350.00	125.00
4 Cy Morgan	850.00	350.00	125.00
5 Chief Bender	1,950	780.00	350.00
6 Harry Krause	850.00	350.00	125.00
7 Art Devlin	850.00	350.00	125.00
8 Matty McIntyre	850.00	350.00	125.00
9 Ty Cobb	15,600	5,200	2,600
10 Ed Willetts (Willett)	850.00	350.00	125.00
11 Sam Crawford	1,950	780.00	350.00
12 Christy Matthewson (Mathewson)	9,750	3,000	1,500
13 Hooks Wiltse	850.00	350.00	125.00
14 Larry Doyle	850.00	350.00	125.00
15 Tommy Leach	850.00	350.00	125.00
16 Harry Lord	850.00	350.00	125.00
17 Ed Cicotte	2,730	780.00	350.00
18 Bill Carrigan	850.00	350.00	125.00
19 Vic Willis	1,950	780.00	325.00
20 Johnny Evers	1,950	780.00	325.00
21 Frank Chance	1,950	780.00	325.00
22 Solly Hoffman (Hofman)	850.00	350.00	125.00
23 Eddie Plank	3,120	1,170	650.00
24 Eddie Collins	1,950	780.00	325.00
25 Ed Reulbach	850.00	350.00	125.00

1910 Philadelphia Caramel (E96)

This set of 30 subjects, known by the ACC designation E96, was issued in 1910 by the Philadelphia Caramel Co. The approximately 1-1/2" x 2-5/8" size and front design remained the same, but the two issues can be identified by the backs. The backs of E96 cards are printed in red and carry a checklist of 30 players. There is also a line at the bottom advising "Previous series 25, making total issue 55 cards." Just below that appears

"Philadelphia Caramel Co./Camden, N.J." Blank-back cards printed on thinner stock are not proofs, but rather were cut off a "Base Ball Series" notebook cover. They are valued about 25-50 percent of a corresponding regular-issue card.

	NM	EX	VG
Complete Set (30):	38,500	15,500	9,500
Common Player:	1,100	400.00	150.00
1 Harry Davis	1,100	400.00	150.00
2 Connie Mack	2,000	1,000	500.00
3 Ira Thomas	1,100	400.00	150.00
4 Home Run Baker	2,000	800.00	400.00
5 Red Dooin	1,100	400.00	150.00
6 George McQuillan	1,100	400.00	150.00
7 Ed Konetchy	1,100	400.00	150.00
8 Ed Karger	1,100	400.00	150.00
9 Mike Mowrey	1,100	400.00	150.00
10 Red Murray	1,100	400.00	150.00
11 Nap Lajoie	2,700	1,100	550.00
12 Claude Rossman	1,100	400.00	150.00
13 Nap Rucker	1,100	400.00	150.00
14 Hugh Jennings	2,000	800.00	400.00
15 Wild Bill Donovan	1,100	400.00	150.00
16 Jim Delahanty	1,100	400.00	150.00
17 George Mullin	1,100	400.00	150.00
18 Frank Arrelanes (Arellanes)	1,100	400.00	150.00
19 Tubby Spencer	1,100	400.00	150.00
20 Johnny Kling	1,100	400.00	150.00
21 Jack Pfister (Pfiester)	1,500	750.00	300.00
22 Mordecai Brown	2,500	1,250	500.00
23 Joe Tinker	2,500	1,250	500.00
24 Fred Clark (Clarke)	2,000	800.00	350.00
25 George Gibson	1,100	400.00	150.00
26 Babe Adams	1,100	400.00	150.00
27 Red Ames	1,100	400.00	150.00
28 Rube Marquard	2,000	800.00	350.00
29 Buck Herzog	1,100	400.00	150.00
30 Chief Myers (Meyers)	1,100	400.00	150.00

1913 Philadelphia Caramel Proofs

The attribution of these cards to Philadelphia Caramel is speculative, since no advertising is found on their blank backs. The three known pieces, however, have pictures and color identical to the players' cards in the 1910 E96 Philadelphia Caramel issue. These proofs differ only in the team designations. Nominally 1-1/2" x 2-5/8", the known examples were hand-cut from a sheet and are, at present, each unique. The Kling card was offered at auction in 2003 without meeting a $500 reserve.

Frank Chance (New York, A.L.)
Harry Davis (Cleveland)
Johnny Kling (Boston, A.L.)

1913 Philadelphia Evening Telegraph Postcards

The attributed date of issue is speculative, about midway through Phillies manager Red Dooin's tenure. Issued by one of the city's daily newspapers, these 3-1/2" x 5-1/2" black-and-white postcards picture the managers of the Phils and A's in large portrait photos. The postcard-style back has ornate typography and embellishments.

1913 Philadelphia Evening Times Supplements

		NM	EX	VG
Complete Set (2):		1,100	550.00	325.00
Common Card:		500.00	250.00	150.00
(1)	Charles Dooin	500.00	250.00	150.00
(2)	Connie Mack	650.00	325.00	200.00

The checklist comprised almost entirely of Connie Mack's A's and John McGraw's Giants suggests this series of newspaper supplements was issued around World Series time. The blank-backed, sepia-toned pictures have posed action photos, are printed on light cardboard stock and measure about 7-1/2" x 9-1/2". This checklist may be incomplete.

		NM	EX	VG
Common Player:		200.00	100.00	60.00
(1)	Home Run Baker	400.00	200.00	120.00
(2)	Jack Barry	200.00	100.00	60.00
(3)	Chief Bender	400.00	200.00	120.00
(4)	George Burns	200.00	100.00	60.00
(5)	Ty Cobb	1,200	600.00	360.00
(6)	Eddie Collins	400.00	200.00	120.00
(7)	Al Demaree	200.00	100.00	60.00
(8)	Larry Doyle	200.00	100.00	60.00
(9)	Walter Johnson	800.00	400.00	240.00
(10)	Rube Marquard	400.00	200.00	120.00
(11)	Christy Mathewson	800.00	400.00	240.00
(12)	Stuffy McInnis	200.00	100.00	60.00
(13)	Chief Meyers	200.00	100.00	60.00
(14)	Rube Oldring	200.00	100.00	60.00
(15)	Eddie Plank	400.00	200.00	120.00
(16)	Jeff Tesreau	200.00	100.00	60.00

1950 Philadelphia Inquirer Fightin' Phillies

As the Whiz Kids battled to a National League pennant the "Philadelphia Inquirer" instituted a set of cut-out baseball cards in the Sunday rotogravure editions during September. The 4-7/8" x 6-7/8" cards have colored portrait photos surrounded with a white border. A facsimile autograph is printed across the chest. In the bottom border are the player's formal name, position, career summary and the line, "Inquirer Fightin' Phillies Album." Backs have whatever articles or ads were on the next page. The unnumbered cards are printed here in alphabetical order.

		NM	EX	VG
Complete Set (24):		350.00	175.00	105.00
Common Player:		15.00	7.50	4.50
(1)	Richie Ashburn	35.00	17.50	10.50

(2)	James Henry Bloodworth	15.00	7.50	4.50
(3)	Ralph Joseph Caballero	15.00	7.50	4.50
(4)	Milo Candini	15.00	7.50	4.50
(5)	Emory Church	15.00	7.50	4.50
(6)	Sylvester Urban Donnelly	15.00	7.50	4.50
(7)	Delmer Ennis	15.00	7.50	4.50
(8)	Mike Mitchel Goliat (Mitchell)	15.00	7.50	4.50
(9)	Granville Wilbur Hamner	15.00	7.50	4.50
(10)	Kenneth Alphonse Heintzelman	15.00	7.50	4.50
(11)	Stanley Ernst Hollmig	15.00	7.50	4.50
(12)	Kenneth W. Johnson	15.00	7.50	4.50
(13)	Willie Edward Jones	15.00	7.50	4.50
(14)	Stanley Edward Lopata	15.00	7.50	4.50
(15)	Russell Charles Meyer	15.00	7.50	4.50
(16)	Robert Miller	15.00	7.50	4.50
(17)	William Beck Nicholson	15.00	7.50	4.50
(18)	Robin Evan Roberts	35.00	17.50	10.50
(19)	Andrew Wasal Seminick	15.00	7.50	4.50
(20)	Kenneth Joseph Silvestri	15.00	7.50	4.50
(21)	Curtis Thomas Simmons	15.00	7.50	4.50
(22)	Richard Alan Sisler	15.00	7.50	4.50
(23)	Edward Stephen Waitkus	15.00	7.50	4.50
(24)	Dick Whitman	15.00	7.50	4.50

1954 Philadelphia Inquirer Album of Baseball Stars

A series of four baseball players from each of Philadelphia's teams appeared on a pair of pages in the Colorama color rotogravure section of the Sunday. Philadelphia Inquirer. Each picture is about 6-3/4" x 9-3/4" and was separated from the other three on its "ALBUM OF SPORTS" page by a black dotted line, indicative of an intention for them to be cut out and saved. Under the portrait is a brief career summary. Backs have other newspaper content as printed each Sunday.

		NM	EX	VG
Complete Set (8):		75.00	37.50	22.50
Common Player:		8.00	4.00	2.50
	JULY 25			
(1)	Richie Ashburn	25.00	12.50	7.50
(2)	Jim Finigan	8.00	4.00	2.50
(3)	Gran Hamner	8.00	4.00	2.50
(4)	Bill Shantz	8.00	4.00	2.50
	SEPT. 12			
(1)	Smoky Burgess	10.00	5.00	3.00
(2)	Arnold Portocarrero	8.00	4.00	2.50
(3)	Robin Roberts	16.00	8.00	4.75
(4)	Curt Simmons	10.00	5.00	3.00

1940 Philadelphia Phillies Photo Pack

This set of 25 photos show players in poses on the field with the Quaker figure and "PHILADELPHIA NATIONAL LEAGUE BASE BALL CLUB" around it in a circular logo in the upper right hand corner. Size is 6" x 8-1/2".

		NM	EX	VG
Complete Set (25):		150.00	75.00	30.00
Common Player:		7.50	3.75	2.25
(1)	Morrie Arnovich	7.50	3.75	2.25
(2)	Bill Atwood	7.50	3.75	2.25
(3)	Walter Beck	7.50	3.75	2.25
(4)	Stan Benjamin	7.50	3.75	2.25
(5)	Bob Bragan	7.50	3.75	2.25
(6)	Roy Bruner	7.50	3.75	2.25
(7)	Kirby Higbie	7.50	3.75	2.25
(8)	Si Johnson	7.50	3.75	2.25
(9)	Syl Johnson	7.50	3.75	2.25
(10)	Chuck Klein	7.50	3.75	2.25
(11)	Ed Levy	7.50	3.75	2.25
(12)	Dan Litwhiler	7.50	3.75	2.25
(13)	Hans Lobert	7.50	3.75	2.25
(14)	Herschel Martin	7.50	3.75	2.25
(15)	Joe Marty	7.50	3.75	2.25
(16)	Maerril May	7.50	3.75	2.25
(17)	Walk Millies	7.50	3.75	2.25
(18)	Hugh Mulcahy	7.50	3.75	2.25
(19)	Ike Pearson	7.50	3.75	2.25
(20)	Doc Prothro	7.50	3.75	2.25
(21)	George Scharen	7.50	3.75	2.25
(22)	Clyde Smoll	7.50	3.75	2.25
(23)	Gus Suhr	7.50	3.75	2.25
(24)	Ben Warren	7.50	3.75	2.25
(25)	Del Young	7.50	3.75	2.25

1943 Philadelphia Phillies Photo Pack

Like many teams in that era, the Phillies issued souvenir photo packs for sale at the stadium and by mail-order. This team issue is in a 6" x 8-1/2", blank-back, black-and-white format. The player picture is bordered in white with the player

name in all-caps in the bottom border. From the large number of players known, it is evident that the composition of the photo packs was changed from time to time as the team roster changed. It is possible this checklist is not complete. The unnumbered pictures have been listed here alphabetically.

		NM	EX	VG
Complete Set (40):		300.00	150.00	90.00
Common Player:		8.00	4.00	2.50
(1)	Buster Adams	8.00	4.00	2.50
(2)	Walter Beck	8.00	4.00	2.50
(3)	Stan Benjamin	8.00	4.00	2.50
(4)	Cy Blanton	8.00	4.00	2.50
(5)	Bobby Bragan	8.00	4.00	2.50
(6)	Charlie Brewster	8.00	4.00	2.50
(7)	Paul Busby	8.00	4.00	2.50
(8)	Ben Culp	8.00	4.00	2.50
(9)	Babe Dahlgren	8.00	4.00	2.50
(10)	Lloyd Dietz	8.00	4.00	2.50
(11)	Nick Etten	8.00	4.00	2.50
(12)	George Eyrich	8.00	4.00	2.50
(13)	Charlie Fuchs	8.00	4.00	2.50
(14)	Al Glossop	8.00	4.00	2.50
(15)	Al Gerheauser	8.00	4.00	2.50
(16)	"Bucky" Harris	12.00	6.00	3.50
(17)	Frank Hoerst	8.00	4.00	2.50
(18)	Si Johnson	8.00	4.00	2.50
(19)	Chuck Klein	15.00	7.50	4.50
(20)	Ernie Koy	8.00	4.00	2.50
(21)	Tex Kraus	8.00	4.00	2.50
(22)	Danny Litwhiler	8.00	4.00	2.50
(23)	Mickey Livingston	8.00	4.00	2.50
(24)	Hans Lobert	8.00	4.00	2.50
(25)	Henry Marnie	8.00	4.00	2.50
(26)	Merrill May	8.00	4.00	2.50
(27)	Rube Melton	8.00	4.00	2.50
(28)	Danny Murtaugh	10.00	5.00	3.00
(29)	Sam Nahem	8.00	4.00	2.50
(30)	Earl Naylor	8.00	4.00	2.50
(31)	Ron Northey	8.00	4.00	2.50
(32)	Tommy Padden	8.00	4.00	2.50
(33)	Ike Pearson	8.00	4.00	2.50
(34)	Johnny Podgajny	8.00	4.00	2.50
(35)	Schoolboy Rowe	10.00	5.00	3.00
(36)	Glen Stewart	8.00	4.00	2.50
(37)	Coaker Triplett	8.00	4.00	2.50
(38)	Lloyd Waner	15.00	7.50	4.50
(39)	Ben Warren	8.00	4.00	2.50
(40)	Jimmy Wasdall	8.00	4.00	2.50

1958 Philadelphia Phillies Picture Pack

This set of 5" x 7" blank-backed, black-and-white player pictures was most likely issued in 1958, though it is also possible the set was issued in 1957 (or both). This team-issue set differs from the contemporary Jay Publishing picture packs in that it does not have the city name in the identication line, only the player name in all-caps and "Phillies." The unnumbered pictures are listed here alphabetically.

		NM	EX	VG
Complete Set (12):		75.00	40.00	22.50
Common Player:		7.50	3.75	2.25
(1)	Harry Anderson	7.50	3.75	2.25
(2)	Richie Ashburn	15.00	7.50	4.50
(3)	Bob Bowman	7.50	3.75	2.25
(4)	Turk Farrell	7.50	3.75	2.25
(5)	Chico Fernandez	7.50	3.75	2.25
(6)	Granny Hamner	7.50	3.75	2.25
(7)	Stan Lopata	7.50	3.75	2.25
(8)	Rip Repulski	7.50	3.75	2.25
(9)	Robin Roberts	15.00	7.50	4.50
(10)	Jack Sanford	7.50	3.75	2.25
(11)	Curt Simmons	7.50	3.75	2.25
(12)	Mayo Smith	7.50	3.75	2.25

1958-60 Philadelphia Phillies Team Issue

Thus far 22 different cards have been discovered in this format; it is likely the checklist here is not yet complete. Like many teams, the Phillies issued these cards to players and staff to honor fan requests for photos and autographs. The cards are 3-1/4" x 5-1/2" and have black-and-white portrait photos with white borders. Backs are blank. The unnumbered cards are listed here alphabetically.

		NM	EX	VG
Common Player:		6.00	3.00	1.75
(1)	Harry Anderson	6.00	3.00	1.75
(2)	Richie Ashburn	12.00	6.00	3.50
(3)	Ed Bouchee	6.00	3.00	1.75
(4)	Smoky Burgess	7.50	3.75	2.25
(5)	Johnny Callison	8.00	4.00	2.50
(6)	Jim Coker	6.00	3.00	1.75
(7)	Clay Dalrymple	6.00	3.00	1.75
(8)	Del Ennis	7.50	3.75	2.25
(9)	Tony Gonzalez	6.00	3.00	1.75
(10)	Granny Hamner	6.00	3.00	1.75
(11)	Willie Jones	6.00	3.00	1.75
(12)	Stan Lopata	6.00	3.00	1.75
(13)	Art Mahaffey	6.00	3.00	1.75
(14)	Gene Mauch	6.00	3.00	1.75
(15)	Bob Morgan	6.00	3.00	1.75
(16)	Wally Post	6.00	3.00	1.75
(17)	Robin Roberts	12.00	6.00	3.50
(18)	Eddie Sawyer	6.00	3.00	1.75
(19)	Andy Seminick	6.00	3.00	1.50
(20)	Ray Semproch	6.00	3.00	1.75
(21)	Chris Short	6.00	3.00	1.75
(22)	Curt Simmons	8.00	4.00	2.50
(23)	Earl Torgeson	6.00	3.00	1.75

1964 Philadelphia Phillies Player Pins

Only four players are checklisted in this series, but it is expected more will be added in the future. These pinbacks are 2-3/16" in diameter and have black-and-white player portraits on front, on a white background. The player's name is printed at bottom in block letters.

		NM	EX	VG
Common Player:		45.00	22.50	13.50
(1)	Dick Allen	90.00	45.00	27.50
(2)	Jim Bunning	90.00	45.00	27.50
(3)	Chris Short	45.00	22.50	13.50
(4)	Roy Sievers	45.00	22.50	13.50

1965 Go! Phillies Go! Pins

These large (3-1/2" diameter) pinback buttons feature a dozen members of the '65 Phils. Player portraits are on a white background and have had the cap and pinstripes colored in red. At top, the title is printed in red and blue. The facsimile autograph at bottom is printed in blue.

		NM	EX	VG
Complete Set (12):		750.00	375.00	225.00
Common Player:		50.00	25.00	15.00
(1)	Rich Allen	100.00	50.00	30.00
(2)	Ruben Amaro	50.00	25.00	15.00
(3)	Bo Belinsky	65.00	32.50	20.00
(4)	Jim Bunning	100.00	50.00	30.00
(5)	Johnny Callison	65.00	32.50	20.00
(6)	Wes Covington	50.00	25.00	15.00
(7)	Ray Culp	50.00	25.00	15.00
(8)	Cookie Rojas	50.00	25.00	15.00
(9)	Chris Short	50.00	25.00	15.00
(10)	Dick Stuart	50.00	25.00	15.00
(11)	Tony Taylor	50.00	25.00	15.00
(12)	Bobby Wine	50.00	25.00	15.00

1965 Philadelphia Phillies Tiles

These decorative heavy ceramic tiles feature color portraits and facsimile autographs on a white background. In 6" x 6" format the tiles were made in England, but decorated in the U.S. They appear to have been originally issued with cork backing and some have been seen with a hangar attached on back.

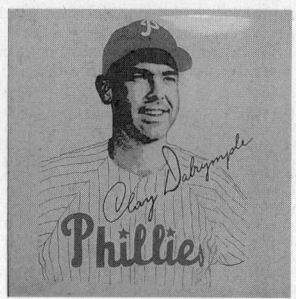

		NM	EX	VG
Complete Set (12):		600.00	300.00	180.00
Common Player:		40.00	20.00	12.00
(1)	Richie Allen	100.00	50.00	30.00
(2)	Bo Belinsky	60.00	30.00	18.00
(3)	Jim Bunning	125.00	65.00	35.00
(4)	Johnny Callison	60.00	30.00	18.00
(5)	Wes Covington	40.00	20.00	12.00
(6)	Clay Dalrymple	40.00	20.00	12.00
(7)	Gene Mauch	40.00	20.00	12.00
(8)	Cookie Rojas	40.00	20.00	12.00
(9)	Tony Taylor	40.00	20.00	12.00
(10)	Chris Short	40.00	20.00	12.00
(11)	Dick Stuart	40.00	20.00	12.00
(12)	Bobby Wine	40.00	20.00	12.00

1967 Philadelphia Phillies Safe Driving

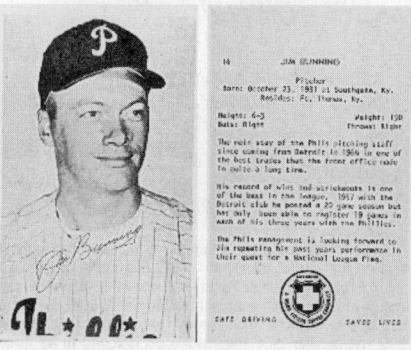

The honor of producing the only safety set of the 1960s goes to the Phillies for this traffic safety set. Measuring 2-3/4" x 4-1/2", the cards have a black-and-white front featuring the standard publicity photo of the player, with a facsimile autograph superimposed. Backs are printed in blue and include a few career and biographical details, along with the player's uniform number, by which the set is checklisted here. At bottom is a circle and shield design with the safety message.

		NM	EX	VG
Complete Set (13):		95.00	47.00	28.00
Common Player:		8.00	4.00	2.50
4	Gene Mauch	8.00	4.00	2.50
6	Johnny Callison	10.00	5.00	3.00
10	Bill White	10.00	5.00	3.00
11	Clay Dalrymple	8.00	4.00	2.50
12	Johnny Briggs	8.00	4.00	2.50
14	Jim Bunning	20.00	10.00	6.00
15	Dick Allen	18.00	9.00	5.50
16	Cookie Rojas	8.00	4.00	2.50
24	Dick Groat	10.00	5.00	3.00
25	Tony Gonzalez	8.00	4.00	2.50
37	Dick Ellsworth	8.00	4.00	2.50
41	Chris Short	8.00	4.00	2.50
46	Larry Jackson	8.00	4.00	2.50

1975 Philadelphia Phillies Photocards

JOE HOERNER

These 3-1/4" x 5-1/2" blank-back, black-and-white cards feature player portrait photos with only the player name in the white border at bottom. Fronts have a semi-gloss finish. It is likely the checklist, presented here alphabetically, is incomplete.

		NM	EX	VG
Common Player:		3.00	1.50	.90
(1)	Tom Hilgendorf	3.00	1.50	.90
(2)	Terry Harmon	3.00	1.50	.90
(3)	Joe Hoerner	3.00	1.50	.90
(4)	Tommy Hutton	3.00	1.50	.90
(5)	Jim Lonborg	4.00	2.00	1.25
(6)	John Oates	3.00	1.50	.90

1961 Phillies Cigar Mickey Mantle

This 6-1/2" x 9" blank-back color photo card of Mickey Mantle was part of a redemption program for Phillies cigars. For $3.39 and 20 cigar bands, a person could receive a Mickey Mantle model baseball glove and this "autographed" (facsimile) photo.

	NM	EX	VG
Mickey Mantle	125.00	62.50	37.50

1912 Photo Art Shop Boston Red Sox

Two postcards are currently known to have been produced, according to the legend on the back, by The Photo Art Shop of Swampscott, Mass. The standard-size (about 3-1/2" x 5-1/2") cards are printed in black-and-white. A vertically formatted card shows opposing World Series aces Joe Wood and Walter Johnson. A horizontal team-photo card has each player's last name printed over his picture and describes the team as "Champions of the American League". The Red Sox went on to defeat the Giants in the World Series.

	NM	EX	VG
Joe Wood, Walter Johnson	1,800	900.00	540.00
1912 Boston Red Sox	900.00	450.00	275.00

1964 Photo Linen Emblems

The attributed date of issue is only approximate. About 3-1/2" x 4-1/2", these sew-on patches feature black-and-white photos with an embroidered red border. The patches were sold in a cello-wrapped package. The checklist presented here in alphabetical order is not complete.

		NM	EX	VG
Complete Set (10):		625.00	300.00	180.00
Common Player:		30.00	15.00	9.00
(1)	Yogi Berra	50.00	25.00	15.00
(2)	Clete Boyer	30.00	15.00	9.00
(3)	Elston Howard	30.00	15.00	9.00
(4)	Sandy Koufax	175.00	87.00	52.00
(5)	Tony Kubek	30.00	15.00	9.00

		NM	EX	VG
(6)	Mickey Mantle	250.00	125.00	75.00
(7)	Roger Maris	90.00	45.00	27.00
(8)	Joe Pepitone	30.00	15.00	9.00
(9)	Bobby Richardson	30.00	15.00	9.00
(10)	Tom Tresh	30.00	15.00	9.00

1972 Photo Sports Co. L.A. Dodgers

This is the first known issue of a sports novelty marketed by Photo Sports Co., Los Angeles. The company is best known to collectors for its 1974 McDonald's promotional "Foto Balls" with player discs. The Dodgers set is similar in concept with a hinged plastic baseball which opens to reveal player discs. A "keyhole" punched at the bottom of the discs keeps them in place within the ball. The Dodgers never rolled out the project and surviving sets are extremely rare. Discs are 2-5/8" diameter with borderless color photos on front. Backs have player stats and the team logo. The unnumbered discs are checklisted here in alphabetical order.

		NM	EX	VG
Complete Set (Ball and Discs):		300.00	150.00	90.00
Common Player:		16.00	8.00	4.75
(1)	Red Adams	16.00	8.00	4.75
(2)	Walt Alston	35.00	17.50	10.50
(3)	Willie Crawford	16.00	8.00	4.75
(4)	Willie Davis	24.00	12.00	7.25
(5)	Al Downing	16.00	8.00	4.75
(6)	Jim Gilliam	24.00	12.00	7.25
(7)	Bill Grabarkewitz	16.00	8.00	4.75
(8)	Jim Lefebvre	16.00	8.00	4.75
(9)	Pete Mikkelsen	16.00	8.00	4.75
(10)	Manny Mota	18.00	9.00	5.50
(11)	Claude Osteen	16.00	8.00	4.75
(12)	Wes Parker	16.00	8.00	4.75
(13)	Duke Sims	16.00	8.00	4.75
(14)	Bill Singer	16.00	8.00	4.75
(15)	Bill Sudakis	16.00	8.00	4.75
(16)	Don Sutton	30.00	15.00	9.00
(17)	Bob Valentine	18.00	9.00	5.50
(18)	Maury Wills	22.00	11.00	6.50

1953 Pictsweet Milwaukee Braves

STAR CATCHER
OF THE MILWAUKEE BRAVES
WALKER COOPER

This black-and-white mini-poster (8-1/2" x 11-1/4") depicts a player holding a package of frozen vegetables. They were probably intended for grocery store window or aisle display. Backs are blank. It's unknown how many players are in the set. See also, Top Taste Bread.

		NM	EX	VG
Common Player:		150.00	75.00	45.00
(1)	"Bullet Bill" Bruton	150.00	75.00	45.00
(2)	Walker Cooper	150.00	75.00	45.00
(3)	Sid Gordon	150.00	75.00	45.00
(4)	Charlie Grimm	150.00	75.00	45.00
(5)	Sibby Sisti	150.00	75.00	45.00
(6)	Max Surkont	150.00	75.00	45.00

1970 Pictures of Champions Baltimore Orioles

12
DAVE MAY

Pictures of Champions

Issued in 1970 in the Baltimore area, this 16-card set pictures members of the Baltimore Orioles. The 2-1/8" x 2-3/4" cards feature black and white player photos on orange card stock. The method of distribution is unknown.

		NM	EX	VG
Complete Set (16):		80.00	40.00	25.00
Common Player:		2.00	1.00	.60
4	Earl Weaver	7.50	3.75	2.25
5	Brooks Robinson	25.00	12.50	7.50
7	Mark Belanger	2.00	1.00	.60
8	Andy Etchebarren	2.00	1.00	.60
9	Don Buford	2.00	1.00	.60
10	Ellie Hendricks	2.00	1.00	.60
12	Dave May	2.00	1.00	.60
15	Dave Johnson	2.00	1.00	.60
16	Dave McNally	2.00	1.00	.60
20	Frank Robinson	20.00	10.00	6.00
22	Jim Palmer	20.00	10.00	6.00
24	Pete Richert	2.00	1.00	.60
29	Dick Hall	2.00	1.00	.60
35	Mike Cuellar	2.00	1.00	.60
39	Eddie Watt	2.00	1.00	.60
40	Dave Leonhard	2.00	1.00	.60

1909-11 Piedmont Cigarettes

In both T205 and T206, Piedmont is the brand found most often on the cards' backs. In T205, Piedmonts backs are printed in blue with either Factory 25 and 42 designation, the latter of which is much scarcer but commands little premium, more due to collector indifference than relative scarcity. In T206, the familiar blue Piedmont logo is found in all three series. In the "150 Subjects" and "350 Subjects" series, only Factory 25 (Va.) is seen. In the "350-460 Subjects" series, both Factory 25 and Factory 42 (N.C.) are seen. The latter is much scarcer and commands a premium over the more common Factory 25 version.

FACTORY 42 OVERPRINTS PREMIUM:
Common Players: 5-7X
Hall of Famers: 2X
(See T205, T206)

1914 Piedmont Art Stamps (T330-2)

This series of "Piedmont Art Stamps" looks like a fragile version of the more popular T205 Gold Border tobacco cards of 1911, employing the same basic design on front. The Piedmont stamps measure 1-1/2" x 2-5/8". Though the backs advertise "100 designs," more than 110 different players are known. And, because some of the players are pictured in two separate poses, there are actually 118 different stamps known, with new discoveries still being made. All but three of the subjects in the Piedmont set were taken from the T205 set; the exceptions being Joe Wood, Walt Blair and Bill Killifer. Because of their fragile composition, examples of Piedmont Art Stamps in Near Mint or better condition are very scarce. The back of the stamps offered a "handsome" album in exchange for 25 Piedmont coupons. The set has an American Card Catalog designation of T330-2. Gaps have been left in the assigned numbering to accommodate future additions.

		NM	EX	VG
Common Player:		150.00	60.00	30.00
(1)	Leon K. Ames	150.00	60.00	30.00

(2)	Jimmy Archer	150.00	60.00	30.00
(3)	Jimmy Austin	150.00	60.00	30.00
(4)	Home Run Baker	450.00	180.00	90.00
(5)	Cy Barger (Full "B" on cap.)	150.00	60.00	30.00
(6)	Cy Barger (Partial "B" on cap.)	150.00	60.00	30.00
(7)	Jack Barry	150.00	60.00	30.00
(8)	Johnny Bates	150.00	60.00	30.00
(9)	Fred Beck	150.00	60.00	30.00
(10)	Beals Becker	150.00	60.00	30.00
(11)	Chief Bender	450.00	180.00	90.00
(12)	Bob Bescher	150.00	60.00	30.00
(13)	Joe Birmingham	150.00	60.00	30.00
(14)	Walt Blair	150.00	60.00	30.00
(15)	Roger Bresnahan	450.00	180.00	90.00
(16)	Al Bridwell	150.00	60.00	30.00
(17)	Mordecai Brown	450.00	180.00	90.00
(18)	Bobby Byrne	150.00	60.00	30.00
(19)	Howie Camnitz	150.00	60.00	30.00
(20)	Bill Carrigan	150.00	60.00	30.00
(21)	Frank Chance	450.00	180.00	90.00
(22)	Hal Chase ("Chase" on front.)	250.00	100.00	50.00
(23)	Hal Chase ("Hal Chase" on front.)	300.00	120.00	60.00
(24)	Ed Cicotte	375.00	150.00	75.00
(25)	Fred Clarke	450.00	180.00	90.00
(26)	Ty Cobb	5,500	2,200	1,100
(27)	Eddie Collins (Mouth closed.)	450.00	180.00	90.00
(28)	Eddie Collins (Mouth open.)	450.00	180.00	90.00
(29)	Otis "Doc" Crandall	150.00	60.00	30.00
(30)	Bill Dahlen	150.00	60.00	30.00
(31)	Jake Daubert	150.00	60.00	30.00
(32)	Jim Delahanty	150.00	60.00	30.00
(33)	Josh Devore	150.00	60.00	30.00
(34)	Red Dooin	150.00	60.00	30.00
(35)	Mickey Doolan	150.00	60.00	30.00
(36)	Tom Downey	150.00	60.00	30.00
(37)	Larry Doyle	150.00	60.00	30.00
(38)	Dick Egan	150.00	60.00	30.00
(39)	Kid Elberfield (Elberfeld)	150.00	60.00	30.00
(40)	Clyde Engle	150.00	60.00	30.00
(41)	Louis Evans	150.00	60.00	30.00
(42)	Johnny Evers	450.00	180.00	90.00
(43)	Ray Fisher	150.00	60.00	30.00
(44)	Art Fletcher	150.00	60.00	30.00
(45)	Russ Ford (Dark cap.)	150.00	60.00	30.00
(46)	Russ Ford (White cap.)	150.00	60.00	30.00
(47)	Art Fromme	150.00	60.00	30.00
(48)	George Gibson	150.00	60.00	30.00
(49)	William Goode (Wilbur Good)	150.00	60.00	30.00
(51)	Eddie Grant	225.00	90.00	45.00
(52)	Clark Griffith	450.00	180.00	90.00
(53)	Bob Groom	150.00	60.00	30.00
(54)	Bob Harmon	150.00	60.00	30.00
(55)	Arnold Hauser	150.00	60.00	30.00
(56)	Buck Herzog	150.00	60.00	30.00
(57)	Dick Hoblitzell	150.00	60.00	30.00
(58)	Miller Huggins	450.00	180.00	90.00
(59)	John Hummel	150.00	60.00	30.00
(60)	Hughie Jennings	450.00	180.00	90.00
(61)	Walter Johnson	750.00	300.00	150.00
(62)	Davy Jones	150.00	60.00	30.00
(63)	Bill Killifer (Killefer)	150.00	60.00	30.00
(64)	Jack Knight	150.00	60.00	30.00
(65)	Ed Konetchy	150.00	60.00	30.00
(66)	Frank LaPorte	150.00	60.00	30.00
(67)	Thomas Leach	150.00	60.00	30.00
(68)	Edgar Lennox	150.00	60.00	30.00
(69)	Hans Lobert	150.00	60.00	30.00
(70)	Harry Lord	150.00	60.00	30.00
(71)	Sherry Magee	150.00	60.00	30.00
(72)	Rube Marquard	450.00	180.00	90.00
(73)	Christy Mathewson	1,250	500.00	250.00
(74)	George McBride	150.00	60.00	30.00
(76)	J.J. McGraw	450.00	180.00	90.00
(77)	Larry McLean	150.00	60.00	30.00
(78)	Fred Merkle	150.00	60.00	30.00
(79)	Chief Meyers	150.00	60.00	30.00
(80)	Clyde Milan	150.00	60.00	30.00
(81)	Dots Miller	150.00	60.00	30.00
(82)	Mike Mitchell	150.00	60.00	30.00
(83)	Pat Moran	150.00	60.00	30.00
(84)	George Moriarity (Moriarty)	150.00	60.00	30.00
(85)	George Mullin	150.00	60.00	30.00
(86)	Danny Murphy	150.00	60.00	30.00
(87)	Jack "Red" Murray	150.00	60.00	30.00
(88)	Tom Needham	150.00	60.00	30.00
(89)	Rebel Oakes	150.00	60.00	30.00
(90)	Rube Oldring	150.00	60.00	30.00
(91)	Fred Parent	150.00	60.00	30.00
(92)	Dode Paskert	150.00	60.00	30.00
(93)	Jack Quinn	150.00	60.00	30.00
(94)	Ed Reulbach	150.00	60.00	30.00
(95)	Lewis Ritchie	150.00	60.00	30.00
(96)	Jack Rowan	150.00	60.00	30.00
(97)	Nap Rucker	150.00	60.00	30.00
(98)	Germany Schaefer	150.00	60.00	30.00
(99)	Wildfire Schulte	150.00	60.00	30.00
(101)	Jim Scott	150.00	60.00	30.00
(102)	Fred Snodgrass	150.00	60.00	30.00
(103)	Tris Speaker	600.00	240.00	120.00
(104)	Oscar Stamage (Stanage)	150.00	60.00	30.00
(105)	George Stovall	150.00	60.00	30.00
(106)	George Suggs	150.00	60.00	30.00
(107)	Jeff Sweeney	150.00	60.00	30.00
(108)	Ira Thomas	150.00	60.00	30.00
(109)	Joe Tinker	450.00	180.00	90.00
(110)	Terry Turner	150.00	60.00	30.00
(111)	Hippo Vaughn	150.00	60.00	30.00
(112)	Heinie Wagner	150.00	60.00	30.00
(113)	Bobby Wallace (No cap.)	450.00	180.00	90.00
(114)	Bobby Wallace (With cap.)	450.00	180.00	90.00
(115)	Ed Walsh	450.00	180.00	90.00
(116)	Zach Wheat	450.00	180.00	90.00
(117)	Irwin "Kaiser" Wilhelm	150.00	60.00	30.00
(118)	Ed Willett	150.00	60.00	30.00
(119)	Owen Wilson	150.00	60.00	30.00
(120)	Hooks Wiltse	150.00	60.00	30.00
(121)	Joe Wood	150.00	60.00	30.00

1939 Piel's Beer Coasters

New York Giants manager Bill Terry was the only baseball player among a trio of local celebrities endoring the beer brand in this series of approximately 4" diameter bar coasters. The printing is in black-and-red.

	NM	EX	VG
Bill Terry	30.00	15.00	9.00

1913-1915 Pinkerton Score/Photo/Post Cards

The picture portions of the T5 Pinkerton cabinets have also been seen in other formats, in printed rather than photographic presentation. The most desirable of these have backs printed for use as baseball scorecards. These measure a nominal 3-1/2" x 5-1/2", give or take 1/4". They are believed to have been printed some years after the cabinet cards. It is unknown to what extent the checklist of T5 can be found in this format. Postcard-style backs have also been seen for some Pinkerton pictures, as well as blank-backed versions; they are considerably discounted from the scorecard type. Confirmed examples are listed here.

		NM	EX	VG
Common Player:		250.00	125.00	75.00
SCORECARD BACKS				
153	Hughie Jennings	500.00	250.00	150.00
159	Ty Cobb	2,500	1,250	750.00
203	King Cole	250.00	125.00	75.00
205	Heinie Zimmerman	250.00	125.00	75.00
206	Wildfire Schulte	250.00	125.00	75.00
208	Joe Tinker	500.00	250.00	150.00
251	Christy Mathewson	1,500	750.00	450.00
252	Fred Merkle	250.00	125.00	75.00
260	Larry Doyle	250.00	125.00	75.00
303	Red Dooin	250.00	125.00	75.00
420	R.C. Hoblitzell	250.00	125.00	75.00
424	Mike Mitchell	250.00	125.00	75.00
505	Connie Mack	500.00	250.00	150.00
511	Eddie Collins	500.00	250.00	150.00
512	Frank Baker	500.00	250.00	150.00
872	Hans Wagner	800.00	400.00	240.00
POSTCARD OR BLANK BACKS				
159	Ty Cobb	1,500	750.00	450.00
203	King Cole	150.00	75.00	45.00
206	Frank Schulte	150.00	75.00	45.00
208	Joe Tinker	250.00	125.00	75.00
251	Christy Mathewson	350.00	175.00	105.00
260	Larry Doyle	150.00	75.00	45.00
264	Chief Myers (Meyers)	150.00	75.00	45.00
419	Clark Griffith	250.00	125.00	75.00
424	Mike Mitchell	150.00	75.00	45.00
501	Chas. Bender	250.00	125.00	75.00
511	Eddie Collins	250.00	125.00	75.00
512	Frank Baker	250.00	125.00	75.00
627	Napoleon Lajoie	250.00	125.00	75.00
855	Fred Clarke	250.00	125.00	75.00
865	Babe Adams	150.00	75.00	45.00
872	Hans Wagner	600.00	300.00	180.00

1912 Pirate Cigarettes (T215)

This set can be considerd a British version of the T215 Red Cross Type 1 set. Distributed by Pirate brand cigarettes of Bristol and London, England, the fronts of the cards are identical to the Red Cross cards, but the green backs carry advertising for Pirate Cigarettes. It is believed that the Pirate cards were printed for distribution to U.S. servicemen in the South Seas. There is reason to believe the "standard" tobacco card length of 2-5/8" (width 1-7/16") may not be universally applicable to the Pirate cards, possibly because of packaging considerations.

		NM	EX	VG
Common Player:		11,000	5,500	3,300
(1)	Red Ames	11,000	5,500	3,300
(2)	Home Run Baker	16,000	8,000	4,800
(3)	Neal Ball	11,000	5,500	3,300
(4)	Chief Bender	16,000	8,000	4,800
(5)	Al Bridwell	11,000	5,500	3,300
(6)	Bobby Byrne (St. Louis)	11,000	5,500	3,300
(7)	Mordecai Brown (Chicago on shirt.)	16,000	8,000	4,800
(8)	Howie Camnitz	11,000	5,500	3,300
(9)	Frank Chance	9,800	4,900	2,950
(10)	Hal Chase	14,500	7,250	4,350
(11)	Eddie Collins	16,000	8,000	4,800
(12)	Doc Crandall	11,000	5,500	3,300
(13)	Sam Crawford	16,000	8,000	4,800
(14)	Birdie Cree	11,000	5,500	3,300
(15)	Harry Davis	11,000	5,500	3,300
(16)	Josh Devore	11,000	5,500	3,300
(17)	Mike Donlin	11,000	5,500	3,300
(18)	Mickey Doolan (Batting)	11,000	5,500	3,300
(19)	Mickey Doolan (Fielding)	11,000	5,500	3,300
(20)	Patsy Dougherty	11,000	5,500	3,300
(21)	Larry Doyle (Batting)	11,000	5,500	3,300
(22)	Larry Doyle (Portrait)	11,000	5,500	3,300
(23)	Jean Dubuc	11,000	5,500	3,300
(24)	Kid Elberfeld	11,000	5,500	3,300
(25)	Steve Evans	11,000	5,500	3,300
(26)	Johnny Evers	16,000	8,000	4,800
(27)	Russ Ford	11,000	5,500	3,300
(28)	Art Fromme	11,000	5,500	3,300
(29)	Clark Griffith	16,000	8,000	4,800
(30)	Bob Groom	11,000	5,500	3,300
(31)	Topsy Hartsel	11,000	5,500	3,300
(32)	Buck Herzog	11,000	5,500	3,300
(33)	Dick Hoblitzell	11,000	5,500	3,300
(34)	Solly Hofman	11,000	5,500	3,300
(35)	Del Howard	11,000	5,500	3,300
(36)	Miller Huggins (Hands at mouth.)	16,000	8,000	4,800
(37)	Miller Huggins (Portrait)	16,000	8,000	4,800
(38)	John Hummel	11,000	5,500	3,300
(39)	Hughie Jennings (Both hands showing.)	16,000	8,000	4,800
(40)	Hughie Jennings (One hand showing.)	16,000	8,000	4,800
(41)	Walter Johnson	35,000	17,500	10,500
(42)	Joe Kelley	16,000	8,000	4,800
(43)	Ed Konetchy	11,000	5,500	3,300
(44)	Harry Krause	11,000	5,500	3,300
(45)	Nap Lajoie	16,000	8,000	4,800
(46)	Joe Lake	11,000	5,500	3,300
(47)	Lefty Leifield	11,000	5,500	3,300
(48)	Harry Lord	11,000	5,500	3,300
(49)	Sherry Magee	11,000	5,500	3,300
(50)	Rube Marquard (Pitching)	16,000	8,000	4,800
(51)	Rube Marquard (Portrait)	16,000	8,000	4,800
(52)	Christy Mathewson (Black cap.)	20,000	10,000	5,000
(53)	Joe McGinnity	16,000	8,000	4,800
(54)	John McGraw (Glove at side.)	16,000	8,000	4,800
(55)	John McGraw (Portrait)	16,000	8,000	4,800
(56)	Harry McIntyre (Chicago)	11,000	5,500	3,300
(57)	Harry McIntyre (Brooklyn & Chicago)	11,000	5,500	3,300
(58)	Matty McIntyre (Detroit)	11,000	5,500	3,300
(59)	Larry McLean	11,000	5,500	3,300
(60)	Fred Merkle	11,000	5,500	3,300
(61)	Chief Meyers	11,000	5,500	3,300
(62)	Mike Mitchell	11,000	5,500	3,300
(63)	Dots Miller	11,000	5,500	3,300
(64)	Mike Mowrey	11,000	5,500	3,300
(65)	George Mullin	11,000	5,500	3,300
(66)	Danny Murphy	11,000	5,500	3,300
(67)	Red Murray	11,000	5,500	3,300
(68)	Rebel Oakes	11,000	5,500	3,300
(69)	Rube Oldring	11,000	5,500	3,300
(70)	Charley O'Leary	11,000	5,500	3,300
(71)	Dode Paskert	11,000	5,500	3,300
(72)	Barney Pelty	11,000	5,500	3,300
(73)	Billy Purtell	11,000	5,500	3,300
(74)	Jack Quinn	11,000	5,500	3,300
(75)	Ed Reulbach	11,000	5,500	3,300
(76)	Nap Rucker	11,000	5,500	3,300
(77)	Germany Schaefer	11,000	5,500	3,300
(78)	Wildfire Schulte	11,000	5,500	3,300
(79)	Jimmy Sheckard	11,000	5,500	3,300
(80)	Frank Smith	11,000	5,500	3,300
(81)	Tris Speaker	18,000	9,000	5,400
(82)	Jake Stahl	11,000	5,500	3,300
(83)	Harry Steinfeldt	11,000	5,500	3,300
(84)	Gabby Street	11,000	5,500	3,300
(85)	Ed Summers	11,000	5,500	3,300
(86)	Jeff Sweeney	11,000	5,500	3,300
(87)	Lee Tannehill	11,000	5,500	3,300
(88)	Ira Thomas	11,000	5,500	3,300
(89)	Joe Tinker	16,000	8,000	4,800
(90)	Heinie Wagner	11,000	5,500	3,300
(91)	Jack Warhop	11,000	5,500	3,300
(92)	Zack Wheat	16,000	8,000	4,800
(93)	Ed Willetts (Willett)	11,000	5,500	3,300
(94)	Owen Wilson	11,000	5,500	3,300
(95)	Hooks Wiltse (Pitching)	11,000	5,500	3,300
(96)	Hooks Wiltse (Portrait)	11,000	5,500	3,300

1910 Pittsburgh Gazette Times Honus Wagner Postcard

Describing him as "The Worlds' Greatest Base Ball Player," the local newspaper published this black-and-white standard size, typically marked, photographic postcard picturing the Flying Dutchman and landmarks from his Carnegie, Pa., hometown.

	NM	EX	VG
Honus Wagner	650.00	325.00	200.00

1904 Pittsburg Leader Honus Wagner Schedule

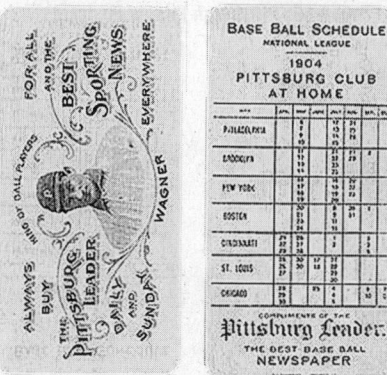

This 3-3/4" x 1-3/4" celluloid pocket schedule for the 1904 Pirates features on its front a black-and-white photographic portrait of the "KING OF BALL PLAYERS," Honus Wagner. Much of the remainder of the front and back printing is in regal purple typography.

	NM	EX	VG
Honus Wagner	3,500	1,750	1,100

1908 Pittsburgh Pirates Vignette Postcards

It has been reliably reported that 15 postcards and an album were produced for this souvenir issue sold at Pittsburgh's Exhibition Field. Only Pirates are pictured in this series of black-and-white standard-format postcards published locally by J.B. Coyle. Cards have an irregularly shaped posed photo of the player at center with his last name (or nickname), position and "PGH-08" crudely printed in white. Divided postcard backs have a stamp box and publisher's credit line. The incomplete checklist presented here is alphabetically arranged. Later editions of the American Card Catalog listed this set as PC800.

		NM	EX	VG
Common Player:		250.00	125.00	75.00
(1)	Abby (Ed Abbaticchio)	250.00	125.00	75.00
(2)	Howie Camnitz	250.00	125.00	75.00
(3)	Fred Clarke	350.00	175.00	105.00
(4)	George Gibson	250.00	125.00	75.00
(5)	Tommy Leach	250.00	125.00	75.00
(6)	Dan Moeller	250.00	125.00	75.00
(10)	Allen Storke	250.00	125.00	75.00
(14)	Honus Wagner	1,000	500.00	300.00
(15)	Owen Wilson	250.00	125.00	75.00

1909 Pittsburgh Pirates Extension Postcard

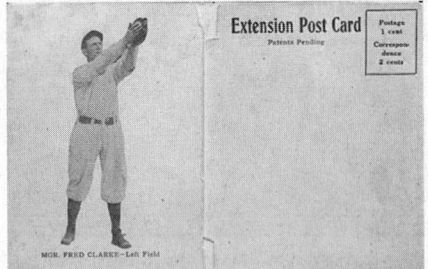

One of many novelty souvenirs commemorating the Bucs' World Championship season of 1909 was this uniquely formatted postcard. Picturing manager Fred Clarke on front, the 3-1/4" x 5-1/2" postcard opens up accordian fashion to a length of 14", revealing small action photos of 17 players each on a white background and identified by last name and position.

	NM	EX	VG
1909 Pittsburgh Pirates	3,000	1,500	900.00

1950-60s Pittsburgh Pirates Postcards

 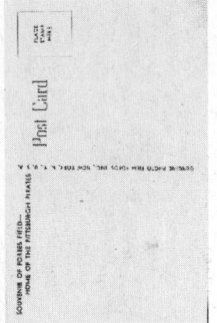

This listing encompasses the issues of several different postcard publishers who supplied black-and-white cards to the players for use in answering fan mail. Several different types of card stock are found, both matte and glossy. Some cards have postcard markings on back, others do not, especially those picturing players in the 1960s style sleeveless style uniforms. Because it is likely other players and poses will be reported, a description of each pose is included.

		NM	EX	VG
Common Player:		15.00	7.50	4.50
(1)	Gair Allie (Ready to hit.)	15.00	7.50	4.50
(2)	Toby Atwell (Squatting w/glove.)	15.00	7.50	4.50
(3)	Tony Bartirome (Stretching at 1B.)	15.00	7.50	4.50
(4)	Carlos Bernier (Batting)	15.00	7.50	4.50
(5)	Ron Blackburn (Pitching, left leg up.)	15.00	7.50	4.50
(6)	Ron Brand (Kneeling w/glove.)	15.00	7.50	4.50
(7)	Jim Bunning (Pitching, to letters.)	25.00	12.50	7.50
(8)	Don (Swede) Carlson (Pitching, by wall.)	15.00	7.50	4.50
(9)	Pete Castiglione (Ready to hit.)	15.00	7.50	4.50
(10)	Pete Castiglione (Kneeling w/bat.)	15.00	7.50	4.50
(12)	Cliff Chambers (Pitching, leg up.)	15.00	7.50	4.50
(13)	Bob Chesnes (Follow-through.)	15.00	7.50	4.50
(14)	Roberto Clemente (Kneeling w/bat.)	125.00	65.00	35.00
(15)	Dick Cole (Fielding)	15.00	7.50	4.50
(16)	Dale Coogan (Ready to hit.)	15.00	7.50	4.50
(18)	Bobby Del Greco (Batting follow-through.)	15.00	7.50	4.50
(20)	Elroy Face (Follow-through, cloth cap, sleeves.)	17.50	8.75	5.25
(21)	Elroy Face (Follow-through, cloth cap, no sleeves.)	17.50	8.75	5.25
(22)	Elroy Face (Follow-through, helmet, sleeves.)	17.50	8.75	5.25
(23)	Elroy Face (Follow-through, helmet, no sleeves.)	17.50	8.75	5.25

		NM	EX	VG
(24)	Hank Foiles (Squatting)	15.00	7.50	4.50
(25)	Gene Freese (Ready to hit.)	15.00	7.50	4.50
(26)	Bob Friend (Follow-through.)	15.00	7.50	4.50
(27)	Bob Friend (Pitching, leg up.)	15.00	7.50	4.50
(28)	Bob Friend (Standing in dugout.)	15.00	7.50	4.50
(29)	Dick Groat (Ready to hit.)	17.50	8.75	5.25
(30)	Fred Haney (Arms folded.)	15.00	7.50	4.50
(31)	John Hetki (Follow-through.)	15.00	7.50	4.50
(32)	Johnny Hopp (Stretching at 1B.)	15.00	7.50	4.50
(34)	Ralph Kiner (Batting, two decks.)	25.00	12.50	7.50
(35)	Nellie King (Follow-through.)	15.00	7.50	4.50
(36)	Ron Kline (Follow-through.)	15.00	7.50	4.50
(37)	Ron Kline (Pitching, leg up.)	15.00	7.50	4.50
(38)	Ted Kluszewski (Kneeling with bat.)	20.00	10.00	6.00
(39)	Ted Kluszewski (Pose to chest.)	20.00	10.00	6.00
(41)	Nick Koback (Kneeling)	15.00	7.50	4.50
(42)	Clem Koshorek (Fielding)	15.00	7.50	4.50
(43)	Danny Kravitz (Ready to hit.)	15.00	7.50	4.50
(44)	Vern Law (Follow-through, bleachers.)	17.50	8.75	5.25
(45)	Vern Law (Follow-through, trees.)	17.50	8.75	5.25
(46)	Vern Law (Follow-through, right foot cut off.)	17.50	8.75	5.25
(47)	Vern Law (Kneeling)	17.50	8.75	5.25
(48)	Vern Law (Pitching, leg up.)	17.50	8.75	5.25
(49)	Lenny Levy (Catching)	15.00	7.50	4.50
(50)	Lenny Levy (Standing in dugout.)	15.00	7.50	4.50
(51)	Dale Long (Batting)	15.00	7.50	4.50
(52)	Dale Long (Kneeling w/bat.)	15.00	7.50	4.50
(53)	Jerry Lynch (Batting, sleeves.)	15.00	7.50	4.50
(54)	Jerry Lynch (Batting, no sleeves.)	15.00	7.50	4.50
(55)	Bill MacDonald (Pitching, leg up.)	15.00	7.50	4.50
(56)	Bill Mazeroski (Fielding, ball in glove, horizontal.)	25.00	12.50	7.50
(57)	Bill Mazeroski (Fielding, ball in hand.)	25.00	12.50	7.50
(58)	Danny Murtaugh (Fielding)	15.00	7.50	4.50
(59)	Danny Murtaugh (Portrait, helmet.)	15.00	7.50	4.50
(60)	George "Red" Munger (Pitching)	15.00	7.50	4.50
(61)	Johnny O'Brien (Jumping)	15.00	7.50	4.50
(63)	Danny O'Connell (Batting)	15.00	7.50	4.50
(64)	Bob Oldis (Portrait to belt.)	15.00	7.50	4.50
(65)	Laurin Pepper (Follow-through.)	15.00	7.50	4.50
(66)	Pete Peterson (Catching)	15.00	7.50	4.50
(68)	Buddy Pritchard (Batting)	15.00	7.50	4.50
(69)	Bob Purkey (Follow-through.)	15.00	7.50	4.50
(70)	Bob Purkey (Portrait)	15.00	7.50	4.50
(71)	Mel Queen (Pitching, leg up.)	15.00	7.50	4.50
(72)	Curt Raydon (Follow-through, horizontal.)	15.00	7.50	4.50
(74)	Dino Restelli (Batting)	15.00	7.50	4.50
(75)	Stan Rojek (Batting)	15.00	7.50	4.50
(76)	Stan Rojek (Standing in dugout.)	15.00	7.50	4.50
(78)	Tom Saffell (Batting)	15.00	7.50	4.50
(80)	Don Schwall (Pitching, no cap.)	15.00	7.50	4.50
(81)	Bob Skinner (Batting)	15.00	7.50	4.50
(82)	Bob Smith (Follow-through.)	15.00	7.50	4.50
(83)	Paul Smith (Batting)	15.00	7.50	4.50
(84)	Art Swanson (Hands on hips.)	15.00	7.50	4.50
(86)	Frank Thomas (Batting, cap.)	17.50	8.75	5.25
(87)	Frank Thomas (Batting, helmet.)	17.50	8.75	5.25
(90)	Bill Virdon (Batting, matte.)	17.50	8.75	5.25
(91)	Bill Virdon (Batting, glossy.)	17.50	8.75	5.25
(92)	Bill Virdon (Kneeling)	17.50	8.75	5.25
(93)	Harry Walker (Portrait)	15.00	7.50	4.50
(94)	Lee Walls (Batting, glove in pocket.)	15.00	7.50	4.50
(95)	Lee Walls (Batting, trees.)	15.00	7.50	4.50
(96)	Jim Walsh (Follow-through, horizontal.)	15.00	7.50	4.50
(97)	Preston Ward (Batting, #44 in background.)	15.00	7.50	4.50
(98)	Preston Ward (Batting, no #44.)	15.00	7.50	4.50
(99)	Fred Waters (Pitching, leg up.)	15.00	7.50	4.50
(100)	Bill Werle (Pitching)	15.00	7.50	4.50

1950 Pittsburgh Pirates Photo Pack

The player photos in this picture pack that was sold at Forbes Field measure 6-1/2" x 9" and are printed in black-and-

white on heavy, blank-backed paper. A facsimile "autograph" is printed on front of each picture, though all were written in the same hand. Several of the photos from this set were the basis for the color paintings found on 1951 Bowman cards. The unnumbered pictures are checklisted here alphabetically.

		NM	EX	VG
Complete Set (26):		250.00	125.00	75.00
Common Player:		12.00	6.00	3.50
(1)	Ted Beard	12.00	6.00	3.50
(2)	Gus Bell	20.00	10.00	6.00
(3)	Pete Castiglione	12.00	6.00	3.50
(4)	Cliff Chambers	12.00	6.00	3.50
(5)	Dale Coogan	12.00	6.00	3.50
(6)	Murry Dickson	12.00	6.00	3.50
(7)	Bob Dillinger	12.00	6.00	3.50
(8)	Froilan Fernandez	12.00	6.00	3.50
(9)	Johnny Hopp	12.00	6.00	3.50
(10)	Ralph Kiner	30.00	15.00	9.00
(11)	Vernon Law	20.00	10.00	6.00
(12)	Vic Lombardi	12.00	6.00	3.50
(13)	Bill MacDonald	12.00	6.00	3.50
(14)	Clyde McCullough	12.00	6.00	3.50
(15)	Bill Meyer	12.00	6.00	3.50
(16)	Ray Mueller	12.00	6.00	3.50
(17)	Danny Murtaugh	12.00	6.00	3.50
(18)	Jack Phillips	12.00	6.00	3.50
(19)	Mel Queen	12.00	6.00	3.50
(20)	Stan Rojek	12.00	6.00	3.50
(21)	Henry Schenz	12.00	6.00	3.50
(22)	George Strickland	12.00	6.00	3.50
(23)	Earl Turner	12.00	6.00	3.50
(24)	Jim Walsh	12.00	6.00	3.50
(25)	Bill Werle	12.00	6.00	3.50
(26)	Wally Westlake	12.00	6.00	3.50

1967 Pittsburgh Pirates Autograph Cards

A souvenir stand item introduced by the Pirates in 1967 was a series of color player cards bearing facsimile autographs. The 3-1/4" x 4-1/4" cards identify the player with a line of type beneath the photo giving name, position and uniform number. Backs are blank. The cards are checklisted here in alphabetical order.

		NM	EX	VG
Complete Set (24):		100.00	50.00	30.00
Common Player:		4.00	2.00	1.25
	SERIES A	.00	.00	.00
(1)	Gene Alley	4.00	2.00	1.25
(2)	Steve Blass	4.00	2.00	1.25
(3)	Roberto Clemente	35.00	17.50	10.00
(4)	Donn Clendenon	5.00	2.50	1.50
(5)	Roy Face	5.00	2.50	1.50
(6)	Jesse Gonder	4.00	2.00	1.25
(7)	Jerry May	4.00	2.00	1.25
(8)	Manny Mota	5.00	2.50	1.50
(9)	Jose Pagan	4.00	2.00	1.25
(10)	Dennis Ribant	4.00	2.00	1.25
(11)	Tommie Sisk	4.00	2.00	1.25
(12)	Bob Veale	4.00	2.00	1.25
	SERIES B	.00	.00	.00
(13)	Matty Alou	4.00	2.00	1.25
(14)	Woody Fryman	4.00	2.00	1.25
(15)	Vernon Law	5.00	2.50	1.50
(16)	Bill Mazeroski	17.50	8.75	5.25
(17)	Al McBean	4.00	2.00	1.25
(18)	Pete Mikkelsen	4.00	2.00	1.25
(19)	Jim Pagliaroni	4.00	2.00	1.25
(20)	Juan Pizarro	4.00	2.00	1.25
(21)	Andy Rodgers	4.00	2.00	1.25
(22)	Willie Stargell	15.00	7.50	4.50
(23)	Harry Walker	4.00	2.00	1.25
(24)	Maury Wills	6.50	3.25	2.00

1968 Pittsburgh Pirates Autograph Cards

These team-issued autograph cards were sold in packages at Forbes Field. The 3-1/4" x 4-1/4" cards feature a color player photo and facsimile autograph. They are blank-backed. Cards were issued in Series A and Series B, with header cards in each series providing a checklist. Cards are listed here by series according to the uniform number found on the card.

		NM	EX	VG
Complete Set (26):		45.00	22.00	13.50
Common Player:		2.00	1.00	.60
	SERIES A			
7	Larry Shepard	2.00	1.00	.60
11	Jose Pagan	2.00	1.00	.60
12	Jerry May	2.00	1.00	.60
14	Jim Bunning	7.50	3.75	2.25
15	Manny Mota	2.00	1.00	.60
17	Donn Clendenon	3.00	1.50	.90
21	Roberto Clemente	15.00	7.50	4.50
22	Gene Alley	2.00	1.00	.60
25	Tommie Sisk	2.00	1.00	.60
26	Roy Face	2.00	1.00	.60
28	Steve Blass	2.00	1.00	.60
39	Bob Veale	2.00	1.00	.60
--	Checklist Card, Series A	2.00	1.00	.60
	SERIES B			
8	Willie Stargell	8.00	4.00	2.50
9	Bill Mazeroski	9.00	4.50	2.75
10	Gary Kolb	2.00	1.00	.60
18	Matty Alou	2.50	1.25	.70
27	Ronnie Kline	2.00	1.00	.60
29	Juan Pizzaro	2.00	1.00	.60
30	Maury Wills	4.00	2.00	1.25
34	Al McBean	2.00	1.00	.60
35	Manny Sanguillen	2.00	1.00	.60
38	Bob Moose	2.00	1.00	.60
40	Dave Wickersham	2.00	1.00	.60
--	Jim Shellenback	2.00	1.00	.60
--	Checklist Card, Series B	2.00	1.00	.60

1969 Pittsburgh Pirates Autograph Cards

BRUCE DEL CANTON (Pitcher) #43

Sold in Series A with a blue header card/checklist and Series B with a pink header card/checklist, these team-issue autograph cards were available at Forbes Field. Identical in format to the previous year's issue, the 3-1/4" x 4-1/4" cards are blank-backed and feature a color player photo on front with a facsimile autograph in the wide white bottom border. Cards are checklisted here by series and uniform number (found on card fronts) within series.

		NM	EX	VG
Complete Set:		50.00	25.00	15.00
Common Player:		2.00	1.00	.60
	Series A			
2	Fred Patek	2.00	1.00	.60
4	Larry Shepard	2.00	1.00	.60
8	Willie Stargell	6.00	3.00	1.75
9	Bill Mazeroski	9.00	4.50	2.75
10	Gary Kolb	2.00	1.00	.60
23	Luke Walker	2.00	1.00	.60
28	Steve Blass	2.00	1.00	.60
29	Al Oliver	4.00	2.00	1.25
35	Manny Sanguillen	2.50	1.25	.70
38	Bob Moose	2.00	1.00	.60
39	Bob Veale	2.00	1.00	.60
42	Chuck Hartenstein	2.00	1.00	.60
	Series B			
7	Bill Virdon	2.50	1.25	.70
11	Jose Pagan	2.00	1.00	.60
12	Jerry May	2.00	1.00	.60
14	Jim Bunning	7.50	3.75	2.25
18	Matty Alou	2.50	1.25	.70
20	Richie Hebner	3.00	1.50	.90
21	Roberto Clemente	15.00	7.50	4.50
22	Gene Alley	2.00	1.00	.60
32	Vernon Law	2.50	1.25	.70
36	Carl Taylor	2.00	1.00	.60
40	Dock Ellis	2.50	1.25	.70
43	Bruce Dal Canton	2.00	1.00	.60

1970 Pittsburgh Pirates (Andersen)

Boston baseball photographer Mike Andersen is believed to have produced this collectors' issue of Pirates cards. Nearly identical in format to his 1969-70 Oakland A's issues, the '70 Pirates measures 2-1/4" x 3-5/8" with black-and-white player poses at center. Player identification and 1969 stats are in the bottom border. Backs are blank. Cards are checklisted here alphabetically.

		NM	EX	VG
Complete Set (12):		40.00	20.00	12.00
Common Player:		2.00	1.00	.60
(1)	Gene Alley	2.00	1.00	.60
(2)	Dave Cash	2.00	1.00	.60
(3)	Dock Ellis	2.00	1.00	.60
(4)	Dave Giusti	2.00	1.00	.60
(5)	Jerry May	2.00	1.00	.60
(6)	Bill Mazeroski	12.00	6.00	3.50
(7)	Al Oliver	4.00	2.00	1.25
(8)	Jose Pagan	2.00	1.00	.60
(9)	Fred Patek	2.00	1.00	.60
(10)	Bob Robertson	2.00	1.00	.60
(11)	Manny Sanguillen	2.00	1.00	.60
(12)	Willie Stargell	12.00	6.00	3.50

1970 Pittsburgh Pirates Autograph Cards

MATTY ALOU [Outfielder] #18

Retaining the 3-1/4" x 4-1/4" format from previous years, these team-issued autograph cards can be distinguished from the 1968-69 issues by the Three Rivers Stadium photo background on each card. The Pirates moved from Forbes Field in June, 1970. The set is checklisted here by uniform number without regard to Series A and B.

		NM	EX	VG
Complete Set (25):		90.00	45.00	27.50
Common Player:		3.00	1.50	.80
2	Fred Patek	3.00	1.50	.80
5	Dave Ricketts	3.00	1.50	.80
8	Willie Stargell	12.00	6.00	3.50
9	Bill Mazeroski	12.00	6.00	3.50
10	Richie Hebner	3.00	1.50	.90
11	Jose Pagan	3.00	1.50	.80
12	Jerry May	3.00	1.50	.80
16	Al Oliver	5.00	2.50	1.50
17	Dock Ellis	3.00	1.50	.80
18	Matty Alou	3.00	1.50	.80
19	Joe Gibbon	3.00	1.50	.80
21	Roberto Clemente	25.00	12.50	7.50
22	Gene Alley	3.00	1.50	.80
22	Orlando Pena	3.00	1.50	.80
23	Luke Walker	3.00	1.50	.80
25	John Jeter	3.00	1.50	.80
25	Bob Robertson	3.00	1.50	.80
30	Dave Cash	3.00	1.50	.80
31	Dave Giusti	3.00	1.50	.80
35	Manny Sanguillen	3.00	1.50	.90
36	Dick Calpaert (Colpaert)	3.00	1.50	.80
38	Bob Moose	3.00	1.50	.80
39	Bob Veale	3.00	1.50	.80
40	Danny Murtaugh	3.00	1.50	.80
50	Jim Nelson	3.00	1.50	.80

1971 Pittsburgh Pirates Autograph Cards

DAVE GIUSTI (Pitcher) #31

The '71 team-issued Pirates autograph cards are distinguished by the appearance of mustard-yellow caps on the players' portraits. Otherwise the blank-back 3-1/4" x 4-1/2" photocards are identical in format to those of earlier seasons. Players are checklisted here alphabetically within series.

		NM	EX	VG
Complete Set (20):		45.00	22.50	13.50
Common Player:		2.00	1.00	.60
	Series A			
(1)	Gene Alley	2.00	1.00	.60
(2)	Nelson Briles	2.00	1.00	.60
(3)	Dave Cash	2.00	1.00	.60
(4)	Dock Ellis	2.00	1.00	.60
(5)	Mudcat Grant	2.50	1.25	.70
(6)	Bill Mazeroski	9.00	4.50	2.75
(7)	Jim Nelson	2.00	1.00	.60
(8)	Al Oliver	4.00	2.00	1.25
(9)	Manny Sanguillen	2.50	1.25	.70
(10)	Luke Walker	2.00	1.00	.60
	Series B			
(11)	Steve Blass	2.00	1.00	.60
(12)	Bob Clemente	15.00	7.50	4.50
(13)	Dave Giusti	2.00	1.00	.60
(14)	Richie Hebner	2.50	1.25	.70
(15)	Bob Johnson	2.00	1.00	.60
(16)	Bob Moose	2.00	1.00	.60
(17)	Jose Pagan	2.00	1.00	.60
(18)	Bob Robertson	2.00	1.00	.60
(19)	Willie Stargell	8.00	4.00	2.50
(20)	Bob Veale	2.00	1.00	.60

1973 Pittsburgh Post-Gazette Pirates

This set of Pirates pictures was printed on newspaper stock one per day in the sports section of the daily paper. The black-bordered black-and-white photos are 5-1/4" x 9-1/4". At top is "'73 Pirate Album" and a short career summary. At bottom are 1972 and career stats. The first six pictures are unnumbered, the others are numbered alphabetically.

		NM	EX	VG
Complete Set (25):		125.00	60.00	35.00
Common Player:		6.00	3.00	1.75
	Gene Alley	6.00	3.00	1.75
	Steve Blass	6.00	3.00	1.75
	Nellie Briles	6.00	3.00	1.75
	Dave Cash	6.00	3.00	1.75
	Roberto Clemente	40.00	20.00	12.00
	Gene Clines	6.00	3.00	1.75
6	Vic Davalillo	6.00	3.00	1.75
7	Dock Ellis	6.00	3.00	1.75
8	Dave Giusti	6.00	3.00	1.75
9	Richie Hebner	6.00	3.00	1.75
10	Jackie Hernandez	6.00	3.00	1.75
11	Ramon Hernandez	6.00	3.00	1.75
12	Bob Johnson	6.00	3.00	1.75
13	Bruce Kison	6.00	3.00	1.75
14	Milt May	6.00	3.00	1.75
15	Bob Miller	6.00	3.00	1.75
16	Bob Moose	6.00	3.00	1.75
17	Al Oliver	7.50	3.75	2.25
18	Bob Robertson	6.00	3.00	1.75
19	Charlie Sands	6.00	3.00	1.75
20	Manny Sanguillen	6.00	3.00	1.75
21	Willie Stargell	12.00	6.00	3.50
22	Rennie Stennett	6.00	3.00	1.75
23	Luke Walker	6.00	3.00	1.75
24	Bill Virdon	7.50	3.75	2.25

1972 Pittsburgh Press "Buc-A-Day" Pirates

BUC-A-DAY ... No. 6
Bill Mazeroski
WILLIAM STANLEY MAZEROSKI (28)

Through the month of March 1972, the daily Pittsburgh Press carried a "Buc-A-Day" feature highlighting members of the team. The feature was intended to be cut out of the paper and saved. Individual pieces measure 3-3/8" wide and vary in length from 9-1/4" to 11-1/16" depending on the length of the biographical information provided. Each player is pictured in a black-and-white photo in street clothes. Some are pictured with golf clubs, fishing poles, with their children, etc. Because of the nature of their distribution and their fragile nature, complete sets are very scarce.

		NM	EX	VG
Complete Set (25):		100.00	50.00	30.00
Common Player:		2.50	1.25	.70
1	Willie Stargell	7.50	3.75	2.25
2	Steve Blass	2.50	1.25	.70
3	Al Oliver	3.00	1.50	.90
4	Bob Moose	2.50	1.25	.70
5	Dave Cash	2.50	1.25	.70
6	Bill Mazeroski	7.50	3.75	2.25
7	Bob Robertson	2.50	1.25	.70
8	Nellie Briles	2.50	1.25	.70
9	Manny Sanguillen	3.00	1.50	.90
10	Vic Davalillo	2.50	1.25	.70
11	Dave Giusti	2.50	1.25	.70
12	Luke Walker	2.50	1.25	.70
13	Gene Clines	2.50	1.25	.70
14	Milt May	2.50	1.25	.70
15	Bob Robertson	2.50	1.25	.70
16	Roberto Clemente	15.00	7.50	4.50
17	Gene Alley	2.50	1.25	.70
18	Bruce Kison	2.50	1.25	.70
19	Jose Pagan	2.50	1.25	.70
20	Dock Ellis	2.50	1.25	.70
21	Richie Hebner	2.50	1.25	.70
22	Bob Miller	2.50	1.25	.70
23	Jackie Hernandez	2.50	1.25	.70
24	Rennie Stennett	2.50	1.25	.70
25	Bob Veale	2.50	1.25	.70

1948 Pittsburgh Provision & Packing Co.

The attributed date is totally arbitrary, based on the photo shown. Also unknown are the scope of the issue and its manner of distribution. Hobby history would suggest the card was created to promote Wagner's ties to the meat company as a spokesman, or perhaps the card was created for Wagner to distribute at appearances on behalf of the packing company. The dark green-printed card measures about 4" x 2-1/2" and is printed on rather thin cardboard. It is not known whether similar cards exist for other players.

	NM	EX	VG
Honus Wagner	400.00	200.00	120.00

1936 Pittsburgh Sun-Telegraph Sport Stamps

Similar to several contemporary issues, the Sport Stamps were printed in a single edition of the daily newspaper. Thirteen players were printed for each of the 16 Major League teams. About 2" x 3", depending on the length of the biography and how well they were cut off the paper, they are printed in black-and-white. A tightly cropped player portrait is centered on a 1-3/4" x 2-1/4" stamp design with the paper's name above and the player's name, position and team below. This checklist is incomplete.

		NM	EX	VG
Complete Set (208):		.00	.00	.00
Common Player:		12.00	6.00	3.50
(1)	Ralph Birkofer	12.00	6.00	3.50
(2)	Cy Blanton	12.00	6.00	3.50
(3)	Bill Brubaker	12.00	6.00	3.50
(4)	Guy Bush	12.00	6.00	3.50
(5)	Ty Cobb	25.00	12.50	7.50
(6)	Jerome "Dizzy" Dean	25.00	12.50	7.50
(7)	Joe DiMaggio	75.00	37.00	22.00
(8)	Hank Greenberg	25.00	12.50	7.50
(9)	Waite Hoyt	20.00	10.00	6.00
(10)	Carl Hubbell	20.00	10.00	6.00
(11)	Woody Jensen	12.00	6.00	3.50
(12)	Red Lucas	12.00	6.00	3.50
(13)	Joe Medwick	20.00	10.00	6.00
(13)	Tommy Padden	12.00	6.00	3.50
(14)	Casey Stengel	20.00	10.00	6.00
(15)	Clarence Strass	12.00	6.00	3.50
(16)	Gus Suhr	12.00	6.00	3.50
(17)	Bill Swift	12.00	6.00	3.50
(18)	John Tising	12.00	6.00	3.50
(19)	Al Todd	12.00	6.00	3.50
(20)	Pie Traynor	20.00	10.00	6.00
(21)	Honus Wagner	25.00	12.50	7.50
(22)	Lloyd Waner	20.00	10.00	6.00
(23)	Paul Waner	20.00	10.00	6.00
(24)	Jim Weaver	12.00	6.00	3.50
(25)	Floyd Young	12.00	6.00	3.50

1954 Plankinton Milwaukee Braves Playing Tips

This set of "How to Play Better Baseball" poster booklets was apparently distributed in packages of hot dogs on a regional basis. Folded, the booklet measures 2-7/8" x 4-3/8" and has a black-and-white player portrait photo with a red background. When opened, the booklet forms an 11" x 17" poster offering big league tips from Braves players. The tips are well illustrated with many photos. There is a booklet for each position as well as one for right- and left-handed pitchers, a coach and even a team trainer.

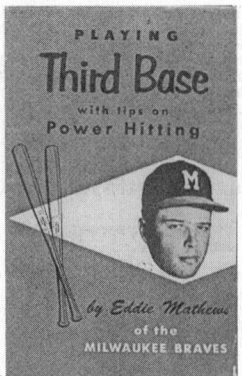

		NM	EX	VG
Complete Set (12):		800.00	400.00	240.00
Common Player:		75.00	37.50	22.50
1	Joe Adcock	90.00	45.00	27.50
2	Danny O'Connell	75.00	37.50	22.50
3	Eddie Mathews	150.00	75.00	45.00
4	Johnny Logan	75.00	37.50	22.50
5	Bobby Thomson	90.00	45.00	27.50
6	Bill Bruton	75.00	37.50	22.50
7	Andy Pafko	75.00	37.50	22.50
8	Del Crandall	75.00	37.50	22.50
9	Warren Spahn	150.00	75.00	45.00
10	Gene Conley	75.00	37.50	22.50
11	Charlie Grimm	75.00	37.50	22.50
12	Joe Taylor	75.00	37.50	22.50

1939 Play Ball Samples

Each of the first 115 cards in the 1939 Play Ball set can be found with red overprinting on the back indicating sample card status. The overprint reads: FREE / SAMPLE CARD / GET YOUR PICTURES OF / LEADING BASEBALL PLAYERS. / THREE PICTURE CARDS PACKED / IN EACH PACKAGE OF / "PLAY BALL AMERICA" / BUBBLE GUM. / AT YOUR CANDY STORE / 1c." Collectors will pay a small premium for a type card of a common player. Sample cards of most star players sell for about double the price of the regular-issue cards, while DiMaggio and Williams samples sell for about the same price as their regular-issue cards.

		NM	EX	VG
Common Player:		35.00	17.50	10.00
26	Joe DiMaggio	1,300	650.00	390.00
92	Ted Williams	1,400	700.00	420.00

1939 Play Ball (R334)

With the issue of this card set by Gum Inc., a new era of baseball cards was born. Although the cards are black-and-white, the photos on front are of better quality than previously seen, and the 2-1/2" x 3-1/8" size was larger than virtually all of the tobacco and caramel cards of the early 20th Century. Card backs feature full player names, "Joseph Paul DiMaggio" instead of "Joe DiMaggio" and extensive biographies. Players are listed here by their most commonly used name. There are 161 cards in the set; card #126 was never issued. The complete set price does not include all back variations found in the low-numbered series. Many of the cards between #2-115 (indicated with an asterisk) can be found with the player name either in all capital letters, or in both upper- and lower-case letters. Minor differences in typography, along with variations in details of the biographical data, or within the wording of the career summary may be found on those cards that exist in two

versions. No premium currently attaches to either version, though the cards with name in upper- and lower-case are somewhat scarcer.

		NM	EX	VG
Complete Set (161):		10,000	4,750	2,750
Common Player (1-115):		25.00	12.50	7.50
Common Player (116-162):		55.00	27.50	16.50
1	Jake Powell	135.00	15.00	7.50
2	Lee Grissom	25.00	12.50	7.50
3	Red Ruffing (*)	100.00	50.00	30.00
4	Eldon Auker (*)	25.00	12.50	7.50
5	Luke Sewell (*)	25.00	12.50	7.50
6	Leo Durocher (*)	100.00	50.00	30.00
7	Bobby Doerr (*)	100.00	50.00	30.00
8	Cotton Pippen	25.00	12.50	7.50
9	Jim Tobin (*)	25.00	12.50	7.50
10	Jimmie DeShong	25.00	12.50	7.50
11	Johnny Rizzo	25.00	12.50	7.50
12	Hersh Martin	25.00	12.50	7.50
13	Luke Hamlin (*)	25.00	12.50	7.50
14	Jim Tabor (*)	25.00	12.50	7.50
15	Paul Derringer (*)	25.00	12.50	7.50
16	Johnny Peacock	25.00	12.50	7.50
17	Emerson Dickman	25.00	12.50	7.50
18	Harry Danning (*)	25.00	12.50	7.50
19	Paul Dean	50.00	25.00	15.00
20	Joe Heving	25.00	12.50	7.50
21	Dutch Leonard (*)	25.00	12.50	7.50
22	Bucky Walters (*)	25.00	12.50	7.50
23	Burgess Whitehead	25.00	12.50	7.50
24	Dick Coffman (*)	25.00	12.50	7.50
25	George Selkirk (*)	25.00	12.50	7.50
26	Joe DiMaggio (*)	1,400	575.00	300.00
27	Fritz Ostermueller (*)	25.00	12.50	7.50
28	Syl Johnson	25.00	12.50	7.50
29	Jack Wilson (*)	25.00	12.50	7.50
30	Bill Dickey (*)	175.00	85.00	55.00
31	Sammy West (*)	25.00	12.50	7.50
32	Bob Seeds	25.00	12.50	7.50
33	Del Young	25.00	12.50	7.50
34	Frank Demaree (*)	25.00	12.50	7.50
35	Bill Jurges (*)	25.00	12.50	7.50
36	Frank McCormick (*)	25.00	12.50	7.50
37	Spud Davis	25.00	12.50	7.50
38	Billy Myers (*)	25.00	12.50	7.50
39	Rick Ferrell (*)	100.00	50.00	30.00
40	Jim Bagby Jr.	25.00	12.50	7.50
41	Lon Warneke (*)	25.00	12.50	7.50
42	Arndt Jorgens	25.00	12.50	7.50
43	Mel Almada	35.00	17.50	10.00
44	Don Heffner	25.00	12.50	7.50
45	Pinky May (*)	25.00	12.50	7.50
46	Morrie Arnovich (*)	40.00	20.00	12.00
47	Buddy Lewis (*)	25.00	12.50	7.50
48	Lefty Gomez (*)	100.00	50.00	30.00
49	Eddie Miller	25.00	12.50	7.50
50	Charlie Gehringer (*)	110.00	55.00	35.00
51	Mel Ott (*)	135.00	65.00	40.00
52	Tommy Henrich (*)	60.00	30.00	18.00
53	Carl Hubbell (*)	125.00	65.00	35.00
54	Harry Gumbert (*)	25.00	12.50	7.50
55	Arky Vaughan (*)	100.00	50.00	30.00
56	Hank Greenberg (*)	250.00	125.00	75.00
57	Buddy Hassett (*)	25.00	12.50	7.50
58	Lou Chiozza	25.00	12.50	7.50
59	Ken Chase	25.00	12.50	7.50
60	Schoolboy Rowe (*)	25.00	12.50	7.50
61	Tony Cuccinello (*)	25.00	12.50	7.50
62	Tom Carey	25.00	12.50	7.50
63	Heinie Mueller	25.00	12.50	7.50
64	Wally Moses (*)	25.00	12.50	7.50
65	Harry Craft (*)	25.00	12.50	7.50
66	Jimmy Ripple	25.00	12.50	7.50
67	Eddie Joost	25.00	12.50	7.50
68	Fred Sington	25.00	12.50	7.50
69	Elbie Fletcher	25.00	12.50	7.50
70	Fred Frankhouse	25.00	12.50	7.50
71	Monte Pearson (*)	25.00	12.50	7.50
72	Debs Garms (*)	25.00	12.50	7.50
73	Hal Schumacher (*)	25.00	12.50	7.50
74	Cookie Lavagetto (*)	25.00	12.50	7.50
75	Frenchy Bordagaray (*)	25.00	12.50	7.50
76	Goody Rosen	40.00	20.00	12.00
77	Lew Riggs	25.00	12.50	7.50
78	Moose Solters (*)	25.00	12.50	7.50
79	Joe Moore (*)	25.00	12.50	7.50
80	Pete Fox (*)	25.00	12.50	7.50
81	Babe Dahlgren (*)	25.00	12.50	7.50
82	Chuck Klein (*)	100.00	50.00	30.00
83	Gus Suhr (*)	25.00	12.50	7.50
84	Skeeter Newsome	25.00	12.50	7.50
85	Johnny Cooney	25.00	12.50	7.50
86	Dolph Camilli (*)	25.00	12.50	7.50
87	Milt Shoffner	25.00	12.50	7.50
88	Charlie Keller	35.00	17.50	10.00
89	Lloyd Waner (*)	100.00	50.00	30.00
90	Bob Klinger (*)	25.00	12.50	7.50
91	Jack Knott (*)	25.00	12.50	7.50
92	Ted Williams (*)	2,100	1,000	500.00
93	Charley Gelbert	25.00	12.50	7.50
94	Heinie Manush	100.00	50.00	30.00
95	Whit Wyatt (*)	25.00	12.50	7.50
96	Babe Phelps (*)	25.00	12.50	7.50
97	Bob Johnson (*)	25.00	12.50	7.50
98	Pinky Whitney	25.00	12.50	7.50
99	Wally Berger (*)	25.00	12.50	7.50
100	Buddy Myer (*)	25.00	12.50	7.50
101	Doc Cramer (*)	25.00	12.50	7.50
102	Pep Young (*)	25.00	12.50	7.50
103	Moe Berg	140.00	75.00	45.00
104	Tommy Bridges (*)	25.00	12.50	7.50
105	Eric McNair (*)	25.00	12.50	7.50
106	Dolly Stark	50.00	25.00	15.00
107	Joe Vosmik	25.00	12.50	7.50
108	Frankie Hayes (*)	25.00	12.50	7.50
109	Myril Hoag (*)	25.00	12.50	7.50
110	Freddie Fitzsimmons	25.00	12.50	7.50

		NM	EX	VG
111	Van Lingle Mungo (*)	35.00	17.50	10.00
112	Paul Waner (*)	100.00	50.00	30.00
113	Al Schacht	50.00	25.00	15.00
114	Cecil Travis (*)	25.00	12.50	7.50
115	Red Kress (*)	25.00	12.50	7.50
116	Gene Desautels	55.00	27.50	16.50
117	Wayne Ambler	55.00	27.50	16.50
118	Lynn Nelson	55.00	27.50	16.50
119	Will Hershberger	55.00	27.50	16.50
120	Rabbit Warstler	55.00	27.50	16.50
121	Bill Posedel	55.00	27.50	16.50
122	George McQuinn	55.00	27.50	16.50
123	Peaches Davis	55.00	27.50	16.50
124	Jumbo Brown	55.00	27.50	16.50
125	Cliff Melton	55.00	27.50	16.50
126	Not Issued			
127	Gil Brack	55.00	27.50	16.50
128	Joe Bowman	55.00	27.50	16.50
129	Bill Swift	55.00	27.50	16.50
130	Bill Brubaker	55.00	27.50	16.50
131	Mort Cooper	55.00	27.50	16.50
132	Jimmy Brown	55.00	27.50	16.50
133	Lynn Myers	55.00	27.50	16.50
134	Tot Pressnell	55.00	27.50	16.50
135	Mickey Owen	55.00	27.50	16.50
136	Roy Bell	55.00	27.50	16.50
137	Pete Appleton	55.00	27.50	16.50
138	George Case	55.00	27.50	16.50
139	Vito Tamulis	55.00	27.50	16.50
140	Ray Hayworth	55.00	27.50	16.50
141	Pete Coscarart	55.00	27.50	16.50
142	Ira Hutchinson	55.00	27.50	16.50
143	Earl Averill	225.00	110.00	65.00
144	Zeke Bonura	55.00	27.50	16.50
145	Hugh Mulcahy	55.00	27.50	16.50
146	Tom Sunkel	55.00	27.50	16.50
147	George Coffman	55.00	27.50	16.50
148	Bill Trotter	55.00	27.50	16.50
149	Max West	55.00	27.50	16.50
150	Jim Walkup	55.00	27.50	16.50
151	Hugh Casey	55.00	27.50	16.50
152	Roy Weatherly	55.00	27.50	16.50
153	Dizzy Trout	55.00	27.50	16.50
154	Johnny Hudson	55.00	27.50	16.50
155	Jimmy Outlaw	55.00	27.50	16.50
156	Ray Berres	55.00	27.50	16.50
157	Don Padgett	55.00	27.50	16.50
158	Bud Thomas	55.00	27.50	16.50
159	Red Evans	55.00	27.50	16.50
160	Gene Moore Jr.	55.00	27.50	16.50
161	Lonny Frey	60.00	27.50	17.50
162	Whitey Moore	200.00	30.00	17.50

1940 Play Ball (R335)

216. JOSEPH ANTON MARTY
Outfielder Philadelphia Phillies
Born: Sacramento, Cal.   Sept. 1, 1913
Bats: Right   Throws: Right
Height: 6'   Weight: 180 lbs.

One of the few Chicago players able to hit Yankee pitching in the 1938 World Series was Joe Marty. Marty came to bat 12 times in that Series and collected 6 hits for a batting mark of .500. One of those hits was a homer; another a double, and he drove in 5 runs. Marty has not yet hit the heights expected of him in the majors, but he has shown flashes of greatness, especially in that Series, and this is only his fourth major league season. The Cubs traded him to the Phils in May of last year, and he should prove a valuable asset to them. Despite a low batting mark last year, Marty drove in 14 runs.

PLAY BALL
Millions of young folks asked for SUPERMAN CARD GUM. Now it's on the way too. This new Adventure and Taste Thrill awaits you at your dealers. Ask for it! Watch for it!
© 1940, GUM, INC., Phila., Pa.

Following the success of its initial effort in 1939, Gum Inc. issued a bigger and better set in 1940. The 240 black-and-white cards are once again in 2-1/2" x 3-1/8" size, but the front photos are enclosed by a frame with the player's name. Backs again offer extensive biographies and are dated. A number of former stars were issued along with contemporary players, and many Hall of Famers are included. The final 60 cards of the set are more difficult to obtain.

		NM	EX	VG
Complete Set (240):		22,500	11,000	6,500
Common Player (1-180):		35.00	17.50	10.00
Common Player (181-240):		60.00	30.00	18.00
1	Joe DiMaggio	3,000	1,100	675.00
2	"Art" Jorgens	35.00	17.50	10.00
3	"Babe" Dahlgren	35.00	17.50	10.00
4	"Tommy" Henrich	60.00	30.00	18.00
5	"Monte" Pearson	35.00	17.50	10.00
6	"Lefty" Gomez	130.00	65.00	40.00
7	"Bill" Dickey	160.00	80.00	45.00
8	"Twinkletoes" Selkirk	35.00	17.50	10.00
9	"Charley" Keller	35.00	17.50	10.00
10	"Red" Ruffing	130.00	65.00	40.00
11	"Jake" Powell	35.00	17.50	10.00
12	"Johnny" Schulte	35.00	17.50	10.00
13	"Jack" Knott	35.00	17.50	10.00
14	"Rabbit" McNair	35.00	17.50	10.00
15	George Case	35.00	17.50	10.00
16	Cecil Travis	35.00	17.50	10.00
17	"Buddy" Myer	35.00	17.50	10.00
18	"Charley" Gelbert	35.00	17.50	10.00
19	Ken Chase	35.00	17.50	10.00
20	"Buddy" Lewis	35.00	17.50	10.00
21	"Rick" Ferrell	130.00	65.00	40.00
22	"Sammy" West	35.00	17.50	10.00
23	"Dutch" Leonard	35.00	17.50	10.00
24	Frank "Blimp" Hayes	35.00	17.50	10.00
25	"Cherokee" Bob Johnson	35.00	17.50	10.00
26	"Wally" Moses	35.00	17.50	10.00
27	"Ted" Williams	1,950	550.00	280.00
28	"Gene" Desautels	35.00	17.50	10.00
29	"Doc" Cramer	35.00	17.50	10.00
30	"Moe" Berg	160.00	80.00	45.00
31	Jack Wilson	35.00	17.50	10.00

		NM	EX	VG
32	"Jim" Bagby	35.00	17.50	10.00
33	"Fritz" Ostermueller	35.00	17.50	10.00
34	John Peacock	35.00	17.50	10.00
35	"Joe" Heving	35.00	17.50	10.00
36	"Jim" Tabor	35.00	17.50	10.00
37	Emerson Dickman	35.00	17.50	10.00
38	"Bobby" Doerr	130.00	65.00	40.00
39	"Tom" Carey	35.00	17.50	10.00
40	"Hank" Greenberg	450.00	225.00	135.00
41	"Charley" Gehringer	180.00	90.00	55.00
42	"Bud" Thomas	35.00	17.50	10.00
43	Pete Fox	35.00	17.50	10.00
44	"Dizzy" Trout	35.00	17.50	10.00
45	"Red" Kress	35.00	17.50	10.00
46	Earl Averill	130.00	65.00	40.00
47	"Old Os" Vitt	35.00	17.50	10.00
48	"Luke" Sewell	35.00	17.50	10.00
49	"Stormy Weather" Weatherly	35.00	17.50	10.00
50	"Hal" Trosky	35.00	17.50	10.00
51	"Don" Heffner	35.00	17.50	10.00
52	Myril Hoag	35.00	17.50	10.00
53	"Mac" McQuinn	35.00	17.50	10.00
54	"Bill" Trotter	35.00	17.50	10.00
55	"Slick" Coffman	35.00	17.50	10.00
56	"Eddie" Miller	35.00	17.50	10.00
57	Max West	35.00	17.50	10.00
58	"Bill" Posedel	35.00	17.50	10.00
59	"Rabbit" Warstler	35.00	17.50	10.00
60	John Cooney	35.00	17.50	10.00
61	"Tony" Cuccinello	35.00	17.50	10.00
62	"Buddy" Hassett	35.00	17.50	10.00
63	"Pete" Cascarart (Coscarart)	35.00	17.50	10.00
64	"Van" Mungo	40.00	20.00	12.00
65	"Fitz" Fitzsimmons	35.00	17.50	10.00
66	"Babe" Phelps	35.00	17.50	10.00
67	"Whit" Wyatt	35.00	17.50	10.00
68	"Dolph" Camilli	35.00	17.50	10.00
69	"Cookie" Lavagetto	35.00	17.50	10.00
70	"Hot Potato" Hamlin	35.00	17.50	10.00
71	Mel Almada	40.00	20.00	12.00
72	"Chuck" Dressen	35.00	17.50	10.00
73	"Bucky" Walters	35.00	17.50	10.00
74	"Duke" Derringer	35.00	17.50	10.00
75	"Buck" McCormick	35.00	17.50	10.00
76	"Lonny" Frey	35.00	17.50	10.00
77	"Bill" Hershberger	60.00	30.00	18.00
78	"Lew" Riggs	35.00	17.50	10.00
79	"Wildfire" Craft	35.00	17.50	10.00
80	"Bill" Myers	35.00	17.50	10.00
81	"Wally" Berger	35.00	17.50	10.00
82	"Hank" Gowdy	35.00	17.50	10.00
83	"Clif" Melton (Cliff)	35.00	17.50	10.00
84	"Jo-Jo" Moore	35.00	17.50	10.00
85	"Hal" Schumacher	35.00	17.50	10.00
86	Harry Gumbert	35.00	17.50	10.00
87	Carl Hubbell	160.00	80.00	45.00
88	"Mel" Ott	225.00	110.00	65.00
89	"Bill" Jurges	35.00	17.50	10.00
90	Frank Demaree	35.00	17.50	10.00
91	Bob "Suitcase" Seeds	35.00	17.50	10.00
92	"Whitey" Whitehead	35.00	17.50	10.00
93	Harry "The Horse" Danning	35.00	17.50	10.00
94	"Gus" Suhr	35.00	17.50	10.00
95	"Mul" Mulcahy	35.00	17.50	10.00
96	"Heinie" Mueller	35.00	17.50	10.00
97	"Morry" Arnovich	35.00	17.50	10.00
98	"Pinky" May	35.00	17.50	10.00
99	"Syl" Johnson	35.00	17.50	10.00
100	"Hersh" Martin	35.00	17.50	10.00
101	"Del" Young	35.00	17.50	10.00
102	"Chuck" Klein	130.00	65.00	40.00
103	"Elbie" Fletcher	35.00	17.50	10.00
104	"Big Poison" Waner	130.00	65.00	40.00
105	"Little Poison" Waner	130.00	65.00	40.00
106	"Pep" Young	35.00	17.50	10.00
107	"Arky" Vaughan	130.00	65.00	40.00
108	"Johnny" Rizzo	35.00	17.50	10.00
109	Don Padgett	35.00	17.50	10.00
110	"Tom" Sunkel	35.00	17.50	10.00
111	"Mickey" Owen	35.00	17.50	10.00
112	"Jimmy" Brown	35.00	17.50	10.00
113	"Mort" Cooper	35.00	17.50	10.00
114	"Lon" Warneke	35.00	17.50	10.00
115	"Mike" Gonzales (Gonzalez)	40.00	20.00	12.00
116	"Al" Schacht	60.00	30.00	18.00
117	"Dolly" Stark	75.00	37.50	22.50
118	"Schoolboy" Hoyt	130.00	65.00	40.00
119	"Ol Pete" Alexander	130.00	65.00	40.00
120	Walter "Big Train" Johnson	275.00	135.00	80.00
121	Atley Donald	35.00	17.50	10.00
122	"Sandy" Sundra	35.00	17.50	10.00
123	"Hildy" Hildebrand	35.00	17.50	10.00
124	"Colonel" Combs	120.00	60.00	35.00
125	"Art" Fletcher	35.00	17.50	10.00
126	"Jake" Solters	35.00	17.50	10.00
127	"Muddy" Ruel	35.00	17.50	10.00
128	"Pete" Appleton	35.00	17.50	10.00
129	"Bucky" Harris	120.00	60.00	35.00
130	"Deerfoot" Milan	35.00	17.50	10.00
131	"Zeke" Bonura	35.00	17.50	10.00
132	Connie Mack	120.00	60.00	35.00
133	"Jimmie" Foxx	300.00	150.00	90.00
134	"Joe" Cronin	130.00	65.00	40.00
135	"Line Drive" Nelson	35.00	17.50	10.00
136	"Cotton" Pippen	35.00	17.50	10.00
137	"Bing" Miller	35.00	17.50	10.00
138	"Beau" Bell	35.00	17.50	10.00
139	Elden Auker (Eldon)	35.00	17.50	10.00
140	"Dick" Coffman	35.00	17.50	10.00
141	"Casey" Stengel	175.00	85.00	50.00
142	"Highpockets" Kelly	120.00	60.00	35.00
143	"Gene" Moore	35.00	17.50	10.00
144	"Joe" Vosmik	35.00	17.50	10.00
145	"Vito" Tamulis	35.00	17.50	10.00
146	"Tot" Pressnell	35.00	17.50	10.00
147	"Johnny" Hudson	35.00	17.50	10.00
148	"Hugh" Casey	35.00	17.50	10.00
149	"Pinky" Shoffner	35.00	17.50	10.00

		NM	EX	VG
150	"Whitey" Moore	35.00	17.50	10.00
151	Edwin Joost	35.00	17.50	10.00
152	Jimmy Wilson	35.00	17.50	10.00
153	"Bill" McKechnie	120.00	60.00	35.00
154	"Jumbo" Brown	35.00	17.50	10.00
155	"Ray" Hayworth	35.00	17.50	10.00
156	"Daffy" Dean	65.00	32.50	20.00
157	"Lou" Chiozza	35.00	17.50	10.00
158	"Stonewall" Jackson	120.00	60.00	35.00
159	"Pancho" Snyder	35.00	17.50	10.00
160	"Hans" Lobert	35.00	17.50	10.00
161	"Debs" Garms	35.00	17.50	10.00
162	Joe Bowman	35.00	17.50	10.00
163	"Spud" Davis	35.00	17.50	10.00
164	"Ray" Berres	35.00	17.50	10.00
165	"Bob" Klinger	35.00	17.50	10.00
166	"Bill" Brubaker	35.00	17.50	10.00
167	"Frankie" Frisch	130.00	65.00	40.00
168	"Honus" Wagner	300.00	150.00	90.00
169	"Gabby" Street	35.00	17.50	10.00
170	"Tris" Speaker	135.00	70.00	40.00
171	Harry Heilmann	120.00	60.00	35.00
172	"Chief" Bender	120.00	60.00	35.00
173	"Larry" Lajoie	120.00	60.00	35.00
174	"Johnny" Evers	120.00	60.00	35.00
175	"Christy" Mathewson	250.00	125.00	75.00
176	"Heinie" Manush	130.00	65.00	40.00
177	Frank "Homerun" Baker	120.00	60.00	35.00
178	Max Carey	120.00	60.00	35.00
179	George Sisler	120.00	60.00	35.00
180	"Mickey" Cochrane	130.00	65.00	40.00
181	"Spud" Chandler	60.00	30.00	18.00
182	"Knick" Knickerbocker	60.00	30.00	18.00
183	Marvin Breuer	60.00	30.00	18.00
184	"Mule" Haas	60.00	30.00	18.00
185	"Joe" Kuhel	60.00	30.00	18.00
186	Taft Wright	60.00	30.00	18.00
187	"Jimmy" Dykes	60.00	30.00	18.00
188	"Joe" Krakauskas	60.00	30.00	18.00
189	"Jim" Bloodworth	60.00	30.00	18.00
190	"Charley" Berry	60.00	30.00	18.00
191	John Babich	60.00	30.00	18.00
192	"Dick" Siebert	60.00	30.00	18.00
193	"Chubby" Dean	60.00	30.00	18.00
194	Sam Chapman	60.00	30.00	18.00
195	"Dee" Miles	60.00	30.00	18.00
196	"Nonny" Nonnenkamp	60.00	30.00	18.00
197	"Lou" Finney	60.00	30.00	18.00
198	"Denny" Galehouse	60.00	30.00	18.00
199	"Pinky" Higgins	60.00	30.00	18.00
200	"Soupy" Campbell	60.00	30.00	18.00
201	Barney McCosky	60.00	30.00	18.00
202	Al Milnar	60.00	30.00	18.00
203	"Bad News" Hale	60.00	30.00	18.00
204	Harry Eisenstat	75.00	37.50	22.50
205	"Rollie" Hemsley	60.00	30.00	18.00
206	"Chet" Laabs	60.00	30.00	18.00
207	"Gus" Mancuso	60.00	30.00	18.00
208	Lee Gamble	60.00	30.00	18.00
209	"Hy" Vandenberg	60.00	30.00	18.00
210	"Bill" Lohrman	60.00	30.00	18.00
211	"Pop" Joiner	60.00	30.00	18.00
212	"Babe" Young	60.00	30.00	18.00
213	John Rucker	60.00	30.00	18.00
214	"Ken" O'Dea	60.00	30.00	18.00
215	"Johnnie" McCarthy	60.00	30.00	18.00
216	"Joe" Marty	60.00	30.00	18.00
217	Walter Beck	60.00	30.00	18.00
218	"Wally" Millies	60.00	30.00	18.00
219	Russ Bauers	60.00	30.00	18.00
220	Mace Brown	60.00	30.00	18.00
221	Lee Handley	60.00	30.00	18.00
222	"Max" Butcher	60.00	30.00	18.00
223	Hugh "Ee-Yah" Jennings	140.00	70.00	40.00
224	"Pie" Traynor	140.00	70.00	40.00
225	"Shoeless Joe" Jackson	2,900	1,250	700.00
226	Harry Hooper	140.00	70.00	40.00
227	"Pop" Haines	140.00	70.00	40.00
228	"Charley" Grimm	60.00	30.00	18.00
229	"Buck" Herzog	60.00	30.00	18.00
230	"Red" Faber	140.00	70.00	40.00
231	"Dolf" Luque	75.00	37.50	22.50
232	"Goose" Goslin	140.00	70.00	40.00
233	"Moose" Earnshaw	60.00	30.00	18.00
234	Frank "Husk" Chance	140.00	70.00	40.00
235	John J. McGraw	140.00	70.00	40.00
236	"Sunny Jim" Bottomley	140.00	70.00	40.00
237	"Wee Willie" Keeler	140.00	70.00	40.00
238	"Poosh 'Em Up Tony" Lazzeri	175.00	85.00	50.00
239	George Uhle	60.00	30.00	18.00
240	"Bill" Atwood	120.00	40.00	20.00

1940 Play Ball Colorized Proofs

64. VAN LINGLE MUNGO
Pitcher   Brooklyn Dodgers

PLAY BALL

Probably created as part of the process which resulted in the introduction of color cards in 1941, these 1940 Play Balls have very muted color tones. It is unknown how many other players' cards from 1940 PB were created or survive in this form. The Mungo and Dean cards, authenticated and graded Excellent by SGC, sold in a 12/04 auction for $2,221.

64 "Van" Mungo
76 "Lonny" Frey
90 Frank Demaree
141 "Casey" Stengel
156 "Daffy" Dean

1941 Play Ball (R336)

1941 Play Ball Paper Version

While the backs are quite similar to the black-and-white cards Gum Inc. issued in 1940, the card fronts in the 1941 set are printed in color. Many of the card photos, however, are just colorized versions of the player's 1940 card. The cards are still in the 2-1/2" x 3-1/8" size, but only 72 cards are included in the set. Card numbers 49-72 are rarer than the lower-numbered cards. The cards were printed in sheets of 12, and can still be found that way. Cards #1-48 can be found with or without the 1941 copyright date at lower-left; cards 49-72 are not found with the 1941 date. Some believe this indicates that a revised (no copyright) version of the low numbers and all of the high numbers were issued in 1942.

	NM	EX	VG
Complete Set (72):	15,000	7,500	4,500
Common Player (1-48):	75.00	37.50	22.50
Common Player (49-72):	100.00	50.00	30.00
1 "Eddie" Miller	340.00	60.00	25.00
2 Max West	110.00	37.50	22.50
3 "Bucky" Walters	75.00	37.50	22.50
4 "Duke" Derringer	75.00	37.50	22.50
5 "Buck" McCormick	75.00	37.50	22.50
6 Carl Hubbell	260.00	130.00	75.00
7 "The Horse" Danning	75.00	37.50	22.50
8 "Mel" Ott	340.00	170.00	100.00
9 "Pinky" May	75.00	37.50	22.50
10 "Arky" Vaughan	190.00	95.00	55.00
11 Debs Garms	75.00	37.50	22.50
12 "Jimmy" Brown	75.00	37.50	22.50
13 "Jimmie" Foxx	500.00	250.00	150.00
14 "Ted" Williams	2,200	1,000	400.00
15 "Joe" Cronin	190.00	95.00	55.00
16 "Hal" Trosky	75.00	37.50	22.50
17 "Stormy" Weatherly	75.00	37.50	22.50
18 "Hank" Greenberg	500.00	250.00	150.00
19 "Charley" Gehringer	250.00	125.00	75.00
20 "Red" Ruffing	190.00	95.00	55.00
21 "Charlie" Keller	150.00	75.00	45.00
22 "Indian Bob" Johnson	75.00	37.50	22.50
23 "Mac" McQuinn	75.00	37.50	22.50
24 "Dutch" Leonard	75.00	37.50	22.50
25 "Gene" Moore	75.00	37.50	22.50
26 Harry "Gunboat" Gumbert	75.00	37.50	22.50
27 "Babe" Young	75.00	37.50	22.50
28 "Joe" Marty	75.00	37.50	22.50
29 Jack Wilson	75.00	37.50	22.50
30 "Lou" Finney	75.00	37.50	22.50
31 "Joe" Kuhel	75.00	37.50	22.50
32 Taft Wright	75.00	37.50	22.50
33 "Happy" Milnar	75.00	37.50	22.50
34 "Rollie" Hemsley	75.00	37.50	22.50
35 "Pinky" Higgins	75.00	37.50	22.50
36 Barney McCosky	75.00	37.50	22.50
37 "Soupy" Campbell	75.00	37.50	22.50
38 Atley Donald	75.00	37.50	22.50
39 "Tommy" Henrich	150.00	75.00	45.00
40 "Johnny" Babich	75.00	37.50	22.50
41 Frank "Blimp" Hayes	75.00	37.50	22.50
42 "Wally" Moses	75.00	37.50	22.50
43 Albert "Bronk" Brancato	75.00	37.50	22.50
44 Sam Chapman	75.00	37.50	22.50
45 Elden Auker (Eldon)	75.00	37.50	22.50
46 "Sid" Hudson	75.00	37.50	22.50
47 "Buddy" Lewis	75.00	37.50	22.50
48 Cecil Travis	75.00	37.50	22.50
49 "Babe" Dahlgren	100.00	50.00	30.00
50 "Johnny" Cooney	100.00	50.00	30.00
51 "Dolph" Camilli	100.00	50.00	30.00
52 Kirby Higbe	100.00	50.00	30.00
53 Luke "Hot Potato" Hamlin	100.00	50.00	30.00
54 "Pee Wee" Reese	600.00	300.00	180.00
55 "Whit" Wyatt	100.00	50.00	30.00
56 "Vandy" Vander Meer	100.00	50.00	30.00
57 "Moe" Arnovich	125.00	65.00	35.00
58 "Frank" Demaree	100.00	50.00	30.00
59 "Bill" Jurges	100.00	50.00	30.00
60 "Chuck" Klein	300.00	150.00	90.00
61 "Vince" DiMaggio	300.00	150.00	90.00
62 "Elbie" Fletcher	100.00	50.00	30.00
63 "Dom" DiMaggio	400.00	200.00	120.00
64 "Bobby" Doerr	300.00	150.00	90.00
65 "Tommy" Bridges	100.00	50.00	30.00
66 Harland Clift (Harlond)	100.00	50.00	30.00
67 "Walt" Judnich	100.00	50.00	30.00
68 "Jack" Knott	100.00	50.00	30.00
69 George Case	100.00	50.00	30.00
70 "Bill" Dickey	350.00	175.00	100.00
71 "Joe" DiMaggio	3,000	1,300	700.00
72 "Lefty" Gomez	425.00	180.00	60.00

As cardboard became a critical commodity during the months prior to the United States' entry into WWII, Play Ball experimented by issuing a version of the first 24 cards in the 1941 set on paper sheets of 12, comprising the color-printed layer of the regular cards and the backs. These paper versions, understandably, did not stand up to handling as well as the cardboard cards and survivors are much scarcer today.

	NM	EX	VG
Complete Set (24):	10,000	5,000	3,000
Common Player:	160.00	55.00	30.00
Complete Sheet 1-12:	3,000	700.00	325.00
Complete Sheet 13-24:	7,000	3,500	2,100
1 Eddie Miller	160.00	55.00	30.00
2 Max West	160.00	55.00	30.00
3 Bucky Walters	160.00	55.00	30.00
4 "Duke" Derringer	160.00	55.00	30.00
5 "Buck" McCormick	160.00	55.00	30.00
6 Carl Hubbell	600.00	210.00	120.00
7 "The Horse" Danning	160.00	55.00	30.00
8 Mel Ott	650.00	225.00	130.00
9 "Pinky" May	160.00	55.00	30.00
10 "Arky" Vaughan	400.00	140.00	80.00
11 Debs Garms	160.00	55.00	30.00
12 "Jimmy" Brown	160.00	55.00	30.00
13 Jimmie Foxx	1,100	385.00	220.00
14 Ted Williams	3,200	1,125	640.00
15 Joe Cronin	400.00	140.00	80.00
16 Hal Trosky	160.00	55.00	30.00
17 Roy Weatherly	160.00	55.00	30.00
18 Hank Greenberg	1,100	385.00	220.00
19 Charley Gehringer	600.00	210.00	120.00
20 "Red" Ruffing	400.00	140.00	80.00
21 Charlie Keller	180.00	65.00	35.00
22 Bob Johnson	160.00	55.00	30.00
23 "Mac" McQuinn	160.00	55.00	30.00
24 Dutch Leonard	160.00	55.00	30.00

1976 Playboy Press Who Was Harry Steinfeldt?

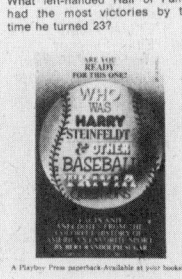

(Babe Ruth)

This 12-card set was issued in 1976 by Playboy Press to promote author Bert Randolph Sugar's book "Who Was Harry Steinfeldt? & Other Baseball Trivia Questions." (Steinfeldt was the third baseman in the Cubs' famous infield that featured Hall of Famers Tinker, Evers and Chance). The black and white cards measure the standard 2-1/2" x 3-1/2" with a player photo on the front and a trivia question and ad for the book on the back.

	NM	EX	VG
Complete Set (12):	150.00	75.00	45.00
Common Player:	9.00	4.50	2.75
(1) Frankie Baumholtz	9.00	4.50	2.75
(2) Jim Bouton	12.00	6.00	3.50
(3) Tony Conigliaro	9.00	4.50	2.75
(4) Don Drysdale	17.50	8.75	5.25
(5) Hank Greenberg	15.00	7.50	4.50
(6) Walter Johnson	25.00	12.50	7.50
(7) Billy Loes	9.00	4.50	2.75
(8) Johnny Mize	15.00	7.50	4.50
(9) Frank "Lefty" O'Doul	12.00	6.00	3.50
(10) Babe Ruth	50.00	25.00	15.00
(11) Johnny Sain	9.00	4.50	2.75
(12) Jim Thorpe	40.00	20.00	12.00

1947 Pleetwood Slacks Jackie Robinson

The date of issue cited is conjectural. This card, about 5" x 8", depicts Jackie Robinson in a coat and tie in a black-and-white photo on front, along with a facsimile autograph. In a strip at bottom is his name and an endorsement for "Pleetwood Slacks." The back is blank. The card was probably used as an autograph vehicle for personal appearances by Robinson at clothing stores.

	NM	EX	VG
Jackie Robinson	600.00	300.00	180.00

1910-12 Plow Boy Tobacco

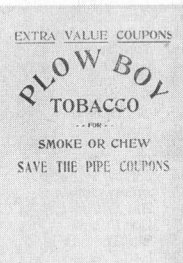

Plowboy Tobacco, a product of the Spaulding & Merrick Co., issued a set of cabinet-size cards in the Chicago area featuring members of the Cubs and White Sox. From the checklist, it appears the bulk of the set was originally issued in 1910 with a few additional cards appearing over the next several years. Measuring approximately 5-3/4" x 8", the Plow Boys feature sepia-toned player photos in poses not found on other tobacco issues. The player's name appears in the lower-left corner, while the team name appears in the lower-right. Two different backs are known. One consists of a simple advertisement for Plow Boy Tobacco, while a second, more difficult, variety includes a list of premiums available in exchange for coupons. The set is among the rarest of all 20th Century tobacco issues.

	NM	EX	VG
Common Player:	3,650	1,450	725.00
Premium Back: 1.5X			
(1) Jimmy Archer	3,650	1,450	725.00
(2) Ginger Beaumont	3,650	1,450	725.00
(3) Lena Blackburne	3,650	1,450	725.00
(4) Bruno Block	3,650	1,450	725.00
(5) Ping Bodie	3,650	1,450	725.00
(6) Mordecai Brown	5,500	2,200	1,100
(7) Al Carson	3,650	1,450	725.00
(8) Frank Chance	5,500	2,200	1,100
(9) Ed Cicotte	5,250	2,100	1,050
(10) King Cole	3,650	1,450	725.00
(11) Shano Collins	3,650	1,450	725.00
(12) George Davis	5,500	2,200	1,100
(13) Patsy Dougherty	3,650	1,450	725.00
(14) Johnny Evers	5,500	2,200	1,100
(15) Chick Gandel (Gandil)	5,250	2,100	1,050
(16) Ed Hahn	3,650	1,450	725.00
(17) Solly Hoffman (Hofman)	3,650	1,450	725.00
(18) Del Howard	3,650	1,450	725.00
(19) Bill Jones	3,650	1,450	725.00
(20) Johnny Kling	3,650	1,450	725.00
(21) Rube Kroh	3,650	1,450	725.00
(22) Frank Lange	3,650	1,450	725.00
(23) Fred Luderus	3,650	1,450	725.00
(24) Harry McIntyre (McIntire)	3,650	1,450	725.00
(25) Ward Miller	3,650	1,450	725.00
(26) Charlie Mullen	3,650	1,450	725.00
(27) Tom Needham	3,650	1,450	725.00
(28) Fred Olmstead	3,650	1,450	725.00
(29) Orval Overall	3,650	1,450	725.00
(30) Fred Parent	3,650	1,450	725.00
(31) Fred Payne	3,650	1,450	725.00
(32) Francis "Big Jeff" Pfeffer	3,650	1,450	725.00
(33) Jake Pfeister	3,650	1,450	725.00
(34) Billy Purtell	3,650	1,450	725.00
(35) Ed Reulbach	3,650	1,450	725.00
(36) Lew Richie	3,650	1,450	725.00
(37) Jimmy Scheckard (Sheckard)	3,650	1,450	725.00
(38) Wildfire Schulte	3,650	1,450	725.00
(39a) Jim Scot (Name incorrect.)	3,650	1,450	725.00
(39b) Jim Scott (Name correct.)	3,650	1,450	725.00
(40) Frank Smith	3,650	1,450	725.00
(41) Harry Steinfeldt	3,650	1,450	725.00
(42) Billy Sullivan	3,650	1,450	725.00
(43) Lee Tannehill	3,650	1,450	725.00
(44) Joe Tinker	5,500	2,200	1,100

		NM	EX	VG
(45)	Ed Walsh	5,500	2,200	1,100
(46)	Doc White	3,650	1,450	725.00
(47)	Irv Young	3,650	1,450	725.00
(48)	Rollie Zeider	3,650	1,450	725.00
(49)	Heinie Zimmerman	3,650	1,450	725.00

1912 Plow's Candy (E300)

PLOW'S CANDY COLLECTION

DELEHANTY
DETROIT AMERICANS

An extremely rare candy issue, cards in this 1912 set measure 3" x 4" and feature sepia-toned photos surrounded by a wide border. The player's name and team appear in the border below the photo, while the words "Plow's Candy Collection" appear at the top. The backs are blank. Not even known to exist until the late 1960s, this set has been assigned the designation of E300 and additions to the checklist continue to appear every few years.

		NM	EX	VG
Common Player:		3,000	1,500	900.00
(1)	Babe Adams	3,000	1,500	900.00
(2)	Home Run Baker	4,800	2,400	1,440
(3)	Cy Barger	3,000	1,500	900.00
(4)	Jack Barry	3,000	1,150	900.00
(5)	Johnny Bates	3,000	1,500	900.00
(7)	Joe Benz	3,000	1,150	900.00
(8)	Bill Berger (Bergen)	3,000	1,500	900.00
(9)	Roger Bresnahan	4,800	2,400	1,440
(10)	Mordecai Brown	4,800	2,400	1,440
(11)	Donie Bush	3,000	1,500	900.00
(12)	Bobby Byrne	3,000	1,500	900.00
(13)	Nixey Callahan	3,000	1,500	900.00
(14)	Hal Chase	4,500	2,250	1,350
(15)	Fred Clarke	4,800	2,400	1,440
(16)	Ty Cobb	40,000	16,500	9,900
(17)	King Cole	3,000	1,500	900.00
(18)	Eddie Collins	4,800	2,400	1,440
(19)	Jack Coombs	3,000	1,500	900.00
(20)	Bill Dahlen	3,000	1,500	900.00
(21)	Bert Daniels	3,000	1,500	900.00
(22)	Harry Davis	3,000	1,500	900.00
(23)	Jim Delehanty	3,000	1,500	900.00
(24)	Josh Devore	3,000	1,500	900.00
(25)	Wild Bill Donovan	3,000	1,500	900.00
(26)	Red Dooin	3,000	1,500	900.00
(27)	Larry Doyle	3,000	1,500	900.00
(28)	Johnny Evers	4,800	2,400	1,440
(29)	Russ Ford	3,000	1,500	900.00
(30)	Del Gainor	3,000	1,500	900.00
(31)	Vean Gregg	3,000	1,500	900.00
(32)	Bob Harmon	3,000	1,500	900.00
(33)	Arnold Hauser	3,000	1,500	900.00
(34)	Dick Hoblitzelle (Hoblitzell)	3,000	1,500	900.00
(35)	Solly Hofman	3,000	1,500	900.00
(36)	Miller Huggins	4,800	2,400	1,440
(37)	John Hummel	3,000	1,500	900.00
(38)	Walter Johnson	7,200	3,600	2,160
(39)	Johnny Kling	3,000	1,500	900.00
(41)	Nap Lajoie	5,400	2,700	1,620
(42)	Jack Lapp	3,000	1,500	900.00
(43)	Fred Luderus	3,000	1,500	900.00
(44)	Sherry Magee	3,000	1,500	900.00
(45)	Rube Marquard	4,800	2,400	1,440
(46)	Christy Mathewson	25,000	4,500	2,700
(47)	Stuffy McInnes (McInnis)	3,000	1,500	900.00
(48)	Larry McLean	3,000	1,500	900.00
(49)	Fred Merkle	3,000	1,500	900.00
(50)	Cy Morgan	3,000	1,500	900.00
(51)	George Moriarty	3,000	1,500	900.00
(52)	Mike Mowrey	3,000	1,500	900.00
(53)	Chief Myers (Meyers)	3,000	1,500	900.00
(54)	Rube Oldring	3,000	1,500	900.00
(55)	Marty O'Toole	3,000	1,500	900.00
(56)	Eddie Plank	5,400	2,700	1,620
(57)	Nap Rucker	3,000	1,500	900.00
(58)	Slim Sallee	3,000	1,500	900.00
(59)	Boss Schmidt	3,000	1,500	900.00
(60)	Jimmy Sheckard	3,000	1,500	900.00
(61)	Tris Speaker	5,400	2,700	1,620
(62)	Billy Sullivan	3,000	1,500	900.00
(63)	Ira Thomas	3,000	1,500	900.00
(64)	Joe Tinker	4,800	2,400	1,440
(65)	John Titus	3,000	1,500	900.00
(66)	Hippo Vaughan (Vaughn)	3,000	1,500	900.00
(67)	Honus Wagner	50,000	15,000	9,000
(68)	Ed Walsh	4,800	2,400	1,440
(69)	Bob Williams	3,000	1,500	900.00

1915 PM1 Ornate-Frame Pins

Little is known about these tiny (approximately 1-1/16" x 1") pins, such as who issued them, when and how they were distributed and how many are in the set. The pins feature a sepia-tone player photo surrounded by an ornate gilded metal frame. The player's name is usually printed in a black strip at

the bottom of the photo. The pins were originally sold for 19 cents. Gaps have been left in the assigned numbering for future additions to the checklist.

		NM	EX	VG
Common Pin:		450.00	225.00	125.00
(1a)	Jimmy Archer	450.00	225.00	125.00
(1b)	Jimmy Archer (No name.)	575.00	285.00	175.00
(2)	Frank Baker	1,100	550.00	330.00
(3)	Jack Barry	450.00	225.00	135.00
(4a)	Chief Bender (No name.)	1,100	550.00	330.00
(4b)	Chief Bender (With name.)	1,100	550.00	330.00
(5)	Frank Chance	1,100	550.00	330.00
(6)	Ty Cobb	5,500	2,750	1,650
(7)	Jake Daubert	450.00	225.00	125.00
(8)	Al Demaree	450.00	225.00	125.00
(9a)	Johnny Evers (Name only.)	1,100	550.00	330.00
(9b)	Johnny Evers (Name and city.)	1,100	550.00	330.00
(10)	Rube Foster	450.00	225.00	125.00
(11)	Dick Hoblitzell	450.00	225.00	125.00
(12)	Walter Johnson	2,000	1,000	600.00
(13)	Benny Kauff	450.00	225.00	125.00
(14)	Johnny Kling (No name.)	450.00	225.00	135.00
(15)	Ed Konetchy	450.00	225.00	125.00
(16)	Nap Lajoie	1,100	550.00	330.00
(17)	Sherry Magee	450.00	225.00	135.00
(18)	Rube Marquard	1,100	550.00	330.00
(19)	Christy Mathewson	2,500	1,250	750.00
(21)	John McGraw	1,100	550.00	330.00
(22)	Ed Reulbach	450.00	225.00	135.00
(23)	Eppa Rixey	1,100	550.00	330.00
(24)	Babe Ruth	15,000	7,500	4,500
(25)	Tris Speaker (Batting, facing forward.)	1,100	550.00	330.00
(26)	Tris Speaker (Batting, side view.)	1,100	550.00	330.00
(27)	Jeff Tesreau	450.00	225.00	135.00
(28)	Joe Tinker	1,100	550.00	330.00
(29)	Honus Wagner	2,750	1,350	825.00

1928 PM6 Baseball Player Pins

The method of distribution for these small (3/8" diameter) pin-backs is unknown, but it has been reported they were given away in cereal boxes. The black-and-white photographic pins have the player name in a black arc at bottom. The extent of the checklist is unknown.

		NM	EX	VG
Common Player:		375.00	185.00	110.00
(1)	Grover Alexander	450.00	225.00	135.00
(2)	Ty Cobb	900.00	450.00	275.00
(3)	Bucky Harris	350.00	175.00	100.00
(4)	Rogers Hornsby	550.00	275.00	165.00
(5)	Walter Johnson	600.00	300.00	180.00
(6)	Babe Ruth	1,200	600.00	360.00
(7)	Geo. Sisler	350.00	175.00	100.00
(8)	Tris Speaker	450.00	225.00	135.00

1940 PM10 Baseball Player Pins

This was the first of two issues that share a nearly identical format. The 1-3/4" celluloid pin-back buttons feature a black-and-white player photo surrounded by a white border. The player's name is in black capital letters at bottom, and his team nickname in the same type size and style at top. These pins were originally sold at ballparks and other souvenir outlets. The checklist, arranged here in alphabetical order, is not complete.

	NM	EX	VG
Common Player:	30.00	15.00	9.00
Dick Bartell	30.00	15.00	9.00
Dolph Camilli	30.00	15.00	9.00
Bill Dickey	50.00	25.00	15.00
Joe DiMaggio	275.00	135.00	85.00
Lou Gehrig	700.00	350.00	210.00
Lou Gehrig (Black border, "NEVER FORGOTTEN" at top.)	650.00	325.00	195.00
Lefty Gomez	50.00	25.00	15.00
Carl Hubbell	100.00	50.00	30.00
Cliff Melton	30.00	15.00	9.00
Pete Reiser	30.00	15.00	9.00
Dixie Walker	30.00	15.00	9.00
Whitlow Wyatt	30.00	15.00	9.00

1951 PM10 Baseball Player Pins

This was the second of two issues that share a nearly identical format. The 1-3/4" celluloid pin-back buttons feature a black-and-white player photo surrounded by a white border. The player's name is in black capital letters at bottom, and full team name in the same type size and style at top. These pins were originally sold at ballparks and other souvenir outlets. The checklist, arranged here in alphabetical order, is likely not complete. Note that the woeful Pittsburgh Pirates represent more than half the known players in this issue.

	NM	EX	VG
Common Player:	50.00	25.00	15.00
Luke Easter	75.00	37.50	22.50
Ned Garver	50.00	25.00	15.00
Monte Irvin	100.00	50.00	30.00
Ralph Kiner	100.00	50.00	30.00
Bob Lemon	100.00	50.00	30.00
Willie Mays	175.00	87.00	52.00
Clyde McCullouhg (McCullough)	50.00	25.00	15.00
Billy Meyer	50.00	25.00	15.00
Danny Murtaugh	50.00	25.00	15.00
Don Newcombe	50.00	25.00	15.00
Saul Rogovin	50.00	25.00	15.00
Stan Rojek	50.00	25.00	15.00
Hank Thompson	50.00	25.00	15.00
Bill Werle	50.00	25.00	15.00

1950s-60s PM10 Baseball Player Pins - Name at Bottom

Issued over a period of years in a variety of styles, these celluloid pinback buttons have in common their approximately 1-3/4" diameter and the appearance of the player name at bottom. Black-and-white player portrait photos are found on a variety of backgrounds. In this checklist, the color of the background is listed, where known, immediately after the team name (where known). Other distinguishing characteristics may also be noted. The pins were usually originally sold with a red, white and blue swallow-tailed silk pennant attached and a brass chain with a baseball, bat or glove charms, or similar plastic toys. Values shown are for pins alone. The checklist here is incomplete.

	NM	EX	VG
Common Player:	20.00	10.00	6.00
Hank Aaron (Blue, script name, team above.)	100.00	50.00	30.00
Sandy Amoros (Brooklyn, blue.)	60.00	30.00	18.00
Harry Anderson (Phillies, photo.)	125.00	65.00	35.00
John Antonelli (NY cap, "floating head.")	20.00	10.00	6.00
John Antonelli (SF cap, ring around photo.)	20.00	10.00	6.00
Luis Aparicio (White Sox, white.)	75.00	37.00	22.00
Ernest Banks (Cubs, white, no cap logo.)	475.00	235.00	140.00
Bo Belinsky (Phillies, white.)	40.00	20.00	12.00
Gus Bell (White)	20.00	10.00	6.00
Gus Bell ("CINCINNATI REDLEGS" beneath name.)	100.00	50.00	30.00
Larry Berra (White)	90.00	45.00	27.00
Larry Berra (Blue)	100.00	50.00	30.00
Yogi Berra	80.00	40.00	24.00
Joe Black (Brooklyn, photo.)	40.00	20.00	12.00
Joe Black (Brooklyn, white, facing front.)	40.00	20.00	12.00
Joe Black (Brooklyn, white, facing his left.)	25.00	12.50	7.50
Don Bollweg (A's, photo.)	20.00	10.00	6.00
Lou Boudreau (Photo, script name.)	60.00	30.00	18.00
Lou Boudreau (Red Sox, white.)	50.00	25.00	15.00
Jackie Brandt (Orioles, photo.)	40.00	20.00	12.00
Eddie Bressoud	20.00	10.00	6.00
Bill Bruton (Braves, white.)	100.00	50.00	30.00
Jim Bunning (Phillies)	40.00	20.00	12.00
Roy Campanella (Brooklyn, blue.)	90.00	45.00	27.50
Roy Campanella (Brooklyn, yellow.)	80.00	40.00	24.00
Roy Campanella (Brooklyn, white, cap backwards.)	75.00	37.50	22.50
Roy Campanella (Brooklyn, white, name across photo.)	60.00	30.00	18.00
Roy Campanella (Brooklyn, white, name under photo.)	60.00	30.00	18.00
Roy Campanella (Brooklyn, white, name in strip.)	100.00	50.00	30.00
Roy Campanella (Brooklyn, white circle border, team at top.)	250.00	125.00	75.00
Chico Carrasquel (Name in script, team at top.)	50.00	25.00	15.00
Phil Cavarretta (Cubs, script name, stars above.)	150.00	75.00	45.00
Orlando Cepeda (Gray)	30.00	15.00	9.00
Orlando Cepeda (S.F., name in strip, photo.)	30.00	15.00	9.00
Gerry Coleman (Dark)	40.00	20.00	12.00
Gerry Coleman (Light)	40.00	20.00	12.00
Tony Conigliaro (Red Sox, gray.)	40.00	20.00	12.00
Morton Cooper (Cardinals, white/black background.)	40.00	20.00	12.00
Billy Cox (Brooklyn, white, neck-to-cap.)	95.00	47.50	28.00
Billy Cox (Brooklyn, white, chest-to-cap.)	60.00	30.00	18.00
Alvin Dark (NY cap, "floating head.")	20.00	10.00	6.00
Jerome (Dizzy) Dean (Black)	90.00	45.00	27.50
Dom DiMaggio (White)	40.00	20.00	12.00
Dom DiMaggio (Dark)	40.00	20.00	12.00
Joe DiMaggio (Black)	475.00	235.00	140.00
Joe DiMaggio (Dark blue, name beyond shoulders.)	250.00	125.00	75.00
Joe DiMaggio (Light blue, name within shoulders.)	150.00	75.00	45.00
Joe DiMaggio (Light blue, name "ear to ear" - modern fantasy, no collectible value.)			
Joe DiMaggio (Green border.)	325.00	160.00	100.00
Joe DiMaggio (White, name in strip.)	200.00	100.00	60.00
Joe DiMaggio (White, name not in strip.)	215.00	100.00	65.00
Joe DiMaggio (Yellow, "YANKEES" under name.)	350.00	175.00	100.00
Larry Doby (Dark)	60.00	30.00	18.00
Larry Doby (Indians, white.)	90.00	45.00	27.50
Carl Erskine (Brooklyn, white.)	75.00	37.50	22.50
Bob Feller (Indians, white.)	80.00	40.00	24.00
Bob Feller (Brown, name in script.)	325.00	160.00	100.00
Whitey Ford	80.00	40.00	24.00
Whitey Ford (White, name in strip, 3-1/2".)	200.00	100.00	60.00
Nelson Fox (White Sox, fox figures at top.)	350.00	175.00	100.00
Carl Furillo (Brooklyn, blue.)	75.00	37.50	22.50
Carl Furillo (Brooklyn, gray.)	65.00	32.50	20.00
Carl Furillo (Brooklyn, photo, dark sleeves.)	100.00	50.00	30.00
Carl Furillo (Brooklyn, photo, no sleeves.)	115.00	60.00	35.00
Ned Garver (Browns, white, belly-to-cap.)	30.00	15.00	9.00
Ned Garver (Browns, white, chest-to-cap.)	30.00	15.00	9.00
Junior Gilliam (Brooklyn, white.)	100.00	50.00	30.00
Junior Gilliam (Brooklyn, photo.)	100.00	50.00	30.00

	NM	EX	VG
Ruben Gomez (SF cap, ring around photo.)	30.00	15.00	9.00
Billy Goodman (White)	100.00	50.00	30.00
Ron Hansen (Orioles, photo.)	40.00	20.00	12.00
Gabby Hartnett (Cubs, black.)	40.00	20.00	12.00
Mike Hegan (Indians, white border, script name.)	450.00	225.00	135.00
Tom Henrich (Gray)	40.00	20.00	12.00
Mike Higgins (Red Sox, dark.)	45.00	22.50	13.50
Gil Hodges (Brooklyn, blue.)	100.00	50.00	30.00
Gil Hodges (Brooklyn, red/orange.)	50.00	25.00	15.00
Gil Hodges (Brooklyn, photo.)	40.00	20.00	12.00
Gil Hodges (Brooklyn, white, name across photo.)	60.00	30.00	18.00
Gil Hodges (Brooklyn, white, name in strip.)	200.00	100.00	60.00
Gil Hodges (Brooklyn, white, name under photo.)	40.00	20.00	12.00
Gil Hodges (Mets, 3-1/2", name in strip.)	150.00	75.00	45.00
Roger Homsby (Rogers) (Browns, white circle border.)	150.00	75.00	45.00
Monte Irvin (Giants, dark.)	80.00	40.00	24.00
Ransom Jackson (Cubs, stars above.)	150.00	75.00	45.00
Forrest "Spook" Jacobs (Gray)	20.00	10.00	6.00
Forrest "Spook" Jacobs (A's, photo.)	20.00	10.00	6.00
Jackie Jensen (Dark)	50.00	25.00	15.00
Jackie Jensen (White)	50.00	25.00	15.00
Ed Joost (A's, photo.)	20.00	10.00	6.00
Harmon Killebrew ("W" on cap, photo.)	375.00	185.00	110.00
Ralph Kiner (Color, facsimile autograph.)	40.00	20.00	12.00
Ralph Kiner (Cubs, hearts above.)	600.00	300.00	180.00
Ted Kluszewski (Dark, name overprinted horizontally.)	200.00	100.00	60.00
Ted Kluszewski (Reds, white, name in strip.)	40.00	20.00	12.00
Ed Kranepool (White)	50.00	25.00	15.00
Big Bill Lee (Cubs, black/gray.)	20.00	10.00	6.00
Bob Lemon (Light)	40.00	20.00	12.00
Whitey Lockman (NY cap, gray.)	25.00	12.50	7.50
Peanuts Lowrey (Cardinals, white.)	25.00	12.50	7.50
Sal Maglie (Brooklyn, photo.)	50.00	25.00	15.00
Frank Malzone	40.00	20.00	12.00
Mickey Mantle (White, batting to waist, name from elbow to armpit.)	275.00	135.00	80.00
Mickey Mantle (White, batting to waist, name from wrist to shoulder.)	300.00	150.00	90.00
Mickey Mantle (Blue, batting, left hand not visible, 1-3/4".)	350.00	175.00	100.00
Mickey Mantle (Baseball background, name in strip.)	200.00	100.00	60.00
Mickey Mantle (Blue, name in strip.) (Modern replicas are commonly encountered.)	250.00	125.00	75.00
Mickey Mantle (Blue, name in strip, looking over left shoulder, 3-1/2".)	150.00	75.00	45.00
Mickey Mantle (Yellow, name in strip, looking over left shoulder, 3-1/2".)	300.00	150.00	90.00
Mickey Mantle (White, portrait.)	300.00	150.00	90.00
Mickey Mantle (Blue, portrait, 3-1/2".)	1,750	875.00	525.00
Juan Marichal (SF cap, uncentered black border.)	60.00	30.00	18.00
Marty Marion (Browns, white circle border.)	300.00	150.00	90.00
Roger Maris (Blue, bat behind head, name in white strip, 3-1/2".)	100.00	50.00	30.00
Roger Maris (White, looking over shoulder, no cap insignia.)	125.00	60.00	35.00
Roger Maris (Orange, bat behind head, 3-1/2".)	100.00	50.00	30.00
Roger Maris (Yellow, bat behind head, 1-3/4".)	75.00	37.50	22.50
Roger Maris (Yellow, blue or purple, bat behind head, 2-1/4" - modern replica, no collectible value.)			
Roger Maris (Yellow, bat behind head, 3-1/2".)	100.00	50.00	30.00
Willie Mays (S.F. Giants, gray.)	325.00	160.00	97.00
Willie Mays (Photo, N.Y. cap.)	300.00	150.00	90.00
Willie Mays (Photo, grass background, S.F. cap.)	300.00	150.00	90.00
Willie Mays (Photo, stadium background, S.F. cap.)	300.00	150.00	90.00
Willie Mays (White, N.Y. cap.)	230.00	115.00	70.00
Willie Mays (White, S.F. cap.)	150.00	75.00	45.00
Willie McCovey (Pats on shoulder, no cap logo.)	200.00	100.00	60.00
Willie McCovey (SF cap, name in ear-to-ear white stripe.)	40.00	20.00	12.00
Gil McDougald (Yankees, gray.)	45.00	22.50	13.50
"Vinegar Bend" Mizell (Cardinals, white.)	30.00	15.00	9.00
Bill Monbouquette	40.00	20.00	12.00
Don Mueller (White, "floating head.")	40.00	20.00	12.00
Bobby Murcer (White)	30.00	15.00	9.00
Stan Musial (Cardinals, white, MUSIAL at bottom, "STAN" THE MAN at top.)	125.00	65.00	40.00

	NM	EX	VG
Stan Musial (Cardinals, white, piping shows.)	100.00	50.00	30.00
Stan Musial (Cardinals, white, no piping.)	100.00	50.00	30.00
Stan Musial (White, team name above photo, facsimile autograph.) (Modern replica exists in 2-3/16" size; no collectible value.)	100.00	50.00	30.00
Stan Musial (Yellow)	125.00	65.00	35.00
Don Newcombe (Brooklyn, blue.)	450.00	225.00	135.00
Don Newcombe (Brooklyn, white, name in strip.)	30.00	15.00	9.00
Don Newcombe (Brooklyn, white, name under photo.)	30.00	20.00	12.00
Don Newcombe (Brooklyn, white circle border, team at top.)	60.00	30.00	18.00
Don Newcombe (Yellow)	50.00	25.00	15.00
Dan O'Connell (SF cap, ring around photo.)	40.00	20.00	12.00
Andy Pafko (Brooklyn, black.)	30.00	15.00	9.00
Joe Page (White)	50.00	25.00	15.00
Leroy (Satchel) Paige (White)	175.00	85.00	50.00
Mel Parnell (Red Sox, white.)	45.00	22.50	13.50
Joe Pepitone (White)	30.00	15.00	9.00
Johnny Pesky (Red Sox, white.)	100.00	50.00	30.00
Billy Pierce (Name in serif type.)	40.00	20.00	12.00
Jimmy Piersall (Light)	50.00	25.00	15.00
Johnny Podres (Brooklyn, white.)	45.00	22.00	13.50
Wally Post ("CINCINNATI REDLEGS" beneath name.)	50.00	25.00	15.00
Vic Power (A's, photo.)	25.00	12.50	7.50
Dick Radatz (Red Sox, gray.)	30.00	15.00	9.00
Vic Raschi (Yankees, white.)	60.00	30.00	18.00
PeeWee Reese (Brooklyn, gray, name in strip.)	200.00	100.00	60.00
"Pee Wee" Reese (Brooklyn, gray, name across photo.)	60.00	30.00	18.00
"Pee Wee" Reese (Brooklyn, white, large photo.)	125.00	65.00	35.00
"Pee Wee" Reese (Brooklyn, white, small photo.)	100.00	50.00	30.00
"Pee Wee" Reese (Brooklyn, photo, name in strip.)	60.00	30.00	18.00
Bill Rigney (NY cap, dark background.)	20.00	10.00	6.00
Phil Rizzuto (White)	80.00	40.00	24.00
Robin Roberts (Phillies, photo.)	50.00	25.00	15.00
Frank Robinson ("Cincinnati Redlegs" at bottom.)	250.00	125.00	75.00
Jackie Robinson (Brooklyn, blue.)	300.00	150.00	90.00
Jackie Robinson (Brooklyn, yellow.)	190.00	95.00	55.00
Jackie Robinson (Brooklyn, white, chest-to-cap.)	200.00	100.00	60.00
Jackie Robinson (Brooklyn, white, neck-to-cap.)	250.00	125.00	75.00
Jackie Robinson (Brooklyn, white, name across bottom, facing his left.)	200.00	100.00	60.00
Jackie Robinson (Brooklyn, gray, name across photo, facing his left.)	200.00	100.00	60.00
Jackie Robinson (Brooklyn, white, name in strip, cap logo not visible.)	600.00	300.00	180.00
Jackie Robinson (Brooklyn, photo.)	275.00	135.00	80.00
Preacher Roe (Brooklyn, wind-up pose.)	90.00	45.00	27.50
Al Rosen (Light background.)	40.00	20.00	12.00
Charles Herbert Ruffing (Yankees, gray.)	40.00	20.00	12.00
Pete Runnels	40.00	20.00	12.00
Ron Santo (Cubs, white.)	40.00	20.00	12.00
Hank Sauer (Cubs, script name, stars above.)	150.00	75.00	45.00
Chuck Schilling	40.00	20.00	12.00
George Scott (White, "floating head.")	20.00	10.00	6.00
Bobby Shantz (A's, white.)	30.00	15.00	9.00
Frank Shea (Yankees, gray.)	50.00	25.00	15.00
Harry Simpson (Indians, white, team name at top, script name at bottom.)	650.00	325.00	195.00
Enos Slaughter (Cardinals, white.)	50.00	25.00	15.00
Enos Slaughter (Cardinals, black.)	50.00	25.00	15.00
Roy Smalley (Cubs, script name, stars above.)	150.00	75.00	45.00
Duke Snider (Brooklyn, white.)	80.00	40.00	24.00
Duke Snider (Brooklyn, blue.)	65.00	35.00	20.00
Duke Snider (Brooklyn, blue, 3-1/2".)	200.00	100.00	60.00
Duke Snider (Brooklyn, gray.)	75.00	37.50	22.50
Duke Snider (Brooklyn, photo.)	150.00	75.00	45.00
Gerald Staley (Cardinals, white.)	20.00	10.00	6.00
Bobby Thomson (NY cap, white, uniform shows.)	40.00	20.00	12.00
Bobby Thomson (NY cap, white, "floating head.")	30.00	15.00	9.00
Gus Triandos (Orioles, photo.)	40.00	20.00	12.00
Robt. Lee Trice (A's, photo.)	25.00	12.50	7.50
Sam White (Red Sox, white.)	30.00	15.00	9.00
James Hoyt Wilhelm (Orioles)	200.00	100.00	60.00
Ted Williams (Name beneath bust, white.)	200.00	100.00	60.00

	NM	EX	VG
Ted Williams (Name in strip, black.)	450.00	225.00	135.00
Ted Williams (Name in strip, white.)	400.00	200.00	120.00
Ted Williams (Name in strip, photo, belt-up.)	90.00	45.00	27.50
Ted Williams (Name in strip, photo, close-up.)	100.00	50.00	30.00
Carl Yastrzemski	100.00	50.00	30.00

1950s-60s PM10 Baseball Player Pins - Name at Top

This series of baseball player pins is similar to contemporary issues in its 1-3/4" (unless otherwise noted) black-and-white celluloid format, but differs in that the player name appears at top. Players known in the series indicate the buttons were issued over a period of several years, probably for sale in stadium concession stands and other souvenir outlets. The alphabetical checklist here is not complete.

	NM	EX	VG
Common Player:	60.00	30.00	18.00
Felipe Alou (Script name.)	40.00	20.00	12.00
Luis Arroyo	20.00	10.00	6.00
Hank Bauer	60.00	30.00	18.00
Yogi Berra	135.00	67.00	40.00
Johnny Blanchard	60.00	30.00	18.00
Cletis Boyer	75.00	37.00	22.00
Roy Campanella (2-1/4")	450.00	225.00	135.00
Andy Carey (2", Yankees, white)	125.00	65.00	37.50
Joe Collins	60.00	30.00	18.00
Del Crandall (2-1/8")	40.00	20.00	12.00
Whitey Ford (2")	150.00	75.00	45.00
Whitey Ford (3-1/2" diameter)	400.00	200.00	120.00
Carl Furillo (2", Brooklyn, white)	75.00	37.00	22.00
Junior Gilliam	75.00	37.00	22.00
Ruben Gomez	40.00	20.00	12.00
Ken Harrelson (Red Sox, white.)	50.00	25.00	15.00
Don Hoak (Brooklyn, white.)	60.00	30.00	18.00
Elston Howard	75.00	37.00	22.00
Jackie Jensen (Red Sox, white.)	75.00	37.00	22.00
Clem Labine (Brooklyn, white.)	60.00	30.00	18.00
Billy Loes (2", Brooklyn, white)	130.00	65.00	40.00
Ed Lopat	60.00	30.00	18.00
Hector Lopez	40.00	20.00	12.00
Frank Malzone (Red Sox, white.)	50.00	25.00	15.00
Mickey Mantle (1-5/8")	500.00	250.00	150.00
Mickey Mantle (2-1/4")	300.00	150.00	90.00
Roger Maris (2", yellow)	150.00	75.00	45.00
Roger Maris (2-1/4", white)	3.00	1.00	1.00
Billy Martin	75.00	37.00	22.00
Willie Mays (2-1/4", white)	450.00	225.00	135.00
Gil McDougald (2", Yankees, white)	100.00	50.00	30.00
Bill Monbouquette (Red Sox, white.)	50.00	25.00	15.00
Walt Moryn (1-1/2", Brooklyn, white)	250.00	125.00	75.00
Don Newcombe (2", Brooklyn, white)	125.00	62.00	37.00
Irv Noren	60.00	30.00	18.00
Johnny Podres (2", Brooklyn, white)	60.00	30.00	18.00
Allie Reynolds	60.00	30.00	18.00
Jackie Robinson (2-1/16", Brooklyn, white)	1,600	800.00	475.00
Preacher Roe (Brooklyn, white.)	60.00	30.00	18.00
Pete Runnels (Red Sox, white.)	50.00	25.00	15.00
Chuck Schilling (Red Sox, white.)	50.00	25.00	15.00
Bill Skowron	60.00	30.00	18.00
Enos Slaughter	60.00	30.00	18.00
Duke Snider (2-1/4", Brooklyn, white)	135.00	67.00	40.00
Warren Spahn	120.00	60.00	36.00
Don Thompson (2", Brooklyn, white)	200.00	100.00	60.00
Bob Turley	60.00	30.00	18.00
Ted Williams (1-3/4", name in strip at top, team in strip at bottom)	80.00	40.00	25.00
Gene Woodling	60.00	30.00	18.00
Carl Yastrzemski	200.00	100.00	60.00
Don Zimmer (Brooklyn, white.)	75.00	37.50	22.50

1956 PM15 Yellow Basepath Pins

These pins were issued circa 1956; the sponsor of this 32-pin set is not indicated. The set, which has been assigned the American Card Catalog designation PM15, is commonly called "Yellow Basepaths" because of the design of the pin,

which features a black-and-white player photo set inside a green infield with yellow basepaths. The unnumbered pins measure 7/8" in diameter.

	NM	EX	VG
Complete Set (32):	4,500	2,250	1,350
Common Player:	85.00	40.00	25.00
(1) Hank Aaron	400.00	200.00	120.00
(2) Joe Adcock	85.00	40.00	25.00
(3) Luis Aparicio	140.00	70.00	40.00
(4) Richie Ashburn	150.00	75.00	45.00
(5) Gene Baker	85.00	40.00	25.00
(6) Ernie Banks	225.00	110.00	65.00
(7) Yogi Berra	245.00	120.00	75.00
(8) Bill Bruton	85.00	40.00	25.00
(9) Larry Doby	140.00	70.00	40.00
(10) Bob Friend	85.00	40.00	25.00
(11) Nellie Fox	140.00	70.00	40.00
(12) Ted Greengrass (Jim)	85.00	40.00	25.00
(13) Steve Gromek	85.00	40.00	25.00
(14) Johnny Groth	85.00	40.00	25.00
(15) Gil Hodges	200.00	100.00	60.00
(16) Al Kaline	150.00	75.00	45.00
(17) Ted Kluzewski (Kluszewski)	140.00	70.00	40.00
(18) Johnny Logan	85.00	40.00	25.00
(19) Dale Long	85.00	40.00	25.00
(20) Mickey Mantle	600.00	300.00	180.00
(21) Ed Matthews (Mathews)	150.00	75.00	45.00
(22) Minnie Minoso	100.00	50.00	30.00
(23) Stan Musial	350.00	175.00	100.00
(24) Don Newcombe	140.00	70.00	40.00
(25) Bob Porterfield	85.00	40.00	25.00
(26) Pee Wee Reese	200.00	100.00	60.00
(27) Robin Roberts	140.00	70.00	40.00
(28) Red Schoendienst	140.00	70.00	40.00
(29) Duke Snider	225.00	110.00	65.00
(30) Vern Stephens	85.00	40.00	25.00
(31) Gene Woodling	100.00	50.00	30.00
(32) Gus Zernial	85.00	40.00	25.00

1909-11 Polar Bear Tobacco

The most distinctive advertising-back found on 1909-11 T206 is that of Polar Bear with its dark blue background and white topography. A more conventional style of ad was used on 1911 T205 cards, also printed in blue. Because the cards were packaged loose among the tobacco leaves in Polar Bear pouches, stains on surviving cards are frequently seen. Polar Bear is among the most common brands found in both series.

PREMIUMS:
T205: 1X
T206: 1-1.5X
(See T205, T206 for checklists and card values.)

1889 Police Gazette Cabinets

Issued in the late 1880s through early 1890s as a premium by Police Gazette, a popular newspaper of the day, these cabinet cards are very rare. The 4-1/4" x 6-1/2" cards consist of sepia-toned photographs mounted on cardboard of various colors. Only about two dozen players are currently known. Some photographs correspond to those used in the S.F. Hess card series and many players are depicted in suit and tie, rather than baseball uniform. Each card displays the name of the player beneath his portrait, along with the signature of "Richard K. Fox" and a line identifying him as "Editor and Proprietor / Police Gazette / Franklin Square, New York."

	NM	EX	VG
Common Player:	16,000	8,000	4,800
Hick Carpenter	16,000	8,000	4,800
Fred Carroll	16,000	8,000	4,800
Bob Clark	16,000	8,000	4,800
John Coleman	16,000	8,000	4,800
Roger Conner (Connor)	20,000	10,000	6,000
Pete Conway	16,000	8,000	4,800
John Corkhill	16,000	8,000	4,800
Jerry Denny	16,000	8,000	4,800
Jas. A. Donohue (Donahue)	16,000	8,000	4,800
Buck Ewing	20,000	10,000	6,000
Bob Ferguson	16,000	8,000	4,800
Jocko Fields	16,000	8,000	4,800
Elmer Foster	16,000	8,000	4,800
Charlie Getzein (Getzien)	16,000	8,000	4,800
Pebbly Jack Glasscock	16,000	8,000	4,800
Bill Gleason	16,000	8,000	4,800
George Gore	16,000	8,000	4,800
Tim Keefe	20,000	10,000	6,000
Gus Krock	16,000	8,000	4,800
A.J. Maul	16,000	8,000	4,800
Ed Morris	16,000	8,000	4,800
Tip O'Neil (O'Neill)	16,000	8,000	4,800
N. (Fred) Pfeffer	16,000	8,000	4,800
Danny Richardson	16,000	8,000	4,800
A.B. Sanders	16,000	8,000	4,800
Charley (Pop) Smith	16,000	8,000	4,800
Elmer Smith	16,000	8,000	4,800
Harry Staley	16,000	8,000	4,800
William Swett (San Francisco)	20,000	10,000	6,000
George Tebeau	16,000	8,000	4,800
John Tener	18,000	9,000	5,400
Billy Terry (Adonis)	16,000	8,000	4,800
Sam Thompson	20,000	10,000	6,000
Curt Welch	16,000	8,000	4,800
Wheeler C. Wikoff (Wykoff) (Pres. American Association)	16,000	8,000	4,800

1895 Police Gazette Supplement

The 12 captains of the National League's teams, collectively termed "Our Baseball Heroes," are pictured in sepia lithographic portraits surrounding a colorful baseball action scene on this supplement issued with the June 1 edition of the men's newspaper. Overall the supplement measures about 21-1/2" x 15-1/2" and is the most impressive of the baseball items issued by the paper prior to the turn of the 20th Century.

	NM	EX	VG
Supplement:	15,000	7,000	4,000
Cap Anson			
Jack Boyle			
Ed Cartwright			
George Davis			
Buck Ewing			
Jack Glasscock			
Mike Griffin			
Connie Mack			
Doggie Miller			
Billy Nash			
Patsy Tebeau			
Wilbert Robinson			

1901-1917 Police Gazette Supplements

Each issue of the weekly men's magazine included a large-format (about 11-1/4" x 16-1/4") blank-backed, black-and-white supplement. In keeping with the publication's editorial focus at the time, the pictures featured baseball players, boxers, other atheletes, actresses and female models. The photos appear in a frame design and measure about 8-1/2" x 12-1/2". The supplements are designated as such by a line of type at top or bottom that names the publication, issue number and issue date. The subject is identified in capital letters beneath the photo and there are a few lines of information at bottom. The magazine sometimes printed the same pictures in nearly identical format within its regular pages. These can be differentiated from the supplements in that they are on pink paper, have advertising or other editorial material on back and are not marked as supplements. Such pages do not enjoy the same popularity and value as the supplements. In this possibly incomplete checklist, the card number shown is the issue number in which the supplement was inserted. The player name or title may not always exactly correspond to that printed on the piece. Because of their large size, the supplements are often found trimmed to remove evidence of corner creases and edge damage. This checklist includes only the baseball subjects.

		NM	EX	VG
Common Player:		100.00	50.00	30.00
1901				
	George Davis (Issue date unknown.)	200.00	100.00	60.00
1251	Christy Mathewson	2,000	1,000	600.00
1903				
1351	Roy Thomas	100.00	50.00	30.00
1353	Red Dooin	100.00	50.00	30.00
1357	Tommy Leach	100.00	50.00	30.00
1359	John McGraw	200.00	100.00	60.00
1361	Cy Seymour	100.00	50.00	30.00
1363	Joe McGinnity	200.00	100.00	60.00
1365	Jack Cronin	100.00	50.00	30.00
1904				
1400	Dan McGann	100.00	50.00	30.00
1403	Red Ames	100.00	50.00	30.00
1407	Jack Warner	100.00	50.00	30.00
1411	Frank Bowerman	100.00	50.00	30.00
1413	Roger Bresnahan	200.00	100.00	60.00
1905				
1450	Joe McGinnity	200.00	100.00	60.00
1451	Napoleon Lajoie	250.00	125.00	75.00
1452	Hans Wagner	1,250	625.00	375.00
1453	Malachi Kittredge	100.00	50.00	30.00
1457	Jack Chesbro	200.00	100.00	60.00
1459	Roger Bresnahan	200.00	100.00	60.00
1461	1905 Pittsburg Team	900.00	450.00	275.00
1463	Willie Keeler	200.00	100.00	60.00
1465	Sam Mertes	100.00	50.00	30.00
1466	Dave Fultz	100.00	50.00	30.00
1467	Carlisle University Team	150.00	75.00	45.00
1468	Bill Hogg	100.00	50.00	30.00
1906				
1502	Aleck Smith	100.00	50.00	30.00
1504	Jack Kleinow	100.00	50.00	30.00
1505	Rube Waddell	200.00	100.00	60.00
1507	Clark Griffith	200.00	100.00	60.00
1510	Nap Shea	100.00	50.00	30.00
1516	Jimmy Casey	100.00	50.00	30.00
1518	Hal Chase	200.00	100.00	60.00
1907				
1548	Harry Davis	100.00	50.00	30.00
1549	Mike Powers	100.00	50.00	30.00
1551	Willie Keeler, Jack Kleinow	150.00	75.00	45.00
1554	Eddie Plank	250.00	125.00	75.00
1557	George Moriarty	100.00	50.00	30.00
1559	Bill Dahlen	100.00	50.00	30.00
1562	Cecil Ferguson	100.00	50.00	30.00
1564	Sammy Strang	100.00	50.00	30.00
1567	Hal Chase, Charlie Armbrucster	150.00	75.00	45.00
1571	Mordecai Brown	200.00	100.00	60.00
1572	Danny Hoffman	100.00	50.00	30.00
1908				
1607	Harry Bay	100.00	50.00	30.00
1613	Harry Lunn	100.00	50.00	30.00
1615	Charley Hemphill	100.00	50.00	30.00
1909				
1655	Buck Herzog	100.00	50.00	30.00
1657	Al Bridwell	100.00	50.00	30.00
1660	Hans Lobert	100.00	50.00	30.00
1663	Bugs Raymond	100.00	50.00	30.00
1664	Harry Coveleski	100.00	50.00	30.00
1665	Chief Meyers	100.00	50.00	30.00
1667	Orval Overall	100.00	50.00	30.00
1673	Al Burch	100.00	50.00	30.00
1674	Mike Donlin	100.00	50.00	30.00
1676	Del Howard	100.00	50.00	30.00
1678	Dick Morris (Amateur)	100.00	50.00	30.00
1910				
1716	Jack Warhop	100.00	50.00	30.00
1717	George Mullen (Mullin)	100.00	50.00	30.00
1720	Russ Ford	100.00	50.00	30.00
1721	Owen Bush	100.00	50.00	30.00
1722	Sherry Magee	100.00	50.00	30.00
1724	Jack Dalton	100.00	50.00	30.00
1726	Bert Daniels	100.00	50.00	30.00
1727	Birdie Cree	100.00	50.00	30.00
1729	Josh Devore	100.00	50.00	30.00
1730	Louis Drucke	100.00	50.00	30.00

		NM	EX	VG
1911				
1771	Christy Mathewson	750.00	375.00	225.00
1779	Arthur Wilson	100.00	50.00	30.00
1782	Hans Wagner, Roger Bresnahan	750.00	375.00	225.00
1791	Home Run Baker	200.00		60.00
1912				
1812	Zach Wheat	200.00	100.00	60.00
1814	Rube Marquard	200.00	100.00	60.00
1821	Tex Erwin	100.00	50.00	30.00
1823	Heinie Zimmerman	100.00	50.00	30.00
1825	Jake Stahl	100.00	50.00	30.00
1913				
1856	Frank Chance	200.00	100.00	60.00
1861	Joe Wood	125.00	62.50	37.50
1867	Jim Thorpe	3,000	1,500	900.00
1872	Jake Daubert	100.00	50.00	30.00
1877	Nap Rucker	100.00	50.00	30.00
1883	Joe Jackson	2,000	1,000	600.00
1888	Walter Johnson	750.00	375.00	225.00
1914				
1920	Ty Cobb	1,500	750.00	450.00
1926	Sam Crawford	200.00	100.00	60.00
1932	Dave Robertson	100.00	50.00	30.00
1938	Fritz Maisel	100.00	50.00	30.00
1942	Boston N.L. Team	200.00	100.00	60.00
1943	Philadelphia A.L. Team	200.00	100.00	60.00
1915				
1961	Ray Caldwell	100.00	50.00	30.00
1966	Rabbit Maranville	200.00	100.00	60.00
1970	Sherry Magee	100.00	50.00	30.00
1975	Hans Lobert	100.00	50.00	30.00
1982	Eddie Collins	200.00	100.00	60.00
1985	Dick Hoblitzell	100.00	50.00	30.00
1989	Grover Alexander	500.00	250.00	150.00
1916				
2011	Larry Doyle	100.00	50.00	30.00
2018	Fred Luderus	100.00	50.00	30.00
2020	Jimmy Archer	100.00	50.00	30.00
2023	Dick Rudolph	100.00	50.00	30.00
2026	Benny Kauff	100.00	50.00	30.00
2029	Sam Crawford	200.00	100.00	60.00
2035	Nick Cullop	100.00	50.00	30.00
2040	Clarence Mitchell	100.00	50.00	30.00
2042	George Sisler	200.00	100.00	60.00
2046	Pol Perritt	100.00	50.00	30.00
1917				
2064	Ping Bodie	100.00	50.00	30.00
2070	Benny Kauff	100.00	50.00	30.00
2074	Hans Lobert	100.00	50.00	30.00
2078	Harry Coveleskie (Coveleski)	100.00	50.00	30.00
2081	Jack Coombs	100.00	50.00	30.00

1914 Polo Grounds Game (WG4)

Called the "Polo Grounds Game" for the green-and-white photo of that stadium on each card's back, this set was officially issued as "All Star Card Base Ball" by The Card Baseball Co. of Norfolk, Va. Fronts of the round-cornered 2-1/2" x 3-1/2" cards have a black-and-white player photo and a baseball play scenario that is used to play the game. The set as issued includes 30 different players cards and 24 duplicate cards on which different game plays are displayed. The unnumbered cards are checklisted here alphabetically.

		NM	EX	VG
Complete Boxed Set (54):		6,650	3,325	2,000
Complete Set (30):		3,000	1,500	900.00
Common Player:		40.00	20.00	12.00
(1)	Jimmy Archer	40.00	20.00	12.00
(2)	Frank Baker	125.00	50.00	30.00
(3)	Frank Chance	125.00	50.00	30.00
(4)	Larry Cheney	40.00	20.00	12.00
(5)	Ty Cobb	1,000	275.00	165.00
(6)	Eddie Collins	100.00	50.00	30.00
(7)	Larry Doyle	40.00	20.00	12.00
(8)	Art Fletcher	40.00	20.00	12.00
(9)	Claude Hendrix	40.00	20.00	12.00
(10)	Joe Jackson	1,500	385.00	230.00
(11)	Hughie Jennings	125.00	50.00	30.00
(12)	Nap Lajoie	125.00	50.00	30.00
(13)	Jimmy Lavender	40.00	20.00	12.00
(14)	Fritz Maisel	40.00	20.00	12.00
(15)	Rabbit Maranville	125.00	50.00	30.00
(16)	Rube Marquard	125.00	50.00	30.00
(17)	Matty (Christy Mathewson)	500.00	100.00	60.00
(18)	John McGraw	125.00	50.00	30.00
(19)	Stuffy McInnis	40.00	20.00	12.00
(20)	Chief Meyers	40.00	20.00	12.00
(21)	Red Murray	40.00	20.00	12.00
(22)	Ed Plank	150.00	50.00	30.00

		NM	EX	VG
(23)	Nap Rucker	40.00	20.00	12.00
(24)	Reb Russell	40.00	20.00	12.00
(25)	Wildfire Schulte	40.00	20.00	12.00
(26)	Jim Scott	40.00	20.00	12.00
(27)	Tris Speaker	175.00	62.00	37.00
(28)	Honus Wagner	750.00	175.00	105.00
(29)	Ed Walsh	125.00	50.00	30.00
(30)	Joe Wood	100.00	30.00	18.00

1915 Postaco Stamps

A small find of these early stamps in complete sheets of 12 in the mid-1990s made the issue collectible, rather than impossibly rare. Individual stamps are 1-3/4" x 2-1/8" and feature black-and-white player portraits set against a bright background of either yellow or red-orange. The player name, position (in most cases), team and league are designated at the bottom of the picture. In the black frame between the picture and the perforated white border is a copyright symbol and "Postaco." Backs are, of course, blank. Stamps are checklisted here in alphabetical order within color group.

		NM	EX	VG
Complete Set, Sheets (3):		3,000	1,500	900.00
Complete Set, Singles (36):		2,500	1,250	750.00
Common Player:		30.00	15.00	9.00
Red-Orange Background				
(1)	Home Run Baker	100.00	50.00	30.00
(2)	Chief Bender	100.00	50.00	30.00
(3)	George Burns	40.00	20.00	12.00
(4)	John Evers	100.00	50.00	30.00
(5)	Max Flack	40.00	20.00	12.00
(6)	Hank Gawdy (Gowdy)	40.00	20.00	12.00
(7)	Claude Ray Hendrix	40.00	20.00	12.00
(8)	Walter Johnson	200.00	100.00	60.00
(9)	Nap Lajoie	100.00	50.00	30.00
(10)	Hans Lobert	40.00	20.00	12.00
(11)	Sherwood Magee	40.00	20.00	12.00
(12)	Rabbit Maranville	100.00	50.00	30.00
(13)	Christy Mathewson	250.00	125.00	75.00
(14)	George McBride	40.00	20.00	12.00
(15)	John McGraw	100.00	50.00	30.00
(16)	Fred Merkle	40.00	20.00	12.00
(17)	Jack Miller	40.00	20.00	12.00
(18)	Emiliano Palmero	40.00	20.00	12.00
(19)	Pol Perritt	40.00	20.00	12.00
(20)	Richard Pratt	40.00	20.00	12.00
(21)	Richard Rudolph	40.00	20.00	12.00
(22)	Butch Schmidt	40.00	20.00	12.00
(23)	Joe Tinker	100.00	50.00	30.00
(24)	Honus Wagner	300.00	150.00	90.00
Yellow Background				
(25)	G.C. Alexander	100.00	50.00	30.00
(26)	J.P. Archer	30.00	15.00	9.00
(27)	Ty Cobb	300.00	150.00	90.00
(28)	Eugene Cocreham	30.00	15.00	9.00
(29)	E.S. Cottrell	30.00	15.00	9.00
(30)	Josh Devore	30.00	15.00	9.00
(31)	A. Hartzell (Roy)	30.00	15.00	9.00
(32)	Wm. H. James (middle initial actually L)	30.00	15.00	9.00
(33)	Connie Mack	75.00	37.50	22.50
(34)	M. McHale	30.00	15.00	9.00
(35)	Geo. T. Stallings	30.00	15.00	9.00
(36)	Ed. Sweeney	30.00	15.00	9.00

1930 Post Cereal Famous North Americans

CHRISTY MATHEWSON (1880-1925) — Greatest of all baseball pitchers.

The year of issue is unconfirmed. Mathewson is the only baseball player from a group of cereal-box cards printed in panels of four and featuring presidents, generals, Indian chiefs, explorers, etc. The front is printed in red and blue, the back is blank. The card measures about 2-5/8" x 3-1/2".

	NM	EX	VG
Christy Mathewson	600.00	300.00	180.00

1960 Post Cereal

These cards were issued on the backs of Grape Nuts Flakes cereal and measure an oversized 7" x 8-3/4". The nine cards in the set include five baseball players two football

(Frank Gifford and John Unitas) and two basketball players (Bob Cousy and Bob Pettit). The full-color photos are bordered by a wood frame design. The cards covered the entire back of the cereal box and are blank backed. Card fronts include the player's name, team and a facsimile autograph. A panel on the side of the box has biographical information.

		NM	EX	VG
Common Player:				
(1)	Don Drysdale	400.00	200.00	120.00
(2)	Al Kaline	400.00	200.00	120.00
(3)	Harmon Killebrew	400.00	200.00	120.00
(4)	Ed Mathews	400.00	200.00	120.00
(5)	Mickey Mantle	2,500	1,250	750.00

1961 Post Cereal

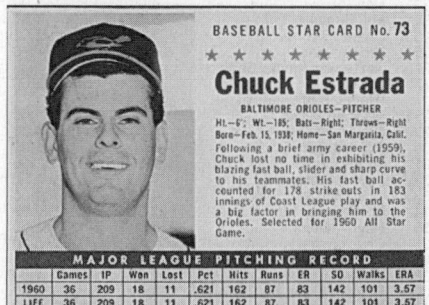

Two hundred different players are included in this set, but with variations the number of different cards exceeds 350. Cards were issued singly and in various panel configurations on the backs of cereal boxes, as well as on thinner stock in 10-card team sheets available from Post via a mail-in offer. Because of placement on less popular sizes and brands of cereal, or because they were issued only on box backs or company sheets, some cards were issued in significantly smaller quantities, making their prices much higher than other comparable players in the set. Well-cut individual cards measure about 3-1/2" x 2-1/2". All cards are numbered in the upper-left corner. Card fronts have full-color portrait photos of the player, along with biographical information and 1960 and career statistics. Backs are blank. The complete set price includes only the most common variation of each player.

		NM	EX	VG
Complete Set (200):		1,600	650.00	375.00
Common Player:		4.00	2.00	1.25
1a	Yogi Berra (Box)	40.00	16.00	10.00
1b	Yogi Berra (Company)	25.00	10.00	6.00
2a	Elston Howard (Box)	7.50	3.00	2.00
2b	Elston Howard (Company)	7.50	3.00	2.00
3a	Bill Skowron (Box)	7.50	3.00	2.00
3b	Bill Skowron (Company)	7.50	3.00	2.00
4a	Mickey Mantle (Box)	160.00	65.00	40.00
4b	Mickey Mantle (Company)	110.00	45.00	25.00
5	Bob Turley (Company)	40.00	16.00	10.00
6a	Whitey Ford (Box)	20.00	8.00	5.00
6b	Whitey Ford (Company)	12.50	5.00	3.00
7a	Roger Maris (Box)	35.00	15.00	9.00
7b	Roger Maris (Company)	35.00	15.00	9.00
8a	Bobby Richardson (Box)	15.00	6.00	4.00
8b	Bobby Richardson (Company)	10.00	4.00	2.50
9a	Tony Kubek (Box)	25.00	10.00	6.25
9b	Tony Kubek (Company)	35.00	15.00	9.00
10	Gil McDougald (Box)	60.00	25.00	15.00
11	Cletis Boyer (Box)	6.00	2.50	1.50
12a	Hector Lopez (Box)	12.50	5.00	3.00
12b	Hector Lopez (Company)	7.50	3.00	2.00
13	Bob Cerv (Box)	4.00	1.50	1.00
14	Ryne Duren (Box)	4.00	1.50	1.00
15	Bobby Shantz (Box)	4.00	1.50	1.00
16	Art Ditmar (Box)	4.00	1.50	1.00
17	Jim Coates (Box)	4.00	1.50	1.00
18	John Blanchard (Box)	4.00	1.50	1.00
19a	Luis Aparicio (Box)	7.50	3.00	2.00
19b	Luis Aparicio (Company)	15.00	6.00	4.00
20a	Nelson Fox (Box)	22.50	9.00	5.75
20b	Nelson Fox (Company)	20.00	8.00	5.00
21a	Bill Pierce (Box)	20.00	8.00	5.00
21b	Bill Pierce (Company)	9.00	3.50	2.25
22a	Early Wynn (Box)	17.50	7.00	4.50
22b	Early Wynn (Company)	25.00	10.00	6.25
23	Bob Shaw (Box)	125.00	50.00	30.00
24a	Al Smith (Box)	20.00	8.00	5.00
24b	Al Smith (Company)	17.50	7.00	4.50
25a	Minnie Minoso (Box)	15.00	6.00	4.00

		NM	EX	VG
25b	Minnie Minoso (Company)	10.00	4.00	2.50
26a	Roy Sievers (Box)	4.00	1.50	1.00
26b	Roy Sievers (Company)	7.50	3.00	2.00
27a	Jim Landis (Box)	15.00	6.00	3.75
27b	Jim Landis (Company)	7.50	3.00	2.00
28a	Sherman Lollar (Box)	4.00	1.50	1.00
28b	Sherman Lollar (Company)	7.50	3.00	2.00
29	Gerry Staley (Box)	4.00	1.50	1.00
30a	Gene Freese (Box, White Sox.)	4.00	1.50	1.00
30b	Gene Freese (Company, Reds.)	9.00	3.50	2.25
31	Ted Kluszewski (Box)	15.00	6.00	4.00
32	Turk Lown (Box)	4.00	1.50	1.00
33a	Jim Rivera (Box)	4.00	1.50	1.00
33b	Jim Rivera (Company)	7.50	3.00	2.00
34	Frank Baumann (Box)	4.00	1.50	1.00
35a	Al Kaline (Box)	25.00	10.00	6.25
35b	Al Kaline (Company)	30.00	12.00	7.50
36a	Rocky Colavito (Box)	30.00	12.00	7.50
36b	Rocky Colavito (Company)	22.50	9.00	5.75
37a	Charley Maxwell (Box)	20.00	8.00	5.00
37b	Charley Maxwell (Company)	15.00	6.00	3.75
38a	Frank Lary (Box)	4.00	1.50	1.00
38b	Frank Lary (Company)	9.00	3.50	2.00
39a	Jim Bunning (Box)	20.00	8.00	5.00
39b	Jim Bunning (Company)	15.00	6.00	4.00
40a	Norm Cash (Box)	4.00	1.50	1.00
40b	Norm Cash (Company)	12.50	5.00	3.00
41a	Frank Bolling (Box, Tigers.)	15.00	6.00	3.75
41b	Frank Bolling (Company, Braves.)	9.00	3.50	2.00
42a	Don Mossi (Box)	10.00	4.00	2.50
42b	Don Mossi (Company)	9.00	3.50	2.00
43a	Lou Berberet (Box)	10.00	4.00	2.50
43b	Lou Berberet (Company)	9.00	3.50	2.00
44	Dave Sisler (Box)	4.00	1.50	1.00
45	Ed Yost (Box)	4.00	1.50	1.00
46	Pete Burnside (Box)	4.00	1.50	1.00
47a	Pete Runnels (Box)	20.00	8.00	5.00
47b	Pete Runnels (Company)	17.50	7.00	4.50
48a	Frank Malzone (Box)	12.50	5.00	3.00
48b	Frank Malzone (Company)	7.50	3.00	2.00
49a	Vic Wertz (Box)	15.00	6.00	3.75
49b	Vic Wertz (Company)	20.00	8.00	5.00
50a	Tom Brewer (Box)	4.00	1.50	1.00
50b	Tom Brewer (Company)	7.50	3.00	2.00
51a	Willie Tasby (Box, no sold line.)	7.50	3.00	2.00
51b	Willie Tasby (Company, sold line.)	15.00	6.00	4.00
52a	Russ Nixon (Box)	4.00	1.50	1.00
52b	Russ Nixon (Company)	7.50	3.00	2.00
53a	Don Buddin (Box)	4.00	1.50	1.00
53b	Don Buddin (Company)	7.50	3.00	2.00
54a	Bill Monbouquette (Box)	4.00	1.50	1.00
54b	Bill Monbouquette (Company)	7.50	3.00	2.00
55a	Frank Sullivan (Box, Red Sox.)	4.00	1.50	1.00
55b	Frank Sullivan (Company, Phillies.)	25.00	10.00	6.25
56a	Haywood Sullivan (Box)	4.00	1.50	1.00
56b	Haywood Sullivan (Company)	7.50	3.00	2.00
57a	Harvey Kuenn (Box, Indians.)	25.00	10.00	6.25
57b	Harvey Kuenn (Company, Giants.)	9.00	3.50	2.00
58a	Gary Bell (Box)	7.50	3.00	2.00
58b	Gary Bell (Company)	7.50	3.00	2.00
59a	Jim Perry (Box)	4.00	1.50	1.00
59b	Jim Perry (Company)	7.50	3.00	2.00
60a	Jim Grant (Box)	4.00	1.50	1.00
60b	Jim Grant (Company)	20.00	8.00	5.00
61a	Johnny Temple (Box)	4.00	1.50	1.00
61b	Johnny Temple (Company)	7.50	3.00	2.00
62a	Paul Foytack (Box)	4.00	1.50	1.00
62b	Paul Foytack (Company)	7.50	3.00	2.00
63a	Vic Power (Box)	15.00	6.00	3.75
63b	Vic Power (Company)	7.50	3.00	2.00
64a	Tito Francona (Box)	4.00	1.50	1.00
64b	Tito Francona (Company)	7.50	3.00	2.00
65a	Ken Aspromonte (Box, no sold line.)	9.00	3.50	2.00
65b	Ken Aspromonte (Company, sold line.)	9.00	3.50	2.00
66	Bob Wilson (Box)	4.00	1.50	1.00
67a	John Romano (Box)	4.00	1.50	1.00
67b	John Romano (Company)	7.50	3.00	2.00
68a	Jim Gentile (Box)	4.00	1.50	1.00
68b	Jim Gentile (Company)	9.00	3.50	2.00
69a	Gus Triandos (Box)	4.00	1.50	1.00
69b	Gus Triandos (Company)	9.00	3.50	2.00
70	Gene Woodling (Box)	30.00	12.00	7.50
71a	Milt Pappas (Box)	4.00	1.50	1.00
71b	Milt Pappas (Company)	17.50	7.00	4.50
72a	Ron Hansen (Box)	4.00	1.50	1.00
72b	Ron Hansen (Company)	9.00	3.50	2.00
73	Chuck Estrada (Company)	110.00	45.00	27.50
74a	Steve Barber (Box)	12.00	4.75	3.00
74b	Steve Barber (Company)	9.00	3.50	2.00
75a	Brooks Robinson (Box)	35.00	15.00	9.00
75b	Brooks Robinson (Company)	35.00	15.00	9.00
76a	Jackie Brandt (Box)	4.00	1.50	1.00
76b	Jackie Brandt (Company)	9.00	3.50	2.00
77a	Marv Breeding (Box)	4.00	1.50	1.00
77b	Marv Breedding (Company)	9.00	3.50	2.00
78	Hal Brown (Box)	4.00	1.50	1.00
79	Billy Klaus (Box)	4.00	1.50	1.00
80a	Hoyt Wilhelm (Box)	7.50	3.00	2.00
80b	Hoyt Wilhelm (Company)	12.50	5.00	3.00
81a	Jerry Lumpe (Box)	9.00	3.50	2.00
81b	Jerry Lumpe (Company)	7.50	3.00	2.00
82a	Norm Siebern (Box)	4.00	1.50	1.00
82b	Norm Siebern (Company)	7.50	3.00	2.00
83a	Bud Daley (Box)	15.00	6.00	4.00
83b	Bud Daley (Company)	25.00	10.00	6.25
84a	Bill Tuttle (Box)	4.00	1.50	1.00
84b	Bill Tuttle (Company)	7.50	3.00	2.00

		NM	EX	VG
85a	Marv Throneberry (Box)	4.00	1.50	1.00
85b	Marv Throneberry (Company)	7.50	3.00	2.00
86a	Dick Williams (Box)	15.00	6.00	3.75
86b	Dick Williams (Company)	7.50	3.00	2.00
87a	Ray Herbert (Box)	4.00	1.50	1.00
87b	Ray Herbert (Company)	7.50	3.00	2.00
88a	Whitey Herzog (Box)	4.00	1.50	1.00
88b	Whitey Herzog (Company)	7.50	3.00	2.00
89a	Ken Hamlin (Box, no sold line.)	4.00	1.50	1.00
89b	Ken Hamlin (Company, sold line.)	9.00	3.50	2.00
90a	Hank Bauer (Box)	15.00	6.00	3.75
90b	Hank Bauer (Company)	9.00	3.50	2.00
91a	Bob Allison (Box, Minneapolis.)	9.00	3.50	2.00
91b	Bob Allison (Company, Minnesota.)	20.00	8.00	5.00
92a	Harmon Killebrew (Box, Minneapolis.)	50.00	20.00	12.50
92b	Harmon Killebrew (Company, Minnesota.)	60.00	24.00	15.00
93a	Jim Lemon (Box, Minneapolis.)	65.00	25.00	15.00
93b	Jim Lemon (Company, Minnesota.)	30.00	12.00	7.50
94	Chuck Stobbs (Company)	150.00	60.00	35.00
95a	Reno Bertoia (Box, Minneapolis.)	4.00	1.50	1.00
95b	Reno Bertoia (Company, Minnesota.)	20.00	8.00	5.00
96a	Billy Gardner (Box, Minneapolis.)	4.00	1.50	1.00
96b	Billy Gardner (Company, Minnesota.)	20.00	8.00	5.00
97a	Earl Battey (Box, Minneapolis.)	6.00	2.50	1.50
97b	Earl Battey (Company, Minnesota.)	20.00	8.00	5.00
98a	Pedro Ramos (Box, Minneapolis.)	4.00	1.50	1.00
98b	Pedro Ramos (Company, Minnesota.)	20.00	8.00	5.00
99a	Camilio Pascual (Camilo) (Box, Minneapolis.)	4.00	1.50	1.00
99b	Camilio Pascual (Camilo) (Company, Minnesota.)	20.00	8.00	5.00
100a	Billy Consolo (Box, Minneapolis.)	4.00	1.50	1.00
100b	Billy Consolo (Company, Minnesota.)	22.50	9.00	5.75
101a	Warren Spahn (Box)	35.00	14.00	9.00
101b	Warren Spahn (Company)	25.00	10.00	6.00
102a	Lew Burdette (Box)	4.00	1.50	1.00
102b	Lew Burdette (Company)	7.50	3.00	2.00
103a	Bob Buhl (Box)	4.00	1.50	1.00
103b	Bob Buhl (Company)	12.50	5.00	3.25
104a	Joe Adcock (Box)	12.50	5.00	3.25
104b	Joe Adcock (Company)	7.50	3.00	2.00
105a	John Logan (Box)	6.00	2.50	1.50
105b	John Logan (Company)	15.00	6.00	4.00
106	Ed Mathews (Company)	40.00	16.00	10.00
107a	Hank Aaron (Box)	30.00	12.00	7.50
107b	Hank Aaron (Company)	30.00	12.00	7.50
108a	Wes Covington (Box)	4.00	1.50	1.00
108b	Wes Covington (Company)	7.50	3.00	2.00
109a	Bill Bruton (Box, Braves.)	25.00	10.00	6.25
109b	Bill Bruton (Company, Tigers.)	12.50	5.00	3.00
110a	Del Crandall (Box)	6.00	2.50	1.50
110b	Del Crandall (Company)	7.50	3.00	2.00
111	Red Schoendienst (Box)	12.50	5.00	3.00
112	Juan Pizarro (Box)	4.00	1.50	1.00
113	Chuck Cottier (Box)	15.00	6.00	4.00
114	Al Spangler (Cox)	4.00	1.50	1.00
115a	Dick Farrell (Box)	25.00	10.00	6.25
115b	Dick Farrell (Company)	7.50	3.00	2.00
116a	Jim Owens (Box)	15.00	6.00	3.75
116b	Jim Owens (Company)	7.50	3.00	2.00
117a	Robin Roberts (Box)	12.50	5.00	3.00
117b	Robin Roberts (Company)	12.50	5.00	3.00
118a	Tony Taylor (Box)	4.00	1.50	1.00
118b	Tony Taylor (Company)	7.50	3.00	2.00
119a	Lee Walls (Box)	4.00	1.50	1.00
119b	Lee Walls (Company)	7.50	3.00	2.00
120a	Tony Curry (Box)	4.00	1.50	1.00
120b	Tony Curry (Company)	7.50	3.00	2.00
121a	Pancho Herrera (Box)	4.00	1.50	1.00
121b	Pancho Herrera (Company)	7.50	3.00	2.00
122a	Ken Walters (Box)	4.00	1.50	1.00
122b	Ken Walters (Company)	7.50	3.00	2.00
123a	John Callison (Box)	4.00	1.50	1.00
123b	John Callison (Company)	7.50	3.00	2.00
124a	Gene Conley (Box, Phillies.)	4.00	1.50	1.00
124b	Gene Conley (Company, Red Sox.)	20.00	8.00	5.00
125a	Bob Friend (Box)	5.00	2.00	1.25
125b	Bob Friend (Company)	7.50	3.00	2.00
126a	Vernon Law (Box)	5.00	2.00	1.25
126b	Vernon Law (Company)	7.50	3.00	2.00
127a	Dick Stuart (Box)	4.00	1.50	1.00
127b	Dick Stuart (Company)	7.50	3.00	2.00
128a	Bill Mazeroski (Box)	20.00	8.00	5.00
128b	Bill Mazeroski (Company)	12.50	5.00	3.00
129a	Dick Groat (Box)	4.00	1.50	1.00
129b	Dick Groat (Company)	10.00	4.00	2.50
130a	Don Hoak (Box)	4.00	1.50	1.00
130b	Don Hoak (Company)	7.50	3.00	2.00
131a	Bob Skinner (Box)	4.00	1.50	1.00
131b	Bob Skinner (Company)	7.50	3.00	2.00
132a	Bob Clemente (Box)	50.00	20.00	12.50
132b	Bob Clemente (Company)	70.00	28.00	17.50
133	Roy Face (Box)	15.00	6.00	4.00
134	Harvey Haddix (Box)	10.00	4.00	2.50
135	Bill Virdon (Box)	40.00	16.00	10.00
136a	Gino Cimoli (Box)	4.00	1.50	1.00
136b	Gino Cimoli (Company)	7.50	3.00	2.00
137	Rocky Nelson (Box)	6.00	2.50	1.50
138a	Smoky Burgess (Box)	4.00	1.50	1.00
138b	Smoky Burgess (Company)	7.50	3.00	2.00

		NM	EX	VG
139	Hal Smith (Box)	6.00	2.50	1.50
140	Wilmer Mizell (Box)	12.00	4.75	3.00
141a	Mike McCormick (Box)	4.00	1.50	1.00
141b	Mike McCormick (Company)	7.50	3.00	2.00
142a	John Antonelli (Box, Giants.)	4.00	1.50	1.00
142b	John Antonelli (Company, Indians.)	9.00	3.50	2.00
143a	Sam Jones (Box)	5.00	2.00	1.25
143b	Sam Jones (Company)	7.50	3.00	2.00
144a	Orlando Cepeda (Box)	22.50	9.00	5.75
144b	Orlando Cepeda (Company)	12.50	5.00	3.00
145a	Willie Mays (Box)	55.00	22.50	13.50
145b	Willie Mays (Company)	45.00	18.00	10.00
146a	Willie Kirkland (Box, Giants.)	60.00	24.00	15.00
146b	Willie Kirkland (Company, Indians.)	25.00	10.00	6.25
147a	Willie McCovey (Box)	20.00	8.00	5.00
147b	Willie McCovey (Company)	25.00	10.00	6.00
148a	Don Blasingame (Box)	4.00	1.50	1.00
148b	Don Blasingame (Company)	7.50	3.00	2.00
149a	Jim Davenport (Box)	4.00	1.50	1.00
149b	Jim Davenport (Company)	7.50	3.00	2.00
150a	Hobie Landrith (Box)	4.00	1.50	1.00
150b	Hobie Landrith (Company)	7.50	3.00	2.00
151	Bob Schmidt (Box)	9.00	3.50	2.00
152a	Ed Bressoud (Box)	4.00	1.50	1.00
152b	Ed Bressoud (Company)	7.50	3.00	2.00
153a	Andre Rodgers (Box, no traded line.)	9.00	3.50	2.00
153b	Andre Rodgers (Box, traded line.)	4.00	1.50	1.00
154	Jack Sanford (Box)	20.00	8.00	5.00
155	Billy O'Dell (Box)	4.00	1.50	1.00
156a	Norm Larker (Box)	7.50	3.00	2.00
156b	Norm Larker (Company)	7.50	3.00	2.00
157a	Charlie Neal (Box)	4.00	1.50	1.00
157b	Charlie Neal (Company)	7.50	3.00	2.00
158a	Jim Gilliam (Box)	7.50	3.00	2.00
158b	Jim Gilliam (Company)	7.50	3.00	2.00
159a	Wally Moon (Box)	20.00	8.00	5.00
159b	Wally Moon (Company)	12.00	4.75	3.00
160a	Don Drysdale (Box)	20.00	8.00	5.00
160b	Don Drysdale (Company)	20.00	8.00	5.00
161a	Larry Sherry (Box)	4.00	1.50	1.00
161b	Larry Sherry (Company)	7.50	3.00	2.00
162	Stan Williams (Box)	7.50	3.00	2.00
163	Mel Roach (Box)	55.00	22.50	13.50
164a	Maury Wills (Box)	20.00	8.00	5.00
164b	Maury Wills (Company)	35.00	14.00	9.00
165	Tom Davis (Box)	4.00	1.50	1.00
166a	John Roseboro (Box)	4.00	1.50	1.00
166b	John Roseboro (Company)	7.50	3.00	2.00
167a	Duke Snider (Box)	15.00	6.00	3.75
167b	Duke Snider (Company)	20.00	8.00	5.00
168a	Gil Hodges (Box)	7.50	3.00	2.00
168b	Gil Hodges (Company)	12.50	5.00	3.00
169	John Podres (Box)	4.00	1.50	1.00
170	Ed Roebuck (Box)	4.00	1.50	1.00
171a	Ken Boyer (Box)	15.00	6.00	3.75
171b	Ken Boyer (Company)	7.50	3.00	2.00
172a	Joe Cunningham (Box)	12.50	5.00	3.00
172b	Joe Cunningham (Company)	9.00	3.50	2.00
173a	Daryl Spencer (Box)	4.00	1.50	1.00
173b	Daryl Spencer (Company)	7.50	3.00	2.00
174a	Larry Jackson (Box)	12.50	5.00	3.00
174b	Larry Jackson (Company)	7.50	3.00	2.00
175a	Lindy McDaniel (Box)	7.50	3.00	2.00
175b	Lindy McDaniel (Company)	7.50	3.00	2.00
176a	Bill White (Box)	4.00	1.50	1.00
176b	Bill White (Company)	7.50	3.00	2.00
177a	Alex Grammas (Box)	20.00	8.00	5.00
177b	Alex Grammas (Company)	7.50	3.00	2.00
178a	Curt Flood (Box)	4.00	1.50	1.00
178b	Curt Flood (Company)	12.50	5.00	3.00
179a	Ernie Broglio (Box)	4.00	1.50	1.00
179b	Ernie Broglio (Company)	8.00	3.25	2.00
180a	Hal Smith (Box)	8.00	3.25	2.00
180b	Hal Smith (Company)	12.50	5.00	3.00
181a	Vada Pinson (Box)	20.00	8.00	5.00
181b	Vada Pinson (Company)	7.50	3.00	2.00
182a	Frank Robinson (Box)	30.00	12.00	7.50
182b	Frank Robinson (Company)	35.00	15.00	9.00
183	Roy McMillan (Box)	100.00	40.00	25.00
184a	Bob Purkey (Box)	4.00	1.50	1.00
184b	Bob Purkey (Company)	7.50	3.00	2.00
185a	Ed Kasko (Box)	7.50	3.00	2.00
185b	Ed Kasko (Company)	7.50	3.00	2.00
186a	Gus Bell (Box)	4.00	1.50	1.00
186b	Gus Bell (Company)	7.50	3.00	2.00
187a	Jerry Lynch (Box)	4.00	1.50	1.00
187b	Jerry Lynch (Company)	7.50	3.00	2.00
188a	Ed Bailey (Box)	4.00	1.50	1.00
188b	Ed Bailey (Company)	7.50	3.00	2.00
189a	Jim O'Toole (Box)	4.00	1.50	1.00
189b	Jim O'Toole (Company)	7.50	3.00	2.00
190a	Billy Martin (Box, no sold line.)	6.00	2.50	1.50
190b	Billy Martin (Company, sold line.)	12.50	5.00	3.00
191a	Ernie Banks (Box)	35.00	15.00	9.00
191b	Ernie Banks (Company)	20.00	8.00	5.00
192a	Richie Ashburn (Box)	12.50	5.00	3.00
192b	Richie Ashburn (Company)	22.50	9.00	5.75
193a	Frank Thomas (Box)	100.00	40.00	25.00
193b	Frank Thomas (Company)	40.00	16.00	10.00
194a	Don Cardwell (Box)	6.00	2.50	1.50
194b	Don Cardwell (Company)	7.50	3.00	2.00
195a	George Altman (Box)	15.00	6.00	3.75
195b	George Altman (Company)	7.50	3.00	2.00
196a	Ron Santo (Box)	6.00	2.50	1.50
196b	Ron Santo (Company)	30.00	12.00	7.50
197a	Glen Hobbie (Box)	4.00	1.50	1.00
197b	Glen Hobbie (Company)	7.50	3.00	2.00
198a	Sam Taylor (Box)	4.00	1.50	1.00
198b	Sam Taylor (Company)	7.50	3.00	2.00
199a	Jerry Kindall (Box)	8.00	3.25	2.00
199b	Jerry Kindall (Company)	7.50	3.00	2.00
200a	Don Elston (Box)	12.00	4.75	3.00
200b	Don Elston (Company)	7.50	3.00	2.00

1961 Post Cereal Company Sheets

Via a mail-in offer, sheets of 10 cards from each team could be ordered from the cereal company. Known to collectors as "company" cards, the sheets were issued in a perforated format on cardboard that is somewhat thinner than box-back cards. Sheet cards have perforations on one, two, or three sides, depending on their original placement on the sheet. Because of player movements between the time the box-back cards and sheet cards were printed, some cards are only found on the mail-in sheets, while others could not be obtained via the mail-in offer, and some are shown on the sheets of the "wrong" team.

		NM	EX	VG
Complete Set (16):		5,250	2,625	1,575
Common Team:		300.00	150.00	90.00
(1)	Baltimore Orioles	300.00	150.00	90.00
(2)	Boston Red Sox	300.00	150.00	90.00
(3)	Chicago Cubs	300.00	150.00	90.00
(4)	Chicago White Sox	300.00	150.00	90.00
(5)	Cincinnati Reds	300.00	150.00	90.00
(6)	Cleveland Indians	300.00	150.00	90.00
(7)	Detroit Tigers	300.00	150.00	90.00
(8)	Kansas City Athletics	300.00	150.00	90.00
(9)	Los Angeles Dodgers	375.00	185.00	110.00
(10)	Milwaukee Braves	375.00	185.00	110.00
(11)	Minnesota Twins	475.00	235.00	140.00
(12)	New York Yankees	600.00	300.00	180.00
(13)	Philadelphia Phillies	300.00	150.00	90.00
(14)	Pittsburgh Pirates	375.00	185.00	110.00
(15)	San Francisco Giants	375.00	185.00	110.00
(16)	St. Louis Cardinals	300.00	150.00	90.00

1961 Post Cereal Display Pinwheel

Designed for use in grocery stores to promote sales of Post cereal with baseball cards on the back, this display features double-sided, oversize (about 8-1/2" x 6") examples of nine of the cards arranged in a circle. At center was a cardboard cutout of a youngster and accommodation for an electric motor.

	NM	EX	VG
Complete Display:	6,500	3,750	2,000

Ken Boyer, Lew Burdette, Roy Face, Whitey Ford, Nellie Fox, Jim Gentile, Jim Lemon, Willie Mays, Pete Runnels

1962 Post Cereal

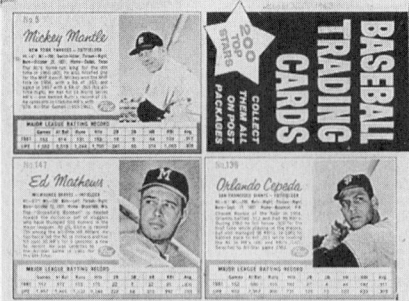

Like the 1961 Post set, there are 200 players pictured in this set of 3-1/2" x 2-1/2" cards. Differences include a Post logo on the card fronts and the player's name in script lettering. Cards are again blank backed and were issued in panels of five to seven cards on cereal boxes. American League players are numbered 1-100 and National League players 101-200. With variations there are 210 cards known. Some of the '62 cards, usually those printed on the backs of less popular brands or sizes, were issued in smaller quantities and sell for more than players of star caliber. The cards of Mickey Mantle and Roger Maris were reproduced in a special two-card panel for a Life magazine insert. The card stock for this insert is slightly thinner, with white margins. The 1962 Post Canadian and Jell-O sets have virtually the same checklist as this set. The complete set price does not include the scarcer variations. The #5 Mickey Mantle card has been extensively counterfeited in recent years by pasting a reproduction of the Life

magazine promo card (no lines in the stats area) to a piece of blank cardboard. All genuine cereal-box Mantle cards have a grid of lines in the stats area.

		NM	EX	VG
Complete Set (200):		1,000	500.00	250.00
Common Player:		4.00	1.50	1.00
April 13 Life magazine w/ad panel:		100.00	50.00	25.00
1	Bill Skowron	10.00	4.00	2.50
2	Bobby Richardson	12.50	5.00	3.00
3	Cletis Boyer	7.50	3.00	2.00
4	Tony Kubek	9.00	3.50	2.00
5a	Mickey Mantle (From box, no printing on back.)	70.00	35.00	17.50
5b	Mickey Mantle (From ad, printing on back.)	50.00	25.00	12.50
6a	Roger Maris (From box, no printing on back.)	35.00	14.00	9.00
6b	Roger Maris (From ad, printing on back.)	30.00	12.00	7.50
7	Yogi Berra	27.50	11.00	7.00
8	Elston Howard	20.00	8.00	5.00
9	Whitey Ford	22.50	9.00	6.00
10	Ralph Terry	10.00	4.00	2.50
11	John Blanchard	4.00	1.50	1.00
12	Luis Arroyo	20.00	8.00	5.00
13	Bill Stafford	4.00	1.50	1.00
14a	Norm Cash (Throws: Right)	30.00	12.00	7.50
14b	Norm Cash (Throws: Left)	10.00	4.00	2.50
15	Jake Wood	7.50	3.00	2.00
16	Steve Boros	10.00	4.00	2.50
17	Chico Fernandez	4.00	1.50	1.00
18	Bill Bruton	4.00	1.50	1.00
19	Rocky Colavito	16.00	6.50	4.00
20	Al Kaline	20.00	8.00	5.00
21	Dick Brown	4.00	1.50	1.00
22	Frank Lary	4.00	1.50	1.00
23	Don Mossi	4.00	1.50	1.00
24	Phil Regan	4.00	1.50	1.00
25	Charley Maxwell	7.50	3.00	2.00
26	Jim Bunning	30.00	12.00	7.50
27a	Jim Gentile (Home: Baltimore)	4.00	1.50	1.00
27b	Jim Gentile (Home: San Lorenzo)	6.00	2.50	1.50
28	Marv Breeding	4.00	1.50	1.00
29	Brooks Robinson	17.50	7.00	4.50
30	Ron Hansen	4.00	1.50	1.00
31	Jackie Brandt	4.00	1.50	1.00
32	Dick Williams	4.00	1.50	1.00
33	Gus Triandos	4.00	1.50	1.00
34	Milt Pappas	7.50	3.00	2.00
35	Hoyt Wilhelm	15.00	6.00	3.50
36	Chuck Estrada	12.50	5.00	3.00
37	Vic Power	4.00	1.50	1.00
38	Johnny Temple	4.00	1.50	1.00
39	Bubba Phillips	4.00	1.50	1.00
40	Tito Francona	9.00	3.50	2.00
41	Willie Kirkland	4.00	1.50	1.00
42	John Romano	4.00	1.50	1.00
43	Jim Perry	4.00	1.50	1.00
44	Woodie Held	4.00	1.50	1.00
45	Chuck Essegian	4.00	1.50	1.00
46	Roy Sievers	4.00	1.50	1.00
47	Nellie Fox	7.50	3.00	2.00
48	Al Smith	4.00	1.50	1.00
49	Luis Aparicio	12.50	5.00	3.25
50	Jim Landis	7.50	3.00	2.00
51	Minnie Minoso	10.00	4.00	2.50
52	Andy Carey	7.50	3.00	2.00
53	Sherman Lollar	4.00	1.50	1.00
54	Bill Pierce	7.50	3.00	2.00
55	Early Wynn	50.00	20.00	12.50
56	Chuck Schilling	7.50	3.00	2.00
57	Pete Runnels	15.00	6.00	3.75
58	Frank Malzone	4.00	1.50	1.00
59	Don Buddin	4.00	1.50	1.00
60	Gary Geiger	25.00	10.00	6.25
61	Carl Yastrzemski	40.00	20.00	10.00
62	Jackie Jensen	7.50	3.00	2.00
63	Jim Pagliaroni	4.00	1.50	1.00
64	Don Schwall	4.00	1.50	1.00
65	Dale Long	4.00	1.50	1.00
66	Chuck Cottier	4.00	1.50	1.00
67	Billy Klaus	9.00	3.50	2.00
68	Coot Veal	9.00	3.50	2.00
69	Marty Keough	60.00	30.00	15.00
70	Willie Tasby	9.00	3.50	2.00
71	Gene Woodling	4.00	1.50	1.00
72	Gene Green	4.00	1.50	1.00
73	Dick Donovan	4.00	1.50	1.00
74	Steve Bilko	4.00	1.50	1.00
75	Rocky Bridges	4.00	1.50	1.00
76	Eddie Yost	4.00	1.50	1.00
77	Leon Wagner	4.00	1.50	1.00
78	Albie Pearson	7.50	3.00	2.00
79	Ken Hunt	4.00	1.50	1.00
80	Earl Averill	4.00	1.50	1.00
81	Ryne Duren	4.00	1.50	1.00
82	Ted Kluszewski	6.00	2.50	1.50
83	Bob Allison	90.00	35.00	20.00
84	Billy Martin	9.00	3.50	2.00
85	Harmon Killebrew	40.00	16.00	10.00
86	Zoilo Versalles	20.00	8.00	5.00
87	Lenny Green	10.00	4.00	2.50
88	Bill Tuttle	4.00	1.50	1.00
89	Jim Lemon	4.00	1.50	1.00
90	Earl Battey	4.00	1.50	1.00
91	Camilo Pascual	4.00	1.50	1.00
92	Norm Siebern	55.00	27.50	13.75
93	Jerry Lumpe	4.00	1.50	1.00
94	Dick Howser	4.00	1.50	1.00
95a	Gene Stephens (Born: Jan. 5)	4.00	1.50	1.00
95b	Gene Stephens (Born: Jan. 20)	20.00	8.00	5.00
96	Leo Posada	4.00	1.50	1.00
97	Joe Pignatano	7.50	3.00	2.00
98	Jim Archer	4.00	1.50	1.00
99	Haywood Sullivan	4.00	1.50	1.00

1962 Post Cereal - Canadian

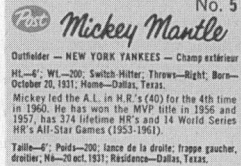

This Post set is scarce due to the much more limited distribution in Canada. Most cards were printed on the back of the cereal boxes and contain a full-color player photo with biography and statistics given in both French and English. Card backs are blank. Cards measure 3-1/2" x 2-1/2". This 200-card set is very similar to the Post Cereal cards printed in the United States. The Post logo appears at the upper-left corner of the Canadian issue. Several cards are scarce because of limited distribution and there are two Whitey Ford cards, the corrected version being the most scarce. The complete set price does not include the scarcer variations. Certain cereal brands had the cards packaged inside the box on perforated panels, and will be found with perforated edges on one side or other.

		NM	EX	VG
	Complete Set (200):	5,000	2,005	1,250
	Common Player:	8.00	3.25	2.00
1	Bill Skowron	35.00	15.00	9.00
2	Bobby Richardson	12.00	4.75	3.00
3	Cletis Boyer	10.00	4.00	2.50
4	Tony Kubek	12.00	4.75	3.00
5a	Mickey Mantle (Stats list 153 hits.)	215.00	85.00	55.00
5b	Mickey Mantle (163 hits; first line of bio ends: "4th time in")	120.00	50.00	30.00
5c	Mickey Mantle (163 hits; first line of bio ends: "4th time")	125.00	50.00	30.00
6a	Roger Maris (First line of French bio has large "P" in "Pour les circuits.")	65.00	25.00	15.00
6b	Roger Maris (French text reads, "Residence." Small "p" in "pour.")	55.00	22.50	13.50
6c	Roger Maris (French text reads, "a," not "Residence." Small "p" in "pour.")	55.00	22.50	13.50
7	Yogi Berra	40.00	16.00	10.00
8	Elston Howard	12.00	4.75	3.00
9a	Whitey Ford (Dodgers)	55.00	22.50	13.50
9b	Whitey Ford (Yankees)	80.00	32.00	20.00
10	Ralph Terry	95.00	38.00	24.00
11	John Blanchard	8.00	3.25	2.00
12	Luis Arroyo	8.00	3.25	2.00
13	Bill Stafford	8.00	3.25	2.00
14	Norm Cash	10.00	4.00	2.50
15	Jake Wood	8.00	3.25	2.00
16	Steve Boros	8.00	3.25	2.00
17	Chico Fernandez	8.00	3.25	2.00
18	Bill Bruton	8.00	3.25	2.00
19a	Rocky Colavito (Script name large.)	17.50	7.00	4.50
19b	Rocky Colavito (Script name small.)	17.50	7.00	4.50
20	Al Kaline	85.00	35.00	20.00
21	Dick Brown	12.00	4.75	3.00
22a	Frank Lary ("Residence-Northport, Alabama.")	17.50	7.00	4.50
22b	Frank Lary ("a Northport, Alabama.")	65.00	25.00	15.00
23	Don Mossi	8.00	3.25	2.00
24	Phil Regan	8.00	3.25	2.00
25	Charley Maxwell	8.00	3.25	2.00
26	Jim Bunning	25.00	10.00	6.25
27a	Jim Gentile (French bio begins "Le 8 mai, Jim ...")	13.50	5.50	3.50
27b	Jim Gentile (Begins, "Le 8 mai 1961, Jim ...")	13.50	5.50	3.50
28	Marv Breeding	17.50	7.00	4.50
29	Brooks Robinson	50.00	20.00	12.50
30	Ron Hansen	8.00	3.25	2.00
31	Jackie Brandt	8.00	3.25	2.00
32	Dick Williams	55.00	22.50	13.50
33	Gus Triandos	10.00	4.00	2.50
34	Milt Pappas	10.00	4.00	2.50
35	Hoyt Wilhelm	95.00	38.00	24.00
36	Chuck Estrada	8.00	3.25	2.00
37	Vic Power	8.00	3.25	2.00
38	Johnny Temple	8.00	3.25	2.00
39	Bubba Phillips	55.00	22.50	13.50
40	Tito Francona	55.00	22.50	13.50
41	Willie Kirkland	13.50	5.50	3.50
42	John Romano	13.50	5.50	3.50
43	Jim Perry	10.00	4.00	2.50
44	Woodie Held	8.00	3.25	2.00
45	Chuck Essegian	8.00	3.25	2.00
46	Roy Sievers	40.00	16.00	10.00
47	Nellie Fox	25.00	10.00	6.25
48	Al Smith	8.00	3.25	2.00
49	Luis Aparicio	100.00	40.00	25.00
50	Jim Landis	13.50	5.50	3.50
51	Minnie Minoso	55.00	22.50	13.50
52	Andy Carey	12.00	4.75	3.00
53	Sherman Lollar	8.00	3.25	2.00
54	Bill Pierce	10.00	4.00	2.50
55	Early Wynn	30.00	12.00	7.50
56	Chuck Schilling	10.00	4.00	2.50
57	Pete Runnels	10.00	4.00	2.50
58	Frank Malzone	8.00	3.25	2.00
59	Don Buddin	12.00	4.75	3.00
60	Gary Geiger	8.00	3.25	2.00
61	Carl Yastrzemski	60.00	25.00	15.00
62	Jackie Jensen	40.00	16.00	10.00
63	Jim Pagliaroni	8.00	3.25	2.00
64	Don Schwall	25.00	10.00	6.25
65	Dale Long	20.00	8.00	5.00
66	Chuck Cottier	8.00	3.25	2.00
67	Billy Klaus	8.00	3.25	2.00
68	Coot Veal	8.00	3.25	2.00
69	Marty Keough	8.00	3.25	2.00
70	Willie Tasby	125.00	50.00	30.00
71	Gene Woodling (Photo reversed.)	10.00	4.00	2.50
72	Gene Green	12.00	4.75	3.00
73	Dick Donovan	8.00	3.25	2.00
74	Steve Bilko	13.50	5.50	3.50
75	Rocky Bridges	12.00	4.75	3.00
76	Eddie Yost	8.00	3.25	2.00
77	Leon Wagner	65.00	25.00	15.00
78	Albie Pearson	13.50	5.50	3.50
79	Ken Hunt	8.00	3.25	2.00
80	Earl Averill	8.00	3.25	2.00
81	Ryne Duren	10.00	4.00	2.50
82	Ted Kluszewski	30.00	12.00	7.50
83	Bob Allison	13.50	5.50	3.50
84	Billy Martin	17.50	7.00	4.50
85	Harmon Killebrew	125.00	50.00	30.00
86	Zoilo Versalles	8.00	3.25	2.00
87	Lenny Green	95.00	38.00	24.00
88	Bill Tuttle	8.00	3.25	2.00
89	Jim Lemon	8.00	3.25	2.00
90	Earl Battey	13.50	5.50	3.50
91	Camilo Pascual	10.00	4.00	2.50
92	Norm Siebern	8.00	3.25	2.00
93	Jerry Lumpe	8.00	3.25	2.00
94	Dick Howser	80.00	32.00	20.00
95	Gene Stephens	8.00	3.25	2.00
96	Leo Posada	8.00	3.25	2.00
97	Joe Pignatano	8.00	3.25	2.00
98	Jim Archer	8.00	3.25	2.00
99	Haywood Sullivan	125.00	50.00	30.00
100	Art Ditmar	25.00	10.00	6.25
101	Gil Hodges	35.00	15.00	9.00
102	Charlie Neal	8.00	3.25	2.00
103	Daryl Spencer	8.00	3.25	2.00
104	Maury Wills	17.50	7.00	4.50
105	Tommy Davis	55.00	22.50	13.50
106	Willie Davis	12.00	4.75	3.00
107	John Rosboro (Roseboro)	10.00	4.00	2.50
108	John Podres	10.00	4.00	2.50
109	Sandy Koufax	80.00	32.00	20.00
110	Don Drysdale	35.00	15.00	9.00
111	Larry Sherry	55.00	22.50	13.50
112	Jim Gilliam	55.00	22.50	13.50
113	Norm Larker	8.00	3.25	2.00
114	Duke Snider	30.00	12.00	7.50
115	Stan Williams	13.50	5.50	3.50
116	Gordy Coleman	8.00	3.25	2.00
117	Don Blasingame	160.00	65.00	40.00
118	Gene Freese	40.00	16.00	10.00
119	Ed Kasko	13.50	5.50	3.50
120	Gus Bell	8.00	3.25	2.00
121	Vada Pinson	10.00	4.00	2.50
122	Frank Robinson	50.00	20.00	12.50
123	Bob Purkey	55.00	22.50	13.50
124	Joey Jay	8.00	3.25	2.00
125	Jim Brosnan	17.50	7.00	4.50
126	Jim O'Toole	8.00	3.25	2.00
127	Jerry Lynch	15.00	6.00	3.75
128	Wally Post	135.00	55.00	35.00
129	Ken Hunt	8.00	3.25	2.00
130	Jerry Zimmerman	8.00	3.25	2.00
131	Willie McCovey	40.00	16.00	10.00
132	Jose Pagan	12.00	4.75	3.00
133	Felipe Alou	10.00	4.00	2.50
134	Jim Davenport	8.00	3.25	2.00
135	Harvey Kuenn	10.00	4.00	2.50
136	Orlando Cepeda	25.00	10.00	6.25
137	Ed Bailey	75.00	30.00	18.50
138	Sam Jones	55.00	22.50	13.50
139	Mike McCormick	8.00	3.25	2.00
140	Juan Marichal	35.00	15.00	9.00
141	Jack Sanford	8.00	3.25	2.00
142a	Willie Mays (Big head.)	80.00	32.00	20.00
142b	Willie Mays (Small head.)	60.00	24.00	15.00
143	Stu Miller	8.00	3.25	2.00
144	Joe Amalfitano	100.00	40.00	25.00
145	Joe Adcock	13.50	5.50	3.50
146	Frank Bolling	13.50	5.50	3.50
147	Ed Mathews	30.00	12.00	7.50
148	Roy McMillan	24.00	9.50	6.00
149a	Hank Aaron (Script name large.)	80.00	32.00	20.00
149b	Hank Aaron (Script name small.)	60.00	24.00	15.00
150	Gino Cimoli	8.00	3.25	2.00
151	Frank Thomas	8.00	3.25	2.00
152	Joe Torre	25.00	10.00	6.25
153	Lou Burdette	25.00	10.00	6.25
154	Bob Buhl	10.00	4.00	2.50
155	Carlton Willey	12.00	4.75	3.00
156	Lee Maye	8.00	3.25	2.00
157	Al Spangler	8.00	3.25	2.00
158	Bill White	10.00	4.00	2.50
159	Ken Boyer	40.00	16.00	10.00
160	Joe Cunningham	8.00	3.25	2.00
161	Carl Warwick	55.00	22.50	13.50
162	Carl Sawatski	8.00	3.25	2.00
163	Lindy McDaniel	8.00	3.25	2.00
164	Ernie Broglio	8.00	3.25	2.00
165	Larry Jackson	8.00	3.25	2.00
166	Curt Flood	25.00	10.00	6.25
167	Curt Simmons	17.50	7.00	4.50

100	Art Ditmar	6.00	2.50	1.50
101	Gil Hodges	50.00	25.00	12.50
102	Charlie Neal	4.00	1.50	1.00
103	Daryl Spencer	25.00	10.00	6.00
104	Maury Wills	4.00	1.50	1.00
105	Tommy Davis	4.00	1.50	1.00
106	Willie Davis	4.00	1.50	1.00
107	John Roseboro	7.50	3.00	2.00
108	John Podres	4.00	1.50	1.00
109a	Sandy Koufax (Blue lines around stats.)	375.00	187.50	93.75
109b	Sandy Koufax (Red lines around stats.)	30.00	15.00	7.50
110	Don Drysdale	20.00	8.00	5.00
111	Larry Sherry	4.00	1.50	1.00
112	Jim Gilliam	7.50	3.00	2.00
113	Norm Larker	65.00	32.50	16.25
114	Duke Snider	20.00	8.00	5.00
115	Stan Williams	4.00	1.50	1.00
116	Gordy Coleman	55.00	27.50	13.75
117	Don Blasingame	12.50	5.00	3.00
118	Gene Freese	4.00	1.50	1.00
119	Ed Kasko	4.00	1.50	1.00
120	Gus Bell	4.00	1.50	1.00
121	Vada Pinson	7.50	3.00	2.00
122	Frank Robinson	50.00	20.00	12.50
123	Bob Purkey	4.00	1.50	1.00
124a	Joey Jay (Blue lines around stats.)	225.00	90.00	55.00
124b	Joey Jay (Red lines around stats.)	6.00	2.50	1.50
125	Jim Brosnan	45.00	22.50	11.25
126	Jim O'Toole	4.00	1.50	1.00
127	Jerry Lynch	55.00	27.50	13.75
128	Wally Post	4.00	1.50	1.00
129	Ken Hunt	4.00	1.50	1.00
130	Jerry Zimmerman	4.00	1.50	1.00
131	Willie McCovey	55.00	27.50	13.75
132	Jose Pagan	4.00	1.50	1.00
133	Felipe Alou	4.00	1.50	1.00
134	Jim Davenport	4.00	1.50	1.00
135	Harvey Kuenn	4.00	1.50	1.00
136	Orlando Cepeda	15.00	6.00	3.75
137	Ed Bailey	4.00	1.50	1.00
138	Sam Jones	4.00	1.50	1.00
139	Mike McCormick	4.00	1.50	1.00
140	Juan Marichal	55.00	27.50	13.75
141	Jack Sanford	4.00	1.50	1.00
142	Willie Mays	35.00	17.50	8.75
143	Stu Miller (Photo actually Chuck Hiller.)	5.00	2.00	1.25
144	Joe Amalfitano	35.00	14.00	9.00
145a	Joe Adock (Name incorrect.)	65.00	32.50	16.25
145b	Joe Adcock (Name correct.)	4.00	1.50	1.00
146	Frank Bolling	4.00	1.50	1.00
147	Ed Mathews	17.50	7.00	4.50
148	Roy McMillan	4.00	1.50	1.00
149	Hank Aaron	40.00	20.00	10.00
150	Gino Cimoli	4.00	1.50	1.00
151	Frank Thomas	4.00	1.50	1.00
152	Joe Torre	25.00	10.00	6.25
153	Lou Burdette	4.00	1.50	1.00
154	Bob Buhl	10.00	4.00	2.50
155	Carlton Willey	20.00	8.00	5.00
156	Lee Maye	20.00	8.00	5.00
157	Al Spangler	7.50	3.00	2.00
158	Bill White	30.00	15.00	7.50
159	Ken Boyer	6.00	2.50	1.50
160	Joe Cunningham	4.00	1.50	1.00
161	Carl Warwick	4.00	1.50	1.00
162	Carl Sawatski	4.00	1.50	1.00
163	Lindy McDaniel	4.00	1.50	1.00
164	Ernie Broglio	4.00	1.50	1.00
165	Larry Jackson	4.00	1.50	1.00
166	Curt Flood	4.00	1.50	1.00
167	Curt Simmons	4.00	1.50	1.00
168	Alex Grammas	4.00	1.50	1.00
169	Dick Stuart	10.00	4.00	2.50
170	Bill Mazeroski	20.00	8.00	5.00
171	Don Hoak	20.00	8.00	5.00
172	Dick Groat	4.00	1.50	1.00
173a	Roberto Clemente (Blue lines around stats.)	350.00	175.00	87.50
173b	Roberto Clemente (Red lines around stats.)	30.00	15.00	7.50
174	Bob Skinner	4.00	1.50	1.00
175	Bill Virdon	4.00	1.50	1.00
176	Smoky Burgess	9.00	3.50	2.25
177	Elroy Face	4.00	1.50	1.00
178	Bob Friend	4.00	1.50	1.00
179	Vernon Law	4.00	1.50	1.00
180	Harvey Haddix	4.00	1.50	1.00
181	Hal Smith	7.50	3.00	2.00
182	Ed Bouchee	4.00	1.50	1.00
183	Don Zimmer	4.00	1.50	1.00
184	Ron Santo	7.50	3.00	2.00
185	Andre Rodgers	4.00	1.50	1.00
186	Richie Ashburn	12.50	5.00	3.00
187a	George Altman (Last line is "...1955.")")	6.00	2.50	1.50
187b	George Altman (Last line is "...1955.")	7.50	3.00	2.00
188	Ernie Banks	17.50	7.00	4.50
189	Sam Taylor	25.00	10.00	6.25
190	Don Elston	7.50	3.00	2.00
191	Jerry Kindall	4.00	1.50	1.00
192	Pancho Herrera	4.00	1.50	1.00
193	Tony Taylor	4.00	1.50	1.00
194	Ruben Amaro	9.00	3.50	2.00
195	Don Demeter	4.00	1.50	1.00
196	Bobby Gene Smith	4.00	1.50	1.00
197	Clay Dalrymple	4.00	1.50	1.00
198	Robin Roberts	10.00	4.00	2.50
199	Art Mahaffey	4.00	1.50	1.00
200	John Buzhardt	4.00	1.50	1.00

168	Alex Grammas	8.00	3.25	2.00
169	Dick Stuart	25.00	10.00	6.25
170	Bill Mazeroski	40.00	16.00	10.00
171	Don Hoak	8.00	3.25	2.00
172	Dick Groat	17.50	7.00	4.50
173	Roberto Clemente	100.00	40.00	25.00
174	Bob Skinner	8.00	3.25	2.00
175	Bill Virdon	10.00	4.00	2.50
176	Smoky Burgess	40.00	16.00	10.00
177	Elroy Face	17.50	7.00	4.50
178	Bob Friend	10.00	4.00	2.50
179	Vernon Law	10.00	4.00	2.50
180	Harvey Haddix	10.00	4.00	2.50
181	Hal Smith	85.00	35.00	20.00
182	Ed Bouchee	100.00	40.00	25.00
183	Don Zimmer	10.00	4.00	2.50
184	Ron Santo	13.50	5.50	3.50
185	Andre Rogers (Rodgers)	8.00	3.25	2.00
186	Richie Ashburn	30.00	12.00	7.50
187	George Altman	8.00	3.25	2.00
188	Ernie Banks	40.00	16.00	10.00
189	Sam Taylor	30.00	12.00	7.50
190	Don Elston	8.00	3.25	2.00
191	Jerry Kindall	8.00	3.25	2.00
192	Pancho Herrera	8.00	3.25	2.00
193	Tony Taylor	8.00	3.25	2.00
194	Ruben Amaro	8.00	3.25	2.00
195	Don Demeter	55.00	22.50	13.50
196	Bobby Gene Smith	8.00	3.25	2.00
197	Clay Dalrymple	8.00	3.25	2.00
198	Robin Roberts	45.00	18.00	11.00
199	Art Mahaffey	8.00	3.25	2.00
200	John Buzhardt	10.00	4.00	2.50

1963 Post Cereal

Another 200-player, 3-1/2" x 2-1/2" set that, with variations, totals more than 205 cards. Numerous color variations also exist due to the different cereal boxes on which the cards were printed. More than any of the other 1960s Post baseball issues, the set is rife with short-prints and other scarcities which make it more difficult to complete than earlier years' sets. The 1963 Post cards are almost identical to the '63 Jell-O set, which is a slight 1/4" narrower. Cards are blank-backed, with a color player photo, biographies and statistics on the numbered card fronts. No Post logo appears on the '63 cards. The complete set price does not include the scarcer variations. An album to hold the cards was given away at grocery stores in a display featuring Mickey Mantle.

		NM	EX	VG
Complete Set (200):		3,300	1,650	825.00
Common Player:		2.00	.80	.50
1	Vic Power	6.00	2.50	1.50
2	Bernie Allen	6.00	2.50	1.50
3	Zoilo Versalles	7.50	3.00	2.00
4	Rich Rollins	5.00	2.00	1.25
5	Harmon Killebrew	25.00	10.00	6.00
6	Lenny Green	30.00	15.00	7.50
7	Bob Allison	9.00	3.50	2.00
8	Earl Battey	12.50	5.00	3.00
9	Camilo Pascual	15.00	6.00	3.50
10a	Jim Kaat (Light pole in background.)	15.00	6.00	3.50
10b	Jim Kaat (No light pole.)	10.00	4.00	2.50
11	Jack Kralick	7.50	3.00	2.00
12	Bill Skowron	15.00	6.00	3.50
13	Bobby Richardson	15.00	6.00	3.50
14	Cletis Boyer	6.00	2.50	1.50
15	Mickey Mantle	300.00	120.00	75.00
16	Roger Maris	115.00	45.00	30.00
17	Yogi Berra	30.00	12.00	7.50
18	Elston Howard	13.50	5.50	3.00
19	Whitey Ford	15.00	6.00	3.50
20	Ralph Terry	6.00	2.50	1.50
21	John Blanchard	10.00	4.00	2.50
22	Bill Stafford	5.00	2.00	1.25
23	Tom Tresh	9.00	3.50	2.00
24	Steve Bilko	15.00	6.00	3.50
25	Bill Moran	5.00	2.00	1.25
26a	Joe Koppe (1962 Avg. is .277)	17.50	7.00	4.50
26b	Joe Koppe (1962 Avg. is .227)	45.00	22.50	11.25
27	Felix Torres	7.50	3.00	2.00
28a	Leon Wagner (Lifetime Avg. is .278.)	15.00	6.00	3.50
28b	Leon Wagner (Lifetime Avg. is .272.)	25.00	10.00	6.00
29	Albie Pearson	5.00	2.00	1.25
30	Lee Thomas (Photo actually George Thomas.)	70.00	35.00	17.50
31	Bob Rodgers	5.00	2.00	1.25
32	Dean Chance	5.00	2.00	1.25
33	Ken McBride	7.50	3.00	2.00
34	George Thomas (Photo actually Lee Thomas.)	9.00	3.50	2.00
35	Joe Cunningham	5.00	2.00	1.25
36a	Nelson Fox (No bat showing.)	30.00	12.00	7.50
36b	Nelson Fox (Part of bat showing.)	25.00	10.00	6.00
37	Luis Aparicio	15.00	6.00	3.75
38	Al Smith	40.00	20.00	10.00
39	Floyd Robinson	90.00	45.00	22.50
40	Jim Landis	5.00	2.00	1.25
41	Charlie Maxwell	5.00	2.00	1.25
42	Sherman Lollar	5.00	2.00	1.25
43	Early Wynn	9.00	3.50	2.00
44	Juan Pizarro	5.00	2.00	1.25
45	Ray Herbert	5.00	2.00	1.25
46	Norm Cash	25.00	10.00	6.25
47	Steve Boros	5.00	2.00	1.25
48	Dick McAuliffe	35.00	15.00	9.00
49	Bill Bruton	12.50	5.00	3.00
50	Rocky Colavito	25.00	10.00	6.25
51	Al Kaline	25.00	10.00	6.25
52	Dick Brown	5.00	2.00	1.25
53	Jim Bunning	95.00	42.50	21.25
54	Hank Aguirre	5.00	2.00	1.25
55	Frank Lary	5.00	2.00	1.25
56	Don Mossi	7.50	3.00	2.00
57	Jim Gentile	9.00	3.50	2.00
58	Jackie Brandt	7.50	3.00	2.00
59	Brooks Robinson	25.00	10.00	6.00
60	Ron Hansen	5.00	2.00	1.25
61	Jerry Adair	160.00	80.00	40.00
62	John (Boog) Powell	15.00	6.00	3.75
63	Russ Snyder	5.00	2.00	1.25
64	Steve Barber	7.50	3.00	2.00
65	Milt Pappas	5.00	2.00	1.25
66	Robin Roberts	10.00	4.00	2.50
67	Tito Francona	5.00	2.00	1.25
68	Jerry Kindall	12.50	5.00	3.00
69	Woodie Held	5.00	2.00	1.25
70	Bubba Phillips	25.00	10.00	6.00
71	Chuck Essegian	5.00	2.00	1.25
72	Willie Kirkland	5.00	2.00	1.25
73	Al Luplow	5.00	2.00	1.25
74	Ty Cline	5.00	2.00	1.25
75	Dick Donovan	5.00	2.00	1.25
76	John Romano	5.00	2.00	1.25
77	Pete Runnels	6.00	2.50	1.50
78	Ed Bressoud	5.00	2.00	1.25
79	Frank Malzone	10.00	4.00	2.50
80	Carl Yastrzemski	275.00	137.50	68.75
81	Gary Geiger	5.00	2.00	1.25
82	Lou Clinton	5.00	2.00	1.25
83	Earl Wilson	7.50	3.00	2.00
84	Bill Monbouquette	5.00	2.00	1.25
85	Norm Siebern	5.00	2.00	1.25
86	Jerry Lumpe	75.00	37.50	18.75
87	Manny Jimenez	75.00	37.50	18.75
88	Gino Cimoli	9.00	3.50	2.00
89	Ed Charles	5.00	2.00	1.25
90	Ed Rakow	5.00	2.00	1.25
91	Bob Del Greco	5.00	2.00	1.25
92	Haywood Sullivan	5.00	2.00	1.25
93	Chuck Hinton	5.00	2.00	1.25
94	Ken Retzer	12.50	5.00	3.00
95	Harry Bright	5.00	2.00	1.25
96	Bob Johnson	7.50	3.00	2.00
97	Dave Stenhouse	20.00	8.00	5.00
98	Chuck Cottier	25.00	10.00	6.25
99	Tom Cheney	7.50	3.00	2.00
100	Claude Osteen	35.00	15.00	9.00
101	Orlando Cepeda	7.50	3.00	2.00
102	Charley Hiller	7.50	3.00	2.00
103	Jose Pagan	5.00	2.00	1.25
104	Jim Davenport	5.00	2.00	1.25
105	Harvey Kuenn	15.00	6.00	3.50
106	Willie Mays	35.00	17.50	8.75
107	Felipe Alou	7.50	3.00	2.00
108	Tom Haller	75.00	37.50	18.75
109	Juan Marichal	10.00	4.00	2.50
110	Jack Sanford	5.00	2.00	1.25
111	Bill O'Dell	5.00	2.00	1.25
112	Willie McCovey	12.50	5.00	3.00
113	Lee Walls	10.00	4.00	2.50
114	Jim Gilliam	15.00	6.00	3.50
115	Maury Wills	17.50	7.00	4.50
116	Ron Fairly	5.00	2.00	1.25
117	Tommy Davis	5.00	2.00	1.25
118	Duke Snider	25.00	10.00	6.25
119	Willie Davis	225.00	90.00	55.00
120	John Roseboro	5.00	2.00	1.25
121	Sandy Koufax	35.00	17.50	8.75
122	Stan Williams	9.00	3.50	2.00
123	Don Drysdale	20.00	8.00	5.00
124a	Daryl Spencer (No arm showing.)	7.50	3.00	2.00
124b	Daryl Spencer (Part of arm showing.)	15.00	6.00	3.50
125	Gordy Coleman	7.50	3.00	2.00
126	Don Blasingame	5.00	2.00	1.25
127	Leo Cardenas	5.00	2.00	1.25
128	Eddie Kasko	150.00	75.00	37.50
129	Jerry Lynch	35.00	15.00	9.75
130	Vada Pinson	15.00	6.00	3.50
131a	Frank Robinson (No stripes on cap.)	30.00	12.00	7.50
131b	Frank Robinson (Stripes on cap.)	45.00	22.50	11.25
132	John Edwards	15.00	6.00	3.50
133	Joey Jay	5.00	2.00	1.25
134	Bob Purkey	5.00	2.00	1.25
135	Marty Keough	15.00	6.00	3.50
136	Jim O'Toole	5.00	2.00	1.25
137	Dick Stuart	7.50	3.00	2.00
138	Bill Mazeroski	12.50	5.00	3.00
139	Dick Groat	6.00	2.50	1.50
140	Don Hoak	25.00	10.00	6.00
141	Bob Skinner	25.00	10.00	6.25
142	Bill Virdon	5.00	2.00	1.25
143	Roberto Clemente	35.00	17.50	8.75
144	Smoky Burgess	15.00	6.00	3.50
145	Bob Friend	5.00	2.00	1.25
146	Al McBean	5.00	2.00	1.25
147	El Roy Face (Elroy)	20.00	8.00	5.00
148	Joe Adcock	13.50	5.50	3.50
149	Frank Bolling	5.00	2.00	1.25
150	Roy McMillan	7.50	3.00	2.00
151	Eddie Mathews	22.50	9.00	5.75
152	Hank Aaron	40.00	20.00	10.00
153	Del Crandall	25.00	10.00	6.25
154a	Bob Shaw (Third sentence has "In 1959" twice.)	10.00	4.00	2.50
154b	Bob Shaw (Third sentence has "In 1959" once.)	9.00	3.50	2.00
155	Lew Burdette	20.00	8.00	5.00
156	Joe Torre	7.50	3.00	2.00
157	Tony Cloninger	5.00	2.00	1.25
158a	Bill White (Ht. 6')	6.00	2.50	1.50
158b	Bill White (Ht. 6'0")	6.00	2.50	1.50
159	Julian Javier	5.00	2.00	1.25
160	Ken Boyer	7.50	3.00	2.00
161	Julio Gotay	5.00	2.00	1.25
162	Curt Flood	85.00	42.50	21.25
163	Charlie James	9.00	3.50	2.00
164	Gene Oliver	5.00	2.00	1.25
165	Ernie Broglio	15.00	6.00	3.50
166	Bob Gibson	45.00	18.00	11.00
167a	Lindy McDaniel (Asterisk before trade line.)	10.00	4.00	2.50
167b	Lindy McDaniel (No asterisk before trade line.)	12.50	5.00	3.25
168	Ray Washburn	5.00	2.00	1.25
169	Ernie Banks	17.50	7.00	4.50
170	Ron Santo	25.00	10.00	6.25
171	George Altman	7.50	3.00	2.00
172	Billy Williams	100.00	50.00	25.00
173	Andre Rodgers	10.00	4.00	2.50
174	Ken Hubbs	25.00	10.00	6.00
175	Don Landrum	5.00	2.00	1.25
176	Dick Bertell	20.00	8.00	5.00
177	Roy Sievers	7.50	3.00	2.00
178	Tony Taylor	12.50	5.00	3.50
179	John Callison	5.00	2.00	1.25
180	Don Demeter	5.00	2.00	1.25
181	Tony Gonzalez	25.00	10.00	6.25
182	Wes Covington	35.00	15.00	9.00
183	Art Mahaffey	5.00	2.00	1.25
184	Clay Dalrymple	7.50	3.00	2.00
185	Al Spangler	6.00	2.50	1.50
186	Roman Mejias	7.50	3.00	2.00
187	Bob Aspromonte	350.00	175.00	87.50
188	Norm Larker	25.00	10.00	6.00
189	Johnny Temple	7.50	3.00	2.00
190	Carl Warwick	15.00	6.00	3.50
191	Bob Lillis	9.00	3.50	2.00
192	Dick Farrell	5.00	2.00	1.25
193	Gil Hodges	15.00	6.00	3.50
194	Marv Throneberry	7.50	3.00	2.00
195	Charlie Neal	30.00	12.00	7.50
196	Frank Thomas	175.00	87.50	43.75
197	Richie Ashburn	35.00	15.00	9.00
198	Felix Mantilla	10.00	4.00	2.50
199	Rod Kanehl	45.00	22.50	11.25
200	Roger Craig	10.00	4.00	2.50

1963 Post/Jell-O Album

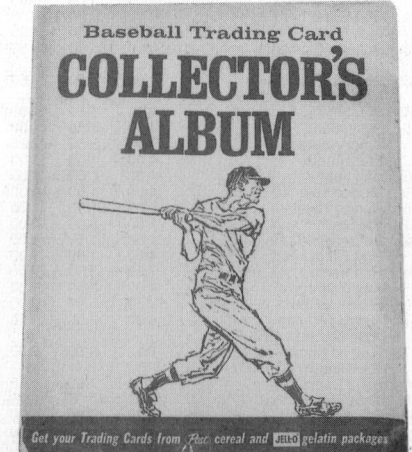

The baseball history and other printed matter in this 26-page 8-1/2" x 11" album seems to point to 1963 as the issue date, though 1962 would not be impossible. Each major league team has a page on which the box-back cards from Post cereals and Jell-O could be pasted. The front cover is printed in red-and-white while the interior pages are in black-and-white.

	NM	EX	VG
Post/Jell-O Album	90.00	45.00	25.00

1978 Post Cereal Steve Garvey Baseball Tips

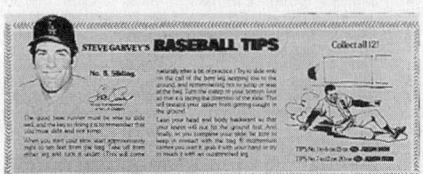

These 7-1/8" x 2-5/8" cut-out panels bordered in red "baseball" stitching were printed on the backs of 15-oz. (#1-6) and 20-oz. (#7-12) packages of Post Raisin Brand cereal. The panels have a green background with black-and-white artwork of a generic player illustrating the tip and a color portrait of Garvey.

		NM	EX	VG
Complete Set (12):		30.00	15.00	9.00
Common Panel:		3.00	1.50	.90
1	The Batting Stance	3.00	1.50	.90
2	Bunting	3.00	1.50	.90
3	Rounding First Base	3.00	1.50	.90
4	The Grip in Throwing	3.00	1.50	.90
5	Fielding a Pop-Up	3.00	1.50	.90
6	Proper Fielding Stances	3.00	1.50	.90
7	On-Deck Observation	3.00	1.50	.90
8	Sliding	3.00	1.50	.90
9	Hitting to the Opposite Field	3.00	1.50	.90
10	Throwing From the Outfield	3.00	1.50	.90
11	Mental Preparation for Each Play	3.00	1.50	.90
12	Total Conditioning	3.00	1.50	.90

1978 Post-Intelligencer 1969 Pilot Profiles

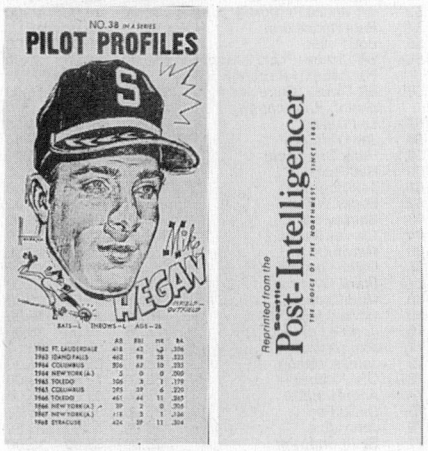

This series of cards of the one-year American League team states on its back they are reprinted from the Seattle Post-Intelligencer newspaper. The 2-3/8" x 5" cards are printed in black-and-white on semi-gloss cardboard. Fronts feature a pencil caricature of the player and include major and minor league stats. A card number is at top. Backs have the newspaper's ad. The cards were a collectors' issue produced by long-time minor league card maker Frank Caruso, with the paper's permission. The cartoons originally ran in a 3" x 6-3/8" format within the pages of the newspaper and are themselves highly collectible, with values about 2X-3X those of the reprints listed here. Reprint sets were originally sold for $6.

		NM	EX	VG
Complete Set (39):		100.00	50.00	30.00
Common Player:		4.00	3.00	1.50
1	Don Mincher	4.00	3.00	1.50
2	Tommy Harper	5.00	2.50	1.50
3	Ray Oyler	4.00	3.00	1.50
4	Jerry McNertney	4.00	3.00	1.50
5	Not Issued			
6	Tommy Davis	5.00	2.50	1.50
7	Gary Bell	4.00	3.00	1.50
8	Chico Salmon	4.00	3.00	1.50
9	Jack Aker	4.00	3.00	1.50
10	Rich Rollins	4.00	3.00	1.50
11	Diego Segui	4.00	3.00	1.50
12	Steve Barber	5.00	2.50	1.50
13	Wayne Comer	4.00	3.00	1.50
14	John Kennedy	4.00	3.00	1.50
15	Buzz Stephen	4.00	3.00	1.50
16	Jim Gosger	4.00	3.00	1.50
17	Mike Ferraro	4.00	3.00	1.50
18	Marty Pattin	4.00	3.00	1.50
19	Gerry Schoen	4.00	3.00	1.50
20	Steve Hovely	4.00	3.00	1.50
21	Frank Crosetti	5.00	2.50	1.50
22	Charles Bates	4.00	3.00	1.50
23	Jose Vidal	4.00	3.00	1.50
24	Bob Richmond	4.00	3.00	1.50
25	Lou Piniella	6.00	3.00	1.75
26	John Miklos	4.00	3.00	1.50
27	John Morris	4.00	3.00	1.50
28	Larry Haney	4.00	3.00	1.50
29	Mike Marshall	5.00	2.50	1.50
30	Marv Staehle	4.00	3.00	1.50
31	Gus Gil	4.00	3.00	1.50
32	Sal Maglie	5.00	2.50	1.50
33	Ron Plaza	4.00	3.00	1.50
34	Ed O'Brien	4.00	3.00	1.50
35	Jim Bouton	6.00	3.00	1.75
36	Bill Stafford	4.00	3.00	1.50
37	Darrell Brandon	4.00	3.00	1.50
38	Mike Hegan	4.00	3.00	1.50
39	Dick Baney	4.00	3.00	1.50

1910 Doc Powers Day Postcard

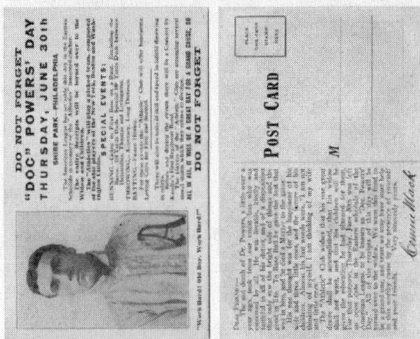

To announce to fans the forthcoming "'Doc' Powers' Day" benefit game, the Philadelphia A's produced this standard-sized (about 5-1/2" x 3-1/2") black-and-white postcard. Front has a photo of the late A's catcher and information about the special events to be held June 30. On back is a message over the facsimile autograph of Connie Mack asking fans to remember the widow and children of their fallen star.

	NM	EX	VG
Doc Powers	750.00	375.00	225.00

1975 Praeger Publishers Ty Cobb

 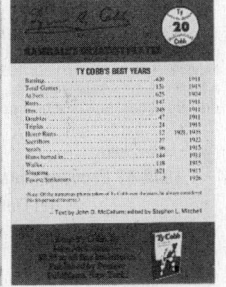

This set was produced by Washington state collector Stephen Mitchell in conjunction with Praeger Publishers of New York to promote the book "Ty Cobb" by John McCallum. Slightly larger than the current 2-1/2" x 3-1/2" standard, the cards featured black-and-white photos on front surrounded by a woodgrain-effect frame and with a plaque at bottom bearing the card title. Backs have an excerpt from the book, an ad for the book and a facsimile autograph. Cards are numbered in a baseball at upper-right. Sets originally sold for $3.25.

		NM	EX	VG
Complete Set (20):		25.00	12.50	7.50
Common Card:		2.00	1.00	.60
1	Ty Breaks In	3.00	1.50	.90
2	Four Inches of the Plate	2.00	1.00	.60
3	Slashing into Third	2.00	1.00	.60
4	Inking Another Contract	2.00	1.00	.60
5	Captain Tyrus R. Cobb	2.00	1.00	.60
6	Ty with "The Big Train" (With Walter Johnson.)	4.00	2.00	1.25
7	The End of an Era (With Babe Ruth.)	6.00	3.00	1.75
8	All-Time Centerfielder	2.00	1.00	.60
9	Ty Could "Walk 'em down"	2.00	1.00	.60
10	Menacing Batsman	2.00	1.00	.60
11	With Brother Paul	2.00	1.00	.60
12	Thomas Edison, Cobb Fan	3.00	1.50	.90
13	Ty Tangles with Muggsy McGraw	2.50	1.25	.70
14	Author McCallum with Cy Young	2.00	1.00	.60
15	Speaker - DiMaggio - Cobb	5.00	2.50	1.50
16	Ted Gets a Lesson (With Ted Williams.)	5.00	2.50	1.50
17	Five for Five!	2.00	1.00	.60
18	"I have but one regret ..."	2.00	1.00	.60
19	Excellence: The Cobb Standard	2.00	1.00	.60
20	His Favorite Photo	3.00	1.50	.90

1954 Preferred Products Milwaukee Braves

Sold as a 12-piece set in an envelope marked "Braves Team Autographed Portraits," this portfolio was one of several issued in the team's early years in Milwaukee. The artwork is apparently by Scott Douglas, whose copyright appears on the outer envelope. The same pictures can be found on Preferred Product felt patches and t-shirts. These 8" x 10" portraits are printed in sepia on cream-colored heavy textured paper and feature facsimile autographs. Backs are blank. The unnumbered portraits are checklisted here alphabetically.

		NM	EX	VG
Complete Set (12):		300.00	150.00	90.00
Common Player:		25.00	12.50	7.50
(1)	Joe Adcock	25.00	12.50	7.50
(2)	Bill Bruton	25.00	12.50	7.50
(3)	Bob Buhl	25.00	12.50	7.50
(4)	Lew Burdette	25.00	12.50	7.50
(5)	Del Crandall	25.00	12.50	7.50
(6)	Johnny Logan	25.00	12.50	7.50
(7)	Ed Mathews	40.00	20.00	12.00
(8)	Danny O'Connell	25.00	12.50	7.50
(9)	Andy Pafko	25.00	12.50	7.50
(10)	Jim Pendleton	25.00	12.50	7.50
(11)	Warren Spahn	40.00	20.00	12.00
(12)	Bob Thomson	25.00	12.50	7.50

1954 Preferred Products Milwaukee Braves Patches

While they are not so identified, the use of the same portraits and facsimile autographs found on the company's player pictures pinpoint this as a Preferred Products issue, as does a paper tag enclosed in the cellophane wrapper in which the patch was sold. The patches are of heavy felt, with blue or sepia pictures and red "stitching" on the baseball background. At 4-7/8" in diameter, they were intended to be sewn to jackets, etc. While only a handful of players have been confirmed to date, it is possible, even likely, that all 12 of the players from the picture set were also issued in this format.

		NM	EX	VG
Common Player:		175.00	85.00	50.00
(1)	Joe Adcock	175.00	85.00	50.00
(2)	Bill Bruton	175.00	85.00	50.00
(3)	Lew Burdette	175.00	85.00	50.00
(5)	Del Crandall	175.00	85.00	50.00
(6)	Johnny Logan	175.00	85.00	50.00
(7)	Eddie Mathews	125.00	65.00	35.00
(8)	Danny O'Connell	175.00	85.00	50.00
(9)	Andy Pafko	175.00	85.00	50.00
(11)	Warren Spahn	125.00	65.00	35.00

1957-60 Preferred Products Milwaukee Braves

Similar in format to the company's 1954 issue, these 8" x 10" portraits are printed in sepia on cream-colored heavy textured paper with player names printed beneath. Backs are blank. The unnumbered portraits are checklisted here alphabetically, but the list may not be complete.

		NM	EX	VG
Common Player:		25.00	12.50	7.50
(1)	Hank Aaron	100.00	50.00	30.00
(2)	Joe Adcock	25.00	12.50	7.50
(3)	Bill Bruton	25.00	12.50	7.50
(4)	Lew Burdette	25.00	12.50	7.50
(5)	Wes Covington	25.00	12.50	7.50

(6)	Johnny Logan	25.00	12.50	7.50
(7)	Carl Sawatski	25.00	12.50	7.50
(8)	Red Schoendienst	35.00	17.50	10.50
(9)	Frank Torre	25.00	12.50	7.50

1950 Prest-O-lite

The attributed date of issue is approximate for this multi-sport promotional postcard issue. Besides the two baseball players, football stars Doak Walker and Leon Hart also exist. The black-and-white, approximately 3-1/2" x 5-1/2" cards on front have a borderless action pose with a salutation and facsimile autograph. The postcard-style divided back has a preprinted message over the player's facsimile autograph, asking the recipient to view ads for the battery manufacturer in various magazines.

	NM	EX	VG
Tommy Henrich	200.00	100.00	60.00
Ted Williams	400.00	200.00	120.00

1914 Pritchard Publishing Giants/ Yankees Stamps

These colorful large-format (about 1-7/8" x 2-5/8") stamps are copyrighted 1914 by Pritchard Publishing Co., New York. All players are N.Y. Giants or Yankees. A similar issue of Yale baseball players is listed in the minor league section. The unnumbered stamps are listed alphabetically by team.

		NM	EX	VG
Common Player:		200.00	100.00	60.00
	N.Y. GIANTS			
(1)	Bob Bescher	200.00	100.00	60.00
(2)	George Burns	200.00	100.00	60.00
(3)	Josh Devore	200.00	100.00	60.00
(4)	Larry Doyle	200.00	100.00	60.00
(5)	Art Fletcher	200.00	100.00	60.00
(6)	Christy Mathewson	900.00	450.00	270.00
(7)	Fred Merkle	200.00	100.00	60.00
(8)	Chief Meyers	200.00	100.00	60.00
(9)	Red Murray	200.00	100.00	60.00
(10)	Fred Snodgrass	200.00	100.00	60.00
	N.Y. YANKEES			
(1)	Ray Caldwell	200.00	100.00	60.00
(2)	Les Channell	200.00	100.00	60.00
(3)	Roy Hartzell	200.00	100.00	60.00
(4)	Bill Holden	200.00	100.00	60.00
(5)	Fritz Maisel	200.00	100.00	60.00
(6)	Roger Peckinpaugh	200.00	100.00	60.00
(7)	Jeff Sweeney	200.00	100.00	60.00
(8)	Jimmy Walsh	200.00	100.00	60.00
(9)	Harry Williams	200.00	100.00	60.00

1956 Prize Frankies Cleveland Indians

Though the back of the cards says 24 Indians' cards were issued, only one player has ever been seen - and precious few of him. The 2-1/4" x 3 3/8" cards have a black-and-white photo on front with the player's name and number in black in the white border at bottom. Backs have an Indian logo and instructions to redeem complete sets of the cards for a pair of box seats. It is unlikely this alone accounts for the scarcity of the cards. More likely this card was made as a prototype for a promotion that never materialized.

	NM	EX	VG
10 Vic Wertz	600.00	300.00	180.00

1924 Proctor's Theatre Babe Ruth

This 1-5/8" x 2-7/8" black-and-white card was issued to promote a vaudeville appearance by Babe Ruth in upstate New York during November 1924. The front has a photo with a facsimile autograph inscribed, "To My Mount Vernon Admirers." Back has details of his appearance.

	NM	EX	VG
Babe Ruth	9,000	4,500	2,700

1946-47 Propagandas Montiel Los Reyes del Deporte

The 180 athletes in this issue of "Sporting Kings" cards are featured in a couple of different styles. Most cards from #1-101 have only the athlete's photo on front, surrounded by a yellow or orange border. Most cards #100-180 also have the card number and player ID on front, with a chest-to-cap photo set a colored frame. All are roughly 2-1/8" x 3-1/8". Backs have biographical data, the issuer's name and, sometimes, an ad for a Cuban novelty store or radio program. Most examples in the hobby today were once pasted in the colorful album accompanying the issue and it is rare to find cards in better than VG condition. The set opens with a run of boxers, then a group of Cuban baseball stars of the past and present, former big league greats and contemporary major leaguers, plus a few wrestlers. Cards #100-180 (except 101) feature players from the Florida International League, a Class B circuit within Organized Baseball with teams in Havana, Miami, Miami Beach, Lakeland and Tampa included. Curiously, the West Palm Beach team is not represented.

		NM	EX	VG
Complete Set (180):		20,000	8,800	4,000
Common Baseball Player:		45.00	20.00	9.00
Album:		300.00	135.00	60.00
1	John L. Sullivan (Boxer)	135.00	60.00	27.50
2	James J. Corbett (Boxer)	85.00	37.50	17.50
3	Bob Fitzsimmons (Boxer)	70.00	30.00	15.00
4	James J. Jeffries (Boxer)	85.00	37.50	17.50
5	Tommy Burns (Boxer)	70.00	30.00	15.00
6	Jack Johnson (Boxer)	90.00	40.00	18.00
7	Jess Willard (Boxer)	75.00	35.00	15.00
8	Jack Dempsey (Boxer)	135.00	60.00	27.50
9	Gene Tunney (Boxer)	75.00	35.00	15.00
10	Max Schmeling (Boxer)	75.00	35.00	15.00
11	Jack Sharkey (Boxer)	70.00	30.00	15.00
12	Primo Carnera (Boxer)	70.00	30.00	15.00
13	Max Baer (Boxer)	70.00	30.00	15.00
14	James J. Braddock (Boxer)	70.00	30.00	15.00
15	Joe Louis (Boxer)	135.00	60.00	27.50
16	Georges Carpentier (Boxer)	70.00	30.00	15.00
17	Tommy Loughran (Boxer)	70.00	30.00	15.00
18	Tony Zale (Boxer)	70.00	30.00	15.00
19	Johnny Dundee (Boxer)	55.00	25.00	10.00
20	Billy Conn (Boxer)	70.00	30.00	15.00
21	Holman Williams (Boxer)	55.00	25.00	10.00
22	Kid Tuncro (Tunero) (Boxer)	55.00	25.00	10.00
23	Lazaro Salazar	300.00	135.00	60.00
24	Napoleon Reyes	120.00	55.00	25.00
25	Roberto Estalella	110.00	50.00	22.50
26	Juan Oliva (Boxer)	55.00	25.00	10.00
27	Gilberto Torres	75.00	35.00	15.00
28	Heberto Blanco	75.00	35.00	15.00
29	Adolfo Luque	375.00	175.00	75.00
30	Luis Galvani (Boxer)	55.00	25.00	10.00
31	Miguel Angel Gonzalez	195.00	90.00	40.00
32	Chuck Klein	110.00	50.00	22.50
33	Joe Legon (Boxer)	55.00	25.00	10.00
34	Carlos Blanco	75.00	35.00	15.00
35	Santos Amaro	225.00	100.00	45.00
36	Kid Chocolate (Boxer)	85.00	37.50	17.50
37	Henry Armstrong (Boxer)	55.00	25.00	10.00
38	Silvio Garcia	300.00	135.00	60.00
39	Martin Dihigo	3,000	1,350	600.00
40	Fermin Guerra	120.00	55.00	25.00
41	Babe Ruth	1,250	560.00	250.00
42	Ty Cobb	450.00	200.00	90.00
43	Alejandro Crespo	75.00	35.00	15.00
44	Ted Williams	900.00	400.00	180.00
45	Jose Maria Fernandez	85.00	37.50	17.50
46	Dom DiMaggio	110.00	50.00	22.50
47	Julio Rojo	75.00	35.00	15.00
48	Armando Marsans	110.00	50.00	22.50
49	Dick Sisler	75.00	35.00	15.00
50	Antonio Rodriguez	75.00	35.00	15.00
51	Joscito Rodriguez	75.00	35.00	15.00
52	Antonio Ordenana	80.00	35.00	15.00
53	Armandito Pi (Boxer)	55.00	25.00	10.00
54	Paul Derringer	75.00	35.00	15.00
55	Bob Feller	185.00	85.00	37.50
56a	Bill Dickey (Photo is Gabby Hartnett.) (Light cap.)	150.00	65.00	30.00
56b	Bill Dickey (Corrected photo.) (Dark cap.)	225.00	100.00	45.00
57	Lou Gehrig	750.00	335.00	150.00
58	Joe DiMaggio	1,575	710.00	315.00
59	Hank Greenberg	165.00	75.00	35.00
60	Red Ruffing	110.00	50.00	22.50
61	Tex Hughson	75.00	35.00	15.00
62	Bucky Walters	75.00	35.00	15.00
63	Stanley Hack	75.00	35.00	15.00
64	Stanley Musial	600.00	275.00	125.00
65	Melvin Ott	135.00	60.00	27.50
66	Dutch Leonard	75.00	35.00	15.00
67	Frank Overmire	75.00	35.00	15.00
68	Mort Cooper	75.00	35.00	15.00
69	Edward Miller	75.00	35.00	15.00
70	Jimmie Foxx	165.00	75.00	35.00
71	Joseph Cronin	110.00	50.00	22.50
72	James Vernon	75.00	35.00	15.00
73	Carl Hubbell	165.00	75.00	35.00
74	Andrew Pafko	75.00	35.00	15.00
75	David Ferris	75.00	35.00	15.00
76	John Mize	110.00	50.00	22.50
77	Spud Chandler	75.00	35.00	15.00
78	Joseph Medwick	110.00	50.00	22.50
79	Christy Mathewson	450.00	200.00	90.00
80	Nelson Potter	75.00	35.00	15.00
81	James Tabor	75.00	35.00	15.00
82	Martin Marion	75.00	35.00	15.00
83	Rip Sewell	75.00	35.00	15.00
84	Philip Cavaretta (Cavarretta)	75.00	35.00	15.00
85	Al Lopez	110.00	50.00	22.50
86	Rudy York	75.00	35.00	15.00
87	Walter Masterson	75.00	35.00	15.00
88	Roger Wolff	75.00	35.00	15.00
89	Jacob Early	75.00	35.00	15.00
90	Oswald Bluege	75.00	35.00	15.00
91	Zoco Godoy (Wrestler)	45.00	20.00	9.00
92	John Kelly Lewis	75.00	35.00	15.00
93	Well Stewart (Wrestler)	45.00	20.00	9.00
94	Bruce Campbell	75.00	35.00	15.00
95	Sherrod Robertson	75.00	35.00	15.00
96	Rose Evans (Wrestler)	45.00	20.00	9.00
97	Maurice "El Angel" Tillet (Wrestler)	45.00	20.00	9.00
98	Nicholas Altrock	75.00	35.00	15.00
99	Helen Willis (Tennis)	70.00	30.00	15.00
100	Borrest Smith	45.00	20.00	9.00
101	Merito Acosta	80.00	35.00	15.00
102	Oscar Rodriguez	45.00	20.00	9.00
103	Octavio Rubert	45.00	20.00	9.00
104	Antonio Lorenzo	45.00	20.00	9.00
105	Agustin del Toro	45.00	20.00	9.00
106	Hector Arago	45.00	20.00	9.00
107	Agustin de la Ville	45.00	20.00	9.00
108	Valeriano (Lilo) Fano	45.00	20.00	9.00
109	Orlando Moreno	45.00	20.00	9.00
110	"Bicho" Dunabeitia	45.00	20.00	9.00
111	Rafael Rivas	45.00	20.00	9.00
112	Jose Traspuestro	45.00	20.00	9.00
113	Mario Diaz	45.00	20.00	9.00
114	Armando Valdes	45.00	20.00	9.00
115	Alberto Matos	45.00	20.00	9.00
116	Humberto Baez	45.00	20.00	9.00
117	Orlando (Tango) Suarez	45.00	20.00	9.00
118	Manuel (Chino) Hidalgo	45.00	20.00	9.00
119	Fernando Rodriguez	45.00	20.00	9.00
120	Jose Cendan	45.00	20.00	9.00
121	Francisco Gallardo	45.00	20.00	9.00
122	Orlando Mejido	45.00	20.00	9.00
123	Julio (Jiqui) Moreno	45.00	20.00	9.00
124	Efrain Vinajcras	45.00	20.00	9.00
125	Luis Suarez	45.00	20.00	9.00
126	Oscar del Calvo	45.00	20.00	9.00

		NM	EX	VG
127	Julio Gomez	45.00	20.00	9.00
128	Ernesto Morillas	45.00	20.00	9.00
129	Leonardo Goicochea	45.00	20.00	9.00
130	Max Rosenfeld	300.00	135.00	60.00
131	Oscar Garmendia	45.00	20.00	9.00
132	Fernando Solis	45.00	20.00	9.00
133	Oliverio Ortiz	55.00	25.00	10.00
134	Osmaro Blanco	45.00	20.00	9.00
135	Oral Ratliff	45.00	20.00	9.00
136	Deo Grose	45.00	20.00	9.00
137	Homer Daugherty	45.00	20.00	9.00
138	Frank Matthews	45.00	20.00	9.00
139	Roger LaFrance	45.00	20.00	9.00
140	Harold Cowan	45.00	20.00	9.00
141	Richard Henton	45.00	20.00	9.00
142	Banks McDowell	45.00	20.00	9.00
143	Harold Graham	45.00	20.00	9.00
144	Jack Sweeting	45.00	20.00	9.00
145	Bill Wixted	45.00	20.00	9.00
146	Larry Graham	45.00	20.00	9.00
147	Ralph Brown	45.00	20.00	9.00
148	Felipe Jimenez	45.00	20.00	9.00
149	John Ippolito	45.00	20.00	9.00
150	Joe Benito	45.00	20.00	9.00
151	Bernardo Fernandez	45.00	20.00	9.00
152	Buckey Winkler	45.00	20.00	9.00
153	Carl Armstrong	45.00	20.00	9.00
154	Jack Bearden	45.00	20.00	9.00
155	George Bucci	45.00	20.00	9.00
156	John Pere (Pare)	45.00	20.00	9.00
157	Mickey O'Brien	45.00	20.00	9.00
158	Lamar Murphy	45.00	20.00	9.00
159	Devon Chaptman (Choptman)	45.00	20.00	9.00
160	Hal Johnson	45.00	20.00	9.00
161	"Bitsy" Mott	45.00	20.00	9.00
162	Charles Cuellar	45.00	20.00	9.00
163	Chester Covington	45.00	20.00	9.00
164	Howard Ermisch	45.00	20.00	9.00
165	Bill Lewis	45.00	20.00	9.00
166	Roy Knepper	45.00	20.00	9.00
167	Bull Enos	45.00	20.00	9.00
168	Joe Wilder	45.00	20.00	9.00
169	Jake Baker	45.00	20.00	9.00
170	Joe Bodner	45.00	20.00	9.00
171	Jackie Myer	45.00	20.00	9.00
172	Mel Fisher	45.00	20.00	9.00
173	Larry Baldwin	45.00	20.00	9.00
174	Richard Farkas	45.00	20.00	9.00
175	Alston McGahgin	45.00	20.00	9.00
176	Ray Weiss	45.00	20.00	9.00
177	Paul Waner	400.00	180.00	80.00
178	Frank Miller	45.00	20.00	9.00
179	John Sabatie	45.00	20.00	9.00
180	John Maire	45.00	20.00	9.00

1966 Pro's Pizza Chicago Cubs

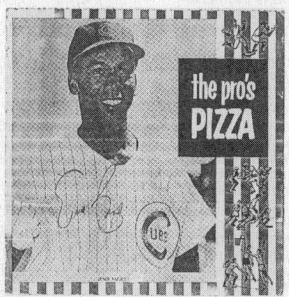

These black-and-white player cards were printed on boxes in which individual-serving pizzas were sold, reportedly only at Wrigley Field. The panel measures 6" x 6" and has a black-and-white player photo at left, with his name in a white strip at bottom. At right are drawn sports action scenes and toward the top is a black box with "the pro's PIZZA" in white. The backs are blank. The unnumbered pieces are listed here alphabetically. The example pictured was autographed by the player, no facsimile signature was printed originally.

		NM	EX	VG
Complete Set (15):		3,250	1,600	975.00
Common Player:		160.00	80.00	50.00
(1)	Ted Abernathy	160.00	80.00	50.00
(2)	Joe Amalfitano	160.00	80.00	50.00
(3)	George Altman	160.00	80.00	50.00
(4)	Ernie Banks	650.00	325.00	200.00
(5)	Ernie Broglio	160.00	80.00	50.00
(6)	Billy Connors	160.00	80.00	50.00
(7)	Dick Ellsworth	160.00	80.00	50.00
(8)	Bill Hoeft	160.00	80.00	50.00
(9)	Ken Holtzman	160.00	80.00	50.00
(10)	Randy Hundley	160.00	80.00	50.00
(11)	Ferguson Jenkins	325.00	160.00	100.00
(12)	Chris Krug	160.00	80.00	50.00
(13)	Ron Santo	245.00	120.00	75.00
(14)	Carl Warwick	160.00	80.00	50.00
(15)	Billy Williams	400.00	200.00	120.00

1967 Pro's Pizza - B & W

For a second year, Chicago players - Cubs and White Sox - were featured on boxes of individual-serving pizza reportedly sold only at the ballparks. The panel on which the player photos (black-and-white) are printed measures 4-3/4" x 5-3/4" and is similar in design to the 1966 issue, except there is a vertical perforation allowing most of the player photo to be torn away in a 3-1/16" x 5-3/4" size. Cards are unnumbered and listed here alphabetically. Values are for unseparated panels. Those separated at the perforation line are worth 60-75%.

		NM	EX	VG
Complete Set (10):		1,500	750.00	450.00
Common Player:		125.00	65.00	35.00
(1)	Ernie Banks	325.00	160.00	100.00
(2)	Glenn Beckert	125.00	65.00	35.00
(3)	Byron Browne	125.00	65.00	35.00
(4)	Don Buford	125.00	65.00	35.00
(5)	Joel Horlen	125.00	65.00	35.00
(6)	Randy Hundley	125.00	65.00	35.00
(7)	Don Kessinger	125.00	65.00	35.00
(8)	Gary Peters	125.00	65.00	35.00
(9)	Ron Santo	175.00	85.00	50.00
(10)	Billy Williams	200.00	100.00	60.00

1967 Pro's Pizza - Color

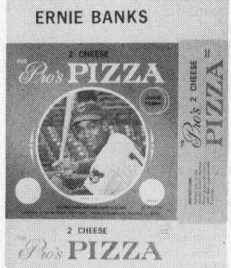

Only Chicago Cubs are included in this set of cards printed on the top of individual serving pizza boxes, reportedly sold only at Wrigley Field. The color player poses are printed in a 4-3/4" diameter circle on top of the box, with the player's name in a white panel at bottom. The player's name was also printed in large black letters on one side of the box. Values shown here are for the unnumbered cards are for the complete box top. A similar issue of Chicago Bears players was also produced.

		NM	EX	VG
Complete Set (12):		5,000	2,500	1,500
Common Player:		400.00	200.00	120.00
(1)	Joe Amalfitano	400.00	200.00	120.00
(2)	Ernie Banks	1,100	550.00	330.00
(3)	Glenn Beckert	400.00	200.00	120.00
(4)	John Boccabella	400.00	200.00	120.00
(5)	Bill Hands	400.00	200.00	120.00
(6)	Ken Holtzman	400.00	200.00	120.00
(7)	Randy Hundley	400.00	200.00	120.00
(8)	Ferguson Jenkins	675.00	335.00	200.00
(9)	Don Kessinger	400.00	200.00	120.00
(10)	Adolfo Phillips	400.00	200.00	120.00
(11)	Ron Santo	600.00	300.00	180.00
(12)	Billy Williams	850.00	425.00	255.00

1972 Pro Star Promotions

This set of postcard-sized (3-1/2" x 5-1/2") color photocards features players from 14 major league teams, with a heavy emphasis on Montreal Expos. Uniforms in the photos have had team logos removed. Cards have a facsimile autograph on front. In the white border at bottom is the player name, league, copyright notice and "Printed in Canada." The unnumbered cards are checklisted here in alphabetical order.

	NM	EX	VG
Complete Set (40):	275.00	135.00	85.00
Common Player:	3.00	1.50	.90

		NM	EX	VG
(1)	Hank Aaron	17.50	8.75	5.25
(2)	Bob Bailey	3.00	1.50	.90
(3)	Johnny Bench	12.50	6.25	3.75
(4)	Vida Blue	3.00	1.50	.90
(5)	John Boccabella	3.00	1.50	.90
(6)	Roberto Clemente	20.00	10.00	6.00
(7)	Boots Day	3.00	1.50	.90
(8)	Jim Fairey	3.00	1.50	.90
(9)	Tim Foli	3.00	1.50	.90
(10)	Ron Hunt	3.00	1.50	.90
(11)	Catfish Hunter	7.50	3.75	2.25
(12)	Reggie Jackson	15.00	7.50	4.50
(13)	Fergy Jenkins	10.00	5.00	3.00
(14)	Mike Jorgensen	3.00	1.50	.90
(15)	Al Kaline	12.50	6.25	3.75
(16)	Harmon Killebrew	12.50	6.25	3.75
(17)	Mickey Lolich	3.00	1.50	.90
(18)	Juan Marichal	7.50	3.75	2.25
(19)	Willie Mays	17.50	8.75	5.25
(20)	Willie McCovey	10.00	5.00	3.00
(21)	Ernie McAnally	3.00	1.50	.90
(22)	Dave McNally	3.00	1.50	.90
(23)	Bill Melton	3.00	1.50	.90
(24)	Carl Morton	3.00	1.50	.90
(25)	Bobby Murcer	3.00	1.50	.90
(26)	Fritz Peterson	3.00	1.50	.90
(27)	Boog Powell	6.00	3.00	1.75
(28)	Steve Renko	3.00	1.50	.90
(29)	Merv Rettenmund	3.00	1.50	.90
(30)	Brooks Robinson	12.50	6.25	3.75
(31)	Frank Robinson	12.50	6.25	3.75
(32)	Pete Rose	17.50	8.75	5.25
(33)	Tom Seaver	12.50	6.25	3.75
(34)	Ken Singleton	3.00	1.50	.90
(35)	Willie Stargell	10.00	5.00	3.00
(36)	Bill Stoneman	3.00	1.50	.90
(37)	Joe Torre	6.00	3.00	1.75
(38)	Checklist - American League	1.50	.70	.45
(39)	Checklist - National League	1.50	.70	.45
(40)	Checklist - Montreal Expos	1.50	.70	.45

1971 Pro Stars Publications Montreal Expos

Posed action photos of the Expos are featured on this postcard-size (3-1/2" x 5-1/2") issue. The color photos are surrounded by a white border and have a facsimile autograph. Printed in the bottom border is, "Copyright Pro Stars Publications 1971 Printed in Canada." Backs are blank. The unnumbered cards are checklisted here in alphabetical order.

		NM	EX	VG
Complete Set (28):		175.00	85.00	50.00
Common Player:		6.00	3.00	1.80
(1)	Bob Bailey	6.00	3.00	1.80
(2)	John Bateman	6.00	3.00	1.80
(3)	John Boccabella	6.00	3.00	1.80
(4)	Ron Brand	6.00	3.00	1.80
(5)	Boots Day	6.00	3.00	1.80
(6)	Jim Fairey	6.00	3.00	1.80
(7)	Ron Fairly	7.50	3.75	2.25
(8)	Jim Gosger	6.00	3.00	1.80
(9)	Don Hahn	6.00	3.00	1.80
(10)	Ron Hunt	6.00	3.00	1.80
(11)	Mack Jones	6.00	3.00	1.80
(12)	Coco Laboy	6.00	3.00	1.80
(13)	Mike Marshall	7.50	3.75	2.25
(14)	Clyde Mashore	6.00	3.00	1.80
(15)	Gene Mauch	7.50	3.75	2.25
(16)	Dan McGinn	6.00	3.00	1.80
(17)	Carl Morton	6.00	3.00	1.80
(18)	John O'Donoghue	6.00	3.00	1.80
(19)	Adolfo Phillips	6.00	3.00	1.80
(20)	Claude Raymond	6.00	3.00	1.80
(21)	Howie Reed	6.00	3.00	1.80
(22)	Steve Renko	6.00	3.00	1.80
(23)	Rusty Staub	10.00	5.00	3.00
(24)	Bill Stoneman	6.00	3.00	1.80
(25)	John Strohmayer	6.00	3.00	1.80
(26)	Gary Sutherland	6.00	3.00	1.80
(27)	Mike Wegener	6.00	3.00	1.80
(28)	Bobby Wine	6.00	3.00	1.80

1950s Publix Markets

It is not known whether this is a one-card set or whether similar cards exist for other players. Without information on other subjects it is impossible to date the issue more precisely. The black-and-white card is printed on thin, semi-gloss cardboard in 4" x 4-3/4" format. The front has a facsimile autograph. The back has a message to Little Leaguers from the Red Sox pitcher and a list of sponsors, along with the Publix logo.

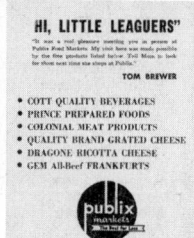

	NM	EX	VG
Tom Brewer	150.00	75.00	45.00

1972 Puerto Rican League Stickers

Often mistakenly called "minor league" cards, this issue consists of 231 ungummed stickers pertinent to the Puerto Rican winter baseball league. A colorful album was available in which to paste the stickers, though obviously stickers that have evidence of glue or torn paper have little collector value. Besides individual player photos, there are stickers of "old-timers" and groups of stickers which make up composite photos of all-star teams and of the island's god of baseball, Roberto Clemente. Team emblem stickers are also included. Many big league stars who were either beginning or ending their pro careers can be found in the set, including some current and future Hall of Famers. Stickers have color photos on the front, with backs printed in Spanish. They measure 2-1/4" x 3".

	NM	EX	VG
Complete Set (231):	1,000	500.00	300.00
Complete Set in Album:	1,200	600.00	350.00
Common Player:	5.00	2.50	1.50
Album:	200.00	100.00	60.00
Unopened Pack:	50.00		

		NM	EX	VG
1	Santurce All-Star Team Composite Photo	10.00	5.00	3.00
2	Santurce All-Star Team Composite Photo	10.00	5.00	3.00
3	Santurce All-Star Team Composite Photo	10.00	5.00	3.00
4	Santurce All-Star Team Composite Photo	10.00	5.00	3.00
5	Santurce All-Star Team Composite Photo	10.00	5.00	3.00
6	Santurce All-Star Team Composite Photo	10.00	5.00	3.00
7	Santurce All-Star Team Composite Photo	10.00	5.00	3.00
8	Santurce All-Star Team Composite Photo	10.00	5.00	3.00
9	Santurce All-Star Team Composite Photo	10.00	5.00	3.00
10	Ponce All-Star Team Composite Photo	10.00	5.00	3.00
11	Ponce All-Star Team Composite Photo	10.00	5.00	3.00
12	Ponce All-Star Team Composite Photo	10.00	5.00	3.00
13	Ponce All-Star Team Composite Photo	10.00	5.00	3.00
14	Ponce All-Star Team Composite Photo	10.00	5.00	3.00
15	Ponce All-Star Team Composite Photo	10.00	5.00	3.00
16	Ponce All-Star Team Composite Photo	10.00	5.00	3.00
17	Ponce All-Star Team Composite Photo	10.00	5.00	3.00
18	Ponce All-Star Team Composite Photo	10.00	5.00	3.00
19	Arecibo Team Emblem	5.00	2.50	1.50
20	Caguas-Guayana Team Emblem	5.00	2.50	1.50
21	Mayaguez Team Emblem	5.00	2.50	1.50
22	Ponce Team Emblem	5.00	2.50	1.50
23	San Juan Team Emblem	5.00	2.50	1.50
24	Santurce Team Emblem	5.00	2.50	1.50
25	Steve Boros	5.00	2.50	1.50
26	Luis Isaac	5.00	2.50	1.50
27	Emmanuel Toledo	5.00	2.50	1.50
28	Gregorio Perez	5.00	2.50	1.50
29	Rosario Llanos	5.00	2.50	1.50
30	Jose Geigel	5.00	2.50	1.50
31	Eduardo Figueroa	5.00	2.50	1.50
32	Julian Muniz	5.00	2.50	1.50
33	Fernando Gonzalez	5.00	2.50	1.50
34	Bennie Ayala	5.00	2.50	1.50
35	Miguel Villaran	5.00	2.50	1.50
36	Efrain Vazquez	5.00	2.50	1.50
37	Ramon Ariles	5.00	2.50	1.50
38	Angel Alcaraz	5.00	2.50	1.50
39	Henry Cruz	5.00	2.50	1.50
40	Jose Silva	5.00	2.50	1.50
41	Jose Alcaide	5.00	2.50	1.50
42	Pepe Mangual	5.00	2.50	1.50
43	Mike Jackson	5.00	2.50	1.50
44	Lynn McGlothen	5.00	2.50	1.50
45	Frank Ortenzio	5.00	2.50	1.50
46	Norm Angelini	5.00	2.50	1.50
47	Richard Coggins	5.00	2.50	1.50
48	Lance Clemons	5.00	2.50	1.50
49	Mike Kelleher	5.00	2.50	1.50
50	Ken Wright	5.00	2.50	1.50
51	Buck Martinez	5.00	2.50	1.50
52	Billy De Mars	5.00	2.50	1.50
53	Elwood Huyke	5.00	2.50	1.50
54	Pedro Garcia	5.00	2.50	1.50
55	Bob Boone	15.00	7.50	4.50
56	Jose Laboy	5.00	2.50	1.50
57	Eduardo Rodriguez	5.00	2.50	1.50
58	Jesus Hernaiz	5.00	2.50	1.50
59	Joaquin Quintana	5.00	2.50	1.50
60	Domingo Figueroa	5.00	2.50	1.50
61	Juan Lopez	5.00	2.50	1.50
62	Luis Alvarado	5.00	2.50	1.50
63	Otoniel Velez	5.00	2.50	1.50
64	Mike Schmidt	300.00	150.00	90.00
65	Felix Millan	5.00	2.50	1.50
66	Guillermo Montanez	5.00	2.50	1.50
67	Ivan de Jesus	7.50	3.75	2.25
68	Sixto Lezcano	5.00	2.50	1.50
69	Jerry Morales	5.00	2.50	1.50
70	Bombo Rivera	5.00	2.50	1.50
71	Mike Ondina	5.00	2.50	1.50
72	Grant Jackson	5.00	2.50	1.50
73	Roger Freed	5.00	2.50	1.50
74	Steve Rogers	5.00	2.50	1.50
75	Mac Scarce	5.00	2.50	1.50
76	Mike Jorgensen	5.00	2.50	1.50
77	Jerry Crider	5.00	2.50	1.50
78	Fred Beene	5.00	2.50	1.50
79	Carl Ermer	5.00	2.50	1.50
80	Luis Marquez	5.00	2.50	1.50
81	Hector Valle	5.00	2.50	1.50
82	Ramon Vega	5.00	2.50	1.50
83	Cirito Cruz	5.00	2.50	1.50
84	Fernando Vega	5.00	2.50	1.50
85	Porfiro Sanchez	5.00	2.50	1.50
86	Jose Sevillano	5.00	2.50	1.50
87	Felix Rango	5.00	2.50	1.50
88	Enrique Rivera	5.00	2.50	1.50
89	Wildredo Rios	5.00	2.50	1.50
90	Javier Andino	5.00	2.50	1.50
91	Milton Ramirez	5.00	2.50	1.50
92	Max Oliveras	5.00	2.50	1.50
93	Jose Calero	5.00	2.50	1.50
94	Esteban Vazquez	5.00	2.50	1.50
95	Hector Cruz	5.00	2.50	1.50
96	Felix Arce	5.00	2.50	1.50
97	Gilberto Rivera	5.00	2.50	1.50
98	Rafael Rodriguez	5.00	2.50	1.50
99	Julio Gonzalez	5.00	2.50	1.50
100	Rosendo Cedeno	5.00	2.50	1.50
101	Pedro Cintron	5.00	2.50	1.50
102	Osvaldo Ortiz	5.00	2.50	1.50
103	Frank Verdi	5.00	2.50	1.50
104	Carlos Santiago	5.00	2.50	1.50
105	Ramon Conde	5.00	2.50	1.50
106	Pat Corrales	5.00	2.50	1.50
107	Jose Morales	5.00	2.50	1.50
108	Jack Whillock	5.00	2.50	1.50
109	Raul Mercado	5.00	2.50	1.50
110	Bonifacio Aponte	5.00	2.50	1.50
111	Angel Alicea	5.00	2.50	1.50
112	Santos Alomar	10.00	5.00	3.00
113	Francisco Libran	5.00	2.50	1.50
114	Edwin Pacheco	5.00	2.50	1.50
115	Luis Gonzalez	5.00	2.50	1.50
116	Juan Rios	5.00	2.50	1.50
117	Jorge Roque	5.00	2.50	1.50
118	Carlos Velez	5.00	2.50	1.50
119	David Gonzalez	5.00	2.50	1.50
120	Jose Cruz	7.50	3.75	2.25
121	Luis Melendez	5.00	2.50	1.50
122	Jose Ortiz	5.00	2.50	1.50
123	David Rosello	5.00	2.50	1.50
124	Juan Veintidos	5.00	2.50	1.50
125	Arnaldo Nazario	5.00	2.50	1.50
126	Dave Lemonds	5.00	2.50	1.50
127	Jim Magnuson	5.00	2.50	1.50
128	Tom Kelley	7.50	3.75	2.25
129	Chris Zachary	5.00	2.50	1.50
130	Hal Breeden	5.00	2.50	1.50
131	Jackie Hernandez	5.00	2.50	1.50
132	Rick Gossage	30.00	15.00	9.00
133	Frank Luchessi	5.00	2.50	1.50
134	Nino Escalera	5.00	2.50	1.50
135	Julio Navarro	5.00	2.50	1.50
136	Manny Sanguillen	15.00	7.50	4.50
137	Bob Johnson	5.00	2.50	1.50
138	Chuck Coggins	5.00	2.50	1.50
139	Orlando Gomez	5.00	2.50	1.50
140	William Melendez	5.00	2.50	1.50
141	Jose Del Moral	5.00	2.50	1.50
142	Jacinto Camacho	5.00	2.50	1.50
143	Emiliano Rivera	5.00	2.50	1.50
144	Luis Peraza	5.00	2.50	1.50
145	Carlos Velazquez	5.00	2.50	1.50
146	Luis Raul Garcia	5.00	2.50	1.50
147	Eliseo Rodriguez	5.00	2.50	1.50
148	Santiago Rosario	5.00	2.50	1.50
149	Ruben Castillo	5.00	2.50	1.50
150	Sergio Ferrer	5.00	2.50	1.50
151	Jose Pagan	5.00	2.50	1.50
152	Raul Colon	5.00	2.50	1.50
153	Robert Rauch	5.00	2.50	1.50
154	Luis Rosado	5.00	2.50	1.50
155	Francisco Lopez	5.00	2.50	1.50
156	Richard Zisk	5.00	2.50	1.50
157	Orlando Alvarez	5.00	2.50	1.50
158	Jaime Rosario	5.00	2.50	1.50
159	Rosendo Torres	5.00	2.50	1.50
160	Jim McKee	5.00	2.50	1.50
161	Mike Nagy	5.00	2.50	1.50
162	Brent Strom	5.00	2.50	1.50
163	Tom Walker	5.00	2.50	1.50
164	Angel Davila	5.00	2.50	1.50
165	Jose Cruz	5.00	2.50	1.50
166	Frank Robinson	25.00	12.50	7.50
167	German Rivera	5.00	2.50	1.50
168	Reinaldo Oliver	5.00	2.50	1.50
169	Geraldo Rodriguez	5.00	2.50	1.50
170	Elrod Hendricks	5.00	2.50	1.50
171	Gilberto Flores	5.00	2.50	1.50
172	Ruben Gomez	5.00	2.50	1.50
173	Juan Pizarro	5.00	2.50	1.50
174	William De Jesus	5.00	2.50	1.50
175	Rogelio Morel	5.00	2.50	1.50
176	Victor Agosto	5.00	2.50	1.50
177	Esteban Texidor	5.00	2.50	1.50
178	Ramon Hernandez	5.00	2.50	1.50
179	Gilberto Rondon Olivo	5.00	2.50	1.50
180	Juan Beniquez	5.00	2.50	1.50
181	Arturo Miranda	5.00	2.50	1.50
182	Manuel Ruiz	5.00	2.50	1.50
183	Julio Gotay	5.00	2.50	1.50
184	Arsenio Rodriguez	5.00	2.50	1.50
185	Luis Delgado	5.00	2.50	1.50
186	Jorge Rivera	5.00	2.50	1.50
187	Willie Crawford	5.00	2.50	1.50
188	Angel Mangual	5.00	2.50	1.50
189	Mike Strahler	5.00	2.50	1.50
190	Doyle Alexander	5.00	2.50	1.50
191	Bob Reynolds	5.00	2.50	1.50
192	Ron Cey	7.50	3.75	2.25
193	Jerr Da Vanon	5.00	2.50	1.50
194	Don Baylor	12.50	6.25	3.75
195	Tony Perez	25.00	12.50	7.50
196	Lloyd Allen	5.00	2.50	1.50
197	Orlando Cepeda	20.00	10.00	6.00
198	Roberto Clemente Composite Photo	15.00	7.50	4.50
199	Roberto Clemente Composite Photo	15.00	7.50	4.50
200	Roberto Clemente Composite Photo	15.00	7.50	4.50
201	Roberto Clemente Composite Photo	15.00	7.50	4.50
202	Roberto Clemente Composite Photo	15.00	7.50	4.50
203	Roberto Clemente Composite Photo	15.00	7.50	4.50
204	Roberto Clemente Composite Photo	15.00	7.50	4.50
205	Roberto Clemente Composite Photo	15.00	7.50	4.50
206	Roberto Clemente Composite Photo	15.00	7.50	4.50
207	Jaime Almendro	5.00	2.50	1.50
208	Jose R. Santiago	5.00	2.50	1.50
209	Luis Cabrera	5.00	2.50	1.50
210	Jorge Tirado	5.00	2.50	1.50
211	Radames Lopez	5.00	2.50	1.50
212	Juan Vargas	5.00	2.50	1.50
213	Francisco Coimbre	5.00	2.50	1.50
214	Freddie Thon	5.00	2.50	1.50
215	Manuel Alvarez	5.00	2.50	1.50
216	Luis Olmo	5.00	2.50	1.50
217	Jose Santiago	7.50	3.75	2.25
218	Hiram Bithorn	12.50	6.25	3.75
219	Willard Brown	30.00	15.00	9.00
220	Robert Thurman	10.00	5.00	3.00
221	Buster Clarkson	7.50	3.75	2.25
222	Satchel Paige	40.00	20.00	12.00
223	Raymond Brown	30.00	15.00	9.00
224	Alonso Perry	7.50	3.75	2.25
225	Quincy Trouppe	12.50	6.25	3.75
226	Santiago Muratti	5.00	2.50	1.50
227	Johnny Davis	5.00	2.50	1.50
228	Lino Suarez	5.00	2.50	1.50
229	Demetrio Pesante	5.00	2.50	1.50
230	Luis Arroyo	5.00	2.50	1.50
231	Jose Garcia	5.00	2.50	1.50

1905 Harry Pulliam Cigar Label

The attributed dated is speculative. Pulliam was the first president of the modern National League. These colorful gold-leaf highlighted lithographed cigar box labels measure 4-1/4" square with clipped corners. Since all examples seen appear to be unused it is believed that the cigar brand never materialized, possibly having been aborted when Pulliam commited suicide in 1909.

	NM	EX	VG
Harry Pulliam	100.00	50.00	30.00

1910 Punch Cigars

By virtue of its age, scarcity and checklist, this is among the most popular of the Cuban card sets. Issued contemporary with a visit by the Detroit Tigers and Philadelphia A's for an exhibition series in Cuba, these cards feature an approximately 1-1/4" x 1-7/8" black-and-white portrait photo attached to a decorative cardboard backing of about 1-3/4" x 2-1/4". Known cards include a dozen each of the Major League teams and, it is speculated, an equal number from Cuba's professional Almendares and Havana clubs; though the complete checklist remains unknown. The scarcity of surviving specimens may be traced to the copy on the original cardboard backing that offers an album for anybody turning in a complete set. Only a tiny percentage of Punch cards are known with their cardboard backing attached. Because most cards seen to date have been in wretched condition, no values are quoted above VG condition. Cards with backing should command a 3X premium.

	NM	EX	VG
Common Cuban Player:			750.00
Common Major Leaguer:			1,125
ALMENDARES			
(1) Armando Cabanas			1,125
(2) Alfredo Cabrera			750.00
(3) Gervasio Gonzalez			1,500
(4) Eleadoro Hidalgo			1,500
(5) Armando Marzans (Marsans)			2,250
(6) Jose Mendez			30,000
(7) Evaristo Pia (Trainer)			750.00
(8) Carlos Roggers (Royer)			1,125
(9) Rogelio Valdes			750.00
			500.00
HAVANA			
(1) P. (Pete) Hill			5,250
(2) Carlos Moran			2,250
(3) Agustin Molina			4,500
(4) Luis Padron			2,250
(5) Agustin Parpetti			1,500
			500.00
DETROIT TIGERS			
(1) Joe Casey			1,125
(2) Ty Cobb			11,250
(3) Sam Crawford			5,250
(4) Tom Jones			1,125
(5) Matty McIntyre			1,125
(6) George Moriarty			1,125
(7) George Mullin			1,125
(8) Charley O'Leary			1,125
(9) Germany Schaefer			1,125
(10) Oscar Stanage			1,125
(11) Ed Summers			1,125
(12) Ed Willetts (Willett)			1,125
			500.00
PHILADELPHIA A'S			
(1) Jack Barry			1,125
(2) Chief Bender			5,250
(3) Jack Coombs			1,125
(4) Harry Davis			1,125
(5) Claude Derrick			1,125
(6) Topsy Hartsel			1,125
(7) Jack Lapp			1,125
(8) Bris Lord			1,125
(9) Stuffy McInnis			1,125
(10) Danny Murphy			1,125
(11) Eddie Plank			6,000
(12) Ira Thomas			1,125

1966 Pure Oil Atlanta Braves

 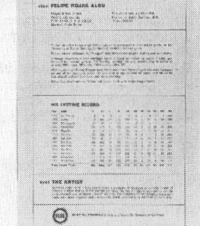

In their first year in Atlanta a set of Braves premium pictures done by noted portrait artist Nicholas Volpe was sponsored by Pure Oil. The 8-1/2" x 11" pictures were given away with gas purchases. Fronts featured a large pastel portrait and smaller full-figure action picture of the player set against a black background. A facsimile player autograph was pencilled at the bottom, along with the artist's signature. The player's name was printed in black in the white bottom border. Backs

are printed in black-and-white and include biographical and career notes, full major and minor league stats, a short biography of the artist and the sponsoring company's logo. The unnumbered cards are checklisted here alphabetically.

	NM	EX	VG
Complete Set (12):	75.00	37.50	22.00
Common Player:	5.00	2.50	1.50
(1) Hank Aaron	25.00	12.50	7.50
(2) Felipe Alou	6.00	3.00	1.75
(3) Frank Bolling	5.00	2.50	1.50
(4) Bobby Bragan	5.00	2.50	1.50
(5) Rico Carty	5.00	2.50	1.50
(6) Tony Cloninger	5.00	2.50	1.50
(7) Mack Jones	5.00	2.50	1.50
(8) Denny LeMaster	5.00	2.50	1.50
(9) Eddie Mathews	15.00	7.50	4.50
(10) Denis Menke	5.00	2.50	1.50
(11) Lee Thomas	5.00	2.50	1.50
(12) Joe Torre	7.50	3.75	2.25

1933 PX3 Double Header Coins

Issued by Gum Inc. circa 1933, this unnumbered set consists of 43 metal discs approximately 1-1/4" in diameter. The front lists the player's name and team beneath his picture. The numbers "1" or "2" also appear inside a small circle at the bottom of the disc, and the wrapper advised collectors to "put 1 and 2 together and make a double header." Some players are found in more than one color. The set is designated as PX3 in the American Card Catalog.

	NM	EX	VG
Complete Set (43):	1,750	875.00	525.00
Common Player:	40.00	20.00	12.00
(1) Sparky Adams	40.00	20.00	12.00
(2) Dale Alexander	40.00	20.00	12.00
(3) Earl Averill	75.00	37.00	22.00
(4) Dick Bartell	40.00	20.00	12.00
(5) Walter Berger	40.00	20.00	12.00
(6) Jim Bottomley	75.00	37.00	22.00
(7) Lefty Brandt	40.00	20.00	12.00
(8) Owen Carroll	40.00	20.00	12.00
(9) Lefty Clark	40.00	20.00	12.00
(10) Mickey Cochrane	75.00	37.00	22.00
(11) Joe Cronin	75.00	37.00	22.00
(12) Jimmy Dykes	40.00	20.00	12.00
(13) George Earnshaw	40.00	20.00	12.00
(14) Wes Ferrell	40.00	20.00	12.00
(15) Neal Finn	40.00	20.00	12.00
(16) Lew Fonseca	40.00	20.00	12.00
(17) Jimmy Foxx	100.00	50.00	30.00
(18) Frankie Frisch	75.00	37.00	22.00
(19) Chick Fullis	40.00	20.00	12.00
(20) Charley Gehringer	75.00	37.00	22.00
(21) Goose Goslin	75.00	37.00	22.00
(22) Johnny Hodapp	40.00	20.00	12.00
(23) Frank Hogan	40.00	20.00	12.00
(24) Si Johnson	40.00	20.00	12.00
(25) Joe Judge	40.00	20.00	12.00
(26) Chuck Klein	75.00	37.00	22.00
(27) Al Lopez	75.00	37.00	22.00
(28) Ray Lucas	40.00	20.00	12.00
(29) Red Lucas	40.00	20.00	12.00
(30) Ted Lyons	75.00	37.00	22.00
(31) Firpo Marberry	40.00	20.00	12.00
(32) Oscar Melillo	40.00	20.00	12.00
(33) Lefty O'Doul	50.00	25.00	15.00
(34) George Pipgras	40.00	20.00	12.00
(35) Flint Rhem	40.00	20.00	12.00
(36) Sam Rice	75.00	37.00	22.00
(37) Muddy Ruel	40.00	20.00	12.00
(38) Harry Seibold	40.00	20.00	12.00
(39) Al Simmons	75.00	37.00	22.00
(40) Joe Vosmik	40.00	20.00	12.00
(41) Gerald Walker	40.00	20.00	12.00
(42) Pinky Whitney	40.00	20.00	12.00
(43) Hack Wilson	75.00	37.00	22.00

Q

1934 Quaker Oats Babe Ruth Premium Photo (8x10)

Members of the cereal company's Babe Ruth Baseball Club could obtain this souvenir photo among many other promotional items endorsed by the slugger. This 8" x 10" black-and-white photo has a facsimile autograph and is inscribed, "To My Pal." Advertising for Quaker Oats appears in the white border at bottom.

	NM	EX	VG
Babe Ruth	600.00	350.00	150.00

1954 Quaker Sports Oddities

Available both as cereal-box premiums and a mail-away set, this issue of horizontal-format 3-1/2" x 2-1/2, round-corner cards depicts "Odd but True" moments in sports. Fronts of the multi-sports set feature portrait and action color art. Backs describe the sports oddity.

	NM	EX	VG
Complete Set (27):	200.00	100.00	60.00
Common Card:	3.00	1.50	.90
1 Johnny Miller (Football)	4.00	2.00	1.25
2 Fred Snite Jr. (Golf)	3.00	1.50	.90
3 George Quam (Handball)	3.00	1.50	.90
4 John B. Maypole (Speed boating.)	3.00	1.50	.90
5 Harold (Bunny) Leavitt (Basketball)	5.00	2.50	1.50
6 Wake Forest College (Football)	5.00	2.50	1.50
7 Amos Alonzo Stagg (Football)	20.00	10.00	6.00
8 Catherine Fellmuth (Bowling)	3.00	1.50	.90
9 Bill Wilson (Golf)	3.00	1.50	.90
10 Chicago Blackhawks (Hockey)	20.00	10.00	6.00
11 Betty Robinson (Track)	3.00	1.50	.90
12 Dartmouth College/ University of Utah (Basketball)	5.00	2.50	1.50
13 Ab Jenkins (Auto racing.)	3.00	1.50	.90
14 Capt. Eddie Rickenbacker (Auto racing.)	5.00	2.50	1.50
15 Jackie LaVine (Swimming)	3.00	1.50	.90
16 Jack Riley (Wrestling)	3.00	1.50	.90
17 Carl Stockton (Biking)	3.00	1.50	.90
18 Jimmy Smilgoff (Baseball)	3.00	1.50	.90
19 George Halas (Football)	20.00	10.00	6.00
20 Joyce Rosenbom (Basketball)	5.00	2.50	1.50
21 Squatters Rights (Baseball)	3.00	1.50	.90
22 Richard Dwyer (Skating)	3.00	1.50	.90
23 Harlem Globetrotters (Basketball)	25.00	12.50	7.50
24 Everett Dean (Basketball)	3.00	1.50	.90
25 Texas U./Northwestern U. (Football)	5.00	2.50	1.50
26 Bronko Nagurski (Football)	25.00	12.50	7.50
27 Yankee Stadium (Baseball)	20.00	10.00	6.00

R

1909 Ramly Cigarettes (T204)

While issued with both Ramly and T.T.T. brand Turkish tobacco cigarettes, the cards in this set take their name from the more common of the two brands. By whatever name, the set is one of the more interesting and attractive of the early 20th Century. The 2" x 2-1/2" cards carry black-and-white photographic portraits with impressive gold embossed frames and borders on the front. Toward the bottom appears the player's last name, position, team and league. The backs carry only the most basic information on the cigarette company. The complete set price does not include the scarce variations of some players' cards on which the photos are square and surrounded by a heavy gold frame with white borders.

		NM	EX	VG
	Complete Set (121):	125,000	50,000	25,000
	Common Player:	1,000	250.00	125.00
	T.T.T.: 4-5X			
(1)	Whitey Alperman	1,000	250.00	125.00
(2a)	John Anderson	1,000	250.00	125.00
	(Photo inside oval frame.)			
(2b)	John Anderson	22,500	9,000	4,500
	(Photo inside square frame.)			
(3)	Jimmy Archer	1,000	250.00	125.00
(4)	Frank Arrelanes (Arellanes)	1,000	250.00	125.00
(5)	Jim Ball	1,000	250.00	125.00
(6)	Neal Ball	1,000	250.00	125.00
(7a)	Frank C. Bancroft (Photo inside oval frame.)	1,000	250.00	125.00
(7b)	Frank C. Bancroft (Photo inside square frame.)	30,000	12,000	6,000
(8)	Johnny Bates	1,000	250.00	125.00
(9)	Fred Beebe	1,000	250.00	125.00
(10)	George Bell	1,000	250.00	125.00
(11)	Chief Bender	3,440	1,375	690.00
(12)	Walter Blair	1,000	250.00	125.00
(13)	Cliff Blankenship	1,000	250.00	125.00
(14)	Frank Bowerman	1,000	250.00	125.00
(15a)	Wm. Bransfield (Photo inside oval frame.)	1,000	250.00	125.00
(15b)	Wm. Bransfield (Photo inside square frame.)	22,500	9,000	4,500
(16)	Roger Bresnahan	3,440	1,375	690.00
(17)	Al Bridwell	1,000	250.00	125.00
(18)	Mordecai Brown	3,440	1,375	690.00
(19)	Fred Burchell	1,000	250.00	125.00
(20a)	Jesse C. Burkett (Photo inside oval frame.)	15,625	6,250	3,125
(20b)	Jesse C. Burkett (Photo inside square frame.)	22,500	9,000	4,500
(21)	Bobby Byrnes (Byrne)	1,000	250.00	125.00
(22)	Bill Carrigan	1,000	250.00	125.00
(23)	Frank Chance	3,440	1,375	690.00
(24)	Charlie Chech	1,000	250.00	125.00
(25)	Ed Cicotte (Cicotte)	3,000	1,200	600.00
(26)	Otis Clymer	1,000	250.00	125.00
(27)	Andy Coakley	1,000	250.00	125.00
(28)	Jimmy Collins	3,440	1,375	690.00
(29)	Ed. Collins	3,440	1,375	690.00
(30)	Wid Conroy	1,005	250.00	125.00
(31)	Jack Coombs	1,000	250.00	125.00
(32)	Doc Crandall	1,000	250.00	125.00
(33)	Lou Criger	1,000	250.00	125.00
(34)	Harry Davis	1,000	250.00	125.00
(35)	Art Devlin	1,000	250.00	125.00
(36a)	Wm. H. Dineen (Dinneen) (Photo inside oval frame.)	1,000	250.00	125.00
(36b)	Wm. H. Dineen (Dinneen) (Photo inside square frame.)	22,500	9,000	4,500
(37)	Pat Donahue	1,000	250.00	125.00
(38)	Mike Donlin	1,000	250.00	125.00
(39)	Wild Bill Donovan	1,000	250.00	125.00
(40)	Gus Dorner	1,000	250.00	125.00
(41)	Joe Dunn	1,000	250.00	125.00
(42)	Kid Elberfield (Elberfeld)	1,000	250.00	125.00
(43)	Johnny Evers	3,440	1,375	690.00
(44)	Bob Ewing	1,000	250.00	125.00
(45)	Cecil Ferguson	1,000	250.00	125.00
(46)	Hobe Ferris	1,000	250.00	125.00
(47)	Jerry Freeman	1,000	250.00	125.00
(48)	Art Fromme	1,000	250.00	125.00
(49)	Bob Ganley	1,000	250.00	125.00
(50)	Doc Gessler	1,000	250.00	125.00
(51)	Peaches Graham	1,000	250.00	125.00
(52)	Clark Griffith	3,440	1,375	690.00
(53)	Roy Hartzell	1,000	250.00	125.00
(54)	Charlie Hemphill	1,000	250.00	125.00
(55)	Dick Hoblitzel (Hoblitzell)	1,000	250.00	125.00
(56a)	Geo. Howard (Photo inside oval frame.)	1,000	250.00	125.00
(56b)	Geo. Howard (Photo inside square frame.)	22,500	9,000	4,500
(57)	Harry Howell	1,000	250.00	125.00
(58)	Miller Huggins	3,440	1,375	690.00
(59)	John Hummell (Hummel)	1,000	250.00	125.00
(60)	Walter Johnson	50,000	20,000	10,000
(61)	Thos. Jones	1,000	250.00	125.00
(62)	Mike Kahoe	1,000	250.00	125.00
(63)	Ed Kargar	1,000	250.00	125.00
(64)	Wee Willie Keeler	3,440	1,375	690.00
(65)	Red Kleinon (Kleinow)	1,000	250.00	125.00
(66)	Jack Knight	1,000	250.00	125.00
(67)	Ed Konetchey	1,000	250.00	125.00
(68)	Vive Lindaman	1,000	250.00	125.00
(69)	Hans Loebert (Lobert)	1,000	250.00	125.00
(70)	Harry Lord	1,000	250.00	125.00
(71)	Harry Lumley	1,000	250.00	125.00
(72)	Johnny Lush	1,000	250.00	125.00
(73)	Rube Manning	1,000	250.00	125.00
(74)	Jimmy McAleer	1,000	250.00	125.00
(75)	Amby McConnell	1,000	250.00	125.00
(76)	Moose McCormick	1,000	250.00	125.00
(77)	Harry McIntyre	1,000	250.00	125.00
(78)	Larry McLean	1,000	250.00	125.00
(79)	Fred Merkle	1,000	250.00	125.00
(80)	Clyde Milan	1,000	250.00	125.00
(81)	Mike Mitchell	1,005	250.00	125.00
(82a)	Pat Moran (Photo inside oval frame.)	1,000	250.00	125.00
(82b)	Pat Moran (Photo inside square frame.)	22,500	9,000	4,500
(83)	Cy Morgan	1,000	250.00	125.00
(84)	Tim Murname (Murnane)	1,005	250.00	125.00
(85)	Danny Murphy	1,000	250.00	125.00
(86)	Red Murray	1,000	250.00	125.00
(87)	Doc Newton	1,000	250.00	125.00
(88)	Simon Nichols (Nicholls)	1,000	250.00	125.00
(89)	Harry Niles	1,000	250.00	125.00

		NM	EX	VG
(90)	Bill O'Hare (O'Hara)	1,000	250.00	125.00
(91)	Charley O'Leary	1,000	250.00	125.00
(92)	Dode Paskert	1,000	250.00	125.00
(93)	Barney Pelty	1,000	250.00	125.00
(94)	Jake Pfeister	1,000	250.00	125.00
(95)	Ed Plank	9,375	3,750	1,875
(96)	Jack Powell	1,000	250.00	125.00
(97)	Bugs Raymond	1,000	250.00	125.00
(98)	Tom Reilly	1,000	250.00	125.00
(99)	Claude Ritchey	1,000	250.00	125.00
(100)	Nap Rucker	1,000	250.00	125.00
(101)	Ed Ruelbach (Reulbach)	1,000	250.00	125.00
(102)	Slim Sallee	1,000	250.00	125.00
(103)	Germany Schaefer	1,005	250.00	125.00
(104)	Jimmy Schekard (Sheckard)	1,000	250.00	125.00
(105)	Admiral Schlei	1,000	250.00	125.00
(106)	Wildfire Schulte	1,000	400.00	200.00
(107)	Jimmy Sebring	1,000	250.00	125.00
(108)	Bill Shipke	1,000	250.00	125.00
(109)	Charlie Smith	1,000	250.00	125.00
(110)	Tubby Spencer	1,000	250.00	125.00
(111)	Jake Stahl	1,000	250.00	125.00
(112)	Jim Stephens	1,000	250.00	125.00
(113)	Harry Stienfeldt (Steinfeldt)	1,000	250.00	125.00
(114)	Gabby Street	1,000	250.00	125.00
(115)	Bill Sweeney	1,000	250.00	125.00
(116)	Fred Tenney	1,000	250.00	125.00
(117)	Ira Thomas	1,000	250.00	125.00
(118)	Joe Tinker	3,440	1,375	690.00
(119)	Bob Unglane (Unglaub)	1,000	250.00	125.00
(120)	Heinie Wagner	1,000	250.00	125.00
(121)	Bobby Wallace	3,440	1,375	690.00

1910 Ramly Team Composite Premiums

Pittsburg Nationals 1910.

At least two versions of coupons found in boxes of Ramly (and possibly T.T.T.) cigarettes offered a large-format (about 23" x 18-1/2") black-and-white photogravure premium featuring a composite of player portraits for five, or six, popular teams of the era. Players are identified in the bottom border, which also has a credit line for the tobacco company. To date, only the 1909 pennant winners' premiums have been confirmed as surviving.

(1)	Boston Red Sox (Unconfirmed)	.00	.00	.00
(2)	Boston Rustlers	.00	.00	.00
(3)	Detroit Tigers	.00	.00	.00
(4)	New York Giants (Unconfirmed)	.00	.00	.00
(5)	Philadelphia A's (unconfirmed)	.00	.00	.00
(6)	Pittsburgh Pirates (5/04 auction, trimmed, $3,163)	.00	.00	.00

1881 Randall Studio Cabinets

What the players of the 1881 Boston Beaneaters were doing posing in their Sunday best suits at the Detroit studio of Randall the photographer is open to speculation, as is the question of whether other teams' players were also photographed on these cabinets. These cabinets are about 4-1/4" x 6-1/2" and blank-backed. On most of them the player name and city and in small type on the portrait.

		NM	EX	VG
	Common Player:	2,000	1,000	600.00
(1)	Tommy Bond	2,000	1,000	600.00
(2)	Tom Deasley	2,000	1,000	600.00
(3)	John Morrill	2,000	1,000	600.00
(4)	John Richmond	2,000	1,000	600.00
(5)	Ezra Sutton	2,000	1,000	600.00
(6)	Jim Whitney	2,000	1,000	600.00

1950s-70s Rawlings Advisory Staff Photos

Advisory staff photos were a promtional item which debuted in the early 1950s, flourished in the Sixties and died in the early 1970s. Generally 8" x 10" (sometimes a little larger), these black-and-white (a few later were color) glossy photos picture players who had contracted with a major baseball equipment company to endorse and use their product. Usually the product - most often a glove - was prominently displayed in the photo. The pictures were often displayed in the windows of sporting goods stores or the walls of sports departments and were sometimes made available to customers. Because the companies tended to stick with players over the years, some photos were reissued, sometimes with and sometimes without a change of team, pose or style. All advisory staff photos of the era are checklisted here in alphabetical order. A pose description is given for each known picture. The photos are checklisted here in alphabetical order. It is unlikely this list is complete. In general, Rawlings advisory staff photos feature a white box within the photo which contains the glove-company logo and a facsimile autograph of the player. Gaps have been left in the checklist numbering to accommodate possible additions.

		NM	EX	VG
	Common Player:	25.00	12.50	7.50
(1)	Joe Adcock (Braves, kneeling.)	35.00	17.50	10.50
(2)	Joe Adcock (Braves, locker room.)	25.00	12.50	7.50
(3)	Joe Adcock (Braves, upper body.)	25.00	12.50	7.50
(4)	Hank Aguirre (Tigers, glove on knee.)	25.00	12.50	7.50
(5)	Bobby Avila (Indians, upper body.)	25.00	12.50	7.50
(6)	Bob Bailey (Pirates, kneeling.)	25.00	12.50	7.50
(7)	Ed Bailey (Reds, gearing up in dugout.)	25.00	12.50	7.50
(8)	Ed Bailey (Giants, catching crouch.)	25.00	12.50	7.50
(9)	Earl Battey (Twins, catching crouch.)	25.00	12.50	7.50
(10)	Earl Battey (Twins, kneeling w/bat.)	25.00	12.50	7.50
(11)	Johnny Bench (Crouching, no catcher's gear.)	45.00	22.00	13.50
(12)	Dick Bertell (Cubs, catching crouch.)	25.00	12.50	7.50
(13)	John Blanchard (Yankees, catching crouch.)	25.00	12.50	7.50
(14)	John Blanchard (Yankees, dugout step.)	25.00	12.50	7.50
(15)	"Clete" Boyer (Yankees, fielding.)	25.00	12.50	7.50
(16)	Ken Boyer (Cardinals, in front of locker.)	25.00	12.50	7.50
(17)	Ken Boyer (Cardinals, b/w, kneeling.)	25.00	12.50	7.50
(18)	Ken Boyer (Mets, b/w, full-length.)	25.00	12.50	7.50
(19)	Ken Boyer (Mets, color, leaning on bat.)	25.00	12.50	7.50
(20)	Ken Boyer (White Sox, upper body.)	30.00	15.00	9.00
(21)	Lew Burdette (Braves, beginning wind-up.)	25.00	12.50	7.50
(22)	Lew Burdette (Braves, upper body w/ball.)	35.00	17.50	10.50
(23)	Bob Cerv (A's, at bat rack.)	25.00	12.50	7.50
(24)	Gordon Coleman (Reds, kneeling w/bat.)	25.00	12.50	7.50
(25)	Tony Conigliaro (Red Sox, glove at chest.)	45.00	22.00	13.50
(26)	Wes Covington (Braves, upper body.)	25.00	12.50	7.50
(27)	Joe Cunningham (White Sox, glove at knee.)	25.00	12.50	7.50
(28)	Joe Cunningham (Cardinals, chest-up.)	25.00	12.50	7.50
(29)	Tommy Davis (Dodgers, dugout step.)	25.00	12.50	7.50
(30)	Don Demeter (Dodgers, upper body.)	25.00	12.50	7.50
(31)	Don Demeter (Phillies, hands on knees.)	25.00	12.50	7.50
(32)	Dick Dietz (Giants, catching pose.)	25.00	12.50	7.50
(33)	Tito Francona (Indians, sitting w/glove.)	25.00	12.50	7.50
(34)	Steve Garvey (Dodgers, horizontal, pose and action.)	25.00	12.50	7.50
(35)	Mudcat Grant (Indians, horizontal, upper body.)	25.00	12.50	7.50
(36)	Dick Groat (Pirates, b/w, full-length.)	25.00	12.50	7.50
(37)	Dick Groat (Pirates, b/w, upper body.)	25.00	12.50	7.50
(38)	Dick Groat (Cardinals, b/w, kneeling w/bat.)	25.00	12.50	7.50
(39)	Dick Groat (Cardinals, b/w, kneeling.)	25.00	12.50	7.50
(40)	Harvey Haddix (Pirates, kneeling.)	25.00	12.50	7.50
(41)	Harvey Haddix (Pirates, locker room.)	25.00	12.50	7.50
(42)	Ken Holtzman (Cubs, hands on knees.)	25.00	12.50	7.50
(43)	Ken Holtzman (A's, horizontal, two poses.)	25.00	12.50	7.50
(44)	Elston Howard (Yankees, catching crouch.)	30.00	15.00	9.00
(45)	Al Hrabosky (Cardinals, upper body.)	25.00	12.50	7.50
(46)	Larry Jackson (Cubs, kneeling.)	25.00	12.50	7.50

		NM	EX	VG
(47)	Larry Jackson (Cardinals, fielding.)	25.00	12.50	7.50
(48)	Larry Jackson (Cardinals, full-length on mound.)	25.00	12.00	7.50
(49)	Reggie Jackson (A's, full-length.)	40.00	20.00	12.00
(50)	Joey Jay (Reds, dugout step, glove on rail.)	25.00	12.50	7.50
(51)	Fergie Jenkins (Cubs, hands on knees.)	25.00	12.50	7.50
(52)	Ed Kranepool (Mets, color, batting.)	25.00	12.50	7.50
(53)	Tony Kubek (Full-length, fielding.)	25.00	12.50	7.50
(54)	Tony Kubek (Kneeling, no bat.)	25.00	12.50	7.50
(55)	Tony Kubek (Kneeling w/bat.)	25.00	12.50	7.50
(56)	Tony Kubek (Horizontal, upper body.)	25.00	12.50	7.50
(57)	Vern Law (Locker room.)	25.00	12.50	7.50
(58)	Jim Lefebvre (Dodgers, kneeling, bat on shoulder.)	25.00	12.50	7.50
(59)	Sherman Lollar (White Sox, throwing from crouch.)	25.00	12.50	7.50
(60)	Art Mahaffey (Phillies, upper body.)	25.00	12.50	7.50
(61)	Mickey Mantle (Upper body, road uniform.)	150.00	75.00	45.00
(62)	Mickey Mantle (Leaning, hands on knees.)	100.00	50.00	30.00
(63)	Mickey Mantle (Seated w/bat, glove on knee.)	130.00	65.00	40.00
(64)	Mickey Mantle (Kneeling)	150.00	75.00	45.00
(65)	Mickey Mantle (Seated at locker, pointing to glove.)	150.00	75.00	45.00
(66)	Eddie Mathews (Braves, full-length.)	45.00	22.00	13.50
(67)	Eddie Mathews (Braves, sepia, upper body.)	45.00	22.00	13.50
(68)	Eddie Mathews (Braves, upper body, glove in front.)	45.00	22.00	13.50
(69)	Eddie Mathews (Braves, upper body, looking at glove.)	45.00	22.00	13.50
(70)	Dal Maxvill (Cardinals, bat on shoulder.)	25.00	12.50	7.50
(71)	Dal Maxvill (Cardinals, fielding.)	25.00	12.50	7.50
(72)	Charlie Maxwell (Tigers, horizontal, upper body.)	25.00	12.50	7.50
(73)	Tim McCarver (Cardinals, catching crouch.)	25.00	12.50	7.50
(74)	Lindy McDaniel (Cardinals, b/w, on dugout steps.)	25.00	12.50	7.50
(75)	Dave McNally (Orioles, upper body.)	25.00	12.50	7.50
(76)	Wilmer Mizell (Cardinals, upper body.)	25.00	12.50	7.50
(77)	Wally Moon (Dodgers, kneeling.)	25.00	12.50	7.50
(78)	Wally Moon (Dodgers, standing.)	25.00	12.50	7.50
(79)	Stan Musial (Upper body.)	50.00	25.00	15.00
(80)	Stan Musial (Horizontal, batting.)	50.00	25.00	15.00
(81)	Stan Musial (Full-length holding glove and bat.)	50.00	25.00	15.00
(82)	Stan Musial (Kneeling on bat.)	50.00	25.00	15.00
(83)	Stan Musial (Kneeling on bat, glove on ground.)	50.00	25.00	15.00
(84)	Stan Musial (Kneeling, glove in front, Busch Stadium.)	50.00	25.00	15.00
(85)	Stan Musial (Full-length, hands on knees.)	80.00	40.00	24.00
(86)	Stan Musial (Socks to cap, white background, in proposed '56 road uniform.)	125.00	62.00	37.00
(87)	Charlie Neal (Dodgers, kneeling.)	25.00	12.50	7.50
(88)	Charlie Neal (Dodgers, looking into glove.)	25.00	12.50	7.50
(89)	Rocky Nelson (Pirates, kneeling.)	25.00	12.50	7.50
(90)	Rocky Nelson (Pirates, fielding.)	25.00	12.50	7.50
(91)	Amos Otis (Royals, upper body.)	25.00	12.50	7.50
(92)	Jim Perry (Indians, pitching.)	25.00	12.50	7.50
(93)	Boog Powell (Orioles, full-length.)	25.00	12.50	7.50
(94)	Rick Reichardt (Angels, full-length.)	25.00	12.50	7.50
(95)	Brooks Robinson (Dugout step.)	45.00	22.00	13.50
(96)	Brooks Robinson (Throwing)	45.00	22.00	13.50
(97)	Brooks Robinson (Standing w/glove.)	45.00	22.00	13.50
(98)	Brooks Robinson (Tying shoe.)	45.00	22.00	13.50
(99)	John Romano (Indians, adjusting shinguard.)	25.00	12.50	7.50
(100)	Manny Sanguillen (Pirates, catching crouch.)	25.00	12.50	7.50
(101)	Chuck Schilling (Full-length.)	25.00	12.50	7.50
(102)	Herb Score (Indians, pitching.)	25.00	12.50	7.50
(103)	Norm Siebern (A's, vest.)	25.00	12.50	7.50
(104)	Norm Siebern (A's, jersey.)	25.00	12.50	7.50
(105)	Roy Sievers (Senators, full-length.)	25.00	12.50	7.50
(106)	Roy Sievers (White Sox, drinking fountain.)	25.00	12.50	7.50
(107)	Roy Sievers (Phillies, kneeling.)	25.00	12.50	7.50
(108)	Bob Skinner (Pirates, upper body.)	25.00	12.50	7.50
(109)	Duke Snider (Brooklyn Dodgers, full-length.)	45.00	22.00	13.50

		NM	EX	VG
(111)	Duke Snider (L.A. Dodgers, upper body.)	45.00	22.00	13.50
(112)	Warren Spahn (Braves, b/w, wind-up.)	45.00	22.00	13.50
(114)	Willie Stargell (Upper body.)	35.00	17.50	10.50
(115)	Willie Stargell (Full-length.)	35.00	17.50	10.50
(116)	Tom Tresh (Yankees, fielding.)	25.00	12.50	7.50
(117)	Tom Tresh (Yankees, full-length.)	25.00	12.50	7.50
(119)	Bob Turley (Yankees, upper body.)	25.00	12.50	7.50
(120)	Bob Turley (At water fountain.)	25.00	12.50	7.50
(121)	Bill White (Cardinals, glove over rail.)	25.00	12.50	7.50
(122)	Bill White (Phillies, b/w, full-length.)	25.00	12.50	7.50
(123)	Bill White (Phillies, color, full-length.)	25.00	12.50	7.50
(124)	Billy Williams (Cubs, full-length.)	35.00	17.50	10.50
(126)	Steve Yeager (Dodgers, upper body.)	25.00	12.50	7.50

1952 Rawlings Stan Musial Premium Photo

In this black-and-white, blank-backed premium photo, Musial is shown in a batting stance superimposed over a game-action photo at Sportsman's Park. A white facsimile autograph is at lower-right. The wide bottom border of the 5" x 7" picture has the Rawlings logoscript and address.

	NM	EX	VG
Stan Musial	40.00	20.00	12.00

1954 Rawlings Stan Musial

The date of issue is speculation although the picture is certainly from 1955 or earlier. This 5-1/2" x 7-1/2" colorized photo is actually part of a cardboard Rawlings glove box. The panel at lower-right of the card identifies it as "A GENUINE RAWLINGS FACSIMILE AUTOGRAPH PICTURE." Back is blank.

	NM	EX	VG
Stan Musial	300.00	150.00	90.00

1955 Rawlings Stan Musial

Though missing from Topps and Bowman card sets from 1954-57, Cardinals superstar Stan Musial wasn't entirely unavailable on baseball cards. About 1955 he appeared on a series of six cards found on boxes of Rawlings baseball gloves carrying Musial's endorsement. The cards feature black-and-white photos of Musial set against a blue background. Because the cards were part of a display box, they are blank-backed.

Depending on the position on the box, the cards measure approximately 2" x 3" (#1A and 2A) or 2-1/2" x 3-3/4" (#1-4). Cards are numbered in a yellow star at upper left.

		NM	EX	VG
Complete Set (6):		2,500	1,250	750.00
Complete Box:		3,000	1,500	900.00
Common Card:		450.00	225.00	125.00
1	Stan Musial (Portrait)	450.00	225.00	125.00
1A	Stan Musial (Portrait with bat.)	450.00	225.00	125.00
2	Stan Musial (Kneeling)	450.00	225.00	125.00
2A	Stan Musial (Portrait)	450.00	225.00	125.00
3	Stan Musial (Swinging, horizontal.)	450.00	225.00	125.00
4	Stan Musial (Batting pose.)	450.00	225.00	125.00

1963 Rawlings Stan Musial Premium

This premium was available by mail and commemorates the career of long-time Rawlings spokesman Stan Musial upon his retirement. The package contains an approximately 9" x 10" color portrait photo of Musial with a facsimile autograph, a sheet illustrated with four portraits of Musial during his career and listing his many records, and a note from the company indicating future availability of Musial gloves.

	NM	EX	VG
Complete Package: Stan Musial	60.00	30.00	18.00

1964 Rawlings Glove Box

Measuring about 2-3/8" x 4" when properly cut off the glove boxes on which they were printed, these full-color cards show stars of the day posing with their Rawlings glove prominently displayed. The blank-backed unnumbered cards are checklisted here alphabetically. The quality of cutting should be considered in grading these cards. In actuality, the cards were not meant to be cut from the boxes, but rather to show which premium photo was packed inside the glove box. Two cards of each player appear on the box.

		NM	EX	VG
Complete Set (8):		450.00	225.00	135.00
Common Player:		25.00	12.50	7.50
Complete Box:		750.00	375.00	225.00
(1)	Ken Boyer	35.00	17.50	10.50
(2)	Tommy Davis	25.00	12.50	7.50
(3)	Dick Groat	25.00	12.50	7.50
(4)	Mickey Mantle	200.00	100.00	60.00
(5)	Brooks Robinson	60.00	30.00	18.00
(6)	Warren Spahn	50.00	25.00	15.00
(7)	Tom Tresh	25.00	12.50	7.50
(8)	Billy Williams	45.00	22.00	13.50

1964-66 Rawlings Premium Photos

One premium photo was inserted into each baseball glove box sold by Rawlings beginning in 1964 and continuing at least into 1966, when some changes in players and pictures were added. The 8" x 9-1/2" full-color photos were advertised on the outside of the boxes in miniature form. Each of the photos pictures a player posed with his Rawlings leather prominently displayed. A black facsimile autograph is printed on the front.

		NM	EX	VG
	Complete Set (12):	600.00	300.00	180.00
	Common Player:	20.00	10.00	6.00
(1a)	Ken Boyer (Cardinals, 1964.)	25.00	12.50	7.50
(1b)	Ken Boyer (Mets, 1966.)	25.00	12.50	7.50
(2)	Tommy Davis	20.00	10.00	6.00
(3)	Dick Groat	20.00	10.00	6.00
(4a)	Mickey Mantle (No undershirt, 1964.)	150.00	75.00	45.00
(4b)	Mickey Mantle (Black undershirt, 1966.)	150.00	75.00	45.00
(5a)	Brooks Robinson (Full-bird cap, 1964.)	70.00	35.00	21.00
(5b)	Brooks Robinson (Bird's-head cap, 1966.)	85.00	42.00	25.00
(6)	Warren Spahn	75.00	37.00	22.00
(7)	Tom Tresh	20.00	10.00	6.00
(8)	Bill White (1966)	20.00	10.00	6.00
(9)	Billy Williams	50.00	25.00	15.00

1965 Rawlings MVP Premiums

The American and National League MVPs are featured in this pair of 8-1/8" x 10-1/4" premium pictures sponsored by the sporting goods manufacturer. The manner of their distribution is unknown. Printed on thin card stock, the premiums feature the artwork of Amadee Wohlschlaeger.

		NM	EX	VG
	Complete Set (2):	125.00	65.00	40.00
(1)	Ken Boyer	65.00	35.00	20.00
(2)	Brooks Robinson	75.00	40.00	25.00

1969 Rawlings

How these cards were distributed is not certain today, nor is the extent of the series known. The approximately 3" x 5" black-and-white cards feature a portrait photo on front, with a wide white border at bottom that holds a facsimile autograph. The back has complete major and minor league stats, career highlights and a Rawlings ad.

	NM	EX	VG
Reggie Jackson	900.00	450.00	275.00
Mickey Mantle	2,500	1,250	750.00

1930 Ray-O-Print Photo Kits

This was one of several contemporary kits for do-it-your-self production of photo prints. The outfits were produced by M.P. & Co., of New York. The novelty kit consists of a 4-1/8" x 2-1/2" kraft paper envelope with production instructions printed on the outside and the name of the subject rubber-stamped on one end. Inside was a film negative, a piece of light-sensitive photo paper (each 1-7/8" x 2-15/16") and a tin stand for exposing and displaying the photo. Values shown are for complete kits. Individual components would be pro-rated, with the negative being the most valuable of the pieces. Anyone with a negative could make unlimited prints today, and even make them look old; collectors should use caution in purchasing prints alone.

	NM	EX	VG
Complete Set (8):	1,000	500.00	300.00
Common Kit:	125.00	67.00	38.00

Card: 20 Percent		.00	.00	.00
(1)	Lou Gehrig	250.00	125.00	75.00
(2)	Babe Ruth	400.00	200.00	120.00
(3)	Jack Dempsey (Boxer)	100.00	50.00	30.00
(4)	Herbert Hoover (President)	75.00	37.00	22.00
(5)	"Lindy" (Charles Lindbergh) (Aviator)	150.00	75.00	45.00
(6)	Mary Pickford (Actress)	50.00	25.00	15.00
(7)	Will Rogers (Humorist)	50.00	25.00	15.00
(8)	We (Charles Lindbergh) (W/ plane, Spirit of St. Louis.)	150.00	75.00	45.00

1899 Henry Reccius Cigars Honus Wagner

The date of this card's issue is probable, though it could have been issued anytime between 1897-99 during Wagner's stay in Louisville. The 3-3/8" x 4-11/16" card is printed in black-on-orange with an oval photograph of Wagner at center. Advertising for the company that marketed cigars under his name is around the border. The back has a lengthy pro-trade union poem. Only one example of the card is known. It was graded by PSA sometime after 1998 and given a Poor-Fair designation. The card was auctioned in November, 2001, for $21,850, and again in April, 2006, for $52,040.

Honus Wagner

1912 Recruit Little Cigars

This is the most common of the back advertisements found in T207. Factory 606 (Maryland) backs are much scarcer than those with Factory 240 (Pennsylvania), but currently carry little premium on that basis. Back printing is usually found in black, but several examples have been authenticated with brown ink printing on back. Their value is undetermined.

(See 1912 T207.)

1976 Red Barn Discs

The scarcest among the several regional sponsors of player disc sets issued in 1976 are those of the Red Barn family restaurant chain in Southeastern Wisconsin. The discs are 3-3/8" diameter with a black-and-white player portrait photo in the center of the baseball design. A line of red stars is above, while the left and right panels feature one of several bright colors. Produced by Michael Schecter Associates under license from the Major League Baseball Players Association, the player photos have had uniform and cap logos removed. Backs are printed in red and purple. The unnumbered checklist here is presented in alphabetical order.

		NM	EX	VG
	Complete Set (70):	500.00	250.00	150.00
	Common Player:	8.00	4.00	2.50
(1)	Henry Aaron	65.00	32.00	19.50
(2)	Johnny Bench	25.00	12.50	7.50
(3)	Vida Blue	8.00	4.00	2.50
(4)	Larry Bowa	8.00	4.00	2.50
(5)	Lou Brock	20.00	10.00	6.00
(6)	Jeff Burroughs	8.00	4.00	2.50
(7)	John Candelaria	8.00	4.00	2.50
(8)	Jose Cardenal	8.00	4.00	2.50
(9)	Rod Carew	20.00	10.00	6.00
(10)	Steve Carlton	25.00	12.50	7.50
(11)	Dave Cash	8.00	4.00	2.50
(12)	Cesar Cedeno	8.00	4.00	2.50
(13)	Ron Cey	8.00	4.00	2.50
(14)	Carlton Fisk	20.00	10.00	6.00
(15)	Tito Fuentes	8.00	4.00	2.50
(16)	Steve Garvey	12.00	6.00	3.50
(17)	Ken Griffey	8.00	4.00	2.50
(18)	Don Gullett	8.00	4.00	2.50
(19)	Willie Horton	8.00	4.00	2.50
(20)	Al Hrabosky	8.00	4.00	2.50
(21)	Catfish Hunter	20.00	10.00	6.00
(22)	Reggie Jackson	40.00	20.00	12.00
(23)	Randy Jones	8.00	4.00	2.50
(24)	Jim Kaat	8.00	4.00	2.50
(25)	Don Kessinger	8.00	4.00	2.50
(26)	Dave Kingman	8.00	4.00	2.50
(27)	Jerry Koosman	8.00	4.00	2.50
(28)	Mickey Lolich	8.00	4.00	2.50
(29)	Greg Luzinski	8.00	4.00	2.50
(30)	Fred Lynn	10.00	5.00	3.00
(31)	Bill Madlock	8.00	4.00	2.50
(32)	Carlos May	8.00	4.00	2.50
(33)	John Mayberry	8.00	4.00	2.50
(34)	Bake McBride	8.00	4.00	2.50
(35)	Doc Medich	8.00	4.00	2.50
(36)	Andy Messersmith	8.00	4.00	2.50
(37)	Rick Monday	8.00	4.00	2.50
(38)	John Montefusco	8.00	4.00	2.50
(39)	Jerry Morales	8.00	4.00	2.50
(40)	Joe Morgan	20.00	10.00	6.00
(41)	Thurman Munson	15.00	7.50	4.50
(42)	Bobby Murcer	8.00	4.00	2.50
(43)	Al Oliver	8.00	4.00	2.50
(44)	Jim Palmer	20.00	10.00	6.00
(45)	Dave Parker	8.00	4.00	2.50
(46)	Tony Perez	20.00	10.00	6.00
(47)	Jerry Reuss	8.00	4.00	2.50
(48)	Brooks Robinson	25.00	12.50	7.50
(49)	Frank Robinson	25.00	12.50	7.50
(50)	Steve Rogers	8.00	4.00	2.50
(51)	Pete Rose	65.00	32.00	19.50
(52)	Nolan Ryan	100.00	50.00	30.00
(53)	Manny Sanguillen	8.00	4.00	2.50
(54)	Mike Schmidt	45.00	22.00	13.50
(55)	Tom Seaver	25.00	12.50	7.50
(56)	Ted Simmons	8.00	4.00	2.50
(57)	Reggie Smith	8.00	4.00	2.50
(58)	Willie Stargell	20.00	10.00	6.00
(59)	Rusty Staub	12.00	6.00	3.50
(60)	Rennie Stennett	8.00	4.00	2.50
(61)	Don Sutton	20.00	10.00	6.00
(62)	Andy Thornton	8.00	4.00	2.50
(63)	Luis Tiant	8.00	4.00	2.50
(64)	Joe Torre	12.00	6.00	3.50
(65)	Mike Tyson	8.00	4.00	2.50
(66)	Bob Watson	8.00	4.00	2.50
(67)	Wilbur Wood	8.00	4.00	2.50
(68)	Jimmy Wynn	8.00	4.00	2.50
(69)	Carl Yastrzemski	25.00	12.50	7.50
(70)	Richie Zisk	8.00	4.00	2.50

1912 Red Cross Tobacco (T207)

Among the rarest back variations known in the tobacco card series is the Red Cross back on T207. Only a handful of examples have ever been seen. Determination of values is an inexact science.

	NM	EX	VG

(See T207 for checklist. A Fair-condition "common" was bid to $3,500 in a 12/00 auction but was not sold.)
Russell Blackburne (4/02 auction G-VG)
George Weaver 10,187
(9/02 auction - Fair)

1910-12 Red Cross Tobacco Type 1 (T215)

The T215 set issued by Red Cross Tobacco is another of the Louisiana regional sets closely related to the T206 "White Border" tobacco cards. Very similar to the T213 Coupon cards, the Red Cross Tobacco cards are found in two distinct types, both featuring color player lithographs and measuring approximately 1-1/2" x 2-5/8", the standard tobacco card size. Type 1 Red Cross cards, issued from 1910 to 1912, have brown captions; while Type 2 cards, most of which appear to be from 1912-13, have blue printing. The backs of both types are identical, displaying the Red Cross name and emblem, which can be used to positively identify the set and differentiate it from the other Louisiana sets of the same period. Several variations have been found, most of them involving caption changes. Gaps have been left in the assigned numbering to accommodate future additions to these checklists.

		NM	EX	VG
Common Player:		825.00	330.00	165.00
(1)	Red Ames	825.00	330.00	165.00
(2)	Home Run Baker	2,500	1,000	500.00
(3)	Neal Ball	825.00	330.00	165.00
(4)	Chief Bender	2,500	1,000	500.00
	(No trees in background.)			
(5)	Chief Bender	2,500	1,000	500.00
	(Trees in background.)			
(6)	Al Bridwell	825.00	330.00	165.00
(7)	Bobby Byrne	825.00	330.00	165.00
(8)	Howie Camnitz	825.00	330.00	165.00
(9)	Frank Chance	2,500	1,000	500.00
(10)	Hal Chase	1,875	750.00	375.00
(11)	Ty Cobb	9,375	3,750	1,875
(12)	Eddie Collins	2,500	1,000	500.00
(13)	Wid Conroy	825.00	330.00	165.00
(14)	Doc Crandall	825.00	330.00	165.00
(15)	Sam Crawford	2,500	1,000	500.00
(16)	Birdie Cree	825.00	330.00	165.00
(17)	Harry Davis	825.00	330.00	165.00
(18)	Josh Devore	825.00	330.00	165.00
(19)	Mike Donlin	825.00	330.00	165.00
(20)	Mickey Doolan	825.00	330.00	165.00
(21)	Patsy Dougherty	825.00	330.00	165.00
(22)	Larry Doyle (Batting)	825.00	330.00	165.00
(23)	Larry Doyle (Portrait)	825.00	330.00	165.00
(24)	Kid Elberfeld	825.00	330.00	165.00
(25)	Russ Ford	825.00	330.00	165.00
(26)	Art Fromme	825.00	330.00	165.00
(27)	Clark Griffith	2,500	1,000	500.00
(28)	Topsy Hartsel	825.00	330.00	165.00
(29)	Dick Hoblitzell	825.00	330.00	165.00
(30)	Solly Hofman	825.00	330.00	165.00
(31)	Del Howard	825.00	330.00	165.00
(32)	Miller Huggins	2,500	1,000	500.00
	(Hands at mouth.)			
(33)	Miller Huggins (Portrait)	2,500	1,000	500.00
(34)	John Hummel	825.00	330.00	165.00
(35)	Hughie Jennings	2,500	1,000	500.00
	(Both hands showing.)			
(36)	Hughie Jennings	2,500	1,000	500.00
	(One hand showing.)			
(37)	Walter Johnson	4,375	1,750	875.00
(38)	Ed Konetchy	825.00	330.00	165.00
(39)	Harry Krause	825.00	330.00	165.00
(41)	Nap Lajoie	2,500	1,000	500.00
(42)	Joe Lake	825.00	330.00	165.00
(43)	Arlie Latham	825.00	330.00	165.00
(44)	Tommy Leach	825.00	330.00	165.00
(45)	Lefty Leifield	825.00	330.00	165.00
(46)	Harry Lord	825.00	330.00	165.00
(47)	Sherry Magee	825.00	330.00	165.00
(48)	Rube Marquard (Pitching)	2,500	1,000	500.00
(49)	Rube Marquard (Portrait)	2,500	1,000	500.00
(51)	Christy Mathewson	6,250	2,500	1,250
	(Dark cap.)			
(52)	Christy Mathewson	6,250	2,500	1,250
	(White cap.)			
(53)	Joe McGinnity	2,500	1,000	500.00
(54)	John McGraw (Glove at hip.)	2,500	1,000	500.00
(55)	John McGraw (Portrait)	2,500	1,000	500.00
(56)	Harry McIntyre	825.00	330.00	165.00
(57)	Fred Merkle	825.00	330.00	165.00
(58)	Chief Meyers	825.00	330.00	165.00
(59)	Dots Miller	825.00	330.00	165.00
(61)	Mike Mowrey	825.00	330.00	165.00
(62)	Danny Murphy	825.00	330.00	165.00
(63)	Red Murray	825.00	330.00	165.00
(64)	Rebel Oakes	825.00	330.00	165.00
(65)	Charley O'Leary	825.00	330.00	165.00
(66)	Dode Paskert	825.00	330.00	165.00
(67)	Barney Pelty	825.00	330.00	165.00
(68)	Jack Quinn	825.00	330.00	165.00
(69)	Ed Reulbach	825.00	330.00	165.00
(71)	Nap Rucker	825.00	330.00	165.00
(72)	Germany Schaefer	825.00	330.00	165.00
(73)	Wildfire Schulte	825.00	330.00	165.00
(74)	Jimmy Sheckard	825.00	330.00	165.00
(75)	Frank Smith	825.00	330.00	165.00
(76)	Frank Smither (Smith)	825.00	330.00	165.00
(77)	Tris Speaker	3,125	1,250	625.00
(78)	Jake Stahl	825.00	330.00	165.00
(79)	Harry Steinfeldt	825.00	330.00	165.00
(81)	Gabby Street (Catching)	825.00	330.00	165.00
(82)	Gabby Street (Portrait)	825.00	330.00	165.00
(83)	Jeff Sweeney	825.00	330.00	165.00
(84)	Lee Tannehill	825.00	330.00	165.00
(85)	Joe Tinker	2,500	1,000	500.00
	(Bat off shoulder.)			
(86)	Joe Tinker (Bat on shoulder.)	2,500	1,000	500.00
(87)	Heinie Wagner	825.00	330.00	165.00
(88)	Jack Warhop	825.00	330.00	165.00
(89)	Zach Wheat	2,500	1,000	500.00
(91)	Doc White	825.00	330.00	165.00
(92)	Ed Willetts (Willett)	825.00	330.00	165.00
(93)	Owen Wilson	825.00	330.00	165.00
(94)	Hooks Wiltse (pitching)	825.00	330.00	165.00
(95)	Hooks Wiltse (portrait)	825.00	330.00	165.00
(96)	Cy Young	6,250	2,500	1,250

1912-13 Red Cross Tobacco Type 2 (T215)

		NM	EX	VG
Common Player:		825.00	330.00	165.00
(1)	Red Ames	825.00	330.00	165.00
(2)	Neal Ball	825.00	330.00	165.00
(3)	Home Run Baker	2,375	950.00	475.00
(4)	Chief Bender	2,375	950.00	475.00
	(No trees in background.)			
(5)	Chief Bender	2,375	950.00	475.00
	(Trees in background.)			
(6)	Roger Bresnahan	2,375	950.00	475.00
(7)	Al Bridwell	825.00	330.00	165.00
(8)	Mordecai Brown	2,375	950.00	475.00
(9)	Bobby Byrne	825.00	330.00	165.00
(10)	Howie Camnitz	825.00	330.00	165.00
(11)	Frank Chance	2,375	950.00	475.00
(12)	Hal Chase	1,500	600.00	300.00
(13)	Ty Cobb	9,375	3,750	1,875
(14)	Eddie Collins	2,375	950.00	475.00
(15)	Doc Crandall	825.00	330.00	165.00
(16)	Sam Crawford	2,375	950.00	475.00
(17)	Birdie Cree	825.00	330.00	165.00
(18)	Harry Davis	825.00	330.00	165.00
(19)	Josh Devore	825.00	330.00	165.00
(21)	Mike Donlin	825.00	330.00	165.00
(22)	Mickey Doolan (Batting)	825.00	330.00	165.00
(23)	Mickey Doolan (Fielding)	825.00	330.00	165.00
(24)	Patsy Dougherty	825.00	330.00	165.00
(25)	Larry Doyle (Batting)	825.00	330.00	165.00
(26)	Larry Doyle (Portrait)	825.00	330.00	165.00
(27)	Jean Dubuc	825.00	330.00	165.00
(28)	Kid Elberfeld	825.00	330.00	165.00
(29)	Johnny Evers	2,375	950.00	475.00
(30)	Russ Ford	825.00	330.00	165.00
(31)	Art Fromme	825.00	330.00	165.00
(32)	Clark Griffith	2,375	950.00	475.00
(33)	Bob Groom	825.00	330.00	165.00
(34)	Topsy Hartsel	825.00	330.00	165.00
(35)	Buck Herzog	825.00	330.00	165.00
(36)	Dick Hoblitzell	825.00	330.00	165.00
(37)	Solly Hofman	825.00	330.00	165.00
(38)	Miller Huggins	2,375	950.00	475.00
	(Hands at mouth.)			
(39)	Miller Huggins (Portrait)	2,375	950.00	475.00
(41)	John Hummel	825.00	330.00	165.00
(42)	Hughie Jennings	2,375	950.00	475.00
(43)	Walter Johnson	3,125	1,250	625.00
(44)	Joe Kelley	2,375	950.00	475.00
(45)	Ed Konetchy	825.00	330.00	165.00
(46)	Harry Krause	825.00	330.00	165.00
(47)	Nap Lajoie	2,375	950.00	475.00
(48)	Joe Lake	825.00	330.00	165.00
(49)	Tommy Leach	825.00	330.00	165.00
(50)	Lefty Leifield	825.00	330.00	165.00
(51)	Harry Lord	825.00	330.00	165.00
(52)	Sherry Magee	825.00	330.00	165.00
(53)	Rube Marquard (Pitching)	2,375	950.00	475.00
(54)	Rube Marquard (Portrait)	2,375	950.00	475.00
(55)	Christy Mathewson	3,440	1,375	690.00
(56)	John McGraw (Glove at side.)	2,300	950.00	475.00
(57)	John McGraw (Portrait)	2,375	950.00	475.00
(58)	Harry McIntire	825.00	330.00	165.00
(59)	Larry McLean	825.00	330.00	165.00
(61)	Fred Merkle	825.00	330.00	165.00
(62)	Dots Miller	825.00	330.00	165.00
(63)	Mike Mitchell	825.00	330.00	165.00
(64)	Mike Mowrey	825.00	330.00	165.00
(65)	George Mullin	825.00	330.00	165.00
(66)	Danny Murphy	825.00	330.00	165.00
(67)	Red Murray	825.00	330.00	165.00
(68)	Rebel Oakes	825.00	330.00	165.00
(69)	Rube Oldring	825.00	330.00	165.00
(70)	Charley O'Leary	825.00	330.00	165.00
(71)	Dode Paskert	825.00	330.00	165.00
(72)	Barney Pelty	825.00	330.00	165.00
(73)	Billy Purtell	825.00	330.00	165.00
(74)	Ed Reulbach	825.00	330.00	165.00
(75)	Nap Rucker	825.00	330.00	165.00
(76)	Germany Schaefer (Chicago)	825.00	330.00	165.00
(77)	Germany Schaefer (Washington)	825.00	330.00	165.00
(78)	Wildfire Schulte	825.00	330.00	165.00
(79)	Frank Smith	825.00	330.00	165.00
(80)	Frank Smither (Smith)	825.00	330.00	165.00
(82)	Tris Speaker	2,375	950.00	475.00
(83)	Jake Stahl	825.00	330.00	165.00
(84)	Harry Steinfeldt	825.00	330.00	165.00
(85)	Ed Summers	825.00	330.00	165.00
(86)	Jeff Sweeney	825.00	330.00	165.00
(87)	Ira Thomas	825.00	330.00	165.00
(88)	Joe Tinker (Bat off shoulder.)	2,375	950.00	475.00
(89)	Joe Tinker (Bat on shoulder.)	2,375	950.00	475.00
(90)	Heinie Wagner	825.00	330.00	165.00
(91)	Jack Warhop	825.00	330.00	165.00
(92)	Doc White	825.00	330.00	165.00
(93)	Hooks Wiltse (Pitching)	825.00	330.00	165.00
(94)	Hooks Wiltse (Portrait)	825.00	330.00	165.00

1954 Red Heart Dog Food

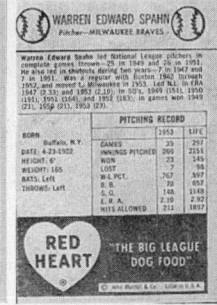

This set of 33 cards was issued in three color-coded series by the Red Heart Dog Food Co. Card fronts feature hand-colored photos on either a blue, green or red background. The 11 red-background cards are scarcer than the 11-card blue or green series. Backs of the 2-5/8" x 3-3/4" cards contain biographical and statistical information along with a Red Heart ad. Each 11-card series was available via a mail-in offer. As late as the early 1970s, the company was still sending cards to collectors who requested them.

		NM	EX	VG
Complete Set (33):		2,150	900.00	450.00
Common Player:		30.00	15.00	9.00
(1)	Richie Ashburn	100.00	40.00	20.00
(2)	Frankie Baumholtz	40.00	16.00	8.00
(3)	Gus Bell	30.00	15.00	9.00
(4)	Billy Cox	40.00	16.00	8.00
(5)	Alvin Dark	30.00	15.00	9.00
(6)	Carl Erskine	75.00	30.00	15.00
(7)	Ferris Fain	40.00	16.00	8.00
(8)	Dee Fondy	30.00	15.00	9.00
(9)	Nelson Fox	85.00	35.00	17.50
(10)	Jim Gilliam	50.00	20.00	10.00
(11)	Jim Hegan	40.00	16.00	8.00
(12)	George Kell	85.00	42.50	21.25
(13)	Ted Kluszewski	65.00	25.00	13.00
(14)	Ralph Kiner	60.00	24.00	12.00
(15)	Harvey Kuenn	30.00	12.00	6.00
(16)	Bob Lemon	55.00	22.50	11.00
(17)	Sherman Lollar	30.00	15.00	9.00
(18)	Mickey Mantle	500.00	250.00	125.00
(19)	Billy Martin	65.00	25.00	13.00
(20)	Gil McDougald	55.00	22.50	11.00
(21)	Roy McMillan	30.00	15.00	9.00
(22)	Minnie Minoso	50.00	20.00	10.00
(23)	Stan Musial	300.00	150.00	75.00
(24)	Billy Pierce	40.00	16.00	8.00
(25)	Al Rosen	45.00	18.00	9.00
(26)	Hank Sauer	30.00	15.00	9.00
(27)	Red Schoendienst	75.00	30.00	15.00
(28)	Enos Slaughter	65.00	25.00	13.00
(29)	Duke Snider	200.00	100.00	50.00
(30)	Warren Spahn	65.00	25.00	13.00
(31)	Sammy White	30.00	15.00	9.00
(32)	Eddie Yost	30.00	12.00	6.00
(33)	Gus Zernial	30.00	12.00	6.00

1952 Red Man Tobacco

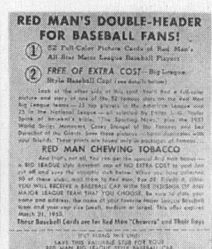

This was the first national set of tobacco cards produced since the golden days of tobacco sets in the early part of the century. There are 52 cards in the set, with 25 top players and one manager from each league. Player selection was made by editor J.G. Taylor Spink of The Sporting News. Cards measure 3-1/2" x 4", including a 1/2" tab at the bottom of each card. These tabs were redeemable for a free baseball cap from Red Man. Cards are harder to find with tabs intact, and thus more valuable in that form. Values quoted here are for cards with tabs. Cards with the tabs removed would be valued about 25-35 percent of the quoted figures. Card fronts are full-color paintings with biographical information inset in the portrait area. Card backs contain company advertising. Cards are numbered and dated only on the tabs. The 1952 Red Man cards can be found with either of two expiration dates on back, March 31 or June 1, 1953; neither commands a premium.

	NM	EX	VG
Complete Set, W/Tab (52):	10,000	4,000	2,000
Common Player, W/Tab:	100.00	40.00	20.00
Complete Set, No Tab (52):	2,250	550.00	275.00
Common Player, No Tab:	20.00	8.00	4.00

WITH TAB

1A	Casey Stengel	250.00	100.00	50.00
1N	Leo Durocher	200.00	80.00	40.00
2A	Roberto Avila	100.00	40.00	20.00
2N	Richie Ashburn	240.00	95.00	45.00
3A	Larry "Yogi" Berra	375.00	150.00	75.00
3N	Ewell Blackwell	120.00	45.00	25.00
4A	Gil Coan	100.00	40.00	20.00
4N	Cliff Chambers	100.00	40.00	20.00
5A	Dom DiMaggio	140.00	55.00	27.50
5N	Murry Dickson	100.00	40.00	20.00
6A	Larry Doby	215.00	85.00	45.00
6N	Sid Gordon	100.00	40.00	20.00
7A	Ferris Fain	100.00	40.00	20.00
7N	Granny Hamner	100.00	40.00	20.00
8A	Bob Feller	325.00	130.00	65.00
8N	Jim Hearn	100.00	40.00	20.00
9A	Nelson Fox	215.00	85.00	45.00
9N	Monte Irvin	215.00	85.00	45.00
10A	Johnny Groth	100.00	40.00	20.00
10N	Larry Jansen	100.00	40.00	20.00
11A	Jim Hegan	100.00	40.00	20.00
11N	Willie Jones	100.00	40.00	20.00
12A	Eddie Joost	100.00	40.00	20.00
12N	Ralph Kiner	215.00	85.00	45.00
13A	George Kell	215.00	85.00	45.00
13N	Whitey Lockman	100.00	40.00	20.00
14A	Gil McDougald	100.00	40.00	20.00
14N	Sal Maglie	100.00	40.00	20.00
15A	Orestes Minoso	100.00	40.00	20.00
15N	Willie Mays	600.00	240.00	120.00
16A	Bill Pierce	100.00	40.00	20.00
16N	Stan Musial	575.00	230.00	115.00
17A	Bob Porterfield	100.00	40.00	20.00
17N	Pee Wee Reese	340.00	135.00	65.00
18A	Eddie Robinson	100.00	40.00	20.00
18N	Robin Roberts	215.00	85.00	45.00
19A	Saul Rogovin	100.00	40.00	20.00
19N	Al Schoendienst	215.00	85.00	45.00
20A	Bobby Shantz	100.00	40.00	20.00
20N	Enos Slaughter	215.00	85.00	45.00
21A	Vern Stephens	100.00	40.00	20.00
21N	Duke Snider	275.00	110.00	55.00
22A	Vic Wertz	100.00	40.00	20.00
22N	Warren Spahn	215.00	85.00	45.00
23A	Ted Williams	1,800	725.00	360.00
23N	Eddie Stanky	100.00	40.00	20.00
24A	Early Wynn	215.00	85.00	45.00
24N	Bobby Thomson	100.00	40.00	20.00
25A	Eddie Yost	100.00	40.00	20.00
25N	Earl Torgeson	100.00	40.00	20.00
26A	Gus Zernial	100.00	40.00	20.00
26N	Wes Westrum	100.00	40.00	20.00

NO TAB

1A	Casey Stengel	45.00	18.00	9.00
1N	Leo Durocher	35.00	14.00	7.00
2A	Roberto Avila	20.00	8.00	4.00
2N	Richie Ashburn	55.00	22.00	11.00
3A	Larry "Yogi" Berra	85.00	35.00	17.50
3N	Ewell Blackwell	25.00	10.00	5.00
4A	Gil Coan	20.00	8.00	4.00
4N	Cliff Chambers	20.00	8.00	4.00
5A	Dom DiMaggio	30.00	12.00	6.00
5N	Murry Dickson	20.00	8.00	4.00
6A	Larry Doby	45.00	18.00	9.00
6N	Sid Gordon	20.00	8.00	4.00
7A	Ferris Fain	20.00	8.00	4.00
7N	Granny Hamner	20.00	8.00	4.00
8A	Bob Feller	80.00	32.00	16.00
8N	Jim Hearn	20.00	8.00	4.00
9A	Nelson Fox	50.00	20.00	10.00
9N	Monte Irvin	45.00	18.00	9.00
10A	Johnny Groth	20.00	8.00	4.00
10N	Larry Jansen	20.00	8.00	4.00
11A	Jim Hegan	20.00	8.00	4.00
11N	Willie Jones	20.00	8.00	4.00
12A	Eddie Joost	20.00	8.00	4.00
12N	Ralph Kiner	45.00	18.00	9.00
13A	George Kell	45.00	18.00	9.00
13N	Whitey Lockman	20.00	8.00	4.00
14A	Gil McDougald	25.00	10.00	5.00
14N	Sal Maglie	20.00	8.00	4.00
15A	Orestes Minoso	30.00	12.00	6.00
15N	Willie Mays	200.00	80.00	40.00
16A	Bill Pierce	20.00	8.00	4.00
16N	Stan Musial	175.00	70.00	35.00
17A	Bob Porterfield	20.00	8.00	4.00
17N	Pee Wee Reese	70.00	28.00	14.00
18A	Eddie Robinson	20.00	8.00	4.00
18N	Robin Roberts	45.00	18.00	9.00
19A	Saul Rogovin	20.00	8.00	4.00
19N	Al Schoendienst	45.00	18.00	9.00
20A	Bobby Shantz	20.00	8.00	4.00
20N	Enos Slaughter	45.00	18.00	9.00
21A	Vern Stephens	20.00	8.00	4.00
21N	Duke Snider	85.00	35.00	17.50
22A	Vic Wertz	20.00	8.00	4.00
22N	Warren Spahn	45.00	18.00	9.00
23A	Ted Williams	375.00	150.00	75.00
23N	Eddie Stanky	20.00	8.00	4.00
24A	Early Wynn	45.00	18.00	9.00
24N	Bobby Thomson	20.00	8.00	4.00
25A	Eddie Yost	20.00	8.00	4.00
25N	Earl Torgeson	20.00	8.00	4.00
26A	Gus Zernial	20.00	8.00	4.00
26N	Wes Westrum	20.00	8.00	4.00

1953 Red Man Tobacco

This was the chewing tobacco company's second annual set of 3-1/2" x 4" cards, including the tabs at the bottom of the cards. Formats for front and back are similar to the '52 edition. The 1953 Red Man cards, however, include card numbers within the player biographical section, and the card backs are headlined "New for '53." Once again, cards with intact tabs (which were redeemable for a free cap) are more valuable.

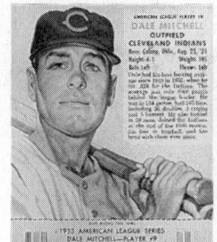

Prices below are for cards with tabs. Cards with tabs removed are worth about 25-35 percent of the stated values. Each league is represented by 25 players and a manager on the full-color cards, a total of 52. Values quoted here are for cards with tabs. Cards with the tabs removed would be valued about 35-40 percent of the quoted figures. The 1953 Red Man cards can be found with either of two expiration dates on back, March 31 or May 31, 1954; neither commands a premium.

	NM	EX	VG
Complete Set, W/Tab (52):	5,500	2,200	1,100
Common Player:	60.00	24.00	12.00
Complete Set, No Tab (52):	1,400	550.00	275.00
Common Player, No Tab:	12.50	5.00	2.50

WITH TAB

1A	Casey Stengel	150.00	60.00	30.00
1N	Charlie Dressen	75.00	30.00	15.00
2A	Hank Bauer	75.00	30.00	15.00
2N	Bobby Adams	60.00	24.00	12.00
3A	Larry "Yogi" Berra	300.00	120.00	60.00
3N	Richie Ashburn	125.00	50.00	25.00
4A	Walt Dropo	60.00	24.00	12.00
4N	Joe Black	100.00	40.00	20.00
5A	Nelson Fox	125.00	50.00	25.00
5N	Roy Campanella	300.00	120.00	60.00
6A	Jackie Jensen	75.00	30.00	15.00
6N	Ted Kluszewski	95.00	38.00	20.00
7A	Eddie Joost	60.00	24.00	12.00
7N	Whitey Lockman	60.00	24.00	12.00
8A	George Kell	125.00	50.00	25.00
8N	Sal Maglie	60.00	24.00	12.00
9A	Dale Mitchell	60.00	24.00	12.00
9N	Andy Pafko	60.00	24.00	12.00
10A	Phil Rizzuto	225.00	90.00	45.00
10N	Pee Wee Reese	250.00	100.00	50.00
11A	Eddie Robinson	60.00	24.00	12.00
11N	Robin Roberts	125.00	50.00	25.00
12A	Gene Woodling	70.00	28.00	14.00
12N	Red Schoendienst	125.00	50.00	25.00
13A	Gus Zernial	60.00	24.00	12.00
13N	Enos Slaughter	125.00	50.00	25.00
14A	Early Wynn	125.00	50.00	25.00
14N	Edwin "Duke" Snider	300.00	120.00	60.00
15A	Joe Dobson	60.00	24.00	12.00
15N	Ralph Kiner	125.00	50.00	25.00
16A	Billy Pierce	60.00	24.00	12.00
16N	Hank Sauer	60.00	24.00	12.00
17A	Bob Lemon	125.00	50.00	25.00
17N	Del Ennis	60.00	24.00	12.00
18A	Johnny Mize	145.00	60.00	30.00
18N	Granny Hamner	60.00	24.00	12.00
19A	Bob Porterfield	60.00	24.00	12.00
19N	Warren Spahn	145.00	60.00	30.00
20A	Bobby Shantz	60.00	24.00	12.00
20N	Wes Westrum	60.00	24.00	12.00
21A	"Mickey" Vernon	60.00	24.00	12.00
21N	Hoyt Wilhelm	125.00	50.00	25.00
22A	Dom DiMaggio	75.00	30.00	15.00
22N	Murry Dickson	60.00	24.00	12.00
23A	Gil McDougald	70.00	28.00	14.00
23N	Warren Hacker	60.00	24.00	12.00
24A	Al Rosen	70.00	28.00	14.00
24N	Gerry Staley	60.00	24.00	12.00
25A	Mel Parnell	60.00	24.00	12.00
25N	Bobby Thomson	60.00	24.00	12.00
26A	Roberto Avila	60.00	24.00	12.00
26N	Stan Musial	700.00	280.00	140.00

NO TAB

1A	Casey Stengel	35.00	14.00	7.00
1N	Charlie Dressen	17.50	7.00	3.50
2A	Hank Bauer	17.50	7.00	3.50
2N	Bobby Adams	12.50	5.00	2.50
3A	Larry "Yogi" Berra	65.00	26.00	13.00
3N	Richie Ashburn	40.00	16.00	8.00
4A	Walt Dropo	12.50	5.00	2.50
4N	Joe Black	20.00	8.00	4.00
5A	Nelson Fox	40.00	16.00	8.00
5N	Roy Campanella	65.00	26.00	13.00
6A	Jackie Jensen	20.00	8.00	4.00
6N	Ted Kluszewski	25.00	10.00	5.00
7A	Eddie Joost	12.50	5.00	2.50
7N	Whitey Lockman	12.50	5.00	2.50
8A	George Kell	40.00	16.00	8.00
8N	Sal Maglie	15.00	6.00	3.00
9A	Dale Mitchell	12.50	5.00	2.50
9N	Andy Pafko	12.50	5.00	2.50
10A	Phil Rizzuto	50.00	20.00	10.00
10N	Pee Wee Reese	60.00	24.00	12.00
11A	Eddie Robinson	12.50	5.00	2.50
11N	Robin Roberts	40.00	16.00	8.00
12A	Gene Woodling	15.00	6.00	3.00
12N	Red Schoendienst	40.00	16.00	8.00
13A	Gus Zernial	12.50	5.00	2.50
13N	Enos Slaughter	40.00	16.00	8.00
14A	Early Wynn	40.00	16.00	8.00
14N	Edwin "Duke" Snider	75.00	30.00	15.00
15A	Joe Dobson	12.50	5.00	2.50
15N	Ralph Kiner	40.00	16.00	8.00
16A	Billy Pierce	15.00	6.00	3.00
16N	Hank Sauer	12.50	5.00	2.50
17A	Bob Lemon	40.00	16.00	8.00
17N	Del Ennis	12.50	5.00	2.50
18A	Johnny Mize	40.00	16.00	8.00
18N	Granny Hamner	12.50	5.00	2.50
19A	Bob Porterfield	12.50	5.00	2.50
19N	Warren Spahn	45.00	18.00	9.00
20A	Bobby Shantz	12.50	5.00	2.50
20N	Wes Westrum	12.50	5.00	2.50
21A	"Mickey" Vernon	12.50	5.00	2.50
21N	Hoyt Wilhelm	35.00	14.00	7.00
22A	Dom DiMaggio	25.00	10.00	5.00
22N	Murry Dickson	12.50	5.00	2.50
23A	Gil McDougald	15.00	6.00	3.00
23N	Warren Hacker	12.50	5.00	2.50
24A	Al Rosen	17.50	7.00	3.50
24N	Gerry Staley	12.50	5.00	2.50
25A	Mel Parnell	12.50	5.00	2.50
25N	Bobby Thomson	12.50	5.00	2.50
26A	Roberto Avila	12.50	5.00	2.50
26N	Stan Musial	125.00	50.00	25.00

1954 Red Man Tobacco

 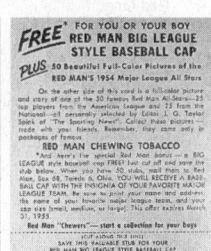

In 1954, the Red Man set eliminated managers from the set, and issued only 25 player cards for each league. There are, however, four variations which bring the total set size to 54 full-color cards. Two cards exist for Gus Bell and Enos Slaughter, while American Leaguers George Kell, Sam Mele and Dave Philley are each shown with two different teams. Complete set prices quoted below do not include the scarcer of the variation pairs. Cards measure 3-1/2" x 4" with tabs intact. Cards without tabs are worth about 25-35 percent of the values quoted below. Formats for the cards remain virtually unchanged, with card numbers included within the player information boxes as well as on the tabs. Cards can be found with either of two expiration dates on back, March 31 or May 31, 1955; neither commands a premium.

	NM	EX	VG
Complete Set, W/Tab (50):	4,000	1,600	800.00
Common Player, W/Tab:	45.00	18.00	9.00
Complete Set, No Tab (50):	1,400	550.00	275.00
Common Player, No Tab:	15.00	6.00	3.00

WITH TAB

1A	Bobby Avila	45.00	18.00	9.00
1N	Richie Ashburn	90.00	36.00	18.00
2A	Jim Busby	45.00	18.00	9.00
2N	Billy Cox	55.00	22.00	11.00
3A	Nelson Fox	90.00	36.00	18.00
3N	Del Crandall	45.00	18.00	9.00
4Aa	George Kell (Boston)	125.00	50.00	25.00
4Ab	George Kell (Chicago)	180.00	70.00	35.00
4N	Carl Erskine	60.00	24.00	12.00
5A	Sherman Lollar	45.00	18.00	9.00
5N	Monte Irvin	90.00	36.00	18.00
6Aa	Sam Mele (Baltimore)	90.00	36.00	18.00
6Ab	Sam Mele (Chicago)	110.00	44.00	22.00
6N	Ted Kluszewski	100.00	40.00	20.00
7A	Orestes Minoso	65.00	26.00	13.00
7N	Don Mueller	45.00	18.00	9.00
8A	Mel Parnell	45.00	18.00	9.00
8N	Andy Pafko	45.00	18.00	9.00
9Aa	Dave Philley (Cleveland)	75.00	30.00	15.00
9Ab	Dave Philley (Philadelphia)	145.00	60.00	30.00
9N	Del Rice	45.00	18.00	9.00
10A	Billy Pierce	45.00	18.00	9.00
10N	Al Schoendienst	90.00	36.00	18.00
11A	Jim Piersall	60.00	24.00	12.00
11N	Warren Spahn	100.00	40.00	20.00
12A	Al Rosen	50.00	20.00	10.00
12N	Curt Simmons	45.00	18.00	9.00
13A	"Mickey" Vernon	45.00	18.00	9.00
13N	Roy Campanella	215.00	85.00	45.00
14A	Sammy White	45.00	18.00	9.00
14N	Jim Gilliam	60.00	24.00	12.00
15A	Gene Woodling	60.00	24.00	12.00
15N	"Pee Wee" Reese	160.00	64.00	32.00
16A	Ed "Whitey" Ford	140.00	56.00	28.00
16N	Edwin "Duke" Snider	215.00	85.00	45.00
17A	Phil Rizzuto	140.00	56.00	28.00
17N	Rip Repulski	45.00	18.00	9.00
18A	Bob Porterfield	45.00	18.00	9.00
18N	Robin Roberts	90.00	36.00	18.00
19A	Al "Chico" Carrasquel	45.00	18.00	9.00
19Na	Enos Slaughter	215.00	85.00	45.00
19Nb	Gus Bell	190.00	75.00	35.00
20A	Larry "Yogi" Berra	200.00	80.00	40.00
20N	Johnny Logan	45.00	18.00	9.00
21A	Bob Lemon	90.00	36.00	18.00
21N	Johnny Antonelli	45.00	18.00	9.00
22A	Ferris Fain	45.00	18.00	9.00
22N	Gil Hodges	90.00	36.00	18.00
23A	Hank Bauer	50.00	20.00	10.00
23N	Eddie Mathews	100.00	40.00	20.00
24A	Jim Delsing	45.00	18.00	9.00
24N	Lew Burdette	45.00	18.00	9.00
25A	Gil McDougald	55.00	22.00	11.00
25N	Willie Mays	425.00	170.00	85.00

NO TAB

1A	Bobby Avila	15.00	6.00	3.00
1N	Richie Ashburn	35.00	14.00	7.00
2A	Jim Busby	15.00	6.00	3.00
2N	Billy Cox	20.00	8.00	4.00
3A	Nelson Fox	35.00	14.00	7.00
3N	Del Crandall	15.00	6.00	3.00
4Aa	George Kell (Boston)	50.00	20.00	10.00
4Ab	George Kell (Chicago)	65.00	26.00	13.00
4N	Carl Erskine	22.50	9.00	4.50
5A	Sherman Lollar	15.00	6.00	3.00
5N	Monte Irvin	35.00	14.00	7.00
6Aa	Sam Mele (Baltimore)	30.00	12.00	6.00
6Ab	Sam Mele (Chicago)	55.00	22.00	11.00
6N	Ted Kluszewski	30.00	12.00	6.00
7A	Orestes Minoso	25.00	10.00	5.00
7N	Don Mueller	15.00	6.00	3.00
8A	Mel Parnell	15.00	6.00	3.00
8N	Andy Pafko	15.00	6.00	3.00
9Aa	Dave Philley (Cleveland)	30.00	12.00	6.00
9Ab	Dave Philley (Philadelphia)	65.00	26.00	13.00
9N	Del Rice	15.00	6.00	3.00
10A	Billy Pierce	15.00	6.00	3.00
10N	Al Schoendienst	35.00	14.00	7.00
11A	Jim Piersall	20.00	8.00	4.00
11N	Warren Spahn	35.00	14.00	7.00
12A	Al Rosen	20.00	8.00	4.00
12N	Curt Simmons	15.00	6.00	3.00
13A	"Mickey" Vernon	15.00	6.00	3.00
13N	Roy Campanella	65.00	26.00	13.00
14A	Sammy White	15.00	6.00	3.00
14N	Jim Gilliam	22.50	9.00	4.50
15A	Gene Woodling	22.50	9.00	4.50
15N	"Pee Wee" Reese	55.00	22.00	11.00
16A	Ed "Whitey" Ford	45.00	18.00	9.00
16N	Edwin "Duke" Snider	65.00	26.00	13.00
17A	Phil Rizzuto	50.00	20.00	10.00
17N	Rip Repulski	15.00	6.00	3.00
18A	Bob Porterfield	15.00	6.00	3.00
18N	Robin Roberts	35.00	14.00	7.00
19A	Al "Chico" Carrasquel	20.00	8.00	4.00
19Na	Enos Slaughter	70.00	28.00	14.00
19Nb	Gus Bell	70.00	28.00	14.00
20A	Larry "Yogi" Berra	65.00	26.00	13.00
20N	Johnny Logan	15.00	6.00	3.00
21A	Bob Lemon	35.00	14.00	7.00
21N	Johnny Antonelli	15.00	6.00	3.00
22A	Ferris Fain	15.00	6.00	3.00
22N	Gil Hodges	35.00	14.00	7.00
23A	Hank Bauer	20.00	8.00	4.00
23N	Eddie Mathews	35.00	14.00	7.00
24A	Jim Delsing	15.00	6.00	3.00
24N	Lew Burdette	15.00	6.00	3.00
25A	Gil McDougald	20.00	8.00	4.00
25N	Willie Mays	130.00	55.00	25.00

1955 Red Man Tobacco

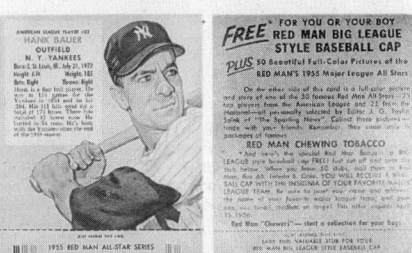

These 50 cards are quite similar to the 1954 edition, with card fronts virtually unchanged except for the data in the biographical box on the color picture area. This set of 3-1/2" x 4" cards includes 25 players from each league, with no known variations. As with all Red Man sets, those cards complete with the redeemable tabs are more valuable. Values quoted below are for cards with tabs. Cards with the tabs removed are worth about 25-35 percent of those figures. Each card can be found with two different expiration dates on back, April 15 or June 15, 1956; neither version commands a premium.

	NM	EX	VG
Complete Set, W/Tab (50):	3,750	1,500	750.00
Common Player, W/Tab:	60.00	24.00	12.00
Complete Set, No Tab (50):	900.00	360.00	180.00
Common Player, No Tab:	10.00	4.00	2.00

WITH TAB

1A	Ray Boone	60.00	24.00	12.00
1N	Richie Ashburn	95.00	38.00	19.00
2A	Jim Busby	60.00	24.00	12.00
2N	Del Crandall	60.00	24.00	12.00
3A	Ed "Whitey" Ford	125.00	50.00	25.00
3N	Gil Hodges	90.00	36.00	18.00
4A	Nelson Fox	90.00	36.00	18.00
4N	Brooks Lawrence	60.00	24.00	12.00
5A	Bob Grim	60.00	24.00	12.00
5N	Johnny Logan	60.00	24.00	12.00
6A	Jack Harshman	60.00	24.00	12.00
6N	Sal Maglie	60.00	24.00	12.00
7A	Jim Hegan	60.00	24.00	12.00
7N	Willie Mays	250.00	100.00	50.00
8A	Bob Lemon	90.00	36.00	18.00
8N	Don Mueller	60.00	24.00	12.00
9A	Irv Noren	60.00	24.00	12.00
9N	Bill Sarni	60.00	24.00	12.00
10A	Bob Porterfield	60.00	24.00	12.00
10N	Warren Spahn	90.00	36.00	18.00
11A	Al Rosen	75.00	30.00	15.00
11N	Henry Thompson	60.00	24.00	12.00
12A	"Mickey" Vernon	60.00	24.00	12.00
12N	Hoyt Wilhelm	90.00	36.00	18.00
13A	Vic Wertz	60.00	24.00	12.00

(second column top)

13N	Johnny Antonelli	60.00	24.00	12.00
14A	Early Wynn	90.00	36.00	18.00
14N	Carl Erskine	75.00	30.00	15.00
15A	Bobby Avila	60.00	24.00	12.00
15N	Granny Hamner	60.00	24.00	12.00
16A	Larry "Yogi" Berra	165.00	65.00	35.00
16N	Ted Kluszewski	75.00	30.00	15.00
17A	Joe Coleman	60.00	24.00	12.00
17N	Pee Wee Reese	125.00	50.00	25.00
18A	Larry Doby	90.00	36.00	18.00
18N	Al Schoendienst	90.00	36.00	18.00
19A	Jackie Jensen	65.00	26.00	13.00
19N	Duke Snider	165.00	65.00	35.00
20A	Pete Runnels	60.00	24.00	12.00
20N	Frank Thomas	60.00	24.00	12.00
21A	Jim Piersall	60.00	24.00	12.00
21N	Ray Jablonski	60.00	24.00	12.00
22A	Hank Bauer	65.00	26.00	13.00
22N	James "Dusty" Rhodes	60.00	24.00	12.00
23A	"Chico" Carrasquel	60.00	24.00	12.00
23N	Gus Bell	60.00	24.00	12.00
24A	Orestes Minoso	75.00	30.00	15.00
24N	Curt Simmons	60.00	24.00	12.00
25A	Sandy Consuegra	60.00	24.00	12.00
25N	Marvin Grissom	60.00	24.00	12.00

NO TAB

1A	Ray Boone	10.00	4.00	2.00
1N	Richie Ashburn	30.00	12.00	6.00
2A	Jim Busby	10.00	4.00	2.00
2N	Del Crandall	10.00	4.00	2.00
3A	Ed "Whitey" Ford	35.00	14.00	7.00
3N	Gil Hodges	30.00	12.00	6.00
4A	Nelson Fox	30.00	12.00	6.00
4N	Brooks Lawrence	10.00	4.00	2.00
5A	Bob Grim	10.00	4.00	2.00
5N	Johnny Logan	10.00	4.00	2.00
6A	Jack Harshman	10.00	4.00	2.00
6N	Sal Maglie	10.00	4.00	2.00
7A	Jim Hegan	10.00	4.00	2.00
7N	Willie Mays	100.00	40.00	20.00
8A	Bob Lemon	30.00	12.00	6.00
8N	Don Mueller	10.00	4.00	2.00
9A	Irv Noren	10.00	4.00	2.00
9N	Bill Sarni	10.00	4.00	2.00
10A	Bob Porterfield	10.00	4.00	2.00
10N	Warren Spahn	30.00	12.00	6.00
11A	Al Rosen	13.50	5.50	2.75
11N	Henry Thompson	10.00	4.00	2.00
12A	"Mickey" Vernon	10.00	4.00	2.00
12N	Hoyt Wilhelm	30.00	12.00	6.00
13A	Vic Wertz	10.00	4.00	2.00
13N	Johnny Antonelli	10.00	4.00	2.00
14A	Early Wynn	30.00	12.00	6.00
14N	Carl Erskine	15.00	6.00	3.00
15A	Bobby Avila	10.00	4.00	2.00
15N	Granny Hamner	10.00	4.00	2.00
16A	Larry "Yogi" Berra	50.00	20.00	10.00
16N	Ted Kluszewski	20.00	8.00	4.00
17A	Joe Coleman	10.00	4.00	2.00
17N	Pee Wee Reese	50.00	20.00	10.00
18A	Larry Doby	30.00	12.00	6.00
18N	Al Schoendienst	30.00	12.00	6.00
19A	Jackie Jensen	13.50	5.50	2.75
19N	Duke Snider	55.00	22.00	11.00
20A	Pete Runnels	10.00	4.00	2.00
20N	Frank Thomas	10.00	4.00	2.00
21A	Jim Piersall	13.50	5.50	2.75
21N	Ray Jablonski	10.00	4.00	2.00
22A	Hank Bauer	13.50	5.50	2.75
22N	James "Dusty" Rhodes	10.00	4.00	2.00
23A	"Chico" Carrasquel	10.00	4.00	2.00
23N	Gus Bell	10.00	4.00	2.00
24A	Orestes Minoso	15.00	6.00	3.00
24N	Curt Simmons	10.00	4.00	2.00
25A	Sandy Consuegra	10.00	4.00	2.00
25N	Marvin Grissom	10.00	4.00	2.00

1952-1954 Red Man Posters

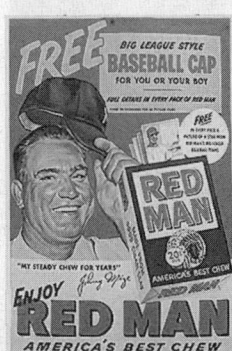

These colorful lithographed paper posters, 11" x 15-1/2", were intended as point-of-purchase displays to encourage sales of the chewing tobacco and offer a baseball cap in exchange for the tabs found on the bottom of each card. The posters were reproduced in 11" x 16" format on cardboard in the 1980s.

		NM	EX	VG
1952	Ralph Kiner (11" x 15")	200.00	100.00	60.00
1953	Enos Slaughter (11" x 15")	300.00	150.00	90.00
1954	Johnny Mize (12" x 15-1/2")	325.00	160.00	95.00

"1952-54" Red Man Posters

Some 30 years after the original 11" x 15-1/2" paper posters were used to advertise Red Man chewing tobacco and the

(third column top)

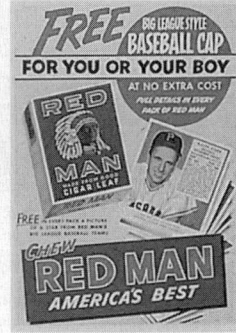

baseball cards and caps available as premiums, three of the pieces were reproduced. Posters which are printed on cardboard and in a 11" x 16" size are modern reproductions with only decorative, rather than collectible, value.

NO COLLECTOR VALUE
1952 Ralph Kiner
1953 Enos Slaughter
1954 Johnny Mize

1976 Redpath Sugar Expos

Among the more unusual baseball collectibles of the late 1970s are the Montreal Expos sugar packs produced by Redpath Sugar for distribution in Quebec. About 1-1/2" x 2-3/4" in size, the sugar packs feature color portraits of the players on front, along with bi-lingual personal information and a uniform number. Backs have a color team logo and career highlights. Uncut sheets or the packaging are known which indicate several players were double- or triple-printed. The checklist here is arranged by uniform number.

		NM	EX	VG
Complete Set (36):		75.00	37.00	22.00
Common Player:		2.00	1.00	.60
1	Osvaldo Jose Virgil	2.00	1.00	.60
5	Peter Mackanin, Jr.	2.00	1.00	.60
6	Karl Otto Kuehl	2.00	1.00	.60
8	Gary Edmund Carter	15.00	7.50	4.50
9	Barry Clifton Foote	2.00	1.00	.60
11	Jose Manuel Mangual	2.00	1.00	.60
14	Lawrence Eugene Doby	6.00	3.00	1.75
15	Larry Alton Parrish	2.00	1.00	.60
16	Michael Jorgensen	2.00	1.00	.60
17	Andre Thornton	4.00	2.00	1.25
18	Joseph Thomas Kerrigan	2.00	1.00	.60
19	Timothy John Foli (DP)	2.00	1.00	.60
20	James Lawrence Lyttle, Jr.	2.00	1.00	.60
21	Frederick John Scherman, Jr.	2.00	1.00	.60
22	Ellis Clarence Valentine	2.00	1.00	.60
26	Donald Joseph Stanhouse	2.00	1.00	.60
27	Dale Albert Murray	2.00	1.00	.60
31	Clayton Laws Kirby, Jr.	2.00	1.00	.60
33	Robert David Lang	2.00	1.00	.60
34	Jose Manuel Morales	2.00	1.00	.60
35	Woodrow Thompson Fryman	3.00	1.50	.90
36	Steven John Dunning	2.00	1.00	.60
37	Jerome Cardell White	2.00	1.00	.60
38	Jesus Maria Frias (Andujar)	2.00	1.00	.60
39	Daniel Dean Warthen	2.00	1.00	.60
40	Donald George Carrithers (3P)	2.00	1.00	.60
41	Ronald Jacques Piche	2.00	1.00	.60
43	James Edward Dwyer	2.00	1.00	.60
44	Jesus Rivera (Torres), Jr.	2.00	1.00	.60
45	Stephen Douglas Rogers (DP)	2.00	1.00	.60
46	Marion Danne Adair	2.00	1.00	.60
47	Wayne Allen Granger	2.00	1.00	.60
48	Lawrence Donald Bearnarth	2.00	1.00	.60
---	Roland Wayne Garrett	2.00	1.00	.60
---	Charles Gilbert Taylor	2.00	1.00	.60
---	Delbert Bernard Unser	2.00	1.00	.60

1977 Redpath Sugar Expos

One of the more obscure regional Canadian issues, this 30-player set features members of the Expos and was printed on sugar packets distributed in the Montreal area in 1977. The front of the packet features a color photo of the player with his name, uniform number, position, height and weight listed in both English and French. A line identifying Redpath Sugar appears alongside the photo. The backs display the Expos logo and brief player highlights (again printed in both French and English). The set has been seen in uncut sheets, revealing that the packets of Steve Rogers and David Cash, Jr. were double printed.

		NM	EX	VG
	Complete Set (30):	75.00	37.00	22.00
	Common Player:	1.50	.70	.45
1	Osvaldo Jose Virgil	1.50	.70	.45
2	James Thomas Brewer	1.50	.70	.45
3	James Barton Vernon	1.50	.70	.45
4	Chris Edward Speier	1.50	.70	.45
5	Peter Mackanin Jr.	1.50	.70	.45
6	William Frederick Gardner	1.50	.70	.45
8	Gary Edmund Carter	15.00	7.50	4.50
9	Barry Clifton Foote	1.50	.70	.45
10	Andre Dawson	6.00	3.00	1.75
11	Ronald Wayne Garrett	1.50	.70	.45
14	Samuel Elias Mejias	1.50	.70	.45
15	Larry Alton Parrish	2.00	1.00	.60
16	Michael Jorgensen	1.50	.70	.45
17	Ellis Clarence Valentine	1.50	.70	.45
18	Joseph Thomas Kerrigan	1.50	.70	.45
20	William Henry McEnaney	1.50	.70	.45
23	Richard Hirshfield Williams	2.00	1.00	.60
24	Atanasio Rigal Perez	3.00	1.50	.90
25	Delbert Bernard Unser	1.50	.70	.45
26	Donald Joseph Stanhouse	1.50	.70	.45
30	David Cash, Jr.	1.50	.70	.45
31	Jackie Gene Brown	1.50	.70	.45
34	Jose Manual Morales	1.50	.70	.45
35	Gerald Ellis Hannahs	1.50	.70	.45
38	Jesus Maria Frias (Andujar)	1.50	.70	.45
39	Daniel Dean Warthen	1.50	.70	.45
42	William Cecil Glenn Atkinson	1.50	.70	.45
45	Stephen Douglas Rogers	2.25	1.25	.70
48	Jeffrey Michael Terpko	1.50	.70	.45
49	Warren Livingston Cromartie	1.50	.70	.45

1886 Red Stocking Cigars

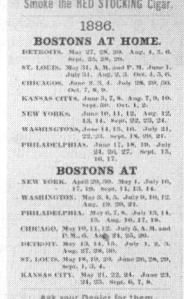

This set of Boston Red Stockings schedule cards was issued in 1886, and the three known cards measure 6-1/2" x 3-3/4". The cards were printed in black and red. One side carries the 1886 Boston schedule, while the other side features a full-length player drawing. Both sides include advertising for "Red Stocking" cigars. Only three different players are known.

		NM	EX	VG
	Complete Set (3):	55,000	27,500	16,500
	Common Player:	45,000	16,000	10,000
(1)	C.G. Buffington	45,000	16,000	10,000
(2)	Capt. John F. Morrill	45,000	16,000	10,000
(3)	Charles Radbourn	100,000	10,000	5,000

1972 Regent Glove Hang Tag

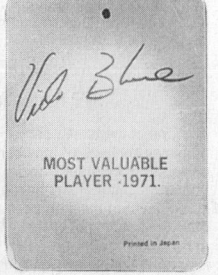

This 2-1/4" x 3" card was distributed as an attachment to baseball gloves sold at retail outlets. A hole punched at top allowed the card to be strung to the glove. Front has a blue background and black-and-white portrait photo of 1971 MVP Vida Blue. His facsimile autograph is on back.

	NM	EX	VG
Vida Blue	15.00	7.50	4.50

1964-68 Requena N.Y. Yankees Postcards

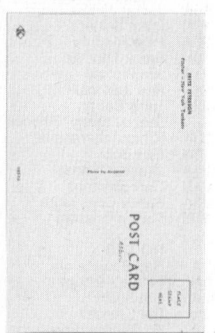

Over a period of several years in the 1960s a series of Yankee color player postcards was issued with the identifier "Photo by Requena." Similar in format, the 3-1/2" x 5-1/2" cards have borderless color photos on front. Except for facsimile autographs on some players' cards, there are no other front graphics. Backs are printed in dark green with player ID at upper-left, a "K"-within-diamond Kodachrome logo at bottom-left, a card number centered at bottom, the Requena line vertically at center and standard postcard markings at right.

		NM	EX	VG
	Complete Set (17):	300.00	150.00	90.00
	Common Player:	15.00	7.50	4.50
66443	Phil Linz	15.00	7.50	4.50
66880	Clete Boyer	15.00	7.50	4.50
66881	Jim Bouton	20.00	10.00	6.00
66882	Tom Tresh	20.00	10.00	6.00
66883	Joe Pepitone	20.00	10.00	6.00
66884	Tony Kubek	20.00	10.00	6.00
66885	Elston Howard	20.00	10.00	6.00
66886	Ralph Terry	15.00	7.50	4.50
66887	Bill Stafford	15.00	7.50	4.50
66888	Whitey Ford	30.00	15.00	9.00
66889	Bob Richardson	20.00	10.00	6.00
69891	Yogi Berra (Signature at top.)	30.00	15.00	9.00
69891	Yogi Berra (Signature at bottom.)	30.00	15.00	9.00
74284	John Blanchard	15.00	7.50	4.50
78909	Pedro Ramos	15.00	7.50	4.50
78910	Mel Stottlemyre	15.00	7.50	4.50
98553	Fritz Peterson	15.00	7.50	4.50
10146 1	Steve Barber	15.00	7.50	4.50

1964-66 Requena N.Y. Yankees 8x10s

Many of the same Yankees players and poses which appear in the standard (3-1/2" x 5-1/2") Requena postcard series can also be found, along with additional subjects, in an 8" x 10" blank-back format. The large format cards are listed here in alphabetical order.

		NM	EX	VG
	Complete Set (21):	300.00	150.00	90.00
	Common Player:	9.00	4.50	2.75
(1)	Yogi Berra	20.00	10.00	6.00
(2)	John Blanchard	9.00	4.50	2.75
(3)	Jim Bouton	12.50	6.25	3.75
(4)	Clete Boyer	9.00	4.50	2.75
(5)	Al Downing	9.00	4.50	2.75
(6)	Whitey Ford	20.00	10.00	6.00
(7)	Ralph Houk	9.00	4.50	2.75
(8)	Elston Howard	12.50	6.25	3.75
(9)	Tony Kubek	12.50	6.25	3.75
(10)	Phil Linz	9.00	4.50	2.75
(11)	Mickey Mantle	35.00	17.50	10.00
(12)	Mickey Mantle, Roger Maris	30.00	15.00	9.00
(13a)	Roger Maris (Facsimile autograph.)	25.00	12.50	7.50
(13b)	Roger Maris (No facsimile autograph.)	25.00	12.50	7.50
(14)	Joe Pepitone	12.50	6.25	3.75
(15)	Pedro Ramos	9.00	4.50	2.75
(16)	Bobby Richardson	12.50	6.25	3.75
(17)	Bill Stafford	9.00	4.50	2.75
(18)	Mel Stottlemyre	9.00	4.50	2.75
(19)	Ralph Terry	9.00	4.50	2.75
(20)	Tom Tresh	12.50	6.25	3.75

1953 R.G. Dun Cigars Milwaukee Braves

This series of counter cards was issued by a cigar company and features the radio schedule for the 1953 Braves. The cards are printed in red and black on cream cardboard and measure 10" x 9-1/2". They are unnumbered and blank-backed. The cards have vertical slits from bottom to about 1/3 the height of the cards, probably so they could be inserted into some type of counter display for Dun cigars. It's unknown how many players were represented in the series.

		NM	EX	VG
	Common Player:	35.00	17.50	10.00
(1)	Lew Burdette	35.00	17.50	10.00
(2)	Jim Wilson	35.00	17.50	10.00

1935 Rice-Stix (UM7)

This two-card set was distributed in packages of shirts from a St. Louis firm. Measuring about 2-1/4" x 3", the cards feature color painting of the pitchers on front, along with a facsimile autograph and photo credits. Backs have a short career summary and an ad for the issuer.

		NM	EX	VG
	Complete Set (2):	1,800	725.00	450.00
(1)	Dizzy Dean	1,200	475.00	300.00
(2)	Paul Dean	625.00	250.00	150.00

1927 Rinkeydink Stamps

These 1-1/4" x 1-1/2" pieces are not actually stamps, but rather are printed on newsprint with unrelated matter on back. The printing is in red, green and black and each stamp has a "denomination" of 2 in a baseball design at top. The "stamps" were featured in the heading of the "Winnie Winkle" comic strip in the Sunday funnies section of newspapers.

		NM	EX	VG
	Complete Set (10):	450.00	225.00	135.00
	Common Player:	30.00	15.00	9.00
(1)	Grover C. Alexander	40.00	20.00	12.00
(2)	Ty Cobb	75.00	37.50	22.00
(3)	Eddie Collins	30.00	15.00	9.00
(4)	Bucky Harris	30.00	15.00	9.00
(5)	Rogers Hornsby	40.00	20.00	12.00
(6)	Walter Johnson	50.00	25.00	15.00
(7)	George Kelly	30.00	15.00	9.00
(8)	Herb Pennock	30.00	15.00	9.00
(9)	Babe Ruth	100.00	50.00	30.00
(10)	Tris Speaker	40.00	20.00	12.00

1933 Rittenhouse Candy (E285)

Designed to resemble a set of playing cards, this set, issued circa 1933 by the Rittenhouse Candy Company of Philadelphia, carries the ACC designation E285 and is generally considered to be the last of the E-card issues. Each card measures 1-7/16" x 2-1/4" and features a small player photo in the center of the playing card design. Cards are known printed in red, orange, blue and green. The backs of the cards usually consist of just one large letter and were part of a promotion in which collectors were instructed to find enough different letters to spell "Rittenhouse Candy Co." Other backs explaining the contest and the prizes available were also issued, as were backs with numbers. Because it was designed as a deck of playing cards, the set is complete at 52 cards, featuring 46 different players (six are pictured on two cards each).

		NM	EX	VG
Complete Set (52):		9,000	3,600	1,800
Common Player:		100.00	40.00	20.00
(1)	Dick Bartell	100.00	40.00	20.00
(2)	Walter Berger	100.00	40.00	20.00
(3)	Max Bishop	100.00	40.00	20.00
(4)	James Bottomley	200.00	80.00	40.00
(5)	Fred Brickell	100.00	40.00	20.00
(6)	Sugar Cain	100.00	40.00	20.00
(7)	Ed. Cihocki	100.00	40.00	20.00
(8)	Phil Collins	100.00	40.00	20.00
(9)	Roger Cramer	100.00	40.00	20.00
(10)	Hughie Critz	100.00	40.00	20.00
(11)	Joe Cronin	200.00	80.00	40.00
(12)	Hazen (Kiki) Cuyler	200.00	80.00	40.00
(13)	Geo. Davis	100.00	40.00	20.00
(14)	Spud Davis	100.00	40.00	20.00
(15)	Jimmy Dykes	100.00	40.00	20.00
(16)	George Earnshaw	100.00	40.00	20.00
(17)	Jumbo Elliot	100.00	40.00	20.00
(18)	Lou Finney	100.00	40.00	20.00
(19)	Jimmy Foxx	275.00	110.00	55.00
(20)	Frankie Frisch (3 of Spades)	200.00	80.00	40.00
(21)	Frankie Frisch (7 of Spades)	200.00	80.00	40.00
(22)	Robert (Lefty) Grove	225.00	90.00	45.00
(23)	Mule Haas	100.00	40.00	20.00
(24)	Chick Hafey	200.00	80.00	40.00
(25)	Chas. Leo Hartnett	200.00	80.00	40.00
(26)	Babe Herman	110.00	45.00	25.00
(27)	Wm. Herman	200.00	80.00	40.00
(28)	Kid Higgins	100.00	40.00	20.00
(29)	Rogers Hornsby	235.00	95.00	45.00
(30)	Don Hurst (Jack of Diamonds)	100.00	40.00	20.00
(31)	Don Hurst (6 of Spades)	100.00	40.00	20.00
(32)	Chuck Klein	200.00	80.00	40.00
(33)	Leroy Mahaffey	100.00	40.00	20.00
(34)	Gus Mancuso	100.00	40.00	20.00
(35)	Rabbit McNair	100.00	40.00	20.00
(36)	Bing Miller	100.00	40.00	20.00
(37)	Frank (Lefty) O'Doul	115.00	45.00	25.00
(38)	Mel Ott	200.00	80.00	40.00
(39)	Babe Ruth (Ace of Spades)	1,000	400.00	200.00
(40)	Babe Ruth (King of Clubs)	1,000	400.00	200.00
(41)	Al Simmons	200.00	80.00	40.00
(42)	Bill Terry	200.00	80.00	40.00
(43)	Pie Traynor	200.00	80.00	40.00
(44)	Rube Wallberg (Walberg)	100.00	40.00	20.00
(45)	Lloyd Waner	200.00	80.00	40.00
(46)	Paul Waner	200.00	80.00	40.00
(47)	Lloyd Warner (Waner)	200.00	80.00	40.00
(48)	Paul Warner (Waner)	200.00	80.00	40.00
(49)	Pinkey Whitney	100.00	40.00	20.00
(50)	Dib Williams	100.00	40.00	20.00
(51)	Hack Wilson (9 of Spades)	200.00	80.00	40.00
(52)	Hack Wilson (9 of Clubs)	200.00	80.00	40.00

1948 R.K.O. Theaters Babe Ruth Premium

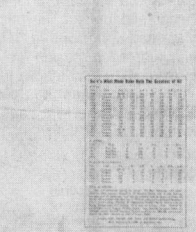

The attributed date is speculative, based on the similarity of the back copy to the 1948 American Association Babe Ruth memorial card. Apparently issued as a premium at moviehouses, this 8" x 9-1/2" picture is printed on thin cardboard. On front is a

sepia action photo of Ruth in the 1932 World Series. In the bottom border is the R.K.O. attribution. Back has biographical details, career highlights and complete major league stats.

	NM	EX	VG
Babe Ruth	400.00	200.00	125.00

1951 Roadmaster Photos

Black-and-white glossy photos of at least two major league stars were available as a premium from Roadmaster bicycles. Contemporary ads said that for a dime, an 8" x 10" photo could be obtained. The photos show the uniformed players seated on Roadmaster bikes inside a ballpark. There is a facsimile autograph on each. Backs are blank. It's possible other player photos may yet be seen.

		NM	EX	VG
(1)	Bob Feller	200.00	100.00	60.00
(2)	Pee Wee Reese	250.00	125.00	75.00

1947 Jackie Robinson Pins

In his historic debut season with the Brooklyn Dodgers, a number of celluloid pinback buttons featuring Jackie Robinson were issued. Ranging in size from about 1-1/4" to 1-3/4", the pins usually feature a black-and-white portrait photo at center and were originally sold with a silk pennant and plastic or pot-metal baseball charms attached.

		NM	EX	VG
(1)	Brooklyn 1947 Dodgers Congratulations "Jackie" (1-1/4" white background)	600.00	300.00	180.00
(2)	HI TEAMMATES (1-3/8", batting, blue background)	250.00	125.00	75.00
(3)	I'M FOR JACKIE (Blue type on white ball, no photo.)	200.00	100.00	60.00
(4)	I'm Rooting for Jackie Robinson (1-3/4", red border)	275.00	135.00	80.00
(5)	I'm Rooting for Jackie Robinson (1-1/4", white background)	350.00	175.00	100.00
(6)	I'm Rooting for Jackie Robinson (1-3/4", gray background)	300.00	150.00	90.00
(7)	JACKIE ROBINSON / DODGERS (1-3/4", b/w photo batting in pinstripes and plain cap)	400.00	200.00	125.00
(8)	JACKIE ROBINSON / DODGERS (1-1/4", white background)	200.00	100.00	60.00
(9)	Jackie Robinson Outstanding Rookie (3-3/8" white border)	200.00	100.00	60.00
(10)	19 Rookie of the Year 47 (1-3/4" red border)(Modern reproductions exist.)	325.00	160.00	100.00

1950s Jackie Robinson WNBC Photocard

This black-and-white 5-3/4" x 7-1/2" photocard pictures Robinson in his post-playing days career as a broadcaster for the NBC radio network's flagship station in New York.

	NM	EX	VG
Jackie Robinson	35.00	17.50	10.50

1911 Rochester Baking Philadelphia A's (D359)

The 1911 Rochester Baking set, an 18-card Philadelphia Athletics set, is among the scarcest of early 20th Century bakery issues. The set commemorates the Athletics' 1910 Championship season, and, except for pitcher Jack Coombs, the checklist includes nearly all key members of the club, including manager Connie Mack. The cards are the standard size for the era, 1-1/2" x 2-5/8". The front of each card features a player portrait set against a colored background. The player's name and the word "Athletics" appear at the bottom, while "World's Champions 1910" is printed along the top. The backs of the cards advertise the set as the "Athletics Series." Collectors should be aware that the same checklist was used for a similar Athletics set issued by Williams Baking and Cullivan's Firesdie tobacco (T208), and also that blank-backed versions are also known to exist, but these are classified as E104 cards in the American Card Catalog.

		NM	EX	VG
Complete Set (18):		85,000	35,000	17,000
Common Player:		3,200	1,600	800.00
(1)	Home Run Baker	7,000	3,500	1,750
(2)	Jack Barry	3,200	1,600	800.00
(3)	Chief Bender	7,000	3,500	1,750
(4)	Eddie Collins	7,000	3,500	1,750
(5)	Harry Davis	3,200	1,600	800.00
(6)	Jimmy Dygert	3,200	1,600	800.00
(7)	Topsy Hartsel	3,200	1,600	800.00
(8)	Harry Krause	3,200	1,600	800.00
(9)	Jack Lapp	3,200	1,600	800.00
(10)	Paddy Livingston	3,200	1,600	800.00
(11)	Bris Lord	3,200	1,600	800.00
(12)	Connie Mack	14,000	7,900	4,575
(13)	Cy Morgan	3,200	1,600	800.00
(14)	Danny Murphy	3,200	1,600	800.00
(15)	Rube Oldring	3,200	1,600	800.00
(16)	Eddie Plank	14,000	7,900	4,575
(17)	Amos Strunk	3,200	1,600	800.00
(18)	Ira Thomas	3,200	1,600	800.00

1955 Rodeo Meats Athletics

This set of 2-1/2" x 3-1/2" color cards was issued by a local meat company to commemorate the first year of the Athletics in Kansas City. There are 38 different players included in the set, with nine players known to apppear in two different variations for a total of 47 cards in the set. Most variations are in background colors, although Bobby Shantz is also listed incorrectly as "Schantz" on one variation. The cards are unnumbered, with the Rodeo logo and player name on the fronts, and an ad for a scrapbook album listed on the backs.

		NM	EX	VG
Complete Set (47):		12,500	6,250	3,750
Common Player:		225.00	110.00	45.00
Album:		550.00	275.00	125.00
(1)	Joe Astroth	225.00	110.00	45.00
(2)	Harold Bevan	275.00	135.00	55.00
(3)	Charles Bishop	275.00	135.00	55.00
(4)	Don Bollweg	275.00	135.00	55.00
(5)	Lou Boudreau	600.00	300.00	120.00
(6)	Cloyd Boyer (Blue background.)	275.00	135.00	55.00
(7)	Cloyd Boyer (Pink background.)	225.00	110.00	45.00

		NM	EX	VG
(8)	Ed Burtschy	275.00	135.00	55.00
(9)	Art Ceccarelli	225.00	110.00	45.00
(10)	Joe DeMaestri (Pea green background.)	275.00	135.00	55.00
(11)	Joe DeMaestri (Light green background.)	225.00	110.00	45.00
(12)	Art Ditmar	225.00	110.00	45.00
(13)	John Dixon	275.00	135.00	55.00
(14)	Jim Finigan	225.00	110.00	45.00
(15)	Marion Fricano	275.00	135.00	55.00
(16)	Tom Gorman	275.00	135.00	55.00
(17)	John Gray	225.00	110.00	45.00
(18)	Ray Herbert	225.00	110.00	45.00
(19)	Forest "Spook" Jacobs (Forrest)	275.00	135.00	55.00
(20)	Alex Kellner	275.00	135.00	55.00
(21)	Harry Kraft (Craft)	225.00	110.00	45.00
(22)	Jack Littrell	225.00	110.00	45.00
(23)	Hector Lopez	275.00	135.00	55.00
(24)	Oscar Melillo	225.00	110.00	45.00
(25)	Arnold Portocarrero (Purple background.)	275.00	135.00	55.00
(26)	Arnold Portocarrero (Gray background.)	225.00	110.00	45.00
(27)	Vic Power (Pink background.)	275.00	135.00	55.00
(28)	Vic Power (Yellow background.)	250.00	125.00	50.00
(29)	Vic Raschi	275.00	135.00	55.00
(30)	Bill Renna (Dark pink background.)	275.00	135.00	55.00
(31)	Bill Renna (Light pink background.)	225.00	110.00	45.00
(32)	Al Robertson	275.00	135.00	55.00
(33)	Johnny Sain	275.00	135.00	55.00
(34a)	Bobby Schantz (Incorrect spelling.)	900.00	450.00	180.00
(34b)	Bobby Shantz (Correct spelling.)	300.00	150.00	60.00
(35)	Wilmer Shantz (Orange background.)	275.00	135.00	55.00
(36)	Wilmer Shantz (Purple background.)	225.00	110.00	45.00
(37)	Harry Simpson	225.00	110.00	45.00
(38)	Enos Slaughter	650.00	325.00	130.00
(39)	Lou Sleater	225.00	110.00	45.00
(40)	George Susce	225.00	110.00	45.00
(41)	Bob Trice	275.00	135.00	55.00
(42)	Elmer Valo (Yellow background.)	275.00	135.00	55.00
(43)	Elmer Valo (Green background.)	225.00	110.00	45.00
(44)	Bill Wilson (Yellow background.)	275.00	135.00	55.00
(45)	Bill Wilson (Purple background.)	225.00	110.00	45.00
(46)	Gus Zernial	250.00	125.00	50.00

1956 Rodeo Meats Athletics

Gus Zernial

Rodeo Meats issued another Kansas City Athletics set in 1956, but this one was a much smaller 13-card set. The 2-1/2" x 3-1/2" cards are again unnumbered, with the player name and Rodeo logo on the fronts. Card backs feature some of the same graphics and copy as the 1955 cards, but the album offer is omitted. The full-color cards were only available in packages of Rodeo hot dogs.

		NM	EX	VG
Complete Set (12):		2,750	1,100	550.00
Common Player:		200.00	80.00	40.00
(1)	Joe Astroth	200.00	80.00	40.00
(2)	Lou Boudreau	350.00	140.00	70.00
(3)	Joe DeMaestri	200.00	80.00	40.00
(4)	Art Ditmar	200.00	80.00	40.00
(5)	Jim Finigan	200.00	80.00	40.00
(6)	Hector Lopez	200.00	80.00	40.00
(7)	Vic Power	200.00	80.00	40.00
(8)	Bobby Shantz	225.00	90.00	45.00
(9)	Harry Simpson	200.00	80.00	40.00
(10)	Enos Slaughter	475.00	190.00	95.00
(11)	Elmer Valo	200.00	80.00	40.00
(12)	Gus Zernial	200.00	80.00	40.00

1976 Rodeo Meats Athletics Commemorative

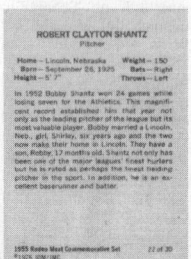

Bobby Shantz

This collectors' issue essentially reprints many of the 1955-56 Rodeo Meats cards in a 2-1/2" x 3-1/2" black-and-white format. Fronts have player photos, the Rodeo logo and the player name in the white border at bottom. Backs, instead of the original Rodeo ads, have player identification, biographical information and career summary, along with a reprint notice.

		NM	EX	VG
Complete Set (30):		20.00	10.00	6.00
Common Player:		2.00	1.00	.60
1	Header Card	.50	.25	.15
2	Checklist Card	.50	.25	.15
3	Joe Astroth	2.00	1.00	.60
4	Lou Boudreau	3.00	1.50	.90
5	Cloyd Boyer	2.00	1.00	.60
6	Art Ceccarelli	2.00	1.00	.60
7	Harry Craft	2.00	1.00	.60
8	Joe DeMaestri	2.00	1.00	.60
9	Art Ditmar	2.00	1.00	.60
10	Jim Finigan	2.00	1.00	.60
11	Ray Herbert	2.00	1.00	.60
12	Tom Gorman	2.00	1.00	.60
13	Alex Kellner	2.00	1.00	.60
14	Jack Littrell	2.00	1.00	.60
15	Hector Lopez	2.00	1.00	.60
16	Oscar Melillo	2.00	1.00	.60
17	Arnie Portocarrero	2.00	1.00	.60
18	Vic Power	2.50	1.25	.70
19	Vic Raschi	2.50	1.25	.70
20	Bill Renna	2.00	1.00	.60
21	Johnny Sain	2.50	1.25	.70
22	Bobby Shantz	2.50	1.25	.70
23	Wilmer Shantz	2.00	1.00	.60
24	Harry Simpson	2.50	1.25	.70
25	Enos Slaughter	4.00	2.00	1.25
26	Lou Sleator	2.00	1.00	.60
27	George Susce	2.00	1.00	.60
28	Elmer Valo	2.00	1.00	.60
29	Bill Wilson	2.00	1.00	.60
30	Gus Zernial	2.50	1.25	.70

1930s Rogers Peet Sport Album

18.— HERB PENNOCK

This is one of the scarcest multi-sport issues of the 1930s. It was the promotion of a New York-Boston chain of stores (boys' clothing?) in the form of a frequent customer program. Boys visiting the store with a parent could receive a set of four cards to be placed in a 14-page 4-1/2" x 7-1/4" album. Individual cards are about 1-7/8" x 2-1/2" and feature black-and-white photos with a white border. The athlete's name and card number are printed in the bottom border. Numbers correspond to spaces in the album. Only the "Baseball Stars" from the issue are checklisted here. Others include hockey, football, track, swimming, golf, tennis, aviation, etc.

		NM	EX	VG
Complete Set (44):		7,500	3,750	2,250
Complete Set in Album:		5,000	2,500	1,500
Common Sticker:		30.00	15.00	9.00
Album:		500.00	250.00	150.00
5	Dazzy Vance	225.00	110.00	65.00
13	Walter Johnson	650.00	325.00	195.00
16	Rogers Hornsby	450.00	225.00	135.00
18	Herb Pennock	225.00	110.00	65.00
28	Lou Gehrig	2,400	1,200	725.00
34	Ty Cobb	1,100	550.00	330.00
38	Tris Speaker	450.00	225.00	135.00
48	Babe Ruth	2,600	1,300	780.00

1960s Rogers Printing Co. Postcards

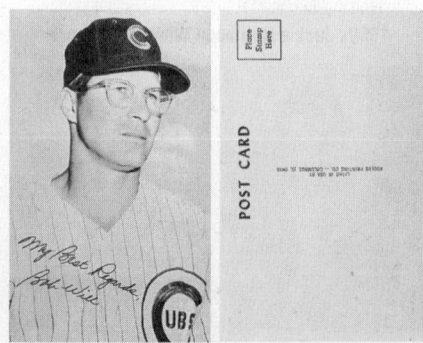

The extent to which this Columbus, Ohio, firm may have provided baseball players with postcards to answer fan mail requests is unknown. At present, only a single card is known, that of Bob Wills, who played his entire major league career (1957-63) with the Cubs. The card is printed in black-and-white on glossy stock in a 3-1/2" x 5-1/2" format. A facsimile autograph message is printed on front. Postcard-style backs have the imprint of the printer.

	NM	EX	VG
Bob Will	3.00	1.50	.90

1970 Rold Gold Pretzels

The 1970 Rold Gold Pretzels set of 15 cards honors the "Greatest Players Ever" in the first 100 years of baseball as chosen by the Baseball Writers of America. The cards, which measure 2-1/4" x 3-1/2" in size, feature a simulated 3-D effect. The set was re-released in 1972 by Kellogg's in packages of Danish-Go-Rounds. Rold Gold cards can be differentiated from the Kellogg's cards of 1972 by the 1970 copyright date found on the card reverse.

		NM	EX	VG
Complete Set (15):		50.00	25.00	15.00
Common Player:		2.00	1.00	.60
1	Walter Johnson	6.00	3.00	1.75
2	Rogers Hornsby	3.00	1.50	.90
3	John McGraw	2.00	1.00	.60
4	Mickey Cochrane	2.00	1.00	.60
5	George Sisler	2.00	1.00	.60
6	Babe Ruth ("Greatest Ever")	15.00	7.50	4.50
7	Robert "Lefty" Grove	2.00	1.00	.60
8	Harold "Pie" Traynor	2.00	1.00	.60
9	Honus Wagner	7.50	3.75	2.25
10	Eddie Collins	2.00	1.00	.60
11	Tris Speaker	3.00	1.50	.90
12	Cy Young	5.00	2.50	1.50
13	Lou Gehrig	10.00	5.00	3.00
14	Babe Ruth ("Greatest Right Fielder")	15.00	7.50	4.50
15	Ty Cobb	9.00	4.50	2.75

1908-1909 Rose Company Postcards

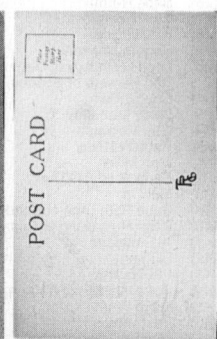

Among the most ornate and attractive baseball cards of the pre-1910 period is the set of postcards produced by The Rose Co., between 1908-09. The 3-1/2" x 5-1/2" cards feature a black-and-white player portrait photo at center, surrounded by an embossed round gold frame. The player's surname and (usually) team are in a white panel under the photo. The background of the card's front is green and includes crossed bats and a baseball, a diamond diagram and pictures of a fielder and batter. The postcard-format back is printed in black-and-white with a TRC logo at bottom-center. The unnumbered postcards are checklisted here alphabetically; including 11 minor league players from Scranton in the New York State League. It is possible future discoveries will be added to this checklist; gaps have been left in the numbering to accommodate them.

		NM	EX	VG
Common Player:		2,400	1,000	500.00
(1)	Ed Abbaticchio	2,400	1,000	500.00
(2)	Bill Abstein	2,400	1,000	500.00
(3)	Whitey Alperman	2,400	1,000	500.00
(4)	Nick Altrock	2,400	1,000	500.00
(5)	John Anderson	2,400	1,000	500.00
(6)	Shad Barry	2,400	1,000	500.00
(7)	Ginger Beaumont	2,400	1,000	500.00
(8)	Heinie Beckendorf	2,400	1,000	500.00
(9)	Fred Beebe	2,400	1,000	500.00

No.	Player			
(10)	Harry Bemis	2,400	1,000	500.00
(11)	Chief Bender	6,000	3,400	1,750
(12)	Bills	2,400	1,000	500.00
(13)	Joe Birmingham	2,400	1,000	500.00
(14)	Frank Bowerman	2,400	1,000	500.00
(15)	Bill Bradley	2,400	1,000	500.00
(16)	Kitty Bransfield	2,400	1,000	500.00
(17)	Roger Bresnahan	6,000	3,400	1,750
(18)	Al Bridwell	2,400	1,000	500.00
(19)	Buster Brown (Philadelphia) (Photo actually Mordecai Brown.)	2,400	1,000	500.00
(20)	Samuel Brown (Boston)	2,400	1,000	500.00
(21)	Mordecai Brown (Chicago)	6,000	3,400	1,750
(22)	Bobby Byrne	2,400	1,000	500.00
(23)	Howie Camnitz	2,400	1,000	500.00
(24)	Billy Campbell	2,400	1,000	500.00
(26)	Frank Chance	6,000	3,400	1,750
(27)	Hal Chase	2,400	1,000	500.00
(28)	Charlie Chech	2,400	1,000	500.00
(29)	Jack Chesbro	6,000	3,400	1,750
(30)	Fred Clarke (Pittsburg)	6,000	3,400	1,750
(31)	Nig Clarke (Cleveland)	2,400	1,000	500.00
(32)	Otis Clymer	2,400	1,000	500.00
(33a)	Andy Coakley (Cincinnati)	2,400	1,000	500.00
(33b)	Andy Coakley (No team name.)	2,400	1,000	500.00
(34)	Ty Cobb	24,000	13,600	7,000
(35)	Jimmy Collins	6,000	3,400	1,750
(36)	Wid Conroy	2,400	1,000	500.00
(37)	Jack Coombs	2,400	1,000	500.00
(38)	Frank Corridon	2,400	1,000	500.00
(39)	Bill Coughlin	2,400	1,000	500.00
(40)	Sam Crawford	6,000	3,400	1,750
(41a)	Lou Criger (Boston)	2,400	1,000	500.00
(41b)	Lou Criger (No team.)	2,400	1,000	500.00
(42)	Bill Dahlen	2,400	1,000	500.00
(43)	Harry Davis	2,400	1,000	500.00
(44)	Joe Delahanty (St. Louis)	2,400	1,000	500.00
(45)	Frank Delehanty (Delahanty) (Washington; team actually N.Y., A.L.)	2,400	1,000	500.00
(46)	Art Devlin	2,400	1,000	500.00
(47)	Mike Donlin	2,400	1,000	500.00
(48)	Jiggs Donohue (Donahue)	2,400	1,000	500.00
(49)	Wild Bill Donovan	2,400	1,000	500.00
(51)	Red Dooin	2,400	1,000	500.00
(52)	Mickey Doolan	2,400	1,000	500.00
(53)	Larry Doyle	2,400	1,000	500.00
(54)	Jimmy Dygert	2,400	1,000	500.00
(55)	Kid Elberfeld	2,400	1,000	500.00
(56)	Eley	2,400	1,000	500.00
(57)	Johnny Evers	6,000	3,400	1,750
(58)	Bob Ewing	2,400	1,000	500.00
(59)	George Ferguson	2,400	1,000	500.00
(60)	Hobe Ferris	2,400	1,000	500.00
(61)	Jerry Freeman	2,400	1,000	500.00
(62)	Bob Ganley	2,400	1,000	500.00
(63)	John Ganzel	2,400	1,000	500.00
(64)	Doc Gessler	2,400	1,000	500.00
(65)	George Gibson	2,400	1,000	500.00
(66)	Billy Gilbert	2,400	1,000	500.00
(67)	Fred Glade	2,400	1,000	500.00
(68)	Ralph Glaze	2,400	1,000	500.00
(69)	Graham	2,400	1,000	500.00
(70)	Eddie Grant	2,400	1,000	500.00
(71)	Groh	2,400	1,000	500.00
(72)	Charley Hale (Hall)	2,400	1,000	500.00
(73)	Halligan	2,400	1,000	500.00
(74)	Topsy Hartsel	2,400	1,000	500.00
(75)	Charlie Hemphill	2,400	1,000	500.00
(76)	Bill Hinchman	2,400	1,000	500.00
(77)	Art Hoelskoetter	2,400	1,000	500.00
(78)	Danny Hoffman	2,400	1,000	500.00
(79)	Solly Hofmann	2,400	1,000	500.00
(80)	Houser	2,400	1,000	500.00
(81)	Harry Howell	2,400	1,000	500.00
(82)	Miller Huggins	6,000	3,400	1,750
(83)	Rudy Hulswitt	2,400	1,000	500.00
(84)	John Hummel	2,400	1,000	500.00
(85a)	Frank Isbel (Isbell)(Chicago)	2,400	1,000	500.00
(85b)	Frank Isbel (Isbell) (No team.)	2,400	1,000	500.00
(86)	Walter Johnson	12,000	6,800	3,500
(87)	Fielder Jones (Chicago)	2,400	1,000	500.00
(88)	Tom Jones (St. Louis)	2,400	1,000	500.00
(89)	Tim Jordan	2,400	1,000	500.00
(90)	Addie Joss	12,000	6,800	3,500
(91)	Johnny Kane	2,400	1,000	500.00
(92)	Ed Karger	2,400	1,000	500.00
(93)	Wee Willie Keeler	6,000	3,400	1,750
(94)	Kellogg	2,400	1,000	500.00
(95)	Ed Killian	2,400	1,000	500.00
(96)	Malachi Kittredge (Kittridge)	2,400	1,000	500.00
(97)	Red Kleinow	2,400	1,000	500.00
(98)	Johnny Kling	2,400	1,000	500.00
(99)	Otto Knabe	2,400	1,000	500.00
(101)	John Knight	2,400	1,000	500.00
(102)	Ed Konetchy	2,400	1,000	500.00
(103)	Nap Lajoie	12,000	6,800	3,500
(104)	Frank LaPorte	2,400	1,000	500.00
(105)	Tommy Leach	2,400	1,000	500.00
(106)	Glenn Leibhardt (Liebhardt)	2,400	1,000	500.00
(107)	Phil Lewis	2,400	1,000	500.00
(108)	Vive Lindamann (Lindaman)	2,400	1,000	500.00
(109)	Hans Lobert	2,400	1,000	500.00
(110)	Harry Lord	2,400	1,000	500.00
(111)	Harry Lumley	2,400	1,000	500.00
(112)	Johnny Lush	2,400	1,000	500.00
(113)	Nick Maddox	2,400	1,000	500.00
(114)	Sherry Magee	2,400	1,000	500.00
(115)	Billy Maloney	2,400	1,000	500.00
(116)	Christy Mathewson	12,000	6,800	3,500
(117)	George McBride	2,400	1,000	500.00
(118)	Joe McGinnity	6,000	3,400	1,750
(119)	Stoney McGlynn	2,400	1,000	500.00
(120)	Harry McIntyre (McIntire)(Brooklyn)	2,400	1,000	500.00
(121)	Matty McIntyre (Detroit)	2,400	1,000	500.00
(122)	Larry McLean	2,400	1,000	500.00
(123)	George McQuillen (McQuillan)	2,400	1,000	500.00
(124)	Clyde Milan	2,400	1,000	500.00
(126)	Mike Mitchell	2,400	1,000	500.00
(127)	Moran	2,400	1,000	500.00
(128)	Mike Mowrey	2,400	1,000	500.00
(129)	George Mullin	2,400	1,000	500.00
(130)	Danny Murphy	2,400	1,000	500.00
(131)	J.J. Murray	2,400	1,000	500.00
(132)	Doc Newton	2,400	1,000	500.00
(133)	Simon Nicholls	2,400	1,000	500.00
(134)	Harry Niles	2,400	1,000	500.00
(135)	Rebel Oakes	2,400	1,000	500.00
(136)	Rube Oldring	2,400	1,000	500.00
(137)	Charley O'Leary	2,400	1,000	500.00
(138)	Patsy O'Rourke	2,400	1,000	500.00
(139)	Al Orth	2,400	1,000	800.00
(140)	Fred Osborne (Osborn)	2,400	1,000	500.00
(141)	Orval Overall	2,400	1,000	500.00
(142)	Freddy Parent	2,400	1,000	500.00
(143)	George Paskert	2,400	1,000	500.00
(144)	Case Patten	2,400	1,000	500.00
(145)	Deacon Phillippi (Phillippe)	2,400	1,000	500.00
(146)	Eddie Plank	12,000	6,800	3,500
(147)	Jack Powell	2,400	1,000	500.00
(148)	Tex Pruiett	2,400	1,000	500.00
(149)	Ed Reulbach	2,400	1,000	500.00
(151)	Bob Rhoades (Rhoads)	2,400	1,000	500.00
(152)	Claude Ritchey	2,400	1,000	500.00
(153)	Claude Rossman	2,400	1,000	500.00
(154)	Nap Rucker	2,400	1,000	500.00
(155)	Germany Schaefer	2,400	1,000	500.00
(156)	George Schlei	2,400	1,000	500.00
(157)	Boss Schmidt	2,400	1,000	500.00
(158)	Ossie Schreck	2,400	1,000	500.00
(159)	Wildfire Schulte	2,400	1,000	500.00
(160)	Schultz	2,400	1,000	500.00
(161)	Socks Seybold	2,400	1,000	500.00
(162)	Cy Seymour	2,400	1,000	500.00
(163)	Spike Shannon	2,400	1,000	500.00
(164)	Jimmy Sheckard	2,400	1,000	500.00
(165)	Tommy Sheehan	2,400	1,000	500.00
(166)	Bill Shipke	2,400	1,000	500.00
(167)	Jimmy Slagle	2,400	1,000	500.00
(168)	Charlie Smith (Chicago)	2,400	1,000	500.00
(169)	Frank Smith (Washington)	2,400	1,000	500.00
(170)	Bob Spade	2,400	1,000	500.00
(171)	Tully Sparks	2,400	1,000	500.00
(172)	Tris Speaker	6,000	3,400	1,750
(173)	Tubby Spencer	2,400	1,000	500.00
(174)	Jake Stahl	2,400	1,000	500.00
(176)	Steele	2,400	1,000	500.00
(177)	Harry Steinfeldt	2,400	1,000	500.00
(178)	George Stone	2,400	1,000	500.00
(179)	George Stovall	2,400	1,000	500.00
(180)	Billy Sullivan	2,400	1,000	500.00
(181)	Ed Summers	2,400	1,000	500.00
(182)	Bill Sweeney	2,400	1,000	500.00
(183)	Lee Tannehill	2,400	1,000	500.00
(184)	Dummy Taylor	2,400	1,000	500.00
(185)	Fred Tenney	2,400	1,000	500.00
(186)	Ira Thomas (No team.)	2,400	1,000	500.00
(187)	Roy Thomas (Pittsburg)	2,400	1,000	500.00
(188)	Jack Thoney	2,400	1,000	500.00
(189)	Joe Tinker	6,000	3,400	1,750
(190)	John Titus	2,400	1,000	500.00
(191)	Terry Turner	2,400	1,000	500.00
(192)	Bob Unglaub	2,400	1,000	500.00
(193)	Rube Waddell	6,000	3,400	1,750
(194)	Heinie Wagner (Boston)	2,400	1,000	500.00
(195)	Honus Wagner (Pittsburg)	24,000	13,600	7,000
(196)	Ed Walsh	6,000	3,400	1,750
(197)	Jack Warner	2,400	1,000	500.00
(198a)	Jake Weimer (Cincinnati)	2,400	1,000	500.00
(198b)	Jake Weimer (No team.)	2,400	1,000	500.00
(199)	Doc White	2,400	1,000	500.00
(201)	Jimmy Williams	2,400	1,000	500.00
(202)	Chief Wilson	2,400	1,000	500.00
(203)	Hooks Wiltse	2,400	1,000	500.00
(204)	George Winter	2,400	1,000	500.00
(205)	Cy Young (Boston)	12,000	6,800	3,500
(206)	Harley Young (Pittsburg)	2,400	1,000	500.00

1905 Rotograph Postcards

Only New York players have been seen on this series of 3-1/4" x 5-3/8" black-and-white or blue-and-white duotone postcards. Cards have player portrait photos with a white strip at bottom identifying the player; a "Rotograph / Series" notation is at left. Backs have typical postcard markings. This checklist may not be complete. The set was listed in the American Card Catalog under the number PC782.

		NM	EX	VG
Common Player:		800.00	400.00	250.00
(1)	Geo. Brown (Browne)	800.00	400.00	250.00
(2)	J.D. Chesbro	1,000	500.00	300.00
(3)	Wm. F. Dahlen	800.00	400.00	250.00
(4)	Clark Griffill (Griffith)	1,350	675.00	405.00
(5)	Joseph McGinnity	1,000	500.00	300.00
(6)	John McGraw	1,500	750.00	450.00
(7)	A. Puttmann	800.00	400.00	250.00
(8)	Luther Taylor	1,250	625.00	375.00

1977 Jim Rowe 4-on-1 Exhibits

This collectors' edition set harkens back to the four-player cards issued in the 1930s by Exhibit Supply Co. The 1977 version is printed in black on yellow in a 3-1/4" x 5-1/2" format. Backs are blank. Each of the four player photos on front is identified by name. The cards are checklisted here in order of team name.

		NM	EX	VG
Complete Set (16):		90.00	45.00	27.00
Common Card:		5.00	2.50	1.50
(1)	Boston Braves (Al Lopez, Rabbit Maranville, Warren Spahn, Casey Stengel)	5.00	2.50	1.50
(2)	Boston Red Sox (Joe Cronin, Herb Pennock, Babe Ruth, Ted Williams)	15.00	7.50	4.50
(3)	Brooklyn Dodgers (Max Carey, Burleigh Grimes, Joe Medwick, Dazzy Vance)	5.00	2.50	1.50
(4)	Chicago Cubs (Kiki Cuyler, Gabby Hartnett, Billy Herman, Freddy Lindstrom)	5.00	2.50	1.50
(5)	Chicago White Sox (Luke Appling, Red Faber, Ted Lyons, Red Ruffing)	5.00	2.50	1.50
(6)	Cincinnati Reds (Chick Hafey, George Kelly, Bill McKechnie, Edd Roush)	5.00	2.50	1.50
(7)	Cleveland Indians (Earl Averill, Lou Boudreau, Bob Feller, Bob Lemon)	5.00	2.50	1.50
(8)	Detroit Tigers (Ty Cobb, Charlie Gehringer, Goose Goslin, Hank Greenberg)	11.00	5.50	3.25
(9)	New York Giants (Dave Bancroft, Carl Hubbell, Mel Ott, Bill Terry)	5.00	2.50	1.50
(10)	New York Yankees (Bill Dickey, Joe DiMaggio, Lou Gehrig, Lefty Gomez)	12.00	6.00	3.50
(11)	Philadelphia Athletics (Mickey Cochrane, Eddie Collins, Lefty Grove, Al Simmons)	5.00	2.50	1.50
(12)	Philadelphia Phillies (Grover Alexander, Jimmie Foxx, Eppa Rixey, Robin Roberts)	5.00	2.50	1.50
(13)	Pittsburgh Pirates (Pie Traynor, Honus Wagner, Lloyd Waner, Paul Waner)	6.00	3.00	1.75
(14)	St. Louis Browns (Jim Bottomley, Earle Combs, Rogers Hornsby, George Sisler)	5.00	2.50	1.50
(15)	St. Louis Cardinals (Dizzy Dean, Frankie Frisch, Jesse Haines, Stan Musial)	5.00	2.50	1.50
(16)	Washington Senators (Bucky Harris, Walter Johnson, Heinie Manush, Sam Rice)	6.00	3.00	1.75

1977 Jim Rowe 1929 Cubs Postcards

Originally retailed for $3 per set, these collector-issue postcards feature on front borderless black-and-white photos in 3-1/2" x 5-7/16" format. Backs are standard Kodak postcard style, with no mention of the issuer. The player name is usually found penned at top.

		NM	EX	VG
Complete Set (13):		30.00	20.00	12.00
Common Player:		3.00	1.50	.90
(1)	Guy Bush	3.00	1.50	.90
(2)	Kiki Cuyler	3.00	1.50	.90
(3)	Woody English	3.00	1.50	.90
(4)	Charlie Grimm	3.00	1.50	.90
(5)	Gabby Hartnett	3.00	1.50	.90

		NM	EX	VG
(6)	Rogers Hornsby	3.00	1.50	.90
(7)	Pat Malone	3.00	1.50	.90
(8)	Norman McMillan	3.00	1.50	.90
(9)	Charlie Root	3.00	1.50	.90
(10)	Riggs Stephenson	3.00	1.50	.90
(11)	Zach Taylor	3.00	1.50	.90
(12)	Hack Wilson	3.00	1.50	.90
(13)	Team photo	3.00	1.50	.90

1977 Jim Rowe 1956 Braves Postcards

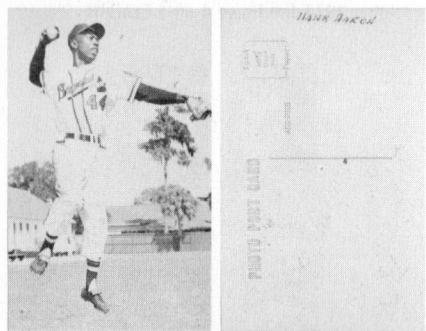

Originally retailed for $4 per set, these collector-issue postcards feature on front borderless black-and-white photos in 3-1/2" x 5-7/16" format. Backs are standard Kodak postcard style, with no mention of the issuer. The player name is usually found penned at top.

		NM	EX	VG
Complete Set (16):		35.00	17.50	10.50
Common Player:		3.00	1.50	.90
(1)	Hank Aaron	4.00	2.00	1.25
(2)	Joe Adcock	3.00	1.50	.90
(3)	Bill Bruton	3.00	1.50	.90
(4)	Bob Buhl	3.00	1.50	.90
(5)	Lew Burdette	3.00	1.50	.90
(6)	Gene Conley	3.00	1.50	.90
(7)	Del Crandall	3.00	1.50	.90
(8)	Charlie Grimm	3.00	1.50	.90
(9)	Fred Haney	3.00	1.50	.90
(10)	Joey Jay	3.00	1.50	.90
(11)	Johnny Logan	3.00	1.50	.90
(12)	Chet Nichols	3.00	1.50	.90
(13)	Danny O'Connell	3.00	1.50	.90
(14)	Andy Pafko	3.00	1.50	.90
(15)	Warren Spahn	3.00	1.50	.90
(16)	Bobby Thomson	3.00	1.50	.90

1978 Royal Crown Cola Iron-Ons

These iron-on color transfers were available in team strips of five players for 50 cents and six bottle cap liners. Because they were licensed only by the Players' Association, and not MLB, the approximately 4-1/4" x 6-1/4" transfers do not show team logos or nicknames.

		NM	EX	VG
Complete Set (130):		750.00	375.00	225.00
Common Player:		6.00	3.00	1.75
	Atlanta Strip	25.00	12.50	7.50
(1)	Jeff Burroughs	6.00	3.00	1.75
(2)	Gary Matthews	6.00	3.00	1.75
(3)	Phil Niekro	7.50	3.75	2.25
(4)	Biff Pocoroba	6.00	3.00	1.75
(5)	Dick Ruthven	6.00	3.00	1.75
	Baltimore Strip	50.00	25.00	15.00
(6)	Al Bumbry	6.00	3.00	1.75
(7)	Lee May	6.00	3.00	1.75
(8)	Eddie Murray	30.00	15.00	9.00
(9)	Jim Palmer	15.00	7.50	4.50
(10)	Ken Singleton	6.00	3.00	1.75
	Boston Strip	40.00	20.00	12.00
(11)	Bill Campbell	6.00	3.00	1.75
(12)	Fred Lynn	6.00	3.00	1.75
(13)	Jim Rice	7.50	3.75	2.25
(14)	George Scott	6.00	3.00	1.75
(15)	Carl Yastrzemski	25.00	12.50	7.50
	California Strip	75.00	37.50	22.50
(16)	Dave Chalk	6.00	3.00	1.75
(17)	Bobby Grich	6.00	3.00	1.75
(18)	Joe Rudi	6.00	3.00	1.75
(19)	Nolan Ryan	60.00	30.00	18.00
(20)	Frank Tanana	6.00	3.00	1.75

		NM	EX	VG
	Chicago (Cubs) Strip	30.00	15.00	9.00
(21)	Bill Buckner	6.00	3.00	1.75
(22)	Dave Kingman	6.00	3.00	1.75
(23)	Steve Ontiveros	6.00	3.00	1.75
(24)	Bruce Sutter	7.50	3.75	2.25
(25)	Manny Trillo	6.00	3.00	1.75
	Chicago (White Sox) Strip	25.00	12.50	7.50
(26)	Ron Blomberg	6.00	3.00	1.75
(27)	Bobby Bonds	6.00	3.00	1.75
(28)	Ralph Garr	6.00	3.00	1.75
(29)	Jorge Orta	6.00	3.00	1.75
(30)	Eric Soderholm	6.00	3.00	1.75
	Cincinnati Strip			
(31)	Johnny Bench	15.00	7.50	4.50
(32)	Unknown	.00	.00	.00
(33)	Joe Morgan	15.00	7.50	4.50
(34)	Unknown			
(35)	Pete Rose	40.00	20.00	12.00
	Cleveland Strip	25.00	12.50	7.50
(36)	Buddy Bell	6.00	3.00	1.75
(37)	Wayne Garland	6.00	3.00	1.75
(38)	Johnny Grubb	6.00	3.00	1.75
(39)	Rick Manning	6.00	3.00	1.75
(40)	Andre Thornton	6.00	3.00	1.75
	Detroit Strip	25.00	12.50	7.50
(41)	Mark Fidrych	6.00	3.00	1.75
(42)	John Hiller	6.00	3.00	1.75
(43)	Ron LeFlore	6.00	3.00	1.75
(44)	Milt May	6.00	3.00	1.75
(45)	Jason Thompson	6.00	3.00	1.75
	Houston Strip	25.00	12.50	7.50
(46)	Enos Cabell	6.00	3.00	1.75
(47)	Cesar Cedeno	6.00	3.00	1.75
(48)	Joe Ferguson	6.00	3.00	1.75
(49)	J.R. Richard	6.00	3.00	1.75
(50)	Bobby Watson	6.00	3.00	1.75
	Kansas City Strip	45.00	22.50	13.50
(51)	George Brett	30.00	15.00	9.00
(52)	Al Cowens	6.00	3.00	1.75
(53)	Hal McRae	6.00	3.00	1.75
(54)	Amos Otis	6.00	3.00	1.75
(55)	Fred Patek	6.00	3.00	1.75
	Los Angeles Strip	30.00	15.00	9.00
(56)	Ron Cey	6.00	3.00	1.75
(57)	Steve Garvey	7.50	3.75	2.25
(58)	Tommy John	6.00	3.00	1.75
(59)	Bill Russell	6.00	3.00	1.75
(60)	Don Sutton	7.50	3.75	2.25
	Milwaukee Strip	30.00	15.00	9.00
(61)	Sal Bando	6.00	3.00	1.75
(62)	Ray Fosse	6.00	3.00	1.75
(63)	Larry Hisle	6.00	3.00	1.75
(64)	Sixto Lezcano	6.00	3.00	1.75
(65)	Robin Yount	15.00	7.50	4.50
	Minnesota Strip	30.00	15.00	9.00
(66)	Rod Carew	15.00	7.50	4.50
(67)	Dan Ford	6.00	3.00	1.75
(68)	Dave Goltz	6.00	3.00	1.75
(69)	Roy Smalley	6.00	3.00	1.75
(70)	Butch Wynegar	6.00	3.00	1.75
	Montreal Strip	30.00	15.00	9.00
(71)	Dave Cash	6.00	3.00	1.75
(72)	Andre Dawson	7.50	3.75	2.25
(73)	Tony Perez	7.50	3.75	2.25
(74)	Steve Rogers	6.00	3.00	1.75
(75)	Ellis Valentine	6.00	3.00	1.75
	New York (Mets) Strip	25.00	12.50	7.50
(76)	Steve Henderson	6.00	3.00	1.75
(77)	Jerry Koosman	6.00	3.00	1.75
(78)	Elliott Maddox	6.00	3.00	1.75
(79)	Willie Montanez	6.00	3.00	1.75
(80)	Lenny Randle	6.00	3.00	1.75
	New York (Yankees) Strip	30.00	15.00	9.00
(81)	Sparky Lyle	6.00	3.00	1.75
(82)	Thurman Munson	7.50	3.75	2.25
(83)	Lou Piniella	6.00	3.00	1.75
(84)	Willie Randolph	6.00	3.00	1.75
(85)	Mickey Rivers	6.00	3.00	1.75
	Oakland Strip	25.00	12.50	7.50
(86)	Wayne Gross	6.00	3.00	1.75
(87)	Rick Langford	6.00	3.00	1.75
(88)	Bill North	6.00	3.00	1.75
(89)	Mitchell Page	6.00	3.00	1.75
(90)	Gary Thomasson	6.00	3.00	1.75
	Philadelphia Strip	60.00	30.00	18.00
(91)	Larry Bowa	6.00	3.00	1.75
(92)	Steve Carlton	15.00	7.50	4.50
(93)	Greg Luzinski	6.00	3.00	1.75
(94)	Garry Maddox	6.00	3.00	1.75
(95)	Mike Schmidt	35.00	17.50	10.50
	Pittsburgh Strip	30.00	15.00	9.00
(96)	John Candelaria	6.00	3.00	1.75
(97)	Dave Parker	6.00	3.00	1.75
(98)	Bill Robinson	6.00	3.00	1.75
(99)	Willie Stargell	15.00	7.50	4.50
(100)	Rennie Stennett	6.00	3.00	1.75
	San Diego Strip	35.00	17.50	10.00
(101)	Rollie Fingers	7.50	3.75	2.25
(102)	Oscar Gamble	6.00	3.00	1.75
(103)	Randy Jones	6.00	3.00	1.75
(104)	Gene Tenace	6.00	3.00	1.75
(105)	Dave Winfield	15.00	7.50	4.50
	San Francisco Strip	30.00	15.00	9.00
(106)	Vida Blue	6.00	3.00	1.75
(107)	Gary Lavelle	6.00	3.00	1.75
(108)	Bill Madlock	6.00	3.00	1.75
(109)	Willie McCovey	15.00	7.50	4.50
(110)	John Montefusco	6.00	3.00	1.75
	Seattle Strip	25.00	12.50	7.50
(111)	Bruce Bochte	6.00	3.00	1.75
(112)	Ruppert Jones	6.00	3.00	1.75
(113)	Dan Meyer	6.00	3.00	1.75
(114)	Lee Stanton	6.00	3.00	1.75
(115)	Bill Stein	6.00	3.00	1.75
	St. Louis Strip	30.00	15.00	9.00
(116)	Lou Brock	15.00	7.50	4.50
(117)	Bob Forsch	6.00	3.00	1.75
(118)	Ken Reitz	6.00	3.00	1.75

		NM	EX	VG
(119)	Ted Simmons	6.00	3.00	1.75
(120)	Garry Templeton	6.00	3.00	1.75
	Texas Strip	25.00	12.50	7.50
(121)	Mike Hargrove	6.00	3.00	1.75
(122)	Toby Harrah	6.00	3.00	1.75
(123)	Jon Matlack	6.00	3.00	1.75
(124)	Jim Sundberg	6.00	3.00	1.75
(125)	Richie Zisk	6.00	3.00	1.75
	Toronto Strip	25.00	12.50	7.50
(126)	Doug Ault	6.00	3.00	1.75
(127)	Bob Bailor	6.00	3.00	1.75
(128)	Jerry Garvin	6.00	3.00	1.75
(129)	Roy Howell	6.00	3.00	1.75
(130)	Al Woods	6.00	3.00	1.75

1950 Royal Desserts

This set was issued one per box on the backs of various Royal Dessert products over a period of three years. The basic set contains 24 players, however a number of variations create the much higher total for the set. In 1950, Royal issued cards with two different tints - black and white with red, or blue and white with red. Over the next two years, various sentences of the cards' biographies were updated; up to three times in some cases. Some players from the set left the majors after 1950 and others were apparently never updated, but the 23 biography updates that do exist, added to the original 24 cards issued in 1950, give the set a total of 47 cards. The 2-5/8" x 3-1/4" cards are blank-backed with personal and playing biographies alongside the card front photos. Some sample cards can be found with advertising for the desserts on back; they are valued at about double regular card prices. A comb-bound album with seven pages to hold 14 cards was also issued in a 3-1/4" x 3-3/8" format with "Royal Stars" and a crown logo printed in red on white.

		NM	EX	VG
Common Player:		125.00	55.00	25.00
Album:		200.00	90.00	40.00
1a	Stan Musial (2nd paragraph begins "Musial's 207...")	525.00	235.00	100.00
1b	Stan Musial (2nd paragraph begins "Musial batted...")	525.00	235.00	100.00
2a	Pee Wee Reese (2nd paragraph begins "Pee Wee's...)	330.00	150.00	65.00
2b	Pee Wee Reese (2nd paragraph begins "Captain...")	330.00	150.00	65.00
2c	Pee Wee Reese (Ad card.)	330.00	150.00	65.00
3a	George Kell (2nd paragraph ends "...in 1945, '46.")	200.00	90.00	40.00
3b	George Kell (2nd paragraph ends "...two base hits, 56.")	200.00	90.00	40.00
3c	George Kell (Ad card.)	200.00	90.00	40.00
4a	Dom DiMaggio (2nd paragraph ends "...during 1947.")	165.00	75.00	35.00
4b	Dom DiMaggio (2nd paragraph ends "...with 11.")	165.00	75.00	35.00
5a	Warren Spahn (2nd paragraph ends "...shutouts 7.")	265.00	120.00	55.00
5b	Warren Spahn (2nd paragraph ends "...with 191.")	265.00	120.00	55.00
6a	Andy Pafko (2nd paragraph ends "...7 games.")	125.00	56.00	25.00
6b	Andy Pafko (2nd paragraph ends "...National League.")	125.00	55.00	25.00
6c	Andy Pafko (2nd paragraph ends "...weighs 190.")	125.00	55.00	25.00
7a	Andy Seminick (2nd paragraph ends "...as outfield.")	125.00	55.00	25.00
7b	Andy Seminick (2nd paragraph ends "...since 1916.")	125.00	55.00	25.00
7c	Andy Seminick (2nd paragraph ends "...in the outfield.")	125.00	55.00	25.00
7d	Andy Seminick (2nd paragraph ends "...right handed.")	125.00	55.00	25.00
8a	Lou Brissie (2nd paragraph ends "...when pitching.")	125.00	55.00	25.00
8b	Lou Brissie (2nd paragraph ends "...weighs 215.")	125.00	55.00	25.00
9a	Ewell Blackwell (2nd paragraph begins "Despite recent illness...")	145.00	65.00	30.00
9b	Ewell Blackwell (2nd paragraph begins "Blackwell's...")	145.00	65.00	30.00

		NM	EX	VG
10a	Bobby Thomson (2nd paragraph begins "In 1949...")	165.00	75.00	35.00
10b	Bobby Thomson (2nd paragraph begins "Thomson is...")	165.00	75.00	35.00
11a	Phil Rizzuto (2nd paragraph ends "...one 1942 game.")	330.00	150.00	65.00
11b	Phil Rizzuto (2nd paragraph ends "...Most Valuable Player.")	330.00	150.00	65.00
12	Tommy Henrich	155.00	70.00	30.00
13	Joe Gordon	125.00	55.00	25.00
14a	Ray Scarborough (Senators)	125.00	55.00	25.00
14b	Ray Scarborough (White Sox, 2nd paragraph ends "...military service.")	125.00	55.00	25.00
14c	Ray Scarborough (White Sox, 2nd paragraph ends "...the season.")	125.00	55.00	25.00
14d	Ray Scarborough (Red Sox)	125.00	55.00	25.00
15a	Stan Rojek (Pirates)	125.00	55.00	25.00
15b	Stan Rojek (Browns)	125.00	55.00	25.00
16	Luke Appling	180.00	80.00	35.00
17	Willard Marshall	125.00	55.00	25.00
18	Alvin Dark	125.00	55.00	25.00
19a	Dick Sisler (2nd paragraph ends "...service record.")	125.00	55.00	25.00
19b	Dick Sisler (2nd paragraph ends "...National League flag.")	125.00	55.00	25.00
19c	Dick Sisler (2nd paragraph ends "...Nov. 2, 1920.")	125.00	55.00	25.00
19d	Dick Sisler (2nd paragraph ends "...from '46 to '48.")	125.00	55.00	25.00
20a	Johnny Ostrowski (White Sox)	125.00	55.00	25.00
20b	Johnny Ostrowski (Senators)	125.00	55.00	25.00
21a	Virgil Trucks (2nd paragraph ends "...in military service.")	125.00	55.00	25.00
21b	Virgil Trucks (2nd paragraph ends "...that year.")	125.00	55.00	25.00
21c	Virgil Trucks (2nd paragraph ends "...for military service.")	125.00	55.00	25.00
22	Eddie Robinson	125.00	55.00	25.00
23	Nanny Fernandez	125.00	55.00	25.00
24	Ferris Fain	125.00	55.00	25.00

1952 Royal Desserts

This set, issued as a premium by Royal Desserts in 1952, consists of 16 unnumbered black and white cards, each measuring 5" x 7". The cards include the inscription "To A Royal Fan" along with the player's facsimile autograph. Backs are blank.

		NM	EX	VG
Complete Set (16):		1,400	625.00	275.00
Common Player:		55.00	25.00	10.00
(1)	Ewell Blackwell	55.00	25.00	10.00
(2)	Leland V. Brissie Jr.	55.00	25.00	10.00
(3)	Alvin Dark	55.00	25.00	10.00
(4)	Dom DiMaggio	100.00	45.00	20.00
(5)	Ferris Fain	55.00	25.00	10.00
(6)	George Kell	100.00	45.00	20.00
(7)	Stan Musial	280.00	125.00	55.00
(8)	Andy Pafko	55.00	25.00	10.00
(9)	Pee Wee Reese	175.00	80.00	35.00
(10)	Phil Rizzuto	160.00	70.00	30.00
(11)	Eddie Robinson	55.00	25.00	10.00
(12)	Ray Scarborough	55.00	25.00	10.00
(13)	Andy Seminick	55.00	25.00	10.00
(14)	Dick Sisler	55.00	25.00	10.00
(15)	Warren Spahn	140.00	65.00	25.00
(16)	Bobby Thomson	80.00	35.00	15.00

1920 Babe Ruth "Headin' Home"

This was one of several series of promotional cards issued to advertise the Bambino's starring role in the 1920 silent film, "Headin' Home." The black-and-white cards measure about 1-1/2" x 2-7/16". They feature borderless photos with the three-line caption: BABE RUTH / IN / "HEADIN' HOME." The cards are frequently found miscut with a portion of another card showing at one or more of the edges. Backs may be blank or carry the advertising of a local theater.

		NM	EX	VG
Complete Set (6):		16,000	8,000	4,750
Common Card:		3,000	1,500	900.00
(1)	Babe Ruth (Bat at shoulder, crotch-to-cap.)	3,000	1,500	900.00
(2)	Babe Ruth (Bat extended to his right.)	3,000	1,500	900.00
(3)	Babe Ruth (Bat on shoulder, full-length.)	3,000	1,500	900.00
(4)	Babe Ruth (Follow-through, bat head-high.)	3,000	1,500	900.00
(5)	Babe Ruth (Follow-through, bat below waist.)	3,000	1,500	900.00
(6)	Babe Ruth (Horizontal card, holding bat.)	3,000	1,500	900.00

1920 Babe Ruth "Headin' Home" Theater Cards

 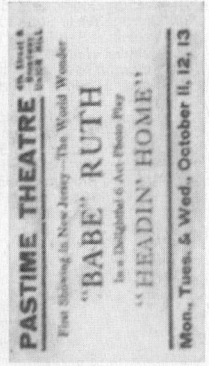

To promote the showing of "Headin' Home," a silent movie starring Babe Ruth, theaters had these cards printed up with details of show dates. Fronts of the 1-3/4" x 3-1/4" cards have a sepia photo of Ruth swinging the bat. On back is an advertisement from a local theater. This is one of the first cards ever to picture Ruth as a N.Y. Yankee.

	NM	EX	VG
Babe Ruth (Both hands on bat.)	2,750	1,375	825.00
Babe Ruth (One hand on bat.)	2,750	1,375	825.00

1920 Babe Ruth "Headin' Home" (Tex Rickard)

Taking advantage of the Babe's enormous popularity in the pinstripes of his new team, he was given a starring role in a 1920 silent movie titled "Headin' Home." To promote the flick, a small set of cards was issued. The 1-7/8" x 3-1/4" black-and-white cards have posed photos of Ruth on front. Dropped out in white in the lower portion of the photo is his name and movie title. Backs have an ad for the movie (some cards are known with blank backs, as well). Tex Rickard was the Ebbets Field announcer for the Brooklyn Dodgers for over 30 years.

		NM	EX	VG
Common Card:		5,000	2,500	1,500
(1)	Babe Ruth (Bat on shoulder, crotch to cap.)	5,000	2,500	1,500
(2)	Babe Ruth (Bat on shoulder, full-length.)	5,000	2,500	1,500
(3)	Babe Ruth (Batting follow-through.)	5,000	2,500	1,500

1920s Babe Ruth Postcard

There is no indication of publisher or specific date of issue on this standard-size, typically marked black-and-white photo postcard which pictures the Babe in street clothes informally posed with a cane chair. The number "210" near the bottom of the photo indicates it was part of a series. The horizontal divided back has typical postcard markings.

	NM	EX	VG
210 Babe Ruth	750.00	375.00	225.00

1920s Babe Ruth Underwear Premium Photo

While the product itself and the boxes and display pieces are collectibles in their own right, among the scarcest pieces associated with the Babe Ruth brand underwear is this approximately 8" x 10" premium photo which was apparently only included in some forms of packaging. The blank-back photo shows a buff Babe in the product and has a facsimile autograph on his right bicep.

	NM	EX	VG
Babe Ruth	500.00	250.00	150.00

1927 "Babe Comes Home" Strip Cards (R94)

This strip card set of unknown scope (at least 75 known) was cataloged as "Movie Stars and Scenes (R94)" in the American Card Catalog. At least two of the cards depict Babe Ruth as "Babe Dugan" in scenes from his silent film. Cards are nominally about 2-7/8" x 2-5/16" and can be found printed in black-and-white or as red, blue or green duotones. The name of the movie is printed in white at bottom. Backs and blank.

	NM	EX	VG
Babe Ruth (In suit w/police.)	1,350	675.00	400.00
Babe Ruth (In uniform, locker room.)	1,350	675.00	400.00

1928 Babe Ruth Home Run Candy Club Membership Card

 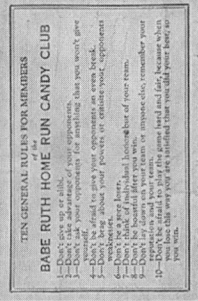

In conjunction with his candy bar, Ruth created the "Babe Ruth Home Run Candy Club," and issued this membership card. Front has a black-and-white portrait photo. Back of the 2-3/4" x 4" card has 10 rules of sportsmanship for members. The card folds open to reveal a membership certificate with a facsimile autograph.

	NM	EX	VG
Babe Ruth	2,500	1,250	750.00

1928 George Ruth Candy Co.

This circa 1928 issue features sepia-toned photos of Babe Ruth. According to the back of the cards, it was issued by the Geo. H. Ruth Candy Co. Cards measure 1-7/8" x 4" and picture Ruth during a 1924 promotional West Coast tour and in scenes from the movie "Babe Comes Home." The cards are numbered and include photo captions at the bottom. The

② "BABE" RUTH
Knocked out 60 Home
Runs in 1927.
His Candy Helped Him.

backs of most cards contain an offer to exchange the six cards for an autographed baseball, which may explain their scarcity today. Cards have been seen with the address to mail for exchange as Cleveland and as San Francisco. Cards can also be found with blank backs. This issue was deceptively counterfeited in the early 21st Century.

		NM	EX	VG
Complete Set (6):		7,000	3,150	1,400
Common Card:		1,250	650.00	300.00
Wrapper:		3,500	2,000	1,250
1	"Babe" Ruth ("King of them all...")	1,250	650.00	300.00
2	"Babe" Ruth ("Knocked out 60 Home Runs...")	1,250	650.00	300.00
3	"Babe" Ruth ("The only player...")	1,250	650.00	300.00
4	"Babe" Ruth ("The Popular Bambino...")	1,250	650.00	300.00
5	"Babe" Ruth ("A favorite with the Kiddies...")	1,250	650.00	300.00
6	"Babe" Ruth ("The King of Swat...")	1,250	650.00	300.00

1948 Babe Ruth Memorial Pin

Likely issued following Ruth's death in 1948, this 1-3/4" celluloid pinback has a black-and-white photo of Ruth swinging a bat on a black background with his name in capital letters in a white arc below.

	NM	EX	VG
Babe Ruth	300.00	150.00	90.00

1936 R311 Glossy Finish

The cards in this 28-card set, which was available as a premium in 1936, measure 6" x 8" and were printed on a glossy cardboard. The photos are either black and white or sepia-toned and include a facsimile autograph. The unnumbered set includes individual players and team photos. The Boston Red Sox team card can be found in two varieties; one shows the sky above the building on the card's right side, while the other does not. Some of the cards are scarcer than others in the set and command a premium. Babe Ruth is featured on the Boston Braves team card.

		NM	EX	VG
Complete Set (27):		3,750	1,850	1,100
Common Player:		60.00	30.00	18.00
(1)	Earl Averill	100.00	50.00	30.00
(2)	James L. "Jim" Bottomley	100.00	50.00	30.00
(3)	Gordon S. "Mickey" Cochrane	100.00	50.00	30.00
(4)	Joe Cronin	100.00	50.00	30.00
(5)	Jerome "Dizzy" Dean	150.00	75.00	45.00
(6)	Jimmy Dykes	60.00	30.00	18.00
(7)	Jimmy Foxx	125.00	65.00	35.00
(8)	Frankie Frisch	100.00	50.00	30.00
(9)	Henry "Hank" Greenberg	120.00	60.00	35.00
(10)	Mel Harder (SP)	120.00	60.00	35.00
(11)	Pepper Martin (SP)	225.00	110.00	65.00
(12)	Lynwood "Schoolboy" Rowe (SP)	120.00	60.00	35.00
(13)	William "Bill" Terry	100.00	50.00	30.00
(14)	Harold "Pie" Traynor	100.00	50.00	30.00
(15)	Amer. League All-Stars - 1935	275.00	135.00	80.00
(16)	American League Pennant Winners - 1934 (Detroit Tigers)	125.00	65.00	35.00
(17)	Boston Braves - 1935	300.00	150.00	90.00
(18a)	Boston Red Sox (Sky visible above building at right.)	100.00	50.00	30.00
(18b)	Boston Red Sox (No sky visible.)	180.00	90.00	55.00
(19)	Brooklyn Dodgers - 1935 (SP)	225.00	110.00	65.00
(20)	Chicago White Sox - 1935	100.00	50.00	30.00
(21)	Columbus Red Birds (1934 Pennant Winners of American Association)(SP)	150.00	75.00	45.00
(22)	National League All-Stars - 1935	180.00	90.00	55.00
(23)	National League Champions - 1935 (Chicago Cubs)	100.00	50.00	30.00
(24)	New York Yankees - 1935	180.00	90.00	55.00
(25)	Pittsburgh Pirates - 1935 (SP)	200.00	100.00	60.00
(26)	St. Louis Browns - 1935	100.00	50.00	30.00
(27)	The World Champions, 1934 (St. Louis Cardinals)	100.00	50.00	30.00

1936 R311 Leather Finish

This set of 15 unnumbered cards, issued as a premium in 1936, is distinctive because of its uneven, leather-like surface. The cards measure 6" x 8" and display a facsimile autograph on the black and white photo surrounded by a plain border. The cards are unnumbered and include individual player photos, multiplayer photos and team photos of the 1935 pennant winners.

		NM	EX	VG
Complete Set (15):		2,750	1,325	825.00
Common Player:		90.00	45.00	25.00
(1)	Frank Crosetti, Joe DiMaggio, Tony Lazzeri	825.00	410.00	245.00
(2)	Paul Derringer	90.00	45.00	25.00
(3)	Wes Ferrell	90.00	45.00	25.00
(4)	Jimmy (Jimmie) Foxx	180.00	90.00	55.00
(5)	Charlie Gehringer	165.00	80.00	50.00
(6)	Mel Harder	90.00	45.00	25.00
(7)	Gabby Hartnett	165.00	80.00	50.00
(8)	Rogers Hornsby	190.00	95.00	55.00
(9)	Connie Mack	165.00	80.00	50.00
(10)	Van Mungo	90.00	45.00	25.00
(11)	Steve O'Neill	90.00	45.00	25.00
(12)	Charles Ruffing	165.00	80.00	50.00
(13)	Arky Vaughan, Honus Wagner	245.00	120.00	75.00
(14)	American League Pennant Winners - 1935 (Detroit Tigers)	165.00	80.00	50.00
(15)	National League Pennant Winners - 1935 (Chicago Cubs)	165.00	80.00	50.00

1936 R312

Gordon Cochrane

The 50 cards in this set of 4" x 5-3/8" point-of-purchase premiums are black-and-white photos that have been tinted in soft pastel colors. The set includes 25 individual player portraits, 14 multi-player cards and 11 action photos. Six of the action photos include facsimile autographs, while the other five have printed legends. The Allen card is scarcer than the others in the set.

		NM	EX	VG
Complete Set (50):		8,500	4,250	2,500
Common Player:		90.00	35.00	20.00
(1)	John Thomas Allen	90.00	35.00	20.00
(2)	Nick Altrock, Al Schact	140.00	55.00	35.00
(3)	Ollie Bejma, Rolly Hemsley	90.00	35.00	20.00
(4)	Les Bell, Zeke Bonura	90.00	35.00	20.00
(5)	Cy Blanton	90.00	35.00	20.00
(6)	Cliff Bolton, Earl Whitehill	90.00	35.00	20.00
(7)	Frenchy Bordagaray, George Earnshaw	90.00	35.00	20.00
(8)	Mace Brown	90.00	35.00	20.00
(9)	Dolph Camilli	90.00	35.00	20.00
(10)	Phil Cavaretta (Cavarretta), Frank Demaree, Augie Galan, Stan Hack, Gabby Hartnett, Billy Herman, Billy Jurges, Chuck Klein, Fred Lindstrom	185.00	75.00	45.00
(11)	Phil Cavaretta (Cavarretta), Stan Hack, Billy Herman, Billy Jurges	185.00	75.00	45.00
(12)	Gordon Cochrane	185.00	75.00	45.00
(13)	Jim Collins, Stan Hack	90.00	35.00	20.00
(14)	Rip Collins	90.00	35.00	20.00
(15)	Joe Cronin, Buckey Harris (Bucky)	125.00	50.00	30.00
(16)	Alvin Crowder	90.00	35.00	20.00
(17)	Kiki Cuyler	185.00	75.00	45.00
(18)	Kiki Cuyler, Tris Speaker, Danny Taylor	225.00	90.00	55.00
(19)	"Bill" Dickey	185.00	75.00	45.00
(20)	Joe DiMagio (DiMaggio)	2,200	850.00	550.00
(21)	"Chas." Dressen	90.00	35.00	20.00
(22)	Rick Ferrell, Russ Van Atta	125.00	50.00	30.00
(23)	Pete Fox, Goose Goslin, "Jo Jo" White	165.00	65.00	40.00
(24)	Jimmey Foxx, Luke Sewell	215.00	85.00	55.00
(25)	Benny Frey	90.00	35.00	20.00
(26)	Augie Galan, "Pie" Traynor	165.00	65.00	40.00
(27)	Lefty Gomez, Myril Hoag	165.00	65.00	40.00
(28)	"Hank" Greenberg	185.00	75.00	45.00
(29)	Lefty Grove, Connie Mack	250.00	100.00	65.00
(30)	Muel Haas (Mule), Mike Kreevich, Dixie Walker	90.00	35.00	20.00
(31)	Mel Harder	90.00	35.00	20.00
(32)	Gabby Hartnett (Mickey Cochrane, Frank Demaree, Ernie Quigley (ump) in photo)	165.00	65.00	40.00
(33)	Gabby Hartnett, Lonnie Warnecke (Warneke)	135.00	55.00	35.00
(34)	Roger Hornsby (Rogers)	250.00	100.00	65.00
(35)	Rogers Hornsby, Allen Sothoren (Sothoron)	185.00	75.00	45.00
(36)	Ernie Lombardi	185.00	75.00	45.00
(37)	Al Lopez	185.00	75.00	45.00
(38)	Pepper Martin	110.00	45.00	25.00
(39)	"Johnny" Mize	185.00	75.00	45.00
(40)	Van L. Mungo	100.00	40.00	25.00
(41)	Bud Parmelee	90.00	35.00	20.00
(42)	Schoolboy Rowe	90.00	35.00	20.00
(43)	Chas. Ruffing	185.00	75.00	45.00
(44)	Eugene Schott	90.00	35.00	20.00
(45)	Casey Stengel	185.00	75.00	45.00
(46)	Bill Sullivan	90.00	35.00	20.00
(47)	Bill Swift	90.00	35.00	20.00
(48)	Floyd Vaughan, Hans Wagner	225.00	90.00	55.00
(49)	L. Waner, P. Waner, Big Jim Weaver	215.00	85.00	55.00
(50)	Ralph Winegarner	90.00	35.00	20.00

1936 R313

(See 1936 National Chicle "Fine Pens.)

1936 R314

(See 1936 Goudey "Wide Pen" Premiums.)

1929-1930 R315

Bob Shawkey "Yankees"
Andrew Reese "Giants"

Apparently issued over a period of at least two years, based on observed player/team combinations, the 58 cards in this set can be found in either black-and-white or yellow-and-black. The unnumbered, blank-backed cards measure a nominal 3-1/4" x 5-1/4" though original cutting variances abound. The cards feature either portraits or posed action photos. The set includes several different types of cards, depending on the caption. Cards can be found with the player's name and team inside a white box in a lower corner; other cards add the position and team in small type in the bottom border; a third type has the player's name in hand lettering near the bottom; and the final type includes the position and team printed in small type along the bottom border.

		NM	EX	VG
Complete Set (46):		6,000	2,400	1,200
Common Player:		45.00	20.00	10.00
(1)	Earl Averill	90.00	35.00	25.00
(2)	"Benny" Bengough	45.00	20.00	10.00
(3)	Laurence Benton (Lawrence)	45.00	20.00	10.00
(4)	"Max" Bishop	45.00	20.00	10.00
(5)	"Sunny Jim" Bottomley	90.00	35.00	20.00
(6)	Bill Cissell	45.00	20.00	10.00
(7)	Bud Clancey (Clancy)	45.00	20.00	10.00
(8)	"Freddy" Fitzsimmons	45.00	20.00	10.00
(9)	"Jimmy" Foxx	260.00	100.00	65.00
(10)	"Johnny" Fredericks (Frederick)	45.00	20.00	10.00
(11)	Frank Frisch	110.00	45.00	25.00
(12)	"Lou" Gehrig	1,500	600.00	375.00
(13)	"Goose" Goslin	90.00	35.00	20.00
(14)	Burleigh Grimes	90.00	35.00	20.00
(15)	"Lefty" Grove	110.00	45.00	25.00
(16)	"Mule" Haas	45.00	20.00	10.00
(17)	Harvey Hendricks (Hendrick)	45.00	20.00	10.00
(18)	"Babe" Herman	60.00	25.00	15.00
(19)	"Roger" Hornsby (Rogers)	135.00	55.00	35.00
(20)	Karl Hubbell (Carl)	90.00	35.00	20.00
(21)	"Stonewall" Jackson	90.00	35.00	20.00
(22)	Smead Jolley	45.00	20.00	10.00
(23)	"Chuck" Klein	90.00	35.00	20.00
(24)	Mark Koenig	45.00	20.00	10.00
(25)	"Tony" Lazerri (Lazzeri)	90.00	35.00	20.00
(26)	Fred Leach	45.00	20.00	10.00
(27)	"Freddy" Lindstrom	90.00	35.00	20.00
(28)	Fred Marberry	45.00	20.00	10.00
(29)	"Bing" Miller	45.00	20.00	10.00
(30)	"Bob" O'Farrell	45.00	20.00	10.00
(31)	Frank O'Doul	75.00	30.00	18.50
(32)	"Herbie" Pennock	90.00	35.00	20.00
(33)	George Pipgras	45.00	20.00	10.00
(34)	Andrew Reese	45.00	20.00	10.00
(35)	Carl Reynolds	45.00	20.00	10.00
(36)	"Babe" Ruth	1,600	640.00	400.00
(37)	"Bob" Shawkey	45.00	20.00	10.00
(38)	Art Shires	45.00	20.00	10.00
(39)	"Al" Simmons	90.00	35.00	20.00
(40)	"Riggs" Stephenson	45.00	20.00	10.00
(41)	"Bill" Terry	90.00	35.00	20.00
(42)	"Pie" Traynor	90.00	35.00	20.00
(43)	"Dazzy" Vance	90.00	35.00	20.00
(44)	Paul Waner	90.00	35.00	20.00
(45)	Hack Wilson	90.00	35.00	20.00
(46)	"Tom" Zachary	45.00	20.00	10.00

1929 R316

(See Kashin Publications.)

1929 R316 5x7 Photos

There is nothing concrete to connect this set of player photos with the Kashin Publications card set which carried the R316 designation in the American Card Catalog except that these 4-7/8" x 6-3/4" heavy-paper pictures use the same photos and graphics as the smaller cards. It is thought that the photos may be the work of Charles M. Conlon and that the 5x7s may have some connection to the Spalding sporting goods company for whom he worked. Pictures feature white borders and facsimile autographs on front, along with the player's city and league on two lines of type at bottom. While the photos are all the same as seen on R316, the city/league designation on some of the photos is sometimes in black instead of white as on the card, or vice versa. Because almost every card from R316 is known in the 5x7 series, it is reasonable to expect that pictures of Frank Hogan and Jimmy Welsh may also exist. A number of players in the 5x7 set do not appear in the Kashin Publications set, and are noted here with an asterisk.

		NM	EX	VG
Complete Set (111):		7,000	3,500	2,100
Common Player:		50.00	25.00	15.00
(1)	Dale Alexander	50.00	25.00	15.00
(2)	Ethan N. Allen	50.00	25.00	15.00
(3)	Ray Benge (*)	50.00	25.00	15.00
(4)	Larry Benton	50.00	25.00	15.00
(5)	Moe Berg	65.00	32.50	20.00
(6)	Max Bishop	50.00	25.00	15.00
(7)	Del Bissonette	50.00	25.00	15.00
(8)	Lucerne A. Blue	50.00	25.00	15.00
(9)	James Bottomley	75.00	37.50	22.50

		NM	EX	VG
(10)	Raymond B. Bressler (*)	50.00	25.00	15.00
(11)	Fred Brickell (*)	50.00	25.00	15.00
(12)	Guy T. Bush	50.00	25.00	15.00
(13)	Harold G. Carlson	50.00	25.00	15.00
(14)	Owen Carroll	50.00	25.00	15.00
(15)	Chalmers W. Cissell (Chalmer)	50.00	25.00	15.00
(16)	Mickey Cochrane (*)	85.00	45.00	25.00
(17)	Earl (Earle) Combs	75.00	37.50	22.50
(18)	Hugh M. Critz	50.00	25.00	15.00
(19)	H.J. DeBerry	50.00	25.00	15.00
(20)	Pete Donohue	50.00	25.00	15.00
(21)	Taylor Douthit	50.00	25.00	15.00
(22)	Chas. W. Dressen	50.00	25.00	15.00
(23)	Clise Dudley (*)	50.00	25.00	15.00
(24)	Jimmy Dykes	50.00	25.00	15.00
(25)	Howard Ehmke	50.00	25.00	15.00
(26)	Elwood English	50.00	25.00	15.00
(27)	Urban Faber	75.00	37.50	22.50
(28)	Fred Fitzsimmons	50.00	25.00	15.00
(29)	Lewis A. Fonseca	50.00	25.00	15.00
(30)	Horace H. Ford	50.00	25.00	15.00
(31)	Jimmy Foxx	85.00	45.00	25.00
(32)	Frank Frisch	75.00	37.50	22.50
(33)	Lou Gehrig	335.00	165.00	100.00
(34)	Charles Gehringer	75.00	37.50	22.50
(35)	Walter Gilbert (*)	50.00	25.00	15.00
(36)	Leon Goslin	75.00	37.50	22.50
(37)	George Grantham	50.00	25.00	15.00
(38)	Burleigh Grimes	75.00	37.50	22.50
(39)	Robert Grove	85.00	45.00	25.00
(40)	Bump Hadley	50.00	25.00	15.00
(41)	Charlie Hafey	75.00	37.50	22.50
(42)	Jesse J. Haines	75.00	37.50	22.50
(43)	Harvey Hendrick	50.00	25.00	15.00
(44)	Floyd C. Herman	50.00	25.00	15.00
(45)	Andy High	50.00	25.00	15.00
(46)	Urban J. Hodapp	50.00	25.00	15.00
(47)	Frank Hogan (Existence not confirmed.)			
(48)	Rogers Hornsby	90.00	45.00	25.00
(49)	Waite Hoyt	75.00	37.50	22.50
(50)	Willis Hudlin	50.00	25.00	15.00
(51)	Frank O. Hurst	50.00	25.00	15.00
(52)	Charlie Jamieson	50.00	25.00	15.00
(53)	Roy C. Johnson	50.00	25.00	15.00
(54)	Percy Jones	50.00	25.00	15.00
(55)	Sam Jones	50.00	25.00	15.00
(56)	Joseph Judge	50.00	25.00	15.00
(57)	Willie Kamm	50.00	25.00	15.00
(58)	Charles Klein	75.00	37.50	22.50
(59)	Mark Koenig	50.00	25.00	15.00
(60)	Ralph Kress	50.00	25.00	15.00
(61)	Fred M. Leach	50.00	25.00	15.00
(62)	Carl Lind (*)	50.00	25.00	15.00
(63)	Fred Lindstrom	75.00	37.50	22.50
(64)	Ad Liska	50.00	25.00	15.00
(65)	Fred Lucas (Red)	50.00	25.00	15.00
(66)	Fred Maguire	50.00	25.00	15.00
(67)	Perce L. Malone	50.00	25.00	15.00
(68)	Fred Manush (Henry)	75.00	37.50	22.50
(69)	Walter Maranville	75.00	37.50	22.50
(70)	Earl McNeely (*)	50.00	25.00	15.00
(71)	Douglas McWeeney (McWeeny)	50.00	25.00	15.00
(72)	Oscar Melillo	50.00	25.00	15.00
(73)	Alex Metzler (*)	50.00	25.00	15.00
(74)	Ed "Bing" Miller	50.00	25.00	15.00
(75)	Clarence Mitchell (*)	50.00	25.00	15.00
(76)	Ed Morgan (*)	50.00	25.00	15.00
(77)	Chas. S. Myer (*)	50.00	25.00	15.00
(78)	Frank O'Doul	65.00	32.50	20.00
(79)	Melvin Ott	85.00	45.00	25.00
(80)	Herbert Pennock	75.00	37.50	22.50
(81)	William W. Regan	50.00	25.00	15.00
(82)	Harry F. Rice	50.00	25.00	15.00
(83)	Sam Rice	75.00	37.50	22.50
(84)	Lance Richbourgh (Richbourg)	50.00	25.00	15.00
(85)	Eddie Rommel	50.00	25.00	15.00
(86)	Chas. H. Root	50.00	25.00	15.00
(87)	Ed Roush	75.00	37.50	22.50
(88)	Harold Ruel (Herold)	50.00	25.00	15.00
(89)	Charles Ruffing	75.00	37.50	22.50
(90)	Jack Russell	50.00	25.00	15.00
(91)	Babe Ruth	425.00	210.00	125.00
(92)	Fred Schulte	50.00	25.00	15.00
(93)	Harry Seibold	50.00	25.00	15.00
(94)	Joe Sewell	75.00	37.50	22.50
(95)	Luke Sewell	50.00	25.00	15.00
(96)	Art Shires	50.00	25.00	15.00
(97)	Al Simmons	75.00	37.50	22.50
(98)	Bob Smith	50.00	25.00	15.00
(99)	Riggs Stephenson	50.00	25.00	15.00
(100)	Wm. H. Terry	75.00	37.50	22.50
(101)	Alphonse Thomas	50.00	25.00	15.00
(102)	Lafayette F. Thompson	50.00	25.00	15.00
(103)	Phil Todt	50.00	25.00	15.00
(104)	Harold J. Traynor	75.00	37.50	22.50
(105)	Dazzy Vance	75.00	37.50	22.50
(106)	Lloyd Waner	75.00	37.50	22.50
(107)	Paul Waner	75.00	37.50	22.50
(108)	Jimmy Welsh (Existence unconfirmed.)			
(109)	Earl Whitehill	50.00	25.00	15.00
(110)	A.C. Whitney	50.00	25.00	15.00
(111)	Claude Willoughby	50.00	25.00	15.00
(112)	Hack Wilson	75.00	37.50	22.50
(113)	Tom Zachary	50.00	25.00	15.00

1933 R337

(See 1933 Eclipse Import.)

1948 R346 Blue Tint

Issued circa 1948-49, the cards in this set derive their name from the distinctive blue coloring used to tint the black-

and-white photos. The cards have blank backs and measure 2" x 2-5/8". The set has a high percentage of New York players and was originally issued in strips of six or eight cards each and therefore would have been more appropriately cataloged as a "W" strip card set. The set includes several variations of team desginations. It appears that all cards #25-48, along with possibly some of the team variations can also be found in black-and-white, rather than blue printing. The complete set price does not include the variations. Proof cards have been found with printing on the back indicating they were photographed by Al Weinstein of Brooklyn.

		NM	EX	VG
Complete Set (48):		1,300	650.00	375.00
Common Player:		15.00	7.50	4.50
Black-and-White: 1.5-3X				
1	Bill Johnson	15.00	7.50	4.50
2a	Leo Durocher (Brooklyn)	30.00	15.00	9.00
2b	Leo Durocher (New York)	30.00	15.00	9.00
3	Marty Marion	20.00	10.00	6.00
4	Ewell Blackwell	15.00	7.50	4.50
5	John Lindell	15.00	7.50	4.50
6	Larry Jansen	15.00	7.50	4.50
7	Ralph Kiner	30.00	15.00	9.00
8	Chuck Dressen	15.00	7.50	4.50
9	Bobby Brown	15.00	7.50	4.50
10	Luke Appling	30.00	15.00	9.00
11	Bill Nicholson	15.00	7.50	4.50
12	Phil Masi	15.00	7.50	4.50
13	Frank Shea	15.00	7.50	4.50
14	Bob Dillinger	15.00	7.50	4.50
15	Pete Suder	15.00	7.50	4.50
16	Joe DiMaggio	225.00	110.00	65.00
17	John Corriden	15.00	7.50	4.50
18a	Mel Ott (New York)	40.00	20.00	12.00
18b	Mel Ott (No team.)	40.00	20.00	12.00
19	Warren Rosar	15.00	7.50	4.50
20	Warren Spahn	35.00	17.50	10.00
21	Allie Reynolds	20.00	10.00	6.00
22	Lou Boudreau	30.00	15.00	9.00
23	Harry Majeski (Hank)(Photo actually Randy Gumpert.)	15.00	7.50	4.50
24	Frank Crosetti	15.00	7.50	4.50
25	Gus Niarhos	15.00	7.50	4.50
26	Bruce Edwards	15.00	7.50	4.50
27	Rudy York	15.00	7.50	4.50
28	Don Black	15.00	7.50	4.50
29	Lou Gehrig	225.00	110.00	65.00
30	Johnny Mize	30.00	15.00	9.00
31	Ed Stanky	15.00	7.50	4.50
32	Vic Raschi	20.00	10.00	6.00
33	Cliff Mapes	15.00	7.50	4.50
34	Enos Slaughter	30.00	15.00	9.00
35	Hank Greenberg	35.00	17.50	10.00
36	Jackie Robinson	125.00	65.00	40.00
37	Frank Hiller	15.00	7.50	4.50
38	Bob Elliot (Elliott)	15.00	7.50	4.50
39	Harry Walker	15.00	7.50	4.50
40	Ed Lopat	15.00	7.50	4.50
41	Bobby Thomson	20.00	10.00	6.00
42	Tommy Henrich	20.00	10.00	6.00
43	Bobby Feller	35.00	17.50	10.00
44	Ted Williams	100.00	50.00	30.00
45	Dixie Walker	15.00	7.50	4.50
46	Johnnie Vander Meer	20.00	10.00	6.00
47	Clint Hartung	15.00	7.50	4.50
(48)	Charlie Keller	20.00	10.00	6.00

1950 R423

These tiny (5/8" x 7/8") cards are numbered roughly in alphabetical order from 1 through 120. They were issued in 13-card perforated strips from vending machines. The black-and-white cards are printed on thin stock and include the player's name beneath his photo. The backs - most commonly printed in orange, but sometimes purple or green - display a rough drawing of a baseball infield with tiny figures at the various positions. It appears the cards were intended to be used to play a game of baseball. Many of the cards were printed on more than one strip, creating varying levels of scarcity not necessarily reflected in pricing.

		NM	EX	VG
	Complete Set (119):	850.00	425.00	250.00
	Common Player:	6.00	3.00	1.75
1	Richie Ashburn	12.50	6.25	3.75
2	Grover Alexander	10.00	5.00	3.00
3	Frank Baumholtz	6.00	3.00	1.75
4	Ralph Branca	6.00	3.00	1.75
5	Yogi Berra	15.00	7.50	4.50
6	Ewell Blackwell	7.50	3.75	2.25
7	Lou Boudreau	7.50	3.75	2.25
8	Harry Brecheen	6.00	3.00	1.75
9	Chico Carrasquel	6.00	3.00	1.75
10	Jerry Coleman	6.00	3.00	1.75
11	Walker Cooper	6.00	3.00	1.75
12	Roy Campanella	17.50	8.75	5.25
13	Phil Cavaretta (Cavarretta)	6.00	3.00	1.75
14a	Ty Cobb (W/ facsimile autograph.)	30.00	15.00	9.00
14b	Ty Cobb (No facsimile autograph.)	40.00	20.00	12.00
15	Mickey Cochrane	7.50	3.75	2.25
16	Ed Collins	7.50	3.75	2.25
17	Frank Crosetti	7.50	3.75	2.25
18	Larry Doby	7.50	3.75	2.25
19	Walter Dropo	6.00	3.00	1.75
20	Alvin Dark	6.00	3.00	1.75
21	Dizzy Dean	17.50	8.75	5.25
22	Bill Dickey	15.00	7.50	4.50
23	Murray Dickson (Murry)	6.00	3.00	1.75
24	Dom DiMaggio	7.50	3.75	2.25
25	Joe DiMaggio	50.00	25.00	15.00
26	Leo Durocher	7.50	3.75	2.25
27	Luke Easter	6.00	3.00	1.75
28	Bob Elliott	6.00	3.00	1.75
29	Del Ennis	6.00	3.00	1.75
30	Ferris Fain	6.00	3.00	1.75
31	Bob Feller	15.00	7.50	4.50
32	Frank Frisch	7.50	3.75	2.25
33	Billy Goodman	6.00	3.00	1.75
34	Lefty Gomez	7.50	3.75	2.25
35	Lou Gehrig	40.00	20.00	12.00
36	Joe Gordon	6.00	3.00	1.75
37	Sid Gordon	6.00	3.00	1.75
38	Hank Greenberg	15.00	7.50	4.50
39	Lefty Grove	10.00	5.00	3.00
40	Art Houtteman	6.00	3.00	1.75
41	Sid Hudson	6.00	3.00	1.75
42	Ken Heintzelman	6.00	3.00	1.75
43	Gene Hermanski	6.00	3.00	1.75
44	Jim Hearn	6.00	3.00	1.75
45	Gil Hodges	12.50	6.25	3.75
46	Harry Heilman (Heilmann)	7.50	3.75	2.25
47	Tommy Henrich	7.50	3.75	2.25
48	Roger Hornsby (Rogers)	10.00	5.00	3.00
49	Carl Hubbell	10.00	5.00	3.00
50	Edwin Joost	6.00	3.00	1.75
51	John Jorgensen	6.00	3.00	1.75
52	Larry Jansen	6.00	3.00	1.75
53	Nippy Jones	6.00	3.00	1.75
54	Walter Johnson	12.50	6.25	3.75
55	Ellis Kinder	6.00	3.00	1.75
56	Jim Konstanty	6.00	3.00	1.75
57	George Kell	7.50	3.75	2.25
58	Ralph Kiner	7.50	3.75	2.25
59	Bob Lemon	7.50	3.75	2.25
60	Whitey Lockman	6.00	3.00	1.75
61	Ed Lopat	7.50	3.75	2.25
62	Tony Lazzeri	7.50	3.75	2.25
63	Cass Michaels	6.00	3.00	1.75
64	Cliff Mapes	6.00	3.00	1.75
65	Willard Marshall	6.00	3.00	1.75
66	Clyde McCullough	6.00	3.00	1.75
67	Connie Mack	7.50	3.75	2.25
68	Christy Mathewson	17.50	8.75	5.25
69	Joe Medwick	7.50	3.75	2.25
70	Johnny Mize	7.50	3.75	2.25
71	Terry Moore	6.00	3.00	1.75
72	Stan Musial	20.00	10.00	6.00
73	Hal Newhouser	7.50	3.75	2.25
74	Don Newcombe	7.50	3.75	2.25
75	Lefty O'Doul	7.50	3.75	2.25
76	Mel Ott	10.00	5.00	3.00
77	Mel Parnell	6.00	3.00	1.75
78	Johnny Pesky	6.00	3.00	1.75
79	Gerald Priddy	6.00	3.00	1.75
80	Dave Philley	6.00	3.00	1.75
81	Bob Porterfield	6.00	3.00	1.75
82	Andy Pafko	6.00	3.00	1.75
83	Howie Pollet	6.00	3.00	1.75
84	Herb Pennock	7.50	3.75	2.25
85	Al Rosen	7.50	3.75	2.25
86	Pee Wee Reese	15.00	7.50	4.50
87	Del Rice	6.00	3.00	1.75
88	Vic Raschi	7.50	3.75	2.25
89	Allie Reynolds	7.50	3.75	2.25
90	Phil Rizzuto	15.00	7.50	4.50
91	Jackie Robinson	35.00	17.50	10.50
92	Babe Ruth	40.00	20.00	12.00
93	Casey Stengel	15.00	7.50	4.50
94	Vern Stephens	6.00	3.00	1.75
95	Duke Snider	15.00	7.50	4.50
96	Enos Slaughter	7.50	3.75	2.25
97	Al Schoendienst	7.50	3.75	2.25
98	Gerald Staley	6.00	3.00	1.75
99	Clyde Shoun	6.00	3.00	1.75
100	Unknown	.00	.00	.00
101	Hank Sauer	6.00	3.00	1.75
102	Al Simmons	7.50	3.75	2.25
103	George Sisler	7.50	3.75	2.25
104	Tris Speaker	12.50	6.25	3.75
105	Ed Stanky	6.00	3.00	1.75
106	Virgil Trucks	6.00	3.00	1.75
107	Henry Thompson	6.00	3.00	1.75
108	Bobby Thomson	7.50	3.75	2.25
109	Dazzy Vance	7.50	3.75	2.25
110	Lloyd Waner	7.50	3.75	2.25
111	Paul Waner	7.50	3.75	2.25
112	Gene Woodling	7.50	3.75	2.25
113	Ted Williams	35.00	17.50	10.50
114	Vic Wertz	6.00	3.00	1.75
115	Wes Westrom (Westrum)	6.00	3.00	1.75
116	Johnny Wyrostek	6.00	3.00	1.75
117	Eddie Yost	6.00	3.00	1.75
118	Allen Zarilla	6.00	3.00	1.75
119	Gus Zernial	6.00	3.00	1.75
120	Sam Zoldack (Zoldak)	6.00	3.00	1.75

S

1936 S and S Game

Small black-and-white player photos are featured on the fronts of this 52-card game set. Measuring about 2-1/4" x 3-1/2", with rounded corners, the cards feature plain green or cream-colored backs. Besides the player photo on front, there are a few biographical details and stats, and a pair of game scenarios. The cards are unnumbered and are checklisted here alphabetically. The complete game included a special scoreboard, at least two "directions" cards and a contest card.

		NM	EX	VG
	Complete Set (52):	1,000	500.00	300.00
	Complete Boxed Set:	1,250	625.00	375.00
	Common Player:	12.50	6.25	3.75
(1)	Luke Appling	30.00	15.00	9.00
(2)	Earl Averill	30.00	15.00	9.00
(3)	Zeke Bonura	12.50	6.25	3.75
(4)	Dolph Camilli	12.50	6.25	3.75
(5)	Ben Cantwell	12.50	6.25	3.75
(6)	Phil Cavaretta (Cavarretta)	12.50	6.25	3.75
(7)	Rip Collins	12.50	6.25	3.75
(8)	Joe Cronin	30.00	15.00	9.00
(9)	Frank Crosetti	20.00	10.00	6.00
(10)	Kiki Cuyler	30.00	15.00	9.00
(11)	Virgil Davis	12.50	6.25	3.75
(12)	Frank Demaree	12.50	6.25	3.75
(13)	Paul Derringer	12.50	6.25	3.75
(14)	Bill Dickey	50.00	25.00	15.00
(15)	Woody English	12.50	6.25	3.75
(16)	Fred Fitzsimmons	12.50	6.25	3.75
(17)	Richard Ferrell	30.00	15.00	9.00
(18)	Pete Fox	12.50	6.25	3.75
(19)	Jimmy (Jimmie) Foxx	60.00	30.00	18.00
(20)	Larry French	12.50	6.25	3.75
(21)	Frank Frisch	30.00	15.00	9.00
(22)	August Galan	12.50	6.25	3.75
(23)	Chas. Gehringer	30.00	15.00	9.00
(24)	John Gill	12.50	6.25	3.75
(25)	Charles Grimm	12.50	6.25	3.75
(26)	Mule Haas	12.50	6.25	3.75
(27)	Stanley Hack	12.50	6.25	3.75
(28)	Bill Hallahan	12.50	6.25	3.75
(29)	Melvin Harder	12.50	6.25	3.75
(30)	Gabby Hartnett	30.00	15.00	9.00
(31)	Ray Hayworth	12.50	6.25	3.75
(32)	Ralston Hemsley	12.50	6.25	3.75
(33)	Bill Herman	30.00	15.00	9.00
(34)	Frank Higgins	12.50	6.25	3.75
(35)	Carl Hubbell	40.00	20.00	12.00
(36)	Bill Jurges	12.50	6.25	3.75
(37)	Vernon Kennedy	12.50	6.25	3.75
(38)	Chuck Klein	30.00	15.00	9.00
(39)	Mike Kreevich	12.50	6.25	3.75
(40)	Bill Lee	12.50	6.25	3.75
(41)	Jos. Medwick	30.00	15.00	9.00
(42)	Van Mungo	12.50	6.25	3.75
(43)	James O'Dea	12.50	6.25	3.75
(44)	Mel Ott	50.00	25.00	15.00
(45)	Rip Radcliff	12.50	6.25	3.75
(46)	Pie Traynor	30.00	15.00	9.00
(47)	Arky Vaughan (Vaughn)	30.00	15.00	9.00
(48)	Joe Vosmik	12.50	6.25	3.75
(49)	Lloyd Waner	30.00	15.00	9.00
(50)	Paul Waner	30.00	15.00	9.00
(51)	Lon Warneke	12.50	6.25	3.75
(52)	Floyd Young	12.50	6.25	3.75

1948-50 Safe-T-Card

The earliest known safety issue is this series sponsored by a children's television show which was in turn sponsored by a Washington, D.C. auto dealer. Player selection and team indications on the cards point to a three-year (1948-50) range of issue dates for the cards. Minor differences in typography and information printed on the front probably differentiate the years of issue. All cards are about 2-1/2" x 3-1/2" with rounded corners. Fronts feature rather crude black-and-white drawings

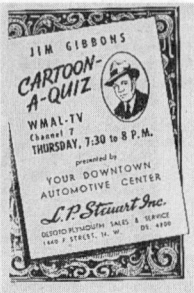

of the players with a facsimile autograph superimposed. A safety message is at top and, on most cards, the player's position and team are printed at bottom. Backs are printed in one of several colors and have a picture of the TV host and an ad for the program and its sponsors. The set is checklisted here alphabetically, though it's possible other cards may be added in the future. Only the baseball players from the set are listed here. Cards featuring football, basketball and other sports figures were also produced, along with cards for team executives, sports reporters and broadcasters.

		NM	EX	VG
	Complete (Baseball) Set (21):	2,925	1,450	875.00
	Common Player:	125.00	65.00	35.00
(1)	Ossie Bluege	125.00	65.00	35.00
(2)	Gil Coan	125.00	65.00	35.00
(3)	Sam Dente	125.00	65.00	35.00
(4)	Jake Early	125.00	65.00	35.00
(5)	Al Evans	125.00	65.00	35.00
(6)	Calvin Griffith	250.00	125.00	75.00
(7)	Clark Griffith	150.00	75.00	45.00
(8)	Bucky Harris	150.00	75.00	45.00
(9)	Sid Hudson	125.00	65.00	35.00
(10)	Joe Kuhel	125.00	65.00	35.00
(11)	Bob Lemon	150.00	75.00	45.00
(12)	Bill McGowan	400.00	200.00	120.00
(13)	George McQuinn	125.00	65.00	35.00
(14)	Don Newcombe	250.00	125.00	75.00
(15)	Joe Ostrowski	125.00	65.00	35.00
(16)	Sam Rice	150.00	75.00	45.00
(17)	Bert Shepard	150.00	75.00	45.00
(18)	Ray Scarborough	125.00	65.00	35.00
(19)	Mickey Vernon	125.00	65.00	35.00
(20)	Early Wynn	150.00	75.00	45.00
(21)	Eddie Yost	125.00	65.00	35.00

1976 Safelon Discs

One of several regional sponsors of player disc sets in 1976, Safelon, of New York, advertised its "Super Star Lunch Bags" in red and purple on the backs of its discs. The discs are 3-3/8" diameter with a black-and-white player portrait photo in the center of the baseball design. A line of red stars is above, while the left and right panels feature one of several bright colors. Produced by Michael Schechter Associates under license from the Major League Baseball Players Association, the player photos have had uniform and cap logos removed. The unnumbered checklist here is presented in alphabetical order.

		NM	EX	VG
	Complete Set (70):	100.00	50.00	30.00
	Common Player:	3.00	1.50	.90
(1)	Henry Aaron	20.00	10.00	6.00
(2)	Johnny Bench	8.00	4.00	2.50
(3)	Vida Blue	3.00	1.50	.90
(4)	Larry Bowa	3.00	1.50	.90
(5)	Lou Brock	6.00	3.00	1.75
(6)	Jeff Burroughs	3.00	1.50	.90
(7)	John Candelaria	3.00	1.50	.90
(8)	Jose Cardenal	3.00	1.50	.90
(9)	Rod Carew	6.00	3.00	1.75
(10)	Steve Carlton	6.00	3.00	1.75
(11)	Dave Cash	3.00	1.50	.90
(12)	Cesar Cedeno	3.00	1.50	.90
(13)	Ron Cey	3.00	1.50	.90
(14)	Carlton Fisk	6.00	3.00	1.75
(15)	Tito Fuentes	3.00	1.50	.90
(16)	Steve Garvey	4.00	2.00	1.25
(17)	Ken Griffey	3.00	1.50	.90
(18)	Don Gullett	3.00	1.50	.90
(19)	Willie Horton	3.00	1.50	.90
(20)	Al Hrabosky	3.00	1.50	.90
(21)	Catfish Hunter	6.00	3.00	1.75
(22)	Reggie Jackson (A's)	12.00	6.00	3.50
(23)	Randy Jones	3.00	1.50	.90
(24)	Jim Kaat	3.00	1.50	.90
(25)	Don Kessinger	3.00	1.50	.90
(26)	Dave Kingman	3.00	1.50	.90
(27)	Jerry Koosman	3.00	1.50	.90
(28)	Mickey Lolich	3.00	1.50	.90
(29)	Greg Luzinski	3.00	1.50	.90
(30)	Fred Lynn	3.00	1.50	.90

(31)	Bill Madlock	3.00	1.50	.90
(32)	Carlos May (White Sox)	3.00	1.50	.90
(33)	John Mayberry	3.00	1.50	.90
(34)	Bake McBride	3.00	1.50	.90
(35)	Doc Medich	3.00	1.50	.90
(36)	Andy Messersmith	3.00	1.50	.90
(37)	Rick Monday	3.00	1.50	.90
(38)	John Montefusco	3.00	1.50	.90
(39)	Jerry Morales	3.00	1.50	.90
(40)	Joe Morgan	6.00	3.00	1.75
(41)	Thurman Munson	5.00	2.50	1.50
(42)	Bobby Murcer	3.00	1.50	.90
(43)	Al Oliver	3.00	1.50	.90
(44)	Jim Palmer	6.00	3.00	1.75
(45)	Dave Parker	3.00	1.50	.90
(46)	Tony Perez	6.00	3.00	1.75
(47)	Jerry Reuss	3.00	1.50	.90
(48)	Brooks Robinson	9.00	4.50	2.75
(49)	Frank Robinson	9.00	4.50	2.75
(50)	Steve Rogers	3.00	1.50	.90
(51)	Pete Rose	15.00	7.50	4.50
(52)	Nolan Ryan	40.00	20.00	12.00
(53)	Manny Sanguillen	3.00	1.50	.90
(54)	Mike Schmidt	12.00	6.00	3.50
(55)	Tom Seaver	9.00	4.50	2.75
(56)	Ted Simmons	3.00	1.50	.90
(57)	Reggie Smith	3.00	1.50	.90
(58)	Willie Stargell	6.00	3.00	1.75
(59)	Rusty Staub	3.00	1.50	.90
(60)	Rennie Stennett	3.00	1.50	.90
(61)	Don Sutton	6.00	3.00	1.75
(62)	Andy Thornton (Cubs)	3.00	1.50	.90
(63)	Luis Tiant	3.00	1.50	.90
(64)	Joe Torre	3.00	1.50	.90
(65)	Mike Tyson	3.00	1.50	.90
(66)	Bob Watson	3.00	1.50	.90
(67)	Wilbur Wood	3.00	1.50	.90
(68)	Jimmy Wynn	3.00	1.50	.90
(69)	Carl Yastrzemski	9.00	4.50	2.75
(70)	Richie Zisk	3.00	1.50	.90

1977 Saga Discs

Virtually identical in format to the several locally sponsored disc sets of the previous year, these 3-3/8" diameter player discs were given away with the purchase of school lunches in the Philadelphia area. They are the scarcest of the 1977 disc sets. Discs once again feature black-and-white player portrait photos in the center of a baseball design. The left and right panels are in one of several bright colors. Licensed by the Players Association through Mike Schechter Associates, the player photos carry no uniform logos. Backs are printed in orange with background art of a sunrise over the mountains. The unnumbered discs are checklisted here alphabetically.

		NM	EX	VG
	Complete Set (70):	850.00	425.00	250.00
	Common Player:	12.50	6.25	3.75
(1)	Sal Bando	12.50	6.25	3.75
(2)	Buddy Bell	12.50	6.25	3.75
(3)	Johnny Bench	40.00	20.00	12.00
(4)	Larry Bowa	12.50	6.25	3.75
(5)	Steve Braun	12.50	6.25	3.75
(6)	George Brett	125.00	62.00	37.00
(7)	Lou Brock	35.00	17.50	10.50
(8)	Jeff Burroughs	12.50	6.25	3.75
(9)	Bert Campaneris	12.50	6.25	3.75
(10)	John Candelaria	12.50	6.25	3.75
(11)	Jose Cardenal	12.50	6.25	3.75
(12)	Rod Carew	35.00	17.50	10.50
(13)	Steve Carlton	35.00	17.50	10.50
(14)	Dave Cash	12.50	6.25	3.75
(15)	Cesar Cedeno	12.50	6.25	3.75
(16)	Ron Cey	12.50	6.25	3.75
(17)	Dave Concepcion	12.50	6.25	3.75
(18)	Dennis Eckersley	35.00	17.50	10.50
(19)	Mark Fidrych	17.50	8.75	5.25
(20)	Rollie Fingers	35.00	17.50	10.50
(21)	Carlton Fisk	35.00	17.50	10.50
(22)	George Foster	12.50	6.25	3.75
(23)	Wayne Garland	12.50	6.25	3.75
(24)	Ralph Garr	12.50	6.25	3.75
(25)	Steve Garvey	25.00	12.50	7.50
(26)	Cesar Geronimo	12.50	6.25	3.75
(27)	Bobby Grich	12.50	6.25	3.75
(28)	Ken Griffey Sr.	12.50	6.25	3.75
(29)	Don Gullett	12.50	6.25	3.75
(30)	Mike Hargrove	12.50	6.25	3.75
(31)	Al Hrabosky	12.50	6.25	3.75
(32)	Jim Hunter	35.00	17.50	10.50
(33)	Reggie Jackson	50.00	25.00	15.00
(34)	Randy Jones	12.50	6.25	3.75
(35)	Dave Kingman	15.00	7.50	4.50
(36)	Jerry Koosman	12.50	6.25	3.75
(37)	Dave LaRoche	12.50	6.25	3.75
(38)	Greg Luzinski	12.50	6.25	3.75
(39)	Fred Lynn	12.50	6.25	3.75
(40)	Bill Madlock	12.50	6.25	3.75
(41)	Rick Manning	12.50	6.25	3.75
(42)	Jon Matlock	12.50	6.25	3.75
(43)	John Mayberry	12.50	6.25	3.75
(44)	Hal McRae	12.50	6.25	3.75

(45)	Andy Messersmith	12.50	6.25	3.75
(46)	Rick Monday	12.50	6.25	3.75
(47)	John Montefusco	12.50	6.25	3.75
(48)	Joe Morgan	35.00	17.50	10.50
(49)	Thurman Munson	30.00	15.00	9.00
(50)	Bobby Murcer	12.50	6.25	3.75
(51)	Bill North	12.50	6.25	3.75
(52)	Jim Palmer	35.00	17.50	10.50
(53)	Tony Perez	35.00	17.50	10.50
(54)	Jerry Reuss	12.50	6.25	3.75
(55)	Brooks Robinson	40.00	20.00	12.00
(56)	Pete Rose	110.00	55.00	33.00
(57)	Joe Rudi	12.50	6.25	3.75
(58)	Nolan Ryan	135.00	67.00	40.00
(59)	Manny Sanguillen	12.50	6.25	3.75
(60)	Mike Schmidt	75.00	37.00	22.00
(61)	Tom Seaver	40.00	20.00	12.00
(62)	Bill Singer	12.50	6.25	3.75
(63)	Willie Stargell	35.00	17.50	10.50
(64)	Rusty Staub	15.00	7.50	4.50
(65)	Luis Tiant	12.50	6.25	3.75
(66)	Bob Watson	12.50	6.25	3.75
(67)	Butch Wynegar	12.50	6.25	3.75
(68)	Carl Yastrzemski	40.00	20.00	12.00
(69)	Robin Yount	35.00	17.50	10.50
(70)	Richie Zisk	12.50	6.25	3.75

1978 Saga Discs

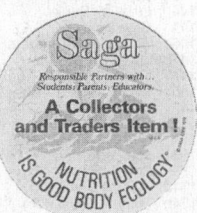

One player from each major league team was selected for inclusion in this disc set distributed by Saga, a provider of school lunches; discs were given one per lunch purchase at selected schools. The 3-3/8" diameter discs have a sepia-toned player portrait photo at center within a white diamond and surrounded by a brightly colored border with four colored stars at top. Licensed by the Players Association through Michael Schechter Associates, the photos have had uniform logos removed. Backs are nearly identical to the previous year, but printed in red. The unnumbered Saga discs are checklisted here according to the numbers found on the Big T/Tastee Freeze versions.

		NM	EX	VG
	Complete Set (26):	130.00	65.00	40.00
	Common Player:	6.00	3.00	1.75
(1)	Buddy Bell	6.00	3.00	1.75
(2)	Jim Palmer	12.50	6.25	3.75
(3)	Steve Garvey	7.50	3.75	2.25
(4)	Jeff Burroughs	6.00	3.00	1.75
(5)	Greg Luzinski	6.00	3.00	1.75
(6)	Lou Brock	12.50	6.25	3.75
(7)	Thurman Munson	10.00	5.00	3.00
(8)	Rod Carew	12.50	6.25	3.75
(9)	George Brett	50.00	25.00	15.00
(10)	Tom Seaver	15.00	7.50	4.50
(11)	Willie Stargell	12.50	6.25	3.75
(12)	Jerry Koosman	6.00	3.00	1.75
(13)	Bill North	6.00	3.00	1.75
(14)	Richie Zisk	6.00	3.00	1.75
(15)	Bill Madlock	6.00	3.00	1.75
(16)	Carl Yastrzemski	15.00	7.50	4.50
(17)	Dave Cash	6.00	3.00	1.75
(18)	Bob Watson	6.00	3.00	1.75
(19)	Dave Kingman	6.50	3.25	2.00
(20)	Gene Tenance (Tenace)	6.00	3.00	1.75
(21)	Ralph Garr	6.00	3.00	1.75
(22)	Mark Fidrych	6.50	3.25	2.00
(23)	Frank Tanana	6.00	3.00	1.75
(24)	Larry Hisle	6.00	3.00	1.75
(25)	Bruce Bochte	6.00	3.00	1.75
(26)	Bob Bailor	6.00	3.00	1.75

1962 John Sain Spinner Promotional Postcard

The attributed date of issue is approximate. This 3-7/16" x 5-7/16" color postcard was issued to promote the John Sain Spinner, a device to teach pitching mechanics. The front pictures the Yankees pitching coach in four views demonstrating

the device, which is itself pictured at top. Black-and-white back is in traditional postcard divided-back format with information on the spinner and ordering information.

	NM	EX	VG
John Sain	15.00	7.50	4.50

1962 Salada-Junket Coins

These 1-3/8" diameter plastic coins were issued in packages of Salada Tea and Junket Pudding mix. There are 221 different players available, with variations bringing the total of different coins to 265. Each coin has a paper color photo inserted in the front which contains the player's name and position plus the coin number. The plastic rims come in six different colors, coded by team. Production began with 180 coins, but the addition of the New York Mets and Houston Colt .45's to the National League allowed the company to expand the set's size. Twenty expansion players were added along with 21 other players. Several players' coins were dropped after the initial 180 run, causing some scarcities. Embossed green plastic shields into which 10 coins could be placed were available via a mail-in offer. About 9" x 10-1/2", the shields have a banner near the top with the team name. Many of the players in the 180 series can be found with variations in the placement of the front typography relative to the colored portrait. Though these variations seem to affect a tiny percentage of some players' 180 coins, they are in most cases too difficult to distinguish except by direct comparison between specimens and are of interest only to the most dedicated Salada collectors.

		NM	EX	VG
	Complete Set, no variations (221):	3,000	1,500	900.00
	Complete Set, w/ variations (265):	6,500	3,250	2,000
	Complete Boxed Presentation Set (180):	1,900	950.00	575.00
	Complete Boxed Presentation Set (200):	2,600	1,300	800.00
	Uncut Sheet (180):	1,800	900.00	550.00
	Common Player (1-180):	4.00	2.00	1.25
	Common Player (181-221):	10.00	5.00	3.00
	Team Shield (Empty):	60.00	30.00	18.00
1	Jim Gentile	5.00	2.50	1.50
2	Bill Pierce	65.00	32.50	20.00
3a	Chico Fernandez (Light blue jersey piping.)	4.00	2.00	1.25
3b	Chico Fernandez (Dark blue jersey piping.)	12.00	6.00	3.50
4	Tom Brewer	15.00	7.50	4.50
5	Woody Held	4.00	2.00	1.25
6	Ray Herbert	22.50	11.00	7.00
7a	Ken Aspromonte (Angels)	10.00	5.00	3.00
7b	Ken Aspromonte (Indians)	10.00	5.00	3.00
8	Whitey Ford	20.00	10.00	6.00
9	Jim Lemon	4.00	2.00	1.25
10	Billy Klaus	4.00	2.00	1.25
11	Steve Barber	27.50	13.50	8.25
12	Nellie Fox	17.50	8.75	5.25
13	Jim Bunning	15.00	7.50	4.50
14	Frank Malzone	5.00	2.50	1.50
15	Tito Francona	4.00	2.00	1.25
16	Bobby Del Greco	4.00	2.00	1.25
17a	Steve Bilko (Red shirt buttons.)	9.00	4.50	2.75
17b	Steve Bilko (White shirt buttons.)	9.00	4.50	2.75
18	Tony Kubek	35.00	17.50	10.00
19	Earl Battey	4.00	2.00	1.25
20	Chuck Cottier	4.00	2.00	1.25
21	Willie Tasby	4.00	2.00	1.25
22	Bob Allison	6.00	3.00	1.75
23	Roger Maris	25.00	12.50	7.50
24a	Earl Averill (Red shirt buttons.)	9.00	4.50	2.75
24b	Earl Averill (White shirt buttons.)	5.00	2.50	1.50
25	Jerry Lumpe	4.00	2.00	1.25
26	Jim Grant	17.50	8.75	5.25
27	Carl Yastrzemski	30.00	15.00	9.00
28a	Rocky Colavito (Light blue jersey piping.)	20.00	10.00	6.00
28b	Rocky Colavito (Dark blue jersey piping.)	12.50	6.25	3.75
29	Al Smith	4.00	2.00	1.25
30	Jim Busby	30.00	15.00	9.00
31	Dick Howser	4.00	2.00	1.25
32	Jim Perry	4.00	2.00	1.25
33	Yogi Berra	25.00	12.50	7.50
34a	Ken Hamlin (Red shirt buttons.)	7.00	3.50	2.00
34b	Ken Hamlin (White shirt buttons.)	4.00	2.00	1.25
35	Dale Long	4.00	2.00	1.25
36	Harmon Killebrew	20.00	10.00	6.00
37a	Dick Brown (Light blue jersey piping.)	12.00	6.00	3.50
37b	Dick Brown (Dark blue jersey piping.)	4.00	2.00	1.25
38	Gary Geiger	4.00	2.00	1.25
39a	Minnie Minoso (White Sox)	20.00	10.00	6.00
39b	Minnie Minoso (Cardinals)	9.00	4.50	2.75
40	Brooks Robinson	20.00	10.00	6.00
41	Mickey Mantle	70.00	35.00	20.00

No.	Player	NM	EX	VG
42	Bennie Daniels	4.00	2.00	1.25
43	Billy Martin	12.00	6.00	3.50
44	Vic Power	5.00	2.50	1.50
45	Joe Pignatano	4.00	2.00	1.25
46a	Ryne Duren (Red shirt buttons.)	9.00	4.50	2.75
46b	Ryne Duren (White shirt buttons.)	8.00	4.00	2.50
47a	Pete Runnels (2B)	12.00	6.00	3.50
47b	Pete Runnels (1B)	7.50	3.75	2.25
48a	Dick Williams (Name on right.)	1,800	900.00	550.00
48b	Dick Williams (Name on left.)	4.00	2.00	1.25
49	Jim Landis	4.00	2.00	1.25
50	Steve Boros	4.00	2.00	1.25
51a	Zoilo Versalles (Red shirt buttons.)	7.00	3.50	2.00
51b	Zoilo Versalles (White shirt buttons.)	7.00	3.50	2.00
52a	Johnny Temple (Indians)	12.50	6.25	3.75
52b	Johnny Temple (Orioles)	5.00	2.50	1.50
53a	Jackie Brandt (Oriole)	15.00	7.50	4.50
53b	Jackie Brandt (Orioles)	1,600	800.00	475.00
54	Joe McClain	4.00	2.00	1.25
55	Sherman Lollar	5.00	2.50	1.50
56	Gene Stephens	4.00	2.00	1.25
57a	Leon Wagner (Red shirt buttons.)	7.00	3.50	2.00
57b	Leon Wagner (White shirt buttons.)	5.00	2.50	1.50
58	Frank Lary	6.00	3.00	1.75
59	Bill Skowron	10.00	5.00	3.00
60	Vic Wertz	20.00	10.00	6.00
61	Willie Kirkland	4.00	2.00	1.25
62	Leo Posada	4.00	2.00	1.25
63a	Albie Pearson (Red shirt buttons.)	9.00	4.50	2.75
63b	Albie Pearson (White shirt buttons.)	8.00	4.00	2.50
64	Bobby Richardson	15.00	7.50	4.50
65a	Marv Breeding (SS)	9.00	4.50	2.75
65b	Marv Breeding (2B)	12.00	6.00	3.50
66	Roy Sievers	70.00	35.00	20.00
67	Al Kaline	25.00	12.50	7.50
68a	Don Buddin (Red Sox)	15.00	7.50	4.50
68b	Don Buddin (Colts)	5.00	2.50	1.50
69a	Lenny Green (Red shirt buttons.)	8.00	4.00	2.50
69b	Lenny Green (White shirt buttons.)	6.00	3.00	1.75
70	Gene Green	40.00	20.00	12.00
71	Luis Aparicio	12.00	6.00	3.50
72	Norm Cash	16.00	8.00	4.75
73	Jackie Jensen	20.00	10.00	6.00
74	Bubba Phillips	6.00	3.00	1.75
75	Jim Archer	4.00	2.00	1.25
76a	Ken Hunt (Red shirt buttons.)	9.00	4.50	2.75
76b	Ken Hunt (White shirt buttons.)	4.00	2.00	1.25
77	Ralph Terry	4.00	2.00	1.25
78	Camilo Pascual	4.00	2.00	1.25
79	Marty Keough	27.50	13.50	8.25
80	Cletis Boyer	10.00	5.00	3.00
81	Jim Pagliaroni	4.00	2.00	1.25
82a	Gene Leek (Red shirt buttons.)	9.00	4.50	2.75
82b	Gene Leek (White shirt buttons.)	4.00	2.00	1.25
83	Jake Wood	5.00	2.50	1.50
84	Coot Veal	25.00	12.50	7.50
85	Norm Siebern	5.00	2.50	1.50
86a	Andy Carey (White Sox)	25.00	12.50	7.50
86b	Andy Carey (Phillies)	9.00	4.50	2.75
87a	Bill Tuttle (Red shirt buttons.)	9.00	4.50	2.75
87b	Bill Tuttle (White shirt buttons.)	25.00	12.50	7.50
88a	Jimmy Piersall (Indians)	20.00	10.00	6.00
88b	Jimmy Piersall (Senators)	20.00	10.00	6.00
89	Ron Hansen	25.00	12.50	7.50
90a	Chuck Stobbs (Red shirt buttons.)	8.00	4.00	2.50
90b	Chuck Stobbs (White shirt buttons.)			1.25
91a	Ken McBride (Red shirt buttons.)	9.00	4.50	2.75
91b	Ken McBride (White shirt buttons.)	7.50	3.75	2.25
92	Bill Bruton	4.00	2.00	1.25
93	Gus Triandos	4.00	2.00	1.25
94	John Romano	4.00	2.00	1.25
95	Elston Howard	10.00	5.00	3.00
96	Gene Woodling	6.00	3.00	1.75
97a	Early Wynn (Pitching pose.)	45.00	22.00	13.50
97b	Early Wynn (Portrait)	15.00	7.50	4.50
98	Milt Pappas	4.00	2.00	1.25
99	Bill Monbouquette	4.00	2.00	1.25
100	Wayne Causey	4.00	2.00	1.25
101	Don Elston	4.00	2.00	1.25
102a	Charlie Neal (Dodgers)	12.00	6.00	3.50
102b	Charlie Neal (Mets)	4.00	2.00	1.25
103	Don Blasingame	4.00	2.00	1.25
104	Frank Thomas	30.00	15.00	9.00
105	Wes Covington	4.00	2.00	1.25
106	Chuck Hiller	5.00	2.50	1.50
107	Don Hoak	4.00	2.00	1.25
108a	Bob Lillis (Cardinals)	27.50	13.50	8.25
108b	Bob Lillis (Colts)	4.00	2.00	1.25
109	Sandy Koufax	30.00	15.00	9.00
110	Gordy Coleman	4.00	2.00	1.25
111	Ed Matthews (Mathews)	20.00	10.00	6.00
112	Art Mahaffey	4.00	2.00	1.25
113a	Ed Bailey (Partial left shoulder; "C" level w/ear.)	1,400	700.00	425.00
113b	Ed Bailey (Full left shoulder; second button red.)	10.00	5.00	3.00
113c	Ed Bailey (Full left shoulder; second button white.)	4.00	2.00	1.25
114	Smoky Burgess	7.00	3.50	2.00
115	Bill White	6.00	3.00	1.75
116	Ed Bouchee	25.00	12.50	7.50
117	Bob Buhl	8.00	4.00	2.50
118	Vada Pinson	4.00	2.00	1.25
119	Carl Sawatski	4.00	2.00	1.25
120	Dick Stuart	6.00	3.00	1.75
121	Harvey Kuenn	40.00	20.00	12.00
122	Pancho Herrera	4.00	2.00	1.25
123a	Don Zimmer (Cubs)	12.50	6.25	3.75
123b	Don Zimmer (Mets)	5.00	2.50	1.50
124	Wally Moon	6.00	3.00	1.75
125	Joe Adcock	9.00	4.50	2.75
126	Joey Jay	4.00	2.00	1.25
127a	Maury Wills (Blue "3" on shirt.)	10.00	5.00	3.00
127b	Maury Wills (Red "3" on shirt.)	10.00	5.00	3.00
128	George Altman	4.00	2.00	1.25
129a	John Buzhardt (Phillies)	30.00	15.00	9.00
129b	John Buzhardt (White Sox)	10.00	5.00	3.00
130	Felipe Alou	4.00	2.00	1.25
131	Bill Mazeroski	15.00	7.50	4.50
132	Ernie Broglio	4.00	2.00	1.25
133	John Roseboro	4.00	2.00	1.25
134	Mike McCormick	4.00	2.00	1.25
135a	Chuck Smith (Phillies)	15.00	7.50	4.50
135b	Chuck Smith (White Sox)	10.00	5.00	3.00
136	Ron Santo	12.00	6.00	3.50
137	Gene Freese	4.00	2.00	1.25
138	Dick Groat	5.00	2.50	1.50
139	Curt Flood	4.00	2.00	1.25
140	Frank Bolling	4.00	2.00	1.25
141	Clay Dalrymple	4.00	2.00	1.25
142	Willie McCovey	16.00	8.00	4.75
143	Bob Skinner	4.00	2.00	1.25
144	Lindy McDaniel	4.00	2.00	1.25
145	Glen Hobbie	4.00	2.00	1.25
146a	Gil Hodges (Dodgers)	30.00	15.00	9.00
146b	Gil Hodges (Mets)	22.50	11.00	6.75
147	Eddie Kasko	4.00	2.00	1.25
148	Gino Cimoli	25.00	12.50	7.50
149	Willie Mays	30.00	15.00	9.00
150	Roberto Clemente	55.00	27.50	16.50
151	Red Schoendienst	15.00	7.50	4.50
152	Joe Torre	5.00	2.50	1.50
153	Bob Purkey	4.00	2.00	1.25
154a	Tommy Davis (3B)	7.50	3.75	2.25
154b	Tommy Davis (OF)	12.00	6.00	3.50
155a	Andre Rogers (Incorrect spelling, 1B.)	7.50	3.75	2.25
155b	Andre Rodgers (Correct spelling, SS.)	12.00	6.00	3.50
156	Tony Taylor	4.00	2.00	1.25
157	Bob Friend	4.00	2.00	1.25
158a	Gus Bell (Redlegs)	20.00	10.00	6.00
158b	Gus Bell (Mets)	4.00	2.00	1.25
159	Roy McMillan	4.00	2.00	1.25
160	Carl Warwick	4.00	2.00	1.25
161	Willie Davis	4.00	2.00	1.25
162	Sam Jones	60.00	30.00	18.00
163	Ruben Amaro	6.00	3.00	1.75
164	Sam Taylor	4.00	2.00	1.25
165	Frank Robinson	15.00	7.50	4.50
166	Lou Burdette	5.00	2.50	1.50
167	Ken Boyer	13.50	6.75	4.00
168	Bill Virdon	4.00	2.00	1.25
169	Jim Davenport	4.00	2.00	1.25
170	Don Demeter	4.00	2.00	1.25
171	Richie Ashburn	40.00	20.00	12.00
172	John Podres	8.00	4.00	2.50
173a	Joe Cunningham (Cardinals)	30.00	15.00	9.00
173b	Joe Cunningham (White Sox)	12.50	6.25	3.75
174	ElRoy Face	5.00	2.50	1.50
175	Orlando Cepeda	12.00	6.00	3.50
176a	Bobby Gene Smith (Phillies)	15.00	7.50	4.50
176b	Bobby Gene Smith (Mets)	6.00	3.00	1.75
177a	Ernie Banks (OF)	25.00	12.50	7.50
177b	Ernie Banks (SS)	20.00	10.00	6.00
178a	Daryl Spencer (3B)	20.00	10.00	6.00
178b	Daryl Spencer (1B)	12.00	6.00	3.50
179	Bob Schmidt	25.00	12.50	7.50
180	Hank Aaron	35.00	17.50	10.50
181	Hobie Landrith	4.00	2.00	1.25
182a	Ed Broussard (Bressoud)	400.00	200.00	120.00
182b	Ed Bressoud	25.00	12.50	7.50
183	Felix Mantilla	10.00	5.00	3.00
184	Dick Farrell	10.00	5.00	3.00
185	Bob Miller	10.00	5.00	3.00
186	Don Taussig	15.00	7.50	4.50
187	Pumpsie Green	10.00	5.00	3.00
188	Bobby Shantz	10.00	5.00	3.00
189	Roger Craig	10.00	5.00	3.00
190	Hal Smith	10.00	5.00	3.00
191	John Edwards	10.00	5.00	3.00
192	John DeMerit	10.00	5.00	3.00
193	Joe Amalfitano	10.00	5.00	3.00
194	Norm Larker	10.00	5.00	3.00
195	Al Heist	10.00	5.00	3.00
196	Al Spangler	10.00	5.00	3.00
197	Alex Grammas	10.00	5.00	3.00
198	Gerry Lynch	10.00	5.00	3.00
199	Jim McKnight	15.00	7.50	4.50
200	Jose Pagen (Pagan)	10.00	5.00	3.00
201	Junior Gilliam	20.00	10.00	6.00
202	Art Ditmar	10.00	5.00	3.00
203	Pete Daley	10.00	5.00	3.00
204	Johnny Callison	20.00	10.00	6.00
205	Stu Miller	10.00	5.00	3.00
206	Russ Snyder	10.00	5.00	3.00
207	Billy Williams	25.00	12.50	7.50
208	Walter Bond	10.00	5.00	3.00
209	Joe Koppe	10.00	5.00	3.00
210	Don Schwall	16.00	8.00	4.75
211	Billy Gardner	15.00	7.50	4.50
212	Chuck Estrada	10.00	5.00	3.00
213	Gary Bell	15.00	7.50	4.50
214	Floyd Robinson	10.00	5.00	3.00
215	Duke Snider	25.00	12.50	7.50
216	Lee Maye	10.00	5.00	3.00
217	Howie Bedell	10.00	5.00	3.00
218	Bob Will	10.00	5.00	3.00
219	Dallas Green	15.00	7.50	4.50
220	Carroll Hardy	15.00	7.50	4.50
221	Danny O'Connell	10.00	5.00	3.00

1962 Salada-Junket Coins - Clip Back

A very rare version of the Salada Tea/Junket Dessert plastic coins exists in a clip-back format. An extruded tab at back center would allow the coin to be slid onto a cap bill or shirt flap as a decoration. With the exception of Averill (Angels), all clip-back Saladas confirmed thus far depict Boston Red Sox players. It has been reported that the clip-back coins were created for use in Opening Day stadium promotions by the Red Sox, Yankees and Mets.

No.	Player	NM	EX	VG
14	Frank Malzone	450.00	225.00	135.00
24	Earl Averill	450.00	225.00	135.00
27	Carl Yastrzemski	600.00	300.00	180.00
38	Gary Geiger	450.00	225.00	135.00
47	Pete Runnels	450.00	225.00	135.00
73	Jackie Jensen	450.00	225.00	135.00
81	Jim Pagliaroni	450.00	225.00	135.00
99	Bill Monbouquette	450.00	225.00	135.00
182	Ed Broussard (Bressoud)	450.00	225.00	135.00
187	Pumpsie Green	450.00	225.00	135.00
210	Don Schwall	450.00	225.00	135.00
220	Carroll Hardy	450.00	225.00	135.00

1963 Salada-Junket Coins

A much smaller set of baseball coins was issued by Salada/Junket in 1963. The 63 coins issued were called "All-Star Baseball Coins" and included most of the top players of the day. Unlike 1962, the coins were made of metal and measured a slightly larger 1-1/2" diameter. American League players have blue rims on their coins, while National Leaguers are rimmed in red. Coin fronts contain no printing on the full-color player photos, while backs list coin number, player name, team and position, along with brief statistics and the sponsors' logos.

No.	Player	NM	EX	VG
	Complete Set (63):	650.00	325.00	200.00
	Common Player:	6.00	3.00	1.75
1	Don Drysdale	12.50	6.25	3.75
2	Dick Farrell	6.00	3.00	1.75
3	Bob Gibson	12.50	6.25	3.75
4	Sandy Koufax	35.00	17.50	10.00
5a	Juan Marichal (No buttons.)	12.50	6.25	3.75
5b	Juan Marichal (Jersey buttons.)	10.00	5.00	3.00
6	Bob Purkey	6.00	3.00	1.75
7	Bob Shaw	6.00	3.00	1.75
8	Warren Spahn	12.50	6.25	3.75
9	Johnny Podres	7.50	3.75	2.25
10	Art Mahaffey	6.00	3.00	1.75
11	Del Crandall	6.00	3.00	1.75
12	John Roseboro	6.00	3.00	1.75
13	Orlando Cepeda	10.00	5.00	3.00
14	Bill Mazeroski	10.00	5.00	3.00
15	Ken Boyer	7.50	3.75	2.25
16	Dick Groat	6.00	3.00	1.75
17	Ernie Banks	15.00	7.50	4.50
18	Frank Bolling	6.00	3.00	1.75
19	Jim Davenport	6.00	3.00	1.75
20	Maury Wills	7.50	3.75	2.25
21	Tommy Davis	6.00	3.00	1.75
22	Willie Mays	35.00	17.50	10.00
23	Roberto Clemente	45.00	22.50	13.50
24	Henry Aaron	30.00	15.00	9.00
25	Felipe Alou	7.50	3.75	2.25
26	Johnny Callison	6.00	3.00	1.75
27	Richie Ashburn	12.50	6.25	3.75
28	Eddie Mathews	12.50	6.25	3.75
29	Frank Robinson	10.00	5.00	3.00
30	Billy Williams	10.00	5.00	3.00
31	George Altman	6.00	3.00	1.75
32	Hank Aguirre	6.00	3.00	1.75
33	Jim Bunning	10.00	5.00	3.00
34	Dick Donovan	6.00	3.00	1.75
35	Bill Monbouquette	6.00	3.00	1.75
36	Camilo Pascual	6.00	3.00	1.75
37	David Stenhouse	6.00	3.00	1.75
38	Ralph Terry	6.00	3.00	1.75
39	Hoyt Wilhelm	10.00	5.00	3.00
40	Jim Kaat	7.50	3.75	2.25
41	Ken McBride	6.00	3.00	1.75
42	Ray Herbert	6.00	3.00	1.75
43	Milt Pappas	6.00	3.00	1.75
44	Earl Battey	6.00	3.00	1.75
45	Elston Howard	7.50	3.75	2.25

46	John Romano	6.00	3.00	1.75
47	Jim Gentile	6.00	3.00	1.75
48	Billy Moran	6.00	3.00	1.75
49	Rich Rollins	6.00	3.00	1.75
50	Luis Aparicio	10.00	5.00	3.00
51	Norm Siebern	6.00	3.00	1.75
52	Bobby Richardson	7.50	3.75	2.25
53	Brooks Robinson	15.00	7.50	4.50
54	Tom Tresh	7.50	3.75	2.25
55	Leon Wagner	6.00	3.00	1.75
56	Mickey Mantle	85.00	45.00	25.00
57	Roger Maris	25.00	12.50	7.50
58	Rocky Colavito	20.00	10.00	6.00
59	Lee Thomas	6.00	3.00	1.75
60	Jim Landis	6.00	3.00	1.75
61	Pete Runnels	6.00	3.00	1.75
62	Yogi Berra	22.50	11.00	6.75
63	Al Kaline	15.00	7.50	4.50

1961 Sam's Family Restaurants Roger Maris

This postcard was issued to commemorate the presentation of Roger Maris' historic 61st home run ball back to the slugger. Pictured with Maris on this color 3-1/2" x 5-1/2" postcard is Sam Gordon, owner of a chain of family restaurants in northern California. Gordon purchased the ball from the fan who caught it, Sal Durante, and flew Durante and his wife, and Maris to Sacramento where he paid $5,000 for the ball and presented it to Maris, who later donated it to the Hall of Fame. On front is a borderless color photo of the presentation. Back has the historical details and the traditional postcard indicia.

		NM	EX	VG
61	Roger Maris, Sam Gordon	50.00	25.00	15.00

1886 W.H. Sanders New York Baseball Club (H812)

This rare 19th Century baseball issue can be classified under the general category of "trade" cards, a popular advertising vehicle of the period. The cards measure 3" x 4-3/4" and feature blue line-drawing portraits of members of the "New York Base Ball Club," which is printed along the top. As was common with this type of trade card, the bottom was left blank to accomodate various messages. The known examples of this set carry ads for local tobacco merchants and other businesses. The portraits are all based on the photographs used in the 1886 Old Judge set. The cards, which have been assigned an ACC designation of H812, are printed on thin paper rather than cardboard.

(See 1889 New York Baseball Club for checklist and values.)

1969 San Diego Padres Premium Pictures

Unlike most of the contemporary large-format (8-1/2" x 11") premium pictures, this issue carries no advertising and appears to have been a team-issue in the Padres inaugural year. Fronts feature large portraits and smaller action pictures of the player against a dark background with a facsimile autograph at the bottom and the player's name printed in the white bottom border. The signature of the artist appears in the lower-left corner. The artwork was done by Nicholas Volpe, who produced many similar items for teams in all sports in the '60s, '70s

and '80s. Backs have a large team logo at center and a sketch of the artist at bottom. There is evidence to suggest that the picture of Cito Gaston is scarcer than the other seven.

		NM	EX	VG
Complete Set (8):		60.00	30.00	18.00
Common Player:		7.50	3.75	2.25
(1)	Ollie Brown	7.50	3.75	2.25
(2)	Tommy Dean	7.50	3.75	2.25
(3)	Al Ferrara	7.50	3.75	2.25
(4)	Clarence Gaston	10.00	5.00	3.00
(5)	Preston Gomez	7.50	3.75	2.25
(6)	Johnny Podres	9.00	4.50	2.75
(7)	Al Santorini	7.50	3.75	2.25
(8)	Ed Spiezio	7.50	3.75	2.25

1977 San Diego Padres Schedule Cards

Members of the 1977 San Diego Padres, players and management, are featured in this set. The 2-1/4" x 3-3/8" cards are printed in brown on thin white stock. Fronts have a player photo with a pinstripe around and the team and player name at bottom. Backs have the team logo at top, a list of promotional dates in the center and ticket information at bottom. While some card backs state "One in a Series of 40 Player Photos," more than 80 variations are known, including some poses with blank backs. The unnumbered cards are checklisted here in alphabetical order, within three types differentiated by back printing.

		NM	EX	VG
Complete Set (89):		60.00	30.00	18.00
Common Player:		1.00	.50	.30
Type 1 - "Series of 40"				
(1)	Bill Almon	1.00	.50	.30
(2)	Joe Amalfitano	1.00	.50	.30
(3)	Buzzy Bavasi (General Manager)	1.00	.50	.30
(4)	Vic Bernal	1.00	.50	.30
(5)	Mike Champion	1.00	.50	.30
(6)	Billy Champion, Bill Almon	1.00	.50	.30
(7)	Roger Craig	1.00	.50	.30
(8)	John D'Acquisto	1.00	.50	.30
(9)	Bob Davis	1.00	.50	.30
(10)	Rollie Fingers	3.00	1.50	.90
(11)	Dave Freisleben	1.00	.50	.30
(12)	Tom Griffin	1.00	.50	.30
(13)	George Hendrick	1.00	.50	.30
(14)	Enzo Hernandez	1.00	.50	.30
(15)	Mike Ivie	1.00	.50	.30
(16)	Randy Jones (Follow-through.)	1.00	.50	.30
(17)	Randy Jones (Cy Young Award)	1.00	.50	.30
(18)	John McNamara	1.00	.50	.30
(19)	Luis Melendez	1.00	.50	.30
(20)	Butch Metzger	1.00	.50	.30
(21)	Bob Owchinko	1.00	.50	.30
(22)	Doug Rader	1.00	.50	.30
(23)	Merv Rettenmund	1.00	.50	.30
(24)	Gene Richards	1.00	.50	.30
(25)	Dave Roberts	1.00	.50	.30
(26)	Rick Sawyer	1.00	.50	.30
(27)	Bob Shirley	1.00	.50	.30
(28)	Bob Skinner	1.00	.50	.30
(29)	Dan Spillner	1.00	.50	.30
(30)	Brent Strom	1.00	.50	.30
(31)	Gary Sutherland	1.00	.50	.30
(32)	Gene Tenace	1.00	.50	.30
(33)	Dave Tomlin	1.00	.50	.30
(34)	Jerry Turner	1.00	.50	.30
(35)	Bobby Valentine	1.00	.50	.30
(36)	Dan Wehrmeister	1.00	.50	.30
(37)	Whitey Wietelmann	1.00	.50	.30
(38)	Don Williams	1.00	.50	.30
(39)	Dave Winfield (One bat.)	10.00	5.00	3.00

		NM	EX	VG
(40)	Dave Winfield (Two bats.)	5.00	2.50	1.50
Type 2 - No "Series of 40"				
(1)	Bill Almon	1.00	.50	.30
(2)	Matty Alou	1.00	.50	.30
(3)	Steve Arlin (Glove to chest.)	1.00	.50	.30
(4)	Steve Arlin (Follow-through.)	1.00	.50	.30
(5)	Bob Barton	1.00	.50	.30
(6)	Glenn Beckert	1.50	.75	.45
(7)	Ollie Brown	1.00	.50	.30
(8)	Dave Campbell (Bat on shoulder.)	1.00	.50	.30
(9)	Dave Campbell (Kneeling)	1.00	.50	.30
(10)	Enzo Hernandez, Nate Colbert	1.00	.50	.30
(11)	Nate Colbert	1.00	.50	.30
(12)	Colbert and Friend (With child.)	1.00	.50	.30
(13)	Jerry Coleman (Announcer)	1.00	.50	.30
(14)	Willie Davis	1.00	.50	.30
(15)	Jim Eakle ("TUBA MAN")	1.00	.50	.30
(16)	Rollie Fingers	3.00	1.50	.90
(17)	Cito Gaston (Bare hands.)	1.00	.50	.30
(18)	Cito Gaston (Batting gloves.)	1.00	.50	.30
(19)	Johnny Grubb	1.00	.50	.30
(20)	George Hendrick	1.00	.50	.30
(21)	Mike Ivie	1.00	.50	.30
(22)	Fred Kendall (Batting)	1.00	.50	.30
(23)	Fred Kendall (Holding ball.)	1.00	.50	.30
(24)	Clay Kirby (Follow-through.)	1.00	.50	.30
(25)	Clay Kirby (Glove to chest.)	1.00	.50	.30
(26)	Dave Marshall	1.00	.50	.30
(27)	Willie McCovey (Moustache)	5.00	2.50	1.50
(28)	John McNamara	1.00	.50	.30
(29)	Bob Miller	1.00	.50	.30
(30)	Fred Norman (Arms above head.)	1.00	.50	.30
(31)	Fred Norman (Kneeling)	1.00	.50	.30
(32)	Gene Richards	1.00	.50	.30
(33)	Ballard Smith (General Manager)	1.00	.50	.30
(34)	Ed Spiezio	1.00	.50	.30
(35)	Derrell (Darrel) Thomas (Glasses)	1.00	.50	.30
(36)	Derrel Thomas (No glasses.)	1.00	.50	.30
(37)	Bobby Tolan (Batting)	1.00	.50	.30
(38)	Bobby Tolan (Kneeling)	1.00	.50	.30
(39)	Jerry Turner	1.00	.50	.30
(40)	Dave Winfield	5.00	2.50	1.50
Type 3 - Blank back				
(1)	Nate Colbert	1.00	.50	.30
(2)	Dave Freisleben	1.00	.50	.30
(3)	Mike Ivie	1.00	.50	.30
(4)	Randy Jones and Bowie Kuhn	1.00	.50	.30
(5)	Mike Kilkenny	1.00	.50	.30
(6)	Ray Kroc (Owner)	1.00	.50	.30
(7)	Willie McCovey	5.00	2.50	1.50
(8)	John McNamara (Facing his right.)	1.00	.50	.30
(9)	Dave Winfield	7.50	3.75	2.25

1932 Sanella Margarine

One of several "foreign" Babe Ruth cards issued during his prime was included in a 112-card set produced as premiums for Sanella margarine in Germany. Ruth is the only major league ballplayer in the set. Cards are in full color, measuring 2-3/4" x 4-1/8". Backs of the unnumbered cards are printed in German. Three types of backs can be found on the Ruth card. Type 1 has the Sanella name nearly centered. The Type 2 back has the brand name printed closer to the bottom of the card, with only four lines of type under it. Type 3 is a variation of Type 2 on which the appropriate page number (83) of the accompanying album is mentioned on the line immediately above "Handbuch des Sports" near the top. Type 1 cards also mention the page number; current hobby data suggests that no Sanellas with centered logos do not mention the page. One card was given with the purchase of each 1/2 pound of margarine and the album could be ordered by mail. See also Astra Margarine.

		NM	EX	VG
Type 1	Babe Ruth (Centered w/83)	200.00	100.00	60.00
Type 2	Babe Ruth (At bottom)	140.00	70.00	42.00
Type 3	Babe Ruth (At bottom w/83.)	200.00	100.00	60.00

1958 San Francisco Call-Bulletin Giants

These unnumbered cards, picturing members of the San Francisco Giants, were inserted in copies of the San Francisco Call-Bulletin newspaper as part of a promotional contest. The 25 cards in the set measure 2" x 4" and were printed on orange paper. The top of the card contains a black and white player photo, while the bottom contains a perforated stub with a serial number used to win prizes. (Cards without the stub intact are approximately 50 percent of the prices

GIANT SCHEDULE

April 15, 16 (N), 17—Los Angeles
April 22 (N), 23, 24—St. Louis
April 25 (N), 26 (Sat.), 27 (Sun.)—Chicago
April 29, 30, May 1 (N), 2 (Sat.)—Phila.
May 4 (2) (Sun.), 5, 6 (N), 7—Pittsburgh
May 9 (N), 10 (Sat.), 11 (Sun.)—L.A.
June 3, (N), 4—Cincinnati
June 6 (N), 7 (Sat.), 8 (Sun.)—Cin.
June 10 (N), 11, 12—Pittsburgh
June 13 (N), 14 (Sat.), 15 (Sun.)—Phila.
June 17 (N), 18—Cincinnati
July 1, 2, 3—Chicago
July 4 (N), 5 (Sat.), 6 (Sun.)—St. Louis
July 10 (N), 11—Cincinnati
July 12 (Sat.), 13, 14—Milwaukee
July 15 (N), 16, 17—Philadelphia
July 18 (N), 19 (Sat.), 20 (Sun.)—Pittsburgh
Aug. 12 (N), 13, 14—Chicago
Aug. 15 (N), 16, 17 (Sun.)—Chicago
Aug. 19, 20, 21, 22 (N), 23 (Sat.)—Cin.
Aug. 24 (Sun.) 25, 26, 27 (N), 28—Milwaukee

This Stub Is Valuable!
Play—
GIANT PAYOFF
See Call-Bulletin
For Winning Numbers
DIAL KJBS—1100
"Clues" Pay Double

GIANT PAYOFF
A Family Fun Game
CASH & MERCHANDISE
PRIZES DAILY
Watch The Call-Bulletin For Daily
List of Winning Numbers — Dial
KJBS for "Clue" Words.

N192106

Willie Mays, Outfielder

listed.) The contest name, "Giant Payoff," appears prominently on both sides of the stub. The back of the card contains a 1958 Giants schedule.

		NM	EX	VG
Complete Set (25):		1,800	900.00	550.00
Common Player:		25.00	12.50	7.50
(1)	Johnny Antonelli	25.00	12.50	7.50
(2)	Curt Barclay	25.00	12.50	7.50
(3)	Tom Bowers (SP)	400.00	200.00	120.00
(4)	Ed Bressoud (SP)	150.00	75.00	45.00
(5)	Orlando Cepeda	250.00	125.00	75.00
(6)	Ray Crone	25.00	12.50	7.50
(7)	Jim Davenport	25.00	12.50	7.50
(8)	Paul Giel	25.00	12.50	7.50
(9)	Ruben Gomez	25.00	12.50	7.50
(10)	Marv Grissom	25.00	12.50	7.50
(11)	Ray Jablonski (SP)	150.00	75.00	45.00
(12)	Willie Kirkland (SP)	150.00	75.00	45.00
(13)	Whitey Lockman	25.00	12.50	7.50
(14)	Willie Mays	250.00	125.00	75.00
(15)	Mike McCormick	25.00	12.50	7.50
(16)	Stu Miller	25.00	12.50	7.50
(17)	Ramon Monzant	25.00	12.50	7.50
(18)	Danny O'Connell	25.00	12.50	7.50
(19)	Bill Rigney	25.00	12.50	7.50
(20)	Hank Sauer	25.00	12.50	7.50
(21)	Bob Schmidt	25.00	12.50	7.50
(22)	Daryl Spencer	25.00	12.50	7.50
(23)	Valmy Thomas	25.00	12.50	7.50
(24)	Bobby Thomson	45.00	22.50	13.50
(25)	Allan Worthington	25.00	12.50	7.50

1971-1982 San Francisco Giants Autograph Cards

RANDY MOFFITT
Randy Moffitt

Chris Arnold — Infielder
Chris Arnold

Giants autograph card courtesy of
Redwood City Tribune

For more than 10 years the Giants issued a number of different types of cards bearing facsimile autographs that the players could use to respond to fan mail. The cards vary in size from 3" x 5" to 3" x 6" and have a black-and-white photo (usually a portrait). The cards are blank-backed. Besides the cards with pre-printed autographs, a number of special cards in similar format were issued without facsimile signature. The listings are presented here in two major styles, those with player name in all-capital letters and those with names in upper and lower case.

		NM	EX	VG
Common Player:		6.00	3.00	1.75

NAME IN ALL-CAPITAL LETTERS
TYPE 1 - Name only, letters 1/8" wide.

(1)	Doyle Alexander	6.00	3.00	1.75
(2)	Gary Alexander	6.00	3.00	1.75
(3)	Joe Altobelli	6.00	3.00	1.75
(4)	Rob Andrews (Portrait)	6.00	3.00	1.75
(5)	Rob Andrews (Fielding)	6.00	3.00	1.75
(6)	Jim Barr (Pitching)	6.00	3.00	1.75
(7)	Dave Bergman	6.00	3.00	1.75
(8)	Vida Blue (Portrait)	8.00	4.00	2.50
(9)	Vida Blue (Pitching)	8.00	4.00	2.50
(10)	Bill Bordley	6.00	3.00	1.75
(11)	Fred Breining	6.00	3.00	1.75
(12)	Dave Bristol	6.00	3.00	1.75

(13)	Enos Cabell	6.00	3.00	1.75
(14)	Jack Clark (Ready to bat.)	8.00	4.00	2.50
(15)	Jack Clark (Swinging bat.)	8.00	4.00	2.50
(16)	Terry Cornutt	6.00	3.00	1.75
(17)	Heity Cruz	6.00	3.00	1.75
(18)	John Curtis	6.00	3.00	1.75
(19)	Jim Dwyer	6.00	3.00	1.75
(20)	Randy Elliott	6.00	3.00	1.75
(21)	Darrell Evans (Portrait)	8.00	4.00	2.50
(22)	Darrell Evans (Batting)	8.00	4.00	2.50
(23)	Tim Foli (Fielding)	6.00	3.00	1.75
(24)	Tom Griffin	6.00	3.00	1.75
(25)	Ed Halicki (Portrait)	6.00	3.00	1.75
(26)	Ed Halicki (Pitching)	6.00	3.00	1.75
(27)	Vic Harris	6.00	3.00	1.75
(28)	Dave Heaverlo (Action)	6.00	3.00	1.75
(29)	Tom Heintzelman	6.00	3.00	1.75
(30)	Larry Herndon	6.00	3.00	1.75
(31)	Marc Hill	6.00	3.00	1.75
(32)	Al Holland	6.00	3.00	1.75
(33)	Mike Ivie (Looks to side.)	6.00	3.00	1.75
(34)	Mike Ivie (Looks to front.)	6.00	3.00	1.75
(35)	Skip James	6.00	3.00	1.75
(36)	Bob Knepper	6.00	3.00	1.75
(37)	Gary Lavelle (Portrait)	6.00	3.00	1.75
(38)	Gary Lavelle (Pitching)	6.00	3.00	1.75
(39)	Johnnie Lemaster (Fielding)	6.00	3.00	1.75
(40)	Dennis Littlejohn	6.00	3.00	1.75
(41)	Bill Madlock	8.00	4.00	2.50
	(Picture reversed.)			
(42)	Bill Madlock (Corrected)	8.00	4.00	2.50
(43)	Jerry Martin	6.00	3.00	1.75
(44)	Milt May	6.00	3.00	1.75
(45)	Willie McCovey (Portrait)	15.00	7.50	4.50
(46)	Willie McCovey (Batting)	15.00	7.50	4.50
(47)	Lynn McGlothen (Pitching)	6.00	3.00	1.75
(48)	Roger Metzger	6.00	3.00	1.75
(49)	Greg Minton	6.00	3.00	1.75
(50)	Randy Moffitt (Portrait)	6.00	3.00	1.75
(51)	Randy Moffitt (Pitching)	6.00	3.00	1.75
(52)	John Montefusco (To neck.)	6.00	3.00	1.75
(53)	John Montefusco (To letters.)	6.00	3.00	1.75
(54)	Joe Morgan	15.00	7.50	4.50
(55)	Rich Murray	6.00	3.00	1.75
(56)	Phil Nastu	6.00	3.00	1.75
(57)	Bill North	6.00	3.00	1.75
(58)	Joe Pettini	6.00	3.00	1.75
(59)	Allen Ripley	6.00	3.00	1.75
(60)	Dave Roberts	6.00	3.00	1.75
(61)	Frank Robinson	20.00	10.00	6.00
(62)	Mike Sadek (To neck.)	6.00	3.00	1.75
(63)	Mike Sadek (To letters.)	6.00	3.00	1.75
(64)	Billy Smith	6.00	3.00	1.75
(65)	Rennie Stennett	6.00	3.00	1.75
(66)	Joe Strain	6.00	3.00	1.75
(67)	John Tamargo	6.00	3.00	1.75
(68)	Derrel Thomas (Throwing)	6.00	3.00	1.75
(69)	Gary Thomasson	6.00	3.00	1.75
(70)	Max Venable	6.00	3.00	1.75
(71)	Terry Whitfield	6.00	3.00	1.75
(72)	Ed Whitson	6.00	3.00	1.75
(73)	Charlie Williams	6.00	3.00	1.75
(74)	Jim Wohlford	6.00	3.00	1.75

TYPE 2 - Name only, letters 1/16" wide.

(1)	Jim Barr (Mouth closed.)	6.00	3.00	1.75
(2)	Jim Barr (Mouth open, fence.)	6.00	3.00	1.75
(3)	Jim Barr (Mouth open, no fence.)	6.00	3.00	1.75
(4)	Bobby Bonds	9.00	4.50	2.75
(5)	Tom Bradley	6.00	3.00	1.75
(6)	Ron Bryant	6.00	3.00	1.75
(7)	Don Carrithers (To neck.)	6.00	3.00	1.75
(8)	Don Carrithers (To letters.)	6.00	3.00	1.75
(9)	Pete Falcone	6.00	3.00	1.75
(10)	Charlie Fox	6.00	3.00	1.75
(11)	Tito Fuentes (To neck.)	6.00	3.00	1.75
(12)	Tito Fuentes (To letters.)	6.00	3.00	1.75
(13)	Alan Gallagher	6.00	3.00	1.75
(14)	Russ Gibson	6.00	3.00	1.75
(15)	Ed Goodson	6.00	3.00	1.75
(16)	Ed Halicki (Pitching)	6.00	3.00	1.75
(17)	Marc Hill	6.00	3.00	1.75
(18)	Jim Howarth	6.00	3.00	1.75
(19)	Jerry Johnson	6.00	3.00	1.75
(20)	Von Joshua	6.00	3.00	1.75
(21)	Gary Lavelle (Pitching)	6.00	3.00	1.75
(22)	Garry Maddox	6.00	3.00	1.75
(23)	Juan Marichal	15.00	7.50	4.50
(24)	Gary Matthews	8.00	4.00	2.50
(25)	Randy Moffitt	6.00	3.00	1.75
(26)	Willie McCovey	15.00	7.50	4.50
(27)	Willie Montanez	6.00	3.00	1.75
(28)	John Montefusco (Pitching)	6.00	3.00	1.75
(29)	Bobby Murcer (Batting)	8.00	4.00	2.50
(30)	Dave Rader	6.00	3.00	1.75
(31)	Ken Reitz (Batting)	6.00	3.00	1.75
(32)	Bill Rigney	6.00	3.00	1.75
(33)	Mike Sadek	6.00	3.00	1.75
(34)	Elias Sosa	6.00	3.00	1.75
(35)	Chris Speier (To neck.)	6.00	3.00	1.75
(36)	Chris Speier (To shoulders.)	6.00	3.00	1.75
(37)	Steve Stone	8.00	4.00	2.50
(38)	Derrel Thomas	6.00	3.00	1.75
(39)	Gary Thomasson	6.00	3.00	1.75
(40)	Jim Willoughby	6.00	3.00	1.75

TYPE 3 - 25th Anniversary Logo

(1)	Jim Barr	6.00	3.00	1.75
(2)	Bob Brenly	6.00	3.00	1.75
(3)	Don Buford (1-1/2" autograph)	6.00	3.00	1.75
(4)	Don Buford (2-1/2" autograph)	6.00	3.00	1.75
(5)	Jim Davenport	6.00	3.00	1.75
(6)	Chili Davis	8.00	4.00	2.50
(7)	Alan Fowlkes	6.00	3.00	1.75
(8)	Rich Gale	6.00	3.00	1.75
(9)	Atlee Hammaker	6.00	3.00	1.75
(10)	Al Holland	6.00	3.00	1.75

(11)	Duane Kuiper	6.00	3.00	1.75
(12)	Bill Laskey	6.00	3.00	1.75
(13)	Jim Lefebvre	6.00	3.00	1.75
(14)	Johnnie Lemaster	6.00	3.00	1.75
(15)	Jeff Leonard (Chain in background.)	8.00	4.00	2.50
(16)	Jeff Leonard (No chain.)	8.00	4.00	2.50
(17)	Renie Martin	6.00	3.00	1.75
(18)	Willie McCovey	15.00	7.50	4.50
(19)	Don McMahon (2-3/8" autograph)	6.00	3.00	1.75
(20)	Don McMahon (2-5/8" autograph)	6.00	3.00	1.75
(21)	Greg Minton	6.00	3.00	1.75
(22)	Joe Morgan	15.00	7.50	4.50
(23)	Tom O'Malley	6.00	3.00	1.75
(24)	Frank Robinson	20.00	10.00	6.00
(25)	Mike Sadek	6.00	3.00	1.75
(26)	Reggie Smith	6.00	3.00	1.75
(27)	Guy Sularz	6.00	3.00	1.75
(28)	Champ Summers	6.00	3.00	1.75
(29)	John Van Ornum (2" autograph)	6.00	3.00	1.75
(30)	John Van Ornum (2-1/4" autograph)	6.00	3.00	1.75
(31)	Jim Wohlford	6.00	3.00	1.75

TYPE 4 - Position after name, no autograph

(1)	Chris Speier	6.00	3.00	1.75

TYPE 5 - Courtesy Chevrolet, no autograph

(1)	Bobby Bonds	9.00	4.50	2.75
(2)	Dick Dietz	6.00	3.00	1.75
(3)	Tito Fuentes	6.00	3.00	1.75
(4)	Ken Henderson	6.00	3.00	1.75

TYPE 6 - West Valley Bicycles, no autograph

(1)	Alan Gallagher	6.00	3.00	1.75

TYPE 7 - Best Chevrolet, no autograph

(1)	Tito Fuentes	6.00	3.00	1.75
(2)	Chris Speier	6.00	3.00	1.75

TYPE 8 - Redwood City Tribune, no autograph

(1)	Jim Barr	6.00	3.00	1.75

NAME IN UPPER- AND LOWER CASE LETTERS
TYPE A - Name only

(1)	John D'Acquisto	6.00	3.00	1.75
(2)	Mike Caldwell	6.00	3.00	1.75
(3)	Ed Goodson	6.00	3.00	1.75
(4)	Dave Kingman	8.00	4.00	2.50
(5)	Steve Ontiveros	6.00	3.00	1.75
(6)	Mike Phillips	6.00	3.00	1.75
(7)	"Wes" Westrum	6.00	3.00	1.75
(8)	Charlie Williams	6.00	3.00	1.75

TYPE B - Team after name, no autograph

(1)	Rich Robertson	6.00	3.00	1.75

TYPE C - Courtesy Chevrolet, no autograph

(1)	Rich Robertson	6.00	3.00	1.75

TYPE D - Position after name

(1)	Garry Maddox	6.00	3.00	1.75

TYPE E - Redwood City Tribune, no logo, no autograph

(1)	Chris Arnold	6.00	3.00	1.75
(2)	Jim Barr	6.00	3.00	1.75
(3)	Jim Howarth	6.00	3.00	1.75
(4)	Garry Maddox	6.00	3.00	1.75
(5)	Dave Rader	6.00	3.00	1.75
(6)	Chris Speier	6.00	3.00	1.75

TYPE F - Redwood City Tribune, with newspaper logo, no autograph

(1)	Chris Arnold	6.00	3.00	1.75
(2)	Jim Barr	6.00	3.00	1.75
(3)	Ed Goodson	6.00	3.00	1.75

TYPE G - Name only, old Giants logo

(1)	Dave Kingman	8.00	4.00	2.50
(2)	Juan Marichal	15.00	7.50	4.50

1977 San Francisco Giants Team Issue

SKIP JAMES
Infielder

These 3-1/2" x 5" blank-back cards feature black-and-white player photos surrounded by an orange frame with black borders. The manager, coaches and instructors are featured along with players in the issue. The unnumbered cards are checklisted here in alphabetical order.

	NM	EX	VG
Complete Set (25):	15.00	7.50	4.50

Common Player:		1.50	.75	.45
(1)	Joe Altobelli	1.50	.75	.45
(2)	Jim Barr	1.50	.75	.45
(3)	Jack Clark	2.50	1.25	.70
(4)	Terry Cornutt	1.50	.75	.45
(5)	Rob Dressler	1.50	.75	.45
(6)	Darrell Evans	2.50	1.25	.70
(7)	Frank Funk	1.50	.75	.45
(8)	Ed Halicki	1.50	.75	.45
(9)	Tom Haller	1.50	.75	.45
(10)	Marc Hill	1.50	.75	.45
(11)	Skip James	1.50	.75	.45
(12)	Bob Knepper	1.50	.75	.45
(13)	Gary Lavelle	1.50	.75	.45
(14)	Bill Madlock	1.75	.90	.50
(15)	Willie McCovey	6.00	3.00	1.75
(16)	Randy Moffitt	1.50	.75	.45
(17)	John Montefusco	1.50	.75	.45
(18)	Marty Perez	1.50	.75	.45
(19)	Frank Riccelli	1.50	.75	.45
(20)	Mike Sadek	1.50	.75	.45
(21)	Hank Sauer	1.50	.75	.45
(22)	Chris Speier	1.50	.75	.45
(23)	Gary Thomasson	1.50	.75	.45
(24)	Tommy Toms	1.50	.75	.45
(25)	Bobby Winkles	1.50	.75	.45

1979 San Francisco Giants Police

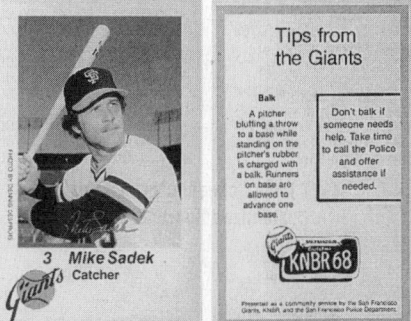

3 Mike Sadek
Catcher

Each of the full-color cards measures 2-5/8" x 4-1/8" and is numbered by player uniform number. The set includes players and coaches. The player's name, position and facsimile autograph are on front, along with the Giants logo. Backs have a "Tip from the Giants" and sponsor logos for the Giants and radio station KNBR, all printed in orange and black. Half of the set was distributed as a ballpark promotion, while the other cards were available from police agencies in several San Francisco Bay area counties.

		NM	EX	VG
Complete Set (29):		10.00	5.00	3.00
Common Player:		.50	.25	.15
1	Dave Bristol	.50	.25	.15
2	Marc Hill	.50	.25	.15
3	Mike Sadek	.50	.25	.15
5	Tom Haller	.50	.25	.15
6	Joe Altobelli	.50	.25	.15
8	Larry Shepard	.50	.25	.15
9	Heity Cruz	.50	.25	.15
10	Johnnie LeMaster	.50	.25	.15
12	Jim Davenport	.50	.25	.15
14	Vida Blue	.75	.40	.25
15	Mike Ivie	.50	.25	.15
16	Roger Metzger	.50	.25	.15
17	Randy Moffitt	.50	.25	.15
18	Bill Madlock	.60	.30	.20
21	Rob Andrews	.50	.25	.15
22	Jack Clark	.75	.40	.25
25	Dave Roberts	.50	.25	.15
26	John Montefusco	.50	.25	.15
28	Ed Halicki	.50	.25	.15
30	John Tamargo	.50	.25	.15
31	Larry Herndon	.50	.25	.15
36	Bill North	.50	.25	.15
39	Bob Knepper	.50	.25	.15
40	John Curtis	.50	.25	.15
41	Darrell Evans	.75	.40	.25
43	Tom Griffin	.50	.25	.15
44	Willie McCovey	5.00	2.50	1.50
46	Gary Lavelle	.50	.25	.15
49	Max Venable	.50	.25	.15

1980 San Francisco Giants Police

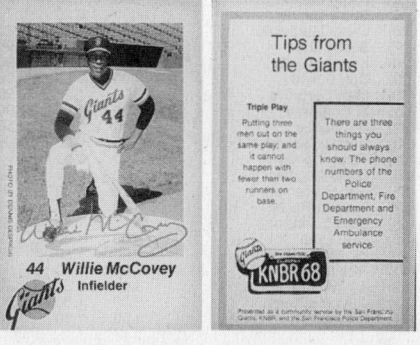

44 Willie McCovey
Infielder

The 1980 Giants police set is virtually identical in format to its 1979 forerunner, with radio station KNBR and the San Francisco Police Department once again co-sponsors. The 2-5/8" x 4-1/8" cards feature full-color photos and facsimile autographs. Backs are in the team's orange and black colors. The set includes players and coaches, with each card numbered by uniform number. As in 1979, half the cards were distributed as a stadium promotion, with the remainder available only from police officers.

		NM	EX	VG
Complete Set (31):		9.00	4.50	2.75
Common Player:		.50	.25	.15
1	Dave Bristol	.50	.25	.15
2	Marc Hill	.50	.25	.15
3	Mike Sadek	.50	.25	.15
5	Jim Lefebvre	.50	.25	.15
6	Rennie Stennett	.50	.25	.15
7	Milt May	.50	.25	.15
8	Vern Benson	.50	.25	.15
9	Jim Wohlford	.50	.25	.15
10	Johnnie LeMaster	.50	.25	.15
12	Jim Davenport	.50	.25	.15
14	Vida Blue	.75	.40	.25
15	Mike Ivie	.50	.25	.15
16	Roger Metzger	.50	.25	.15
17	Randy Moffitt	.50	.25	.15
19	Al Holland	.50	.25	.15
20	Joe Strain	.50	.25	.15
22	Jack Clark	.50	.25	.15
26	John Montefusco	.50	.25	.15
28	Ed Halicki	.50	.25	.15
31	Larry Herndon	.50	.25	.15
32	Ed Whitson	.50	.25	.15
36	Bill North	.50	.25	.15
38	Greg Minton	.50	.25	.15
39	Bob Knepper	.50	.25	.15
41	Darrell Evans	.60	.30	.20
42	John Van Ornum	.50	.25	.15
43	Tom Griffin	.50	.25	.15
44	Willie McCovey	4.00	2.00	1.25
45	Terry Whitfield	.50	.25	.15
46	Gary Lavelle	.50	.25	.15
47	Don McMahon	.50	.25	.15

1940s Sarra Trade Cards

While the cards are undated, one of the uniforms shown places its issue between 1940-1950. These ad cards are about 3-1/2" x 5-3/8" and printed in sepia on thick cream-colored paper stock. The backs picture examples of the company's personal care products, including cologne, available in sizes up to one quart!

	NM	EX	VG
Ralph Kiner	250.00	125.00	75.00
Stan Musial	350.00	175.00	100.00
Babe Ruth	550.00	275.00	165.00

1938 Sawyer Biscuit Cubs/White Sox

In the late 1930s, a local baker ran a promotion by which fans could redeem a coupon found in its product along with a dime for a matted black-and-white portrait photo of a favorite Chicago ballplayer. The photo was delivered in a thick textured maroon frame about 4-3/4" x 5-3/4" in size that had a punch-out stand on back. The Sawyer company name is not found on the actual photo, but is seen on the envelope and cover letter which are sometimes found with the pictures. It is unknown whether the list presented here is complete.

		NM	EX	VG
Common Player:		600.00	300.00	180.00
CHICAGO CUBS				
(1)	Jim Asbell	600.00	300.00	180.00
(2)	Clay Bryant	600.00	300.00	180.00

(3)	Tex Carleton	600.00	300.00	180.00
(4)	Phil Cavarretta	600.00	300.00	180.00
(5)	Rip Collins	600.00	300.00	180.00
(6)	Jerome "Dizzy" Dean	1,200	600.00	360.00
(7)	Frank Demaree	600.00	300.00	180.00
(8)	Al Epperly	600.00	300.00	180.00
(9)	Larry French	600.00	300.00	180.00
(10)	Augie Galan	600.00	300.00	180.00
(11)	Bob Garbark	600.00	300.00	180.00
(12)	Charlie Grimm	600.00	300.00	180.00
(13)	Stan Hack	650.00	325.00	195.00
(14)	Gabby Hartnett	750.00	375.00	225.00
(15)	Billy Herman	750.00	375.00	225.00
(16)	Bill Jurges	600.00	300.00	180.00
(17)	Tony Lazzeri	750.00	375.00	225.00
(18)	Bill Lee	600.00	300.00	180.00
(19)	Bob Logan	600.00	300.00	180.00
(20)	Joe Marty	600.00	300.00	180.00
(21)	Ken O'Dea	600.00	300.00	180.00
(22)	Carl Reynolds	600.00	300.00	180.00
(23)	Charlie Root	600.00	300.00	180.00
(24)	Jack Russell	600.00	300.00	180.00
CHICAGO WHITE SOX				
(1)	Luke Appling	750.00	375.00	225.00
(2)	Boze Berger	600.00	300.00	180.00
(3)	Clint Brown	600.00	300.00	180.00
(4)	Frog Dietrich	600.00	300.00	180.00
(5)	Jimmie Dykes	600.00	300.00	180.00
(6)	Frank Gabler	600.00	300.00	180.00
(7)	Jackie Hayes	600.00	300.00	180.00
(8)	Jack Knott	600.00	300.00	180.00
(9)	Mike Kreevich	600.00	300.00	180.00
(10)	Joe Kuhel	600.00	300.00	180.00
(11)	Thornton Lee	600.00	300.00	180.00
(12)	Ted Lyons	750.00	375.00	225.00
(13)	Marv Owen	600.00	300.00	180.00
(14)	Tony Rensa	600.00	300.00	180.00
(15)	Dunc Rigney	600.00	300.00	180.00
(16)	Larry Rosenthal	600.00	300.00	180.00
(17)	Norm Schlueter	600.00	300.00	180.00
(18)	Luke Sewell	600.00	300.00	180.00
(19)	Henk Steinbacher	600.00	300.00	180.00
(20)	Monty Stratton	625.00	310.00	185.00
(21)	Gee Gee Walker	600.00	300.00	180.00
(22)	Porkshops Whitehead	600.00	300.00	180.00
BROADCASTER				
	Bob Elson	600.00	300.00	180.00

1921-22 Schapira Bros. Big Show Candy

The players known, with the teams on which they are pictured, can pinpoint the issue date no closer than 1921-22. Nominally about 1-3/4" or 1-7/8" x 2-3/8" (size varies because the cards were printed without borders in sheet form, and are often found crudely cut), the cards were one of several types of insert cards and toys found in boxes of Schapira's "Big Show" candy. The cards have black-and-white borderless photos on which the player name is (usually) printed diagonally in script at lower right. Most cards have an Underwood & Underwood credit line on front, as well. Backs are blank. The unnumbered cards are listed here alphabetically, though the checklist may not be complete. Most cards are found with a horizontal crease at center, possibly to get them into the tight-fitting candy box.

		NM	EX	VG
Common Player:		200.00	100.00	60.00
(1)	George J. Burns	200.00	80.00	40.00
(2)	Ty Cobb	1,800	725.00	350.00
(3)	Stan Coveleski	250.00	100.00	50.00
(4)	(Jake) Daubert	200.00	80.00	40.00
(5)	Joe Dugan	200.00	80.00	40.00
(6)	Jimmy Dykes	200.00	80.00	40.00
(7)	Walter Holke	200.00	80.00	40.00
(8)	Walter Johnson	600.00	240.00	120.00
(9)	Joe Judge	200.00	80.00	40.00
(10)	Dick Kerr	200.00	80.00	40.00
(11)	Rabbit Maranville	250.00	100.00	50.00
(12)	Bob Meusel	200.00	80.00	40.00
(13)	Hy Meyers (Myers)	200.00	80.00	40.00
(14)	O'Neil (Mickey?)	200.00	80.00	40.00
(15)	Roger Peckinpaugh	200.00	80.00	40.00
(16)	Edd Rousch (Roush)	250.00	100.00	50.00
(17)	Ray Schalk	200.00	80.00	40.00
(18)	Everett Scott	200.00	80.00	40.00
(19)	Aaron Ward	200.00	80.00	40.00

1921 Schapira Bros. Candy Babe Ruth

The date assigned to this rare candy issue is a best guess based on the uniform in which the Babe is shown on the various cards. The blank-back cards measure between

1-5/8" and 1-3/4" in width, and are 2-1/2" tall. Printed in red, white and blue the cards were printed on a candy box and come in two types. Apparently each box contained a portrait card of Ruth which offered "a base ball autographed by Babe Ruth" for 250 of the pictures, plus one of five action photos. The portrait card would thus be much more common than any particular action pose, unless great numbers of them were redeemed. The cards illustrated here are not front and back, but show a typical action card and the portrait card. The unnumbered cards are checklisted here in alphabetical order based on the card's caption.

		NM	EX	VG
Complete Set (6):		5,500	2,200	1,100
(1)	Cleared the Bags (Babe Ruth)	1,000	400.00	200.00
(2)	Home Run (Babe Ruth)	1,000	400.00	200.00
(3)	Over the Fence (Babe Ruth)	1,000	400.00	200.00
(4)	They Passed Him (Babe Ruth)	1,000	400.00	200.00
(5)	Waiting for a High One (Babe Ruth)	1,000	400.00	200.00
(6a)	Babe Ruth (Portrait) (Arrows point to top of ball.)	900.00	360.00	180.00
(6b)	Babe Ruth (No arrows.)	900.00	360.00	180.00

1975 Michael Schechter Associates Test Discs

Prior to rolling out its 70-disc set in 1976, Michael Schecter Associates issued this sample set of discs the previous year. Slightly larger, at 3-9/16" diameter, than the '76 issues, the '75 sample discs share a similar format. Fronts have a black-and-white player photo from which uniform logo details have been removed due to lack of licensing by Major League Baseball. Backs are blank. The Seaver and Bench discs are considerably scarcer than the other four players in the set.

		NM	EX	VG
Complete Set (6):		175.00	90.00	55.00
Common Player:		6.00	3.00	1.75
(1)	Hank Aaron	15.00	7.50	4.50
(2)	Johnny Bench	60.00	30.00	18.00
(3)	Catfish Hunter	6.00	3.00	1.75
(4)	Fred Lynn	6.00	3.00	1.75
(5)	Pete Rose	10.00	5.00	3.00
(6)	Tom Seaver	100.00	50.00	30.00

1976 Michael Schechter Associates Discs

Following its test issue of 1975, Michael Schechter Associates ran out its baseball player disc issues on a large scale in 1976. While most were sold with specific sponsor advertising on back, they were also made available with blank backs. The discs are 3-3/8" diameter with a black-and-white player portrait photo in the center of the baseball design. A line of red stars is above, while the left and right panels feature one of several bright colors. Produced by MSA under license from the Major League Players Association, the player photos have had uniform and cap logos removed. The unnumbered discs are presented in alphabetical order.

		NM	EX	VG
Complete Set (70):		60.00	30.00	18.00
Common Player:		.50	.25	.15
(1)	Henry Aaron	12.50	6.25	3.75

(2)	Johnny Bench	6.00	3.00	1.75
(3)	Vida Blue	.50	.25	.15
(4)	Larry Bowa	.50	.25	.15
(5)	Lou Brock	4.50	2.25	1.25
(6)	Jeff Burroughs	.50	.25	.15
(7)	John Candelaria	.50	.25	.15
(8)	Jose Cardenal	.50	.25	.15
(9)	Rod Carew	6.00	3.00	1.75
(10)	Steve Carlton	4.50	2.25	1.25
(11)	Dave Cash	.50	.25	.15
(12)	Cesar Cedeno	.50	.25	.15
(13)	Ron Cey	.50	.25	.15
(14)	Carlton Fisk	4.50	2.25	1.25
(15)	Tito Fuentes	.50	.25	.15
(16)	Steve Garvey	3.00	1.50	.90
(17)	Ken Griffey	.50	.25	.15
(18)	Don Gullett	.50	.25	.15
(19)	Willie Horton	.50	.25	.15
(20)	Al Hrabosky	.50	.25	.15
(21)	Catfish Hunter	4.50	2.25	1.25
(22)	Reggie Jackson (A's)	9.00	4.50	2.75
(23)	Randy Jones	.50	.25	.15
(24)	Jim Kaat	.50	.25	.15
(25)	Don Kessinger	.50	.25	.15
(26)	Dave Kingman	.50	.25	.15
(27)	Jerry Koosman	.50	.25	.15
(28)	Mickey Lolich	.60	.30	.20
(29)	Greg Luzinski	.50	.25	.15
(30)	Fred Lynn	.50	.25	.15
(31)	Bill Madlock	.50	.25	.15
(32)	Carlos May (White Sox)	.50	.25	.15
(33)	John Mayberry	.50	.25	.15
(34)	Bake McBride	.50	.25	.15
(35)	Doc Medich	.50	.25	.15
(36)	Andy Messersmith	.50	.25	.15
(37)	Rick Monday	.50	.25	.15
(38)	John Montefusco	.50	.25	.15
(39)	Jerry Morales	.50	.25	.15
(40)	Joe Morgan	4.50	2.25	1.25
(41)	Thurman Munson	4.50	2.25	1.25
(42)	Bobby Murcer	.50	.25	.15
(43)	Al Oliver	.50	.25	.15
(44)	Jim Palmer	4.50	2.25	1.25
(45)	Dave Parker	.50	.25	.15
(46)	Tony Perez	4.50	2.25	1.25
(47)	Jerry Reuss	.50	.25	.15
(48)	Brooks Robinson	6.00	3.00	1.75
(49)	Frank Robinson	6.00	3.00	1.75
(50)	Steve Rogers	.50	.25	.15
(51)	Pete Rose	10.00	5.00	3.00
(52)	Nolan Ryan	15.00	7.50	4.50
(53)	Manny Sanguillen	.50	.25	.15
(54)	Mike Schmidt	10.00	5.00	3.00
(55)	Tom Seaver	6.00	3.00	1.75
(56)	Ted Simmons	.50	.25	.15
(57)	Reggie Smith	.50	.25	.15
(58)	Willie Stargell	4.50	2.25	1.25
(59)	Rusty Staub	.75	.40	.25
(60)	Rennie Stennett	.50	.25	.15
(61)	Don Sutton	4.50	2.25	1.25
(62)	Andy Thornton	.50	.25	.15
(63)	Luis Tiant	.50	.25	.15
(64)	Joe Torre	.50	.25	.15
(65)	Mike Tyson	.50	.25	.15
(66)	Bob Watson	.50	.25	.15
(67)	Wilbur Wood	.50	.25	.15
(68)	Jimmy Wynn	.50	.25	.15
(69)	Carl Yastrzemski	6.00	3.00	1.75
(70)	Richie Zisk	.50	.25	.15

1977 Michael Schechter Associates Cup Lids

One of MSA's early baseball novelty issues was a set of drink-cup lids. The 3-1/2" diameter pieces are made of pressed and waxed cardboard. They are 3/16" thick and have a 3/8" die-cut hole for inserting a straw. Design is similar to other MSA issues of the era, with a black-and-white player portrait photo at center of a simulated baseball design. Personal data is printed in colored panels at left and right, and there is a row of colored stars above the photo. Player caps do not show team insignia because the issue was licensed only by the players' union, and not the owners. The unnumbered lids are checklisted here in alphabetical order.

		NM	EX	VG
Complete Set (49):		700.00	350.00	225.00
Common Player:		10.00	5.00	3.00
(1)	Sal Bando	10.00	5.00	3.00
(2)	Johnny Bench	30.00	15.00	9.00
(3)	Larry Bowa	10.00	5.00	3.00
(4)	Steve Braun	10.00	5.00	3.00
(5)	George Brett	100.00	50.00	30.00
(6)	Lou Brock	30.00	15.00	9.00
(7)	Bert Campaneris	10.00	5.00	3.00
(8)	Bill Campbell	10.00	5.00	3.00
(9)	Jose Cardenal	10.00	5.00	3.00

(10)	Rod Carew	30.00	15.00	9.00
(11)	Dave Cash	10.00	5.00	3.00
(12)	Cesar Cedeno	10.00	5.00	3.00
(13)	Chris Chambliss	10.00	5.00	3.00
(14)	Dave Concepcion	10.00	5.00	3.00
(15)	Mark Fidrych	10.00	5.00	3.00
(16)	Rollie Fingers	20.00	10.00	6.00
(17)	George Foster	10.00	5.00	3.00
(18)	Wayne Garland	10.00	5.00	3.00
(19)	Steve Garvey	20.00	10.00	6.00
(20)	Cesar Geronimo	10.00	5.00	3.00
(21)	Bobby Grich	10.00	5.00	3.00
(22)	Don Gullett	10.00	5.00	3.00
(23)	Mike Hargrove	10.00	5.00	3.00
(24)	Catfish Hunter	20.00	10.00	6.00
(25)	Randy Jones	10.00	5.00	3.00
(26)	Dave Kingman	15.00	7.50	4.50
(27)	Dave LaRoche	10.00	5.00	3.00
(28)	Greg Luzinski	10.00	5.00	3.00
(29)	Fred Lynn	10.00	5.00	3.00
(30)	Jon Matlack	10.00	5.00	3.00
(31)	Bake McBride	10.00	5.00	3.00
(32)	Joe Morgan	25.00	12.50	7.50
(33)	Phil Niekro	20.00	10.00	6.00
(34)	Jim Palmer	25.00	12.50	7.50
(35)	Dave Parker	10.00	5.00	3.00
(36)	Fred Patek	10.00	5.00	3.00
(37)	Mickey Rivers	10.00	5.00	3.00
(38)	Brooks Robinson	30.00	15.00	9.00
(39)	Pete Rose	75.00	37.00	22.00
(40)	Nolan Ryan	100.00	50.00	30.00
(41)	Tom Seaver (1976)	60.00	30.00	18.00
(42)	Mike Schmidt	50.00	25.00	15.00
(43)	Bill Singer	10.00	5.00	3.00
(44)	Chris Speier	10.00	5.00	3.00
(45)	Willie Stargell	25.00	12.50	7.50
(46)	Luis Tiant	12.50	6.25	3.75
(47)	Butch Wynegar	10.00	5.00	3.00
(48)	Robin Yount	20.00	10.00	6.00
(49)	Richie Zisk	10.00	5.00	3.00

1977 Mike Schechter Associates Customized Sports Discs

Virtually identical in format to the several locally sponsored disc sets of the previous year, these 3-3/8" diameter player discs once again feature black-and-white player portrait photos in the center of a baseball design. The left and right panels are in one of several bright colors. Licensed by the Players' Association, the photos carry no uniform logos. Backs of the discs are printed in dark blue and carry an ad from MSA for "Customized Sports Discs" and novelties for which Schechter held the licenses. The unnumbered discs are checklisted here alphabetically.

		NM	EX	VG
Complete Set (70):		350.00	175.00	100.00
Common Player:		3.00	1.50	.90
(1)	Sal Bando	3.00	1.50	.90
(2)	Buddy Bell	3.00	1.50	.90
(3)	Johnny Bench	20.00	10.00	6.00
(4)	Larry Bowa	3.00	1.50	.90
(5)	Steve Braun	3.00	1.50	.90
(6)	George Brett	125.00	62.00	37.00
(7)	Lou Brock	15.00	7.50	4.50
(8)	Jeff Burroughs	3.00	1.50	.90
(9)	Bert Campaneris	3.00	1.50	.90
(10)	John Candelaria	3.00	1.50	.90
(11)	Jose Cardenal	3.00	1.50	.90
(12)	Rod Carew	20.00	10.00	6.00
(13)	Steve Carlton	20.00	10.00	6.00
(14)	Dave Cash	3.00	1.50	.90
(15)	Cesar Cedeno	3.00	1.50	.90
(16)	Ron Cey	3.00	1.50	.90
(17)	Dave Concepcion	3.00	1.50	.90
(18)	Dennis Eckersley	15.00	7.50	4.50
(19)	Mark Fidrych	6.00	3.00	1.75
(20)	Rollie Fingers	15.00	7.50	4.50
(21)	Carlton Fisk	15.00	7.50	4.50
(22)	George Foster	3.00	1.50	.90
(23)	Wayne Garland	3.00	1.50	.90
(24)	Ralph Garr	3.00	1.50	.90
(25)	Steve Garvey	12.50	6.25	3.75
(26)	Cesar Geronimo	3.00	1.50	.90
(27)	Bobby Grich	3.00	1.50	.90
(28)	Ken Griffey Sr.	3.00	1.50	.90
(29)	Don Gullett	3.00	1.50	.90
(30)	Mike Hargrove	3.00	1.50	.90
(31)	Al Hrabosky	3.00	1.50	.90
(32)	Jim Hunter	15.00	7.50	4.50
(33)	Reggie Jackson	30.00	15.00	9.00
(34)	Randy Jones	3.00	1.50	.90
(35)	Dave Kingman	5.00	2.50	1.50
(36)	Jerry Koosman	3.00	1.50	.90
(37)	Dave LaRoche	3.00	1.50	.90
(38)	Greg Luzinski	3.00	1.50	.90
(39)	Fred Lynn	3.00	1.50	.90
(40)	Bill Madlock	3.00	1.50	.90
(41)	Rick Manning	3.00	1.50	.90
(42)	Jon Matlack	3.00	1.50	.90
(43)	John Mayberry	3.00	1.50	.90
(44)	Hal McRae	3.00	1.50	.90

(45)	Andy Messersmith	3.00	1.50	.90
(46)	Rick Monday	3.00	1.50	.90
(47)	John Montefusco	3.00	1.50	.90
(48)	Joe Morgan	15.00	7.50	4.50
(49)	Thurman Munson	12.50	6.25	3.75
(50)	Bobby Murcer	3.00	1.50	.90
(51)	Bill North	3.00	1.50	.90
(52)	Jim Palmer	15.00	7.50	4.50
(53)	Tony Perez	15.00	7.50	4.50
(54)	Jerry Reuss	3.00	1.50	.90
(55)	Brooks Robinson	20.00	10.00	6.00
(56)	Pete Rose	75.00	37.00	22.00
(57)	Joe Rudi	3.00	1.50	.90
(58)	Nolan Ryan	125.00	62.00	37.00
(59)	Manny Sanguillen	3.00	1.50	.90
(60)	Mike Schmidt	100.00	50.00	30.00
(61)	Tom Seaver	20.00	10.00	6.00
(62)	Bill Singer	3.00	1.50	.90
(63)	Willie Stargell	15.00	7.50	4.50
(64)	Rusty Staub	5.00	2.50	1.50
(65)	Luis Tiant	3.00	1.50	.90
(66)	Bob Watson	3.00	1.50	.90
(67)	Butch Wynegar	3.00	1.50	.90
(68)	Carl Yastrzemski	20.00	10.00	6.00
(69)	Robin Yount	15.00	7.50	4.50
(70)	Richie Zisk	3.00	1.50	.90

1915 Schmelzer's Sporting Goods Pins

The date of issue attributed is speculative, based on the limited checklist currently available. These pin-back celluloid buttons measure about 1-1/4" in diameter. A color lithographed figure of a generic ballplayer shares the front with a smaller inset black-and-white photo of an actual player and a fancy script position designation. The player's last name appears at the bottom of the photo. Issuer identification is on back. It is presumed at least one pinback was issued for each of the nine positions.

		NM	EX	VG
	Common Player:	350.00	175.00	105.00
RF	"Ty" Cobb	26,250	13,125	7,500
3B	Charlie Deal	5,625	2,813	1,688
C	Hank Gowdy	5,625	2,813	1,688
LF	Hoffman	5,625	2,813	1,688
CF	Joe Jackson	12,000	6,000	3,600
P	Christy Mathewson	6,750	3,375	2,025
SS	Rabbit Maranville	5,625	2,813	1,688
1B	Butch Schmidt	5,625	2,813	1,688

1921 C. Shulz Baseball Card Game

While this catalog generally does not attempt to list game cards which do not depict actual ballplayers, this set is considered exceptional due to its format similarity to the popularly collected 1922 American Caramel issue known as E120. Backs of the game cards are printed in blue on white and reproduce the border design of the National League cards of E120. The unnamed photo of Heinie Groh on back is identical to that on E120, except uniform lettering has been airbrushed away on the game card. Backs are printed in red with a ball-game situation. The credit line on back reads, "Instructions Copyrighted 1921 by C. Schulz." The game cards measure about 2-1/2" x 3-1/2".

	NM	EX	VG
Common Card:	35.00	17.50	10.00

1949 Schumacher Service Station

Because some of these cards have been found with the advertising of Schumacher Service Station (location unknown) printed in red on the back, the issue is so designated for cataloging purposes. Given that the (living) players from this set were with their respective teams in 1949-1950, the issue date

could be either year. Measuring 2-5/8" x 3-9/16", the cards are black-and-white on the front. It is unknown whether other players were issued in this series.

		NM	EX	VG
	Complete Set (9):	2,200	1,100	650.00
	Common Player:	200.00	100.00	60.00
(1)	Joe Garagiola	250.00	125.00	75.00
(2)	Marty Marion	225.00	110.00	65.00
(3)	Les Moss	200.00	100.00	60.00
(4)	George (Red) Munger	200.00	100.00	60.00
(5)	Don Newcomb (Newcombe)	250.00	125.00	75.00
(6)	Howard Pollet	200.00	100.00	60.00
(7)	George Herman (Babe) Ruth	600.00	300.00	180.00
(8)	Red Schoendienst	250.00	125.00	75.00
(9)	Vernon Stephens	200.00	100.00	60.00

1935 Schutter-Johnson (R332)

This 50-card set was issued by the Schutter-Johnson Candy Corp. of Chicago and Brooklyn circa 1930 and features drawings of major league players offering baseball playing tips. The cards measure 2-1/4" x 2-7/8". The drawings on the front are set against a red background while the backs are titled "Major League Secrets" and give the player's advice on some aspect of the game. The Schutter-Johnson name appears at the bottom.

		NM	EX	VG
	Complete Set (50):	17,500	7,000	3,500
	Common Player:	200.00	100.00	50.00
1	Al Simmons	350.00	140.00	70.00
2	Lloyd Waner	275.00	110.00	55.00
3	Kiki Cuyler	275.00	110.00	55.00
4	Frank Frisch	275.00	110.00	55.00
5	Chick Hafey	275.00	110.00	55.00
6	Bill Klem (Umpire)	450.00	180.00	90.00
7	Rogers Hornsby	300.00	120.00	60.00
8	Carl Mays	200.00	100.00	50.00
9	Chas. Wrigley (Umpire)	275.00	110.00	55.00
10	Christy Mathewson	900.00	360.00	180.00
11	Bill Dickey	275.00	110.00	55.00
12	Walter Berger	200.00	100.00	50.00
13	George Earnshaw	200.00	100.00	50.00
14	Hack Wilson	275.00	110.00	55.00
15	Charley Grimm	200.00	100.00	50.00
16	Lloyd Waner, Paul Waner	275.00	110.00	55.00
17	Chuck Klein	275.00	110.00	55.00
18	Woody English	200.00	100.00	50.00
19	Grover Alexander	300.00	120.00	60.00
20	Lou Gehrig	2,000	800.00	400.00
21	Wes Ferrell	200.00	100.00	50.00
22	Carl Hubbell	300.00	120.00	60.00
23	Pie Traynor	275.00	110.00	55.00
24	Gus Mancuso	200.00	100.00	50.00
25	Ben Cantwell	200.00	100.00	50.00
26	Babe Ruth	2,350	940.00	470.00
27	"Goose" Goslin	275.00	110.00	55.00
28	Earle Combs	275.00	110.00	55.00
29	"Kiki" Cuyler	275.00	110.00	55.00
30	Jimmy Wilson	200.00	100.00	50.00
31	Dizzy Dean	450.00	180.00	90.00
32	Mickey Cochrane	275.00	110.00	55.00
33	Ted Lyons	275.00	110.00	55.00
34	Si Johnson	200.00	100.00	50.00
35	Dizzy Dean	450.00	180.00	90.00
36	Pepper Martin	225.00	90.00	45.00
37	Joe Cronin	275.00	110.00	55.00
38	Gabby Hartnett	275.00	110.00	55.00
39	Oscar Melillo	200.00	100.00	50.00
40	Ben Chapman	200.00	100.00	50.00
41	John McGraw	275.00	110.00	55.00
42	Babe Ruth	2,350	940.00	470.00
43	"Red" Lucas	200.00	100.00	50.00
44	Charley Root	200.00	100.00	50.00
45	Dazzy Vance	275.00	110.00	55.00
46	Hugh Critz	200.00	100.00	50.00
47	"Firpo" Marberry	200.00	100.00	50.00
48	Grover Alexander	300.00	120.00	60.00
49	Lefty Grove	325.00	130.00	65.00
50	Heinie Meine	200.00	100.00	50.00

1888 "Scrapps Tobacco" Die-Cuts

The origin of these die-cut, embossed player busts is not known, but they were apparently part of a book of "punch-outs" issued in the late 1880s. When out of their original album, they apparently resembled scraps of paper, presumably leading to their unusual name. An earlier theory that they were issued by "Scrapps Tobacco" has since been discounted after research indicated there never was such a company. The die-cuts include 18 different players - nine members of the American Association St. Louis Browns and nine from the National League Detroit Wolverines. Although they vary slightly in size, the player busts are generally about 2" wide and 3" high. The drawings for the St. Louis player busts were taken from the Old Judge "Brown's Champions" set. The player's name appears along the bottom.

		NM	EX	VG
	Complete Set (18):	35,000	14,000	7,000
	Common Player:	1,800	725.00	360.00
(1)	C.W. Bennett	1,800	725.00	360.00
(2)	D. Brouthers	2,400	960.00	480.00
(3)	A.J. Bushong	1,800	725.00	360.00
(4)	Robert L. Caruthers	1,800	725.00	360.00
(5)	Charles Comiskey	2,400	960.00	480.00
(6)	F. Dunlap	1,800	725.00	360.00
(7)	David L. Foutz	1,800	725.00	360.00
(8)	C.H. Getzen (Getzien)	1,800	725.00	360.00
(9)	Wm. Gleason	1,800	725.00	360.00
(10)	E. Hanlon	2,400	960.00	500.00
(11)	Walter A. Latham	1,800	725.00	360.00
(12)	James O'Neill	1,800	725.00	360.00
(13)	H. Richardson	1,800	725.00	360.00
(14)	Wm. Robinson	2,400	960.00	480.00
(15)	J.C. Rowe	1,800	725.00	360.00
(16)	S. Thompson	2,400	960.00	480.00
(17)	Curtis Welch	1,800	725.00	360.00
(18)	J.L. White	1,800	725.00	360.00

1949 Sealtest Phillies Stickers

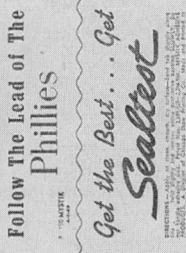

This regional Phillies set was issued in the Philadelphia area in 1949 by Sealtest Dairy. It consisted of 12 large (3-1/2" by 4-1/4") sticker cards with peel-off backs. The front of the unnumbered cards featured an action photo with facsimile autograph, while the back has an advertisement for Sealtest products. The same format, photos and checklist were also used for the Lummis Peanut Butter card set issued in Philadelphia the same year.

		NM	EX	VG
	Complete Set (12):	2,800	1,400	850.00
	Common Player:	250.00	125.00	75.00
(1)	Rich Ashburn	700.00	350.00	210.00
(2)	Hank Borowy	250.00	125.00	75.00
(3)	Del Ennis	260.00	130.00	78.00
(4)	Granny Hamner	250.00	125.00	75.00
(5)	Puddinhead Jones	250.00	125.00	75.00
(6)	Russ Meyer	250.00	125.00	75.00
(7)	Bill Nicholson	250.00	125.00	75.00
(8)	Robin Roberts	700.00	350.00	210.00
(9)	"Schoolboy" Rowe	250.00	125.00	75.00
(10)	Andy Seminick	250.00	125.00	75.00
(11)	Curt Simmons	300.00	150.00	90.00
(12)	Eddie Waitkus	250.00	125.00	75.00

1946 Sears St. Louis Browns/Cardinals Postcards

One of the more popular issues of the immediate post-war period are the black-and-white postcards of St. Louis Browns and Cardinals players issued by Sears in East St. Louis. The 3-1/2" x 5-3/8" postcards have posed player portraits on front with the player's name and Sears "Compliments of" line in the white border beneath. Backs are stamped "POST CARD / ACTUAL PHO-TOGRAPH." The cards were reported to have been issued in groups of five on a bi-weekly basis, sold both at the Sears store and through the mail. The unnumbered cards are checklisted here alphabetically within team.

		NM	EX	VG
Complete Set (69):		8,000	4,000	2,400
Common Player:		100.00	50.00	30.00
	St. Louis Browns Set (33):	3,000	1,500	900.00
(1)	John Berardino	200.00	100.00	60.00
(2)	Frank Biscan	100.00	50.00	30.00
(3)	Mark Christman	100.00	50.00	30.00
(4)	Babe Dahlgren	100.00	50.00	30.00
(5)	Bob Dillinger	100.00	50.00	30.00
(6)	Stanley Ferens	100.00	50.00	30.00
(7)	Denny Galehouse	100.00	50.00	30.00
(8)	Joe Grace	100.00	50.00	30.00
(9)	Jeff Heath	100.00	50.00	30.00
(10)	Henry Helf	100.00	50.00	30.00
(11)	Fred Hoffman	100.00	50.00	30.00
(12)	Walt Judnich	100.00	50.00	30.00
(13)	Ellis Kinder	100.00	50.00	30.00
(14)	Jack Kramer	100.00	50.00	30.00
(15)	Chet Laabs	100.00	50.00	30.00
(16)	Al LaMacchia	125.00	65.00	35.00
(17)	John Lucadello	100.00	50.00	30.00
(18)	Frank Mancuso	100.00	50.00	30.00
(19)	Glenn McQuillen	100.00	50.00	30.00
(20)	John Miller	100.00	50.00	30.00
(21)	Al Milnar	150.00	75.00	45.00
(22)	Bob Muncrief	100.00	50.00	30.00
(23)	Nelson Potter	100.00	50.00	30.00
(24)	Ken Sears	100.00	50.00	30.00
(25)	Len Schulte	100.00	50.00	30.00
(26)	Luke Sewell	100.00	50.00	30.00
(27)	Joe Schultz	100.00	50.00	30.00
(28)	Tex Shirley	100.00	50.00	30.00
(29)	Vern Stephens	100.00	50.00	30.00
(30)	Chuck Stevens	100.00	50.00	30.00
(31)	Zack Taylor	100.00	50.00	30.00
(32)	Al Zarilla	100.00	50.00	30.00
(33)	Sam Zoldak	100.00	50.00	30.00
	St. Louis Cardinals Set (36):	5,000	2,500	1,500
(1)	Buster Adams	100.00	50.00	30.00
(2)	Red Barrett	100.00	50.00	30.00
(3)	Johnny Beazley	100.00	50.00	30.00
(4)	Al Brazle	100.00	50.00	30.00
(5)	Harry Brecheen	100.00	50.00	30.00
(6)	Ken Burkhart	100.00	50.00	30.00
(7)	Joffre Cross	100.00	50.00	30.00
(8)	Murray Dickson	100.00	50.00	30.00
(9)	George Dockins	100.00	50.00	30.00
(10)	Blix Donnelly	150.00	75.00	45.00
(11)	Erv Dusak	100.00	50.00	30.00
(12)	Eddie Dyer	100.00	50.00	30.00
(13)	Bill Endicott	100.00	50.00	30.00
(14)	Joe Garagiola	400.00	200.00	120.00
(15)	Mike Gonzales (Gonzalez)	125.00	65.00	35.00
(16)	Lou Klein	100.00	50.00	30.00
(17)	Clyde Kluttz	100.00	50.00	30.00
(18)	Howard Krist	100.00	50.00	30.00
(19)	George Kurowski	100.00	50.00	30.00
(20)	Danny Litwhiler	100.00	50.00	30.00
(21)	Marty Marion	150.00	75.00	45.00
(22)	Fred Martin	100.00	50.00	30.00
(23)	Terry Moore	125.00	65.00	35.00
(24)	Stan Musial	1,000	500.00	300.00
(25)	Ken O'Dea	100.00	50.00	30.00
(26)	Howard Pollet	100.00	50.00	30.00
(27)	Del Rice	100.00	50.00	30.00
(28)	Red Schoendienst	300.00	150.00	90.00
(29)	Walt Sessi	100.00	50.00	30.00
(30)	Dick Sisler	100.00	50.00	30.00
(31)	Enos Slaughter	300.00	150.00	90.00
(32)	Max Surkont	100.00	50.00	30.00
(33)	Harry Walker	100.00	50.00	30.00
(34)	Buzzy Wares	100.00	50.00	30.00
(35)	Ernie White	100.00	50.00	30.00
(36)	Ted Wilks	100.00	50.00	30.00

1969 Seattle Pilots Premium Pictures

This set of 8-1/2" x 11" premium pictures is based on the artwork of John Wheeldon, who did contemporary issues for the Mets, Twins and Red Sox, as well. The pastels feature large portraits and smaller action pictures with a large facsimile autograph at bottom. Backs are in black-and-white and feature biographical data, comprehensive career summary and complete minor and major league stats. There is a self-portrait and biographical sketch of the artist on back, as well. The premiums were given away at selected Pilots home games during their lone season in Seattle. They were later sold for 25 cents each in the concession stand. The unnumbered pictures are checklisted here in alphabetical order.

		NM	EX	VG
Complete Set (8):		75.00	37.00	22.00
Common Player:		8.00	4.00	2.50
(1)	Wayne Comer	8.00	4.00	2.50
(2)	Tommy Harper	10.00	5.00	3.00
(3)	Mike Hegan	8.00	4.00	2.50
(4)	Jerry McNertney	8.00	4.00	2.50
(5)	Don Mincher	8.00	4.00	2.50
(6)	Ray Oyler	8.00	4.00	2.50
(7)	Marty Pattin	8.00	4.00	2.50
(8)	Diego Segui	8.00	4.00	2.50

1963 Mickey Sego S.F. Giants

These self-framing pictures feature the artwork of Mickey Sego, but the method of their distribution is unknown. Measuring 7" x 8-1/2", the pieces have a dark frame around a large black-and-white portrait and smaller cartoon drawing of the player. There are also a few words about the player's career. A simulated plaque at the bottom of the frame bears a facsimile autograph. Each picture has a hole at top for hanging.

		NM	EX	VG
Common Player:		15.00	7.50	4.50
(1)	Chuck Hiller	15.00	7.50	4.50
(2)	Harvey Kuenn	20.00	10.00	6.00
(3)	Willie Mays	85.00	42.00	25.00
(4)	Billy Pierce	17.50	8.75	5.25

1914 Lawrence Semon Postcards

Seven players are currently known in this series, but it's possible others remain to be reported. The approximately 3-1/2" x 5-1/2" postcards feature on their fronts either portrait or action drawings of star players by Lawrence Semon. A few biographical and career details are printed at bottom, which has allowed the assignment of 1914 as the year of issue. Backs are standard postcard style. The unnumbered cards are checklisted here alphabetically.

		NM	EX	VG
Common Player:		250.00	125.00	75.00
(1)	George Burns	250.00	125.00	75.00
(2)	Frank Chance	500.00	250.00	150.00

(3)	Ty Cobb	2,500	1,250	750.00
(4)	Walter Johnson	2,250	1,125	675.00
(5)	Cornelius McGillicuddy (Connie Mack)	400.00	200.00	120.00
(6)	Richard (Rube) Marquard	400.00	200.00	120.00
(7)	John J. McGraw	400.00	200.00	120.00

1946-1947 Sensacion Premiums

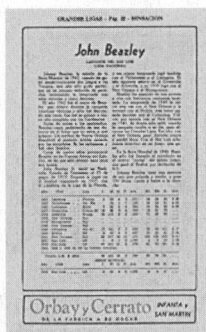

Two types of baseball premium pictures were issued by the magazine "Sensacion" during the winter league season of 1946-47. One series of 27 features Cuban stars (some of whom played in the Major Leagues), while a series of 11 Major League stars was also issued. Printed in color on newspaper stock, the pictures measure about 7-3/4" x 11". Fronts have large portraits or posed action photos with the player name in a fancy bottom border. Backs have lengthy career summaries and full stats, along with a small ad. The premiums were issued in magazines as well as in a complete album of each type. They are numbered according to the apparent order of their appearance.

		NM	EX	VG
Complete Set, Cubans (27):		1,500	750.00	450.00
Complete Set, Major Leaguers (11):		600.00	300.00	175.00
Common Cuban Player:		30.00	15.00	9.00
Common Major Leaguer:		45.00	22.50	13.50
	Estrellas del Base Ball Cubano			
(1)	Napoleon Reyes	45.00	22.50	13.50
(2)	Fermin Guerra	30.00	15.00	9.00
(3)	Gilberto Torres	30.00	15.00	9.00
(4)	Martin Dihigo	750.00	375.00	225.00
(5)	Lazaro Salazar	100.00	50.00	30.00
(6)	Silvio Garcia	100.00	50.00	30.00
(7)	Pollo Rodriguez	30.00	15.00	9.00
(8)	Herberto Blanco	30.00	15.00	9.00
(9)	Andres Fleitas	30.00	15.00	9.00
(10)	Jorge J. Torres	30.00	15.00	9.00
(11)	Salvador Hernandez	30.00	15.00	9.00
(12)	Agapito Mayor	30.00	15.00	9.00
(13)	Tomas de la Cruz	30.00	15.00	9.00
(14)	Gilberto Valdivia	30.00	15.00	9.00
(15)	Julio Moreno	30.00	15.00	9.00
(16)	Regino Otero	30.00	15.00	9.00
(17)	Claro Duany	50.00	25.00	15.00
(18)	Pedro Jimenez	30.00	15.00	9.00
(19)	Tony Castanos	30.00	15.00	9.00
(20)	Alberto Hernandez	30.00	15.00	9.00
(21)	Hector Rodriguez	40.00	20.00	12.00
(22)	Carlos Blanco	30.00	15.00	9.00
(23)	Roberto Ortiz	50.00	25.00	15.00
(24)	Rene Monteagudo	30.00	15.00	9.00
(25)	Pedro Pages	30.00	15.00	9.00
(26)	Conrado Marrero	40.00	20.00	12.00
(27)	Chino Hidalgo	30.00	15.00	9.00
	Estrellas de las Grandes Ligas			
(1)	Stan Musial	150.00	75.00	45.00
(2)	Jim (Mickey) Vernon	50.00	25.00	15.00
(3)	Dave Ferris	45.00	22.50	13.50
(4)	Johnny Pesky	45.00	22.50	13.50
(5)	Howie Pollett	45.00	22.50	13.50
(6)	Ted Williams	200.00	100.00	60.00
(7)	Johnny Hopp	45.00	22.50	13.50
(8)	Dom DiMaggio	75.00	37.00	22.00
(9)	Tex Hughson	45.00	22.50	13.50
(10)	Johnny Beazley	45.00	22.00	13.50
(11)	Tommy Holmes	45.00	22.50	13.50

1977 Sertoma Stars

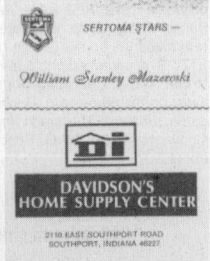

This collectors' issue was produced by an Indianapolis service club. The 3" x 4" cards are printed in black on a textured yellow stock. Fronts have borderless player poses, many of which were lifted from earlier-issued cards. Backs have the Sertoma logo, set name and player name at top. Beneath a squiggly line is a business-card size ad for different members of the organization.

		NM	EX	VG
Complete Set (24):		45.00	22.50	13.50
Common Player:		2.00	1.00	.60
(1)	Hank Aaron	10.00	5.00	3.00
(2)	Bob Allison	2.00	.75	.60
(3)	Clete Boyer	2.00	.75	.60
(4)	Don Buford	2.00	.75	.60
(5)	Rod Carew	3.00	1.50	.90
(6)	Rico Carty	2.00	.75	.60
(7)	Roberto Clemente	15.00	7.50	4.50
(8)	Jim Ray Hart	2.00	.75	.60
(9)	Dave Johnson	2.00	.75	.60
(10)	Harmon Killebrew	3.00	1.50	.90
(11)	Mickey Mantle	20.00	10.00	6.00
(12)	Juan Marichal	3.00	1.50	.90
(13)	Bill Mazeroski	3.00	1.50	.90
(14)	Joe Morgan	3.00	1.50	.90
(15)	Phil Niekro	2.50	1.25	.70
(16)	Tony Oliva	2.00	1.00	.60
(17)	Gaylord Perry	2.50	1.25	.70
(18)	Boog Powell	2.00	1.00	.60
(19)	Brooks Robinson	3.50	1.75	1.00
(20)	Frank Robinson	3.50	1.75	1.00
(21)	John Roseboro	2.00	.75	.60
(22)	Rusty Staub	2.00	.75	.60
(23)	Joe Torre	2.00	1.00	.60
(24)	Jim Wynn	2.00	.75	.60

1977 Sertoma Stars - Puzzle Backs

This collectors set was issued in conjunction with the Indianapolis Sports Collectors Convention in 1977. The set was sold for $3 with proceeds benefiting the local Sertoma (Service to Mankind) Club's charity works. Cards measure 2-3/4" x 4-1/8". A 2-1/2" black circle at center contains a black-and-white player photo. The background on front is yellow, with red and black printing. Backs are borderless and form an old Pittsburgh Pirates team photo puzzle. Sets were originally sold for $3.50.

		NM	EX	VG
Complete Set (25):		75.00	37.50	22.50
Common Player:		2.00	1.00	.60
(1)	Bernie Allen	2.00	1.00	.60
(2)	Home Run Baker	2.00	1.00	.60
(3)	Ted Beard	2.00	1.00	.60
(4)	Don Buford	2.00	1.00	.60
(5)	Eddie Cicotte	4.00	2.00	1.25
(6)	Roberto Clemente	20.00	10.00	6.00
(7)	Dom Dallessandro	2.00	1.00	.60
(8)	Carl Erskine	2.00	1.00	.60
(9)	Nellie Fox	6.00	3.00	1.75
(10)	Lou Gehrig	20.00	10.00	6.00
(11)	Joe Jackson	20.00	10.00	6.00
(12)	Len Johnston	2.00	1.00	.60
(13)	Benny Kauff	2.00	1.00	.60
(14)	Dick Kenworthy	2.00	1.00	.60
(15)	Harmon Killebrew	6.00	3.00	1.75
(16)	"Lefty Bob" Logan	2.00	1.00	.60
(17)	Willie Mays	15.00	7.50	4.50
(18)	Satchel Paige	9.00	4.50	2.75
(19)	Edd Roush	2.00	1.00	.60
(20)	Chico Ruiz	2.00	1.00	.60
(21)	Babe Ruth	20.00	10.00	6.00
(22)	Herb Score	2.00	1.00	.60
(23)	George Sisler	2.00	1.00	.60
(24)	Buck Weaver	5.00	2.50	1.50
(25)	Early Wynn	2.00	1.00	.60

1961 7-11

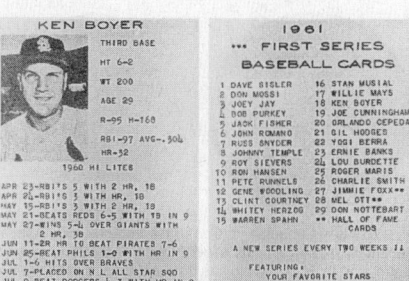

The first of 7-11's baseball card issues was a crude attempt which was abruptly halted. The checklist for the 30-card set indicated that it was the first of planned series to be issued two weeks apart. No follow-up to the first series was ever distributed. The 2-7/16" x 3-3/8" cards are printed on pink cardboard stock, with blank backs. Small black-and-white player portraits appear in the upper-left, with the player name at top, team name at bottom and card number in the lower-right corner. There are a few biographical bits and stats to the right of the photo, and several lines of 1960 season highlights below. The cards were sold seven for a nickel in vending machines.

		NM	EX	VG
Complete Set (30):		2,400	1,200	725.00
Common Player:		50.00	25.00	15.00
1	Dave Sisler	50.00	25.00	15.00
2	Don Mossi	50.00	25.00	15.00
3	Joey Jay	50.00	25.00	15.00
4	Bob Purkey	50.00	25.00	15.00
5	Jack Fisher	50.00	25.00	15.00
6	John Romano	50.00	25.00	15.00
7	Russ Snyder	50.00	25.00	15.00
8	Johnny Temple	50.00	25.00	15.00
9	Roy Sievers	50.00	25.00	15.00
10	Ron Hansen	50.00	25.00	15.00
11	Pete Runnels	50.00	25.00	15.00
12	Gene Woodling	50.00	25.00	15.00
13	Clint Courtney	50.00	25.00	15.00
14	Whitey Herzog	50.00	25.00	15.00
15	Warren Spahn	120.00	60.00	35.00
16	Stan Musial	250.00	125.00	75.00
17	Willie Mays	400.00	200.00	120.00
18	Ken Boyer	60.00	30.00	18.00
19	Joe Cunningham	50.00	25.00	15.00
20	Orlando Cepeda	90.00	45.00	27.00
21	Gil Hodges	125.00	65.00	35.00
22	Yogi Berra	150.00	75.00	45.00
23	Ernie Banks	200.00	100.00	60.00
24	Lou Burdette	50.00	25.00	15.00
25	Roger Maris	250.00	125.00	75.00
26	Charlie Smith	50.00	25.00	15.00
27	Jimmie Foxx	50.00	25.00	15.00
28	Mel Ott	50.00	25.00	15.00
29	Don Nottebart	50.00	25.00	15.00
----	Checklist	50.00	25.00	15.00

1975 Shakey's Pizza West Coast Greats

This collectors' issue was sponsored by Seattle area Shakey's Pizza restaurants in conjunction with the 1975 convention of the Washington State Sports Collectors Assn. Two thousand sets were produced featuring players who were born and/or played on the West Coast. The first 1,000 attendees at the convention were given a free sample of card #1, DiMaggio. Cards are 2-3/4" x about 3-5/8". Fronts have a black-and-white photo at center with black and red graphics. A large Shakey's logo is at lower-left. The card number, player name, position and connection to the West Coast are printed at lower-right. Backs are in red and white with the pizza chain's logo and a list of four Seattle-area locations.

		NM	EX	VG
Complete Set (18):		30.00	15.00	9.00
Common Player:		4.00	2.00	1.25
1	Joe DiMaggio	15.00	7.50	4.50
2	Paul Waner	4.00	2.00	1.25
3	Lefty Gomez	4.00	2.00	1.25
4	Earl Averill	4.00	2.00	1.25
5	Ernie Lombardi	4.00	2.00	1.25
6	Joe Cronin	4.00	2.00	1.25
7	George Burns	4.00	2.00	1.25
8	Casey Stengel	5.00	2.50	1.50
9	Wahoo Sam Crawford	4.00	2.00	1.25
10	Ted Williams	12.50	6.25	3.75
11	Fred Hutchinson	4.00	2.00	1.25
12	Duke Snider	7.50	3.75	2.25
13	Hal Chase	4.00	2.00	1.25
14	Bobby Doerr	4.00	2.00	1.25
15	Arky Vaughan	4.00	2.00	1.25
16	Tony Lazzeri	4.00	2.00	1.25
17	Lefty O'Doul	4.00	2.00	1.25
18	Stan Hack	4.00	2.00	1.25

1976 Shakey's Pizza Hall of Fame

Between 1975-77 the Washington State Sports Collectors Assn. worked with the Shakey's pizza chain in the Seattle area to produce and distribute several sets of "old timers" cards. Generally one card from the set was given away to hobbyists attending the club's annual convention, with other cards available at the pizza places. Complete sets were also widely sold within the hobby. Interpretation of whether these are "legitimate" cards or a collector issue is up to each collector. The 1976 cards were issued in four series: Hall of Fame, Greatest Players, Immortals and All-Time Greats. The format was identical, with the (approximately) 2-1/2" x 3-1/2" cards featuring

black-and-white player photos on front, surrounded by a red frame and bright blue border. Backs are in red, black and white with large Shakey's ads at top and bottom. Also on back are player biographies and career stats. The cards were issued in order of the players' induction into the Hall of Fame. All four series are skip-numbered. Cards of Sam Thompson and Robin Roberts were re-issued in Series 2 to correct errors.

		NM	EX	VG
Complete Set (160):		100.00	50.00	30.00
Complete Set, no coupons (158):		75.00	37.50	22.00
Common Player:		2.00	1.00	.60
Series 1 - Baseball's Hall of Fame		35.00	17.50	10.50
A	Earl Averill ($1 off pizza coupon on back; card show giveaway)	4.00	2.00	1.25
1	Ty Cobb	7.50	3.75	2.25
3	Walter Johnson	3.00	1.50	.90
12	Connie Mack	2.00	1.00	.60
18	Lou Gehrig	9.00	4.50	2.75
20	George Sisler	2.00	1.00	.60
21	Cap Anson	2.00	1.00	.60
36	Mike "King" Kelly	2.00	1.00	.60
41	Jack Chesbro	2.00	1.00	.60
50	Mickey Cochrane	2.00	1.00	.60
52	Lefty Grove	2.00	1.00	.60
54	Herb Pennock	2.00	1.00	.60
55	Pie Traynor	2.00	1.00	.60
56	Charlie Gehringer	2.00	1.00	.60
57	Three-Finger Brown	2.00	1.00	.60
58	Kid Nichols	2.00	1.00	.60
59	Jimmie Foxx	2.00	1.00	.60
64	Al Simmons	2.00	1.00	.60
72	Rabbit Maranville	2.00	1.00	.60
73	Bill Terry	2.00	1.00	.60
80	Joe Cronin	2.00	1.00	.60
83	Joe McCarthy	2.00	1.00	.60
86	Bill Hamilton	2.00	1.00	.60
88	Jackie Robinson	7.50	3.75	2.25
89	Bill McKechnie	2.00	1.00	.60
93	Sam Rice	2.00	1.00	.60
95	Luke Appling	2.00	1.00	.60
103	Ted Williams	7.50	3.75	2.25
104	Casey Stengel	2.00	1.00	.60
107	Lloyd Waner	2.00	1.00	.60
108	Joe Medwick	2.00	1.00	.60
115	Lou Boudreau	2.00	1.00	.60
122	Harry Hooper	2.00	1.00	.60
127	Yogi Berra	3.00	1.50	.90
129	Lefty Gomez	2.00	1.00	.60
131	Sandy Koufax	7.50	3.75	2.25
143	Jocko Conlan	2.00	1.00	.60
144	Whitey Ford	2.00	1.00	.60
146	Sam Thompson	2.00	1.00	.60
147	Earl Averill	2.00	1.00	.60
149	Billy Herman	2.00	1.00	.60
154	Cal Hubbard	2.00	1.00	.60
156	Fred Lindstrom	2.00	1.00	.60
157	Robin Roberts	2.00	1.00	.60
Series 2 - Baseball's Greatest Players		35.00	17.50	10.50
A	Earl Averill (Card show giveaway, coupon on back.)	2.00	1.00	.60
4	Christy Mathewson	3.00	1.50	.90
6	Nap Lajoie	2.00	1.00	.60
7	Tris Speaker	2.00	1.00	.60
9	Morgan Bulkeley	2.00	1.00	.60
10	Ban Johnson	2.00	1.00	.60
11	John McGraw	2.00	1.00	.60
14	Grover Alexander	2.00	1.00	.60
17	Eddie Collins	2.00	1.00	.60
19	Willie Keeler	2.00	1.00	.60
22	Charles Comiskey	2.00	1.00	.60
24	Buck Ewing	2.00	1.00	.60
31	Fred Clarke	2.00	1.00	.60
32	Jimmy Collins	2.00	1.00	.60
34	Hugh Duffy	2.00	1.00	.60
35	Hugh Jennings	2.00	1.00	.60
38	Wilbert Robinson	2.00	1.00	.60
40	Frank Chance	2.00	1.00	.60
42	John Evers	2.00	1.00	.60
43	Clark Griffith	2.00	1.00	.60
47	Joe Tinker	2.00	1.00	.60
51	Frank Frisch	2.00	1.00	.60
53	Carl Hubbell	2.00	1.00	.60
65	Ed Barrow	2.00	1.00	.60
66	Chief Bender	2.00	1.00	.60
67	Tommy Connolly	2.00	1.00	.60
74	Joe DiMaggio	12.50	6.25	3.75
75	Gabby Hartnett	2.00	1.00	.60
78	Home Run Baker	2.00	1.00	.60
81	Hank Greenberg	3.00	1.50	.90
87	Bob Feller	2.00	1.00	.60
90	Edd Roush	2.00	1.00	.60
109	Kiki Cuyler	2.00	1.00	.60
111	Roy Campanella	4.00	2.00	1.25
113	Stan Coveleski	2.00	1.00	.60

116	Earle Combs	2.00	1.00	.60
120	Jake Beckley	2.00	1.00	.60
125	Satchel Paige	4.00	2.00	1.25
128	Josh Gibson	3.00	1.50	.90
135	Roberto Clemente	10.00	5.00	3.00
141	Cool Papa Bell	2.00	1.00	.60
142	Jim Bottomley	2.00	1.00	.60
146	Sam Thompson	2.00	1.00	.60
150	Judy Johnson	2.00	1.00	.60
152	Oscar Charleston	2.00	1.00	.60
158	Robin Roberts	2.00	1.00	.60
	Series 3 - Baseball's Immortals	25.00	12.50	7.50
5	Honus Wagner	3.50	1.75	1.00
13	George Wright	2.00	1.00	.60
15	Alexander Cartwright	2.00	1.00	.60
16	Henry Chadwick	2.00	1.00	.60
23	Candy Cummings	2.00	1.00	.60
25	Old Hoss Radbourne	2.00	1.00	.60
26	Al Spalding	2.00	1.00	.60
28	Judge Landis	2.00	1.00	.60
29	Roger Bresnahan	2.00	1.00	.60
30	Dan Brouthers	2.00	1.00	.60
33	Ed Delahanty	2.00	1.00	.60
37	Jim O'Rourke	2.00	1.00	.60
39	Jesse Burkett	2.00	1.00	.60
44	Tommy McCarthy	2.00	1.00	.60
45	Joe McGinnity	2.00	1.00	.60
46	Eddie Plank	2.00	1.00	.60
49	Ed Walsh	2.00	1.00	.60
61	Harry Heilmann	2.00	1.00	.60
68	Bill Klem	2.00	1.00	.60
70	Harry Wright	2.00	1.00	.60
85	Max Carey	2.00	1.00	.60
91	John Clarkson	2.00	1.00	.60
92	Elmer Flick	2.00	1.00	.60
96	Red Faber	2.00	1.00	.60
97	Burleigh Grimes	2.00	1.00	.60
98	Miller Huggins	2.00	1.00	.60
99	Tim Keefe	2.00	1.00	.60
101	Monte Ward	2.00	1.00	.60
102	Pud Galvin	2.00	1.00	.60
110	Goose Goslin	2.00	1.00	.60
114	Waite Hoyt	2.00	1.00	.60
117	Ford Frick	2.00	1.00	.60
118	Jesse Haines	2.00	1.00	.60
126	George Weiss	2.00	1.00	.60
130	William Harridge	2.00	1.00	.60
132	Buck Leonard	2.00	1.00	.60
133	Early Wynn	2.00	1.00	.60
136	Billy Evans	2.00	1.00	.60
137	Monte Irvin	2.00	1.00	.60
138	George Kelly	2.00	1.00	.60
140	Mickey Welch	2.00	1.00	.60
148	Bucky Harris	2.00	1.00	.60
151	Ralph Kiner	2.00	1.00	.60
153	Roger Connor	2.00	1.00	.60
	Series 4 - Ball's All-Time Greats	20.00	10.00	6.00
2	Babe Ruth	12.50	6.25	3.75
8	Cy Young	2.50	1.25	.70
27	Rogers Hornsby	2.00	1.00	.60
48	Rube Waddell	2.00	1.00	.60
62	Paul Waner	2.00	1.00	.60
63	Dizzy Dean	2.50	1.25	.70
69	Bobby Wallace	2.00	1.00	.60
71	Bill Dickey	2.00	1.00	.60
77	Dazzy Vance	2.00	1.00	.60
79	Ray Schalk	2.00	1.00	.60
82	Sam Crawford	2.00	1.00	.60
84	Zack Wheat	2.00	1.00	.60
94	Eppa Rixey	2.00	1.00	.60
100	Heinie Manush	2.00	1.00	.60
105	Red Ruffing	2.00	1.00	.60
106	Branch Rickey	2.00	1.00	.60
112	Stan Musial	5.00	2.50	1.50
119	Dave Bancroft	2.00	1.00	.60
121	Chick Hafey	2.00	1.00	.60
123	Joe Kelley	2.00	1.00	.60
124	Rube Marquard	2.00	1.00	.60
134	Ross Youngs	2.00	1.00	.60
139	Warren Spahn	2.00	1.00	.60
145	Mickey Mantle	16.00	8.00	4.75
155	Bob Lemon	2.00	1.00	.60

1977 Shakey's All-Time Superstars

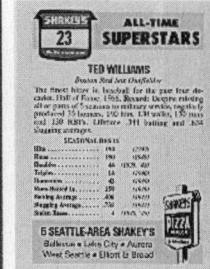

This set of baseball's all-time greatest (at least through the 1950s) was the final production of the Washington State Sports Collectors Assn. and local Shakey's restaurants. About 2-3/8" x 3", the cards feature black-and-white player photos at center with a red border around. A facsimile autograph appears in blue on the photo. Backs are similar to earlier Shakey's issues, with large logos for the pizza chain, player information and "Seasonal Bests" stats, all printed in red and black on white. Several special cards were produced for distribution at the 1977 annual convention and other venues.

		NM	EX	VG
	Complete Set (28):	35.00	17.50	10.00
	Complete Set (25):	25.00	12.50	7.50
	Common Player:	2.00	1.00	.60
	Welcome to WSSCA Show Card (Collectibles collage.)	3.00	1.50	.90
A	Earl Averill	3.00	1.50	.90
B	John Mize ($1 coupon on back)	3.00	1.50	.90
C	Robert Lee Johnson	3.00	1.50	.90
1	Connie Mack	2.00	1.00	.60
2	John J. McGraw	2.00	1.00	.60
3	Denton T. (Cy) Young	4.00	2.00	1.25
4	Walter Johnson	4.00	2.00	1.25
5	G.C. Alexander	2.00	1.00	.60
6	Christy Mathewson	4.00	2.00	1.25
7	Lefty Grove	2.00	1.00	.60
8	Mickey Cochrane	2.00	1.00	.60
9	Bill Dickey	2.00	1.00	.60
10	Lou Gehrig	7.50	3.75	2.25
11	George Sisler	2.00	1.00	.60
12	Cap Anson	2.00	1.00	.60
13	Jimmie Foxx	2.00	1.00	.60
14	Rogers Hornsby	2.00	1.00	.60
15	Nap Lajoie	2.00	1.00	.60
16	Eddie Collins	2.00	1.00	.60
17	Pie Traynor	2.00	1.00	.60
18	Honus Wagner	4.00	2.00	1.25
19	Ty Cobb	7.50	3.75	2.25
20	Babe Ruth	10.00	5.00	3.00
21	Joe Jackson	10.00	5.00	3.00
22	Tris Speaker	2.00	1.00	.60
23	Ted Williams	6.00	3.00	1.75
24	Joe DiMaggio	7.50	3.75	2.25
25	Stan Musial	5.00	2.50	1.50
---	WSSCA Club Information Card	4.00	2.00	1.25

1952 Shelby Bicycles

The year of issue stated is conjectural, based on the familiar picture of Berra used for this promotional photo. The photo shows Yogi kneeling in full catcher's gear, except mask, ready to throw the ball; it is seen on his '50 Bowman card, among others. The blank-back, black-and-white photos are 5" x 7" with a white border all around. Scripted at bottom is, "Ride Shelby / The Winner's Bike / Sincerely / Yogi Berra."

	NM	EX	VG
Yogi Berra	150.00	75.00	45.00

1958-1959 Shillito's Boys' Shop Cincinnati Reds

This rare regional set was issued by a Cincinnati-area chain department store. The 2-1/2" x 3-1/2" black-and-white glossy cards are essentially a version of contemporary team-issued photos except for the presence (usually) on the otherwise blank back of a purple "SHILLITO'S / BOYS' SHOPS" rubber-stamp. Some cards have been seen wuthout the ad on back. The unnumbered pictures are listed here in alphabetical order.

		NM	EX	VG
	Complete Set (23):	3,500	1,750	1,050
	Common Player:	200.00	100.00	60.00
(1)	Tom Acker	200.00	100.00	60.00
(2)	Ed Bailey	200.00	100.00	60.00
(3)	Gus Bell	200.00	100.00	60.00
(4)	John "Dutch" Dotterer	200.00	100.00	60.00
(5)	Walt Dropo	200.00	100.00	60.00
(6)	Del Ennis	200.00	100.00	60.00
(7)	Jay Hook	200.00	100.00	60.00
(8)	Hal Jeffcoat	200.00	100.00	60.00
(9)	Eddie Kasko	200.00	100.00	60.00
(10)	Brooks Lawrence	200.00	100.00	60.00
(11)	Jerry Lynch	200.00	100.00	60.00
(12)	Roy McMillan	200.00	100.00	60.00
(13)	Eddie Miksis	200.00	100.00	60.00
(14)	Don Newcombe	230.00	115.00	69.00
(15)	Joe Nuxhall	250.00	125.00	75.00
(16)	Jim O'Toole	200.00	100.00	60.00
(17)	Vada Pinson	250.00	125.00	75.00
(18)	Bob Purkey	200.00	100.00	60.00
(19)	Frank Robinson	500.00	250.00	150.00
(20)	Frank Thomas	200.00	100.00	60.00
(21)	Johnny Temple	200.00	100.00	60.00
(22)	Bob Thurman	200.00	100.00	60.00
(23)	Pete Whisenant	200.00	100.00	60.00

1974 Shillito's Pete Rose

PETE ROSE, 3rd Base CINCINNATI REDS

Probably issued in conjunction with an autograph-signing appearance at the Cincinnati department store, this picture could have been issued in either 1974 or 1975. The glossy black-and-white, blank-back photo measures 5-1/2" x 8". The autograph on the example shown is genuine, the photo does not have a facsimile signature.

	NM	EX	VG
Pete Rose	150.00	75.00	45.00

1976 Shillito's Kahn's Reds Clubhouse

Though the format for each photo differs, this series of Reds player photos was issued under the sponsorship of the Shillito's department store and Kahn's meats. In about 5" x 7-3/16" format, the blank-back photos are black-and-white with at least one (Bench) having red highlights. The pictures were given out at player autograph appearances at various Shillito's locations between June 21 and August 13. Youngsters enrolled in the club received a membership card, probably entitling them to an autograph at each event. With five dates specifically mentioned, it is likely at least one more photo exists in this series.

		NM	EX	VG
	Common Player:	.00	.00	.00
(1)	Johnny Bench (Kenwood Plaza)	100.00	50.00	30.00
(2)	Dave Concepcion (Kahn's - WLW Radio)	30.00	15.00	9.00
(3)	Doug Flynn (No sponsor.)	12.00	6.00	3.50
(4)	George Foster (Four sponsors listed.)	15.00	7.50	4.50
(5)	Pete Rose (Shillito's)	100.00	50.00	30.00
---	Membership Card	10.00	5.00	3.00

1962 Shirriff Coins

This is a Canadian version of the better-known Salada-Junket plastic player coins issued in the U.S. Backs specify an issue of 200; 21 of the players from the Salada set were not issued by Shirriff. Because the Canadian coins were produced after the U.S. version they are not found with all the variations known in Salada, nor the differing levels of scarcity. Shirriff coins were packed in bags of potato chips, with each coin sealed in a clear cellophane wrapper. Although the Canadian coins are much scarcer than the U.S., significantly less demand keeps prices lower, as well.

		NM	EX	VG
	Complete Set (200):	1,600	800.00	525.00
	Common Player:	6.00	3.00	1.75
1	Jim Gentile	7.00	3.50	2.00
2	Not Issued (Bill Pierce)			
3	Chico Fernandez (Light blue piping.)	6.00	3.00	1.75
4	Not Issued (Tom Brewer)			
5	Woody Held	6.00	3.00	1.75
6	Not Issued (Ray Herbert)	.00	.00	.00
7	Ken Aspromonte (Indians)	6.00	3.00	1.75
8	Whitey Ford	40.00	20.00	12.00
9	Jim Lemon	6.00	3.00	1.75
10	Billy Klaus	6.00	3.00	1.75
11	Not Issued (Steve Barber)			
12	Nellie Fox	25.00	12.50	7.50
13	Jim Bunning	25.00	12.50	7.50
14	Frank Malzone	6.00	3.00	1.75
15	Tito Francona	6.00	3.00	1.75
16	Bobby Del Greco	6.00	3.00	1.75
17	Steve Bilko	6.00	3.00	1.75
18	Not Issued (Tony Kubek)			
19	Earl Battey	6.00	3.00	1.75
20	Chuck Cottier	6.00	3.00	1.75
21	Willie Tasby	6.00	3.00	1.75
22	Bob Allison	7.00	3.50	2.00
23	Roger Maris	40.00	20.00	12.00
24	Earl Averill	6.00	3.00	1.75
25	Jerry Lumpe	6.00	3.00	1.75
26	Not Issued (Jim Grant)			
27	Carl Yastrzemski	50.00	25.00	15.00
28	Rocky Colavito (Blue piping.)	20.00	10.00	6.00
29	Al Smith	6.00	3.00	1.75
30	Not Issued (Jim Busby)			
31	Dick Howser	6.00	3.00	1.75
32	Jim Perry	6.00	3.00	1.75
33	Yogi Berra	50.00	25.00	15.00
34	Ken Hamlin	6.00	3.00	1.75
35	Dale Long	6.00	3.00	1.75
36	Harmon Killebrew	35.00	17.50	10.50
37	Dick Brown	6.00	3.00	1.75
38	Gary Geiger	6.00	3.00	1.75
39	Minnie Minoso (Cardinals)	9.00	4.50	2.75
40	Brooks Robinson	35.00	17.50	10.50
41	Mickey Mantle	180.00	90.00	54.00
42	Bennie Daniels	6.00	3.00	1.75
43	Billy Martin	15.00	7.50	4.50
44	Vic Power	7.00	3.50	2.00
45	Joe Pignatano	6.00	3.00	1.75
46	Ryne Duren	7.00	3.50	2.00
47	Pete Runnels (1B)	6.00	3.00	1.75
48	Dick Williams	6.00	3.00	1.75
49	Jim Landis	6.00	3.00	1.75
50	Steve Boros	6.00	3.00	1.75
51	Zoilo Versalles	7.00	3.50	2.00
52	Johnny Temple (Orioles)	6.00	3.00	1.75
53	Jackie Brandt	6.00	3.00	1.75
54	Joe McClain	6.00	3.00	1.75
55	Sherman Lollar	6.00	3.00	1.75
56	Gene Stephens	6.00	3.00	1.75
57	Leon Wagner	6.00	3.00	1.75
58	Frank Lary	6.00	3.00	1.75
59	Bill Skowron	12.00	6.00	3.50
60	Not Issued (Vic Wertz)			
61	Willie Kirkland	6.00	3.00	1.75
62	Leo Posada	6.00	3.00	1.75
63	Albie Pearson	7.00	3.50	2.00
64	Bobby Richardson	15.00	7.50	4.50
65	Marv Breeding (SS)	6.00	3.00	1.75
66	Not Issued (Roy Sievers)			
67	Al Kaline	35.00	17.50	10.50
68	Don Buddin (Colts)	6.00	3.00	1.75
69	Lenny Green (White top button.)	6.00	3.00	1.75
70	Not Issued (Gene Green)			
71	Luis Aparicio	25.00	12.50	7.50
72	Norm Cash	12.00	6.00	3.50
73	Not Issued (Jackie Jensen)			
74	Bubba Phillips	6.00	3.00	1.75
75	Jim Archer	6.00	3.00	1.75
76	Ken Hunt	6.00	3.00	1.75
77	Ralph Terry	6.00	3.00	1.75
78	Camilo Pascual	6.00	3.00	1.75
79	Not Issued (Marty Keough)			
80	Cletis Boyer	9.00	4.50	2.75
81	Jim Pagliaroni	6.00	3.00	1.75
82	Gene Leek	6.00	3.00	1.75
83	Jake Wood	6.00	3.00	1.75
84	Not Issued (Coot Veal)			
85	Norm Siebern	6.00	3.00	1.75
86	Andy Carey (Phillies)	6.00	3.00	1.75
87	Bill Tuttle (White top button.)	6.00	3.00	1.75
88	Jimmy Piersall	6.00	3.00	1.75
89	Not Issued (Ron Hansen)			
90	Chuck Stobbs	6.00	3.00	1.75
91	Ken McBride	6.00	3.00	1.75
92	Bill Bruton	6.00	3.00	1.75
93	Gus Triandos	6.00	3.00	1.75
94	John Romano	6.00	3.00	1.75
95	Elston Howard	12.00	6.00	3.50
96	Gene Woodling	6.00	3.00	1.75
97	Early Wynn (Portrait)	20.00	10.00	6.00
98	Milt Pappas	6.00	3.00	1.75
99	Bill Monbouquette	6.00	3.00	1.75
100	Wayne Causey	6.00	3.00	1.75
101	Don Elston	6.00	3.00	1.75
102	Charlie Neal	6.00	3.00	1.75
103	Don Blasingame	6.00	3.00	1.75
104	Not Issued (Frank Thomas)			
105	Wes Covington	6.00	3.00	1.75
106	Chuck Hiller	6.00	3.00	1.75
107	Don Hoak	6.00	3.00	1.75
108	Bob Lillis (Colts)	6.00	3.00	1.75
109	Sandy Koufax	65.00	32.00	19.50
110	Gordy Coleman	6.00	3.00	1.75
111	Ed Matthews (Mathews)	30.00	15.00	9.00
112	Art Mahaffey	6.00	3.00	1.75
113	Ed Bailey (Name above ear.)	6.00	3.00	1.75
114	Smoky Burgess	7.00	3.50	2.00
115	Bill White	7.00	3.50	2.00
116	Not Issued (Ed Bouchee)			
117	Bob Buhl	6.00	3.00	1.75
118	Vada Pinson	7.00	3.50	2.00
119	Carl Sawatski	6.00	3.00	1.75
120	Dick Stuart	7.00	3.50	2.00
121	Not Issued (Harvey Kuenn)			
122	Pancho Herrera	6.00	3.00	1.75
123	Don Zimmer	7.00	3.50	2.00
124	Wally Moon	7.00	3.50	2.00
125	Joe Adcock	6.00	3.00	1.75
126	Joey Jay	6.00	3.00	1.75
127	Maury Wills (Red 3 on uniform.)	12.00	6.00	3.50
128	George Altman	6.00	3.00	1.75
129	John Buzhardt	6.00	3.00	1.75
130	Felipe Alou	7.00	3.50	2.00
131	Bill Mazeroski	25.00	12.50	7.50
132	Ernie Broglio	6.00	3.00	1.75
133	John Roseboro	7.00	3.50	2.00
134	Mike McCormick	6.00	3.00	1.75
135	Chuck Smith (White Sox)	6.00	3.00	1.75
136	Ron Santo	12.00	6.00	3.50
137	Gene Freese	6.00	3.00	1.75
138	Dick Groat	7.00	3.50	2.00
139	Curt Flood	7.00	3.50	2.00
140	Frank Bolling	6.00	3.00	1.75
141	Clay Dalrymple	6.00	3.00	1.75
142	Willie McCovey	30.00	15.00	9.00
143	Bob Skinner	6.00	3.00	1.75
144	Lindy McDaniel	6.00	3.00	1.75
145	Glen Hobbie	6.00	3.00	1.75
146	Gil Hodges	20.00	10.00	6.00
147	Eddie Kasko	6.00	3.00	1.75
148	Not Issued (Gino Cimoli)			
149	Willie Mays	75.00	37.00	22.00
150	Roberto Clemente	90.00	45.00	27.00
151	Red Schoendienst	25.00	12.50	7.50
152	Joe Torre	9.00	4.50	2.75
153	Bob Purkey	6.00	3.00	1.75
154	Tommy Davis (3B)	7.50	3.75	2.25
155	Andre Rogers (Rodgers)	6.00	3.00	1.75
156	Tony Taylor	6.00	3.00	1.75
157	Bob Friend	6.00	3.00	1.75
158	Gus Bell	6.00	3.00	1.75
159	Roy McMillan	6.00	3.00	1.75
160	Carl Warwick	6.00	3.00	1.75
161	Willie Davis	6.00	3.00	1.75
162	Not Issued (Sam Jones)			
163	Ruben Amaro	6.00	3.00	1.75
164	Sam Taylor	6.00	3.00	1.75
165	Frank Robinson	35.00	17.50	10.50
166	Lou Burdette	6.00	3.00	1.75
167	Ken Boyer	10.00	5.00	3.00
168	Bill Virdon	6.00	3.00	1.75
169	Jim Davenport	6.00	3.00	1.75
170	Don Demeter	6.00	3.00	1.75
171	Not Issued (Richie Ashburn)			
172	John Podres	7.50	3.75	2.25
173	Joe Cunningham (White Sox)	6.00	3.00	1.75
174	ElRoy Face	6.00	3.00	1.75
175	Orlando Cepeda	25.00	12.50	7.50
176	Bobby Gene Smith	6.00	3.00	1.75
177	Ernie Banks (SS)	50.00	25.00	15.00
178	Daryl Spencer (1B)	6.00	3.00	1.75
179	Not Issued (Bob Schmidt)			
180	Hank Aaron	75.00	37.00	22.00
181	Hobie Landrith	6.00	3.00	1.75
182	Ed Bressoud	6.00	3.00	1.75
183	Felix Mantilla	6.00	3.00	1.75
184	Dick Farrell	6.00	3.00	1.75
185	Bob Miller	6.00	3.00	1.75
186	Don Taussig	6.00	3.00	1.75
187	Pumpsie Green	6.00	3.00	1.75
188	Bobby Shantz	7.50	3.75	2.25
189	Roger Craig	6.00	3.00	1.75
190	Hal Smith	6.00	3.00	1.75
191	John Edwards	6.00	3.00	1.75
192	John DeMerit	6.00	3.00	1.75
193	Joe Amalfitano	6.00	3.00	1.75
194	Norm Larker	6.00	3.00	1.75
195	Al Heist	6.00	3.00	1.75
196	Al Spangler	6.00	3.00	1.75
197	Alex Grammas	6.00	3.00	1.75
198	Gerry Lynch	6.00	3.00	1.75
199	Jim McKnight	6.00	3.00	1.75
200	Jose Pagen (Pagan)	6.00	3.00	1.75
201	Junior Gilliam	7.50	3.75	2.25
202	Art Ditmar	6.00	3.00	1.75
203	Pete Daley	6.00	3.00	1.75
204	Johnny Callison	6.00	3.00	1.75
205	Stu Miller	6.00	3.00	1.75
206	Russ Snyder	6.00	3.00	1.75
207	Billy Williams	25.00	12.50	7.50
208	Walter Bond	6.00	3.00	1.75
209	Joe Koppe	6.00	3.00	1.75
210	Don Schwall	6.00	3.00	1.75
211	Billy Gardner	6.00	3.00	1.75
212	Chuck Estrada	6.00	3.00	1.75
213	Gary Bell	6.00	3.00	1.75
214	Floyd Robinson	6.00	3.00	1.75
215	Duke Snider	35.00	17.50	10.50
216	Lee Maye	6.00	3.00	1.75
217	Howie Bedell	6.00	3.00	1.75
218	Bob Will	6.00	3.00	1.75
219	Dallas Green	7.50	3.75	2.25
220	Carroll Hardy	6.00	3.00	1.75
221	Danny O'Connell	6.00	3.00	1.75

1928 Shonen Kulubu Babe Ruth Postcard

This card, which the Japanese inscription describes as picturing Babe Ruth hitting his first home run of 1926, was part of a multi-sport premium issue by the Japanese magazine Shonen Kubulu ("Youth Club"). The front has a colorized black-and-white photo, with blue inscriptions at right. Back is in blue with standard international postcard indicia.

	NM	EX	VG
Babe Ruth	500.00	250.00	150.00

1889 G. Waldon Smith Boston Beaneaters Cabinets

Whether the scope of this issue encompassed a greater portion of the 1889 Boston National Leaguers or just the four currently known players is presently unknown. Boston photographer G. Waldon Smith immortalized the players in a series of 4-1/4" x 6-1/2" cabinet cards. Each card features a capless, chest-up portrait of a mustachioed ballplayer. The studio's name and location are printed in red at bottom. The players are not identified on the pieces. The 1889 pictures can be differentiated from the 1890 issue by the ornateness of the studio address; the earlier is in plain type, the later is more ornate and includes the state abbreviation.

		NM	EX	VG
	Common Player:	3,600	1,800	1,080
(1)	Tom Brown	3,600	1,800	1,080
(2)	Harry Ganzel	3,600	1,800	1,080
(3)	Billy Nash	3,600	1,800	1,080
(4)	Pop Smith	3,600	1,800	1,080
(6)	The Boston Base Ball Club (Team photo, 21" x 18".)	18,000	9,000	5,400

1890 G. Waldon Smith Cabinets

As little as is known about the 1889 Smith baseball cabinets, the 1890 issue is even less well documented. Only a single player is currently recorded, Tom Brown, who also appears in the 1889 issue. In 1890, Brown was a member of the Boston Players League team; whether or not his teammates or those of the Boston National League club can be found in this issue remains unknown. Like the 1889 cabinets, size is about 4-1/4" x 6-1/2" and no player identification is presented. The 1890 cabinets can be differentiated from the 1889s by the more elaborate presentation of the studio address at bottom-right, including the state abbreviation.

	NM	EX	VG
Tom Brown	3,000	1,500	900.00
Boston Base Ball Club / Players' League (Team photo, 22" x 18".)	20,000	10,000	6,000

1904 G. Waldon Smith Cabinets

Following a move down Tremont St. to No. 164A, this Boston photographer was still producing baseball player cabinet photos. Like his earlier photos, the circa 1904 pieces have black-and-white photographs mounted on stiff 4-1/4" x 6-1/2" cardboard backings. The only currently known picture in this series is a full-length portrait of Kip Selbach. Others almost certainly exist.

	NM	EX	VG
Kip Selbach	2,500	1,250	750.00

1909 W.W. Smith Postcards

THE MIGHTY HONUS

Only two subjects are known in this series of postcards issued contemporary with the 1909 World Series between the Tigers and Pirates, though it is possible a card of Ty Cobb might have also been issued. The 3-1/2" x 5-1/2" black-and-white cards have pencil portraits by W.W. Smith. Backs have standard postcard markings.

		NM	EX	VG
Complete Set (2):		1,000	500.00	300.00
(1)	The Mighty Honus (Honus Wagner)	750.00	375.00	225.00
(2)	Two of a Kind (Ty Cobb, Honus Wagner)	3,000	1,500	900.00

1957 Sohio Gas Indians/Reds

In 1957 Sohio (Standard Oil of Ohio) gas stations in Ohio issued sets of Cleveland Indians and Cincinnati Reds photocards and team albums. The blank-backed cards are 5" x 7" and printed in black-and-white with one perforated edge. The cards have a facsimile autograph as the only identification. The unnumbered cards are checklisted here alphabetically within team.

		NM	EX	VG
Complete Set (36):		650.00	325.00	195.00
Common Player:		10.00	5.00	3.00
CLEVELAND INDIANS				
Complete Set (18):		300.00	150.00	90.00
(1)	Bob Avila	10.00	5.00	3.00
(2)	Jim Busby	10.00	5.00	3.00
(3)	Chico Carrasquel	10.00	5.00	3.00
(4)	Rocky Colavito	75.00	37.00	22.00
(5)	Mike Garcia	10.00	5.00	3.00
(6)	Jim Hegan	10.00	5.00	3.00
(7)	Bob Lemon	20.00	10.00	6.00
(8)	Roger Maris	150.00	75.00	45.00
(9)	Don Mossi	10.00	5.00	3.00
(10)	Ray Narleski	10.00	5.00	3.00
(11)	Russ Nixon	10.00	5.00	3.00
(12)	Herb Score	15.00	7.50	4.50
(13)	Al Smith	10.00	5.00	3.00
(14)	George Strickland	10.00	5.00	3.00
(15)	Bob Usher	10.00	5.00	3.00
(16)	Vic Wertz	10.00	5.00	3.00
(17)	Gene Woodling	10.00	5.00	3.00
(18)	Early Wynn	20.00	10.00	6.00
----	Cleveland Indians Album	60.00	30.00	18.00
CINCINNATI REDS				
Complete Set (18):		325.00	160.00	97.00
(1)	Ed Bailey	10.00	5.00	3.00
(2)	Gus Bell	10.00	5.00	3.00
(3)	Rocky Bridges	10.00	5.00	3.00
(4)	Smoky Burgess	10.00	5.00	3.00
(5)	Hersh Freeman	10.00	5.00	3.00
(6)	Alex Grammas	10.00	5.00	3.00
(7)	Don Gross	10.00	5.00	3.00
(8)	Warren Hacker	10.00	5.00	3.00
(9)	Don Hoak	10.00	5.00	3.00
(10)	Hal Jeffcoat	10.00	5.00	3.00
(11)	Johnny Klippstein	10.00	5.00	3.00
(12)	Ted Kluszewski	60.00	30.00	18.00
(13)	Brooks Lawrence	10.00	5.00	3.00
(14)	Roy McMillan	10.00	5.00	3.00
(15)	Joe Nuxhall	12.50	6.25	3.75
(16)	Wally Post	10.00	5.00	3.00
(17)	Frank Robinson	150.00	75.00	45.00
(18)	Johnny Temple	10.00	5.00	3.00
----	Cincinnati Redlegs Album	60.00	30.00	18.00

1969 Solon Kansas City Royals

LOU PINIELLA
Outfielder

This collectors' issue is believed to have originated with Illinois hobbyist Bob Solon. The black-and-white, blank-back cards feature members of the expansion Royals. The border beneath the posed photos features a team logo and player identification at bottom. Cards measure 2-1/8" x 3-5/8". The checklist here is arranged alphabetically, as the cards are unnumbered.

		NM	EX	VG
Complete Set (15):		16.00	8.00	4.75
Common Player:		2.00	1.00	.60
(1)	Jerry Adair	2.00	1.00	.60
(2)	Wally Bunker	2.00	1.00	.60
(3)	Moe Drabowsky	3.00	1.50	.90
(4)	Dick Drago	2.00	1.00	.60
(5)	Joe Foy	2.00	1.00	.60
(6)	Joe Gordon	2.00	1.00	.60
(7)	Chuck Harrison	2.00	1.00	.60
(8)	Mike Hedlund	2.00	1.00	.60
(9)	Jack Hernandez	2.00	1.00	.60
(10)	Pat Kelly	2.00	1.00	.60
(11)	Roger Nelson	2.00	1.00	.60
(12)	Bob Oliver	2.00	1.00	.60
(13)	Lou Piniella	6.00	3.00	1.75
(14)	Ellie Rodriguez	2.00	1.00	.60
(15)	Dave Wickersham	2.00	1.00	.60

1905 Souvenir Post Card Shop of Cleveland

Formal portraits of the 1905 Cleveland Naps are featured in this set of black-and-white postcards. The 3-1/4" x 5-1/2" cards have a wide white border at bottom which carries the legend, "SOUVENIR POST CARD SHOP OF CLEVELAND." The player name is in white at the bottom of the photo. Backs have postage rate information and a notice, "NOTHING BUT ADDRESS ON THIS SIDE."

		NM	EX	VG
Complete Set (19):		16,500	8,250	5,000
Common Player:		950.00	475.00	285.00
(1)	Harry Bay	950.00	475.00	285.00
(2)	Harry Bemis	950.00	475.00	285.00
(3)	Bill Bernhard	950.00	475.00	285.00
(4)	Bill Bradley	950.00	475.00	285.00
(5)	Fred Buelow	950.00	475.00	285.00
(6)	Charles C. Carr	950.00	475.00	285.00
(7)	Frank Donahue	950.00	475.00	285.00
(8)	Elmer Flick	1,425	710.00	425.00
(9)	Otto Hess	950.00	475.00	285.00
(10)	Jay Jackson	950.00	475.00	285.00
(11)	Addie Joss	2,750	1,375	825.00
(12)	Nick Kahl	950.00	475.00	285.00
(13)	Napoleon Lajoie	2,000	1,000	600.00
(14)	Earl Moore	950.00	475.00	285.00
(15)	Robert Rhoads	950.00	475.00	285.00
(16)	George Stovall	950.00	475.00	285.00
(17)	Terry Turner	950.00	475.00	285.00
(18)	Ernest Vinson	950.00	475.00	285.00
(19)	Team Portraits Composite	1,500	750.00	450.00

1909-11 Sovereign Cigarettes

Premiums shown are for common-player cards. Hall of Famers or other high-demand cards generally realize little or no premium with Sovereign back. On T205s, the backs are printed in green.

PREMIUMS
T205: 1.25X
T206 150 Subjects: 1X
T206 350 Subjects: 1.5X
T206 460 Subjects: 1.5X
(See T205, T206 for checklists and base card values.)

1949 Spalding Joe DiMaggio Glove Premium Photos

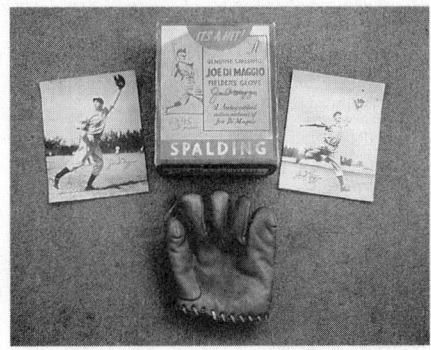

The attributed date is only approximate. Lucky youngsters who received a Spalding Joe DiMaggio fielder's glove also got a pair of 8" x 10" black-and-white posed action photos of the Yankee Clipper. Each blank-back, borderless photo has a facsimile autograph.

		NM	EX	VG
(1)	Joe DiMaggio (No ball in photo.)	125.00	65.00	40.00
(2)	Joe DiMaggio (Ball in photo.)	125.00	65.00	40.00

1950s-70s Spalding Advisory Staff Photos

Advisory staff photos were a promtional item which debuted in the early 1950s, flourished in the 1960s and died in the early 1970s. Generally 8" x 10" (sometimes a little larger), these black-and-white (a few later were color) glossy photos picture players who had contracted with a major baseball equipment company to endorse and use their product. Usually the product - most often a glove - was prominently displayed in the photo. The pictures were often displayed in the windows of sporting goods stores or the walls of sports departments and were sometimes made available to customers. Because the companies tended to stick with players over the years, some photos were reissued, sometimes with and sometimes without a change of team, pose or typography. Spalding staff photos of the era are checklisted here in alphabetical order. Team designation and pose description is given for each known picture. The photos are checklisted here in alphabetical order. It is unlikely this list is complete. Several arrangements of typography in the bottom border are seen for Spalding advisory staff pictures.

		NM	EX	VG
Common Player:		12.00	6.00	3.50
(1)	Richie Allen (Phillies, batting helmet.)	20.00	10.00	6.00
(2)	Gene Alley (Pirates, upper body.)	12.00	6.00	3.50

		NM	EX	VG
(3)	Mike Andrews (Red Sox, upper body.)	12.00	6.00	3.50
(4)	Bob Aspromonte (Dodgers, upper body.)	12.00	6.00	3.50
(5)	Sal Bando (A's, upper body.)	12.00	6.00	3.50
(7)	Steve Barber (Orioles, chest-to-cap.)	12.00	6.00	3.50
(8)	John Bateman (Colt .45s, upper body.)	12.00	6.00	3.50
(9)	Yogi Berra (Yankees, batting.)	30.00	15.00	9.00
(10)	Yogi Berra (Mets, upper body.)	30.00	15.00	9.00
(11)	Don Bessent (Brooklyn, follow-through.)	20.00	10.00	6.00
(12a)	Frank Bolling (Tigers, fielding.)	15.00	7.50	4.50
(12b)	Frank Bolling (Braves, chest up.)	15.00	7.50	4.50
(13)	Jim Bouton (Yankees, upper body.)	15.00	7.50	4.50
(14)	Jim Bunning (Phillies, upper body.)	20.00	10.00	6.00
(16)	John Callison (Phillies, batson shoulder.)	12.00	6.00	3.50
(17)	Rocky Colavito (Tigers, batting.)	25.00	12.50	7.50
(18)	Roger Craig (Brooklyn, follow-through.)	15.00	7.50	4.50
(19)	Clay Dalrymple (Phillies, upper body.)	12.00	6.00	3.50
(20)	Alvin Dark (Cardinals, batting follow-through.)	20.00	10.00	6.00
(21)	Don Drysdale (Dodgers, pitching follow-through.)	25.00	12.50	7.50
(22)	Sam Esposito (White Sox, hands on knees.)	12.00	6.00	3.50
(23)	Ron Fairly (Dodgers, upper body.)	12.00	6.00	3.50
(24)	Dick Farrell (Phillies, follow-through.)	25.00	12.50	7.50
(25)	Whitey Ford (Yankees, hands over head.)	30.00	15.00	9.00
(26)	Jim Fregosi (L.A. Angels, upper body.)	15.00	7.50	4.50
(27)	Jim Fregosi (California Angels, upper body, looking front.)	15.00	7.50	4.50
(28)	Jim Fregosi (California Angels, upper body, looking right.)	15.00	7.50	4.50
(29)	Jim Fregosi (Angels, green borders, b/w portrait.)	15.00	7.50	4.50
(30)	Bob Gibson (Color, stretch position.)	25.00	12.50	7.50
(33)	Tom Haller (Giants, catching crouch.)	12.00	6.00	3.50
(34)	Richie Hebner (Pirates, full-length.)	12.00	6.00	3.50
(35)	Mike Hegan (Brewers, upper body.)	12.00	6.00	3.50
(36)	Jim Hickman (Mets, upper body.)	12.00	6.00	3.50
(37)	Ken Hunt (Reds, follow-through.)	20.00	10.00	6.00
(38)	Jerry Koosman (Mets, ready to pitch.)	15.00	7.50	4.50
(39)	Jerry Koosman (Mets, upper body.)	15.00	7.50	4.50
(40)	Don Larsen (Yankees, follow-through.)	25.00	12.50	7.50
(41)	Charlie Lau (Braves, upper body.)	15.00	7.50	4.50
(42)	Mickey Lolich (Tigers, upper body, ready to pitch.)	15.00	7.50	4.50
(43)	Jerry Lumpe (Tigers, belt-up.)	12.00	6.00	3.50
(45)	Roger Maris (Yankees, batting.)	30.00	15.00	9.00
(46)	Roger Maris (Yankees, full-length.)	30.00	15.00	9.00
(47)	Roger Maris (Cardinals, "picture-frame," b/w photo.)	30.00	15.00	9.00
(49)	Dick McAuliffe (Tigers, portrait.)	12.00	6.00	3.50
(50)	Bill Monbouquette (Red Sox, wind-up.)	12.00	6.00	3.50
(51)	Bobby Murcer (Yankees, upper body.)	12.00	6.00	3.50
(53)	Jim Northrup (Tigers, batting.)	12.00	6.00	3.50
(56)	Jim Pagliaroni (Pirates, batting.)	12.00	6.00	3.50
(58)	Jim Palmer (Upper body.)	25.00	12.50	7.50
(60)	Joe Pepitone (Yankees, batting.)	15.00	7.50	4.50
(61)	Gary Peters (White Sox, green borders, b/w portrait.)	12.00	6.00	3.50
(62)	Rico Petrocelli (Red Sox, upper body.)	12.00	6.00	3.50
(64)	Joe Pignatano (A's, hands on hips.)	12.00	6.00	3.50
(66)	Bob Rodgers (Angels, portrait.)	12.00	6.00	3.50
(67)	Rich Rollins (Twins, arms crossed.)	12.00	6.00	3.50
(69)	Nolan Ryan (Angels, color, pitching.)	75.00	37.00	22.00
(72)	Tom Seaver (Mets, waist-to-cap.)	30.00	15.00	9.00
(73)	Tom Seaver (Mets, color, pitching.)	30.00	15.00	9.00
(75)	Mel Stottlemyre (Yankees, rust borders, b/w pitching pose.)	12.00	6.00	3.50
(76)	Dick Stuart (Pirates, batting.)	15.00	7.50	4.50
(78)	Joe Torre (Braves, upper body.)	15.00	7.50	4.50
(79)	Joe Torre (Cardinals, red borders, b/w portrait.)	15.00	7.50	4.50
(85)	Pete Ward (White Sox, portrait.)	12.00	6.00	3.50

		NM	EX	VG
(86)	Fred Whitfield (Indians, portrait.)	12.00	6.00	3.50
(87)	Maury Wills (Dodgers, chest-to-cap.)	15.00	7.50	4.50
(88)	Maury Wills (No team, full-length batting.)	12.00	6.00	3.50
(90)	Carl Yastrzemski (Kneeling w/ bats.)	30.00	15.00	9.00
(91)	Carl Yastrzemski (Picture-frame border, b/w portrait.)	30.00	15.00	9.00

1969 Spare-Time Products Minnesota Twins Discs

The intended use and manner of distribution of these 8" uniface color discs is unknown. The hard composition discs have a baseball design on which is centered a player portrait. A facsimile autograph is at bottom and there is a hole at top for hanging. Copyright information appears at lower-right.

		NM	EX	VG
Complete Set (8):		400.00	200.00	125.00
Common Player:		30.00	15.00	9.00
(1)	Dave Boswell	30.00	22.00	9.00
(2)	Leo Cardenas	30.00	15.00	9.00
(3)	Dean Chance	30.00	15.00	9.00
(4)	Jim Kaat	45.00	22.00	13.50
(5)	Tony Oliva (SP)	150.00	75.00	45.00
(6)	Ron Perranoski	30.00	22.00	9.00
(7)	Jim Perry	30.00	15.00	9.00
(8)	John Roseboro	30.00	15.00	9.00

1948 Speedway 79 Tiger of the Week Photos

This set of blank-back, black-and-white 8" x 10" photos was issued by one of the Tigers radio sponsors. One photo, bearing a facsimile autograph on front, was given away each week to honor the outstanding Tigers performer. The photos have no markings identifying the issuer and they are unnumbered. They are checklisted here alphabetically.

		NM	EX	VG
Complete Set (14):		350.00	175.00	100.00
Common Player:		30.00	15.00	9.00
(1)	Neil Berry	30.00	15.00	9.00
(2)	"Hoot" Evers	30.00	15.00	9.00
(3)	Ted Gray	30.00	15.00	9.00
(4)	Art Houtteman	30.00	15.00	9.00
(5)	Fred Hutchinson	30.00	15.00	9.00
(6)	George Kell	50.00	25.00	15.00
(7)	Eddie Lake	30.00	15.00	9.00
(8)	Johnny Lipon	30.00	15.00	9.00
(9)	Hal Newhouser	50.00	25.00	15.00
(10)	Dizzy Trout	30.00	15.00	9.00
(11)	Virgil Trucks	30.00	15.00	9.00
(12)	George Vico	30.00	15.00	9.00
(13)	Dick Wakefield	30.00	15.00	9.00
(14)	Bill Wertz	30.00	15.00	9.00

1936 Spencer Shoes Jimmie Foxx Premium Photo

The attributed date is speculative, based on the uniform in which the player is pictured on this 7" x 9", blank-back, black-and-white premium photo. The picture has a facsimile autograph at left. At bottom-right in script is, "Courtesy of Spencer Shoes."

	NM	EX	VG
Jimmie Foxx	350.00	175.00	105.00

1953-55 Spic and Span Braves

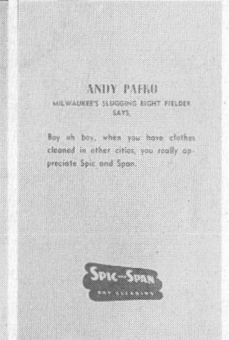

The first of several regional issues from a Milwaukee dry cleaner, the 1953-55 Spic and Span Braves set consists of black-and-white cards, 3-1/4" x 5-1/2". The fronts of the card have a facsimile autograph beneath the player photo. Cards are found with blank backs or with a Spic and Span advertising message on the back. Blank-backed cards are believed to have been issued by Wisco gas stations.

		NM	EX	VG
Complete Set (29):		1,800	900.00	540.00
Common Player:		50.00	25.00	15.00
(1)	Hank Aaron	600.00	300.00	180.00
(2)	Joe Adcock	50.00	25.00	15.00
(3)	John Antonelli	50.00	25.00	15.00
(4)	Vern Bickford	50.00	25.00	15.00
(5)	Bill Bruton	50.00	25.00	15.00
(6)	Bob Buhl	50.00	25.00	15.00
(7)	Lew Burdette	50.00	25.00	15.00
(8)	Dick Cole	50.00	25.00	15.00
(9)	Walker Cooper	50.00	25.00	15.00
(10)	Del Crandall	50.00	25.00	15.00
(11)	George Crowe	50.00	25.00	15.00
(12)	Jack Dittmer	50.00	25.00	15.00
(13)	Sid Gordon	50.00	25.00	15.00
(14)	Ernie Johnson	50.00	25.00	15.00
(15)	Dave Jolly	50.00	25.00	15.00
(16)	Don Liddle	50.00	25.00	15.00
(17)	John Logan	50.00	25.00	15.00
(18)	Ed Mathews	200.00	100.00	60.00
(19)	Chet Nichols	50.00	25.00	15.00
(20)	Dan O'Connell	50.00	25.00	15.00
(21)	Andy Pafko	50.00	25.00	15.00
(22)	Jim Pendleton	50.00	25.00	15.00
(23)	Ebba St. Claire	50.00	25.00	15.00
(24)	Warren Spahn	200.00	100.00	60.00
(25)	Max Surkont	50.00	25.00	15.00
(26)	Bob Thomson	75.00	37.50	22.00
(27)	Bob Thorpe	50.00	25.00	15.00
(28)	Roberto Vargas	50.00	25.00	15.00
(29)	Jim Wilson	50.00	25.00	15.00

1953-57 Spic and Span Braves 7x10 Photos

This regional set was issued by Spic and Span Dry Cleaners of Milwaukee over a four-year period and consists of large (7" x 10") photos of Braves players. Of all the various Spic and Span sets, this one seems to be the easiest to find. The fronts feature a player photo with a facsimile autograph below. The Spic and Span logo also appears on the fronts, while the backs are blank. A header card picturing Milwaukee County Stadium also exists.

		NM	EX	VG
Complete Set (14):		335.00	165.00	100.00
Common Player:		25.00	12.50	7.50
(1)	Joe Adcock	25.00	12.50	7.50
(2)	William H. Bruton	25.00	12.50	7.50
(3)	Robert Buhl	25.00	12.50	7.50
(4)	Lou Burdette	25.00	12.50	7.50
(5)	Del Crandall	25.00	12.50	7.50
(6)	Jack Dittmer	25.00	12.50	7.50
(7)	Johnny Logan	25.00	12.50	7.50

		NM	EX	VG
(8)	Edwin L. Mathews, Jr.	75.00	37.50	22.00
(9)	Chet Nichols	25.00	12.50	7.50
(10)	Danny O'Connell	25.00	12.50	7.50
(11)	Andy Pafko	25.00	12.50	7.50
(12)	Warren E. Spahn	75.00	37.50	22.00
(13)	Bob Thomson	35.00	17.50	10.00
(14)	Milwaukee County Stadium	35.00	17.50	10.00

1954 Spic and Span Braves

Player selection points to 1954 as the date of this issue, making it contemporary with several other card sets produced by the chain of Wisconsin dry cleaners. These cards are printed in blue on 5-1/2" x 8-1/2" yellow cardstock. Fronts have player portraits by an artist signed as "Warmth," facsimile autographs, a promotional quote from the player and the sponsor's logo. Backs are blank. It is not known whether the set is complete at 13.

		NM	EX	VG
Complete Set (13):		1,200	600.00	350.00
Common Player:		75.00	37.50	22.50
(1)	Joe Adcock	90.00	45.00	27.50
(2)	William H. Bruton	75.00	37.50	22.50
(3)	Robert Buhl	75.00	37.50	22.50
(4)	Lou Burdette	75.00	37.50	22.50
(5)	Del Crandall	75.00	37.50	22.50
(6)	Jack Dittmer	75.00	37.50	22.50
(7)	Johnny Logan	75.00	37.50	22.50
(8)	Edwin L. Mathews Jr.	225.00	110.00	70.00
(9)	Chet Nichols	75.00	37.50	22.50
(10)	Danny O'Connell	75.00	37.50	22.50
(11)	Andy Pafko	75.00	37.50	22.50
(12)	Warren E. Spahn	225.00	110.00	70.00
(13)	Bob Thomson	90.00	45.00	27.50

1954-56 Spic and Span Braves

Issued during the three-year period from 1954-1956, this Spic and Span set consists of 18 postcard-size (4" x 6") cards. The front of the cards include a facsimile autograph printed in white and the Spic and Span logo.

		NM	EX	VG
Complete Set (18):		1,350	675.00	400.00
Common Player:		35.00	17.50	10.00
(1)	Hank Aaron	400.00	200.00	120.00
(2)	Joe Adcock	35.00	17.50	10.00
(3)	William H. Bruton	35.00	17.50	10.00
(4)	Robert Buhl	35.00	17.50	10.00
(5)	Lou Burdette	35.00	17.50	10.00
(6)	Gene Conley	35.00	17.50	10.00
(7)	Del Crandall	35.00	17.50	10.00
(8)	Ray Crone	35.00	17.50	10.00
(9)	Jack Dittmer	35.00	17.50	10.00
(10)	Ernie Johnson	35.00	17.50	10.00
(11)	Dave Jolly	35.00	17.50	10.00
(12)	Johnny Logan	35.00	17.50	10.00
(13)	Edwin L. Mathews, Jr.	225.00	110.00	70.00
(14)	Chet Nichols	35.00	17.50	10.00
(15)	Danny O'Connell	35.00	17.50	10.00
(16)	Andy Pafko	35.00	17.50	10.00
(17)	Warren E. Spahn	220.00	110.00	70.00
(18)	Bob Thomson	60.00	30.00	18.00

1955 Spic and Span Braves Die-Cuts

This 17-card, die-cut set is the rarest of all the Spic and Span issues. The stand-ups, which measure approximately 7-1/2" x 7", picture the players in action poses and were designed to be

punched out, allowing them to stand up. Most cards were used in this fashion, making better-condition cards very rare today. The front of the card includes a facsimile autograph and the Spic and Span logo.

		NM	EX	VG
Complete Set (18):		4,400	2,200	1,250
Common Player:		175.00	90.00	55.00
(1)	Hank Aaron	900.00	450.00	275.00
(2)	Joe Adcock	175.00	90.00	55.00
(3)	Bill Bruton	175.00	90.00	55.00
(4)	Bob Buhl	175.00	90.00	55.00
(5)	Lew Burdette	175.00	90.00	55.00
(6)	Gene Conley	175.00	90.00	55.00
(7)	Del Crandall	175.00	90.00	55.00
(8)	Jack Dittmer	175.00	90.00	55.00
(9)	Ernie Johnson	175.00	90.00	55.00
(10)	Dave Jolly	175.00	90.00	55.00
(11)	John Logan	175.00	90.00	55.00
(12)	Ed Mathews	450.00	225.00	135.00
(13)	Chet Nichols	175.00	90.00	55.00
(14)	Dan O'Connell	175.00	90.00	55.00
(15)	Andy Pafko	175.00	90.00	55.00
(16)	Warren Spahn	450.00	225.00	135.00
(17)	Bob Thomson	225.00	110.00	65.00
(18)	Jim Wilson	175.00	90.00	55.00

1957 Spic and Span Braves

This 20-card set was issued in 1957, the year the Braves were World Champions and is a highly desirable set. The cards measure 4" x 5" and have a wide white border surrounding the player photo. A blue Spic and Span logo appears in the lower-right corner and the card includes a salutation and facsimile autograph, also in blue.

		NM	EX	VG
Complete Set (20):		1,250	625.00	375.00
Common Player:		25.00	12.50	7.50
(1)	Hank Aaron	400.00	200.00	120.00
(2)	Joe Adcock	25.00	12.50	7.50
(3)	Bill Bruton	25.00	12.50	7.50
(4)	Bob Buhl	25.00	12.50	7.50
(5)	Lew Burdette	25.00	12.50	7.50
(6)	Gene Conley	25.00	12.50	7.50
(7)	Wes Covington (SP)	50.00	25.00	15.00
(8)	Del Crandall	25.00	12.50	7.50
(9)	Ray Crone	25.00	12.50	7.50
(10)	Fred Haney	25.00	12.50	7.50
(11)	Ernie Johnson	25.00	12.50	7.50
(12)	John Logan	25.00	12.50	7.50
(13)	Felix Mantilla (SP)	50.00	25.00	15.00
(14)	Ed Mathews	85.00	45.00	25.00
(15)	Dan O'Connell	25.00	12.50	7.50
(16)	Andy Pafko	25.00	12.50	7.50
(17)	Red Schoendienst (SP)	110.00	55.00	35.00
(18)	Warren Spahn	85.00	45.00	25.00
(19)	Bob Thomson	45.00	22.50	13.50
(20)	Bob Trowbridge (SP)	50.00	25.00	15.00

1960 Spic and Span Braves

Spic and Span's final Milwaukee Braves issue consists of 26 cards, each measuring 2-3/4" x 3-1/8". The fronts contain a white-bordered photo with no printing, while the backs include a facsimile autograph and the words "Photographed and Autographed Exclusively for Spic and Span." The 1960 set includes the only known variation in the Spic and Span sets; a "flopped" negative error showing catcher Del Crandall batting left-handed was later corrected.

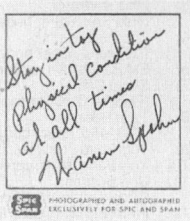

		NM	EX	VG
Complete Set (26):		1,650	825.00	500.00
Common Player:		35.00	17.50	10.00
(1)	Hank Aaron	650.00	325.00	200.00
(2)	Joe Adcock	35.00	17.50	10.00
(3)	Bill Bruton	35.00	17.50	10.00
(4)	Bob Buhl	35.00	17.50	10.00
(5)	Lew Burdette	35.00	17.50	10.00
(6)	Chuck Cottier	35.00	17.50	10.00
(7a)	Del Crandall (Photo reversed.)	60.00	30.00	18.00
(7b)	Del Crandall (Correct photo.)	35.00	17.50	10.00
(8)	Chuck Dressen	35.00	17.50	10.00
(9)	Joey Jay	35.00	17.50	10.00
(10)	John Logan	35.00	17.50	10.00
(11)	Felix Mantilla	35.00	17.50	10.00
(12)	Ed Mathews	125.00	65.00	35.00
(13)	Lee Maye	35.00	17.50	10.00
(14)	Don McMahon	35.00	17.50	10.00
(15)	George Myatt	35.00	17.50	10.00
(16)	Andy Pafko	35.00	17.50	10.00
(17)	Juan Pizarro	35.00	17.50	10.00
(18)	Mel Roach	35.00	17.50	10.00
(19)	Bob Rush	35.00	17.50	10.00
(20)	Bob Scheffing	35.00	17.50	10.00
(21)	Red Schoendienst	90.00	45.00	27.50
(22)	Warren Spahn	125.00	65.00	35.00
(23)	Al Spangler	35.00	17.50	10.00
(24)	Frank Torre	35.00	17.50	10.00
(25)	Carl Willey	35.00	17.50	10.00
(26)	Whit Wyatt	35.00	17.50	10.00

1964-67 Sport Hobbyist Famous Card Series

These very early collectors issues were produced over a period of several years in the mid-1960s during Frank Nagy's ownership of the "Sport Hobbyist" magazine. The 2-1/4" x 3-3/4" black-and-white cards picture on their fronts reproductions of rare and famous baseball cards from Nagy's unequaled collection, including eight of the very rare Tarzan Bread issue of the mid-1930s which few collectors even today have seen. Backs have identification of the pictured card, utilizing the then-standard "American Card Catalog" set designations.

		NM	EX	VG
Complete Set (30):		90.00	45.00	27.50
Common Player:		5.00	2.50	1.50
1	T206 Honus Wagner	12.50	6.25	3.75
2	T212 Henley	5.00	2.50	1.50
3	C46 Simmons	5.00	2.50	1.50
4	M116 Christy Mathewson	5.00	2.50	1.50
5	M101-5 Jack Barry	5.00	2.50	1.50
6	T204 Mordecai Brown	5.00	2.50	1.50
7	D322 Tip Top Bread Webb	5.00	2.50	1.50
8	S74 Lou Criger	5.00	2.50	1.50
9	R333 DeLong Kiki Cuyler	5.00	2.50	1.50
10	R319 Nap Lajoie	7.50	3.75	2.25
11	T205 John McGraw	5.00	2.50	1.50
12	E107 Addie Joss	5.00	2.50	1.50
13	W502 George Sisler	5.00	2.50	1.50
14	Allen & Ginter N29 Buck Ewing	5.00	2.50	1.50
15	E90 Chief Bender	5.00	2.50	1.50
16	E104 George Mullin	5.00	2.50	1.50
17	E95 Fred Merkle	5.00	2.50	1.50
18	E121 Walter Schang	5.00	2.50	1.50
19	Allen & Ginter N28 Tim Keefe	5.00	2.50	1.50
20	E120 Harold (Muddy) Ruel	5.00	2.50	1.50
21	D382 Irving (Jack) Burns	5.00	2.50	1.50
22	D382 George Connally	5.00	2.50	1.50
23	D382 Myril Hoag	5.00	2.50	1.50
24	D382 Willie Kamm	5.00	2.50	1.50
25	D382 Dutch Leonard	5.00	2.50	1.50
26	D382 Clyde Manion	5.00	2.50	1.50
27	D382 Johnny Vergez	5.00	2.50	1.50
28	D382 Tom Zachary	5.00	2.50	1.50
29	E145 Ty Cobb	7.50	3.75	2.25
30	Playing Card, Richardson	5.00	2.50	1.50

1971 Sport Hobbyist Famous Card Series

A new series of collector cards, designed as the first-ever attempt to reproduce the T206 tobacco set, was begun under the hobby paper's new ownership but quickly abandoned. The 2" x 3" cards have a black-and-white picture of a card at center, surrounded by a red frame (except Bescher, which has a black frame). Backs identify the card and include a card number.

	NM	EX	VG
Complete Set (21):	90.00	45.00	27.50
Common Card:	5.00	2.50	1.50
31 T206 Abbaticchio	5.00	2.50	1.50
32 T206 Barbeau	5.00	2.50	1.50
33 T206 Burch	5.00	2.50	1.50
34 T206 M. Brown	5.00	2.50	1.50
35 T206 Chase	5.00	2.50	1.50
36 T206 Ball	5.00	2.50	1.50
37 T206 Abstein	5.00	2.50	1.50
38 T206 Bowerman	5.00	2.50	1.50
39 T206 Chase	5.00	2.50	1.50
40 T206 Criss	5.00	2.50	1.50
41 T206 Beck	5.00	2.50	1.50
42 T206 Bresnahan	5.00	2.50	1.50
43 T206 Bradley	5.00	2.50	1.50
44 T206 Berger	5.00	2.50	1.50
45 T206 Bransfield	5.00	2.50	1.50
46 T206 Bescher	5.00	2.50	1.50
47 T206 Bell	5.00	2.50	1.50
48 T206 Bergen	5.00	2.50	1.50
49 T206 Bender	5.00	2.50	1.50
50 T206 Bush	5.00	2.50	1.50
51 T206 Chesbro	5.00	2.50	1.50

1975 Sport Hobbyist

This was one of several series of collectors issues produced in the 1960s and 1970s by the Sport Hobbyist, one of the card hobby's earliest periodicals. This series features the past greats of the game in postcard size (3-1/2" x 5-1/2"). Cards are found either blank-backed or with an ad offering various new-card products. Fronts of cards numbered through 115 have watercolor portraits in an oval frame. A box below offers a career summary. Higher number cards feature photos and/or artwork, sometimes with a caption, and sometimes with no identification. Cards are numbered with an SH prefix. Each series of 18 were originally sold for $1.50.

	NM	EX	VG
Complete Set (48):	150.00	75.00	45.00
Common Player:	5.00	2.50	1.50
98 Lou Gehrig	15.00	7.50	4.50
99 Ty Cobb	12.50	6.25	3.75
100 Joe DiMaggio	15.00	7.50	4.50
101 Mel Ott	5.00	2.50	1.50
102 Carl Hubbell	5.00	2.50	1.50
103 Babe Ruth	20.00	10.00	6.00
104 Rogers Hornsby	7.50	3.75	2.25
105 Tris Speaker	7.50	3.75	2.25
106 Hank Greenberg	7.50	3.75	2.25
107 Jimmy (Jimmie) Foxx	7.50	3.75	2.25
108 Ted Williams	15.00	7.50	4.50
109 Mickey Cochrane	5.00	2.50	1.50
110 Bob Feller	7.50	3.75	2.25
111 Cy Young	9.00	4.50	2.75
112 George Sissler (Sisler)	5.00	2.50	1.50
113 Honus Wagner	9.00	4.50	2.75
114 Lefty Grove	5.00	2.50	1.50
115 Dizzy Dean	7.50	3.75	2.25
116 Babe Ruth (Farewell address.)	9.00	4.50	2.75
117 Jackie Robinson	7.50	3.75	2.25
118 Mike Kelly (Woodcut.)	5.00	2.50	1.50
119 Honus Wagner (Portrait and action.)	5.00	2.50	1.50
120 Babe Ruth (W/mascot Ray Kelly.)	9.00	4.50	2.75
121 Babe Ruth (Photos/artwork.)	5.00	2.50	1.50
122 John M. Ward (Newsboy cabinet.)	5.00	2.50	1.50
123 Babe Ruth (Photos/artwork.)	5.00	2.50	1.50
124 Babe Ruth (Artwork)	5.00	2.50	1.50
125 Hall of Fame Dedication, 1939	5.00	2.50	1.50
126 Babe Ruth (At microphone.)	5.00	2.50	1.50
127 Babe Ruth, Jacob Ruppert	7.50	3.75	2.25
128 Stan Musial	7.50	3.75	2.25
129 Babe Ruth (W/others.)	5.00	2.50	1.50
130 George Kell	5.00	2.50	1.50
131 Luke Appling	5.00	2.50	1.50
132 Cecil Travis	5.00	2.50	1.50
133 Larry "Yogi" Berra	7.50	3.75	2.25
134 Harry Heilman (Heilmann)	5.00	2.50	1.50
135 Johnny Mize	5.00	2.50	1.50
136 Christy Mathewson	7.50	3.75	2.25
137 Ralph Kiner	5.00	2.50	1.50
138 Bill Dickey	5.00	2.50	1.50
139 Hank Sauer	5.00	2.50	1.50
140 Hank Greenberg	7.50	3.75	2.25
141 Charlie Gehringer	5.00	2.50	1.50
142 Walter Evers	5.00	2.50	1.50
143 John Pepper Martin	5.00	2.50	1.50
144 Vern Stephens	5.00	2.50	1.50
145 Bobbie (Bobby) Doerr	5.00	2.50	1.50

1975 Sport Hobbyist Team Composites

This was one of several series of collectors issues produced in the 1960s and 1970s by the Sport Hobbyist, one of the card hobby's earliest periodicals. This series features black-and-white postcard size (about 3-1/2" x 5-1/4") reproductions of team composite photos from the 1931 Spalding Guide. Cards are blank-backed. Most of the cards are numbered, with an SH prefix, though some are not.

	NM	EX	VG
Common Card:	6.00	3.00	1.80
70 Chicago Cubs	6.00	3.00	1.80
71 Philadelphia Athletics	6.00	3.00	1.80
72 N.Y. Giants	6.00	3.00	1.80
73			
74 Pittsburgh Pirates	6.00	3.00	1.80
75 Chicago Cubs	6.00	3.00	1.80
76			
77 Boston Braves	6.00	3.00	1.80
78 Cincinnati Reds	6.00	3.00	1.80
79 Brooklyn Dodgers	6.00	3.00	1.80
80			
81 Philadelphia A's	6.00	3.00	1.80
82 Cleveland Indians	6.00	3.00	1.80
83 Detroit Tigers	6.00	3.00	1.80
84 Chicago White Sox	6.00	3.00	1.80
85 Chicago White Sox	6.00	3.00	1.80
86 Boston Red Sox	6.00	3.00	1.80
87 Boston Red Sox	6.00	3.00	1.80
88 N.Y. Yankees	10.00	5.00	3.00
89 Cleveland Indians	6.00	3.00	1.80
90 St. Louis Browns	6.00	3.00	1.80
91 Washington Senators	6.00	3.00	1.80
92 Boston Braves	6.00	3.00	1.80
93 St. Louis Browns	6.00	3.00	1.80
94 Washington Senators	6.00	3.00	1.80
95 Philadelphia Phillies	6.00	3.00	1.80
96 Cincinnati Reds	6.00	3.00	1.80
97 Philadelphia Phillies	6.00	3.00	1.80
UNNUMBERED			
--- Brooklyn Dodgers	6.00	3.00	1.80
--- Detroit Tigers	6.00	3.00	1.80
--- N.Y. Yankees	10.00	5.00	3.00
--- Pittsburgh Pirates	6.00	3.00	1.80

1888-1889 Sporting Extra World Tour Imperial Cabinets

These large-format (about 9-3/4" x 6-1/2") imperial cabinet cards were issued in conjunction with "Spalding's World Base Ball Tour" of 1888-1889, though their method of distribution is unknown. The cards feature team portraits on a heavy cardboard, gilt-edge mount. At top is the name of the sponsoring cigarette brand, at bottom is the team name, printed in red. Backs are blank. Each of the cards that appeared in a 12/05 auction is believed unique.

(1) THE ALL AMERICA B.B. TOURISTS

(2) THE CHICAGO B.B. TOURISTS
Pair sold in 12/05 auction for $27,709.

1902-11 Sporting Life Cabinets (W600)

From 1902 through 1911, Sporting Life, a weekly newspaper published in Philadelphia, produced and sold a lengthy run of 5" x 7-1/2" "Cabinet Phototypes of Well-known Baseball Players." They were collectively given the catalog number of W600 in "The American Card Catalog." Because many players were issued with different team designations as they moved about over the years, and because there are new discoveries from this issue being made even today, it is likely this checklist will remain in flux for some time to come. For that reason, gaps in the assigned card numbers in this checklist have been left to accommodate additions. Several different styles and colors of mattes were used over the years, with many players issued in more than one of them. Many of the earliest cabinets picture the players in suit-and-tie, while later issues show them in uniform. Where verified, cabinets showing players in street clothes are noted. The black-and-white player portraits are mounted on heavy cardboard mattes. The player's name, position, team and league are printed beneath the photo. Backs are blank. Each cabinet was issued in a transparent envelope. They were originally given away for three two-cents stamps and a coupon found in the paper; later they were offered for sale for 10 cents apiece; 12 for a dollar. The checklist here is presented in alphabetical order. Most of the names are as presented in contemporary ads from the newspaper; rife with misspellings and misidentifications, and may or may not represent the actual spelling shown on the cards. The year shown in parentheses indicates the first year the player was issued with that team. Because these cards were sold individually upon fan request, this is an issue in which the superstars of the day are more common than the benchwarmers. It is also likely that some of the cards on this list were never issued or do not survive.

		NM	EX	VG
Common Player:		2,400	1,200	720.00
(1)	Edward Abbatichio (Abbaticchio) (Boston NL, 1903.)	3,600	1,800	1,100
(2)	Edward Abbaticchio (Pittsburg, 1907.)	2,400	1,200	720.00
(3)	William Abstein (St. Louis AL, 1910.)	2,400	1,200	720.00
(4)	Charles B. Adams (Pittsburg, 1909.)	2,400	1,200	720.00
(5)	C.A. Alperman (Brooklyn, 1906.)	2,400	1,200	720.00
(6)	David Altizer (Washington, 1907.)	2,400	1,200	720.00
(7)	Nick Altrock (Chicago AL, 1903.)	4,300	2,150	1,300
(8)	Leon Ames (New York, NL, 1904.)	2,400	1,200	720.00
(9)	John Anderson (St. Louis AL, 1902, street.)	3,600	1,800	1,100
(10)	John Anderson (New York AL, 1904.)	2,400	1,200	720.00
(11)	John Anderson (Washington, 1905.)	2,400	1,200	720.00
(12)	Frank Arelanes (Arellanes) (Boston AL, 1910.)	2,400	1,200	720.00
(13)	Charles Armbruster (Boston AL, 1906.)	2,400	1,200	720.00
(14)	William R. Armour (Detroit, 1906.)	2,400	1,200	720.00
(15)	Harry Arndt (St. Louis NL, 1906.)	2,400	1,200	720.00
(16)	Harry J. Aubrey (Boston NL, 1903.)	3,600	1,800	1,100
(17)	James Austin (New York AL, 1910.)	2,400	1,200	720.00
(18)	Charles Babb (New York NL, 1903.)	3,600	1,800	1,100
(19)	Charles Babb (Brooklyn, 1904.)	2,400	1,200	720.00
(20)	William Bailey (St. Louis AL, 1910.)	2,400	1,200	720.00
(21)	Frank Baker (Philadelphia AL, 1910.)	6,500	3,250	1,950
(22)	J. Barbeau (Cleveland, 1906.)	2,400	1,200	720.00
(23)	G.O. Barclay (Boston NL, 1904.)	2,400	1,200	720.00
(24)	Edward Barger (First name Eros.) (Brooklyn, 1910.)	2,400	1,200	720.00
(25)	James Barrett (Detroit, 1902, street.)	3,600	1,800	1,100
(26)	James Barrett (Boston AL, 1906.)	2,400	1,200	720.00
(27)	John C. Barry (Philadelphia NL, 1902.)	3,600	1,800	1,100

No.	Name (Team, Year)			
(28)	John C. Barry (Chicago NL, 1904.)	2,400	1,200	720.00
(29)	John C. Barry (Cincinnati, 1905.)	2,400	1,200	720.00
(30)	John C. Barry (St. Louis NL, 1906.)	2,400	1,200	720.00
(31)	John J. Barry (Philadelphia AL, 1910.)	2,400	1,200	720.00
(32)	Harry L. Barton (Philadelphia AL, 1905.)	2,400	1,200	720.00
(33)	Henry Batch (Brooklyn, 1906.)	2,400	1,200	720.00
(34)	Joseph Bates (Johnny) (Boston NL, 1907.)	2,400	1,200	720.00
(35)	Harry Bay (Cleveland, 1903.)	3,600	1,800	1,100
(36)	Clarence H. Beaumont (Pittsburg, 1902, street.)	3,600	1,800	1,100
(37)	Clarence H. Beaumont (Pittsburg, 1902, uniform.)	3,600	1,800	1,100
(38)	Clarence H. Beaumont (Boston NL, 1907.)	2,400	1,200	720.00
(39)	Fred Beck (Boston NL, 1910.)	2,400	1,200	720.00
(40)	Harry Beckendorf (Detroit, 1910.)	2,400	1,200	720.00
(41)	Jacob Beckley (Cincinnati, 1902.)	7,900	4,000	2,375
(42)	Jacob Beckley (St. Louis NL, 1904.)	6,500	3,250	1,950
(43)	Fred L. Beebe (St. Louis NL, 1906.)	2,400	1,200	720.00
(44)	George C. Bell (Brooklyn, 1910.)	2,400	1,200	720.00
(45)	Harry Bemis (Cleveland, 1903.)	3,600	1,800	1,100
(46)	Charles Bender (Philadelphia AL, 1903, street.)	7,900	4,000	2,375
(47)	Charles Bender (Philadelphia AL, 1903, uniform.)	7,900	4,000	2,375
(48)	Justin J. Bennett (St. Louis NL, 1907.)	2,400	1,200	720.00
(49)	William Bergen (Brooklyn, 1904.)	2,400	1,200	720.00
(50)	Charles Berger (Cleveland, 1907.)	2,400	1,200	720.00
(51)	William Bernhardt (Bernhard) (Cleveland, 1902, street.)	3,600	1,800	1,100
(52)	Robert Bescher (Cincinnati, 1910.)	2,400	1,200	720.00
(53)	Walter Beville (Henry "Monte")(New York, AL 1903.)	3,600	1,800	1,100
(54)	Walter Beville (Henry "Monte") (Detroit, 1904.)	2,400	1,200	720.00
(55)	Russell Blackburne (Chicago AL, 1910.)	2,400	1,200	720.00
(56)	Elmer Bliss (St. Louis NL, 1910.)	2,400	1,200	720.00
(57)	Frank Bowerman (New York NL, 1903.)	3,600	1,800	1,100
(58)	Frank (William J.) Bradley (Cleveland, 1903.)	3,600	1,800	1,100
(59)	William J. Bradley (Cleveland, 1903.)	3,600	1,800	1,100
(60)	David L. Brain (St. Louis NL, 1903.)	3,600	1,800	1,100
(61)	David L. Brain (Pittsburg, 1905.)	2,400	1,200	720.00
(62)	David L. Brain (Boston NL, 1906.)	2,400	1,200	720.00
(63)	William Bransfield (Pittsburg, 1902, street.)	3,600	1,800	1,100
(64)	William Bransfield (Pittsburg, 1902, uniform.)	3,600	1,800	1,100
(65)	William Bransfield (Philadelphia NL, 1905.)	2,400	1,200	720.00
(66)	Roger Bresnahan (New York NL, 1903.)	7,900	4,000	2,375
(67)	Roger Bresnahan (St. Louis NL, 1909.)	6,500	3,250	1,950
(68)	Albert Bridwell (Boston NL, 1906.)	2,400	1,200	720.00
(69)	Herbert Briggs (Chicago NL, 1905.)	2,400	1,200	720.00
(70)	Herbert Briggs (Brooklyn, 1906.)	2,400	1,200	720.00
(71)	Charles E. Brown (St. Louis NL, 1906.)	2,400	1,200	720.00
(72)	Charles E. Brown (Philadelphia NL, 1907.)	2,400	1,200	720.00
(73)	Mordecai Brown (Chicago NL, 1904.)	6,500	3,250	1,950
(74)	Samuel Brown (Boston NL, 1907.)	2,400	1,200	720.00
(75)	George Browne (New York NL, 1903.)	3,600	1,800	1,100
(76)	Fred Buelow (Detroit, 1903.)	3,600	1,800	1,100
(77)	Fred Buelow (Cleveland, 1904.)	2,400	1,200	720.00
(78)	James T. Burke (St. Louis NL, 1903.)	3,600	1,800	1,100
(79)	James T. Burke (Philadelphia AL, 1906.)	2,400	1,200	720.00
(80)	Jesse Burkett (St. Louis AL, 1903.)	43,200	21,600	12,960
(81)	Jesse Burkett (Boston AL, 1905.)	6,500	3,250	1,950
(82)	James J. Callahan (Chicago AL, 1903.)	3,600	1,800	1,100
(83)	Howard Camnitz (Pittsburg, 1910.)	2,400	1,200	720.00
(84)	Wirt V. Cannell (Virgin Wirt) (Boston NL, 1903.)	3,600	1,800	1,100
(85)	Joseph Cantillion (Washington, 1907.)	2,400	1,200	720.00
(86)	George Carey (Washington, 1903.)	3,600	1,800	1,100
(87)	P.J. Carney (Boston NL, 1903.)	3,600	1,800	1,100
(88)	Charles C. Carr (Cleveland, 1904.)	2,400	1,200	720.00
(89)	Charles C. Carr (Cincinnati, 1906.)	2,400	1,200	720.00
(90)	William Carrigan (Boston AL, 1910.)	2,400	1,200	720.00
(91)	James P. Casey (Chicago NL, 1902, street.)	3,600	1,800	1,100
(92)	James P. Casey (Brooklyn, 1906.)	2,400	1,200	720.00
(93)	Joseph Cassidy (Washington, 1904.)	2,400	1,200	720.00
(94)	Luis Castro (Philadelphia AL, 1902, street.)	2,400	1,200	720.00
(95)	Frank Chance (Chicago NL, 1902, street.)	7,900	4,000	2,375
(96)	Frank Chance (Chicago NL, 1902, uniform.)	7,900	4,000	2,375
(97)	Harold Chase (New York AL, 1906.)	5,000	2,600	1,400
(98)	John Chesbro (Pittsburg, 1902, street.)	7,900	4,000	2,375
(99)	John Chesbro (New York AL, 1903, uniform.)	7,900	4,000	2,375
(100)	Edw. V. Cicotte (Boston AL, 1910.)	6,500	3,250	1,950
(101)	William Clark (Clarke) (Washington, 1903.)	3,600	1,800	1,100
(102)	William Clark (Clarke) (New York NL, 1905.)	2,400	1,200	720.00
(103)	Fred Clarke (Pittsburg, 1902, street.)	7,900	4,000	2,375
(104)	Fred Clarke (Pittsburg, 1902, uniform.)	7,900	4,000	2,375
(104)	Justin J. Clarke (Cleveland, 1906.)	2,400	1,200	720.00
(105)	Thomas Clarke (Cincinnati, 1910.)	2,400	1,200	720.00
(106)	Walter Clarkson (New York AL, 1906.)	2,400	1,200	720.00
(107)	Walter Clarkson (Cleveland, 1907.)	2,400	1,200	720.00
(108)	Otis Clymer (Pittsburg, 1905.)	2,400	1,200	720.00
(109)	Otis Clymer (Washington, 1907.)	2,400	1,200	720.00
(110)	Andrew Coakley (Philadelphia AL, 1905.)	2,400	1,200	720.00
(111)	Andrew Coakley (Cincinnati, 1907.)	2,400	1,200	720.00
(112)	Tyrus R. Cobb (Detroit, 1907.)	21,600	10,800	6,500
(115)	Edward Collins (Philadelphia AL, 1907.)	6,500	3,250	1,950
(116)	James Collins (Boston AL, 1902, uniform.)	7,200	3,600	2,150
(117)	W.M. Congalton (Cleveland, 1906.)	2,400	1,200	720.00
(118)	W.A. Congalton (Boston AL, 1907.)	2,400	1,200	720.00
(119)	William Conroy (New York AL, 1903.)	3,600	1,800	1,100
(120)	Richard Cooley (Boston NL, 1902, street.)	3,600	1,800	1,100
(121)	Richard Cooley (Detroit, 1905.)	2,400	1,200	720.00
(122)	John W. Coombs (Philadelphia AL, 1910.)	2,400	1,200	720.00
(123)	T.W. Corcoran (Cincinnati, 1904.)	2,400	1,200	720.00
(124)	T.W. Corcoran (New York NL, 1907.)	2,400	1,200	720.00
(125)	Frank J. Corridon (Philadelphia NL, 1907.)	2,400	1,200	720.00
(126)	William Coughlin (Washington, 1903.)	3,600	1,800	1,100
(127)	William Coughlin (Detroit, 1904.)	2,400	1,200	720.00
(128)	Ernest Courtney (Philadelphia NL, 1905.)	2,400	1,200	720.00
(129)	Otis Crandall (New York NL, 1910.)	2,400	1,200	720.00
(130)	Samuel Crawford (Cincinnati, 1902, street.)	7,900	4,000	2,375
(131)	Samuel Crawford (Detroit, 1903.)	7,900	4,000	2,375
(132)	Burde Cree (Birdie) (New York AL, 1911.)	2,400	1,200	720.00
(134)	Louis Criger (Boston AL, 1903.)	3,600	1,800	1,100
(135)	Dode Criss (St. Louis AL, 1910.)	2,400	1,200	720.00
(136)	John Cronin (New York NL, 1903.)	3,600	1,800	1,100
(137)	John Cronin (Brooklyn, 1904.)	2,400	1,200	720.00
(138)	Lafayette Cross (Philadelphia AL, 1902, street.)	3,600	1,800	1,100
(139)	Lafayette Cross (Washington, 1906.)	2,400	1,200	720.00
(140)	Monte Cross (Philadelphia AL, 1902.)	3,600	1,800	1,100
(142)	Clarence Currie (St. Louis NL, 1903.)	3,600	1,800	1,100
(143)	Clarence Currie (Chicago NL, 1903.)	3,600	1,800	1,100
(145)	William Dahlen (Brooklyn, 1902, street.)	4,300	2,150	1,300
(146)	William Dahlen (New York NL, 1904.)	2,400	1,200	720.00
(147)	Thomas Daly (Chicago AL, 1903, street.)	3,600	1,800	1,100
(148)	Thomas Daly (Cincinnati, 1903.)	3,600	1,800	1,100
(148)	George Davis (Chicago AL, 1902.)	7,900	4,000	2,375
(150)	Harry Davis (Philadelphia AL, 1902, street.)	3,600	1,800	1,100
(152)	Edward J. Delahanty (Washington, 1902, street.)	19,400	9,700	5,825
(153)	James Delahanty (Boston NL, 1904.)	2,400	1,200	720.00
(154)	James Delahanty (Cincinnati, 1906.)	2,400	1,200	720.00
(155)	James Delahanty (St. Louis AL, 1907.)	2,400	1,200	720.00
(156)	James Delahanty (Washington, 1907.)	2,400	1,200	720.00
(158)	Arthur Devlin (New York NL, 1905.)	2,400	1,200	720.00
(159)	Joshua Devore (New York NL, 1911.)	2,400	1,200	720.00
(160)	Charles Dexter (Boston NL, 1903.)	3,600	1,800	1,100
(161)	Frank Dillon (Brooklyn, 1903.)	3,600	1,800	1,100
(162)	William Dinneen (Boston AL, 1903.)	3,600	1,800	1,100
(163)	William Dineen (St. Louis AL, 1907.)	2,400	1,200	720.00
(164)	John Dobbs (Brooklyn, 1903.)	3,600	1,800	1,100
(164)	Edward Doheny (Pittsburg, 1903.)	3,600	1,800	1,100
(165)	Harry Dolan (Patrick Henry "Cozy")(Cincinnati, 1904.)	2,400	1,200	720.00
(166)	Harry Dolan (Patrick Henry "Cozy")(Boston NL, 1905.)	2,400	1,200	720.00
(167)	Frank Donahue (St. Louis AL, 1903.)	3,600	1,800	1,100
(168)	Frank Donahue (Cleveland, 1903.)	3,600	1,800	1,100
(169)	Frank Donahue (Detroit, 1906.)	2,400	1,200	720.00
(170)	J. "Jiggs" Donahue (Chicago AL, 1903.)	3,600	1,800	1,100
(171)	Michael Donlin (Cincinnati, 1902, street.)	3,600	1,800	1,100
(172)	Michael Donlin (New York NL, 1904.)	2,400	1,200	720.00
(173)	P.J. (Patrick) Donovan (St. Louis NL, 1902, street.)	3,600	1,800	1,100
(174)	Patrick J. Donovan (Washington, 1904.)	2,400	1,200	720.00
(175)	Patrick J. Donovan (Brooklyn, 1906, street.)	2,400	1,200	720.00
(176)	William Donovan (Detroit, 1903.)	3,600	1,800	1,100
(177)	Charles Dooin (Philadelphia NL, 1903.)	3,600	1,800	1,100
(178)	Michael Doolin (Doolan) (Philadelphia NL, 1906.)	3,600	1,800	1,100
(180)	Thomas Doran (Boston AL, 1904.)	2,400	1,200	720.00
(181)	Thomas Doran (Detroit, 1905.)	2,400	1,200	720.00
(182)	August Dorner (Boston NL, 1907.)	2,400	1,200	720.00
(183)	Patrick Dougherty (Boston AL, 1903.)	3,600	1,800	1,100
(184)	Patrick Dougherty (New York AL, 1904.)	2,400	1,200	720.00
(185)	Patrick Dougherty (Chicago AL, 1906.)	2,400	1,200	720.00
(186)	William Douglas (Douglass) (Philadelphia NL, 1902.)	3,600	1,800	1,100
(187)	Thomas Downey (Cincinnati, 1910.)	2,400	1,200	720.00
(188)	J.W. Downs (Detroit, 1907.)	2,400	1,200	720.00
(189)	Joe Doyle (New York AL, 1907.)	2,400	1,200	720.00
(190)	John Doyle (Brooklyn, 1903.)	3,600	1,800	1,100
(191)	John Doyle (Philadelphia NL, 1904.)	2,400	1,200	720.00
(192)	Larry J. Doyle (New York NL, 1908.)	2,400	1,200	720.00
(194)	Louis Drill (Washington, 1903.)	3,600	1,800	1,100
(195)	Louis Drill (Detroit, 1904.)	2,400	1,200	720.00
(196)	Hugh Duffy (Philadelphia NL, 1905.)	6,500	3,250	1,950
(197)	William Duggleby (Philadelphia NL, 1903.)	3,600	1,800	1,100
(198)	William Duggleby (Pittsburg, 1907.)	2,400	1,200	720.00
(199)	August Dundon (Chicago AL, 1904.)	2,400	1,200	720.00
(200)	Edward Dunkle (Washington, 1903.)	3,600	1,800	1,100
(201)	James Dunleavy (John) (St. Louis NL, 1904.)	2,400	1,200	720.00
(202)	John Dunn (New York NL, 1903.)	3,600	1,800	1,100
(203)	James H. Dygert (Philadelphia AL, 1905.)	2,400	1,200	720.00
(204)	Malcolm Eason (Brooklyn, 1906.)	2,400	1,200	720.00
(205)	Harry Eells (Cleveland, 1906.)	2,400	1,200	720.00
(206)	Richard J. Egan (Cincinnati, 1910.)	2,400	1,200	720.00
(207)	Norman Elberfeld (Detroit, 1903.)	3,600	1,800	1,100
(208)	Norman Elberfeld (New York AL, 1903.)	3,600	1,800	1,100
(209)	Claude Elliott (New York NL, 1904.)	2,400	1,200	720.00
(210)	George W. Ellis (St. Louis NL, 1910.)	2,400	1,200	720.00
(212)	John Eubank (Detroit, 1906.)	2,400	1,200	720.00
(213)	John Evers (Chicago NL, 1903.)	7,900	4,000	2,375
(214)	Robert Ewing (George L.) (Cincinnati, 1904.)	2,400	1,200	720.00
(216)	Fred Falkenberg (Washington, 1906.)	2,400	1,200	720.00
(217)	Charles Farrell (Brooklyn, 1902, street.)	3,600	1,800	1,100
(218)	Charles Farrell (Boston AL, 1903.)	3,600	1,800	1,100
(219)	John S. Farrell (St. Louis NL, 1903.)	3,600	1,800	1,100

No.	Name / (Team, Year)			
(220)	Cecil Ferguson (George) (New York NL, 1906.)	2,400	1,200	720.00
(221)	Hobe Ferris (Boston AL, 1903.)	3,600	1,800	1,100
(222)	Thomas S. Fisher (Middle initial C.)(Boston NL, 1904.)	2,400	1,200	720.00
(223)	Patrick Flaherty (Chicago AL, 1903.)	3,600	1,800	1,100
(224)	Patrick Flaherty (Pittsburg, 1904.)	2,400	1,200	720.00
(225)	Patrick Flaherty (Boston NL, 1907.)	2,400	1,200	720.00
(226)	Elmer Flick (Cleveland, 1903.)	7,900	4,000	2,375
(227)	John Flynn (Pittsburg, 1910.)	2,400	1,200	720.00
(229)	William Foxen (Chicago NL, 1910.)	2,400	1,200	720.00
(231)	Charles Fraser (Philadelphia NL, 1903, street.)	3,600	1,800	1,100
(232)	Charles Fraser (Boston NL, 1905.)	2,400	1,200	720.00
(233)	Charles Fraser (Chicago NL, 1907.)	2,400	1,200	720.00
(234)	John ("Buck") Freeman (Boston AL, 1902.)	4,300	2,150	1,300
(235)	William Friel (St. Louis AL, 1903.)	3,600	1,800	1,100
(236)	Arthur Fromme (Cincinnati, 1910.)	2,400	1,200	720.00
(237)	David L. Fultz (Philadelphia AL, 1902, street.)	3,600	1,800	1,100
(238)	David L. Fultz (New York AL, 1903.)	3,600	1,800	1,100
(240)	Robert S. Ganley (Pittsburg, 1906.)	2,400	1,200	720.00
(241)	Robert S. Ganley (Washington, 1907.)	2,400	1,200	720.00
(242)	John Ganzell (Ganzel) (New York AL, 1903.)	3,600	1,800	1,100
(243)	John Ganzel (Ganzell) (Cincinnati, 1907.)	2,400	1,200	720.00
(244)	Virgil Garvin (Brooklyn, 1903.)	3,600	1,800	1,100
(245)	Harry L. Gaspar (Cincinnati, 1910.)	2,400	1,200	720.00
(246)	Philip Geier (Boston NL, 1904.)	2,400	1,200	720.00
(247)	Harry Gessler (Brooklyn, 1903.)	3,600	1,800	1,100
(248)	Harry Gessler (Chicago NL, 1906.)	2,400	1,200	720.00
(250)	George Gibson (Pittsburg, 1905.)	2,400	1,200	720.00
(251)	Norwood Gibson (Boston AL, 1903.)	3,600	1,800	1,100
(252)	William Gilbert (New York NL, 1903.)	3,600	1,800	1,100
(253)	Frederick Glade (St. Louis AL, 1904.)	2,400	1,200	720.00
(254)	Harry Gleason (Boston AL, 1903.)	3,600	1,800	1,100
(255)	Harry Gleason (St. Louis AL, 1904.)	2,400	1,200	720.00
(256)	William Gleason (Philadelphia NL, 1903.)	3,600	1,800	1,100
(258)	William Gochnauer (John Gochnaur) (Cleveland, 1903.)	3,600	1,800	1,100
(259)	Michael Grady (St. Louis NL, 1904.)	2,400	1,200	720.00
(260)	Edward L. Grant (Philadelphia NL, 1910.)	3,450	1,725	1,050
(262)	Daniel Green (Chicago AL, 1903.)	3,600	1,800	1,100
(263)	E.W. Greminger (Boston NL, 1903.)	3,600	1,800	1,100
(264)	E.W. Greminger (Detroit, 1904.)	2,400	1,200	720.00
(265)	Clarke Griffith (Clark) (Chicago AL, 1902.)	7,900	4,000	2,375
(266)	Clarke Griffith (Clark) (New York AL, 1903.)	7,900	4,000	2,375
(267)	Myron Grimshaw (Boston AL, 1906.)	2,400	1,200	720.00
(269)	James Hackett (St. Louis NL, 1903.)	3,600	1,800	1,100
(270)	Edgar Hahn (Chicago AL, 1906.)	2,400	1,200	720.00
(271)	Frank Hahn (Cincinnati, 1902, street.)	2,400	1,200	720.00
(272)	Frank Hahn (New York AL, 1905.)	2,400	1,200	720.00
(273)	Charles Hall (Cincinnati, 1907.)	2,400	1,200	720.00
(274)	William H. Hallman (Philadelphia NL, 1903.)	3,600	1,800	1,100
(275)	William H. Hallman (Pittsburg, 1906.)	2,400	1,200	720.00
(276)	Edward Hanlon (Brooklyn, 1905, street.)	6,500	3,250	1,950
(277)	Edward Hanlon (Cincinnati, 1906.)	6,500	3,250	1,950
(278)	Richard Harley (Chicago NL, 1903.)	3,600	1,800	1,100
(279)	Robert Harmon (St. Louis NL, 1910.)	2,400	1,200	720.00
(280)	Charles Harper (Cincinnati, 1903.)	3,600	1,800	1,100
(281)	Charles Harper (Chicago NL, 1906.)	2,400	1,200	720.00
(282)	Joseph Harris (Boston AL, 1906.)	2,400	1,200	720.00
(283)	Harry Hart (Chicago AL, 1906.)	2,400	1,200	720.00
(284)	Frederick L. Hartzell (Hartsel) (Philadelphia AL, 1902.)	3,600	1,800	1,100
(285)	Roy A. Hartzell (St. Louis AL, 1906.)	2,400	1,200	720.00
(287)	J.E. Heidrick (St. Louis AL, 1903.)	3,600	1,800	1,100
(288)	Charles Hemphill (St. Louis AL, 1903.)	3,600	1,800	1,100
(289)	Weldon Henley (Philadelphia AL, 1903, street.)	3,600	1,800	1,100
(290)	Otto Hess (Cleveland, 1904.)	2,400	1,200	720.00
(291)	Edward Heydon (Mike)(Washington, 1906.)	2,400	1,200	720.00
(292)	Charles Hickman (Cleveland, 1903.)	3,600	1,800	1,100
(293)	Charles Hickman (Detroit, 1904.)	2,400	1,200	720.00
(294)	Charles Hickman (Washington, 1905.)	2,400	1,200	720.00
(295)	Charles Hickman (Chicago AL, 1907.)	2,400	1,200	720.00
(296)	Hunter Hill (St. Louis AL, 1903.)	3,600	1,800	1,100
(297)	Hunter Hill (Washington, 1904.)	2,400	1,200	720.00
(298)	Homer Hillebrand (Pittsburg, 1905.)	2,400	1,200	720.00
(299)	Harry Hinchman (Cleveland, 1907.)	2,400	1,200	720.00
(300)	William Hinchman (Cleveland, 1907.)	2,400	1,200	720.00
(303)	R. C. Hoblitzel (Cincinnati, 1910.)	2,400	1,200	720.00
(304)	Daniel Hoffman (Philadelphia AL, 1903.)	3,600	1,800	1,100
(305)	Daniel Hoffman (New York AL, 1906.)	2,400	1,200	720.00
(306)	Arthur Hofman (Chicago NL, 1906.)	2,400	1,200	720.00
(307)	William Hogg (New York AL, 1906.)	2,400	1,200	720.00
(308)	A. Holesketter (St. Louis NL, 1907.)	2,400	1,200	720.00
(309)	William Holmes (James Wm. "Ducky") (Chicago AL, 1903.)	3,600	1,800	1,100
(310)	George Howard (Pittsburg, 1905.)	2,400	1,200	720.00
(311)	George Howard (Boston NL, 1906.)	2,400	1,200	720.00
(312)	Harry Howell (Baltimore, 1902, street.)	3,600	1,800	1,100
(313)	Harry Howell (New York AL, 1903, street.)	3,600	1,800	1,100
(314)	Harry Howell (St. Louis AL, 1904.)	2,400	1,200	720.00
(315)	Miller Huggins (Cincinnati, 1906.)	6,500	3,250	1,950
(316)	James Hughes (Brooklyn, 1902, street.)	3,600	1,800	1,100
(317)	Thomas Hughes (Boston AL, 1902.)	3,600	1,800	1,100
(318)	Thomas Hughes (New York AL, 1904.)	2,400	1,200	720.00
(319)	Thomas Hughes (Washington, 1904.)	2,400	1,200	720.00
(320)	John Hulseman (Frank Huelsman) (Washington, 1904.)	2,400	1,200	720.00
(321)	Rudolph Hulswitt (Philadelphia NL, 1903.)	3,600	1,800	1,100
(322)	John Hummell (Hummel)(Brooklyn, 1906.)	2,400	1,200	720.00
(323)	Berthold J. Husting (Philadelphia AL, 1902, street.)	3,600	1,800	1,100
(324)	Hamilton Hyatt (Pittsburg, 1909.)	2,400	1,200	720.00
(325)	Frank Isbell (Chicago AL, 1903.)	3,600	1,800	1,100
(326)	Fred Jacklitsch (Brooklyn, 1903, street.)	3,600	1,800	1,100
(327)	Fred Jacklitsch (Philadelphia NL, 1907.)	2,400	1,200	720.00
(328)	James Jackson (Cleveland, 1906.)	2,400	1,200	720.00
(329)	Harry Jacobson (Albert "Beany") (Washington, 1904.)	2,400	1,200	720.00
(330)	Harry Jacobson (Albert "Beany") (St. Louis AL, 1906.)	2,400	1,200	720.00
(331)	Harry Jacobson (Albert "Beany")(Boston AL, 1907.)	2,400	1,200	720.00
(333)	Hugh Jennings (Philadelphia NL, 1902.)	7,900	4,000	2,375
(334)	Hugh Jennings (Detroit, 1907.)	6,500	3,250	1,950
(335)	Charles Jones (Washington, 1905.)	2,400	1,200	720.00
(336)	David Jones (Chicago NL, 1904.)	2,400	1,200	720.00
(337)	David Jones (Detroit, 1906.)	2,400	1,200	720.00
(338)	Fielder Jones (Chicago AL, 1902.)	3,600	1,800	1,100
(339)	Oscar Jones (Brooklyn, 1903.)	3,600	1,800	1,100
(340)	Thomas Jones (St. Louis AL, 1904.)	2,400	1,200	720.00
(341)	Otto Jordan ("Dutch") (Brooklyn, 1903.)	3,600	1,800	1,100
(342)	Otto Jordan ("Dutch") (Cleveland, 1905.)	2,400	1,200	720.00
(343)	Tim Jordan (Brooklyn, 1906.)	2,400	1,200	720.00
(344)	Adrian Joss (Cleveland, 1903.)	8,600	4,300	2,600
(345)	Michael Kahoe (St. Louis AL, 1903.)	3,600	1,800	1,100
(346)	Michael Kahoe (Philadelphia NL, 1905.)	2,400	1,200	720.00
(347)	Michael Kahoe (Chicago NL, 1907.)	2,400	1,200	720.00
(348)	Michael Kahoe (Washington, 1907.)	2,400	1,200	720.00
(349)	Edward Karger (Edwin) (Boston AL, 1910.)	2,400	1,200	720.00
(350)	Robert Keefe (New York AL, 1906.)	2,400	1,200	720.00
(351)	William Keeler (Brooklyn, 1902, street.)	7,900	4,000	2,375
(352)	William Keeler (New York, AL 1903, street.)	7,900	4,000	2,375
(353)	William Keister (Philadelphia NL, 1903.)	3,600	1,800	1,100
(355)	Joseph J. Kelley (Cincinnati, 1902, street.)	13,000	6,500	3,900
(356)	William Kennedy (Pittsburg, 1903, street.)	3,600	1,800	1,100
(357)	Edward Killian (Detroit, 1904.)	2,400	1,200	720.00
(358)	James Kissinger (Chas. "Rube" Kisinger) (Detroit, 1903.)	3,600	1,800	1,100
(359)	Frank Kitson (Brooklyn, 1902, street.)	3,600	1,800	1,100
(360)	Frank Kitson (Detroit, 1903.)	3,600	1,800	1,100
(361)	Frank Kitson (Washington, 1906.)	2,400	1,200	720.00
(362)	Frank Kitson (New York AL, 1907.)	2,400	1,200	720.00
(363)	Malachi Kittridge (Washington, 1903.)	3,600	1,800	1,100
(365)	John Kleinow (New York AL, 1905, street.)	2,400	1,200	720.00
(366)	John Kleinow (New York AL, 1905, uniform.)	2,400	1,200	720.00
(367)	John Kling (Chicago NL, 1903.)	3,600	1,800	1,100
(368)	F. Otto Knabe (Philadelphia NL, 1910.)	2,400	1,200	720.00
(369)	John Knight (Philadelphia AL, 1905.)	2,400	1,200	720.00
(370)	John Knight (Boston AL, 1907.)	2,400	1,200	720.00
(371)	Bernard Koehler (St. Louis AL, 1906.)	2,400	1,200	720.00
(372)	Edward Konetchy (St. Louis NL, 1907.)	2,400	1,200	720.00
(373)	Harry Krause (Philadelphia AL, 1910.)	2,400	1,200	720.00
(374)	Otto Krueger (Pittsburg, 1903.)	3,600	1,800	1,100
(375)	Otto Krueger (Philadelphia NL, 1905.)	2,400	1,200	720.00
(376)	George LaChance (Boston AL, 1903.)	3,600	1,800	1,100
(377)	Napoleon Lajoie (Cleveland, 1902, street.)	7,900	4,000	2,375
(378)	Napoleon Lajoie (Cleveland, 1902, uniform.)	7,900	4,000	2,375
(379)	Joseph Lake (St. Louis AL, 1910.)	2,400	1,200	720.00
(380)	Frank Laporte (LaPorte) (New York AL, 1906.)	2,400	1,200	720.00
(381)	Louis Laroy (LeRoy)	2,400	1,200	720.00
(382)	William Lauder (New York NL, 1903.)	3,600	1,800	1,100
(383)	Thomas Leach (Pittsburg, 1902.)	3,600	1,800	1,100
(384)	Wyatt Lee (Washington, 1903.)	3,600	1,800	1,100
(385)	Wyatt Lee (Pittsburg, 1904.)	2,400	1,200	720.00
(386)	Samuel Leever (Pittsburg, 1902, street.)	3,600	1,800	1,100
(387)	Samuel Leever (Pittsburg, 1902, uniform.)	2,400	1,200	720.00
(388)	Philip Lewis (Brooklyn, 1908.)	2,400	1,200	720.00
(389)	Vive A. Lindaman (Boston NL, 1906.)	2,400	1,200	720.00
(390)	Paddy Livingstone (Livingston) (Philadelphia AL, 1910.)	2,400	1,200	720.00
(391)	John Lobert (Cincinnati, 1907.)	2,400	1,200	720.00
(392)	Herman Long (Boston NL, 1902.)	3,600	1,800	1,100
(393)	Herman Long (Detroit, 1903.)	3,600	1,800	1,100
(394)	Herman Long (New York AL, 1903.)	3,600	1,800	1,100
(395)	Briscoe Lord (Philadelphia AL, 1905.)	2,400	1,200	720.00
(396)	Harry D. Lord (Chicago AL, 1910.)	2,400	1,200	720.00
(397)	Robert H. Lowe (Detroit, 1907.)	2,400	1,200	720.00
(398)	Harry Lumley (Brooklyn, 1904.)	2,400	1,200	720.00
(399)	Carl Lundgren (Chicago NL, 1903.)	3,600	1,800	1,100
(400)	John Lush (Chicago NL, 1903.)	2,400	1,200	720.00
(401)	William L. Lush (Detroit, 1903.)	3,600	1,800	1,100
(402)	William L. Lush (Cleveland, 1904.)	2,400	1,200	720.00
(403)	Michael M. Lynch (Pittsburg, 1906.)	2,400	1,200	720.00
(404)	Michael M. Lynch (New York NL, 1907.)	2,400	1,200	720.00
(405)	Connie Mack (Philadelphia AL, 1902, street.)	7,900	4,000	2,375
(406)	Nick Maddox (Pittsburg, 1909.)	2,400	1,200	720.00
(407)	Sherwood Magee (Philadelphia NL, 1905.)	2,400	1,200	720.00
(408)	George H. Magoon (Chicago AL, 1903.)	3,600	1,800	1,100
(409)	John Malarkey (Boston NL, 1903.)	3,600	1,800	1,100
(410)	William Maloney (Chicago NL, 1906.)	2,400	1,200	720.00
(411)	William Maloney (Brooklyn, 1906.)	2,400	1,200	720.00
(412)	William R. Marshall (New York NL, 1905.)	2,400	1,200	720.00
(413)	William R. Marshall (St. Louis NL, 1906.)	2,400	1,200	720.00

No.	Player	C1	C2	C3
(414)	William R. Marshall (Brooklyn, 1909.)	2,400	1,200	720.00
(415)	Christopher Matthewson (Mathewson) (New York NL, 1902, street.)	21,600	10,800	6,500
(416a)	Christopher Matthewson (Mathewson) (New York NL, 1902, uniform.)	19,400	9,700	5,825
(416b)	Christopher Mathewson (New York, NL, uniform, corrected.)	17,280	8,600	5,200
(417)	James A. McAleer (St. Louis AL, 1906.)	2,400	1,200	720.00
(418)	Louis McAllister (Lewis) (Detroit, 1903.)	3,600	1,800	1,100
(419)	John McCarthy (Cleveland, 1903.)	3,600	1,800	1,100
(420)	John McCarthy (Chicago NL, 1903.)	3,600	1,800	1,100
(421)	John McCarthy (Brooklyn, 1906.)	2,400	1,200	720.00
(422)	John J. McCloskey (St. Louis NL, 1906.)	2,400	1,200	720.00
(423)	Ambrose McConnell (Boston AL, 1910.)	2,400	1,200	720.00
(424)	George W. McQuillan (Philadelphia NL, 1907.)	2,400	1,200	720.00
(425)	Barry McCormick (St. Louis NL, 1903.)	3,600	1,800	1,100
(426)	Barry McCormick (Washington, 1903.)	3,600	1,800	1,100
(427)	Michael McCormick (Brooklyn, 1904.)	2,400	1,200	720.00
(428)	Charles McFarland (St. Louis NL, 1903.)	3,600	1,800	1,100
(429)	Charles McFarland (Pittsburg, 1906.)	2,400	1,200	720.00
(430)	Edward McFarland (Chicago AL, 1902, street.)	3,600	1,800	1,100
(431)	Herm McFarland (Hermas) (New York AL, 1903.)	3,600	1,800	1,100
(432)	John McFetridge (Philadelphia NL, 1903.)	3,600	1,800	1,100
(433)	Dan McGann (New York NL, 1903.)	3,600	1,800	1,100
(434)	Joseph McGinnity (New York NL, 1902, street.)	7,900	4,000	2,375
(435)	Joseph McGinnity (New York NL, 1902, uniform.)	7,900	4,000	2,375
(436)	John J. McGraw (Infielder, New York NL, 1902, street.)	7,900	4,000	2,375
(437)	John J. McGraw (Manager, New York NL, 1902, street.)	7,900	4,000	2,375
(438)	James McGuire (Detroit, 1903.)	2,400	1,200	720.00
(439)	James McGuire (New York AL, 1904.)	2,400	1,200	720.00
(440)	James McGuire (Boston AL, 1907.)	2,400	1,200	720.00
(441)	Harry McIntyre (McIntire) (Brooklyn, 1905.)	2,400	1,200	720.00
(442)	Matty McIntyre (Detroit, 1904, street.)	2,400	1,200	720.00
(443)	John B. McLean (Cincinnati, 1910.)	2,400	1,200	720.00
(444)	John Menefee (Chicago NL, 1903.)	3,600	1,800	1,100
(445)	Fred Merkle (New York NL, 1908.)	2,400	1,200	720.00
(446)	Samuel Mertes (New York NL, 1903.)	3,600	1,800	1,100
(447)	Samuel Mertes (St. Louis NL, 1906.)	2,400	1,200	720.00
(448)	Samuel Mertes (Boston NL, 1907.)	2,400	1,200	720.00
(451)	Clyde Milan (Washington, 1910.)	2,400	1,200	720.00
(452)	John B. Miller (Pittsburg, 1909.)	2,400	1,200	720.00
(453)	Roscoe Miller (New York NL, 1903.)	3,600	1,800	1,100
(454)	Roscoe Miller (Pittsburg, 1903.)	3,600	1,800	1,100
(455)	William Milligan (New York NL, 1904.)	2,400	1,200	720.00
(456)	Frederick Mitchell (Philadelphia NL, 1903, street.)	3,600	1,800	1,100
(457)	Frederick Mitchell (Brooklyn, 1904.)	2,400	1,200	720.00
(458)	M.F. Mitchell (Cincinnati, 1910.)	2,400	1,200	720.00
(461)	Earl Moore (Cleveland, 1903.)	3,600	1,800	1,100
(462)	Earl Moore (New York AL, 1907.)	2,400	1,200	720.00
(463)	Charles P. Moran (Middle initial V.) (Washington, 1904.)	2,400	1,200	720.00
(464)	Charles P. Moran (Middle initial V.) (St. Louis AL, 1904.)	2,400	1,200	720.00
(465)	Patrick J. Moran (Boston NL, 1902, street.)	3,600	1,800	1,100
(466)	Patrick J. Moran (Chicago NL, 1906.)	2,400	1,200	720.00
(467)	Lewis Moren (Philadelphia NL, 1910.)	2,400	1,200	720.00
(468)	Harry R. Morgan (Philadelphia AL, 1910.)	2,400	1,200	720.00
(469)	Eugene Moriarty (George) (New York AL, 1906.)	2,400	1,200	720.00
(470)	John Morrissey (Cincinnati, 1903.)	3,600	1,800	1,100
(471)	Michael Mowery (Cincinnati, 1907.)	2,400	1,200	720.00
(472)	George Mullin (Detroit, 1903.)	3,600	1,800	1,100
(473)	Daniel Murphy (Philadelphia AL, 1902, street.)	3,600	1,800	1,100
(474)	John J. Murray (St. Louis NL, 1907.)	2,400	1,200	720.00
(475)	William Murray (Boston NL, 1907.)	2,400	1,200	720.00
(477)	Joseph Nealon (Jim) (Pittsburg, 1906.)	2,400	1,200	720.00
(478)	Daniel Needham (Thomas) (Boston NL, 1904.)	2,400	1,200	720.00
(479)	Eustace J. Newton (New York AL, 1906.)	2,400	1,200	720.00
(481)	Simon Nicholls (Philadelphia AL, 1907.)	2,400	1,200	720.00
(482)	Harry Niles (St. Louis AL, 1906.)	2,400	1,200	720.00
(483)	George Nill (Washington, 1906.)	2,400	1,200	720.00
(484)	George Nill (Cleveland, 1907.)	2,400	1,200	720.00
(485)	Pete Noonan (St. Louis NL, 1906.)	2,400	1,200	720.00
(486)	John O'Brien (Boston AL, 1903.)	3,600	1,800	1,100
(487)	Peter O'Brien (St. Louis AL, 1906.)	2,400	1,200	720.00
(488)	Peter O'Brien (Cleveland, 1907.)	2,400	1,200	720.00
(489)	Peter O'Brien (Washington, 1907.)	2,400	1,200	720.00
(490)	John O'Connor (Pittsburg, 1902.)	3,600	1,800	1,100
(491)	John O'Connor (New York AL, 1903.)	3,600	1,800	1,100
(492)	John O'Connor (St. Louis AL, 1904.)	2,400	1,200	720.00
(493)	Reuben Oldring (Philadelphia AL, 1906.)	2,400	1,200	720.00
(494)	Charles O'Leary (Detroit, 1904.)	2,400	1,200	720.00
(495)	John J. O'Neil (O'Neill) (St. Louis NL, 1903.)	3,000	1,500	900.00
(496)	John J. O'Neil (O'Neill) (Chicago NL, 1904.)	2,400	1,200	720.00
(497)	John O'Neil (O'Neill) (Boston NL, 1903.)	2,400	1,200	720.00
(498)	Michael J. O'Neil (O'Neill) (St. Louis NL, 1903.)	3,600	1,800	1,100
(499)	Michael J. O'Neil (O'Neill)(Brooklyn, 1906.)	2,400	1,200	720.00
(500)	Albert Orth (Washington, 1903.)	3,600	1,800	1,100
(501)	Albert Orth (New York AL, 1904.)	2,400	1,200	720.00
(502)	Orville Overall (Orval) (Chicago NL, 1906.)	2,400	1,200	720.00
(503)	Frank Owen (Chicago AL, 1903.)	3,600	1,800	1,100
(504)	Richard Padden (St. Louis AL, 1903.)	3,600	1,800	1,100
(505)	Frederick Parent (Boston AL, 1902.)	3,600	1,800	1,100
(506)	Frederick Parent (Chicago AL, 1908.)	2,400	1,200	720.00
(508)	George Paskert (Cincinnati, 1910.)	2,400	1,200	720.00
(509)	James Pastorious (Brooklyn, 1906.)	2,400	1,200	720.00
(510)	Case Patten (Washington, 1903.)	3,600	1,800	1,100
(511)	Roy Patterson (Chicago AL, 1903.)	3,600	1,800	1,100
(512)	Frederick Payne (Detroit, 1903.)	2,400	1,200	720.00
(513)	Henry Peitz (Cincinnati, 1904.)	2,400	1,200	720.00
(514)	Henry Peitz (Pittsburg, 1905.)	2,400	1,200	720.00
(515)	Barney Pelty (St. Louis AL, 1904.)	2,400	1,200	720.00
(516)	Frank Pfeiffer ("Big Jeff" Pfeffer)(Chicago NL, 1905.)	2,400	1,200	720.00
(517)	Frank Pfeiffer ("Big Jeff" Pfeffer)(Boston NL, 1906.)	2,400	1,200	720.00
(518)	John Pfiester (Chicago NL, 1907.)	2,400	1,200	720.00
(519)	Edward Phelps (Pittsburg, 1903.)	3,600	1,800	1,100
(520)	Edward Phelps (Cincinnati, 1905.)	2,400	1,200	720.00
(521)	Charles Phillippe (Pittsburg, 1903.)	3,600	1,800	1,100
(522)	William Phillips (Cincinnati, 1902, street.)	3,600	1,800	1,100
(523)	Wiley Piatt (Boston NL, 1903.)	3,600	1,800	1,100
(524)	Oliver Pickering (Philadelphia AL, 1903.)	3,600	1,800	1,100
(525)	Oliver Pickering (St. Louis AL, 1906.)	2,400	1,200	720.00
(526)	Charles Pittinger (Boston NL, 1903.)	3,600	1,800	1,100
(527)	Charles Pittinger (Philadelphia NL, 1905.)	2,400	1,200	720.00
(528)	Edward S. Plank (Philadelphia AL, 1902 street.)	7,900	4,000	2,375
(529)	Edward S. Plank (Philadelphia AL, 1902, uniform.)	7,900	4,000	2,375
(530)	Edward Poole (Cincinnati, 1903.)	3,600	1,800	1,100
(531)	Edward Poole (Brooklyn, 1904.)	2,400	1,200	720.00
(532)	John Powell (St. Louis AL, 1903.)	3,600	1,800	1,100
(533)	John Powell (New York AL, 1904.)	2,400	1,200	720.00
(534)	Maurice R. Powers (Michael) (Philadelphia AL, 1902, street.)	3,600	1,800	1,100
(535)	William Purtell (Boston AL, 1910.)	2,400	1,200	720.00
(536)	Ambrose Puttmann (New York AL, 1905.)	2,400	1,200	720.00
(539)	Thomas Raub (Chicago NL, 1903.)	3,600	1,800	1,100
(540)	Frederick Raymer (Boston NL, 1904.)	2,400	1,200	720.00
(541)	William Reidy (Brooklyn, 1903.)	3,600	1,800	1,100
(542)	Ed Reulbach (Chicago NL, 1907.)	2,400	1,200	720.00
(543)	R.B. Rhoades (Rhoads) (Cleveland, 1903.)	3,600	1,800	1,100
(544)	Lewis Richie (Chicago NL, 1910.)	2,400	1,200	720.00
(545)	Branch Rickey (New York AL, 1907.)	6,500	3,250	1,950
(546)	Claude Ritchey (Pittsburg, 1902, street.)	3,600	1,800	1,100
(547)	Claude Ritchey (Boston NL, 1907.)	2,400	1,200	720.00
(548)	Louis Ritter (Lewis) (Brooklyn, 1903.)	3,600	1,800	1,100
(549)	Clyde Robinson (Detroit, 1904.)	2,400	1,200	720.00
(550)	George Rohe (Chicago AL, 1906.)	2,400	1,200	720.00
(553)	Claude Rossman (Cleveland, 1906.)	2,400	1,200	720.00
(554)	Claude Rossman (Detroit, 1907.)	2,400	1,200	720.00
(555)	Frank Roth (Philadelphia NL, 1903.)	3,600	1,800	1,100
(556)	Frank Roth (St. Louis AL, 1905.)	2,400	1,200	720.00
(557)	Frank Roth (Chicago AL, 1906.)	2,400	1,200	720.00
(558)	John A. Rowan (Cincinnati, 1910.)	2,400	1,200	720.00
(559)	James Ryan (Washington, 1902, street.)	3,600	1,800	1,100
(562)	Harry Sallee (St. Louis NL, 1910.)	2,400	1,200	720.00
(563)	Herman Schaefer (Detroit, 1907.)	2,400	1,200	720.00
(564)	George Schlei (Cincinnati, 1906.)	2,400	1,200	720.00
(565)	Charles Schmidt (Detroit, 1906.)	2,400	1,200	720.00
(566)	Harry Schmidt (Henry) (Brooklyn, 1903.)	3,600	1,800	1,100
(567)	Osee F. Schreckengost (Ossee) (Philadelphia AL, 1902, street.)	3,600	1,800	1,100
(568)	Osee F. Schreckengost (Ossee) (Philadelphia AL, 1902, uniform.)	3,600	1,800	1,100
(569)	Frank Schulte (Chicago NL, 1905.)	2,400	1,200	720.00
(570)	Al Schweitzer (St. Louis AL, 1910.)	2,400	1,200	720.00
(571)	James Sebring (Pittsburg, 1903.)	3,600	1,800	1,100
(572)	James Sebring (Cincinnati, 1904.)	2,400	1,200	720.00
(573)	James Sebring (Chicago NL, 1905.)	2,400	1,200	720.00
(575)	Albert Selbach (Washington, 1903.)	3,600	1,800	1,100
(576)	Albert Selbach (Boston AL, 1904.)	2,400	1,200	720.00
(577)	Ralph O. "Socks" Seybold (Philadelphia AL, 1902, street.)	3,600	1,800	1,100
(578)	J. Bentley Seymour (Cincinnati, 1903.)	3,600	1,800	1,100
(579)	J. Bentley Seymour (New York NL, 1906.)	2,400	1,200	720.00
(580)	Arthur Shafer (New York NL, 1910.)	2,400	1,200	720.00
(581)	W.P. Shannon (St. Louis NL, 1904.)	2,400	1,200	720.00
(582)	W.P. Shannon (New York NL, 1906.)	2,400	1,200	720.00
(583)	Daniel Shay (St. Louis NL, 1904.)	2,400	1,200	720.00
(586)	David Shean (Boston NL, 1910.)	2,400	1,200	720.00
(587)	James Sheckard (Brooklyn, 1902, street.)	3,600	1,800	1,100
(588)	James Sheckard (Chicago NL, 1906.)	2,400	1,200	720.00
(589)	Edward Siever (Detroit, 1903.)	3,600	1,800	1,100
(590)	Edward Siever (St. Louis AL, 1903.)	3,600	1,800	1,100
(591)	James Slagle (Chicago NL, 1903.)	3,600	1,800	1,100
(592)	John Slattery (Chicago AL, 1903.)	3,600	1,800	1,100
(593)	Alexander Smith ("Broadway Aleck")(Boston AL, 1903.)	3,600	1,800	1,100
(594)	Alexander Smith ("Broadway Aleck")(Chicago NL, 1904.)	2,400	1,200	720.00
(595)	Alexander Smith ("Broadway Aleck") (New York NL, 1906.)	2,400	1,200	720.00
(596)	Charles Smith (Boston AL, 1910.)	2,400	1,200	720.00
(597)	Edward Smith (St. Louis AL, 1906.)	2,400	1,200	720.00
(598)	Frank Smith (Chicago AL, 1904.)	2,400	1,200	720.00
(599)	Harry Smith (Pittsburg, 1902, street.)	3,600	1,800	1,100
(600)	Heinie Smith (Detroit, 1903, street.)	3,600	1,800	1,100
(602)	Homer Smoot (St. Louis NL, 1903.)	3,600	1,800	1,100
(603)	Homer Smoot (Cincinnati, 1906.)	2,400	1,200	720.00
(604)	Frank Sparks (T. Frank "Tully") (Philadelphia, NL, 1903 .)	3,600	1,800	1,100
(605)	Charles ("Chic") Stahl (Boston AL, 1903.)	4,000	1,950	1,200
(606)	Jacob G. Stahl (Washington, 1904.)	2,400	1,200	720.00

		NM	EX	VG
(607)	Jacob G. Stahl (Washington)	2,400	1,200	720.00
(609)	J.B. Stanley (Boston NL, 1903.)	3,600	1,800	1,100
(610)	J.B. Stanley (Washington, 1905.)	2,400	1,200	720.00
(611)	Harry Steinfeldt (Cincinnati, 1902, street.)	3,600	1,800	1,100
(612)	Harry Steinfeldt (Chicago NL, 1905.)	2,400	1,200	720.00
(615)	James Stephens (St. Louis AL, 1910.)	2,400	1,200	720.00
(616)	George Stone (St. Louis AL, 1905.)	2,400	1,200	720.00
(617)	George Stovall (Cleveland, 1904.)	2,400	1,200	720.00
(618)	Jesse Stovall (Detroit, 1904.)	2,400	1,200	720.00
(619)	Samuel Strang (Brooklyn, 1903.)	3,600	1,800	1,100
(620)	Samuel Strang (New York NL, 1905.)	2,400	1,200	720.00
(621)	Elmer Stricklett (Brooklyn, 1906.)	2,400	1,200	720.00
(622)	Willie Sudhoff (St. Louis AL, 1903.)	3,600	1,800	1,100
(623)	Willie Sudhoff (Washington, 1906.)	2,400	1,200	720.00
(624)	Joseph Sugden (St. Louis AL, 1903.)	3,600	1,800	1,100
(625)	George Suggs (Cincinnati, 1910.)	2,400	1,200	720.00
(628)	William D. Sullivan (Middle initial J.)(Chicago AL, 1902.)	3,600	1,800	1,100
(629)	Edgar Summers (Detroit, 1909.)	2,400	1,200	720.00
(630)	William J. Sweeney (Boston NL, 1910.)	2,400	1,200	720.00
(632)	Jesse Tannehill (New York AL, 1903.)	3,600	1,800	1,100
(633)	Jesse Tannehill (Boston AL, 1904.)	2,400	1,200	720.00
(634)	Lee Tannehill (Chicago AL, 1903.)	3,600	1,800	1,100
(636)	John Taylor (Chicago NL, 1902.)	3,600	1,800	1,100
(637)	John Taylor (St. Louis NL, 1904.)	2,400	1,200	720.00
(638)	Luther H. Taylor (New York NL, 1903.)	7,900	4,000	2,375
(639)	Fred Tenney (Boston NL, 1903.)	3,600	1,800	1,100
(640)	Ira Thomas (New York AL, 1906.)	2,400	1,200	720.00
(641)	Roy Thomas (Philadelphia NL, 1903.)	3,600	1,800	1,100
(642)	John Thoney (Cleveland, 1903.)	3,600	1,800	1,100
(643)	John Thoney (Washington, 1904.)	2,400	1,200	720.00
(644)	John Thoney (New York AL, 1904.)	2,400	1,200	720.00
(645)	Joseph B. Tinker (Chicago NL, 1903.)	7,900	4,000	2,375
(646)	John Townsend (Washington, 1903.)	3,600	1,800	1,100
(647)	John Townsend (Cleveland, 1906.)	2,400	1,200	720.00
(648)	Terrence Turner (Cleveland, 1904.)	2,400	1,200	720.00
(650)	Robert Unglaub (Boston AL, 1905.)	2,400	1,200	720.00
(652)	George Van Haltren (New York NL, 1902, street.)	4,300	2,150	1,300
(653)	George Van Haltren (New York NL, 1902, uniform.)	4,300	2,150	1,300
(654)	Fred Veil (Pittsburg, 1903.)	3,600	1,800	1,100
(655)	Ernest Vinson (Cleveland, 1905.)	2,400	1,200	720.00
(656)	Ernest Vinson (Chicago AL, 1905.)	2,400	1,200	720.00
(660)	George Edward "Rube" Waddell (Philadelphia AL, 1902, street.)	7,900	4,000	2,375
(661)	George Edward Waddell (St. Louis AL, 1908.)	6,500	3,250	1,950
(663)	Charles Wagner (Boston AL, 1910.)	2,400	1,200	720.00
(664)	John ("Hans") Wagner (Pittsburg, 1902, street.)	19,400	9,700	5,825
(665)	John ("Hans") Wagner (Pittsburg, 1905, uniform.)	11,520	5,750	3,450
(666)	Robert Wallace (St. Louis AL, 1902.)	7,900	4,000	2,375
(668)	Edward A. Walsh (Chicago AL, 1904.)	6,500	3,250	1,950
(670)	John Warner (New York NL, 1903.)	3,600	1,800	1,100
(671)	John Warner (St. Louis NL, 1905.)	2,400	1,200	720.00
(672)	John Warner (Detroit, 1905.)	2,400	1,200	720.00
(673)	John Warner (Washington, 1906.)	2,400	1,200	720.00
(674)	Arthur Weaver (Pittsburg, 1903.)	3,600	1,800	1,100
(675)	Arthur Weaver (St. Louis AL, 1905.)	2,400	1,200	720.00
(676)	Jacob Weimer (Chicago NL, 1903.)	3,600	1,800	1,100
(677)	Jacob Weimer (Cincinnati, 1906.)	2,400	1,200	720.00
(678)	G. Harry White (G. Harris "Doc") (Chicago AL, 1903.)	3,600	1,800	1,100
(679)	Robert Wicker (Chicago NL, 1903.)	3,600	1,800	1,100
(680)	Robert Wicker (Cincinnati, 1906.)	2,400	1,200	720.00
(681)	Fredrick Wilhelm (Irvin "Kaiser") (Pittsburg, 1903.)	3,600	1,800	1,100

		NM	EX	VG
(682)	Fredrick Wilhelm (Irvin "Kaiser")(Boston NL, 1904.)	2,400	1,200	720.00
(683)	Edgar Willett (Detroit, 1907.)	2,400	1,200	720.00
(684)	James Williams (Baltimore, 1902, street.)	3,600	1,800	1,100
(685)	James Williams (New York AL, 1903, street.)	3,600	1,800	1,100
(686)	James Williams (New York AL, 1903, uniform.)	3,600	1,800	1,100
(687)	Otto G. Williams (Chicago NL, 1904.)	2,400	1,200	720.00
(688)	Otto G. Williams (Philadelphia AL, 1905.)	2,400	1,200	720.00
(689)	Otto G. Williams (Washington, 1906.)	2,400	1,200	720.00
(692)	Victor J. Willis (Boston NL, 1903.)	7,900	4,000	2,375
(693)	Victor J. Willis (Pittsburg, 1906.)	6,500	2,350	1,950
(694)	Howard P. Wilson (Philadelphia AL, 1902, street.)	3,600	1,800	1,100
(695)	Howard P. Wilson (Washington, 1903.)	3,600	1,800	1,100
(696)	Howard P. Wilson (Cleveland, 1906.)	2,400	1,200	720.00
(698)	J. Owen Wilson (Pittsburg, 1910.)	2,400	1,200	720.00
(699)	George Wiltse (New York NL, 1904.)	2,400	1,200	720.00
(700)	Louis Wiltse (Lewis) (Baltimore, 1902.)	3,600	1,800	1,100
(701)	Louis Wiltse (Lewis) (New York AL, 1903.)	3,600	1,800	1,100
(702)	George Winters (Winter) (Boston AL, 1902, street.)	3,600	1,800	1,100
(705)	William Wolfe (Wilbert) (Washington, 1904.)	2,400	1,200	720.00
(706)	Harry Wolverton (Philadelphia NL, 1902, street.)	3,600	1,800	1,100
(707)	Harry Wolverton (Boston NL, 1905.)	2,400	1,200	720.00
(708)	Robert Wood (Detroit, 1904.)	2,400	1,200	720.00
(710)	Eugene Wright (Clarence Eugene)(Cleveland, 1903.)	3,600	1,800	1,100
(711)	Eugene Wright (Clarence Eugene) (St. Louis AL, 1903.)	3,600	1,800	1,100
(712)	Joseph Yeager (Detroit, 1902, street.)	3,600	1,800	1,100
(713)	Joseph Yeager (New York AL, 1905.)	2,400	1,200	720.00
(714)	Joseph Yeager (St. Louis AL, 1907.)	2,400	1,200	720.00
(715)	Denton ("Cy") Young (Boston AL, 1902.)	19,400	9,700	5,825
(716)	Irving Young (Boston NL, 1905.)	2,400	1,200	720.00
(717)	David Zearfoss (St. Louis NL, 1904.)	2,400	1,200	720.00
(718)	Charles Zimmer (Pittsburg, 1902.)	3,600	1,800	1,100
(719)	Charles Zimmer (Philadelphia NL, 1903.)	3,600	1,800	1,100
(720)	H. Zimmerman (Chicago NL, 1910.)	2,400	1,200	720.00

TRAP SHOOTERS

(T1)	Neas Apgar	950.00	500.00	300.00
(T2)	Chas. W. Budd	950.00	500.00	300.00
(T3)	W.R. Crosby	950.00	500.00	300.00
(T4)	J.A.R. Elliott	950.00	500.00	300.00
(T5)	J.S. Fanning	950.00	500.00	300.00
(T6)	Fred Gilbert	950.00	500.00	300.00
(T7)	Rolla O. Heikes	950.00	500.00	300.00
(T8)	H.C. Hirschy	950.00	500.00	300.00
(T9)	Tom A. Marshall	950.00	500.00	300.00
(T10)	Harvey McMurchy	950.00	500.00	300.00
(T11)	Ralph Trimble	950.00	500.00	300.00

1902 Sporting Life Team Composites (W601)

Printed on heavy 13" x 14" paper and featuring a composite of player photos arranged around that of the manager and a notice of league championship status, these prints were offered to readers of the weekly sports paper for six cents in postage stamps or 50 cents per dozen. The art was often found on the covers of "Sporting Life." While the prints were issued in 1902, they specify the teams as champions "for 1903." The Buck Weaver shown on the Butte composite is not the future Black Sox shortstop.

		NM	EX	VG
Complete Set:		4,500	2,200	1,350
Common Team:		300.00	150.00	90.00
(1)	Philadelphia, American League	500.00	250.00	150.00
(2)	Pittsburg, National League	500.00	250.00	150.00
(3)	Albany, New York State League	300.00	150.00	90.00

(4)	Butte, Pacific Northwest League	400.00	200.00	120.00
(5)	Indianapolis, American Association	400.00	200.00	120.00
(6)	Kansas City, Western League	400.00	200.00	120.00
(7)	Manchester, New England League	300.00	150.00	90.00
(8)	Nashville, Southern League	350.00	175.00	105.00
(9)	New Haven, Connecticut League	300.00	150.00	90.00
(10)	Rockford, Illinois-Indiana-Iowa League	300.00	150.00	90.00
(11)	Toronto, Eastern League	400.00	200.00	120.00

1903 Sporting Life Team Composites (W601)

Portraits of the individual players, usually identified by name and position, surround the manager's portrait in this series of team composites sold by Sporting Life newspaper. The 1903 series is the first in which all major league team composites were available. The 13" x 14" pictures are printed on heavy enamel paper and were sold for six cents in postage stamps, 50 cents per dozen. In some years bound portfolio complete sets were also offered, as were some of the more popular minor league teams. Notations of league and World Championships were incorporated into the design where appropriate. While issued in 1903, the pictures of league championship teams carry the notation "For 1904."

		NM	EX	VG
Complete Set (25):		5,550	2,700	1,650
Common (Major League) Team:		400.00	200.00	120.00
(1)	Boston, National League	400.00	200.00	120.00
(2)	Brooklyn, National League	400.00	200.00	120.00
(3)	Chicago, National League	600.00	300.00	180.00
(4)	Cincinnati, National League	400.00	200.00	120.00
(5)	New York, National League	500.00	250.00	150.00
(6)	Philadelphia, National League	400.00	200.00	120.00
(7)	Pittsburgh, National League	500.00	250.00	150.00
(8)	St. Louis, National League	400.00	200.00	120.00
(9)	Boston, American League	450.00	225.00	135.00
(10)	Chicago, American League	400.00	200.00	120.00
(11)	Cleveland, American League	400.00	200.00	120.00
(12)	Detroit, American League	400.00	200.00	120.00
(13)	New York, American League	450.00	225.00	135.00
(14)	Philadelphia, American League	450.00	225.00	135.00
(15)	St. Louis, American League	400.00	200.00	120.00
(16)	Washington, American League	400.00	200.00	120.00
(17)	Ft. Wayne, Central League	250.00	125.00	75.00
(18)	Holyoke, Connecticut League	250.00	125.00	75.00
(19)	Jersey City, Eastern League	300.00	150.00	90.00
(20)	Los Angeles, Pacific Coast League	300.00	150.00	90.00
(21)	Lowell, New England League	250.00	125.00	75.00
(22)	Memphis, Southern League	250.00	125.00	75.00
(23)	Schenectady, New York State League	250.00	125.00	75.00
(24)	Sedalia, Missouri Valley League	250.00	125.00	75.00
(25)	St. Paul, American Association	300.00	150.00	90.00

1904 Sporting Life Team Composites (W601)

Portraits of the individual players, usually identified by name and position, surround the manager's portrait in this series of team composites sold by Sporting Life newspaper. The 13" x 14" pictures are printed on heavy enamel paper and were sold for a dime apiece postpaid. In some years bound portfolio complete sets were also offered, as were some of the more popular minor league teams. Notations of league and World Championships were incorporated into the design where appropriate.

		NM	EX	VG
Complete Set (24):		5,550	2,700	1,650
Common (Major League) Team:		400.00	200.00	120.00
(1)	Boston, National League	400.00	200.00	120.00
(2)	Brooklyn, National League	400.00	200.00	120.00
(3)	Chicago, National League	600.00	300.00	180.00
(4)	Cincinnati, National League	400.00	200.00	120.00
(5)	New York, National League	500.00	250.00	150.00
(6)	Philadelphia, National League	400.00	200.00	120.00
(7)	Pittsburgh, National League	550.00	275.00	165.00
(8)	St. Louis, National League	400.00	200.00	120.00
(9)	Boston, American League	450.00	225.00	135.00
(10)	Chicago, American League	400.00	200.00	120.00
(11)	Cleveland, American League	400.00	200.00	120.00
(12)	Detroit, American League	400.00	200.00	120.00
(13)	New York, American League	450.00	225.00	135.00
(14)	Philadelphia, American League	450.00	225.00	135.00
(15)	St. Louis, American League	400.00	200.00	120.00

(16)	Washington, American League	400.00	200.00	120.00
(17)	Buffalo, Eastern League	300.00	150.00	90.00
(18)	Ft. Wayne, Central League	200.00	100.00	60.00
(19)	Haverhill, New England League	200.00	100.00	60.00
(20)	Macon, South Atlantic League	200.00	100.00	60.00
(21)	Memphis, Southern League	200.00	100.00	60.00
(22)	Springfield, Indiana-Illinois-Iowa League	200.00	100.00	60.00
(23)	St. Paul, American Association	250.00	125.00	75.00
(24)	Syracuse, New York League (1903 Indiana-Illinois-Iowa League Champs)	200.00	100.00	60.00

1905 Sporting Life Team Composites (W601)

Portraits of the individual players, usually identified by name and position, surround the manager's portrait in this series of team composites sold by Sporting Life newspaper. The 13" x 14" pictures are printed on heavy enamel paper and were sold for a dime apiece postpaid. In some years bound portfolio complete sets were also offered, as were some of the more popular minor league teams. Notations of league and World Championships were incorporated into the design where appropriate.

		NM	EX	VG
Complete Set (23):		5,500	2,700	1,650
Common (Major League) Team:		400.00	200.00	120.00
(1)	Boston, National League	400.00	200.00	120.00
(2)	Brooklyn, National League	400.00	200.00	120.00
(3)	Chicago, National League	600.00	300.00	180.00
(4)	Cincinnati, National League	400.00	200.00	120.00
(5)	New York, National League	450.00	225.00	135.00
(6)	Philadelphia, National League	400.00	200.00	120.00
(7)	Pittsburg, National League	750.00	375.00	225.00
(8)	St. Louis, National League	400.00	200.00	120.00
(9)	Boston, American League	400.00	200.00	120.00
(10)	Chicago, American League	400.00	200.00	120.00
(11)	Cleveland, American League	400.00	200.00	120.00
(12)	Detroit, American League	400.00	200.00	120.00
(13)	New York, American League	600.00	300.00	180.00
(14)	Philadelphia, American League	600.00	300.00	180.00
(15)	St. Louis, American League	400.00	200.00	120.00
(16)	Washington, American League	400.00	200.00	120.00
(17)	A., J. & G., New York League	200.00	100.00	60.00
(18)	Columbus, American Association	250.00	125.00	75.00
(19)	Concord, New England League	200.00	100.00	60.00
(20)	Des Moines, Western League	200.00	100.00	60.00
(21)	Macon, South Atlantic League	200.00	100.00	60.00
(22)	New Orleans, Southern League	250.00	125.00	75.00
(23)	Providence, Eastern League	250.00	125.00	75.00

1906-07 Sporting Life Team Composite Postcards

A miniature version of the Sporting Life's team composite lithographs was utilized to create a postcard set. In 3-5/8" x 5-7/16" format, the postcards have a composite of player portraits surrounding that of the manager, with a wide white right margin. Backs have standard postcard indicia. Some cards have been found with backs containing an ad offering either league's set for 10 cents in stamps.

		NM	EX	VG
Complete Set (16):		13,500	6,750	4,150
Common Team:		675.00	335.00	200.00
(1)	Boston, National League	675.00	335.00	200.00
(2)	Brooklyn, National League	900.00	450.00	270.00
(3)	Chicago, National League	900.00	450.00	270.00
(4)	Cincinnati, National League	850.00	425.00	255.00
(5)	New York, National League	850.00	425.00	255.00
(6)	Philadelphia, National League	675.00	335.00	200.00
(7)	Pittsburg, National League	1,000	500.00	300.00
(8)	St. Louis, National League	675.00	335.00	200.00
(9)	Boston, American League	700.00	350.00	210.00
(10)	Chicago, American League	750.00	375.00	225.00
(11)	Cleveland, American League	1,100	550.00	330.00
(12)	Detroit, American League	1,200	600.00	360.00
(13)	New York, American League	1,100	550.00	330.00
(14)	Philadelphia, American League	900.00	450.00	270.00
(15)	St. Louis, American League	900.00	450.00	270.00
(16)	Washington, American League	800.00	400.00	240.00

1906 Sporting Life Team Composites (W601)

Originally sold as a string-bound "Premier Art Portfolio" containing 24 major and minor league team composite pictures, single pieces from this premium issue are not uncommonly found as they were later offered individually for 10 cents apiece. The individual pieces measure 13" x 14" and are printed in black-and-white on heavy enameled paper. Individual player pictures are arranged around a baseball containing the manager's picture. Each player is identified beneath his photo by name and position. By 1906 the year printed on the pictures corresponds to the year of issue.

		NM	EX	VG
Complete Set (24):		12,000	6,000	3,500
Common Major League Team:		550.00	275.00	165.00
Common Minor League Team:		300.00	150.00	90.00
(1)	Boston, National League	750.00	375.00	225.00
(2)	Brooklyn, National League	550.00	275.00	165.00
(3)	Chicago, National League	800.00	400.00	240.00
(4)	Cincinnati, National League	550.00	275.00	165.00
(5)	New York, National League	650.00	325.00	195.00
(6)	Philadelphia, National League	675.00	335.00	200.00
(7)	Pittsburg, National League	650.00	325.00	195.00
(8)	St. Louis, National League	550.00	275.00	165.00
(9)	Boston, American League	800.00	400.00	240.00
(10)	Chicago, American League	650.00	325.00	195.00
(11)	Cleveland, American League	1,200	600.00	360.00
(12)	Detroit, American League	1,200	600.00	360.00
(13)	New York, American League	800.00	400.00	240.00
(14)	Philadelphia, American League	800.00	400.00	240.00
(15)	St. Louis, American League	550.00	275.00	165.00
(16)	Washington, American League	550.00	275.00	165.00
(17)	National League president, managers	600.00	300.00	180.00
(18)	American League president, managers	600.00	300.00	180.00
(19)	Birmingham, Southern League	300.00	150.00	90.00
(20)	Buffalo, Eastern League	300.00	150.00	90.00
(21)	Columbus, American Assoc.	300.00	150.00	90.00
(22)	Grand Rapids, Central League	300.00	150.00	90.00
(23)	Norwich, Connecticut League	300.00	150.00	90.00
(24)	Scranton, New York League	300.00	150.00	90.00

1907 Sporting Life Team Composites (W601)

Portraits of the individual players, usually identified by name and position, surround the manager's portrait in this series of team composites sold by Sporting Life newspaper. The 13" x 14" pictures are printed on heavy enamel paper and were sold for a dime apiece postpaid. In some years bound portfolio complete sets were also offered, as were some of the more popular minor league teams. Notations of league and World Championships were incorporated into the design where appropriate.

		NM	EX	VG
Complete Set (23):		5,500	2,700	1,600
Common (Major League) Team:		400.00	200.00	120.00
(1)	Boston, National League	400.00	200.00	120.00
(2)	Brooklyn, National League	400.00	200.00	120.00
(3)	Chicago, National League	500.00	250.00	150.00
(4)	Cincinnati, National League	400.00	200.00	120.00
(5)	New York, National League	500.00	250.00	150.00
(6)	Philadelphia, National League	400.00	200.00	120.00
(7)	Pittsburg, National League	450.00	225.00	135.00
(8)	St. Louis, National League	400.00	200.00	120.00
(9)	Boston, American League	400.00	200.00	120.00
(10)	Chicago, American League	400.00	200.00	120.00
(11)	Cleveland, American League	400.00	200.00	120.00
(12)	Detroit, American League	600.00	300.00	180.00
(13)	New York, American League	450.00	225.00	135.00
(14)	Philadelphia, American League	400.00	200.00	120.00
(15)	St. Louis, American League	400.00	200.00	120.00
(16)	Washington, American League	500.00	250.00	150.00
(17)	Toronto, Eastern League	300.00	150.00	90.00
(18)	Columbus, American Assoc.	300.00	150.00	90.00
(19)	Williamsport, Tri-State League	200.00	100.00	60.00
(20)	Albany, New York League	200.00	100.00	60.00
(21)	Atlanta, Southern League	200.00	100.00	60.00
(22)	Holyoke, Connecticut League	200.00	100.00	60.00
(23)	Norfolk, Virginia League	200.00	100.00	60.00

1908 Sporting Life Team Composites (W601)

Portraits of the individual players, usually identified by name and position, surround the manager's portrait in this series of team composites sold by Sporting Life newspaper. The 13" x 14" pictures are printed on heavy enamel paper and were sold for a dime apiece postpaid. In some years bound portfolio complete sets were also offered, as were some of the more popular minor league teams. Notations of league and World Championships were incorporated into the design where appropriate.

		NM	EX	VG
Complete Set (16):		4,500	2,250	1,350
Common Team:		400.00	200.00	120.00
(1)	Boston, National League	400.00	200.00	120.00
(2)	Brooklyn, National League	400.00	200.00	120.00
(3)	Chicago, National League	500.00	250.00	150.00
(4)	Cincinnati, National League	400.00	200.00	120.00
(5)	New York, National League	425.00	210.00	125.00
(6)	Philadelphia, National League	400.00	200.00	120.00
(7)	Pittsburgh, National League	450.00	225.00	135.00
(8)	St. Louis, National League	400.00	200.00	120.00
(9)	Boston, American League	400.00	200.00	120.00
(10)	Chicago, American League	400.00	200.00	120.00
(11)	Cleveland, American League	400.00	200.00	120.00
(12)	Detroit, American League	600.00	300.00	180.00
(13)	New York, American League	450.00	225.00	135.00
(14)	Philadelphia, American League	400.00	200.00	120.00
(15)	St. Louis, American League	400.00	200.00	120.00
(16)	Washington, American League	450.00	225.00	135.00

1909 Sporting Life Team Composites (W601)

Portraits of the individual players, usually identified by name and position, surround the manager's portrait in this series of team composites sold by Sporting Life newspaper. The 13" x 14" pictures are printed on heavy enamel paper and were sold for a dime apiece postpaid. In some years bound portfolio complete sets were also offered, as were some of the more popular minor league teams. Notations of league and World Championships were incorporated into the design where appropriate.

		NM	EX	VG
Complete Set (16):		6,500	3,250	1,850
Common Team:		600.00	300.00	180.00
(1)	Boston, National League	600.00	300.00	180.00
(2)	Brooklyn, National League	600.00	300.00	180.00
(3)	Chicago, National League	750.00	375.00	225.00
(4)	Cincinnati, National League	600.00	300.00	180.00
(5)	New York, National League	675.00	335.00	200.00
(6)	Philadelphia, National League	600.00	300.00	180.00
(7)	Pittsburgh, National League	1,125	560.00	335.00
(8)	St. Louis, National League	1,000	500.00	300.00

		NM	EX	VG
(9)	Boston, American League	600.00	300.00	180.00
(10)	Chicago, American League	600.00	300.00	180.00
(11)	Cleveland, American League	600.00	300.00	180.00
(12)	Detroit, American League	900.00	450.00	270.00
(13)	New York, American League	675.00	335.00	200.00
(14)	Philadelphia, American League	600.00	300.00	180.00
(15)	St. Louis, American League	600.00	300.00	180.00
(16)	Washington, American League	675.00	335.00	200.00

1910 Sporting Life Team Composites (W601)

After several years of issuing composite team photos for all major league teams (and some minor league teams), Sporting Life in 1910 began issuing them only for the league and World's Champions. Like the others, they are 13" x 14", printed on heavy enamel paper with individual player portrait photos surrounding the manager at center.

		NM	EX	VG
Complete Set (2):		1,200	600.00	350.00
Common Team:		300.00	150.00	90.00
(1)	Chicago Cubs (N.L. Champs)	450.00	225.00	135.00
(2)	Philadelphia Athletics (World's Champions)	750.00	375.00	225.00

1910-11 Sporting Life (M116)

Hans Wagner, Pitts. Nationals

WHEN YOU THINK OF
BASE BALL
THINK OF
SPORTING LIFE
FOR 27 YEARS THE RECOGNIZED AUTHORITY ON ALL BASE BALL MATTERS
TO-DAY IT IS
LARGER, BRIGHTER AND BETTER THAN EVER!
PUBLISHED EVERY SATURDAY 5¢ the Copy
AT ALL NEWSDEALERS.

This set of nominally 1-1/2" x 2-5/8" (individual card sizes vary even moreso than typically found on early 20th Century cards, notably with the "high numbers" often found somewhat larger) cards was offered to subscribers to "Sporting Life," a major competitor of "The Sporting News" in the early part of the century. The cards were issued in 24 series of 12 cards each, sold by mail for four cents per series. Card fronts feature color-tinted black-and-white portrait photos with the name and team printed below. Backs have various ads for the weekly paper. The last three 24-card series are scarcer than the earlier cards. These 72 cards have "Over 300 subjects" printed on back. Values in this checklist are adjusted according to that scarcity. The scarce blue-background cards appear to have been a second printing of the first two 12-card series which no doubt sold out quickly in the original pastel-background version due to the popularity of the players included. The 12 players in the Third Series can be found in an original printing with the ad on back printed in black, and a later version with a blue back. Each of the Third Series cards also exhibits on front subtle differences in the size and coloring of the player portrait. The complete set price does not include variations. Early series cards with over 300 subjects back should have 30% premium.

		NM	EX	VG
Common Player:		360.00	180.00	110.00
(1)	Ed Abbaticchio	360.00	180.00	110.00
(2a)	Babe Adams (Black back.)	360.00	180.00	110.00
(2b)	Babe Adams (Blue back.)	520.00	260.00	155.00
(3)	Red Ames	1,000	500.00	300.00
(4)	Jimmy Archer	1,000	500.00	300.00
(5)	Frank Arrelanes (Arellanes)	360.00	180.00	110.00
(6)	Tommy Atkins	1,000	500.00	300.00
(7)	Jimmy Austin	1,000	500.00	300.00
(8)	Les Bachman (Backman)	360.00	180.00	110.00
(9)	Bill Bailey	360.00	180.00	110.00
(10a)	Home Run Baker (Black back.)	1,600	800.00	480.00
(10b)	Home Run Baker (Blue back.)	2,400	1,200	720.00
(11)	Cy Barger	360.00	180.00	110.00
(12)	Jack Barry	360.00	180.00	110.00
(13a)	Johnny Bates (Philadelphia)	360.00	180.00	110.00
(13b)	Johnny Bates (Cincinnati) (A G-VG example sold at auction 4/06 for $22,987.)			
(14)	Ginger Beaumont	360.00	180.00	110.00
(15)	Fred Beck	360.00	180.00	110.00
(16)	Heinie Beckendorf	360.00	180.00	110.00
(17)	Fred Beebe	360.00	180.00	110.00
(18)	George Bell	360.00	180.00	110.00
(19)	Harry Bemis	360.00	180.00	110.00
(20a)	Chief Bender (Blue background.)	2,400	1,200	720.00
(20b)	Chief Bender (Pastel background.)	1,600	800.00	480.00
(21)	Bill Bergen	360.00	180.00	110.00
(22)	Heinie Berger	360.00	180.00	110.00
(23)	Bob Bescher	360.00	180.00	110.00
(24)	Joe Birmingham	360.00	180.00	110.00
(25)	Lena Blackburn (Blackburne)	360.00	180.00	110.00
(26)	John Bliss	1,000	500.00	300.00
(27)	Bruno Block	1,000	500.00	300.00
(28)	Bill Bradley	360.00	180.00	110.00
(29)	Kitty Bransfield	360.00	180.00	110.00
(30a)	Roger Bresnahan (Blue)	2,400	1,200	720.00
(30b)	Roger Bresnahan (Pastel)	1,600	800.00	480.00
(31)	Al Bridwell	360.00	180.00	110.00
(32)	Buster Brown (Boston)	360.00	180.00	110.00
(33a)	Mordecai Brown (Blue, Chicago.)	2,400	1,200	720.00
(33b)	Mordecai Brown (Pastel, Chicago.)	1,600	800.00	480.00
(34)	Al Burch	360.00	180.00	110.00
(35)	Donie Bush	360.00	180.00	110.00
(36)	Bobby Byrne	360.00	180.00	110.00
(37)	Howie Camnitz	360.00	180.00	110.00
(38)	Vin Campbell	1,000	500.00	300.00
(39)	Bill Carrigan	360.00	180.00	110.00
(40a)	Frank Chance (Blue)	2,400	1,200	720.00
(40b)	Frank Chance (Pastel)	1,600	800.00	480.00
(41)	Chappy Charles	360.00	180.00	110.00
(42a)	Hal Chase (Blue)	1,600	800.00	480.00
(42b)	Hal Chase (Pastel)	1,100	550.00	330.00
(43)	Ed Cicotte	1,800	900.00	540.00
(44a)	Fred Clarke (Pittsburgh, black back.)	1,600	800.00	480.00
(44b)	Fred Clarke (Pittsburgh, blue back.)	2,400	1,200	720.00
(45)	Nig Clarke (Cleveland)	360.00	180.00	110.00
(46)	Tommy Clarke (Cincinnati)	1,000	500.00	300.00
(47a)	Ty Cobb (Blue)	6,000	3,000	1,800
(47b)	Ty Cobb (Pastel)	18,000	9,000	5,400
(48a)	Eddie Collins (Blue)	2,400	1,200	720.00
(48b)	Eddie Collins (Pastel)	1,600	800.00	480.00
(49)	Ray Collins	1,000	500.00	300.00
(50)	Wid Conroy	360.00	180.00	110.00
(51)	Jack Coombs	360.00	180.00	110.00
(52)	Frank Corridon	360.00	180.00	110.00
(53)	Harry Coveleskie (Coveleski)	2,000	1,000	600.00
(54)	Doc Crandall	360.00	180.00	110.00
(55a)	Sam Crawford (Blue)	2,400	1,200	720.00
(55b)	Sam Crawford (Pastel)	1,600	800.00	480.00
(56)	Birdie Cree	360.00	180.00	110.00
(57)	Lou Criger	360.00	180.00	110.00
(58)	Dode Criss	1,000	500.00	300.00
(59)	Cliff Curtis	1,000	500.00	300.00
(60)	Bill Dahlen	360.00	180.00	110.00
(61)	Bill Davidson	1,000	500.00	300.00
(62a)	Harry Davis (Blue)	1,000	500.00	300.00
(62b)	Harry Davis (Pastel)	360.00	180.00	110.00
(63)	Jim Delehanty (Delahanty)	360.00	180.00	110.00
(64)	Ray Demmitt	1,000	500.00	300.00
(65)	Rube Dessau	1,000	500.00	300.00
(66a)	Art Devlin (Black back.)	360.00	180.00	110.00
(66b)	Art Devlin (Blue back.)	520.00	260.00	155.00
(67)	Josh Devore	1,000	500.00	300.00
(68)	Pat Donahue	360.00	180.00	110.00
(69)	Patsy Donovan	1,000	500.00	300.00
(70a)	Wild Bill Donovan (Blue)	1,000	500.00	300.00
(70b)	Wild Bill Donovan (Pastel)	360.00	180.00	110.00
(71a)	Red Dooin (Blue)	1,000	500.00	300.00
(71b)	Red Dooin (Pastel)	360.00	180.00	110.00
(72)	Mickey Doolan	360.00	180.00	110.00
(73)	Patsy Dougherty	360.00	180.00	110.00
(74)	Tom Downey	360.00	180.00	110.00
(75)	Jim Doyle	360.00	180.00	110.00
(76a)	Larry Doyle (Blue)	1,000	500.00	300.00
(76b)	Larry Doyle (Pastel)	360.00	180.00	110.00
(77)	Hugh Duffy	1,600	800.00	480.00
(78)	Jimmy Dygert	360.00	180.00	110.00
(79)	Dick Eagan (Egan)	360.00	180.00	110.00
(80)	Kid Elberfeld	360.00	180.00	110.00
(81)	Rube Ellis	360.00	180.00	110.00
(82)	Clyde Engle	360.00	180.00	110.00
(83)	Tex Erwin	1,000	500.00	300.00
(84)	Steve Evans	1,000	500.00	300.00
(85a)	Johnny Evers (Black back.)	1,600	800.00	480.00
(85b)	Johnny Evers (Blue back.)	2,400	1,200	720.00
(86)	Bob Ewing	360.00	180.00	110.00
(87)	Cy Falkenberg	360.00	180.00	110.00
(88)	George Ferguson	360.00	180.00	110.00
(89)	Art Fletcher	1,000	500.00	300.00
(90)	Elmer Flick	1,600	800.00	480.00
(91)	John Flynn	1,000	500.00	300.00
(92)	Russ Ford	1,000	500.00	300.00
(93)	Eddie Foster	1,000	500.00	300.00
(94)	Bill Foxen	360.00	180.00	110.00
(95)	John Frill	1,000	500.00	300.00
(96)	Sam Frock	1,000	500.00	300.00
(97)	Art Fromme	360.00	180.00	110.00
(98)	Earl Gardner (New York)	1,000	500.00	300.00
(99)	Larry Gardner (Boston)	1,000	500.00	300.00
(100)	Harry Gaspar	1,000	500.00	300.00
(101)	Doc Gessler	360.00	180.00	110.00
(102a)	George Gibson (Blue)	1,000	500.00	300.00
(102b)	George Gibson (Pastel)	360.00	180.00	110.00
(103)	Bill Graham (St. Louis)	360.00	180.00	110.00
(104)	Peaches Graham (Boston)	360.00	180.00	110.00
(105)	Eddie Grant	360.00	180.00	110.00
(106)	Clark Griffith	1,600	800.00	480.00
(107)	Ed Hahn	360.00	180.00	110.00
(108)	Charley Hall	360.00	180.00	110.00
(109)	Bob Harmon	1,000	500.00	300.00
(110)	Topsy Hartsel	360.00	180.00	110.00
(111)	Roy Hartzell	360.00	180.00	110.00
(112)	Heinie Heitmuller	360.00	180.00	110.00
(113)	Buck Herzog	360.00	180.00	110.00
(114)	Dick Hoblitzel (Hoblitzell)	360.00	180.00	110.00
(115)	Danny Hoffman	360.00	180.00	110.00
(116)	Solly Hofman	360.00	180.00	110.00
(117)	Harry Hooper	1,600	800.00	480.00
(118)	Harry Howell	360.00	180.00	110.00
(119)	Miller Huggins	1,600	800.00	480.00
(120)	Long Tom Hughes	1,000	500.00	300.00
(121)	Rudy Hulswitt	360.00	180.00	110.00
(122)	John Hummel	360.00	180.00	110.00
(123)	George Hunter	360.00	180.00	110.00
(124)	Ham Hyatt	360.00	180.00	110.00
(125)	Fred Jacklitsch	360.00	180.00	110.00
(126a)	Hughie Jennings (Blue)	2,400	1,200	720.00
(126b)	Hughie Jennings (Pastel)	1,600	800.00	480.00
(127)	Walter Johnson	7,000	3,500	2,100
(128a)	Davy Jones (Blue)	1,000	500.00	300.00
(128b)	Davy Jones (Pastel)	360.00	180.00	110.00
(129)	Tom Jones	360.00	180.00	110.00
(130a)	Tim Jordan (Blue)	1,000	500.00	300.00
(130b)	Tim Jordan (Pastel)	360.00	180.00	110.00
(131)	Addie Joss	1,800	900.00	540.00
(132)	Johnny Kane	360.00	180.00	110.00
(133)	Ed Karger	360.00	180.00	110.00
(134)	Red Killifer (Killefer)	1,000	500.00	300.00
(135)	Johnny Kling	360.00	180.00	110.00
(136)	Otto Knabe	360.00	180.00	110.00
(137)	John Knight	1,000	500.00	300.00
(138)	Ed Konetchy	360.00	180.00	110.00
(139)	Harry Krause	360.00	180.00	110.00
(140)	Rube Kroh	360.00	180.00	110.00
(141)	Art Krueger	1,600	800.00	480.00
(142a)	Nap Lajoie (Blue)	2,400	1,200	720.00
(142b)	Nap Lajoie (Pastel)	1,600	800.00	480.00
(143)	Fred Lake (Boston)	360.00	180.00	110.00
(144)	Joe Lake (St. Louis)	1,000	500.00	300.00
(145)	Frank LaPorte	360.00	180.00	110.00
(146)	Jack Lapp	1,000	500.00	300.00
(147)	Chick Lathers	1,000	500.00	300.00
(148a)	Tommy Leach (Blue)	1,000	500.00	300.00
(148b)	Tommy Leach (Pastel)	360.00	180.00	110.00
(149)	Sam Leever	360.00	180.00	110.00
(150)	Lefty Leifeld	360.00	180.00	110.00
(151)	Ed Lennox	360.00	180.00	110.00
(152)	Fred Linke (Link)	1,000	500.00	300.00
(153)	Paddy Livingstone (Livingston)	360.00	180.00	110.00
(154)	Hans Lobert	1,000	500.00	300.00
(155)	Bris Lord	360.00	180.00	110.00
(156a)	Harry Lord (Blue)	1,000	500.00	300.00
(156b)	Harry Lord (Pastel)	360.00	180.00	110.00
(157)	Johnny Lush	360.00	180.00	110.00
(158)	Connie Mack	1,600	800.00	480.00
(159)	Tom Madden	1,000	500.00	300.00
(160)	Nick Maddox	360.00	180.00	110.00
(161)	Sherry Magee	360.00	180.00	110.00
(162a)	Christy Mathewson (Blue)	10,000	5,000	3,000
(162b)	Christy Mathewson (Pastel)	5,400	2,700	1,625
(163)	Al Mattern	360.00	180.00	110.00
(164)	Jimmy McAleer	360.00	180.00	110.00
(165)	George McBride	1,000	500.00	300.00
(166a)	Amby McConnell (Boston)	360.00	180.00	110.00
(166b)	Amby McConnell (Chicago)	10,000	5,000	3,000
(167)	Pryor McElveen	360.00	180.00	110.00
(168)	John McGraw	1,600	800.00	480.00
(169)	Deacon McGuire	360.00	180.00	110.00
(170)	Stuffy McInnes (McInnis)	1,000	500.00	300.00
(171)	Harry McIntire (McIntyre)	360.00	180.00	110.00
(172)	Matty McIntyre	360.00	180.00	110.00
(173)	Larry McLean	360.00	180.00	110.00
(174)	Tommy McMillan	360.00	180.00	110.00
(175a)	George McQuillan (Blue, Philadelphia.)	1,000	500.00	300.00
(175b)	George McQuillan (Pastel, Philadelphia.)	360.00	180.00	110.00
(175c)	George McQuillan (Cincinnati)	5,000	2,500	1,500
(176)	Paul Meloan	1,000	500.00	300.00
(177)	Fred Merkle	360.00	180.00	110.00
(178)	Clyde Milan	360.00	180.00	110.00
(179)	Dots Miller (Pittsburgh)	360.00	180.00	110.00
(180)	Warren Miller (Washington)	1,000	500.00	300.00
(181)	Fred Mitchell	1,000	500.00	300.00
(182)	Mike Mitchell	360.00	180.00	110.00
(183)	Earl Moore	360.00	180.00	110.00
(184)	Pat Moran	360.00	180.00	110.00
(185a)	Lew Moren (Black back.)	520.00	260.00	155.00
(185b)	Lew Moren (Blue back.)	360.00	180.00	110.00
(186)	Cy Morgan	360.00	180.00	110.00
(187)	George Moriarty	360.00	180.00	110.00
(188)	Mike Mowery (Mowrey)	1,000	500.00	300.00
(189a)	George Mullin (Black back.)	360.00	180.00	110.00
(189b)	George Mullin (Blue back.)	520.00	260.00	155.00
(190)	Danny Murphy	360.00	180.00	110.00
(191)	Red Murray	360.00	180.00	110.00
(192)	Chief Myers (Meyers)	1,000	500.00	300.00
(193)	Tom Needham	360.00	180.00	110.00
(194)	Harry Niles	360.00	180.00	110.00
(195)	Rebel Oakes	1,000	500.00	300.00
(196)	Jack O'Connor	360.00	180.00	110.00
(197)	Paddy O'Connor	360.00	180.00	110.00
(198)	Bill O'Hara	360.00	180.00	110.00
(199)	Rube Oldring	360.00	180.00	110.00
(200)	Charley O'Leary	360.00	180.00	110.00
(201)	Orval Overall	360.00	180.00	110.00
(202)	Freddy Parent	360.00	180.00	110.00
(203)	Dode Paskert	1,000	500.00	300.00
(204)	Fred Payne	1,000	500.00	300.00
(205)	Barney Pelty	360.00	180.00	110.00
(206)	Hub Pernoll	1,000	500.00	300.00
(207)	George Perring	1,000	500.00	300.00
(208)	Big Jeff Pfeffer	1,000	500.00	300.00

		NM	EX	VG
(209)	Jack Pfiester	360.00	180.00	110.00
(210)	Art Phelan	1,000	500.00	300.00
(211)	Ed Phelps	360.00	180.00	110.00
(212)	Deacon Phillippe	360.00	180.00	110.00
(213)	Eddie Plank	4,800	2,400	1,450
(214)	Jack Powell	360.00	180.00	110.00
(215)	Billy Purtell	360.00	180.00	110.00
(216)	Farmer Ray	1,000	500.00	300.00
(217)	Bugs Raymond	360.00	180.00	110.00
(218)	Doc Reisling	360.00	180.00	110.00
(219)	Ed Reulbach	360.00	180.00	110.00
(220)	Lew Richie	360.00	180.00	110.00
(221)	Jack Rowan	360.00	180.00	110.00
(222a)	Nap Rucker (Black back.)	360.00	180.00	110.00
(222b)	Nap Rucker (Blue back.)	520.00	260.00	155.00
(223)	Slim Sallee	360.00	180.00	110.00
(224)	Doc Scanlon	360.00	180.00	110.00
(225)	Germany Schaefer	1,000	500.00	300.00
(226)	Lou Schettler	360.00	180.00	110.00
(227)	Admiral Schlei	360.00	180.00	110.00
(228)	Boss Schmidt	360.00	180.00	110.00
(229)	Wildfire Schulte	360.00	180.00	110.00
(230)	Al Schweitzer	360.00	180.00	110.00
(231)	Jim Scott	1,000	500.00	300.00
(232a)	Cy Seymour (N.Y.)	360.00	180.00	110.00
(232b)	Cy Seymour (Baltimore) (Two known; 4/04 auction $18,000+ Fair-Good.)			
(233)	Tillie Shafer	360.00	180.00	110.00
(234)	Bud Sharpe	1,000	500.00	300.00
(235)	Dave Shean	1,000	500.00	300.00
(236)	Jimmy Sheckard	360.00	180.00	110.00
(237)	Mike Simon	1,000	500.00	300.00
(238)	Charlie Smith (Boston)	1,000	500.00	300.00
(239)	Frank Smith (Chicago)	360.00	180.00	110.00
(240)	Harry Smith (Boston)	360.00	180.00	110.00
(241)	Fred Snodgrass	360.00	180.00	110.00
(242)	Bob Spade	360.00	180.00	110.00
(243)	Tully Sparks	360.00	180.00	110.00
(244)	Tris Speaker	3,000	1,500	900.00
(245)	Jake Stahl	360.00	180.00	110.00
(246)	George Stallings	360.00	180.00	110.00
(247)	Oscar Stanage	360.00	180.00	110.00
(248)	Harry Steinfeldt	360.00	180.00	110.00
(249)	Jim Stephens	360.00	180.00	110.00
(250)	George Stone	360.00	180.00	110.00
(251)	George Stovall	360.00	180.00	110.00
(252)	Gabby Street	360.00	180.00	110.00
(253)	Sailor Stroud	1,000	500.00	300.00
(254)	Amos Strunk	1,000	500.00	300.00
(255)	George Suggs	360.00	180.00	110.00
(256)	Billy Sullivan	360.00	180.00	110.00
(257a)	Ed Summers (Black back.)	360.00	180.00	110.00
(257b)	Ed Summers (Blue back.)	520.00	260.00	155.00
(258)	Bill Sweeney (Boston)	360.00	180.00	110.00
(259)	Jeff Sweeney (New York)	1,000	500.00	300.00
(260)	Lee Tannehill	360.00	180.00	110.00
(261a)	Fred Tenney (Blue)	1,000	500.00	300.00
(261b)	Fred Tenney (Pastel)	360.00	180.00	110.00
(262a)	Ira Thomas (Blue)	1,000	500.00	300.00
(262b)	Ira Thomas (Pastel)	360.00	180.00	110.00
(263)	Jack Thoney	360.00	180.00	110.00
(264a)	Joe Tinker (Black back.)	1,600	800.00	480.00
(264b)	Joe Tinker (Blue back.)	2,400	1,200	720.00
(265)	John Titus	1,000	500.00	300.00
(266)	Terry Turner	360.00	180.00	110.00
(267)	Bob Unglaub	360.00	180.00	110.00
(268a)	Rube Waddell (Black back.)	1,600	800.00	480.00
(268b)	Rube Waddell (Blue back.)	2,400	1,200	720.00
(269a)	Hans Wagner (Pittsburgh, blue.)	9,000	5,500	3,000
(269b)	Hans Wagner (Pittsburgh, pastel.)	7,000	3,500	2,000
(270)	Heinie Wagner (Boston)	360.00	180.00	110.00
(271)	Bobby Wallace	1,600	800.00	480.00
(272)	Ed Walsh (Chicago)	1,600	800.00	480.00
(273a)	Jimmy Walsh (Gray background, Philadelphia.)	1,400	700.00	420.00
(273b)	Jimmy Walsh (White background, Philadelphia.)	1,400	700.00	420.00
(274)	Doc White	360.00	180.00	110.00
(275)	Kaiser Wilhelm	360.00	180.00	110.00
(276)	Ed Willett	360.00	180.00	110.00
(277)	Vic Willis	1,600	800.00	480.00
(278)	Art Wilson (New York)	1,000	500.00	300.00
(279)	Owen Wilson (Pittsburgh)	360.00	180.00	110.00
(280)	Hooks Wiltse	360.00	180.00	110.00
(281)	Harry Wolter	360.00	180.00	110.00
(282)	Smokey Joe Wood	2,700	1,350	810.00
(283)	Ralph Works	360.00	180.00	110.00
(284a)	Cy Young (Black back.)	3,600	1,800	1,100
(284b)	Cy Young (Blue back.)	4,800	2,400	1,500
(285)	Irv Young	360.00	180.00	110.00
(286)	Heinie Zimmerman	1,000	500.00	300.00
(287)	Dutch Zwilling	360.00	180.00	110.00

1911 Sporting Life Cabinets (M110)

This set of 5-5/8" x 7-1/2" premium photos is similar to, but much scarcer than, the contemporary T3 Turkey Red cab-inets. Like those, the Sporting Life cabinets feature a pastel player picture surrounded by a gray frame with a "gold" name-plate at bottom. Backs have advertising for the weekly sports paper printed in blue.

		NM	EX	VG
Complete Set (6):		90,000	35,000	17,500
Common Player:		5,500	2,200	1,325
(1)	Frank Chance	10,000	4,000	2,000
(2)	Hal Chase	8,000	3,200	1,600
(3)	Ty Cobb	25,000	10,000	5,000
(4)	Napoleon Lajoie	10,000	4,000	2,000
(5)	Christy Mathewson	20,000	8,000	4,000
(6)	Honus Wagner	35,000	17,500	8,750

1911 Sporting Life Team Composites (W601)

After several years of issuing composite team photos for all major league teams (and some minor league teams), Sporting Life in 1910 began issuing them only for the league and World's Champions. Like the others, they are 13" x 14", printed on heavy enamel paper with individual player portrait photos surrounding the manager at center.

		NM	EX	VG
Complete Set (2):		1,200	600.00	350.00
Common Team:		300.00	150.00	90.00
(1)	New York Giants (N.L. Champs)	600.00	300.00	180.00
(2)	Philadelphia Athletics (World's Champions)	750.00	375.00	225.00

1899-1900 Sporting News Supplements (M101-1)

For much of 1899 and 1900, the weekly issues of The Sporting News included a baseball player portrait supplement. About 8-3/4" x 11", the pictures offered vignetted photos of the era's stars on a glossy paper stock. Virtually all pictures were formal head-and-shoulders portraits; some in uniform, some in civilian clothes. A handful of players are depicted in full-length poses. The pictures were produced for the sports paper by National Copper Plate Co., (which issued its own set of prints listed elsewhere in this catalog). The TSN supplements have a logotype above the photo and the date in which it was included in the paper. Full player name and team/year are printed at bottom. Backs have a small box offering career information. Besides offering the pictures with weekly issues, portfolios of 50 could be had by starting or renewing a sub-scription for $2 a year.

		NM	EX	VG
Complete Set (62):		90,000	36,000	18,000
Common Player:		1,125	450.00	225.00
1899				
(1)	William Lange (Apr. 22)	1,125	450.00	225.00
(2)	Hugh Duffy (Apr. 29)	1,875	750.00	375.00
(3)	Charles A. Nichols (May 6)	1,875	750.00	375.00
(4)	Martin Bergen (May 13)	1,125	450.00	225.00
(5)	Michael Griffin (May 20)	1,125	450.00	225.00
(6)	Wilbert Robinson (May 27)	1,875	750.00	375.00
(7)	Clark C. Griffith (June 3)	1,875	750.00	375.00
(8)	John J. Doyle (June 10)	1,125	450.00	225.00
(9)	R.J. Wallace (June 17)	1,875	750.00	375.00
(10)	John O'Connor (June 24)	1,125	450.00	225.00
(11)	Louis Criger (July 1)	1,125	450.00	225.00
(12)	Jerry H. Nops (July 8)	1,125	450.00	225.00
(13)	William Kennedy (July 15)	1,125	450.00	225.00
(14)	P.J. Donovan (July 22)	1,125	450.00	225.00
(15)	William H. Keeler (July 29)	1,875	750.00	375.00
(16)	John J. McGraw (Aug. 5)	1,875	750.00	375.00
(17)	James Hughes (Aug. 12)	1,125	450.00	225.00
(18)	John Wagner (Aug. 19)	11,250	4,500	2,250
(19)	Victor G. Willis (Aug. 26)	1,875	750.00	375.00
(20)	James J. Collins (Sept. 2)	1,875	750.00	375.00
(21)	Eugene DeMontreville (Sept. 9)	1,125	450.00	225.00

		NM	EX	VG
(22)	Joseph J. Kelley (Sept. 16)	1,875	750.00	375.00
(23)	Frank L. Donahue (Francis R. "Red")(Sept. 23)	1,125	450.00	225.00
(24)	Edward J. Delehanty (Delahanty)(Sept. 30)	1,125	450.00	225.00
(25)	Fred C. Clark (Clarke)(Oct. 7)	1,875	750.00	375.00
(26)	Napoleon Lajoie (Oct. 14)	1,875	750.00	375.00
(27)	Edward Hanlon (Oct. 21)	1,875	750.00	375.00
(28)	Charles Stahl (Oct. 28)	1,125	450.00	225.00
(29)	Lave N. Cross (Nov. 4)	1,125	450.00	225.00
(30)	Elmer H. Flick (Nov. 11)	1,875	750.00	375.00
(31)	Frank LeRoy Chance (Nov. 18)	1,875	750.00	375.00
(32)	George S. Davis (Nov. 25)	1,875	750.00	375.00
(33)	Hugh J. Jennings (Dec. 2)	1,875	750.00	375.00
(34)	Denton T. Young (Dec. 9)	3,750	1,500	750.00
1900				
(35)	George E. Waddell (Apr. 14)	1,875	750.00	375.00
(36)	John Dunn (Apr. 21)	1,125	450.00	225.00
(37)	Clarence Beaumont (Apr. 28)	1,125	450.00	225.00
(38)	James T. McGuire (May 5)	1,125	450.00	225.00
(39)	William H. Dineen (May 12)	1,125	450.00	225.00
(40)	James T. Williams (May 19)	1,125	450.00	225.00
(41)	Thomas W. Corcoran (May 26)	1,125	450.00	225.00
(42)	John Freeman (June 2)	1,125	450.00	225.00
(43)	Henry Peitz (June 9)	1,125	450.00	225.00
(44)	Charles Phillippe (June 16)	1,125	450.00	225.00
(45)	Frank Hahn (June 23)	1,125	450.00	225.00
(46)	J. Emmet Heidrick (June 30)	1,125	450.00	225.00
(47)	Joseph McGinnity (July 7)	1,875	750.00	375.00
(48)	John D. Chesbro (July 14)	1,875	750.00	375.00
(49)	William R. Hamilton (July 21)	1,125	450.00	225.00
(50)	Samuel Leever (July 28)	1,125	450.00	225.00
(51)	Mike Donlin (Aug. 4)	1,125	450.00	225.00
(52)	William F. Dahlen (Aug. 11)	1,125	450.00	225.00
(53)	Frederick Tenney (Aug. 18)	1,125	450.00	225.00
(54)	Edward P. Scott (Aug. 25)	1,125	450.00	225.00
(55)	Edward M. Lewis (Sept. 1)	1,125	450.00	225.00
(56)	Theodore Breitenstein (Sept. 8)	1,125	450.00	225.00
(57)	Herman C. Long (Sept. 15)	1,125	450.00	225.00
(58)	Jesse Tannehill (Sept. 22)	1,125	450.00	225.00
(59)	Burt E. Jones (Sept. 29)	1,125	450.00	225.00
(60)	J. Callahan (Nixey)(Oct. 6)	1,125	450.00	225.00
(61)	Claude Ritchey (Oct. 13)	1,125	450.00	225.00
(62)	Roy Thomas (Oct. 20)	1,125	450.00	225.00

1909-1913 Sporting News Supplements (M101-2)

Among the finest large-format baseball collectibles pub-lished in the early part of the 20th Century was the 100-piece series of sepia-toned supplements issued by The Sporting News. Initially issued in a size of about 7-1/2" x 10", by late 1909 the size evolved to about 8-1/2" x 10" with the team pho-tos issued in a 16" x 10" format. The series was begun with the insertion of a supplement in the July 22, 1909, issue of TSN. One supplement was issued with each week's paper through April 7, 1910. There were several gaps over the course of the next several years, until the final piece was issued with the TSN dated Dec. 11, 1913. Most of the supplements feature full-length poses of the players. Each is labeled "Supplement to The Sporting News" with the issue date at top. At bottom is a box with the player's name and team. Backs are usually blank, but some supplements are found with colored advertis-ing on back for various other collectibles from the newspaper. The TSN supplements were printed on heavy paper and are usually found with corner creases or other signs of wear.

		NM	EX	VG
Complete Set (100):		25,000	12,500	7,500
Common Player:		80.00	40.00	25.00
Ad backs: 3X				
1909				
(1)	Roger Bresnahan (7/22)	600.00	300.00	180.00
(2)	Denton Young, Louis Criger (7/29)	450.00	225.00	135.00
(3)	Christopher Mathewson (8/5)	1,000	500.00	300.00
(4)	Tyrus R. Cobb (8/12)	1,200	600.00	360.00
(5)	Napoleon Lajoie (8/19)	550.00	275.00	165.00
(6)	Sherwood N. Magee (8/26)	80.00	40.00	25.00
(7)	Frank L. Chance (9/2)	500.00	250.00	150.00
(8)	Edward Walsh (9/9)	500.00	250.00	150.00
(9)	Nap Rucker (9/16)	80.00	40.00	25.00
(10)	Honus Wagner (9/23)	1,000	500.00	300.00
(11)	Hugh Jennings (9/30)	550.00	275.00	165.00
(12)	Fred C. Clarke (10/7)	550.00	275.00	165.00
(13)	Byron Bancroft Johnson (10/14)	550.00	275.00	165.00
(14)	Charles A. Comiskey (10/21)	550.00	275.00	165.00
(15)	Edward Collins (10/28)	550.00	275.00	165.00
(16)	James A. McAleer (11/4)	160.00	80.00	50.00
(17)	Pittsburgh Team (11/11)	350.00	175.00	100.00
(18)	Detroit Team (11/18)	350.00	175.00	100.00

(19)	George Bell (11/25)	160.00	80.00	50.00
(20)	Tris Speaker (12/2)	650.00	325.00	195.00
(21)	Mordecai Brown (12/9)	550.00	275.00	165.00
(22)	Hal Chase (12/16)	550.00	275.00	165.00
(23)	Thomas W. Leach (12/23)	160.00	80.00	50.00
(24)	Owen Bush (12/30)	160.00	80.00	50.00

1910

(25)	John J. Evers (1/6)	400.00	200.00	120.00
(26)	Harry Krause (1/13)	80.00	40.00	25.00
(27)	Chas. B. Adams (1/20)	80.00	40.00	25.00
(28)	Addie Joss (1/27)	400.00	200.00	120.00
(29)	Orval Overall (2/3)	80.00	40.00	25.00
(30)	Samuel E. Crawford (2/10)	400.00	200.00	120.00
(31)	Fred Merkle (2/17)	90.00	45.00	25.00
(32)	George Mullin (2/24)	80.00	40.00	25.00
(33)	Edward Konetchy (3/3)	80.00	40.00	25.00
(34)	George Gibson, Arthur Raymond (3/10)	80.00	40.00	25.00
(35)	Ty Cobb, Hans Wagner (3/17)	2,000	1,000	600.00
(36)	Connie Mack (3/24)	400.00	200.00	120.00
(37)	Wm. Evans, "Silk" O'Loughlin, William Klem, Wm. Johnston (3/31)	550.00	275.00	165.00
(38)	Edward Plank (4/7)	325.00	160.00	95.00
(39)	Walter Johnson, Charles E. Street (9/1)	500.00	250.00	150.00
(40)	John C. Kling (9/8)	80.00	40.00	25.00
(41)	Frank Baker (9/15)	400.00	200.00	120.00
(42)	Charles S. Dooin (9/22)	80.00	40.00	25.00
(43)	Wm. F. Carrigan (9/29)	80.00	40.00	25.00
(44)	John B. McLean (10/6)	80.00	40.00	25.00
(45)	John W. Coombs (10/13)	80.00	40.00	25.00
(46)	Jos. B. Tinker (10/20)	350.00	175.00	100.00
(47)	John I. Taylor (10/27)	80.00	40.00	25.00
(48)	Russell Ford (11/3)	80.00	40.00	25.00
(49)	Leonard L. Cole (11/10)	80.00	40.00	25.00
(50)	Harry Lord (11/17)	80.00	40.00	25.00
(51)	Philadelphia-A Team (11/24)	130.00	65.00	40.00
(52)	Chicago-N Team (12/1)	130.00	65.00	40.00
(53)	Charles A. Bender (12/8)	400.00	200.00	120.00
(54)	Arthur Hofman (12/15)	80.00	40.00	25.00
(55)	Bobby Wallace (12/21)	325.00	160.00	95.00
(56)	Jno. J. McGraw (12/28)	325.00	160.00	95.00

1911

(57)	Harry H. Davis (1/5)	80.00	40.00	25.00
(58)	James P. Archer (1/12)	80.00	40.00	25.00
(59)	Ira Thomas (1/19)	80.00	40.00	25.00
(60)	Robert Byrnes (1/26)	80.00	40.00	25.00
(61)	Clyde Milan (2/2)	80.00	40.00	25.00
(62)	John T. Meyer (2/9)(Meyers)	80.00	40.00	25.00
(63)	Robert Bescher (2/16)	80.00	40.00	25.00
(64)	John J. Barry (2/23)	80.00	40.00	25.00
(65)	Frank Schulte (3/2)	80.00	40.00	25.00
(66)	C. Harris White (3/9)	80.00	40.00	25.00
(67)	Lawrence Doyle (3/16)	80.00	40.00	25.00
(68)	Joe Jackson (3/23)	2,500	1,250	750.00
(69)	Martin O'Toole, William Kelly (10/26)	80.00	40.00	25.00
(70)	Vean Gregg (11/2)	80.00	40.00	25.00
(71)	Richard W. Marquard (11/9)	325.00	160.00	95.00
(72)	John E. McInnis (11/16)	80.00	40.00	25.00
(73)	Grover C. Alexander (11/23)	350.00	175.00	100.00
(74)	Del Gainor (11/30)	80.00	40.00	25.00
(75)	Fred Snodgrass (12/7)	80.00	40.00	25.00
(76)	James J. Callahan (12/14)	80.00	40.00	25.00
(77)	Robert Harmon (12/21)	80.00	40.00	25.00
(78)	George Stovall (12/28)	80.00	40.00	25.00

1912

(79)	Zack D. Wheat (1/4)	325.00	160.00	95.00
(80)	Frank "Ping" Bodie (1/11)	80.00	40.00	25.00
(81)	Boston-A Team (10/10)	130.00	65.00	40.00
(82)	New York-N Team (10/17)	130.00	65.00	40.00
(83)	Jake Stahl (10/24)	80.00	40.00	25.00
(84)	Joe Wood (10/31)	275.00	135.00	80.00
(85)	Charles Wagner (11/7)	80.00	40.00	25.00
(86)	Lew Ritchie (11/14)	80.00	40.00	25.00
(87)	Clark Griffith (11/21)	325.00	160.00	95.00
(88)	Arnold Hauser (11/28)	80.00	40.00	25.00
(89)	Charles Herzog (12/5)	80.00	40.00	25.00
(90)	James Lavender (12/12)	80.00	40.00	25.00
(91)	Jeff Tesreau (12/19)	80.00	40.00	25.00
(92)	August Herrmann (12/26)	110.00	55.00	30.00

1913

(93)	Jake Daubert (10/23)	80.00	40.00	25.00
(94)	Heinie Zimmerman (10/30)	80.00	40.00	25.00
(95)	Ray Schalk (11/6)	325.00	160.00	95.00
(96)	Hans Lobert (11/13)	80.00	40.00	25.00
(97)	Albert W. Demaree (11/20)	80.00	40.00	25.00
(98)	Arthur Fletcher (11/27)	80.00	40.00	25.00
(99)	Charles A. Somers (12/4)	80.00	40.00	25.00
(100)	Joe Birmingham (12/11)	80.00	40.00	25.00

1913 Sporting News Postcards (M101-3)

This six-card set was issued as a premium by the weekly sports newspaper. The 3-1/2" x 5-1/2" cards have borderless front photos printed in duotone color. Along with the player and team names at bottom is a "Published by The Sporting News" tag line. Postcard-format backs are in black-and-white. The unnumbered cards are checklisted here alphabetically.

		NM	EX	VG
Complete Set (6):		4,250	2,125	1,275
Common Player:		275.00	135.00	80.00
(1)	Roger Bresnahan	450.00	225.00	135.00
(2)	Ty Cobb	2,000	1,000	600.00
(3)	Eddie Collins	450.00	225.00	135.00
(4)	Vean Gregg	275.00	135.00	80.00
(5)	Walter Johnson, Gabby Street	750.00	375.00	225.00
(6)	Rube Marquard	450.00	225.00	135.00

1916 The Sporting News (M101-5)

(Though listed in catalogs for more than 25 years, it is now believed M101-5 cards with Sporting News backs do not exist.)

1916 The Sporting News (M101-4)

The "update" version of the promotional premium issued by The Sporting News is nearly identical to the earlier cards. The 200 black-and-white cards once again are printed with player photo, name, position, team and card number on front and advertising on the backs. The set checklist and, generally, values are the same for sets issued by several other businesses around the country. Most of the players included on the 1-5/8" x 3" cards also appear in the prior edition. Despite being labeled in the American Card Catalog as M101-4, this version was issued after the M101-5 version, with the first advertising appearing in August 1916. Cards could be ordered in series of 20 for a dime, or the complete set was free with a $2 subscription. The complete set price does not include variations.

		NM	EX	VG
Complete Set (200):		60,000	30,000	18,000
Common Player:		95.00	50.00	30.00
1	Babe Adams	110.00	50.00	30.00
2	Sam Agnew	95.00	50.00	30.00
3	Eddie Ainsmith	95.00	50.00	30.00
4	Grover Alexander	600.00	300.00	180.00
5	Leon Ames	95.00	50.00	30.00
6	Jimmy Archer	95.00	50.00	30.00
7	Jimmy Austin	95.00	50.00	30.00
8	H.D. Baird	95.00	50.00	30.00
9	J. Franklin Baker	390.00	190.00	115.00
10	Dave Bancroft	390.00	190.00	115.00
11	Jack Barry	95.00	50.00	30.00
12	Zinn Beck	95.00	50.00	30.00
13	"Chief" Bender	390.00	190.00	115.00
14	Joe Benz	95.00	50.00	30.00
15	Bob Bescher	95.00	50.00	30.00
16	Al Betzel	95.00	50.00	30.00
17	Mordecai Brown	390.00	190.00	115.00
18	Eddie Burns	95.00	50.00	30.00
19	George Burns	95.00	50.00	30.00
20	Geo. J. Burns	95.00	50.00	30.00
21	Joe Bush	95.00	50.00	30.00
22	"Donie" Bush	95.00	50.00	30.00
23	Art Butler	95.00	50.00	30.00
24	Bobbie Byrne	95.00	50.00	30.00
25	Forrest Cady	95.00	50.00	30.00
26	Jimmy Callahan	95.00	50.00	30.00
27	Ray Caldwell	95.00	50.00	30.00
28	Max Carey	390.00	190.00	115.00
29	George Chalmers	95.00	50.00	30.00
30	Ray Chapman	95.00	50.00	30.00
31	Larry Cheney	95.00	50.00	30.00
32	Eddie Cicotte	390.00	190.00	115.00
33	Tom Clarke	95.00	50.00	30.00
34	Eddie Collins	390.00	190.00	155.00
35	"Shauno" Collins	95.00	50.00	30.00
36	Charles Comiskey	390.00	190.00	115.00
37	Joe Connolly	95.00	50.00	30.00
38	Ty Cobb	4,800	2,400	1,440
39	Harry Coveleskie (Coveleski)	95.00	50.00	30.00
40	Gavvy Cravath	95.00	50.00	30.00
41	Sam Crawford	390.00	190.00	115.00
42	Jean Dale	95.00	50.00	30.00
43	Jake Daubert	95.00	50.00	30.00
44	Charles Deal	95.00	50.00	30.00
45	Al Demaree	95.00	50.00	30.00
46	Josh Devore	95.00	50.00	30.00
47	William Doak	95.00	50.00	30.00
48	Bill Donovan	95.00	50.00	30.00
49	Charles Dooin	95.00	50.00	30.00
50	Mike Doolan	95.00	50.00	30.00
51	Larry Doyle	95.00	50.00	30.00
52	Jean Dubuc	95.00	50.00	30.00

53	Oscar Dugey	95.00	50.00	30.00
54	Johnny Evers	390.00	190.00	115.00
55	Urban Faber	390.00	190.00	115.00
56	"Hap" Felsch	1,000	285.00	170.00
57	Bill Fischer	95.00	50.00	30.00
58	Ray Fisher	95.00	50.00	30.00
59	Max Flack	95.00	50.00	30.00
60	Art Fletcher	95.00	50.00	30.00
61	Eddie Foster	95.00	50.00	30.00
62	Jacques Fournier	95.00	50.00	30.00
63	Del Gainer (Gainor)	95.00	50.00	30.00
64	"Chic" Gandil	1,000	190.00	115.00
65	Larry Gardner	95.00	50.00	30.00
66	Joe Gedeon	95.00	50.00	30.00
67	Gus Getz	95.00	50.00	30.00
68	Geo. Gibson	95.00	50.00	30.00
69	Wilbur Good	95.00	50.00	30.00
70	Hank Gowdy	95.00	50.00	30.00
71	John Graney	95.00	50.00	30.00
72	Clark Griffith	390.00	190.00	115.00
73	Tom Griffith	95.00	50.00	30.00
74	Heinie Groh	95.00	50.00	30.00
75	Earl Hamilton	95.00	50.00	30.00
76	Bob Harmon	95.00	50.00	30.00
77	Roy Hartzell	95.00	50.00	30.00
78	Claude Hendrix	95.00	50.00	30.00
79	Olaf Henriksen	95.00	50.00	30.00
80	John Henry	95.00	50.00	30.00
81	"Buck" Herzog	95.00	50.00	30.00
82	Hugh High	95.00	50.00	30.00
83	Dick Hoblitzell	95.00	50.00	30.00
84	Harry Hooper	390.00	190.00	115.00
85	Ivan Howard	95.00	50.00	30.00
86	Miller Huggins	390.00	190.00	115.00
87	Joe Jackson	15,000	5,400	3,240
88	William James	95.00	50.00	30.00
89	Harold Janvrin	95.00	50.00	30.00
90	Hugh Jennings	390.00	190.00	115.00
91	Walter Johnson	1,140	570.00	345.00
92	Fielder Jones	95.00	50.00	30.00
93	Joe Judge	95.00	50.00	30.00
94	Bennie Kauff	95.00	50.00	30.00
95	Wm. Killefer Jr.	95.00	50.00	30.00
96	Ed. Konetchy	95.00	50.00	30.00
97	Napoleon Lajoie	390.00	190.00	115.00
98	Jack Lapp	95.00	50.00	30.00
99	John Lavan	95.00	50.00	30.00
100	Jimmy Lavender	95.00	50.00	30.00
101	"Nemo" Leibold	95.00	50.00	30.00
102	H.B. Leonard	95.00	50.00	30.00
103	Duffy Lewis	95.00	50.00	30.00
104	Hans Lobert	95.00	50.00	30.00
105	Tom Long	95.00	50.00	30.00
106	Fred Luderus	95.00	50.00	30.00
107	Connie Mack	390.00	190.00	115.00
108	Lee Magee	95.00	50.00	30.00
109	Sherwood Magee	95.00	50.00	30.00
110	Al. Mamaux	95.00	50.00	30.00
111	Leslie Mann	95.00	50.00	30.00
112	"Rabbit" Maranville	390.00	190.00	115.00
113	Rube Marquard	390.00	190.00	115.00
114	J. Erskine Mayer	150.00	80.00	45.00
115	George McBride	95.00	50.00	30.00
116	John J. McGraw	390.00	190.00	115.00
117	Jack McInnis	95.00	50.00	30.00
118	Fred Merkle	95.00	50.00	30.00
119	Chief Meyers	95.00	50.00	30.00
120	Clyde Milan	95.00	50.00	30.00
121	John Miller	95.00	50.00	30.00
122	Otto Miller	95.00	50.00	30.00
123	Willie Mitchell	95.00	50.00	30.00
124	Fred Mollwitz	95.00	50.00	30.00
125	Pat Moran	95.00	50.00	30.00
126	Ray Morgan	95.00	50.00	30.00
127	Geo. Moriarty	95.00	50.00	30.00
128	Guy Morton	95.00	50.00	30.00
129	Mike Mowrey	95.00	50.00	30.00
130	Ed. Murphy	95.00	50.00	30.00
131	"Hy" Myers	95.00	50.00	30.00
132	J.A. Niehoff	95.00	50.00	30.00
133	Rube Oldring	95.00	50.00	30.00
134	Oliver O'Mara	95.00	50.00	30.00
135	Steve O'Neill	95.00	50.00	30.00
136	"Dode" Paskert	95.00	50.00	30.00
137	Roger Peckinpaugh	95.00	50.00	30.00
138	Walter Pipp	95.00	50.00	30.00
139	Derril Pratt (Derrill)	95.00	50.00	30.00
140	Pat Ragan	95.00	50.00	30.00
141	Bill Randen	95.00	50.00	30.00
142	Eppa Rixey	390.00	190.00	115.00
143	Davey Robertson	95.00	50.00	30.00
144	Wilbert Robinson	390.00	190.00	115.00
145	Bob Roth	95.00	50.00	30.00
146	Ed. Roush	390.00	190.00	115.00
147	Clarence Rowland	95.00	50.00	30.00
148	"Nap" Rucker	95.00	50.00	30.00
149	Dick Rudolph	95.00	50.00	30.00
150	Reb Russell	95.00	50.00	30.00
151	Babe Ruth	30,000	15,000	9,000
152	Vic Saier	95.00	50.00	30.00
153	"Slim" Sallee	95.00	50.00	30.00
154	Ray Schalk	390.00	190.00	115.00
155	Walter Schang	95.00	50.00	30.00
156	Frank Schulte	95.00	50.00	30.00
157	Everett Scott	95.00	50.00	30.00
158	Jim Scott	95.00	50.00	30.00
159	Tom Seaton	95.00	50.00	30.00
160	Howard Shanks	95.00	50.00	30.00
161	Bob Shawkey	95.00	50.00	30.00
162	Ernie Shore	95.00	50.00	30.00
163	Burt Shotton	95.00	50.00	30.00
164	Geo. Sisler	390.00	190.00	115.00
165	J. Carlisle Smith	95.00	50.00	30.00
166	Fred Snodgrass	95.00	50.00	30.00
167	Geo. Stallings	95.00	50.00	30.00
168a	Oscar Stanage (Catching)	95.00	50.00	30.00
168b	Oscar Stanage (Portrait to thighs.)	900.00	450.00	270.00

		NM	EX	VG
169	Charles Stengel	390.00	190.00	115.00
170	Milton Stock	95.00	50.00	30.00
171	Amos Strunk	95.00	50.00	30.00
172	Billy Sullivan	95.00	50.00	30.00
173	"Jeff" Tesreau	95.00	50.00	30.00
174	Joe Tinker	390.00	190.00	115.00
175	Fred Toney	95.00	50.00	30.00
176	Terry Turner	95.00	50.00	30.00
177	George Tyler	95.00	50.00	30.00
178	Jim Vaughn	95.00	50.00	30.00
179	Bob Veach	95.00	50.00	30.00
180	James Viox	95.00	50.00	30.00
181	Oscar Vitt	95.00	50.00	30.00
182	Hans Wagner	2,500	660.00	395.00
183	Clarence Walker	95.00	50.00	30.00
184	Ed. Walsh	390.00	190.00	115.00
185	W. Wambsganss	95.00	50.00	30.00
	(Photo actually Fritz Coumbe.)			
186	Buck Weaver	1,000	285.00	170.00
187	Carl Weilman	95.00	50.00	30.00
188	Zach Wheat	390.00	190.00	115.00
189	Geo. Whitted	95.00	50.00	30.00
190	Fred Williams	95.00	50.00	30.00
191	Art Wilson	95.00	50.00	30.00
192	J. Owen Wilson	95.00	50.00	30.00
193	Ivy Wingo	95.00	50.00	30.00
194	"Mel" Wolfgang	95.00	50.00	30.00
195	Joe Wood	500.00	120.00	75.00
196	Steve Yerkes	95.00	50.00	30.00
197	"Pep" Young	95.00	50.00	30.00
198	Rollie Zeider	95.00	50.00	30.00
199	Heiny Zimmerman	95.00	50.00	30.00
200	Ed. Zwilling	95.00	50.00	30.00

1919 Sporting News (M101-6)

(The issue listed in previous editions as 1919 Sporting News Supplements (M101-6) is now listed as 1917-1920 Felix Mendelsohn.)

1926 Sporting News Supplements (M101-7)

This set of 11 player photos was issued as a post-World Series weekly supplement by The Sporting News in 1926. Sepia-toned portrait or posed photos are featured on the 7" x 10" supplements. The player's name and team are printed at the bottom, while a line indentifying The Sporting News and the date appear in the upper left corner. The unnumbered set includes a half-dozen Hall of Famers. Large-format (10" x 14-1/4") team photos of the 1926 Yankees (October 28) and Cardinals were also issued in the weeks preceding the start of issue for the weekly player supplements.

		NM	EX	VG
Complete Set (13):		2,000	800.00	400.00
Common Player:		40.00	16.00	8.00
(1)	Hazen "Kiki" Cuyler	100.00	40.00	20.00
(2)	Rogers Hornsby	125.00	50.00	25.00
(3)	Tony Lazzeri	100.00	40.00	20.00
(4)	Harry E. Manush (Henry)	100.00	40.00	20.00
(5)	John Mostil	40.00	16.00	8.00
(6)	Harry Rice	40.00	16.00	8.00
(7)	George Herman "Babe" Ruth	1,200	480.00	240.00
(8)	Al Simmons	100.00	40.00	20.00
(9)	Harold "Pie" Traynor	100.00	40.00	20.00
(10)	George Uhle	40.00	16.00	8.00
(11)	Glenn Wright	40.00	16.00	8.00
(12)	1926 Cardinals Team Photo	100.00	40.00	20.00
(13)	1926 Yankees Team Photo	200.00	80.00	40.00

1927-1928 Sporting News Ad-Back Supplements (M101-7)

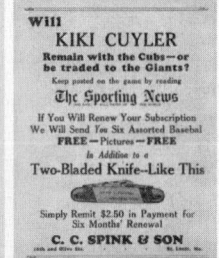

Evidently faced with a surplus of player supplements from its 1926 issue, The Sporting News recycled at least some of them in subsequent years as subscription sales advertising. Fronts of the supplements differ in that the sports paper's logo

and the original issue date from 1926 have been removed from the upper-left border. Instead of blank backs, however, the re-issues have color (blue or red seen to date) advertising on back. Respond-by dates in 1927 have been seen rubber-stamped on the back of some pieces, while that of Kiki Cuyler mentions his team as being the Cubs, who he joined in 1928.

	NM	EX	VG
Kiki Cuyler	300.00	125.00	65.00
Babe Ruth	1,500	600.00	300.00

1932 Sporting News Supplements (M101-8)

This issue of player-picture supplements from TSN is unusual not only in its brevity - only four were issued - but also in that the pictures have printed matter on back, consisting of player personal data and complete major/minor league stats. Only the Grimm piece has an issue date: Sept. 1, 1932. The pictures are on thin card stock in an 8-1/4" x 10-1/2" format. Fronts have a black-and-white photo with the player named in the wide bottom border.

		NM	EX	VG
Complete Set (4):		2,000	1,000	600.00
Common Player:		240.00	120.00	72.00
(1)	Jerome H. (Dizzy) Dean	900.00	450.00	270.00
(2)	Vernon Gomez	600.00	300.00	180.00
(3)	Charles John Grimm	250.00	125.00	75.00
(4)	Lonnie Warneke	250.00	125.00	75.00

1939 Sporting News Supplements (M101-9)

These dated supplements feature a trio of team photos and two star players as individuals. The team pictures are about 15" x 10-1/2" and comprise double-page spreads; the single players are 7-1/2" x 10".

		NM	EX	VG
Complete Set (5):		800.00	400.00	240.00
Common:		150.00	75.00	45.00
(1)	Joseph DiMaggio (Oct. 26)	200.00	100.00	60.00
(2)	Robert Feller (Nov. 9)	150.00	75.00	45.00
(3)	Cincinnati Reds Team (Nov. 2)	150.00	75.00	45.00
(4)	N.Y. Yankees Team (Oct. 19)	200.00	100.00	60.00
(5)	St. Louis Cardinals Team (Nov. 16)	150.00	75.00	45.00

1888 Sporting Times (M117)

Examples of these cards, issued in 1888 and 1889 by the Sporting Times weekly newspaper, are very rare. The complete set price includes all variations. The cabinet-size cards (7-1/4" x 4-1/2") feature line drawings of players in action poses on soft cardboard stock. The cards came in a variety of pastel colors surrounded by a 1/4" white border. The player's last name is printed on each drawing, as are the words "Courtesy Sporting Times New York." A pair of crossed bats and a baseball appear along the bottom of the card. Twenty-seven different players are known to exist. The drawing of Cap Anson is the same one used in the N28 Allen & Ginter series, and some of the other drawings are based on photos used in the popular Old Judge series.

		NM	EX	VG
Common Player:		15,000	10,000	6,000
(1)	Cap Anson	35,000	17,500	10,000
(2)	Jersey Bakely	15,000	10,000	6,000
(3)	Dan Brouthers	25,000	12,500	7,500
(4)	Doc Bushong	15,000	10,000	6,000
(5)	Jack Clements	15,000	10,000	6,000
(6)	Charlie Comiskey	25,000	12,500	7,500
(7)	Jerry Denny	15,000	10,000	6,000
(8)	Buck Ewing	25,000	12,500	7,500
(9)	Dude Esterbrook	15,000	10,000	6,000
(10)	Jay Faatz	15,000	10,000	6,000
(11)	Pud Galvin	25,000	12,500	7,500
(12)	Jack Glasscock	15,000	10,000	6,000
(13)	Tim Keefe	25,000	12,500	7,500
(14)	King Kelly	30,000	15,000	9,000
(15)	Matt Kilroy	15,000	10,000	6,000
(16)	Arlie Latham	15,000	10,000	6,000
(17)	Doggie Miller	15,000	10,000	6,000
(18)	Hank O'Day	15,000	10,000	6,000
(19)	Fred Pfeffer	15,000	10,000	6,000
(20)	Henry Porter	15,000	10,000	6,000
(21)	Toad Ramsey	15,000	10,000	6,000
(22)	Long John Reilly	15,000	10,000	6,000
(23)	Mike Smith	15,000	10,000	6,000
(24)	Harry Stovey	15,000	10,000	6,000
(25)	Sam Thompson	25,000	12,500	7,500
(26)	John Ward	25,000	12,500	7,500
(27)	Mickey Welch	25,000	12,500	7,500

1933 Sport Kings (R338)

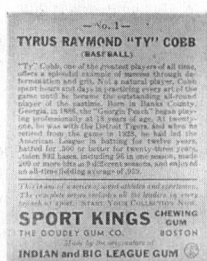

This 48-card set features athletes at the top of several sports such as boxing, football, skiing, dogsled racing, and swimming, as well as three hall-of-fame baseball players. the cards measure 2-3/8" x 2-7/8" and feature waist-up portrait artwork.

		NM	EX	VG
Complete Set (48):		30,000	15,000	9,000
Common Player (1-24):		200.00	100.00	60.00
Common Player (25-48):		250.00	125.00	75.00
1	Ty Cobb	6,000	3,000	1,800
2	Babe Ruth	7,000	3,500	2,100
3	Nat Holman	200.00	100.00	60.00
4	Harold "Red" Grange	1,000	500.00	300.00
5	Ed Wachter	200.00	100.00	60.00
6	Jim Thorpe	1,000	500.00	300.00
7	Bobby Walthour, Jr.	200.00	100.00	60.00
8	Walter Hagen	500.00	250.00	150.00
9	Ed Blood	200.00	100.00	60.00
10	Anton Lekang	200.00	100.00	60.00
11	Charles Jewtraw	200.00	100.00	60.00
12	Bobby McLean	200.00	100.00	60.00
13	LaVerne Fatour	200.00	100.00	60.00
14	Jim Londos	200.00	100.00	60.00
15	Reggie McNamara	200.00	100.00	60.00
16	William Tilden	200.00	100.00	60.00
17	Jack Dempsey	500.00	250.00	150.00
18	Gene Tunney	200.00	100.00	60.00
19	Eddie Shore	500.00	250.00	150.00
20	Duke Kahanamoku	200.00	100.00	60.00
21	Johnny Weissmuller	500.00	250.00	150.00
22	Gene Sarazen	500.00	250.00	150.00
23	Vincent Richards	200.00	100.00	60.00
24	Howie Morenz	500.00	250.00	150.00
25	Ralph Snoddy	250.00	125.00	75.00
26	James R. Wedell	250.00	125.00	75.00
27	Roscoe Turner	250.00	125.00	75.00
28	Jimmy Doolittle	250.00	125.00	75.00
29	Ace Bailey	250.00	125.00	75.00
30	Ching Johnson	250.00	125.00	75.00
31	Bobby Walthour, Jr.	250.00	125.00	75.00
32	Joe Lopchick	250.00	125.00	75.00
33	Eddie Burke	250.00	125.00	75.00
34	Irving Jaffee	250.00	125.00	75.00
35	Knute Rockne	1,000	500.00	300.00
36	Willie Hoppe	250.00	125.00	75.00
37	Helene Madison	250.00	125.00	75.00
38	Bobby Jones	3,000	1,500	900.00
39	Jack Westrope	250.00	125.00	75.00
40	Don George	250.00	125.00	75.00
41	Jim Browning	250.00	125.00	75.00
42	Carl Hubbell	500.00	250.00	150.00
43	Primo Carnera	250.00	125.00	75.00
44	Max Baer	250.00	125.00	75.00

		NM	EX	VG
45	Babe Didrickson	500.00	250.00	150.00
46	Ellsworth Vines	250.00	125.00	75.00
47	J. Hubert Stevens	250.00	125.00	75.00
48	Leonhard Seppala	250.00	125.00	75.00

1947 Sport Magazine Premium

This 8-1/2" x 11", blank-back, paper-stock picture appears to have been a premium issued in conjunction with Sport magazine's premiere issue in March 1947, perhaps as a send-away offer. The picture has a black-and-white portrait photo on a bright orange background, surrounded with a white border. In the lower-left corner is "March '47." "15 Sport" appears at lower-right.

		NM	EX	VG
15	Joe DiMaggio	35.00	17.50	10.50

1953 Sport Magazine All-Star Portfolio

This set of 5-3/8" x 7" glossy color pictures was used by Sport Magazine as a subscription premium. Featuring the outstanding photography of Ozzie Sweet, all but the Bob Mathias pictures are portraits, surrounded with a white border and the player name at bottom. Backs are blank. The heavy cardboard mailing envelope contains short athlete biographies.

		NM	EX	VG
	Complete Set (10):	175.00	85.00	50.00
	Common Player:	20.00	10.00	6.00
(1)	Joe Black	25.00	12.50	7.50
(2)	Robert Cousy (Basketball)	20.00	10.00	6.00
(3)	Elroy Hirsch (Football)	20.00	10.00	6.00
(4)	Rocky Marciano (Boxing)	30.00	15.00	9.00
(5)	Robert Bruce Mathias (Track and field.)	20.00	10.00	6.00
(6)	Stanley Frank Musial	45.00	22.50	13.50
(7)	John Olszewski (Football)	20.00	10.00	6.00
(8)	Allie Pierce Reynolds	20.00	10.00	6.00
(9)	Robin Evan Roberts	30.00	15.00	9.00
(10)	Robert Clayton Shantz	20.00	10.00	6.00

1968-69 Sports Cards for Collectors

These Myron Aronstein-drawn 3-1/2" x 4-1/4" postcards feature 78 pre-1950 players. Cards 1-36 feature blank backs, and 37-78 have brief biographical and statistical data. The last four are checklists.

		NM	EX	VG
	Complete Set (82):	100.00	50.00	30.00
	Common Player:	2.00	1.00	.60
1	Babe Ruth	15.00	7.50	5.00
2	Rube Marquard	2.00	1.00	.60
3	Zack Wheat	2.00	1.00	.60
4	John Clarkson	2.00	1.00	.60
5	Honus Wagner	2.00	1.00	.60
6	Johnny Evers	2.00	1.00	.60
7	Bill Dickey	2.00	1.00	.60
8	Elmer Smith	2.00	1.00	.60
9	Ty Cobb	10.00	5.00	3.00
10	Jack Chesbro	2.00	1.00	.60
11	George Gibson	2.00	1.00	.60
12	Bullet Joe Bush	2.00	1.00	.60
13	George Mullin	2.00	1.00	.60
14	Buddy Meyer	2.00	1.00	.60
15	Jimmy Collins	2.00	1.00	.60
16	Bill Wambsganss	2.00	1.00	.60
17	Jack Barry	2.00	1.00	.60
18	Dickie Kerr	2.00	1.00	.60
19	Connie Mack	2.00	1.00	.60
20	Rabbit Maranville	2.00	1.00	.60
21	Roger Peckinpaugh	2.00	1.00	.60
22	Mickey Cochrane	2.00	1.00	.60
23	George Kelly	2.00	1.00	.60
24	Frank "Home Rune" Baker	2.00	1.00	.60
25	Wally Schang	2.00	1.00	.60
26	Eddie Plank	2.00	1.00	.60
27	Bill Donovan	2.00	1.00	.60
28	Red Faber	2.00	1.00	.60
29	Hack Wilson	2.00	1.00	.60
30	Mordecai "3 Finger" Brown	2.00	1.00	.60
31	Fred Merkle	2.00	1.00	.60
32	Heinie Groh	2.00	1.00	.60
33	Stuffy McInnis	2.00	1.00	.60
34	Hal Chase	2.00	1.00	.60
35	Judge Kenesaw Mountain Landis	2.00	1.00	.60
36	Chief Bender	2.00	1.00	.60
37	Fred Snodgrass	2.00	1.00	.60
38	Tony Lazzeri	2.00	1.00	.60
39	John McGraw	2.00	1.00	.60
40	Mel Ott	10.00	5.00	3.00
41	Grover Alexander	2.00	1.00	.60
42	Rube Waddell	2.00	1.00	.60
43	Wilbert Robinson	2.00	1.00	.60
44	Cap Anson	2.00	1.00	.60
45	Eddie Cicotte	2.00	1.00	.60
46	Hank Gowdy	2.00	1.00	.60
47	Frankie Frisch	2.00	1.00	.60
48	Charles Comiskey	2.00	1.00	.60
49	Clyde Milan	2.00	1.00	.60
50	Jimmy Wilson	2.00	1.00	.60
51	Christy Mathewson	10.00	5.00	3.00
52	Tim Keefe	2.00	1.00	.60
53	Abner Doubleday	2.00	1.00	.60
54	Ed Walsh	2.00	1.00	.60
55	Jim Thorpe	10.00	5.00	3.00
56	Roger Bresnahan	2.00	1.00	.60
57	Frank Chance	2.00	1.00	.60
58	Heinie Manush	2.00	1.00	.60
59	Max Carey	2.00	1.00	.60
60	Joe Tinker	2.00	1.00	.60
61	Benny Kauff	2.00	1.00	.60
62	Fred Clarke	2.00	1.00	.60
63	Smokey Joe Wood	2.00	1.00	.60
64	George Burns	2.00	1.00	.60
65	Walter Johnson	10.00	5.00	3.00
66	Ferdie Schupp	2.00	1.00	.60
67	Jimmy McAleer	2.00	1.00	.60
68	Larry Gardner	2.00	1.00	.60
69	Buck Ewing	2.00	1.00	.60
70	George Sisler	2.00	1.00	.60
71	Charley Robertson	2.00	1.00	.60
72	Bill Dineen	2.00	1.00	.60
73	Kid Gleason	2.00	1.00	.60
74	Jim Bottomley	2.00	1.00	.60
75	Sam Crawford	2.00	1.00	.60
76	Kid Nichols	2.00	1.00	.60
77	Dick Rudolph	2.00	1.00	.60
78	Bill Klem	2.00	1.00	.60
79	Checklist			
80	Checklist			
81	Checklist			
82	Checklist			

1970 Sports Cards for Collectors Old Timer Postcards

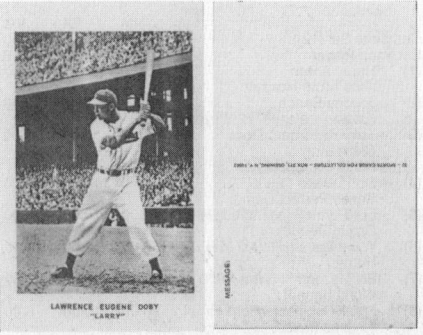

The date of issue given here is approximate. This collectors issue "Old Timer Postcard Series" features black-and-white photos bordered in white in a 3-1/2" x 5-1/2" format. Player identification in the bottom border usually offers his complete name on one line and his nickname below. Backs are divided by a card number and the name and address of the issuer. At left is a space for "MESSAGE:."

		NM	EX	VG
	Complete Set (32):	75.00	37.50	22.00
	Common Player:	4.00	2.00	1.25
1	Babe Ruth, Lou Gehrig	12.00	6.00	3.50
2	Larry Doby	6.00	3.00	1.75
3	Mike Garcia	4.00	2.00	1.25
4	Bob Feller	10.00	5.00	3.00
5	Early Wynn	4.00	2.00	1.25
6	Burleigh Grimes	4.00	2.00	1.25
7	Rabbit Maranville	4.00	2.00	1.25
8	Babe Ruth	15.00	7.50	4.50
9	Lou Gehrig	12.00	6.00	3.50
10	Joe DiMaggio	12.00	6.00	3.50
11	Ty Cobb	10.00	5.00	3.00
12	Lou Boudreau	4.00	2.00	1.25
13	Jimmie Foxx	4.00	2.00	1.25
14	Casey Stengel	6.00	3.00	1.75
15	Kenesaw M. Landis	4.00	2.00	1.25
16	Max Carey	4.00	2.00	1.25
17	Wilbert Robinson	4.00	2.00	1.25
18	Paul Richards	4.00	2.00	1.25
19	Zack Wheat	4.00	2.00	1.25
20	Rube Marquard	4.00	2.00	1.25
21	Dave Bancroft	4.00	2.00	1.25
22	Bobby Thomson	4.00	2.00	1.25
23	Mel Ott	4.00	2.00	1.25
24	Bobo Newsom	4.00	2.00	1.25
25	Johnny Mize	4.00	2.00	1.25
26	Walker Cooper	4.00	2.00	1.25
27	Fred "Dixie" Walker	4.00	2.00	1.25
28	Augie Galan	4.00	2.00	1.25
29	"Snuffy" Sturnweiss (Stirmweiss)	4.00	2.00	1.25
30	Floyd Caves "Babe" Herman	4.00	2.00	1.25
31	Babe Ruth	15.00	7.50	4.50
32	Babe Ruth	15.00	7.50	4.50

1970 Sports Cards for Collectors Sports Stuff

This set includes 10 Myron Aronsten-drawn 3-1/2" x 4-1/4" postcards depicting pre-1920 baseball luminaries, trivia, and legends.

		NM	EX	VG
	Complete Set (10):	20.00	10.00	6.00
	Common Player:	2.00	1.00	.60
1	Manager Trivia	2.00	1.00	.60
2	1914 Miracle Braves	2.00	1.00	.60
3	1919 Black Sox	2.00	1.00	.60
4	Eddie Plank, Fred Clarke, Roger Bresnahan, Babe Ruth	5.00	2.50	1.50
5	Bobby Lowe	2.00	1.00	.60
6	$100,000 Athletics Infield	2.00	1.00	.60
7	Joe Bush, Eddie Plank, Chief Bender	2.00	1.00	.60
8	Joe Tinker, Johnny Evers, Frank Chance	2.00	1.00	.60
9	Wilbert Robinson, John McGraw, Roger Peckinpaugh	2.00	1.00	.60
10	Ty Cobb	5.00	2.50	1.50

1977-79 Sportscaster

This massive set of full-color cards includes players from dozens of different sports - some of them very obscure - among more than 2,000 different subjects, making it one of the biggest sets of trading cards ever issued. Available by mail subscription from 1977 through 1979, the Sportscaster cards are large, measuring 4-3/4" x 6-1/4". Subscribers were mailed one series of 24 cards for $1.89 plus postage every month or so. The set has an international flavor to it, including such sports as rugby, soccer, lawn bowling, fencing, karate, bicycling, curling, skiing, bullfighting, auto racing, mountain climbing, hang gliding, yachting, sailing, badminton, bobsledding, etc. Each card has a series of icons in the upper-right corner to assist collectors in the various methods of sorting. Most popular among American collectors are the baseball, football and basketball stars in the set, which includes the 140 baseball subjects listed here. The checklist includes many Hall of Famers. Backs contain detailed write-ups of the player featured. Because the set was issued in series, and many collectors dropped out of the program before the end, cards in the higher series are especially scarce. This accounts for prices on some of the superstar cards, issued in early series, being lower than for some of the lesser-known players. The cards of Aaron and Bench are quite common because they were mailed to large numbers of persons as samples to introduce the program. The cards were also sold in several European countries and can be found with backs printed in French, Swedish and other languages.

		NM	EX	VG
	Complete (Baseball) Set (140):	350.00	175.00	100.00
	Common Player:	1.00	.50	.30
(1)	Henry Aaron	4.00	2.00	1.25
(2)	Danny Ainge	30.00	15.00	9.00
(3)	Emmett Ashford (Umpire)	2.50	1.25	.70
(4)	Ernie Banks	2.75	1.50	.80
(5)	Johnny Bench	7.50	3.75	2.25
(6)	Vida Blue	1.75	.90	.50
(7)	Bert Blyleven	1.25	.60	.40
(8)	Bobby Bonds	3.25	1.75	1.00
(9)	Lyman Bostock	1.25	.60	.40
(10)	George Brett	5.00	2.50	1.50
(11)	Lou Brock	3.25	1.75	1.00
(12)	Jeff Burroughs	1.25	.60	.40
(13)	Roy Campanella	8.00	4.00	2.50
(14)	John Candelaria	1.25	.60	.40
(15)	Rod Carew	3.25	1.75	1.00
(16)	Steve Carlton	4.00	2.00	1.25
(17)	Ron Cey	1.00	.50	.30
(18)	Roberto Clemente	10.00	5.00	3.00
(19)	Steve Dembowski	2.25	1.25	.70
(20)	Joe DiMaggio	5.00	2.50	1.50
(21)	Dennis Eckersley	4.00	2.00	1.25
(22)	Mark Fidrych	1.75	.90	.50
(23)	Carlton Fisk	6.00	3.00	1.75
(24)	Mike Flanagan	3.00	1.50	.90
(25)	Steve Garvey	5.00	2.50	1.50

(26)	Ron Guidry	3.00	1.50	.90
(27)	Gil Hodges	4.00	2.00	1.25
(28)	Catfish Hunter	4.00	2.00	1.25
(29)	Tommy John	1.25	.60	.40
(30)	Randy Jones	1.00	.50	.30
(31)	Dave Kingman	1.75	.90	.50
(32)	Sandy Koufax	6.00	3.00	1.75
(33)	Tommy Lasorda	6.50	3.25	2.00
(34)	Ron LeFlore	1.25	.60	.40
(35)	Greg Luzinski	1.00	.50	.30
(36)	Billy Martin	3.25	1.75	1.00
(37)	Willie Mays	4.00	2.00	1.25
(38)	Lee Mazzilli	5.00	2.50	1.50
(39)	Willie McCovey	3.75	2.00	1.25
(40)	Joe Morgan	2.75	1.50	.80
(41)	Thurman Munson	4.00	2.00	1.25
(42)	Stan Musial	5.00	2.50	1.50
(43)	Phil Niekro	4.00	2.00	1.25
(44)	Jim Palmer	3.00	1.50	.90
(45)	Dave Parker	1.75	.90	.50
(46)	Freddie Patek	1.25	.60	.40
(47)	Gaylord Perry	2.25	1.25	.70
(48)	Jim Piersall	2.75	1.50	.80
(49)	Vada Pinson	1.25	.60	.40
(50)	Rick Reuschel	1.25	.60	.40
(51)	Jim Rice	6.00	3.00	1.75
(52)	J.R. Richard	2.25	1.25	.70
(53)	Brooks Robinson	3.75	2.00	1.25
(54)	Frank Robinson	5.00	2.50	1.50
(55)	Jackie Robinson	5.00	2.50	1.50
(56)	Pete Rose	6.00	3.00	1.75
(57)	Joe Rudi	1.00	.50	.30
(58)	Babe Ruth	6.00	3.00	1.75
(59)	Nolan Ryan	7.00	3.50	2.00
(60)	Tom Seaver	3.75	2.00	1.25
(61)	Warren Spahn	3.75	2.00	1.25
(62)	Monty Stratton	2.25	1.25	.70
(63)	Craig Swan	1.75	.90	.50
(64)	Frank Tanana	1.00	.50	.30
(65)	Ron Taylor	2.25	1.25	.70
(66)	Garry Templeton	1.00	.50	.30
(67)	Gene Tenace	1.00	.50	.30
(68)	Bobby Thomson	1.75	.90	.50
(69)	Andre Thornton	1.25	.60	.40
(70)	Johnny VanderMeer	1.75	.90	.50
(71)	Ted Williams	7.00	3.50	2.00
(72)	Maury Wills	1.00	.50	.30
(73)	Hack Wilson	3.25	1.75	1.00
(74)	Dave Winfield (Hitting)	8.00	4.00	2.50
(75)	Dave Winfield (Portrait)	4.00	2.00	1.25
(76)	Cy Young	2.75	1.50	.80
(77)	The 1927 Yankees	2.75	1.50	.80
(78)	1969 Mets	6.50	3.25	2.00
(79)	All-Star Game (Steve Garvey, Joe Morgan)	2.75	1.50	.80
(80)	Amateur Draft (Rick Monday)	1.25	.60	.40
(81)	At-A-Glance Reference (Tom Seaver)	5.00	2.50	1.50
(82)	Babe Ruth Baseball (Ed Figueroa)	6.50	3.25	2.00
(83)	Baltimore Memorial Stadium	3.00	1.50	.90
(84)	Boston's Fenway Park	5.00	2.50	1.50
(85)	Brother vs. Brother (Joe Niekro)	2.75	1.50	.80
(86)	Busch Memorial Stadium	2.50	1.25	.70
(87)	Candlestick Park	2.00	1.00	.60
(88)	Cape Cod League (Jim Beattie)	6.00	3.00	1.75
(89)	A Century and a Half of Baseball (Johnny Bench)	1.75	.90	.50
(90)	Cy Young Award (Tom Seaver)	2.75	1.50	.80
(91)	The Dean Brothers (Dizzy Dean, Paul Dean)	5.00	2.50	1.50
(92)	Designated Hitter (Rusty Staub)	2.25	1.25	.70
(93)	Dodger Stadium	2.75	1.50	.80
(94)	Perfect Game (Don Larsen)	3.25	1.75	1.00
(95)	The Double Steal (Davey Lopes)	5.00	2.50	1.50
(96)	Fenway Park	4.00	2.00	1.25
(97)	The Firemen (Goose Gossage)	4.00	2.00	1.25
(98)	Forever Blowing Bubbles (Davey Lopes)	2.00	1.00	.60
(99)	The Forsch Brothers (Bob Forsch, Ken Forsch)	5.00	2.50	1.50
(100)	Four Home Runs In A Game (Mike Schmidt)	6.50	3.25	2.00
(101)	400-Homer Club (Duke Snider)	5.00	2.50	1.50
(102)	Great Moments (Bob Gibson)	3.25	1.75	1.00
(103)	Great Moments (Ferguson Jenkins)	2.25	1.25	.70
(104)	Great Moments (Mickey Lolich)	1.75	.90	.50
(105)	Great Moments (Carl Yastrzemski)	3.25	1.75	1.00
(106)	Hidden Ball Trick (Carl Yastrzemski)	2.75	1.50	.80
(107)	Hit And Run (George Foster)	1.25	.60	.40
(108)	Hitting The Cutoff Man	1.00	.50	.30
(109)	Hitting Pitchers (Don Drysdale)	3.25	1.75	1.00
(110)	Infield Fly Rule (Bobby Grich)	1.25	.60	.40
(111)	Instruction (Rod Carew)	2.75	1.50	.80
(112)	Interference (Johnny Bench)	2.75	1.50	.80
(113)	Iron Mike (Pitching Machine)	2.75	1.50	.80
(114)	Keeping Score	1.75	.90	.50
(115)	Like Father, Like Son (Roy Smalley)	3.75	2.00	1.25
(116)	Lingo I (Gary Carter)	1.75	.90	.50
(117)	Lingo II (Earl Weaver)	2.75	1.50	.80
(118)	Little Leagues To Big Leagues (Hector Torres)	1.75	.90	.50
(119)	Maris and Mantle (Mickey Mantle, Roger Maris)	4.00	2.00	1.25
(120)	Measurements (Memorial Stadium)	1.00	.50	.30

(121)	The Money Game (Dennis Eckersley)	6.00	3.00	1.75
(122)	NCAA Tournament (Aggies-Longhorns)	1.75	.90	.50
(123)	The Oakland A's, 1971-75	3.00	1.50	.90
(124)	The Perfect Game (Sandy Koufax)	3.50	1.75	1.00
(125)	Pickoff (Luis Tiant)	1.25	.60	.40
(126)	The Presidential Ball (William Howard Taft)	1.75	.90	.50
(127)	Relief Pitching (Mike Marshall)	1.25	.60	.40
(128)	The Rules (Hank Aaron)	2.75	1.50	.80
(129)	Rundown (Mets vs. Astros)	1.75	.90	.50
(130)	7th Game of the World Series (Bert Campaneris)	2.25	1.25	.70
(131)	Shea Stadium	2.50	1.25	.70
(132)	The 3000 Hit Club (Roberto Clemente)	8.00	4.00	2.50
(133)	Training Camps (Orioles)	2.75	1.50	.80
(134)	Triple Crown (Carl Yastrzemski)	16.00	8.00	4.75
(135)	Triple Play (Rick Burleson)	2.75	1.50	.80
(136)	Triple Play (Bill Wambsganss)	1.75	.90	.50
(137)	Umpires Strike	1.75	.90	.50
(138)	Veterans Stadium	2.50	1.25	.70
(139)	Wrigley Marathon (Mike Schmidt)	8.00	4.00	2.50
(140)	Yankee Stadium	1.00	.50	.30
	Beyond Sports (Baseball) Set: (6):	.00	.00	.00
(1)	Clemente Award (Andre Thornton)	5.00	2.50	1.50
(2)	Clowns (Al Schact, Nick Altrock)	4.00	2.00	1.25
(3)	Fellowship of Christian Athletes (Don Kessinger)	4.00	2.00	1.25
(4)	High School Record Book (David Clyde)	2.50	1.25	.70
(5)	Hutchinson Award (Al Kaline)	40.00	20.00	12.00
(6)	Walkie-Talkie (Yogi Berra)	5.00	2.50	1.50

1977 Sports Challenge Records

Taped highlights and an interview with the player are featured on this series of 33-1/3 RPM records. The 6" diameter records have a centerhole to be punched out to play the record. Fronts have a stylized picture of the player, his name and a title. Backs describe the highlight and give other career details.

		NM	EX	VG
	Complete Set (12):	250.00	125.00	75.00
	Common Player:	20.00	10.00	6.00
(1)	Henry Aaron (Hits 715th Homer)	45.00	22.50	13.50
(2)	Johnny Bench (Beats Pirates in '72 Playoff)	30.00	15.00	9.00
(3)	Jerry Koosman, Donn Clendenon (1969 Miracle Mets)	20.00	10.00	6.00
(4)	Don Larsen ('56 World Series Perfect Game)	20.00	10.00	6.00
(5)	Fred Lynn (Has Incredible Day in Detroit)	20.00	10.00	6.00
(6)	Willie Mays (Hits 1st Met Homer)	35.00	17.50	10.50
(7)	Bill Mazeroski (Wins 1960 World Series)	25.00	12.50	7.50
(8)	Frank Robinson (Homers 1st Time as Indian)	20.00	10.00	6.00
(9)	Nolan Ryan (4th No Hitter)	45.00	22.50	13.50
(10)	Tom Seaver (Cubs Ruin Perfect Game)	25.00	12.50	7.50
(11)	Bobby Thomson (Shot Heard 'Round the World)	20.00	10.00	6.00
(12)	Ted Williams (Last Time at Bat in Boston)	35.00	17.50	10.50

1926 Sports Co. of America Champions

Little was known of these small (1-1/2" x 2-1/4") black-and-white cards until an original store display was discovered in the late 1980s. Carrying a copyright date of November

1926, from Sports Co. of America, a San Francisco publishing firm, these cards were produced for A. G. Spalding & Bros., the sporting goods firm. Each card was issued in a wax paper baggie with a like-sized red, white and blue "Sport-Scrip" which was serial numbered for use in a candy prize drawing at the store or could be redeemed for 10 cents on Spalding equipment. The cards themselves feature ornately framed photos at center, with "CHAMPIONS" in a cartouche at top and the player's name and sport in a second ornate frame at bottom. Most backs have biographical data and career notes, but some are seen with advertising offering an album for the pieces. Nearly 50 baseball players are known from a list of over 175 male and female athletes from sports as diverse as fishing, chess and balloon racing. The unnumbered baseball players from the set are checklisted here in alphabetical order.

		NM	EX	VG
	Common Baseball Player:	45.00	20.00	10.00
	Ad Back: 2X			
(1)	"Babe" Adams	45.00	20.00	10.00
(2)	Grover Alexander	275.00	110.00	55.00
(3)	Nick Altrock	45.00	20.00	10.00
(4)	Dave Bancroft	220.00	90.00	45.00
(5)	Jesse Barnes	45.00	20.00	10.00
(6)	Oswald Bluege	45.00	20.00	10.00
(7)	Jim Bottomley	220.00	90.00	45.00
(8)	Max Carey	220.00	90.00	45.00
(9)	Ty Cobb	825.00	330.00	165.00
(10)	Mickey Cochrane	220.00	90.00	45.00
(11)	Eddie Collins	220.00	90.00	45.00
(12)	Stan Coveleskie (Coveleski)	220.00	90.00	45.00
(13)	Kiki Cuyler	220.00	90.00	45.00
(14)	Hank DeBerry	45.00	20.00	10.00
(15)	Jack Fournier	45.00	20.00	10.00
(16)	Goose Goslin	220.00	90.00	45.00
(17)	Charlie Grimm	45.00	20.00	10.00
(18)	Bucky Harris	220.00	90.00	45.00
(19)	Gabby Hartnett	220.00	90.00	45.00
(20)	Fred Hofmann	45.00	20.00	10.00
(21)	Rogers Hornsby	275.00	110.00	55.00
(22)	Waite Hoyt	220.00	90.00	45.00
(23)	Walter Johnson	715.00	290.00	145.00
(24)	Joe Judge	45.00	20.00	10.00
(25)	Willie Kamm	45.00	20.00	10.00
(26)	Tony Lazzeri	220.00	90.00	45.00
(27)	Rabbit Maranville	220.00	90.00	45.00
(28)	Fred Marberry	45.00	20.00	10.00
(29)	Rube Marquard	220.00	90.00	45.00
(30)	"Stuffy" McInnis	45.00	20.00	10.00
(31)	"Babe" Pinelli	45.00	20.00	10.00
(32)	Wally Pipp	45.00	20.00	10.00
(33)	Sam Rice	220.00	90.00	45.00
(34)	Emory Rigney	45.00	20.00	10.00
(35)	Dutch Ruether	45.00	20.00	10.00
(36a)	Babe Ruth (1926 Copyright)	2,000	705.00	350.00
(36b)	Babe Ruth (1927 Copyright)	4,000	1,320	660.00
(37)	Ray Schalk	220.00	90.00	45.00
(38)	Joey Sewell	220.00	90.00	45.00
(39)	Urban Shocker	45.00	20.00	10.00
(40)	Al Simmons	220.00	90.00	45.00
(41)	George Sisler	220.00	90.00	45.00
(42)	Tris Speaker	275.00	110.00	55.00
(43)	Pie Traynor	220.00	90.00	45.00
(44)	George Uhle	45.00	20.00	10.00
(45)	Paul Waner	220.00	90.00	45.00
(46)	Aaron L. Ward	45.00	20.00	10.00
(47)	Ken Williams	45.00	20.00	10.00
(48)	Glenn Wright	45.00	20.00	10.00
(49)	Emil Yde	45.00	20.00	10.00

1946-49 Sports Exchange All-Star Picture File

Produced and sold (originally at 50 cents per series) by "The Trading Post," one of the first card collectors' publications, over a period which spanned several years in the late 1940s, this 113-card set was issued in 12 series. Most of the series were nine cards each, printed in black-and-white, unnumbered and blank-backed in a 7" x 10" format. The first 27 cards carry no series designation but were advertised as Series 1A and 1B and Series 2. Series 3 features 11 cards and is printed in sepia tones rather than black-and-white. The fourth series is also unmarked. The final two series consist of 12 cards each, printed two per sheet in smaller format. The photos are labeled as originating with the International News Service. Most of the same players and photos appearing in this set are also found in the Sports Exchange Baseball Miniatures set. Because this was one of the first baseball card sets issued after World War II, it contains cards of several players not found in other issues. The set carries a W603 designation in the "American Card Catalog." Cards are listed alphabetically within series in the checklist which follows.

	NM	EX	VG
Complete Set (113):	2,750	1,350	825.00
Common Card:	15.00	7.50	4.50

SERIES 1A

(1)	Phil Cavaretta	15.00	7.50	4.50
(2)	Walker Cooper	15.00	7.50	4.50
(3)	Dave Ferriss	15.00	7.50	4.50
(4)	Les Fleming	15.00	7.50	4.50
(5)	Whitey Kurowski	15.00	7.50	4.50
(6)	Marty Marion	20.00	10.00	6.00
(7)	Rip Sewell	15.00	7.50	4.50
(8)	Eddie Stanky	20.00	10.00	6.00
(9)	Dixie Walker	15.00	7.50	4.50

SERIES 1B

(10)	Bill Dickey	40.00	20.00	12.00
(11)	Bobby Doerr	30.00	15.00	9.00
(12)	Bob Feller	40.00	20.00	12.00
(13)	Hank Greenberg	75.00	37.00	22.00
(14)	George McQuinn	15.00	7.50	4.50
(15)	Ray Mueller	15.00	7.50	4.50
(16)	Hal Newhouser	30.00	15.00	9.00
(17)	Dick Wakefield	15.00	7.50	4.50
(18)	Ted Williams	150.00	75.00	45.00

SERIES 2

(19)	Al Benton	15.00	7.50	4.50
(20)	Lou Boudreau	30.00	15.00	9.00
(21)	Spud Chandler	15.00	7.50	4.50
(22)	Jeff Heath	15.00	7.50	4.50
(23)	Kirby Higbe	15.00	7.50	4.50
(24)	Tex Hughson	15.00	7.50	4.50
(25)	Stan Musial	175.00	90.00	55.00
(26)	Howie Pollet	15.00	7.50	4.50
(27)	Enos Slaughter	40.00	20.00	12.00

SERIES 3

(28)	Harry Brecheen	15.00	7.50	4.50
(29)	Dom DiMaggio	30.00	15.00	9.00
(30)	Del Ennis	15.00	7.50	4.50
(31)	Al Evans	15.00	7.50	4.50
(32)	Johnny Lindell	15.00	7.50	4.50
(33)	Johnny Mize	35.00	17.50	10.50
(34)	Johnny Pesky	15.00	7.50	4.50
(35)	Pete Reiser	15.00	7.50	4.50
(36a)	Aaron Robinson (Throwing)	15.00	7.50	4.50
(36b)	Aaron Robinson (Fielding)	15.00	7.50	4.50
(37)	1946 Boston Red Sox Team	30.00	15.00	9.00
(38)	1946 St. Louis Cardinals Team	30.00	15.00	9.00

SERIES 4

(39)	Jimmie Foxx	45.00	22.00	13.50
(40)	Frank Frisch	30.00	15.00	9.00
(41)	Lou Gehrig	150.00	75.00	45.00
(42)	Lefty Grove	35.00	17.50	10.50
(43)	Bill Hallahan	15.00	7.50	4.50
(44)	Rogers "Rajah" Hornsby	45.00	22.00	13.50
(45)	Carl Hubbell	30.00	15.00	9.00
(46)	Babe Ruth	250.00	125.00	75.00
(47)	Hack Wilson	30.00	15.00	9.00

SERIES 5

(48)	Eddie Dyer	15.00	7.50	4.50
(49)	Charlie Grimm	15.00	7.50	4.50
(50)	Billy Herman	30.00	15.00	9.00
(51)	Ted Lyons	30.00	15.00	9.00
(52)	Lefty O'Doul	25.00	12.50	7.50
(53)	Steve O'Neill	15.00	7.50	4.50
(54)	Herb Pennock	30.00	15.00	9.00
(55)	Luke Sewell	15.00	7.50	4.50
(56)	Billy Southworth	15.00	7.50	4.50

SERIES 6

(57)	Ewell Blackwell	25.00	12.50	7.50
(58)	Jimmy Outlaw	15.00	7.50	4.50
(59)	Andy Pafko	15.00	7.50	4.50
(60)	Pee Wee Reese	75.00	37.00	22.00
(61)	Phil Rizzuto	60.00	30.00	18.00
(62)	Buddy Rosar	15.00	7.50	4.50
(63)	Johnny Sain	25.00	12.50	7.50
(64)	Dizzy Trout	15.00	7.50	4.50
(65)	Harry Walker	15.00	7.50	4.50

SERIES 7

(66)	Floyd Bevens	15.00	7.50	4.50
(67)	Hugh Casey	15.00	7.50	4.50
(68)	Sam Chapman	15.00	7.50	4.50
(69)	Joe DiMaggio	150.00	75.00	45.00
(70)	Tommy Henrich	25.00	12.50	7.50
(71)	Ralph Kiner	30.00	15.00	9.00
(72)	Cookie Lavagetto	15.00	7.50	4.50
(73)	Vic Lombardi	15.00	7.50	4.50
(74)	Cecil Travis	15.00	7.50	4.50

SERIES 8

(75)	Nick Altrock	20.00	10.00	6.00
(76)	Mark Christman	15.00	7.50	4.50
(77)	Earle Combs	30.00	15.00	9.00
(78)	Travis Jackson	30.00	15.00	9.00
(79)	Bob Muncrief	15.00	7.50	4.50
(80)	Earl Neale	25.00	12.50	7.50
(81)	Joe Page	15.00	7.50	4.50
(82)	Honus Wagner	75.00	37.00	22.00
(83)	Mickey Witek	15.00	7.50	4.50

SERIES 9

(84)	George Case	15.00	7.50	4.50
(85)	Jake Early	15.00	7.50	4.50
(86)	Carl Furillo	30.00	15.00	9.00
(87)	Augie Galan	15.00	7.50	4.50
(88)	Bert Haas	15.00	7.50	4.50
(89)	Johnny Hopp	15.00	7.50	4.50
(90)	Ray Lamanno	15.00	7.50	4.50
(91)	Buddy Lewis	15.00	7.50	4.50
(92)	Warren Spahn	40.00	20.00	12.00

SERIES 10

(93)	Lu Blue	15.00	7.50	4.50
q94)	Bruce Edwards	15.00	7.50	4.50
(95)	Elbie Fletcher	15.00	7.50	4.50
(96)	Joe Gordon	15.00	7.50	4.50
(97)	Tommy Holmes	15.00	7.50	4.50
(98)	Billy Johnson	15.00	7.50	4.50
(99)	Phil Masi	15.00	7.50	4.50
(100)	Red Munger	15.00	7.50	4.50
(101)	Vern Stephens	15.00	7.50	4.50

SERIES 11

(102)	Ralph Branca, Ken Keltner	20.00	10.00	6.00
(103)	Mickey Cochrane, Bob Dillinger	40.00	20.00	12.00
(104)	Dizzy Dean, Eddie Joost	80.00	40.00	24.00
(105)	Joe Jackson, Wally Westlake	400.00	200.00	120.00
(106)	Larry Jansen, Yogi Berra	80.00	40.00	24.00
(107)	Peanuts Lowrey, Heinie Manush	40.00	20.00	12.00

SERIES 12

(108)	Gene Bearden, Dale Mitchell	45.00	22.00	13.50
(109)	Steve Gromek, Earl Torgeson	45.00	22.00	13.50
(110)	Jim Hegan, Mickey Vernon	45.00	22.00	13.50
(111)	Bob Lemon, Red Rolfe	100.00	50.00	30.00
(112)	Billy Meyer, Ben Chapman	45.00	22.00	13.50
(113)	Sibbi Sisti, Zach Taylor	45.00	22.00	13.50

1947 Sports Exchange Baseball Miniatures

Heinie Manush

Produced and sold (originally at $1 per series) by one of the hobby's first periodicals, "The Trading Post," this 108-card set was released in three series, designated by red, green and gold borders. The blank-back, unnumbered cards are printed in black-and-white and were sold in sheets of six. When cut from the sheets, individual cards in the red- and green-bordered series measure 2-1/2" x 3", while the gold-bordered cards measure 2-1/2" x 3-1/8". The set is checklisted here alphabetically within series. The set carries an American Card Catalog designation of W602.

	NM	EX	VG
Complete Set (108):	4,750	2,400	1,400
Common Player:	15.00	7.50	4.50

GREEN BORDER SERIES

(1)	Nick Altrock	20.00	10.00	6.00
(2)	Floyd Bevens	15.00	7.50	4.50
(3)	Ewell Blackwell	20.00	10.00	6.00
(4)	Lou Boudreau	35.00	17.50	10.50
(5)	Harry Brecheen	15.00	7.50	4.50
(6)	Hugh Casey	15.00	7.50	4.50
(7)	Phil Cavaretta	15.00	7.50	4.50
(8)	Sam Chapman	15.00	7.50	4.50
(9)	Mark Christman	15.00	7.50	4.50
(10)	Bill Dickey	40.00	20.00	12.00
(11)	Dom DiMaggio	25.00	12.50	7.50
(12)	Joe DiMaggio	400.00	200.00	120.00
(13)	Eddie Dyer	15.00	7.50	4.50
(14)	Frank Frisch	40.00	20.00	12.00
(15)	Lou Gehrig	275.00	135.00	82.00
(16)	Charlie Grimm	15.00	7.50	4.50
(17)	Lefty Grove	40.00	20.00	12.00
(18)	Tommy Henrich	20.00	10.00	6.00
(19)	Ralph Kiner	35.00	17.50	10.50
(20)	Cookie Lavagetto	15.00	7.50	4.50
(21)	Vic Lombardi	15.00	7.50	4.50
(22)	Ted Lyons	35.00	17.50	10.50
(23)	Bob Muncrief	15.00	7.50	4.50
(24)	Stan Musial	160.00	80.00	48.00
(25)	Steve O'Neill	15.00	7.50	4.50
(26)	Jimmy Outlaw	15.00	7.50	4.50
(27)	Joe Page	15.00	7.50	4.50
(28)	Pee Wee Reese	65.00	32.00	19.50
(29)	Phil Rizzuto	65.00	32.00	19.50
(30)	Buddy Rosar	15.00	7.50	4.50
(31)	Johnny Sain	20.00	10.00	6.00
(32)	Billy Southworth	15.00	7.50	4.50
(33)	Cecil Travis	15.00	7.50	4.50
(34)	Honus Wagner	90.00	45.00	27.00
(35)	Harry Walker	15.00	7.50	4.50
(36)	Mickey Witek	15.00	7.50	4.50

RED BORDER SERIES

(37)	Yogi Berra	80.00	40.00	24.00
(38)	Lu Blue	15.00	7.50	4.50
(39)	Ben Chapman	15.00	7.50	4.50
(40)	Mickey Cochrane	35.00	17.50	10.50
(41)	Earle Combs	35.00	17.50	10.50
(42)	Dizzy Dean	95.00	47.00	28.00
(43)	Bob Dillinger	15.00	7.50	4.50
(44)	Bobby Doerr	35.00	17.50	10.50
(45)	Al Evans	15.00	7.50	4.50
(46)	Jimmy (Jimmie) Foxx	50.00	25.00	15.00
(47)	Joe Gordon	15.00	7.50	4.50
(48)	Bill Hallahan	15.00	7.50	4.50
(49)	Tommy Holmes	15.00	7.50	4.50
(50)	Rogers Hornsby	50.00	25.00	15.00
(51)	Carl Hubbell	45.00	22.00	13.50
(52)	Travis Jackson	35.00	17.50	10.50
(53)	Bill Johnson	15.00	7.50	4.50
(54)	Ken Keltner	15.00	7.50	4.50
(55)	Whitey Kurowski	15.00	7.50	4.50
(56)	Ray Lamanno	15.00	7.50	4.50
(57)	Johnny Lindell	15.00	7.50	4.50
(58)	Peanuts Lowrey	15.00	7.50	4.50
(59)	Phil Masi	15.00	7.50	4.50
(60)	Earl Neale	20.00	10.00	6.00
(61)	Hal Newhouser	35.00	17.50	10.50

	NM	EX	VG
(62)	Lefty O'Doul	25.00	12.50	7.50
(63)	Herb Pennock	35.00	17.50	10.50
(64)	Red Rolfe	35.00	17.50	10.50
(65)	Babe Ruth	450.00	225.00	135.00
(66)	Luke Sewell	15.00	7.50	4.50
(67)	Rip Sewell	15.00	7.50	4.50
(68)	Warren Spahn	60.00	30.00	18.00
(69)	Vern Stephens	15.00	7.50	4.50
(70)	Dizzy Trout	15.00	7.50	4.50
(71)	Wally Westlake	15.00	7.50	4.50
(72)	Hack Wilson	50.00	25.00	15.00

GOLD BORDER SERIES

(73)	Al Benton	30.00	15.00	9.00
(74)	Ralph Branca	25.00	12.50	7.50
(75)	George Case	30.00	15.00	9.00
(76)	Spud Chandler	30.00	15.00	9.00
(77)	Jake Early	30.00	15.00	9.00
(78)	Bruce Edwards	30.00	15.00	9.00
(79)	Del Ennis	30.00	15.00	9.00
(80)	Bob Feller	80.00	40.00	24.00
(81)	Dave Ferriss	30.00	15.00	9.00
(82)	Les Fleming	30.00	15.00	9.00
(83)	Carl Furillo	150.00	75.00	45.00
(84)	Augie Galan	30.00	15.00	9.00
(85)	Hank Greenberg	100.00	50.00	30.00
(86)	Bert Haas	30.00	15.00	9.00
(87)	Jeff Heath	30.00	15.00	9.00
(88)	Billy Herman	60.00	30.00	18.00
(89)	Kirby Higbe	30.00	15.00	9.00
(90)	Tex Hughson	30.00	15.00	9.00
(91)	Johnny Hopp	30.00	15.00	9.00
(92)	Joe Jackson	650.00	325.00	195.00
(93)	Larry Jansen	30.00	15.00	9.00
(94)	Eddie Joost	30.00	15.00	9.00
(95)	Buddy Lewis	30.00	15.00	9.00
(96)	Heinie Manush	60.00	30.00	18.00
(97)	Marty Marion	30.00	15.00	9.00
(98)	George McQuinn	30.00	15.00	9.00
(99)	Johnny Mize	60.00	30.00	18.00
(100)	Red Munger	30.00	15.00	9.00
(101)	Andy Pafko	30.00	15.00	9.00
(102)	Johnny Pesky	30.00	15.00	9.00
(103)	Howie Pollet	30.00	15.00	9.00
(104)	Pete Reiser	30.00	15.00	9.00
(105)	Aaron Robinson	30.00	15.00	9.00
(106)	Enos Slaughter	60.00	30.00	18.00
(107)	Dixie Walker	30.00	15.00	9.00
(108)	Ted Williams (Photo actually Bobby Doerr.)	200.00	100.00	60.00

1963 Sports "Hall of Fame" Busts

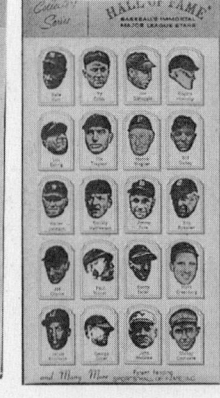

Licensed by the National Baseball Hall of Fame, this set of 20 plastic player busts was produced by Sports "Hall of Fame," Inc., of New York. Each six-inch statue has a white player figure atop a wood-look pedestal with a plaque providing career details. The busts were sold in a red, white and gold display box with photos of the players on the back. Though the box back promised "Many More," only the 20 players pictured were ever issued. Retail price at issue was $1-1.25. The first 12 busts are more common than the final eight, with Foxx and Greenberg especially scarce. Values quoted are for busts alone, add $25 for accompanying box and $50 or more for unopened box with cellophane.

	NM	EX	VG
Complete Set (20):	3,000	1,500	900.00
Common Player:	75.00	35.00	20.00
(1)	Babe Ruth	110.00	55.00	30.00
(2)	Ty Cobb	90.00	45.00	25.00
(3)	Joe DiMaggio	110.00	55.00	30.00
(4)	Rogers Hornsby	80.00	40.00	24.00
(5)	Lou Gehrig	100.00	50.00	30.00
(6)	Pie Traynor	75.00	35.00	20.00
(7)	Honus Wagner	150.00	75.00	45.00
(8)	Bill Dickey	110.00	55.00	30.00
(9)	Walter Johnson	135.00	65.00	40.00
(10)	Christy Mathewson	110.00	55.00	30.00
(11)	Jimmie Foxx	335.00	165.00	100.00
(12)	Tris Speaker	75.00	35.00	20.00
(13)	Joe Cronin	180.00	90.00	50.00
(14)	Paul Waner	165.00	80.00	45.00
(15)	Bobby Feller	225.00	110.00	65.00
(16)	Hank Greenberg	275.00	135.00	80.00
(17)	Jackie Robinson	260.00	130.00	75.00
(18)	George Sisler	200.00	100.00	60.00
(19)	John McGraw	200.00	100.00	60.00
(20)	Mickey Cochrane	200.00	100.00	60.00

1954 Sports Illustrated Topps Foldouts

To illustrate a feature about baseball card collecting in its very first issue, Sports Illustrated included a three-page fold-out featuring 27 contemporary Topps cards. Printed on glossy paper stock in full color, the paper cards are exact front and back reproductions of the real thing. The foldout panel is found in the Aug. 16, 1954, issue of SI which features on its cover a photo of Eddie Mathews at bat during a night game. The magazine's second issue also contains a 27-card foldout of New York Yankees cards in full color, and supplements them with black-and-white "cards" in the general style of '54 Topps for those Yankees who appeared only on Bowman cards or on no cards in 1954. The August 23 issue of SI features a stand of golf clubs on its cover. Surviving examples of SI issue #2 are actually scarcer than the debut issue. Singles of the paper cards are rarely encountered. In 2001, SI reprinted 50,000 copies of issue #1 as a subscription premium. These copies are unmarked as reprints and difficult to distinguish from the originals. Many surviving original copies have a mail-in subscription offer card which the reprint does not.

		NM	EX	VG
	Aug. 16, 1954 Issue (Original)	250.00	125.00	75.00
	Aug. 16, 1954 Issue (2001 Reprint)	30.00	15.00	9.00
1	Ted Williams			
2	Gus Zernial			
4	Hank Sauer			
6	Pete Runnels			
7	Ted Kluszewski			
9	Harvey Haddix			
10	Jackie Robinson			
15	Al Rosen			
24	Granny Hamner			
25	Harvey Kuenn			
26	Ray Jablonski			
27	Ferris Fain			
29	Jim Hegan			
30	Ed Mathews			
32	Duke Snider			
34	Jim Rivera			
40	Mel Parnell			
45	Richie Ashburn			
70	Larry Doby			
77	Ray Boone			
85	Bob Turley			
90	Willie Mays			
100	Bob Keegan			
102	Gil Hodges			
119	Johnny Antonelli			
137	Wally Moon			
235	Vern Law			
	Aug. 23, 1954 Issue	350.00	175.00	100.00
5	Ed Lopat			
17	Phil Rizzuto			
37	Whitey Ford			
50	Yogi Berra			
56	Willie Miranda			
62	Eddie Robinson			
83	Joe Collins			
96	Charlie Silvera			
101	Gene Woodling			
105	Andy Carey			
130	Hank Bauer			
175	Johnny Sain			
205	Bob Kuzava			
230	Bill Skowron			
239	Harry Byrd			
	Bob Cerv			
	Jerry Coleman			
	Tom Gorman			
	Bob Grim			
	Mickey Mantle			
	Jim McDonald			
	Gil McDougald			
	Tom Morgan			
	Irv Noren			
	Allie Reynolds			
	Enos Slaughter			

1955 Sports Illustrated Topps Foldouts

SI kicked off the 1955 baseball season by including a page of 1955 Topps card reproductions in its April 11 and April 18 issues. Unlike the tri-fold panels of 1954, the 1955 issues contain only eight reproductions per magazine. Printed in full size in full color on glossy magazine paper, the pages are exact front and back replicas of regular-issue 1955 Topps cards. The April 11 issue features on its cover Willie Mays, Leo Durocher and Lorraine Day (Mrs. D.); the April 18 issue has Al Rosen at bat. Surviving examples of these 1955 SI issues are scarce and the paper cards are seldom seen as singles.

		NM	EX	VG
	April 11, 1955 Issue	200.00	100.00	60.00
1	Dusty Rhodes			
26	Dick Groat			
28	Ernie Banks			
31	Warren Spahn			
56	Ray Jablonski			
67	Wally Moon			
79	Danny Schell			
90	Karl Spooner			
	April 18, 1955 Issue	60.00	30.00	18.00
8	Hal Smith			
10	Bob Keegan			
11	Ferris Fain			
16	Roy Sievers			
38	Bob Turley			
70	Al Rosen			
77	Arnie Portocarrero			
106	Frank Sullivan			

1968-70 Sports Illustrated Posters

Between 1968-70, Sports Illustrated issued a series of baseball player posters. The 2' x 3' blank-back posters have borderless color action or posed photos. In an upper corner are the player identification, copyright, poster number, etc., in small type. Values for the posters issued in 1969 and 1970 are higher than those produced in 1968. Current market values reflect the fact that many superstars' posters were sold in larger quantities than those of journeymen players and survive in greater numbers. The posters are listed here alphabetically within year of issue. Original selling price of the posters was $1.50 each, plus postage.

		NM	EX	VG
	Complete Set (86):	2,500	1,250	750.00
	Common Player:	10.00	5.00	3.00
	1968			
(1)	Hank Aaron	45.00	22.50	13.50
(2)	Rich Allen	30.00	15.00	9.00
(3)	Gene Alley	15.00	7.50	4.50
(4)	Felipe Alou	15.00	7.50	4.50
(5)	Max Alvis	10.00	5.00	3.00
(6)	Bob Aspromonte	10.00	5.00	3.00
(7)	Ernie Banks (Photo actually Billy Williams.)	35.00	17.50	10.50
(8)	Clete Boyer	12.50	6.25	3.75
(9)	Lou Brock	15.00	7.50	4.50
(10)	John Callison	15.00	7.50	4.50
(11)	Campy Campaneris	12.50	6.25	3.75
(12)	Leo Cardenas	12.50	6.25	3.75
(13)	Paul Casanova	17.50	8.75	5.25
(14)	Orlando Cepeda	17.50	8.75	5.25
(15)	Roberto Clemente	185.00	95.00	55.00
(16)	Tony Conigliaro	20.00	10.00	6.00
(17)	Willie Davis	15.00	7.50	4.50
(18)	Don Drysdale	17.50	8.75	5.25
(19)	Al Ferrara	12.50	6.25	3.75
(20)	Curt Flood	15.00	7.50	4.50
(21)	Bill Freehan	30.00	15.00	9.00
(22)	Jim Fregosi	10.00	5.00	3.00
(23)	Bob Gibson	15.00	7.50	4.50
(24)	Bud Harrelson (Photo actually Ken Harrelson.)	20.00	10.00	6.00
(25)	Joe Horlen	10.00	5.00	3.00
(26)	Tony Horton	15.00	7.50	4.50
(27)	Tommy John	12.50	6.25	3.75
(28)	Al Kaline	40.00	20.00	12.00
(29)	Harmon Killebrew	17.50	8.75	5.25
(30)	Jim Lonborg	17.50	8.75	5.25
(31)	Jim Maloney	12.50	6.25	3.75
(32)	Mickey Mantle	185.00	92.00	55.00
(33)	Juan Marichal	17.50	8.75	5.25
(34)	Willie Mays	110.00	55.00	35.00
(35)	Bill Mazeroski	25.00	12.50	7.50
(36)	Tim McCarver	17.50	8.75	5.25
(37)	Mike McCormick	15.00	7.50	4.50
(38)	Willie McCovey	45.00	22.50	13.50
(39a)	Don Mincher (Angels)	15.00	7.50	4.50
(39b)	Don Mincher (Pilots)	20.00	10.00	6.00
(40)	Rick Monday	12.50	6.25	3.75
(41)	Tony Oliva	15.00	7.50	4.50
(42)	Rick Reichardt	10.00	5.00	3.00
(43)	Brooks Robinson	175.00	90.00	50.00
(44)	Frank Robinson	75.00	37.50	22.00
(45)	Pete Rose	100.00	50.00	30.00
(46)	Ron Santo	17.50	8.75	5.25
(47)	Tom Seaver	130.00	65.00	39.00
(48)	Chris Short	15.00	7.50	4.50
(49)	Reggie Smith	12.50	6.25	3.75
(50)	Rusty Staub	17.50	8.75	5.25
(51)	Mel Stottlemyre	20.00	10.00	6.00
(52)	Ron Swoboda	25.00	12.50	7.50
(53)	Cesar Tovar	15.00	7.50	4.50
(54)	Earl Wilson	17.50	8.75	5.25
(55)	Jim Wynn	10.00	5.00	3.00
(56)	Carl Yastrzemski	25.00	12.50	7.50
	1969			
(1)	Tommie Agee	17.50	8.75	5.25
(2)	Mike Andrews	12.50	6.25	3.75
(3)	Ernie Banks (Batting)	15.00	7.50	4.50
(4a)	Gary Bell (Indians)	20.00	10.00	6.00
(4b)	Gary Bell (Pilots)	20.00	10.00	6.00
(5a)	Tommy Davis (White Sox)	17.50	8.75	5.25
(5b)	Tommy Davis (Pilots)	20.00	10.00	6.00
(6)	Frank Howard	20.00	10.00	6.00
(7)	Reggie Jackson	95.00	47.00	28.00
(8)	Fergie Jenkins	45.00	22.00	13.50
(9)	Let's Go Mets (Tommie Agee, Jerry Grote, Cleon Jones, Jerry Koosman, Ed Kranepool, Tom Seaver, Ron Swoboda)	20.00	10.00	6.00
(10)	Denny McLain	15.00	7.50	4.50
(11)	Bobby Murcer	45.00	22.00	13.50
(12)	John Odom	17.50	8.75	5.25
(13)	Rico Petrocelli	17.50	8.75	5.25
(14)	Boog Powell	20.00	10.00	6.00
(15)	Roy White	25.00	12.50	7.50
	1970			
(1)	Glenn Beckert	17.50	8.75	5.25
(2)	Bobby Bonds	20.00	10.00	6.00
(3)	Rod Carew	17.50	8.75	5.25
(4)	Mike Cuellar	17.50	8.75	5.25
(5)	Mike Epstein	15.00	7.50	4.50
(6)	Ken Holtzman	15.00	7.50	4.50
(7)	Cleon Jones	15.00	7.50	4.50
(8)	Mickey Lolich	15.00	7.50	4.50
(9)	Sam McDowell	20.00	10.00	6.00
(10)	Phil Niekro	35.00	17.50	10.50
(11)	Wes Parker	17.50	8.75	5.25
(12)	Tony Perez	25.00	12.50	7.50
(13)	Bill Singer	10.00	5.00	3.00
(14)	Walt Williams	20.00	10.00	6.00

1968 Sports Memorabilia All Time Baseball Team

This is one of the earliest collectors' issue baseball card sets created for distribution solely within the hobby. The 2-1/2" x 3-1/2" cards feature the artwork of Art Ouelette done in sepia tones on a white background and surrounded by a yellow border. Backs have career information, copyright and player identification. Issue price was $2.50.

		NM	EX	VG
	Complete Set (15):	35.00	17.50	10.00
	Common Player:	2.00	1.00	.60
1	Checklist	.50	.25	.15
2	"Connie" Mack	2.00	1.00	.60
3	Walter Johnson	4.00	2.00	1.25
4	Warren Spahn	2.00	1.00	.60
5	Christy Mathewson	4.00	2.00	1.25
6	Lefty Grove	2.00	1.00	.60
7	Mickey Cochrane	2.00	1.00	.60
8	Bill Dickey	2.00	1.00	.60
9	"Tris" Speaker	2.50	1.25	.75
10	"Ty" Cobb	6.00	3.00	2.00
11	"Babe" Ruth	10.00	5.00	3.00
12	"Lou" Gehrig	7.50	3.75	2.25
13	Rogers Hornsby	2.50	1.25	.75
14	"Honus" Wagner	5.00	2.50	1.50
15	"Pie" Traynor	2.00	1.00	.60

1960 Sports Novelties Inc. Genuine Baseball Photos

(See 1960 Leaf for checklist and price guide.)

1960s Sports Pix Premiums

Roger Maris

These black-and-white blank-back pictures were distributed as a premium for Sports Pix magazine in the early 1960s. Two sizes are known: A smaller (about 8" x 10") style was issued in the early 1960s, while a larger (about 8-1/2" x 10-1/2") format was produced after 1963. Both styles have the photo bordered in white, with the player name centered at bottom. In the bottom-right corner is a three-line credit to the magazine and its Washington, D.C. address. Gaps have been left in the assigned numbering to accommodate future additions.

		NM	EX	VG
	Common Player:	10.00	5.00	3.00
(1)	Ty Cobb (Large)	7.50	3.75	2.25
(2)	Mickey Cochrane (Large)	3.00	1.50	.90
(3)	Rocky Colavito (Large)	5.00	2.50	1.50
(3)	Joe Cronin (Large)	3.00	1.50	.90
(4)	Bill Dickey (Large)	3.00	2.00	1.00
(5)	Joe DiMaggio (Large, glossy, w/caption.)	7.50	3.75	2.25
(7)	Bob Feller (Large)	3.00	2.00	1.00
(8)	Lou Gehrig (Large)	7.50	3.75	2.25
(9)	Charlie Gehringer (Large)	3.00	2.00	1.00
(11)	"Lefty" Grove (Large)	.00	2.00	1.00
(12)	Rogers Hornsby (Large)	3.00	2.00	1.00
(13)	Walter Johnson (Large)	5.00	2.50	1.50
(14)	Sandy Koufax (Small)	5.00	2.50	1.50
(15)	Sandy Koufax (Large)	5.00	2.50	1.50
(16)	Mickey Mantle (Large)	15.00	7.50	4.50
(17)	Mickey Mantle (Small)	15.00	7.50	4.50
(18)	Roger Maris (Large)	4.50	2.25	1.25
(19)	Willie Mays (Large)	7.50	3.75	2.25
(20)	Willie Mays (Small)	7.50	3.75	2.25
(21)	John McGraw (Large)	3.00	2.00	1.00
(22)	Stan Musial (Large)	5.00	2.50	1.50
(24)	Babe Ruth (Large)	7.50	3.75	2.25
(25)	George Sisler (Large)	3.00	2.00	1.00
(26)	Warren Spahn (Large)	3.00	2.00	1.00
(27)	"Casey" Stengel (Large)	3.00	2.00	1.00
(28)	"Pie" Traynor (Large)	3.00	2.00	1.00
(30)	"Honus" Wagner (Large)	4.50	2.25	1.25
(32)	Ted Williams (Large)	7.50	3.75	2.25

1979 Sports Reading Series

This set of large-format (about 8-1/2" x 14") was designed to encourage youthful readers. The black-and-white cards have one or more photos and lengthy text describing the player and/or action depicted.

		NM	EX	VG
	Complete Set (50):	250.00	125.00	75.00
	Common Player:	5.00	2.50	1.50
1	Carlos May	5.00	2.50	1.50
2	Babe Ruth	10.00	5.00	3.00
3	Eddie Gaedel	6.00	3.00	1.75
4	Cesar Gutierrez	5.00	2.50	1.50
5	Ted Williams	7.50	3.75	2.25
6	Pete Gray	6.00	3.00	1.75
7	Hank Aaron	7.50	3.75	2.25
8	Lou Brock	5.00	2.50	1.50
9	Virgil Trucks	5.00	2.50	1.50
10	Cesar Tovar	5.00	2.50	1.50
11	Wrigley Field	5.00	2.50	1.50
12	Ron Guidry	5.00	2.50	1.50
13	Bill Davis	5.00	2.50	1.50
14	Jimmy Piersall	5.00	2.50	1.50
15	Eddie Gaedel	6.00	3.00	1.75
16	Reggie Jackson	7.50	3.75	2.25
17	Mark Fidrych	5.00	2.50	1.50
18	Sandy Koufax	7.50	3.75	2.25
19	Dale Long	5.00	2.50	1.50
20	Herb Score	5.00	2.50	1.50
21	Dizzy Dean, Daffy Dean	5.00	2.50	1.50
22	Stan Musial	7.50	3.75	2.25
23	1903 N.Y. Giants	5.00	2.50	1.50
24	Pete Rose	7.50	3.75	2.25
25	Cy Young	5.00	2.50	1.50
26	Ferguson Jenkins	5.00	2.50	1.50
27	Minnie Minoso	5.00	2.50	1.50
28	Mort Cooper, Walker Cooper	5.00	2.50	1.50
29	Jim Thorpe	7.50	3.75	2.25
30	Lefty Grove	5.00	2.50	1.50
31	Roberto Clemente	9.00	4.50	2.75
32	Pres. Coolidge Throws Out First Ball	5.00	2.50	1.50
33	Lou Gehrig	7.50	3.75	2.25
34	Nolan Ryan	10.00	5.00	3.00
35	1969 N.Y. Mets	5.00	2.50	1.50
36	Yankee Stadium	5.00	2.50	1.50
37	Jackie Robinson	7.50	3.75	2.25
38	Carl Hubbell	5.00	2.50	1.50
39	Willie Mays	7.50	3.75	2.25
40	Mike Schmidt	6.00	3.00	1.75
41	Harvey Haddix	5.00	2.50	1.50
42	Pete Reiser	5.00	2.50	1.50

43	Gary Cooper (Pride of the Yankees)	5.00	2.50	1.50
44	Jackie Robinson	7.50	3.75	2.25
45	Walter Johnson	5.00	2.50	1.50
46	Hall of Fame	5.00	2.50	1.50
47	Jose Morales	5.00	2.50	1.50
48	Rod Carew	5.00	2.50	1.50
49	Lou Boudreau	5.00	2.50	1.50
50	Hank Greenberg	5.00	2.50	1.50

1950 Sport Stars Luckee Key Charms

This series of 1-3/8" square, diamond-format aluminum tags depicts on front an action picture of a player along with his facsimile autograph. A good luck and sportsmanship message appears on back. The charms are holed at the top to accomodate a beaded chain. While the charms themselves are not so marked, they were produced by Ralpat Co., of Cleveland, and sold on an approximately 3" x 5" cardboard backing card which has a line-art portrait of the player, his name, "Sport Stars" and "Luckee Key Charm." Values shown are for complete card/charm combinations. The metal charms themselves would be valued at about 35-50 percent.

		NM	EX	VG
	Complete Set (5):	150.00	75.00	45.00
	Common Player:	15.00	7.50	4.50
(1)	Ewell Blackwell	15.00	7.50	4.50
(2)	Bob Feller	30.00	15.00	9.00
(3)	Ralph Kiner	20.00	10.00	6.00
(4)	Hal Newhouser	17.50	8.75	5.25
(5)	Ted Williams	100.00	50.00	30.00

1976 Sportstix

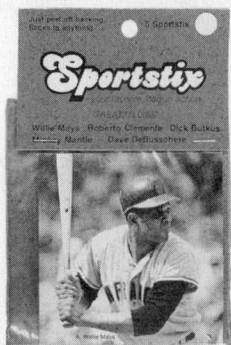

These peel-off player stickers were sold in five-piece plastic packs, with specific contents noted on the header. Stickers are found in three formats: 3-1/2" square, 3-1/2" square with clipped corners and 3" diameter round. The set includes 10 numbered current players and three retired baseball superstars identified as A, B and D. Stickers have full-color player pictures on front with no border. The player's name and sticker number are printed in black. Backs are blank. Besides the baseball players, there were stickers for football and basketball players, in a total issue of 30.

		NM	EX	VG
	Complete Baseball Set (13):	40.00	20.00	12.00
	Common Player:	1.00	.50	.30
A	Willie Mays	10.00	5.00	3.00
C	Roberto Clemente	12.50	6.25	3.75
D	Mickey Mantle	15.00	7.50	4.50
1	Dave Kingman	1.00	.50	.30
2	Steve Busby	1.00	.50	.30
3	Bill Madlock	1.00	.50	.30
4	Jeff Burroughs	1.00	.50	.30
5	Ted Simmons	1.00	.50	.30
6	Randy Jones	1.00	.50	.30
7	Buddy Bell	1.00	.50	.30
8	Dave Cash	1.00	.50	.30
9	Jerry Grote	1.00	.50	.30
10	Davey Lopes	1.00	.50	.30

1975 SSPC Promo Cards

The six players in this sample set can each be found with three different backs. Some backs are similar to the cards issued in 1976, with player data and career summary. Some

cards will have an ad message on back offering the complete 1976 SSPC set and team sets. Still others have blank backs. All cards are in 2-1/2" x 3-1/2" format with color photos on front surrounded by a white border and no extraneous graphics. Blank-back versions are worth 2-4X the values quoted here.

		NM	EX	VG
	Complete Set (6):	15.00	7.50	4.50
	Common Player:	1.50	.75	.45
(1)	Hank Aaron	4.00	2.00	1.25
(2)	Catfish Hunter	2.00	1.00	.60
(3)	Dave Kingman	1.50	.75	.45
(4)	Mickey Mantle	7.50	3.75	2.25
(5)	Willie Mays	4.00	2.00	1.25
(6)	Tom Seaver	3.00	1.50	.90

1975 SSPC Sample Cards

The Winter 1975 issue of "Collector's Quarterly" magazine (an advertising vehicle for Mike Aronstein, SSPC's principal) contained a two-page cardboard insert previewing the 1976 SSPC set. The cards could be cut apart into singles and represented something of a traded set, as each player or manager changed teams between the end of the 1975 season and the start of 1976. The cards have the players pictured on front in their old uniforms, with their new teams identified on back. Backs of the 2-1/2" x 3-1/2" cards are printed in red and black with a player biography and uniform number. "SAMPLE CARD 1975" is printed around the uniform number. A card number is in the lower-left corner, with 1975 copyright at bottom-right.

		NM	EX	VG
	Complete Set, Uncut Sheet:	25.00	12.50	7.50
	Complete Set, Singles (18):	20.00	10.00	6.00
	Common Card:	1.50	.75	.45
1	Harry Parker	1.50	.75	.45
2	Jim Bibby	1.50	.75	.45
3	Mike Wallace	1.50	.75	.45
4	Tony Muser	1.50	.75	.45
5	Yogi Berra	7.50	3.75	2.25
6	Preston Gomez	1.50	.75	.45
7	Jack McKeon	1.50	.75	.45
8	Sam McDowell	1.50	.70	.45
9	Gaylord Perry	4.00	2.00	1.25
10	Fred Stanley	1.50	.75	.45
11	Willie Davis	1.50	.70	.45
12	Don Hopkins	1.50	.75	.45
13	Whitey Herzog	1.50	.75	.45
14	Ray Sadecki	1.50	.75	.45
15	Stan Bahnsen	1.50	.75	.45
16	Bob Oliver	1.50	.75	.45
17	Denny Doyle	1.50	.75	.45
18	Deron Johnson	1.50	.70	.45

1975 SSPC

This set, produced by the Sport Star Publishing Company in 1975 as a collectors' issue (though not actually issued until 1976), was withdrawn from the market because of legal entanglements. Because SSPC agreed never to reprint the issue, some collectors feel it has an air of legitimacy. The complete set contains 630 full-color cards, each 2-1/2" x 3-1/2" in size. The cards look similar to 1953 Bowmans, with only the player picture (no identification) on the fronts. Card backs are in a vertical format, with personal stats, brief biographies, uniform and card numbers printed in a variety of colors. Sets originally sold for $9.99.

		NM	EX	VG
	Complete Set (630):	60.00	30.00	18.00
	Common Player:	.10	.05	.03
1	Lee William (Buzz) Capra	.10	.05	.03
2	Thomas Ross House	.10	.05	.03
3	Maximino Leon	.10	.05	.03
4	Carl Wendle Morton	.10	.05	.03
5	Philip Henry Niekro	1.50	.70	.45
6	Michael Wayne Thompson	.10	.05	.03
7	Elias Sosa (Martinez)	.10	.05	.03
8	Larvell Blanks	.10	.05	.03
9	Darrell Wayne Evans	.10	.05	.03
10	Rodney Joe Gilbreath	.10	.05	.03
11	Michael Ken-Wai Lum	.10	.05	.03
12	Craig George Robinson	.10	.05	.03
13	Earl Craig Williams, Jr.	.10	.05	.03
14	Victor Crosby Correll	.10	.05	.03
15	Biff Pocoroba	.10	.05	.03
16	Johnny B. (Dusty) Baker, Jr.	.35	.20	.11
17	Ralph Allen Garr	.10	.05	.03
18	Clarence Edward (Cito) Gaston	.10	.05	.03
19	David LaFrance May	.10	.05	.03
20	Rowland Johnnie Office	.10	.05	.03
21	Robert Brooks Beall	.10	.05	.03
22	George Lee (Sparky) Anderson	1.00	.50	.30
23	John Eugene Billingham	.10	.05	.03
24	Pedro Rodriguez Borbon	.10	.05	.03
25	Clay Palmer Carroll	.10	.05	.03
26	Patrick Leonard Darcy	.10	.05	.03
27	Donald Edward Gullett	.10	.05	.03
28	Clayton Laws Kirby	.10	.05	.03
29	Gary Lynn Nolan	.10	.05	.03
30	Fredie Hubert Norman	.10	.05	.03
31	Johnny Lee Bench	2.50	1.25	.70
32	William Francis Plummer	.10	.05	.03
33	Darrel Lee Chaney	.10	.05	.03
34	David Ismael Concepcion	.10	.05	.03
35	Terrence Michael Crowley	.10	.05	.03
36	Daniel Driessen	.10	.05	.03
37	Robert Douglas Flynn, Jr.	.10	.05	.03
38	Joe Leonard Morgan	2.00	1.00	.60
39	Atanasio Rigal (Tony) Perez	1.50	.70	.45
40	George Kenneth (Ken) Griffey	.35	.20	.11
41	Peter Edward Rose	5.00	2.50	1.50
42	Edison Rosanda Armbrister	.10	.05	.03
43	John Christopher Vukovich	.10	.05	.03
44	George Arthur Foster	.10	.05	.03
45	Cesar Francisco Geronimo	.10	.05	.03
46	Mervin Weldon Rettenmund	.10	.05	.03
47	James Frederick Crawford	.10	.05	.03
48	Kenneth Roth Forsch	.10	.05	.03
49	Douglas James Konieczny	.10	.05	.03
50	Joseph Franklin Niekro	.10	.05	.03
51	Clifford Johnson	.10	.05	.03
52	Alfred Henry (Skip) Jutze	.10	.05	.03
53	Milton Scott May	.10	.05	.03
54	Robert Patrick Andrews	.10	.05	.03
55	Kenneth George Boswell	.10	.05	.03
56	Tommy Vann Helms	.10	.05	.03
57	Roger Henry Metzger	.10	.05	.03
58	Lawrence William Milbourne	.10	.05	.03
59	Douglas Lee Rader	.10	.05	.03
60	Robert Jose Watson	.10	.05	.03
61	Enos Milton Cabell, Jr.	.10	.05	.03
62	Jose Delan Cruz	.10	.05	.03
63	Cesar Cedeno	.10	.05	.03
64	Gregory Eugene Gross	.10	.05	.03
65	Wilbur Leon Howard	.10	.05	.03
66	Alphonso Erwin Downing	.10	.05	.03
67	Burt Carlton Hooton	.10	.05	.03
68	Charles Oliver Hough	.10	.05	.03
69	Thomas Edward John	.25	.13	.08
70	John Alexander Messersmith	.10	.05	.03
71	Douglas James Rau	.10	.05	.03
72	Richard Alan Rhoden	.10	.05	.03
73	Donald Howard Sutton	1.50	.70	.45
74	Frederick Steven Auerbach	.10	.05	.03
75	Ronald Charles Cey	.10	.05	.03
76	Ivan De Jesus	.10	.05	.03
77	Steven Patrick Garvey	1.00	.50	.30
78	Leonadus Lacy	.10	.05	.03
79	David Earl Lopes	.10	.05	.03
80	Kenneth Lee McMullen	.10	.05	.03
81	Joseph Vance Ferguson	.10	.05	.03
82	Paul Ray Powell	.10	.05	.03
83	Stephen Wayne Yeager	.10	.05	.03
84	Willie Murphy Crawford	.10	.05	.03
85	Henry Cruz	.10	.05	.03
86	Charles Fuqua Manuel	.10	.05	.03
87	Manuel Mota	.10	.05	.03
88	Thomas Marian Paciorek	.10	.05	.03
89	James Sherman Wynn	.10	.05	.03
90	Walter Emmons Alston	1.00	.50	.30
91	William Joseph Buckner	.10	.05	.03
92	James Leland Barr	.10	.05	.03
93	Ralph Michael (Mike) Caldwell	.10	.05	.03
94	John Francis D'Acquisto	.10	.05	.03
95	David Wallace Heaverlo	.10	.05	.03
96	Gary Robert Lavelle	.10	.05	.03
97	John Joseph Montefusco, Jr.	.10	.05	.03
98	Charles Prosek Williams	.10	.05	.03
99	Christopher Paul Arnold	.10	.05	.03

		NM	EX	VG
100	Mark Kevin Hill (Marc)	.10	.05	.03
101	David Martin Rader	.10	.05	.03
102	Charles Bruce Miller	.10	.05	.03
103	Guillermo Naranjo (Willie) Montanez	.10	.05	.03
104	Steven Robert Ontiveros	.10	.05	.03
105	Chris Edward Speier	.10	.05	.03
106	Derrel Osbon Thomas	.10	.05	.03
107	Gary Leah Thomasson	.10	.05	.03
108	Glenn Charles Adams	.10	.05	.03
109	Von Everett Joshua	.10	.05	.03
110	Gary Nathaniel Matthews	.10	.05	.03
111	Bobby Ray Murcer	.10	.05	.03
112	Horace Arthur Speed III	.10	.05	.03
113	Wesley Noreen Westrum	.10	.05	.03
114	Richard Nevin Folkers	.10	.05	.03
115	Alan Benton Foster	.10	.05	.03
116	David James Freisleben	.10	.05	.03
117	Daniel Vincent Frisella	.10	.05	.03
118	Randall Leo Jones	.10	.05	.03
119	Daniel Ray Spillner	.10	.05	.03
120	Howard Lawrence (Larry) Hardy	.10	.05	.03
121	Cecil Randolph (Randy) Hundley	.10	.05	.03
122	Fred Lyn Kendall	.10	.05	.03
123	John Francis McNamara	.10	.05	.03
124	Rigoberto (Tito) Fuentes	.10	.05	.03
125	Enzo Octavio Hernandez	.10	.05	.03
126	Stephen Michael Huntz	.10	.05	.03
127	Michael Wilson Ivie	.10	.05	.03
128	Hector Epitacio Torres	.10	.05	.03
129	Theodore Rodger Kubiak	.10	.05	.03
130	John Maywood Grubb, Jr.	.10	.05	.03
131	John Henry Scott	.10	.05	.03
132	Robert Tolan	.10	.05	.03
133	David Mark Winfield	2.50	1.25	.70
134	William Joseph Gogolewski	.10	.05	.03
135	Danny L. Osborn	.10	.05	.03
136	James Lee Kaat	.25	.13	.08
137	Claude Wilson Osteen	.10	.05	.03
138	Cecil Lee Upshaw, Jr.	.10	.05	.03
139	Wilbur Forrester Wood, Jr.	.10	.05	.03
140	Lloyd Cecil Allen	.10	.05	.03
141	Brian Jay Downing	.10	.05	.03
142	James Sarkis Essian, Jr.	.10	.05	.03
143	Russell Earl (Bucky) Dent	.50	.25	.15
144	Jorge Orta	.10	.05	.03
145	Lee Edward Richard	.10	.05	.03
146	William Allen Stein	.10	.05	.03
147	Kenneth Joseph Henderson	.10	.05	.03
148	Carlos May	.10	.05	.03
149	Nyls Wallace Rex Nyman	.10	.05	.03
150	Robert Pasquali Coluccio, Jr.	.10	.05	.03
151	Charles William Tanner, Jr.	.10	.05	.03
152	Harold Patrick (Pat) Kelly	.10	.05	.03
153	Jerry Wayne Hairston Sr.	.10	.05	.03
154	Richard Fred (Pete) Varney, Jr.	.10	.05	.03
155	William Edwin Melton	.10	.05	.03
156	Richard Michael Gossage	.50	.25	.15
157	Terry Jay Forster	.10	.05	.03
158	Richard Michael Hinton	.10	.05	.03
159	Nelson Kelley Briles	.10	.05	.03
160	Alan James Fitzmorris	.10	.05	.03
161	Stephen Bernard Mingori	.10	.05	.03
162	Martin William Pattin	.10	.05	.03
163	Paul William Splittorff, Jr.	.10	.05	.03
164	Dennis Patrick Leonard	.10	.05	.03
165	John Albert (Buck) Martinez	.10	.05	.03
166	Gorrell Robert (Bob) Stinson III	.10	.05	.03
167	George Howard Brett	7.50	3.75	2.25
168	Harmon Clayton Killebrew, Jr.	2.50	1.25	.70
169	John Claiborn Mayberry	.10	.05	.03
170	Freddie Joe Patek	.10	.05	.03
171	Octavio (Cookie) Rojas	.10	.05	.03
172	Rodney Darrell Scott	.10	.05	.03
173	Tolia (Tony) Solaita	.10	.05	.03
174	Frank White, Jr.	.10	.05	.03
175	Alfred Edward Cowens, Jr.	.10	.05	.03
176	Harold Abraham McRae	.10	.05	.03
177	Amos Joseph Otis	.10	.05	.03
178	Vada Edward Pinson, Jr.	.50	.25	.15
179	James Eugene Wohlford	.10	.05	.03
180	James Douglas Bird	.10	.05	.03
181	Mark Alan Littell	.10	.05	.03
182	Robert McClure	.10	.05	.03
183	Steven Lee Busby	.10	.05	.03
184	Francis Xavier Healy	.10	.05	.03
185	Dorrel Norman Elvert (Whitey) Herzog	.10	.05	.03
186	Andrew Earl Hassler	.10	.05	.03
187	Lynn Nolan Ryan, Jr.	7.50	3.75	2.25
188	William Robert Singer	.10	.05	.03
189	Frank Daryl Tanana	.10	.05	.03
190	Eduardo Figueroa	.10	.05	.03
191	David S. Collins	.10	.05	.03
192	Richard Hirshfeld Williams	.10	.05	.03
193	Eliseo Rodriguez	.10	.05	.03
194	David Lee Chalk	.10	.05	.03
195	Winston Enriquillo Llenas	.10	.05	.03
196	Rudolph Bart Meoli	.10	.05	.03
197	Orlando Ramirez	.10	.05	.03
198	Gerald Peter Remy	.10	.05	.03
199	Billy Edward Smith	.10	.05	.03
200	Bruce Anton Bochte	.10	.05	.03
201	Joseph Michael Lahoud, Jr.	.10	.05	.03
202	Morris Nettles, Jr.	.10	.05	.03
203	John Milton (Mickey) Rivers	.10	.05	.03
204	Leroy Bobby Stanton	.10	.05	.03
205	Victor Albury	.10	.05	.03
206	Thomas Henry Burgmeier	.10	.05	.03
207	William Franklin Butler	.10	.05	.03
208	William Richard Campbell	.10	.05	.03
209	Alton Ray Corbin	.10	.05	.03
210	George Henry (Joe) Decker, Jr.	.10	.05	.03
211	James Michael Hughes	.10	.05	.03

		NM	EX	VG
212	Edward Norman Bane (Photo actually Mike Pazik.)	.10	.05	.03
213	Glenn Dennis Borgmann	.10	.05	.03
214	Rodney Cline Carew	2.50	1.25	.70
215	Stephen Robert Brye	.10	.05	.03
216	Darnell Glenn (Dan) Ford	.10	.05	.03
217	Antonio Oliva	.35	.20	.11
218	David Allan Goltz	.10	.05	.03
219	Rikalbert Blyleven	.25	.13	.08
220	Larry Eugene Hisle	.10	.05	.03
221	Stephen Russell Braun, III	.10	.05	.03
222	Jerry Wayne Terrell	.10	.05	.03
223	Eric Thane Soderholm	.10	.05	.03
224	Philip Anthony Roof	.10	.05	.03
225	Danny Leon Thompson	.10	.05	.03
226	James William Colborn	.10	.05	.03
227	Thomas Andrew Murphy	.10	.05	.03
228	Eduardo Rodriguez	.10	.05	.03
229	James Michael Slaton	.10	.05	.03
230	Edward Nelson Sprague	.10	.05	.03
231	Charles William Moore, Jr.	.10	.05	.03
232	Darrell Ray Porter	.10	.05	.03
233	Kurt Anthony Bevacqua	.10	.05	.03
234	Pedro Garcia	.10	.05	.03
235	James Michael (Mike) Hegan	.10	.05	.03
236	Donald Wayne Money	.10	.05	.03
237	George C. Scott, Jr.	.10	.05	.03
238	Robin R. Yount	5.00	2.50	1.50
239	Henry Louis Aaron	5.00	2.50	1.50
240	Robert Walker Ellis	.10	.05	.03
241	Sixto Lezcano	.10	.05	.03
242	Robert Vance Mitchell	.10	.05	.03
243	James Gorman Thomas, III	.10	.05	.03
244	William Edward Travers	.10	.05	.03
245	Peter Sven Broberg	.10	.05	.03
246	William Howard Sharp	.10	.05	.03
247	Arthur Bobby Lee Darwin	.10	.05	.03
248	Rick Gerald Austin (Photo actually Larry Anderson.)	.10	.05	.03
249	Lawrence Dennis Anderson (Photo actually Rick Austin.)	.10	.05	.03
250	Thomas Antony Bianco	.10	.05	.03
251	DeLancy LaFayette Currence	.10	.05	.03
252	Steven Raymond Foucault	.10	.05	.03
253	William Alfred Hands, Jr.	.10	.05	.03
254	Steven Lowell Hargan	.10	.05	.03
255	Ferguson Arthur Jenkins	1.50	.70	.45
256	Bob Mitchell Sheldon	.10	.05	.03
257	James Umbarger	.10	.05	.03
258	Clyde Wright	.10	.05	.03
259	William Roger Fahey	.10	.05	.03
260	James Howard Sundberg	.10	.05	.03
261	Leonardo Alfonso Cardenas	.10	.05	.03
262	James Louis Fregosi	.10	.05	.03
263	Dudley Michael (Mike) Hargrove	.10	.05	.03
264	Colbert Dale (Toby) Harrah	.10	.05	.03
265	Roy Lee Howell	.10	.05	.03
266	Leonard Shenoff Randle	.10	.05	.03
267	Roy Frederick Smalley III	.10	.05	.03
268	James Lloyd Spencer	.10	.05	.03
269	Jeffrey Alan Burroughs	.10	.05	.03
270	Thomas Alan Grieve	.10	.05	.03
271	Joseph Lovitto, Jr.	.10	.05	.03
272	Frank Joseph Lucchesi	.10	.05	.03
273	David Earl Nelson	.10	.05	.03
274	Ted Lyle Simmons	.10	.05	.03
275	Louis Clark Brock	2.00	1.00	.60
276	Ronald Ray Fairly	.10	.05	.03
277	Arnold Ray (Bake) McBride	.10	.05	.03
278	Carl Reginald (Reggie) Smith	.10	.05	.03
279	William Henry Davis	.10	.05	.03
280	Kenneth John Reitz	.10	.05	.03
281	Charles William (Buddy) Bradford	.10	.05	.03
282	Luis Antonio Melendez	.10	.05	.03
283	Michael Ray Tyson	.10	.05	.03
284	Ted Crawford Sizemore	.10	.05	.03
285	Mario Miguel Guerrero	.10	.05	.03
286	Larry Lintz	.10	.05	.03
287	Kenneth Victor Rudolph	.10	.05	.03
288	Richard Arlin Billings	.10	.05	.03
289	Jerry Wayne Mumphrey	.10	.05	.03
290	Michael Sherman Wallace	.10	.05	.03
291	Alan Thomas Hrabosky	.10	.05	.03
292	Kenneth Lee Reynolds	.10	.05	.03
293	Michael Douglas Garman	.10	.05	.03
294	Robert Herbert Forsch	.10	.05	.03
295	John Allen Denny	.10	.05	.03
296	Harold R. Rasmussen	.10	.05	.03
297	Lynn Everratt McGlothen (Everett)	.10	.05	.03
298	Michael Roswell Barlow	.10	.05	.03
299	Gregory John Terlecky	.10	.05	.03
300	Albert Fred (Red) Schoendienst	1.00	.50	.30
301	Ricky Eugene Reuschel	.10	.05	.03
302	Steven Michael Stone	.10	.05	.03
303	William Gordon Bonham	.10	.05	.03
304	Oscar Joseph Zamora	.10	.05	.03
305	Kenneth Douglas Frailing	.10	.05	.03
306	Milton Edward Wilcox	.10	.05	.03
307	Darold Duane Knowles	.10	.05	.03
308	Rufus James (Jim) Marshall	.10	.05	.03
309	Bill Madlock, Jr.	.10	.05	.03
310	Jose Domec Cardenal	.10	.05	.03
311	Robert James (Rick) Monday, Jr.	.10	.05	.03
312	Julio Ruben (Jerry) Morales	.10	.05	.03
313	Timothy Kenneth Hosley	.10	.05	.03
314	Gene Taylor Hiser	.10	.05	.03
315	Donald Eulon Kessinger	.10	.05	.03
316	Jesus Manuel (Manny) Trillo	.10	.05	.03
317	Ralph Pierre (Pete) LaCock, Jr.	.10	.05	.03
318	George Eugene Mitterwald	.10	.05	.03
319	Steven Eugene Swisher	.10	.05	.03
320	Robert Walter Sperring	.10	.05	.03

No.	Name			
321	Victor Lanier Harris	.10	.05	.03
322	Ronald Ray Dunn	.10	.05	.03
323	Jose Manuel Morales	.10	.05	.03
324	Peter MacKanin, Jr.	.10	.05	.03
325	James Charles Cox	.10	.05	.03
326	Larry Alton Parrish	.10	.05	.03
327	Michael Jorgensen	.10	.05	.03
328	Timothy John Foli	.10	.05	.03
329	Harold Noel Breeden	.10	.05	.03
330	Nathan Colbert, Jr.	.10	.05	.03
331	Jesus Maria (Pepe) Frias	.10	.05	.03
332	James Patrick (Pat) Scanlon	.10	.05	.03
333	Robert Sherwood Bailey	.10	.05	.03
334	Gary Edmund Carter	2.00	1.00	.60
335	Jose Mauel (Pepe) Mangual	.10	.05	.03
336	Lawrence David Biittner	.10	.05	.03
337	James Lawrence Lyttle, Jr.	.10	.05	.03
338	Gary Roenicke	.10	.05	.03
339	Anthony Scott	.10	.05	.03
340	Jerome Cardell White	.10	.05	.03
341	James Edward Dwyer	.10	.05	.03
342	Ellis Clarence Valentine	.10	.05	.03
343	Frederick John Scherman, Jr.	.10	.05	.03
344	Dennis Herman Blair	.10	.05	.03
345	Woodrow Thompson Fryman	.10	.05	.03
346	Charles Gilbert Taylor	.10	.05	.03
347	Daniel Dean Warthen	.10	.05	.03
348	Donald George Carrithers	.10	.05	.03
349	Stephen Douglas Rogers	.10	.05	.03
350	Dale Albert Murray	.10	.05	.03
351	Edwin Donald (Duke) Snider	3.00	1.50	.90
352	Ralph George Houk	.10	.05	.03
353	John Frederick Hiller	.10	.05	.03
354	Michael Stephen Lolich	.10	.05	.03
355	David Lawrence Lemancyzk	.10	.05	.03
356	Lerrin Harris LaGrow	.10	.05	.03
357	Fred Arroyo	.10	.05	.03
358	Joseph Howard Coleman	.10	.05	.03
359	Benjamin A. Oglivie	.10	.05	.03
360	Willie Wattison Horton	.10	.05	.03
361	John Clinton Knox	.10	.05	.03
362	Leon Kauffman Roberts	.10	.05	.03
363	Ronald LeFlore	.10	.05	.03
364	Gary Lynn Sutherland	.10	.05	.03
365	Daniel Thomas Meyer	.10	.05	.03
366	Aurelio Rodriguez	.10	.05	.03
367	Thomas Martin Veryzer	.10	.05	.03
368	Lavern Jack Pierce	.10	.05	.03
369	Eugene Richard Michael	.10	.05	.03
370	Robert (Billy) Baldwin	.10	.05	.03
371	William James Gates Brown	.10	.05	.03
372	Mitchell Jack (Mickey) Stanley	.10	.05	.03
373	Terryal Gene Humphrey	.10	.05	.03
374	Doyle Lafayette Alexander	.10	.05	.03
375	Miguel Angel (Mike) Cuellar	.10	.05	.03
376	Marcus Wayne Garland	.10	.05	.03
377	Ross Albert Grimsley III	.10	.05	.03
378	Grant Dwight Jackson	.10	.05	.03
379	Dyar K. Miller	.10	.05	.03
380	James Alvin Palmer	2.00	1.00	.60
381	Michael Augustine Torrez	.10	.05	.03
382	Michael Henry Willis	.10	.05	.03
383	David Edwin Duncan	.10	.05	.03
384	Elrod Jerome Hendricks	.10	.05	.03
385	James Neamon Hutto Jr.	.10	.05	.03
386	Robert Michael Bailor	.10	.05	.03
387	Douglas Vernon DeCinces	.10	.05	.03
388	Robert Anthony Grich	.10	.05	.03
389	Lee Andrew May	.10	.05	.03
390	Anthony Joseph Muser	.10	.05	.03
391	Timothy C. Nordbrook	.10	.05	.03
392	Brooks Calbert Robinson, Jr.	2.50	1.25	.70
393	Royle Stillman	.10	.05	.03
394	Don Edward Baylor	.10	.05	.03
395	Paul L.D. Blair	.10	.05	.03
396	Alonza Benjamin Bumbry	.10	.05	.03
397	Larry Duane Harlow	.10	.05	.03
398	Herman Thomas (Tommy) Davis, Jr.	.10	.05	.03
399	James Thomas Northrup	.10	.05	.03
400	Kenneth Wayne Singleton	.10	.05	.03
401	Thomas Michael Shopay	.10	.05	.03
402	Fredrick Michael Lynn	.75	.40	.25
403	Carlton Ernest Fisk	2.00	1.00	.60
404	Cecil Celester Cooper	.10	.05	.03
405	James Edward Rice	1.00	.50	.30
406	Juan Jose Beniquez	.10	.05	.03
407	Robert Dennis Doyle	.10	.05	.03
408	Dwight Michael Evans	.10	.05	.03
409	Carl Michael Yastrzemski	3.00	1.50	.90
410	Richard Paul Burleson	.10	.05	.03
411	Bernardo Carbo	.10	.05	.03
412	Douglas Lee Griffin, Jr.	.10	.05	.03
413	Americo P. Petrocelli	.10	.05	.03
414	Robert Edward Montgomery	.10	.05	.03
415	Timothy P. Blackwell	.10	.05	.03
416	Richard Alan Miller	.10	.05	.03
417	Darrell Dean Johnson	.10	.05	.03
418	Jim Scott Burton	.10	.05	.03
419	James Arthur Willoughby	.10	.05	.03
420	Rogelio (Roger) Moret	.10	.05	.03
421	William Francis Lee, III	.10	.05	.03
422	Richard Anthony Drago	.10	.05	.03
423	Diego Pablo Segui	.10	.05	.03
424	Luis Clemente Tiant	.10	.05	.03
425	James Augustus (Catfish) Hunter	1.50	.70	.45
426	Richard Clyde Sawyer	.10	.05	.03
427	Rudolph May Jr.	.10	.05	.03
428	Richard William Tidrow	.10	.05	.03
429	Albert Walter (Sparky) Lyle	.10	.05	.03
430	George Francis (Doc) Medich	.10	.05	.03
431	Patrick Edward Dobson, Jr.	.10	.05	.03
432	David Percy Pagan	.10	.05	.03
433	Thurman Lee Munson	2.00	1.00	.60
434	Carroll Christopher Chambliss	.10	.05	.03
435	Roy Hilton White	.10	.05	.03
436	Walter Allen Williams	.10	.05	.03
437	Graig Nettles	.10	.05	.03
438	John Rikard (Rick) Dempsey	.10	.05	.03
439	Bobby Lee Bonds	.25	.13	.08
440	Edward Martin Hermann (Herrmann)	.10	.05	.03
441	Santos Alomar	.10	.05	.03
442	Frederick Blair Stanley	.10	.05	.03
443	Terry Bertland Whitfield	.10	.05	.03
444	Richard Alan Bladt	.10	.05	.03
445	Louis Victor Piniella	.50	.25	.15
446	Richard Allen Coggins	.10	.05	.03
447	Edwin Albert Brinkman	.10	.05	.03
448	James Percy Mason	.10	.05	.03
449	Larry Murray	.10	.05	.03
450	Ronald Mark Blomberg	.10	.05	.03
451	Elliott Maddox	.10	.05	.03
452	Kerry Dineen	.10	.05	.03
453	Alfred Manuel (Billy) Martin	.50	.25	.15
454	Dave Bergman	.10	.05	.03
455	Otoniel Velez	.10	.05	.03
456	Joseph Walter Hoerner	.10	.05	.03
457	Frank Edwin (Tug) McGraw, Jr.	.10	.05	.03
458	Henry Eugene (Gene) Garber	.10	.05	.03
459	Steven Norman Carlton	2.00	1.00	.60
460	Larry Richard Christenson	.10	.05	.03
461	Thomas Gerald Underwood	.10	.05	.03
462	James Reynold Lonborg	.10	.05	.03
463	John William (Jay) Johnstone, Jr.	.10	.05	.03
464	Lawrence Robert Bowa	.10	.05	.03
465	David Cash, Jr.	.10	.05	.03
466	Ollie Lee Brown	.10	.05	.03
467	Gregory Michael Luzinski	.10	.05	.03
468	Johnny Lane Oates	.10	.05	.03
469	Michael Allen Anderson	.10	.05	.03
470	Michael Jack Schmidt	4.00	2.00	1.25
471	Robert Raymond Boone	.10	.05	.03
472	Thomas George Hutton	.10	.05	.03
473	Richard Anthony Allen	.50	.25	.15
474	Antonio Taylor	.10	.05	.03
475	Jerry Lindsey Martin	.10	.05	.03
476	Daniel Leonard Ozark	.10	.05	.03
477	Richard David Ruthven	.10	.05	.03
478	James Richard Todd, Jr.	.10	.05	.03
479	Paul Aaron Lindblad	.10	.05	.03
480	Roland Glen Fingers	1.50	.70	.45
481	Vida Blue, Jr.	.10	.05	.03
482	Kenneth Dale Holtzman	.10	.05	.03
483	Richard Allen Bosman	.10	.05	.03
484	Wilfred Charles (Sonny) Siebert	.10	.05	.03
485	William Glenn Abbott	.10	.05	.03
486	Stanley Raymond Bahnsen	.10	.05	.03
487	Michael Norris	.10	.05	.03
488	Alvin Ralph Dark	.10	.05	.03
489	Claudell Washington	.10	.05	.03
490	Joseph Oden Rudi	.10	.05	.03
491	William Alex North	.10	.05	.03
492	Dagoberto Blanco (Bert) Campaneris	.10	.05	.03
493	Fury Gene Tenace	.10	.05	.03
494	Reginald Martinez Jackson	4.00	2.00	1.25
495	Philip Mason Garner	.10	.05	.03
496	Billy Leo Williams	2.00	1.00	.60
497	Salvatore Leonard Bando	.10	.05	.03
498	James William Holt	.10	.05	.03
499	Teodoro Noel Martinez	.10	.05	.03
500	Raymond Earl Fosse	.10	.05	.03
501	Matthew Alexander	.10	.05	.03
502	Wallace Larry Haney	.10	.05	.03
503	Angel Luis Mangual	.10	.05	.03
504	Fred Ray Beene	.10	.05	.03
505	Thomas William Buskey	.10	.05	.03
506	Dennis Lee Eckersley	2.00	1.00	.60
507	Roric Edward Harrison	.10	.05	.03
508	Donald Harris Hood	.10	.05	.03
509	James Lester Kern	.10	.05	.03
510	David Eugene LaRoche	.10	.05	.03
511	Fred Ingels (Fritz) Peterson	.10	.05	.03
512	James Michael Strickland	.10	.05	.03
513	Michael Richard (Rick) Waits	.10	.05	.03
514	Alan Dean Ashby	.10	.05	.03
515	John Charles Ellis	.10	.05	.03
516	Rick Cerone	.10	.05	.03
517	David Gus (Buddy) Bell	.10	.05	.03
518	John Anthony Brohamer, Jr.	.10	.05	.03
519	Ricardo Adolfo Jacobo Carty	.10	.05	.03
520	Edward Carlton Crosby	.10	.05	.03
521	Frank Thomas Duffy	.10	.05	.03
522	Duane Eugene Kuiper (Photo actually Rick Manning.)	.10	.05	.03
523	Joseph Anthony Lis	.10	.05	.03
524	John Wesley (Boog) Powell	.50	.25	.15
525	Frank Robinson	2.50	1.25	.70
526	Oscar Charles Gamble	.10	.05	.03
527	George Andrew Hendrick	.10	.05	.03
528	John Lee Lowenstein	.10	.05	.03
529	Richard Eugene Manning (photo actually Duane Kuiper)	.10	.05	.03
530	Tommy Alexander Smith	.10	.05	.03
531	Leslie Charles (Charlie) Spikes	.10	.05	.03
532	Steve Jack Kline	.10	.05	.03
533	Edward Emil Kranepool	.10	.05	.03
534	Michael Vail	.10	.05	.03
535	Delbert Bernard Unser	.10	.05	.03
536	Felix Bernardo Martinez Millan	.10	.05	.03
537	Daniel Joseph (Rusty) Staub	.25	.13	.08
538	Jesus Maria Rojas Alou	.10	.05	.03
539	Ronald Wayne Garrett	.10	.05	.03
540	Michael Dwaine Phillips	.10	.05	.03
541	Joseph Paul Torre	.10	.05	.03
542	David Arthur Kingman	.10	.05	.03
543	Eugene Anthony Clines	.10	.05	.03
544	Jack Seale Heidemann	.10	.05	.03
545	Derrel McKinley (Bud) Harrelson	.10	.05	.03
546	John Hardin Stearns	.10	.05	.03
547	John David Milner	.10	.05	.03
548	Robert John Apodaca	.10	.05	.03
549	Claude Edward (Skip) Lockwood Jr.	.10	.05	.03
550	Kenneth George Sanders	.10	.05	.03
551	George Thomas (Tom) Seaver	3.00	1.50	.90
552	Ricky Alan Baldwin	.10	.05	.03
553	Jonathan Trumpbour Matlack	.10	.05	.03
554	Henry Gaylon Webb	.10	.05	.03
555	Randall Lee Tate	.10	.05	.03
556	Tom Edward Hall	.10	.05	.03
557	George Heard Stone Jr.	.10	.05	.03
558	Craig Steven Swan	.10	.05	.03
559	Gerald Allen Cram	.10	.05	.03
560	Roy J. Staiger	.10	.05	.03
561	Kenton C. Tekulve	.10	.05	.03
562	Jerry Reuss	.10	.05	.03
563	John R. Candelaria	.10	.05	.03
564	Lawrence C. Demery	.10	.05	.03
565	David John Giusti Jr.	.10	.05	.03
566	James Phillip Rooker	.10	.05	.03
567	Ramon Gonzalez Hernandez	.10	.05	.03
568	Bruce Eugene Kison	.10	.05	.03
569	Kenneth Alven Brett (Alvin)	.10	.05	.03
570	Robert Ralph Moose Jr.	.10	.05	.03
571	Manuel Jesus Sanguillen	.10	.05	.03
572	David Gene Parker	.10	.05	.03
573	Wilver Dornel Stargell	2.00	1.00	.60
574	Richard Walter Zisk	.10	.05	.03
575	Renaldo Antonio Stennett	.10	.05	.03
576	Albert Oliver Jr.	.25	.13	.08
577	William Henry Robinson Jr.	.10	.05	.03
578	Robert Eugene Robertson	.10	.05	.03
579	Richard Joseph Hebner	.10	.05	.03
580	Edgar Leon Kirkpatrick	.10	.05	.03
581	Don Robert (Duffy) Dyer	.10	.05	.03
582	Craig Reynolds	.10	.05	.03
583	Franklin Fabian Taveras	.10	.05	.03
584	William Larry Randolph	.10	.05	.03
585	Arthur H. Howe	.10	.05	.03
586	Daniel Edward Murtaugh	.10	.05	.03
587	Charles Richard (Rich) McKinney	.10	.05	.03
588	James Edward Goodson	.10	.05	.03
589	George Brett, Al Cowans/ Checklist	1.50	.70	.45
590	Keith Hernandez, Lou Brock/ Checklist	.15	.08	.05
591	Jerry Koosman, Duke Snider/ Checklist	.25	.13	.08
592	John Knox, Maury Wills/ Checklist	.10	.05	.03
593a	Catfish Hunter, Noland Ryan/ Checklist	4.00	2.00	1.25
593b	Catfish Hunter, Nolan Ryan/ Checklist	3.00	1.50	.90
594	Pee Wee Reese, Ralph Branca, Carl Erskine	1.00	.50	.30
595	Willie Mays, Herb Score/ Checklist	1.00	.50	.30
596	Larry Eugene Cox	.10	.05	.03
597	Eugene William Mauch	.10	.05	.03
598	William Frederick (Whitey) Wietelmann	.10	.05	.03
599	Wayne Kirby Simpson	.10	.05	.03
600	Melvin Erskine Thomason	.10	.05	.03
601	Issac Bernard (Ike) Hampton	.10	.05	.03
602	Kenneth S. Crosby	.10	.05	.03
603	Ralph Emanuel Rowe	.10	.05	.03
604	James Vernon Tyrone	.10	.05	.03
605	Michael Dennis Kelleher	.10	.05	.03
606	Mario Mendoza	.10	.05	.03
607	Michael George Rogodzinski	.10	.05	.03
608	Robert Collins Gallagher	.10	.05	.03
609	Jerry Martin Koosman	.10	.05	.03
610	Joseph Filmore Frazier	.10	.05	.03
611	Karl Kuehl	.10	.05	.03
612	Frank J. LaCorte	.10	.05	.03
613	Raymond Douglas Bare	.10	.05	.03
614	Billy Arnold Muffett	.10	.05	.03
615	William Harry Laxton	.10	.05	.03
616	Willie Howard Mays	5.00	2.50	1.50
617	Philip Joseph Cavaretta (Cavarretta)	.10	.05	.03
618	Theodore Bernard Kluszewski	.50	.25	.15
619	Elston Gene Howard	.10	.05	.03
620	Alexander Peter Grammas	.10	.05	.03
621	James Barton (Mickey) Vernon	.10	.05	.03
622	Richard Allan Sisler	.10	.05	.03
623	Harvey Haddix, Jr.	.10	.05	.03
624	Bobby Brooks Winkles	.10	.05	.03
625	John Michael Pesky	.10	.05	.03
626	James Houston Davenport	.10	.05	.03
627	David Allen Tomlin	.10	.05	.03
628	Roger Lee Craig	.10	.05	.03
629	John Joseph Amalfitano	.10	.05	.03
630	James Harrison Reese	.25	.13	.08

1975 SSPC Mets/Yankees

Team sets of the New York clubs were issued by SSPC bearing a 1975 copyright date and in the same "pure card" format as most of the company's other issues. The 2-1/2" x 3-1/2" cards have a posed color photo on front with a thin white border and no extraneous graphics - not even the player's name. Backs are printed in red and blue with personal data and a career summary, along with the player's full formal name. The checklist lists the player as he is best known. Issue price was $1.25 per team set.

		NM	EX	VG
	Complete Set (45):	15.00	7.50	4.50
	Common Player:	.25	.13	.08
	New York Mets Team Set:	9.00	4.50	2.75
1	John Milner	.25	.13	.08
2	Henry Webb	.25	.13	.08
3	Tom Hall	.25	.13	.08
4	Del Unser	.25	.13	.08
5	Wayne Garrett	.25	.13	.08
6	Jesus Alou	.25	.13	.08
7	Rusty Staub	.40	.20	.12
8	John Stearns	.25	.13	.08
9	Dave Kingman	.75	.40	.25
10	Ed Kranepool	.35	.20	.11
11	Cleon Jones	.40	.20	.12
12	Tom Seaver	4.00	2.00	1.25
13	George Stone	.25	.13	.08
14	Jerry Koosman	.35	.20	.11
15	Bob Apodaca	.25	.13	.08
16	Felix Millan	.25	.13	.08
17	Gene Clines	.25	.13	.08
18	Mike Phillips	.25	.13	.08
19	Yogi Berra	3.00	1.50	.90
20	Joe Torre	1.50	.70	.45
21	Jon Matlack	.25	.13	.08
22	Ricky Baldwin	.25	.13	.08
	New York Yankees Team Set:	9.00	4.50	2.75
1	Catfish Hunter	1.00	.50	.30
2	Bobby Bonds	.35	.20	.11
3	Ed Brinkman	.25	.13	.08
4	Ron Blomberg	.25	.13	.08
5	Thurman Munson	3.50	1.75	1.00
6	Roy White	.35	.20	.11
7	Larry Gura	.25	.13	.08
8	Ed Hermann	.25	.13	.08
9	Bill Virdon	.25	.13	.08
10	Elliott Maddox	.25	.13	.08
11	Lou Piniella	.50	.25	.15
12	Rick Dempsey	.25	.13	.08
13	Fred Stanley	.25	.13	.08
14	Chris Chambliss	.25	.13	.08
15	Doc Medich	.25	.13	.08
16	Pat Dobson	.25	.13	.08
17	Alex Johnson	.25	.13	.08
18	Jim Mason	.25	.13	.08
19	Sandy Alomar	.25	.13	.08
20	Graig Nettles	.50	.25	.15
21	Walt Williams	.25	.13	.08
22	Sparky Lyle	.35	.20	.11
23	Dick Tidrow	.25	.13	.08

1975 SSPC Puzzle Backs

A large black-and-white puzzle picture of Nolan Ryan and Catfish Hunter can be assembled with the backs of these cards. Fronts of the 3-9/16" x 4-1/4" cards have a color player pose with a white border. The player's name, position and team are printed at bottom. Fronts have a glossy surface. The SSPC identification only appears around the border of the puzzle. The unnumbered cards are checklisted here alphabetically. Issue price was $2.

		NM	EX	VG
	Complete Set, Uncut Sheet:	40.00	20.00	12.00
	Complete Set (24):	20.00	10.00	6.00
	Common Player:	.30	.15	.09
(1)	Hank Aaron	4.00	2.00	1.25
(2)	Johnny Bench	1.75	.90	.50
(3)	Bobby Bonds	.35	.20	.11
(4)	Jeff Burroughs	.30	.15	.09
(5)	Rod Carew	1.75	.90	.50
(6)	Dave Cash	.30	.15	.09
(7)	Cesar Cedeno	.30	.15	.09
(8)	Bucky Dent	.30	.15	.09
(9)	Rollie Fingers	1.25	.60	.40
(10)	Steve Garvey	1.00	.50	.30
(11)	John Grubb	.30	.15	.09
(12)	Reggie Jackson	2.00	1.00	.60
(13)	Jim Kaat	.30	.15	.09
(14)	Greg Luzinski	.30	.15	.09
(15)	Fred Lynn	.50	.25	.15
(16)	Bill Madlock	.30	.15	.09
(17)	Andy Messersmith	.30	.15	.09
(18)	Thurman Munson	1.50	.70	.45
(19)	Jim Palmer	1.25	.60	.40
(20)	Dave Parker	.30	.15	.09
(21)	Jim Rice	.50	.25	.15
(22)	Pete Rose	4.00	2.00	1.25
(23)	Tom Seaver	1.75	.90	.50
(24)	Chris Speier	.30	.15	.09

1975 SSPC Superstars

Nearly four dozen of the game's contemporary and former stars are featured in this set. Like other SSPC issues of 1975, fronts of the 2-1/2" x 3-1/2" cards have posed color photos with a white border. There are no other graphics, not even the player's name. The horizontal backs feature the player's full formal name (checklist here uses popular name) along with personal data, career summary and stats. Issue price was $4.

		NM	EX	VG
	Complete Set (42):	25.00	12.50	7.50
	Common Player:	.25	.13	.08
1	Wilbur Wood	.25	.13	.08
2	Johnny Sain	.25	.13	.08
3	Bill Melton	.25	.13	.08
4	Dick Allen	.50	.25	.15
5	Jim Palmer	1.00	.50	.30
6	Brooks Robinson	1.50	.70	.45
7	Tommy Davis	.25	.13	.08
8	Frank Robinson	1.50	.70	.45
9	Vada Pinson (Nolan Ryan in background of photo.)	1.00	.50	.30
10	Nolan Ryan	4.00	2.00	1.25
11	Reggie Jackson	3.00	1.50	.90
12	Vida Blue	.25	.13	.08
13	Sal Bando	.25	.13	.08
14	Bert Campaneris	.25	.13	.08
15	Tom Seaver	2.00	1.00	.60
16	Bud Harrelson	.25	.13	.08
17	Jerry Koosman	.25	.13	.08
18	Dave Nelson	.25	.13	.08
19	Ted Williams	3.50	1.75	1.00
20	Tony Oliva	.35	.20	.11
21	Mickey Lolich	.25	.13	.08
22	Amos Otis	.25	.13	.08
23	Carl Yastrzemski	2.00	1.00	.60
24	Mike Cuellar	.25	.13	.08
25	Doc Medich	.25	.13	.08
26	Cesar Cedeno	.25	.13	.08
27	Jeff Burroughs	.25	.13	.08
28	Ted Williams, Sparky Lyle	.75	.40	.25
29	Johnny Bench	2.00	1.00	.60
30	Gaylord Perry	1.00	.50	.30
31	John Mayberry	.25	.13	.08
32	Rod Carew	1.00	.50	.30
33	Whitey Ford	2.00	1.00	.60
34	Al Kaline	2.00	1.00	.60
35	Willie Mays	3.50	1.75	1.00
36	Warren Spahn	1.00	.50	.30
37	Mickey Mantle	5.00	2.50	1.50
38	Norm Cash	.35	.20	.11
39	Steve Busby	.25	.13	.08
40	Yogi Berra	2.00	1.00	.60
41	Harvey Kuenn	.25	.13	.08
42	Felipe Alou, Jesus Alou, Matty Alou	.60	.30	.20

1976 SSPC Yankees Old Timers Day

JOE DIMAGGIO

The Spring 1976 edition of "Collectors Quarterly" maga-zine contained a nine-card sheet of players who had appeared at an old timers' games in Yankees Stadium. The sheet could be cut into individual 2-1/2" x 3-1/2" cards with a color player photo and name on front. Backs form a black-and-white puz-zle picture of Joe DiMaggio, Mickey Mantle, Whitey Ford, and Billy Martin. Cards are checklisted here alphabetically.

		NM	EX	VG
	Complete Magazine:	25.00	12.50	7.50
	Complete Set, Singles:	15.00	7.50	4.50
	Common Player:	.35	.20	.11
(1)	Earl Averill	.35	.20	.11
(2)	Joe DiMaggio	6.00	3.00	1.75
(3)	Tommy Henrich	.35	.20	.11
(4)	Billy Herman	.35	.20	.11
(5)	Monte Irvin	.35	.20	.11
(6)	Jim Konstanty	.35	.20	.11
(7)	Mickey Mantle	7.50	3.75	2.25
(8)	Pee Wee Reese	3.00	1.50	.90
(9)	Bobby Thompson (Thomson)	.50	.25	.15

1976 SSPC 1887 World Series

The history of the 1887 "World Series" between the Detroit Wolverines of the National League and the St. Louis Browns of the American Association is told on the backs of this collector's issue. The 2-1/2" x 3-1/2" cards were printed on a pair of uncut sheets inserted in the Fall 1976 issue of "Col-lectors Quarterly" magazine. Fronts of the cards reproduce in full color the Scrapps tobacco die-cut cards originally issued in 1888. Backs recount the individual players' performances in the series as well as giving a career summary; they are printed in red and black. Detroit won the Series, a best-of-15 contest.

		NM	EX	VG
	Complete Magazine:	15.00	7.50	4.50
	Complete Set, Singles:	12.00	6.00	3.50
	Common Player:	.75	.40	.25
1	Bob Caruthers	.75	.40	.25
2	David Foutz	.75	.40	.25
3	W.A. Latham	.75	.40	.25
4	Charles H. Getzin (Getzien)	.75	.40	.25
5	J.C. Rowe	.75	.40	.25
6	Fred Dunlap	.75	.40	.25
7	James O'Neill	.75	.40	.25
8	Curtis Welch	.75	.40	.25
9	William Gleason	.75	.40	.25
10	Sam Thompson	.75	.40	.25
11	Ned Hanlon	.75	.40	.25
12	Dan Brothers (Brouthers)	.75	.40	.25
13	Albert Bushong	.75	.40	.25
14	Charles Comiskey	.75	.40	.25
15	Wm. Robinson	.75	.40	.25
16	Charles Bennett	.75	.40	.25
17	Hardy Richardson	.75	.40	.25
18	Deacon White	.75	.40	.25

1976 SSPC 1963 New York Mets

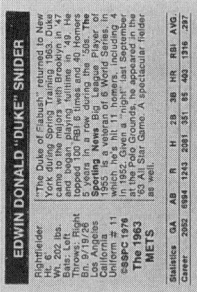

Issued in the Summer 1976 issue of "Collectors Quar-terly" magazine as a two-page uncut sheet, this 18-card issue features the 1963 Mets. Like contemporary collectors' issues from SSPC, the cards feature white-bordered color photos on front with no other graphics or player identification. Backs are printed in black-and-white, contain player biographical data, a career summary and uniform number, by which the checklist is arranged. Size is standard 2-1/2" x 3-1/2".

		NM	EX	VG
	Complete Magazine:	25.00	12.50	7.50
	Complete Set, Singles (18):	15.00	7.50	4.50
	Common Player:	1.00	.50	.30
1	Duke Carmel	1.00	.50	.30
5	Norman Burt Sherry	1.00	.50	.30
7	Casey Stengel	5.00	2.50	1.50
9	Jim Hickman	1.00	.50	.30
10	Rod Kanehl	1.00	.50	.30
11	Duke Snider	7.50	3.75	2.25
12	Jesse Gonder	1.00	.50	.30

		NM	EX	VG
16	Dick Smith	1.00	.50	.30
17	Clarence Coleman	1.00	.50	.30
18	Pumpsie Green	1.00	.50	.30
23	Joe Christopher	1.00	.50	.30
36	Tracy Stallard	1.00	.50	.30
39	Steve Dillon	1.00	.50	.30
40	Rich Moran	1.00	.50	.30
41	Grover Powell	1.00	.50	.30
43	Ted Schreiber	1.00	.50	.30
53	Ernest White	1.00	.50	.30
56	Ed Bauta	1.00	.50	.30

1978 SSPC All Star Gallery

A series of team "Photo Fact Cards" was produced by Sports Stars Publishing Co., for insertion into its 48-page "All Star Gallery" magazine, sold for $2. Fully licensed by MLB and the Players Union, the 27 cards in each team set are printed on a triple-fold 24" x 10-7/8" cardboard sheet stapled into the center of the magazine. Cards are not perforated, though the back of each nine-card panel has dotted lines to guide the cutting of 2-1/2" x 3-1/2" single cards from the sheet. Fronts are full-color poses with no extraneous graphics. Backs are in black-and-white with a few vital data, a career summary, uniform number and a card number from within the overall issue of 270. Only eight teams are represented in the All-Star Gallery magazine series. The Yankees (#001-027) and Phillies cards (#028-054) issued with other magazines that year may be considered part of the All-Star Gallery issue.

		NM	EX	VG
	Complete Set, Magazines (8):	135.00	65.00	40.00
	Complete Set, Singles (216):	125.00	60.00	35.00
	Common Player:	.50	.25	.15
	Los Angeles Dodgers Magazine:	15.00	7.50	4.50
0055	Burt Hooton	.50	.25	.15
0056	Bill Russell	.50	.25	.15
0057	Dusty Baker	.60	.30	.20
0058	Reggie Smith	.50	.25	.15
0059	Dick Rhoden	.50	.25	.15
0060	Jerry Grote	.50	.25	.15
0061	Bill Butler	.50	.25	.15
0062	Ron Cey	.50	.25	.15
0063	Ron Cey	.50	.25	.15
0064	Ted Martinez	.50	.25	.15
0065	Ed Goodson	.50	.25	.15
0066	Vic Davalillo	.50	.25	.15
0067	Davey Lopes	.50	.25	.15
0068	Terry Forster	.50	.25	.15
0069	Lee Lacy	.50	.25	.15
0070	Mike Garman	.50	.25	.15
0071	Steve Garvey	1.50	.70	.45
0072	Johnny Oates	.50	.25	.15
0073	Steve Yeager	.50	.25	.15
0074	Rafael Landestoy	.50	.25	.15
0075	Tommy John	.60	.30	.20
0076	Glenn Burke	.50	.25	.15
0077	Rick Monday	.50	.25	.15
0078	Doug Rau	.50	.25	.15
0079	Manny Mota	.50	.25	.15
0080	Don Sutton	2.00	1.00	.60
0081	Charlie Hough	.50	.25	.15
	Texas Rangers Magazine:	12.50	6.25	3.75
0082	Mike Hargrove	.50	.25	.15
0083	Jim Sundberg	.50	.25	.15
0084	Fergie Jenkins	2.00	1.00	.60
0085	Paul Lindblad	.50	.25	.15
0086	Sandy Alomar	.50	.25	.15
0087	John Lowenstein	.50	.25	.15
0088	Claudell Washington	.50	.25	.15
0089	Toby Harrah	.50	.25	.15
0090	Jim Umbarger	.50	.25	.15
0091	Len Barker	.50	.25	.15
0092	Dave May	.50	.25	.15
0093	Kurt Bevacqua	.50	.25	.15
0094	Jim Mason	.50	.25	.15
0095	Bump Wills	.50	.25	.15
0096	Dock Ellis	.50	.25	.15
0097	Bill Fahey	.50	.25	.15
0098	Richie Zisk	.50	.25	.15
0099	Jon Matlack	.50	.25	.15
0100	John Ellis	.50	.25	.15
0101	Bert Campaneris	.50	.25	.15
0102	Doc Medich	.50	.25	.15
0103	Juan Beniquez	.50	.25	.15
0104	Bill Hunter	.50	.25	.15
0105	Doyle Alexander	.50	.25	.15
0106	Roger Moret	.50	.25	.15
0107	Mike Jorgensen	.50	.25	.15
0108	Al Oliver	.60	.30	.20
	Cincinnati Reds Magazine:	15.00	7.50	4.50
0109	Fred Norman	.50	.25	.15
0110	Ray Knight	.50	.25	.15
0111	Pedro Borbon	.50	.25	.15
0112	Bill Bonham	.50	.25	.15

0113	George Foster	.60	.30	.20
0114	Doug Bair	.50	.25	.15
0115	Cesar Geronimo	.50	.25	.15
0116	Tom Seaver	3.50	1.75	1.00
0117	Mario Soto	.50	.25	.15
0118	Ken Griffey	.50	.25	.15
0119	Mike Lum	.50	.25	.15
0120	Tom Hume	.50	.25	.15
0121	Joe Morgan	2.50	1.25	.70
0122	Manny Sarmiento	.50	.25	.15
0123	Dan Driessen	.50	.25	.15
0124	Ed Armbrister	.50	.25	.15
0125	John Summers	.50	.25	.15
0126	Fred Auerbach	.50	.25	.15
0127	Doug Capilla	.50	.25	.15
0128	Johnny Bench	3.50	1.75	1.00
0129	Sparky Anderson	1.50	.70	.45
0130	Raul Ferreyra	.50	.25	.15
0131	Dale Murray	.50	.25	.15
0132	Pete Rose	7.50	3.75	2.25
0133	Dave Concepcion	.50	.25	.15
0134	Junior Kennedy	.50	.25	.15
0135	Dave Collins	.50	.25	.15
	Chicago White Sox Magazine:	12.50	6.25	3.75
0136	Mike Eden	.50	.25	.15
0137	Lamar Johnson	.50	.25	.15
0138	Ron Schueler	.50	.25	.15
0139	Bob Lemon	.75	.40	.25
0140	Thad Bosley	.50	.25	.15
0141	Bobby Bonds	.60	.30	.20
0142	Wilbur Wood	.50	.25	.15
0143	Jorge Orta	.50	.25	.15
0144	Francisco Barrios	.50	.25	.15
0145	Greg Pryor	.50	.25	.15
0146	Chet Lemon	.50	.25	.15
0147	Mike Squires	.50	.25	.15
0148	Eric Soderholm	.50	.25	.15
0149	Reggie Sanders	.50	.25	.15
0150	Kevin Bell	.50	.25	.15
0151	Alan Bannister	.50	.25	.15
0152	Henry Cruz	.50	.25	.15
0153	Larry Doby	2.00	1.00	.60
0154	Don Kessinger	.50	.25	.15
0155	Ralph Garr	.50	.25	.15
0156	Bill Nahorodny	.50	.25	.15
0157	Ron Blomberg	.50	.25	.15
0158	Bob Molinaro	.50	.25	.15
0159	Junior Moore	.50	.25	.15
0160	Minnie Minoso	1.50	.70	.45
0161	Lerrin LaGrow	.50	.25	.15
0162	Wayne Nordhagen	.50	.25	.15
	Boston Red Sox Magazine:	20.00	10.00	6.00
0163	Ramon Aviles	.50	.25	.15
0164	Bob Stanley	.50	.25	.15
0165	Reggie Cleveland	.50	.25	.15
0166	John Brohamer	.50	.25	.15
0167	Bill Lee	.50	.25	.15
0168	Jim Burton	.50	.25	.15
0169	Bill Campbell	.50	.25	.15
0170	Mike Torrez	.50	.25	.15
0171	Dick Drago	.50	.25	.15
0172	Butch Hobson	.50	.25	.15
0173	Bob Bailey	.50	.25	.15
0174	Fred Lynn	.50	.25	.15
0175	Rick Burleson	.50	.25	.15
0176	Luis Tiant	.50	.25	.15
0177	Ted Williams	6.00	3.00	1.75
0178	Dennis Eckersley	2.00	1.00	.60
0179	Don Zimmer	.50	.25	.15
0180	Carlton Fisk	2.50	1.25	.70
0181	Dwight Evans	.50	.25	.15
0182	Fred Kendall	.50	.25	.15
0183	George Scott	.50	.25	.15
0184	Frank Duffy	.50	.25	.15
0185	Bernie Carbo	.50	.25	.15
0186	Jerry Remy	.50	.25	.15
0187	Carl Yastrzemski	4.00	2.00	1.25
0188	Allen Ripley	.50	.25	.15
0189	Jim Rice	.90	.45	.25
	California Angels Magazine:	20.00	10.00	6.00
0190	Ken Landreaux	.50	.25	.15
0191	Paul Hartzell	.50	.25	.15
0192	Ken Brett	.50	.25	.15
0193	Dave Garcia	.50	.25	.15
0194	Bobby Grich	.50	.25	.15
0195	Lyman Bostock	.50	.25	.15
0196	Isaac Hampton	.50	.25	.15
0197	Dave LaRoche	.50	.25	.15
0198	Dave Chalk	.50	.25	.15
0199	Rick Miller	.50	.25	.15
0200	Floyd Rayford	.50	.25	.15
0201	Willie Aikens	.50	.25	.15
0202	Balor Moore	.50	.25	.15
0203	Nolan Ryan	10.00	5.00	3.00
0204	Dan Goodwin	.50	.25	.15
0205	Ron Fairly	.50	.25	.15
0206	Dyar Miller	.50	.25	.15
0207	Carney Lansford	.50	.25	.15
0208	Don Baylor	.60	.30	.20
0209	Gil Flores	.50	.25	.15
0210	Terry Humphrey	.50	.25	.15
0211	Frank Tanana	.50	.25	.15
0212	Chris Knapp	.50	.25	.15
0213	Ron Jackson	.50	.25	.15
0214	Joe Rudi	.50	.25	.15
0215	Tony Solaita	.50	.25	.15
0216	Steve Mulliniks	.50	.25	.15
	Kansas City Royals Magazine:	20.00	10.00	6.00
0217	George Brett	6.00	3.00	1.75
0218	Doug Bird	.50	.25	.15
0219	Hal McRae	.50	.25	.15
0220	Dennis Leonard	.50	.25	.15
0221	Darrell Porter	.50	.25	.15
0222	Randy McGilberry	.50	.25	.15
0223	Pete LaCock	.50	.25	.15
0224	Whitey Herzog	.50	.25	.15

0225	Andy Hassler	.50	.25	.15
0226	Joe Lahoud	.50	.25	.15
0227	Amos Otis	.50	.25	.15
0228	Al Hrabosky	.50	.25	.15
0229	Clint Hurdle	.50	.25	.15
0230	Paul Splittorff	.50	.25	.15
0231	Marty Pattin	.50	.25	.15
0232	Frank White	.50	.25	.15
0233	John Wathan	.50	.25	.15
0234	Freddie Patek	.50	.25	.15
0235	Rich Gale	.50	.25	.15
0236	U.L. Washington	.50	.25	.15
0237	Larry Gura	.50	.25	.15
0238	Jim Colburn	.50	.25	.15
0239	Tom Poquette	.50	.25	.15
0240	Al Cowens	.50	.25	.15
0241	Willie Wilson	.50	.25	.15
0242	Steve Mingori	.50	.25	.15
0243	Jerry Terrell	.50	.25	.15
	Chicago Cubs Magazine:	12.50	6.25	3.75
0244	Larry Biittner	.50	.25	.15
0245	Rick Reuschel	.50	.25	.15
0246	Dave Rader	.50	.25	.15
0247	Paul Reuschel	.50	.25	.15
0248	Hector Cruz	.50	.25	.15
0249	Woody Fryman	.50	.25	.15
0250	Steve Ontiveros	.50	.25	.15
0251	Mike Gordon	.50	.25	.15
0252	Dave Kingman	.50	.25	.15
0253	Gene Clines	.50	.25	.15
0254	Bruce Sutter	2.00	1.00	.60
0255	Guillermo Hernandez	.50	.25	.15
0256	Ivan DeJesus	.50	.25	.15
0257	Greg Gross	.50	.25	.15
0258	Larry Cox	.50	.25	.15
0259	Joe Wallis	.50	.25	.15
0260	Dennis Lamp	.50	.25	.15
0261	Ray Burris	.50	.25	.15
0262	Bill Caudill	.50	.25	.15
0263	Donnie Moore	.50	.25	.15
0264	Bill Buckner	.60	.30	.20
0265	Bobby Murcer	.60	.30	.20
0266	Dave Roberts	.50	.25	.15
0267	Mike Krukow	.50	.25	.15
0268	Herman Franks	.50	.25	.15
0269	Mike Kelleher	.50	.25	.15
0270	Rudy Meoli	.50	.25	.15

1978 SSPC Baseball the Phillies Way

This team set was produced on a tri-fold insert in an SSPC magazine titled, "Baseball the Phillies Way." The magazine offered playing tips. Cards are in the contemporary SSPC format of a posed front photo with a white border and no other graphics. Backs are printed in red, white and black with player ID, career data and card numbers between 0028-0054, continuing the sequence begun with the Yankees yearbook team set which continues with the All-Star Gallery set. Cards could be cut from the sheets into 2-1/2" x 3-1/2" singles.

		NM	EX	VG
	Complete Magazine:	15.00	7.50	4.50
	Complete Set, Singles (27):	12.00	6.00	3.50
	Common Player:	.50	.25	.15
0028	Garry Maddox	.50	.25	.15
0029	Steve Carlton	2.50	1.25	.70
0030	Ron Reed	.50	.25	.15
0031	Greg Luzinski	.50	.25	.15
0032	Bobby Wine	.50	.25	.15
0033	Bob Boone	1.50	.70	.45
0034	Carroll Beringer	.50	.25	.15
0035	Dick Hebner	.50	.25	.15
0036	Ray Ripplemeyer	.50	.25	.15
0037	Tony Harmon	.50	.25	.15
0038	Gene Garber	.50	.25	.15
0039	Ted Sizemore	.50	.25	.15
0040	Barry Foote	.50	.25	.15
0041	Tony Taylor	.50	.25	.15
0042	Tug McGraw	.75	.40	.25
0043	Jay Johnstone	.65	.35	.20
0044	Randy Lerch	.50	.25	.15
0045	Billy DeMars	.50	.25	.15
0046	Mike Schmidt	5.00	2.50	1.50
0047	Larry Christenson	.50	.25	.15
0048	Tim McCarver	1.00	.50	.30
0049	Larry Bowa	.65	.35	.20
0050	Danny Ozark	.50	.25	.15
0051	Jerry Martin	.50	.25	.15
0052	Jim Lonborg	.50	.25	.15
0053	Bake McBride	.50	.25	.15
0054	Warren Brusstar	.50	.25	.15

1978 SSPC Yankees Yearbook

This team set was printed on a tri-fold insert found both in the 1978 Yankees yearbook and a magazine titled "Diary of a Champion Yankee," produced by SSPC. The nine cards on each sheet could be cut apart into 2-1/2" x 3-1/2" singles.

Cards follow the basic SSPC format of a posed color photo on front with a white border and no graphic elements. Backs have player identification, career summary and "CHAMPIONSHIP SEASON" highlights, printed in black and blue on white. Cards are numbered from 0001-0027, and may be considered part of the larger All-Star Gallery issue.

		NM	EX	VG
Complete Magazine:		12.50	6.25	3.75
Complete Set, Singles (27):		10.00	5.00	3.00
Common Player:		.50	.25	.15
0001	Thurman Munson	3.00	1.50	.90
0002	Cliff Johnson	.50	.25	.15
0003	Lou Piniella	.75	.40	.25
0004	Dell Alston	.50	.25	.15
0005	Yankee Stadium	1.00	.50	.30
0006	Ken Holtzman	.50	.25	.15
0007	Chris Chambliss	.50	.25	.15
0008	Roy White	.60	.30	.20
0009	Ed Figueroa	.50	.25	.15
0010	Dick Tidrow	.50	.25	.15
0011	Sparky Lyle	.60	.30	.20
0012	Fred Stanley	.50	.25	.15
0013	Mickey Rivers	.50	.25	.15
0014	Billy Martin	.75	.40	.25
0015	George Zeber	.50	.25	.15
0016	Ken Clay	.50	.25	.15
0017	Ron Guidry	.75	.40	.25
0018	Don Gullett	.50	.25	.15
0019	Fran Healy	.50	.25	.15
0020	Paul Blair	.50	.25	.15
0021	Mickey Klutts	.50	.25	.15
0022	Yankee team	.50	.25	.15
0023	Catfish Hunter	1.50	.70	.45
0024	Bucky Dent	.75	.40	.25
0025	Graig Nettles	.75	.40	.25
0026	Reggie Jackson	3.00	1.50	.90
0027	Willie Randolph	.60	.30	.20

1889 "The Stage" Stars of the Diamond

Titled "Stars of the Diamond" and issued weekly between May 25-Aug. 31, 1889, these numbered supplements were printed in "The Stage" newspaper, a Philadelphia-based publication. Two types of supplements are found, those picturing New York players in uniforms (from Joseph Hall photos), and those picturing members of the Philadelphia National League and American Association teams in street clothes. The black-and-white portraits are printed in a 9" x 12" format on newsprint, making surviving examples very rare today.

		NM	EX	VG
Common Player:		250.00	125.00	75.00
1	Charles Buffington	250.00	125.00	75.00
2	John Clements	250.00	125.00	75.00
3	Harry D. Stovey	250.00	125.00	75.00
4	"Gus" Weyhing	250.00	125.00	75.00
5	L.M. Cross	250.00	125.00	75.00
6	Edward Seward	250.00	125.00	75.00
7	Wm. Robinson (Wilbert)	375.00	185.00	110.00
8	Denny Lyons	375.00	185.00	110.00
9	A.B. Sanders	250.00	125.00	75.00
10	William Schriver	250.00	125.00	75.00
11	Daniel M. Casey	250.00	125.00	75.00
12	"Tim" Keefe	375.00	185.00	110.00
13	"Buck" Ewing	375.00	185.00	110.00
14	John Ward	375.00	185.00	110.00

1953 Stahl-Meyer Franks

These nine cards, issued in packages of hot dogs by a New York area meat company, feature three players from each of the New York teams of the day - Dodgers Giants and Yankees. Cards in the set measure 3-1/4" x 4-1/2". The card fronts in this unnumbered set feature color photos with player name and facsimile autograph. The backs list both biographical and statistical information on half the card and a ticket offer

promotion on the other half. The card corners are cut diagonally, although some cards (apparently cut from sheets) with square corners have been seen. Cards are white-bordered.

		NM	EX	VG
Complete Set (9):		20,000	9,000	4,000
Common Player:		500.00	225.00	100.00
(1)	Hank Bauer	550.00	245.00	110.00
(2)	Roy Campanella	2,000	900.00	400.00
(3)	Gil Hodges	1,250	560.00	250.00
(4)	Monte Irvin	750.00	335.00	150.00
(5)	Whitey Lockman	500.00	225.00	100.00
(6)	Mickey Mantle	13,500	6,100	2,750
(7)	Phil Rizzuto	1,250	560.00	250.00
(8)	Duke Snider	2,000	900.00	400.00
(9)	Bobby Thomson	650.00	290.00	130.00

1954 Stahl-Meyer Franks

 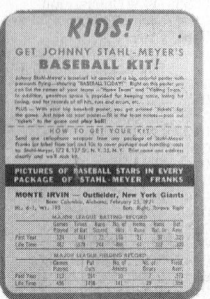

The 1954 set of Stahl-Meyer Franks was increased to 12 cards which retained the 3-1/4" x 4-1/2" size. The most prominent addition to the '54 set was New York Giants slugger Willie Mays. The card fronts are identical in format to the previous year's set. However, the backs are different as they are designed on a vertical format. The backs also contain an advertisement for a "Johnny Stahl-Meyer Baseball Kit." The cards in the set are unnumbered.

		NM	EX	VG
Complete Set (12):		30,000	13,500	6,000
Common Player:		650.00	290.00	130.00
(1)	Hank Bauer	750.00	335.00	150.00
(2)	Carl Erskine	750.00	335.00	150.00
(3)	Gil Hodges	2,000	900.00	400.00
(4)	Monte Irvin	1,000	450.00	200.00
(5)	Whitey Lockman	650.00	290.00	130.00
(6)	Gil McDougald	750.00	335.00	150.00
(7)	Mickey Mantle	12,000	5,400	2,400
(8)	Willie Mays	8,500	3,825	1,700
(9)	Don Mueller	650.00	290.00	130.00
(10)	Don Newcombe	750.00	335.00	150.00
(11)	Phil Rizzuto	2,000	900.00	400.00
(12)	Duke Snider	2,000	900.00	400.00

1955 Stahl-Meyer Franks

 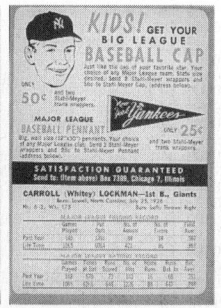

Eleven of the 12 players in the 1955 set are the same as those featured in 1954. The exception is the New York Giants Dusty Rhodes, who replaced Willie Mays on the 3-1/4" x 4-1/2" cards. The card fronts are again full-color photos bordered in yellow with diagonal corners, and four players from each of the three New York teams are featured. The backs offer a new promotion, with a drawing of Mickey Mantle and advertisements selling pennants and caps. Player statistics are still included on the vertical card backs. The cards in the set are unnumbered.

		NM	EX	VG
Complete Set (12):		20,000	9,000	4,000
Common Player:		500.00	225.00	100.00
(1)	Hank Bauer	600.00	275.00	125.00
(2)	Carl Erskine	600.00	275.00	125.00
(3)	Gil Hodges	1,500	675.00	300.00
(4)	Monte Irvin	800.00	360.00	160.00
(5)	Whitey Lockman	500.00	225.00	100.00
(6)	Mickey Mantle	12,000	5,400	2,400
(7)	Gil McDougald	600.00	275.00	125.00
(8)	Don Mueller	500.00	225.00	100.00
(9)	Don Newcombe	500.00	225.00	100.00
(10)	Jim Rhodes	500.00	225.00	100.00
(11)	Phil Rizzuto	1,500	675.00	300.00
(12)	Duke Snider	1,500	675.00	300.00

1916 Standard Biscuit (D350-1)

 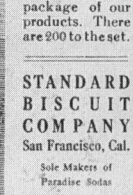

The range of cards in this issue is uncertain as examples can be found corresponding to the checklists of both of the 1916 sets known as M101-5 and M101-4 Blank Backs. Standard Biscuit cards in this format are also known that correspond to neither M101-5 nor M101-4. The approximately 1-5/8" x 3" black-and-white cards usually command a modest premium from collectors seeking to enhance a type collection or superstar collection. A trial checklist is begun herewith. Since D350-1 can be found corresponding to both M101-4 and M101-5, they have two different numerical checklists and should be split into D350-1a & D350-1b.

		NM	EX	VG
Common Player:		90.00	45.00	30.00
1	Babe Adams	90.00	45.00	30.00
3	Ed Ainsmith	90.00	45.00	30.00
6	Jimmy Archer	90.00	45.00	30.00
12	Beals Becker	90.00	45.00	30.00
13	Joe Benz	90.00	45.00	30.00
14	Bob Bescher	90.00	45.00	30.00
15	Al Betzel	90.00	45.00	30.00
18	Eddie Burns	90.00	45.00	30.00
27	George Chalmers	90.00	45.00	30.00
37	Joe Connolly	90.00	45.00	30.00
39	Harry Coveleskie (Coveleski)	90.00	45.00	30.00
42	Sam Crawford	400.00	200.00	130.00
48	William Doak	90.00	45.00	30.00
50	Charles Dooin	90.00	45.00	30.00
60	Max Flack	90.00	45.00	30.00
61	Art Fletcher	90.00	45.00	30.00
63	Jacques Fournier	90.00	45.00	30.00
64	"Chic" Gandil	900.00	450.00	300.00
66	Joe Gedeon	90.00	45.00	30.00
68	George Gibson	90.00	45.00	30.00
69	Wilbur Good	90.00	45.00	30.00
71	John Graney	90.00	45.00	30.00
72	Tom Griffith	90.00	45.00	30.00
73	Heinie Groh	90.00	45.00	30.00
75	Bob Harmon	90.00	45.00	30.00
77	Claude Hendrix	90.00	45.00	30.00
79	John Henry	90.00	45.00	30.00
80	Buck Herzog	90.00	45.00	30.00
82	Dick Hoblitzell	90.00	45.00	30.00
84	Ivan Howard	90.00	45.00	30.00
87	Joe Jackson	10,000	5,000	3,300
89	Hugh Jennings	400.00	200.00	130.00
131	Les Nunamaker	90.00	45.00	30.00
137	E.J. Pfeffer	90.00	45.00	30.00
164	Ernie Shore	90.00	45.00	30.00
172a	Milton Stock	90.00	45.00	30.00
172b	Billy Sullivan	90.00	45.00	30.00
176	Jim Thorpe	17,500	8,750	5,775
184	Honus Wagner	2,700	1,350	510.00
186	Bobby Wallace	600.00	300.00	200.00
191	Fred Williams	90.00	45.00	30.00
195	Joe Wood	350.00	175.00	115.00
196	Joe Wood	350.00	175.00	115.00
199	Heiny Zimmerman	90.00	45.00	30.00

1917 Standard Biscuit (D350-2)

 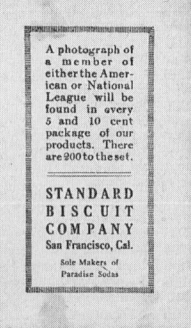

The 200 cards in this set are more commonly found with the advertising of Collins-McCarthy Candy Co. on the back. The cards measure about 2" x 3-1/4" and are printed in black-

and-white. Though the Standard Biscuit cards are scarcer than the Collins-McCarthy version, collectors do not attach much premium to them.

		NM	EX	VG
	Complete Set (200):	70,000	35,000	21,000
	Common Player:	150.00	75.00	45.00
1	Sam Agnew	150.00	75.00	45.00
2	Grover Alexander	1,000	700.00	300.00
3	W.S. Alexander (W.E.)	150.00	75.00	45.00
4	Leon Ames	150.00	75.00	45.00
5	Fred Anderson	150.00	75.00	45.00
6	Ed Appleton	150.00	75.00	45.00
7	Jimmy Archer	150.00	75.00	45.00
8	Jimmy Austin	150.00	75.00	45.00
9	Jim Bagby	150.00	75.00	45.00
10	H.D. Baird	150.00	75.00	45.00
11	J. Franklin Baker	1,000	700.00	300.00
12	Dave Bancroft	1,000	700.00	300.00
13	Jack Barry	150.00	75.00	45.00
14	Joe Benz	150.00	75.00	45.00
15	Al Betzel	150.00	75.00	45.00
16	Ping Bodie	150.00	75.00	45.00
17	Joe Boehling	150.00	75.00	45.00
18	Eddie Burns	150.00	75.00	45.00
19	George Burns	150.00	75.00	45.00
20	Geo. J. Burns	150.00	75.00	45.00
21	Joe Bush	150.00	75.00	45.00
22	Owen Bush	150.00	75.00	45.00
23	Bobby Byrne	150.00	75.00	45.00
24	Forrest Cady	150.00	75.00	45.00
25	Max Carey	1,000	700.00	300.00
26	Ray Chapman	200.00	100.00	60.00
27	Larry Cheney	150.00	75.00	45.00
28	Eddie Cicotte	1,000	700.00	300.00
29	Tom Clarke	150.00	75.00	45.00
30	Ty Cobb	5,000	3,000	2,000
31	Eddie Collins	1,000	700.00	300.00
32	"Shauno" Collins (Shano)	150.00	75.00	45.00
33	Fred Coumbe	150.00	75.00	45.00
34	Harry Coveleskie (Coveleski)	150.00	75.00	45.00
35	Gavvy Cravath	150.00	75.00	45.00
36	Sam Crawford	1,000	700.00	300.00
37	Geo. Cutshaw	150.00	75.00	45.00
38	Jake Daubert	150.00	75.00	45.00
39	Geo. Dauss	150.00	75.00	45.00
40	Charles Deal	150.00	75.00	45.00
41	"Wheezer" Dell	150.00	75.00	45.00
42	William Doak	150.00	75.00	45.00
43	Bill Donovan	150.00	75.00	45.00
44	Larry Doyle	150.00	75.00	45.00
45	Johnny Evers	1,000	700.00	300.00
46	Urban Faber	1,000	700.00	300.00
47	"Hap" Felsch	1,000	700.00	300.00
48	Bill Fischer	150.00	75.00	45.00
49	Ray Fisher	150.00	75.00	45.00
50	Art Fletcher	150.00	75.00	45.00
51	Eddie Foster	150.00	75.00	45.00
52	Jacques Fournier	150.00	75.00	45.00
53	Del Gainer (Gainor)	150.00	75.00	45.00
54	Bert Gallia	150.00	75.00	45.00
55	"Chic" Gandil (Chick)	1,000	700.00	300.00
56	Larry Gardner	150.00	75.00	45.00
57	Joe Gedeon	150.00	75.00	45.00
58	Gus Getz	150.00	75.00	45.00
59	Frank Gilhooley	150.00	75.00	45.00
60	Wm. Gleason	150.00	75.00	45.00
61	M.A. Gonzales (Gonzalez)	165.00	80.00	50.00
62	Hank Gowdy	150.00	75.00	45.00
63	John Graney	150.00	75.00	45.00
64	Tom Griffith	150.00	75.00	45.00
65	Heinie Groh	150.00	75.00	45.00
66	Bob Groom	150.00	75.00	45.00
67	Louis Guisto	150.00	75.00	45.00
68	Earl Hamilton	150.00	75.00	45.00
69	Harry Harper	150.00	75.00	45.00
70	Grover Hartley	150.00	75.00	45.00
71	Harry Heilmann	5,000	4,000	2,000
72	Claude Hendrix	150.00	75.00	45.00
73	Olaf Henriksen	150.00	75.00	45.00
74	John Henry	150.00	75.00	45.00
75	"Buck" Herzog	150.00	75.00	45.00
76	Hugh High	150.00	75.00	45.00
77	Dick Hoblitzell	150.00	75.00	45.00
78	Walter Holke	150.00	75.00	45.00
79	Harry Hooper	1,000	700.00	300.00
80	Rogers Hornsby	20,000	12,500	7,000
81	Ivan Howard	150.00	75.00	45.00
82	Joe Jackson	16,500	8,500	5,000
83	Harold Janvrin	150.00	75.00	45.00
84	William James	150.00	75.00	45.00
85	C. Jamieson	150.00	75.00	45.00
86	Hugh Jennings	1,000	700.00	300.00
87	Walter Johnson	3,000	2,000	1,000
88	James Johnston	150.00	75.00	45.00
89	Fielder Jones	150.00	75.00	45.00
90	Joe Judge	150.00	75.00	45.00
91	Hans Lobert	150.00	75.00	45.00
92	Benny Kauff	150.00	75.00	45.00
93	Wm. Killefer Jr.	150.00	75.00	45.00
94	Ed. Konetchy	150.00	75.00	45.00
95	John Lavan	150.00	75.00	45.00
96	Jimmy Lavender	150.00	75.00	45.00
97	"Nemo" Leibold	150.00	75.00	45.00
98	H.B. Leonard	150.00	75.00	45.00
99	Duffy Lewis	150.00	75.00	45.00
100	Tom Long	150.00	75.00	45.00
101	Wm. Louden	150.00	75.00	45.00
102	Fred Luderus	150.00	75.00	45.00
103	Lee Magee	150.00	75.00	45.00
104	Sherwood Magee	150.00	75.00	45.00
105	Al Mamaux	150.00	75.00	45.00
106	Leslie Mann	150.00	75.00	45.00
107	"Rabbit" Maranville	1,000	700.00	300.00
108	Rube Marquard	1,000	700.00	300.00
109	Armando Marsans	165.00	85.00	50.00
110	J. Erskine Mayer	175.00	85.00	50.00
111	George McBride	150.00	75.00	45.00
112	Lew McCarty	150.00	75.00	45.00
113	John J. McGraw	1,000	700.00	300.00
114	Jack McInnis	150.00	75.00	45.00
115	Lee Meadows	150.00	75.00	45.00
116	Fred Merkle	150.00	75.00	45.00
117	"Chief" Meyers	150.00	75.00	45.00
118	Clyde Milan	150.00	75.00	45.00
119	Otto Miller	150.00	75.00	45.00
120	Clarence Mitchell	150.00	75.00	45.00
121	Ray Morgan	150.00	75.00	45.00
122	Guy Morton	150.00	75.00	45.00
123	"Mike" Mowrey	150.00	75.00	45.00
124	Elmer Myers	150.00	75.00	45.00
125	"Hy" Myers	150.00	75.00	45.00
126	A.E. Neale	175.00	85.00	50.00
127	Arthur Nehf	150.00	75.00	45.00
128	J.A. Niehoff	150.00	75.00	45.00
129	Steve O'Neill	150.00	75.00	45.00
130	"Dode" Paskert	150.00	75.00	45.00
131	Roger Peckinpaugh	150.00	75.00	45.00
132	"Pol" Perritt	150.00	75.00	45.00
133	"Jeff" Pfeffer	150.00	75.00	45.00
134	Walter Pipp	150.00	75.00	45.00
135	Derril Pratt (Derrill)	150.00	75.00	45.00
136	Bill Rariden	150.00	75.00	45.00
137	E.C. Rice	350.00	175.00	100.00
138	Wm. A. Ritter (Wm. H.)	150.00	75.00	45.00
139	Eppa Rixey	1,000	700.00	300.00
140	Davey Robertson	150.00	75.00	45.00
141	"Bob" Roth	150.00	75.00	45.00
142	Ed. Roush	1,000	700.00	300.00
143	Clarence Rowland	150.00	75.00	45.00
144	Dick Rudolph	150.00	75.00	45.00
145	William Rumler	150.00	75.00	45.00
146	Reb Russell	150.00	75.00	45.00
147	"Babe" Ruth	12,500	6,250	3,750
148	Vic Saier	150.00	75.00	45.00
149	"Slim" Sallee	150.00	75.00	45.00
150	Ray Schalk	1,000	700.00	300.00
151	Walter Schang	150.00	75.00	45.00
152	Frank Schulte	150.00	75.00	45.00
153	Ferd Schupp	150.00	75.00	45.00
154	Everett Scott	150.00	75.00	45.00
155	Hank Severeid	150.00	75.00	45.00
156	Howard Shanks	150.00	75.00	45.00
157	Bob Shawkey	150.00	75.00	45.00
158	Jas. Sheckard	150.00	75.00	45.00
159	Ernie Shore	150.00	75.00	45.00
160	C.H. Shorten	150.00	75.00	45.00
161	Burt Shotton	150.00	75.00	45.00
162	Geo. Sisler	1,000	700.00	300.00
163	Elmer Smith	150.00	75.00	45.00
164	J. Carlisle Smith	150.00	75.00	45.00
165	Fred Snodgrass	150.00	75.00	45.00
166	Tris Speaker	2,000	1,500	1,000
167	Oscar Stanage	150.00	75.00	45.00
168	Charles Stengel	1,000	700.00	500.00
169	Milton Stock	150.00	75.00	45.00
170	Amos Strunk	150.00	75.00	45.00
171	"Zeb" Terry	150.00	75.00	45.00
172	"Jeff" Tesreau	150.00	75.00	45.00
173	Chester Thomas	150.00	75.00	45.00
174	Fred Toney	150.00	75.00	45.00
175	Terry Turner	150.00	75.00	45.00
176	George Tyler	150.00	75.00	45.00
177	Jim Vaughn	150.00	75.00	45.00
178	Bob Veach	150.00	75.00	45.00
179	Oscar Vitt	150.00	75.00	45.00
180	Hans Wagner	3,500	1,750	1,050
181	Clarence Walker	150.00	75.00	45.00
182	Jim Walsh	150.00	75.00	45.00
183	Al Walters	150.00	75.00	45.00
184	W. Wambsganss	150.00	75.00	45.00
185	Buck Weaver	1,000	500.00	300.00
186	Carl Weilman	150.00	75.00	45.00
187	Zack Wheat	1,000	700.00	300.00
188	Geo. Whitted	150.00	75.00	45.00
189	Joe Wilhoit	150.00	75.00	45.00
190	Claude Williams	750.00	375.00	225.00
191	Fred Williams	150.00	75.00	45.00
192	Art Wilson	150.00	75.00	45.00
193	Lawton Witt	150.00	75.00	45.00
194	Joe Wood	150.00	75.00	45.00
195	William Wortman	150.00	75.00	45.00
196	Steve Yerkes	150.00	75.00	45.00
197	Earl Yingling	150.00	75.00	45.00
198	"Pep" (Ralph) Young	150.00	75.00	45.00
199	Rollie Zeider	150.00	75.00	45.00
200	Henry Zimmerman	150.00	75.00	45.00

1921 Standard Biscuit (D350-3)

A photograph of a member of either the American or National League will be found in every 5 and 10 cent package of our products. There are 80 to the set.

STANDARD BISCUIT COMPANY
San Francisco, Cal.
Sole Makers of Paradise Sodas

It is unknown to what extent this scarcest of the three Standard Biscuit advertising issues actually parallels the E121 Series of 80, on which American Caramel Co. backs are more

commonly found. This uncertainty contributes to the relatively low premium value (about 2X) attached to the Standard Biscuit versions. Backs have been seen in two styles; one mentions "80 to the set," the other mentions "contains 80 photographs." Cards are printed in black-and-white in a size of about 2" x 3-1/4". A checklist has been started here in an effort to better understand the issue.

PREMIUM: 2X

(3)	Jim Bagby
(4a)	J. Franklin Baker
(12)	Max Carey (Hands at hips.)
(14)	Ty Cobb (Throwing, looking front.)
(15b)	Ty Cobb (Throwing, looking right, manager on front.)
(16)	Eddie Collins
(19)	Dave Davenport
(37)	Tom Griffith
(40)	John Henry
(41)	Clarence Hodge
(52)	James Johnston
(61)	Al Mamaux
(62)	"Rabbit" Maranville
(83)	Eppa Rixey, Jr.
(86)	Babe Ruth
(90)	Ray Schalk
(103)	Chester Thomas
(109)	Jim Vaughn (Dark cap.)
(113)	Oscar Vitt
(116)	Zach Wheat
(120)	Joe Wood

1910 Standard Caramel Co. (E93)

This 30-card set issued in 1910 by Standard Caramel Co. of Lancaster, Pa., is closely related to several other candy sets from this period which share the same format and, in many cases, the same player poses. The cards measure 1-1/2" x 2-3/4" and utilize tinted black-and-white player photos. The back of each card contains an alphabetical checklist of the set plus a line indicating it was manufactured by Standard Caramel Co., Lancaster, Pa. The set carries the ACC designation of E93.

		NM	EX	VG
	Complete Set (30):	100,000	40,000	20,000
	Common Player:	1,500	600.00	300.00
(1)	Red Ames	1,500	600.00	300.00
(2)	Chief Bender	3,000	1,200	600.00
(3)	Mordecai Brown	3,000	1,200	600.00
(4)	Frank Chance	3,000	1,200	600.00
(5)	Hal Chase	2,200	880.00	440.00
(6)	Fred Clarke	3,000	1,200	600.00
(7)	Ty Cobb	15,000	6,000	3,000
(8)	Eddie Collins	3,000	1,200	600.00
(9)	Harry Coveleskie (Coveleski)	1,500	600.00	300.00
(10)	Jim Delehanty	2,000	1,000	500.00
(11)	Wild Bill Donovan	1,500	600.00	300.00
(12)	Red Dooin	1,500	600.00	300.00
(13)	Johnny Evers	3,000	1,200	600.00
(14)	George Gibson	1,500	600.00	300.00
(15)	Clark Griffith	3,000	1,200	600.00
(16)	Hugh Jennings	3,000	1,200	600.00
(17)	Davy Jones	1,500	600.00	300.00
(18)	Addie Joss	3,300	1,320	660.00
(19)	Nap Lajoie	3,000	120.00	600.00
(20)	Tommy Leach	1,500	600.00	300.00
(21)	Christy Mathewson	8,000	3,200	1,600
(22)	John McGraw	3,000	1,200	600.00
(23)	Jim Pastorious	1,500	600.00	300.00
(24)	Deacon Phillippi (Phillippe)	1,500	600.00	300.00
(25)	Eddie Plank	5,000	2,000	1,000
(26)	Joe Tinker	3,000	1,200	600.00
(27)	Rube Waddell	3,000	1,200	600.00
(28)	Honus Wagner	12,000	4,800	2,400
(29)	Hooks Wiltse	1,500	600.00	300.00
(30)	Cy Young	8,000	3,500	1,750

1960-70s Stan Musial & Biggie's Restaurant

These black-and-white photocards were prepared for Musial's use while glad-handing patrons at his St. Louis eatery. The pictures have a facsimile autograph. A "Compliments of . . ." message is printed in the bottom border. Backs are blank.

		NM	EX	VG
(1)	Stan Musial (Batting pose, 5" x 7".)	10.00	5.00	3.00
(2)	Stan Musial (Batting pose, 3-1/2" x 5-1/2".)	10.00	5.00	3.00
(3)	Stan Musial (Standing w/glove, 5" x 7".)	10.00	5.00	3.00

1952 Star-Cal Decals Type 1

The Meyercord Co., of Chicago issued two sets of baseball player decals in 1952. The Type I Star-Cal Decal set consists of 68 different major leaguers, each pictured on a large (4-1/8" x 6-1/8") decal. The player's name and facsimile autograph appear on the decal, along with the decal number listed on the checklist here. Values shown are for decals complete with outer directions envelope.

		NM	EX	VG
Complete Set (68):		7,500	3,750	2,250
Common Player:		45.00	22.50	13.50
70A	Allie Reynolds	50.00	25.00	15.00
70B	Ed Lopat	50.00	25.00	15.00
70C	Yogi Berra	200.00	100.00	60.00
70D	Vic Raschi	50.00	25.00	15.00
70E	Jerry Coleman	45.00	22.50	13.50
70F	Phil Rizzuto	110.00	55.00	35.00
70G	Mickey Mantle	1,750	875.00	525.00
71A	Mel Parnell	45.00	22.50	13.50
71B	Ted Williams	400.00	200.00	120.00
71C	Ted Williams	400.00	200.00	120.00
71D	Vern Stephens	45.00	22.50	13.50
71E	Billy Goodman	45.00	22.50	13.50
71F	Dom DiMaggio	50.00	25.00	15.00
71G	Dick Gernert	45.00	22.50	13.50
71H	Hoot Evers	45.00	22.50	13.50
72A	George Kell	50.00	25.00	15.00
72B	Hal Newhouser	50.00	25.00	15.00
72C	Hoot Evers	45.00	22.50	13.50
72D	Vic Wertz	45.00	22.50	13.50
72E	Fred Hutchinson	45.00	22.50	13.50
72F	Johnny Groth	45.00	22.50	13.50
73A	Al Zarilla	45.00	22.50	13.50
73B	Billy Pierce	45.00	22.50	13.50
73C	Eddie Robinson	45.00	22.50	13.50
73D	Chico Carrasquel	50.00	25.00	15.00
73E	Minnie Minoso	50.00	25.00	15.00
73F	Jim Busby	45.00	22.50	13.50
73G	Nellie Fox	55.00	27.50	16.50
73H	Sam Mele	45.00	22.50	13.50
74A	Larry Doby	55.00	27.50	16.50
74B	Al Rosen	50.00	25.00	15.00
74C	Bob Lemon	55.00	27.00	16.50
74D	Jim Hegan	45.00	22.50	13.50
74E	Bob Feller	90.00	45.00	27.00
74F	Dale Mitchell	45.00	22.50	13.50
75A	Ned Garver	45.00	22.50	13.50
76A	Gus Zernial	45.00	22.50	13.50
76B	Ferris Fain	45.00	22.50	13.50
76C	Bobby Shantz	45.00	22.50	13.50
77A	Richie Ashburn	60.00	30.00	18.00
77B	Ralph Kiner	55.00	27.50	16.50
77C	Curt Simmons	45.00	22.50	13.50
78A	Bobby Thomson	55.00	27.50	16.50
78B	Alvin Dark	45.00	22.50	13.50
78C	Sal Maglie	45.00	22.50	13.50
78D	Larry Jansen	45.00	22.50	13.50
78E	Willie Mays	425.00	210.00	125.00
78F	Monte Irvin	55.00	27.50	16.50
78G	Whitey Lockman	45.00	22.50	13.50
79A	Gil Hodges	90.00	45.00	27.00
79B	Pee Wee Reese	110.00	55.00	35.00
79C	Roy Campanella	110.00	55.00	35.00
79D	Don Newcombe	55.00	27.50	16.50
79E	Duke Snider	110.00	55.00	35.00
79F	Preacher Roe	50.00	25.00	15.00
79G	Jackie Robinson	350.00	175.00	105.00
80A	Eddie Miksis	45.00	22.50	13.50
80B	Dutch Leonard	45.00	22.50	13.50
80C	Randy Jackson	45.00	22.50	13.50
80D	Bob Rush	45.00	22.50	13.50
80E	Hank Sauer	45.00	22.50	13.50
80F	Phil Cavarretta	45.00	22.50	13.50
80G	Warren Hacker	45.00	22.50	13.50
81A	Red Schoendienst	55.00	27.50	16.50
81B	Wally Westlake	45.00	22.50	13.50
81C	Cliff Chambers	45.00	22.50	13.50
81D	Enos Slaughter	55.00	27.50	16.50
81E	Stan Musial	275.00	135.00	85.00
81F	Stan Musial	275.00	135.00	85.00
81G	Jerry Staley	45.00	22.50	13.50

1952 Star-Cal Decals Type 2

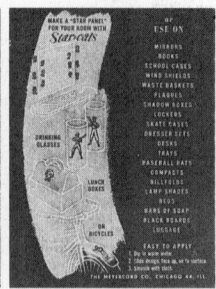

Also produced by Chicago's Meyercord Co. in 1952, these Star-Cal Decals are similar to the Type I variety, except the decal sheets are smaller, measuring 4-1/8" x 3-1/16", and each sheet features two players instead of one.

		NM	EX	VG
Complete Set (32):		3,000	1,500	900.00
Common Player:		45.00	22.50	13.50
84A	Vic Raschi, Allie Reynolds	80.00	40.00	25.00
84B	Yogi Berra, Ed Lopat	165.00	80.00	50.00
84C	Jerry Coleman, Phil Rizzuto	135.00	65.00	40.00
85A	Ted Williams, Ted Williams	450.00	225.00	135.00
85B	Dom DiMaggio, Mel Parnell	60.00	30.00	18.00
85C	Billy Goodman, Vern Stephens	45.00	22.50	13.50
86A	George Kell, Hal Newhouser	80.00	40.00	25.00
86B	Hoot Evers, Vic Wertz	45.00	22.50	13.50
86C	Johnny Groth, Fred Hutchinson	45.00	22.50	13.50
87A	Eddie Robinson, Eddie Robinson	45.00	22.50	13.50
87B	Chico Carrasquel, Minnie Minoso	60.00	30.00	18.00
87C	Nellie Fox, Billy Pierce	65.00	32.50	20.00
87D	Jim Busby, Al Zarilla	45.00	22.50	13.50
88A	Jim Hegan, Bob Lemon	65.00	32.50	20.00
88B	Larry Doby, Bob Feller	165.00	80.00	50.00
88C	Dale Mitchell, Al Rosen	45.00	22.50	13.50
89A	Ned Garver, Ned Garver	45.00	22.50	13.50
89B	Ferris Fain, Gus Zernial	45.00	22.50	13.50
89C	Richie Ashburn, Richie Ashburn	75.00	37.50	22.00
89D	Ralph Kiner, Ralph Kiner	75.00	37.50	22.00
90A	Monty Irvin, Willie Mays (Monte)	300.00	150.00	90.00
90B	Larry Jansen, Sal Maglie	45.00	22.50	13.50
90C	Al Dark, Bobby Thomson	55.00	27.50	16.50
91A	Gil Hodges, Pee Wee Reese	225.00	110.00	65.00
91B	Roy Campanella, Jackie Robinson	300.00	150.00	90.00
91C	Preacher Roe, Duke Snider	200.00	100.00	60.00
92A	Phil Cavarretta, Dutch Leonard	45.00	22.50	13.50
92B	Randy Jackson, Eddie Miksis	45.00	22.50	13.50
92C	Bob Rush, Hank Sauer	45.00	22.50	13.50
93A	Stan Musial, Stan Musial	350.00	175.00	105.00
93B	Red Schoendienst, Enos Slaughter	90.00	45.00	27.00
93C	Cliff Chambers, Wally Westlake	45.00	22.50	13.50

1976 Star Market Red Sox

Only Red Sox are featured in this set issued by the Star Market chain in the Boston area. Players are photographed hatless in jerseys which feature the Massachusetts Bicentennial logo. Pictures measure 5-7/8" x 9" and have a 3/16" white border all around. A facsimile autograph is printed on the front in black. Backs are blank. The unnumbered pictures are checklisted here alphabetically.

		NM	EX	VG
Complete Set (16):		35.00	17.50	10.00
Common Player:		1.50	.75	.45
(1)	Rick Burleson	1.50	.75	.45
(2)	Reggie Cleveland	1.50	.75	.45
(3)	Cecil Cooper	2.50	1.25	.70
(4)	Denny Doyle	1.50	.75	.45
(5)	Dwight Evans	2.50	1.25	.70
(6)	Carlton Fisk	5.00	2.50	1.50
(7)	Tom House	1.50	.75	.45
(8)	Fergie Jenkins	4.00	2.00	1.25
(9)	Bill Lee	1.50	.75	.45
(10)	Fred Lynn	2.50	1.25	.70
(11)	Rick Miller	1.50	.75	.45
(12)	Rico Petrocelli	2.50	1.25	.70
(13)	Jim Rice	3.50	1.75	1.00
(14)	Luis Tiant	2.50	1.25	.70
(15)	Rick Wise	1.50	.75	.45
(16)	Carl Yastrzemski	10.00	5.00	3.00

1928 Star Player Candy

WALLY SCHANG

Little is known about the origin of this set. The producer is not identified, but experienced collectors generally refer to it as the Star Player Candy set, possibly because it was distributed with a product of that name. The cards measure 1-7/8" x 2-7/8", are sepia-toned, blank-backed and printed on thin paper. The player's name (but no team designation) appears in the border below the photo in brown capital letters. To date the checklist of baseball players numbers 73, but more may exist, and cards of football players have also been found.

		NM	EX	VG
Common Player:		900.00	360.00	180.00
(1)	Dave Bancroft	2,000	800.00	400.00
(2)	Emile Barnes	900.00	360.00	180.00
(3)	L.A. Blue	900.00	360.00	180.00
(4)	Garland Buckeye	900.00	360.00	180.00
(5)	George Burns	900.00	360.00	180.00
(6)	Guy T. Bush	900.00	360.00	180.00
(7)	Owen T. Carroll	900.00	360.00	180.00
(8)	Chalmer Cissell	900.00	360.00	180.00
(9)	Ty Cobb	20,000	8,000	4,000
(10)	Gordon Cochrane	2,000	800.00	400.00
(11)	Richard Coffman	900.00	360.00	180.00
(12)	Eddie Collins	2,000	800.00	400.00
(13)	Stanley Coveleskie (Coveleski)	2,000	800.00	400.00
(14)	Hugh Critz	900.00	360.00	180.00
(15)	Hazen Cuyler	2,000	800.00	400.00
(16)	Charles Dressen	900.00	360.00	180.00
(17)	Joe Dugan	900.00	360.00	180.00
(18)	Elwood English	900.00	360.00	180.00
(19)	Bib Falk (Bibb)	900.00	360.00	180.00
(20)	Ira Flagstead	900.00	360.00	180.00
(21)	Bob Fothergill	900.00	360.00	180.00
(22)	Frank T. Frisch	2,000	800.00	400.00
(23)	Foster Ganzel	900.00	360.00	180.00
(24)	Lou Gehrig	22,500	9,000	4,500
(25)	Chas. Gihringer (Gehringer)	2,000	800.00	400.00
(26)	George Gerken	900.00	360.00	180.00
(27)	Grant Gillis	900.00	360.00	180.00
(28)	Miguel Gonzales (Gonzalez)	900.00	360.00	180.00
(29)	Sam Gray	900.00	360.00	180.00
(30)	Chas. J. Grimm	900.00	360.00	180.00
(31)	Robert M. Grove	2,250	900.00	450.00
(32)	Chas. J. Hafey	2,000	800.00	400.00
(33)	Jesse Haines	2,000	800.00	400.00
(34)	Chas. L. Hartnett	2,000	800.00	400.00
(35)	Clifton Heathcote	900.00	360.00	180.00
(36)	Harry Heilmann	2,000	800.00	400.00
(37)	John Heving	900.00	360.00	180.00
(38)	Waite Hoyt	2,000	800.00	400.00
(39)	Chas. Jamieson	900.00	360.00	180.00
(40)	Joe Judge	900.00	360.00	180.00
(41)	Willie Kamm	900.00	360.00	180.00
(42)	George Kelly	2,000	800.00	400.00
(43)	Tony Lazzeri	2,000	800.00	400.00
(44)	Adolfo Luque	900.00	360.00	180.00
(45)	Ted Lyons	2,000	800.00	400.00
(46)	Hugh McMullen	900.00	360.00	180.00
(47)	Bob Meusel	900.00	360.00	180.00
(48)	Wilcey Moore (Wilcy)	900.00	360.00	180.00
(49)	Ed C. Morgan	900.00	360.00	180.00
(50)	Buddy Myer	900.00	360.00	180.00
(51)	Herb Pennock	2,000	800.00	400.00
(52)	Everett Purdy	900.00	360.00	180.00
(53)	William Regan	900.00	360.00	180.00
(54)	Eppa Rixey	2,000	800.00	400.00
(55)	Charles Root	900.00	360.00	180.00
(56)	Jack Rothrock	900.00	360.00	180.00
(57)	Harold Ruel (Herold)	900.00	360.00	180.00
(58)	Babe Ruth	32,500	13,000	6,500

		NM	EX	VG
(59)	Wally Schang	900.00	360.00	180.00
(60)	Joe Sewell	2,000	800.00	400.00
(61)	Luke Sewell	900.00	360.00	180.00
(62)	Joe Shaute	900.00	360.00	180.00
(63)	George Sisler	2,000	800.00	400.00
(64)	Tris Speaker	2,500	1,000	500.00
(65)	Riggs Stephenson	900.00	360.00	180.00
(66)	Jack Tavener	900.00	360.00	180.00
(67)	Al Thomas	900.00	360.00	180.00
(68)	Harold J. Traynor	2,000	800.00	400.00
(69)	George Uhle	900.00	360.00	180.00
(70)	Dazzy Vance	2,000	800.00	400.00
(71)	Cy Williams	900.00	360.00	180.00
(72)	Ken Williams	900.00	360.00	180.00
(73)	Lewis R. Wilson	2,000	800.00	400.00

1929 Star Player Candy

21

BABE RUTH, "Sultan of Swat," has reigned supreme as home run king for eight consecutive years. His record of 60 home runs in one season will probably remain unbroken for some years to come.

BABE RUTH

The actual year of issue can only be approximated from the write-ups on the cards' backs. Only two players can be checklisted thus far, though the numbers on the backs would seem to indicate an issue of at least 32. The 1-7/8" x 2-7/8" cards are printed in sepia with wide borders on front and player name below the photo. Unlike the 1928 Star Candy issue, this series has printed and numbered backs.

		NM	EX	VG
21	Babe Ruth	20,000	10,000	6,000
32	Lou Gehrig	22,500	11,250	6,750

1892 J.U. Stead Studio Cabinets

J.U. STEAD.   383 5th Ave., N.Y.

Only members of the N.Y. Giants are thus far known in this series of cabinet cards from New York City photographer J.U. Stead. About standard cabinet size (4-1/2" x 6-1/2") the cards have black-and-white portraits. On the thick cardboard mount's bottom border is the name and address of the studio. Backs repeat that information and have three lines of type at bottom extolling "Instantaneous Photographs." Unless the player name was pencilled on the card by a previous owner, the players are not otherwise identified. Fortunately, the plethora of contemporary issues from other sources makes matching names and photos fairly easy. The issue date attributed is speculative.

	NM	EX	VG
Common Player:	3,000	1,500	900.00
Roger Connor	6,000	2,000	1,200
Willie Keeler	10,000	3,750	2,250
Mike Tiernan	3,000	1,500	900.00

1909-16 Max Stein Postcards (PC758)

Issued over a period of several years these sepia-toned photo postcards depict most of the stars of the day. In standard 3-1/2" x 5-1/2" format they have typical postcard indicia on the back. Some cards have been seen with a "United States Pub." legend on the back. Most of the subjects played in Stein's Chicago location. Besides the baseball players listed here, the series also included "Statesmen, etc.," "Aeroplanes and Flyers, Fighters, etc.," and, "Dancing Girls," according to advertising found on the back of some cards. Wholesale prices when issued were 35 cents per hundred, $2.75 per thousand.

		NM	EX	VG
Common Player:		200.00	80.00	40.00
Advertising Back: 1.5X				
(1)	Ping Bodie	200.00	80.00	40.00
(2)	Frank Chance	400.00	160.00	80.00
(3)	Ty Cobb	2,250	900.00	450.00
(4)	Johnny Evers	400.00	160.00	80.00
(5)	Rube Marquard	400.00	160.00	80.00
(6)	Christy Mathewson	1,200	480.00	240.00
(7)	John McGraw	400.00	160.00	80.00
(8)	Chief Meyers	200.00	80.00	40.00
(9)	Marty O'Toole	200.00	80.00	40.00
(10)	Wildfire Schulte	200.00	80.00	40.00
(11)	Tris Speaker	450.00	180.00	90.00
(12)	Jake Stahl	200.00	80.00	40.00
(13)	Jim Thorpe	2,500	1,000	500.00
(14)	Joe Tinker	400.00	160.00	80.00
(15)	Honus Wagner	1,500	600.00	300.00
(16)	Ed Walsh	400.00	160.00	80.00
(17)	Buck Weaver	1,750	700.00	350.00
(18)	Joe Wood	200.00	80.00	40.00
(19)	Heinie Zimmerman	200.00	80.00	40.00
(20)	Chicago Cubs (Jimmy Archer, Roger Bresnahan, Johnny Evers, Mike Hechinger, Tom Needham)	200.00	80.00	40.00
(21)	Chicago Cubs (Bill Clymer, Wilbur Good, Ward Miller, Mike Mitchell, Wildfire Schulte)	200.00	80.00	40.00
(22)	Boston Americans Team Photo	200.00	80.00	40.00
(23)	1916 Chicago Cubs Team Photo	300.00	120.00	60.00
(24)	1916 Cincinnati Reds Team Photo	200.00	80.00	40.00
(25)	New York Nationals Team Photo	200.00	80.00	40.00
(26)	Johnny Coulon, Jess Willard (Boxers)	200.00	80.00	40.00

1904 Stenzel's Rooter Buttons

The extent of the checklist for this rare Cincinnati 1-1/4" pinback celluloid button issue is unknown. According to a paper label found in the back of well-preserved examples, the buttons are the issue of "Jake Stenzel B.B. Exchange located opposite Ball Park." Fronts have "STENZEL'S ROOTER BUTTON" at top and a player portrait photo at center with last name and position below.

		NM	EX	VG
(1)	Mike Donlin	750.00	375.00	225.00
(2)	Bob Ewing	600.00	300.00	180.00
(3)	Jack Harper	600.00	300.00	180.00
(4)	Joe Kelley	1,750	875.00	525.00
(5)	Win Kellum	600.00	300.00	180.00
(6)	Peaches O'Neil (O'Neill)	900.00	450.00	275.00
(7)	Heinie Pietz (Peitz)	600.00	300.00	180.00
(8)	Admiral Schlei	600.00	300.00	180.00
(9)	Cy Seymour	600.00	300.00	180.00
(10)	Jack Sutthoff	600.00	300.00	180.00
(11)	Sam Woodruff	600.00	300.00	180.00

1911 Stevens Firearms Philadelphia Athletics

PENNANT WINNERS 1911

Baseball: Philadelphia Athletics
Trap Shooting: Stevens Repeating Shotgun
Rifle Shooting: Stevens Rifle

Murphy, Right Field, Philadelphia Athletics.

STEVENS FIREARMS for sale by

Riding on the coattails of the A's American League pennant (and eventual World Series) win, Stevens Firearms created this set of cards to promote its rifles and shotguns. About

6-3/16" x 3-7/16", the blank-back, medium-weight cards have a black-and-white posed action photo at left with the player identified by name, position and team. At top right is advertising, at bottom-right is a box where local retailers' addresses could be stamped or printed. Cards have been seen printed on several different colors of stock. In actuality, these are really ink blotters from the old fountain pen days as opposed to "cards." Other players are likely to have been issued.

		NM	EX	VG
Common Player:		1,000	500.00	300.00
(1)	Frank Baker	1,500	750.00	450.00
(2)	Chief Bender	1,500	750.00	450.00
(3)	Bris Lord	1,000	500.00	300.00
(4)	Connie Mack	1,500	750.00	450.00
(5)	Danny Murphy	1,000	500.00	300.00
(6)	Rube Oldring	1,000	500.00	300.00
(7)	Harry Davis	1,000	500.00	300.00
(8)	Ira Thomas	1,000	500.00	300.00

1888-1889 Stevens Studio Australian Tour Cabinets

After the 1888 season, Albert Spalding toured to Australia with a group of major league players to increase interest in baseball Down Under (as well as to increase demand for the baseball equipment his firm sold). Prior to departure, many of the players gathered at Stevens Studio in Chicago for portrait photos to be made into cabinet cards, presumably for sale as souvenirs on the junket. Vignetted portraits present the players in their Sunday best. Below a decorative dividing line is "Spalding's Australian Base Ball Tour / Stevens 1888-89 Chicago." Back has a large ornate ad for the photographer. The full extent of the checklist is unknown.

	NM	EX	VG
Common Player:	3,500	1,750	1,000
Cap Anson	10,000	5,000	3,000
Jim Donnelly	3,500	1,750	1,000
Jim Fogarty	3,500	1,750	1,000
Ned Williamson	3,500	1,750	1,000

1890 Stevens Studio Chicago Pirates Cabinets

The single-season players' revolution that spawned the Players League is marked with this issue of cabinet cards from the Stevens studio of Chicago. Only members of the Chicago Pirates P.L. team have been seen in this issue, all in street clothes and identified by a name penned on the front. A composite-photo card is also known, providing reasonable expectations that more individual player cabinets will be discovered. The studio advertising on back is ornately printed in maroon.

		NM	EX	VG
Common Player:		1,800	900.00	550.00
(1)	Charles Comiskey	3,850	1,925	1,100
(2)	Hugh Duffy	3,850	1,925	1,100
(3)	Silver Flint	1,800	900.00	550.00
(4)	Jimmy Ryan	1,800	900.00	550.00
(5)	Team Composite	10,000	5,000	3,000

1890 Stevens Studio Chicago White Stockings Cabinets

Cabinet cards in the standard 4-1/4" x 6-1/2" format of at least three of the 1890 Chicago National Leaguers, as well as a team composite picture are known to have been produced by the Stevens Art Studio. Fronts have vignetted portraits of the players in dress clothes. Backs have an ornate ad for the photographer, which includes the note, "DUPLICATES OF THIS PICTURE CAN BE HAD AT ANY TIME, AT REDUCED

RATES." Player names are often found penned on the cards, as the photos are otherwise unidentified. At least two styles of cardboard mounts are seen with the White Stockings cabinets. The extent of the checklist is also unknown.

		NM	EX	VG
Common Player:		1,800	900.00	550.00
(1)	Cap Anson	8,250	4,125	2,475
(2)	Mike Sullivan	1,800	900.00	550.00
(3)	Pat Wright	1,800	900.00	550.00
(4)	1890 Chicago White Stockings	4,400	2,200	1,325

1941 St. Louis Browns Team Issue (W753)

Measuring 2-1/8" x 2-5/8", this unnumbered boxed set of cards features the St. Louis Browns in black-and-white portrait photos on front. Backs have player name, position and personal and statistical information. There are also cards for coaches and one of the the club's two managers that season (Luke Sewell). As the Browns weren't much of a team in 1941 (or in most seasons for that matter) there are no major stars in the set. The issue was cataloged as W753 in the ACC.

		NM	EX	VG
Complete Set (30):		850.00	425.00	250.00
Common Player:		35.00	17.50	10.00
Box:		75.00	35.00	25.00
(1)	Johnny Allen	35.00	17.50	10.00
(2)	Elden Auker (Eldon)	35.00	17.50	10.00
(3)	Donald L Barnes	35.00	17.50	10.00
(4)	Johnny Berardino	50.00	25.00	15.00
(5)	George Caster	35.00	17.50	10.00
(6)	Harlond Benton (Darky) Clift	35.00	17.50	10.00
(7)	Roy J. Cullenbine	35.00	17.50	10.00
(8)	William O. DeWitt (Vice-President)	35.00	17.50	10.00
(9)	Roberto Estalella	35.00	17.50	10.00
(10)	Richard Benjamin (Rick) Ferrell	60.00	30.00	18.00
(11)	Dennis W. Galehouse	35.00	17.50	10.00
(12)	Joseph L. Grace	35.00	17.50	10.00
(13)	Frank Grube	35.00	17.50	10.00
(14)	Robert A. Harris	35.00	17.50	10.00
(15)	Donald Henry Heffner	35.00	17.50	10.00
(16)	Fred Hofmann	35.00	17.50	10.00
(17)	Walter Franklin Judnich	35.00	17.50	10.00
(18)	John Henry (Jack) Kramer	35.00	17.50	10.00
(19)	Chester (Chet) Laabs	35.00	17.50	10.00
(20)	John Lucadello	35.00	17.50	10.00
(21)	George Hartley McQuinn	35.00	17.50	10.00
(22)	Robert Cleveland Muncrief, Jr.	35.00	17.50	10.00
(23)	John Niggeling	35.00	17.50	10.00
(24)	Fred Raymond (Fritz) Ostermueller	35.00	17.50	10.00
(25)	James Luther (Luke) Sewell	35.00	17.50	10.00
(26)	Alan Cochran Strange (Cochrane)	35.00	17.50	10.00
(27)	Robert Virgil (Bob) Swift	35.00	17.50	10.00
(28)	James W. (Zack) Taylor	35.00	17.50	10.00
(29)	William Felix (Bill) Trotter	35.00	17.50	10.00
(30)	Presentation Card/Order Form	10.00	5.00	3.00

1952 St. Louis Browns Postcards

This series of player postcards features black-and-white glossy photos on front with a white border. The cards bear no player identification and were evidently intended for use in honoring fan requests for autographs. The 1952 issue can be differentiated from that of 1953 by the absence of a stamp box on back. The unnumbered cards are checklisted here alphabetically, though the list may be incomplete. Multiple player names indicate known different poses.

	NM	EX	VG
Common Player:	50.00	25.00	15.00

(1)	Tommy Byrne	50.00	25.00	15.00
(2)	Bob Cain	50.00	25.00	15.00
(3)	Bob Cain	50.00	25.00	15.00
(4)	Clint Courtney	50.00	25.00	15.00
(5)	Jim Delsing	50.00	25.00	15.00
(6)	Jim Dyck	50.00	25.00	15.00
(7)	Jim Dyck	50.00	25.00	15.00
(8)	Ned Garver	50.00	25.00	15.00
(9)	Marty Marion	60.00	30.00	18.00
(10)	Cass Michaels	50.00	25.00	15.00
(11)	Bob Nieman	50.00	25.00	15.00
(12)	Satchel Paige	200.00	100.00	60.00
(13)	Duane Pillette	50.00	25.00	15.00
(14)	Jim Rivera	50.00	25.00	15.00
(15)	Bill Veeck	75.00	37.00	22.00
(16)	Bobby Young	50.00	25.00	15.00

1953 St. Louis Browns Postcards

This series of player postcards from the team's final year in St. Louis features black-and-white glossy photos on front with a white border. The cards bear no player identification and were evidently intended for use in honoring fan requests for autographs. The 1953 issue can be differentiated from that of 1952 by the presence of a stamp box on back identifying the issuer as Deorite Peerless. The unnumbered cards are checklisted here alphabetically though the list is likely incomplete.

		NM	EX	VG
Common Player:		50.00	25.00	15.00
(1)	Connie Berry	50.00	25.00	15.00
(2)	Mike Blyzka	50.00	25.00	15.00
(3)	Harry Brecheen	50.00	25.00	15.00
(4)	Bob Cain	50.00	25.00	15.00
(5)	Clint Courtney	50.00	25.00	15.00
(6)	Jim Dyck	50.00	25.00	15.00
(7)	Hank Edwards	50.00	25.00	15.00
(8)	Ned Garver	50.00	25.00	15.00
(9)	Johnny Groth	50.00	25.00	15.00
(11)	Bobo Holloman	50.00	25.00	15.00
(12)	Billy Hunter	50.00	25.00	15.00
(13)	Dick Kokos	50.00	25.00	15.00
(14)	Dick Kryhoski	50.00	25.00	15.00
(15)	Max Lanier	50.00	25.00	15.00
(16)	Don Larsen	75.00	37.50	22.00
(17)	Don Lenhardt	50.00	25.00	15.00
(18)	Dick Littlefield	50.00	25.00	15.00
(19)	Marty Marion	60.00	30.00	18.00
(21)	Babe Martin	50.00	25.00	15.00
(22)	Willy Miranda	50.00	25.00	15.00
(23)	Les Moss	50.00	25.00	15.00
(24)	Bill Norman	50.00	25.00	15.00
(25)	Satchel Paige (Kneeling)	200.00	100.00	60.00
(26)	Satchel Paige (Pitching)	200.00	100.00	60.00
(27)	Duane Pillette	50.00	25.00	15.00
(28)	Bob Scheffing	50.00	25.00	15.00
(29)	Roy Sievers	60.00	30.00	18.00
(31)	Marlin Stuart	50.00	25.00	15.00
(32)	Virgil Trucks	65.00	32.00	19.50
(33)	Bill Veeck	75.00	37.00	22.00
(34)	Vic Wertz	50.00	25.00	15.00
(35)	Bobby Young	50.00	25.00	12.00

1941 St. Louis Cardinals Team Issue (W754)

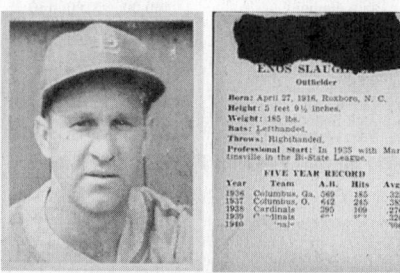

A companion set to W753, this time featuring the National League team in St. Louis. Cards measure 2-1/8" x 2-5/8" and are unnumbered. Like the Browns set, this issue features black-and-white portrait photos on front and the individual's name, position and personal and statistical information on back. One interesting addition to the set is a card of Branch Rickey which, coupled with cards of Enos Slaughter and Johnny Mize, gives the set a bit more appeal than the Browns set. ACC designation is W754.

	NM	EX	VG
Complete Set (30):	1,000	500.00	300.00

Common Player:		35.00	17.50	10.00
Box:		75.00	35.00	25.00
(1)	Sam Breadon	35.00	17.50	10.00
(2)	James Brown	35.00	17.50	10.00
(3)	Morton Cooper	35.00	17.50	10.00
(4)	William Walker Cooper	35.00	17.50	10.00
(5)	Estel Crabtree	35.00	17.50	10.00
(6)	Frank Crespi	35.00	17.50	10.00
(7)	William Crouch	35.00	17.50	10.00
(8)	Miguel Mike Gonzalez	50.00	25.00	15.00
(9)	Harry Gumbert	35.00	17.50	10.00
(10)	John Hopp	35.00	17.50	10.00
(11)	Ira Hutchinson	35.00	17.50	10.00
(12)	Howard Krist	35.00	17.50	10.00
(13)	Edward E. Lake	35.00	17.50	10.00
(14)	Hubert Max Lanier	35.00	17.50	10.00
(15)	Gus Mancuso	35.00	17.50	10.00
(16)	Martin Marion	55.00	27.50	16.50
(17)	Steve Mesner	35.00	17.50	10.00
(18)	John Mize	100.00	50.00	30.00
(19)	Capt. Terry Moore	50.00	25.00	15.00
(20)	Sam Nahem	35.00	17.50	10.00
(21)	Don Padgett	35.00	17.50	10.00
(22)	Branch Rickey (Vice-President)	60.00	30.00	18.00
(23)	Clyde Shoun	35.00	17.50	10.00
(24)	Enos Slaughter	100.00	50.00	30.00
(25)	William H. (Billy) Southworth	35.00	17.50	10.00
(26)	Herman Coaker Triplett	35.00	17.50	10.00
(27)	Clyde Buzzy Wares	35.00	17.50	10.00
(28)	Lon Warneke	35.00	17.50	10.00
(29)	Ernest White	35.00	17.50	10.00
(30)	Presentation Card/Order Form	10.00	5.00	3.00

1966 St. Louis Cardinals Busch Stadium Immortals Coins

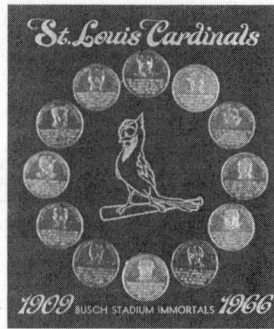

A dozen all-time great Cardinals are included in this set of commemorative medallions. Each 1-1/2" bright bronze "coin" has a portrait and career summary. The coins were issued in a 9" x 10-1/2" cardinal-red cardboard holder with gold logo and graphics.

		NM	EX	VG
Complete Board/Coin Set:		75.00	37.50	22.50
Common Player:		7.50	3.75	2.25
(1)	Dizzy Dean	10.00	5.00	3.00
(2)	Frank Frisch	7.50	3.75	2.25
(3)	Chick Hafey	7.50	3.75	2.25
(4)	Jesse Haines	7.50	3.75	2.25
(5)	Marty Marion	7.50	3.75	2.25
(6)	Joe Medwick	7.50	3.75	2.25
(7)	Johnny Mize	7.50	3.75	2.25
(8)	Terry Moore	7.50	3.75	2.25
(9)	Stan Musial	15.00	7.50	4.50
(10)	Red Schoendienst	7.50	3.75	2.25
(11)	George Sisler	7.50	3.75	2.25
(12)	Enos Slaughter	7.50	3.75	2.25

1953 Stop & Shop Boston Red Sox

Four of the early 1950s Red Sox appear in this series issued by a Boston grocery chain. The cards may have been distributed in conjunction with players' in-store appearances. The cards measure 3-3/4" x 5" and are printed in black-and-white. A facsimile autograph appears on the front. Backs have the sponsor's advertising. The unnumbered cards are checklisted here alphabetically. See also 1953 First National Super Market Boston Red Sox.

		NM	EX	VG
Complete Set (4):		3,000	1,500	900.00
Common Player:		750.00	375.00	225.00
(1)	Billy Goodman	750.00	375.00	225.00
(2)	Ellis Kinder	750.00	375.00	225.00
(3)	Mel Parnell	750.00	375.00	225.00
(4)	Sammy White	750.00	375.00	225.00

1888 Sub Rosa Cigarettes Girl Baseball Players (N508)

(See 1888 Allen & Ginter Girl Baseball Players.)

1916 Successful Farming

Best known for its use as a promotional medium for The Sporting News (M101-5), this 200-card set can be found with ads on the back for several local and regional businesses. Among them is Successful Farming magazine of Des Moines, Iowa. Type card collectors and superstar collectors can expect to pay a modest premium for individual cards with the magazine's advertising. Cards measure about 1-5/8" x 3" and are printed in black-and-white.

PREMIUM: 2-3X
(See 1916 Sporting News M101-5 for checklist and base card values.)

1976 Sugar Daddy Sports World

Two baseball related cards were issued as part of this multi-sport candy insert set. Each card is titled "BASEBALL" and they detail the 1974 and 1975 World Series and depict a player - though not naming him - in action. The cards are 1" x 2-3/4" and have a white-bordered color photo on front. Backs include various advertising details.

		NM	EX	VG
Complete Set (25):		60.00	30.00	18.00
12	Pete Rose (Series 1, 1974 World Series)	25.00	12.50	7.50
25	Bobby Murcer (Series 2, 1975 World Series)	17.50	9.00	5.00

1962 Sugardale Weiners

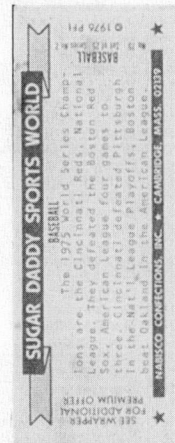

The Sugardale Meats set of black and white cards measure 5-1/8" x 3-3/4". The 22-card set includes 18 Cleveland Indians and four Pittsburgh Pirates players. The Indians cards

are numbered from 1-19 with card number 6 not issued. The Pirates cards are lettered from A to D. The card fronts contain a relatively small player photo, with biographical information and Sugardale logo. The backs are printed in red and offer playing tips and another company logo. Card number 10 (Bob Nieman) is considerably more scarce than other cards in the set.

		NM	EX	VG
Complete Set (22):		10,000	4,000	2,000
Common Player:		325.00	130.00	65.00
A	Dick Groat	325.00	130.00	65.00
B	Roberto Clemente	3,250	1,300	650.00
C	Don Hoak	325.00	130.00	65.00
D	Dick Stuart	325.00	130.00	65.00
1	Barry Latman	325.00	130.00	65.00
2	Gary Bell	325.00	130.00	65.00
3	Dick Donovan	325.00	130.00	65.00
4	Frank Funk	325.00	130.00	65.00
5	Jim Perry	325.00	130.00	65.00
6	Not Issued			
7	Johnny Romano	325.00	130.00	65.00
8	Ty Cline	325.00	130.00	65.00
9	Tito Francona	325.00	130.00	65.00
10	Bob Nieman (SP)	1,200	480.00	240.00
11	Willie Kirkland	325.00	130.00	65.00
12	Woodie Held	325.00	130.00	65.00
13	Jerry Kindall	325.00	130.00	65.00
14	Bubba Phillips	325.00	130.00	65.00
15	Mel Harder	325.00	130.00	65.00
16	Salty Parker	325.00	130.00	65.00
17	Ray Katt	325.00	130.00	65.00
18	Mel McGaha	325.00	130.00	65.00
19	Pedro Ramos	325.00	130.00	65.00

1963 Sugardale Weiners

Sugardale Meats again featured Cleveland and Pittsburgh players in its 1963 set, which grew to 31 cards. The black and white cards again measure 5-1/8" x 3-3/4", and consist of 28 Indians and five Pirates players. Card formats are virtually identical to the 1962 cards, with the only real difference being the information included in the player biographies. The cards are numbered 1-38, with numbers 6, 21, 22 and 29-32 not issued. Cards for Bob Skinner (#35) and Jim Perry (#5) are scarce as these two players were traded during the season and their cards withdrawn from distribution. The red card backs again offer playing tips.

		NM	EX	VG
Complete Set (31):		10,000	4,000	2,000
Common Player:		325.00	130.00	65.00
A	Don Cardwell	325.00	130.00	65.00
B	Robert R. Skinner (SP)	600.00	240.00	120.00
C	Donald B. Schwall	325.00	130.00	65.00
D	Jim Pagliaroni	325.00	130.00	65.00
E	Dick Schofield	325.00	130.00	65.00
1	Barry Latman	325.00	130.00	65.00
2	Gary Bell	325.00	130.00	65.00
3	Dick Donovan	325.00	130.00	65.00
4	Joe Adcock	400.00	160.00	80.00
5	Jim Perry (SP)	600.00	240.00	120.00
6	Not Issued			
7	Johnny Romano	325.00	130.00	65.00
8	Mike de la Hoz	325.00	130.00	65.00
9	Tito Francona	325.00	130.00	65.00
10	Gene Green	325.00	130.00	65.00
11	Willie Kirkland	325.00	130.00	65.00
12	Woodie Held	325.00	130.00	65.00
13	Jerry Kindall	325.00	130.00	65.00
14	Max Alvis	325.00	130.00	65.00
15	Mel Harder	325.00	130.00	65.00
16	George Strickland	325.00	130.00	65.00
17	Elmer Valo	325.00	130.00	65.00
18	Birdie Tebbetts	325.00	130.00	65.00
19	Pedro Ramos	325.00	130.00	65.00
20	Al Luplow	325.00	130.00	65.00
21	Not Issued			
22	Not Issued			
23	Jim Grant	325.00	130.00	65.00
24	Victor Davalillo	325.00	130.00	65.00
25	Jerry Walker	325.00	130.00	65.00
26	Sam McDowell	400.00	160.00	80.00
27	Fred Whitfield	325.00	130.00	65.00
28	Jack Kralick	325.00	130.00	65.00
29	Not Issued			
30	Not Issued			
31	Not Issued			
32	Not Issued			
33	Bob Allen	325.00	130.00	65.00

1933 Sulima Cigarettes

This is one of several early 1930s German cigarette cards to picture Babe Ruth. In this case he is pictured on the 1-5/8" x 2-3/8" black-and-white card with American comedic actor

Harold Lloyd. The card is part of a numbered set of 272 movie star cards. Backs are printed in German. The card is identical in format to the Josetti cigarette cards.

		NM	EX	VG
151	Babe Ruth, Harold Lloyd	1,100	550.00	330.00

1936 Sunday Advertiser Sport Stamps

(See 1936 Boston American Sport Stamps.)

1974 Sun-Glo Pop Al Kaline

This 2-1/4" x 4-1/2" card was issued as an attachment to bottles of soda pop. The blank-back card features a modishly dressed portrait of the former Tigers great and his endorsement for the soda. Cards are printed in black on various brightly colored backgrounds.

	NM	EX	VG
Al Kaline	6.00	3.00	1.75

1969 Sunoco Cubs/Brewers Pins

Fans in Southern Wisconsin and Northern Illinois could acquire 1-1/8" lithographed steel baseball player pins of the Cubs and Brewers at participating Sunoco gas stations. The blue-and-white (Cubs) or red-and-white (Brewers) pins have black-and-white player portrait photos at center on which cap logos have been removed. The Brewers pins are somewhat scarcer than those of the Cubs.

		NM	EX	VG
Complete Set (18):		100.00	50.00	30.00
Common Player:		4.00	2.00	1.25
Chicago Cubs Team Set:		65.00	32.50	20.00
(1)	Ernie Banks	25.00	12.50	7.50
(2)	Glenn Beckert	4.00	2.00	1.25
(3)	Jim Hickman	4.00	2.00	1.25
(4)	Randy Hundley	4.00	2.00	1.25
(5)	Ferguson Jenkins	7.50	3.75	2.25
(6)	Don Kessinger	6.00	3.00	1.75
(7)	Joe Pepitone	6.00	3.00	1.75
(8)	Ron Santo	10.00	5.00	3.00
(9)	Billy Williams	12.50	6.25	3.75
Milwaukee Brewers Team Set:		50.00	25.00	15.00
(1)	Tommy Harper	6.00	3.00	1.75
(2)	Mike Hegan	6.00	3.00	1.75

		NM	EX	VG
(3)	Lew Krausse	6.00	3.00	1.75
(4)	Ted Kubiak	6.00	3.00	1.75
(5)	Marty Pattin	6.00	3.00	1.75
(6)	Phil Roof	6.00	3.00	1.75
(7)	Ken Sanders	6.00	3.00	1.75
(8)	Ted Savage	6.00	3.00	1.75
(9)	Danny Walton	6.00	3.00	1.75

1931 Sun Pictures Photo Kits

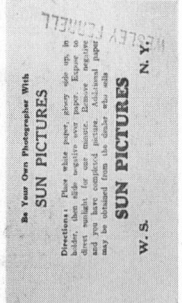

One of several contemporary kits for do-it-yourself production of photos, this issue was produced in New York City by a firm identified only as "W.S." A complete outfit consists of a 4-1/4" x 2-1/2" pink or kraft paper envelope with the name of the subject inside rubber-stamped on one end, a film negative, a piece of photo paper and a stand for producing/displaying the photo. The negative and resulting print measure 2-5/16" x 3-1/4". The set is listed in the American Card Catalog as W626. Prices shown are for complete kits; individual pieces would be pro-rated, with the negative the most valuable component. Because individual prints can be easily made even today, they have little collectible value. Only the baseball players are listed here.

		NM	EX	VG
Common Player Kit:		125.00	62.00	37.50
(1)	George Earnshaw	125.00	62.00	37.50
(2)	Wesley Ferrell	125.00	62.00	38.00
(3)	Lefty Grove	250.00	125.00	75.00
(4)	Leo Hartnett	225.00	112.00	67.00
(5)	Tony Lazzeri	250.00	125.00	75.00
(6)	Herb Pennock	225.00	112.00	67.00
(7)	Babe Ruth	2,400	1,200	725.00
(8)	Al Simmons	225.00	112.00	67.00
(9)	Dazzy Vance	225.00	112.00	67.00
(10)	Hack Wilson	250.00	125.00	75.00

1960s Sunny Ayr Farms Johnny Callison

In the absence of other player cardsm, it is impossible to date this issue any more precisely than Callison's tenure with the Phillies which encompassed the 1960s. The 3-1/2" x 5-1/2" black-and-white card had a facsimile autograph on front. The divided back is printed in red.

	NM	EX	VG
Johnny Callison	100.00	50.00	30.00

1970 Superballs

Manufactured by Chemtoy (though not credited on the balls), these high-bouncing hard rubber balls are composed of see-through material in which is imbedded a disc with a baseball player's portrait and identification. About 1-1/8" in diameter, the balls identify the player by name, team and position and include a four-digit number. In this checklist, the balls are listed alphabetically for lack of access to a complete list of the actual numbers. It is also possible the checklist in incomplete.

		NM	EX	VG
Complete Set (286):		1,650	825.00	500.00
Common Player:		5.00	2.50	1.50
(1)	Hank Aaron	40.00	20.00	12.00
(2)	Jerry Adair	5.00	2.50	1.50
(3)	Tommie Agee	5.00	2.50	1.50
(4)	Bernie Allen	5.00	2.50	1.50
(5)	Lloyd Allen	5.00	2.50	1.50
(6)	Gene Alley	5.00	2.50	1.50
(7)	Bob Allison	5.00	2.50	1.50
(8)	Sandy Alomar	5.00	2.50	1.50
(9)	Jesus Alou	5.00	2.50	1.50
(10)	Matty Alou	5.00	2.50	1.50
(11)	Max Alvis	5.00	2.50	1.50
(12)	Mike Andrews	5.00	2.50	1.50
(13)	Luis Aparicio	17.50	8.75	5.25
(14)	Jose Arcia	5.00	2.50	1.50
(15)	Bob Aspromonte	5.00	2.50	1.50
(16)	Jose Azcue	5.00	2.50	1.50
(17)	Bob Bailey	5.00	2.50	1.50
(18)	Jack Baldschun	5.00	2.50	1.50
(19)	Sal Bando	5.00	2.50	1.50
(20)	Ernie Banks	25.00	12.50	7.50
(21)	John Bateman	5.00	2.50	1.50
(22)	Glenn Beckert	5.00	2.50	1.50
(23)	Mark Belanger	5.00	2.50	1.50
(24)	Ken Berry	5.00	2.50	1.50
(25)	Paul Blair	5.00	2.50	1.50
(26)	Curt Blefary	5.00	2.50	1.50
(27)	John Boccabella	5.00	2.50	1.50
(28)	Bobby Bonds	5.00	2.50	1.50
(29)	John Boozer	5.00	2.50	1.50
(30)	Ken Boswell	5.00	2.50	1.50
(31)	Clete Boyer	5.00	2.50	1.50
(32)	Gene Brabender	5.00	2.50	1.50
(33)	Ron Brand	5.00	2.50	1.50
(34)	Jim Brewer	5.00	2.50	1.50
(35)	Johnny Briggs	5.00	2.50	1.50
(36)	Nelson Briles	5.00	2.50	1.50
(37)	Ed Brinkman	5.00	2.50	1.50
(38)	Lou Brock	17.50	8.75	5.25
(39)	Don Buford	5.00	2.50	1.50
(40)	Tom Burgmeier	5.00	2.50	1.50
(41)	Bill Butler	5.00	2.50	1.50
(42)	Johnny Callison	5.00	2.50	1.50
(43)	Bert Campaneris	5.00	2.50	1.50
(44)	Jim Campanis	5.00	2.50	1.50
(45)	Chris Cannizzaro	5.00	2.50	1.50
(46)	Jose Cardenal	5.00	2.50	1.50
(47)	Leo Cardenas	5.00	2.50	1.50
(48)	Rod Carew	20.00	10.00	6.00
(49)	Clay Carroll	5.00	2.50	1.50
(50)	Rico Carty	5.00	2.50	1.50
(51)	Paul Casanova	5.00	2.50	1.50
(52)	Norm Cash	10.00	5.00	3.00
(53)	Orlando Cepeda	17.50	8.75	5.25
(54)	Billy Champion	5.00	2.50	1.50
(55)	Dean Chance	5.00	2.50	1.50
(56a)	Roberto Clemente (Red insert.)	60.00	30.00	18.00
(56b)	Roberto Clemente (Blue insert.)	50.00	25.00	15.00
(57)	Tony Cloninger	5.00	2.50	1.50
(58)	Nate Colbert	5.00	2.50	1.50
(59)	Joe Coleman	5.00	2.50	1.50
(60)	Kevin Collins	5.00	2.50	1.50
(61)	Wayne Comer	5.00	2.50	1.50
(62)	Tony Conigliaro	10.00	5.00	3.00
(63)	Billy Cowan	5.00	2.50	1.50
(64)	Casey Cox	5.00	2.50	1.50
(65)	Willie Crawford	5.00	2.50	1.50
(66)	Mike Cuellar	5.00	2.50	1.50
(67)	Al Dark	5.00	2.50	1.50
(68)	Vic Davalillo	5.00	2.50	1.50
(69)	Jim Davenport	5.00	2.50	1.50
(70)	Willie Davis	5.00	2.50	1.50
(71)	Tommy Dean	5.00	2.50	1.50
(72)	Larry Dierker	5.00	2.50	1.50
(73)	Dick Dietz	5.00	2.50	1.50
(74)	Moe Drabowsky	5.00	2.50	1.50
(75)	Leo Durocher	13.50	6.75	4.00
(76)	Johnny Edwards	5.00	2.50	1.50
(77)	Dock Ellis	5.00	2.50	1.50
(78)	Dick Ellsworth	5.00	2.50	1.50
(79)	Mike Epstein	5.00	2.50	1.50
(80)	Andy Etchebarren	5.00	2.50	1.50
(81)	Ron Fairly	5.00	2.50	1.50
(82)	Al Ferrara	5.00	2.50	1.50
(83)	Rollie Fingers	13.50	6.75	4.00
(84)	Mike Fiore	5.00	2.50	1.50
(85)	Eddie Fisher	5.00	2.50	1.50
(86)	Jack Fisher	5.00	2.50	1.50
(87)	Ray Fosse	5.00	2.50	1.50
(88)	Bill Freehan	5.00	2.50	1.50
(89)	Jim Fregosi	5.00	2.50	1.50
(90)	Tito Fuentes	5.00	2.50	1.50
(91)	Vern Fuller	5.00	2.50	1.50
(92)	Woody Fryman	5.00	2.50	1.50
(93)	Len Gabrielson	5.00	2.50	1.50
(94)	Gary Gentry	5.00	2.50	1.50
(95)	Jake Gibbs	5.00	2.50	1.50
(96)	Russ Gibson	5.00	2.50	1.50
(97)	Billy Grabarkewitz	5.00	2.50	1.50
(98)	Dick Green	5.00	2.50	1.50
(99)	Tom Griffin	5.00	2.50	1.50
(100)	Jerry Grote	5.00	2.50	1.50
(101)	Tom Haller	5.00	2.50	1.50
(102)	Steve Hamilton	5.00	2.50	1.50
(103)	Ron Hansen	5.00	2.50	1.50
(104)	Tommy Harmon	5.00	2.50	1.50
(105)	Tommy Harper	5.00	2.50	1.50
(106)	Bud Harrelson	5.00	2.50	1.50
(107)	Jim Ray Hart	5.00	2.50	1.50
(108)	Richie Hebner	5.00	2.50	1.50
(109)	Mike Hedlund	5.00	2.50	1.50
(110)	Mike Hegan	5.00	2.50	1.50
(111)	Tommy Helms	5.00	2.50	1.50
(112)	Angel Hermoso	5.00	2.50	1.50
(113)	Ed Herrmann	5.00	2.50	1.50
(114)	Mike Hershberger	5.00	2.50	1.50
(115)	Jim Hickman	5.00	2.50	1.50
(116)	Jim Hicks	5.00	2.50	1.50
(117)	Chuck Hinton	5.00	2.50	1.50
(118)	Larry Hisle	5.00	2.50	1.50
(119)	Gil Hodges	13.50	6.75	4.00
(120)	Ken Holtzman	5.00	2.50	1.50
(121)	Joel Horlen	5.00	2.50	1.50
(122)	Willie Horton	5.00	2.50	1.50
(123)	Ralph Houk	5.00	2.50	1.50
(124)	Frank Howard	7.50	3.75	2.25
(125)	Randy Hundley	5.00	2.50	1.50
(126)	Ron Hunt	5.00	2.50	1.50
(127)	Jim Hunter	13.50	6.75	4.00
(128)	Steve Huntz	5.00	2.50	1.50
(129)	Al Jackson	5.00	2.50	1.50
(130)	Reggie Jackson	35.00	17.50	10.50
(131)	Pat Jarvis	5.00	2.50	1.50
(132)	Julian Javier	5.00	2.50	1.50
(133)	Tommy John	10.00	5.00	3.00
(134)	Dave Johnson	5.00	2.50	1.50
(135)	Jerry Johnson	5.00	2.50	1.50
(136)	Jay Johnstone	5.00	2.50	1.50
(137)	Cleon Jones	5.00	2.50	1.50
(138)	Dalton Jones	5.00	2.50	1.50
(139)	Jim Kaat	7.50	3.75	2.25
(140)	Al Kaline	20.00	10.00	6.00
(141)	Dick Kelley	5.00	2.50	1.50
(142)	Pat Kelly	5.00	2.50	1.50
(143)	John Kennedy	5.00	2.50	1.50
(144)	Joe Keough	5.00	2.50	1.50
(145)	Don Kessinger	5.00	2.50	1.50
(146)	Harmon Killebrew	20.00	10.00	6.00
(147)	Clay Kirby	5.00	2.50	1.50
(148)	Darold Knowles	5.00	2.50	1.50
(149)	Jerry Koosman	5.00	2.50	1.50
(150)	Andy Kosco	5.00	2.50	1.50
(151)	Ed Kranepool	5.00	2.50	1.50
(152)	Lew Krausse	5.00	2.50	1.50
(153)	Coco Laboy	5.00	2.50	1.50
(154)	Hal Lanier	5.00	2.50	1.50
(155)	George Lauzerique	5.00	2.50	1.50
(156)	Denny Lemaster	5.00	2.50	1.50
(157)	Bob Locker	5.00	2.50	1.50
(158)	Mickey Lolich	5.00	2.50	1.50
(159)	Jim Lonborg	5.00	2.50	1.50
(160)	Mike Lum	5.00	2.50	1.50
(161)	Jim Maloney	5.00	2.50	1.50
(162)	Juan Marichal	13.50	6.75	4.00
(163)	Dal Maxvill	5.00	2.50	1.50
(164)	Carlos May	5.00	2.50	1.50
(165)	Lee May	5.00	2.50	1.50
(166)	Willie Mays	40.00	20.00	12.00
(167)	Bill Mazeroski	17.50	8.75	5.25
(168)	Dick McAuliffe	5.00	2.50	1.50
(169)	Mike McCormick	5.00	2.50	1.50
(170)	Willie McCovey	20.00	10.00	6.00
(171)	Denny McLain	5.00	2.50	1.50
(172)	Jerry McNertney	5.00	2.50	1.50
(173)	Bill Melton	5.00	2.50	1.50
(174)	Denis Menke	5.00	2.50	1.50
(175)	Jim Merritt	5.00	2.50	1.50
(176)	Gene Michael	5.00	2.50	1.50
(177)	Pete Mikkelsen	5.00	2.50	1.50
(178)	Felix Millan	5.00	2.50	1.50
(179)	Norm Miller	5.00	2.50	1.50
(180)	Don Mincher	5.00	2.50	1.50
(181)	George Mitterwald	5.00	2.50	1.50
(182)	Rick Monday	5.00	2.50	1.50
(183)	Don Money	5.00	2.50	1.50
(184)	Bob Moose	5.00	2.50	1.50
(185)	Dave Morehead	5.00	2.50	1.50
(186)	Joe Morgan	20.00	10.00	6.00
(187)	Bobby Mercer (Murcer)	7.50	3.75	2.25
(188)	Ivan Murrell	5.00	2.50	1.50
(189)	Phil Niekro	13.50	6.75	4.00
(190)	Jim Northrup	5.00	2.50	1.50
(191)	Tony Oliva	10.00	5.00	3.00
(192)	Al Oliver	5.00	2.50	1.50
(193)	Claude Osteen	5.00	2.50	1.50
(194)	Jose Pagan	5.00	2.50	1.50
(195)	Jim Pagliaroni	5.00	2.50	1.50
(196)	Jim Palmer	20.00	10.00	6.00
(197)	Lowell Palmer	5.00	2.50	1.50
(198)	Milt Pappas	5.00	2.50	1.50
(199)	Marty Pattin	5.00	2.50	1.50
(200)	Roberto Pena	5.00	2.50	1.50
(201)	Joe Pepitone	7.50	3.75	2.25
(202)	Tony Perez	17.50	8.75	5.25
(203)	Gaylord Perry	13.50	6.75	4.00
(204)	Jim Perry	5.00	2.50	1.50
(205)	Fritz Peterson	5.00	2.50	1.50
(206)	Rico Petroceli (Petrocelli)	5.00	2.50	1.50
(207)	Lefty Phillips	5.00	2.50	1.50
(208)	Tom Phoebus	5.00	2.50	1.50
(209)	Lou Piniella	7.50	3.75	2.25
(210)	Vada Pinson	7.50	3.75	2.25
(211)	Boog Powell	10.00	5.00	3.00
(212)	Frank Quillici	5.00	2.50	1.50
(213)	Doug Rader	5.00	2.50	1.50
(214)	Ron Reed	5.00	2.50	1.50
(215)	Rich Reese	5.00	2.50	1.50
(216)	Rick Reichardt	5.00	2.50	1.50
(217)	Phil Regan	5.00	2.50	1.50
(218)	Roger Repoz	5.00	2.50	1.50
(219)	Juan Rios	5.00	2.50	1.50
(220)	Brooks Robinson	20.00	10.00	6.00
(221)	Frank Robinson	20.00	10.00	6.00
(222)	Cookie Rojas	5.00	2.50	1.50
(223)	Rich Rollins	5.00	2.50	1.50
(224)	Pete Rose	40.00	20.00	12.00
(225)	Gary Ross	5.00	2.50	1.50
(226)	Joe Rudi	5.00	2.50	1.50
(227)	Manny Sanguillen	5.00	2.50	1.50
(228)	Jose Santiago	5.00	2.50	1.50
(229)	Ron Santo	10.00	5.00	3.00

		NM	EX	VG
(230)	Tom Satriano	5.00	2.50	1.50
(231)	Richie Scheinblum	5.00	2.50	1.50
(232)	Red Schoendienst	13.50	6.75	4.00
(233)	George Scott	5.00	2.50	1.50
(234)	Tom Seaver	20.00	10.00	6.00
(235)	Norm Siebern	5.00	2.50	1.50
(236)	Sonny Siebert	5.00	2.50	1.50
(237)	Duke Sims	5.00	2.50	1.50
(238)	Tommie Sisk	5.00	2.50	1.50
(239)	Ted Sizemore	5.00	2.50	1.50
(240)	Mayo Smith	5.00	2.50	1.50
(241)	Reggie Smith	5.00	2.50	1.50
(242)	Willie Smith	5.00	2.50	1.50
(243)	Russ Snyder	5.00	2.50	1.50
(244)	Joe Sparma	5.00	2.50	1.50
(245)	Lee Stange	5.00	2.50	1.50
(246)	Mickey Stanley	5.00	2.50	1.50
(247)	Willie Stargell	17.50	8.75	5.25
(248)	Rusty Staub	7.50	3.75	2.25
(249)	Ron Stone	5.00	2.50	1.50
(250)	Bill Stoneman	5.00	2.50	1.50
(251)	Mel Stottlemyre	5.00	2.50	1.50
(252)	Ed Stroud	5.00	2.50	1.50
(253)	Bill Sudakis	5.00	2.50	1.50
(254)	Gary Sutherland	5.00	2.50	1.50
(255)	Ron Swoboda	5.00	2.50	1.50
(256)	Carl Taylor	5.00	2.50	1.50
(257)	Tony Taylor	5.00	2.50	1.50
(258)	Bob Tillman	5.00	2.50	1.50
(259)	Bobby Tolan	5.00	2.50	1.50
(260)	Cesar Tovar	5.00	2.50	1.50
(261)	Jeff Torborg	5.00	2.50	1.50
(262)	Joe Torre	10.00	5.00	3.00
(263)	Hector Torres	5.00	2.50	1.50
(264)	Tom Tresh	7.50	3.75	2.25
(265)	Ted Uhlaender	5.00	2.50	1.50
(266)	Del Unser	5.00	2.50	1.50
(267)	Bob Veale	5.00	2.50	1.50
(268)	Zoilo Versalles	5.00	2.50	1.50
(269)	Bill Voss	5.00	2.50	1.50
(270)	Pete Ward	5.00	2.50	1.50
(271)	Greg Washburn	5.00	2.50	1.50
(272)	Eddie Watt	5.00	2.50	1.50
(273)	Ramon Webster	5.00	2.50	1.50
(274)	Al Weis	5.00	2.50	1.50
(275)	Roy White	5.00	2.50	1.50
(276)	Billy Williams	17.50	8.75	5.25
(277)	Ted Williams	30.00	15.00	9.00
(278)	Walt Williams	5.00	2.50	1.50
(279)	Billy Wilson	5.00	2.50	1.50
(280)	Don Wilson	5.00	2.50	1.50
(281)	Earl Wilson	5.00	2.50	1.50
(282)	Rick Wise	5.00	2.50	1.50
(283)	Bobby Wine	5.00	2.50	1.50
(284)	Wilbur Wood	5.00	2.50	1.50
(285)	Woody Woodward	5.00	2.50	1.50
(286)	Billy Wynne	5.00	2.50	1.50

1980 Superstar

SUPERSTAR

SUPERSTAR

WILLIE HOWARD MAYS
Centerfielder, New York and
San Francisco Giants

In 1951 Willie Mays was the National League Rookie-of-the-Year and played in the World Series for the New York Giants. After several brilliant years with the Giants, in both New York and San Francisco, Willie was traded to the New York Mets in 1972. The following year, Willie ended his memorable career, by again appearing in the fall classic.

Willie lead the New York Giants to a stunning World Series Championship over the heavily favored Cleveland Indians in 1954. Ironically, although he had 660 lifetime homers to place him third on the all-time list he never homered in the World Series.

This collectors' issue, probably produced by Card Collectors Closet in Springfield, Mass., included up to five cards each of the most famous former players. The 2-1/2" x 3-1/2" cards have black-and-white photos on front, with yellow, white and blue graphics. Backs are in black-and-white with career narrative. The set sold originally for $3.50.

		NM	EX	VG
Complete Set (45):		20.00	10.00	6.00
Common Player:		.75	.35	.20
1	Babe Ruth	1.25	.60	.40
2	Roberto Clemente	1.00	.50	.30
3	Roberto Clemente	1.00	.50	.30
4	Roberto Clemente	1.00	.50	.30
5	Lou Gehrig, Joe DiMaggio	.75	.35	.20
6	Mickey Mantle, Roger Maris	1.75	.90	.40
7	Roger Maris, Yogi Berra, Mickey Mantle	1.25	.60	.40
8	Whitey Ford, Sandy Koufax	.75	.35	.20
9	Babe Ruth	1.25	.60	.40
10	Roger Maris, Mickey Mantle	1.75	.90	.40
11	Ted Williams, Stan Musial, Willie Mays	.75	.35	.20
12	Mickey Mantle, Hank Aaron	1.25	.60	.40
13	Sandy Koufax	.75	.35	.20
14	Sandy Koufax	.75	.35	.20
15	Thurman Munson	.75	.35	.20
16	Sandy Koufax	.75	.35	.20
17	Sandy Koufax	.75	.35	.20
18	Willie Mays	.75	.35	.20
19	Willie Mays	.75	.35	.20
20	Willie Mays	.75	.35	.20
21	Willie Mays	.75	.35	.20
22	Ted Williams	.75	.35	.20
23	Ted Williams	.75	.35	.20
24	Ted Williams	.75	.35	.20
25	Ted Williams	.75	.35	.20
26	Lou Gehrig	.75	.35	.20

27	Lou Gehrig	.75	.35	.20
28	Lou Gehrig	.75	.35	.20
29	Lou Gehrig	.75	.35	.20
30	Mickey Mantle	2.00	1.00	.60
31	Mickey Mantle	2.00	1.00	.60
32	Mickey Mantle	2.00	1.00	.60
33	Mickey Mantle	2.00	1.00	.60
34	Hank Aaron	.75	.35	.20
35	Joe DiMaggio	.75	.35	.20
36	Joe DiMaggio	.75	.35	.20
37	Joe DiMaggio	.75	.35	.20
38	Joe DiMaggio	.75	.35	.20
39	Roberto Clemente	1.00	.50	.30
40	Babe Ruth	1.25	.60	.40
41	Babe Ruth	1.25	.60	.40
42	Babe Ruth	1.25	.60	.40
43	Hank Aaron	.75	.35	.20
44	Hank Aaron	.75	.35	.20
45	Hank Aaron	.75	.35	.20

1970 Super Valu Minnesota Twins

One of many Minnesota Twins regional issues from the team's first decade, this set of player portraits was painted by noted celebrity artist John Wheeldon. Individual player pictures were given away at Super Valu grocery stores. The premiums feature large portraits and smaller action pictures, painted in pastels, against a pastel background. A facsimile autograph is printed below the pictures and the player's name is printed in the bottom border. At 7-3/4" x 9-3/8", the Twins portraits are somewhat smaller than similar contemporary issues. Backs are printed in black-and-white and include a self-portrait and biography of the artist. Player information includes biographical bits, a lengthy career summary and complete major and minor league stats. Team and sponsor logo are also included on the unnumbered card backs. The set is checklisted here alphabetically.

		NM	EX	VG
Complete Set (12):		90.00	45.00	27.50
Common Player:		6.00	3.00	1.75
(1)	Brant Alyea	6.00	3.00	1.75
(2)	Leo Cardenas	6.00	3.00	1.75
(3)	Rod Carew	20.00	10.00	6.00
(4)	Jim Kaat	9.00	4.50	2.75
(5)	Harmon Killebrew	20.00	10.00	6.00
(6)	George Mitterwald	6.00	3.00	1.75
(7)	Tony Oliva	9.00	4.50	2.75
(8)	Ron Perranoski	6.00	3.00	1.75
(9)	Jim Perry	6.00	3.00	1.75
(10)	Rich Reese	6.00	3.00	1.75
(11)	Luis Tiant	7.50	3.75	2.25
(12)	Cesar Tovar	6.00	3.00	1.75

1874 Suppards & Fennemore Cabinets

Only members of the hometown 1874 Athletics (National Association) have been reported in this issue of cabinet cards from the Philadelphia studio. The 4-1/4" x 6-1/2" cards have full-length poses on front. Backs carry an ornate ad for the photographer. The players are not identified on the cards, unless an earlier owner has written the name. Thus far the team's most famous player, Cap Anson, has not been reported.

		NM	EX	VG
Common Player:		3,750	1,875	1,125
(1)	Joe Battin (Bat on shoulder.)	3,750	1,875	1,125
(2)	John Clapp (Cap on floor to his right.)	3,750	1,875	1,125
(3)	Wes Fisler (Bat at right side, no cap on front.)	3,750	1,875	1,125
(4)	Dick McBride (Ball in hands at waist.)	3,750	1,875	1,125
(5)	Mike McGeary (Bat in crook of arm.)	3,750	1,875	1,125
(6)	John McMullin (Bat at his left, cap on floor at left.)	3,750	1,875	1,125
(7)	Tim Murnane (Bat at his right, cap on floor at left.)	4,050	2,025	1,200

1966 Swap-N-Save Album

While this 4" x 9" album pictures 1965 and 1966 Topps cards in full color on front and back, it is not connected with Topps. The album's interior pages feature die-cuts which allow the central panel to be removed so both front and back of each card can be viewed. Informational pages include team rosters.

	NM	EX	VG
Album:	80.00	40.00	20.00

1909-11 Sweet Caporal

Among the most common of the American Tobacco Co. brands advertising on the backs of 1909-11 T206 and 1911 T205 is Sweet Caporal. T206s can be found with factory designations of No. 25, No. 30, No. 42 (overprinted), No. 649 and No. 649 (overprinted). In T205, Sweet Cap backs can be found printed in red (no factory number, or No. 42) or black, No. 25, No. 42.

(See T205, T206.)

1909-12 Sweet Caporal Domino Discs (PX7)

Domino Discs, distributed by Sweet Caporal Cigarettes from 1909 to 1912, are among the more obscure 20th Century tobacco issues. Although the disc set contains many of the same players - some even pictured in the same poses - as the later Sweet Caporal pin set, the discs have always lagged behind the pins in collector appeal. The Domino Discs, so called because each disc has a large, white domino printed on the back, measure approximately 1-1/8" in diameter and are made of thin cardboard surrounded by a metal rim. The fronts of the discs contain a player portrait set against a background of either red, green or blue. The words "Sweet Caporal Cigarettes" appear on the front along with the player's last name and team. There are 129 different major leaguers featured in the set. Each player can be found with two picture variations involving uniform or cap details, or just the size of the portrait. Also known to exist as part of the set is a disc which pictures a generic player and contains the words "Home Team" against a red background on one side and "Visiting Team" with a green background on the reverse. Because each of the players can theoretically be found in two pictures, with three different background colors and with varying numbers of dots on the dominoes, there is almost an impossible number of variations available. Collectors, however, generally collect the discs without regard to background color or domino arrangement. The Domino Disc set was assigned the designation PX7 in the American Card Catalog.

		NM	EX	VG
Complete Set (129):		10,000	5,000	3,000
Common Player:		60.00	30.00	18.00
(1)	Red Ames	60.00	30.00	18.00
(2)	Jimmy Archer	60.00	30.00	18.00
(3)	Jimmy Austin	60.00	30.00	18.00
(4)	Home Run Baker	130.00	65.00	40.00
(5)	Neal Ball	60.00	30.00	18.00
(6)	Cy Barger	60.00	30.00	18.00
(7)	Jack Barry	60.00	30.00	18.00
(8)	Johnny Bates	60.00	30.00	18.00
(9)	Beals Becker	60.00	30.00	18.00

(10)	George Bell	60.00	30.00	18.00
(11)	Chief Bender	130.00	65.00	40.00
(12)	Bill Bergen	60.00	30.00	18.00
(13)	Bob Bescher	60.00	30.00	18.00
(14)	Joe Birmingham	60.00	30.00	18.00
(15)	Roger Bresnahan	130.00	65.00	40.00
(16)	Al Bridwell	60.00	30.00	18.00
(17)	Mordecai Brown	130.00	65.00	40.00
(18)	Bobby Byrne	60.00	30.00	18.00
(19)	Nixey Callahan	60.00	30.00	18.00
(20)	Howie Camnitz	60.00	30.00	18.00
(21)	Bill Carrigan	60.00	30.00	18.00
(22)	Frank Chance	130.00	65.00	40.00
(23)	Hal Chase	60.00	30.00	18.00
(24)	Ed Cicotte	60.00	30.00	18.00
(25)	Fred Clarke	130.00	65.00	40.00
(26a)	Ty Cobb ("D" on cap.)	600.00	300.00	180.00
(26b)	Ty Cobb (No "D" on cap.)	600.00	300.00	180.00
(27)	Eddie Collins	130.00	65.00	40.00
(28)	Doc Crandall	60.00	30.00	18.00
(29)	Birdie Cree	60.00	30.00	18.00
(30)	Bill Dahlen	60.00	30.00	18.00
(31)	Jim Delahanty	60.00	30.00	18.00
(32)	Art Devlin	60.00	30.00	18.00
(33)	Josh Devore	60.00	30.00	18.00
(34)	Red Dooin	60.00	30.00	18.00
(35)	Mickey Doolan	60.00	30.00	18.00
(36)	Patsy Dougherty	60.00	30.00	18.00
(37)	Tom Downey	60.00	30.00	18.00
(38)	Larry Doyle	60.00	30.00	18.00
(39)	Louis Drucke	60.00	30.00	18.00
(40)	Clyde Engle	60.00	30.00	18.00
(41)	Tex Erwin	60.00	30.00	18.00
(42)	Steve Evans	60.00	30.00	18.00
(43)	Johnny Evers	130.00	65.00	40.00
(44)	Cecil Ferguson	60.00	30.00	18.00
(45)	Russ Ford	60.00	30.00	18.00
(46)	Art Fromme	60.00	30.00	18.00
(47)	Harry Gaspar	60.00	30.00	18.00
(48)	George Gibson	60.00	30.00	18.00
(49)	Eddie Grant	65.00	32.50	20.00
(50)	Clark Griffith	130.00	65.00	40.00
(51)	Bob Groom	60.00	30.00	18.00
(52)	Bob Harmon	60.00	30.00	18.00
(53)	Topsy Hartsel	60.00	30.00	18.00
(54)	Arnold Hauser	60.00	30.00	18.00
(55)	Dick Hoblitzell	60.00	30.00	18.00
(56)	Danny Hoffman	60.00	30.00	18.00
(57)	Miller Huggins	130.00	65.00	40.00
(58)	John Hummel	60.00	30.00	18.00
(59)	Hugh Jennings	130.00	65.00	40.00
(60)	Walter Johnson	350.00	175.00	100.00
(61)	Ed Karger	60.00	30.00	18.00
(62a)	Jack Knight (Yankees)	60.00	30.00	18.00
(62b)	Jack Knight (Senators)	60.00	30.00	18.00
(63)	Ed Konetchy	60.00	30.00	18.00
(64)	Harry Krause	60.00	30.00	18.00
(65)	Frank LaPorte	60.00	30.00	18.00
(66)	Nap Lajoie	130.00	65.00	40.00
(67)	Tommy Leach	60.00	30.00	18.00
(68)	Sam Leever	60.00	30.00	18.00
(69)	Lefty Leifield	60.00	30.00	18.00
(70)	Paddy Livingston	60.00	30.00	18.00
(71)	Hans Lobert	60.00	30.00	18.00
(72)	Harry Lord	60.00	30.00	18.00
(73)	Nick Maddox	60.00	30.00	18.00
(74)	Sherry Magee	60.00	30.00	18.00
(75)	Rube Marquard	130.00	65.00	40.00
(76)	Christy Mathewson	400.00	200.00	120.00
(77)	Al Mattern	60.00	30.00	18.00
(78)	George McBride	60.00	30.00	18.00
(79)	John McGraw	130.00	65.00	40.00
(80)	Harry McIntire	60.00	30.00	18.00
(81)	Matty McLean	60.00	30.00	18.00
(82)	Larry McLean	60.00	30.00	18.00
(83)	Fred Merkle	60.00	30.00	18.00
(84)	Chief Meyers	60.00	30.00	18.00
(85)	Clyde Milan	60.00	30.00	18.00
(86)	Dots Miller	60.00	30.00	18.00
(87)	Mike Mitchell	60.00	30.00	18.00
(88a)	Pat Moran (Cubs)	60.00	30.00	18.00
(88b)	Pat Moran (Phillies)	60.00	30.00	18.00
(89)	George Mullen (Mullin)	60.00	30.00	18.00
(90)	Danny Murphy	60.00	30.00	18.00
(91)	Red Murray	60.00	30.00	18.00
(92)	Tom Needham	60.00	30.00	18.00
(93)	Rebel Oakes	60.00	30.00	18.00
(94)	Rube Oldring	60.00	30.00	18.00
(95)	Fred Parent	60.00	30.00	18.00
(96)	Dode Paskert	60.00	30.00	18.00
(97)	Barney Pelty	60.00	30.00	18.00
(98)	Eddie Phelps	60.00	30.00	18.00
(99)	Deacon Phillippe	60.00	30.00	18.00
(100)	Jack Quinn	60.00	30.00	18.00
(101)	Ed Reulbach	60.00	30.00	18.00
(102)	Lew Richie	60.00	30.00	18.00
(103)	Jack Rowan	60.00	30.00	18.00
(104)	Nap Rucker	60.00	30.00	18.00
(105a)	Doc Scanlon (Scanlan) (Superbas)	60.00	30.00	18.00
(105b)	Doc Scanlon (Scanlan) (Phillies)	60.00	30.00	18.00
(106)	Germany Schaefer	60.00	30.00	18.00
(107)	Boss Schmidt	60.00	30.00	18.00
(108)	Wildfire Schulte	60.00	30.00	18.00
(109)	Jimmy Sheckard	60.00	30.00	18.00
(110)	Hap Smith	60.00	30.00	18.00
(111)	Tris Speaker	150.00	75.00	45.00
(112)	Harry Stovall	60.00	30.00	18.00
(113a)	Gabby Street (Senators)	60.00	30.00	18.00
(113b)	Gabby Street (Yankees)	60.00	30.00	18.00
(114)	George Suggs	60.00	30.00	18.00
(115)	Ira Thomas	60.00	30.00	18.00
(116)	Joe Tinker	130.00	65.00	40.00
(117)	John Titus	60.00	30.00	18.00
(118)	Terry Turner	60.00	30.00	18.00
(119)	Heinie Wagner	60.00	30.00	18.00
(120)	Bobby Wallace	130.00	65.00	40.00
(121)	Ed Walsh	130.00	65.00	40.00
(122)	Jack Warhop	60.00	30.00	18.00
(123)	Zach Wheat	130.00	65.00	40.00
(124)	Doc White	60.00	30.00	18.00
(125a)	Art Wilson (Dark cap, Pirates.)	60.00	30.00	18.00
(125b)	Art Wilson (Dark cap, Giants.)	60.00	30.00	18.00
(126a)	Owen Wilson (White cap, Giants.)	60.00	30.00	18.00
(126b)	Owen Wilson (White cap, Pirates.)	60.00	30.00	18.00
(127)	Hooks Wiltse	60.00	30.00	18.00
(128)	Harry Wolter	60.00	30.00	18.00
(129)	Cy Young	400.00	200.00	120.00

1910-12 Sweet Caporal Pins (P2)

Expanding its premiums to include more than just trading cards, the American Tobacco Co. issued a series of baseball pins circa 1910-12. The sepia-colored pins measure 7/8" in diameter. The set includes 152 different players, but because of numerous "large letter" and "small letter" variations, collectors generally consider the set complete at 205 different pins. Fifty of the players are pictured on a second pin that usually displays the same photo but has the player's name and team designation printed in larger letters. Three players (Bresnahan, Mullin and Wallace) have three pins each. It is now generally accepted that there are 153 pins with "small letters" and another 52 "large letter" variations in a complete set. Research among advanced collectors has shown that 19 of the pins, including six of the "large letter" variations, are considered more difficult to find. The back of each pin has a variously colored paper insert advertising Sweet Caporal Cigarettes. The red backings are generally less common. The Sweet Caporal pins are closely related to the popular T205 Gold Border tobacco cards, also issued by the American Tobacco Co. about the same time. All but nine of the players featured in the pin set were also pictured on T205 cards, and in nearly all cases the photos are identical. The Sweet Caporal pins are designated as P2 in the American Card Catalog. The complete set price includes all variations.

		NM	EX	VG
Complete Set (204):		10,000	5,000	3,000
Common Player:		30.00	15.00	9.00
(1)	Ed Abbaticchio	30.00	15.00	9.00
(2)	Red Ames	30.00	15.00	9.00
(3a)	Jimmy Archer (Small letters.)	30.00	15.00	9.00
(3b)	Jimmy Archer (Large letters.)	35.00	17.50	10.00
(4a)	Jimmy Austin (Small letters.)	30.00	15.00	9.00
(4b)	Jimmy Austin (Large letters.)	35.00	17.50	10.00
(5)	Home Run Baker	90.00	45.00	27.00
(6)	Neal Ball	30.00	15.00	9.00
(7)	Cy Barger	30.00	15.00	9.00
(8)	Jack Barry	30.00	15.00	9.00
(9)	Johnny Bates	30.00	15.00	9.00
(10)	Beals Becker	30.00	15.00	9.00
(11)	Fred Beebe	30.00	15.00	9.00
(12a)	George Bell (Small letters.)	30.00	15.00	9.00
(12b)	George Bell (Large letters.)	35.00	17.50	10.00
(13a)	"Chief" Bender (Small letters.)	90.00	45.00	27.00
(13b)	"Chief" Bender (Large letters.)	100.00	50.00	30.00
(14)	Bill Bergen	30.00	15.00	9.00
(15)	Bob Bescher	30.00	15.00	9.00
(16)	Joe Birmingham	30.00	15.00	9.00
(17)	Kitty Bransfield	65.00	32.50	20.00
(18a)	Roger Bresnahan (Mouth closed, small letters.)	90.00	45.00	27.00
(18b)	Roger Bresnahan (Mouth closed, large letters.)	100.00	50.00	30.00
(19)	Roger Bresnahan (Mouth open.)	90.00	45.00	27.00
(20)	Al Bridwell	30.00	15.00	9.00
(21a)	Mordecai Brown (Small letters.)	90.00	45.00	27.00
(21b)	Mordecai Brown (Large letters.)	100.00	50.00	30.00
(22)	Bobby Byrne	30.00	15.00	9.00
(23)	Nixey Callahan	30.00	15.00	9.00
(24a)	Howie Camnitz (Small letters.)	30.00	15.00	9.00
(24b)	Howie Camnitz (Large letters.)	35.00	17.50	10.00
(25a)	Bill Carrigan (Small letters.)	30.00	15.00	9.00
(25b)	Bill Carrigan (Large letters.)	35.00	17.50	10.00
(26a)	Frank Chance (Small letters.)	90.00	45.00	27.00
(26b)	Frank Chance (Large letters.)	100.00	50.00	30.00
(27)	Hal Chase (Small letters.)	50.00	25.00	15.00
(28)	Hal Chase (Large letters.)	90.00	45.00	27.00
(29)	Ed Cicotte	90.00	45.00	27.00
(30a)	Fred Clarke (Small letters.)	90.00	45.00	27.00
(30b)	Fred Clarke (Large letters.)	100.00	50.00	30.00
(31a)	Ty Cobb (Small letters, "D" on cap.)	600.00	300.00	180.00
(31b)	Ty Cobb (Large letters, no "D" on cap.)	675.00	335.00	200.00
(32a)	Eddie Collins (Small letters.)	90.00	45.00	27.00
(32b)	Eddie Collins (Large letters.)	100.00	50.00	30.00
(33)	Doc Crandall	30.00	15.00	9.00
(34)	Birdie Cree	65.00	32.50	20.00
(35)	Bill Dahlen	30.00	15.00	9.00

(36)	Jim Delahanty	30.00	15.00	9.00
(37)	Art Devlin	30.00	15.00	9.00
(38)	Josh Devore	30.00	15.00	9.00
(39)	Wild Bill Donovan	65.00	32.50	20.00
(40a)	Red Dooin (Small letters.)	30.00	15.00	9.00
(40b)	Red Dooin (Large letters.)	35.00	17.50	10.00
(41a)	Mickey Doolan (Small letters.)	30.00	15.00	9.00
(41b)	Mickey Doolan (Large letters.)	35.00	17.50	10.00
(42)	Patsy Dougherty	30.00	15.00	9.00
(43a)	Tom Downey. (Small letters.)	30.00	15.00	9.00
(43b)	Tom Downey (Large letters.)	35.00	17.50	10.00
(44a)	Larry Doyle (Small letters.)	30.00	15.00	9.00
(44b)	Larry Doyle (Large letters.)	35.00	17.50	10.00
(45)	Louis Drucke	30.00	15.00	9.00
(46a)	Hugh Duffy (Small letters.)	90.00	45.00	27.00
(46b)	Hugh Duffy (Large letters.)	100.00	50.00	30.00
(47)	Jimmy Dygert	30.00	15.00	9.00
(48a)	Kid Elberfeld (Small letters.)	30.00	15.00	9.00
(48b)	Kid Elberfeld (Large letters.)	35.00	17.50	10.00
(49a)	Clyde Engle (Small letters.)	30.00	15.00	9.00
(49b)	Clyde Engle (Large letters.)	35.00	17.50	10.00
(50)	Tex Erwin	30.00	15.00	9.00
(51)	Steve Evans	30.00	15.00	9.00
(52)	Johnny Evers	90.00	45.00	27.00
(53)	Cecil Ferguson	30.00	15.00	9.00
(54)	John Flynn	30.00	15.00	9.00
(55a)	Russ Ford (Small letters.)	30.00	15.00	9.00
(55b)	Russ Ford (Large letters.)	35.00	17.50	10.00
(56)	Art Fromme	30.00	15.00	9.00
(57)	Harry Gaspar	30.00	15.00	9.00
(58a)	George Gibson (Small letters.)	30.00	15.00	9.00
(58b)	George Gibson (Large letters.)	35.00	17.50	10.00
(59)	Eddie Grant	65.00	32.50	20.00
(60)	Dolly Gray	30.00	15.00	9.00
(61a)	Clark Griffith (Small letters.)	90.00	45.00	27.00
(61b)	Clark Griffith (Large letters.)	100.00	50.00	30.00
(62)	Bob Groom	30.00	15.00	9.00
(63)	Bob Harmon	30.00	15.00	9.00
(64)	Topsy Hartsel	30.00	15.00	9.00
(65)	Arnold Hauser	65.00	32.50	20.00
(66)	Ira Hemphill	30.00	15.00	9.00
(67a)	Buck Herzog (Small letters.)	30.00	15.00	9.00
(67b)	Buck Herzog (Large letters.)	35.00	17.50	10.00
(68)	Dick Hoblitzell	30.00	15.00	9.00
(69)	Danny Hoffman	30.00	15.00	9.00
(70)	Harry Hooper	90.00	45.00	27.00
(71a)	Miller Huggins (Small letters.)	90.00	45.00	27.00
(71b)	Miller Huggins (Large letters.)	100.00	50.00	30.00
(72)	John Hummel	30.00	15.00	9.00
(73)	Hugh Jennings (Small letters.)	90.00	45.00	27.00
(74)	Hugh Jennings (Large letters.)	100.00	50.00	30.00
(75a)	Walter Johnson (Small letters.)	225.00	110.00	65.00
(75b)	Walter Johnson (Large letters.)	275.00	135.00	85.00
(76)	Tom Jones	65.00	32.50	20.00
(77)	Ed Karger	30.00	15.00	9.00
(78)	Ed Killian	65.00	32.50	20.00
(79a)	Jack Knight (Small letters.)	30.00	15.00	9.00
(79b)	Jack Knight (Large letters.)	35.00	17.50	10.00
(80)	Ed Konetchy	30.00	15.00	9.00
(81)	Harry Krause	30.00	15.00	9.00
(82)	Rube Kroh	30.00	15.00	9.00
(83)	Nap Lajoie	90.00	45.00	27.00
(84a)	Frank LaPorte (Small letters.)	30.00	15.00	9.00
(84b)	Frank LaPorte (Large letters.)	35.00	17.50	10.00
(85)	Arlie Latham	30.00	15.00	9.00
(86a)	Tommy Leach (Small letters.)	30.00	15.00	9.00
(86b)	Tommy Leach (Large letters.)	35.00	17.50	10.00
(87)	Sam Leever	30.00	15.00	9.00
(88)	Lefty Leifield	30.00	15.00	9.00
(89)	Hans Lobert	30.00	15.00	9.00
(90a)	Harry Lord (Small letters.)	30.00	15.00	9.00
(90b)	Harry Lord (Large letters.)	35.00	17.50	10.00
(91)	Paddy Livingston	30.00	15.00	9.00
(92)	Nick Maddox	30.00	15.00	9.00
(93)	Sherry Magee	30.00	15.00	9.00
(94)	Rube Marquard	90.00	45.00	27.00
(95a)	Christy Mathewson (Small letters.)	225.00	110.00	65.00
(95b)	Christy Mathewson (Large letters.)	275.00	135.00	80.00
(96a)	Al Mattern (Small letters.)	30.00	15.00	9.00
(96b)	Al Mattern (Large letters.)	35.00	17.50	10.00
(97)	George McBride	30.00	15.00	9.00
(98a)	John McGraw (Small letters.)	90.00	45.00	27.00
(98b)	John McGraw (Large letters.)	100.00	50.00	30.00
(99)	Harry McIntire (Cubs)	30.00	15.00	9.00
(100a)	Matty McIntire (White Sox, small letters.)	30.00	15.00	9.00
(100b)	Matty McIntire (White Sox, large letters.)	35.00	17.50	10.00
(101a)	John McLean (Small letters.)	30.00	15.00	9.00
(101b)	John McLean (Large letters.)	35.00	17.50	10.00
(102)	Fred Merkle	30.00	15.00	9.00
(103)	Chief Meyers	30.00	15.00	9.00
(104)	Clyde Milan	30.00	15.00	9.00
(105)	Dots Miller	30.00	15.00	9.00
(106)	Mike Mitchell	30.00	15.00	9.00
(107)	Pat Moran	30.00	15.00	9.00
(108a)	George Mullen (Mullin) (Small letters.)	30.00	15.00	9.00
(108b)	George Mullen (Large letters, white cap.)	90.00	45.00	27.00
(109)	Danny Murphy	30.00	15.00	9.00
(110a)	Red Murray (Small letters.)	35.00	17.50	10.00
(110b)	Red Murray (Large letters.)	30.00	15.00	9.00
(111)	Tom Needham	65.00	32.50	20.00
(112a)	Rebel Oakes (Small letters.)	30.00	15.00	9.00
(112b)	Rebel Oakes (Large letters.)	35.00	17.50	10.00
(113)	Rube Oldring	30.00	15.00	9.00
(114)	Charley O'Leary	30.00	15.00	9.00
(115)	Orval Overall	65.00	32.50	20.00
(116)	Fred Parent	30.00	15.00	9.00
(117a)	Dode Paskert (Small letters.)	30.00	15.00	9.00
(117b)	Dode Paskert (Large letters.)	35.00	17.50	10.00
(118)	Barney Pelty	30.00	15.00	9.00
(119)	Jake Pfeister	30.00	15.00	9.00
(120)	Eddie Phelps	30.00	15.00	9.00
(121)	Deacon Phillippe	30.00	15.00	9.00

		NM	EX	VG
(122)	Jack Quinn	30.00	15.00	9.00
(123)	Ed Reulbach	30.00	15.00	9.00
(124)	Lew Richie	30.00	15.00	9.00
(125)	Jack Rowan	30.00	15.00	9.00
(126a)	Nap Rucker (Small letters.)	30.00	15.00	9.00
(126b)	Nap Rucker (Large letters.)	35.00	17.50	10.00
(127)	Doc Scanlon (Scanlan)	65.00	32.50	20.00
(128)	Germany Schaefer	30.00	15.00	9.00
(129)	Jimmy Scheckard (Sheckard)	30.00	15.00	9.00
(130a)	Boss Schmidt (Small letters.)	30.00	15.00	9.00
(130b)	Boss Schmidt (Large letters.)	35.00	17.50	10.00
(131)	Wildfire Schulte	30.00	15.00	9.00
(132)	Hap Smith	30.00	15.00	9.00
(133a)	Tris Speaker (Small letters.)	150.00	75.00	45.00
(133b)	Tris Speaker (Large letters.)	175.00	85.00	50.00
(134)	Oscar Stanage	30.00	15.00	9.00
(135)	Harry Steinfeldt	30.00	15.00	9.00
(136)	George Stone	30.00	15.00	9.00
(137a)	George Stoval (Stovall) (Small letters.)	30.00	15.00	9.00
(137b)	George Stoval (Stovall) (Large letters.)	35.00	17.50	10.00
(138a)	Gabby Street (Small letters.)	30.00	15.00	9.00
(138b)	Gabby Street (Large letters.)	35.00	17.50	10.00
(139)	George Suggs	30.00	15.00	9.00
(140a)	Ira Thomas (Small letters.)	30.00	15.00	9.00
(140b)	Ira Thomas (Large letters.)	35.00	17.50	10.00
(141a)	Joe Tinker (Small letters.)	90.00	45.00	27.00
(141b)	Joe Tinker (Large letters.)	100.00	50.00	30.00
(142a)	John Titus (Small letters.)	30.00	15.00	9.00
(142b)	John Titus (Large letters.)	35.00	17.50	10.00
(143)	Terry Turner	30.00	15.00	9.00
(144)	Heinie Wagner	30.00	15.00	9.00
(145a)	Bobby Wallace (With cap, small letters.)	90.00	45.00	27.00
(145b)	Bobby Wallace (With cap, large letters.)	100.00	50.00	30.00
(146)	Bobby Wallace (Without cap.)	90.00	45.00	27.00
(147)	Ed Walsh	90.00	45.00	27.00
(148)	Jack Warhop	30.00	15.00	9.00
(149a)	Zach Wheat (Small letters.)	90.00	45.00	27.00
(149b)	Zach Wheat (Large letters.)	100.00	50.00	30.00
(150)	Doc White	30.00	15.00	9.00
(151)	Art Wilson (Giants)	30.00	15.00	9.00
(152)	Owen Wilson (Pirates)	30.00	15.00	9.00
(153)	Hooks Wiltse	30.00	15.00	9.00
(154)	Harry Wolter	30.00	15.00	9.00
(155a)	"Cy" Young ("C" on cap.)	200.00	100.00	60.00
(155b)	Old Cy Young (Plain cap.)	225.00	110.00	65.00

1928 Sweetman

(27) TY COBB

The cards of this St. Louis firm share the format - about 1-3/8" x 2-1/2", black-and-white with card number in parentheses to the left of player name on front - and checklist with the 1928 York Caramels Type 2 issue, but are less frequently encountered. Backs of the Sweetman cards offer an album for 15 cents in stamps. The type of business is which Sweetman Co., Inc., was engaged in is unknown.

		NM	EX	VG
Complete Set (60):		25,000	12,500	7,500
Common Player:		250.00	125.00	75.00
1	Burleigh Grimes	400.00	200.00	120.00
2	Walter Reuther (Ruether)	250.00	125.00	75.00
3	Joe Dugan	250.00	125.00	75.00
4	Red Faber	400.00	200.00	120.00
5	Gabby Hartnett	400.00	200.00	120.00
6	Babe Ruth	6,000	3,000	1,800
7	Bob Meusel	250.00	125.00	75.00
8	Herb Pennock	400.00	200.00	120.00
9	George Burns	250.00	125.00	75.00
10	Joe Sewell	400.00	200.00	120.00
11	George Uhle	250.00	125.00	75.00
12	Bob O'Farrell	250.00	125.00	75.00
13	Rogers Hornsby	500.00	250.00	150.00
14	"Pie" Traynor	400.00	200.00	120.00
15	Clarence Mitchell	250.00	125.00	75.00
16	Eppa Jepha Rixey	400.00	200.00	120.00
17	Carl Mays	300.00	150.00	90.00
18	Adolfo Luque	250.00	125.00	75.00
19	Dave Bancroft	400.00	200.00	120.00
20	George Kelly	400.00	200.00	120.00
21	Earl (Earle) Combs	400.00	200.00	120.00
22	Harry Heilmann	400.00	200.00	120.00
23	Ray W. Schalk	400.00	200.00	120.00
24	Johnny Mostil	250.00	125.00	75.00
25	Hack Wilson	400.00	200.00	120.00
26	Lou Gehrig	4,000	2,000	1,200
27	Ty Cobb	4,000	2,000	1,200
28	Tris Speaker	500.00	250.00	150.00
29	Tony Lazzeri	400.00	200.00	120.00

		NM	EX	VG
30	Waite Hoyt	400.00	200.00	120.00
31	Sherwood Smith	250.00	125.00	75.00
32	Max Carey	400.00	200.00	120.00
33	Eugene Hargrave	250.00	125.00	75.00
34	Miguel L. Gonzales (Miguel A. Gonzalez)	250.00	125.00	75.00
35	Joe Judge	250.00	125.00	75.00
36	E.C. (Sam) Rice	400.00	200.00	120.00
37	Earl Sheely	250.00	125.00	75.00
38	Sam Jones	250.00	125.00	75.00
39	Bib (Bibb) A. Falk	250.00	125.00	75.00
40	Willie Kamm	250.00	125.00	75.00
41	Stanley Harris	400.00	200.00	120.00
42	John J. McGraw	400.00	200.00	120.00
43	Artie Nehf	250.00	125.00	75.00
44	Grover Alexander	500.00	250.00	150.00
45	Paul Waner	400.00	200.00	120.00
46	William H. Terry	400.00	200.00	120.00
47	Glenn Wright	250.00	125.00	75.00
48	Earl Smith	250.00	125.00	75.00
49	Leon (Goose) Goslin	400.00	200.00	120.00
50	Frank Frisch	400.00	200.00	120.00
51	Joe Harris	250.00	125.00	75.00
52	Fred (Cy) Williams	250.00	125.00	75.00
53	Eddie Roush	400.00	200.00	120.00
54	George Sisler	400.00	200.00	120.00
55	Ed. Rommel	250.00	125.00	75.00
56	Rogers Peckinpaugh (Roger)	250.00	125.00	75.00
57	Stanley Coveleskie (Coveleski)	400.00	200.00	120.00
58	Lester Bell	250.00	125.00	75.00
59	Clyde Barnhart	250.00	125.00	75.00
60	John P. McInnis	250.00	125.00	75.00

1948 Swell Babe Ruth Story

The Philadelphia Gum Co., in 1948, created a card set about the movie "The Babe Ruth Story," which starred William Bendix and Claire Trevor. The set, whose American Card Catalog designation is R421, contains 28 black and white, numbered cards which measure 2" x 2-1/2". The Babe Ruth Story set was originally intended to consist of sixteen cards. Twelve additional cards (#'s 17-28) were added when Ruth died before the release of the film. The card backs include an offer for an autographed photo of William Bendix, starring as the Babe, for five Swell Bubble Gum wrappers and five cents.

		NM	EX	VG
Complete Set (28):		2,750	1,100	550.00
Common Card (1-16):		45.00	20.00	10.00
Common Card (17-28):		125.00	55.00	30.00
1	"The Babe Ruth Story" in the Making	150.00	65.00	35.00
2	Batboy Becomes the Babe (William Bendix)	45.00	20.00	10.00
3	Claire Hodgson (Claire Trevor)	45.00	20.00	10.00
4	Babe Ruth and Claire Hodgson	45.00	20.00	10.00
5	Brother Mathias (Charles Bickford)	45.00	20.00	10.00
6	Phil Conrad (Sam Levene)	45.00	20.00	10.00
7	Nightclub Singer (Gertrude Niesen)	45.00	20.00	10.00
8	Baseball's Famous Deal, Jack Dunn (William Frawley)	45.00	20.00	10.00
9	Mr. and Mrs. Babe Ruth	45.00	20.00	10.00
10	Babe Ruth, Claire Ruth and Brother Mathias	45.00	20.00	10.00
11	Babe Ruth and Miller Huggins (Fred Lightner)	45.00	20.00	10.00
12	Babe at Bed of Ill Boy Johnny Sylvester (Gregory Marshall)	45.00	20.00	10.00
13	Sylvester Family Listening to Game	45.00	20.00	10.00
14	"When a Feller Needs a Friend" (With dog at police station)	45.00	20.00	10.00
15	Dramatic Home Run	45.00	20.00	10.00
16	The Homer That Set the Record - #60 (#60)	75.00	34.00	18.50
17	"The Slap That Started Baseball's Famous Career"	125.00	55.00	30.00
18	The Babe Plays Santa Claus	125.00	55.00	30.00
19	Meeting of Owner and Manager	125.00	55.00	30.00
20	"Broken Window Paid Off"	125.00	55.00	30.00
21	Babe in a Crowd of Autograph Collectors	200.00	90.00	50.00
22	Charley Grimm, William Bendix	125.00	55.00	30.00
23	Ted Lyons, William Bendix	125.00	55.00	30.00
24	Lefty Gomez, William Bendix, Bucky Harris	150.00	65.00	35.00
25	Babe Ruth, William Bendix	400.00	180.00	100.00
26	Babe Ruth, William Bendix	400.00	180.00	100.00
27	Babe Ruth, Claire Trevor	400.00	180.00	100.00
28	William Bendix, Babe Ruth, Claire Trevor	400.00	180.00	100.00

1948 Swell Sport Thrills

This is a set of black-and-white cards which depicts memorable events in baseball history. The cards measure 2-1/2" x 3" and have a picture frame border and event title on the card fronts. The card backs describe the event in detail. Twenty cards were produced in this set by the Swell Gum Co. of Philadelphia. Each card is numbered, and card numbers 9, 11, 16 and 20 are considered more difficult to obtain.

		NM	EX	VG
Complete Set (20):		1,500	675.00	375.00
Common Player:		30.00	13.50	7.00
1	Greatest Single Inning (Mickey Cochrane, Jimmy (Jimmie) Foxx, George Haas, Bing Miller, Al Simmons)	85.00	37.50	20.00
2	Amazing Record (Pete Reiser)	30.00	13.50	7.00
3	Dramatic Debut (Jackie Robinson)	175.00	80.00	45.00
4	Greatest Pitcher (Walter Johnson)	75.00	35.00	17.50
5	Three Strikes Not Out! (Tommy Henrich, Mickey Owen)	30.00	13.50	7.00
6	Home Run Wins Series (Bill Dickey)	35.00	16.00	9.00
7	Never Say Die Pitcher (Hal Schumacher)	30.00	13.50	7.00
8	Five Strikeouts! (Carl Hubbell)	40.00	18.00	10.00
9	Greatest Catch! (Al Gionfriddo)	55.00	25.00	13.50
10	No Hits! No Runs! (Johnny VanderMeer)	30.00	13.50	7.00
11	Bases Loaded! (Tony Lazzeri, Bob O'Farrell)	35.00	16.00	9.00
12	Most Dramatic Home Run (Lou Gehrig, Babe Ruth)	200.00	90.00	50.00
13	Winning Run (Tommy Bridges, Mickey Cochrane, Goose Goslin)	30.00	13.50	7.00
14	Great Slugging (Lou Gehrig)	225.00	100.00	55.00
15	Four Men to Stop Him! (Jim Bagby, Al Smith)	50.00	22.50	12.50
16	Three Run Homer in Ninth! (Joe DiMaggio, Joe Gordon, Ted Williams)	200.00	90.00	50.00
17	Football Block! (Whitey Kurowski, Johnny Lindell)	30.00	13.50	7.00
18	Home Run to Fame (Pee Wee Reese)	85.00	37.50	20.00
19	Strikeout Record! (Bob Feller)	50.00	22.50	12.50
20	Rifle Arm! (Carl Furillo)	50.00	22.50	12.50

1957 Swift Meats

One of the really different baseball card issues of the 50s was the set of 18 3-D baseball player figures which could be punched out and assembled from cards included in packages of hot dogs. The unpunched cards measure approximately 3-1/2" x 4". Prices below are for unpunched cards. Values for assembled figures are problematical.

		NM	EX	VG
Complete Set, Singles (18):		1,500	750.00	450.00
Complete Set w/ Mailer, Playing Board:		2,650	1,300	775.00
Common Player:		60.00	30.00	18.00
1	John Podres	60.00	30.00	18.00
2	Gus Triandos	60.00	30.00	18.00
3	Dale Long	60.00	30.00	18.00
4	Billy Pierce	60.00	30.00	18.00
5	Ed Bailey	60.00	30.00	18.00
6	Vic Wertz	60.00	30.00	18.00
7	Nelson Fox	130.00	65.00	40.00
8	Ken Boyer	75.00	37.50	22.50
9	Gil McDougald	75.00	37.50	22.50
10	Junior Gilliam	75.00	37.50	22.50
11	Eddie Yost	60.00	30.00	18.00
12	Johnny Logan	60.00	30.00	18.00
13	Hank Aaron	200.00	100.00	60.00
14	Bill Tuttle	60.00	30.00	18.00
15	Jackie Jensen	60.00	30.00	18.00
16	Frank Robinson	200.00	100.00	60.00

		NM	EX	VG
17	Richie Ashburn	130.00	65.00	40.00
18	Rocky Colavito	200.00	100.00	60.00

1951 Sylvania Leo Durocher Postcard

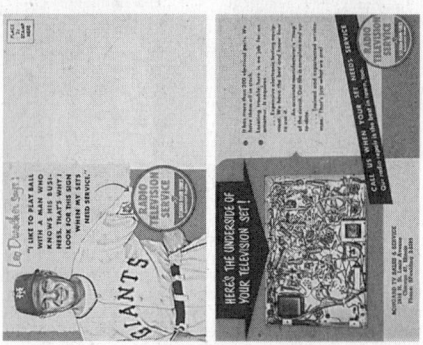

The N.Y. Giants manager endorses Sylvania radio/television service on this large-format (8-1/2" x 5-1/2") postcard. Color artwork features Durocher with a quotation endorsing Sylvania parts and service.

	NM	EX	VG
Leo Durocher	50.00	25.00	15.00

1910-11 S74 Silks - White

BASEBALL-ACTRESS SERIES ON SATIN

Useful in making pillow covers and other fancy articles for home decoration.

To remove satin from this paper back, loosen at corner and pull gently—moistening if necessary.

OLD MILL CIGARETTES,

Designated as S74 in the "American Card Catalog," these delicate fabric collectibles are popular with advanced collectors. The silks were issued as premiums with several different brands of cigarettes: Turkey Red, Old Mill, Red Sun, and, rarely, Helmar. The satin-like silks can be found in two different styles, either "white" or "colored." The white silks measure 1-7/8" x 3" and were originally issued with a brown paper backing that carried an advertisement for one of the cigarette brands. The backing also advised that the silks were "useful in making pillow covers and other fancy articles for home decoration." Many undoubtedly were used for such purposes, making silks with the paper backing still intact more difficult to find. White silks must have the backing intact to command top values shown here. Ninety-two subjects are known in the "white" silks. The silks feature the player pictures found in the popular T205 Gold Border tobacco card set.

		NM	EX	VG
	Complete Set (92):	16,000	6,400	4,150
	Common Player:	135.00	55.00	35.00
	No Paper Backing: 50 Percent			
(1)	Home Run Baker	300.00	120.00	75.00
(2)	Cy Barger	135.00	55.00	35.00
(3)	Jack Barry	135.00	55.00	35.00
(4)	Johnny Bates	135.00	55.00	35.00
(5)	Fred Beck	135.00	55.00	35.00
(6)	Beals Becker	135.00	55.00	35.00
(7)	George Bell	135.00	55.00	35.00
(8)	Chief Bender	300.00	120.00	75.00
(9)	Roger Bresnahan	300.00	120.00	75.00
(10)	Al Bridwell	135.00	55.00	35.00
(11)	Mordecai Brown	300.00	120.00	75.00
(12)	Bobby Byrne	135.00	55.00	35.00
(13)	Howie Camnitz	135.00	55.00	35.00
(14)	Bill Carrigan	135.00	55.00	35.00
(15)	Frank Chance	300.00	120.00	75.00
(16)	Hal Chase	250.00	100.00	60.00
(17)	Fred Clarke	300.00	120.00	75.00
(18)	Ty Cobb	1,350	550.00	350.00
(19)	Eddie Collins	300.00	120.00	75.00
(20)	Doc Crandall	135.00	55.00	35.00
(21)	Lou Criger	135.00	55.00	35.00
(22)	Jim Delahanty	135.00	55.00	35.00
(23)	Art Devlin	135.00	55.00	35.00
(24)	Red Dooin	135.00	55.00	35.00
(25)	Mickey Doolan	135.00	55.00	35.00
(26)	Larry Doyle	135.00	55.00	35.00
(27)	Jimmy Dygert	135.00	55.00	35.00
(28)	Kid Elberfield (Elberfeld)	135.00	55.00	35.00
(29)	Steve Evans	135.00	55.00	35.00
(30)	Johnny Evers	300.00	120.00	75.00
(31)	Bob Ewing	135.00	55.00	35.00
(32)	Art Fletcher	135.00	55.00	35.00
(33)	John Flynn	135.00	55.00	35.00
(34)	Bill Foxen	135.00	55.00	35.00
(35)	George Gibson	135.00	55.00	35.00
(36)	Peaches Graham (Cubs)	135.00	55.00	35.00
(37)	Peaches Graham (Rustlers)	135.00	55.00	35.00

(38)	Clark Griffith	300.00	120.00	75.00
(39)	Topsy Hartsel	135.00	55.00	35.00
(40)	Arnold Hauser	135.00	55.00	35.00
(41)	Charlie Hemphill	135.00	55.00	35.00
(42)	Davy Jones	135.00	55.00	35.00
(43)	Jack Knight	135.00	55.00	35.00
(44)	Ed Konetchy	135.00	55.00	35.00
(45)	Harry Krause	135.00	55.00	35.00
(46)	Tommy Leach	135.00	55.00	35.00
(47)	Rube Marquard	300.00	120.00	75.00
(48)	Christy Mathewson	650.00	260.00	160.00
(49)	Al Mattern	135.00	55.00	35.00
(50)	Amby McConnell	135.00	55.00	35.00
(51)	John McGraw	300.00	120.00	75.00
(52)	Harry McIntire (McIntyre)	135.00	55.00	35.00
(53)	Fred Merkle	135.00	55.00	35.00
(54)	Chief Meyers	135.00	55.00	35.00
(55)	Dots Miller	135.00	55.00	35.00
(56)	Danny Murphy	135.00	55.00	35.00
(57)	Red Murray	135.00	55.00	35.00
(58)	Tom Needham	135.00	55.00	35.00
(59)	Rebel Oakes	135.00	55.00	35.00
(60)	Rube Oldring	135.00	55.00	35.00
(61)	Orval Overall	135.00	55.00	35.00
(62)	Fred Parent	135.00	55.00	35.00
(63)	Fred Payne	135.00	55.00	35.00
(64)	Barney Pelty	135.00	55.00	35.00
(65)	Deacon Phillippe	135.00	55.00	35.00
(66)	Jack Quinn	135.00	55.00	35.00
(67)	Bugs Raymond	135.00	55.00	35.00
(68)	Ed Reulbach	135.00	55.00	35.00
(69)	Doc Scanlon (Scanlan)	135.00	55.00	35.00
(70)	Germany Schaefer	135.00	55.00	35.00
(71)	Geo. Schlei	135.00	55.00	35.00
(72)	Wildfire Schulte	135.00	55.00	35.00
(73)	Dave Shean	135.00	55.00	35.00
(74)	Jimmy Sheckard	135.00	55.00	35.00
(75)	Tony Smith (Superbas)	135.00	55.00	35.00
(76)	Harry Smith (Rustlers)	500.00	200.00	125.00
(77)	Fred Snodgrass	135.00	55.00	35.00
(78)	Tris Speaker	350.00	140.00	87.00
(79)	Harry Steinfeldt (Cubs)	135.00	55.00	35.00
(80)	Harry Steinfeldt (Rustlers)	135.00	55.00	35.00
(81)	George Stone	135.00	55.00	35.00
(82)	Gabby Street	135.00	55.00	35.00
(83)	Ed Summers	135.00	55.00	35.00
(84)	Lee Tannehill	135.00	55.00	35.00
(85)	Joe Tinker	300.00	120.00	75.00
(86)	John Titus	135.00	55.00	35.00
(87)	Terry Turner	135.00	55.00	35.00
(88)	Bobby Wallace	300.00	120.00	75.00
(89)	Doc White	135.00	55.00	35.00
(90)	Ed Willett	135.00	55.00	35.00
(91)	Art Wilson	135.00	55.00	35.00
(92)	Harry Wolter	135.00	55.00	35.00

1911 S74 Silks - Colored

Factory No. 7, 3rd Dist. N.Y.

TIGERS

Ty Cobb

TURKEY RED CIGARETTES

Designated as S74 in the "American Card Catalog," these delicate fabric collectibles are popular with advanced collectors. The silks were issued as premiums with several different brands of cigarettes: Turkey Red, Old Mill, Helmar, and, rarely, Red Sun. The satin-like silks can be found in two different styles, either "white" or "colored." The S74 "colored" silks, as their name indicates, were issued in a variety of colors. They are slightly larger than the white version, measuring 1-7/8" x 3-1/2", and were issued without a paper backing, carrying the cigarette brand name on the lower front of the fabric. (No color silks advertising the Helmar brand are known to exist.) In the colored silks, 120 subjects are known. The silks feature the same player pictures found in the popular T205 Gold Border tobacco card set.

		NM	EX	VG
	Complete Set (120):	20,000	8,000	5,000
	Common Player:	150.00	60.00	35.00
(1)	Red Ames	150.00	60.00	35.00
(2)	Jimmy Archer	150.00	60.00	35.00
(3)	Home Run Baker	300.00	120.00	70.00
(4)	Cy Barger	150.00	60.00	35.00
(5)	Jack Barry	150.00	60.00	35.00
(6)	Johnny Bates	150.00	60.00	35.00
(7)	Beals Becker	150.00	60.00	35.00
(8)	George Bell	150.00	60.00	35.00
(9)	Chief Bender	300.00	120.00	70.00
(10)	Bill Bergen	150.00	60.00	35.00
(11)	Bob Bescher	150.00	60.00	35.00
(12)	Roger Bresnahan (Mouth closed.)	300.00	120.00	70.00

(13)	Roger Bresnahan (Mouth open.)	300.00	120.00	70.00
(14)	Al Bridwell	150.00	60.00	35.00
(15)	Mordecai Brown	300.00	120.00	70.00
(16)	Bobby Byrne	150.00	60.00	35.00
(17)	Howie Camnitz	150.00	60.00	35.00
(18)	Bill Carrigan	150.00	60.00	35.00
(19)	Frank Chance	300.00	120.00	70.00
(20)	Hal Chase	225.00	90.00	55.00
(21)	Ed Cicotte	300.00	120.00	70.00
(22)	Fred Clarke	300.00	120.00	70.00
(23)	Ty Cobb	1,200	480.00	290.00
(24)	Eddie Collins	300.00	120.00	70.00
(25)	Doc Crandall	150.00	60.00	35.00
(26)	Bill Dahlen	150.00	60.00	35.00
(27)	Jake Daubert	150.00	60.00	35.00
(28)	Jim Delahanty	150.00	60.00	35.00
(29)	Art Devlin	150.00	60.00	35.00
(30)	Josh Devore	150.00	60.00	35.00
(31)	Red Dooin	150.00	60.00	35.00
(32)	Mickey Doolan	150.00	60.00	35.00
(33)	Tom Downey	150.00	60.00	35.00
(34)	Larry Doyle	150.00	60.00	35.00
(35)	Hugh Duffy	300.00	120.00	70.00
(36)	Jimmy Dygert	150.00	60.00	35.00
(37)	Kid Elberfield (Elberfeld)	150.00	60.00	35.00
(38)	Steve Evans	150.00	60.00	35.00
(39)	Johnny Evers	300.00	120.00	70.00
(40)	Bob Ewing	150.00	60.00	35.00
(41)	Art Fletcher	150.00	60.00	35.00
(42)	John Flynn	150.00	60.00	35.00
(43)	Russ Ford	150.00	60.00	35.00
(44)	Bill Foxen	150.00	60.00	35.00
(45)	Art Fromme	150.00	60.00	35.00
(46)	George Gibson	150.00	60.00	35.00
(47)	Peaches Graham	150.00	60.00	35.00
(48)	Eddie Grant	150.00	60.00	35.00
(49)	Clark Griffith	300.00	120.00	70.00
(50)	Topsy Hartsel	150.00	60.00	35.00
(51)	Arnold Hauser	150.00	60.00	35.00
(52)	Charlie Hemphill	150.00	60.00	35.00
(53)	Dick Hoblitzell	150.00	60.00	35.00
(54)	Miller Huggins	300.00	120.00	70.00
(55)	John Hummel	150.00	60.00	35.00
(56)	Walter Johnson	600.00	240.00	145.00
(57)	Davy Jones	150.00	60.00	35.00
(58)	Johnny Kling	150.00	60.00	35.00
(59)	Jack Knight	150.00	60.00	35.00
(60)	Ed Konetchy	150.00	60.00	35.00
(61)	Harry Krause	150.00	60.00	35.00
(62)	Tommy Leach	150.00	60.00	35.00
(63)	Lefty Leifield	150.00	60.00	35.00
(64)	Hans Lobert	150.00	60.00	35.00
(65)	Rube Marquard	300.00	120.00	70.00
(66)	Christy Mathewson	750.00	300.00	180.00
(67)	Al Mattern	150.00	60.00	35.00
(68)	Amby McConnell	150.00	60.00	35.00
(69)	John McGraw	300.00	120.00	70.00
(70)	Harry McIntire (McIntyre)	150.00	60.00	35.00
(71)	Fred Merkle	150.00	60.00	35.00
(72)	Chief Meyers	150.00	60.00	35.00
(73)	Dots Miller	150.00	60.00	35.00
(74)	Mike Mitchell	150.00	60.00	35.00
(75)	Pat Moran	150.00	60.00	35.00
(76)	George Moriarty	150.00	60.00	35.00
(77)	George Mullin	150.00	60.00	35.00
(78)	Danny Murphy	150.00	60.00	35.00
(79)	Red Murray	150.00	60.00	35.00
(80)	Tom Needham	150.00	60.00	35.00
(81)	Rebel Oakes	150.00	60.00	35.00
(82)	Rube Oldring	150.00	60.00	35.00
(83)	Orval Overall	150.00	60.00	35.00
(84)	Fred Parent	150.00	60.00	35.00
(85)	Dode Paskert	150.00	60.00	35.00
(86)	Fred Payne	150.00	60.00	35.00
(87)	Barney Pelty	150.00	60.00	35.00
(88)	Deacon Phillippe	150.00	60.00	35.00
(89)	Jack Quinn	150.00	60.00	35.00
(90)	Bugs Raymond	150.00	60.00	35.00
(91)	Ed Reulbach	150.00	60.00	35.00
(92)	Jack Rowan	150.00	60.00	35.00
(93)	Nap Rucker	150.00	60.00	35.00
(94)	Doc Scanlon (Scanlan)	150.00	60.00	35.00
(95)	Germany Schaefer	150.00	60.00	35.00
(96)	Geo. Schlei	150.00	60.00	35.00
(97)	Wildfire Schulte	150.00	60.00	35.00
(98)	Dave Shean	150.00	60.00	35.00
(99)	Jimmy Sheckard	150.00	60.00	35.00
(100)	Happy Smith	150.00	60.00	35.00
(101)	Fred Snodgrass	150.00	60.00	35.00
(102)	Tris Speaker	400.00	160.00	95.00
(103)	Jake Stahl	150.00	60.00	35.00
(104)	Harry Steinfeldt	150.00	60.00	35.00
(105)	George Stone	150.00	60.00	35.00
(106)	Gabby Street	150.00	60.00	35.00
(107)	Ed Summers	150.00	60.00	35.00
(108)	Lee Tannehill	150.00	60.00	35.00
(109)	Joe Tinker	300.00	120.00	70.00
(110)	John Titus	150.00	60.00	35.00
(111)	Terry Turner	150.00	60.00	35.00
(112)	Bobby Wallace	300.00	120.00	70.00
(113)	Zack Wheat	300.00	120.00	70.00
(114)	Doc White (White Sox)	150.00	60.00	35.00
(115)	Kirby White (Pirates)	150.00	60.00	35.00
(116)	Ed Willett	150.00	60.00	35.00
(117)	Owen Wilson	150.00	60.00	35.00
(118)	Hooks Wiltse	150.00	60.00	35.00
(119)	Harry Wolter	150.00	60.00	35.00
(120)	Cy Young	750.00	300.00	180.00

1912 S81 Silks

The 1912 S81 "Silks," so-called because they featured pictures of baseball players on a satin-like fabric rather than paper or cardboard, are closely related to the better-known T3 Turkey Red cabinet cards of the same era. The silks, which featured 25 of the day's top baseball players among its other various subjects, were available as a premium with Helmar "Turkish Trophies" cigarettes. According to an advertising sheet, one silk could be obtained for 25 Helmar coupons. The silks measure about 6-3/4" x 8-3/4" and, with a few exceptions, used the same pictures featured on the popular Turkey Red cards. Five players (Rube Marquard, Rube Benton, Marty O'Toole, Grover Alexander and Russ Ford) appear in the "Silks" set that were not included in the T3 set. In addition, an error involving the Frank Baker card was corrected for the "Silks" set. (In the T3 set, Baker's card actually pictured Jack Barry.) Several years ago a pair of New England collectors found a small stack of Christy Mathewson "Silks," making his, by far, the most common. Otherwise, the "Silks" are generally so rare that it is difficult to determine the relative scarcity of the others. Baseball enthusiasts are usually only attracted to the 25 baseball players in the "Silks" premium set, but it is interesting to note that the promotion also offered dozens of other subjects, including "beautiful women in bathing and athletic costumes, charming dancers in gorgeous attire, natiional flags and generals on horseback."

		NM	EX	VG
Complete Set (25):		145,000	50,000	27,500
Common Player:		3,000	1,000	575.00
86	Rube Marquard	6,500	2,275	1,225
87	Marty O'Toole	3,000	1,000	575.00
88	Rube Benton	3,000	1,000	575.00
89	Grover Alexander	9,000	3,150	1,700
90	Russ Ford	3,000	1,000	575.00
91	John McGraw	6,500	2,275	1,225
92	Nap Rucker	3,000	1,000	575.00
93	Mike Mitchell	3,000	1,000	575.00
94	Chief Bender	6,500	2,275	1,225
95	Home Run Baker	6,500	2,275	1,225
96	Nap Lajoie	6,500	2,275	1,225
97	Joe Tinker	6,500	2,275	1,225
98	Sherry Magee	3,000	1,000	575.00
99	Howie Camnitz	3,000	1,000	575.00
100	Eddie Collins	6,500	2,275	1,225
101	Red Dooin	3,000	1,000	575.00
102	Ty Cobb	15,000	5,250	2,850
103	Hugh Jennings	6,500	2,275	1,225
104	Roger Bresnahan	6,500	2,275	1,225
105	Jake Stahl	3,000	1,000	575.00
106	Tris Speaker	8,000	2,800	1,525
107	Ed Walsh	6,500	2,275	1,225
108	Christy Mathewson	6,000	2,100	1,150
109	Johnny Evers	6,500	2,275	1,225
110	Walter Johnson	12,000	4,200	2,275

1912 S110 Baseball Player Silks Pillow Case

Closely related to the S81 silks, and issued as a premuim for 100 coupons, this approximately 23" x 23" pillow case shares the same designs as the individual silks of the players thereon. Cross-stich borders for the player images on the cloth pillow case would indicate the silks were meant to be sewn on as they were acquired. Besides the baseball players pillow cases, similar premiums are known for the other Turkey Red/Helmar silks -- Indians, generals, etc.

		NM	EX	VG
(1)	Home Run Baker, Ty Cobb, Walter Johnson, Christy Mathewson, Tris Speaker	8,500	4,250	2,550
(2)	Home Run Baker, Ty Cobb, Christy Mathewson, Marty O'Toole, Tris Speaker	8,000	4,000	2,400

T

1928 Tabacalera la Morena

Believed to have been issued in El Salvador in the late 1920s, the extent of this card issue is not yet known. It is possible other American baseball players are included in the issue. Approximately 1-7/8" x 2-5/8", the cards are printed in black-and-white with some color tints added. The borderless front that includes the card number at bottom. Backs are printed in Spanish and repeat the card number along with player identification and a few words about the pictured players. An ad at bottom attributes the card (roughly): "Courtesy of Rich Brown Tobacco, the Champion among Consumers."

		NM	EX	VG
96	St. Louis Cardinals Team	100.00	50.00	30.00
97	Everett Scott	50.00	25.00	15.00
98	Babe Ruth	900.00	450.00	270.00
100	Lou Gehrig, Babe Ruth	500.00	250.00	150.00
101	George Kelly	100.00	50.00	30.00
103	Earl Webb	50.00	25.00	15.00
105	Ty Cobb, Babe Ruth	300.00	150.00	90.00
106	Jim Bottomley	100.00	50.00	30.00
107	Christy Mathewson, John McGraw	150.00	75.00	45.00
109	John J. Mc. Graw	100.00	50.00	30.00
110	Ullmann	50.00	25.00	15.00
111	Lee Todd, P Todd	50.00	25.00	15.00
114	St. Louis Cardinals/Brooklyn Robins	50.00	25.00	15.00
120	St. Louis Cardinals/Brooklyn Robins	50.00	25.00	15.00

1916 Tango Eggs

Unknown until the discovery of a hoard of "fewer than 500" cards in 1991, this 20-card set was produced for L. Frank & Co. of New Orleans to be distributed in an as-yet unknown manner in connection with its Tango brand eggs. Similar in size (1-7/16" x 2-3/4") and format to contemporary caramel cards, the Tango set features familiar player pictures from those issues. In fact, several of the Tango cards have player designations which differ from the same pictures used in the E106 American Caramel issue of 1915. The Tango cards feature a glossy front surface, and are brightly colored. The hoard varied greatly in the number of each player's card. Some were found in quantities as low as one, while some were represented by more than 50 specimens. Because several of the cards exist in only a single specimen, no price for a complete set is quoted.

		NM	EX	VG
Common Player:		240.00	95.00	50.00
(1)	Bob Bescher	240.00	95.00	50.00
(2)	Roger Bresnahan (Four known.)	2,400	960.00	480.00
(3)	Al Bridwell (Fewer than 10 known.)	870.00	350.00	175.00
(4)	Hal Chase	1,080	430.00	215.00
(5)	Ty Cobb (One known, VG, value undetermined.)			
(6)	Eddie Collins	1,920	770.00	385.00
(7)	Sam Crawford (Fewer than five known.)	2,400	960.00	480.00

		NM	EX	VG
(8)	Red Dooin	430.00	175.00	85.00
(9)	Johnny Evers (One known, G/VG, value undetermined.)			
(10)	Happy Felsch (Picture actually Ray Demmitt.) (2-3 known)	2,880	1,150	575.00
(11)	Hughie Jennings (20 known)	660.00	265.00	135.00
(12)	George McQuillen	510.00	205.00	100.00
(13)	Billy Meyer (Picture actually Fred Jacklitsch.)	450.00	180.00	90.00
(14)	Ray Morgan (Picture actually Mike Doolan.) (2-3 known)	1,920	770.00	385.00
(15)	Danny Murphy	270.00	110.00	55.00
(16)	Germany Schaefer (1-2 known)	2,400	960.00	480.00
(17)	Joe Tinker (Unconfirmed)	2,880	1,150	575.00
(18)	Honus Wagner (None confirmed.)			
(19)	Buck Weaver (Picture actually Joe Tinker.)	1,500	600.00	300.00
(20)	Heinie Zimmerman (Fewer than 10 known.)	870.00	350.00	175.00

1934 Tarzan Bread (D382)

Among the rarest issues of the 1930s is this set sponsored by an unusually named brand of bread from a bakery whose location is unknown. The cards are printed in black-and-white in 2-1/4" x 3-1/4" format. Borderless front photos have the player name in capital letters. Backs have the sponsor's name and a short career summary. The checklist here, almost certainly incomplete, is arranged alphabetically; the cards are unnumbered.

		NM	EX	VG
Common Player:		2,200	1,100	650.00
(1)	Sparky Adams	2,200	1,100	650.00
(2)	Walter Betts	2,200	1,100	650.00
(3)	Ed Brandt	2,200	1,100	650.00
(4)	Tommy Bridges	2,200	1,100	650.00
(5)	Irving "Jack" Burns	2,200	1,100	650.00
(6)	Bruce Campbell	2,200	1,100	650.00
(7)	Tex Carleton	2,200	1,100	650.00
(8)	Dick Coffman	2,200	1,100	650.00
(9)	George Connally	2,200	1,100	650.00
(10)	Tony Cuccinello	2,200	1,100	650.00
(11)	Debs Garms	2,200	1,100	650.00
(12)	Milt Gaston	2,200	1,100	650.00
(13)	Bill Hallahan	2,200	1,100	650.00
(14)	Myril Hoag	2,200	1,100	650.00
(15)	Chief Hogsett	2,200	1,100	650.00
(16)	Arndt Jorgens	2,200	1,100	650.00
(17)	Willie Kamm	2,200	1,100	650.00
(18)	Dutch Leonard	2,200	1,100	650.00
(19)	Clyde Manion	2,200	1,100	650.00
(20)	Eric McNair	2,200	1,100	650.00
(21)	Oscar Melillo	2,200	1,100	650.00
(22)	Bob O'Farrell	2,200	1,100	650.00
(23)	Gus Suhr	2,200	1,100	650.00
(24)	Evar Swanson	2,200	1,100	650.00
(25)	Billy Urbanski	2,200	1,100	650.00
(26)	Johnny Vergez	2,200	1,100	650.00
(27)	Robert Worthington	2,200	1,100	650.00
(28)	Tom Zachary	2,200	1,100	650.00

1969 Tasco All-Star Collection Caricatures

This set of large - 11-1/2" x 16" - player posters features colorful caricatures with an emphasis on Tigers players, befitting the Detroit address of the publisher. Licensed by MLBPA, the pictures are listed here alphabetically. They were originally sold for less than $1 apiece.

		NM	EX	VG
Complete Set (46):		450.00	225.00	135.00
Common Player:		7.50	3.75	2.25
(1)	Hank Aaron	35.00	17.50	10.50
(2)	Richie Allen	12.50	6.25	3.75

(3)	Luis Aparicio	17.50	8.75	5.25
(4)	Ernie Banks	25.00	12.50	7.50
(5)	Glenn Beckert	7.50	3.75	2.25
(6)	Johnny Bench	20.00	10.00	6.00
(7)	Norm Cash	10.00	5.00	3.00
(8)	Danny Cater	7.50	3.75	2.25
(9)	Pat Dobson	7.50	3.75	2.25
(10)	Don Drysdale	17.50	8.75	5.25
(11)	Bill Freehan	7.50	3.75	2.25
(12)	Jim Fregosi	7.50	3.75	2.25
(13)	Bob Gibson	17.50	8.75	5.25
(14)	Bill Hands	7.50	3.75	2.25
(15)	Ken Holtzman	7.50	3.75	2.25
(16)	Willie Horton	7.50	3.75	2.25
(17)	Frank Howard	9.00	4.50	2.75
(18)	Randy Hundley	7.50	3.75	2.25
(19)	Ferguson Jenkins	17.50	8.75	5.25
(20)	Al Kaline	25.00	12.50	7.50
(21)	Don Kessinger	7.50	3.75	2.25
(22)	Jerry Koosman	7.50	3.75	2.25
(23)	Mickey Lolich	7.50	3.75	2.25
(24)	Juan Marichal	17.50	8.75	5.25
(25)	Willie Mays	35.00	17.50	10.50
(26)	Bill Mazeroski	17.50	8.75	5.25
(27)	Dick McAuliffe	7.50	3.75	2.25
(28)	Denny McLain	7.50	3.75	2.25
(29)	Dave McNally	7.50	3.75	2.25
(30)	Jim Northrup	7.50	3.75	2.25
(31)	Tony Oliva	9.00	4.50	2.75
(32)	Adolfo Phillips	7.50	3.75	2.25
(33)	Jim Price	7.50	3.75	2.25
(34)	Brooks Robinson	20.00	10.00	6.00
(35)	Pete Rose	35.00	17.50	10.50
(36)	Ron Santo	15.00	7.50	4.50
(37)	Joe Sparma	7.50	3.75	2.25
(38)	Mickey Stanley	7.50	3.75	2.25
(39)	Mel Stottlemyre	7.50	3.75	2.25
(40)	Luis Tiant	7.50	3.75	2.25
(41)	Joe Torre	9.00	4.50	2.75
(42)	Dick Tracewski	7.50	3.75	2.25
(43)	Don Wert	7.50	3.75	2.25
(44)	Billy Williams	17.50	8.75	5.25
(45)	Earl Wilson	7.50	3.75	2.25
(46)	Carl Yastrzemski	25.00	12.50	7.50

1970 Tasco Caricatures

JIM "CATFISH" HUNTER

This group of colorful player caricatures was sold in a four-pack featuring two each baseball and football players. The 8-1/2" x 10-7/8" blank-back pictures have central images surrounded by colorful borders.

		NM	EX	VG
Complete Set (4):		150.00	75.00	45.00
Common Player:		40.00	20.00	12.00
(1)	Jim "Catfish" Hunter	40.00	20.00	12.00
(2)	Al Kaline	50.00	25.00	15.00
(3)	Joe Namath	75.00	37.00	22.00
(4)	O.J. Simpson	50.00	25.00	15.00

1933 Tattoo Orbit (R305)

IRVING D. HADLEY

Pitcher
St. Louis "Browns"

Born July 5, 1904
Height, 5 ft. 10½ in.
Weight, 190 lbs.

Found in 1¢ packages of Tattoo gum, these 2" x 2-1/4" cards were produced by the Orbit Gum Co., of Chicago, a subsidiary of Wrigley's. Fronts feature a black-and-white photo which is tinted to give the skin some color. Stylized ballpark backgrounds are separated from the photograph by a black line. The rest of the background is printed in vivid red, yellow and green. Backs have player identification and vitals. Cards of Bump Hadley and George Blaeholder are the most elusive, followed by those of Ivy Andrews and Rogers Hornsby.

		NM	EX	VG
Complete Set (60):		20,000	8,000	4,000
Common Player:		250.00	100.00	60.00
(1)	Dale Alexander	250.00	100.00	60.00
(2)	Ivy Paul Andrews	900.00	360.00	225.00
(3)	Earl Averill	400.00	160.00	100.00
(4)	Richard Bartell	250.00	100.00	60.00
(5)	Walter Berger	250.00	100.00	60.00
(6)	George F. Blaeholder	1,000	400.00	250.00

(7)	Irving J. Burns	250.00	100.00	60.00
(8)	Guy T. Bush	250.00	100.00	60.00
(9)	Bruce D. Campbell	250.00	100.00	60.00
(10)	William Cissell	250.00	100.00	60.00
(11)	Lefty Clark	250.00	100.00	60.00
(12)	Mickey Cochrane	400.00	160.00	100.00
(13)	Phil Collins	250.00	100.00	60.00
(14)	Hazen Kiki Cuyler	400.00	160.00	100.00
(15)	Dizzy Dean	575.00	230.00	145.00
(16)	Jimmy Dykes	250.00	100.00	60.00
(17)	George L. Earnshaw	250.00	100.00	60.00
(18)	Woody English	250.00	100.00	60.00
(19)	Lewis A. Fonseca	250.00	100.00	60.00
(20)	Jimmy Foxx	750.00	300.00	185.00
(21)	Burleigh A. Grimes	400.00	160.00	100.00
(22)	Charles John Grimm	250.00	100.00	60.00
(23)	Robert M. Grove	500.00	200.00	125.00
(24)	Frank Grube	250.00	100.00	60.00
(25)	George W. Haas	250.00	100.00	60.00
(26)	Irving D. Hadley	1,000	400.00	250.00
(27)	Chick Hafey	400.00	160.00	100.00
(28)	Jesse Joseph Haines	400.00	160.00	100.00
(29)	William Hallahan	250.00	100.00	60.00
(30)	Melvin Harder	250.00	100.00	60.00
(31)	Gabby Hartnett	400.00	160.00	100.00
(32)	Babe Herman	250.00	100.00	60.00
(33)	William Herman	400.00	160.00	100.00
(34)	Rogers Hornsby	1,200	480.00	300.00
(35)	Roy C. Johnson	250.00	100.00	60.00
(36)	J. Smead Jolley	250.00	100.00	60.00
(37)	William Jurges	250.00	100.00	60.00
(38)	William Kamm	250.00	100.00	60.00
(39)	Mark A. Koenig	250.00	100.00	60.00
(40)	James J. Levey	450.00	180.00	110.00
(41)	Ernie Lombardi	400.00	160.00	100.00
(42)	Red Lucas	250.00	100.00	60.00
(43)	Ted Lyons	400.00	160.00	100.00
(44)	Connie Mack	400.00	160.00	100.00
(45)	Pat Malone	250.00	100.00	60.00
(46)	Pepper Martin	300.00	125.00	75.00
(47)	Marty McManus	250.00	100.00	60.00
(48)	Frank J. O'Doul	350.00	140.00	87.00
(49)	Richard Porter	250.00	100.00	60.00
(50)	Carl N. Reynolds	250.00	100.00	60.00
(51)	Charles Henry Root	250.00	100.00	60.00
(52)	Robert Seeds	250.00	100.00	60.00
(53)	Al H. Simmons	400.00	160.00	100.00
(54)	Jackson Riggs Stephenson	250.00	100.00	60.00
(55)	Bud Tinning	250.00	100.00	60.00
(56)	Joe Vosmik	250.00	100.00	60.00
(57)	Rube Walberg	250.00	100.00	60.00
(58)	Paul Waner	400.00	160.00	100.00
(59)	Lonnie Warneke	250.00	100.00	60.00
(60)	Arthur C. Whitney	250.00	100.00	60.00

1933 Tattoo Orbit (R308)

LEE ROY MAHAFFEY
PHILADELPHIA
ATHLETICS • 175

This obscure set of cards, issued with Tattoo Orbit gum, is numbered from 151 through 207, with a few of the numbers still unknown. Most surviving examples measure 1-7/8" x 1-1/4," but larger pieces (2-1/2" x 3-7/8") are also known with the same players and numbers. The player pictures on the cards "developed" when moistened and rubbed with a piece of blotting paper. Besides the baseball players, there were also pictures of movie stars and other celebrities.

		NM	EX	VG
Common Player:		200.00	90.00	50.00
Large-Format: 4X				
151	Vernon Gomez	500.00	225.00	125.00
152	Kiki Cuyler	500.00	225.00	125.00
153	Jimmy Foxx	850.00	380.00	210.00
154	Al Simmons	500.00	225.00	125.00
155	Chas. J. Grimm	200.00	90.00	50.00
156	William Jurges	200.00	90.00	50.00
157	Chuck Klein	500.00	225.00	125.00
158	Richard Bartell	200.00	90.00	50.00
159	Pepper Martin	275.00	125.00	69.00
160	Earl Averill	500.00	225.00	125.00
161	William Dickey	500.00	225.00	125.00
162	Wesley Ferrell	200.00	90.00	50.00
163	Oral Hildebrand	200.00	90.00	50.00
164	Wm. Kamm	200.00	90.00	50.00
165	Earl Whitehill	200.00	90.00	50.00
166	Charles Fullis	200.00	90.00	50.00
167	Jimmy Dykes	200.00	90.00	50.00
168	Ben Cantwell	200.00	90.00	50.00
169	George Earnshaw	200.00	90.00	50.00
170	Jackson Stephenson	200.00	90.00	50.00
171	Randolph Moore	200.00	90.00	50.00
172	Ted Lyons	500.00	225.00	125.00
173	Goose Goslin	500.00	225.00	125.00
174	E. Swanson	200.00	90.00	50.00
175	Lee Roy Mahaffey	200.00	90.00	50.00

176	Joe Cronin	500.00	225.00	125.00
177	Tom Bridges	200.00	90.00	50.00
178	Henry Manush	500.00	225.00	125.00
179	Walter Stewart	200.00	90.00	50.00
180	Frank Pytlak	200.00	90.00	50.00
181	Dale Alexander	200.00	90.00	50.00
182	Robert Grove	600.00	270.00	150.00
183	Charles Gehringer	500.00	225.00	125.00
184	Lewis Fonseca	200.00	90.00	50.00
185	Alvin Crowder	200.00	90.00	50.00
186	Mickey Cochrane	500.00	225.00	125.00
187	Max Bishop	200.00	90.00	50.00
188	Connie Mack	500.00	225.00	125.00
189	Guy Bush	200.00	90.00	50.00
190	Charlie Root	200.00	90.00	50.00
191a	Burleigh Grimes	500.00	225.00	125.00
191b	Gabby Hartnett	500.00	225.00	125.00
192	Pat Malone	200.00	90.00	50.00
193	Woody English	200.00	90.00	50.00
194	Lonnie Warneke	200.00	90.00	50.00
195	Babe Herman	275.00	125.00	69.00
196	Unknown			
197	Unknown			
198	Unknown			
199	Unknown			
200	Gabby Hartnett	500.00	225.00	125.00
201	Paul Waner	500.00	225.00	125.00
202	Dizzy Dean	750.00	335.00	185.00
203	Unknown			
204	Unknown			
205	Jim Bottomley	500.00	225.00	125.00
206	Unknown			
207	Charles Hafey	500.00	225.00	125.00
208	Unknown			
209	Unknown			
210	Unknown			

1907-09 H.M. Taylor Detroit Tigers Postcards

Various players and groups of players are featured in this issue of hometown heroes from H. M. Taylor in Detroit. The 5-1/2" x 3-1/2" black-and-white cards have white borders on front. Undivided backs have a gothic "Post Card" at top, a one-cent stamp box and, at bottom-left, "Rights reserved by H. M. Taylor, Detroit."

		NM	EX	VG
Complete Set (7):		5,000	2,500	1,500
Common Card:		525.00	260.00	150.00
(1)	Tyrus Cobb (At bat.)	1,800	900.00	550.00
(2)	Bill Coughlin (Batting)	525.00	260.00	150.00
(3)	Sam Crawford (Ready for the Ball.)	750.00	375.00	225.00
(4)	Detroit Club (Team photo.)	850.00	425.00	250.00
(5)	Wild Bill Donovan (Floral horseshoe presented at Philadelphia.)	525.00	260.00	150.00
(6)	Hughie Jennings ("WEE'AH")	525.00	260.00	150.00
(7)	Hughie Jennings, Wild Bill Donovan, Frank Chance (In dugout.)	525.00	260.00	150.00

1972 TCMA The 1930's

96
THE
1930'S
LOPEZ,
Alfonso Raymond
"Al"

1928, '30 thru '35
Brooklyn Dodgers

© THE CARD MEMORABILIA ASSOCIATES 1976
TCMA   A.MAWALK, N.Y.

Extending to over 500 cards, this was one of TCMA's first ventures into the business of creating collectors' edition card sets of former players. Over the length of the series there were a number of style differences. The set was issued in 21 series of 24 cards each. All cards were printed in black-and-white (except for Series 18-19 printed in blue) and feature player photos on usually borderless fronts. Dimensions were about 2" x 2-3/4" for most series, with Series 15-16 in a 2-1/2" x 3-1/2" format. Except for a TCMA copyright line on some of the earlier cards, there is no other printing on front. Backs have player identification, team affiliations, TCMA copyright and, after #72, a card number. Production is reported as 1,000 sets. Blank-bank versions and uncut panels of 12 exist.

		NM	EX	VG
	Complete Set (504):	400.00	200.00	120.00
	Common Player:	3.00	1.50	.90
(1)	Roy Bell	3.00	1.50	.90
(2)	Max Bishop	3.00	1.50	.90
(3)	Bob Boken	3.00	1.50	.90
(4)	Cliff Bolton	3.00	1.50	.90
(5)	John Broaca	3.00	1.50	.90
(6)	Bill Brubaker	3.00	1.50	.90
(7)	Slick Castleman	3.00	1.50	.90
(8)	Dick Coffman	3.00	1.50	.90
(9)	Phil Collins	3.00	1.50	.90
(10)	Earle Combs	3.00	1.50	.90
(11)	Doc Cramer	3.00	1.50	.90
(12)	Joe Cronin	3.00	1.50	.90
(13)	Jack Crouch	3.00	1.50	.90
(14)	Tony Cuccinello	3.00	1.50	.90
(15)	Babe Dahlgren	3.00	1.50	.90
(16)	Spud Davis	3.00	1.50	.90
(17)	Dizzy Dean	6.00	3.00	1.75
(18)	Paul Dean	3.00	1.50	.90
(19)	Bill Dickey	3.00	1.50	.90
(20)	Joe DiMaggio	10.00	5.00	3.00
(21)	George Earnshaw	3.00	1.50	.90
(22)	Woody English	3.00	1.50	.90
(23)	Woody English	3.00	1.50	.90
(24)	Hal Finney	3.00	1.50	.90
(25)	Freddie Fitzsimmons, Bump Hadley	3.00	1.50	.90
(26)	Tony Freitas	3.00	1.50	.90
(27)	Frank Frisch	3.00	1.50	.90
(28)	Milt Gaston	3.00	1.50	.90
(29)	Sid Gautreaux	3.00	1.50	.90
(30)	Charlie Gehringer	3.00	1.50	.90
(31)	Charley Gelbert	3.00	1.50	.90
(32)	Lefty Gomez	3.00	1.50	.90
(33)	Lefty Grove	5.00	2.50	1.50
(34)	Chick Hafey	3.00	1.50	.90
(35)	Jesse Haines	3.00	1.50	.90
(36)	Bill Hallahan	3.00	1.50	.90
(37)	Bucky Harris	3.00	1.50	.90
(38)	Ed Heusser	3.00	1.50	.90
(39)	Carl Hubbell	3.00	1.50	.90
(40)	Carl Hubbell	3.00	1.50	.90
(41)	Jimmy Jordan	3.00	1.50	.90
(42)	Joe Judge	3.00	1.50	.90
(43)	Len Koenecke	3.00	1.50	.90
(44)	Mark Koenig	3.00	1.50	.90
(45)	Cookie Lavagetto	3.00	1.50	.90
(46)	Roxie Lawson	3.00	1.50	.90
(47)	Tony Lazzeri	3.00	1.50	.90
(48)	Gus Mancuso	3.00	1.50	.90
(49)	John McCarthy	3.00	1.50	.90
(50)	Joe Medwick	3.00	1.50	.90
(51)	Cliff Melton	3.00	1.50	.90
(52)	Terry Moore	3.00	1.50	.90
(53)	John Murphy	3.00	1.50	.90
(54)	Ken O'Dea	3.00	1.50	.90
(55)	Bob O'Farrell	3.00	1.50	.90
(56)	Manuel Onis	3.00	1.50	.90
(57)	Monte Pearson	3.00	1.50	.90
(58)	Paul Richards	3.00	1.50	.90
(59)	Max Rosenfeld	6.00	3.00	1.75
(60)	Red Ruffing	3.00	1.50	.90
(61)	Red Ruffing	3.00	1.50	.90
(62)	Hal Schumacher	3.00	1.50	.90
(63)	George Selkirk	3.00	1.50	.90
(64)	Joe Shaute	3.00	1.50	.90
(65)	Gordon Slade	3.00	1.50	.90
(66)	Lindo Storti	3.00	1.50	.90
(67)	Smokey Sundra	3.00	1.50	.90
(68)	Bill Terry	3.00	1.50	.90
(69)	Jack Tising	3.00	1.50	.90
(70)	Sandy Vance	3.00	1.50	.90
(71)	Rube Walberg	3.00	1.50	.90
(72)	Sammy West	3.00	1.50	.90
73	Vito Tamulis	3.00	1.50	.90
74	Kemp Wicker	3.00	1.50	.90
75	Bob Seeds	3.00	1.50	.90
76	Jack Saltzgaver	3.00	1.50	.90
77	Walter Brown	3.00	1.50	.90
78	Spud Chandler	3.00	1.50	.90
79	Myril Hoag	3.00	1.50	.90
80	Joe Glenn	3.00	1.50	.90
81	Lefty Gomez	3.00	1.50	.90
82	Arndt Jorgens	3.00	1.50	.90
83	Jesse Hill	3.00	1.50	.90
84	Red Rolfe	3.00	1.50	.90
85	Wes Ferrell	3.00	1.50	.90
86	Joe Morrissey	3.00	1.50	.90
87	Tony Piet	3.00	1.50	.90
88	Fred Walker	3.00	1.50	.90
89	Bill Dietrich	3.00	1.50	.90
90	Lyn Lary	3.00	1.50	.90
91	Lyn Lary	3.00	1.50	.90
92	Lyn Lary	3.00	1.50	.90
93	Lyn Lary	3.00	1.50	.90
94	Buzz Boyle	3.00	1.50	.90
95	Tony Malinosky	3.00	1.50	.90
96	Al Lopez	3.00	1.50	.90
97	Linus Frey	3.00	1.50	.90
98	Tony Malinosky	3.00	1.50	.90
99	Owen Carroll	3.00	1.50	.90
100	Buddy Hassett	3.00	1.50	.90
101	Gib Brack	3.00	1.50	.90
102	Sam Leslie	3.00	1.50	.90
103	Fred Heimach	3.00	1.50	.90
104	Burleigh Grimes	3.00	1.50	.90
105	Ray Benge	3.00	1.50	.90
106	Joe Stripp	3.00	1.50	.90
107	Joe Becker	3.00	1.50	.90
108	Oscar Melillo	3.00	1.50	.90
109	Charley O'Leary, Rogers Hornsby	3.00	1.50	.90
110	Luke Appling	3.00	1.50	.90
111	Stan Hack	3.00	1.50	.90
112	Ray Hayworth	3.00	1.50	.90
113	Charles Wilson	3.00	1.50	.90
114	Hal Trosky	3.00	1.50	.90
115	Wes Ferrell	3.00	1.50	.90
116	Lyn Lary	3.00	1.50	.90
117	Milt Gaston	3.00	1.50	.90
118	Eldon Auker	3.00	1.50	.90
119	Heinie Manush	3.00	1.50	.90
120	Jimmie Foxx	6.00	3.00	1.75
121	Don Heffner	3.00	1.50	.90
122	George Pipgras	3.00	1.50	.90
123	Bump Hadley	3.00	1.50	.90
124	Tommy Henrich	3.00	1.50	.90
125	Joe McCarthy	3.00	1.50	.90
126	Joe Sewell	3.00	1.50	.90
127	Frank Crosetti	3.00	1.50	.90
128	Fred Walker	3.00	1.50	.90
129	Ted Kleinhans	3.00	1.50	.90
130	Jake Powell	3.00	1.50	.90
131	Ben Chapman	3.00	1.50	.90
132	John Murphy	3.00	1.50	.90
133	Lon Warneke	3.00	1.50	.90
134	Augie Galan	3.00	1.50	.90
135	Gene Lillard	3.00	1.50	.90
136	Stan Hack	3.00	1.50	.90
137	Frank Demaree	3.00	1.50	.90
138	Tony Piet	3.00	1.50	.90
139	Tony Piet	3.00	1.50	.90
140	Don Brennan	3.00	1.50	.90
141	Hal Schumacher, Lefty Gomez	3.00	1.50	.90
142	Bump Hadley	3.00	1.50	.90
143	Ollie Bejma	3.00	1.50	.90
144	Jim Bottomley	3.00	1.50	.90
145	Clay Bryant	3.00	1.50	.90
146	Charlie Grimm	3.00	1.50	.90
147	Flea Clifton	3.00	1.50	.90
148	Rollie Stiles	3.00	1.50	.90
149	Al Simmons	3.00	1.50	.90
150	Al Simmons	3.00	1.50	.90
151	Lyn Lary	3.00	1.50	.90
152	Roy Weatherly	3.00	1.50	.90
153	Whit Wyatt	3.00	1.50	.90
154	Oscar Vitt	3.00	1.50	.90
155	Jack Kroner	3.00	1.50	.90
156	Ted Lyons	3.00	1.50	.90
157	Joe Malay	3.00	1.50	.90
158	John McCarthy	3.00	1.50	.90
159	Hy Vandenberg	3.00	1.50	.90
160	Hank Leiber	3.00	1.50	.90
161	Joe Moore	3.00	1.50	.90
162	Cliff Melton	3.00	1.50	.90
163	Harry Danning	3.00	1.50	.90
164	Ray Harrell	3.00	1.50	.90
165	Bruce Ogrodowski	3.00	1.50	.90
166	Leo Durocher	3.00	1.50	.90
167	Leo Durocher	3.00	1.50	.90
168	William Walker	3.00	1.50	.90
169	Alvin Crowder	3.00	1.50	.90
170	Gus Suhr	3.00	1.50	.90
171	Monty Stratton	4.50	2.25	1.25
172	Boze Berger	3.00	1.50	.90
173	John Whitehead	3.00	1.50	.90
174	Joe Heving	3.00	1.50	.90
175	Merv Shea	3.00	1.50	.90
176	Ed Durham	3.00	1.50	.90
177	Buddy Myer	3.00	1.50	.90
178	Earl Whitehill	3.00	1.50	.90
179	Joe Cronin	3.00	1.50	.90
180	Zeke Bonura	3.00	1.50	.90
181	John Knott	3.00	1.50	.90
182	John Allen	3.00	1.50	.90
183	William Knickerbocker	3.00	1.50	.90
184	Earl Averill	3.00	1.50	.90
185	Bob Feller	4.50	2.25	1.25
186	Steve O'Neill	3.00	1.50	.90
187	Bruce Campbell	3.00	1.50	.90
188	Ivy Andrews	3.00	1.50	.90
189	Ivy Andrews	3.00	1.50	.90
190	Muddy Ruel	3.00	1.50	.90
191	Art Scharein	3.00	1.50	.90
192	Merv Shea	3.00	1.50	.90
193	George Myatt	3.00	1.50	.90
194	Bill Werber	3.00	1.50	.90
195	Red Lucas	3.00	1.50	.90
196	Hugh Luby	3.00	1.50	.90
197	Vic Sorrell	3.00	1.50	.90
198	Mickey Cochrane	3.00	1.50	.90
199	Rudy York	3.00	1.50	.90
200	Ray Mack	3.00	1.50	.90
201	Vince DiMaggio	4.50	2.25	1.25
202	Mel Ott	4.50	2.25	1.25
203	John Lucadello	3.00	1.50	.90
204	Debs Garms	3.00	1.50	.90
205	John Murphy, Pat Malone, Bump Hadley, Kemp Wicker, John Broaca	3.00	1.50	.90
206	Stan Sperry	3.00	1.50	.90
207	Hal Schumacher	3.00	1.50	.90
208	Blondy Ryan	3.00	1.50	.90
209	Bob Seeds	3.00	1.50	.90
210	Danny MacFayden	3.00	1.50	.90
211	Fran Healy	3.00	1.50	.90
212	Al Spohrer	3.00	1.50	.90
213	Ed Linke	3.00	1.50	.90
214	Joe Schultz	3.00	1.50	.90
215	Casey Stengel	3.00	1.50	.90
216	Casey Stengel	3.00	1.50	.90
217	Phil Hensick	3.00	1.50	.90
218	Rollie Hemsley	3.00	1.50	.90
219	Ace Parker	4.50	2.25	1.25
220	Henry Helf	3.00	1.50	.90
221	Bill Schuster	3.00	1.50	.90
222	Heinie Schuble	3.00	1.50	.90
223	John Salveson	3.00	1.50	.90
224	Robert Grace	3.00	1.50	.90
225	Sig Gryska	3.00	1.50	.90
226	Mickey Haslin	3.00	1.50	.90
227	Randy Gumpert	3.00	1.50	.90
228	Frank Gustine	3.00	1.50	.90
229	Marv Gudat	3.00	1.50	.90
230	Bob Logan	3.00	1.50	.90
231	Marvin Owen	3.00	1.50	.90
232	Bucky Walters	3.00	1.50	.90
233	Marty Hopkins	3.00	1.50	.90
234	Jimmy Dykes	3.00	1.50	.90
235	Lefty O'Doul	3.00	1.50	.90
236	Larry Rosenthal	3.00	1.50	.90
237	Mickey Haslin	3.00	1.50	.90
238	Eugene Schott	3.00	1.50	.90
239	Sad Sam Jones	3.00	1.50	.90
240	Edwin Rommel	3.00	1.50	.90
241	Rip Collins	3.00	1.50	.90
242	Rosy Ryan	3.00	1.50	.90
243	James Bucher	3.00	1.50	.90
244	Ethan Allen	3.00	1.50	.90
245	Dick Bartell	3.00	1.50	.90
246	Henry Leiber	3.00	1.50	.90
247	Lou Chiozza	3.00	1.50	.90
248	Babe Herman	3.00	1.50	.90
249	Tommy Henrich	3.00	1.50	.90
250	Thornton Lee	3.00	1.50	.90
251	Joe Kuhel	3.00	1.50	.90
252	George Pipgras	3.00	1.50	.90
253	Luke Sewell	3.00	1.50	.90
254	Tony Lazzeri	3.00	1.50	.90
255	Ival Goodman	3.00	1.50	.90
256	George Rensa	3.00	1.50	.90
257	Hal Newhouser	3.00	1.50	.90
258	Rogers Hornsby	5.00	2.50	1.50
259	Tuck Stainback	3.00	1.50	.90
260	Vance Page	3.00	1.50	.90
261	Art Scharein	3.00	1.50	.90
262	Mike Ryba	3.00	1.50	.90
263	James Lindsey	3.00	1.50	.90
264	Ed Parsons	3.00	1.50	.90
265	Elon Hogsett	3.00	1.50	.90
266	Bud Hafey	3.00	1.50	.90
267	John Gill	3.00	1.50	.90
268	Owen Bush	3.00	1.50	.90
269	Ethan Allen	3.00	1.50	.90
270	Jim Bagby	3.00	1.50	.90
271	Bill Atwood	3.00	1.50	.90
272	Phil Cavarretta	3.00	1.50	.90
273	Travis Jackson	3.00	1.50	.90
274	Ted Olson	3.00	1.50	.90
275	Boze Berger	3.00	1.50	.90
276	Norb Kleinke	3.00	1.50	.90
277	Rip Radcliff	3.00	1.50	.90
278	Mule Haas	3.00	1.50	.90
279	Julius Solters	3.00	1.50	.90
280	Ivey Shiver	3.00	1.50	.90
281	Wes Schulmerich	3.00	1.50	.90
282	Ray Kolp	3.00	1.50	.90
283	Si Johnson	3.00	1.50	.90
284	Al Hollingsworth	3.00	1.50	.90
285	D'Arcy Flowers	3.00	1.50	.90
286	Adam Comorosky	3.00	1.50	.90
287	Allen Cooke	3.00	1.50	.90
288	Clyde Kimsey	3.00	1.50	.90
289	Fred Ostermueller	3.00	1.50	.90
290	Angelo Giuliani	3.00	1.50	.90
291	John Wilson	3.00	1.50	.90
292	George Dickman	3.00	1.50	.90
293	Jim DeShong	3.00	1.50	.90
294	Red Evans	3.00	1.50	.90
295	Curtis Davis	3.00	1.50	.90
296	Charlie Berry	3.00	1.50	.90
297	George Gibson	3.00	1.50	.90
298	Fern Bell	3.00	1.50	.90
299	Irv Bartling	3.00	1.50	.90
300	Babe Barna	3.00	1.50	.90
301	Henry Johnson	3.00	1.50	.90
302	Harlond Clift	3.00	1.50	.90
303	Lu Blue	3.00	1.50	.90
304	George Hockette	3.00	1.50	.90
305	Walt Bashore	3.00	1.50	.90
306	Walter Beck	3.00	1.50	.90
307	Jewel Ens	3.00	1.50	.90
308	Doc Prothro	3.00	1.50	.90
309	Morrie Arnovich	3.00	1.50	.90
310	Bill Killefer	3.00	1.50	.90
311	Pete Appleton	3.00	1.50	.90
312	Fred Archer	3.00	1.50	.90
313	Bill Lohrman	3.00	1.50	.90
314	Fred Haney	3.00	1.50	.90
315	Jimmy Ripple	3.00	1.50	.90
316	Johnny Kerr	3.00	1.50	.90
317	Harry Gumbert	3.00	1.50	.90
318	Samuel Derringer	3.00	1.50	.90
319	Firpo Marberry	3.00	1.50	.90
320	Waite Hoyt	3.00	1.50	.90
321	Rick Ferrell	3.00	1.50	.90
322	Hank Greenberg	6.00	3.00	1.75
323	Carl Reynolds	3.00	1.50	.90
324	Roy Johnson	3.00	1.50	.90
325	Gil English	3.00	1.50	.90
326	Al Smith	3.00	1.50	.90
327	Dolph Camilli	3.00	1.50	.90
328	Oscar Grimes	3.00	1.50	.90
329	Ray Berres	3.00	1.50	.90
330	Norm Schlueter	3.00	1.50	.90
331	Joe Vosmik	3.00	1.50	.90
332	Jimmy Dykes	3.00	1.50	.90
333	Vern Washington	3.00	1.50	.90
334	"Bad News" Hale	3.00	1.50	.90
335	Lew Fonseca	3.00	1.50	.90
336	Mike Kreevich	3.00	1.50	.90
337	Bob Johnson	3.00	1.50	.90
338	"Jeep" Handley	3.00	1.50	.90
339	Gabby Hartnett	3.00	1.50	.90
340	Freddie Lindstrom	3.00	1.50	.90
341	Bert Haas	3.00	1.50	.90
342	Elbie Fletcher	3.00	1.50	.90
343	Tom Hafey	3.00	1.50	.90
344	Rip Collins	3.00	1.50	.90
345	John Babich	3.00	1.50	.90
346	Joe Beggs	3.00	1.50	.90

No.	Player	NM	EX	VG
347	Bobo Newsom	3.00	1.50	.90
348	Wally Berger	3.00	1.50	.90
349	Bud Thomas	3.00	1.50	.90
350	Tom Heath	3.00	1.50	.90
351	Cecil Travis	3.00	1.50	.90
352	Jack Redmond	3.00	1.50	.90
353	Fred Schulte	3.00	1.50	.90
354	Pat Malone	3.00	1.50	.90
355	Hugh Critz	3.00	1.50	.90
356	Frank Pytlak	3.00	1.50	.90
357	Glenn Liebhardt	3.00	1.50	.90
358	Al Milnar	3.00	1.50	.90
359	Al Benton	3.00	1.50	.90
360	Moe Berg	6.00	3.00	1.75
361	Al Brancato	3.00	1.50	.90
362	Mark Christman	3.00	1.50	.90
363	Fabian Gaffke	3.00	1.50	.90
364	George Gill	3.00	1.50	.90
365	Oral Hildebrand	3.00	1.50	.90
366	Lou Fette	3.00	1.50	.90
367	Tex Carleton	3.00	1.50	.90
368	Don Gutteridge	3.00	1.50	.90
369	Pete Fox	3.00	1.50	.90
370	George Blaeholder	3.00	1.50	.90
371	George Caster	3.00	1.50	.90
372	Joe Cascarella	3.00	1.50	.90
373	Jimmy Hitchcock	3.00	1.50	.90
374	Frank Croucher	3.00	1.50	.90
375	LeRoy Parmelee	3.00	1.50	.90
376	Joe Mulligan	3.00	1.50	.90
377	John Welch	3.00	1.50	.90
378	Donald McNair	3.00	1.50	.90
379	Frenchy Bordagaray	3.00	1.50	.90
380	Denny Galehouse	3.00	1.50	.90
381	Robert Harris	3.00	1.50	.90
382	Max Butcher	3.00	1.50	.90
383	Sam Byrd	3.00	1.50	.90
384	Pete Coscarart	3.00	1.50	.90
385	George Case	3.00	1.50	.90
386	John Hudson	3.00	1.50	.90
387	Frank Crespi	3.00	1.50	.90
388	Gene Desautels	3.00	1.50	.90
389	Bill Cissell	3.00	1.50	.90
390	John Burns	3.00	1.50	.90
391	Larry Benton	3.00	1.50	.90
392	James Holbrook	3.00	1.50	.90
393	Ernie Koy	3.00	1.50	.90
394	Bobby Doerr	3.00	1.50	.90
395	Harry Boyles	3.00	1.50	.90
396	Pinky Higgins	3.00	1.50	.90
397	Mel Almada	3.00	1.50	.90
398	Carl Fischer	3.00	1.50	.90
399	Rabbit Maranville, Johnny Evers, Hank Gowdy	3.00	1.50	.90
400	Lou Gehrig	10.00	5.00	3.00
401	Lincoln Blakely	3.00	1.50	.90
402	James Henry	3.00	1.50	.90
403	Ed Holley	3.00	1.50	.90
404	Elmer Hodgin	3.00	1.50	.90
405	Bob Garbark	3.00	1.50	.90
406	John Burnett	3.00	1.50	.90
407	David Harris	3.00	1.50	.90
408	Johnny Dickshot	3.00	1.50	.90
409	Ray Mueller	3.00	1.50	.90
410	John Welaj	3.00	1.50	.90
411	Les McCrabb	3.00	1.50	.90
412	George Uhle	3.00	1.50	.90
413	Leo Mangum	3.00	1.50	.90
414	Howard Maple	3.00	1.50	.90
415	Syl Johnson	3.00	1.50	.90
416	Hershel Martin	3.00	1.50	.90
417	Joe Martin	3.00	1.50	.90
418	Phil Masi	3.00	1.50	.90
419	Bobby Mattick	3.00	1.50	.90
420	Marshall Mauldin	3.00	1.50	.90
421	Frank May	3.00	1.50	.90
422	Merrill May	3.00	1.50	.90
423	Bill McAfee	3.00	1.50	.90
424	Benny McCoy	3.00	1.50	.90
425	Charlie George	3.00	1.50	.90
426	Roy Hughes	3.00	1.50	.90
427	Bill Kerksieck	3.00	1.50	.90
428	Wes Kingdon	3.00	1.50	.90
429	Lynn King	3.00	1.50	.90
430	Harry Kinzy	3.00	1.50	.90
431	Harry Kimberlin	3.00	1.50	.90
432	Bob Klinger	3.00	1.50	.90
433	Wilfred Knothe	3.00	1.50	.90
434	Lou Finney	3.00	1.50	.90
435	Roy Johnson	3.00	1.50	.90
436	Woody Jensen	3.00	1.50	.90
437	George Jeffcoat	3.00	1.50	.90
438	Roy Joiner	3.00	1.50	.90
439	Baxter Jordan	3.00	1.50	.90
440	Edwin Joost	3.00	1.50	.90
441	Bubber Jonnard	3.00	1.50	.90
442	Bucky Jacobs	3.00	1.50	.90
443	Art Jacobs	3.00	1.50	.90
444	Orville Jorgens	3.00	1.50	.90
445	Hal Kelleher	3.00	1.50	.90
446	Harry Kelley	3.00	1.50	.90
447	Ken Keltner	3.00	1.50	.90
448	Paul Kardon	3.00	1.50	.90
449	Alex Kampouris	3.00	1.50	.90
450	Willie Kamm	3.00	1.50	.90
451	Bob Kahle	3.00	1.50	.90
452	Billy Jurges	3.00	1.50	.90
453	Ken Jungles	3.00	1.50	.90
454	John Juelich	3.00	1.50	.90
455	John Marcum	3.00	1.50	.90
456	Walt Masterson	3.00	1.50	.90
457	Clint Brown	3.00	1.50	.90
458	Buddy Lewis	3.00	1.50	.90
459	Watty Clark	3.00	1.50	.90
460	Johnny Cooney	3.00	1.50	.90
461	Mel Harder	3.00	1.50	.90
462	Justin McLaughlin	3.00	1.50	.90
463	Frank Grube	3.00	1.50	.90
464	Jeff Heath	3.00	1.50	.90
465	Cliff Heathcote	3.00	1.50	.90
466	Harvey Hendrick	3.00	1.50	.90
467	Johnny Hodapp	3.00	1.50	.90
468	Bob Holland	3.00	1.50	.90
469	Otto Huber	3.00	1.50	.90
470	Rudy Hulswitt	3.00	1.50	.90
471	Roy Johnson	3.00	1.50	.90
472	Smead Jolley	3.00	1.50	.90
473	Rollie Hemsley, Bob Smith, John Moore	3.00	1.50	.90
474	John Jones	3.00	1.50	.90
475	Harry Kelley	3.00	1.50	.90
476	George Kelly	3.00	1.50	.90
477	Chuck Klein	3.00	1.50	.90
478	Joe Krakauskas	3.00	1.50	.90
479	Mike Kreevich	3.00	1.50	.90
480	Dick Lanahan	3.00	1.50	.90
481	Emil "Dutch" Leonard	3.00	1.50	.90
482	Harl Maggert	3.00	1.50	.90
483	Cyrus Malis	3.00	1.50	.90
484	Dario Lodigiani	3.00	1.50	.90
485	Walt Masterson	3.00	1.50	.90
486	Rabbit Maranville	3.00	1.50	.90
487	Ed Marshall	3.00	1.50	.90
488	Tim McKeithan	3.00	1.50	.90
489	Patrick McLaughlin	3.00	1.50	.90
490	Bob McNamara	3.00	1.50	.90
491	Steve Mesner	3.00	1.50	.90
492	Clarence Mitchell	3.00	1.50	.90
493	Mal Moss	3.00	1.50	.90
494	Joe Murray	3.00	1.50	.90
495	Pete Naktenis	3.00	1.50	.90
496	Bill Nicholson	3.00	1.50	.90
497	John Rigney	3.00	1.50	.90
498	Clyde Sukeforth	3.00	1.50	.90
499	Evar Swanson	3.00	1.50	.90
500	Dan Taylor	3.00	1.50	.90
501	Sloppy Thurston	3.00	1.50	.90
502	Forrest Wright	3.00	1.50	.90
503	Ray Lucas	3.00	1.50	.90
504	Nig Lipscomb	3.00	1.50	.90

1973-80 TCMA All-Time Greats Postcards

HANK GREENBERG

One of the longest collectors' series issued by TCMA in the 1970s was this set of player postcards. Measuring 3-1/2" x 5-1/2" the black-and-white cards have large photos on front, bordered in black and highlighted with banners and baseball equipment. Backs have postcard markings. Six series of cards were issued between 1973-80 and the unnumbered cards are checklisted here in alphabetical order within series.

		NM	EX	VG
Complete Set (156):		150.00	75.00	45.00
Common Player:		3.00	1.50	.90
SERIES 1				
(1)	Luke Appling	3.00	1.50	.90
(2)	Mickey Cochrane	3.00	1.50	.90
(3)	Eddie Collins	3.00	1.50	.90
(4)	Kiki Cuyler	3.00	1.50	.90
(5)	Bill Dickey	3.00	1.50	.90
(6)	Joe DiMaggio	7.50	3.75	2.25
(7)	Bob Feller	3.00	1.50	.90
(8)	Frank Frisch	3.00	1.50	.90
(9)	Lou Gehrig	7.50	3.75	2.25
(10)	Goose Goslin	3.00	1.50	.90
(11)	Chick Hafey	3.00	1.50	.90
(12)	Gabby Hartnett	3.00	1.50	.90
(13)	Rogers Hornsby	4.00	2.00	1.25
(14)	Ted Lyons	3.00	1.50	.90
(15)	Connie Mack	3.00	1.50	.90
(16)	Heinie Manush	3.00	1.50	.90
(17)	Rabbit Maranville	3.00	1.50	.90
(18)	Ducky Medwick	3.00	1.50	.90
(19)	Al Simmons	3.00	1.50	.90
(20)	Bill Terry	3.00	1.50	.90
(21)	Pie Traynor	3.00	1.50	.90
(22)	Dazzy Vance	3.00	1.50	.90
(23)	Cy Young	5.00	2.50	1.50
(24)	Gabby Hartnett, Babe Ruth	6.00	3.00	1.75
SERIES 2				
(1)	Roger Bresnahan	3.00	1.50	.90
(2)	Dizzy Dean	4.00	2.00	1.25
(3)	Buck Ewing & mascot	3.00	1.50	.90
(4)	Jimmie Foxx	4.50	2.25	1.25
(5)	Hank Greenberg	4.50	2.25	1.25
(6)	Burleigh Grimes	3.00	1.50	.90
(7)	Harry Heilmann	3.00	1.50	.90
(8)	Waite Hoyt	3.00	1.50	.90
(9)	Walter Johnson	5.00	2.50	1.50
(10)	George Kelly	3.00	1.50	.90
(11)	Christy Mathewson	5.00	2.50	1.50
(12)	John McGraw	3.00	1.50	.90
(13)	Stan Musial	4.00	2.00	1.25
(14)	Mel Ott	3.00	1.50	.90
(15)	Satchel Paige	6.00	3.00	1.75
(16)	Sam Rice	3.00	1.50	.90
(17)	Edd Roush	3.00	1.50	.90
(18)	Red Ruffing	3.00	1.50	.90
(19)	Casey Stengel	3.00	1.50	.90
(20)	Honus Wagner	6.00	3.00	1.75
(21)	Lloyd Waner	3.00	1.50	.90
(22)	Paul Waner	3.00	1.50	.90
(23)	Harry Wright	3.00	1.50	.90
(24)	Ross Youngs	3.00	1.50	.90
SERIES 3				
(1)	Home Run Baker	3.00	1.50	.90
(2)	Chief Bender	3.00	1.50	.90
(3)	Jim Bottomley	3.00	1.50	.90
(4)	Lou Boudreau	3.00	1.50	.90
(5)	Mordecai Brown	3.00	1.50	.90
(6)	Roy Campanella	3.50	1.75	1.00
(7)	Max Carey	3.00	1.50	.90
(8)	Ty Cobb	7.50	3.75	2.25
(9)	Earle Combs	3.00	1.50	.90
(10)	Jocko Conlan	3.00	1.50	.90
(11)	Hugh Duffy	3.00	1.50	.90
(12)	Red Faber	3.00	1.50	.90
(13)	Lefty Grove	3.00	1.50	.90
(14)	Judge K.M. Landis	3.00	1.50	.90
(15)	Eddie Plank	3.00	1.50	.90
(16)	Hoss Radbourne	3.00	1.50	.90
(17)	Eppa Rixey	3.00	1.50	.90
(18)	Jackie Robinson	6.00	3.00	1.75
(19)	Babe Ruth	7.50	3.75	2.25
(20)	George Sisler	3.00	1.50	.90
(21)	Zack Wheat	3.00	1.50	.90
(22)	Ted Williams	6.00	3.00	1.75
(23)	Mel Ott, Babe Ruth	6.00	3.00	1.75
(24)	Tris Speaker, Wilbert Robinson	3.00	1.50	.90
SERIES 4				
(1)	Grover C. Alexander	3.50	1.75	1.00
(2)	Cap Anson	3.00	1.50	.90
(3)	Earl Averill	3.00	1.50	.90
(4)	Ed Barrow	3.00	1.50	.90
(5)	Yogi Berra	3.50	1.75	1.00
(6)	Roberto Clemente	6.00	3.00	1.75
(7)	Jimmy Collins	3.00	1.50	.90
(8)	Whitey Ford	3.50	1.75	1.00
(9)	Ford Frick	3.00	1.50	.90
(10)	Vernon Gomez	3.00	1.50	.90
(11)	Bucky Harris	3.00	1.50	.90
(12)	Billy Herman	3.00	1.50	.90
(13)	Carl Hubbell	3.00	1.50	.90
(14)	Miller Huggins	3.00	1.50	.90
(15)	Monte Irvin	3.00	1.50	.90
(16)	Ralph Kiner	3.00	1.50	.90
(17)	Bill Klem	3.00	1.50	.90
(18)	Sandy Koufax	6.00	3.00	1.75
(19)	Napoleon Lajoie	3.00	1.50	.90
(20)	Bob Lemon	3.00	1.50	.90
(21)	Mickey Mantle	7.50	3.75	2.25
(22)	Rube Marquard	3.00	1.50	.90
(23)	Joe McCarthy	3.00	1.50	.90
(24)	Bill McKechnie	3.00	1.50	.90
(25)	Herb Pennock	3.00	1.50	.90
(26)	Warren Spahn	3.00	1.50	.90
(27)	Joe Tinker	3.00	1.50	.90
(28)	Early Wynn	3.00	1.50	.90
(29)	Joe Cronin, Honus Wagner, Bill Terry	3.00	1.50	.90
(30)	Jimmie Foxx, Lou Gehrig	6.00	3.00	1.75
(31)	Hank Greenberg, Ralph Kiner	3.00	1.50	.90
(32)	Walter Johnson, Connie Mack	3.00	1.50	.90
(33)	Connie Mack, Bob Feller	3.00	1.50	.90
(34)	Mel Ott, Lou Gehrig	6.00	3.00	1.75
(35)	Al Simmons, Tris Speaker, Ty Cobb	3.00	1.50	.90
(36)	Ted Williams, Lou Boudreau	3.00	1.50	.90
SERIES 5				
(1)	Dave Bancroft	3.00	1.50	.90
(2)	Ernie Banks	3.50	1.75	1.00
(3)	Frank Chance	3.00	1.50	.90
(4)	Stan Coveleski	3.00	1.50	.90
(5)	Billy Evans	3.00	1.50	.90
(6)	Clark Griffith	3.00	1.50	.90
(7)	Jesse Haines	3.00	1.50	.90
(8)	Will Harridge	3.00	1.50	.90
(9)	Harry Hooper	3.00	1.50	.90
(10)	Cal Hubbard	3.00	1.50	.90
(11)	Hugh Jennings	3.00	1.50	.90
(12)	Wee Willie Keeler	3.00	1.50	.90
(13)	Fred Lindstrom	3.00	1.50	.90
(14)	Pop Lloyd	3.00	1.50	.90
(15)	Al Lopez	3.00	1.50	.90
(16)	Robin Roberts	3.00	1.50	.90
(17)	Amos Rusie	3.00	1.50	.90
(18)	Ray Schalk	3.00	1.50	.90
(19)	Joe Sewell	3.00	1.50	.90
(20)	Rube Waddell	3.00	1.50	.90
(21)	George Weiss	3.00	1.50	.90
(22)	Dizzy Dean, Gabby Hartnett	3.00	1.50	.90
(23)	Joe DiMaggio, Mickey Mantle	7.50	3.75	2.25
(24)	Ted Williams, Joe DiMaggio	6.00	3.00	1.75
SERIES 6				
(1)	Jack Chesbro	3.00	1.50	.90
(2)	Tom Connolly	3.00	1.50	.90
(3)	Sam Crawford	3.00	1.50	.90
(4)	Elmer Flick	3.00	1.50	.90
(5)	Charlie Gehringer	3.00	1.50	.90
(6)	Warren Giles	3.00	1.50	.90
(7)	Ban Johnson	3.00	1.50	.90
(8)	Addie Joss	3.00	1.50	.90
(9)	Al Kaline	3.00	1.50	.90
(10)	Willie Mays	6.00	3.00	1.75
(11)	Joe McGinnity	3.00	1.50	.90
(12)	Larry McPhail (MacPhail)	3.00	1.50	.90
(13)	Branch Rickey	3.00	1.50	.90
(14)	Wilbert Robinson	3.00	1.50	.90
(15)	Duke Snider	3.00	1.50	.90
(16)	Tris Speaker	4.00	2.00	1.25

		NM	EX	VG
(17)	Bobby Wallace	3.00	1.50	.90
(18)	Hack Wilson	.45	.25	.14
(19)	Yogi Berra, Casey Stengel	4.00	2.00	1.25
(20)	Warren Giles, Roberto Clemente	4.50	2.25	1.25
(21)	Mickey Mantle, Willie Mays	6.00	3.00	1.75
(22)	John McGraw, Babe Ruth	6.00	3.00	1.75
(23)	Satchel Paige, Bob Feller	5.00	2.50	1.50
(24)	Paul Waner, Lloyd Waner	4.00	2.00	1.25

1973 TCMA All Time New York Yankees Team

Outfield-Mickey Mantle

Printed in black-and-white in 3-1/2" x 5-1/2" format, these cards have borderless photos on front with a white strip at bottom in which the player's position and name appear. Backs list the all-time roster but are not numbered or dated. Production was 1,000 sets.

		NM	EX	VG
Complete Set (12):		25.00	12.50	7.50
Common Player:		3.50	1.75	1.00
(1)	Bill Dickey	3.50	1.75	1.00
(2)	Joe DiMaggio	10.00	5.00	3.00
(3)	Whitey Ford	5.00	2.50	1.50
(4)	Lou Gehrig	10.00	5.00	3.00
(5)	Tony Lazzeri	3.50	1.75	1.00
(6)	Mickey Mantle	15.00	7.50	4.50
(7)	Johnny Murphy	3.50	1.75	1.00
(8)	Phil Rizzuto	5.00	2.50	1.50
(9)	Red Rolfe	3.50	1.75	1.00
(10)	Red Ruffing	3.50	1.75	1.00
(11)	Babe Ruth	10.00	5.00	3.00
(12)	Casey Stengel	3.50	1.75	1.00

1973 TCMA Autographs & Drawings Postcards

These black-and-white postcards feature drawings of the players, along with facsimile autographs.

		NM	EX	VG
Complete Set (12):		50.00	25.00	15.00
Common Player:		5.00	2.50	1.50
1	Mickey Cockran (Cochrane)	5.00	2.50	1.50
2	Christy Mathewson	5.00	2.50	1.50
3	Roberto Clemente	10.00	5.00	3.00
4	Rogers Hornsby	5.00	2.50	1.50
5	Pie Traynor	5.00	2.50	1.50
6	Frankie Frisch	5.00	2.50	1.50
7	Ty Cobb	7.50	3.75	2.25
8	Connie Mack	5.00	2.50	1.50
9	Babe Ruth	10.00	5.00	3.00
10	Lou Gehrig	8.00	4.00	2.50
11	Gil Hodges	5.00	2.50	1.50
12	Jackie Robinson	8.00	4.00	2.50

1973-1974 TCMA Autograph Series

These postcard-size black-and-white cards have borderless front photos with a wide white strip at bottom to accommodate an autograph. They are blank-backed.

		NM	EX	VG
Complete Set (36):		125.00	65.00	35.00
Common Player:		4.00	2.00	1.20
1	Satchel Paige	7.50	3.75	2.25
2	Phil Rizzuto	6.00	3.00	1.75
3	Sid Gordon	4.00	2.00	1.20
4	Ernie Lombardi	4.00	2.00	1.20
5	Jesse Haines	4.00	2.00	1.20
6	Joe Gordon	4.00	2.00	1.20
7	Bill Terry	4.00	2.00	1.20
8	Bill Dickey	6.00	3.00	1.75
9	Joe DiMaggio	12.00	6.00	3.50
10	Carl Hubbell	5.00	2.50	1.50
11	Fred Lindstrom	4.00	2.00	1.20
12	Ted Lyons	4.00	2.00	1.20
13	Red Ruffing	4.00	2.00	1.20
14	Joe Gordon	4.00	2.00	1.20
15	Bob Feller	6.00	3.00	1.75
16	Yogi Berra	7.50	3.75	2.25
17	Ford Frick, Whitey Ford	5.00	2.50	1.50
18	Sandy Koufax	12.00	6.00	3.50
19	Ted Williams	10.00	5.00	3.00
20	Warren Spahn	5.00	2.50	1.50
21	Al Rosen	4.00	2.00	1.20
22	Luke Appling	4.00	2.00	1.20
23	Joe Bush	4.00	2.00	1.20
24	Joe Medwick	4.00	2.00	1.20
25	Lou Boudreau	4.00	2.00	1.20
26	Ralph Kiner	4.00	2.00	1.20
27	Lloyd Waner	4.00	2.00	1.20
28	Pee Wee Reese	7.50	3.75	2.25
29	Duke Snider	7.50	3.75	2.25
30	Sal Maglie	4.00	2.00	1.20
31	Monte Irvin	4.00	2.00	1.20
32	Lefty Gomez	4.00	2.00	1.20
33	George Kelly	4.00	2.00	1.20
34	Joe Adcock	4.00	2.00	1.20
35	Max Carey	4.00	2.00	1.20
36	Rube Marquard	4.00	2.00	1.20

1973 TCMA "Bobo"

The major league travels of Bobo Newsom are chronicled in this set of 3-1/2" x 5-1/2" black-and-white cards depicting the pitcher in the uniforms of the nine teams for whom he played between 1929-53.

		NM	EX	VG
Complete Set (10):		25.00	12.50	7.50
Common Card:		4.00	2.00	1.25
(1)	Bobo Newsom (A's)	4.00	2.00	1.25
(2)	Bobo Newsom (A's, with Bobby Shantz.)	4.00	2.00	1.25
(3)	Bobo Newsom (Browns)	4.00	2.00	1.25
(4)	Bobo Newsom (Cubs)	4.00	2.00	1.25
(5)	Bobo Newsom (Dodgers, with Leo Durocher.)	4.00	2.00	1.25
(6)	Bobo Newsom (Giants)	4.00	2.00	1.25
(7)	Bobo Newsom (Red Sox)	4.00	2.00	1.25
(8)	Bobo Newsom (Senators, with Ossie Bluege.)	4.00	2.00	1.25
(9)	Bobo Newsom (Tigers, with Paul Derringer.)	4.00	2.00	1.25
(10)	Bobo Newsom (Yankees, with Vic Rashi, Bucky Harris.)	4.00	2.00	1.25

1973 TCMA Giants 1886

		NM	EX	VG
Complete Set (15):		40.00	20.00	12.00
Common Player:		2.00	1.00	.60
1	Roger Connor	2.00	1.00	.60
2	Larry Corcoran	2.00	1.00	.60
3	Tom Deasley	2.00	1.00	.60
4	Mike Dorgan	2.00	1.00	.60
5	Dude Esterbrook	2.00	1.00	.60
6	Buck Ewing	2.00	1.00	.60
7	Joe Gerhardt	2.00	1.00	.60
8	Pete Gillespie	2.00	1.00	.60
9	Tim Keefe	2.00	1.00	.60
10	Jim Mutrie	2.00	1.00	.60
11	Jim O'Rourke	2.00	1.00	.60
12	Daniel Richardson	2.00	1.00	.60
13	John M. Ward	2.00	1.00	.60
14	Mickey Welch	2.00	1.00	.60
15	Bat Boy	2.00	1.00	.60

1973 TCMA Pudge Gautreaux

This custom-published postcard of the Brooklyn Dodgers catcher (1936-37) was printed in black-and-white in a 3-1/2" x 6" format. The issue date is approximate.

	NM	EX	VG
Sid "Pudge" Gautreaux	4.00	2.00	1.25

1973-78 TCMA League Leaders

One of TCMA's earliest major series of collectors cards was this run of postcard-size (3-1/2" x 5-1/2") black-and-whites honoring various statistical leaders in each league from the 1920s through the 1950s. Backs have a list of the leaders by year within decade, with one of them pictured on the front. The unnumbered cards are checklisted here in alphabetical order within decade, as they were issued.

		NM	EX	VG
Complete Set (96):		190.00	95.00	55.00
Common Player:		5.00	2.50	1.50
	Complete Set, The 1920s	50.00	25.00	15.00
(1)	Grover C. Alexander	5.00	2.50	1.50
(2)	Jim Bagby, Sr.	5.00	2.50	1.50
(3)	Jim Bottomley	5.00	2.50	1.50
(4)	Eddie Collins	5.00	2.50	1.50
(5)	Earle Combs	5.00	2.50	1.50
(6)	Kiki Cuyler	5.00	2.50	1.50
(7)	Urban "Red" Faber	5.00	2.50	1.50
(8)	Johnny Frederick	5.00	2.50	1.50
(9)	Charlie Gehringer	5.00	2.50	1.50
(10)	Goose Goslin	5.00	2.50	1.50
(11)	Rogers Hornsby	5.00	2.50	1.50
(12)	Walter Johnson	6.00	3.00	1.75
(13)	Freddie Lindstrom	5.00	2.50	1.50
(14)	Bob Meusel	5.00	2.50	1.50
(15)	Charlie Root	5.00	2.50	1.50
(16)	Babe Ruth, Rogers Hornsby	7.50	3.75	2.25
(17)	Al Simmons, Babe Ruth	7.50	3.75	2.25
(18)	Tris Speaker	5.00	2.50	1.50
(19)	Dazzy Vance	5.00	2.50	1.50
(20)	Lloyd Waner	5.00	2.50	1.50
(21)	Cy Williams	5.00	2.50	1.50
(22)	Ken Williams	5.00	2.50	1.50
(23)	Hack Wilson	5.00	2.50	1.50
(24)	Ross Youngs	5.00	2.50	1.50
	Complete Set, The 1930s	50.00	25.00	15.00
(1)	Johnny Allen	5.00	2.50	1.50
(2)	Beau Bell	5.00	2.50	1.50
(3)	Cy Blanton	5.00	2.50	1.50
(4)	Ben Chapman	5.00	2.50	1.50
(5)	Joe Cronin	5.00	2.50	1.50
(6)	Dizzy Dean	6.50	3.25	2.00
(7)	Joe DiMaggio	20.00	10.00	6.00
(8)	Jimmie Foxx	5.00	2.50	1.50
(9)	Lou Gehrig	15.00	7.50	4.50
(10)	Charlie Gehringer	5.00	2.50	1.50
(11)	Lefty Gomez	5.00	2.50	1.50
(12)	Ival Goodman	5.00	2.50	1.50
(13)	Lefty Grove	5.00	2.50	1.50
(14)	Billy Herman	5.00	2.50	1.50
(15)	Ernie Lombardi	5.00	2.50	1.50
(16)	Chuck Klein	5.00	2.50	1.50
(17)	Heinie Manush	5.00	2.50	1.50
(18)	Pepper Martin	5.00	2.50	1.50
(19)	Joe Medwick	5.00	2.50	1.50
(20)	Van Mungo	5.00	2.50	1.50
(21)	Mel Ott	5.00	2.50	1.50

		NM	EX	VG
(22)	Bill Terry	5.00	2.50	1.50
(23)	Hal Trosky	5.00	2.50	1.50
(24)	Arky Vaughan	5.00	2.50	1.50
	Complete Set, The 1940s	50.00	25.00	15.00
(1)	Gene Bearden	5.00	2.50	1.50
(2)	Lou Boudreau	5.00	2.50	1.50
(3)	George Case	5.00	2.50	1.50
(4)	Phil Cavarretta	5.00	2.50	1.50
(5)	Bob Feller	6.00	3.00	1.75
(6)	Boo Ferriss	5.00	2.50	1.50
(7)	Hank Greenberg	9.00	4.50	2.75
(8)	Jeff Heath	5.00	2.50	1.50
(9)	Tommy Holmes	5.00	2.50	1.50
(10)	Larry Jansen	5.00	2.50	1.50
(11)	George Kell	5.00	2.50	1.50
(12)	Ralph Kiner	5.00	2.50	1.50
(13)	Marty Marion	5.00	2.50	1.50
(14)	Johnny Mize	5.00	2.50	1.50
(15)	Stan Musial	10.00	5.00	3.00
(16)	Bill Nicholson	5.00	2.50	1.50
(17)	Johnny Pesky	5.00	2.50	1.50
(18)	Jackie Robinson	10.00	5.00	3.00
(19)	Enos Slaughter	5.00	2.50	1.50
(20)	Snuffy Stirnweiss	5.00	2.50	1.50
(21)	Bill Voiselle	5.00	2.50	1.50
(22)	Bucky Walters	5.00	2.50	1.50
(23)	Ted Williams	10.00	5.00	3.00
(24)	Ted Williams, Joe DiMaggio	10.00	5.00	3.00
	Complete Set, The 1950s	50.00	25.00	15.00
(1)	Luis Aparicio	5.00	2.50	1.50
(2)	Ernie Banks	5.00	2.50	1.50
(3)	Bill Bruton	5.00	2.50	1.50
(4)	Lew Burdette	5.00	2.50	1.50
(5)	Rocky Colavito	5.00	2.50	1.50
(6)	Dom DiMaggio	5.00	2.50	1.50
(7)	Ferris Fain	5.00	2.50	1.50
(8)	Whitey Ford	5.00	2.50	1.50
(9)	Don Hoak	5.00	2.50	1.50
(10)	Sam Jethroe	5.00	2.50	1.50
(11)	Ted Kluszewski	5.00	2.50	1.50
(12)	Harvey Kuenn	5.00	2.50	1.50
(13)	Bob Lemon	5.00	2.50	1.50
(14)	Mickey Mantle	30.00	15.00	9.00
(15)	Willie Mays	15.00	7.50	4.50
(16)	Willie Mays, Bobby Avila	5.00	2.50	1.50
(17)	Minnie Minoso	5.00	2.50	1.50
(18)	Don Newcombe	5.00	2.50	1.50
(19)	Robin Roberts	5.00	2.50	1.50
(20)	Hank Sauer	5.00	2.50	1.50
(21)	Bobby Shantz	5.00	2.50	1.50
(22)	Roy Sievers	5.00	2.50	1.50
(23)	Duke Snider	6.00	3.00	1.75
(24)	Mickey Vernon	5.00	2.50	1.50

1973 TCMA Sports Scoop Hall of Fame

This set of large-format (3-1/2" x 5-1/2") black-and-white cards was produced by TCMA for the collectors' magazine Sports Scoop, which was promoting the players to be inducted into the Hall of Fame. Backs have information about the player's career and HoF credentials.

		NM	EX	VG
	Complete Set (12):	20.00	10.00	6.00
	Common Player:	2.00	1.00	.60
(1)	Earl Averill	2.50	1.25	.70
(2)	Ben Chapman	2.00	1.00	.60
(3)	Doc Cramer	2.00	1.00	.60
(4)	Spud Davis	2.00	1.00	.60
(5)	Babe Herman	2.00	1.00	.60
(6)	Billy Herman	2.50	1.25	.70
(7)	Chuck Klein	2.50	1.25	.70
(8)	Bob Meusel	2.00	1.00	.60
(9)	Johnny Mize	3.00	1.50	.90
(10)	Joe Sewell	2.50	1.25	.70
(11)	Enos Slaughter	3.00	1.50	.90
(12)	Hal Trosky	2.00	1.00	.60

1973 TCMA 1874 Philadelphia Athletics

This early collectors' issue reproduces woodcuts of the A's as they appeared in the July 25, 1874, edition of Harper's Weekly. The 3-1/16" x 4-1/2" cards are printed in black-and-white with the player name and position in the white border at bottom. Identical backs credit the pictures' original source and state "TCMA Reprint 1973." The unnumbered cards are checklisted here alphabetically.

		NM	EX	VG
	Complete Set (9):	25.00	12.50	7.50
	Common Player:	3.00	1.50	.90
(1)	Cap Anson	10.00	5.00	3.00
(2)	Joseph Battin	3.00	1.50	.90
(3)	John Clapp	3.00	1.50	.90
(4)	Wes Fisler	3.00	1.50	.90
(5)	Count Gedney	3.00	1.50	.90
(6)	Dick McBride	3.00	1.50	.90

(7)	Mike McGeary	3.00	1.50	.90
(8)	J.F. McMullen	3.00	1.50	.90
(9)	Ezra Sutton	3.00	1.50	.90

1973 TCMA 1890 Base-ball Season

This set commemorates the baseball "war" of 1890 when many National League players - stars and journeymen alike - defected to a new player-owned league called, appropriately enough, the Players League. Fronts of these 3-1/8" x 4-1/2" black-and-white cards feature reproductions of woodcuts originally printed in Harper's Weekly. Backs have information about the teams in each league. The unnumbered cards are checklisted here in alphabetical order. Original issue price of the set was $3.

		NM	EX	VG
	Complete Set (30):	48.00	24.00	14.50
	Common Player:	2.00	1.00	.60
(1)	Cap Anson	2.00	1.00	.60
(2)	Dan Brouthers	2.00	1.00	.60
(3)	Thomas E. Burns	2.00	1.00	.60
(4)	John Clarkson	2.00	1.00	.60
(5)	C.A. Comiskey	2.00	1.00	.60
(6)	Roger Connor	2.00	1.00	.60
(7)	E.N. Crane	2.00	1.00	.60
(8)	Jeremiah Denny	2.00	1.00	.60
(9)	William B. Ewing	2.00	1.00	.60
(10)	D.L. Foutz	2.00	1.00	.60
(11)	John W. Glasscock	2.00	1.00	.60
(12)	W. Hallman	2.00	1.00	.60
(13)	Edward Hanlon	2.00	1.00	.60
(14)	Timothy J. Keefe	2.00	1.00	.60
(15)	M.J. Kelly	2.00	1.00	.60
(16)	M. Kilroy	2.00	1.00	.60
(17)	W.A. Latham	2.00	1.00	.60
(18)	J.A. McPhee	2.00	1.00	.60
(19)	Joseph Mulvey	2.00	1.00	.60
(20)	W.D. O'Brien	2.00	1.00	.60
(21)	David Orr	2.00	1.00	.60
(22)	John G. Reilly	2.00	1.00	.60
(23)	S.L. Thompson	2.00	1.00	.60
(24)	M. Tiernan	2.00	1.00	.60
(25)	John M. Ward	2.00	1.00	.60
(26)	M. Welsh (Welch)	2.00	1.00	.60
(27)	A. Weyhing	2.00	1.00	.60
(28)	Charles Zimmer	2.00	1.00	.60
(29)	A dive for second base	1.00	.50	.30
(30)	Brotherhood Players Header Card	1.00	.50	.30

1973 TCMA 1930's No Hit Pitchers and 6 for 6 Hitters

These large-format (3-1/2" x 5-1/2") cards feature the no-hit pitchers and 6-for-6 hitters of the 1930s. Borderless front photos are in black-and-white. On back of the pitchers' cards is a list of the decade's no-hitters, the date, score and opposing team. A similar list of the 6-for-6 hitters is on the back of their cards. The cards are unnumbered.

		NM	EX	VG
	Complete Set (12):	40.00	20.00	12.00
	Common Player:	4.00	2.00	1.25
	PITCHERS	.00	.00	.00
(1)	Paul Dean	6.00	3.00	1.75
(2)	Bill Dietrich	4.00	2.00	1.25
(3)	Vern Kennedy	4.00	2.00	1.25
(4)	Monte Pearson	4.00	2.00	1.25
(5)	Johnny Vander Meer	5.00	2.50	1.50
	HITTERS	.00	.00	.00
(6)	Jim Bottomley	6.00	3.00	1.75
(7)	Bruce Campbell	4.00	2.00	1.25
(8)	Doc Cramer	4.00	2.00	1.25
(9)	Myril Hoag	4.00	2.00	1.25
(10)	Cookie Lavagetto	4.00	2.00	1.25
(11)	Terry Moore	5.00	2.50	1.50
(12)	Henry Steinbacher	4.00	2.00	1.25

1973 TCMA 1941 Brooklyn Dodgers

These 3-3/8" x 2-1/2" cards are printed in blue-and-white. The unnumbered cards do not have player names on front.

		NM	EX	VG
	Complete Set (32):	50.00	25.00	15.00
	Common Player:	2.00	1.00	.60
(1)	Title Card	1.00	.50	.30
(2)	John Allen	2.00	1.00	.60
(3)	Mace Brown	2.00	1.00	.60
(4)	Dolph Camilli	2.00	1.00	.60
(5)	Hugh Casey	2.00	1.00	.60
(6)	Curt Davis	2.00	1.00	.60
(7)	Tom Drake	2.00	1.00	.60
(8)	Leo Durocher	4.00	2.00	1.25
(9)	Fred Fitzsimmons	2.00	1.00	.60
(10)	Herman Franks	2.00	1.00	.60

(11)	Augie Galan	2.00	1.00	.60
(12)	Tony Giuliani	2.00	1.00	.60
(13)	Luke Hamlin	2.00	1.00	.60
(14)	Billy Herman	4.00	2.00	1.25
(15)	Kirby Higbe	2.00	1.00	.60
(16)	Alex Kampouris	2.00	1.00	.60
(17)	Newt Kimball	2.00	1.00	.60
(18)	Cookie Lavagetto	2.00	1.00	.60
(19)	Ducky Medwick	4.00	2.00	1.25
(20)	Van Mungo	2.00	1.00	.60
(21)	Mickey Owen	2.00	1.00	.60
(22)	Babe Phelps	2.00	1.00	.60
(23)	Pee Wee Reese	8.00	4.00	2.50
(24)	Pete Reiser	2.00	1.00	.60
(25)	Lew Riggs	2.00	1.00	.60
(26)	Bill Swift	2.00	1.00	.60
(27)	Vito Tamulis	2.00	1.00	.60
(28)	Joe Vosmik	2.00	1.00	.60
(29)	Dixie Walker	2.00	1.00	.60
(30)	Paul Waner	4.00	2.00	1.25
(31)	Jimmy Wasdell	2.00	1.00	.60
(32)	Whit Wyatt	2.00	1.00	.60

1973 TCMA Stan Martucci Postcards

This set of postcards was custom-produced by TCMA for card dealer Stan Martucci who apparently used them as "ride alongs" when filling orders. Approximately 3-1/2" x 5-1/2", the fronts have borderless, unidentified black-and-white photos of popular former stars. The back is in standard postcard format and had the player identified at top-left and a note from Martucci in the message area.

		NM	EX	VG
	Complete Set (16):	15.00	7.50	4.50
	Common Player:	1.00	.50	.30
(1)	Joe Cronin	1.00	.50	.30
(2)	Dizzy Dean	2.00	1.00	.60
(3)	Joe DiMaggio	5.00	2.50	1.50
(4)	Jimmie Foxx	2.00	1.00	.60
(5)	Lou Gehrig	5.00	2.50	1.50
(6)	Charlie Gehringer	1.00	.50	.30
(7)	Lefty Gomez	1.00	.50	.30
(8)	Lefty Grove	1.00	.50	.30
(9)	Carl Hubbell	1.00	.50	.30
(10)	Ted Lyons	1.00	.50	.30
(11)	Heinie Manush	1.00	.50	.30
(12)	Joe Medwick	1.00	.50	.30
(13)	Mel Ott	1.00	.50	.30
(14)	Red Ruffing	1.00	.50	.30
(15)	Bill Terry	1.00	.50	.30
(16)	Paul Waner	1.00	.50	.30

1974 TCMA Nicknames

Nicknames of notable ballplayers of the 1930s-40s are featured in this early collectors' set. Fronts of the 2-5/16" x 3-1/2" cards have a black-and-white photo with the player's nickname in the bottom border and "Nicknames" in the top border, both printed in red. Backs have a card number, the player's full name, position and the teams and years he played in the major leagues. The set originally sold for $3.

		NM	EX	VG
	Complete Set (28):	40.00	20.00	12.00
	Common Player:	3.00	1.50	.90
1	Rapid Robert Feller	4.50	2.25	1.25
2	Babe Dahlgren	3.00	1.50	.90
3	Spud Chandler	3.00	1.50	.90
4	Ducky Medwick	3.00	1.50	.90
5	Silent Cal Benge	3.00	1.50	.90
6	Goose Goslin	3.00	1.50	.90
7	Mule Haas	3.00	1.50	.90
8	Dizzy Dean	6.00	3.00	1.75
9	Cowboy Harrell	3.00	1.50	.90
10	Buzz Boyle	3.00	1.50	.90
11	Coonskin Davis	3.00	1.50	.90
12	Moose Solters	3.00	1.50	.90
13	Sad Sam Jones	3.00	1.50	.90
14	Bad News Hale	3.00	1.50	.90
15	Bucky Harris	3.00	1.50	.90
16	Lord Jim Jordan	3.00	1.50	.90
17	Zeke Bonura	3.00	1.50	.90
18	Heave-o Hafey	3.00	1.50	.90
19	Spud Davis	3.00	1.50	.90
20	Bing Miller	3.00	1.50	.90
21	Preacher Roe	3.00	1.50	.90
22	Wild Bill Hallahan	3.00	1.50	.90
23	Indian Bob Johnson	3.00	1.50	.90
24	Flash Gordon	3.00	1.50	.90
25	Tot Pressnell	3.00	1.50	.90
26	Hot Potato Hamlin	3.00	1.50	.90
27	Old Reliable Henrich	3.00	1.50	.90
28	Tom Hafey	3.00	1.50	.90

1974 TCMA Sports Nostalgia Store Postcards

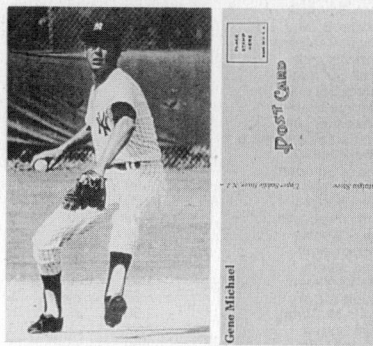

To celebrate the opening of one of the first, if not the first, sports collectors' retail stores, TCMA issued a set of four 3-1/2" x 5-1/2" black-and-white postcards. The set includes one current N.Y. Yankees player and three former boxers. The set was issued in an edition of 1,000.

		NM	EX	VG
Complete Set (4):		20.00	10.00	6.00
Common Card:		5.00	2.50	1.50
(1)	Gene Michael	7.50	3.75	2.25
(2)	Emile Griffith	5.00	2.50	1.50
(3)	Floyd Patterson	5.00	2.50	1.50
(4)	Willie Pep	5.00	2.50	1.50

1974 TCMA Stadium Postcards

These 5" x 3-1/2" black-and-white postcards are not numbered and are listed here alphabetically.

		NM	EX	VG
Complete Set (12):		35.00	17.50	10.50
Common Card:		4.00	2.00	1.20
(1)	Baltimore Stadium	4.00	2.00	1.20
(2)	Boston Braves Field	4.00	2.00	1.20
(3)	Crosley Field	4.00	2.00	1.20
(4)	Ebbet's (Ebbets) Field	6.00	3.00	1.75
(5)	Forbes Field	4.00	2.00	1.20
(6)	Griffith Field	4.00	2.00	1.20
(7)	Milwaukee County Stadium	4.00	2.00	1.20
(8)	Narvin (Navin) Field	4.00	2.00	1.20
(9)	Polo Grounds	4.00	2.00	1.20
(10)	Shea Stadium	4.00	2.00	1.20
(11)	Wrigley Field	5.00	2.50	1.50
(12)	Yankee Stadium	7.50	3.75	2.25

1974-75 TCMA St. Louis Browns

Some of baseball's most loveable losers from about the 1930s through the team's flight to Baltimore in 1953 are presented in this multi-series collectors' issue. Cards are printed in a 2-1/4" x 3-7/8" format, with brown ink used on front and on back of Series 1 and 2; Series 3 cards have black ink on back. Some cards have player identification on front, some only on back. All cards have a TCMA copyright date line and a few player stats for his years with the Brownies. The unnumbered cards are checklisted here alphabetically by series.

		NM	EX	VG
Complete Set (108):		80.00	40.00	20.00
Common Player:		1.50	.75	.45
	Series 1 - 1974	25.00	12.50	7.50
(1)	Ethan Allen	1.50	.75	.45
(2)	Mel Almada	2.00	1.00	.60
(3)	Ed Baecht	1.50	.75	.45
(4)	John Berardino	4.00	2.00	1.25
(5)	Emil Bildilli	1.50	.75	.45
(6)	John Blake	1.50	.75	.45
(7)	Julio Bonetti	1.50	.75	.45
(8)	Earl Caldwell	1.50	.75	.45
(9)	Scoops Carey	1.50	.75	.45
(10)	Stinky Davis	1.50	.75	.45
(11)	Fred Haney	1.50	.75	.45
(12)	Jeff Heath	1.50	.75	.45
(13)	Don Heffner	1.50	.75	.45
(14)	Rollie Hemsley	1.50	.75	.45
(15)	Oral Hildebrand	1.50	.75	.45
(16)	Elon Hogsett	1.50	.75	.45
(17)	Ben Huffman	1.50	.75	.45
(18)	Sig Jakucki	1.50	.75	.45
(19)	Billy Knickerbocker	1.50	.75	.45
(20)	John Knott	1.50	.75	.45
(21)	Jack Kramer	1.50	.75	.45
(22)	Red Kress	1.50	.75	.45
(23)	Chet Laabs	1.50	.75	.45
(24)	Gerard "Nig" Lipscomb	1.50	.75	.45
(25)	John Lucadello	1.50	.75	.45
(26)	Mel Mazzera	1.50	.75	.45
(27)	Red McQuillen	1.50	.75	.45
(28)	George McQuinn	1.50	.75	.45
(29)	Oscar Melillo	1.50	.75	.45
(30)	Howard Mills	1.50	.75	.45
(31)	Bob Muncrief	1.50	.75	.45
(32)	Hank Thompson	1.50	.75	.45
(33)	Russell "Sheriff" Van Atta	1.50	.75	.45
(34)	Joe Vosmik	1.50	.75	.45
(35)	Jim Walkup	1.50	.75	.45
(36)	Sam West	1.50	.75	.45
	Series 2 - 1974	30.00	15.00	9.00
(37)	Floyd Baker	1.50	.75	.45
(38)	John Bassler	1.50	.75	.45
(39)	Ollie Bejma	1.50	.75	.45
(40)	Jim Bottomley	2.00	1.00	.60
(41)	Willard Brown	4.50	2.25	1.25
(42)	Bob Dillinger	1.50	.75	.45
(43)	Owen "Red" Friend	1.50	.75	.45
(44)	Eddie Gaedel	5.00	2.50	1.50
(45)	Dennis Galehouse	1.50	.75	.45
(46)	Joseph Gallagher	1.50	.75	.45
(47)	Ned Garver	1.50	.75	.45
(48)	Robert Harris	1.50	.75	.45
(49)	Al Hollingsworth	1.50	.75	.45
(50)	Walter Judnich	1.50	.75	.45
(51)	William "Lefty" Kennedy	1.50	.75	.45
(52)	Lou Kretlow	1.50	.75	.45
(53)	Martin Marion	1.50	.70	.45
(54)	Les Moss	1.50	.75	.45
(55)	Louis "Bobo" Newsom	1.50	.75	.45
(56)	Fritz Ostermueller	1.50	.75	.45
(57)	Joe Ostrowski	1.50	.75	.45
(58)	Edward Pellagrini	1.50	.75	.45
(59)	Duane Pillette	1.50	.75	.45
(60)	Nelson Potter	1.50	.75	.45
(61)	Raymond "Rip" Radcliff	1.50	.75	.45
(62)	Harry Rice	1.50	.75	.45
(63)	Jim Rivera	1.50	.75	.45
(64)	John "Fred" Sanford	1.50	.75	.45
(65)	Luke Sewell	1.50	.75	.45
(66)	Al Shirley	1.50	.75	.45
(67)	Junior Stephens	1.50	.75	.45
(68)	Thomas Turner	1.50	.75	.45
(69)	Ken Wood	1.50	.75	.45
(70)	Allen "Zeke" Zarilla	1.50	.75	.45
(71)	Samuel "Sad Sam" Zoldak	1.50	.75	.45
(72)	1944 Infield	1.50	.75	.45
	Series 3 - 1975	30.00	15.00	9.00
(73)	Bow-Wow Arft	1.50	.75	.45
(74)	Matthew Batts	1.50	.75	.45
(75)	Tommy Byrne	1.50	.75	.45
(76)	Skippy Byrnes	1.50	.75	.45
(77)	Raymond Coleman	1.50	.75	.45
(78)	Scrap Iron Courtney	1.50	.75	.45
(79)	James Delsing	1.50	.75	.45
(80)	William "Kid" DeMars	1.50	.75	.45
(81)	Clifford "Mule" Fannin	1.50	.75	.45
(82)	Tom Fine	1.50	.75	.45
(83)	Pete Gray	5.00	2.50	1.50
(84)	Red Hayworth	1.50	.75	.45
(85)	Procopio Herrera	1.50	.70	.45
(86)	Fred Hoffman	1.50	.75	.45
(87)	Walter "Union Man" Holke	1.50	.75	.45
(88)	Hal Hudson	1.50	.70	.45
(89)	Richard Kokos	1.50	.75	.45
(90)	Michael Kreevich	1.50	.75	.45
(91)	Richard Kryhoski	1.50	.75	.45
(92)	Paul "Peanuts" Lehner	1.50	.75	.45
(93)	Footsie Lenhardt	1.50	.75	.45
(94)	Joe Lutz	1.50	.75	.45
(95)	Robert Mahoney	1.50	.75	.45
(96)	Frank Mancuso	1.50	.75	.45
(97)	Clifford Mapes	1.50	.75	.45
(98)	Cass Michaels	1.50	.75	.45
(99)	Frank "Stubby" Overmire	1.50	.75	.45
(100)	Satchel Paige	5.00	2.50	1.50
(101)	Roy Sievers	1.50	.75	.45
(102)	Louis Sleator	1.50	.75	.45
(103)	Richard Starr	1.50	.75	.45
(104)	Thomas "Muscles" Upton	1.50	.75	.45
(105)	Jerome Witte	1.50	.75	.45
(106)	Robert Young	1.50	.75	.45
(107)	1951 Browns	1.50	.75	.45
(108)	1952 Browns	1.50	.75	.45

1974 TCMA The Babe Postcards

This set of black-and-white postcards features photos of Ruth with contemporary players and managers. Cards measure 5-1/2" x 3-1/2" and have standard postcard indicia on the backs.

		NM	EX	VG
Complete Set (6):		20.00	10.00	6.00
Common Card:		5.00	2.50	1.50
1	Babe Ruth, Bill Terry	5.00	2.50	1.50
2	Babe Ruth, Walter Johnson	5.00	2.50	1.50
3	Babe Ruth, Lou Gehrig, Joe McCarthy	5.00	2.50	1.50
4	Babe Ruth, Miller Huggins	5.00	2.50	1.50
5	Babe Ruth, Tony Lazzeri	5.00	2.50	1.50
6	Babe Ruth and 1934 All-Stars	5.00	2.50	1.50

1974 TCMA 1890 Brooklyn Club

The National League champion Brooklyn Bridegrooms are featured in this collectors issue. Fronts of the 3-1/2" x 3-3/4" black-and-white cards picture the players in dress suits with ornate designs around the border. The design was copied from an 1890 Brooklyn scorecard/yearbook. Backs have biographical information and career highlights, also copied from the earlier publication. The back also includes a 1974 TCMA reprint notice. The unnumbered cards are checklisted here in alphabetical order.

		NM	EX	VG
Complete Set (16):		30.00	15.00	9.00
Common Player:		3.00	1.50	.90
(1)	Thomas P. Burns	3.00	1.50	.90
(2)	Albert J. Bushong	3.00	1.50	.90
(3)	Robert Lee Caruthers	3.00	1.50	.90
(4)	Robert H. Clark	3.00	1.50	.90
(5)	Hubbert Collins	3.00	1.50	.90
(6)	John S. Corkhill	3.00	1.50	.90
(7)	Thomas P. Daly	3.00	1.50	.90
(8)	D.L. Foutz	3.00	1.50	.90
(9)	Michael F. Hughes	3.00	1.50	.90
(10)	Thomas J. Lovett	3.00	1.50	.90
(11)	W.H. McGunnigle	3.00	1.50	.90
(12)	Wm. D. O'Brien	3.00	1.50	.90
(13)	George Burton Pinkney	3.00	1.50	.90
(14)	George J. Smith	3.00	1.50	.90
(15)	George T. Stallings	3.00	1.50	.90
(16)	Wm. H. Terry	3.00	1.50	.90

1974 TCMA 1910-14 Philadelphia Athletics Postcards

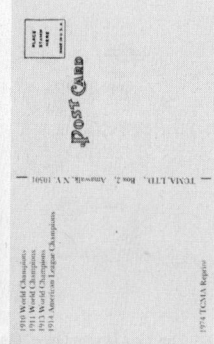

This series of collectors' issue postcards (about 3-1/2" x 5-3/4") was issued in two forms; printed front and back in black-and-white or in blue-and-white. While numbered between 501 and 518, only 12 cards were issued. The cards are reproductions of the images from the 1911 Pinkerton cabinets (T5). The postcard-format backs have a "1974 TCMA Reprint" notice along with the list of the dynasty's league and world championships.

		NM	EX	VG
Complete Set (12):		10.00	5.00	3.00
Common Player:		1.00	.50	.30
501	Chas. Bender	1.50	.70	.45
502	John Coombs	1.00	.50	.30
503	Eddie Plank	1.50	.70	.45
504	Amos Strunk	1.00	.50	.30
506	Ira Thomas	1.00	.50	.30
508	Stuffy McInnis	1.00	.50	.30
510	Rube Oldring	1.00	.50	.30
511	Eddie Collins	1.50	.70	.45
512	Frank Baker	1.50	.70	.45
515	Jack Barry	1.00	.50	.30
516	Jack Lapp	1.00	.50	.30
518	Danny Murphy	1.00	.50	.30

1974 TCMA 1929-31 Athletics

	1929 - 1931 PHILADELPHIA ATHLETICS
	JAMES JOSEPH DYKES

	1929	1930	1931
Games	119	125	101
AB	401	435	355
Hits	131	131	97
Runs	76	69	48
HR	13	6	3
RBI	79	73	46
BA	.327	.301	.273

TCMA 1974

Jimmy Dykes   Inf.

Stars of the Philadelphia A's dynasty which won two World Series and an A.L. pennant from 1929-31 are featured in this collectors issue. The 2-5/8" x 4" cards have black-and-white player photos at center. Printed in green in the white border at top is "1929-31 Athletics." At bottom, printed in black, is the player's name and position. Backs are in black-and-white with stats for 1929, 1930 and 1931, as appropriate. The unnumbered cards are checklisted here in alphabetical order.

		NM	EX	VG
	Complete Set (29):	30.00	15.00	9.00
	Common Player:	2.00	1.00	.60
(1)	Max Bishop	2.00	1.00	.60
(2)	Joe Boley	2.00	1.00	.60
(3)	George Burns	2.00	1.00	.60
(4)	Mickey Cochrane	3.00	1.50	.90
(5)	Eddie Collins, Lew Krausse	2.00	1.00	.60
(6)	"Doc" Cramer	2.00	1.00	.60
(7)	Jimmy Dykes	2.00	1.00	.60
(8)	George Earnshaw	2.00	1.00	.60
(9)	Howard Ehmke	2.00	1.00	.60
(10)	Lou Finney, John Heving	2.00	1.00	.60
(11)	Jimmie Foxx	4.00	2.00	1.25
(12)	Walt French, Waite Hoyt	2.00	1.00	.60
(13)	"Lefty" Grove	3.00	1.50	.90
(14)	"Mule" Haas	2.00	1.00	.60
(15)	Sammy Hale	2.00	1.00	.60
(16)	"Pinky" Higgins, Phil Todt	2.00	1.00	.60
(17)	Earle Mack, Connie Mack	2.00	1.00	.60
(18)	Roy Mahaffey	2.00	1.00	.60
(19)	Eric McNair	2.00	1.00	.60
(20)	Bing Miller	2.00	1.00	.60
(21)	Jim Moore, Jim Peterson	2.00	1.00	.60
(22)	Jack Quinn	2.00	1.00	.60
(23)	Eddie Rommel	2.00	1.00	.60
(24)	Wally Schang	2.50	1.25	.70
(25)	Al Simmons	2.50	1.25	.70
(26)	Homer Summa	2.00	1.00	.60
(27)	Rube Walberg	2.00	1.00	.60
(28)	"Dib" Williams	2.00	1.00	.60
(29)	Team Photo Card (10" x 5")	10.00	5.00	3.00

1974 TCMA 1934 St. Louis Cardinals

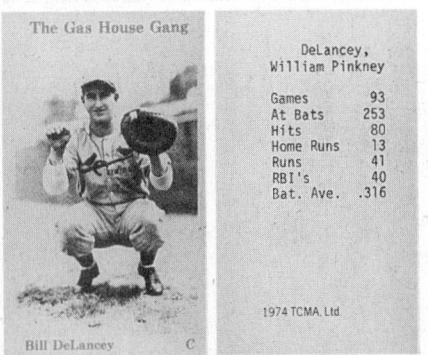

The Gas House Gang

	DeLancey, William Pinkney
Games	93
At Bats	253
Hits	80
Home Runs	13
Runs	41
RBI's	40
Bat. Ave.	.316

1974 TCMA. Ltd.

Bill DeLancey   C

The "Gas House Gang" (as some of these cards are designated) is featured in this collectors' issue. Cards are 2-1/4" x 3-5/8" (#27-31 are 4-1/2" x 3-3/4") and feature black-and-white photos on front with red typography. Backs have a few stats in black-and-white. Some cards have a title at top reading "1934 Cardinals." The unnumbered cards are checklisted here in alphabetical order.

		NM	EX	VG
	Complete Set (31):	50.00	25.00	15.00
	Common Player:	2.00	1.00	.60
(1)	"Tex" Carleton	2.00	1.00	.60
(2)	"Ripper" Collins	2.00	1.00	.60
(3)	"Pat" Crawford	2.00	1.00	.60
(4)	"Spud" Davis	2.00	1.00	.60
(5)	"Daffy" Dean	2.50	1.25	.70
(6)	"Dizzy" Dean	4.00	2.00	1.25
(7)	Bill DeLancey	2.00	1.00	.60
(8)	Leo Durocher	2.50	1.25	.70
(9)	Frank Frisch	2.50	1.25	.70
(10)	"Chick" Fullis	2.00	1.00	.60
(11)	"Mike" Gonzalez	2.50	1.25	.70
(12)	"Pop" Haines	2.50	1.25	.70
(13)	Bill Hallahan	2.00	1.00	.60
(14)	Francis Healey (Healy)	2.00	1.00	.60
(15)	Jim Lindsey	2.00	1.00	.60
(16)	"Pepper" Martin	2.50	1.25	.70
(17)	"Ducky" Medwick	2.50	1.25	.70
(18)	Jim Mooney	2.00	1.00	.60
(19)	Ernie Orsatti	2.00	1.00	.60
(20)	Flint Rhem	2.00	1.00	.60
(21)	John Rothrock	2.00	1.00	.60
(22)	"Dazzy" Vance	2.50	1.25	.70
(23)	Bill Walker	2.00	1.00	.60
(24)	"Buzzy" Wares	2.00	1.00	.60
(25)	"Whitey" Whitehead	2.00	1.00	.60
(26)	Jim Winford	2.00	1.00	.60
(27)	"Daffy" & "Dizzy" (Daffy Dean, Dizzy Dean)	6.00	3.00	1.75
(28)	Dizzy & Leo Celebrate (Dizzy Dean, Leo Durocher)	4.00	2.00	1.25
(29)	Durocher Scores (Leo Durocher) (1934 World Series)	4.00	2.00	1.25
(30)	Medwick Out Cochrane Catcher (Mickey Cochrane, Ducky Medwick) (1934 World Series)	4.00	2.00	1.25
(31)	1934 St. Louis Cardinals World Champions	4.00	2.00	1.25

1974 TCMA 1934-5 Detroit Tigers

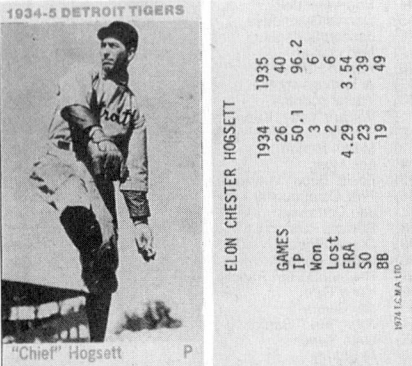

1934-5 DETROIT TIGERS

	ELON CHESTER HOGSETT	1934	1935
GAMES		26	40
IP		50.1	96.2
Won		3	6
Lost		2	6
ERA		4.29	3.54
SO		23	39
BB		19	49

1974 TCMA LTD.

"Chief" Hogsett   P

Members of the 1934 A.L. Champion and 1935 World's Champion teams are featured in this collectors issue team set. Except for a pair of large-format (4-1/4" x 3-3/4") cards, the cards measure about 2-1/8" x 3-5/8". Fronts have black-and-white photos. Above and below the photo are white stripes with the set title, player name and position. Backs are in black-and-white with 1934 and/or 1935 stats. The unnumbered cards are checklisted here alphabetically.

		NM	EX	VG
	Complete Set (36):	35.00	17.50	10.00
	Common Player:	2.00	1.00	.60
(1)	Eldon Auker	2.00	1.00	.60
(2)	Del Baker	2.00	1.00	.60
(3)	Tommy Bridges	2.00	1.00	.60
(4)	"Flea" Clifton	2.00	1.00	.60
(5)	Mickey Cochrane	4.00	2.00	1.25
(6)	"General" Crowder	2.00	1.00	.60
(7)	Frank Doljack	2.00	1.00	.60
(8)	Carl Fischer	2.00	1.00	.60
(9)	Pete Fox	2.00	1.00	.60
(10)	Vic Frasier	2.00	1.00	.60
(11)	Charlie Gehringer	4.00	2.00	1.25
(12)	Goose Goslin	2.00	1.00	.60
(13)	Hank Greenberg	5.00	2.50	1.50
(14)	Luke Hamlin	2.00	1.00	.60
(15)	Clyde Hatter	2.00	1.00	.60
(16)	Ray Hayworth	2.00	1.00	.60
(17)	"Chief" Hogsett	2.00	1.00	.60
(18)	Roxie Lawson	2.00	1.00	.60
(19)	"Firpo" Marberry	2.00	1.00	.60
(20)	Chet Morgan	2.00	1.00	.60
(21)	Marv Owen	2.00	1.00	.60
(22)	"Cy" Perkins	2.00	1.00	.60
(23)	"Red" Phillips	2.00	1.00	.60
(24)	Frank Reiber	2.00	1.00	.60
(25)	Billy Rogell	2.00	1.00	.60
(26)	"Schoolboy" Rowe	2.00	1.00	.60
(27)	"Heinie" Schuble	2.00	1.00	.60
(28)	Hugh Shelley	2.00	1.00	.60
(29)	Vic Sorrell	2.00	1.00	.60
(30)	Joe Sullivan	2.00	1.00	.60
(31)	"Gee" Walker	2.00	1.00	.60
(32)	"Hub" Walker	2.00	1.00	.60
(33)	"Jo-Jo" White	2.00	1.00	.60
(34)	Rudy York	2.00	1.00	.60
(35)	1934 Pitchers (Eldon Auker, Firpo Marberry, Tommy Bridges, Schoolboy Rowe) (4-1/4" x 3-3/4")	5.00	2.50	1.50
(36)	1935 Outfield (Goose Goslin, Jo-Jo White, Pete Fox) (4-1/4" x 3-3/4")	5.00	2.50	1.50

1974 TCMA 1936-37 New York Giants

This is the rarest of the TCMA Great Teams sets. Fewer than half of the 1,000 sets got into the hands of customers before legal action by Dick Bartell forced the company to halt sales and destroy more than 500 sets. The 2-5/8" x 3-3/8" cards are printed in black-and-orange. They are unnumbered and checklisted here in alphabetical order.

		NM	EX	VG
	Complete Set (36):	90.00	45.00	27.50
	Common Player:	2.50	1.25	.75
(1)	Title card	1.00	.50	.30
(2)	Tom Baker	2.50	1.25	.75
(3)	Dick Bartell	2.50	1.25	.75
(4)	Wally Berger	2.50	1.25	.75
(5)	Don Brennan	2.50	1.25	.75
(6)	Walter Brown	2.50	1.25	.75
(7)	Clyde Castleman	2.50	1.25	.75
(8)	Lou Chiozza	2.50	1.25	.70
(9)	Dick Coffman	2.50	1.25	.75
(10)	Harry Danning	2.50	1.25	.75
(11)	George Davis	2.50	1.25	.75
(12)	Charlie English	2.50	1.25	.75
(13)	Freddie Fitzsimmons	2.50	1.25	.75
(14)	Frank Gabler	2.50	1.25	.75
(15)	Harry Gumbert	2.50	1.25	.75
(16)	Mickey Haslin	2.50	1.25	.75
(17)	Carl Hubbell	6.00	3.00	1.75
(18)	Travis Jackson	4.00	2.00	1.25
(19)	Mark Koenig	2.50	1.25	.75
(20)	Hank Leiber	2.50	1.25	.75
(21)	Sam Leslie	2.50	1.25	.75
(22)	Bill Lohrman	2.50	1.25	.75
(23)	Eddie Mayo	2.50	1.25	.75
(24)	John McCarthy	2.50	1.25	.75
(25)	Cliff Melton	2.50	1.25	.75
(26)	Jo Jo Moore	2.50	1.25	.75
(27)	Mel Ott	6.00	3.00	1.75
(28)	Jimmy Ripple	2.50	1.25	.75
(29)	Hal Schumacher	2.50	1.25	.75
(30)	Al Smith	2.50	1.25	.75
(31)	Roy Spencer	2.50	1.25	.75
(32)	Bill Terry	5.00	2.50	1.50
(33)	Hy Vandenberg	2.50	1.25	.75
(34)	Phil Weintraub	2.50	1.25	.75
(35)	Burgess Whitehead	2.50	1.25	.75
(36)	Babe Young	2.50	1.25	.75

1974 TCMA 1936-1939 Yankee Dynasty

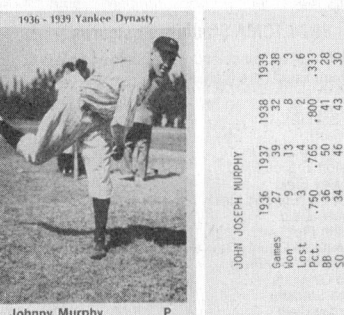

1936 - 1939 Yankee Dynasty

	JOHN JOSEPH MURPHY	1936	1937	1938	1939
Games		27	39	32	38
Won		9	13	8	3
Lost		3	4	2	6
BB		.750	.765	.800	.333
SO		36	46	43	28
ERA		3.38	4.17	4.24	4.40

TCMA Ltd.

Johnny Murphy   P

Many of the players who participated in one or more of the Yankees' four consecutive World Champion seasons in the late 1930s are included in this collectors' edition. Cards are 2-3/4" x 4" and feature black-and-white photos on front. In the white borders at top and bottom, the set name and player identification are printed in blue. Backs have stats for each season and are printed in black-and-white on a white background. A virtual reprint of this set was made circa 1983 with two player cards added and a brown background on back. The unnumbered cards are checklisted here alphabetically.

		NM	EX	VG
	Complete Set (56):	75.00	37.50	22.50
	Complete Set (51):	45.00	22.50	13.50
	Common Player:	2.00	1.00	.60
(1)	"Poison Ivy" Andrews	2.00	1.00	.60
(2)	Joe Beggs	2.00	1.00	.60
(3)	Marv Breuer	2.00	1.00	.60
(4)	Johnny Broaca	2.00	1.00	.60
(5)	"Jumbo" Brown	2.00	1.00	.60
(6)	"Spud" Chandler	2.00	1.00	.60
(7)	Ben Chapman	2.00	1.00	.60
(8)	Earle Combs	2.00	1.00	.60
(9)	Frankie Crosetti	2.00	1.00	.60
(10)	"Babe" Dahlgren	2.00	1.00	.60
(11)	Bill Dickey	2.50	1.25	.70
(12)	Joe DiMaggio	10.00	5.00	3.00
(13)	Atley Donald	2.00	1.00	.60
(14)	Wes Ferrell	2.00	1.00	.60
(15)	Artie Fletcher	2.00	1.00	.60
(16)	Joe Gallagher	2.00	1.00	.60
(17)	Lou Gehrig	10.00	5.00	3.00
(18)	Joe Glenn	2.00	1.00	.60
(19)	"Lefty" Gomez	2.00	1.00	.60
(20)	Joe Gordon	2.00	1.00	.60
(21)	"Bump" Hadley	2.00	1.00	.60
(22)	Don Heffner	2.00	1.00	.60
(23)	Tommy Henrich	2.00	1.00	.60
(24)	Oral Hildebrand	2.00	1.00	.60
(25)	Myril Hoag	2.00	1.00	.60
(26)	Roy Johnson	2.00	1.00	.60
(27)	Arndt Jorgens	2.00	1.00	.60
(28)	Charlie Keller	2.00	1.00	.60
(29)	Ted Kleinhans	2.00	1.00	.60
(30)	Billy Knickerbocker	2.00	1.00	.60
(31)	Tony Lazzeri	2.50	1.25	.70
(32)	Frank Makosky	2.00	1.00	.60
(33)	"Pat" Malone	2.00	1.00	.60
(34)	Johnny Murphy	2.00	1.00	.60
(35)	"Monty" Pearson	2.00	1.00	.60
(36)	"Jake" Powell	2.00	1.00	.60
(37)	"Red" Rolfe	2.00	1.00	.60
(38)	"Buddy" Rosar	2.00	1.00	.60
(39)	"Red" Ruffing	2.50	1.25	.70
(40)	Marius Russo	2.00	1.00	.60
(41)	"Jack" Saltzgaver	2.00	1.00	.60
(42)	Paul Schreiber	2.00	1.00	.60
(43)	Johnny Schulte	2.00	1.00	.60
(44)	Bob Seeds	2.00	1.00	.60

(45)	"Twinkletoes" Selkirk	2.00	1.00	.60
(46)	Lee Stine	2.00	1.00	.60
(47)	Steve Sundra	2.00	1.00	.60
(48)	"Sandy" Vance	2.00	1.00	.60
(49)	Dixie Walker	2.00	1.00	.60
(50)	Kemp Wicker	2.00	1.00	.60
(51)	Joe McCarthy, Jacob Ruppert	2.00	1.00	.60

5-1/2" x 4" FEATURE CARDS

(52)	Joe DiMaggio, Frank Crosetti, Tony Lazzeri, Bill Dickey, Lou Gehrig, Jake Powell, George Selkirk	5.00	2.50	1.50
(53)	Lou Gehrig, Joe DiMaggio	7.50	3.75	2.25
(54)	Gehrig Hits Another	6.00	3.00	1.75
(55)	Red Rolfe, Tony Lazzeri, Lou Gehrig, Frank Crosetti	5.00	2.50	1.50
(56)	World Champions - 1936	6.00	3.00	1.75

1974 TCMA 1952 Brooklyn Dodgers

The National League champion '52 Dodgers are featured in this collectors issue. Nominally 2-3/4" x 3-3/8", the cards are often found with minor variations in size. Fronts are printed in red and blue with a white border. The only identification on front is the player's first name or nickname. Backs are in black-and-white with the player's full name, position, uniform number, 1952 stats and TCMA copyright. Cards are checklisted here in alphabetical order.

		NM	EX	VG
	Complete Set (40):	25.00	15.00	7.50
	Common Player:	2.00	1.00	.60
(1)	Header/Team History Card (Jackie Robinson, Gil Hodges, Roy Campanella, Billy Cox, Pee Wee Reese)	2.00	1.00	.60
(2)	Cal Abrams	2.00	1.00	.60
(3)	Sandy Amoros	2.00	1.00	.60
(4)	Joe Black	2.00	1.00	.60
(5)	Ralph Branca	2.00	1.00	.60
(6)	Rocky Bridges	2.00	1.00	.60
(7)	Roy Campanella	4.00	2.00	1.25
(8)	Billy Cox	2.00	1.00	.60
(9)	Chuck Dressen	2.00	1.00	.60
(10)	Carl Erskine	2.00	1.00	.60
(11)	Carl Furillo	3.00	1.50	.90
(12)	Billy Herman	2.00	1.00	.60
(13)	Gil Hodges	4.00	2.00	1.25
(14)	Tommy Holmes	2.00	1.00	.60
(15)	Jim Hughes	2.00	1.00	.60
(16)	Clyde King	2.00	1.00	.60
(17)	Clem Labine	2.00	1.00	.60
(18)	Joe Landrum	2.00	1.00	.60
(19)	Cookie Lavagetto	2.00	1.00	.60
(20)	Ken Lehman	2.00	1.00	.60
(21)	Steve Lembo	2.00	1.00	.60
(22)	Billy Loes	2.00	1.00	.60
(23)	Ray Moore	2.00	1.00	.60
(24)	Bobby Morgan	2.00	1.00	.60
(25)	Ron Negray	2.00	1.00	.60
(26)	Rocky Nelson	2.00	1.00	.60
(27)	Andy Pafko	2.00	1.00	.60
(28)	Jake Pitler	2.00	1.00	.60
(29)	Bud Podbielan	2.00	1.00	.60
(30)	Pee Wee Reese	4.00	2.00	1.25
(31)	Jackie Robinson	7.50	3.75	2.25
(32)	Preacher Roe	2.00	1.00	.60
(33)	Johnny Rutherford	2.00	1.00	.60
(34)	Johnny Schmitz	2.00	1.00	.60
(35)	George Shuba	2.00	1.00	.60
(36)	Duke Snider	4.00	2.00	1.25
(37)	Chris Van Cuyk	2.00	1.00	.60
(38)	Ben Wade	2.00	1.00	.60
(39)	Rube Walker	2.00	1.00	.60
(40)	Dick Williams	2.00	1.00	.60

1975 TCMA All Time Brooklyn/Los Angeles Dodgers

A picked team of former Dodgers stars is featured in this collectors issue team set. Cards are in black-and-white in the standard 2-1/2" x 3-1/2" format. Fronts have player identification in the border beneath the photo. Backs have a checklist by position and a TCMA copyright line. The unnumbered cards are checklisted here in the order presented on back.

		NM	EX	VG
	Complete Set (12):	36.00	18.00	11.00
	Common Player:	2.25	1.25	.70
(1)	Gil Hodges	3.00	1.50	.90
(2)	Jackie Robinson	10.00	5.00	3.00
(3)	Pee Wee Reese	3.00	1.50	.90
(4)	Junior Gilliam	2.25	1.25	.70
(5)	Duke Snider	3.00	1.50	.90
(6)	Dixie Walker	2.25	1.25	.70
(7)	Zack Wheat	2.25	1.25	.70
(8)	Roy Campanella	4.00	2.00	1.25
(9)	Don Drysdale	3.00	1.50	.90
(10)	Sandy Koufax	8.00	4.00	2.50
(11)	Hugh Casey	2.25	1.25	.70
(12)	Walter Alston	2.25	1.25	.70

1975 TCMA All-Time Greats

This is a smaller - both in size and number - version of TCMA's Hall of Famer postcard set issued between 1973-80. These collectors' edition cards measure 2-3/8" x 3-3/4" and were issued in strips of six. Two printings with blue-and-white fronts and red backs, the second in black-and-white, blank-backed. Surrounding the photo on front is a blue or black border with baseball equipment ornamentation. The unnumbered cards are checklisted here in alphabetical order.

		NM	EX	VG
	Complete Set (39):	40.00	20.00	12.00
	Common Player:	2.00	1.00	.60
(1)	"Luke" Appling	2.00	1.00	.60
(2)	Roger Bresnahan	2.00	1.00	.60
(3)	Ty Cobb	8.00	4.00	2.50
(4)	Mickey Cochrane	2.00	1.00	.60
(5)	Eddie Collins	2.00	1.00	.60
(6)	Kiki Cuyler	2.00	1.00	.60
(7)	Dizzy Dean	4.00	2.00	1.25
(8)	Bill Dickey	2.00	1.00	.60
(9)	Joe DiMaggio	8.00	4.00	2.50
(10)	Bob Feller	2.00	1.00	.60
(11)	Elmer Flick	2.00	1.00	.60
(12)	Frank Frisch	2.00	1.00	.60
(13)	Lou Gehrig	8.00	4.00	2.50
(14)	Hank Greenberg	4.00	2.00	1.25
(15)	Goose Goslin	2.00	1.00	.60
(16)	Chick Hafey	2.00	1.00	.60
(17)	Gabby Hartnett	2.00	1.00	.60
(18)	Harry Heilmann	2.00	1.00	.60
(19)	Rogers Hornsby	2.00	1.00	.60
(20)	Waite Hoyt	2.00	1.00	.60
(21)	Walter Johnson	4.00	2.00	1.25
(22)	George Kelly	2.00	1.00	.60
(23)	Ted Lyons	2.00	1.00	.60
(24)	Connie Mack	2.00	1.00	.60
(25)	Mickey Mantle	10.00	5.00	3.00
(26)	Rabbit Maranville	2.00	1.00	.60
(27)	Mel Ott	2.00	1.00	.60
(28)	Edd Roush	2.00	1.00	.60
(29)	Red Ruffing	2.00	1.00	.60
(30)	Babe Ruth	10.00	5.00	3.00
(31)	Al Simmons	2.00	1.00	.60
(32)	Casey Stengel	2.00	1.00	.60
(33)	Pie Traynor	2.00	1.00	.60
(34)	Dazzy Vance	2.00	1.00	.60
(35)	Honus Wagner	4.00	2.00	1.25
(36)	Lloyd Waner	2.00	1.00	.60
(37)	Paul Waner	2.00	1.00	.60
(38)	Ted Williams	6.00	3.00	1.75
(39)	Harry Wright	2.00	1.00	.60

1975 TCMA All Time New York Giants

An all-time line-up of Giants is presented in this collector issue. Fronts of the 2-1/2" x 3-1/2" cards are black-and-white player photos with the player's name and position printed in red in the white bottom border. Backs are in black-and-white and present the all-time roster. The unnumbered cards are checklisted here alphabetically.

		NM	EX	VG
	Complete Set (12):	30.00	15.00	9.00
	Common Player:	2.00	1.00	.60
(1)	Alvin Dark	2.00	1.00	.60
(2)	Frankie Frisch	2.00	1.00	.60
(3)	Carl Hubbell	2.00	1.00	.60
(4)	Freddie Lindstrom	2.00	1.00	.60
(5)	Christy Mathewson	4.00	2.00	1.25
(6)	Willie Mays	15.00	7.50	4.50
(7)	John McGraw	2.00	1.00	.60
(8)	Mel Ott	2.00	1.00	.60
(9)	Bill Terry	2.00	1.00	.60
(10)	Bobby Thomson	2.00	1.00	.60
(11)	Wes Westrum	2.00	1.00	.60
(12)	Hoyt Wilhelm	2.00	1.00	.60

1975 TCMA All Time New York Yankees

The best players on the best team in baseball history are featured in this collectors' edition. Cards measure 2-1/2" x 3-3/4" and feature black-and-white photos on front, with white borders. Player name and position are printed in a white strip toward the bottom of the picture. Backs have a list of the all-time team. The unnumbered cards are listed here in that order.

		NM	EX	VG
	Complete Set (12):	15.00	7.50	4.50
	Common Player:	2.00	1.00	.60
(1)	Lou Gehrig	4.00	2.00	1.25
(2)	Tony Lazzeri	2.00	1.00	.60
(3)	Red Rolfe	2.00	1.00	.60
(4)	Phil Rizzuto	2.50	1.25	.70
(5)	Babe Ruth	5.00	2.50	1.50
(6)	Mickey Mantle	6.00	3.00	1.75
(7)	Joe DiMaggio	4.00	2.00	1.25
(8)	Bill Dickey	2.00	1.00	.60
(9)	Red Ruffing	2.00	1.00	.60
(10)	Whitey Ford	2.50	1.25	.70
(11)	Johnny Murphy	2.00	1.00	.60
(12)	Casey Stengel	2.00	1.00	.60

1975 TCMA Larry French Postcards

The career of National League pitcher Larry French is recounted in this set of 3-1/2" x 5-1/2" black-and-white postcard-size cards. Fronts have photos of him with the Pirates, Cubs and Dodgers. Backs have a continuing biography.

		NM	EX	VG
	Complete Set (6):	15.00	7.50	4.50
	Common Card:	3.00	1.50	.90
1	Larry French (Pittsburgh Pirates)	3.00	1.50	.90
2	Larry French (Chicago Cubs)	3.00	1.50	.90
3	Larry French (W/Bill Lee, Charlie Root, Tuck Stainback .)	3.00	1.50	.90
4	Larry French (W/Charlie Grimm, Fred Lindstrom.)	3.00	1.50	.90
5	Larry French (Brooklyn Dodgers)	3.00	1.50	.90
6	Larry French (W/Mickey Owen.)	3.00	1.50	.90

1975 TCMA Guam WW2

This set of 3-1/2" x 5-1/2" black-and-white cards details the connection between Major League Baseball and the Pacific island of Guam during WWII. Some cards picture players in the their military uniforms, others shown them in baseball uniforms. Backs contain a narrative of the series.

	NM	EX	VG
Complete Set (18):	25.00	12.50	7.50
Common Card:	1.00	.50	.30
1 Phil Rizzuto, Terry Moore	5.00	2.50	1.50
2 Gab Gab Guam 1945	1.00	.50	.30
3 Team Photo	1.00	.50	.30
4 Merrill May, Pee Wee Reese, Johnny Vander Meer	2.50	1.25	.70
5 Team Photo	1.00	.50	.30
6 Team Photo	1.00	.50	.30
7 Del Ennis	2.00	1.00	.60
8 Mace Brown	2.00	1.00	.60
9 Pee Wee Reese, Joe Gordon, Bill Dickey	3.50	1.75	1.00
10 Glenn McQuillen	2.00	1.00	.60
11 Mike Budnick	2.00	1.00	.60
12 Team Photo	1.00	.50	.30
13 "Skeets" Dickey	2.00	1.00	.60
14 Connie Ryan	2.00	1.00	.60
15 Hal White	2.00	1.00	.60
16 Mickey Cochrane	7.50	3.75	2.25
17 Barney McCosky	2.00	1.00	.60
18 Ben Huffman	2.00	1.00	.60

1975 TCMA 1913 Philadelphia Athletics

Members of the World Champion A's of 1913 are featured in this collectors' edition card set. In an unusual 3-1/8" x 5-11/16" format, the cards have black-and-white photos on front, with white borders and player identification at bottom. Backs feature season statistics. The unnumbered cards are checklisted here alphabetically.

	NM	EX	VG
Complete Set (16):	20.00	10.00	6.00
Common Player:	3.00	1.50	.90
(1) Home Run Baker	3.00	1.50	.90
(2) Jack Barry	3.00	1.50	.90
(3) Chief Bender	3.00	1.50	.90
(4) Joe Bush	3.00	1.50	.90
(5) Eddie Collins	3.00	1.50	.90
(6) Jack Coombs	3.00	1.50	.90
(7) Jack Lapp	3.00	1.50	.90
(8) Connie Mack	3.00	1.50	.90
(9) Stuffy McInnis	3.00	1.50	.90
(10) Dan Murphy	3.00	1.50	.90
(11) Eddie Murphy	3.00	1.50	.90
(12) Rube Oldring	3.00	1.50	.90
(13) William Orr	3.00	1.50	.90
(14) Ed Plank	3.00	1.50	.90
(15) Walter Schang	3.00	1.50	.90
(16) Amos Strunk	3.00	1.50	.90

1975 TCMA 1919 Chicago White Sox

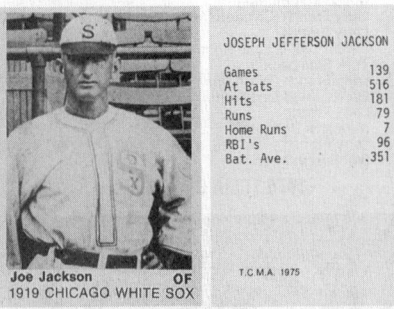

The infamous Black Sox who threw the 1919 World Series, and their teammates, are featured in this collectors' edition. The 2-1/2" x 3-1/2" cards are printed in black-and-white. Fronts have player photos with identification in the white border at bottom. Backs have 1919 season stats. The unnumbered cards are checklisted here alphabetically.

	NM	EX	VG
Complete Set (28):	35.00	17.50	10.00
Common Player:	1.00	.50	.30
(1) Joe Benz	1.00	.50	.30
(2) Eddie Cicotte	3.50	1.75	1.00
(3) Eddie Collins	2.50	1.25	.70
(4) Shano Collins	1.00	.50	.30
(5) Dave Danforth	1.00	.50	.30
(6) Red Faber	1.00	.40	.25
(7) Happy Felsch	3.50	1.75	1.00

(8) Chick Gandil	5.00	2.50	1.50
(9) Kid Gleason	1.00	.50	.30
(10) Joe Jackson	10.00	5.00	3.00
(11) Bill James	1.00	.50	.30
(12) Dickie Kerr	1.00	.50	.30
(13) Nemo Leibold	1.00	.50	.30
(14) Byrd Lynn	1.00	.50	.30
(15) Erskine Mayer	2.00	1.00	.60
(16) Harvey McClellan	1.00	.50	.30
(17) Fred McMullin	4.00	2.00	1.25
(18) Eddie Murphy	1.00	.50	.30
(19) Pat Ragan	1.00	.50	.30
(20) Swede Risberg	4.00	2.00	1.25
(21) Charlie Robertson	1.00	.50	.30
(22) Reb Russell	1.00	.50	.30
(23) Ray Schalk	1.00	.40	.25
(24) Buck Weaver	6.00	3.00	1.75
(25) Roy Wilkinson	1.00	.50	.30
(26) Lefty Williams	4.00	2.00	1.25
(27) Frank Shellenback, Grover Lowdermilk, Joe Jenkins, Dickie Kerr, Ray Schalk	1.00	.50	.30
(28) Team Photo (4-3/4" x 3-1/2")	7.50	3.75	2.25

1975 TCMA 1924-1925 Washington Senators

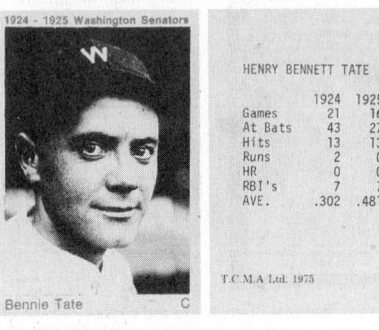

The back-to-back American League champion Senators of 1924-25 are featured in this collectors' edition card set. Cards measure 2-3/8" x 3-7/16". Fronts have black-and-white photos with blue captions and white borders. Backs have player stats for the two seasons. The unnumbered cards are checklisted here in alphabetical order.

	NM	EX	VG
Complete Set (42):	30.00	15.00	9.00
Common Player:	1.50	.75	.45
(1) Spencer Adams	1.50	.75	.45
(2) Nick Altrock	1.50	.75	.45
(3) Ossie Bluege	1.50	.75	.45
(4) Stan Coveleski	1.50	.75	.45
(5) Alex Ferguson	1.50	.75	.45
(6) Showboat Fisher	1.50	.75	.45
(7) Goose Goslin	1.50	.75	.45
(8) Bart Griffith	1.50	.75	.45
(9) Pinky Hargrave	1.50	.75	.45
(10) Bucky Harris	1.50	.75	.45
(11) Joe Harris	1.50	.75	.45
(12) Tex Jeanes	1.50	.75	.45
(13) Walter Johnson	4.00	2.00	1.25
(14) Joe Judge	1.50	.75	.45
(15) Wade Lefler	1.50	.75	.45
(16) Nemo Leibold	1.50	.75	.45
(17) Firpo Marberry	1.50	.75	.45
(18) Joe Martina	1.50	.75	.45
(19) Wid Matthews	1.50	.75	.45
(20) Mike McNally	1.50	.75	.45
(21) Earl McNeely	1.50	.75	.45
(22) Ralph Miller	1.50	.75	.45
(23) George Mogridge	1.50	.75	.45
(24) Buddy Myer	1.50	.75	.45
(25) Curly Ogden	1.50	.75	.45
(26) Roger Peckinpaugh	1.50	.75	.45
(27) Spencer Pumpelly	1.50	.75	.45
(28) Sam Rice	1.50	.75	.45
(29) Muddy Ruel	1.50	.75	.45
(30) Dutch Ruether	1.50	.75	.45
(31) Allen Russell	1.50	.75	.45
(32) Everett Scott	1.50	.75	.45
(33) Hank Severeid	1.50	.75	.45
(34) Mule Shirley	1.50	.75	.45
(35) Byron Speece	1.50	.75	.45
(36) Benny Tate	1.50	.75	.45
(37) Bobby Veach	1.50	.75	.45
(38) Tom Zachary	1.50	.75	.45
(39) Paul Zahniser	1.50	.75	.45
	5" x 3-1/2" FEATURE CARDS		
(40) Bucky Harris, Bill McKechnie	2.00	1.00	.60
(41) Ossie Bluege, Roger Peckinpaugh, Bucky Harris, Joe Judge	2.00	1.00	.60
(42) Tom Zachary, Firpo Marberry, Alex Ferguson, Walter Johnson	2.50	1.25	.70

1975 TCMA 1927 New York Yankees

One of the greatest teams in baseball history is featured in this set of collectors' cards. The 2-1/2" x 3-1/2" cards have black-and-white photos with a white border. At top is the team identification, at bottom is player name and position. The back has the player's 1927 season stats. The unnumbered cards are checklisted here alphabetically.

	NM	EX	VG
Complete Set (30):	40.00	20.00	12.00
Common Player:	2.00	1.00	.60
(1) Walter Beall	2.00	1.00	.60
(2) Benny Bengough	2.00	1.00	.60
(3) Pat Collins	2.00	1.00	.60
(4) Earle Combs	2.00	1.00	.60
(5) Joe Dugan	2.00	1.00	.60
(6) Cedric Durst	2.00	1.00	.60
(7) Mike Gazella	2.00	1.00	.60
(8) Lou Gehrig	7.50	3.75	2.25
(9) Joe Giard	2.00	1.00	.60
(10) Johnny Grabowski	2.00	1.00	.60
(11) Waite Hoyt	2.00	1.00	.60
(12) Miller Huggins	2.00	1.00	.60
(13) Mark Koenig	2.00	1.00	.60
(14) Tony Lazzeri	2.00	1.00	.60
(15) Bob Meusel	2.00	1.00	.60
(16) Wilcy Moore	2.00	1.00	.60
(17) Ray Morehart	2.00	1.00	.60
(18) Ben Paschal	2.00	1.00	.60
(19) Herb Pennock	2.00	1.00	.60
(20) George Pipgras	2.00	1.00	.60
(21) Dutch Ruether	2.00	1.00	.60
(22) Jacob Ruppert	2.00	1.00	.60
(23) Babe Ruth	12.00	6.00	3.50
(24) Bob Shawkey	2.00	1.00	.60
(25) Urban Shocker	2.00	1.00	.60
(26) Myles Thomas	2.00	1.00	.60
(27) Julie Wera	2.00	1.00	.60
(28) Yankee Coaches and Manager (Charlie O'Leary, Miller Huggins, Artie Fletcher)	2.00	1.00	.60
(29) Yankee Stadium	3.00	1.50	.90
(30) Yankees infield (Lou Gehrig, Tony Lazzeri, Mark Koenig, Joe Dugan) (5" x 3-5/8")	9.00	4.50	2.75

1975 TCMA 1942-46 St. Louis Cardinals

This collectors' issue set features players and staff from the Cards' war-years dynasty. In 2-1/2" x 3-5/8" format, the cards have black-and-white photos with red printing on front. The unnumbered cards have statistics on back.

	NM	EX	VG
Complete Set (66):	40.00	20.00	12.00
Common Player:	1.00	.50	.30
(1) Buster Adams	1.00	.50	.30
(2) Red Barrett	1.00	.50	.30
(3) John Beazley	1.00	.50	.30
(4) Al Brazle	1.00	.50	.30
(5) Harry Brecheen	1.00	.50	.30
(6) Jimmy Brown	1.00	.50	.30
(7) Ken Burkhart	1.00	.50	.30
(8) Bud Byerly	1.00	.50	.30
(9) Mort Cooper	1.00	.50	.30
(10) Walker Cooper	1.00	.50	.30
(11) Estel Crabtree	1.00	.50	.30
(12) Creepy Crespi	1.00	.50	.30
(13) Jeff Cross	1.00	.50	.30
(14) Frank Demaree	1.00	.50	.30
(15) Murrey Dickson (Murry)	1.00	.50	.30
(16) Blix Donnelly	1.00	.50	.30
(17) Erv Dusak	1.00	.50	.30
(18) Eddie Dyer	1.00	.50	.30
(19) Bill Endicott	1.00	.50	.30
(20) George Fallon	1.00	.50	.30
(21) Joe Garagiola	3.00	1.50	.90
(22) Debs Garms	1.00	.50	.30
(23) Mike Gonzalez	1.25	.60	.30
(24) Johnny Grodzicki	1.00	.50	.30
(25) Harry Gumbert	1.00	.50	.30
(26) Johnny Hopp	1.00	.50	.30
(27) Nippy Jones	1.00	.50	.30
(28) Lou Klein	1.00	.50	.30
(29) Clyde Kluttz	1.00	.50	.30
(30) Howie Krist	1.00	.50	.30

		NM	EX	VG
(31)	Whitey Kurowski	1.00	.50	.30
(32)	Max Lanier	1.00	.50	.30
(33)	Danny Litwhiler	1.00	.50	.30
(34)	Bill Lohrman	1.00	.50	.30
(35)	Marty Marion	1.50	.70	.45
(36)	Freddie Martin	1.00	.50	.30
(37)	Pepper Martin	2.00	1.00	.60
(38)	Terry Moore	1.00	.50	.30
(39)	Red Munger	1.00	.50	.30
(40)	Stan Musial	5.00	2.50	1.50
(41)	Sam Narron	1.00	.50	.30
(42)	Ken O'Dea	1.00	.50	.30
(43)	Howie Pollet	1.00	.50	.30
(44)	Del Rice	1.00	.50	.30
(45)	Ray Sanders	1.00	.50	.30
(46)	Fred Schmidt	1.00	.50	.30
(47)	Red Schoendienst	3.00	1.50	.90
(48)	Walt Sessi	1.00	.50	.30
(49)	Clyde Shoun	1.00	.50	.30
(50)	Dick Sisler	1.00	.50	.30
(51)	Enos Slaughter	3.00	1.50	.90
(52)	Billy Southworth	1.00	.50	.30
(53)	Coaker Triplett	1.00	.50	.30
(54)	Emil Verban	1.00	.50	.30
(55)	Harry Walker	1.00	.50	.30
(56)	Buzzy Wares	1.00	.50	.30
(57)	Lon Warneke	1.00	.50	.30
(58)	Ernie White	1.00	.50	.30
(59)	Del Wilber	1.00	.50	.30
(60)	Ted Wilks	1.00	.50	.30
(61)	Leo Durocher, Eddie Dyer	1.00	.50	.30
(62)	Stan Musial, Billy Southworth, Johnny Hopp	1.00	.50	.30
(63)	Stan Musial, Billy Southworth, Ray Sanders	1.00	.50	.30
(64)	Red Ruffing, Johnny Beazley	1.00	.50	.30
(65)	1942 St. Louis Cardinals (5" x 3-1/2")	3.00	1.50	.90
(66)	Sportsman's Park (5" x 3-1/2")	2.50	1.25	.70

1975 TCMA 1946 Boston Red Sox

Ben Steiner 3b
1946 BOSTON RED SOX

BENJAMIN SAUNDERS STEINER

Games 3
At Bats 4
Hits 1
Runs 1
Home Runs 0
Runs Batted In 0
Batting Average .250

TCMA, Ltd. 1975

The Red Sox American League champions of 1946 are featured in this collectors' issue. Blue-and-white player photos appear on front, with the player's name and position in black below. At bottom-front is the team name in red. Backs of the 2-1/2" x 3-1/2" cards have the player's 1946 stats. The unnumbered cards are checklisted here in alphabetical order.

		NM	EX	VG
	Complete Set (43):	45.00	22.50	13.50
	Common Player:	1.50	.75	.45
(1)	Jim Bagby	1.50	.75	.45
(2)	Del Baker	1.50	.75	.45
(3)	Mace Brown	1.50	.75	.45
(4)	Bill Butland	1.50	.75	.45
(5)	Paul Campbell	1.50	.75	.45
(6)	Tom Carey	1.50	.75	.45
(7)	Joe Cronin	2.00	1.00	.60
(8)	Leon Culberson	1.50	.75	.45
(9)	Tom Daly	1.50	.75	.45
(10)	Dom DiMaggio	2.50	1.25	.70
(11)	Joe Dobson	1.50	.75	.45
(12)	Bobby Doerr	1.50	.75	.45
(13)	Clem Dreisewerd	1.50	.75	.45
(14)	"Boo" Ferriss	1.50	.75	.45
(15)	Andy Gilbert	1.50	.75	.45
(16)	Don Gutteridge	1.50	.75	.45
(17)	Mickey Harris	1.50	.75	.45
(18)	Randy Heflin	1.50	.75	.45
(19)	"Pinky" Higgins	1.50	.75	.45
(20)	"Tex" Hughson	1.50	.75	.45
(21)	Earl Johnson	1.50	.75	.45
(22)	Bob Klinger	1.50	.75	.45
(23)	Johnny Lazor	1.50	.75	.45
(24)	Tom McBride	1.50	.75	.45
(25)	Ed McGah	1.50	.75	.45
(26)	"Catfish" Metkovich	1.50	.75	.45
(27)	Wally Moses	1.50	.75	.45
(28)	Roy Partee	1.50	.75	.45
(29)	Eddie Pellagrini	1.50	.75	.45
(30)	Johnny Pesky	1.50	.75	.45
(31)	Frank Pytlak	1.50	.75	.45
(32)	"Rip" Russell	1.50	.75	.45
(33)	Mike Ryba	1.50	.75	.45
(34)	Ben Steiner	1.50	.70	.45
(35)	Charlie Wagner	1.50	.75	.45
(36)	Hal Wagner	1.50	.75	.45
(37)	Ted Williams	7.50	3.75	2.25
(38)	Larry Woodall	1.50	.75	.45
(39)	Rudy York	1.50	.75	.45
(40)	Bill Zuber	1.50	.75	.45
(41)	Team Photo	2.00	1.00	.60
(42)	Larry Woodall, Hal Wagner, Del Baker	1.50	.75	.45
(43)	Rudy York, Wally Moses, Dom DiMaggio, Bobby Doerr, Charlie Wagner (5" x 3-1/2")	4.00	2.00	1.25

1975 TCMA 1950 Philadelphia Phillies/Whiz Kids

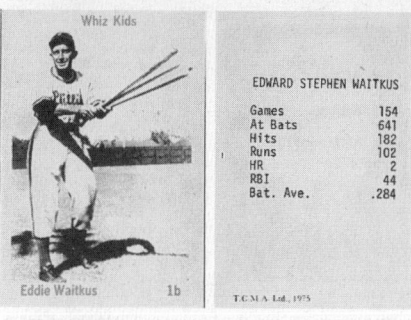

Whiz Kids

Eddie Waitkus 1b

EDWARD STEPHEN WAITKUS

Games 154
At Bats 641
Hits 182
Runs 102
HR 2
RBI 44
Bat. Ave. .284

T.C.M.A. Ltd. 1975

The National League Champion "Whiz Kids" are featured in this collectors' issue. The 2-1/2" x 3-1/2" cards have black-and-white photos on front with the player's name and position in red at bottom and either "Whiz Kids" or "1950 Philadelphia Phillies" in red at top. Black-and-white backs have 1950 season stats. The unnumbered cards are checklisted here alphabetically. The large-format multiple-player card was issued coincidentally with the set.

		NM	EX	VG
	Complete Set (32):	45.00	22.50	13.50
	Common Player:	2.00	1.00	.60
(1)	Richie Ashburn	11.00	5.50	3.25
(2)	Benny Bengough	2.00	1.00	.60
(3)	Jimmy Bloodworth	2.00	1.00	.60
(4)	Hank Borowy	2.00	1.00	.60
(5)	"Putsy" Caballero	2.00	1.00	.60
(6)	"Bubba" Church	2.00	1.00	.60
(7)	Dusty Cooke	2.00	1.00	.60
(8)	Blix Donnelly	2.00	1.00	.60
(9)	Del Ennis	2.00	1.00	.60
(10)	Mike Goliat	2.00	1.00	.60
(11)	Granny Hamner	2.00	1.00	.60
(12)	Ken Heintzelman	2.00	1.00	.60
(13)	Stan Hollmig	2.00	1.00	.60
(14)	Ken Johnson	2.00	1.00	.60
(15)	"Puddin-Head" Jones	2.00	1.00	.60
(16)	Jim Konstanty	2.00	1.00	.60
(17)	Stan Lopata	2.00	1.00	.60
(18)	Jackie Mayo	2.00	1.00	.60
(19)	Russ Meyer	2.00	1.00	.60
(20)	Bob Miller	2.00	1.00	.60
(21)	Bill Nicholson	2.00	1.00	.60
(22)	Cy Perkins	2.00	1.00	.60
(23)	Robin Roberts	11.00	5.50	3.25
(24)	Eddie Sawyer	2.00	1.00	.60
(25)	Andy Seminick	2.00	1.00	.60
(26)	Ken Silvestri	2.00	1.00	.60
(27)	Curt Simmons	2.00	1.00	.60
(28)	Dick Sisler	2.00	1.00	.60
(29)	"Jocko" Thompson	2.00	1.00	.60
(30)	Eddie Waitkus	2.00	1.00	.60
(31)	Dick Whitman	2.00	1.00	.60
(32)	Russ Meyer, Hank Borowy, Bill Nicholson, Willie Jones (4-7/8" x 3-1/2")	15.00	7.50	4.50

1975 TCMA 1951 New York Giants

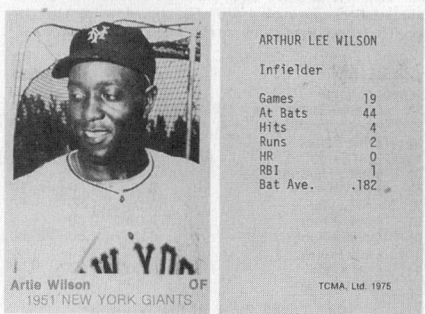

Artie Wilson OF
1951 NEW YORK GIANTS

ARTHUR LEE WILSON

Infielder

Games 19
At Bats 44
Hits 4
Runs 2
HR 0
RBI 1
Bat. Ave. .182

TCMA. Ltd. 1975

The National League Champion Giants of 1951 are honored in this collectors' issue card set. The 2-1/2" x 3-1/2" cards have black-and-white photos on front, with player name, team and position in the bottom border in red-orange ink. Backs are black-and-white with 1951 stats. The unnumbered cards are listed here in alphabetical order.

		NM	EX	VG
	Complete Set (34):	35.00	17.50	10.00
	Common Player:	1.50	.75	.45
(1)	George Bamberger	1.50	.75	.45
(2)	Roger Bowman	1.50	.75	.45
(3)	Al Corwin	1.50	.75	.45
(4)	Alvin Dark	2.00	1.00	.60
(5)	Allen Gettel	1.50	.75	.45
(6)	Clint Hartung	1.50	.75	.45
(7)	Jim Hearn	1.50	.75	.45
(8)	Monte Irvin	2.00	1.00	.60
(9)	Larry Jansen	1.50	.75	.45
(10)	Sheldon Jones	1.50	.75	.45
(11)	"Spider" Jorgensen	1.50	.75	.45
(12)	Monte Kennedy	1.50	.75	.45
(13)	Alex Konikowski	1.50	.70	.45
(14)	Dave Koslo	1.50	.75	.45
(15)	Jack Kramer	1.50	.75	.45
(16)	Whitey Lockman	1.50	.75	.45
(17)	"Lucky" Lohrke	1.50	.75	.45
(18)	Sal Maglie	1.50	.70	.45
(19)	Jack Maguire	1.50	.70	.45
(20)	Willie Mays	10.00	5.00	3.00
(21)	Don Mueller	1.50	.75	.45
(22)	Ray Noble	1.50	.75	.45
(23)	Earl Rapp	1.50	.75	.45
(24)	Bill Rigney	1.50	.75	.45
(25)	George Spencer	1.50	.75	.45
(26)	Eddie Stanky	1.50	.70	.45
(27)	Hank Thompson	1.50	.75	.45
(28)	Bobby Thomson	2.50	1.20	.70
(29)	Wes Westrum	1.50	.75	.45
(30)	Davey Williams	1.50	.75	.45
(31)	Artie Wilson	1.50	.75	.45
(32)	Sal Yvars	1.50	.75	.45
(33)	Leo Durocher, Willie Mays (3-5/8" x 5")	7.00	3.50	2.00
(34)	Durocher and coaches (3-5/8" x 5")	3.00	1.50	.90

1975 TCMA 1954 Cleveland Indians

Art Houtteman P

1954 CLEVELAND INDIANS

ARTHUR JOSEPH HOUTTEMAN

Games 32
IP 188
Won 15
Lost 7
Pct. 6.82
BB 59
SO 68
ERA 3.35

T.C.M.A. 1975

The American League Champions of 1954 are featured in this collectors' issue. Individual player cards are 2-1/2" x 3-1/2" printed in black-and-white. Backs have 1954 season stats. Three large-format (3-3/4" x 5-1/8") multi-player cards were issued with the complete set. The unnumbered cards are checklisted here alphabetically.

		NM	EX	VG
	Complete Set (39):	35.00	17.50	10.00
	Common Player:	1.50	.75	.45
(1)	Bobby Avila	2.00	1.00	.60
(2)	Bob Chakales	1.50	.75	.45
(3)	Tony Cuccinello	1.50	.75	.45
(4)	Sam Dente	1.50	.75	.45
(5)	Larry Doby	3.50	1.75	1.00
(6)	Luke Easter	2.00	1.00	.60
(7)	Bob Feller	5.00	2.50	1.50
(8)	Mike Garcia	2.00	1.00	.60
(9)	Joe Ginsberg	1.50	.75	.45
(10)	Bill Glynn	1.50	.75	.45
(11)	Mickey Grasso	1.50	.75	.45
(12)	Mel Harder	1.50	.75	.45
(13)	Jim Hegan	1.50	.75	.45
(14)	Bob Hooper	1.50	.75	.45
(15)	Dave Hoskins	1.50	.75	.45
(16)	Art Houtteman	1.50	.75	.45
(17)	Bob Kennedy	1.50	.75	.45
(18)	Bob Lemon	2.50	1.25	.70
(19)	Al Lopez	2.50	1.25	.70
(20)	Hank Majeski	1.50	.75	.45
(21)	Dale Mitchell	1.50	.75	.45
(22)	Don Mossi	1.50	.75	.45
(23)	Hal Naragon	1.50	.75	.45
(24)	Ray Narleski	1.50	.75	.45
(25)	Rocky Nelson	1.50	.75	.45
(26)	Hal Newhouser	2.50	1.25	.70
(27)	Dave Philley	1.50	.75	.45
(28)	Dave Pope	1.50	.75	.45
(29)	Rudy Regalado	1.50	.75	.45
(30)	Al Rosen	2.00	1.00	.60
(31)	Jose Santiago	1.50	.75	.45
(32)	Al Smith	1.50	.75	.45
(33)	George Strickland	1.50	.75	.45
(34)	Vic Wertz	1.50	.75	.45
(35)	Wally Westlake	1.50	.75	.45
(36)	Early Wynn	2.50	1.25	.70
(37)	Large Format Cards	1.50	.75	.45
(38)	Al Lopez and Coaches	5.00	2.50	1.50
(39)	Al Lopez and Pitchers	5.00	2.50	1.50
	Indians Outfielders	5.00	2.50	1.50

1975 TCMA/ASCCA Ad Card

To promote the American Sports Card Collectors Association Show in New York City, this 3-1/2" x 5-1/2" black-and-white card done in the format of the All-Time Greats postcards was issued. The front pictures two of the game's greatest pitchers and offers a discount on show admission. The back provides a detailed description of the show.

	NM	EX	VG
Dizzy Dean, Lefty Grove	6.00	3.00	1.80

1976 TCMA DiMaggio Brothers Postcard

This black-and-white postcard was issued singly circa the mid-1970s. It measures approximately 3-1/2" x 5-1/2".

	NM	EX	VG
Dom DiMaggio, Joe DiMaggio, Vince DiMaggio	12.00	6.00	3.50

1976 TCMA Larry Rosenthal

This custom-published card of the long-time American League outfielder (1936-1945) was printed in red, black and white in a 2-5/8" x 4-5/8" format. The issue date is approximate.

	NM	EX	VG
Larry Rosenthal	6.00	3.00	2.00

1976 TCMA Umpires

American League

Don Denkinger Umpire

Eight of the better-known umpires of the era apparently commissioned TCMA to produce cards for them. The cards are black-and-white in the standard 2-1/2" x 3-1/2" format.

	NM	EX	VG
Complete Set (8):	25.00	12.50	7.50
Common Card:	4.00	2.00	1.25
(1) Larry Barnett	4.00	2.00	1.25
(2) Al Clark	4.00	2.00	1.25
(3) Nick Colosi	4.00	2.00	1.25
(4) Don Denkinger	4.00	2.00	1.25
(5) Art Frantz	4.00	2.00	1.25
(6) Marty Springstead	4.00	2.00	1.25
(7) Ed Sudol	4.00	2.00	1.25
(8) Bill Williams	4.00	2.00	1.25

1976 TCMA 1911 N.Y. Highlanders Postcard

This black-and-white postcard was issued singly circa the mid-1970s. It measures approximately 6" x 3-1/2".

	NM	EX	VG
1911 N.Y. Highlanders Team Photo	12.00	6.00	3.50

1976 TCMA 1938 Chicago Cubs

AUGUST JOHN GALAN

Games	110
At Bats	395
Hits	113
Runs	52
Home Runs	6
RBI	69
Bat. Ave.	.286

1938 CHICAGO CUBS
NATIONAL LEAGUE CHAMPIONS
1976 TCMA LTD.

Augie Galan OF

The National League Champion Chicago Cubs of 1938 are featured in this collectors issue. The 2-1/2" x 3-1/2" cards have black-and-white player photos on front with the player's name and position in blue at bottom. Backs are in black-and-white with season stats. The unnumbered cards are checklisted here alphabetically.

	NM	EX	VG
Complete Set (33):	40.00	20.00	12.00
Common Player:	2.00	1.00	.60
(1) Jim Asbell	2.00	1.00	.60
(2) Clay Bryant	2.00	1.00	.60
(3) Tex Carleton	2.00	1.00	.60
(4) Phil Cavarretta	2.00	1.00	.60
(5) Ripper Collins	2.00	1.00	.60
(6) "Red" Corriden	2.00	1.00	.60
(7) Dizzy Dean	7.50	3.75	2.25
(8) Frank Demaree	2.00	1.00	.60
(9) Al Epperly	2.00	1.00	.60
(10) Larry French	2.00	1.00	.60
(11) Augie Galan	2.00	1.00	.60
(12) Bob Garbark	2.00	1.00	.60
(13) Charlie Grimm	2.00	1.00	.60
(14) Stan Hack	2.00	1.00	.60
(15) Gabby Hartnett	3.00	1.50	.90
(16) Billy Herman	3.00	1.50	.90
(17) Kirby Higbe	2.00	1.00	.60
(18) Hardrock Johnson	2.00	1.00	.60
(19) Billy Jurges	2.00	1.00	.60
(20) Newt Kimball	2.00	1.00	.60
(21) Tony Lazzeri	3.00	1.50	.90
(22) Bill Lee	2.00	1.00	.60
(23) Bob Logan	2.00	1.00	.60
(24) Joe Marty	2.00	1.00	.60
(25) Bobby Mattick	2.00	1.00	.60
(26) Steve Mesner	2.00	1.00	.60
(27) Ken O'Dea	2.00	1.00	.60
(28) Vance Page	2.00	1.00	.60
(29) Carl Reynolds	2.00	1.00	.60
(30) Charlie Root	2.00	1.00	.60
(31) Jack Russell	2.00	1.00	.60
(32) Coaker Triplett	2.00	1.00	.60
(33) Team History Card	.70	.35	.20

1977 TCMA All-Time White Sox

Ray Schalk C

All-Time Chicago White Sox	
Eddie Robinson	1B
Eddie Collins	2B
Willie Kamm	3B
Luke Appling	SS
Ray Schalk	C
Al Simmons	LF
Johnny Mostil	CF
Harry Hooper	RF
Ted Lyons	RHP
Billy Pierce	LHP
Gerry Staley	RP
Al Lopez	Mgr

Because this is one of the few early TCMA issues not to have a date printed on the back, the quoted year of issue is approximate. Fronts of the 2-1/2" x 3-1/2" cards have black-and-white player photos with name and position printed in red in the bottom border. Black-and-white backs have an all-time team roster of position players, pitchers and manager. The unnumbered cards are checklisted here in alphabetical order.

	NM	EX	VG
Complete Set (12):	24.00	12.00	7.25
Common Player:	2.00	1.00	.60
(1) Luke Appling	2.50	1.25	.70
(2) Eddie Collins	2.50	1.25	.70
(3) Harry Hooper	2.00	1.00	.60
(4) Willie Kamm	2.00	1.00	.60
(5) Al Lopez	2.00	1.00	.60
(6) Ted Lyons	2.00	1.00	.60
(7) Johnny Mostil	2.00	1.00	.60
(8) Billy Pierce	2.00	1.00	.60
(9) Eddie Robinson	2.00	1.00	.60
(10) Ray Schalk	2.00	1.00	.60
(11) Al Simmons	2.00	1.00	.60
(12) Gerry Staley	2.00	1.00	.60

1977 TCMA Chicago Cubs All Time Team

Chicago Cubs

ALL TIME TEAM

RF - Kiki Cuyler

Chicago Cubs All Time Team	
1B - Charlie Grimm	
2B - Rogers Hornsby	
SS - Ernie Banks	
3B - Ron Santo	
C - Gabby Hartnett	
LF - Billy Williams	
RF - Kiki Cuyler	
CF - Hack Wilson	
RHP - Charlie Root	
LHR - Larry French	
RP - Emil Kush	
MGR - Charlie Grimm	
INF - Billy Herman	

The best of the Cubs are presented in this collectors issue. An all-time great at each position is featured on the 2-1/2" x 3-1/2" card. Fronts have black-and-white photos with orange graphics. Backs are in black-and-white and list the team by position. The unnumbered cards are checklisted here in that order.

	NM	EX	VG
Complete Set (12):	30.00	15.00	9.00
Common Player:	3.00	1.50	.90
(1) Charlie Grimm	3.00	1.50	.90
(2) Rogers Hornsby	4.00	2.00	1.25
(3) Ernie Banks	4.00	2.00	1.25
(4) Ron Santo	3.00	1.50	.90
(5) Gabby Hartnett	3.00	1.50	.90
(6) Billy Williams	3.00	1.50	.90
(7) Kiki Cuyler	3.00	1.50	.90
(8) Hack Wilson	4.00	2.00	1.25
(9) Charlie Root	3.00	1.50	.90
(10) Larry French	3.00	1.50	.90
(11) Emil Kush	3.00	1.50	.90
(12) Billy Herman	3.00	1.50	.90

1977 TCMA Stars of the Twenties

GABBY HARTNETT

CHICAGO

Six players are featured on this 22" x 11" triple-folder which was glued into issues of the Summer, 1977, "Baseball Quarterly" magazine from TCMA. The pictures feature artwork by John Anderson in sepia tones on heavy cream-colored textured paper stock. The pictures are back-to-back in pairs as listed here, with individual pictures varying in width from 7-1/4" to 7-1/2".

	NM	EX	VG
Complete Foldout:	10.00	5.00	3.00
Common Pair:	3.00	1.50	.90
(1/2) Joe Bush, Gabby Hartnett	3.00	1.50	.90
(3/4) Jim Bottomley, "Mule" Haas	3.00	1.50	.90
(5/6) Sam Rice, Buddy Myer	3.00	1.50	.90

1977-80 TCMA The War Years

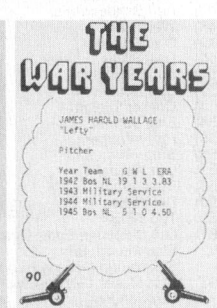

THE WAR YEARS

JAMES HAROLD WALLACE "Lefty"
Pitcher

Year	Team	G	W	L	ERA
1942	Bos NL	19	1	3	3.83
1943	Military Service.				
1944	Military Service.				
1945	Bos NL	5	1	0	4.50

90

The decimated major league rosters circa 1942-46 are reflected in this collectors' card set. The 2-1/2" x 3-1/2" cards have black-and-white player photos on front, with a white border around. There is no typography on front. Backs have player identification, stats and the set title. Series 1, cards #1-45 was issued in 1977 and is much scarcer than Series 2, #46-90, which was issued in 1980.

	NM	EX	VG
Complete Set (90):	140.00	70.00	42.50
Common Player:	2.00	1.00	.60
1 Samuel Narron	3.00	1.50	.90
2 Raymond Mack	3.00	1.50	.90
3 Arnold (Mickey) Owen	3.00	1.50	.90
4 John Peacock	3.00	1.50	.90
5 Paul (Dizzy) Trout	3.00	1.50	.90
6 George (Birdie) Tebbetts	3.00	1.50	.90
7 Alfred Todd	3.00	1.50	.90
8 Harlond Clift	3.00	1.50	.90
9 Don G.N. (Gil) Torres	3.00	1.50	.90
10 Alfonso Lopez	4.00	2.00	1.25
11 Ulysses (Tony) Lupien	3.00	1.50	.90
12 Lucius Appling	4.00	2.00	1.25
13 James (Pat) Seery	3.00	1.50	.90
14 Phil Masi	3.00	1.50	.90
15 Thomas Turner	3.00	1.50	.90
16 Nicholas Piccuito	3.00	1.50	.90
17 Mel Ott	7.50	3.75	2.25
18 Thadford Treadway	3.00	1.50	.90
19 Sam Naham (Neham)	3.00	1.50	.90
20 Truett (Rip) Sewell	3.00	1.50	.90
21 Roy Partee	3.00	1.50	.90
22 Richard Siebert	3.00	1.50	.90
23 Francis (Red) Barrett	3.00	1.50	.90
24 Paul O'Dea	3.00	1.50	.90
25 Lou Parisse	3.00	1.50	.90
26 Martin Marion	4.00	2.00	1.25
27 Eugene Moore	3.00	1.50	.90
28 Walter Beck	3.00	1.50	.90
29 Donald Manno	3.00	1.50	.90
30 Harold Newhouser	4.00	2.00	1.25
31 August Mancuso	3.00	1.50	.90
32 Merrill May	3.00	1.50	.90
33 Gerald Priddy	3.00	1.50	.90
34 Herman Besse	3.00	1.50	.90
35 Luis Olmo	3.00	1.50	.90
36 Robert O'Neill	3.00	1.50	.90
37 John Barrett	3.00	1.50	.90
38 Gordon Maltzberger	3.00	1.50	.90
39 William Nicholson	3.00	1.50	.90
40 Ron Northey	3.00	1.50	.90
41 Howard Pollet	3.00	1.50	.90
42 Aloysius Piechota	3.00	1.50	.90
43 Albert Shepard	7.50	3.75	2.25
44 Alfred Anderson	3.00	1.50	.90
45 Damon Phillips	3.00	1.50	.90
46 Herman Franks	2.00	1.00	.60
47 Aldon Wilke	2.00	1.00	.60
48 Max Macon	2.00	1.00	.60
49 Lester Webber	2.00	1.00	.60
50 Robert Swift	2.00	1.00	.60
51 Philip Weintraub	2.00	1.00	.60
52 Nicholas Strincevich	2.00	1.00	.60
53 Michael Tresh	2.00	1.00	.60
54 William Trotter	2.00	1.00	.60
55 1943 Yankees (Spud Chandler, Frank Crosetti, Bill Dickey, Nick Etten, Joe Gordon, Billy Johnson, Charlie Keller, John Lindell, Bud Metheny)	4.00	2.00	1.25
56 John Sturm	2.00	1.00	.60
57 Silas Johnson	2.00	1.00	.60
58 Donald Kolloway	2.00	1.00	.60
59 Cecil Vaughn (Vaughan)	2.00	1.00	.60
60 St. Louis Browns Bombers (Harlond Clift, Walt Judnich, Chet Laabs)	3.00	1.50	.90
61 Harold Wagner	2.00	1.00	.60
62 Alva Javery	2.00	1.00	.60

		NM	EX	VG
63	1941 Boston Bees Pitchers (George Barnicle, Ed Carnett, Art Johnson, Frank LaManna, Casey Stengel, Bob Williams)	3.00	1.50	.90
64	Adolph Camilli	2.00	1.00	.60
65	Myron McCormick	2.00	1.00	.60
66	Richard Wakefield	2.00	1.00	.60
67	James (Mickey) Vernon	3.00	1.50	.90
68	John Vander Meer	3.00	1.50	.90
69	James McDonnell	4.00	2.00	1.25
70	Thomas Jordan	2.00	1.00	.60
71	Maurice Van Robays	2.00	1.00	.60
72	Charles Stanceau	2.00	1.00	.60
73	Samuel Zoldak	2.00	1.00	.60
74	Raymond Starr	2.00	1.00	.60
75	Roger Wolff	2.00	1.00	.60
76	Cecil Travis	2.00	1.00	.60
77	Arthur Johnson	2.00	1.00	.60
78	Louis (Lewis) Riggs	2.00	1.00	.60
79	Peter Suder	2.00	1.00	.60
80	Thomas Warren	2.00	1.00	.60
81	John Welaj	2.00	1.00	.60
82	Gerald Walker	2.00	1.00	.60
83	Dewey Williams	2.00	1.00	.60
84	Leonard Merullo	2.00	1.00	.60
85	John Johnson	2.00	1.00	.60
86	Eugene Thompson	2.00	1.00	.60
87	William Zuber	2.00	1.00	.60
88	Earl Johnson	2.00	1.00	.60
89	Norman Young	2.00	1.00	.60
90	James Wallace	2.00	1.00	.60

1977 TCMA 1920 Cleveland Indians

The World Champion Indians are pictured on this collectors' issue team set. In standard 2-1/2" x 3-1/2" size with black-and-white photos, the cards are unnumbered. Some of the players are pictured in their 1921 uniforms with the "World Champions" lettering.

		NM	EX	VG
	Complete Set (22):	25.00	12.50	7.50
	Common Player:	2.00	1.00	.60
(1)	Jim Bagby	2.00	1.00	.60
(2)	George Burns	2.00	1.00	.60
(3)	Ray Caldwell	2.00	1.00	.60
(4)	Ray Chapman	3.00	1.50	.90
(5)	Stan Coveleski	2.50	1.25	.70
(6)	Joe Evans	2.00	1.00	.60
(7)	Larry Gardner	2.00	1.00	.60
(8)	Jack Graney	2.00	1.00	.60
(9)	Charlie Jamieson	2.00	1.00	.60
(10)	Doc Johnston	2.00	1.00	.60
(11)	Harry Lunte	2.00	1.00	.60
(12)	Duster Mails	2.00	1.00	.60
(13)	Guy Morton	2.00	1.00	.60
(14)	Les Nunamaker	2.00	1.00	.60
(15)	Steve O'Neill	2.00	1.00	.60
(16)	Joe Sewell	2.50	1.25	.70
(17)	Elmer Smith	2.00	1.00	.60
(18)	Tris Speaker	4.00	2.00	1.25
(19)	George Uhle	2.00	1.00	.60
(20)	Bill Wambsganss	2.50	1.25	.70
(21)	Joe Wood	2.50	1.25	.70
(22)	World Series Foes (Wilbert Robinson, Tris Speaker) (5-1/2" x 3)	4.00	2.00	1.25

1977 TCMA 1927 Yankees 50th Anniversary

Henry Louis Gehrig
First Baseman
Ht. 6-0 Wt. 200
Ba. Left Th. Left
Bn. 6/19/03
Dd. 6/2/41

Even though Babe Ruth is probably best-remembered for his 50 home runs in 1927, it was Gehrig who won the American League's Most Valuable Player award that year. While Ruth led the majors in homers and runs scored in '27, Gehrig was tops in RBI, total bases, doubles and, of course, games played. He also led the '27 Yankees in batting with a .373 mark. The "Iron Horse" was voted into the Hall of Fame by a special vote in 1939, shortly after his brilliant career was cut short by a fatal illness.

As an insert in its inaugural issue of "Baseball Quarterly" magazine dated Winter, 1977, TCMA included a 16-3/4" x 11" cardboard panel with 18 black-and-white cards featuring members of the 1927 N.Y. Yankees. Measuring about 2-1/2" x 3-3/8" if cut apart, the individual cards have unadorned photos on front framed in black with a white border. Backs have player identification, a 50th anniversary logo, career summary and 1927 and career stats. The unnumbered cards are listed here in alphabetical order.

		NM	EX	VG
	Complete Panel:	35.00	17.50	10.50
	Complete Set (18):	25.00	12.50	7.50
	Common Player:	2.00	1.00	.60
(1)	Bernard Oliver Bengough	2.00	1.00	.60
(2)	Tharon Patrick Collins	2.00	1.00	.60
(3)	Earle Bryan Combs	2.00	1.00	.60
(4)	Joseph Anthony Dugan	2.00	1.00	.60
(5)	Henry Louis Gehrig	6.00	3.00	1.75
(6)	John Patrick Grabowski	2.00	1.00	.60
(7)	Waite Charles Hoyt	2.00	1.00	.60
(8)	Miller James Huggins	2.00	1.00	.60
(9)	Mark Anthony Koenig	2.00	1.00	.60
(10)	Anthony Michael Lazzeri	2.00	1.00	.60
(11)	Robert Williams Meusel	2.00	1.00	.60
(12)	William Wilcy Moore	2.00	1.00	.60
(13)	Herbert Jeffries Pennock	2.00	1.00	.60

		NM	EX	VG
(14)	George William Pipgras	2.00	1.00	.60
(15)	Walter Henry Ruether	2.00	1.00	.60
(16)	George Herman Ruth	8.00	4.00	2.50
(17)	James Robert Shawkey	2.00	1.00	.60
(18)	Urban James Shocker	2.00	1.00	.60

1977 TCMA 1939-40 Cincinnati Reds

The National League Champion Reds of 1939 and the World's Champion team of 1940 are featured in this collectors' issue. The 2-1/2" x 3-1/2" cards have black-and-white photos on front surrounded by red borders. Backs, also in black-and-white, have 1939 and/or 1940 season stats.

		NM	EX	VG
	Complete Set (45):	35.00	17.50	10.00
	Common Player:	1.50	.75	.45
1	Vince DiMaggio	2.50	1.25	.70
2	Wally Berger	1.50	.75	.45
3	Nolan Richardson (Nolen)	1.50	.75	.45
4	Ernie Lombardi	2.50	1.25	.70
5	Ival Goodman	1.50	.75	.45
6	Jim Turner	1.50	.75	.45
7	Bucky Walters	1.50	.75	.45
8	Jimmy Ripple	1.50	.75	.45
9	Hank Johnson	1.50	.75	.45
10	Bill Baker	1.50	.75	.45
11	Al Simmons	2.00	1.00	.60
12	Johnny Hutchings	1.50	.75	.45
13	Peaches Davis	1.50	.75	.45
14	Willard Hershberger	2.50	1.25	.70
15	Bill Werber	1.50	.75	.45
16	Harry Craft	1.50	.75	.45
17	Milt Galatzer	1.50	.75	.45
18	Dick West	1.50	.75	.45
19	Art Jacobs	1.50	.75	.45
20	Joe Beggs	1.50	.75	.45
21	Frenchy Bordagaray	1.50	.75	.45
22	Lee Gamble	1.50	.75	.45
23	Lee Grissom	1.50	.75	.45
24	Eddie Joost	1.50	.75	.45
25	Milt Shofner	1.50	.75	.45
26	Morrie Arnovich	1.50	.75	.45
27	Pete Naktenis	1.50	.75	.45
28	Jim Weaver	1.50	.75	.45
29	Mike McCormick	1.50	.75	.45
30	John Niggeling	1.50	.75	.45
31	Les Scarsella	1.50	.75	.45
32	Lonny Frey	1.50	.75	.45
33	Bill Myers	1.50	.75	.45
34	Frank McCormick	1.50	.75	.45
35	Lew Riggs	1.50	.75	.45
36	Nino Bongiovanni	1.50	.75	.45
37	Johnny Rizzo	1.50	.75	.45
38	Wes Livengood	1.50	.75	.45
39	Junior Thompson	1.50	.75	.45
40	Mike Dejan	1.50	.75	.45
41	Jimmy Wilson	1.50	.75	.45
42	Paul Derringer	1.50	.75	.45
43	Johnny Vander Meer	2.00	1.00	.60
44	Whitey Moore	1.50	.75	.45
45	Bill McKechnie	2.00	1.00	.60

1977 TCMA 1960 Pittsburgh Pirates

The World's Champions Pirates are featured on this collector issue. The 2-1/2" x 3-1/2" cards have black-and-white photos on front surrounded by orange borders. Backs, also in black-and-white, have a card number, player name and position at top and season stats.

		NM	EX	VG
	Complete Set (42):	100.00	50.00	30.00
	Common Player:	3.00	1.50	.90
1	Danny Murtaugh	3.00	1.50	.90
2	Dick Stuart	4.00	2.00	1.25
3	Bill Mazeroski	10.00	5.00	3.00
4	Dick Groat	4.00	2.00	1.25
5	Don Hoak	3.00	1.50	.90

		NM	EX	VG
6	Roberto Clemente	20.00	10.00	6.00
7	Bill Virdon	3.00	1.50	.90
8	Bob Skinner	3.00	1.50	.90
9	Smoky Burgess	3.00	1.50	.90
10	Gino Cimoli	3.00	1.50	.90
11	Rocky Nelson	3.00	1.50	.90
12	Hal Smith	3.00	1.50	.90
13	Dick Schofield	3.00	1.50	.90
14	Joe Christopher	3.00	1.50	.90
15	Gene Baker	3.00	1.50	.90
16	Bob Oldis	3.00	1.50	.90
17	Vern Law	3.00	1.50	.90
18	Bob Friend	3.00	1.50	.90
19	Wilmer Mizell	3.00	1.50	.90
20	Harvey Haddix	3.00	1.50	.90
21	Roy Face	3.00	1.50	.90
22	Fred Green	3.00	1.50	.90
23	Joe Gibbon	3.00	1.50	.90
24	Clem Labine	3.00	1.50	.90
25	Paul Giel	3.00	1.50	.90
26	Tom Cheney	3.00	1.50	.90
27	Earl Francis	3.00	1.50	.90
28	Jim Umbricht	3.00	1.50	.90
29	George Witt	3.00	1.50	.90
30.	Bennie Daniels	3.00	1.50	.90
31	Don Gross	3.00	1.50	.90
32	Diomedes Olivo	4.00	2.00	1.25
33	Roman Mejias	3.00	1.50	.90
34	R.C. Stevens	3.00	1.50	.90
35	Mickey Vernon	3.00	1.50	.90
36	Danny Kravitz	3.00	1.50	.90
37	Harry Bright	3.00	1.50	.90
38	Dick Barone	3.00	1.50	.90
39	Bill Burwell	3.00	1.50	.90
40	Lenny Levy	4.00	2.00	1.25
41	Sam Narron	3.00	1.50	.90
42	Team Card (Bob Friend)	3.00	1.50	.90

1977 TCMA/ASCCA Ad Card

To promote the American Sports Card Collectors Association Show in New York City, this 2-1/2" x 3-1/2" black-and-white, gold highlighted card was issued. The front pictures Babe Ruth and offers a 25-cent discount on show admission. The back provides a detailed description of the show.

	NM	EX	VG
Babe Ruth	6.00	3.00	1.80

1977-84 TCMA/Renata Galasso

This issue of six 45-card series is in similar format but with different players, checklists and copyright dates produced by TCMA and marketed by Renata Galasso. In 2-1/2" x 3-1/2" format the cards have black-and-white photos on front. Backs are printed in red and blue and include a career summary, large Galasso ad and TCMA dateline.

		NM	EX	VG
	Complete Set (270):	50.00	25.00	15.00
	Common Player:	.25	.13	.08
	SERIES 1 - 1977	12.50	6.25	3.75
1	Joe DiMaggio	4.00	2.00	1.25
2	Ralph Kiner	.25	.13	.08
3	Don Larsen	.25	.13	.08
4	Robin Roberts	.25	.13	.08
5	Roy Campanella	.50	.25	.15
6	Smoky Burgess	.25	.13	.08
7	Mickey Mantle	6.00	3.00	1.75
8	Willie Mays	3.00	1.50	.90
9	George Kell	.25	.13	.08
10	Ted Williams	3.00	1.50	.90
11	Carl Furillo	.25	.13	.08
12	Bob Feller	.25	.13	.08
13	Casey Stengel	.25	.13	.08
14	Richie Ashburn	.25	.13	.08
15	Gil Hodges	.25	.13	.08
16	Stan Musial	.75	.40	.25
17	Don Newcombe	.25	.13	.08
18	Jackie Jensen	.25	.13	.08
19	Lou Boudreau	.25	.13	.08
20	Jackie Robinson	2.00	1.00	.60
21	Billy Goodman	.25	.13	.08
22	Satchel Paige	1.00	.50	.30
23	Hoyt Wilhelm	.25	.13	.08
24	Duke Snider	.25	.13	.08
25	Whitey Ford	.25	.13	.08
26	Monte Irvin	.25	.13	.08
27	Hank Sauer	.25	.13	.08
28	Sal Maglie	.25	.13	.08
29	Ernie Banks	.25	.13	.08
30	Billy Pierce	.25	.13	.08
31	Pee Wee Reese	.25	.13	.08
32	Al Lopez	.25	.13	.08
33	Allie Reynolds	.25	.13	.08
34	Eddie Mathews	.25	.13	.08
35	Al Rosen	.25	.13	.08
36	Early Wynn	.25	.13	.08

#	Player			
37	Phil Rizzuto	.25	.13	.08
38	Warren Spahn	.25	.13	.08
39	Bobby Thomson	.25	.13	.08
40	Enos Slaughter	.25	.13	.08
41	Roberto Clemente	4.00	2.00	1.25
42	Luis Aparicio	.25	.13	.08
43	Roy Sievers	.25	.13	.08
44	Hank Aaron	4.00	2.00	1.25
45	Mickey Vernon	.25	.13	.08
	SERIES 2 - 1979	10.00	5.00	3.00
46	Lou Gehrig	3.00	1.50	.90
47	Lefty O'Doul	.25	.13	.08
48	Chuck Klein	.25	.13	.08
49	Paul Waner	.25	.13	.08
50	Mel Ott	.25	.13	.08
51	Riggs Stephenson	.25	.13	.08
52	Dizzy Dean	.50	.25	.15
53	Frankie Frisch	.25	.13	.08
54	Red Ruffing	.25	.13	.08
55	Lefty Grove	.25	.13	.08
56	Heinie Manush	.25	.13	.08
57	Jimmie Foxx	.25	.13	.08
58	Al Simmons	.25	.13	.08
59	Charlie Root	.25	.13	.08
60	Goose Goslin	.25	.13	.08
61	Mickey Cochrane	.25	.13	.08
62	Gabby Hartnett	.25	.13	.08
63	Ducky Medwick	.25	.13	.08
64	Ernie Lombardi	.25	.13	.08
65	Joe Cronin	.25	.13	.08
66	Pepper Martin	.25	.13	.08
67	Jim Bottomley	.25	.13	.08
68	Bill Dickey	.25	.13	.08
69	Babe Ruth	5.00	2.50	1.50
70	Joe McCarthy	.25	.13	.08
71	Doc Cramer	.25	.13	.08
72	Kiki Cuyler	.25	.13	.08
73	Johnny Vander Meer	.25	.13	.08
74	Paul Derringer	.25	.13	.08
75	Freddie Fitzsimmons	.25	.13	.08
76	Lefty Gomez	.25	.13	.08
77	Arky Vaughan	.25	.13	.08
78	Stan Hack	.25	.13	.08
79	Earl Averill	.25	.13	.08
80	Luke Appling	.25	.13	.08
81	Mel Harder	.25	.13	.08
82	Hank Greenberg	.25	.13	.08
83	Schoolboy Rowe	.25	.13	.08
84	Billy Herman	.25	.13	.08
85	Gabby Street	.25	.13	.08
86	Lloyd Waner	.25	.13	.08
87	Jocko Conlan	.25	.13	.08
88	Carl Hubbell	.25	.13	.08
89	Series 1 checklist	.25	.13	.08
90	Series 2 checklist	.25	.13	.08
	SERIES 3 - 1980	7.50	3.75	2.25
91	Babe Ruth	3.00	1.50	.90
92	Rogers Hornsby	.25	.13	.08
93	Edd Roush	.25	.13	.08
94	George Sisler	.25	.13	.08
95	Harry Heilmann	.25	.13	.08
96	Tris Speaker	.25	.13	.08
97	Burleigh Grimes	.25	.13	.08
98	John McGraw	.25	.13	.08
99	Eppa Rixey	.25	.13	.08
100	Ty Cobb	1.00	.50	.30
101	Zack Wheat	.25	.13	.08
102	Pie Traynor	.25	.13	.08
103	Max Carey	.25	.13	.08
104	Dazzy Vance	.25	.13	.08
105	Walter Johnson	.50	.25	.15
106	Herb Pennock	.25	.13	.08
107	Joe Sewell	.25	.13	.08
108	Sam Rice	.25	.13	.08
109	Earle Combs	.25	.13	.08
110	Ted Lyons	.25	.13	.08
111	Eddie Collins	.25	.13	.08
112	Bill Terry	.25	.13	.08
113	Hack Wilson	.25	.13	.08
114	Rabbit Maranville	.25	.13	.08
115	Charlie Grimm	.25	.13	.08
116	Tony Lazzeri	.25	.13	.08
117	Waite Hoyt	.25	.13	.08
118	Stan Coveleski	.25	.13	.08
119	George Kelly	.25	.13	.08
120	Jimmy Dykes	.25	.13	.08
121	Red Faber	.25	.13	.08
122	Dave Bancroft	.25	.13	.08
123	Judge Landis	.25	.13	.08
124	Branch Rickey	.25	.13	.08
125	Jesse Haines	.25	.13	.08
126	Carl Mays	.25	.13	.08
127	Fred Lindstrom	.25	.13	.08
128	Miller Huggins	.25	.13	.08
129	Sad Sam Jones	.25	.13	.08
130	Joe Judge	.25	.13	.08
131	Ross Young (Youngs)	.25	.13	.08
132	Bucky Harris	.25	.13	.08
133	Bob Meusel	.25	.13	.08
134	Billy Evans	.25	.13	.08
135	1927 N.Y. Yankees Team Photo/Checklist	.50	.25	.15
	SERIES 4 - 1981	7.50	3.75	2.25
136	Ty Cobb	1.00	.50	.30
137	Nap Lajoie	.25	.13	.08
138	Tris Speaker	.25	.13	.08
139	Heinie Groh	.25	.13	.08
140	Sam Crawford	.25	.13	.08
141	Clyde Milan	.25	.13	.08
142	Chief Bender	.25	.13	.08
143	Big Ed Walsh	.25	.13	.08
144	Walter Johnson	.50	.25	.15
145	Connie Mack	.25	.13	.08
146	Hal Chase	.25	.13	.08
147	Hugh Duffy	.25	.13	.08
148	Honus Wagner	.50	.25	.15
149	Tom Connolly	.25	.13	.08
150	Clark Griffith	.25	.13	.08
151	Zack Wheat	.25	.13	.08
152	Christy Mathewson	.50	.25	.15
153	Grover C. Alexander	.25	.13	.08
154	Joe Jackson	3.00	1.50	.90
155	Home Run Baker	.25	.13	.08
156	Ed Plank	.25	.13	.08
157	Larry Doyle	.25	.13	.08
158	Rube Marquard	.25	.13	.08
159	Johnny Evers	.25	.13	.08
160	Joe Tinker	.25	.13	.08
161	Frank Chance	.25	.13	.08
162	Wilbert Robinson	.25	.13	.08
163	Roger Peckinpaugh	.25	.13	.08
164	Fred Clarke	.25	.13	.08
165	Babe Ruth	3.00	1.50	.90
166	Wilbur Cooper	.25	.13	.08
167	Germany Schaefer	.25	.13	.08
168	Addie Joss	.25	.13	.08
169	Cy Young	.50	.25	.15
170	Ban Johnson	.25	.13	.08
171	Joe Judge	.25	.13	.08
172	Harry Hooper	.25	.13	.08
173	Bill Klem	.25	.13	.08
174	Ed Barrow	.25	.13	.08
175	Ed Cicotte	.25	.13	.08
176	Hughie Jennings	.25	.13	.08
177	Ray Schalk	.25	.13	.08
178	Nick Altrock	.25	.13	.08
179	Roger Bresnahan	.25	.13	.08
180	$100,000 Infield	.25	.13	.08
	SERIES 5 - 1983	7.50	3.75	2.25
181	Lou Gehrig	3.00	1.50	.90
182	Eddie Collins	.25	.13	.08
183	Art Fletcher	.25	.13	.08
184	Jimmie Foxx	.25	.13	.08
185	Lefty Gomez	.25	.13	.08
186	Oral Hildebrand	.25	.13	.08
187	General Crowder	.25	.13	.08
188	Bill Dickey	.25	.13	.08
189	Wes Ferrell	.25	.13	.08
190	Al Simmons	.25	.13	.08
191	Tony Lazzeri	.25	.13	.08
192	Sam West	.25	.13	.08
193	Babe Ruth	3.00	1.50	.90
194	Connie Mack	.25	.13	.08
195	Lefty Grove	.25	.13	.08
196	Eddie Rommel	.25	.13	.08
197	Ben Chapman	.25	.13	.08
198	Joe Cronin	.25	.13	.08
199	Rich Ferrell (Rick)	.25	.13	.08
200	Charlie Gehringer	.25	.13	.08
201	Jimmy Dykes	.25	.13	.08
202	Earl Averill	.25	.13	.08
203	Pepper Martin	.25	.13	.08
204	Bill Terry	.25	.13	.08
205	Pie Traynor	.25	.13	.08
206	Gabby Hartnett	.25	.13	.08
207	Frank Frisch	.25	.13	.08
208	Carl Hubbell	.25	.13	.08
209	Paul Waner	.25	.13	.08
210	Woody English	.25	.13	.08
211	Bill Hallahan	.25	.13	.08
212	Dick Bartell	.25	.13	.08
213	Bill McKechnie	.25	.13	.08
214	Max Carey	.25	.13	.08
215	John McGraw	.25	.13	.08
216	Jimmie Wilson	.25	.13	.08
217	Chick Hafey	.25	.13	.08
218	Chuck Klein	.25	.13	.08
219	Lefty O'Doul	.25	.13	.08
220	Wally Berger	.25	.13	.08
221	Hal Schumacher	.25	.13	.08
222	Lon Warneke	.25	.13	.08
223	Tony Cuccinello	.25	.13	.08
(224)	1933 A.L. All-Stars	.50	.25	.15
(225)	1933 N.L. All-Stars	.50	.25	.15
	SERIES 6 - 1984	15.00	7.50	4.50
226	Roger Maris	.75	.40	.25
227	Babe Ruth	3.00	1.50	.90
228	Jackie Robinson	2.00	1.00	.60
229	Pete Gray	.75	.40	.25
230	Ted Williams	3.00	1.50	.90
231	Hank Aaron	3.00	1.50	.90
232	Mickey Mantle	5.00	2.50	1.50
233	Gil Hodges	.25	.13	.08
234	Walter Johnson	.50	.25	.15
235	Joe DiMaggio	3.00	1.50	.90
236	Lou Gehrig	3.00	1.50	.90
237	Stan Musial	.75	.40	.25
238	Mickey Cochrane	.25	.13	.08
239	Denny McLain	.25	.13	.08
240	Carl Hubbell	.25	.13	.08
241	Harvey Haddix	.25	.13	.08
242	Christy Mathewson	.50	.25	.15
243	Johnny VanderMeer	.25	.13	.08
244	Sandy Koufax	3.00	1.50	.90
245	Willie Mays	3.00	1.50	.90
246	Don Drysdale	.25	.13	.08
247	Bobby Richardson	.25	.13	.08
248	Hoyt Wilhelm	.25	.13	.08
249	Yankee Stadium	.25	.13	.08
250	Bill Terry	.25	.13	.08
251	Roy Campanella	.50	.25	.15
252	Roberto Clemente	3.00	1.50	.90
253	Casey Stengel	.25	.13	.08
254	Ernie Banks	.50	.25	.15
255	Bobby Thomson	.25	.13	.08
256	Mel Ott	.25	.13	.08
257	Tony Oliva	.25	.13	.08
258	Satchel Paige	1.00	.50	.30
259	Joe Jackson	3.00	1.50	.90
260	Larry Lajoie	.25	.13	.08
261	Bill Mazeroski	.25	.13	.08
262	Bill Wambsganss	.25	.13	.08
263	Willie McCovey	.25	.13	.08
264	Warren Spahn	.25	.13	.08
265	Lefty Gomez	.25	.13	.08
266	Dazzy Vance	.25	.13	.08
267	Sam Crawford	.25	.13	.08
268	Tris Speaker	.25	.13	.08
269	Lou Brock	.25	.13	.08
270	Cy Young	.25	.13	.08

1978 TCMA Baseball Nostalgia Postcard

TCMA produced this card for Baseball Nostalgia, Inc., a Cooperstown, N.Y., hobby shop, in an edition of 500. The card pictures a Cooperstown resident who taught at the local high school following a short (1934-36) major league pitching career. The 3-1/2" x 5-1/2" black-and-white card has standard postcard markings on back.

	NM	EX	VG
Vernon "Whitey" Wilshere	6.00	3.00	1.80

1978 TCMA The 1960's

Nearly 300 players of the 1960s are featured in this collectors issue. Fronts of the 2-1/2" x 3-1/2" cards have a color photo with a black frameline and white border. There are no other graphics. Backs are printed in green and include a lengthy career summary. On some cards the set's title, "The 1960's" is printed at top. Several mistakes in card numbering are noted in the accompanying checklist.

		NM	EX	VG
Complete Set (293):		40.00	20.00	12.00
Common Player:		.25	.13	.08
1	Smoky Burgess	.25	.13	.08
2	Juan Marichal	1.00	.50	.30
3	Don Drysdale	1.00	.50	.30
4	Jim Gentile	.25	.13	.08
5	Roy Face	.25	.13	.08
6	Joe Pepitone	.25	.13	.08
7	Joe Christopher	.25	.13	.08
8	Wayne Causey	.25	.13	.08
9	Frank Bolling	.25	.13	.08
10	Jim Maloney	.25	.13	.08
11	Roger Maris	2.50	1.25	.70
12	Bill White	.25	.13	.08
13	Roberto Clemente	7.50	3.75	2.25
14	Bob Saverine	.25	.13	.08
15	Barney Schultz	.25	.13	.08
16	Albie Pearson	.25	.13	.08
17	Denny Lemaster	.25	.13	.08
18	Ernie Broglio	.25	.13	.08
19	Bobby Klaus	.25	.13	.08
20	Tony Cloninger	.25	.13	.08
21	Whitey Ford	1.50	.70	.45
22	Ron Santo	.60	.30	.20
23	Jim Duckworth	.25	.13	.08
24	Willie Davis	.25	.13	.08
25	Ed Charles	.25	.13	.08
26	Bob Allison	.25	.13	.08
27	Fritz Ackley	.25	.13	.08
28	Ruben Amaro	.25	.13	.08
29	Johnny Callison	.25	.13	.08
30	Greg Bollo	.25	.13	.08
31	Felix Millan	.25	.13	.08
32	Camilo Pascual	.25	.13	.08
33	Jackie Brandt	.25	.13	.08
34	Don Lock	.25	.13	.08
35	Chico Ruiz	.25	.13	.08
36	Joe Azcue	.25	.13	.08
37	Ed Bailey	.25	.13	.08
38	Pete Ramos	.25	.13	.08
39	Eddie Bressoud	.25	.13	.08
40	Al Kaline	1.50	.70	.45
41	Ron Brand	.25	.13	.08
42	Bob Lillis	.25	.13	.08
43	Not Issued (See #125.)			
44	Buster Narum	.25	.13	.08
45	Jim Gilliam	.25	.13	.08
46	Claude Raymond	.25	.13	.08

47	Billy Bryan	.25	.13	.08
48	Marshall Bridges	.25	.13	.08
49	Norm Cash	.45	.25	.14
50	Orlando Cepeda	1.00	.50	.30
51	Lee Maye	.25	.13	.08
52	Andre Rodgers	.25	.13	.08
53	Ken Berry	.25	.13	.08
54	Don Mincher	.25	.13	.08
55	Jerry Lumpe	.25	.13	.08
56	Milt Pappas	.25	.13	.08
57	Steve Barber	.25	.13	.08
58	Denis Menke	.25	.13	.08
59	Larry Maxie	.25	.13	.08
60	Bob Gibson	1.00	.50	.30
61	Larry Bearnarth	.25	.13	.08
62	Bill Mazeroski	1.00	.50	.30
63	Bob Rodgers	.25	.13	.08
64	Jerry Arrigo	.25	.13	.08
65	Joe Nuxhall	.25	.13	.08
66	Dean Chance	.25	.13	.08
67	Ken Boyer	.60	.30	.20
68	John Odom	.25	.13	.08
69	Chico Cardenas	.25	.13	.08
70	Maury Wills	.35	.20	.11
71	Tony Oliva	.45	.25	.14
72	Don Nottebart	.25	.13	.08
73	Joe Adcock	.25	.13	.08
74	Felipe Alou	.25	.13	.08
75	Matty Alou	.25	.13	.08
76	Dick Radatz	.25	.13	.08
77	Jim Bouton	.25	.13	.08
78	John Blanchard	.25	.13	.08
79	Juan Pizarro	.25	.13	.08
80	Boog Powell	.45	.25	.14
81	Earl Robinson	.25	.13	.08
82	Bob Chance	.25	.13	.08
83	Max Alvis	.25	.13	.08
84	Don Blasingame	.25	.13	.08
85	Tom Cheney	.25	.13	.08
86	Jerry Arrigo	.25	.13	.08
87	Tommy Davis	.25	.13	.08
88	Steve Boros	.25	.13	.08
89	Don Cardwell	.25	.13	.08
90	Harmon Killebrew	1.50	.70	.45
91	Jim Pagliaroni	.25	.13	.08
92	Jim O'Toole	.25	.13	.08
93	Dennis Bennett	.25	.13	.08
94	Dick McAuliffe	.25	.13	.08
95	Dick Brown	.25	.13	.08
96	Joe Amalfitano	.25	.13	.08
97	Phil Linz	.25	.13	.08
98	Not Issued (See #165.)	.25	.13	.08
99	Dave Nicholson	.25	.13	.08
100	Hoyt Wilhelm	1.00	.50	.30
101	Don Leppert	.25	.13	.08
102	Jose Pagan	.25	.13	.08
103	Sam McDowell	.25	.13	.08
104	Jack Baldschun	.25	.13	.08
105	Jim Perry	.25	.13	.08
106	Hal Reniff	.25	.13	.08
107	Lee Maye	.25	.13	.08
108	Joe Adcock	.25	.13	.08
109	Bob Bolin	.25	.13	.08
110	Don Leppert	.25	.13	.08
111	Bill Monbouquette	.25	.13	.08
112	Bobby Richardson	.45	.25	.14
113	Earl Battey	.25	.13	.08
114	Bob Veale	.25	.13	.08
115	Lou Jackson	.25	.13	.08
116	Frank Kreutzer	.25	.13	.08
117	Jerry Zimmerman	.25	.13	.08
118	Don Schwall	.25	.13	.08
119	Rich Rollins	.25	.13	.08
120	Pete Ward	.25	.13	.08
121	Moe Drabowsky	.25	.13	.08
122	Jesse Gonder	.25	.13	.08
123	Hal Woodeshick	.25	.13	.08
124	John Herrnstein	.25	.13	.08
125a	Gary Peters (Should be #43.)	.25	.13	.08
125b	Leon Wagner	.25	.13	.08
126	Dwight Siebler	.25	.13	.08
027	Gary Kroll	.25	.13	.08
128	Tony Horton	.25	.13	.08
129	John DeMerit	.25	.13	.08
130	Sandy Koufax	6.00	3.00	1.75
131	Jim Davenport	.25	.13	.08
132	Wes Covington	.25	.13	.08
133	Tony Taylor	.25	.13	.08
134	Jack Kralick	.25	.13	.08
135	Bill Pleis	.25	.13	.08
136	Russ Snyder	.25	.13	.08
137	Joe Torre	.75	.40	.25
138	Ted Wills	.25	.13	.08
139	Wes Stock	.25	.13	.08
140	Frank Robinson	1.50	.70	.45
141	Dave Stenhouse	.25	.13	.08
142	Ron Hansen	.25	.13	.08
143	Don Elston	.25	.13	.08
144	Del Crandall	.25	.13	.08
145	Bennie Daniels	.25	.13	.08
146	Vada Pinson	.45	.25	.14
147	Bill Spanswick	.25	.13	.08
148	Earl Wilson	.25	.13	.08
149	Ty Cline	.25	.13	.08
150	Dick Groat	.25	.13	.08
151	Jim Duckworth	.25	.13	.08
152	Jimmie Schaffer	.25	.13	.08
153	George Thomas	.25	.13	.08
154	Wes Stock	.25	.13	.08
155	Mike White	.25	.13	.08
156	John Podres	.25	.13	.08
157	Willie Crawford	.25	.13	.08
158	Fred Gladding	.25	.13	.08
159	John Wyatt	.25	.13	.08
160	Bob Friend	.25	.13	.08
161	Ted Uhlaender	.25	.13	.08
162	Dick Stigman	.25	.13	.08
163	Don Wert	.25	.13	.08
164	Eddie Bressoud	.25	.13	.08
165a	Ed Roebuck (Should be #98.)	.25	.13	.08
165b	Leon Wagner	.25	.13	.08
166	Al Spangler	.25	.13	.08
167	Bob Sadowski	.25	.13	.08
168	Ralph Terry	.25	.13	.08
169	Jimmie Schaffer	.25	.13	.08
170a	Jim Fregosi (Should be #180.)	.25	.13	.08
170b	Dick Hall	.25	.13	.08
171	Al Spangler	.25	.13	.08
172	Bob Tillman	.25	.13	.08
173	Ed Bailey	.25	.13	.08
174	Cesar Tovar	.25	.13	.08
175	Morrie Stevens	.25	.13	.08
176	Floyd Weaver	.25	.13	.08
177	Frank Malzone	.25	.13	.08
178	Norm Siebern	.25	.13	.08
179	Dick Phillips	.25	.13	.08
180	Not Issued (See #170.)	.25	.13	.08
181	Bobby Wine	.25	.13	.08
182	Masanori Murakami	.75	.40	.25
183	Chuck Schilling	.25	.13	.08
184	Jimmie Schaffer	.25	.13	.08
185	John Roseboro	.25	.13	.08
186	Jake Wood	.25	.13	.08
187	Dallas Green	.25	.13	.08
188	Tom Haller	.25	.13	.08
189	Chuck Cottier	.25	.13	.08
190	Brooks Robinson	1.50	.70	.45
191	Ty Cline	.25	.13	.08
192	Bubba Phillips	.25	.13	.08
193	Al Jackson	.25	.13	.08
194	Herm Starrette	.25	.13	.08
195	Dave Wickersham	.25	.13	.08
196	Vic Power	.25	.13	.08
197	Ray Culp	.25	.13	.08
198	Don Demeter	.25	.13	.08
199	Dick Schofield	.25	.13	.08
200	Stephen Grant	.25	.13	.08
201	Roger Craig	.25	.13	.08
202	Dick Farrell	.25	.13	.08
203	Clay Dalrymple	.25	.13	.08
204	Jim Duffalo	.25	.13	.08
205	Tito Francona	.25	.13	.08
206	Tony Conigliaro	.45	.25	.14
207	Jim King	.25	.13	.08
208	Joe Gibbon	.25	.13	.08
209	Arnold Earley	.25	.13	.08
210	Denny McLain	.25	.13	.08
211	Don Larsen	.25	.13	.08
212	Ron Hunt	.25	.13	.08
213	Deron Johnson	.25	.13	.08
214	Harry Bright	.25	.13	.08
215	Ernie Fazio	.25	.13	.08
216	Joey Jay	.25	.13	.08
217	Jim Coates	.25	.13	.08
218	Jerry Kindall	.25	.13	.08
219	Joe Gibbon	.25	.13	.08
220	Frank Howard	.35	.20	.11
221	Howie Koplitz	.25	.13	.08
222	Larry Jackson	.25	.13	.08
223	Dale Long	.25	.13	.08
224	Jimmy Dykes	.25	.13	.08
225	Hank Aguirre	.25	.13	.08
226	Earl Francis	.25	.13	.08
227	Vic Wertz	.25	.13	.08
228	Larry Haney	.25	.13	.08
229	Tony LaRussa	.45	.25	.14
230	Moose Skowron	.35	.20	.11
231a	Tito Francona (Should be #235.)			
231b	Lee Thomas	.25	.13	.08
232	Ken Johnson	.25	.13	.08
233	Dick Howser	.25	.13	.08
234	Bobby Knoop	.25	.13	.08
235	Not Issued (See #231.)	.25	.13	.08
236	Elston Howard	.35	.20	.11
237	Donn Clendenon	.25	.13	.08
238	Jesse Gonder	.25	.13	.08
239	Vern Law	.25	.13	.08
240	Curt Flood	.25	.13	.08
241	Dal Maxvill	.25	.13	.08
242	Roy Sievers	.25	.13	.08
243	Jim Brewer	.25	.13	.08
244	Harry Craft	.25	.13	.08
245	Dave Eilers	.25	.13	.08
246	Dave DeBusschere	.25	.13	.08
247	Ken Harrelson	.25	.13	.08
248	Not Issued (See #249.)	.25	.13	.08
249a	Jim Duffalo	.25	.13	.08
249b	Eddie Kasko (Should be #248.)	.25	.13	.08
250	Luis Aparicio	1.00	.50	.30
251	Ron Kline	.25	.13	.08
252	Chuck Hinton	.25	.13	.08
253	Frank Lary	.25	.13	.08
254	Stu Miller	.25	.13	.08
255	Ernie Banks	2.00	1.00	.60
256	Dick Farrell	.25	.13	.08
257	Bud Daley	.25	.13	.08
258	Luis Arroyo	.25	.13	.08
259	Bob Del Greco	.25	.13	.08
260	Ted Williams	6.00	3.00	1.75
261	Mike Epstein	.25	.13	.08
262	Mickey Mantle	10.00	5.00	3.00
263	Jim LeFebvre	.25	.13	.08
264	Pat Jarvis	.25	.13	.08
265	Chuck Hinton	.25	.13	.08
266	Don Larsen	.25	.13	.08
267	Jim Coates	.25	.13	.08
268	Gary Kolb	.25	.13	.08
269	Jim Ray Hart	.25	.13	.08
270	Dave McNally	.25	.13	.08
271	Jerry Kindall	.25	.13	.08
272	Hector Lopez	.25	.13	.08
273	Claude Osteen	.25	.13	.08
274	Jack Aker	.25	.13	.08
275	Mike Shannon	.25	.13	.08
276	Lew Burdette	.25	.13	.08
277	Mack Jones	.25	.13	.08
278	Art Shamsky	.25	.13	.08
279	Bob Johnson	.25	.13	.08
280	Willie Mays	6.00	3.00	1.75
281	Rich Nye	.25	.13	.08
282	Bill Cowan	.25	.13	.08
283	Gary Kolb	.25	.13	.08
284	Woody Held	.25	.13	.08
285	Bill Freehan	.25	.13	.08
286	Larry Jackson	.25	.13	.08
287	Mike Hershberger	.25	.13	.08
288	Julian Javier	.25	.13	.08
289	Charley Smith	.25	.13	.08
290	Hank Aaron	6.00	3.00	1.75
291	John Boccabella	.25	.13	.08
292	Charley James	.25	.13	.08
293	Sammy Ellis	.25	.13	.08

1978 TCMA 1941 Brooklyn Dodgers

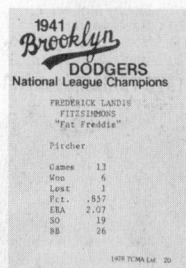

Freddie Fitzsimmons • Pitcher

The National League Champion Brooklyn Dodgers are featured in the collectors' edition card set. Measuring 2-1/2" x 3-1/2", the cards have blue duotone player photos on front with the name and position overprinted in black at bottom. A white border surrounds the photo. Backs are in black-and-white with a large championship logo and a few stats from the 1941 season.

		NM	EX	VG
	Complete Set (43):	25.00	12.50	7.50
	Common Player:	1.50	.75	.45
1	Mickey Owen	2.50	1.25	.70
2	Pee Wee Reese	7.50	3.75	2.25
3	Hugh Casey	1.50	.75	.45
4	Larry French	1.50	.75	.45
5	Tom Drake	1.50	.75	.45
6	Ed Albosta	1.50	.75	.45
7	Tommy Tatum	1.50	.75	.45
8	Paul Waner	3.50	1.75	1.00
9	Van Lingle Mungo	2.50	1.25	.70
10	Bill Swift	1.50	.75	.45
11	Dolph Camilli	2.50	1.25	.70
12	Pete Coscarart	1.50	.75	.45
13	Vito Tamulis	1.50	.75	.45
14	John Allen	1.50	.75	.45
15	Lee Grissom	1.50	.75	.45
16	Billy Herman	2.50	1.25	.70
17	Joe Vosmik	1.50	.75	.45
18	Babe Phelps	1.50	.75	.45
19	Mace Brown	1.50	.75	.45
20	Freddie Fitzsimmons	1.50	.75	.45
21	Angelo Guiliani	1.50	.75	.45
22	Lewis Riggs	1.50	.75	.45
23	Jimmy Wasdell	1.50	.75	.45
24	Herman Franks	1.50	.75	.45
25	Alex Kampouris	1.50	.75	.45
26	Kirby Higbe	1.50	.75	.45
27	Joe Medwick	2.50	1.25	.70
28	Newt Kimball	1.50	.75	.45
29	Curt Davis	1.50	.75	.45
30	Augie Galan	1.50	.75	.45
31	Luke Hamlin	1.50	.75	.45
32	Cookie Lavagetto	1.50	.75	.45
33	Joe Gallagher	1.50	.75	.45
34	Whitlow Wyatt	1.50	.75	.45
35	Dixie Walker	1.50	.75	.45
36	Pete Reiser	1.50	.75	.45
37	Leo Durocher	2.50	1.25	.70
38	Pee Wee Reese, Joe Medwick (3" x 5")	4.50	2.25	1.25
39	Dixie Walker, Joe Medwick, Dolph Camilli, Pete Reiser (3" x 5")	4.50	2.25	1.25
40	Team photo	3.00	1.50	.90
41	Kemp Wicker	1.50	.75	.45
42	George Pfister	2.00	1.00	.60
43	Chuck Dressen	1.50	.75	.45

1979 TCMA All Time Tigers

ALL TIME DETROIT TIGER TEAM	
Hank Greenberg	1B
Charlie Gehringer	2B
George Kell	3B
Billy Rogell	SS
Ty Cobb	OF
Harry Heilmann	OF
Al Kaline	OF
Mickey Cochrane	C
Denny McLain	RHP
Hal Newhouser	LHP
Terry Fox	RP
Steve O'Neil	Mgr

PITCHER — TERRY FOX

T.C.M.A. Ltd. 1979

Utilizing a format similar to its several minor league team sets of the same year, this collectors' issue from TCMA features an "All Time" Tigers team selection of position players, pitchers and manager. The 2-1/2" x 3-1/2" cards have black-and-white photos on front with the player's name and position in an orange "wave" at bottom; the whole is surrounded by a white border. Backs are in black-and-white and detail the all-time line-up. The unnumbered cards are checklisted here alphabetically.

	NM	EX	VG
Complete Set (12):	20.00	10.00	6.00
Common Player:	1.50	.70	.45
(1) Ty Cobb	6.00	3.00	1.75
(2) Mickey Cochrane	1.50	.70	.45
(3) Terry Fox	1.50	.70	.45
(4) Charlie Gehringer	2.50	1.25	.70
(5) Hank Greenberg	5.00	2.50	1.50
(6) Harry Heilmann	1.50	.70	.45
(7) Al Kaline	5.00	2.50	1.50
(8) George Kell	1.50	.70	.45
(9) Denny McLain	1.50	.70	.45
(10) Hal Newhouser	1.50	.70	.45
(11) Steve O'Neil (O'Neill)	1.50	.70	.45
(12) Billy Rogell	1.50	.70	.45

1979 TCMA Baseball History Series: The Fifties

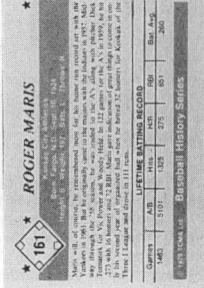

The "pure" format of the 1953 Bowman set was borrowed in this collectors' issue featuring the stars and journeymen of baseball in the 1950s. The 2-1/2" x 3-1/2" cards have color photos on front with white borders. Backs are in red and black with personal data and career summary and stats. Each set originally sold by TCMA came with two large-format (5" x 3-1/2") team-photo cards.

		NM	EX	VG
	Complete Set (291):	35.00	17.50	10.00
	Common Player:	.25	.13	.08
1	Joe DiMaggio	7.50	3.75	2.25
2	Yogi Berra	1.50	.70	.45
3	Warren Spahn	.75	.40	.25
4	Robin Roberts	.60	.30	.20
5	Ernie Banks	1.50	.70	.45
6	Willie Mays	5.00	2.50	1.50
7	Mickey Mantle	10.00	5.00	3.00
8	Roy Campanella	1.50	.70	.45
9	Stan Musial	4.00	2.00	1.25
10	Ted Williams	5.00	2.50	1.50
11	Ed Bailey	.25	.13	.08
12	Ted Kluszewski	.60	.30	.20
13	Ralph Kiner	.60	.30	.20
14	Dick Littlefield	.25	.13	.08
15	Nellie Fox	.60	.30	.20
16	Billy Pierce	.25	.13	.08
17	Richie Ashburn	.60	.30	.20
18	Del Ennis	.25	.13	.08
19	Bob Lemon	.50	.25	.15
20	Early Wynn	.50	.25	.15
21	Joe Collins	.25	.13	.08
22	Hank Bauer	.25	.13	.08
23	Roberto Clemente	6.00	3.00	1.75
24	Frank Thomas	.25	.13	.08
25	Alvin Dark	.25	.13	.08
26	Whitey Lockman	.25	.13	.08
27	Larry Doby	.60	.30	.20
28	Bob Feller	.75	.40	.25
29	Willie Jones	.25	.13	.08
30	Granny Hamner	.25	.13	.08
31	Clem Labine	.25	.13	.08
32	Ralph Branca	.25	.13	.08
33	Jack Harshman	.25	.13	.08
34	Dick Donovan	.25	.13	.08
35	Tommy Henrich	.25	.13	.08
36	Jerry Coleman	.25	.13	.08
37	Billy Hoeft	.25	.13	.08
38	Johnny Groth	.25	.13	.08
39	Harvey Haddix	.25	.13	.08
40	Gerry Staley	.25	.13	.08
41	Dale Long	.25	.13	.08
42	Vern Law	.25	.13	.08
43	Dodger Power	1.50	.70	.45
44	Sam Jethroe	.25	.13	.08
45	Vic Wertz	.25	.13	.08
46	Wes Westrum	.25	.13	.08
47	Dee Fondy	.25	.13	.08
48	Gene Baker	.25	.13	.08
49	Sandy Koufax	5.00	2.50	1.50
50	Billy Loes	.25	.13	.08
51	Chuck Diering	.25	.13	.08
52	Joe Ginsberg	.25	.13	.08
53	Jim Konstanty	.25	.13	.08
54	Curt Simmons	.25	.13	.08
55	Alex Kellner	.25	.13	.08
56	Charlie Dressen	.25	.13	.08
57	Frank Sullivan	.25	.13	.08
58	Mel Parnell	.25	.13	.08
59	Bobby Hofman	.25	.13	.08
60	Bill Connelly	.25	.13	.08
61	Corky Valentine	.25	.13	.08
62	Johnny Klippstein	.25	.13	.08
63	Chuck Tanner	.25	.13	.08
64	Dick Drott	.25	.13	.08
65	Dean Stone	.25	.13	.08
66	Jim Busby	.25	.13	.08
67	Sid Gordon	.25	.13	.08
68	Del Crandall	.25	.13	.08
69	Walker Cooper	.25	.13	.08
70	Hank Sauer	.25	.13	.08
71	Gil Hodges	.75	.40	.25
72	Duke Snider	1.00	.50	.30
73	Sherman Lollar	.25	.13	.08
74	Chico Carrasquel	.25	.13	.08
75	Gus Triandos	.25	.13	.08
76	Bob Harrison	.25	.13	.08
77	Eddie Waitkus	.25	.13	.08
78	Ken Heintzelman	.25	.13	.08
79	Harry Simpson	.25	.13	.08
80	Luke Easter	.25	.13	.08
81	Ed Dick	.25	.13	.08
82	Jim DePaola	.25	.13	.08
83	Billy Cox	.25	.13	.08
84	Pee Wee Reese	1.00	.50	.30
85	Virgil Trucks	.25	.13	.08
86	George Kell	.50	.25	.15
87	Mickey Vernon	.25	.13	.08
88	Eddie Yost	.25	.13	.08
89	Gus Bell	.25	.13	.08
90	Wally Post	.25	.13	.08
91	Ed Lopat	.25	.13	.08
92	Dick Wakefield	.25	.13	.08
93	Solly Hemus	.25	.13	.08
94	Al "Red" Schoendienst	.60	.30	.20
95	Sammy White	.25	.13	.08
96	Billy Goodman	.25	.13	.08
97	Jim Hearn	.25	.13	.08
98	Ruben Gomez	.25	.13	.08
99	Marty Marion	.25	.13	.08
100	Bill Virdon	.25	.13	.08
101	Chuck Stobbs	.25	.13	.08
102	Ron Samford	.25	.13	.08
103	Bill Tuttle	.25	.13	.08
104	Harvey Kuenn	.25	.13	.08
105	Joe Cunningham	.25	.13	.08
106	Bill Sarni	.25	.13	.08
107	Jack Kramer	.25	.13	.08
108	Eddie Stanky	.25	.13	.08
109	Carmen Mauro	.25	.13	.08
110	Wayne Belardi	.25	.13	.08
111	Preston Ward	.25	.13	.08
112	Jack Shepard	.25	.13	.08
113	Buddy Kerr	.25	.13	.08
114	Vern Bickford	.25	.13	.08
115	Ellis Kinder	.25	.13	.08
116	Walt Dropo	.25	.13	.08
117	Duke Maas	.25	.13	.08
118	Billy Hunter	.25	.13	.08
119	Ewell Blackwell	.25	.13	.08
120	Hershell Freeman	.25	.13	.08
121	Freddie Martin	.25	.13	.08
122	Erv Dusak	.25	.13	.08
123	Roy Hartsfield	.25	.13	.08
124	Willard Marshall	.25	.13	.08
125	Jack Sanford	.25	.13	.08
126	Herm Wehmeier	.25	.13	.08
127	Hal Smith	.25	.13	.08
128	Jim Finigan	.25	.13	.08
129	Bob Hale	.25	.13	.08
130	Jim Wilson	.25	.13	.08
131	Bill Wight	.25	.13	.08
132	Mike Fornieles	.25	.13	.08
133	Steve Gromek	.25	.13	.08
134	Herb Score	.35	.20	.11
135	Ryne Duren	.25	.13	.08
136	Bob Turley	.25	.13	.08
137	Wally Moon	.25	.13	.08
138	Fred Hutchinson	.25	.13	.08
139	Jim Hegan	.25	.13	.08
140	Dale Mitchell	.25	.13	.08
141	Walt Moryn	.25	.13	.08
142	Cal Neeman	.25	.13	.08
143	Billy Martin	.50	.25	.15
144	Phil Rizzuto	1.00	.50	.30
145	Preacher Roe	.25	.13	.08
146	Carl Erskine	.25	.13	.08
147	Vic Power	.25	.13	.08
148	Elmer Valo	.25	.13	.08
149	Don Mueller	.25	.13	.08
150	Hank Thompson	.25	.13	.08
151	Stan Lopata	.25	.13	.08
152	Dick Sisler	.25	.13	.08
153	Willard Schmidt	.25	.13	.08
154	Roy McMillan	.25	.13	.08
155	Gil McDougald	.25	.13	.08
156	Gene Woodling	.25	.13	.08
157	Eddie Mathews	.75	.40	.25
158	Johnny Logan	.25	.13	.08
159	Dan Bankhead	.25	.13	.08
160	Joe Black	.25	.13	.08
161	Roger Maris	1.50	.70	.45
162	Bob Cerv	.25	.13	.08
163	Paul Minner	.25	.13	.08
164	Bob Rush	.25	.13	.08
165	Gene Hermanski	.25	.13	.08
166	Harry Brecheen	.25	.13	.08
167	Davey Williams	.25	.13	.08
168	Monte Irvin	.60	.30	.20
169	Clint Courtney	.25	.13	.08
170	Sandy Consuegra	.25	.13	.08
171	Bobby Shantz	.25	.13	.08
172	Harry Byrd	.25	.13	.08
173	Marv Throneberry	.25	.13	.08
174	Woody Held	.25	.13	.08
175	Al Rosen	.25	.13	.08
176	Rance Pless	.25	.13	.08
177	Steve Bilko	.25	.13	.08
178	Joe Presko	.25	.13	.08
179	Ray Boone	.25	.13	.08
180	Jim Lemon	.25	.13	.08
181	Andy Pafko	.25	.13	.08
182	Don Newcombe	.35	.20	.11
183	Frank Lary	.25	.13	.08
184	Al Kaline	.75	.40	.25
185	Allie Reynolds	.25	.13	.08
186	Vic Raschi	.25	.13	.08
187	Dodger Braintrust	.50	.25	.15
188	Jim Piersall	.25	.13	.08
189	George Wilson	.25	.13	.08
190	Jim "Dusty" Rhodes	.25	.13	.08
191	Duane Pillette	.25	.13	.08
192	Dave Philley	.25	.13	.08
193	Bobby Morgan	.25	.13	.08
194	Russ Meyer	.25	.13	.08
195	Hector Lopez	.25	.13	.08
196	Arnie Portocarrero	.25	.13	.08
197	Joe Page	.25	.13	.08
198	Tommy Byrne	.25	.13	.08
199	Ray Monzant	.25	.13	.08
200	John "Windy" McCall	.25	.13	.08
201	Leo Durocher	.50	.25	.15
202	Bobby Thomson	.35	.20	.11
203	Jack Banta	.25	.13	.08
204	Joe Pignatano	.25	.13	.08
205	Carlos Paula	.25	.13	.08
206	Roy Sievers	.25	.13	.08
207	Mickey McDermott	.25	.13	.08
208	Ray Scarborough	.25	.13	.08
209	Bill Miller	.25	.13	.08
210	Bill Skowron	.25	.13	.08
211	Bob Nieman	.25	.13	.08
212	Al Pilarcik	.25	.13	.08
213	Jerry Priddy	.25	.13	.08
214	Frank House	.25	.13	.08
215	Don Mossi	.25	.13	.08
216	Rocky Colavito	.60	.30	.20
217	Brooks Lawrence	.25	.13	.08
218	Ted Wilks	.25	.13	.08
219	Zack Monroe	.25	.13	.08
220	Art Ditmar	.25	.13	.08
221	Cal McLish	.25	.13	.08
222	Gene Bearden	.25	.13	.08
223	Norm Siebern	.25	.13	.08
224	Bob Wiesler	.25	.13	.08
225	Foster Castleman	.25	.13	.08
226	Daryl Spencer	.25	.13	.08
227	Dick Williams	.25	.13	.08
228	Don Zimmer	.25	.13	.08
229	Jackie Jensen	.25	.13	.08
230	Billy Johnson	.25	.13	.08
231	Dave Koslo	.25	.13	.08
232	Al Corwin	.25	.13	.08
233	Erv Palica	.25	.13	.08
234	Bob Milliken	.25	.13	.08
235	Ray Katt	.25	.13	.08
236	Sammy Calderone	.25	.13	.08
237	Don Demeter	.25	.13	.08
238	Karl Spooner	.25	.13	.08
239	The Veteran and The Rookie	.50	.25	.15
240	Enos Slaughter	.50	.25	.15
241	Dick Kryhoski	.25	.13	.08
242	Art Houtteman	.25	.13	.08
243	Andy Carey	.25	.13	.08
244	Tony Kubek	.35	.20	.11
245	Mike McCormick	.25	.13	.08
246	Bob Schmidt	.25	.13	.08
247	Nelson King	.25	.13	.08
248	Bob Skinner	.25	.13	.08
249	Dick Bokelmann	.25	.13	.08
250	Eddie Kazak	.25	.13	.08
251	Billy Klaus	.25	.13	.08
252	Norm Zauchin	.25	.13	.08
253	Art Schult	.25	.13	.08
254	Bob Martyn	.25	.13	.08
255	Larry Jansen	.25	.13	.08
256	Sal Maglie	.25	.13	.08
257	Bob Darnell	.25	.13	.08
258	Ken Lehman	.25	.13	.08
259	Jim Blackburn	.25	.13	.08
260	Bob Purkey	.25	.13	.08
261	Harry Walker	.25	.13	.08
262	Joe Garagiola	.35	.20	.11
263	Gus Zernial	.25	.13	.08
264	Walter "Hoot" Evers	.25	.13	.08
265	Mark Freeman	.25	.13	.08
266	Charlie Silvera	.25	.13	.08
267	Johnny Podres	.25	.13	.08
268	Jim Hughes	.25	.13	.08
269	Al Worthington	.25	.13	.08
270	Hoyt Wilhelm	.50	.25	.15
271	Elston Howard	.25	.13	.08
272	Don Larsen	.40	.20	.12
273	Don Hoak	.25	.13	.08
274	Chico Fernandez	.25	.13	.08
275	Gail Harris	.25	.13	.08
276	Valmy Thomas	.25	.13	.08
277	George Shuba	.25	.13	.08
278	Al "Rube" Walker	.25	.13	.08
279	Willard Ramsdell	.25	.13	.08
280	Lindy McDaniel	.25	.13	.08
281	Bob Wilson	.25	.13	.08
282	Chuck Templeton	.25	.13	.08
283	Eddie Robinson	.25	.13	.08
284	Bob Porterfield	.25	.13	.08
285	Larry Miggins	.25	.13	.08
286	Minnie Minoso	.25	.13	.08
287	Lou Boudreau	.50	.25	.15
288	Jim Davenport	.25	.13	.08
289	Bob Miller	.25	.13	.08
290	Jim Gilliam	.25	.13	.08
291	Jackie Robinson	4.00	2.00	1.25
Bonus 1955 Brooklyn Dodgers		10.00	5.00	3.00
1	Team Card			
Bonus 1957 Milwaukee Braves		10.00	5.00	3.00
2	Team			

1979 TCMA Japan Pro Baseball

Stars of Japan's Pacific and Central "major" leagues are featured in this collectors' issue. More than a dozen Americans playing or managing in Japan at the time are included in the set, as well as several Japanese Hall of Famers including home-run king Sadaharu Oh. Cards feature a color posed portrait with a light blue semi-circle at bottom containing the team and player name in royal blue. Backs are printed in red and black on white and have a few personal data, 1978 and career stats, plus league and team logos and TCMA copyright. Cards are nominally standard 2-1/2" x 3-1/2" in size, but actual size varies a bit due to cutting discrepancies.

		NM	EX	VG
Complete Set (90):		50.00	25.00	15.00
Common Player:		.50	.25	.15
1	Sadaharu Oh	15.00	7.50	4.50
2	Jinten Haku	.50	.25	.15
3	Toshizo Sakamoto	.50	.25	.15
4	Tony Muser	1.00	.50	.30
5	Makoto Matsubara	.50	.25	.15
6	Masayuki Nakaysuka	.50	.25	.15
7	Daisuke Yamashita	.50	.25	.15
8	Koji Yamamoto	.50	.25	.15
9	Sachio Kinugasa	4.00	2.00	1.25
10	Bernie Williams	.60	.30	.20
11	Bobby Marcano	.60	.30	.20
12	Koichi Tabuchi	.50	.25	.15
13	Katsuya Nomura	3.00	1.50	.90
14	Jack Maloof	.60	.30	.20
15	Masahiro Doi	.50	.25	.15
16	Hiroyuki Yamazaki	.50	.25	.15
17	Vernon Law	2.00	1.00	.60
18	Dave Hilton	.60	.30	.20
19	Katsuo Osugi	.50	.25	.15
20	Tsutomu Wakamatsu	.50	.25	.15
21	John Scott	.60	.30	.20
22	Toru Sugiura	.50	.25	.15
23	Akihiko Kondo	.50	.25	.15
24	Shintaro Mizutani	.50	.25	.15
25	Tatsuro Hirooka	.50	.25	.15
26	Kojiro Ikegaya	.50	.25	.15
27	Yutaka Enatsu	1.50	.70	.45
28	Tomehiro Kaneda	.50	.25	.15
29	Yoshihiko Takahashi	.50	.25	.15
30	Jitsuo Mizutani	.60	.30	.20
31	Adrian Garrett	.60	.30	.20
32	Jim Lyttle	.60	.30	.20
33	Takeshi Koba	.50	.25	.15
34	Sam Ewing	.60	.30	.20
35	Kazumi Takahashi	.50	.25	.15
36	Kazushi Saeki	.50	.25	.15
37	Masanori Murakami	7.50	3.75	2.25
38	Toshiro Kato	.50	.25	.15
39	Junichi Kashiwabara	.50	.25	.15
40	Masaru Tomita	.50	.25	.15
41	Bobby Mitchell	.60	.30	.20
42	Mikio Sendoh	.50	.25	.15
43	Chris Arnold	.60	.30	.20
44	Charlie Manuel	.60	.30	.20
45	Keiji Suzuki	.50	.25	.15
46	Toru Ogawa	.50	.25	.15
47	Shigeru Ishiwata	.50	.25	.15
48	Kyosuke Sasaki	.50	.25	.15
49	Iwao Ikebe	.50	.25	.15
50	Kaoru Betto	.50	.25	.15
51	Gene Martin	.60	.30	.20
52	Felix Millan	1.00	.50	.30
53	Mitsuo Motoi	.50	.25	.15
54	Tomio Tashiro	.50	.25	.15
55	Shigeo Nagashima	7.50	3.75	2.25
56	Yoshikazu Takagi	.50	.25	.15
57	Keiichi Nagasaki	.50	.25	.15
58	Rick Krueger	.60	.30	.20
59	John Sipin	.60	.30	.20
60	Osao Shibata	.50	.25	.15
61	Isao Harimoto	.50	.25	.15
62	Shigeru Takada	.50	.25	.15
63	Michiyo Arito	.50	.25	.15
64	Hisao Niura	.50	.25	.15
65	Teruhide Sakurai	.50	.25	.15
66	Yoshito Oda	.50	.25	.15
67	Leron Lee	.60	.30	.20
68	Carlos May	.60	.30	.20
69	Frank Ortenzio	.60	.30	.20
70	Leon Lee	.60	.30	.20
71	Mitsuru Fujiwara	.50	.25	.15
72	Senichi Hoshino	.50	.25	.15
73	Tatsuhiko Kimata	.50	.25	.15
74	Morimichi Takagi	.50	.25	.15
75	Yasunori Oshima	.50	.25	.15
76	Yasushi Tao	.50	.25	.15
77	Wayne Garrett	.60	.30	.20
78	Bob Jones	.60	.30	.20
79	Toshiro Naka	.50	.25	.15
80	Don Blasingame	3.00	1.50	.90
81	Mike Reinbach	.60	.30	.20
82	Masashi Takenouchi	.50	.25	.15
83	Masayuki Kakefu	.50	.25	.15
84	Katsuhiro Nakamura	.50	.25	.15
85	Shigeru Kobayashi	.50	.25	.15
86	Lee Stanton	.60	.30	.20
87	Takenori Emoto	.50	.25	.15
88	Sohachi Aniya	.50	.25	.15
89	Wally Yonamine	4.00	2.00	1.25
90	Kazuhiro Yamauchi	.50	.25	.15

1979 TCMA 1927 New York Yankees

Perhaps the finest baseball team of all time is featured in this collectors' set. The sepia oval photos at center are surrounded by black-and-white graphics of baseball equipment and other ornamentation. Player name and position are in a strip beneath the photo. Backs have personal data and a career summary. The cards are in standard 2-1/2" x 3-1/2".

		NM	EX	VG
Complete Set (32):		20.00	10.00	6.00
Common Player:		1.00	.50	.30
1	Babe Ruth	6.00	3.00	1.75
2	Lou Gehrig	4.00	2.00	1.25
3	Tony Lazzeri	1.00	.50	.30
4	Mark Koenig	1.00	.50	.30
5	Julie Wera	1.00	.50	.30
6	Ray Morehart	1.00	.50	.30
7	Art Fletcher	1.00	.50	.30
8	Joe Dugan	1.00	.50	.30
9	Charley O'Leary	1.00	.50	.30
10	Bob Meusel	1.00	.50	.30
11	Earle Combs	1.00	.50	.30
12	Cedric Durst	1.00	.50	.30
13	Johnny Grabowski	1.00	.50	.30
14	Mike Gazella	1.00	.50	.30
15	Pat Collins	1.00	.50	.30
16	Waite Hoyt	1.00	.50	.30
17	Myles Thomas	1.00	.50	.30
18	Benny Bengough	1.00	.50	.30
19	Herb Pennock	1.00	.50	.30
20	Wilcy Moore	1.00	.50	.30
21	Urban Shocker	1.00	.50	.30
22	Dutch Ruether	1.00	.50	.30
23	George Pipgras	1.00	.50	.30
24	Jacob Ruppert	1.00	.50	.30
25	Eddie Bennett	1.00	.50	.30
26	Ed Barrow	1.00	.50	.30
27	Ben Paschal	1.00	.50	.30
28	Miller Huggins	1.00	.50	.30
29	Joe Giard	1.00	.50	.30
30	Bob Shawkey	1.00	.50	.30
31	Walter Beall	1.00	.50	.30
32	Don Miller	1.00	.50	.30

1980 TCMA All-Time Teams

In 1980, TCMA began a new series of sets featuring 11 all-time great players and a manager from several of the 26 teams. In standard 2-1/2" x 3-1/2" format, most of the cards utilize black-and-white player photos, though some more recent stars are pictured in color. Several decorative borders, varying by team, surround the front photos. On most team sets there is an "All Time" designation at top, with the player name and (usually) position at bottom. Backs are fairly uniform, printed in blue or black, and offering a few biographical details and career highlights or a checklist. Besides hobby sales, these old-timers' sets were also sold in several major retail chains.

(Team sets listed individually.)

1980 TCMA All Time Brooklyn Dodgers

		NM	EX	VG
Complete Set (12):		6.00	3.00	1.80
Common Player:		.50	.25	.15
1	Gil Hodges	1.00	.50	.30
2	Jim Gilliam	.50	.25	.15
3	Pee Wee Reese	1.00	.50	.30
4	Jackie Robinson	3.00	1.50	.90
5	Sandy Koufax	3.00	1.50	.90
6	Zach Wheat	.50	.25	.15
7	Dixie Walker	.50	.25	.15
8	Hugh Casey	.50	.25	.15
9	Dazzy Vance	.50	.25	.15
10	Duke Snider	1.00	.50	.30
11	Roy Campanella	1.50	.70	.45
12	Walter Alston	.50	.25	.15

1980 TCMA All Time Cubs

 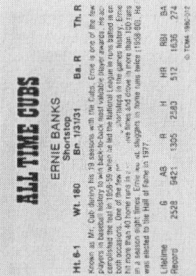

		NM	EX	VG
Complete Set (12):		6.00	3.00	1.80
Common Player:		.50	.25	.15
1	Billy Williams	1.50	.70	.45
2	Charlie Root	.50	.25	.15
3	Ron Santo	1.50	.70	.45
4	Larry French	.50	.25	.15
5	Gabby Hartnett	.50	.25	.15
6	Emil Kush	.50	.25	.15
7	Charlie Grimm	.50	.25	.15
8	Kiki Cuyler	.50	.25	.15
9	Billy Herman	.50	.25	.15
10	Hack Wilson	1.00	.50	.30
11	Rogers Hornsby	1.00	.50	.30
12	Ernie Banks	4.00	2.00	1.25

1980 TCMA All Time N.Y. Giants

ALL TIME N.Y. GIANTS
BILL TERRY

Bill Terry, nicknamed "Memphis Bill" was one of the greatest hitters in baseball history. Over his fourteen year career he maintained a .341 batting average. Although he was not known as a slugger, he knocked home one hundred or more runs in six consecutive years. Terry is best remembered as the last .400 hitter in the National League, as he batted .401 in 1930. Terry, a Hall of Fame selection in 1954, also succeeded John McGraw as the Giant's manager. He led them to three pennants over a ten year period.

© TCMA Ltd. 1980-0007

		NM	EX	VG
Complete Set (12):		6.00	3.00	1.80
Common Player:		.50	.25	.15
1	Willie Mays	4.00	2.00	1.25
2	Wes Westrum	.50	.25	.15
3	Carl Hubbell	.50	.25	.15
4	Hoyt Wilhelm	.50	.25	.15
5	Bobby Thomson	1.00	.50	.30
6	Frankie Frisch	.50	.25	.15
7	Bill Terry	.50	.25	.15
8	Alvin Dark	.50	.25	.15
9	Mel Ott	1.00	.50	.30
10	Christy Mathewson	2.50	1.25	.70
11	Freddie Lindstrom	.50	.25	.15
12	John McGraw	.50	.25	.15

1980 TCMA All Time Tigers

Sets printed with blue or red borders.

		NM	EX	VG
Complete Set (12):		6.00	3.00	1.80
Common Player:		.50	.25	.15
1	George Kell	.50	.25	.15
2	Billy Rogell	.50	.25	.15
3	Ty Cobb	4.00	2.00	1.25
4	Hank Greenberg	2.50	1.25	.70
5	Al Kaline	1.50	.70	.45
6	Charlie Gehringer	.75	.40	.25
7	Harry Heilmann	.50	.25	.15
8	Hal Newhouser	.50	.25	.15
9	Steve O'Neill	.50	.25	.15
10	Denny McLain	.50	.25	.15
11	Mickey Cochrane	.50	.25	.15
12	John Hiller	.50	.25	.15

1980 TCMA All Time White Sox

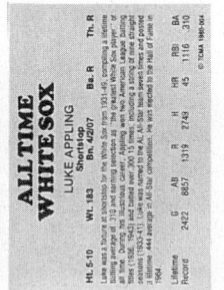

		NM	EX	VG
Complete Set (12):		6.00	3.00	1.80
Common Player:		.50	.25	.15
1	Ted Lyons	.50	.25	.15
2	Eddie Collins	2.00	1.00	.60
3	Al Lopez	.75	.40	.25
4	Luke Appling	2.00	1.00	.60
5	Billy Pierce	.75	.40	.25
6	Willie Kamm	.50	.25	.15
7	Johnny Mostil	.50	.25	.15
8	Al Simmons	.75	.40	.25
9	Ray Schalk	.50	.25	.15
10	Gerry Staley	.50	.25	.15
11	Harry Hooper	.50	.25	.15
12	Eddie Robinson	.50	.25	.15

1980 TCMA All Time Yankees

1B	Lou Gehrig
2B	Tony Lazzeri
3B	Red Rolfe
SS	Phil Rizzuto
OF	Babe Ruth
OF	Mickey Mantle
OF	Joe DiMaggio
C	Bill Dickey
P	Red Ruffing
P	Whitey Ford
RP	Johnny Murphy
Mgr	Casey Stengel

		NM	EX	VG
Complete Set (12):		16.00	8.00	4.75
Common Player:		.50	.25	.15
1	Lou Gehrig	4.00	2.00	1.25
2	Tony Lazzeri	.50	.25	.15
3	Red Rolfe	.50	.25	.15
4	Phil Rizzuto	1.00	.50	.30
5	Babe Ruth	4.00	2.00	1.25
6	Mickey Mantle	5.00	2.50	1.50
7	Joe DiMaggio	4.00	2.00	1.25
8	Bill Dickey	.75	.40	.25
9	Red Ruffing	.50	.25	.15
10	Whitey Ford	1.00	.50	.30
11	Johnny Murphy	.50	.25	.15
12	Casey Stengel	.75	.40	.25

1980 TCMA 1914 Miracle (Boston) Braves

The 1914 Boston Braves team which went from dead last in the National League in mid-July to winning the pennant by 10-1/2 games and sweeping the Philadelphia A's in the World Series is featured on this collectors' issue. In standard 2-1/2" x 3-1/2" format, the cards feature sepia photos in fancy borders. Backs have details of the person's contribution to the "Miracle," along with stats and biographical data.

		NM	EX	VG
Complete Set (32):		30.00	15.00	9.00
Common Player:		1.00	.50	.30
1	Joe Connolly	1.00	.50	.30
2	Lefty Tyler	1.00	.50	.30
3	Tom Hughes	1.00	.50	.30
4	Hank Gowdy	1.00	.50	.30
5	Gene Cochreham (Cocreham)	1.25	.60	.40
6	Larry Gilbert	1.00	.50	.30
7	George Davis	1.00	.50	.30
8	Hub Perdue	1.00	.50	.30
9	Otto Hess	1.00	.50	.30
10	Clarence Kraft	1.25	.60	.40
11	Tommy Griffith	1.00	.50	.30
12	1914 World Series	1.00	.50	.30
13	Oscar Dugey	1.00	.50	.30
14	Josh Devore	1.00	.50	.30
15	George Stallings	1.00	.50	.30
16	Rabbit Maranville	1.50	.70	.45
17	Paul Strand	1.00	.50	.30
18	Charlie Deal	1.00	.50	.30
19	Dick Rudolph	1.00	.50	.30
20	Butch Schmidt	1.00	.50	.30
21	Johnny Evers	2.00	1.00	.60
22	Dick Crutcher	1.25	.60	.40
23	Possum Whitted	1.00	.50	.30
24	Fred Mitchell	1.00	.50	.30
25	Herbie Moran	1.00	.50	.30
26	Bill James	1.00	.50	.30
27	Ted Cather	1.00	.50	.30
28	Red Smith	1.00	.50	.30
29	Les Mann	1.00	.50	.30
30	Herbie Moran, Wally Schrang (Schang)	1.00	.50	.30
31	Not Issued			
32	Johnny Evers (1914 MVP)	1.00	.50	.30
33	Jim Gaffney	1.25	.60	.40

1980 TCMA 1950 Philadelphia Phillies/Whiz Kids

The National League Champions of 1950 are featured in this collectors' issue team-set. The 2-1/2" x 3-1/2" cards have black-and-white player photo surrounded by red borders. Backs are in black-and-white with player personal data, career summary and 1950 and lifetime stats.

		NM	EX	VG
Complete Set (31):		20.00	10.00	6.00
Common Player:		.60	.30	.20
1	Ken Silvestri	.50	.25	.15
2	Hank Borowy	.50	.25	.15
3	Bob Miller	.50	.25	.15
4	Jocko Thompson	.50	.25	.15
5	Curt Simmons	.50	.25	.15
6	Dick Sisler	.50	.25	.15
7	Eddie Waitkus	.50	.25	.15
8	Dick Whitman	.50	.25	.15
9	Andy Seminick	.50	.25	.15
10	Richie Ashburn	5.00	2.50	1.50
11	Bubba Church	.50	.25	.15
12	Jackie Mayo	.50	.25	.15
13	Eddie Sawyer	.50	.25	.15
14	Benny Bengough	.50	.25	.15
15	Jim Konstanty	.50	.25	.15
16	Robin Roberts	5.00	2.50	1.50
17	Del Ennis	.50	.25	.15
18	Dusty Cooke	.50	.25	.15
19	Mike Goliat	.50	.25	.15
20	Russ Meyer	.50	.25	.15
21	Granny Hamner	.50	.25	.15
22	Stan Lopata	.50	.25	.15
23	Willie Jones	.50	.25	.15
24	Stan Hollmig	.50	.25	.15
25	Jimmy Bloodworth	.50	.25	.15
26	Ken Johnson	.50	.25	.15
27	Bill Nicholson	.50	.25	.15
28	Ken Heintzelman	.50	.25	.15
29	Blix Donnelly	.50	.25	.15
30	Putsy Caballero	.50	.25	.15
31	Cy Perkins	.50	.25	.15

1980 TCMA 1957 Milwaukee Braves

The World Champion Milwaukee Braves are featured in this collectors' issue. The 2-1/2" x 3-1/2" cards have blue-and-white player photos with white borders, blue typography and

red graphics. Backs are in blue-and-white with a few bits of player data, career information and stats, along with a TCMA copyright line.

		NM	EX	VG
Complete Set (42):		30.00	15.00	9.00
Common Player:		.50	.25	.15
1	Don McMahon	.50	.25	.15
2	Joey Jay	.75	.40	.25
3	Phil Paine	.50	.25	.15
4	Bob Trowbridge	.50	.25	.15
5	Bob Buhl	.50	.25	.15
6	Lew Burdette	.75	.40	.25
7	Ernie Johnson	.50	.25	.15
8	Ray Crone	.50	.25	.15
9	Taylor Phillips	.50	.25	.15
10	Johnny Logan	.50	.25	.15
11	Frank Torre	.50	.25	.15
12	John DeMerit	.50	.25	.15
13	Red Murff	.50	.25	.15
14	Nippy Jones	.50	.25	.15
15	Bobby Thomson	.75	.40	.25
16	Chuck Tanner	.50	.25	.15
17	Charlie Root	.50	.25	.15
18	Juan Pizarro	.50	.25	.15
19	Hawk Taylor	.50	.25	.15
20	Mel Roach	.50	.25	.15
21	Bob Hazle	.75	.40	.25
22	Del Rice	.50	.25	.15
23	Felix Mantilla	.50	.25	.15
24	Andy Pafko	.50	.25	.15
25	Del Crandall	.75	.40	.25
26	Wes Covington	.50	.25	.15
27	Eddie Mathews	5.00	2.50	1.50
28	Joe Adcock	.75	.40	.25
29	Dick Cole	.50	.25	.15
30	Carl Sawatski	.50	.25	.15
31	Warren Spahn	5.00	2.50	1.50
32	Hank Aaron	10.00	5.00	3.00
33	Bob Keely	.50	.25	.15
34	Johnny Riddle	.50	.25	.15
35	Connie Ryan	.50	.25	.15
36	Harry Hanebrink	.50	.25	.15
37	Danny O'Connell	.50	.25	.15
38	Fred Haney	.50	.25	.15
39	Dave Jolly	.50	.25	.15
40	Red Schoendienst	3.50	1.75	1.00
41	Gene Conley	.50	.25	.15
42	Bill Bruton	.50	.25	.15

1980 TCMA 1959 L.A. Dodgers

This collectors' issue features the members of the 1959 World Champion L.A. Dodgers. The 2-1/2" x 3-1/2" cards can be found printed in either black-and-white or blue-and-white on front and back. Fronts have player photos with white borders. Backs have personal data, 1959 and career stats and a few sentences about the player's performance in the championship season.

		NM	EX	VG
Complete Set (40):		40.00	20.00	12.00
Common Player:		1.00	.50	.30
1	Joe Pignatano	1.00	.50	.30
2	Carl Furillo	1.50	.70	.45
3	Bob Lillis	1.00	.50	.30
4	Chuck Essegian	1.00	.50	.30
5	Dick Gray	1.00	.50	.30
6	Rip Repulski	1.00	.50	.30
7	Jim Baxes	1.00	.50	.30
8	Frank Howard	2.50	1.25	.70
9	Solly Drake	1.00	.50	.30
10	Sandy Amoros	1.50	.70	.45
11	Norm Sherry	1.50	.70	.45
12	Tommy Davis	1.50	.70	.45
13	Jim Gilliam	1.50	.70	.45
14	Duke Snider	5.00	2.50	1.50
15	Maury Wills	2.50	1.25	.70

		NM	EX	VG
16	Don Demeter	1.00	.50	.30
17	Wally Moon	1.50	.70	.45
18	John Roseboro	1.50	.70	.45
19	Ron Fairly	1.50	.70	.45
20	Norm Larker	1.50	.70	.45
21	Charlie Neal	1.50	.70	.45
22	Don Zimmer	1.50	.70	.45
23	Chuck Dressen	1.00	.50	.30
24	Gil Hodges	4.00	2.00	1.25
25	Joe Becker	1.00	.50	.30
26	Walter Alston	1.50	.70	.45
27	Greg Mulleavy	1.00	.50	.30
28	Don Drysdale	4.00	2.00	1.25
29	Johnny Podres	1.50	.70	.45
30	Sandy Koufax	7.50	3.75	2.25
31	Roger Craig	1.50	.70	.45
32	Danny McDevitt	1.00	.50	.30
33	Bill Harris	1.00	.50	.30
34	Larry Sherry	1.00	.50	.30
35	Stan Williams	1.50	.70	.45
36	Clem Labine	1.50	.70	.45
37	Chuck Churn	1.00	.50	.30
38	Johnny Klippstein	1.00	.50	.30
39	Carl Erskine	1.50	.70	.45
40	Fred Kipp	1.00	.50	.30

1980 TCMA 1960 Pittsburgh Pirates

The World Champion 1960 Pirates are featured in this collectors issue team-set. Black-and-white player photos are bordered in gold on the fronts of the 2-1/2" x 3-1/2" cards. Backs are in black-and-white with personal data, career summary and stats for the 1960 season and career. The Cimoli error card #39 was pulled from distribution and replaced with the unnumbered corrected version.

		NM	EX	VG
Complete Set (41):		30.00	15.00	9.00
(No #39 Cimoli error.)				
Common Player:		.50	.25	.15
1	Clem Labine	.50	.25	.15
2	Bob Friend	.75	.40	.25
3	Roy Face	.75	.40	.25
4	Vern Law	.75	.40	.25
5	Harvey Haddix	.75	.40	.25
6	Vinegar Bend Mizell	.50	.25	.15
7	Bill Burwell	.50	.25	.15
8	Diomedes Olivo	.50	.25	.15
9	Don Gross	.50	.25	.15
10	Fred Green	.50	.25	.15
11	Jim Umbricht	.50	.25	.15
12	George Witt	.50	.25	.15
13	Tom Cheney	.50	.25	.15
14	Bennie Daniels	.50	.25	.15
15	Earl Francis	.50	.25	.15
16	Joe Gibbon	.50	.25	.15
17	Paul Giel	.50	.25	.15
18	Danny Kravitz	.50	.25	.15
19	R.C. Stevens	.50	.25	.15
20	Roman Mejias	.50	.25	.15
21	Dick Barone	.50	.25	.15
22	Sam Narron	.50	.25	.15
23	Harry Bright	.50	.25	.15
24	Mickey Vernon	.50	.25	.15
25	Bob Skinner	.60	.30	.20
26	Smoky Burgess	.60	.30	.20
27	Bill Virdon	.60	.30	.20
28	Not Issued			
29	Don Hoak	.60	.30	.20
30	Bill Mazeroski	6.00	3.00	1.75
31	Dick Stuart	1.50	.70	.45
32	Dick Groat	1.50	.70	.45
33	Bob Oldis	.50	.25	.15
34	Gene Baker	.50	.25	.15
35	Joe Christopher	.50	.25	.15
36	Dick Schofield	.60	.30	.20
37	Hal Smith	.50	.25	.15
38	Rocky Nelson	.50	.25	.15
39	Gino Cimoli	6.00	3.00	1.75
	(Photo actually Dick Schofield.)			
40	Danny Murtaugh	.50	.25	.15
41	Lenny Levy	.50	.25	.15
---	Gino Cimoli	.50	.25	.15
---	Roberto Clemente	12.00	6.00	3.50

1980 TCMA 1961 Cincinnati Reds

Virtually every member of the World Champion Cincinnati Reds team of 1961 is included in this collectors issue. Fronts of the 2-1/2" x 3-1/2" cards feature black-and-white player poses with red graphics. Backs are in black-and-white with personal data, 1961 and career stats and a short career summary.

		NM	EX	VG
Complete Set (41):		30.00	15.00	9.00
Common Player:		1.00	.50	.30
1	Eddie Kasko	1.00	.50	.30
2	Wally Post	1.00	.50	.30
3	Vada Pinson	2.50	1.25	.70
4	Frank Robinson	7.50	3.75	2.25
5	Pete Whisenant	1.00	.50	.30
6	Reggie Otero	1.00	.50	.30
7	Dick Sisler	1.00	.50	.30
8	Jim Turner	1.00	.50	.30
9	Fred Hutchinson	1.00	.50	.30
10	Gene Freese	1.00	.50	.30
11	Gordy Coleman	1.00	.50	.30
12	Don Blasingame	1.00	.50	.30
13	Gus Bell	1.00	.50	.30
14	Leo Cardenas	1.00	.50	.30
15	Elio Chacon	1.00	.50	.30
16	Dick Gernert	1.00	.50	.30
17	Jim Baumer	1.00	.50	.30
18	Willie Jones	1.00	.50	.30
19	Joe Gaines	1.00	.50	.30
20	Cliff Cook	1.00	.50	.30
21	Harry Anderson	1.00	.50	.30
22	Jerry Zimmerman	1.00	.50	.30
23	Johnny Edwards	1.00	.50	.30
24	Bob Schmidt	1.00	.50	.30
25	Darrell Johnson	1.00	.50	.30
26	Ed Bailey	1.00	.50	.30
27	Joey Jay	1.00	.50	.30
28	Jim O'Toole	1.00	.50	.30
29	Bob Purkey	1.00	.50	.30
30	Jim Brosnan	1.00	.50	.30
31	Ken Hunt	1.00	.50	.30
32	Ken Johnson	1.00	.50	.30
33	Jim Mahoney	1.00	.50	.30
34	Bill Henry	1.00	.50	.30
35	Jerry Lynch	1.00	.50	.30
36	Hal Bevan	1.00	.50	.30
37	Howie Nunn	1.00	.50	.30
38	Sherman Jones	1.00	.50	.30
39	Jay Hook	1.00	.50	.30
40	Claude Osteen	1.00	.50	.30
41	Marshall Bridges	1.00	.50	.30

1980 TCMA/Sports Nostalgia Store Babe Ruth

The same photo on the Babe Ruth card which appeared in TCMA's 1927 N.Y. Yankees set from 1979 was utilized by Sports Nostalgia as an advertising medium. On the back of the ad card is store information and an offer to redeem the card there for a free picture of Ruth. Production was 500 cards.

	NM	EX	VG
Babe Ruth	7.50	3.75	2.25

1978 Allen P. Terach Immortals of Baseball

These souvenir cards were issued as the first of what was intended to be a series honoring baseball's greatest players. No succeeding issues were forthcoming. The images on the 9" x 6-1/2" blank-back cards are printed in black-and-white and sepia. Fine print at the bottom states the card is part of an edition of 3,500. Issue price was just under $5 apiece.

		NM	EX	VG
	Souvenir Card:			
1	Babe Ruth, Joe DiMaggio	9.00	4.50	2.75
2	Ty Cobb, Stan Musial	6.00	3.00	1.75

1914 Texas Tommy Type 1 (E224)

Designated as E224 in the American Card Catalog these cards measure about 2-3/8" x 3-1/2". Fronts feature sepia-toned action photos with the player's name in capital letters and his team below in parenthesis. The back carries a lengthy player biography and most cards, although not all, include year-by-year statistics at the bottom. The words "Texas Tommy" appear at the top. Texas Tommy was a candy bar

brand from the Cardinet Candy Co., Oakland, Calif. The candy bar took its name from a popular dance of the era. Most examples of this set have been found in northern California. There is also a second variety of the set, smaller in size (1-7/8" x 3"), which have borderless pictures and a glossy finish. Gaps have been left in the assigned numbers on this checklist to accomodate future additions.

		NM	EX	VG
	Common Player:	5,850	2,925	1,755
(1)	Jimmy Archer	5,850	2,925	1,755
(2)	Jimmy Austin	5,850	2,925	1,755
(3)	Home Run Baker	9,750	4,875	2,925
(4)	Chief Bender	9,750	4,875	2,925
(5)	Bob Bescher	5,850	2,925	1,755
(6)	Ping Bodie	5,850	2,925	1,755
(7)	Donie Bush	5,850	2,925	1,755
(8)	Bobby Byrne	5,850	2,925	1,755
(9)	Nixey Callanan (Callahan)	5,850	2,925	1,755
(10)	Howie Camnitz	5,850	2,925	1,755
(11)	Frank Chance	9,750	4,875	2,925
(12)	Hal Chase	8,450	4,225	2,535
(13)	Ty Cobb	45,500	22,750	13,000
(14)	Jack Coombs	5,850	2,925	1,755
(15)	Sam Crawford	9,750	4,875	2,925
(16)	Birdie Cree	5,850	2,925	1,755
(17)	Al Demaree	5,850	2,925	1,755
(18)	Red Dooin	5,850	2,925	1,755
(19)	Larry Doyle	5,850	2,925	1,755
(20)	Johnny Evers	9,750	4,875	2,925
(21)	Vean Gregg	5,850	2,925	1,755
(22)	Bob Harmon	5,850	2,925	1,755
(23)	Joe Jackson	58,500	29,250	17,550
(24)	Walter Johnson	19,500	9,750	5,850
(25)	Otto Knabe	5,850	2,925	1,755
(26)	Nap Lajoie	9,750	4,875	2,925
(27)	Harry Lord	5,850	2,925	1,755
(28)	Connie Mack	9,750	4,875	2,925
(29)	Armando Marsans	5,850	2,925	1,755
(30)	Christy Mathewson	9,750	4,875	2,925
(31)	George McBride	5,850	2,925	1,755
(32)	John McGraw	9,750	4,875	2,925
(33)	Stuffy McInnis	5,850	2,925	1,755
(34)	Chief Meyers	5,850	2,925	1,755
(35)	Earl Moore	5,850	2,925	1,755
(36)	Mike Mowrey	5,850	2,925	1,755
(37)	Rebel Oakes	5,850	2,925	1,755
(38)	Marty O'Toole	5,850	2,925	1,755
(39)	Eddie Plank	13,000	6,500	3,900
(41)	Bud Ryan	5,850	2,925	1,755
(42)	Tris Speaker	16,250	8,125	4,875
(43)	Jake Stahl	5,850	2,925	1,755
(44)	Oscar Strange (Stanage)	5,850	2,925	1,755
(45)	Bill Sweeney	5,850	2,925	1,755
(46)	Honus Wagner	39,000	19,500	11,700
(47)	Ed Walsh	9,750	4,875	2,925
(48)	Zach Wheat	9,750	4,875	2,925
(49)	Harry Wolter	5,850	2,925	1,755
(50)	Joe Wood	7,150	3,575	2,145
(51)	Steve Yerkes	5,850	2,925	1,755
(52)	Heinie Zimmerman	5,850	2,925	1,755

1914 Texas Tommy Type 2 (E224)

Type 2 Texas Tommy cards are smaller in size, at about 1-7/8" x 3" to 3-1/16", have a glossy front surface and are blank-backed. Their only real link to the Type 1 Texas Tommy cards is the shared front on those players who appear in both checklists.

		NM	EX	VG
Common Player:		6,000	3,000	1,800
(1)	Ping Bodie	6,000	3,000	1,800
(2)	Larry Doyle	6,000	3,000	1,800
(3)	Vean Gregg	6,000	3,000	1,800
(4)	Harry Hooper	7,800	3,900	2,340
(5)	Walter Johnson	12,000	6,000	3,600
(6)	Connie Mack	7,800	3,900	2,340
(7)	Rube Marquard	7,800	3,900	2,340
(8)	Christy Mathewson	14,400	7,200	4,320
(9)	John McGraw	7,800	3,900	2,340
(10)	Chief Meyers	6,000	3,000	1,800
(11)	Fred Snodgrass	6,000	3,000	1,800
(12)	Jake Stahl	6,000	3,000	1,800
(13)	Honus Wagner	16,200	8,100	4,860
(14)	Joe Wood	6,600	3,300	1,980
(15)	Steve Yerkes	6,000	3,000	1,800

1928 Tharp's Ice Cream

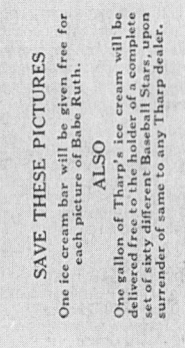

(6) BABE RUTH

Sharing the same format and checklist with several other contemporary ice cream sets this 60-card set includes all of the top stars of the day. Cards are printed in black-and-white on a 1-3/8" x 2-1/2" format. There appears to have been two different types issued, but the extent of each version is unknown. The variations are found in the player's name and card number which can appear either in a strip within the frame of the photo, or printed in the border beneath the photo. Card backs have a redemption offer that includes an ice cream bar in exchange for a Babe Ruth card, or a gallon of ice cream for a complete set of 60.

		NM	EX	VG
Complete Set (60):		20,000	8,000	4,000
Common Player:		115.00	90.00	20.00
1	Burleigh Grimes	225.00	90.00	45.00
2	Walter Reuther (Ruether)	115.00	45.00	20.00
3	Joe Dugan	115.00	45.00	20.00
4	Red Faber	225.00	90.00	45.00
5	Gabby Hartnett	225.00	90.00	45.00
6a	Babe Ruth (Portrait)	7,500	3,000	1,500
6b	Babe Ruth (Throwing)	7,500	3,000	1,500
7	Bob Meusel	115.00	45.00	20.00
8	Herb Pennock	225.00	90.00	45.00
9	George Burns	115.00	45.00	20.00
10	Joe Sewell	225.00	90.00	45.00
11	George Uhle	115.00	45.00	20.00
12	Bob O'Farrell	115.00	45.00	20.00
13	Rogers Hornsby	350.00	140.00	70.00
14	"Pie" Traynor	225.00	90.00	45.00
15	Clarence Mitchell	115.00	45.00	20.00
16a	Eppa Jepha Rixey	225.00	90.00	45.00
16b	Eppa Rixey	225.00	90.00	45.00
17	Carl Mays	115.00	45.00	20.00
18	Adolfo Luque	125.00	50.00	25.00
19	Dave Bancroft	225.00	90.00	45.00
20	George Kelly	225.00	90.00	45.00
21	Earl (Earle) Combs	225.00	90.00	45.00
22	Harry Heilmann	225.00	90.00	45.00
23a	Ray W. Schalk	225.00	90.00	45.00
23b	Ray Schalk	225.00	90.00	45.00
24	Johnny Mostil	115.00	45.00	20.00
25	Hack Wilson	225.00	90.00	45.00
26	Lou Gehrig	2,500	1,000	500.00
27	Ty Cobb	1,500	600.00	300.00
28	Tris Speaker	350.00	140.00	70.00
29	Tony Lazzeri	225.00	90.00	45.00
30	Waite Hoyt	225.00	90.00	45.00
31	Sherwood Smith	115.00	45.00	20.00
32	Max Carey	225.00	90.00	45.00
33	Eugene Hargrave	115.00	45.00	20.00
34	Miguel L. Gonzalez (Middle initial A.)	125.00	50.00	25.00
35	Joe Judge	115.00	45.00	20.00
36	E.C. (Sam) Rice	225.00	90.00	45.00
37	Earl Sheely	115.00	45.00	20.00
38	Sam Jones	115.00	45.00	20.00
39	Bib (Bibb) A. Falk	115.00	45.00	20.00
40	Willie Kamm	115.00	45.00	20.00
41	Stanley Harris	225.00	90.00	45.00
42	John J. McGraw	225.00	90.00	45.00
43	Artie Nehf	115.00	45.00	20.00
44	Grover Alexander	700.00	280.00	140.00
45	Paul Waner	225.00	90.00	45.00
46	William H. Terry (Photo actually Zeb Terry.)	225.00	90.00	45.00
47	Glenn Wright	115.00	45.00	20.00
48	Earl Smith	115.00	45.00	20.00
49	Leon (Goose) Goslin	225.00	90.00	45.00
50	Frank Frisch	225.00	90.00	45.00
51	Joe Harris	115.00	45.00	20.00

		NM	EX	VG
52	Fred (Cy) Williams	115.00	45.00	20.00
53	Eddie Roush	225.00	90.00	45.00
54	George Sisler	225.00	90.00	45.00
55	Ed. Rommel	115.00	45.00	20.00
56	Rogers Peckinpaugh (Roger)	115.00	45.00	20.00
57	Stanley Coveleskie (Coveleski)	225.00	90.00	45.00
58	Lester Bell	115.00	45.00	20.00
59	L. Waner	225.00	90.00	45.00
60	John P. McInnis	115.00	45.00	20.00

1978 The Card Coach Milwaukee Braves Greats

Stars of the Milwaukee Braves from the early 1950s through the early 1960s are featured in this collectors' issue. The 2-1/2" x 3-1/2" cards have black-and-white player photos on front with the player name in the white border at bottom. Backs are also in black-and-white with personal data, career summary and stats. Cards are numbered by uniform number.

		NM	EX	VG
Complete Set (15):		10.00	5.00	3.00
Common Player:		2.00	1.00	.60
1	Del Crandall	2.00	1.00	.60
4	Red Schoendienst	2.00	1.00	.60
8	Bob Uecker	2.50	1.25	.70
9	Joe Adcock	2.00	1.00	.60
10	Bob Buhl	2.00	1.00	.60
15	Joe Torre	2.50	1.25	.70
16	Carlton Willey	2.00	1.00	.60
21	Warren Spahn	3.00	1.50	.90
22	Johnny Logan	2.00	1.00	.60
33	Lew Burdette	2.00	1.00	.60
34	Billy Bruton	2.00	1.00	.60
41	Eddie Mathews	3.00	1.50	.90
43	Wes Covington	2.00	1.00	.60
44	Hank Aaron	7.50	3.75	2.25
48	Andy Pafko (Checklist)	2.00	1.00	.60

1971 Ticketron L.A. Dodgers/S.F. Giants

Essentially large team schedule cards with promotional dates noted and an ad for the ticket service, the Ticketron Dodgers/Giants cards of 1971 are similar in format. Each has a color photo on front with facsimile autograph. The Dodgers cards are 4" x 6" with no borders on fronts; the 3-3/4" x 5-3/4" Giants cards have a white border. Backs are white with red and blue printing. The unnumbered cards are checklisted here alphabetically within team.

		NM	EX	VG
Complete Dodgers Set (20):		75.00	37.00	22.00
Complete Giants Set (10):		150.00	75.00	45.00
Common Dodger Player:		3.00	1.50	.90
Common Giant Player:		6.00	3.00	1.75
LOS ANGELES DODGERS				
(1)	Richie Allen	15.00	7.50	4.50
(2)	Walter Alston	6.00	3.00	1.75
(3)	Jim Brewer	3.00	1.50	.90
(4)	Willie Crawford	3.00	1.50	.90
(5)	Willie Davis	4.50	2.25	1.25
(6)	Steve Garvey	20.00	10.00	6.00
(7)	Bill Grabarkewitz	3.00	1.50	.90
(8)	Jim Lefebvre	3.00	1.50	.90
(9)	Pete Mikkelsen	3.00	1.50	.90
(10)	Joe Moeller	3.00	1.50	.90
(11)	Manny Mota	4.50	2.25	1.25
(12)	Claude Osteen	3.00	1.50	.90
(13)	Wes Parker	3.00	1.50	.90
(14)	Bill Russell	4.50	2.25	1.25
(15)	Duke Sims	3.00	1.50	.90
(16)	Bill Singer	3.00	1.50	.90
(17)	Bill Sudakis	3.00	1.50	.90
(18)	Don Sutton	20.00	10.00	6.00
(19)	Maury Wills	7.50	3.75	2.25
(20)	Jerry Doggett, Vin Scully	3.00	1.50	.90

SAN FRANSICO GIANTS

		NM	EX	VG
(1)	Bobby Bonds	9.00	4.50	2.75
(2)	Dick Dietz	6.00	3.00	1.75
(3)	Charles Fox	6.00	3.00	1.75
(4)	Tito Fuentes	6.00	3.00	1.75
(5)	Ken Henderson	6.00	3.00	1.75
(6)	Juan Marichal	20.00	10.00	6.00
(7)	Willie Mays	60.00	30.00	18.00
(8)	Willie McCovey	25.00	12.50	7.50
(9)	Don McMahon	3.00	1.50	.90
(10)	Gaylord Perry	15.00	7.50	4.50

1972 Ticketron Phillies

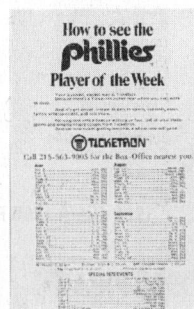

The Phillies' main off-site ticket outlet produced this set of schedule cards. Fronts are in horizontal 6" x 3-7/8" format with a color player photo at center. Backs are in black-and-white and include a Phillies home schedule and sponsor advertising. Because he was traded to the Expos in mid-season, the card of Tim McCarver is scarcer than the others.

		NM	EX	VG
Complete Set (10):		95.00	47.00	28.00
Common Player:		8.00	4.00	2.50
(1)	Mike Anderson	8.00	4.00	2.50
(2)	Larry Bowa	8.00	4.00	2.50
(3)	Steve Carlton	15.00	7.50	4.50
(4)	Deron Johnson	8.00	4.00	2.50
(5)	Frank Lucchesi	8.00	4.00	2.50
(6)	Greg Luzinski	10.00	5.00	3.00
(7)	Tim McCarver	35.00	17.50	10.50
(8)	Don Money	8.00	4.00	2.50
(9)	Willie Montanez	8.00	4.00	2.50
(10)	Dick Selma	8.00	4.00	2.50

1959 Ticoa Tires Frank Malzone

This black-and-white J.D. McCarthy postcard of the former Red Sox infielder was issued in conjunction with Malzone's endorsement of the Boston area tire store chain. The card measures 3-1/4" x 5-1/2" and has a blue facsimile autograph on front. A similar promotional postcard is listed under Molinari's Restaurant.

	NM	EX	VG
Frank Malzone	25.00	12.50	7.50

1910 Tip-Top Bread Pittsburgh Pirates (D322)

The previous season's World Champion Pittsburgh Pirates are featured in this issue. The cards have an unusual - for the era - nearly square (1-13/16" x 2-3/8") format. Fronts have pastel paintings of the subjects with identification in the white border below as "World's Champions." Backs have a checklist, ad for the bakery and offer to send the complete set of cards for 50 bread labels.

		NM	EX	VG
	Complete Set (25):	90,000	45,000	27,000
	Common Player:	2,000	1,000	600.00
1	Barney Dreyfuss (President)	10,000	7,000	4,000
2	William H. Locke (Secretary)	2,000	1,000	600.00
3	Fred Clarke	7,000	4,000	2,000
4	Honus Wagner	50,000	30,000	15,000
5	Tom Leach	2,000	1,000	600.00
6	George Gibson	2,000	1,000	600.00
7	Dots Miller	2,000	1,000	600.00
8	Howie Camnitz	2,000	1,000	600.00
9	Babe Adams	2,000	1,000	600.00
10	Lefty Leifield	2,000	1,000	600.00
11	Nick Maddox	2,000	1,000	600.00
12	Deacon Philippe	2,000	1,000	600.00
13	Bobby Byrne	2,000	1,000	600.00
14	Ed Abbaticchio	2,000	1,000	600.00
15	Lefty Webb	2,000	1,000	600.00
16	Vin Campbell	2,000	1,000	600.00
17	Owen Wilson	2,000	1,000	600.00
18	Sam Leever	2,000	1,000	600.00
19	Mike Simon	2,000	1,000	600.00
20	Ham Hyatt	2,000	1,000	600.00
21	Paddy O'Connor	2,000	1,000	600.00
22	John Flynn	2,350	1,000	600.00
23	Kirby White	2,000	1,000	600.00
24	Tip Top Boy Mascot	6,000	3,000	2,000
25	Forbes Field	4,000	2,000	1,500

1939 Tip-Top Bread Joe DiMaggio Pin

This 1-1/4" black-and-white photo portrait pin has a white background and printed endorsement for the Ward's brand. Similar pins were issued of boxer Billy Conn and hockey star Eddie Shore.

	NM	EX	VG
Joe DiMaggio	600.00	300.00	180.00

1947 Tip Top Bread

This 163-card set actually consists of a group of regional issues, some of which are scarcer than others. The 2-1/4" x 3" cards are borderless at top and sides, with a black-and-white player photo below which is a white strip containing the player identification. Backs carry an illustrated advertisement. The set is known for a quantity of obscure players, many of whom played during the talent-lean World War II seasons.

		NM	EX	VG
	Complete Set (163):	16,000	6,400	3,200
	Common Player:	60.00	25.00	12.50
(1)	Bill Ayers	60.00	25.00	12.50
(2)	Floyd Baker	100.00	40.00	20.00
(3)	Charles Barrett	100.00	40.00	20.00
(4)	Eddie Basinski	60.00	25.00	12.50
(5)	John Berardino	100.00	40.00	20.00
(6)	Larry Berra	500.00	200.00	100.00
(7)	Bill Bevens	100.00	40.00	20.00
(8)	Robert Blattner	60.00	25.00	12.50
(9)	Ernie Bonham	60.00	25.00	12.50
(10)	Bob Bragan	80.00	32.00	16.00
(11)	Ralph Branca	125.00	50.00	25.00
(12)	Alpha Brazle	60.00	25.00	12.50
(13)	Bobbie Brown (Bobby)	100.00	40.00	20.00
(14)	Mike Budnick	60.00	25.00	12.50
(15)	Ken Burkhart	60.00	25.00	12.50
(16)	Thomas Byrne	100.00	40.00	20.00
(17)	Earl Caldwell	100.00	40.00	20.00
(18)	"Hank" Camelli	100.00	40.00	20.00
(19)	Hugh Casey	80.00	32.00	16.00
(20)	Phil Cavarretta	100.00	40.00	20.00
(21)	Bob Chipman	100.00	40.00	20.00
(22)	Lloyd Christopher	100.00	40.00	20.00
(23)	Bill Cox	60.00	25.00	12.50

		NM	EX	VG
(24)	Bernard Creger	60.00	25.00	12.50
(25)	Frank Crosetti	100.00	40.00	20.00
(26)	Joffre Cross	60.00	25.00	12.50
(27)	Leon Culberson	100.00	40.00	20.00
(28)	Dick Culler	100.00	40.00	20.00
(29)	Dom DiMaggio	200.00	80.00	40.00
(30)	George Dickey	100.00	40.00	20.00
(31)	Chas. E. Diering	60.00	25.00	12.50
(32)	Joseph Dobson	100.00	40.00	20.00
(33)	Bob Doerr	260.00	105.00	52.00
(34)	Ervin Dusak	60.00	25.00	12.50
(35)	Bruce Edwards	60.00	24.00	12.00
(36)	Walter "Hoot" Evers	130.00	52.00	26.00
(37)	Clifford Fannin	60.00	25.00	12.50
(38)	"Nanny" Fernandez	100.00	40.00	20.00
(39)	Dave "Boo" Ferriss	100.00	40.00	20.00
(40)	Elbie Fletcher	60.00	25.00	12.50
(41)	Dennis Galehouse	60.00	25.00	12.50
(42)	Joe Garagiola	225.00	90.00	45.00
(43)	Sid Gordon	60.00	25.00	12.50
(44)	John Gorsica	100.00	40.00	20.00
(45)	Hal Gregg	60.00	24.00	12.00
(46)	Frank Gustine	60.00	25.00	12.50
(47)	Stanley Hack	100.00	40.00	20.00
(48)	Mickey Harris	100.00	40.00	20.00
(49)	Clinton Hartung	60.00	25.00	12.50
(50)	Joe Hatten	60.00	24.00	12.00
(51)	Frank Hayes	100.00	40.00	20.00
(52)	"Jeff" Heath	60.00	25.00	12.50
(53)	Tom Henrich	130.00	52.00	26.00
(54)	Gene Hermanski	60.00	24.00	12.00
(55)	Kirby Higbe	60.00	25.00	12.50
(56)	Ralph Hodgin	100.00	40.00	20.00
(57)	Tex Hughson	100.00	40.00	20.00
(58)	Fred Hutchinson	150.00	60.00	30.00
(59)	LeRoy Jarvis	60.00	25.00	12.50
(60)	"Si" Johnson	100.00	40.00	20.00
(61)	Don Johnson	100.00	40.00	20.00
(62)	Earl Johnson	80.00	32.00	16.00
(63)	John Jorgensen	60.00	24.00	12.00
(64)	Walter Judnick (Judnich)	60.00	25.00	12.50
(65)	Tony Kaufmann	60.00	25.00	12.50
(66)	George Kell	260.00	105.00	52.00
(67)	Charlie Keller	100.00	40.00	20.00
(68)	Bob Kennedy	100.00	40.00	20.00
(69)	Montia Kennedy	60.00	25.00	12.50
(70)	Ralph Kiner	140.00	56.00	28.00
(71)	Dave Koslo	60.00	25.00	12.50
(72)	Jack Kramer	60.00	25.00	12.50
(73)	Joe Kuhel	100.00	40.00	20.00
(74)	George Kurowski	60.00	25.00	12.50
(75)	Emil Kush	100.00	40.00	20.00
(76)	"Eddie" Lake	100.00	40.00	20.00
(77)	Harry Lavagetto	80.00	32.00	16.00
(78)	Bill Lee	100.00	40.00	20.00
(79)	Thornton Lee	60.00	25.00	12.50
(80)	Paul Lehner	60.00	25.00	12.50
(81)	John Lindell	100.00	40.00	20.00
(82)	Danny Litwhiler	100.00	40.00	20.00
(83)	"Mickey" Livingston	100.00	40.00	20.00
(84)	Carroll Lockman	60.00	25.00	12.50
(85)	Jack Lohrke	60.00	25.00	12.50
(86)	Ernie Lombardi	140.00	56.00	28.00
(87)	Vic Lombardi	60.00	24.00	12.00
(88)	Edmund Lopat	130.00	52.00	26.00
(89)	Harry Lowrey	100.00	40.00	20.00
(90)	Marty Marion	80.00	32.00	16.00
(91)	Willard Marshall	60.00	25.00	12.50
(92)	Phil Masi	100.00	40.00	20.00
(93)	Edward J. Mayo	100.00	40.00	20.00
(94)	Clyde McCullough	100.00	40.00	20.00
(95)	Frank Melton	100.00	40.00	20.00
(96)	Cass Michaels	100.00	40.00	20.00
(97)	Ed Miksis	100.00	40.00	20.00
(98)	Arthur Mills	100.00	40.00	20.00
(99)	Johnny Mize	140.00	56.00	28.00
(100)	Lester Moss	60.00	25.00	12.50
(101)	"Pat" Mullin	100.00	40.00	20.00
(102)	"Bob" Muncrief	60.00	25.00	12.50
(103)	George Munger	60.00	25.00	12.50
(104)	Fritz Ostermueller	60.00	25.00	12.50
(105)	James P. Outlaw	100.00	40.00	20.00
(106)	Frank "Stub" Overmire	100.00	40.00	20.00
(107)	Andy Pafko	100.00	40.00	20.00
(108)	Joe Page	100.00	40.00	20.00
(109)	Roy Partee	100.00	40.00	20.00
(110)	Johnny Pesky	100.00	40.00	20.00
(111)	Nelson Potter	60.00	25.00	12.50
(112)	Mel Queen	100.00	40.00	20.00
(113)	Marion Rackley	60.00	24.00	12.00
(114)	Al Reynolds	125.00	50.00	25.00
(115)	Del Rice	60.00	25.00	12.50
(116)	Marv Rickert	100.00	40.00	20.00
(117)	John Rigney	100.00	40.00	20.00
(118)	Phil Rizzuto	375.00	150.00	75.00
(119)	Aaron Robinson	100.00	40.00	20.00
(120)	"Preacher" Roe	80.00	32.00	16.00
(121)	Carvel Rowell	100.00	40.00	20.00
(122)	Jim Russell	60.00	25.00	12.50
(123)	Rip Russell	100.00	40.00	20.00
(124)	Connie Ryan	100.00	40.00	20.00
(125)	John Sain	100.00	40.00	20.00
(126)	Ray Sanders	100.00	40.00	20.00
(127)	Fred Sanford	60.00	25.00	12.50
(128)	Johnny Schmitz	100.00	40.00	20.00
(129)	Joe Schultz	60.00	25.00	12.50
(130)	"Rip" Sewell	60.00	25.00	12.50
(131)	Dick Sisler	60.00	25.00	12.50
(132)	"Sibby" Sisti	100.00	40.00	20.00
(133)	Enos Slaughter	130.00	52.00	26.00
(134)	"Billy" Southworth	100.00	40.00	20.00
(135)	Warren Spahn	475.00	190.00	95.00
(136)	Verne Stephens (Vern)	60.00	25.00	12.50
(137)	George Sternweiss (Stirnweiss)	100.00	40.00	20.00
(138)	Ed Stevens	60.00	24.00	12.00
(139)	Nick Strincevich	60.00	25.00	12.50
(140)	"Bobby" Sturgeon	100.00	40.00	20.00

		NM	EX	VG
(141)	Robt. "Bob" Swift	100.00	40.00	20.00
(142)	Geo. "Birdie" Tibbetts (Tebbetts)	100.00	40.00	20.00
(143)	"Mike" Tresh	100.00	40.00	20.00
(144)	Ken Trinkle	60.00	25.00	12.50
(145)	Paul "Diz" Trout	100.00	40.00	20.00
(146)	Virgil "Fire" Trucks	100.00	40.00	20.00
(147)	Thurman Tucker	100.00	40.00	20.00
(148)	Bill Voiselle	60.00	25.00	12.50
(149)	Hal Wagner	100.00	40.00	20.00
(150)	Honus Wagner	475.00	190.00	95.00
(151)	Eddy Waitkus	100.00	40.00	20.00
(152)	Richard "Dick" Wakefield	100.00	40.00	20.00
(153)	Jack Wallaesa	100.00	40.00	20.00
(154)	Charles Wensloff	100.00	40.00	20.00
(155)	Ted Wilks	60.00	25.00	12.50
(156)	Mickey Witek	60.00	25.00	12.50
(157)	"Jerry" Witte	60.00	25.00	12.50
(158)	Ed Wright	100.00	40.00	20.00
(159)	Taft Wright	100.00	40.00	20.00
(160)	Henry Wyse	100.00	40.00	20.00
(161)	"Rudy" York	100.00	40.00	20.00
(162)	Al Zarilla	60.00	25.00	12.50
(163)	Bill Zuber	125.00	50.00	25.00

1952 Tip Top Bread Labels

This unnumbered set of bread end-labels consists of 48 different labels, including two of Phil Rizzuto. The player's photo, name and team appear inside a star, with the words "Tip Top" printed above. The labels measure approximately 2-1/2" x 2-3/4". An advertising message appears in red on back. A large fold-out sheet to collect and display the labels was also issued. Each space is labeled with a player name and basic information, and is die-cut to allow the label to be slid in.

		NM	EX	VG
	Complete Set (48):	20,000	9,000	4,500
	Common Player:	400.00	180.00	100.00
	Display Sheet:	250.00	125.00	75.00
(1)	Hank Bauer	450.00	200.00	110.00
(2)	Yogi Berra	700.00	315.00	175.00
(3)	Ralph Branca	450.00	200.00	110.00
(4)	Lou Brissie	400.00	180.00	100.00
(5)	Roy Campanella	700.00	315.00	175.00
(6)	Phil Cavarreta (Cavarretta)	400.00	180.00	100.00
(7)	Murray Dickson (Murry)	400.00	180.00	100.00
(8)	Ferris Fain	400.00	180.00	100.00
(9)	Carl Furillo	450.00	200.00	110.00
(10)	Ned Garver	400.00	180.00	100.00
(11)	Sid Gordon	400.00	180.00	100.00
(12)	John Groth	400.00	180.00	100.00
(13)	Gran Hamner	400.00	180.00	100.00
(14)	Jim Hearn	400.00	180.00	100.00
(15)	Gene Hermanski	400.00	180.00	100.00
(16)	Gil Hodges	550.00	245.00	135.00
(17)	Larry Jansen	400.00	180.00	100.00
(18)	Eddie Joost	400.00	180.00	100.00
(19)	George Kell	500.00	225.00	125.00
(20)	Dutch Leonard	400.00	180.00	100.00
(21)	Whitey Lockman	400.00	180.00	100.00
(22)	Ed Lopat	450.00	200.00	110.00
(23)	Sal Maglie	400.00	180.00	100.00
(24)	Mickey Mantle	4,500	2,000	1,125
(25)	Gil McDougald	450.00	200.00	110.00
(26)	Dale Mitchell	400.00	180.00	100.00
(27)	Don Mueller	400.00	180.00	100.00
(28)	Andy Pafko	400.00	180.00	100.00
(29)	Bob Porterfield	400.00	180.00	100.00
(30)	Ken Raffensberger	400.00	180.00	100.00
(31)	Allie Reynolds	450.00	200.00	110.00
(32a)	Phil Rizzuto (Rizzuto) ("NY" shows on shirt.)	600.00	275.00	150.00
(32b)	Phil Rizutto (Rizzuto) (No "NY" visible on shirt.)	600.00	275.00	150.00
(33)	Robin Roberts	550.00	245.00	135.00
(34)	Saul Rogovin	400.00	180.00	100.00
(35)	Ray Scarborough	400.00	180.00	100.00
(36)	Red Schoendienst	500.00	225.00	125.00
(37)	Dick Sisler	400.00	180.00	100.00
(38)	Enos Slaughter	500.00	225.00	125.00
(39)	Duke Snider	600.00	275.00	150.00
(40)	Warren Spahn	600.00	275.00	150.00
(41)	Vern Stephens	400.00	180.00	100.00
(42)	Earl Torgeson	400.00	180.00	100.00
(43)	Mickey Vernon	400.00	180.00	100.00
(44)	Ed Waitkus	400.00	180.00	100.00
(45)	Wes Westrum	400.00	180.00	100.00
(46)	Eddie Yost	400.00	180.00	100.00
(47)	Al Zarilla	400.00	180.00	100.00

1887 Tobin Lithographs Color

The Tobin lithographs, measuring about 3" x 4-1/2", are typical of the "trade" cards that were popular advertising vehicles in the late 19th Century. Found in both black-and-white and color, the lithos include 10 cards depicting caricature action drawings of popular baseball players of the era. Each cartoon-like drawing is accompanied by a colorful caption along with the player's name in parenthesis below. The team affiliation is printed in the upper-left corner, while a large space in the upper-right corner was left blank to accomodate advertising messages. As a result, Tobin cards can be found with ads for various products and services or left blank. Similarly the backs of the cards are also found either blank or with advertising. The set takes its name from the manufacturer, whose name ("Tobin N.Y.") appears in the lower-right corner of each card.

		NM	EX	VG
Complete Set (10):		6,650	2,650	1,325
Common Player:		675.00	275.00	135.00
(1)	"Go It Old Boy" (Ed Andrews)	675.00	275.00	135.00
(2)	"Oh, Come Off!" (Cap Anson)	1,325	525.00	275.00
(3)	"Watch Me Soak it" (Dan Brouthers)	800.00	325.00	160.00
(4)	"Not Onto It" (Charlie Ferguson)	675.00	275.00	135.00
(5)	"Struck By A Cyclone" (Pebbly Jack Glasscock)	675.00	275.00	135.00
(6)	"An Anxious Moment" (Paul Hines)	675.00	275.00	135.00
(7)	"Where'l You Have It?" (Tim Keefe)	800.00	325.00	160.00
(8)	"The Flower Of The Flock" (Our Own Kelly)	1,000	400.00	200.00
(9)	"A Slide For Home" (Jim M'Cormick) (McCormick)	675.00	275.00	135.00
(10)	"Ain't It A Daisy?" (Smiling Mickey Welch)	800.00	325.00	160.00

1887 Tobin Lithographs B/W

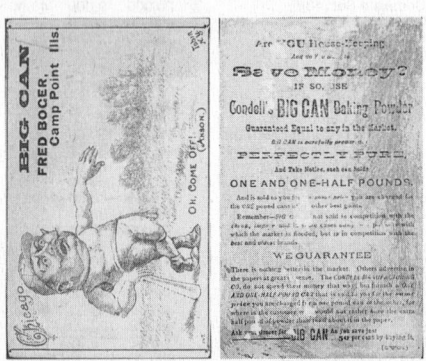

The black-and-white Tobin Lithographs were likely created to offer 19th Century advertisers a lower-cost venue than the lavishly colored version of the same cards. It appears, however, that most advertisers opted for the color type and/or that the color cards were saved more often because the black-and-white cards are today many times scarcer than their color counterparts. Despite the disparity in rarity, the black-and-whites carry only a modest premium value over the color, again probably attributable to the grander overall appearance of the colored cards.

		NM	EX	VG
Complete Set (10):		12,500	5,000	2,500
Common Player:		1,250	500.00	250.00
(1)	"Go It Old Boy" (Ed Andrews)	1,250	500.00	250.00
(2)	"Oh, Come Off!" (Cap Anson)	2,500	1,000	500.00
(3)	"Watch Me Soak it" (Dan Brouthers)	1,500	600.00	300.00
(4)	"Not Onto It" (Charlie Ferguson)	1,250	500.00	250.00
(5)	"Struck By A Cyclone" (Pebbly Jack Glasscock)	1,250	500.00	250.00
(6)	"An Anxious Moment" (Paul Hines)	1,250	500.00	250.00
(7)	"Where'l You Have It?" (Tim Keefe)	1,500	600.00	300.00
(8)	"The Flower Of The Flock" (Our Own Kelly)	1,900	760.00	380.00
(9)	"A Slide For Home" (Jim M'Cormick) (McCormick)	1,250	500.00	250.00
(10)	"Ain't It A Daisy?" (Smiling Mickey Welch)	1,500	600.00	300.00

1948-1949 Toleteros

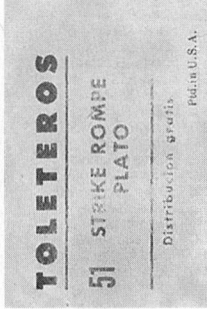

HILTON SMITH

This was the first of three annual issues during the Puerto Rican League winter seasons. Cards are about 1-1/2" x 2-1/4", printed in sepia on thin cardboard. Backs are printed in black-and-white and have a "play" designation for use in a card game. They are numbered, but the numbers are not unique to specific players. Several of the cards were issued in photographic format, rather than printed. It is believed these are scarcer than the regular cards and may account for most of the seven cards which are not currently checklisted. They are designated here with a (P) notation. This checklist is presented alphabetically. An album was issued with the set, and like most contemporary Caribbean issues, cards are usually found in well-used condition with evidence of past mounting. Toleteros is roughly translated as "sluggers."

		NM	EX	VG
Complete Set (168):				
Value Undetermined				
Common Player:		150.00	75.00	45.00
Album:				
(1)	Yuyo Acosta	150.00	75.00	45.00
(2)	Hector Agosto	150.00	75.00	45.00
(3)	Alberto Alberdeston	150.00	75.00	45.00
(4)	Alberto Alicea	150.00	75.00	45.00
(5)	Jaime Almendro	150.00	75.00	45.00
(6)	Guinea Alomar	150.00	75.00	45.00
(7)	Pedro Alomar	150.00	75.00	45.00
(8)	Alfredo Alonso	150.00	75.00	45.00
(9)	Yiyo Alonso	150.00	75.00	45.00
(10)	Pablo Andino	150.00	75.00	45.00
(11)	Jueyito Andrade	150.00	75.00	45.00
(12)	Paday Anglero	150.00	75.00	45.00
(13)	Luis Arroyo	200.00	100.00	60.00
(14)	Pedro J. Arroyo	150.00	75.00	45.00
(15)	Joe Atkins (P)	300.00	150.00	90.00
(16)	Eugene Baker	300.00	150.00	90.00
(17)	Dan Bankhead	300.00	150.00	90.00
(18)	Bennett	150.00	75.00	45.00
(19)	Carlos Bernier	200.00	100.00	60.00
(20)	Hiram Bithorn	250.00	125.00	75.00
(21)	Efrain Blasini	150.00	75.00	45.00
(22)	Oswaldo Brau	150.00	75.00	45.00
(23)	Johnny Britton	150.00	75.00	45.00
(25)	George Brown	150.00	75.00	45.00
(26)	Willard Brown	4,500	2,250	1,350
(27)	Jose Burgos	150.00	75.00	45.00
(28)	Tommy Butts	1,200	600.00	360.00
(29)	Joe Buzas	150.00	75.00	45.00
(30)	Luis R. Cabrera	150.00	75.00	45.00
(31)	Marzo Cabrera	150.00	75.00	45.00
(32)	Eugenio Camara	150.00	75.00	45.00
(33)	Juan Carrero	150.00	75.00	45.00
(34)	Medina Chapman	150.00	75.00	45.00
(35)	Fernando Clara	150.00	75.00	45.00
(36)	Buster Clarkson (P)	800.00	400.00	240.00
(37)	Francisco Coimbre	1,000	500.00	300.00
(38)	Eugene Collins	400.00	200.00	120.00
(39)	Cefo Conde	150.00	75.00	45.00
(40)	Johnny Cox	150.00	75.00	45.00
(41)	Vitin Cruz	150.00	75.00	45.00
(42)	Johnny Davis	500.00	250.00	150.00
(43)	Piper Davis	500.00	250.00	150.00
(44)	Felle Delgado	150.00	75.00	45.00
(45)	Luke Easter	500.00	250.00	150.00
(46)	Howard Easterling	600.00	300.00	180.00
(47)	Saturnino Escalera	150.00	75.00	45.00
(49)	Teggy Espinosa	150.00	75.00	45.00
(50)	Coco Ferrer	150.00	75.00	45.00
(51)	Wilmer Fields	400.00	200.00	120.00
(52)	Tite Figueroa	150.00	75.00	45.00
(53)	Oscar Mir Flores	150.00	75.00	45.00
(54)	Jesus M. Freyre	150.00	75.00	45.00
(55)	Cinque Garcia	150.00	75.00	45.00
(56)	Alfonso Gerard	150.00	75.00	45.00
(57)	Jim Gilliam (P)	800.00	400.00	240.00
(58)	Charlie Glock	150.00	75.00	45.00
(59)	Ruben Gomez	250.00	125.00	75.00
(60)	David Gonzalez	150.00	75.00	45.00
(61)	Gely Goyco	150.00	75.00	45.00
(62)	Jack Graham	150.00	75.00	45.00
(63)	Roberto Griffith	600.00	300.00	180.00
(64)	Jesus Guilbe	150.00	75.00	45.00
(65)	Juan Guilbe	150.00	75.00	45.00
(66)	Hector Haddock	150.00	75.00	45.00
(67)	Sam Hairston	200.00	100.00	60.00
(68)	Van Harrington	150.00	75.00	45.00
(69)	Luman Harris	150.00	75.00	45.00
(70)	Manuel Hernandez	150.00	75.00	45.00
(71)	Efrain Hidalgo	150.00	75.00	45.00
(72)	Dixie Howell	150.00	75.00	45.00
(73)	Jim Lamarque (P)	800.00	400.00	240.00
(75)	Carlos Lanauze	150.00	75.00	45.00

		NM	EX	VG
(76)	Ramon Lasa	150.00	75.00	45.00
(77)	Lee Layton	150.00	75.00	45.00
(78)	Liebould	150.00	75.00	45.00
(79)	Royce Lint	150.00	75.00	45.00
(80)	Radames Lopez	150.00	75.00	45.00
(81)	Louis Louden	250.00	125.00	75.00
(82)	Robert Lynn	150.00	75.00	45.00
(83)	Caro Maldonado	150.00	75.00	45.00
(84)	Canena Marquez	500.00	250.00	150.00
(85)	Antonio Marrero	150.00	75.00	45.00
(86)	Gilberto Marrero	150.00	75.00	45.00
(87)	Humberto Marti	150.00	75.00	45.00
(88)	Millito Martinez	150.00	75.00	45.00
(89)	Jose E. Montalvo	150.00	75.00	45.00
(90)	Luis Morales	150.00	75.00	45.00
(91)	Willie Morales	150.00	75.00	45.00
(92)	Howard Moss	150.00	75.00	45.00
(93)	Chaguin Muratti	150.00	75.00	45.00
(94)	Domingo Navarro	150.00	75.00	45.00
(95)	Millito Navarro	200.00	100.00	60.00
(97)	Alfredo Olivencia	150.00	75.00	45.00
(98)	Guayubin Olivo	200.00	100.00	60.00
(99)	Noel Oquendo	150.00	75.00	45.00
(100)	Otoniel Ortiz	150.00	75.00	45.00
(101)	Rafaelito Ortiz	150.00	75.00	45.00
(102)	Alberto Padilla	150.00	75.00	45.00
(103)	Fernando Diaz Pedroso	200.00	100.00	60.00
(104)	Victor Pellot (Power)	250.00	125.00	75.00
(105)	Pedro Pena	150.00	75.00	45.00
(106)	Pepin Pereira	150.00	75.00	45.00
(107)	Ismael Perez	150.00	75.00	45.00
(108)	Juan Perez	150.00	75.00	45.00
(109)	Palomo Perez	150.00	75.00	45.00
(110)	Villodas Perez	150.00	75.00	45.00
(111)	Alonso Perry	500.00	250.00	150.00
(112)	Jose Polanco	150.00	75.00	45.00
(113)	Bill Powell	200.00	100.00	60.00
(114)	Tomas Quinones	200.00	100.00	60.00
(115)	R. Cuebas Quintana	150.00	75.00	45.00
(116)	Milton Ralat	150.00	75.00	45.00
(117)	Otto Ralat	150.00	75.00	45.00
(118)	Fernando Ramos	150.00	75.00	45.00
(119)	Xavier Rescigno	150.00	75.00	45.00
(121)	Miguel L. Rivera	150.00	75.00	45.00
(122)	Charlie Rivero	150.00	75.00	45.00
(123)	Bienvenido Rodriguez	150.00	75.00	45.00
(124)	Pedro Rodriguez	150.00	75.00	45.00
(125)	Anastasio Rosario	150.00	75.00	45.00
(126)	Jorge Rosas	150.00	75.00	45.00
(127)	Cafe Salaberrios	150.00	75.00	45.00
(128)	Wilfredo Salas	150.00	75.00	45.00
(129)	Juan Sanchez	150.00	75.00	45.00
(130)	Carlos M. Santiago	150.00	75.00	45.00
(131)	Jose G. Santiago (P)	400.00	200.00	120.00
(132)	Ed Sauer	150.00	75.00	45.00
(133)	George Scales	1,200	600.00	360.00
(134)	Kermit Schmidt	150.00	75.00	45.00
(135)	Ken Sears (P)	400.00	200.00	120.00
(136)	Herbert Sewell (Souell)	250.00	125.00	75.00
(137)	Dwain Sloat	150.00	75.00	45.00
(138)	Eugene Smith	200.00	100.00	60.00
(139)	Hilton Smith	20,000	10,000	6,000
(140)	John Ford Smith	400.00	200.00	120.00
(141)	Fernando Sola	150.00	75.00	45.00
(142)	Ismael Solla	150.00	75.00	45.00
(143)	Francisco Sostre	150.00	75.00	45.00
(144)	Earl Taborn	200.00	100.00	60.00
(145)	Freddie Thon	150.00	75.00	45.00
(146)	Bob Thurman	400.00	200.00	120.00
(147)	Griffin Tirado	150.00	75.00	45.00
(148)	Leon Tirado	150.00	75.00	45.00
(149)	Pedro J. Toro	150.00	75.00	45.00
(150)	Bin Torres	150.00	75.00	45.00
(151)	Carmelo Torres	150.00	75.00	45.00
(152)	Onofre Torres	150.00	75.00	45.00
(153)	Penpen Torres	150.00	75.00	45.00
(154)	Quincy Trouppe	1,000	500.00	300.00
(155)	Foca Valentin	150.00	75.00	45.00
(156)	Roberto Vargas	150.00	75.00	45.00
(157)	Tetelo Vargas	1,000	500.00	300.00
(158)	Rafael Vasquez	150.00	75.00	45.00
(159)	Guillermo Vega	150.00	75.00	45.00
(160)	Jose L. Velazquez	150.00	75.00	45.00
(161)	Laru Velazquez	150.00	75.00	45.00
(162)	Vicente Villafane	150.00	75.00	45.00
(165)	Luis Villodas	200.00	100.00	60.00
(166)	Jesse Williams	200.00	100.00	60.00
(167)	Artie Wilson	500.00	250.00	150.00
(168)	Rogelio Wiscovich	150.00	75.00	45.00

1949-1950 Toleteros

LEON DAY

The second of three annual issues during the Puerto Rican League winter seasons, these cards are similar in format to the previous year's set. Front photos are printed in black-and-white, and the backs are printed in red. Cards are about 1-1/2" x 2-1/4", printed on thin cardboard with a light gloss. Backs have a "play" designation for use in a card game and are numbered, though the numbers are not unique to specific players. This checklist is presented alphabetically. Some players can be found in two different poses. Where the variations are known, they are described parenthetically; where the poses are not known, an asterisk is shown. Players with a (P) designation were produced on photographic, rather than printed stock and are scarcer than the regular cards. An album was issued with the set, and like most contemporary Caribbean issues, cards are usually found in well-used condition with evidence of past mounting. Toleteros is roughly translated as "sluggers."

		NM	EX	VG
Complete Set (216):				
Value Undetermined				
Common Player:		100.00	50.00	30.00
Album:		600.00	300.00	180.00
(1)	Hector Agosto	100.00	50.00	30.00
(2)	Alberto Alberdeston	100.00	50.00	30.00
(3)	Alberto Alicea	100.00	50.00	30.00
(4)	Jaime Almendro (*)	100.00	50.00	30.00
(5)	Guinea Alomar	100.00	50.00	30.00
(6)	Pedro Alomar	100.00	50.00	30.00
(7)	Alfredo Alonso	100.00	50.00	30.00
(8)	Yiyo Alonso	100.00	50.00	30.00
(9)	Ismael Alvarado	100.00	50.00	30.00
(10)	Manuel Alvarez (*)	100.00	50.00	30.00
(11)	Pablo Andino	100.00	50.00	30.00
(12)	Jueyito Andrade	100.00	50.00	30.00
(13)	Paday Anglero	100.00	50.00	30.00
(14)	Luis Arroyo (*)	125.00	65.00	40.00
(15)	Pedro J. Arroyo	100.00	50.00	30.00
(16)	Eugene Baker	150.00	75.00	45.00
(17)	Dan Bankhead	150.00	75.00	45.00
(18)	Sammy Bankhead	300.00	150.00	90.00
(19)	Ramon Bayron	100.00	50.00	30.00
(20)	Carlos Bernier	125.00	65.00	40.00
(21)	Hiram Bithorn	200.00	100.00	60.00
(22)	Efrain Blasini	100.00	50.00	30.00
(23)	Anil Bonilla (*)	100.00	50.00	30.00
(24)	Stan Bread (Breard)	100.00	50.00	30.00
(25)	Chester Brewer	1,000	500.00	300.00
(26)	Johnny Britton	100.00	50.00	30.00
(27)	George Brown	100.00	50.00	30.00
(28)	Willard Brown (*)	3,600	1,800	1,075
(29)	J.A. Burgos (*)	100.00	50.00	30.00
(30)	Tommy Butts	300.00	150.00	90.00
(31)	Joe Buzas	100.00	50.00	30.00
(32)	Rafael Cabezudo	100.00	50.00	30.00
(33)	Luis R. Cabrera	100.00	50.00	30.00
(34)	Marzo Cabrera	100.00	50.00	30.00
(35)	Manolete Caceres (*)	100.00	50.00	30.00
(36)	Eugenio Camara	100.00	50.00	30.00
(37)	Maximo Casals	100.00	50.00	30.00
(38)	Rafael Casanovas	100.00	50.00	30.00
(39)	Nino Zurdo Castro	100.00	50.00	30.00
(40)	Perucho Cepeda (*)	500.00	250.00	150.00
(41)	Medina Chapman	100.00	50.00	30.00
(42)	T. Gomez Checo	100.00	50.00	30.00
(43)	Buster Clarkson	300.00	150.00	90.00
(44)	Francisco Coimbre	400.00	200.00	120.00
(45a)	Eugene Collins (Chest-up.)	200.00	100.00	60.00
(45b)	Eugene Collins (Waist-up.)	200.00	100.00	60.00
(46)	Luis Colmenero	100.00	50.00	30.00
(47)	Luis Colon	100.00	50.00	30.00
(48)	Monchile Concepcion (*)	125.00	65.00	40.00
(49)	Cefo Conde	100.00	50.00	30.00
(50)	Omar Cordero	100.00	50.00	30.00
(51)	Johnny Cox	100.00	50.00	30.00
(52)	Vitin Cruz	100.00	50.00	30.00
(53)	Johnny Davis	400.00	200.00	120.00
(54)	Lomax Davis	125.00	65.00	40.00
(55)	Piper Davis	200.00	100.00	60.00
(56)	Leon Day	12,000	6,000	3,600
(57)	Felle Delgado	100.00	50.00	30.00
(58)	Carmelo Delpin	100.00	50.00	30.00
(59)	Ruben Diaz	100.00	50.00	30.00
(60)	Lucius Easter	300.00	150.00	90.00
(61)	Howard Easterling	200.00	100.00	60.00
(62)	Saturnino Escalera	100.00	50.00	30.00
(63)	Teggy Espinosa	100.00	50.00	30.00
(64)	George Fallon	100.00	50.00	30.00
(65)	Coco Ferrer (*)	100.00	50.00	30.00
(66)	Walter Fialla (Fiala)	100.00	50.00	30.00
(67)	Wilmer Fields (*)	300.00	150.00	90.00
(68)	Tite Figueroa	100.00	50.00	30.00
(69)	Oscar Mir Flores	100.00	50.00	30.00
(70)	Jesus M. Freyre	100.00	50.00	30.00
(71)	Les Fusselman (Fusselman)	100.00	50.00	30.00
(72)	Cinque Garcia	100.00	50.00	30.00
(73)	Alfonso Gerard	100.00	50.00	30.00
(74)	Alban Glossopp (Glossop)	100.00	50.00	30.00
(75)	Ruben Gomez (*)	150.00	75.00	45.00
(76)	Faelo Gonzalez (P)	200.00	100.00	60.00
(77)	Rafael Gonzalez	100.00	50.00	30.00
(78)	Gely Goyco	100.00	50.00	30.00
(79)	Jack Graham	100.00	50.00	30.00
(80)	Bill Greason	125.00	65.00	40.00
(81)	Felo Guilbe	100.00	50.00	30.00
(82)	Jesus Guilbe	100.00	50.00	30.00
(83)	Juan Guilbe	100.00	50.00	30.00
(84)	Hector Haddock	100.00	50.00	30.00
(85)	Sam Hairston	150.00	75.00	45.00
(86)	Luman Harris	100.00	50.00	30.00
(87a)	Vic Harris (Black background.)	1,000	500.00	300.00
(87b)	Vic Harris (Outdoors background.)	1,000	500.00	300.00
(88)	Angel Hernaiz (P)	200.00	100.00	60.00
(89)	Manuel Hernandez	100.00	50.00	30.00
(90)	Efrain Hidalgo	100.00	50.00	30.00
(91)	Dixie Howell	100.00	50.00	30.00
(92)	Roy Hughes (*)	100.00	50.00	30.00
(93)	Natalio Irizarry	100.00	50.00	30.00
(94)	Walter James	100.00	50.00	30.00
(95)	Cecyl Kayser (P)	300.00	150.00	90.00
(96)	Jack Krauss	100.00	50.00	30.00
(97)	Jim Lamarque	200.00	100.00	60.00
(98)	Carlos Lanauze	100.00	50.00	30.00
(99)	Ramon Lasa	100.00	50.00	30.00
(100)	Rafael Lastra	100.00	50.00	30.00
(101)	Lee Layton	100.00	50.00	30.00
(102)	Lettish	100.00	50.00	30.00
(103)	Johnny Logan	100.00	50.00	30.00
(104)	Radames Lopez	100.00	50.00	30.00
(105)	Louis Louden	150.00	75.00	45.00
(106)	Robert Lynn	100.00	50.00	30.00
(107)	Al Lyons	100.00	50.00	30.00
(108)	Cirico Machuca	100.00	50.00	30.00
(109)	Caro Maldonado	100.00	50.00	30.00
(110)	Clifford Mapes	100.00	50.00	30.00
(111)	Jim Markland (P)	200.00	100.00	60.00
(112)	Canena Marquez	200.00	100.00	60.00
(113)	Leo Marquez	100.00	50.00	30.00
(114)	Antonio Marrero (*)	100.00	50.00	30.00
(115)	Gilberto Marrero	100.00	50.00	30.00
(116)	Humberto Marti	100.00	50.00	30.00
(117)	Achin Matos	100.00	50.00	30.00
(118)	Booker McDaniels	150.00	75.00	45.00
(119)	George McQuillen	100.00	50.00	30.00
(120)	Agustin Medina	100.00	50.00	30.00
(121)	John Medina	100.00	50.00	30.00
(122)	Vicente Medina	100.00	50.00	30.00
(123)	Henry Miller (P)	300.00	150.00	90.00
(124)	Jose E. Montalvo	100.00	50.00	30.00
(125)	Luis A. Morales (*)	100.00	50.00	30.00
(126)	Pedroso Morales	100.00	50.00	30.00
(127)	Willie Morales	100.00	50.00	30.00
(128)	Howard Moss	100.00	50.00	30.00
(129)	Gallego Munoz	100.00	50.00	30.00
(130)	Digno Navarro	100.00	50.00	30.00
(131)	Domingo Navarro	100.00	50.00	30.00
(132)	Millito Navarro	125.00	65.00	40.00
(133)	Earl Naylor (P)	200.00	100.00	60.00
(134)	Alfredo Olivencia	100.00	50.00	30.00
(135)	Guayubin Olivo	125.00	65.00	40.00
(136)	Noel Oquendo	100.00	50.00	30.00
(137)	Otoniel Ortiz	100.00	50.00	30.00
(138)	Rafaelito Ortiz	100.00	50.00	30.00
(139)	Alberto Padilla	100.00	50.00	30.00
(140)	Miguel Payano (P)	200.00	100.00	60.00
(141)	Fernando Diaz Pedroso (*)	125.00	65.00	40.00
(142)	Victor Pellot (Power)	150.00	75.00	45.00
(143)	Pedro Pena	100.00	50.00	30.00
(144)	Pepin Pereira (*)	100.00	50.00	30.00
(145)	Ismael Perez	100.00	50.00	30.00
(146)	Juan Perez	100.00	50.00	30.00
(147)	Palomo Perez	100.00	50.00	30.00
(148)	Rogelio Perez	100.00	50.00	30.00
(149)	Villodas Perez	100.00	50.00	30.00
(150)	Alonso Perry	200.00	100.00	60.00
(151)	Russ Peters	100.00	50.00	30.00
(152)	Jose Polanco	100.00	50.00	30.00
(153)	Bill Powell	100.00	50.00	30.00
(154)	Thomas Quinones (*)	125.00	65.00	40.00
(155)	Milton Ralat	100.00	50.00	30.00
(156)	Otto Ralat	100.00	50.00	30.00
(157)	Fernando Ramos	100.00	50.00	30.00
(158)	Lionel Richards	100.00	50.00	30.00
(159)	Reinoso Reinoso	100.00	50.00	30.00
(160)	Xavier Rescigno	100.00	50.00	30.00
(161)	Miguel L. Rivera	100.00	50.00	30.00
(162)	Bienvenido Rodriguez	100.00	50.00	30.00
(163)	Pedro Rodriguez	100.00	50.00	30.00
(164)	Jose M. Roque	100.00	50.00	30.00
(165)	Fachy Rosado	100.00	50.00	30.00
(166)	Jorge Rosas	100.00	50.00	30.00
(167)	Ramon Salgado (*)	100.00	50.00	30.00
(168)	Juan Sanchez	100.00	50.00	30.00
(169)	Carlos M. Santiago	100.00	50.00	30.00
(170)	Jose G. Santiago	100.00	50.00	30.00
(171)	Ed Sauer (*)	100.00	50.00	30.00
(172)	George Scales	800.00	400.00	240.00
(173)	Kermit Schmidt (*)	100.00	50.00	30.00
(174)	Ken Sears	100.00	50.00	30.00
(175)	Dick Seay	700.00	350.00	210.00
(176)	Jose Seda	100.00	50.00	30.00
(177)	Barney Serrell	200.00	100.00	60.00
(178)	McDuffie Sevilla (*)	100.00	50.00	30.00
(179)	Dwain Sloat	100.00	50.00	30.00
(180)	Eugene Smith	125.00	65.00	40.00
(181)	Hilton Smith	12,000	6,000	3,600
(182)	John Ford Smith	150.00	75.00	45.00
(183)	Jerome Snider	100.00	50.00	30.00
(184)	Ismael Solla	100.00	50.00	30.00
(185)	Francisco Sostre	100.00	50.00	30.00
(186)	Herb Souell	100.00	50.00	30.00
(187)	Luis St. Clair	100.00	50.00	30.00
(188)	Tetelo Sterling	100.00	50.00	30.00
(189)	Lonnie Summers	125.00	65.00	40.00
(190)	Jim Tabor (*)	100.00	50.00	30.00
(191)	Earl Taborn	100.00	50.00	30.00
(192)	Israel Ten (*)	100.00	50.00	30.00
(193)	Leo Thomas	100.00	50.00	30.00
(194)	Freddie Thon	100.00	50.00	30.00
(195)	Bob Thurman (*)	200.00	100.00	60.00
(196)	Griffin Tirado (*)	100.00	50.00	30.00
(197)	Leon Tirado	100.00	50.00	30.00
(198)	Bin Torres	100.00	50.00	30.00
(199)	Carmelo Torres	100.00	50.00	30.00
(200)	Indian Torres	100.00	50.00	30.00
(201)	Quincy Trouppe	700.00	350.00	210.00
(202)	Hector Trussa	100.00	50.00	30.00
(203)	Foca Valentin	100.00	50.00	30.00
(204)	Roberto Vargas	100.00	50.00	30.00
(205)	Tetelo Vargas	300.00	150.00	90.00
(206)	Rafael Vazquez	100.00	50.00	30.00
(207)	Guillermo Vega	100.00	50.00	30.00
(208)	Jose L. Velazquez	100.00	50.00	30.00
(209)	Vicente Villafane (*)	100.00	50.00	30.00
(210)	Luis Villodas	100.00	50.00	30.00
(211)	Curley Williams (P)	300.00	150.00	90.00
(212)	Marvin Williams (P)	300.00	150.00	90.00
(213)	Artie Wilson	300.00	150.00	90.00
(214)	Robert Wilson (*)	100.00	50.00	30.00
(215)	Rogelio Wiscovich	100.00	50.00	30.00
(216)	Rafael Zavala	100.00	50.00	30.00

1950-1951 Toleteros

JOSHUA GIBSON

The last of three annual issues during the Puerto Rican League winter seasons, these cards are similar in format to the previous years' sets, with the principal difference being that the approximately 1-3/4" x 2-1/2" cards are printed in color rather than black-and-white. Most are printed on thin cardboard, but some are produced on photographic stock and believed to be scarcer than the others. Those are designated with a (P) in the checklist. Unlike the previous years' issues, backs are blank. This checklist is presented alphabetically. An album was issued with the set, and like most contemporary Caribbean issues, cards are usually found in well-used condition with evidence of past mounting. Toleteros is roughly translated as "sluggers."

		NM	EX	VG
Complete Set (192):				
Value Undetermined				
Common Player:		60.00	30.00	18.00
Album:		300.00	150.00	90.00
(1)	Hector Agosto	60.00	30.00	18.00
(2)	Robert Alexander	60.00	30.00	18.00
(3)	Alberto Alicea	60.00	30.00	18.00
(4)	Jaime Almendro (Blue Senadores.)	60.00	30.00	18.00
(5)	Jaime Almendro (Red Senadores.)	60.00	30.00	18.00
(6)	Pedro Alomar	60.00	30.00	18.00
(7)	Ismael Alvarado (Ponce)	60.00	30.00	18.00
(8)	Ismael Alvarado (Aguadilla)	60.00	30.00	18.00
(9)	Jueyito Andrade	60.00	30.00	18.00
(10)	Nick Andromidas	60.00	30.00	18.00
(11)	Pacay Anglero	60.00	30.00	18.00
(12)	Luis (Tite) Arroyo	75.00	37.50	22.50
(13)	Pedro J. Arroyo	60.00	30.00	18.00
(14)	Dan Bankhead	100.00	50.00	30.00
(15)	Babe Barna	60.00	30.00	18.00
(16)	Carlos Bernier	75.00	37.50	22.50
(17)	John Bero	60.00	30.00	18.00
(18)	Wayne Blackburn	60.00	30.00	18.00
(19)	Efrain Blasini	60.00	30.00	18.00
(20)	Bill Boyd	75.00	37.50	22.50
(21)	Stan Breard	60.00	30.00	18.00
(22)	Willard Brown	4,000	2,000	1,200
(23)	Lou Burdette (P)	125.00	65.00	35.00
(24)	Jose A. Burgos	60.00	30.00	18.00
(25)	Rafael Cabezudo	60.00	30.00	18.00
(26)	Luis R. Cabrera	60.00	30.00	18.00
(27)	Marzo Cabrera	60.00	30.00	18.00
(28)	Manolete Caceres	60.00	30.00	18.00
(29)	Rafael Casanova	60.00	30.00	18.00
(30)	Medina Chapman	60.00	30.00	18.00
(31)	Al Cihosky (P)	125.00	65.00	35.00
(32)	Mike Clark	60.00	30.00	18.00
(33)	Buster Clarkson (Santurce)	250.00	125.00	75.00
(34)	Buster Clarkson (Ponce)	250.00	125.00	75.00
(35)	Francisco Coimbre	300.00	150.00	90.00
(36)	Rafael Colmenero	60.00	30.00	18.00
(37)	Luis Colon	60.00	30.00	18.00
(38)	Monchile Concepcion	75.00	37.50	22.50
(39)	Cefo Conde	60.00	30.00	18.00
(40)	Omar Cordero	60.00	30.00	18.00
(41)	William Costa	60.00	30.00	18.00
(42)	Clinton Courtney	75.00	37.50	22.50
(43)	George Crowe	75.00	37.50	22.50
(44)	Johnny Davis (Mayaguez)	150.00	75.00	45.00
(45)	Johnny Davis (San Juan)	150.00	75.00	45.00
(46)	Piper Davis	200.00	100.00	60.00
(47)	Ellis Deal	75.00	37.50	22.50
(48)	Felle Delgado	60.00	30.00	18.00
(49)	Luke Easter	175.00	85.00	30.00
(50)	Jaime A. Escalera	60.00	30.00	18.00
(51)	Saturnino Escalera	60.00	30.00	18.00
(52)	Luis Ferbe	60.00	30.00	18.00
(53)	L.E. Fernandez	60.00	30.00	18.00
(54)	Coco Ferrer	60.00	30.00	18.00
(55)	Walter Fialla (Fiala)	60.00	30.00	18.00
(56)	Wilmer Fields	150.00	75.00	45.00
(57)	Jose A. Figueroa	75.00	37.50	22.50
(58)	Oscar Mir Flores	60.00	30.00	18.00
(59)	Jesus M. Freyre	60.00	30.00	18.00
(60)	Dominic Galata	60.00	30.00	18.00
(61)	Felipe Garcia	60.00	30.00	18.00
(62)	Alfonso Gerard	60.00	30.00	18.00
(63)	Al Gerheauser (P)	125.00	60.00	35.00
(64)	Joshua Gibson	75,000	37,500	20,000
(65)	Jim Gilliam	150.00	75.00	45.00
(66)	Ruben Gomez	75.00	37.50	22.50
(67)	Rafael Gonzalez	60.00	30.00	18.00

		NM	EX	VG
(68)	Felo Guilbe (Ponce)	60.00	30.00	18.00
(69)	Felo Guilbe (San Juan)	60.00	30.00	18.00
(70)	Juan Guilbe	60.00	30.00	18.00
(71)	Hector Haddock	60.00	30.00	18.00
(72)	Red Hardy (P)	125.00	60.00	35.00
(73)	Van Harrington (P)	125.00	60.00	35.00
(74)	Ray Hathaway	60.00	30.00	18.00
(75)	Ralston Hemsley	75.00	37.50	22.50
(76)	Angel Hernaiz	60.00	30.00	18.00
(77)	Rudy Hernandez	60.00	30.00	18.00
(78)	Don Hoak	100.00	50.00	30.00
(79)	Rogers Hornsby	500.00	250.00	150.00
(80)	Dixie Howell	60.00	30.00	18.00
(81)	Natalio Irizarry (P)	125.00	60.00	35.00
(82)	Walter James	60.00	30.00	18.00
(83)	Stan Karpinsky (P)	125.00	60.00	35.00
(84)	Cecyl Kayser	100.00	50.00	30.00
(85)	Carlos Lanauze	60.00	30.00	18.00
(86)	Rafael Lastra	60.00	30.00	18.00
(87)	Quique Leon	60.00	30.00	18.00
(88)	George Lerchen (P)	125.00	60.00	35.00
(89)	Lou Limmer	60.00	30.00	18.00
(90)	Royce Lint	60.00	30.00	18.00
(91)	Al Lyons	60.00	30.00	18.00
(92)	Glenn MacQuillen	60.00	30.00	18.00
(93)	Jim Markland	60.00	30.00	18.00
(94)	Luis A. Marquez	225.00	110.00	65.00
(95)	Bob Marquis	60.00	30.00	18.00
(96)	Antonio Marrero	60.00	30.00	18.00
(97)	Humberto Marti	60.00	30.00	18.00
(98)	Vicente Medina	60.00	30.00	18.00
(99)	M. Monserrate Jr.	60.00	30.00	18.00
(100)	Jose E. Montalvo (Blue Senadores.)	60.00	30.00	18.00
(101)	Jose E. Montalvo (Red Senadores.)	60.00	30.00	18.00
(102)	Luis Morales	60.00	30.00	18.00
(103)	Pedroso Morales	60.00	30.00	18.00
(104)	Willie Morales	60.00	30.00	18.00
(105)	Luis M. Munoz (Blue Senadores.)	60.00	30.00	18.00
(106)	Luis M. Munoz (Red Senadores.)	60.00	30.00	18.00
(107)	Napier	60.00	30.00	18.00
(108)	Digno Navarro	60.00	30.00	18.00
(109)	Ernest Nevel	60.00	30.00	18.00
(110)	Alfredo Olivencia	60.00	30.00	18.00
(111)	L. Rodriguez Olmo	75.00	37.50	22.50
(112)	Noel Oquendo	60.00	30.00	18.00
(113)	Otoniel Ortiz	60.00	30.00	18.00
(114)	Rafaelito Ortiz	60.00	30.00	18.00
(115)	Roy Partlow	175.00	85.00	50.00
(116)	Miguel Payano (Red Senadores.)	60.00	30.00	18.00
(117)	Miguel Payano (Mayaguez)	60.00	30.00	18.00
(118)	Fernando Pedroso	75.00	37.50	22.50
(119)	Victor Pellot (Power)	100.00	50.00	30.00
(120)	Pedro Pena	60.00	30.00	18.00
(121)	Jose Pereira	60.00	30.00	18.00
(122)	Ismael Perez	60.00	30.00	18.00
(123)	Juan Perez	60.00	30.00	18.00
(124)	Villodas Perez	60.00	30.00	18.00
(125)	Alonso Perry	225.00	110.00	65.00
(126)	Alonso Perry	225.00	110.00	65.00
(127)	Jose D. Polanco	60.00	30.00	18.00
(128)	A. Portocarrero	60.00	30.00	18.00
(129)	Bill Powell	75.00	37.50	22.50
(130)	Tomas Quinones	75.00	37.50	22.50
(131)	Milton Ralat	60.00	30.00	18.00
(132)	Fernando Ramos	60.00	30.00	18.00
(133)	Henry Rementeria	60.00	30.00	18.00
(134)	Luis Renta	60.00	30.00	18.00
(135)	Herminio Reyes	60.00	30.00	18.00
(136)	Lionel Richards	60.00	30.00	18.00
(137)	Gene Richardson	75.00	37.50	22.50
(138)	Jim Rivera	60.00	30.00	18.00
(139)	Miguel A. Rivera	60.00	30.00	18.00
(140)	Roberto Rivera	60.00	30.00	18.00
(141)	Jack Robinson	60.00	30.00	18.00
(142)	Ministro Rodriguez	60.00	30.00	18.00
(143)	Pedro Rodriguez	60.00	30.00	18.00
(144)	Jorge Rosas	60.00	30.00	18.00
(145)	Miguel Ruiz	60.00	30.00	18.00
(146)	Ramon Salgado	60.00	30.00	18.00
(147)	Juan Sanchez	60.00	30.00	18.00
(148)	Carlos M. Santiago	60.00	30.00	18.00
(149)	Jose G. Santiago	60.00	30.00	18.00
(150)	George Scales	600.00	300.00	180.00
(151)	Scarpatte	60.00	30.00	18.00
(152)	Kermit Schmidt (Ponce)	60.00	30.00	18.00
(153)	Kermit Schmidt (Red Senadores.)	60.00	30.00	18.00
(154)	Ken Sears	60.00	30.00	18.00
(155)	Dick Seay	300.00	150.00	90.00
(156)	Pedro Seda	60.00	30.00	18.00
(157)	McDuffie Sevilla	60.00	30.00	18.00
(158)	Vincent Shuppe	60.00	30.00	18.00
(159)	William Skowron	150.00	75.00	45.00
(160)	Dwain Sloat	60.00	30.00	18.00
(161)	John Ford Smith	175.00	85.00	50.00
(162)	Francisco Sostre	60.00	30.00	18.00
(163)	Jose St. Clair (Looking forward.)	60.00	30.00	18.00
(164)	Jose St. Clair (Looking left.)	60.00	30.00	18.00
(165)	Luis St. Clair	60.00	30.00	18.00
(166)	Jimmy Starks	75.00	37.50	22.50
(167)	Israel Ten	60.00	30.00	18.00
(168)	Leo Thomas	60.00	30.00	18.00
(169)	Valmy Thomas (P)	150.00	75.00	45.00
(170)	Freddie Thon	60.00	30.00	18.00
(171)	Bob Thurman	175.00	85.00	50.00
(172)	Miguel A. Tineo	60.00	30.00	18.00
(173)	Griffin Tirado (Blue background.)	60.00	30.00	18.00
(174)	Griffin Tirado (Trees in background.)	60.00	30.00	18.00
(175)	Bin Torres	60.00	30.00	18.00
(176)	Clarkson Torres	60.00	30.00	18.00

		NM	EX	VG
(177)	Manuel Traboux	60.00	30.00	18.00
(178)	Gilberto Valentin	60.00	30.00	18.00
(179)	Roberto Vargas	60.00	30.00	18.00
(180)	Tetelo Vargas	350.00	175.00	100.00
(181)	Rafael Vazquez	60.00	30.00	18.00
(182)	Guillermo Vega	60.00	30.00	18.00
(183)	Jose L. Velazquez	60.00	30.00	18.00
(184)	Vicente Villafane	60.00	30.00	18.00
(185)	Luis Villodas	75.00	37.50	22.50
(186)	Curley Williams (P)	150.00	75.00	45.00
(187)	Artie Wilson	225.00	110.00	65.00
(188)	Robert Wilson (P)	150.00	75.00	45.00
(189)	Jerry Witte (P)	125.00	60.00	35.00
(190)	Pete Wojey	60.00	30.00	18.00
(191)	Andres Zabala	60.00	30.00	18.00
(192)	Rafael Zavala	60.00	30.00	18.00

1950-1951 Toleteros In Action

90. Piper intenta sacar a Tetelo- SAFE

		NM	EX	VG
	Complete Set (178):	6,500	3,250	2,000
	Common Card:	50.00	25.00	15.00
1	Pellot fildea con elegencia. (Victor Pellot (Power)	60.00	30.00	18.00
2	Burgos conecta hit de piernas. (Jose Burgos)	50.00	25.00	15.00
3	OUT por medio paso.	50.00	25.00	15.00
4	Te gusta el mamabo, Canena? (Canena Marquez)	65.00	32.50	20.00
5	OUT!!	50.00	25.00	15.00
6	Lanauze se eleva tras la bola. (Carlos Lanauze)	50.00	25.00	15.00
7	Simpson se escurre en tercera. . .	50.00	25.00	15.00
8	Si no se la cae la bola. . .	50.00	25.00	15.00
9	Escalera realiza brillante cogida. (Saturnino Escalera)	50.00	25.00	15.00
10	Lucha Grecoromana?	50.00	25.00	15.00
11	Gallego a punto deslizarse. . (Gallego Munoz)	50.00	25.00	15.00
12	Parece. . .pero no lo empuja. . .	50.00	25.00	15.00
13	Ramos da out a Felo en primera. (Fernando Ramos)	50.00	25.00	15.00
14	El Chiquitin y El Magnifico.	50.00	25.00	15.00
15	Limmer llege de pie tras triple. (Lou Limmer)	50.00	25.00	15.00
16	Arroyo toca a Costa. . .OUT. (Luis Arroyo)	50.00	25.00	15.00
17	Thon a salvo en tercera. (Freddie Thon)	50.00	25.00	15.00
18	Thurman hacia home Scales lo felicita. (Bob Thurman, George Scales)	65.00	32.50	20.00
19	Not Issued			
20	Not Issued			
21	Coca trata de escurrirse - OUT. (Coco Ferrer)	50.00	25.00	15.00
22	Thurman out a manos de Lanauze (Bob Thurman, Carlos Lanauze)	65.00	32.50	20.00
23	Santiago felicita a Atkins (Carlos M. Santiago, Joe Atkins)	50.00	25.00	15.00
24	Griffin captura a Miller en home. (Griffin Tirado, Henry Miller)	50.00	25.00	15.00
25	"Detente Villodas": Escalera. (Luis Villodas, Saturnino Escalera)	50.00	25.00	15.00
26	Felo se desliza. . .SAFE. (Felo Guilbe)	50.00	25.00	15.00
27	Gallego llega safe a Home. (Gallego Munoz)	50.00	25.00	15.00
28	Que pena! Se cayo la bola. . .	50.00	25.00	15.00
29	Easterling esperando la bola - OUT. (Howard Easterling)	50.00	25.00	15.00
30	Pitcher McDuffie anotando. (McDuffie Sevilla)	50.00	25.00	15.00
31	El raudo Roberto se desliza - SAFE. (Roberto Vargas)	50.00	25.00	15.00
32	Harris felicita Brown tras homerun (Willard Brown)	200.00	100.00	60.00
33	Burgos intenta sacar Easter - SAFE. (Jose Burgos, Luke Easter)	65.00	32.50	20.00
34	Los Leones felicitan a Clarkson. (Buster Clarkson)	65.00	32.50	20.00
35	Otoniel realiza dificil cogida. . . (Otoniel Ortiz)	50.00	25.00	15.00
36	Thurman safe en tercera. . . (Bob Thurman)	65.00	32.50	20.00
37	Bernier safe en home. (Carlos Bernier)	50.00	25.00	15.00
38	Chifflan Clark se va de homerun. (Chiflan Clark)	50.00	25.00	15.00
39	El gran Easter llega tras homerun. (Luke Easter)	65.00	32.50	20.00

		NM	EX	VG
40	Se cae bola a Fields; Graham safe. (Wilmer Fields, Jack Graham)	60.00	30.00	18.00
41	Otoniel trata sacar Taborn - SAFE. (Otoniel Ortiz, Earl Taborn)	50.00	25.00	15.00
42	McQuillen se desliza tercera - SAFE. (George McQuillen)	50.00	25.00	15.00
43	Uno, dos y tres. . .Y anota Coimbre (Francisco Coimbre)	90.00	45.00	27.50
44	Carlos Manuel llega trade. . .OUT. (Carlos M. Santiago)	50.00	25.00	15.00
45	Aprieta el paso, Griffin. . . (Griffin Tirado)	50.00	25.00	15.00
46	Pepe Lucas saca out a Resbaloso. (Pepe Lucas)	50.00	25.00	15.00
47	"No hay quien pase", dice Howell (Dixie Howell)	50.00	25.00	15.00
48	Y que dice el Umpiere?	50.00	25.00	15.00
49	Pedroso intenta robo home - OUT. (Fernando Pedroso)	50.00	25.00	15.00
50	Se formo el nudo. . .	50.00	25.00	15.00
51	Cogelo con calma, Leo. . . (Leo Thomas)	50.00	25.00	15.00
52	Tetelo galopando hacia primera. . . (Tetelo Vargas)	90.00	45.00	27.50
53	Haciendose burla?	50.00	25.00	15.00
54	Los tiburones felicitan. . .	50.00	25.00	15.00
55	La No. 29 de Bernier. (Carlos Bernier)	50.00	25.00	15.00
56	Jockey entra facilmente a primera.	50.00	25.00	15.00
57	Buzas felicita a Collins. (Joe Buzas, Eugene Collins)	50.00	25.00	15.00
58	Ya es tarde, Jose Enrique. . .	50.00	25.00	15.00
59	Lomax Davis entra tras homerun (Lomax Davis)	50.00	25.00	15.00
60	Haddock no puede sacar Villafane. (Hector Haddock)	50.00	25.00	15.00
61	Otoniel Ortiz se va de hom,erun. . . (Otoniel Ortiz)	50.00	25.00	15.00
62	Otra mas para Bernier (Carlos Bernier)	50.00	25.00	15.00
63	Montalvo se desliza en tercera (?) (Jose E. Montalvo)	50.00	25.00	15.00
64	Willie es todo ojos. . . (Willie Morales)	50.00	25.00	15.00
65	La Mucura esta llegando. . . (Johnny Davis)	60.00	30.00	18.00
66	Chapman da out espectacular. (Medina Chapman)	50.00	25.00	15.00
67	McQuilen pisa plato tras homerun (George McQuillen)	50.00	25.00	15.00
68	"Coimbre, Safe". . .dice el Umpire. (Francisco Coimbre)	90.00	45.00	27.50
69	Llega Perry despues de Homerun. . . (Alonso Perry)	65.00	32.50	20.00
70	Griffin, ya es tuyo. . . (Griffin Tirado)	50.00	25.00	15.00
71	Fields pisa plato tras Homerun. . . (Wilmer Fields)	50.00	25.00	15.00
72	EL HOMBRE ESE. . . (Willard Brown)	200.00	100.00	60.00
73	Jockey se desliza violentamente. . .	50.00	25.00	15.00
74	Montalvo esperando a Tite - OUT. (Jose E. Montalvo)	50.00	25.00	15.00
75	Perry anota transqueando. . . (Alonso Perry)	65.00	32.50	20.00
76	Fields pivotea para double-play. (Wilmer Fields)	60.00	30.00	18.00
77	Andando en la cuerda, Piper? (Piper Davis)	65.00	32.50	20.00
78	Montalvo en pie de combate. . . (Jose E. Montalvo)	50.00	25.00	15.00
79	EN GRAN EXPECTATIVA. . .	50.00	25.00	15.00
80	Indios reciben Gachito tras homer	50.00	25.00	15.00
81	Butts esquiva la bola - SAFE. (Pee Wee Butts)	50.00	25.00	15.00
82	Otro para el Gaucho Davis. . (Johnny Davis)	60.00	30.00	18.00
83	Los leones se alborotan. . . (Piper Davis)	60.00	30.00	18.00
84	Lanauze safe en home. . . (Carlos Lanauze)	50.00	25.00	15.00
85	Lanauze se alarga - OUT. (Carlos Lanauze)	50.00	25.00	15.00
86	Thurman llega tras homerun. (Bob Thurman)	65.00	32.50	20.00
87	Sauer roba home espectacularmente (Ed Sauer)	50.00	25.00	15.00
88	PERRY SE ESTIRA. . .OUT. (Alonso Perry)	65.00	32.50	20.00
89	Clarkson conecta otro homerun. (Buster Clarkson)	65.00	32.50	20.00
90	Piper intenta sacar a Tetelo - SAFE (Tetelo Vargas, Piper Davis)	90.00	45.00	27.50
91	QUE QUE USTED DICE. . .?	50.00	25.00	15.00
92	Bernier se roba el home. . . (Carlos Bernier)	50.00	25.00	15.00
93	UNA ESCENA DE RUTINA. . (Willard Brown)	200.00	100.00	60.00
94	Taborn trata de esquvarse - OUT. (Earl Taborn)	50.00	25.00	15.00
95	Pita Marti safe en tercera. (Humberto Marti)	50.00	25.00	15.00
96	PIE CONTRA PIE. . .(?)	50.00	25.00	15.00
97	NO QUIERE NI VERLO. . .	50.00	25.00	15.00
98	SUDOR Y ARENA. . .	50.00	25.00	15.00
99	Jueyito safe en primera. (Jueyito Andrade)	50.00	25.00	15.00
100	QUIEN LLEGO PRIMERO?	50.00	25.00	15.00
101	LLEGO TARDE EL TIRO..SAFE.	50.00	25.00	15.00

		NM	EX	VG
102	Escalera se estira. . .pero es SAFE. (Saturnino Escalera)	50.00	25.00	15.00
103	Howell aspera. . .Almendro observa. (Dixie Howell)	50.00	25.00	15.00
104	A todo vapor hacia tercera. . .	50.00	25.00	15.00
105	Buena cogida, pero es SAFE.	50.00	25.00	15.00
106	El arbitro observa. . .SAFE.	50.00	25.00	15.00
107	SAFE EN HOME.	50.00	25.00	15.00
108	Regreso a tiempo. . .SAFE.	50.00	25.00	15.00
109	Canena es felicitados tras Homer. (Canena Marquez)	65.00	32.50	20.00
110	"COC SAFE", canta el umpiere. (Coco Ferrer)	50.00	25.00	15.00
111	Taft Wright jonronen. . . (Taft Wright)	50.00	25.00	15.00
112	Esta solo. . .pero siempre gana.	50.00	25.00	15.00
113	????????, CANTE!	50.00	25.00	15.00
114	Casanovas quieto en tercera. . . (Rafael Casanovas)	50.00	25.00	15.00
115	Wilson espera pero no llega. . .SAFE. (Artie Wilson)	65.00	32.50	20.00
116	FELLE FELICITA MONTALVO (Felle Delgado, Jose E. Montalvo)	50.00	25.00	15.00
117	El tigre tambien se desliza. . .Safe.	50.00	25.00	15.00
118	Limmer se adelanta. . .Montalvo out. (Lou Limmer, Jose E. Montalvo)	50.00	25.00	15.00
119	TIRO MALO. . .BUTTS SAFE. (Pee Wee Butts)	50.00	25.00	15.00
120	SAFE EN TERCERA.	50.00	25.00	15.00
121	EL JIBARO CONECTA HIT. . .	50.00	25.00	15.00
122	Chapman no puede alcanzarla. . . (Medina Chapman)	50.00	25.00	15.00
123	Guinea Alomar da OUT en Home. (Guinea Alomar)	50.00	25.00	15.00
124	INDIO ANOTA EN SLIDE. . .	50.00	25.00	15.00
125	Miller saca a Serrel en primera. (Henry Miller, Barney Serrell)	50.00	25.00	15.00
126	El gran COIMBRE llega SAFE. (Francisco Coimbre)	90.00	45.00	27.50
127	El arbitro tome impulsa. . .OUT!	50.00	25.00	15.00
128	TROUPPE DA OUT EN HOME. (Quincy Trouppe)	90.00	45.00	27.50
129	BANKHEAD OUT EN PRIMERA. (Bankhead)	60.00	30.00	18.00
130	Tiene que pensarlo bien. . .	50.00	25.00	15.00
131	Escalera a salvo en tercera. . . (Saturnino Escalera)	50.00	25.00	15.00
132	DOS MANOS QUE BUSCAN. . .	50.00	25.00	15.00
133	FIGUEROA SE DESLIZA - SAFE (Tite Figueroa)	50.00	25.00	15.00
134	VIENE LA BOLA. . .OUT.	50.00	25.00	15.00
135	Esperando el tiro. . .OUT.	50.00	25.00	15.00
136	KAYSER SAFE EN PRIMERA. (Cecyl Kayser)	50.00	25.00	15.00
137	COCO FERRER DA OUT. (Coco Ferrer)	50.00	25.00	15.00
138	Lo atajaron a tiempo. . .OUT.	50.00	25.00	15.00
139	Limmer da su primer homer. (Lou Limmer)	50.00	25.00	15.00
140	Starks y Blasini alegan. . . (Jimmy Starks, Efrain Blasini)	50.00	25.00	15.00
141	BARNA SE VA DE HOMERUN. (Babe Barna)	50.00	25.00	15.00
142	"La antesala del gran choque. . . (George Scales)	60.00	30.00	18.00
143	"QUIETO". DICE EL UMPIRE.	50.00	25.00	15.00
144	LO SACARON POR UN PELO. . .	50.00	25.00	15.00
145	Un recibimiento poco agradable.	50.00	25.00	15.00
146	Montalvo se desliza. . .OUT. (Jose E. Montalvo)	50.00	25.00	15.00
147	ALOMAR OUT EN HOME. . . (Alomar)	50.00	25.00	15.00
148	EASTER SAFE EN HOME. . . (Luke Easter)	65.00	32.50	20.00
149	Grillo se anota hit de piernas. . .	50.00	25.00	15.00
150	BARNA SAFE EN TERCERA. (Babe Barna)	50.00	25.00	15.00
151	Esta en la base pero es OUT.	50.00	25.00	15.00
152	TYBOR DA OUT A TABORN. (Jim Tabor, Earl Taborn)	50.00	25.00	15.00
153	BUTTS OUT EN PRIMERA. (Pee Wee Butts)	50.00	25.00	15.00
154	Viene la bola. . .Hernaiz SAFE. (Angel Hernaiz)	50.00	25.00	15.00
155	VILLODAS LO ESPERA. . .OUT. (Luis Villodas)	50.00	25.00	15.00
156	TYBOR SACA A COCA FERRER. (Jim Tabor, Coco Ferrer)	50.00	25.00	15.00
157	LO FUSILAN EN TERCERA.	50.00	25.00	15.00
158	BLOQUEADO. . .	50.00	25.00	15.00
159	"Estoy firme en base", dice Coco. (Coco Ferrer)	50.00	25.00	15.00
160	Ruben Gomez se tira slide. . .SAFE. (Ruben Gomez)	50.00	25.00	15.00
161	HOWELL OUT EN PRIMERA. (Dixie Howell)	50.00	25.00	15.00
162	SAFE EN HOME.	50.00	25.00	15.00
163	PERRY ES ESCURRE. . .SAFE. (Alonso Perry)	65.00	32.50	20.00
164	PEDROSO SE LESIONA. (Fernando Pedroso)	50.00	25.00	15.00
165	LA APOTEOSIS DEL TRIUNFO.	50.00	25.00	15.00
166	Ruben jonroneo ganar su juego. (Ruben Gomez)	50.00	25.00	15.00
167	Primer homerun CANENA 1950-51 (Canena Marquez)	65.00	32.50	20.00
168	GOLPE DE IZQUIRDA? SAFE.	50.00	25.00	15.00
169	PELLOT OUT EN HOME. (Victor Pellot-(Power))	65.00	32.50	20.00
170	Muchos ojos tras Scales y Mullens. (George Scales)	60.00	30.00	18.00
171	Nube de polvo en el Castillo. . .	50.00	25.00	15.00
172	Bero participa carnaval jonrones. (John Bero)	50.00	25.00	15.00
173	Lanauze completa out a Butts. (Carlos Lanauze, Pee Wee Butts)	50.00	25.00	15.00
174	SE LE ESCAPO LA PILDORA.	50.00	25.00	15.00
175	EL UMPIRE DECIDIRA. . .	50.00	25.00	15.00
176	Llego tarde el HOMBRE ESE. (Willard Brown)	200.00	100.00	60.00
177	THON SE DESLIZA. . .SAFE. (Freddie Thon)	50.00	25.00	15.00
178	AL REVES, PERO SAFE. . .	50.00	25.00	15.00
179	Hughes no puede sacar al corredor. (Roy Hughes)	50.00	25.00	15.00
180	"Chiflan Safe". . .dice el Umpiere. (Chiflan Clark)	50.00	25.00	15.00

1909-11 Tolstoi Cigarettes

PREMIUMS:
Commons: 1.5-2X
Hall of Famers: 1-2X
(See T206 for checklist and base values.)

1887 Tomlinson Studios Cabinets

The extent to which this Detroit photographer promulgated individual player cabinet cards of the 1887 Wolverines is unknown. However, since the portrait on the known Bennett card is the same as that found on a team-composite cabinet card, it is not unreasonable to expect that each of the other 13 players pictured on the team card may have been issued individually. The cabinet is in the typical 4-1/4" x 6-1/2" format, with blank back.

	NM	EX	VG
C.W. Bennett (Portrait)	5,000	2,500	1,500
C.W. Bennett (Batting)	5,000	2,500	1,500
Jimmy Manning	5,000	2,500	1,500

1909 Topping & Co. Detroit Tigers Postcards

This set of postcards features the members of the 1909 American League Champion Detroit Tigers. About 3-1/2" x 5-1/2" in size, vertically formatted fronts have black-and-white player portraits at center within a yellow six-pointed star. "Tiger Stars" appears in script in a yellow stripe at top, while the player name and position are in a similar strip at bottom. Black trim surrounds the design elements. Backs are black-and-white with standard postcard markings and a credit line for Topping and Publishers Co., Detroit. The unnumbered cards are listed here alphabetically.

		NM	EX	VG
	Complete Set (21):	12,000	6,000	3,500
	Common Player:	400.00	200.00	120.00
(1)	Henry Beckendorf	400.00	200.00	120.00
(2)	Donie Bush	400.00	200.00	120.00
(3)	Ty Cobb	3,500	1,750	1,000
(4)	Sam Crawford	1,000	500.00	300.00
(5)	Jim Delehanty	400.00	200.00	120.00
(6)	Bill Donovan	400.00	200.00	120.00
(7)	Hughie Jennings	400.00	200.00	120.00
(8)	Davy Jones	400.00	200.00	120.00
(9)	Tom Jones	400.00	200.00	120.00
(10)	Ed Killian	400.00	200.00	120.00
(11)	Matty McIntyre	400.00	200.00	120.00
(12)	George Moriarty	400.00	200.00	120.00
(13)	George Mullin	400.00	200.00	120.00
(14)	Charley O'Leary	400.00	200.00	120.00
(15)	Germany Schaefer	400.00	200.00	120.00
(16)	Charlie Schmidt	400.00	200.00	120.00
(17)	George Speer	400.00	200.00	120.00
(18)	Oscar Stanage	400.00	200.00	120.00
(19)	Eddie Summers	400.00	200.00	120.00
(20)	Ed Willett	400.00	200.00	120.00
(21)	Ralph Works	400.00	200.00	120.00

1948 Topps Magic Photos

The first Topps baseball cards appeared as a subset of 19 cards from an issue of 252 "Magic Photos." The set takes its name from the self-developing nature of the cards. The cards were blank on the front when first taken from the wrapper. By spitting on the wrapper and holding it to the card while exposing it to light the black-and-white photo appeared. Measuring 7/8" x 1-1/2," the cards are very similar to Topps 1955 and 1956 "Hocus Focus" issues.

		NM	EX	VG
	Complete Set (19):	2,400	1,200	725.00
	Common Card:	60.00	30.00	18.00
1	Lou Boudreau	75.00	37.50	22.50
2	Cleveland Indians	60.00	30.00	18.00
3	Bob Eliott	75.00	37.50	22.50
4	Cleveland Indians 4-3	60.00	30.00	18.00
5	Cleveland Indians 4-1	60.00	30.00	18.00
6	Babe Ruth	450.00	225.00	135.00
7	Tris Speaker	90.00	45.00	27.50
8	Rogers Hornsby	90.00	45.00	27.50
9	Connie Mack	75.00	37.50	22.50
10	Christy Mathewson	150.00	75.00	45.00
11	Hans Wagner	100.00	50.00	30.00
12	Grover Alexander	90.00	45.00	27.50
13	Ty Cobb	275.00	135.00	80.00
14	Lou Gehrig	275.00	135.00	80.00
15	Walter Johnson	125.00	65.00	35.00
16	Cy Young	125.00	65.00	35.00
17	George Sisler	75.00	37.50	22.50
18	Tinker and Evers	125.00	65.00	35.00
19	Third Base Cleveland Indians	75.00	37.50	22.50

1951 Topps Red Backs

Like the Blue Backs, the Topps Red Backs which were sold at the same time came two to a package for 1¢. Their black-and-white photographs appear on a red, white, blue and yellow background. The back printing is red on white. Their 2" x 2-5/8" size is the same as Blue Backs. Also identical is the set size (52 cards) and the game situations to be found on the fronts of the cards, for use in playing a card game of baseball.

Red Backs are more common than the Blue Backs by virtue of a 1980s discovery of a large hoard of unopened boxes. Red Backs are also known to have been sold in a plastic-bagged set along with a foldout paper game board for 29 cents.

		NM	EX	VG
	Complete Set (52):	1,000	500.00	300.00
	Common Player:	12.00	6.00	3.50
	Wax Pack (2):	100.00		
1	Larry (Yogi) Berra	150.00	75.00	37.50
2	Sid Gordon	12.00	6.00	3.50
3	Ferris Fain	12.00	6.00	3.50
4	Verne Stephens	12.00	6.00	3.50
5	Phil Rizzuto	60.00	30.00	15.00
6	Allie Reynolds	30.00	15.00	7.50
7	Howie Pollet	12.00	6.00	3.50
8	Early Wynn	35.00	17.50	8.75
9	Roy Sievers	12.00	6.00	3.50
10	Mel Parnell	12.00	6.00	3.50
11	Gene Hermanski	12.00	6.00	3.50
12	Jim Hegan	12.00	6.00	3.50
13	Dale Mitchell	12.00	6.00	3.50
14	Wayne Terwilliger	12.00	6.00	3.50
15	Ralph Kiner	35.00	17.50	8.75
16	Preacher Roe	30.00	15.00	7.50
17	Dave Bell	12.00	6.00	3.50
18	Gerry Coleman	20.00	10.00	5.00
19	Dick Kokos	12.00	6.00	3.50
20	Dominick DiMaggio	30.00	15.00	7.50
21	Larry Jansen	12.00	6.00	3.50
22	Bob Feller	50.00	25.00	14.00
23	Ray Boone	12.00	6.00	3.50
24	Hank Bauer	20.00	10.00	5.00
25	Cliff Chambers	12.00	6.00	3.50
26	Luke Easter	20.00	10.00	5.00
27	Wally Westlake	12.00	6.00	3.50
28	Elmer Valo	12.00	6.00	3.50
29	Bob Kennedy	12.00	6.00	3.50
30	Warren Spahn	50.00	25.00	14.00
31	Gil Hodges	40.00	20.00	11.00
32	Henry Thompson	12.00	6.00	3.50
33	William Werle	12.00	6.00	3.50
34	Grady Hatton	12.00	6.00	3.50
35	Al Rosen	20.00	10.00	5.00
36a	Gus Zernial (Chicago in bio.)	25.00	15.00	10.00
36b	Gus Zernial (Philadelphia in bio.)	25.00	12.50	8.00
37	Wes Westrum	12.00	6.00	3.50
38	Ed (Duke) Snider	60.00	30.00	18.00
39	Ted Kluszewski	30.00	15.00	7.50
40	Mike Garcia	12.00	6.00	3.50
41	Whitey Lockman	12.00	6.00	3.50
42	Ray Scarborough	12.00	6.00	3.50
43	Maurice McDermott	12.00	6.00	3.50
44	Sid Hudson	12.00	6.00	3.50
45	Andy Seminick	12.00	6.00	3.50
46	Billy Goodman	12.00	6.00	3.50
47	Tommy Glaviano	12.00	6.00	3.50
48	Eddie Stanky	12.00	6.00	3.50
49	Al Zarilla	12.00	6.00	3.50
50	Monte Irvin	40.00	20.00	10.00
51	Eddie Robinson	12.00	6.00	3.50
52a	Tommy Holmes (Boston in bio.)	50.00	25.00	15.00
52b	Tommy Holmes (Hartford in bio.)	25.00	12.50	8.00

1951 Topps Blue Backs

Sold two cards in a package with a piece of candy for 1¢, the Topps Blue Backs are considerably scarcer than their Red Back counterparts. The 2" x 2-5/8" cards carry a black-and-white player photograph on a red, white, yellow and green background along with the player's name and other information including their 1950 record on the front. The back is printed in blue on a white background. The 52-card set has varied baseball situations on them, making the playing of a rather elementary game of baseball possible. Although scarce, Blue Backs were printed on thick cardboard and have survived quite well over the years. There are, however, few stars in the set.

		NM	EX	VG
	Complete Set (52):	2,000	1,000	600.00
	Common Player:	30.00	15.00	8.00
	Wax Pack (2):	200.00		
1	Eddie Yost	40.00	20.00	10.00
2	Henry (Hank) Majeski	30.00	15.00	8.00
3	Richie Ashburn	200.00	100.00	50.00
4	Del Ennis	30.00	15.00	8.00
5	Johnny Pesky	30.00	15.00	8.00
6	Albert (Red) Schoendienst	100.00	50.00	25.00
7	Gerald Staley	30.00	15.00	8.00
8	Dick Sisler	30.00	15.00	8.00
9	Johnny Sain	40.00	20.00	10.00
10	Joe Page	30.00	15.00	8.00
11	Johnny Groth	30.00	15.00	8.00
12	Sam Jethroe	30.00	15.00	8.00
13	James (Mickey) Vernon	30.00	15.00	8.00
14	George Munger	30.00	15.00	8.00
15	Eddie Joost	30.00	15.00	8.00
16	Murry Dickson	30.00	15.00	8.00
17	Roy Smalley	30.00	15.00	8.00
18	Ned Garver	30.00	15.00	8.00
19	Phil Masi	30.00	15.00	8.00
20	Ralph Branca	40.00	20.00	10.00
21	Billy Johnson	30.00	15.00	8.00
22	Bob Kuzava	30.00	15.00	8.00
23	Paul (Dizzy) Trout	30.00	15.00	8.00
24	Sherman Lollar	30.00	15.00	8.00
25	Sam Mele	30.00	15.00	8.00
26	Chico Carrasquel	30.00	15.00	8.00
27	Andy Pafko	30.00	15.00	8.00
28	Harry (The Cat) Brecheen	30.00	15.00	8.00
29	Granville Hamner	30.00	15.00	8.00
30	Enos (Country) Slaughter	100.00	50.00	25.00
31	Lou Brissie	30.00	15.00	8.00
32	Bob Elliott	30.00	15.00	8.00
33	Don Lenhardt	30.00	15.00	8.00
34	Earl Torgeson	30.00	15.00	8.00
35	Tommy Byrne	30.00	15.00	8.00
36	Cliff Fannin	30.00	15.00	8.00
37	Bobby Doerr	100.00	50.00	25.00
38	Irv Noren	30.00	15.00	8.00
39	Ed Lopat	40.00	20.00	10.00
40	Vic Wertz	30.00	15.00	8.00
41	Johnny Schmitz	30.00	15.00	8.00
42	Bruce Edwards	30.00	15.00	8.00
43	Willie (Puddin' Head) Jones	30.00	15.00	8.00
44	Johnny Wyrostek	30.00	15.00	8.00
45	Bill Pierce	30.00	15.00	8.00
46	Gerry Priddy	30.00	15.00	8.00
47	Herman Wehmeier	30.00	15.00	8.00
48	Billy Cox	30.00	15.00	8.00
49	Henry (Hank) Sauer	30.00	15.00	8.00
50	Johnny Mize	100.00	50.00	25.00
51	Eddie Waitkus	30.00	15.00	8.00
52	Sam Chapman	30.00	15.00	8.00

1951 Topps Connie Mack's All-Stars

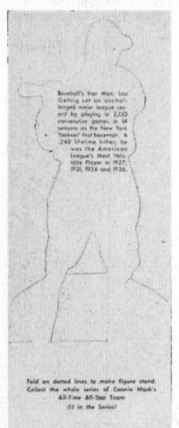

A set of die-cut, 2-1/16" x 5-1/4" cards, all 11 players are Hall of Famers. The cards feature a black-and-white action player photograph printed on a red background with a colored name plaque underneath. Like the "Current All-Stars," with which they were issued, the background could be folded, making it possible for the card to stand up. This practice, however, resulted in the card's mutilation and lowers its condition in the eyes of today's collectors. Connie Mack All-Stars are scarce today and, despite being relatively expensive, retain a certain popularity as one of Topps first issues.

		NM	EX	VG
	Complete Set (11):	16,000	8,000	4,750
	Common Player:	525.00	260.00	155.00
(1)	Grover Cleveland Alexander	900.00	450.00	275.00
(2)	Gordon Stanley Cochrane	600.00	300.00	180.00
(3)	Edward Trowbridge Collins	600.00	300.00	180.00
(4)	James J. Collins	600.00	300.00	180.00
(5)	Lou Gehrig	4,500	2,250	1,350
(6)	Walter Johnson	1,000	500.00	300.00
(7)	Connie Mack	600.00	300.00	180.00
(8)	Christopher Mathewson	1,125	560.00	335.00
(9)	George Herman Ruth	5,500	2,750	1,650
(10)	Tris Speaker	600.00	300.00	180.00
(11)	Honus Wagner	1,250	625.00	375.00

1951 Topps Major League All-Stars

The Topps Major League All-Stars are very similar to the Connie Mack All-Stars of the same year. The 2-1/16" x 5-1/4"

cards have a black-and-white photograph on a red die-cut background. Most of the background could be folded over so that the card would stand up. A plaque at the base carries brief biographical information. The set was to contain 11 cards, but only eight were actually issued in gum packs. Those of Konstanty, Roberts and Stanky were not issued and are very rare, with only a handful of each known. A big problem with the set is that if the card was used as it was intended it was folded and, thus, damaged from a collector's viewpoint. That makes top quality examples of any players difficult to find and quite expensive.

		NM	EX	VG
	Complete Set (11):	14,000	7,000	4,200
	Common Player:	1,025	510.00	305.00
(1)	Yogi Berra	3,000	1,500	900.00
(2)	Larry Doby	1,900	950.00	575.00
(3)	Walt Dropo	900.00	450.00	270.00
(4)	"Hoot" Evers	900.00	450.00	270.00
(5)	George Clyde Kell	1,600	800.00	480.00
(6)	Ralph Kiner	1,600	800.00	480.00
(7)	Jim Konstanty	30,000	15,000	9,000
(8)	Bob Lemon	1,600	800.00	480.00
(9)	Phil Rizzuto	2,750	1,375	825.00
(10)	Robin Roberts	35,000	17,500	10,500
(11)	Ed Stanky	30,000	15,000	9,000

1951 Topps Teams

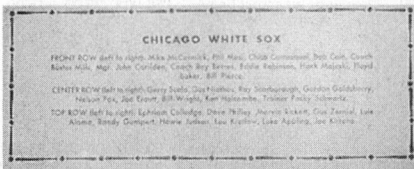

An innovative issue for 1951, the Topps team cards were a nine-card set, 5-1/4" x 2-1/16", which carry a black-and-white picture of a major league team surrounded by a yellow border on the front. The back identifies team members with red printing on white cardboard. There are two versions of each card, with and without the date "1950" in the banner that carries the team name. Undated versions are valued slightly higher than the cards with dates. Strangely only nine teams were issued. Scarcity varies, with the Cardinals and Red Sox being the most difficult to obtain.

		NM	EX	VG
(1a)	Boston Red Sox (1950)	475.00	235.00	140.00
(1b)	Boston Red Sox (Undated)	500.00	250.00	150.00
(2a)	Brooklyn Dodgers (1950)	375.00	185.00	110.00
(2b)	Brooklyn Dodgers (Undated)	400.00	200.00	120.00
(3a)	Chicago White Sox (1950)	275.00	135.00	80.00
(3b)	Chicago White Sox (Undated)	250.00	125.00	75.00
(4a)	Cincinnati Reds (1950)	300.00	150.00	90.00
(4b)	Cincinnati Reds (Undated)	325.00	160.00	95.00
(5a)	New York Giants (1950)	300.00	150.00	90.00
(5b)	New York Giants (Undated)	325.00	160.00	95.00
(6a)	Philadelphia Athletics (1950)	225.00	110.00	65.00
(6b)	Philadelphia Athletics (Undated)	250.00	125.00	75.00
(7a)	Philadelphia Phillies (1950)	225.00	110.00	65.00
(7b)	Philadelphia Phillies (Undated)	400.00	200.00	120.00
(8a)	St. Louis Cardinals (1950)	400.00	200.00	120.00
(8b)	St. Louis Cardinals (Undated)	425.00	210.00	125.00
(9a)	Washington Senators (1950)	250.00	125.00	75.00
(9b)	Washington Senators (Undated)	300.00	150.00	90.00

1952 Topps

At 407 cards, the 1952 Topps set was the largest set of its day, both in number of cards and physical dimensions of the cards. Cards are 2-5/8" x 3-3/4" with a colorized black-

and-white photo on front. Major baseball card innovations presented in the set include the first-ever use of color team logos as part of the design, and the inclusion of stats for the previous season and career on the backs. The first 80 cards in the set can be found with backs printed entirely in black or black and red. While "Black Backs" used to command a significant premium over the "Red Back" version, that differential has diminished in recent years to the point of insignificance. Several cards in the #1-80 range can be found with noticeable color differences on front depending on whether they are Red Back or Black Back. Cards #311-407, known as the "high numbers," were distributed in limited areas and are extremely rare.

		NM	EX	VG
	Complete Set (407):	120,000	55,000	30,000
	Common Player (1-250):	45.00	22.50	13.50
	Common Player (251-310):	60.00	30.00	18.00
	Common Player (311-407):	275.00	135.00	80.00
1	Andy Pafko	6,000	500.00	190.00
2	*James E. Runnels*	900.00	40.00	20.00
3	Hank Thompson	45.00	22.50	13.50
4	Don Lenhardt	45.00	22.50	13.50
5	Larry Jansen	45.00	22.50	13.50
6	Grady Hatton	45.00	22.50	13.50
7	Wayne Terwilliger	55.00	27.50	16.50
8	Fred Marsh	45.00	22.50	13.50
9	Bobby Hogue	55.00	27.50	16.50
10	Al Rosen	80.00	40.00	20.00
11	Phil Rizzuto	600.00	300.00	180.00
12	Monty Basgall	45.00	22.50	13.50
13	Johnny Wyrostek	45.00	22.50	13.50
14	Bob Elliott	45.00	22.50	13.50
15	Johnny Pesky	45.00	22.50	13.50
16	Gene Hermanski	45.00	22.50	13.50
17	Jim Hegan	45.00	22.50	13.50
18	Merrill Combs	45.00	22.50	13.50
19	Johnny Bucha	45.00	22.50	13.50
20	*Billy Loes*	150.00	75.00	37.50
21	Ferris Fain	60.00	30.00	18.00
22	Dom DiMaggio	125.00	75.00	45.00
23	Billy Goodman	45.00	22.50	13.50
24	Luke Easter	60.00	30.00	18.00
25	Johnny Groth	45.00	22.50	13.50
26	Monty Irvin	150.00	75.00	37.50
27	Sam Jethroe	45.00	22.50	13.50
28	Jerry Priddy	45.00	22.50	13.50
29	Ted Kluszewski	150.00	75.00	37.50
30	Mel Parnell	45.00	22.50	13.50
31	Gus Zernial	100.00	50.00	25.00
32	Eddie Robinson	45.00	22.50	13.50
33	Warren Spahn	300.00	150.00	75.00
34	Elmer Valo	45.00	22.50	13.50
35	Hank Sauer	45.00	22.50	13.50
36	Gil Hodges	300.00	150.00	75.00
37	Duke Snider	500.00	250.00	125.00
38	Wally Westlake	45.00	22.50	13.50
39	"Dizzy" Trout	45.00	22.50	13.50
40	Irv Noren	45.00	22.50	13.50
41	Bob Wellman	45.00	22.50	13.50
42	Lou Kretlow	45.00	22.50	13.50
43	Ray Scarborough	45.00	22.50	13.50
44	Con Dempsey	45.00	22.50	13.50
45	Eddie Joost	45.00	22.50	13.50
46	Gordon Goldsberry	45.00	22.50	13.50
47	Willie Jones	45.00	22.50	13.50
48a	Joe Page (Wrong (Sain) back.)	1,800	900.00	540.00
48b	Joe Page (Correct back.)	125.00	90.00	45.00
49a	Johnny Sain (Wrong (Page) back.)	2,000	1,000	600.00
49b	Johnny Sain (Correct back.)	150.00	75.00	50.00
50	Marv Rickert	45.00	22.50	13.50
51	Jim Russell	55.00	27.50	16.50
52	Don Mueller	45.00	22.50	13.50
53	Chris Van Cuyk	55.00	27.50	16.50
54	Leo Kiely	45.00	22.50	13.50
55	Ray Boone	45.00	22.50	13.50
56	Tommy Glaviano	45.00	22.50	13.50
57	Ed Lopat	90.00	45.00	25.00
58	Bob Mahoney	45.00	22.50	13.50
59	Robin Roberts	200.00	100.00	60.00
60	Sid Hudson	45.00	22.50	13.50
61	"Tookie" Gilbert	45.00	22.50	13.50
62	Chuck Stobbs	45.00	22.50	13.50
63	Howie Pollet	45.00	22.50	13.50
64	Roy Sievers	45.00	22.50	13.50
65	Enos Slaughter	160.00	80.00	40.00
66	"Preacher" Roe	100.00	50.00	35.00
67	Allie Reynolds	120.00	60.00	35.00
68	Cliff Chambers	45.00	22.50	13.50
69	Virgil Stallcup	45.00	22.50	13.50
70	Al Zarilla	45.00	22.50	13.50
71	Tom Upton	45.00	22.50	13.50
72	Karl Olson	45.00	22.50	13.50
73	William Werle	45.00	22.50	13.50
74	Andy Hansen	45.00	22.50	13.50
75	Wes Westrum	45.00	22.50	13.50
76	Eddie Stanky	45.00	22.50	13.50
77	Bob Kennedy	45.00	22.50	13.50
78	Ellis Kinder	45.00	22.50	13.50
79	Gerald Staley	45.00	22.50	13.50
80	Herman Wehmeier	45.00	22.50	13.50
81	Vernon Law	45.00	22.50	13.50
82	Duane Pillette	45.00	22.50	13.50
83	Billy Johnson	45.00	22.50	13.50
84	Vern Stephens	45.00	22.50	13.50
85	Bob Kuzava	55.00	27.50	16.50
86	Ted Gray	45.00	22.50	13.50
87	Dale Coogan	45.00	22.50	13.50
88	Bob Feller	175.00	87.00	52.00
89	Johnny Lipon	45.00	22.50	13.50
90	Mickey Grasso	45.00	22.50	13.50
91	Al Schoendienst	140.00	70.00	40.00
92	Dale Mitchell	45.00	22.50	13.50
93	Al Sima	45.00	22.50	13.50
94	Sam Mele	45.00	22.50	13.50
95	Ken Holcombe	45.00	22.50	13.50
96	Willard Marshall	45.00	22.50	13.50
97	Earl Torgeson	45.00	22.50	13.50
98	Bill Pierce	55.00	27.50	16.50
99	Gene Woodling	80.00	40.00	24.00
100	Del Rice	45.00	22.50	13.50
101	Max Lanier	45.00	22.50	13.50
102	Bill Kennedy	45.00	22.50	13.50
103	Cliff Mapes	45.00	22.50	13.50
104	Don Kolloway	45.00	22.50	13.50
105	John Pramesa	45.00	22.50	13.50
106	Mickey Vernon	45.00	22.50	13.50
107	Connie Ryan	45.00	22.50	13.50
108	Jim Konstanty	45.00	22.50	13.50
109	Ted Wilks	45.00	22.50	13.50
110	Dutch Leonard	45.00	22.50	13.50
111	Harry Lowrey	45.00	22.50	13.50
112	Henry Majeski	45.00	22.50	13.50
113	Dick Sisler	45.00	22.50	13.50
114	Willard Ramsdell	45.00	22.50	13.50
115	George Munger	45.00	22.50	13.50
116	Carl Scheib	45.00	22.50	13.50
117	Sherman Lollar	45.00	22.50	13.50
118	Ken Raffensberger	45.00	22.50	13.50
119	Maurice McDermott	45.00	22.50	13.50
120	Bob Chakales	45.00	22.50	13.50
121	Gus Niarhos	45.00	22.50	13.50
122	Jack Jensen	100.00	50.00	30.00
123	Eddie Yost	45.00	22.50	13.50
124	Monte Kennedy	45.00	22.50	13.50
125	Bill Rigney	45.00	22.50	13.50
126	Fred Hutchinson	45.00	22.50	13.50
127	Paul Minner	45.00	22.50	13.50
128	Don Bollweg	55.00	27.50	16.50
129	Johnny Mize	140.00	70.00	35.00
130	Sheldon Jones	45.00	22.50	13.50
131	Morrie Martin	45.00	22.50	13.50
132	Clyde Kluttz	45.00	22.50	13.50
133	Al Widmar	45.00	22.50	13.50
134	Joe Tipton	45.00	22.50	13.50
135	Dixie Howell	45.00	22.50	13.50
136	Johnny Schmitz	45.00	22.50	13.50
137	*Roy McMillan*	50.00	25.00	15.00
138	Bill MacDonald	45.00	22.50	13.50
139	Ken Wood	45.00	22.50	13.50
140	John Antonelli	45.00	22.50	13.50
141	Clint Hartung	45.00	22.50	13.50
142	Harry Perkowski	45.00	22.50	13.50
143	Les Moss	45.00	22.50	13.50
144	Ed Blake	45.00	22.50	13.50
145	Joe Haynes	45.00	22.50	13.50
146	Frank House	45.00	22.50	13.50
147	Bob Young	45.00	22.50	13.50
148	Johnny Klippstein	45.00	22.50	13.50
149	Dick Kryhoski	45.00	22.50	13.50
150	Ted Beard	45.00	22.50	13.50
151	*Wally Post*	55.00	27.50	16.50
152	Al Evans	45.00	22.50	13.50
153	Bob Rush	45.00	22.50	13.50
154	Joe Muir	45.00	22.50	13.50
155	Frank Overmire	55.00	27.50	16.50
156	Frank Hiller	45.00	22.50	13.50
157	Bob Usher	45.00	22.50	13.50
158	Eddie Waitkus	45.00	22.50	13.50
159	Saul Rogovin	45.00	22.50	13.50
160	Owen Friend	45.00	22.50	13.50
161	Bud Byerly	45.00	22.50	13.50
162	Del Crandall	45.00	22.50	13.50
163	Stan Rojek	45.00	22.50	13.50
164	Walt Dubiel	45.00	22.50	13.50
165	Eddie Kazak	45.00	22.50	13.50
166	Paul LaPalme	45.00	22.50	13.50
167	Bill Howerton	45.00	22.50	13.50
168	*Charlie Silvera*	75.00	37.50	22.50
169	Howie Judson	45.00	22.50	13.50
170	Gus Bell	65.00	32.50	20.00
171	Ed Erautt	45.00	22.50	13.50
172	Eddie Miksis	45.00	22.50	13.50
173	Roy Smalley	45.00	22.50	13.50
174	Clarence Marshall	45.00	22.50	13.50
175	*Billy Martin*	500.00	250.00	125.00
176	Hank Edwards	45.00	22.50	13.50
177	Bill Wight	45.00	22.50	13.50
178	Cass Michaels	45.00	22.50	13.50
179	Frank Smith	45.00	22.50	13.50
180	*Charley Maxwell*	60.00	30.00	18.00
181	Bob Swift	45.00	22.50	13.50
182	Billy Hitchcock	45.00	22.50	13.50
183	Erv Dusak	45.00	22.50	13.50
184	Bob Ramazzotti	45.00	22.50	13.50
185	Bill Nicholson	45.00	22.50	13.50
186	Walt Masterson	45.00	22.50	13.50
187	Bob Miller	45.00	22.50	13.50
188	Clarence Podbielan	45.00	22.50	13.50
189	Pete Reiser	45.00	22.50	13.50
190	Don Johnson	45.00	22.50	13.50
191	Yogi Berra	800.00	400.00	250.00
192	Myron Ginsberg	45.00	22.50	13.50
193	Harry Simpson	45.00	22.50	13.50
194	Joe Hatten	45.00	22.50	13.50
195	*Orestes Minoso*	175.00	87.50	43.75
196	Solly Hemus	45.00	22.50	13.50
197	George Strickland	45.00	22.50	13.50
198	Phil Haugstad	50.00	25.00	15.00
199	George Zuverink	45.00	22.50	13.50
200	Ralph Houk	75.00	50.00	25.00
201	Alex Kellner	45.00	22.50	13.50
202	Joe Collins	60.00	30.00	18.00
203	Curt Simmons	45.00	22.50	13.50
204	Ron Northey	45.00	22.50	13.50
205	Clyde King	45.00	22.50	13.50
206	Joe Ostrowski	55.00	27.50	16.50
207	Mickey Harris	45.00	22.50	13.50
208	Marlin Stuart	45.00	22.50	13.50
209	Howie Fox	45.00	22.50	13.50
210	Dick Fowler	45.00	22.50	13.50
211	Ray Coleman	45.00	22.50	13.50
212	Ned Garver	45.00	22.50	13.50
213	Nippy Jones	45.00	22.50	13.50
214	Johnny Hopp	55.00	27.50	16.50
215	Hank Bauer	95.00	45.00	25.00
216	Richie Ashburn	225.00	112.50	56.25
217	George Stirnweiss	45.00	22.50	13.50
218	Clyde McCullough	45.00	22.50	13.50
219	Bobby Shantz	55.00	27.50	16.50
220	Joe Presko	45.00	22.50	13.50
221	Granny Hamner	45.00	22.50	13.50
222	"Hoot" Evers	45.00	22.50	13.50
223	Del Ennis	45.00	22.50	13.50
224	Bruce Edwards	45.00	22.50	13.50
225	Frank Baumholtz	45.00	22.50	13.50
226	Dave Philley	45.00	22.50	13.50
227	Joe Garagiola	100.00	50.00	25.00
228	Al Brazle	45.00	22.50	13.50
229	Gene Bearden	45.00	22.50	13.50
230	Matt Batts	45.00	22.50	13.50
231	Sam Zoldak	45.00	22.50	13.50
232	Billy Cox	90.00	45.00	25.00
233	*Bob Friend*	75.00	37.50	22.50
234	Steve Souchock	45.00	22.50	13.50
235	Walt Dropo	45.00	22.50	13.50
236	Ed Fitz Gerald	45.00	22.50	13.50
237	Jerry Coleman	60.00	30.00	18.00
238	Art Houtteman	45.00	22.50	13.50
239	*Rocky Bridges*	45.00	22.50	13.50
240	Jack Phillips	45.00	22.50	13.50
241	Tommy Byrne	45.00	22.50	13.50
242	Tom Poholsky	45.00	22.50	13.50
243	Larry Doby	100.00	50.00	25.00
244	Vic Wertz	45.00	22.50	13.50
245	Sherry Robertson	45.00	22.50	13.50
246	George Kell	100.00	50.00	25.00
247	Randy Gumpert	45.00	22.50	13.50
248	Frank Shea	45.00	22.50	13.50
249	Bobby Adams	45.00	22.50	13.50
250	Carl Erskine	100.00	50.00	25.00
251	Chico Carrasquel	95.00	47.50	27.50
252	Vern Bickford	60.00	30.00	18.00
253	Johnny Berardino	75.00	37.50	22.50
254	Joe Dobson	60.00	30.00	18.00
255	Clyde Vollmer	60.00	30.00	18.00
256	Pete Suder	60.00	30.00	18.00
257	Bobby Avila	60.00	30.00	18.00
258	Steve Gromek	60.00	30.00	18.00
259	Bob Addis	60.00	30.00	18.00
260	Pete Castiglione	60.00	30.00	18.00
261	Willie Mays	2,200	1,100	660.00
262	Virgil Trucks	60.00	30.00	18.00
263	Harry Brecheen	60.00	30.00	18.00
264	Roy Hartsfield	60.00	30.00	18.00
265	Chuck Diering	60.00	30.00	18.00
266	Murry Dickson	60.00	30.00	18.00
267	Sid Gordon	60.00	30.00	18.00
268	Bob Lemon	125.00	62.50	31.25
269	Willard Nixon	60.00	30.00	18.00
270	Lou Brissie	60.00	30.00	18.00
271	Jim Delsing	60.00	30.00	18.00
272	Mike Garcia	60.00	30.00	18.00
273	Erv Palica	70.00	35.00	20.00
274	Ralph Branca	125.00	62.50	31.25
275	Pat Mullin	60.00	30.00	18.00
276	Jim Wilson	60.00	30.00	18.00
277	Early Wynn	175.00	85.00	50.00
278	Al Clark	60.00	30.00	18.00
279	Ed Stewart	60.00	30.00	18.00
280	Cloyd Boyer	60.00	30.00	18.00
281	Tommy Brown	60.00	30.00	18.00
282	Birdie Tebbetts	60.00	30.00	18.00
283	Phil Masi	60.00	30.00	18.00
284	Hank Arft	60.00	30.00	18.00
285	Cliff Fannin	60.00	30.00	18.00
286	Joe De Maestri	60.00	30.00	18.00
287	Steve Bilko	60.00	30.00	18.00
288	Chet Nichols	60.00	30.00	18.00
289	Tommy Holmes	60.00	30.00	18.00
290	Joe Astroth	60.00	30.00	18.00
291	Gil Coan	60.00	30.00	18.00
292	Floyd Baker	60.00	30.00	18.00
293	Sibby Sisti	60.00	30.00	18.00
294	Walker Cooper	60.00	30.00	18.00
295	Phil Cavarretta	60.00	30.00	18.00
296	"Red" Rolfe	60.00	30.00	18.00
297	Andy Seminick	60.00	30.00	18.00
298	Bob Ross	60.00	30.00	18.00
299	Ray Murray	60.00	30.00	18.00
300	Barney McCosky	60.00	30.00	18.00
301	Bob Porterfield	60.00	30.00	18.00
302	Max Surkont	60.00	30.00	18.00
303	Harry Dorish	60.00	30.00	18.00
304	Sam Dente	60.00	30.00	18.00
305	Paul Richards	60.00	30.00	18.00
306	Lou Sleator	60.00	30.00	18.00
307a	Frank Campos (Black star on back to right of "TOPPS BASEBALL.") (Graded "Very Good" example auctioned 4/096 for $3,231.))			

		NM	EX	VG
307b	Frank Campos (Red star on back to right of "TOPPS BASEBALL.")	60.00	30.00	18.00
308	Luis Aloma	60.00	30.00	18.00
309	Jim Busby	60.00	30.00	18.00
310	George Metkovich	125.00	30.00	18.00
311	Mickey Mantle (DP)	29,500	17,000	8,000
312	Jackie Robinson (DP)	2,200	1,100	550.00
313	Bobby Thomson (DP)	340.00	170.00	85.00
314	Roy Campanella	2,500	1,250	625.00
315	Leo Durocher	600.00	300.00	150.00
316	Davey Williams	275.00	135.00	80.00
317	Connie Marrero	275.00	135.00	80.00
318	Hal Gregg	275.00	135.00	80.00
319	Al Walker	300.00	150.00	90.00
320	John Rutherford	300.00	150.00	90.00
321	*Joe Black*	400.00	200.00	100.00
322	Randy Jackson	275.00	135.00	80.00
323	Bubba Church	275.00	135.00	80.00
324	Warren Hacker	275.00	135.00	80.00
325	Bill Serena	275.00	135.00	80.00
326	George Shuba	400.00	200.00	100.00
327	Archie Wilson	275.00	135.00	80.00
328	Bob Borkowski	275.00	135.00	80.00
329	Ivan Delock	275.00	135.00	80.00
330	Turk Lown	275.00	135.00	80.00
331	Tom Morgan	275.00	135.00	80.00
332	Tony Bartirome	275.00	135.00	80.00
333	Pee Wee Reese	1,800	900.00	450.00
334	Wilmer Mizell	275.00	135.00	80.00
335	Ted Lepcio	275.00	135.00	80.00
336	Dave Koslo	275.00	135.00	80.00
337	Jim Hearn	275.00	135.00	80.00
338	Sal Yvars	275.00	135.00	80.00
339	Russ Meyer	275.00	135.00	80.00
340	Bob Hooper	275.00	135.00	80.00
341	Hal Jeffcoat	275.00	135.00	80.00
342	*Clem Labine*	500.00	250.00	125.00
343	Dick Gernert	275.00	135.00	80.00
344	Ewell Blackwell	275.00	135.00	80.00
345	Sam White	275.00	135.00	80.00
346	George Spencer	275.00	135.00	80.00
347	Joe Adcock	375.00	187.50	100.00
348	Bob Kelly	275.00	135.00	80.00
349	Bob Cain	275.00	135.00	80.00
350	Cal Abrams	275.00	135.00	80.00
351	Al Dark	300.00	150.00	90.00
352	Karl Drews	275.00	135.00	80.00
353	Bob Del Greco	275.00	135.00	80.00
354	Fred Hatfield	275.00	135.00	80.00
355	Bobby Morgan	300.00	150.00	90.00
356	Toby Atwell	275.00	135.00	80.00
357	Smoky Burgess	350.00	175.00	100.00
358	John Kucab	275.00	135.00	80.00
359	Dee Fondy	275.00	135.00	80.00
360	George Crowe	275.00	135.00	80.00
361	Bill Posedel	275.00	135.00	80.00
362	Ken Heintzelman	275.00	135.00	80.00
363	Dick Rozek	275.00	135.00	80.00
364	Clyde Sukeforth	275.00	135.00	80.00
365	"Cookie" Lavagetto	275.00	135.00	80.00
366	Dave Madison	275.00	135.00	80.00
367	Bob Thorpe	275.00	135.00	80.00
368	Ed Wright	275.00	135.00	80.00
369	*Dick Groat*	400.00	200.00	120.00
370	Billy Hoeft	275.00	135.00	80.00
371	Bob Hofman	275.00	135.00	80.00
372	*Gil McDougald*	500.00	250.00	150.00
373	Jim Turner	375.00	187.50	100.00
374	Al Benton	275.00	135.00	80.00
375	Jack Merson	275.00	135.00	80.00
376	Faye Throneberry	275.00	135.00	80.00
377	Chuck Dressen	275.00	135.00	80.00
378	Les Fusselman	275.00	135.00	80.00
379	Joe Rossi	275.00	135.00	80.00
380	Clem Koshorek	275.00	135.00	80.00
381	Milton Stock	275.00	135.00	80.00
382	Sam Jones	275.00	135.00	80.00
383	Del Wilber	275.00	135.00	80.00
384	Frank Crosetti	500.00	250.00	125.00
385	Herman Franks	275.00	135.00	80.00
386	Eddie Yuhas	275.00	135.00	80.00
387	Billy Meyer	275.00	135.00	80.00
388	Bob Chipman	275.00	135.00	80.00
389	Ben Wade	300.00	150.00	90.00
390	Glenn Nelson	300.00	150.00	90.00
391	Ben Chapman (Photo actually Sam Chapman.)	275.00	135.00	80.00
392	*Hoyt Wilhelm*	900.00	450.00	225.00
393	Ebba St. Claire	275.00	135.00	80.00
394	Billy Herman	450.00	225.00	120.00
395	Jake Pitler	300.00	150.00	90.00
396	*Dick Williams*	450.00	225.00	120.00
397	Forrest Main	275.00	135.00	80.00
398	Hal Rice	275.00	135.00	80.00
399	Jim Fridley	275.00	135.00	80.00
400	Bill Dickey	1,100	550.00	330.00
401	Bob Schultz	275.00	135.00	80.00
402	Earl Harrist	275.00	135.00	80.00
403	Bill Miller	300.00	150.00	90.00
404	Dick Brodowski	275.00	135.00	80.00
405	Eddie Pellagrini	275.00	135.00	80.00
406	*Joe Nuxhall*	450.00	225.00	120.00
407	*Eddie Mathews*	10,000	3,600	1,525

1952 Topps "Canadian"

Perhaps because the "gray back" 1954 Topps cards have long been known as the "Canadian" issue, there is growing hobby support for the belief that a similar abbreviated set was printed in Canada for distribution there. The cards differ from the regular 1952 Topps of the same numerical range in that they are printed on a gray-backed cardboard stock, distinctly different from the cream-colored stock found on most '52 Topps #131-190. Additionally, the fronts of most, but not all, of the "Canadian" cards have colors which are subjectively

darker or more muted than the the "U.S.A." versions. The market is just beginning to differentiate values between the two types, though the gray-backs are considered scarcer.

		NM	EX	VG
Complete Set (60):		5,000	2,500	1,500
Common Player:		80.00	40.00	24.00
131	Morrie Martin	80.00	40.00	24.00
132	Clyde Kluttz	80.00	40.00	24.00
133	Al Widmar	80.00	40.00	24.00
134	Joe Tipton	80.00	40.00	24.00
135	Dixie Howell	80.00	40.00	24.00
136	Johnny Schmitz	85.00	42.50	25.00
137	Roy McMillan	80.00	40.00	24.00
138	Bill MacDonald	80.00	40.00	24.00
139	Ken Wood	80.00	40.00	24.00
140	John Antonelli	80.00	40.00	24.00
141	Clint Hartung	80.00	40.00	24.00
142	Harry Perkowski	80.00	40.00	24.00
143	Les Moss	80.00	40.00	24.00
144	Ed Blake	80.00	40.00	24.00
145	Joe Haynes	80.00	40.00	24.00
146	Frank House	80.00	40.00	24.00
147	Bob Young	80.00	40.00	24.00
148	Johnny Klippstein	80.00	40.00	24.00
149	Dick Kryhoski	80.00	40.00	24.00
150	Ted Beard	80.00	40.00	24.00
151	Wally Post	80.00	40.00	24.00
152	Al Evans	80.00	40.00	24.00
153	Bob Rush	80.00	40.00	24.00
154	Joe Muir	80.00	40.00	24.00
155	Frank Overmire	85.00	42.50	25.00
156	Frank Hiller	80.00	40.00	24.00
157	Bob Usher	80.00	40.00	24.00
158	Eddie Waitkus	80.00	40.00	24.00
159	Saul Rogovin	80.00	40.00	24.00
160	Owen Friend	80.00	40.00	24.00
161	Bud Byerly	80.00	40.00	24.00
162	Del Crandall	80.00	40.00	24.00
163	Stan Rojek	80.00	40.00	24.00
164	Walt Dubiel	80.00	40.00	24.00
165	Eddie Kazak	80.00	40.00	24.00
166	Paul LaPalme	80.00	40.00	24.00
167	Bill Howerton	80.00	40.00	24.00
168	Charlie Silvera	100.00	50.00	30.00
169	Howie Judson	80.00	40.00	24.00
170	Gus Bell	100.00	50.00	30.00
171	Ed Erautt	80.00	40.00	24.00
172	Eddie Miksis	80.00	40.00	24.00
173	Roy Smalley	80.00	40.00	24.00
174	Clarence Marshall	80.00	40.00	24.00
175	Billy Martin	500.00	250.00	150.00
176	Hank Edwards	80.00	40.00	24.00
177	Bill Wight	80.00	40.00	24.00
178	Cass Michaels	80.00	40.00	24.00
179	Frank Smith	80.00	40.00	24.00
180	Charley Maxwell	80.00	40.00	24.00
181	Bob Swift	80.00	40.00	24.00
182	Billy Hitchcock	80.00	40.00	24.00
183	Erv Dusak	80.00	40.00	24.00
184	Bob Ramazzotti	80.00	40.00	24.00
185	Bill Nicholson	80.00	40.00	24.00
186	Walt Masterson	80.00	40.00	24.00
187	Bob Miller	80.00	40.00	24.00
188	Clarence Podbielan	80.00	40.00	24.00
189	Pete Reiser	80.00	40.00	24.00
190	Don Johnson	80.00	40.00	24.00

1953 Topps

The 1953 Topps set reflects the company's continuing legal battles with Bowman. The set, originally intended to consist of 280 cards, is lacking six numbers (253, 261, 267, 268, 271 and 275) that represent players whose contracts were lost to the competition. The 2-5/8" x 3-3/4" cards feature painted player pictures. A color team logo appears at a bottom panel (red for American League and black for National). Card backs contain the first baseball-card trivia questions along with brief

statistics and player biographies. In the red panel at the top, which lists the player's personal data, cards from the 2nd Series (#86-165 plus 10, 44, 61, 72 and 81) can be found with that data printed in either black or white, black being the marginally scarcer variety. Eighty-five cards between #1-165 were printed in noticeably larger quantities than the others, and are indicated in these listings with a double-print (DP) notation. Cards #221-280, the high numbers, were printed late in the season, in smaller quantities than the earlier series. Among the high numbers, even scarcer short-printed (SP) cards are interspersed in the series.

		NM	EX	VG
Complete Set (274):		27,500	9,250	5,250
Common Player (1-165):		30.00	15.00	9.00
Common Player (166-220):		35.00	17.50	10.00
Common Player (221-280):		60.00	30.00	18.00
Short-print Player (221-280):		90.00	45.00	27.50
1	Jackie Robinson (DP)	900.00	450.00	270.00
2	Luke Easter (DP)	40.00	20.00	12.00
3	George Crowe	40.00	20.00	12.00
4	Ben Wade	45.00	22.50	13.50
5	Joe Dobson	40.00	20.00	12.00
6	Sam Jones	40.00	20.00	12.00
7	Bob Borkowski (DP)	30.00	15.00	9.00
8	Clem Koshorek (DP)	30.00	15.00	9.00
9	Joe Collins	45.00	22.50	13.50
10	Smoky Burgess (SP)	70.00	35.00	20.00
11	Sal Yvars	40.00	20.00	12.00
12	Howie Judson (DP)	30.00	15.00	9.00
13	Connie Marrero (DP)	30.00	15.00	9.00
14	Clem Labine (DP)	60.00	30.00	18.00
15	Bobo Newsom (DP)	30.00	15.00	9.00
16	Harry Lowrey (DP)	30.00	15.00	9.00
17	Billy Hitchcock	40.00	20.00	12.00
18	Ted Lepcio (DP)	30.00	15.00	9.00
19	Mel Parnell (DP)	30.00	15.00	9.00
20	Hank Thompson	40.00	20.00	12.00
21	Billy Johnson	40.00	20.00	12.00
22	Howie Fox	40.00	20.00	12.00
23	Toby Atwell (DP)	30.00	15.00	9.00
24	Ferris Fain	40.00	20.00	12.00
25	Ray Boone	40.00	20.00	12.00
26	Dale Mitchell (DP)	30.00	15.00	9.00
27	Roy Campanella (DP)	300.00	150.00	75.00
28	Eddie Pellagrini	40.00	20.00	12.00
29	Hal Jeffcoat	40.00	20.00	12.00
30	Willard Nixon	40.00	20.00	12.00
31	Ewell Blackwell	55.00	27.50	16.50
32	Clyde Vollmer	40.00	20.00	12.00
33	Bob Kennedy (DP)	30.00	15.00	9.00
34	George Shuba	60.00	30.00	18.00
35	Irv Noren (DP)	35.00	17.50	10.00
36	Johnny Groth (DP)	30.00	15.00	9.00
37	Ed Mathews (DP)	275.00	187.50	100.00
38	Jim Hearn (DP)	30.00	15.00	9.00
39	Eddie Miksis	40.00	20.00	12.00
40	John Lipon	40.00	20.00	12.00
41	Enos Slaughter	80.00	40.00	24.00
42	Gus Zernial (DP)	30.00	15.00	9.00
43	Gil McDougald	75.00	37.50	22.50
44	Ellis Kinder (DP)	75.00	37.50	22.50
45	Grady Hatton (DP)	30.00	15.00	9.00
46	Johnny Klippstein (DP)	30.00	15.00	9.00
47	Bubba Church (DP)	30.00	15.00	9.00
48	Bob Del Greco (DP)	30.00	15.00	9.00
49	Faye Throneberry (DP)	30.00	15.00	9.00
50	Chuck Dressen (DP)	40.00	20.00	12.00
51	Frank Campos (DP)	30.00	15.00	9.00
52	Ted Gray (DP)	30.00	15.00	9.00
53	Sherman Lollar (DP)	30.00	15.00	9.00
54	Bob Feller (DP)	175.00	87.50	50.00
55	Maurice McDermott (DP)	30.00	15.00	9.00
56	Gerald Staley (DP)	30.00	15.00	9.00
57	Carl Scheib	40.00	20.00	12.00
58	George Metkovich	40.00	20.00	12.00
59	Karl Drews (DP)	30.00	15.00	9.00
60	Cloyd Boyer (DP)	30.00	15.00	9.00
61	Early Wynn (SP)	125.00	62.50	31.25
62	Monte Irvin (DP)	100.00	50.00	30.00
63	Gus Niarhos (DP)	30.00	15.00	9.00
64	Dave Philley	40.00	20.00	12.00
65	Earl Harrist	40.00	20.00	12.00
66	Orestes Minoso	70.00	35.00	20.00
67	Roy Sievers (DP)	30.00	15.00	9.00
68	Del Rice	40.00	20.00	12.00
69	Dick Brodowski	40.00	20.00	12.00
70	Ed Yuhas	40.00	20.00	12.00
71	Tony Bartirome	40.00	20.00	12.00
72	Fred Hutchinson (SP)	75.00	37.50	22.50
73	Eddie Robinson	40.00	20.00	12.00
74	Joe Rossi	40.00	20.00	12.00
75	Mike Garcia	40.00	20.00	12.00
76	Pee Wee Reese	200.00	100.00	60.00
77	Johnny Mize	75.00	37.50	22.50
78	Al Schoendienst	100.00	50.00	30.00
79	Johnny Wyrostek	40.00	20.00	12.00
80	Jim Hegan	40.00	20.00	12.00
81	Joe Black (SP)	80.00	40.00	20.00
82	Mickey Mantle	3,000	1,200	525.00
83	Howie Pollet	40.00	20.00	12.00
84	Bob Hooper (DP)	30.00	15.00	9.00
85	Bobby Morgan (DP)	35.00	17.50	10.00
86	Billy Martin	175.00	87.50	43.75
87	Ed Lopat	60.00	30.00	18.00
88	Willie Jones (DP)	30.00	15.00	9.00
89	Chuck Stobbs (DP)	30.00	15.00	9.00
90	Hank Edwards (DP)	30.00	15.00	9.00
91	Ebba St. Claire (DP)	30.00	15.00	9.00
92	Paul Minner (DP)	30.00	15.00	9.00
93	Hal Rice (DP)	30.00	15.00	9.00
94	William Kennedy (DP)	30.00	15.00	9.00
95	Willard Marshall (DP)	30.00	15.00	9.00
96	Virgil Trucks	40.00	20.00	12.00
97	Don Kolloway (DP)	30.00	15.00	9.00
98	Cal Abrams (DP)	30.00	15.00	9.00

#	Player	NM	EX	VG
99	Dave Madison	40.00	20.00	12.00
100	Bill Miller	40.00	20.00	12.00
101	Ted Wilks	40.00	20.00	12.00
102	Connie Ryan (DP)	30.00	15.00	9.00
103	Joe Astroth (DP)	30.00	15.00	9.00
104	Yogi Berra	400.00	200.00	100.00
105	Joe Nuxhall (DP)	35.00	17.50	10.00
106	John Antonelli	40.00	20.00	12.00
107	Danny O'Connell (DP)	30.00	15.00	9.00
108	Bob Porterfield (DP)	30.00	15.00	9.00
109	Alvin Dark	40.00	20.00	12.00
110	Herman Wehmeier (DP)	30.00	15.00	9.00
111	Hank Sauer (DP)	30.00	15.00	9.00
112	Ned Garver (DP)	30.00	15.00	9.00
113	Jerry Priddy	40.00	20.00	12.00
114	Phil Rizzuto	250.00	125.00	62.50
115	George Spencer	40.00	20.00	12.00
116	Frank Smith (DP)	30.00	15.00	9.00
117	Sid Gordon (DP)	30.00	15.00	9.00
118	Gus Bell (DP)	30.00	15.00	9.00
119	John Sain	75.00	37.50	22.50
120	Davey Williams	40.00	20.00	12.00
121	Walt Dropo	40.00	20.00	12.00
122	Elmer Valo	40.00	20.00	12.00
123	Tommy Byrne (DP)	30.00	15.00	9.00
124	Sibby Sisti (DP)	30.00	15.00	9.00
125	Dick Williams (DP)	35.00	17.50	10.00
126	Bill Connelly (DP)	30.00	15.00	9.00
127	Clint Courtney (DP)	30.00	15.00	9.00
128	Wilmer Mizell (DP)	30.00	15.00	9.00
129	Keith Thomas	40.00	20.00	12.00
130	Turk Lown (DP)	30.00	15.00	9.00
131	Harry Byrd (DP)	30.00	15.00	9.00
132	Tom Morgan	45.00	22.50	13.50
133	Gil Coan	40.00	20.00	12.00
134	Rube Walker	45.00	22.50	13.50
135	Al Rosen (DP)	45.00	22.50	13.50
136	Ken Heintzelman (DP)	30.00	15.00	9.00
137	John Rutherford (DP)	35.00	17.50	10.00
138	George Kell	55.00	27.50	16.50
139	Sammy White	40.00	20.00	12.00
140	Tommy Glaviano	40.00	20.00	12.00
141	Allie Reynolds (DP)	75.00	37.50	22.50
142	Vic Wertz	40.00	20.00	12.00
143	Billy Pierce	40.00	20.00	12.00
144	Bob Schultz (DP)	30.00	15.00	9.00
145	Harry Dorish (DP)	30.00	15.00	9.00
146	Granville Hamner	40.00	20.00	12.00
147	Warren Spahn	200.00	100.00	50.00
148	Mickey Grasso	40.00	20.00	12.00
149	Dom DiMaggio (DP)	65.00	32.50	20.00
150	Harry Simpson (DP)	30.00	15.00	9.00
151	Hoyt Wilhelm	100.00	50.00	25.00
152	Bob Adams (DP)	30.00	15.00	9.00
153	Andy Seminick (DP)	30.00	15.00	9.00
154	Dick Groat	40.00	20.00	12.00
155	Dutch Leonard	40.00	20.00	12.00
156	Jim Rivera (DP)	30.00	15.00	9.00
157	Bob Addis (DP)	30.00	15.00	9.00
158	*John Logan*	40.00	20.00	12.00
159	Wayne Terwilliger (DP)	30.00	15.00	9.00
160	Bob Young	40.00	20.00	12.00
161	Vern Bickford (DP)	30.00	15.00	9.00
162	Ted Kluszewski	80.00	40.00	24.00
163	Fred Hatfield (DP)	30.00	15.00	9.00
164	Frank Shea (DP)	30.00	15.00	9.00
165	Billy Hoeft	40.00	20.00	12.00
166	Bill Hunter	35.00	17.50	10.00
167	Art Schult	35.00	17.50	10.00
168	Willard Schmidt	35.00	17.50	10.00
169	Dizzy Trout	35.00	17.50	10.00
170	Bill Werle	35.00	17.50	10.00
171	Bill Glynn	35.00	17.50	10.00
172	Rip Repulski	35.00	17.50	10.00
173	Preston Ward	35.00	17.50	10.00
174	Billy Loes	45.00	22.50	13.50
175	Ron Kline	35.00	17.50	10.00
176	*Don Hoak*	40.00	20.00	12.00
177	Jim Dyck	35.00	17.50	10.00
178	Jim Waugh	35.00	17.50	10.00
179	Gene Hermanski	35.00	17.50	10.00
180	Virgil Stallcup	35.00	17.50	10.00
181	Al Zarilla	35.00	17.50	10.00
182	Bob Hofman	35.00	17.50	10.00
183	*Stu Miller*	35.00	17.50	10.00
184	*Hal Brown*	35.00	17.50	10.00
185	*Jim Pendleton*	35.00	17.50	10.00
186	Charlie Bishop	35.00	17.50	10.00
187	Jim Fridley	35.00	17.50	10.00
188	*Andy Carey*	60.00	30.00	18.00
189	Ray Jablonski	35.00	17.50	10.00
190	Dixie Walker	35.00	17.50	10.00
191	Ralph Kiner	75.00	37.50	18.75
192	Wally Westlake	35.00	17.50	10.00
193	Mike Clark	35.00	17.50	10.00
194	Eddie Kazak	35.00	17.50	10.00
195	Ed McGhee	35.00	17.50	10.00
196	Bob Keegan	35.00	17.50	10.00
197	Del Crandall	35.00	17.50	10.00
198	Forrest Main	35.00	17.50	10.00
199	Marion Fricano	35.00	17.50	10.00
200	Gordon Goldsberry	35.00	17.50	10.00
201	Paul La Palme	35.00	17.50	10.00
202	Carl Sawatski	35.00	17.50	10.00
203	Cliff Fannin	35.00	17.50	10.00
204	Dick Bokelmann	35.00	17.50	10.00
205	Vern Benson	35.00	17.50	10.00
206	*Ed Bailey*	35.00	17.50	10.00
207	Whitey Ford	300.00	150.00	75.00
208	Jim Wilson	35.00	17.50	10.00
209	Jim Greengrass	35.00	17.50	10.00
210	*Bob Cerv*	45.00	22.20	13.50
211	J.W. Porter	35.00	17.50	10.00
212	Jack Dittmer	35.00	17.50	10.00
213	Ray Scarborough	35.00	17.50	10.00
214	*Bill Bruton*	35.00	17.50	10.00
215	*Gene Conley*	35.00	17.50	10.00
216	Jim Hughes	40.00	20.00	12.00

#	Player	NM	EX	VG
217	Murray Wall	35.00	17.50	10.00
218	Les Fusselman	35.00	17.50	10.00
219	Pete Runnels (Picture actually Don Johnson.)	35.00	17.50	10.00
220	Satchell Paige	900.00	450.00	270.00
221	Bob Milliken (SP)	100.00	50.00	30.00
222	Vic Janowicz	100.00	50.00	30.00
223	John O'Brien	60.00	30.00	18.00
224	Lou Sleater	60.00	30.00	18.00
225	Bobby Shantz (SP)	90.00	45.00	27.50
226	Ed Erautt (SP)	90.00	45.00	27.50
227	Morris Martin (SP)	90.00	45.00	27.50
228	Hal Newhouser (SP)	150.00	75.00	37.50
229	Rocky Krsnich (SP)	90.00	45.00	27.50
230	Johnny Lindell	60.00	30.00	18.00
231	Solly Hemus	60.00	30.00	18.00
232	Dick Kokos (SP)	90.00	45.00	27.50
233	Al Aber (SP)	90.00	45.00	27.50
234	Ray Murray	60.00	30.00	18.00
235	John Hetki	60.00	30.00	18.00
236	Harry Perkowski	60.00	30.00	18.00
237	Clarence Podbielan	60.00	30.00	18.00
238	Cal Hogue	60.00	30.00	18.00
239	Jim Delsing (SP)	90.00	45.00	27.50
240	Freddie Marsh (SP)	90.00	45.00	27.50
241	Al Sima	60.00	30.00	18.00
242	Charlie Silvera (SP)	100.00	50.00	30.00
243	Carlos Bernier	60.00	30.00	18.00
244	Willie Mays (SP)	2,500	1,000	400.00
245	Bill Norman	90.00	45.00	27.50
246	*Roy Face*	75.00	37.50	22.50
247	Mike Sandlock	60.00	30.00	18.00
248	Gene Stephens	60.00	30.00	18.00
249	Ed O'Brien (SP)	90.00	45.00	27.50
250	Bob Wilson (SP)	90.00	45.00	27.50
251	Sid Hudson (SP)	90.00	45.00	27.50
252	Henry Foiles (SP)	90.00	45.00	27.50
253	Not Issued			
254	Preacher Roe	100.00	50.00	25.00
255	Dixie Howell (SP)	100.00	50.00	25.00
256	Les Peden (SP)	90.00	45.00	27.50
257	Bob Boyd (SP)	90.00	45.00	27.50
258	*Jim Gilliam* (SP)	400.00	200.00	100.00
259	Roy McMillan	60.00	30.00	18.00
260	Sam Calderone (SP)	90.00	45.00	27.50
261	Not Issued			
262	Bob Oldis (SP)	90.00	45.00	27.50
263	*Johnny Podres* (SP)	300.00	150.00	90.00
264	Gene Woodling	95.00	47.50	27.50
265	Jackie Jensen (SP)	125.00	62.50	31.25
266	Bob Cain (SP)	90.00	45.00	27.50
267	Not Issued			
268	Not Issued			
269	Duane Pillette (SP)	90.00	45.00	27.50
270	Vern Stephens (SP)	90.00	45.00	27.50
271	Not Issued			
272	Bill Antonello (SP)	100.00	50.00	30.00
273	*Harvey Haddix* (SP)	125.00	62.50	31.25
274	John Riddle (SP)	90.00	45.00	27.50
275	Not Issued			
276	Ken Raffensberger (SP)	90.00	45.00	27.50
277	Don Lund (SP)	90.00	45.00	27.50
278	Willie Miranda (SP)	90.00	45.00	27.50
279	Joe Coleman	60.00	30.00	18.00
280	*Milt Bolling* (SP)	350.00	175.00	87.50

1954 Topps

The first issue to use two player pictures on the front, the 1954 Topps set remains popular today. Solid color backgrounds frame both color portraits and black-and-white action pictures of the player. The player's name, position, team and team logo appear at the top. Backs include an "Inside Baseball" cartoon regarding the player as well as statistics and biography. The 250-card, 2-5/8" x 3-3/4" set includes manager and coaches cards. A gray-back version of cards #1-50 is known, distinguished by the use of dark gray cardboard on back. These are often attributed to Canadian issue and carry a modest premium.

	NM	EX	VG
Complete Set (250):	9,250	4,000	2,400
Common Player (1-50):	20.00	10.00	6.00
Common Player (51-75):	35.00	17.50	10.00
Common Player (76-250):	20.00	10.00	6.00
1 Ted Williams	800.00	400.00	200.00
2 Gus Zernial	35.00	10.00	6.00
3 Monte Irvin	60.00	30.00	18.00
4 Hank Sauer	20.00	10.00	6.00
5 Ed Lopat	25.00	12.50	7.50
6 Pete Runnels	20.00	10.00	6.00
7 Ted Kluszewski	35.00	17.50	10.00
8 Bobby Young	20.00	10.00	6.00
9 Harvey Haddix	20.00	10.00	6.00
10 Jackie Robinson	300.00	150.00	90.00
11 Paul Smith	20.00	10.00	6.00

#	Player	NM	EX	VG
12	Del Crandall	20.00	10.00	6.00
13	Billy Martin	100.00	50.00	25.00
14	Preacher Roe	35.00	17.50	10.00
15	Al Rosen	30.00	15.00	9.00
16	Vic Janowicz	25.00	12.50	7.50
17	Phil Rizzuto	125.00	62.50	31.25
18	Walt Dropo	20.00	10.00	6.00
19	Johnny Lipon	20.00	10.00	6.00
20	Warren Spahn	150.00	75.00	37.50
21	Bobby Shantz	20.00	10.00	6.00
22	Jim Greengrass	20.00	10.00	6.00
23	Luke Easter	25.00	12.50	7.50
24	Granny Hamner	20.00	10.00	6.00
25	*Harvey Kuenn*	35.00	17.50	10.00
26	Ray Jablonski	20.00	10.00	6.00
27	Ferris Fain	20.00	10.00	6.00
28	Paul Minner	20.00	10.00	6.00
29	Jim Hegan	20.00	10.00	6.00
30	Ed Mathews	100.00	50.00	25.00
31	Johnny Klippstein	20.00	10.00	6.00
32	Duke Snider	200.00	100.00	50.00
33	Johnny Schmitz	20.00	10.00	6.00
34	Jim Rivera	20.00	10.00	6.00
35	Junior Gilliam	35.00	17.50	10.00
36	Hoyt Wilhelm	40.00	20.00	12.00
37	Whitey Ford	200.00	100.00	50.00
38	Eddie Stanky	20.00	10.00	6.00
39	Sherm Lollar	20.00	10.00	6.00
40	Mel Parnell	20.00	10.00	6.00
41	Willie Jones	20.00	10.00	6.00
42	Don Mueller	20.00	10.00	6.00
43	Dick Groat	20.00	10.00	6.00
44	Ned Garver	20.00	10.00	6.00
45	Richie Ashburn	80.00	40.00	20.00
46	Ken Raffensberger	20.00	10.00	6.00
47	Ellis Kinder	20.00	10.00	6.00
48	Billy Hunter	20.00	10.00	6.00
49	Ray Murray	20.00	10.00	6.00
50	Yogi Berra	300.00	150.00	75.00
51	Johnny Lindell	35.00	17.50	10.00
52	*Vic Power*	40.00	20.00	12.00
53	Jack Dittmer	35.00	17.50	10.00
54	Vern Stephens	35.00	17.50	10.00
55	Phil Cavarretta	35.00	17.50	10.00
56	Willie Miranda	35.00	17.50	10.00
57	Luis Aloma	35.00	17.50	10.00
58	Bob Wilson	35.00	17.50	10.00
59	Gene Conley	35.00	17.50	10.00
60	Frank Baumholtz	35.00	17.50	10.00
61	Bob Cain	35.00	17.50	10.00
62	Eddie Robinson	40.00	20.00	12.00
63	Johnny Pesky	35.00	17.50	10.00
64	Hank Thompson	35.00	17.50	10.00
65	Bob Swift	35.00	17.50	10.00
66	Ted Lepcio	35.00	17.50	10.00
67	Jim Willis	35.00	17.50	10.00
68	Sammy Calderone	35.00	17.50	10.00
69	Bud Podbielan	35.00	17.50	10.00
70	Larry Doby	75.00	37.50	18.75
71	Frank Smith	35.00	17.50	10.00
72	Preston Ward	35.00	17.50	10.00
73	Wayne Terwilliger	35.00	17.50	10.00
74	Bill Taylor	35.00	17.50	10.00
75	Fred Haney	35.00	17.50	10.00
76	Bob Scheffing	20.00	10.00	6.00
77	Ray Boone	20.00	10.00	6.00
78	Ted Kazanski	20.00	10.00	6.00
79	Andy Pafko	20.00	10.00	6.00
80	Jackie Jensen	30.00	15.00	9.00
81	Dave Hoskins	20.00	10.00	6.00
82	Milt Bolling	20.00	10.00	6.00
83	Joe Collins	25.00	12.50	7.50
84	Dick Cole	20.00	10.00	6.00
85	*Bob Turley*	35.00	17.50	10.00
86	Billy Herman	45.00	22.50	13.50
87	Roy Face	20.00	10.00	6.00
88	Matt Batts	20.00	10.00	6.00
89	Howie Pollet	20.00	10.00	6.00
90	Willie Mays	450.00	225.00	135.00
91	Bob Oldis	20.00	10.00	6.00
92	Wally Westlake	20.00	10.00	6.00
93	Sid Hudson	20.00	10.00	6.00
94	*Ernie Banks*	1,000	500.00	300.00
95	Hal Rice	20.00	10.00	6.00
96	Charlie Silvera	25.00	12.50	7.50
97	Jerry Lane	20.00	10.00	6.00
98	Joe Black	60.00	30.00	20.00
99	Bob Hofman	20.00	10.00	6.00
100	Bob Keegan	20.00	10.00	6.00
101	Gene Woodling	50.00	25.00	15.00
102	Gil Hodges	90.00	45.00	22.50
103	*Jim Lemon*	25.00	12.50	7.50
104	Mike Sandlock	20.00	10.00	6.00
105	Andy Carey	25.00	12.50	7.50
106	Dick Kokos	20.00	10.00	6.00
107	Duane Pillette	20.00	10.00	6.00
108	Thornton Kipper	20.00	10.00	6.00
109	Bill Bruton	20.00	10.00	6.00
110	Harry Dorish	20.00	10.00	6.00
111	Jim Delsing	20.00	10.00	6.00
112	Bill Renna	20.00	10.00	6.00
113	Bob Boyd	20.00	10.00	6.00
114	Dean Stone	20.00	10.00	6.00
115	"Rip" Repulski	20.00	10.00	6.00
116	Steve Bilko	20.00	10.00	6.00
117	Solly Hemus	20.00	10.00	6.00
118	Carl Scheib	20.00	10.00	6.00
119	Johnny Antonelli	20.00	10.00	6.00
120	Roy McMillan	20.00	10.00	6.00
121	Clem Labine	45.00	22.50	13.50
122	Johnny Logan	20.00	10.00	6.00
123	Bobby Adams	20.00	10.00	6.00
124	Marion Fricano	20.00	10.00	6.00
125	Harry Perkowski	20.00	10.00	6.00
126	Ben Wade	25.00	12.50	7.50
127	Steve O'Neill	20.00	10.00	6.00
128	*Hank Aaron*	1,800	900.00	450.00
129	Forrest Jacobs	20.00	10.00	6.00

		NM	EX	VG
130	Hank Bauer	40.00	20.00	10.00
131	Reno Bertoia	20.00	10.00	6.00
132	*Tom Lasorda*	250.00	125.00	62.50
133	Del Baker	20.00	10.00	6.00
134	Cal Hogue	20.00	10.00	6.00
135	Joe Presko	20.00	10.00	6.00
136	Connie Ryan	20.00	10.00	6.00
137	*Wally Moon*	35.00	17.50	10.00
138	Bob Borkowski	20.00	10.00	6.00
139	Ed O'Brien, Johnny O'Brien	60.00	30.00	15.00
140	Tom Wright	20.00	10.00	6.00
141	*Joe Jay*	40.00	20.00	12.00
142	Tom Poholsky	20.00	10.00	6.00
143	Rollie Hemsley	20.00	10.00	6.00
144	Bill Werle	20.00	10.00	6.00
145	Elmer Valo	20.00	10.00	6.00
146	Don Johnson	20.00	10.00	6.00
147	John Riddle	20.00	10.00	6.00
148	Bob Trice	20.00	10.00	6.00
149	Jim Robertson	20.00	10.00	6.00
150	Dick Kryhoski	20.00	10.00	6.00
151	Alex Grammas	20.00	10.00	6.00
152	Mike Blyzka	20.00	10.00	6.00
153	Rube Walker	25.00	12.50	7.50
154	Mike Fornieles	20.00	10.00	6.00
155	Bob Kennedy	20.00	10.00	6.00
156	Joe Coleman	20.00	10.00	6.00
157	Don Lenhardt	20.00	10.00	6.00
158	"Peanuts" Lowrey	20.00	10.00	6.00
159	Dave Philley	20.00	10.00	6.00
160	"Red" Kress	20.00	10.00	6.00
161	John Hetki	20.00	10.00	6.00
162	Herman Wehmeier	20.00	10.00	6.00
163	Frank House	20.00	10.00	6.00
164	Stu Miller	20.00	10.00	6.00
165	Jim Pendleton	20.00	10.00	6.00
166	Johnny Podres	45.00	22.50	13.50
167	Don Lund	20.00	10.00	6.00
168	Morrie Martin	20.00	10.00	6.00
169	Jim Hughes	25.00	12.50	7.50
170	*Jim Rhodes*	40.00	20.00	12.00
171	Leo Kiely	20.00	10.00	6.00
172	Hal Brown	20.00	10.00	6.00
173	Jack Harshman	20.00	10.00	6.00
174	Tom Qualters	20.00	10.00	6.00
175	*Frank Leja*	25.00	12.50	7.50
176	Bob Keely	20.00	10.00	6.00
177	Bob Milliken	25.00	12.50	7.50
178	Bill Glynn (Glynn)	20.00	10.00	6.00
179	Gair Allie	20.00	10.00	6.00
180	Wes Westrum	20.00	10.00	6.00
181	Mel Roach	20.00	10.00	6.00
182	Chuck Harmon	20.00	10.00	6.00
183	Earle Combs	25.00	12.50	7.50
184	Ed Bailey	20.00	10.00	6.00
185	Chuck Stobbs	20.00	10.00	6.00
186	Karl Olson	20.00	10.00	6.00
187	"Heinie" Manush	25.00	12.50	7.50
188	Dave Jolly	20.00	10.00	6.00
189	Bob Ross	20.00	10.00	6.00
190	Ray Herbert	20.00	10.00	6.00
191	*Dick Schofield*	25.00	12.50	7.50
192	"Cot" Deal	20.00	10.00	6.00
193	Johnny Hopp	20.00	10.00	6.00
194	Bill Sarni	20.00	10.00	6.00
195	Bill Consolo	20.00	10.00	6.00
196	Stan Jok	20.00	10.00	6.00
197	"Schoolboy" Rowe	20.00	10.00	6.00
198	Carl Sawatski	20.00	10.00	6.00
199	"Rocky" Nelson	20.00	10.00	6.00
200	Larry Jansen	20.00	10.00	6.00
201	*Al Kaline*	700.00	350.00	175.00
202	*Bob Purkey*	20.00	10.00	6.00
203	Harry Brecheen	20.00	10.00	6.00
204	Angel Scull	20.00	10.00	6.00
205	Johnny Sain	30.00	15.00	9.00
206	Ray Crone	20.00	10.00	6.00
207	Tom Oliver	20.00	10.00	6.00
208	Grady Hatton	20.00	10.00	6.00
209	Charlie Thompson	25.00	12.50	7.50
210	*Bob Buhl*	20.00	10.00	6.00
211	Don Hoak	25.00	12.50	7.50
212	Mickey Micelotta	20.00	10.00	6.00
213	John Fitzpatrick	20.00	10.00	6.00
214	Arnold Portocarrero	20.00	10.00	6.00
215	Ed McGhee	20.00	10.00	6.00
216	Al Sima	20.00	10.00	6.00
217	Paul Schreiber	20.00	10.00	6.00
218	Fred Marsh	20.00	10.00	6.00
219	Charlie Kress	20.00	10.00	6.00
220	Ruben Gomez	20.00	10.00	6.00
221	Dick Brodowski	20.00	10.00	6.00
222	Bill Wilson	20.00	10.00	6.00
223	Joe Haynes	20.00	10.00	6.00
224	Dick Weik	20.00	10.00	6.00
225	Don Liddle	20.00	10.00	6.00
226	Jehosie Heard	20.00	10.00	6.00
227	Buster Mills	20.00	10.00	6.00
228	Gene Hermanski	20.00	10.00	6.00
229	Bob Talbot	20.00	10.00	6.00
230	Bob Kuzava	25.00	12.50	7.50
231	Roy Smalley	20.00	10.00	6.00
232	Lou Limmer	20.00	10.00	6.00
233	Augie Galan	20.00	10.00	6.00
234	*Jerry Lynch*	20.00	10.00	6.00
235	Vern Law	20.00	10.00	6.00
236	Paul Penson	20.00	10.00	6.00
237	Mike Ryba	20.00	10.00	6.00
238	Al Aber	20.00	10.00	6.00
239	*Bill Skowron*	90.00	45.00	22.50
240	Sam Mele	20.00	10.00	6.00
241	Bob Miller	20.00	10.00	6.00
242	Curt Roberts	20.00	10.00	6.00
243	Ray Blades	20.00	10.00	6.00
244	Leroy Wheat	20.00	10.00	6.00
245	Roy Sievers	20.00	10.00	6.00
246	Howie Fox	20.00	10.00	6.00
247	Eddie Mayo	20.00	10.00	6.00
248	*Al Smith*	20.00	10.00	6.00
249	Wilmer Mizell	20.00	10.00	6.00
250	Ted Williams	700.00	200.00	100.00

1954 Topps "Canadian"

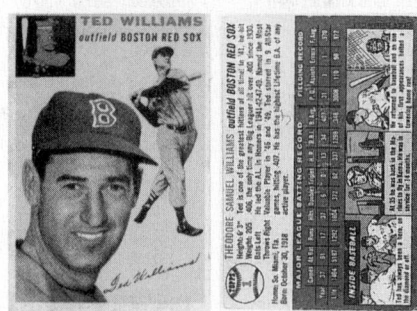

This version of the first 50 cards from 1954 Topps has long been known as the "Canadian" issue. It is widely believed that the abbreviated set was intended solely for Canadian distribution. The cards differ from the regular 1954 Topps in that they are printed on a gray-backed cardboard stock, distinctly different from the white stock found on most '54 Topps. Later series white-back Topps cards were sold in Canada in O-Pee-Chee marked wrappers at four for a nickel as opposed to six for five cents in the U.S.

		NM	EX	VG
	Complete Set (50):	5,500	2,750	1,750
	Common Player:	40.00	20.00	12.00
1	Ted Williams	1,500	700.00	450.00
2	Gus Zernial	60.00	20.00	12.00
3	Monte Irvin	115.00	55.00	35.00
4	Hank Sauer	40.00	20.00	12.00
5	Ed Lopat	50.00	25.00	15.00
6	Pete Runnels	40.00	20.00	12.00
7	Ted Kluszewski	75.00	35.00	22.50
8	Bobby Young	40.00	20.00	12.00
9	Harvey Haddix	40.00	20.00	12.00
10	Jackie Robinson	525.00	250.00	150.00
11	Paul Smith	40.00	20.00	12.00
12	Del Crandall	40.00	20.00	12.00
13	Billy Martin	225.00	100.00	65.00
14	Preacher Roe	75.00	35.00	22.50
15	Al Rosen	85.00	40.00	25.00
16	Vic Janowicz	45.00	22.00	13.50
17	Phil Rizzuto	225.00	110.00	65.00
18	Walt Dropo	40.00	20.00	12.00
19	Johnny Lipon	40.00	20.00	12.00
20	Warren Spahn	215.00	100.00	60.00
21	Bobby Shantz	45.00	22.50	13.50
22	Jim Greengrass	40.00	20.00	12.00
23	Luke Easter	40.00	20.00	12.00
24	Granny Hamner	40.00	20.00	12.00
25	Harvey Kuenn	75.00	35.00	22.50
26	Ray Jablonski	40.00	20.00	12.00
27	Ferris Fain	40.00	20.00	12.00
28	Paul Minner	40.00	20.00	12.00
29	Jim Hegan	40.00	20.00	12.00
30	Ed Mathews	165.00	80.00	47.50
31	Johnny Klippstein	40.00	20.00	12.00
32	Duke Snider	315.00	150.00	90.00
33	Johnny Schmitz	40.00	20.00	12.00
34	Jim Rivera	40.00	20.00	12.00
35	Junior Gilliam	85.00	40.00	25.00
36	Hoyt Wilhelm	115.00	55.00	32.50
37	Whitey Ford	215.00	100.00	60.00
38	Eddie Stanky	45.00	22.50	13.50
39	Sherm Lollar	40.00	20.00	12.00
40	Mel Parnell	40.00	20.00	12.00
41	Willie Jones	40.00	20.00	12.00
42	Don Mueller	40.00	20.00	12.00
43	Dick Groat	40.00	20.00	12.00
44	Ned Garver	40.00	20.00	12.00
45	Richie Ashburn	140.00	70.00	40.00
46	Ken Raffensberger	40.00	20.00	12.00
47	Ellis Kinder	40.00	20.00	12.00
48	Billy Hunter	40.00	20.00	12.00
49	Ray Murray	40.00	20.00	12.00
50	Yogi Berra	365.00	175.00	100.00

1954 Topps Look 'N See

Among the 135 historical figures in this set is only one baseball player - Babe Ruth. These 2-1/16" x 2-15/16" cards feature colorful portrait paintings on the front and biographies on the back. The answer to a trivia question on back can be discovered by laying a piece of red cellophane over the question box.

		NM	EX	VG
	Complete Set (135):	3,000	1,500	900.00
	Common Card:	4.00	2.00	1.25
15	Babe Ruth	150.00	75.00	45.00

1954 Topps Scoops

World - and sports - history from the mid-18th Century through October 1953, is chronicled in this 156-card set. Four baseball subjects are presented in the set. Cards are 2-1/16" x 2-15/16" and feature on the front a color painting with a dated caption box at bottom. Originally a black scratch-off ink covered the caption box (cards with the black ink removed can still be considered Mint as those with the ink currently command little premium value). Backs feature a simulated newspaper front page with banner headline and picture, along with a description of the event.

		NM	EX	VG
	Complete Set (156):	3,000	1,500	800.00
	Common Card:	6.00	3.00	1.75
27	Bob Feller Strikeout King, Oct. 2, 1938 (Bob Feller)	60.00	30.00	18.00
41	Babe Ruth Sets Record, Sept. 30, 1927 (Babe Ruth)	250.00	125.00	75.00
130	Braves Go to Milwaukee	40.00	20.00	12.00
154	26-Inning Tie Game May 1, 1920	60.00	30.00	18.00

1955 Topps

The 1955 Topps set is numerically the smallest of the regular annual issues. The 3-3/4" x 2-5/8" cards mark the first time that Topps used a horizontal format for the entire set. While that format was new, the design was not; they are very similar to the 1954 cards to the point many pictures appeared in both years. Although it was slated for a 210-card set, the 1955 Topps set turned out to be only 206 cards with numbers 175, 186, 203 and 209 never being released. The scarce high numbers in this set begin with #161.

		NM	EX	VG
	Complete Set (206):	8,000	3,750	2,250
	Common Player (1-150):	20.00	10.00	6.00
	Common Player (151-160):	25.00	12.50	7.50
	Common Player (161-210):	45.00	22.50	13.50
1	"Dusty" Rhodes	125.00	62.50	31.25
2	Ted Williams	500.00	250.00	150.00
3	Art Fowler	20.00	10.00	6.00
4	Al Kaline	150.00	75.00	45.00
5	Jim Gilliam	60.00	30.00	15.00
6	Stan Hack	25.00	12.50	7.50
7	Jim Hegan	20.00	10.00	6.00
8	Hal Smith	20.00	10.00	6.00
9	Bob Miller	20.00	10.00	6.00
10	Bob Keegan	20.00	10.00	6.00
11	Ferris Fain	20.00	10.00	6.00
12	"Jake" Thies	20.00	10.00	6.00
13	Fred Marsh	20.00	10.00	6.00
14	Jim Gilliam	20.00	10.00	6.00
15	Jim Pendleton	20.00	10.00	6.00
16	Roy Sievers	20.00	10.00	6.00
17	Bobby Hofman	20.00	10.00	6.00
18	Russ Kemmerer	20.00	10.00	6.00
19	Billy Herman	40.00	20.00	10.00
20	Andy Carey	25.00	12.50	7.50
21	Alex Grammas	20.00	10.00	6.00
22	Bill Skowron	35.00	17.50	10.00
23	Jack Parks	20.00	10.00	6.00
24	Hal Newhouser	20.00	10.00	6.00
25	Johnny Podres	40.00	20.00	12.00
26	Dick Groat	20.00	10.00	6.00
27	*Billy Gardner*	20.00	10.00	6.00
28	Ernie Banks	250.00	125.00	62.50
29	Herman Wehmeier	20.00	10.00	6.00
30	Vic Power	20.00	10.00	6.00
31	Warren Spahn	150.00	75.00	37.50

#	Player	NM	EX	VG
32	Ed McGhee	20.00	10.00	6.00
33	Tom Qualters	20.00	10.00	6.00
34	Wayne Terwilliger	20.00	10.00	6.00
35	Dave Jolly	20.00	10.00	6.00
36	Leo Kiely	20.00	10.00	6.00
37	*Joe Cunningham*	20.00	10.00	6.00
38	Bob Turley	27.50	13.50	8.25
39	Bill Glynn	20.00	10.00	6.00
40	Don Hoak	25.00	12.50	7.50
41	Chuck Stobbs	20.00	10.00	6.00
42	"Windy" McCall	20.00	10.00	6.00
43	Harvey Haddix	20.00	10.00	6.00
44	"Corky" Valentine	20.00	10.00	6.00
45	Hank Sauer	20.00	10.00	6.00
46	Ted Kazanski	20.00	10.00	6.00
47	Hank Aaron	325.00	160.00	97.00
48	Bob Kennedy	20.00	10.00	6.00
49	J.W. Porter	20.00	10.00	6.00
50	Jackie Robinson	475.00	237.50	118.75
51	Jim Hughes	25.00	12.50	7.50
52	Bill Tremel	20.00	10.00	6.00
53	Bill Taylor	20.00	10.00	6.00
54	Lou Limmer	20.00	10.00	6.00
55	"Rip" Repulski	20.00	10.00	6.00
56	Ray Jablonski	20.00	10.00	6.00
57	*Billy O'Dell*	20.00	10.00	6.00
58	Jim Rivera	20.00	10.00	6.00
59	Gair Allie	20.00	10.00	6.00
60	Dean Stone	20.00	10.00	6.00
61	"Spook" Jacobs	20.00	10.00	6.00
62	Thornton Kipper	20.00	10.00	6.00
63	Joe Collins	25.00	12.50	7.50
64	*Gus Triandos*	25.00	12.50	7.50
65	Ray Boone	20.00	10.00	6.00
66	Ron Jackson	20.00	10.00	6.00
67	Wally Moon	20.00	10.00	6.00
68	Jim Davis	20.00	10.00	6.00
69	Ed Bailey	20.00	10.00	6.00
70	Al Rosen	40.00	20.00	12.00
71	Ruben Gomez	20.00	10.00	6.00
72	Karl Olson	20.00	10.00	6.00
73	Jack Shepard	20.00	10.00	6.00
74	Bob Borkowski	20.00	10.00	6.00
75	*Sandy Amoros*	50.00	25.00	12.50
76	Howie Pollet	20.00	10.00	6.00
77	Arnold Portocarrero	20.00	10.00	6.00
78	Gordon Jones	20.00	10.00	6.00
79	Danny Schell	20.00	10.00	6.00
80	Bob Grim	25.00	12.50	7.50
81	Gene Conley	20.00	10.00	6.00
82	Chuck Harmon	20.00	10.00	6.00
83	Tom Brewer	20.00	10.00	6.00
84	*Camilo Pascual*	35.00	17.50	10.00
85	*Don Mossi*	35.00	17.50	10.00
86	Bill Wilson	20.00	10.00	6.00
87	Frank House	20.00	10.00	6.00
88	*Bob Skinner*	20.00	10.00	6.00
89	*Joe Frazier*	20.00	10.00	6.00
90	*Karl Spooner*	25.00	12.50	7.50
91	Milt Bolling	20.00	10.00	6.00
92	*Don Zimmer*	50.00	25.00	12.50
93	Steve Bilko	20.00	10.00	6.00
94	Reno Bertoia	20.00	10.00	6.00
95	Preston Ward	20.00	10.00	6.00
96	Charlie Bishop	20.00	10.00	6.00
97	Carlos Paula	20.00	10.00	6.00
98	Johnny Riddle	20.00	10.00	6.00
99	Frank Leja	25.00	12.50	7.50
100	Monte Irvin	40.00	20.00	12.00
101	Johnny Gray	20.00	10.00	6.00
102	Wally Westlake	20.00	10.00	6.00
103	Charlie White	20.00	10.00	6.00
104	Jack Harshman	20.00	10.00	6.00
105	Chuck Diering	20.00	10.00	6.00
106	*Frank Sullivan* (Several variations exist in the size, shape and density of the dot over the "i" in the facsimile autograph.)	20.00	10.00	6.00
107	Curt Roberts	20.00	10.00	6.00
108	"Rube" Walker	25.00	12.50	7.50
109	Ed Lopat	30.00	15.00	9.00
110	Gus Zernial	20.00	10.00	6.00
111	Bob Milliken	25.00	12.50	7.50
112	Nelson King	20.00	10.00	6.00
113	Harry Brecheen	20.00	10.00	6.00
114	Lou Ortiz	20.00	10.00	6.00
115	Ellis Kinder	20.00	10.00	6.00
116	Tom Hurd	20.00	10.00	6.00
117	Mel Roach	20.00	10.00	6.00
118	Bob Purkey	20.00	10.00	6.00
119	Bob Lennon	20.00	10.00	6.00
120	Ted Kluszewski	45.00	22.50	13.50
121	Bill Renna	20.00	10.00	6.00
122	Carl Sawatski	20.00	10.00	6.00
123	*"Sandy" Koufax*	775.00	385.00	230.00
124	*Harmon Killebrew*	275.00	135.00	82.00
125	Ken Boyer	80.00	40.00	24.00
126	Dick Hall	20.00	10.00	6.00
127	*Dale Long*	20.00	10.00	6.00
128	Ted Lepcio	20.00	10.00	6.00
129	Elvin Tappe	20.00	10.00	6.00
130	Mayo Smith	20.00	10.00	6.00
131	Grady Hatton	20.00	10.00	6.00
132	Bob Trice	20.00	10.00	6.00
133	Dave Hoskins	20.00	10.00	6.00
134	Joe Jay	20.00	10.00	6.00
135	Johnny O'Brien	20.00	10.00	6.00
136	"Bunky" Stewart	20.00	10.00	6.00
137a	Harry Elliott (Last line in bio is, "the Cards in '53.")	20.00	10.00	6.00
137b	Harry Elliott (Last line in bio ends, "the Cards in (crescent mark).")			6.00
137c	Harry Elliott (Last line in bio ends, "the Cards in.")	20.00	10.00	6.00
138	Ray Herbert	20.00	10.00	6.00
139	Steve Kraly	25.00	12.50	7.50

#	Player	NM	EX	VG
140	Mel Parnell	20.00	10.00	6.00
141	Tom Wright	20.00	10.00	6.00
142	Jerry Lynch	20.00	10.00	6.00
143	Dick Schofield	20.00	10.00	6.00
144	*Joe Amalfitano*	20.00	10.00	6.00
145	Elmer Valo	20.00	10.00	6.00
146	*Dick Donovan*	20.00	10.00	6.00
147	Laurin Pepper	20.00	10.00	6.00
148	Hal Brown	20.00	10.00	6.00
149	Ray Crone	20.00	10.00	6.00
150	Mike Higgins	20.00	10.00	6.00
151	"Red" Kress	25.00	12.50	7.50
152	*Harry Agganis*	100.00	50.00	25.00
153	"Bud" Podbielan	25.00	12.50	7.50
154	Willie Miranda	25.00	12.50	7.50
155	Ed Mathews	200.00	100.00	50.00
156	Joe Black	60.00	30.00	18.00
157	Bob Miller	25.00	12.50	7.50
158	Tom Carroll	35.00	17.50	10.50
159	Johnny Schmitz	25.00	12.50	7.50
160	Ray Narleski	25.00	12.50	7.50
161	*Chuck Tanner*	50.00	25.00	15.00
162	Joe Coleman	45.00	22.50	13.50
163	Faye Throneberry	45.00	22.50	13.50
164	*Roberto Clemente*	2,000	1,000	600.00
165	Don Johnson	45.00	22.50	13.50
166	Hank Bauer	75.00	37.50	18.75
167	Tom Casagrande	45.00	22.50	13.50
168	Duane Pillette	45.00	22.50	13.50
169	Bob Oldis	45.00	22.50	13.50
170	Jim Pearce	45.00	22.50	13.50
171	Dick Brodowski	45.00	22.50	13.50
172	Frank Baumholtz	45.00	22.50	13.50
173	Bob Kline	45.00	22.50	13.50
174	Rudy Minarcin	45.00	22.50	13.50
175	Not Issued			
176	Norm Zauchin	45.00	22.50	13.50
177	Jim Robertson	45.00	22.50	13.50
178	Bobby Adams	45.00	22.50	13.50
179	Jim Bolger	45.00	22.50	13.50
180	Clem Labine	60.00	30.00	18.00
181	Roy McMillan	45.00	22.50	13.50
182	Humberto Robinson	45.00	22.50	13.50
183	Tony Jacobs	45.00	22.50	13.50
184	Harry Perkowski	45.00	22.50	13.50
185	Don Ferrarese	45.00	22.50	13.50
186	Not Issued			
187	Gil Hodges	175.00	87.50	43.75
188	Charlie Silvera	50.00	25.00	15.00
189	Phil Rizzuto	175.00	87.50	43.75
190	Gene Woodling	40.00	20.00	12.00
191	Ed Stanky	45.00	22.50	13.50
192	Jim Delsing	45.00	22.50	13.50
193	Johnny Sain	50.00	25.00	12.50
194	Willie Mays	600.00	300.00	150.00
195	Ed Roebuck	50.00	25.00	15.00
196	Gale Wade	45.00	22.50	13.50
197	Al Smith	45.00	22.50	13.50
198	Yogi Berra	300.00	150.00	75.00
199	Bert Hamric	50.00	25.00	15.00
200	Jack Jensen	60.00	30.00	18.00
201	Sherm Lollar	45.00	22.50	13.50
202	Jim Owens	45.00	22.50	13.50
203	Not Issued			
204	Frank Smith	45.00	22.50	13.50
205	Gene Freese	45.00	22.50	13.50
206	Pete Daley	45.00	22.50	13.50
207	Bill Consolo	45.00	22.50	13.50
208	Ray Moore	45.00	22.50	13.50
209	Not Issued			
210	Duke Snider	600.00	130.00	80.00

1955 Topps Doubleheaders

This set is a throwback to the 1911 T201 Mecca Double Folders. The cards are perforated through the middle, allowing them to be folded. Open, there is a color painting of a player set against a stadium background. When folded, a different player and stadium appears; both players share the same lower legs and feet. Backs have abbreviated career histories and stats. Placed side by side in reverse numerical order, the backgrounds form a continuous stadium scene. When open the cards measure 2-1/16" x 4-7/8". The 66 cards in the set mean 132 total players, all of whom also appeared in the lower numbers of the regular 1955 Topps set.

	NM	EX	VG
Complete Set (66):	4,000	2,000	1,200
Common Card:	45.00	22.50	13.50
Wax Pack:	240.00	.00	.00

#	Players	NM	EX	VG
1-2	Al Rosen, Chuck Diering	60.00	25.00	15.00
3-4	Monte Irvin, Russ Kemmerer	60.00	30.00	18.00
5-6	Ted Kazanski, Gordon Jones	45.00	22.50	13.50
7-8	Bill Taylor, Billy O'Dell	45.00	22.50	13.50
9-10	J.W. Porter, Thornton Kipper	45.00	22.50	13.50
11-12	Curt Roberts, Arnie Portocarrero	45.00	22.50	13.50
13-14	Wally Westlake, Frank House	45.00	22.50	13.50
15-16	Rube Walker, Lou Limmer	45.00	22.50	13.50
17-18	Dean Stone, Charlie White	45.00	22.50	13.50
19-20	Karl Spooner, Jim Hughes	50.00	25.00	15.00
21-22	Bill Skowron, Frank Sullivan	60.00	30.00	18.00
23-24	Jack Shepard, Stan Hack	45.00	22.50	13.50
25-26	Jackie Robinson, Don Hoak	325.00	160.00	100.00
27-28	Dusty Rhodes, Jim Davis	45.00	22.50	13.50
29-30	Vic Power, Ed Bailey	45.00	22.50	13.50
31-32	Howie Pollet, Ernie Banks	200.00	100.00	60.00
33-34	Jim Pendleton, Gene Conley	45.00	22.50	13.50
35-36	Karl Olson, Andy Carey	45.00	22.50	13.50
37-38	Wally Moon, Joe Cunningham	45.00	22.50	13.50
39-40	Fred Marsh, "Jake" Thies	45.00	22.50	13.50
41-42	Ed Lopat, Harvey Haddix	45.00	22.50	13.50
43-44	Leo Kiely, Chuck Stobbs	45.00	22.50	13.50
45-46	Al Kaline, "Corky" Valentine	225.00	110.00	65.00
47-48	"Spook" Jacobs, Johnny Gray	45.00	22.50	13.50
49-50	Ron Jackson, Jim Finigan	45.00	22.50	13.50
51-52	Ray Jablonski, Bob Keegan	45.00	22.50	13.50
53-54	Billy Herman, Sandy Amoros	60.00	30.00	18.00
55-56	Chuck Harmon, Bob Skinner	45.00	22.50	13.50
57-58	Dick Hall, Bob Grim	45.00	22.50	13.50
59-60	Bill Glynn, Bob Miller	45.00	22.50	13.50
61-62	Billy Gardner, John Hetki	45.00	22.50	13.50
63-64	Bob Borkowski, Bob Turley	45.00	22.50	13.50
65-66	Joe Collins, Jack Harshman	45.00	22.50	13.50
67-68	Jim Hegan, Jack Parks	45.00	22.50	13.50
69-70	Ted Williams, Hal Smith	425.00	210.00	125.00
71-72	Gair Allie, Grady Hatton	45.00	22.50	13.50
73-74	Jerry Lynch, Harry Brecheen	45.00	22.50	13.50
75-76	Tom Wright, "Bunky" Stewart	45.00	22.50	13.50
77-78	Dave Hoskins, Ed McGhee	45.00	22.50	13.50
79-80	Roy Sievers, Art Fowler	45.00	22.50	13.50
81-82	Danny Schell, Gus Triandos	45.00	22.50	13.50
83-84	Joe Frazier, Don Mossi	45.00	22.50	13.50
85-86	Elmer Valo, Hal Brown	45.00	22.50	13.50
87-88	Bob Kennedy, "Windy" McCall	45.00	22.50	13.50
89-90	Ruben Gomez, Jim Rivera	45.00	22.50	13.50
91-92	Lou Ortiz, Milt Bolling	45.00	22.50	13.50
93-94	Carl Sawatski, Elvin Tappe	45.00	22.50	13.50
95-96	Dave Jolly, Bobby Hofman	45.00	22.50	13.50
97-98	Preston Ward, Don Zimmer	45.00	22.50	13.50
99-100	Bill Renna, Dick Groat	45.00	22.50	13.50
101-102	Bill Wilson, Bill Tremel	45.00	22.50	13.50
103-104	Hank Sauer, Camilo Pascual	45.00	22.50	13.50
105-106	Hank Aaron, Ray Herbert	400.00	200.00	120.00
107-108	Alex Grammas, Tom Qualters	45.00	22.50	13.50
109-110	Hal Newhouser, Charlie Bishop	60.00	30.00	18.00
111-112	Harmon Killebrew, John Podres	225.00	110.00	65.00
113-114	Ray Boone, Bob Purkey	45.00	22.50	13.50
115-116	Dale Long, Ferris Fain	45.00	22.50	13.50
117-118	Steve Bilko, Bob Milliken	45.00	22.50	13.50
119-120	Mel Parnell, Tom Hurd	45.00	22.50	13.50
121-122	Ted Kluszewski, Jim Owens	60.00	30.00	18.00
123-124	Gus Zernial, Bob Trice	45.00	22.50	13.50
125-126	"Rip" Repulski, Ted Lepcio	45.00	22.50	13.50
127-128	Warren Spahn, Tom Brewer	150.00	75.00	45.00
129-130	Jim Gilliam, Ellis Kinder	60.00	30.00	18.00
131-132	Herm Wehmeier, Wayne Terwilliger	45.00	22.50	13.50

1955 Topps Hocus Focus

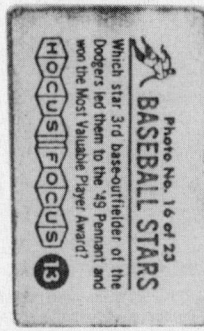

This set is a direct descendant of the 1948 "Topps Magic Photo" issue. Again, the baseball players were part of a larger overall series covering several topical areas. The cards, 7/8 x 1-3/8", state on the back that they are a series of 23, though only 14 are known. The photos on these cards were developed by wetting the card's surface and exposing it to light. Prices below are for cards with well-developed pictures. Cards with poorly developed photos are worth significantly less.

		NM	EX	VG
Common Player:		255.00	125.00	76.00
1	Babe Ruth	3,500	1,750	1,000
2	Lou Gehrig	3,500	1,750	1,000
3	Dick Groat	275.00	135.00	80.00
4	Ed Lopat	400.00	200.00	120.00
5	Hank Sauer	250.00	125.00	75.00
6	"Dusty" Rhodes	250.00	125.00	75.00
7	Ted Williams	1,950	975.00	585.00
8	Harvey Haddix	250.00	125.00	75.00
9	Ray Boone	250.00	125.00	75.00
10	Al Rosen	450.00	225.00	135.00
11	Unknown			

		NM	EX	VG
12	Warren Spahn	600.00	300.00	180.00
13	Jim Rivera	250.00	125.00	75.00
14	Ted Kluszewski	600.00	300.00	180.00
15	Gus Zernial	250.00	125.00	75.00
16	Jackie Robinson	1,750	875.00	525.00
17	Unknown			
18	Johnny Schmitz	250.00	125.00	75.00
19	Unknown			
20	Karl Spooner	275.00	135.00	80.00
21	Ed Mathews	600.00	300.00	180.00
22	Unknown			
23	Unknown			

1955 Topps Stamps

An extremely rare and enigmatic test issue, these stamps are the same size as Topps' 1955 card issue and have a blank, gummed back. Most of the specimens currently known are imperforate along one of the sides. All of the known examples have counterparts in the regular set which range from card #6 through 108. The unnumbered stamps are checklisted here alphabetically, with gaps left in the numbering to accommodate future discoveries.

		NM	EX	VG
Common Player:		750.00	375.00	225.00
(1)	Ray Boone	750.00	375.00	225.00
(2)	Joe Cunningham	750.00	375.00	225.00
(3)	Jim Davis	750.00	375.00	225.00
(4)	Chuck Diering	750.00	375.00	225.00
(5)	Ruben Gomez	750.00	375.00	225.00
(6)	Alex Grammas	750.00	375.00	225.00
(7)	Stan Hack	750.00	375.00	225.00
(8)	Harvey Haddix	750.00	375.00	225.00
(9)	Bobby Hofman	750.00	375.00	225.00
(11)	Ray Jablonski	750.00	375.00	225.00
(12)	Dave Jolly	750.00	375.00	225.00
(13)	Ted Kazanski	750.00	375.00	225.00
(14)	Don Mossi	775.00	385.00	230.00
(15)	Jim Pendleton	750.00	375.00	225.00
(16)	Howie Pollet	750.00	375.00	225.00
(17)	Jack Shepard	750.00	375.00	225.00
(18)	Bob Skinner	750.00	375.00	225.00
(19)	Bill Skowron	975.00	485.00	290.00
(20)	Karl Spooner	775.00	385.00	230.00
(21)	Bill Tremel	750.00	375.00	225.00
(22)	Corky Valentine	750.00	375.00	225.00
(23)	Rube Walker	775.00	385.00	230.00
(24)	Charlie White	750.00	375.00	225.00

1956 Topps

This set is similar in format to the 1955 Topps set, again using both a portrait and an "action" picture. Some portraits are the same as those used in 1955 (and even 1954). Innovations found in the 1956 Topps set of 2-5/8" x 3-3/4" cards include team cards introduced as part of a regular set. Additionally, there are two unnumbered checklist cards (the complete set price quoted below does not include the checklist cards). Finally, there are cards of the two league presidents, William Harridge and Warren Giles. On the backs, a three-panel cartoon depicts big moments from the player's career while biographical information appears above the cartoon and the statistics below. Card backs for numbers 1-180 can be found with either white or gray cardboard. Some hobbyists feel a premium is warranted for gray backs between #1-100 and white backs from #101-180.

		NM	EX	VG
Complete Set (340):		9,000	4,250	2,550
Common Player (1-180):		15.00	7.50	4.50
Common Player (181-340):		20.00	10.00	6.00
1	William Harridge	125.00	25.00	15.00
2	Warren Giles	65.00	12.00	6.00
3	Elmer Valo	15.00	7.50	4.50
4	Carlos Paula	15.00	7.50	4.50

		NM	EX	VG
5	Ted Williams	550.00	275.00	137.50
6	Ray Boone	15.00	7.50	4.50
7	Ron Negray	15.00	7.50	4.50
8	Walter Alston	45.00	22.50	13.50
9	Ruben Gomez	15.00	7.50	4.50
10	Warren Spahn	125.00	62.50	31.25
11a	Chicago Cubs - 1955	80.00	40.00	20.00
11b	Chicago Cubs	60.00	30.00	18.00
	(No date, name centered.)			
11c	Chicago Cubs	70.00	35.00	20.00
	(No date, name at left.)			
12	Andy Carey	20.00	10.00	6.00
13	Roy Face	15.00	7.50	4.50
14	Ken Boyer	25.00	12.50	7.50
15	Ernie Banks	125.00	62.50	31.25
16	*Hector Lopez*	20.00	10.00	6.00
17	Gene Conley	15.00	7.50	4.50
18	Dick Donovan	15.00	7.50	4.50
19	Chuck Diering	15.00	7.50	4.50
20	Al Kaline	125.00	62.50	31.25
21	Joe Collins	20.00	10.00	6.00
22	Jim Finigan	15.00	7.50	4.50
23	Freddie Marsh	20.00	10.00	6.00
24	Dick Groat	20.00	10.00	6.00
25	Ted Kluszewski	35.00	17.50	10.00
26	Grady Hatton	15.00	7.50	4.50
27	Nelson Burbrink	15.00	7.50	4.50
28	Bobby Hofman	15.00	7.50	4.50
29	Jack Harshman	15.00	7.50	4.50
30	Jackie Robinson	300.00	150.00	75.00
31	Hank Aaron	400.00	200.00	100.00
32	Frank House	15.00	7.50	4.50
33	Roberto Clemente	450.00	225.00	112.50
34	Tom Brewer	15.00	7.50	4.50
35	Al Rosen	20.00	10.00	6.00
36	Rudy Minarcin	15.00	7.50	4.50
37	Alex Grammas	15.00	7.50	4.50
38	Bob Kennedy	15.00	7.50	4.50
39	Don Mossi	15.00	7.50	4.50
40	Bob Turley	25.00	12.50	7.50
41	Hank Sauer	15.00	7.50	4.50
42	Sandy Amoros	25.00	12.50	7.50
43	Ray Moore	15.00	7.50	4.50
44	"Windy" McCall	15.00	7.50	4.50
45	Gus Zernial	15.00	7.50	4.50
46	Gene Freese	15.00	7.50	4.50
47	Art Fowler	15.00	7.50	4.50
48	Jim Hegan	15.00	7.50	4.50
49	*Pedro Ramos*	20.00	10.00	6.00
50	"Dusty" Rhodes	15.00	7.50	4.50
51	Ernie Oravetz	15.00	7.50	4.50
52	Bob Grim	20.00	10.00	6.00
53	Arnold Portocarrero	15.00	7.50	4.50
54	Bob Keegan	15.00	7.50	4.50
55	Wally Moon	15.00	7.50	4.50
56	Dale Long	15.00	7.50	4.50
57	"Duke" Maas	15.00	7.50	4.50
58	Ed Roebuck	20.00	10.00	6.00
59	Jose Santiago	15.00	7.50	4.50
60	Mayo Smith	15.00	7.50	4.50
61	Bill Skowron	35.00	17.50	10.00
62	Hal Smith	15.00	7.50	4.50
63	*Roger Craig*	27.50	13.50	8.00
64	Luis Arroyo	15.00	7.50	4.50
65	Johnny O'Brien	15.00	7.50	4.50
66	Bob Speake	15.00	7.50	4.50
67	Vic Power	15.00	7.50	4.50
68	Chuck Stobbs	15.00	7.50	4.50
69	Chuck Tanner	15.00	7.50	4.50
70	Jim Rivera	15.00	7.50	4.50
71	Frank Sullivan	15.00	7.50	4.50
72a	Philadelphia Phillies - 1955	100.00	50.00	25.00
72b	Philadelphia Phillies	40.00	20.00	12.00
	(No date, name centered.)			
72c	Philadelphia Phillies	60.00	30.00	18.00
	(No date, name at left.)			
73	Wayne Terwilliger	15.00	7.50	4.50
74	Jim King	15.00	7.50	4.50
75	Roy Sievers	15.00	7.50	4.50
76	Ray Crone	15.00	7.50	4.50
77	Harvey Haddix	15.00	7.50	4.50
78	Herman Wehmeier	15.00	7.50	4.50
79	Sandy Koufax	350.00	175.00	87.50
80	Gus Triandos	15.00	7.50	4.50
81	Wally Westlake	15.00	7.50	4.50
82	Bill Renna	15.00	7.50	4.50
83	Karl Spooner	20.00	10.00	6.00
84	"Babe" Birrer	15.00	7.50	4.50
85a	Cleveland Indians - 1955	85.00	42.50	25.00
85b	Cleveland Indians	50.00	25.00	15.00
	(No date, name centered.)			
85c	Cleveland Indians	80.00	40.00	20.00
	(No date, name at left.)			
86	Ray Jablonski	15.00	7.50	4.50
87	Dean Stone	15.00	7.50	4.50
88	Johnny Kucks	20.00	10.00	6.00
89	Norm Zauchin	15.00	7.50	4.50
90a	Cincinnati Redlegs - 1955	100.00	50.00	30.00
90b	Cincinnati Redlegs	45.00	22.50	13.50
	(No date, name centered.)			
90c	Cincinnati Redlegs	90.00	45.00	27.50
	(No date, name at left.)			
91	Gail Harris	15.00	7.50	4.50
92	"Red" Wilson	15.00	7.50	4.50
93	George Susce, Jr.	15.00	7.50	4.50
94	Ronnie Kline	15.00	7.50	4.50
95a	Milwaukee Braves - 1955	100.00	50.00	25.00
95b	Milwaukee Braves (No date, name centered.)	60.00	30.00	18.00
95c	Milwaukee Braves (No date, name at left.)	55.00	27.50	16.50
96	Bill Tremel	15.00	7.50	4.50
97	Jerry Lynch	15.00	7.50	4.50
98	Camilo Pascual	15.00	7.50	4.50
99	Don Zimmer	30.00	15.00	9.00
100a	Baltimore Orioles - 1955	100.00	50.00	25.00
100b	Baltimore Orioles (No date, name centered.)	100.00	50.00	25.00

		NM	EX	VG
100c	Baltimore Orioles	100.00	50.00	25.00
	(No date, name at left.)			
101	Roy Campanella	150.00	75.00	37.50
102	Jim Davis	15.00	7.50	4.50
103	Willie Miranda	15.00	7.50	4.50
104	Bob Lennon	15.00	7.50	4.50
105	Al Smith	15.00	7.50	4.50
106	Joe Astroth	15.00	7.50	4.50
107	Ed Mathews	100.00	50.00	25.00
108	Laurin Pepper	15.00	7.50	4.50
109	Enos Slaughter	32.50	16.00	10.00
110	Yogi Berra	180.00	90.00	45.00
111	Boston Red Sox	35.00	17.50	10.00
112	Dee Fondy	15.00	7.50	4.50
113	Phil Rizzuto	150.00	75.00	37.50
114	Jim Owens	15.00	7.50	4.50
115	Jackie Jensen	20.00	10.00	6.00
116	Eddie O'Brien	15.00	7.50	4.50
117	Virgil Trucks	15.00	7.50	4.50
118	"Nellie" Fox	50.00	25.00	15.00
119	*Larry Jackson*	15.00	7.50	4.50
120	Richie Ashburn	50.00	25.00	15.00
121	Pittsburgh Pirates	65.00	32.50	20.00
122	Willard Nixon	15.00	7.50	4.50
123	Roy McMillan	15.00	7.50	4.50
124	Don Kaiser	15.00	7.50	4.50
125	"Minnie" Minoso	30.00	15.00	9.00
126	Jim Brady	15.00	7.50	4.50
127	Willie Jones	15.00	7.50	4.50
128	Eddie Yost	15.00	7.50	4.50
129	"Jake" Martin	15.00	7.50	4.50
130	Willie Mays	350.00	175.00	87.50
131	Bob Roselli	15.00	7.50	4.50
132	Bobby Avila	15.00	7.50	4.50
133	Ray Narleski	15.00	7.50	4.50
134	St. Louis Cardinals	25.00	12.50	7.50
135	Mickey Mantle	1,000	500.00	300.00
136	Johnny Logan	15.00	7.50	4.50
137	Al Silvera	15.00	7.50	4.50
138	Johnny Antonelli	15.00	7.50	4.50
139	Tommy Carroll	20.00	10.00	6.00
140	*Herb Score*	35.00	17.50	10.00
141	Joe Frazier	15.00	7.50	4.50
142	Gene Baker	15.00	7.50	4.50
143	Jim Piersall	20.00	10.00	6.00
144	Leroy Powell	15.00	7.50	4.50
145	Gil Hodges	55.00	27.50	16.50
146	Washington Nationals	40.00	20.00	12.00
147	Earl Torgeson	15.00	7.50	4.50
148	Alvin Dark	15.00	7.50	4.50
149	"Dixie" Howell	15.00	7.50	4.50
150	"Duke" Snider	150.00	75.00	37.50
151	"Spook" Jacobs	15.00	7.50	4.50
152	Billy Hoeft	15.00	7.50	4.50
153	Frank Thomas	15.00	7.50	4.50
154	Dave Pope	15.00	7.50	4.50
155	Harvey Kuenn	20.00	10.00	6.00
156	Wes Westrum	15.00	7.50	4.50
157	Dick Brodowski	15.00	7.50	4.50
158	Wally Post	15.00	7.50	4.50
159	Clint Courtney	15.00	7.50	4.50
160	Billy Pierce	15.00	7.50	4.50
161	Joe De Maestri	15.00	7.50	4.50
162	"Gus" Bell	15.00	7.50	4.50
163	Gene Woodling	15.00	7.50	4.50
164	Harmon Killebrew	150.00	75.00	37.50
165	"Red" Schoendienst	35.00	17.50	10.00
166	Brooklyn Dodgers	200.00	100.00	50.00
167	Harry Dorish	15.00	7.50	4.50
168	Sammy White	15.00	7.50	4.50
169	Bob Nelson	15.00	7.50	4.50
170	Bill Virdon	15.00	7.50	4.50
171	Jim Wilson	15.00	7.50	4.50
172	*Frank Torre*	20.00	10.00	6.00
173	Johnny Podres	30.00	15.00	9.00
174	Glen Gorbous	15.00	7.50	4.50
175	Del Crandall	15.00	7.50	4.50
176	Alex Kellner	15.00	7.50	4.50
177	Hank Bauer	30.00	15.00	9.00
178	Joe Black	20.00	10.00	6.00
179	Harry Chiti	15.00	7.50	4.50
180	Robin Roberts	40.00	20.00	12.00
181	Billy Martin	100.00	50.00	25.00
182	Paul Minner	20.00	10.00	6.00
183	Stan Lopata	20.00	10.00	6.00
184	Don Bessent	25.00	12.50	7.50
185	Bill Bruton	20.00	10.00	6.00
186	Ron Jackson	20.00	10.00	6.00
187	Early Wynn	55.00	27.50	16.50
188	Chicago White Sox	60.00	30.00	15.00
189	Ned Garver	20.00	10.00	6.00
190	Carl Furillo	45.00	22.50	13.50
191	Frank Lary	20.00	10.00	6.00
192	"Smoky" Burgess	20.00	10.00	6.00
193	Wilmer Mizell	20.00	10.00	6.00
194	Monte Irvin	55.00	27.50	16.50
195	George Kell	45.00	22.50	13.50
196	Tom Poholsky	20.00	10.00	6.00
197	Granny Hamner	20.00	10.00	6.00
198	Ed Fitzgerald	20.00	10.00	6.00
199	Hank Thompson	20.00	10.00	6.00
200	Bob Feller	120.00	60.00	30.00
201	"Rip" Repulski	20.00	10.00	6.00
202	Jim Hearn	20.00	10.00	6.00
203	Bill Tuttle	20.00	10.00	6.00
204	Art Swanson	20.00	10.00	6.00
205	"Whitey" Lockman	20.00	10.00	6.00
206	Erv Palica	20.00	10.00	6.00
207	Jim Small	20.00	10.00	6.00
208	Elston Howard	45.00	22.50	13.50
209	Max Surkont	20.00	10.00	6.00
210	Mike Garcia	20.00	10.00	6.00
211	Murry Dickson	20.00	10.00	6.00
212	Johnny Temple	20.00	10.00	6.00
213	Detroit Tigers	60.00	30.00	18.00
214	Bob Rush	20.00	10.00	6.00
215	Tommy Byrne	25.00	12.50	7.50
216	Jerry Schoonmaker	20.00	10.00	6.00

		NM	EX	VG
217	Billy Klaus	20.00	10.00	6.00
218	Joe Nuxall (Nuxhall)	25.00	12.50	7.50
219	Lew Burdette	20.00	10.00	6.00
220	Del Ennis	20.00	10.00	6.00
221	Bob Friend	20.00	10.00	6.00
222	Dave Philley	20.00	10.00	6.00
223	Randy Jackson	25.00	12.50	7.50
224	"Bud" Podbielan	20.00	10.00	6.00
225	Gil McDougald	35.00	17.50	10.00
226	New York Giants	50.00	25.00	15.00
227	Russ Meyer	20.00	10.00	6.00
228	"Mickey" Vernon	20.00	10.00	6.00
229	Harry Brecheen	20.00	10.00	6.00
230	"Chico" Carrasquel	20.00	10.00	6.00
231	Bob Hale	20.00	10.00	6.00
232	"Toby" Atwell	20.00	10.00	6.00
233	Carl Erskine	30.00	15.00	9.00
234	"Pete" Runnels	20.00	10.00	6.00
235	Don Newcombe	55.00	27.50	16.50
236	Kansas City Athletics	35.00	17.50	10.00
237	Jose Valdivielso	20.00	10.00	6.00
238	Walt Dropo	20.00	10.00	6.00
239	Harry Simpson	20.00	10.00	6.00
240	"Whitey" Ford	125.00	62.50	31.25
241	Don Mueller	20.00	10.00	6.00
242	Hershell Freeman	20.00	10.00	6.00
243	Sherm Lollar	20.00	10.00	6.00
244	Bob Buhl	20.00	10.00	6.00
245	Billy Goodman	20.00	10.00	6.00
246	Tom Gorman	20.00	10.00	6.00
247	Bill Sarni	20.00	10.00	6.00
248	Bob Porterfield	20.00	10.00	6.00
249	Johnny Klippstein	20.00	10.00	6.00
250	Larry Doby	45.00	22.50	13.50
251	New York Yankees	250.00	125.00	75.00
252	Vernon Law	20.00	10.00	6.00
253	Irv Noren	25.00	12.50	7.50
254	George Crowe	20.00	10.00	6.00
255	Bob Lemon	35.00	17.50	10.00
256	Tom Hurd	20.00	10.00	6.00
257	Bobby Thomson	25.00	12.50	7.50
258	Art Ditmar	20.00	10.00	6.00
259	Sam Jones	20.00	10.00	6.00
260	"Pee Wee" Reese	150.00	75.00	37.50
261	Bobby Shantz	20.00	10.00	6.00
262	Howie Pollet	20.00	10.00	6.00
263	Bob Miller	20.00	10.00	6.00
264	Ray Monzant	20.00	10.00	6.00
265	Sandy Consuegra	20.00	10.00	6.00
266	Don Ferrarese	20.00	10.00	6.00
267	Bob Nieman	20.00	10.00	6.00
268	Dale Mitchell	20.00	10.00	6.00
269	Jack Meyer	20.00	10.00	6.00
270	Billy Loes	25.00	12.50	7.50
271	Foster Castleman	20.00	10.00	6.00
272	Danny O'Connell	20.00	10.00	6.00
273	Walker Cooper	20.00	10.00	6.00
274	Frank Baumholtz	20.00	10.00	6.00
275	Jim Greengrass	20.00	10.00	6.00
276	George Zuverink	20.00	10.00	6.00
277	Daryl Spencer	20.00	10.00	6.00
278	Chet Nichols	20.00	10.00	6.00
279	Johnny Groth	20.00	10.00	6.00
280	Jim Gilliam	45.00	22.50	13.50
281	Art Houtteman	20.00	10.00	6.00
282	Warren Hacker	20.00	10.00	6.00
283	Hal Smith	20.00	10.00	6.00
284	Ike Delock	20.00	10.00	6.00
285	Eddie Miksis	20.00	10.00	6.00
286	Bill Wight	20.00	10.00	6.00
287	Bobby Adams	20.00	10.00	6.00
288	Bob Cerv (SP)	45.00	22.50	13.50
289	Hal Jeffcoat	20.00	10.00	6.00
290	Curt Simmons	20.00	10.00	6.00
291	Frank Kellert	20.00	10.00	6.00
292	*Luis Aparicio*	150.00	75.00	37.50
293	Stu Miller	20.00	10.00	6.00
294	Ernie Johnson	20.00	10.00	6.00
295	Clem Labine	30.00	15.00	9.00
296	Andy Seminick	20.00	10.00	6.00
297	Bob Skinner	20.00	10.00	6.00
298	Johnny Schmitz	20.00	10.00	6.00
299	Charley Neal (SP)	35.00	17.50	10.00
300	Vic Wertz	20.00	10.00	6.00
301	Marv Grissom	20.00	10.00	6.00
302	Eddie Robinson	25.00	12.50	7.50
303	Jim Dyck	20.00	10.00	6.00
304	Frank Malzone	20.00	10.00	6.00
305	Brooks Lawrence	20.00	10.00	6.00
306	Curt Roberts	20.00	10.00	6.00
307	Hoyt Wilhelm	40.00	20.00	12.00
308	"Chuck" Harmon	20.00	10.00	6.00
309	*Don Blasingame*	25.00	12.50	7.50
310	Steve Gromek	20.00	10.00	6.00
311	Hal Naragon	20.00	10.00	6.00
312	Andy Pafko	20.00	10.00	6.00
313	Gene Stephens	20.00	10.00	6.00
314	Hobie Landrith	20.00	10.00	6.00
315	Milt Bolling	20.00	10.00	6.00
316	Jerry Coleman	25.00	12.50	7.50
317	Al Aber	20.00	10.00	6.00
318	Fred Hatfield	20.00	10.00	6.00
319	Jack Crimian	20.00	10.00	6.00
320	Joe Adcock	20.00	10.00	6.00
321	Jim Konstanty	25.00	12.50	7.50
322	Karl Olson	20.00	10.00	6.00
323	Willard Schmidt	20.00	10.00	6.00
324	"Rocky" Bridges	20.00	10.00	6.00
325	Don Liddle	20.00	10.00	6.00
326	Connie Johnson	20.00	10.00	6.00
327	Bob Wiesler	20.00	10.00	6.00
328	Preston Ward	20.00	10.00	6.00
329	Lou Berberet	20.00	10.00	6.00
330	Jim Busby	20.00	10.00	6.00
331	Dick Hall	20.00	10.00	6.00
332	Don Larsen	55.00	27.50	16.50
333	"Rube" Walker	25.00	12.50	7.50
334	Bob Miller	20.00	10.00	6.00
335	Don Hoak	20.00	10.00	6.00
336	Ellis Kinder	20.00	10.00	6.00
337	Bobby Morgan	20.00	10.00	6.00
338	Jim Delsing	20.00	10.00	6.00
339	Rance Pless	20.00	10.00	6.00
340	Mickey McDermott	45.00	15.00	8.00
----	Checklist 1/3	250.00	125.00	62.50
----	Checklist 2/4	250.00	125.00	62.50

1956 Topps Hocus Focus

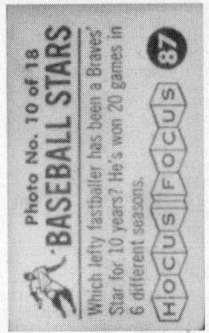

Following its 1955 issue with a somewhat larger format (1" x 1-5/8") the following year, the baseball players in this set are part of a larger overall series covering several topical areas. Cards backs specify an issue of 18 baseball stars. The black-and-white photos on these cards were developed by wetting the card's surface and exposing to light. Prices below are for cards with well-developed pictures. Cards with poorly developed photos are worth significantly less.

		NM	EX	VG
	Complete Set (18):	7,000	3,500	2,100
	Common Player:	220.00	110.00	66.00
1	Dick Groat	225.00	110.00	65.00
2	Ed Lopat	425.00	210.00	125.00
3	Hank Sauer	225.00	110.00	65.00
4	"Dusty" Rhodes	225.00	110.00	65.00
5	Ted Williams	1,600	800.00	480.00
6	Harvey Haddix	225.00	110.00	65.00
7	Ray Boone	225.00	110.00	65.00
8	Al Rosen	250.00	125.00	75.00
9	Mayo Smith	225.00	110.00	65.00
10	Warren Spahn	550.00	275.00	165.00
11	Jim Rivera	225.00	110.00	65.00
12	Ted Kluszewski	450.00	225.00	135.00
13	Gus Zernial	225.00	110.00	65.00
14	Jackie Robinson	1,350	675.00	400.00
15	Hal Smith	225.00	110.00	65.00
16	Johnny Schmitz	225.00	110.00	65.00
17	"Spook" Jacobs	225.00	110.00	65.00
18	Mel Parnell	225.00	110.00	65.00

1956 Topps Pins

One of Topps first specialty issues, the 60-pin set of ballplayers issued in 1956 contains a high percentage of bigname stars which, combined with the scarcity of the pins, makes collecting a complete set extremely challenging. Compounding the situation is the fact that some pins are seen far less often than others, though the reason is unknown. Chuck Stobbs, Hector Lopez and Chuck Diering are unaccountably scarce. Measuring 1-1/8" in diameter, the pins utilize the same portraits found on 1956 Topps baseball cards. The photos are set against a solid color background. The pins were sold in a box picturing the Ted Williams pin, with a piece of bubblegum for five cents.

		NM	EX	VG
	Complete Set (60):	3,600	1,800	1,100
	Common Player:	40.00	20.00	12.00
	Box:	500.00	250.00	150.00
(1)	Hank Aaron	200.00	100.00	60.00
(2)	Sandy Amoros	50.00	25.00	15.00
(3)	Luis Arroyo	40.00	20.00	12.00
(4)	Ernie Banks	150.00	75.00	45.00
(5)	Yogi Berra	150.00	75.00	45.00
(6)	Joe Black	60.00	30.00	18.00
(7)	Ray Boone	40.00	20.00	12.00
(8)	Ken Boyer	45.00	22.50	13.50
(9)	Joe Collins	45.00	22.50	13.50
(10)	Gene Conley	40.00	20.00	12.00
(11)	Chuck Diering	275.00	135.00	85.00
(12)	Dick Donovan	40.00	20.00	12.00
(13)	Jim Finigan	40.00	20.00	12.00
(14)	Art Fowler	40.00	20.00	12.00
(15)	Ruben Gomez	40.00	20.00	12.00
(16)	Dick Groat	40.00	20.00	12.00
(17)	Harvey Haddix	40.00	20.00	12.00

		NM	EX	VG
(18)	Jack Harshman	40.00	20.00	12.00
(19)	Grady Hatton	40.00	20.00	12.00
(20)	Jim Hegan	40.00	20.00	12.00
(21)	Gil Hodges	100.00	50.00	30.00
(22)	Bobby Hofman	40.00	20.00	12.00
(23)	Frank House	40.00	20.00	12.00
(24)	Jackie Jensen	45.00	22.50	13.50
(25)	Al Kaline	100.00	50.00	30.00
(26)	Bob Kennedy	40.00	20.00	12.00
(27)	Ted Kluszewski	85.00	42.50	25.00
(28)	Dale Long	40.00	20.00	12.00
(29)	Hector Lopez	400.00	200.00	120.00
(30)	Ed Mathews	100.00	50.00	30.00
(31)	Willie Mays	200.00	100.00	60.00
(32)	Roy McMillan	40.00	20.00	12.00
(33)	Willie Miranda	40.00	20.00	12.00
(34)	Wally Moon	40.00	20.00	12.00
(35)	Don Mossi	40.00	20.00	12.00
(36)	Ron Negray	40.00	20.00	12.00
(37)	Johnny O'Brien	40.00	20.00	12.00
(38)	Carlos Paula	40.00	20.00	12.00
(39)	Vic Power	40.00	20.00	12.00
(40)	Jim Rivera	40.00	20.00	12.00
(41)	Phil Rizzuto	150.00	75.00	45.00
(42)	Jackie Robinson	180.00	90.00	55.00
(43)	Al Rosen	45.00	22.50	13.50
(44)	Hank Sauer	40.00	20.00	12.00
(45)	Roy Sievers	40.00	20.00	12.00
(46)	Bill Skowron	45.00	22.50	13.50
(47)	Al Smith	40.00	20.00	12.00
(48)	Hal Smith	40.00	20.00	12.00
(49)	Mayo Smith	40.00	20.00	12.00
(50)	Duke Snider	125.00	65.00	35.00
(51)	Warren Spahn	100.00	50.00	30.00
(52)	Karl Spooner	45.00	22.50	13.50
(53)	Chuck Stobbs	225.00	110.00	65.00
(54)	Frank Sullivan	40.00	20.00	12.00
(55)	Bill Tremel	40.00	20.00	12.00
(56)	Gus Triandos	40.00	20.00	12.00
(57)	Bob Turley	50.00	25.00	15.00
(58)	Herman Wehmeier	40.00	20.00	12.00
(59)	Ted Williams	225.00	110.00	65.00
(60)	Gus Zernial	40.00	20.00	12.00

1957 Topps

For 1957, Topps reduced the size of its cards to the now-standard 2-1/2" x 3-1/2." Set size was increased to 407 cards. Another change came in the form of the use of real color photographs as opposed to the hand-colored black and whites of previous years. For the first time since 1954, there were also cards with more than one player. The two, "Dodger Sluggers" and "Yankees' Power Hitters" began a trend toward the increased use of multiple-player cards. Another first-time innovation, found on the backs, is complete players statistics. The scarce cards in the set are not the highest numbers, but rather numbers 265-352. Four unnumbered checklist cards were issued along with the set. They are quite expensive and are not included in the complete set prices quoted below.

		NM	EX	VG
	Complete Set (407):	12,500	6,000	3,500
	Common Player (1-264):	12.00	6.00	3.50
	Common Player (265-352):	25.00	12.50	7.50
	Common Player (353-407):	12.00	6.00	3.50
1	Ted Williams	600.00	300.00	150.00
2	Yogi Berra	200.00	100.00	50.00
3	Dale Long	12.00	6.00	3.50
4	Johnny Logan	12.00	6.00	3.50
5	Sal Maglie	20.00	10.00	6.00
6	Hector Lopez	12.00	6.00	3.50
7	Luis Aparicio	40.00	20.00	12.00
8	Don Mossi	12.00	6.00	3.50
9	Johnny Temple	12.00	6.00	3.50
10	Willie Mays	400.00	200.00	100.00
11	George Zuverink	12.00	6.00	3.50
12	Dick Groat	12.00	6.00	3.50
13	Wally Burnette	12.00	6.00	3.50
14	Bob Nieman	12.00	6.00	3.50
15	Robin Roberts	50.00	25.00	15.00
16	Walt Moryn	12.00	.6.00	3.50
17	Billy Gardner	12.00	6.00	3.50
18	*Don Drysdale*	250.00	125.00	62.50
19	Bob Wilson	12.00	6.00	3.50
20	Hank Aaron (Photo reversed.)	325.00	162.50	81.25
21	Frank Sullivan	12.00	6.00	3.50
22	Jerry Snyder (Photo actually Ed Fitz Gerald.)	12.00	6.00	3.50
23	Sherman Lollar	12.00	6.00	3.50
24	*Bill Mazeroski*	80.00	40.00	20.00
25	Whitey Ford	150.00	75.00	37.50
26	Bob Boyd	12.00	6.00	3.50
27	Ted Kazanski	12.00	6.00	3.50
28	Gene Conley	12.00	6.00	3.50
29	*Whitey Herzog*	15.00	7.50	4.50
30	Pee Wee Reese	75.00	37.50	22.50

#	Name				#	Name				#	Name			
31	Ron Northey	12.00	6.00	3.50	148	Don Mueller	12.00	6.00	3.50	264	Bob Turley	25.00	12.50	7.50
32	Hersh Freeman	12.00	6.00	3.50	149	Bob Kennedy	12.00	6.00	3.50	265	Harvey Haddix	25.00	12.50	7.50
33	Jim Small	12.00	6.00	3.50	150	Bob Friend	12.00	6.00	3.50	266	Ken Kuhn	25.00	12.50	7.50
34	Tom Sturdivant	15.00	7.50	4.50	151	Willie Miranda	12.00	6.00	3.50	267	Danny Kravitz	25.00	12.50	7.50
35	*Frank Robinson*	300.00	150.00	75.00	152	Jack Harshman	12.00	6.00	3.50	268	Jackie Collum	25.00	12.50	7.50
36	Bob Grim	15.00	7.50	4.50	153	Karl Olson	12.00	6.00	3.50	269	Bob Cerv	25.00	12.50	7.50
37	Frank Torre	12.00	6.00	3.50	154	Red Schoendienst	30.00	15.00	9.00	270	Washington Senators Team	45.00	22.50	13.50
38	Nellie Fox	40.00	20.00	12.00	155	Jim Brosnan	12.00	6.00	3.50	271	Danny O'Connell	25.00	12.50	7.50
39	Al Worthington	12.00	6.00	3.50	156	Gus Triandos	12.00	6.00	3.50	272	Bobby Shantz	40.00	20.00	12.00
40	Early Wynn	30.00	15.00	9.00	157	Wally Post	12.00	6.00	3.50	273	Jim Davis	25.00	12.50	7.50
41	Hal Smith	12.00	6.00	3.50	158	Curt Simmons	12.00	6.00	3.50	274	Don Hoak	25.00	12.50	7.50
42	Dee Fondy	12.00	6.00	3.50	159	Solly Drake	12.00	6.00	3.50	275	Cleveland Indians Team	40.00	20.00	12.00
43	Connie Johnson	12.00	6.00	3.50	160	Billy Pierce	12.00	6.00	3.50	276	Jim Pyburn	25.00	12.50	7.50
44	Joe DeMaestri	12.00	6.00	3.50	161	Pittsburgh Pirates Team	20.00	10.00	6.00	277	Johnny Podres	40.00	20.00	12.00
45	Carl Furillo	40.00	20.00	12.00	162	Jack Meyer	12.00	6.00	3.50	278	Fred Hatfield	25.00	12.50	7.50
46	Bob Miller	12.00	6.00	3.50	163	Sammy White	12.00	6.00	3.50	279	Bob Thurman	25.00	12.50	7.50
47	Don Blasingame	12.00	6.00	3.50	164	Tommy Carroll	15.00	7.50	4.50	280	Alex Kellner	25.00	12.50	7.50
48	Bill Bruton	12.00	6.00	3.50	165	Ted Kluszewski	80.00	40.00	20.00	281	Gail Harris	25.00	12.50	7.50
49	Daryl Spencer	12.00	6.00	3.50	166	Roy Face	12.00	6.00	3.50	282	Jack Dittmer	25.00	12.50	7.50
50	Herb Score	25.00	12.50	7.50	167	Vic Power	12.00	6.00	3.50	283	*Wes Covington*	25.00	12.50	7.50
51	Clint Courtney	12.00	6.00	3.50	168	Frank Lary	12.00	6.00	3.50	284	Don Zimmer	40.00	20.00	12.00
52	Lee Walls	12.00	6.00	3.50	169	Herb Plews	12.00	6.00	3.50	285	Ned Garver	25.00	12.50	7.50
53	Clem Labine	20.00	10.00	6.00	170	Duke Snider	150.00	75.00	37.50	286	*Bobby Richardson*	120.00	60.00	30.00
54	Elmer Valo	12.00	6.00	3.50	171	Boston Red Sox Team	32.50	16.00	10.00	287	Sam Jones	25.00	12.50	7.50
55	Ernie Banks	130.00	65.00	32.50	172	Gene Woodling	12.00	6.00	3.50	288	Ted Lepcio	25.00	12.50	7.50
56	Dave Sisler	12.00	6.00	3.50	173	Roger Craig	15.00	7.50	4.50	289	Jim Bolger	25.00	12.50	7.50
57	Jim Lemon	12.00	6.00	3.50	174	Willie Jones	12.00	6.00	3.50	290	Andy Carey	35.00	17.50	10.00
58	Ruben Gomez	12.00	6.00	3.50	175	Don Larsen	35.00	17.50	10.00	291	Windy McCall	20.00	10.00	6.00
59	Dick Williams	12.00	6.00	3.50	176a	Gene Baker	12.00	6.00	3.50	292	Billy Klaus	25.00	12.50	7.50
60	Billy Hoeft	12.00	6.00	3.50	176b	Gene Baker (Error on back, "EUGENF W. BAKEP.")	800.00	400.00	240.00	293	Ted Abernathy	25.00	12.50	7.50
61	Dusty Rhodes	12.00	6.00	3.50						294	Rocky Bridges	25.00	12.50	7.50
62	Billy Martin	40.00	20.00	12.00	177	Eddie Yost	12.00	6.00	3.50	295	Joe Collins	35.00	17.50	10.50
63	Ike Delock	12.00	6.00	3.50	178	Don Bessent	15.00	7.50	4.50	296	Johnny Klippstein	25.00	12.50	7.50
64	Pete Runnels	12.00	6.00	3.50	179	Ernie Oravetz	12.00	6.00	3.50	297	Jack Crimian	25.00	12.50	7.50
65	Wally Moon	12.00	6.00	3.50	180	Gus Bell	12.00	6.00	3.50	298	Irv Noren	25.00	12.50	7.50
66	Brooks Lawrence	12.00	6.00	3.50	181	Dick Donovan	12.00	6.00	3.50	299	Chuck Harmon	25.00	12.50	7.50
67	Chico Carrasquel	12.00	6.00	3.50	182	Hobie Landrith	12.00	6.00	3.50	300	Mike Garcia	25.00	12.50	7.50
68	Ray Crone	12.00	6.00	3.50	183	Chicago Cubs Team	25.00	12.50	7.50	301	Sam Esposito	25.00	12.50	7.50
69	Roy McMillan	12.00	6.00	3.50	184	*Tito Francona*	12.00	6.00	3.50	302	Sandy Koufax	350.00	175.00	87.50
70	Richie Ashburn	45.00	22.50	13.50	185	Johnny Kucks	15.00	7.50	4.50	303	Billy Goodman	25.00	12.50	7.50
71	Murry Dickson	12.00	6.00	3.50	186	Jim King	12.00	6.00	3.50	304	Joe Cunningham	25.00	12.50	7.50
72	Bill Tuttle	12.00	6.00	3.50	187	Virgil Trucks	12.00	6.00	3.50	305	Chico Fernandez	25.00	12.50	7.50
73	George Crowe	12.00	6.00	3.50	188	Felix Mantilla	12.00	6.00	3.50	306	*Darrell Johnson*	35.00	17.50	10.00
74	Vito Valentinetti	12.00	6.00	3.50	189	Willard Nixon	12.00	6.00	3.50	307	Jack Phillips	25.00	12.50	7.50
75	Jim Piersall	15.00	7.50	4.50	190	Randy Jackson	15.00	7.50	4.50	308	Dick Hall	25.00	12.50	7.50
76	Bob Clemente	300.00	150.00	75.00	191	Joe Margoneri	12.00	6.00	3.50	309	Jim Busby	25.00	12.50	7.50
77	Paul Foytack	12.00	6.00	3.50	192	Jerry Coleman	15.00	7.50	4.50	310	Max Surkont	25.00	12.50	7.50
78	Vic Wertz	12.00	6.00	3.50	193	Del Rice	12.00	6.00	3.50	311	Al Pilarcik	25.00	12.50	7.50
79	*Lindy McDaniel*	15.00	7.50	4.50	194	Hal Brown	12.00	6.00	3.50	312	*Tony Kubek*	90.00	45.00	22.50
80	Gil Hodges	45.00	22.50	13.50	195	Bobby Avila	12.00	6.00	3.50	313	Mel Parnell	25.00	12.50	7.50
81	Herm Wehmeier	12.00	6.00	3.50	196	Larry Jackson	12.00	6.00	3.50	314	Ed Bouchee	25.00	12.50	7.50
82	Elston Howard	30.00	15.00	9.00	197	Hank Sauer	12.00	6.00	3.50	315	Lou Berberet	25.00	12.50	7.50
83	Lou Skizas	12.00	6.00	3.50	198	Detroit Tigers Team	20.00	10.00	6.00	316	Billy O'Dell	25.00	12.50	7.50
84	Moe Drabowsky	12.00	6.00	3.50	199	Vernon Law	12.00	6.00	3.50	317	New York Giants Team	60.00	30.00	15.00
85	Larry Doby	40.00	20.00	12.00	200	Gil McDougald	25.00	12.50	7.50	318	Mickey McDermott	25.00	12.50	7.50
86	Bill Sarni	12.00	6.00	3.50	201	Sandy Amoros	25.00	12.50	7.50	319	*Gino Cimoli*	30.00	15.00	9.00
87	Tom Gorman	12.00	6.00	3.50	202	Dick Gernert	12.00	6.00	3.50	320	Neil Chrisley	25.00	12.50	7.50
88	Harvey Kuenn	12.00	6.00	3.50	203	Hoyt Wilhelm	25.00	12.50	7.50	321	Red Murff	25.00	12.50	7.50
89	Roy Sievers	12.00	6.00	3.50	204	Kansas City A's Team	20.00	10.00	6.00	322	Cincinnati Redlegs Team	45.00	22.50	13.50
90	Warren Spahn	100.00	50.00	25.00	205	Charley Maxwell	12.00	6.00	3.50	323	Wes Westrum	25.00	12.50	7.50
91	Mack Burk	12.00	6.00	3.50	206	Willard Schmidt	12.00	6.00	3.50	324	Brooklyn Dodgers Team	125.00	62.50	31.25
92	Mickey Vernon	12.00	6.00	3.50	207	Billy Hunter	12.00	6.00	3.50	325	Frank Bolling	25.00	12.50	7.50
93	Hal Jeffcoat	12.00	6.00	3.50	208	Lew Burdette	12.00	6.00	3.50	326	Pedro Ramos	25.00	12.50	7.50
94	Bobby Del Greco	12.00	6.00	3.50	209	Bob Skinner	12.00	6.00	3.50	327	Jim Pendleton	25.00	12.50	7.50
95	Mickey Mantle	750.00	375.00	225.00	210	Roy Campanella	150.00	75.00	37.50	328	*Brooks Robinson*	400.00	200.00	100.00
96	Hank Aguirre	12.00	6.00	3.50	211	Camilo Pascual	12.00	6.00	3.50	329	Chicago White Sox Team	45.00	22.50	13.50
97	New York Yankees Team	100.00	50.00	25.00	212	*Rocky Colavito*	125.00	62.50	31.25	330	Jim Wilson	25.00	12.50	7.50
98	Al Dark	12.00	6.00	3.50	213	Les Moss	12.00	6.00	3.50	331	Ray Katt	25.00	12.50	7.50
99	Bob Keegan	12.00	6.00	3.50	214	Philadelphia Phillies Team	25.00	12.50	7.50	332	Bob Bowman	25.00	12.50	7.50
100	League Presidents (Warren Giles, William Harridge)	60.00	30.00	18.00	215	Enos Slaughter	35.00	17.50	10.00	333	Ernie Johnson	25.00	12.50	7.50
					216	Marv Grissom	12.00	6.00	3.50	334	Jerry Schoonmaker	25.00	12.50	7.50
101	Chuck Stobbs	12.00	6.00	3.50	217	Gene Stephens	12.00	6.00	3.50	335	Granny Hamner	25.00	12.50	7.50
102	Ray Boone	12.00	6.00	3.50	218	Ray Jablonski	12.00	6.00	3.50	336	*Haywood Sullivan*	25.00	12.50	7.50
103	Joe Nuxhall	12.00	6.00	3.50	219	Tom Acker	12.00	6.00	3.50	337	Rene Valdes (Valdez)	30.00	15.00	9.00
104	Hank Foiles	12.00	6.00	3.50	220	Jackie Jensen	17.50	8.75	5.25	338	*Jim Bunning*	150.00	75.00	37.50
105	Johnny Antonelli	12.00	6.00	3.50	221	Dixie Howell	12.00	6.00	3.50	339	Bob Speake	25.00	12.50	7.50
106	Ray Moore	12.00	6.00	3.50	222	Alex Grammas	12.00	6.00	3.50	340	Bill Wight	25.00	12.50	7.50
107	Jim Rivera	12.00	6.00	3.50	223	Frank House	12.00	6.00	3.50	341	Don Gross	25.00	12.50	7.50
108	Tommy Byrne	15.00	7.50	4.50	224	Marv Blaylock	12.00	6.00	3.50	342	Gene Mauch	25.00	12.50	7.50
109	Hank Thompson	12.00	6.00	3.50	225	Harry Simpson	12.00	6.00	3.50	343	Taylor Phillips	25.00	12.50	7.50
110	Bill Virdon	12.00	6.00	3.50	226	Preston Ward	12.00	6.00	3.50	344	Paul LaPalme	25.00	12.50	7.50
111	Hal Smith	12.00	6.00	3.50	227	Jerry Staley	12.00	6.00	3.50	345	Paul Smith	25.00	12.50	7.50
112	Tom Brewer	12.00	6.00	3.50	228	Smoky Burgess	12.00	6.00	3.50	346	Dick Littlefield	25.00	12.50	7.50
113	Wilmer Mizell	12.00	6.00	3.50	229	George Susce	12.00	6.00	3.50	347	Hal Naragon	25.00	12.50	7.50
114	Milwaukee Braves Team	30.00	15.00	9.00	230	George Kell	25.00	12.50	7.50	348	Jim Hearn	25.00	12.50	7.50
115	Jim Gilliam	27.50	13.50	8.25	231	Solly Hemus	12.00	6.00	3.50	349	Nelson King	25.00	12.50	7.50
116	Mike Fornieles	12.00	6.00	3.50	232	Whitey Lockman	12.00	6.00	3.50	350	Eddie Miksis	25.00	12.50	7.50
117	Joe Adcock	12.00	6.00	3.50	233	Art Fowler	12.00	6.00	3.50	351	Dave Hillman	25.00	12.50	7.50
118	Bob Porterfield	12.00	6.00	3.50	234	Dick Cole	12.00	6.00	3.50	352	Ellis Kinder	25.00	12.50	7.50
119	Stan Lopata	12.00	6.00	3.50	235	Tom Poholsky	12.00	6.00	3.50	353	Cal Neeman	12.00	6.00	3.50
120	Bob Lemon	35.00	17.50	10.00	236	Joe Ginsberg	12.00	6.00	3.50	354	Rip Coleman	12.00	6.00	3.50
121	*Cletis Boyer*	30.00	15.00	9.00	237	Foster Castleman	12.00	6.00	3.50	355	Frank Malzone	12.00	6.00	3.50
122	Ken Boyer	20.00	10.00	6.00	238	Eddie Robinson	12.00	6.00	3.50	356	Faye Throneberry	12.00	6.00	3.50
123	Steve Ridzik	12.00	6.00	3.50	239	Tom Morgan	12.00	6.00	3.50	357	Earl Torgeson	12.00	6.00	3.50
124	Dave Philley	12.00	6.00	3.50	240	Hank Bauer	30.00	15.00	9.00	358	Jerry Lynch	12.00	6.00	3.50
125	Al Kaline	100.00	50.00	25.00	241	Joe Lonnett	12.00	6.00	3.50	359	Tom Cheney	12.00	6.00	3.50
126	Bob Wiesler	12.00	6.00	3.50	242	Charley Neal	15.00	7.50	4.50	360	Johnny Groth	12.00	6.00	3.50
127	Bob Buhl	12.00	6.00	3.50	243	St. Louis Cardinals Team	20.00	10.00	6.00	361	Curt Barclay	12.00	6.00	3.50
128	Ed Bailey	12.00	6.00	3.50	244	Billy Loes	12.00	6.00	3.50	362	Roman Mejias	12.00	6.00	3.50
129	Saul Rogovin	12.00	6.00	3.50	245	Rip Repulski	12.00	6.00	3.50	363	Eddie Kasko	12.00	6.00	3.50
130	Don Newcombe	25.00	12.50	7.50	246	Jose Valdivielso	12.00	6.00	3.50	364	*Cal McLish*	12.00	6.00	3.50
131	Milt Bolling	12.00	6.00	3.50	247	Turk Lown	12.00	6.00	3.50	365	Ossie Virgil	15.00	7.50	4.50
132	Art Ditmar	12.00	6.00	3.50	248	Jim Finigan	12.00	6.00	3.50	366	Ken Lehman	12.00	6.00	3.50
133	Del Crandall	12.00	6.00	3.50	249	Dave Pope	12.00	6.00	3.50	367	Ed FitzGerald	12.00	6.00	3.50
134	Don Kaiser	12.00	6.00	3.50	250	Ed Mathews	55.00	27.50	16.50	368	Bob Purkey	12.00	6.00	3.50
135	Bill Skowron	30.00	15.00	9.00	251	Baltimore Orioles Team	20.00	10.00	6.00	369	Milt Graff	12.00	6.00	3.50
136	Jim Hegan	12.00	6.00	3.50	252	Carl Erskine	20.00	10.00	6.00	370	Warren Hacker	12.00	6.00	3.50
137	Bob Rush	12.00	6.00	3.50	253	Gus Zernial	12.00	6.00	3.50	371	Bob Lennon	12.00	6.00	3.50
138	Minnie Minoso	25.00	12.50	7.50	254	Ron Negray	12.00	6.00	3.50	372	Norm Zauchin	12.00	6.00	3.50
139	Lou Kretlow	12.00	6.00	3.50	255	Charlie Silvera	12.00	6.00	3.50	373	Pete Whisenant	12.00	6.00	3.50
140	Frank Thomas	12.00	6.00	3.50	256	Ronnie Kline	12.00	6.00	3.50	374	Don Cardwell	12.00	6.00	3.50
141	Al Aber	12.00	6.00	3.50	257	Walt Dropo	12.00	6.00	3.50	375	*Jim Landis*	12.00	6.00	3.50
142	Charley Thompson	12.00	6.00	3.50	258	Steve Gromek	12.00	6.00	3.50	376	Don Elston	15.00	7.50	4.50
143	Andy Pafko	12.00	6.00	3.50	259	Eddie O'Brien	12.00	6.00	3.50	377	Andre Rodgers	12.00	6.00	3.50
144	Ray Narleski	12.00	6.00	3.50	260	Del Ennis	12.00	6.00	3.50	378	Elmer Singleton	12.00	6.00	3.50
145	Al Smith	12.00	6.00	3.50	261	Bob Chakales	12.00	6.00	3.50	379	Don Lee	12.00	6.00	3.50
146	Don Ferrarese	12.00	6.00	3.50	262	Bobby Thomson	15.00	7.50	4.50	380	Walker Cooper	12.00	6.00	3.50
147	Al Walker	15.00	7.50	4.50	263	George Strickland	12.00	6.00	3.50	381	Dean Stone	12.00	6.00	3.50

#	Name	NM	EX	VG
382	Jim Brideweser	12.00	6.00	3.50
383	*Juan Pizarro*	12.00	6.00	3.50
384	Bobby Gene Smith	12.00	6.00	3.50
385	Art Houtteman	12.00	6.00	3.50
386	Lyle Luttrell	12.00	6.00	3.50
387	*Jack Sanford*	12.00	6.00	3.50
388	Pete Daley	12.00	6.00	3.50
389	Dave Jolly	12.00	6.00	3.50
390	Reno Bertoia	12.00	6.00	3.50
391	*Ralph Terry*	15.00	7.50	4.50
392	Chuck Tanner	12.00	6.00	3.50
393	Raul Sanchez	12.00	6.00	3.50
394	Luis Arroyo	12.00	6.00	3.50
395	Bubba Phillips	12.00	6.00	3.50
396	Casey Wise	12.00	6.00	3.50
397	Roy Smalley	12.00	6.00	3.50
398	Al Cicotte	15.00	7.50	4.50
399	Billy Consolo	12.00	6.00	3.50
400	Dodgers' Sluggers (Roy Campanella, Carl Furillo, Gil Hodges, Duke Snider)	250.00	125.00	62.50
401	*Earl Battey*	15.00	7.50	4.50
402	Jim Pisoni	12.00	6.00	3.50
403	Dick Hyde	12.00	6.00	3.50
404	Harry Anderson	12.00	6.00	3.50
405	Duke Maas	12.00	6.00	3.50
406	Bob Hale	12.00	6.00	3.50
407	Yankees' Power Hitters (Mickey Mantle, Yogi Berra)	500.00	250.00	125.00
----	Checklist Series 1-2 (Big Blony ad on back)	600.00	300.00	180.00
----	Checklist Series 1-2 (Bazooka ad on back)	600.00	300.00	180.00
----	Checklist Series 2-3 (Big Blony)	625.00	310.00	185.00
----	Checklist Series 2-3 (Bazooka)	625.00	310.00	185.00
----	Checklist Series 3-4 (Twin Blony)	1,300	650.00	390.00
----	Checklist Series 3-4 (Bazooka)	1,300	650.00	390.00
----	Checklist Series 4-5 (Twin Blony)	1,950	975.00	585.00
----	Checklist Series 4-5 (Bazooka)	1,950	975.00	585.00
----	Contest May 4	100.00	50.00	25.00
----	Contest May 25	135.00	65.00	40.00
----	Contest June 22	145.00	75.00	45.00
----	Contest July 19	200.00	100.00	60.00
----	Lucky Penny insert card	150.00	75.00	37.50

1958 Topps

Topps continued to expand its set size in 1958 with the release of a 494-card set. One card (#145) was not issued after Ed Bouchee was suspended from baseball. Cards retained the 2-1/2" x 3-1/2" size. There are a number of variations, including player or team names found in either yellow or white lettering on 33 cards between numbers 2-108 (higher priced yellow-letter variations checklisted below are not included in the complete set prices). The number of multiple-player cards was increased. A major innovation is the addition of 20 "All-Star" cards. For the first time, checklists were incorporated into the numbered series, on the backs of team cards.

#	Name	NM	EX	VG
	Complete Set (494):	8,500	4,250	2,500
	Common Player (1-495):	9.00	4.50	2.57
1	Ted Williams	600.00	175.00	80.00
2a	Bob Lemon (Yellow team.)	80.00	40.00	24.00
2b	Bob Lemon (White team.)	30.00	15.00	9.00
3	Alex Kellner	9.00	4.50	2.57
4	Hank Foiles	9.00	4.50	2.57
5	Willie Mays	325.00	162.50	81.25
6	George Zuverink	9.00	4.50	2.57
7	Dale Long	9.00	4.50	2.57
8a	Eddie Kasko (Yellow name.)	60.00	30.00	18.00
8b	Eddie Kasko (White name.)	9.00	4.50	2.57
9	Hank Bauer	20.00	10.00	6.00
10	Lou Burdette	9.00	4.50	2.57
11a	Jim Rivera (Yellow team.)	60.00	30.00	18.00
11b	Jim Rivera (White team.)	9.00	4.50	2.57
12	George Crowe	9.00	4.50	2.57
13a	Billy Hoeft (Yellow name.)	60.00	30.00	18.00
13b	Billy Hoeft (White name, orange triangle by foot.)	9.00	4.50	2.57
13c	Billy Hoeft (White name, red triangle by foot.)	9.00	4.50	2.57
14	Rip Repulski	9.00	4.50	2.57
15	Jim Lemon	9.00	4.50	2.57
16	Charley Neal	9.00	4.50	2.57
17	Felix Mantilla	9.00	4.50	2.57
18	Frank Sullivan	9.00	4.50	2.57
19	1957 Giants Team	40.00	20.00	12.00
20a	Gil McDougald (Yellow name.)	75.00	37.50	22.00
20b	Gil McDougald (White name.)	20.00	10.00	6.00
21	Curt Barclay	9.00	4.50	2.57

#	Name	NM	EX	VG
22	Hal Naragon	9.00	4.50	2.57
23a	Bill Tuttle (Yellow name.)	60.00	30.00	18.00
23b	Bill Tuttle (White name.)	9.00	4.50	2.57
24a	Hobie Landrith (Yellow name.)	60.00	30.00	18.00
24b	Hobie Landrith (White name.)	9.00	4.50	2.57
25	Don Drysdale	100.00	50.00	25.00
26	Ron Jackson	9.00	4.50	2.57
27	Bud Freeman	9.00	4.50	2.57
28	Jim Busby	9.00	4.50	2.57
29	Ted Lepcio	9.00	4.50	2.57
30a	Hank Aaron (Yellow name.)	425.00	210.00	125.00
30b	Hank Aaron (White name.)	225.00	112.50	56.25
31	Tex Clevenger	9.00	4.50	2.57
32a	J.W. Porter (Yellow name.)	60.00	30.00	18.00
32b	J.W. Porter (White name.)	9.00	4.50	2.57
33a	Cal Neeman (Yellow team.)	60.00	30.00	18.00
33b	Cal Neeman (White team.)	9.00	4.50	2.57
34	Bob Thurman	9.00	4.50	2.57
35a	Don Mossi (Yellow team.)	60.00	30.00	18.00
35b	Don Mossi (White team.)	9.00	4.50	2.57
36	Ted Kazanski	9.00	4.50	2.57
37	*Mike McCormick* (Photo actually Ray Monzant.)	9.00	4.50	2.57
38	Dick Gernert	9.00	4.50	2.57
39	Bob Martyn	9.00	4.50	2.57
40	George Kell	20.00	10.00	6.00
41	Dave Hillman	9.00	4.50	2.57
42	*John Roseboro*	25.00	12.50	7.50
43	Sal Maglie	12.50	6.25	3.75
44	Wash. Senators Team	20.00	10.00	6.00
45	Dick Groat	9.00	4.50	2.57
46a	Lou Sleater (Yellow name.)	60.00	30.00	18.00
46b	Lou Sleater (White name.)	9.00	4.50	2.57
47	*Roger Maris*	500.00	250.00	125.00
48	Chuck Harmon	9.00	4.50	2.57
49	Smoky Burgess	9.00	4.50	2.57
50a	Billy Pierce (Yellow team.)	60.00	30.00	18.00
50b	Billy Pierce (White team.)	9.00	4.50	2.57
51	Del Rice	9.00	4.50	2.57
52a	Bob Clemente (Yellow team.)	500.00	250.00	125.00
52b	Bob Clemente (White team.)	300.00	150.00	75.00
53a	Morrie Martin (Yellow name.)	60.00	30.00	18.00
53b	Morrie Martin (White name.)	9.00	4.50	2.57
54	*Norm Siebern*	12.50	6.25	3.75
55	Chico Carrasquel	9.00	4.50	2.57
56	Bill Fischer	9.00	4.50	2.57
57a	Tim Thompson (Yellow name.)	60.00	30.00	18.00
57b	Tim Thompson (White name.)	9.00	4.50	2.57
58a	Art Schult (Yellow team.)	60.00	30.00	18.00
58b	Art Schult (White team.)	9.00	4.50	2.57
59	Dave Sisler	9.00	4.50	2.57
60a	Del Ennis (Yellow name.)	60.00	30.00	18.00
60b	Del Ennis (White name.)	9.00	4.50	2.57
61a	Darrell Johnson (Yellow name.)	100.00	50.00	30.00
61b	Darrell Johnson (White name.)	15.00	7.50	4.50
62	Joe DeMaestri	9.00	4.50	2.57
63	Joe Nuxhall	9.00	4.50	2.57
64	Joe Lonnett	9.00	4.50	2.57
65a	Von McDaniel (Yellow name.)	60.00	30.00	18.00
65b	Von McDaniel (White name.)	9.00	4.50	2.57
66	Lee Walls	9.00	4.50	2.57
67	Joe Ginsberg	9.00	4.50	2.57
68	Daryl Spencer	9.00	4.50	2.57
69	Wally Burnette	9.00	4.50	2.57
70a	Al Kaline (Yellow name.)	250.00	125.00	62.50
70b	Al Kaline (White name.)	100.00	50.00	25.00
71	1957 Dodgers Team	80.00	40.00	20.00
72	Bud Byerly (Photo actually Hal Griggs.)	9.00	4.50	2.57
73	Pete Daley	9.00	4.50	2.57
74	Roy Face	9.00	4.50	2.57
75	Gus Bell	9.00	4.50	2.57
76a	Dick Farrell (Yellow team.)	60.00	30.00	18.00
76b	Dick Farrell (White team.)	9.00	4.50	2.57
77a	Don Zimmer (Yellow team.)	80.00	40.00	24.00
77b	Don Zimmer (White team.)	15.00	7.50	4.50
78a	Ernie Johnson (Yellow team.)	60.00	30.00	18.00
78b	Ernie Johnson (White team.)	9.00	4.50	2.57
79a	Dick Williams (Yellow team.)	60.00	30.00	18.00
79b	Dick Williams (White team.)	9.00	4.50	2.57
80	Dick Drott	9.00	4.50	2.57
81a	*Steve Boros* (Yellow team.)	60.00	30.00	18.00
81b	*Steve Boros* (White team.)	9.00	4.50	2.57
82	Ronnie Kline	9.00	4.50	2.57
83	*Bob Hazle*	9.00	4.50	2.57
84	Billy O'Dell	9.00	4.50	2.57
85a	Luis Aparicio (Yellow name.)	140.00	70.00	40.00
85b	Luis Aparicio (White name.)	30.00	15.00	9.00
86	Valmy Thomas	9.00	4.50	2.57
87	Johnny Kucks	10.00	5.00	3.00
88	Duke Snider	45.00	22.50	13.50
89	Billy Klaus	9.00	4.50	2.57
90	Robin Roberts	30.00	15.00	9.00
91	Chuck Tanner	9.00	4.50	2.57
92a	Clint Courtney (Yellow name.)	60.00	30.00	18.00
92b	Clint Courtney (White name.)	9.00	4.50	2.57
93	Sandy Amoros	12.00	6.00	3.50
94	Bob Skinner	9.00	4.50	2.57
95	Frank Bolling	9.00	4.50	2.57
96	Joe Durham	9.00	4.50	2.57
97a	Larry Jackson (Yellow name.)	60.00	30.00	18.00
97b	Larry Jackson (White name.)	9.00	4.50	2.57
98a	Billy Hunter (Yellow name.)	60.00	30.00	18.00
98b	Billy Hunter (White name.)	9.00	4.50	2.57
99	Bobby Adams	9.00	4.50	2.57
100a	Early Wynn (Yellow name.)	90.00	45.00	27.50
100b	Early Wynn (White name.)	20.00	10.00	6.00
101a	Bobby Richardson (Yellow name.)	100.00	50.00	30.00
101b	Bobby Richardson (White name.)	30.00	15.00	9.00
102	George Strickland	9.00	4.50	2.57
103	Jerry Lynch	9.00	4.50	2.57
104	Jim Pendleton	9.00	4.50	2.57
105	Billy Gardner	9.00	4.50	2.57
106	Dick Schofield	9.00	4.50	2.57
107	Ossie Virgil	9.00	4.50	2.57

#	Name	NM	EX	VG
108a	Jim Landis (Yellow team.)	60.00	30.00	18.00
108b	Jim Landis (White team.)	9.00	4.50	2.57
109	Herb Plews	9.00	4.50	2.57
110	Johnny Logan	9.00	4.50	2.57
111	Stu Miller	9.00	4.50	2.57
112	Gus Zernial	9.00	4.50	2.57
113	Jerry Walker	9.00	4.50	2.57
114	Irv Noren	9.00	4.50	2.57
115	Jim Bunning	20.00	10.00	6.00
116	Dave Philley	9.00	4.50	2.57
117	Frank Torre	9.00	4.50	2.57
118	Harvey Haddix	9.00	4.50	2.57
119	Harry Chiti	9.00	4.50	2.57
120	Johnny Podres	12.00	6.00	3.50
121	Eddie Miksis	9.00	4.50	2.57
122	Walt Moryn	9.00	4.50	2.57
123	Dick Tomanek	9.00	4.50	2.57
124	Bobby Usher	9.00	4.50	2.57
125	Al Dark	9.00	4.50	2.57
126	Stan Palys	9.00	4.50	2.57
127	Tom Sturdivant	10.00	5.00	3.00
128	*Willie Kirkland*	9.00	4.50	2.57
129	Jim Derrington	9.00	4.50	2.57
130	Jackie Jensen	10.00	5.00	3.00
131	Bob Henrich	9.00	4.50	2.57
132	Vernon Law	9.00	4.50	2.57
133	Russ Nixon	9.00	4.50	2.57
134	Phila. Phillies Team	16.00	8.00	4.75
135	Mike Drabowsky	9.00	4.50	2.57
136	Jim Finnigan	9.00	4.50	2.57
137	Russ Kemmerer	9.00	4.50	2.57
138	Earl Torgeson	9.00	4.50	2.57
139	George Brunet	9.00	4.50	2.57
140	Wes Covington	9.00	4.50	2.57
141	Ken Lehman	9.00	4.50	2.57
142	Enos Slaughter	25.00	12.50	7.50
143	Billy Muffett	9.00	4.50	2.57
144	Bobby Morgan	9.00	4.50	2.57
145	Not Issued			
146	Dick Gray	9.00	4.50	2.57
147	*Don McMahon*	9.00	4.50	2.57
148	Billy Consolo	9.00	4.50	2.57
149	Tom Acker	9.00	4.50	2.57
150	Mickey Mantle	1,000	500.00	250.00
151	Buddy Pritchard	9.00	4.50	2.57
152	Johnny Antonelli	9.00	4.50	2.57
153	Les Moss	9.00	4.50	2.57
154	Harry Byrd	9.00	4.50	2.57
155	Hector Lopez	9.00	4.50	2.57
156	Dick Hyde	9.00	4.50	2.57
157	Dee Fondy	9.00	4.50	2.57
158	Cleve. Indians Team	25.00	12.50	7.50
159	Taylor Phillips	10.00	5.00	3.00
160	Don Hoak	9.00	4.50	2.57
161	Don Larsen	25.00	12.50	7.50
162	Gil Hodges	30.00	15.00	9.00
163	Jim Wilson	9.00	4.50	2.57
164	Bob Taylor	9.00	4.50	2.57
165	Bob Nieman	9.00	4.50	2.57
166	Danny O'Connell	9.00	4.50	2.57
167	Frank Baumann	9.00	4.50	2.57
168	Joe Cunningham	9.00	4.50	2.57
169	Ralph Terry	9.00	4.50	2.57
170	Vic Wertz	9.00	4.50	2.57
171	Harry Anderson	9.00	4.50	2.57
172	Don Gross	9.00	4.50	2.57
173	Eddie Yost	9.00	4.50	2.57
174	K.C. Athletics Team	20.00	10.00	6.00
175	*Marv Throneberry*	25.00	12.50	7.50
176	Bob Buhl	9.00	4.50	2.57
177	Al Smith	9.00	4.50	2.57
178	Ted Kluszewski	20.00	10.00	6.00
179	Willy Miranda	9.00	4.50	2.57
180	Lindy McDaniel	9.00	4.50	2.57
181	Willie Jones	9.00	4.50	2.57
182	Joe Caffie	9.00	4.50	2.57
183	Dave Jolly	9.00	4.50	2.57
184	Elvin Tappe	9.00	4.50	2.57
185	Ray Boone	9.00	4.50	2.57
186	Jack Meyer	9.00	4.50	2.57
187	Sandy Koufax	275.00	137.50	68.75
188	Milt Bolling (Photo actually Lou Berberet.)	9.00	4.50	2.57
189	George Susce	9.00	4.50	2.57
190	Red Schoendienst	20.00	10.00	6.00
191	Art Ceccarelli	9.00	4.50	2.57
192	Milt Graff	9.00	4.50	2.57
193	*Jerry Lumpe*	12.50	6.25	3.75
194	Roger Craig	9.00	4.50	2.57
195	Whitey Lockman	9.00	4.50	2.57
196	Mike Garcia	9.00	4.50	2.57
197	Haywood Sullivan	9.00	4.50	2.57
198	Bill Virdon	9.00	4.50	2.57
199	Don Blasingame	9.00	4.50	2.57
200	Bob Keegan	9.00	4.50	2.57
201	Jim Bolger	9.00	4.50	2.57
202	*Woody Held*	9.00	4.50	2.57
203	Al Walker	9.00	4.50	2.57
204	Leo Kiely	9.00	4.50	2.57
205	Johnny Temple	9.00	4.50	2.57
206	Bob Shaw	9.00	4.50	2.57
207	Solly Hemus	9.00	4.50	2.57
208	Cal McLish	9.00	4.50	2.57
209	Bob Anderson	9.00	4.50	2.57
210	Wally Moon	9.00	4.50	2.57
211	Pete Burnside	9.00	4.50	2.57
212	Bubba Phillips	9.00	4.50	2.57
213	Red Wilson	9.00	4.50	2.57
214	Willard Schmidt	9.00	4.50	2.57
215	Jim Gilliam	12.50	6.25	3.75
216	St. Louis Cards Team	25.00	12.50	7.50
217	Jack Harshman	9.00	4.50	2.57
218	Dick Rand	9.00	4.50	2.57
219	Camilo Pascual	9.00	4.50	2.57
220	Tom Brewer	9.00	4.50	2.57
221	Jerry Kindall	9.00	4.50	2.57
222	Bud Daley	9.00	4.50	2.57
223	Andy Pafko	9.00	4.50	2.57

#	Player	NM	EX	VG
224	Bob Grim	10.00	5.00	3.00
225	Billy Goodman	9.00	4.50	2.57
226	Bob Smith (Photo actually Bobby Gene Smith.)	9.00	4.50	2.57
227	Gene Stephens			2.57
228	Duke Maas	9.00	4.50	2.57
229	Frank Zupo	9.00	4.50	2.57
230	Richie Ashburn	30.00	15.00	9.00
231	Lloyd Merritt	9.00	4.50	2.57
232	Reno Bertoia	9.00	4.50	2.57
233	Mickey Vernon	9.00	4.50	2.57
234	Carl Sawatski	9.00	4.50	2.57
235	Tom Gorman	9.00	4.50	2.57
236	Ed FitzGerald	9.00	4.50	2.57
237	Bill Wight	9.00	4.50	2.57
238	Bill Mazeroski	30.00	15.00	9.00
239	Chuck Stobbs	9.00	4.50	2.57
240	Moose Skowron	20.00	10.00	6.00
241	Dick Littlefield	9.00	4.50	2.57
242	Johnny Klippstein	9.00	4.50	2.57
243	Larry Raines	9.00	4.50	2.57
244	*Don Demeter*	9.00	4.50	2.57
245	*Frank Lary*	9.00	4.50	2.57
246	New York Yankees Team	100.00	50.00	25.00
247	Casey Wise	9.00	4.50	2.57
248	Herm Wehmeier	9.00	4.50	2.57
249	Ray Moore	9.00	4.50	2.57
250	Roy Sievers	9.00	4.50	2.57
251	Warren Hacker	9.00	4.50	2.57
252	Bob Trowbridge	9.00	4.50	2.57
253	Don Mueller	9.00	4.50	2.57
254	Alex Grammas	9.00	4.50	2.57
255	Bob Turley	25.00	12.50	7.50
256	Chicago White Sox Team	20.00	10.00	6.00
257	Hal Smith	9.00	4.50	2.57
258	Carl Erskine	17.50	8.75	5.25
259	Al Pilarcik	9.00	4.50	2.57
260	Frank Malzone	9.00	4.50	2.57
261	Turk Lown	9.00	4.50	2.57
262	Johnny Groth	9.00	4.50	2.57
263	Eddie Bressoud	9.00	4.50	2.57
264	Jack Sanford	9.00	4.50	2.57
265	Pete Runnels	9.00	4.50	2.57
266	Connie Johnson	9.00	4.50	2.57
267	Sherm Lollar	9.00	4.50	2.57
268	Granny Hamner	9.00	4.50	2.57
269	Paul Smith	9.00	4.50	2.57
270	Warren Spahn	80.00	40.00	20.00
271	Billy Martin	20.00	10.00	6.00
272	Ray Crone	9.00	4.50	2.57
273	Hal Smith	9.00	4.50	2.57
274	Rocky Bridges	9.00	4.50	2.57
275	Elston Howard	20.00	10.00	6.00
276	Bobby Avila	9.00	4.50	2.57
277	Virgil Trucks	9.00	4.50	2.57
278	Mack Burk	9.00	4.50	2.57
279	Bob Boyd	9.00	4.50	2.57
280	Jim Piersall	9.00	4.50	2.57
281	Sam Taylor	9.00	4.50	2.57
282	Paul Foytack	9.00	4.50	2.57
283	Ray Shearer	9.00	4.50	2.57
284	Ray Katt	9.00	4.50	2.57
285	Frank Robinson	100.00	50.00	25.00
286	Gino Cimoli	9.00	4.50	2.57
287	Sam Jones	9.00	4.50	2.57
288	Harmon Killebrew	100.00	50.00	25.00
289	Series Hurling Rivals (Lou Burdette, Bobby Shantz)	25.00	12.50	7.50
290	Dick Donovan	9.00	4.50	2.57
291	Don Landrum	9.00	4.50	2.57
292	Ned Garver	9.00	4.50	2.57
293	Gene Freese	9.00	4.50	2.57
294	Hal Jeffcoat	9.00	4.50	2.57
295	Minnie Minoso	20.00	10.00	6.00
296	*Ryne Duren*	50.00	25.00	15.00
297	Don Buddin	9.00	4.50	2.57
298	Jim Hearn	9.00	4.50	2.57
299	Harry Simpson	9.00	4.50	2.57
300	League Presidents (Warren Giles, William Harridge)	35.00	17.50	10.00
301	Randy Jackson	9.00	4.50	2.57
302	Mike Baxes	9.00	4.50	2.57
303	Neil Chrisley	9.00	4.50	2.57
304	Tigers' Big Bats (Al Kaline, Harvey Kuenn)	35.00	17.50	10.00
305	Clem Labine	12.50	6.25	3.75
306	Whammy Douglas	9.00	4.50	2.57
307	Brooks Robinson	100.00	50.00	25.00
308	Paul Giel	9.00	4.50	2.57
309	Gail Harris	9.00	4.50	2.57
310	Ernie Banks	125.00	62.50	31.25
311	Bob Purkey	9.00	4.50	2.57
312	Boston Red Sox Team	25.00	12.50	7.50
313	Bob Rush	9.00	4.50	2.57
314	Dodgers' Boss & Power (Duke Snider, Walter Alston)	35.00	17.50	10.00
315	Bob Friend	9.00	4.50	2.57
316	Tito Francona	9.00	4.50	2.57
317	*Albie Pearson*	10.00	5.00	3.00
318	Frank House	9.00	4.50	2.57
319	Lou Skizas	9.00	4.50	2.57
320	Whitey Ford	80.00	40.00	20.00
321	Sluggers Supreme (Ted Kluszewski, Ted Williams)	100.00	50.00	25.00
322	Harding Peterson	9.00	4.50	2.57
323	Elmer Valo	9.00	4.50	2.57
324	Hoyt Wilhelm	20.00	10.00	6.00
325	Joe Adcock	9.00	4.50	2.57
326	Bob Miller	9.00	4.50	2.57
327	Chicago Cubs Team	20.00	10.00	6.00
328	Ike Delock	9.00	4.50	2.57
329	Bob Cerv	9.00	4.50	2.57
330	Ed Bailey	9.00	4.50	2.57
331	Pedro Ramos	9.00	4.50	2.57
332	Jim King	9.00	4.50	2.57
333	Andy Carey	10.00	5.00	3.00
334	Mound Aces (Bob Friend, Billy Pierce)	12.00	6.00	3.00
335	Ruben Gomez	9.00	4.50	2.57
336	Bert Hamric	9.00	4.50	2.57
337	Hank Aguirre	9.00	4.50	2.57
338	Walt Dropo	9.00	4.50	2.57
339	Fred Hatfield	9.00	4.50	2.57
340	Don Newcombe	25.00	12.50	7.50
341	Pittsburgh Pirates Team	30.00	15.00	9.00
342	Jim Brosnan	9.00	4.50	2.57
343	*Orlando Cepeda*	100.00	50.00	25.00
344	Bob Porterfield	9.00	4.50	2.57
345	Jim Hegan	9.00	4.50	2.57
346	Steve Bilko	9.00	4.50	2.57
347	Don Rudolph	9.00	4.50	2.57
348	Chico Fernandez	9.00	4.50	2.57
349	Murry Dickson	9.00	4.50	2.57
350	Ken Boyer	12.50	6.25	3.75
351	Braves' Fence Busters (Hank Aaron, Joe Adcock, Del Crandall, Eddie Mathews)	60.00	30.00	18.00
352	Herb Score	12.50	6.25	3.75
353	Stan Lopata	9.00	4.50	2.57
354	Art Ditmar	10.00	5.00	3.00
355	Bill Bruton	9.00	4.50	2.57
356	Bob Malkmus	9.00	4.50	2.57
357	Danny McDevitt	9.00	4.50	2.57
358	Gene Baker	9.00	4.50	2.57
359	Billy Loes	9.00	4.50	2.57
360	Roy McMillan	9.00	4.50	2.57
361	Mike Fornieles	9.00	4.50	2.57
362	Ray Jablonski	9.00	4.50	2.57
363	Don Elston	9.00	4.50	2.57
364	Earl Battey	9.00	4.50	2.57
365	Tom Morgan	9.00	4.50	2.57
366	Gene Green	9.00	4.50	2.57
367	Jack Urban	9.00	4.50	2.57
368	Rocky Colavito	50.00	25.00	15.00
369	Ralph Lumenti	9.00	4.50	2.57
370	Yogi Berra	120.00	60.00	30.00
371	Marty Keough	9.00	4.50	2.57
372	Don Cardwell	9.00	4.50	2.57
373	Joe Pignatano	9.00	4.50	2.57
374	Brooks Lawrence	9.00	4.50	2.57
375	Pee Wee Reese	45.00	22.50	13.50
376	Charley Rabe	9.00	4.50	2.57
377a	Milwaukee Braves Team (Alphabetical checklist.)	20.00	10.00	6.00
377b	Milwaukee Braves Team (Numerical checklist.)	140.00	70.00	40.00
378	Hank Sauer	9.00	4.50	2.57
379	Ray Herbert	9.00	4.50	2.57
380	Charley Maxwell	9.00	4.50	2.57
381	Hal Brown	9.00	4.50	2.57
382	Al Cicotte	10.00	5.00	3.00
383	Lou Berberet	9.00	4.50	2.57
384	John Goryl	9.00	4.50	2.57
385	Wilmer Mizell	9.00	4.50	2.57
386	Birdie's Young Sluggers (Ed Bailey, Frank Robinson, Birdie Tebbetts)	20.00	10.00	6.00
387	Wally Post	9.00	4.50	2.57
388	Billy Moran	9.00	4.50	2.57
389	Bill Taylor	9.00	4.50	2.57
390	Del Crandall	9.00	4.50	2.57
391	Dave Melton	9.00	4.50	2.57
392	Bennie Daniels	9.00	4.50	2.57
393	Tony Kubek	20.00	10.00	6.00
394	*Jim Grant*	10.00	5.00	3.00
395	Willard Nixon	9.00	4.50	2.57
396	Dutch Dotterer	9.00	4.50	2.57
397a	Detroit Tigers Team (Alphabetical checklist.)	15.00	7.50	4.50
397b	Detroit Tigers Team (Numerical checklist.)	125.00	65.00	35.00
398	Gene Woodling	9.00	4.50	2.57
399	Marv Grissom	9.00	4.50	2.57
400	Nellie Fox	25.00	12.50	7.50
401	Don Bessent	9.00	4.50	2.57
402	Bobby Gene Smith	9.00	4.50	2.57
403	Steve Korcheck	9.00	4.50	2.57
404	Curt Simmons	9.00	4.50	2.57
405	Ken Aspromonte	9.00	4.50	2.57
406	Vic Power	9.00	4.50	2.57
407	Carlton Willey	9.00	4.50	2.57
408a	Baltimore Orioles Team (Alphabetical checklist.)	15.00	7.50	4.50
408b	Baltimore Orioles Team (Numerical checklist.)	125.00	65.00	35.00
409	Frank Thomas	9.00	4.50	2.57
410	Murray Wall	9.00	4.50	2.57
411	*Tony Taylor*	9.00	4.50	2.57
412	Jerry Staley	9.00	4.50	2.57
413	*Jim Davenport*	9.00	4.50	2.57
414	Sammy White	9.00	4.50	2.57
415	Bob Bowman	9.00	4.50	2.57
416	Foster Castleman	9.00	4.50	2.57
417	Carl Furillo	15.00	7.50	4.50
418	World Series Foes (Hank Aaron, Mickey Mantle)	400.00	200.00	100.00
419	Bobby Shantz	15.00	7.50	4.50
420	*Vada Pinson*	20.00	10.00	6.00
421	Dixie Howell	9.00	4.50	2.57
422	Norm Zauchin	9.00	4.50	2.57
423	Phil Clark	9.00	4.50	2.57
424	Larry Doby	20.00	10.00	6.00
425	Sam Esposito	9.00	4.50	2.57
426	Johnny O'Brien	9.00	4.50	2.57
427	Al Worthington	9.00	4.50	2.57
428a	Cincinnati Redlegs Team (Alphabetical checklist.)	15.00	7.50	4.50
428b	Cincinnati Redlegs Team (Numerical checklist.)	125.00	65.00	35.00
429	Gus Triandos	9.00	4.50	2.57
430	Bobby Thomson	12.00	6.00	3.50
431	Gene Conley	9.00	4.50	2.57
432	John Powers	9.00	4.50	2.57
433	Pancho Herrera	9.00	4.50	2.57
433a	Pancho Herrera (Printing error, no "a" in Herrera.)	4,000	2,000	1,200
434	Harvey Kuenn	9.00	4.50	2.57
435	Ed Roebuck	9.00	4.50	2.57
436	Rival Fence Busters (Willie Mays, Duke Snider)	80.00	40.00	20.00
437	Bob Speake	9.00	4.50	2.57
438	Whitey Herzog	9.00	4.50	2.57
439	Ray Narleski	9.00	4.50	2.57
440	Ed Mathews	80.00	40.00	20.00
441	Jim Marshall	9.00	4.50	2.57
442	Phil Paine	9.00	4.50	2.57
443	Billy Harrell (SP)	15.00	7.50	4.50
444	Danny Kravitz	9.00	4.50	2.57
445	Bob Smith	9.00	4.50	2.57
446	Carroll Hardy (SP)	15.00	7.50	4.50
447	Ray Monzant	9.00	4.50	2.57
448	*Charlie Lau*	13.50	7.00	4.00
449	Gene Fodge	9.00	4.50	2.57
450	Preston Ward (SP)	15.00	7.50	4.50
451	Joe Taylor	9.00	4.50	2.57
452	Roman Mejias	9.00	4.50	2.57
453	Tom Qualters	9.00	4.50	2.57
454	Harry Hanebrink	9.00	4.50	2.57
455	Hal Griggs (Photo actually Bud Byerly.)	9.00	4.50	2.57
456	Dick Brown	9.00	4.50	2.57
457	*Milt Pappas*	10.00	5.00	3.00
458	Julio Becquer	9.00	4.50	2.57
459	Ron Blackburn	9.00	4.50	2.57
460	Chuck Essegian	9.00	4.50	2.57
461	Ed Mayer	9.00	4.50	2.57
462	Gary Geiger (SP)	15.00	7.50	4.50
463	Vito Valentinetti	9.00	4.50	2.57
464	*Curt Flood*	30.00	15.00	9.00
465	Arnie Portocarrero	9.00	4.50	2.57
466	Pete Whisenant	9.00	4.50	2.57
467	Glen Hobbie	9.00	4.50	2.57
468	Bob Schmidt	9.00	4.50	2.57
469	Don Ferrarese	9.00	4.50	2.57
470	R.C. Stevens	9.00	4.50	2.57
471	Lenny Green	9.00	4.50	2.57
472	Joe Jay	9.00	4.50	2.57
473	Bill Renna	9.00	4.50	2.57
474	Roman Semproch	9.00	4.50	2.57
475	All-Star Managers (Fred Haney, Casey Stengel)	30.00	15.00	9.00
476	Stan Musial (All-Star)	35.00	17.50	10.00
477	Bill Skowron (All-Star)	15.00	7.50	4.50
478	Johnny Temple (All-Star)	10.00	5.00	3.00
479	Nellie Fox (All-Star)	15.00	7.50	4.50
480	Eddie Mathews (All-Star)	25.00	12.50	7.50
481	Frank Malzone (All-Star)	10.00	5.00	3.00
482	Ernie Banks (All-Star)	30.00	15.00	9.00
483	Luis Aparicio (All-Star)	20.00	10.00	6.00
484	Frank Robinson (All-Star)	30.00	15.00	9.00
485	Ted Williams (All-Star)	150.00	75.00	37.50
486	Willie Mays (All-Star)	75.00	37.50	18.75
487	Mickey Mantle (All-Star)(Triple Print)	200.00	100.00	50.00
488	Hank Aaron (All-Star)	55.00	27.50	16.50
489	Jackie Jensen (All-Star)	12.00	6.00	3.50
490	Ed Bailey (All-Star)	10.00	5.00	3.00
491	Sherman Lollar (All-Star)	10.00	5.00	3.00
492	Bob Friend (All-Star)	10.00	5.00	3.00
493	Bob Turley (All-Star)	15.00	7.50	4.50
494	Warren Spahn (All-Star)	25.00	12.50	7.50
495	Herb Score (All-Star)	15.00	7.50	4.50
----	Contest Card (All-Star Game, July 8)	70.00	35.00	20.00
----	Felt Emblems Insert Card	45.00	22.50	13.50

1959 Topps

These 2-1/2" x 3-1/2" cards have a round photograph on front with a solid-color background above and below and a white border. A facsimile autograph is found across the photo. The 572-card set marks the largest set issued to that time. Card numbers below 507 have red and green printing on back with the card number in white in a green box. On high number cards beginning with #507, the printing is black and red and the card number is in a black box. Specialty cards include multiple-player cards, team cards with checklists on back, "All-Star" cards, "Baseball Thrills," and 31 "Rookie Stars." There is also a card of the commissioner, Ford Frick, and one of Roy Campanella in a wheelchair. A handful of cards can be found with and without lines added to the biographies on back indicating trades or demotions; those without the added lines are scarcer and more valuable and are not included in the complete set price. Card numbers 199-286 can be found with either white or gray backs, with the gray stock being the less common.

		NM	EX	VG
	Complete Set (572):	11,500	3,250	1,900
	Common Player (1-506):	7.00	3.50	2.00
	Common Player (507-572):	15.00	7.50	4.50
1	Ford Frick	80.00	40.00	20.00
2	Eddie Yost	12.00	3.50	

#	Name			
3	Don McMahon	7.00	3.50	2.00
4	Albie Pearson	7.00	3.50	2.00
5	Dick Donovan	7.00	3.50	2.00
6	Alex Grammas	7.00	3.50	2.00
7	Al Pilarcik	7.00	3.50	2.00
8	Philadelphia Phillies Team (SP)	90.00	45.00	27.50
9	Paul Giel	7.00	3.50	2.00
10	Mickey Mantle	1,000.	500.00	250.00
11	Billy Hunter	7.00	3.50	2.00
12	Vern Law	7.00	3.50	2.00
13	Dick Gernert	7.00	3.50	2.00
14	Pete Whisenant	7.00	3.50	2.00
15	Dick Drott	7.00	3.50	2.00
16	Joe Pignatano	7.00	3.50	2.00
17	Danny's All-Stars (Ted Kluszewski, Danny Murtaugh, Frank J. Thomas)	13.50	7.00	4.00
18	Jack Urban	7.00	3.50	2.00
19	Ed Bressoud	7.00	3.50	2.00
20	Duke Snider	40.00	20.00	12.00
21	Connie Johnson	7.00	3.50	2.00
22	Al Smith	7.00	3.50	2.00
23	Murry Dickson	7.00	3.50	2.00
24	Red Wilson	7.00	3.50	2.00
25	Don Hoak	7.00	3.50	2.00
26	Chuck Stobbs	7.00	3.50	2.00
27	Andy Pafko	7.00	3.50	2.00
28	Red Worthington	7.00	3.50	2.00
29	Jim Bolger	7.00	3.50	2.00
30	Nellie Fox	30.00	15.00	9.00
31	Ken Lehman	7.00	3.50	2.00
32	Don Buddin	7.00	3.50	2.00
33	Ed Fitz Gerald	7.00	3.50	2.00
34	Pitchers Beware (Al Kaline, Charlie Maxwell)	25.00	12.50	7.50
35	Ted Kluszewski	17.50	8.75	5.25
36	Hank Aguirre	7.00	3.50	2.00
37	Gene Green	7.00	3.50	2.00
38	Morrie Martin	7.00	3.50	2.00
39	Ed Bouchee	7.00	3.50	2.00
40a	Warren Spahn (Born 1931.)	100.00	50.00	25.00
40b	Warren Spahn (Born 1931, "3" partially obscured.)	100.00	50.00	25.00
40c	Warren Spahn (Born 1921.)	50.00	25.00	12.50
41	Bob Martyn	7.00	3.50	2.00
42	Murray Wall	7.00	3.50	2.00
43	Steve Bilko	7.00	3.50	2.00
44	Vito Valentinetti	7.00	3.50	2.00
45	Andy Carey	9.00	4.50	2.75
46	Bill Henry	7.00	3.50	2.00
47	Jim Finigan	7.00	3.50	2.00
48	Baltimore Orioles Team	17.50	8.75	5.25
49	Bill Hall	7.00	3.50	2.00
50	Willie Mays	175.00	87.50	43.75
51	Rip Coleman	7.00	3.50	2.00
52	Coot Veal	7.00	3.50	2.00
53	Stan Williams	20.00	10.00	6.00
54	Mel Roach	7.00	3.50	2.00
55	Tom Brewer	7.00	3.50	2.00
56	Carl Sawatski	7.00	3.50	2.00
57	Al Cicotte	7.00	3.50	2.00
58	Eddie Miksis	7.00	3.50	2.00
59	Irv Noren	7.00	3.50	2.00
60	Bob Turley	15.00	7.50	4.50
61	Dick Brown	7.00	3.50	2.00
62	Tony Taylor	7.00	3.50	2.00
63	Jim Hearn	7.00	3.50	2.00
64	Joe DeMaestri	7.00	3.50	2.00
65	Frank Torre	7.00	3.50	2.00
66	Joe Ginsberg	7.00	3.50	2.00
67	Brooks Lawrence	7.00	3.50	2.00
68	Dick Schofield	7.00	3.50	2.00
69	San Francisco Giants Team	17.50	8.75	5.25
70	Harvey Kuenn	7.00	3.50	2.00
71	Don Bessent	7.00	3.50	2.00
72	Bill Renna	7.00	3.50	2.00
73	Ron Jackson	7.00	3.50	2.00
74	Directing the Power (Cookie Lavagetto, Jim Lemon, Roy Sievers)	9.00	4.50	2.75
75	Sam Jones	7.00	3.50	2.00
76	Bobby Richardson	25.00	12.50	7.50
77	John Goryl	7.00	3.50	2.00
78	Pedro Ramos	7.00	3.50	2.00
79	Harry Chiti	7.00	3.50	2.00
80	Minnie Minoso	15.00	7.50	4.50
81	Hal Jeffcoat	7.00	3.50	2.00
82	Bob Boyd	7.00	3.50	2.00
83	Bob Smith	7.00	3.50	2.00
84	Reno Bertoia	7.00	3.50	2.00
85	Harry Anderson	7.00	3.50	2.00
86	Bob Keegan	7.00	3.50	2.00
87	Danny O'Connell	7.00	3.50	2.00
88	Herb Score	15.00	7.50	4.50
89	Billy Gardner	7.00	3.50	2.00
90	Bill Skowron (SP)	60.00	30.00	18.00
91	Herb Moford	7.00	3.50	2.00
92	Dave Philley	7.00	3.50	2.00
93	Julio Becquer	7.00	3.50	2.00
94	Chicago White Sox Team	17.50	8.75	5.25
95	Carl Willey	7.00	3.50	2.00
96	Lou Berberet	7.00	3.50	2.00
97	Jerry Lynch	7.00	3.50	2.00
98	Arnie Portocarrero	7.00	3.50	2.00
99	Ted Kazanski	7.00	3.50	2.00
100	Bob Cerv	7.00	3.50	2.00
101	Alex Kellner	7.00	3.50	2.00
102	Felipe Alou	25.00	12.50	7.50
103	Billy Goodman	7.00	3.50	2.00
104	Del Rice	7.00	3.50	2.00
105	Lee Walls	7.00	3.50	2.00
106	Hal Woodeshick	7.00	3.50	2.00
107	Norm Larker	10.00	5.00	3.00
108	Zack Monroe	9.00	4.50	2.75
109	Bob Schmidt	7.00	3.50	2.00
110	George Witt	7.00	3.50	2.00
111	Cincinnati Red Legs Team	16.00	8.00	4.75
112	Billy Consolo	7.00	3.50	2.00
113	Taylor Phillips	7.00	3.50	2.00
114	Earl Battey	7.00	3.50	2.00
115	Mickey Vernon	7.00	3.50	2.00
116	Bob Allison	13.50	7.00	4.00
117	John Blanchard	15.00	7.50	4.50
118	John Buzhardt	7.00	3.50	2.00
119	John Callison	12.50	6.25	3.75
120	Chuck Coles	7.00	3.50	2.00
121	Bob Conley	7.00	3.50	2.00
122	Bennie Daniels	7.00	3.50	2.00
123	Don Dillard	7.00	3.50	2.00
124	Dan Dobbek	7.00	3.50	2.00
125	Ron Fairly	13.50	6.75	4.00
126	Eddie Haas	7.00	3.50	2.00
127	Kent Hadley	7.00	3.50	2.00
128	Bob Hartman	7.00	3.50	2.00
129	Frank Herrera	7.00	3.50	2.00
130	Lou Jackson	7.00	3.50	2.00
131	Deron Johnson	10.00	5.00	3.00
132	Don Lee	7.00	3.50	2.00
133	Bob Lillis	7.00	3.50	2.00
134	Jim McDaniel	7.00	3.50	2.00
135	Gene Oliver	7.00	3.50	2.00
136	Jim O'Toole	7.50	3.75	2.25
137	Dick Ricketts	7.00	3.50	2.00
138	John Romano	7.00	3.50	2.00
139	Ed Sadowski	7.00	3.50	2.00
140	Charlie Secrest	7.00	3.50	2.00
141	Joe Shipley	7.00	3.50	2.00
142	Dick Stigman	7.00	3.50	2.00
143	Willie Tasby	7.00	3.50	2.00
144	Jerry Walker	7.00	3.50	2.00
145	Dom Zanni	7.00	3.50	2.00
146	Jerry Zimmerman	7.00	3.50	2.00
147	Cubs' Clubbers (Ernie Banks, Dale Long, Walt Moryn)	20.00	10.00	6.00
148	Mike McCormick	7.00	3.50	2.00
149	Jim Bunning	20.00	10.00	6.00
150	Stan Musial	150.00	75.00	37.50
151	Bob Malkmus	7.00	3.50	2.00
152	Johnny Klippstein	7.00	3.50	2.00
153	Jim Marshall	7.00	3.50	2.00
154	Ray Herbert	7.00	3.50	2.00
155	Enos Slaughter	20.00	10.00	6.00
156	Ace Hurlers (Billy Pierce, Robin Roberts)	12.50	6.25	3.75
157	Felix Mantilla	7.00	3.50	2.00
158	Walt Dropo	7.00	3.50	2.00
159	Bob Shaw	7.00	3.50	2.00
160	Dick Groat	7.00	3.50	2.00
161	Frank Baumann	7.00	3.50	2.00
162	Bobby G. Smith	7.00	3.50	2.00
163	Sandy Koufax	160.00	80.00	40.00
164	Johnny Groth	7.00	3.50	2.00
165	Bill Bruton	7.00	3.50	2.00
166	Destruction Crew (Rocky Colavito, Larry Doby, Minnie Minoso)	20.00	10.00	6.00
167	Duke Maas	7.00	3.50	2.00
168	Carroll Hardy	7.00	3.50	2.00
169	Ted Abernathy	7.00	3.50	2.00
170	Gene Woodling	7.00	3.50	2.00
171	Willard Schmidt	7.00	3.50	2.00
172	Kansas City Athletics Team	16.00	8.00	4.75
173	Bill Monbouquette	7.00	3.50	2.00
174	Jim Pendleton	7.00	3.50	2.00
175	Dick Farrell	7.00	3.50	2.00
176	Preston Ward	7.00	3.50	2.00
177	Johnny Briggs	7.00	3.50	2.00
178	Ruben Amaro	7.00	3.50	2.00
179	Don Rudolph	7.00	3.50	2.00
180	Yogi Berra	100.00	50.00	25.00
181	Bob Porterfield	7.00	3.50	2.00
182	Milt Graff	7.00	3.50	2.00
183	Stu Miller	7.00	3.50	2.00
184	Harvey Haddix	7.00	3.50	2.00
185	Jim Busby	7.00	3.50	2.00
186	Mudcat Grant	7.00	3.50	2.00
187	Bubba Phillips	7.00	3.50	2.00
188	Juan Pizarro	7.00	3.50	2.00
189	Neil Chrisley	7.00	3.50	2.00
190	Bill Virdon	7.00	3.50	2.00
191	Russ Kemmerer	7.00	3.50	2.00
192	Charley Beamon	7.00	3.50	2.00
193	Sammy Taylor	7.00	3.50	2.00
194	Jim Brosnan	7.00	3.50	2.00
195	Rip Repulski	7.00	3.50	2.00
196	Billy Moran	7.00	3.50	2.00
197	Ray Semproch	7.00	3.50	2.00
198	Jim Davenport	7.00	3.50	2.00
199	Leo Kiely	7.00	3.50	2.00
200	Warren Giles	20.00	10.00	6.00
201	Tom Acker	7.00	3.50	2.00
202	Roger Maris	120.00	60.00	30.00
203	Ozzie Virgil	7.00	3.50	2.00
204	Casey Wise	7.00	3.50	2.00
205	Don Larsen	17.50	8.75	5.25
206	Carl Furillo	17.50	8.75	5.25
207	George Strickland	7.00	3.50	2.00
208	Willie Jones	7.00	3.50	2.00
209	Lenny Green	7.00	3.50	2.00
210	Ed Bailey	7.00	3.50	2.00
211	Bob Blaylock	7.00	3.50	2.00
212	Fence Busters (Hank Aaron, Eddie Mathews)	80.00	40.00	20.00
213	Jim Rivera	7.00	3.50	2.00
214	Marcelino Solis	7.00	3.50	2.00
215	Jim Lemon	7.00	3.50	2.00
216	Andre Rodgers	7.00	3.50	2.00
217	Carl Erskine	12.50	6.25	3.75
218	Roman Mejias	7.00	3.50	2.00
219	George Zuverink	7.00	3.50	2.00
220	Frank Malzone	7.00	3.50	2.00
221	Bob Bowman	7.00	3.50	2.00
222	Bobby Shantz	15.00	7.50	4.50
223	St. Louis Cardinals Team	20.00	10.00	6.00
224	Claude Osteen	7.50	3.75	2.25
225	Johnny Logan	7.00	3.50	2.00
226	Art Ceccarelli	7.00	3.50	2.00
227	Hal Smith	7.00	3.50	2.00
228	Don Gross	7.00	3.50	2.00
229	Vic Power	7.00	3.50	2.00
230	Bill Fischer	7.00	3.50	2.00
231	Ellis Burton	7.00	3.50	2.00
232	Eddie Kasko	7.00	3.50	2.00
233	Paul Foytack	7.00	3.50	2.00
234	Chuck Tanner	7.00	3.50	2.00
235	Valmy Thomas	7.00	3.50	2.00
236	Ted Bowsfield	7.00	3.50	2.00
237	Run Preventers (Gil McDougald, Bobby Richardson, Bob Turley)	20.00	10.00	6.00
238	Gene Baker	7.00	3.50	2.00
239	Bob Trowbridge	7.00	3.50	2.00
240	Hank Bauer	13.50	7.00	4.00
241	Billy Muffett	7.00	3.50	2.00
242	Ron Samford	7.00	3.50	2.00
243	Marv Grissom	7.00	3.50	2.00
244	Dick Gray	7.00	3.50	2.00
245	Ned Garver	7.00	3.50	2.00
246	J.W. Porter	7.00	3.50	2.00
247	Don Ferrarese	7.00	3.50	2.00
248	Boston Red Sox Team	16.00	8.00	4.75
249	Bobby Adams	7.00	3.50	2.00
250	Billy O'Dell	7.00	3.50	2.00
251	Cletis Boyer	15.00	7.50	4.50
252	Ray Boone	7.00	3.50	2.00
253	Seth Morehead	7.00	3.50	2.00
254	Zeke Bella	7.00	3.50	2.00
255	Del Ennis	7.00	3.50	2.00
256	Jerry Davie	7.00	3.50	2.00
257	Leon Wagner	9.00	4.50	2.75
258	Fred Kipp	7.00	3.50	2.00
259	Jim Pisoni	7.00	3.50	2.00
260	Early Wynn	20.00	10.00	6.00
261	Gene Stephens	7.00	3.50	2.00
262	Hitters' Foes (Don Drysdale, Clem Labine, Johnny Podres)	20.00	10.00	6.00
263	Buddy Daley	7.00	3.50	2.00
264	Chico Carrasquel	7.00	3.50	2.00
265	Ron Kline	7.00	3.50	2.00
266	Woody Held	7.00	3.50	2.00
267	John Romonosky	7.00	3.50	2.00
268	Tito Francona	7.00	3.50	2.00
269	Jack Meyer	7.00	3.50	2.00
270	Gil Hodges	20.00	10.00	6.00
271	Orlando Pena	7.00	3.50	2.00
272	Jerry Lumpe	9.00	4.50	2.75
273	Joe Jay	7.00	3.50	2.00
274	Jerry Kindall	7.00	3.50	2.00
275	Jack Sanford	7.00	3.50	2.00
276	Pete Daley	7.00	3.50	2.00
277	Turk Lown	7.00	3.50	2.00
278	Chuck Essegian	7.00	3.50	2.00
279	Ernie Johnson	7.00	3.50	2.00
280	Frank Bolling	7.00	3.50	2.00
281	Walt Craddock	7.00	3.50	2.00
282	R.C. Stevens	7.00	3.50	2.00
283	Russ Heman	7.00	3.50	2.00
284	Steve Korcheck	7.00	3.50	2.00
285	Joe Cunningham	7.00	3.50	2.00
286	Dean Stone	7.00	3.50	2.00
287	Don Zimmer	12.50	6.25	3.75
288	Dutch Dotterer	7.00	3.50	2.00
289	Johnny Kucks	9.00	4.50	2.75
290	Wes Covington	7.00	3.50	2.00
291	Pitching Partners (Camilo Pascual, Pedro Ramos)	9.00	4.50	2.75
292	Dick Williams	7.00	3.50	2.00
293	Ray Moore	7.00	3.50	2.00
294	Hank Foiles	7.00	3.50	2.00
295	Billy Martin	17.50	8.75	5.25
296	Ernie Broglio	7.00	3.50	2.00
297	Jackie Brandt	7.00	3.50	2.00
298	Tex Clevenger	7.00	3.50	2.00
299	Billy Klaus	7.00	3.50	2.00
300	Richie Ashburn	25.00	12.50	7.50
301	Earl Averill	7.00	3.50	2.00
302	Don Mossi	7.00	3.50	2.00
303	Marty Keough	7.00	3.50	2.00
304	Chicago Cubs Team	16.00	8.00	4.75
305	Curt Raydon	7.00	3.50	2.00
306	Jim Gilliam	12.00	6.00	3.50
307	Curt Barclay	7.00	3.50	2.00
308	Norm Siebern	9.00	4.50	2.75
309	Sal Maglie	7.00	3.50	2.00
310	Luis Aparicio	25.00	12.50	7.50
311	Norm Zauchin	7.00	3.50	2.00
312	Don Newcombe	9.00	4.50	2.75
313	Frank House	7.00	3.50	2.00
314	Don Cardwell	7.00	3.50	2.00
315	Joe Adcock	7.00	3.50	2.00
316a	Ralph Lumenti (No optioned statement.)	75.00	37.50	22.50
316b	Ralph Lumenti (Optioned statement.)	7.00	3.50	2.00
317	N.L. Hitting Kings (Richie Ashburn, Willie Mays)	45.00	22.50	13.50
318	Rocky Bridges	7.00	3.50	2.00
319	Dave Hillman	7.00	3.50	2.00
320	Bob Skinner	7.00	3.50	2.00
321a	Bob Giallombardo (No optioned statement.)	75.00	37.50	22.50
321b	Bob Giallombardo (Optioned statement.)	7.00	3.50	2.00
322a	Harry Hanebrink (No trade statement.)	90.00	45.00	27.50
322b	Harry Hanebrink (Trade statement.)	7.00	3.50	2.00
323	Frank Sullivan	7.00	3.50	2.00
324	Don Demeter	7.00	3.50	2.00
325	Ken Boyer	13.50	7.00	4.00
326	Marv Throneberry	10.00	5.00	3.00

327	*Gary Bell*	7.00	3.50	2.00
328	Lou Skizas	7.00	3.50	2.00
329	Detroit Tigers Team	17.50	8.75	5.25
330	Gus Triandos	7.00	3.50	2.00
331	Steve Boros	7.00	3.50	2.00
332	Ray Monzant	7.00	3.50	2.00
333	Harry Simpson	7.00	3.50	2.00
334	Glen Hobbie	7.00	3.50	2.00
335	Johnny Temple	7.00	3.50	2.00
336a	Billy Loes (No trade statement.)	75.00	37.50	22.50
336b	Billy Loes (Trade statement.)	7.00	3.50	2.00
337	George Crowe	7.00	3.50	2.00
338	*George Anderson* (Sparky)	30.00	15.00	9.00
339	Roy Face	7.00	3.50	2.00
340	Roy Sievers	7.00	3.50	2.00
341	Tom Qualters	7.00	3.50	2.00
342	Ray Jablonski	7.00	3.50	2.00
343	Billy Hoeft	7.00	3.50	2.00
344	Russ Nixon	7.00	3.50	2.00
345	Gil McDougald	12.50	6.25	3.75
346	Batter Bafflers (Tom Brewer, Dave Sisler)	9.00	4.50	2.75
347	Bob Buhl	7.00	3.50	2.00
348	Ted Lepcio	7.00	3.50	2.00
349	Hoyt Wilhelm	15.00	7.50	4.50
350	Ernie Banks	80.00	40.00	20.00
351	Earl Torgeson	7.00	3.50	2.00
352	Robin Roberts	20.00	10.00	6.00
353	Curt Flood	12.00	6.00	3.50
354	Pete Burnside	7.00	3.50	2.00
355	Jim Piersall	9.00	4.50	2.75
356	Bob Mabe	7.00	3.50	2.00
357	*Dick Stuart*	10.00	5.00	3.00
358	Ralph Terry	7.00	3.50	2.00
359	*Bill White*	12.50	6.25	3.75
360	Al Kaline	35.00	17.50	10.00
361	Willard Nixon	7.00	3.50	2.00
362a	Dolan Nichols (No optioned statement.)	80.00	40.00	24.00
362b	Dolan Nichols (Optioned statement.)	7.00	3.50	2.00
363	Bobby Avila	7.00	3.50	2.00
364	Danny McDevitt	7.00	3.50	2.00
365	Gus Bell	7.00	3.50	2.00
366	Humberto Robinson	7.00	3.50	2.00
367	Cal Neeman	7.00	3.50	2.00
368	Don Mueller	7.00	3.50	2.00
369	Dick Tomanek	7.00	3.50	2.00
370	Pete Runnels	7.00	3.50	2.00
371	Dick Brodowski	7.00	3.50	2.00
372	Jim Hegan	7.00	3.50	2.00
373	Herb Plews	7.00	3.50	2.00
374	Art Ditmar	9.00	4.50	2.75
375	Bob Nieman	7.00	3.50	2.00
376	Hal Naragon	7.00	3.50	2.00
377	Johnny Antonelli	7.00	3.50	2.00
378	Gail Harris	7.00	3.50	2.00
379	Bob Miller	7.00	3.50	2.00
380	Hank Aaron	160.00	80.00	40.00
381	Mike Baxes	7.00	3.50	2.00
382	Curt Simmons	7.00	3.50	2.00
383	Words of Wisdom (Don Larsen, Casey Stengel)	16.00	8.00	4.75
384	Dave Sisler	7.00	3.50	2.00
385	Sherm Lollar	7.00	3.50	2.00
386	Jim Delsing	7.00	3.50	2.00
387	Don Drysdale	25.00	12.50	7.50
388	Bob Will	7.00	3.50	2.00
389	Joe Nuxhall	7.00	3.50	2.00
390	Orlando Cepeda	25.00	12.50	7.50
391	Milt Pappas	7.00	3.50	2.00
392	Whitey Herzog	7.00	3.50	2.00
393	Frank Lary	7.00	3.50	2.00
394	Randy Jackson	7.00	3.50	2.00
395	Elston Howard	15.00	7.50	4.50
396	Bob Rush	7.00	3.50	2.00
397	Washington Senators Team	16.00	8.00	4.75
398	Wally Post	7.00	3.50	2.00
399	Larry Jackson	7.00	3.50	2.00
400	Jackie Jensen	10.00	5.00	3.00
401	Ron Blackburn	7.00	3.50	2.00
402	Hector Lopez	7.00	3.50	2.00
403	Clem Labine	12.50	6.25	3.75
404	Hank Sauer	7.00	3.50	2.00
405	Roy McMillan	7.00	3.50	2.00
406	Solly Drake	7.00	3.50	2.00
407	Moe Drabowsky	7.00	3.50	2.00
408	Keystone Combo (Luis Aparicio, Nellie Fox)	20.00	10.00	6.00
409	Gus Zernial	7.00	3.50	2.00
410	Billy Pierce	7.00	3.50	2.00
411	Whitey Lockman	7.00	3.50	2.00
412	Stan Lopata	7.00	3.50	2.00
413	Camillo (Camilo) Pascual	7.00	3.50	2.00
414	Dale Long	7.00	3.50	2.00
415	Bill Mazeroski	20.00	10.00	6.00
416a	Haywood Sullivan (No circle around copyright symbol, no period after "A" in "U.S.A.")	15.00	7.50	4.50
416b	Haywood Sullivan (No circle around copyright symbol, period added after "A" in "U.S.A.")	7.00	3.50	2.00
416c	Haywood Sullivan (Circle around copyright symbol, period after "A" in "U.S.A.")	7.00	3.50	2.00
417	Virgil Trucks	7.00	3.50	2.00
418	Gino Cimoli	7.00	3.50	2.00
419	Milwaukee Braves Team	16.00	8.00	4.75
420	Rocky Colavito	20.00	10.00	6.00
421	Herm Wehmeier	7.00	3.50	2.00
422	Hobie Landrith	7.00	3.50	2.00
423	Bob Grim	7.00	3.50	2.00
424	Ken Aspromonte	7.00	3.50	2.00
425	Del Crandall	7.00	3.50	2.00
426	Jerry Staley	7.00	3.50	2.00
427	Charlie Neal	7.00	3.50	2.00
428	Buc Hill Aces (Roy Face, Bob Friend, Ron Kline, Vern Law)	9.00	4.50	2.75
429	Bobby Thomson	9.00	4.50	2.75
430	Whitey Ford	40.00	20.00	12.00
431	Whammy Douglas	7.00	3.50	2.00
432	Smoky Burgess	7.00	3.50	2.00
433	Billy Harrell	7.00	3.50	2.00
434	Hal Griggs	7.00	3.50	2.00
435	Frank Robinson	30.00	15.00	9.00
436	Granny Hamner	7.00	3.50	2.00
437	Ike Delock	7.00	3.50	2.00
438	Sam Esposito	7.00	3.50	2.00
439	Brooks Robinson	30.00	15.00	9.00
440	Lou Burdette	7.00	3.50	2.00
441	John Roseboro	7.00	3.50	2.00
442	Ray Narleski	7.00	3.50	2.00
443	Daryl Spencer	7.00	3.50	2.00
444	*Ronnie Hansen*	7.00	3.50	2.00
445	Cal McLish	7.00	3.50	2.00
446	Rocky Nelson	7.00	3.50	2.00
447	Bob Anderson	7.00	3.50	2.00
448	Vada Pinson	7.00	3.50	2.00
449	Tom Gorman	7.00	3.50	2.00
450	Ed Mathews	45.00	22.50	13.50
451	Jimmy Constable	7.00	3.50	2.00
452	Chico Fernandez	7.00	3.50	2.00
453	Les Moss	7.00	3.50	2.00
454	Phil Clark	7.00	3.50	2.00
455	Larry Doby	15.00	7.50	4.50
456	Jerry Casale	7.00	3.50	2.00
457	Los Angeles Dodgers Team	20.00	10.00	6.00
458	Gordon Jones	7.00	3.50	2.00
459	Bill Tuttle	7.00	3.50	2.00
460	Bob Friend	7.00	3.50	2.00
461	Mantle Hits 42nd Homer For Crown (Mickey Mantle)	100.00	50.00	30.00
462	Colavito's Great Catch Saves Game (Rocky Colavito)	12.50	6.25	3.75
463	Kaline Becomes Youngest Batting Champ (Al Kaline)	15.00	7.50	4.50
464	Mays' Catch Makes Series History (Willie Mays)	35.00	17.50	10.00
465	Sievers Sets Homer Mark (Roy Sievers)	7.00	3.50	2.00
466	Pierce All-Star Starter (Billy Pierce)	7.00	3.50	2.00
467	Aaron Clubs World Series Homer (Hank Aaron)	25.00	12.50	7.50
468	Snider's Play Brings L.A. Victory (Duke Snider)	15.00	7.50	4.50
469	Hustler Banks Wins M.V.P. Award (Ernie Banks)	16.00	8.00	5.00
470	Musial Raps Out 3,000th Hit (Stan Musial)	25.00	12.50	7.50
471	Tom Sturdivant	9.00	4.50	2.75
472	Gene Freese	7.00	3.50	2.00
473	Mike Fornieles	7.00	3.50	2.00
474	Moe Thacker	7.00	3.50	2.00
475	Jack Harshman	7.00	3.50	2.00
476	Cleveland Indians Team	16.00	8.00	4.75
477	Barry Latman	7.00	3.50	2.00
478	Bob Clemente	175.00	87.50	43.75
479	Lindy McDaniel	7.00	3.50	2.00
480	Red Schoendienst	20.00	10.00	6.00
481	Charley Maxwell	7.00	3.50	2.00
482	Russ Meyer	7.00	3.50	2.00
483	Clint Courtney	7.00	3.50	2.00
484	Willie Kirkland	7.00	3.50	2.00
485	Ryne Duren	10.00	5.00	3.00
486	Sammy White	7.00	3.50	2.00
487	Hal Brown	7.00	3.50	2.00
488	Walt Moryn	7.00	3.50	2.00
489	John C. Powers	7.00	3.50	2.00
490	Frank Thomas	7.00	3.50	2.00
491	Don Blasingame	7.00	3.50	2.00
492	Gene Conley	7.00	3.50	2.00
493	Jim Landis	7.00	3.50	2.00
494	Don Pavletich	7.00	3.50	2.00
495	Johnny Podres	11.00	5.50	3.25
496	Wayne Terwilliger	7.00	3.50	2.00
497	Hal R. Smith	7.00	3.50	2.00
498	Dick Hyde	7.00	3.50	2.00
499	Johnny O'Brien	7.00	3.50	2.00
500	Vic Wertz	7.00	3.50	2.00
501	Bobby Tiefenauer	7.00	3.50	2.00
502	Al Dark	7.00	3.50	2.00
503	Jim Owens	7.00	3.50	2.00
504	Ossie Alvarez	7.00	3.50	2.00
505	Tony Kubek	20.00	10.00	6.00
506	Bob Purkey	7.00	3.50	2.00
507	Bob Hale	15.00	7.50	4.50
508	Art Fowler	15.00	7.50	4.50
509	*Norm Cash*	80.00	40.00	20.00
510	New York Yankees Team	125.00	62.50	31.25
511	George Susce	15.00	7.50	4.50
512	George Altman	15.00	7.50	4.50
513	Tom Carroll	15.00	7.50	4.50
514	*Bob Gibson*	320.00	160.00	80.00
515	Harmon Killebrew	120.00	60.00	30.00
516	Mike Garcia	15.00	7.50	4.50
517	Joe Koppe	15.00	7.50	4.50
518	*Mike Cuellar*	20.00	10.00	6.00
519	Infield Power (Dick Gernert, Frank Malzone, Pete Runnels)	17.50	8.75	5.25
520	Don Elston	15.00	7.50	4.50
521	Gary Geiger	15.00	7.50	4.50
522	Gene Snyder	15.00	7.50	4.50
523	Harry Bright	15.00	7.50	4.50
524	Larry Osborne	15.00	7.50	4.50
525	Jim Coates	17.50	8.75	5.25
526	Bob Speake	15.00	7.50	4.50
527	Solly Hemus	15.00	7.50	4.50
528	Pittsburgh Pirates Team	40.00	20.00	12.00
529	*George Bamberger*	15.00	7.50	4.50
530	Wally Moon	15.00	7.50	4.50
531	Ray Webster	15.00	7.50	4.50
532	Mark Freeman	15.00	7.50	4.50
533	Darrell Johnson	17.50	8.75	5.25
534	Faye Throneberry	15.00	7.50	4.50
535	Ruben Gomez	15.00	7.50	4.50
536	Dan Kravitz	15.00	7.50	4.50
537	Rodolfo Arias	15.00	7.50	4.50
538	Chick King	15.00	7.50	4.50
539	Gary Blaylock	15.00	7.50	4.50
540	Willy Miranda	15.00	7.50	4.50
541	Bob Thurman	15.00	7.50	4.50
542	*Jim Perry*	30.00	15.00	9.00
543	Corsair Outfield Trio (Roberto Clemente, Bob Skinner, Bill Virdon)	100.00	50.00	25.00
544	Lee Tate	15.00	7.50	4.50
545	Tom Morgan	15.00	7.50	4.50
546	Al Schroll	15.00	7.50	4.50
547	Jim Baxes	15.00	7.50	4.50
548	Elmer Singleton	15.00	7.50	4.50
549	Howie Nunn	15.00	7.50	4.50
550	Roy Campanella (Symbol of Courage)	150.00	75.00	37.50
551	Fred Haney (All-Star)	15.00	7.50	4.50
552	Casey Stengel (All-Star)	25.00	12.50	7.50
553	Orlando Cepeda (All-Star)	25.00	12.50	7.50
554	Bill Skowron (All-Star)	22.50	11.00	6.75
555	Bill Mazeroski (All-Star)	25.00	12.50	7.50
556	Nellie Fox (All-Star)	27.50	13.50	8.25
557	Ken Boyer (All-Star)	20.00	10.00	6.00
558	Frank Malzone (All-Star)	15.00	7.50	4.50
559	Ernie Banks (All-Star)	45.00	22.50	13.50
560	Luis Aparicio (All-Star)	20.00	10.00	6.00
561	Hank Aaron (All-Star)	150.00	75.00	37.50
562	Al Kaline (All-Star)	30.00	15.00	9.00
563	Willie Mays (All-Star)	125.00	62.50	31.25
564	Mickey Mantle (All-Star)	300.00	150.00	75.00
565	Wes Covington (All-Star)	15.00	7.50	4.50
566	Roy Sievers (All-Star)	15.00	7.50	4.50
567	Del Crandall (All-Star)	15.00	7.50	4.50
568	Gus Triandos (All-Star)	15.00	7.50	4.50
569	Bob Friend (All-Star)	15.00	7.50	4.50
570	Bob Turley (All-Star)	17.50	8.75	5.25
571	Warren Spahn (All-Star)	27.50	13.50	8.25
572	Billy Pierce (All-Star)	150.00	10.00	6.00
----	Elect Your Favorite Rookie Insert (Paper stock, September 29 date on back.)	200.00	100.00	60.00
----	Felt Pennants Insert (paper stock)	30.00	15.00	9.00

1960 Topps

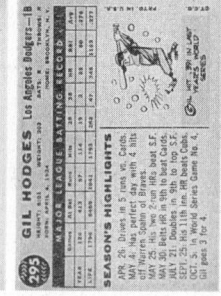

In 1960, Topps opted for a horizontal format in standard 3-1/2" x 2-1/2" size. Basic fronts have a large color portrait or pose at right and black-and-white action photograph at left. After a one-year hiatus, backs returned to the use of lifetime statistics along with a cartoon and short career summary or previous season highlights. Specialty cards in the 572-card set are multi-player cards, managers and coaches cards, and highlights of the 1959 World Series. Two groups of rookie cards are included. The first are numbers 117-148, which are the Sport Magazine rookies. The second group is called "Topps All-Star Rookies." Finally, there is a run of All-Star cards to close out the set in the scarcer high numbers. Cards #375-440 can be found with backs printed on either white or grey cardboard, with the white stock being the less common. Team cards have checklists on the back.

	NM	EX	VG
Complete Set (572):	6,500	3,250	2,000
Common Player (1-440):	6.00	3.00	1.75
Common Player (441-506):	9.00	4.50	2.75
Common Player (507-572):	15.00	7.50	4.50
1 Early Wynn	40.00	10.00	6.00
2 Roman Mejias	20.00	4.00	1.75
3 Joe Adcock	6.00	3.00	1.75
4 Bob Purkey	6.00	3.00	1.75
5 Wally Moon	6.00	3.00	1.75
6 Lou Berberet	6.00	3.00	1.75
7 Master and Mentor (Willie Mays, Bill Rigney)	20.00	10.00	6.00
8 Bud Daley	6.00	3.00	1.75
9 Faye Throneberry	6.00	3.00	1.75
10 Ernie Banks	70.00	35.00	17.50
11 Norm Siebern	6.00	3.00	1.75
12 Milt Pappas	6.00	3.00	1.75
13 Wally Post	6.00	3.00	1.75
14 Jim Grant	6.00	3.00	1.75
15 Pete Runnels	6.00	3.00	1.75
16 Ernie Broglio	6.00	3.00	1.75
17 Johnny Callison	6.00	3.00	1.75
18 Los Angeles Dodgers Team	35.00	17.50	10.00
19 Felix Mantilla	6.00	3.00	1.75
20 Roy Face	6.00	3.00	1.75
21 Dutch Dotterer	6.00	3.00	1.75
22 Rocky Bridges	6.00	3.00	1.75
23 Eddie Fisher	6.00	3.00	1.75

#	Player			
24	Dick Gray	6.00	3.00	1.75
25	Roy Sievers	6.00	3.00	1.75
26	Wayne Terwilliger	6.00	3.00	1.75
27	Dick Drott	6.00	3.00	1.75
28	Brooks Robinson	40.00	20.00	12.00
29	Clem Labine	8.00	4.00	2.50
30	Tito Francona	6.00	3.00	1.75
31	Sammy Esposito	6.00	3.00	1.75
32	Sophomore Stalwarts (Jim O'Toole, Vada Pinson)	9.00	4.50	2.75
33	Tom Morgan	6.00	3.00	1.75
34	George Anderson (Sparky)	20.00	10.00	6.00
35	Whitey Ford	35.00	17.50	10.00
36	Russ Nixon	6.00	3.00	1.75
37	Bill Bruton	6.00	3.00	1.75
38	Jerry Casale	6.00	3.00	1.75
39	Earl Averill	6.00	3.00	1.75
40	Joe Cunningham	6.00	3.00	1.75
41	Barry Latman	6.00	3.00	1.75
42	Hobie Landrith	6.00	3.00	1.75
43	Washington Senators Team	15.00	7.50	4.50
44	Bobby Locke	6.00	3.00	1.75
45	Roy McMillan	6.00	3.00	1.75
46	Jack Fisher	6.00	3.00	1.75
47	Don Zimmer	12.00	6.00	3.50
48	Hal Smith	6.00	3.00	1.75
49	Curt Raydon	6.00	3.00	1.75
50	Al Kaline	50.00	25.00	12.50
51	Jim Coates	6.00	3.00	1.75
52	Dave Philley	6.00	3.00	1.75
53	Jackie Brandt	6.00	3.00	1.75
54	Mike Fornieles	6.00	3.00	1.75
55	Bill Mazeroski	20.00	10.00	6.00
56	Steve Korcheck	6.00	3.00	1.75
57	Win-Savers (Turk Lown, Gerry Staley)	6.00	3.00	1.75
58	Gino Cimoli	6.00	3.00	1.75
59	Juan Pizarro	6.00	3.00	1.75
60	Gus Triandos	6.00	3.00	1.75
61	Eddie Kasko	6.00	3.00	1.75
62	Roger Craig	6.00	3.00	1.75
63	George Strickland	6.00	3.00	1.75
64	Jack Meyer	6.00	3.00	1.75
65	Elston Howard	15.00	7.50	4.50
66	Bob Trowbridge	6.00	3.00	1.75
67	Jose Pagan	6.00	3.00	1.75
68	Dave Hillman	6.00	3.00	1.75
69	Billy Goodman	6.00	3.00	1.75
70	Lou Burdette	6.00	3.00	1.75
71	Marty Keough	6.00	3.00	1.75
72	Detroit Tigers Team	15.00	7.50	4.50
73	Bob Gibson	50.00	25.00	15.00
74	Walt Moryn	6.00	3.00	1.75
75	Vic Power	6.00	3.00	1.75
76	Bill Fischer	6.00	3.00	1.75
77	Hank Foiles	6.00	3.00	1.75
78	Bob Grim	6.00	3.00	1.75
79	Walt Dropo	6.00	3.00	1.75
80	Johnny Antonelli	6.00	3.00	1.75
81	Russ Snyder	6.00	3.00	1.75
82	Ruben Gomez	6.00	3.00	1.75
83	Tony Kubek	25.00	12.50	7.50
84	Hal Smith	6.00	3.00	1.75
85	Frank Lary	6.00	3.00	1.75
86	Dick Gernert	6.00	3.00	1.75
87	John Romonosky	6.00	3.00	1.75
88	John Roseboro	6.00	3.00	1.75
89	Hal Brown	6.00	3.00	1.75
90	Bobby Avila	6.00	3.00	1.75
91	Bennie Daniels	6.00	3.00	1.75
92	Whitey Herzog	6.00	3.00	1.75
93	Art Schult	6.00	3.00	1.75
94	Leo Kiely	6.00	3.00	1.75
95	Frank Thomas	6.00	3.00	1.75
96	Ralph Terry	7.50	3.75	2.25
97	Ted Lepcio	6.00	3.00	1.75
98	Gordon Jones	6.00	3.00	1.75
99	Lenny Green	6.00	3.00	1.75
100	Nellie Fox	20.00	10.00	6.00
101	Bob Miller	6.00	3.00	1.75
102	Kent Hadley	6.00	3.00	1.75
103	Dick Farrell	6.00	3.00	1.75
104	Dick Schofield	6.00	3.00	1.75
105	Larry Sherry	12.00	6.00	3.50
106	Billy Gardner	6.00	3.00	1.75
107	Carl Willey	6.00	3.00	1.75
108	Pete Daley	6.00	3.00	1.75
109	Cletis Boyer	13.50	6.75	4.00
110	Cal McLish	6.00	3.00	1.75
111	Vic Wertz	6.00	3.00	1.75
112	Jack Harshman	6.00	3.00	1.75
113	Bob Skinner	6.00	3.00	1.75
114	Ken Aspromonte	6.00	3.00	1.75
115	Fork and Knuckler (Roy Face, Hoyt Wilhelm)	9.00	4.50	2.75
116	Jim Rivera	6.00	3.00	1.75
117	Tom Borland	6.00	3.00	1.75
118	Bob Bruce	6.00	3.00	1.75
119	Chico Cardenas	6.00	3.00	1.75
120	Duke Carmel	6.00	3.00	1.75
121	Camilo Carreon	6.00	3.00	1.75
122	Don Dillard	6.00	3.00	1.75
123	Dan Dobbek	6.00	3.00	1.75
124	Jim Donohue	6.00	3.00	1.75
125	Dick Ellsworth	6.00	3.00	1.75
126	Chuck Estrada	6.00	3.00	1.75
127	Ronnie Hansen	6.00	3.00	1.75
128	Bill Harris	6.00	3.00	1.75
129	Bob Hartman	6.00	3.00	1.75
130	Frank Herrera	6.00	3.00	1.75
131	Ed Hobaugh	6.00	3.00	1.75
132	Frank Howard	20.00	10.00	6.00
133	Manuel Javier	6.00	3.00	1.75
134	Deron Johnson	7.50	3.75	2.25
135	Ken Johnson	6.00	3.00	1.75
136	Jim Kaat	20.00	10.00	6.00
137	Lou Klimchock	6.00	3.00	1.75
138	Art Mahaffey	6.00	3.00	1.75
139	Carl Mathias	6.00	3.00	1.75
140	Julio Navarro	6.00	3.00	1.75
141	Jim Proctor	6.00	3.00	1.75
142	Bill Short	6.00	3.00	1.75
143	Al Spangler	6.00	3.00	1.75
144	Al Stieglitz	6.00	3.00	1.75
145	Jim Umbricht	6.00	3.00	1.75
146	Ted Wieand	6.00	3.00	1.75
147	Bob Will	6.00	3.00	1.75
148	Carl Yastrzemski	225.00	112.50	56.25
149	Bob Nieman	6.00	3.00	1.75
150	Billy Pierce	6.00	3.00	1.75
151	San Francisco Giants Team	15.00	7.50	4.50
152	Gail Harris	6.00	3.00	1.75
153	Bobby Thomson	7.50	3.75	2.25
154	Jim Davenport	6.00	3.00	1.75
155	Charlie Neal	6.00	3.00	1.75
156	Art Ceccarelli	6.00	3.00	1.75
157	Rocky Nelson	6.00	3.00	1.75
158	Wes Covington	6.00	3.00	1.75
159	Jim Piersall	8.00	4.00	2.50
160	Rival All-Stars (Ken Boyer, Mickey Mantle)	150.00	75.00	37.50
161	Ray Narleski	6.00	3.00	1.75
162	Sammy Taylor	6.00	3.00	1.75
163	Hector Lopez	6.00	3.00	1.75
164	Cincinnati Reds Team	15.00	7.50	4.50
165	Jack Sanford	6.00	3.00	1.75
166	Chuck Essegian	6.00	3.00	1.75
167	Valmy Thomas	6.00	3.00	1.75
168	Alex Grammas	6.00	3.00	1.75
169	Jake Striker	6.00	3.00	1.75
170	Del Crandall	6.00	3.00	1.75
171	Johnny Groth	6.00	3.00	1.75
172	Willie Kirkland	6.00	3.00	1.75
173	Billy Martin	10.00	5.00	3.00
174	Cleveland Indians Team	15.00	7.50	4.50
175	Pedro Ramos	6.00	3.00	1.75
176	Vada Pinson	10.00	5.00	3.00
177	Johnny Kucks	6.00	3.00	1.75
178	Woody Held	6.00	3.00	1.75
179	Rip Coleman	6.00	3.00	1.75
180	Harry Simpson	6.00	3.00	1.75
181	Billy Loes	6.00	3.00	1.75
182	Glen Hobbie	6.00	3.00	1.75
183	Eli Grba	6.00	3.00	1.75
184	Gary Geiger	6.00	3.00	1.75
185	Jim Owens	6.00	3.00	1.75
186	Dave Sisler	6.00	3.00	1.75
187	Jay Hook	6.00	3.00	1.75
188	Dick Williams	6.00	3.00	1.75
189	Don McMahon	6.00	3.00	1.75
190	Gene Woodling	6.00	3.00	1.75
191	Johnny Klippstein	6.00	3.00	1.75
192	Danny O'Connell	6.00	3.00	1.75
193	Dick Hyde	6.00	3.00	1.75
194	Bobby Gene Smith	6.00	3.00	1.75
195	Lindy McDaniel	6.00	3.00	1.75
196	Andy Carey	6.00	3.00	1.75
197	Ron Kline	6.00	3.00	1.75
198	Jerry Lynch	6.00	3.00	1.75
199	Dick Donovan	6.00	3.00	1.75
200	Willie Mays	125.00	62.50	31.25
201	Larry Osborne	6.00	3.00	1.75
202	Fred Kipp	6.00	3.00	1.75
203	Sammy White	6.00	3.00	1.75
204	Ryne Duren	7.50	3.75	2.25
205	Johnny Logan	6.00	3.00	1.75
206	Claude Osteen	6.00	3.00	1.75
207	Bob Boyd	6.00	3.00	1.75
208	Chicago White Sox Team	15.00	7.50	4.50
209	Ron Blackburn	6.00	3.00	1.75
210	Harmon Killebrew	30.00	15.00	9.00
211	Taylor Phillips	6.00	3.00	1.75
212	Walt Alston	12.00	6.00	3.50
213	Chuck Dressen	6.00	3.00	1.75
214	Jimmie Dykes	6.00	3.00	1.75
215	Bob Elliott	6.00	3.00	1.75
216	Joe Gordon	6.00	3.00	1.75
217	Charley Grimm	6.00	3.00	1.75
218	Solly Hemus	6.00	3.00	1.75
219	Fred Hutchinson	6.00	3.00	1.75
220	Billy Jurges	6.00	3.00	1.75
221	Cookie Lavagetto	6.00	3.00	1.75
222	Al Lopez	10.00	5.00	3.00
223	Danny Murtaugh	6.00	3.00	1.75
224	Paul Richards	6.00	3.00	1.75
225	Bill Rigney	6.00	3.00	1.75
226	Eddie Sawyer	6.00	3.00	1.75
227	Casey Stengel	17.50	8.75	5.25
228	Ernie Johnson	6.00	3.00	1.75
229	Joe Morgan	6.00	3.00	1.75
230	Mound Magicians (Bob Buhl, Lou Burdette, Warren Spahn)	17.50	8.75	5.25
231	Hal Naragon	6.00	3.00	1.75
232	Jim Busby	6.00	3.00	1.75
233	Don Elston	6.00	3.00	1.75
234	Don Demeter	6.00	3.00	1.75
235	Gus Bell	6.00	3.00	1.75
236	Dick Ricketts	6.00	3.00	1.75
237	Elmer Valo	6.00	3.00	1.75
238	Danny Kravitz	6.00	3.00	1.75
239	Joe Shipley	6.00	3.00	1.75
240	Luis Aparicio	17.50	8.75	5.25
241	Albie Pearson	6.00	3.00	1.75
242	St. Louis Cardinals Team	15.00	7.50	4.50
243	Bubba Phillips	6.00	3.00	1.75
244	Hal Griggs	6.00	3.00	1.75
245	Eddie Yost	6.00	3.00	1.75
246	Lee Maye	6.00	3.00	1.75
247	Gil McDougald	12.00	6.00	3.50
248	Del Rice	6.00	3.00	1.75
249	Earl Wilson	6.00	3.00	1.75
250	Stan Musial	100.00	50.00	25.00
251	Bobby Malkmus	6.00	3.00	1.75
252	Ray Herbert	6.00	3.00	1.75
253	Eddie Bressoud	6.00	3.00	1.75
254	Arnie Portocarrero	6.00	3.00	1.75
255	Jim Gilliam	10.00	5.00	3.00
256	Dick Brown	6.00	3.00	1.75
257	Gordy Coleman	6.00	3.00	1.75
258	Dick Groat	6.00	3.00	1.75
259	George Altman	6.00	3.00	1.75
260	Power Plus (Rocky Colavito, Tito Francona)	11.00	5.50	3.25
261	Pete Burnside	6.00	3.00	1.75
262	Hank Bauer	7.50	3.75	2.25
263	Darrell Johnson	6.00	3.00	1.75
264	Robin Roberts	12.50	6.25	3.75
265	Rip Repulski	6.00	3.00	1.75
266	Joe Jay	6.00	3.00	1.75
267	Jim Marshall	6.00	3.00	1.75
268	Al Worthington	6.00	3.00	1.75
269	Gene Green	6.00	3.00	1.75
270	Bob Turley	10.00	5.00	3.00
271	Julio Becquer	6.00	3.00	1.75
272	Fred Green	6.00	3.00	1.75
273	Neil Chrisley	6.00	3.00	1.75
274	Tom Acker	6.00	3.00	1.75
275	Curt Flood	9.00	4.50	2.75
276	Ken McBride	6.00	3.00	1.75
277	Harry Bright	6.00	3.00	1.75
278	Stan Williams	6.00	3.00	1.75
279	Chuck Tanner	6.00	3.00	1.75
280	Frank Sullivan	6.00	3.00	1.75
281	Ray Boone	6.00	3.00	1.75
282	Joe Nuxhall	6.00	3.00	1.75
283	John Blanchard	7.50	3.75	2.25
284	Don Gross	6.00	3.00	1.75
285	Harry Anderson	6.00	3.00	1.75
286	Ray Semproch	6.00	3.00	1.75
287	Felipe Alou	7.50	3.75	2.25
288	Bob Mabe	6.00	3.00	1.75
289	Willie Jones	6.00	3.00	1.75
290	Jerry Lumpe	6.00	3.00	1.75
291	Bob Keegan	6.00	3.00	1.75
292	Dodger Backstops (Joe Pignatano, John Roseboro)	7.50	3.75	2.25
293	Gene Conley	6.00	3.00	1.75
294	Tony Taylor	6.00	3.00	1.75
295	Gil Hodges	15.00	7.50	4.50
296	Nelson Chittum	6.00	3.00	1.75
297	Reno Bertoia	6.00	3.00	1.75
298	George Witt	6.00	3.00	1.75
299	Earl Torgeson	6.00	3.00	1.75
300	Hank Aaron	140.00	70.00	35.00
301	Jerry Davie	6.00	3.00	1.75
302	Philadelphia Phillies Team	15.00	7.50	4.50
303	Billy O'Dell	6.00	3.00	1.75
304	Joe Ginsberg	6.00	3.00	1.75
305	Richie Ashburn	15.00	7.50	4.50
306	Frank Baumann	6.00	3.00	1.75
307	Gene Oliver	6.00	3.00	1.75
308	Dick Hall	6.00	3.00	1.75
309	Bob Hale	6.00	3.00	1.75
310	Frank Malzone	6.00	3.00	1.75
311	Raul Sanchez	6.00	3.00	1.75
312	Charlie Lau	6.00	3.00	1.75
313	Turk Lown	6.00	3.00	1.75
314	Chico Fernandez	6.00	3.00	1.75
315	Bobby Shantz	11.00	5.50	3.25
316	Willie McCovey	150.00	75.00	37.50
317	Pumpsie Green	7.50	3.75	2.25
318	Jim Baxes	6.00	3.00	1.75
319	Joe Koppe	6.00	3.00	1.75
320	Bob Allison	6.00	3.00	1.75
321	Ron Fairly	6.00	3.00	1.75
322	Willie Tasby	6.00	3.00	1.75
323	Johnny Romano	6.00	3.00	1.75
324	Jim Perry	7.50	3.75	2.25
325	Jim O'Toole	6.00	3.00	1.75
326	Bob Clemente	175.00	87.50	43.75
327	Ray Sadecki	6.00	3.00	1.75
328	Earl Battey	6.00	3.00	1.75
329	Zack Monroe	6.00	3.00	1.75
330	Harvey Kuenn	6.00	3.00	1.75
331	Henry Mason	6.00	3.00	1.75
332	New York Yankees Team	37.50	18.50	11.00
333	Danny McDevitt	6.00	3.00	1.75
334	Ted Abernathy	6.00	3.00	1.75
335	Red Schoendienst	12.50	6.25	3.75
336	Ike Delock	6.00	3.00	1.75
337	Cal Neeman	6.00	3.00	1.75
338	Ray Monzant	6.00	3.00	1.75
339	Harry Chiti	6.00	3.00	1.75
340	Harvey Haddix	6.00	3.00	1.75
341	Carroll Hardy	6.00	3.00	1.75
342	Casey Wise	6.00	3.00	1.75
343	Sandy Koufax	125.00	62.50	31.25
344	Clint Courtney	6.00	3.00	1.75
345	Don Newcombe	7.50	3.75	2.25
346	J.C. Martin (Photo actually Gary Peters.)	6.00	3.00	1.75
347	Ed Bouchee	6.00	3.00	1.75
348	Barry Shetrone	6.00	3.00	1.75
349	Moe Drabowsky	6.00	3.00	1.75
350	Mickey Mantle	425.00	210.00	125.00
351	Don Nottebart	6.00	3.00	1.75
352	Cincy Clouters (Gus Bell, Jerry Lynch, Frank Robinson)	12.00	6.00	3.50
353	Don Larsen	8.00	4.00	2.50
354	Bob Lillis	6.00	3.00	1.75
355	Bill White	6.00	3.00	1.75
356	Joe Amalfitano	6.00	3.00	1.75
357	Al Schroll	6.00	3.00	1.75
358	Joe De Maestri	6.00	3.00	1.75
359	Buddy Gilbert	6.00	3.00	1.75
360	Herb Score	7.50	3.75	2.25
361	Bob Oldis	6.00	3.00	1.75
362	Russ Kemmerer	6.00	3.00	1.75
363	Gene Stephens	6.00	3.00	1.75
364	Paul Foytack	6.00	3.00	1.75
365	Minnie Minoso	12.50	6.25	3.75
366	Dallas Green	9.00	4.50	2.75
367	Bill Tuttle	6.00	3.00	1.75
368	Daryl Spencer	6.00	3.00	1.75

No.	Player	NM	EX	VG
369	Billy Hoeft	6.00	3.00	1.75
370	Bill Skowron	17.50	8.75	5.25
371	Bud Byerly	6.00	3.00	1.75
372	Frank House	6.00	3.00	1.75
373	Don Hoak	6.00	3.00	1.75
374	Bob Buhl	6.00	3.00	1.75
375	Dale Long	6.00	3.00	1.75
376	Johnny Briggs	6.00	3.00	1.75
377	Roger Maris	100.00	50.00	25.00
378	Stu Miller	6.00	3.00	1.75
379	Red Wilson	6.00	3.00	1.75
380	Bob Shaw	6.00	3.00	1.75
381	Milwaukee Braves Team	16.00	8.00	4.75
382	Ted Bowsfield	6.00	3.00	1.75
383	Leon Wagner	6.00	3.00	1.75
384	Don Cardwell	6.00	3.00	1.75
385	World Series Game 1 (Neal Steals Second)	10.00	5.00	3.00
386	World Series Game 2 (Neal Belts 2nd Homer)	10.00	5.00	3.00
387	World Series Game 3 (Furillo Breaks Up Game)	10.00	5.00	3.00
388	World Series Game 4 (Hodges' Winning Homer)	10.00	5.00	3.00
389	World Series Game 5 (Luis Swipes Base)	12.00	6.00	3.50
390	World Series Game 6 (Scrambling After Ball)	10.00	5.00	3.00
391	World Series Summary (The Champs Celebrate)	10.00	5.00	3.00
392	Tex Clevenger	6.00	3.00	1.75
393	Smoky Burgess	6.00	3.00	1.75
394	Norm Larker	6.00	3.00	1.75
395	Hoyt Wilhelm	13.50	6.75	4.00
396	Steve Bilko	6.00	3.00	1.75
397	Don Blasingame	6.00	3.00	1.75
398	Mike Cuellar	6.00	3.00	1.75
399	Young Hill Stars (Jack Fisher, Milt Pappas, Jerry Walker)	6.00	3.00	1.75
400	Rocky Colavito	20.00	10.00	6.00
401	Bob Duliba	6.00	3.00	1.75
402	Dick Stuart	6.00	3.00	1.75
403	Ed Sadowski	6.00	3.00	1.75
404	Bob Rush	6.00	3.00	1.75
405	Bobby Richardson	25.00	12.50	7.50
406	Billy Klaus	6.00	3.00	1.75
407	*Gary Peters* (Photo actually J.C. Martin.)	6.00	3.00	1.75
408	Carl Furillo	11.00	5.50	3.25
409	Ron Samford	6.00	3.00	1.75
410	Sam Jones	6.00	3.00	1.75
411	Ed Bailey	6.00	3.00	1.75
412	Bob Anderson	6.00	3.00	1.75
413	Kansas City Athletics Team	15.00	7.50	4.50
414	Don Williams	6.00	3.00	1.75
415	Bob Cerv	6.00	3.00	1.75
416	Humberto Robinson	6.00	3.00	1.75
417	Chuck Cottier	6.00	3.00	1.75
418	Don Mossi	6.00	3.00	1.75
419	George Crowe	6.00	3.00	1.75
420	Ed Mathews	25.00	12.50	7.50
421	Duke Maas	6.00	3.00	1.75
422	Johnny Powers	6.00	3.00	1.75
423	Ed Fitz Gerald	6.00	3.00	1.75
424	Pete Whisenant	6.00	3.00	1.75
425	Johnny Podres	10.00	5.00	3.00
426	Ron Jackson	6.00	3.00	1.75
427	Al Grunwald	6.00	3.00	1.75
428	Al Smith	6.00	3.00	1.75
429	American League Kings (Nellie Fox, Harvey Kuenn)	12.50	6.25	3.75
430	Art Ditmar	6.00	3.00	1.75
431	Andre Rodgers	6.00	3.00	1.75
432	Chuck Stobbs	6.00	3.00	1.75
433	Irv Noren	6.00	3.00	1.75
434	Brooks Lawrence	6.00	3.00	1.75
435	Gene Freese	6.00	3.00	1.75
436	Marv Throneberry	6.00	3.00	1.75
437	Bob Friend	6.00	3.00	1.75
438	Jim Coker	6.00	3.00	1.75
439	Tom Brewer	6.00	3.00	1.75
440	Jim Lemon	6.00	3.00	1.75
441	Gary Bell	9.00	4.50	2.75
442	Joe Pignatano	9.00	4.50	2.75
443	Charlie Maxwell	9.00	4.50	2.75
444	Jerry Kindall	9.00	4.50	2.75
445	Warren Spahn	35.00	17.50	10.00
446	Ellis Burton	9.00	4.50	2.75
447	Ray Moore	9.00	4.50	2.75
448	*Jim Gentile*	15.00	7.50	4.50
449	Jim Brosnan	9.00	4.50	2.75
450	Orlando Cepeda	30.00	15.00	9.00
451	Curt Simmons	9.00	4.50	2.75
452	Ray Webster	9.00	4.50	2.75
453	Vern Law	9.00	4.50	2.75
454	Hal Woodeshick	9.00	4.50	2.75
455	Baltimomre Orioles Coaches (Harry Brecheen, Lum Harris, Eddie Robinson)	9.00	4.50	2.75
456	Boston Red Sox Coaches (Del Baker, Billy Herman, Sal Maglie, Rudy York)	15.00	7.50	4.50
457	Chicago Cubs Coaches (Lou Klein, Charlie Root, Elvin Tappe)	9.00	4.50	2.75
458	Chicago White Sox Coaches (Ray Berres, Johnny Cooney, Tony Cuccinello, Don Gutteridge)	9.00	4.50	2.75
459	Cincinnati Reds Coaches (Cot Deal, Wally Moses, Reggie Otero)	9.00	4.50	2.75
460	Cleveland Indians Coaches (Mel Harder, Red Kress, Bob Lemon, Jo-Jo White)	10.00	5.00	3.00
461	Detroit Tigers Coaches (Luke Appling, Tom Ferrick, Billy Hitchcock)	10.00	5.00	3.00
462	Kansas City A's Coaches (Walker Cooper, Fred Fitzsimmons, Don Heffner)	9.00	4.50	2.75
463	L.A. Dodgers Coaches (Joe Becker, Bobby Bragan, Greg Mulleavy, Pete Reiser)	9.00	4.50	2.75
464	Milwaukee Braves Coaches (George Myatt, Andy Pafko, Bob Scheffing, Whitlow Wyatt)	9.00	4.50	2.75
465	N.Y. Yankees Coaches (Frank Crosetti, Bill Dickey, Ralph Houk, Ed Lopat)	20.00	10.00	6.00
466	Phila. Phillies Coaches (Dick Carter, Andy Cohen, Ken Silvestri)	9.00	4.50	2.75
467	Pitts. Pirates Coaches (Bill Burwell, Sam Narron, Frank Oceak, Mickey Vernon)	9.00	4.50	2.75
468	St. Louis Cards Coaches (Ray Katt, Johnny Keane, Howie Pollet, Harry Walker)	9.00	4.50	2.75
469	San Fran. Giants Coaches (Salty Parker, Bill Posedel, Wes Westrum)	9.00	4.50	2.75
470	Wash. Senators Coaches (Ellis Clary, Sam Mele, Bob Swift)	9.00	4.50	2.75
471	Ned Garver	9.00	4.50	2.75
472	Al Dark	9.00	4.50	2.75
473	Al Cicotte	9.00	4.50	2.75
474	Haywood Sullivan	9.00	4.50	2.75
475	Don Drysdale	35.00	17.50	10.00
476	Lou Johnson	9.00	4.50	2.75
477	Don Ferrarese	9.00	4.50	2.75
478	Frank Torre	9.00	4.50	2.75
479	Georges Maranda	9.00	4.50	2.75
480	Yogi Berra	90.00	45.00	22.50
481	Wes Stock	9.00	4.50	2.75
482	Frank Bolling	9.00	4.50	2.75
483	Camilo Pascual	9.00	4.50	2.75
484	Pittsburgh Pirates Team	25.00	12.50	7.50
485	Ken Boyer	15.00	7.50	4.50
486	Bobby Del Greco	9.00	4.50	2.75
487	Tom Sturdivant	9.00	4.50	2.75
488	Norm Cash	15.00	7.50	4.50
489	Steve Ridzik	9.00	4.50	2.75
490	Frank Robinson	40.00	20.00	12.00
491	Mel Roach	9.00	4.50	2.75
492	Larry Jackson	9.00	4.50	2.75
493	Duke Snider	50.00	25.00	12.50
494	Baltimore Orioles Team	20.00	10.00	6.00
495	Sherm Lollar	9.00	4.50	2.75
496	Bill Virdon	9.00	4.50	2.75
497	John Tsitouris	9.00	4.50	2.75
498	Al Pilarcik	9.00	4.50	2.75
499	Johnny James	9.00	4.50	2.75
500	Johnny Temple	9.00	4.50	2.75
501	Bob Schmidt	9.00	4.50	2.75
502	Jim Bunning	20.00	10.00	6.00
503	Don Lee	9.00	4.50	2.75
504	Seth Morehead	9.00	4.50	2.75
505	Ted Kluszewski	15.00	7.50	4.50
506	Lee Walls	9.00	4.50	2.75
507	Dick Stigman	15.00	7.50	4.50
508	Billy Consolo	15.00	7.50	4.50
509	*Tommy Davis*	20.00	10.00	6.00
510	Jerry Staley	15.00	7.50	4.50
511	Ken Walters	15.00	7.50	4.50
512	Joe Gibbon	15.00	7.50	4.50
513	Chicago Cubs Team	20.00	10.00	6.00
514	*Steve Barber*	17.50	8.75	5.25
515	Stan Lopata	15.00	7.50	4.50
516	Marty Kutyna	15.00	7.50	4.50
517	Charley James	15.00	7.50	4.50
518	*Tony Gonzalez*	15.00	7.50	4.50
519	Ed Roebuck	15.00	7.50	4.50
520	Don Buddin	15.00	7.50	4.50
521	Mike Lee	15.00	7.50	4.50
522	Ken Hunt	15.00	7.50	4.50
523	*Clay Dalrymple*	15.00	7.50	4.50
524	Bill Henry	15.00	7.50	4.50
525	Marv Breeding	15.00	7.50	4.50
526	Paul Giel	15.00	7.50	4.50
527	Jose Valdivielso	15.00	7.50	4.50
528	Ben Johnson	15.00	7.50	4.50
529	Norm Sherry	17.50	8.75	5.25
530	Mike McCormick	15.00	7.50	4.50
531	Sandy Amoros	15.00	7.50	4.50
532	Mike Garcia	15.00	7.50	4.50
533	Lu Clinton	15.00	7.50	4.50
534	Ken MacKenzie	15.00	7.50	4.50
535	Whitey Lockman	15.00	7.50	4.50
536	Wynn Hawkins	15.00	7.50	4.50
537	Boston Red Sox Team	25.00	12.50	7.50
538	Frank Barnes	15.00	7.50	4.50
539	Gene Baker	15.00	7.50	4.50
540	Jerry Walker	15.00	7.50	4.50
541	Tony Curry	15.00	7.50	4.50
542	Ken Hamlin	15.00	7.50	4.50
543	Elio Chacon	15.00	7.50	4.50
544	Bill Monbouquette	15.00	7.50	4.50
545	Carl Sawatski	15.00	7.50	4.50
546	Hank Aguirre	15.00	7.50	4.50
547	*Bob Aspromonte*	17.50	8.75	5.25
548	*Don Mincher*	15.00	7.50	4.50
549	John Buzhardt	15.00	7.50	4.50
550	Jim Landis	15.00	7.50	4.50
551	Ed Rakow	15.00	7.50	4.50
552	Walt Bond	15.00	7.50	4.50
553	Bill Skowron (All-Star)	20.00	10.00	6.00
554	Willie McCovey (All-Star)	35.00	17.50	10.00
555	Nellie Fox (All-Star)	20.00	10.00	6.00
556	Charlie Neal (All-Star)	17.50	8.75	5.25
557	Frank Malzone (All-Star)	17.50	8.75	5.25
558	Eddie Mathews (All-Star)	25.00	12.50	7.50
559	Luis Aparicio (All-Star)	20.00	10.00	6.00
560	Ernie Banks (All-Star)	35.00	17.50	10.00
561	Al Kaline (All-Star)	30.00	15.00	9.00
562	Joe Cunningham (All-Star)	17.50	8.75	5.25
563	Mickey Mantle (All-Star)	275.00	137.50	68.75
564	Willie Mays (All-Star)	100.00	50.00	25.00
565	Roger Maris (All-Star)	100.00	50.00	25.00
566	Hank Aaron (All-Star)	100.00	50.00	25.00
567	Sherm Lollar (All-Star)	17.50	8.75	5.25
568	Del Crandall (All-Star)	17.50	8.75	5.25
569	Camilo Pascual (All-Star)	17.50	8.75	5.25
570	Don Drysdale (All-Star)	25.00	12.50	7.50
571	Billy Pierce (All-Star)	17.50	8.75	5.25
572	Johnny Antonelli (All-Star)	25.00	9.00	5.25
----	Elect Your Favorite Rookie Insert (Paper stock, no date on back.)	30.00	15.00	9.00
----	Hot Iron Transfer Insert (Paper stock.)	30.00	15.00	9.00

1960 Topps Proofs

KENT HADLEY
NEW YORK YANKEES — FIRST BASE

Subsequent to a pair of December 1959 trades, the 1960 Topps cards of three players were significantly changed. Whether the change occurred prior to regular production printing and packaging or while the cards were still in the proofing stage is unknown. The changes affect the cards of Gino Cimoli, Kent Hadley and, reportedly, Marv Throneberry. In the very rare versions each player's card has at bottom left the logo of his team prior to the trade. The common regular-issue version has the new team logo. The front of Hadley's rare card names his team as the Yankees, while Cimoli's rare version says Cardinals.

		NM	EX	VG
58	Gino Cimoli (Cardinals logo.) (No recent sales.)			
102	Kent Hadley (A's logo.) (Nov., 1999 auction record.)	13,500	.00	.00
436	Marv Throneberry (Yankees logo.) (Existence not confirmed.)			

1960 Topps Tattoos

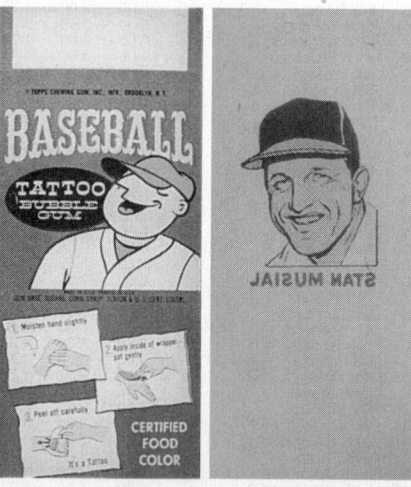

BASEBALL TATTOO BUBBLE GUM

STAN MUSIAL

Probably the least popular of all Topps products among parents and teachers, the Tattoos were printed on the reverse of the wrappers of Topps "Tattoo Bubble Gum." The entire wrapper was 1-9/16" x 3-1/2." The owner moistened their skin and applied the back of the wrapper to the wet spot, producing a colorful "tattoo" (although often blurred by running colors). The set offered 96 tattoo possibilities of which 55 were players, 16 teams, 15 action pictures and 10 autographed balls. Because the packaged gum slides easily in and out of the "sealed" wrapper, allowing the tattoo to be easily seen, unopened packs command little premium.

	NM	EX	VG
Complete Set (96):	2,750	1,350	825.00
Common Player:	20.00	10.00	6.00
Common Non-player:	12.00	6.00	3.50
(1) Hank Aaron	150.00	75.00	45.00
(2) Bob Allison	20.00	10.00	6.00
(3) John Antonelli	20.00	10.00	6.00
(4) Richie Ashburn	40.00	20.00	12.00
(5) Ernie Banks	65.00	32.00	19.50
(6) Yogi Berra	60.00	30.00	18.00
(7) Lew Burdette	20.00	10.00	6.00

(8)	Orlando Cepeda	35.00	17.50	10.50
(9)	Rocky Colavito	35.00	17.50	10.50
(10)	Joe Cunningham	20.00	10.00	6.00
(11)	Buddy Daley	20.00	10.00	6.00
(12)	Don Drysdale	40.00	20.00	12.00
(13)	Ryne Duren	20.00	10.00	6.00
(14)	Roy Face	20.00	10.00	6.00
(15)	Whitey Ford	60.00	30.00	18.00
(16)	Nellie Fox	35.00	17.50	10.50
(17)	Tito Francona	20.00	10.00	6.00
(18)	Gene Freese	20.00	10.00	6.00
(19)	Jim Gilliam	20.00	10.00	6.00
(20)	Dick Groat	20.00	10.00	6.00
(21)	Ray Herbert	20.00	10.00	6.00
(22)	Glen Hobbie	20.00	10.00	6.00
(23)	Jackie Jensen	20.00	10.00	6.00
(24)	Sam Jones	20.00	10.00	6.00
(25)	Al Kaline	60.00	30.00	18.00
(26)	Harmon Killebrew	40.00	20.00	12.00
(27)	Harvey Kuenn	20.00	10.00	6.00
(28)	Frank Lary	20.00	10.00	6.00
(29)	Vernon Law	20.00	10.00	6.00
(30)	Frank Malzone	20.00	10.00	6.00
(31)	Mickey Mantle	300.00	150.00	90.00
(32)	Roger Maris	75.00	37.00	22.00
(33)	Ed Mathews	40.00	20.00	12.00
(34)	Willie Mays	150.00	75.00	45.00
(35)	Cal Mclish	20.00	10.00	6.00
(36)	Wally Moon	20.00	10.00	6.00
(37)	Walt Moryn	20.00	10.00	6.00
(38)	Don Mossi	20.00	10.00	6.00
(39)	Stan Musial	100.00	50.00	30.00
(40)	Charlie Neal	20.00	10.00	6.00
(41)	Don Newcombe	20.00	10.00	6.00
(42)	Milt Pappas	20.00	10.00	6.00
(43)	Camilo Pascual	20.00	10.00	6.00
(44)	Billie (Billy) Pierce	20.00	10.00	6.00
(45)	Robin Roberts	35.00	17.50	10.50
(46)	Frank Robinson	40.00	20.00	12.00
(47)	Pete Runnels	20.00	10.00	6.00
(48)	Herb Score	20.00	10.00	6.00
(49)	Warren Spahn	35.00	17.50	10.50
(50)	Johnny Temple	20.00	10.00	6.00
(51)	Gus Triandos	20.00	10.00	6.00
(52)	Jerry Walker	20.00	10.00	6.00
(53)	Bill White	20.00	10.00	6.00
(54)	Gene Woodling	20.00	10.00	6.00
(55)	Early Wynn	35.00	17.50	10.50
(56)	Chicago Cubs Logo	15.00	7.50	4.50
(57)	Cincinnati Reds Logo	15.00	7.50	4.50
(58)	Los Angeles Dodgers Logo	15.00	7.50	4.50
(59)	Milwaukee Braves Logo	15.00	7.50	4.50
(60)	Philadelphia Phillies Logo	15.00	7.50	4.50
(61)	Pittsburgh Pirates Logo	20.00	10.00	6.00
(62)	San Francisco Giants Logo	15.00	7.50	4.50
(63)	St. Louis Cardinals Logo	15.00	7.50	4.50
(64)	Baltimore Orioles Logo	15.00	7.50	4.50
(65)	Boston Red Sox Logo	15.00	7.50	4.50
(66)	Chicago White Sox Logo	15.00	7.50	4.50
(67)	Cleveland Indians Logo	15.00	7.50	4.50
(68)	Detroit Tigers Logo	15.00	7.50	4.50
(69)	Kansas City Athletics Logo	15.00	7.50	4.50
(70)	New York Yankees Logo	20.00	10.00	6.00
(71)	Washington Senators Logo	15.00	7.50	4.50
(72)	Autograph (Richie Ashburn)	20.00	10.00	6.00
(73)	Autograph (Rocky Colavito)	25.00	12.50	7.50
(74)	Autograph (Roy Face)	15.00	7.50	4.50
(75)	Autograph (Jackie Jensen)	15.00	7.50	4.50
(76)	Autograph (Harmon Killebrew)	25.00	12.50	7.50
(77)	Autograph (Mickey Mantle)	100.00	50.00	30.00
(78)	Autograph (Willie Mays)	50.00	25.00	15.00
(79)	Autograph (Stan Musial)	50.00	25.00	15.00
(80)	Autograph (Billy Pierce)	15.00	7.50	4.50
(81)	Autograph (Jerry Walker)	15.00	7.50	4.50
(82)	Run-Down	12.00	6.00	3.50
(83)	Out At First	12.00	6.00	3.50
(84)	The Final Word	12.00	6.00	3.50
(85)	Twisting Foul	12.00	6.00	3.50
(86)	Out At Home	12.00	6.00	3.50
(87)	Circus Catch	12.00	6.00	3.50
(88)	Great Catch	12.00	6.00	3.50
(89)	Stolen Base	12.00	6.00	3.50
(90)	Grand Slam Homer	12.00	6.00	3.50
(91)	Double Play	12.00	6.00	3.50
(92)	Left-Handed Follow Thru	12.00	6.00	3.50
(93)	Left-Handed High Leg Kick	12.00	6.00	3.50
(94)	Right-handed pitcher	12.00	6.00	3.50
(95)	Right-handed batter	12.00	6.00	3.50
(96)	Left-handed batter	12.00	6.00	3.50

1950s-60s Topps "PROMOTIONAL SAMPLES"

 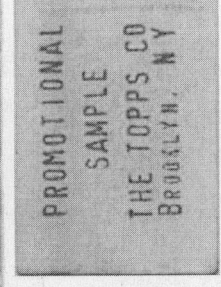

These mini sample cards are fantasy items created in the late 1990s to defraud collectors. Often sold grouped in an older frame or otherwise made to look old, they are pictures which have been cut out of the "Topps Baseball Cards" books or the team-issued Surf books which reproduced Topps cards

in about 1-1/4" x 1-3/4" format. The color glossy pictures were then glued to a cardboard back which has been rubber-stamped "PROMOTIONAL / SAMPLE / THE TOPPS CO / BROOKLYN, N.Y." There were no legitimate miniature Topps promotional or sample cards produced.

(No Collectible Value.)

1961 Topps

Except for some of the specialty cards, Topps returned to a vertical format with their 1961 cards. The set is numbered through 589, however, only 587 cards were printed. No numbers 426, 587 and 588 were issued. Two cards numbered 463 exist (one a Braves team card and one a player card of Jack Fisher). Actually, the Braves team card is checklisted as #426. Designs for 1961 are basically large color portraits; the backs return to extensive statistics. A three-panel cartoon highlighting the player's career appears on the card backs. Innovations include numbered checklists, cards for statistical leaders, and 10 "Baseball Thrills" cards. The scarce high numbers are card numbers 523-589.

		NM	EX	VG
	Complete Set (587):	7,500	3,750	2,250
	Common Player (1-522):	6.00	3.00	1.75
	Common Player (523-589):	20.00	10.00	6.00
1	Dick Groat	25.00	6.00	2.00
2	Roger Maris	250.00	125.00	62.50
3	John Buzhardt	6.00	3.00	1.75
4	Lenny Green	6.00	3.00	1.75
5	Johnny Romano	6.00	3.00	1.75
6	Ed Roebuck	6.00	3.00	1.75
7	Chicago White Sox Team	10.00	5.00	3.00
8	Dick Williams	6.00	3.00	1.75
9	Bob Purkey	6.00	3.00	1.75
10	Brooks Robinson	50.00	25.00	12.50
11	Curt Simmons	6.00	3.00	1.75
12	Moe Thacker	6.00	3.00	1.75
13	Chuck Cottier	6.00	3.00	1.75
14	Don Mossi	6.00	3.00	1.75
15	Willie Kirkland	6.00	3.00	1.75
16	Billy Muffett	6.00	3.00	1.75
17	1st Series Checklist (1-88)	12.00	6.00	3.50
18	Jim Grant	6.00	3.00	1.75
19	Cletis Boyer	10.00	5.00	3.00
20	Robin Roberts	15.00	7.50	4.50
21	*Zoilo Versalles*	12.50	6.25	3.75
22	Clem Labine	6.00	3.00	1.75
23	Don Demeter	6.00	3.00	1.75
24	Ken Johnson	6.00	3.00	1.75
25	Reds' Heavy Artillery (Gus Bell, Vada Pinson, Frank Robinson)	15.00	7.50	4.50
26	Wes Stock	6.00	3.00	1.75
27	Jerry Kindall	6.00	3.00	1.75
28	Hector Lopez	6.00	3.00	1.75
29	Don Nottebart	6.00	3.00	1.75
30	Nellie Fox	20.00	10.00	6.00
31	Bob Schmidt	6.00	3.00	1.75
32	Ray Sadecki	6.00	3.00	1.75
33	Gary Geiger	6.00	3.00	1.75
34	Wynn Hawkins	6.00	3.00	1.75
35	*Ron Santo*	50.00	25.00	12.50
36	Jack Kralick	6.00	3.00	1.75
37	Charlie Maxwell	6.00	3.00	1.75
38	Bob Lillis	6.00	3.00	1.75
39	Leo Posada	6.00	3.00	1.75
40	Bob Turley	10.00	5.00	3.00
41	N.L. Batting Leaders (Roberto Clemente, Dick Groat, Norm Larker, Willie Mays)	20.00	10.00	6.00
42	A.L. Batting Leaders (Minnie Minoso, Pete Runnels, Bill Skowron, Al Smith)	9.00	4.50	2.75
43	N.L. Home Run Leaders (Hank Aaron, Ernie Banks, Ken Boyer, Eddie Mathews)	17.50	8.75	5.25
44	A.L. Home Run Leaders (Rocky Colavito, Jim Lemon, Mickey Mantle, Roger Maris)	75.00	37.50	18.75
45	N.L. E.R.A. Leaders (Ernie Broglio, Don Drysdale, Bob Friend, Mike McCormick, Stan Williams)	7.00	3.50	2.00
46	A.L. E.R.A. Leaders (Frank Baumann, Hal Brown, Jim Bunning, Art Ditmar)	9.00	4.50	2.75
47a	N.L. Pitching Leaders (Ernie Broglio, Lou Burdette, Vern Law, Warren Spahn) (Vertical black bar in Burdette's box to right of 19.)	12.00	6.00	3.50

		NM	EX	VG
47b	N.L. Pitching Leaders (Ernie Broglio, Lew Burdette, Vern Law, Warren Spahn) (No black bar.)	12.00	6.00	3.50
48	A.L. Pitching Leaders (Bud Daley, Art Ditmar, Chuck Estrada, Frank Lary, Milt Pappas, Jim Perry)	7.00	3.50	2.00
49	N.L. Strikeout Leaders (Ernie Broglio, Don Drysdale, Sam Jones, Sandy Koufax)	16.00	8.00	4.75
50	A.L. Strikeout Leaders (Jim Bunning, Frank Lary, Pedro Ramos, Early Wynn)	12.00	6.00	3.50
51	Detroit Tigers Team	10.00	5.00	3.00
52	George Crowe	6.00	3.00	1.75
53	Russ Nixon	6.00	3.00	1.75
54	Earl Francis	6.00	3.00	1.75
55	Jim Davenport	6.00	3.00	1.75
56	Russ Kemmerer	6.00	3.00	1.75
57	Marv Throneberry	6.00	3.00	1.75
58	Joe Schaffernoth	6.00	3.00	1.75
59	Jim Woods	6.00	3.00	1.75
60	Woodie Held	6.00	3.00	1.75
61	Ron Piche	6.00	3.00	1.75
62	Al Pilarcik	6.00	3.00	1.75
63	Jim Kaat	9.00	4.50	2.75
64	Alex Grammas	6.00	3.00	1.75
65	Ted Kluszewski	10.00	5.00	3.00
66	Bill Henry	6.00	3.00	1.75
67	Ossie Virgil	6.00	3.00	1.75
68	Deron Johnson	6.00	3.00	1.75
69	Earl Wilson	6.00	3.00	1.75
70	Bill Virdon	6.00	3.00	1.75
71	Jerry Adair	6.00	3.00	1.75
72	Stu Miller	6.00	3.00	1.75
73	Al Spangler	6.00	3.00	1.75
74	Joe Pignatano	6.00	3.00	1.75
75	Lindy Shows Larry (Larry Jackson, Lindy McDaniel)	6.00	3.00	1.75
76	Harry Anderson	6.00	3.00	1.75
77	Dick Stigman	6.00	3.00	1.75
78	Lee Walls	6.00	3.00	1.75
79	Joe Ginsberg	6.00	3.00	1.75
80	Harmon Killebrew	25.00	12.50	7.50
81	Tracy Stallard	6.00	3.00	1.75
82	Joe Christopher	6.00	3.00	1.75
83	Bob Bruce	6.00	3.00	1.75
84	Lee Maye	6.00	3.00	1.75
85	Jerry Walker	6.00	3.00	1.75
86	Los Angeles Dodgers Team	11.00	5.50	3.25
87	Joe Amalfitano	6.00	3.00	1.75
88	Richie Ashburn	15.00	7.50	4.50
89	Billy Martin	9.00	4.50	2.75
90	Jerry Staley	6.00	3.00	1.75
91	Walt Moryn	6.00	3.00	1.75
92	Hal Naragon	6.00	3.00	1.75
93	Tony Gonzalez	6.00	3.00	1.75
94	Johnny Kucks	6.00	3.00	1.75
95	Norm Cash	12.50	6.25	3.75
96	Billy O'Dell	6.00	3.00	1.75
97	Jerry Lynch	6.00	3.00	1.75
98a	2nd Series Checklist (9-176) ("Checklist" in red on front.)	12.00	6.00	3.50
98b	2nd Series Checklist (89-176) ("Checklist" in yellow, 98 on back in black.)	12.00	6.00	3.50
98c	2nd Series Checklist (89-176) ("Checklist" in yellow, 98 on back in white.)	12.00	6.00	3.50
99	Don Buddin	6.00	3.00	1.75
100	Harvey Haddix	6.00	3.00	1.75
101	Bubba Phillips	6.00	3.00	1.75
102	Gene Stephens	6.00	3.00	1.75
103	Ruben Amaro	6.00	3.00	1.75
104	John Blanchard	7.50	3.75	2.25
105	Carl Willey	6.00	3.00	1.75
106	Whitey Herzog	6.00	3.00	1.75
107	Seth Morehead	6.00	3.00	1.75
108	Dan Dobbek	6.00	3.00	1.75
109	Johnny Podres	7.50	3.75	2.25
110	Vada Pinson	9.00	4.50	2.75
111	Jack Meyer	6.00	3.00	1.75
112	Chico Fernandez	6.00	3.00	1.75
113	Mike Fornieles	6.00	3.00	1.75
114	Hobie Landrith	6.00	3.00	1.75
115	Johnny Antonelli	6.00	3.00	1.75
116	Joe DeMaestri	6.00	3.00	1.75
117	Dale Long	6.00	3.00	1.75
118	Chris Cannizzaro	6.00	3.00	1.75
119	A's Big Armor (Hank Bauer, Jerry Lumpe, Norm Siebern)	9.00	4.50	2.75
120	Ed Mathews	20.00	10.00	6.00
121	Eli Grba	6.00	3.00	1.75
122	Chicago Cubs Team	10.00	5.00	3.00
123	Billy Gardner	6.00	3.00	1.75
124	J.C. Martin	6.00	3.00	1.75
125	Steve Barber	6.00	3.00	1.75
126	Dick Stuart	6.00	3.00	1.75
127	Ron Kline	6.00	3.00	1.75
128	Rip Repulski	6.00	3.00	1.75
129	Ed Hobaugh	6.00	3.00	1.75
130	Norm Larker	6.00	3.00	1.75
131	Paul Richards	6.00	3.00	1.75
132	Al Lopez	12.50	6.25	3.75
133	Ralph Houk	25.00	12.50	7.50
134	Mickey Vernon	6.00	3.00	1.75
135	Fred Hutchinson	6.00	3.00	1.75
136	Walt Alston	12.50	6.25	3.75
137	Chuck Dressen	6.00	3.00	1.75
138	Danny Murtaugh	6.00	3.00	1.75
139	Solly Hemus	6.00	3.00	1.75
140	Gus Triandos	6.00	3.00	1.75
141	*Billy Williams*	60.00	30.00	15.00
142	Luis Arroyo	6.00	3.00	1.75
143	Russ Snyder	6.00	3.00	1.75
144	Jim Coker	6.00	3.00	1.75
145	Bob Buhl	6.00	3.00	1.75

#	Name			
146	Marty Keough	6.00	3.00	1.75
147	Ed Rakow	6.00	3.00	1.75
148	Julian Javier	6.00	3.00	1.75
149	Bob Oldis	6.00	3.00	1.75
150	Willie Mays	120.00	60.00	30.00
151	Jim Donohue	6.00	3.00	1.75
152	Earl Torgeson	6.00	3.00	1.75
153	Don Lee	6.00	3.00	1.75
154	Bobby Del Greco	6.00	3.00	1.75
155	Johnny Temple	6.00	3.00	1.75
156	Ken Hunt	6.00	3.00	1.75
157	Cal McLish	6.00	3.00	1.75
158	Pete Daley	6.00	3.00	1.75
159	Baltimore Orioles Team	10.00	5.00	3.00
160	Whitey Ford	50.00	25.00	12.50
161	Sherman Jones	6.00	3.00	1.75
162	Jay Hook	6.00	3.00	1.75
163	Ed Sadowski	6.00	3.00	1.75
164	Felix Mantilla	6.00	3.00	1.75
165	Gino Cimoli	6.00	3.00	1.75
166	Danny Kravitz	6.00	3.00	1.75
167	San Francisco Giants Team	10.00	5.00	3.00
168	Tommy Davis	6.00	3.00	1.75
169	Don Elston	6.00	3.00	1.75
170	Al Smith	6.00	3.00	1.75
171	Paul Foytack	6.00	3.00	1.75
172	Don Dillard	6.00	3.00	1.75
173	Beantown Bombers (Jackie Jensen, Frank Malzone, Vic Wertz)	9.00	4.50	2.75
174	Ray Semproch	6.00	3.00	1.75
175	Gene Freese	6.00	3.00	1.75
176	Ken Aspromonte	6.00	3.00	1.75
177	Don Larsen	7.50	3.75	2.25
178	Bob Nieman	6.00	3.00	1.75
179	Joe Koppe	6.00	3.00	1.75
180	Bobby Richardson	15.00	7.50	4.50
181	Fred Green	6.00	3.00	1.75
182	*Dave Nicholson*	6.00	3.00	1.75
183	Andre Rodgers	6.00	3.00	1.75
184	Steve Bilko	6.00	3.00	1.75
185	Herb Score	6.00	3.00	1.75
186	Elmer Valo	6.00	3.00	1.75
187	Billy Klaus	6.00	3.00	1.75
188	Jim Marshall	6.00	3.00	1.75
189a	3rd Series Checklist (177-264) (No "4" on player at left.)	10.00	5.00	3.00
189b	3rd Series Checklist (177-264) ("4" shows on player on left)	10.00	5.00	3.00
190	Stan Williams	6.00	3.00	1.75
191	Mike de la Hoz	6.00	3.00	1.75
192	Dick Brown	6.00	3.00	1.75
193	Gene Conley	6.00	3.00	1.75
194	Gordy Coleman	6.00	3.00	1.75
195	Jerry Casale	6.00	3.00	1.75
196	Ed Bouchee	6.00	3.00	1.75
197	Dick Hall	6.00	3.00	1.75
198	Carl Sawatski	6.00	3.00	1.75
199	Bob Boyd	6.00	3.00	1.75
200	Warren Spahn	40.00	20.00	10.00
201	Pete Whisenant	6.00	3.00	1.75
202	Al Neiger	6.00	3.00	1.75
203	Eddie Bressoud	6.00	3.00	1.75
204	Bob Skinner	6.00	3.00	1.75
205	Bill Pierce	6.00	3.00	1.75
206	Gene Green	6.00	3.00	1.75
207	Dodger Southpaws (Sandy Koufax, Johnny Podres)	20.00	10.00	6.00
208	Larry Osborne	6.00	3.00	1.75
209	Ken McBride	6.00	3.00	1.75
210	Pete Runnels	6.00	3.00	1.75
211	Bob Gibson	25.00	12.50	7.50
212	Haywood Sullivan	6.00	3.00	1.75
213	*Bill Stafford*	6.00	3.00	1.75
214	Danny Murphy	6.00	3.00	1.75
215	Gus Bell	6.00	3.00	1.75
216	Ted Bowsfield	6.00	3.00	1.75
217	Mel Roach	6.00	3.00	1.75
218	Hal Brown	6.00	3.00	1.75
219	Gene Mauch	6.00	3.00	1.75
220	Al Dark	6.00	3.00	1.75
221	Mike Higgins	6.00	3.00	1.75
222	Jimmie Dykes	6.00	3.00	1.75
223	Bob Scheffing	6.00	3.00	1.75
224	Joe Gordon	6.00	3.00	1.75
225	Bill Rigney	6.00	3.00	1.75
226	Harry Lavagetto	6.00	3.00	1.75
227	Juan Pizarro	6.00	3.00	1.75
228	New York Yankees Team	60.00	30.00	15.00
229	Rudy Hernandez	6.00	3.00	1.75
230	Don Hoak	6.00	3.00	1.75
231	Dick Drott	6.00	3.00	1.75
232	Bill White	6.00	3.00	1.75
233	Joe Jay	6.00	3.00	1.75
234	Ted Lepcio	6.00	3.00	1.75
235	Camilo Pascual	6.00	3.00	1.75
236	Don Gile	6.00	3.00	1.75
237	Billy Loes	6.00	3.00	1.75
238	Jim Gilliam	7.50	3.75	2.25
239	Dave Sisler	6.00	3.00	1.75
240	Ron Hansen	6.00	3.00	1.75
241	Al Cicotte	6.00	3.00	1.75
242	Hal W. Smith	6.00	3.00	1.75
243	Frank Lary	6.00	3.00	1.75
244	Chico Cardenas	6.00	3.00	1.75
245	Joe Adcock	6.00	3.00	1.75
246	Bob Davis	6.00	3.00	1.75
247	Billy Goodman	6.00	3.00	1.75
248	Ed Keegan	6.00	3.00	1.75
249	Cincinnati Reds Team	10.00	5.00	3.00
250	Buc Hill Aces (Roy Face, Vern Law)	9.00	4.50	2.75
251	Bill Bruton	6.00	3.00	1.75
252	Bill Short	6.00	3.00	1.75
253	Sammy Taylor	6.00	3.00	1.75
254	Ted Sadowski	6.00	3.00	1.75
255	Vic Power	6.00	3.00	1.75
256	Billy Hoeft	6.00	3.00	1.75
257	Carroll Hardy	6.00	3.00	1.75
258	Jack Sanford	6.00	3.00	1.75
259	John Schaive	6.00	3.00	1.75
260	Don Drysdale	25.00	12.50	7.50
261	Charlie Lau	6.00	3.00	1.75
262	Tony Curry	6.00	3.00	1.75
263	Ken Hamlin	6.00	3.00	1.75
264	Glen Hobbie	6.00	3.00	1.75
265	Tony Kubek	15.00	7.50	4.50
266	Lindy McDaniel	6.00	3.00	1.75
267	Norm Siebern	6.00	3.00	1.75
268	Ike DeLock (Delock)	6.00	3.00	1.75
269	Harry Chiti	6.00	3.00	1.75
270	Bob Friend	6.00	3.00	1.75
271	Jim Landis	6.00	3.00	1.75
272	Tom Morgan	6.00	3.00	1.75
273a	4th Series Checklist (265-352) (Copyright ends opposite fifth name.)	12.00	6.00	3.50
273b	4th Series Checklist (265-352) (Copyright ends opposite top name.)	12.00	6.00	3.50
274	Gary Bell	6.00	3.00	1.75
275	Gene Woodling	6.00	3.00	1.75
276	Ray Rippelmeyer	6.00	3.00	1.75
277	Hank Foiles	6.00	3.00	1.75
278	Don McMahon	6.00	3.00	1.75
279	Jose Pagan	6.00	3.00	1.75
280	Frank Howard	9.00	4.50	2.75
281	Frank Sullivan	6.00	3.00	1.75
282	Faye Throneberry	6.00	3.00	1.75
283	Bob Anderson	6.00	3.00	1.75
284	Dick Gernert	6.00	3.00	1.75
285	Sherm Lollar	6.00	3.00	1.75
286	George Witt	6.00	3.00	1.75
287	Carl Yastrzemski	45.00	22.50	13.50
288	Albie Pearson	6.00	3.00	1.75
289	Ray Moore	6.00	3.00	1.75
290	Stan Musial	100.00	50.00	25.00
291	Tex Clevenger	6.00	3.00	1.75
292	Jim Baumer	6.00	3.00	1.75
293	Tom Sturdivant	6.00	3.00	1.75
294	Don Blasingame	6.00	3.00	1.75
295	Milt Pappas	6.00	3.00	1.75
296	Wes Covington	6.00	3.00	1.75
297	Kansas City Athletics Team	10.00	5.00	3.00
298	Jim Golden	6.00	3.00	1.75
299	Clay Dalrymple	6.00	3.00	1.75
300	Mickey Mantle	650.00	325.00	162.50
301	Chet Nichols	6.00	3.00	1.75
302	Al Heist	6.00	3.00	1.75
303	Gary Peters	6.00	3.00	1.75
304	Rocky Nelson	6.00	3.00	1.75
305	Mike McCormick	6.00	3.00	1.75
306	World Series Game 1 (Virdon Saves Game)	9.00	4.50	2.75
307	World Series Game 2 (Mantle Slams 2 Homers)	75.00	37.50	18.75
308	World Series Game 3 (Richardson Is Hero)	20.00	10.00	6.00
309	World Series Game 4 (Cimoli Safe In Crucial Play)	9.00	4.50	2.75
310	World Series Game 5 (Face Saves The Day)	10.00	5.00	3.00
311	World Series Game 6 (Ford Pitches Second Shutout)	15.00	7.50	4.50
312	World Series Game 7 (Mazeroski's Homer Wins It!)	25.00	12.50	7.50
313	World Series (The Winners Celebrate)	12.50	6.25	3.75
314	Bob Miller	6.00	3.00	1.75
315	Earl Battey	6.00	3.00	1.75
316	Bobby Gene Smith	6.00	3.00	1.75
317	*Jim Brewer*	6.00	3.00	1.75
318	Danny O'Connell	6.00	3.00	1.75
319	Valmy Thomas	6.00	3.00	1.75
320	Lou Burdette	6.00	3.00	1.75
321	Marv Breeding	6.00	3.00	1.75
322	Bill Kunkel	6.00	3.00	1.75
323	Sammy Esposito	6.00	3.00	1.75
324	Hank Aguirre	6.00	3.00	1.75
325	Wally Moon	6.00	3.00	1.75
326	Dave Hillman	6.00	3.00	1.75
327	*Matty Alou*	12.50	6.25	3.75
328	Jim O'Toole	6.00	3.00	1.75
329	Julio Becquer	6.00	3.00	1.75
330	Rocky Colavito	15.00	7.50	4.50
331	Ned Garver	6.00	3.00	1.75
332	Dutch Dotterer (Photo actually Tommy Dotterer.)	6.00	3.00	1.75
333	Fritz Brickell	6.00	3.00	1.75
334	Walt Bond	6.00	3.00	1.75
335	Frank Bolling	6.00	3.00	1.75
336	Don Mincher	6.00	3.00	1.75
337	Al's Aces (Al Lopez, Herb Score, Early Wynn)	9.00	4.50	2.75
338	Don Landrum	6.00	3.00	1.75
339	Gene Baker	6.00	3.00	1.75
340	Vic Wertz	6.00	3.00	1.75
341	Jim Owens	6.00	3.00	1.75
342	Clint Courtney	6.00	3.00	1.75
343	Earl Robinson	6.00	3.00	1.75
344	Sandy Koufax	100.00	50.00	25.00
345	Jim Piersall	7.50	3.75	2.25
346	Howie Nunn	6.00	3.00	1.75
347	St. Louis Cardinals Team	10.00	5.00	3.00
348	Steve Boros	6.00	3.00	1.75
349	Danny McDevitt	6.00	3.00	1.75
350	Ernie Banks	50.00	25.00	12.50
351	Jim King	6.00	3.00	1.75
352	Bob Shaw	6.00	3.00	1.75
353	Howie Bedell	6.00	3.00	1.75
354	Billy Harrell	6.00	3.00	1.75
355	Bob Allison	6.00	3.00	1.75
356	Ryne Duren	7.50	3.75	2.25
357	Daryl Spencer	6.00	3.00	1.75
358	Earl Averill	6.00	3.00	1.75
359	Dallas Green	7.50	3.75	2.25
360	Frank Robinson	25.00	12.50	7.50
361a	5th Series Checklist (353-429) ("Topps Baseball" in black on front.)	10.00	5.00	3.00
361b	5th Series Checklist (353-429) ("Topps Baseball" in yellow.)	12.00	6.00	3.50
362	Frank Funk	6.00	3.00	1.75
363	John Roseboro	6.00	3.00	1.75
364	Moe Drabowsky	6.00	3.00	1.75
365	Jerry Lumpe	6.00	3.00	1.75
366	Eddie Fisher	6.00	3.00	1.75
367	Jim Rivera	6.00	3.00	1.75
368	Bennie Daniels	6.00	3.00	1.75
369	Dave Philley	6.00	3.00	1.75
370	Roy Face	6.00	3.00	1.75
371	Bill Skowron (SP)	50.00	25.00	12.50
372	Bob Hendley	6.00	3.00	1.75
373	Boston Red Sox Team	10.00	5.00	3.00
374	Paul Giel	6.00	3.00	1.75
375	Ken Boyer	13.50	6.75	4.00
376	Mike Roarke	6.00	3.00	1.75
377	Ruben Gomez	6.00	3.00	1.75
378	Wally Post	6.00	3.00	1.75
379	Bobby Shantz	6.00	3.00	1.75
380	Minnie Minoso	9.00	4.50	2.75
381	Dave Wickersham	6.00	3.00	1.75
382	Frank Thomas	6.00	3.00	1.75
383	Frisco First Liners (Mike McCormick, Billy O'Dell, Jack Sanford)	7.50	3.75	2.25
384	Chuck Essegian	6.00	3.00	1.75
385	Jim Perry	6.00	3.00	1.75
386	Joe Hicks	6.00	3.00	1.75
387	Duke Maas	6.00	3.00	1.75
388	Bob Clemente	150.00	75.00	37.50
389	Ralph Terry	6.00	3.00	1.75
390	Del Crandall	6.00	3.00	1.75
391	Winston Brown	6.00	3.00	1.75
392	Reno Bertoia	6.00	3.00	1.75
393	Batter Bafflers (Don Cardwell, Glen Hobbie)	7.50	3.75	2.25
394	Ken Walters	6.00	3.00	1.75
395	Chuck Estrada	6.00	3.00	1.75
396	Bob Aspromonte	6.00	3.00	1.75
397	Hal Woodeshick	6.00	3.00	1.75
398	Hank Bauer	7.50	3.75	2.25
399	Cliff Cook	6.00	3.00	1.75
400	Vern Law	6.00	3.00	1.75
401	Babe Ruth Hits 60th Homer	50.00	25.00	15.00
402	Larsen Pitches Perfect Game (SP)	25.00	12.50	7.50
403	Brooklyn-Boston Play 26-Inning Tie	6.00	3.00	1.75
404	Hornsby Tops N.L. with .424 Average	9.00	4.50	2.75
405	Gehrig Benched After 2,130 Games	75.00	37.50	18.75
406	Mantle Blasts 565 ft. Home Run	100.00	50.00	25.00
407	Jack Chesbro Wins 41st Game	6.00	3.00	1.75
408	Mathewson Strikes Out 267 Batters (SP)	17.50	8.75	5.25
409	Johnson Hurls 3rd Shutout In 4 Days	9.00	4.50	2.75
410	Haddix Pitches 12 Perfect Innings	7.50	3.75	2.25
411	Tony Taylor	6.00	3.00	1.75
412	Larry Sherry	6.00	3.00	1.75
413	Eddie Yost	6.00	3.00	1.75
414	Dick Donovan	6.00	3.00	1.75
415	Hank Aaron	125.00	62.50	31.25
416	*Dick Howser* (SP)	12.50	6.25	3.75
417	*Juan Marichal*	100.00	50.00	25.00
418	Ed Bailey	6.00	3.00	1.75
419	Tom Borland	6.00	3.00	1.75
420	Ernie Broglio	6.00	3.00	1.75
421	Ty Cline (SP)	12.50	6.25	3.75
422	Bud Daley	6.00	3.00	1.75
423	Charlie Neal (SP)	12.50	6.25	3.75
424	Turk Lown	6.00	3.00	1.75
425	Yogi Berra	85.00	42.50	21.25
426	Not Issued (See #463.)			
427	Dick Ellsworth	6.00	3.00	1.75
428	Ray Barker (SP)	12.50	6.25	3.75
429	Bill Kaline	50.00	25.00	12.50
430	Bill Mazeroski (SP)	50.00	25.00	12.50
431	Chuck Stobbs	6.00	3.00	1.75
432	Coot Veal	6.00	3.00	1.75
433	Art Mahaffey	6.00	3.00	1.75
434	Tom Brewer	6.00	3.00	1.75
435	Orlando Cepeda	15.00	7.50	4.50
436	*Jim Maloney* (SP)	20.00	10.00	6.00
437a	6th Series Checklist (430-506) (#440 is Louis Aparicio)	12.00	6.00	3.50
437b	6th Series Checklist (430-506) (#440 is Luis Aparicio)	10.00	5.00	3.00
438	Curt Flood	7.50	3.75	2.25
439	*Phil Regan*	6.00	3.00	1.75
440	Luis Aparicio	15.00	7.50	4.50
441	Dick Bertell	6.00	3.00	1.75
442	Gordon Jones	6.00	3.00	1.75
443	Duke Snider	30.00	15.00	9.00
444	Joe Nuxhall	6.00	3.00	1.75
445	Frank Malzone	6.00	3.00	1.75
446	Bob "Hawk" Taylor	6.00	3.00	1.75
447	Harry Bright	6.00	3.00	1.75
448	Del Rice	6.00	3.00	1.75
449	*Bobby Bolin*	6.00	3.00	1.75
450	Jim Lemon	6.00	3.00	1.75
451	Power For Ernie (Ernie Broglio, Daryl Spencer, Bill White)	7.50	3.75	2.25
452	Bob Allen	6.00	3.00	1.75
453	Dick Schofield	6.00	3.00	1.75

454	Pumpsie Green	6.00	3.00	1.75
455	Early Wynn	12.50	6.25	3.75
456	Hal Bevan	6.00	3.00	1.75
457	Johnny James	6.00	3.00	1.75
458	Willie Tasby	6.00	3.00	1.75
459	Terry Fox	6.00	3.00	1.75
460	Gil Hodges	12.50	6.25	3.75
461	Smoky Burgess	6.00	3.00	1.75
462	Lou Klimchock	6.00	3.00	1.75
463a	Milwaukee Braves Team	10.00	5.00	3.00
	(Should be card #426.)			
463b	Jack Fisher	6.00	3.00	1.75
464	*Leroy Thomas*	6.00	3.00	1.75
465	Roy McMillan	6.00	3.00	1.75
466	Ron Moeller	6.00	3.00	1.75
467	Cleveland Indians Team	10.00	5.00	3.00
468	Johnny Callison	6.00	3.00	1.75
469	Ralph Lumenti	6.00	3.00	1.75
470	Roy Sievers	6.00	3.00	1.75
471	Phil Rizzuto (MVP)	30.00	15.00	7.50
472	Yogi Berra (MVP)	50.00	25.00	12.50
473	Bobby Shantz (MVP)	7.50	3.75	2.25
474	Al Rosen (MVP)	7.50	3.75	2.25
475	Mickey Mantle (MVP)	220.00	110.00	55.00
476	Jackie Jensen (MVP)	7.50	3.75	2.25
477	Nellie Fox (MVP)	17.50	8.75	5.25
478	Roger Maris (MVP)	60.00	30.00	15.00
479	Jim Konstanty (MVP)	6.00	3.00	1.75
480	Roy Campanella (MVP)	40.00	20.00	10.00
481	Hank Sauer (MVP)	6.00	3.00	1.75
482	Willie Mays (MVP)	50.00	25.00	12.50
483	Don Newcombe (MVP)	7.50	3.75	2.25
484	Hank Aaron (MVP)	50.00	25.00	12.50
485	Ernie Banks (MVP)	20.00	10.00	6.00
486	Dick Groat (MVP)	7.50	3.75	2.25
487	Gene Oliver	6.00	3.00	1.75
488	Joe McClain	6.00	3.00	1.75
489	Walt Dropo	6.00	3.00	1.75
490	Jim Bunning	12.50	6.25	3.75
491	Philadelphia Phillies Team	10.00	5.00	3.00
492	Ron Fairly	6.00	3.00	1.75
493	Don Zimmer	7.50	3.75	2.25
494	Tom Cheney	6.00	3.00	1.75
495	Elston Howard	15.00	7.50	4.50
496	Ken MacKenzie	6.00	3.00	1.75
497	Willie Jones	6.00	3.00	1.75
498	Ray Herbert	6.00	3.00	1.75
499	*Chuck Schilling*	6.00	3.00	1.75
500	Harvey Kuenn	6.00	3.00	1.75
501	John DeMerit	6.00	3.00	1.75
502	Clarence Coleman	6.00	3.00	1.75
503	Tito Francona	6.00	3.00	1.75
504	Billy Consolo	6.00	3.00	1.75
505	Red Schoendienst	12.50	6.25	3.75
506	*Willie Davis*	13.50	6.75	4.00
507	Pete Burnside	6.00	3.00	1.75
508	Rocky Bridges	6.00	3.00	1.75
509	Camilo Carreon	6.00	3.00	1.75
510	Art Ditmar	6.00	3.00	1.75
511	Joe Morgan	6.00	3.00	1.75
512	Bob Will	6.00	3.00	1.75
513	Jim Brosnan	6.00	3.00	1.75
514	Jake Wood	6.00	3.00	1.75
515	Jackie Brandt	6.00	3.00	1.75
516a	7th Series Checklist	12.00	6.00	3.50
	(507-587) (Second "C" of			
	"CHECK" above #13's cap.)			
516b	7th Series Checklist	12.00	6.00	3.50
	(506-587) (Second "C" of			
	"CHECK" covers top of			
	#13's cap.)			
517	Willie McCovey	40.00	20.00	10.00
518	Andy Carey	6.00	3.00	1.75
519	Jim Pagliaroni	6.00	3.00	1.75
520	Joe Cunningham	6.00	3.00	1.75
521	Brother Battery (Larry	10.00	5.00	3.00
	Sherry, Norm Sherry)			
522	Dick Farrell	6.00	3.00	1.75
523	Joe Gibbon	20.00	10.00	6.00
524	Johnny Logan	20.00	10.00	6.00
525	*Ron Perranoski*	60.00	30.00	15.00
526	R.C. Stevens	20.00	10.00	6.00
527	Gene Leek	20.00	10.00	6.00
528	Pedro Ramos	20.00	10.00	6.00
529	Bob Roselli	20.00	10.00	6.00
530	Bobby Malkmus	20.00	10.00	6.00
531	Jim Coates	20.00	10.00	6.00
532	Bob Hale	20.00	10.00	6.00
533	Jack Curtis	20.00	10.00	6.00
534	Eddie Kasko	20.00	10.00	6.00
535	Larry Jackson	20.00	10.00	6.00
536	Bill Tuttle	20.00	10.00	6.00
537	Bobby Locke	20.00	10.00	6.00
538	Chuck Hiller	20.00	10.00	6.00
539	Johnny Klippstein	20.00	10.00	6.00
540	Jackie Jensen	22.50	11.00	7.00
541	Roland Sheldon	20.00	10.00	6.00
542	Minnesota Twins Team	40.00	20.00	10.00
543	Roger Craig	20.00	10.00	6.00
544	George Thomas	20.00	10.00	6.00
545	Hoyt Wilhelm	60.00	30.00	15.00
546	Marty Kutyna	20.00	10.00	6.00
547	Leon Wagner	20.00	10.00	6.00
548	Ted Wills	20.00	10.00	6.00
549	Hal R. Smith	20.00	10.00	6.00
550	Frank Baumann	20.00	10.00	6.00
551	George Altman	20.00	10.00	6.00
552	Jim Archer	20.00	10.00	6.00
553	Bill Fischer	20.00	10.00	6.00
554	Pittsburgh Pirates Team	75.00	37.50	18.75
555	Sam Jones	20.00	10.00	6.00
556	Ken R. Hunt	20.00	10.00	6.00
557	Jose Valdivielso	20.00	10.00	6.00
558	Don Ferrarese	20.00	10.00	6.00
559	Jim Gentile	60.00	30.00	15.00
560	Barry Latman	20.00	10.00	6.00
561	Charley James	20.00	10.00	6.00
562	Bill Monbouquette	20.00	10.00	6.00

563	Bob Cerv	20.00	10.00	6.00
564	Don Cardwell	20.00	10.00	6.00
565	Felipe Alou	25.00	12.50	6.25
566	Paul Richards (All-Star)	20.00	10.00	6.00
567	Danny Murtaugh (All-Star)	20.00	10.00	6.00
568	Bill Skowron (All-Star)	25.00	12.50	7.50
569	Frank Herrera (All-Star)	20.00	10.00	6.00
570	Nellie Fox (All-Star)	50.00	25.00	12.50
571	Bill Mazeroski (All-Star)	50.00	25.00	12.50
572	Brooks Robinson (All-Star)	60.00	30.00	15.00
573	Ken Boyer (All-Star)	22.50	11.00	6.75
574	Luis Aparicio (All-Star)	50.00	25.00	12.50
575	Ernie Banks (All-Star)	100.00	50.00	25.00
576	Roger Maris (All-Star)	150.00	75.00	37.50
577	Hank Aaron (All-Star)	160.00	80.00	40.00
578	Mickey Mantle (All-Star)	500.00	250.00	125.00
579	Willie Mays (All-Star)	160.00	80.00	40.00
580	Al Kaline (All-Star)	80.00	40.00	20.00
581	Frank Robinson (All-Star)	90.00	45.00	22.50
582	Earl Battey (All-Star)	20.00	10.00	6.00
583	Del Crandall (All-Star)	20.00	10.00	6.00
584	Jim Perry (All-Star)	20.00	10.00	6.00
585	Bob Friend (All-Star)	20.00	10.00	6.00
586	Whitey Ford (All-Star)	100.00	50.00	25.00
587	Not Issued			
588	Not Issued			
589	Warren Spahn (All-Star)	100.00	50.00	25.00

1961 Topps Dice Game

One of the more obscure Topps test issues that may have never actually been issued is the 1961 Topps Dice Game. Eighteen black and white cards, each measuring 2-1/2" x 3-1/2" in size, comprise the set. Interestingly, there are no identifying marks, such as copyrights or trademarks, to indicate the set was produced by Topps. The card backs contain various baseball plays that occur when a certain pitch is called and a specific number of the dice is rolled.

		NM	EX	VG
	Common Player:	1,850	925.00	550.00
(1)	Earl Battey	1,850	925.00	550.00
(2)	Del Crandall	1,850	925.00	550.00
(3)	Jim Davenport	1,850	925.00	550.00
(4)	Don Drysdale	4,500	2,250	1,350
(5)	Dick Groat	1,850	925.00	550.00
(6)	Al Kaline	7,500	3,750	2,250
(7)	Tony Kubek	3,250	1,625	975.00
(8)	Mickey Mantle	45,000	22,500	13,500
(9)	Willie Mays	20,000	8,500	5,100
(10)	Bill Mazeroski	4,500	2,250	1,350
(11)	Stan Musial	20,000	10,000	6,000
(12)	Camilo Pascual	1,850	925.00	550.00
(13)	Bobby Richardson	3,500	1,750	1,050
(14)	Brooks Robinson	7,500	3,750	2,250
(15)	Frank Robinson	7,500	3,750	2,250
(16)	Norm Siebern	1,850	925.00	550.00
(17)	Leon Wagner	1,850	925.00	550.00
(18)	Bill White	1,850	925.00	550.00

1961 Topps Magic Rub-Offs

Not too different in concept from the tattoos of the previous year, the Topps Magic Rub-Off was designed to leave impressions of team themes or individual players when properly applied. Measuring 2-1/16" x 3-1/16", the Magic Rub-Off was not designed specifically for application to the owner's skin. The set features team themes that are a far cry from official logos, and the players (one per team) seem to have been included for their nicknames.

	NM	EX	VG
Complete Set (36):	200.00	100.00	60.00
Common Player:	6.00	3.00	1.75

(1)	Baltimore Orioles Pennant	6.00	3.00	1.75
(2)	Ernie "Bingo" Banks	15.00	7.50	4.50
(3)	Yogi Berra	15.00	7.50	4.50
(4)	Boston Red Sox Pennant	6.00	3.00	1.75
(5)	Jackie "Ozark" Brandt	6.00	3.00	1.75
(6)	Jim "Professor" Brosnan	6.00	3.00	1.75
(7)	Chicago Cubs Pennant	6.00	3.00	1.75
(8)	Chicago White Sox Pennant	6.00	3.00	1.75
(9)	Cincinnati Red Legs Pennant	6.00	3.00	1.75
(10)	Cleveland Indians Pennant	6.00	3.00	1.75
(11)	Detroit Tigers Pennant	6.00	3.00	1.75
(12)	Henry "Dutch" Dotterer	6.00	3.00	1.75
(13)	Joe "Flash" Gordon	6.00	3.00	1.75
(14)	Harvey "The Kitten" Haddix	6.00	3.00	1.75
(15)	Frank "Pancho" Hererra	6.00	3.00	1.75
(16)	Frank "Tower" Howard	7.50	3.75	2.25
(17)	"Sad" Sam Jones	6.00	3.00	1.75
(18)	Kansas City Athletics Pennant	6.00	3.00	1.75
(19)	Los Angeles Angels Pennant	7.50	3.75	2.25
(20)	Los Angeles Dodgers Pennant	7.50	3.75	2.25
(21)	Omar "Turk" Lown	6.00	3.00	1.75
(22)	Billy "The Kid" Martin	7.50	3.75	2.25
(23)	Duane "Duke" Mass (Maas)	6.00	3.00	1.75
(24)	Charlie "Paw Paw" Maxwell	6.00	3.00	1.75
(25)	Milwaukee Braves Pennant	6.00	3.00	1.75
(26)	Minnesota Twins Pennant	7.50	3.75	2.25
(27)	"Farmer" Ray Moore	6.00	3.00	1.75
(28)	Walt "Moose" Moryn	6.00	3.00	1.75
(29)	New York Yankees Pennant	9.00	4.50	2.75
(30)	Philadelphia Phillies Pennant	6.00	3.00	1.75
(31)	Pittsburgh Pirates Pennant	6.00	3.00	1.75
(32)	John "Honey" Romano	6.00	3.00	1.75
(33)	"Pistol Pete" Runnels	6.00	3.00	1.75
(34)	St. Louis Cardinals Pennant	6.00	3.00	1.75
(35)	San Francisco Giants Pennant	6.00	3.00	1.75
(36)	Washington Senators Pennant	9.00	4.50	2.75

1961 Topps Stamps

Issued as an added insert to 1961 Topps wax packs these 1-3/8" x 1-3/16" stamps were desiegnd to be collected and placed in an album which could be bought for an additional 10¢. Packs of cards contained two stamps. There are 208 stamps in a complete set which depict 207 different players (Al Kaline appears twice). There are 104 players on brown stamps and 104 on green. While there are many Hall of Famers on the stamps, prices remain low because there is relatively little interest in what is a non-card set.

		NM	EX	VG
	Complete Set (208):	750.00	375.00	225.00
	Common Player:	2.00	1.00	.60
	Stamp Album (Green):	65.00	30.00	20.00
(1)	Hank Aaron	20.00	10.00	6.00
(2)	Joe Adcock	2.00	1.00	.60
(3)	Hank Aguirre	2.00	1.00	.60
(4)	Bob Allison	2.00	1.00	.60
(5)	George Altman	2.00	1.00	.60
(6)	Bob Anderson	2.00	1.00	.60
(7)	Johnny Antonelli	2.00	1.00	.60
(8)	Luis Aparicio	12.00	6.00	3.50
(9)	Luis Arroyo	2.00	1.00	.60
(10)	Richie Ashburn	13.50	6.75	4.00
(11)	Ken Aspromonte	2.00	1.00	.60
(12)	Ed Bailey	2.00	1.00	.60
(13)	Ernie Banks	13.50	6.75	4.00
(14)	Steve Barber	2.00	1.00	.60
(15)	Earl Battey	2.00	1.00	.60
(16)	Hank Bauer	2.00	1.00	.60
(17)	Gus Bell	2.00	1.00	.60
(18)	Yogi Berra	13.50	6.75	4.00
(19)	Reno Bertoia	2.00	1.00	.60
(20)	John Blanchard	2.00	1.00	.60
(21)	Don Blasingame	2.00	1.00	.60
(22)	Frank Bolling	2.00	1.00	.60
(23)	Steve Boros	2.00	1.00	.60
(24)	Ed Bouchee	2.00	1.00	.60
(25)	Bob Boyd	2.00	1.00	.60
(26)	Cletis Boyer	2.00	1.00	.60
(27)	Ken Boyer	3.00	1.50	.90
(28)	Jackie Brandt	2.00	1.00	.60
(29)	Marv Breeding	2.00	1.00	.60
(30)	Eddie Bressoud	2.00	1.00	.60
(31)	Jim Brewer	2.00	1.00	.60
(32)	Tom Brewer	2.00	1.00	.60
(33)	Jim Brosnan	2.00	1.00	.60
(34)	Bill Bruton	2.00	1.00	.60
(35)	Bob Buhl	2.00	1.00	.60
(36)	Jim Bunning	10.00	5.00	3.00
(37)	Smoky Burgess	2.00	1.00	.60
(38)	John Buzhardt	2.00	1.00	.60
(39)	Johnny Callison	2.00	1.00	.60
(40)	Chico Cardenas	2.00	1.00	.60
(41)	Andy Carey	2.00	1.00	.60
(42)	Jerry Casale	2.00	1.00	.60
(43)	Norm Cash	2.00	1.00	1.25

(44)	Orlando Cepeda	10.00	5.00	3.00
(45)	Bob Cerv	2.00	1.00	.60
(46)	Harry Chiti	2.00	1.00	.60
(47)	Gene Conley	2.00	1.00	.60
(48)	Wes Covington	2.00	1.00	.60
(49)	Del Crandall	2.00	1.00	.60
(50)	Tony Curry	2.00	1.00	.60
(51)	Bud Daley	2.00	1.00	.60
(52)	Pete Daley	2.00	1.00	.60
(53)	Clay Dalrymple	2.00	1.00	.60
(54)	Jim Davenport	2.00	1.00	.60
(55)	Tommy Davis	2.00	1.00	.60
(56)	Bobby Del Greco	2.00	1.00	.60
(57)	Ike Delock	2.00	1.00	.60
(58)	Art Ditmar	2.00	1.00	.60
(59)	Dick Donovan	2.00	1.00	.60
(60)	Don Drysdale	13.50	6.75	4.00
(61)	Dick Ellsworth	2.00	1.00	.60
(62)	Don Elston	2.00	1.00	.60
(63)	Chuck Estrada	2.00	1.00	.60
(64)	Roy Face	2.00	1.00	.60
(65)	Dick Farrell	2.00	1.00	.60
(66)	Chico Fernandez	2.00	1.00	.60
(67)	Curt Flood	2.00	1.00	.60
(68)	Whitey Ford	13.50	6.75	4.00
(69)	Tito Francona	2.00	1.00	.60
(70)	Gene Freese	2.00	1.00	.60
(71)	Bob Friend	2.00	1.00	.60
(72)	Billy Gardner	2.00	1.00	.60
(73)	Ned Garver	2.00	1.00	.60
(74)	Gary Geiger	2.00	1.00	.60
(75)	Jim Gentile	2.00	1.00	.60
(76)	Dick Gernert	2.00	1.00	.60
(77)	Tony Gonzalez	2.00	1.00	.60
(78)	Alex Grammas	2.00	1.00	.60
(79)	Jim Grant	2.00	1.00	.60
(80)	Dick Groat	2.00	1.00	.60
(81)	Dick Hall	2.00	1.00	.60
(82)	Ron Hansen	2.00	1.00	.60
(83)	Bob Hartman	2.00	1.00	.60
(84)	Woodie Held	2.00	1.00	.60
(85)	Ray Herbert	2.00	1.00	.60
(86)	Frank Herrera	2.00	1.00	.60
(87)	Whitey Herzog	2.00	1.00	.60
(88)	Don Hoak	2.00	1.00	.60
(89)	Elston Howard	5.00	2.50	1.50
(90)	Frank Howard	4.00	2.00	1.25
(91)	Ken Hunt	2.00	1.00	.60
(92)	Larry Jackson	2.00	1.00	.60
(93)	Julian Javier	2.00	1.00	.60
(94)	Joe Jay	2.00	1.00	.60
(95)	Jackie Jensen	2.00	1.00	.60
(96)	Jim Kaat	2.50	1.25	.70
(97a)	Al Kaline (Green)	25.00	12.50	7.50
(97b)	Al Kaline (Brown)	15.00	7.50	4.50
(98)	Eddie Kasko	2.00	1.00	.60
(99)	Russ Kemmerer	2.00	1.00	.60
(100)	Harmon Killebrew	13.50	6.75	4.00
(101)	Billy Klaus	2.00	1.00	.60
(102)	Ron Kline	2.00	1.00	.60
(103)	Johnny Klippstein	2.00	1.00	.60
(104)	Ted Kluszewski	10.00	5.00	3.00
(105)	Tony Kubek	5.00	2.50	1.50
(106)	Harvey Kuenn	2.00	1.00	.60
(107)	Jim Landis	2.00	1.00	.60
(108)	Hobie Landrith	2.00	1.00	.60
(109)	Norm Larker	2.00	1.00	.60
(110)	Frank Lary	2.00	1.00	.60
(111)	Barry Latman	2.00	1.00	.60
(112)	Vern Law	2.00	1.00	.60
(113)	Jim Lemon	2.00	1.00	.60
(114)	Sherman Lollar	2.00	1.00	.60
(115)	Dale Long	2.00	1.00	.60
(116)	Jerry Lumpe	2.00	1.00	.60
(117)	Jerry Lynch	2.00	1.00	.60
(118)	Art Mahaffey	2.00	1.00	.60
(119)	Frank Malzone	2.00	1.00	.60
(120)	Felix Mantilla	2.00	1.00	.60
(121)	Mickey Mantle	60.00	30.00	18.00
(122)	Juan Marichal	13.50	6.75	4.00
(123)	Roger Maris	25.00	12.50	7.50
(124)	Billy Martin	5.00	2.50	1.50
(125)	J.C. Martin	2.00	1.00	.60
(126)	Ed Mathews	13.50	6.75	4.00
(127)	Charlie Maxwell	2.00	1.00	.60
(128)	Willie Mays	20.00	10.00	6.00
(129)	Bill Mazeroski	12.00	6.00	3.50
(130)	Mike McCormick	2.00	1.00	.60
(131)	Willie McCovey	13.50	6.75	4.00
(132)	Lindy McDaniel	2.00	1.00	.60
(133)	Roy McMillan	2.00	1.00	.60
(134)	Minnie Minoso	3.00	1.50	.90
(135)	Bill Monbouquette	2.00	1.00	.60
(136)	Wally Moon	2.00	1.00	.60
(137)	Stan Musial	20.00	10.00	6.00
(138)	Charlie Neal	2.00	1.00	.60
(139)	Rocky Nelson	2.00	1.00	.60
(140)	Russ Nixon	2.00	1.00	.60
(141)	Billy O'Dell	2.00	1.00	.60
(142)	Jim O'Toole	2.00	1.00	.60
(143)	Milt Pappas	2.00	1.00	.60
(144)	Camilo Pascual	2.00	1.00	.60
(145)	Jim Perry	2.00	1.00	.60
(146)	Bubba Phillips	2.00	1.00	.60
(147)	Bill Pierce	2.00	1.00	.60
(148)	Jim Piersall	2.00	1.00	.60
(149)	Vada Pinson	3.00	1.50	.90
(150)	Johnny Podres	2.50	1.25	.70
(151)	Wally Post	2.00	1.00	.60
(152)	Vic Powers (Power)	2.00	1.00	.60
(153)	Pedro Ramos	2.00	1.00	.60
(154)	Robin Roberts	10.00	5.00	3.00
(155)	Brooks Robinson	13.50	6.75	4.00
(156)	Frank Robinson	13.50	6.75	4.00
(157)	Ed Roebuck	2.00	1.00	.60
(158)	John Romano	2.00	1.00	.60
(159)	John Roseboro	2.00	1.00	.60
(160)	Pete Runnels	2.00	1.00	.60

(161)	Ed Sadowski	2.00	1.00	.60
(162)	Jack Sanford	2.00	1.00	.60
(163)	Ron Santo	3.00	1.50	.90
(164)	Ray Semproch	2.00	1.00	.60
(165)	Bobby Shantz	2.00	1.00	.60
(166)	Bob Shaw	2.00	1.00	.60
(167)	Larry Sherry	2.00	1.00	.60
(168)	Norm Siebern	2.00	1.00	.60
(169)	Roy Sievers	2.00	1.00	.60
(170)	Curt Simmons	2.00	1.00	.60
(171)	Dave Sisler	2.00	1.00	.60
(172)	Bob Skinner	2.00	1.00	.60
(173)	Al Smith	2.00	1.00	.60
(174)	Hal Smith	2.00	1.00	.60
(175)	Hal Smith	2.00	1.00	.60
(176)	Duke Snider	13.50	6.75	4.00
(177)	Warren Spahn	13.50	6.75	4.00
(178)	Daryl Spencer	2.00	1.00	.60
(179)	Bill Stafford	2.00	1.00	.60
(180)	Jerry Staley	2.00	1.00	.60
(181)	Gene Stephens	2.00	1.00	.60
(182)	Chuck Stobbs	2.00	1.00	.60
(183)	Dick Stuart	2.00	1.00	.60
(184)	Willie Tasby	2.00	1.00	.60
(185)	Sammy Taylor	2.00	1.00	.60
(186)	Tony Taylor	2.00	1.00	.60
(187)	Johnny Temple	2.00	1.00	.60
(188)	Marv Throneberry	2.00	1.00	.60
(189)	Gus Triandos	2.00	1.00	.60
(190)	Bob Turley	2.00	1.00	.60
(191)	Bill Tuttle	2.00	1.00	.60
(192)	Zoilo Versalles	2.00	1.00	.60
(193)	Bill Virdon	2.00	1.00	.60
(194)	Lee Walls	2.00	1.00	.60
(195)	Vic Wertz	2.00	1.00	.60
(196)	Pete Whisenant	2.00	1.00	.60
(197)	Bill White	2.00	1.00	.60
(198)	Hoyt Wilhelm	10.00	5.00	3.00
(199)	Bob Will	2.00	1.00	.60
(200)	Carl Willey	2.00	1.00	.60
(201)	Billy Williams	12.00	6.00	3.50
(202)	Dick Williams	2.00	1.00	.60
(203)	Stan Williams	2.00	1.00	.60
(204)	Gene Woodling	2.00	1.00	.60
(205)	Early Wynn	10.00	5.00	3.00
(206)	Carl Yastrzemski	13.50	6.75	4.00
(207)	Eddie Yost	2.00	1.00	.60

1961 Topps Stamps Panels

BILLY MARTIN — CINCINNATI REDS — 2nd BASE

WHITEY HERZOG — KANSAS CITY A's — OUTFIELD

Some advanced collectors pursue the 1961 Topps stamps in the form of the two-stamp panels in which they were issued. The 208 different stamps which make up the issue can be found on 182 different two-stamp panels. The unnumbered stamps are listed here alphabetically according to the name of the player which appears on the left end of the panel. Values shown are for complete panels of two players stamps plus the attached tab at left.

		NM	EX	VG
Complete Panel Set (182):		3,000	1,500	900.00
Common Panel:		9.00	4.50	2.75
(1)	Hank Aguirre/Bob Boyd	9.00	4.50	2.75
(2)	Bob Allison/Orlando Cepeda	20.00	10.00	6.00
(3)	Bob Allison/Early Wynn	20.00	10.00	6.00
(4)	George Altman/Andy Carey	9.00	4.50	2.75
(5)	George Altman/Lindy McDaniel	9.00	4.50	2.75
(6)	Johnny Antonelli/Ken Hunt	9.00	4.50	2.75
(7)	Richie Ashburn/Don Drysdale	30.00	15.00	9.00
(8)	Richie Ashburn/Joe Jay	25.00	12.50	7.50
(9)	Ken Aspromonte/Chuck Estrada	9.00	4.50	2.75
(10)	Ken Aspromonte/Jerry Lynch	9.00	4.50	2.75
(11)	Ed Bailey/Marv Breeding	9.00	4.50	2.75
(12)	Ed Bailey/Smoky Burgess	9.00	4.50	2.75
(13)	Ernie Banks/Chico Fernandez	30.00	15.00	9.00
(14)	Ernie Banks/Pedro Ramos	30.00	15.00	9.00
(15)	Steve Barber/Eddie Kasko	9.00	4.50	2.75
(16)	Steve Barber/Roy Sievers	9.00	4.50	2.75
(17)	Earl Battey/Art Ditmar	9.00	4.50	2.75
(18)	Earl Battey/Bill White	9.00	4.50	2.75
(19)	Gus Bell/Gary Geiger	9.00	4.50	2.75
(20)	Gus Bell/Early Wynn	20.00	10.00	6.00
(21)	John Blanchard/Dick Donovan	9.00	4.50	2.75
(22)	John Blanchard/Ray Semproch	9.00	4.50	2.75
(23)	Don Blasingame/Elston Howard	12.00	6.00	3.50
(24)	Don Blasingame/Charlie Maxwell	9.00	4.50	2.75
(25)	Frank Bolling/Luis Aparicio	20.00	10.00	6.00
(26)	Frank Bolling/Whitey Herzog	9.00	4.50	2.75
(27)	Steve Boros/Ike Delock	9.00	4.50	2.75
(28)	Steve Boros/Russ Nixon	9.00	4.50	2.75
(29)	Ed Bouchee/Larry Sherry	9.00	4.50	2.75
(30)	Ed Bouchee/Willie Tasby	9.00	4.50	2.75
(31)	Cletis Boyer/Johnny Klippstein	9.00	4.50	2.75
(32)	Jim Brewer/Vern Law	9.00	4.50	2.75
(33)	Jim Brewer/Camilo Pascual	9.00	4.50	2.75
(34)	Tom Brewer/Tommy Davis	9.00	4.50	2.75

(35)	Tom Brewer/Larry Sherry	9.00	4.50	2.75
(36)	Jim Brosnan/Roy McMillan	9.00	4.50	2.75
(37)	Jim Brosnan/Calr Willey	9.00	4.50	2.75
(38)	Bill Bruton/Ken Boyer	12.00	6.00	3.50
(39)	Bill Bruton/Mickey Mantle	200.00	100.00	60.00
(40)	Bob Buhl/Willie Mays	60.00	30.00	18.00
(41)	Bob Buhl/Roy Sievers	9.00	4.50	2.75
(42)	Jim Bunning/Bob Boyd	20.00	10.00	6.00
(43)	Jim Bunning/Ron Hansen	20.00	10.00	6.00
(44)	John Buzhardt/Brooks Robinson	30.00	15.00	9.00
(45)	John Buzhardt/Dick Williams	9.00	4.50	2.75
(46)	Johnny Callison/Jim Landis	9.00	4.50	2.75
(47)	Johnny Callison/Ed Roebuck	9.00	4.50	2.75
(48)	Harry Chiti/Jackie Brandt	9.00	4.50	2.75
(49)	Harry Chiti/Gene Conley	9.00	4.50	2.75
(50)	Del Crandall/Billy Gardner	9.00	4.50	2.75
(51)	Bud Daley/Al Kaline	30.00	15.00	9.00
(52)	Bud Daley/Dave Sisler	9.00	4.50	2.75
(53)	Pete Daley/Dick Ellsworth	9.00	4.50	2.75
(54)	Pete Daley/Hal (R.) Smith	9.00	4.50	2.75
(55)	Clay Dalrymple/Norm Larker	9.00	4.50	2.75
(56)	CLay Dalrymple/Stan Williams	9.00	4.50	2.75
(57)	Jim Davenport/Reno Bertoia	9.00	4.50	2.75
(58)	Jim Davenport/Jerry Lynch	9.00	4.50	2.75
(59)	Bobby Del Greco/Roy Face	9.00	4.50	2.75
(60)	Bobby Del Greco/Frank Howard	12.00	6.00	3.50
(61)	Gene Freese/Wes Covington	9.00	4.50	2.75
(62)	Gene Freese/Vada Pinson	9.00	4.50	2.75
(63)	Bob Friend/Hank Aaron	60.00	30.00	18.00
(64)	Bob Friend/Lee Walls	9.00	4.50	2.75
(65)	Jim Gentile/Chuck Estrada	9.00	4.50	2.75
(66)	Jim Gentile/Billy O'Dell	9.00	4.50	2.75
(67)	Dick Gernert/Russ Nixon	9.00	4.50	2.75
(68)	Alex Grammas/Eddie Bressoud	9.00	4.50	2.75
(69)	Frank Herrera/Joe Jay	9.00	4.50	2.75
(70)	Frank Herrera/Jim Landis	9.00	4.50	2.75
(71)	Julian Javier/Eddie Kasko	9.00	4.50	2.75
(72)	Jackie Jensen/Hank Bauer	15.00	7.50	4.50
(73)	Jackie Jensen/Mickey Mantle	200.00	100.00	60.00
(74)	Al Kaline/Dick Hall	30.00	15.00	9.00
(75)	Al Kaline/Ray Herbert	30.00	15.00	9.00
(76)	Russ Kemmerer/Ed Sadowski	9.00	4.50	2.75
(77)	Harmon Killebrew/Bill Stafford	30.00	15.00	9.00
(78)	Harmon Killebrew/Bill White	30.00	15.00	9.00
(79)	Billy Klaus/Bob Anderson	9.00	4.50	2.75
(80)	Ron Kline/Juan Marichal	20.00	10.00	6.00
(81)	Ron Kline/Curt Simmons	9.00	4.50	2.75
(82)	Tony Kubek/Reno Bertoia	12.00	6.00	3.50
(83)	Frank Lary/Andy Carey	9.00	4.50	2.75
(84)	Barry Latman/Hank Bauer	9.00	4.50	2.75
(85)	Jim Lemon/Tony Curry	9.00	4.50	2.75
(86)	Jim Lemon/Dick Williams	9.00	4.50	2.75
(87)	Sherm Lollar/Willie Mays	60.00	30.00	18.00
(88)	Sherm Lollar/Duke Snider	30.00	15.00	9.00
(89)	Dale Long/Bob Anderson	9.00	4.50	2.75
(90)	Dale Long/Don Elston	9.00	4.50	2.75
(91)	Art Mahaffey/Vada Pinson	9.00	4.50	2.75
(92)	Art Mahaffey/Robin Roberts	20.00	10.00	6.00
(93)	Frank Malzone/Dick Hall	9.00	4.50	2.75
(94)	Frank Malzone/Bob Hartman	9.00	4.50	2.75
(95)	Felix Mantilla/Billy Gardner	9.00	4.50	2.75
(96)	Felix Mantilla/Gary Geiger	9.00	4.50	2.75
(97)	Roger Maris/Johnny Klippstein	45.00	22.00	13.50
(98)	Roger Maris/Ray Semproch	45.00	22.00	13.50
(99)	Billy Martin/Hank Aaron	60.00	30.00	18.00
(100)	Billy Martin/Whitey Herzog	15.00	7.50	4.50
(101)	J.C. Martin/Bob Cerv	9.00	4.50	2.75
(102)	J.C. Martin/Eddie Yost	9.00	4.50	2.75
(103)	Ed Mathews/Chico Cardenas	30.00	15.00	9.00
(104)	Bill Mazeroski/Joe Adcock	20.00	10.00	6.00
(105)	Bill Mazeroski/Elston Howard	20.00	10.00	6.00
(106)	Mike McCormick/Rocky Nelson	9.00	4.50	2.75
(107)	Mike McCormick/Curt Simmons	9.00	4.50	2.75
(108)	Wille McCovey/Smoky Burgess	30.00	15.00	9.00
(109)	Minnie Minoso/Ted Kluszewski	15.00	7.50	4.50
(110)	Minnie Minoso/Eddie Yost	12.00	6.00	3.50
(111)	Bikl Monbouquette/Tony Curry	9.00	4.50	2.75
(112)	Bill Monbouquette/Sammy Taylor	9.00	4.50	2.75
(113)	Wally Moon/Roy Face	9.00	4.50	2.75
(114)	Stan Musial/Rocky Nelson	60.00	30.00	18.00
(115)	Charlie Neal/Marv Breeding	9.00	4.50	2.75
(116)	Charlie Neal/Jim Grant	9.00	4.50	2.75
(117)	Jim O'Toole/Chico Cardenas	9.00	4.50	2.75
(118)	Jim O'Toole/Roy McMillan	9.00	4.50	2.75
(119)	Milt Pappas/Tito Francona	9.00	4.50	2.75
(120)	Milt Pappas/Jim Piersall	9.00	4.50	2.75
(121)	Jim Perry/Bob Cerv	9.00	4.50	2.75
(122)	Jim Perry/Ken Hunt	9.00	4.50	2.75
(123)	Bubba Phillips/Art Ditmar	9.00	4.50	2.75
(124)	Bubba Phillips/Jim Kaat	15.00	7.50	4.50
(125)	Johnny Podres/Dick Farrell	9.00	4.50	2.75
(126)	Wally Post/Dick Farrell	9.00	4.50	2.75
(127)	Wally Post/Robin Roberts	20.00	10.00	6.00
(128)	Frank Robinson/Jim Grant	30.00	15.00	9.00
(129)	Frank Robinson/Don Hoak	30.00	15.00	9.00
(130)	John Romano/Al Kaline	30.00	15.00	9.00
(131)	John Roseboro/Dick Groat	9.00	4.50	2.75
(132)	Pete Runnels/Larry Jackson	9.00	4.50	2.75
(133)	Jack Sanford/Whitey Ford	30.00	15.00	9.00
(134)	Jack Sanford/Pedro Ramos	9.00	4.50	2.75
(135)	Ron Santo/Harvey Kuenn	15.00	7.50	4.50
(136)	Ron Santo/Vern Law	15.00	7.50	4.50
(137)	Bobby Shantz/Joe Adcock	9.00	4.50	2.75
(138)	Bobby Shantz/Dick Groat	9.00	4.50	2.75
(139)	Bob Shaw/Jerry Casale	9.00	4.50	2.75
(140)	Bob Shaw/Ned Garver	9.00	4.50	2.75
(141)	Norm Siebern/Tony Gonzalez	9.00	4.50	2.75
(142)	Norm Siebern/Woodie Held	9.00	4.50	2.75
(143)	Bob Skinner/Hobie Landrith	9.00	4.50	2.75

		NM	EX	VG
(144)	Bob Skinner/Juan Marichal	20.00	10.00	6.00
(145)	Al Smith/Don Drysdale	25.00	12.50	7.50
(146)	Hal (W.) Smith/ Eddie Bressoud	9.00	4.50	2.75
(147)	Hal (W.) Smith/Harvey Kuenn	9.00	4.50	2.75
(148)	Daryl Spencer/Norm Cash	9.00	4.50	2.75
(149)	Daryl Spencer/ Vic Powers (Power)	9.00	4.50	2.75
(150)	Jerry Staley/Ned Garver	9.00	4.50	2.75
(151)	Jerry Staley/Ed Sadowski	9.00	4.50	2.75
(152)	Gene Stephens/Gene Conley	9.00	4.50	2.75
(153)	Gene Stephens/Ike Delock	9.00	4.50	2.75
(154)	Chuck Stobbs/Ken Boyer	12.00	6.00	3.50
(155)	Chuck Stobbs/Curt Flood	9.00	4.50	2.75
(156)	Dick Stuart/Whitey Ford	30.00	15.00	9.00
(157)	Dick Stuart/Larry Jackson	9.00	4.50	2.75
(158)	Tony Taylor/Frank Howard	12.00	6.00	3.50
(159)	Tony Taylor/Norm Larker	9.00	4.50	2.75
(160)	Johnny Temple/Norm Cash	9.00	4.50	2.75
(161)	Johnny Temple/Dave Sisler	9.00	4.50	2.75
(162)	Marv Throneberry/Yogi Berra	45.00	22.00	13.50
(163)	Marv Throneberry/ Tommy Davis	9.00	4.50	2.75
(164)	Gus Triandos/Sammy Taylor	9.00	4.50	2.75
(165)	Bob Turley/Luis Aparicio	20.00	10.00	6.00
(166)	Bill Tuttle/Jerry Casale	9.00	4.50	2.75
(167)	Bill Tuttle/Bill Pierce	9.00	4.50	2.75
(168)	Zoilo Versalles/Bill Stafford	9.00	4.50	2.75
(169)	Bill Virdon/Yogi Berra	30.00	15.00	9.00
(170)	Vic Wertz/Bob Hartman	9.00	4.50	2.75
(171)	Vic Wertz/Jerry Lumpe	9.00	4.50	2.75
(172)	Pete Whisenant/Luis Arroyo	9.00	4.50	2.75
(173)	Pete Whisenant/Dick Donovan	9.00	4.50	2.75
(174)	Hoyt Wilhelm/Ron Hansen	20.00	10.00	6.00
(175)	Hoyt Wilhelm/Jim Piersall	20.00	10.00	6.00
(176)	Bob Will/Tony Gonzalez	9.00	4.50	2.75
(177)	Bob Will/Lindy McDaniel	9.00	4.50	2.75
(178)	Billy Williams/Warren Spahn	30.00	15.00	9.00
(179)	Billy Williams/Carl Willey	25.00	12.50	7.50
(180)	Gene Woodling/Don Elston	9.00	4.50	2.75
(181)	Gene Woodling/Hal (R.) Smith	9.00	4.50	2.75
(182)	Carl Yastrzemski/Jerry Lumpe	60.00	30.00	18.00

1962 Topps

The 1962 Topps set established another plateau for set size with 598 cards. The 2-1/2" x 3-1/2" cards feature a photograph set against a woodgrain background. The lower-right corner has been made to look like it is curling away. Many established specialty cards dot the set including statistical leaders, multi-player cards, team cards, checklists, World Series cards and All-Stars. Of note is that 1962 was the first year of the multi-player rookie card. There is a nine-card "In Action" subset and a 10-card run of special Babe Ruth cards. Photo variations of several cards in the 2nd Series (#110-196) exist. All cards in the 2nd Series can be found with two distinct printing variations, an early printing with the cards containing a very noticeable greenish tint, having been corrected to clear photos in subsequent print runs. The complete set price in the checklist that follows does not include the higher-priced variations. Among the high numbers (#523-598) certain cards were "short-printed," produced in lesser quantities. These cards carry a higher value and are indicated in the checklist by the notation (SP) after the player name.

		NM	EX	VG
Complete Set (598):		5,500	2,750	1,650
Common Player (1-446):		4.00	2.00	1.25
Common Player (447-522):		7.00	3.50	2.00
Common Player (523-598):		10.00	5.00	3.00
1	Roger Maris	500.00	250.00	125.00
2	Jim Brosnan	4.00	2.00	1.25
3	Pete Runnels	4.00	2.00	1.25
4	John DeMerit	4.00	2.00	1.25
5	Sandy Koufax	150.00	75.00	37.50
6	Marv Breeding	4.00	2.00	1.25
7	Frank Thomas	4.00	2.00	1.25
8	Ray Herbert	4.00	2.00	1.25
9	Jim Davenport	4.00	2.00	1.25
10	Bob Clemente	200.00	100.00	50.00
11	Tom Morgan	4.00	2.00	1.25
12	Harry Craft	4.00	2.00	1.25
13	Dick Howser	4.00	2.00	1.25
14	Bill White	4.00	2.00	1.25
15	Dick Donovan	4.00	2.00	1.25
16	Darrell Johnson	4.00	2.00	1.25
17	Johnny Callison	4.00	2.00	1.25
18	Managers' Dream (Mickey Mantle, Willie Mays).	200.00	100.00	50.00
19	*Ray Washburn*	4.00	2.00	1.25
20	Rocky Colavito	15.00	7.50	4.50
21	Jim Kaat	6.00	3.00	1.75
22a	1st Series Checklist (1-88) (Numbers 121-176 on back.)	6.00	3.00	1.75
22b	1st Series Checklist (1-88) (Numbers 33-88 on back.)	9.00	4.50	2.75
23	Norm Larker	4.00	2.00	1.25
24	Detroit Tigers Team	7.00	3.50	2.00
25	Ernie Banks	65.00	32.50	16.25
26	Chris Cannizzaro	4.00	2.00	1.25
27	Chuck Cottier	4.00	2.00	1.25
28	Minnie Minoso	9.00	4.50	2.75
29	Casey Stengel	13.50	6.75	4.00
30	Ed Mathews	25.00	12.50	7.50
31	*Tom Tresh*	13.50	6.75	4.00
32	John Roseboro	4.00	2.00	1.25
33	Don Larsen	4.00	2.00	1.25
34	Johnny Temple	4.00	2.00	1.25
35	*Don Schwall*	4.00	2.00	1.25
36	Don Leppert	4.00	2.00	1.25
37	Tribe Hill Trio (Barry Latman, Jim Perry, Dick Stigman)	6.00	3.00	1.75
38	Gene Stephens	4.00	2.00	1.25
39	Joe Koppe	4.00	2.00	1.25
40	Orlando Cepeda	16.00	8.00	4.75
41	Cliff Cook	4.00	2.00	1.25
42	Jim King	4.00	2.00	1.25
43	Los Angeles Dodgers Team	10.00	5.00	3.00
44	Don Taussig	4.00	2.00	1.25
45	Brooks Robinson	25.00	12.50	7.50
46	*Jack Baldschun*	4.00	2.00	1.25
47	Bob Will	4.00	2.00	1.25
48	Ralph Terry	4.00	2.00	1.25
49	Hal Jones	4.00	2.00	1.25
50	Stan Musial	100.00	50.00	25.00
51	A.L. Batting Leaders (Norm Cash, Elston Howard, Al Kaline, Jim Piersall)	12.50	6.25	3.75
52	N.L. Batting Leaders (Ken Boyer, Roberto Clemente, Wally Moon, Vada Pinson)	15.00	7.50	4.50
53	A.L. Home Run Leaders (Jim Gentile, Harmon Killebrew, Mickey Mantle, Roger Maris)	100.00	50.00	25.00
54	N.L. Home Run Leaders (Orlando Cepeda, Willie Mays, Frank Robinson)	12.50	6.25	3.75
55	A.L. E.R.A. Leaders (Dick Donovan, Don Mossi, Milt Pappas, Bill Stafford)	6.00	3.00	1.75
56	N.L. E.R.A. Leaders (Mike McCormick, Jim O'Toole, Curt Simmons, Warren Spahn)	7.00	3.50	2.00
57	A.L. Win Leaders (Steve Barber, Jim Bunning, Whitey Ford, Frank Lary)	10.00	5.00	3.00
58	N.L. Win Leaders (Joe Jay, Jim O'Toole, Warren Spahn)	7.00	3.50	2.00
59	A.L. Strikeout Leaders (Jim Bunning, Whitey Ford, Camilo Pascual, Juan Pizzaro)	7.50	3.75	2.25
60	N.L. Strikeout Leaders (Don Drysdale, Sandy Koufax, Jim O'Toole, Stan Williams)	16.00	8.00	4.75
61	St. Louis Cardinals Team	7.00	3.50	2.00
62	Steve Boros	4.00	2.00	1.25
63	*Tony Cloninger*	7.00	3.50	2.00
64	Russ Snyder	4.00	2.00	1.25
65	Bobby Richardson	15.00	7.50	4.50
66	Cuno Barragon (Barragan)	4.00	2.00	1.25
67	Harvey Haddix	4.00	2.00	1.25
68	Ken L. Hunt	4.00	2.00	1.25
69	Phil Ortega	4.00	2.00	1.25
70	Harmon Killebrew	25.00	12.50	7.50
71	Dick LeMay	4.00	2.00	1.25
72	Bob's Pupils (Steve Boros, Bob Scheffing, Jake Wood)	4.50	2.25	1.25
73	Nellie Fox	16.00	8.00	4.75
74	Bob Lillis	4.00	2.00	1.25
75	Milt Pappas	4.00	2.00	1.25
76	Howie Bedell	4.00	2.00	1.25
77	Tony Taylor	4.00	2.00	1.25
78	Gene Green	4.00	2.00	1.25
79	Ed Hobaugh	4.00	2.00	1.25
80	Vada Pinson	7.00	3.50	2.00
81	Jim Pagliaroni	4.00	2.00	1.25
82	Deron Johnson	4.00	2.00	1.25
83	Larry Jackson	4.00	2.00	1.25
84	Lenny Green	4.00	2.00	1.25
85	Gil Hodges	15.00	7.50	4.50
86	*Donn Clendenon*	6.00	3.00	1.75
87	Mike Roarke	4.00	2.00	1.25
88	Ralph Houk	10.00	5.00	3.00
89	Barney Schultz	4.00	2.00	1.25
90	Jim Piersall	6.00	3.00	1.75
91	J.C. Martin	4.00	2.00	1.25
92	Sam Jones	4.00	2.00	1.25
93	John Blanchard	5.00	2.50	1.50
94	Jay Hook	4.00	2.00	1.25
95	Don Hoak	4.00	2.00	1.25
96	Eli Grba	4.00	2.00	1.25
97	Tito Francona	4.00	2.00	1.25
98	2nd Series Checklist (89-176)	6.00	3.00	1.75
99	*John Powell* (Boog)	20.00	10.00	6.00
100	Warren Spahn	50.00	25.00	12.50
101	Carroll Hardy	4.00	2.00	1.25
102	Al Schroll	4.00	2.00	1.25
103	Don Blasingame	4.00	2.00	1.25
104	Ted Savage	4.00	2.00	1.25
105	Don Mossi	4.00	2.00	1.25
106	Carl Sawatski	4.00	2.00	1.25
107	Mike McCormick	4.00	2.00	1.25
108	Willie Davis	5.00	2.50	1.50
109	Bob Shaw	4.00	2.00	1.25
110	Bill Skowron	22.50	11.00	7.00
111	Dallas Green	4.00	2.00	1.25
112	Hank Foiles	4.00	2.00	1.25
113	Chicago White Sox Team	7.00	3.50	2.00
114	Howie Koplitz	4.00	2.00	1.25
115	Bob Skinner	4.00	2.00	1.25
116	Herb Score	4.00	2.00	1.25
117	Gary Geiger	4.00	2.00	1.25
118	Julian Javier	4.00	2.00	1.25
119	Danny Murphy	4.00	2.00	1.25
120	Bob Purkey	4.00	2.00	1.25
121	Billy Hitchcock	4.00	2.00	1.25
122	Norm Bass	4.00	2.00	1.25
123	Mike de la Hoz	4.00	2.00	1.25
124	Bill Pleis	4.00	2.00	1.25
125	Gene Woodling	4.00	2.00	1.25
126	Al Cicotte	4.00	2.00	1.25
127	Pride of the A's (Hank Bauer, Jerry Lumpe, Norm Siebern)	4.50	2.25	1.25
128	Art Fowler	4.00	2.00	1.25
129a	Lee Walls (Pinstriped jersey.)	20.00	10.00	6.00
129b	Lee Walls (Plain jersey.)	6.00	3.00	1.75
130	Frank Bolling	4.00	2.00	1.25
131	*Pete Richert*	4.00	2.00	1.25
132a	Los Angeles Angels Team (With inset photos.)	13.50	6.75	4.00
132b	Los Angeles Angels Team (No inset photos.)	7.00	3.50	2.00
133	Felipe Alou	9.00	4.50	2.75
134a	Billy Hoeft (Green sky.)	15.00	7.50	4.50
134b	Billy Hoeft (Blue sky.)	12.00	6.00	3.50
135	Babe as a Boy (Babe Ruth)	20.00	10.00	6.00
136	Babe Joins Yanks (Babe Ruth)	20.00	10.00	6.00
137	Babe and Mgr. Huggins (Babe Ruth)	20.00	10.00	6.00
138	The Famous Slugger (Babe Ruth)	20.00	10.00	6.00
139a	Hal Reniff (Pitching)	30.00	15.00	7.50
139b	Hal Reniff (Portrait)	15.00	7.50	4.50
139c	Babe Hits 60 (Babe Ruth) (Pole in background at left.)	50.00	25.00	12.50
139d	Babe Hits 60 (Babe Ruth) (No pole.)	35.00	17.50	10.00
140	Gehrig and Ruth (Babe Ruth)	35.00	17.50	10.00
141	Twilight Years (Babe Ruth)	20.00	10.00	6.00
142	Coaching for the Dodgers (Babe Ruth)	20.00	10.00	6.00
143	Greatest Sports Hero (Babe Ruth)	20.00	10.00	6.00
144	Farewell Speech (Babe Ruth)	20.00	10.00	6.00
145	Barry Latman	4.00	2.00	1.25
146	Don Demeter	4.00	2.00	1.25
147a	Bill Kunkel (Ball in hand.)	17.50	8.75	5.25
147b	Bill Kunkel (Portrait)	12.00	6.00	3.50
148	Wally Post	4.00	2.00	1.25
149	Bob Duliba	4.00	2.00	1.25
150	Al Kaline	50.00	25.00	12.50
151	Johnny Klippstein	4.00	2.00	1.25
152	Mickey Vernon	4.00	2.00	1.25
153	Pumpsie Green	4.00	2.00	1.25
154	Lee Thomas	4.00	2.00	1.25
155	Stu Miller	4.00	2.00	1.25
156	Merritt Ranew	4.00	2.00	1.25
157	Wes Covington	4.00	2.00	1.25
158	Milwaukee Braves Team	7.00	3.50	2.00
159	Hal Reniff	4.00	2.00	1.25
160	Dick Stuart	4.00	2.00	1.25
161	Frank Baumann	4.00	2.00	1.25
162	Sammy Drake	4.00	2.00	1.25
163	Hot Corner Guardians (Cletis Boyer, Billy Gardner)	10.00	5.00	3.00
164	Hal Naragon	4.00	2.00	1.25
165	Jackie Brandt	4.00	2.00	1.25
166	Don Lee	4.00	2.00	1.25
167	*Tim McCarver*	17.50	8.75	5.25
168	Leo Posada	4.00	2.00	1.25
169	Bob Cerv	4.00	2.00	1.25
170	Ron Santo	12.50	6.25	3.75
171	Dave Sisler	4.00	2.00	1.25
172	Fred Hutchinson	4.00	2.00	1.25
173	Chico Fernandez	4.00	2.00	1.25
174a	Carl Willey (With cap.)	15.00	7.50	4.50
174b	Carl Willey (No cap.)	8.00	4.00	2.50
175	Frank Howard	5.00	2.50	1.50
176a	Eddie Yost (Batting)	15.00	7.50	4.50
176b	Eddie Yost (Portrait)	4.00	2.00	1.25
177	Bobby Shantz	4.00	2.00	1.25
178	Camilo Carreon	4.00	2.00	1.25
179	Tom Sturdivant	4.00	2.00	1.25
180	Bob Allison	4.00	2.00	1.25
181	Paul Brown	4.00	2.00	1.25
182	Bob Nieman	4.00	2.00	1.25
183	Roger Craig	4.00	2.00	1.25
184	Haywood Sullivan	4.00	2.00	1.25
185	Roland Sheldon	4.00	2.00	1.25
186	*Mack Jones*	4.00	2.00	1.25
187	Gene Conley	4.00	2.00	1.25
188	Chuck Hiller	4.00	2.00	1.25
189	Dick Hall	4.00	2.00	1.25
190a	Wally Moon (With cap.)	20.00	10.00	6.00
190b	Wally Moon (No cap.)	6.00	3.00	1.75
191	Jim Brewer	4.00	2.00	1.25
192a	3rd Series Checklist (177- 264) (192 is Check List, 3)	7.00	3.50	2.00
192b	3rd Series Checklist (177- 264) (192 is Check List 3)	8.00	4.00	2.50
193	Eddie Kasko	4.00	2.00	1.25
194	*Dean Chance*	12.50	6.25	3.75
195	Joe Cunningham	4.00	2.00	1.25
196	Terry Fox	4.00	2.00	1.25
197	Daryl Spencer	4.00	2.00	1.25
198	Johnny Keane	4.00	2.00	1.25
199	*Gaylord Perry*	80.00	40.00	20.00
200	Mickey Mantle	650.00	325.00	162.50
201	Ike Delock	4.00	2.00	1.25
202	Carl Warwick	4.00	2.00	1.25
203	Jack Fisher	4.00	2.00	1.25
204	Johnny Weekly	4.00	2.00	1.25
205	Gene Freese	4.00	2.00	1.25
206	Washington Senators Team	7.00	3.50	2.00
207	Pete Burnside	4.00	2.00	1.25
208	Billy Martin	12.00	6.00	3.50
209	*Jim Fregosi*	15.00	7.50	4.50
210	Roy Face	6.00	3.00	1.75
211	Midway Masters (Frank Bolling, Roy McMillan)	4.50	2.25	1.25

#	Name			
212	Jim Owens	4.00	2.00	1.25
213	Richie Ashburn	20.00	10.00	6.00
214	Dom Zanni	4.00	2.00	1.25
215	Woody Held	4.00	2.00	1.25
216	Ron Kline	4.00	2.00	1.25
217	Walt Alston	10.00	5.00	3.00
218	*Joe Torre*	55.00	27.50	16.50
219	*Al Downing*	12.00	6.00	3.50
220	Roy Sievers	4.00	2.00	1.25
221	Bill Short	4.00	2.00	1.25
222	Jerry Zimmerman	4.00	2.00	1.25
223	Alex Grammas	4.00	2.00	1.25
224	Don Rudolph	4.00	2.00	1.25
225	Frank Malzone	4.00	2.00	1.25
226	San Francisco Giants Team	7.00	3.50	2.00
227	Bobby Tiefenauer	4.00	2.00	1.25
228	Dale Long	4.00	2.00	1.25
229	Jesus McFarlane	4.00	2.00	1.25
230	Camilo Pascual	4.00	2.00	1.25
231	Ernie Bowman	4.00	2.00	1.25
232	World Series Game 1 (Yanks Win Opener)	8.00	4.00	2.50
233	World Series Game 2 (Jay Ties It Up)	10.00	5.00	3.00
234	World Series Game 3 (Maris Wins It In the 9th)	22.50	11.00	7.00
235	World Series Game 4 (Ford Sets New Mark)	17.50	8.75	5.25
236	World Series Game 5 (Yanks Crush Reds in Finale)	7.00	3.50	2.00
237	World Series (The Winners Celebrate)	10.00	5.00	3.00
238	Norm Sherry	4.00	2.00	1.25
239	Cecil Butler	4.00	2.00	1.25
240	George Altman	4.00	2.00	1.25
241	Johnny Kucks	4.00	2.00	1.25
242	Mel McGaha	4.00	2.00	1.25
243	Robin Roberts	15.00	7.50	4.50
244	Don Gile	4.00	2.00	1.25
245	Ron Hansen	4.00	2.00	1.25
246	Art Ditmar	4.00	2.00	1.25
247	Joe Pignatano	4.00	2.00	1.25
248	Bob Aspromonte	4.00	2.00	1.25
249	Ed Keegan	4.00	2.00	1.25
250	Norm Cash	12.00	6.00	3.50
251	New York Yankees Team	50.00	25.00	12.50
252	Earl Francis	4.00	2.00	1.25
253	Harry Chiti	4.00	2.00	1.25
254	Gordon Windhorn	4.00	2.00	1.25
255	Juan Pizarro	4.00	2.00	1.25
256	Elio Chacon	4.00	2.00	1.25
257	Jack Spring	4.00	2.00	1.25
258	Marty Keough	4.00	2.00	1.25
259	Lou Klimchock	4.00	2.00	1.25
260	Bill Pierce	4.00	2.00	1.25
261	George Alusik	4.00	2.00	1.25
262	Bob Schmidt	4.00	2.00	1.25
263	The Right Pitch (Joe Jay, Bob Purkey, Jim Turner)	4.50	2.25	1.25
264	Dick Ellsworth	4.00	2.00	1.25
265	Joe Adcock	4.00	2.00	1.25
266	John Anderson	4.00	2.00	1.25
267	Dan Dobbek	4.00	2.00	1.25
268	Ken McBride	4.00	2.00	1.25
269	Bob Oldis	4.00	2.00	1.25
270	Dick Groat	4.00	2.00	1.25
271	Ray Rippelmeyer	4.00	2.00	1.25
272	Earl Robinson	4.00	2.00	1.25
273	Gary Bell	4.00	2.00	1.25
274	Sammy Taylor	4.00	2.00	1.25
275	Norm Siebern	4.00	2.00	1.25
276	Hal Kostad	4.00	2.00	1.25
277	4th Series Checklist (265-352)	7.00	3.50	2.00
278	Ken Johnson	4.00	2.00	1.25
279	Hobie Landrith	4.00	2.00	1.25
280	Johnny Podres	7.50	3.75	2.25
281	*Jake Gibbs*	7.50	3.75	2.25
282	Dave Hillman	4.00	2.00	1.25
283	Charlie Smith	4.00	2.00	1.25
284	Ruben Amaro	4.00	2.00	1.25
285	Curt Simmons	4.00	2.00	1.25
286	Al Lopez	9.00	4.50	2.75
287	George Witt	4.00	2.00	1.25
288	Billy Williams	35.00	17.50	8.75
289	Mike Krsnich	4.00	2.00	1.25
290	Jim Gentile	6.00	3.00	1.75
291	Hal Stowe	4.00	2.00	1.25
292	Jerry Kindall	4.00	2.00	1.25
293	Bob Miller	4.00	2.00	1.25
294	Philadelphia Phillies Team	7.50	3.75	2.25
295	Vern Law	4.00	2.00	1.25
296	Ken Hamlin	4.00	2.00	1.25
297	Ron Perranoski	4.00	2.00	1.25
298	Bill Tuttle	4.00	2.00	1.25
299	*Don Wert*	4.00	2.00	1.25
300	Willie Mays	250.00	125.00	62.50
301	Galen Cisco	4.00	2.00	1.25
302	*John Edwards*	4.00	2.00	1.25
303	Frank Torre	4.00	2.00	1.25
304	Dick Farrell	4.00	2.00	1.25
305	Jerry Lumpe	4.00	2.00	1.25
306	Redbird Rippers (Larry Jackson, Lindy McDaniel)	5.00	2.50	1.50
307	Jim Grant	4.00	2.00	1.25
308	Neil Chrisley	4.00	2.00	1.25
309	Moe Morhardt	4.00	2.00	1.25
310	Whitey Ford	50.00	25.00	12.50
311	Kubek Makes The Double Play (Tony Kubek)	12.00	6.00	3.50
312	Spahn Shows No-Hit Form (Warren Spahn)	15.00	7.50	4.50
313	Maris Blasts 61st (Roger Maris)	75.00	37.50	18.75
314	Colavito's Power (Rocky Colavito)	11.00	5.50	3.25
315	Ford Tosses a Curve (Whitey Ford)	20.00	10.00	6.00

#	Name			
316	Killebrew Sends One into Orbit (Harmon Killebrew)	20.00	10.00	6.00
317	Musial Plays 21st Season (Stan Musial)	17.50	8.75	5.25
318	The Switch Hitter Connects (Mickey Mantle)	150.00	75.00	37.50
319	McCormick Shows His Stuff (Mike McCormick)	6.00	3.00	1.75
320	Hank Aaron	175.00	87.50	43.75
321	Lee Stange	4.00	2.00	1.25
322	Al Dark	4.00	2.00	1.25
323	Don Landrum	4.00	2.00	1.25
324	Joe McClain	4.00	2.00	1.25
325	Luis Aparicio	15.00	7.50	4.50
326	Tom Parsons	4.00	2.00	1.25
327	Ozzie Virgil	4.00	2.00	1.25
328	Ken Walters	4.00	2.00	1.25
329	Bob Bolin	4.00	2.00	1.25
330	Johnny Romano	4.00	2.00	1.25
331	Moe Drabowsky	4.00	2.00	1.25
332	Don Buddin	4.00	2.00	1.25
333	Frank Cipriani	4.00	2.00	1.25
334	Boston Red Sox Team	9.00	4.50	2.75
335	Bill Bruton	4.00	2.00	1.25
336	Billy Muffett	4.00	2.00	1.25
337	Jim Marshall	4.00	2.00	1.25
338	Billy Gardner	4.00	2.00	1.25
339	Jose Valdivielso	4.00	2.00	1.25
340	Don Drysdale	50.00	25.00	12.50
341	Mike Hershberger	4.00	2.00	1.25
342	Ed Rakow	4.00	2.00	1.25
343	Albie Pearson	4.00	2.00	1.25
344	Ed Bauta	4.00	2.00	1.25
345	Chuck Schilling	4.00	2.00	1.25
346	Jack Kralick	4.00	2.00	1.25
347	Chuck Hinton	4.00	2.00	1.25
348	Larry Burright	4.00	2.00	1.25
349	Paul Foytack	4.00	2.00	1.25
350	Frank Robinson	50.00	25.00	12.50
351	Braves' Backstops (Del Crandall, Joe Torre)	12.00	6.00	3.50
352	Frank Sullivan	4.00	2.00	1.25
353	Bill Mazeroski	20.00	10.00	6.00
354	Roman Mejias	4.00	2.00	1.25
355	Steve Barber	4.00	2.00	1.25
356	Tom Haller	4.00	2.00	1.25
357	Jerry Walker	4.00	2.00	1.25
358	Tommy Davis	4.00	2.00	1.25
359	Bobby Locke	4.00	2.00	1.25
360	Yogi Berra	80.00	40.00	20.00
361	Bob Hendley	4.00	2.00	1.25
362	Ty Cline	4.00	2.00	1.25
363	Bob Roselli	4.00	2.00	1.25
364	Ken Hunt	4.00	2.00	1.25
365	Charley Neal	4.00	2.00	1.25
366	Phil Regan	4.00	2.00	1.25
367	5th Checklist (353-429)	8.00	4.00	2.50
368	Bob Tillman	4.00	2.00	1.25
369	Ted Bowsfield	4.00	2.00	1.25
370	Ken Boyer	7.50	3.75	2.25
371	Earl Battey	4.00	2.00	1.25
372	Jack Curtis	4.00	2.00	1.25
373	Al Heist	4.00	2.00	1.25
374	Gene Mauch	4.00	2.00	1.25
375	Ron Fairly	4.00	2.00	1.25
376	Bud Daley	4.00	2.00	1.25
377	Johnny Orsino	4.00	2.00	1.25
378	Bennie Daniels	4.00	2.00	1.25
379	Chuck Essegian	4.00	2.00	1.25
380	Lou Burdette	4.00	2.00	1.25
381	Chico Cardenas	4.00	2.00	1.25
382	Dick Williams	4.00	2.00	1.25
383	Ray Sadecki	4.00	2.00	1.25
384	Kansas City Athletics Team	8.00	4.00	2.50
385	Early Wynn	12.00	6.00	3.50
386	Don Mincher	4.00	2.00	1.25
387	*Lou Brock*	120.00	60.00	30.00
388	Ryne Duren	4.00	2.00	1.25
389	Smoky Burgess	4.00	2.00	1.25
390	Orlando Cepeda (All-Star)	10.00	5.00	3.00
391	Bill Mazeroski (All-Star)	12.00	6.00	3.50
392	Ken Boyer (All-Star)	7.00	3.50	2.00
393	Roy McMillan (All-Star)	4.00	2.00	1.25
394	Hank Aaron (All-Star)	60.00	30.00	15.00
395	Willie Mays (All-Star)	50.00	25.00	12.50
396	Frank Robinson (All-Star)	13.50	6.75	4.00
397	John Roseboro (All-Star)	4.00	2.00	1.25
398	Don Drysdale (All-Star)	13.50	6.75	4.00
399	Warren Spahn (All-Star)	13.50	6.75	4.00
400	Elston Howard	15.00	7.50	4.50
401	AL & NL Homer Kings (Roger Maris, Orlando Cepeda)	60.00	30.00	15.00
402	Gino Cimoli	4.00	2.00	1.25
403	Chet Nichols	4.00	2.00	1.25
404	Tim Harkness	4.00	2.00	1.25
405	Jim Perry	4.00	2.00	1.25
406	Bob Taylor	4.00	2.00	1.25
407	Hank Aguirre	4.00	2.00	1.25
408	Gus Bell	4.00	2.00	1.25
409	Pittsburgh Pirates Team	11.00	5.50	3.25
410	Al Smith	4.00	2.00	1.25
411	Danny O'Connell	4.00	2.00	1.25
412	Charlie James	4.00	2.00	1.25
413	Matty Alou	4.00	2.00	1.25
414	Joe Gaines	4.00	2.00	1.25
415	Bill Virdon	4.00	2.00	1.25
416	Bob Scheffing	4.00	2.00	1.25
417	Joe Azcue	4.00	2.00	1.25
418	Andy Carey	4.00	2.00	1.25
419	Bob Bruce	4.00	2.00	1.25
420	Gus Triandos	4.00	2.00	1.25
421	Ken MacKenzie	4.00	2.00	1.25
422	Steve Bilko	4.00	2.00	1.25
423	Rival League Relief Aces (Roy Face, Hoyt Wilhelm)	9.00	4.50	2.75
424	Al McBean	4.00	2.00	1.25
425	Carl Yastrzemski	125.00	62.50	31.25
426	Bob Farley	4.00	2.00	1.25

#	Name			
427	Jake Wood	4.00	2.00	1.25
428	Joe Hicks	4.00	2.00	1.25
429	Bill O'Dell	4.00	2.00	1.25
430	Tony Kubek	15.00	7.50	4.50
431	*Bob Rodgers*	4.00	2.00	1.25
432	Jim Pendleton	4.00	2.00	1.25
433	Jim Archer	4.00	2.00	1.25
434	Clay Dalrymple	4.00	2.00	1.25
435	Larry Sherry	4.00	2.00	1.25
436	Felix Mantilla	4.00	2.00	1.25
437	Ray Moore	4.00	2.00	1.25
438	Dick Brown	4.00	2.00	1.25
439	Jerry Buchek	4.00	2.00	1.25
440	Joe Jay	4.00	2.00	1.25
441a	6th Series Checklist (430-506) (Large "CHECKLIST.")	9.00	4.50	2.75
441b	6th Series Checklist (430-506) (Small "CHECKLIST.")	9.00	4.50	2.75
442	Wes Stock	4.00	2.00	1.25
443	Del Crandall	4.00	2.00	1.25
444	Ted Wills	4.00	2.00	1.25
445	Vic Power	4.00	2.00	1.25
446	Don Elston	4.00	2.00	1.25
447	Willie Kirkland	7.00	3.50	2.00
448	Joe Gibbon	7.00	3.50	2.00
449	Jerry Adair	7.00	3.50	2.00
450	Jim O'Toole	7.00	3.50	2.00
451	*Jose Tartabull*	7.00	3.50	2.00
452	Earl Averill	7.00	3.50	2.00
453	Cal McLish	7.00	3.50	2.00
454	Floyd Robinson	7.00	3.50	2.00
455	Luis Arroyo	7.00	3.50	2.00
456	Joe Amalfitano	7.00	3.50	2.00
457	Lou Clinton	7.00	3.50	2.00
458a	Bob Buhl ("M" on cap)	17.50	8.75	5.25
458b	Bob Buhl (Plain cap.)	15.00	7.50	4.50
459	Ed Bailey	7.00	3.50	2.00
460	Jim Bunning	20.00	10.00	6.00
461	*Ken Hubbs*	15.00	7.50	4.50
462a	Willie Tasby ("W" on cap)	17.50	8.75	5.25
462b	Willie Tasby (Plain cap.)	16.00	8.00	4.75
463	Hank Bauer	9.00	4.50	2.75
464	*Al Jackson*	7.00	3.50	2.00
465	Cincinnati Reds Team	11.00	5.50	3.25
466	Norm Cash (All-Star)	13.50	6.75	4.00
467	Chuck Schilling (All-Star)	7.00	3.50	2.00
468	Brooks Robinson (All-Star)	15.00	7.50	4.50
469	Luis Aparicio (All-Star)	11.00	5.50	3.25
470	Al Kaline (All-Star)	20.00	10.00	6.00
471	Mickey Mantle (All-Star)	225.00	112.50	56.25
472	Rocky Colavito (All-Star)	12.00	6.00	3.50
473	Elston Howard (All-Star)	10.00	5.00	3.00
474	Frank Lary (All-Star)	7.00	3.50	2.00
475	Whitey Ford (All-Star)	15.00	7.50	4.50
476	Baltimore Orioles Team	12.50	6.25	3.75
477	Andre Rodgers	7.00	3.50	2.00
478	Don Zimmer	12.50	6.25	3.75
479	*Joel Horlen*	7.00	3.50	2.00
480	Harvey Kuenn	7.00	3.50	2.00
481	Vic Wertz	7.00	3.50	2.00
482	Sam Mele	7.00	3.50	2.00
483	Don McMahon	7.00	3.50	2.00
484	Dick Schofield	7.00	3.50	2.00
485	Pedro Ramos	7.00	3.50	2.00
486	Jim Gilliam	12.00	6.00	3.50
487	Jerry Lynch	7.00	3.50	2.00
488	Hal Brown	7.00	3.50	2.00
489	Julio Gotay	7.00	3.50	2.00
490	Clete Boyer	13.50	6.75	4.00
491	Leon Wagner	7.00	3.50	2.00
492	Hal Smith	7.00	3.50	2.00
493	Danny McDevitt	7.00	3.50	2.00
494	Sammy White	7.00	3.50	2.00
495	Don Cardwell	7.00	3.50	2.00
496	Wayne Causey	7.00	3.50	2.00
497	Ed Bouchee	7.00	3.50	2.00
498	Jim Donohue	7.00	3.50	2.00
499	Zoilo Versalles	7.00	3.50	2.00
500	Duke Snider	60.00	30.00	15.00
501	Claude Osteen	7.00	3.50	2.00
502	Hector Lopez	7.00	3.50	2.00
503	Danny Murtaugh	7.00	3.50	2.00
504	Eddie Bressoud	7.00	3.50	2.00
505	Juan Marichal	40.00	20.00	10.00
506	Charley Maxwell	7.00	3.50	2.00
507	Ernie Broglio	7.00	3.50	2.00
508	Gordy Coleman	7.00	3.50	2.00
509	*Dave Giusti*	7.00	3.50	2.00
510	Jim Lemon	7.00	3.50	2.00
511	Bubba Phillips	7.00	3.50	2.00
512	Mike Fornieles	7.00	3.50	2.00
513	Whitey Herzog	7.00	3.50	2.00
514	Sherm Lollar	7.00	3.50	2.00
515	Stan Williams	7.00	3.50	2.00
516a	7th Series Checklist (507-598) (Boxes are yellow.)	9.00	4.50	2.75
516b	7th Series Checklist (507-598) (Boxes are white.)	9.00	4.50	2.75
517	Dave Wickersham	7.00	3.50	2.00
518	Lee Maye	7.00	3.50	2.00
519	Bob Johnson	7.00	3.50	2.00
520	Bob Friend	7.00	3.50	2.00
521	Jacke Davis	7.00	3.50	2.00
522	Lindy McDaniel	7.00	3.50	2.00
523	Russ Nixon (SP)	15.00	7.50	4.50
524	Howie Nunn (SP)	15.00	7.50	4.50
525	George Thomas	10.00	5.00	3.00
526	Hal Woodeshick (SP)	15.00	7.50	4.50
527	*Dick McAuliffe*	10.00	5.00	3.00
528	Turk Lown	10.00	5.00	3.00
529	John Schaive (SP)	10.00	5.00	3.00
530	Bob Gibson (SP)	125.00	112.50	56.25
531	Bobby G. Smith	10.00	5.00	3.00
532	Dick Stigman	10.00	5.00	3.00
533	Charley Lau (SP)	15.00	7.50	4.50
534	Tony Gonzalez (SP)	15.00	7.50	4.50
535	Ed Roebuck	10.00	5.00	3.00
536	Dick Gernert	10.00	5.00	3.00

#	Player	NM	EX	VG
537	Cleveland Indians Team	20.00	10.00	6.00
538	Jack Sanford	10.00	5.00	3.00
539	Billy Moran	10.00	5.00	3.00
540	Jim Landis (SP)	15.00	7.50	4.50
541	Don Nottebart (SP)	15.00	7.50	4.50
542	Dave Philley	10.00	5.00	3.00
543	Bob Allen (SP)	15.00	7.50	4.50
544	Willie McCovey (SP)	120.00	60.00	30.00
545	Hoyt Wilhelm (SP)	50.00	25.00	12.50
546	Moe Thacker (SP)	15.00	7.50	4.50
547	Don Ferrarese	10.00	5.00	3.00
548	Bobby Del Greco	10.00	5.00	3.00
549	Bill Rigney (SP)	15.00	7.50	4.50
550	Art Mahaffey (SP)	15.00	7.50	4.50
551	Harry Bright	10.00	5.00	3.00
552	Chicago Cubs Team (SP)	50.00	25.00	12.50
553	Jim Coates	10.00	5.00	3.00
554	Bubba Morton (SP)	15.00	7.50	4.50
555	John Buzhardt (SP)	15.00	7.50	4.50
556	Al Spangler	10.00	5.00	3.00
557	Bob Anderson (SP)	15.00	7.50	4.50
558	John Goryl	10.00	5.00	3.00
559	Mike Higgins	10.00	5.00	3.00
560	Chuck Estrada (SP)	15.00	7.50	4.50
561	Gene Oliver (SP)	15.00	7.50	4.50
562	Bill Henry	10.00	5.00	3.00
563	Ken Aspromonte	10.00	5.00	3.00
564	Bob Grim	10.00	5.00	3.00
565	Jose Pagan	10.00	5.00	3.00
566	Marty Kutyna (SP)	15.00	7.50	4.50
567	Tracy Stallard (SP)	15.00	7.50	4.50
568	Jim Golden	10.00	5.00	3.00
569	Ed Sadowski (SP)	15.00	7.50	4.50
570	Bill Stafford	10.00	5.00	3.00
571	Billy Klaus (SP)	15.00	7.50	4.50
572	Bob Miller (SP)	15.00	7.50	4.50
573	Johnny Logan	10.00	5.00	3.00
574	Dean Stone	10.00	5.00	3.00
575	Red Schoendienst	25.00	12.50	7.50
576	Russ Kemmerer (SP)	15.00	7.50	4.50
577	Dave Nicholson (SP)	15.00	7.50	4.50
578	Jim Duffalo	10.00	5.00	3.00
579	Jim Schaffer (SP)	15.00	7.50	4.50
580	Bill Monbouquette	10.00	5.00	3.00
581	Mel Roach	10.00	5.00	3.00
582	Ron Piche	10.00	5.00	3.00
583	Larry Osborne	10.00	5.00	3.00
584	Minnesota Twins Team (SP)	50.00	25.00	12.50
585	Glen Hobbie (SP)	15.00	7.50	4.50
586	Sammy Esposito (SP)	15.00	7.50	4.50
587	Frank Funk (SP)	15.00	7.50	4.50
588	Birdie Tebbetts	10.00	5.00	3.00
589	Bob Turley	17.50	8.75	5.25
590	Curt Flood	17.50	8.75	5.25
591	Rookie Parade Pitchers (*Sam McDowell, Ron Nischwitz, Art Quirk, Dick Radatz, Ron Taylor*)	75.00	37.50	18.75
592	Rookie Parade Pitchers (Bo Belinsky, Joe Bonikowski, Jim Bouton, Dan Pfister, Dave Stenhouse)	75.00	37.50	18.75
593	Rookie Parade Pitchers (*Craig Anderson, Jack Hamilton, Jack Lamabe, Bob Moorhead, Bob Veale*)	40.00	20.00	12.00
594	Rookie Parade Catchers (*Doug Camilli, Doc Edwards, Don Pavletich, Ken Retzer, Bob Uecker*)	75.00	37.50	18.75
595	Rookie Parade Infielders (Ed Charles, Marlin Coughtry, Bob Sadowski, Felix Torres)	25.00	12.50	7.50
596	Rookie Parade Infielders (*Bernie Allen, Phil Linz, Joe Pepitone, Rich Rollins*)	80.00	40.00	20.00
597	Rookie Parade Infielders (Rod Kanehl, Jim McKnight, Denis Menke, Amado Samuel)	40.00	20.00	12.00
598	Rookie Parade Outfielders (*Howie Goss, Jim Hickman, Manny Jimenez, Al Luplow, Ed Olivares*)	80.00	40.00	20.00

1962 Topps Baseball Bucks

Issued in their own one-cent package, "Baseball Bucks" measure 4-1/8" x 1-3/4", were printed in black on green paper and designed to resemble dollar bills. The center player portrait has a banner underneath with the player's name. His home park is shown on the right and there is some biographical information at left. The back features a large denomination, with the player's league and team logo on either side.

Poorly centered examples of this issue are the rule, rather than the exception. Sixty-two of the players appear on facsimile $1 notes. There are 24 $5 stars and 10 $10 superstars. Baseball Bucks are graded without regard to the vertical fold with which they were issued.

		NM	EX	VG
	Complete Set (96):	2,000	1,000	600.00
	Common Player:	7.50	3.75	2.25
	Wax Pack:	175.00		
(1)	Hank Aaron ($5)	50.00	25.00	15.00
(2)	Joe Adcock	7.50	3.75	2.25
(3)	George Altman	7.50	3.75	2.25
(4)	Jim Archer	7.50	3.75	2.25
(5)	Richie Ashburn ($5)	40.00	20.00	12.00
(6)	Ernie Banks ($10)	45.00	22.00	13.50
(7)	Earl Battey	7.50	3.75	2.25
(8)	Gus Bell	7.50	3.75	2.25
(9)	Yogi Berra ($5)	40.00	20.00	12.00
(10)	Ken Boyer ($10)	15.00	7.50	4.50
(11)	Jackie Brandt	7.50	3.75	2.25
(12)	Jim Bunning	15.00	7.50	4.50
(13)	Lou Burdette ($5)	7.50	3.75	2.25
(14)	Don Cardwell	7.50	3.75	2.25
(15)	Norm Cash ($5)	15.00	7.50	4.50
(16)	Orlando Cepeda ($5)	30.00	15.00	9.00
(17)	Roberto Clemente ($5)	200.00	100.00	60.00
(18)	Rocky Colavito ($5)	25.00	12.50	7.50
(19)	Chuck Cottier	7.50	3.75	2.25
(20)	Roger Craig	7.50	3.75	2.25
(21)	Bennie Daniels	7.50	3.75	2.25
(22)	Don Demeter	7.50	3.75	2.25
(23)	Don Drysdale	30.00	15.00	9.00
(24)	Chuck Estrada	7.50	3.75	2.25
(25)	Dick Farrell	7.50	3.75	2.25
(26)	Whitey Ford ($10)	40.00	20.00	12.00
(27)	Nellie Fox ($5)	30.00	15.00	9.00
(28)	Tito Francona	7.50	3.75	2.25
(29)	Bob Friend	7.50	3.75	2.25
(30)	Jim Gentile ($5)	7.50	3.75	2.25
(31)	Dick Gernert	7.50	3.75	2.25
(32)	Lenny Green	7.50	3.75	2.25
(33)	Dick Groat	7.50	3.75	2.25
(34)	Woody Held	7.50	3.75	2.25
(35)	Don Hoak	7.50	3.75	2.25
(36)	Gil Hodges ($5)	25.00	12.50	7.50
(37)	Frank Howard	10.00	5.00	3.00
(38)	Elston Howard	10.00	5.00	3.00
(39)	Dick Howser	7.50	3.75	2.25
(40)	Ken Hunt	7.50	3.75	2.25
(41)	Larry Jackson	7.50	3.75	2.25
(42)	Joe Jay	7.50	3.75	2.25
(43)	Al Kaline	30.00	15.00	9.00
(44)	Harmon Killebrew ($5)	40.00	20.00	12.00
(45)	Sandy Koufax ($5)	75.00	37.00	22.00
(46)	Harvey Kuenn	7.50	3.75	2.25
(47)	Jim Landis	7.50	3.75	2.25
(48)	Norm Larker	7.50	3.75	2.25
(49)	Frank Lary ($5)	7.50	3.75	2.25
(50)	Jerry Lumpe	7.50	3.75	2.25
(51)	Art Mahaffey	7.50	3.75	2.25
(52)	Frank Malzone	7.50	3.75	2.25
(53)	Felix Mantilla	7.50	3.75	2.25
(54)	Mickey Mantle ($10)	350.00	175.00	105.00
(55)	Roger Maris ($10)	45.00	22.00	13.50
(56)	Ed Mathews ($10)	35.00	17.50	10.50
(57)	Willie Mays ($10)	65.00	32.00	19.50
(58)	Ken McBride	7.50	3.75	2.25
(59)	Mike McCormick	7.50	3.75	2.25
(60)	Stu Miller	7.50	3.75	2.25
(61)	Minnie Minoso	10.00	5.00	3.00
(62)	Wally Moon ($5)	7.50	3.75	2.25
(63)	Stan Musial ($10)	60.00	30.00	18.00
(64)	Danny O'Connell	7.50	3.75	2.25
(65)	Jim O'Toole	7.50	3.75	2.25
(66)	Camilo Pascual ($5)	7.50	3.75	2.25
(67)	Jim Perry	7.50	3.75	2.25
(68)	Jimmy Piersall ($5)	12.00	6.00	3.50
(69)	Vada Pinson ($5)	12.00	6.00	3.50
(70)	Juan Pizarro	7.50	3.75	2.25
(71)	Johnny Podres	10.00	5.00	3.00
(72)	Vic Power ($5)	7.50	3.75	2.25
(73)	Bob Purkey	7.50	3.75	2.25
(74)	Pedro Ramos	7.50	3.75	2.25
(75)	Brooks Robinson ($5)	30.00	15.00	9.00
(76)	Floyd Robinson	7.50	3.75	2.25
(77)	Frank Robinson ($10)	35.00	17.50	10.50
(78)	Johnny Romano	7.50	3.75	2.25
(79)	Pete Runnels ($5)	7.50	3.75	2.25
(80)	Don Schwall	7.50	3.75	2.25
(81)	Bobby Shantz ($5)	7.50	3.75	2.25
(82)	Norm Siebern	7.50	3.75	2.25
(83)	Roy Sievers ($5)	7.50	3.75	2.25
(84)	Hal (W.) Smith	7.50	3.75	2.25
(85)	Warren Spahn ($10)	40.00	20.00	12.00
(86)	Dick Stuart	7.50	3.75	2.25
(87)	Tony Taylor	7.50	3.75	2.25
(88)	Lee Thomas	7.50	3.75	2.25
(89)	Gus Triandos	7.50	3.75	2.25
(90)	Leon Wagner	7.50	3.75	2.25
(91)	Jerry Walker	7.50	3.75	2.25
(92)	Bill White	7.50	3.75	2.25
(93)	Billy Williams	15.00	7.50	4.50
(94)	Gene Woodling	7.50	3.75	2.25
(95)	Early Wynn ($5)	15.00	7.50	4.50
(96)	Carl Yastrzemski	40.00	20.00	12.00

1962 Topps Stamps

An artistic improvement over the somewhat drab Topps stamps of the previous year, the 1962 stamps, 1-3/8" x 1-7/8", had color player photographs set on red or yellow backgrounds. As in 1961, they were issued in two-stamp panels as insert with Topps baseball cards. A change from 1961 was the inclusion of team emblems in the set. A complete set consists of 201 stamps; Roy Sievers was originally portrayed on the wrong team - Athletics - and was later corrected to the Phillies.

CARL YASTRZEMSKI
BOST. RED SOX   OUTFIELD

		NM	EX	VG
	Complete Set (200):	800.00	400.00	240.00
	Common Player:	3.00	1.50	.90
	Stamp Album (Red):	60.00	30.00	18.00
(1)	Hank Aaron	15.00	7.50	4.50
(2)	Jerry Adair	3.00	1.50	.90
(3)	Joe Adcock	3.00	1.50	.90
(4)	Bob Allison	3.00	1.50	.90
(5)	Felipe Alou	4.00	2.00	1.25
(6)	George Altman	3.00	1.50	.90
(7)	Joe Amalfitano	3.00	1.50	.90
(8)	Ruben Amaro	3.00	1.50	.90
(9)	Luis Aparicio	6.00	3.00	1.75
(10)	Jim Archer	3.00	1.50	.90
(11)	Bob Aspromonte	3.00	1.50	.90
(12)	Ed Bailey	3.00	1.50	.90
(13)	Jack Baldschun	3.00	1.50	.90
(14)	Ernie Banks	9.00	4.50	2.75
(15)	Earl Battey	3.00	1.50	.90
(16)	Gus Bell	3.00	1.50	.90
(17)	Yogi Berra	12.00	6.00	3.50
(18)	Dick Bertell	3.00	1.50	.90
(19)	Steve Bilko	3.00	1.50	.90
(20)	Frank Bolling	3.00	1.50	.90
(21)	Steve Boros	3.00	1.50	.90
(22)	Ted Bowsfield	3.00	1.50	.90
(23)	Clete Boyer	3.00	1.50	.90
(24)	Ken Boyer	4.00	2.00	1.25
(25)	Jackie Brandt	3.00	1.50	.90
(26)	Bill Bruton	3.00	1.50	.90
(27)	Jim Bunning	6.00	3.00	1.75
(28)	Lou Burdette	3.00	1.50	.90
(29)	Smoky Burgess	3.00	1.50	.90
(30)	Johnny Callizon (Callison)	3.00	1.50	.90
(31)	Don Cardwell	3.00	1.50	.90
(32)	Camilo Carreon	3.00	1.50	.90
(33)	Norm Cash	4.00	2.00	1.25
(34)	Orlando Cepeda	6.00	3.00	1.75
(35)	Roberto Clemente	20.00	10.00	6.00
(36)	Ty Cline	3.00	1.50	.90
(37)	Rocky Colavito	6.00	3.00	1.75
(38)	Gordon Coleman	3.00	1.50	.90
(39)	Chuck Cottier	3.00	1.50	.90
(40)	Roger Craig	3.00	1.50	.90
(41)	Del Crandall	3.00	1.50	.90
(42)	Pete Daley	3.00	1.50	.90
(43)	Clay Dalrymple	3.00	1.50	.90
(44)	Bennie Daniels	3.00	1.50	.90
(45)	Jim Davenport	3.00	1.50	.90
(46)	Don Demeter	3.00	1.50	.90
(47)	Dick Donovan	3.00	1.50	.90
(48)	Don Drysdale	10.00	5.00	3.00
(49)	John Edwards	3.00	1.50	.90
(50)	Dick Ellsworth	3.00	1.50	.90
(51)	Chuck Estrada	3.00	1.50	.90
(52)	Roy Face	3.00	1.50	.90
(53)	Ron Fairly	3.00	1.50	.90
(54)	Dick Farrell	3.00	1.50	.90
(55)	Whitey Ford	12.00	6.00	3.50
(56)	Mike Fornieles	3.00	1.50	.90
(57)	Nellie Fox	7.00	3.50	2.00
(58)	Tito Francona	3.00	1.50	.90
(59)	Gene Freese	3.00	1.50	.90
(60)	Bob Friend	3.00	1.50	.90
(61)	Gary Geiger	3.00	1.50	.90
(62)	Jim Gentile	3.00	1.50	.90
(63)	Tony Gonzalez	3.00	1.50	.90
(64)	Lenny Green	3.00	1.50	.90
(65)	Dick Groat	3.00	1.50	.90
(66)	Ron Hansen	3.00	1.50	.90
(67)	Al Heist	3.00	1.50	.90
(68)	Woody Held	3.00	1.50	.90
(69)	Ray Herbert	3.00	1.50	.90
(70)	Chuck Hinton	3.00	1.50	.90
(71)	Don Hoak	3.00	1.50	.90
(72)	Glen Hobbie	3.00	1.50	.90
(73)	Gil Hodges	6.00	3.00	1.75
(74)	Jay Hook	3.00	1.50	.90
(75)	Elston Howard	4.00	2.00	1.25
(76)	Frank Howard	3.00	1.50	.90
(77)	Dick Howser	3.00	1.50	.90
(78)	Ken Hunt	3.00	1.50	.90
(79)	Larry Jackson	3.00	1.50	.90
(80)	Julian Javier	3.00	1.50	.90
(81)	Joe Jay	3.00	1.50	.90
(82)	Bob Johnson	3.00	1.50	.90
(83)	Sam Jones	3.00	1.50	.90
(84)	Al Kaline	9.00	4.50	2.75
(85)	Eddie Kasko	3.00	1.50	.90
(86)	Harmon Killebrew	10.00	5.00	3.00
(87)	Sandy Koufax	15.00	7.50	4.50
(88)	Jack Kralick	3.00	1.50	.90
(89)	Tony Kubek	4.00	2.00	1.25
(90)	Harvey Kuenn	3.00	1.50	.90
(91)	Jim Landis	3.00	1.50	.90
(92)	Hobie Landrith	3.00	1.50	.90
(93)	Frank Lary	3.00	1.50	.90

(94)	Barry Latman	3.00	1.50	.90
(95)	Jerry Lumpe	3.00	1.50	.90
(96)	Art Mahaffey	3.00	1.50	.90
(97)	Frank Malzone	3.00	1.50	.90
(98)	Felix Mantilla	3.00	1.50	.90
(99)	Mickey Mantle	50.00	25.00	15.00
(100)	Juan Marichal	6.00	3.00	1.75
(101)	Roger Maris	13.50	6.75	4.00
(102)	J.C. Martin	3.00	1.50	.90
(103)	Ed Mathews	9.00	4.50	2.75
(104)	Willie Mays	15.00	7.50	4.50
(105)	Bill Mazeroski	6.00	3.00	1.75
(106)	Ken McBride	3.00	1.50	.90
(107)	Tim McCarver	3.00	1.50	.90
(108)	Joe McClain	3.00	1.50	.90
(109)	Mike McCormick	3.00	1.50	.90
(110)	Lindy McDaniel	3.00	1.50	.90
(111)	Roy McMillan	3.00	1.50	.90
(112)	Bob L. Miller	3.00	1.50	.90
(113)	Stu Miller	3.00	1.50	.90
(114)	Minnie Minoso	6.00	3.00	1.75
(115)	Bill Monbouquette	3.00	1.50	.90
(116)	Wally Moon	3.00	1.50	.90
(117)	Don Mossi	3.00	1.50	.90
(118)	Stan Musial	15.00	7.50	4.50
(119)	Russ Nixon	3.00	1.50	.90
(120)	Danny O'Connell	3.00	1.50	.90
(121)	Jim O'Toole	3.00	1.50	.90
(122)	Milt Pappas	3.00	1.50	.90
(123)	Camilo Pascual	3.00	1.50	.90
(124)	Albie Pearson	3.00	1.50	.90
(125)	Jim Perry	3.00	1.50	.90
(126)	Bubba Phillips	3.00	1.50	.90
(127)	Jimmy Piersall	3.00	1.50	.90
(128)	Vada Pinson	3.00	1.50	.90
(129)	Juan Pizarro	3.00	1.50	.90
(130)	Johnny Podres	3.00	1.50	.90
(131)	Leo Posada	3.00	1.50	.90
(132)	Vic Power	3.00	1.50	.90
(133)	Bob Purkey	3.00	1.50	.90
(134)	Pedro Ramos	3.00	1.50	.90
(135)	Bobby Richardson	3.00	1.50	.90
(136)	Brooks Robinson	10.00	5.00	3.00
(137)	Floyd Robinson	3.00	1.50	.90
(138)	Frank Robinson	10.00	5.00	3.00
(139)	Bob Rodgers	3.00	1.50	.90
(140)	Johnny Romano	3.00	1.50	.90
(141)	John Roseboro	3.00	1.50	.90
(142)	Pete Runnels	3.00	1.50	.90
(143)	Ray Sadecki	3.00	1.50	.90
(144)	Ron Santo	3.00	1.50	.90
(145)	Chuck Schilling	3.00	1.50	.90
(146)	Barney Schultz	3.00	1.50	.90
(147)	Don Schwall	3.00	1.50	.90
(148)	Bobby Shantz	3.00	1.50	.90
(149)	Bob Shaw	3.00	1.50	.90
(150)	Norm Siebern	3.00	1.50	.90
(151a)	Roy Sievers (Kansas City)	3.00	1.50	.90
(151b)	Roy Sievers (Philadelphia)	3.00	1.50	.90
(152)	Bill Skowron	4.00	2.00	1.25
(153)	Hal (W.) Smith	3.00	1.50	.90
(154)	Duke Snider	12.00	6.00	3.50
(155)	Warren Spahn	9.00	4.50	2.75
(156)	Al Spangler	3.00	1.50	.90
(157)	Daryl Spencer	3.00	1.50	.90
(158)	Gene Stephens	3.00	1.50	.90
(159)	Dick Stuart	3.00	1.50	.90
(160)	Haywood Sullivan	3.00	1.50	.90
(161)	Tony Taylor	3.00	1.50	.90
(162)	George Thomas	3.00	1.50	.90
(163)	Lee Thomas	3.00	1.50	.90
(164)	Bob Tiefenauer	3.00	1.50	.90
(165)	Joe Torre	6.00	3.00	1.75
(166)	Gus Triandos	3.00	1.50	.90
(167)	Bill Tuttle	3.00	1.50	.90
(168)	Zoilo Versalles	3.00	1.50	.90
(169)	Bill Virdon	3.00	1.50	.90
(170)	Leon Wagner	3.00	1.50	.90
(171)	Jerry Walker	3.00	1.50	.90
(172)	Lee Walls	3.00	1.50	.90
(173)	Bill White	3.00	1.50	.90
(174)	Hoyt Wilhelm	4.00	2.00	1.25
(175)	Billy Williams	6.00	3.00	1.75
(176)	Jake Wood	3.00	1.50	.90
(177)	Gene Woodling	3.00	1.50	.90
(178)	Early Wynn	4.00	2.00	1.25
(179)	Carl Yastrzemski	12.00	6.00	3.50
(180)	Don Zimmer	3.00	1.50	.90
(181)	Baltimore Orioles Logo	3.00	1.50	.90
(182)	Boston Red Sox Logo	3.00	1.50	.90
(183)	Chicago Cubs Logo	3.00	1.50	.90
(184)	Chicago White Sox Logo	3.00	1.50	.90
(185)	Cincinnati Reds Logo	3.00	1.50	.90
(186)	Cleveland Indians Logo	3.00	1.50	.90
(187)	Detroit Tigers Logo	3.00	1.50	.90
(188)	Houston Colts Logo	3.00	1.50	.90
(189)	Kansas City Athletics Logo	3.00	1.50	.90
(190)	Los Angeles Angels Logo	3.00	1.50	.90
(191)	Los Angeles Dodgers Logo	3.00	1.50	.90
(192)	Milwaukee Braves Logo	3.00	1.50	.90
(193)	Minnesota Twins Logo	3.00	1.50	.90
(194)	New York Mets Logo	3.00	1.50	.90
(195)	New York Yankees Logo	6.00	3.00	1.75
(196)	Philadelphia Phillies Logo	3.00	1.50	.90
(197)	Pittsburgh Pirates Logo	3.00	1.50	.90
(198)	St. Louis Cardinals Logo	3.00	1.50	.90
(199)	San Francisco Giants Logo	3.00	1.50	.90
(200)	Washington Senators Logo	3.00	1.50	.90

1962 Topps Stamps Panels

Some advanced collectors pursue the 1962 Topps stamps in the form of the two-stamp panels in which they were issued. The 200 stamps which make up the issue can be found on 245 different two-stamp panels, flanked at left by a smaller tab advertising the accompanying album. The

unnumbered stamps are listed here alphabetically according to the name of the player or team which apears on the left end of the panel. Values shown are for full three-piece panels.

		NM	EX	VG
Complete Panel Set (245):		2,750	1,375	825.00
Common Panel:		4.00	2.00	1.25
(1)	Hank Aaron/Ted Bowsfield	35.00	17.50	10.50
(2)	Jerry Adair/Tony Gonzalez	8.00	4.00	2.50
(3)	Joe Adcock/George Thomas	8.00	4.00	2.50
(4)	Bob Allison/Jim Davenport	8.00	4.00	2.50
(5)	Felipe Alou/Mickey Mantle	100.00	50.00	30.00
(6)	Felipe Alou/Chuck Schilling	9.00	4.50	2.75
(7)	George Altman/ Rocky Colavito	10.00	5.00	3.00
(8)	George Altman/Don Schwall	8.00	4.00	2.50
(9)	Joe Amalfitano/Jim Gentile	8.00	4.00	2.50
(10)	Joe Amalfitano/Vic Power	8.00	4.00	2.50
(11)	Ruben Amaro/ Carl Yastrzemski	30.00	15.00	9.00
(12)	Luis Aparicio/Dick Farrell	10.00	5.00	3.00
(13)	Luis Aparicio/Al Heist	10.00	5.00	3.00
(14)	Bob Aspromonte/Al Kaline	15.00	7.50	4.50
(15)	Ed Bailey/Jim Piersall	8.00	4.00	2.50
(16)	Ernie Banks/Milt Pappas	20.00	10.00	6.00
(17)	Earl Battey/Bob Clemente	35.00	17.50	10.50
(18)	Earl Battey/Ed Mathews	12.00	6.00	3.50
(19)	Gus Bell/Steve Boros	8.00	4.00	2.50
(20)	Gus Bell/Ty Cline	8.00	4.00	2.50
(21)	Yogi Berra/Roy Face	20.00	10.00	6.00
(22)	Yogi Berra/Jack Kralick	15.00	7.50	4.50
(23)	Dick Bertell/Hoyt Wilhelm	10.00	5.00	3.00
(24)	Dick Bertell/Don Zimmer	9.00	4.50	2.75
(25)	Steve Bilko/Ruben Amaro	8.00	4.00	2.50
(26)	Steve Bilko/Roy Sievers	8.00	4.00	2.50
(27)	Frank Bolling/Nellie Fox	10.00	5.00	3.00
(28)	Steve Boros/Art Mahaffey	8.00	4.00	2.50
(29)	Clete Boyer/Chuck Cottier	9.00	4.50	2.75
(30)	Ken Boyer/Bob Friend	9.00	4.50	2.75
(31)	Jackie Brandt/Frank Robinson	15.00	7.50	4.50
(32)	Bill Bruton/Ernie Banks	20.00	10.00	6.00
(33)	Bill Bruton/Jay Hook	8.00	4.00	2.50
(34)	Jim Bunning/Bob Miller	10.00	5.00	3.00
(35)	Jim Bunning/Jim O'Toole	10.00	5.00	3.00
(36)	Jim Bunning/Daryl Spencer	10.00	5.00	3.00
(37)	Lou Burdette/Ed Mathews	12.00	6.00	3.50
(38)	Lou Burdette/Willie Mays	35.00	17.50	10.50
(39)	Smoky Burgess/ Bobby Richardson	9.00	4.50	2.75
(40)	Johnny Callizon (Callison)/ Barry Latman	9.00	4.50	2.75
(41)	Johnny Callizon (Callison)/Frank Malzone	9.00	4.50	2.75
(42)	Johnny Callizon (Callison)/ Willie Mays	35.00	17.50	10.50
(43)	Don Cardwell/Hoyt Wilhelm	10.00	5.00	3.00
(44)	Norm Cash/Dick Bertell	9.00	4.50	2.75
(45)	Norm Cash/Don Cardwell	9.00	4.50	2.75
(46)	Norm Cash/Dick Howser	9.00	4.50	2.75
(47)	Ty Cline/Art Mahaffey	8.00	4.00	2.50
(48)	Rocky Colavito/Sam Jones	10.00	5.00	3.00
(49)	Gordon Coleman/Pete Daley	8.00	4.00	2.50
(50)	Gordon Coleman/ Danny O'Connell	8.00	4.00	2.50
(51)	Roger Craig/Ted Bowsfield	8.00	4.00	2.50
(52)	Roger Craig/Minnie Minoso	9.00	4.50	2.75
(53)	Del Crandall/Clete Boyer	9.00	4.50	2.75
(54)	Del Crandall/Ray Sadecki	8.00	4.00	2.50
(55)	Pete Daley/Bob Friend	8.00	4.00	2.50
(56)	Pete Daley/Mike McCormick	8.00	4.00	2.50
(57)	Clay Dalrymple/Woody Held	8.00	4.00	2.50
(58)	Clay Dalrymple/Pedro Ramos	8.00	4.00	2.50
(59)	Bennie Daniels/Jerry Walker	8.00	4.00	2.50
(60)	Jim Davenport/ Harmon Killebrew	15.00	7.50	4.50
(61)	Don Demeter/ Haywood Sullivan	8.00	4.00	2.50
(62)	Don Demeter/Gus Triandos	8.00	4.00	2.50
(63)	Don Demeter/Lee Walls	8.00	4.00	2.50
(64)	Dick Donovan/Jerry Adair	8.00	4.00	2.50
(65)	Dick Donovan/Jim Perry	8.00	4.00	2.50
(66)	Dick Donovan/Vada Pinson	9.00	4.50	2.75
(67)	John Edwards/Jerry Walker	8.00	4.00	2.50
(68)	Dick Ellsworth/Glen Hobbie	8.00	4.00	2.50
(69)	Dick Ellsworth/Pete Runnels	8.00	4.00	2.50
(70)	Chuck Estrada/Don Drysdale	12.00	6.00	3.50
(71)	Chuck Estrada/Al Kaline	15.00	7.50	4.50
(72)	Roy Face/Minnie Minoso	9.00	4.50	2.75
(73)	Ron Fairly/Jim Landis	8.00	4.00	2.50
(74)	Dick Farrell/Frank Lary	8.00	4.00	2.50
(75)	Whitey Ford/Joe Torre	15.00	7.50	4.50
(76)	Nellie Fox/Willie Mays	35.00	17.50	10.50
(77)	Tito Francona/Ken Boyer	9.00	4.50	2.75
(78)	Tito Francona/Bob Johnson	8.00	4.00	2.50
(79)	Gene Freese/Bob Allison	8.00	4.00	2.50
(80)	Gene Freese/Ernie Banks	15.00	7.50	4.50
(81)	Gary Geiger/ Bobby Richardson	9.00	4.50	2.75
(82)	Jim Gentile/Hal W. Smith	8.00	4.00	2.50
(83)	Dick Groat/Joe McClain	8.00	4.00	2.50
(84)	Al Heist/Frank Lary	8.00	4.00	2.50
(85)	Woody Held/Orlando Cepeda	10.00	5.00	3.00

(86)	Ray Herbert/Frank Bolling	8.00	4.00	2.50
(87)	Ray Herbert/Eddie Kasko	8.00	4.00	2.50
(88)	Chuck Hinton/Dick Groat	8.00	4.00	2.50
(89)	Chuck Hinton/Stu Miller	8.00	4.00	2.50
(90)	Don Hoak/Bob Allison	8.00	4.00	2.50
(91)	Gil Hodges/Bennie Daniels	10.00	5.00	3.00
(92)	Gil Hodges/John Edwards	10.00	5.00	3.00
(93)	Elston Howard/Bob Clemente	35.00	17.50	10.50
(94)	Dick Howser/Don Zimmer	9.00	4.50	2.75
(95)	Ken Hunt/Lenny Green	8.00	4.00	2.50
(96)	Larry Jackson/Smoky Burgess	8.00	4.00	2.50
(97)	Larry Jackson/Gary Geiger	8.00	4.00	2.50
(98)	Joe Jay/Johnny Romano	8.00	4.00	2.50
(99)	Bob Johnson/Bob Friend	8.00	4.00	2.50
(100)	Al Kaline/Don Hoak	15.00	7.50	4.50
(101)	Eddie Kasko/Nellie Fox	10.00	5.00	3.00
(102)	Sandy Koufax/Joe Adcock	30.00	15.00	9.00
(103)	Sandy Koufax/Hobie Landrith	30.00	15.00	9.00
(104)	Sandy Koufax/Bob Shaw	30.00	15.00	9.00
(105)	Jack Kralick/Minnie Minoso	9.00	4.50	2.75
(106)	Harvey Kuenn/Ken Hunt	8.00	4.00	2.50
(107)	Havey Kuenn/Gene Woodling	8.00	4.00	2.50
(108)	Hobie Landrith/Mike Fornieles	8.00	4.00	2.50
(109)	Barry Latman/Tony Kubek	9.00	4.50	2.75
(110)	Barry Latman/Johnny Podres	8.00	4.00	2.50
(111)	Frank Malzone/Johnny Podres	8.00	4.00	2.50
(112)	Frank Malzone/Duke Snider	15.00	7.50	4.50
(113)	Felix Mantilla/Camilo Carreon	8.00	4.00	2.50
(114)	Mickey Mantle/Hank Aaron	125.00	62.00	37.00
(115)	Mickey Mantle/Dick Stuart	110.00	55.00	33.00
(116)	Juan Marichal/Bill Bruton	12.00	6.00	3.50
(117)	Juan Marichal/Gene Freese	12.00	6.00	3.50
(118)	Juan Marichal/Don Hoak	12.00	6.00	3.50
(119)	Roger Maris/Lou Burdette	20.00	10.00	6.00
(120)	Roger Maris/Nellie Fox	20.00	10.00	6.00
(121)	Roger Maris/Lee Thomas	20.00	10.00	6.00
(122)	J.C. Martin/Felix Mantilla	8.00	4.00	2.50
(123)	J.C. Martin/Barney Schultz	8.00	4.00	2.50
(124)	Willie Mays/Tony Kubek	35.00	17.50	10.50
(125)	Bill Mazeroski/Earl Battey	10.00	5.00	3.00
(126)	Bill Mazeroski/Elston Howard	10.00	5.00	3.00
(127)	Bill Mazeroski/Early Wynn	12.00	6.00	3.50
(128)	Ken McBride/Joe Torre	9.00	4.50	2.75
(129)	Tim McCarver/Bill Tuttle	9.00	4.50	2.75
(130)	Lindy McDaniel/Jim Piersall	8.00	4.00	2.50
(131)	Roy McMillan/Bob Allison	8.00	4.00	2.50
(132)	Roy McMillan/Albie Pearson	8.00	4.00	2.50
(133)	Roy McMillan/Leon Wagner	8.00	4.00	2.50
(134)	Bob Miller/Ron Hansen	8.00	4.00	2.50
(135)	Stu Miller/Joe McCain	8.00	4.00	2.50
(136)	Bill Monbouquette/Don Hoak	8.00	4.00	2.50
(137)	Bill Monbouquette/Joe Torre	9.00	4.50	2.75
(138)	Wally Moon/Frank Malzone	8.00	4.00	2.50
(139)	Wally Moon/Juan Pizarro	8.00	4.00	2.50
(140)	Wally Moon/Brooks Robinson	20.00	10.00	6.00
(141)	Don Mossi/Bill Bruton	8.00	4.00	2.50
(142)	Don Mossi/Johnny Romano	8.00	4.00	2.50
(143)	Don Mossi/Al Spangler	8.00	4.00	2.50
(144)	Stan Musial/Whitey Ford	30.00	15.00	9.00
(145)	Stan Musial/Joe Torre	30.00	15.00	9.00
(146)	Russ Nixon/Ed Bailey	8.00	4.00	2.50
(147)	Russ Nixon/Lindy McDaniel	8.00	4.00	2.50
(148)	Danny O'Connell/ Mike McCormick	8.00	4.00	2.50
(149)	Jim O'Toole/Ron Hansen	8.00	4.00	2.50
(150)	Jim O'Toole/Gene Stephens	8.00	4.00	2.50
(151)	Camilo Pascual/Pete Daley	8.00	4.00	2.50
(152)	Camilo Pascual/Tim McCarver	9.00	4.50	2.75
(153)	Camilo Pascual/Bill Virdon	8.00	4.00	2.50
(154)	Albie Pearson/Julian Javier	8.00	4.00	2.50
(155)	Jim Perry/Frank Howard	8.00	4.00	2.50
(156)	Bubba Phillips/Don Drysdale	12.00	6.00	3.50
(157)	Vada Pinson/Tony Gonzalez	9.00	4.50	2.75
(158)	Vada Pinson/Frank Howard	9.00	4.50	2.75
(159)	Juan Pizarro/Jack Baldschun	8.00	4.00	2.50
(160)	Johnny Podres/Jim Archer	8.00	4.00	2.50
(161)	Leo Posada/Milt Pappas	8.00	4.00	2.50
(162)	Leo Posada/Johnny Romano	8.00	4.00	2.50
(163)	Vic Power/Hal W. Smith	8.00	4.00	2.50
(164)	Bob Purkey/Harmon Killebrew	15.00	7.50	4.50
(165)	Pedro Ramos/ Orlando Cepeda	10.00	5.00	3.00
(166)	Brooks Robinson/ Jack Baldschun	15.00	7.50	4.50
(167)	Brooks Robinson/Duke Snider	20.00	10.00	6.00
(168)	Floyd Robinson/Ron Fairly	8.00	4.00	2.50
(169)	Floyd Robinson/Tony Taylor	8.00	4.00	2.50
(170)	Bob Rodgers/Hank Aaron	35.00	17.50	10.50
(171)	Bob Rodgers/Roger Craig	8.00	4.00	2.50
(172)	Bob Rodgers/Johnny Romano	8.00	4.00	2.50
(173)	Johnny Romano/ Minnie Minoso	9.00	4.50	2.75
(174)	John Roseboro/ Bob Aspromonte		2.50	
(175)	John Roseboro/ Chuck Estrada		2.50	
(176)	John Roseboro/Bubba Phillips	8.00	4.00	2.50
(177)	Ray Sadecki/Chuck Cottier	8.00	4.00	2.50
(178)	Ron Santo/Ernie Banks	20.00	10.00	6.00
(179)	Ron Santo/Joe Jay	9.00	4.50	2.75
(180)	Ron Santo/Leo Posada	9.00	4.50	2.75
(181)	Chuck Schilling/Hank Aaron	35.00	17.50	10.50
(182)	Chuck Schilling/Dick Stuart	8.00	4.00	2.50
(183)	Barney Schultz/ Camilo Carreon	8.00	4.00	2.50
(184)	Don Schwall/Sam Jones	8.00	4.00	2.50
(185)	Bobby Shantz/Pete Runnels	8.00	4.00	2.50
(186)	Bob Shaw/Mike Fornieles	8.00	4.00	2.50
(187)	Bob Shaw/George Thomas	8.00	4.00	2.50
(188)	Norm Siebern/Dick Ellsworth	8.00	4.00	2.50
(189)	Norm Siebern/Bobby Shantz	8.00	4.00	2.50
(190)	Norm Siebern/Early Wynn	10.00	5.00	3.00
(191)	Roy Sievers/Carl Yastrzemski	30.00	15.00	9.00
(192)	Bill Skowron/Jim Davenport	9.00	4.50	2.75
(193)	Bill Skowron/Bob Purkey	9.00	4.50	2.75
(194)	Warren Spahn/Whitey Ford	20.00	10.00	6.00
(195)	Al Spangler/Jim Archer	8.00	4.00	2.50

No.	Name	NM	EX	VG
(196)	Al Spangler/Jay Hook	8.00	4.00	2.50
(197)	Daryl Spencer/Gene Stephens	8.00	4.00	2.50
(198)	Haywood Sullivan/Jerry Lumpe	8.00	4.00	2.50
(199)	Haywood Sullivan/Billy Williams	10.00	5.00	3.00
(200)	Tony Taylor/Jim Landis	8.00	4.00	2.50
(201)	Lee Thomas/Ed Mathews	12.00	6.00	3.50
(202)	Bob Tiefenauer/Jackie Brandt	8.00	4.00	2.50
(203)	Bob Tiefenauer/Jake Wood	8.00	4.00	2.50
(204)	Gus Triandos/Billy Williams	10.00	5.00	3.00
(205)	Zoilo Versalles/Whitey Ford	12.50	6.25	3.75
(206)	Zoilo Versalles/Stan Musial	30.00	15.00	9.00
(207)	Zoilo Veraalles/Warren Spahn	12.00	6.00	3.50
(208)	Bill Virdon/Bob Friend	8.00	4.00	2.50
(209)	Bill Virdon/Bill Tuttle	8.00	4.00	2.50
(210)	Leon Wagner/Jim Davenport	8.00	4.00	2.50
(211)	Leon Wagner/Julian Javier	8.00	4.00	2.50
(212)	Lee Walls/Jerry Lumpe	8.00	4.00	2.50
(213)	Bill White/Al Kaline	15.00	7.50	4.50
(214)	Bill White/Ken McBride	8.00	4.00	2.50
(215)	Bill White/Bill Monbouquette	8.00	4.00	2.50
(216)	Jake Wood/Frank Robinson	12.00	6.00	3.50
(217)	Gene Woodling/Lenny Green	8.00	4.00	2.50
(218)	Early Wynn/Glen Hobbie	10.00	5.00	3.00
(219)	Early Wynn/Ed Mathews	15.00	7.50	4.50
(220)	Angels/Athletics	8.00	4.00	2.50
(221)	Angels/Colts	9.00	4.50	2.75
(222)	Angels/Orioles	8.00	4.00	2.50
(223)	Athletics/Mets	10.00	5.00	3.00
(224)	Athletics/Pirates	9.00	4.50	2.75
(225)	Cardinals/Indians	9.00	4.50	2.75
(226)	Colts/Mets	12.00	6.00	3.50
(227)	Colts/Twins	9.00	4.50	2.75
(228)	Cubs/Senators	9.00	4.50	2.75
(229)	Giants/Red Sox	9.00	4.50	2.75
(230)	Giants/Tigers	9.00	4.50	2.75
(231)	Giants/White Sox	12.00	6.00	3.50
(232)	Indians/Reds	9.00	4.50	2.75
(233)	Mets/Dodgers	10.00	5.00	3.00
(234)	Orioles/Pirates	9.00	4.50	2.75
(235)	Phillies/Senators	9.00	4.50	2.75
(236)	Red Sox/Braves	9.00	4.50	2.75
(237)	Red Sox/Phillies	9.00	4.50	2.75
(238)	Reds/Indians	9.00	4.50	2.75
(239)	Reds/Yankees	12.50	6.25	3.75
(240)	Tigers/Braves	9.00	4.50	2.75
(241)	Twins/Dodgers	12.50	6.25	3.75
(242)	White Sox/Cubs	10.00	5.00	3.00
(243)	White Sox/Phillies	10.00	5.00	3.00
(244)	Yankees/Cardinals	12.50	6.25	3.75
(245)	Yankees/Reds	12.50	6.25	3.75

1963 Topps

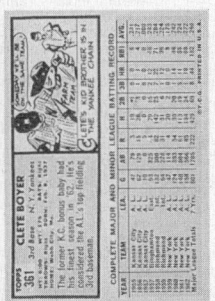

Although the number of cards dropped to 576, the 1963 Topps set is among the most popular of the 1960s. A color photo dominates the 2-1/2" x 3-1/2" card, but a colored circle at the bottom carries a black and white portrait as well. A colored band gives the player's name, team and position. The backs again feature career statistics and a cartoon, career summary and brief biographical details. The set is somewhat unlike those immediately preceding it in that there are fewer specialty cards. The major groupings are statistical leaders, World Series highlights and rookies. It is one rookie which makes the set special - Pete Rose. As one of the most avidly sought cards in history and a high-numbered card at that, the Rose rookie card accounts for much of the value of a complete set.

		NM	EX	VG
	Complete Set (576):	5,500	2,750	1,375
	Common Player (1-446):	4.00	2.00	1.25
	Common Player (447-576):	12.50	6.25	3.25
1	N.L. Batting Leaders (Hank Aaron, Bill White, Frank Robinson, Tommy Davis, Stan Musial)	40.00	20.00	10.00
2	A.L. Batting Leaders (Chuck Hinton, Mickey Mantle, Floyd Robinson, Pete Runnels, Norm Siebern)	40.00	20.00	10.00
3	N.L. Home Run Leaders (Hank Aaron, Ernie Banks, Orlando Cepeda, Willie Mays, Frank Robinson)	40.00	20.00	12.00
4	A.L. Home Run Leaders (Norm Cash, Rocky Colavito, Jim Gentile, Harmon Killebrew, Roger Maris, Leon Wagner)	20.00	10.00	6.00
5	N.L. E.R.A. Leaders (Don Drysdale, Bob Gibson, Sandy Koufax, Bob Shaw, Bob Purkey)	17.50	8.75	5.25

No.	Name	NM	EX	VG
6	A.L. E.R.A. Leaders (Hank Aguirre, Dean Chance, Eddie Fisher, Whitey Ford, Robin Roberts)	10.00	5.00	3.00
7	N.L. Pitching Leaders (Don Drysdale, Joe Jay, Art Mahaffey, Billy O'Dell, Bob Purkey, Jack Sanford)	12.00	6.00	3.50
8	A.L. Pitching Leaders (Jim Bunning, Dick Donovan, Ray Herbert, Camilo Pascual, Ralph Terry)	10.00	5.00	3.00
9	N.L. Strikeout Leaders (Don Drysdale, Dick Farrell, Bob Gibson, Sandy Koufax, Billy O'Dell)	20.00	10.00	6.00
10	A.L. Strikeout Leaders (Jim Bunning, Jim Kaat, Camilo Pascual, Juan Pizarro, Ralph Terry)	9.00	4.50	2.75
11	Lee Walls	4.00	2.00	1.25
12	Steve Barber	4.00	2.00	1.25
13	Philadelphia Phillies Team	7.00	3.50	2.00
14	Pedro Ramos	4.00	2.00	1.25
15	Ken Hubbs	10.00	5.00	3.00
16	Al Smith	4.00	2.00	1.25
17	Ryne Duren	4.00	2.00	1.25
18	Buc Blasters (Smoky Burgess, Roberto Clemente, Bob Skinner, Dick Stuart)	75.00	37.50	18.75
19	Pete Burnside	4.00	2.00	1.25
20	Tony Kubek	12.50	6.25	3.75
21	Marty Keough	4.00	2.00	1.25
22	Curt Simmons	4.00	2.00	1.25
23	Ed Lopat	4.00	2.00	1.25
24	Bob Bruce	4.00	2.00	1.25
25	Al Kaline	50.00	25.00	12.50
26	Ray Moore	4.00	2.00	1.25
27	Choo Choo Coleman	4.00	2.00	1.25
28	Mike Fornieles	4.00	2.00	1.25
29a	1962 Rookie Stars (Sammy Ellis, Ray Culp, John Boozer, Jesse Gonder)	6.00	3.00	1.75
29b	1963 Rookie Stars (Sammy Ellis, Ray Culp, John Boozer, Jesse Gonder)	4.00	2.00	1.25
30	Harvey Kuenn	4.00	2.00	1.25
31	Cal Koonce	4.00	2.00	1.25
32	Tony Gonzalez	4.00	2.00	1.25
33	Bo Belinsky	4.00	2.00	1.25
34	Dick Schofield	4.00	2.00	1.25
35	John Buzhardt	4.00	2.00	1.25
36	Jerry Kindall	4.00	2.00	1.25
37	Jerry Lynch	4.00	2.00	1.25
38	Bud Daley	4.00	2.00	1.25
39	Los Angeles Angels Team	7.00	3.50	2.00
40	Vic Power	4.00	2.00	1.25
41	Charlie Lau	4.00	2.00	1.25
42	Stan Williams	4.00	2.00	1.25
43	Veteran Masters (Casey Stengel, Gene Woodling)	7.50	3.75	2.25
44	Terry Fox	4.00	2.00	1.25
45	Bob Aspromonte	4.00	2.00	1.25
46	Tommie Aaron	5.00	2.50	1.50
47	Don Lock	4.00	2.00	1.25
48	Birdie Tebbetts	4.00	2.00	1.25
49	Dal Maxvill	4.00	2.00	1.25
50	Bill Pierce	4.00	2.00	1.25
51	George Alusik	4.00	2.00	1.25
52	Chuck Schilling	4.00	2.00	1.25
53	Joe Moeller	4.00	2.00	1.25
54a	1962 Rookie Stars (Nelson Mathews, Harry Fanok, Jack Cullen, Dave DeBusschere)	10.00	5.00	3.00
54b	1963 Rookie Stars (Jack Cullen, Dave DeBusschere, Harry Fanok, Nelson Mathews)	8.00	4.00	2.50
55	Bill Virdon	4.00	2.00	1.25
56	Dennis Bennett	4.00	2.00	1.25
57	Billy Moran	4.00	2.00	1.25
58	Bob Will	4.00	2.00	1.25
59	Craig Anderson	4.00	2.00	1.25
60	Elston Howard	9.00	4.50	2.75
61	Ernie Bowman	4.00	2.00	1.25
62	Bob Hendley	4.00	2.00	1.25
63	Cincinnati Reds Team	7.00	3.50	2.00
64	Dick McAuliffe	4.00	2.00	1.25
65	Jackie Brandt	4.00	2.00	1.25
66	Mike Joyce	4.00	2.00	1.25
67	Ed Charles	4.00	2.00	1.25
68	Friendly Foes (Gil Hodges, Duke Snider)	15.00	7.50	4.50
69	Bud Zipfel	4.00	2.00	1.25
70	Jim O'Toole	4.00	2.00	1.25
71	Bobby Wine	4.00	2.00	1.25
72	Johnny Romano	4.00	2.00	1.25
73	Bobby Bragan	4.00	2.00	1.25
74	Denver Lemaster	4.00	2.00	1.25
75	Bob Allison	4.00	2.00	1.25
76	Earl Wilson	4.00	2.00	1.25
77	Al Spangler	4.00	2.00	1.25
78	Marv Throneberry	4.00	2.00	1.25
79	1st Series Checklist (1-88)	6.00	3.00	1.75
80	Jim Gilliam	6.00	3.00	1.75
81	Jimmie Schaffer	4.00	2.00	1.25
82	Ed Rakow	4.00	2.00	1.25
83	Charley James	4.00	2.00	1.25
84	Ron Kline	4.00	2.00	1.25
85	Tom Haller	4.00	2.00	1.25
86	Charley Maxwell	4.00	2.00	1.25
87	Bob Veale	4.00	2.00	1.25
88	Ron Hansen	4.00	2.00	1.25
89	Dick Stigman	4.00	2.00	1.25
90	Gordy Coleman	4.00	2.00	1.25
91	Dallas Green	4.00	2.00	1.25
92	Hector Lopez	4.00	2.00	1.25

No.	Name	NM	EX	VG
93	Galen Cisco	4.00	2.00	1.25
94	Bob Schmidt	4.00	2.00	1.25
95	Larry Jackson	4.00	2.00	1.25
96	Lou Clinton	4.00	2.00	1.25
97	Bob Duliba	4.00	2.00	1.25
98	George Thomas	4.00	2.00	1.25
99	Jim Umbricht	4.00	2.00	1.25
100	Joe Cunningham	4.00	2.00	1.25
101	Joe Gibbon	4.00	2.00	1.25
102a	2nd Series Checklist (89-176) ("Checklist" in red on yellow.)	6.00	3.00	1.75
102b	2nd Series Checklist (89-176) ("Checklist" in white on red.)	10.00	5.00	3.00
103	Chuck Essegian	4.00	2.00	1.25
104	Lew Krausse	4.00	2.00	1.25
105	Ron Fairly	4.00	2.00	1.25
106	Bob Bolin	4.00	2.00	1.25
107	Jim Hickman	4.00	2.00	1.25
108	Hoyt Wilhelm	15.00	7.50	4.50
109	Lee Maye	4.00	2.00	1.25
110	Rich Rollins	4.00	2.00	1.25
111	Al Jackson	4.00	2.00	1.25
112	Dick Brown	4.00	2.00	1.25
113	Don Landrum (Photo actally Ron Santo.)	4.00	2.00	1.25
114	Dan Osinski	4.00	2.00	1.25
115	Carl Yastrzemski	40.00	20.00	12.00
116	Jim Brosnan	4.00	2.00	1.25
117	Jacke Davis	4.00	2.00	1.25
118	Sherm Lollar	4.00	2.00	1.25
119	Bob Lillis	4.00	2.00	1.25
120	Roger Maris	80.00	40.00	20.00
121	Jim Hannan	4.00	2.00	1.25
122	Julio Gotay	4.00	2.00	1.25
123	Frank Howard	4.00	2.00	1.25
124	Dick Howser	4.00	2.00	1.25
125	Robin Roberts	15.00	7.50	4.50
126	Bob Uecker	17.50	8.75	5.25
127	Bill Tuttle	4.00	2.00	1.25
128	Matty Alou	4.00	2.00	1.25
129	Gary Bell	4.00	2.00	1.25
130	Dick Groat	4.00	2.00	1.25
131	Washington Senators Team	7.00	3.50	2.00
132	Jack Hamilton	4.00	2.00	1.25
133	Gene Freese	4.00	2.00	1.25
134	Bob Scheffing	4.00	2.00	1.25
135	Richie Ashburn	15.00	7.50	4.50
136	Ike Delock	4.00	2.00	1.25
137	Mack Jones	4.00	2.00	1.25
138	Pride of N.L. (Willie Mays, Stan Musial)	80.00	40.00	20.00
139	Earl Averill	4.00	2.00	1.25
140	Frank Lary	4.00	2.00	1.25
141	Manny Mota		3.00	1.75
142	World Series Game 1 (Yanks' Ford Wins Series Opener)	11.00	5.50	3.25
143	World Series Game 2 (Sanford Flashes Shutout Magic)	5.00	2.50	1.50
144	World Series Game 3 (Maris Sparks Yankee Rally)	12.00	6.00	3.50
145	World Series Game 4 (Hiller Blasts Grand Slammer)	5.00	2.50	1.50
146	World Series Game 5 (Tresh's Homer Defeats Giants)	6.00	3.00	1.75
147	World Series Game 6 (Pierce Stars in 3-Hit Victory)	6.00	3.00	1.75
148	World Series Game 7 (Yanks Celebrate as Terry Wins)	7.00	3.50	2.00
149	Marv Breeding	4.00	2.00	1.25
150	Johnny Podres	6.00	3.00	1.75
151	Pittsburgh Pirates Team	10.00	5.00	3.00
152	Ron Nischwitz	4.00	2.00	1.25
153	Hal Smith	4.00	2.00	1.25
154	Walt Alston	7.50	3.75	2.25
155	Bill Stafford	4.00	2.00	1.25
156	Roy McMillan	4.00	2.00	1.25
157	Diego Segui	4.00	2.00	1.25
158	1963 Rookie Stars (Rogelio Alvarez, Tommy Harper, Dave Roberts, Bob Saverine)	6.00	3.00	1.75
159	Jim Pagliaroni	4.00	2.00	1.25
160	Juan Pizarro	4.00	2.00	1.25
161	Frank Torre	4.00	2.00	1.25
162	Minnesota Twins Team	7.00	3.50	2.00
163	Don Larsen	4.00	2.00	1.25
164	Bubba Morton	4.00	2.00	1.25
165	Jim Kaat	5.00	2.50	1.50
166	Johnny Keane	4.00	2.00	1.25
167	Jim Fregosi	4.00	2.00	1.25
168	Russ Nixon	4.00	2.00	1.25
169	1963 Rookie Stars (Dick Egan, Julio Navarro, Gaylord Perry, Tommie Sisk)	17.50	8.75	5.25
170	Joe Adcock	4.00	2.00	1.25
171	Steve Hamilton	4.00	2.00	1.25
172	Gene Oliver	4.00	2.00	1.25
173	Bombers' Best (Tom Tresh, Mickey Mantle, Bobby Richardson)	150.00	75.00	37.50
174	Larry Burright	4.00	2.00	1.25
175	Bob Buhl	4.00	2.00	1.25
176	Jim King	4.00	2.00	1.25
177	Bubba Phillips	4.00	2.00	1.25
178	Johnny Edwards	4.00	2.00	1.25
179	Ron Piche	4.00	2.00	1.25
180	Bill Skowron	10.00	5.00	3.00
181	Sammy Esposito	4.00	2.00	1.25
182	Albie Pearson	4.00	2.00	1.25
183	Joe Pepitone	10.00	5.00	3.00
184	Vern Law	4.00	2.00	1.25
185	Chuck Hiller	4.00	2.00	1.25
186	Jerry Zimmerman	4.00	2.00	1.25
187	Willie Kirkland	4.00	2.00	1.25
188	Eddie Bressoud	4.00	2.00	1.25
189	Dave Giusti	4.00	2.00	1.25

#	Player			
190	Minnie Minoso	6.00	3.00	1.75
191	3rd Series Checklist (177-264)	8.00	4.00	2.50
192	Clay Dalrymple	4.00	2.00	1.25
193	Andre Rodgers	4.00	2.00	1.25
194	Joe Nuxhall	4.00	2.00	1.25
195	Manny Jimenez	4.00	2.00	1.25
196	Doug Camilli	4.00	2.00	1.25
197	Roger Craig	4.00	2.00	1.25
198	Lenny Green	4.00	2.00	1.25
199	Joe Amalfitano	4.00	2.00	1.25
200	Mickey Mantle	650.00	325.00	162.50
201	Cecil Butler	4.00	2.00	1.25
202	Boston Red Sox Team	7.00	3.50	2.00
203	Chico Cardenas	4.00	2.00	1.25
204	Don Nottebart	4.00	2.00	1.25
205	Luis Aparicio	15.00	7.50	4.50
206	Ray Washburn	4.00	2.00	1.25
207	Ken Hunt	4.00	2.00	1.25
208	1963 Rookie Stars (Ron Herbel, John Miller, Ron Taylor, Wally Wolf)	4.00	2.00	1.25
209	Hobie Landrith	4.00	2.00	1.25
210	Sandy Koufax	150.00	75.00	37.50
211	Fred Whitfield	4.00	2.00	1.25
212	Glen Hobbie	4.00	2.00	1.25
213	Billy Hitchcock	4.00	2.00	1.25
214	Orlando Pena	4.00	2.00	1.25
215	Bob Skinner	4.00	2.00	1.25
216	Gene Conley	4.00	2.00	1.25
217	Joe Christopher	4.00	2.00	1.25
218	Tiger Twirlers (Jim Bunning, Frank Lary, Don Mossi)	7.50	3.75	2.25
219	Chuck Cottier	4.00	2.00	1.25
220	Camilo Pascual	4.00	2.00	1.25
221	Cookie Rojas	4.00	2.00	1.25
222	Chicago Cubs Team	7.00	3.50	2.00
223	Eddie Fisher	4.00	2.00	1.25
224	Mike Roarke	4.00	2.00	1.25
225	Joe Jay	4.00	2.00	1.25
226	Julian Javier	4.00	2.00	1.25
227	Jim Grant	4.00	2.00	1.25
228	1963 Rookie Stars (Max Alvis, Bob Bailey, Ed Kranepool, Tony Oliva)	50.00	25.00	12.50
229	Willie Davis	4.00	2.00	1.25
230	Pete Runnels	4.00	2.00	1.25
231	Eli Grba (Photo actually Ryne Duren.)	4.00	2.00	1.25
232	Frank Malzone	4.00	2.00	1.25
233	Casey Stengel	15.00	7.50	4.50
234	Dave Nicholson	4.00	2.00	1.25
235	Billy O'Dell	4.00	2.00	1.25
236	Bill Bryan	4.00	2.00	1.25
237	Jim Coates	4.00	2.00	1.25
238	Lou Johnson	4.00	2.00	1.25
239	Harvey Haddix	4.00	2.00	1.25
240	Rocky Colavito	17.50	8.75	5.25
241	Billy Smith	4.00	2.00	1.25
242	Power Plus (Hank Aaron, Ernie Banks)	60.00	30.00	15.00
243	Don Leppert	4.00	2.00	1.25
244	John Tsitouris	4.00	2.00	1.25
245	Gil Hodges	12.50	6.25	3.75
246	Lee Stange	4.00	2.00	1.25
247	New York Yankees Team	50.00	25.00	12.50
248	Tito Francona	4.00	2.00	1.25
249	Leo Burke	4.00	2.00	1.25
250	Stan Musial	100.00	50.00	25.00
251	Jack Lamabe	4.00	2.00	1.25
252	Ron Santo	13.50	6.75	4.00
253	1963 Rookie Stars (Len Gabrielson, Pete Jernigan, Deacon Jones, John Wojcik)	4.00	2.00	1.25
254	Mike Hershberger	4.00	2.00	1.25
255	Bob Shaw	4.00	2.00	1.25
256	Jerry Lumpe	4.00	2.00	1.25
257	Hank Aguirre	4.00	2.00	1.25
258	Alvin Dark	4.00	2.00	1.25
259	Johnny Logan	4.00	2.00	1.25
260	Jim Gentile	4.00	2.00	1.25
261	Bob Miller	4.00	2.00	1.25
262	Ellis Burton	4.00	2.00	1.25
263	Dave Stenhouse	4.00	2.00	1.25
264	Phil Linz	4.00	2.00	1.25
265	Vada Pinson	7.00	3.50	2.00
266	Bob Allen	4.00	2.00	1.25
267	Carl Sawatski	4.00	2.00	1.25
268	Don Demeter	4.00	2.00	1.25
269	Don Mincher	4.00	2.00	1.25
270	Felipe Alou	5.00	2.50	1.50
271	Dean Stone	4.00	2.00	1.25
272	Danny Murphy	4.00	2.00	1.25
273	Sammy Taylor	4.00	2.00	1.25
274	6th Series Checklist (265-352)	8.00	4.00	2.50
275	Ed Mathews	25.00	12.50	7.50
276	Barry Shetrone	4.00	2.00	1.25
277	Dick Farrell	4.00	2.00	1.25
278	Chico Fernandez	4.00	2.00	1.25
279	Wally Moon	4.00	2.00	1.25
280	Bob Rodgers	4.00	2.00	1.25
281	Tom Sturdivant	4.00	2.00	1.25
282	Bob Del Greco	4.00	2.00	1.25
283	Roy Sievers	4.00	2.00	1.25
284	Dave Sisler	4.00	2.00	1.25
285	Dick Stuart	4.00	2.00	1.25
286	Stu Miller	4.00	2.00	1.25
287	Dick Bertell	4.00	2.00	1.25
288	Chicago White Sox Team	8.00	4.00	2.50
289	Hal Brown	4.00	2.00	1.25
290	Bill White	4.00	2.00	1.25
291	Don Rudolph	4.00	2.00	1.25
292	Pumpsie Green	4.00	2.00	1.25
293	Bill Pleis	4.00	2.00	1.25
294	Bill Rigney	4.00	2.00	1.25
295	Ed Roebuck	4.00	2.00	1.25
296	Doc Edwards	4.00	2.00	1.25
297	Jim Golden	4.00	2.00	1.25
298	Don Dillard	4.00	2.00	1.25
299	1963 Rookie Stars (Tom Butters, Bob Dustal, Dave Morehead, Dan Schneider)	4.00	2.00	1.25
300	Willie Mays	160.00	80.00	40.00
301	Bill Fischer	4.00	2.00	1.25
302	Whitey Herzog	4.00	2.00	1.25
303	Earl Francis	4.00	2.00	1.25
304	Harry Bright	4.00	2.00	1.25
305	Don Hoak	4.00	2.00	1.25
306	Star Receivers (Earl Battey, Elston Howard)	5.00	2.50	1.50
307	Chet Nichols	4.00	2.00	1.25
308	Camilo Carreon	4.00	2.00	1.25
309	Jim Brewer	4.00	2.00	1.25
310	Tommy Davis	6.00	3.00	1.75
311	Joe McClain	4.00	2.00	1.25
312	Houston Colt .45s Team	13.50	6.75	4.00
313	Ernie Broglio	4.00	2.00	1.25
314	John Goryl	4.00	2.00	1.25
315	Ralph Terry	4.00	2.00	1.25
316	Norm Sherry	4.00	2.00	1.25
317	Sam McDowell	5.00	2.50	1.50
318	Gene Mauch	4.00	2.00	1.25
319	Joe Gaines	4.00	2.00	1.25
320	Warren Spahn	60.00	30.00	15.00
321	Gino Cimoli	4.00	2.00	1.25
322	Bob Turley	4.00	2.00	1.25
323	Bill Mazeroski	20.00	10.00	6.00
324	1963 Rookie Stars (Vic Davalillo, Phil Roof, Pete Ward, George Williams)	6.00	3.00	1.75
325	Jack Sanford	4.00	2.00	1.25
326	Hank Foiles	4.00	2.00	1.25
327	Paul Foytack	4.00	2.00	1.25
328	Dick Williams	4.00	2.00	1.25
329	Lindy McDaniel	4.00	2.00	1.25
330	Chuck Hinton	4.00	2.00	1.25
331	Series Foes (Bill Pierce, Bill Stafford)	7.00	3.50	2.00
332	Joel Horlen	4.00	2.00	1.25
333	Carl Warwick	4.00	2.00	1.25
334	Wynn Hawkins	4.00	2.00	1.25
335	Leon Wagner	4.00	2.00	1.25
336	Ed Bauta	4.00	2.00	1.25
337	Los Angeles Dodgers Team	15.00	7.50	4.50
338	Russ Kemmerer	4.00	2.00	1.25
339	Ted Bowsfield	4.00	2.00	1.25
340	Yogi Berra	100.00	50.00	25.00
341a	Jack Baldschun (White slash across body in inset photo.)	8.00	4.00	2.50
341b	Jack Baldschun (Slash repaired with red/mottling.)	4.00	2.00	1.25
342	Gene Woodling	4.00	2.00	1.25
343	Johnny Pesky	4.00	2.00	1.25
344	Don Schwall	4.00	2.00	1.25
345	Brooks Robinson	60.00	30.00	15.00
346	Billy Hoeft	4.00	2.00	1.25
347	Joe Torre	17.50	8.75	5.25
348	Vic Wertz	4.00	2.00	1.25
349	Zoilo Versalles	4.00	2.00	1.25
350	Bob Purkey	4.00	2.00	1.25
351	Al Luplow	4.00	2.00	1.25
352	Ken Johnson	4.00	2.00	1.25
353	Billy Williams	20.00	10.00	6.00
354	Dom Zanni	4.00	2.00	1.25
355	Dean Chance	4.00	2.00	1.25
356	John Schaive	4.00	2.00	1.25
357	George Altman	4.00	2.00	1.25
358	Milt Pappas	4.00	2.00	1.25
359	Haywood Sullivan	4.00	2.00	1.25
360	Don Drysdale	50.00	25.00	12.50
361	Clete Boyer	9.00	4.50	2.75
362	5th Series Checklist (353-429)	9.00	4.50	2.75
363	Dick Radatz	4.00	2.00	1.25
364	Howie Goss	4.00	2.00	1.25
365	Jim Bunning	13.50	6.75	4.00
366	Tony Taylor	4.00	2.00	1.25
367	Tony Cloninger	4.00	2.00	1.25
368	Ed Bailey	4.00	2.00	1.25
369	Jim Lemon	4.00	2.00	1.25
370	Dick Donovan	4.00	2.00	1.25
371	Rod Kanehl	4.00	2.00	1.25
372	Don Lee	4.00	2.00	1.25
373	Jim Campbell	4.00	2.00	1.25
374	Claude Osteen	4.00	2.00	1.25
375	Ken Boyer	10.00	5.00	3.00
376	Johnnie Wyatt	4.00	2.00	1.25
377	Baltimore Orioles Team	9.00	4.50	2.75
378	Bill Henry	4.00	2.00	1.25
379	Bob Anderson	4.00	2.00	1.25
380	Ernie Banks	100.00	50.00	25.00
381	Frank Baumann	4.00	2.00	1.25
382	Ralph Houk	6.00	3.00	1.75
383	Pete Richert	4.00	2.00	1.25
384	Bob Tillman	4.00	2.00	1.25
385	Art Mahaffey	4.00	2.00	1.25
386	1963 Rookie Stars (John Bateman, Larry Bearnarth, Ed Kirkpatrick, Garry Roggenburk)	5.00	2.50	1.50
387	Al McBean	4.00	2.00	1.25
388	Jim Davenport	4.00	2.00	1.25
389	Frank Sullivan	4.00	2.00	1.25
390	Hank Aaron	185.00	92.50	46.25
391	Bill Dailey	4.00	2.00	1.25
392	Tribe Thumpers (Tito Francona, Johnny Romano)	4.50	2.25	1.25
393	Ken MacKenzie	4.00	2.00	1.25
394	Tim McCarver	9.00	4.50	2.75
395	Don McMahon	4.00	2.00	1.25
396	Joe Koppe	4.00	2.00	1.25
397	Kansas City Athletics Team	9.00	4.50	2.75
398	Boog Powell	12.50	6.25	3.75
399	Dick Ellsworth	4.00	2.00	1.25
400	Frank Robinson	60.00	30.00	15.00
401	Jim Bouton	12.00	6.00	3.50
402	Mickey Vernon	4.00	2.00	1.25
403	Ron Perranoski	4.00	2.00	1.25
404	Bob Oldis	4.00	2.00	1.25
405	Floyd Robinson	4.00	2.00	1.25
406	Howie Koplitz	4.00	2.00	1.25
407	1963 Rookie Stars (Larry Elliot, Frank Kostro, Chico Ruiz, Dick Simpson)	4.00	2.00	1.25
408	Billy Gardner	4.00	2.00	1.25
409	Roy Face	4.00	2.00	1.25
410	Earl Battey	4.00	2.00	1.25
411	Jim Constable	4.00	2.00	1.25
412	Dodgers' Big Three (Johnny Podres, Don Drysdale, Sandy Koufax)	50.00	25.00	12.50
413	Jerry Walker	4.00	2.00	1.25
414	Ty Cline	4.00	2.00	1.25
415	Bob Gibson	60.00	30.00	15.00
416	Alex Grammas	4.00	2.00	1.25
417	San Francisco Giants Team	9.00	4.50	2.75
418	Johnny Orsino	4.00	2.00	1.25
419	Tracy Stallard	4.00	2.00	1.25
420	Bobby Richardson	12.50	6.25	3.75
421	Tom Morgan	4.00	2.00	1.25
422	Fred Hutchinson	4.00	2.00	1.25
423	Ed Hobaugh	4.00	2.00	1.25
424	Charley Smith	4.00	2.00	1.25
425	Smoky Burgess	4.00	2.00	1.25
426	Barry Latman	4.00	2.00	1.25
427	Bernie Allen	4.00	2.00	1.25
428	Carl Boles	4.00	2.00	1.25
429	Lou Burdette	4.00	2.00	1.25
430	Norm Siebern	4.00	2.00	1.25
431a	6th Series Checklist (430-506) ("Checklist" in black on front.)	8.00	4.00	2.50
431b	6th Series Checklist (430-506) ("Checklist" in white.)	20.00	10.00	6.00
432	Roman Mejias	4.00	2.00	1.25
433	Denis Menke	4.00	2.00	1.25
434	Johnny Callison	4.00	2.00	1.25
435	Woody Held	4.00	2.00	1.25
436	Tim Harkness	4.00	2.00	1.25
437	Bill Bruton	4.00	2.00	1.25
438	Wes Stock	4.00	2.00	1.25
439	Don Zimmer	6.00	3.00	1.75
440	Juan Marichal	25.00	12.50	7.50
441	Lee Thomas	4.00	2.00	1.25
442	J.C. Hartman	4.00	2.00	1.25
443	Jim Piersall	7.00	3.50	2.00
444	Jim Maloney	4.00	2.00	1.25
445	Norm Cash	9.00	4.50	2.75
446	Whitey Ford	60.00	30.00	15.00
447	Felix Mantilla	12.50	6.25	3.25
448	Jack Kralick	12.50	6.25	3.25
449	Jose Tartabull	12.50	6.25	3.25
450	Bob Friend	12.50	6.25	3.25
451	Cleveland Indians Team	20.00	10.00	6.00
452	Barney Schultz	12.50	6.25	3.25
453	Jake Wood	12.50	6.25	3.25
454a	Art Fowler (Card # on orange background.)	12.50	6.25	3.25
454b	Art Fowler (Card # on white background.)	30.00	15.00	9.00
455	Ruben Amaro	12.50	6.25	3.25
456	Jim Coker	12.50	6.25	3.25
457	Tex Clevenger	12.50	6.25	3.25
458	Al Lopez	20.00	10.00	6.00
459	Dick LeMay	12.50	6.25	3.25
460	Del Crandall	12.50	6.25	3.25
461	Norm Bass	12.50	6.25	3.25
462	Wally Post	12.50	6.25	3.25
463	Joe Schaffernoth	12.50	6.25	3.25
464	Ken Aspromonte	12.50	6.25	3.25
465	Chuck Estrada	12.50	6.25	3.25
466	1963 Rookie Stars (Bill Freehan, Tony Martinez, Nate Oliver, Jerry Robinson)	60.00	30.00	15.00
467	Phil Ortega	12.50	6.25	3.25
468	Carroll Hardy	12.50	6.25	3.25
469	Jay Hook	12.50	6.25	3.25
470	Tom Tresh (SP)	40.00	20.00	10.00
471	Ken Retzer	12.50	6.25	3.25
472	Lou Brock	75.00	37.50	18.75
473	New York Mets Team	75.00	37.50	18.75
474	Jack Fisher	12.50	6.25	3.25
475	Gus Triandos	12.50	6.25	3.25
476	Frank Funk	12.50	6.25	3.25
477	Donn Clendenon	12.50	6.25	3.25
478	Paul Brown	12.50	6.25	3.25
479	Ed Brinkman	12.50	6.25	3.25
480	Bill Monbouquette	12.50	6.25	3.25
481	Bob Taylor	12.50	6.25	3.25
482	Felix Torres	12.50	6.25	3.25
483	Jim Owens	12.50	6.25	3.25
484	Dale Long (SP)	15.00	7.50	4.50
485	Jim Landis	12.50	6.25	3.25
486	Ray Sadecki	12.50	6.25	3.25
487	John Roseboro	12.50	6.25	3.25
488	Jerry Adair	12.50	6.25	3.25
489	Paul Toth	12.50	6.25	3.25
490	Willie McCovey	100.00	50.00	25.00
491	Harry Craft	12.50	6.25	3.25
492	Dave Wickersham	12.50	6.25	3.25
493	Walt Bond	12.50	6.25	3.25
494	Phil Regan	12.50	6.25	3.25
495	Frank Thomas (SP)	15.00	7.50	4.50
496	1963 Rookie Stars (Carl Bouldin, Steve Dalkowski, Fred Newman, Jack Smith)	20.00	10.00	6.00
497	Bennie Daniels	12.50	6.25	3.25
498	Eddie Kasko	12.50	6.25	3.25
499	J.C. Martin	12.50	6.25	3.25
500	Harmon Killebrew (SP)	150.00	75.00	37.50
501	Joe Azcue	12.50	6.25	3.25
502	Daryl Spencer	12.50	6.25	3.25
503	Milwaukee Braves Team	15.00	7.50	4.50
504	Bob Johnson	12.50	6.25	3.25
505	Curt Flood	15.00	7.50	4.50
506	Gene Green	12.50	6.25	3.25

		NM	EX	VG
507	Roland Sheldon	12.50	6.25	3.25
508	Ted Savage	12.50	6.25	3.25
509a	7th Series Checklist (507-576) (Copyright centered.)	17.50	8.75	5.25
509b	7th Series Checklist (509-576) (Copyright to right.)	17.50	8.75	5.25
510	Ken McBride	12.50	6.25	3.25
511	Charlie Neal	12.50	6.25	3.25
512	Cal McLish	12.50	6.25	3.25
513	Gary Geiger	12.50	6.25	3.25
514	Larry Osborne	12.50	6.25	3.25
515	Don Elston	12.50	6.25	3.25
516	Purnal Goldy	12.50	6.25	3.25
517	Hal Woodeshick	12.50	6.25	3.25
518	Don Blasingame	12.50	6.25	3.25
519	Claude Raymond	12.50	6.25	3.25
520	Orlando Cepeda	30.00	15.00	9.00
521	Dan Pfister	12.50	6.25	3.25
522	1963 Rookie Stars (Mel Nelson, Gary Peters, Art Quirk, Jim Roland)			
523	Bill Kunkel	12.50	6.25	3.25
524	St. Louis Cardinals Team	20.00	10.00	6.00
525	Nellie Fox	50.00	25.00	12.50
526	Dick Hall	12.50	6.25	3.25
527	Ed Sadowski	12.50	6.25	3.25
528	Carl Willey	12.50	6.25	3.25
529	Wes Covington	12.50	6.25	3.25
530	Don Mossi	12.50	6.25	3.25
531	Sam Mele	12.50	6.25	3.25
532	Steve Boros	12.50	6.25	3.25
533	Bobby Shantz	12.50	6.25	3.25
534	Ken Walters	12.50	6.25	3.25
535	Jim Perry	12.50	6.25	3.25
536	Norm Larker	12.50	6.25	3.25
537	1963 Rookie Stars (Pedro Gonzalez, Ken McMullen, Pete Rose, Al Weis)	900.00	450.00	225.00
538	George Brunet	12.50	6.25	3.25
539	Wayne Causey	12.50	6.25	3.25
540	Bob Clemente	250.00	125.00	62.00
541	Ron Moeller	12.50	6.25	3.25
542	Lou Klimchock	12.50	6.25	3.25
543	Russ Snyder	12.50	6.25	3.25
544	1963 Rookie Stars (Duke Carmel, Bill Haas, Dick Phillips, Rusty Staub)	50.00	25.00	12.50
545	Jose Pagan	12.50	6.25	3.25
546	Hal Reniff	12.50	6.25	3.25
547	Gus Bell	12.50	6.25	3.25
548	Tom Satriano	12.50	6.25	3.25
549	1963 Rookie Stars (Marcelino Lopez, Pete Lovrich, Elmo Plaskett, Paul Ratliff)	13.00	6.50	3.25
550	Duke Snider	75.00	37.50	18.75
551	Billy Klaus	12.50	6.25	3.25
552	Detroit Tigers Team	50.00	25.00	12.50
553	1963 Rookie Stars (Brock Davis, Jim Gosger, John Herrnstein, Willie Stargell)	120.00	60.00	30.00
554	Hank Fischer	12.50	6.25	3.25
555	John Blanchard	15.00	7.50	3.75
556	Al Worthington	12.50	6.25	3.25
557	Cuno Barragan	12.50	6.25	3.25
558	1963 Rookie Stars (Bill Faul, Ron Hunt, Bob Lipski, Al Moran)	13.00	6.50	3.25
559	Danny Murtaugh	12.50	6.25	3.25
560	Ray Herbert	12.50	6.25	3.25
561	Mike de la Hoz	12.50	6.25	3.25
562	1963 Rookie Stars (Randy Cardinal, Dave McNally, Don Rowe, Ken Rowe)	25.00	12.50	7.50
563	Mike McCormick	12.50	6.25	3.25
564	George Banks	12.50	6.25	3.25
565	Larry Sherry	12.50	6.25	3.25
566	Cliff Cook	12.50	6.25	3.25
567	Jim Duffalo	12.50	6.25	3.25
568	Bob Sadowski	12.50	6.25	3.25
569	Luis Arroyo	12.50	6.25	3.25
570	Frank Bolling	12.50	6.25	3.25
571	Johnny Klippstein	12.50	6.25	3.25
572	Jack Spring	12.50	6.25	3.25
573	Coot Veal	12.50	6.25	3.25
574	Hal Kolstad	12.50	6.25	3.25
575	Don Cardwell	12.50	6.25	3.25
576	Johnny Temple	13.50	5.00	3.00

1963 Topps Famous Americans Stamps

Actually marketed as "Stamp Gum," this obscure test issue features 80 perforated stamps depicting great Americans from all walks of life, including two baseball players. The 2-9/16" x 1-3/8" stamps are printed in black, blue and yellow and combine a photographic portrait with a cartoon drawing. Centering is often a problem with these pieces. Only the baseball players are listed here.

		NM	EX	VG
50	Babe Ruth	300.00	150.00	90.00
60	Lou Gehrig	250.00	125.00	75.00

1963 Topps Mickey Mantle Plaque

Advertised as a "mask" on high-number 1963 Topps wax wrappers, this is actually a plastic plaque. About 6" x 8", the plaque features a color picture of Mantle in embossed plastic with a faux wood frame, also embossed plastic, around it. A holed tab at top allows hanging.

	NM	EX	VG
Mickey Mantle	3,500	1,750	1,050

1963 Topps Peel-Offs

Measuring 1-1/4" x 2-3/4", Topps Peel-Offs were an insert with 1963 Topps baseball cards. There are 46 players in the unnumbered set, each pictured in a color photo inside an oval with the player's name, team and position in a band below. The back of the Peel-Off is removable, leaving a sticky surface that made the Peel-Off a popular decorative item among youngsters of the day. Naturally, that makes them quite scarce today. The stickers can be found both blank-backed (much scarcer) and with instructions printed on the peel-off backing.

		NM	EX	VG
	Complete Set (46):	525.00	275.00	160.00
	Common Player:	4.00	2.00	1.25
(1)	Hank Aaron	35.00	17.50	10.00
(2)	Luis Aparicio	12.50	6.25	3.75
(3)	Richie Ashburn	17.50	8.75	5.25
(4)	Bob Aspromonte	4.00	2.00	1.25
(5)	Ernie Banks	22.50	11.00	6.75
(6)	Ken Boyer	7.50	3.75	2.25
(7)	Jim Bunning	10.00	5.00	3.00
(8)	Johnny Callison	4.00	2.00	1.25
(9)	Orlando Cepeda	10.00	5.00	3.00
(10)	Roberto Clemente	40.00	20.00	12.00
(11)	Rocky Colavito	9.00	4.50	2.75
(12)	Tommy Davis	4.00	2.00	1.25
(13)	Dick Donovan	4.00	2.00	1.25
(14)	Don Drysdale	15.00	7.50	4.50
(15)	Dick Farrell	4.00	2.00	1.25
(16)	Jim Gentile	4.00	2.00	1.25
(17)	Ray Herbert	4.00	2.00	1.25
(18)	Chuck Hinton	4.00	2.00	1.25
(19)	Ken Hubbs	7.50	3.75	2.25
(20)	Al Jackson	4.00	2.00	1.25
(21)	Al Kaline	17.50	8.75	5.25
(22)	Harmon Killebrew	17.50	8.75	5.25
(23)	Sandy Koufax	40.00	20.00	12.00
(24)	Jerry Lumpe	4.00	2.00	1.25
(25)	Art Mahaffey	4.00	2.00	1.25
(26)	Mickey Mantle	100.00	50.00	30.00
(27)	Willie Mays	35.00	17.50	10.00
(28)	Bill Mazeroski	12.50	6.25	3.75
(29)	Bill Monbouquette	4.00	2.00	1.25
(30)	Stan Musial	35.00	17.50	10.00
(31)	Camilo Pascual	4.00	2.00	1.25
(32)	Bob Purkey	4.00	2.00	1.25
(33)	Bobby Richardson	9.00	4.50	2.75
(34)	Brooks Robinson	17.50	8.75	5.25
(35)	Floyd Robinson	4.00	2.00	1.25
(36)	Frank Robinson	17.50	8.75	5.25
(37)	Bob Rodgers	4.00	2.00	1.25
(38)	Johnny Romano	4.00	2.00	1.25
(39)	Jack Sanford	4.00	2.00	1.25
(40)	Norm Siebern	4.00	2.00	1.25
(41)	Warren Spahn	17.50	8.75	5.25
(42)	Dave Stenhouse	4.00	2.00	1.25
(43)	Ralph Terry	4.00	2.00	1.25
(44)	Lee Thomas	4.00	2.00	1.25
(45)	Bill White	4.00	2.00	1.25
(46)	Carl Yastrzemski	20.00	10.00	6.00

1963 Topps Valentine Foldees

Featuring the artwork of 1960s cartoonist Jack Davis, this set of specialty cards had the left and right panels of the 4-1/2" x 2-3/8" pieces slit to allow either the top or the bottom half of the portrait to be folded over the central panel to create funny combinations. There were 55 cards in the series; Babe Ruth is the only baseball player included.

		NM	EX	VG
	Complete Set (55):	150.00	75.00	45.00
6	Babe Ruth	25.00	12.50	7.50

1964 Topps

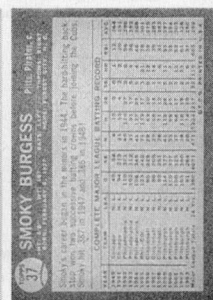

The 1964 Topps set is a 587-card issue of 2-1/2" x 3-1/2" cards which is considered by many as being among the company's best efforts. Card fronts feature a large color photo which blends into a top panel which contains the team name, while a panel below the picture carries the player's name and position. An interesting innovation on the back is a baseball quiz question which required the rubbing of a white panel to reveal the answer. As in 1963, specialty cards remained modest in number with a 12-card set of statistical leaders, a few multi-player cards, rookies and World Series highlights. An interesting card is an "In Memoriam" card for Ken Hubbs who was killed in an airplane crash.

		NM	EX	VG
	Complete Set (587):	4,250	2,125	1,250
	Common Player (1-370):	3.50	1.75	1.00
	Common Player (371-522):	6.00	3.00	1.75
	Common Player (523-587):	9.00	4.50	2.75
1	N.L. E.R.A. Leaders (Dick Ellsworth, Bob Friend, Sandy Koufax)	25.00	12.50	6.25
2	A.L. E.R.A. Leaders (Camilo Pascual, Gary Peters, Juan Pizarro)	12.00	3.00	2.00
3	N.L. Pitching Leaders (Sandy Koufax, Jim Maloney, Juan Marichal, Warren Spahn)	20.00	10.00	6.00
4a	A.L. Pitching Leaders (Jim Bouton, Whitey Ford, Camilo Pascual) (Apostrophe after "Pitching" on back.)	17.50	8.75	5.25
4b	A.L. Pitching Leaders (Jim Bouton, Whitey Ford, Camilo Pascual) (No apostrophe.)	17.50	8.75	5.25
5	N.L. Strikeout Leaders (Don Drysdale, Sandy Koufax, Jim Maloney)	20.00	10.00	6.00
6	A.L. Strikeout Leaders (Jim Bunning, Camilo Pascual, Dick Stigman)	12.50	6.25	3.75
7	N.L. Batting Leaders (Hank Aaron, Roberto Clemente, Tommy Davis, Dick Groat)	16.00	8.00	4.75
8	A.L. Batting Leaders (Al Kaline, Rich Rollins, Carl Yastrzemski)	12.50	6.25	3.75

#	Card			
9	N.L. Home Run Leaders (Hank Aaron, Orlando Cepeda, Willie Mays, Willie McCovey)	25.00	12.50	6.25
10	A.L. Home Run Leaders (Bob Allison, Harmon Killebrew, Dick Stuart)	12.00	6.00	3.50
11	N.L. R.B.I. Leaders (Hank Aaron, Ken Boyer, Bill White)	12.50	6.25	3.75
12	A.L. R.B.I. Leaders (Al Kaline, Harmon Killebrew, Dick Stuart)	13.50	6.75	4.00
13	Hoyt Wilhelm	15.00	7.50	4.50
14	Dodgers Rookies (Dick Nen, Nick Willhite)	3.50	1.75	1.00
15	Zoilo Versalles	3.50	1.75	1.00
16	John Boozer	3.50	1.75	1.00
17	Willie Kirkland	3.50	1.75	1.00
18	Billy O'Dell	3.50	1.75	1.00
19	Don Wart	3.50	1.75	1.00
20	Bob Friend	3.50	1.75	1.00
21	Yogi Berra	50.00	25.00	12.50
22	Jerry Adair	3.50	1.75	1.00
23	Chris Zachary	3.50	1.75	1.00
24	Carl Sawatski	3.50	1.75	1.00
25	Bill Monbouquette	3.50	1.75	1.00
26	Gino Cimoli	3.50	1.75	1.00
27	New York Mets Team	7.50	3.75	2.25
28	Claude Osteen	3.50	1.75	1.00
29	Lou Brock	40.00	20.00	10.00
30	Ron Perranoski	3.50	1.75	1.00
31	Dave Nicholson	3.50	1.75	1.00
32	Dean Chance	3.50	1.75	1.00
33	Reds Rookies (Sammy Ellis, Mel Queen)	3.50	1.75	1.00
34	Jim Perry	3.50	1.75	1.00
35	Ed Mathews	20.00	10.00	6.00
36	Hal Reniff	3.50	1.75	1.00
37	Smoky Burgess	3.50	1.75	1.00
38	Jim Wynn	5.00	2.50	1.50
39	Hank Aguirre	3.50	1.75	1.00
40	Dick Groat	3.50	1.75	1.00
41	Friendly Foes (Willie McCovey, Leon Wagner)	10.00	5.00	3.00
42	Moe Drabowsky	3.50	1.75	1.00
43	Roy Sievers	3.50	1.75	1.00
44	Duke Carmel	3.50	1.75	1.00
45	Milt Pappas	3.50	1.75	1.00
46	Ed Brinkman	3.50	1.75	1.00
47	Giants Rookies (Jesus Alou, Ron Herbel)	5.00	2.50	1.75
48	Bob Perry	3.50	1.75	1.00
49	Bill Henry	3.50	1.75	1.00
50	Mickey Mantle	550.00	275.00	137.50
51	Pete Richert	3.50	1.75	1.00
52	Chuck Hinton	3.50	1.75	1.00
53	Denis Menke	3.50	1.75	1.00
54	Sam Mele	3.50	1.75	1.00
55	Ernie Banks	45.00	22.50	11.25
56	Hal Brown	3.50	1.75	1.00
57	Tim Harkness	3.50	1.75	1.00
58	Don Demeter	3.50	1.75	1.00
59	Ernie Broglio	3.50	1.75	1.00
60	Frank Malzone	3.50	1.75	1.00
61	Angel Backstops (Bob Rodgers, Ed Sadowski)	3.50	1.75	1.00
62	Ted Savage	3.50	1.75	1.00
63	Johnny Orsino	3.50	1.75	1.00
64	Ted Abernathy	3.50	1.75	1.00
65	Felipe Alou	4.50	2.25	1.25
66	Eddie Fisher	3.50	1.75	1.00
67	Detroit Tigers Team	6.00	3.00	1.75
68	Willie Davis	3.50	1.75	1.00
69	Clete Boyer	10.00	5.00	3.00
70	Joe Torre	12.00	6.00	3.50
71	Jack Spring	3.50	1.75	1.00
72	Chico Cardenas	3.50	1.75	1.00
73	Jimmie Hall	3.50	1.75	1.00
74	Pirates Rookies (Tom Butters, Bob Priddy)	3.50	1.75	1.00
75	Wayne Causey	3.50	1.75	1.00
76	1st Series Checklist (1-88)	5.00	2.50	1.50
77	Jerry Walker	3.50	1.75	1.00
78	Merritt Ranew	3.50	1.75	1.00
79	Bob Heffner	3.50	1.75	1.00
80	Vada Pinson	9.00	4.50	2.75
81	All-Star Vets (Nellie Fox, Harmon Killebrew)	12.50	6.25	3.75
82	Jim Davenport	3.50	1.75	1.00
83	Gus Triandos	3.50	1.75	1.00
84	Carl Willey	3.50	1.75	1.00
85	Pete Ward	3.50	1.75	1.00
86	Al Downing	3.50	1.75	1.00
87	St. Louis Cardinals Team	6.00	3.00	1.75
88	John Roseboro	3.50	1.75	1.00
89	Boog Powell	7.50	3.75	2.25
90	Earl Battey	3.50	1.75	1.00
91	Bob Bailey	3.50	1.75	1.00
92	Steve Ridzik	3.50	1.75	1.00
93	Gary Geiger	3.50	1.75	1.00
94	Braves Rookies (Jim Britton, Larry Maxie)	3.50	1.75	1.00
95	George Altman	3.50	1.75	1.00
96	Bob Buhl	3.50	1.75	1.00
97	Jim Fregosi	3.50	1.75	1.00
98	Bill Bruton	3.50	1.75	1.00
99	Al Stanek	3.50	1.75	1.00
100	Elston Howard	12.50	6.25	3.75
101	Walt Alston	6.00	3.00	1.75
102	2nd Series Checklist (89-176)	6.00	3.00	1.75
103	Curt Flood	5.00	2.50	1.50
104	Art Mahaffey	3.50	1.75	1.00
105	Woody Held	3.50	1.75	1.00
106	Joe Nuxhall	3.50	1.75	1.00
107	White Sox Rookies (Bruce Howard, Frank Kreutzer)	3.50	1.75	1.00
108	John Wyatt	3.50	1.75	1.00
109	Rusty Staub	10.00	5.00	3.00
110	Albie Pearson	3.50	1.75	1.00
111	Don Elston	3.50	1.75	1.00
112	Bob Tillman	3.50	1.75	1.00
113	Grover Powell	3.50	1.75	1.00
114	Don Lock	3.50	1.75	1.00
115	Frank Bolling	3.50	1.75	1.00
116	Twins Rookies (Tony Oliva, Jay Ward)	9.00	4.50	2.75
117	Earl Francis	3.50	1.75	1.00
118	John Blanchard	5.00	2.50	1.50
119	Gary Kolb	3.50	1.75	1.00
120	Don Drysdale	17.50	8.75	5.25
121	Pete Runnels	3.50	1.75	1.00
122	Don McMahon	3.50	1.75	1.00
123	Jose Pagan	3.50	1.75	1.00
124	Orlando Pena	3.50	1.75	1.00
125	Pete Rose	250.00	125.00	62.50
126	Russ Snyder	3.50	1.75	1.00
127	Angels Rookies (Aubrey Gatewood, Dick Simpson)	3.50	1.75	1.00
128	Mickey Lolich	12.50	6.25	3.75
129	Amado Samuel	3.50	1.75	1.00
130	Gary Peters	3.50	1.75	1.00
131	Steve Boros	3.50	1.75	1.00
132	Milwaukee Braves Team	6.00	3.00	1.75
133	Jim Grant	3.50	1.75	1.00
134	Don Zimmer	5.00	2.50	1.50
135	Johnny Callison	3.50	1.75	1.00
136	World Series Game 1 (Koufax Strikes Out 15)	30.00	15.00	9.00
137	World Series Game 2 (Davis Sparks Rally)	9.00	4.50	2.75
138	World Series Game 3 (L.A. Takes 3rd Straight)	9.00	4.50	2.75
139	World Series Game 4 (Sealing Yanks' Doom)	7.00	3.50	2.00
140	World Series (The Dodgers Celebrate)	7.00	3.50	2.00
141	Danny Murtaugh	3.50	1.75	1.00
142	John Bateman	3.50	1.75	1.00
143	Bubba Phillips	3.50	1.75	1.00
144	Al Worthington	3.50	1.75	1.00
145	Norm Siebern	3.50	1.75	1.00
146	Indians Rookies (Bob Chance, Tommy John)	17.50	8.75	5.25
147	Ray Sadecki	3.50	1.75	1.00
148	J.C. Martin	3.50	1.75	1.00
149	Paul Foytack	3.50	1.75	1.00
150	Willie Mays	120.00	60.00	30.00
151	K.C. Athletics Team	6.00	3.00	1.75
152	Denver Lemaster	3.50	1.75	1.00
153	Dick Williams	3.50	1.75	1.00
154	Dick Tracewski	3.50	1.75	1.00
155	Duke Snider	15.00	7.50	4.50
156	Bill Dailey	3.50	1.75	1.00
157	Gene Mauch	3.50	1.75	1.00
158	Ken Johnson	3.50	1.75	1.00
159	Charlie Dees	3.50	1.75	1.00
160	Ken Boyer	8.00	4.00	2.50
161	Dave McNally	3.50	1.75	1.00
162	Hitting Area (Vada Pinson, Dick Sisler)	5.00	2.50	1.50
163	Donn Clendenon	3.50	1.75	1.00
164	Bud Daley	3.50	1.75	1.00
165	Jerry Lumpe	3.50	1.75	1.00
166	Marty Keough	3.50	1.75	1.00
167	Senators Rookies (Mike Brumley, Lou Piniella)	27.50	13.50	8.25
168	Al Weis	3.50	1.75	1.00
169	Del Crandall	3.50	1.75	1.00
170	Dick Radatz	3.50	1.75	1.00
171	Ty Cline	3.50	1.75	1.00
172	Cleveland Indians Team	6.00	3.00	1.75
173	Ryne Duren	3.50	1.75	1.00
174	Doc Edwards	3.50	1.75	1.00
175	Billy Williams	17.50	8.75	5.25
176	Tracy Stallard	3.50	1.75	1.00
177	Harmon Killebrew	25.00	12.50	6.25
178	Hank Bauer	4.50	2.25	1.25
179	Carl Warwick	3.50	1.75	1.00
180	Tommy Davis	3.50	1.75	1.00
181	Dave Wickersham	3.50	1.75	1.00
182	Sox Sockers (Chuck Schilling, Carl Yastrzemski)	17.50	8.75	5.25
183	Ron Taylor	3.50	1.75	1.00
184	Al Luplow	3.50	1.75	1.00
185	Jim O'Toole	3.50	1.75	1.00
186	Roman Mejias	3.50	1.75	1.00
187	Ed Roebuck	3.50	1.75	1.00
188	3rd Series Checklist (177-264)	5.00	2.50	1.50
189	Bob Hendley	3.50	1.75	1.00
190	Bobby Richardson	12.50	6.25	3.75
191	Clay Dalrymple	3.50	1.75	1.00
192	Cubs Rookies (John Boccabella, Billy Cowan)	3.50	1.75	1.00
193	Jerry Lynch	3.50	1.75	1.00
194	John Goryl	3.50	1.75	1.00
195	Floyd Robinson	3.50	1.75	1.00
196	Jim Gentile	3.50	1.75	1.00
197	Frank Lary	3.50	1.75	1.00
198	Len Gabrielson	3.50	1.75	1.00
199	Joe Azcue	3.50	1.75	1.00
200	Sandy Koufax	125.00	62.50	31.25
201	Orioles Rookies (Sam Bowens, Wally Bunker)	3.50	1.75	1.00
202	Galen Cisco	3.50	1.75	1.00
203	John Kennedy	3.50	1.75	1.00
204	Matty Alou	3.50	1.75	1.00
205	Nellie Fox	12.50	6.25	3.75
206	Steve Hamilton	3.50	1.75	1.00
207	Fred Hutchinson	3.50	1.75	1.00
208	Wes Covington	3.50	1.75	1.00
209	Bob Allen	3.50	1.75	1.00
210	Carl Yastrzemski	35.00	17.50	10.00
211	Jim Coker	3.50	1.75	1.00
212	Pete Lovrich	3.50	1.75	1.00
213	Los Angeles Angels Team	6.00	3.00	1.75
214	Ken McMullen	3.50	1.75	1.00
215	Ray Herbert	3.50	1.75	1.00
216	Mike de la Hoz	3.50	1.75	1.00
217	Jim King	3.50	1.75	1.00
218	Hank Fischer	3.50	1.75	1.00
219	Young Aces (Jim Bouton, Al Downing)	8.00	4.00	2.50
220	Dick Ellsworth	3.50	1.75	1.00
221	Bob Saverine	3.50	1.75	1.00
222	Bill Pierce	3.50	1.75	1.00
223	George Banks	3.50	1.75	1.00
224	Tommie Sisk	3.50	1.75	1.00
225	Roger Maris	60.00	30.00	15.00
226	Colts Rookies (Gerald Grote, Larry Yellen)	5.00	2.50	1.50
227	Barry Latman	3.50	1.75	1.00
228	Felix Mantilla	3.50	1.75	1.00
229	Charley Lau	3.50	1.75	1.00
230	Brooks Robinson	40.00	20.00	10.00
231	Dick Calmus	3.50	1.75	1.00
232	Al Lopez	6.00	3.00	1.75
233	Hal Smith	3.50	1.75	1.00
234	Gary Bell	3.50	1.75	1.00
235	Ron Hunt	3.50	1.75	1.00
236	Bill Faul	3.50	1.75	1.00
237	Chicago Cubs Team	6.50	3.25	2.00
238	Roy McMillan	3.50	1.75	1.00
239	Herm Starrette	3.50	1.75	1.00
240	Bill White	3.50	1.75	1.00
241	Jim Owens	3.50	1.75	1.00
242	Harvey Kuenn	3.50	1.75	1.00
243	Phillies Rookies (Richie Allen, John Herrnstein)	17.50	8.75	5.25
244	Tony LaRussa	17.50	8.75	5.25
245	Dick Stigman	3.50	1.75	1.00
246	Manny Mota	3.50	1.75	1.00
247	Dave DeBusschere	5.00	2.50	1.50
248	Johnny Pesky	3.50	1.75	1.00
249	Doug Camilli	3.50	1.75	1.00
250	Al Kaline	40.00	20.00	10.00
251	Choo Choo Coleman	3.50	1.75	1.00
252	Ken Aspromonte	3.50	1.75	1.00
253	Wally Post	3.50	1.75	1.00
254	Don Hoak	3.50	1.75	1.00
255	Lee Thomas	3.50	1.75	1.00
256	Johnny Weekly	3.50	1.75	1.00
257	San Francisco Giants Team	6.00	3.00	1.75
258	Garry Roggenburk	3.50	1.75	1.00
259	Harry Bright	3.50	1.75	1.00
260	Frank Robinson	40.00	20.00	10.00
261	Jim Hannan	3.50	1.75	1.00
262	Cardinals Rookies (Harry Fanok, Mike Shannon)	9.00	4.50	2.75
263	Chuck Estrada	3.50	1.75	1.00
264	Jim Landis	3.50	1.75	1.00
265	Jim Bunning	12.50	6.25	3.75
266	Gene Freese	3.50	1.75	1.00
267	Wilbur Wood	5.00	2.50	1.50
268	Bill's Got It (Danny Murtaugh, Bill Virdon)	3.50	1.75	1.00
269	Ellis Burton	3.50	1.75	1.00
270	Rich Rollins	3.50	1.75	1.00
271	Bob Sadowski	3.50	1.75	1.00
272	Jake Wood	3.50	1.75	1.00
273	Mel Nelson	3.50	1.75	1.00
274	4th Series Checklist (265-352)	6.00	3.00	1.75
275	John Tsitouris	3.50	1.75	1.00
276	Jose Tartabull	3.50	1.75	1.00
277	Ken Retzer	3.50	1.75	1.00
278	Bobby Shantz	3.50	1.75	1.00
279	Joe Koppe	3.50	1.75	1.00
280	Juan Marichal	12.50	6.25	3.75
281	Yankees Rookies (Jake Gibbs, Tom Metcalf)	5.00	2.50	1.50
282	Bob Bruce	3.50	1.75	1.00
283	Tommy McCraw	3.50	1.75	1.00
284	Dick Schofield	3.50	1.75	1.00
285	Robin Roberts	12.50	6.25	3.75
286	Don Landrum	3.50	1.75	1.00
287	Red Sox Rookies (Tony Conigliaro, Bill Spanswick)	50.00	25.00	12.50
288	Al Moran	3.50	1.75	1.00
289	Frank Funk	3.50	1.75	1.00
290	Bob Allison	3.50	1.75	1.00
291	Phil Ortega	3.50	1.75	1.00
292	Mike Roarke	3.50	1.75	1.00
293	Phillies Team	6.00	3.00	1.75
294	Ken Hunt	3.50	1.75	1.00
295	Roger Craig	3.50	1.75	1.00
296	Ed Kirkpatrick	3.50	1.75	1.00
297	Ken MacKenzie	3.50	1.75	1.00
298	Harry Craft	3.50	1.75	1.00
299	Bill Stafford	3.50	1.75	1.00
300	Hank Aaron	125.00	62.50	31.25
301	Larry Brown	3.50	1.75	1.00
302	Dan Pfister	3.50	1.75	1.00
303	Jim Campbell	3.50	1.75	1.00
304	Bob Johnson	3.50	1.75	1.00
305	Jack Lamabe	3.50	1.75	1.00
306	Giant Gunners (Orlando Cepeda, Willie Mays)	40.00	20.00	10.00
307	Joe Gibbon	3.50	1.75	1.00
308	Gene Stephens	3.50	1.75	1.00
309	Paul Toth	3.50	1.75	1.00
310	Jim Gilliam	5.00	2.50	1.50
311	Tom Brown	3.50	1.75	1.00
312	Tigers Rookies (Fritz Fisher, Fred Gladding)	3.50	1.75	1.00
313	Chuck Hiller	3.50	1.75	1.00
314	Jerry Buchek	3.50	1.75	1.00
315	Bo Belinsky	3.50	1.75	1.00
316	Gene Oliver	3.50	1.75	1.00
317	Al Smith	3.50	1.75	1.00
318	Twins Team	6.00	3.00	1.75
319	Paul Brown	3.50	1.75	1.00
320	Rocky Colavito	12.50	6.25	3.75
321	Bob Lillis	3.50	1.75	1.00
322	George Brunet	3.50	1.75	1.00

		NM	EX	VG
323	John Buzhardt	3.50	1.75	1.00
324	Casey Stengel	12.50	6.25	3.75
325	Hector Lopez	3.50	1.75	1.00
326	Ron Brand	3.50	1.75	1.00
327	Don Blasingame	3.50	1.75	1.00
328	Bob Shaw	3.50	1.75	1.00
329	Russ Nixon	3.50	1.75	1.00
330	Tommy Harper	3.50	1.75	1.00
331	A.L. Bombers (Norm Cash, Al Kaline, Mickey Mantle, Roger Maris)	150.00	75.00	37.50
332	Ray Washburn	3.50	1.75	1.00
333	Billy Moran	3.50	1.75	1.00
334	Lew Krausse	3.50	1.75	1.00
335	Don Mossi	3.50	1.75	1.00
336	Andre Rodgers	3.50	1.75	1.00
337	Dodgers Rookies (Al Ferrara, Jeff Torborg)	6.00	3.00	1.75
338	Jack Kralick	3.50	1.75	1.00
339	Walt Bond	3.50	1.75	1.00
340	Joe Cunningham	3.50	1.75	1.00
341	Jim Roland	3.50	1.75	1.00
342	Willie Stargell	30.00	15.00	7.50
343	Senators Team	6.00	3.00	1.75
344	Phil Linz	3.50	1.75	1.00
345	Frank Thomas	3.50	1.75	1.00
346	Joe Jay	3.50	1.75	1.00
347	Bobby Wine	3.50	1.75	1.00
348	Ed Lopat	3.50	1.75	1.00
349	Art Fowler	3.50	1.75	1.00
350	Willie McCovey	20.00	10.00	6.00
351	Dan Schneider	3.50	1.75	1.00
352	Eddie Bressoud	3.50	1.75	1.00
353	Wally Moon	3.50	1.75	1.00
354	Dave Giusti	3.50	1.75	1.00
355	Vic Power	3.50	1.75	1.00
356	Reds Rookies (Bill McCool, Chico Ruiz)	3.50	1.75	1.00
357	Charley James	3.50	1.75	1.00
358	Ron Kline	3.50	1.75	1.00
359	Jim Schaffer	3.50	1.75	1.00
360	Joe Pepitone	4.50	2.25	1.25
361	Jay Hook	3.50	1.75	1.00
362	5th Series Checklist (353-429)	6.00	3.00	1.75
363	Dick McAuliffe	3.50	1.75	1.00
364	Joe Gaines	3.50	1.75	1.00
365	Cal McLish	3.50	1.75	1.00
366	Nelson Mathews	3.50	1.75	1.00
367	Fred Whitfield	3.50	1.75	1.00
368	White Sox Rookies (Fritz Ackley, Don Buford)	5.50	2.75	1.75
369	Jerry Zimmerman	3.50	1.75	1.00
370	Hal Woodeshick	3.50	1.75	1.00
371	Frank Howard	7.50	3.75	2.25
372	Howie Koplitz	6.00	3.00	1.75
373	Pittsburgh Pirates Team	11.00	5.50	3.25
374	Bobby Bolin	6.00	3.00	1.75
375	Ron Santo	20.00	10.00	6.00
376	Dave Morehead	6.00	3.00	1.75
377	Bob Skinner	6.00	3.00	1.75
378	Braves Rookies (Jack Smith, Woody Woodward)	6.00	3.00	1.75
379	Tony Gonzalez	6.00	3.00	1.75
380	Whitey Ford	40.00	20.00	10.00
381	Bob Taylor	6.00	3.00	1.75
382	Wes Stock	6.00	3.00	1.75
383	Bill Rigney	6.00	3.00	1.75
384	Ron Hansen	6.00	3.00	1.75
385	Curt Simmons	6.00	3.00	1.75
386	Lenny Green	6.00	3.00	1.75
387	Terry Fox	6.00	3.00	1.75
388	Athletics Rookies (John O'Donoghue, George Williams)	6.00	3.00	1.75
389	Jim Umbricht	6.00	3.00	1.75
390	Orlando Cepeda	17.50	8.75	5.25
391	Sam McDowell	6.00	3.00	1.75
392	Jim Pagliaroni	6.00	3.00	1.75
393	Casey Teaches (Ed Kranepool, Casey Stengel)	12.50	6.25	3.75
394	Bob Miller	6.00	3.00	1.75
395	Tom Tresh	13.50	6.75	4.00
396	Dennis Bennett	6.00	3.00	1.75
397	Chuck Cottier	6.00	3.00	1.75
398	Mets Rookies (Bill Haas, Dick Smith)	6.00	3.00	1.75
399	Jackie Brandt	6.00	3.00	1.75
400	Warren Spahn	35.00	17.50	8.75
401	Charlie Maxwell	6.00	3.00	1.75
402	Tom Sturdivant	6.00	3.00	1.75
403	Cincinnati Reds Team	10.00	5.00	3.00
404	Tony Martinez	6.00	3.00	1.75
405	Ken McBride	6.00	3.00	1.75
406	Al Spangler	6.00	3.00	1.75
407	Bill Freehan	6.00	3.00	1.75
408	Cubs Rookies (Fred Burdette, Jim Stewart)	6.00	3.00	1.75
409	Bill Fischer	6.00	3.00	1.75
410	Dick Stuart	6.00	3.00	1.75
411	Lee Walls	6.00	3.00	1.75
412	Ray Culp	6.00	3.00	1.75
413	Johnny Keane	6.00	3.00	1.75
414	Jack Sanford	6.00	3.00	1.75
415	Tony Kubek	12.50	6.25	3.75
416	Lee Maye	6.00	3.00	1.75
417	Don Cardwell	6.00	3.00	1.75
418	Orioles Rookies (Darold Knowles, Les Narum)	6.00	3.00	1.75
419	Ken Harrelson	9.00	4.50	2.75
420	Jim Maloney	6.00	3.00	1.75
421	Camilo Carreon	6.00	3.00	1.75
422	Jack Fisher	6.00	3.00	1.75
423	Tops in N.L. (Hank Aaron, Willie Mays)	125.00	62.50	31.50
424	Dick Bertell	6.00	3.00	1.75
425	Norm Cash	12.00	6.00	3.50
426	Bob Rodgers	6.00	3.00	1.75
427	Don Rudolph	6.00	3.00	1.75
428	Red Sox Rookies (Archie Skeen, Pete Smith)	6.00	3.00	1.75
429	Tim McCarver	12.50	6.25	3.75
430	Juan Pizarro	6.00	3.00	1.75
431	George Alusik	6.00	3.00	1.75
432	Ruben Amaro	6.00	3.00	1.75
433	New York Yankees Team	40.00	20.00	10.00
434	Don Nottebart	6.00	3.00	1.75
435	Vic Davalillo	6.00	3.00	1.75
436	Charlie Neal	6.00	3.00	1.75
437	Ed Bailey	6.00	3.00	1.75
438	6th Series Checklist (430-506)	11.00	5.50	3.25
439	Harvey Haddix	6.00	3.00	1.75
440	Bob Clemente	200.00	100.00	50.00
441	Bob Duliba	6.00	3.00	1.75
442	Pumpsie Green	6.00	3.00	1.75
443	Chuck Dressen	6.00	3.00	1.75
444	Larry Jackson	6.00	3.00	1.75
445	Bill Skowron	9.00	4.50	2.75
446	Julian Javier	6.00	3.00	1.75
447	Ted Bowsfield	6.00	3.00	1.75
448	Cookie Rojas	6.00	3.00	1.75
449	Deron Johnson	6.00	3.00	1.75
450	Steve Barber	6.00	3.00	1.75
451	Joe Amalfitano	6.00	3.00	1.75
452	Giants Rookies (Gil Garrido, Jim Hart)	7.50	3.75	2.25
453	Frank Baumann	6.00	3.00	1.75
454	Tommie Aaron	6.00	3.00	1.75
455	Bernie Allen	6.00	3.00	1.75
456	Dodgers Rookies (Wes Parker, John Werhas)	6.00	3.00	1.75
457	Jesse Gonder	6.00	3.00	1.75
458	Ralph Terry	6.00	3.00	1.75
459	Red Sox Rookies (Pete Charton, Dalton Jones)	6.00	3.00	1.75
460	Bob Gibson	30.00	15.00	7.50
461	George Thomas	6.00	3.00	1.75
462	Birdie Tebbetts	6.00	3.00	1.75
463	Don Leppert	6.00	3.00	1.75
464	Dallas Green	6.00	3.00	1.75
465	Mike Hershberger	6.00	3.00	1.75
466	Athletics Rookies (Dick Green, Aurelio Monteagudo)	6.00	3.00	1.75
467	Bob Aspromonte	6.00	3.00	1.75
468	Gaylord Perry	40.00	20.00	10.00
469	Cubs Rookies (Fred Norman, Sterling Slaughter)	6.00	3.00	1.75
470	Jim Bouton	10.00	5.00	3.00
471	Gates Brown	6.50	3.25	2.00
472	Vern Law	6.00	3.00	1.75
473	Baltimore Orioles Team	9.00	4.50	3.75
474	Larry Sherry	6.00	3.00	1.75
475	Ed Charles	6.00	3.00	1.75
476	Braves Rookies (Rico Carty, Dick Kelley)	9.00	4.50	2.75
477	Mike Joyce	6.00	3.00	1.75
478	Dick Howser	6.00	3.00	1.75
479	Cardinals Rookies (Dave Bakenhaster, Johnny Lewis)	6.00	3.00	1.75
480	Bob Purkey	6.00	3.00	1.75
481	Chuck Schilling	6.00	3.00	1.75
482	Phillies Rookies (John Briggs, Danny Cater)	6.00	3.00	1.75
483	Fred Valentine	6.00	3.00	1.75
484	Bill Pleis	6.00	3.00	1.75
485	Tom Haller	6.00	3.00	1.75
486	Bob Kennedy	6.00	3.00	1.75
487	Mike McCormick	6.00	3.00	1.75
488	Yankees Rookies (Bob Meyer, Pete Mikkelsen)	6.00	3.00	1.75
489	Julio Navarro	6.00	3.00	1.75
490	Ron Fairly	6.00	3.00	1.75
491	Ed Rakow	6.00	3.00	1.75
492	Colts Rookies (Jim Beauchamp, Mike White)	6.00	3.00	1.75
493	Don Lee	6.00	3.00	1.75
494	Al Jackson	6.00	3.00	1.75
495	Bill Virdon	6.00	3.00	1.75
496	Chicago White Sox Team	9.00	4.50	2.75
497	Jeoff Long	6.00	3.00	1.75
498	Dave Stenhouse	6.00	3.00	1.75
499	Indians Rookies (Chico Salmon, Gordon Seyfried)	6.00	3.00	1.75
500	Camilo Pascual	6.00	3.00	1.75
501	Bob Veale	6.00	3.00	1.75
502	Angels Rookies (Bobby Knoop, Bob Lee)	6.00	3.00	1.75
503	Earl Wilson	6.00	3.00	1.75
504	Claude Raymond	6.00	3.00	1.75
505	Stan Williams	6.00	3.00	1.75
506	Bobby Bragan	6.00	3.00	1.75
507	John Edwards	6.00	3.00	1.75
508	Diego Segui	6.00	3.00	1.75
509	Pirates Rookies (Gene Alley, Orlando McFarlane)	6.00	3.00	1.75
510	Lindy McDaniel	6.00	3.00	1.75
511	Lou Jackson	6.00	3.00	1.75
512	Tigers Rookies (Willie Horton, Joe Sparma)	22.50	11.00	6.75
513	Don Larsen	6.00	3.00	1.75
514	Jim Hickman	6.00	3.00	1.75
515	Johnny Romano	6.00	3.00	1.75
516	Twins Rookies (Jerry Arrigo, Dwight Siebler)	6.00	3.00	1.75
517a	7th Series Checklist (507-587) (Wrong numbering on back.)	15.00	7.50	4.50
517b	7th Series Checklist (507-587) (Correct numbering on back.)	11.00	5.50	3.25
518	Carl Bouldin	6.00	3.00	1.75
519	Charlie Smith	6.00	3.00	1.75
520	Jack Baldschun	6.00	3.00	1.75
521	Tom Satriano	6.00	3.00	1.75
522	Bobby Tiefenauer	6.00	3.00	1.75
523	Lou Burdette	9.00	4.50	2.75
524	Reds Rookies (Jim Dickson, Bobby Klaus)	9.00	4.50	2.75
525	Al McBean	9.00	4.50	2.75
526	Lou Clinton	9.00	4.50	2.75
527	Larry Bearnarth	9.00	4.50	2.75
528	Athletics Rookies (Dave Duncan, Tom Reynolds)	9.00	4.50	2.75
529	Al Dark	9.00	4.50	2.75
530	Leon Wagner	9.00	4.50	2.75
531	L.A. Dodgers Team	17.50	8.75	5.25
532	Twins Rookies (Bud Bloomfield, Joe Nossek)	9.00	4.50	2.75
533	Johnny Klippstein	9.00	4.50	2.75
534	Gus Bell	9.00	4.50	2.75
535	Phil Regan	9.00	4.50	2.75
536	Mets Rookies (Larry Elliot, John Stephenson)	9.00	4.50	2.75
537	Dan Osinski	9.00	4.50	2.75
538	Minnie Minoso	13.50	6.75	4.00
539	Roy Face	9.00	4.50	2.75
540	Luis Aparicio	35.00	17.50	10.00
541	Braves Rookies (Phil Niekro, Phil Roof)	75.00	37.50	18.75
542	Don Mincher	9.00	4.50	2.75
543	Bob Uecker	40.00	20.00	10.00
544	Colts Rookies (Steve Hertz, Joe Hoerner)	9.00	4.50	2.75
545	Max Alvis	9.00	4.50	2.75
546	Joe Christopher	9.00	4.50	2.75
547	Gil Hodges	15.00	7.50	4.50
548	N.L. Rookies (Wayne Schurr, Paul Speckenbach)	9.00	4.50	2.75
549	Joe Moeller	9.00	4.50	2.75
550	Ken Hubbs - In Memoriam	30.00	15.00	7.50
551	Billy Hoeft	9.00	4.50	2.75
552	Indians Rookies (Tom Kelley, Sonny Siebert)	11.00	5.50	3.25
553	Jim Brewer	9.00	4.50	2.75
554	Hank Foiles	9.00	4.50	2.75
555	Lee Stange	9.00	4.50	2.75
556	Mets Rookies (Steve Dillon, Ron Locke)	9.00	4.50	2.75
557	Leo Burke	9.00	4.50	2.75
558	Don Schwall	9.00	4.50	2.75
559	Dick Phillips	9.00	4.50	2.75
560	Dick Farrell	9.00	4.50	2.75
561	Phillies Rookies (Dave Bennett, Rick Wise)	11.00	5.50	3.25
562	Pedro Ramos	9.00	4.50	2.75
563	Dal Maxvill	9.00	4.50	2.75
564	A.L. Rookies (Joe McCabe, Jerry McNertney)	9.00	4.50	2.75
565	Stu Miller	9.00	4.50	2.75
566	Ed Kranepool	9.00	4.50	2.75
567	Jim Kaat	12.50	6.25	3.75
568	N.L. Rookies (Phil Gagliano, Cap Peterson)	9.00	4.50	2.75
569	Fred Newman	9.00	4.50	2.75
570	Bill Mazeroski	40.00	20.00	10.00
571	Gene Conley	9.00	4.50	2.75
572	A.L. Rookies (Dick Egan, Dave Gray)	9.00	4.50	2.75
573	Jim Duffalo	9.00	4.50	2.75
574	Manny Jimenez	9.00	4.50	2.75
575	Tony Cloninger	9.00	4.50	2.75
576	Mets Rookies (Jerry Hinsley, Bill Wakefield)	9.00	4.50	2.75
577	Gordy Coleman	9.00	4.50	2.75
578	Glen Hobbie	9.00	4.50	2.75
579	Boston Red Sox Team	17.50	8.75	5.25
580	Johnny Podres	11.00	5.50	3.25
581	Yankees Rookies (Pedro Gonzalez, Archie Moore)	9.00	4.50	2.75
582	Rod Kanehl	9.00	4.50	2.75
583	Tito Francona	9.00	4.50	2.75
584	Joel Horlen	9.00	4.50	2.75
585	Tony Taylor	9.00	4.50	2.75
586	Jim Piersall	10.00	5.00	3.00
587	Bennie Daniels	12.00	6.00	3.50

1964 Topps Coins

The 164 metal coins in this set were issued by Topps as inserts in the company's baseball card wax packs. The series is divided into two principal types, 120 "regular" coins and 44 All-Star coins. The 1 1/2" diameter coins feature a full-color background for the player photos in the "regular" series, while the players in the All-Star series are featured against plain red or blue backgrounds. There are two variations each of the Mantle, Causey and Hinton coins among the All-Star subset.

		NM	EX	VG
	Complete Set (164):	1,125	550.00	325.00
	Common Player:	6.00	3.00	1.75
1	Don Zimmer	6.00	3.00	1.75
2	Jim Wynn	6.00	3.00	1.75
3	Johnny Orsino	6.00	3.00	1.75
4	Jim Bouton	7.50	3.75	2.25
5	Dick Groat	6.00	3.00	1.75
6	Leon Wagner	6.00	3.00	1.75
7	Frank Malzone	6.00	3.00	1.75
8	Steve Barber	6.00	3.00	1.75
9	Johnny Romano	6.00	3.00	1.75
10	Tom Tresh	7.50	3.75	2.25

		NM	EX	VG
11	Felipe Alou	6.00	3.00	1.75
12	Dick Stuart	6.00	3.00	1.75
13	Claude Osteen	6.00	3.00	1.75
14	Juan Pizarro	6.00	3.00	1.75
15	Donn Clendenon	6.00	3.00	1.75
16	Jimmie Hall	6.00	3.00	1.75
17	Larry Jackson	6.00	3.00	1.75
18	Brooks Robinson	15.00	7.50	4.50
19	Bob Allison	6.00	3.00	1.75
20	Ed Roebuck	6.00	3.00	1.75
21	Pete Ward	6.00	3.00	1.75
22	Willie McCovey	12.50	6.25	3.75
23	Elston Howard	7.00	3.50	2.00
24	Diego Segui	6.00	3.00	1.75
25	Ken Boyer	7.00	3.50	2.00
26	Carl Yastrzemski	20.00	10.00	6.00
27	Bill Mazeroski	12.50	6.25	3.75
28	Jerry Lumpe	6.00	3.00	1.75
29	Woody Held	6.00	3.00	1.75
30	Dick Radatz	6.00	3.00	1.75
31	Luis Aparicio	10.00	5.00	3.00
32	Dave Nicholson	6.00	3.00	1.75
33	Ed Mathews	15.00	7.50	4.50
34	Don Drysdale	15.00	7.50	4.50
35	Ray Culp	6.00	3.00	1.75
36	Juan Marichal	10.00	5.00	3.00
37	Frank Robinson	15.00	7.50	4.50
38	Chuck Hinton	6.00	3.00	1.75
39	Floyd Robinson	6.00	3.00	1.75
40	Tommy Harper	6.00	3.00	1.75
41	Ron Hansen	6.00	3.00	1.75
42	Ernie Banks	20.00	10.00	6.00
43	Jesse Gonder	6.00	3.00	1.75
44	Billy Williams	10.00	5.00	3.00
45	Vada Pinson	7.00	3.50	2.00
46	Rocky Colavito	9.00	4.50	2.75
47	Bill Monbouquette	6.00	3.00	1.75
48	Max Alvis	6.00	3.00	1.75
49	Norm Siebern	6.00	3.00	1.75
50	John Callison	6.00	3.00	1.75
51	Rich Rollins	6.00	3.00	1.75
52	Ken McBride	6.00	3.00	1.75
53	Don Lock	6.00	3.00	1.75
54	Ron Fairly	6.00	3.00	1.75
55	Roberto Clemente	30.00	15.00	9.00
56	Dick Ellsworth	6.00	3.00	1.75
57	Tommy Davis	6.00	3.00	1.75
58	Tony Gonzalez	6.00	3.00	1.75
59	Bob Gibson	15.00	7.50	4.50
60	Jim Maloney	6.00	3.00	1.75
61	Frank Howard	7.00	3.50	2.00
62	Jim Pagliaroni	6.00	3.00	1.75
63	Orlando Cepeda	10.00	5.00	3.00
64	Ron Perranoski	6.00	3.00	1.75
65	Curt Flood	6.00	3.00	1.75
66	Al McBean	6.00	3.00	1.75
67	Dean Chance	6.00	3.00	1.75
68	Ron Santo	7.50	3.75	2.25
69	Jack Baldschun	6.00	3.00	1.75
70	Milt Pappas	6.00	3.00	1.75
71	Gary Peters	6.00	3.00	1.75
72	Bobby Richardson	7.50	3.75	2.25
73	Lee Thomas	6.00	3.00	1.75
74	Hank Aguirre	6.00	3.00	1.75
75	Carl Willey	6.00	3.00	1.75
76	Camilo Pascual	6.00	3.00	1.75
77	Bob Friend	6.00	3.00	1.75
78	Bill White	6.00	3.00	1.75
79	Norm Cash	7.50	3.75	2.25
80	Willie Mays	30.00	15.00	9.00
81	Duke Carmel	6.00	3.00	1.75
82	Pete Rose	35.00	17.50	10.50
83	Hank Aaron	30.00	15.00	9.00
84	Bob Aspromonte	6.00	3.00	1.75
85	Jim O'Toole	6.00	3.00	1.75
86	Vic Davalillo	6.00	3.00	1.75
87	Bill Freehan	6.00	3.00	1.75
88	Warren Spahn	15.00	7.50	4.50
89	Ron Hunt	6.00	3.00	1.75
90	Denis Menke	6.00	3.00	1.75
91	Turk Farrell	6.00	3.00	1.75
92	Jim Hickman	6.00	3.00	1.75
93	Jim Bunning	9.00	4.50	2.75
94	Bob Hendley	6.00	3.00	1.75
95	Ernie Broglio	6.00	3.00	1.75
96	Rusty Staub	7.00	3.50	2.00
97	Lou Brock	10.00	5.00	3.00
98	Jim Fregosi	6.00	3.00	1.75
99	Jim Grant	6.00	3.00	1.75
100	Al Kaline	15.00	7.50	4.50
101	Earl Battey	6.00	3.00	1.75
102	Wayne Causey	6.00	3.00	1.75
103	Chuck Schilling	6.00	3.00	1.75
104	Boog Powell	7.50	3.75	2.25
105	Dave Wickersham	6.00	3.00	1.75
106	Sandy Koufax	30.00	15.00	9.00
107	John Bateman	6.00	3.00	1.75
108	Ed Brinkman	6.00	3.00	1.75
109	Al Downing	6.00	3.00	1.75
110	Joe Azcue	6.00	3.00	1.75
111	Albie Pearson	6.00	3.00	1.75
112	Harmon Killebrew	15.00	7.50	4.50
113	Tony Taylor	6.00	3.00	1.75
114	Alvin Jackson	6.00	3.00	1.75
115	Billy O'Dell	6.00	3.00	1.75
116	Don Demeter	6.00	3.00	1.75
117	Ed Charles	6.00	3.00	1.75
118	Joe Torre	7.50	3.75	2.25
119	Don Nottebart	6.00	3.00	1.75
120	Mickey Mantle	65.00	32.00	19.50
121	Joe Pepitone (All-Star)	7.50	3.75	2.25
122	Dick Stuart (All-Star)	6.00	3.00	1.75
123	Bobby Richardson (All-Star)	7.50	3.75	2.25
124	Jerry Lumpe (All-Star)	6.00	3.00	1.75
125	Brooks Robinson (All-Star)	12.50	6.25	3.75
126	Frank Malzone (All-Star)	6.00	3.00	1.75
127	Luis Aparicio (All-Star)	9.00	4.50	2.75
128	Jim Fregosi (All-Star)	6.00	3.00	1.75

		NM	EX	VG
129	Al Kaline (All-Star)	12.50	6.25	3.75
130	Leon Wagner (All-Star)	6.00	3.00	1.75
131a	Mickey Mantle (All-Star, lefthanded.)	45.00	22.00	13.50
131b	Mickey Mantle (All-Star, righthanded.)	50.00	25.00	15.00
132	Albie Pearson (All-Star)	6.00	3.00	1.75
133	Harmon Killebrew (All-Star)	12.50	6.25	3.75
134	Carl Yastrzemski (All-Star)	17.50	8.75	5.25
135	Elston Howard (All-Star)	7.00	3.50	2.00
136	Earl Battey (All-Star)	6.00	3.00	1.75
137	Camilo Pascual (All-Star)	6.00	3.00	1.75
138	Jim Bouton (All-Star)	7.00	3.50	2.00
139	Whitey Ford (All-Star)	15.00	7.50	4.50
140	Gary Peters (All-Star)	6.00	3.00	1.75
141	Bill White (All-Star)	6.00	3.00	1.75
142	Orlando Cepeda (All-Star)	9.00	4.50	2.75
143	Bill Mazeroski (All-Star)	10.00	5.00	3.00
144	Tony Taylor (All-Star)	6.00	3.00	1.75
145	Ken Boyer (All-Star)	7.00	3.50	2.00
146	Ron Santo (All-Star)	7.50	3.75	2.25
147	Dick Groat (All-Star)	6.00	3.00	1.75
148	Roy McMillan (All-Star)	6.00	3.00	1.75
149	Hank Aaron (All-Star)	27.50	13.50	8.25
150	Roberto Clemente (All-Star)	27.50	13.50	8.25
151	Willie Mays (All-Star)	27.50	13.50	8.25
152	Vada Pinson (All-Star)	7.00	3.50	2.00
153	Tommy Davis (All-Star)	6.00	3.00	1.75
154	Frank Robinson (All-Star)	12.50	6.25	3.75
155	Joe Torre (All-Star)	7.50	3.75	2.25
156	Tim McCarver (All-Star)	6.00	3.00	1.75
157	Juan Marichal (All-Star)	10.00	5.00	3.00
158	Jim Maloney (All-Star)	6.00	3.00	1.75
159	Sandy Koufax (All-Star)	27.50	13.50	8.25
160	Warren Spahn (All-Star)	12.50	6.25	3.75
161a	Wayne Causey (All-Star, N.L. on back.)	20.00	10.00	6.00
161b	Wayne Causey (All-Star, A.L. on back.)	6.00	3.00	1.75
162a	Chuck Hinton (All-Star, N.L. on back.)	20.00	10.00	6.00
162b	Chuck Hinton (All-Star, A.L. on back.)	6.00	3.00	1.75
163	Bob Aspromonte (All-Star)	6.00	3.00	1.75
164	Ron Hunt (All-Star)	6.00	3.00	1.75

1964 Topps Giants

Measuring 3-1/8" x 5-1/4" the Topps Giants were the company's first postcard-size issue. The cards feature large color photographs surrounded by white borders with a white baseball containing the player's name, position and team. Card backs carry another photo of the player surrounded by a newspaper-style explanation of the depicted career highlight. The 60-card set contains primarily players which means it's an excellent place to find inexpensive cards of Hall of Famers. The '64 Giants were not printed in equal quantity and seven of the cards, including Sandy Koufax and Willie Mays, are significantly scarcer than the remainder of the set.

		NM	EX	VG
	Complete Set (60):	300.00	150.00	75.00
	Common Player:	3.00	1.50	.90
1	Gary Peters	3.00	1.50	.90
2	Ken Johnson	3.00	1.50	.90
3	Sandy Koufax (SP)	40.00	20.00	10.00
4	Bob Bailey	3.00	1.50	.90
5	Milt Pappas	3.00	1.50	.90
6	Ron Hunt	3.00	1.50	.90
7	Whitey Ford	10.00	5.00	3.00
8	Roy McMillan	3.00	1.50	.90
9	Rocky Colavito	6.00	3.00	1.75
10	Jim Bunning	6.00	3.00	1.75
11	Roberto Clemente	30.00	15.00	7.50
12	Al Kaline	9.00	4.50	2.75
13	Nellie Fox	7.00	3.50	2.00
14	Tony Gonzalez	3.00	1.50	.90
15	Jim Gentile	3.00	1.50	.90
16	Dean Chance	3.00	1.50	.90
17	Dick Ellsworth	3.00	1.50	.90
18	Jim Fregosi	3.00	1.50	.90
19	Dick Groat	3.00	1.50	.90
20	Chuck Hinton	3.00	1.50	.90
21	Elston Howard	4.50	2.25	1.25
22	Dick Farrell	3.00	1.50	.90
23	Albie Pearson	3.00	1.50	.90
24	Frank Howard	4.00	2.00	1.25
25	Mickey Mantle	60.00	30.00	15.00
26	Joe Torre	5.00	2.50	1.50
27	Ed Brinkman	3.00	1.50	.90
28	Bob Friend (SP)	12.50	6.25	3.75
29	Frank Robinson	8.00	4.00	2.50
30	Bill Freehan	3.00	1.50	.90

		NM	EX	VG
31	Warren Spahn	8.00	4.00	2.50
32	Camilo Pascual	3.00	1.50	.90
33	Pete Ward	3.00	1.50	.90
34	Jim Maloney	3.00	1.50	.90
35	Dave Wickersham	3.00	1.50	.90
36	Johnny Callison	3.00	1.50	.90
37	Juan Marichal	7.00	3.50	2.00
38	Harmon Killebrew	9.00	4.50	2.75
39	Luis Aparicio	7.00	3.50	2.00
40	Dick Radatz	3.00	1.50	.90
41	Bob Gibson	7.00	3.50	2.00
42	Dick Stuart (SP)	15.00	7.50	4.50
43	Tommy Davis	3.00	1.50	.90
44	Tony Oliva	3.50	1.75	1.00
45	Wayne Causey (SP)	15.00	7.50	4.50
46	Max Alvis	3.00	1.50	.90
47	Galen Cisco (SP)	13.50	6.75	4.00
48	Carl Yastrzemski	9.00	4.50	2.75
49	Hank Aaron	35.00	17.50	8.75
50	Brooks Robinson	9.00	4.50	2.75
51	Willie Mays (SP)	50.00	25.00	12.50
52	Billy Williams	8.00	4.00	2.50
53	Juan Pizarro	3.00	1.50	.90
54	Leon Wagner	3.00	1.50	.90
55	Orlando Cepeda	7.00	3.50	2.00
56	Vada Pinson	3.50	1.75	1.00
57	Ken Boyer	3.50	1.75	1.00
58	Ron Santo	5.00	2.50	1.50
59	John Romano	3.00	1.50	.90
60	Bill Skowron (SP)	20.00	10.00	5.00

1964 Topps Photo Tatoos

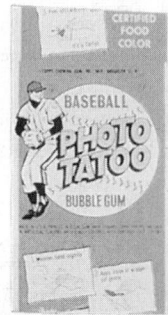

Apparently not content to leave the skin of American children without adornment, Topps jumped back into the tattoo field in 1964 with the release of a new series, measuring 1-9/16" x 3-1/2". The picture side for the 20 team tattoos gives the team logo and name.

		NM	EX	VG
	Complete Set (79):	3,000	1,500	900.00
	Common Player:	15.00	7.50	4.50
	Unopened Pack:	160.00		
(1)	Hank Aaron	135.00	65.00	40.00
(2)	Hank Aguirre	15.00	7.50	4.50
(3)	Max Alvis	15.00	7.50	4.50
(4)	Ernie Banks	80.00	40.00	24.00
(5)	Steve Barber	15.00	7.50	4.50
(6)	Ken Boyer	20.00	10.00	6.00
(7)	Johnny Callison	15.00	7.50	4.50
(8)	Norm Cash	20.00	10.00	6.00
(9)	Wayne Causey	15.00	7.50	4.50
(10)	Orlando Cepeda	50.00	25.00	15.00
(11)	Rocky Colavito	50.00	25.00	15.00
(12)	Ray Culp	15.00	7.50	4.50
(13)	Vic Davalillo	15.00	7.50	4.50
(14)	Moe Drabowsky	15.00	7.50	4.50
(15)	Dick Ellsworth	15.00	7.50	4.50
(16)	Curt Flood	15.00	7.50	4.50
(17)	Bill Freehan	15.00	7.50	4.50
(18)	Jim Fregosi	15.00	7.50	4.50
(19)	Bob Friend	15.00	7.50	4.50
(20)	Dick Groat	15.00	7.50	4.50
(21)	Woody Held	15.00	7.50	4.50
(22)	Frank Howard	20.00	10.00	6.00
(23)	Al Jackson	15.00	7.50	4.50
(24)	Larry Jackson	15.00	7.50	4.50
(25)	Ken Johnson	15.00	7.50	4.50
(26)	Al Kaline	60.00	30.00	18.00
(27)	Harmon Killebrew (Green background.)	60.00	30.00	18.00
(28)	Harmon Killebrew (Red background.)	60.00	30.00	18.00
(29)	Sandy Koufax (Horizontal band.)	135.00	65.00	40.00
(30)	Sandy Koufax (Diagonal band.)	145.00	75.00	45.00
(31)	Don Lock	15.00	7.50	4.50
(32)	Frank Malzone	15.00	7.50	4.50
(33)	Mickey Mantle (Diagonal yellow band.)	325.00	160.00	100.00
(34)	Mickey Mantle (Red triangle.)	325.00	160.00	100.00
(35)	Eddie Mathews	60.00	30.00	18.00
(36)	Willie Mays (Yellow background encompasses head.)	135.00	65.00	40.00
(37)	Willie Mays (Yellow background ears-to-chin.)	135.00	65.00	40.00
(38)	Bill Mazeroski	60.00	30.00	18.00
(39)	Ken McBride	15.00	7.50	4.50
(40)	Bill Monbouquette	15.00	7.50	4.50
(41)	Dave Nicholson	15.00	7.50	4.50
(42)	Claude Osteen	15.00	7.50	4.50
(43)	Milt Pappas	15.00	7.50	4.50

		NM	EX	VG
(44)	Camilio Pascual	15.00	7.50	4.50
(45)	Albie Pearson	15.00	7.50	4.50
(46)	Ron Perranoski	15.00	7.50	4.50
(47)	Gary Peters	15.00	7.50	4.50
(48)	Boog Powell	20.00	10.00	6.00
(49)	Frank Robinson	60.00	30.00	18.00
(50)	John Romano	15.00	7.50	4.50
(51)	Norm Siebern	15.00	7.50	4.50
(52)	Warren Spahn	60.00	30.00	18.00
(53)	Dick Stuart	15.00	7.50	4.50
(54)	Lee Thomas	15.00	7.50	4.50
(55)	Joe Torre	25.00	12.50	7.50
(56)	Pete Ward	15.00	7.50	4.50
(57)	Carlton Willey	15.00	7.50	4.50
(58)	Billy Williams	60.00	30.00	18.00
(59)	Carl Yastrzemski	75.00	37.50	22.50
(60)	Baltimore Orioles Logo	20.00	10.00	6.00
(61)	Boston Red Sox Logo	20.00	10.00	6.00
(62)	Chicago Cubs Logo	20.00	10.00	6.00
(63)	Chicago White Sox Logo	20.00	10.00	6.00
(64)	Cincinnati Reds Logo	20.00	10.00	6.00
(65)	Cleveland Indians Logo	20.00	10.00	6.00
(66)	Detroit Tigers Logo	20.00	10.00	6.00
(67)	Houston Colts Logo	25.00	12.50	7.50
(68)	Kansas City Athletics Logo	20.00	10.00	6.00
(69)	Los Angeles Angels Logo	20.00	10.00	6.00
(70)	Los Angeles Dodgers Logo	20.00	10.00	6.00
(71)	Milwaukee Braves Logo	20.00	10.00	6.00
(72)	Minnesota Twins Logo	20.00	10.00	6.00
(73)	New York Mets Logo	25.00	12.50	7.50
(74)	New York Yankees Logo	25.00	12.50	7.50
(75)	Philadelphia Phillies Logo	20.00	10.00	6.00
(76)	Pittsburgh Pirates Logo	20.00	10.00	6.00
(77)	St. Louis Cardinals Logo	20.00	10.00	6.00
(78)	San Francisco Giants Logo	20.00	10.00	6.00
(79)	Washington Senators Logo	20.00	10.00	6.00

1964 Topps Rookie All-Star Banquet

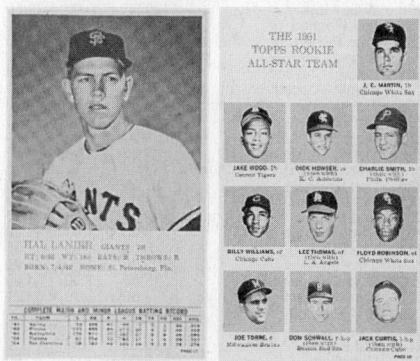

Since 1959, Topps has sponsored a formal post-season banquet to honor its annual Rookie All-Star team. In 1964, the gum company deviated from the tradition dinner program by issuing a 36-card boxed set. Each of the cards is printed in black-and-white, with red or light blue graphic highlights. The first seven cards in the set feature Topps staff and baseball dignitaries involved in the selection of the rookie team. Cards #8-12 are composite photos of the 1959-63 Rookie All-Star team. Cards #13-34A showcase the '64 honorees. Each player's card is matched with a card from the team's public relations officer extolling the rookie's virtues. Each card in this unique dinner program measures 3" x 5-1/4" and is numbered as a "PAGE" in the lower-right corner.

		NM	EX	VG
	Complete Boxed Set (36):	2,800	1,400	850.00
	Common Player:	17.50	8.75	5.25
1	"6th Annual Topps Rookie All-Star Team Awards" Header Card	17.50	8.75	5.25
2	The Baseball World Votes (Tommy Davis, Jeff Torborg, Ron Santo, Billy Williams.)	17.50	8.75	5.25
3	The Baseball World Votes (Six more clubhouse scenes.)	17.50	8.75	5.25
4	Topps Rookie All-Star Team Honorary Election Committee (Photos of media and Hall of Famers Hank Greenberg and Fran Frisch.)	55.00	27.00	16.50
5	Topps Rookie All-Star Team Honorary Election Committee (Photos of five media, Topps' VP Joel Shorin and Jackie Robinson.)	120.00	60.00	35.00
6	Executive Director of the Committee and His Associates (Topps' Cy Berger, three others.)	17.50	8.75	5.25
7	Topps Salutes Joe Garagiola (Joe Garagiola)	95.00	45.00	25.00
8	The 1959 Topps Rookie All-Star Team (Willie McCovey, Pumpsie Green, Joe Koppe, Jim Baxes, Bobby Allison, Ron Fairly, Willie Tasby, John Romano, Jim Perry, Jim O'Toole)	225.00	110.00	65.00
9	The 1960 Topps Rookie All-Star Team (Jim Gentile, Julian Javier, Ron Hansen, Ron Santo, Tommy Davis, Frank Howard, Tony Curry, Jimmie Coker, Chuck Estrada, Dick Stigman)	225.00	110.00	65.00
10	The 1961 Topps Rookie All-Star Team (J.C. Martin, Jake Wood, Dick Howser, Charlie Smith, Billy Williams, Lee Thomas, Floyd Robinson, Joe Torre, Don Schwall, Jack Curtis)	185.00	90.00	55.00
11	The 1962 Topps Rookie All-Star Team (Fred Whitfield, Bernie Allen, Tom Tresh, Ed Charles, Manny Jiminez, Al Luplow, Boog Powell, Buck Rodgers, Dean Chance, Al Jackson)	185.00	90.00	55.00
12	The 1963 Topps Rookie All-Star Team (Pete Rose, Rusty Staub, Al Weis, Pete Ward, Jimmie Hall, Vic Davalillo, Tommy Harper, Jesse Gonder, Ray Culp, Gary Peters)	1,400	700.00	425.00
13	1964 Topps Rookie All-Star Team Header Card	17.50	8.75	5.25
14	Ed Uhas, Cleveland Indians PR	17.50	8.75	5.25
15	Bob Chance	135.00	65.00	40.00
16	Garry Schumacher, S.F. Giants PR	17.50	8.75	5.25
17	Hal Lanier	135.00	65.00	40.00
18	Larry Shenk, Phillies PR	17.50	8.75	5.25
19	Richie Allen	300.00	150.00	90.00
20	Jim Schaaf, Athletics PR	17.50	8.75	5.25
21	Bert Campaneris	160.00	80.00	45.00
22	Ernie Johnson, Braves PR	17.50	8.75	5.25
23	Rico Carty	160.00	80.00	45.00
24	Bill Crowley, Red Sox PR	17.50	8.75	5.25
25	Tony Conigliaro	345.00	175.00	100.00
26	Tom Mee, Twins PR	17.50	8.75	5.25
27	Tony Oliva	210.00	100.00	60.00
28	Burt Hawkins, Senators PR	17.50	8.75	5.25
29	Mike Brumley	135.00	65.00	40.00
30	Hank Zureick, Reds PR	17.50	8.75	5.25
31	Bill McCool	135.00	65.00	40.00
32	Rob Brown, Orioles PR	17.50	8.75	5.25
33	Wally Bunker	135.00	65.00	40.00
34	"5th Annual Topps Minor League Player of the Year" Header Card	17.50	8.75	5.25
34A	Luis Tiant (Minor League Player of the Year)	160.00	80.00	45.00
35	Rookie All-Star Trophy	17.50	8.75	5.25

1964 Topps Stand-Ups

These 2-1/2" x 3-1/2" cards were the first since the All-Star sets of 1951 to be die-cut. This made it possible for a folded card to stand on display. The 77-cards in the set feature color photographs of the player with yellow and green backgrounds. Directions for folding are on the yellow top background, and when folded only the green background remains. Of the 77 cards, 55 were double-printed while 22 were single-printed, making them twice as scarce.

		NM	EX	VG
	Complete Set (77):	2,400	1,200	600.00
	Common Player:	12.00	6.00	3.50
	Wax Pack (1):	600.00		
(1)	Hank Aaron	180.00	90.00	45.00
(2)	Hank Aguirre	12.00	6.00	3.50
(3)	George Altman	12.00	6.00	3.50
(4)	Max Alvis	12.00	6.00	3.50
(5)	Bob Aspromonte	12.00	6.00	3.50
(6)	Jack Baldschun (SP)	20.00	10.00	6.00
(7)	Ernie Banks	100.00	50.00	25.00
(8)	Steve Barber	12.00	6.00	3.50
(9)	Earl Battey	12.00	6.00	3.50
(10)	Ken Boyer	20.00	10.00	6.00
(11)	Ernie Broglio	12.00	6.00	3.50
(12)	Johnny Callison	12.00	6.00	3.50
(13)	Norm Cash (SP)	65.00	32.50	16.25
(14)	Wayne Causey	12.00	6.00	3.50
(15)	Orlando Cepeda	27.50	13.50	8.25
(16)	Ed Charles	12.00	6.00	3.50
(17)	Roberto Clemente	240.00	120.00	60.00
(18)	Donn Clendenon (SP)	20.00	10.00	6.00
(19)	Rocky Colavito	25.00	12.50	7.50
(20)	Ray Culp (SP)	20.00	10.00	6.00
(21)	Tommy Davis	12.00	6.00	3.50
(22)	Don Drysdale (SP)	140.00	70.00	35.00
(23)	Dick Ellsworth	12.00	6.00	3.50
(24)	Dick Farrell	12.00	6.00	3.50
(25)	Jim Fregosi	12.00	6.00	3.50
(26)	Bob Friend	12.00	6.00	3.50
(27)	Jim Gentile	12.00	6.00	3.50
(28)	Jesse Gonder (SP)	20.00	10.00	6.00
(29)	Tony Gonzalez (SP)	20.00	10.00	6.00
(30)	Dick Groat	12.50	6.25	3.75
(31)	Woody Held	12.00	6.00	3.50
(32)	Chuck Hinton	12.00	6.00	3.50
(33)	Elston Howard	20.00	10.00	6.00
(34)	Frank Howard (SP)	27.50	13.50	8.25
(35)	Ron Hunt	12.00	6.00	3.50
(36)	Al Jackson	12.00	6.00	3.50
(37)	Ken Johnson	12.00	6.00	3.50
(38)	Al Kaline	100.00	50.00	25.00
(39)	Harmon Killebrew	100.00	50.00	25.00
(40)	Sandy Koufax	200.00	100.00	50.00
(41)	Don Lock (SP)	20.00	10.00	6.00
(42)	Jerry Lumpe (SP)	20.00	10.00	6.00
(43)	Jim Maloney	12.00	6.00	3.50
(44)	Frank Malzone	12.00	6.00	3.50
(45)	Mickey Mantle	550.00	275.00	137.50
(46)	Juan Marichal (SP)	120.00	60.00	30.00
(47)	Ed Mathews (SP)	150.00	75.00	37.50
(48)	Willie Mays	300.00	150.00	75.00
(49)	Bill Mazeroski	22.50	11.00	7.00
(50)	Ken McBride	12.00	6.00	3.50
(51)	Willie McCovey (SP)	120.00	60.00	30.00
(52)	Claude Osteen	12.00	6.00	3.50
(53)	Jim O'Toole	12.00	6.00	3.50
(54)	Camilo Pascual	12.00	6.00	3.50
(55)	Albie Pearson (SP)	20.00	10.00	6.00
(56)	Gary Peters	12.00	6.00	3.50
(57)	Vada Pinson	15.00	7.50	4.50
(58)	Juan Pizarro	12.00	6.00	3.50
(59)	Boog Powell	20.00	10.00	6.00
(60)	Bobby Richardson	20.00	10.00	6.00
(61)	Brooks Robinson	100.00	50.00	25.00
(62)	Floyd Robinson	12.00	6.00	3.50
(63)	Frank Robinson	100.00	50.00	25.00
(64)	Ed Roebuck (SP)	20.00	10.00	6.00
(65)	Rich Rollins	12.00	6.00	3.50
(66)	Johnny Romano	12.00	6.00	3.50
(67)	Ron Santo (SP)	50.00	25.00	12.50
(68)	Norm Siebern	12.00	6.00	3.50
(69)	Warren Spahn (SP)	150.00	75.00	37.50
(70)	Dick Stuart (SP)	20.00	10.00	6.00
(71)	Lee Thomas	12.00	6.00	3.50
(72)	Joe Torre	30.00	15.00	9.00
(73)	Pete Ward	12.00	6.00	3.50
(74)	Bill White (SP)	25.00	12.50	7.50
(75)	Billy Williams (SP)	120.00	60.00	30.00
(76)	Hal Woodeshick (SP)	20.00	10.00	6.00
(77)	Carl Yastrzemski (SP)	500.00	250.00	125.00

1965 Topps

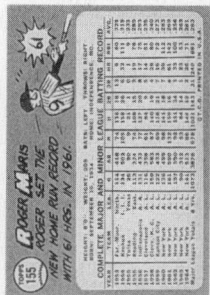

The 1965 Topps set features a large color photograph of the player surrounded by a colored, round-cornered frame and a white border. The bottom of the 2-1/2" x 3-1/2" cards includes a pennant with a color team logo and name over the left side of a rectangle which features the player's name and position. Backs feature statistics and, if space allowed, a cartoon and headline about the player. There are no multi-player cards in the 1965 set other than the usual team cards and World Series highlights. Rookie cards include team, as well as league groupings from two to four players per card. Also present in the 598-card set are statistical leaders. Certain cards in the high-number series (#523-598) were produced in lesser quantities than the rest of the series. Known as "short-prints," and valued somewhat higher than the other high numbers, they are indicated in the checklist by an (SP) after the player name.

		NM	EX	VG
	Complete Set (598):	4,000	2,000	1,200
	Common Player (1-370):	3.00	1.50	.90
	Common Player (371-598):	6.00	3.00	1.75
1	A.L. Batting Leaders (Elston Howard, Tony Oliva, Brooks Robinson)	25.00	12.50	6.25
2	N.L. Batting Leaders (Hank Aaron, Rico Carty, Roberto Clemente)	20.00	10.00	5.00
3	A.L. Home Run Leaders (Harmon Killebrew, Mickey Mantle, Boog Powell)	40.00	20.00	10.00
4	N.L. Home Run Leaders (Johnny Callison, Orlando Cepeda, Jim Hart, Willie Mays, Billy Williams)	20.00	10.00	6.00
5	A.L. RBI Leaders (Harmon Killebrew, Mickey Mantle, Brooks Robinson, Dick Stuart)	35.00	17.50	10.00
6	N.L. RBI Leaders (Ken Boyer, Willie Mays, Ron Santo)	13.50	6.75	4.00
7	A.L. ERA Leaders (Dean Chance, Joel Horlen)	3.50	1.75	1.00
8	N.L. ERA Leaders (Don Drysdale, Sandy Koufax)	20.00	10.00	5.00

#	Name			
9	A.L. Pitching Leaders (Wally Bunker, Dean Chance, Gary Peters, Juan Pizarro, Dave Wickersham)	3.50	1.75	1.00
10	N.L. Pitching Leaders (Larry Jackson, Juan Marichal, Ray Sadecki)	4.50	2.25	1.25
11	A.L. Strikeout Leaders (Dean Chance, Al Downing, Camilo Pascual)	3.50	1.75	1.00
12	N.L. Strikeout Leaders (Don Drysdale, Bob Gibson, Bob Veale)	12.00	6.00	3.50
13	Pedro Ramos	3.00	1.50	.90
14	Len Gabrielson	3.00	1.50	.90
15	Robin Roberts	12.50	6.25	3.75
16	Astros Rookies (*Sonny Jackson, Joe Morgan*)	60.00	30.00	15.00
17	Johnny Romano	3.00	1.50	.90
18	Bill McCool	3.00	1.50	.90
19	Gates Brown	3.00	1.50	.90
20	Jim Bunning	10.00	5.00	3.00
21	Don Blasingame	3.00	1.50	.90
22	Charlie Smith	3.00	1.50	.90
23	Bob Tiefenauer	3.00	1.50	.90
24	Twins Team	7.50	3.75	2.25
25	Al McBean	3.00	1.50	.90
26	Bobby Knoop	3.00	1.50	.90
27	Dick Bertell	3.00	1.50	.90
28	Barney Schultz	3.00	1.50	.90
29	Felix Mantilla	3.00	1.50	.90
30	Jim Bouton	4.50	2.25	1.25
31	Mike White	3.00	1.50	.90
32	Herman Franks	3.00	1.50	.90
33	Jackie Brandt	3.00	1.50	.90
34	Cal Koonce	3.00	1.50	.90
35	Ed Charles	3.00	1.50	.90
36	Bobby Wine	3.00	1.50	.90
37	Fred Gladding	3.00	1.50	.90
38	Jim King	3.00	1.50	.90
39	Gerry Arrigo	3.00	1.50	.90
40	Frank Howard	4.50	2.25	1.25
41	White Sox Rookies (*Bruce Howard, Marv Staehle*)	3.00	1.50	.90
42	Earl Wilson	3.00	1.50	.90
43	Mike Shannon	3.00	1.50	.90
44	Wade Blasingame	3.00	1.50	.90
45	Roy McMillan	3.00	1.50	.90
46	Bob Lee	3.00	1.50	.90
47	Tommy Harper	3.00	1.50	.90
48	Claude Raymond	3.00	1.50	.90
49	Orioles Rookies (*Curt Blefary, John Miller*)	3.00	1.50	.90
50	Juan Marichal	13.50	6.75	4.00
51	Billy Bryan	3.00	1.50	.90
52	Ed Roebuck	3.00	1.50	.90
53	Dick McAuliffe	3.00	1.50	.90
54	Joe Gibbon	3.00	1.50	.90
55	Tony Conigliaro	12.00	6.00	3.50
56	Ron Kline	3.00	1.50	.90
57	Cards Team	7.50	3.75	2.25
58	Fred Talbot	3.00	1.50	.90
59	Nate Oliver	3.00	1.50	.90
60	Jim O'Toole	3.00	1.50	.90
61	Chris Cannizzaro	3.00	1.50	.90
62	Jim Katt (Kaat)	3.50	1.75	1.00
63	Ty Cline	3.00	1.50	.90
64	Lou Burdette	3.00	1.50	.90
65	Tony Kubek	11.00	5.50	3.25
66	Bill Rigney	3.00	1.50	.90
67	Harvey Haddix	3.00	1.50	.90
68	Del Crandall	3.00	1.50	.90
69	Bill Virdon	3.00	1.50	.90
70	Bill Skowron	3.50	1.75	1.00
71	John O'Donoghue	3.00	1.50	.90
72	Tony Gonzalez	3.00	1.50	.90
73	Dennis Ribant	3.00	1.50	.90
74	Red Sox Rookies (*Rico Petrocelli, Jerry Stephenson*)	13.50	6.75	4.00
75	Deron Johnson	3.00	1.50	.90
76	Sam McDowell	3.00	1.50	.90
77	Doug Camilli	3.00	1.50	.90
78	Dal Maxvill	3.00	1.50	.90
79a	1st Series Checklist (1-88) (61 is C. Cannizzaro)	3.50	1.75	1.00
79b	1st Series Checklist (1-88) (61 is Cannizzaro)	7.00	3.50	2.00
80	Turk Farrell	3.00	1.50	.90
81	Don Buford	3.00	1.50	.90
82	Braves Rookies (*Santos Alomar, John Braun*)	4.50	2.25	1.25
83	George Thomas	3.00	1.50	.90
84	Ron Herbel	3.00	1.50	.90
85	Willie Smith	3.00	1.50	.90
86	Les Narum	3.00	1.50	.90
87	Nelson Mathews	3.00	1.50	.90
88	Jack Lamabe	3.00	1.50	.90
89	Mike Hershberger	3.00	1.50	.90
90	Rich Rollins	3.00	1.50	.90
91	Cubs Team	7.50	3.75	2.25
92	Dick Howser	3.00	1.50	.90
93	Jack Fisher	3.00	1.50	.90
94	Charlie Lau	3.00	1.50	.90
95	Bill Mazeroski	12.50	6.25	3.75
96	Sonny Siebert	3.00	1.50	.90
97	Pedro Gonzalez	3.00	1.50	.90
98	Bob Miller	3.00	1.50	.90
99	Gil Hodges	9.00	4.50	2.75
100	Ken Boyer	4.50	2.25	1.25
101	Fred Newman	3.00	1.50	.90
102	Steve Boros	3.00	1.50	.90
103	Harvey Kuenn	3.00	1.50	.90
104	2nd Series Checklist (89-176)	4.00	2.00	1.25
105	Chico Salmon	3.00	1.50	.90
106	Gene Oliver	3.00	1.50	.90
107	Phillies Rookies (*Pat Corrales, Costen Shockley*)	4.00	2.00	1.25
108	Don Mincher	3.00	1.50	.90
109	Walt Bond	3.00	1.50	.90
110	Ron Santo	12.00	6.00	3.50
111	Lee Thomas	3.00	1.50	.90
112	Derrell Griffith	3.00	1.50	.90
113	Steve Barber	3.00	1.50	.90
114	Jim Hickman	3.00	1.50	.90
115	Bobby Richardson	20.00	10.00	5.00
116	Cardinals Rookies (*Dave Dowling, Bob Tolan*)	3.00	1.50	.90
117	Wes Stock	3.00	1.50	.90
118	*Hal Lanier*	3.00	1.50	.90
119	John Kennedy	3.00	1.50	.90
120	Frank Robinson	40.00	20.00	10.00
121	Gene Alley	3.00	1.50	.90
122	Bill Pleis	3.00	1.50	.90
123	Frank Thomas	3.00	1.50	.90
124	Tom Satriano	3.00	1.50	.90
125	Juan Pizarro	3.00	1.50	.90
126	Dodgers Team	7.50	3.75	2.25
127	Frank Lary	3.00	1.50	.90
128	Vic Davalillo	3.00	1.50	.90
129	Bennie Daniels	3.00	1.50	.90
130	Al Kaline	40.00	20.00	10.00
131	Johnny Keane	4.00	2.00	1.25
132	World Series Game 1 (Cards Take Opener)	10.00	5.00	3.00
133	World Series Game 2 (Stottlemyre Wins)	15.00	7.50	3.75
134	World Series Game 3 (Mantle's Clutch HR)	60.00	30.00	15.00
135	World Series Game 4 (Boyer's Grand-Slam)	10.00	5.00	3.00
136	World Series Game 5 (10th Inning Triumph)	7.00	3.50	2.00
137	World Series Game 6 (Bouton Wins Again)	10.00	5.00	3.00
138	World Series Game 7 (Gibson Wins Finale)	15.00	7.50	4.50
139	World Series (The Cards Celebrate)	9.00	4.50	2.75
140	Dean Chance	3.00	1.50	.90
141	Charlie James	3.00	1.50	.90
142	Bill Monbouquette	3.00	1.50	.90
143	Pirates Rookies (John Gelnar, Jerry May)	3.00	1.50	.90
144	Ed Kranepool	3.00	1.50	.90
145	*Luis Tiant*	20.00	10.00	5.00
146	Ron Hansen	3.00	1.50	.90
147	Dennis Bennett	3.00	1.50	.90
148	Willie Kirkland	3.00	1.50	.90
149	Wayne Schurr	3.00	1.50	.90
150	Brooks Robinson	40.00	20.00	10.00
151	Athletics Team	7.50	3.75	2.25
152	Phil Ortega	3.00	1.50	.90
153	Norm Cash	9.00	4.50	2.75
154	Bob Humphreys	3.00	1.50	.90
155	Roger Maris	50.00	25.00	15.00
156	Bob Sadowski	3.00	1.50	.90
157	Zoilo Versalles	3.00	1.50	.90
158	Dick Sisler	3.00	1.50	.90
159	Jim Duffalo	3.00	1.50	.90
160	Bob Clemente	200.00	100.00	50.00
161	Frank Baumann	3.00	1.50	.90
162	Russ Nixon	3.00	1.50	.90
163	John Briggs	3.00	1.50	.90
164	Al Spangler	3.00	1.50	.90
165	Dick Ellsworth	3.00	1.50	.90
166	Indians Rookies (*Tommie Agee, George Culver*)	9.00	4.50	2.75
167	Bill Wakefield	3.00	1.50	.90
168	Dick Green	3.00	1.50	.90
169	Dave Vineyard	3.00	1.50	.90
170	Hank Aaron	160.00	80.00	40.00
171	Jim Roland	3.00	1.50	.90
172	Jim Piersall	6.00	3.00	1.75
173	Tigers Team	8.00	4.00	2.50
174	Joe Jay	3.00	1.50	.90
175	Bob Aspromonte	3.00	1.50	.90
176	Willie McCovey	20.00	10.00	5.00
177	Pete Mikkelsen	3.00	1.50	.90
178	Dalton Jones	3.00	1.50	.90
179	Hal Woodeshick	3.00	1.50	.90
180	Bob Allison	3.00	1.50	.90
181	Senators Rookies (*Don Loun, Joe McCabe*)	3.00	1.50	.90
182	Mike de la Hoz	3.00	1.50	.90
183	Dave Nicholson	3.00	1.50	.90
184	John Boozer	3.00	1.50	.90
185	Max Alvis	3.00	1.50	.90
186	Billy Cowan	3.00	1.50	.90
187	Casey Stengel	12.50	6.25	3.75
188	Sam Bowens	3.00	1.50	.90
189	3rd Series Checklist (177-264)	6.50	3.25	2.00
190	Bill White	3.00	1.50	.90
191	Phil Regan	3.00	1.50	.90
192	Jim Coker	3.00	1.50	.90
193	Gaylord Perry	12.00	6.00	3.50
194	Angels Rookies (*Bill Kelso, Rick Reichardt*)	3.00	1.50	.90
195	Bob Veale	3.00	1.50	.90
196	Ron Fairly	3.00	1.50	.90
197	Diego Segui	3.00	1.50	.90
198	Smoky Burgess	3.00	1.50	.90
199	Bob Heffner	3.00	1.50	.90
200	Joe Torre	12.00	6.00	3.50
201	Twins Rookies (*Cesar Tovar, Sandy Valdespino*)	3.00	1.50	.90
202	Leo Burke	3.00	1.50	.90
203	Dallas Green	3.00	1.50	.90
204	Russ Snyder	3.00	1.50	.90
205	Warren Spahn	30.00	15.00	7.50
206	Willie Horton	3.00	1.50	.90
207	Pete Rose	160.00	80.00	40.00
208	Tommy John	6.00	3.00	1.75
209	Pirates Team	7.50	3.75	2.25
210	Jim Fregosi	3.00	1.50	.90
211	Steve Ridzik	3.00	1.50	.90
212	Ron Brand	3.00	1.50	.90
213	Jim Davenport	3.00	1.50	.90
214	Bob Purkey	3.00	1.50	.90
215	Pete Ward	3.00	1.50	.90
216	Al Worthington	3.00	1.50	.90
217	Walt Alston	9.00	4.50	2.75
218	Dick Schofield	3.00	1.50	.90
219	Bob Meyer	3.00	1.50	.90
220	Billy Williams	25.00	12.50	7.50
221	John Tsitouris	3.00	1.50	.90
222	Bob Tillman	3.00	1.50	.90
223	Dan Osinski	3.00	1.50	.90
224	Bob Chance	3.00	1.50	.90
225	Bo Belinsky	3.00	1.50	.90
226	Yankees Rookies (*Jake Gibbs, Elvio Jimenez*)	9.00	4.50	2.75
227	Bobby Klaus	3.00	1.50	.90
228	Jack Sanford	3.00	1.50	.90
229	Lou Clinton	3.00	1.50	.90
230	Ray Sadecki	3.00	1.50	.90
231	Jerry Adair	3.00	1.50	.90
232	*Steve Blass*	3.00	1.50	.90
233	Don Zimmer	6.00	3.00	1.75
234	White Sox Team	7.50	3.75	2.25
235	Chuck Hinton	3.00	1.50	.90
236	*Dennis McLain*	20.00	10.00	5.00
237	Bernie Allen	3.00	1.50	.90
238	Joe Moeller	3.00	1.50	.90
239	Doc Edwards	3.00	1.50	.90
240	Bob Bruce	3.00	1.50	.90
241	Mack Jones	3.00	1.50	.90
242	George Brunet	3.00	1.50	.90
243	Reds Rookies (*Ted Davidson, Tommy Helms*)	3.00	1.50	.90
244	Lindy McDaniel	3.00	1.50	.90
245	Joe Pepitone	10.00	5.00	3.00
246	Tom Butters	3.00	1.50	.90
247	Wally Moon	3.00	1.50	.90
248	Gus Triandos	3.00	1.50	.90
249	Dave McNally	3.00	1.50	.90
250	Willie Mays	150.00	75.00	37.50
251	Billy Herman	7.50	3.75	2.25
252	Pete Richert	3.00	1.50	.90
253	Danny Cater	3.00	1.50	.90
254	Roland Sheldon	3.00	1.50	.90
255	Camilo Pascual	3.00	1.50	.90
256	Tito Francona	3.00	1.50	.90
257	Jim Wynn	3.00	1.50	.90
258	Larry Bearnarth	3.00	1.50	.90
259	Tigers Rookies (*Jim Northrup, Ray Oyler*)	4.00	2.00	1.25
260	Don Drysdale	20.00	10.00	6.00
261	Duke Carmel	3.00	1.50	.90
262	Bud Daley	3.00	1.50	.90
263	Marty Keough	3.00	1.50	.90
264	Bob Buhl	3.00	1.50	.90
265	Jim Pagliaroni	3.00	1.50	.90
266	*Bert Campaneris*	15.00	7.50	4.50
267	Senators Team	7.50	3.75	2.25
268	Ken McBride	3.00	1.50	.90
269	Frank Bolling	3.00	1.50	.90
270	Milt Pappas	3.00	1.50	.90
271	Don Wert	3.00	1.50	.90
272	Chuck Schilling	3.00	1.50	.90
273	4th Series Checklist (265-352)	7.50	3.75	2.25
274	Lum Harris	3.00	1.50	.90
275	Dick Groat	3.00	1.50	.90
276	Hoyt Wilhelm	12.50	6.25	3.75
277	Johnny Lewis	3.00	1.50	.90
278	Ken Retzer	3.00	1.50	.90
279	Dick Tracewski	3.00	1.50	.90
280	Dick Stuart	3.00	1.50	.90
281	Bill Stafford	3.00	1.50	.90
282	Giants Rookies (*Dick Estelle, Masanori Murakami*)	20.00	10.00	6.00
283	Fred Whitfield	3.00	1.50	.90
284	Nick Willhite	3.00	1.50	.90
285	Ron Hunt	3.00	1.50	.90
286	Athletic Rookies (*Jim Dickson, Aurelio Monteagudo*)	3.00	1.50	.90
287	Gary Kolb	3.00	1.50	.90
288	Jack Hamilton	3.00	1.50	.90
289	Gordy Coleman	3.00	1.50	.90
290	Wally Bunker	3.00	1.50	.90
291	Jerry Lynch	3.00	1.50	.90
292	Larry Yellen	3.00	1.50	.90
293	Angels Team	7.50	3.75	2.25
294	Tim McCarver	8.00	4.00	2.50
295	Dick Radatz	3.00	1.50	.90
296	Tony Taylor	3.00	1.50	.90
297	Dave DeBusschere	4.00	2.00	1.25
298	Jim Stewart	3.00	1.50	.90
299	Jerry Zimmerman	3.00	1.50	.90
300	Sandy Koufax	100.00	50.00	25.00
301	Birdie Tebbetts	3.00	1.50	.90
302	Al Stanek	3.00	1.50	.90
303	Johnny Orsino	3.00	1.50	.90
304	Dave Stenhouse	3.00	1.50	.90
305	Rico Carty	3.00	1.50	.90
306	Bubba Phillips	3.00	1.50	.90
307	Barry Latman	3.00	1.50	.90
308	Mets Rookies (*Cleon Jones, Tom Parsons*)	8.00	4.00	2.50
309	Steve Hamilton	3.00	1.50	.90
310	Johnny Callison	3.00	1.50	.90
311	Orlando Pena	3.00	1.50	.90
312	Joe Nuxhall	3.00	1.50	.90
313	Jimmie Schaffer	3.00	1.50	.90
314	Sterling Slaughter	3.00	1.50	.90
315	Frank Malzone	3.00	1.50	.90
316	Reds Team	7.00	3.50	2.00
317	Don McMahon	3.00	1.50	.90
318	Matty Alou	3.00	1.50	.90
319	Ken McMullen	3.00	1.50	.90
320	Bob Gibson	30.00	15.00	7.50
321	Rusty Staub	7.50	3.75	2.25
322	Rick Wise	3.00	1.50	.90
323	Hank Bauer	3.00	1.50	.90

#	Player			
324	Bobby Locke	3.00	1.50	.90
325	Donn Clendenon	3.00	1.50	.90
326	Dwight Siebler	3.00	1.50	.90
327	Denis Menke	3.00	1.50	.90
328	Eddie Fisher	3.00	1.50	.90
329	Hawk Taylor	3.00	1.50	.90
330	Whitey Ford	50.00	25.00	12.50
331	Dodgers Rookies (Al Ferrara, John Purdin)	3.00	1.50	.90
332	Ted Abernathy	3.00	1.50	.90
333	Tommie Reynolds	3.00	1.50	.90
334	Vic Roznovsky	3.00	1.50	.90
335	Mickey Lolich	6.00	3.00	1.75
336	Woody Held	3.00	1.50	.90
337	Mike Cuellar	3.00	1.50	.90
338	Phillies Team	7.50	3.75	2.25
339	Ryne Duren	3.00	1.50	.90
340	Tony Oliva	15.00	7.50	4.50
341	Bobby Bolin	3.00	1.50	.90
342	Bob Rodgers	3.00	1.50	.90
343	Mike McCormick	3.00	1.50	.90
344	Wes Parker	3.00	1.50	.90
345	Floyd Robinson	3.00	1.50	.90
346	Bobby Bragan	3.00	1.50	.90
347	Roy Face	3.00	1.50	.90
348	George Banks	3.00	1.50	.90
349	Larry Miller	3.00	1.50	.90
350	Mickey Mantle	650.00	325.00	162.50
351	Jim Perry	3.00	1.50	.90
352	*Alex Johnson*	3.50	1.75	1.00
353	Jerry Lumpe	3.00	1.50	.90
354	Cubs Rookies (Billy Ott, Jack Warner)	3.00	1.50	.90
355	Vada Pinson	8.00	4.00	2.50
356	Bill Spanswick	3.00	1.50	.90
357	Carl Warwick	3.00	1.50	.90
358	Albie Pearson	3.00	1.50	.90
359	Ken Johnson	3.00	1.50	.90
360	Orlando Cepeda	20.00	10.00	6.00
361	5th Series Checklist (353-429)	9.00	4.50	2.75
362	Don Schwall	3.00	1.50	.90
363	Bob Johnson	3.00	1.50	.90
364	Galen Cisco	3.00	1.50	.90
365	Jim Gentile	3.00	1.50	.90
366	Dan Schneider	3.00	1.50	.90
367	Leon Wagner	3.00	1.50	.90
368	White Sox Rookies (Ken Berry, Joel Gibson)	3.00	1.50	.90
369	Phil Linz	3.00	1.50	.90
370	Tommy Davis	3.00	1.50	.90
371	Frank Kreutzer	7.50	3.75	2.25
372	Clay Dalrymple	7.50	3.75	2.25
373	Curt Simmons	7.50	3.75	2.25
374	Angels Rookies (Jose Cardenal, Dick Simpson)	9.00	4.50	2.75
375	Dave Wickersham	7.50	3.75	2.25
376	Jim Landis	7.50	3.75	2.25
377	Willie Stargell	20.00	10.00	6.00
378	Chuck Estrada	7.50	3.75	2.25
379	Giants Team	10.00	5.00	3.00
380	Rocky Colavito	12.00	6.00	3.50
381	Al Jackson	7.50	3.75	2.25
382	J.C. Martin	7.50	3.75	2.25
383	Felipe Alou	9.00	4.50	2.75
384	Johnny Klippstein	7.50	3.75	2.25
385	Carl Yastrzemski	40.00	20.00	10.00
386	Cubs Rookies (Paul Jaeckel, Fred Norman)	7.50	3.75	2.25
387	Johnny Podres	9.00	4.50	2.75
388	John Blanchard	7.50	3.75	2.25
389	Don Larsen	7.50	3.75	2.25
390	Bill Freehan	7.50	3.75	2.25
391	Mel McGaha	7.50	3.75	2.25
392	Bob Friend	7.50	3.75	2.25
393	Ed Kirkpatrick	7.50	3.75	2.25
394	Jim Hannan	7.50	3.75	2.25
395	Jim Hart	7.50	3.75	2.25
396	Frank Bertaina	7.50	3.75	2.25
397	Jerry Buchek	7.50	3.75	2.25
398	Reds Rookies (Dan Neville, Art Shamsky)	7.50	3.75	2.25
399	Ray Herbert	7.50	3.75	2.25
400	Harmon Killebrew	50.00	25.00	12.50
401	Carl Willey	7.50	3.75	2.25
402	Joe Amalfitano	7.50	3.75	2.25
403	Red Sox Team	10.00	5.00	3.00
404	Stan Williams	7.50	3.75	2.25
405	John Roseboro	7.50	3.75	2.25
406	Ralph Terry	7.50	3.75	2.25
407	Lee Maye	7.50	3.75	2.25
408	Larry Sherry	7.50	3.75	2.25
409	Astros Rookies (*Jim Beauchamp, Larry Dierker*)	9.00	4.50	2.75
410	Luis Aparicio	17.50	8.75	5.25
411	Roger Craig	7.50	3.75	2.25
412	Bob Bailey	7.50	3.75	2.25
413	Hal Reniff	7.50	3.75	2.25
414	Al Lopez	12.50	6.25	3.75
415	Curt Flood	12.50	6.25	3.75
416	Jim Brewer	7.50	3.75	2.25
417	Ed Brinkman	7.50	3.75	2.25
418	Johnny Edwards	7.50	3.75	2.25
419	Ruben Amaro	7.50	3.75	2.25
420	Larry Jackson	7.50	3.75	2.25
421	Twins Rookies (Gary Dotter, Jay Ward)	7.50	3.75	2.25
422	Aubrey Gatewood	7.50	3.75	2.25
423	Jesse Gonder	7.50	3.75	2.25
424	Gary Bell	7.50	3.75	2.25
425	Wayne Causey	7.50	3.75	2.25
426	Braves Team	10.00	5.00	3.00
427	Bob Saverine	7.50	3.75	2.25
428	Bob Shaw	7.50	3.75	2.25
429	Don Demeter	7.50	3.75	2.25
430	Gary Peters	7.50	3.75	2.25
431	Cardinals Rookies (Nelson Briles, Wayne Spiezio)	9.00	4.50	2.75
432	Jim Grant	7.50	3.75	2.25
433	John Bateman	7.50	3.75	2.25
434	Dave Morehead	7.50	3.75	2.25
435	Willie Davis	7.50	3.75	2.25
436	Don Elston	7.50	3.75	2.25
437	Chico Cardenas	7.50	3.75	2.25
438	Harry Walker	7.50	3.75	2.25
439	Moe Drabowsky	7.50	3.75	2.25
440	Tom Tresh	12.50	6.25	3.75
441	Denver Lemaster	7.50	3.75	2.25
442	Vic Power	7.50	3.75	2.25
443	6th Series Checklist (430-506)	9.00	4.50	2.75
444	Bob Hendley	7.50	3.75	2.25
445	Don Lock	7.50	3.75	2.25
446	Art Mahaffey	7.50	3.75	2.25
447	Julian Javier	7.50	3.75	2.25
448	Lee Stange	7.50	3.75	2.25
449	Mets Rookies (Jerry Hinsley, Gary Kroll)	7.50	3.75	2.25
450	Elston Howard	12.00	6.00	3.50
451	Jim Owens	7.50	3.75	2.25
452	Gary Geiger	7.50	3.75	2.25
453	Dodgers Rookies (Willie Crawford, John Werhas)	7.50	3.75	2.25
454	Ed Rakow	7.50	3.75	2.25
455	Norm Siebern	7.50	3.75	2.25
456	Bill Henry	7.50	3.75	2.25
457	Bob Kennedy	7.50	3.75	2.25
458	John Buzhardt	7.50	3.75	2.25
459	Frank Kostro	7.50	3.75	2.25
460	Richie Allen	25.00	12.50	6.25
461	Braves Rookies (Clay Carroll, Phil Niekro)	30.00	15.00	7.50
462	Lew Krausse (Photo actually Pete Lovrich.)	7.50	3.75	2.25
463	Manny Mota	7.50	3.75	2.25
464	Ron Piche	7.50	3.75	2.25
465	Tom Haller	7.50	3.75	2.25
466	Senators Rookies (Pete Craig, Dick Nen)	7.50	3.75	2.25
467	Ray Washburn	7.50	3.75	2.25
468	Larry Brown	7.50	3.75	2.25
469	Don Nottebart	7.50	3.75	2.25
470	Yogi Berra	60.00	30.00	15.00
471	Billy Hoeft	7.50	3.75	2.25
472	Don Pavletich	7.50	3.75	2.25
473	Orioles Rookies (*Paul Blair, Dave Johnson*)	12.50	6.25	3.75
474	Cookie Rojas	7.50	3.75	2.25
475	Clete Boyer	10.00	5.00	3.00
476	Billy O'Dell	7.50	3.75	2.25
477	Cardinals Rookies (*Fritz Ackley, Steve Carlton*)	175.00	87.50	43.75
478	Wilbur Wood	7.50	3.75	2.25
479	Ken Harrelson	7.50	3.75	2.25
480	Joel Horlen	7.50	3.75	2.25
481	Indians Team	10.00	5.00	3.00
482	Bob Priddy	7.50	3.75	2.25
483	George Smith	7.50	3.75	2.25
484	Ron Perranoski	7.50	3.75	2.25
485	Nellie Fox	15.00	7.50	4.50
486	Angels Rookies (Tom Egan, Pat Rogan)	7.50	3.75	2.25
487	Woody Woodward	7.50	3.75	2.25
488	Ted Wills	7.50	3.75	2.25
489	Gene Mauch	7.50	3.75	2.25
490	Earl Battey	7.50	3.75	2.25
491	Tracy Stallard	7.50	3.75	2.25
492	Gene Freese	7.50	3.75	2.25
493	Tigers Rookies (Bruce Brubaker, Bill Roman)	7.50	3.75	2.25
494	Jay Ritchie	7.50	3.75	2.25
495	Joe Christopher	7.50	3.75	2.25
496	Joe Cunningham	7.50	3.75	2.25
497	Giants Rookies (Ken Henderson, Jack Hiatt)	7.50	3.75	2.25
498	Gene Stephens	7.50	3.75	2.25
499	Stu Miller	7.50	3.75	2.25
500	Ed Mathews	30.00	15.00	7.50
501	Indians Rookies (Ralph Gagliano, Jim Rittwage)	7.50	3.75	2.25
502	Don Cardwell	7.50	3.75	2.25
503	Phil Gagliano	7.50	3.75	2.25
504	Jerry Grote	7.50	3.75	2.25
505	Ray Culp	7.50	3.75	2.25
506	Sam Mele	7.50	3.75	2.25
507	Sammy Ellis	7.50	3.75	2.25
508a	7th Series Checklist (507-598) (Large print on front.)	9.00	4.50	2.75
508b	7th Series Checklist (507-598) (Small print on front.)	9.00	4.50	2.75
509	Red Sox Rookies (Bob Guindon, Gerry Vezendy)	7.50	3.75	2.25
510	Ernie Banks	80.00	40.00	20.00
511	Ron Locke	7.50	3.75	2.25
512	Cap Peterson	7.50	3.75	2.25
513	Yankees Team	30.00	15.00	7.50
514	Joe Azcue	7.50	3.75	2.25
515	Vern Law	7.50	3.75	2.25
516	Al Weis	7.50	3.75	2.25
517	Angels Rookies (Paul Schaal, Jack Warner)	7.50	3.75	2.25
518	Ken Rowe	7.50	3.75	2.25
519	Bob Uecker	20.00	10.00	5.00
520	Tony Cloninger	7.50	3.75	2.25
521	Phillies Rookies (Dave Bennett, Morrie Stevens)	7.50	3.75	2.25
522	Hank Aguirre	7.50	3.75	2.25
523	Mike Brumley	9.00	4.50	2.75
524	Dave Giusti (SP)	9.00	4.50	2.75
525	Eddie Bressoud	7.50	3.75	2.25
526	Athletics Rookies (*Catfish Hunter, Rene Lachemann, Skip Lockwood, Johnny Odom*) (SP)	80.00	40.00	20.00
527	Jeff Torborg (SP)	9.00	4.50	2.75
528	George Altman	7.50	3.75	2.25
529	Jerry Fosnow (SP)	9.00	4.50	2.75
530	Jim Maloney	7.50	3.75	2.25
531	Chuck Hiller	7.50	3.75	2.25
532	Hector Lopez	9.00	4.50	2.75
533	Mets Rookies (*Jim Bethke, Tug McGraw, Dan Napolean, Ron Swoboda*) (SP)	25.00	12.50	6.25
534	John Herrnstein	7.50	3.75	2.25
535	Jack Kralick	9.00	4.50	2.75
536	Andre Rodgers (SP)	9.00	4.50	2.75
537	Angels Rookies (**Marcelino Lopez, Rudy May, Phil Roof**)	9.00	4.50	2.75
538	Chuck Dressen (SP)	9.00	4.50	2.75
539	Herm Starrette	7.50	3.75	2.25
540	Lou Brock (SP)	25.00	12.50	6.25
541	White Sox Rookies (Greg Bollo, Bob Locker)	7.50	3.75	2.25
542	Lou Klimchock	7.50	3.75	2.25
543	Ed Connolly (SP)	9.00	4.50	2.75
544	Howie Reed	7.50	3.75	2.25
545	Jesus Alou (SP)	9.00	4.50	2.75
546	Indians Rookies (**Ray Barker, Bill Davis, Mike Hedlund, Floyd Weaver**)	7.50	3.75	2.25
547	Jake Wood	9.00	4.50	2.75
548	Dick Stigman	7.50	3.75	2.25
549	Cubs Rookies (Glenn Beckert, Roberto Pena) (SP)	12.00	6.00	3.50
550	*Mel Stottlemyre* (SP)	25.00	12.50	6.25
551	Mets Team	16.00	8.00	4.75
552	Julio Gotay	7.50	3.75	2.25
553	Houston Rookies (**Dan Coombs, Jack McClure, Gene Ratliff**)	7.50	3.75	2.25
554	Chico Ruiz	9.00	4.50	2.75
555	Jack Baldschun (SP)	9.00	4.50	2.75
556	Red Schoendienst	12.50	6.25	3.75
557	Jose Santiago	7.50	3.75	2.25
558	Tommie Sisk	7.50	3.75	2.25
559	Ed Bailey (SP)	9.00	4.50	2.75
560	Boog Powell (SP)	10.00	5.00	3.00
561	Dodgers Rookies (**Dennis Daboll, Mike Kekich, Jim Lefebvre, Hector Valle**)	12.00	6.00	3.50
562	Billy Moran	7.50	3.75	2.25
563	Julio Navarro	7.50	3.75	2.25
564	Mel Nelson	7.50	3.75	2.25
565	Ernie Broglio (SP)	9.00	4.50	2.75
566	Yankees Rookies (**Gil Blanco, Art Lopez, Ross Moschitto**) (SP)	10.00	5.00	3.00
567	Tommie Aaron	7.50	3.75	2.25
568	Ron Taylor (SP)	9.00	4.50	2.75
569	Gino Cimoli (SP)	9.00	4.50	2.75
570	Claude Osteen (SP)	9.00	4.50	2.75
571	Ossie Virgil (SP)	9.00	4.50	2.75
572	Orioles team (SP)	15.00	7.50	4.50
573	Red Sox Rookies (**Jim Lonborg, Gerry Moses, Mike Ryan, Bill Schlesinger**) (SP)	13.50	6.75	4.00
574	Roy Sievers	7.50	3.75	2.25
575	Jose Pagan	7.50	3.75	2.25
576	Terry Fox (SP)	9.00	4.50	2.75
577	A.L. Rookies (**Jim Buschhorn, Darold Knowles, Richie Scheinblum**) (SP)	9.00	4.50	2.75
578	Camilo Carreon (SP)	9.00	4.50	2.75
579	Dick Smith (SP)	9.00	4.50	2.75
580	Jimmie Hall (SP)	9.00	4.50	2.75
581	N.L. Rookies (**Kevin Collins, Tony Perez, Dave Ricketts**) (SP)	80.00	40.00	20.00
582	Bob Schmidt (SP)	9.00	4.50	2.75
583	Wes Covington (SP)	9.00	4.50	2.75
584	Harry Bright	7.50	3.75	2.25
585	Hank Fischer	7.50	3.75	2.25
586	Tommy McCraw (SP)	9.00	4.50	2.75
587	Joe Sparma	7.50	3.75	2.25
588	Lenny Green	7.50	3.75	2.25
589	Giants Rookies (**Frank Linzy, Bob Schroder**) (SP)	9.00	4.50	2.75
590	Johnnie Wyatt	7.50	3.75	2.25
591	Bob Skinner (SP)	9.00	4.50	2.75
592	Frank Bork (SP)	9.00	4.50	2.75
593	Tigers Rookies (**Jackie Moore, John Sullivan**) (SP)	9.00	4.50	2.75
594	Joe Gaines	7.50	3.75	2.25
595	Don Lee	7.50	3.75	2.25
596	Don Landrum (SP)	9.00	4.50	2.75
597	Twins Rookies (**Joe Nossek, Dick Reese, John Sevcik**)	7.00	3.50	2.00
598	Al Downing (SP)	25.00	6.00	3.00

1965 Topps Embossed

Inserted in regular packs, the 2-1/8" x 3-1/2" Topps Embossed cards feature a 3-D profile portrait on gold foil-like cardboard (some collectors report finding the cards with silver cardboard). The player's name, team and position are below the portrait - which is good, because most of the embossed portraits are otherwise unrecognizeable. There is a gold border with American League players framed in blue and National Leaguers in red.

		NM	EX	VG
	Complete Set (72):	400.00	140.00	60.00
	Common Player:	4.00	1.50	.60
1	Carl Yastrzemski	15.00	5.25	2.25
2	Ron Fairly	4.00	1.50	.60
3	Max Alvis	4.00	1.50	.60
4	Jim Ray Hart	4.00	1.50	.60
5	Bill Skowron	5.00	1.75	.70
6	Ed Kranepool	4.00	1.50	.60
7	Tim McCarver	5.00	1.75	.70
8	Sandy Koufax	25.00	9.00	4.00
9	Donn Clendenon	4.00	1.50	.60
10	John Romano	4.00	1.50	.60
11	Mickey Mantle	60.00	20.00	9.00
12	Joe Torre	6.00	2.00	.90
13	Al Kaline	15.00	5.25	2.25
14	Al McBean	4.00	1.50	.60
15	Don Drysdale	10.00	3.50	1.50
16	Brooks Robinson	12.50	4.50	2.00
17	Jim Bunning	9.00	3.25	1.25
18	Gary Peters	4.00	1.50	.60
19	Roberto Clemente	40.00	14.00	6.00
20	Milt Pappas	4.00	1.50	.60
21	Wayne Causey	4.00	1.50	.60
22	Frank Robinson	12.50	4.50	2.00
23	Bill Mazeroski	9.00	3.25	1.25
24	Diego Segui	4.00	1.50	.60
25	Jim Bouton	4.00	1.50	.60
26	Ed Mathews	10.00	3.50	1.50
27	Willie Mays	25.00	9.00	4.00
28	Ron Santo	6.00	2.00	.90
29	Boog Powell	6.00	2.00	.90
30	Ken McBride	4.00	1.50	.60
31	Leon Wagner	4.00	1.50	.60
32	John Callison	4.00	1.50	.60
33	Zoilo Versalles	4.00	1.50	.60
34	Jack Baldschun	4.00	1.50	.60
35	Ron Hunt	4.00	1.50	.60
36	Richie Allen	6.00	2.00	.90
37	Frank Malzone	4.00	1.50	.60
38	Bob Allison	4.00	1.50	.60
39	Jim Fregosi	4.00	1.50	.60
40	Billy Williams	9.00	3.25	1.25
41	Bill Freehan	4.00	1.50	.60
42	Vada Pinson	5.00	1.75	.70
43	Bill White	4.00	1.50	.60
44	Roy McMillan	4.00	1.50	.60
45	Orlando Cepeda	9.00	3.25	1.25
46	Rocky Colavito	7.50	2.75	1.25
47	Ken Boyer	5.00	1.75	.70
48	Dick Radatz	4.00	1.50	.60
49	Tommy Davis	4.00	1.50	.60
50	Walt Bond	4.00	1.50	.60
51	John Orsino	4.00	1.50	.60
52	Joe Christopher	4.00	1.50	.60
53	Al Spangler	4.00	1.50	.60
54	Jim King	4.00	1.50	.60
55	Mickey Lolich	4.00	1.50	.60
56	Harmon Killebrew	10.00	3.50	1.50
57	Bob Shaw	4.00	1.50	.60
58	Ernie Banks	15.00	5.25	2.25
59	Hank Aaron	25.00	9.00	4.00
60	Chuck Hinton	4.00	1.50	.60
61	Bob Aspromonte	4.00	1.50	.60
62	Lee Maye	4.00	1.50	.60
63	Joe Cunningham	4.00	1.50	.60
64	Pete Ward	4.00	1.50	.60
65	Bobby Richardson	6.00	2.00	.90
66	Dean Chance	4.00	1.50	.60
67	Dick Ellsworth	4.00	1.50	.60
68	Jim Maloney	4.00	1.50	.60
69	Bob Gibson	9.00	3.25	1.25
70	Earl Battey	4.00	1.50	.60
71	Tony Kubek	5.00	1.75	.70
72	Jack Kralick	4.00	1.50	.60

1965 Topps Push-Pull

PUSH·PULL   PUSH·PULL

Part of a 36-card set combining sports and non-sport subjects, the Push-Pull novelties have a louvered shutter attached to a tab at the bottom. When the tab is moved, from position to position, each of the underlying photos is revealed

in turn. The cards measure 2-1/2" x 4-11/16". Backs are printed in black-and-white and contain biographical data. Three of the cards in the set feature baseball players.

		NM	EX	VG
	Complete Set (36):	3,650	1,800	1,050
(1)	Lou Gehrig, Babe Ruth	500.00	250.00	150.00
(2)	Casey Stengel Wins/Loses	75.00	37.00	22.00
(3)	Yogi Berra, Mickey Mantle	950.00	475.00	285.00

1965 Topps Transfers

Issued as strips of three players each as inserts in 1965, the Topps Transfers were 2" x 3" portraits of players. The transfers have blue or red bands at the top and bottom with the team name and position in the top band and the player's name in the bottom. As is so often the case, the superstars in the transfer set can be quite expensive, but like many of Topps non-card products, the common transfers are neither terribly expensive or popular today.

		NM	EX	VG
	Complete Set (72):	750.00	375.00	225.00
	Common Player:	6.00	3.00	1.75
(1)	Hank Aaron	50.00	25.00	15.00
(2)	Richie Allen	12.00	6.00	3.50
(3)	Bob Allison	6.00	3.00	1.75
(4)	Max Alvis	6.00	3.00	1.75
(5)	Luis Aparicio	17.50	8.75	5.25
(6)	Bob Aspromonte	6.00	3.00	1.75
(7)	Walt Bond	6.00	3.00	1.75
(8)	Jim Bouton	9.00	4.50	2.75
(9)	Ken Boyer	10.00	5.00	3.00
(10)	Jim Bunning	17.50	8.75	5.25
(11)	John Callison	6.00	3.00	1.75
(12)	Rico Carty	6.00	3.00	1.75
(13)	Wayne Causey	6.00	3.00	1.75
(14)	Orlando Cepeda	17.50	8.75	5.25
(15)	Bob Chance	6.00	3.00	1.75
(16)	Dean Chance	6.00	3.00	1.75
(17)	Joe Christopher	6.00	3.00	1.75
(18)	Roberto Clemente	60.00	30.00	18.00
(19)	Rocky Colavito	15.00	7.50	4.50
(20)	Tony Conigliaro	10.00	5.00	3.00
(21)	Tommy Davis	6.00	3.00	1.75
(22)	Don Drysdale	17.50	8.75	5.25
(23)	Bill Freehan	6.00	3.00	1.75
(24)	Jim Fregosi	6.00	3.00	1.75
(25)	Bob Gibson	17.50	8.75	5.25
(26)	Dick Groat	6.00	3.00	1.75
(27)	Tom Haller	6.00	3.00	1.75
(28)	Chuck Hinton	6.00	3.00	1.75
(29)	Elston Howard	9.00	4.50	2.75
(30)	Ron Hunt	6.00	3.00	1.75
(31)	Al Jackson	6.00	3.00	1.75
(32)	Al Kaline	25.00	12.50	7.50
(33)	Harmon Killebrew	20.00	10.00	6.00
(34)	Jim King	6.00	3.00	1.75
(35)	Ron Kline	6.00	3.00	1.75
(36)	Bobby Knoop	6.00	3.00	1.75
(37)	Sandy Koufax	45.00	22.00	13.50
(38)	Ed Kranepool	6.00	3.00	1.75
(39)	Jim Maloney	6.00	3.00	1.75
(40)	Mickey Mantle	90.00	45.00	27.00
(41)	Juan Marichal	17.50	8.75	5.25
(42)	Lee Maye	6.00	3.00	1.75
(43)	Willie Mays	50.00	25.00	15.00
(44)	Bill Mazeroski	17.50	8.75	5.25
(45)	Tony Oliva	7.50	3.75	2.25
(46)	Jim O'Toole	6.00	3.00	1.75
(47)	Milt Pappas	6.00	3.00	1.75
(48)	Camilo Pascual	6.00	3.00	1.75
(49)	Gary Peters	6.00	3.00	1.75
(50)	Vada Pinson	6.00	3.00	1.75
(51)	Juan Pizarro	6.00	3.00	1.75
(52)	Boog Powell	10.00	5.00	3.00
(53)	Dick Radatz	6.00	3.00	1.75
(54)	Bobby Richardson	10.00	5.00	3.00
(55)	Brooks Robinson	20.00	10.00	6.00
(56)	Frank Robinson	20.00	10.00	6.00
(57)	Bob Rodgers	6.00	3.00	1.75
(58)	John Roseboro	6.00	3.00	1.75
(59)	Ron Santo	12.00	6.00	3.50
(60)	Diego Segui	6.00	3.00	1.75
(61)	Bill Skowron	9.00	4.50	2.75
(62)	Al Spangler	6.00	3.00	1.75
(63)	Dick Stuart	6.00	3.00	1.75
(64)	Luis Tiant	6.00	3.00	1.75
(65)	Joe Torre	12.00	6.00	3.50
(66)	Bob Veale	6.00	3.00	1.75
(67)	Leon Wagner	6.00	3.00	1.75
(68)	Pete Ward	6.00	3.00	1.75
(69)	Bill White	6.00	3.00	1.75
(70)	Dave Wickersham	6.00	3.00	1.75
(71)	Billy Williams	17.50	8.75	5.25
(72)	Carl Yastrzemski	25.00	12.50	7.50

1966 Topps

In 1966, Topps produced another 598-card set. The 2-1/2" x 3-1/2" cards feature the traditional color photograph with a diagonal strip in the upper left-hand corner carrying the team name. A band at the bottom carries the player's name and position. Multi-player cards returned in 1966 after a year's hiatus. The statistical leader cards feature the categorical leader and two runners-up. Most team managers have cards as well. The 1966 set features a handful of cards found with or without a notice of the player's sale or trade to another team. Cards without the notice bring higher prices and are not included in the complete set prices. Some cards in the high series (#523-598) were short-printed - produced in lesser quantities than the rest of the series. They are valued somewhat higher than the others and are indicated in the checklist by an (SP) notation following the player name.

		NM	EX	VG
	Complete Set (598):	4,600	2,300	1,375
	Common Player (1-370):	4.00	2.00	1.25
	Common Player (371-446):	7.50	3.75	2.25
	Common Player (447-522):	9.00	4.50	2.75
	Common Player (523-598):	12.50	6.25	3.75
1	Willie Mays	250.00	125.00	62.50
2	Ted Abernathy	4.00	2.00	1.25
3	Sam Mele	4.00	2.00	1.25
4	Ray Culp	4.00	2.00	1.25
5	Jim Fregosi	4.00	2.00	1.25
6	Chuck Schilling	4.00	2.00	1.25
7	Tracy Stallard	4.00	2.00	1.25
8	Floyd Robinson	4.00	2.00	1.25
9	Clete Boyer	8.00	4.00	2.50
10	Tony Cloninger	4.00	2.00	1.25
11	Senators Rookies (Brant Alyea, Pete Craig)	4.00	2.00	1.25
12	John Tsitouris	4.00	2.00	1.25
13	Lou Johnson	4.00	2.00	1.25
14	Norm Siebern	4.00	2.00	1.25
15	Vern Law	4.00	2.00	1.25
16	Larry Brown	4.00	2.00	1.25
17	Johnny Stephenson	4.00	2.00	1.25
18	Roland Sheldon	4.00	2.00	1.25
19	Giants Team	7.50	3.75	2.25
20	Willie Horton	4.00	2.00	1.25
21	Don Nottebart	4.00	2.00	1.25
22	Joe Nossek	4.00	2.00	1.25
23	Jack Sanford	4.00	2.00	1.25
24	*Don Kessinger*	7.50	3.75	2.25
25	Pete Ward	4.00	2.00	1.25
26	Ray Sadecki	4.00	2.00	1.25
27	Orioles Rookies (Andy Etchebarren, Darold Knowles)	6.00	3.00	1.75
28	Phil Niekro	15.00	7.50	4.50
29	Mike Brumley	4.00	2.00	1.25
30	Pete Rose	80.00	40.00	20.00
31	Jack Cullen	4.00	2.00	1.25
32	Adolfo Phillips	4.00	2.00	1.25
33	Jim Pagliaroni	4.00	2.00	1.25
34	1st Series Checklist (1-88)	7.50	3.75	2.25
35	Ron Swoboda	4.00	2.00	1.25
36	Jim Hunter	15.00	7.50	4.50
37	Billy Herman	6.00	3.00	1.75
38	Ron Nischwitz	4.00	2.00	1.25
39	Ken Henderson	4.00	2.00	1.25
40	Jim Grant	4.00	2.00	1.25
41	Don LeJohn	4.00	2.00	1.25
42	Aubrey Gatewood	4.00	2.00	1.25
43a	Don Landrum (No button on pants.)	4.00	2.00	1.25
43b	Don Landrum (Partial button on pants.)	6.00	3.00	1.75
43c	Don Landrum (Full button on pants.)	6.00	3.00	1.75
44	Indians Rookies (Bill Davis, Tom Kelley)	4.00	2.00	1.25
45	Jim Gentile	4.00	2.00	1.25
46	Howie Koplitz	4.00	2.00	1.25
47	J.C. Martin	4.00	2.00	1.25
48	Paul Blair	4.00	2.00	1.25
49	Woody Woodward	4.00	2.00	1.25
50	Mickey Mantle	400.00	200.00	100.00
51	Gordon Richardson	4.00	2.00	1.25
52	Power Plus (Johnny Callison, Wes Covington)	4.00	2.00	1.25
53	Bob Duliba	4.00	2.00	1.25
54	Jose Pagan	4.00	2.00	1.25
55	Ken Harrelson	4.00	2.00	1.25
56	Sandy Valdespino	4.00	2.00	1.25
57	Jim Lefebvre	4.00	2.00	1.25
58	Dave Wickersham	4.00	2.00	1.25
59	Reds Team	7.00	3.50	2.00
60	Curt Flood	4.00	2.00	1.25
61	Bob Bolin	4.00	2.00	1.25
62a	Merritt Ranew (No sold statement.)	20.00	10.00	6.00

No.	Player			
62b	Merritt Ranew (With sold statement.)	4.00	2.00	1.25
63	Jim Stewart	4.00	2.00	1.25
64	Bob Bruce	4.00	2.00	1.25
65	Leon Wagner	4.00	2.00	1.25
66	Al Weis	4.00	2.00	1.25
67	Mets Rookies (Cleon Jones, Dick Selma)	4.00	2.00	1.25
68	Hal Reniff	4.00	2.00	1.25
69	Ken Hamlin	4.00	2.00	1.25
70	Carl Yastrzemski	25.00	12.50	6.25
71	Frank Carpin	4.00	2.00	1.25
72	Tony Perez	25.00	12.50	6.25
73	Jerry Zimmerman	4.00	2.00	1.25
74	Don Mossi	4.00	2.00	1.25
75	Tommy Davis	4.00	2.00	1.25
76	Red Schoendienst	7.50	3.75	2.25
77	Johnny Orsino	4.00	2.00	1.25
78	Frank Linzy	4.00	2.00	1.25
79	Joe Pepitone	8.00	4.00	2.50
80	Richie Allen	6.00	3.00	1.75
81	Ray Oyler	4.00	2.00	1.25
82	Bob Hendley	4.00	2.00	1.25
83	Albie Pearson	4.00	2.00	1.25
84	Braves Rookies (Jim Beauchamp, Dick Kelley)	4.00	2.00	1.25
85	Eddie Fisher	4.00	2.00	1.25
86	John Bateman	4.00	2.00	1.25
87	Dan Napoleon	4.00	2.00	1.25
88	Fred Whitfield	4.00	2.00	1.25
89	Ted Davidson	4.00	2.00	1.25
90	Luis Aparicio	15.00	7.50	4.50
91a	Bob Uecker (No trade statement.)	60.00	30.00	18.00
91b	Bob Uecker (With trade statement.)	20.00	10.00	6.00
92	Yankees Team	15.00	7.50	4.50
93	Jim Lonborg	4.00	2.00	1.25
94	Matty Alou	4.00	2.00	1.25
95	Pete Richert	4.00	2.00	1.25
96	Felipe Alou	6.00	3.00	1.75
97	Jim Merritt	4.00	2.00	1.25
98	Don Demeter	4.00	2.00	1.25
99	Buc Belters (Donn Clendenon, Willie Stargell)	8.00	4.00	2.50
100	Sandy Koufax	100.00	50.00	25.00
101a	2nd Series Checklist (89-176) (115 is Spahn)	12.50	6.25	3.75
101b	2nd Series Checklist (89-176) (115 is Henry)	7.50	3.75	2.25
102	Ed Kirkpatrick	4.00	2.00	1.25
103a	Dick Groat (No trade statement.)	15.00	7.50	3.75
103b	Dick Groat (With trade statement.)	4.00	2.00	1.25
104a	Alex Johnson (No trade statement.)	20.00	10.00	6.00
104b	Alex Johnson (With trade statement.)	4.00	2.00	1.25
105	Milt Pappas	4.00	2.00	1.25
106	Rusty Staub	6.00	3.00	1.75
107	Athletics Rookies (Larry Stahl, Ron Tompkins)	4.00	2.00	1.25
108	Bobby Klaus	4.00	2.00	1.25
109	Ralph Terry	4.00	2.00	1.25
110	Ernie Banks	25.00	12.50	6.25
111	Gary Peters	4.00	2.00	1.25
112	Manny Mota	4.00	2.00	1.25
113	Hank Aguirre	4.00	2.00	1.25
114	Jim Gosger	4.00	2.00	1.25
115	Bill Henry	4.00	2.00	1.25
116	Walt Alston	6.00	3.00	1.75
117	Jake Gibbs	4.00	2.00	1.25
118	Mike McCormick	4.00	2.00	1.25
119	Art Shamsky	4.00	2.00	1.25
120	Harmon Killebrew	15.00	7.50	3.75
121	Ray Herbert	4.00	2.00	1.25
122	Joe Gaines	4.00	2.00	1.25
123	Pirates Rookies (Frank Bork, Jerry May)	4.00	2.00	1.25
124	Tug McGraw	4.00	2.00	1.25
125	Lou Brock	20.00	10.00	6.00
126	*Jim Palmer*	100.00	50.00	25.00
127	Ken Berry	4.00	2.00	1.25
128	Jim Landis	4.00	2.00	1.25
129	Jack Kralick	4.00	2.00	1.25
130	Joe Torre	6.00	3.00	1.75
131	Angels Team	7.50	3.75	2.25
132	Orlando Cepeda	15.00	7.50	4.50
133	Don McMahon	4.00	2.00	1.25
134	Wes Parker	4.00	2.00	1.25
135	Dave Morehead	4.00	2.00	1.25
136	Woody Held	4.00	2.00	1.25
137	Pat Corrales	4.00	2.00	1.25
138	Roger Repoz	4.00	2.00	1.25
139	Cubs Rookies (Byron Browne, Don Young)	4.00	2.00	1.25
140	Jim Maloney	4.00	2.00	1.25
141	Tom McCraw	4.00	2.00	1.25
142	Don Dennis	4.00	2.00	1.25
143	Jose Tartabull	4.00	2.00	1.25
144	Don Schwall	4.00	2.00	1.25
145	Bill Freehan	4.00	2.00	1.25
146	George Altman	4.00	2.00	1.25
147	Lum Harris	4.00	2.00	1.25
148	Bob Johnson	4.00	2.00	1.25
149	Dick Nen	4.00	2.00	1.25
150	Rocky Colavito	12.00	6.00	3.50
151	Gary Wagner	4.00	2.00	1.25
152	Frank Malzone	4.00	2.00	1.25
153	Rico Carty	4.00	2.00	1.25
154	Chuck Hiller	4.00	2.00	1.25
155	Marcelino Lopez	4.00	2.00	1.25
156	D P Combo (Hal Lanier, Dick Schofield)	4.00	2.00	1.25
157	Rene Lachemann	4.00	2.00	1.25
158	Jim Brewer	4.00	2.00	1.25
159	Chico Ruiz	4.00	2.00	1.25
160	Whitey Ford	35.00	17.50	8.75
161	Jerry Lumpe	4.00	2.00	1.25
162	Lee Maye	4.00	2.00	1.25
163	Tito Francona	4.00	2.00	1.25
164	White Sox Rookies (Tommie Agee, Marv Staehle)	4.00	2.00	1.25
165	Don Lock	4.00	2.00	1.25
166	Chris Krug	4.00	2.00	1.25
167	Boog Powell	6.00	3.00	1.75
168	Dan Osinski	4.00	2.00	1.25
169	Duke Sims	4.00	2.00	1.25
170	Cookie Rojas	4.00	2.00	1.25
171	Nick Willhite	4.00	2.00	1.25
172	Mets Team	6.00	3.00	1.75
173	Al Spangler	4.00	2.00	1.25
174	Ron Taylor	4.00	2.00	1.25
175	Bert Campaneris	4.00	2.00	1.25
176	Jim Davenport	4.00	2.00	1.25
177	Hector Lopez	4.00	2.00	1.25
178	Bob Tillman	4.00	2.00	1.25
179	Cardinals Rookies (Dennis Aust, Bob Tolan)	4.00	2.00	1.25
180	Vada Pinson	7.50	3.75	2.25
181	Al Worthington	4.00	2.00	1.25
182	Jerry Lynch	4.00	2.00	1.25
183a	3rd Series Checklist (177-264) (Large print on front.)	7.50	3.75	2.25
183b	3rd Series Checklist (177-264) (Small print on front.)	9.00	4.50	2.75
184	Denis Menke	4.00	2.00	1.25
185	Bob Buhl	4.00	2.00	1.25
186	Ruben Amaro	4.00	2.00	1.25
187	Chuck Dressen	4.00	2.00	1.25
188	Al Luplow	4.00	2.00	1.25
189	John Roseboro	4.00	2.00	1.25
190	Jimmie Hall	4.00	2.00	1.25
191	Darrell Sutherland	4.00	2.00	1.25
192	Vic Power	4.00	2.00	1.25
193	Dave McNally	4.00	2.00	1.25
194	Senators Team	6.00	3.00	1.75
195	Joe Morgan	25.00	12.50	7.50
196	Don Pavletich	4.00	2.00	1.25
197	Sonny Siebert	4.00	2.00	1.25
198	*Mickey Stanley*	6.00	3.00	1.75
199	Chisox Clubbers (Floyd Robinson, Johnny Romano, Bill Skowron)	6.00	3.00	1.75
200	Ed Mathews	20.00	10.00	6.00
201	Jim Dickson	4.00	2.00	1.25
202	Clay Dalrymple	4.00	2.00	1.25
203	Jose Santiago	4.00	2.00	1.25
204	Cubs Team	7.50	3.75	2.25
205	Tom Tresh	9.00	4.50	2.75
206	Alvin Jackson	4.00	2.00	1.25
207	Frank Quilici	4.00	2.00	1.25
208	Bob Miller	4.00	2.00	1.25
209	Tigers Rookies (*Fritz Fisher, John Hiller*)	4.00	2.00	1.25
210	Bill Mazeroski	17.50	8.75	5.25
211	Frank Kreutzer	4.00	2.00	1.25
212	Ed Kranepool	4.00	2.00	1.25
213	Fred Newman	4.00	2.00	1.25
214	Tommy Harper	4.00	2.00	1.25
215	N.L. Batting Leaders (Hank Aaron, Roberto Clemente, Willie Mays)	35.00	17.50	8.75
216	A.L. Batting Leaders (Vic Davalillo, Tony Oliva, Carl Yastrzemski)	16.00	8.00	4.75
217	N.L. Home Run Leaders (Willie Mays, Willie McCovey, Billy Williams)	15.00	7.50	3.75
218	A.L. Home Run Leaders (Norm Cash, Tony Conigliaro, Willie Horton)	12.50	6.25	3.75
219	N.L. RBI Leaders (Deron Johnson, Willie Mays, Frank Robinson)	15.00	7.50	3.75
220	A.L. RBI Leaders (Rocky Colavito, Willie Horton, Tony Oliva)	12.00	6.00	3.50
221	N.L. ERA Leaders (Sandy Koufax, Vern Law, Juan Marichal)	15.00	7.50	4.50
222	A.L. ERA Leaders (Eddie Fisher, Sam McDowell, Sonny Siebert)	6.00	3.00	1.75
223	N.L. Pitching Leaders (Tony Cloninger, Don Drysdale, Sandy Koufax)	16.00	8.00	4.75
224	A.L. Pitching Leaders (Jim Grant, Jim Kaat, Mel Stottlemyre)	9.00	4.50	2.75
225	N.L. Strikeout Leaders (Bob Gibson, Sandy Koufax, Bob Veale)	15.00	7.50	4.50
226	A.L. Strikeout Leaders (Mickey Lolich, Sam McDowell, Denny McLain, Sonny Siebert)	10.00	5.00	3.00
227	Russ Nixon	4.00	2.00	1.25
228	Larry Dierker	4.00	2.00	1.25
229	Hank Bauer	4.50	2.25	1.25
230	Johnny Callison	4.00	2.00	1.25
231	Floyd Weaver	4.00	2.00	1.25
232	Glenn Beckert	4.00	2.00	1.25
233	Dom Zanni	4.00	2.00	1.25
234	Yankees Rookies (*Rich Beck, Roy White*)	15.00	7.50	4.50
235	Don Cardwell	4.00	2.00	1.25
236	Mike Hershberger	4.00	2.00	1.25
237	Billy O'Dell	4.00	2.00	1.25
238	Dodgers Team	9.00	4.50	2.75
239	Orlando Pena	4.00	2.00	1.25
240	Earl Battey	4.00	2.00	1.25
241	Dennis Ribant	4.00	2.00	1.25
242	Jesus Alou	4.00	2.00	1.25
243	Nelson Briles	4.00	2.00	1.25
244	Astros Rookies (Chuck Harrison, Sonny Jackson)	4.00	2.00	1.25
245	John Buzhardt	4.00	2.00	1.25
246	Ed Bailey	4.00	2.00	1.25
247	Carl Warwick	4.00	2.00	1.25
248	Pete Mikkelsen	4.00	2.00	1.25
249	Bill Rigney	4.00	2.00	1.25
250	Sam Ellis	4.00	2.00	1.25
251	Ed Brinkman	4.00	2.00	1.25
252	Denver Lemaster	4.00	2.00	1.25
253	Don Wert	4.00	2.00	1.25
254	Phillies Rookies (Fergie Jenkins, Bill Sorrell)	60.00	30.00	15.00
255	Willie Stargell	20.00	10.00	6.00
256	Lew Krausse	4.00	2.00	1.25
257	Jeff Torborg	4.00	2.00	1.25
258	Dave Giusti	4.00	2.00	1.25
259	Red Sox Team	7.50	3.75	2.25
260	Bob Shaw	4.00	2.00	1.25
261	Ron Hansen	4.00	2.00	1.25
262	Jack Hamilton	4.00	2.00	1.25
263	Tom Egan	4.00	2.00	1.25
264	Twins Rookies (Andy Kosco, Ted Uhlaender)	4.00	2.00	1.25
265	Stu Miller	4.00	2.00	1.25
266	Pedro Gonzalez	4.00	2.00	1.25
267	Joe Sparma	4.00	2.00	1.25
268	John Blanchard	4.00	2.00	1.25
269	Don Heffner	4.00	2.00	1.25
270	Claude Osteen	4.00	2.00	1.25
271	Hal Lanier	4.00	2.00	1.25
272	Jack Baldschun	4.00	2.00	1.25
273	Astro Aces (Bob Aspromonte, Rusty Staub)	6.00	3.00	1.75
274	Buster Narum	4.00	2.00	1.25
275	Tim McCarver	7.50	3.75	2.25
276	Jim Bouton	6.00	3.00	1.75
277	George Thomas	4.00	2.00	1.25
278	Calvin Koonce	4.00	2.00	1.25
279a	4th Series Checklist (265-352) (Player's cap black.)	7.00	3.50	2.00
279b	4th Series Checklist (265-352) (Player's cap red.)	7.50	3.75	2.25
280	Bobby Knoop	4.00	2.00	1.25
281	Bruce Howard	4.00	2.00	1.25
282	Johnny Lewis	4.00	2.00	1.25
283	Jim Perry	4.00	2.00	1.25
284	Bobby Wine	4.00	2.00	1.25
285	Luis Tiant	4.00	2.00	1.25
286	Gary Geiger	4.00	2.00	1.25
287	Jack Aker	4.00	2.00	1.25
288	Dodgers Rookies (*Bill Singer, Don Sutton*)	60.00	30.00	15.00
289	Larry Sherry	4.00	2.00	1.25
290	Ron Santo	12.50	6.25	3.75
291	Moe Drabowsky	4.00	2.00	1.25
292	Jim Coker	4.00	2.00	1.25
293	Mike Shannon	4.00	2.00	1.25
294	Steve Ridzik	4.00	2.00	1.25
295	Jim Hart	4.00	2.00	1.25
296	Johnny Keane	4.00	2.00	1.25
297	Jim Owens	4.00	2.00	1.25
298	Rico Petrocelli	6.00	3.00	1.75
299	Lou Burdette	4.00	2.00	1.25
300	Bob Clemente	150.00	75.00	37.50
301	Greg Bollo	4.00	2.00	1.25
302	Ernie Bowman	4.00	2.00	1.25
303a	Indians Team (Dot between "PLACE" and "AMERICAN.")	6.00	3.00	1.75
303b	Indians Team (No dot.)	6.00	3.00	1.75
304	John Herrnstein	4.00	2.00	1.25
305	Camilo Pascual	4.00	2.00	1.25
306	Ty Cline	4.00	2.00	1.25
307	Clay Carroll	4.00	2.00	1.25
308	Tom Haller	4.00	2.00	1.25
309	Diego Segui	4.00	2.00	1.25
310	Frank Robinson	30.00	15.00	7.50
311	Reds Rookies (Tommy Helms, Dick Simpson)	4.00	2.00	1.25
312	Bob Saverine	4.00	2.00	1.25
313	Chris Zachary	4.00	2.00	1.25
314	Hector Valle	4.00	2.00	1.25
315	Norm Cash	11.00	5.50	3.25
316	Jack Fisher	4.00	2.00	1.25
317	Dalton Jones	4.00	2.00	1.25
318	Harry Walker	4.00	2.00	1.25
319	Gene Freese	4.00	2.00	1.25
320	Bob Gibson	30.00	15.00	9.00
321	Rick Reichardt	4.00	2.00	1.25
322	Bill Faul	4.00	2.00	1.25
323	Ray Barker	4.00	2.00	1.25
324	John Boozer	4.00	2.00	1.25
325	Vic Davalillo	4.00	2.00	1.25
326a	Braves Team (Dot between "PLACE" and "NATIONAL.")	7.50	3.75	2.25
326b	Braves Team (No dot.)	7.50	3.75	2.25
327	Bernie Allen	4.00	2.00	1.25
328	Jerry Grote	4.00	2.00	1.25
329	Pete Charton	4.00	2.00	1.25
330	Ron Fairly	4.00	2.00	1.25
331	Ron Herbel	4.00	2.00	1.25
332	Billy Bryan	4.00	2.00	1.25
333	Senators Rookies (Joe Coleman, Jim French)	4.00	2.00	1.25
334	Marty Keough	4.00	2.00	1.25
335	Juan Pizarro	4.00	2.00	1.25
336	Gene Alley	4.00	2.00	1.25
337	Fred Gladding	4.00	2.00	1.25
338	Dal Maxvill	4.00	2.00	1.25
339	Del Crandall	4.00	2.00	1.25
340	Dean Chance	4.00	2.00	1.25
341	Wes Westrum	4.00	2.00	1.25
342	Bob Humphreys	4.00	2.00	1.25
343	Joe Christopher	4.00	2.00	1.25
344	Steve Blass	4.00	2.00	1.25
345	Bob Allison	4.00	2.00	1.25
346	Mike de la Hoz	4.00	2.00	1.25
347	Phil Regan	4.00	2.00	1.25

No.	Player	NM	EX	VG
348	Orioles Team	8.00	4.00	2.50
349	Cap Peterson	4.00	2.00	1.25
350	Mel Stottlemyre	6.00	3.00	1.75
351	Fred Valentine	4.00	2.00	1.25
352	Bob Aspromonte	4.00	2.00	1.25
353	Al McBean	4.00	2.00	1.25
354	Smoky Burgess	4.00	2.00	1.25
355	Wade Blasingame	4.00	2.00	1.25
356	Red Sox Rookies (Owen Johnson, Ken Sanders)	4.00	2.00	1.25
357	Gerry Arrigo	4.00	2.00	1.25
358	Charlie Smith	4.00	2.00	1.25
359	Johnny Briggs	4.00	2.00	1.25
360	Ron Hunt	4.00	2.00	1.25
361	Tom Satriano	4.00	2.00	1.25
362	Gates Brown	4.00	2.00	1.25
363	5th Series Checklist (353-429)	9.00	4.50	2.75
364	Nate Oliver	4.00	2.00	1.25
365	Roger Maris	50.00	25.00	12.50
366	Wayne Causey	4.00	2.00	1.25
367	Mel Nelson	4.00	2.00	1.25
368	Charlie Lau	4.00	2.00	1.25
369	Jim King	4.00	2.00	1.25
370	Chico Cardenas	4.00	2.00	1.25
371	Lee Stange	7.50	3.75	2.25
372	Harvey Kuenn	7.50	3.75	2.25
373	Giants Rookies (Dick Estelle, Jack Hiatt)	7.50	3.75	2.25
374	Bob Locker	7.50	3.75	2.25
375	Donn Clendenon	7.50	3.75	2.25
376	Paul Schaal	7.50	3.75	2.25
377	Turk Farrell	7.50	3.75	2.25
378	Dick Tracewski	7.50	3.75	2.25
379	Cards Team	10.00	5.00	3.00
380	Tony Conigliaro	12.50	6.25	3.75
381	Hank Fischer	7.50	3.75	2.25
382	Phil Roof	7.50	3.75	2.25
383	Jackie Brandt	7.50	3.75	2.25
384	Al Downing	7.50	3.75	2.25
385	Ken Boyer	10.00	5.00	3.00
386	Gil Hodges	11.00	5.50	3.25
387	Howie Reed	7.50	3.75	2.25
388	Don Mincher	7.50	3.75	2.25
389	Jim O'Toole	7.50	3.75	2.25
390	Brooks Robinson	40.00	20.00	10.00
391	Chuck Hinton	7.50	3.75	2.25
392	Cubs Rookies (*Bill Hands, Randy Hundley*)	12.00	6.00	3.50
393	George Brunet	7.50	3.75	2.25
394	Ron Brand	7.50	3.75	2.25
395	Len Gabrielson	7.50	3.75	2.25
396	Jerry Stephenson	7.50	3.75	2.25
397	Bill White	7.50	3.75	2.25
398	Danny Cater	7.50	3.75	2.25
399	Ray Washburn	7.50	3.75	2.25
400	Zoilo Versalles	7.50	3.75	2.25
401	Ken McMullen	7.50	3.75	2.25
402	Jim Hickman	7.50	3.75	2.25
403	Fred Talbot	7.50	3.75	2.25
404a	Pirates Team (Dot between "PLACE" and "NATIONAL.")	12.50	6.25	3.75
404b	Pirates Team (No dot.)	12.50	6.25	3.75
405	Elston Howard	9.00	4.50	2.75
406	Joe Jay	7.50	3.75	2.25
407	John Kennedy	7.50	3.75	2.25
408	Lee Thomas	7.50	3.75	2.25
409	Billy Hoeft	7.50	3.75	2.25
410	Al Kaline	40.00	20.00	10.00
411	Gene Mauch	7.50	3.75	2.25
412	Sam Bowens	7.50	3.75	2.25
413	John Romano	7.50	3.75	2.25
414	Dan Coombs	7.50	3.75	2.25
415	Max Alvis	7.50	3.75	2.25
416	Phil Ortega	7.50	3.75	2.25
417	Angels Rookies (Jim McGlothlin, Ed Sukla)	7.50	3.75	2.25
418	Phil Gagliano	7.50	3.75	2.25
419	Mike Ryan	7.50	3.75	2.25
420	Juan Marichal	15.00	7.50	3.75
421	Roy McMillan	7.50	3.75	2.25
422	Ed Charles	7.50	3.75	2.25
423	Ernie Broglio	7.50	3.75	2.25
424	Reds Rookies (Lee May, Darrell Osteen)	10.00	5.00	3.00
425	Bob Veale	7.50	3.75	2.25
426	White Sox Team	10.00	5.00	3.00
427	John Miller	7.50	3.75	2.25
428	Sandy Alomar	7.50	3.75	2.25
429	Bill Monbouquette	7.50	3.75	2.25
430	Don Drysdale	20.00	10.00	6.00
431	Walt Bond	7.50	3.75	2.25
432	Bob Heffner	7.50	3.75	2.25
433	Alvin Dark	7.50	3.75	2.25
434	Willie Kirkland	7.50	3.75	2.25
435	Jim Bunning	15.00	7.50	4.50
436	Julian Javier	7.50	3.75	2.25
437	Al Stanek	7.50	3.75	2.25
438	Willie Smith	7.50	3.75	2.25
439	Pedro Ramos	7.50	3.75	2.25
440	Deron Johnson	7.50	3.75	2.25
441	Tommie Sisk	7.50	3.75	2.25
442	Orioles Rookies (Ed Barnowski, Eddie Watt)	7.50	3.75	2.25
443	Bill Wakefield	7.50	3.75	2.25
444a	6th Series Checklist (430-506) (456 is R. Sox Rookies)	7.50	3.75	2.25
444b	6th Series Checklist (430-506) (456 is Red Sox Rookies)	9.00	4.50	2.75
445	Jim Kaat	9.00	4.50	2.75
446	Mack Jones	7.50	3.75	2.25
447	Dick Ellsworth (Photo actually Ken Hubbs.)	12.50	6.25	3.75
448	Eddie Stanky	9.00	4.50	2.75
449	Joe Moeller	9.00	4.50	2.75
450	Tony Oliva	15.00	7.50	4.50
451	Barry Latman	9.00	4.50	2.75
452	Joe Azcue	9.00	4.50	2.75
453	Ron Kline	9.00	4.50	2.75
454	Jerry Buchek	9.00	4.50	2.75
455	Mickey Lolich	9.00	4.50	2.75
456	Red Sox Rookies (Darrell Brandon, Joe Foy)	9.00	4.50	2.75
457	Joe Gibbon	9.00	4.50	2.75
458	Manny Jiminez (Jimenez)	9.00	4.50	2.75
459	Bill McCool	9.00	4.50	2.75
460	Curt Blefary	9.00	4.50	2.75
461	Roy Face	9.00	4.50	2.75
462	Bob Rodgers	9.00	4.50	2.75
463	Phillies Team	12.00	6.00	3.50
464	Larry Bearnarth	9.00	4.50	2.75
465	Don Buford	9.00	4.50	2.75
466	Ken Johnson	9.00	4.50	2.75
467	Vic Roznovsky	9.00	4.50	2.75
468	Johnny Podres	9.00	4.50	2.75
469	Yankees Rookies (Bobby Murcer, Dooley Womack)	30.00	15.00	7.50
470	Sam McDowell	9.00	4.50	2.75
471	Bob Skinner	9.00	4.50	2.75
472	Terry Fox	9.00	4.50	2.75
473	Rich Rollins	9.00	4.50	2.75
474	Dick Schofield	9.00	4.50	2.75
475	Dick Radatz	9.00	4.50	2.75
476	Bobby Bragan	9.00	4.50	2.75
477	Steve Barber	9.00	4.50	2.75
478	Tony Gonzalez	9.00	4.50	2.75
479	Jim Hannan	9.00	4.50	2.75
480	Dick Stuart	9.00	4.50	2.75
481	Bob Lee	9.00	4.50	2.75
482	Cubs Rookies (John Boccabella, Dave Dowling)	9.00	4.50	2.75
483	Joe Nuxhall	9.00	4.50	2.75
484	Wes Covington	9.00	4.50	2.75
485	Bob Bailey	9.00	4.50	2.75
486	Tommy John	9.00	4.50	2.75
487	Al Ferrara	9.00	4.50	2.75
488	George Banks	9.00	4.50	2.75
489	Curt Simmons	9.00	4.50	2.75
490	Bobby Richardson	20.00	10.00	5.00
491	Dennis Bennett	9.00	4.50	2.75
492	Athletics Team	12.00	6.00	3.50
493	Johnny Klippstein	9.00	4.50	2.75
494	Gordon Coleman	9.00	4.50	2.75
495	Dick McAuliffe	9.00	4.50	2.75
496	Lindy McDaniel	9.00	4.50	2.75
497	Chris Cannizzaro	9.00	4.50	2.75
498	Pirates Rookies (Woody Fryman, Luke Walker)	9.00	4.50	2.75
499	Wally Bunker	9.00	4.50	2.75
500	Hank Aaron	125.00	62.50	31.25
501	John O'Donoghue	9.00	4.50	2.75
502	Lenny Green	9.00	4.50	2.75
503	Steve Hamilton	9.00	4.50	2.75
504	Grady Hatton	9.00	4.50	2.75
505	Jose Cardenal	9.00	4.50	2.75
506	Bo Belinsky	9.00	4.50	2.75
507	John Edwards	9.00	4.50	2.75
508	*Steve Hargan*	9.00	4.50	2.75
509	Jake Wood	9.00	4.50	2.75
510	Hoyt Wilhelm	16.00	8.00	4.75
511	Giants Rookies (*Bob Barton, Tito Fuentes*)	9.00	4.50	2.75
512	Dick Stigman	9.00	4.50	2.75
513	Camilo Carreon	9.00	4.50	2.75
514	Hal Woodeshick	9.00	4.50	2.75
515	Frank Howard	9.00	4.50	2.75
516	Eddie Bressoud	9.00	4.50	2.75
517a	7th Series Checklist (507-598) (529 is W. Sox Rookies)	11.00	5.50	3.25
517b	7th Series Checklist (507-598) (529 is White Sox Rookies)	13.50	6.75	4.00
518	Braves Rookies (Herb Hippauf, Arnie Umbach)	9.00	4.50	2.75
519	Bob Friend	9.00	4.50	2.75
520	Jim Wynn	9.00	4.50	2.75
521	John Wyatt	9.00	4.50	2.75
522	Phil Linz	9.00	4.50	2.75
523	Bob Sadowski	12.50	6.25	3.75
524	Giants Rookies (Ollie Brown, Don Mason) (SP)	16.00	8.00	4.75
525	Gary Bell (SP)	16.00	8.00	4.75
526	Twins Team (SP)	75.00	37.50	18.75
527	Julio Navarro	12.50	6.25	3.75
528	Jesse Gonder (SP)	16.00	8.00	4.75
529	White Sox Rookies (Lee Elia, Dennis Higgins, Bill Voss)	12.50	6.25	3.75
530	Robin Roberts	40.00	20.00	10.00
531	Joe Cunningham	12.50	6.25	3.75
532	Aurelio Monteagudo (SP)	16.00	8.00	4.75
533	Jerry Adair (SP)	16.00	8.00	4.75
534	Mets Rookies (Dave Eilers, Rob Gardner)	12.50	6.25	3.75
535	Willie Davis (SP)	16.00	8.00	4.75
536	Dick Egan	12.50	6.25	3.75
537	Herman Franks	12.50	6.25	3.75
538	Bob Allen (SP)	16.00	8.00	4.75
539	Astros Rookies (Bill Heath, Carroll Sembera)	12.50	6.25	3.75
540	Denny McLain (SP)	50.00	25.00	15.00
541	Gene Oliver (SP)	16.00	8.00	4.75
542	George Smith	12.50	6.25	3.75
543	Roger Craig (SP)	16.00	8.00	4.75
544	Cardinals Rookies (Joe Hoerner, George Kernek, Jimmy Williams) (SP)	16.00	8.00	4.75
545	Dick Green (SP)	16.00		4.75
546	Dwight Siebler	12.50	6.25	3.75
547	*Horace Clarke* (SP)	45.00	22.50	11.25
548	Gary Kroll (SP)	16.00	8.00	4.75
549	Senators Rookies (Al Closter, Casey Cox)	12.50	6.25	3.75
550	Willie McCovey (SP)	100.00	50.00	25.00
551	Bob Purkey (SP)	16.00	8.00	4.75
552	Birdie Tebbetts (SP)	16.00	8.00	4.75
553	Major League Rookies (Pat Garrett, Jackie Warner)	12.50	6.25	3.75
554	Jim Northrup (SP)	16.00	8.00	4.75
555	Ron Perranoski (SP)	16.00	8.00	4.75
556	Mel Queen (SP)	16.00	8.00	4.75
557	Felix Mantilla (SP)	16.00	8.00	4.75
558	Red Sox Rookies (*Guido Grilli, Pete Magrini, George Scott*)	20.00	10.00	6.00
559	Roberto Pena (SP)	16.00	8.00	4.75
560	Joel Horlen	12.50	6.25	3.75
561	Choo Choo Coleman (SP)	25.00	12.50	6.25
562	Russ Snyder	12.50	6.25	3.75
563	Twins Rookies (Pete Cimino, Cesar Tovar)	12.50	6.25	3.75
564	Bob Chance (SP)	16.00	8.00	4.75
565	Jimmy Piersall (SP)	35.00	17.50	8.75
566	Mike Cuellar (SP)	16.00	8.00	4.75
567	Dick Howser (SP)	16.00	8.00	4.75
568	Athletics Rookies (Paul Lindblad, Ron Stone)	12.50	6.25	3.75
569	Orlando McFarlane (SP)	16.00	8.00	4.75
570	Art Mahaffey (SP)	16.00	8.00	4.75
571	Dave Roberts (SP)	16.00	8.00	4.75
572	Bob Priddy	12.50	6.25	3.75
573	Derrell Griffith	12.50	6.25	3.75
574	Mets Rookies (Bill Hepler, Bill Murphy)	12.50	6.25	3.75
575	Earl Wilson	12.50	6.25	3.75
576	Dave Nicholson (SP)	16.00	8.00	4.75
577	Jack Lamabe (SP)	16.00	8.00	4.75
578	Chi Chi Olivo (SP)	16.00	8.00	4.75
579	Orioles Rookies (Frank Bertaina, Gene Brabender, Dave Johnson)	20.00	10.00	5.00
580	Billy Williams (SP)	40.00	20.00	10.00
581	Tony Martinez	12.50	6.25	3.75
582	Garry Roggenburk	12.50	6.25	3.75
583	Tigers Team	75.00	37.50	22.50
584	Yankees Rookies (*Frank Fernandez, Fritz Peterson*)	15.00	7.50	4.50
585	Tony Taylor	12.50	6.25	3.75
586	Claude Raymond (SP)	16.00	8.00	4.75
587	Dick Bertell	12.50	6.25	3.75
588	Athletics Rookies (Chuck Dobson, Ken Suarez)	12.50	6.25	3.75
589	Lou Klimchock (SP)	16.00	8.00	4.75
590	Bill Skowron (SP)	30.00	15.00	7.50
591	N.L. Rookies (Grant Jackson, Bart Shirley) (SP)	16.00	8.00	4.75
592	Andre Rodgers	12.50	6.25	3.75
593	Doug Camilli (SP)	16.00	8.00	4.75
594	Chico Salmon	12.50	6.25	3.75
595	Larry Jackson	12.50	6.25	3.75
596	Astros Rookies (Nate Colbert, Greg Sims) (SP)	20.00	10.00	6.00
597	John Sullivan	12.50	6.25	3.75
598	Gaylord Perry (SP)	170.00	85.00	42.50

1966 Topps Comic Book Foldees

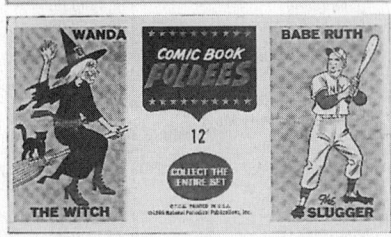

Comic book heroes and other fictional characters were the focus of this set of 44 "foldees." The pictures on the left and right ends of the 4-1/2" x 2-3/8" cards were cut through the middle to allow them to be folded over the central picture and each other to create funny combinations. Babe Ruth, in a rather generic drawing, is the only baseball player represented in the issue. A version of the set exists which carries a "T.G.C. PRINTED IN CANADA" copyright line; it is valued similarly.

	NM	EX	VG
Complete set (44):	100.00	50.00	30.00
12 Babe Ruth	20.00	10.00	7.25

1966 Topps Punch-Outs

Only a handful of surviving examples of this issue are known. It is believed they represent a prototype for the 1967 Topps Punch-Outs which were themselves issued only on a test basis. The cards are blank-backed, measuring about 2-1/2" x 4-5/8" and perforated at center to allow the American League and National League to be separated for game play. A team captain is pictured in black-and-white on each half of the card. The A.L. side has a red background with 35 yellow baseballs to be punched out to determine game action. Background on the N.L. side is blue. Because of their rarity and lack of recent sales records, valuations for most pieces are not provided. This checklist is likely incomplete.

		NM	EX	VG
(1)	Ernie Banks, Mel Stottlemyre			
(2)	Johnny Callison, Jim Grant			
(3)	Donn Clendenon, Al Kaline			
(4)	Curt Flood, Bill Skowron			
(5)	Jim Ray Hart, Mickey Mantle			
(6)	Juan Marichal, Rich Rollins			
(7)	Sandy Koufax, Carl Yastrzemski (12/04 auction)	6,700		
(8)	John Roseboro, Bobby Richardson			
(9)	Willie Stargell, Felix Mantilla			
(10)	Willie Mays, Tony Conigliaro			
(11)	Joe Torre, Harmon Killebrew			

1966 Topps Rub-Offs

Returning to a concept last tried in 1961, Topps tried an expanded version of Rub-Offs in 1966. Measuring 2-1/16" x 3", the Rub-Offs are in vertical format for the 100 players and horizontal for the 20 team pennants. The player Rub-Offs feature a color photo. Cutting procedures left well-centered examples the distinct minority.

		NM	EX	VG
Complete Set (120):		800.00	265.00	120.00
Common Player:		5.00	1.50	.75
(1)	Hank Aaron	30.00	11.00	5.00
(2)	Jerry Adair	5.00	1.50	.75
(3)	Richie Allen	6.00	2.00	.90
(4)	Jesus Alou	5.00	1.50	.75
(5)	Max Alvis	5.00	1.50	.75
(6)	Bob Aspromonte	5.00	1.50	.75
(7)	Ernie Banks	15.00	5.00	2.50
(8)	Earl Battey	5.00	1.50	.75
(9)	Curt Blefary	5.00	1.50	.75
(10)	Ken Boyer	6.00	2.00	.90
(11)	Bob Bruce	5.00	1.50	.75
(12)	Jim Bunning	10.00	3.50	1.50
(13)	Johnny Callison	5.00	1.50	.75
(14)	Bert Campaneris	5.00	1.50	.75
(15)	Jose Cardenal	5.00	1.50	.75
(16)	Dean Chance	5.00	1.50	.75
(17)	Ed Charles	5.00	1.50	.75
(18)	Bob Clemente	35.00	12.00	5.00
(19)	Tony Cloninger	5.00	1.50	.75
(20)	Rocky Colavito	6.00	2.00	.90
(21)	Tony Conigliaro	6.50	2.25	1.00
(22)	Vic Davilillo	5.00	1.50	.75
(23)	Willie Davis	5.00	1.50	.75
(24)	Don Drysdale	10.00	3.50	1.50
(25)	Sammy Ellis	5.00	1.50	.75
(26)	Dick Ellsworth	5.00	1.50	.75
(27)	Ron Fairly	5.00	1.50	.75
(28)	Dick Farrell	5.00	1.50	.75
(29)	Eddie Fisher	5.00	1.50	.75
(30)	Jack Fisher	5.00	1.50	.75
(31)	Curt Flood	5.00	1.50	.75
(32)	Whitey Ford	15.00	5.25	2.25
(33)	Bill Freehan	5.00	1.50	.75
(34)	Jim Fregosi	5.00	1.50	.75
(35)	Bob Gibson	10.00	3.50	1.50
(36)	Jim Grant	5.00	1.50	.75
(37)	Jimmie Hall	5.00	1.50	.75
(38)	Ken Harrelson	5.00	1.50	.75
(39)	Jim Hart	5.00	1.50	.75
(40)	Joel Horlen	5.00	1.50	.75
(41)	Willie Horton	5.00	1.50	.75
(42)	Frank Howard	6.00	2.00	.90
(43)	Deron Johnson	5.00	1.50	.75
(44)	Al Kaline	12.50	4.50	2.00
(45)	Harmon Killebrew	10.00	3.50	1.50
(46)	Bobby Knoop	5.00	1.50	.75
(47)	Sandy Koufax	30.00	10.00	5.00
(48)	Ed Kranepool	5.00	1.50	.75
(49)	Gary Kroll	5.00	1.50	.75
(50)	Don Landrum	5.00	1.50	.75
(51)	Vernon Law	5.00	1.50	.75
(52)	Johnny Lewis	5.00	1.50	.75
(53)	Don Lock	5.00	1.50	.75
(54)	Mickey Lolich	5.00	1.50	.75

		NM	EX	VG
(55)	Jim Maloney	5.00	1.50	.75
(56)	Felix Mantilla	5.00	1.50	.75
(57)	Mickey Mantle	55.00	20.00	8.00
(58)	Juan Marichal	10.00	3.50	1.50
(59)	Ed Mathews	10.00	3.50	1.50
(60)	Willie Mays	30.00	10.00	5.00
(61)	Bill Mazeroski	10.00	3.50	1.50
(62)	Dick McAuliffe	5.00	1.50	.75
(63)	Tim McCarver	6.00	2.00	.90
(64)	Willie McCovey	10.00	3.50	1.50
(65)	Sammy McDowell	5.00	1.50	.75
(66)	Ken McMullen	5.00	1.50	.75
(67)	Denis Menke	5.00	1.50	.75
(68)	Bill Monbouquette	5.00	1.50	.75
(69)	Joe Morgan	10.00	3.50	1.50
(70)	Fred Newman	5.00	1.50	.75
(71)	John O'Donoghue	5.00	1.50	.75
(72)	Tony Oliva	6.00	2.00	.90
(73)	Johnny Orsino	5.00	1.50	.75
(74)	Phil Ortega	5.00	1.50	.75
(75)	Milt Pappas	5.00	1.50	.75
(76)	Dick Radatz	5.00	1.50	.75
(77)	Bobby Richardson	6.50	2.25	1.00
(78)	Pete Richert	5.00	1.50	.75
(79)	Brooks Robinson	12.50	4.50	2.00
(80)	Floyd Robinson	5.00	1.50	.75
(81)	Frank Robinson	12.50	4.50	2.00
(82)	Cookie Rojas	5.00	1.50	.75
(83)	Pete Rose	25.00	9.00	4.00
(84)	John Roseboro	5.00	1.50	.75
(85)	Ron Santo	6.50	2.25	1.00
(86)	Bill Skowron	5.00	1.75	.70
(87)	Willie Stargell	10.00	3.50	1.50
(88)	Mel Stottlemyre	5.00	1.50	.75
(89)	Dick Stuart	5.00	1.50	.75
(90)	Ron Swoboda	5.00	1.50	.75
(91)	Fred Talbot	5.00	1.50	.75
(92)	Ralph Terry	5.00	1.50	.75
(93)	Joe Torre	6.50	2.25	1.00
(94)	Tom Tresh	5.00	1.50	.75
(95)	Bob Veale	5.00	1.50	.75
(96)	Pete Ward	5.00	1.50	.75
(97)	Bill White	5.00	1.50	.75
(98)	Billy Williams	10.00	3.50	1.50
(99)	Jim Wynn	5.00	1.50	.75
(100)	Carl Yastrzemski	15.00	5.25	2.25
(101)	Angels Pennant	7.00	2.50	1.00
(102)	Astros Pennant	7.00	2.50	1.00
(103)	Athletics Pennant	7.00	2.50	1.00
(104)	Braves Pennant	7.00	2.50	1.00
(105)	Cards Pennant	7.00	2.50	1.00
(106)	Cubs Pennant	7.00	2.50	1.00
(107)	Dodgers Pennant	7.00	2.50	1.00
(108)	Giants Pennant	7.00	2.50	1.00
(109)	Indians Pennant	7.00	2.50	1.00
(110)	Mets Pennant	7.00	2.50	1.00
(111)	Orioles Pennant	7.00	2.50	1.00
(112)	Phillies Pennant	7.00	2.50	1.00
(113)	Pirates Pennant	7.00	2.50	1.00
(114)	Red Sox Pennant	7.00	2.50	1.00
(115)	Reds Pennant	7.00	2.50	1.00
(116)	Senators Pennant	7.00	2.50	1.00
(117)	Tigers Pennant	7.00	2.50	1.00
(118)	Twins Pennant	7.00	2.50	1.00
(119)	White Sox Pennant	7.00	2.50	1.00
(120)	Yankees Pennant	9.00	3.25	1.25

1967 Topps

This 609-card set of 2-1/2" x 3-1/2" cards marked the largest set up to that time for Topps. Card fronts feature large color photographs bordered by white. The player's name and position are printed at the top with the team at the bottom. Across the front of the card with the exception of #254 (Milt Pappas) there is a facsimile autograph. The backs were the first to be done vertically, although they continued to carry familiar statistical and biographical information. The only subsets are statistical leaders and World Series highlights. Rookie cards are grouped by team or league with two players per card. The high numbers (#534-609) in '67 are quite scarce, and while it is known that some are even scarcer, by virtue of having been short-printed in relation to the rest of the series, there is no general agreement on which cards are involved. Cards in the high series which are generally believed to have been double-printed - and thus worth somewhat less than the other cards in the series - are indicated in the checklist by a (DP) notation following the player name.

	NM	EX	VG
Complete Set (609):	4,500	2,250	1,350
Common Player (1-370):	2.00	1.00	.60
Common Player (371-457):	4.00	2.00	1.25
Common Player (458-533):	7.00	3.50	2.00
Common Player (534-609):	12.00	6.00	3.50

1	The Champs (Hank Bauer, Brooks Robinson, Frank Robinson)	20.00	9.00	5.00
2	Jack Hamilton	2.00	1.00	.60
3	Duke Sims	2.00	1.00	.60
4	Hal Lanier	2.00	1.00	.60
5	Whitey Ford	30.00	15.00	7.50
6	Dick Simpson	2.00	1.00	.60
7	Don McMahon	2.00	1.00	.60
8	Chuck Harrison	2.00	1.00	.60
9	Ron Hansen	2.00	1.00	.60
10	Matty Alou	2.00	1.00	.60
11	Barry Moore	2.00	1.00	.60
12	Dodgers Rookies (Jimmy Campanis, Bill Singer)	2.00	1.00	.60
13	Joe Sparma	2.00	1.00	.60
14	Phil Linz	2.00	1.00	.60
15	Earl Battey	2.00	1.00	.60
16	Bill Hands	2.00	1.00	.60
17	Jim Gosger	2.00	1.00	.60
18	Gene Oliver	2.00	1.00	.60
19	Jim McGlothlin	2.00	1.00	.60
20	Orlando Cepeda	10.00	5.00	2.50
21	Dave Bristol	2.00	1.00	.60
22	Gene Brabender	2.00	1.00	.60
23	Larry Elliot	2.00	1.00	.60
24	Bob Allen	2.00	1.00	.60
25	Elston Howard	7.00	3.50	2.00
26a	Bob Priddy (No trade statement.)	25.00	12.50	6.25
26b	Bob Priddy (With trade statement.)	2.00	1.00	.60
27	Bob Saverine	2.00	1.00	.60
28	Barry Latman	2.00	1.00	.60
29	Tommy McCraw	2.00	1.00	.60
30	Al Kaline	20.00	10.00	6.00
31	Jim Brewer	2.00	1.00	.60
32	Bob Bailey	2.00	1.00	.60
33	Athletics Rookies (Sal Bando, Randy Schwartz)	4.00	2.00	1.25
34	Pete Cimino	2.00	1.00	.60
35	Rico Carty	2.00	1.00	.60
36	Bob Tillman	2.00	1.00	.60
37	Rick Wise	2.00	1.00	.60
38	Bob Johnson	2.00	1.00	.60
39	Curt Simmons	2.00	1.00	.60
40	Rick Reichardt	2.00	1.00	.60
41	Joe Hoerner	2.00	1.00	.60
42	Mets Team	8.00	4.00	2.50
43	Chico Salmon	2.00	1.00	.60
44	Joe Nuxhall	2.00	1.00	.60
45a	Roger Maris (Cards on front.)	50.00	25.00	12.50
45b	Roger Maris (Yankees on front, blank-back proof.)	1,275	637.50	318.75
46	Lindy McDaniel	2.00	1.00	.60
47	Ken McMullen	2.00	1.00	.60
48	Bill Freehan	2.00	1.00	.60
49	Roy Face	2.00	1.00	.60
50	Tony Oliva	6.00	3.00	1.75
51	Astros Rookies (Dave Adlesh, Wes Bales)	2.00	1.00	.60
52	Dennis Higgins	2.00	1.00	.60
53	Clay Dalrymple	2.00	1.00	.60
54	Dick Green	2.00	1.00	.60
55	Don Drysdale	20.00	10.00	6.00
56	Jose Tartabull	2.00	1.00	.60
57	*Pat Jarvis*	2.00	1.00	.60
58a	Paul Schaal (Bat green above name.)	15.00	7.50	4.50
58b	Paul Schaal (Bat natural above name.)	2.00	1.00	.60
59	Ralph Terry	2.00	1.00	.60
60	Luis Aparicio	15.00	7.50	4.50
61	Gordy Coleman	2.00	1.00	.60
62a	1st Series Check List (1-109) (Frank Robinson) (Copyright symbol beneath T of Tribe.)	7.00	3.50	2.00
62b	1st Series Check List (1-109) (Frank Robinson) (Copyright symbol beneath r of Tribe.)	7.00	3.50	2.00
63	Cards Clubbers (Lou Brock, Curt Flood)	12.00	6.00	3.50
64	Fred Valentine	2.00	1.00	.60
65	Tom Haller	2.00	1.00	.60
66	Manny Mota	2.00	1.00	.60
67	Ken Berry	2.00	1.00	.60
68	Bob Buhl	2.00	1.00	.60
69	Vic Davalillo	2.00	1.00	.60
70	Ron Santo	6.00	3.00	1.75
71	Camilo Pascual	2.00	1.00	.60
72	Tigers Rookies (George Korince, John Matchick) (Korince photo actually James M. Brown.)	2.00	1.00	.60
73	Rusty Staub	3.00	1.50	.90
74	Wes Stock	2.00	1.00	.60
75	George Scott	2.00	1.00	.60
76	Jim Barbieri	2.00	1.00	.60
77	Dooley Womack	2.00	1.00	.60
78	Pat Corrales	2.00	1.00	.60
79	Bubba Morton	2.00	1.00	.60
80	Jim Maloney	2.00	1.00	.60
81	Eddie Stanky	2.00	1.00	.60
82	Steve Barber	2.00	1.00	.60
83	Ollie Brown	2.00	1.00	.60
84	Tommie Sisk	2.00	1.00	.60
85	Johnny Callison	2.00	1.00	.60
86a	Mike McCormick (No trade statement.)	30.00	15.00	9.00
86b	Mike McCormick (With trade statement.)	2.00	1.00	.60
87	George Altman	2.00	1.00	.60
88	Mickey Lolich	2.00	1.00	.60
89	*Felix Millan*	2.00	1.00	.60
90	Jim Nash	2.00	1.00	.60
91	Johnny Lewis	2.00	1.00	.60
92	Ray Washburn	2.00	1.00	.60

No.	Player			
93	Yankees Rookies (**Stan Bahnsen, Bobby Murcer**)	12.00	6.00	3.50
94	Ron Fairly	2.00	1.00	.60
95	Sonny Siebert	2.00	1.00	.60
96	Art Shamsky	2.00	1.00	.60
97	Mike Cuellar	2.00	1.00	.60
98	Rich Rollins	2.00	1.00	.60
99	Lee Stange	2.00	1.00	.60
100	Frank Robinson	20.00	10.00	6.00
101	Ken Johnson	2.00	1.00	.60
102	Phillies Team	3.50	1.75	1.00
103a	2nd Series Check List (110-196) (Mickey Mantle) (170: Line after D)	25.00	12.50	7.50
103b	2nd Series Check List (110-196) (Mickey Mantle) (170: Period after D)	25.00	12.50	7.50
104	Minnie Rojas	2.00	1.00	.60
105	Ken Boyer	5.00	2.50	1.50
106	Randy Hundley	2.00	1.00	.60
107	Joel Horlen	2.00	1.00	.60
108	Alex Johnson	2.00	1.00	.60
109	Tribe Thumpers (Rocky Colavito, Leon Wagner)	9.00	4.50	2.75
110	Jack Aker	2.00	1.00	.60
111	John Kennedy	2.00	1.00	.60
112	Dave Wickersham	2.00	1.00	.60
113	Dave Nicholson	2.00	1.00	.60
114	Jack Baldschun	2.00	1.00	.60
115	Paul Casanova	2.00	1.00	.60
116	Herman Franks	2.00	1.00	.60
117	Darrell Brandon	2.00	1.00	.60
118	Bernie Allen	2.00	1.00	.60
119	Wade Blasingame	2.00	1.00	.60
120	Floyd Robinson	2.00	1.00	.60
121	Ed Bressoud	2.00	1.00	.60
122	George Brunet	2.00	1.00	.60
123	Pirates Rookies (Jim Price, Luke Walker)	2.00	1.00	.60
124	Jim Stewart	2.00	1.00	.60
125	Moe Drabowsky	2.00	1.00	.60
126	Tony Taylor	2.00	1.00	.60
127	John O'Donoghue	2.00	1.00	.60
128a	Ed Spiezio (Most of "SPIE" missing at top.)	75.00	37.50	22.50
128b	Ed Spiezio (Lettering all there.)	2.00	1.00	.60
129	Phil Roof	2.00	1.00	.60
130	Phil Regan	2.00	1.00	.60
131	Yankees Team	9.00	4.50	2.75
132	Ozzie Virgil	2.00	1.00	.60
133	Ron Kline	2.00	1.00	.60
134	Gates Brown	2.00	1.00	.60
135	Deron Johnson	2.00	1.00	.60
136	Carroll Sembera	2.00	1.00	.60
137	Twins Rookies (Ron Clark, Jim Ollom)	2.00	1.00	.60
138	Dick Kelley	2.00	1.00	.60
139	Dalton Jones	2.00	1.00	.60
140	Willie Stargell	20.00	10.00	6.00
141	John Miller	2.00	1.00	.60
142	Jackie Brandt	2.00	1.00	.60
143	Sox Sockers (Don Buford, Pete Ward)	2.00	1.00	.60
144	Bill Hepler	2.00	1.00	.60
145	Larry Brown	2.00	1.00	.60
146	Steve Carlton	40.00	20.00	10.00
147	Tom Egan	2.00	1.00	.60
148	Adolfo Phillips	2.00	1.00	.60
149a	Joe Moeller (White streak between "M" and cap.)	30.00	15.00	9.00
149b	Joe Moeller (No white streak.)	2.00	1.00	.60
150	Mickey Mantle	400.00	200.00	100.00
151	World Series Game 1 (Moe Mows Down 11)	6.00	3.00	1.75
152	World Series Game 2 (Palmer Blanks Dodgers)	11.00	5.50	3.25
153	World Series Game 3 (Blair's Homer Defeats L.A.)	6.00	3.00	1.75
154	World Series Game 4 (Orioles Win 4th Straight)	6.00	3.00	1.75
155	World Series (The Winners Celebrate)	7.50	3.75	2.25
156	Ron Herbel	2.00	1.00	.60
157	Danny Cater	2.00	1.00	.60
158	Jimmy Coker	2.00	1.00	.60
159	Bruce Howard	2.00	1.00	.60
160	Willie Davis	2.00	1.00	.60
161	Dick Williams	2.00	1.00	.60
162	Billy O'Dell	2.00	1.00	.60
163	Vic Roznovsky	2.00	1.00	.60
164	Dwight Siebler	2.00	1.00	.60
165	Cleon Jones	2.00	1.00	.60
166	Ed Mathews	20.00	10.00	6.00
167	Senators Rookies (Joe Coleman, Tim Cullen)	2.00	1.00	.60
168	Ray Culp	2.00	1.00	.60
169	Horace Clarke	2.00	1.00	.60
170	Dick McAuliffe	2.00	1.00	.60
171	Calvin Koonce	2.00	1.00	.60
172	Bill Heath	2.00	1.00	.60
173	Cards Team	5.00	2.50	1.50
174	Dick Radatz	2.00	1.00	.60
175	Bobby Knoop	2.00	1.00	.60
176	Sammy Ellis	2.00	1.00	.60
177	Tito Fuentes	2.00	1.00	.60
178	John Buzhardt	2.00	1.00	.60
179	Braves Rookies (Cecil Upshaw, Chas. Vaughan)	2.00	1.00	.60
180	Curt Blefary	2.00	1.00	.60
181	Terry Fox	2.00	1.00	.60
182	Ed Charles	2.00	1.00	.60
183	Jim Pagliaroni	2.00	1.00	.60
184	George Thomas	2.00	1.00	.60
185	**Ken Holtzman**	4.00	2.00	1.25
186	Mets Maulers (Ed Kranepool, Ron Swoboda)	3.50	1.75	1.00
187	Pedro Ramos	2.00	1.00	.60
188	Ken Harrelson	2.00	1.00	.60
189	Chuck Hinton	2.00	1.00	.60
190	Turk Farrell	2.00	1.00	.60
191a	3rd Series Check List (197-283) (Willie Mays) (214 is Dick Kelley)	9.00	4.50	2.75
191b	3rd Series Check List (197-283) (Willie Mays) (214 is Tom Kelley)	12.00	6.00	3.50
192	Fred Gladding	2.00	1.00	.60
193	Jose Cardenal	2.00	1.00	.60
194	Bob Allison	2.00	1.00	.60
195	Al Jackson	2.00	1.00	.60
196	Johnny Romano	2.00	1.00	.60
197	Ron Perranoski	2.00	1.00	.60
198	Chuck Hiller	2.00	1.00	.60
199	Billy Hitchcock	2.00	1.00	.60
200	Willie Mays	125.00	62.50	31.25
201	Hal Reniff	2.00	1.00	.60
202	Johnny Edwards	2.00	1.00	.60
203	Al McBean	2.00	1.00	.60
204	Orioles Rookies (Mike Epstein, Tom Phoebus)	2.00	1.00	.60
205	Dick Groat	2.00	1.00	.60
206	Dennis Bennett	2.00	1.00	.60
207	John Orsino	2.00	1.00	.60
208	Jack Lamabe	2.00	1.00	.60
209	Joe Nossek	2.00	1.00	.60
210	Bob Gibson	25.00	12.50	6.25
211	Twins Team	6.00	3.00	1.75
212	Chris Zachary	2.00	1.00	.60
213	*Jay Johnstone*	4.00	2.00	1.25
214	Tom Kelley	2.00	1.00	.60
215	Ernie Banks	25.00	12.50	7.50
216	Bengal Belters (Norm Cash, Al Kaline)	15.00	7.50	4.50
217	Rob Gardner	2.00	1.00	.60
218	Wes Parker	2.00	1.00	.60
219	Clay Carroll	2.00	1.00	.60
220	Jim Hart	2.00	1.00	.60
221	Woody Fryman	2.00	1.00	.60
222	Reds Rookies (Lee May, Darrell Osteen)	2.00	1.00	.60
223	Mike Ryan	2.00	1.00	.60
224	Walt Bond	2.00	1.00	.60
225	Mel Stottlemyre	4.00	2.00	1.25
226	Julian Javier	2.00	1.00	.60
227	Paul Lindblad	2.00	1.00	.60
228	Gil Hodges	9.00	4.50	2.75
229	Larry Jackson	2.00	1.00	.60
230	Boog Powell	6.00	3.00	1.75
231	John Bateman	2.00	1.00	.60
232	Don Buford	2.00	1.00	.60
233	A.L. ERA Leaders (Steve Hargan, Joel Horlen, Gary Peters)	3.00	1.50	.90
234	N.L. ERA Leaders (Mike Cuellar, Sandy Koufax, Juan Marichal)	12.00	6.00	3.50
235	A.L. Pitching Leaders (Jim Kaat, Denny McLain, Earl Wilson)	3.50	1.75	1.00
236	N.L. Pitching Leaders (Bob Gibson, Sandy Koufax, Juan Marichal, Gaylord Perry)	15.00	7.50	3.75
237	A.L. Strikeout Leaders (Jim Kaat, Sam McDowell, Earl Wilson)	3.50	1.75	1.00
238	N.L. Strikeout Leaders (Jim Bunning, Sandy Koufax, Bob Veale)	12.00	6.00	3.50
239	A.L. Batting Leaders (Al Kaline, Tony Oliva, Frank Robinson)	15.00	7.50	3.75
240	N.L. Batting Leaders (Felipe Alou, Matty Alou, Rico Carty)	11.00	5.50	3.25
241	A.L. RBI Leaders (Harmon Killebrew, Boog Powell, Frank Robinson)	11.00	5.50	3.25
242	N.L. RBI Leaders (Hank Aaron, Richie Allen, Bob Clemente)	15.00	7.50	3.75
243	A.L. Home Run Leaders (Harmon Killebrew, Boog Powell, Frank Robinson)	11.00	5.50	3.25
244	N.L. Home Run Leaders (Hank Aaron, Richie Allen, Willie Mays)	15.00	7.50	4.50
245	Curt Flood	5.00	2.50	1.50
246	Jim Perry	2.00	1.00	.60
247	Jerry Lumpe	2.00	1.00	.60
248	Gene Mauch	2.00	1.00	.60
249	Nick Willhite	2.00	1.00	.60
250	Hank Aaron	100.00	50.00	25.00
251	Woody Held	2.00	1.00	.60
252a	Bob Bolin (White streak between Bob and Bolin.)	60.00	30.00	18.00
252b	Bob Bolin (No white streak.)	2.00	1.00	.60
253	Indians Rookies (Bill Davis, Gus Gil)	2.00	1.00	.60
254	Milt Pappas	2.00	1.00	.60
255	Frank Howard	2.50	1.25	.70
256	Bob Hendley	2.00	1.00	.60
257	Charley Smith	2.00	1.00	.60
258	Lee Maye	2.00	1.00	.60
259	Don Dennis	2.00	1.00	.60
260	Jim Lefebvre	2.00	1.00	.60
261	John Wyatt	2.00	1.00	.60
262	Athletics Team	6.00	3.00	1.75
263	Hank Aguirre	2.00	1.00	.60
264	Ron Swoboda	2.00	1.00	.60
265	Lou Burdette	2.00	1.00	.60
266	Pitt Power (Donn Clendenon, Willie Stargell)	12.00	6.00	3.50
267	Don Schwall	2.00	1.00	.60
268	John Briggs	2.00	1.00	.60
269	Don Nottebart	2.00	1.00	.60
270	Zoilo Versalles	2.00	1.00	.60
271	Eddie Watt	2.00	1.00	.60
272	Cubs Rookies (Bill Connors, Dave Dowling)	2.00	1.00	.60
273	Dick Lines	2.00	1.00	.60
274	Bob Aspromonte	2.00	1.00	.60
275	Fred Whitfield	2.00	1.00	.60
276	Bruce Brubaker	2.00	1.00	.60
277	Steve Whitaker	2.00	1.00	.60
278	4th Series Check List (284-370) (Jim Kaat)	7.00	3.50	2.00
279	Frank Linzy	2.00	1.00	.60
280	Tony Conigliaro	9.00	4.50	2.75
281	Bob Rodgers	2.00	1.00	.60
282	Johnny Odom	2.00	1.00	.60
283	Gene Alley	2.00	1.00	.60
284	Johnny Podres	3.00	1.50	.90
285	Lou Brock	10.00	5.00	2.50
286	Wayne Causey	2.00	1.00	.60
287	Mets Rookies (Greg Goossen, Bart Shirley)	2.00	1.00	.60
288	Denver Lemaster	2.00	1.00	.60
289	Tom Tresh	6.00	3.00	1.75
290	Bill White	2.00	1.00	.60
291	Jim Hannan	2.00	1.00	.60
292	Don Pavletich	2.00	1.00	.60
293	Ed Kirkpatrick	2.00	1.00	.60
294	Walt Alston	7.00	3.50	2.00
295	Sam McDowell	2.00	.70	.60
296	Glenn Beckert	2.00	1.00	.60
297	Dave Morehead	2.00	1.00	.60
298	Ron Davis	2.00	1.00	.60
299	Norm Siebern	2.00	1.00	.60
300	Jim Kaat	4.00	2.00	1.25
301	Jesse Gonder	2.00	1.00	.60
302	Orioles Team	6.00	3.00	1.75
303	Gil Blanco	2.00	1.00	.60
304	Phil Gagliano	2.00	1.00	.60
305	Earl Wilson	2.00	1.00	.60
306	*Bud Harrelson*	7.00	3.50	2.00
307	Jim Beauchamp	2.00	1.00	.60
308	Al Downing	2.00	1.00	.60
309	Hurlers Beware (Richie Allen, Johnny Callison)	6.00	3.00	1.75
310	Gary Peters	2.00	1.00	.60
311	Ed Brinkman	2.00	1.00	.60
312	Don Mincher	2.00	1.00	.60
313	Bob Lee	2.00	1.00	.60
314	Red Sox Rookies (**Mike Andrews, Reggie Smith**)	12.00	6.00	3.50
315	Billy Williams	15.00	7.50	3.75
316	Jack Kralick	2.00	1.00	.60
317	Cesar Tovar	2.00	1.00	.60
318	Dave Giusti	2.00	1.00	.60
319	Paul Blair	2.00	1.00	.60
320	Gaylord Perry	15.00	7.50	4.50
321	Mayo Smith	2.00	1.00	.60
322	Jose Pagan	2.00	1.00	.60
323	Mike Hershberger	2.00	1.00	.60
324	Hal Woodeshick	2.00	1.00	.60
325	Chico Cardenas	2.00	1.00	.60
326	Bob Uecker	12.00	6.00	3.50
327	Angels Team	6.00	3.00	1.75
328	Clete Boyer	4.00	2.00	1.25
329	Charlie Lau	2.00	1.00	.60
330	Claude Osteen	2.00	1.00	.60
331	Joe Foy	2.00	1.00	.60
332	Jesus Alou	2.00	1.00	.60
333	Fergie Jenkins	10.00	5.00	2.50
334	Twin Terrors (Bob Allison, Harmon Killebrew)	15.00	7.50	4.50
335	Bob Veale	2.00	1.00	.60
336	Joe Azcue	2.00	1.00	.60
337	Joe Morgan	17.50	8.75	5.25
338	Bob Locker	2.00	1.00	.60
339	Chico Ruiz	2.00	1.00	.60
340	Joe Pepitone	4.00	2.00	1.25
341	Giants Rookies (Dick Dietz, Bill Sorrell)	2.00	1.00	.60
342	Hank Fischer	2.00	1.00	.60
343	Tom Satriano	2.00	1.00	.60
344	Ossie Chavarria	2.00	1.00	.60
345	Stu Miller	2.00	1.00	.60
346	Jim Hickman	2.00	1.00	.60
347	Grady Hatton	2.00	1.00	.60
348	Tug McGraw	3.00	1.50	.90
349	Bob Chance	2.00	1.00	.60
350	Joe Torre	7.00	3.50	2.00
351	Vern Law	2.00	1.00	.60
352	Ray Oyler	2.00	1.00	.60
353	Bill McCool	2.00	1.00	.60
354	Cubs Team	6.00	3.00	1.75
355	Carl Yastrzemski	60.00	30.00	15.00
356	Larry Jaster	2.00	1.00	.60
357	Bill Skowron	5.00	2.50	1.50
358	Ruben Amaro	2.00	1.00	.60
359	Dick Ellsworth	2.00	1.00	.60
360	Leon Wagner	2.00	1.00	.60
361	5th Series Check List (371-457) (Roberto Clemente)	9.00	4.50	2.75
362	Darold Knowles	2.00	1.00	.60
363	Dave Johnson	2.00	1.00	.60
364	Claude Raymond	2.00	1.00	.60
365	John Roseboro	2.00	1.00	.60
366	Andy Kosco	2.00	1.00	.60
367	Angels Rookies (Bill Kelso, Don Wallace)	2.00	1.00	.60
368	Jack Hiatt	2.00	1.00	.60
369	Jim Hunter	20.00	10.00	5.00
370	Tommy Davis	2.00	1.00	.60
371	Jim Lonborg	4.00	2.00	1.25
372	Mike de la Hoz	4.00	2.00	1.25
373	White Sox Rookies (Duane Josephson, Fred Klages)	4.00	2.00	1.25
374a	Mel Queen (Rule under stats totals nearly gone.)	4.00	2.00	1.25
374b	Mel Queen (Full rule.)	4.00	2.00	1.25
375	Jake Gibbs	4.00	2.00	1.25
376	Don Lock	4.00	2.00	1.25

		NM	EX	VG
377	Luis Tiant	4.00	2.00	1.25
378	Tigers Team	7.00	3.50	2.00
379	Jerry May	4.00	2.00	1.25
380	Dean Chance	4.00	2.00	1.25
381	Dick Schofield	4.00	2.00	1.25
382	Dave McNally	4.00	2.00	1.25
383	Ken Henderson	4.00	2.00	1.25
384	Cards Rookies	4.00	2.00	1.25
	(Jim Cosman, Dick Hughes)			
385	Jim Fregosi	4.00	2.00	1.25
386	Dick Selma	4.00	2.00	1.25
387	Cap Peterson	4.00	2.00	1.25
388	Arnold Earley	4.00	2.00	1.25
389	Al Dark	4.00	2.00	1.25
390	Jim Wynn	4.00	2.00	1.25
391	Wilbur Wood	4.00	2.00	1.25
392	Tommy Harper	4.00	2.00	1.25
393	Jim Bouton	7.00	3.50	2.00
394	Jake Wood	4.00	2.00	1.25
395	Chris Short	4.00	2.00	1.25
396	Atlanta Aces (Tony Cloninger, Denis Menke)	7.00	3.50	2.00
397	Willie Smith	4.00	2.00	1.25
398	Jeff Torborg	4.00	2.00	1.25
399	Al Worthington	4.00	2.00	1.25
400	Roberto Clemente	125.00	62.50	31.25
401	Jim Coates	4.00	2.00	1.25
402a	Phillies Rookies (Grant Jackson, Billy Wilson) (Incomplete line under Wilson's stats.)	6.50	3.25	2.00
402b	Grant Jackson, Billy Wilson (Complete line.)	4.00	2.00	1.25
403	Dick Nen	4.00	2.00	1.25
404	Nelson Briles	4.00	2.00	1.25
405	Russ Snyder	4.00	2.00	1.25
406	Lee Elia	4.00	2.00	1.25
407	Reds Team	7.00	3.50	2.00
408	Jim Northrup	4.00	2.00	1.25
409	Ray Sadecki	4.00	2.00	1.25
410	Lou Johnson	4.00	2.00	1.25
411	Dick Howser	4.00	2.00	1.25
412	Astros Rookies (*Norm Miller, Doug Rader*)	5.00	2.50	1.50
413	Jerry Grote	4.00	2.00	1.25
414	Casey Cox	4.00	2.00	1.25
415	Sonny Jackson	4.00	2.00	1.25
416	Roger Repoz	4.00	2.00	1.25
417a	Bob Bruce (RBAVES on back.)	20.00	10.00	5.00
417b	Bob Bruce (Corrected)	4.00	2.00	1.25
418	Sam Mele	4.00	2.00	1.25
419	Don Kessinger	4.00	2.00	1.25
420	Denny McLain	7.00	3.50	2.00
421	Dal Maxvill	4.00	2.00	1.25
422	Hoyt Wilhelm	15.00	7.50	4.50
423	Fence Busters (Willie Mays, Willie McCovey)	25.00	12.50	7.50
424	Pedro Gonzalez	4.00	2.00	1.25
425	Pete Mikkelsen	4.00	2.00	1.25
426	Lou Clinton	4.00	2.00	1.25
427a	Ruben Gomez (Stats totals line nearly gone.)	12.00	6.00	3.50
427b	Ruben Gomez (Full stats totals line.)	4.00	2.00	1.25
428	Dodgers Rookies (*Tom Hutton, Gene Michael*)	6.00	3.00	1.75
429	Garry Roggenburk	4.00	2.00	1.25
430	Pete Rose	90.00	45.00	22.50
431	Ted Uhlaender	4.00	2.00	1.25
432	Jimmie Hall	4.00	2.00	1.25
433	Al Luplow	4.00	2.00	1.25
434	Eddie Fisher	4.00	2.00	1.25
435	Mack Jones	4.00	2.00	1.25
436	Pete Ward	4.00	2.00	1.25
437	Senators Team	7.00	3.50	2.00
438	Chuck Dobson	4.00	2.00	1.25
439	Byron Browne	4.00	2.00	1.25
440	Steve Hargan	4.00	2.00	1.25
441	Jim Davenport	4.00	2.00	1.25
442	Yankees Rookies (Bill Robinson, Joe Verbanic)	6.00	3.00	1.75
443	Tito Francona	4.00	2.00	1.25
444	George Smith	4.00	2.00	1.25
445	Don Sutton	15.00	7.50	4.50
446	Russ Nixon	4.00	2.00	1.25
447a	Bo Belinsky (1966 S.D. stats nearly gone.)	6.00	3.00	1.75
447b	Bo Belinsky (Full 1966 S.D. stats line.)	4.00	2.00	1.25
448	Harry Walker	4.00	2.00	1.25
449	Orlando Pena	4.00	2.00	1.25
450	Richie Allen	12.00	6.00	3.50
451	Fred Newman	4.00	2.00	1.25
452	Ed Kranepool	4.00	2.00	1.25
453	Aurelio Monteagudo	4.00	2.00	1.25
454a	6th Series Check List (458-533) (Juan Marichal) (Left ear shows.)	9.00	4.50	2.75
454b	6th Series Check List (458-533) (Juan Marichal) (No left ear.)	12.00	6.00	3.50
455	Tommie Agee	4.00	2.00	1.25
456	Phil Niekro	15.00	7.50	4.50
457	Andy Etchebarren	4.00	2.00	1.25
458	Lee Thomas	7.00	3.50	2.00
459	Senators Rookies (Dick Bosman, Pete Craig)	7.00	3.50	2.00
460	Harmon Killebrew	60.00	30.00	15.00
461	Bob Miller	7.00	3.50	2.00
462	Bob Barton	7.00	3.50	2.00
463	Hill Aces (Sam McDowell, Sonny Siebert)	11.00	5.50	3.25
464	Dan Coombs	7.00	3.50	2.00
465	Willie Horton	7.00	3.50	2.00
466	Bobby Wine	7.00	3.50	2.00
467	Jim O'Toole	7.00	3.50	2.00
468	Ralph Houk	7.00	3.50	2.00

		NM	EX	VG
469	Len Gabrielson	7.00	3.50	2.00
470	Bob Shaw	7.00	3.50	2.00
471	Rene Lachemann	7.00	3.50	2.00
472	Pirates Rookies (John Gelnar, George Spriggs)	7.00	3.50	2.00
473	Jose Santiago	7.00	3.50	2.00
474	Bob Tolan	7.00	3.50	2.00
475	Jim Palmer	75.00	37.50	18.75
476	Tony Perez (SP)	40.00	20.00	12.00
477	Braves Team	11.00	5.50	3.25
478	Bob Humphreys	7.00	3.50	2.00
479	Gary Bell	7.00	3.50	2.00
480	Willie McCovey	30.00	15.00	7.50
481	Leo Durocher	12.00	6.00	3.50
482	Bill Monbouquette	7.00	3.50	2.00
483	Jim Landis	7.00	3.50	2.00
484	Jerry Adair	7.00	3.50	2.00
485	Tim McCarver	15.00	7.50	3.75
486	Twins Rookies (Rich Reese, Bill Whitby)	7.00	3.50	2.00
487	Tom Reynolds	7.00	3.50	2.00
488	Gerry Arrigo	7.00	3.50	2.00
489	Doug Clemens	7.00	3.50	2.00
490	Tony Cloninger	7.00	3.50	2.00
491	Sam Bowens	7.00	3.50	2.00
492	Pirates Team	15.00	7.50	3.75
493	Phil Ortega	7.00	3.50	2.00
494	Bill Rigney	7.00	3.50	2.00
495	Fritz Peterson	7.00	3.50	2.00
496	Orlando McFarlane	7.00	3.50	2.00
497	Ron Campbell	7.00	3.50	2.00
498	Larry Dierker	7.00	3.50	2.00
499	Indians Rookies (George Culver, Jose Vidal)	7.00	3.50	2.00
500	Juan Marichal	20.00	10.00	5.00
501	Jerry Zimmerman	7.00	3.50	2.00
502	Derrell Griffith	7.00	3.50	2.00
503	Dodgers Team	15.00	7.50	3.75
504	Orlando Martinez	7.00	3.50	2.00
505	Tommy Helms	7.00	3.50	2.00
506	Smoky Burgess	7.00	3.50	2.00
507	Orioles Rookies (Ed Barnowski, Larry Haney)	7.00	3.50	2.00
508	Dick Hall	7.00	3.50	2.00
509	Jim King	7.00	3.50	2.00
510	Bill Mazeroski	20.00	10.00	6.00
511	Don Wert	7.00	3.50	2.00
512	Red Schoendienst	15.00	7.50	4.50
513	Marcelino Lopez	7.00	3.50	2.00
514	John Werhas	7.00	3.50	2.00
515	Bert Campaneris	7.00	3.50	2.00
516	Giants Team	17.50	8.75	5.25
517	Fred Talbot	7.00	3.50	2.00
518	Denis Menke	7.00	3.50	2.00
519	Ted Davidson	7.00	3.50	2.00
520	Max Alvis	7.00	3.50	2.00
521	Bird Bombers (Curt Blefary, Boog Powell)	7.50	3.75	2.25
522	John Stephenson	7.00	3.50	2.00
523	Jim Merritt	7.00	3.50	2.00
524	Felix Mantilla	7.00	3.50	2.00
525	Ron Hunt	7.00	3.50	2.00
526	Tigers Rookies (Pat Dobson, George Korince)	11.00	5.50	3.25
527	Dennis Ribant	7.00	3.50	2.00
528	Rico Petrocelli	12.50	6.25	3.75
529	Gary Wagner	7.00	3.50	2.00
530	Felipe Alou	12.00	6.00	3.50
531	7th Series Check List (534-609) (Brooks Robinson)	12.00	6.00	3.50
532	Jim Hicks	7.00	3.50	2.00
533	Jack Fisher	7.00	3.50	2.00
534	Hank Bauer (DP)	8.00	4.00	2.50
535	Donn Clendenon	12.00	6.00	3.50
536	Cubs Rookies (Joe Niekro, Paul Popovich)	25.00	12.50	6.25
537	Chuck Estrada (DP)	8.00	4.00	2.50
538	J.C. Martin	12.00	6.00	3.50
539	Dick Egan (DP)	8.00	4.00	2.50
540	Norm Cash	50.00	25.00	12.50
541	Joe Gibbon	12.00	6.00	3.50
542	Athletics Rookies (Rick Monday, Tony Pierce) (DP)	12.50	6.25	3.75
543	Dan Schneider	12.00	6.00	3.50
544	Indians Team	20.00	10.00	5.00
545	Jim Grant	12.00	6.00	3.50
546	Woody Woodward	12.00	6.00	3.50
547	Red Sox Rookies (Russ Gibson, Bill Rohr) (DP)	8.00	4.00	2.50
548	Tony Gonzalez (DP)	8.00	4.00	2.50
549	Jack Sanford	12.00	6.00	3.50
550	Vada Pinson (DP)	12.00	6.00	3.50
551	Doug Camilli (DP)	8.00	4.00	2.50
552	Ted Savage	12.00	6.00	3.50
553	Yankees Rookies (Mike Hegan, Thad Tillotson)	30.00	15.00	7.50
554	Andre Rodgers (DP)	8.00	4.00	2.50
555	Don Cardwell	12.00	6.00	3.50
556	Al Weis (DP)	8.00	4.00	2.50
557	Al Ferrara	12.00	6.00	3.50
558	Orioles Rookies (Mark Belanger, Bill Dillman)	45.00	22.50	13.50
559	Dick Tracewski (DP)	8.00	4.00	2.50
560	Jim Bunning	45.00	22.50	11.25
561	Sandy Alomar	12.00	6.00	3.50
562	Steve Blass (DP)	8.00	4.00	2.50
563	Joe Adcock	15.00	7.50	4.50
564	Astros Rookies (Alonzo Harris, Aaron Pointer) (DP)	8.00	4.00	2.50
565	Lew Krausse	12.00	6.00	3.50
566	Gary Geiger (DP)	8.00	4.00	2.50
567	Steve Hamilton	12.00	6.00	3.50
568	John Sullivan	12.00	6.00	3.50
569	A.L. Rookies (*Hank Allen, Rod Carew*) (DP)	300.00	150.00	75.00
570	Maury Wills	50.00	25.00	12.50
571	Larry Sherry	12.00	6.00	3.50
572	Don Demeter	12.00	6.00	3.50

		NM	EX	VG
573	White Sox Team (Indians team stats on back)	20.00	10.00	5.00
574	Jerry Buchek	12.00	6.00	3.50
575	*Dave Boswell*	12.00	6.00	3.50
576	N.L. Rookies (Norm Gigon, Ramon Hernandez)	12.00	6.00	3.50
577	Bill Short	12.00	6.00	3.50
578	John Boccabella	12.00	6.00	3.50
579	Bill Henry	12.00	6.00	3.50
580	Rocky Colavito	150.00	75.00	37.50
581	Mets Rookies (*Bill Denehy, Tom Seaver*)	600.00	300.00	150.00
582	Jim Owens (DP)	8.00	4.00	2.50
583	Ray Barker	12.00	6.00	3.50
584	Jim Piersall	20.00	10.00	6.00
585	Wally Bunker	12.00	6.00	3.50
586	Manny Jimenez	12.00	6.00	3.50
587	N.L. Rookies (Don Shaw, Gary Sutherland)	12.00	6.00	3.50
588	Johnny Klippstein (DP)	8.00	4.00	2.50
589	Dave Ricketts (DP)	8.00	4.00	2.50
590	Pete Richert	12.00	6.00	3.50
591	Ty Cline	12.00	6.00	3.50
592	N.L. Rookies (Jim Shellenback, Ron Willis)	12.00	6.00	3.50
593	Wes Westrum	12.00	6.00	3.50
594	Dan Osinski	12.00	6.00	3.50
595	Cookie Rojas	12.00	6.00	3.50
596	Galen Cisco (DP)	8.00	4.00	2.50
597	Ted Abernathy	12.00	6.00	3.50
598	White Sox Rookies (Ed Stroud, Walt Williams)	12.00	6.00	3.50
599	Bob Duliba (DP)	8.00	4.00	2.50
600	Brooks Robinson (SP)	250.00	125.00	62.50
601	Bill Bryan (DP)	8.00	4.00	2.50
602	Juan Pizarro	12.00	6.00	3.50
603	Athletics Rookies (Tim Talton, Ramon Webster)	12.00	6.00	3.50
604	Red Sox Team	100.00	50.00	25.00
605	Mike Shannon	50.00	25.00	12.50
606	Ron Taylor	12.00	6.00	3.50
607	Mickey Stanley	25.00	12.50	7.50
608	Cubs Rookies (Rich Nye, John Upham) (DP)	8.00	4.00	2.50
609	Tommy John	80.00	40.00	20.00

1967 Topps Discs

Similar to the more common 28-piece set of 1968, this set of all-stars is known only in proof form, evidently intended to be pressed onto a pin-back button issue which never materialized. Printed on blank-backed silver foil about 2-3/8" square, the pieces have a 2-1/4" diameter center with color player portrait with name and position printed in black across the chest. Some pieces have a team name to the left and right of the player's picture. "JAPAN" is printed in tiny black letters at top-left, apparently intended to be folded under the rim of the button. The unnumbered discs are checklisted here alphabetically.

		NM	EX	VG
Complete Set (24):		12,500	6,250	3,750
Common Player:		185.00	90.00	55.00
(1)	Hank Aaron	1,400	700.00	420.00
(2)	Johnny Callison	185.00	90.00	55.00
(3)	Bert Campaneris	185.00	90.00	55.00
(4)	Leo Cardenas	185.00	90.00	55.00
(5)	Orlando Cepeda	600.00	300.00	180.00
(6)	Roberto Clemente	1,850	925.00	555.00
(7)	Frank Howard	210.00	105.00	63.00
(8)	Cleon Jones	185.00	90.00	55.00
(9)	Bobby Knoop	185.00	90.00	55.00
(10)	Sandy Koufax	1,150	575.00	345.00
(11)	Mickey Mantle	2,800	1,400	840.00
(12)	Juan Marichal	600.00	300.00	180.00
(13)	Willie Mays	1,400	700.00	420.00
(14)	Sam McDowell	185.00	90.00	55.00
(15)	Denny McLain	210.00	105.00	63.00
(16)	Joe Morgan	600.00	300.00	180.00
(17)	Tony Oliva	185.00	90.00	55.00
(18)	Boog Powell	225.00	110.00	67.00
(19)	Brooks Robinson	750.00	375.00	225.00
(20)	Frank Robinson	750.00	375.00	225.00
(21)	Johnny Romano	185.00	90.00	55.00
(22)	Ron Santo	210.00	105.00	63.00
(23)	Joe Torre	450.00	225.00	135.00
(24)	Carl Yastrzemski	750.00	375.00	225.00

1967 Topps S.F. Giants Discs

One of several prototypes for pinback button sets which were never issued. Generally found in the form of a silver-foil cardboard square, about 2-3/8" a side, the 2-1/4" round center features color player photos or team booster slogans. The player's name and position are printed across his chest, the team name at top. At top-left is a tiny black "JAPAN." The unnumbered discs are checklisted here alphabetically.

		NM	EX	VG
Complete Set (24):		8,000	4,000	2,400
Common Player:		185.00	92.00	55.00
(1)	Jesus Alou	185.00	92.00	55.00
(2)	Bob Bolin	185.00	92.00	55.00
(3)	Ollie Brown	185.00	92.00	55.00
(4)	Jim Davenport	185.00	92.00	55.00
(5)	Herman Franks	185.00	92.00	55.00
(6)	Len Gabrielson	185.00	92.00	55.00
(7)	Joe Gibbon	185.00	92.00	55.00
(8)	Tom Haller	185.00	92.00	55.00
(9)	Jim Ray Hart	185.00	92.00	55.00
(10)	Ron Herbel	185.00	92.00	55.00
(11)	Hal Lanier	185.00	92.00	55.00
(12)	Frank Linzy	185.00	92.00	55.00
(13)	Juan Marichal	925.00	460.00	275.00
(14)	Willie Mays	1,625	810.00	485.00
(15)	Willie McCovey	925.00	460.00	275.00
(16)	Lindy McDaniel	185.00	92.00	55.00
(17)	Gaylord Perry	825.00	410.00	245.00
(18)	Cap Peterson	185.00	92.00	55.00
(19)	Bob Priddy	185.00	92.00	55.00
(20)	Happiness is a Giant Win	115.00	57.00	34.00
(21)	I Love the Giants	115.00	57.00	34.00
(22)	Let's Go Giants	115.00	57.00	34.00
(23)	Willie Mays for Mayor (Willie Mays)	700.00	350.00	210.00
(24)	S.F. Giants Logo	115.00	57.00	34.00

1967 Topps Pin-Ups

The 5" x 7" "All Star Pin-ups" were wax pack inserts. They feature a full color picture with the player's name, position and team in a circle in one of the lower corners on the front. The numbered set consists of 32 players (generally big names). Because the large paper pin-ups had to be folded several times to fit into the wax packs, the factory-created folds are not considered when grading unless paper separations have developed along the seams. At least one of the pin-ups (Clemente) has been seen in an unnumbered version printed on better-quality sticker stock and not having fold lines.

		NM	EX	VG
Complete Set (32):		150.00	65.00	35.00
Common Player:		2.00	.70	.30
1	Boog Powell	2.50	.90	.40
2	Bert Campaneris	2.00	.70	.30
3	Brooks Robinson	9.00	3.25	1.25
4	Tommie Agee	2.00	.70	.30
5	Carl Yastrzemski	9.00	3.25	1.25
6	Mickey Mantle	40.00	14.00	6.00
7	Frank Howard	2.50	.90	.40
8	Sam McDowell	2.00	.70	.30
9	Orlando Cepeda	6.00	2.00	.90
10	Chico Cardenas	2.00	.70	.30
11	Roberto Clemente	20.00	7.00	3.00
12	Willie Mays	15.00	5.25	2.25
13	Cleon Jones	2.00	.70	.30
14	John Callison	2.00	.70	.30
15	Hank Aaron	15.00	5.25	2.25
16	Don Drysdale	7.50	2.75	1.25
17	Bobby Knoop	2.00	.70	.30
18	Tony Oliva	2.50	.90	.40
19	Frank Robinson	9.00	3.25	1.25
20	Denny McLain	2.50	.90	.40
21	Al Kaline	9.00	3.25	1.25
22	Joe Pepitone	3.00	1.00	.45
23	Harmon Killebrew	7.50	2.75	1.25
24	Leon Wagner	2.00	.70	.30
25	Joe Morgan	7.50	2.75	1.25
26	Ron Santo	3.00	1.00	.45
27	Joe Torre	4.50	1.50	.70
28	Juan Marichal	6.00	2.00	.90
29	Matty Alou	2.00	.70	.30
30	Felipe Alou	2.00	.70	.30
31	Ron Hunt	2.00	.70	.30
32	Willie McCovey	7.50	2.75	1.25

1967 Topps Punch-Outs

This test issue was reportedly released around Maryland in cello packs containing two perforated strips of three game cards each. Cards are printed in black, white and red and measure 2-1/2" x 4-2/3". Backs have instructions on how to play a baseball game by punching out the small squares. Only the "Team Captain" is pictured on the card; each captain can be found with at least two different line-ups on his team, creating a large number of collectible variations. Variations in some player photos have also been noted. The unnumbered issue is checklisted here in alphabetical order. Note, punch-outs of the following players are now believed not to exist: Campaneris, Gibson, Grote, McMillan, and Brooks Robinson.

		NM	EX	VG
Complete Set (91):		19,000	9,500	5,750
Common Player:		80.00	40.00	24.00
(1)	Hank Aaron	1,500	750.00	450.00
(2)	Richie Allen	150.00	75.00	45.00
(3)	Gene Alley	80.00	40.00	24.00
(4)	Felipe Alou	90.00	45.00	27.00
(5)	Matty Alou	80.00	40.00	24.00
(6)	Max Alvis	80.00	40.00	24.00
(7)	Luis Aparicio	200.00	100.00	60.00
(8)	Steve Barber	80.00	40.00	24.00
(9)	Earl Battey	80.00	40.00	24.00
(10)	Clete Boyer	80.00	40.00	24.00
(11)	Ken Boyer	100.00	50.00	30.00
(12)	Lou Brock	200.00	100.00	60.00
(13)	Jim Bunning	175.00	87.00	52.00
(14)	Johnny Callison	80.00	40.00	24.00
(15)	Bert Campaneris (Believed not to exist.)	80.00	40.00	24.00
(16)	Leo Cardenas	80.00	40.00	24.00
(17)	Rico Carty	80.00	40.00	24.00
(18)	Norm Cash	90.00	45.00	27.00
(19)	Orlando Cepeda	175.00	87.00	52.00
(20)	Ed Charles	80.00	40.00	24.00
(21a)	Roberto Clemente (Plain background photo.)	1,500	750.00	450.00
(21b)	Roberto Clemente (Stadium background photo.)	2,000	1,000	600.00
(22)	Donn Clendenon	80.00	40.00	24.00
(23)	Rocky Colavito	150.00	75.00	45.00
(24)	Tony Conigliaro	90.00	45.00	27.00
(25)	Willie Davis	80.00	40.00	24.00
(26)	Johnny Edwards	80.00	40.00	24.00
(27)	Andy Etchebarren	80.00	40.00	24.00
(28)	Curt Flood	80.00	40.00	24.00
(29)	Bill Freehan	80.00	40.00	24.00
(30)	Jim Fregosi	80.00	40.00	24.00
(31)	Bob Gibson (Believed not to exist.)	300.00	150.00	90.00
(32)	Dick Green	80.00	40.00	24.00
(33)	Dick Groat	80.00	40.00	24.00
(34)	Jerry Grote (Believed not to exist.)	80.00	40.00	24.00
(35)	Tom Haller	80.00	40.00	24.00
(36)	Jim Ray Hart	80.00	40.00	24.00
(37)	Mike Hershberger	80.00	40.00	24.00
(38)	Elston Howard	100.00	50.00	30.00
(39)	Frank Howard	90.00	45.00	27.00
(40)	Ron Hunt	80.00	40.00	24.00
(41)	Sonny Jackson	80.00	40.00	24.00
(42)	Cleon Jones	80.00	40.00	24.00
(43)	Jim Kaat	100.00	50.00	30.00
(44)	Al Kaline	400.00	200.00	120.00
(45)	Harmon Killebrew	300.00	150.00	90.00
(46)	Bobby Knoop	80.00	40.00	24.00
(47)	Sandy Koufax	1,500	750.00	450.00
(48)	Ed Kranepool	80.00	40.00	24.00
(49)	Jim Lefebvre	80.00	40.00	24.00
(50)	Don Lock	80.00	40.00	24.00
(51)	Jerry Lumpe	80.00	40.00	24.00
(52)	Mickey Mantle	2,400	1,200	720.00
(53)	Juan Marichal	175.00	87.00	52.00
(54)	Willie Mays	1,500	750.00	450.00
(55)	Bill Mazeroski	175.00	87.00	52.00
(56)	Dick McAuliffe	80.00	40.00	24.00
(57)	Tim McCarver	90.00	45.00	27.00
(58)	Willie McCovey	200.00	100.00	60.00
(59)	Denny McLain	90.00	45.00	27.00
(60)	Roy McMillan (Believed not to exist.)	80.00	40.00	24.00
(61)	Denis Menke	80.00	40.00	24.00
(62)	Joe Morgan	200.00	100.00	60.00
(63)	Tony Oliva	90.00	45.00	27.00
(64)	Joe Pepitone	100.00	50.00	30.00
(65)	Gaylord Perry	175.00	87.00	52.00
(66)	Vada Pinson	90.00	45.00	27.00
(67)	Boog Powell	100.00	50.00	30.00
(68)	Rick Reichardt	80.00	40.00	24.00
(69)	Brooks Robinson (Believed not to exist.)	400.00	200.00	120.00
(70)	Floyd Robinson	80.00	40.00	24.00
(71)	Frank Robinson	400.00	200.00	120.00
(72)	Johnny Romano	80.00	40.00	24.00
(73)	Pete Rose	1,250	625.00	375.00
(74)	John Roseboro	80.00	40.00	24.00
(75)	Ron Santo	100.00	50.00	30.00
(76)	Chico Salmon	80.00	40.00	24.00
(77)	George Scott	80.00	40.00	24.00
(78)	Sonny Siebert	80.00	40.00	24.00
(79)	Russ Snyder	80.00	40.00	24.00
(80)	Willie Stargell	200.00	100.00	60.00
(81)	Mel Stottlemyre	80.00	40.00	24.00
(82)	Joe Torre	120.00	60.00	36.00
(83)	Cesar Tovar	80.00	40.00	24.00
(84)	Tom Tresh	90.00	45.00	27.00
(85)	Zoilo Versalles	80.00	40.00	24.00
(86)	Leon Wagner	80.00	40.00	24.00
(87)	Bill White	80.00	40.00	24.00
(88)	Fred Whitfield	80.00	40.00	24.00
(89)	Billy Williams	175.00	87.00	52.00
(90)	Jimmy Wynn	80.00	40.00	24.00
(91)	Carl Yastrzemski	450.00	225.00	135.00

1967 Topps Stand-Ups

Never actually issued, no more than a handful of each of these rare test issues have made their way into the hobby market. Designed so that the color photo of the player's head could be popped out of the black background and placed into a punch-out base to create a stand-up display, examples of these 3-1/8" x 5-1/4" cards can be found either on thick stock, die-cut around the portrait and with a die-cut stand, or as thin-stock proofs without the die-cutting. Blank-backed, there are 24 cards in the set, numbered on the front at bottom left.

		NM	EX	VG
Complete Set, Thick (24):		75,000	37,500	22,500
Complete Set, Thin (24):		60,000	30,000	18,000
Common Player, Thick:		1,250	625.00	375.00
Common Player, Thin:		1,000	500.00	300.00
THICK STOCK, DIE-CUT				
1	Pete Rose	4,750	2,375	1,425
2	Gary Peters	1,250	625.00	375.00
3	Frank Robinson	2,400	1,200	720.00
4	Jim Lonborg	1,250	625.00	375.00
5	Ron Swoboda	1,250	625.00	375.00
6	Harmon Killebrew	2,100	1,050	630.00
7	Roberto Clemente	8,500	4,250	2,550
8	Mickey Mantle	12,500	6,250	3,750
9	Jim Fregosi	1,250	625.00	375.00
10	Al Kaline	3,000	1,500	900.00
11	Don Drysdale	2,500	1,250	750.00
12	Dean Chance	1,250	625.00	375.00
13	Orlando Cepeda	1,750	875.00	525.00
14	Tim McCarver	1,400	700.00	420.00
15	Frank Howard	1,400	700.00	420.00
16	Max Alvis	1,250	625.00	375.00
17	Rusty Staub	1,400	700.00	420.00
18	Richie Allen	1,400	700.00	420.00
19	Willie Mays	8,500	4,250	2,550
20	Hank Aaron	8,500	4,250	2,550
21	Carl Yastrzemski	7,000	3,500	2,100
22	Ron Santo	1,400	700.00	420.00
23	Catfish Hunter	1,750	875.00	525.00
24	Jim Wynn	1,250	625.00	375.00
THIN STOCK, PROOFS				
1	Pete Rose	3,750	1,875	1,125
2	Gary Peters	1,000	500.00	300.00
3	Frank Robinson	1,900	950.00	570.00
4	Jim Lonborg	1,000	500.00	300.00
5	Ron Swoboda	1,000	500.00	300.00
6	Harmon Killebrew	1,650	825.00	495.00
7	Roberto Clemente	6,500	3,250	1,950
8	Mickey Mantle	10,000	5,000	3,000
9	Jim Fregosi	1,000	500.00	300.00
10	Al Kaline	2,500	1,250	750.00
11	Don Drysdale	2,000	1,000	600.00
12	Dean Chance	1,000	500.00	300.00
13	Orlando Cepeda	1,400	700.00	420.00
14	Tim McCarver	1,100	550.00	330.00
15	Frank Howard	1,100	550.00	330.00
16	Max Alvis	1,000	500.00	300.00
17	Rusty Staub	1,100	550.00	330.00
18	Richie Allen	1,100	550.00	330.00
19	Willie Mays	7,000	3,500	2,100

		NM	EX	VG
20	Hank Aaron	7,000	3,500	2,100
21	Carl Yastrzemski	5,500	2,750	1,650
22	Ron Santo	1,100	550.00	330.00
23	Catfish Hunter	1,400	700.00	420.00
24	Jim Wynn	1,000	500.00	300.00

1967 Topps Pirates Stickers

Considered a "test" issue, this 33-sticker set of 2-1/2" x 3-1/2" stickers is very similar to the Red Sox stickers which were produced the same year. Player stickers have a color picture (often just the player's head) and the player's name in large "comic book" letters. Besides the players, there are other topics such as "I Love the Pirates," "Bob Clemente for Mayor," and a number of similar sentiments. The stickers have blank backs and are rather scarce.

		NM	EX	VG
Complete Set (33):		750.00	375.00	225.00
Common Player:		15.00	7.50	4.50
1	Gene Alley	15.00	7.50	4.50
2	Matty Alou	15.00	7.50	4.50
3	Dennis Ribant	15.00	7.50	4.50
4	Steve Blass	15.00	7.50	4.50
5	Juan Pizarro	15.00	7.50	4.50
6	Bob Clemente	175.00	85.00	50.00
7	Donn Clendenon	15.00	7.50	4.50
8	Roy Face	15.00	7.50	4.50
9	Woody Fryman	15.00	7.50	4.50
10	Jesse Gonder	15.00	7.50	4.50
11	Vern Law	15.00	7.50	4.50
12	Al McBean	15.00	7.50	4.50
13	Jerry May	15.00	7.50	4.50
14	Bill Mazeroski	35.00	17.50	10.00
15	Pete Mikkelsen	15.00	7.50	4.50
16	Manny Mota	15.00	7.50	4.50
17	Billy O'Dell	15.00	7.50	4.50
18	Jose Pagan	15.00	7.50	4.50
19	Jim Pagliaroni	15.00	7.50	4.50
20	Johnny Pesky	15.00	7.50	4.50
21	Tommie Sisk	15.00	7.50	4.50
22	Willie Stargell	60.00	30.00	18.00
23	Bob Veale	15.00	7.50	4.50
24	Harry Walker	15.00	7.50	4.50
25	I Love The Pirates	20.00	10.00	6.00
26	Let's Go Pirates	20.00	10.00	6.00
27	Bob Clemente For Mayor	100.00	50.00	30.00
28	National League Batting Champion (Matty Alou)	15.00	7.50	4.50
29	Happiness Is A Pirate Win	20.00	10.00	6.00
30	Donn Clendenon Is My Hero	15.00	7.50	4.50
31	Pirates' Home Run Champion (Willie Stargell)	30.00	15.00	9.00
32	Pirates Logo	20.00	10.00	6.00
33	Pirates Pennant	25.00	12.50	7.50

1967 Topps Red Sox Stickers

Like the 1967 Pirates Stickers, the Red Sox Stickers were part of the same test procedure. The Red Sox Stickers have the same 2-1/2" x 3-1/2" dimensions, color picture and large player's name on the front. A set is complete at 33 stickers. The majority are players, but themes such as "Let's Go Red Sox" are also included.

		NM	EX	VG
Complete Set (33):		500.00	250.00	150.00
Common Player:		10.00	5.00	3.00
1	Dennis Bennett	10.00	5.00	3.00
2	Darrell Brandon	10.00	5.00	3.00
3	Tony Conigliaro	35.00	17.50	10.00
4	Don Demeter	10.00	5.00	3.00
5	Hank Fischer	10.00	5.00	3.00

		NM	EX	VG
6	Joe Foy	10.00	5.00	3.00
7	Mike Andrews	10.00	5.00	3.00
8	Dalton Jones	10.00	5.00	3.00
9	Jim Lonborg	10.00	5.00	3.00
10	Don McMahon	10.00	5.00	3.00
11	Dave Morehead	10.00	5.00	3.00
12	George Smith	10.00	5.00	3.00
13	Rico Petrocelli	15.00	7.50	4.50
14	Mike Ryan	10.00	5.00	3.00
15	Jose Santiago	10.00	5.00	3.00
16	George Scott	10.00	5.00	3.00
17	Sal Maglie	10.00	5.00	3.00
18	Reggie Smith	10.00	5.00	3.00
19	Lee Stange	10.00	5.00	3.00
20	Jerry Stephenson	10.00	5.00	3.00
21	Jose Tartabull	10.00	5.00	3.00
22	George Thomas	10.00	5.00	3.00
23	Bob Tillman	10.00	5.00	3.00
24	Johnnie Wyatt	10.00	5.00	3.00
25	Carl Yastrzemski	90.00	45.00	27.50
26	Dick Williams	10.00	5.00	3.00
27	I Love The Red Sox	12.50	6.25	3.75
28	Let's Go Red Sox	12.50	6.25	3.75
29	Carl Yastrzemski For Mayor	50.00	25.00	15.00
30	Tony Conigliaro Is My Hero	27.50	13.50	8.25
31	Happiness Is A Boston Win	12.50	6.25	3.75
32	Red Sox Logo	15.00	7.50	4.50
33	Red Sox Pennant	20.00	10.00	6.00

1967 Topps Who Am I?

A cartoon caption and goofy facial features were printed on the front of these 2-1/2" x 3-1/2" cards and were designed to be scratched off to reveal the portrait, name and claim to fame of the person beneath. This 44-card set includes all manner of U.S. and international historical figures, including four baseball players. Backs are printed in red and have a large question mark with several hints printed thereon. Unscratched cards are much rarer than scratched cards, though they carry only about a 50 percent premium.

		NM	EX	VG
Complete Set (44):		850.00	425.00	250.00
Wax Pack:		350.00		
12	Babe Ruth	100.00	50.00	30.00
22	Mickey Mantle	225.00	110.00	65.00
33	Willie Mays	100.00	50.00	30.00
41	Sandy Koufax	100.00	50.00	30.00

1968 Topps

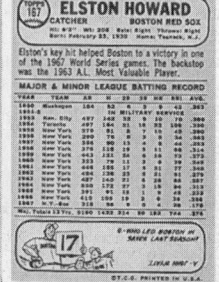

In 1968, Topps returned to a 598-card set of 2-1/2" x 3-1/2" cards. It is not, however, more of the same by way of appearance as the cards feature a color photograph on a background of what appears to be a burlap fabric. The player's name is below the photo but on the unusual background. A colored circle on the lower right carries the team and position. Backs were also changed, while retaining the vertical format introduced the previous year, with stats in the middle and cartoon at the bottom. The set features many of the old favorite subsets, including statistical leaders, World Series highlights, multi-player cards, checklists, rookie cards and the return of All-Star cards. Most checklist cards are double-printed, once in the series preceding the series it lists and once within the series it lists; subtle variations between the pairs are listed where known.

		NM	EX	VG
Complete Set (598):		3,000	1,500	900.00
Common Player (1-457):		2.00	1.00	.60
Common Player (458-598):		5.00	2.50	1.50
1	N.L. Batting Leaders (Matty Alou, Roberto Clemente, Tony Gonzalez)	15.00	7.50	3.75
2	A.L. Batting Leaders (Al Kaline, Frank Robinson, Carl Yastrzemski)	15.00	7.50	3.75

		NM	EX	VG
3	N.L. RBI Leaders (Hank Aaron, Orlando Cepeda, Roberto Clemente)	15.00	7.50	3.75
4	A.L. RBI Leaders (Harmon Killebrew, Frank Robinson, Carl Yastrzemski)	12.00	6.00	3.50
5	N.L. Home Run Leaders (Hank Aaron, Willie McCovey, Ron Santo, Jim Wynn)	20.00	10.00	6.00
6	A.L. Home Run Leaders (Frank Howard, Harmon Killebrew, Carl Yastrzemski)	12.00	6.00	3.50
7	N.L. ERA Leaders (Jim Bunning, Phil Niekro, Chris Short)	7.00	3.50	2.00
8	A.L. ERA Leaders (Joe Horlen, Gary Peters, Sonny Siebert)	2.00	1.00	.60
9	N.L. Pitching Leaders (Jim Bunning, Fergie Jenkins, Mike McCormick, Claude Osteen)	7.00	3.50	2.00
10a	A.L. Pitching Leaders (Dean Chance, Jim Lonborg, Earl Wilson) ("Lonberg" on back.)	9.00	4.50	2.75
10b	A.L. Pitching Leaders (Dean Chance, Jim Lonborg, Earl Wilson) ("Lonborg" on back.)	7.00	3.50	2.00
11	N.L. Strikeout Leaders (Jim Bunning, Fergie Jenkins, Gaylord Perry)	7.00	3.50	2.00
12	A.L. Strikeout Leaders (Dean Chance, Jim Lonborg, Sam McDowell)	7.00	3.50	2.00
13	Chuck Hartenstein	2.00	1.00	.60
14	Jerry McNertney	2.00	1.00	.60
15	Ron Hunt	2.00	1.00	.60
16	Indians Rookies (Lou Piniella, Richie Scheinblum)	5.00	2.50	1.50
17	Dick Hall	2.00	1.00	.60
18	Mike Hershberger	2.00	1.00	.60
19	Juan Pizarro	2.00	1.00	.60
20	Brooks Robinson	20.00	10.00	5.00
21	Ron Davis	2.00	1.00	.60
22	Pat Dobson	2.00	1.00	.60
23	Chico Cardenas	2.00	1.00	.60
24	Bobby Locke	2.00	1.00	.60
25	Julian Javier	2.00	1.00	.60
26	Darrell Brandon	2.00	1.00	.60
27	Gil Hodges	7.50	3.75	2.25
28	Ted Uhlaender	2.00	1.00	.60
29	Joe Verbanic	2.00	1.00	.60
30	Joe Torre	8.00	4.00	2.50
31	Ed Stroud	2.00	1.00	.60
32	Joe Gibbon	2.00	1.00	.60
33	Pete Ward	2.00	1.00	.60
34	Al Ferrara	2.00	1.00	.60
35	Steve Hargan	2.00	1.00	.60
36	Pirates Rookies (**Bob Moose, Bob Robertson**)	2.00	1.00	.60
37	Billy Williams	13.50	6.75	4.00
38	Tony Pierce	2.00	1.00	.60
39	Cookie Rojas	2.00	1.00	.60
40	Denny McLain	20.00	10.00	5.00
41	Julio Gotay	2.00	1.00	.60
42	Larry Haney	2.00	1.00	.60
43	Gary Bell	2.00	1.00	.60
44	Frank Kostro	2.00	1.00	.60
45	Tom Seaver	50.00	25.00	12.50
46	Dave Ricketts	2.00	1.00	.60
47	Ralph Houk	2.50	1.25	.70
48	Ted Davidson	2.00	1.00	.60
49a	Ed Brinkman (Yellow team.)	50.00	25.00	12.50
49b	Ed Brinkman (White team.)	2.00	1.00	.60
50	Willie Mays	60.00	30.00	15.00
51	Bob Locker	2.00	1.00	.60
52	Hawk Taylor	2.00	1.00	.60
53	Gene Alley	2.00	1.00	.60
54	Stan Williams	2.00	1.00	.60
55	Felipe Alou	5.00	2.50	1.50
56	Orioles Rookies (Dave Leonhard, Dave May)	2.00	1.00	.60
57	Dan Schneider	2.00	1.00	.60
58	Ed Mathews	15.00	7.50	3.75
59	Don Lock	2.00	1.00	.60
60	Ken Holtzman	2.00	1.00	.60
61	Reggie Smith	2.00	1.00	.60
62	Chuck Dobson	2.00	1.00	.60
63	Dick Kenworthy	2.00	1.00	.60
64	Jim Merritt	2.00	1.00	.60
65	John Roseboro	2.00	1.00	.60
66a	Casey Cox (Yellow team.)	75.00	37.50	18.75
66b	Casey Cox (White team.)	2.00	1.00	.60
67	1st Series Check List (1-109) (Jim Kaat)	5.00	2.50	1.50
68	Ron Willis	2.00	1.00	.60
69	Tom Tresh	6.00	3.00	1.75
70	Bob Veale	2.00	1.00	.60
71	Vern Fuller	2.00	1.00	.60
72	Tommy John	5.00	2.50	1.50
73	Jim Hart	2.00	1.00	.60
74	Milt Pappas	2.00	1.00	.60
75	Don Mincher	2.00	1.00	.60
76	Braves Rookies (**Jim Britton, Ron Reed**)	2.00	1.00	.60
77	**Don Wilson**	2.00	1.00	.60
78	Jim Northrup	2.00	1.00	.60
79	Ted Kubiak	2.00	1.00	.60
80	Rod Carew	50.00	25.00	12.50
81	Larry Jackson	2.00	1.00	.60
82	Sam Bowens	2.00	1.00	.60
83	John Stephenson	2.00	1.00	.60
84	Bob Tolan	2.00	1.00	.60
85	Gaylord Perry	9.00	4.50	2.75
86	Willie Stargell	12.00	6.00	3.50
87	Dick Williams	2.00	1.00	.60
88	Phil Regan	2.00	1.00	.60

No.	Player			
89	Jake Gibbs	2.00	1.00	.60
90	Vada Pinson	5.00	2.50	1.50
91	Jim Ollom	2.00	1.00	.60
92	Ed Kranepool	2.00	1.00	.60
93	Tony Cloninger	2.00	1.00	.60
94	Lee Maye	2.00	1.00	.60
95	Bob Aspromonte	2.00	1.00	.60
96	Senators Rookies (Frank Coggins, Dick Nold)	2.00	1.00	.60
97	Tom Phoebus	2.00	1.00	.60
98	Gary Sutherland	2.00	1.00	.60
99	Rocky Colavito	7.00	3.50	2.00
100	Bob Gibson	20.00	10.00	5.00
101	Glenn Beckert	2.00	1.00	.60
102	Jose Cardenal	2.00	1.00	.60
103	Don Sutton	9.00	4.50	2.75
104	Dick Dietz	2.00	1.00	.60
105	Al Downing	2.00	1.00	.60
106	Dalton Jones	2.00	1.00	.60
107	2nd Series Check List (110-196) (Juan Marichal)	5.00	2.50	1.50
108	Don Pavletich	2.00	1.00	.60
109	Bert Campaneris	2.00	1.00	.60
110	Hank Aaron	80.00	40.00	20.00
111	Rich Reese	2.00	1.00	.60
112	Woody Fryman	2.00	1.00	.60
113	Tigers Rookies (Tom Matchick, Daryl Patterson)	2.00	1.00	.60
114	Ron Swoboda	2.00	1.00	.60
115	Sam McDowell	2.00	1.00	.60
116	Ken McMullen	2.00	1.00	.60
117	Larry Jaster	2.00	1.00	.60
118	Mark Belanger	2.00	1.00	.60
119	Ted Savage	2.00	1.00	.60
120	Mel Stottlemyre	5.00	2.50	1.50
121	Jimmie Hall	2.00	1.00	.60
122	Gene Mauch	2.00	1.00	.60
123	Jose Santiago	2.00	1.00	.60
124	Nate Oliver	2.00	1.00	.60
125	Joe Horlen	2.00	1.00	.60
126	Bobby Etheridge	2.00	1.00	.60
127	Paul Lindblad	2.00	1.00	.60
128	Astros Rookies (Tom Dukes, Alonzo Harris)	2.00	1.00	.60
129	Mickey Stanley	2.00	1.00	.60
130	Tony Perez	10.00	5.00	3.00
131	Frank Bertaina	2.00	1.00	.60
132	Bud Harrelson	2.00	1.00	.60
133	Fred Whitfield	2.00	1.00	.60
134	Pat Jarvis	2.00	1.00	.60
135	Paul Blair	2.00	1.00	.60
136	Randy Hundley	2.00	1.00	.60
137	Twins Team	5.00	2.50	1.50
138	Ruben Amaro	2.00	1.00	.60
139	Chris Short	2.00	1.00	.60
140	Tony Conigliaro	5.00	2.50	1.50
141	Dal Maxvill	2.00	1.00	.60
142	White Sox Rookies (Buddy Bradford, Bill Voss)	2.00	1.00	.60
143	Pete Cimino	2.00	1.00	.60
144	Joe Morgan	12.00	6.00	3.50
145	Don Drysdale	15.00	7.50	4.50
146	Sal Bando	2.00	1.00	.60
147	Frank Linzy	2.00	1.00	.60
148	Dave Bristol	2.00	1.00	.60
149	Bob Saverine	2.00	1.00	.60
150	Roberto Clemente	100.00	50.00	25.00
151	World Series Game 1 (Brock Socks 4 Hits in Opener)	6.00	3.00	1.75
152	World Series Game 2 (Yaz Smashes Two Homers)	12.00	6.00	3.00
153	World Series Game 3 (Briles Cools Off Boston)	3.00	1.50	.90
154	World Series Game 4 (Gibson Hurls Shutout)	9.00	4.50	2.75
155	World Series Game 5 (Lonborg Wins Again)	6.00	3.00	1.75
156	World Series Game 6 (Petrocelli Socks Two Homers)	6.00	3.00	1.75
157	World Series Game 7 (St. Louis Wins It)	6.00	3.00	1.75
158	1967 World Series (The Cardinals Celebrate)	5.00	2.50	1.50
159	Don Kessinger	2.00	1.00	.60
160	Earl Wilson	2.00	1.00	.60
161	Norm Miller	2.00	1.00	.60
162	Cards Rookies (*Hal Gilson, Mike Torrez*)	2.00	1.00	.60
163	Gene Brabender	2.00	1.00	.60
164	Ramon Webster	2.00	1.00	.60
165	Tony Oliva	5.00	2.50	1.50
166	Claude Raymond	2.00	1.00	.60
167	Elston Howard	5.00	2.50	1.50
168	Dodgers Team	5.00	2.50	1.50
169	Bob Bolin	2.00	1.00	.60
170	Jim Fregosi	2.00	1.00	.60
171	Don Nottebart	2.00	1.00	.60
172	Walt Williams	2.00	1.00	.60
173	John Boozer	2.00	1.00	.60
174	Bob Tillman	2.00	1.00	.60
175	Maury Wills	2.00	1.00	.60
176	Bob Allen	2.00	1.00	.60
177	Mets Rookies (*Jerry Koosman, Nolan Ryan*)	600.00	300.00	150.00
178	Don Wert	2.00	1.00	.60
179	Bill Stoneman	2.00	1.00	.60
180	Curt Flood	3.00	1.50	.90
181	Jerry Zimmerman	2.00	1.00	.60
182	Dave Giusti	2.00	1.00	.60
183	Bob Kennedy	2.00	1.00	.60
184	Lou Johnson	2.00	1.00	.60
185	Tom Haller	2.00	1.00	.60
186	Eddie Watt	2.00	1.00	.60
187	Sonny Jackson	2.00	1.00	.60
188	Cap Peterson	2.00	1.00	.60
189	Bill Landis	2.00	1.00	.60
190	Bill White	2.00	1.00	.60
191	Dan Frisella	2.00	1.00	.60
192a	3rd Series Check List (197-283) (Carl Yastrzemski) ("To increase the..." on back.)	6.00	3.00	1.75
192b	3rd Series Check List (197-283) (Carl Yastrzemski) ("To increase your..." on back.)	6.00	3.00	1.75
193	Jack Hamilton	2.00	1.00	.60
194	Don Buford	2.00	1.00	.60
195	Joe Pepitone	5.00	2.50	1.50
196	Gary Nolan	2.00	1.00	.60
197	Larry Brown	2.00	1.00	.60
198	Roy Face	2.00	1.00	.60
199	A's Rookies (Darrell Osteen, Roberto Rodriguez)	2.00	1.00	.60
200	Orlando Cepeda	11.00	5.50	3.25
201	*Mike Marshall*	3.00	1.50	.90
202	Adolfo Phillips	2.00	1.00	.60
203	Dick Kelley	2.00	1.00	.60
204	Andy Etchebarren	2.00	1.00	.60
205	Juan Marichal	9.00	4.50	2.75
206	Cal Ermer	2.00	1.00	.60
207	Carroll Sembera	2.00	1.00	.60
208	Willie Davis	2.00	1.00	.60
209	Tim Cullen	2.00	1.00	.60
210	Gary Peters	2.00	1.00	.60
211	J.C. Martin	2.00	1.00	.60
212	Dave Morehead	2.00	1.00	.60
213	Chico Ruiz	2.00	1.00	.60
214	Yankees Rookies (Stan Bahnsen, Frank Fernandez)	2.00	1.00	.60
215	Jim Bunning	9.00	4.50	2.75
216	Bubba Morton	2.00	1.00	.60
217	Turk Farrell	2.00	1.00	.60
218	Ken Suarez	2.00	1.00	.60
219	Rob Gardner	2.00	1.00	.60
220	Harmon Killebrew	15.00	7.50	3.75
221	Braves Team	5.00	2.50	1.50
222	Jim Hardin	2.00	1.00	.60
223	Ollie Brown	2.00	1.00	.60
224	Jack Aker	2.00	1.00	.60
225	Richie Allen	6.00	3.00	1.75
226	Jimmie Price	2.00	1.00	.60
227	Joe Hoerner	2.00	1.00	.60
228	Dodgers Rookies (**Jack Billingham**, Jim Fairey)	2.00	1.00	.60
229	Fred Klages	2.00	1.00	.60
230	Pete Rose	50.00	25.00	12.50
231	Dave Baldwin	2.00	1.00	.60
232	Denis Menke	2.00	1.00	.60
233	George Scott	2.00	1.00	.60
234	Bill Monbouquette	2.00	1.00	.60
235	Ron Santo	6.00	3.00	1.75
236	Tug McGraw	2.00	1.00	.60
237	Alvin Dark	2.00	1.00	.60
238	Tom Satriano	2.00	1.00	.60
239	Bill Henry	2.00	1.00	.60
240	Al Kaline	40.00	20.00	10.00
241	Felix Millan	2.00	1.00	.60
242	Moe Drabowsky	2.00	1.00	.60
243	Rich Rollins	2.00	1.00	.60
244	John Donaldson	2.00	1.00	.60
245	Tony Gonzalez	2.00	1.00	.60
246	Fritz Peterson	2.00	1.00	.60
247	Reds Rookies (**Johnny Bench**, Ron Tompkins)	125.00	62.50	31.25
248	Fred Valentine	2.00	1.00	.60
249	Bill Singer	2.00	1.00	.60
250	Carl Yastrzemski	20.00	10.00	6.00
251	*Manny Sanguillen*	4.50	2.25	1.25
252	Angels Team	5.00	2.50	1.50
253	Dick Hughes	2.00	1.00	.60
254	Cleon Jones	2.00	1.00	.60
255	Dean Chance	2.00	1.00	.60
256	Norm Cash	7.00	3.50	2.00
257	Phil Niekro	9.00	4.50	2.75
258	Cubs Rookies (Jose Arcia, Bill Schlesinger)	2.00	1.00	.60
259	Ken Boyer	5.00	2.50	1.50
260	Jim Wynn	2.00	1.00	.60
261	Dave Duncan	2.00	1.00	.60
262	Rick Wise	2.00	1.00	.60
263	Horace Clarke	2.00	1.00	.60
264	Ted Abernathy	2.00	1.00	.60
265	Tommy Davis	2.00	1.00	.60
266	Paul Popovich	2.00	1.00	.60
267	Herman Franks	2.00	1.00	.60
268	Bob Humphreys	2.00	1.00	.60
269	Bob Tiefenauer	2.00	1.00	.60
270	Matty Alou	2.00	1.00	.60
271	Bobby Knoop	2.00	1.00	.60
272	Ray Culp	2.00	1.00	.60
273	Dave Johnson	2.00	1.00	.60
274	Mike Cuellar	2.00	1.00	.60
275	Tim McCarver	5.00	2.50	1.50
276	Jim Roland	2.00	1.00	.60
277	Jerry Buchek	2.00	1.00	.60
278a	4th Series Check List (284-370) (Orlando Cepeda) (Copyright at right.)	5.00	2.50	1.50
278b	4th Series Check List (284-370) (Orlando Cepeda) (Copyright at left.)	5.50	2.75	1.75
279	Bill Hands	2.00	1.00	.60
280	Mickey Mantle	400.00	200.00	100.00
281	Jim Campanis	2.00	1.00	.60
282	Rick Monday	2.00	1.00	.60
283	Mel Queen	2.00	1.00	.60
284	John Briggs	2.00	1.00	.60
285	Dick McAuliffe	2.00	1.00	.60
286	Cecil Upshaw	2.00	1.00	.60
287	White Sox Rookies (Mickey Abarbanel, Cisco Carlos)	2.00	1.00	.60
288	Dave Wickersham	2.00	1.00	.60
289	Woody Held	2.00	1.00	.60
290	Willie McCovey	15.00	7.50	3.75
291	Dick Lines	2.00	1.00	.60
292	Art Shamsky	2.00	1.00	.60
293	Bruce Howard	2.00	1.00	.60
294	Red Schoendienst	7.00	3.50	2.00
295	Sonny Siebert	2.00	1.00	.60
296	Byron Browne	2.00	1.00	.60
297	Russ Gibson	2.00	1.00	.60
298	Jim Brewer	2.00	1.00	.60
299	Gene Michael	2.00	1.00	.60
300	Rusty Staub	2.50	1.25	.70
301	Twins Rookies (George Mitterwald, Rick Renick)	2.00	1.00	.60
302	Gerry Arrigo	2.00	1.00	.60
303	Dick Green	2.00	1.00	.60
304	Sandy Valdespino	2.00	1.00	.60
305	Minnie Rojas	2.00	1.00	.60
306	Mike Ryan	2.00	1.00	.60
307	John Hiller	2.00	1.00	.60
308	Pirates Team	6.00	3.00	1.75
309	Ken Henderson	2.00	1.00	.60
310	Luis Aparicio	11.00	5.50	3.25
311	Jack Lamabe	2.00	1.00	.60
312	Curt Blefary	2.00	1.00	.60
313	Al Weis	2.00	1.00	.60
314	Red Sox Rookies (Bill Rohr, George Spriggs)	2.00	1.00	.60
315	Zoilo Versalles	2.00	1.00	.60
316	Steve Barber	2.00	1.00	.60
317	Ron Brand	2.00	1.00	.60
318	Chico Salmon	2.00	1.00	.60
319	George Culver	2.00	1.00	.60
320	Frank Howard	2.50	1.25	.70
321	Leo Durocher	6.00	3.00	1.75
322	Dave Boswell	2.00	1.00	.60
323	Deron Johnson	2.00	1.00	.60
324	Jim Nash	2.00	1.00	.60
325	Manny Mota	2.00	1.00	.60
326	Dennis Ribant	2.00	1.00	.60
327	Tony Taylor	2.00	1.00	.60
328	Angels Rookies (Chuck Vinson, Jim Weaver)	2.00	1.00	.60
329	Duane Josephson	2.00	1.00	.60
330	Roger Maris	50.00	25.00	12.50
331	Dan Osinski	2.00	1.00	.60
332	Doug Rader	2.00	1.00	.60
333	Ron Herbel	2.00	1.00	.60
334	Orioles Team	5.00	2.50	1.50
335	Bob Allison	2.00	1.00	.60
336	John Purdin	2.00	1.00	.60
337	Bill Robinson	2.00	1.00	.60
338	Bob Johnson	2.00	1.00	.60
339	Rich Nye	2.00	1.00	.60
340	Max Alvis	2.00	1.00	.60
341	Jim Lemon	2.00	1.00	.60
342	Ken Johnson	2.00	1.00	.60
343	Jim Gosger	2.00	1.00	.60
344	Donn Clendenon	2.00	1.00	.60
345	Bob Hendley	2.00	1.00	.60
346	Jerry Adair	2.00	1.00	.60
347	George Brunet	2.00	1.00	.60
348	Phillies Rookies (Larry Colton, Dick Thoenen)	2.00	1.00	.60
349	Ed Spiezio	2.00	1.00	.60
350	Hoyt Wilhelm	9.00	4.50	2.75
351	Bob Barton	2.00	1.00	.60
352	Jackie Hernandez	2.00	1.00	.60
353	Mack Jones	2.00	1.00	.60
354	Pete Richert	2.00	1.00	.60
355	Ernie Banks	20.00	10.00	6.00
356a	5th Series Check List (371-457) (Ken Holtzman) (Top of cap away from black circle.)	5.00	2.50	1.50
356b	5th Series Check List (371-457) (Ken Holtzman) (Top of cap near black circle.)	5.00	2.50	1.50
357	Len Gabrielson	2.00	1.00	.60
358	Mike Epstein	2.00	1.00	.60
359	Joe Moeller	2.00	1.00	.60
360	Willie Horton	2.00	1.00	.60
361	Harmon Killebrew (All-Star)	7.50	3.75	2.25
362	Orlando Cepeda (All-Star)	5.00	2.50	1.50
363	Rod Carew (All-Star)	6.50	3.25	2.00
364	Joe Morgan (All-Star)	6.00	3.00	1.75
365	Brooks Robinson (All-Star)	7.50	3.75	2.25
366	Ron Santo (All-Star)	5.00	2.50	1.50
367	Jim Fregosi (All-Star)	2.00	1.00	.60
368	Gene Alley (All-Star)	2.00	1.00	.60
369	Carl Yastrzemski (All-Star)	7.50	3.75	2.25
370	Hank Aaron (All-Star)	25.00	12.50	6.25
371	Tony Oliva (All-Star)	2.50	1.25	.70
372	Lou Brock (All-Star)	6.00	3.00	1.75
373	Frank Robinson (All-Star)	7.50	3.75	2.25
374	Roberto Clemente (All-Star)	25.00	12.50	6.25
375	Bill Freehan (All-Star)	2.00	1.00	.60
376	Tim McCarver (All-Star)	3.00	1.50	.90
377	Joe Horlen (All-Star)	2.00	1.00	.60
378	Bob Gibson (All-Star)	7.00	3.50	2.00
379	Gary Peters (All-Star)	2.00	1.00	.60
380	Ken Holtzman (All-Star)	2.00	1.00	.60
381	Boog Powell	3.00	1.50	.90
382	Ramon Hernandez	2.00	1.00	.60
383	Steve Whitaker	2.00	1.00	.60
384	Red Rookies (*Bill Henry, Hal McRae*)	6.00	3.00	1.75
385	Jim Hunter	10.00	5.00	3.00
386	Greg Goossen	2.00	1.00	.60
387	Joe Foy	2.00	1.00	.60
388	Ray Washburn	2.00	1.00	.60
389	Jay Johnstone	2.00	1.00	.60
390	Bill Mazeroski	10.00	5.00	3.00
391	Bob Priddy	2.00	1.00	.60
392	Grady Hatton	2.00	1.00	.60
393	Jim Perry	2.00	1.00	.60
394	Tommie Aaron	2.00	1.00	.60
395	Camilo Pascual	2.00	1.00	.60
396	Bobby Wine	2.00	1.00	.60
397	Vic Davalillo	2.00	1.00	.60
398	Jim Grant	2.00	1.00	.60
399	Ray Oyler	2.00	1.00	.60

#	Player			
400a	Mike McCormick (White team.)	150.00	75.00	37.50
400b	Mike McCormick (Yellow team.)	2.00	1.00	.60
401	Mets Team	5.00	2.50	1.50
402	Mike Hegan	2.00	1.00	.60
403	John Buzhardt	2.00	1.00	.60
404	Floyd Robinson	2.00	1.00	.60
405	Tommy Helms	2.00	1.00	.60
406	Dick Ellsworth	2.00	1.00	.60
407	Gary Kolb	2.00	1.00	.60
408	Steve Carlton	20.00	10.00	5.00
409	Orioles Rookies (Frank Peters, Ron Stone)	2.00	1.00	.60
410	Fergie Jenkins	10.00	5.00	3.00
411	Ron Hansen	2.00	1.00	.60
412	Clay Carroll	2.00	1.00	.60
413	Tommy McCraw	2.00	1.00	.60
414	Mickey Lolich	2.00	1.00	.60
415	Johnny Callison	2.00	1.00	.60
416	Bill Rigney	2.00	1.00	.60
417	Willie Crawford	2.00	1.00	.60
418	Eddie Fisher	2.00	1.00	.60
419	Jack Hiatt	2.00	1.00	.60
420	Cesar Tovar	2.00	1.00	.60
421	Ron Taylor	2.00	1.00	.60
422	Rene Lachemann	2.00	1.00	.60
423	Fred Gladding	2.00	1.00	.60
424	White Sox Team	5.00	2.50	1.50
425	Jim Maloney	2.00	1.00	.60
426	Hank Allen	2.00	1.00	.60
427	Dick Calmus	2.00	1.00	.60
428	Vic Roznovsky	2.00	1.00	.60
429	Tommie Sisk	2.00	1.00	.60
430	Rico Petrocelli	2.00	1.00	.60
431	Dooley Womack	2.00	1.00	.60
432	Indians Rookies (Bill Davis, Jose Vidal)	2.00	1.00	.60
433	Bob Rodgers	2.00	1.00	.60
434	Ricardo Joseph	2.00	1.00	.60
435	Ron Perranoski	2.00	1.00	.60
436	Hal Lanier	2.00	1.00	.60
437	Don Cardwell	2.00	1.00	.60
438	Lee Thomas	2.00	1.00	.60
439	Luman Harris	2.00	1.00	.60
440	Claude Osteen	2.00	1.00	.60
441	Alex Johnson	2.00	1.00	.60
442	Dick Bosman	2.00	1.00	.60
443	Joe Azcue	2.00	1.00	.60
444	Jack Fisher	2.00	1.00	.60
445	Mike Shannon	2.00	1.00	.60
446	Ron Kline	2.00	1.00	.60
447	Tigers Rookies (George Korince, Fred Lasher)	2.00	1.00	.60
448	Gary Wagner	2.00	1.00	.60
449	Gene Oliver	2.00	1.00	.60
450	Jim Kaat	2.50	1.25	.70
451	Al Spangler	2.00	1.00	.60
452	Jesus Alou	2.00	1.00	.60
453	Sammy Ellis	2.00	1.00	.60
454a	6th Series Check List (458-533) (Frank Robinson) (Neck chain shows.)	6.00	3.00	1.75
454b	6th Series Check List (458-533) (Frank Robinson) (No neck chain.)	6.00	3.00	1.75
455	Rico Carty	2.00	1.00	.60
456	John O'Donoghue	2.00	1.00	.60
457	Jim Lefebvre	2.00	1.00	.60
458	Lew Krausse	5.00	2.50	1.50
459	Dick Simpson	5.00	2.50	1.50
460	Jim Lonborg	5.00	2.50	1.50
461	Chuck Hiller	5.00	2.50	1.50
462	Barry Moore	5.00	2.50	1.50
463	Jimmie Schaffer	5.00	2.50	1.50
464	Don McMahon	5.00	2.50	1.50
465	Tommie Agee	5.00	2.50	1.50
466	Bill Dillman	5.00	2.50	1.50
467	Dick Howser	5.00	2.50	1.50
468	Larry Sherry	5.00	2.50	1.50
469	Ty Cline	5.00	2.50	1.50
470	Bill Freehan	5.00	2.50	1.50
471	Orlando Pena	5.00	2.50	1.50
472	Walt Alston	8.00	4.00	2.50
473	Al Worthington	5.00	2.50	1.50
474	Paul Schaal	5.00	2.50	1.50
475	Joe Niekro	5.00	2.50	1.50
476	Woody Woodward	5.00	2.50	1.50
477	Phillies Team	6.00	3.00	1.75
478	Dave McNally	5.00	2.50	1.50
479	Phil Gagliano	5.00	2.50	1.50
480	Manager's Dream (Chico Cardenas, Roberto Clemente, Tony Oliva)	75.00	37.50	18.75
481	John Wyatt	5.00	2.50	1.50
482	Jose Pagan	5.00	2.50	1.50
483	Darold Knowles	5.00	2.50	1.50
484	Phil Roof	5.00	2.50	1.50
485	Ken Berry	5.00	2.50	1.50
486	Cal Koonce	5.00	2.50	1.50
487	Lee May	5.00	2.50	1.50
488	Dick Tracewski	5.00	2.50	1.50
489	Wally Bunker	5.00	2.50	1.50
490	Super Stars (Harmon Killebrew, Mickey Mantle, Willie Mays)	140.00	70.00	35.00
491	Denny Lemaster	5.00	2.50	1.50
492	Jeff Torborg	5.00	2.50	1.50
493	Jim McGlothlin	5.00	2.50	1.50
494	Ray Sadecki	5.00	2.50	1.50
495	Leon Wagner	5.00	2.50	1.50
496	Steve Hamilton	5.00	2.50	1.50
497	Cards Team	6.00	3.00	1.75
498	Bill Bryan	5.00	2.50	1.50
499	Steve Blass	5.00	2.50	1.50
500	Frank Robinson	25.00	12.50	7.50
501	John Odom	5.00	2.50	1.50
502	Mike Andrews	5.00	2.50	1.50
503	Al Jackson	5.00	2.50	1.50
504	Russ Snyder	5.00	2.50	1.50
505	Joe Sparma	5.00	2.50	1.50
506	Clarence Jones	5.00	2.50	1.50
507	Wade Blasingame	5.00	2.50	1.50
508	Duke Sims	5.00	2.50	1.50
509	Dennis Higgins	5.00	2.50	1.50
510	Ron Fairly	5.00	2.50	1.50
511	Bill Kelso	5.00	2.50	1.50
512	Grant Jackson	5.00	2.50	1.50
513	Hank Bauer	5.00	2.50	1.50
514	Al McBean	5.00	2.50	1.50
515	Russ Nixon	5.00	2.50	1.50
516	Pete Mikkelsen	5.00	2.50	1.50
517	Diego Segui	5.00	2.50	1.50
518a	7th Series Check List (534-598) (Clete Boyer) (539 is Maj. L. Rookies)	6.00	3.00	1.75
518b	7th Series Check List (534-598) (Clete Boyer) (539 is Amer. L. Rookies)	10.00	5.00	3.00
519	Jerry Stephenson	5.00	2.50	1.50
520	Lou Brock	15.00	7.50	3.75
521	Don Shaw	5.00	2.50	1.50
522	Wayne Causey	5.00	2.50	1.50
523	John Tsitouris	5.00	2.50	1.50
524	Andy Kosco	5.00	2.50	1.50
525	Jim Davenport	5.00	2.50	1.50
526	Bill Denehy	5.00	2.50	1.50
527	Tito Francona	5.00	2.50	1.50
528	Tigers Team	45.00	22.50	11.25
529	Bruce Von Hoff	5.00	2.50	1.50
530	Bird Belters (Brooks Robinson, Frank Robinson)	25.00	12.50	6.25
531	Chuck Hinton	5.00	2.50	1.50
532	Luis Tiant	5.00	2.50	1.50
533	Wes Parker	5.00	2.50	1.50
534	Bob Miller	5.00	2.50	1.50
535	Danny Cater	5.00	2.50	1.50
536	Bill Short	5.00	2.50	1.50
537	Norm Siebern	5.00	2.50	1.50
538	Manny Jimenez	5.00	2.50	1.50
539	Major League Rookies (Mike Ferraro, Jim Ray)	5.00	2.50	1.50
540	Nelson Briles	5.00	2.50	1.50
541	Sandy Alomar	5.00	2.50	1.50
542	John Boccabella	5.00	2.50	1.50
543	Bob Lee	5.00	2.50	1.50
544	Mayo Smith	5.00	2.50	1.50
545	Lindy McDaniel	5.00	2.50	1.50
546	Roy White	4.50	2.25	1.25
547	Dan Coombs	5.00	2.50	1.50
548	Bernie Allen	5.00	2.50	1.50
549	Orioles Rookies (Curt Motton, Roger Nelson)	5.00	2.50	1.50
550	Clete Boyer	5.00	2.50	1.50
551	Darrell Sutherland	5.00	2.50	1.50
552	Ed Kirkpatrick	5.00	2.50	1.50
553	Hank Aguirre	5.00	2.50	1.50
554	A's Team	6.00	3.00	1.75
555	Jose Tartabull	5.00	2.50	1.50
556	Dick Selma	5.00	2.50	1.50
557	Frank Quilici	5.00	2.50	1.50
558	John Edwards	5.00	2.50	1.50
559	Pirates Rookies (Carl Taylor, Luke Walker)	5.00	2.50	1.50
560	Paul Casanova	5.00	2.50	1.50
561	Lee Elia	5.00	2.50	1.50
562	Jim Bouton	6.00	3.00	1.75
563	Ed Charles	5.00	2.50	1.50
564	Eddie Stanky	5.00	2.50	1.50
565	Larry Dierker	5.00	2.50	1.50
566	Ken Harrelson	5.00	2.50	1.50
567	Clay Dalrymple	5.00	2.50	1.50
568	Willie Smith	5.00	2.50	1.50
569	N.L. Rookies (Ivan Murrell, Les Rohr)	5.00	2.50	1.50
570	Rick Reichardt	5.00	2.50	1.50
571	Tony LaRussa	6.00	3.00	1.75
572	Don Bosch	5.00	2.50	1.50
573	Joe Coleman	5.00	2.50	1.50
574	Reds Team	7.50	3.75	2.25
575	Jim Palmer	35.00	17.50	8.75
576	Dave Adlesh	5.00	2.50	1.50
577	Fred Talbot	5.00	2.50	1.50
578	Orlando Martinez	5.00	2.50	1.50
579	N.L. Rookies (*Larry Hisle, Mike Lum*)	5.00	2.50	1.50
580	Bob Bailey	5.00	2.50	1.50
581	Garry Roggenburk	5.00	2.50	1.50
582	Jerry Grote	5.00	2.50	1.50
583	Gates Brown	6.00	3.00	1.75
584	Larry Shepard	5.00	2.50	1.50
585	Wilbur Wood	5.00	2.50	1.50
586	Jim Pagliaroni	5.00	2.50	1.50
587	Roger Repoz	5.00	2.50	1.50
588	Dick Schofield	5.00	2.50	1.50
589	Twins Rookies (Ron Clark, Moe Ogier)	5.00	2.50	1.50
590	Tommy Harper	5.00	2.50	1.50
591	Dick Nen	5.00	2.50	1.50
592	John Bateman	5.00	2.50	1.50
593	Lee Stange	5.00	2.50	1.50
594	Phil Linz	5.00	2.50	1.50
595	Phil Ortega	5.00	2.50	1.50
596	Charlie Smith	5.00	2.50	1.50
597	Bill McCool	5.00	2.50	1.50
598	Jerry May	10.00	5.00	2.50

1968 Topps Action All-Star Stickers

Another of the many Topps test issues of the late 1960s, Action All-Star stickers were sold in a strip of three, with bubblegum, for 10 cents. The strip is comprised of three 3-1/4" x 5-1/4" panels, perforated at the joints for separation. The numbered central panel contains a large photo of a star player. The top and bottom panels each contain smaller pictures of

three players. While there are 16 numbered center panels, only 12 of them are different; panels 13-16 are double-prints. Similarly, the triple-player panels at top and bottom of stickers 13-16 repeat panels from #1-4. Prices below are for stickers which have all three panels still joined. Individual panels are priced signicantly lower.

		NM	EX	VG
Complete Set (16):		3,850	1,900	1,150
Common Panel:		100.00	50.00	30.00
1	Orlando Cepeda, Joe Horlen, Al Kaline, Bill Mazeroski, Claude Osteen, Mel Stottlemyre, Carl Yastrzemski	300.00	150.00	90.00
2	Don Drysdale, Harmon Killebrew, Mike McCormick, Tom Phoebus, George Scott, Ron Swoboda, Pete Ward	125.00	65.00	35.00
3	Hank Aaron, Paul Casanova, Jim Maloney, Joe Pepitone, Rick Reichardt, Frank Robinson, Tom Seaver	115.00	55.00	35.00
4	Bob Aspromonte, Johnny Callison, Dean Chance, Jim Lefebvre, Jim Lonborg, Frank Robinson, Ron Santo	150.00	75.00	45.00
5	Bert Campaneris, Al Downing, Willie Horton, Ed Kranepool, Willie Mays, Pete Rose, Ron Santo	375.00	185.00	110.00
6	Max Alvis, Ernie Banks, Al Kaline, Tim McCarver, Rusty Staub, Walt Williams, Carl Yastrzemski	300.00	150.00	90.00
7	Rod Carew, Tony Gonzalez, Steve Hargan, Mickey Mantle, Willie McCovey, Rick Monday, Billy Williams	500.00	250.00	150.00
8	Clete Boyer, Jim Bunning, Tony Conigliaro, Mike Cuellar, Joe Horlen, Ken McMullen, Don Mincher	100.00	50.00	30.00
9	Orlando Cepeda, Bob Clemente, Jim Fregosi, Harmon Killebrew, Willie Mays, Chris Short, Earl Wilson	300.00	150.00	90.00
10	Hank Aaron, Bob Gibson, Bud Harrelson, Jim Hunter, Mickey Mantle, Gary Peters, Vada Pinson	375.00	185.00	110.00
11	Don Drysdale, Bill Freehan, Frank Howard, Ferguson Jenkins, Tony Oliva, Bob Veale, Jim Wynn	235.00	115.00	70.00
12	Richie Allen, Bob Clemente, Sam McDowell, Jim McGlothlin, Tony Perez, Brooks Robinson, Joe Torre	850.00	425.00	255.00
13	Dean Chance, Don Drysdale, Jim Lefebvre, Tom Phoebus, Frank Robinson, George Scott, Carl Yastrzemski	300.00	150.00	90.00
14	Paul Casanova, Orlando Cepeda, Joe Horlen, Harmon Killebrew, Bill Mazeroski, Rick Reichardt, Tom Seaver	175.00	85.00	50.00
15	Bob Aspromonte, Johnny Callison, Jim Lonborg, Mike McCormick, Frank Robinson, Ron Swoboda, Pete Ward	125.00	62.00	37.00
16	Hank Aaron, Al Kaline, Jim Maloney, Claude Osteen, Joe Pepitone, Ron Santo, Mel Stottlemyre	225.00	110.00	65.00

1968 Topps "Batter Up" Game

The same cards which were issued as pack inserts in 1968 Topps were sold in a much scarcer boxed-set form. Packaged in a colorful cardboard box with game rules on back, the set is labeled "Batter Up" and can be found in versions with 10 or 15 original retail price.

	NM	EX	VG
Complete Boxed Set:	275.00	85.00	45.00

(See 1968 Topps Game for individual card checklist and values.)

1968 Topps Deckle Edge Proofs

While most Topps proofs are so rare as to preclude their listing in this catalog, the 1968 Deckle Edge test set is an exception. Usually found in the form of a 7-3/4" x 11" uncut sheet of nine black-and-white cards, single cards are sometimes encountered. The blank-backed sheet and cards can be found with the players' facsimile autographs printed in red, black or blue. Unnumbered cards are checklisted here alphabetically.

	NM	EX	VG
Complete Set, Singles (9):	700.00	350.00	225.00
Uncut Sheet:	700.00	350.00	225.00
Common Player:	50.00	25.00	15.00
(1) Dave Adlesh	50.00	25.00	15.00
(2) Hank Aguirre	50.00	25.00	15.00
(3) Sandy Alomar	50.00	25.00	15.00
(4) Sonny Jackson	50.00	25.00	15.00
(5) Bob Johnson	50.00	25.00	15.00
(6) Claude Osteen	50.00	25.00	15.00
(7) Juan Pizarro	50.00	25.00	15.00
(8) Hal Woodeshick	50.00	25.00	15.00
(9) Carl Yastrzemski	400.00	200.00	120.00

1968 Topps Discs

One of the scarcer Topps baseball collectibles, this set was apparently a never-completed test issue. These full-color, cardboard discs, which measure approximately 2-1/4" in diameter, were probably intended to be made into a pin set but production was never completed and no actual pins are known to exist. Uncut sheets of the player discs have been found. The discs include a player portrait photo with the name beneath and (usually) the city and team nickname along the sides.

	NM	EX	VG
Complete Set (28):	8,000	4,000	2,400
Common Player:	125.00	65.00	35.00
(1) Hank Aaron	625.00	310.00	185.00
(2) Richie Allen	140.00	75.00	40.00
(3) Gene Alley	125.00	65.00	35.00
(4) Rod Carew	350.00	175.00	100.00

(5) Orlando Cepeda	300.00	150.00	90.00
(6) Dean Chance	125.00	65.00	35.00
(7) Roberto Clemente	850.00	425.00	255.00
(8) Tommy Davis	125.00	65.00	35.00
(9) Bill Freehan	125.00	65.00	35.00
(10) Jim Fregosi	125.00	65.00	35.00
(11) Steve Hargan	125.00	65.00	35.00
(12) Frank Howard	125.00	65.00	35.00
(13) Al Kaline	350.00	175.00	100.00
(14) Harmon Killebrew	350.00	175.00	100.00
(15) Mickey Mantle	1,750	875.00	525.00
(16) Willie Mays	625.00	310.00	185.00
(17) Mike McCormick	125.00	65.00	35.00
(18) Rick Monday	125.00	65.00	35.00
(19) Claude Osteen	125.00	65.00	35.00
(20) Gary Peters	125.00	65.00	35.00
(21) Brooks Robinson	350.00	175.00	100.00
(22) Frank Robinson	350.00	175.00	100.00
(23) Pete Rose	550.00	275.00	165.00
(24) Ron Santo	150.00	75.00	45.00
(25) Rusty Staub	135.00	70.00	40.00
(26) Joe Torre	125.00	65.00	35.00
(27) Bob Veale	125.00	65.00	35.00
(28) Carl Yastrzemski	350.00	175.00	100.00

1968 Topps Game

A throwback to the Red and Blue Back sets of 1951, the 33-cards in the 1968 Topps Game set, inserted into packs of regular '68 Topps cards or purchases as a complete boxed set, enable the owner to play a game of baseball based on the game situations on each card. Also on the 2-1/4" x 3-1/4" cards were a color photograph of a player and his facsimile autograph. One redeeming social value of the set (assuming you're not mesmerized by the game) is that it affords an inexpensive way to get big-name cards as the set is loaded with stars, but not at all popular with collectors.

	NM	EX	VG
Complete Set (33):	115.00	55.00	35.00
Common Player:	2.00	1.00	.60
1 Mateo Alou	2.00	1.00	.60
2 Mickey Mantle	30.00	15.00	9.00
3 Carl Yastrzemski	10.00	5.00	3.00
4 Henry Aaron	12.00	6.00	3.50
5 Harmon Killebrew	9.00	4.50	2.75
6 Roberto Clemente	15.00	7.50	4.50
7 Frank Robinson	9.00	4.50	2.75
8 Willie Mays	12.00	6.00	3.50
9 Brooks Robinson	9.00	4.50	2.75
10 Tommy Davis	2.00	1.00	.60
11 Bill Freehan	2.00	1.00	.60
12 Claude Osteen	2.00	1.00	.60
13 Gary Peters	2.00	1.00	.60
14 Jim Lonborg	2.00	1.00	.60
15 Steve Hargan	2.00	1.00	.60
16 Dean Chance	2.00	1.00	.60
17 Mike McCormick	2.00	1.00	.60
18 Tim McCarver	3.00	1.50	.90
19 Ron Santo	6.00	3.00	1.75
20 Tony Gonzalez	2.00	1.00	.60
21 Frank Howard	3.00	1.50	.90
22 George Scott	2.00	1.00	.60
23 Rich Allen	6.00	3.00	1.75
24 Jim Wynn	2.00	1.00	.60
25 Gene Alley	2.00	1.00	.60
26 Rick Monday	2.00	1.00	.60
27 Al Kaline	9.00	4.50	2.75
28 Rusty Staub	3.00	1.50	.90
29 Rod Carew	9.00	4.50	2.75
30 Pete Rose	12.00	6.00	3.50
31 Joe Torre	6.00	3.00	1.75
32 Orlando Cepeda	6.00	3.00	1.75
33 Jim Fregosi	2.00	1.00	.60

1968 Topps Plaks

Among the scarcest Topps test issues of the late 1960s, the "All Star Baseball Plaks" were plastic busts of two dozen stars of the era which came packaged like model airplane parts. The busts had to be snapped off a sprue and could be inserted into a base which carried the player's name. Packed with the plastic plaks was one of two checklist cards which featured six color photos per side. The 2-1/8" x 4" checklist cards are popular with superstar collectors and are considerably easier to find today than the actual plaks. Wax packs of three plaks and two sticks of bubblegum were sold for a dime.

	NM	EX	VG
Complete Set (24):	9,000	4,500	2,750
Common Player:	100.00	50.00	30.00
1 Max Alvis	100.00	50.00	30.00
2 Dean Chance	100.00	50.00	30.00
3 Jim Fregosi	100.00	50.00	30.00
4 Frank Howard	125.00	62.00	37.00
5 Jim Hunter	250.00	125.00	75.00
6 Al Kaline	400.00	200.00	120.00
7 Harmon Killebrew	400.00	200.00	120.00
8 Jim Lonborg	100.00	50.00	30.00
9 Mickey Mantle	1,850	925.00	555.00
10 Gary Peters	100.00	50.00	30.00
11 Frank Robinson	400.00	200.00	120.00
12 Carl Yastrzemski	450.00	225.00	135.00
13 Hank Aaron	750.00	375.00	225.00
14 Richie Allen	125.00	62.00	37.00
15 Orlando Cepeda	300.00	150.00	90.00
16 Roberto Clemente	1,350	675.00	400.00
17 Tommy Davis	100.00	50.00	30.00
18 Don Drysdale	400.00	200.00	120.00
19 Willie Mays	750.00	375.00	225.00
20 Tim McCarver	125.00	62.00	37.00
21 Ron Santo	125.00	62.00	37.00
22 Rusty Staub	125.00	62.00	37.00
23 Pete Rose	650.00	325.00	195.00
24 Jim Wynn	100.00	50.00	30.00
--- Checklist Card 1-12	1,000	500.00	300.00
--- Checklist Card 13-24	1,500	750.00	450.00

1968 Topps Posters

Yet another innovation from the creative minds at Topps appeared in 1968; a set of color player posters. Measuring 9-3/4" x 18-1/8," each poster was sold separately with its own piece of gum, rather than as an insert. The posters feature a large color photograph with a star at the bottom containing the player's name, position and team. There are 24 different posters which were folded numerous times to fit into the package they were sold in. Unless the paper has split at the folds, they are not considered in grading.

	NM	EX	VG
Complete Set (24):	650.00	325.00	200.00
Common Player:	15.00	7.50	4.50
Unopened Pack:	175.00	.00	.00
1 Dean Chance	15.00	7.50	4.50
2 Max Alvis	15.00	7.50	4.50
3 Frank Howard	17.50	8.75	5.25
4 Jim Fregosi	15.00	7.50	4.50
5 Catfish Hunter	20.00	10.00	6.00
6 Roberto Clemente	60.00	30.00	18.00
7 Don Drysdale	25.00	12.50	7.50
8 Jim Wynn	15.00	7.50	4.50
9 Al Kaline	25.00	12.50	7.50
10 Harmon Killebrew	25.00	12.50	7.50
11 Jim Lonborg	15.00	7.50	4.50
12 Orlando Cepeda	20.00	10.00	6.00
13 Gary Peters	15.00	7.50	4.50
14 Hank Aaron	50.00	25.00	15.00
15 Richie Allen	17.50	8.75	5.25
16 Carl Yastrzemski	30.00	15.00	9.00
17 Ron Swoboda	15.00	7.50	4.50
18 Mickey Mantle	80.00	40.00	24.00
19 Tim McCarver	15.00	7.50	4.50
20 Willie Mays	50.00	25.00	15.00
21 Ron Santo	17.50	8.75	5.25
22 Rusty Staub	17.50	8.75	5.25
23 Pete Rose	50.00	25.00	15.00
24 Frank Robinson	25.00	12.50	7.50

1968 Tipps From Topps Book

While the Bazooka brand is not referenced in this booklet, it presents the baseball playing tips that appeared on box backs of Bazooka gum. The player photo and cartoon tips are printed in blue in the interior pages of the 5-7/8" x 3" book. The front and back covers are black, white and green. The manner of distribution for this premium is not known.

	NM	EX	VG
Tipps From Topps Book	150.00	75.00	45.00

1968 Topps 3-D Prototype

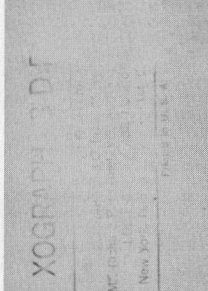

Apparently produced as a prototype for the 3-D cards which Topps issued as a test in 1968, this prototype card is 2-1/4" x 3-1/4" with square corners. The team name is in red block letters at top. The back carries a rubber-stamped notice which identifies the card as a "Xograph 3-D" product from New York City.

	NM	EX	VG
Brooks Robinson	20,000	10,000	6,000

1968 Topps 3-D

These very rare test-issue cards measure 2-1/4" x 3-1/2" with rounded corners and blank backs. They simulate a three-dimensional effect with backgrounds purposely blurred, in front of which is a sharp color player photograph. The outer layer is a thin coating of ribbed plastic. The special process gives the picture the illusion of depth when the card is moved or tilted. As this was done two years before Kellogg's began its 3-D cards, this test issue really was breaking new ground. Production and distribution were limited, making the cards very tough to find. Some cards, said to have been the first produced, are stamped on back with a notice from Visual Panographics of New York. "This is an experimental XOGRAPH card produced as a limited edition. Not for public circulation or distribution. Not for resale. To be returned to:".

	NM	EX	VG
Complete Set (12):	17,500	8,750	5,250
Common Player:	500.00	250.00	150.00

Wrapper:			
(1)	Bob Clemente	900.00	450.00	275.00
	Willie Davis	12,000	6,000	3,600
(2)	Willie Davis	500.00	250.00	150.00
(3)	Ron Fairly	500.00	250.00	150.00
(4)	Curt Flood	650.00	325.00	200.00
(5)	Jim Lonborg	500.00	250.00	150.00
(6)	Jim Maloney	500.00	250.00	150.00
(7)	Tony Perez	1,000	500.00	300.00
(8)	Boog Powell	750.00	375.00	225.00
(9)	Bill Robinson	500.00	250.00	150.00
(10)	Rusty Staub	750.00	375.00	225.00
(11)	Mel Stottlemyre	500.00	250.00	150.00
(12)	Ron Swoboda	500.00	250.00	150.00

1968 Topps/Milton Bradley

As part of a Win-A-Card trading card board game, Milton Bradley contracted with Topps to print 132 special versions of its 1968 baseball cards, 1967 football cards and hot rod cards. The baseball cards can be differentiated from regular-issue 1968 Topps in that the yellow ink on back is much lighter and brighter than the dark yellow/gold ink usually found on back. Also, some of the card fronts will show evidence of the white-bordered football and hot rod cards at one or more edges. Collectors currently will pay only a small premium for the MB version, but that gap is likely to widen in the future.

		NM	EX	VG
Complete (Baseball) Set (76):				
Common Player:				
7	N.L. ERA Leaders (Jim Bunning, Phil Niekro, Chris Short)	7.00	3.50	2.00
8	A.L. ERA Leaders (Joe Horlen, Gary Peters, Sonny Siebert)	2.00	1.00	.60
10	A.L. Pitching Leaders (Dean Chance, Jim Lonborg, Earl Wilson)	9.00	4.50	2.75
13	Chuck Hartenstein	2.00	1.00	.60
16	Indians Rookies (Lou Piniella, Richie Scheinblum)	4.00	2.00	1.25
17	Dick Hall	2.00	1.00	.60
18	Mike Hershberger	2.00	1.00	.60
19	Juan Pizarro	2.00	1.00	.60
20	Brooks Robinson	15.00	7.50	4.50
24	Bobby Locke	2.00	1.00	.60
26	Darrell Brandon	2.00	1.00	.60
34	Al Ferrara	2.00	1.00	.60
36	Pirates Rookies (**Bob Moose, Bob Robertson**)	2.00	1.00	.60
38	Tony Pierce	2.00	1.00	.60
43	Gary Bell	2.00	1.00	.60
44	Frank Kostro	2.00	1.00	.60
45	Tom Seaver	30.00	15.00	9.00
48	Ted Davidson	2.00	1.00	.60
49	Ed Brinkman (Yellow team.)	50.00	25.00	15.00
53	Gene Alley	2.00	1.00	.60
57	Dan Schneider	2.00	1.00	.60
58	Ed Mathews	13.50	6.75	4.00
60	Ken Holtzman	2.00	1.00	.60
61	Reggie Smith	2.00	1.00	.60
62	Chuck Dobson	2.00	1.00	.60
64	Jim Merritt	2.00	1.00	.60
66	Casey Cox (Yellow team.)	50.00	25.00	15.00
68	Ron Willis	2.00	1.00	.60
72	Tommy John	4.00	2.00	1.25
74	Milt Pappas	2.00	1.00	.60
77	**Don Wilson**	2.00	1.00	.60
78	Jim Northrup	2.00	1.00	.60
80	Rod Carew	17.50	8.75	5.25
81	Larry Jackson	2.00	1.00	.60
85	Gaylord Perry	9.00	4.50	2.75
89	Jake Gibbs	2.00	1.00	.60
94	Lee Maye	2.00	1.00	.60
98	Gary Sutherland	2.00	1.00	.60
99	Rocky Colavito	7.00	3.50	2.00
100	Bob Gibson	17.50	8.75	5.25
105	Al Downing	2.00	1.00	.60
106	Dalton Jones	2.00	1.00	.60
107	2nd Series Check List (110-196) (Juan Marichal)	4.00	2.00	1.25
108	Don Pavletich	2.00	1.00	.60
110	Hank Aaron	40.00	20.00	12.00
112	Woody Fryman	2.00	1.00	.60
113	Tigers Rookies (Tom Matchick, Daryl Patterson)	2.00	1.00	.60
117	Larry Jaster	2.00	1.00	.60
118	Mark Belanger	2.00	1.00	.60
119	Ted Savage	2.00	1.00	.60
120	Mel Stottlemyre	4.00	2.00	1.25
121	Jimmie Hall	2.00	1.00	.60
124	Nate Oliver	2.00	1.00	.60
127	Paul Lindblad	2.00	1.00	.60
128	Astros Rookies (Tom Dukes, Alonzo Harris)	2.00	1.00	.60
129	Mickey Stanley	2.00	1.00	.60
133	Randy Hundley	2.00	1.00	.60
139	Chris Short	2.00	1.00	.60
143	Pete Cimino	2.00	1.00	.60
146	Sal Bando	2.00	1.00	.60
149	Bob Saverine	2.00	1.00	.60
155	World Series Game 5 (Lonborg Wins Again)	6.00	3.00	1.75
156	World Series Game 6 (Petrocelli Socks Two Homers)	6.00	3.00	1.75
165	Tony Oliva	4.00	2.00	1.25
168	Dodgers Team	5.00	2.50	1.50
172	Walt Williams	2.00	1.00	.60
175	Maury Wills	2.00	1.00	.60
176	Bob Allen	2.00	1.00	.60
177	Mets Rookies (**Jerry Koosman, Nolan Ryan**)	335.00	190.00	95.00
179	Bill Stoneman	2.00	1.00	.60
180	Curt Flood	3.00	1.50	.90

185	Tom Haller	2.00	1.00	.60
189	Bill Landis	2.00	1.00	.60
191	Dan Frisella	2.00	1.00	.60
193	Jack Hamilton	2.00	1.00	.60
195	Joe Pepitone	4.00	2.00	1.25

1969 Topps

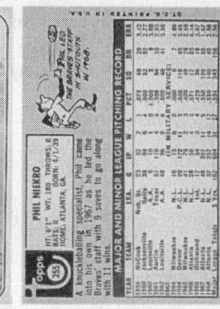

The 1969 Topps set broke yet another record for quantity as the issue is officially a whopping 664 cards. With substantial numbers of variations, the number of possible cards runs closer to 700. The design of the 2-1/2" x 3-1/2" cards in the set feature a color photo with the team name printed in block letters underneath. A circle contains the player's name and position. Card backs returned to a horizontal format. Despite the size of the set, it contains no team cards. It does, however, have multi-player cards, All-Stars, statistical leaders, and World Series highlights. Most significant among the varieties are white and yellow letter cards from the run of #'s 440-511. The complete set prices below do not include the scarcer and more expensive "white letter" variations.

		NM	EX	VG
Complete Set (664):		3,150	1,550	925.00
Common Player (1-588):		2.00	1.00	.60
Common Player (589-664):		3.00	1.50	.90
1	A.L. Batting Leaders (Danny Cater, Tony Oliva, Carl Yastrzemski)	10.00	5.00	2.50
2	N.L. Batting Leaders (Felipe Alou, Matty Alou, Pete Rose)	15.00	7.50	4.50
3	A.L. RBI Leaders (Ken Harrelson, Frank Howard, Jim Northrup)	2.50	1.25	.75
4	N.L. RBI Leaders (Willie McCovey, Ron Santo, Billy Williams)	10.00	5.00	2.50
5	A.L. Home Run Leaders (Ken Harrelson, Willie Horton, Frank Howard)	6.00	3.00	1.75
6	N.L. Home Run Leaders (Richie Allen, Ernie Banks, Willie McCovey)	8.00	4.00	2.50
7	A.L. ERA Leaders (Sam McDowell, Dave McNally, Luis Tiant)	3.00	1.50	.90
8	N.L. ERA Leaders (Bobby Bolin, Bob Gibson, Bob Veale)	4.00	2.00	1.25
9	A.L. Pitching Leaders (Denny McLain, Dave McNally, Mel Stottlemyre, Luis Tiant)	4.00	2.00	1.25
10	N.L. Pitching Leaders (Bob Gibson, Fergie Jenkins, Juan Marichal)	5.00	2.50	1.50
11	A.L. Strikeout Leaders (Sam McDowell, Denny McLain, Luis Tiant)	3.00	1.50	.90
12	N.L. Strikeout Leaders (Bob Gibson, Fergie Jenkins, Bill Singer)	5.00	2.50	1.50
13	Mickey Stanley	2.00	1.00	.60
14	Al McBean	2.00	1.00	.60
15	Boog Powell	3.00	1.50	.90
16	Giants Rookies (Cesar Gutierrez, Rich Robertson)	2.00	1.00	.60
17	Mike Marshall	2.00	1.00	.60
18	Dick Schofield	2.00	1.00	.60
19	Ken Suarez	2.00	1.00	.60
20	Ernie Banks	25.00	12.50	7.50
21	Jose Santiago	2.00	1.00	.60
22	Jesus Alou	2.00	1.00	.60
23	Lew Krausse	2.00	1.00	.60
24	Walt Alston	4.00	2.00	1.25
25	Roy White	2.00	1.00	.60
26	Clay Carroll	2.00	1.00	.60
27	Bernie Allen	2.00	1.00	.60
28	Mike Ryan	2.00	1.00	.60
29	Dave Morehead	2.00	1.00	.60
30	Bob Allison	2.00	1.00	.60
31	Mets Rookies (**Gary Gentry, Amos Otis**)	3.00	1.50	.90
32	Sammy Ellis	2.00	1.00	.60
33	Wayne Causey	2.00	1.00	.60
34	Gary Peters	2.00	1.00	.60
35	Joe Morgan	10.00	5.00	3.00
36	Luke Walker	2.00	1.00	.60
37	Curt Motton	2.00	1.00	.60
38	Zoilo Versalles	2.00	1.00	.60
39	Dick Hughes	2.00	1.00	.60
40	Mayo Smith	2.00	1.00	.60
41	Bob Barton	2.00	1.00	.60
42	Tommy Harper	2.00	1.00	.60
43	Joe Niekro	2.00	1.00	.60
44	Danny Cater	2.00	1.00	.60

#	Player			
45	Maury Wills	2.00	1.00	.60
46	Fritz Peterson	2.00	1.00	.60
47a	Paul Popovich (Emblem visible thru airbrush.)	15.00	7.50	4.50
47b	Paul Popovich (Helmet emblem completely airbrushed.)	2.00	1.00	.60
48	Brant Alyea	2.00	1.00	.60
49a	Royals Rookies (Steve Jones, Eliseo Rodriguez) (Rodriguez on front.)	15.00	7.50	4.50
49b	Royals Rookies (Steve Jones, Eliseo Rodriguez) (Rodriquez on front.)	2.00	1.00	.60
50	Roberto Clemente	60.00	30.00	15.00
51	Woody Fryman	2.00	1.00	.60
52	Mike Andrews	2.00	1.00	.60
53	Sonny Jackson	2.00	1.00	.60
54	Cisco Carlos	2.00	1.00	.60
55	Jerry Grote	2.00	1.00	.60
56	Rich Reese	2.00	1.00	.60
57	1st Series Check List (1-109) (Denny McLain)	4.00	2.00	1.25
58	Fred Gladding	2.00	1.00	.60
59	Jay Johnstone	2.00	1.00	.60
60	Nelson Briles	2.00	1.00	.60
61	Jimmie Hall	2.00	1.00	.60
62	Chico Salmon	2.00	1.00	.60
63	Jim Hickman	2.00	1.00	.60
64	Bill Monbouquette	2.00	1.00	.60
65	Willie Davis	2.00	1.00	.60
66	Orioles Rookies (**Mike Adamson, Merv Rettenmund**)	2.00	1.00	.60
67	Bill Stoneman	2.00	1.00	.60
68	Dave Duncan	2.00	1.00	.60
69	Steve Hamilton	2.00	1.00	.60
70	Tommy Helms	2.00	1.00	.60
71	Steve Whitaker	2.00	1.00	.60
72	Ron Taylor	2.00	1.00	.60
73	Johnny Briggs	2.00	1.00	.60
74	Preston Gomez	2.00	1.00	.60
75	Luis Aparicio	9.00	4.50	2.75
76	Norm Miller	2.00	1.00	.60
77a	Ron Perranoski (LA visible thru airbrush.)	10.00	5.00	2.50
77b	Ron Perranoski (Cap emblem completely airbrushed.)	2.00	1.00	.60
78	Tom Satriano	2.00	1.00	.60
79	Milt Pappas	2.00	1.00	.60
80	Norm Cash	6.00	3.00	1.75
81	Mel Queen	2.00	1.00	.60
82	Pirates Rookies (**Rich Hebner, Al Oliver**)	10.00	5.00	3.00
83	Mike Ferraro	2.00	1.00	.60
84	Bob Humphreys	2.00	1.00	.60
85	Lou Brock	20.00	10.00	6.00
86	Pete Richert	2.00	1.00	.60
87	Horace Clarke	2.00	1.00	.60
88	Rich Nye	2.00	1.00	.60
89	Russ Gibson	2.00	1.00	.60
90	Jerry Koosman	2.00	1.00	.60
91	Al Dark	2.00	1.00	.60
92	Jack Billingham	2.00	1.00	.60
93	Joe Foy	2.00	1.00	.60
94	Hank Aguirre	2.00	1.00	.60
95	Johnny Bench	60.00	30.00	15.00
96	Denver Lemaster	2.00	1.00	.60
97	Buddy Bradford	2.00	1.00	.60
98	Dave Giusti	2.00	1.00	.60
99a	Twins Rookies (**Danny Morris, Graig Nettles**) (Black loop above "Twins.")	13.50	6.75	4.00
99b	Twins Rookies (**Danny Morris, Graig Nettles**) (No black loop.)	10.00	5.00	2.50
100	Hank Aaron	60.00	30.00	15.00
101	Daryl Patterson	2.00	1.00	.60
102	Jim Davenport	2.00	1.00	.60
103	Roger Repoz	2.00	1.00	.60
104	Steve Blass	2.00	1.00	.60
105	Rick Monday	2.00	1.00	.60
106	Jim Hannan	2.00	1.00	.60
107a	2nd Series Check List (110-218) (Bob Gibson) (161 is Jim Purdin)	4.00	2.00	1.25
107b	2nd Series Check List (110-218) (Bob Gibson) (161 is John Purdin)	6.00	3.00	1.75
108	Tony Taylor	2.00	1.00	.60
109	Jim Lonborg	2.00	1.00	.60
110	Mike Shannon	2.00	1.00	.60
111	Johnny Morris	2.00	1.00	.60
112	J.C. Martin	2.00	1.00	.60
113	Dave May	2.00	1.00	.60
114	Yankees Rookies (Alan Closter, John Cumberland)			
115	Bill Hands	2.00	1.00	.60
116	Chuck Harrison	2.00	1.00	.60
117	Jim Fairey	2.00	1.00	.60
118	Stan Williams	2.00	1.00	.60
119	Doug Rader	2.00	1.00	.60
120	Pete Rose	40.00	20.00	10.00
121	Joe Grzenda	2.00	1.00	.60
122	Ron Fairly	2.00	1.00	.60
123	Wilbur Wood	2.00	1.00	.60
124	Hank Bauer	2.00	1.00	.60
125	Ray Sadecki	2.00	1.00	.60
126	Dick Tracewski	2.00	1.00	.60
127	Kevin Collins	2.00	1.00	.60
128	Tommie Aaron	2.00	1.00	.60
129	Bill McCool	2.00	1.00	.60
130	Carl Yastrzemski	25.00	12.50	7.50
131	Chris Cannizzaro	2.00	1.00	.60
132	Dave Baldwin	2.00	1.00	.60
133	Johnny Callison	2.00	1.00	.60

#	Player			
134	Jim Weaver	2.00	1.00	.60
135	Tommy Davis	2.00	1.00	.60
136	Cards Rookies (Steve Huntz, Mike Torrez)	2.00	1.00	.60
137	Wally Bunker	2.00	1.00	.60
138	John Bateman	2.00	1.00	.60
139	Andy Kosco	2.00	1.00	.60
140	Jim Lefebvre	2.00	1.00	.60
141	Bill Dillman	2.00	1.00	.60
142	Woody Woodward	2.00	1.00	.60
143	Joe Nossek	2.00	1.00	.60
144	Bob Hendley	2.00	1.00	.60
145	Max Alvis	2.00	1.00	.60
146	Jim Perry	2.00	1.00	.60
147	Leo Durocher	5.00	2.50	1.50
148	Lee Stange	2.00	1.00	.60
149	Ollie Brown	2.00	1.00	.60
150	Denny McLain	5.00	2.50	1.50
151a	Clay Dalrymple (Phillies)	15.00	7.50	3.75
151b	Clay Dalrymple (Orioles)	2.00	1.00	.60
152	Tommie Sisk	2.00	1.00	.60
153	Ed Brinkman	2.00	1.00	.60
154	Jim Britton	2.00	1.00	.60
155	Pete Ward	2.00	1.00	.60
156	Astros Rookies (Hal Gilson, Leon McFadden)	2.00	1.00	.60
157	Bob Rodgers	2.00	1.00	.60
158	Joe Gibbon	2.00	1.00	.60
159	Jerry Adair	2.00	1.00	.60
160	Vada Pinson	3.00	1.50	.90
161	John Purdin	2.00	1.00	.60
162	World Series Game 1 (Gibson Fans 17; Sets New Record)	15.00	7.50	4.50
163	World Series Game 2 (Tiger Homers Deck The Cards)	6.00	3.00	1.75
164	World Series Game 3 (McCarver's Homer Puts St. Louis Ahead)	7.00	3.50	2.00
165	World Series Game 4 (Brock's Lead-Off HR Starts Cards' Romp)	7.00	3.50	2.00
166	World Series Game 5 (Kaline's Key Hit Sparks Tiger Rally)	7.00	3.50	2.00
167	World Series Game 6 (Tiger 10-Run Inning Ties Mark)	6.00	3.00	1.75
168	World Series Game 7 (Lolich Series Hero Outduels Gibson)	9.00	4.50	2.75
169	World Series (Tigers Celebrate Their Victory)	12.00	6.00	3.50
170	Frank Howard	3.00	1.50	.90
171	Glenn Beckert	2.00	1.00	.60
172	Jerry Stephenson	2.00	1.00	.60
173	White Sox Rookies (Bob Christian, Gerry Nyman)	2.00	1.00	.60
174	Grant Jackson	2.00	1.00	.60
175	Jim Bunning	8.00	4.00	2.50
176	Joe Azcue	2.00	1.00	.60
177	Ron Reed	2.00	1.00	.60
178	Ray Oyler	2.00	1.00	.60
179	Don Pavletich	2.00	1.00	.60
180	Willie Horton	2.00	1.00	.60
181	Mel Nelson	2.00	1.00	.60
182	Bill Rigney	2.00	1.00	.60
183	Don Shaw	2.00	1.00	.60
184	Roberto Pena	2.00	1.00	.60
185	Tom Phoebus	2.00	1.00	.60
186	John Edwards	2.00	1.00	.60
187	Leon Wagner	2.00	1.00	.60
188	Rick Wise	2.00	1.00	.60
189	Red Sox Rookies (Joe Lahoud, John Thibdeau)	2.00	1.00	.60
190	Willie Mays	80.00	40.00	20.00
191	Lindy McDaniel	2.00	1.00	.60
192	Jose Pagan	2.00	1.00	.60
193	Don Cardwell	2.00	1.00	.60
194	Ted Uhlaender	2.00	1.00	.60
195	John Odom	2.00	1.00	.60
196	Lum Harris	2.00	1.00	.60
197	Dick Selma	2.00	1.00	.60
198	Willie Smith	2.00	1.00	.60
199	Jim French	2.00	1.00	.60
200	Bob Gibson	15.00	7.50	4.50
201	Russ Snyder	2.00	1.00	.60
202	Don Wilson	2.00	1.00	.60
203	Dave Johnson	2.00	1.00	.60
204	Jack Hiatt	2.00	1.00	.60
205	Rick Reichardt	2.00	1.00	.60
206	Phillies Rookies (Larry Hisle, Barry Lersch)	2.00	1.00	.60
207	Roy Face	2.00	1.00	.60
208a	Donn Clendenon (Expos)	20.00	10.00	5.00
208b	Donn Clendenon (Houston)	2.00	1.00	.60
209	Larry Haney (Photo reversed.)	2.00	1.00	.60
210	Felix Millan	2.00	1.00	.60
211	Galen Cisco	2.00	1.00	.60
212	Tom Tresh	6.00	3.00	1.75
213	Gerry Arrigo	2.00	1.00	.60
214	3rd Series Check List (219-327)	4.00	2.00	1.25
215	Rico Petrocelli	2.00	1.00	.60
216	Don Sutton	8.00	4.00	2.50
217	John Donaldson	2.00	1.00	.60
218	John Roseboro	2.00	1.00	.60
219	**Freddie Patek**			
220	Sam McDowell	2.00	1.00	.60
221	Art Shamsky	2.00	1.00	.60
222	Duane Josephson	2.00	1.00	.60
223	Tom Dukes	2.00	1.00	.60
224	Angels Rookies (Bill Harrelson, Steve Kealey)	2.00	1.00	.60
225	Don Kessinger	2.00	1.00	.60
226	Bruce Howard	2.00	1.00	.60
227	Frank Johnson	2.00	1.00	.60
228	Dave Leonhard	2.00	1.00	.60
229	Don Lock	2.00	1.00	.60

#	Player			
230	Rusty Staub	3.00	1.50	.90
231	Pat Dobson	2.00	1.00	.60
232	Dave Ricketts	2.00	1.00	.60
233	Steve Barber	2.00	1.00	.60
234	Dave Bristol	2.00	1.00	.60
235	Jim Hunter	15.00	7.50	3.75
236	Manny Mota	2.00	1.00	.60
237	**Bobby Cox**	12.00	6.00	3.50
238	Ken Johnson	2.00	1.00	.60
239	Bob Taylor	2.00	1.00	.60
240	Ken Harrelson	2.00	1.00	.60
241	Jim Brewer	2.00	1.00	.60
242	Frank Kostro	2.00	1.00	.60
243	Ron Kline	2.00	1.00	.60
244	Indians Rookies (**Ray Fosse**, George Woodson)	3.50	1.75	1.00
245	Ed Charles	2.00	1.00	.60
246	Joe Coleman	2.00	1.00	.60
247	Gene Oliver	2.00	1.00	.60
248	Bob Priddy	2.00	1.00	.60
249	Ed Spiezio	2.00	1.00	.60
250	Frank Robinson	20.00	10.00	5.00
251	Ron Herbel	2.00	1.00	.60
252	Chuck Cottier	2.00	1.00	.60
253	Jerry Johnson	2.00	1.00	.60
254	Joe Schultz	2.00	1.00	.60
255	Steve Carlton	20.00	10.00	5.00
256	Gates Brown	2.00	1.00	.60
257	Jim Ray	2.00	1.00	.60
258	Jackie Hernandez	2.00	1.00	.60
259	Bill Short	2.00	1.00	.60
260	**Reggie Jackson**	300.00	150.00	75.00
261	Bob Johnson	2.00	1.00	.60
262	Mike Kekich	2.00	1.00	.60
263	Jerry May	2.00	1.00	.60
264	Bill Landis	2.00	1.00	.60
265	Chico Cardenas	2.00	1.00	.60
266	Dodgers Rookies (Alan Foster, Tom Hutton)	2.00	1.00	.60
267	Vicente Romo	2.00	1.00	.60
268	Al Spangler	2.00	1.00	.60
269	Al Weis	2.00	1.00	.60
270	Mickey Lolich	2.00	1.00	.60
271	Larry Stahl	2.00	1.00	.60
272	Ed Stroud	2.00	1.00	.60
273	Ron Willis	2.00	1.00	.60
274	Clyde King	2.00	1.00	.60
275	Vic Davalillo	2.00	1.00	.60
276	Gary Wagner	2.00	1.00	.60
277	**Rod Hendricks**	2.00	1.00	.60
278	Gary Geiger	2.00	1.00	.60
279	Roger Nelson	2.00	1.00	.60
280	Alex Johnson	2.00	1.00	.60
281	Ted Kubiak	2.00	1.00	.60
282	Pat Jarvis	2.00	1.00	.60
283	Sandy Alomar	2.00	1.00	.60
284	Expos Rookies (Jerry Robertson, Mike Wegener)	2.00	1.00	.60
285	Don Mincher	2.00	1.00	.60
286	**Dock Ellis**	3.00	1.50	.90
287	Jose Tartabull	2.00	1.00	.60
288	Ken Holtzman	2.00	1.00	.60
289	Bart Shirley	2.00	1.00	.60
290	Jim Kaat	3.00	1.50	.90
291	Vern Fuller	2.00	1.00	.60
292	Al Downing	2.00	1.00	.60
293	Dick Dietz	2.00	1.00	.60
294	Jim Lemon	2.00	1.00	.60
295	Tony Perez	12.00	6.00	3.00
296	**Andy Messersmith**	3.00	1.50	.90
297	Deron Johnson	2.00	1.00	.60
298	Dave Nicholson	2.00	1.00	.60
299	Mark Belanger	2.00	1.00	.60
300	Felipe Alou	4.00	2.00	1.25
301	Darrell Brandon	2.00	1.00	.60
302	Jim Pagliaroni	2.00	1.00	.60
303	Cal Koonce	2.00	1.00	.60
304	Padres Rookies (**Bill Davis, Clarence Gaston**)	4.00	2.00	1.25
305	Dick McAuliffe	2.00	1.00	.60
306	Jim Grant	2.00	1.00	.60
307	Gary Kolb	2.00	1.00	.60
308	Wade Blasingame	2.00	1.00	.60
309	Walt Williams	2.00	1.00	.60
310	Tom Haller	2.00	1.00	.60
311	**Sparky Lyle**	6.00	3.00	1.75
312	Lee Elia	2.00	1.00	.60
313	Bill Robinson	2.00	1.00	.60
314	4th Series Check List (328-425) (Don Drysdale)	5.00	2.50	1.50
315	Eddie Fisher	2.00	1.00	.60
316	Hal Lanier	2.00	1.00	.60
317	Bruce Look	2.00	1.00	.60
318	Jack Fisher	2.00	1.00	.60
319	Ken McMullen	2.00	1.00	.60
320	Dal Maxvill	2.00	1.00	.60
321	Jim McAndrew	2.00	1.00	.60
322	Jose Vidal	2.00	1.00	.60
323	Larry Miller	2.00	1.00	.60
324	Tigers Rookies (Les Cain, Dave Campbell)	2.00	1.00	.60
325	Jose Cardenal	2.00	1.00	.60
326	Gary Sutherland	2.00	1.00	.60
327	Willie Crawford	2.00	1.00	.60
328	Joe Horlen	2.00	1.00	.60
329	Rick Joseph	2.00	1.00	.60
330	Tony Conigliaro	6.00	3.00	1.75
331	Braves Rookies (**Gil Garrido, Tom House**)	2.00	1.00	.60
332	Fred Talbot	2.00	1.00	.60
333	Ivan Murrell	2.00	1.00	.60
334	Phil Roof	2.00	1.00	.60
335	Bill Mazeroski	10.00	5.00	3.00
336	Jim Roland	2.00	1.00	.60
337	Marty Martinez	2.00	1.00	.60
338	**Del Unser**	2.00	1.00	.60

#	Name			
339	Reds Rookies (Steve Mingori, Jose Pena)	2.00	1.00	.60
340	Dave McNally	2.00	1.00	.60
341	Dave Adlesh	2.00	1.00	.60
342	Bubba Morton	2.00	1.00	.60
343	Dan Frisella	2.00	1.00	.60
344	Tom Matchick	2.00	1.00	.60
345	Frank Linzy	2.00	1.00	.60
346	Wayne Comer	2.00	1.00	.60
347	Randy Hundley	2.00	1.00	.60
348	Steve Hargan	2.00	1.00	.60
349	Dick Williams	2.00	1.00	.60
350	Richie Allen	4.00	2.00	1.25
351	Carroll Sembera	2.00	1.00	.60
352	Paul Schaal	2.00	1.00	.60
353	Jeff Torborg	2.00	1.00	.60
354	Nate Oliver	2.00	1.00	.60
355	Phil Niekro	8.00	4.00	2.50
356	Frank Quilici	2.00	1.00	.60
357	Carl Taylor	2.00	1.00	.60
358	Athletics Rookies (George Lauzerique, Roberto Rodriguez)	2.00	1.00	.60
359	Dick Kelley	2.00	1.00	.60
360	Jim Wynn	2.00	1.00	.60
361	Gary Holman	2.00	1.00	.60
362	Jim Maloney	2.00	1.00	.60
363	Russ Nixon	2.00	1.00	.60
364	Tommie Agee	2.00	1.00	.60
365	Jim Fregosi	2.00	1.00	.60
366	Bo Belinsky	2.00	1.00	.60
367	Lou Johnson	2.00	1.00	.60
368	Vic Roznovsky	2.00	1.00	.60
369	Bob Skinner	2.00	1.00	.60
370	Juan Marichal	8.00	4.00	2.50
371	Sal Bando	2.00	1.00	.60
372	Adolfo Phillips	2.00	1.00	.60
373	Fred Lasher	2.00	1.00	.60
374	Bob Tillman	2.00	1.00	.60
375	Harmon Killebrew	20.00	10.00	6.00
376	Royals Rookies (*Mike Fiore, Jim Rooker*)	2.00	1.00	.60
377	Gary Bell	2.00	1.00	.60
378	Jose Herrera	2.00	1.00	.60
379	Ken Boyer	2.00	1.00	.60
380	Stan Bahnsen	2.00	1.00	.60
381	Ed Kranepool	2.00	1.00	.60
382	Pat Corrales	2.00	1.00	.60
383	Casey Cox	2.00	1.00	.60
384	Larry Shepard	2.00	1.00	.60
385	Orlando Cepeda	10.00	5.00	3.00
386	Jim McGlothlin	2.00	1.00	.60
387	Bobby Klaus	2.00	1.00	.60
388	Tom McCraw	2.00	1.00	.60
389	Dan Coombs	2.00	1.00	.60
390	Bill Freehan	2.00	1.00	.60
391	Ray Culp	2.00	1.00	.60
392	Bob Burda	2.00	1.00	.60
393	Gene Brabender	2.00	1.00	.60
394	Pilots Rookies (Lou Piniella, Marv Staehle)	4.00	2.00	1.25
395	Chris Short	2.00	1.00	.60
396	Jim Campanis	2.00	1.00	.60
397	Chuck Dobson	2.00	1.00	.60
398	Tito Francona	2.00	1.00	.60
399	Bob Bailey	2.00	1.00	.60
400	Don Drysdale	15.00	7.50	4.50
401	Jake Gibbs	2.00	1.00	.60
402	Ken Boswell	2.00	1.00	.60
403	Bob Miller	2.00	1.00	.60
404	Cubs Rookies (Vic LaRose, Gary Ross)	2.00	1.00	.60
405	Lee May	2.00	1.00	.60
406	Phil Ortega	2.00	1.00	.60
407	Tom Egan	2.00	1.00	.60
408	Nate Colbert	2.00	1.00	.60
409	Bob Moose	2.00	1.00	.60
410	Al Kaline	15.00	7.50	3.75
411	Larry Dierker	2.00	1.00	.60
412	5th Series Check List (426-512) (Mickey Mantle)	20.00	10.00	5.00
413	Roland Sheldon	2.00	1.00	.60
414	Duke Sims	2.00	1.00	.60
415	Ray Washburn	2.00	1.00	.60
416	Willie McCovey (All-Star)	7.00	3.50	2.00
417	Ken Harrelson (All-Star)	2.00	1.00	.60
418	Tommy Helms (All-Star)	2.00	1.00	.60
419	Rod Carew (All-Star)	8.00	4.00	2.50
420	Ron Santo (All-Star)	4.00	2.00	1.25
421	Brooks Robinson (All-Star)	9.00	4.50	2.75
422	Don Kessinger (All-Star)	2.00	1.00	.60
423	Bert Campaneris (All-Star)	2.00	1.00	.60
424	Pete Rose (All-Star)	25.00	12.50	6.25
425	Carl Yastrzemski (All-Star)	15.00	7.50	3.75
426	Curt Flood (All-Star)	3.00	1.50	.90
427	Tony Oliva (All-Star)	3.00	1.50	.90
428	Lou Brock (All-Star)	7.00	3.50	2.00
429	Willie Horton (All-Star)	2.00	1.00	.60
430	Johnny Bench (All-Star)	15.00	7.50	3.75
431	Bill Freehan (All-Star)	2.00	1.00	.60
432	Bob Gibson (All-Star)	8.00	4.00	2.50
433	Denny McLain (All-Star)	3.00	1.50	.90
434	Jerry Koosman (All-Star)	2.00	1.00	.60
435	Sam McDowell (All-Star)	2.00	1.00	.60
436	Gene Alley	2.00	1.00	.60
437	Luis Alcaraz	2.00	1.00	.60
438	Gary Waslewski	2.00	1.00	.60
439	White Sox Rookies (Ed Herrmann, Dan Lazar)	2.00	1.00	.60
440a	Willie McCovey (Last name in white.)	150.00	75.00	45.00
440b	Willie McCovey (Last name in yellow.)	15.00	7.50	3.75
441a	Dennis Higgins (Last name in white.)	60.00	30.00	18.00
441b	Dennis Higgins (Last name in yellow.)	2.00	1.00	.60
442	Ty Cline	2.00	1.00	.60
443	Don Wert	2.00	1.00	.60
444a	Joe Moeller (Last name in white.)	60.00	30.00	18.00
444b	Joe Moeller (Last name in yellow.)	2.00	1.00	.60
445	Bobby Knoop	2.00	1.00	.60
446	Claude Raymond	2.00	1.00	.60
447a	Ralph Houk (Last name in white.)	80.00	40.00	24.00
447b	Ralph Houk (Last name in yellow.)	5.00	2.50	1.50
448	Bob Tolan	2.00	1.00	.60
449	Paul Lindblad	2.00	1.00	.60
450	Billy Williams	15.00	7.50	3.75
451a	Rich Rollins (First name in white.)	60.00	30.00	18.00
451b	Rich Rollins (First name in yellow.)	2.00	1.00	.60
452a	Al Ferrara (First name in white.)	60.00	30.00	18.00
452b	Al Ferrara (First name in yellow.)	2.00	1.00	.60
453	Mike Cuellar	2.00	1.00	.60
454a	Phillies Rookies (*Larry Colton, Don Money*) (Names in white.)	60.00	30.00	18.00
454b	Phillies Rookies (*Larry Colton, Don Money*) (Names in yellow.)			
455	Sonny Siebert	2.00	1.00	.60
456	Bud Harrelson	2.00	1.00	.60
457	Dalton Jones	2.00	1.00	.60
458	Curt Blefary	2.00	1.00	.60
459	Dave Boswell	2.00	1.00	.60
460	Joe Torre	5.00	2.50	1.50
461a	Mike Epstein (Last name in white.)	60.00	30.00	18.00
461b	Mike Epstein (Last name in yellow.)	2.00	1.00	.60
462	Red Schoendienst	7.00	3.50	2.00
463	Dennis Ribant	2.00	1.00	.60
464a	Dave Marshall (Last name in white.)	60.00	30.00	18.00
464b	Dave Marshall (Last name in yellow.)	2.00	1.00	.60
465	Tommy John	4.00	2.00	1.25
466	John Boccabella	2.00	1.00	.60
467	Tom Reynolds	2.00	1.00	.60
468a	Pirates Rookies (Bruce Dal Canton, Bob Robertson) (Names in white.)	60.00	30.00	18.00
468b	Pirates Rookies (Bruce Dal Canton, Bob Robertson) (Names in yellow.)	2.00	1.00	.60
469	Chico Ruiz	2.00	1.00	.60
470a	Mel Stottlemyre (Last name in white.)	60.00	30.00	18.00
470b	Mel Stottlemyre (Last name in yellow.)	3.00	1.50	.90
471a	Ted Savage (Last name in white.)	60.00	30.00	18.00
471b	Ted Savage (Last name in yellow.)	2.00	1.00	.60
472	Jim Price	2.00	1.00	.60
473a	Jose Arcia (First name in white.)	60.00	30.00	18.00
473b	Jose Arcia (First name in yellow.)	2.00	1.00	.60
474	Tom Murphy	2.00	1.00	.60
475	Tim McCarver	3.00	1.50	.90
476a	Red Sox Rookies (*Ken Brett*, Gerry Moses) (Names in white.)	60.00	30.00	18.00
476b	Red Sox Rookies (*Ken Brett*, Gerry Moses) (Names in yellow.)	3.00	1.50	.90
477	Jeff James	2.00	1.00	.60
478	Don Buford	2.00	1.00	.60
479	Richie Scheinblum	2.00	1.00	.60
480	Tom Seaver	70.00	35.00	17.50
481	Bill Melton	2.00	1.00	.60
482a	Jim Gosger (Last name in white.)	60.00	30.00	18.00
482b	Jim Gosger (First name in white.)	2.00	1.00	.60
483	Ted Abernathy	2.00	1.00	.60
484	Joe Gordon	2.00	1.00	.60
485a	Gaylord Perry (Last name in white.)	90.00	45.00	27.50
485b	Gaylord Perry (Last name in yellow.)	8.00	4.00	2.50
486a	Paul Casanova (Last name in white.)	60.00	30.00	18.00
486b	Paul Casanova (Last name in yellow.)	2.00	1.00	.60
487	Denis Menke	2.00	1.00	.60
488	Joe Sparma	2.00	1.00	.60
489	Clete Boyer	3.00	1.50	.90
490	Matty Alou	2.00	1.00	.60
491a	Twins Rookies (Jerry Crider, George Mitterwald) (Names in white.)	60.00	30.00	18.00
491b	Twins Rookies (Jerry Crider, George Mitterwald) (Names in yellow.)	2.00	1.00	.60
492	Tony Cloninger	2.00	1.00	.60
493a	Wes Parker (Last name in white.)	60.00	30.00	18.00
493b	Wes Parker (Last name in yellow.)	2.00	1.00	.60
494	Ken Berry	2.00	1.00	.60
495	Bert Campaneris	2.00	1.00	.60
496	Larry Jaster	2.00	1.00	.60
497	Julian Javier	2.00	1.00	.60
498	Juan Pizarro	2.00	1.00	.60
499	Astros Rookies (Don Bryant, Steve Shea)	2.00	1.00	.60
500a	Mickey Mantle (Last name in white.)	2,000	1,000	500.00
500b	Mickey Mantle (Last name in yellow.)	400.00	200.00	100.00
501a	Tony Gonzalez (First name in white.)	60.00	30.00	18.00
501b	Tony Gonzalez (First name in yellow.)	2.00	1.00	.60
502	Minnie Rojas	2.00	1.00	.60
503	Larry Brown	2.00	1.00	.60
504	6th Series Check List (513-588) (Brooks Robinson)	7.00	3.50	2.00
505a	Bobby Bolin (Last name in white.)	60.00	30.00	18.00
505b	Bobby Bolin (Last name in yellow.)	2.00	1.00	.60
506	Paul Blair	2.00	1.00	.60
507	Cookie Rojas	2.00	1.00	.60
508	Moe Drabowsky	2.00	1.00	.60
509	Manny Sanguillen	2.00	1.00	.60
510	Rod Carew	30.00	15.00	7.50
511a	Diego Segui (First name in white.)	60.00	30.00	18.00
511b	Diego Segui (First name in yellow.)	2.00	1.00	.60
512	Cleon Jones	2.00	1.00	.60
513	Camilo Pascual	2.00	1.00	.60
514	Mike Lum	2.00	1.00	.60
515	Dick Green	2.00	1.00	.60
516	Earl Weaver	9.00	4.50	2.75
517	Mike McCormick	2.00	1.00	.60
518	Fred Whitfield	2.00	1.00	.60
519	Yankees Rookies (Len Boehmer, Gerry Kenney)	2.00	1.00	.60
520	Bob Veale	2.00	1.00	.60
521	George Thomas	2.00	1.00	.60
522	Joe Hoerner	2.00	1.00	.60
523	Bob Chance	2.00	1.00	.60
524	Expos Rookies (Jose Laboy, Floyd Wicker)	2.00	1.00	.60
525	Earl Wilson	2.00	1.00	.60
526	Hector Torres	2.00	1.00	.60
527	Al Lopez	6.00	3.00	1.75
528	Claude Osteen	2.00	1.00	.60
529	Ed Kirkpatrick	2.00	1.00	.60
530	Cesar Tovar	2.00	1.00	.60
531	Dick Farrell	2.00	1.00	.60
532	Bird Hill Aces (Mike Cuellar, Jim Hardin, Dave McNally, Tom Phoebus)	3.50	1.75	1.00
533	Nolan Ryan	250.00	125.00	62.50
534	Jerry McNertney	2.00	1.00	.60
535	Phil Regan	2.00	1.00	.60
536	Padres Rookies (*Danny Breeden, Dave Roberts*)	2.00	1.00	.60
537	Mike Paul	2.00	1.00	.60
538	Charlie Smith	2.00	1.00	.60
539	Ted Shows How (Mike Epstein, Ted Williams)	13.50	6.75	4.00
540	Curt Flood	3.00	1.50	.90
541	Joe Verbanic	2.00	1.00	.60
542	Bob Aspromonte	2.00	1.00	.60
543	Fred Newman	2.00	1.00	.60
544	Tigers Rookies (Mike Kilkenny, Ron Woods)	2.00	1.00	.60
545	Willie Stargell	12.00	6.00	3.00
546	Jim Nash	2.00	1.00	.60
547	Billy Martin	6.00	3.00	1.75
548	Bob Locker	2.00	1.00	.60
549	Ron Brand	2.00	1.00	.60
550	Brooks Robinson	25.00	12.50	7.50
551	Wayne Granger	2.00	1.00	.60
552	Dodgers Rookies (*Ted Sizemore, Bill Sudakis*)	3.00	1.50	.90
553	Ron Davis	2.00	1.00	.60
554	Frank Bertaina	2.00	1.00	.60
555	Jim Hart	2.00	1.00	.60
556	A's Stars (Sal Bando, Bert Campaneris, Danny Cater)	3.00	1.50	.90
557	Frank Fernandez	2.00	1.00	.60
558	*Tom Burgmeier*	2.00	1.00	.60
559	Cards Rookies (Joe Hague, Jim Hicks)	2.00	1.00	.60
560	Luis Tiant	2.00	1.00	.60
561	Ron Clark	2.00	1.00	.60
562	*Bob Watson*	4.00	2.00	1.25
563	Marty Pattin	2.00	1.00	.60
564	Gil Hodges	7.00	3.50	2.00
565	Hoyt Wilhelm	8.00	4.00	2.50
566	Ron Hansen	2.00	1.00	.60
567a	Pirates Rookies (Elvio Jimenez, Jim Shellenback) (No black outline around title letters.)	45.00	22.50	13.50
567b	Pirates Rookies (Elvio Jiminez, Jim Shellenback) (Title letters outlined in black.)	2.00	1.00	.60
568	Cecil Upshaw	2.00	1.00	.60
569	Billy Harris	2.00	1.00	.60
570	Ron Santo	15.00	7.50	3.75
571	Cap Peterson	2.00	1.00	.60
572	Giants Heroes (Juan Marichal, Willie McCovey)	9.00	4.50	2.75
573	Jim Palmer	10.00	5.00	2.50
574	George Scott	2.00	1.00	.60
575	Bill Singer	2.00	1.00	.60
576	Phillies Rookies (Ron Stone, Bill Wilson)	2.00	1.00	.60
577	Mike Hegan	2.00	1.00	.60
578	Don Bosch	2.00	1.00	.60
579	*Dave Nelson*	2.00	1.00	.60
580	Jim Northrup	2.00	1.00	.60
581	Gary Nolan	2.00	1.00	.60
582a	7th Series Check List (589-664) (Tony Oliva) (Red circle on back.)	4.50	2.25	1.25

		NM	EX	VG
582b	7th Series Check List (589-664) (Tony Oliva) (White circle on back.)	3.00	1.50	.90
583	*Clyde Wright*	2.00	1.00	.60
584	Don Mason	2.00	1.00	.60
585	Ron Swoboda	2.00	1.00	.60
586	Tim Cullen	2.00	1.00	.60
587	*Joe Rudi*	5.00	2.50	1.50
588	Bill White	3.00	1.50	.90
589	Joe Pepitone	6.00	3.00	1.75
590	Rico Carty	3.00	1.50	.90
591	Mike Hedlund	3.00	1.50	.90
592	Padres Rookies (Rafael Robles, Al Santorini)	3.00	1.50	.90
593	Don Nottebart	3.00	1.50	.90
594	Dooley Womack	3.00	1.50	.90
595	Lee Maye	3.00	1.50	.90
596	Chuck Hartenstein	3.00	1.50	.90
597	A.L. Rookies (Larry Burchart, *Rollie Fingers*, Bob Floyd)	35.00	17.50	8.75
598	Ruben Amaro	3.00	1.50	.90
599	John Boozer	3.00	1.50	.90
600	Tony Oliva	6.00	3.00	1.75
601	Tug McGraw	4.00	2.00	1.25
602	Cubs Rookies (Alec Distaso, Jim Qualls, Don Young)	3.00	1.50	.90
603	Joe Keough	3.00	1.50	.90
604	Bobby Etheridge	3.00	1.50	.90
605	Dick Ellsworth	3.00	1.50	.90
606	Gene Mauch	3.00	1.50	.90
607	Dick Bosman	3.00	1.50	.90
608	Dick Simpson	3.00	1.50	.90
609	Phil Gagliano	3.00	1.50	.90
610	Jim Hardin	3.00	1.50	.90
611	Braves Rookies (Bob Didier, Walt Hriniak, Gary Neibauer)	3.00	1.50	.90
612	Jack Aker	3.00	1.50	.90
613	Jim Beauchamp	3.00	1.50	.90
614	Astros Rookies (Tom Griffin, Skip Guinn)	3.00	1.50	.90
615	Len Gabrielson	3.00	1.50	.90
616	Don McMahon	3.00	1.50	.90
617	Jesse Gonder	3.00	1.50	.90
618	Ramon Webster	3.00	1.50	.90
619	Royals Rookies (Bill Butler, *Pat Kelly*, Juan Rios)	3.00	1.50	.90
620	Dean Chance	3.00	1.50	.90
621	Bill Voss	3.00	1.50	.90
622	Dan Osinski	3.00	1.50	.90
623	Hank Allen	3.00	1.50	.90
624	N.L. Rookies (Darrel Chaney, Duffy Dyer, Terry Harmon)	3.00	1.50	.90
625	Mack Jones	3.00	1.50	.90
626	Gene Michael	3.00	1.50	.90
627	George Stone	3.00	1.50	.90
628	Red Sox Rookies (*Bill Conigliaro*, Syd O'Brien, Fred Wenz)	4.00	2.00	1.25
629	Jack Hamilton	3.00	1.50	.90
630	*Bobby Bonds*	25.00	12.50	7.50
631	John Kennedy	3.00	1.50	.90
632	Jon Warden	3.00	1.50	.90
633	Harry Walker	3.00	1.50	.90
634	Andy Etchebarren	3.00	1.50	.90
635	George Culver	3.00	1.50	.90
636	Woodie Held	3.00	1.50	.90
637	Padres Rookies (Jerry DaVanon, Clay Kirby, Frank Reberger)	3.00	1.50	.90
638	Ed Sprague	3.00	1.50	.90
639	Barry Moore	3.00	1.50	.90
640	Fergie Jenkins	15.00	7.50	3.75
641	N.L. Rookies (Bobby Darwin, Tommy Dean, John Miller)	3.00	1.50	.90
642	John Hiller	3.00	1.50	.90
643	Billy Cowan	3.00	1.50	.90
644	Chuck Hinton	3.00	1.50	.90
645	George Brunet	3.00	1.50	.90
646	Expos Rookies (*Dan McGinn, Carl Morton*)	3.00	1.50	.90
647	Dave Wickersham	3.00	1.50	.90
648	Bobby Wine	3.00	1.50	.90
649	Al Jackson	3.00	1.50	.90
650	Ted Williams	25.00	12.50	6.25
651	Gus Gil	3.00	1.50	.90
652	Eddie Watt	3.00	1.50	.90
653	*Aurelio Rodriguez* (Photo actually batboy Leonard Garcia.)	6.00	3.00	1.75
654	White Sox Rookies (*Carlos May*, Rich Morales, Don Secrist)	3.50	1.75	1.00
655	Mike Hershberger	3.00	1.50	.90
656	Dan Schneider	3.00	1.50	.90
657	Bobby Murcer	6.00	3.00	1.75
658	A.L. Rookies (Bill Burbach, Tom Hall, Jim Miles)	3.00	1.50	.90
659	Johnny Podres	3.00	1.50	.90
660	Reggie Smith	3.00	1.50	.90
661	Jim Merritt	3.00	1.50	.90
662	Royals Rookies (Dick Drago, Bob Oliver, George Spriggs)	3.00	1.50	.90
663	Dick Radatz	4.50	2.25	1.25
664	Ron Hunt	13.50	3.00	1.00

1969 Topps Decals

Designed as an insert for 1969 regular issue card packs, these decals are virtually identical in format to the '69 cards. The 48 decals in the set measure 1" x 2-1/2", although they are mounted on white paper backing which measures 1-3/4" x 2-1/8." In March 2001, a hoard consisting of two original 10,000-piece rolls - 833 each of half the players in the set - was sold at auction. The players represented in that find are indicated in these listings with an asterisk.

		NM	EX	VG
Complete Set (48):		350.00	175.00	100.00
Common Player:		4.00	2.00	1.25
(1)	Hank Aaron	25.00	12.50	7.50
(2)	Richie Allen	7.00	3.50	2.00
(3)	Felipe Alou	5.00	2.50	1.50
(4)	Matty Alou	4.00	2.00	1.25
(5)	Luis Aparicio	9.00	4.50	2.75
(6)	Bob Clemente	30.00	15.00	9.00
(7)	Donn Clendenon	4.00	2.00	1.25
(8)	Tommy Davis (*)	4.00	2.00	1.25
(9)	Don Drysdale (*)	10.00	5.00	3.00
(10)	Joe Foy (*)	4.00	2.00	1.25
(11)	Jim Fregosi	4.00	2.00	1.25
(12)	Bob Gibson (*)	10.00	5.00	3.00
(13)	Tony Gonzalez	4.00	2.00	1.25
(14)	Tom Haller	4.00	2.00	1.25
(15)	Ken Harrelson	4.00	2.00	1.25
(16)	Tommy Helms	4.00	2.00	1.25
(17)	Willie Horton (*)	4.00	2.00	1.25
(18)	Frank Howard	4.50	2.25	1.25
(19)	Reggie Jackson (*)	20.00	10.00	6.00
(20)	Fergie Jenkins	9.00	4.50	2.75
(21)	Harmon Killebrew (*)	10.00	5.00	3.00
(22)	Jerry Koosman (*)	4.00	2.00	1.25
(23)	Mickey Mantle	40.00	20.00	12.00
(24)	Willie Mays (*)	20.00	10.00	6.00
(25)	Tim McCarver	4.50	2.25	1.25
(26)	Willie McCovey	10.00	5.00	3.00
(27)	Sam McDowell (*)	4.00	2.00	1.25
(28)	Denny McLain (*)	4.00	2.00	1.25
(29)	Dave McNally (*)	4.00	2.00	1.25
(30)	Don Mincher	4.00	2.00	1.25
(31)	Rick Monday	4.00	2.00	1.25
(32)	Tony Oliva (*)	4.50	2.25	1.25
(33)	Camilo Pascual	4.00	2.00	1.25
(34)	Rick Reichardt (*)	4.00	2.00	1.25
(35)	Frank Robinson (*)	10.00	5.00	3.00
(36)	Pete Rose (*)	20.00	10.00	6.00
(37)	Ron Santo (*)	5.00	2.50	1.50
(38)	Tom Seaver (*)	12.00	6.00	3.50
(39)	Dick Selma (*)	4.00	2.00	1.25
(40)	Chris Short (*)	4.00	2.00	1.25
(41)	Rusty Staub	4.00	2.00	1.25
(42)	Mel Stottlemyre	4.00	2.00	1.25
(43)	Luis Tiant (*)	4.00	2.00	1.25
(44)	Pete Ward	4.00	2.00	1.25
(45)	Hoyt Wilhelm (*)	7.50	3.75	2.25
(46)	Maury Wills (*)	4.00	2.00	1.25
(47)	Jim Wynn	4.00	2.00	1.25
(48)	Carl Yastrzemski (*)	12.00	6.00	3.50

1969 Topps Deckle Edge

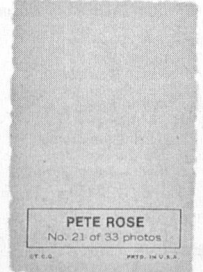

These 2-1/4" x 3-1/4" cards take their name from their borders which have a scalloped effect. Fronts have a black-and-white player photo along with a blue facsimile autograph. Backs have the player's name and the card number in light blue ink in a small box at the bottom of the card. While there are only 33 numbered cards, there are actually 35 possible players; both Jim Wynn and Hoyt Wilhelm cards are found as #11 while cards of Joe Foy and Rusty Staub as #22. Straight-edged proof cards are sometimes found but these were never formally issued; they carry a premium.

		NM	EX	VG
Complete Set (33):		80.00	40.00	25.00
Common Player:		1.00	.50	.30
Proofs: 6-8X				
1	Brooks Robinson	9.00	4.50	2.75
2	Boog Powell	1.50	.70	.45
3	Ken Harrelson	1.00	.50	.30
4	Carl Yastrzemski	9.00	4.50	2.75
5	Jim Fregosi	1.00	.50	.30
6	Luis Aparicio	7.50	3.75	2.25
7	Luis Tiant	1.00	.50	.30
8	Denny McLain	1.00	.50	.30
9	Willie Horton	1.00	.50	.30
10	Bill Freehan	1.00	.50	.30
11a	Hoyt Wilhelm	6.00	3.00	1.75
11b	Jim Wynn	12.00	6.00	3.50
12	Rod Carew	7.50	3.75	2.25
13	Mel Stottlemyre	1.00	.50	.30
14	Rick Monday	1.00	.50	.30
15	Tommy Davis	1.00	.50	.30
16	Frank Howard	1.50	.70	.45
17	Felipe Alou	1.00	.50	.30
18	Don Kessinger	1.00	.50	.30
19	Ron Santo	2.00	1.00	.60
20	Tommy Helms	1.00	.50	.30
21	Pete Rose	15.00	7.50	4.50
22a	Rusty Staub	2.00	1.00	.60
22b	Joe Foy	9.00	4.50	2.75
23	Tom Haller	1.00	.50	.30
24	Maury Wills	1.00	.50	.30
25	Jerry Koosman	1.00	.50	.30
26	Richie Allen	3.00	1.50	.90
27	Roberto Clemente	20.00	10.00	6.00
28	Curt Flood	1.00	.50	.30
29	Bob Gibson	7.50	3.75	2.25
30	Al Ferrara	1.00	.50	.30
31	Willie McCovey	7.50	3.75	2.25
32	Juan Marichal	6.00	3.00	1.75
33	Willie Mays	15.00	7.50	4.50

1969 Topps Stamps

Topps continued to refine its efforts at baseball stamps in 1969 with the release of 240 player stamps, each measuring 1" x 1-7/16". Each stamp has a color photo along with the player's name, position and team. Unlike prior stamp issues, the 1969 stamps have 24 separate albums (one per team). The stamps were issued in strips of 12, many players appearing on two different strips.

		NM	EX	VG
Complete Sheet Set (24):		200.00	100.00	60.00
Common Sheet:		5.00	2.50	1.50
Complete Stamp Album Set (24):		80.00	40.00	20.00
Single Stamp Album:		3.00	1.50	.90
Unopened Pack:		50.00	.00	.00
(1)	Tommie Agee, Sandy Alomar, Jose Cardenal, Dean Chance, Joe Foy, Jim Grant, Don Kessinger, Mickey Mantle, Jerry May, Bob Rodgers, Cookie Rojas, Gary Sutherland	55.00	27.50	16.50
(2)	Jesus Alou, Mike Andrews, Larry Brown, Moe Drabowsky, Alex Johnson, Lew Krausse, Jim Lefebvre, Dal Maxvill, John Odom, Claude Osteen, Rick Reichardt, Luis Tiant	5.00	2.50	1.50
(3)	Hank Aaron, Matty Alou, Max Alvis, Nelson Briles, Eddie Fisher, Bud Harrelson, Willie Horton, Randy Hundley, Larry Jaster, Jim Kaat, Gary Peters, Pete Ward	20.00	10.00	6.00
(4)	Don Buford, John Callison, Tommy Davis, Jackie Hernandez, Fergie Jenkins, Lee May, Denny McLain, Bob Oliver, Roberto Pena, Tony Perez, Joe Torre, Tom Tresh	7.50	3.75	2.25
(5)	Jim Bunning, Dean Chance, Joe Foy, Sonny Jackson, Don Kessinger, Rick Monday, Gaylord Perry, Roger Repoz, Cookie Rojas, Mel Stottlemyre, Leon Wagner, Jim Wynn	7.50	3.75	2.25
(6)	Felipe Alou, Gerry Arrigo, Bob Aspromonte, Gary Bell, Clay Dalrymple, Jim Fregosi, Tony Gonzalez, Duane Josephson, Dick McAuliffe, Tony Oliva, Brooks Robinson, Willie Stargell	20.00	10.00	6.00
(7)	Steve Barber, Donn Clendenon, Joe Coleman, Vic Davalillo, Russ Gibson, Jerry Grote, Tom Haller, Andy Kosco, Willie McCovey, Don Mincher, Joe Morgan, Don Wilson	7.50	3.75	2.25

(8)	George Brunet, Don Buford, John Callison, Danny Cater, Tommy Davis, Willie Davis, John Edwards, Jim Hart, Mickey Lolich, Willie Mays, Roberto Pena, Mickey Stanley	25.00	12.50	7.50
(9)	Ernie Banks, Glenn Beckert, Ken Berry, Horace Clarke, Roberto Clemente, Larry Dierker, Len Gabrielson, Jake Gibbs, Jerry Koosman, Sam McDowell, Tom Satriano, Bill Singer	25.00	12.50	7.50
(10)	Gene Alley, Lou Brock, Larry Brown, Moe Drabowsky, Frank Howard, Tommie John, Roger Nelson, Claude Osteen, Phil Regan, Rick Reichardt, Tony Taylor, Roy White	7.50	3.75	2.25
(11)	Bob Allison, John Bateman, Don Drysdale, Dave Johnson, Harmon Killebrew, Jim Maloney, Bill Mazeroski, Gerry McNertney, Ron Perranoski, Rico Petrocelli, Pete Rose, Billy Williams	35.00	17.50	10.50
(12)	Bernie Allen (Senators), Jose Arcia, Stan Bahnsen, Sal Bando, Jim Davenport, Tito Francona, Dick Green, Ron Hunt, Mack Jones, Vada Pinson, George Scott, Don Wert	5.00	2.50	1.50
(13)	Gerry Arrigo, Bob Aspromonte, Joe Azcue, Curt Blefary, Orlando Cepeda, Bill Freehan, Jim Fregosi, Dave Giusti, Duane Josephson, Tim McCarver, Jose Santiago, Bob Tolan	7.50	3.75	2.25
(14)	Jerry Adair, Johnny Bench, Clete Boyer, John Briggs, Bert Campaneris, Woody Fryman, Ron Kline, Bobby Knoop, Ken McMullen, Adolfo Phillips, John Roseboro, Tom Seaver	20.00	10.00	6.00
(15)	Norm Cash, Ron Fairly, Bob Gibson, Bill Hands, Cleon Jones, Al Kaline, Paul Schaal, Mike Shannon, Duke Sims, Reggie Smith, Steve Whitaker, Carl Yastrzemski	15.00	7.50	4.50
(16)	Steve Barber, Paul Casanova, Dick Dietz, Russ Gibson, Jerry Grote, Tom Haller, Ed Kranepool, Juan Marichal, Denis Menke, Jim Nash, Bill Robinson, Frank Robinson	15.00	7.50	4.50
(17)	Bobby Bolin, Ollie Brown, Rod Carew, Mike Epstein, Bud Harrelson, Larry Jaster, Dave McNally, Willie Norton, Milt Pappas, Gary Peters, Paul Popovich, Stan Williams	7.50	3.75	2.25
(18)	Ted Abernathy, Bob Allison, Ed Brinkman, Don Drysdale, Jim Hardin, Julian Javier, Hal Lanier, Jim McGlothlin, Ron Perranoski, Rich Rollins, Ron Santo, Billy Williams	15.00	7.50	4.50
(19)	Richie Allen, Luis Aparicio, Wally Bunker, Curt Flood, Ken Harrelson, Jim Hunter, Denver Lemaster, Felix Millan, Jim Northrop (Northrup), Art Shamsky, Larry Stahl, Ted Uhlaender	7.50	3.75	2.25
(20)	Bob Bailey, Johnny Bench, Woody Fryman, Jim Hannan, Ron Kline, Al McBean, Camilo Pascual, Joe Pepitone, Doug Rader, Ron Reed, John Roseboro, Sonny Siebert	7.50	3.75	2.25
(21)	Jack Aker, Tommy Harper, Tommy Helms, Dennis Higgins, Jim Hunter, Don Lock, Lee Maye, Felix Millan, Jim Northrop (Northrup), Larry Stahl, Don Sutton, Zoilo Versalles	7.50	3.75	2.25
(22)	Norm Cash, Ed Charles, Joe Horlen, Pat Jarvis, Jim Lonborg, Manny Mota, Boog Powell, Dick Selma, Mike Shannon, Duke Sims, Steve Whitaker, Hoyt Wilhelm	7.50	3.75	2.25
(23)	Bernie Allen (Senator), Ray Culp, Al Ferrara, Tito Francona, Dick Green, Ron Hunt, Ray Oyler, Tom Phoebus, Rusty Staub, Bob Veale, Maury Wills, Wilbur Wood	5.00	2.50	1.50
(24)	Ernie Banks, Mark Belanger, Steve Blass, Horace Clarke, Bob Clemente, Larry Dierker, Dave Duncan, Chico Salmon, Chris Short, Ron Swoboda, Cesar Tovar, Rick Wise	20.00	10.00	6.00

1969 Topps Super

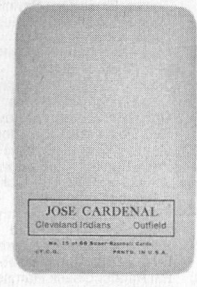

These 2-1/4" x 3-1/4" cards are not the bigger "Super" cards which would be seen in following years. Rather, what enabled Topps to dub them "Super Baseball Cards" is their high-gloss finish which enhances the bright color photograph used on their fronts. The only other design element on the front is a facsimile autograph. The backs contain a box at the bottom which carries the player's name, team, position, a copyright line and the card number. Another unusual feature is that the cards have rounded corners, although square-cornered proof cards are also known, completely printed on front and back.

		NM	EX	VG
	Complete Set (66):	6,000	3,000	1,800
	Common Player:	20.00	10.00	6.00
	Proofs: 2-3X			
1	Dave McNally	20.00	10.00	6.00
2	Frank Robinson	175.00	85.00	50.00
3	Brooks Robinson	175.00	85.00	50.00
4	Ken Harrelson	20.00	10.00	6.00
5	Carl Yastrzemski	250.00	125.00	75.00
6	Ray Culp	20.00	10.00	6.00
7	James Fregosi	20.00	10.00	6.00
8	Rick Reichardt	20.00	10.00	6.00
9	Vic Davalillo	20.00	10.00	6.00
10	Luis Aparicio	100.00	50.00	30.00
11	Pete Ward	20.00	10.00	6.00
12	Joe Horlen	20.00	10.00	6.00
13	Luis Tiant	20.00	10.00	6.00
14	Sam McDowell	20.00	10.00	6.00
15	Jose Cardenal	20.00	10.00	6.00
16	Willie Horton	20.00	10.00	6.00
17	Denny McLain	20.00	10.00	6.00
18	Bill Freehan	20.00	10.00	6.00
19	Harmon Killebrew	175.00	85.00	50.00
20	Tony Oliva	20.00	10.00	6.00
21	Dean Chance	20.00	10.00	6.00
22	Joe Foy	20.00	10.00	6.00
23	Roger Nelson	20.00	10.00	6.00
24	Mickey Mantle	1,100	550.00	350.00
25	Mel Stottlemyre	20.00	10.00	6.00
26	Roy White	20.00	10.00	6.00
27	Rick Monday	20.00	10.00	6.00
28	Reggie Jackson	400.00	200.00	120.00
29	Bert Campaneris	20.00	10.00	6.00
30	Frank Howard	20.00	10.00	6.00
31	Camilo Pascual	20.00	10.00	6.00
32	Tommy Davis	20.00	10.00	6.00
33	Don Mincher	20.00	10.00	6.00
34	Henry Aaron	400.00	200.00	120.00
35	Felipe Alou	20.00	10.00	6.00
36	Joe Torre	50.00	25.00	15.00
37	Fergie Jenkins	100.00	50.00	30.00
38	Ronald Santo	35.00	17.50	10.00
39	Billy Williams	100.00	50.00	30.00
40	Tommy Helms	20.00	10.00	6.00
41	Pete Rose	400.00	200.00	120.00
42	Joe Morgan	100.00	50.00	30.00
43	Jim Wynn	20.00	10.00	6.00
44	Curt Blefary	20.00	10.00	6.00
45	Willie Davis	20.00	10.00	6.00
46	Don Drysdale	135.00	65.00	40.00
47	Tom Haller	20.00	10.00	6.00
48	Rusty Staub	35.00	17.50	10.00
49	Maurice Wills	20.00	10.00	6.00
50	Cleon Jones	20.00	10.00	6.00
51	Jerry Koosman	20.00	10.00	6.00
52	Tom Seaver	175.00	87.00	52.00
53	Rich Allen	45.00	22.50	13.50
54	Chris Short	20.00	10.00	6.00
55	Cookie Rojas	20.00	10.00	6.00
56	Mateo Alou	20.00	10.00	6.00
57	Steve Blass	20.00	10.00	6.00
58	Roberto Clemente	500.00	250.00	150.00
59	Curt Flood	20.00	10.00	6.00
60	Bob Gibson	125.00	65.00	35.00
61	Tim McCarver	35.00	17.50	10.00
62	Dick Selma	20.00	10.00	6.00
63	Ollie Brown	20.00	10.00	6.00
64	Juan Marichal	100.00	50.00	30.00
65	Willie Mays	400.00	200.00	120.00
66	Willie McCovey	120.00	60.00	36.00

1969 Topps Team Posters

Picking up where the 1968 posters left off, the 1969 poster is larger at about 12" x 20". The posters each have a team focus with a large pennant carrying the team name, along with nine or 10 photos of players. Each of the photos has a facsimile autograph. The size of posters meant they had to be folded to fit in their packages. These original folds are not considered when grading, unless the paper has split on those seams.

		NM	EX	VG
	Complete Set (24):	2,250	1,125	675.00
	Common Poster:	55.00	27.50	16.00
	Unopened Pack:	190.00		
1	Detroit Tigers (Norm Cash, Bill Freehan, Willie Horton, Al Kaline, Mickey Lolich, Dick McAuliffe, Denny McLain, Jim Northrup, Mickey Stanley, Don Wert, Earl Wilson)	125.00	65.00	35.00
2	Atlanta Braves (Hank Aaron, Felipe Alou, Clete Boyer, Rico Carty, Tito Francona, Sonny Jackson, Pat Jarvis, Felix Millan, Phil Niekro, Milt Pappas, Joe Torre)	90.00	45.00	27.00
3	Boston Red Sox (Mike Andrews, Tony Conigliaro, Ray Culp, Russ Gibson, Ken Harrelson, Jim Lonborg, Rico Petrocelli, Jose Santiago, George Scott, Reggie Smith, Carl Yastrzemski)	100.00	50.00	30.00
4	Chicago Cubs (Ernie Banks, Glenn Beckert, Bill Hands, Jim Hickman, Ken Holtzman, Randy Hundley, Fergie Jenkins, Don Kessinger, Adolfo Phillips, Ron Santo, Billy Williams)	90.00	45.00	27.00
5	Baltimore Orioles (Mark Belanger, Paul Blair, Don Buford, Andy Etchebarren, Jim Hardin, Dave Johnson, Dave McNally, Tom Phoebus, Boog Powell, Brooks Robinson, Frank Robinson)	80.00	40.00	24.00
6	Houston Astros (Curt Blefary, Donn Clendenon, Larry Dierker, John Edwards, Denny Lemaster, Denis Menke, Norm Miller, Joe Morgan, Doug Rader, Don Wilson, Jim Wynn)	55.00	27.50	16.00
7	Kansas City Royals (Jerry Adair, Wally Bunker, Mike Fiore, Joe Foy, Jackie Hernandez, Pat Kelly, Dave Morehead, Roger Nelson, Dave Nicholson, Eliseo Rodriguez, Steve Whitaker)	55.00	27.50	16.00
8	Philadelphia Phillies (Richie Allen, Johnny Callison, Woody Fryman, Larry Hisle, Don Money, Cookie Rojas, Mike Ryan, Chris Short, Tony Taylor, Bill White, Rick Wise)	60.00	30.00	18.00
9	Seattle Pilots (Jack Aker, Steve Barber, Gary Bell, Tommy Davis, Jim Gosger, Tommy Harper, Gerry McNertney, Don Mincher, Ray Oyler, Rich Rollins, Chico Salmon)	150.00	75.00	45.00
10	Montreal Expos (Bob Bailey, John Bateman, Jack Billingham, Jim Grant, Larry Jaster, Mack Jones, Manny Mota, Rusty Staub, Gary Sutherland, Jim Williams, Maury Wills)	50.00	25.00	15.00
11	Chicago White Sox (Sandy Alomar, Luis Aparicio, Ken Berry, Buddy Bradford, Joe Horlen, Tommy John, Duane Josephson, Tom McCraw, Bill Melton, Pete Ward, Wilbur Wood)	55.00	27.50	16.00
12	San Diego Padres (Jose Arcia, Danny Breeden, Ollie Brown, Bill Davis, Ron Davis, Tony Gonzalez, Dick Kelley, Al McBean, Roberto Pena, Dick Selma, Ed Spiezio)	55.00	27.50	16.00
13	Cleveland Indians (Max Alvis, Joe Azcue, Jose Cardenal, Vern Fuller, Lou Johnson, Sam McDowell, Sonny Siebert, Duke Sims, Russ Snyder, Luis Tiant, Zoilo Versalles)	75.00	37.00	22.00

		NM	EX	VG
14	San Francisco Giants (Bobby Bolin, Jim Davenport, Dick Dietz, Jim Hart, Ron Hunt, Hal Lanier, Juan Marichal, Willie Mays, Willie McCovey, Gaylord Perry, Charlie Smith)	125.00	65.00	35.00
15	Minnesota Twins (Bob Allison, Chico Cardenas, Rod Carew, Dean Chance, Jim Kaat, Harmon Killebrew, Tony Oliva, Jim Perry, John Roseboro, Cesar Tovar, Ted Uhlaender)	100.00	50.00	30.00
16	Pittsburgh Pirates (Gene Alley, Matty Alou, Steve Blass, Jim Bunning, Bob Clemente, Rich Hebner, Jerry May, Bill Mazeroski, Bob Robertson, Willie Stargell, Bob Veale)	135.00	65.00	40.00
17	California Angels (Ruben Amaro, George Brunet, Bob Chance, Vic Davalillo, Jim Fregosi, Bobby Knoop, Jim McGlothlin, Rick Reichardt, Roger Repoz, Bob Rodgers, Hoyt Wilhelm)	60.00	30.00	18.00
18	St. Louis Cardinals (Nelson Briles, Lou Brock, Orlando Cepeda, Curt Flood, Bob Gibson, Julian Javier, Dal Maxvill, Tim McCarver, Vada Pinson, Mike Shannon, Ray Washburn)	75.00	37.50	22.00
19	New York Yankees (Stan Bahnsen, Horace Clarke, Bobby Cox, Jake Gibbs, Mickey Mantle, Joe Pepitone, Fritz Peterson, Bill Robinson, Mel Stottlemyre, Tom Tresh, Roy White)	165.00	82.00	49.00
20	Cincinnati Reds (Gerry Arrigo, Johnny Bench, Tommy Helms, Alex Johnson, Jim Maloney, Lee May, Gary Nolan, Tony Perez, Pete Rose, Bob Tolan, Woody Woodward)	110.00	55.00	33.00
21	Oakland Athletics (Sal Bando, Bert Campaneris, Danny Cater, Dick Green, Mike Hershberger, Jim Hunter, Reggie Jackson, Rick Monday, Jim Nash, John Odom, Jim Pagliaroni)	100.00	50.00	30.00
22	Los Angeles Dodgers (Willie Crawford, Willie Davis, Don Drysdale, Ron Fairly, Tom Haller, Andy Kosco, Jim Lefebvre, Claude Osteen, Paul Popovich, Bill Singer, Bill Sudakis)	80.00	40.00	24.00
23	Washington Senators (Bernie Allen, Brant Alyea, Ed Brinkman, Paul Casanova, Joe Coleman, Mike Epstein, Jim Hannan, Frank Howard, Ken McMullen, Camilo Pascual, Del Unser)	80.00	40.00	24.00
24	New York Mets (Tommie Agee, Ken Boswell, Ed Charles, Jerry Grote, Bud Harrelson, Cleon Jones, Jerry Koosman, Ed Kranepool, Jim McAndrew, Tom Seaver, Ron Swoboda)	150.00	75.00	45.00

1969 Topps 4-On-1 Mini Stickers

Another in the long line of Topps test issues, the 4-on-1s are 2-1/2" x 3-1/2" cards with blank backs featuring a quartet of miniature stickers in the design of the same cards from the 1969 Topps regular set. There are 25 different cards, for a total of 100 different stickers. As they are not common, Mint cards bring fairly strong prices on today's market. As the set was drawn from the 3rd Series of the regular cards, it includes some rookie stickers and World Series highlight stickers.

		NM	EX	VG
	Complete Set (25):	2,250	1,125	675.00
	Common 4-in-1:	50.00	25.00	15.00
	Unopened Pack:	375.00		
(1)	Jerry Adair, Willie Mays, Johnny Morris, Don Wilson	400.00	200.00	120.00
(2)	Tommie Aaron, Jim Britton, Donn Clendenon, Woody Woodward	50.00	25.00	15.00
(3)	Tommy Davis, Don Pavletich, Vada Pinson, World Series Game 4 (Lou Brock)	75.00	37.50	22.00
(4)	Max Alvis, Glenn Beckert, Ron Fairly, Rick Wise	50.00	25.00	15.00
(5)	Johnny Callison, Jim French, Lum Harris, Dick Selma	50.00	25.00	15.00
(6)	Bob Gibson, Larry Haney, Rick Reichardt, World Series Game 3 (Tim McCarver)	125.00	65.00	35.00
(7)	Wally Bunker, Don Cardwell, Joe Gibbon, Astros Rookies (Gilsen, McFadden)	50.00	25.00	15.00
(8)	Ollie Brown, Jim Bunning, Andy Kosco, Ron Reed	50.00	25.00	15.00
(9)	Bill Dillman, Jim Lefebvre, John Purdin, John Roseboro	50.00	25.00	15.00
(10)	Bill Hands, Chuck Harrison, Lindy McDaniel, Felix Millan	50.00	25.00	15.00
(11)	Jack Hiatt, Dave Johnson, Mel Nelson, Tommie Sisk	50.00	25.00	15.00
(12)	Clay Dalrymple, Leo Durocher, John Odom, Wilbur Wood	50.00	25.00	15.00
(13)	Hank Bauer, Kevin Collins, Ray Oyler, Russ Snyder	50.00	25.00	15.00
(14)	Gerry Arrigo, Jim Perry, Red Sox Rookies (Lahoud, Thibdeau), World Series Game 7 (Mickey Lolich)	50.00	25.00	15.00
(15)	Bill McCool, Roberto Pena, Doug Rader, World Series Game 2 (Willie Horton)	75.00	37.50	22.00
(16)	Ed Brinkman, Roy Face, Willie Horton, Bob Rodgers	50.00	25.00	15.00
(17)	Dave Baldwin, J.C. Martin, Dave May, Ray Sadecki	50.00	25.00	15.00
(18)	Jose Pagan, Tom Phoebus, Mike Shannon, World Series Game 1 (Bob Gibson)	50.00	25.00	15.00
(19)	Pete Rose, Lee Stange, Don Sutton, Ted Uhlaender	500.00	250.00	150.00
(20)	Joe Grzenda, Frank Howard, Dick Tracewski, Jim Weaver	50.00	25.00	15.00
(21)	Joe Azcue, Grant Jackson, Denny McLain, White Sox Rookies (Christman, Nyman)	50.00	25.00	15.00
(22)	John Edwards, Jim Fairey, Phillies Rookies, Stan Williams	50.00	25.00	15.00
(23)	John Bateman, Willie Smith, Leon Wagner, World Series Summary	50.00	25.00	15.00
(24)	Chris Cannizzaro, Bob Hendley, World Series Game 5 (Al Kaline), Yankees Rookies (Closter, Cumberland)	50.00	25.00	15.00
(25)	Joe Nossek, Rico Petrocelli, Carl Yastrzemski, Cardinals Rookies (Huntz, Torrez)	350.00	175.00	105.00

1969 Topps Bowie Kuhn

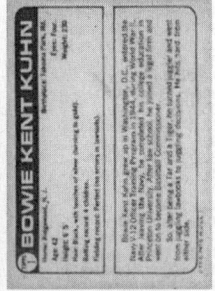

Following Kuhn's election as Commissioner in February 1969, Topps produced this special card, presumably for his personal use. In standard 2-1/2" x 3-1/2" format, but printed on thinner than usual card stock, the front has a photo of Kuhn's face composited with the drawing of a crowned baseball player sitting on top of the world. The horizontal back has a few personal data and a career summary.

		NM	EX	VG
1	Bowie Kuhn	90.00	45.00	27.50

1970 Topps

Topps established another set size record by coming out with 720 cards in 1970. The 2-1/2" x 3-1/2" cards have a color photo with a thin white frame. The photos have the player's team overprinted at the top, while the player's name in script and his position are at the bottom. A gray border surrounds the front. Card backs follow the normal design pattern, although they are more readable than some issues of the past. Team cards returned and were joined with many of the usual specialty cards. The World Series highlights were joined by cards with playoff highlights. Statistical leaders and All-Stars are also included in the set. High-numbered cards provide the most expensive cards in the set.

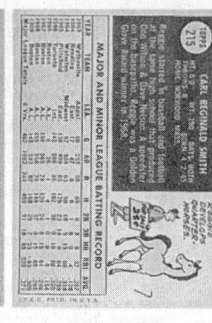

		NM	EX	VG
	Complete Set (720):	2,400	1,200	725.00
	Common Player (1-546):	1.50	.75	.45
	Common Player (547-633):	4.00	2.00	1.00
	Common Player (634-720):	8.00	4.00	2.25
1	World Champions (Mets Team)	25.00	12.50	7.50
2	Diego Segui	1.50	.75	.45
3	Darrel Chaney	1.50	.75	.45
4	Tom Egan	1.50	.75	.45
5	Wes Parker	1.50	.75	.45
6	Grant Jackson	1.50	.75	.45
7	Indians Rookies (Gary Boyd, Russ Nagelson)	1.50	.75	.45
8	Jose Martinez	1.50	.75	.45
9	1st Series Check List (1-132)	8.00	4.00	2.50
10	Carl Yastrzemski	20.00	10.00	5.00
11	Nate Colbert	1.50	.75	.45
12	John Hiller	1.50	.75	.45
13	Jack Hiatt	1.50	.75	.45
14	Hank Allen	1.50	.75	.45
15	Larry Dierker	1.50	.75	.45
16	Charlie Metro	1.50	.75	.45
17	Hoyt Wilhelm	6.00	3.00	1.75
18	Carlos May	1.50	.75	.45
19	John Boccabella	1.50	.75	.45
20	Dave McNally	1.50	.75	.45
21	Athletics Rookies (*Vida Blue, Gene Tenace*)	5.00	2.50	1.25
22	Ray Washburn	1.50	.75	.45
23	Bill Robinson	1.50	.75	.45
24	Dick Selma	1.50	.75	.45
25	Cesar Tovar	1.50	.75	.45
26	Tug McGraw	1.50	.75	.45
27	Chuck Hinton	1.50	.75	.45
28	Billy Wilson	1.50	.75	.45
29	Sandy Alomar	1.50	.75	.45
30	Matty Alou	1.50	.75	.45
31	Marty Pattin	1.50	.75	.45
32	Harry Walker	1.50	.75	.45
33	Don Wert	1.50	.75	.45
34	Willie Crawford	1.50	.75	.45
35	Joe Horlen	1.50	.75	.45
36	Reds Rookies (*Danny Breeden, Bernie Carbo*)	1.50	.75	.45
37	Dick Drago	1.50	.75	.45
38	Mack Jones	1.50	.75	.45
39	Mike Nagy	1.50	.75	.45
40	Rich Allen	3.00	1.50	.90
41	George Lauzerique	1.50	.75	.45
42	Tito Fuentes	1.50	.75	.45
43	Jack Aker	1.50	.75	.45
44	Roberto Pena	1.50	.75	.45
45	Dave Johnson	1.50	.75	.45
46	Ken Rudolph	1.50	.75	.45
47	Bob Miller	1.50	.75	.45
48	Gil Garrido (Gil)	1.50	.75	.45
49	Tim Cullen	1.50	.75	.45
50	Tommie Agee	1.50	.75	.45
51	Bob Christian	1.50	.75	.45
52	Bruce Dal Canton	1.50	.75	.45
53	John Kennedy	1.50	.75	.45
54	Jeff Torborg	1.50	.75	.45
55	John Odom	1.50	.75	.45
56	Phillies Rookies (Joe Lis, Scott Reid)	1.50	.75	.45
57	Pat Kelly	1.50	.75	.45
58	Dave Marshall	1.50	.75	.45
59	Dick Ellsworth	1.50	.75	.45
60	Jim Wynn	1.50	.75	.45
61	N.L. Batting Leaders (Roberto Clemente, Cleon Jones, Pete Rose)	15.00	7.50	3.75
62	A.L. Batting Leaders (Rod Carew, Tony Oliva, Reggie Smith)	6.00	3.00	1.75
63	N.L. RBI Leaders (Willie McCovey, Tony Perez, Ron Santo)	5.00	2.50	1.50
64	A.L. RBI Leaders (Reggie Jackson, Harmon Killebrew, Boog Powell)	10.00	5.00	3.00
65	N.L. Home Run Leaders (Hank Aaron, Lee May, Willie McCovey)	10.00	5.00	3.00
66	A.L. Home Run Leaders (Frank Howard, Reggie Jackson, Harmon Killebrew)	8.00	4.00	2.50
67	N.L. ERA Leaders (Steve Carlton, Bob Gibson, Juan Marichal)	8.00	4.00	2.50
68	A.L. ERA Leaders (Dick Bosman, Mike Cuellar, Jim Palmer)	4.00	2.00	1.25
69	N.L. Pitching Leaders (Fergie Jenkins, Juan Marichal, Phil Niekro, Tom Seaver)	10.00	5.00	3.00

No.	Player			
70	A.L. Pitching Leaders (Dave Boswell, Mike Cuellar, Dennis McLain, Dave McNally, Jim Perry, Mel Stottlemyre)	4.00	2.00	1.25
71	N.L. Strikeout Leaders (Bob Gibson, Fergie Jenkins, Bill Singer)	6.00	3.00	1.75
72	A.L. Strikeout Leaders (Mickey Lolich, Sam McDowell, Andy Messersmith)	4.00	2.00	1.25
73	Wayne Granger	1.50	.75	.45
74	Angels Rookies (Greg Washburn, Wally Wolf)	1.50	.75	.45
75	Jim Kaat	1.50	.75	.45
76	Carl Taylor	1.50	.75	.45
77	Frank Linzy	1.50	.75	.45
78	Joe Lahoud	1.50	.75	.45
79	Clay Kirby	1.50	.75	.45
80	Don Kessinger	1.50	.75	.45
81	Dave May	1.50	.75	.45
82	Frank Fernandez	1.50	.75	.45
83	Don Cardwell	1.50	.75	.45
84	Paul Casanova	1.50	.75	.45
85	Max Alvis	1.50	.75	.45
86	Lum Harris	1.50	.75	.45
87	Steve Renko	1.50	.75	.45
88	Pilots Rookies (Dick Baney, Miguel Fuentes)	1.50	.75	.45
89	Juan Rios	1.50	.75	.45
90	Tim McCarver	3.00	1.50	.90
91	Rich Morales	1.50	.75	.45
92	George Culver	1.50	.75	.45
93	Rick Renick	1.50	.75	.45
94	Fred Patek	1.50	.75	.45
95	Earl Wilson	1.50	.75	.45
96	Cards Rookies (*Leron Lee, Jerry Reuss*)	3.00	1.50	.90
97	Joe Moeller	1.50	.75	.45
98	Gates Brown	1.50	.75	.45
99	Bobby Pfeil	1.50	.75	.45
100	Mel Stottlemyre	1.50	.75	.45
101	Bobby Floyd	1.50	.75	.45
102	Joe Rudi	1.50	.75	.45
103	Frank Reberger	1.50	.75	.45
104	Gerry Moses	1.50	.75	.45
105	Tony Gonzalez	1.50	.75	.45
106	Darold Knowles	1.50	.75	.45
107	Bobby Etheridge	1.50	.75	.45
108	Tom Burgmeier	1.50	.75	.45
109	Expos Rookies (Garry Jestadt, Carl Morton)	1.50	.75	.45
110	Bob Moose	1.50	.75	.45
111	Mike Hegan	1.50	.75	.45
112	Dave Nelson	1.50	.75	.45
113	Jim Ray	1.50	.75	.45
114	Gene Michael	1.50	.75	.45
115	Alex Johnson	1.50	.75	.45
116	Sparky Lyle	1.50	.75	.45
117	Don Young	1.50	.75	.45
118	George Mitterwald	1.50	.75	.45
119	Chuck Taylor	1.50	.75	.45
120	Sal Bando	1.50	.75	.45
121	Orioles Rookies (*Fred Beene, Terry Crowley*)	1.50	.75	.45
122	George Stone	1.50	.75	.45
123	Don Gutteridge	1.50	.75	.45
124	Larry Jaster	1.50	.75	.45
125	Deron Johnson	1.50	.75	.45
126	Marty Martinez	1.50	.75	.45
127	Joe Coleman	1.50	.75	.45
128a	2nd Series Check List (133-263) (226 is R Perranoski)	5.00	2.50	1.50
128b	2nd Series Check List (133-263) (226 is R. Perranoski)	5.00	2.50	1.50
129	Jimmie Price	1.50	.75	.45
130	Ollie Brown	1.50	.75	.45
131	Dodgers Rookies (Ray Lamb, Bob Stinson)	1.50	.75	.45
132	Jim McGlothlin	1.50	.75	.45
133	Clay Carroll	1.50	.75	.45
134	Danny Walton	1.50	.75	.45
135	Dick Dietz	1.50	.75	.45
136	Steve Hargan	1.50	.75	.45
137	Art Shamsky	1.50	.75	.45
138	Joe Foy	1.50	.75	.45
139	Rich Nye	1.50	.75	.45
140	Reggie Jackson	50.00	25.00	12.50
141	Pirates Rookies (*Dave Cash*, Johnny Jeter)	1.50	.75	.45
142	Fritz Peterson	1.50	.75	.45
143	Phil Gagliano	1.50	.75	.45
144	Ray Culp	1.50	.75	.45
145	Rico Carty	1.50	.75	.45
146	Danny Murphy	1.50	.75	.45
147	Angel Hermoso	1.50	.75	.45
148	Earl Weaver	4.00	2.00	1.25
149	Billy Champion	1.50	.75	.45
150	Harmon Killebrew	10.00	5.00	3.00
151	Dave Roberts	1.50	.75	.45
152	Ike Brown	1.50	.75	.45
153	Gary Gentry	1.50	.75	.45
154	Senators Rookies (Jan Dukes, Jim Miles)	1.50	.75	.45
155	Denis Menke	1.50	.75	.45
156	Eddie Fisher	1.50	.75	.45
157	Manny Mota	1.50	.75	.45
158	Jerry McNertney	1.50	.75	.45
159	Tommy Helms	1.50	.75	.45
160	Phil Niekro	6.00	3.00	1.75
161	Richie Scheinblum	1.50	.75	.45
162	Jerry Johnson	1.50	.75	.45
163	Syd O'Brien	1.50	.75	.45
164	Ty Cline	1.50	.75	.45
165	Ed Kirkpatrick	1.50	.75	.45
166	Al Oliver	2.00	1.00	.60
167	Bill Burbach	1.50	.75	.45
168	Dave Watkins	1.50	.75	.45
169	Tom Hall	1.50	.75	.45
170	Billy Williams	8.00	4.00	2.50
171	Jim Nash	1.50	.75	.45
172	Braves Rookies (**Ralph Garr**, Garry Hill)	2.00	1.00	.60
173	Jim Hicks	1.50	.75	.45
174	Ted Sizemore	1.50	.75	.45
175	Dick Bosman	1.50	.75	.45
176	Jim Hart	1.50	.75	.45
177	Jim Northrup	1.50	.75	.45
178	Denny Lemaster	1.50	.75	.45
179	Ivan Murrell	1.50	.75	.45
180	Tommy John	2.00	1.00	.60
181	Sparky Anderson	6.00	3.00	1.75
182	Dick Hall	1.50	.75	.45
183	Jerry Grote	1.50	.75	.45
184	Ray Fosse	1.50	.75	.45
185	Don Mincher	1.50	.75	.45
186	Rick Joseph	1.50	.75	.45
187	Mike Hedlund	1.50	.75	.45
188	Manny Sanguillen	1.50	.75	.45
189	Yankees Rookies (*Dave McDonald, Thurman Munson*)	100.00	50.00	25.00
190	Joe Torre	6.00	3.00	1.75
191	Vicente Romo	1.50	.75	.45
192	Jim Qualls	1.50	.75	.45
193	Mike Wegener	1.50	.75	.45
194	Chuck Manuel	1.50	.75	.45
195	N.L.C.S. Game 1 (Seaver Wins Opener!)	10.00	5.00	3.00
196	N.L.C.S. Game 2 (Mets Show Muscle!)	6.00	3.00	1.75
197	N.L.C.S. Game 3 (Ryan Saves the Day!)	25.00	12.50	6.25
198	Mets Celebrate (We're Number One!)(Nolan Ryan)	15.00	7.50	4.50
199	A.L.C.S. Game 1 (Orioles Win A Squeaker!)	4.00	2.00	1.25
200	A.L.C.S. Game 2 (Powell Scores Winning Run!)	4.00	2.00	1.25
201	A.L.C.S. Game 3 (Birds Wrap It Up!)	3.00	1.50	.90
202	Oriole Celebrate (Sweep Twins In Three!)	3.00	1.50	.90
203	Rudy May	1.50	.75	.45
204	Len Gabrielson	1.50	.75	.45
205	Bert Campaneris	1.50	.75	.45
206	Clete Boyer	1.50	.75	.45
207	Tigers Rookies (Norman McRae, Bob Reed)	1.50	.75	.45
208	Fred Gladding	1.50	.75	.45
209	Ken Suarez	1.50	.75	.45
210	Juan Marichal	6.00	3.00	1.75
211	Ted Williams	20.00	10.00	5.00
212	Al Santorini	1.50	.75	.45
213	Andy Etchebarren	1.50	.75	.45
214	Ken Boswell	1.50	.75	.45
215	Reggie Smith	1.50	.75	.45
216	Chuck Hartenstein	1.50	.75	.45
217	Ron Hansen	1.50	.75	.45
218	Ron Stone	1.50	.75	.45
219	Jerry Kenney	1.50	.75	.45
220	Steve Carlton	10.00	5.00	3.00
221	Ron Brand	1.50	.75	.45
222	Jim Rooker	1.50	.75	.45
223	Nate Oliver	1.50	.75	.45
224	Steve Barber	1.50	.75	.45
225	Lee May	1.50	.75	.45
226	Ron Perranoski	1.50	.75	.45
227	Astros Rookies (**John Mayberry**, Bob Watkins)	1.50	.75	.45
228	Aurelio Rodriguez	1.50	.75	.45
229	Rich Robertson	1.50	.75	.45
230	Brooks Robinson	15.00	7.50	3.75
231	Luis Tiant	1.50	.75	.45
232	Bob Didier	1.50	.75	.45
233	Lew Krausse	1.50	.75	.45
234	Tommy Dean	1.50	.75	.45
235	Mike Epstein	1.50	.75	.45
236	Bob Veale	1.50	.75	.45
237	Russ Gibson	1.50	.75	.45
238	Jose Laboy	1.50	.75	.45
239	Ken Berry	1.50	.75	.45
240	Fergie Jenkins	6.00	3.00	1.75
241	Royals Rookies (Al Fitzmorris, Scott Northey)	1.50	.75	.45
242	Walter Alston	4.00	2.00	1.25
243	Joe Sparma	1.50	.75	.45
244a	3rd Series Check List (264-372) (Red bat on front.)	6.00	3.00	1.75
244b	3rd Series Check List (264-372) (Brown bat on front.)	6.00	3.00	1.75
245	Leo Cardenas	1.50	.75	.45
246	Jim McAndrew	1.50	.75	.45
247	Lou Klimchock	1.50	.75	.45
248	Jesus Alou	1.50	.75	.45
249	Bob Locker	1.50	.75	.45
250	Willie McCovey	10.00	5.00	3.00
251	Dick Schofield	1.50	.75	.45
252	Lowell Palmer	1.50	.75	.45
253	Ron Woods	1.50	.75	.45
254	Camilo Pascual	1.50	.75	.45
255	*Jim Spencer*	1.50	.75	.45
256	Vic Davalillo	1.50	.75	.45
257	Dennis Higgins	1.50	.75	.45
258	Paul Popovich	1.50	.75	.45
259	Tommie Reynolds	1.50	.75	.45
260	Claude Osteen	1.50	.75	.45
261	Curt Motton	1.50	.75	.45
262	Padres Rookies (Jerry Morales, Jim Williams)	1.50	.75	.45
263	Duane Josephson	1.50	.75	.45
264	Rich Hebner	1.50	.75	.45
265	Randy Hundley	1.50	.75	.45
266	Wally Bunker	1.50	.75	.45
267	Twins Rookies (Herman Hill, Paul Ratliff)	1.50	.75	.45
268	Claude Raymond	1.50	.75	.45
269	Cesar Gutierrez	1.50	.75	.45
270	Chris Short	1.50	.75	.45
271	Greg Goossen	1.50	.75	.45
272	Hector Torres	1.50	.75	.45
273	Ralph Houk	4.00	2.00	1.25
274	Gerry Arrigo	1.50	.75	.45
275	Duke Sims	1.50	.75	.45
276	Ron Hunt	1.50	.75	.45
277	Paul Doyle	1.50	.75	.45
278	Tommie Aaron	1.50	.75	.45
279	*Bill Lee*	1.50	.75	.45
280	Donn Clendenon	1.50	.75	.45
281	Casey Cox	1.50	.75	.45
282	Steve Huntz	1.50	.75	.45
283	Angel Bravo	1.50	.75	.45
284	Jack Baldschun	1.50	.75	.45
285	Paul Blair	1.50	.75	.45
286	Dodgers Rookies (**Bill Buckner**, Jack Jenkins)	6.00	3.00	1.75
287	Fred Talbot	1.50	.75	.45
288	Larry Hisle	1.50	.75	.45
289	Gene Brabender	1.50	.75	.45
290	Rod Carew	10.00	5.00	3.00
291	Leo Durocher	4.00	2.00	1.25
292	Eddie Leon	1.50	.75	.45
293	Bob Bailey	1.50	.75	.45
294	Jose Azcue	1.50	.75	.45
295	Cecil Upshaw	1.50	.75	.45
296	Woody Woodward	1.50	.75	.45
297	Curt Blefary	1.50	.75	.45
298	Ken Henderson	1.50	.75	.45
299	Buddy Bradford	1.50	.75	.45
300	Tom Seaver	25.00	12.50	7.50
301	Chico Salmon	1.50	.75	.45
302	Jeff James	1.50	.75	.45
303	Brant Alyea	1.50	.75	.45
304	*Bill Russell*	4.00	2.00	1.25
305	World Series Game 1 (Buford Belts Leadoff Homer!)	4.00	2.00	1.25
306	World Series Game 2 (Clendenon's HR Breaks Ice!)	4.00	2.00	1.25
307	World Series Game 3 (Agee's Catch Saves The Day!)	4.00	2.00	1.25
308	World Series Game 4 (Martin's Bunt Ends Deadlock!)	4.00	2.00	1.25
309	World Series Game 5 (Koosman Shuts The Door!)	4.00	2.00	1.25
310	World Series Celebration (Mets Whoop It Up!)	8.00	4.00	2.50
311	Dick Green	1.50	.75	.45
312	Mike Torrez	1.50	.75	.45
313	Mayo Smith	1.50	.75	.45
314	Bill McCool	1.50	.75	.45
315	Luis Aparicio	8.00	4.00	2.50
316	Skip Guinn	1.50	.75	.45
317	Red Sox Rookies (Luis Alvarado, Billy Conigliaro)	1.50	.75	.45
318	Willie Smith	1.50	.75	.45
319	Clayton Dalrymple	1.50	.75	.45
320	Jim Maloney	1.50	.75	.45
321	Lou Piniella	3.00	1.50	.90
322	Luke Walker	1.50	.75	.45
323	Wayne Comer	1.50	.75	.45
324	Tony Taylor	1.50	.75	.45
325	Dave Boswell	1.50	.75	.45
326	Bill Voss	1.50	.75	.45
327	Hal King	1.50	.75	.45
328	George Brunet	1.50	.75	.45
329	Chris Cannizzaro	1.50	.75	.45
330	Lou Brock	10.00	5.00	3.00
331	Chuck Dobson	1.50	.75	.45
332	Bobby Wine	1.50	.75	.45
333	Bobby Murcer	3.00	1.50	.90
334	Phil Regan	1.50	.75	.45
335	Bill Freehan	1.50	.75	.45
336	Del Unser	1.50	.75	.45
337	Mike McCormick	1.50	.75	.45
338	Paul Schaal	1.50	.75	.45
339	Johnny Edwards	1.50	.75	.45
340	Tony Conigliaro	4.00	2.00	1.25
341	Bill Sudakis	1.50	.75	.45
342	Wilbur Wood	1.50	.75	.45
343a	4th Series Check List (373-459) (Red bat on front.)	5.00	2.50	1.50
343b	4th Series Check List (373-459) (Brown bat on front.)	5.00	2.50	1.50
344	Marcelino Lopez	1.50	.75	.45
345	Al Ferrara	1.50	.75	.45
346	Red Schoendienst	4.00	2.00	1.25
347	Russ Snyder	1.50	.75	.45
348	Mets Rookies (Jesse Hudson, Mike Jorgensen)	1.50	.75	.45
349	Steve Hamilton	1.50	.75	.45
350	Roberto Clemente	60.00	30.00	15.00
351	Tom Murphy	1.50	.75	.45
352	Bob Barton	1.50	.75	.45
353	Stan Williams	1.50	.75	.45
354	Amos Otis	1.50	.75	.45
355	Doug Rader	1.50	.75	.45
356	Fred Lasher	1.50	.75	.45
357	Bob Burda	1.50	.75	.45
358	*Pedro Borbon*	1.50	.75	.45
359	Phil Roof	1.50	.75	.45
360	Curt Flood	2.00	1.00	.60
361	Ray Jarvis	1.50	.75	.45
362	Joe Hague	1.50	.75	.45
363	Tom Shopay	1.50	.75	.45
364	Dan McGinn	1.50	.75	.45
365	Zoilo Versalles	1.50	.75	.45
366	Barry Moore	1.50	.75	.45
367	Mike Lum	1.50	.75	.45
368	Ed Herrmann	1.50	.75	.45
369	Alan Foster	1.50	.75	.45
370	Tommy Harper	1.50	.75	.45
371	Rod Gaspar	1.50	.75	.45
372	Dave Giusti	1.50	.75	.45

#	Player			
373	Roy White	2.50	1.25	.75
374	Tommie Sisk	1.50	.75	.45
375	Johnny Callison	1.50	.75	.45
376	Lefty Phillips	1.50	.75	.45
377	Bill Butler	1.50	.75	.45
378	Jim Davenport	1.50	.75	.45
379	Tom Tischinski	1.50	.75	.45
380	Tony Perez	8.00	4.00	2.50
381	Athletics Rookies (Bobby Brooks, Mike Olivo)	1.50	.75	.45
382	Jack DiLauro	1.50	.75	.45
383	Mickey Stanley	1.50	.75	.45
384	Gary Neibauer	1.50	.75	.45
385	George Scott	1.50	.75	.45
386	Bill Dillman	1.50	.75	.45
387	Baltimore Orioles Team	3.00	1.50	.90
388	Byron Browne	1.50	.75	.45
389	Jim Shellenback	1.50	.75	.45
390	Willie Davis	1.50	.75	.45
391	Larry Brown	1.50	.75	.45
392	Walt Hriniak	1.50	.75	.45
393	John Gelnar	1.50	.75	.45
394	Gil Hodges	6.00	3.00	1.75
395	Walt Williams	1.50	.75	.45
396	Steve Blass	1.50	.75	.45
397	Roger Repoz	1.50	.75	.45
398	Bill Stoneman	1.50	.75	.45
399	New York Yankees Team	8.00	4.00	2.50
400	Denny McLain	1.50	.70	.45
401	Giants Rookies (John Harrell, Bernie Williams)	1.50	.75	.45
402	Ellie Rodriguez	1.50	.75	.45
403	Jim Bunning	6.00	3.00	1.75
404	Rich Reese	1.50	.75	.45
405	Bill Hands	1.50	.75	.45
406	Mike Andrews	1.50	.75	.45
407	Bob Watson	1.50	.75	.45
408	Paul Lindblad	1.50	.75	.45
409	Bob Tolan	1.50	.75	.45
410	Boog Powell	5.00	2.50	1.50
411	Los Angeles Dodgers Team	6.00	3.00	1.75
412	Larry Burchart	1.50	.75	.45
413	Sonny Jackson	1.50	.75	.45
414	Paul Edmondson	1.50	.75	.45
415	Julian Javier	1.50	.75	.45
416	Joe Verbanic	1.50	.75	.45
417	John Bateman	1.50	.75	.45
418	John Donaldson	1.50	.75	.45
419	Ron Taylor	1.50	.75	.45
420	Ken McMullen	1.50	.75	.45
421	Pat Dobson	1.50	.75	.45
422	Kansas City Royals Team	3.00	1.50	.90
423	Jerry May	1.50	.75	.45
424	Mike Kilkenny	1.50	.75	.45
425	Bobby Bonds	3.00	1.50	.90
426	Bill Rigney	1.50	.75	.45
427	Fred Norman	1.50	.75	.45
428	Don Buford	1.50	.75	.45
429	Cubs Rookies (Randy Bobb, Jim Cosman)	1.50	.75	.45
430	A. Messersmith	1.50	.75	.45
431	Ron Swoboda	1.50	.75	.45
432a	5th Series Check List (460-546) ("Baseball" on front in yellow.)	4.00	2.00	1.25
432b	5th Series Check List (460-546) ("Baseball" on front in white.)	4.00	2.00	1.25
433	Ron Bryant	1.50	.75	.45
434	Felipe Alou	2.50	1.25	.75
435	Nelson Briles	1.50	.75	.45
436	Philadelphia Phillies Team	3.00	1.50	.90
437	Danny Cater	1.50	.75	.45
438	Pat Jarvis	1.50	.75	.45
439	Lee Maye	1.50	.75	.45
440	Bill Mazeroski	8.00	4.00	2.50
441	John O'Donoghue	1.50	.75	.45
442	Gene Mauch	1.50	.75	.45
443	Al Jackson	1.50	.75	.45
444	White Sox Rookies (Bill Farmer, John Matias)	1.50	.75	.45
445	Vada Pinson	2.00	1.00	.60
446	*Billy Grabarkewitz*	1.50	.75	.45
447	Lee Stange	1.50	.75	.45
448	Houston Astros Team	3.00	1.50	.90
449	Jim Palmer	8.00	4.00	2.50
450	Willie McCovey (All-Star)	6.00	3.00	1.75
451	Boog Powell (All-Star)	2.00	1.00	.60
452	Felix Millan (All-Star)	1.50	.75	.45
453	Rod Carew (All-Star)	6.00	3.00	1.75
454	Ron Santo (All-Star)	3.00	1.50	.90
455	Brooks Robinson (All-Star)	6.00	3.00	1.75
456	Don Kessinger (All-Star)	1.50	.75	.45
457	Rico Petrocelli (All-Star)	1.50	.75	.45
458	Pete Rose (All-Star)	15.00	7.50	3.75
459	Reggie Jackson (All-Star)	10.00	5.00	3.00
460	Matty Alou (All-Star)	1.50	.75	.45
461	Carl Yastrzemski (All-Star)	10.00	5.00	3.00
462	Hank Aaron (All-Star)	25.00	12.50	7.50
463	Frank Robinson (All-Star)	8.00	4.00	2.50
464	Johnny Bench (All-Star)	15.00	7.50	3.75
465	Bill Freehan (All-Star)	1.50	.75	.45
466	Juan Marichal (All-Star)	6.00	3.00	1.75
467	Denny McLain (All-Star)	1.50	.70	.45
468	Jerry Koosman (All-Star)	1.50	.75	.45
469	Sam McDowell (All-Star)	1.50	.75	.45
470	Willie Stargell	10.00	5.00	3.00
471	Chris Zachary	1.50	.75	.45
472	Atlanta Braves Team	3.00	1.50	.90
473	Don Bryant	1.50	.75	.45
474	Dick Kelley	1.50	.75	.45
475	Dick McAuliffe	1.50	.75	.45
476	Don Shaw	1.50	.75	.45
477	Orioles Rookies (Roger Freed, Al Severinsen)	1.50	.75	.45
478	Bob Heise	1.50	.75	.45
479	Dick Woodson	1.50	.75	.45
480	Glenn Beckert	1.50	.75	.45

#	Player			
481	Jose Tartabull	1.50	.75	.45
482	Tom Hilgendorf	1.50	.75	.45
483	Gail Hopkins	1.50	.75	.45
484	Gary Nolan	1.50	.75	.45
485	Jay Johnstone	1.50	.75	.45
486	Terry Harmon	1.50	.75	.45
487	Cisco Carlos	1.50	.75	.45
488	J.C. Martin	1.50	.75	.45
489	Eddie Kasko	1.50	.75	.45
490	Bill Singer	1.50	.75	.45
491	Graig Nettles	3.00	2.00	.90
492	Astros Rookies (Keith Lampard, Scipio Spinks)	1.50	.75	.45
493	Lindy McDaniel	1.50	.75	.45
494	Larry Stahl	1.50	.75	.45
495	Dave Morehead	1.50	.75	.45
496	Steve Whitaker	1.50	.75	.45
497	Eddie Watt	1.50	.75	.45
498	Al Weis	1.50	.75	.45
499	Skip Lockwood	1.50	.75	.45
500	Hank Aaron	50.00	25.00	12.50
501	Chicago White Sox Team	3.00	1.50	.90
502	Rollie Fingers	8.00	4.00	2.50
503	Dal Maxvill	1.50	.75	.45
504	Don Pavletich	1.50	.75	.45
505	Ken Holtzman	1.50	.75	.45
506	Ed Stroud	1.50	.75	.45
507	Pat Corrales	1.50	.75	.45
508	Joe Niekro	1.50	.75	.45
509	Montreal Expos Team	3.00	1.50	.90
510	Tony Oliva	3.50	1.75	1.00
511	Joe Hoerner	1.50	.75	.45
512	Billy Harris	1.50	.75	.45
513	Preston Gomez	1.50	.75	.45
514	Steve Hovley	1.50	.75	.45
515	Don Wilson	1.50	.75	.45
516	Yankees Rookies (John Ellis, Jim Lyttle)	1.50	.75	.45
517	Joe Gibbon	1.50	.75	.45
518	Bill Melton	1.50	.75	.45
519	Don McMahon	1.50	.75	.45
520	Willie Horton	1.50	.75	.45
521	Cal Koonce	1.50	.75	.45
522	California Angels Team	3.00	1.50	.90
523	Jose Pena	1.50	.75	.45
524	Alvin Dark	1.50	.75	.45
525	Jerry Adair	1.50	.75	.45
526	Ron Herbel	1.50	.75	.45
527	Don Bosch	1.50	.75	.45
528	Elrod Hendricks	1.50	.75	.45
529	Bob Aspromonte	1.50	.75	.45
530	Bob Gibson	15.00	7.50	3.75
531	Ron Clark	1.50	.75	.45
532	Danny Murtaugh	1.50	.75	.45
533	Buzz Stephen	1.50	.75	.45
534	Minnesota Twins Team	3.00	1.50	.90
535	Andy Kosco	1.50	.75	.45
536	Mike Kekich	1.50	.75	.45
537	Joe Morgan	10.00	5.00	3.00
538	Bob Humphreys	1.50	.75	.45
539	Phillies Rookies (**Larry Bowa**, Dennis Doyle)	6.00	3.00	1.75
540	Gary Peters	1.50	.75	.45
541	Bill Heath	1.50	.75	.45
542a	6th Series Check List (547-633) (Gray bat on front.)	5.00	2.50	1.50
542b	6th Series Check List (547-633) (Brown bat on front.)	5.00	2.50	1.50
543	Clyde Wright	1.50	.75	.45
544	Cincinnati Reds Team	5.00	2.50	1.50
545	Ken Harrelson	1.50	.75	.45
546	Ron Reed	1.50	.75	.45
547	Rick Monday	4.00	2.00	1.25
548	Howie Reed	3.00	1.50	.90
549	St. Louis Cardinals Team	6.00	3.00	1.75
550	Frank Howard	5.00	2.50	1.50
551	Dock Ellis	4.00	2.00	1.25
552	Royals Rookies (Don O'Riley, Dennis Paepke, Fred Rico)	4.00	2.00	1.25
553	Jim Lefebvre	4.00	2.00	1.25
554	Tom Timmermann	4.00	2.00	1.25
555	Orlando Cepeda	15.00	7.50	3.75
556	Dave Bristol	4.00	2.00	1.25
557	Ed Kranepool	4.00	2.00	1.25
558	Vern Fuller	4.00	2.00	1.25
559	Tommy Davis	4.00	2.00	1.25
560	Gaylord Perry	8.00	4.00	2.50
561	Tom McCraw	4.00	2.00	1.25
562	Ted Abernathy	4.00	2.00	1.25
563	Boston Red Sox Team	8.00	4.00	2.50
564	Johnny Briggs	4.00	2.00	1.25
565	Jim Hunter	8.00	4.00	2.50
566	Gene Alley	4.00	2.00	1.25
567	Bob Oliver	4.00	2.00	1.25
568	Stan Bahnsen	4.00	2.00	1.25
569	Cookie Rojas	4.00	2.00	1.25
570	Jim Fregosi	5.00	2.50	1.50
571	Jim Brewer	4.00	2.00	1.25
572	Frank Quilici	4.00	2.00	1.25
573	Padres Rookies (Mike Corkins, Rafael Robles, Ron Slocum)	4.00	2.00	1.25
574	Bobby Bolin	4.00	2.00	1.25
575	Cleon Jones	4.00	2.00	1.25
576	Milt Pappas	4.00	2.00	1.25
577	Bernie Allen	4.00	2.00	1.25
578	Tom Griffin	4.00	2.00	1.25
579	Detroit Tigers Team	8.00	4.00	2.50
580	Pete Rose	50.00	25.00	15.00
581	Tom Satriano	4.00	2.00	1.25
582	Mike Paul	4.00	2.00	1.25
583	Hal Lanier	4.00	2.00	1.25
584	Al Downing	5.00	2.50	1.50
585	Rusty Staub	6.00	3.00	1.75
586	Rickey Clark	4.00	2.00	1.25
587	Jose Arcia	4.00	2.00	1.25

#	Player			
588a	7th Series Check List (634-720) (666 is Adolpho Phillips)	6.00	3.00	1.75
588b	7th Series Check List (634-720) (666 is Adolfo Phillips)	6.00	3.00	1.75
589	Joe Keough	4.00	2.00	1.25
590	Mike Cuellar	4.00	2.00	1.25
591	Mike Ryan	4.00	2.00	1.25
592	Daryl Patterson	4.00	2.00	1.25
593	Chicago Cubs Team	8.00	4.00	2.50
594	Jake Gibbs	4.00	2.00	1.25
595	Maury Wills	4.00	2.00	1.25
596	Mike Hershberger	4.00	2.00	1.25
597	Sonny Siebert	4.00	2.00	1.25
598	Joe Pepitone	5.00	2.50	1.50
599	Senators Rookies (Gene Martin, Dick Stelmaszek, Dick Such)	4.00	2.00	1.25
600	Willie Mays	80.00	40.00	20.00
601	Pete Richert	4.00	2.00	1.25
602	Ted Savage	4.00	2.00	1.25
603	Ray Oyler	4.00	2.00	1.25
604	Clarence Gaston	6.00	3.00	1.75
605	Rick Wise	4.00	2.00	1.25
606	Chico Ruiz	4.00	2.00	1.25
607	Gary Waslewski	4.00	2.00	1.25
608	Pittsburgh Pirates Team	8.00	4.00	2.50
609	*Buck Martinez*	6.00	3.00	1.75
610	Jerry Koosman	6.00	3.00	1.75
611	Norm Cash	6.00	3.00	1.75
612	Jim Hickman	4.00	2.00	1.25
613	Dave Baldwin	4.00	2.00	1.25
614	Mike Shannon	4.00	2.00	1.25
615	Mark Belanger	4.00	2.00	1.25
616	Jim Merritt	4.00	2.00	1.25
617	Jim French	4.00	2.00	1.25
618	Billy Wynne	4.00	2.00	1.25
619	Norm Miller	4.00	2.00	1.25
620	Jim Perry	4.00	2.00	1.25
621	Braves Rookies (**Darrell Evans**, Rick Kester, Mike McQueen)	10.00	5.00	3.00
622	Don Sutton	8.00	4.00	2.50
623	Horace Clarke	4.00	2.00	1.25
624	Clyde King	4.00	2.00	1.25
625	Dean Chance	4.00	2.00	1.25
626	Dave Ricketts	4.00	2.00	1.25
627	Gary Wagner	4.00	2.00	1.25
628	Wayne Garrett	4.00	2.00	1.25
629	Merv Rettenmund	4.00	2.00	1.25
630	Ernie Banks	50.00	25.00	12.50
631	Oakland Athletics Team	8.00	4.00	2.50
632	Gary Sutherland	4.00	2.00	1.25
633	Roger Nelson	4.00	2.00	1.25
634	Bud Harrelson	8.00	4.00	2.50
635	Bob Allison	8.00	4.00	2.50
636	Jim Stewart	8.00	4.00	2.50
637	Cleveland Indians Team	12.00	6.00	3.50
638	Frank Bertaina	8.00	4.00	2.50
639	Dave Campbell	8.00	4.00	2.50
640	Al Kaline	50.00	25.00	12.50
641	Al McBean	8.00	4.00	2.50
642	Angels Rookies (Greg Garrett, Gordon Lund, Jarvis Tatum)	8.00	4.00	2.50
643	Jose Pagan	8.00	4.00	2.50
644	Gerry Nyman	8.00	4.00	2.50
645	Don Money	8.00	4.00	2.50
646	Jim Britton	8.00	4.00	2.50
647	Tom Matchick	8.00	4.00	2.50
648	Larry Haney	8.00	4.00	2.50
649	Jimmie Hall	8.00	4.00	2.50
650	Sam McDowell	10.00	5.00	3.00
651	Jim Gosger	8.00	4.00	2.50
652	Rich Rollins	10.00	5.00	3.00
653	Moe Drabowsky	8.00	4.00	2.50
654	N.L. Rookies (Boots Day, **Oscar Gamble**, Angel Mangual)	10.00	5.00	3.00
655	John Roseboro	8.00	4.00	2.50
656	Jim Hardin	8.00	4.00	2.50
657	San Diego Padres Team	15.00	7.50	4.50
658	Ken Tatum	8.00	4.00	2.50
659	Pete Ward	8.00	4.00	2.50
660	Johnny Bench	75.00	37.50	18.75
661	Jerry Robertson	8.00	4.00	2.50
662	Frank Lucchesi	8.00	4.00	2.50
663	Tito Francona	8.00	4.00	2.50
664	Bob Robertson	8.00	4.00	2.50
665	Jim Lonborg	8.00	4.00	2.50
666	Adolfo Phillips	8.00	4.00	2.50
667	Bob Meyer	8.00	4.00	2.50
668	Bob Tillman	8.00	4.00	2.50
669	White Sox Rookies (Bart Johnson, Dan Lazar, Mickey Scott)	8.00	4.00	2.50
670	Ron Santo	20.00	10.00	5.00
671	Jim Campanis	10.00	5.00	3.00
672	Leon McFadden	8.00	4.00	2.50
673	Ted Uhlaender	8.00	4.00	2.50
674	Dave Leonhard	8.00	4.00	2.50
675	Jose Cardenal	10.00	5.00	3.00
676	Washington Senators Team	15.00	7.50	4.50
677	Woodie Fryman	8.00	4.00	2.50
678	Dave Duncan	15.00	7.50	4.50
679	Ray Sadecki	8.00	4.00	2.50
680	Rico Petrocelli	10.00	5.00	3.00
681	Bob Garibaldi	8.00	4.00	2.50
682	Dalton Jones	8.00	4.00	2.50
683	Reds Rookies (Vern Geishert, Hal McRae, Wayne Simpson)	10.00	5.00	3.00
684	Jack Fisher	8.00	4.00	2.50
685	Tom Haller	8.00	4.00	2.50
686	Jackie Hernandez	8.00	4.00	2.50
687	Bob Priddy	8.00	4.00	2.50
688	Ted Kubiak	8.00	4.00	2.50
689	Frank Tepedino	8.00	4.00	2.50
690	Ron Fairly	8.00	4.00	2.50

		NM	EX	VG
691	Joe Grzenda	8.00	4.00	2.50
692	Duffy Dyer	8.00	4.00	2.50
693	Bob Johnson	8.00	4.00	2.50
694	Gary Ross	8.00	4.00	2.50
695	Bobby Knoop	8.00	4.00	2.50
696	San Francisco Giants Team	12.00	6.00	3.00
697	Jim Hannan	8.00	4.00	2.50
698	Tom Tresh	10.00	5.00	3.00
699	Hank Aguirre	8.00	4.00	2.50
700	Frank Robinson	50.00	25.00	12.50
701	Jack Billingham	8.00	4.00	2.50
702	A.L. Rookies (Bob Johnson, Ron Klimkowski, Bill Zepp)	8.00	4.00	2.50
703	Lou Marone	8.00	4.00	2.50
704	Frank Baker	8.00	4.00	2.50
705	Tony Cloninger	8.00	4.00	2.50
706	John McNamara	8.00	4.00	2.50
707	Kevin Collins	8.00	4.00	2.50
708	Jose Santiago	8.00	4.00	2.50
709	Mike Fiore	8.00	4.00	2.50
710	Felix Millan	8.00	4.00	2.50
711	Ed Brinkman	8.00	4.00	2.50
712	Nolan Ryan	225.00	112.50	56.25
713	Seattle Pilots Team	20.00	10.00	6.00
714	Al Spangler	8.00	4.00	2.50
715	Mickey Lolich	8.00	4.00	2.50
716	Cards Rookies (Sal Campisi, **Reggie Cleveland**, Santiago Guzman)	10.00	5.00	3.00
717	Tom Phoebus	8.00	4.00	2.50
718	Ed Spiezio	8.00	4.00	2.50
719	Jim Roland	8.00	4.00	2.50
720	Rick Reichardt	12.00	5.00	2.50

1970 Topps Candy Lids

The 1970 Topps Candy Lids are a test issue that was utilized again in 1973. The set is made up of 24 lids that measure 1-7/8" in diameter and were the tops of small 1.1 oz. tubs of "Baseball Stars Candy." Unlike the 1973 versions, the 1970 lids have no border surrounding the full-color photos. Frank Howard, Tom Seaver and Carl Yastrzemski photos are found on the top (outside) of the candy lid.

		NM	EX	VG
Complete Set (24):		2,800	1,400	840.00
Common Player:		40.00	20.00	12.00
(1)	Hank Aaron	350.00	175.00	105.00
(2)	Rich Allen	75.00	37.00	22.00
(3)	Luis Aparicio	140.00	70.00	42.00
(4)	Johnny Bench	225.00	110.00	67.00
(5)	Ollie Brown	40.00	20.00	12.00
(6)	Willie Davis	40.00	20.00	12.00
(7)	Jim Fregosi	40.00	20.00	12.00
(8)	Mike Hegan	40.00	20.00	12.00
(9)	Frank Howard	60.00	30.00	18.00
(10)	Reggie Jackson	275.00	135.00	82.00
(11)	Fergie Jenkins	130.00	65.00	39.00
(12)	Harmon Killebrew	175.00	87.00	52.00
(13)	Juan Marichal	140.00	70.00	42.00
(14)	Bill Mazeroski	140.00	70.00	42.00
(15)	Tim McCarver	60.00	30.00	18.00
(16)	Sam McDowell	40.00	20.00	12.00
(17)	Denny McLain	60.00	30.00	18.00
(18)	Lou Piniella	45.00	22.00	13.50
(19)	Frank Robinson	175.00	87.00	52.00
(20)	Tom Seaver	200.00	100.00	60.00
(21)	Rusty Staub	60.00	30.00	18.00
(22)	Mel Stottlemyre	40.00	20.00	12.00
(23)	Jim Wynn	40.00	20.00	12.00
(24)	Carl Yastrzemski	225.00	110.00	67.00

1970 Topps Cloth Stickers

The earliest and rarest of the Topps cloth sticker test issues, only 15 subjects are known, and only a single specimen apiece is known for many of them. In the same 2-1/2" x 3-1/2" size, and with the same design as the 1970 Topps

baseball cards, the stickers are blank-backed. The stickers of Denny Lemaster, Dennis Higgins and Rich Nye use photos that are different from their '70 Topps cards. It is quite likely that the checklist presented here is incomplete. The stickers are unnumbered and are checklisted alphabetically.

		NM	EX	VG
Common Player:		1,750	875.00	525.00
(1)	A.L. Playoff Game 2 (Boog Powell)	1,900	950.00	570.00
(2)	Bill Burbach	1,750	875.00	525.00
(3)	Gary Gentry	1,750	875.00	525.00
(4)	Tom Hall	1,750	875.00	525.00
(5)	Chuck Hartenstein	1,750	875.00	525.00
(6)	Dennis Higgins	1,750	875.00	525.00
(7)	Jose Laboy	1,750	875.00	525.00
(8)	Denny Lemaster	1,750	875.00	525.00
(9)	Juan Marichal	2,200	1,100	660.00
(10)	Willie McCovey	1,750	875.00	525.00
(11)	Jerry McNertney	1,750	875.00	525.00
(12)	Curt Motton	1,750	875.00	525.00
(13)	Ivan Murrell	1,750	875.00	525.00
(14)	N.L. Playoff Game 1 (Tom Seaver)	1,750	875.00	525.00
(15)	N.L. Playoff Game 3 (Nolan Ryan)	3,000	1,500	900.00
(16)	Phil Niekro	2,100	1,050	630.00
(17)	Jim Northrup	1,750	875.00	525.00
(18)	Rich Nye	1,750	875.00	525.00
(19)	Ron Perranoski	1,750	875.00	525.00
(20)	Al Santorini	1,750	875.00	525.00

1970 Topps Posters

Helping to ease a price increase, Topps included extremely fragile 8-11/16" x 9-5/8" posters in packs of regular cards. The posters feature color portraits and a smaller black and white "action" pose as well as the player's name, team and position at the top. Although there are Hall of Famers in the 24-poster set, all the top names are not represented. Folds from original packaging are not considered in grading unless they split the paper.

		NM	EX	VG
Complete Set (24):		60.00	30.00	18.00
Common Player:		3.00	1.50	.90
1	Joe Horlen	3.00	1.50	.90
2	Phil Niekro	6.00	3.00	1.75
3	Willie Davis	3.00	1.50	.90
4	Lou Brock	7.00	3.50	2.00
5	Ron Santo	4.00	2.00	1.25
6	Ken Harrelson	3.00	1.50	.90
7	Willie McCovey	7.00	3.50	2.00
8	Rick Wise	3.00	1.50	.90
9	Andy Messersmith	3.00	1.50	.90
10	Ron Fairly	3.00	1.50	.90
11	Johnny Bench	10.00	5.00	3.00
12	Frank Robinson	10.00	5.00	3.00
13	Tommie Agee	3.00	1.50	.90
14	Roy White	3.00	1.50	.90
15	Larry Dierker	3.00	1.50	.90
16	Rod Carew	9.00	4.50	2.75
17	Don Mincher	3.00	1.50	.90
18	Ollie Brown	3.00	1.50	.90
19	Ed Kirkpatrick	3.00	1.50	.90
20	Reggie Smith	3.00	1.50	.90
21	Roberto Clemente	25.00	12.50	7.50
22	Frank Howard	3.00	1.50	.90
23	Bert Campaneris	3.00	1.50	.90
24	Denny McLain	3.00	1.50	.90

1970 Topps Scratch-Offs

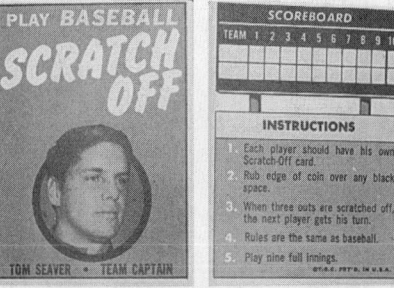

Not having given up on the idea of a game which could be played with baseball cards, Topps provided a new game - the baseball scratch-off - in 1970. Unfolded, cards measure 3-3/8" x 5", and reveal a baseball game played by rubbing the black ink off playing squares to determine the "action." Fronts have

a player picture as "captain," while backs have instructions and a scoreboard. Inserts with white centers are from 1970 while those with red centers are from 1971.

		NM	EX	VG
Complete Set (24):		60.00	30.00	18.00
Common Player:		1.50	.75	.45
(1)	Hank Aaron	12.00	6.00	3.50
(2)	Rich Allen	2.50	1.25	.70
(3)	Luis Aparicio	3.50	1.75	1.00
(4)	Sal Bando	1.50	.75	.45
(5)	Glenn Beckert	1.50	.75	.45
(6)	Dick Bosman	1.50	.75	.45
(7)	Nate Colbert	1.50	.75	.45
(8)	Mike Hegan	1.50	.75	.45
(9)	Mack Jones	1.50	.75	.45
(10)	Al Kaline	4.50	2.25	1.25
(11)	Harmon Killebrew	4.50	2.25	1.25
(12)	Juan Marichal	3.50	1.75	1.00
(13)	Tim McCarver	2.50	1.25	.70
(14)	Sam McDowell	1.50	.75	.45
(15)	Claude Osteen	1.50	.75	.45
(16)	Tony Perez	3.50	1.75	1.00
(17)	Lou Piniella	1.50	.75	.45
(18)	Boog Powell	2.50	1.25	.70
(19)	Tom Seaver	4.50	2.25	1.25
(20)	Jim Spencer	1.50	.75	.45
(21)	Willie Stargell	3.50	1.75	1.00
(22)	Mel Stottlemyre	1.50	.75	.45
(23)	Jim Wynn	1.50	.75	.45
(24)	Carl Yastrzemski	6.00	3.00	1.75

1970 Topps Story Booklets

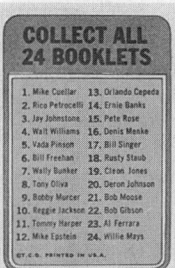

Measuring 2-1/2" x 3-7/16", the Topps Story Booklet was a 1970 regular pack insert. The booklet feature a photo, title and booklet number on the "cover." Inside are six pages of comic book story. The backs give a checklist of other available booklets. Not every star had a booklet as the set is only 24 in number.

		NM	EX	VG
Complete Set (24):		65.00	32.50	20.00
Common Player:		1.50	.75	.45
1	Mike Cuellar	1.50	.75	.45
2	Rico Petrocelli	1.50	.75	.45
3	Jay Johnstone	1.50	.75	.45
4	Walt Williams	1.50	.75	.45
5	Vada Pinson	2.25	1.25	.70
6	Bill Freehan	1.50	.75	.45
7	Wally Bunker	1.50	.75	.45
8	Tony Oliva	2.25	1.25	.70
9	Bobby Murcer	2.00	1.00	.60
10	Reggie Jackson	9.00	4.50	2.75
11	Tommy Harper	1.50	.75	.45
12	Mike Epstein	1.50	.75	.45
13	Orlando Cepeda	4.00	2.00	1.25
14	Ernie Banks	7.00	3.50	2.00
15	Pete Rose	10.00	5.00	3.00
16	Denis Menke	1.50	.75	.45
17	Bill Singer	1.50	.75	.45
18	Rusty Staub	2.00	1.00	.60
19	Cleon Jones	1.50	.75	.45
20	Deron Johnson	1.50	.75	.45
21	Bob Moose	1.50	.75	.45
22	Bob Gibson	5.00	2.50	1.50
23	Al Ferrara	1.50	.75	.45
24	Willie Mays	10.00	5.00	3.00

1970 Topps Super

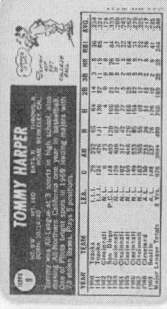

Representing a refinement of the concept begun in 1969, the 1970 Topps Supers had a new 3-1/8" x 5-1/4" size. Printed on thick stock with rounded corners, card fronts feature a borderless color photograph and facsimile autograph. Backs are an enlarged version of the player's regular 1970 Topps card. Probably due to the press sheet configuration, eight of the 42 cards were short-printed. The most elusive is card #38 (Boog Powell). The set was more widely produced than was the case in 1969. Square-cornered proofs, either with blank or printed backs, are known, valued from 1X-2X the regular-card price.

		NM	EX	VG
	Complete Set (42):	250.00	125.00	75.00
	Common Player:	4.00	2.00	1.25
	Unopened Pack:	95.00	.00	.00
	Proofs: 1-2X			
1	Claude Osteen (SP)	10.00	5.00	3.00
2	Sal Bando (SP)	10.00	5.00	3.00
3	Luis Aparicio	9.00	4.50	2.75
4	Harmon Killebrew	15.00	7.50	4.50
5	Tom Seaver (SP)	25.00	12.50	7.50
6	Larry Dierker	4.00	2.00	1.25
7	Bill Freehan	4.00	2.00	1.25
8	Johnny Bench	20.00	10.00	6.00
9	Tommy Harper	4.00	2.00	1.25
10	Sam McDowell	4.00	2.00	1.25
11	Lou Brock	12.00	6.00	3.50
12	Roberto Clemente	40.00	20.00	12.00
13	Willie McCovey	12.00	6.00	3.50
14	Rico Petrocelli	4.00	2.00	1.25
15	Phil Niekro	9.00	4.50	2.75
16	Frank Howard	4.00	2.00	1.25
17	Denny McLain	4.00	2.00	1.25
18	Willie Mays	35.00	17.50	10.00
19	Willie Stargell	12.00	6.00	3.50
20	Joe Horlen	4.00	2.00	1.25
21	Ron Santo	6.00	3.00	1.75
22	Dick Bosman	4.00	2.00	1.25
23	Tim McCarver	5.00	2.50	1.50
24	Henry Aaron	35.00	17.50	10.00
25	Andy Messersmith	4.00	2.00	1.25
26	Tony Oliva	5.00	2.50	1.50
27	Mel Stottlemyre	4.00	2.00	1.25
28	Reggie Jackson	30.00	15.00	9.00
29	Carl Yastrzemski	20.00	10.00	6.00
30	James Fregosi	4.00	2.00	1.25
31	Vada Pinson	5.00	2.50	1.50
32	Lou Piniella	4.00	2.00	1.25
33	Robert Gibson	10.00	5.00	3.00
34	Pete Rose	35.00	17.50	10.00
35	Jim Wynn	4.00	2.00	1.25
36	Ollie Brown (SP)	10.00	5.00	3.00
37	Frank Robinson (SP)	35.00	17.50	10.00
38	Boog Powell (SP)	60.00	30.00	18.00
39	Willie Davis (SP)	10.00	5.00	3.00
40	Billy Williams (SP)	20.00	10.00	6.00
41	Rusty Staub	5.00	2.50	1.50
42	Tommie Agee	4.00	2.00	1.25

1971 Topps

In 1971, Topps again increased the size of its set to 752 cards. These 2-1/2" x 3-1/2" cards feature a large color photo with a thin white frame. Above the picture, in the card's overall black border, is the player's name, team and position. A facsimile autograph completes the front. Backs feature a major change as a black-and-white "snapshot" of the player appears. Abbreviated statistics, a line giving the player's first pro and major league games and a short biography complete the back. Specialty cards in this issue are limited. There are statistical leaders as well as World Series and playoff highlights. High-number cards #644-752 are scarce, with about half of the cards being short-printed.

		NM	EX	VG
	Complete Set (752):	3,000	1,500	900.00
	Common Player (1-523):	2.00	1.00	.60
	Common Player (524-643):	4.00	2.00	1.00
	Common Player (644-752):	6.00	3.00	1.75
1	World Champions (Orioles Team)	15.00	7.50	3.75
2	Dock Ellis	2.00	1.00	.60
3	Dick McAuliffe	2.00	1.00	.60
4	Vic Davalillo	2.00	1.00	.60
5	Thurman Munson	125.00	62.50	31.25
6	Ed Spiezio	2.00	1.00	.60
7	Jim Holt	2.00	1.00	.60
8	Mike McQueen	2.00	1.00	.60
9	George Scott	2.00	1.00	.60
10	Claude Osteen	2.00	1.00	.60
11	*Elliott Maddox*	2.00	1.00	.60
12	Johnny Callison	2.00	1.00	.60
13	White Sox Rookies (Charlie Brinkman, Dick Moloney)	2.00	1.00	.60
14	*Dave Concepcion*	15.00	7.50	4.50
15	Andy Messersmith	2.00	1.00	.60
16	*Ken Singleton*	4.00	2.00	1.25
17	Billy Sorrell	2.00	1.00	.60
18	Norm Miller	2.00	1.00	.60
19	Skip Pitlock	2.00	1.00	.60
20	Reggie Jackson	50.00	25.00	15.00
21	Dan McGinn	2.00	1.00	.60
22	Phil Roof	2.00	1.00	.60
23	Oscar Gamble	2.00	1.00	.60
24	Rich Hand	2.00	1.00	.60
25	Clarence Gaston	2.00	1.00	.60
26	*Bert Blyleven*	20.00	10.00	6.00
27	Pirates Rookies (Fred Cambria, Gene Clines)	2.00	1.00	.60
28	Ron Klimkowski	2.00	1.00	.60
29	Don Buford	2.00	1.00	.60
30	Phil Niekro	8.00	4.00	2.50
31	Eddie Kasko	2.00	1.00	.60
32	Jerry DaVanon	2.00	1.00	.60
33	Del Unser	2.00	1.00	.60
34	Sandy Vance	2.00	1.00	.60
35	Lou Piniella	4.00	2.00	1.25
36	Dean Chance	2.00	1.00	.60
37	Rich McKinney	2.00	1.00	.60
38	*Jim Colborn*	2.00	1.00	.60
39	Tigers Rookies (*Gene Lamont, Lerrin LaGrow*)	2.00	1.00	.60
40	Lee May	2.00	1.00	.60
41	Rick Austin	2.00	1.00	.60
42a	Boots Day (Stadium lights behind ear.)	8.00	4.00	2.50
42b	Boots Day (No stadium lights.)	8.00	4.00	2.50
43	Steve Kealey	2.00	1.00	.60
44	Johnny Edwards	2.00	1.00	.60
45	Jim Hunter	8.00	4.00	2.50
46	Dave Campbell	2.00	1.00	.60
47	Johnny Jeter	2.00	1.00	.60
48	Dave Baldwin	2.00	1.00	.60
49	Don Money	2.00	1.00	.60
50	Willie McCovey	10.00	5.00	3.00
51	Steve Kline	2.00	1.00	.60
52	Braves Rookies (*Oscar Brown, Earl Williams*)	2.00	1.00	.60
53	Paul Blair	2.00	1.00	.60
54	1st Series Checklist (1-132)	5.00	2.50	1.50
55	Steve Carlton	20.00	10.00	6.00
56	Duane Josephson	2.00	1.00	.60
57	Von Joshua	2.00	1.00	.60
58	Bill Lee	2.00	1.00	.60
59	Gene Mauch	2.00	1.00	.60
60	Dick Bosman	2.00	1.00	.60
61	A.L. Batting Leaders (Alex Johnson, Tony Oliva, Carl Yastrzemski)	8.00	4.00	2.50
62	N.L. Batting Leaders (Rico Carty, Manny Sanguillen, Joe Torre)	6.00	3.00	1.75
63	A.L. RBI Leaders (Tony Conigliaro, Frank Howard, Boog Powell)	6.00	3.00	1.75
64	N.L. RBI Leaders (Johnny Bench, Tony Perez, Billy Williams)	8.00	4.00	2.50
65	A.L. Home Run Leaders (Frank Howard, Harmon Killebrew, Carl Yastrzemski)	8.00	4.00	2.50
66	N.L. Home Run Leaders (Johnny Bench, Tony Perez, Billy Williams)	10.00	5.00	3.00
67	A.L. ERA Leaders (Jim Palmer, Diego Segui, Clyde Wright)	6.00	3.00	1.75
68	N.L. ERA Leaders (Tom Seaver, Wayne Simpson, Luke Walker)	6.00	3.00	1.75
69	A.L. Pitching Leaders (Mike Cuellar, Dave McNally, Jim Perry)	3.00	1.50	.90
70	N.L. Pitching Leaders (Bob Gibson, Fergie Jenkins, Gaylord Perry)	8.00	4.00	2.50
71	A.L. Strikeout Leaders (Bob Johnson, Mickey Lolich, Sam McDowell)	3.00	1.50	.90
72	N.L. Strikeout Leaders (Bob Gibson, Fergie Jenkins, Tom Seaver)	8.00	4.00	2.50
73	George Brunet	2.00	1.00	.60
74	Twins Rookies (Pete Hamm, Jim Nettles)	2.00	1.00	.60
75	Gary Nolan	2.00	1.00	.60
76	Ted Savage	2.00	1.00	.60
77	Mike Compton	2.00	1.00	.60
78	Jim Spencer	2.00	1.00	.60
79	Wade Blasingame	2.00	1.00	.60
80	Bill Melton	2.00	1.00	.60
81	Felix Millan	2.00	1.00	.60
82	Casey Cox	2.00	1.00	.60
83	Mets Rookies (*Randy Bobb, Tim Foli*)	2.00	1.00	.60
84	Marcel Lachemann	2.00	1.00	.60
85	Billy Grabarkewitz	2.00	1.00	.60
86	Mike Kilkenny	2.00	1.00	.60
87	Jack Heidemann	2.00	1.00	.60
88	Hal King	2.00	1.00	.60
89	Ken Brett	2.00	1.00	.60
90	Joe Pepitone	2.00	1.00	.60
91	Bob Lemon	4.00	2.00	1.25
92	Fred Wenz	2.00	1.00	.60
93	Senators Rookies (Norm McRae, Denny Riddleberger)	2.00	1.00	.60
94	Don Hahn	2.00	1.00	.60
95	Luis Tiant	2.00	1.00	.60
96	Joe Hague	2.00	1.00	.60
97	Floyd Wicker	2.00	1.00	.60
98	Joe Decker	2.00	1.00	.60
99	Mark Belanger	2.00	1.00	.60
100	Pete Rose	80.00	40.00	20.00
101	Les Cain	2.00	1.00	.60
102	Astros Rookies (*Ken Forsch*, Larry Howard)	2.00	1.00	.60
103	Rich Severson	2.00	1.00	.60
104	Dan Frisella	2.00	1.00	.60
105	Tony Conigliaro	6.00	3.00	1.75
106	Tom Dukes	2.00	1.00	.60
107	Roy Foster	2.00	1.00	.60
108	John Cumberland	2.00	1.00	.60
109	Steve Hovley	2.00	1.00	.60
110	Bill Mazeroski	10.00	5.00	3.00
111	Yankees Rookies (Loyd Colson, Bobby Mitchell)	2.00	1.00	.60
112	Manny Mota	2.00	1.00	.60
113	Jerry Crider	2.00	1.00	.60
114	Billy Conigliaro	2.00	1.00	.60
115	Donn Clendenon	2.00	1.00	.60
116	Ken Sanders	2.00	1.00	.60
117	*Ted Simmons*	8.00	4.00	2.50
118	Cookie Rojas	2.00	1.00	.60
119	Frank Lucchesi	2.00	1.00	.60
120	Willie Horton	2.00	1.00	.60
121	Cubs Rookies (Jim Dunegan, Roe Skidmore)	2.00	1.00	.60
122	Eddie Watt	2.00	1.00	.60
123a	2nd Series Checklist (133-263) (Card # on right, orange helmet.)	5.00	2.50	1.50
123b	2nd Series Checklist (133-263) (Card # on right, red helmet.)	5.00	2.50	1.50
123c	2nd Series Checklist (133-263) (Card # centered.)	5.00	2.50	1.50
124	*Don Gullett*	2.00	1.00	.60
125	Ray Fosse	2.00	1.00	.60
126	Danny Coombs	2.00	1.00	.60
127	*Danny Thompson*	2.00	1.00	.60
128	Frank Johnson	2.00	1.00	.60
129	Aurelio Monteagudo	2.00	1.00	.60
130	Denis Menke	2.00	1.00	.60
131	Curt Blefary	2.00	1.00	.60
132	Jose Laboy	2.00	1.00	.60
133	Mickey Lolich	2.00	1.00	.60
134	Jose Arcia	2.00	1.00	.60
135	Rick Monday	2.00	1.00	.60
136	Duffy Dyer	2.00	1.00	.60
137	Marcelino Lopez	2.00	1.00	.60
138	Phillies Rookies (*Joe Lis, Willie Montanez*)	2.00	1.00	.60
139	Paul Casanova	2.00	1.00	.60
140	Gaylord Perry	8.00	4.00	2.50
141	Frank Quilici	2.00	1.00	.60
142	Mack Jones	2.00	1.00	.60
143	Steve Blass	2.00	1.00	.60
144	Jackie Hernandez	2.00	1.00	.60
145	Bill Singer	2.00	1.00	.60
146	Ralph Houk	2.00	1.00	.60
147	Bob Priddy	2.00	1.00	.60
148	John Mayberry	2.00	1.00	.60
149	Mike Hershberger	2.00	1.00	.60
150	Sam McDowell	2.00	1.00	.60
151	Tommy Davis	2.00	1.00	.60
152	Angels Rookies (Lloyd Allen, Winston Llenas)	2.00	1.00	.60
153	Gary Ross	2.00	1.00	.60
154	Cesar Gutierrez	2.00	1.00	.60
155	Ken Henderson	2.00	1.00	.60
156	Bart Johnson	2.00	1.00	.60
157	Bob Bailey	2.00	1.00	.60
158	Jerry Reuss	2.00	1.00	.60
159	Jarvis Tatum	2.00	1.00	.60
160	Tom Seaver	25.00	12.50	7.50
161	Coins Checklist	4.00	2.00	1.25
162	Jack Billingham	2.00	1.00	.60
163	Buck Martinez	2.00	1.00	.60
164	Reds Rookies (*Frank Duffy, Milt Wilcox*)	2.00	1.00	.60
165	Cesar Tovar	2.00	1.00	.60
166	Joe Hoerner	2.00	1.00	.60
167	Tom Grieve	2.00	1.00	.60
168	Bruce Dal Canton	2.00	1.00	.60
169	Ed Herrmann	2.00	1.00	.60
170	Mike Cuellar	2.00	1.00	.60
171	Bobby Wine	2.00	1.00	.60
172	Duke Sims	2.00	1.00	.60
173	Gil Garrido	2.00	1.00	.60
174	*Dave LaRoche*	2.00	1.00	.60
175	Jim Hickman	2.00	1.00	.60
176	Red Sox Rookies (Doug Griffin, Bob Montgomery)	2.00	1.00	.60
177	Hal McRae	2.00	1.00	.60
178	Dave Duncan	2.00	1.00	.60
179	Mike Corkins	2.00	1.00	.60
180	Al Kaline	20.00	10.00	6.00
181	Hal Lanier	2.00	1.00	.60
182	Al Downing	2.00	1.00	.60
183	Gil Hodges	5.00	2.50	1.25
184	Stan Bahnsen	2.00	1.00	.60
185	Julian Javier	2.00	1.00	.60
186	Bob Spence	2.00	1.00	.60
187	Ted Abernathy	2.00	1.00	.60
188	Dodgers Rookies (*Mike Strahler, Bob Valentine*)	4.00	2.00	1.25
189	George Mitterwald	2.00	1.00	.60
190	Bob Tolan	2.00	1.00	.60
191	Mike Andrews	2.00	1.00	.60
192	Billy Wilson	2.00	1.00	.60
193	*Bob Grich*	5.00	2.50	1.50
194	Mike Lum	2.00	1.00	.60
195	A.L. Playoff Game 1 (Powell Muscles Twins!)	5.00	2.50	1.50
196	A.L. Playoff Game 2 (McNally Makes It Two Straight!)	3.00	1.50	.90
197	A.L. Playoff Game 3 (Palmer Mows 'Em Down!)	6.00	3.00	1.75
198	Orioles Celebrate! (A Team Effort!)	3.00	1.50	.90
199	N.L. Playoff Game 1 (Cline Pinch-Triple Decides It!)	3.00	1.50	.90
200	N.L. Playoff Game 2 (Tolan Scores For Third Time!)	3.00	1.50	.90
201	N.L. Playoff Game 3 (Cline Scores Winning Run!)	3.00	1.50	.90
202	Reds Celebrate! (World Series Bound!)	3.00	1.50	.90

No.	Name			
203	Larry Gura	2.00	1.00	.60
204	Brewers Rookies (George Kopacz, Bernie Smith)	2.00	1.00	.60
205	Gerry Moses	2.00	1.00	.60
206a	3rd Series Checklist (264-393) (Orange helmet.)	6.00	3.00	1.75
206b	3rd Series Checklist (264-393) (Red helmet.)	6.00	3.00	1.75
207	Alan Foster	2.00	1.00	.60
208	Billy Martin	8.00	4.00	2.50
209	Steve Renko	2.00	1.00	.60
210	Rod Carew	15.00	7.50	4.50
211	Phil Hennigan	2.00	1.00	.60
212	Rich Hebner	2.00	1.00	.60
213	Frank Baker	2.00	1.00	.60
214	Al Ferrara	2.00	1.00	.60
215	Diego Segui	2.00	1.00	.60
216	Cards Rookies (Reggie Cleveland, Luis Melendez)	2.00	1.00	.60
217	Ed Stroud	2.00	1.00	.60
218	Tony Cloninger	2.00	1.00	.60
219	Elrod Hendricks	2.00	1.00	.60
220	Ron Santo	8.00	4.00	2.50
221	Dave Morehead	2.00	1.00	.60
222	Bob Watson	2.00	1.00	.60
223	Cecil Upshaw	2.00	1.00	.60
224	Alan Gallagher	2.00	1.00	.60
225	Gary Peters	2.00	1.00	.60
226	Bill Russell	2.00	1.00	.60
227	Floyd Weaver	2.00	1.00	.60
228	Wayne Garrett	2.00	1.00	.60
229	Jim Hannan	2.00	1.00	.60
230	Willie Stargell	15.00	7.50	4.50
231	Indians Rookies (Vince Colbert, John Lowenstein)	2.00	1.00	.60
232	John Strohmayer	2.00	1.00	.60
233	Larry Bowa	2.00	1.00	.60
234	Jim Lyttle	2.00	1.00	.60
235	Nate Colbert	2.00	1.00	.60
236	Bob Humphreys	2.00	1.00	.60
237	Cesar Cedeno	6.00	3.00	1.75
238	Chuck Dobson	2.00	1.00	.60
239	Red Schoendienst	6.00	3.00	1.75
240	Clyde Wright	2.00	1.00	.60
241	Dave Nelson	2.00	1.00	.60
242	Jim Ray	2.00	1.00	.60
243	Carlos May	2.00	1.00	.60
244	Bob Tillman	2.00	1.00	.60
245	Jim Kaat	3.00	1.50	.90
246	Tony Taylor	2.00	1.00	.60
247	Royals Rookies (Jerry Cram, Paul Splittorff)	2.00	1.00	.60
248	Hoyt Wilhelm	8.00	4.00	2.50
249	Chico Salmon	2.00	1.00	.60
250	Johnny Bench	50.00	25.00	12.50
251	Frank Reberger	2.00	1.00	.60
252	Eddie Leon	2.00	1.00	.60
253	Bill Sudakis	2.00	1.00	.60
254	Cal Koonce	2.00	1.00	.60
255	Bob Robertson	2.00	1.00	.60
256	Tony Gonzalez	2.00	1.00	.60
257	Nelson Briles	2.00	1.00	.60
258	Dick Green	2.00	1.00	.60
259	Dave Marshall	2.00	1.00	.60
260	Tommy Harper	2.00	1.00	.60
261	Darold Knowles	2.00	1.00	.60
262	Padres Rookies (Dave Robinson, Jim Williams)	2.00	1.00	.60
263	John Ellis	2.00	1.00	.60
264	Joe Morgan	10.00	5.00	2.50
265a	Jim Northrup (Black "dot" at right of photo.)	2.00	1.00	.60
265b	Jim Northrup (Black "blob" at right of photo.)	2.00	1.00	.60
266	Bill Stoneman	2.00	1.00	.60
267	Rich Morales	2.00	1.00	.60
268	Phillies Team	4.00	2.00	1.25
269	Gail Hopkins	2.00	1.00	.60
270	Rico Carty	2.00	1.00	.60
271	Bill Zepp	2.00	1.00	.60
272	Tommy Helms	2.00	1.00	.60
273	Pete Richert	2.00	1.00	.60
274	Ron Slocum	2.00	1.00	.60
275	Vada Pinson	5.00	2.50	1.50
276	Giants Rookies (Mike Davison, George Foster)	10.00	5.00	2.50
277	Gary Waslewski	2.00	1.00	.60
278	Jerry Grote	2.00	1.00	.60
279	Lefty Phillips	2.00	1.00	.60
280	Fergie Jenkins	10.00	5.00	3.00
281	Danny Walton	2.00	1.00	.60
282	Jose Pagan	2.00	1.00	.60
283	Dick Such	2.00	1.00	.60
284	Jim Gosger	2.00	1.00	.60
285	Sal Bando	2.00	1.00	.60
286	Jerry McNertney	2.00	1.00	.60
287	Mike Fiore	2.00	1.00	.60
288	Joe Moeller	2.00	1.00	.60
289	White Sox Team	4.00	2.00	1.25
290	Tony Oliva	10.00	5.00	2.50
291	George Culver	2.00	1.00	.60
292	Jay Johnstone	2.00	1.00	.60
293	Pat Corrales	2.00	1.00	.60
294	Steve Dunning	2.00	1.00	.60
295	Bobby Bonds	4.00	2.00	1.25
296	Tom Timmermann	2.00	1.00	.60
297	Johnny Briggs	2.00	1.00	.60
298	Jim Nelson	2.00	1.00	.60
299	Ed Kirkpatrick	2.00	1.00	.60
300	Brooks Robinson	20.00	10.00	6.00
301	Earl Wilson	2.00	1.00	.60
302	Phil Gagliano	2.00	1.00	.60
303	Lindy McDaniel	2.00	1.00	.60
304	Ron Brand	2.00	1.00	.60
305	Reggie Smith	2.00	1.00	.60
306a	Jim Nash (Black blob, left center.)	4.00	2.00	1.25
306b	Jim Nash (Blob airbrushed away.)	2.00	1.00	.60
307	Don Wert	2.00	1.00	.60
308	Cards Team	3.00	1.50	.90
309	Dick Ellsworth	2.00	1.00	.60
310	Tommie Agee	2.00	1.00	.60
311	Lee Stange	2.00	1.00	.60
312	Harry Walker	2.00	1.00	.60
313	Tom Hall	2.00	1.00	.60
314	Jeff Torborg	2.00	1.00	.60
315	Ron Fairly	2.00	1.00	.60
316	Fred Scherman	2.00	1.00	.60
317	Athletics Rookies (Jim Driscoll, Angel Mangual)	2.00	1.00	.60
318	Rudy May	2.00	1.00	.60
319	Ty Cline	2.00	1.00	.60
320	Dave McNally	2.00	1.00	.60
321	Tom Matchick	2.00	1.00	.60
322	Jim Beauchamp	2.00	1.00	.60
323	Billy Champion	2.00	1.00	.60
324	Graig Nettles	4.00	2.00	1.25
325	Juan Marichal	8.00	4.00	2.50
326	Richie Scheinblum	2.00	1.00	.60
327	World Series Game 1 (Powell Homers To Opposite Field!)	3.00	1.50	.90
328	World Series Game 2 (Buford Goes 2-For-4!)	2.00	1.00	.60
329	World Series Game 3 (F. Robinson Shows Muscle!)	6.00	3.00	1.75
330	World Series Game 4 (Reds Stay Alive!)	2.00	1.00	.60
331	World Series Game 5 (B. Robinson Commits Robbery!)	8.00	4.00	2.50
332	World Series Celebration! (Convincing Performance!)	5.00	2.50	1.50
333	Clay Kirby	2.00	1.00	.60
334	Roberto Pena	2.00	1.00	.60
335	Jerry Koosman	2.00	1.00	.60
336	Tigers Team	4.00	2.00	1.25
337	Jesus Alou	2.00	1.00	.60
338	Gene Tenace	2.00	1.00	.60
339	Wayne Simpson	2.00	1.00	.60
340	Rico Petrocelli	2.00	1.00	.60
341	Steve Garvey	35.00	17.50	8.75
342	Frank Tepedino	2.00	1.00	.60
343	Pirates Rookies (Ed Acosta, Milt May)	2.00	1.00	.60
344	Ellie Rodriguez	2.00	1.00	.60
345	Joe Horlen	2.00	1.00	.60
346	Lum Harris	2.00	1.00	.60
347	Ted Uhlaender	2.00	1.00	.60
348	Fred Norman	2.00	1.00	.60
349	Rich Reese	2.00	1.00	.60
350	Billy Williams	5.00	2.50	1.25
351	Jim Shellenback	2.00	1.00	.60
352	Denny Doyle	2.00	1.00	.60
353	Carl Taylor	2.00	1.00	.60
354	Don McMahon	2.00	1.00	.60
355	Bud Harrelson	2.00	1.00	.60
356	Bob Locker	2.00	1.00	.60
357	Reds Team	4.00	2.00	1.25
358	Danny Cater	2.00	1.00	.60
359	Ron Reed	2.00	1.00	.60
360	Jim Fregosi	2.00	1.00	.60
361	Don Sutton	8.00	4.00	2.50
362	Orioles Rookies (Mike Adamson, Roger Freed)	2.00	1.00	.60
363	Mike Nagy	2.00	1.00	.60
364	Tommy Dean	2.00	1.00	.60
365	Bob Johnson	2.00	1.00	.60
366	Ron Stone	2.00	1.00	.60
367	Dalton Jones	2.00	1.00	.60
368	Bob Veale	2.00	1.00	.60
369a	4th Series Checklist (394-523) (Orange helmet.)	5.00	2.50	1.50
369b	4th Series Checklist (394-523) (Red helmet, black line above ear.)	6.00	3.00	1.75
369c	4th Series Checklist (394-523) (Red helmet, no line.)	6.00	3.00	1.75
370	Joe Torre	6.00	3.00	1.75
371	Jack Hiatt	2.00	1.00	.60
372	Lew Krausse	2.00	1.00	.60
373	Tom McCraw	2.00	1.00	.60
374	Clete Boyer	2.00	1.00	.60
375	Steve Hargan	2.00	1.00	.60
376	Expos Rookies (Clyde Mashore, Ernie McAnally)	2.00	1.00	.60
377	Greg Garrett	2.00	1.00	.60
378	Tito Fuentes	2.00	1.00	.60
379	Wayne Granger	2.00	1.00	.60
380	Ted Williams	12.00	6.00	3.50
381	Fred Gladding	2.00	1.00	.60
382	Jake Gibbs	2.00	1.00	.60
383	Rod Gaspar	2.00	1.00	.60
384	Rollie Fingers	8.00	4.00	2.50
385	Maury Wills	4.00	2.00	1.25
386	Red Sox Team	4.00	2.00	1.25
387	Ron Herbel	2.00	1.00	.60
388	Al Oliver	2.00	1.00	.60
389	Ed Brinkman	2.00	1.00	.60
390	Glenn Beckert	2.00	1.00	.60
391	Twins Rookies (Steve Brye, Cotton Nash)	2.00	1.00	.60
392	Grant Jackson	2.00	1.00	.60
393	Merv Rettenmund	2.00	1.00	.60
394	Clay Carroll	2.00	1.00	.60
395	Roy White	2.00	1.00	.60
396	Dick Schofield	2.00	1.00	.60
397	Alvin Dark	2.00	1.00	.60
398	Howie Reed	2.00	1.00	.60
399	Jim French	2.00	1.00	.60
400	Hank Aaron	65.00	32.50	16.25
401	Tom Murphy	2.00	1.00	.60
402	Dodgers Team	4.00	2.00	1.25
403	Joe Coleman	2.00	1.00	.60
404	Astros Rookies (Buddy Harris, Roger Metzger)	2.00	1.00	.60
405	Leo Cardenas	2.00	1.00	.60
406	Ray Sadecki	2.00	1.00	.60
407	Joe Rudi	2.00	1.00	.60
408	Rafael Robles	2.00	1.00	.60
409	Don Pavletich	2.00	1.00	.60
410	Ken Holtzman	2.00	1.00	.60
411	George Spriggs	2.00	1.00	.60
412	Jerry Johnson	2.00	1.00	.60
413	Pat Kelly	2.00	1.00	.60
414	Woodie Fryman	2.00	1.00	.60
415	Mike Hegan	2.00	1.00	.60
416	Gene Alley	2.00	1.00	.60
417	Dick Hall	2.00	1.00	.60
418	Adolfo Phillips	2.00	1.00	.60
419	Ron Hansen	2.00	1.00	.60
420	Jim Merritt	2.00	1.00	.60
421	John Stephenson	2.00	1.00	.60
422	Frank Bertaina	2.00	1.00	.60
423	Tigers Rookies (Tim Marting, Dennis Saunders)	2.00	1.00	.60
424	Roberto Rodriquez (Rodriguez)	2.00	1.00	.60
425	Doug Rader	2.00	1.00	.60
426	Chris Cannizzaro	2.00	1.00	.60
427	Bernie Allen	2.00	1.00	.60
428	Jim McAndrew	2.00	1.00	.60
429	Chuck Hinton	2.00	1.00	.60
430	Wes Parker	2.00	1.00	.60
431	Tom Burgmeier	2.00	1.00	.60
432	Bob Didier	2.00	1.00	.60
433	Skip Lockwood	2.00	1.00	.60
434	Gary Sutherland	2.00	1.00	.60
435	Jose Cardenal	2.00	1.00	.60
436	Wilbur Wood	2.00	1.00	.60
437	Danny Murtaugh	2.00	1.00	.60
438	Mike McCormick	2.00	1.00	.60
439	Phillies Rookies (Greg Luzinski, Scott Reid)	5.00	2.50	1.50
440	Bert Campaneris	2.00	1.00	.60
441	Milt Pappas	2.00	1.00	.60
442	Angels Rookies	4.00	2.00	1.25
443	Rich Robertson	2.00	1.00	.60
444	Jimmie Price	2.00	1.00	.60
445	Art Shamsky	2.00	1.00	.60
446	Bobby Bolin	2.00	1.00	.60
447	Cesar Geronimo	3.00	1.50	.90
448	Dave Roberts	2.00	1.00	.60
449	Brant Alyea	2.00	1.00	.60
450	Bob Gibson	15.00	7.50	4.50
451	Joe Keough	2.00	1.00	.60
452	John Boccabella	2.00	1.00	.60
453	Terry Crowley	2.00	1.00	.60
454	Mike Paul	2.00	1.00	.60
455	Don Kessinger	2.00	1.00	.60
456	Bob Meyer	2.00	1.00	.60
457	Willie Smith	2.00	1.00	.60
458	White Sox Rookies (Dave Lemonds, Ron Lolich)	2.00	1.00	.60
459	Jim Lefebvre	2.00	1.00	.60
460	Fritz Peterson	2.00	1.00	.60
461	Jim Hart	2.00	1.00	.60
462	Senators Team	5.00	2.50	1.50
463	Tom Kelley	2.00	1.00	.60
464	Aurelio Rodriguez	2.00	1.00	.60
465	Tim McCarver	6.00	3.00	1.75
466	Ken Berry	2.00	1.00	.60
467	Al Santorini	2.00	1.00	.60
468	Frank Fernandez	2.00	1.00	.60
469	Bob Aspromonte	2.00	1.00	.60
470	Bob Oliver	2.00	1.00	.60
471	Tom Griffin	2.00	1.00	.60
472	Ken Rudolph	2.00	1.00	.60
473	Gary Wagner	2.00	1.00	.60
474	Jim Fairey	2.00	1.00	.60
475	Ron Perranoski	2.00	1.00	.60
476	Dal Maxvill	2.00	1.00	.60
477	Earl Weaver	5.00	2.50	1.50
478	Bernie Carbo	2.00	1.00	.60
479	Dennis Higgins	2.00	1.00	.60
480	Manny Sanguillen	2.00	1.00	.60
481	Daryl Patterson	2.00	1.00	.60
482	Padres Team	5.00	2.50	1.50
483	Gene Michael	2.00	1.00	.60
484	Don Wilson	2.00	1.00	.60
485	Ken McMullen	2.00	1.00	.60
486	Steve Huntz	2.00	1.00	.60
487	Paul Schaal	2.00	1.00	.60
488	Jerry Stephenson	2.00	1.00	.60
489	Luis Alvarado	2.00	1.00	.60
490	Deron Johnson	2.00	1.00	.60
491	Jim Hardin	2.00	1.00	.60
492	Ken Boswell	2.00	1.00	.60
493	Dave May	2.00	1.00	.60
494	Braves Rookies (Ralph Garr, Rick Kester)	2.00	1.00	.60
495	Felipe Alou	3.00	1.50	.90
496	Woody Woodward	2.00	1.00	.60
497	Horacio Pina	2.00	1.00	.60
498	John Kennedy	2.00	1.00	.60
499	5th Series Checklist (524-643)	6.00	3.00	1.75
500	Jim Perry	2.00	1.00	.60
501	Andy Etchebarren	2.00	1.00	.60
502	Cubs Team	5.00	2.50	1.50
503	Gates Brown	2.00	1.00	.60
504	Ken Wright	2.00	1.00	.60
505	Ollie Brown	2.00	1.00	.60
506	Bobby Knoop	2.00	1.00	.60
507	George Stone	2.00	1.00	.60
508	Roger Repoz	2.00	1.00	.60
509	Jim Grant	2.00	1.00	.60
510	Ken Harrelson	2.00	1.00	.60
511	Chris Short	2.00	1.00	.60
512	Red Sox Rookies (Mike Garman, Dick Mills)	2.00	1.00	.60
513	Nolan Ryan	150.00	75.00	37.50
514	Ron Woods	2.00	1.00	.60

#	Player	NM	EX	VG
515	Carl Morton	2.00	1.00	.60
516	Ted Kubiak	2.00	1.00	.60
517	Charlie Fox	2.00	1.00	.60
518	Joe Grzenda	2.00	1.00	.60
519	Willie Crawford	2.00	1.00	.60
520	Tommy John	5.00	2.50	1.50
521	Leron Lee	2.00	1.00	.60
522	Twins Team	4.00	2.00	1.25
523	John Odom	2.00	1.00	.60
524	Mickey Stanley	4.00	2.00	1.25
525	Ernie Banks	50.00	25.00	12.50
526	Ray Jarvis	4.00	2.00	1.25
527	Cleon Jones	4.00	2.00	1.25
528	Wally Bunker	4.00	2.00	1.25
529	N.L. Rookies (Bill Buckner, Enzo Hernandez, Marty Perez)	6.00	3.00	1.75
530	Carl Yastrzemski	25.00	12.50	7.50
531	Mike Torrez	4.00	2.00	1.25
532	Bill Rigney	4.00	2.00	1.25
533	Mike Ryan	4.00	2.00	1.25
534	Luke Walker	4.00	2.00	1.25
535	Curt Flood	5.00	2.50	1.50
536	Claude Raymond	4.00	2.00	1.25
537	Tom Egan	4.00	2.00	1.25
538	Angel Bravo	4.00	2.00	1.25
539	Larry Brown	4.00	2.00	1.25
540	Larry Dierker	4.00	2.00	1.25
541	Bob Burda	4.00	2.00	1.25
542	Bob Miller	4.00	2.00	1.25
543	Yankees Team	8.00	4.00	2.50
544	Vida Blue	5.00	2.50	1.50
545	Dick Dietz	4.00	2.00	1.25
546	John Matias	4.00	2.00	1.25
547	Pat Dobson	4.00	2.00	1.25
548	Don Mason	4.00	2.00	1.25
549	Jim Brewer	4.00	2.00	1.25
550	Harmon Killebrew	20.00	10.00	5.00
551	Frank Linzy	4.00	2.00	1.25
552	Buddy Bradford	4.00	2.00	1.25
553	Kevin Collins	4.00	2.00	1.25
554	Lowell Palmer	4.00	2.00	1.25
555	Walt Williams	4.00	2.00	1.25
556	Jim McGlothlin	4.00	2.00	1.25
557	Tom Satriano	4.00	2.00	1.25
558	Hector Torres	4.00	2.00	1.25
559	A.L. Rookies (Terry Cox, Bill Gogolewski, Gary Jones)	4.00	2.00	1.25
560	Rusty Staub	5.00	2.50	1.50
561	Syd O'Brien	4.00	2.00	1.25
562	Dave Giusti	4.00	2.00	1.25
563	Giants Team	10.00	5.00	3.00
564	Al Fitzmorris	4.00	2.00	1.25
565	Jim Wynn	4.00	2.00	1.25
566	Tim Cullen	4.00	2.00	1.25
567	Walt Alston	6.00	3.00	1.75
568	Sal Campisi	4.00	2.00	1.25
569	Ivan Murrell	4.00	2.00	1.25
570	Jim Palmer	25.00	12.50	7.50
571	Ted Sizemore	4.00	2.00	1.25
572	Jerry Kenney	4.00	2.00	1.25
573	Ed Kranepool	4.00	2.00	1.25
574	Jim Bunning	8.00	4.00	2.50
575	Bill Freehan	4.00	2.00	1.25
576	Cubs Rookies (Brock Davis, Adrian Garrett, Garry Jestadt)	4.00	2.00	1.25
577	Jim Lonborg	4.00	2.00	1.25
578	Ron Hunt	4.00	2.00	1.25
579	Marty Pattin	4.00	2.00	1.25
580	Tony Perez	15.00	7.50	3.75
581	Roger Nelson	4.00	2.00	1.25
582	Dave Cash	4.00	2.00	1.25
583	Ron Cook	4.00	2.00	1.25
584	Indians Team	10.00	5.00	3.00
585	Willie Davis	4.00	2.00	1.25
586	Dick Woodson	4.00	2.00	1.25
587	Sonny Jackson	4.00	2.00	1.25
588	Tom Bradley	4.00	2.00	1.25
589	Bob Barton	4.00	2.00	1.25
590	Alex Johnson	4.00	2.00	1.25
591	Jackie Brown	4.00	2.00	1.25
592	Randy Hundley	4.00	2.00	1.25
593	Jack Aker	4.00	2.00	1.25
594	Cards Rookies (Bob Chlupsa, Al Hrabosky, Bob Stinson)	6.00	3.00	1.75
595	Dave Johnson	4.00	2.00	1.25
596	Mike Jorgensen	4.00	2.00	1.25
597	Ken Suarez	4.00	2.00	1.25
598	Rick Wise	4.00	2.00	1.25
599	Norm Cash	4.00	2.00	1.25
600	Willie Mays	100.00	50.00	30.00
601	Ken Tatum	4.00	2.00	1.25
602	Marty Martinez	4.00	2.00	1.25
603	Pirates Team	8.00	4.00	2.50
604	John Gelnar	4.00	2.00	1.25
605	Orlando Cepeda	10.00	5.00	2.50
606	Chuck Taylor	4.00	2.00	1.25
607	Paul Ratliff	4.00	2.00	1.25
608	Mike Wegener	4.00	2.00	1.25
609	Leo Durocher	8.00	4.00	2.50
610	Amos Otis	4.00	2.00	1.25
611	Tom Phoebus	4.00	2.00	1.25
612	Indians Rookies (Lou Camilli, Ted Ford, Steve Mingori)	4.00	2.00	1.25
613	Pedro Borbon	4.00	2.00	1.25
614	Billy Cowan	4.00	2.00	1.25
615	Mel Stottlemyre	6.00	3.00	1.75
616	Larry Hisle	4.00	2.00	1.25
617	Clay Dalrymple	4.00	2.00	1.25
618	Tug McGraw	4.00	2.00	1.25
619a	6th Series Checklist (644-752) (No copyright on back.)	5.00	2.50	1.50
619b	6th Series Checklist (644-752) (With copyright, no wavy line on helmet brim.)	4.00	2.00	1.25
619c	6th Series Checklist (644-752) (With copyright, wavy line on helmet brim.)			

#	Player	NM	EX	VG
620	Frank Howard	5.00	2.50	1.50
621	Ron Bryant	4.00	2.00	1.25
622	Joe Lahoud	4.00	2.00	1.25
623	Pat Jarvis	4.00	2.00	1.25
624	Athletics Team	10.00	5.00	3.00
625	Lou Brock	25.00	12.50	7.50
626	Freddie Patek	4.00	2.00	1.25
627	Steve Hamilton	4.00	2.00	1.25
628	John Bateman	4.00	2.00	1.25
629	John Hiller	4.00	2.00	1.25
630	Roberto Clemente	150.00	75.00	37.50
631	Eddie Fisher	4.00	2.00	1.25
632	Darrel Chaney	4.00	2.00	1.25
633	A.L. Rookies (Bobby Brooks, Pete Koegel, Scott Northey)	4.00	2.00	1.25
634	Phil Regan	4.00	2.00	1.25
635	Bobby Murcer	15.00	7.50	4.50
636	Denny Lemaster	4.00	2.00	1.25
637	Dave Bristol	4.00	2.00	1.25
638	Stan Williams	4.00	2.00	1.25
639	Tom Haller	4.00	2.00	1.25
640	Frank Robinson	40.00	20.00	12.00
641	Mets Team	10.00	5.00	3.00
642	Jim Roland	4.00	2.00	1.25
643	Rick Reichardt	4.00	2.00	1.25
644	Jim Stewart (SP)	8.00	4.00	2.50
645	Jim Maloney (SP)	8.00	4.00	2.50
646	Bobby Floyd (SP)	8.00	4.00	2.50
647	Juan Pizarro	6.00	3.00	1.75
648	Mets Rookies (*Rich Folkers*, *Ted Martinez*, *Jon Matlack*) (SP)	20.00	10.00	6.00
649	Sparky Lyle (SP)	10.00	5.00	3.00
650	Rich Allen (SP)	30.00	15.00	9.00
651	Jerry Robertson (SP)	8.00	4.00	2.50
652	Braves Team	10.00	5.00	3.00
653	Russ Snyder (SP)	8.00	4.00	2.50
654	Don Shaw (SP)	8.00	4.00	2.50
655	Mike Epstein (SP)	8.00	4.00	2.50
656	Gerry Nyman (SP)	8.00	4.00	2.50
657	Jose Azcue	6.00	3.00	1.75
658	Paul Lindblad (SP)	8.00	4.00	2.50
659	Byron Browne (SP)	8.00	4.00	2.50
660	Ray Culp	6.00	3.00	1.75
661	Chuck Tanner (SP)	8.00	4.00	2.50
662	Mike Hedlund (SP)	8.00	4.00	2.50
663	Marv Staehle	6.00	3.00	1.75
664	Major League Rookies (Archie Reynolds, Bob Reynolds, Ken Reynolds) (SP)	8.00	4.00	2.50
665	Ron Swoboda (SP)	8.00	4.00	2.50
666	Gene Brabender (SP)	8.00	4.00	2.50
667	Pete Ward	6.00	3.00	1.75
668	Gary Neibauer	6.00	3.00	1.75
669	Ike Brown (SP)	8.00	4.00	2.50
670	Bill Hands	6.00	3.00	1.75
671	Bill Voss (SP)	8.00	4.00	2.50
672	Ed Crosby (SP)	8.00	4.00	2.50
673	Gerry Janeski (SP)	8.00	4.00	2.50
674	Expos Team	10.00	5.00	2.50
675	Dave Boswell	6.00	3.00	1.75
676	Tommie Reynolds	6.00	3.00	1.75
677	Jack DiLauro (SP)	8.00	4.00	2.50
678	George Thomas	6.00	3.00	1.75
679	Don O'Riley	6.00	3.00	1.75
680	Don Mincher (SP)	8.00	4.00	2.50
681	Bill Butler	6.00	3.00	1.75
682	Terry Harmon	6.00	3.00	1.75
683	Bill Burbach (SP)	8.00	4.00	2.50
684	Curt Motton	6.00	3.00	1.75
685	Moe Drabowsky	6.00	3.00	1.75
686	Chico Ruiz (SP)	8.00	4.00	2.50
687	Ron Taylor (SP)	8.00	4.00	2.50
688	Sparky Anderson (SP)	25.00	12.50	7.50
689	Frank Baker	6.00	3.00	1.75
690	Bob Moose	6.00	3.00	1.75
691	Bob Heise	6.00	3.00	1.75
692	A.L. Rookies (Hal Haydel, Rogelio Moret, Wayne Twitchell) (SP)	8.00	4.00	2.50
693	Jose Pena (SP)	8.00	4.00	2.50
694	Rick Renick (SP)	8.00	4.00	2.50
695	Joe Niekro	6.00	3.00	1.75
696	Jerry Morales	6.00	3.00	1.75
697	Rickey Clark (SP)	8.00	4.00	2.50
698	Brewers Team (SP)	15.00	7.50	3.75
699	Jim Britton	6.00	3.00	1.75
700	Boog Powell	20.00	10.00	6.00
701	Bob Garibaldi	6.00	3.00	1.75
702	Milt Ramirez	6.00	3.00	1.75
703	Mike Kekich	6.00	3.00	1.75
704	J.C. Martin (SP)	8.00	4.00	2.50
705	Dick Selma (SP)	8.00	4.00	2.50
706	Joe Foy (SP)	8.00	4.00	2.50
707	Fred Lasher	6.00	3.00	1.75
708	Russ Nagelson (SP)	8.00	4.00	2.50
709	Major League Rookies (*Dusty Baker, Don Baylor, Tom Paciorek*) (SP)	75.00	37.50	18.75
710	Sonny Siebert	6.00	3.00	1.75
711	Larry Stahl (SP)	8.00	4.00	2.50
712	Jose Martinez	6.00	3.00	1.75
713	Mike Marshall (SP)	8.00	4.00	2.50
714	Dick Williams (SP)	8.00	4.00	2.50
715	Horace Clarke (SP)	8.00	4.00	2.50
716	Dave Leonhard	6.00	3.00	1.75
717	Tommie Aaron (SP)	8.00	4.00	2.50
718	Billy Wynne	6.00	3.00	1.75
719	Jerry May (SP)	8.00	4.00	2.50
720	Matty Alou	6.00	3.00	1.75
721	John Morris	6.00	3.00	1.75
722	Astros Team (SP)	15.00	7.50	4.50
723	Vicente Romo (SP)	8.00	4.00	2.50
724	Tom Tischinski (SP)	8.00	4.00	2.50
725	Gary Gentry (SP)	8.00	4.00	2.50
726	Paul Popovich (SP)	6.00	3.00	1.75
727	Ray Lamb (SP)	8.00	4.00	2.50

#	Player	NM	EX	VG
728	N.L. Rookies (Keith Lampard, Wayne Redmond, Bernie Williams)	6.00	3.00	1.75
729	Dick Billings	6.00	3.00	1.75
730	Jim Rooker	6.00	3.00	1.75
731	Jim Qualls (SP)	8.00	4.00	2.50
732	Bob Reed	6.00	3.00	1.75
733	Lee Maye (SP)	8.00	4.00	2.50
734	Rob Gardner (SP)	8.00	4.00	2.50
735	Mike Shannon (SP)	8.00	4.00	2.50
736	Mel Queen (SP)	8.00	4.00	2.50
737	Preston Gomez (SP)	8.00	4.00	2.50
738	Russ Gibson (SP)	8.00	4.00	2.50
739	Barry Lersch (SP)	8.00	4.00	2.50
740	Luis Aparicio (SP)	25.00	12.50	7.50
741	Skip Guinn	6.00	3.00	1.75
742	Royals Team	10.00	5.00	3.00
743	John O'Donoghue (SP)	8.00	4.00	2.50
744	Chuck Manuel (SP)	8.00	4.00	2.50
745	Sandy Alomar (SP)	8.00	4.00	2.50
746	Andy Kosco	6.00	3.00	1.75
747	N.L. Rookies (Balor Moore, Al Severinsen, Scipio Spinks)	6.00	3.00	1.75
748	John Purdin (SP)	8.00	4.00	2.50
749	Ken Szotkiewicz	6.00	3.00	1.75
750	Denny McLain (SP)	20.00	10.00	6.00
751	Al Weis (SP)	6.00	3.00	1.75
752	Dick Drago	10.00	5.00	3.00

1971 Topps All-Star Rookies Artist's Proofs

There exists only one set of these artist's proofs for a proposed set of All-Star Rookie cards. The standard-size card fronts are pasted onto 9-1/2" x 6-1/2" cardboard backing. It may have been intended that these be issued in card form for Topps' annual banquet. There is a player for each position on the 1970 All-Rookie Team, plus right- and left-handed pitchers. Players are listed here in alphabetical order.

		NM	EX	VG
Complete Set (10):		1,500	750.00	450.00
Common Player:		200.00	100.00	60.00
(1)	Larry Bowa	350.00	175.00	105.00
(2)	Les Cain	200.00	100.00	60.00
(3)	Bernie Carbo	200.00	100.00	60.00
(4)	Dave Cash	200.00	100.00	60.00
(5)	Billy Conigliaro	200.00	100.00	60.00
(6)	John Ellis	200.00	100.00	60.00
(7)	Roy Foster	200.00	100.00	60.00
(8)	Alan Gallagher	200.00	100.00	60.00
(9)	Carl Morton	200.00	100.00	60.00
(10)	Thurman Munson	750.00	375.00	225.00

1971 Topps Coins

Measuring 1-1/2" in diameter, the latest edition of the Topps coins was a 153-piece set. The coins feature a color photograph surrounded by a colored band on the front. The band carries the player's name, team, position and several stars. Backs have a short biography, the coin number and encouragement to collect the entire set. Back colors differ, with #s 1-51 having a brass back, #s 52-102 chrome backs, and the rest have blue backs. Most of the stars of the period are included in the set.

		NM	EX	VG
Complete Set (153):		500.00	250.00	150.00
Common Player:		2.00	1.00	.60
1	Cito Gaston	2.00	1.00	.60
2	Dave Johnson	2.00	1.00	.60
3	Jim Bunning	8.00	4.00	2.50
4	Jim Spencer	2.00	1.00	.60
5	Felix Millan	2.00	1.00	.60
6	Gerry Moses	2.00	1.00	.60
7	Fergie Jenkins	8.00	4.00	2.50
8	Felipe Alou	2.50	1.25	.70
9	Jim McGlothlin	2.00	1.00	.60
10	Dick McAuliffe	2.00	1.00	.60
11	Joe Torre	5.00	2.50	1.50
12	Jim Perry	2.00	1.00	.60
13	Bobby Bonds	2.00	1.00	.60

14	Danny Cater	2.00	1.00	.60
15	Bill Mazeroski	8.00	4.00	2.50
16	Luis Aparicio	8.00	4.00	2.50
17	Doug Rader	2.00	1.00	.60
18	Vada Pinson	3.00	1.50	.90
19	John Bateman	2.00	1.00	.60
20	Lew Krausse	2.00	1.00	.60
21	Billy Grabarkewitz	2.00	1.00	.60
22	Frank Howard	2.00	1.00	.60
23	Jerry Koosman	2.00	1.00	.60
24	Rod Carew	10.00	5.00	3.00
25	Al Ferrara	2.00	1.00	.60
26	Dave McNally	2.00	1.00	.60
27	Jim Hickman	2.00	1.00	.60
28	Sandy Alomar	2.00	1.00	.60
29	Lee May	2.00	1.00	.60
30	Rico Petrocelli	2.00	1.00	.60
31	Don Money	2.00	1.00	.60
32	Jim Rooker	2.00	1.00	.60
33	Dick Dietz	2.00	1.00	.60
34	Roy White	2.00	1.00	.60
35	Carl Morton	2.00	1.00	.60
36	Walt Williams	2.00	1.00	.60
37	Phil Niekro	8.00	4.00	2.50
38	Bill Freehan	2.00	1.00	.60
39	Julian Javier	2.00	1.00	.60
40	Rick Monday	2.00	1.00	.60
41	Don Wilson	2.00	1.00	.60
42	Ray Fosse	2.00	1.00	.60
43	Art Shamsky	2.00	1.00	.60
44	Ted Savage	2.00	1.00	.60
45	Claude Osteen	2.00	1.00	.60
46	Ed Brinkman	2.00	1.00	.60
47	Matty Alou	2.00	1.00	.60
48	Bob Oliver	2.00	1.00	.60
49	Danny Coombs	2.00	1.00	.60
50	Frank Robinson	10.00	5.00	3.00
51	Randy Hundley	2.00	1.00	.60
52	Cesar Tovar	2.00	1.00	.60
53	Wayne Simpson	2.00	1.00	.60
54	Bobby Murcer	2.00	1.00	.60
55	Tony Taylor	2.00	1.00	.60
56	Tommy John	3.00	1.50	.90
57	Willie McCovey	9.00	4.50	2.75
58	Carl Yastrzemski	13.50	6.75	4.00
59	Bob Bailey	2.00	1.00	.60
60	Clyde Wright	2.00	1.00	.60
61	Orlando Cepeda	8.00	4.00	2.50
62	Al Kaline	10.00	5.00	3.00
63	Bob Gibson	9.00	4.50	2.75
64	Bert Campaneris	2.00	1.00	.60
65	Ted Sizemore	2.00	1.00	.60
66	Duke Sims	2.00	1.00	.60
67	Bud Harrelson	2.00	1.00	.60
68	Jerry McNertney	2.00	1.00	.60
69	Jim Wynn	2.00	1.00	.60
70	Dick Bosman	2.00	1.00	.60
71	Roberto Clemente	30.00	15.00	9.00
72	Rich Reese	2.00	1.00	.60
73	Gaylord Perry	8.00	4.00	2.50
74	Boog Powell	3.00	1.50	.90
75	Billy Williams	9.00	4.50	2.75
76	Bill Melton	2.00	1.00	.60
77	Nate Colbert	2.00	1.00	.60
78	Reggie Smith	2.00	1.00	.60
79	Deron Johnson	2.00	1.00	.60
80	Catfish Hunter	8.00	4.00	2.50
81	Bob Tolan	2.00	1.00	.60
82	Jim Northrup	2.00	1.00	.60
83	Ron Fairly	2.00	1.00	.60
84	Alex Johnson	2.00	1.00	.60
85	Pat Jarvis	2.00	1.00	.60
86	Sam McDowell	2.00	1.00	.60
87	Lou Brock	9.00	4.50	2.75
88	Danny Walton	2.00	1.00	.60
89	Denis Menke	2.00	1.00	.60
90	Jim Palmer	9.00	4.50	2.75
91	Tommie Agee	2.00	1.00	.60
92	Duane Josephson	2.00	1.00	.60
93	Willie Davis	2.00	1.00	.60
94	Mel Stottlemyre	2.00	1.00	.60
95	Ron Santo	5.00	2.50	1.50
96	Amos Otis	2.00	1.00	.60
97	Ken Henderson	2.00	1.00	.60
98	George Scott	2.00	1.00	.60
99	Dock Ellis	2.00	1.00	.60
100	Harmon Killebrew	10.00	5.00	3.00
101	Pete Rose	20.00	10.00	6.00
102	Rick Reichardt	2.00	1.00	.60
103	Cleon Jones	2.00	1.00	.60
104	Ron Perranoski	2.00	1.00	.60
105	Tony Perez	9.00	4.50	2.75
106	Mickey Lolich	2.00	1.00	.60
107	Tim McCarver	3.00	1.50	.90
108	Reggie Jackson	15.00	7.50	4.50
109	Chris Cannizzaro	2.00	1.00	.60
110	Steve Hargan	2.00	1.00	.60
111	Rusty Staub	3.00	1.50	.90
112	Andy Messersmith	2.00	1.00	.60
113	Rico Carty	2.00	1.00	.60
114	Brooks Robinson	10.00	5.00	3.00
115	Steve Carlton	9.00	4.50	2.75
116	Mike Hegan	2.00	1.00	.60
117	Joe Morgan	9.00	4.50	2.75
118	Thurman Munson	8.00	4.00	2.50
119	Don Kessinger	2.00	1.00	.60
120	Joe Horlen	2.00	1.00	.60
121	Wes Parker	2.00	1.00	.60
122	Sonny Siebert	2.00	1.00	.60
123	Willie Stargell	9.00	4.50	2.75
124	Ellie Rodriguez	2.00	1.00	.60
125	Juan Marichal	8.00	4.00	2.50
126	Mike Epstein	2.00	1.00	.60
127	Tom Seaver	10.00	5.00	3.00
128	Tony Oliva	3.00	1.50	.90
129	Jim Merritt	2.00	1.00	.60
130	Willie Horton	2.00	1.00	.60
131	Rick Wise	2.00	1.00	.60

132	Sal Bando	2.00	1.00	.60
133	Ollie Brown	2.00	1.00	.60
134	Ken Harrelson	2.00	1.00	.60
135	Mack Jones	2.00	1.00	.60
136	Jim Fregosi	2.00	1.00	.60
137	Hank Aaron	25.00	12.50	7.50
138	Fritz Peterson	2.00	1.00	.60
139	Joe Hague	2.00	1.00	.60
140	Tommy Harper	2.00	1.00	.60
141	Larry Dierker	2.00	1.00	.60
142	Tony Conigliaro	4.00	2.00	1.25
143	Glenn Beckert	2.00	1.00	.60
144	Carlos May	2.00	1.00	.60
145	Don Sutton	8.00	4.00	2.50
146	Paul Casanova	2.00	1.00	.60
147	Bob Moose	2.00	1.00	.60
148	Leo Cardenas	2.00	1.00	.60
149	Johnny Bench	10.00	5.00	3.00
150	Mike Cuellar	2.00	1.00	.60
151	Donn Clendenon	2.00	1.00	.60
152	Lou Piniella	3.00	1.50	.90
153	Willie Mays	25.00	12.50	7.50

1971 Topps Greatest Moments

This 55-card set features highlights from the careers of top players of the day. The front of the 2-1/2" x 4-3/4" cards features a portrait photo of the player at left and deckle-edge action photo at right. There is a small headline on the white border of the action photo. The player's name and "One of Baseball's Greatest Moments" along with a black border complete the front. The back features a detail from the front photo and the story of the event. The newspaper style presentation includes the name of real newspapers. Relatively scarce, virtually every card in this set is a star or at least an above-average player. Because of their unusual size, 22 of the cards were double-printed, as indicated in the checklist here. Because of endemic centering problems there is a greater than usual value difference between NM and lower-grade cards.

		NM	EX	VG
Complete Set (55):		4,500	2,250	1,350
Common Player:		20.00	10.00	6.00
1	Thurman Munson (DP)	300.00	150.00	90.00
2	Hoyt Wilhelm	75.00	37.50	22.50
3	Rico Carty	65.00	32.50	20.00
4	Carl Morton (DP)	20.00	10.00	6.00
5	Sal Bando (DP)	20.00	10.00	6.00
6	Bert Campaneris (DP)	20.00	10.00	6.00
7	Jim Kaat	70.00	35.00	20.00
8	Harmon Killebrew	225.00	110.00	65.00
9	Brooks Robinson	250.00	125.00	75.00
10	Jim Perry	45.00	22.50	13.50
11	Tony Oliva	125.00	62.50	37.50
12	Vada Pinson	125.00	62.50	37.50
13	Johnny Bench	300.00	150.00	90.00
14	Tony Perez	100.00	50.00	30.00
15	Pete Rose (DP)	145.00	75.00	45.00
16	Jim Fregosi (DP)	20.00	10.00	6.00
17	Alex Johnson (DP)	20.00	10.00	6.00
18	Clyde Wright (DP)	20.00	10.00	6.00
19	Al Kaline (DP)	100.00	50.00	30.00
20	Denny McLain	50.00	25.00	15.00
21	Jim Northrup	45.00	22.50	13.50
22	Bill Freehan	50.00	25.00	15.00
23	Mickey Lolich	60.00	30.00	18.00
24	Bob Gibson (DP)	75.00	37.50	22.50
25	Tim McCarver (DP)	35.00	17.50	10.00
26	Orlando Cepeda (DP)	45.00	22.50	13.50
27	Lou Brock (DP)	60.00	30.00	18.00
28	Nate Colbert (DP)	20.00	10.00	6.00
29	Maury Wills	50.00	25.00	15.00
30	Wes Parker	65.00	32.50	20.00
31	Jim Wynn	55.00	27.50	16.50
32	Larry Dierker	60.00	30.00	18.00
33	Bill Melton	60.00	30.00	18.00
34	Joe Morgan	75.00	37.50	22.50
35	Rusty Staub	65.00	32.50	20.00
36	Ernie Banks (DP)	95.00	47.50	27.50
37	Billy Williams	75.00	37.50	22.50
38	Lou Piniella	80.00	40.00	24.00
39	Rico Petrocelli (DP)	35.00	17.50	10.00
40	Carl Yastrzemski (DP)	95.00	47.50	27.50
41	Willie Mays (DP)	175.00	85.00	55.00
42	Tommy Harper	45.00	22.50	13.50

43	Jim Bunning (DP)	25.00	12.50	7.50
44	Fritz Peterson	60.00	30.00	18.00
45	Roy White	75.00	37.50	22.50
46	Bobby Murcer	165.00	80.00	50.00
47	Reggie Jackson	600.00	300.00	180.00
48	Frank Howard	60.00	30.00	18.00
49	Dick Bosman	50.00	25.00	15.00
50	Sam McDowell (DP)	25.00	12.50	7.50
51	Luis Aparicio (DP)	45.00	22.50	13.50
52	Willie McCovey (DP)	65.00	32.50	20.00
53	Joe Pepitone	65.00	32.50	20.00
54	Jerry Grote	45.00	22.50	13.50
55	Bud Harrelson	90.00	45.00	27.50

1971 Topps Scratch-Offs

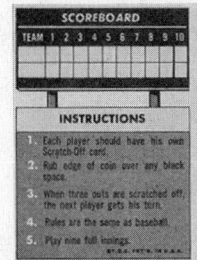

For a second year in 1971, Topps continued its scratch-off baseball card game with the same checklist of 24 players from the previous year. Unfolded, cards measure 3-3/8" x 5", and reveal a baseball game played by rubbing the black ink off squares to determine the "action." Fronts of the cards have a player picture as "captain," while backs have instructions and a scoreboard. Inserts with white centers are from 1970 while those with red centers are from 1971.

		NM	EX	VG
Complete Set (24):		65.00	32.50	20.00
Common Player:		1.50	.75	.45
(1)	Hank Aaron	7.50	3.75	2.25
(2)	Rich Allen	2.00	1.00	.60
(3)	Luis Aparicio	3.50	1.75	1.00
(4)	Sal Bando	1.50	.75	.45
(5)	Glenn Beckert	1.50	.75	.45
(6)	Dick Bosman	1.50	.75	.45
(7)	Nate Colbert	1.50	.75	.45
(8)	Mike Hegan	1.50	.75	.45
(9)	Mack Jones	1.50	.75	.45
(10)	Al Kaline	5.00	2.50	1.50
(11)	Harmon Killebrew	5.00	2.50	1.50
(12)	Juan Marichal	3.50	1.75	1.00
(13)	Tim McCarver	2.00	1.00	.60
(14)	Sam McDowell	1.50	.75	.45
(15)	Claude Osteen	1.50	.75	.45
(16)	Tony Perez	3.50	1.75	1.00
(17)	Lou Piniella	1.50	.75	.45
(18)	Boog Powell	2.00	1.00	.60
(19)	Tom Seaver	5.00	2.50	1.50
(20)	Jim Spencer	1.50	.75	.45
(21)	Willie Stargell	3.50	1.75	1.00
(22)	Mel Stottlemyre	1.50	.75	.45
(23)	Jim Wynn	1.50	.75	.45
(24)	Carl Yastrzemski	5.00	2.50	1.50

1971 Topps Super

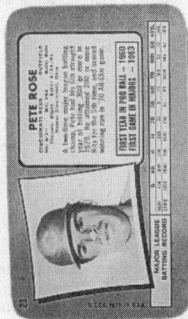

Topps continued to produce its special oversized cards in 1971. Measuring 3-1/8" x 5-1/4" with rounded corners, they feature a borderless color photograph with a facsimile autograph on front. Backs are basically enlargements of the player's regular Topps card. The set size was enlarged to 63 cards in 1971, so there are no short-printed cards as in 1970. Proof cards with square corners and blank backs, measuring about 3-3/8" x 5-1/2", are known.

		NM	EX	VG
Complete Set (63):		300.00	150.00	90.00
Common Player:		3.00	1.50	.90
Wax Pack (3):		50.00		
Proofs: 1-2X				
1	Reggie Smith	3.00	1.50	.90
2	Gaylord Perry	7.50	3.75	2.25
3	Ted Savage	3.00	1.50	.90
4	Donn Clendenon	3.00	1.50	.90
5	Boog Powell	4.50	2.25	1.25
6	Tony Perez	7.50	3.75	2.25
7	Dick Bosman	3.00	1.50	.90
8	Alex Johnson	3.00	1.50	.90

#	Player	NM	EX	VG
9	Rusty Staub	3.50	1.75	1.00
10	Mel Stottlemyre	3.00	1.50	.90
11	Tony Oliva	4.00	2.00	1.25
12	Bill Freehan	3.00	1.50	.90
13	Fritz Peterson	3.00	1.50	.90
14	Wes Parker	3.00	1.50	.90
15	Cesar Cedeno	3.00	1.50	.90
16	Sam McDowell	3.00	1.50	.90
17	Frank Howard	3.00	1.50	.90
18	Dave McNally	3.00	1.50	.90
19	Rico Petrocelli	3.00	1.50	.90
20	Pete Rose	25.00	12.50	7.50
21	Luke Walker	3.00	1.50	.90
22	Nate Colbert	3.00	1.50	.90
23	Luis Aparicio	7.50	3.75	2.25
24	Jim Perry	3.00	1.50	.90
25	Louis Brock	9.00	4.50	2.75
26	Roy White	3.00	1.50	.90
27	Claude Osteen	3.00	1.50	.90
28	Carl W. Morton	3.00	1.50	.90
29	Rico Carty	3.00	1.50	.90
30	Larry Dierker	3.00	1.50	.90
31	Bert Campaneris	3.00	1.50	.90
32	Johnny Bench	10.00	5.00	3.00
33	Felix Millan	3.00	1.50	.90
34	Tim McCarver	3.50	1.75	1.00
35	Ronald Santo	6.00	3.00	1.75
36	Tommie Agee	3.00	1.50	.90
37	Roberto Clemente	40.00	20.00	12.00
38	Reggie Jackson	20.00	10.00	6.00
39	Clyde Wright	3.00	1.50	.90
40	Rich Allen	4.50	2.25	1.25
41	Curt Flood	3.50	1.75	1.00
42	Fergie Jenkins	7.50	3.75	2.25
43	Willie Stargell	9.00	4.50	2.75
44	Henry Aaron	25.00	12.50	7.50
45	Amos Otis	3.00	1.50	.90
46	Willie McCovey	9.00	4.50	2.75
47	William Melton	3.00	1.50	.90
48	Bob Gibson	9.00	4.50	2.75
49	Carl Yastrzemski	12.00	6.00	3.50
50	Glenn Beckert	3.00	1.50	.90
51	Ray Fosse	3.00	1.50	.90
52	Clarence Gaston	3.00	1.50	.90
53	Tom Seaver	10.00	5.00	3.00
54	Al Kaline	10.00	5.00	3.00
55	Jim Northrup	3.00	1.50	.90
56	Willie Mays	25.00	12.50	7.50
57	Sal Bando	3.00	1.50	.90
58	Deron Johnson	3.00	1.50	.90
59	Brooks Robinson	10.00	5.00	3.00
60	Harmon Killebrew	9.00	4.50	2.75
61	Joseph Torre	4.50	2.25	1.25
62	Lou Piniella	4.50	2.25	1.25
63	Tommy Harper	3.00	1.50	.90

1971 Topps Tattoos

Topps once again produced baseball tattoos in 1971. This time, the tattoos came in a variety of sizes, shapes and themes. The sheets of tattoos measure 3-1/2" x 14-1/4". Each sheet contains an assortment of tattoos in two sizes, 1-3/4" x 2-3/8", or 1-3/16" x 1-3/4". There are players, facsimile autographed baseballs, team pennants and assorted baseball cartoon figures carried on the 16 different sheets. Listings below are for complete sheets; with the exception of the biggest-name stars, individual tattoos have little or no collector value.

	NM	EX	VG
Complete Sheet Set (16):	350.00	175.00	100.00
Common Sheet:	10.00	5.00	3.00
Unopened Pack:	25.00		
1 Brooks Robinson Autograph Montreal Expos Pennant San Francisco Giants Pennant (Sal Bando, Dick Bosman, Nate Colbert, Cleon Jones, Juan Marichal)	25.00	12.50	7.50
2 Red Sox Pennant Carl Yastrzemski Autograph New York Mets Pennant (Glenn Beckert, Tommy Harper, Ken Henderson, Fritz Peterson, Bob Robertson, Carl Yastrzemski)	35.00	17.50	10.00

	NM	EX	VG
3 Jim Fregosi Autograph New York Yankees Pennant Philadelphia Phillies Pennant (Orlando Cepeda, Jim Fregosi, Randy Hundley, Reggie Jackson, Jerry Koosman, Jim Palmer)	35.00	17.50	10.00
4 Kansas City Royals Pennant Oakland Athletics Pennant Sam McDowell Autograph (Dick Dietz, Cito Gaston, Dave Johnson, Sam McDowell, Gary Nolan, Amos Otis)	10.00	5.00	3.00
5 Al Kaline Autograph Braves Pennant L.A. Dodgers Pennant (Bill Grabarkewitz, Al Kaline, Lee May, Tom Murphy, Vada Pinson, Manny Sanguillen)	20.00	10.00	6.00
6 Chicago Cubs Pennant Cincinnati Reds Pennant Harmon Kilebrew Autograph (Luis Aparicio, Paul Blair, Chris Cannizzaro, Donn Clendenon, Larry Dieker, Harmon Killebrew)	25.00	12.50	7.50
7 Boog Powell Autograph Cleveland Indians Pennant Milwaukee Brewers Pennant (Rich Allen, Bert Campaneris, Don Money, Boog Powell, Ted Savage, Rusty Staub)	15.00	7.50	4.50
8 Chicago White Sox Pennant Frank Howard Autograph San Diego Padres Pennant (Leo Cardenas, Bill Hands, Frank Howard, Wes Parker, Reggie Smith, Willie Stargell)	10.00	5.00	3.00
9 Detroit Tigers Pennant Henry Aaron Autograph (Hank Aaron, Tommy Agee, Jim Hunter, Dick McAuliffe, Tony Perez, Lou Piniella)	35.00	17.50	10.00
10 Baltimore Orioles Pennant Fergie Jenkins Autograph (Roberto Clemente, Tony Conigliaro, Fergie Jenkins, Thurman Munson, Gary Peters, Joe Torre)	50.00	25.00	15.00
11 Johnny Bench Autograph Washington Senators Pennant (Johnny Bench, Rico Carty, Bill Mazeroski, Bob Oliver, Rico Petrocelli, Frank Robinson)	35.00	17.50	10.00
12 Billy Williams Autograph Houston Astros Pennant (Bill Freehan, Dave McNally, Felix Millan, Mel Stottlemyre, Bob Tolan, Billy Williams)	15.00	7.50	4.50
13 Pittsburgh Pirates Pennant Willie McCovey Autograph (Ray Culp, Bud Harrelson, Mickey Lolich, Willie McCovey, Ron Santo, Roy White)	20.00	10.00	6.00
14 Minnesota Twins Pennant Tom Seaver Autograph (Bill Melton, Jim Perry, Pete Rose, Tom Seaver, Maury Wills, Clyde Wright)	45.00	22.00	13.50
15 Robert Gibson Autograph St. Louis Cardinals Pennant (Rod Carew, Bob Gibson, Alex Johnson, Don Kessinger, Jim Merritt, Rick Monday)	20.00	10.00	6.00
16 Angels Pennant Willie Mays Autograph (Larry Bowa, Mike Cuellar, Ray Fosse, Willie Mays, Carl Morton, Tony Oliva)	25.00	12.50	7.50

1972 Topps

The largest Topps issue of its time appeared in 1972, with the set size reaching the 787 mark. The 2-1/2" x 3-1/2" cards are something special as well. Their fronts have a color photo which is shaped into an arch and surrounded by two different color borders, all of which is inside the overall white border. The player's name is in a white panel below the picture while the team name is above the picture in what might best be described as "superhero" type in a variety of colors. No mention of the player's position appears on the front. Cards backs are tame by comparison, featuring statistics and a trivia question. The set features a record number of specialty cards

including more than six dozen "In Action" (shown as "IA" in checklists below) cards featuring action shots of popular players. There are the usual statistical leaders, playoff and World Series highlights. Other innovations are 16 "Boyhood Photo" cards which depict scrapbook black and white photos of 1972's top players, and a group of cards depicting the trophies which comprise baseball's major awards. Finally, a group of seven "Traded" cards was included which feature a large "Traded" across the front of the card.

		NM	EX	VG
	Complete Set (787):	1,800	900.00	500.00
	Common Player (1-525):	1.50	.70	.45
	Common Player (526-656):	4.00	2.00	1.00
	Common Player (657-787):	12.00	6.00	3.00
1	Pirates Team (World Champions)	8.00	4.00	2.50
2	Ray Culp	1.50	.70	.45
3	Bob Tolan	1.50	.70	.45
4	1st Series Checklist (1-132)	4.00	2.00	1.25
5	John Bateman	1.50	.70	.45
6	Fred Scherman	1.50	.70	.45
7	Enzo Hernandez	1.50	.70	.45
8	Ron Swoboda	1.50	.70	.45
9	Stan Williams	1.50	.70	.45
10	Amos Otis	1.50	.70	.45
11	Bobby Valentine	1.50	.70	.45
12	Jose Cardenal	1.50	.70	.45
13	Joe Grzenda	1.50	.70	.45
14	Phillies Rookies (Mike Anderson, Pete Koegel, Wayne Twitchell)	1.50	.70	.45
15	Walt Williams	1.50	.70	.45
16	Mike Jorgensen	1.50	.70	.45
17	Dave Duncan	1.50	.70	.45
18a	Juan Pizarro (Green under "C" and "S.")	7.50	3.75	2.25
18b	Juan Pizarro (Yellow under "C" and "S.")	1.50	.70	.45
19	Billy Cowan	1.50	.70	.45
20	Don Wilson	1.50	.70	.45
21	Braves Team	3.00	1.50	.90
22	Rob Gardner	1.50	.70	.45
23	Ted Kubiak	1.50	.70	.45
24	Ted Ford	1.50	.70	.45
25	Bill Singer	1.50	.70	.45
26	Andy Etchebarren	1.50	.70	.45
27	Bob Johnson	1.50	.70	.45
28	Twins Rookies (Steve Brye, Bob Gebhard, Hal Haydel)	1.50	.70	.45
29a	Bill Bonham (Green under "C" and "S.")	7.50	3.75	2.25
29b	Bill Bonham (Yellow under "C" and "S.")	1.50	.70	.45
30	Rico Petrocelli	1.50	.70	.45
31	Cleon Jones	1.50	.70	.45
32	Cleon Jones (In Action)	1.50	.70	.45
33	Billy Martin	6.00	3.00	1.75
34	Billy Martin (In Action)	2.00	1.00	.60
35	Jerry Johnson	1.50	.70	.45
36	Jerry Johnson (In Action)	1.50	.70	.45
37	Carl Yastrzemski	10.00	5.00	2.50
38	Carl Yastrzemski (In Action)	5.00	2.50	1.50
39	Bob Barton	1.50	.70	.45
40	Bob Barton (In Action)	1.50	.70	.45
41	Tommy Davis	1.50	.70	.45
42	Tommy Davis (In Action)	1.50	.70	.45
43	Rick Wise	1.50	.70	.45
44	Rick Wise (In Action)	1.50	.70	.45
45a	Glenn Beckert (Green under "C" and "S.")	7.50	3.75	2.25
45b	Glenn Beckert (Yellow under "C" and "S.")	1.50	.70	.45
46	Glenn Beckert (In Action)	1.50	.70	.45
47	John Ellis	1.50	.70	.45
48	John Ellis (In Action)	1.50	.70	.45
49	Willie Mays	50.00	25.00	12.50
50	Willie Mays (In Action)	20.00	10.00	6.00
51	Harmon Killebrew	8.00	4.00	2.50
52	Harmon Killebrew (In Action)	5.00	2.50	1.50
53	Bud Harrelson	1.50	.70	.45
54	Bud Harrelson (In Action)	1.50	.70	.45
55	Clyde Wright	1.50	.70	.45
56	Rich Chiles	1.50	.70	.45
57	Bob Oliver	1.50	.70	.45
58	Ernie McAnally	1.50	.70	.45
59	*Fred Stanley*	1.50	.70	.45
60	Manny Sanguillen	1.50	.70	.45
61	Cubs Rookies (Gene Hiser, Burt Hooton, Earl Stephenson)	1.50	.70	.45
62	Angel Mangual	1.50	.70	.45
63	Duke Sims	1.50	.70	.45
64	Pete Broberg	1.50	.70	.45
65	Cesar Cedeno	1.50	.70	.45
66	Ray Corbin	1.50	.70	.45
67	Red Schoendienst	4.00	2.00	1.25
68	Jim York	1.50	.70	.45
69	Roger Freed	1.50	.70	.45
70	Mike Cuellar	1.50	.70	.45
71	Angels Team	3.00	1.50	.90
72	*Bruce Kison*	1.50	.70	.45
73	Steve Huntz	1.50	.70	.45
74	Cecil Upshaw	1.50	.70	.45
75	Bert Campaneris	1.50	.70	.45
76	Don Carrithers	1.50	.70	.45
77	Ron Theobald	1.50	.70	.45
78	Steve Arlin	1.50	.70	.45
79	Red Sox Rookies (Cecil Cooper, Carlton Fisk, Mike Garman)	60.00	30.00	15.00
80	Tony Perez	6.00	3.00	1.75
81	Mike Hedlund	1.50	.70	.45
82	Ron Woods	1.50	.70	.45
83	Dalton Jones	1.50	.70	.45
84	Vince Colbert	1.50	.70	.45

#	Name			
85	N.L. Batting Leaders (Glenn Beckert, Ralph Garr, Joe Torre)	4.00	2.00	1.25
86	A.L. Batting Leaders (Bobby Murcer, Tony Oliva, Merv Rettenmund)	3.00	1.50	.90
87	N.L. R.B.I. Leaders (Hank Aaron, Willie Stargell, Joe Torre)	6.00	3.00	1.75
88	A.L. R.B.I. Leaders (Harmon Killebrew, Frank Robinson, Reggie Smith)	3.00	1.50	.90
89	N.L. Home Run Leaders (Hank Aaron, Lee May, Willie Stargell)	6.00	3.00	1.75
90	A.L. Home Run Leaders (Norm Cash, Reggie Jackson, Bill Melton)	4.00	2.00	1.25
91	N.L. E.R.A. Leaders (Dave Roberts (picture is Denny Coombs), Tom Seaver, Don Wilson)	2.50	1.25	.70
92	A.L. E.R.A. Leaders (Vida Blue, Jim Palmer, Wilbur Wood)	2.00	1.00	.60
93	N.L. Pitching Leaders (Steve Carlton, Al Downing, Fergie Jenkins, Tom Seaver)	4.00	2.00	1.25
94	A.L. Pitching Leaders (Vida Blue, Mickey Lolich, Wilbur Wood)	1.50	.70	.45
95	N.L. Strikeout Leaders (Fergie Jenkins, Tom Seaver, Bill Stoneman)	4.00	2.00	1.25
96	A.L. Strikeout Leaders (Vida Blue, Joe Coleman, Mickey Lolich)	1.50	.70	.45
97	Tom Kelley	1.50	.70	.45
98	Chuck Tanner	1.50	.70	.45
99	*Ross Grimsley*	1.50	.70	.45
100	Frank Robinson	8.00	4.00	2.50
101	Astros Rookies (*Ray Busse, Bill Grief, J.R. Richard*)	4.00	2.00	1.25
102	Lloyd Allen	1.50	.70	.45
103	2nd Series Checklist (133-263)	2.00	1.00	.60
104	*Toby Harrah*	1.50	.70	.45
105	Gary Gentry	1.50	.70	.45
106	Brewers Team	3.00	1.50	.90
107	*Jose Cruz*	3.00	1.50	.90
108	Gary Waslewski	1.50	.70	.45
109	Jerry May	1.50	.70	.45
110	Ron Hunt	1.50	.70	.45
111	Jim Grant	1.50	.70	.45
112	Greg Luzinski	1.50	.70	.45
113	Rogelio Moret	1.50	.70	.45
114	Bill Buckner	1.50	.70	.45
115	Jim Fregosi	1.50	.70	.45
116	*Ed Farmer*	1.50	.70	.45
117a	Cleo James (Green under "C" and "S.")	7.50	3.75	2.25
117b	Cleo James (Yellow under "C" and "S.")	1.50	.70	.45
118	Skip Lockwood	1.50	.70	.45
119	Marty Perez	1.50	.70	.45
120	Bill Freehan	1.50	.70	.45
121	Ed Sprague	1.50	.70	.45
122	Larry Biittner	1.50	.70	.45
123	Ed Acosta	1.50	.70	.45
124	Yankees Rookies (Alan Closter, Roger Hambright, Rusty Torres)	1.50	.70	.45
125	Dave Cash	1.50	.70	.45
126	Bart Johnson	1.50	.70	.45
127	Duffy Dyer	1.50	.70	.45
128	Eddie Watt	1.50	.70	.45
129	Charlie Fox	1.50	.70	.45
130	Bob Gibson	8.00	4.00	2.50
131	Jim Nettles	1.50	.70	.45
132	Joe Morgan	8.00	4.00	2.50
133	Joe Keough	1.50	.70	.45
134	Carl Morton	1.50	.70	.45
135	Vada Pinson	2.50	1.25	.70
136	Darrel Chaney	1.50	.70	.45
137	Dick Williams	1.50	.70	.45
138	Mike Kekich	1.50	.70	.45
139	Tim McCarver	3.00	1.50	.90
140	Pat Dobson	1.50	.70	.45
141	Mets Rookies (Buzz Capra, Jon Matlack, Leroy Stanton)	1.50	.70	.45
142	*Chris Chambliss*	3.00	1.50	.90
143	Garry Jestadt	1.50	.70	.45
144	Marty Pattin	1.50	.70	.45
145	Don Kessinger	1.50	.70	.45
146	Steve Kealey	1.50	.70	.45
147	*Dave Kingman*	6.00	3.00	1.75
148	Dick Billings	1.50	.70	.45
149	Gary Neibauer	1.50	.70	.45
150	Norm Cash	2.50	1.25	.70
151	Jim Brewer	1.50	.70	.45
152	Gene Clines	1.50	.70	.45
153	Rick Auerbach	1.50	.70	.45
154	Ted Simmons	4.00	2.00	1.25
155	Larry Dierker	1.50	.70	.45
156	Twins Team	3.00	1.50	.90
157	Don Gullett	1.50	.70	.45
158	Jerry Kenney	1.50	.70	.45
159	John Boccabella	1.50	.70	.45
160	Andy Messersmith	1.50	.70	.45
161	Brock Davis	1.50	.70	.45
162	Brewers Rookies (Jerry Bell, Darrell Porter, Bob Reynolds) (Bell and Porter photos transposed.)	1.50	.70	.45
163	Tug McGraw	1.50	.70	.45
164	Tug McGraw (In Action)	1.50	.70	.45
165	*Chris Speier*	1.50	.70	.45
166	Chris Speier (In Action)	1.50	.70	.45

#	Name			
167	Deron Johnson	1.50	.70	.45
168	Deron Johnson (In Action)	1.50	.70	.45
169	Vida Blue	4.00	2.00	1.25
170	Vida Blue (In Action)	2.00	1.00	.60
171	Darrell Evans	3.00	1.50	.90
172	Darrell Evans (In Action)	2.00	1.00	.60
173	Clay Kirby	1.50	.70	.45
174	Clay Kirby (In Action)	1.50	.70	.45
175	Tom Haller	1.50	.70	.45
176	Tom Haller (In Action)	1.50	.70	.45
177	Paul Schaal	1.50	.70	.45
178	Paul Schaal (In Action)	1.50	.70	.45
179	Dock Ellis	1.50	.70	.45
180	Dock Ellis (In Action)	1.50	.70	.45
181	Ed Kranepool	1.50	.70	.45
182	Ed Kranepool (In Action)	1.50	.70	.45
183	Bill Melton	1.50	.70	.45
184	Bill Melton (In Action)	1.50	.70	.45
185	Ron Bryant	1.50	.70	.45
186	Ron Bryant (In Action)	1.50	.70	.45
187	Gates Brown	1.50	.70	.45
188	Frank Lucchesi	1.50	.70	.45
189	Gene Tenace	1.50	.70	.45
190	Dave Giusti	1.50	.70	.45
191	*Jeff Burroughs*	3.00	1.50	.90
192	Cubs Team	4.00	2.00	1.25
193	*Kurt Bevacqua*	1.50	.70	.45
194	Fred Norman	1.50	.70	.45
195	Orlando Cepeda	6.00	3.00	1.75
196	Mel Queen	1.50	.70	.45
197	Johnny Briggs	1.50	.70	.45
198	Dodgers Rookies (*Charlie Hough*, Bob O'Brien, Mike Strahler)	5.00	2.50	1.50
199	Mike Fiore	1.50	.70	.45
200	Lou Brock	8.00	4.00	2.50
201	Phil Roof	1.50	.70	.45
202	Scipio Spinks	1.50	.70	.45
203	*Ron Blomberg*	2.50	1.25	.70
204	Tommy Helms	1.50	.70	.45
205	Dick Drago	1.50	.70	.45
206	Dal Maxvill	1.50	.70	.45
207	Tom Egan	1.50	.70	.45
208	Milt Pappas	1.50	.70	.45
209	Joe Rudi	1.50	.70	.45
210	Denny McLain	3.00	1.50	.90
211	Gary Sutherland	1.50	.70	.45
212	Grant Jackson	1.50	.70	.45
213	Angels Rookies (Art Kusnyer, Billy Parker, Tom Silverio)	1.50	.70	.45
214	Mike McQueen	1.50	.70	.45
215	Alex Johnson	1.50	.70	.45
216	Joe Niekro	1.50	.70	.45
217	Roger Metzger	1.50	.70	.45
218	Eddie Kasko	1.50	.70	.45
219	*Rennie Stennett*	1.50	.70	.45
220	Jim Perry	1.50	.70	.45
221	N.L. Playoffs (Bucs Champs)	4.00	2.00	1.25
222	A.L. Playoffs (Orioles Champs)	5.00	2.50	1.50
223	World Series Game 1	4.00	2.00	1.25
224	World Series Game 2	4.00	2.00	1.25
225	World Series Game 3	4.00	2.00	1.25
226	World Series Game 4 (Roberto Clemente)	10.00	5.00	3.00
227	World Series Game 5	4.00	2.00	1.25
228	World Series Game 6	4.00	2.00	1.25
229	World Series Game 7	4.00	2.00	1.25
230	Series Celebration (On Top of the World)	4.00	2.00	1.25
231	Casey Cox	1.50	.70	.45
232	Giants Rookies (Chris Arnold, Jim Barr, Dave Rader)	1.50	.70	.45
233	Jay Johnstone	1.50	.70	.45
234	Ron Taylor	1.50	.70	.45
235	Merv Rettenmund	1.50	.70	.45
236	Jim McGlothlin	1.50	.70	.45
237	Yankees Team	4.00	2.00	1.25
238	Leron Lee	1.50	.70	.45
239	Tom Timmermann	1.50	.70	.45
240	Rich Allen	3.00	1.50	.90
241	Rollie Fingers	6.00	3.00	1.75
242	Don Mincher	1.50	.70	.45
243	Frank Linzy	1.50	.70	.45
244	Steve Braun	1.50	.70	.45
245	Tommie Agee	1.50	.70	.45
246	Tom Burgmeier	1.50	.70	.45
247	Milt May	1.50	.70	.45
248	Tom Bradley	1.50	.70	.45
249	Harry Walker	1.50	.70	.45
250	Boog Powell	2.00	1.00	.60
251a	3rd Series Checklist (264-394) (Small print on front.)	3.00	1.50	.90
251b	3rd Series Checklist (264-394) (Large print on front.)	3.00	1.50	.90
252	Ken Reynolds	1.50	.70	.45
253	Sandy Alomar	1.50	.70	.45
254	Boots Day	1.50	.70	.45
255	Jim Lonborg	1.50	.70	.45
256	George Foster	2.50	1.25	.70
257	Tigers Rookies (Jim Foor, Tim Hosley, Paul Jata)	1.50	.70	.45
258	Randy Hundley	1.50	.70	.45
259	Sparky Lyle	1.50	.70	.45
260	Ralph Garr	1.50	.70	.45
261	Steve Mingori	1.50	.70	.45
262	Padres Team	3.00	1.50	.90
263	Felipe Alou	2.00	1.00	.60
264	Tommy John	2.00	1.00	.60
265	Wes Parker	1.50	.70	.45
266	Bobby Bolin	1.50	.70	.45
267	Dave Concepcion	2.00	1.00	.60
268	A's Rookies (Dwain Anderson, Chris Floethe)	1.50	.70	.45
269	Don Hahn	1.50	.70	.45
270	Jim Palmer	8.00	4.00	2.50
271	Ken Rudolph	1.50	.70	.45
272	*Mickey Rivers*	2.00	1.00	.60

#	Name			
273	Bobby Floyd	1.50	.70	.45
274	Al Severinsen	1.50	.70	.45
275	Cesar Tovar	1.50	.70	.45
276	Gene Mauch	1.50	.70	.45
277	Elliott Maddox	1.50	.70	.45
278	Dennis Higgins	1.50	.70	.45
279	Larry Brown	1.50	.70	.45
280	Willie McCovey	8.00	4.00	2.50
281	Bill Parsons	1.50	.70	.45
282	Astros Team	4.00	2.00	1.25
283	Darrell Brandon	1.50	.70	.45
284	Ike Brown	1.50	.70	.45
285	Gaylord Perry	6.00	3.00	1.75
286	Gene Alley	1.50	.70	.45
287	Jim Hardin	1.50	.70	.45
288	Johnny Jeter	1.50	.70	.45
289	Syd O'Brien	1.50	.70	.45
290	Sonny Siebert	1.50	.70	.45
291	Hal McRae	2.50	1.25	.70
292	Hal McRae (In Action)	1.50	.70	.45
293	Danny Frisella	1.50	.70	.45
294	Danny Frisella (In Action)	1.50	.70	.45
295	Dick Dietz	1.50	.70	.45
296	Dick Dietz (In Action)	1.50	.70	.45
297	Claude Osteen	1.50	.70	.45
298	Claude Osteen (In Action)	1.50	.70	.45
299	Hank Aaron	50.00	25.00	12.50
300	Hank Aaron (In Action)	25.00	12.50	7.50
301	George Mitterwald	1.50	.70	.45
302	George Mitterwald (In Action)	1.50	.70	.45
303	Joe Pepitone	2.00	1.00	.60
304	Joe Pepitone (In Action)	1.50	.70	.45
305	Ken Boswell	1.50	.70	.45
306	Ken Boswell (In Action)	1.50	.70	.45
307	Steve Renko	1.50	.70	.45
308	Steve Renko (In Action)	1.50	.70	.45
309	Roberto Clemente	50.00	25.00	15.00
310	Roberto Clemente (In Action)	30.00	15.00	9.00
311	Clay Carroll	1.50	.70	.45
312	Clay Carroll (In Action)	1.50	.70	.45
313	Luis Aparicio	6.00	3.00	1.75
314	Luis Aparicio (In Action)	4.00	2.00	1.25
315	Paul Splittorff	1.50	.70	.45
316	Cardinals Rookies (*Jim Bibby*, Santiago Guzman, Jorge Roque)	1.50	.70	.45
317	Rich Hand	1.50	.70	.45
318	Sonny Jackson	1.50	.70	.45
319	Aurelio Rodriguez	1.50	.70	.45
320	Steve Blass	1.50	.70	.45
321	Joe Lahoud	1.50	.70	.45
322	Jose Pena	1.50	.70	.45
323	Earl Weaver	5.00	2.50	1.50
324	Mike Ryan	1.50	.70	.45
325	Mel Stottlemyre	1.50	.70	.45
326	Pat Kelly	1.50	.70	.45
327	*Steve Stone*	3.00	1.50	.90
328	Red Sox Team	5.00	2.50	1.50
329	Roy Foster	1.50	.70	.45
330	Jim Hunter	6.00	3.00	1.75
331	Stan Swanson	1.50	.70	.45
332	Buck Martinez	1.50	.70	.45
333	Steve Barber	1.50	.70	.45
334	Rangers Rookies (Bill Fahey, Jim Mason, Tom Ragland)	1.50	.70	.45
335	Bill Hands	1.50	.70	.45
336	Marty Martinez	1.50	.70	.45
337	Mike Kilkenny	1.50	.70	.45
338	Bob Grich	1.50	.70	.45
339	Ron Cook	1.50	.70	.45
340	Roy White	1.50	.70	.45
341	Joe Torre (Boyhood Photo)	2.50	1.25	.70
342	Wilbur Wood (Boyhood Photo)	1.50	.70	.45
343	Willie Stargell (Boyhood Photo)	2.00	1.00	.60
344	Dave McNally (Boyhood Photo)	1.50	.70	.45
345	Rick Wise (Boyhood Photo)	1.50	.70	.45
346	Jim Fregosi (Boyhood Photo)	1.50	.70	.45
347	Tom Seaver (Boyhood Photo)	3.00	1.50	.90
348	Sal Bando (Boyhood Photo)	1.50	.70	.45
349	Al Fitzmorris	1.50	.70	.45
350	Frank Howard	2.00	1.00	.60
351	Braves Rookies (Jimmy Britton, Tom House, Rick Kester)	1.50	.70	.45
352	Dave LaRoche	1.50	.70	.45
353	Art Shamsky	1.50	.70	.45
354	Tom Murphy	1.50	.70	.45
355	Bob Watson	1.50	.70	.45
356	Gerry Moses	1.50	.70	.45
357	Woodie Fryman	1.50	.70	.45
358	Sparky Anderson	4.00	2.00	1.25
359	Don Pavletich	1.50	.70	.45
360	Dave Roberts	1.50	.70	.45
361	Mike Andrews	1.50	.70	.45
362	Mets Team	4.00	2.00	1.25
363	Ron Klimkowski	1.50	.70	.45
364	Johnny Callison	1.50	.70	.45
365	Dick Bosman	1.50	.70	.45
366	Jimmy Rosario	1.50	.70	.45
367	Ron Perranoski	1.50	.70	.45
368	Danny Thompson	1.50	.70	.45
369	Jim Lefebvre	1.50	.70	.45
370	Don Buford	1.50	.70	.45
371	Denny Lemaster	1.50	.70	.45
372	Royals Rookies (Lance Clemons, Monty Montgomery)	1.50	.70	.45
373	John Mayberry	1.50	.70	.45
374	Jack Heidemann	1.50	.70	.45
375	Reggie Cleveland	1.50	.70	.45
376	Andy Kosco	1.50	.70	.45
377	Terry Harmon	1.50	.70	.45
378	4th Series Checklist (395-525)	3.00	1.50	.90
379	Ken Berry	1.50	.70	.45
380	Earl Williams	1.50	.70	.45
381	White Sox Team	3.00	1.50	.90

No.	Player			
382	Joe Gibbon	1.50	.70	.45
383	Brant Alyea	1.50	.70	.45
384	Dave Campbell	1.50	.70	.45
385	Mickey Stanley	1.50	.70	.45
386	Jim Colborn	1.50	.70	.45
387	Horace Clarke	1.50	.70	.45
388	Charlie Williams	1.50	.70	.45
389	Bill Rigney	1.50	.70	.45
390	Willie Davis	1.50	.70	.45
391	Ken Sanders	1.50	.70	.45
392	Pirates Rookies (*Fred Cambria, Richie Zisk*)	2.00	1.00	.60
393	Curt Motton	1.50	.70	.45
394	Ken Forsch	1.50	.70	.45
395	Matty Alou	1.50	.70	.45
396	Paul Lindblad	1.50	.70	.45
397	Phillies Team	4.00	2.00	1.25
398	Larry Hisle	2.00	1.00	.60
399	Milt Wilcox	1.50	.70	.45
400	Tony Oliva	3.00	1.50	.90
401	Jim Nash	1.50	.70	.45
402	Bobby Heise	1.50	.70	.45
403	John Cumberland	1.50	.70	.45
404	Jeff Torborg	1.50	.70	.45
405	Ron Fairly	1.50	.70	.45
406	*George Hendrick*	2.00	1.00	.60
407	Chuck Taylor	1.50	.70	.45
408	Jim Northrup	1.50	.70	.45
409	Frank Baker	1.50	.70	.45
410	Fergie Jenkins	6.00	3.00	1.75
411	Bob Montgomery	1.50	.70	.45
412	Dick Kelley	1.50	.70	.45
413	White Sox Rookies (Don Eddy, Dave Lemonds)	1.50	.70	.45
414	Bob Miller	1.50	.70	.45
415	Cookie Rojas	1.50	.70	.45
416	Johnny Edwards	1.50	.70	.45
417	Tom Hall	1.50	.70	.45
418	Tom Shopay	1.50	.70	.45
419	Jim Spencer	1.50	.70	.45
420	Steve Carlton	15.00	7.50	4.50
421	Ellie Rodriguez	1.50	.70	.45
422	Ray Lamb	1.50	.70	.45
423	Oscar Gamble	1.50	.70	.45
424	Bill Gogolewski	1.50	.70	.45
425	Ken Singleton	1.50	.70	.45
426	Ken Singleton (In Action)	1.50	.70	.45
427	Tito Fuentes	1.50	.70	.45
428	Tito Fuentes (In Action)	1.50	.70	.45
429	Bob Robertson	1.50	.70	.45
430	Bob Robertson (In Action)	1.50	.70	.45
431	Clarence Gaston	1.50	.70	.45
432	Clarence Gaston (In Action)	1.50	.70	.45
433	Johnny Bench	25.00	12.50	6.25
434	Johnny Bench (In Action)	15.00	7.50	3.75
435	Reggie Jackson	25.00	12.50	7.50
436	Reggie Jackson (In Action)	10.00	5.00	2.50
437	Maury Wills	1.50	.70	.45
438	Maury Wills (In Action)	1.50	.70	.45
439	Billy Williams	8.00	4.00	2.50
440	Billy Williams (In Action)	5.00	2.50	1.50
441	Thurman Munson	25.00	12.50	6.25
442	Thurman Munson (In Action)	10.00	5.00	3.00
443	Ken Henderson	1.50	.70	.45
444	Ken Henderson (In Action)	1.50	.70	.45
445	Tom Seaver	25.00	12.50	7.50
446	Tom Seaver (In Action)	10.00	5.00	2.50
447	Willie Stargell	10.00	5.00	2.50
448	Willie Stargell (In Action)	5.00	2.50	1.50
449	Bob Lemon	4.00	2.00	1.25
450	Mickey Lolich	1.50	.70	.45
451	Tony LaRussa	2.50	1.25	.70
452	Ed Herrmann	1.50	.70	.45
453	Barry Lersch	1.50	.70	.45
454	A's Team	4.00	2.00	1.25
455	Tommy Harper	1.50	.70	.45
456	Mark Belanger	1.50	.70	.45
457	Padres Rookies (*Darcy Fast, Mike Ivie, Derrel Thomas*)	1.50	.70	.45
458	Aurelio Monteagudo	1.50	.70	.45
459	Rick Renick	1.50	.70	.45
460	Al Downing	1.50	.70	.45
461	Tim Cullen	1.50	.70	.45
462	Rickey Clark	1.50	.70	.45
463	Bernie Carbo	1.50	.70	.45
464	Jim Roland	1.50	.70	.45
465	Gil Hodges	4.00	2.00	1.25
466	Norm Miller	1.50	.70	.45
467	Steve Kline	1.50	.70	.45
468	Richie Scheinblum	1.50	.70	.45
469	Ron Herbel	1.50	.70	.45
470	Ray Fosse	1.50	.70	.45
471	Luke Walker	1.50	.70	.45
472	Phil Gagliano	1.50	.70	.45
473	Dan McGinn	1.50	.70	.45
474	Orioles Rookies (*Don Baylor, Roric Harrison, Johnny Oates*)	10.00	5.00	3.00
475	Gary Nolan	1.50	.70	.45
476	Lee Richard	1.50	.70	.45
477	Tom Phoebus	1.50	.70	.45
478a	5th Series Checklist (526-656) (Small print on front.)	2.50	1.25	.70
478b	5th Series Checklist (526-656) (Large printing on front.)	2.50	1.25	.70
479	Don Shaw	1.50	.70	.45
480	Lee May	1.50	.70	.45
481	Billy Conigliaro	1.50	.70	.45
482	Joe Hoerner	1.50	.70	.45
483	Ken Suarez	1.50	.70	.45
484	Lum Harris	1.50	.70	.45
485	Phil Regan	1.50	.70	.45
486	John Lowenstein	1.50	.70	.45
487	Tigers Team	5.00	2.50	1.50
488	Mike Nagy	1.50	.70	.45
489	Expos Rookies (Terry Humphrey, Keith Lampard)	1.50	.70	.45
490	Dave McNally	1.50	.70	.45
491	Lou Piniella (Boyhood Photo)	1.50	.70	.45
492	Mel Stottlemyre (Boyhood Photo)	1.50	.70	.45
493	Bob Bailey (Boyhood Photo)	1.50	.70	.45
494	Willie Horton (Boyhood Photo)	1.50	.70	.45
495	Bill Melton (Boyhood Photo)	1.50	.70	.45
496	Bud Harrelson (Boyhood Photo)	1.50	.70	.45
497	Jim Perry (Boyhood Photo)	1.50	.70	.45
498	Brooks Robinson (Boyhood Photo)	4.00	2.00	1.25
499	Vicente Romo	1.50	.70	.45
500	Joe Torre	5.00	2.50	1.50
501	Pete Hamm	1.50	.70	.45
502	Jackie Hernandez	1.50	.70	.45
503	Gary Peters	1.50	.70	.45
504	Ed Spiezio	1.50	.70	.45
505	Mike Marshall	1.50	.70	.45
506	Indians Rookies (*Terry Ley, Jim Moyer, Dick Tidrow*)	1.50	.70	.45
507	Fred Gladding	1.50	.70	.45
508	Ellie Hendricks	1.50	.70	.45
509	Don McMahon	1.50	.70	.45
510	Ted Williams	20.00	10.00	5.00
511	Tony Taylor	1.50	.70	.45
512	Paul Popovich	1.50	.70	.45
513	Lindy McDaniel	1.50	.70	.45
514	Ted Sizemore	1.50	.70	.45
515	Bert Blyleven	3.00	1.50	.90
516	Oscar Brown	1.50	.70	.45
517	Ken Brett	1.50	.70	.45
518	Wayne Garrett	1.50	.70	.45
519	Ted Abernathy	1.50	.70	.45
520	Larry Bowa	1.50	.70	.45
521	Alan Foster	1.50	.70	.45
522	Dodgers Team	4.00	2.00	1.25
523	Chuck Dobson	1.50	.70	.45
524	Reds Rookies (Ed Armbrister, Mel Behney)	1.50	.70	.45
525	Carlos May	1.50	.70	.45
526	Bob Bailey	4.00	2.00	1.00
527	Dave Leonhard	4.00	2.00	1.00
528	Ron Stone	4.00	2.00	1.00
529	Dave Nelson	4.00	2.00	1.00
530	Don Sutton	10.00	5.00	3.00
531	Freddie Patek	5.00	2.50	1.25
532	Fred Kendall	4.00	2.00	1.00
533	Ralph Houk	6.00	3.00	1.75
534	Jim Hickman	4.00	2.00	1.00
535	Ed Brinkman	4.00	2.00	1.00
536	Doug Rader	4.00	2.00	1.00
537	Bob Locker	4.00	2.00	1.00
538	Charlie Sands	4.00	2.00	1.00
539	*Terry Forster*	5.00	2.50	1.25
540	Felix Millan	4.00	2.00	1.00
541	Roger Repoz	4.00	2.00	1.00
542	Jack Billingham	4.00	2.00	1.00
543	Duane Josephson	4.00	2.00	1.00
544	Ted Martinez	4.00	2.00	1.00
545	Wayne Granger	4.00	2.00	1.00
546	Joe Hague	4.00	2.00	1.00
547	Indians Team	6.00	3.00	1.75
548	Frank Reberger	4.00	2.00	1.00
549	Dave May	4.00	2.00	1.00
550	Brooks Robinson	20.00	10.00	5.00
551	Ollie Brown	4.00	2.00	1.00
552	Ollie Brown (In Action)	4.00	2.00	1.00
553	Wilbur Wood	4.00	2.00	1.00
554	Wilbur Wood (In Action)	4.00	2.00	1.00
555	Ron Santo	8.00	4.00	2.50
556	Ron Santo (In Action)	5.00	2.50	1.25
557	John Odom	4.00	2.00	1.00
558	John Odom (In Action)	4.00	2.00	1.00
559	Pete Rose	40.00	20.00	10.00
560	Pete Rose (In Action)	20.00	10.00	5.00
561	Leo Cardenas	4.00	2.00	1.00
562	Leo Cardenas (In Action)	4.00	2.00	1.00
563	Ray Sadecki	4.00	2.00	1.00
564	Ray Sadecki (In Action)	4.00	2.00	1.00
565	Reggie Smith	4.00	2.00	1.00
566	Reggie Smith (In Action)	4.00	2.00	1.00
567	Juan Marichal	10.00	5.00	3.00
568	Juan Marichal (In Action)	5.00	2.50	1.50
569	Ed Kirkpatrick	4.00	2.00	1.00
570	Ed Kirkpatrick (In Action)	4.00	2.00	1.00
571	Nate Colbert	4.00	2.00	1.00
572	Nate Colbert (In Action)	4.00	2.00	1.00
573	Fritz Peterson	4.00	2.00	1.00
574	Fritz Peterson (In Action)	4.00	2.00	1.00
575	Al Oliver	5.00	2.50	1.25
576	Leo Durocher	5.00	2.50	1.50
577	Mike Paul	4.00	2.00	1.00
578	Billy Grabarkewitz	4.00	2.00	1.00
579	*Doyle Alexander*	5.00	2.50	1.25
580	Lou Piniella	5.00	2.50	1.50
581	Wade Blasingame	4.00	2.00	1.00
582	Expos Team	6.00	3.00	1.75
583	Darold Knowles	4.00	2.00	1.00
584	Jerry McNertney	4.00	2.00	1.00
585	George Scott	4.00	2.00	1.00
586	Denis Menke	4.00	2.00	1.00
587	Billy Wilson	4.00	2.00	1.00
588	Jim Holt	4.00	2.00	1.00
589	Hal Lanier	4.00	2.00	1.00
590	Graig Nettles	4.00	2.00	1.00
591	Paul Casanova	4.00	2.00	1.00
592	Lew Krausse	4.00	2.00	1.00
593	Rich Morales	4.00	2.00	1.00
594	Jim Beauchamp	4.00	2.00	1.00
595	Nolan Ryan	100.00	50.00	30.00
596	Manny Mota	4.00	2.00	1.00
597	Jim Magnuson	4.00	2.00	1.00
598	Hal King	4.00	2.00	1.00
599	Billy Champion	4.00	2.00	1.00
600	Al Kaline	20.00	10.00	5.00
601	George Stone	4.00	2.00	1.00
602	Dave Bristol	4.00	2.00	1.00
603	Jim Ray	4.00	2.00	1.00
604a	6th Series Checklist (657-787) (Copyright on right.)	6.00	3.00	1.75
604b	6th Series Checklist (657-787) (Copyright on left.)	6.00	3.00	1.75
605	Nelson Briles	4.00	2.00	1.00
606	Luis Melendez	4.00	2.00	1.00
607	Frank Duffy	4.00	2.00	1.00
608	Mike Corkins	4.00	2.00	1.00
609	Tom Grieve	4.00	2.00	1.00
610	Bill Stoneman	4.00	2.00	1.00
611	Rich Reese	4.00	2.00	1.00
612	Joe Decker	4.00	2.00	1.00
613	Mike Ferraro	4.00	2.00	1.00
614	Ted Uhlaender	4.00	2.00	1.00
615	Steve Hargan	4.00	2.00	1.00
616	*Joe Ferguson*	3.00	1.50	.90
617	Royals Team	6.00	3.00	1.75
618	Rich Robertson	4.00	2.00	1.00
619	Rich McKinney	4.00	2.00	1.00
620	Phil Niekro	10.00	5.00	3.00
621	Commissioners Award	4.00	2.00	1.00
622	Most Valuable Player Award	4.00	2.00	1.00
623	Cy Young Award	4.00	2.00	1.00
624	Minor League Player Of The Year Award	4.00	2.00	1.00
625	Rookie of the Year Award	4.00	2.00	1.00
626	Babe Ruth Award	4.00	2.00	1.00
627	Moe Drabowsky	4.00	2.00	1.00
628	Terry Crowley	4.00	2.00	1.00
629	Paul Doyle	4.00	2.00	1.00
630	Rich Hebner	4.00	2.00	1.00
631	John Strohmayer	4.00	2.00	1.00
632	Mike Hegan	4.00	2.00	1.00
633	Jack Hiatt	4.00	2.00	1.00
634	Dick Woodson	4.00	2.00	1.00
635	Don Money	4.00	2.00	1.00
636	Bill Lee	4.00	2.00	1.00
637	Preston Gomez	4.00	2.00	1.00
638	Ken Wright	4.00	2.00	1.00
639	J.C. Martin	4.00	2.00	1.00
640	Joe Coleman	4.00	2.00	1.00
641	Mike Lum	4.00	2.00	1.00
642	Denny Riddleberger	4.00	2.00	1.00
643	Russ Gibson	4.00	2.00	1.00
644	Bernie Allen	4.00	2.00	1.00
645	Jim Maloney	4.00	2.00	1.00
646	Chico Salmon	4.00	2.00	1.00
647	Bob Moose	4.00	2.00	1.00
648	Jim Lyttle	4.00	2.00	1.00
649	Pete Richert	4.00	2.00	1.00
650	Sal Bando	4.00	2.00	1.00
651	Reds Team	8.00	4.00	2.50
652	Marcelino Lopez	4.00	2.00	1.00
653	Jim Fairey	4.00	2.00	1.00
654	Horacio Pina	4.00	2.00	1.00
655	Jerry Grote	4.00	2.00	1.00
656	Rudy May	4.00	2.00	1.00
657	Bobby Wine	12.00	6.00	3.00
658	Steve Dunning	12.00	6.00	3.00
659	Bob Aspromonte	12.00	6.00	3.00
660	Paul Blair	12.00	6.00	3.00
661	Bill Virdon	12.00	6.00	3.00
662	Stan Bahnsen	12.00	6.00	3.00
663	Fran Healy	12.00	6.00	3.00
664	Bobby Knoop	12.00	6.00	3.00
665	Chris Short	12.00	6.00	3.00
666	Hector Torres	12.00	6.00	3.00
667	Ray Newman	12.00	6.00	3.00
668	Rangers Team	25.00	12.50	6.25
669	Willie Crawford	12.00	6.00	3.00
670	Ken Holtzman	12.00	6.00	3.00
671	Donn Clendenon	12.00	6.00	3.00
672	Archie Reynolds	12.00	6.00	3.00
673	Dave Marshall	12.00	6.00	3.00
674	John Kennedy	12.00	6.00	3.00
675	Pat Jarvis	12.00	6.00	3.00
676	Danny Cater	12.00	6.00	3.00
677	Ivan Murrell	12.00	6.00	3.00
678	Steve Luebber	12.00	6.00	3.00
679	Astros Rookies (Bob Fenwick, Bob Stinson)	12.00	6.00	3.00
680	Dave Johnson	12.00	6.00	3.00
681	Bobby Pfeil	12.00	6.00	3.00
682	Mike McCormick	12.00	6.00	3.00
683	Steve Hovley	12.00	6.00	3.00
684	Hal Breeden	12.00	6.00	3.00
685	Joe Horlen	12.00	6.00	3.00
686	Steve Garvey	25.00	12.50	7.50
687	Del Unser	12.00	6.00	3.00
688	Cardinals Team	15.00	7.50	3.75
689	Eddie Fisher	12.00	6.00	3.00
690	Willie Montanez	12.00	6.00	3.00
691	Curt Blefary	12.00	6.00	3.00
692	Curt Blefary (In Action)	12.00	6.00	3.00
693	Alan Gallagher	12.00	6.00	3.00
694	Alan Gallagher (In Action)	12.00	6.00	3.00
695	Rod Carew	50.00	25.00	15.00
696	Rod Carew (In Action)	25.00	12.50	7.50
697	Jerry Koosman	15.00	7.50	4.50
698	Jerry Koosman (In Action)	12.00	6.00	3.00
699	Bobby Murcer	13.00	6.50	3.75
700	Bobby Murcer (In Action)	12.00	6.00	3.00
701	Jose Pagan	12.00	6.00	3.00
702	Jose Pagan (In Action)	12.00	6.00	3.00
703	Doug Griffin	12.00	6.00	3.00
704	Doug Griffin (In Action)	12.00	6.00	3.00
705	Pat Corrales	12.00	6.00	3.00
706	Pat Corrales (In Action)	12.00	6.00	3.00
707	Tim Foli	12.00	6.00	3.00
708	Tim Foli (In Action)	12.00	6.00	3.00
709	Jim Kaat	15.00	7.50	4.50
710	Jim Kaat (In Action)	12.00	6.00	3.00
711	Bobby Bonds	12.00	6.00	3.00
712	Bobby Bonds (In Action)	12.00	6.00	3.00
713	Gene Michael	12.00	6.00	3.00

		NM	EX	VG
714	Gene Michael (In Action)	12.00	6.00	3.00
715	Mike Epstein	12.00	6.00	3.00
716	Jesus Alou	12.00	6.00	3.00
717	Bruce Dal Canton	12.00	6.00	3.00
718	Del Rice	12.00	6.00	3.00
719	Cesar Geronimo	12.00	6.00	3.00
720	Sam McDowell	12.00	6.00	3.00
721	Eddie Leon	12.00	6.00	3.00
722	Bill Sudakis	12.00	6.00	3.00
723	Al Santorini	12.00	6.00	3.00
724	A.L. Rookies (John Curtis, Rich Hinton, Mickey Scott)	12.00	6.00	3.00
725	Dick McAuliffe	12.00	6.00	3.00
726	Dick Selma	12.00	6.00	3.00
727	Jose Laboy	12.00	6.00	3.00
728	Gail Hopkins	12.00	6.00	3.00
729	Bob Veale	12.00	6.00	3.00
730	Rick Monday	12.00	6.00	3.00
731	Orioles Team	15.00	7.50	4.50
732	George Culver	12.00	6.00	3.00
733	Jim Hart	12.00	6.00	3.00
734	Bob Burda	12.00	6.00	3.00
735	Diego Segui	12.00	6.00	3.00
736	Bill Russell	12.00	6.00	3.00
737	*Lenny Randle*	12.00	6.00	3.00
738	Jim Merritt	12.00	6.00	3.00
739	Don Mason	12.00	6.00	3.00
740	Rico Carty	12.00	6.00	3.00
741	Major League Rookies (*Tom Hutton, Rick Miller, John Milner*)	12.00	6.00	3.00
742	Jim Rooker	12.00	6.00	3.00
743	Cesar Gutierrez	12.00	6.00	3.00
744	*Jim Slaton*	12.00	6.00	3.00
745	Julian Javier	12.00	6.00	3.00
746	Lowell Palmer	12.00	6.00	3.00
747	Jim Stewart	12.00	6.00	3.00
748	Phil Hennigan	12.00	6.00	3.00
749	Walter Alston	15.00	7.50	4.50
750	Willie Horton	12.00	6.00	3.00
751	Steve Carlton (Traded)	30.00	15.00	9.00
752	Joe Morgan (Traded)	30.00	15.00	9.00
753	Denny McLain (Traded)	15.00	7.50	4.50
754	Frank Robinson (Traded)	25.00	12.50	6.25
755	Jim Fregosi (Traded)	15.00	7.50	4.50
756	Rick Wise (Traded)	12.00	6.00	3.00
757	Jose Cardenal (Traded)	12.00	6.00	3.00
758	Gil Garrido	12.00	6.00	3.00
759	Chris Cannizzaro	12.00	6.00	3.00
760	Bill Mazeroski	20.00	10.00	6.00
761	A.L.-N.L. Rookies (**Ron Cey, Ben Oglivie**, Bernie Williams)	20.00	10.00	6.00
762	Wayne Simpson	12.00	6.00	3.00
763	Ron Hansen	12.00	6.00	3.00
764	Dusty Baker	15.00	7.50	4.50
765	Ken McMullen	12.00	6.00	3.00
766	Steve Hamilton	12.00	6.00	3.00
767	Tom McCraw	12.00	6.00	3.00
768	Denny Doyle	12.00	6.00	3.00
769	Jack Aker	12.00	6.00	3.00
770	Jim Wynn	12.00	6.00	3.00
771	Giants Team	15.00	7.50	3.75
772	Ken Tatum	12.00	6.00	3.00
773	Ron Brand	12.00	6.00	3.00
774	Luis Alvarado	12.00	6.00	3.00
775	Jerry Reuss	12.00	6.00	3.00
776	Bill Voss	12.00	6.00	3.00
777	Hoyt Wilhelm	20.00	10.00	5.00
778	Twins Rookies (Vic Albury, **Rick Dempsey**, Jim Strickland)	15.00	7.50	3.75
779	Tony Cloninger	12.00	6.00	3.00
780	Dick Green	12.00	6.00	3.00
781	Jim McAndrew	12.00	6.00	3.00
782	Larry Stahl	12.00	6.00	3.00
783	Les Cain	12.00	6.00	3.00
784	Ken Aspromonte	12.00	6.00	3.00
785	Vic Davalillo	12.00	6.00	3.00
786	Chuck Brinkman	12.00	6.00	3.00
787	Ron Reed	12.00	6.00	3.00

1972 Topps Candy Lid Test Issue

Between the production of its regular-issue candy lid sets of 1970 and 1973, Topps was working on another issue that survives today in proof form, either as uncropped squares or cut to the 1-7/8" diameter tabbed lid form meant to cover a plastic bucket of bubblegum nuggets. The 1972 proofs are very close to the 1973 issue in format; the principal difference is the player portrait does not have a solid-color border as on the 1973s, and that the pictures of Seaver and Yaz on the front are set against green, rather than orange, stars. The extent of the checklist is unknown.

		NM	EX	VG
Common Player:		100.00	50.00	30.00
(1)	Hank Aaron	900.00	450.00	275.00
(2)	Dick Allen	150.00	75.00	45.00
(3)	Dusty Baker	100.00	50.00	35.00
(4)	Sal Bando	100.00	50.00	30.00
(5)	Johnny Bench	450.00	225.00	135.00

		NM	EX	VG
(6)	Bobby Bonds	100.00	50.00	30.00
(7)	Dick Bosman	100.00	50.00	30.00
(8)	Lou Brock	250.00	125.00	75.00
(9)	Rod Carew	300.00	150.00	90.00
(10)	Steve Carlton	300.00	150.00	90.00
(11)	Nate Colbert	100.00	50.00	30.00
(12)	Willie Davis	100.00	50.00	30.00
(13)	Larry Dierker	100.00	50.00	30.00
(14)	Mike Epstein	100.00	50.00	30.00
(15)	Carlton Fisk	300.00	150.00	90.00
(16)	Tim Foli	100.00	50.00	30.00
(17)	Ray Fosse	100.00	50.00	30.00
(18)	Bill Freehan	100.00	50.00	30.00
(19)	Bob Gibson	300.00	150.00	90.00
(20)	Bud Harrelson	100.00	50.00	30.00
(21)	Catfish Hunter	250.00	125.00	75.00
(22)	Reggie Jackson	650.00	325.00	195.00
(23)	Fergie Jenkins	250.00	125.00	75.00
(24)	Al Kaline	350.00	175.00	100.00
(25)	Harmon Killebrew	350.00	175.00	100.00
(26)	Clay Kirby	100.00	50.00	30.00
(27)	Mickey Lolich	100.00	50.00	30.00
(28)	Greg Luzinski	100.00	50.00	30.00
(29)	Mike Marshall	100.00	50.00	30.00
(30)	Lee May	100.00	50.00	30.00
(31)	John Mayberry	100.00	50.00	30.00
(32)	Willie Mays	900.00	450.00	275.00
(33)	Willie McCovey	250.00	125.00	75.00
(34)	Thurman Munson	300.00	150.00	90.00
(35)	Bobby Murcer	150.00	75.00	45.00
(36)	Gary Nolan	100.00	50.00	30.00
(37)	Amos Otis	100.00	50.00	30.00
(38)	Jim Palmer	250.00	125.00	75.00
(39)	Gaylord Perry	250.00	125.00	75.00
(40)	Lou Piniella	150.00	75.00	45.00
(41)	Brooks Robinson	350.00	175.00	100.00
(42)	Frank Robinson	350.00	175.00	100.00
(43)	Ellie Rodriguez	100.00	50.00	30.00
(44)	Pete Rose	900.00	450.00	275.00
(45)	Nolan Ryan	2,500	1,250	750.00
(46)	Manny Sanguillen	100.00	50.00	30.00
(47)	George Scott	100.00	50.00	30.00
(48)	Tom Seaver	350.00	175.00	100.00
(49)	Chris Speier	100.00	50.00	30.00
(50)	Willie Stargell	250.00	125.00	75.00
(51)	Don Sutton	250.00	125.00	75.00
(52)	Joe Torre	150.00	75.00	45.00
(53)	Billy Williams	250.00	125.00	75.00
(54)	Wilbur Wood	100.00	50.00	30.00
(55)	Carl Yastrzemski	450.00	225.00	135.00

1972 Topps Cloth Stickers

Despite the fact they were never actually issued, examples of this test issue can readily be found within the hobby. The set of 33 contains stickers with designs identical to cards found in three contiguous rows of a regular Topps card sheet that year; thus the inclusion of a meaningless checklist card. Sometimes found in complete 33-sticker strips, or 132-piece sheets, individual stickers nominally measure 2-1/2" x 3-1/2", though dimensions vary according to the care with which they were cut. Stickers are unnumbered and blank-backed; most are found without the original paper backing as the glue used did not hold up well over the years. Eleven of the stickers are prone to miscutting and are identified with an (SP) in the checklist.

		NM	EX	VG
Complete Set (33):		1,300	650.00	390.00
Common Player:		20.00	10.00	6.00
(1)	Hank Aaron	200.00	100.00	60.00
(2)	Luis Aparicio (In Action)(SP)	60.00	30.00	18.00
(3)	Ike Brown	20.00	10.00	6.00
(4)	Johnny Callison	20.00	10.00	6.00
(5)	Checklist 264-319	10.00	5.00	3.00
(6)	Roberto Clemente (In Action)	300.00	150.00	90.00
(7)	Dave Concepcion (SP)	40.00	20.00	12.00
(8)	Ron Cook	20.00	10.00	6.00
(9)	Willie Davis	20.00	10.00	6.00
(10)	Al Fitzmorris	20.00	10.00	6.00
(11)	Bobby Floyd	20.00	10.00	6.00
(12)	Roy Foster	20.00	10.00	6.00
(13)	Jim Fregosi (Boyhood Photo)	20.00	10.00	6.00
(14)	Danny Frisella (In Action)	20.00	10.00	6.00
(15)	Woody Fryman (SP)	25.00	12.50	7.50
(16)	Terry Harmon	20.00	10.00	6.00
(17)	Frank Howard (SP)	40.00	20.00	12.00
(18)	Ron Klimkowski	20.00	10.00	6.00
(19)	Joe Lahoud	20.00	10.00	6.00
(20)	Jim Lefebvre	20.00	10.00	6.00
(21)	Elliott Maddox	20.00	10.00	6.00
(22)	Marty Martinez	20.00	10.00	6.00
(23)	Willie McCovey (SP)	100.00	50.00	30.00
(24)	Hal McRae (SP)	30.00	15.00	9.00
(25)	Syd O'Brien (SP)	25.00	12.50	7.50

		NM	EX	VG
(26)	Red Sox team	25.00	12.50	7.50
(27)	Aurelio Rodriguez	20.00	10.00	6.00
(28)	Al Severinsen	20.00	10.00	6.00
(29)	Art Shamsky (SP)	25.00	12.50	7.50
(30)	Steve Stone (SP)	30.00	15.00	9.00
(31)	Stan Swanson (SP)	25.00	12.50	7.50
(32)	Bob Watson	20.00	10.00	6.00
(33)	Roy White (SP)	30.00	15.00	9.00

1972 Topps Posters

Issued as a separate set, rather than as a wax pack insert, these 9-7/16" x 18" posters feature a borderless full-color picture on the front with the player's name, team and position. Printed on very thin paper, the posters were folded for packaging, causing large creases that cannot be removed. Grading of these posters is done without regard to those packaging folds.

		NM	EX	VG
Complete Set (24):		700.00	350.00	200.00
Common Player:		12.00	6.00	3.50
Wax Pack:		50.00	.00	.00
1	Dave McNally	12.00	6.00	3.50
2	Carl Yastrzemski	45.00	22.50	13.50
3	Bill Melton	12.00	6.00	3.50
4	Ray Fosse	12.00	6.00	3.50
5	Mickey Lolich	12.00	6.00	3.50
6	Amos Otis	12.00	6.00	3.50
7	Tony Oliva	15.00	7.50	4.50
8	Vida Blue	12.00	6.00	3.50
9	Hank Aaron	75.00	37.50	22.00
10	Fergie Jenkins	30.00	15.00	9.00
11	Pete Rose	75.00	37.50	22.00
12	Willie Davis	12.00	6.00	3.50
13	Tom Seaver	40.00	20.00	12.00
14	Rick Wise	12.00	6.00	3.50
15	Willie Stargell	30.00	15.00	9.00
16	Joe Torre	17.50	8.75	5.25
17	Willie Mays	75.00	37.50	22.00
18	Andy Messersmith	12.00	6.00	3.50
19	Wilbur Wood	12.00	6.00	3.50
20	Harmon Killebrew	35.00	17.50	10.00
21	Billy Williams	30.00	15.00	9.00
22	Bud Harrelson	12.00	6.00	3.50
23	Roberto Clemente	125.00	65.00	35.00
24	Willie McCovey	30.00	15.00	9.00

1973 Topps

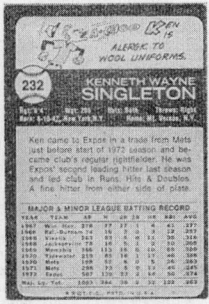

Topps cut back to 660 cards in 1973. The set is interesting for it marks the last time cards were issued by series, a procedure which had produced many a scarce high number card over the years. These 2-1/2" x 3-1/2" cards have a color photo, accented by a silhouette of a player on the front, indicative of his position. Card backs are vertical for the first time since 1968, with the usual statistical and biographical information. Specialty cards begin with card number 1, which depicted Ruth, Mays and Aaron as the all-time home run leaders. It was followed by statistical leaders, although there also were additional all-time leader cards. Also present are playoff and World Series highlights. From the age-and-youth department, the 1973 Topps set has coaches and managers as well as more "Boyhood Photos."

	NM	EX	VG
Complete Set (660):	700.00	350.00	200.00

No.	Player / Description			
	Common Player (1-396):	.75	.40	.25
	Common Player (397-528):	1.00	.50	.30
	Common Player (529-660):	2.00	1.00	.60
	Series 1/2/3 Wax Pack (10):	80.00		
	Series 4 Wax Pack (10):	165.00		
	Series 5 Wax Pack (10+1):	215.00		
1	All Time Home Run Leaders (Hank Aaron, Willie Mays, Babe Ruth)	35.00	17.50	8.75
2	Rich Hebner	.75	.40	.25
3	Jim Lonborg	.75	.40	.25
4	John Milner	.75	.40	.25
5	Ed Brinkman	.75	.40	.25
6	Mac Scarce	.75	.40	.25
7	Texas Rangers Team	1.00	.50	.30
8	Tom Hall	.75	.40	.25
9	Johnny Oates	.75	.40	.25
10	Don Sutton	3.00	1.50	.90
11	Chris Chambliss	.75	.40	.25
12a	Padres Mgr./Coaches (Dave Garcia, Johnny Podres, Bob Skinner, Whitey Wietelmann, Don Zimmer) (Coaches background brown.)	1.00	.50	.30
12b	Padres Mgr./Coaches (Dave Garcia, Johnny Podres, Bob Skinner, Whitey Wietelmann, Don Zimmer) (Coaches background orange.)	1.00	.50	.30
13	George Hendrick	.75	.40	.25
14	Sonny Siebert	.75	.40	.25
15	Ralph Garr	.75	.40	.25
16	Steve Braun	.75	.40	.25
17	Fred Gladding	.75	.40	.25
18	Leroy Stanton	.75	.40	.25
19	Tim Foli	.75	.40	.25
20a	Stan Bahnsen (Small gap in left border.)	1.00	.50	.30
20b	Stan Bahnsen (No gap.)	.75	.40	.25
21	Randy Hundley	.75	.40	.25
22	Ted Abernathy	.75	.40	.25
23	Dave Kingman	1.00	.50	.30
24	Al Santorini	.75	.40	.25
25	Roy White	.75	.40	.25
26	Pittsburgh Pirates Team	2.00	1.00	.60
27	Bill Gogolewski	.75	.40	.25
28	Hal McRae	.75	.40	.25
29	Tony Taylor	.75	.40	.25
30	Tug McGraw	.75	.40	.25
31a	Buddy Bell (Small gap in right border.)	6.00	3.00	1.75
31b	Buddy Bell (No gap.)	6.00	3.00	1.75
32	Fred Norman	.75	.40	.25
33	Jim Breazeale	.75	.40	.25
34	Pat Dobson	.75	.40	.25
35	Willie Davis	.75	.40	.25
36	Steve Barber	.75	.40	.25
37	Bill Robinson	.75	.40	.25
38	Mike Epstein	.75	.40	.25
39	Dave Roberts	.75	.40	.25
40	Reggie Smith	.75	.40	.25
41	Tom Walker	.75	.40	.25
42	Mike Andrews	.75	.40	.25
43	Randy Moffitt	.75	.40	.25
44	Rick Monday	.75	.40	.25
45	Ellie Rodriguez (Photo actually Paul Ratliff.)	.75	.40	.25
46	Lindy McDaniel	.75	.40	.25
47	Luis Melendez	.75	.40	.25
48	Paul Splittorff	.75	.40	.25
49a	Twins Mgr./Coaches (Vern Morgan, Frank Quilici, Bob Rodgers, Ralph Rowe, Al Worthington) (Coaches background brown.)	.75	.40	.25
49b	Twins Mgr./Coaches (Vern Morgan, Frank Quilici, Bob Rodgers, Ralph Rowe, Al Worthington) (Coaches background orange.)	.75	.40	.25
50	Roberto Clemente	50.00	25.00	12.50
51	Chuck Seelbach	.75	.40	.25
52	Denis Menke	.75	.40	.25
53	Steve Dunning	.75	.40	.25
54	Checklist 1-132	1.00	.50	.30
55	Jon Matlack	.75	.40	.25
56	Merv Rettenmund	.75	.40	.25
57	Derrel Thomas	.75	.40	.25
58	Mike Paul	.75	.40	.25
59	Steve Yeager	.75	.40	.25
60	Ken Holtzman	.75	.40	.25
61	Batting Leaders (Rod Carew, Billy Williams)	1.00	.50	.30
62	Home Run Leaders (Dick Allen, Johnny Bench)	1.00	.50	.30
63	Runs Batted In Leaders (Dick Allen, Johnny Bench)	1.00	.50	.30
64	Stolen Base Leaders (Lou Brock, Bert Campaneris)	1.00	.50	.30
65	Earned Run Average Leaders (Steve Carlton, Luis Tiant)	1.00	.50	.30
66	Victory Leaders (Steve Carlton, Gaylord Perry, Wilbur Wood)	1.00	.50	.30
67	Strikeout Leaders (Steve Carlton, Nolan Ryan)	20.00	10.00	6.00
68	Leading Firemen (Clay Carroll, Sparky Lyle)			
69	Phil Gagliano	.75	.40	.25
70	Milt Pappas	.75	.40	.25
71	Johnny Briggs	.75	.40	.25
72	Ron Reed	.75	.40	.25
73	Ed Herrmann	.75	.40	.25
74	Billy Champion	.75	.40	.25
75	Vada Pinson	1.00	.50	.30
76	Doug Rader	.75	.40	.25
77	Mike Torrez	.75	.40	.25
78	Richie Scheinblum	.75	.40	.25
79	Jim Willoughby	.75	.40	.25
80	Tony Oliva ("MINNSEOTA" on front is uncorrected error.)	1.00	.50	.30
81a	Cubs Mgr./Coaches (Hank Aguirre, Ernie Banks, Larry Jansen, Whitey Lockman, Pete Reiser) (Trees in coaches background.)	1.25	.60	.40
81b	Cubs Mgr./Coaches (Hank Aguirre, Ernie Banks, Larry Jansen, Whitey Lockman, Pete Reiser) (Solid orange background.)	1.25	.60	.40
82	Fritz Peterson	.75	.40	.25
83	Leron Lee	.75	.40	.25
84	Rollie Fingers	3.00	1.50	.90
85	Ted Simmons	.75	.40	.25
86	Tom McCraw	.75	.40	.25
87	Ken Boswell	.75	.40	.25
88	Mickey Stanley	.75	.40	.25
89	Jack Billingham	.75	.40	.25
90	Brooks Robinson	10.00	5.00	2.50
91	Los Angeles Dodgers Team	2.00	1.00	.60
92	Jerry Bell	.75	.40	.25
93	Jesus Alou	.75	.40	.25
94	Dick Billings	.75	.40	.25
95	Steve Blass	.75	.40	.25
96	Doug Griffin	.75	.40	.25
97	Willie Montanez	.75	.40	.25
98	Dick Woodson	.75	.40	.25
99	Carl Taylor	.75	.40	.25
100	Hank Aaron	40.00	20.00	12.00
101	Ken Henderson	.75	.40	.25
102	Rudy May	.75	.40	.25
103	Celerino Sanchez	.75	.40	.25
104	Reggie Cleveland	.75	.40	.25
105	Carlos May	.75	.40	.25
106	Terry Humphrey	.75	.40	.25
107	Phil Hennigan	.75	.40	.25
108	Bill Russell	1.00	.50	.30
109	Doyle Alexander	.75	.40	.25
110	Bob Watson	.75	.40	.25
111	Dave Nelson	.75	.40	.25
112	Gary Ross	.75	.40	.25
113	Jerry Grote	.75	.40	.25
114	Lynn McGlothen	.75	.40	.25
115	Ron Santo	2.00	1.00	.60
116a	Yankees Mgr./Coaches (Jim Hegan, Ralph Houk, Elston Howard, Dick Howser, Jim Turner) (Coaches background brown.)	2.00	1.00	.60
116b	Yankees Mgr./Coaches (Jim Hegan, Ralph Houk, Elston Howard, Dick Howser, Jim Turner) (Coaches background orange.)	2.00	1.00	.60
117	Ramon Hernandez	.75	.40	.25
118	John Mayberry	.75	.40	.25
119	Larry Bowa	1.50	.70	.45
120	Joe Coleman	.75	.40	.25
121	Dave Rader	.75	.40	.25
122	Jim Strickland	.75	.40	.25
123	Sandy Alomar	.75	.40	.25
124	Jim Hardin	.75	.40	.25
125	Ron Fairly	.75	.40	.25
126	Jim Brewer	.75	.40	.25
127	Milwaukee Brewers Team	2.00	1.00	.60
128	Ted Sizemore	.75	.40	.25
129	Terry Forster	.75	.40	.25
130	Pete Rose	25.00	12.50	6.25
131a	Red Sox Mgr./Coaches (Doug Camilli, Eddie Kasko, Don Lenhardt, Eddie Popowski, Lee Stange) (Coaches background brown.)	.75	.40	.25
131b	Red Sox Mgr./Coaches (Doug Camilli, Eddie Kasko, Don Lenhardt, Eddie Popowski, Lee Stange) (Coaches background orange.)	.75	.40	.25
132	Matty Alou	.75	.40	.25
133	Dave Roberts	.75	.40	.25
134	Milt Wilcox	.75	.40	.25
135	Lee May	.75	.40	.25
136a	Orioles Mgr./Coaches (George Bamberger, Jim Frey, Billy Hunter, George Staller, Earl Weaver) (Coaches background brown.)	2.00	1.00	.60
136b	Orioles Mgr./Coaches (George Bamberger, Jim Frey, Billy Hunter, George Staller, Earl Weaver) (Coaches background orange.)	2.00	1.00	.60
137	Jim Beauchamp	.75	.40	.25
138	Horacio Pina	.75	.40	.25
139	Carmen Fanzone	.75	.40	.25
140	Lou Piniella	2.00	1.00	.60
141	Bruce Kison	.75	.40	.25
142	Thurman Munson	20.00	10.00	5.00
143	John Curtis	.75	.40	.25
144	Marty Perez	.75	.40	.25
145	Bobby Bonds	2.00	1.00	.60
146	Woodie Fryman	.75	.40	.25
147	Mike Anderson	.75	.40	.25
148	Dave Goltz	.75	.40	.25
149	Ron Hunt	.75	.40	.25
150	Wilbur Wood	1.50	.70	.45
151	Wes Parker	.75	.40	.25
152	Dave May	.75	.40	.25
153	Al Hrabosky	1.50	.70	.45
154	Jeff Torborg	.75	.40	.25
155	Sal Bando	.75	.40	.25
156	Cesar Geronimo	.75	.40	.25
157	Denny Riddleberger	.75	.40	.25
158	Houston Astros Team	2.00	1.00	.60
159	Clarence Gaston	.75	.40	.25
160	Jim Palmer	8.00	4.00	2.00
161	Ted Martinez	.75	.40	.25
162	Pete Broberg	.75	.40	.25
163	Vic Davalillo	.75	.40	.25
164	Monty Montgomery	.75	.40	.25
165	Luis Aparicio	4.00	2.00	1.25
166	Terry Harmon	.75	.40	.25
167	Steve Stone	1.00	.50	.30
168	Jim Northrup	.75	.40	.25
169	Ron Schueler	.75	.40	.25
170	Harmon Killebrew	5.00	2.50	1.25
171	Bernie Carbo	.75	.40	.25
172	Steve Kline	.75	.40	.25
173	Hal Breeden	.75	.40	.25
174	Rich Gossage	12.00	6.00	3.50
175	Frank Robinson	8.00	4.00	2.50
176	Chuck Taylor	.75	.40	.25
177	Bill Plummer	.75	.40	.25
178	Don Rose	.75	.40	.25
179a	A's Mgr./Coaches (Jerry Adair, Vern Hoscheit, Irv Noren, Wes Stock, Dick Williams) (Coaches background brown.)	1.00	.50	.30
179b	A's Mgr./Coaches (Jerry Adair, Vern Hoscheit, Irv Noren, Wes Stock, Dick Williams) (Coaches background orange.)	1.00	.50	.30
180	Fergie Jenkins	5.00	2.50	1.25
181	Jack Brohamer	.75	.40	.25
182	Mike Caldwell	.75	.40	.25
183	Don Buford	.75	.40	.25
184	Jerry Koosman	1.00	.50	.30
185	Jim Wynn	.75	.40	.25
186	Bill Fahey	.75	.40	.25
187	Luke Walker	.75	.40	.25
188	Cookie Rojas	.75	.40	.25
189	Greg Luzinski	1.50	.70	.45
190	Bob Gibson	8.00	4.00	2.00
191	Detroit Tigers Team	2.00	1.00	.60
192	Pat Jarvis	.75	.40	.25
193	Carlton Fisk	10.00	5.00	2.50
194	Jorge Orta	.75	.40	.25
195	Clay Carroll	.75	.40	.25
196	Ken McMullen	.75	.40	.25
197	Ed Goodson	.75	.40	.25
198	Horace Clarke	.75	.40	.25
199	Bert Blyleven	1.50	.70	.45
200	Billy Williams	5.00	2.50	1.50
201	A.L. Playoffs (Hendrick Scores Winning Run.)	1.00	.50	.30
202	N.L. Playoffs (Foster's Run Decides It.)	1.00	.50	.30
203	World Series Game 1 (Tenace The Menace.)	1.00	.50	.30
204	World Series Game 2 (A's Make It Two Straight.)	1.00	.50	.30
205	World Series Game 3 (Reds Win Squeeker.)	1.00	.50	.30
206	World Series Game 4 (Tenace Singles In Ninth.)	1.00	.50	.30
207	World Series Game 5 (Odom Out At Plate.)	1.00	.50	.30
208	World Series Game 6 (Reds' Slugging Ties Series.)	4.00	2.00	1.25
209	World Series Game 7 (Campy Starts Winning Rally.)	1.00	.50	.30
210	A's Win! (World Champions.)	1.50	.70	.45
211	Balor Moore	.75	.40	.25
212	Joe Lahoud	.75	.40	.25
213	Steve Garvey	3.00	1.50	.90
214	Dave Hamilton	.75	.40	.25
215	Dusty Baker	1.00	.50	.30
216	Toby Harrah	.75	.40	.25
217	Don Wilson	.75	.40	.25
218	Aurelio Rodriguez	.75	.40	.25
219	St. Louis Cardinals Team	2.00	1.00	.60
220	Nolan Ryan	50.00	25.00	15.00
221	Fred Kendall	.75	.40	.25
222	Rob Gardner	.75	.40	.25
223	Bud Harrelson	.75	.40	.25
224	Bill Lee	.75	.40	.25
225	Al Oliver	1.00	.50	.30
226	Ray Fosse	.75	.40	.25
227	Wayne Twitchell	.75	.40	.25
228	Bobby Darwin	.75	.40	.25
229	Roric Harrison	.75	.40	.25
230	Joe Morgan	5.00	2.50	1.25
231	Bill Parsons	.75	.40	.25
232	Ken Singleton	.75	.40	.25
233	Ed Kirkpatrick	.75	.40	.25
234	Bill North	.75	.40	.25
235	Jim Hunter	3.00	1.50	.90
236	Tito Fuentes	.75	.40	.25
237a	Braves Mgr./Coaches (Lew Burdette, Jim Busby, Roy Hartsfield, Eddie Mathews, Ken Silvestri) (Coaches background brown.)	1.00	.50	.30
237b	Braves Mgr./Coaches (Lew Burdette, Jim Busby, Roy Hartsfield, Eddie Mathews, Ken Silvestri) (Coaches background orange.)	1.00	.50	.30
238	Tony Muser	.75	.40	.25
239	Pete Richert	.75	.40	.25
240	Bobby Murcer	1.00	.50	.30
241	Dwain Anderson	.75	.40	.25
242	George Culver	.75	.40	.25
243	California Angels Team	2.00	1.00	.60
244	Ed Acosta	.75	.40	.25
245	Carl Yastrzemski	10.00	5.00	3.00
246	Ken Sanders	.75	.40	.25
247	Del Unser	.75	.40	.25

#	Player			
248	Jerry Johnson	.75	.40	.25
249	Larry Biittner	.75	.40	.25
250	Manny Sanguillen	.75	.40	.25
251	Roger Nelson	.75	.40	.25
252a	Giants Mgr./Coaches (Joe Amalfitano, Charlie Fox, Andy Gilbert, Don McMahon, John McNamara) (Coaches background brown.)	.75	.40	.25
252b	Giants Mgr./Coaches (Joe Amalfitano, Charlie Fox, Andy Gilbert, Don McMahon, John McNamara) (Coaches background orange.)	.75	.40	.25
253	Mark Belanger	.75	.40	.25
254	Bill Stoneman	.75	.40	.25
255	Reggie Jackson	12.00	6.00	3.50
256	Chris Zachary	.75	.40	.25
257a	Mets Mgr./Coaches (Yogi Berra, Roy McMillan, Joe Pignatano, Rube Walker, Eddie Yost) (Coaches background brown.)	2.00	1.00	.60
257b	Mets Mgr./Coaches (Yogi Berra, Roy McMillan, Joe Pignatano, Rube Walker, Eddie Yost) (Coaches background orange.)	2.00	1.00	.60
258	Tommy John	1.00	.50	.30
259	Jim Holt	.75	.40	.25
260	Gary Nolan	.75	.40	.25
261	Pat Kelly	.75	.40	.25
262	Jack Aker	.75	.40	.25
263	George Scott	.75	.40	.25
264	Checklist 133-264	1.00	.50	.30
265	Gene Michael	.75	.40	.25
266	Mike Lum	.75	.40	.25
267	Lloyd Allen	.75	.40	.25
268	Jerry Morales	.75	.40	.25
269	Tim McCarver	1.50	.70	.45
270	Luis Tiant	.75	.40	.25
271	Tom Hutton	.75	.40	.25
272	Ed Farmer	.75	.40	.25
273	Chris Speier	.75	.40	.25
274	Darold Knowles	.75	.40	.25
275	Tony Perez	4.00	2.00	1.00
276	Joe Lovitto	.75	.40	.25
277	Bob Miller	.75	.40	.25
278	Baltimore Orioles Team	3.00	1.50	.90
279	Mike Strahler	.75	.40	.25
280	Al Kaline	8.00	4.00	2.50
281	Mike Jorgensen	.75	.40	.25
282	Steve Hovley	.75	.40	.25
283	Ray Sadecki	.75	.40	.25
284	Glenn Borgmann	.75	.40	.25
285	Don Kessinger	.75	.40	.25
286	Frank Linzy	.75	.40	.25
287	Eddie Leon	.75	.40	.25
288	Gary Gentry	.75	.40	.25
289	Bob Oliver	.75	.40	.25
290	Cesar Cedeno	.75	.40	.25
291	Rogelio Moret	.75	.40	.25
292	Jose Cruz	.75	.40	.25
293	Bernie Allen	.75	.40	.25
294	Steve Arlin	.75	.40	.25
295	Bert Campaneris	.75	.40	.25
296	Reds Mgr./Coaches (Sparky Anderson, Alex Grammas, Ted Kluszewski, George Scherger, Larry Shepard)	2.50	1.25	.70
297	Walt Williams	.75	.40	.25
298	Ron Bryant	.75	.40	.25
299	Ted Ford	.75	.40	.25
300	Steve Carlton	10.00	5.00	2.50
301	Billy Grabarkewitz	.75	.40	.25
302	Terry Crowley	.75	.40	.25
303	Nelson Briles	.75	.40	.25
304	Duke Sims	.75	.40	.25
305	Willie Mays	40.00	20.00	12.00
306	Tom Burgmeier	.75	.40	.25
307	Boots Day	.75	.40	.25
308	Skip Lockwood	.75	.40	.25
309	Paul Popovich	.75	.40	.25
310	Dick Allen	1.50	.70	.45
311	Joe Decker	.75	.40	.25
312	Oscar Brown	.75	.40	.25
313	Jim Ray	.75	.40	.25
314	Ron Swoboda	.75	.40	.25
315	John Odom	.75	.40	.25
316	San Diego Padres Team	2.00	1.00	.60
317	Danny Cater	.75	.40	.25
318	Jim McGlothlin	.75	.40	.25
319	Jim Spencer	.75	.40	.25
320	Lou Brock	8.00	4.00	2.00
321	Rich Hinton	.75	.40	.25
322	*Garry Maddox*	1.00	.50	.30
323	Tigers Mgr./Coaches (Art Fowler, Billy Martin, Joe Schultz, Charlie Silvera, Dick Tracewski)	1.00	.50	.30
324	Al Downing	.75	.40	.25
325	Boog Powell	1.00	.50	.30
326	Darrell Brandon	.75	.40	.25
327	John Lowenstein	.75	.40	.25
328	Bill Bonham	.75	.40	.25
329	Ed Kranepool	.75	.40	.25
330	Rod Carew	10.00	5.00	2.50
331	Carl Morton	.75	.40	.25
332	*John Felske*	.75	.40	.25
333	Gene Clines	.75	.40	.25
334	Freddie Patek	.75	.40	.25
335	Bob Tolan	.75	.40	.25
336	Tom Bradley	.75	.40	.25
337	Dave Duncan	1.00	.50	.30
338	Checklist 265-396	1.00	.50	.30
339	Dick Tidrow	.75	.40	.25
340	Nate Colbert	.75	.40	.25
341	Jim Palmer (Boyhood Photo)	1.50	.70	.45

#	Player			
342	Sam McDowell (Boyhood Photo)	.75	.40	.25
343	Bobby Murcer (Boyhood Photo)	.75	.40	.25
344	Jim Hunter (Boyhood Photo)	1.50	.70	.45
345	Chris Speier (Boyhood Photo)	.75	.40	.25
346	Gaylord Perry (Boyhood Photo)	1.50	.70	.45
347	Kansas City Royals Team	2.00	1.00	.60
348	Rennie Stennett	.75	.40	.25
349	Dick McAuliffe	.75	.40	.25
350	Tom Seaver	10.00	5.00	3.00
351	Jimmy Stewart	.75	.40	.25
352	*Don Stanhouse*	.75	.40	.25
353	Steve Brye	.75	.40	.25
354	Billy Parker	.75	.40	.25
355	Mike Marshall	.75	.40	.25
356	White Sox Mgr./Coaches (Joe Lonnett, Jim Mahoney, Al Monchak, Johnny Sain, Chuck Tanner)	.75	.40	.25
357	Ross Grimsley	.75	.40	.25
358	Jim Nettles	.75	.40	.25
359	Cecil Upshaw	.75	.40	.25
360	Joe Rudi (Photo actually Gene Tenace.)	.75	.40	.25
361	Fran Healy	.75	.40	.25
362	Eddie Watt	.75	.40	.25
363	Jackie Hernandez	.75	.40	.25
364	Rick Wise	.75	.40	.25
365	Rico Petrocelli	.75	.40	.25
366	Brock Davis	.75	.40	.25
367	Burt Hooton	.75	.40	.25
368	Bill Buckner	1.00	.50	.30
369	Lerrin LaGrow	.75	.40	.25
370	Willie Stargell	6.00	3.00	1.75
371	Mike Kekich	.75	.40	.25
372	Oscar Gamble	.75	.40	.25
373	Clyde Wright	.75	.40	.25
374	Darrell Evans	1.00	.50	.30
375	Larry Dierker	.75	.40	.25
376	Frank Duffy	.75	.40	.25
377	Expos Mgr./Coaches (Dave Bristol, Larry Doby, Gene Mauch, Cal McLish, Jerry Zimmerman)	1.00	.50	.30
378	Lenny Randle	.75	.40	.25
379	Cy Acosta	.75	.40	.25
380	Johnny Bench	15.00	7.50	3.75
381	Vicente Romo	.75	.40	.25
382	Mike Hegan	.75	.40	.25
383	Diego Segui	.75	.40	.25
384	Don Baylor	3.00	1.50	.90
385	Jim Perry	.75	.40	.25
386	Don Money	.75	.40	.25
387	Jim Barr	.75	.40	.25
388	Ben Oglivie	.75	.40	.25
389	New York Mets Team	4.00	2.00	1.25
390	Mickey Lolich	.75	.40	.25
391	*Lee Lacy*	.75	.40	.25
392	Dick Drago	.75	.40	.25
393	Jose Cardenal	.75	.40	.25
394	Sparky Lyle	.75	.40	.25
395	Roger Metzger	.75	.40	.25
396	Grant Jackson	.75	.40	.25
397	Dave Cash	1.00	.50	.30
398	Rich Hand	1.00	.50	.30
399	George Foster	1.00	.50	.30
400	Gaylord Perry	5.00	2.50	1.50
401	Clyde Mashore	1.00	.50	.30
402	Jack Hiatt	1.00	.50	.30
403	Sonny Jackson	1.00	.50	.30
404	Chuck Brinkman	1.00	.50	.30
405	Cesar Tovar	1.00	.50	.30
406	Paul Lindblad	1.00	.50	.30
407	Felix Millan	1.00	.50	.30
408	Jim Colborn	1.00	.50	.30
409	Ivan Murrell	1.00	.50	.30
410	Willie McCovey	5.00	2.50	1.25
411	Ray Corbin	1.00	.50	.30
412	Manny Mota	1.00	.50	.30
413	Tom Timmermann	1.00	.50	.30
414	Ken Rudolph	1.00	.50	.30
415	Marty Pattin	1.00	.50	.30
416	Paul Schaal	1.00	.50	.30
417	Scipio Spinks	1.00	.50	.30
418	Bobby Grich	1.00	.50	.30
419	Casey Cox	1.00	.50	.30
420	Tommie Agee	1.00	.50	.30
421	Angels Mgr./Coaches (Tom Morgan, Salty Parker, Jimmie Reese, John Roseboro, Bobby Winkles)	1.50	.70	.45
422	Bob Robertson	1.00	.50	.30
423	Johnny Jeter	1.00	.50	.30
424	Denny Doyle	1.00	.50	.30
425	Alex Johnson	1.00	.50	.30
426	Dave LaRoche	1.00	.50	.30
427	Rick Auerbach	1.00	.50	.30
428	Wayne Simpson	1.00	.50	.30
429	Jim Fairey	1.00	.50	.30
430	Vida Blue	1.50	.70	.45
431	Gerry Moses	1.00	.50	.30
432	Dan Frisella	1.00	.50	.30
433	Willie Horton	1.00	.50	.30
434	San Francisco Giants Team	3.00	1.50	.90
435	Rico Carty	1.00	.50	.30
436	Jim McAndrew	1.00	.50	.30
437	John Kennedy	1.00	.50	.30
438	Enzo Hernandez	1.00	.50	.30
439	Eddie Fisher	1.00	.50	.30
440	Glenn Beckert	1.00	.50	.30
441	Gail Hopkins	1.00	.50	.30
442	Dick Dietz	1.00	.50	.30
443	Danny Thompson	1.00	.50	.30
444	Ken Brett	1.00	.50	.30
445	Ken Berry	1.00	.50	.30
446	Jerry Reuss	1.00	.50	.30

#	Player			
447	Joe Hague	1.00	.50	.30
448	John Hiller	1.00	.50	.30
449a	Indians Mgr./Coaches (Ken Aspromonte, Rocky Colavito, Joe Lutz, Warren Spahn) (Spahn's ear pointed.)	1.50	.70	.45
449b	Indians Mgr./Coaches (Ken Aspromonte, Rocky Colavito, Joe Lutz, Warren Spahn) (Spahn's ear round.)	2.00	1.00	.60
450	Joe Torre	3.00	1.50	.90
451	John Vukovich	1.00	.50	.30
452	Paul Casanova	1.00	.50	.30
453	Checklist 397-528	1.25	.60	.40
454	Tom Haller	1.00	.50	.30
455	Bill Melton	1.00	.50	.30
456	Dick Green	1.00	.50	.30
457	John Strohmayer	1.00	.50	.30
458	Jim Mason	1.00	.50	.30
459	Jimmy Howarth	1.00	.50	.30
460	Bill Freehan	1.00	.50	.30
461	Mike Corkins	1.00	.50	.30
462	Ron Blomberg	1.00	.50	.30
463	Ken Tatum	1.00	.50	.30
464	Chicago Cubs Team	4.00	2.00	1.25
465	Dave Giusti	1.00	.50	.30
466	Jose Arcia	1.00	.50	.30
467	Mike Ryan	1.00	.50	.30
468	Tom Griffin	1.00	.50	.30
469	Dan Monzon	1.00	.50	.30
470	Mike Cuellar	1.00	.50	.30
471	All-Time Hit Leader (Ty Cobb)	8.00	4.00	2.00
472	All-Time Grand Slam Leader (Lou Gehrig)	12.00	6.00	3.50
473	All-Time Total Base Leader (Hank Aaron)	8.00	4.00	2.00
474	All-Time RBI Leader (Babe Ruth)	15.00	7.50	3.75
475	All-Time Batting Leader (Ty Cobb)	6.00	3.00	1.50
476	All-Time Shutout Leader (Walter Johnson)	3.00	1.50	.90
477	All-Time Victory Leader (Cy Young)	3.00	1.50	.90
478	All-Time Strikeout Leader (Walter Johnson)	3.00	1.50	.90
479	Hal Lanier	1.00	.50	.30
480	Juan Marichal	6.00	3.00	1.75
481	Chicago White Sox Team	3.00	1.50	.90
482	*Rick Reuschel*	2.00	1.00	.60
483	Dal Maxvill	1.00	.50	.30
484	Ernie McAnally	1.00	.50	.30
485	Norm Cash	1.50	.70	.45
486a	Phillies Mgr./Coaches (Carroll Berringer, Billy DeMars, Danny Ozark, Ray Rippelmeyer, Bobby Wine) (Coaches background brown-red.)	1.00	.50	.30
486b	Phillies Mgr./Coaches (Carroll Beringer, Billy DeMars, Danny Ozark, Ray Rippelmeyer, Bobby Wine) (Coaches background orange.)	1.00	.50	.30
487	Bruce Dal Canton	1.00	.50	.30
488	Dave Campbell	1.00	.50	.30
489	Jeff Burroughs	1.00	.50	.30
490	Claude Osteen	1.00	.50	.30
491	Bob Montgomery	1.00	.50	.30
492	Pedro Borbon	1.00	.50	.30
493	Duffy Dyer	1.00	.50	.30
494	Rich Morales	1.00	.50	.30
495	Tommy Helms	1.00	.50	.30
496	Ray Lamb	1.00	.50	.30
497	Cardinals Mgr./Coaches (Vern Benson, George Kissell, Red Schoendienst, Barney Schultz)	1.50	.70	.45
498	Graig Nettles	1.50	.70	.45
499	Bob Moose	1.00	.50	.30
500	Oakland A's Team	4.00	2.00	1.25
501	Larry Gura	1.00	.50	.30
502	Bobby Valentine	1.00	.50	.30
503	Phil Niekro	5.00	2.50	1.50
504a	Earl Williams (Small gap in each side border.)	1.25	.60	.40
504b	Earl Williams (No gaps in border.)	1.00	.50	.30
505	Bob Bailey	1.00	.50	.30
506	Bart Johnson	1.00	.50	.30
507	Darrel Chaney	1.00	.50	.30
508	Gates Brown	1.00	.50	.30
509	Jim Nash	1.00	.50	.30
510	Amos Otis	1.00	.50	.30
511	Sam McDowell	1.00	.50	.30
512	Dalton Jones	1.00	.50	.30
513	Dave Marshall	1.00	.50	.30
514	Jerry Kenney	1.00	.50	.30
515	Andy Messersmith	1.00	.50	.30
516	Danny Walton	1.00	.50	.30
517a	Pirates Mgr./Coaches (Don Leppert, Bill Mazeroski, Dave Ricketts, Bill Virdon, Mel Wright) (Coaches background brown.)	1.50	.70	.45
517b	Pirates Mgr./Coaches (Don Leppert, Bill Mazeroski, Dave Ricketts, Bill Virdon, Mel Wright) (Coaches background orange.)	1.50	.70	.45
518	Bob Veale	1.00	.50	.30
519	John Edwards	1.00	.50	.30
520	Mel Stottlemyre	1.25	.60	.40
521	Atlanta Braves Team	4.00	2.00	1.25
522	Leo Cardenas	1.00	.50	.30
523	Wayne Granger	1.00	.50	.30
524	Gene Tenace	1.00	.50	.30
525	Jim Fregosi	1.00	.50	.30

No.	Player	NM	EX	VG
526	Ollie Brown	1.00	.50	.30
527	Dan McGinn	1.00	.50	.30
528	Paul Blair	1.00	.50	.30
529	Milt May	2.00	1.00	.60
530	Jim Kaat	4.00	2.00	1.25
531	Ron Woods	2.00	1.00	.60
532	Steve Mingori	2.00	1.00	.60
533	Larry Stahl	2.00	1.00	.60
534	Dave Lemonds	2.00	1.00	.60
535	John Callison	2.00	1.00	.60
536	Philadelphia Phillies Team	6.00	3.00	1.75
537	Bill Slayback	2.00	1.00	.60
538	Jim Hart	2.00	1.00	.60
539	Tom Murphy	2.00	1.00	.60
540	Cleon Jones	2.00	1.00	.60
541	Bob Bolin	2.00	1.00	.60
542	Pat Corrales	2.00	1.00	.60
543	Alan Foster	2.00	1.00	.60
544	Von Joshua	2.00	1.00	.60
545	Orlando Cepeda	6.00	3.00	1.50
546	Jim York	2.00	1.00	.60
547	Bobby Heise	2.00	1.00	.60
548	Don Durham	2.00	1.00	.60
549	Rangers Mgr./Coaches (Chuck Estrada, Whitey Herzog, Chuck Hiller, Jackie Moore)	2.00	1.00	.60
550	Dave Johnson	2.00	1.00	.60
551	Mike Kilkenny	2.00	1.00	.60
552	J.C. Martin	2.00	1.00	.60
553	Mickey Scott	2.00	1.00	.60
554	Dave Concepcion	2.00	1.00	.60
555	Bill Hands	2.00	1.00	.60
556	New York Yankees Team	8.00	4.00	2.00
557	Bernie Williams	2.00	1.00	.60
558	Jerry May	2.00	1.00	.60
559	Barry Lersch	2.00	1.00	.60
560	Frank Howard	3.00	1.50	.90
561	Jim Geddes	2.00	1.00	.60
562	Wayne Garrett	2.00	1.00	.60
563	Larry Haney	2.00	1.00	.60
564	Mike Thompson	2.00	1.00	.60
565	Jim Hickman	2.00	1.00	.60
566	Lew Krausse	2.00	1.00	.60
567	Bob Fenwick	2.00	1.00	.60
568	Ray Newman	2.00	1.00	.60
569	Dodgers Mgr./Coaches (Red Adams, Walt Alston, Monty Basgall, Jim Gilliam, Tom Lasorda)	5.00	2.50	1.50
570	Bill Singer	2.00	1.00	.60
571	Rusty Torres	2.00	1.00	.60
572	Gary Sutherland	2.00	1.00	.60
573	Fred Beene	2.00	1.00	.60
574	Bob Didier	2.00	1.00	.60
575	Dock Ellis	2.00	1.00	.60
576	Montreal Expos Team	5.00	2.50	1.50
577	*Eric Soderholm*	2.00	1.00	.60
578	Ken Wright	2.00	1.00	.60
579	Tom Grieve	2.00	1.00	.60
580	Joe Pepitone	2.00	1.00	.60
581	Steve Kealey	2.00	1.00	.60
582	Darrell Porter	2.00	1.00	.60
583	Bill Greif	2.00	1.00	.60
584	Chris Arnold	2.00	1.00	.60
585	Joe Niekro	2.00	1.00	.60
586	Bill Sudakis	2.00	1.00	.60
587	Rich McKinney	2.00	1.00	.60
588	Checklist 529-660	15.00	7.50	4.50
589	Ken Forsch	2.00	1.00	.60
590	Deron Johnson	2.00	1.00	.60
591	Mike Hedlund	2.00	1.00	.60
592	John Boccabella	2.00	1.00	.60
593	Royals Mgr./Coaches (Galen Cisco, Harry Dunlop, Charlie Lau, Jack McKeon)	2.00	1.00	.60
594	Vic Harris	2.00	1.00	.60
595	Don Gullett	2.00	1.00	.60
596	Boston Red Sox Team	5.00	2.50	1.50
597	Mickey Rivers	2.00	1.00	.60
598	Phil Roof	2.00	1.00	.60
599	Ed Crosby	2.00	1.00	.60
600	Dave McNally	2.00	1.00	.60
601	Rookie Catchers (George Pena, Sergio Robles, Rick Stelmaszek)	3.00	1.50	.90
602	Rookie Pitchers (*Mel Behney, Ralph Garcia, Doug Rau*)	3.00	1.50	.90
603	Rookie Third Basemen (*Terry Hughes, Bill McNulty, Ken Reitz*)	3.00	1.50	.90
604	Rookie Pitchers (Jesse Jefferson, Dennis O'Toole, Bob Strampe)	3.00	1.50	.90
605	Rookie First Basemen (Pat Bourque, **Enos Cabell**, Gonzalo Marquez)	3.00	1.50	.90
606	Rookie Outfielders (**Gary Matthews**, Tom Paciorek, Jorge Roque)	4.00	2.00	1.25
607	Rookie Shortstops (Ray Busse, Pepe Frias, Mario Guerrero)	3.00	1.50	.90
608	Rookie Pitchers (*Steve Busby, Dick Colpaert, George Medich*)	3.00	1.50	.90
609	Rookie Second Basemen (*Larvell Blanks, Pedro Garcia, Dave Lopes*)	5.00	2.50	1.50
610	Rookie Pitchers (Jimmy Freeman, Charlie Hough, Hank Webb)	4.00	2.00	1.25
611	Rookie Outfielders (Rich Coggins, Jim Wohlford, Richie Zisk)	3.00	1.50	.90
612	Rookie Pitchers (Steve Lawson, Bob Reynolds, Brent Strom)	3.00	1.50	.90
613	Rookie Catchers (**Bob Boone**, Mike Ivie, Skip Jutze)	12.00	6.00	3.00
614	Rookie Outfielders (**Al Bumbry, Dwight Evans**, Charlie Spikes)	20.00	10.00	6.00
615	Rookie Third Basemen (***Ron Cey, John Hilton, Mike Schmidt***)	160.00	80.00	40.00
616	Rookie Pitchers (Norm Angelini, Steve Blateric, Mike Garman)	3.00	1.50	.90
617	Rich Chiles	2.00	1.00	.60
618	Andy Etchebarren	2.00	1.00	.60
619	Billy Wilson	2.00	1.00	.60
620	Tommy Harper	2.00	1.00	.60
621	Joe Ferguson	2.00	1.00	.60
622	Larry Hisle	2.00	1.00	.60
623	Steve Renko	2.00	1.00	.60
624	Astros Mgr./Coaches (Leo Durocher, Preston Gomez, Grady Hatton, Hub Kittle, Jim Owens)	3.00	1.50	.90
625	Angel Mangual	2.00	1.00	.60
626	Bob Barton	2.00	1.00	.60
627	Luis Alvarado	2.00	1.00	.60
628	Jim Slaton	2.00	1.00	.60
629	Cleveland Indians Team	5.00	2.50	1.50
630	Denny McLain	6.00	3.00	1.75
631	Tom Matchick	2.00	1.00	.60
632	Dick Selma	2.00	1.00	.60
633	Ike Brown	2.00	1.00	.60
634	Alan Closter	2.00	1.00	.60
635	Gene Alley	2.00	1.00	.60
636	Rick Clark	2.00	1.00	.60
637	Norm Miller	2.00	1.00	.60
638	Ken Reynolds	2.00	1.00	.60
639	Willie Crawford	2.00	1.00	.60
640	Dick Bosman	2.00	1.00	.60
641	Cincinnati Reds Team	5.00	2.50	1.25
642	Jose Laboy	2.00	1.00	.60
643	Al Fitzmorris	2.00	1.00	.60
644	Jack Heidemann	2.00	1.00	.60
645	Bob Locker	2.00	1.00	.60
646	Brewers Mgr./Coaches (Del Crandall, Harvey Kuenn, Joe Nossek, Bob Shaw, Jim Walton)	2.00	1.00	.60
647	George Stone	2.00	1.00	.60
648	Tom Egan	2.00	1.00	.60
649	Rich Folkers	2.00	1.00	.60
650	Felipe Alou	4.00	2.00	1.25
651	Don Carrithers	2.00	1.00	.60
652	Ted Kubiak	2.00	1.00	.60
653	Joe Hoerner	2.00	1.00	.60
654	Minnesota Twins Team	4.00	2.00	1.25
655	Clay Kirby	2.00	1.00	.60
656	John Ellis	2.00	1.00	.60
657	Bob Johnson	2.00	1.00	.60
658	Elliott Maddox	2.00	1.00	.60
659	Jose Pagan	2.00	1.00	.60
660	Fred Scherman	2.00	1.00	.60

1973 Topps Candy Lids

A bit out of the ordinary, the Topps Candy Lids were the top of a product called "Baseball Stars Bubble Gum." The bottom (inside) of the lids carry a color photo of a player with a ribbon containing the name, position and team. The lids are 1-7/8" in diameter. A total of 55 different lids were made, featuring most of the stars of the day.

		NM	EX	VG
Complete Set (55):		750.00	375.00	225.00
Common Player:		6.00	3.00	1.75
Unopened Tub:		135.00	.00	.00
(1)	Hank Aaron	60.00	30.00	18.00
(2)	Dick Allen	7.50	3.75	2.25
(3)	Dusty Baker	6.00	3.00	1.75
(4)	Sal Bando	6.00	3.00	1.75
(5)	Johnny Bench	30.00	15.00	9.00
(6)	Bobby Bonds	6.00	3.00	1.75
(7)	Dick Bosman	6.00	3.00	1.75
(8)	Lou Brock	15.00	7.50	4.50
(9)	Rod Carew	25.00	12.50	7.50
(10)	Steve Carlton	25.00	12.50	7.50
(11)	Nate Colbert	6.00	3.00	1.75
(12)	Willie Davis	6.00	3.00	1.75
(13)	Larry Dierker	6.00	3.00	1.75
(14)	Mike Epstein	6.00	3.00	1.75
(15)	Carlton Fisk	15.00	7.50	4.50
(16)	Tim Foli	6.00	3.00	1.75
(17)	Ray Fosse	6.00	3.00	1.75
(18)	Bill Freehan	6.00	3.00	1.75
(19)	Bob Gibson	25.00	12.50	7.50
(20)	Bud Harrelson	6.00	3.00	1.75
(21)	Catfish Hunter	15.00	7.50	4.50
(22)	Reggie Jackson	40.00	20.00	12.00
(23)	Fergie Jenkins	15.00	7.50	4.50
(24)	Al Kaline	30.00	15.00	9.00
(25)	Harmon Killebrew	30.00	15.00	9.00
(26)	Clay Kirby	6.00	3.00	1.75
(27)	Mickey Lolich	6.00	3.00	1.75
(28)	Greg Luzinski	6.00	3.00	1.75
(29)	Mike Marshall	6.00	3.00	1.75
(30)	Lee May	6.00	3.00	1.75
(31)	John Mayberry	6.00	3.00	1.75
(32)	Willie Mays	60.00	30.00	18.00
(33)	Willie McCovey	15.00	7.50	4.50
(34)	Thurman Munson	25.00	12.50	7.50
(35)	Bobby Murcer	12.50	6.25	3.75
(36)	Gary Nolan	6.00	3.00	1.75
(37)	Amos Otis	6.00	3.00	1.75
(38)	Jim Palmer	15.00	7.50	4.50
(39)	Gaylord Perry	15.00	7.50	4.50
(40)	Lou Piniella	7.50	3.75	2.25
(41)	Brooks Robinson	30.00	15.00	9.00
(42)	Frank Robinson	30.00	15.00	9.00
(43)	Ellie Rodriguez	6.00	3.00	1.75
(44)	Pete Rose	50.00	25.00	15.00
(45)	Nolan Ryan	200.00	100.00	60.00
(46)	Manny Sanguillen	6.00	3.00	1.75
(47)	George Scott	6.00	3.00	1.75
(48)	Tom Seaver	25.00	12.50	7.50
(49)	Chris Speier	6.00	3.00	1.75
(50)	Willie Stargell	15.00	7.50	4.50
(51)	Don Sutton	15.00	7.50	4.50
(52)	Joe Torre	7.50	3.75	2.25
(53)	Billy Williams	15.00	7.50	4.50
(54)	Wilbur Wood	6.00	3.00	1.75
(55)	Carl Yastrzemski	35.00	17.50	10.50

1973 Topps Comics

Strictly a test issue, if ever publicly distributed at all (most are found without any folding which would have occurred had they actually been used to wrap a piece of bubblegum), the 24 players in the 1973 Topps Comics issue appear on 4-5/8" x 3-7/16" waxed paper wrappers. The inside of the wrapper combines a color photo and facsimile autograph with a comic-style presentation of the player's career highlights. The Comics share a checklist with the 1973 Topps Pin-Ups, virtually all star players.

		NM	EX	VG
Complete Set (24):		15,000	7,500	4,500
Common Player:		200.00	100.00	60.00
(1)	Hank Aaron	1,100	550.00	330.00
(2)	Dick Allen	375.00	185.00	110.00
(3)	Johnny Bench	675.00	335.00	200.00
(4)	Steve Carlton	550.00	275.00	165.00
(5)	Nate Colbert	200.00	100.00	60.00
(6)	Willie Davis	200.00	100.00	60.00
(7)	Mike Epstein	200.00	100.00	60.00
(8)	Reggie Jackson	1,100	550.00	330.00
(9)	Harmon Killebrew	550.00	275.00	165.00
(10)	Mickey Lolich	200.00	100.00	60.00
(11)	Mike Marshall	200.00	100.00	60.00
(12)	Lee May	200.00	100.00	60.00
(13)	Willie McCovey	550.00	275.00	165.00
(14)	Bobby Murcer	300.00	150.00	90.00
(15)	Gaylord Perry	525.00	260.00	155.00
(16)	Lou Piniella	300.00	150.00	90.00
(17)	Brooks Robinson	900.00	450.00	270.00
(18)	Nolan Ryan	3,500	1,750	1,000
(19)	George Scott	200.00	100.00	60.00
(20)	Tom Seaver	750.00	375.00	225.00
(21)	Willie Stargell	550.00	275.00	165.00
(22)	Joe Torre	300.00	150.00	90.00
(23)	Billy Williams	525.00	260.00	155.00
(24)	Carl Yastrzemski	1,100	550.00	330.00

1973 Topps Pin-Ups

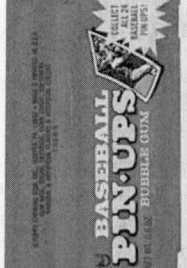

Another test issue of 1973, the 24 Topps Pin-Ups include the same basic format and the same checklist of star-caliber players as the Comics test issue of the same year. The 3-7/16" x 4-5/8" Pin-Ups are actually the inside of a wrapper for a piece of bubblegum. The color player photo features a decorative lozenge inserted at bottom with the player's name, team and position. There is also a facsimile autograph. Curiously, neither the Pin-Ups nor the Comics of 1973 bear team logos on the players' caps.

		NM	EX	VG
Complete Set (24):		9,000	4,500	2,750
Common Player:		250.00	125.00	75.00
(1)	Hank Aaron	800.00	400.00	240.00
(2)	Dick Allen	300.00	150.00	90.00
(3)	Johnny Bench	600.00	300.00	180.00
(4)	Steve Carlton	500.00	250.00	150.00
(5)	Nate Colbert	250.00	125.00	75.00
(6)	Willie Davis	250.00	125.00	75.00
(7)	Mike Epstein	265.00	130.00	80.00
(8)	Reggie Jackson	800.00	400.00	240.00
(9)	Harmon Killebrew	550.00	275.00	165.00
(10)	Mickey Lolich	265.00	130.00	80.00
(11)	Mike Marshall	250.00	125.00	75.00
(12)	Lee May	250.00	125.00	75.00
(13)	Willie McCovey	550.00	275.00	165.00
(14)	Bobby Murcer	300.00	150.00	90.00
(15)	Gaylord Perry	500.00	250.00	150.00
(16)	Lou Piniella	300.00	150.00	90.00
(17)	Brooks Robinson	600.00	300.00	180.00
(18)	Nolan Ryan	900.00	450.00	270.00
(19)	George Scott	250.00	125.00	75.00
(20)	Tom Seaver	600.00	300.00	180.00
(21)	Willie Stargell	550.00	275.00	165.00
(22)	Joe Torre	275.00	135.00	82.00
(23)	Billy Williams	550.00	275.00	165.00
(24)	Carl Yastrzemski	650.00	325.00	195.00

1973 Topps Team Checklists

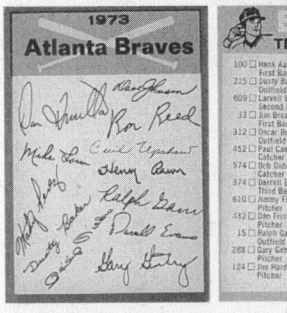

This is a 24-card unnumbered set of 2-1/2" x 3-1/2" cards that is generally believed to have been included with the high-numbered series in 1973, while also being made available in a mail-in offer. The front of the cards have the team name at the top and a white panel with various facsimile autographs takes up the rest of the space except for a blue border. Backs feature the team name and checklist. Relatively scarce, these somewhat mysterious cards are not included by many in their collections despite their obvious relationship to the regular set.

		NM	EX	VG
Complete Set (24):		100.00	50.00	30.00
Common Checklist:		3.50	1.75	1.00
(1)	Atlanta Braves	3.50	1.75	1.00
(2)	Baltimore Orioles	3.50	1.75	1.00
(3)	Boston Red Sox	5.00	2.50	1.50
(4)	California Angels	3.50	1.75	1.00
(5)	Chicago Cubs	3.50	1.75	1.00
(6)	Chicago White Sox	3.50	1.75	1.00
(7)	Cincinnati Reds	5.00	2.50	1.50
(8)	Cleveland Indians	3.50	1.75	1.00
(9)	Detroit Tigers	6.00	3.00	1.75
(10)	Houston Astros	3.50	1.75	1.00
(11)	Kansas City Royals	3.50	1.75	1.00
(12)	Los Angeles Dodgers	3.50	1.75	1.00
(13)	Milwaukee Brewers	3.50	1.75	1.00
(14)	Minnesota Twins	3.50	1.75	1.00
(15)	Montreal Expos	3.50	1.75	1.00
(16)	New York Mets	6.00	3.00	1.75
(17)	New York Yankees	6.00	3.00	1.75
(18)	Oakland A's	6.00	3.00	1.75
(19)	Philadelphia Phillies	3.50	1.75	1.00
(20)	Pittsburgh Pirates	3.50	1.75	1.00
(21)	St. Louis Cardinals	3.50	1.75	1.00
(22)	San Diego Padres	3.50	1.75	1.00
(23)	San Francisco Giants	3.50	1.75	1.00
(24)	Texas Rangers	3.50	1.75	1.00

1973 Topps 1953 Reprints

Long before Topps reprinted virtually the entire 1953 set in its "Archives" program in 1991, selected cards from the '53 set had been reprinted in a rare eight-card issue. Some sources say the cards were produced as table favors at a

Topps banquet, while at least one contemporary hobby periodical said they were sold on a test-issue basis in Brooklyn. It was said only 300 of the sets were made. Unlike the original cards in 2-5/8" x 3-3/4" format, the test issue cards are modern standard 2-1/2" x 3-1/2". Three of the players in the issue were misidentified. Card backs feature a career summary written as though in 1953; the backs are formatted differently than original 1953 Topps cards and are printed in black-and-white.

		NM	EX	VG
Complete Set (8):		750.00	375.00	225.00
Common Player:		35.00	17.50	10.00
1	Satchell Paige	225.00	110.00	65.00
2	Jackie Robinson	300.00	150.00	90.00
3	Carl Furillo (Picture actually Bill Antonello.)	50.00	25.00	15.00
4	Al Rosen (Picture actually Jim Fridley.)	35.00	17.50	10.00
5	Hal Newhouser	40.00	20.00	12.00
6	Clyde McCullough (Picture actually Vic Janowicz.)	35.00	17.50	10.00
7	"Peanuts" Lowrey		17.50	10.00
8	Johnny Mize	85.00	42.50	25.00

1974 Topps

Issued all at once at the beginning of the year, rather than by series throughout the baseball season as had been done since 1952, this 660-card '74 Topps set features a famous group of error cards. At the time the cards were printed, it was uncertain whether the San Diego Padres would move to Washington, D.C., and by the time a decision was made some Padres cards had appeared with a "Washington, Nat'l League" designation on the front. A total of 15 cards were affected, and those with the Washington designation bring prices well in excess of regular cards of the same players (the Washington variations are not included in the complete set prices quoted below). The 2-1/2" x 3-1/2" cards feature color photos (frequently game-action shots) along with the player's name, team and position. Specialty cards abound, starting with a Hank Aaron tribute and running through the usual managers, statistical leaders, playoff and World Series highlights, multi-player rookie cards and All-Stars.

		NM	EX	VG
Unopened Factory Set (704):		600.00	.00	.00
Complete Set (660):		350.00	175.00	100.00
Common Player:		.40	.20	.10
Wax Pack (2):		9.00		
Wax Pack (8+1 - B.T.C.):		50.00		
Wax Box (36):		2,000		
Wax Pack (12+1 - B.T.C.):		75.00		
Wax Box (24):		1,875		
Cello Pack: (22):		115.00		
Rack Pack: (42):		250.00		
Vending Box (500):		925.00		
1	Hank Aaron (All-Time Home Run King)	50.00	25.00	15.00
2	Hank Aaron (Aaron Special 1954-57)	10.00	5.00	3.00
3	Hank Aaron (Aaron Special 1958-61)	10.00	5.00	3.00
4	Hank Aaron (Aaron Special 1962-65)	10.00	5.00	3.00
5	Hank Aaron (Aaron Special 1966-69)	10.00	5.00	3.00
6	Hank Aaron (Aaron Special 1970-73)	10.00	5.00	3.00
7	Jim Hunter	4.00	2.00	1.25
8	George Theodore	.40	.20	.10
9	Mickey Lolich	.40	.20	.09
10	Johnny Bench	20.00	10.00	6.00
11	Jim Bibby	.40	.20	.10
12	Dave May	.40	.20	.10
13	Tom Hilgendorf	.40	.20	.10
14	Paul Popovich	.40	.20	.10
15	Joe Torre	2.00	1.00	.60
16	Baltimore Orioles Team	2.00	1.00	.60
17	Doug Bird	.40	.20	.10
18	Gary Thomasson	.40	.20	.10
19	Gerry Moses	.40	.20	.10
20	Nolan Ryan	40.00	20.00	12.00
21	Bob Gallagher	.40	.20	.10
22	Cy Acosta	.40	.20	.10
23	Craig Robinson	.40	.20	.10
24	John Hiller	.40	.20	.10
25	Ken Singleton	.40	.20	.10
26	*Bill Campbell*	.40	.20	.10
27	George Scott	.40	.20	.10
28	Manny Sanguillen	.40	.20	.10
29	Phil Niekro	4.00	2.00	1.25
30	Bobby Bonds	.40	.20	.09
31	Astros Mgr./Coaches (Roger Craig, Preston Gomez, Grady Hatton, Hub Kittle, Bob Lillis)	.40	.20	.09

32a	John Grubb (Washington)	3.00	1.50	.90
32b	John Grubb (San Diego)	.40	.20	.10
33	Don Newhauser	.40	.20	.10
34	Andy Kosco	.40	.20	.10
35	Gaylord Perry	4.00	2.00	1.25
36	St. Louis Cardinals Team	2.00	1.00	.60
37	Dave Sells	.40	.20	.10
38	Don Kessinger	.40	.20	.10
39	Ken Suarez	.40	.20	.10
40	Jim Palmer	6.00	3.00	1.75
41	Bobby Floyd	.40	.20	.10
42	Claude Osteen	.40	.20	.10
43	Jim Wynn	.40	.20	.10
44	Mel Stottlemyre	.75	.40	.25
45	Dave Johnson	.40	.20	.10
46	Pat Kelly	.40	.20	.10
47	*Dick Ruthven*	.40	.20	.10
48	Dick Sharon	.40	.20	.10
49	Steve Renko	.40	.20	.10
50	Rod Carew	6.00	3.00	1.75
51	Bobby Heise	.40	.20	.10
52	Al Oliver	.50	.25	.15
53a	Fred Kendall (Washington)	3.00	1.50	.90
53b	Fred Kendall (San Diego)	.40	.20	.10
54	*Elias Sosa*	.40	.20	.10
55	Frank Robinson	8.00	4.00	2.50
56	New York Mets Team	1.50	.70	.45
57	Darold Knowles	.40	.20	.10
58	Charlie Spikes	.40	.20	.10
59	Ross Grimsley	.40	.20	.10
60	Lou Brock	8.00	4.00	2.50
61	Luis Aparicio	4.00	2.00	1.25
62	Bob Locker	.40	.20	.10
63	Bill Sudakis	.40	.20	.10
64	Doug Rau	.40	.20	.10
65	Amos Otis	.40	.20	.10
66	Sparky Lyle	.40	.20	.10
67	Tommy Helms	.40	.20	.10
68	Grant Jackson	.40	.20	.10
69	Del Unser	.40	.20	.10
70	Dick Allen	.75	.40	.25
71	Danny Frisella	.40	.20	.10
72	Aurelio Rodriguez	.40	.20	.10
73	Mike Marshall	.40	.20	.10
74	Minnesota Twins Team	1.00	.50	.30
75	Jim Colborn	.40	.20	.10
76	Mickey Rivers	.40	.20	.10
77a	Rich Troedson (Washington)	3.00	1.50	.90
77b	Rich Troedson (San Diego)	.40	.20	.10
78	Giants Mgr./Coaches (Joe Amalfitano, Charlie Fox, Andy Gilbert, Don McMahon, John McNamara)	.40	.20	.10
79	Gene Tenace	.40	.20	.10
80	Tom Seaver	10.00	5.00	3.00
81	Frank Duffy	.40	.20	.10
82	Dave Giusti	.40	.20	.10
83	Orlando Cepeda	4.00	2.00	1.25
84	Rick Wise	.40	.20	.10
85	Joe Morgan	6.00	3.00	1.75
86	Joe Ferguson	.40	.20	.10
87	Fergie Jenkins	4.00	2.00	1.25
88	Freddie Patek	.40	.20	.10
89	Jackie Brown	.40	.20	.10
90	Bobby Murcer	.50	.25	.15
91	Ken Forsch	.40	.20	.10
92	Paul Blair	.40	.20	.10
93	Rod Gilbreath	.40	.20	.10
94	Detroit Tigers Team	1.00	.50	.30
95	Steve Carlton	8.00	4.00	2.50
96	*Jerry Hairston Sr.*	.40	.20	.10
97	Bob Bailey	.40	.20	.10
98	Bert Blyleven	.75	.40	.25
99	Brewers Mgr./Coaches (Del Crandall, Harvey Kuenn, Joe Nossek, Jim Walton, Al Widmar)	.40	.20	.10
100	Willie Stargell	8.00	4.00	2.50
101	Bobby Valentine	.40	.20	.10
102a	Bill Greif (Washington)	3.00	1.50	.90
102b	Bill Greif (San Diego)	.40	.20	.10
103	Sal Bando	.40	.20	.10
104	Ron Bryant	.40	.20	.10
105	Carlton Fisk	10.00	5.00	3.00
106	Harry Parker	.40	.20	.10
107	Alex Johnson	.40	.20	.10
108	Al Hrabosky	.40	.20	.10
109	Bob Grich	.40	.20	.10
110	Billy Williams	5.00	2.50	1.50
111	Clay Carroll	.40	.20	.10
112	Dave Lopes	.40	.20	.10
113	Dick Drago	.40	.20	.10
114	California Angels Team	1.00	.50	.30
115	Willie Horton	.40	.20	.10
116	Jerry Reuss	.40	.20	.10
117	Ron Blomberg	.40	.20	.10
118	Bill Lee	.40	.20	.10
119	Phillies Mgr./Coaches (Carroll Beringer, Bill DeMars, Danny Ozark, Ray Ripplemeyer, Bobby Wine)	.40	.20	.10
120	Wilbur Wood	.40	.20	.10
121	Larry Lintz	.40	.20	.10
122	Jim Holt	.40	.20	.10
123	Nelson Briles	.40	.20	.10
124	Bob Coluccio	.40	.20	.10
125a	Nate Colbert (Washington)	3.00	1.50	.90
125b	Nate Colbert (San Diego)	.40	.20	.10
126	Checklist 1-132	.75	.40	.25
127	Tom Paciorek	.40	.20	.10
128	John Ellis	.40	.20	.10
129	Chris Speier	.40	.20	.10
130	Reggie Jackson	15.00	7.50	4.50
131	Bob Boone	1.50	.70	.45
132	Felix Millan	.40	.20	.10
133	*David Clyde*	.40	.20	.10
134	Denis Menke	.40	.20	.10
135	Roy White	.40	.20	.10

#	Player			
136	Rick Reuschel	.40	.20	.10
137	Al Bumbry	.40	.20	.10
138	Ed Brinkman	.40	.20	.10
139	Aurelio Monteagudo	.40	.20	.10
140	Darrell Evans	.75	.40	.25
141	Pat Bourque	.40	.20	.10
142	Pedro Garcia	.40	.20	.10
143	Dick Woodson	.40	.20	.10
144	Dodgers Mgr./Coaches (Red Adams, Walter Alston, Monty Basgall, Jim Gilliam, Tom Lasorda)	1.00	.50	.30
145	Dock Ellis	.40	.20	.10
146	Ron Fairly	.40	.20	.10
147	Bart Johnson	.40	.20	.10
148a	Dave Hilton (Washington)	3.00	1.50	.90
148b	Dave Hilton (San Diego)	.40	.20	.10
149	Mac Scarce	.40	.20	.10
150	John Mayberry	.40	.20	.10
151	Diego Segui	.40	.20	.10
152	Oscar Gamble	.40	.20	.10
153	Jon Matlack	.40	.20	.10
154	Houston Astros Team	1.50	.70	.45
155	Bert Campaneris	.40	.20	.10
156	Randy Moffitt	.40	.20	.10
157	Vic Harris	.40	.20	.10
158	Jack Billingham	.40	.20	.10
159	Jim Ray Hart	.40	.20	.10
160	Brooks Robinson	6.00	3.00	1.75
161	*Ray Burris*	.50	.20	.10
162	Bill Freehan	.40	.20	.10
163	Ken Berry	.40	.20	.10
164	Tom House	.40	.20	.10
165	Willie Davis	.40	.20	.10
166	Royals Mgr./Coaches (Galen Cisco, Harry Dunlop, Charlie Lau, Jack McKeon)	.40	.20	.10
167	Luis Tiant	1.00	.50	.30
168	Danny Thompson	.40	.20	.10
169	*Steve Rogers*	.40	.20	.10
170	Bill Melton	.40	.20	.10
171	Eduardo Rodriguez	.40	.20	.10
172	Gene Clines	.40	.20	.10
173a	*Randy Jones* (Washington)	3.00	1.50	.90
173b	*Randy Jones* (San Diego)	.40	.20	.10
174	Bill Robinson	.40	.20	.10
175	Reggie Cleveland	.40	.20	.10
176	John Lowenstein	.40	.20	.10
177	Dave Roberts	.40	.20	.10
178	Garry Maddox	.40	.20	.10
179	Mets Mgr./Coaches (Yogi Berra, Roy McMillan, Joe Pignatano, Rube Walker, Eddie Yost)	1.50	.70	.45
180	Ken Holtzman	.40	.20	.10
181	Cesar Geronimo	.40	.20	.10
182	Lindy McDaniel	.40	.20	.10
183	Johnny Oates	.40	.20	.10
184	Texas Rangers Team	1.00	.50	.30
185	Jose Cardenal	.40	.20	.10
186	Fred Scherman	.40	.20	.10
187	Don Baylor	1.00	.50	.30
188	Rudy Meoli	.40	.20	.10
189	Jim Brewer	.40	.20	.10
190	Tony Oliva	1.50	.70	.45
191	Al Fitzmorris	.40	.20	.10
192	Mario Guerrero	.40	.20	.10
193	Tom Walker	.40	.20	.10
194	Darrell Porter	.40	.20	.10
195	Carlos May	.40	.20	.10
196	Jim Fregosi	.75	.40	.25
197a	Vicente Romo (Washington)	3.00	1.50	.90
197b	Vicente Romo (San Diego)	.40	.20	.10
198	Dave Cash	.40	.20	.10
199	Mike Kekich	.40	.20	.10
200	Cesar Cedeno	.40	.20	.10
201	Batting Leaders (Rod Carew, Pete Rose)	6.00	3.00	1.75
202	Home Run Leaders (Reggie Jackson, Willie Stargell)	4.00	2.00	1.25
203	RBI Leaders (Reggie Jackson, Willie Stargell)	4.00	2.00	1.25
204	Stolen Base Leaders (Lou Brock, Tommy Harper)	1.50	.70	.45
205	Victory Leaders (Ron Bryant, Wilbur Wood)	1.00	.50	.30
206	Earned Run Average Leaders (Jim Palmer, Tom Seaver)	2.00	1.00	.60
207	Strikeout Leaders (Nolan Ryan, Tom Seaver)	10.00	5.00	3.00
208	Leading Firemen (John Hiller, Mike Marshall)	1.00	.50	.30
209	Ted Sizemore	.40	.20	.10
210	Bill Singer	.40	.20	.10
211	Chicago Cubs Team	1.00	.50	.30
212	Rollie Fingers	4.00	2.00	1.25
213	Dave Rader	.40	.20	.10
214	Billy Grabarkewitz	.40	.20	.10
215	Al Kaline	8.00	4.00	2.50
216	Ray Sadecki	.40	.20	.10
217	Tim Foli	.40	.20	.10
218	Johnny Briggs	.40	.20	.10
219	Doug Griffin	.40	.20	.10
220	Don Sutton	4.00	2.00	1.25
221	White Sox Mgr./Coaches (Joe Lonnett, Jim Mahoney, Alex Monchak, Johnny Sain, Chuck Tanner)	.40	.20	.10
222	Ramon Hernandez	.40	.20	.10
223	Jeff Burroughs	.40	.20	.10
224	Roger Metzger	.40	.20	.10
225	Paul Splittorff	.40	.20	.10
226a	Washington Nat'l. Team	8.00	4.00	2.50
226b	San Diego Padres Team	2.00	1.00	.60
227	Mike Lum	.40	.20	.10
228	Ted Kubiak	.40	.20	.10
229	Fritz Peterson	.40	.20	.10
230	Tony Perez	4.00	2.00	1.25
231	Dick Tidrow	.40	.20	.10
232	Steve Brye	.40	.20	.10
233	Jim Barr	.40	.20	.10
234	John Milner	.40	.20	.10
235	Dave McNally	.40	.20	.10
236	Cardinals Mgr./Coaches (Vern Benson, George Kissell, Johnny Lewis, Red Schoendienst, Barney Schultz)	.75	.40	.25
237	Ken Brett	.40	.20	.10
238	Fran Healy	.40	.20	.10
239	Bill Russell	.40	.20	.10
240	Joe Coleman	.40	.20	.10
241a	Glenn Beckert (Washington)	3.00	1.50	.90
241b	Glenn Beckert (San Diego)	.40	.20	.10
242	Bill Gogolewski	.40	.20	.10
243	Bob Oliver	.40	.20	.10
244	Carl Morton	.40	.20	.10
245	Cleon Jones	.40	.20	.10
246	Oakland A's Team	2.00	1.00	.60
247	Rick Miller	.40	.20	.10
248	Tom Hall	.40	.20	.10
249	George Mitterwald	.40	.20	.10
250a	Willie McCovey (Washington)	20.00	10.00	6.00
250b	Willie McCovey (San Diego)	15.00	7.50	4.50
251	Graig Nettles	1.50	.70	.45
252	*Dave Parker*	8.00	4.00	2.50
253	John Boccabella	.40	.20	.10
254	Stan Bahnsen	.40	.20	.10
255	Larry Bowa	1.00	.50	.30
256	Tom Griffin	.40	.20	.10
257	Buddy Bell	.40	.20	.10
258	Jerry Morales	.40	.20	.10
259	Bob Reynolds	.40	.20	.10
260	Ted Simmons	.75	.40	.25
261	Jerry Bell	.40	.20	.10
262	Ed Kirkpatrick	.40	.20	.10
263	Checklist 133-264	1.00	.50	.30
264	Joe Rudi	.40	.20	.10
265	Tug McGraw	.40	.20	.10
266	Jim Northrup	.40	.20	.10
267	Andy Messersmith	.40	.20	.10
268	Tom Grieve	.40	.20	.10
269	Bob Johnson	.40	.20	.10
270	Ron Santo	3.00	1.50	.90
271	Bill Hands	.40	.20	.10
272	Paul Casanova	.40	.20	.10
273	Checklist 265-396	.75	.40	.25
274	Fred Beene	.40	.20	.10
275	Ron Hunt	.40	.20	.10
276	Angels Mgr./Coaches (Tom Morgan, Salty Parker, Jimmie Reese, John Roseboro, Bobby Winkles)	.40	.20	.10
277	Gary Nolan	.40	.20	.10
278	Cookie Rojas	.40	.20	.10
279	Jim Crawford	.40	.20	.10
280	Carl Yastrzemski	10.00	5.00	3.00
281	San Francisco Giants Team	1.00	.50	.30
282	Doyle Alexander	.40	.20	.10
283	Mike Schmidt	15.00	7.50	4.50
284	Dave Duncan	.40	.20	.10
285	Reggie Smith	.40	.20	.10
286	Tony Muser	.40	.20	.10
287	Clay Kirby	.40	.20	.10
288	*Gorman Thomas*	2.00	1.00	.60
289	Rick Auerbach	.40	.20	.10
290	Vida Blue	1.00	.50	.30
291	Don Hahn	.40	.20	.10
292	Chuck Seelbach	.40	.20	.10
293	Milt May	.40	.20	.10
294	Steve Foucault	.40	.20	.10
295	Rick Monday	.40	.20	.10
296	Ray Corbin	.40	.20	.10
297	Hal Breeden	.40	.20	.10
298	Roric Harrison	.40	.20	.10
299	Gene Michael	.40	.20	.10
300	Pete Rose	20.00	10.00	6.00
301	Bob Montgomery	.40	.20	.10
302	Rudy May	.40	.20	.10
303	George Hendrick	.40	.20	.10
304	Don Wilson	.40	.20	.10
305	Tito Fuentes	.40	.20	.10
306	Orioles Mgr./Coaches (George Bamberger, Jim Frey, Billy Hunter, George Staller, Earl Weaver)	2.00	1.00	.60
307	Luis Melendez	.40	.20	.10
308	Bruce Dal Canton	.40	.20	.10
309a	Dave Roberts (Washington)	3.00	1.50	.90
309b	Dave Roberts (San Diego)	.40	.20	.10
310	Terry Forster	.40	.20	.10
311	Jerry Grote	.40	.20	.10
312	Deron Johnson	.40	.20	.10
313	Berry Lersch	.40	.20	.10
314	Milwaukee Brewers Team	1.00	.50	.30
315	Ron Cey	.50	.25	.15
316	Jim Perry	.40	.20	.10
317	Richie Zisk	.40	.20	.10
318	Jim Merritt	.40	.20	.10
319	Randy Hundley	.40	.20	.10
320	Dusty Baker	1.00	.50	.30
321	Steve Braun	.40	.20	.10
322	Ernie McAnally	.40	.20	.10
323	Richie Scheinblum	.40	.20	.10
324	Steve Kline	.40	.20	.10
325	Tommy Harper	.40	.20	.10
326	Reds Mgr./Coaches (Sparky Anderson, Alex Grammas, Ted Kluszewski, George Scherger, Larry Shepard)	2.00	1.00	.60
327	Tom Timmermann	.40	.20	.10
328	Skip Jutze	.40	.20	.10
329	Mark Belanger	.40	.20	.10
330	Juan Marichal	4.00	2.00	1.25
331	All-Star Catchers (Johnny Bench, Carlton Fisk)	4.00	2.00	1.25
332	All-Star First Basemen (Hank Aaron, Dick Allen)	6.00	3.00	1.75
333	All-Star Second Basemen (Rod Carew, Joe Morgan)	3.00	1.50	.90
334	All-Star Third Basemen (Brooks Robinson, Ron Santo)	2.00	1.00	.60
335	All-Star Shortstops (Bert Campaneris, Chris Speier)	1.00	.50	.30
336	All-Star Left Fielders (Bobby Murcer, Pete Rose)	5.00	2.50	1.50
337	All-Star Center Fielders (Cesar Cedeno, Amos Otis)	.75	.40	.25
338	All-Star Right Fielders (Reggie Jackson, Billy Williams)	4.00	2.00	1.25
339	All-Star Pitchers (Jim Hunter, Rick Wise)	2.00	1.00	.60
340	Thurman Munson	8.00	4.00	2.50
341	*Dan Driessen*	.40	.20	.10
342	Jim Lonborg	.40	.20	.10
343	Kansas City Royals Team	1.00	.50	.30
344	Mike Caldwell	.40	.20	.10
345	Bill North	.40	.20	.10
346	Ron Reed	.40	.20	.10
347	Sandy Alomar	.40	.20	.10
348	Pete Richert	.40	.20	.10
349	John Vukovich	.40	.20	.10
350	Bob Gibson	6.00	3.00	1.75
351	Dwight Evans	1.00	.50	.30
352	Bill Stoneman	.40	.20	.10
353	Rich Coggins	.40	.20	.10
354	Cubs Mgr./Coaches (Hank Aguirre, Whitey Lockman, Jim Marshall, J.C. Martin, Al Spangler)	.40	.20	.10
355	Dave Nelson	.40	.20	.10
356	Jerry Koosman	.40	.20	.10
357	Buddy Bradford	.40	.20	.10
358	Dal Maxvill	.40	.20	.10
359	Brent Strom	.40	.20	.10
360	Greg Luzinski	1.00	.50	.30
361	Don Carrithers	.40	.20	.10
362	Hal King	.40	.20	.10
363	New York Yankees Team	2.00	1.00	.60
364a	Clarence Gaston (Washington)	3.00	1.50	.90
364b	Clarence Gaston (San Diego)	.40	.20	.10
365	Steve Busby	.40	.20	.10
366	Larry Hisle	.40	.20	.10
367	Norm Cash	1.00	.50	.30
368	Manny Mota	.40	.20	.10
369	Paul Lindblad	.40	.20	.10
370	Bob Watson	.40	.20	.10
371	Jim Slaton	.40	.20	.10
372	Ken Reitz	.40	.20	.10
373	John Curtis	.40	.20	.10
374	Marty Perez	.40	.20	.10
375	Earl Williams	.40	.20	.10
376	Jorge Orta	.40	.20	.10
377	Ron Woods	.40	.20	.10
378	Burt Hooton	.40	.20	.10
379	Rangers Mgr./Coaches (Art Fowler, Frank Lucchesi, Billy Martin, Jackie Moore, Charlie Silvera)	.45	.25	.15
380	Bud Harrelson	.40	.20	.10
381	Charlie Sands	.40	.20	.10
382	Bob Moose	.40	.20	.10
383	Philadelphia Phillies Team	1.00	.50	.30
384	Chris Chambliss	.75	.40	.25
385	Don Gullett	.40	.20	.10
386	Gary Matthews	.40	.20	.10
387a	Rich Morales (Washington)	3.00	1.50	.90
387b	Rich Morales (San Diego)	.40	.20	.10
388	Phil Roof	.40	.20	.10
389	Gates Brown	.40	.20	.10
390	Lou Piniella	2.00	1.00	.60
391	Billy Champion	.40	.20	.10
392	Dick Green	.40	.20	.10
393	Orlando Pena	.40	.20	.10
394	Ken Henderson	.40	.20	.10
395	Doug Rader	.40	.20	.10
396	Tommy Davis	.40	.20	.10
397	George Stone	.40	.20	.10
398	Duke Sims	.40	.20	.10
399	Mike Paul	.40	.20	.10
400	Harmon Killebrew	6.00	3.00	1.75
401	Elliott Maddox	.40	.20	.10
402	Jim Rooker	.40	.20	.10
403	Red Sox Mgr./Coaches (Don Bryant, Darrell Johnson, Eddie Popowski, Lee Stange, Don Zimmer)	.40	.20	.10
404	Jim Howarth	.40	.20	.10
405	Ellie Rodriguez	.40	.20	.10
406	Steve Arlin	.40	.20	.10
407	Jim Wohlford	.40	.20	.10
408	Charlie Hough	1.00	.50	.30
409	Ike Brown	.40	.20	.10
410	Pedro Borbon	.40	.20	.10
411	Frank Baker	.40	.20	.10
412	Chuck Taylor	.40	.20	.10
413	Don Money	.40	.20	.10
414	Checklist 397-528	2.00	1.00	.60
415	Gary Gentry	.40	.20	.10
416	Chicago White Sox Team	1.00	.50	.30
417	Rich Folkers	.40	.20	.10
418	Walt Williams	.40	.20	.10
419	Wayne Twitchell	.40	.20	.10
420	Ray Fosse	.40	.20	.10
421	Dan Fife	.40	.20	.10
422	Gonzalo Marquez	.40	.20	.10
423	Fred Stanley	.40	.20	.10
424	Jim Beauchamp	.40	.20	.10
425	Pete Broberg	.40	.20	.10
426	Rennie Stennett	.40	.20	.10
427	Bobby Bolin	.40	.20	.10

428	Gary Sutherland	.40	.20	.10
429	Dick Lange	.40	.20	.10
430	Matty Alou	.40	.20	.10
431	*Gene Garber*	.40	.20	.10
432	Chris Arnold	.40	.20	.10
433	Lerrin LaGrow	.40	.20	.10
434	Ken McMullen	.40	.20	.10
435	Dave Concepcion	1.00	.50	.30
436	Don Hood	.40	.20	.10
437	Jim Lyttle	.40	.20	.10
438	Ed Herrmann	.40	.20	.10
439	Norm Miller	.40	.20	.10
440	Jim Kaat	1.50	.70	.45
441	Tom Ragland	.40	.20	.10
442	Alan Foster	.40	.20	.10
443	Tom Hutton	.40	.20	.10
444	Vic Davalillo	.40	.20	.10
445	George Medich	.40	.20	.10
446	Len Randle	.40	.20	.10
447	Twins Mgr./Coaches (Vern Morgan, Frank Quilici, Bob Rodgers, Ralph Rowe)	.40	.20	.10
448	Ron Hodges	.40	.20	.10
449	Tom McCraw	.40	.20	.10
450	Rich Hebner	.40	.20	.10
451	Tommy John	1.00	.50	.30
452	Gene Hiser	.40	.20	.10
453	Balor Moore	.40	.20	.10
454	Kurt Bevacqua	.40	.20	.10
455	Tom Bradley	.40	.20	.10
456	*Dave Winfield*	50.00	25.00	15.00
457	Chuck Goggin	.40	.20	.10
458	Jim Ray	.40	.20	.10
459	Cincinnati Reds Team	1.50	.70	.45
460	Boog Powell	1.00	.50	.30
461	John Odom	.40	.20	.10
462	Luis Alvarado	.40	.20	.10
463	Pat Dobson	.40	.20	.10
464	Jose Cruz	.40	.20	.10
465	Dick Bosman	.40	.20	.10
466	Dick Billings	.40	.20	.10
467	Winston Llenas	.40	.20	.10
468	Pepe Frias	.40	.20	.10
469	Joe Decker	.40	.20	.10
470	A.L. Playoffs (Reggie Jackson)	4.00	2.00	1.25
471	N.L. Playoffs (Jon Matlack)	.50	.25	.15
472	World Series Game 1 (Darold Knowles)	.50	.25	.15
473	World Series Game 2 (Willie Mays)	6.00	3.00	1.75
474	World Series Game 3	1.00	.50	.30
475	World Series Game 4	1.00	.50	.30
476	World Series Game 5	1.00	.50	.30
477	World Series Game 6 (Reggie Jackson)	4.00	2.00	1.25
478	World Series Game 7	1.50	.75	.45
479	A's Celebrate (Win 2nd Consecutive Championship!)	1.00	.50	.30
480	Willie Crawford	.40	.20	.10
481	Jerry Terrell	.40	.20	.10
482	Bob Didier	.40	.20	.10
483	Atlanta Braves Team	1.00	.50	.30
484	Carmen Fanzone	.40	.20	.10
485	Felipe Alou	.50	.25	.15
486	Steve Stone	.40	.20	.10
487	Ted Martinez	.40	.20	.10
488	Andy Etchebarren	.40	.20	.10
489	Pirates Mgr./Coaches (Don Leppert, Bill Mazeroski, Danny Murtaugh, Don Osborn, Bob Skinner)	.75	.40	.25
490	Vada Pinson	1.00	.50	.30
491	Roger Nelson	.40	.20	.10
492	Mike Rogodzinski	.40	.20	.10
493	Joe Hoerner	.40	.20	.10
494	Ed Goodson	.40	.20	.10
495	Dick McAuliffe	.40	.20	.10
496	Tom Murphy	.40	.20	.10
497	Bobby Mitchell	.40	.20	.10
498	Pat Corrales	.40	.20	.10
499	Rusty Torres	.40	.20	.10
500	Lee May	.75	.40	.25
501	Eddie Leon	.40	.20	.10
502	Dave LaRoche	.40	.20	.10
503	Eric Soderholm	.40	.20	.10
504	Joe Niekro	.75	.40	.25
505	Bill Buckner	.75	.40	.25
506	Ed Farmer	.40	.20	.10
507	Larry Stahl	.40	.20	.10
508	Montreal Expos Team	1.00	.50	.30
509	Jesse Jefferson	.40	.20	.10
510	Wayne Garrett	.40	.20	.10
511	Toby Harrah	.40	.20	.10
512	Joe Lahoud	.40	.20	.10
513	Jim Campanis	.40	.20	.10
514	Paul Schaal	.40	.20	.10
515	Willie Montanez	.40	.20	.10
516	Horacio Pina	.40	.20	.10
517	Mike Hegan	.40	.20	.10
518	Derrel Thomas	.40	.20	.10
519	Bill Sharp	.40	.20	.10
520	Tim McCarver	1.50	.70	.45
521	Indians Mgr./Coaches (Ken Aspromonte, Clay Bryant, Tony Pacheco)	.40	.20	.10
522	J.R. Richard	1.00	.50	.30
523	Cecil Cooper	1.00	.50	.30
524	Bill Plummer	.40	.20	.10
525	Clyde Wright	.40	.20	.10
526	Frank Tepedino	.40	.20	.10
527	Bobby Darwin	.40	.20	.10
528	Bill Bonham	.40	.20	.10
529	Horace Clarke	.40	.20	.10
530	Mickey Stanley	.40	.20	.10
531	Expos Mgr./Coaches (Dave Bristol, Larry Doby, Gene Mauch, Cal McLish, Jerry Zimmerman)	.40	.20	.10

532	Skip Lockwood	.40	.20	.10
533	Mike Phillips	.40	.20	.10
534	Eddie Watt	.40	.20	.10
535	Bob Tolan	.40	.20	.10
536	Duffy Dyer	.40	.20	.10
537	Steve Mingori	.40	.20	.10
538	Cesar Tovar	.40	.20	.10
539	Lloyd Allen	.40	.20	.10
540	Bob Robertson	.40	.20	.10
541	Cleveland Indians Team	1.00	.50	.30
542	Rich Gossage	4.00	2.00	1.25
543	Danny Cater	.40	.20	.10
544	Ron Schueler	.40	.20	.10
545	Billy Conigliaro	.40	.20	.10
546	Mike Corkins	.40	.20	.10
547	Glenn Borgmann	.40	.20	.10
548	Sonny Siebert	.40	.20	.10
549	Mike Jorgensen	.40	.20	.10
550	Sam McDowell	.40	.20	.10
551	Von Joshua	.40	.20	.10
552	Denny Doyle	.40	.20	.10
553	Jim Willoughby	.40	.20	.10
554	Tim Johnson	.40	.20	.10
555	Woodie Fryman	.40	.20	.10
556	Dave Campbell	.40	.20	.10
557	Jim McGlothlin	.40	.20	.10
558	Bill Fahey	.40	.20	.10
559	Darrel Chaney	.40	.20	.10
560	Mike Cuellar	.40	.20	.10
561	Ed Kranepool	.40	.20	.10
562	Jack Aker	.40	.20	.10
563	Hal McRae	.75	.40	.25
564	Mike Ryan	.40	.20	.10
565	Milt Wilcox	.40	.20	.10
566	Jackie Hernandez	.40	.20	.10
567	Boston Red Sox Team	1.50	.75	.45
568	Mike Torrez	.40	.20	.10
569	Rick Dempsey	.40	.20	.10
570	Ralph Garr	.40	.20	.10
571	Rich Hand	.40	.20	.10
572	Enzo Hernandez	.40	.20	.10
573	Mike Adams	.40	.20	.10
574	Bill Parsons	.40	.20	.10
575	Steve Garvey	2.00	1.00	.60
576	Scipio Spinks	.40	.20	.10
577	Mike Sadek	.40	.20	.10
578	Ralph Houk	.75	.40	.25
579	Cecil Upshaw	.40	.20	.10
580	Jim Spencer	.40	.20	.10
581	Fred Norman	.40	.20	.10
582	*Bucky Dent*	2.00	1.00	.60
583	Marty Pattin	.40	.20	.10
584	Ken Rudolph	.40	.20	.10
585	Merv Rettenmund	.40	.20	.10
586	Jack Brohamer	.40	.20	.10
587	*Larry Christenson*	.40	.20	.10
588	Hal Lanier	.40	.20	.10
589	Boots Day	.40	.20	.10
590	Rogelio Moret	.40	.20	.10
591	Sonny Jackson	.40	.20	.10
592	Ed Bane	.40	.20	.10
593	Steve Yeager	.40	.20	.10
594	Leroy Stanton	.40	.20	.10
595	Steve Blass	.40	.20	.10
596	Rookie Pitchers (**Wayne Garland, Fred Holdsworth, Mark Littell, Dick Pole**)			
597	Rookie Shortstops (*Dave Chalk, John Gamble, Pete Mackanin, Manny Trillo*)	1.00	.50	.30
598	Rookie Outfielders (*Dave Augustine, Ken Griffey, Steve Ontiveros, Jim Tyrone*)	10.00	5.00	3.00
599a	Rookie Pitchers (Ron Diorio, Dave Freisleben, Frank Riccelli, Greg Shanahan) (Freisleben- Washington)	1.00	.50	.30
599b	Rookie Pitchers (Ron Diorio, Dave Freisleben, Frank Riccelli, Greg Shanahan) (Freisleben- San Diego large print.)	3.00	1.50	.90
599c	Rookie Pitchers (Ron Diorio, Dave Freisleben, Frank Riccelli, Greg Shanahan) (Freisleben- San Diego small print.)	5.00	2.50	1.50
600	Rookie Infielders (**Ron Cash, Jim Cox, Bill Madlock, Reggie Sanders**)	5.00	1.50	
601	Rookie Outfielders (**Ed Armbrister, Rich Bladt, Brian Downing, Bake McBride**)	2.00	1.00	.60
602	Rookie Pitchers (Glenn Abbott, Rick Henninger, Craig Swan, Dan Vossler)	.75	.40	.25
603	Rookie Catchers (Barry Foote, Tom Lundstedt, Charlie Moore, Sergio Robles)	.75	.40	.25
604	Rookie Infielders (*Terry Hughes, John Knox, Andy Thornton, Frank White*)	4.00	2.00	1.25
605	Rookie Pitchers (*Vic Albury, Ken Frailing, Kevin Kobel, Frank Tanana*)	3.00	1.50	.90
606	Rookie Outfielders (Jim Fuller, Wilbur Howard, Tommy Smith, Otto Velez)	.75	.40	.25
607	Rookie Shortstops (*Leo Foster, Tom Heintzelman, Dave Rosello, Frank Taveras*)	.75	.40	.25
608a	Rookie Pitchers (Bob Apodaca, Dick Baney, John D'Acquisto, Mike Wallace) (Apodaca incorrect)	1.50	.75	.45

608b	Rookie Pitchers (Bob Apodaca, Dick Baney, John D'Acquisto, Mike Wallace) (Corrected)	.75	.40	.25
609	Rico Petrocelli	1.00	.50	.30
610	Dave Kingman	.75	.40	.25
611	Rick Stelmaszek	.40	.20	.10
612	Luke Walker	.40	.20	.10
613	Dan Monzon	.40	.20	.10
614	Adrian Devine	.40	.20	.10
615	Johnny Jeter	.40	.20	.10
616	Larry Gura	.40	.20	.10
617	Ted Ford	.40	.20	.10
618	Jim Mason	.40	.20	.10
619	Mike Anderson	.40	.20	.10
620	Al Downing	.40	.20	.10
621	Bernie Carbo	.40	.20	.10
622	Phil Gagliano	.40	.20	.10
623	Celerino Sanchez	.40	.20	.10
624	Bob Miller	.40	.20	.10
625	Ollie Brown	.40	.20	.10
626	Pittsburgh Pirates Team	1.00	.50	.30
627	Carl Taylor	.40	.20	.10
628	Ivan Murrell	.40	.20	.10
629	Rusty Staub	.75	.40	.25
630	Tommie Agee	.40	.20	.10
631	Steve Barber	.40	.20	.10
632	George Culver	.40	.20	.10
633	Dave Hamilton	.40	.20	.10
634	Braves Mgr./Coaches (Jim Busby, Eddie Mathews, Connie Ryan, Ken Silvestri, Herm Starrette)	2.00	1.00	.60
635	John Edwards	.40	.20	.10
636	Dave Goltz	.40	.20	.10
637	Checklist 529-660	1.00	.50	.30
638	Ken Sanders	.40	.20	.10
639	Joe Lovitto	.40	.20	.10
640	Milt Pappas	.40	.20	.10
641	Chuck Brinkman	.40	.20	.10
642	Terry Harmon	.40	.20	.10
643	Los Angeles Dodgers Team	2.50	1.25	.75
644	Wayne Granger	.40	.20	.10
645	Ken Boswell	.40	.20	.10
646	George Foster	.75	.40	.25
647	*Juan Beniquez*	.40	.20	.10
648	Terry Crowley	.40	.20	.10
649	Fernando Gonzalez	.40	.20	.10
650	Mike Epstein	.40	.20	.10
651	Leron Lee	.40	.20	.10
652	Gail Hopkins	.40	.20	.10
653	Bob Stinson	.40	.20	.10
654a	Jesus Alou (No position.)	4.00	2.00	1.25
654b	Jesus Alou ("Outfield")	.40	.20	.10
655	Mike Tyson	.40	.20	.10
656	Adrian Garrett	.40	.20	.10
657	Jim Shellenback	.40	.20	.10
658	Lee Lacy	.40	.20	.10
659	Joe Lis	.40	.20	.10
660	Larry Dierker	1.50	.70	.45

1974 Topps Traded

Appearing late in the season, these 2-1/2" x 3-1/2" cards share the format of the regular-issue Topps cards. The major change is a large yellow panel with the word "Traded" in red, added below the player photo. Backs feature a "Baseball News" design that contains the details of the trade. Card numbers correspond to the player's regular card number in 1974 except that the suffix "T" is added. The set consists of 43 player cards and a checklist. In most cases, Topps did not obtain pictures of the players in their new uniforms. Instead, the Topps artists simply provided the needed changes to existing photos.

	NM	EX	VG
Complete Set (44):	25.00	12.50	7.50
Common Player:	.50	.25	.15
23T Craig Robinson	.50	.25	.15
42T Claude Osteen	.50	.25	.15
43T Jim Wynn	.50	.25	.15
51T Bobby Heise	.50	.25	.15
59T Ross Grimsley	.50	.25	.15
62T Bob Locker	.50	.25	.15
63T Bill Sudakis	.50	.25	.15
73T Mike Marshall	.50	.25	.15
123T Nelson Briles	.50	.25	.15
139T Aurelio Monteagudo	.50	.25	.15
151T Diego Segui	.50	.25	.15
165T Willie Davis	.50	.25	.15
175T Reggie Cleveland	.50	.25	.15
182T Lindy McDaniel	.50	.25	.15
186T Fred Scherman	.50	.25	.15
249T George Mitterwald	.50	.25	.15
262T Ed Kirkpatrick	.50	.25	.15
269T Bob Johnson	.50	.25	.15
270T Ron Santo	3.00	1.50	.90

313T	Barry Lersch	.50	.25	.15
319T	Randy Hundley	.50	.25	.15
330T	Juan Marichal	4.00	2.00	1.25
348T	Pete Richert	.50	.25	.15
373T	John Curtis	.50	.25	.15
390T	Lou Piniella	2.00	1.00	.60
428T	Gary Sutherland	.50	.25	.15
454T	Kurt Bevacqua	.50	.25	.15
458T	Jim Ray	.50	.25	.15
485T	Felipe Alou	.75	.40	.25
486T	Steve Stone	.75	.40	.25
496T	Tom Murphy	.50	.25	.15
516T	Horacio Pina	.50	.25	.15
534T	Eddie Watt	.50	.25	.15
538T	Cesar Tovar	.50	.25	.15
544T	Ron Schueler	.50	.25	.15
579T	Cecil Upshaw	.50	.25	.15
585T	Merv Rettenmund	.50	.25	.15
612T	Luke Walker	.50	.25	.15
616T	Larry Gura	.50	.25	.15
618T	Jim Mason	.50	.25	.15
630T	Tommie Agee	.50	.25	.15
648T	Terry Crowley	.50	.25	.15
649T	Fernando Gonzalez	.50	.25	.15
----	Traded Checklist	.50	.25	.15

1974 Topps Action Emblem Cloth Stickers

This enigmatic Topps test issue has never found favor with collectors because no actual ballplayers are pictured. In fact, official team logos are not used either, negating the necessity of licensing from either Major League Baseball or the Players Association. The 2-1/2" x 3-1/2" cloth stickers were sold with a rub-off baseball game card in a Topps white test wrapper with a sticker describing them as "Topps Baseball Action Emblems Cloth Stickers." Each sticker features a generic ballplayer on front with a city (not team) name. At bottom is a pennant with another major league city named and a generic baseball symbol at its left. Backs are blank. This issue can be found in either a cloth sticker version or cardboard version. The cardboard pieces are worth about 4X the cloth type.

		NM	EX	VG
Complete Set (24):		900.00	450.00	275.00
Common Sticker:		40.00	20.00	12.00
Wax Pack:		75.00		
Cardboard: 4X				
(1)	Atlanta/Baltimore	40.00	20.00	12.00
(2)	Baltimore/Montreal	40.00	20.00	12.00
(3)	Boston/Oakland	40.00	20.00	12.00
(4)	California/St. Louis	40.00	20.00	12.00
(5)	Chicago/Houston	40.00	20.00	12.00
(6)	Chicago/Pittsburgh	40.00	20.00	12.00
(7)	Cincinnati/Minnesota	40.00	20.00	12.00
(8)	Cleveland/San Diego	40.00	20.00	12.00
(9)	Detroit/New York	40.00	20.00	12.00
(10)	Houston/Chicago	40.00	20.00	12.00
(11)	Kansas City/Philadelphia	40.00	20.00	12.00
(12)	Los Angeles/Milwaukee	40.00	20.00	12.00
(13)	Milwaukee/New York	40.00	20.00	12.00
(14)	Minnesota/California	40.00	20.00	12.00
(15)	Montreal/San Francisco	40.00	20.00	12.00
(16)	New York/Cincinnati	40.00	20.00	12.00
(17)	New York/Texas	40.00	20.00	12.00
(18)	Oakland/Boston	40.00	20.00	12.00
(19)	Philadelphia/Los Angeles	40.00	20.00	12.00
(20)	Pittsburgh/Cleveland	40.00	20.00	12.00
(21)	St. Louis/Kansas City	40.00	20.00	12.00
(22)	San Diego/Detroit	40.00	20.00	12.00
(23)	San Francisco/Chicago	40.00	20.00	12.00
(24)	Texas/Atlanta	40.00	20.00	12.00

1974 Topps Deckle Edge

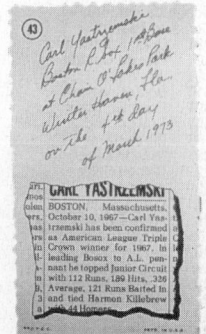

These borderless 2-7/8" x 5" cards feature a black-and-white photograph with a blue facsimile autograph on the front. The backs have in handwritten script the player's name, team, position and the date and location of the picture. Below is a mock newspaper clipping providing a detail from the player's career. Backs can be found in either gray or white (somewhat scarcer). The cards take their names from their specially cut edges which give them a scalloped appearance. The 72-card set was a test issue and received rather limited distribution around Massachusetts. The cards were sold three per pack for five cents with a piece of gum, or in two-card pack with no gum. Proof versions with straight edges and white or gray backs are known; they are slightly larger, at about 3-1/8" x 5-1/4".

		NM	EX	VG
Complete Set (72):		5,000	2,500	1,500
Common Player:		20.00	10.00	6.00
White Backs: 1.5X				
Proofs: .75-1X				
Wax Pack (5):		375.00		
1	Amos Otis	20.00	10.00	6.00
2	Darrell Evans	20.00	10.00	6.00
3	Bob Gibson	135.00	65.00	40.00
4	David Nelson	20.00	10.00	6.00
5	Steve Carlton	135.00	65.00	40.00
6	Catfish Hunter	90.00	45.00	27.50
7	Thurman Munson	135.00	65.00	40.00
8	Bob Grich	20.00	10.00	6.00
9	Tom Seaver	150.00	75.00	45.00
10	Ted Simmons	20.00	10.00	6.00
11	Bobby Valentine	20.00	10.00	6.00
12	Don Sutton	90.00	45.00	27.50
13	Wilbur Wood	20.00	10.00	6.00
14	Doug Rader	20.00	10.00	6.00
15	Chris Chambliss	20.00	10.00	6.00
16	Pete Rose	275.00	135.00	80.00
17	John Hiller	20.00	10.00	6.00
18	Burt Hooton	20.00	10.00	6.00
19	Tim Foli	20.00	10.00	6.00
20	Lou Brock	100.00	50.00	30.00
21	Ron Bryant	20.00	10.00	6.00
22	Manuel Sanguillen	20.00	10.00	6.00
23	Bobby Tolan	20.00	10.00	6.00
24	Greg Luzinski	20.00	10.00	6.00
25	Brooks Robinson	150.00	75.00	45.00
26	Felix Millan	20.00	10.00	6.00
27	Luis Tiant	20.00	10.00	6.00
28	Willie McCovey	100.00	50.00	30.00
29	Chris Speier	20.00	10.00	6.00
30	George Scott	20.00	10.00	6.00
31	Willie Stargell	100.00	50.00	30.00
32	Rod Carew	135.00	65.00	40.00
33	Charlie Spikes	20.00	10.00	6.00
34	Nate Colbert	20.00	10.00	6.00
35	Richie Hebner	20.00	10.00	6.00
36	Bobby Bonds	20.00	10.00	6.00
37	Buddy Bell	20.00	10.00	6.00
38	Claude Osteen	20.00	10.00	6.00
39	Rich Allen	55.00	27.50	16.50
40	Bill Russell	20.00	10.00	6.00
41	Nolan Ryan	900.00	450.00	275.00
42	Willie Davis	20.00	10.00	6.00
43	Carl Yastrzemski	160.00	80.00	45.00
44	Jon Matlack	20.00	10.00	6.00
45	Jim Palmer	135.00	65.00	40.00
46	Bert Campaneris	20.00	10.00	6.00
47	Bert Blyleven	20.00	10.00	6.00
48	Jeff Burroughs	20.00	10.00	6.00
49	Jim Colborn	20.00	10.00	6.00
50	Dave Johnson	20.00	10.00	6.00
51	John Mayberry	20.00	10.00	6.00
52	Don Kessinger	20.00	10.00	6.00
53	Joe Coleman	20.00	10.00	6.00
54	Tony Perez	90.00	45.00	27.50
55	Jose Cardenal	20.00	10.00	6.00
56	Paul Splittorff	20.00	10.00	6.00
57	Henry Aaron	275.00	135.00	80.00
58	David May	20.00	10.00	6.00
59	Fergie Jenkins	90.00	45.00	27.50
60	Ron Blomberg	20.00	10.00	6.00
61	Reggie Jackson	175.00	85.00	50.00
62	Tony Oliva	40.00	20.00	12.00
63	Bobby Murcer	45.00	22.50	13.50
64	Carlton Fisk	100.00	50.00	30.00
65	Steve Rogers	20.00	10.00	6.00
66	Frank Robinson	150.00	75.00	45.00
67	Joe Ferguson	20.00	10.00	6.00
68	Bill Melton	20.00	10.00	6.00
69	Bob Watson	20.00	10.00	6.00
70	Larry Bowa	20.00	10.00	6.00
71	Johnny Bench	150.00	75.00	45.00
72	Willie Horton	20.00	10.00	6.00

1974 Topps Puzzles

One of many test issues by Topps in the mid-1970s, the 12-player jigsaw puzzle set was an innovation which never caught on with collectors. The 40-piece puzzles (4-3/4" x 7-1/2") feature color photos with a decorative lozenge at bottom naming the player, team and position. The 25-cent or 29-cent puzzles came in individual wrappers picturing Tom Seaver. Centering, particularly of the Ryan puzzle, is a plague with the puzzles, accounting for the greater than usual spread betwerrn NM and lower- grade values.

		NM	EX	VG
Complete Set (12):		2,000	700.00	300.00
Common Player:		65.00	32.50	20.00
Wax Pack:		225.00		
Wrapper:		20.00		
(1)	Hank Aaron	250.00	90.00	35.00
(2)	Dick Allen	75.00	30.00	15.00
(3)	Johnny Bench	125.00	44.00	18.50
(4)	Bobby Bonds	65.00	25.00	10.00
(5)	Bob Gibson	125.00	44.00	18.50
(6)	Reggie Jackson	200.00	70.00	30.00
(7)	Bobby Murcer	65.00	25.00	10.00
(8)	Jim Palmer	100.00	35.00	15.00
(9)	Nolan Ryan	650.00	225.00	100.00
(10)	Tom Seaver	125.00	44.00	18.50
(11)	Willie Stargell	100.00	35.00	15.00
(12)	Carl Yastrzemski	250.00	87.00	37.00

1974 Topps Stamps

Topps continued to market baseball stamps in 1974 through the release of 240 unnumbered stamps featuring color player portraits. The player's name, team and position are found in an oval at the bottom of the 1" x 1-1/2" stamps. The stamps, sold separately rather than issued as an insert, came in panels of 12. Two dozen team albums designed to hold 10 stamps were also issued.

		NM	EX	VG
Complete Sheet Set (24):		90.00	45.00	25.00
Common Sheet:		2.00	1.00	.60
Complete Stamp Album Set (24):		300.00	150.00	90.00
Single Stamp Album:		5.00	2.50	1.50
(1)	Hank Aaron, Luis Aparicio, Bob Bailey, Johnny Bench, Ron Blomberg, Bob Boone, Lou Brock, Bud Harrelson, Randy Jones, Dave Rader, Nolan Ryan, Joe Torre	15.00	7.50	4.50
(2)	Buddy Bell, Steve Braun, Jerry Grote, Tommy Helms, Bill Lee, Mike Lum, Dave May, Brooks Robinson, Bill Russell, Del Unser, Wilbur Wood, Carl Yastrzemski	9.00	4.50	2.75
(3)	Jerry Bell, Jim Colborn, Toby Harrah, Ken Henderson, John Hiller, Randy Hundley, Don Kessinger, Jerry Koosman, Dave Lopes, Felix Millan, Thurman Munson, Ted Simmons	6.00	3.00	1.75
(4)	Jerry Bell, Bill Buckner, Jim Colborn, Ken Henderson, Don Kessinger, Felix Millan, George Mitterwald, Dave Roberts, Ted Simmons, Jim Slaton, Charlie Spikes, Paul Splittorff	2.00	1.00	.60
(5)	Glenn Beckert, Jim Bibby, Bill Buckner, Jim Lonborg, George Mitterwald, Dave Parker, Dave Roberts, Jim Slaton, Reggie Smith, Charlie Spikes, Paul Splittorff, Bob Watson	2.00	1.00	.60
(6)	Paul Blair, Bobby Bonds, Ed Brinkman, Norm Cash, Mike Epstein, Tommy Harper, Mike Marshall, Phil Niekro, Cookie Rojas, George Scott, Mel Stottlemyre, Jim Wynn	2.00	1.00	.60
(7)	Jack Billingham, Reggie Cleveland, Bobby Darwin, Dave Duncan, Tim Foli, Ed Goodson, Cleon Jones, Mickey Lolich, George Medich, John Milner, Rick Monday, Bobby Murcer	2.00	1.00	.60

(8)	Steve Carlton, Orlando Cepeda, Joe Decker, Reggie Jackson, Dave Johnson, John Mayberry, Bill Melton, Roger Metzger, Dave Nelson, Jerry Reuss, Jim Spencer, Bobby Valentine	10.00	5.00	3.00
(9)	Dan Driessen, Pedro Garcia, Grant Jackson, Al Kaline, Clay Kirby, Carlos May, Willie Montanez, Rogelio Moret, Jim Palmer, Doug Rader, J. R. Richard, Frank Robinson	7.50	3.75	2.25
(10)	Pedro Garcia, Ralph Garr, Wayne Garrett, Ron Hunt, Al Kaline, Fred Kendall, Carlos May, Jim Palmer, Doug Rader, Frank Robinson, Rick Wise, Richie Zisk	7.50	3.75	2.25
(11)	Dusty Baker, Larry Bowa, Steve Busby, Chris Chambliss, Dock Ellis, Cesar Geronimo, Fran Healy, Deron Johnson, Jorge Orta, Joe Rudi, Mickey Stanley, Rennie Stennett	2.00	1.00	.60
(12)	Bob Coluccio, Ray Corbin, John Ellis, Oscar Gamble, Dave Giusti, Bill Greif, Alex Johnson, Mike Jorgensen, Andy Messersmith, Bill Robinson, Elias Sosa, Willie Stargell	2.00	1.00	.60
(13)	Ron Bryant, Nate Colbert, Jose Cruz, Dan Driessen, Billy Grabarkewitz, Don Gullett, Willie Horton, Grant Jackson, Clay Kirby, Willie Montanez, Rogelio Moret, J. R. Richard	2.00	1.00	.60
(14)	Carlton Fisk, Bill Freehan, Bobby Grich, Vic Harris, George Hendrick, Ed Herrmann, Jim Holt, Ken Holtzman, Fergie Jenkins, Lou Piniella, Steve Rogers, Ken Singleton	5.00	2.50	1.50
(15)	Stan Bahnsen, Sal Bando, Mark Belanger, David Clyde, Willie Crawford, Burt Hooton, Jon Matlack, Tim McCarver, Joe Morgan, Gene Tenace, Dick Tidrow, Dave Winfield	7.50	3.75	2.25
(16)	Hank Aaron, Stan Bahnsen, Bob Bailey, Johnny Bench, Bob Boone, Jon Matlack, Tim McCarver, Joe Morgan, Dave Rader, Gene Tenace, Dick Tidrow, Joe Torre	10.00	5.00	3.00
(17)	John Boccabella, Frank Duffy, Darrell Evans, Sparky Lyle, Lee May, Don Money, Bill North, Ted Sizemore, Chris Speier, Wayne Twitchell, Billy Williams, Earl Williams	2.00	1.00	.60
(18)	John Boccabella, Bobby Darwin, Frank Duffy, Dave Duncan, Tim Foli, Cleon Jones, Mickey Lolich, Sparky Lyle, Lee May, Rick Monday, Bill North, Billy Williams	2.00	1.00	.60
(19)	Don Baylor, Vida Blue, Tom Bradley, Jose Cardenal, Ron Cey, Greg Luzinski, Johnny Oates, Tony Oliva, Al Oliver, Tony Perez, Darrell Porter, Roy White	3.00	1.50	.90
(20)	Pedro Borbon, Rod Carew, Roric Harrison, Jim Hunter, Ed Kirkpatrick, Garry Maddox, Gene Michael, Rick Miller, Claude Osteen, Amos Otis, Rich Reuschel, Mike Tyson	5.00	2.50	1.50
(21)	Sandy Alomar, Bert Campaneris, Dave Concepcion, Tommy Davis, Joe Ferguson, Tito Fuentes, Jerry Morales, Carl Morton, Gaylord Perry, Vada Pinson, Dave Roberts, Elias Rodriguez	2.00	1.00	.60
(22)	Dick Allen, Jeff Burroughs, Joe Coleman, Terry Forster, Bob Gibson, Harmon Killebrew, Tug McGraw, Bob Oliver, Steve Renko, Pete Rose, Luis Tiant, Otto Velez	12.00	6.00	3.50
(23)	Johnny Briggs, Willie Davis, Jim Fregosi, Rich Hebner, Pat Kelly, Dave Kingman, Willie McCovey, Graig Nettles, Freddie Patek, Marty Pattin, Manny Sanguillen, Richie Scheinblum	5.00	2.50	1.50
(24)	Bert Blyleven, Nelson Briles, Cesar Cedeno, Ron Fairly, Johnny Grubb, Dave McNally, Aurelio Rodriguez, Ron Santo, Tom Seaver, Bill Singer, Bill Sudakis, Don Sutton	6.00	3.00	1.75

1974 Topps Team Checklists

This set is a repeat of the 1973 set in the form of 24 unnumbered 2-1/2" x 3-1/2" checklist cards. Cards feature a team name on the front at the top with a white panel and a number of facsimile autographs below. Backs feature the team name and a checklist. The big difference between the 1973 and 1974 checklists is that the 1973s have blue borders

 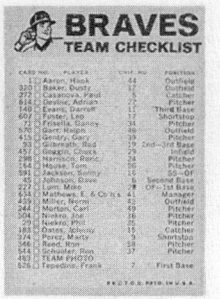

while the 1974s have red borders. The 1974s were inserted into packages of the regular issue Topps cards and were also available in uncut sheet form as a wrapper redemption.

	NM	EX	VG
Complete Set (24):	25.00	12.50	7.50
Common Checklist:	1.50	.75	.45
Uncut Sheet:	25.00	12.50	7.50
(1) Atlanta Braves	1.50	.75	.45
(2) Baltimore Orioles	1.50	.75	.45
(3) Boston Red Sox	1.50	.75	.45
(4) California Angels	1.50	.75	.45
(5) Chicago Cubs	1.50	.75	.45
(6) Chicago White Sox	1.50	.75	.45
(7) Cincinnati Reds	1.50	.75	.45
(8) Cleveland Indians	1.50	.75	.45
(9) Detroit Tigers	1.50	.75	.45
(10) Houston Astros	1.50	.75	.45
(11) Kansas City Royals	1.50	.75	.45
(12) Los Angeles Dodgers	1.50	.75	.45
(13) Milwaukee Brewers	1.50	.75	.45
(14) Minnesota Twins	1.50	.75	.45
(15) Montreal Expos	1.50	.75	.45
(16) New York Mets	1.50	.75	.45
(17) New York Yankees	1.50	.75	.45
(18) Oakland A's	1.50	.75	.45
(19) Philadelphia Phillies	1.50	.75	.45
(20) Pittsburgh Pirates	1.50	.75	.45
(21) St. Louis Cardinals	1.50	.75	.45
(22) San Diego Padres	1.50	.75	.45
(23) San Francisco Giants	1.50	.75	.45
(24) Texas Rangers	1.50	.75	.45

1975 Topps

 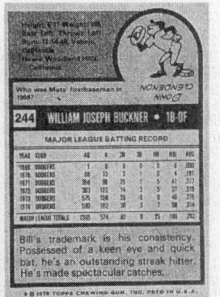

What was once seen as the strongest rookie card crop of any modern card set made this a collector favorite from the outset. Featuring the most colorful designs since 1972, cards feature large front photos with facsimile autographs. Red-and-green backs include a cartoon trivia fact and complete stats. A subset of 1951-74 MVP cards which reproduces or creates contemporary cards of past stars is one of several special features of the set, as are a group of four-on-one rookie cards. While the cards were all issued at one time, the first 132 cards have been discovered to have been printed in somewhat lesser quantities than the rest of the issue. This scarcity is not noted among the mini-version of the set which was produced as a test issue. Team/manager cards are sometimes found on thinner, white cardboard stock; these are a special version produced for a mail-in offer.

	NM	EX	VG
Complete Set (660):	650.00	325.00	162.50
Common Player:	.40	.20	.10
Mini Stars/Rookies: 1-1.5X			
Wax Pack (10):	40.00		
Wax Box (36):	2,400		
Cello Pack (18):	85.00		
Rack Pack (42):	190.00		
Vending Box (500):	.00		
1 Hank Aaron ('74 Highlights)	30.00	15.00	9.00
2 Lou Brock ('74 Highlights)	2.00	1.00	.60
3 Bob Gibson ('74 Highlights)	2.00	1.00	.60
4 Al Kaline ('74 Highlights)	4.00	2.00	1.25
5 Nolan Ryan ('74 Highlights)	12.00	6.00	3.50
6 Mike Marshall ('74 Highlights)	.40	.20	.10
7 Dick Bosman, Steve Busby, Nolan Ryan ('74 Highlights)	8.00	4.00	2.50
8 Rogelio Moret	.40	.20	.10
9 Frank Tepedino	.40	.20	.10
10 Willie Davis	.40	.20	.10
11 Bill Melton	.40	.20	.10
12 David Clyde	.40	.20	.10
13 Gene Locklear	.40	.20	.10
14 Milt Wilcox	.40	.20	.10
15 Jose Cardenal	.40	.20	.10
16 Frank Tanana	.40	.20	.10

17	Dave Concepcion	.40	.20	.10
18	Tigers team (Ralph Houk)	1.50	.70	.45
19	Jerry Koosman	.40	.20	.10
20	Thurman Munson	12.00	6.00	3.00
21	Rollie Fingers	3.00	1.50	.90
22	Dave Cash	.40	.20	.10
23	Bill Russell	.75	.40	.25
24	Al Fitzmorris	.40	.20	.10
25	Lee May	.75	.40	.25
26	Dave McNally	.40	.20	.10
27	Ken Reitz	.40	.20	.10
28	Tom Murphy	.40	.20	.10
29	Dave Parker	1.50	.70	.45
30	Bert Blyleven	1.50	.70	.45
31	Dave Rader	.40	.20	.10
32	Reggie Cleveland	.40	.20	.10
33	Dusty Baker	1.50	.70	.45
34	Steve Renko	.40	.20	.10
35	Ron Santo	2.00	1.00	.60
36	Joe Lovitto	.40	.20	.10
37	Dave Freisleben	.40	.20	.10
38	Buddy Bell	.75	.40	.25
39	Andy Thornton	.75	.40	.25
40	Bill Singer	.40	.20	.10
41	Cesar Geronimo	.40	.20	.10
42	Joe Coleman	.40	.20	.10
43	Cleon Jones	.40	.20	.10
44	Pat Dobson	.40	.20	.10
45	Joe Rudi	.40	.20	.10
46	Phillies Team (Danny Ozark)	1.50	.70	.45
47	Tommy John	1.50	.70	.45
48	Freddie Patek	.40	.20	.10
49	Larry Dierker	.75	.40	.25
50	Brooks Robinson	10.00	5.00	2.50
51	*Bob Forsch*	.75	.40	.25
52	Darrell Porter	.75	.40	.25
53	Dave Giusti	.40	.20	.10
54	Eric Soderholm	.40	.20	.10
55	Bobby Bonds	1.50	.70	.45
56	Rick Wise	.40	.20	.10
57	Dave Johnson	.75	.40	.25
58	Chuck Taylor	.40	.20	.10
59	Ken Henderson	.40	.20	.10
60	Fergie Jenkins	3.00	1.50	.90
61	Dave Winfield	12.00	6.00	3.50
62	Fritz Peterson	.40	.20	.10
63	Steve Swisher	.40	.20	.10
64	Dave Chalk	.40	.20	.10
65	Don Gullett	.40	.20	.10
66	Willie Horton	.40	.20	.10
67	Tug McGraw	.75	.40	.25
68	Ron Blomberg	.40	.20	.10
69	John Odom	.40	.20	.10
70	Mike Schmidt	20.00	10.00	6.00
71	Charlie Hough	.75	.40	.25
72	Royals Team (Jack McKeon)	1.00	.50	.30
73	J.R. Richard	.40	.20	.10
74	Mark Belanger	.40	.20	.10
75	Ted Simmons	1.00	.50	.30
76	Ed Sprague	.40	.20	.10
77	Richie Zisk	.40	.20	.10
78	Ray Corbin	.40	.20	.10
79	Gary Matthews	.40	.20	.10
80	Carlton Fisk	6.00	3.00	1.75
81	Ron Reed	.40	.20	.10
82	Pat Kelly	.40	.20	.10
83	Jim Merritt	.40	.20	.10
84	Enzo Hernandez	.40	.20	.10
85	Bill Bonham	.40	.20	.10
86	Joe Lis	.40	.20	.10
87	George Foster	1.00	.50	.30
88	Tom Egan	.40	.20	.10
89	Jim Ray	.40	.20	.10
90	Rusty Staub	1.00	.50	.30
91	Dick Green	.40	.20	.10
92	Cecil Upshaw	.40	.20	.10
93	Dave Lopes	1.00	.50	.30
94	Jim Lonborg	.75	.40	.25
95	John Mayberry	.75	.40	.25
96	Mike Cosgrove	.40	.20	.10
97	Earl Williams	.40	.20	.10
98	Rich Folkers	.40	.20	.10
99	Mike Hegan	.40	.20	.10
100	Willie Stargell	5.00	2.50	1.25
101	Expos Team (Gene Mauch)	1.00	.50	.30
102	Joe Decker	.40	.20	.10
103	Rick Miller	.40	.20	.10
104	Bill Madlock	.75	.40	.25
105	Buzz Capra	.40	.20	.10
106	*Mike Hargrove*	2.00	1.00	.60
107	Jim Barr	.40	.20	.10
108	Tom Hall	.40	.20	.10
109	George Hendrick	.40	.20	.10
110	Wilbur Wood	.40	.20	.10
111	Wayne Garrett	.40	.20	.10
112	Larry Hardy	.40	.20	.10
113	Elliott Maddox	.40	.20	.10
114	Dick Lange	.40	.20	.10
115	Joe Ferguson	.40	.20	.10
116	Lerrin LaGrow	.40	.20	.10
117	Orioles Team (Earl Weaver)	3.00	1.50	.90
118	Mike Anderson	.40	.20	.10
119	Tommy Helms	.40	.20	.10
120	Steve Busby (Photo actually Fran Healy.)	.40	.20	.10
121	Bill North	.40	.20	.10
122	Al Hrabosky	.75	.40	.25
123	Johnny Briggs	.40	.20	.10
124	Jerry Reuss	.75	.40	.25
125	Ken Singleton	.75	.40	.25
126	Checklist 1-132	2.00	1.00	.60
127	Glen Borgmann	.40	.20	.10
128	Bill Lee	.40	.20	.10
129	Rick Monday	.40	.20	.10
130	Phil Niekro	3.00	1.50	.90
131	Toby Harrah	.40	.20	.10
132	Randy Moffitt	.40	.20	.10
133	Dan Driessen	.40	.20	.10

#	Player			
134	Ron Hodges	.40	.20	.10
135	Charlie Spikes	.40	.20	.10
136	Jim Mason	.40	.20	.10
137	Terry Forster	.40	.20	.10
138	Del Unser	.40	.20	.10
139	Horacio Pina	.40	.20	.10
140	Steve Garvey	2.00	1.00	.60
141	Mickey Stanley	.40	.20	.10
142	Bob Reynolds	.40	.20	.10
143	*Cliff Johnson*	.40	.20	.10
144	Jim Wohlford	.40	.20	.10
145	Ken Holtzman	.40	.20	.10
146	Padres Team (John McNamara)	1.00	.50	.30
147	Pedro Garcia	.40	.20	.10
148	Jim Rooker	.40	.20	.10
149	Tim Foli	.40	.20	.10
150	Bob Gibson	5.00	2.50	1.50
151	Steve Brye	.40	.20	.10
152	Mario Guerrero	.40	.20	.10
153	Rick Reuschel	.40	.20	.10
154	Mike Lum	.40	.20	.10
155	Jim Bibby	.40	.20	.10
156	Dave Kingman	1.00	.50	.30
157	Pedro Borbon	.40	.20	.10
158	Jerry Grote	.40	.20	.10
159	Steve Arlin	.40	.20	.10
160	Graig Nettles	1.00	.50	.30
161	Stan Bahnsen	.40	.20	.10
162	Willie Montanez	.40	.20	.10
163	Jim Brewer	.40	.20	.10
164	Mickey Rivers	.40	.20	.10
165	Doug Rader	.40	.20	.10
166	Woodie Fryman	.40	.20	.10
167	Rich Coggins	.40	.20	.10
168	Bill Greif	.40	.20	.10
169	Cookie Rojas	.40	.20	.10
170	Bert Campaneris	.40	.20	.10
171	Ed Kirkpatrick	.40	.20	.10
172	Red Sox Team (Darrell Johnson)	1.50	.70	.45
173	Steve Rogers	.40	.20	.10
174	Bake McBride	.40	.20	.10
175	Don Money	.40	.20	.10
176	Burt Hooton	.40	.20	.10
177	Vic Correll	.40	.20	.10
178	Cesar Tovar	.40	.20	.10
179	Tom Bradley	.40	.20	.10
180	Joe Morgan	6.00	3.00	1.50
181	Fred Beene	.40	.20	.10
182	Don Hahn	.40	.20	.10
183	Mel Stottlemyre	.40	.20	.10
184	Jorge Orta	.40	.20	.10
185	Steve Carlton	6.00	3.00	1.50
186	Willie Crawford	.40	.20	.10
187	Denny Doyle	.40	.20	.10
188	Tom Griffin	.40	.20	.10
189	1951-MVPs (Yogi Berra, Roy Campanella)	3.00	1.50	.90
190	1952-MVPs (Hank Sauer, Bobby Shantz)	1.00	.50	.30
191	1953-MVPs (Roy Campanella, Al Rosen)	1.50	.70	.45
192	1954-MVPs (Yogi Berra, Willie Mays)	4.00	2.00	1.25
193	1955-MVPs (Yogi Berra, Roy Campanella)	3.00	1.50	.90
194	1956-MVPs (Mickey Mantle, Don Newcombe)	8.00	4.00	2.00
195	1957-MVPs (Hank Aaron, Mickey Mantle)	10.00	5.00	2.50
196	1958-MVPs (Ernie Banks, Jackie Jensen)	2.50	1.25	.70
197	1959-MVPs (Ernie Banks, Nellie Fox)	2.00	1.00	.60
198	1960-MVPs (Dick Groat, Roger Maris)	1.50	.70	.45
199	1961-MVPs (Roger Maris, Frank Robinson)	2.00	1.00	.60
200	1962-MVPs (Mickey Mantle, Maury Wills)	8.00	4.00	2.50
201	1963-MVPs (Elston Howard, Sandy Koufax)	2.50	1.25	.70
202	1964-MVPs (Ken Boyer, Brooks Robinson)	1.00	.50	.30
203	1965-MVPs (Willie Mays, Zoilo Versalles)	2.00	1.00	.60
204	1966-MVPs (Roberto Clemente, Frank Robinson)	5.00	2.50	1.50
205	1967-MVPs (Orlando Cepeda, Carl Yastrzemski)	1.50	.70	.45
206	1968-MVPs (Bob Gibson, Denny McLain)	1.50	.70	.45
207	1969-MVPs (Harmon Killebrew, Willie McCovey)	2.00	1.00	.60
208	1970-MVPs (Johnny Bench, Boog Powell)	2.00	1.00	.60
209	1971-MVPs (Vida Blue, Joe Torre)	1.00	.50	.30
210	1972-MVPs (Rich Allen, Johnny Bench)	2.00	1.00	.60
211	1973-MVPs (Reggie Jackson, Pete Rose)	4.00	2.00	1.25
212	1974-MVPs (Jeff Burroughs, Steve Garvey)	1.00	.50	.30
213	Oscar Gamble	.40	.20	.10
214	Harry Parker	.40	.20	.10
215	Bobby Valentine	.40	.20	.10
216	Giants Team (Wes Westrum)	1.00	.50	.30
217	Lou Piniella	1.50	.70	.45
218	Jerry Johnson	.40	.20	.10
219	Ed Herrmann	.40	.20	.10
220	Don Sutton	3.00	1.50	.90
221	Aurelio Rodriguez (Rodriguez)	.40	.20	.10
222	Dan Spillner	.40	.20	.10
223	*Robin Yount*	50.00	25.00	15.00
224	Ramon Hernandez	.40	.20	.10
225	Bob Grich	.75	.40	.25
226	Bill Campbell	.40	.20	.10
227	Bob Watson	.40	.20	.10
228	*George Brett*	80.00	40.00	20.00
229	Barry Foote	.40	.20	.10
230	Jim Hunter	5.00	2.50	1.25
231	Mike Tyson	.40	.20	.10
232	Diego Segui	.40	.20	.10
233	Billy Grabarkewitz	.40	.20	.10
234	Tom Grieve	.40	.20	.10
235	Jack Billingham	.40	.20	.10
236	Angels Team (Dick Williams)	1.00	.50	.30
237	Carl Morton	.40	.20	.10
238	Dave Duncan	.75	.40	.25
239	George Stone	.40	.20	.10
240	Garry Maddox	.40	.20	.10
241	Dick Tidrow	.40	.20	.10
242	Jay Johnstone	.40	.20	.10
243	Jim Kaat	1.50	.70	.45
244	Bill Buckner	.75	.40	.25
245	Mickey Lolich	1.00	.50	.30
246	Cardinals Team (Red Schoendienst)	1.00	.50	.30
247	Enos Cabell	.40	.20	.10
248	Randy Jones	.40	.20	.10
249	Danny Thompson	.40	.20	.10
250	Ken Brett	.40	.20	.10
251	Fran Healy	.40	.20	.10
252	Fred Scherman	.40	.20	.10
253	Jesus Alou	.40	.20	.10
254	Mike Torrez	.40	.20	.10
255	Dwight Evans	1.00	.50	.30
256	Billy Champion	.40	.20	.10
257	Checklist 133-264	2.00	1.00	.60
258	Dave LaRoche	.40	.20	.10
259	Len Randle	.40	.20	.10
260	Johnny Bench	12.00	6.00	3.00
261	Andy Hassler	.40	.20	.10
262	Rowland Office	.40	.20	.10
263	Jim Perry	.40	.20	.10
264	John Milner	.40	.20	.10
265	Ron Bryant	.40	.20	.10
266	Sandy Alomar	.40	.20	.10
267	Dick Ruthven	.40	.20	.10
268	Hal McRae	.75	.40	.25
269	Doug Rau	.40	.20	.10
270	Ron Fairly	.40	.20	.10
271	Jerry Moses	.40	.20	.10
272	Lynn McGlothen	.40	.20	.10
273	Steve Braun	.40	.20	.10
274	Vicente Romo	.40	.20	.10
275	Paul Blair	.40	.20	.10
276	White Sox Team (Chuck Tanner)	1.00	.50	.30
277	Frank Taveras	.40	.20	.10
278	Paul Lindblad	.40	.20	.10
279	Milt May	.40	.20	.10
280	Carl Yastrzemski	10.00	5.00	3.00
281	Jim Slaton	.40	.20	.10
282	Jerry Morales	.40	.20	.10
283	Steve Foucault	.40	.20	.10
284	Ken Griffey	2.00	1.00	.60
285	Ellie Rodriguez	.40	.20	.10
286	Mike Jorgensen	.40	.20	.10
287	Roric Harrison	.40	.20	.10
288	Bruce Ellingsen	.40	.20	.10
289	Ken Rudolph	.40	.20	.10
290	Jon Matlack	.40	.20	.10
291	Bill Sudakis	.40	.20	.10
292	Ron Schueler	.40	.20	.10
293	Dick Sharon	.40	.20	.10
294	*Geoff Zahn*	.40	.20	.10
295	Vada Pinson	1.50	.70	.45
296	Alan Foster	.40	.20	.10
297	Craig Kusick	.40	.20	.10
298	Johnny Grubb	.40	.20	.10
299	Bucky Dent	1.00	.50	.30
300	Reggie Jackson	12.00	6.00	3.50
301	Dave Roberts	.40	.20	.10
302	*Rick Burleson*	.75	.40	.25
303	Grant Jackson	.40	.20	.10
304	Pirates Teamz (Danny Murtaugh)	1.50	.70	.45
305	Jim Colborn	.40	.20	.10
306	Batting Leaders (Rod Carew, Ralph Garr)	1.50	.70	.45
307	Home Run Leaders (Dick Allen, Mike Schmidt)	3.00	1.50	.90
308	Runs Batted In Leaders (Johnny Bench, Jeff Burroughs)	1.50	.70	.45
309	Stolen Base Leaders (Lou Brock, Bill North)	1.50	.70	.45
310	Victory Leaders (Jim Hunter, Fergie Jenkins, Andy Messersmith, Phil Niekro)	1.50	.70	.45
311	Earned Run Average Leaders (Buzz Capra, Jim Hunter)	1.50	.70	.45
312	Strikeout Leaders (Steve Carlton, Nolan Ryan)	10.00	5.00	3.00
313	Leading Firemen (Terry Forster, Mike Marshall)	1.00	.50	.30
314	Buck Martinez	.40	.20	.10
315	Don Kessinger	.40	.20	.10
316	Jackie Brown	.40	.20	.10
317	Joe Lahoud	.40	.20	.10
318	Ernie McAnally	.40	.20	.10
319	Johnny Oates	.40	.20	.10
320	Pete Rose	25.00	12.50	7.50
321	Rudy May	.40	.20	.10
322	Ed Goodson	.40	.20	.10
323	Fred Holdsworth	.40	.20	.10
324	Ed Kranepool	.40	.20	.10
325	Tony Oliva	1.50	.70	.45
326	Wayne Twitchell	.40	.20	.10
327	Jerry Hairston Sr.	.40	.20	.10
328	Sonny Siebert	.40	.20	.10
329	Ted Kubiak	.40	.20	.10
330	Mike Marshall	.40	.20	.10
331	Indians Team (Frank Robinson)	1.50	.75	.45
332	Fred Kendall	.40	.20	.10
333	Dick Drago	.40	.20	.10
334	*Greg Gross*	.40	.20	.10
335	Jim Palmer	4.00	2.00	1.25
336	Rennie Stennett	.40	.20	.10
337	Kevin Kobel	.40	.20	.10
338	Rick Stelmaszek	.40	.20	.10
339	Jim Fregosi	1.00	.50	.30
340	Paul Splittorff	.40	.20	.10
341	Hal Breeden	.40	.20	.10
342	Leroy Stanton	.40	.20	.10
343	Danny Frisella	.40	.20	.10
344	Ben Oglivie	1.00	.50	.30
345	Clay Carroll	.40	.20	.10
346	Bobby Darwin	.40	.20	.10
347	Mike Caldwell	.40	.20	.10
348	Tony Muser	.40	.20	.10
349	Ray Sadecki	.40	.20	.10
350	Bobby Murcer	.75	.40	.25
351	Bob Boone	1.50	.70	.45
352	Darold Knowles	.40	.20	.10
353	Luis Melendez	.40	.20	.10
354	Dick Bosman	.40	.20	.10
355	Chris Cannizzaro	.40	.20	.10
356	Rico Petrocelli	.75	.40	.25
357	Ken Forsch	.40	.20	.10
358	Al Bumbry	.40	.20	.10
359	Paul Popovich	.40	.20	.10
360	George Scott	.40	.20	.10
361	Dodgers Team (Walter Alston)	1.50	.75	.45
362	Steve Hargan	.40	.20	.10
363	Carmen Fanzone	.40	.20	.10
364	Doug Bird	.40	.20	.10
365	Bob Bailey	.40	.20	.10
366	Ken Sanders	.40	.20	.10
367	Craig Robinson	.40	.20	.10
368	Vic Albury	.40	.20	.10
369	Merv Rettenmund	.40	.20	.10
370	Tom Seaver	10.00	5.00	3.00
371	Gates Brown	.40	.20	.10
372	John D'Acquisto	.40	.20	.10
373	Bill Sharp	.40	.20	.10
374	Eddie Watt	.40	.20	.10
375	Roy White	.45	.25	.15
376	Steve Yeager	.40	.20	.10
377	Tom Hilgendorf	.40	.20	.10
378	Derrel Thomas	.40	.20	.10
379	Bernie Carbo	.40	.20	.10
380	Sal Bando	.40	.20	.10
381	John Curtis	.40	.20	.10
382	Don Baylor	1.50	.70	.45
383	Jim York	.40	.20	.10
384	Brewers Team (Del Crandall)	1.50	.70	.45
385	Dock Ellis	.40	.20	.10
386	Checklist 265-396	2.00	1.00	.60
387	Jim Spencer	.40	.20	.10
388	Steve Stone	.75	.40	.25
389	Tony Solaita	.40	.20	.10
390	Ron Cey	1.00	.50	.30
391	Don DeMola	.40	.20	.10
392	Bruce Bochte	.40	.20	.10
393	Gary Gentry	.40	.20	.10
394	Larvell Blanks	.40	.20	.10
395	Bud Harrelson	.40	.20	.10
396	Fred Norman	.40	.20	.10
397	Bill Freehan	.75	.40	.25
398	Elias Sosa	.40	.20	.10
399	Terry Harmon	.40	.20	.10
400	Dick Allen	1.00	.50	.30
401	Mike Wallace	.40	.20	.10
402	Bob Tolan	.40	.20	.10
403	Tom Buskey	.40	.20	.10
404	Ted Sizemore	.40	.20	.10
405	John Montague	.40	.20	.10
406	Bob Gallagher	.40	.20	.10
407	*Herb Washington*	1.00	.50	.30
408	Clyde Wright	.40	.20	.10
409	Bob Robertson	.40	.20	.10
410	Mike Cueller (Cuellar)	.40	.20	.10
411	George Mitterwald	.40	.20	.10
412	Bill Hands	.40	.20	.10
413	Marty Pattin	.40	.20	.10
414	Manny Mota	.40	.20	.10
415	John Hiller	.40	.20	.10
416	Larry Lintz	.40	.20	.10
417	Skip Lockwood	.40	.20	.10
418	Leo Foster	.40	.20	.10
419	Dave Goltz	.40	.20	.10
420	Larry Bowa	1.50	.70	.45
421	Mets Team (Yogi Berra)	2.50	1.25	.70
422	Brian Downing	.40	.20	.10
423	Clay Kirby	.40	.20	.10
424	John Lowenstein	.40	.20	.10
425	Tito Fuentes	.40	.20	.10
426	George Medich	.40	.20	.10
427	Clarence Gaston	.40	.20	.10
428	Dave Hamilton	.40	.20	.10
429	*Jim Dwyer*	.40	.20	.10
430	Luis Tiant	1.00	.50	.30
431	Rod Gilbreath	.40	.20	.10
432	Ken Berry	.40	.20	.10
433	Larry Demery	.40	.20	.10
434	Bob Locker	.40	.20	.10
435	Dave Nelson	.40	.20	.10
436	Ken Frailing	.40	.20	.10
437	*Al Cowens*	.40	.20	.10
438	Don Carrithers	.40	.20	.10
439	Ed Brinkman	.40	.20	.10
440	Andy Messersmith	.40	.20	.10
441	Bobby Heise	.40	.20	.10
442	Maximino Leon	.40	.20	.10
443	Twins Team (Frank Quilici)	1.00	.50	.30
444	Gene Garber	.40	.20	.10
445	Felix Millan	.40	.20	.10
446	Bart Johnson	.40	.20	.10

447	Terry Crowley	.40	.20	.10
448	Frank Duffy	.40	.20	.10
449	Charlie Williams	.40	.20	.10
450	Willie McCovey	5.00	2.50	1.50
451	Rick Dempsey	.40	.20	.10
452	Angel Mangual	.40	.20	.10
453	Claude Osteen	.40	.20	.10
454	Doug Griffin	.40	.20	.10
455	Don Wilson	.40	.20	.10
456	Bob Coluccio	.40	.20	.10
457	Mario Mendoza	.40	.20	.10
458	Ross Grimsley	.40	.20	.10
459	A.L. Championships (Brooks Robinson)	1.00	.50	.30
460	N.L. Championships (Steve Garvey)	1.00	.50	.30
461	World Series Game 1 (Reggie Jackson)	2.00	1.00	.60
462	World Series Game 2 (Joe Ferguson)	.75	.40	.25
463	World Series Game 3 (Rollie Fingers)	1.50	.70	.45
464	World Series Game 4	.75	.40	.25
465	World Series Game 5	.75	.40	.25
466	A's Do It Again! (Win 3rd Straight World Series!)	1.50	.70	.45
467	Ed Halicki	.40	.20	.10
468	Bobby Mitchell	.40	.20	.10
469	Tom Dettore	.40	.20	.10
470	Jeff Burroughs	.40	.20	.10
471	Bob Stinson	.40	.20	.10
472	Bruce Dal Canton	.40	.20	.10
473	Ken McMullen	.40	.20	.10
474	Luke Walker	.40	.20	.10
475	Darrell Evans	1.00	.50	.30
476	*Ed Figueroa*	.40	.20	.10
477	Tom Hutton	.40	.20	.10
478	Tom Burgmeier	.40	.20	.10
479	Ken Boswell	.40	.20	.10
480	Carlos May	.40	.20	.10
481	*Will McEnaney*	.40	.20	.10
482	Tom McCraw	.40	.20	.10
483	Steve Ontiveros	.40	.20	.10
484	Glenn Beckert	.40	.20	.10
485	Sparky Lyle	.40	.20	.10
486	Ray Fosse	.40	.20	.10
487	Astros Team (Preston Gomez)	1.00	.50	.30
488	Bill Travers	.40	.20	.10
489	Cecil Cooper	1.00	.50	.30
490	Reggie Smith	.75	.40	.25
491	Doyle Alexander	.40	.20	.10
492	Rich Hebner	.40	.20	.10
493	Don Stanhouse	.40	.20	.10
494	*Pete LaCock*	.40	.20	.10
495	Nelson Briles	.40	.20	.10
496	Pepe Frias	.40	.20	.10
497	Jim Nettles	.40	.20	.10
498	Al Downing	.40	.20	.10
499	Marty Perez	.40	.20	.10
500	Nolan Ryan	50.00	25.00	15.00
501	Bill Robinson	.40	.20	.10
502	Pat Bourque	.40	.20	.10
503	Fred Stanley	.40	.20	.10
504	Buddy Bradford	.40	.20	.10
505	Chris Speier	.40	.20	.10
506	Leron Lee	.40	.20	.10
507	Tom Carroll	.40	.20	.10
508	Bob Hansen	.40	.20	.10
509	Dave Hilton	.40	.20	.10
510	Vida Blue	.75	.40	.25
511	Rangers Team (Billy Martin)	1.50	.75	.45
512	Larry Milbourne	.40	.20	.10
513	Dick Pole	.40	.20	.10
514	Jose Cruz	.40	.20	.10
515	Manny Sanguillen	.40	.20	.10
516	Don Hood	.40	.20	.10
517	Checklist 397-528	2.00	1.00	.60
518	Leo Cardenas	.40	.20	.10
519	Jim Todd	.40	.20	.10
520	Amos Otis	.40	.20	.10
521	Dennis Blair	.40	.20	.10
522	Gary Sutherland	.40	.20	.10
523	Tom Paciorek	.40	.20	.10
524	John Doherty	.40	.20	.10
525	Tom House	.40	.20	.10
526	Larry Hisle	.40	.20	.10
527	Mac Scarce	.40	.20	.10
528	Eddie Leon	.40	.20	.10
529	Gary Thomasson	.40	.20	.10
530	Gaylord Perry	3.00	1.50	.90
531	Reds Team (Sparky Anderson)	5.00	2.50	1.50
532	Gorman Thomas	.40	.20	.10
533	Rudy Meoli	.40	.20	.10
534	Alex Johnson	.40	.20	.10
535	Gene Tenace	.40	.20	.10
536	Bob Moose	.40	.20	.10
537	Tommy Harper	.40	.20	.10
538	Duffy Dyer	.40	.20	.10
539	Jesse Jefferson	.40	.20	.10
540	Lou Brock	5.00	2.50	1.50
541	Roger Metzger	.40	.20	.10
542	Pete Broberg	.40	.20	.10
543	Larry Biittner	.40	.20	.10
544	Steve Mingori	.40	.20	.10
545	Billy Williams	5.00	2.50	1.50
546	John Knox	.40	.20	.10
547	Von Joshua	.40	.20	.10
548	Charlie Sands	.40	.20	.10
549	Bill Butler	.40	.20	.10
550	Ralph Garr	.40	.20	.10
551	Larry Christenson	.40	.20	.10
552	Jack Brohamer	.40	.20	.10
553	John Boccabella	.40	.20	.10
554	Rich Gossage	1.50	.70	.45
555	Al Oliver	1.00	.50	.30
556	Tim Johnson	.40	.20	.10

557	Larry Gura	.40	.20	.10
558	Dave Roberts	.40	.20	.10
559	Bob Montgomery	.40	.20	.10
560	Tony Perez	5.00	2.50	1.25
561	A's Team (Alvin Dark)	1.00	.50	.30
562	Gary Nolan	.40	.20	.10
563	Wilbur Howard	.40	.20	.10
564	Tommy Davis	.40	.20	.10
565	Joe Torre	2.00	1.00	.60
566	Ray Burris	.40	.20	.10
567	*Jim Sundberg*	1.00	.50	.30
568	Dale Murray	.40	.20	.10
569	Frank White	.40	.20	.10
570	Jim Wynn	.40	.20	.10
571	Dave Lemanczyk	.40	.20	.10
572	Roger Nelson	.40	.20	.10
573	Orlando Pena	.40	.20	.10
574	Tony Taylor	.40	.20	.10
575	Gene Clines	.40	.20	.10
576	Phil Roof	.40	.20	.10
577	John Morris	.40	.20	.10
578	Dave Tomlin	.40	.20	.10
579	Skip Pitlock	.40	.20	.10
580	Frank Robinson	8.00	4.00	2.00
581	Darrel Chaney	.40	.20	.10
582	Eduardo Rodriguez	.40	.20	.10
583	Andy Etchebarren	.40	.20	.10
584	Mike Garman	.40	.20	.10
585	Chris Chambliss	.75	.40	.25
586	Tim McCarver	1.00	.50	.30
587	Chris Ward	.40	.20	.10
588	Rick Auerbach	.40	.20	.10
589	Braves Team (Clyde King)	1.00	.50	.30
590	Cesar Cedeno	.40	.20	.10
591	Glenn Abbott	.40	.20	.10
592	Balor Moore	.40	.20	.10
593	Gene Lamont	.40	.20	.10
594	Jim Fuller	.40	.20	.10
595	Joe Niekro	.40	.20	.10
596	Ollie Brown	.40	.20	.10
597	Winston Llenas	.40	.20	.10
598	Bruce Kison	.40	.20	.10
599	Nate Colbert	.40	.20	.10
600	Rod Carew	6.00	3.00	1.75
601	Juan Beniquez	.40	.20	.10
602	John Vukovich	.40	.20	.10
603	Lew Krausse	.40	.20	.10
604	Oscar Zamora	.40	.20	.10
605	John Ellis	.40	.20	.10
606	Bruce Miller	.40	.20	.10
607	Jim Holt	.40	.20	.10
608	Gene Michael	.40	.20	.10
609	Ellie Hendricks	.40	.20	.10
610	Ron Hunt	.40	.20	.10
611	Yankees Team (Bill Virdon)	2.00	1.00	.60
612	Terry Hughes	.40	.20	.10
613	Bill Parsons	.40	.20	.10
614	Rookie Pitchers (Jack Kucek, Dyar Miller, Vern Ruhle, Paul Siebert)	.40	.20	.10
615	Rookie Pitchers (*Pat Darcy, Dennis Leonard, Tom Underwood, Hank Webb*)	.40	.20	.10
616	Rookie Outfielders (*Dave Augustine, Pepe Mangual, Jim Rice, John Scott*)	20.00	10.00	6.00
617	Rookie Infielders (Mike Cubbage, Doug DeCinces, Reggie Sanders, Manny Trillo)	1.50	.70	.45
618	Rookie Pitchers (*Jamie Easterly, Tom Johnson, Scott McGregor, Rick Rhoden*)	2.00	1.00	.60
619	Rookie Outfielders (Benny Ayala, Nyls Nyman, Tommy Smith, Jerry Turner)	.40	.20	.10
620	Rookie Catchers-Outfielders (*Gary Carter, Marc Hill, Danny Meyer, Leon Roberts*)	20.00	10.00	5.00
621	Rookie Pitchers (John Denny, Rawly Eastwick, Jim Kern, Juan Veintidos)	.50	.25	.15
622	Rookie Outfielders (*Ed Armbrister, Fred Lynn, Tom Poquette, Terry Whitfield*)	8.00	4.00	2.50
623	Rookie Infielders (*Phil Garner, Keith Hernandez, Bob Sheldon, Tom Veryzer*)	10.00	5.00	2.50
624	Rookie Pitchers (Doug Konieczny, Gary Lavelle, Jim Otten, Eddie Solomon)	.40	.20	.10
625	Boog Powell	1.00	.50	.30
626	Larry Haney	.40	.20	.10
627	Tom Walker	.40	.20	.10
628	*Ron LeFlore*	.75	.40	.25
629	Joe Hoerner	.40	.20	.10
630	Greg Luzinski	1.00	.50	.30
631	Lee Lacy	.40	.20	.10
632	Morris Nettles	.40	.20	.10
633	Paul Casanova	.40	.20	.10
634	Cy Acosta	.40	.20	.10
635	Chuck Dobson	.40	.20	.10
636	Charlie Moore	.40	.20	.10
637	Ted Martinez	.40	.20	.10
638	Cubs Team (Jim Marshall)	1.50	.70	.45
639	Steve Kline	.40	.20	.10
640	Harmon Killebrew	6.00	3.00	1.75
641	Jim Northrup	.40	.20	.10
642	Mike Phillips	.40	.20	.10
643	Brent Strom	.40	.20	.10
644	Bill Fahey	.40	.20	.10
645	Danny Cater	.40	.20	.10
646	Checklist 529-660	1.00	.50	.30
647	*Claudell Washington*	.75	.40	.25

648	Dave Pagan	.40	.20	.10
649	Jack Heidemann	.40	.20	.10
650	Dave May	.40	.20	.10
651	John Morlan	.40	.20	.10
652	Lindy McDaniel	.40	.20	.10
653	Lee Richards	.40	.20	.10
654	Jerry Terrell	.40	.20	.10
655	Rico Carty	.40	.20	.10
656	Bill Plummer	.40	.20	.10
657	Bob Oliver	.40	.20	.10
658	Vic Harris	.40	.20	.10
659	Bob Apodaca	.40	.20	.10
660	Hank Aaron	30.00	15.00	9.00

1975 Topps Mini

This popular set was actually a test issue to see how collectors would react to cards which were 20 percent smaller than the standard 2-1/2" x 3-1/2". Other than their 2-1/4" x 3-1/8" size, they are exactly the same front and back as the regular-issue '75 Topps. The experimental cards were sold in Michigan and on the West Coast, where they were quickly gobbled up by collectors, dealers and speculators. While the minis for many years enjoyed a 2X premium over regular 1975 Topps values, that differential has shrunk in recent years.

	NM	EX	VG
Complete Set (660):	425.00	210.00	125.00
Common Player:	.50	.25	.15
Wax Pack (10):	40.00		
Wax Box (36):	1,600		
Cello Pack (18):	100.00		
Rack Pack (42):	200.00		

(Stars and rookies valued 1X to 1.5X regular 1975 Topps.)

1975 Topps Team Checklist Sheet

Via a mail-in wrapper redemption, collectors could receive an uncut sheet of the 24 team photo/checklist cards from the 1975 Topps baseball set. Measuring about 10-1/2" x 20-1/8", the sheet could be cut into individual team cards of standard size. The sheet-cut cards differ from issued versions in that they have white backs and are printed on thinner stock than the pack-issued versions.

	NM	EX	VG
Complete Sheet:	50.00	25.00	15.00

1976 Topps

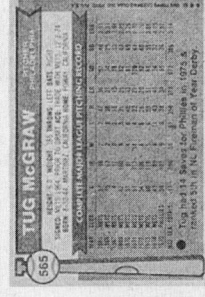

These 2-1/2" x 3-1/2" cards begin a design trend for Topps. The focus was more on the photo quality than in past years with a corresponding trend toward simplicity in the borders. The front of the cards has the player's name and team in two strips while his position is in the lower-left corner under a drawing of a player representing that position. The backs have a bat and ball with the card number on the left; statistics and personal information and career highlights on the right. The 660-card set features a number of specialty sets including record-setting performances, statistical leaders, playoff and World Series highlights, the Sporting News All-Time All-Stars and father and son combinations.

	NM	EX	VG
Complete Set (660):	250.00	125.00	75.00
Common Player:	.40	.20	.10
Wax Pack (6):	30.00		
Wax Box (36 six-card):	1,200		
Wax Pack (10):	50.00		
Wax Box (36 10-card):	2,000		
Cello Pack (18):	60.00		
Cello Box (24):	1,950		
Rack Pack (42):	105.00		
Vending Box (500):	510.00		
1	Hank Aaron (Record Breaker)	20.00	10.00	5.00
2	Bobby Bonds (Record Breaker)	1.50	.70	.45

#	Name			
3	Mickey Lolich (Rzecord Breaker)	.40	.20	.10
4	Dave Lopes (Record Breaker)	.40	.20	.10
5	Tom Seaver (Record Breaker)	3.00	1.50	.90
6	Rennie Stennett (Record Breaker)	.40	.20	.10
7	Jim Umbarger	.40	.20	.10
8	Tito Fuentes	.40	.20	.10
9	Paul Lindblad	.40	.20	.10
10	Lou Brock	5.00	2.50	1.50
11	Jim Hughes	.40	.20	.10
12	Richie Zisk	.40	.20	.10
13	Johnny Wockenfuss	.40	.20	.10
14	Gene Garber	.40	.20	.10
15	George Scott	.40	.20	.10
16	Bob Apodaca	.40	.20	.10
17	New York Yankees Team (Billy Martin)	1.50	.70	.45
18	Dale Murray	.40	.20	.10
19	George Brett	30.00	15.00	7.50
20	Bob Watson	.40	.20	.10
21	Dave LaRoche	.40	.20	.10
22	Bill Russell	1.00	.50	.30
23	Brian Downing	.40	.20	.10
24	Cesar Geronimo	.40	.20	.10
25	Mike Torrez	.40	.20	.10
26	Andy Thornton	.75	.40	.25
27	Ed Figueroa	.40	.20	.10
28	Dusty Baker	1.50	.70	.45
29	Rick Burleson	.40	.20	.10
30	*John Montefusco*	.40	.20	.10
31	Len Randle	.40	.20	.10
32	Danny Frisella	.40	.20	.10
33	Bill North	.40	.20	.10
34	Mike Garman	.40	.20	.10
35	Tony Oliva	1.00	.50	.30
36	Frank Taveras	.40	.20	.10
37	John Hiller	.40	.20	.10
38	Garry Maddox	.40	.20	.10
39	Pete Broberg	.40	.20	.10
40	Dave Kingman	.75	.40	.25
41	*Tippy Martinez*	.75	.40	.25
42	Barry Foote	.40	.20	.10
43	Paul Splittorff	.40	.20	.10
44	Doug Rader	.40	.20	.10
45	Boog Powell	.75	.40	.25
46	Los Angeles Dodgers Team (Walter Alston)	1.00	.50	.30
47	Jesse Jefferson	.40	.20	.10
48	Dave Concepcion	.40	.20	.10
49	Dave Duncan	.40	.20	.10
50	Fred Lynn	.75	.40	.25
51	Ray Burris	.40	.20	.10
52	Dave Chalk	.40	.20	.10
53	Mike Beard	.40	.20	.10
54	Dave Rader	.40	.20	.10
55	Gaylord Perry	3.00	1.50	.90
56	Bob Tolan	.40	.20	.10
57	Phil Garner	.40	.20	.10
58	Ron Reed	.40	.20	.10
59	Larry Hisle	.40	.20	.10
60	Jerry Reuss	.40	.20	.10
61	Ron LeFlore	.40	.20	.10
62	Johnny Oates	.40	.20	.10
63	Bobby Darwin	.40	.20	.10
64	Jerry Koosman	.40	.20	.10
65	Chris Chambliss	.40	.20	.10
66	Father & Son (Buddy Bell, Gus Bell)	.40	.20	.10
67	Father & Son (Bob Boone, Ray Boone)	.40	.20	.12
68	Father & Son (Joe Coleman, Joe Coleman, Jr.)	.40	.20	.10
69	Father & Son (Jim Hegan, Mike Hegan)	.40	.20	.10
70	Father & Son (Roy Smalley, III, Roy Smalley, Jr.)	.40	.20	.10
71	Steve Rogers	.40	.20	.10
72	Hal McRae	.40	.20	.10
73	Baltimore Orioles Team (Earl Weaver)	1.00	.50	.30
74	Oscar Gamble	.40	.20	.10
75	Larry Dierker	.40	.20	.10
76	Willie Crawford	.40	.20	.10
77	Pedro Borbon	.40	.20	.10
78	Cecil Cooper	.40	.20	.10
79	Jerry Morales	.40	.20	.10
80	Jim Kaat	.75	.40	.25
81	Darrell Evans	.75	.40	.25
82	Von Joshua	.40	.20	.10
83	Jim Spencer	.40	.20	.10
84	Brent Strom	.40	.20	.10
85	Mickey Rivers	.40	.20	.10
86	Mike Tyson	.40	.20	.10
87	Tom Burgmeier	.40	.20	.10
88	Duffy Dyer	.40	.20	.10
89	Vern Ruhle	.40	.20	.10
90	Sal Bando	.40	.20	.10
91	Tom Hutton	.40	.20	.10
92	Eduardo Rodriguez	.40	.20	.10
93	Mike Phillips	.40	.20	.10
94	Jim Dwyer	.40	.20	.10
95	Brooks Robinson	6.00	3.00	1.75
96	Doug Bird	.40	.20	.10
97	Wilbur Howard	.40	.20	.10
98	*Dennis Eckersley*	30.00	15.00	7.50
99	Lee Lacy	.40	.20	.10
100	Jim Hunter	4.00	2.00	1.00
101	Pete LaCock	.40	.20	.10
102	Jim Willoughby	.40	.20	.10
103	Biff Pocoroba	.40	.20	.10
104	Cincinnati Reds Team (Sparky Anderson)	1.00	.50	.30
105	Gary Lavelle	.40	.20	.10
106	Tom Grieve	.40	.20	.10
107	Dave Roberts	.40	.20	.10
108	Don Kirkwood	.40	.20	.10
109	Larry Lintz	.40	.20	.10
110	Carlos May	.40	.20	.10
111	Danny Thompson	.40	.20	.10
112	*Kent Tekulve*	.75	.40	.25
113	Gary Sutherland	.40	.20	.10
114	Jay Johnstone	.40	.20	.10
115	Ken Holtzman	.40	.20	.10
116	Charlie Moore	.40	.20	.10
117	Mike Jorgensen	.40	.20	.10
118	Boston Red Sox Team (Darrell Johnson)	1.00	.50	.30
119	Checklist 1-132	1.00	.50	.30
120	Rusty Staub	.75	.40	.25
121	Tony Solaita	.40	.20	.10
122	Mike Cosgrove	.40	.20	.10
123	Walt Williams	.40	.20	.10
124	Doug Rau	.40	.20	.10
125	Don Baylor	1.50	.70	.45
126	Tom Dettore	.40	.20	.10
127	Larvell Blanks	.40	.20	.10
128	Ken Griffey	1.00	.50	.30
129	Andy Etchebarren	.40	.20	.10
130	Luis Tiant	1.00	.50	.30
131	Bill Stein	.40	.20	.10
132	Don Hood	.40	.20	.10
133	Gary Matthews	.40	.20	.10
134	Mike Ivie	.40	.20	.10
135	Bake McBride	.40	.20	.10
136	Dave Goltz	.40	.20	.10
137	Bill Robinson	.40	.20	.10
138	Lerrin LaGrow	.40	.20	.10
139	Gorman Thomas	.75	.40	.25
140	Vida Blue	1.00	.50	.30
141	*Larry Parrish*	1.00	.50	.30
142	Dick Drago	.40	.20	.10
143	Jerry Grote	.40	.20	.10
144	Al Fitzmorris	.40	.20	.10
145	Larry Bowa	1.00	.50	.30
146	George Medich	.40	.20	.10
147	Houston Astros Team (Bill Virdon)	1.00	.50	.30
148	Stan Thomas	.40	.20	.10
149	Tommy Davis	.40	.20	.10
150	Steve Garvey	2.00	1.00	.60
151	Bill Bonham	.40	.20	.10
152	Leroy Stanton	.40	.20	.10
153	Buzz Capra	.40	.20	.10
154	Bucky Dent	.40	.20	.10
155	Jack Billingham	.40	.20	.10
156	Rico Carty	.40	.20	.10
157	Mike Caldwell	.40	.20	.10
158	Ken Reitz	.40	.20	.10
159	Jerry Terrell	.40	.20	.10
160	Dave Winfield	8.00	4.00	2.50
161	Bruce Kison	.40	.20	.10
162	Jack Pierce	.40	.20	.10
163	Jim Slaton	.40	.20	.10
164	Pepe Mangual	.40	.20	.10
165	Gene Tenace	.40	.20	.10
166	Skip Lockwood	.40	.20	.10
167	Freddie Patek	.40	.20	.10
168	Tom Hilgendorf	.40	.20	.10
169	Graig Nettles	.75	.40	.25
170	Rick Wise	.40	.20	.10
171	Greg Gross	.40	.20	.10
172	Texas Rangers Team (Frank Lucchesi)	1.00	.50	.30
173	Steve Swisher	.40	.20	.10
174	Charlie Hough	.75	.40	.25
175	Ken Singleton	.40	.20	.10
176	Dick Lange	.40	.20	.10
177	Marty Perez	.40	.20	.10
178	Tom Buskey	.40	.20	.10
179	George Foster	.75	.40	.25
180	Rich Gossage	1.00	.50	.30
181	Willie Montanez	.40	.20	.10
182	Harry Rasmussen	.40	.20	.10
183	Steve Braun	.40	.20	.10
184	Bill Greif	.40	.20	.10
185	Dave Parker	1.00	.50	.30
186	Tom Walker	.40	.20	.10
187	Pedro Garcia	.40	.20	.10
188	Fred Scherman	.40	.20	.10
189	Claudell Washington	.40	.20	.10
190	Jon Matlack	.40	.20	.10
191	N.L. Batting Leaders (Bill Madlock, Manny Sanguillen, Ted Simmons)	.75	.40	.25
192	A.L. Batting Leaders (Rod Carew, Fred Lynn, Thurman Munson)	1.00	.50	.30
193	N.L. Home Run Leaders (Dave Kingman, Greg Luzinski, Mike Schmidt)	2.00	1.00	.60
194	A.L. Home Run Leaders (Reggie Jackson, John Mayberry, George Scott)	2.00	1.00	.60
195	N.L. RBI Leaders (Johnny Bench, Greg Luzinski, Tony Perez)	1.00	.50	.30
196	A.L. RBI Leaders (Fred Lynn, John Mayberry, George Scott)	.40	.20	.10
197	N.L. Stolen Base Leaders (Lou Brock, Dave Lopes, Joe Morgan)	1.50	.70	.45
198	A.L. Stolen Base Leaders (Amos Otis, Mickey Rivers, Claudell Washington)	.40	.20	.10
199	N.L. Victory Leaders (Randy Jones, Andy Messersmith, Tom Seaver)	2.00	1.00	.60
200	A.L. Victory Leaders (Vida Blue, Jim Hunter, Jim Palmer)	1.00	.50	.30
201	N.L. ERA Leaders (Randy Jones, Andy Messersmith, Tom Seaver)	1.00	.50	.30
202	A.L. ERA Leaders (Dennis Eckersley, Jim Hunter, Jim Palmer)	2.00	1.00	.60
203	N.L. Strikeout Leaders (Andy Messersmith, John Montefusco, Tom Seaver)	1.50	.70	.45
204	A.L. Strikeout Leaders (Bert Blyleven, Gaylord Perry, Frank Tanana)	1.00	.50	.30
205	Major League Leading Firemen (Rich Gossage, Al Hrabosky)	.75	.40	.25
206	Manny Trillo	.40	.20	.10
207	Andy Hassler	.40	.20	.10
208	Mike Lum	.40	.20	.10
209	Alan Ashby	.40	.20	.10
210	Lee May	.40	.20	.10
211	Clay Carroll	.40	.20	.10
212	Pat Kelly	.40	.20	.10
213	Dave Heaverlo	.40	.20	.10
214	Eric Soderholm	.40	.20	.10
215	Reggie Smith	.40	.20	.10
216	Montreal Expos Team (Karl Kuehl)	1.00	.50	.30
217	Dave Freisleben	.40	.20	.10
218	John Knox	.40	.20	.10
219	Tom Murphy	.40	.20	.10
220	Manny Sanguillen	.40	.20	.10
221	Jim Todd	.40	.20	.10
222	Wayne Garrett	.40	.20	.10
223	Ollie Brown	.40	.20	.10
224	Jim York	.40	.20	.10
225	Roy White	.40	.20	.10
226	Jim Sundberg	.40	.20	.10
227	Oscar Zamora	.40	.20	.10
228	John Hale	.40	.20	.10
229	*Jerry Remy*	.40	.20	.10
230	Carl Yastrzemski	8.00	4.00	2.00
231	Tom House	.40	.20	.10
232	Frank Duffy	.40	.20	.10
233	Grant Jackson	.40	.20	.10
234	Mike Sadek	.40	.20	.10
235	Bert Blyleven	1.00	.50	.30
236	Kansas City Royals Team (Whitey Herzog)	1.00	.50	.30
237	Dave Hamilton	.40	.20	.10
238	Larry Biittner	.40	.20	.10
239	John Curtis	.40	.20	.10
240	Pete Rose	20.00	10.00	5.00
241	Hector Torres	.40	.20	.10
242	Dan Meyer	.40	.20	.10
243	Jim Rooker	.40	.20	.10
244	Bill Sharp	.40	.20	.10
245	Felix Millan	.40	.20	.10
246	Cesar Tovar	.40	.20	.10
247	Terry Harmon	.40	.20	.10
248	Dick Tidrow	.40	.20	.10
249	Cliff Johnson	.40	.20	.10
250	Fergie Jenkins	3.00	1.50	.90
251	Rick Monday	.40	.20	.10
252	Tim Nordbrook	.40	.20	.10
253	Bill Buckner	.75	.40	.25
254	Rudy Meoli	.40	.20	.10
255	Fritz Peterson	.40	.20	.10
256	Rowland Office	.40	.20	.10
257	Ross Grimsley	.40	.20	.10
258	Nyls Nyman	.40	.20	.10
259	Darrel Chaney	.40	.20	.10
260	Steve Busby	.40	.20	.10
261	Gary Thomasson	.40	.20	.10
262	Checklist 133-264	1.00	.50	.30
263	*Lyman Bostock*	.75	.40	.25
264	Steve Renko	.40	.20	.10
265	Willie Davis	.40	.20	.10
266	Alan Foster	.40	.20	.10
267	Aurelio Rodriguez	.40	.20	.10
268	Del Unser	.40	.20	.10
269	Rick Austin	.40	.20	.10
270	Willie Stargell	4.00	2.00	1.25
271	Jim Lonborg	.40	.20	.10
272	Rick Dempsey	.40	.20	.10
273	Joe Niekro	.40	.20	.10
274	Tommy Harper	.40	.20	.10
275	*Rick Manning*	.75	.40	.25
276	Mickey Scott	.40	.20	.10
277	Chicago Cubs Team (Jim Marshall)	1.00	.50	.30
278	Bernie Carbo	.40	.20	.10
279	Roy Howell	.40	.20	.10
280	Burt Hooton	.40	.20	.10
281	Dave May	.40	.20	.10
282	Dan Osborn	.40	.20	.10
283	Merv Rettenmund	.40	.20	.10
284	Steve Ontiveros	.40	.20	.10
285	Mike Cuellar	.40	.20	.10
286	Jim Wohlford	.40	.20	.10
287	Pete Mackanin	.40	.20	.10
288	Bill Campbell	.40	.20	.10
289	Enzo Hernandez	.40	.20	.10
290	Ted Simmons	.40	.20	.10
291	Ken Sanders	.40	.20	.10
292	Leon Roberts	.40	.20	.10
293	Bill Castro	.40	.20	.10
294	Ed Kirkpatrick	.40	.20	.10
295	Dave Cash	.40	.20	.10
296	Pat Dobson	.40	.20	.10
297	Roger Metzger	.40	.20	.10
298	Dick Bosman	.40	.20	.10
299	Champ Summers	.40	.20	.10
300	Johnny Bench	10.00	5.00	3.00
301	Jackie Brown	.40	.20	.10
302	Rick Miller	.40	.20	.10
303	Steve Foucault	.40	.20	.10
304	California Angels Team (Dick Williams)	1.00	.50	.30
305	Andy Messersmith	.40	.20	.10
306	Rod Gilbreath	.40	.20	.10
307	Al Bumbry	.40	.20	.10
308	Jim Barr	.40	.20	.10
309	Bill Melton	.40	.20	.10
310	Randy Jones	.40	.20	.10

#	Player			
311	Cookie Rojas	.40	.20	.10
312	Don Carrithers	.40	.20	.10
313	*Dan Ford*	.40	.20	.10
314	Ed Kranepool	.40	.20	.10
315	Al Hrabosky	.40	.20	.10
316	Robin Yount	10.00	5.00	2.50
317	*John Candelaria*	1.00	.50	.30
318	Bob Boone	.75	.40	.25
319	Larry Gura	.40	.20	.10
320	Willie Horton	.40	.20	.10
321	Jose Cruz	.75	.40	.25
322	Glenn Abbott	.40	.20	.10
323	Rob Sperring	.40	.20	.10
324	Jim Bibby	.40	.20	.10
325	Tony Perez	4.00	2.00	1.25
326	Dick Pole	.40	.20	.10
327	Dave Moates	.40	.20	.10
328	Carl Morton	.40	.20	.10
329	Joe Ferguson	.40	.20	.10
330	Nolan Ryan	25.00	12.50	7.50
331	San Diego Padres Team (John McNamara)	1.00	.50	.30
332	Charlie Williams	.40	.20	.10
333	Bob Coluccio	.40	.20	.10
334	Dennis Leonard	.40	.20	.10
335	Bob Grich	.75	.40	.25
336	Vic Albury	.40	.20	.10
337	Bud Harrelson	.40	.20	.10
338	Bob Bailey	.40	.20	.10
339	John Denny	.40	.20	.10
340	Jim Rice	3.00	1.50	.90
341	Lou Gehrig (All Time 1B)	10.00	5.00	3.00
342	Rogers Hornsby (All Time 2B)	2.50	1.25	.70
343	Pie Traynor (All Time 3B)	1.00	.50	.30
344	Honus Wagner (All Time SS)	5.00	2.50	1.50
345	Babe Ruth (All Time OF)	15.00	7.50	4.50
346	Ty Cobb (All Time OF)	10.00	5.00	3.00
347	Ted Williams (All Time OF)	10.00	5.00	3.00
348	Mickey Cochrane (All Time C)	1.00	.50	.30
349	Walter Johnson" (All Time RHP)	4.00	2.00	1.25
350	Lefty Grove (All Time LHP)	1.00	.50	.30
351	Randy Hundley	.40	.20	.10
352	Dave Giusti	.40	.20	.10
353	*Sixto Lezcano*	.75	.40	.25
354	Ron Blomberg	.40	.20	.10
355	Steve Carlton	4.00	2.00	1.25
356	Ted Martinez	.40	.20	.10
357	Ken Forsch	.40	.20	.10
358	Buddy Bell	.40	.20	.10
359	Rick Reuschel	.40	.20	.10
360	Jeff Burroughs	.40	.20	.10
361	Detroit Tigers Team (Ralph Houk)	1.00	.50	.30
362	Will McEnaney	.40	.20	.10
363	*Dave Collins*	.40	.20	.12
364	Elias Sosa	.40	.20	.10
365	Carlton Fisk	5.00	2.50	1.50
366	Bobby Valentine	.40	.20	.10
367	Bruce Miller	.40	.20	.10
368	Wilbur Wood	.40	.20	.10
369	Frank White	.75	.40	.25
370	Ron Cey	.75	.40	.25
371	Ellie Hendricks	.40	.20	.10
372	Rick Baldwin	.40	.20	.10
373	Johnny Briggs	.40	.20	.10
374	Dan Warthen	.40	.20	.10
375	Ron Fairly	.40	.20	.10
376	Rich Hebner	.40	.20	.10
377	Mike Hegan	.40	.20	.10
378	Steve Stone	.40	.20	.10
379	Ken Boswell	.40	.20	.10
380	Bobby Bonds	1.00	.50	.30
381	Denny Doyle	.40	.20	.10
382	Matt Alexander	.40	.20	.10
383	John Ellis	.40	.20	.10
384	Philadelphia Phillies Team (Danny Ozark)	1.00	.50	.30
385	Mickey Lolich	.75	.40	.25
386	Ed Goodson	.40	.20	.10
387	Mike Miley	.40	.20	.10
388	Stan Perzanowski	.40	.20	.10
389	Glenn Adams	.40	.20	.10
390	Don Gullett	.40	.20	.10
391	Jerry Hairston Sr.	.40	.20	.10
392	Checklist 265-396	1.00	.50	.30
393	Paul Mitchell	.40	.20	.10
394	Fran Healy	.40	.20	.10
395	Jim Wynn	.40	.20	.10
396	Bill Lee	.40	.20	.10
397	Tim Foli	.40	.20	.10
398	Dave Tomlin	.40	.20	.10
399	Luis Melendez	.40	.20	.10
400	Rod Carew	5.00	2.50	1.50
401	Ken Brett	.40	.20	.10
402	Don Money	.40	.20	.10
403	Geoff Zahn	.40	.20	.10
404	Enos Cabell	.40	.20	.10
405	Rollie Fingers	3.00	1.50	.90
406	Ed Herrmann	.40	.20	.10
407	Tom Underwood	.40	.20	.10
408	Charlie Spikes	.40	.20	.10
409	Dave Lemanczyk	.40	.20	.10
410	Ralph Garr	.40	.20	.10
411	Bill Singer	.40	.20	.10
412	Toby Harrah	.40	.20	.10
413	Pete Varney	.40	.20	.10
414	Wayne Garland	.40	.20	.10
415	Vada Pinson	1.00	.50	.30
416	Tommy John	1.00	.50	.30
417	Gene Clines	.40	.20	.10
418	Jose Morales	.40	.20	.10
419	Reggie Cleveland	.40	.20	.10
420	Joe Morgan	4.00	2.00	1.25
421	Oakland A's Team	1.00	.50	.30
422	Johnny Grubb	.40	.20	.10
423	Ed Halicki	.40	.20	.10
424	Phil Roof	.40	.20	.10
425	Rennie Stennett	.40	.20	.10
426	Bob Forsch	.40	.20	.10
427	Kurt Bevacqua	.40	.20	.10
428	Jim Crawford	.40	.20	.10
429	Fred Stanley	.40	.20	.10
430	Jose Cardenal	.40	.20	.10
431	Dick Ruthven	.40	.20	.10
432	Tom Veryzer	.40	.20	.10
433	Rick Waits	.40	.20	.10
434	Morris Nettles	.40	.20	.10
435	Phil Niekro	3.00	1.50	.90
436	Bill Fahey	.40	.20	.10
437	Terry Forster	.40	.20	.10
438	Doug DeCinces	.40	.20	.10
439	Rick Rhoden	.40	.20	.10
440	John Mayberry	.40	.20	.10
441	Gary Carter	6.00	3.00	1.75
442	Hank Webb	.40	.20	.10
443	San Francisco Giants Team	1.00	.50	.30
444	Gary Nolan	.40	.20	.10
445	Rico Petrocelli	.40	.20	.10
446	Larry Haney	.40	.20	.10
447	Gene Locklear	.40	.20	.10
448	Tom Johnson	.40	.20	.10
449	Bob Robertson	.40	.20	.10
450	Jim Palmer	4.00	2.00	1.25
451	Buddy Bradford	.40	.20	.10
452	Tom Hausman	.40	.20	.10
453	Lou Piniella	1.50	.70	.45
454	Tom Griffin	.40	.20	.10
455	Dick Allen	.75	.40	.25
456	Joe Coleman	.40	.20	.10
457	Ed Crosby	.40	.20	.10
458	Earl Williams	.40	.20	.10
459	Jim Brewer	.40	.20	.10
460	Cesar Cedeno	.40	.20	.10
461	NL & AL Championships	.75	.40	.25
462	1975 World Series	.75	.40	.25
463	Steve Hargan	.40	.20	.10
464	Ken Henderson	.40	.20	.10
465	Mike Marshall	.40	.20	.10
466	Bob Stinson	.40	.20	.10
467	Woodie Fryman	.40	.20	.10
468	Jesus Alou	.40	.20	.10
469	Rawly Eastwick	.40	.20	.10
470	Bobby Murcer	.75	.40	.25
471	Jim Burton	.40	.20	.10
472	Bob Davis	.40	.20	.10
473	Paul Blair	.40	.20	.10
474	Ray Corbin	.40	.20	.10
475	Joe Rudi	.40	.20	.10
476	Bob Moose	.40	.20	.10
477	Cleveland Indians Team (Frank Robinson)	1.50	.70	.45
478	Lynn McGlothen	.40	.20	.10
479	Bobby Mitchell	.40	.20	.10
480	Mike Schmidt	12.00	6.00	3.00
481	Rudy May	.40	.20	.10
482	Tim Hosley	.40	.20	.10
483	Mickey Stanley	.40	.20	.10
484	Eric Raich	.40	.20	.10
485	Mike Hargrove	.40	.20	.10
486	Bruce Dal Canton	.40	.20	.10
487	Leron Lee	.40	.20	.10
488	Claude Osteen	.40	.20	.10
489	Skip Jutze	.40	.20	.10
490	Frank Tanana	.40	.20	.10
491	Terry Crowley	.40	.20	.10
492	Marty Pattin	.40	.20	.10
493	Derrel Thomas	.40	.20	.10
494	Craig Swan	.40	.20	.10
495	Nate Colbert	.40	.20	.10
496	Juan Beniquez	.40	.20	.10
497	Joe McIntosh	.40	.20	.10
498	Glenn Borgmann	.40	.20	.10
499	Mario Guerrero	.40	.20	.10
500	Reggie Jackson	10.00	5.00	3.00
501	Billy Champion	.40	.20	.10
502	Tim McCarver	1.00	.50	.30
503	Elliott Maddox	.40	.20	.10
504	Pittsburgh Pirates Team (Danny Murtaugh)	1.00	.50	.30
505	Mark Belanger	.40	.20	.10
506	George Mitterwald	.40	.20	.10
507	Ray Bare	.40	.20	.10
508	*Duane Kuiper*	.40	.20	.10
509	Bill Hands	.40	.20	.10
510	Amos Otis	.40	.20	.10
511	Jamie Easterly	.40	.20	.10
512	Ellie Rodriguez	.40	.20	.10
513	Bart Johnson	.40	.20	.10
514	Dan Driessen	.40	.20	.10
515	Steve Yeager	.40	.20	.10
516	Wayne Granger	.40	.20	.10
517	John Milner	.40	.20	.10
518	*Doug Flynn*	.40	.20	.10
519	Steve Brye	.40	.20	.10
520	Willie McCovey	4.00	2.00	1.25
521	Jim Colborn	.40	.20	.10
522	Ted Sizemore	.40	.20	.10
523	Bob Montgomery	.40	.20	.10
524	Pete Falcone	.40	.20	.10
525	Billy Williams	3.00	1.50	.75
526	Checklist 397-528	1.00	.50	.30
527	Mike Anderson	.40	.20	.10
528	Dock Ellis	.40	.20	.10
529	Deron Johnson	.40	.20	.10
530	Don Sutton	3.00	1.50	.90
531	New York Mets Team (Joe Frazier)	1.00	.50	.30
532	Milt May	.40	.20	.10
533	Lee Richard	.40	.20	.10
534	Stan Bahnsen	.40	.20	.10
535	Dave Nelson	.40	.20	.10
536	Mike Thompson	.40	.20	.10
537	Tony Muser	.40	.20	.10
538	Pat Darcy	.40	.20	.10
539	John Balaz	.40	.20	.10
540	Bill Freehan	.40	.20	.10
541	Steve Mingori	.40	.20	.10
542	Keith Hernandez	1.00	.50	.30
543	Wayne Twitchell	.40	.20	.10
544	Pepe Frias	.40	.20	.10
545	Sparky Lyle	.40	.20	.10
546	Dave Rosello	.40	.20	.10
547	Roric Harrison	.40	.20	.10
548	Manny Mota	.40	.20	.10
549	Randy Tate	.40	.20	.10
550	Hank Aaron	25.00	12.50	7.50
551	Jerry DaVanon	.40	.20	.10
552	Terry Humphrey	.40	.20	.10
553	Randy Moffitt	.40	.20	.10
554	Ray Fosse	.40	.20	.10
555	Dyar Miller	.40	.20	.10
556	Minnesota Twins Team (Gene Mauch)	1.00	.50	.30
557	Dan Spillner	.40	.20	.10
558	Clarence Gaston	.40	.20	.10
559	Clyde Wright	.40	.20	.10
560	Jorge Orta	.40	.20	.10
561	Tom Carroll	.40	.20	.10
562	Adrian Garrett	.40	.20	.10
563	Larry Demery	.40	.20	.10
564	Kurt Bevacqua (Bubble Gum Blowing Champ)	.40	.20	.10
565	Tug McGraw	.75	.40	.25
566	Ken McMullen	.40	.20	.10
567	George Stone	.40	.20	.10
568	Rob Andrews	.40	.20	.10
569	Nelson Briles	.40	.20	.10
570	George Hendrick	.40	.20	.10
571	Don DeMola	.40	.20	.10
572	Rich Coggins	.40	.20	.10
573	Bill Travers	.40	.20	.10
574	Don Kessinger	.40	.20	.10
575	Dwight Evans	.75	.40	.25
576	Maximino Leon	.40	.20	.10
577	Marc Hill	.40	.20	.10
578	Ted Kubiak	.40	.20	.10
579	Clay Kirby	.40	.20	.10
580	Bert Campaneris	.40	.20	.10
581	St. Louis Cardinals Team (Red Schoendienst)	1.50	.70	.45
582	Mike Kekich	.40	.20	.10
583	Tommy Helms	.40	.20	.10
584	Stan Wall	.40	.20	.10
585	Joe Torre	1.50	.70	.45
586	Ron Schueler	.40	.20	.10
587	Leo Cardenas	.40	.20	.10
588	Kevin Kobel	.40	.20	.10
589	Rookie Pitchers (Santo Alcala, Mike Flanagan, Joe Pactwa, Pablo Torrealba)	1.00	.50	.30
590	Rookie Outfielders (**Henry Cruz, Chet Lemon, Ellis Valentine, Terry Whitfield**)	.75	.40	.25
591	Rookie Pitchers (Steve Grilli, Craig Mitchell, Jose Sosa, George Throop)	.40	.20	.10
592	Rookie Infielders (*Dave McKay, Willie Randolph, Jerry Royster, Roy Staiger*)	6.00	3.00	1.75
593	Rookie Pitchers (*Larry Anderson, Ken Crosby, Mark Littell, Butch Metzger*)	.40	.20	.10
594	Rookie Catchers & Outfielders (Andy Merchant, Ed Ott, Royle Stillman, Jerry White)	.40	.20	.10
595	Rookie Pitchers (Steve Barr, Art DeFilippis, Randy Lerch, Sid Monge)	.40	.20	.10
596	Rookie Infielders (*Lamar Johnson, Johnny LeMaster, Jerry Manuel, Craig Reynolds*)	.40	.20	.10
597	Rookie Pitchers (Don Aase, Jack Kucek, Frank LaCorte, Mike Pazik)	.40	.20	.10
598	Rookie Outfielders (Hector Cruz, **Jamie Quirk**, Jerry Turner, Joe Wallis)	.40	.20	.10
599	Rookie Pitchers (*Rob Dressler, Ron Guidry, Bob McClure, Pat Zachry*)	10.00	5.00	2.50
600	Tom Seaver	8.00	4.00	2.50
601	Ken Rudolph	.40	.20	.10
602	Doug Konieczny	.40	.20	.10
603	Jim Holt	.40	.20	.10
604	Joe Lovitto	.40	.20	.10
605	Al Downing	.40	.20	.10
606	Milwaukee Brewers Team (Alex Grammas)	1.00	.50	.30
607	Rich Hinton	.40	.20	.10
608	Vic Correll	.40	.20	.10
609	Fred Norman	.40	.20	.10
610	Greg Luzinski	.75	.40	.25
611	Rich Folkers	.40	.20	.10
612	Joe Lahoud	.40	.20	.10
613	Tim Johnson	.40	.20	.10
614	Fernando Arroyo	.40	.20	.10
615	Mike Cubbage	.40	.20	.10
616	Buck Martinez	.40	.20	.10
617	Darold Knowles	.40	.20	.10
618	Jack Brohamer	.40	.20	.10
619	Bill Butler	.40	.20	.10
620	Al Oliver	.75	.40	.25
621	Tom Hall	.40	.20	.10
622	Rick Auerbach	.40	.20	.10
623	Bob Allietta	.40	.20	.10
624	Tony Taylor	.40	.20	.10
625	J.R. Richard	.40	.20	.10
626	Bob Sheldon	.40	.20	.10
627	Bill Plummer	.40	.20	.10
628	John D'Acquisto	.40	.20	.10
629	Sandy Alomar	.40	.20	.10

		NM	EX	VG
630	Chris Speier	.40	.20	.10
631	Atlanta Braves Team (Dave Bristol)	1.00	.50	.30
632	Rogelio Moret	.40	.20	.10
633	*John Stearns*	.40	.20	.10
634	Larry Christenson	.40	.20	.10
635	Jim Fregosi	.40	.20	.10
636	Joe Decker	.40	.20	.10
637	Bruce Bochte	.40	.20	.10
638	Doyle Alexander	.40	.20	.10
639	Fred Kendall	.40	.20	.10
640	Bill Madlock	.75	.40	.25
641	Tom Paciorek	.40	.20	.10
642	Dennis Blair	.40	.20	.10
643	Checklist 529-660	1.00	.50	.30
644	Tom Bradley	.40	.20	.10
645	Darrell Porter	.40	.20	.10
646	John Lowenstein	.40	.20	.10
647	Ramon Hernandez	.40	.20	.10
648	Al Cowens	.40	.20	.10
649	Dave Roberts	.40	.20	.10
650	Thurman Munson	8.00	4.00	2.00
651	John Odom	.40	.20	.10
652	Ed Armbrister	.40	.20	.10
653	*Mike Norris*	.40	.20	.10
654	Doug Griffin	.40	.20	.10
655	Mike Vail	.40	.20	.10
656	Chicago White Sox Team (Chuck Tanner)	1.00	.50	.30
657	*Roy Smalley*	.40	.20	.10
658	Jerry Johnson	.40	.20	.10
659	Ben Oglivie	.40	.20	.10
660	Dave Lopes	1.00	.50	.30

1976 Topps Traded

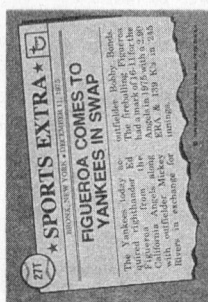

Similar to the Topps Traded set of 1974, the 2-1/2" x 3-1/2" cards feature photos of players traded after the printing deadline. The style of the cards is essentially the same as the regular issue, but with a large "Sports Extra" headline announcing the trade and its date. The backs continue in newspaper style to detail the specifics of the trade. There are 43 player cards and one checklist in the set. Numbers remain the same as the player's regular card, with the addition of a "T" suffix.

		NM	EX	VG
Complete Set (44):		20.00	10.00	6.00
Common Player:		.75	.35	.20
27T	Ed Figueroa	.75	.35	.20
28T	Dusty Baker	1.25	.60	.40
44T	Doug Rader	.75	.35	.20
58T	Ron Reed	.75	.35	.20
74T	Oscar Gamble	.75	.35	.20
80T	Jim Kaat	.75	.35	.20
83T	Jim Spencer	.75	.35	.20
85T	Mickey Rivers	.75	.35	.20
99T	Lee Lacy	.75	.35	.20
120T	Rusty Staub	.75	.35	.20
127T	Larvell Blanks	.75	.35	.20
146T	George Medich	.75	.35	.20
158T	Ken Reitz	.75	.35	.20
208T	Mike Lum	.75	.35	.20
211T	Clay Carroll	.75	.35	.20
231T	Tom House	.75	.35	.20
250T	Fergie Jenkins	3.00	1.50	.90
259T	Darrel Chaney	.75	.35	.20
292T	Leon Roberts	.75	.35	.20
296T	Pat Dobson	.75	.35	.20
309T	Bill Melton	.75	.35	.20
338T	Bob Bailey	.75	.35	.20
380T	Bobby Bonds	.75	.35	.20
383T	John Ellis	.75	.35	.20
385T	Mickey Lolich	.75	.35	.20
401T	Ken Brett	.75	.35	.20
410T	Ralph Garr	.75	.35	.20
411T	Bill Singer	.75	.35	.20
428T	Jim Crawford	.75	.35	.20
434T	Morris Nettles	.75	.35	.20
464T	Ken Henderson	.75	.35	.20
497T	Joe McIntosh	.75	.35	.20
524T	Pete Falcone	.75	.35	.20
527T	Mike Anderson	.75	.35	.20
528T	Dock Ellis	.75	.35	.20
532T	Milt May	.75	.35	.20
554T	Ray Fosse	.75	.35	.20
579T	Clay Kirby	.75	.35	.20
583T	Tommy Helms	.75	.35	.20
592T	Willie Randolph	.75	.35	.20
618T	Jack Brohamer	.75	.35	.20
632T	Rogelio Moret	.75	.35	.20
649T	Dave Roberts	.75	.35	.20
----	Traded Checklist	.75	.35	.20

1976 Topps Cloth Sticker Prototypes

Apparently produced to test different materials for the cloth sticker set which would be issued the following year, these prototypes were never issued. Each of the players can be found on

four different types of material. The blank-backed stickers feature the card fronts as they appeared in the regular 1976 issue. It is unknown whether other players were produced for the test.

	NM	EX	VG
Common Player:	30.00	15.00	9.00
(1a) Bob Apodaca (Silk.)	30.00	15.00	9.00
(1b) Bob Apodaca (Thin felt.)	30.00	15.00	9.00
(1c) Bob Apodaca (Textured felt.)	60.00	30.00	18.00
(1d) Bob Apodaca (Thick felt.)	30.00	15.00	9.00
(2a) Duffy Dyer (Silk)	30.00	15.00	9.00
(2b) Duffy Dyer (Thin felt.)	30.00	15.00	9.00
(2c) Duffy Dyer (Textured felt.)	60.00	30.00	18.00
(2d) Duffy Dyer (Thick felt.)	30.00	15.00	9.00

1976 Topps Team Checklist Sheet

Via a mail-in redemption (50¢ and a wrapper), collectors could receive an uncut sheet of the 24 team photo/checklist cards from the 1976 Topps baseball set. Measuring about 10-1/2" x 20-1/8", the sheet could be cut into individual team cards of standard size, though printed on stock that is lighter than pack-issued versions.

	NM	EX	VG
Complete Sheet:	35.00	17.50	10.00

1976 Topps Joe Garagiola

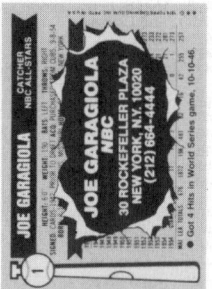

Topps produced this personal business card for long-time NBC announcer and former major leaguer Joe Garagiola. The front is in the format of a 1973 Topps card and has a color portrait. The back resembles the 1976 Topps card, is in black-and-white and provides contact information.

		NM	EX	VG
1	Joe Garagiola	20.00	10.00	6.00

1976 Topps/Dynamite Magazine Panels

In at least one issue of its "Dynamite" kids' magazine, Scholastic Book Club teamed with Topps to insert a six-card panel of its 1976 baseball issue. Values shown are for just the uncut panel; complete magazines would bear a small premium.

		NM	EX	VG
Complete Panel:		20.00	10.00	6.00
469	Rawly Eastwick			
471	Jim Burton			
474	Ray Corbin			
481	Rudy May			
482	Tim Hosley			
522	Ted Sizemore			

1977 Topps

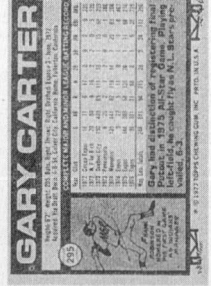

The 1977 Topps Set is a 660-card effort featuring front designs dominated by a color photograph on which there is a facsimile autograph. Above the picture are the player's name, team and position. The backs of the 2-1/2" x 3-1/2" cards

include personal and career statistics along with newspaper-style highlights and a cartoon. Specialty cards include statistical leaders, record performances, a new "Turn Back The Clock" feature which highlighted great past moments and a "Big League Brothers" feature.

		NM	EX	VG
Complete Set (660):		200.00	95.00	55.00
Common Player:		.25	.10	.06
Wax Pack (10):		22.50		
Wax Box (36):		500.00		
Cello Pack (18):		40.00		
Cello Box (24):		1,200		
Rack Pack (39):		65.00		
Rack Box (24):		2,000		
Vending Box (500):		350.00		
1	Batting Leaders (George Brett, Bill Madlock)	6.00	3.00	1.75
2	Home Run Leaders (Graig Nettles, Mike Schmidt)	2.00	1.00	.60
3	RBI Leaders (George Foster, Lee May)	.75	.40	.25
4	Stolen Base Leaders (Dave Lopes, Bill North)	.50	.25	.15
5	Victory Leaders (Randy Jones, Jim Palmer)	1.00	.50	.30
6	Strikeout Leaders (Nolan Ryan, Tom Seaver)	10.00	5.00	3.00
7	ERA Leaders (John Denny, Mark Fidrych)	.50	.25	.15
8	Leading Firemen (Bill Campbell, Rawly Eastwick)	.25	.10	.06
9	Doug Rader	.25	.10	.06
10	Reggie Jackson	8.00	4.00	2.50
11	Rob Dressler	.25	.10	.06
12	Larry Haney	.25	.10	.06
13	Luis Gomez	.25	.10	.06
14	Tommy Smith	.25	.10	.06
15	Don Gullett	.25	.10	.06
16	Bob Jones	.25	.10	.06
17	Steve Stone	.25	.10	.06
18	Indians Team (Frank Robinson)	1.50	.70	.45
19	John D'Acquisto	.25	.10	.06
20	Graig Nettles	.75	.40	.25
21	Ken Forsch	.25	.10	.06
22	Bill Freehan	.25	.10	.06
23	Dan Driessen	.25	.10	.06
24	Carl Morton	.25	.10	.06
25	Dwight Evans	.75	.40	.25
26	Ray Sadecki	.25	.10	.06
27	Bill Buckner	.75	.40	.25
28	Woodie Fryman	.25	.10	.06
29	Bucky Dent	.50	.25	.15
30	Greg Luzinski	.50	.25	.15
31	Jim Todd	.25	.10	.06
32	Checklist 1-132	1.00	.50	.30
33	Wayne Garland	.25	.10	.06
34	Angels Team (Norm Sherry)	1.00	.50	.30
35	Rennie Stennett	.25	.10	.06
36	John Ellis	.25	.10	.06
37	Steve Hargan	.25	.10	.06
38	Craig Kusick	.25	.10	.06
39	Tom Griffin	.25	.10	.06
40	Bobby Murcer	.50	.25	.15
41	Jim Kern	.25	.10	.06
42	Jose Cruz	.25	.10	.06
43	Ray Bare	.25	.10	.06
44	Bud Harrelson	.25	.10	.06
45	Rawly Eastwick	.25	.10	.06
46	Buck Martinez	.25	.10	.06
47	Lynn McGlothen	.25	.10	.06
48	Tom Paciorek	.25	.10	.06
49	Grant Jackson	.25	.10	.06
50	Ron Cey	.50	.25	.15
51	Brewers Team (Alex Grammas)	1.00	.50	.30
52	Ellis Valentine	.25	.10	.06
53	Paul Mitchell	.25	.10	.06
54	Sandy Alomar	.25	.10	.06
55	Jeff Burroughs	.25	.10	.06
56	Rudy May	.25	.10	.06
57	Marc Hill	.25	.10	.06
58	Chet Lemon	.25	.10	.06
59	Larry Christenson	.25	.10	.06
60	Jim Rice	2.00	1.00	.60
61	Manny Sanguillen	.25	.10	.06
62	Eric Raich	.25	.10	.06
63	Tito Fuentes	.25	.10	.06
64	Larry Biittner	.25	.10	.06
65	Skip Lockwood	.25	.10	.06
66	Roy Smalley	.25	.10	.06
67	*Joaquin Andujar*	.50	.25	.15
68	Bruce Bochte	.25	.10	.06
69	Jim Crawford	.25	.10	.06
70	Johnny Bench	8.00	4.00	2.00
71	Dock Ellis	.25	.10	.06
72	Mike Anderson	.25	.10	.06
73	Charlie Williams	.25	.10	.06
74	A's Team (Jack McKeon)	1.00	.50	.30
75	Dennis Leonard	.25	.10	.06
76	Tim Foli	.25	.10	.06
77	Dyar Miller	.25	.10	.06
78	Bob Davis	.25	.10	.06
79	Don Money	.25	.10	.06
80	Andy Messersmith	.25	.10	.06
81	Juan Beniquez	.25	.10	.06
82	Jim Rooker	.25	.10	.06
83	Kevin Bell	.25	.10	.06
84	Ollie Brown	.25	.10	.06
85	Duane Kuiper	.25	.10	.06
86	Pat Zachry	.25	.10	.06
87	Glenn Borgmann	.25	.10	.06
88	Stan Wall	.25	.10	.06
89	*Butch Hobson*	.25	.10	.06
90	Cesar Cedeno	.25	.10	.06
91	John Verhoeven	.25	.10	.06

#	Player			
92	Dave Rosello	.25	.10	.06
93	Tom Poquette	.25	.10	.06
94	Craig Swan	.25	.10	.06
95	Keith Hernandez	.75	.40	.25
96	Lou Piniella	.75	.40	.25
97	Dave Heaverlo	.25	.10	.06
98	Milt May	.25	.10	.06
99	Tom Hausman	.25	.10	.06
100	Joe Morgan	3.00	1.50	.90
101	Dick Bosman	.25	.10	.06
102	Jose Morales	.25	.10	.06
103	Mike Bacsik	.25	.10	.06
104	*Omar Moreno*	.50	.25	.15
105	Steve Yeager	.50	.25	.15
106	Mike Flanagan	.50	.25	.15
107	Bill Melton	.25	.10	.06
108	Alan Foster	.25	.10	.06
109	Jorge Orta	.25	.10	.06
110	Steve Carlton	4.00	2.00	1.25
111	Rico Petrocelli	.50	.25	.15
112	Bill Greif	.25	.10	.06
113	Blue Jays Mgr./Coaches (Roy Hartsfield, Don Leppert, Bob Miller, Jackie Moore, Harry Warner)	.75	.40	.25
114	Bruce Dal Canton	.25	.10	.06
115	Rick Manning	.25	.10	.06
116	Joe Niekro	.25	.10	.06
117	Frank White	.25	.10	.06
118	Rick Jones	.25	.10	.06
119	John Stearns	.25	.10	.06
120	Rod Carew	4.00	2.00	1.00
121	Gary Nolan	.25	.10	.06
122	Ben Oglivie	.25	.10	.06
123	Fred Stanley	.25	.10	.06
124	George Mitterwald	.25	.10	.06
125	Bill Travers	.25	.10	.06
126	Rod Gilbreath	.25	.10	.06
127	Ron Fairly	.25	.10	.06
128	Tommy John	.50	.25	.15
129	Mike Sadek	.25	.10	.06
130	Al Oliver	.75	.40	.25
131	Orlando Ramirez	.25	.10	.06
132	Chip Lang	.25	.10	.06
133	Ralph Garr	.25	.10	.06
134	Padres Team (John McNamara)	.75	.40	.25
135	Mark Belanger	.25	.10	.06
136	*Jerry Mumphrey*	.25	.10	.06
137	Jeff Terpko	.25	.10	.06
138	Bob Stinson	.25	.10	.06
139	Fred Norman	.25	.10	.06
140	Mike Schmidt	10.00	5.00	3.00
141	Mark Littell	.25	.10	.06
142	Steve Dillard	.25	.10	.06
143	Ed Herrmann	.25	.10	.06
144	*Bruce Sutter*	15.00	7.50	4.50
145	Tom Veryzer	.25	.10	.06
146	Dusty Baker	1.00	.50	.30
147	Jackie Brown	.25	.10	.06
148	Fran Healy	.25	.10	.06
149	Mike Cubbage	.25	.10	.06
150	Tom Seaver	6.00	3.00	1.75
151	Johnnie LeMaster	.25	.10	.06
152	Gaylord Perry	2.50	1.25	.70
153	Ron Jackson	.25	.10	.06
154	Dave Giusti	.25	.10	.06
155	Joe Rudi	.25	.10	.06
156	Pete Mackanin	.25	.10	.06
157	Ken Brett	.25	.10	.06
158	Ted Kubiak	.25	.10	.06
159	Bernie Carbo	.25	.10	.06
160	Will McEnaney	.25	.10	.06
161	*Garry Templeton*	1.00	.50	.30
162	Mike Cuellar	.25	.10	.06
163	Dave Hilton	.25	.10	.06
164	Tug McGraw	.25	.10	.06
165	Jim Wynn	.25	.10	.06
166	Bill Campbell	.25	.10	.06
167	Rich Hebner	.25	.10	.06
168	Charlie Spikes	.25	.10	.06
169	Darold Knowles	.25	.10	.06
170	Thurman Munson	6.00	3.00	1.75
171	Ken Sanders	.25	.10	.06
172	John Milner	.25	.10	.06
173	Chuck Scrivener	.25	.10	.06
174	Nelson Briles	.25	.10	.06
175	*Butch Wynegar*	.25	.10	.06
176	Bob Robertson	.25	.10	.06
177	Bart Johnson	.25	.10	.06
178	Bombo Rivera	.25	.10	.06
179	Paul Hartzell	.25	.10	.06
180	Dave Lopes	.50	.25	.15
181	Ken McMullen	.25	.10	.06
182	Dan Spillner	.25	.10	.06
183	Cardinals Team (Vern Rapp)	1.00	.50	.30
184	Bo McLaughlin	.25	.10	.06
185	Sixto Lezcano	.25	.10	.06
186	Doug Flynn	.25	.10	.06
187	Dick Pole	.25	.10	.06
188	Bob Tolan	.25	.10	.06
189	Rick Dempsey	.25	.10	.06
190	Ray Burris	.25	.10	.06
191	Doug Griffin	.25	.10	.06
192	Clarence Gaston	.25	.10	.06
193	Larry Gura	.25	.10	.06
194	Gary Matthews	.25	.10	.06
195	Ed Figueroa	.25	.10	.06
196	Len Randle	.25	.10	.06
197	Ed Ott	.25	.10	.06
198	Wilbur Wood	.25	.10	.06
199	Pepe Frias	.25	.10	.06
200	Frank Tanana	.25	.10	.06
201	Ed Kranepool	.25	.10	.06
202	Tom Johnson	.25	.10	.06
203	Ed Armbrister	.25	.10	.06
204	Jeff Newman	.25	.10	.06
205	Pete Falcone	.25	.10	.06
206	Boog Powell	.75	.40	.25
207	Glenn Abbott	.25	.10	.06
208	Checklist 133-264	.75	.40	.25
209	Rob Andrews	.25	.10	.06
210	Fred Lynn	.50	.25	.15
211	Giants Team (Joe Altobelli)	.75	.40	.25
212	Jim Mason	.25	.10	.06
213	Maximino Leon	.25	.10	.06
214	Darrell Porter	.25	.10	.06
215	Butch Metzger	.25	.10	.06
216	Doug DeCinces	.25	.10	.06
217	Tom Underwood	.25	.10	.06
218	*John Wathan*	.25	.10	.06
219	Joe Coleman	.25	.10	.06
220	Chris Chambliss	.50	.25	.15
221	Bob Bailey	.25	.10	.06
222	Francisco Barrios	.25	.10	.06
223	Earl Williams	.25	.10	.06
224	Rusty Torres	.25	.10	.06
225	Bob Apodaca	.25	.10	.06
226	Leroy Stanton	.25	.10	.06
227	*Joe Sambito*	.25	.10	.06
228	Twins Team (Gene Mauch)	1.00	.50	.30
229	Don Kessinger	.25	.10	.06
230	Vida Blue	.25	.10	.06
231	George Brett (Record Breaker)	6.00	3.00	1.50
232	Minnie Minoso (Record Breaker)	.50	.25	.15
233	Jose Morales (Record Breaker)	.50	.25	.15
234	Nolan Ryan (Record Breaker)	12.00	6.00	3.00
235	Cecil Cooper	.25	.10	.06
236	Tom Buskey	.25	.10	.06
237	Gene Clines	.25	.10	.06
238	Tippy Martinez	.25	.10	.06
239	Bill Plummer	.25	.10	.06
240	Ron LeFlore	.25	.10	.06
241	Dave Tomlin	.25	.10	.06
242	Ken Henderson	.25	.10	.06
243	Ron Reed	.25	.10	.06
244	John Mayberry	.25	.10	.06
245	Rick Rhoden	.25	.10	.06
246	Mike Vail	.25	.10	.06
247	Chris Knapp	.25	.10	.06
248	Wilbur Howard	.25	.10	.06
249	Pete Redfern	.25	.10	.06
250	Bill Madlock	.50	.25	.15
251	Tony Muser	.25	.10	.06
252	Dale Murray	.25	.10	.06
253	John Hale	.25	.10	.06
254	Doyle Alexander	.25	.10	.06
255	George Scott	.25	.10	.06
256	Joe Hoerner	.25	.10	.06
257	Mike Miley	.25	.10	.06
258	Luis Tiant	.50	.25	.15
259	Mets Team (Joe Frazier)	1.00	.50	.30
260	J.R. Richard	.25	.10	.06
261	Phil Garner	.50	.25	.15
262	Al Cowens	.25	.10	.06
263	Mike Marshall	.25	.10	.06
264	Tom Hutton	.25	.10	.06
265	*Mark Fidrych*	5.00	2.50	1.50
266	Derrel Thomas	.25	.10	.06
267	Ray Fosse	.25	.10	.06
268	Rick Sawyer	.25	.10	.06
269	Joe Lis	.25	.10	.06
270	Dave Parker	.50	.25	.15
271	Terry Forster	.25	.10	.06
272	Lee Lacy	.25	.10	.06
273	Eric Soderholm	.25	.10	.06
274	Don Stanhouse	.25	.10	.06
275	Mike Hargrove	.25	.10	.06
276	A.L. Championship (Chambliss' Dramatic Homer Decides It)	.25	.13	.08
277	N.L. Championship (Reds Sweep Phillies 3 In Row)	3.00	1.50	.90
278	Danny Frisella	.25	.10	.06
279	Joe Wallis	.25	.10	.06
280	Jim Hunter	2.50	1.25	.70
281	Roy Staiger	.25	.10	.06
282	Sid Monge	.25	.10	.06
283	Jerry DaVanon	.25	.10	.06
284	Mike Norris	.25	.10	.06
285	Brooks Robinson	4.00	2.00	1.25
286	Johnny Grubb	.25	.10	.06
287	Reds Team (Sparky Anderson)	1.00	.50	.30
288	Bob Montgomery	.25	.10	.06
289	Gene Garber	.25	.10	.06
290	Amos Otis	.25	.10	.06
291	*Jason Thompson*	.25	.10	.06
292	Rogelio Moret	.25	.10	.06
293	Jack Brohamer	.25	.10	.06
294	George Medich	.25	.10	.06
295	Gary Carter	3.00	1.50	.90
296	Don Hood	.25	.10	.06
297	Ken Reitz	.25	.10	.06
298	Charlie Hough	.25	.10	.06
299	Otto Velez	.25	.10	.06
300	Jerry Koosman	.25	.10	.06
301	Toby Harrah	.25	.10	.06
302	Mike Garman	.25	.10	.06
303	Gene Tenace	.25	.10	.06
304	Jim Hughes	.25	.10	.06
305	Mickey Rivers	.25	.10	.06
306	Rick Waits	.25	.10	.06
307	Gary Sutherland	.25	.10	.06
308	Gene Pentz	.25	.10	.06
309	Red Sox Team (Don Zimmer)	1.50	.70	.45
310	Larry Bowa	.50	.25	.15
311	Vern Ruhle	.25	.10	.06
312	Rob Belloir	.25	.10	.06
313	Paul Blair	.25	.10	.06
314	Steve Mingori	.25	.10	.06
315	Dave Chalk	.25	.10	.06
316	Steve Rogers	.25	.10	.06
317	Kurt Bevacqua	.25	.10	.06
318	Duffy Dyer	.25	.10	.06
319	Rich Gossage	.75	.40	.25
320	Ken Griffey	.75	.40	.25
321	Dave Goltz	.25	.10	.06
322	Bill Russell	.50	.25	.15
323	Larry Lintz	.25	.10	.06
324	John Curtis	.25	.10	.06
325	Mike Ivie	.25	.10	.06
326	Jesse Jefferson	.25	.10	.06
327	Astros Team (Bill Virdon)	.75	.40	.25
328	Tommy Boggs	.25	.10	.06
329	Ron Hodges	.25	.10	.06
330	George Hendrick	.25	.10	.06
331	Jim Colborn	.25	.10	.06
332	Elliott Maddox	.25	.10	.06
333	Paul Reuschel	.25	.10	.06
334	Bill Stein	.25	.10	.06
335	Bill Robinson	.25	.10	.06
336	Denny Doyle	.25	.10	.06
337	Ron Schueler	.25	.10	.06
338	Dave Duncan	.25	.10	.06
339	Adrian Devine	.25	.10	.06
340	Hal McRae	.50	.25	.15
341	Joe Kerrigan	.25	.10	.06
342	Jerry Remy	.25	.10	.06
343	Ed Halicki	.25	.10	.06
344	Brian Downing	.25	.10	.06
345	Reggie Smith	.25	.10	.06
346	Bill Singer	.25	.10	.06
347	George Foster	.25	.10	.06
348	Brent Strom	.25	.10	.06
349	Jim Holt	.25	.10	.06
350	Larry Dierker	.25	.10	.06
351	Jim Sundberg	.25	.10	.06
352	Mike Phillips	.25	.10	.06
353	Stan Thomas	.25	.10	.06
354	Pirates Team (Chuck Tanner)	.75	.40	.25
355	Lou Brock	3.00	1.50	.90
356	Checklist 265-396	.75	.40	.25
357	Tim McCarver	.75	.40	.25
358	Tom House	.25	.10	.06
359	Willie Randolph	.75	.40	.25
360	Rick Monday	.25	.10	.06
361	Eduardo Rodriguez	.25	.10	.06
362	Tommy Davis	.25	.10	.06
363	Dave Roberts	.25	.10	.06
364	Vic Correll	.25	.10	.06
365	Mike Torrez	.25	.10	.06
366	Ted Sizemore	.25	.10	.06
367	Dave Hamilton	.25	.10	.06
368	Mike Jorgensen	.25	.10	.06
369	Terry Humphrey	.25	.10	.06
370	John Montefusco	.25	.10	.06
371	Royals Team (Whitey Herzog)	1.00	.50	.30
372	Rich Folkers	.25	.10	.06
373	Bert Campaneris	.25	.10	.06
374	Kent Tekulve	.25	.10	.06
375	Larry Hisle	.25	.10	.06
376	Nino Espinosa	.25	.10	.06
377	Dave McKay	.25	.10	.06
378	Jim Umbarger	.25	.10	.06
379	Larry Cox	.25	.10	.06
380	Lee May	.25	.10	.06
381	Bob Forsch	.25	.10	.06
382	Charlie Moore	.25	.10	.06
383	Stan Bahnsen	.25	.10	.06
384	Darrel Chaney	.25	.10	.06
385	Dave LaRoche	.25	.10	.06
386	Manny Mota	.25	.10	.06
387	Yankees Team (Billy Martin)	2.00	1.00	.60
388	Terry Harmon	.25	.10	.06
389	Ken Kravec	.25	.10	.06
390	Dave Winfield	3.00	1.50	.90
391	Dan Warthen	.25	.10	.06
392	Phil Roof	.25	.10	.06
393	John Lowenstein	.25	.10	.06
394	Bill Laxton	.25	.10	.06
395	Manny Trillo	.25	.10	.06
396	Tom Murphy	.25	.10	.06
397	*Larry Herndon*	.25	.10	.06
398	Tom Burgmeier	.25	.10	.06
399	Bruce Boisclair	.25	.10	.06
400	Steve Garvey	2.00	1.00	.60
401	Mickey Scott	.25	.10	.06
402	Tommy Helms	.25	.10	.06
403	Tom Grieve	.25	.10	.06
404	Eric Rasmussen	.25	.10	.06
405	Claudell Washington	.25	.10	.06
406	Tim Johnson	.25	.10	.06
407	Dave Freisleben	.25	.10	.06
408	Cesar Tovar	.25	.10	.06
409	Pete Broberg	.25	.10	.06
410	Willie Montanez	.25	.10	.06
411	World Series Games 1 & 2 (Joe Morgan, Johnny Bench)	2.00	1.00	.60
412	World Series Games 3 & 4 (Johnny Bench)	2.00	1.00	.60
413	World Series Summary	.75	.40	.25
414	Tommy Harper	.25	.10	.06
415	Jay Johnstone	.25	.10	.06
416	Chuck Hartenstein	.25	.10	.06
417	Wayne Garrett	.25	.10	.06
418	White Sox Team (Bob Lemon)	1.00	.50	.30
419	Steve Swisher	.25	.10	.06
420	Rusty Staub	.50	.25	.15
421	Doug Rau	.25	.10	.06
422	Freddie Patek	.25	.10	.06
423	Gary Lavelle	.25	.10	.06
424	Steve Brye	.25	.10	.06
425	Joe Torre	1.00	.50	.30
426	Dick Drago	.25	.10	.06
427	Dave Rader	.25	.10	.06
428	Rangers Team (Frank Lucchesi)	.75	.40	.25
429	Ken Boswell	.25	.10	.06
430	Fergie Jenkins	2.50	1.25	.70
431	Dave Collins	.25	.10	.06
432	Buzz Capra	.25	.10	.06

		NM	EX	VG
433	Nate Colbert (Turn Back The Clock)	.25	.10	.06
434	Carl Yastrzemski (Turn Back The Clock)	1.50	.70	.45
435	Maury Wills (Turn Back The Clock)	.50	.25	.15
436	Bob Keegan (Turn Back The Clock)	.25	.10	.06
437	Ralph Kiner (Turn Back The Clock)	.75	.40	.25
438	Marty Perez	.25	.10	.06
439	Gorman Thomas	.25	.10	.06
440	Jon Matlack	.25	.10	.06
441	Larvell Blanks	.25	.10	.06
442	Braves Team (Dave Bristol)	1.00	.50	.30
443	Lamar Johnson	.25	.10	.06
444	Wayne Twitchell	.25	.10	.06
445	Ken Singleton	.25	.10	.06
446	Bill Bonham	.25	.10	.06
447	Jerry Turner	.25	.10	.06
448	Ellie Rodriguez	.25	.10	.06
449	Al Fitzmorris	.25	.10	.06
450	Pete Rose	15.00	7.50	4.50
451	Checklist 397-528	1.00	.50	.30
452	Mike Caldwell	.25	.10	.06
453	Pedro Garcia	.25	.10	.06
454	Andy Etchebarren	.25	.10	.06
455	Rick Wise	.25	.10	.06
456	Leon Roberts	.25	.10	.06
457	Steve Luebber	.25	.10	.06
458	Leo Foster	.25	.10	.06
459	Steve Foucault	.25	.10	.06
460	Willie Stargell	4.00	2.00	1.25
461	Dick Tidrow	.25	.10	.06
462	Don Baylor	.30	.15	.10
463	Jamie Quirk	.25	.10	.06
464	Randy Moffitt	.25	.10	.06
465	Rico Carty	.25	.10	.06
466	Fred Holdsworth	.25	.10	.06
467	Phillies Team (Danny Ozark)	.50	.25	.15
468	Ramon Hernandez	.25	.10	.06
469	Pat Kelly	.25	.10	.06
470	Ted Simmons	.50	.25	.15
471	Del Unser	.25	.10	.06
472	Rookie Pitchers (Don Aase, Bob McClure, Gil Patterson (Photo is Sheldon Gill.), Dave Wehrmeister)	.25	.10	.06
473	Rookie Outfielders (*Andre Dawson, Gene Richards, John Scott, Denny Walling*)	20.00	10.00	5.00
474	Rookie Shortstops (Bob Bailor, Kiko Garcia, Craig Reynolds, Alex Taveras)	.25	.10	.06
475	Rookie Pitchers (Chris Batton, Rick Camp, Scott McGregor, Manny Sarmiento)	.25	.10	.06
476	Rookie Catchers (*Gary Alexander, Rick Cerone, Dale Murphy, Kevin Pasley*)	15.00	7.50	3.75
477	Rookie Infielders (Doug Ault, Rich Dauer, Orlando Gonzalez, Phil Mankowski)	.25	.10	.06
478	Rookie Pitchers (Jim Gideon, Leon Hooten, Dave Johnson, Mark Lemongello)	.25	.10	.06
479	Rookie Outfielders (Brian Asselstine, Wayne Gross, Sam Mejias, Alvis Woods)	.25	.10	.06
480	Carl Yastrzemski	6.00	3.00	1.75
481	Roger Metzger	.25	.10	.06
482	Tony Solaita	.25	.10	.06
483	Richie Zisk	.25	.10	.06
484	Burt Hooton	.25	.10	.06
485	Roy White	.25	.10	.06
486	Ed Bane	.25	.10	.06
487	Rookie Pitchers (Larry Anderson, Ed Glynn, Joe Henderson, Greg Terlecky)	.25	.10	.06
488	Rookie Outfielders (*Jack Clark, Ruppert Jones, Lee Mazzilli, Dan Thomas*)	3.00	1.50	.90
489	Rookie Pitchers (*Len Barker, Randy Lerch, Greg Minton, Mike Overy*)	.75	.40	.25
490	Rookie Shortstops (Billy Almon, Mickey Klutts, Tommy McMillan, Mark Wagner)	.25	.10	.06
491	Rookie Pitchers (*Mike Dupree, Dennis Martinez, Craig Mitchell, Bob Sykes*)	3.00	1.50	.90
492	Rookie Outfielders (*Tony Armas, Steve Kemp, Carlos Lopez, Gary Woods*)	.75	.40	.25
493	Rookie Pitchers (Mike Krukow, Jim Otten, Gary Wheelock, Mike Willis)	.25	.10	.06
494	Rookie Infielders (*Juan Bernhardt, Mike Champion, Jim Gantner, Bump Wills*)	1.00	.50	.30
495	Al Hrabosky	.50	.25	.15
496	Gary Thomasson	.25	.10	.06
497	Clay Carroll	.25	.10	.06
498	Sal Bando	.25	.10	.06
499	Pablo Torrealba	.25	.10	.06
500	Dave Kingman	.75	.40	.25
501	Jim Bibby	.25	.10	.06
502	Randy Hundley	.25	.10	.06
503	Bill Lee	.25	.10	.06
504	Dodgers Team (Tom Lasorda)	1.50	.70	.45
505	Oscar Gamble	.50	.25	.15
506	Steve Grilli	.25	.10	.06
507	Mike Hegan	.25	.10	.06
508	Dave Pagan	.25	.10	.06
509	Cookie Rojas	.25	.10	.06
510	John Candelaria	.25	.10	.06
511	Bill Fahey	.25	.10	.06
512	Jack Billingham	.25	.10	.06
513	Jerry Terrell	.25	.10	.06
514	Cliff Johnson	.25	.10	.06
515	Chris Speier	.25	.10	.06
516	Bake McBride	.25	.10	.06
517	*Pete Vuckovich*	.50	.25	.15
518	Cubs Team (Herman Franks)	1.00	.50	.30
519	Don Kirkwood	.25	.10	.06
520	Garry Maddox	.50	.25	.15
521	Bob Grich	.25	.10	.06
522	Enzo Hernandez	.25	.10	.06
523	Rollie Fingers	2.50	1.25	.70
524	Rowland Office	.25	.10	.06
525	Dennis Eckersley	4.00	2.00	1.25
526	Larry Parrish	.25	.10	.06
527	Dan Meyer	.25	.10	.06
528	Bill Castro	.25	.10	.06
529	Jim Essian	.25	.10	.06
530	Rick Reuschel	.25	.10	.06
531	Lyman Bostock	.25	.10	.06
532	Jim Willoughby	.25	.10	.06
533	Mickey Stanley	.25	.10	.06
534	Paul Splittorff	.25	.10	.06
535	Cesar Geronimo	.25	.10	.06
536	Vic Albury	.25	.10	.06
537	Dave Roberts	.25	.10	.06
538	Frank Taveras	.25	.10	.06
539	Mike Wallace	.25	.10	.06
540	Bob Watson	.25	.10	.06
541	John Denny	.25	.10	.06
542	Frank Duffy	.25	.10	.06
543	Ron Blomberg	.25	.10	.06
544	Gary Ross	.25	.10	.06
545	Bob Boone	.25	.10	.06
546	Orioles Team (Earl Weaver)	1.50	.70	.45
547	Willie McCovey	3.00	1.50	.90
548	*Joel Youngblood*	.25	.10	.06
549	Jerry Royster	.25	.10	.06
550	Randy Jones	.25	.10	.06
551	Bill North	.25	.10	.06
552	Pepe Mangual	.25	.10	.06
553	Jack Heidemann	.25	.10	.06
554	Bruce Kimm	.25	.10	.06
555	Dan Ford	.25	.10	.06
556	Doug Bird	.25	.10	.06
557	Jerry White	.25	.10	.06
558	Elias Sosa	.25	.10	.06
559	Alan Bannister	.25	.10	.06
560	Dave Concepcion	.25	.10	.06
561	Pete LaCock	.25	.10	.06
562	Checklist 529-660	.75	.40	.25
563	Bruce Kison	.25	.10	.06
564	Alan Ashby	.25	.10	.06
565	Mickey Lolich	.50	.25	.15
566	Rick Miller	.25	.10	.06
567	Enos Cabell	.25	.10	.06
568	Carlos May	.25	.10	.06
569	Jim Lonborg	.25	.10	.06
570	Bobby Bonds	.75	.40	.25
571	Darrell Evans	.25	.10	.06
572	Ross Grimsley	.25	.10	.06
573	Joe Ferguson	.25	.10	.06
574	Aurelio Rodriguez	.25	.10	.06
575	Dick Ruthven	.25	.10	.06
576	Fred Kendall	.25	.10	.06
577	Jerry Augustine	.25	.10	.06
578	Bob Randall	.25	.10	.06
579	Don Carrithers	.25	.10	.06
580	George Brett	15.00	7.50	3.75
581	Pedro Borbon	.25	.10	.06
582	Ed Kirkpatrick	.25	.10	.06
583	Paul Lindblad	.25	.10	.06
584	Ed Goodson	.25	.10	.06
585	Rick Burleson	.25	.10	.06
586	Steve Renko	.25	.10	.06
587	Rick Baldwin	.25	.10	.06
588	Dave Moates	.25	.10	.06
589	Mike Cosgrove	.25	.10	.06
590	Buddy Bell	.25	.10	.06
591	Chris Arnold	.25	.10	.06
592	Dan Briggs	.25	.10	.06
593	Dennis Blair	.25	.10	.06
594	Biff Pocoroba	.25	.10	.06
595	John Hiller	.25	.10	.06
596	*Jerry Martin*	.25	.10	.06
597	Mariners Mgr./Coaches (Don Bryant, Jim Busby, Darrell Johnson, Vada Pinson, Wes Stock)	1.00	.50	.30
598	Sparky Lyle	.25	.10	.06
599	Mike Tyson	.25	.10	.06
600	Jim Palmer	3.00	1.50	.90
601	Mike Lum	.25	.10	.06
602	Andy Hassler	.25	.10	.06
603	Willie Davis	.25	.10	.06
604	Jim Slaton	.25	.10	.06
605	Felix Millan	.25	.10	.06
606	Steve Braun	.25	.10	.06
607	Larry Demery	.25	.10	.06
608	Roy Howell	.25	.10	.06
609	Jim Barr	.25	.10	.06
610	Jose Cardenal	.25	.10	.06
611	Dave Lemanczyk	.25	.10	.06
612	Barry Foote	.25	.10	.06
613	Reggie Cleveland	.25	.10	.06
614	Greg Gross	.25	.10	.06
615	Phil Niekro	2.50	1.25	.70
616	Tommy Sandt	.25	.10	.06
617	Bobby Darwin	.25	.10	.06
618	Pat Dobson	.25	.10	.06
619	Johnny Oates	.25	.10	.06
620	Don Sutton	2.50	1.25	.70
621	Tigers Team (Ralph Houk)	1.00	.50	.30
622	Jim Wohlford	.25	.10	.06
623	Jack Kucek	.25	.10	.06
624	Hector Cruz	.25	.10	.06
625	Ken Holtzman	.25	.10	.06
626	Al Bumbry	.25	.10	.06
627	Bob Myrick	.25	.10	.06
628	Mario Guerrero	.25	.10	.06
629	Bobby Valentine	.25	.10	.06
630	Bert Blyleven	.75	.40	.25
631	Big League Brothers (George Brett, Ken Brett)	5.00	2.50	1.50
632	Big League Brothers (Bob Forsch, Ken Forsch)	.25	.10	.06
633	Big League Brothers (Carlos May, Lee May)	.25	.10	.06
634	Big League Brothers (Paul Reuschel, Rick Reuschel) (Names switched.)	.25	.10	.06
635	Robin Yount	6.00	3.00	1.50
636	Santo Alcala	.25	.10	.06
637	Alex Johnson	.25	.10	.06
638	Jim Kaat	.50	.25	.15
639	Jerry Morales	.25	.10	.06
640	Carlton Fisk	4.00	2.00	1.25
641	Dan Larson	.25	.10	.06
642	Willie Crawford	.25	.10	.06
643	Mike Pazik	.25	.10	.06
644	Matt Alexander	.25	.10	.06
645	Jerry Reuss	.25	.10	.06
646	Andres Mora	.25	.10	.06
647	Expos Team (Dick Williams)	.75	.40	.25
648	Jim Spencer	.25	.10	.06
649	Dave Cash	.25	.10	.06
650	Nolan Ryan	30.00	15.00	7.50
651	Von Joshua	.25	.10	.06
652	Tom Walker	.25	.10	.06
653	Diego Segui	.25	.10	.06
654	Ron Pruitt	.25	.10	.06
655	Tony Perez	3.00	1.50	.90
656	Ron Guidry	1.00	.50	.30
657	Mick Kelleher	.25	.10	.06
658	Marty Pattin	.25	.10	.06
659	Merv Rettenmund	.25	.10	.06
660	Willie Horton	1.00	.50	.30

1977 Topps Proofs

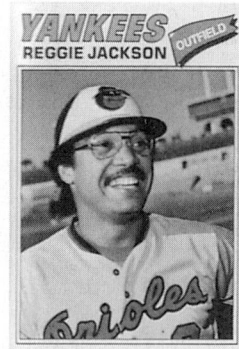

Perhaps the most sought-after Topps proof card is the 1977 blank-back featuring Reggie Jackson in an Orioles uniform but designating his team as the Yankees, with whom he signed as a free agent prior to the 1977 season. Less well-known are a group of other players' cards that have uniform/team variations from the regularly issued versions. All of the handful of known examples were hand-cut from sheets. Backs are blank.

	NM	EX	VG
Don Baylor	350.00	175.00	100.00
Rollie Fingers	900.00	450.00	275.00
Al Fitzmorris	300.00	150.00	90.00
Wayne Garland	300.00	150.00	90.00
Bill Greif	200.00	100.00	60.00
Reggie Jackson (5/04 auction)	6,000		
Pat Kelly	300.00	150.00	90.00
Gary Matthews	450.00	225.00	135.00
Dan Meyer	300.00	150.00	90.00
Bill Singer	200.00	100.00	60.00
Steve Stone	350.00	175.00	100.00
Gene Tenace	425.00	210.00	125.00

1977 Topps Team Checklist Sheet

A redemption offer on packs of 1977 Topps cards offered an uncut sheet of the 26 team/checklist cards by mail. Besides the perforated team cards, the 10-1/2" x 22-1/2" sheet has a card offering collectors a card locker. The cards on the sheet are identical to the single team/checklist cards issued in packs, except they are printed on thinner card stock.

	NM	EX	VG
Uncut Sheet	35.00	17.50	10.50

1977 Topps/Dynamite Magazine Panels

In at least two issues of its "Dynamite" kids' magazine, Scholastic Book Club teamed with Topps to insert a six-card panel of its 1977 baseball issue. Values shown are for just the uncut panel; complete magazines would bear a small premium.

	NM	EX	VG
Complete Panel Set (2):	50.00	25.00	15.00
PANEL 1	25.00	12.50	7.50
215 Butch Metzger			
335 Bill Robinson			
599 Mike Tyson			
625 Ken Holtzman			
630 Bert Blyleven			
641 Dan Larson			
PANEL 2	30.00	15.00	9.00
242 Ken Henderson			
294 George Medich			
415 Jay Johnstone			
535 Cesar Geronimo			
580 George Brett			
626 Al Bumbry			

1977 Topps Cloth Stickers

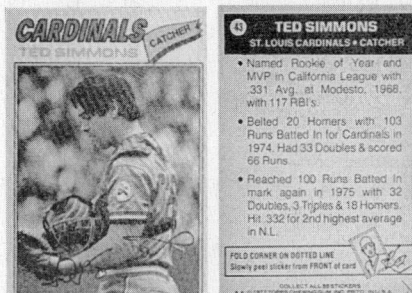

One of the few Topps specialty issues of the late 1970s, the 73-piece set of cloth stickers issued in 1977 includes 55 player stickers and 18 puzzle cards which could be joined to form a photo of the American League or National League All-Star teams. Issued as a separate issue, the 2-1/2" x 3-1/2" stickers have a paper backing which could be removed to allow the cloth to be adhered to a jacket, notebook, etc.

	NM	EX	VG
Complete Set (73):	75.00	37.70	22.50
Common Player:	1.00	.50	.30
Wax Pack:	12.50		
Wax Box (36):	325.00		
1 Alan Ashby	1.00	.50	.30
2 Buddy Bell	1.00	.50	.30
3 Johnny Bench	5.00	2.50	1.50
4 Vida Blue	1.00	.50	.30
5 Bert Blyleven	1.00	.50	.30
6 Steve Braun	1.00	.50	.30
7 George Brett	8.00	4.00	2.50
8 Lou Brock	4.00	2.00	1.25
9 Jose Cardenal	1.00	.50	.30
10 Rod Carew	5.00	2.50	1.50
11 Steve Carlton	4.00	2.00	1.25
12 Dave Cash	1.00	.50	.30
13 Cesar Cedeno	1.00	.50	.30
14 Ron Cey	1.00	.50	.30
15 Mark Fidrych	2.50	1.25	.70
16 Dan Ford	1.00	.50	.30
17 Wayne Garland	1.00	.50	.30
18 Ralph Garr	1.00	.50	.30
19 Steve Garvey	2.00	1.00	.60
20 Mike Hargrove	1.00	.50	.30
21 Catfish Hunter	3.00	1.50	.90
22 Reggie Jackson	8.00	4.00	2.50
23 Randy Jones	1.00	.50	.30
24 Dave Kingman	1.00	.50	.30
25 Bill Madlock	1.00	.50	.30
26 Lee May	1.00	.50	.30
27 John Mayberry	1.00	.50	.30
28 Andy Messersmith	1.00	.50	.30
29 Willie Montanez	1.00	.50	.30
30 John Montefusco	1.00	.50	.30
31 Joe Morgan	4.00	2.00	1.25
32 Thurman Munson	4.00	2.00	1.25
33 Bobby Murcer	1.00	.50	.30
34 Al Oliver	1.00	.50	.30
35 Dave Pagan	1.00	.50	.30
36 Jim Palmer	4.00	2.00	1.25
37 Tony Perez	3.00	1.50	.90
38 Pete Rose	10.00	5.00	3.00
39 Joe Rudi	1.00	.50	.30
40 Nolan Ryan	20.00	10.00	6.00
41 Mike Schmidt	8.00	4.00	2.50
42 Tom Seaver	5.00	2.50	1.50
43 Ted Simmons	1.00	.50	.30
44 Bill Singer	1.00	.50	.30
45 Willie Stargell	4.00	2.00	1.25
46 Rusty Staub	1.25	.60	.40
47 Don Sutton	3.00	1.50	.90
48 Luis Tiant	1.00	.50	.30
49 Bill Travers	1.00	.50	.30
50 Claudell Washington	1.00	.50	.30
51 Bob Watson	1.00	.50	.30

52 Dave Winfield	4.00	2.00	1.25
53 Carl Yastrzemski	7.00	3.50	2.00
54 Robin Yount	4.00	2.00	1.25
55 Richie Zisk	1.00	.50	.30
--- American League	6.00	3.00	1.75
Nine-Piece Puzzle			
--- National League Nine-Piece	6.00	3.00	1.75
Puzzle			

1978 Topps

 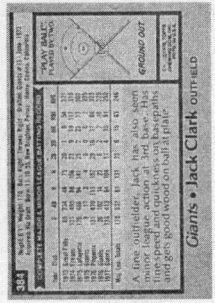

JACK CLARK

At 726 cards, this was the largest issue from Topps since 1972. In design, the color player photo is slightly larger than usual, with the player's name and team at the bottom. In the upper right-hand corner of the 2-1/2" x 3-1/2" cards, there is a small white baseball with the player's position. Most of the starting All-Stars from the previous year had a red, white and blue shield instead of the baseball. Backs feature statistics and a baseball situation which made a card game of baseball possible. Specialty cards include baseball records, statistical leaders and the World Series and playoffs. As one row of cards per sheet had to be double-printed to accommodate the 726-card set size, some cards are more common, yet that seems to have no serious impact on their prices.

	NM	EX	VG
Complete Set (726):	200.00	100.00	45.00
Common Player:	.20	.10	.06
Wax Pack (14):	15.00		
Wax Box (36):	480.00		
Cello Pack (21):	25.00		
Cello Box (24):	475.00		
Rack Pack (39):	35.00		
Rack Box (24):	725.00		
Vending Box (500):	285.00		
1 Lou Brock (Record Breaker)	1.00	.50	.30
2 Sparky Lyle (Record Breaker)	.20	.10	.06
3 Willie McCovey (Record Breaker)	.50	.25	.15
4 Brooks Robinson (Record Breaker)	2.00	1.00	.60
5 Pete Rose (Record Breaker)	6.00	3.00	1.50
6 Nolan Ryan (Record Breaker)	15.00	7.50	3.75
7 Reggie Jackson (Record Breaker)	4.00	2.00	1.25
8 Mike Sadek	.20	.10	.06
9 Doug DeCinces	.20	.10	.06
10 Phil Niekro	3.00	1.50	.90
11 Rick Manning	.20	.10	.06
12 Don Aase	.20	.10	.06
13 Art Howe	.20	.10	.06
14 Lerrin LaGrow	.20	.10	.06
15 Tony Perez	4.00	2.00	1.25
16 Roy White	.20	.10	.06
17 Mike Krukow	.20	.10	.06
18 Bob Grich	.20	.10	.06
19 Darrell Porter	.20	.10	.06
20 Pete Rose	10.00	5.00	2.50
21 Steve Kemp	.20	.10	.06
22 Charlie Hough	.20	.10	.06
23 Bump Wills	.20	.10	.06
24 Don Money	.20	.10	.06
25 Jon Matlack	.20	.10	.06
26 Rich Hebner	.20	.10	.06
27 Geoff Zahn	.20	.10	.06
28 Ed Ott	.20	.10	.06
29 Bob Lacey	.20	.10	.06
30 George Hendrick	.20	.10	.06
31 Glenn Abbott	.20	.10	.06
32 Garry Templeton	.20	.10	.06
33 Dave Lemanczyk	.20	.10	.06
34 Willie McCovey	4.00	2.00	1.25
35 Sparky Lyle	.20	.10	.06
36 *Eddie Murray*	50.00	25.00	12.50
37 Rick Waits	.20	.10	.06
38 Willie Montanez	.20	.10	.06
39 *Floyd Bannister*	.45	.25	.14
40 Carl Yastrzemski	5.00	2.50	1.50
41 Burt Hooton	.20	.10	.06
42 Jorge Orta	.20	.10	.06
43 Bill Atkinson	.20	.10	.06
44 Toby Harrah	.20	.10	.06
45 Mark Fidrych	.30	.15	.09
46 Al Cowens	.20	.10	.06
47 Jack Billingham	.20	.10	.06
48 Don Baylor	.25	.13	.08
49 Ed Kranepool	.20	.10	.06
50 Rick Reuschel	.20	.10	.06
51 Charlie Moore	.20	.10	.06
52 Jim Lonborg	.20	.10	.06
53 Phil Garner	.20	.10	.06
54 Tom Johnson	.20	.10	.06
55 Mitchell Page	.20	.10	.06
56 Randy Jones	.20	.10	.06
57 Dan Meyer	.20	.10	.06
58 Bob Forsch	.20	.10	.06
59 Otto Velez	.20	.10	.06

60 Thurman Munson	5.00	2.50	1.25
61 Larvell Blanks	.20	.10	.06
62 Jim Barr	.20	.10	.06
63 Don Zimmer	.20	.10	.06
64 Gene Pentz	.20	.10	.06
65 Ken Singleton	.20	.10	.06
66 White Sox Team	.30	.15	.09
67 Claudell Washington	.20	.10	.06
68 Steve Foucault	.20	.10	.06
69 Mike Vail	.20	.10	.06
70 Rich Gossage	.20	.10	.06
71 Terry Humphrey	.20	.10	.06
72 Andre Dawson	3.00	1.50	.90
73 Andy Hassler	.20	.10	.06
74 Checklist 1-121	.20	.10	.06
75 Dick Ruthven	.20	.10	.06
76 Steve Ontiveros	.20	.10	.06
77 Ed Kirkpatrick	.20	.10	.06
78 Pablo Torrealba	.20	.10	.06
79 Darrell Johnson (DP)	.20	.10	.06
80 Ken Griffey	.20	.10	.06
81 Pete Redfern	.20	.10	.06
82 Giants Team	.30	.15	.09
83 Bob Montgomery	.20	.10	.06
84 Kent Tekulve	.20	.10	.06
85 Ron Fairly	.20	.10	.06
86 Dave Tomlin	.20	.10	.06
87 John Lowenstein	.20	.10	.06
88 Mike Phillips	.20	.10	.06
89 Ken Clay	.20	.10	.06
90 Larry Bowa	.20	.10	.06
91 Oscar Zamora	.20	.10	.06
92 Adrian Devine	.20	.10	.06
93 Bobby Cox	.40	.20	.12
94 Chuck Scrivener	.20	.10	.06
95 Jamie Quirk	.20	.10	.06
96 Orioles Team	.30	.15	.09
97 Stan Bahnsen	.20	.10	.06
98 Jim Essian	.20	.10	.06
99 *Willie Hernandez*	.30	.15	.09
100 George Brett	15.00	7.50	3.75
101 Sid Monge	.20	.10	.06
102 Matt Alexander	.20	.10	.06
103 Tom Murphy	.20	.10	.06
104 Lee Lacy	.20	.10	.06
105 Reggie Cleveland	.20	.10	.06
106 Bill Plummer	.20	.10	.06
107 Ed Halicki	.20	.10	.06
108 Von Joshua	.20	.10	.06
109 Joe Torre	.55	.30	.15
110 Richie Zisk	.20	.10	.06
111 Mike Tyson	.20	.10	.06
112 Astros Team	.30	.15	.09
113 Don Carrithers	.20	.10	.06
114 Paul Blair	.20	.10	.06
115 Gary Nolan	.20	.10	.06
116 Tucker Ashford	.20	.10	.06
117 John Montague	.20	.10	.06
118 Terry Harmon	.20	.10	.06
119 Denny Martinez	.20	.10	.06
120 Gary Carter	4.00	2.00	1.25
121 Alvis Woods	.20	.10	.06
122 Dennis Eckersley	4.00	2.00	1.25
123 Manny Trillo	.20	.10	.06
124 *Dave Rozema*	.20	.10	.06
125 George Scott	.20	.10	.06
126 Paul Moskau	.20	.10	.06
127 Chet Lemon	.20	.10	.06
128 Bill Russell	.20	.10	.06
129 Jim Colborn	.20	.10	.06
130 Jeff Burroughs	.20	.10	.06
131 Bert Blyleven	.20	.10	.06
132 Enos Cabell	.20	.10	.06
133 Jerry Augustine	.20	.10	.06
134 *Steve Henderson*	.20	.10	.06
135 Ron Guidry	.30	.15	.09
136 Ted Sizemore	.20	.10	.06
137 Craig Kusick	.20	.10	.06
138 Larry Demery	.20	.10	.06
139 Wayne Gross	.20	.10	.06
140 Rollie Fingers	3.00	1.50	.90
141 Ruppert Jones	.20	.10	.06
142 John Montefusco	.20	.10	.06
143 Keith Hernandez	.20	.10	.06
144 Jesse Jefferson	.20	.10	.06
145 Rick Monday	.20	.10	.06
146 Doyle Alexander	.20	.10	.06
147 Lee Mazzilli	.20	.10	.06
148 Andre Thornton	.20	.10	.06
149 Dale Murray	.20	.10	.06
150 Bobby Bonds	.20	.10	.06
151 Milt Wilcox	.20	.10	.06
152 *Ivan DeJesus*	.20	.10	.06
153 Steve Stone	.20	.10	.06
154 Cecil Cooper	.20	.10	.06
155 Butch Hobson	.20	.10	.06
156 Andy Messersmith	.20	.10	.06
157 Pete LaCock	.20	.10	.06
158 Joaquin Andujar	.20	.10	.06
159 Lou Piniella	.30	.15	.09
160 Jim Palmer	4.00	2.00	1.25
161 Bob Boone	.20	.10	.06
162 Paul Thormodsgard	.20	.10	.06
163 Bill North	.20	.10	.06
164 Bob Owchinko	.20	.10	.06
165 Rennie Stennett	.20	.10	.06
166 Carlos Lopez	.20	.10	.06
167 Tim Foli	.20	.10	.06
168 Reggie Smith	.20	.10	.06
169 Jerry Johnson	.20	.10	.06
170 Lou Brock	4.00	2.00	1.25
171 Pat Zachry	.20	.10	.06
172 Mike Hargrove	.20	.10	.06
173 Robin Yount	4.00	2.00	1.25
174 Wayne Garland	.20	.10	.06
175 Jerry Morales	.20	.10	.06
176 Milt May	.20	.10	.06
177 Gene Garber	.20	.10	.06

No.	Player			
178	Dave Chalk	.20	.10	.06
179	Dick Tidrow	.20	.10	.06
180	Dave Concepcion	.20	.10	.06
181	Ken Forsch	.20	.10	.06
182	Jim Spencer	.20	.10	.06
183	Doug Bird	.20	.10	.06
184	Checklist 122-242	.20	.10	.06
185	Ellis Valentine	.20	.10	.06
186	*Bob Stanley*	.20	.10	.06
187	Jerry Royster	.20	.10	.06
188	Al Bumbry	.20	.10	.06
189	Tom Lasorda	.55	.30	.15
190	John Candelaria	.20	.10	.06
191	Rodney Scott	.20	.10	.06
192	Padres Team	.30	.15	.09
193	Rich Chiles	.20	.10	.06
194	Derrel Thomas	.20	.10	.06
195	Larry Dierker	.20	.10	.06
196	Bob Bailor	.20	.10	.06
197	Nino Espinosa	.20	.10	.06
198	Ron Pruitt	.20	.10	.06
199	Craig Reynolds	.20	.10	.06
200	Reggie Jackson	6.00	3.00	1.75
201	Batting Leaders (Rod Carew, Dave Parker)	.50	.25	.15
202	Home Run Leaders (George Foster, Jim Rice)	.25	.13	.08
203	RBI Leaders (George Foster, Larry Hisle)	.20	.10	.06
204	Stolen Base Leaders (Freddie Patek, Frank Taveras)	.20	.10	.06
205	Victory Leaders (Steve Carlton, Dave Goltz, Dennis Leonard, Jim Palmer)	.50	.25	.15
206	Strikeout Leaders (Phil Niekro, Nolan Ryan)	3.00	1.50	.90
207	ERA Leaders (John Candelaria, Frank Tanana)	.20	.10	.06
208	Leading Firemen (Bill Campbell, Rollie Fingers)	.25	.13	.08
209	Dock Ellis	.20	.10	.06
210	Jose Cardenal	.20	.10	.06
211	Earl Weaver (DP)	.50	.25	.15
212	Mike Caldwell	.20	.10	.06
213	Alan Bannister	.20	.10	.06
214	Angels Team	.30	.15	.09
215	Darrell Evans	.25	.13	.08
216	Mike Paxton	.20	.10	.06
217	Rod Gilbreath	.20	.10	.06
218	Marty Pattin	.20	.10	.06
219	Mike Cubbage	.20	.10	.06
220	Pedro Borbon	.20	.10	.06
221	Chris Speier	.20	.10	.06
222	Jerry Martin	.20	.10	.06
223	Bruce Kison	.20	.10	.06
224	Jerry Tabb	.20	.10	.06
225	Don Gullett	.20	.10	.06
226	Joe Ferguson	.20	.10	.06
227	Al Fitzmorris	.20	.10	.06
228	Manny Mota	.20	.10	.06
229	Leo Foster	.20	.10	.06
230	Al Hrabosky	.20	.10	.06
231	Wayne Nordhagen	.20	.10	.06
232	Mickey Stanley	.20	.10	.06
233	Dick Pole	.20	.10	.06
234	Herman Franks	.20	.10	.06
235	Tim McCarver	.30	.15	.09
236	Terry Whitfield	.20	.10	.06
237	Rich Dauer	.20	.10	.06
238	Juan Beniquez	.20	.10	.06
239	Dyar Miller	.20	.10	.06
240	Gene Tenace	.20	.10	.06
241	Pete Vuckovich	.20	.10	.06
242	Barry Bonnell	.20	.10	.06
243	Bob McClure	.20	.10	.06
244	Expos Team	.30	.15	.09
245	Rick Burleson	.20	.10	.06
246	Dan Driessen	.20	.10	.06
247	Larry Christenson	.20	.10	.06
248	Frank White	.20	.10	.06
249	Dave Goltz	.20	.10	.06
250	Graig Nettles	.25	.13	.08
251	Don Kirkwood	.20	.10	.06
252	Steve Swisher	.20	.10	.06
253	Jim Kern	.20	.10	.06
254	Dave Collins	.20	.10	.06
255	Jerry Reuss	.20	.10	.06
256	Joe Altobelli	.20	.10	.06
257	Hector Cruz	.20	.10	.06
258	John Hiller	.20	.10	.06
259	Dodgers Team	.50	.25	.15
260	Bert Campaneris	.20	.10	.06
261	Tim Hosley	.20	.10	.06
262	Rudy May	.20	.10	.06
263	Danny Walton	.20	.10	.06
264	Jamie Easterly	.20	.10	.06
265	Sal Bando	.20	.10	.06
266	*Bob Shirley*	.20	.10	.06
267	Doug Ault	.20	.10	.06
268	Gil Flores	.20	.10	.06
269	Wayne Twitchell	.20	.10	.06
270	Carlton Fisk	4.00	2.00	1.25
271	Randy Lerch	.20	.10	.06
272	Royle Stillman	.20	.10	.06
273	Fred Norman	.20	.10	.06
274	Freddie Patek	.20	.10	.06
275	Dan Ford	.20	.10	.06
276	Bill Bonham	.20	.10	.06
277	Bruce Boisclair	.20	.10	.06
278	Enrique Romo	.20	.10	.06
279	Bill Virdon	.20	.10	.06
280	Buddy Bell	.20	.10	.06
281	Eric Rasmussen	.20	.10	.06
282	Yankees Team	1.00	.50	.30
283	Omar Moreno	.20	.10	.06
284	Randy Moffitt	.20	.10	.06
285	Steve Yeager	.20	.10	.06
286	Ben Oglivie	.20	.10	.06
287	Kiko Garcia	.20	.10	.06
288	Dave Hamilton	.20	.10	.06
289	Checklist 243-363	.20	.10	.06
290	Willie Horton	.20	.10	.06
291	Gary Ross	.20	.10	.06
292	Gene Richard	.20	.10	.06
293	Mike Willis	.20	.10	.06
294	Larry Parrish	.20	.10	.06
295	Bill Lee	.20	.10	.06
296	Biff Pocoroba	.20	.10	.06
297	Warren Brusstar	.20	.10	.06
298	Tony Armas	.20	.10	.06
299	Whitey Herzog	.20	.10	.06
300	Joe Morgan	4.00	2.00	1.25
301	Buddy Schultz	.20	.10	.06
302	Cubs Team	.30	.15	.09
303	Sam Hinds	.20	.10	.06
304	John Milner	.20	.10	.06
305	Rico Carty	.20	.10	.06
306	Joe Niekro	.20	.10	.06
307	Glenn Borgmann	.20	.10	.06
308	Jim Rooker	.20	.10	.06
309	Cliff Johnson	.20	.10	.06
310	Don Sutton	3.00	1.50	.90
311	Jose Baez	.20	.10	.06
312	Greg Minton	.20	.10	.06
313	Andy Etchebarren	.20	.10	.06
314	Paul Lindblad	.20	.10	.06
315	Mark Belanger	.20	.10	.06
316	Henry Cruz	.20	.10	.06
317	Dave Johnson	.20	.10	.06
318	Tom Griffin	.20	.10	.06
319	Alan Ashby	.20	.10	.06
320	Fred Lynn	.20	.10	.06
321	Santo Alcala	.20	.10	.06
322	Tom Paciorek	.20	.10	.06
323	Jim Fregosi (DP)	.20	.10	.06
324	Vern Rapp	.20	.10	.06
325	Bruce Sutter	3.00	1.50	.90
326	Mike Lum	.20	.10	.06
327	Rick Langford	.20	.10	.06
328	Brewers Team	.30	.15	.09
329	John Verhoeven	.20	.10	.06
330	Bob Watson	.20	.10	.06
331	Mark Littell	.20	.10	.06
332	Duane Kuiper	.20	.10	.06
333	Jim Todd	.20	.10	.06
334	John Stearns	.20	.10	.06
335	Bucky Dent	.20	.10	.06
336	Steve Busby	.20	.10	.06
337	Tom Grieve	.20	.10	.06
338	Dave Heaverlo	.20	.10	.06
339	Mario Guerrero	.20	.10	.06
340	Bake McBride	.20	.10	.06
341	Mike Flanagan	.20	.10	.06
342	Aurelio Rodriguez	.20	.10	.06
343	John Wathan (DP)	.20	.10	.06
344	Sam Ewing	.20	.10	.06
345	Luis Tiant	.20	.10	.06
346	Larry Biittner	.20	.10	.06
347	Terry Forster	.20	.10	.06
348	Del Unser	.20	.10	.06
349	Rick Camp (DP)	.20	.10	.06
350	Steve Garvey	2.00	1.00	.60
351	Jeff Torborg	.20	.10	.06
352	Tony Scott	.20	.10	.06
353	Doug Bair	.20	.10	.06
354	Cesar Geronimo	.20	.10	.06
355	Bill Travers	.20	.10	.06
356	Mets Team	.60	.30	.20
357	Tom Poquette	.20	.10	.06
358	Mark Lemongello	.20	.10	.06
359	Marc Hill	.20	.10	.06
360	Mike Schmidt	8.00	4.00	2.00
361	Chris Knapp	.20	.10	.06
362	Dave May	.20	.10	.06
363	Bob Randall	.20	.10	.06
364	Jerry Turner	.20	.10	.06
365	Ed Figueroa	.20	.10	.06
366	Larry Milbourne (DP)	.20	.10	.06
367	Rick Dempsey	.20	.10	.06
368	Balor Moore	.20	.10	.06
369	Tim Nordbrook	.20	.10	.06
370	Rusty Staub	.25	.13	.08
371	Ray Burris	.20	.10	.06
372	Brian Asselstine	.20	.10	.06
373	Jim Willoughby	.20	.10	.06
374a	Jose Morales (Red stitching on position ball.)	.20	.10	.06
374b	Jose Morales (Black overprint on red stitching.)	.20	.10	.06
375	Tommy John	.30	.15	.09
376	Jim Wohlford	.20	.10	.06
377	Manny Sarmiento	.20	.10	.06
378	Bobby Winkles	.20	.10	.06
379	Skip Lockwood	.20	.10	.06
380	Ted Simmons	.20	.10	.06
381	Phillies Team	.35	.20	.11
382	Joe Lahoud	.20	.10	.06
383	Mario Mendoza	.20	.10	.06
384	Jack Clark	.30	.15	.09
385	Tito Fuentes	.20	.10	.06
386	Bob Gorinski	.20	.10	.06
387	Ken Holtzman	.20	.10	.06
388	Bill Fahey (DP)	.20	.10	.06
389	Julio Gonzalez	.20	.10	.06
390	Oscar Gamble	.20	.10	.06
391	Larry Haney	.20	.10	.06
392	Billy Almon	.20	.10	.06
393	Tippy Martinez	.20	.10	.06
394	Roy Howell	.20	.10	.06
395	Jim Hughes	.20	.10	.06
396	Bob Stinson	.20	.10	.06
397	Greg Gross	.20	.10	.06
398	Don Hood	.20	.10	.06
399	Pete Mackanin	.20	.10	.06
400	Nolan Ryan	25.00	12.50	6.25
401	Sparky Anderson	.55	.30	.15
402	Dave Campbell	.20	.10	.06
403	Bud Harrelson	.20	.10	.06
404	Tigers Team	.30	.15	.09
405	Rawly Eastwick	.20	.10	.06
406	Mike Jorgensen	.20	.10	.06
407	Odell Jones	.20	.10	.06
408	Joe Zdeb	.20	.10	.06
409	Ron Schueler	.20	.10	.06
410	Bill Madlock	.20	.10	.06
411	A.L. Championships (Yankees Rally To Defeat Royals)	.50	.25	.15
412	N.L. Championships (Dodgers Overpower Phillies In Four)	.50	.25	.15
413	World Series (Reggie & Yankees Reign Supreme)	2.00	1.00	.60
414	Darold Knowles (DP)	.20	.10	.06
415	Ray Fosse	.20	.10	.06
416	Jack Brohamer	.20	.10	.06
417	Mike Garman	.20	.10	.06
418	Tony Muser	.20	.10	.06
419	Jerry Garvin	.20	.10	.06
420	Greg Luzinski	.20	.10	.06
421	Junior Moore	.20	.10	.06
422	Steve Braun	.20	.10	.06
423	Dave Rosello	.20	.10	.06
424	Red Sox Team	.45	.25	.14
425	Steve Rogers	.20	.10	.06
426	Fred Kendall	.20	.10	.06
427	*Mario Soto*	.35	.20	.11
428	Joel Youngblood	.20	.10	.06
429	Mike Barlow	.20	.10	.06
430	Al Oliver	.30	.15	.09
431	Butch Metzger	.20	.10	.06
432	Terry Bulling	.20	.10	.06
433	Fernando Gonzalez	.20	.10	.06
434	Mike Norris	.20	.10	.06
435	Checklist 364-484	.20	.10	.06
436	Vic Harris (DP)	.20	.10	.06
437	Bo McLaughlin	.20	.10	.06
438	John Ellis	.20	.10	.06
439	Ken Kravec	.20	.10	.06
440	Dave Lopes	.20	.10	.06
441	Larry Gura	.20	.10	.06
442	Elliott Maddox	.20	.10	.06
443	Darrel Chaney	.20	.10	.06
444	Roy Hartsfield	.20	.10	.06
445	Mike Ivie	.20	.10	.06
446	Tug McGraw	.20	.10	.06
447	Leroy Stanton	.20	.10	.06
448	Bill Castro	.20	.10	.06
449	Tim Blackwell	.20	.10	.06
450	Tom Seaver	5.00	2.50	1.50
451	Twins Team	.30	.15	.09
452	Jerry Mumphrey	.20	.10	.06
453	Doug Flynn	.20	.10	.06
454	Dave LaRoche	.20	.10	.06
455	Bill Robinson	.20	.10	.06
456	Vern Ruhle	.20	.10	.06
457	Bob Bailey	.20	.10	.06
458	Jeff Newman	.20	.10	.06
459	Charlie Spikes	.20	.10	.06
460	Jim Hunter	3.00	1.50	.90
461	Rob Andrews	.20	.10	.06
462	Rogelio Moret	.20	.10	.06
463	Kevin Bell	.20	.10	.06
464	Jerry Grote	.20	.10	.06
465	Hal McRae	.20	.10	.06
466	Dennis Blair	.20	.10	.06
467	Alvin Dark	.20	.10	.06
468	*Warren Cromartie*	.20	.10	.06
469	Rick Cerone	.20	.10	.06
470	J.R. Richard	.20	.10	.06
471	Roy Smalley	.20	.10	.06
472	Ron Reed	.20	.10	.06
473	Bill Buckner	.20	.10	.06
474	Jim Slaton	.20	.10	.06
475	Gary Matthews	.20	.10	.06
476	Bill Stein	.20	.10	.06
477	Doug Capilla	.20	.10	.06
478	Jerry Remy	.20	.10	.06
479	Cardinals Team	.30	.15	.09
480	Ron LeFlore	.20	.10	.06
481	Jackson Todd	.20	.10	.06
482	Rick Miller	.20	.10	.06
483	Ken Macha	.20	.10	.06
484	Jim Norris	.20	.10	.06
485	Chris Chambliss	.20	.10	.06
486	John Curtis	.20	.10	.06
487	Jim Tyrone	.20	.10	.06
488	Dan Spillner	.20	.10	.06
489	Rudy Meoli	.20	.10	.06
490	Amos Otis	.20	.10	.06
491	Scott McGregor	.20	.10	.06
492	Jim Sundberg	.20	.10	.06
493	Steve Renko	.20	.10	.06
494	Chuck Tanner	.20	.10	.06
495	Dave Cash	.20	.10	.06
496	*Jim Clancy*	.20	.10	.06
497	Glenn Adams	.20	.10	.06
498	Joe Sambito	.20	.10	.06
499	Mariners Team	.30	.15	.09
500	George Foster	.20	.10	.06
501	Dave Roberts	.20	.10	.06
502	Pat Rockett	.20	.10	.06
503	Ike Hampton	.20	.10	.06
504	Roger Freed	.20	.10	.06
505	Felix Millan	.20	.10	.06
506	Ron Blomberg	.20	.10	.06
507	Willie Crawford	.20	.10	.06
508	Johnny Oates	.20	.10	.06
509	Brent Strom	.20	.10	.06
510	Willie Stargell	4.00	2.00	1.25
511	Frank Duffy	.20	.10	.06
512	Larry Herndon	.20	.10	.06
513	Barry Foote	.20	.10	.06
514	Rob Sperring	.20	.10	.06

#	Player	NM	EX	VG
515	Tim Corcoran	.20	.10	.06
516	Gary Beare	.20	.10	.06
517	Andres Mora	.20	.10	.06
518	Tommy Boggs (DP)	.20	.10	.06
519	Brian Downing	.20	.10	.06
520	Larry Hisle	.20	.10	.06
521	Steve Staggs	.20	.10	.06
522	Dick Williams	.20	.10	.06
523	*Donnie Moore*	.20	.10	.06
524	Bernie Carbo	.20	.10	.06
525	Jerry Terrell	.20	.10	.06
526	Reds Team	.45	.25	.14
527	Vic Correll	.20	.10	.06
528	Rob Picciolo	.20	.10	.06
529	Paul Hartzell	.20	.10	.06
530	Dave Winfield	4.00	2.00	1.25
531	Tom Underwood	.20	.10	.06
532	Skip Jutze	.20	.10	.06
533	Sandy Alomar	.20	.10	.06
534	Wilbur Howard	.20	.10	.06
535	Checklist 485-605	.20	.10	.06
536	Roric Harrison	.20	.10	.06
537	Bruce Bochte	.20	.10	.06
538	Johnnie LeMaster	.20	.10	.06
539	Vic Davalillo	.20	.10	.06
540	Steve Carlton	4.00	2.00	1.25
541	Larry Cox	.20	.10	.06
542	Tim Johnson	.20	.10	.06
543	Larry Harlow	.20	.10	.06
544	Len Randle	.20	.10	.06
545	Bill Campbell	.20	.10	.06
546	Ted Martinez	.20	.10	.06
547	John Scott	.20	.10	.06
548	Billy Hunter (DP)	.20	.10	.06
549	Joe Kerrigan	.20	.10	.06
550	John Mayberry	.20	.10	.06
551	Braves Team	.30	.15	.09
552	Francisco Barrios	.20	.10	.06
553	*Terry Puhl*	.25	.13	.08
554	Joe Coleman	.20	.10	.06
555	Butch Wynegar	.20	.10	.06
556	Ed Armbrister	.20	.10	.06
557	Tony Solaita	.20	.10	.06
558	Paul Mitchell	.20	.10	.06
559	Phil Mankowski	.20	.10	.06
560	Dave Parker	.20	.10	.06
561	Charlie Williams	.20	.10	.06
562	Glenn Burke	.20	.10	.06
563	Dave Rader	.20	.10	.06
564	Mick Kelleher	.20	.10	.06
565	Jerry Koosman	.20	.10	.06
566	Merv Rettenmund	.20	.10	.06
567	Dick Drago	.20	.10	.06
568	Tom Hutton	.20	.10	.06
569	*Lary Sorensen*	.20	.10	.06
570	Dave Kingman	.20	.10	.06
571	Buck Martinez	.20	.10	.06
572	Rick Wise	.20	.10	.06
573	Luis Gomez	.20	.10	.06
574	Bob Lemon	.50	.25	.15
575	Pat Dobson	.20	.10	.06
576	Sam Mejias	.20	.10	.06
577	A's Team	.30	.15	.09
578	Buzz Capra	.20	.10	.06
579	*Rance Mulliniks*	.25	.13	.08
580	Rod Carew	4.00	2.00	1.25
581	Lynn McGlothen	.20	.10	.06
582	Fran Healy	.20	.10	.06
583	George Medich	.20	.10	.06
584	John Hale	.20	.10	.06
585	Woodie Fryman	.20	.10	.06
586	Ed Goodson	.20	.10	.06
587	John Urrea	.20	.10	.06
588	Jim Mason	.20	.10	.06
589	*Bob Knepper*	.20	.10	.06
590	Bobby Murcer	.20	.10	.06
591	George Zeber	.20	.10	.06
592	Bob Apodaca	.20	.10	.06
593	Dave Skaggs	.20	.10	.06
594	Dave Freisleben	.20	.10	.06
595	Sixto Lezcano	.20	.10	.06
596	Gary Wheelock	.20	.10	.06
597	Steve Dillard	.20	.10	.06
598	Eddie Solomon	.20	.10	.06
599	Gary Woods	.20	.10	.06
600	Frank Tanana	.20	.10	.06
601	Gene Mauch	.20	.10	.06
602	Eric Soderholm	.20	.10	.06
603	Will McEnaney	.20	.10	.06
604	Earl Williams	.20	.10	.06
605	Rick Rhoden	.20	.10	.06
606	Pirates Team	.30	.15	.09
607	Fernando Arroyo	.20	.10	.06
608	Johnny Grubb	.20	.10	.06
609	John Denny	.20	.10	.06
610	Garry Maddox	.20	.10	.06
611	Pat Scanlon	.20	.10	.06
612	Ken Henderson	.20	.10	.06
613	Marty Perez	.20	.10	.06
614	Joe Wallis	.20	.10	.06
615	Clay Carroll	.20	.10	.06
616	Pat Kelly	.20	.10	.06
617	Joe Nolan	.20	.10	.06
618	Tommy Helms	.20	.10	.06
619	*Thad Bosley*	.20	.10	.06
620	Willie Randolph	.20	.10	.06
621	Craig Swan	.20	.10	.06
622	Champ Summers	.20	.10	.06
623	Eduardo Rodriguez	.20	.10	.06
624	Gary Alexander	.20	.10	.06
625	Jose Cruz	.20	.10	.06
626	Blue Jays Team	.30	.15	.09
627	Dave Johnson	.20	.10	.06
628	Ralph Garr	.20	.10	.06
629	Don Stanhouse	.20	.10	.06
630	Ron Cey	.20	.10	.06
631	Danny Ozark	.20	.10	.06
632	Rowland Office	.20	.10	.06
633	Tom Veryzer	.20	.10	.06
634	Len Barker	.20	.10	.06
635	Joe Rudi	.20	.10	.06
636	Jim Bibby	.20	.10	.06
637	Duffy Dyer	.20	.10	.06
638	Paul Splittorff	.20	.10	.06
639	Gene Clines	.20	.10	.06
640	Lee May	.20	.10	.06
641	Doug Rau	.20	.10	.06
642	Denny Doyle	.20	.10	.06
643	Tom House	.20	.10	.06
644	Jim Dwyer	.20	.10	.06
645	Mike Torrez	.20	.10	.06
646	Rick Auerbach	.20	.10	.06
647	Steve Dunning	.20	.10	.06
648	Gary Thomasson	.20	.10	.06
649	*Moose Haas*	.20	.10	.06
650	Cesar Cedeno	.20	.10	.06
651	Doug Rader	.20	.10	.06
652	Checklist 606-726	.20	.10	.06
653	Ron Hodges	.20	.10	.06
654	Pepe Frias	.20	.10	.06
655	Lyman Bostock	.20	.10	.06
656	Dave Garcia	.20	.10	.06
657	Bombo Rivera	.20	.10	.06
658	Manny Sanguillen	.20	.10	.06
659	Rangers Team	.30	.15	.09
660	Jason Thompson	.20	.10	.06
661	Grant Jackson	.20	.10	.06
662	Paul Dade	.20	.10	.06
663	Paul Reuschel	.20	.10	.06
664	Fred Stanley	.20	.10	.06
665	Dennis Leonard	.20	.10	.06
666	Billy Smith	.20	.10	.06
667	Jeff Byrd	.20	.10	.06
668	Dusty Baker	.35	.20	.11
669	Pete Falcone	.20	.10	.06
670	Jim Rice	.75	.40	.25
671	Gary Lavelle	.20	.10	.06
672	Don Kessinger	.20	.10	.06
673	Steve Brye	.20	.10	.06
674	*Ray Knight*	1.00	.50	.30
675	Jay Johnstone	.20	.10	.06
676	Bob Myrick	.20	.10	.06
677	Ed Herrmann	.20	.10	.06
678	Tom Burgmeier	.20	.10	.06
679	Wayne Garrett	.20	.10	.06
680	Vida Blue	.20	.10	.06
681	Rob Belloir	.20	.10	.06
682	Ken Brett	.20	.10	.06
683	Mike Champion	.20	.10	.06
684	Ralph Houk	.20	.10	.06
685	Frank Taveras	.20	.10	.06
686	Gaylord Perry	3.00	1.50	.90
687	*Julio Cruz*	.25	.13	.08
688	George Mitterwald	.20	.10	.06
689	Indians Team	.30	.15	.09
690	Mickey Rivers	.20	.10	.06
691	Ross Grimsley	.20	.10	.06
692	Ken Reitz	.20	.10	.06
693	Lamar Johnson	.20	.10	.06
694	Elias Sosa	.20	.10	.06
695	Dwight Evans	.20	.10	.06
696	Steve Mingori	.20	.10	.06
697	Roger Metzger	.20	.10	.06
698	Juan Bernhardt	.20	.10	.06
699	Jackie Brown	.20	.10	.06
700	Johnny Bench	6.00	3.00	1.50
701	Rookie Pitchers (**Tom Hume,** Larry Landreth, Steve McCatty, Bruce Taylor)	.20	.10	.06
702	Rookie Catchers (Bill Nahorodny, Kevin Pasley, Rick Sweet, Don Werner)	.20	.10	.06
703	Rookie Pitchers (**Larry Andersen, Tim Jones, Mickey Mahler, Jack Morris**)	4.00	2.00	1.00
704	Rookie 2nd Basemen (**Garth Iorg, Dave Oliver, Sam Perlozzo, Lou Whitaker**)	6.00	3.00	1.50
705	Rookie Outfielders (**Dave Bergman, Miguel Dilone, Clint Hurdle, Willie Norwood**)	.20	.10	.06
706	Rookie 1st Basemen (**Wayne Cage, Ted Cox, Pat Putnam, Dave Revering**)	.20	.10	.06
707	Rookie Shortstops (**Mickey Klutts, Paul Molitor, Alan Trammell, U.L. Washington**)	50.00	25.00	12.50
708	Rookie Catchers (**Bo Diaz, Dale Murphy, Lance Parrish, Ernie Whitt**)	4.00	2.00	1.00
709	Rookie Pitchers (**Steve Burke, Matt Keough, Lance Rautzhan, Dan Schatzeder**)	.20	.10	.06
710	Rookie Outfielders (Dell Alston, Rick Bosetti, Mike Easler, Keith Smith)	.20	.10	.06
711	Rookie Pitchers (Cardell Camper, Dennis Lamp, Craig Mitchell, Roy Thomas)	.20	.10	.06
712	Bobby Valentine	.20	.10	.06
713	Bob Davis	.20	.10	.06
714	Mike Anderson	.20	.10	.06
715	Jim Kaat	.20	.10	.06
716	Clarence Gaston	.20	.10	.06
717	Nelson Briles	.20	.10	.06
718	Ron Jackson	.20	.10	.06
719	Randy Elliott	.20	.10	.06
720	Fergie Jenkins	3.00	1.50	.90
721	Billy Martin	.50	.25	.15
722	Pete Broberg	.20	.10	.06
723	Johnny Wockenfuss	.20	.10	.06
724	Royals Team	.30	.15	.09
725	Kurt Bevacqua	.20	.10	.06
726	Wilbur Wood	.20	.10	.06

1978 Topps Team Checklist Sheet

A redemption offer on packs of 1978 Topps cards offered an uncut sheet of the 26 team/checklist cards by mail. Besides the team cards, the 10-1/2" x 22-1/2" sheet has a card offering collectors card boxes. The cards on the sheet are identical to the single team/checklist cards issued in packs.

	NM	EX	VG
Uncut Sheet	25.00	12.50	7.50

1978 Topps/Dynamite Magazine Panels

In issue No. 47 of its "Dynamite" kids' magazine, Scholastic Book Club teamed with Topps to insert a six-card panel of its 1978 baseball issue. Three such panels have been found thus far, one of which includes an Eddie Murray rookie card. Values shown are for just the uncut panel; complete magazines would bear a small premium.

		NM	EX	VG
Complete Panel Set (3):		60.00	30.00	18.00
PANEL 1		40.00	20.00	12.00
36	Eddie Murray			
125	George Scott			
141	Ruppert Jones			
150	Bobby Bonds			
490	Amos Otis			
550	John Mayberry			
PANEL 2		10.00	5.00	3.00
21	Steve Kemp			
168	Reggie Smith			
200	Reggie Jackson			
245	Rick Burleson			
332	Duane Kuiper			
440	Davey Lopes			
PANEL 3		15.00	7.50	4.50
44	Toby Harrah			
120	Gary Carter			
130	Jeff Burroughs			
320	Fred Lynn			
335	Bucky Dent			
670	Jim Rice			

1978 Topps/Zest Soap

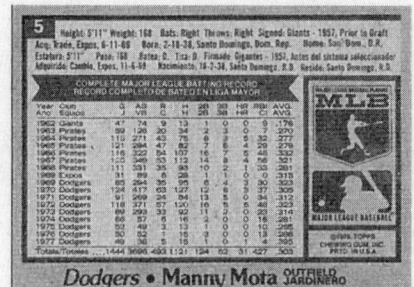

Produced by Topps for a Zest Soap promotion, the five cards in this set are almost identical to the regular issue, except the backs are printed in both Spanish and English, the game feature on back has been replaced by MLB and MLBPA logos and the card numbers are different. The cards measure 2-1/2" x 3-1/2". Because of the player selection and the bilingual backs, it seems obvious that this set was aimed at the Hispanic community. Cards were issued as complete sets in a cello package.

		NM	EX	VG
Complete Set (5):				
Common Player:				
1	Joaquin Andujar	2.00	1.00	.60
2	Bert Campaneris	4.50	2.25	1.25
3	Ed Figueroa	1.50	.70	.45

4	Willie Montanez	1.50	.70	.45
5	Manny Mota	4.50	2.25	1.25

1979 Topps

The size of this issue remained the same as in 1978 with 726 cards making their appearance. Actually, the 2-1/2" x 3-1/2" cards have a relatively minor design change from the previous year. The large color photo still dominates the front, with the player's name, team and position below it. The baseball with the player's position was moved to the lower left and the position replaced by a Topps logo. On the back, the printing color was changed and the game situation was replaced by a quiz called "Baseball Dates". Specialty cards include statistical leaders, major league records set during the season and eight cards devoted to career records. For the first time, rookies were arranged by teams under the heading of "Prospects". The key Ozzie Smith rookie card is usually seen with very poor centering.

		NM	EX	VG
	Complete Set (726):	150.00	75.00	37.50
	Common Player:	.15	.08	.05
	Wax Pack (12):	10.00		
	Wax Box (36):	300.00		
	Cello Pack (18):	12.50		
	Cello Box (24):	325.00		
	Super Cello Pack (28):	.00		
	Super Cello Box (24):	.00		
	Rack Pack (39):	25.00		
	Rack Box (24):	480.00		
	Vending Box (500):	165.00		
1	Batting Leaders	1.00	.50	.30
	(Rod Carew, Dave Parker)			
2	Home Run Leaders	.15	.08	.05
	(George Foster, Jim Rice)			
3	RBI Leaders	.15	.08	.05
	(George Foster, Jim Rice)			
4	Stolen Base Leaders	.15	.08	.05
	(Ron LeFlore, Omar Moreno)			
5	Victory Leaders	.15	.08	.05
	(Ron Guidry, Gaylord Perry)			
6	Strikeout Leaders	4.00	2.00	1.25
	(J.R. Richard, Nolan Ryan)			
7	ERA Leaders	.15	.08	.05
	(Ron Guidry, Craig Swan)			
8	Leading Firemen (Rollie	.20	.10	.06
	Fingers, Rich Gossage)			
9	Dave Campbell	.15	.08	.05
10	Lee May	.15	.08	.05
11	Marc Hill	.15	.08	.05
12	Dick Drago	.15	.08	.05
13	Paul Dade	.15	.08	.05
14	Rafael Landestoy	.15	.08	.05
15	Ross Grimsley	.15	.08	.05
16	Fred Stanley	.15	.08	.05
17	Donnie Moore	.15	.08	.05
18	Tony Solaita	.15	.08	.05
19	Larry Gura	.15	.08	.05
20	Joe Morgan	3.00	1.50	.90
21	Kevin Kobel	.15	.08	.05
22	Mike Jorgensen	.15	.08	.05
23	Terry Forster	.15	.08	.05
24	Paul Molitor	8.00	4.00	2.00
25	Steve Carlton	3.00	1.50	.90
26	Jamie Quirk	.15	.08	.05
27	Dave Goltz	.15	.08	.05
28	Steve Brye	.15	.08	.05
29	Rick Langford	.15	.08	.05
30	Dave Winfield	3.00	1.50	.90
31	Tom House	.15	.08	.05
32	Jerry Mumphrey	.15	.08	.05
33	Dave Rozema	.15	.08	.05
34	Rob Andrews	.15	.08	.05
35	Ed Figueroa	.15	.08	.05
36	Alan Ashby	.15	.08	.05
37	Joe Kerrigan	.15	.08	.05
38	Bernie Carbo	.15	.08	.05
39	Dale Murphy	2.00	1.00	.60
40	Dennis Eckersley	2.50	1.25	.70
41	Twins Team (Gene Mauch)	.25	.13	.08
42	Ron Blomberg	.15	.08	.05
43	Wayne Twitchell	.15	.08	.05
44	Kurt Bevacqua	.15	.08	.05
45	Al Hrabosky	.15	.08	.05
46	Ron Hodges	.15	.08	.05
47	Fred Norman	.15	.08	.05
48	Merv Rettenmund	.15	.08	.05
49	Vern Ruhle	.15	.08	.05
50	Steve Garvey	1.50	.70	.45
51	Ray Fosse	.15	.08	.05
52	Randy Lerch	.15	.08	.05
53	Mick Kelleher	.15	.08	.05
54	Dell Alston	.15	.08	.05
55	Willie Stargell	3.00	1.50	.90
56	John Hale	.15	.08	.05
57	Eric Rasmussen	.15	.08	.05
58	Bob Randall	.15	.08	.05

59	John Denny	.15	.08	.05
60	Mickey Rivers	.15	.08	.05
61	Bo Diaz	.15	.08	.05
62	Randy Moffitt	.15	.08	.05
63	Jack Brohamer	.15	.08	.05
64	Tom Underwood	.15	.08	.05
65	Mark Belanger	.15	.08	.05
66	Tigers Team (Les Moss)	.25	.13	.08
67	Jim Mason	.15	.08	.05
68	Joe Niekro	.15	.08	.05
69	Elliott Maddox	.15	.08	.05
70	John Candelaria	.15	.08	.05
71	Brian Downing	.15	.08	.05
72	Steve Mingori	.15	.08	.05
73	Ken Henderson	.15	.08	.05
74	*Shane Rawley*	.15	.08	.05
75	Steve Yeager	.15	.08	.05
76	Warren Cromartie	.15	.08	.05
77	Dan Briggs	.15	.08	.05
78	Elias Sosa	.15	.08	.05
79	Ted Cox	.15	.08	.05
80	Jason Thompson	.15	.08	.05
81	Roger Erickson	.15	.08	.05
82	Mets Team (Joe Torre)	.75	.40	.25
83	Fred Kendall	.15	.08	.05
84	Greg Minton	.15	.08	.05
85	Gary Matthews	.15	.08	.05
86	Rodney Scott	.15	.08	.05
87	Pete Falcone	.15	.08	.05
88	Bob Molinaro	.15	.08	.05
89	Dick Tidrow	.15	.08	.05
90	Bob Boone	.15	.08	.05
91	Terry Crowley	.15	.08	.05
92	Jim Bibby	.15	.08	.05
93	Phil Mankowski	.15	.08	.05
94	Len Barker	.15	.08	.05
95	Robin Yount	4.00	2.00	1.00
96	Indians Team (Jeff Torborg)	.25	.13	.08
97	Sam Mejias	.15	.08	.05
98	Ray Burris	.15	.08	.05
99	John Wathan	.15	.08	.05
100	Tom Seaver	4.00	2.00	1.00
101	Roy Howell	.15	.08	.05
102	Mike Anderson	.15	.08	.05
103	Jim Todd	.15	.08	.05
104	Johnny Oates	.15	.08	.05
105	Rick Camp	.15	.08	.05
106	Frank Duffy	.15	.08	.05
107	Jesus Alou	.15	.08	.05
108	Eduardo Rodriguez	.15	.08	.05
109	Joel Youngblood	.15	.08	.05
110	Vida Blue	.15	.08	.05
111	Roger Freed	.15	.08	.05
112	Phillies Team (Danny Ozark)	.25	.13	.08
113	Pete Redfern	.15	.08	.05
114	Cliff Johnson	.15	.08	.05
115	Nolan Ryan	20.00	10.00	5.00
116	*Ozzie Smith*	60.00	30.00	15.00
117	Grant Jackson	.15	.08	.05
118	Bud Harrelson	.15	.08	.05
119	Don Stanhouse	.15	.08	.05
120	Jim Sundberg	.15	.08	.05
121	Checklist 1-121	.15	.08	.05
122	Mike Paxton	.15	.08	.05
123	Lou Whitaker	1.00	.50	.30
124	Dan Schatzeder	.15	.08	.05
125	Rick Burleson	.15	.08	.05
126	Doug Bair	.15	.08	.05
127	Thad Bosley	.15	.08	.05
128	Ted Martinez	.15	.08	.05
129	Marty Pattin	.15	.08	.05
130	Bob Watson	.15	.08	.05
131	Jim Clancy	.15	.08	.05
132	Rowland Office	.15	.08	.05
133	Bill Castro	.15	.08	.05
134	Alan Bannister	.15	.08	.05
135	Bobby Murcer	.15	.08	.05
136	Jim Kaat	.15	.08	.05
137	Larry Wolfe	.15	.08	.05
138	Mark Lee	.15	.08	.05
139	Luis Pujols	.15	.08	.05
140	Don Gullett	.15	.08	.05
141	Tom Paciorek	.15	.08	.05
142	Charlie Williams	.15	.08	.05
143	Tony Scott	.15	.08	.05
144	Sandy Alomar	.15	.08	.05
145	Rick Rhoden	.15	.08	.05
146	Duane Kuiper	.15	.08	.05
147	Dave Hamilton	.15	.08	.05
148	Bruce Boisclair	.15	.08	.05
149	Manny Sarmiento	.15	.08	.05
150	Wayne Cage	.15	.08	.05
151	John Hiller	.15	.08	.05
152	Rick Cerone	.15	.08	.05
153	Dennis Lamp	.15	.08	.05
154	Jim Gantner	.15	.08	.05
155	Dwight Evans	.15	.08	.05
156	Buddy Solomon	.15	.08	.05
157	U.L. Washington	.15	.08	.05
158	Joe Sambito	.15	.08	.05
159	Roy White	.15	.08	.05
160	Mike Flanagan	.15	.08	.05
161	Barry Foote	.15	.08	.05
162	Tom Johnson	.15	.08	.05
163	Glenn Burke	.15	.08	.05
164	Mickey Lolich	.15	.08	.05
165	Frank Taveras	.15	.08	.05
166	Leon Roberts	.15	.08	.05
167a	Roger Metzger (Solid vertical black line between first and last names, through "A" of GIANTS.")	.50	.25	.15
167b	Roger Metzger (Partial black line.)	.25	.13	.08
167c	Roger Metzger (No black line.)	.15	.08	.05
168	Dave Freisleben	.15	.08	.05
169	Bill Nahorodny	.15	.08	.05

170	Don Sutton	2.50	1.25	.70
171	Gene Clines	.15	.08	.05
172	Mike Bruhert	.15	.08	.05
173	John Lowenstein	.15	.08	.05
174	Rick Auerbach	.15	.08	.05
175	George Hendrick	.15	.08	.05
176	Aurelio Rodriguez	.15	.08	.05
177	Ron Reed	.15	.08	.05
178	Alvis Woods	.15	.08	.05
179	Jim Beattie	.15	.08	.05
180	Larry Hisle	.15	.08	.05
181	Mike Garman	.15	.08	.05
182	Tim Johnson	.15	.08	.05
183	Paul Splittorff	.15	.08	.05
184	Darrel Chaney	.15	.08	.05
185	Mike Torrez	.15	.08	.05
186	Eric Soderholm	.15	.08	.05
187	Mark Lemongello	.15	.08	.05
188	Pat Kelly	.15	.08	.05
189	*Eddie Whitson*	.25	.13	.08
190	Ron Cey	.15	.08	.05
191	Mike Norris	.15	.08	.05
192	Cardinals Team (Ken Boyer)	.25	.13	.08
193	Glenn Adams	.15	.08	.05
194	Randy Jones	.15	.08	.05
195	Bill Madlock	.15	.08	.05
196	Steve Kemp	.15	.08	.05
197	Bob Apodaca	.15	.08	.05
198	Johnny Grubb	.15	.08	.05
199	Larry Milbourne	.15	.08	.05
200	Johnny Bench	4.00	2.00	1.00
201	Mike Edwards (Record Breaker)	.15	.08	.05
202	Ron Guidry (Record Breaker)	.15	.08	.05
203	J.R. Richard (Record Breaker)	.15	.08	.05
204	Pete Rose (Record Breaker)	1.00	.50	.30
205	John Stearns (Record Breaker)	.15	.08	.05
206	Sammy Stewart (Record Breaker)	.15	.08	.05
207	Dave Lemanczyk	.15	.08	.05
208	Clarence Gaston	.15	.08	.05
209	Reggie Cleveland	.15	.08	.05
210	Larry Bowa	.15	.08	.05
211	Denny Martinez	.15	.08	.05
212	*Carney Lansford*	.60	.30	.20
213	Bill Travers	.15	.08	.05
214	Red Sox Team (Don Zimmer)	.25	.13	.08
215	Willie McCovey	3.00	1.50	.90
216	Wilbur Wood	.15	.08	.05
217	Steve Dillard	.15	.08	.05
218	Dennis Leonard	.15	.08	.05
219	Roy Smalley	.15	.08	.05
220	Cesar Geronimo	.15	.08	.05
221	Jesse Jefferson	.15	.08	.05
222	Bob Beall	.15	.08	.05
223	Kent Tekulve	.15	.08	.05
224	Dave Revering	.15	.08	.05
225	Rich Gossage	.25	.13	.08
226	Ron Pruitt	.15	.08	.05
227	Steve Stone	.15	.08	.05
228	Vic Davalillo	.15	.08	.05
229	Doug Flynn	.15	.08	.05
230	Bob Forsch	.15	.08	.05
231	Johnny Wockenfuss	.15	.08	.05
232	Jimmy Sexton	.15	.08	.05
233	Paul Mitchell	.15	.08	.05
234	Toby Harrah	.15	.08	.05
235	Steve Rogers	.15	.08	.05
236	Jim Dwyer	.15	.08	.05
237	Billy Smith	.15	.08	.05
238	Balor Moore	.15	.08	.05
239	Willie Horton	.15	.08	.05
240	Rick Reuschel	.15	.08	.05
241	Checklist 122-242	.15	.08	.05
242	Pablo Torrealba	.15	.08	.05
243	Buck Martinez	.15	.08	.05
244	Pirates Team (Chuck Tanner)	.25	.13	.08
245	Jeff Burroughs	.15	.08	.05
246	Darrell Jackson	.15	.08	.05
247	Tucker Ashford	.15	.08	.05
248	Pete LaCock	.15	.08	.05
249	Paul Thormodsgard	.15	.08	.05
250	Willie Randolph	.15	.08	.05
251	Jack Morris	.40	.20	.12
252	Bob Stinson	.15	.08	.05
253	Rick Wise	.15	.08	.05
254	Luis Gomez	.15	.08	.05
255	Tommy John	.30	.15	.09
256	Mike Sadek	.15	.08	.05
257	Adrian Devine	.15	.08	.05
258	Mike Phillips	.15	.08	.05
259	Reds Team (Sparky Anderson)	.75	.40	.25
260	Richie Zisk	.15	.08	.05
261	Mario Guerrero	.15	.08	.05
262	Nelson Briles	.15	.08	.05
263	Oscar Gamble	.15	.08	.05
264	*Don Robinson*	.15	.08	.05
265	Don Money	.15	.08	.05
266	Jim Willoughby	.15	.08	.05
267	Joe Rudi	.15	.08	.05
268	Julio Gonzalez	.15	.08	.05
269	Woodie Fryman	.15	.08	.05
270	Butch Hobson	.15	.08	.05
271	Rawly Eastwick	.15	.08	.05
272	Tim Corcoran	.15	.08	.05
273	Jerry Terrell	.15	.08	.05
274	Willie Norwood	.15	.08	.05
275	Junior Moore	.15	.08	.05
276	Jim Colborn	.15	.08	.05
277	Tom Grieve	.15	.08	.05
278	Andy Messersmith	.15	.08	.05
279	Jerry Grote	.15	.08	.05
280	Andre Thornton	.15	.08	.05
281	Vic Correll	.15	.08	.05
282	Blue Jays Team (Roy Hartsfield)	.25	.13	.08

No.	Player			
283	Ken Kravec	.15	.08	.05
284	Johnnie LeMaster	.15	.08	.05
285	Bobby Bonds	.15	.08	.05
286	Duffy Dyer	.15	.08	.05
287	Andres Mora	.15	.08	.05
288	Milt Wilcox	.15	.08	.05
289	Jose Cruz	.15	.08	.05
290	Dave Lopes	.15	.08	.05
291	Tom Griffin	.15	.08	.05
292	Don Reynolds	.15	.08	.05
293	Jerry Garvin	.15	.08	.05
294	Pepe Frias	.15	.08	.05
295	Mitchell Page	.15	.08	.05
296	Preston Hanna	.15	.08	.05
297	Ted Sizemore	.15	.08	.05
298	Rich Gale	.15	.08	.05
299	Steve Ontiveros	.15	.08	.05
300	Rod Carew	3.00	1.50	.90
301	Tom Hume	.15	.08	.05
302	Braves Team (Bobby Cox)	.45	.25	.14
303	Lary Sorensen	.15	.08	.05
304	Steve Swisher	.15	.08	.05
305	Willie Montanez	.15	.08	.05
306	Floyd Bannister	.15	.08	.05
307	Larvell Blanks	.15	.08	.05
308	Bert Blyleven	.15	.08	.05
309	Ralph Garr	.15	.08	.05
310	Thurman Munson	5.00	2.50	1.50
311	Gary Lavelle	.15	.08	.05
312	Bob Robertson	.15	.08	.05
313	Dyar Miller	.15	.08	.05
314	Larry Harlow	.15	.08	.05
315	Jon Matlack	.15	.08	.05
316	Milt May	.15	.08	.05
317	Jose Cardenal	.15	.08	.05
318	*Bob Welch*	1.50	.70	.45
319	Wayne Garrett	.15	.08	.05
320	Carl Yastrzemski	4.00	2.00	1.00
321	Gaylord Perry	2.50	1.25	.70
322	Danny Goodwin	.15	.08	.05
323	Lynn McGlothen	.15	.08	.05
324	Mike Tyson	.15	.08	.05
325	Cecil Cooper	.15	.08	.05
326	Pedro Borbon	.15	.08	.05
327	Art Howe	.15	.08	.05
328	A's Team (Jack McKeon)	.25	.13	.08
329	Joe Coleman	.15	.08	.05
330	George Brett	8.00	4.00	2.00
331	Mickey Mahler	.15	.08	.05
332	Gary Alexander	.15	.08	.05
333	Chet Lemon	.15	.08	.05
334	Craig Swan	.15	.08	.05
335	Chris Chambliss	.15	.08	.05
336	Bobby Thompson	.15	.08	.05
337	John Montague	.15	.08	.05
338	Vic Harris	.15	.08	.05
339	Ron Jackson	.15	.08	.05
340	Jim Palmer	3.00	1.50	.90
341	*Willie Upshaw*	.20	.10	.06
342	Dave Roberts	.15	.08	.05
343	Ed Glynn	.15	.08	.05
344	Jerry Royster	.15	.08	.05
345	Tug McGraw	.15	.08	.05
346	Bill Buckner	.15	.08	.05
347	Doug Rau	.15	.08	.05
348	Andre Dawson	1.50	.70	.45
349	Jim Wright	.15	.08	.05
350	Garry Templeton	.15	.08	.05
351	Wayne Nordhagen	.15	.08	.05
352	Steve Renko	.15	.08	.05
353	Checklist 243-363	.15	.08	.05
354	Bill Bonham	.15	.08	.05
355	Lee Mazzilli	.15	.08	.05
356	Giants Team (Joe Altobelli)	.25	.13	.08
357	Jerry Augustine	.15	.08	.05
358	Alan Trammell	2.00	1.00	.60
359	Dan Spillner	.15	.08	.05
360	Amos Otis	.15	.08	.05
361	Tom Dixon	.15	.08	.05
362	Mike Cubbage	.15	.08	.05
363	Craig Skok	.15	.08	.05
364	Gene Richards	.15	.08	.05
365	Sparky Lyle	.15	.08	.05
366	Juan Bernhardt	.15	.08	.05
367	Dave Skaggs	.15	.08	.05
368	Don Aase	.15	.08	.05
369a	Bump Wills (Blue Jays)	2.00	1.00	.60
369b	Bump Wills (Rangers)	2.00	1.00	.60
370	Dave Kingman	.15	.08	.05
371	Jeff Holly	.15	.08	.05
372	Lamar Johnson	.15	.08	.05
373	Lance Rautzhan	.15	.08	.05
374	Ed Herrmann	.15	.08	.05
375	Bill Campbell	.15	.08	.05
376	Gorman Thomas	.15	.08	.05
377	Paul Moskau	.15	.08	.05
378	Rob Picciolo	.15	.08	.05
379	Dale Murray	.15	.08	.05
380	John Mayberry	.15	.08	.05
381	Astros Team (Bill Virdon)	.25	.13	.08
382	Jerry Martin	.15	.08	.05
383	Phil Garner	.15	.08	.05
384	Tommy Boggs	.15	.08	.05
385	Dan Ford	.15	.08	.05
386	Francisco Barrios	.15	.08	.05
387	Gary Thomasson	.15	.08	.05
388	Jack Billingham	.15	.08	.05
389	Joe Zdeb	.15	.08	.05
390	Rollie Fingers	2.50	1.25	.70
391	Al Oliver	.30	.15	.09
392	Doug Ault	.15	.08	.05
393	Scott McGregor	.15	.08	.05
394	Randy Stein	.15	.08	.05
395	Dave Cash	.15	.08	.05
396	Bill Plummer	.15	.08	.05
397	Sergio Ferrer	.15	.08	.05
398	Ivan DeJesus	.15	.08	.05
399	David Clyde	.15	.08	.05

No.	Player			
400	Jim Rice	.50	.25	.15
401	Ray Knight	.15	.08	.05
402	Paul Hartzell	.15	.08	.05
403	Tim Foli	.15	.08	.05
404	White Sox Team (Don Kessinger)	.25	.13	.08
405	Butch Wynegar	.15	.08	.05
406	Joe Wallis	.15	.08	.05
407	Pete Vuckovich	.15	.08	.05
408	Charlie Moore	.15	.08	.05
409	*Willie Wilson*	2.00	1.00	.60
410	Darrell Evans	.15	.08	.05
411	All-Time Hits Leaders (Ty Cobb, George Sisler)	.50	.25	.15
412	All-Time RBI Leaders (Hank Aaron, Hack Wilson)	.50	.25	.15
413	All-Time Home Run Leaders (Hank Aaron, Roger Maris)	4.50	2.25	1.25
414	All-Time Batting Average Leaders (Ty Cobb, Roger Hornsby)	.50	.25	.15
415	All-Time Stolen Bases Leader (Lou Brock)	.30	.15	.09
416	All-Time Wins Leaders (Jack Chesbro, Cy Young)	.25	.13	.08
417	All-Time Strikeout Leaders (Walter Johnson, Nolan Ryan)	4.50	2.25	1.25
418	All-Time ERA Leaders (Walter Johnson, Dutch Leonard)	.20	.10	.06
419	Dick Ruthven	.15	.08	.05
420	Ken Griffey	.15	.08	.05
421	Doug DeCinces	.15	.08	.05
422	Ruppert Jones	.15	.08	.05
423	Bob Montgomery	.15	.08	.05
424	Angels Team (Jim Fregosi)	.25	.13	.08
425	Rick Manning	.15	.08	.05
426	Chris Speier	.15	.08	.05
427	Andy Replogle	.15	.08	.05
428	Bobby Valentine	.15	.08	.05
429	John Urrea	.15	.08	.05
430	Dave Parker	.15	.08	.05
431	Glenn Borgmann	.15	.08	.05
432	Dave Heaverlo	.15	.08	.05
433	Larry Biittner	.15	.08	.05
434	Ken Clay	.15	.08	.05
435	Gene Tenace	.15	.08	.05
436	Hector Cruz	.15	.08	.05
437	Rick Williams	.15	.08	.05
438	Horace Speed	.15	.08	.05
439	Frank White	.15	.08	.05
440	Rusty Staub	.15	.08	.05
441	Lee Lacy	.15	.08	.05
442	Doyle Alexander	.15	.08	.05
443	Bruce Bochte	.15	.08	.05
444	*Aurelio Lopez*	.15	.08	.05
445	Steve Henderson	.15	.08	.05
446	Jim Lonborg	.15	.08	.05
447	Manny Sanguillen	.15	.08	.05
448	Moose Haas	.15	.08	.05
449	Bombo Rivera	.15	.08	.05
450	Dave Concepcion	.15	.08	.05
451	Royals Team (Whitey Herzog)	.25	.13	.08
452	Jerry Morales	.15	.08	.05
453	Chris Knapp	.15	.08	.05
454	Len Randle	.15	.08	.05
455	Bill Lee	.15	.08	.05
456	Chuck Baker	.15	.08	.05
457	Bruce Sutter	2.50	1.25	.70
458	Jim Essian	.15	.08	.05
459	Sid Monge	.15	.08	.05
460	Graig Nettles	.15	.08	.05
461	Jim Barr	.15	.08	.05
462	Otto Velez	.15	.08	.05
463	Steve Comer	.15	.08	.05
464	Joe Nolan	.15	.08	.05
465	Reggie Smith	.15	.08	.05
466	Mark Littell	.15	.08	.05
467	Don Kessinger	.15	.08	.05
468	Stan Bahnsen	.15	.08	.05
469	Lance Parrish	.30	.15	.09
470	Garry Maddox	.15	.08	.05
471	Joaquin Andujar	.15	.08	.05
472	Craig Kusick	.15	.08	.05
473	Dave Roberts	.15	.08	.05
474	Dick Davis	.15	.08	.05
475	Dan Driessen	.15	.08	.05
476	Tom Poquette	.15	.08	.05
477	Bob Grich	.15	.08	.05
478	Juan Beniquez	.15	.08	.05
479	Padres Team (Roger Craig)	.25	.13	.08
480	Fred Lynn	.15	.08	.05
481	Skip Lockwood	.15	.08	.05
482	Craig Reynolds	.15	.08	.05
483	Checklist 364-484	.15	.08	.05
484	Rick Waits	.15	.08	.05
485	Bucky Dent	.15	.08	.05
486	Bob Knepper	.15	.08	.05
487	Miguel Dilone	.15	.08	.05
488	Bob Owchinko	.15	.08	.05
489	Larry Cox (Photo actually Dave Rader.)	.15	.08	.05
490	Al Cowens	.15	.08	.05
491	Tippy Martinez	.15	.08	.05
492	Bob Bailor	.15	.08	.05
493	Larry Christenson	.15	.08	.05
494	Jerry White	.15	.08	.05
495	Tony Perez	2.00	1.00	.60
496	Barry Bonnell	.15	.08	.05
497	Glenn Abbott	.15	.08	.05
498	Rich Chiles	.15	.08	.05
499	Rangers Team (Pat Corrales)	.25	.13	.08
500	Ron Guidry	.20	.10	.06
501	Junior Kennedy	.15	.08	.05
502	Steve Braun	.15	.08	.05
503	Terry Humphrey	.15	.08	.05
504	*Larry McWilliams*	.15	.08	.05
505	Ed Kranepool	.15	.08	.05
506	John D'Acquisto	.15	.08	.05

No.	Player			
507	Tony Armas	.15	.08	.05
508	Charlie Hough	.15	.08	.05
509	Mario Mendoza	.15	.08	.05
510	Ted Simmons	.15	.08	.05
511	Paul Reuschel	.15	.08	.05
512	Jack Clark	.15	.08	.05
513	Dave Johnson	.15	.08	.05
514	Mike Proly	.15	.08	.05
515	Enos Cabell	.15	.08	.05
516	Champ Summers	.15	.08	.05
517	Al Bumbry	.15	.08	.05
518	Jim Umbarger	.15	.08	.05
519	Ben Oglivie	.15	.08	.05
520	Gary Carter	3.00	1.50	.90
521	Sam Ewing	.15	.08	.05
522	Ken Holtzman	.15	.08	.05
523	John Milner	.15	.08	.05
524	Tom Burgmeier	.15	.08	.05
525	Freddie Patek	.15	.08	.05
526	Dodgers Team (Tom Lasorda)	.60	.30	.20
527	Lerrin LaGrow	.15	.08	.05
528	Wayne Gross	.15	.08	.05
529	Brian Asselstine	.15	.08	.05
530	Frank Tanana	.15	.08	.05
531	Fernando Gonzalez	.15	.08	.05
532	Buddy Schultz	.15	.08	.05
533	Leroy Stanton	.15	.08	.05
534	Ken Forsch	.15	.08	.05
535	Ellis Valentine	.15	.08	.05
536	Jerry Reuss	.15	.08	.05
537	Tom Veryzer	.15	.08	.05
538	Mike Ivie	.15	.08	.05
539	John Ellis	.15	.08	.05
540	Greg Luzinski	.15	.08	.05
541	Jim Slaton	.15	.08	.05
542	Rick Bosetti	.15	.08	.05
543	Kiko Garcia	.15	.08	.05
544	Fergie Jenkins	2.00	1.00	.60
545	John Stearns	.15	.08	.05
546	Bill Russell	.15	.08	.05
547	Clint Hurdle	.15	.08	.05
548	Enrique Romo	.15	.08	.05
549	Bob Bailey	.15	.08	.05
550	Sal Bando	.15	.08	.05
551	Cubs Team (Herman Franks)	.25	.13	.08
552	Jose Morales	.15	.08	.05
553	Denny Walling	.15	.08	.05
554	Matt Keough	.15	.08	.05
555	Biff Pocoroba	.15	.08	.05
556	Mike Lum	.15	.08	.05
557	Ken Brett	.15	.08	.05
558	Jay Johnstone	.15	.08	.05
559	Greg Pryor	.15	.08	.05
560	John Montefusco	.15	.08	.05
561	Ed Ott	.15	.08	.05
562	Dusty Baker	.20	.10	.06
563	Roy Thomas	.15	.08	.05
564	Jerry Turner	.15	.08	.05
565	Rico Carty	.15	.08	.05
566	Nino Espinosa	.15	.08	.05
567	Rich Hebner	.15	.08	.05
568	Carlos Lopez	.15	.08	.05
569	Bob Sykes	.15	.08	.05
570	Cesar Cedeno	.15	.08	.05
571	Darrell Porter	.15	.08	.05
572	Rod Gilbreath	.15	.08	.05
573	Jim Kern	.15	.08	.05
574	Claudell Washington	.15	.08	.05
575	Luis Tiant	.15	.08	.05
576	Mike Parrott	.15	.08	.05
577	Brewers Team (George Bamberger)	.25	.13	.08
578	Pete Broberg	.15	.08	.05
579	Greg Gross	.15	.08	.05
580	Ron Fairly	.15	.08	.05
581	Darold Knowles	.15	.08	.05
582	Paul Blair	.15	.08	.05
583	Julio Cruz	.15	.08	.05
584	Jim Rooker	.15	.08	.05
585	Hal McRae	.15	.08	.05
586	*Bob Horner*	1.00	.50	.30
587	Ken Reitz	.15	.08	.05
588	Tom Murphy	.15	.08	.05
589	Terry Whitfield	.15	.08	.05
590	J.R. Richard	.15	.08	.05
591	Mike Hargrove	.15	.08	.05
592	Mike Krukow	.15	.08	.05
593	Rick Dempsey	.15	.08	.05
594	Bob Shirley	.15	.08	.05
595	Phil Niekro	2.00	1.00	.60
596	Jim Wohlford	.15	.08	.05
597	Bob Stanley	.15	.08	.05
598	Mark Wagner	.15	.08	.05
599	Jim Spencer	.15	.08	.05
600	George Foster	.15	.08	.05
601	Dave LaRoche	.15	.08	.05
602	Checklist 485-605	.15	.08	.05
603	Rudy May	.15	.08	.05
604	Jeff Newman	.15	.08	.05
605	Rick Monday	.15	.08	.05
606	Expos Team (Dick Williams)	.25	.13	.08
607	Omar Moreno	.15	.08	.05
608	Dave McKay	.15	.08	.05
609	Silvio Martinez	.15	.08	.05
610	Mike Schmidt	6.00	3.00	1.75
611	Jim Norris	.15	.08	.05
612	*Rick Honeycutt*	.25	.13	.08
613	Mike Edwards	.15	.08	.05
614	Willie Hernandez	.15	.08	.05
615	Ken Singleton	.15	.08	.05
616	Billy Almon	.15	.08	.05
617	Terry Puhl	.15	.08	.05
618	Jerry Remy	.15	.08	.05
619	*Ken Landreaux*	.15	.08	.05
620	Bert Campaneris	.15	.08	.05
621	Pat Zachry	.15	.08	.05
622	Dave Collins	.15	.08	.05
623	Bob McClure	.15	.08	.05

624	Larry Herndon	.15	.08	.05
625	Mark Fidrych	.20	.10	.06
626	Yankees Team (Bob Lemon)	.60	.30	.20
627	Gary Serum	.15	.08	.05
628	Del Unser	.15	.08	.05
629	Gene Garber	.15	.08	.05
630	Bake McBride	.15	.08	.05
631	Jorge Orta	.15	.08	.05
632	Don Kirkwood	.15	.08	.05
633	Rob Wilfong	.15	.08	.05
634	Paul Lindblad	.15	.08	.05
635	Don Baylor	.30	.15	.09
636	Wayne Garland	.15	.08	.05
637	Bill Robinson	.15	.08	.05
638	Al Fitzmorris	.15	.08	.05
639	Manny Trillo	.15	.08	.05
640	Eddie Murray	10.00	5.00	2.50
641	*Bobby Castillo*	.15	.08	.05
642	Wilbur Howard	.15	.08	.05
643	Tom Hausman	.15	.08	.05
644	Manny Mota	.15	.08	.05
645	George Scott	.15	.08	.05
646	Rick Sweet	.15	.08	.05
647	Bob Lacey	.15	.08	.05
648	Lou Piniella	.25	.13	.08
649	John Curtis	.15	.08	.05
650	Pete Rose	10.00	5.00	2.50
651	Mike Caldwell	.15	.08	.05
652	Stan Papi	.15	.08	.05
653	Warren Brusstar	.15	.08	.05
654	Rick Miller	.15	.08	.05
655	Jerry Koosman	.15	.08	.05
656	Hosken Powell	.15	.08	.05
657	George Medich	.15	.08	.05
658	Taylor Duncan	.15	.08	.05
659	Mariners Team (Darrell Johnson)	.25	.13	.08
660	Ron LeFlore	.15	.08	.05
661	Bruce Kison	.15	.08	.05
662	Kevin Bell	.15	.08	.05
663	Mike Vail	.15	.08	.05
664	Doug Bird	.15	.08	.05
665	Lou Brock	3.00	1.50	.90
666	Rich Dauer	.15	.08	.05
667	Don Hood	.15	.08	.05
668	Bill North	.15	.08	.05
669	Checklist 606-726	.15	.08	.05
670	Jim Hunter	3.00	1.50	.90
671	Joe Ferguson	.15	.08	.05
672	Ed Halicki	.15	.08	.05
673	Tom Hutton	.15	.08	.05
674	Dave Tomlin	.15	.08	.05
675	Tim McCarver	.25	.13	.08
676	Johnny Sutton	.15	.08	.05
677	Larry Parrish	.15	.08	.05
678	Geoff Zahn	.15	.08	.05
679	Derrel Thomas	.15	.08	.05
680	Carlton Fisk	3.00	1.50	.90
681	*John Henry Johnson*	.15	.08	.05
682	Dave Chalk	.15	.08	.05
683	Dan Meyer	.15	.08	.05
684	Jamie Easterly	.15	.08	.05
685	Sixto Lezcano	.15	.08	.05
686	Ron Schueler	.15	.08	.05
687	Rennie Stennett	.15	.08	.05
688	Mike Willis	.15	.08	.05
689	Orioles Team (Earl Weaver)	.60	.30	.20
690	Buddy Bell	.15	.08	.05
691	Dock Ellis	.15	.08	.05
692	Mickey Stanley	.15	.08	.05
693	Dave Rader	.15	.08	.05
694	Burt Hooton	.15	.08	.05
695	Keith Hernandez	.15	.08	.05
696	Andy Hassler	.15	.08	.05
697	Dave Bergman	.15	.08	.05
698	Bill Stein	.15	.08	.05
699	Hal Dues	.15	.08	.05
700	Reggie Jackson	5.00	2.50	1.25
701	Orioles Prospects (*Mark Corey, John Flinn, Sammy Stewart*)	.15	.08	.05
702	Red Sox Prospects (Joel Finch, Garry Hancock, Allen Ripley)	.15	.08	.05
703	Angels Prospects (Jim Anderson, Dave Frost, Bob Slater)	.15	.08	.05
704	White Sox Prospects (*Ross Baumgarten, Mike Colbern, Mike Squires*)	.15	.08	.05
705	Indians Prospects (*Alfredo Griffin*, Tim Norrid, Dave Oliver)	.25	.13	.08
706	Tigers Prospects (Dave Stegman, Dave Tobik, Kip Young)	.15	.08	.05
707	Royals Prospects (Randy Bass, Jim Gaudet, Randy McGilberry)	.15	.08	.05
708	Brewers Prospects (*Kevin Bass, Eddie Romero, Ned Yost*)	.25	.13	.08
709	Twins Prospects (Sam Perlozzo, Rick Sofield, Kevin Stanfield)	.15	.08	.05
710	Yankees Prospects (*Brian Doyle, Mike Heath, Dave Rajsich*)	.20	.10	.06
711	A's Prospects (*Dwayne Murphy, Bruce Robinson, Alan Wirth*)	.15	.08	.05
712	Mariners Prospects (Bud Anderson, Greg Biercevicz, Byron McLaughlin)	.15	.08	.05
713	Rangers Prospects (*Danny Darwin, Pat Putnam, Billy Sample*)	.25	.13	.08

714	Blue Jays Prospects (Victor Cruz, Pat Kelly, Ernie Whitt)	.15	.08	.05
715	Braves Prospects (*Bruce Benedict, Glenn Hubbard, Larry Whisenton*)	.25	.13	.08
716	Cubs Prospects (*Dave Geisel, Karl Pagel, Scot Thompson*)	.15	.08	.05
717	Reds Prospects (*Mike LaCoss, Ron Oester, Harry Spilman*)	.15	.08	.05
718	Astros Prospects (Bruce Bochy, Mike Fischlin, Don Pisker)	.15	.08	.05
719	Dodgers Prospects (*Pedro Guerrero, Rudy Law, Joe Simpson*)	1.50	.70	.45
720	Expos Prospects (*Jerry Fry, Jerry Pirtle, Scott Sanderson*)	.30	.15	.09
721	Mets Prospects (Juan Berenguer, Dwight Bernard, Dan Norman)	.15	.08	.05
722	Phillies Prospects (*Jim Morrison, Lonnie Smith, Jim Wright*)	.50	.25	.15
723	Pirates Prospects (Dale Berra, Eugenio Cotes, Ben Wiltbank)	.15	.08	.05
724	Cardinals Prospects (*Tom Bruno, George Frazier, Terry Kennedy*)	.20	.10	.06
725	Padres Prospects (Jim Beswick, Steve Mura, Broderick Perkins)	.15	.08	.05
726	Giants Prospects (Greg Johnston, Joe Strain, John Tamargo)	.15	.08	.05

1979 Topps Team Checklist Sheet

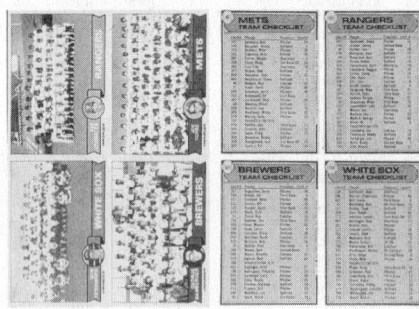

This uncut sheet of 26 team card/checklists was available via a mail-in offer. The sheet was mailed with two folds. The sheet cards are printed on lighter stock.

	NM	EX	VG
Uncut Sheet:	20.00	10.00	6.00

1979 Topps Comics

Issued as the 3" x 3-3/4" wax wrapper for a five-cent piece of bubblegum, this "test" issue was bought up in great quantities by speculators and remains rather common. It is also inexpensive, because the comic-style player representations were not popular with collectors. The set is complete at 33 pieces. Each wax box contains only 11 different players. Original packaging folds are not considered in grading.

		NM	EX	VG
	Complete Set (33):	15.00	7.50	4.50
	Common Player:	.25	.13	.08
	Wax Box (72):	55.00	.00	.00
1	Eddie Murray	1.50	.70	.45
2	Jim Rice	.60	.30	.20
3	Carl Yastrzemski	1.50	.70	.45
4	Nolan Ryan	5.00	2.50	1.50
5	Chet Lemon	.25	.13	.08
6	Andre Thornton	.25	.13	.08
7	Rusty Staub	.25	.13	.08
8	Ron LeFlore	.25	.13	.08
9	George Brett	3.00	1.50	.90
10	Larry Hisle	.25	.13	.08
11	Rod Carew	1.50	.70	.45
12	Reggie Jackson	2.50	1.25	.70
13	Ron Guidry	.25	.13	.08
14	Mitchell Page	.25	.13	.08
15	Leon Roberts	.25	.13	.08
16	Al Oliver	.25	.13	.08
17	John Mayberry	.25	.13	.08
18	Bob Horner	.25	.13	.08
19	Phil Niekro	1.00	.50	.30
20	Dave Kingman	.25	.13	.08

21	John Bench	1.50	.70	.45
22	Tom Seaver	1.50	.70	.45
23	J.R. Richard	.25	.13	.08
24	Steve Garvey	.60	.30	.20
25	Reggie Smith	.25	.13	.08
26	Ross Grimsley	.25	.13	.08
27	Craig Swan	.25	.13	.08
28	Pete Rose	3.50	1.75	1.00
29	Dave Parker	.25	.13	.08
30	Ted Simmons	.25	.13	.08
31	Dave Winfield	1.50	.70	.45
32	Jack Clark	.25	.13	.08
33	Vida Blue	.25	.13	.08

1979 Topps/Dynamite Magazine Panels

In at least two issue of its "Dynamite" kids' magazine, Scholastic Book Club teamed with Topps to insert a six-card panel of its 1979 baseball issue. Complete magazines would bear a small premium.

		NM	EX	VG
	Complete Panel:	20.00	10.00	6.00
2	Home Run Leaders (Jim Rice, George Foster)			
5	Victory Leaders (Ron Guidry, Gaylord Perry)			
6	Strikeout Leaders (Nolan Ryan, J.R. Richard)			
201	Mike Edwards (Record Breaker)			
202	Ron Guidry (Record Breaker)			
203	J.R. Richard (Record Breaker)			
	Complete Panel:	15.00	7.50	4.50
232	Jimmy Sexton			
292	Don Reynolds			
336	Bobby Thompson			
432	Dave Heaverlo			
532	Buddy Schultz			
539	John Ellis			

1980 Topps

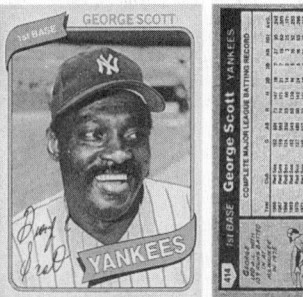

Again numbering 726 cards measuring 2-1/2" x 3-1/2", Topps did make some design changes in 1980. Fronts have the usual color picture with a facsimile autograph. The player's name appears above the picture, while his position is on a pennant at the upper left and his team on another pennant in the lower right. Backs no longer feature games, returning instead to statistics, personal information, a few headlines and a cartoon about the player. Specialty cards include statistical leaders, and previous season highlights. Many rookies again appear in team threesomes.

		NM	EX	VG
	Complete Set (726):	120.00	60.00	30.00
	Common Player:	.15	.08	.05
	Wax Pack (15):	10.00		
	Wax Box (36):	260.00		
	Cello Pack (25):	12.50		
	Cello Box (24):	275.00		
	Super Cello Pack (28):	14.00		
	Super Cello Box (24):	290.00		
	Rack Pack (42):	17.75		
	Rack Box (24):	360.00		
	Vending Box (500):	100.00		
1	Lou Brock, Carl Yastrzemski (Highlights)	1.00	.50	.30
2	Willie McCovey (Highlights)	.30	.15	.09
3	Manny Mota (Highlights)	.15	.08	.05
4	Pete Rose (Highlights)	2.00	1.00	.60
5	Garry Templeton (Highlights)	.15	.08	.05
6	Del Unser (Highlights)	.15	.08	.05
7	Mike Lum	.15	.08	.05
8	Craig Swan	.15	.08	.05
9a	Steve Braun (Name in yellow.)	200.00	100.00	60.00
9b	Steve Braun (Name in red.)	.15	.08	.05
10	Denny Martinez	.15	.08	.05
11	Jimmy Sexton	.15	.08	.05
12	John Curtis	.15	.08	.05
13	Ron Pruitt	.15	.08	.05
14	Dave Cash	.15	.08	.05
15	Bill Campbell	.15	.08	.05

#	Name			
16	Jerry Narron	.15	.08	.05
17	Bruce Sutter	2.00	1.00	.60
18	Ron Jackson	.15	.08	.05
19	Balor Moore	.15	.08	.05
20	Dan Ford	.15	.08	.05
21	Manny Sarmiento	.15	.08	.05
22	Pat Putnam	.15	.08	.05
23	Derrel Thomas	.15	.08	.05
24	Jim Slaton	.15	.08	.05
25	Lee Mazzilli	.15	.08	.05
26	Marty Pattin	.15	.08	.05
27	Del Unser	.15	.08	.05
28	Bruce Kison	.15	.08	.05
29	Mark Wagner	.15	.08	.05
30	Vida Blue	.15	.08	.05
31	Jay Johnstone	.15	.08	.05
32	Julio Cruz	.15	.08	.05
33	Tony Scott	.15	.08	.05
34	Jeff Newman	.15	.08	.05
35	Luis Tiant	.15	.08	.05
36	Rusty Torres	.15	.08	.05
37	Kiko Garcia	.15	.08	.05
38	Dan Spillner	.15	.08	.05
39	Rowland Office	.15	.08	.05
40	Carlton Fisk	2.50	1.25	.70
41	Rangers Team (Pat Corrales)	.25	.13	.08
42	*Dave Palmer*	.15	.08	.05
43	Bombo Rivera	.15	.08	.05
44	Bill Fahey	.15	.08	.05
45	Frank White	.15	.08	.05
46	Rico Carty	.15	.08	.05
47	Bill Bonham	.15	.08	.05
48	Rick Miller	.15	.08	.05
49	Mario Guerrero	.15	.08	.05
50	J.R. Richard	.15	.08	.05
51	Joe Ferguson	.15	.08	.05
52	Warren Brusstar	.15	.08	.05
53	Ben Oglivie	.15	.08	.05
54	Dennis Lamp	.15	.08	.05
55	Bill Madlock	.15	.08	.05
56	Bobby Valentine	.15	.08	.05
57	Pete Vuckovich	.15	.08	.05
58	Doug Flynn	.15	.08	.05
59	Eddy Putman	.15	.08	.05
60	Bucky Dent	.20	.10	.06
61	Gary Serum	.15	.08	.05
62	Mike Ivie	.15	.08	.05
63	Bob Stanley	.15	.08	.05
64	Joe Nolan	.15	.08	.05
65	Al Bumbry	.15	.08	.05
66	Royals Team (Jim Frey)	.25	.13	.08
67	Doyle Alexander	.15	.08	.05
68	Larry Harlow	.15	.08	.05
69	Rick Williams	.15	.08	.05
70	Gary Carter	2.50	1.25	.70
71	John Milner	.15	.08	.05
72	Fred Howard	.15	.08	.05
73	Dave Collins	.15	.08	.05
74	Sid Monge	.15	.08	.05
75	Bill Russell	.15	.08	.05
76	John Stearns	.15	.08	.05
77	*Dave Stieb*	1.00	.50	.30
78	Ruppert Jones	.15	.08	.05
79	Bob Owchinko	.15	.08	.05
80	Ron LeFlore	.15	.08	.05
81	Ted Sizemore	.15	.08	.05
82	Astros Team (Bill Virdon)	.25	.13	.08
83	*Steve Trout*	.15	.08	.05
84	Gary Lavelle	.15	.08	.05
85	Ted Simmons	.15	.08	.05
86	Dave Hamilton	.15	.08	.05
87	Pepe Frias	.15	.08	.05
88	Ken Landreaux	.15	.08	.05
89	Don Hood	.15	.08	.05
90	Manny Trillo	.15	.08	.05
91	Rick Dempsey	.15	.08	.05
92	Rick Rhoden	.15	.08	.05
93	Dave Roberts	.15	.08	.05
94	*Neil Allen*	.15	.08	.05
95	Cecil Cooper	.15	.08	.05
96	A's Team (Jim Marshall)	.25	.13	.08
97	Bill Lee	.15	.08	.05
98	Jerry Terrell	.15	.08	.05
99	Victor Cruz	.15	.08	.05
100	Johnny Bench	3.00	1.50	.90
101	Aurelio Lopez	.15	.08	.05
102	Rich Dauer	.15	.08	.05
103	*Bill Caudill*	.15	.08	.05
104	Manny Mota	.15	.08	.05
105	Frank Tanana	.15	.08	.05
106	*Jeff Leonard*	.25	.13	.08
107	Francisco Barrios	.15	.08	.05
108	Bob Horner	.15	.08	.05
109	Bill Travers	.15	.08	.05
110	Fred Lynn	.15	.08	.05
111	Bob Knepper	.15	.08	.05
112	White Sox Team (Tony LaRussa)	.45	.25	.14
113	Geoff Zahn	.15	.08	.05
114	Juan Beniquez	.15	.08	.05
115	Sparky Lyle	.15	.08	.05
116	Larry Cox	.15	.08	.05
117	Dock Ellis	.15	.08	.05
118	Phil Garner	.15	.08	.05
119	Sammy Stewart	.15	.08	.05
120	Greg Luzinski	.15	.08	.05
121	Checklist 1-121	.15	.08	.05
122	Dave Rosello	.15	.08	.05
123	Lynn Jones	.15	.08	.05
124	Dave Lemanczyk	.15	.08	.05
125	Tony Perez	2.00	1.00	.60
126	Dave Tomlin	.15	.08	.05
127	Gary Thomasson	.15	.08	.05
128	Tom Burgmeier	.15	.08	.05
129	Craig Reynolds	.15	.08	.05
130	Amos Otis	.15	.08	.05
131	Paul Mitchell	.15	.08	.05
132	Biff Pocoroba	.15	.08	.05
133	Jerry Turner	.15	.08	.05
134	Matt Keough	.15	.08	.05
135	Bill Buckner	.15	.08	.05
136	Dick Ruthven	.15	.08	.05
137	*John Castino*	.15	.08	.05
138	Ross Baumgarten	.15	.08	.05
139	*Dane Iorg*	.15	.08	.05
140	Rich Gossage	.25	.13	.08
141	Gary Alexander	.15	.08	.05
142	Phil Huffman	.15	.08	.05
143	Bruce Bochte	.15	.08	.05
144	Steve Comer	.15	.08	.05
145	Darrell Evans	.15	.08	.05
146	Bob Welch	.15	.08	.05
147	Terry Puhl	.15	.08	.05
148	Manny Sanguillen	.15	.08	.05
149	Tom Hume	.15	.08	.05
150	Jason Thompson	.15	.08	.05
151	Tom Hausman	.15	.08	.05
152	John Fulgham	.15	.08	.05
153	Tim Blackwell	.15	.08	.05
154	Lary Sorensen	.15	.08	.05
155	Jerry Remy	.15	.08	.05
156	Tony Brizzolara	.15	.08	.05
157	Willie Wilson	.15	.08	.05
158	Rob Picciolo	.15	.08	.05
159	Ken Clay	.15	.08	.05
160	Eddie Murray	3.00	1.50	.90
161	Larry Christenson	.15	.08	.05
162	Bob Randall	.15	.08	.05
163	Steve Swisher	.15	.08	.05
164a	Greg Pryor (No name.)	200.00	100.00	60.00
164b	Greg Pryor (Name in blue.)	.15	.08	.05
165	Omar Moreno	.15	.08	.05
166	Glenn Abbott	.15	.08	.05
167	Jack Clark	.15	.08	.05
168	Rick Waits	.15	.08	.05
169	Luis Gomez	.15	.08	.05
170	Burt Hooton	.15	.08	.05
171	Fernando Gonzalez	.15	.08	.05
172	Ron Hodges	.15	.08	.05
173	John Henry Johnson	.15	.08	.05
174	Ray Knight	.15	.08	.05
175	Rick Reuschel	.15	.08	.05
176	Champ Summers	.15	.08	.05
177	Dave Heaverlo	.15	.08	.05
178	Tim McCarver	.15	.08	.05
179	*Ron Davis*	.25	.13	.08
180	Warren Cromartie	.15	.08	.05
181	Moose Haas	.15	.08	.05
182	Ken Reitz	.15	.08	.05
183	Jim Anderson	.15	.08	.05
184	Steve Renko	.15	.08	.05
185	Hal McRae	.15	.08	.05
186	Junior Moore	.15	.08	.05
187	Alan Ashby	.15	.08	.05
188	Terry Crowley	.15	.08	.05
189	Kevin Kobel	.15	.08	.05
190	Buddy Bell	.15	.08	.05
191	Ted Martinez	.15	.08	.05
192	Braves Team (Bobby Cox)	.45	.25	.14
193	Dave Goltz	.15	.08	.05
194	Mike Easler	.15	.08	.05
195	John Montefusco	.15	.08	.05
196	Lance Parrish	.15	.08	.05
197	Byron McLaughlin	.15	.08	.05
198	Dell Alston	.15	.08	.05
199	Mike LaCoss	.15	.08	.05
200	Jim Rice	.30	.15	.09
201	Batting Leaders (Keith Hernandez, Fred Lynn)	.15	.08	.05
202	Home Run Leaders (Dave Kingman, Gorman Thomas)	.15	.08	.05
203	Runs Batted In Leaders (Don Baylor, Dave Winfield)	.35	.20	.11
204	Stolen Base Leaders (Omar Moreno, Willie Wilson)	.15	.08	.05
205	Victory Leaders (Mike Flanagan, Joe Niekro, Phil Niekro)	.25	.13	.08
206	Strikeout Leaders (J.R. Richard, Nolan Ryan)	3.50	1.75	1.00
207	ERA Leaders (Ron Guidry, J.R. Richard)	.25	.13	.08
208	Wayne Cage	.15	.08	.05
209	Von Joshua	.15	.08	.05
210	Steve Carlton	2.50	1.25	.70
211	Dave Skaggs	.15	.08	.05
212	Dave Roberts	.15	.08	.05
213	Mike Jorgensen	.15	.08	.05
214	Angels Team (Jim Fregosi)	.25	.13	.08
215	Sixto Lezcano	.15	.08	.05
216	Phil Mankowski	.15	.08	.05
217	Ed Halicki	.15	.08	.05
218	Jose Morales	.15	.08	.05
219	Steve Mingori	.15	.08	.05
220	Dave Concepcion	.15	.08	.05
221	Joe Cannon	.15	.08	.05
222	*Ron Hassey*	.25	.13	.08
223	Bob Sykes	.15	.08	.05
224	Willie Montanez	.15	.08	.05
225	Lou Piniella	.25	.13	.08
226	Bill Stein	.15	.08	.05
227	Len Barker	.15	.08	.05
228	Johnny Oates	.15	.08	.05
229	Jim Bibby	.15	.08	.05
230	Dave Winfield	2.50	1.25	.70
231	Steve McCatty	.15	.08	.05
232	Alan Trammell	.60	.30	.20
233	LaRue Washington	.15	.08	.05
234	Vern Ruhle	.15	.08	.05
235	Andre Dawson	1.00	.50	.30
236	Marc Hill	.15	.08	.05
237	Scott McGregor	.15	.08	.05
238	Rob Wilfong	.15	.08	.05
239	Don Aase	.15	.08	.05
240	Dave Kingman	.15	.08	.05
241	Checklist 122-242	.15	.08	.05
242	Lamar Johnson	.15	.08	.05
243	Jerry Augustine	.15	.08	.05
244	Cardinals Team (Ken Boyer)	.25	.13	.08
245	Phil Niekro	2.00	1.00	.60
246	Tim Foli	.15	.08	.05
247	Frank Riccelli	.15	.08	.05
248	Jamie Quirk	.15	.08	.05
249	Jim Clancy	.15	.08	.05
250	Jim Kaat	.15	.08	.05
251	Kip Young	.15	.08	.05
252	Ted Cox	.15	.08	.05
253	John Montague	.15	.08	.05
254	Paul Dade	.15	.08	.05
255	Dusty Baker	.15	.08	.05
256	Roger Erickson	.15	.08	.05
257	Larry Herndon	.15	.08	.05
258	Paul Moskau	.15	.08	.05
259	Mets Team (Joe Torre)	.60	.30	.20
260	Al Oliver	.20	.10	.06
261	Dave Chalk	.15	.08	.05
262	Benny Ayala	.15	.08	.05
263	Dave LaRoche	.15	.08	.05
264	Bill Robinson	.15	.08	.05
265	Robin Yount	2.50	1.25	.70
266	Bernie Carbo	.15	.08	.05
267	Dan Schatzeder	.15	.08	.05
268	Rafael Landestoy	.15	.08	.05
269	Dave Tobik	.15	.08	.05
270	Mike Schmidt	4.50	2.25	1.25
271	Dick Drago	.15	.08	.05
272	Ralph Garr	.15	.08	.05
273	Eduardo Rodriguez	.15	.08	.05
274	Dale Murphy	1.50	.70	.45
275	Jerry Koosman	.15	.08	.05
276	Tom Veryzer	.15	.08	.05
277	Rick Bosetti	.15	.08	.05
278	Jim Spencer	.15	.08	.05
279	Rob Andrews	.15	.08	.05
280	Gaylord Perry	2.00	1.00	.60
281	Paul Blair	.15	.08	.05
282	Mariners Team (Darrell Johnson)	.25	.13	.08
283	John Ellis	.15	.08	.05
284	Larry Murray	.15	.08	.05
285	Don Baylor	.25	.13	.08
286	Darold Knowles	.15	.08	.05
287	John Lowenstein	.15	.08	.05
288	Dave Rozema	.15	.08	.05
289	Bruce Bochy	.15	.08	.05
290	Steve Garvey	1.00	.50	.30
291	Randy Scarbery	.15	.08	.05
292	Dale Berra	.15	.08	.05
293	Elias Sosa	.15	.08	.05
294	Charlie Spikes	.15	.08	.05
295	Larry Gura	.15	.08	.05
296	Dave Rader	.15	.08	.05
297	Tim Johnson	.15	.08	.05
298	Ken Holtzman	.15	.08	.05
299	Steve Henderson	.15	.08	.05
300	Ron Guidry	.25	.13	.08
301	Mike Edwards	.15	.08	.05
302	Dodgers Team (Tom Lasorda)	.60	.30	.20
303	Bill Castro	.15	.08	.05
304	Butch Wynegar	.15	.08	.05
305	Randy Jones	.15	.08	.05
306	Denny Walling	.15	.08	.05
307	Rick Honeycutt	.15	.08	.05
308	Mike Hargrove	.15	.08	.05
309	Larry McWilliams	.15	.08	.05
310	Dave Parker	.15	.08	.05
311	Roger Metzger	.15	.08	.05
312	Mike Barlow	.15	.08	.05
313	Johnny Grubb	.15	.08	.05
314	*Tim Stoddard*	.15	.08	.05
315	Steve Kemp	.15	.08	.05
316	Bob Lacey	.15	.08	.05
317	Mike Anderson	.15	.08	.05
318	Jerry Reuss	.15	.08	.05
319	Chris Speier	.15	.08	.05
320	Dennis Eckersley	2.00	1.00	.60
321	Keith Hernandez	.15	.08	.05
322	Claudell Washington	.15	.08	.05
323	Mick Kelleher	.15	.08	.05
324	Tom Underwood	.15	.08	.05
325	Dan Driessen	.15	.08	.05
326	Bo McLaughlin	.15	.08	.05
327	Ray Fosse	.15	.08	.05
328	Twins Team (Gene Mauch)	.25	.13	.08
329	Bert Roberge	.15	.08	.05
330	Al Cowens	.15	.08	.05
331	Rich Hebner	.15	.08	.05
332	Enrique Romo	.15	.08	.05
333	Jim Norris	.15	.08	.05
334	Jim Beattie	.15	.08	.05
335	Willie McCovey	2.50	1.25	.70
336	George Medich	.15	.08	.05
337	Carney Lansford	.15	.08	.05
338	Johnny Wockenfuss	.15	.08	.05
339	John D'Acquisto	.15	.08	.05
340	Ken Singleton	.15	.08	.05
341	Jim Essian	.15	.08	.05
342	Odell Jones	.15	.08	.05
343	Mike Vail	.15	.08	.05
344	Randy Lerch	.15	.08	.05
345	Larry Parrish	.15	.08	.05
346	Buddy Solomon	.15	.08	.05
347	*Harry Chappas*	.15	.08	.05
348	Checklist 243-363	.15	.08	.05
349	Jack Brohamer	.15	.08	.05
350	George Hendrick	.15	.08	.05
351	Bob Davis	.15	.08	.05
352	Dan Briggs	.15	.08	.05
353	Andy Hassler	.15	.08	.05
354	Rick Auerbach	.15	.08	.05
355	Gary Matthews	.15	.08	.05
356	Padres Team (Jerry Coleman)	.25	.13	.08
357	Bob McClure	.15	.08	.05
358	Lou Whitaker	.25	.13	.08

#	Name			
359	Randy Moffitt	.15	.08	.05
360	Darrell Porter	.15	.08	.05
361	Wayne Garland	.15	.08	.05
362	Danny Goodwin	.15	.08	.05
363	Wayne Gross	.15	.08	.05
364	Ray Burris	.15	.08	.05
365	Bobby Murcer	.25	.13	.08
366	Rob Dressler	.15	.08	.05
367	Billy Smith	.15	.08	.05
368	*Willie Aikens*	.20	.10	.06
369	Jim Kern	.15	.08	.05
370	Cesar Cedeno	.15	.08	.05
371	Jack Morris	.15	.08	.05
372	Joel Youngblood	.15	.08	.05
373	*Dan Petry*	.20	.10	.06
374	Jim Gantner	.15	.08	.05
375	Ross Grimsley	.15	.08	.05
376	Gary Allenson	.15	.08	.05
377	Junior Kennedy	.15	.08	.05
378	Jerry Mumphrey	.15	.08	.05
379	Kevin Bell	.15	.08	.05
380	Garry Maddox	.15	.08	.05
381	Cubs Team (Preston Gomez)	.25	.13	.08
382	Dave Freisleben	.15	.08	.05
383	Ed Ott	.15	.08	.05
384	Joey McLaughlin	.15	.08	.05
385	Enos Cabell	.15	.08	.05
386	Darrell Jackson	.15	.08	.05
387a	Fred Stanley (Name in yellow.)	260.00	130.00	78.00
387b	Fred Stanley (Name in red.)	.15	.08	.05
388	Mike Paxton	.15	.08	.05
389	Pete LaCock	.15	.08	.05
390	Fergie Jenkins	2.00	1.00	.60
391	Tony Armas	.15	.08	.05
392	Milt Wilcox	.15	.08	.05
393	Ozzie Smith	8.00	4.00	2.00
394	Reggie Cleveland	.15	.08	.05
395	Ellis Valentine	.15	.08	.05
396	Dan Meyer	.15	.08	.05
397	Roy Thomas	.15	.08	.05
398	Barry Foote	.15	.08	.05
399	Mike Proly	.15	.08	.05
400	George Foster	.15	.08	.05
401	Pete Falcone	.15	.08	.05
402	Merv Rettenmund	.15	.08	.05
403	Pete Redfern	.15	.08	.05
404	Orioles Team (Earl Weaver)	.60	.30	.20
405	Dwight Evans	.15	.08	.05
406	Paul Molitor	2.50	1.25	.70
407	Tony Solaita	.15	.08	.05
408	Bill North	.15	.08	.05
409	Paul Splittorff	.15	.08	.05
410	Bobby Bonds	.15	.08	.05
411	Frank LaCorte	.15	.08	.05
412	Thad Bosley	.15	.08	.05
413	Allen Ripley	.15	.08	.05
414	George Scott	.15	.08	.05
415	Bill Atkinson	.15	.08	.05
416	*Tom Brookens*	.15	.08	.05
417	Craig Chamberlain	.15	.08	.05
418	Roger Freed	.15	.08	.05
419	Vic Correll	.15	.08	.05
420	Butch Hobson	.15	.08	.05
421	Doug Bird	.15	.08	.05
422	Larry Milbourne	.15	.08	.05
423	Dave Frost	.15	.08	.05
424	Yankees Team (Dick Howser)	.45	.25	.14
425	Mark Belanger	.15	.08	.05
426	Grant Jackson	.15	.08	.05
427	Tom Hutton	.15	.08	.05
428	Pat Zachry	.15	.08	.05
429	Duane Kuiper	.15	.08	.05
430	Larry Hisle	.15	.08	.05
431	Mike Krukow	.15	.08	.05
432	Willie Norwood	.15	.08	.05
433	Rich Gale	.15	.08	.05
434	Johnnie LeMaster	.15	.08	.05
435	Don Gullett	.15	.08	.05
436	Billy Almon	.15	.08	.05
437	Joe Niekro	.15	.08	.05
438	Dave Revering	.15	.08	.05
439	Mike Phillips	.15	.08	.05
440	Don Sutton	2.00	1.00	.60
441	Eric Soderholm	.15	.08	.05
442	Jorge Orta	.15	.08	.05
443	Mike Parrott	.15	.08	.05
444	Alvis Woods	.15	.08	.05
445	Mark Fidrych	.25	.13	.08
446	Duffy Dyer	.15	.08	.05
447	Nino Espinosa	.15	.08	.05
448	Jim Wohlford	.15	.08	.05
449	Doug Bair	.15	.08	.05
450	George Brett	6.00	3.00	1.50
451	Indians Team (Dave Garcia)	.25	.13	.08
452	Steve Dillard	.15	.08	.05
453	Mike Bacsik	.15	.08	.05
454	Tom Donohue	.15	.08	.05
455	Mike Torrez	.15	.08	.05
456	Frank Taveras	.15	.08	.05
457	Bert Blyleven	.15	.08	.05
458	Billy Sample	.15	.08	.05
459	Mickey Lolich	.15	.08	.05
460	Willie Randolph	.15	.08	.05
461	Dwayne Murphy	.15	.08	.05
462	Mike Sadek	.15	.08	.05
463	Jerry Royster	.15	.08	.05
464	John Denny	.15	.08	.05
465	Rick Monday	.15	.08	.05
466	Mike Squires	.15	.08	.05
467	Jesse Jefferson	.15	.08	.05
468	Aurelio Rodriguez	.15	.08	.05
469	Randy Niemann	.15	.08	.05
470	Bob Boone	.20	.10	.06
471	Hosken Powell	.15	.08	.05
472	Willie Hernandez	.15	.08	.05
473	Bump Wills	.15	.08	.05
474	Steve Busby	.15	.08	.05

#	Name			
475	Cesar Geronimo	.15	.08	.05
476	Bob Shirley	.15	.08	.05
477	Buck Martinez	.15	.08	.05
478	Gil Flores	.15	.08	.05
479	Expos Team (Dick Williams)	.25	.13	.08
480	Bob Watson	.15	.08	.05
481	Tom Paciorek	.15	.08	.05
482	*Rickey Henderson*	55.00	27.50	13.75
483	Bo Diaz	.15	.08	.05
484	Checklist 364-484	.15	.08	.05
485	Mickey Rivers	.15	.08	.05
486	Mike Tyson	.15	.08	.05
487	Wayne Nordhagen	.15	.08	.05
488	Roy Howell	.15	.08	.05
489	Preston Hanna	.15	.08	.05
490	Lee May	.15	.08	.05
491	Steve Mura	.15	.08	.05
492	Todd Cruz	.15	.08	.05
493	Jerry Martin	.15	.08	.05
494	Craig Minetto	.15	.08	.05
495	Bake McBride	.15	.08	.05
496	Silvio Martinez	.15	.08	.05
497	Jim Mason	.15	.08	.05
498	Danny Darwin	.15	.08	.05
499	Giants Team (Dave Bristol)	.25	.13	.08
500	Tom Seaver	3.00	1.50	.90
501	Rennie Stennett	.15	.08	.05
502	Rich Wortham	.15	.08	.05
503	Mike Cubbage	.15	.08	.05
504	Gene Garber	.15	.08	.05
505	Bert Campaneris	.15	.08	.05
506	Tom Buskey	.15	.08	.05
507	Leon Roberts	.15	.08	.05
508	U.L. Washington	.15	.08	.05
509	Ed Glynn	.15	.08	.05
510	Ron Cey	.15	.08	.05
511	Eric Wilkins	.15	.08	.05
512	Jose Cardenal	.15	.08	.05
513	Tom Dixon	.15	.08	.05
514	Steve Ontiveros	.15	.08	.05
515	Mike Caldwell	.15	.08	.05
516	Hector Cruz	.15	.08	.05
517	Don Stanhouse	.15	.08	.05
518	Nelson Norman	.15	.08	.05
519	Steve Nicosia	.15	.08	.05
520	Steve Rogers	.15	.08	.05
521	Ken Brett	.15	.08	.05
522	Jim Morrison	.15	.08	.05
523	Ken Henderson	.15	.08	.05
524	Jim Wright	.15	.08	.05
525	Clint Hurdle	.15	.08	.05
526	Phillies Team (Dallas Green)	.60	.30	.20
527	Doug Rau	.15	.08	.05
528	Adrian Devine	.15	.08	.05
529	Jim Barr	.15	.08	.05
530	Jim Sundberg	.15	.08	.05
531	Eric Rasmussen	.15	.08	.05
532	Willie Horton	.15	.08	.05
533	Checklist 485-605	.15	.08	.05
534	Andre Thornton	.15	.08	.05
535	Bob Forsch	.15	.08	.05
536	Lee Lacy	.15	.08	.05
537	*Alex Trevino*	.15	.08	.05
538	Joe Strain	.15	.08	.05
539	Rudy May	.15	.08	.05
540	Pete Rose	6.00	3.00	1.50
541	Miguel Dilone	.15	.08	.05
542	Joe Coleman	.15	.08	.05
543	Pat Kelly	.15	.08	.05
544	*Rick Sutcliffe*	2.00	1.00	.60
545	Jeff Burroughs	.15	.08	.05
546	Rick Langford	.15	.08	.05
547a	John Wathan (Name in yellow.)	200.00	100.00	60.00
547b	John Wathan (Name in red.)	.15	.08	.05
548	Dave Rajsich	.15	.08	.05
549	Larry Wolfe	.15	.08	.05
550	Ken Griffey	.15	.08	.05
551	Pirates Team (Chuck Tanner)	.25	.13	.08
552	Bill Nahorodny	.15	.08	.05
553	Dick Davis	.15	.08	.05
554	Art Howe	.15	.08	.05
555	Ed Figueroa	.15	.08	.05
556	Joe Rudi	.15	.08	.05
557	Mark Lee	.15	.08	.05
558	Alfredo Griffin	.15	.08	.05
559	Dale Murray	.15	.08	.05
560	Dave Lopes	.15	.08	.05
561	Eddie Whitson	.15	.08	.05
562	Joe Wallis	.15	.08	.05
563	Will McEnaney	.15	.08	.05
564	Rick Manning	.15	.08	.05
565	Dennis Leonard	.15	.08	.05
566	Bud Harrelson	.15	.08	.05
567	Skip Lockwood	.15	.08	.05
568	*Gary Roenicke*	.15	.08	.05
569	Terry Kennedy	.15	.08	.05
570	Roy Smalley	.15	.08	.05
571	Joe Sambito	.15	.08	.05
572	Jerry Morales	.15	.08	.05
573	Kent Tekulve	.15	.08	.05
574	Scot Thompson	.15	.08	.05
575	Ken Kravec	.15	.08	.05
576	Jim Dwyer	.15	.08	.05
577	Blue Jays Team (Bobby Mattick)	.25	.13	.08
578	Scott Sanderson	.15	.08	.05
579	Charlie Moore	.15	.08	.05
580	Nolan Ryan	15.00	7.50	3.75
581	Bob Bailor	.15	.08	.05
582	Brian Doyle	.15	.08	.05
583	Bob Stinson	.15	.08	.05
584	Kurt Bevacqua	.15	.08	.05
585	Al Hrabosky	.15	.08	.05
586	Mitchell Page	.15	.08	.05
587	Garry Templeton	.15	.08	.05
588	Greg Minton	.15	.08	.05
589	Chet Lemon	.15	.08	.05

#	Name			
590	Jim Palmer	2.50	1.25	.70
591	Rick Cerone	.15	.08	.05
592	Jon Matlack	.15	.08	.05
593	Jesus Alou	.15	.08	.05
594	Dick Tidrow	.15	.08	.05
595	Don Money	.15	.08	.05
596	Rick Matula	.15	.08	.05
597a	Tom Poquette (Name in yellow.)	200.00	100.00	60.00
597b	Tom Poquette (Name in red.)	.15	.08	.05
598	Fred Kendall	.15	.08	.05
599	Mike Norris	.15	.08	.05
600	Reggie Jackson	4.00	2.00	1.25
601	Buddy Schultz	.15	.08	.05
602	Brian Downing	.15	.08	.05
603	Jack Billingham	.15	.08	.05
604	Glenn Adams	.15	.08	.05
605	Terry Forster	.15	.08	.05
606	Reds Team (John McNamara)	.25	.13	.08
607	Woodie Fryman	.15	.08	.05
608	Alan Bannister	.15	.08	.05
609	Ron Reed	.15	.08	.05
610	Willie Stargell	2.50	1.25	.70
611	Jerry Garvin	.15	.08	.05
612	Cliff Johnson	.15	.08	.05
613	Randy Stein	.15	.08	.05
614	John Hiller	.15	.08	.05
615	Doug DeCinces	.15	.08	.05
616	Gene Richards	.15	.08	.05
617	Joaquin Andujar	.15	.08	.05
618	Bob Montgomery	.15	.08	.05
619	Sergio Ferrer	.15	.08	.05
620	Richie Zisk	.15	.08	.05
621	Bob Grich	.15	.08	.05
622	Mario Soto	.15	.08	.05
623	Gorman Thomas	.15	.08	.05
624	Lerrin LaGrow	.15	.08	.05
625	Chris Chambliss	.15	.08	.05
626	Tigers Team (Sparky Anderson)	.75	.40	.25
627	Pedro Borbon	.15	.08	.05
628	Doug Capilla	.15	.08	.05
629	Jim Todd	.15	.08	.05
630	Larry Bowa	.15	.08	.05
631	Mark Littell	.15	.08	.05
632	Barry Bonnell	.15	.08	.05
633	Bob Apodaca	.15	.08	.05
634	Glenn Borgmann	.15	.08	.05
635	John Candelaria	.15	.08	.05
636	Toby Harrah	.15	.08	.05
637	Joe Simpson	.15	.08	.05
638	*Mark Clear*	.15	.08	.05
639	Larry Biittner	.15	.08	.05
640	Mike Flanagan	.15	.08	.05
641	Ed Kranepool	.15	.08	.05
642	Ken Forsch	.15	.08	.05
643	John Mayberry	.15	.08	.05
644	Charlie Hough	.15	.08	.05
645	Rick Burleson	.15	.08	.05
646	Checklist 606-726	.15	.08	.05
647	Milt May	.15	.08	.05
648	Roy White	.15	.08	.05
649	Tom Griffin	.15	.08	.05
650	Joe Morgan	2.50	1.25	.70
651	Rollie Fingers	2.00	1.00	.60
652	Mario Mendoza	.15	.08	.05
653	Stan Bahnsen	.15	.08	.05
654	Bruce Boisclair	.15	.08	.05
655	Tug McGraw	.15	.08	.05
656	Larvell Blanks	.15	.08	.05
657	Dave Edwards	.15	.08	.05
658	Chris Knapp	.15	.08	.05
659	Brewers Team (George Bamberger)	.25	.13	.08
660	Rusty Staub	.15	.08	.05
661	Orioles Future Stars (Mark Corey, Dave Ford, Wayne Krenchicki)	.15	.08	.05
662	Red Sox Future Stars (Joel Finch, Mike O'Berry, Chuck Rainey)	.15	.08	.05
663	Angels Future Stars (*Ralph Botting, Bob Clark, Dickie Thon*)	.25	.13	.08
664	White Sox Future Stars (*Mike Colbern, Guy Hoffman, Dewey Robinson*)	.15	.08	.05
665	Indians Future Stars (Larry Andersen, Bobby Cuellar, Sandy Wihtol)	.15	.08	.05
666	Tigers Future Stars (Mike Chris, Al Greene, Bruce Robbins)	.15	.08	.05
667	Royals Future Stars (*Renie Martin, Bill Paschall, Dan Quisenberry*)	1.00	.50	.30
668	Brewers Future Stars (Danny Boitano, Willie Mueller, Lenn Sakata)	.15	.08	.05
669	Twins Future Stars (*Dan Graham, Rick Sofield, Gary Ward*)	.25	.13	.08
670	Yankees Future Stars (Bobby Brown, Brad Gulden, Darryl Jones)	.15	.08	.05
671	A's Future Stars (*Derek Bryant, Brian Kingman, Mike Morgan*)	.50	.25	.15
672	Mariners Future Stars (Charlie Beamon, Rodney Craig, Rafael Vasquez)	.15	.08	.05
673	Rangers Future Stars (Brian Allard, Jerry Don Gleaton, Greg Mahlberg)	.15	.08	.05
674	Blue Jays Future Stars (Butch Edge, Pat Kelly, Ted Wilborn)	.15	.08	.05

675	Braves Future Stars (Bruce Benedict, Larry Bradford, Eddie Miller)	.15	.08	.05
676	Cubs Future Stars (Dave Geisel, Steve Macko, Karl Pagel)	.15	.08	.05
677	Reds Future Stars (Art DeFreites, Frank Pastore, Harry Spilman)	.15	.08	.05
678	Astros Future Stars (*Reggie Baldwin, Alan Knicely, Pete Ladd*)	.15	.08	.05
679	Dodgers Future Stars (*Joe Beckwith, Mickey Hatcher, Dave Patterson*)	.25	.13	.08
680	Expos Future Stars (*Tony Bernazard, Randy Miller, John Tamargo*)	.15	.08	.05
681	Mets Future Stars (*Dan Norman, Jesse Orosco, Mike Scott*)	1.00	.50	.30
682	Phillies Future Stars (*Ramon Aviles, Dickie Noles, Kevin Saucier*)	.15	.08	.05
683	Pirates Future Stars (Dorian Boyland, Alberto Lois, Harry Saferight)	.15	.08	.05
684	Cardinals Future Stars (*George Frazier, Tom Herr, Dan O'Brien*)	.30	.15	.09
685	Padres Future Stars (Tim Flannery, Brian Greer, Jim Wilhelm)	.15	.08	.05
686	Giants Future Stars (Greg Johnston, Dennis Littlejohn, Phil Nastu)	.15	.08	.05
687	Mike Heath	.15	.08	.05
688	Steve Stone	.15	.08	.05
689	Red Sox Team (Don Zimmer)	.25	.13	.08
690	Tommy John	.25	.13	.08
691	Ivan DeJesus	.15	.08	.05
692	Rawly Eastwick	.15	.08	.05
693	Craig Kusick	.15	.08	.05
694	Jim Rooker	.15	.08	.05
695	Reggie Smith	.15	.08	.05
696	Julio Gonzalez	.15	.08	.05
697	David Clyde	.15	.08	.05
698	Oscar Gamble	.15	.08	.05
699	Floyd Bannister	.15	.08	.05
700	Rod Carew	2.50	1.25	.70
701	*Ken Oberkfell*	.15	.08	.05
702	Ed Farmer	.15	.08	.05
703	Otto Velez	.15	.08	.05
704	Gene Tenace	.15	.08	.05
705	Freddie Patek	.15	.08	.05
706	Tippy Martinez	.15	.08	.05
707	Elliott Maddox	.15	.08	.05
708	Bob Tolan	.15	.08	.05
709	Pat Underwood	.15	.08	.05
710	Graig Nettles	.25	.13	.08
711	Bob Galasso	.15	.08	.05
712	Rodney Scott	.15	.08	.05
713	Terry Whitfield	.15	.08	.05
714	Fred Norman	.15	.08	.05
715	Sal Bando	.15	.08	.05
716	Lynn McGlothen	.15	.08	.05
717	Mickey Klutts	.15	.08	.05
718	Greg Gross	.15	.08	.05
719	Don Robinson	.15	.08	.05
720	Carl Yastrzemski	3.00	1.50	.90
721	Paul Hartzell	.15	.08	.05
722	Jose Cruz	.15	.08	.05
723	Shane Rawley	.15	.08	.05
724	Jerry White	.15	.08	.05
725	Rick Wise	.15	.08	.05
726	Steve Yeager	.15	.08	.05

1980 Topps Team Checklist Sheet

This uncut sheet of 26 1980 Topps team cards was available via a mail-in offer. The sheet was mailed with two folds and includes an offer to picture yourself on a baseball card. The sheet cards are printed on lighter card stock.

	NM	EX	VG
Uncut Sheet	15.00	7.50	4.50

1980 Topps N.Y. Yankees Proof

One of the most popular proof cards of the era is this N.Y. Yankees team photo card with an inset photo of manager Billy Martin, who was fired in October, 1979, after punching a marshmellow salesman. By the time the cards were issued, Martin's name and photo had been replaced by rookie manager Dick Howser. The card is blank-backed and usually shows evidence of having been handcut from a proof sheet.

	NM	EX	VG
N.Y. Yankees	200.00	100.00	60.00

1980 Topps Stickers Prototypes

These appear to be prototypes for a Topp sticker issue that never materialized. In 3-1/2" x 2-1/2" format, the pieces have player picture pairs stuck onto a cardboard backing. Backs are blank. It is unknown if the listed examples, all of which are unique, comprise the entirety of the samples.

		NM	EX	VG
Common Card:		125.00	60.00	35.00
(1)	Johnny Bench, Maury Wills	200.00	100.00	60.00
(2)	Nino Espinosa, Ron Cey	125.00	60.00	35.00
(3)	Dwight Evans, Carlton Fisk	150.00	75.00	45.00
(4)	Don (Ron) Guidry, Dave Parker	125.00	60.00	35.00
(5)	Reggie Jackson, J.R. Richard	200.00	100.00	60.00

1980 Topps Superstar 5x7 Photos

In actuality, these cards measure 4-7/8" x 6-7/8". These were another Topps "test" issue that was bought out almost entirely by speculators. The 60 cards have a color photo on the front and a blue ink facsimile autograph. Backs have the player's name, team, position and card number. The issue was printed on different cardboard stocks, with the first on thick cardboard with a white back and the second on thinner cardboard with a gray back. Prices below are for the more common gray backs; white backs are valued 2.5X-3X the figures shown, except for triple-print cards (indicated by "3P" in checklist), which are valued at about 7.5X the gray-back price in the white-back version. The white backs were test marketed in three-card cello packs in selected geographical areas.

		NM	EX	VG
Complete Set, Gray Backs (60):		10.00	5.00	3.00
Complete Set, White Backs (60):		20.00	10.00	6.00
Common Player, Gray Back:		.25	.13	.08
Common Player, White Back:		.75	.40	.25
Wax Box (48):		10.00		
1	Willie Stargell	1.00	.50	.30
2	Mike Schmidt (3P)	1.50	.70	.45
3	Johnny Bench	1.00	.50	.30
4	Jim Palmer	.75	.40	.25
5	Jim Rice	.50	.25	.15
6	Reggie Jackson (3P)	1.50	.70	.45
7	Ron Guidry	.45	.25	.14
8	Lee Mazzilli	.25	.13	.08
9	Don Baylor	.50	.25	.15
10	Fred Lynn	.25	.13	.08
11	Ken Singleton	.25	.13	.08
12	Rod Carew (3P)	.75	.40	.25
13	Steve Garvey (3P)	.50	.25	.15
14	George Brett (3P)	1.50	.70	.45
15	Tom Seaver	1.50	.70	.45
16	Dave Kingman	.25	.13	.08
17	Dave Parker (3P)	.25	.13	.08
18	Dave Winfield	1.00	.50	.30
19	Pete Rose	2.00	1.00	.60
20	Nolan Ryan	4.00	2.00	1.25
21	Graig Nettles	.25	.13	.08
22	Carl Yastrzemski	1.50	.70	.45
23	Tommy John	.40	.20	.12
24	George Foster	.25	.13	.08
25	J.R. Richard	.25	.13	.08
26	Keith Hernandez	.25	.13	.08
27	Bob Horner	.25	.13	.08
28	Eddie Murray	1.50	.70	.45
29	Steve Kemp	.25	.13	.08
30	Gorman Thomas	.25	.13	.08
31	Sixto Lezcano	.25	.13	.08
32	Bruce Sutter	1.00	.50	.30
33	Cecil Cooper	.25	.13	.08
34	Larry Bowa	.25	.13	.08
35	Al Oliver	.35	.20	.11

36	Ted Simmons	.25	.13	.08
37	Garry Templeton	.25	.13	.08
38	Jerry Koosman	.25	.13	.08
39	Darrell Porter	.25	.13	.08
40	Roy Smalley	.25	.13	.08
41	Craig Swan	.25	.13	.08
42	Jason Thompson	.25	.13	.08
43	Andre Thornton	.25	.13	.08
44	Rick Manning	.25	.13	.08
45	Kent Tekulve	.25	.13	.08
46	Phil Niekro	.75	.40	.25
47	Buddy Bell	.25	.13	.08
48	Randy Jones	.25	.13	.08
49	Brian Downing	.25	.13	.08
50	Amos Otis	.25	.13	.08
51	Rick Bosetti	.25	.13	.08
52	Gary Carter	.75	.40	.25
53	Larry Parrish	.25	.13	.08
54	Jack Clark	.25	.13	.08
55	Bruce Bochte	.25	.13	.08
56	Cesar Cedeno	.25	.13	.08
57	Chet Lemon	.25	.13	.08
58	Dave Revering	.25	.13	.08
59	Vida Blue	.25	.13	.08
60	Davey Lopes	.25	.13	.08

1980 Topps Test Coins

These silver-dollar size (1-3/8" diameter) metal coins appear to have been a Topps test issue. The coins have a player portrait at center on obverse. On reverse center is player personal data and a Topps copyright line. Coins have been seen in compositions resembling bronze, silver and gold. Some of the coins have a hole at top.

	NM	EX	VG
Rod Carew	150.00	75.00	45.00
Steve Garvey	150.00	75.00	45.00
Reggie Jackson	300.00	150.00	90.00

1953 Top Taste Bread Milwaukee Braves

This series of black-and-white mini-posters (8-1/2" x 11-1/4") depicts members of the 1953 Braves holding loaves of bread. They were probably intended for grocery store window or bakery aisle display. Backs are blank. It's unknown how many players are in the set. See also, Pictsweet Milwaukee Braves.

		NM	EX	VG
Common Player:		150.00	75.00	45.00
(1)	Lew Burdette	150.00	75.00	45.00
(2)	George Crowe	150.00	75.00	45.00
(3)	Andy Pafko	150.00	75.00	45.00
(4)	Bucky Walters	150.00	75.00	45.00

1976 Towne Club Discs

One of several regional sponsors of player disc sets in 1976 was the Towne Club Pop Centers chain. The discs are 3-3/8" diameter with a black-and-white player portrait photo in the center of the baseball design. A line of red stars is above, while the left and right panels feature one of several bright colors. Produced by Michael Schecter Associates under license from the Major League Baseball Players Association, the player photos have had uniform and cap logos removed. Backs are printed in red. The unnumbered checklist here is presented in alphabetical order.

	NM	EX	VG
Complete Set (70):	50.00	25.00	15.00
Common Player:	1.00	.50	.30
(1) Henry Aaron	10.00	5.00	3.00
(2) Johnny Bench	5.00	2.50	1.50
(3) Vida Blue	1.00	.50	.30
(4) Larry Bowa	1.00	.50	.30
(5) Lou Brock	4.00	2.00	1.25
(6) Jeff Burroughs	1.00	.50	.30
(7) John Candelaria	1.00	.50	.30
(8) Jose Cardenal	1.00	.50	.30
(9) Rod Carew	4.00	2.00	1.25
(10) Steve Carlton	4.00	2.00	1.25
(11) Dave Cash	1.00	.50	.30
(12) Cesar Cedeno	1.00	.50	.30
(13) Ron Cey	1.00	.50	.30
(14) Carlton Fisk	4.00	2.00	1.25
(15) Tito Fuentes	1.00	.50	.30
(16) Steve Garvey	3.00	1.50	.90
(17) Ken Griffey	1.00	.50	.30
(18) Don Gullett	1.00	.50	.30
(19) Willie Horton	1.00	.50	.30
(20) Al Hrabosky	1.00	.50	.30
(21) Catfish Hunter	4.00	2.00	1.25
(22) Reggie Jackson (A's)	7.50	3.75	2.25
(23) Randy Jones	1.00	.50	.30
(24) Jim Kaat	1.00	.50	.30
(25) Don Kessinger	1.00	.50	.30
(26) Dave Kingman	1.00	.50	.30
(27) Jerry Koosman	1.00	.50	.30
(28) Mickey Lolich	1.00	.50	.30
(29) Greg Luzinski	1.00	.50	.30
(30) Fred Lynn	1.00	.50	.30
(31) Bill Madlock	1.00	.50	.30
(32) Carlos May	1.00	.50	.30
(33) John Mayberry	1.00	.50	.30
(34) Bake McBride	1.00	.50	.30
(35) Doc Medich	1.00	.50	.30
(36) Andy Messersmith	1.00	.50	.30
(37) Rick Monday	1.00	.50	.30
(38) John Montefusco	1.00	.50	.30
(39) Jerry Morales	1.00	.50	.30
(40) Joe Morgan	4.00	2.00	1.25
(41) Thurman Munson	5.00	2.50	1.50
(42) Bobby Murcer	1.00	.50	.30
(43) Al Oliver	1.00	.50	.30
(44) Jim Palmer	4.00	2.00	1.25
(45) Dave Parker	1.00	.50	.30
(46) Tony Perez	4.00	2.00	1.25
(47) Jerry Reuss	1.00	.50	.30
(48) Brooks Robinson	5.00	2.50	1.50
(49) Frank Robinson	5.00	2.50	1.50
(50) Steve Rogers	1.00	.50	.30
(51) Pete Rose	10.00	5.00	3.00
(52) Nolan Ryan	20.00	10.00	6.00
(53) Manny Sanguillen	1.00	.50	.30
(54) Mike Schmidt	7.50	3.75	2.25
(55) Tom Seaver	5.00	2.50	1.50
(56) Ted Simmons	1.00	.50	.30
(57) Reggie Smith	1.00	.50	.30
(58) Willie Stargell	4.00	2.00	1.25
(59) Rusty Staub	1.50	.70	.45
(60) Rennie Stennett	1.00	.50	.30
(61) Don Sutton	4.00	2.00	1.25
(62) Andy Thornton	1.00	.50	.30
(63) Luis Tiant	1.00	.50	.30
(64) Joe Torre	2.50	1.25	.70
(65) Mike Tyson	1.00	.50	.30
(66) Bob Watson	1.00	.50	.30
(67) Wilbur Wood	1.00	.50	.30
(68) Jimmy Wynn	1.00	.50	.30
(69) Carl Yastrzemski	6.00	3.00	1.75
(70) Richie Zisk	1.00	.50	.30

1910 Toy Town Post Office

Rather than a card issuer, this enigmatic rubber-stamp has been found on the backs of dozens of 1910-era baseball cards. Measuring 1/2" in diameter the seal is in purple ink. At center is a barred circle with "TOY TOWN" above and "POST OFFICE" below. The stamp was part of a Milton Bradley post office toy set and has been seen on different types of cards that eventually made their way into the hobby. On low-grade cards, the stamp neither greatly adds nor detracts from the value of the card on which it is placed.

(See individual card issuers for base values.)

1965 Trade Bloc Minnesota Twins

These cards were produced as part of a baseball game which was marketed at Metropolitan Stadium for $1. The blank-back cards measure 2-1/4" x 3-1/2" and are printed in either blue or sepia tones. Besides Twins players and staff, the set includes cards of various team souvenir items as well as old Met Stadium. Besides the player photo, cards include a facsimile autograph, stats and personal data. The unnumbered cards are checklisted here in alphabetical order.

	NM	EX	VG
Complete Set (52):	600.00	300.00	175.00
Common Player:	15.00	7.50	4.50
Common Non-player Card:	5.00	2.50	1.50
(1) Bernard Allen	15.00	7.50	4.50
(2) Bob Allison	20.00	10.00	6.00
(3) Earl Battey	15.00	7.50	4.50
(4) Dave Boswell	15.00	7.50	4.50
(5) Gerald Fosnow	15.00	7.50	4.50
(6) James Grant	15.00	7.50	4.50
(7) Calvin Griffith	20.00	10.00	6.00
(8) Jimmie Hall	15.00	7.50	4.50
(9) Jim Kaat	25.00	12.50	7.50
(10) Harmon Killebrew	60.00	30.00	18.00
(11) Jerry Kindall	15.00	7.50	4.50
(12) Johnny Klippstein	15.00	7.50	4.50
(13) Frank Kostro	15.00	7.50	4.50
(14) James Lemon	15.00	7.50	4.50
(15) George "Doc" Lentz	15.00	7.50	4.50
(16) Alfred Martin (Billy)	30.00	15.00	9.00
(17) Sam Mele	15.00	7.50	4.50
(18) Donald Mincher	15.00	7.50	4.50
(19) Harold Naragon	15.00	7.50	4.50
(20) Melvin Nelson	15.00	7.50	4.50
(21) Joseph Nossek	15.00	7.50	4.50
(22) Pedro Oliva (Tony)	40.00	20.00	12.00
(23) Camilo Pascual	20.00	10.00	6.00
(24) James Perry	15.00	7.50	4.50
(25) Bill Pleis	15.00	7.50	4.50
(26) Richard Rollins	15.00	7.50	4.50
(27) John Sain	15.00	7.50	4.50
(28) John Sevcik	15.00	7.50	4.50
(29) Richard Stigman	15.00	7.50	4.50
(30) Sandy Valdespino	15.00	7.50	4.50
(31) Zoilo Versalles	25.00	12.50	7.50
(32) Allan Worthington	15.00	7.50	4.50
(33) Gerald Zimmerman	15.00	7.50	4.50
(34) Metropolitan Stadium	10.00	5.00	3.00
(35) L.A. Angels Logo	5.00	2.50	1.50
(36) K.C. Athletics Logo	5.00	2.50	1.50
(37) Cleveland Indians Logo	5.00	2.50	1.50
(38) Baltimore Orioles Logo	5.00	2.50	1.50
(39) Boston Red Sox Logo	5.00	2.50	1.50
(40) Washington Senators Logo	5.00	2.50	1.50
(41) Detroit Tigers Logo	5.00	2.50	1.50
(42) Minnesota Twins Logo	5.00	2.50	1.50
(43) Chicago White Sox Logo	5.00	2.50	1.50
(44) N.Y. Yankees Logo	5.00	2.50	1.50
(45) Twins Autographed Ball	5.00	2.50	1.50
(46) Twins Autographed Bat	5.00	2.50	1.50
(47) Twins Bobbin' Head Doll	5.00	2.50	1.50
(48) Twins Cap	5.00	2.50	1.50
(49) Twins Pennant	5.00	2.50	1.50
(50) Twins Scorebook	5.00	2.50	1.50
(51) Twins Warmup Jacket	5.00	2.50	1.50
(52) Twins Yearbook	5.00	2.50	1.50

1964 Transfer-ette Chicago Cubs Iron-ons

This novelty item features artist-rendered portraits of Cubs players which were designed to be transferred to t-shirts, notebook covers or other items via an iron-on process. Each package contains three sheets of nine images; one each in blue, black and red. The sheets are about 8-3/8" x 10-3/4" with each player image about 2-1/2" x 2-3/4". According to the packaging, other teams were planned, along with larger two-color player portraits.

	NM	EX	VG
Complete Set:	50.00	25.00	15.00

BLACK SHEET
Ernie Banks
Dick Bertell
John Boccabella
Glen Hobbie
Calvin Koonce
Merritt Ranew
Andre Rodgers
Ron Santo
Jim Stewart
BLUE SHEET
Steve Boros
Lou Brock
Bob Buhl
Ellis Burton
Bill Cowan
Dick Ellsworth
Don Elston
Bob Kennedy
Jimmie Schaffer
RED SHEET
Tom Baker
Jim Brewer
Leo Burke
Larry Jackson
Don Landrum
Paul Toth
Jack Warner
Billy Williams
Chicago Cubs Logo

1964 Transfer-ette Chicago White Sox Iron-ons

This novelty item features artist-rendered portraits of White Sox players which were designed to be transferred to t-shirts, notebook covers or other items via an iron-on process. Each package contains three sheets of nine images; one each in blue, black and red. The sheets are about 8-3/8" x 10-3/4" with each player image about 2-1/2" x 2-3/4". According to the packaging, other teams were planned, along with larger two-color player portraits.

	NM	EX	VG
Complete Set:	40.00	20.00	12.00

BLACK SHEET
Jim Brosnan
Don Buford
John Buzhardt
Joe Cunningham
Jim Golden
Joel Horlen
Charlie Maxwell
Dave Nicholson
Gene Stephens
BLUE SHEET
Fritz Ackley
Frank Bauman (Baumann)
Camilo Carreon
Dave DeBusschere
Ed Fisher
Mike Joyce
J.C. Martin
Tom McCraw
Hoyt Wilhelm
RED SHEET
Ron Hansen
Ray Herbert
Mike Hershberger
Jim Landis
Gary Peters
Floyd Robinson
Pete Ward
Al Weis
White Sox Logo

1969 Transogram

These 2-1/2" x 3-1/2" cards were printed on the back of toy baseball player statue boxes. The cards feature a color photo of the player surrounded by a rounded white border. Below the photo is the player's name in red and his team and other personal details all printed in black. The overall background is yellow. The cards were designed to be cut off the box, but collectors prefer to find the box intact and, better still, with the statue inside. While the cards themselves are not numbered, there is a number on each box's end flap, which is the order in which the cards are checklisted here. Three-player boxes were also sold.

CUT CARD OR STATUE

		NM	EX	VG
(1)	Joe Azcue	12.50	6.25	3.75
(2)	Willie Horton	12.50	6.25	3.75
(3)	Luis Tiant	12.50	6.25	3.75
(4)	Denny McLain	12.50	6.25	3.75
(5)	Jose Cardenal	12.50	6.25	3.75
(6)	Al Kaline	30.00	15.00	9.00
(7)	Tony Oliva	15.00	7.50	4.50
(8)	Blue Moon Odom	12.50	6.25	3.75
(9)	Cesar Tovar	12.50	6.25	3.75
(10)	Rick Monday	12.50	6.25	3.75
(11)	Harmon Killebrew	25.00	12.50	7.50
(12)	Danny Cater	12.50	6.25	3.75
(13)	Brooks Robinson	35.00	17.50	10.00
(14)	Jim Fregosi	12.50	6.25	3.75
(15)	Dave McNally	12.50	6.25	3.75
(16)	Frank Robinson	35.00	17.50	10.00
(17)	Bobby Knoop	12.50	6.25	3.75
(18)	Rick Reichardt	12.50	6.25	3.75
(19)	Carl Yastrzemski	35.00	17.50	10.00
(20)	Pete Ward	12.50	6.25	3.75
(21)	Rico Petrocelli	12.50	6.25	3.75
(22)	Tommy John	15.00	7.50	4.50
(23)	Ken Harrelson	12.50	6.25	3.75
(24)	Luis Aparicio	25.00	12.50	7.50
(25)	Mike Epstein	12.50	6.25	3.75
(26)	Roy White	12.50	6.25	3.75
(27)	Camilo Pascual	12.50	6.25	3.75
(28)	Mel Stottlemyre	12.50	6.25	3.75
(29)	Frank Howard	15.00	7.50	4.50
(30)	Mickey Mantle	185.00	90.00	55.00
(31)	Lou Brock	25.00	12.50	7.50
(32)	Juan Marichal	25.00	12.50	7.50
(33)	Bob Gibson	25.00	12.50	7.50
(34)	Willie Mays	60.00	30.00	18.00
(35)	Tim McCarver	15.00	7.50	4.50
(36)	Willie McCovey	25.00	12.50	7.50
(37)	Don Wilson	12.50	6.25	3.75
(38)	Billy Williams	25.00	12.50	7.50
(39)	Dan Staub (Rusty)	15.00	7.50	4.50
(40)	Ernie Banks	45.00	22.50	13.50
(41)	Jim Wynn	12.50	6.25	3.75
(42)	Ron Santo	15.00	7.50	4.50
(43)	Tom Haller	12.50	6.25	3.75
(44)	Ron Swoboda	12.50	6.25	3.75
(45)	Willie Davis	12.50	6.25	3.75
(46)	Jerry Koosman	12.50	6.25	3.75
(47)	Jim Lefebvre	12.50	6.25	3.75
(48)	Tom Seaver	30.00	15.00	9.00
(49)	Joe Torre (Atlanta)	20.00	10.00	6.00
(50)	Tony Perez	25.00	12.50	7.50
(51)	Felipe Alou	12.50	6.25	3.75
(52)	Lee May	12.50	6.25	3.75
(53)	Hank Aaron	60.00	30.00	18.00
(54)	Pete Rose	60.00	30.00	18.00
(55)	Cookie Rojas	12.50	6.25	3.75
(56)	Roberto Clemente	60.00	30.00	18.00
(57)	Richie Allen	15.00	7.50	4.50
(58)	Matty Alou	12.50	6.25	3.75
(59)	Johnny Callison	12.50	6.25	3.75
(60)	Bill Mazeroski	25.00	12.50	7.50

COMPLETE BOX W/STATUE

(1)	Joe Azcue	85.00	42.50	25.00
(2)	Willie Horton	85.00	42.50	25.00
(3)	Luis Tiant	85.00	42.50	25.00
(4)	Denny McLain	85.00	42.50	25.00
(5)	Jose Cardenal	85.00	42.50	25.00
(6)	Al Kaline	175.00	85.00	50.00
(7)	Tony Oliva	100.00	50.00	30.00
(8)	Blue Moon Odom	85.00	42.50	25.00
(9)	Cesar Tovar	85.00	42.50	25.00
(10)	Rick Monday	85.00	42.50	25.00
(11)	Harmon Killebrew	200.00	100.00	60.00
(12)	Danny Cater	85.00	42.50	25.00
(13)	Brooks Robinson	250.00	125.00	75.00
(14)	Jim Fregosi	85.00	42.50	25.00
(15)	Dave McNally	85.00	42.50	25.00
(16)	Frank Robinson	250.00	125.00	75.00
(17)	Bobby Knoop	85.00	42.50	25.00
(18)	Rick Reichardt	85.00	42.50	25.00
(19)	Carl Yastrzemski	300.00	150.00	90.00
(20)	Pete Ward	85.00	42.50	25.00
(21)	Rico Petrocelli	85.00	42.50	25.00
(22)	Tommy John	120.00	60.00	36.00
(23)	Ken Harrelson	85.00	42.50	25.00
(24)	Luis Aparicio	175.00	85.00	50.00
(25)	Mike Epstein	85.00	42.50	25.00
(26)	Roy White	85.00	42.50	25.00
(27)	Camilo Pascual	85.00	42.50	25.00
(28)	Mel Stottlemyre	85.00	42.50	25.00
(29)	Frank Howard	100.00	50.00	30.00
(30)	Mickey Mantle	850.00	425.00	255.00
(31)	Lou Brock	175.00	85.00	50.00
(32)	Juan Marichal	175.00	85.00	50.00
(33)	Bob Gibson	175.00	85.00	50.00
(34)	Willie Mays	400.00	200.00	120.00
(35)	Tim McCarver	100.00	50.00	30.00
(36)	Willie McCovey	175.00	85.00	50.00
(37)	Don Wilson	85.00	42.50	25.00
(38)	Billy Williams	175.00	85.00	50.00
(39)	Dan Staub (Rusty)	120.00	60.00	36.00
(40)	Ernie Banks	350.00	175.00	100.00
(41)	Jim Wynn	85.00	42.50	25.00
(42)	Ron Santo	120.00	60.00	36.00
(43)	Tom Haller	85.00	42.50	25.00
(44)	Ron Swoboda	85.00	42.50	25.00
(45)	Willie Davis	85.00	42.50	25.00
(46)	Jerry Koosman	120.00	60.00	36.00
(47)	Jim Lefebvre	85.00	42.50	25.00
(48)	Tom Seaver	200.00	100.00	60.00
(49)	Joe Torre (Atlanta)	100.00	50.00	30.00
(50)	Tony Perez	175.00	85.00	50.00
(51)	Felipe Alou	100.00	50.00	30.00
(52)	Lee May	85.00	42.50	25.00
(53)	Hank Aaron	400.00	200.00	120.00
(54)	Pete Rose	400.00	200.00	120.00
(55)	Cookie Rojas	85.00	42.50	25.00
(56)	Roberto Clemente	450.00	225.00	135.00
(57)	Richie Allen	100.00	50.00	30.00
(58)	Matty Alou	85.00	42.50	25.00
(59)	Johnny Callison	85.00	42.50	25.00
(60)	Bill Mazeroski	175.00	85.00	50.00

1970 Transogram

The 1970 Transogram cards were found printed on boxes of three Transogram baseball player statues. The individual player cards are slightly larger than 1969's, at 2-9/16" x 3-1/2". The 30-card set has the same pictures as the 1969 set except for Joe Torre. All players in the '70 set were also in the '69 Transogram issue except for Reggie Jackson, Sam McDowell and Boog Powell. Each box contains a side panel with a series number and 1" x 1-1/4" portrait photos of the players in the series. Prices shown are for cards cut from the box.

		NM	EX	VG
Complete Set (30):		550.00	275.00	175.00
Complete Set, Boxes/Statues (10):		2,255	1,100	650.00
Common Player:		10.00	5.00	3.00
	Series 1 Boxed Set:	400.00	200.00	120.00
(1)	Pete Rose	50.00	25.00	15.00
(2)	Willie Mays	60.00	30.00	18.00
(3)	Cleon Jones	10.00	5.00	3.00
	Series 2 Boxed Set:	160.00	80.00	48.00
(4)	Ron Santo	15.00	7.50	4.50
(5)	Willie Davis	10.00	5.00	3.00
(6)	Willie McCovey	17.50	8.75	5.25
	Series 3 Boxed Set:	275.00	135.00	82.00
(7)	Juan Marichal	17.50	8.75	5.25
(8)	Joe Torre (St. Louis)	15.00	7.50	4.50
(9)	Ernie Banks	30.00	15.00	9.00
	Series 4 Boxed Set:	375.00	185.00	110.00
(10)	Hank Aaron	60.00	30.00	18.00
(11)	Jim Wynn	10.00	5.00	3.00
(12)	Tom Seaver	25.00	12.50	7.50
	Series 5 Boxed Set:	450.00	225.00	135.00
(13)	Bob Gibson	17.50	8.75	5.25
(14)	Roberto Clemente	100.00	50.00	30.00
(15)	Jerry Koosman	10.00	5.00	3.00
	Series 11 Boxed Set:	300.00	150.00	90.00
(16)	Denny McLain	12.50	6.25	3.75
(17)	Reggie Jackson	30.00	15.00	9.00
(18)	Boog Powell	15.00	7.50	4.50
	Series 12 Boxed Set:	175.00	87.00	52.00
(19)	Frank Robinson	25.00	12.50	7.50
(20)	Frank Howard	10.00	5.00	3.00
(21)	Rick Reichardt	10.00	5.00	3.00
	Series 13 Boxed Set:	225.00	110.00	67.00
(22)	Carl Yastrzemski	25.00	12.50	7.50
(23)	Tony Oliva	15.00	7.50	4.50
(24)	Mel Stottlemyre	10.00	5.00	3.00
	Series 14 Boxed Set:	180.00	90.00	54.00
(25)	Al Kaline	25.00	12.50	7.50
(26)	Jim Fregosi	10.00	5.00	3.00
(27)	Sam McDowell	10.00	5.00	3.00
	Series 15 Boxed Set:	180.00	90.00	54.00
(28)	Blue Moon Odom	10.00	5.00	3.00
(29)	Harmon Killebrew	25.00	12.50	7.50
(30)	Rico Petrocelli	10.00	5.00	3.00

1970 Transogram Mets

This Transogram set features members of the World Champion N.Y. Mets. Like the other 1970 Transograms, the issue was packaged in a three-statue cardboard box with cellophane front panel and cards printed on the back. Player cards are 2-9/16" x 3-1/2" and retain the basic format of Transogram cards of 1969-70: a color photo with player name in red and team, position and biographical details in black. Backs are blank. Values shown here are for cards cut from the box. Complete unopened boxes are worth 3-4X the figures shown.

		NM	EX	VG
Complete Boxed Set (5):		1,400	700.00	425.00
Complete Panel Set (5):		650.00	325.00	200.00
Complete Card Set (15):		350.00	175.00	100.00
Common Player:		12.50	6.25	3.75
	Series 21 Boxed Set	225.00	110.00	65.00
	Series 21 Uncut Box/Panel	125.00	65.00	35.00
(1)	Ed Kranepool	12.50	6.25	3.75
(2)	Al Weis	12.50	6.25	3.75
(3)	Tom Seaver	35.00	17.50	10.00
	Series 22 Boxed Set	125.00	65.00	35.00
	Series 22 Uncut Box/Panel	60.00	30.00	18.00
(4)	Ken Boswell	12.50	6.25	3.75
(5)	Jerry Koosman	12.50	6.25	3.75
(6)	Jerry Grote	12.50	6.25	3.75
	Series 23 Boxed Set	125.00	65.00	35.00
	Series 23 Uncut Box/Panel	60.00	30.00	18.00
(7)	Art Shamsky	12.50	6.25	3.75
(8)	Gary Gentry	12.50	6.25	3.75
(9)	Tommie Agee	12.50	6.25	3.75
	Series 24 Boxed Set	685.00	340.00	200.00
	Series 24 Uncut Box/Panel	350.00	175.00	100.00
(10)	Nolan Ryan	225.00	110.00	65.00
(11)	Tug McGraw	12.50	6.25	3.75
(12)	Cleon Jones	12.50	6.25	3.75
	Series 25 Boxed Set	150.00	75.00	45.00
	Series 25 Uncut Box/Panel	60.00	30.00	18.00
(13)	Ron Swoboda	12.50	6.25	3.75
(14)	Bud Harrelson	12.50	6.25	3.75
(15)	Donn Clendenon	12.50	6.25	3.75

1920s Otto Treulich & Son

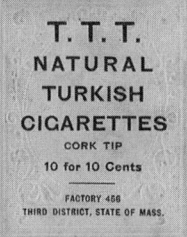

This promotional photocard was issued, according to the blue rubber-stamped advertising on back, by Chicago clothier Otto Treulich & Son. Front of the approximately 2-3/4" x 3-1/2" card has a black-and-white studio portrait of Cubs pitcher Grover Cleveland Alexander, dressed to the nines (presumably in the haberdashery of the sponsor), and bearing a fac-simile autograph.

	NM	EX	VG
Grover Alexander	400.00	200.00	120.00

1909 T.T.T. Cigarettes (T204)

This is one of two brands of cigarette advertising found on the backs of the ornate, gold-trimmed T204 cards. The initials stand for T.T. Tinayens, the Boston firm which also produced Ramly cigarettes, more commonly found mentioned on the cards' backs. In recent years collectors have begun paying a premium as high as 4-5X for the T.T.T. versions.

Premium: 4-5X
(See checklist under Ramly Cigarettes listing.)

1888 Rafael Tuck & Sons Artistic Series Baseball

This series of die-cut color lithographed player figures does not represent actual players, but rather generic figures in late 19th Century uniforms labeled with the names of various major league teams of the era. The actual date of issue is unknown. The cardboard figures were issued in a sheet of 20 with duplicates. Individual figures vary in size with a typical piece about 1-1/2" wide and 2-3/4" high. Players are shown in batting, throwing and fielding poses. The set was lithographed in Germany and published in England by Rafael Tuck & Sons, a famous postcard publisher.

	NM	EX	VG
Complete Set (10):	3,000	1,500	900.00
Common Card:	325.00	160.00	95.00
(1) Baltimore	325.00	160.00	95.00
(2) Boston	325.00	160.00	95.00
(3) Brooklyn	325.00	160.00	95.00
(4) Chicago	325.00	160.00	95.00
(5) Detroit	325.00	160.00	95.00
(6) Indianapolis	325.00	160.00	95.00
(7) New York	325.00	160.00	95.00
(8) Philadelphia	325.00	160.00	95.00
(9) Pittsburgh	325.00	160.00	95.00
(10) St. Louis	325.00	160.00	95.00

1925 Turf Cigarettes

"Sports Records" is the name of a two-series, 50-card issue by Turf Cigarettes. The last card in the set depicts George Sisler (though not named) on the front in a color action scene. Black-and-white back of the card describes Sisler's batting prowess. Like other British tobacco cards of the era, size is 2-5/8" x 1-3/8".

	NM	EX	VG
50 Baseball (George Sisler)	90.00	45.00	25.00

1909-11 Ty Cobb Tobacco (T206)

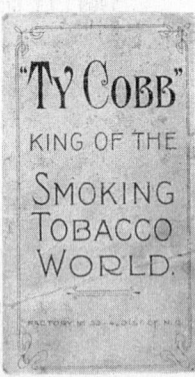

Much rarer than the famed Honus Wagner card from the related cigarette card series known collectively as T206, the Ty Cobb brand tobacco back was known in only about half a dozen collections until June 1997 when a find of five lower-grade specimens was auctioned. Because T206 was generally collected by front design, rather than back, through most of the hobby's history, it has only been in recent years that the value of the "Ty Cobb-back" T206 has begun to approach the other great rarities of the series. The only front known with a Cobb tobacco back is the red-background portrait. Some of the extant examples appear to have been hand-cut from a sheet. In April 2002 a PSA-graded Good example sold at an auction for $18,055. Most recently, an SGC-graded card sold at an auction for $25,000 in May 2005, and another sold at an auction for $24,655 in November 2005.

(See T206, #95b. Approximately 11 known.)

1910-1911 T3 Turkey Red Cabinets

Turkey Red cabinet cards were obtained by mailing in coupons found in Turkey Red, Fez and Old Mill brand cigarettes. Turkey Reds measure 5-3/4" x 8", and feature full-color lithograph fronts with wide gray frames. Backs are known in three styles: 1) checklist with no ordering information, 2) checklist with ordering information, and 3) with an illustrated ad for Turkey Red cigarettes. The checklist backs are found with both low- and high-number cards, the ad backs are only on cards #77-126. The series consists of 25 boxers and 100 baseball players. Coupons issued in the cigarette boxes indicate the first 50 baseball player cards were produced for spring, 1910, delivery, with the 25 boxers produced later that year and the final 50 baseball players issued in 1911.

		NM	EX	VG
Complete Set (130):		160,000	80,000	48,000
Common Player:		1,500	600.00	360.00
Turkey Red Ad Back: 1.5-2X				
1	Mordecai Brown	3,300	1,650	990.00
2	Bill Bergen	1,500	750.00	450.00
3	Tommy Leach	1,500	600.00	360.00
4	Roger Bresnahan	2,550	1,275	765.00
5	Sam Crawford	2,550	1,275	765.00
6	Hal Chase	1,700	850.00	500.00
7	Howie Camnitz	1,500	600.00	360.00
8	Fred Clarke	2,550	1,275	765.00
9	Ty Cobb	35,000	15,000	9,000
10	Art Devlin	1,500	600.00	360.00
11	Bill Dahlen	1,500	600.00	360.00
12	Wild Bill Donovan	1,500	600.00	360.00
13	Larry Doyle	1,500	600.00	360.00
14	Red Dooin	1,500	600.00	360.00
15	Kid Elberfeld	1,500	600.00	360.00
16	Johnny Evers	2,500	1,250	750.00
17	Clark Griffith	2,500	1,250	750.00
18	Hughie Jennings	2,500	1,250	750.00
19	Addie Joss	4,000	1,800	1,100
20	Tim Jordan	1,500	600.00	360.00
21	Red Kleinow	1,500	600.00	360.00
22	Harry Krause	1,500	600.00	360.00
23	Nap Lajoie	4,400	1,500	900.00
24	Mike Mitchell	1,500	600.00	360.00
25	Matty McIntyre	1,500	600.00	360.00
26	John McGraw	3,000	1,500	900.00
27	Christy Mathewson	16,000	5,000	2,500
28a	Harry McIntyre (Brooklyn)	1,500	600.00	360.00
28b	Harry McIntyre (Brooklyn and Chicago)	1,500	600.00	360.00
29	Amby McConnell	2,000	1,000	600.00
30	George Mullin	1,500	600.00	360.00
31	Sherry Magee	1,500	600.00	360.00
32	Orval Overall	1,500	600.00	360.00
33	Jake Pfeister	1,500	600.00	360.00
34	Nap Rucker	1,500	600.00	360.00
35	Joe Tinker	2,600	1,200	750.00
36	Tris Speaker	6,600	3,000	1,800
37	Slim Sallee	1,500	600.00	360.00
38	Jake Stahl	1,500	600.00	360.00
39	Rube Waddell	2,600	1,200	750.00
40	Vic Willis	2,600	1,200	750.00
41	Hooks Wiltse	1,500	600.00	360.00
42	Cy Young	10,000	3,600	2,200
43	Out At Third	1,600	700.00	425.00
44	Trying To Catch Him Napping	1,600	700.00	425.00
45	Jordan & Herzog At First	1,600	700.00	425.00
46	Safe At Third	1,600	700.00	425.00
47	Frank Chance	3,000	1,400	800.00
48	Jack Murray	1,500	600.00	360.00
49	A Close Play At Second	1,600	800.00	450.00
50	Chief Myers	1,500	600.00	360.00
77	Red Ames	1,500	600.00	360.00
78	Home Run Baker	2,600	1,200	750.00
79	George Bell	1,500	600.00	360.00
80	Chief Bender	2,600	1,200	720.00
81	Bob Bescher	1,500	600.00	360.00
82	Kitty Bransfield	1,500	600.00	360.00
83	Al Bridwell	1,500	600.00	360.00
84	George Browne	1,500	600.00	360.00
85	Bill Burns	1,500	600.00	360.00
86	Bill Carrigan	1,500	600.00	360.00
87	Eddie Collins	2,600	1,200	780.00
88	Harry Coveleski	1,500	600.00	360.00
89	Lou Criger	1,500	600.00	360.00
90a	Mickey Doolin (Doolan)	1,600	700.00	400.00
90b	Mickey Doolan (Name correct.)	1,500	600.00	360.00
91	Tom Downey	1,500	600.00	360.00
92	Jimmy Dygert	1,500	600.00	360.00
93	Art Fromme	1,500	600.00	360.00
94	George Gibson	1,500	600.00	360.00
95	Peaches Graham	1,500	600.00	360.00
96	Bob Groom	1,500	600.00	360.00
97	Dick Hoblitzell	1,500	600.00	360.00
98	Solly Hofman	1,500	600.00	360.00

99	Walter Johnson	16,000	5,000	3,000
100	Davy Jones	1,500	600.00	360.00
101	Wee Willie Keeler	2,600	1,200	720.00
102	Johnny Kling	1,500	600.00	360.00
103	Ed Konetchy	1,500	600.00	360.00
104	Ed Lennox	1,500	600.00	360.00
105	Hans Lobert	1,500	600.00	360.00
106	Harry Lord	1,500	600.00	360.00
107	Rube Manning	2,000	1,000	600.00
108	Fred Merkle	1,500	600.00	360.00
109	Pat Moran	1,500	600.00	360.00
110	George McBride	1,500	600.00	360.00
111	Harry Niles	1,500	600.00	360.00
112a	Dode Paskert (Cincinnati)	1,500	600.00	360.00
112b	Dode Paskert (Cincinnati and Philadelphia)	1,500	600.00	360.00
113	Bugs Raymond	1,500	600.00	360.00
114	Bob Rhoades (Rhoads)	12,000	4,000	2,400
115	Admiral Schlei	1,500	600.00	360.00
116	Boss Schmidt	1,500	600.00	360.00
117	Wildfire Schulte	1,500	600.00	360.00
118	Frank Smith	1,500	600.00	360.00
119	George Stone	1,500	600.00	360.00
120	Gabby Street	1,500	600.00	360.00
121	Billy Sullivan	1,500	600.00	360.00
122a	Fred Tenney (New York)	1,500	600.00	360.00
122b	Fred Tenney (New York and Boston)	1,500	600.00	360.00
123	Ira Thomas	1,500	600.00	360.00
124	Bobby Wallace	2,600	1,200	750.00
125	Ed Walsh	2,500	1,300	750.00
126	Owen Wilson	1,500	600.00	360.00

1911 T5 Pinkerton Cabinets

Because they are photographs affixed to a cardboard backing, the cards in the 1911 Pinkerton set are considered "true" cabinet cards. The Pinkerton cabinets are a rather obscure issue, and because of their original method of distribution, it would be virtually impossible to assemble a complete set today. It remains uncertain how many subjects exist in the set. Pinkerton, the parent of Red Man and other tobacco products, offered the cabinets in exchange for coupons found in cigarette packages. According to an original advertising sheet, some 376 different photos were available. A consumer could exchange 10 coupons for the card of his choice. The photos available included players from the 16 major league teams plus teams from the minor league American Association, Southern Michigan Association, and, probably, others. Pinkertons vary in both size and type of mount. The most desirable combination is a 3-3/8" x 5-1/2" photograph affixed to a thick cardboard mount measuring approximately 4-3/4" x 7-3/4". But original Pinkerton cabinets have also been found in different sizes and with less substantial backings. The most attractive mounts are embossed around the picture, but some Pinkertons have a white border surrounding the photograph. Prices listed are for cards with cardboard mounts. Cards with paper mounts are worth about 50-75 percent of listed prices. Some of the Pinkerton photos were reproduced in postcard size printed issues in later years; some with postcard style backs, some with scorecard backs and others are blank-backed (See 1911 Pinkerton).

		NM	EX	VG
Common Player:		1,000	500.00	315.00
Checklist Brochure:		625.00	315.00	190.00
Redemption Coupon:		500.00	250.00	150.00
Blank-Back Card: 5-10 Percent				
Postcard-Back: 10-15 Percent				
101	Jim Stephens	1,000	500.00	315.00
102	Bobby Wallace	2,190	1,095	655.00
103	Joe Lake	1,000	500.00	315.00
104	George Stone	1,000	500.00	315.00
105	Jack O'Connor	1,000	500.00	315.00
106	Bill Abstein	1,000	500.00	315.00
107	Rube Waddell	2,190	1,095	655.00
108	Roy Hartzell	1,000	500.00	315.00
109	Danny Hoffman	1,000	500.00	315.00
110	Dode Cris	1,000	500.00	315.00
111	Al Schweitzer	1,000	500.00	315.00
112	Art Griggs	1,000	500.00	315.00
113	Bill Bailey	1,000	500.00	315.00
114	Pat Newman	1,000	500.00	315.00
115	Harry Howell	1,000	500.00	315.00
116	Hobe Ferris	1,000	500.00	315.00
117	John McAleese	1,000	500.00	315.00
118	Ray Demmitt	1,000	500.00	315.00
119	Red Fisher	1,000	500.00	315.00
120	Frank Truesdale	1,000	500.00	315.00
121	Barney Pelty	1,000	500.00	315.00

#	Player			
123	Ed Killifer (Killefer)	1,000	500.00	315.00
151	Matty McIntyre	1,000	500.00	315.00
152	Jim Delahanty	1,000	500.00	315.00
153	Hughey Jennings	2,190	1,095	655.00
154	Ralph Works	1,000	500.00	315.00
155	George Moriarity (Moriarty)	1,000	500.00	315.00
156	Sam Crawford	2,190	1,095	655.00
157	Boss Schmidt	1,000	500.00	315.00
158	Owen Bush	1,000	500.00	315.00
159	Ty Cobb	8,750	4,375	2,625
160	Bill Donovan	1,000	500.00	315.00
161	Oscar Stanage	1,000	500.00	315.00
162	George Mullen (Mullin)	1,000	500.00	315.00
163	Davy Jones	1,000	500.00	315.00
164	Charley O'Leary	1,000	500.00	315.00
165	Tom Jones	1,000	500.00	315.00
166	Joe Casey	1,000	500.00	315.00
167	Ed Willetts (Willett)	1,000	500.00	315.00
168	Ed Lafeite (Lafitte)	1,000	500.00	315.00
169	Ty Cobb	20,000	4,530	2,720
170	Ty Cobb	20,000	4,530	2,720
201	John Evers	2,190	1,095	655.00
202	Mordecai Brown	2,190	1,095	655.00
203	King Cole	1,000	500.00	315.00
204	Johnny Cane	1,000	500.00	315.00
205	Heinie Zimmerman	1,000	500.00	315.00
206	Wildfire Schulte	1,000	500.00	315.00
207	Frank Chance	2,190	1,095	655.00
208	Joe Tinker	2,190	1,095	655.00
209	Orvall Overall	1,000	500.00	315.00
210	Jimmy Archer	1,000	500.00	315.00
211	Johnny Kling	1,000	500.00	315.00
212	Jimmy Sheckard	1,000	500.00	315.00
213	Harry McIntyre	1,000	500.00	315.00
214	Lew Richie	1,000	500.00	315.00
215	Ed Ruelbach	1,000	500.00	315.00
216	Artie Hoffman (Hofman)	1,000	500.00	315.00
217	Jake Pfeister	1,000	500.00	315.00
218	Harry Steinfeldt	1,000	500.00	315.00
219	Tom Needham	1,000	500.00	315.00
220	Ginger Beaumont	1,000	500.00	315.00
251	Christy Mathewson	10,000	2,815	1,690
252	Fred Merkle	1,000	500.00	315.00
253	Hooks Wiltsie	1,000	500.00	315.00
254	Art Devlin	1,000	500.00	315.00
255	Fred Snodgrass	1,000	500.00	315.00
256	Josh Devore	1,000	500.00	315.00
257	Red Murray	1,000	500.00	315.00
258	Cy Seymour	1,000	500.00	315.00
259	Rube Marquard	2,190	1,095	655.00
260	Larry Doyle	1,000	500.00	315.00
261	Bugs Raymond	1,000	500.00	315.00
262	Doc Crandall	1,000	500.00	315.00
263	Admiral Schlei	1,000	500.00	315.00
264	Chief Myers (Meyers)	1,000	500.00	315.00
265	Bill Dahlen	1,000	500.00	315.00
266	Beals Becker	1,000	500.00	315.00
267	Louis Drucke	1,000	500.00	315.00
301	Fred Luderus	1,000	500.00	315.00
302	John Titus	1,000	500.00	315.00
303	Red Dooin	1,000	500.00	315.00
304	Eddie Stack	1,000	500.00	315.00
305	Kitty Bransfield	1,000	500.00	315.00
306	Sherry Magee	1,000	500.00	315.00
307	Otto Knabe	1,000	500.00	315.00
308	Jimmy "Runt" Walsh	1,000	500.00	315.00
309	Earl Moore	1,000	500.00	315.00
310	Mickey Doolan	1,000	500.00	315.00
311	Ad Brennan	1,000	500.00	315.00
312	Bob Ewing	1,000	500.00	315.00
313	Lou Schettler	1,000	500.00	315.00
351	Joe Willis	1,000	500.00	315.00
352	Rube Ellis	1,000	500.00	315.00
353	Steve Evans	1,000	500.00	315.00
354	Miller Huggins	2,190	1,095	655.00
355	Arnold Hauser	1,000	500.00	315.00
356	Frank Corridon	1,000	500.00	315.00
357	Roger Bresnahan	2,190	1,095	655.00
358	Slim Sallee	1,000	500.00	315.00
359	Mike Mowrey	1,000	500.00	315.00
360	Ed Konetchy	1,000	500.00	315.00
361	Beckman	1,000	500.00	315.00
362	Rebel Oakes	1,000	500.00	315.00
363	Johnny Lush	1,000	500.00	315.00
364	Eddie Phelps	1,000	500.00	315.00
365	Robert Harmon	1,000	500.00	315.00
401	Lou (Pat) Moran	1,000	500.00	315.00
402	George McQuillian (McQuillan)	1,000	500.00	315.00
403	Johnny Bates	1,000	500.00	315.00
404	Eddie Grant	1,000	500.00	315.00
405	Tommy McMillan	1,000	500.00	315.00
406	Tommy Clark (Clarke)	1,000	500.00	315.00
407	Jack Rowan	1,000	500.00	315.00
408	Bob Bescher	1,000	500.00	315.00
409	Fred Beebe	1,000	500.00	315.00
410	Tom Downey	1,000	500.00	315.00
411	George Suggs	1,000	500.00	315.00
412	Hans Lobert	1,000	500.00	315.00
413	Jimmy Phelan	1,000	500.00	315.00
414	Dode Paskert	1,000	500.00	315.00
415	Ward Miller	1,000	500.00	315.00
416	Richard J. Egan	1,000	500.00	315.00
417	Art Fromme	1,000	500.00	315.00
418	Bill Burns	1,000	500.00	315.00
419	Clark Griffith	2,190	1,095	655.00
420	Dick Hoblitzell	1,000	500.00	315.00
421	Harry Gasper	1,000	500.00	315.00
422	Dave Altizer	1,000	500.00	315.00
423	Larry McLean	1,000	500.00	315.00
424	Mike Mitchell	1,000	500.00	315.00
451	John Hummel	1,000	500.00	315.00
452	Tony Smith	1,000	500.00	315.00
453	Bill Davidson	1,000	500.00	315.00
454	Ed Lennox	1,000	500.00	315.00
455	Zach Wheat	2,190	1,095	655.00
457	Elmer Knetzer	1,000	500.00	315.00
458	Rube Dessau	1,000	500.00	315.00
459	George Bell	1,000	500.00	315.00
460	Jake Daubert	1,000	500.00	315.00
461	Doc Scanlan	1,000	500.00	315.00
462	Nap Rucker	1,000	500.00	315.00
463	Cy Barger	1,000	500.00	315.00
464	Kaiser Wilhelm	1,000	500.00	315.00
465	Bill Bergen	1,000	500.00	315.00
466	Tex Erwin	1,000	500.00	315.00
501	Chas. Bender	2,190	1,095	655.00
502	John Coombs	1,000	500.00	315.00
503	Ed Plank	4,000	1,565	935.00
504	Amos Strunk	1,000	500.00	315.00
505	Connie Mack	2,190	1,095	655.00
506	Ira Thomas	1,000	500.00	315.00
507	Biscoe Lord (Briscoe)	1,000	500.00	315.00
508	Stuffy McInnis	1,000	500.00	315.00
509	Jimmy Dygert	1,000	500.00	315.00
510	Rube Oldring	1,000	500.00	315.00
511	Eddie Collins	2,190	1,095	655.00
512	Home Run Baker	2,190	1,095	655.00
513	Harry Krause	1,000	500.00	315.00
514	Harry Davis	1,000	500.00	315.00
515	Jack Barry	1,000	500.00	315.00
516	Jack Lapp	1,000	500.00	315.00
517	Cy Morgan	1,000	500.00	315.00
518	Danny Murphy	1,000	500.00	315.00
519	Topsy Hartsell	1,000	500.00	315.00
520	Paddy Livingston	1,000	500.00	315.00
521	P. Adkins	1,000	500.00	315.00
522	Eddie Collins	2,190	1,095	655.00
523	Paddy Livingston	1,000	500.00	315.00
551	Doc Gessler	1,000	500.00	315.00
552	Bill Cunningham	1,000	500.00	315.00
554	John Henry	1,000	500.00	315.00
555	Jack Lelivelt	1,000	500.00	315.00
556	Bobby Groome	1,000	500.00	315.00
557	Doc Ralston	1,000	500.00	315.00
558	Kid Elberfelt (Elberfeld)	1,000	500.00	315.00
559	Doc Reisling	1,000	500.00	315.00
560	Herman Schaefer	1,000	500.00	315.00
561	Walter Johnson	6,000	2,500	1,500
562	Dolly Gray	1,000	500.00	315.00
563	Wid Conroy	1,000	500.00	315.00
564	Charley Street	1,000	500.00	315.00
565	Bob Unglaub	1,000	500.00	315.00
566	Clyde Milan	1,000	500.00	315.00
567	George Browne	1,000	500.00	315.00
568	George McBride	1,000	500.00	315.00
569	Red Killifer (Killefer)	1,000	500.00	315.00
601	Addie Joss	2,190	1,095	655.00
602	Addie Joss	2,190	1,095	655.00
603	Napoleon Lajoie	2,190	1,095	655.00
604	Nig Clark (Clarke)	1,000	500.00	315.00
605	Cy Falkenberg	1,000	500.00	315.00
606	Harry Bemis	1,000	500.00	315.00
607	George Stovall	1,000	500.00	315.00
608	Fred Blanding	1,000	500.00	315.00
609	Elmer Koestner	1,000	500.00	315.00
610	Ted Easterly	1,000	500.00	315.00
611	Willie Mitchell	1,000	500.00	315.00
612	Hornhorst	1,000	500.00	315.00
613	Elmer Flick	2,190	1,095	655.00
614	Speck Harkness	1,000	500.00	315.00
615	Tuck Turner	1,000	500.00	315.00
616	Joe Jackson	50,000	10,000	6,000
617	Grover Land	1,000	500.00	315.00
618	Gladstone Graney	1,000	500.00	315.00
619	Dave Callahan	1,000	500.00	315.00
620	Ben DeMott	1,000	500.00	315.00
621	Neill Ball (Neal)	1,000	500.00	315.00
622	Dode Birmingham	1,000	500.00	315.00
623	George Kaler (Kahler)	1,000	500.00	315.00
624	Sid Smith	1,000	500.00	315.00
625	Bert Adams	1,000	500.00	315.00
626	Bill Bradley	1,000	500.00	315.00
627	Napoleon Lajoie	2,190	1,095	655.00
651	Bill Corrigan (Carrigan)	1,000	500.00	315.00
652	Joe Woods (Wood)	1,000	500.00	315.00
653	Heinie Wagner	1,000	500.00	315.00
654	Billy Purtell	1,000	500.00	315.00
655	Frank Smith	1,000	500.00	315.00
656	Harry Lord	1,000	500.00	315.00
657	Patsy Donovan	1,000	500.00	315.00
658	Duffy Lewis	1,000	500.00	315.00
659	Jack Kleinow	1,000	500.00	315.00
660	Ed Karger	1,000	500.00	315.00
661	Clyde Engle	1,000	500.00	315.00
662	Ben Hunt	1,000	500.00	315.00
663	Charlie Smith	1,000	500.00	315.00
664	Tris Speaker	3,000	1,155	695.00
665	Tom Madden	1,000	500.00	315.00
666	Larry Gardner	1,000	500.00	315.00
667	Harry Hooper	2,190	1,095	655.00
668	Marty McHale	1,000	500.00	315.00
669	Ray Collins	1,000	500.00	315.00
670	Jake Stahl	1,000	500.00	315.00
701	Dave Shean	1,000	500.00	315.00
702	Roy Miller	1,000	500.00	315.00
703	Fred Beck	1,000	500.00	315.00
704	Bill Collings (Collins)	1,000	500.00	315.00
705	Bill Sweeney	1,000	500.00	315.00
706	Buck Herzog	1,000	500.00	315.00
707	Bud Sharp (Sharpe)	1,000	500.00	315.00
708	Cliff Curtis	1,000	500.00	315.00
709	Al Mattern	1,000	500.00	315.00
710	Buster Brown	1,000	500.00	315.00
711	Bill Rariden	1,000	500.00	315.00
712	Grant	1,000	500.00	315.00
713	Ed Abbaticchio	1,000	500.00	315.00
714	Cecil Ferguson	1,000	500.00	315.00
715	Billy Burke	1,000	500.00	315.00
716	Sam Frock	1,000	500.00	315.00
717	Wilbur Goode (Good)	1,000	500.00	315.00
751	Charlie French	1,000	500.00	315.00
752	Patsy Dougherty	1,000	500.00	315.00
753	Shano Collins	1,000	500.00	315.00
754	Fred Parent	1,000	500.00	315.00
755	Willis Cole	1,000	500.00	315.00
756	Billy Sullivan	1,000	500.00	315.00
757	Rube Sutor (Suter)	1,000	500.00	315.00
758	Chick Gandil	2,315	1,155	695.00
759	Jim Scott	1,000	500.00	315.00
760	Ed Walsh	2,190	1,095	655.00
761	Gavvy Cravath	1,000	500.00	315.00
762	Bobby Messenger	1,000	500.00	315.00
763	Doc White	1,000	500.00	315.00
764	Rollie Zeider	1,000	500.00	315.00
765	Fred Payne	1,000	500.00	315.00
766	Lee Tannehill	1,000	500.00	315.00
767	Eddie Hahn	1,000	500.00	315.00
768	Hugh Duffy	2,190	1,095	655.00
769	Fred Olmstead	1,000	500.00	315.00
770	Lena Blackbourne (Blackburne)	1,000	500.00	315.00
771	Young "Cy" Young	1,000	500.00	315.00
801	Lew Brockett	1,000	500.00	315.00
802	Frank Laporte (LaPorte)	1,000	500.00	315.00
803	Bert Daniels	1,000	500.00	315.00
804	Walter Blair	1,000	500.00	315.00
805	Jack Knight	1,000	500.00	315.00
806	Jimmy Austin	1,000	500.00	315.00
807	Hal Chase	1,190	595.00	355.00
808	Birdie Cree	1,000	500.00	315.00
809	Jack Quinn	1,000	500.00	315.00
810	Walter Manning	1,000	500.00	315.00
811	Jack Warhop	1,000	500.00	315.00
812	Jeff Sweeney	1,000	500.00	315.00
813	Charley Hemphill	1,000	500.00	315.00
814	Harry Wolters	1,000	500.00	315.00
815	Tom Hughes	1,000	500.00	315.00
816	Earl Gardiner (Gardner)	1,000	500.00	315.00
851	John Flynn	1,000	500.00	315.00
852	Bill Powell	1,000	500.00	315.00
853	Honus Wagner	15,000	3,750	2,250
854	Bill Powell	1,000	500.00	315.00
855	Fred Clarke	2,190	1,095	655.00
856	Owen Wilson	1,000	500.00	315.00
857	George Gibson	1,000	500.00	315.00
858	Mike Simon	1,000	500.00	315.00
859	Tommy Leach	1,000	500.00	315.00
860	Lefty Leifeld (Leifield)	1,000	500.00	315.00
861	Nick Maddox	1,000	500.00	315.00
862	Dots Miller	1,000	500.00	315.00
863	Howard Camnitz	1,000	500.00	315.00
864	Deacon Phillippi (Phillippe)	1,000	500.00	315.00
865	Babe Adams	1,000	500.00	315.00
866	Ed Abbaticchio	1,000	500.00	315.00
867	Paddy O'Connor	1,000	500.00	315.00
868	Bobby Byrne	1,000	500.00	315.00
869	Vin Campbell	1,000	500.00	315.00
870	Ham Hyatt	1,000	500.00	315.00
871	Sam Leever	1,000	500.00	315.00
872	Hans Wagner	15,000	3,750	2,250
873	Hans Wagner	15,000	3,750	2,250
874	Bill McKecknie (McKechnie)	2,190	1,095	655.00
875	Kirby White	1,000	500.00	315.00
901	Jimmie Burke	1,000	500.00	315.00
902	Charlie Carr	1,000	500.00	315.00
903	Larry Cheney	1,000	500.00	315.00
904	Chet Chadbourne	1,000	500.00	315.00
905	Dan Howley	1,000	500.00	315.00
906	Jimmie Burke	1,000	500.00	315.00
907	Ray Mowe	1,000	500.00	315.00
908	Billy Milligan	1,000	500.00	315.00
909	Frank Oberlin	1,000	500.00	315.00
910	Ralph Glaze	1,000	500.00	315.00
911	O'Day	1,000	500.00	315.00
912	Kerns	1,000	500.00	315.00
913	Jim Duggan	1,000	500.00	315.00
914	Simmy Murch	1,000	500.00	315.00
915	Frank Delehanty	1,000	500.00	315.00
916	Craig	1,000	500.00	.315.00
917	Jack Coffee (Coffey)	1,000	500.00	315.00
918	Lefty George	1,000	500.00	315.00
919	Otto Williams	1,000	500.00	315.00
920	M. Hayden	1,000	500.00	315.00
951	Joe Cantillion	1,000	500.00	315.00
952	Smith	1,000	500.00	315.00
953	Claud Rossman (Claude)	1,000	500.00	315.00
1001	Tony James	1,000	500.00	315.00
1002	Jack Powell	1,000	500.00	315.00
1003	Wm. J. Harbeau	1,000	500.00	315.00
1004	Homer Smoot	1,000	500.00	315.00
1051	Bill Friel	1,000	500.00	315.00
1052	Bill Friel	1,000	500.00	315.00
1053	Fred Odwell	1,000	500.00	315.00
1054	Alex Reilley	1,000	500.00	315.00
1055	Eugene Packard	1,000	500.00	315.00
1056	Irve Wrattan	1,000	500.00	315.00
1057	"Red" Nelson	1,000	500.00	315.00
1058	George Perring	1,000	500.00	315.00
1059	Glen Liebhardt	1,000	500.00	315.00
1060	Jimmie O'Rourke	1,000	500.00	315.00
1061	Fred Cook	1,000	500.00	315.00
1062	Charles Arbogast	1,000	500.00	315.00
1063	Jerry Downs	1,000	500.00	315.00
1064	"Bunk" Congalton	1,000	500.00	315.00
1065	Fred Carisch	1,000	500.00	315.00
1066	"Red" Sitton	1,000	500.00	315.00
1067	George Kaler (Kahler)	1,000	500.00	315.00
1068	Arthur Kruger	1,000	500.00	315.00
1102	Earl Yingling	1,000	500.00	315.00
1103	Jerry Freeman	1,800	500.00	315.00
1104	Harry Hinchman	1,000	500.00	315.00
1105	Jim Baskette (Toledo)	1,000	500.00	315.00
1106	Denny Sullivan	1,000	500.00	315.00
1107	Carl Robinson	1,000	500.00	315.00
1108	Bill Rodgers	1,000	500.00	315.00
1109	Hi West	1,000	500.00	315.00
1110	Billy Hallman	1,000	500.00	315.00
1111	Wm. Elwert	1,000	500.00	315.00
1112	Piano Legs Hickman	1,000	500.00	315.00
1113	Joe McCarthy	2,190	1,095	655.00
1114	Fred Abbott	1,000	500.00	315.00
1115	Jack Guilligan (Gilligan)	1,000	500.00	315.00

1510	Musser	1,000 500.00 315.00
1613	C. Winger	1,000 500.00 315.00

1911 T201 Mecca Double Folders

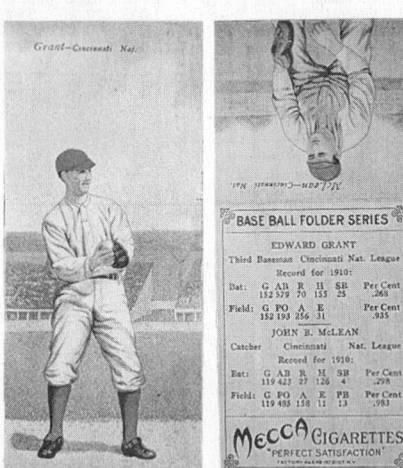

These cards found in packages of Mecca cigarettes feature one player when the card is open, and another when the card is folded; two players sharing the same pair of legs. Mecca Double Folders measure about 2-1/8" to 2-3/16" x 4-11/16". The pictures are color lithographs, the text is printed in black. The cards contain an innovation in the form of the first use of player statistics. The 50-card set contains 100 different players including a number of Hall of Famers. Examples authenticated and graded by major certification firms carry a much larger premium than most other cards of the era.

		NM	EX	VG
	Complete Set (50):	25,000	7,000	2,650
	Common Player:	385.00	85.00	30.00
(1)	William Abstein, John Butler	385.00	85.00	30.00
(2)	Frank Baker, Edward Collins	560.00	180.00	75.00
(3)	Harry Baker, Thomas Downie (Downey)	385.00	85.00	30.00
(4)	James Barrett, Grant McGlynn	385.00	85.00	30.00
(5)	John Barry, John Lapp	385.00	85.00	30.00
(6)	Charles Bender, Reuben Oldring	435.00	135.00	55.00
(7)	William Bergen, Zack Wheat	400.00	130.00	50.00
(8)	Walter Blair, Roy Hartzell	385.00	85.00	30.00
(9)	Roger Bresnahan, Miller Huggins	650.00	200.00	80.00
(10)	Albert Bridwell, Christy Matthewson (Mathewson)	1,200	375.00	150.00
(11)	Mordecai Brown, Arthur Hofman	425.00	140.00	55.00
(12)	Robert Byrne, Fred Clarke	400.00	115.00	45.00
(13)	Frank Chance, John Evers	600.00	200.00	80.00
(14)	Harold Chase, Edward Sweeney	400.00	100.00	40.00
(15)	Edward Cicotte, John Thoney	625.00	140.00	55.00
(16)	Thomas Clarke, Harry Gaspar	385.00	85.00	30.00
(17)	Ty Cobb, Sam Crawford	3,000	1,000	400.00
(18)	Leonard Cole, John Kling	385.00	85.00	30.00
(19)	John Coombs, Ira Thomas	385.00	85.00	30.00
(20)	Jake Daubert, Nap Rucker	385.00	85.00	30.00
(21)	Bill Donovan, Ralph Stroud	385.00	85.00	30.00
(22)	Charles Dooin, John Titus	385.00	85.00	30.00
(23)	Patsy Dougherty, Harry Lord	500.00	165.00	65.00
(24)	Jerry Downs, Fred Odwell	385.00	85.00	30.00
(25)	Larry Doyle, Chief Meyers	385.00	85.00	30.00
(26)	James Dygert, Cy Seymour	385.00	85.00	30.00
(27)	Norman Elberfeld, George McBride	385.00	85.00	30.00
(28)	Fred Falkenberg, Napoleon Lajoie	575.00	190.00	75.00
(29)	Edward Fitzpatrick, Ed Killian	385.00	85.00	30.00
(30)	Russell Ford, Otis Johnson	385.00	85.00	30.00
(31)	Edward Foster, Joseph Ward	385.00	85.00	30.00
(32)	Earl Gardner, Tris Speaker	600.00	200.00	80.00
(33)	George Gibson, Thomas Leach	385.00	85.00	30.00
(34)	George Graham, Al Mattern	385.00	85.00	30.00
(35)	Edward Grant, John McLean	385.00	85.00	30.00
(36)	Arnold Hauser, Ernest Lush	385.00	85.00	30.00
(37)	Charles Herzog, Roy Miller	385.00	85.00	30.00
(38)	Charles Hickman, Harry Hinchman	385.00	85.00	30.00
(39)	Hugh Jennings, Edgar Summers	425.00	140.00	55.00
(40)	Walter Johnson, Charles Street	1,200	400.00	160.00
(41)	Frank LaPorte, James Stephens	385.00	85.00	30.00
(42)	Joseph Lake, Robert Wallace	400.00	130.00	50.00
(43)	Albert Leifield, Mike Simon	385.00	85.00	30.00
(44)	John Lobert, Earl Moore	385.00	85.00	30.00
(45)	Arthur McCabe, Charles Starr	385.00	85.00	30.00
(46)	Lewis McCarty, Joseph McGinnity	400.00	130.00	60.00
(47)	Fred Merkle, George Wiltse	385.00	85.00	30.00
(48)	Frederick Payne, Edward Walsh	400.00	130.00	60.00
(49)	George Stovall, Terrence Turner	385.00	85.00	30.00
(50)	Otto Williams, Orville Woodruff	385.00	85.00	30.00

1912 T202 Hassan Triple Folders

Measuring about 5-1/4" x 2-1/4", Hassan cigarette cards carried the concept of multiple-player cards even further than the double-fold Mecca set of the previous year. Scored so that the player pictures on each end - which are full-color and very close to exact duplicates of T205 "Gold Borders" cards - can fold over the black-and-white action-photo center panel, the Hassan Triple Folder appears like a booklet when closed. The individual player panels are not necessarily related to the action scene. The Hassan Triple Folders feature player biographies on the back of the two individual cards with a description of the action on the back of the center panel. Values depend on the player featured in the center panel, as well as the players featured on the end cards. Moreso than most contemporary cards, the value of NM or better T202s that have been graded by a major certification company as well as the players featured on the end cards. Moreso than most contemporary issues, T202s that have been graded NM or better by a reputable certification company carry a larger premium over ungraded examples.

		NM	EX	VG
	Complete Set (132):	175,000	45,000	20,000
	Common Player:	600.00	175.00	55.00
(1)	A Close Play At The Home Plate (LaPorte, Wallace)	600.00	175.00	55.00
(2)	A Close Play At The Home Plate (Pelty, Wallace)	600.00	175.00	55.00
(3)	A Desperate Slide For Third (Cobb, O'Leary)	5,400	1,850	475.00
(4)	A Great Batsman (Barger, Bergen)	600.00	175.00	55.00
(5)	A Great Batsman (Bergen, Rucker)	600.00	175.00	55.00
(6)	Ambrose McConnell At Bat (Blair, Quinn)	600.00	175.00	55.00
(7)	A Wide Throw Saves Crawford (Mullin, Stanage)	600.00	175.00	55.00
(8)	Baker Gets His Man (Baker, Collins)	1,200	400.00	200.00
(9)	Birmingham Gets To Third (Johnson, Street)	1,250	450.00	175.00
(10)	Birmingham's Home Run (Birmingham, Turner)	600.00	175.00	55.00
(11)	Bush Just Misses Austin (Magee, Moran)	600.00	175.00	55.00
(12)	Carrigan Blocks His Man (Gaspar, McLean)	600.00	175.00	55.00
(13)	Carrigan Blocks His Man (Carrigan, Wagner)	600.00	175.00	55.00
(14)	Catching Him Napping (Bresnahan, Oakes)	600.00	175.00	55.00
(15)	Caught Asleep Off First (Bresnahan, Harmon)	600.00	175.00	55.00
(16)	Chance Beats Out A Hit (Chance, Foxen)	1,200	300.00	125.00
(17)	Chance Beats Out A Hit (Archer, McIntyre)	600.00	175.00	55.00
(18)	Chance Beats Out A Hit (Archer, Overall)	600.00	175.00	55.00
(19)	Chance Beats Out A Hit (Archer, Rowan)	600.00	175.00	55.00
(20)	Chance Beats Out A Hit (Chance, Shean)	1,100	350.00	200.00
(21)	Chase Dives Into Third (Chase, Wolter)	600.00	175.00	55.00
(22)	Chase Dives Into Third (Clarke, Gibson)	600.00	175.00	55.00
(23)	Chase Dives Into Third (Gibson, Phillippe)	600.00	175.00	55.00
(24)	Chase Gets Ball Too Late (Egan, Mitchell)	600.00	175.00	55.00
(25)	Chase Gets Ball Too Late (Chase, Wolter)	600.00	175.00	55.00
(26)	Chase Guarding First (Chase, Wolter)	600.00	175.00	55.00
(27)	Chase Guarding First (Clarke, Gibson)	600.00	175.00	55.00
(28)	Chase Guarding First (Gibson, Leifield)	600.00	175.00	55.00
(29)	Chase Ready For The Squeeze Play (Magee, Paskert)	600.00	175.00	55.00
(30)	Chase Safe At Third (Baker, Barry)	600.00	175.00	55.00
(31)	Chief Bender Waiting For A Good One (Bender, Thomas)	600.00	175.00	55.00
(32)	Clarke Hikes For Home (Bridwell, Kling)	600.00	175.00	55.00

(33)	Close At First (Ball, Stovall)	600.00	175.00	55.00
(34)	Close At The Plate (Payne, Walsh)	600.00	175.00	55.00
(35)	Close At The Plate (Payne, White)	600.00	175.00	55.00
(36)	Close At Third - Speaker (Speaker, Wood)	1,400	500.00	200.00
(37)	Close At Third - Wagner (Carrigan, Wagner)	600.00	175.00	55.00
(38)	Collins Easily Safe (Byrne, Clarke)	600.00	175.00	55.00
(39)	Collins Easily Safe (Baker, Collins)	600.00	175.00	55.00
(40)	Collins Easily Safe (Collins, Murphy)	600.00	175.00	55.00
(41)	Crawford About To Smash One (Stanage, Summers)	600.00	175.00	55.00
(42)	Cree Rolls Home (Daubert, Hummel)	600.00	175.00	55.00
(43)	Davy Jones' Great Slide (Delahanty, Jones)	600.00	175.00	55.00
(44)	Devlin Gets His Man (Devlin (Giants), Mathewson)	1,800	600.00	300.00
(45)	Devlin Gets His Man (Devlin (Rustlers), Mathewson)	3,500	1,200	500.00
(46)	Devlin Gets His Man (Fletcher, Mathewson)	1,900	700.00	300.00
(47)	Devlin Gets His Man (Mathewson, Meyers)	2,000	700.00	300.00
(48)	Donlin Out At First (Camnitz, Gibson)	600.00	175.00	55.00
(49)	Donlin Out At First (Doyle, Merkle)	600.00	175.00	55.00
(50)	Donlin Out At First (Leach, Wilson)	600.00	175.00	55.00
(51)	Donlin Out At First (Dooin, Magee)	600.00	175.00	55.00
(52)	Donlin Out At First (Gibson, Phillippe)	600.00	175.00	55.00
(53)	Dooin Gets His Man (Dooin, Doolan)	600.00	175.00	55.00
(54)	Dooin Gets His Man (Dooin, Lobert)	600.00	175.00	55.00
(55)	Dooin Gets His Man (Dooin, Titus)	600.00	175.00	55.00
(56)	Easy For Larry (Doyle, Merkle)	600.00	175.00	55.00
(57)	Elberfeld Beats The Throw (Elberfeld, Milan)	600.00	175.00	55.00
(58)	Elberfeld Gets His Man (Elberfeld, Milan)	600.00	175.00	55.00
(59)	Engle In A Close Play (Engle, Speaker)	1,300	400.00	200.00
(60)	Evers Makes A Safe Slide (Archer, Evers)	600.00	175.00	55.00
(61)	Evers Makes A Safe Slide (Chance, Evers)	1,700	600.00	300.00
(62)	Evers Makes A Safe Slide (Archer, Overall)	600.00	175.00	55.00
(63)	Evers Makes A Safe Slide (Archer, Reulbach)	600.00	175.00	55.00
(64)	Evers Makes A Safe Slide (Chance, Tinker)	3,000	1,000	400.00
(65)	Fast Work At Third (Cobb, O'Leary)	4,000	1,200	675.00
(66)	Ford Putting Over A Spitter (Ford, Vaughn)	600.00	175.00	55.00
(67)	Ford Putting Over A Spitter (Sweeney, Ford)	600.00	175.00	55.00
(68)	Good Play At Third (Cobb, Moriarity (Moriarty))	5,700	1,600	650.00
(69)	Grant Gets His Man (Grant, Hoblitzell)	600.00	175.00	55.00
(70)	Hal Chase Too Late (McConnell, McIntyre)	600.00	175.00	55.00
(71)	Hal Chase Too Late (McLean, Suggs)	600.00	175.00	55.00
(72)	Harry Lord At Third (Lennox, Tinker)	600.00	175.00	55.00
(73)	Hartzell Covering Third (Dahlen, Scanlan)	600.00	175.00	55.00
(74)	Hartsel Strikes Out (Gray, Groom)	600.00	175.00	55.00
(75)	Held At Third (Lord, Tannehill)	600.00	175.00	55.00
(76)	Jake Stahl Guarding First (Cicotte, Stahl)	1,300	500.00	200.00
(77)	Jim Delahanty At Bat (Delahanty, Jones)	600.00	175.00	55.00
(78)	Just Before The Battle (Ames, Meyers)	600.00	175.00	55.00
(79)	Just Before The Battle (Bresnahan, McGraw)	600.00	175.00	55.00
(80)	Just Before The Battle (Crandall, Meyers)	600.00	175.00	55.00
(81)	Just Before The Battle (Becker, Devore)	600.00	175.00	55.00
(82)	Just Before The Battle (Fletcher, Mathewson)	1,900	700.00	300.00
(83)	Just Before The Battle (Marquard, Meyers)	600.00	175.00	55.00
(84)	Just Before The Battle (Jennings, McGraw)	1,600	300.00	100.00
(85)	Just Before The Battle (Mathewson, Meyers)	1,300	500.00	200.00
(86)	Just Before The Battle (Murray, Snodgrass)	600.00	175.00	55.00
(87)	Just Before The Battle (Meyers, Wiltse)	600.00	175.00	55.00
(88)	Knight Catches A Runner (Johnson, Knight)	1,400	550.00	225.00
(89)	Lobert Almost Caught (Bridwell, Kling)	600.00	175.00	55.00
(90)	Lobert Almost Caught (Kling, Young)	1,950	450.00	225.00
(91)	Lobert Almost Caught (Kling, Mattern)	600.00	175.00	55.00
(92)	Lobert Almost Caught (Kling, Steinfeldt)	600.00	175.00	55.00

		NM	EX	VG
(93)	Lobert Gets Tenney (Dooin, Lobert)	600.00	175.00	55.00
(94)	Lord Catches His Man (Lord, Tannehil)	600.00	175.00	55.00
(95)	McConnell Caught (Needham, Richie)	600.00	175.00	55.00
(96)	McIntyre At Bat (McConnell, McIntyre)	600.00	175.00	55.00
(97)	Moriarty Spiked (Stanage, Willett)	600.00	175.00	55.00
(98)	Nearly Caught (Bates, Bescher)	600.00	175.00	55.00
(99)	Oldring Almost Home (Lord, Oldring)	600.00	175.00	55.00
(100)	Schaefer On First (McBride, Milan)	600.00	175.00	55.00
(101)	Schaefer Steals Second (Griffith, McBride)	600.00	175.00	55.00
(102)	Scoring From Second (Lord, Oldring)	600.00	175.00	55.00
(103)	Scrambling Back To First (Barger, Bergen)	600.00	175.00	55.00
(104)	Scrambling Back To First (Chase, Wolter)	600.00	175.00	55.00
(105)	Speaker Almost Caught (Clarke, Miller)	850.00	325.00	125.00
(106)	Speaker Rounding Third (Speaker, Wood)	1,400	500.00	300.00
(107)	Speaker Scores (Engle, Speaker)	1,400	500.00	200.00
(108)	Stahl Safe (Austin, Stovall)	600.00	175.00	55.00
(109)	Stone About To Swing (Schulte, Sheckard)	600.00	175.00	55.00
(110)	Sullivan Puts Up A High One (Evans, Huggins)	600.00	175.00	55.00
(111)	Sullivan Puts Up A High One (Gray, Groom)	600.00	175.00	55.00
(112)	Sweeney Gets Stahl (Ford, Vaughn)	600.00	175.00	55.00
(113)	Sweeney Gets Stahl (Ford, Sweeney)	600.00	175.00	55.00
(114)	Tenney Lands Safely (Latham, Raymond)	600.00	175.00	55.00
(115)	The Athletic Infield (Baker, Barry)	600.00	175.00	55.00
(116)	The Athletic Infield (Brown, Graham)	600.00	175.00	55.00
(117)	The Athletic Infield (Hauser, Konetchy)	600.00	175.00	55.00
(118)	The Athletic Infield (Krause, Thomas)	600.00	175.00	55.00
(119)	The Pinch Hitter (Egan, Hoblitzell)	600.00	175.00	55.00
(120)	The Scissors Slide (Birmingham, Turner)	600.00	175.00	55.00
(121)	Tom Jones At Bat (Fromme, McLean)	600.00	175.00	55.00
(122)	Tom Jones At Bat (Gaspar, McLean)	600.00	175.00	55.00
(123)	Too Late For Devlin (Ames, Meyers)	600.00	175.00	55.00
(124)	Too Late For Devlin (Crandall, Meyers)	600.00	175.00	55.00
(125)	Too Late For Devlin (Devlin (Giants), Mathewson)	2,000	700.00	300.00
(126)	Too Late For Devlin (Devlin (Rustlers), Mathewson)	3,900	1,400	600.00
(127)	Too Late For Devlin (Marquard, Meyers)	600.00	175.00	55.00
(128)	Too Late For Devlin (Meyers, Wiltse)	600.00	175.00	55.00
(129)	Ty Cobb Steals Third (Cobb, Jennings)	7,000	2,000	1,100
(130)	Ty Cobb Steals Third (Cobb, Moriarty)	5,400	1,850	850.00
(131)	Ty Cobb Steals Third (Austin, Stovall)	2,500	900.00	400.00
(132)	Wheat Strikes Out (Dahlen, Wheat)	1,300	500.00	200.00

1909 T204

(See 1909 Ramly Cigarettes, 1909 T.T.T. Cigarettes.)

1911 T205 Gold Border

Featuring distinctive gold-leaf borders, these cards were issued in a number of different cigarette brands. The cards nominally measure 1-7/16" x 2-5/8" although many cards, even though untrimmed or unaltered, measure somewhat less than those dimensions in length and/or width. American League cards feature a color lithograph of the player inside a stylized baseball diamond. National League cards have head-and-shoulders portraits on a plain background, plus the first-ever use of a facsimile autograph in a major card set. The 12 minor league players in the set feature three-quarter length portraits or action pictures in an elaborate frame of columns and other devices. Card backs of the major leaguers carry the player's full name (another first) and statistics. Card backs of the minor leaguers lack the statistics. The complete set price does not include the scarcer of the letter-suffixed variations. Values shown are for cards with the most common cigarette advertising on back: Piedmont and Sweet Caporal. Cards of other brands may carry a premium (see listings under brand name). The condition of the fragile gold leaf on the borders is an important grading consideration.

		NM	EX	VG
	Common Player	500.00	80.00	25.00
(1)	Edward J. Abbaticchio	500.00	80.00	25.00
(2)	Doc Adkins	1,620	240.00	95.00
(3)	Leon K. Ames	500.00	80.00	25.00
(4)	Jas. P. Archer	500.00	80.00	25.00
(5)	Jimmy Austin	500.00	80.00	25.00
(6)	Bill Bailey	500.00	80.00	25.00
(7)	Home Run Baker	2,340	350.00	140.00
(8)	Neal Ball	500.00	80.00	25.00
(9)	E.B. Barger (Full "B" on cap.)	1,500	220.00	90.00
(10)	E.B. Barger (Partial "B" on cap.)	2,400	360.00	145.00
(11)	Jack Barry	500.00	80.00	25.00
(12)	Emil Batch	1,620	240.00	95.00
(13)	John W. Bates	500.00	80.00	25.00
(14)	Fred Beck	500.00	80.00	25.00
(15)	B. Becker	500.00	80.00	25.00
(16)	George G. Bell	500.00	80.00	25.00
(17)	Chas. Bender	2,100	315.00	120.00
(18)	William Bergen	500.00	80.00	25.00
(19)	Bob Bescher	500.00	80.00	25.00
(20)	Joe Birmingham	500.00	80.00	25.00
(21)	Lena Blackburne	500.00	80.00	25.00
(22)	William E. Bransfield	500.00	80.00	25.00
(23)	Roger P. Bresnahan (Mouth closed.)	1,680	250.00	105.00
(24)	Roger P. Bresnahan (Mouth open.)	3,420	510.00	210.00
(25)	A.H. Bridwell	500.00	80.00	25.00
(26)	Mordecai Brown	1,980	295.00	120.00
(27)	Robert Byrne	500.00	80.00	25.00
(28)	Hick Cady	1,620	240.00	95.00
(29)	H. Camnitz	500.00	80.00	25.00
(30)	Bill Carrigan	500.00	80.00	25.00
(31)	Frank J. Chance	2,280	345.00	140.00
(32a)	Hal Chase (Both ears show, gold diamond frame extends below shoulders.)	1,080	165.00	65.00
(32b)	Hal Chase (Both ears show, gold diamond frame ends at shoulders.)	1,620	240.00	95.00
(33)	Hal Chase (Only left ear shows.)	3,240	480.00	195.00
(34)	Ed Cicotte	2,580	390.00	150.00
(35)	Fred C. Clarke	1,440	215.00	90.00
(36)	Ty Cobb	13,200	3,750	1,080
(37)	Eddie Collins (Mouth closed.)	2,100	315.00	120.00
(38)	Eddie Collins (Mouth open.)	4,680	700.00	285.00
(39)	Jimmy Collins	2,580	390.00	155.00
(40)	Frank J. Corridon	500.00	80.00	25.00
(41a)	Otis Crandall ("t" not crossed in name)	1,020	150.00	60.00
(41b)	Otis Crandall ("t" crossed in name)	1,320	200.00	80.00
(42)	Lou Criger	500.00	80.00	25.00
(43)	W.F. Dahlen	2,200	400.00	175.00
(44)	Jake Daubert	500.00	10.00	25.00
(45)	Jim Delahanty	500.00	80.00	25.00
(46)	Arthur Devlin	500.00	80.00	25.00
(47)	Josh Devore	500.00	80.00	25.00
(48)	W.R. Dickson	500.00	80.00	25.00
(49)	Jiggs Donohue (Donahue)	2,880	435.00	175.00
(50)	Chas. S. Dooin	500.00	80.00	25.00
(51)	Michael J. Doolan	500.00	80.00	25.00
(52a)	Patsy Dougherty (Red sock for team emblem.)	2,500	500.00	200.00
(52b)	Patsy Dougherty (White sock for team emblem.)	1,000	400.00	100.00
(53)	Thomas Downey	500.00	80.00	25.00
(54)	Larry Doyle	500.00	80.00	25.00
(55)	Hugh Duffy	2,820	420.00	170.00
(56)	Jack Dunn	2,640	395.00	155.00
(57)	Jimmy Dygert	500.00	80.00	25.00
(58)	R. Egan	500.00	80.00	25.00
(59)	Kid Elberfeld	500.00	80.00	25.00
(60)	Clyde Engle	500.00	80.00	25.00
(61)	Louis Evans	500.00	80.00	25.00
(62)	John J. Evers	3,300	495.00	200.00
(63)	Robert Ewing	500.00	80.00	25.00
(64)	G.C. Ferguson	500.00	80.00	25.00
(65)	Ray Fisher	2,940	440.00	175.00
(66)	Arthur Fletcher	500.00	80.00	25.00
(67)	John A. Flynn	500.00	80.00	25.00
(68)	Russ Ford (Black cap.)	700.00	80.00	50.00
(69)	Russ Ford (White cap.)	2,220	330.00	135.00
(70)	Wm. A. Foxen	500.00	80.00	25.00
(71)	Jimmy Frick	1,620	240.00	100.00
(72)	Arthur Fromme	500.00	80.00	25.00
(73)	Earl Gardner	700.00	80.00	50.00
(74)	H.L. Gaspar	500.00	80.00	25.00
(75)	George Gibson	500.00	80.00	25.00
(76)	Wilbur Goode	500.00	80.00	25.00
(77)	George F. Graham (Rustlers)	500.00	80.00	25.00
(78)	George F. Graham (Cubs)	1,680	255.00	105.00
(79)	Edward L. Grant	2,400	360.00	145.00
(80a)	Dolly Gray (No stats on back.)	1,000	200.00	50.00
(80b)	Dolly Gray (Stats on back.)	4,800	720.00	290.00
(81)	Clark Griffith	1,800	270.00	110.00
(82)	Bob Groom	500.00	80.00	55.00
(83)	Charlie Hanford	1,620	240.00	100.00
(84)	Bob Harmon (Both ears show.)	500.00	80.00	25.00
(85)	Bob Harmon (Only left ear shows.)	2,520	380.00	150.00
(86)	Topsy Hartsel	500.00	80.00	25.00
(87)	Arnold J. Hauser	500.00	80.00	25.00
(88)	Charlie Hemphill	500.00	80.00	25.00
(89)	C.L. Herzog	500.00	80.00	25.00
(90a)	R. Hoblitzell (No stats on back.) (A PSA-graded EX-MT example was auctioned for $33,000 in 2005.)	500.00	21,600	9,900
(90b)	R. Hoblitzell ("Cin." after 2nd 1908 in stats.)	1,560	235.00	100.00
(90c)	R. Hoblitzel (Name incorrect, no "Cin." after 1908 in stats.)	3,420	510.00	210.00
(90d)	R. Hoblitzell (Name correct, "Cin." after 1908 in stats.)	8,400	1,200	510.00
(91)	Danny Hoffman	500.00	80.00	25.00
(92)	Miller J. Huggins	1,920	290.00	115.00
(93)	John E. Hummel	500.00	80.00	25.00
(94)	Fred Jacklitsch	500.00	80.00	25.00
(95)	Hughie Jennings	1,440	215.00	85.00
(96)	Walter Johnson	8,400	1,320	510.00
(97)	D. Jones	500.00	80.00	25.00
(98)	Tom Jones	500.00	80.00	25.00
(99)	Addie Joss	9,000	1,500	700.00
(100)	Ed Karger	1,600	300.00	100.00
(101)	Ed Killian	500.00	80.00	25.00
(102)	Red Kleinow	1,560	235.00	90.00
(103)	John G. Kling	500.00	80.00	25.00
(104)	Jack Knight	500.00	80.00	25.00
(105)	Ed Konetchy	500.00	80.00	25.00
(106)	Harry Krause	500.00	80.00	25.00
(107)	Floyd M. Kroh	500.00	80.00	25.00
(108)	Frank LaPorte	500.00	80.00	25.00
(109)	Frank Lang (Lange)	500.00	80.00	25.00
(110a)	A. Latham (A. Latham on back.)	700.00	80.00	50.00
(110b)	A. Latham (W.A. Latham on back.)	1,600	300.00	50.00
(111)	Thomas W. Leach	500.00	80.00	25.00
(112)	Watty Lee	1,620	240.00	100.00
(113)	Sam Leever	500.00	80.00	25.00
(114a)	A. Leifield (Initial "A." on front.)	700.00	80.00	50.00
(114b)	A.P. Leifield (Initials "A.P." on front.)	1,600	300.00	50.00
(115)	Edgar Lennox	500.00	80.00	25.00
(116)	Paddy Livingston	500.00	80.00	25.00
(117)	John B. Lobert	500.00	80.00	25.00
(118)	Bris Lord (Athletics)	500.00	80.00	25.00
(119)	Harry Lord (White Sox)	500.00	80.00	25.00
(120)	Jno. C. Lush	500.00	80.00	25.00
(121)	Nick Maddox	500.00	80.00	25.00
(122)	Sherwood R. Magee	870.00	135.00	50.00
(123)	R.W. Marquard	2,280	345.00	140.00
(124)	C. Mathewson	8,820	1,320	495.00
(124a)	Christy Mathewson (1 loss variation (only on Cycle backs).)	20,000	10,000	4,000
(125)	A.A. Mattern	500.00	80.00	25.00
(126)	Sport McAllister	1,620	240.00	100.00
(127)	George McBride	870.00	135.00	55.00
(128)	Amby McConnell	500.00	80.00	25.00
(129)	P.M. McElveen	500.00	80.00	25.00
(130)	J.J. McGraw	2,280	345.00	140.00
(131)	Harry McIntire (Cubs)	500.00	80.00	25.00
(132)	Matty McIntyre (White Sox)	500.00	80.00	25.00
(133)	M.A. McLean (Initials actually J.B.)	500.00	80.00	435.00
(134)	Fred Merkle	500.00	80.00	25.00
(135)	George Merritt	1,620	240.00	100.00
(136)	J.T. Meyers	500.00	80.00	25.00
(137)	Clyde Milan	500.00	80.00	25.00
(138)	J.D. Miller	500.00	80.00	25.00
(139)	M.F. Mitchell	500.00	80.00	25.00
(140a)	P.J. Moran (Stray line of type below stats.)	12,000	1,800	720.00
(140b)	P.J. Moran (No stray line.)	500.00	80.00	25.00
(141)	George Moriarty	500.00	80.00	25.00
(142)	George Mullin	500.00	80.00	25.00
(143)	Danny Murphy	500.00	80.00	25.00
(144)	Jack Murray	500.00	80.00	25.00
(145)	John Nee	1,620	240.00	100.00
(146)	Thomas J. Needham	500.00	80.00	25.00
(147)	Rebel Oakes	500.00	80.00	25.00
(148)	Rube Oldring	500.00	80.00	25.00
(149)	Charley O'Leary	500.00	80.00	25.00
(150)	Fred Olmstead	500.00	80.00	25.00
(151)	Orval Overall	500.00	80.00	25.00
(152)	Freddy Parent	500.00	80.00	25.00
(153)	George Paskert	500.00	80.00	25.00
(154)	Fred Payne	500.00	80.00	25.00
(155)	Barney Pelty	840.00	135.00	55.00
(156)	John Pfeister	500.00	80.00	25.00
(157)	Jimmy Phelan	1,620	240.00	100.00
(158)	E.J. Phelps	500.00	80.00	25.00
(159)	C. Phillippe	500.00	80.00	25.00
(160)	Jack Quinn	500.00	80.00	25.00
(161)	A.L. Raymond	1,600	400.00	200.00
(162)	E.M. Reulbach	500.00	80.00	25.00
(163)	Lewis Richie	500.00	80.00	25.00
(164)	John A. Rowan	3,000	500.00	200.00
(165)	George N. Rucker	500.00	80.00	25.00
(166)	W.D. Scanlan	2,940	440.00	175.00
(167)	Germany Schaefer	500.00	80.00	25.00
(168)	George Schlei	500.00	80.00	25.00
(169)	Boss Schmidt	500.00	80.00	25.00
(170)	F.M. Schulte	500.00	80.00	25.00
(171)	Jim Scott	500.00	80.00	25.00
(172)	B.H. Sharpe	500.00	80.00	25.00
(173)	David Shean (Rustlers)	500.00	80.00	25.00
(174)	David Shean (Cubs)	2,520	380.00	150.00
(175)	Jas. T. Sheckard	500.00	80.00	25.00
(176)	Hack Simmons	500.00	80.00	25.00
(177)	Tony Smith	500.00	80.00	25.00
(178)	Fred C. Snodgrass	500.00	80.00	25.00
(179)	Tris Speaker	5,190	780.00	315.00
(180)	Jake Stahl	1,140	170.00	75.00

Danny Murphy outfielder of the Philadelphia Athletics, has been playing professional ball for a long time, having commenced when only eighteen, and is still going strong. He has been with the Athletics since 1902, playing second base till 1908, and doing it well, but he had to make way for the rapidly rising Collins, and to keep his big bat in the line-up he was shifted to the outfield. Danny kept right on fielding well and slugging when at bat, having made 84 two-baggers, 39 three-baggers and 16 home runs in the last three years.

BASE BALL SERIES — Smoke or Chew Honest LONG CUT ALWAYS THE BEST.

(181)	Oscar Stanage	500.00	80.00	25.00
(182)	Harry Steinfeldt	500.00	80.00	25.00
(183)	George Stone	500.00	80.00	25.00
(184)	George Stovall	500.00	80.00	25.00
(185)	Gabby Street	500.00	80.00	25.00
(186)	George F. Suggs	3,000	500.00	200.00
(187)	Ed Summers	500.00	80.00	25.00
(188)	Jeff Sweeney	2,700	405.00	165.00
(189)	Lee Tannehill	500.00	80.00	25.00
(190)	Ira Thomas	500.00	80.00	25.00
(191)	Joe Tinker	2,160	330.00	135.00
(192)	John Titus	500.00	80.00	25.00
(193)	Terry Turner	2,640	395.00	155.00
(194)	James Vaughn	2,880	435.00	175.00
(195)	Charles Wagner	3,180	475.00	195.00
(196)	Bobby Wallace (With cap.)	1,770	270.00	110.00
(197a)	Bobby Wallace (No cap, one line of 1910 stats.)	18,000	2,700	1,080
(197b)	Bobby Wallace (No cap, two lines of 1910 stats.)	7,800	1,170	470.00
(198)	Ed Walsh	5,400	810.00	330.00
(199)	Z.D. Wheat	2,280	345.00	140.00
(200)	Doc White (White Sox)	500.00	80.00	25.00
(201)	Kirb. White (Pirates)	1,600	300.00	100.00
(202a)	Irvin K. Wilhelm ("suffered" in 18th line of bio. Very scarce, only found with Hassan back.)	9,000	5,000	2,000
(202b)	Irvin K. Wilhelm ("suffe ed" in 18th line of bio)	3,000	300.00	150.00
(203)	Ed Willett	500.00	80.00	25.00
(204)	J. Owen Wilson	500.00	80.00	25.00
(205)	George R. Wiltse (Both ears show.)	500.00	80.00	25.00
(206)	George R. Wiltse (Only right ear shows.)	2,580	390.00	155.00
(207)	Harry Wolter	500.00	80.00	25.00
(208)	Cy Young	11,100	1,650	665.00

1909-11 T206 White Border

The nearly 525 cards which make up the T206 set are the most popular of the early tobacco card issues. Players are depicted in color lithographs surrounded by a white border. The player's last name on the 1-7/16" x 2-5/8" cards appears at the bottom with the city and league, when a city had more than one team. Backs contain an ad for one of 16 brands of cigarettes. There are 389 major leaguer cards and 134 minor leaguer cards in the set, but with front/back varieties the number of potentially different cards runs into the thousands. The set features many expensive cards including a number of pose and/or team variations. Values shown are for cards with the most common advertising on back: Piedmont and Sweet Caporal. Other backs carry a premium depending on scarcity (see listings under brand names). Several popularly collected printing errors have been included in the listings.

		NM	EX	VG
Common Player:		400.00	100.00	50.00
(1)	Ed Abbaticchio (Blue sleeves.)	400.00	100.00	50.00
(2)	Ed Abbaticchio (Brown sleeves.)	400.00	100.00	50.00
(3)	Fred Abbott	400.00	100.00	50.00
(4)	Bill Abstein	400.00	100.00	50.00
(5)	Doc Adkins	400.00	100.00	50.00
(6)	Whitey Alperman	400.00	100.00	50.00
(7)	Red Ames (Hands at chest.)	800.00	200.00	75.00
(8)	Red Ames (Hands above head.)	400.00	100.00	50.00
(9)	Red Ames (Portrait)	400.00	100.00	50.00
(10)	John Anderson	400.00	100.00	50.00
(11)	Frank Arellanes	400.00	100.00	50.00
(12)	Herman Armbruster	400.00	100.00	50.00
(13)	Harry Arndt	400.00	100.00	50.00
(14)	Jake Atz	400.00	100.00	50.00
(15)	Home Run Baker	1,700	350.00	175.00
(16)	Neal Ball (New York)	400.00	100.00	50.00
(17)	Neal Ball (Cleveland)	400.00	100.00	50.00
(18)	Jap Barbeau	400.00	100.00	50.00
(19)	Cy Barger	400.00	100.00	50.00
(20)	Jack Barry (Philadelphia)	400.00	100.00	50.00
(21)	Shad Barry (Milwaukee)	400.00	100.00	50.00
(22)	Jack Bastian	1,300	350.00	125.00
(23)	Emil Batch	400.00	100.00	50.00
(24)	Johnny Bates	400.00	100.00	50.00
(25)	Harry Bay	1,300	350.00	125.00
(26)	Ginger Beaumont	400.00	100.00	50.00
(27)	Fred Beck	400.00	100.00	50.00
(28)	Beals Becker	400.00	100.00	50.00
(29)	Jake Beckley	1,500	300.00	100.00
(30)	George Bell (Hands above head.)	400.00	100.00	50.00

(31)	George Bell (Pitching follow through.)	400.00	100.00	50.00
(32)	Chief Bender (Pitching, no trees in background.)	1,800	300.00	120.00
(33)	Chief Bender (Pitching, trees in background.)	1,900	400.00	140.00
(34)	Chief Bender (Portrait)	1,300	300.00	125.00
(35)	Bill Bergen (Batting)	400.00	100.00	50.00
(36)	Bill Bergen (Catching)	400.00	100.00	50.00
(37)	Heinie Berger	400.00	100.00	50.00
(38)	Bill Bernhard	1,300	400.00	125.00
(39)	Bob Bescher (Hands in air.)	400.00	100.00	50.00
(40)	Bob Bescher (Portrait)	400.00	100.00	50.00
(41)	Joe Birmingham	900.00	200.00	100.00
(42)	Lena Blackburne	400.00	100.00	50.00
(43)	Jack Bliss	400.00	100.00	50.00
(44)	Frank Bowerman	400.00	100.00	50.00
(45)	Bill Bradley (Portrait)	400.00	100.00	50.00
(46)	Bill Bradley (With bat.)	400.00	100.00	50.00
(47)	Dave Brain	400.00	100.00	50.00
(48)	Kitty Bransfield	400.00	100.00	50.00
(49)	Roy Brashear	400.00	100.00	50.00
(50)	Ted Breitenstein	1,300	400.00	125.00
(51)	Roger Bresnahan (Portrait)	1,700	300.00	100.00
(52)	Roger Bresnahan (With bat.)	1,350	400.00	100.00
(53)	Al Bridwell (Portrait, no cap.)	400.00	100.00	50.00
(54)	Al Bridwell (Portrait, with cap.)	400.00	100.00	50.00
(55a)	George Brown (Browne) (Chicago)	400.00	100.00	50.00
(55b)	George Brown (Browne) (Washington)	2,100	400.00	200.00
(56)	Mordecai Brown (Chicago on shirt.)	1,600	300.00	110.00
(57)	Mordecai Brown (Cubs on shirt.)	3,600	700.00	300.00
(58)	Mordecai Brown (Portrait)	1,500	300.00	110.00
(59)	Al Burch (Batting)	1,000	200.00	100.00
(60)	Al Burch (Fielding)	400.00	100.00	50.00
(61)	Fred Burchell	400.00	100.00	50.00
(62)	Jimmy Burke	400.00	100.00	50.00
(63)	Bill Burns	400.00	100.00	50.00
(64)	Donie Bush	400.00	100.00	50.00
(65)	John Butler	400.00	100.00	50.00
(66)	Bobby Byrne	400.00	100.00	50.00
(67)	Howie Camnitz (Arm at side.)	400.00	100.00	50.00
(68)	Howie Camnitz (Arms folded.)	400.00	100.00	50.00
(69)	Howie Camnitz (Hands above head.)	400.00	100.00	50.00
(70)	Billy Campbell	400.00	100.00	50.00
(71)	Scoops Carey	1,300	400.00	125.00
(72)	Charley Carr	400.00	100.00	50.00
(73)	Bill Carrigan	400.00	100.00	50.00
(74)	Doc Casey	400.00	100.00	50.00
(75)	Peter Cassidy	400.00	100.00	50.00
(76)	Frank Chance (Batting)	1,800	300.00	110.00
(77)	Frank Chance (Portrait, red background.)	1,900	400.00	125.00
(78)	Frank Chance (Portrait, yellow background.)	1,400	300.00	110.00
(79)	Bill Chappelle	400.00	100.00	50.00
(80)	Chappie Charles	400.00	100.00	50.00
(81)	Hal Chase (Holding trophy.)	800.00	200.00	100.00
(82)	Hal Chase (Portrait, blue background.)	900.00	200.00	100.00
(83)	Hal Chase (Portrait, pink background.)	1,000	200.00	100.00
(84)	Hal Chase (Throwing, dark cap.)	1,000	200.00	100.00
(85)	Hal Chase (Throwing, white cap.)	1,000	200.00	100.00
(86)	Jack Chesbro	1,900	300.00	125.00
(87)	Ed Cicotte	1,400	300.00	100.00
(88)	Bill Clancy (Clancey)	400.00	100.00	50.00
(89)	Josh Clark (Columbus) (Clarke)	400.00	100.00	50.00
(90)	Fred Clarke (Pittsburgh, holding bat.)	1,200	200.00	100.00
(91)	Fred Clarke (Pittsburgh, portrait.)	1,400	300.00	100.00
(92)	J.J. Clarke (Nig) (Cleveland)	400.00	100.00	50.00
(93)	Bill Clymer	400.00	100.00	50.00
(94)	Ty Cobb (Portrait, green background.)	9,000	2,600	1,500
(95a)	Ty Cobb (Portrait, red background.)	4,500	1,600	900.00
(95b)	Ty Cobb (Portrait, red background, Ty Cobb brand back.)		120,000	72,000
(96)	Ty Cobb (Bat off shoulder.)	9,600	2,300	1,000
(97)	Ty Cobb (Bat on shoulder.)	9,300	1,900	1,000
(98)	Cad Coles	1,300	400.00	125.00
(99)	Eddie Collins (Philadelphia)	1,400	400.00	125.00
(100)	Jimmy Collins (Minneapolis)	1,300	200.00	100.00
(101)	Bunk Congalton	400.00	100.00	50.00
(102)	Wid Conroy (Fielding)	400.00	100.00	50.00
(103)	Wid Conroy (With bat.)	400.00	100.00	50.00
(104)	Harry Covaleski (Coveleski)	400.00	100.00	50.00
(105)	Doc Crandall (Portrait, no cap.)	400.00	100.00	50.00
(106)	Doc Crandall (Portrait, with cap.)	400.00	100.00	50.00
(107)	Bill Cranston	1,300	400.00	125.00
(108)	Gavvy Cravath	400.00	100.00	50.00
(109)	Sam Crawford (Throwing)	1,700	300.00	125.00
(110)	Sam Crawford (With bat.)	1,500	300.00	110.00
(111)	Birdie Cree	400.00	100.00	50.00
(112)	Lou Criger	400.00	100.00	50.00
(113)	Dode Criss	400.00	100.00	50.00
(114)	Monte Cross	400.00	100.00	50.00
(115a)	Bill Dahlen (Boston)	1,000	400.00	125.00
(115b)	Bill Dahlen (Brooklyn)	2,100	400.00	200.00
(116)	Paul Davidson	400.00	100.00	50.00
(117)	George Davis (Chicago)	1,600	300.00	100.00
(118)	Harry Davis (Philadelphia, Davis on front.)	400.00	100.00	50.00
(119)	Harry Davis (Philadelphia, H. Davis on front.)	400.00	100.00	50.00
(120)	Frank Delehanty (Delahanty) (Louisville)	400.00	100.00	50.00

(121)	Jim Delehanty (Delahanty) (Washington)	400.00	100.00	50.00
(122a)	Ray Demmitt (New York)	400.00	100.00	50.00
(122b)	Ray Demmitt (St. Louis)	42,000	13,000	6,500
(123)	Rube Dessau	400.00	100.00	50.00
(124)	Art Devlin	400.00	100.00	50.00
(125)	Josh Devore	400.00	100.00	50.00
(126)	Bill Dineen (Dinneen)	400.00	100.00	50.00
(127)	Mike Donlin (Fielding)	800.00	200.00	100.00
(128)	Mike Donlin (Seated)	800.00	200.00	100.00
(129)	Mike Donlin (With bat.)	400.00	100.00	50.00
(130)	Jiggs Donohue (Donahue)	400.00	100.00	50.00
(131)	Wild Bill Donovan (Portrait)	400.00	100.00	50.00
(132)	Wild Bill Donovan (Throwing)	400.00	100.00	50.00
(133)	Red Dooin	400.00	100.00	50.00
(134)	Mickey Doolan (Batting)	400.00	100.00	50.00
(135)	Mickey Doolan (Fielding)	400.00	100.00	50.00
(136)	Mickey Doolin (Doolan)	400.00	100.00	50.00
(137)	Gus Dorner	400.00	100.00	50.00
(138)	Patsy Dougherty (Arm in air.)	400.00	100.00	50.00
(139)	Patsy Dougherty (Portrait)	400.00	100.00	50.00
(140)	Tom Downey (Batting)	400.00	100.00	50.00
(141)	Tom Downey (Fielding)	400.00	100.00	50.00
(142)	Jerry Downs	400.00	100.00	50.00
(143a)	Joe Doyle (N.Y. Nat'l., hands above head.)			72,000
(143b)	Joe Doyle (N.Y., hands above head.)	2,200	500.00	125.00
(144)	Larry Doyle (N.Y. Nat'l., portrait.)	400.00	100.00	50.00
(145)	Larry Doyle (N.Y. Nat'l., throwing.)	400.00	100.00	50.00
(146)	Larry Doyle (N.Y. Nat'l., with bat.)	400.00	100.00	50.00
(147)	Jean Dubuc	400.00	100.00	50.00
(148)	Hugh Duffy	1,700	300.00	110.00
(149)	Jack Dunn (Baltimore)	400.00	100.00	50.00
(150)	Joe Dunn (Brooklyn)	400.00	100.00	50.00
(151)	Bull Durham	400.00	100.00	50.00
(152)	Jimmy Dygert	400.00	100.00	50.00
(153)	Ted Easterly	400.00	100.00	50.00
(154)	Dick Egan	400.00	100.00	50.00
(155a)	Kid Elberfeld (New York)	400.00	100.00	50.00
(155b)	Kid Elberfeld (Washington, portrait.)	6,600	1,200	500.00
(156)	Kid Elberfeld (Washington, fielding.)	400.00	100.00	50.00
(157)	Roy Ellam	1,300	400.00	125.00
(158)	Clyde Engle	400.00	100.00	50.00
(159)	Steve Evans	400.00	100.00	50.00
(160)	Johnny Evers (Portrait)	3,000	600.00	200.00
(161)	Johnny Evers (With bat, Chicago on shirt.)	1,400	300.00	125.00
(162)	Johnny Evers (With bat, Cubs on shirt.)	1,900	400.00	150.00
(163)	Bob Ewing	400.00	100.00	50.00
(164)	Cecil Ferguson	400.00	100.00	50.00
(165)	Hobe Ferris	400.00	100.00	50.00
(166)	Lou Fiene (Portrait)	400.00	100.00	50.00
(167)	Lou Fiene (Throwing)	400.00	100.00	50.00
(168)	Steamer Flanagan	400.00	100.00	50.00
(169)	Art Fletcher	400.00	100.00	50.00
(170)	Elmer Flick	2,000	400.00	100.00
(171)	Russ Ford	400.00	100.00	50.00
(172)	Ed Foster	1,300	400.00	125.00
(173)	Jerry Freeman	400.00	100.00	50.00
(174)	John Frill	400.00	100.00	50.00
(175)	Charlie Fritz	1,300	400.00	125.00
(176)	Art Fromme	400.00	100.00	50.00
(177)	Chick Gandil	1,200	300.00	100.00
(178)	Bob Ganley	400.00	100.00	50.00
(179)	John Ganzel	400.00	100.00	50.00
(180)	Harry Gasper	400.00	100.00	50.00
(181)	Rube Geyer	400.00	100.00	50.00
(182)	George Gibson	400.00	100.00	50.00
(183)	Billy Gilbert	400.00	100.00	50.00
(184)	Wilbur Goode (Good)	400.00	100.00	50.00
(185)	Bill Graham (St. Louis)	400.00	100.00	50.00
(186)	Peaches Graham (Boston)	400.00	100.00	50.00
(187)	Dolly Gray	400.00	100.00	50.00
(188)	Ed Greminger	1,300	400.00	125.00
(189)	Clark Griffith (Batting)	1,800	300.00	100.00
(190)	Clark Griffith (Portrait)	1,600	300.00	100.00
(191)	Moose Grimshaw	400.00	100.00	50.00
(192)	Bob Groom	400.00	100.00	50.00
(193)	Tom Guiheen	1,300	400.00	125.00
(194)	Ed Hahn	400.00	100.00	50.00
(195)	Bob Hall	400.00	100.00	50.00
(196)	Bill Hallman	400.00	100.00	50.00
(197)	Jack Hannifan (Hannifin)	400.00	100.00	50.00
(198)	Bill Hart (Little Rock)	1,300	400.00	125.00
(199)	Jimmy Hart (Montgomery)	1,300	400.00	125.00
(200)	Topsy Hartsel	400.00	100.00	50.00
(201)	Jack Hayden	400.00	100.00	50.00
(202)	J. Ross Helm	1,300	400.00	125.00
(203)	Charlie Hemphill	400.00	100.00	50.00
(204)	Buck Herzog (Boston)	800.00	200.00	100.00
(205)	Buck Herzog (New York)	400.00	100.00	50.00
(206)	Gordon Hickman	1,300	400.00	125.00
(207)	Bill Hinchman (Cleveland)	400.00	100.00	50.00
(208)	Harry Hinchman (Toledo)	1,300	400.00	125.00
(209)	Dick Hoblitzell	400.00	100.00	50.00
(210)	Danny Hoffman (St. Louis)	400.00	100.00	50.00
(211)	Izzy Hoffman (Providence)	400.00	100.00	50.00
(212)	Solly Hofman	400.00	100.00	50.00
(213)	Bock Hooker	1,300	400.00	125.00
(214)	Del Howard (Chicago)	400.00	100.00	50.00
(215)	Ernie Howard (Savannah)	1,300	400.00	125.00
(216)	Harry Howell (Hand at waist.)	400.00	100.00	50.00
(217)	Harry Howell (Portrait)	400.00	100.00	50.00
(218)	Miller Huggins (Hands at mouth.)	1,400	300.00	100.00
(219)	Miller Huggins (Portrait)	1,200	200.00	100.00
(220)	Rudy Hulswitt	400.00	100.00	50.00
(221)	John Hummel	400.00	100.00	50.00
(222)	George Hunter	400.00	100.00	50.00
(223)	Frank Isbell	400.00	100.00	50.00
(224)	Fred Jacklitsch	400.00	100.00	50.00

(225)	Jimmy Jackson	400.00	100.00	50.00
(226)	Hughie Jennings	1,300	200.00	100.00
	(One hand showing.)			
(227)	Hughie Jennings	1,400	300.00	100.00
	(Both hands showing.)			
(228)	Hughie Jennings (Portrait)	1,300	200.00	125.00
(229)	Walter Johnson	5,400	1,000	400.00
	(Hands at chest.)			
(230)	Walter Johnson (Portrait)	4,800	1,400	700.00
(231)	Fielder Jones	400.00	100.00	50.00
	(Chicago, hands at hips.)			
(232)	Fielder Jones	400.00	100.00	50.00
	(Chicago, portrait.)			
(233)	Davy Jones (Detroit)	400.00	100.00	50.00
(234)	Tom Jones (St. Louis)	400.00	100.00	50.00
(235)	Dutch Jordan (Atlanta)	1,300	400.00	125.00
(236)	Tim Jordan (Brooklyn, batting.)	400.00	100.00	50.00
(237)	Tim Jordan	400.00	100.00	50.00
	(Brooklyn, portrait.)			
(238)	Addie Joss (Pitching)	1,800	300.00	120.00
(239)	Addie Joss (Portrait)	1,500	300.00	125.00
(240)	Ed Karger	400.00	100.00	50.00
(241)	Willie Keeler (Portrait)	2,500	500.00	200.00
(242)	Willie Keeler (W/bat.)	2,500	500.00	200.00
(243)	Joe Kelley	1,300	200.00	100.00
(244)	J.F. Kiernan	1,300	400.00	125.00
(245)	Ed Killian (Pitching)	400.00	100.00	50.00
(246)	Ed Killian (Portrait)	400.00	100.00	50.00
(247)	Frank King	1,300	400.00	125.00
(248)	Rube Kisinger	400.00	100.00	50.00
(249a)	Red Kleinow (Boston)	2,100	400.00	200.00
(249b)	Red Kleinow	400.00	100.00	50.00
	(New York, catching.)			
(250)	Red Kleinow	400.00	100.00	50.00
	(New York, with bat.)			
(251)	Johnny Kling	400.00	100.00	50.00
(252)	Otto Knabe	400.00	100.00	50.00
(253)	Jack Knight (Portrait)	400.00	100.00	50.00
(254)	Jack Knight (With bat.)	400.00	100.00	50.00
(255)	Ed Konetchy	400.00	100.00	50.00
	(Glove above head.)			
(256)	Ed Konetchy	400.00	100.00	50.00
	(Glove near ground.)			
(257)	Harry Krause (Pitching)	400.00	100.00	50.00
(258)	Harry Krause (Portrait)	400.00	100.00	50.00
(259)	Rube Kroh	400.00	100.00	50.00
(260)	Art Kruger (Krueger)	400.00	100.00	50.00
(261)	James Lafitte	1,300	400.00	125.00
(262)	Nap Lajoie (Portrait)	3,600	700.00	300.00
(263)	Nap Lajoie (Throwing)	2,900	500.00	200.00
(264)	Nap Lajoie (With bat.)	3,600	800.00	200.00
(265)	Joe Lake (New York)	400.00	100.00	50.00
(266)	Joe Lake	400.00	100.00	50.00
	(St. Louis, ball in hand.)			
(267)	Joe Lake	400.00	100.00	50.00
	(St. Louis, no ball in hand.)			
(268)	Frank LaPorte	400.00	100.00	50.00
(269)	Arlie Latham	400.00	100.00	50.00
(270)	Bill Lattimore	400.00	100.00	50.00
(271)	Jimmy Lavender	400.00	100.00	50.00
(272)	Tommy Leach (Bending over.)	400.00	100.00	50.00
(273)	Tommy Leach (Portrait)	400.00	100.00	50.00
(274)	Lefty Leifield (Batting)	400.00	100.00	50.00
(275)	Lefty Leifield (Pitching)	400.00	100.00	50.00
(276)	Ed Lennox	400.00	100.00	50.00
(277)	Harry Lentz (Sentz)	1,300	400.00	125.00
(278)	Glenn Liebhardt	400.00	100.00	50.00
(279)	Vive Lindaman	400.00	100.00	50.00
(280)	Perry Lipe	1,300	400.00	125.00
(281)	Paddy Livingstone (Livingston)	400.00	100.00	50.00
(282)	Hans Lobert	400.00	100.00	50.00
(283)	Harry Lord	400.00	100.00	50.00
(284)	Harry Lumley	400.00	100.00	50.00
(285a)	Carl Lundgren (Chicago)	3,800	800.00	300.00
(285b)	Carl Lundgren (Kansas City)	400.00	100.00	50.00
(286)	Nick Maddox	400.00	100.00	50.00
(287a)	Sherry Magie (Magee) (Auction Results: May 08, Heritage SGC30 $13,145. May 08, Robert Edward PSA3 $17,000. May 08, Robert Edward PSA1 $6,500. Aug. 08, Mastro SGC20 $8,500. Jan. 09, eBay PSA 1.5 $7,096. Jan. 09, Sports cards plus PSA 2.5 $12,530.) Values shown represent recent auctions of examples graded by PSA, SGC or GAI. Purchase of ungraded specimens is not recommended.			
	VG-EX - 21,250 / 19,720			
	VG - 15,000			
	GOOD - 12,000			
	FAIR - 3925			
	POOR - 4,500			
(287b)	Sherry Magee (Portrait)	800.00	100.00	60.00
(288)	Sherry Magee (With bat.)	400.00	100.00	50.00
(289)	Bill Malarkey	400.00	100.00	50.00
(290)	Billy Maloney	400.00	100.00	50.00
(291)	George Manion	1,300	400.00	125.00
(292)	Rube Manning (Batting)	400.00	100.00	50.00
(293)	Rube Manning (Pitching)	400.00	100.00	50.00
(294)	Rube Marquard	1,600	300.00	100.00
	(Hands at thighs.)			
(295)	Rube Marquard	1,600	300.00	100.00
	(Follow-through.)			
(296)	Rube Marquard (Portrait)	1,800	300.00	110.00
(297)	Doc Marshall	400.00	100.00	50.00
(298)	Christy Mathewson	2,700	1,000	300.00
	(Dark cap.)			
(299)	Christy Mathewson (Portrait)	5,200	1,100	450.00
(300)	Christy Mathewson	5,100	900.00	400.00
	(White cap.)			
(301)	Al Mattern	400.00	100.00	50.00
(302)	John McAleese	400.00	100.00	50.00
(303)	George McBride	400.00	100.00	50.00
(304)	Pat McCauley	1,300	400.00	125.00
(305)	Moose McCormick	400.00	100.00	50.00
(306)	Pryor McElveen	400.00	100.00	50.00
(307)	Dan McGann	400.00	100.00	50.00
(308)	Jim McGinley	400.00	100.00	50.00
(309)	Iron Man McGinnity	1,400	200.00	100.00
(310)	Stoney McGlynn	400.00	100.00	50.00
(311)	John McGraw (Finger in air.)	2,100	400.00	200.00
(312)	John McGraw (Glove at hip.)	2,000	400.00	110.00
(313)	John McGraw	1,700	300.00	110.00
	(Portrait, no cap.)			
(314)	John McGraw	1,400	300.00	110.00
	(Portrait, with cap.)			
(315)	Harry McIntyre (Brooklyn)	400.00	100.00	50.00
(316)	Harry McIntyre (Brooklyn & Chicago)	400.00	100.00	50.00
(317)	Matty McIntyre (Detroit)	400.00	100.00	50.00
(318)	Larry McLean	400.00	100.00	50.00
(319)	George McQuillan	400.00	100.00	50.00
	(Ball in hand.)			
(320)	George McQuillan (With bat.)	400.00	100.00	60.00
(321)	Fred Merkle (Portrait)	400.00	100.00	60.00
(322)	Fred Merkle (Throwing)	400.00	100.00	50.00
(323)	George Merritt	400.00	100.00	50.00
(324)	Chief Meyers	400.00	100.00	50.00
(325)	Clyde Milan	400.00	100.00	50.00
(326)	Dots Miller (Pittsburgh)	400.00	100.00	50.00
(327)	Molly Miller (Dallas)	1,300	400.00	125.00
(328)	Bill Milligan	400.00	100.00	50.00
(329)	Fred Mitchell (Toronto)	400.00	100.00	50.00
(330)	Mike Mitchell (Cincinnati)	400.00	100.00	50.00
(331)	Dan Moeller	400.00	100.00	50.00
(332)	Carlton Molesworth	1,300	400.00	125.00
(333)	Herbie Moran (Providence)	400.00	100.00	50.00
(334)	Pat Moran (Chicago)	400.00	100.00	50.00
(335)	George Moriarty	400.00	100.00	50.00
(336)	Mike Mowrey	400.00	100.00	50.00
(337)	Dom Mullaney	1,300	400.00	125.00
(338)	George Mullen (Mullin)	400.00	100.00	50.00
(339)	George Mullin (Throwing)	900.00	200.00	100.00
(340)	George Mullin (With bat.)	400.00	100.00	50.00
(341)	Danny Murphy (Batting)	400.00	100.00	50.00
(342)	Danny Murphy (Throwing)	900.00	200.00	100.00
(343)	Red Murray (Batting)	400.00	100.00	50.00
(344)	Red Murray (Portrait)	400.00	100.00	50.00
(345)	Chief Myers (Meyers) (Batting)	400.00	100.00	50.00
(346)	Chief Myers (Meyers) (Fielding)	400.00	100.00	50.00
(347)	Billy Nattress	400.00	100.00	50.00
(348)	Tom Needham	400.00	100.00	50.00
(349)	Simon Nicholls	400.00	100.00	50.00
	(Hands on knees.)			
(350)	Simon Nichols (Nicholls)	400.00	100.00	50.00
	(Batting)			
(351)	Harry Niles	400.00	100.00	50.00
(352)	Rebel Oakes	400.00	100.00	50.00
(353)	Frank Oberlin	400.00	100.00	50.00
(354)	Peter O'Brien	400.00	100.00	50.00
(355a)	Bill O'Hara (New York)	400.00	100.00	50.00
(355b)	Bill O'Hara (St Louis. Recent Auctions: Apr. 08, Robert Edward SGC 20 $1,600. May 08, eBay PSA1 $1,650. July 08, Huggins & Scott SGC 20 $1,200. Oct. 08, Huggins & Scott PSA 4 mk $2,100. Jan. 09, Sports cards plus PSA 6 mc $5,035.)	42,000	13,000	6,500
(356)	Rube Oldring (Batting)	400.00	100.00	50.00
(357)	Rube Oldring (Fielding)	400.00	100.00	50.00
(358)	Charley O'Leary	400.00	100.00	50.00
	(Hands on knees.)			
(359)	Charley O'Leary (Portrait)	400.00	100.00	50.00
(360)	William J. O'Neil	400.00	100.00	50.00
(361)	Al Orth	1,300	400.00	125.00
(362)	William Otey	1,300	400.00	125.00
(363)	Orval Overall	400.00	100.00	50.00
	(Hand face level.)			
(364)	Orval Overall	400.00	100.00	50.00
	(Hands waist level.)			
(365)	Orval Overall (Portrait)	400.00	100.00	50.00
(366)	Frank Owen	400.00	100.00	50.00
(367)	George Paige	1,300	400.00	125.00
(368)	Fred Parent	400.00	100.00	50.00
(369)	Dode Paskert	400.00	100.00	50.00
(370)	Jim Pastorius	400.00	100.00	50.00
(371)	Harry Pattee	900.00	200.00	100.00
(372)	Fred Payne	400.00	100.00	50.00
(373)	Barney Pelty (Horizontal photo.)	900.00	200.00	100.00
(374)	Barney Pelty (Vertical photo.)	400.00	100.00	50.00
(375)	Hub Perdue	1,300	400.00	125.00
(376)	George Perring	400.00	100.00	50.00
(377)	Arch Persons	1,300	400.00	125.00
(378)	Francis (Big Jeff) Pfeffer	400.00	100.00	50.00
(379)	Jake Pfeister (Pfiester)	400.00	100.00	50.00
	(Seated)			
(380)	Jake Pfeister (Pfiester)	400.00	100.00	50.00
	(Throwing)			
(381)	Jimmy Phelan	400.00	100.00	50.00
(382)	Eddie Phelps	400.00	100.00	50.00
(383)	Deacon Phillippe	400.00	100.00	50.00
(384)	Ollie Pickering	400.00	100.00	50.00
(385)	Eddie Plank (Auction results: May 08, Heritage SGC40 $77,675. June 08, Sports Cards Plus GAI3 $34,023. Aug 08, Mastro SGC "A" $17,000. Jan. 09, Sports Cards Plus PSA "A" $15,693. Feb. 09, Goodwin PSA 3 $52,638.) Values shown reflect recent auctions of examples graded by PSA, SGC or GAI. Purchase of ungraded specimens is not recommended.			
	EX-MT - 100,000			
	VG - 60,000			
	GOOD - 35,000			
	POOR - 20,000			
(386)	Phil Poland	400.00	100.00	50.00
(387)	Jack Powell	900.00	200.00	100.00
(388)	Mike Powers	400.00	100.00	60.00
(389)	Billy Purtell	400.00	100.00	50.00
(390)	Ambrose Puttman (Puttmann)	400.00	100.00	50.00
(391)	Lee Quillen (Quillin)	400.00	100.00	50.00
(392)	Jack Quinn	400.00	100.00	50.00
(393)	Newt Randall	400.00	100.00	50.00
(394)	Bugs Raymond	400.00	100.00	50.00
(395)	Ed Reagan	1,300	400.00	125.00
(396)	Ed Reulbach (Glove showing.)	900.00	200.00	100.00
(397)	Ed Reulbach	400.00	100.00	50.00
	(No glove showing.)			
(398)	Dutch Revelle	1,300	400.00	125.00
(399)	Bob Rhoades (Rhoads)	400.00	100.00	50.00
	(Hands at chest.)			
(400)	Bob Rhoades (Rhoads)	900.00	200.00	60.00
	(Right arm extended.)			
(401)	Charlie Rhodes	400.00	100.00	50.00
(402)	Claude Ritchey	400.00	100.00	50.00
(403)	Lou Ritter	400.00	100.00	50.00
(404)	Ike Rockenfeld	1,300	400.00	125.00
(405)	Claude Rossman	400.00	100.00	50.00
(406)	Nap Rucker (Portrait)	400.00	100.00	50.00
(407)	Nap Rucker (Throwing)	400.00	100.00	50.00
(408)	Dick Rudolph	400.00	100.00	50.00
(409)	Ray Ryan	1,300	400.00	125.00
(410)	Germany Schaefer (Detroit)	400.00	100.00	50.00
(411)	Germany Schaefer (Washington)	400.00	100.00	50.00
(412)	George Schirm	400.00	100.00	50.00
(413)	Larry Schlafly	400.00	100.00	50.00
(414)	Admiral Schlei (Batting)	400.00	100.00	50.00
(415)	Admiral Schlei (Catching)	400.00	100.00	50.00
(416)	Admiral Schlei (Portrait)	400.00	100.00	50.00
(417)	Boss Schmidt (Portrait)	400.00	100.00	50.00
(418)	Boss Schmidt (Throwing)	400.00	100.00	50.00
(419)	Ossee Schreck (Schreckengost)	780.00	140.00	55.00
(420)	Wildfire Schulte (Front view.)	1,000	400.00	60.00
(421)	Wildfire Schulte (Back view.)	400.00	100.00	50.00
(422)	Jim Scott	400.00	100.00	50.00
(423)	Charles Seitz	1,300	400.00	125.00
(424)	Cy Seymour (Batting)	400.00	100.00	50.00
(425)	Cy Seymour (Portrait)	400.00	100.00	50.00
(426)	Cy Seymour (Throwing)	400.00	100.00	50.00
(427)	Spike Shannon	400.00	100.00	50.00
(428)	Bud Sharpe	400.00	100.00	50.00
(429)	Shag Shaughnessy	1,300	400.00	125.00
(430)	Al Shaw (St. Louis)	400.00	100.00	50.00
(431)	Hunky Shaw (Providence)	400.00	100.00	50.00
(432)	Jimmy Sheckard	400.00	100.00	50.00
	(Glove showing.)			
(433)	Jimmy Sheckard	400.00	100.00	50.00
	(No glove showing.)			
(434)	Bill Shipke	400.00	100.00	50.00
(435)	Jimmy Slagle	400.00	100.00	50.00
(436)	Carlos Smith (Shreveport)	1,300	400.00	125.00
(437)	Frank Smith (Chicago, F. Smith on front.)	400.00	100.00	50.00
(438a)	Frank Smith (Chicago, white cap.)	400.00	100.00	50.00
(438b)	Frank Smith (Chicago & Boston)	1,700	300.00	125.00
(439)	Happy Smith (Brooklyn)	400.00	100.00	50.00
(440)	Heinie Smith (Buffalo)	400.00	100.00	50.00
(441)	Sid Smith (Atlanta)	1,300	400.00	125.00
(442)	Fred Snodgrass (Batting)	400.00	100.00	50.00
(443)	Fred Snodgrass (Catching)	400.00	100.00	50.00
(444)	Bob Spade	400.00	100.00	50.00
(445)	Tris Speaker	4,500	800.00	325.00
(446)	Tubby Spencer	400.00	100.00	50.00
(447)	Jake Stahl (Glove shows.)	400.00	100.00	50.00
(448)	Jake Stahl (No glove shows.)	400.00	100.00	50.00
(449)	Oscar Stanage	400.00	100.00	50.00
(450)	Dolly Stark	1,300	400.00	125.00
(451)	Charlie Starr	400.00	100.00	50.00
(452)	Harry Steinfeldt (Portrait)	400.00	100.00	50.00
(453)	Harry Steinfeldt (With bat.)	400.00	100.00	50.00
(454)	Jim Stephens	400.00	100.00	50.00
(455)	George Stone	400.00	100.00	50.00
(456)	George Stovall (Batting)	400.00	100.00	50.00
(457)	George Stovall (Portrait)	400.00	100.00	50.00
(458)	Sam Strang	400.00	100.00	50.00
(459)	Gabby Street (Catching)	400.00	100.00	50.00
(460)	Gabby Street (Portrait)	400.00	100.00	50.00
(461)	Billy Sullivan	400.00	100.00	50.00
(462)	Ed Summers	400.00	100.00	50.00
(463)	Bill Sweeney (Boston)	400.00	100.00	50.00
(464)	Jeff Sweeney (New York)	400.00	100.00	50.00
(465)	Jesse Tannehill (Washington)	400.00	100.00	50.00
(466)	Lee Tannehill (Chicago, L. Tannehill on front.)	400.00	100.00	50.00
(467)	Lee Tannehill (Chicago, Tannehill on front.)	400.00	100.00	50.00
(468)	Dummy Taylor	400.00	150.00	60.00
(469)	Fred Tenney	400.00	100.00	50.00
(470)	Tony Thebo	1,300	400.00	125.00
(471)	Ira Thielman	400.00	100.00	50.00
(472)	Ira Thomas	400.00	100.00	50.00
(473)	Woodie Thornton	1,300	400.00	125.00
(474)	Joe Tinker (Bat off shoulder.)	1,800	400.00	110.00
(475)	Joe Tinker (Bat on shoulder.)	1,700	300.00	110.00
(476)	Joe Tinker (Hands on knees.)	1,700	300.00	110.00
(477)	Joe Tinker (Portrait)	1,800	400.00	125.00
(478)	John Titus	400.00	100.00	50.00
(479)	Terry Turner	400.00	100.00	50.00
(480)	Bob Unglaub	400.00	100.00	50.00
(481)	Juan Violat (Viola)	1,300	400.00	125.00
(482)	Rube Waddell (Portrait)	1,800	400.00	125.00
(483)	Rube Waddell (Throwing)	1,800	400.00	110.00
(484)	Heinie Wagner (Bat on left shoulder.)	400.00	100.00	50.00
(485)	Heinie Wagner (Bat on right shoulder.)	400.00	100.00	50.00
(486)	Honus Wagner (Some auction results: May 2008 Heritage Auctions, SGC10 $227,050. May 2008, Robert Edwards BVG1, $270,000. Aug. 2008 Mastro PSA 5 mc $1,620,000. Dec. 2008, Philip Weiss SGC40 $826,000.) Values shown refelct recent auctions of examples graded by PSA, SGC or GAI. Purchase of ungraded specimens is not recommended.			
	NM-MT - 2,800,000			
	VG+ - 456,000			
	VG - 400,000			

GOOD - 350,000
GOOD - 350,000
FAIR - 300,000
POOR - 270,000

(487)	Bobby Wallace	1,500	300.00	100.00
(488)	Ed Walsh	2,300	400.00	200.00
(489)	Jack Warhop	400.00	100.00	50.00
(490)	Jake Weimer	400.00	100.00	50.00
(491)	James Westlake	1,300	400.00	125.00
(492)	Zack Wheat	1,500	300.00	140.00
(493)	Doc White (Chicago, pitching.)	400.00	100.00	50.00
(494)	Doc White (Chicago, portrait.)	400.00	100.00	50.00
(495)	Foley White (Houston)	1,300	400.00	125.00
(496)	Jack White (Buffalo)	400.00	100.00	50.00
(497)	Kaiser Wilhelm (Hands at chest.)	400.00	100.00	50.00
(498)	Kaiser Wilhelm (With bat.)	400.00	100.00	50.00
(499)	Ed Willett	400.00	100.00	50.00
(500)	Ed Willetts (Willett)	400.00	100.00	50.00
(501)	Jimmy Williams	400.00	100.00	50.00
(502)	Vic Willis (Portrait)	1,700	400.00	100.00
(503)	Vic Willis (Throwing)	1,700	300.00	100.00
(504)	Vic Willis (With bat.)	1,200	200.00	100.00
(505)	Owen Wilson	400.00	100.00	50.00
(506)	Hooks Wiltse (Pitching)	400.00	100.00	50.00
(507)	Hooks Wiltse (Portrait, no cap.)	400.00	100.00	50.00
(508)	Hooks Wiltse (Portrait, with cap.)	400.00	100.00	50.00
(509)	Lucky Wright	400.00	100.00	50.00
(510)	Cy Young (Cleveland, glove shows.)	3,800	700.00	350.00
(511)	Cy Young (Cleveland, bare hand shows.)	4,400	800.00	375.00
(512)	Cy Young (Cleveland, portrait.)	8,700	1,600	700.00
(513)	Irv Young (Minneapolis)	400.00	100.00	50.00
(514)	Heinie Zimmerman	400.00	100.00	50.00

1909-11 T206 Errors

SWEENEY, BOSTON NAT'L.

SWEENEY, BOSTON NAT'L.

Because of the complexity of the lithographic process by which T206 cards were printed, a number of significant printing errors - missing colors, broken or missing type, etc. - are known. Early in hobby history some of these errors were collected alongside such true design variations as the "Magie" misspelling and Joe Doyle "N.Y. Nat'l." Because of the continued popularity of T206, some of these errors remain in demand today and can command significant premium values. It should be noted, however, that not all similar errors within T206 bring such high prices; value seems dependent on the length of time the errors have been known in the hobby. Because of the ease with which various typographic elements - "S" in Snodgrass, "o" in Toronto, can be erased, many fakes of this type of error are known; collectors should be wary and consider having the cards professionally authenticated.

		NM	EX	VG
(27)	Beck, no "B"s (Missing red ink.)	1,500	750.00	450.00
(28)	Becker, no "B" (Missing red ink.)	1,500	750.00	450.00
(95a)	Cobb, orange background (Missing red ink.)	4,000	1,500	900.00
(137)	Dopner (Three have been recently found, & authenticated: pricing pending sales.)			
(164)	Ferguson, no "B" (Missing red ink.)	2,300	1,150	700.00
(279)	Lindaman, no "B" (Missing red ink.)	1,500	750.00	450.00
(286)	Maddox, Pittsburg (No team, name, city.)	6,000	3,000	1,800
(297)	Marshall, no "B" (Missing blue ink.)	2,000	1,000	600.00
(329)	Mitchell, "TORONT" (No last "O.")	2,000	1,000	600.00
(343)	Murray (Yellow background.)	1,500	750.00	450.00
(344)	Murr'y (Broken "A" in name, Lenox, Tolstoi, and Old Mill Back.)	7,000	3,500	2,100
(428)	Shappe, Newark (Should be Sharpe.)	4,000	2,000	1,000
(442)	nodgrass - batting (Should be Snodgrass; most of initial "S" missing.)	4,000	2,000	1,000
(443)	nodgrass - catching (All known examples, even those in grading company holders, are altered specimens with no collectible value.)			
(463)	Sweeney, no "B" (Missing magenta ink.)	9,000	4,500	2,700

(484)	Wagner, no "B" (Bat on left shoulder, missing magenta.)	2,500	1,250	750.00
	Common Player (Missing one or more colors.)	500.00	250.00	150.00

1912 T207 Brown Background

Harry Lord

Harry Lord, the brilliant White Sox third baseman, came to Chicago in one of the queerest baseball deals ever recorded. Lord first achieved success in the New England League, where, in 1908, he was lifted to the Boston Americans. Although rated as a wonderful ball player, he fell out with the club management and was traded to Comiskey, who secured a star. Lord played wonderful ball in 1911 and is rated by many as the greatest baseman now playing—a worthy successor to Bradley and Collins. Last season he batted .321, fielded .941 and led his club with stolen bases.

RECRUIT LITTLE CIGARS

LORD-CHICAGO-AMER.

Less popular and even less understood than their T205 and T206 antecedents from American Tobacco, the T207 "Brown Background" series shares the same approximately 1-7/16" x 2-5/8" format with the earlier T-cards. A chocolate background frames the rather drab player drawings, which rely on occasional bit of color on the uniform to break up the predominant earth tones. The cards have beige borders. A white strip below the picture has the player's last name, city and league. Unlike most other cards of its time, T207 has a glossy coating on front which over the years tends to crack and/or "craze" exacerbating the appaearance of creases and other signs of wear. Card backs have the player's full name, career summary and (usually) an ad for one of several brands of cigarettes. Red Cross brand backs are virtually impossible to find, while red Cycle advertising is noticeably scarcer than more common Broadleaf or "anonymous" (no-advertising) versions. Cards with Recruit Little Cigars advertising on back are the most common. There are a number of unaccountably scarce cards in the set, including a higher than usual number of obscure players. The Davis card with blue "C" on cap carried in earlier catalogs has been removed for lack of evidence of its existence. The previously listed Carrigan-Wagner wrongbacks have also been de-listed due to their nature as wrong-back printing errors rather than true variations.

		NM	EX	VG
	Common Player:	220.00	75.00	45.00
	Red Cycle Backs: 1.5X anonymous or broadleaf backs.			
(1)	John B. Adams	1,760	615.00	355.00
(2)	Edward Ainsmith	220.00	75.00	45.00
(3)	Rafael Almeida	1,250	625.00	300.00
(4a)	James Austin (Insignia on shirt.)	440.00	155.00	90.00
(4b)	James Austin (No insignia on shirt.)	220.00	75.00	45.00
(5)	Neal Ball	200.00	75.00	45.00
(6)	Eros Barger	220.00	75.00	45.00
(7)	Jack Barry	250.00	90.00	50.00
(8)	Charles Bauman (Baumann)	1,250	625.00	300.00
(9)	Beals Becker	330.00	110.00	65.00
(10)	Chief (Albert) Bender	525.00	180.00	110.00
(11)	Joseph Benz	1,250	625.00	300.00
(12)	Robert Bescher	220.00	75.00	45.00
(13)	Joe Birmingham	1,250	625.00	300.00
(14)	Russell Blackburne	1,250	625.00	300.00
(15)	Fred Blanding	1,250	625.00	300.00
(16)	Jimmy Block	495.00	170.00	100.00
(17)	Ping Bodie	220.00	75.00	45.00
(18)	Hugh Bradley	220.00	75.00	45.00
(19)	Roger Bresnaham (Bresnahan)	495.00	170.00	100.00
(20)	J.F. Bushelman	1,250	625.00	300.00
(21)	Henry (Hank) Butcher	1,250	625.00	300.00
(22)	Robert M. Byrne	220.00	75.00	45.00
(23)	John James Callahan	220.00	75.00	45.00
(24)	Howard Camnitz	220.00	75.00	45.00
(25)	Max Carey	855.00	305.00	165.00
(26)	Bill Carrigan	220.00	75.00	45.00
(27)	George Chalmers	220.00	75.00	45.00
(28)	Frank Leroy Chance	715.00	250.00	145.00
(29)	Edward Cicotte	1,100	385.00	220.00
(30)	Tom Clarke	220.00	75.00	45.00
(31)	Leonard Cole	220.00	75.00	45.00
(32)	John Collins	305.00	105.00	60.00
(33)	Robert Coulson	220.00	75.00	45.00
(34)	Tex Covington	220.00	75.00	45.00
(35)	Otis Crandall	220.00	75.00	45.00
(36)	William Cunningham	1,250	625.00	300.00
(37)	Dave Danforth	250.00	95.00	50.00
(38)	Bert Daniels	440.00	155.00	90.00
(39)	John Daubert (Jake)	220.00	75.00	45.00
(40)	Harry Davis	250.00	90.00	50.00
(41)	Jim Delehanty	220.00	75.00	45.00
(42)	Claude Derrick	220.00	75.00	45.00
(43)	Arthur Devlin	250.00	95.00	50.00
(44)	Joshua Devore	220.00	75.00	45.00
(45)	Mike Donlin	2,500	1,500	750.00
(46)	Edward Donnelly	1,250	625.00	300.00
(47)	Charles Dooin	220.00	75.00	45.00
(48)	Tom Downey	880.00	310.00	175.00
(49)	Lawrence Doyle	440.00	155.00	90.00

(50)	Del Drake	385.00	135.00	75.00
(51)	Ted Easterly	220.00	75.00	45.00
(52)	George Ellis	660.00	230.00	135.00
(53)	Clyde Engle	360.00	125.00	70.00
(54)	R.E. Erwin	660.00	230.00	135.00
(55)	Louis Evans	220.00	75.00	45.00
(56)	John Ferry	220.00	75.00	45.00
(57a)	Ray Fisher (Blue cap.)	220.00	75.00	45.00
(57b)	Ray Fisher (White cap.)	300.00	150.00	75.00
(58)	Arthur Fletcher	220.00	75.00	45.00
(59)	Jacques Fournier	1,250	625.00	300.00
(60)	Arthur Fromme	250.00	90.00	50.00
(61)	Del Gainor	220.00	75.00	45.00
(62)	William Lawrence Gardner	330.00	110.00	65.00
(63)	Lefty George	440.00	220.00	110.00
(64)	Roy Golden	220.00	75.00	45.00
(65)	Harry Gowdy	220.00	75.00	45.00
(66)	George Graham	660.00	230.00	135.00
(67)	J.G. Graney	825.00	285.00	165.00
(68)	Vean Gregg	1,250	625.00	300.00
(69)	Casey Hageman	440.00	155.00	90.00
(70)	Charlie Hall	440.00	155.00	90.00
(71)	E.S. Hallinan	220.00	75.00	45.00
(72)	Earl Hamilton	220.00	75.00	45.00
(73)	Robert Harmon	220.00	75.00	45.00
(74)	Grover Hartley	440.00	155.00	90.00
(75)	Olaf Henriksen	230.00	110.00	60.00
(76)	John Henry	440.00	155.00	90.00
(77)	Charles Herzog	1,250	625.00	300.00
(78)	Robert Higgins	310.00	110.00	60.00
(79)	Chester Hoff	1,250	625.00	300.00
(80)	William Hogan	310.00	110.00	60.00
(81)	Harry Hooper	1,320	470.00	265.00
(82)	Ben Houser	1,250	625.00	300.00
(83)	Hamilton Hyatt	1,250	625.00	300.00
(84)	Walter Johnson	2,090	730.00	420.00
(85)	George Kaler	220.00	75.00	45.00
(86)	William Kelly	1,250	625.00	300.00
(87)	Jay Kirke	440.00	155.00	90.00
(88)	John Kling	715.00	250.00	145.00
(89)	Otto Knabe	220.00	75.00	45.00
(90)	Elmer Knetzer	220.00	75.00	45.00
(91)	Edward Konetchy	220.00	75.00	45.00
(92)	Harry Krause	220.00	75.00	45.00
(93)	"Red" Kuhn	1,250	625.00	300.00
(94)	Joseph Kutina	1,250	625.00	300.00
(95)	F.H. (Bill) Lange	1,250	625.00	300.00
(96)	Jack Lapp	220.00	75.00	45.00
(97)	W. Arlington Latham	220.00	75.00	45.00
(98)	Thomas W. Leach	220.00	75.00	45.00
(99)	Albert Leifield	220.00	75.00	45.00
(100)	Edgar Lennox	220.00	75.00	45.00
(101)	Duffy Lewis	495.00	170.00	100.00
(102a)	Irving Lewis (No emblem on sleeve.)	20,000	10,000	5,000
(102b)	Irving Lewis (Emblem on sleeve.)	10,450	5,000	3,000
(103)	Jack Lively	220.00	75.00	45.00
(104a)	Paddy Livingston ("A" on shirt.)	1,200	425.00	245.00
(104b)	Paddy Livingston (Big "C" on shirt.)	1,265	440.00	255.00
(104c)	Paddy Livingston (Small "C" on shirt.)	330.00	115.00	65.00
(105)	Briscoe Lord (Philadelphia)	440.00	155.00	90.00
(106)	Harry Lord (Chicago)	440.00	155.00	90.00
(107)	Louis Lowdermilk	10,450	3,660	2,090
(108)	Richard Marquard	605.00	210.00	120.00
(109)	Armando Marsans	770.00	270.00	155.00
(110)	George McBride	310.00	110.00	60.00
(111)	Alexander McCarthy	1,250	625.00	300.00
(112)	Edward McDonald	330.00	110.00	65.00
(113)	John J. McGraw	635.00	220.00	125.00
(114)	Harry McIntire	220.00	75.00	45.00
(115)	Matthew McIntyre	220.00	75.00	45.00
(116)	William McKechnie	2,000	1,000	500.00
(117)	Larry McLean	220.00	75.00	45.00
(118)	Clyde Milan	220.00	75.00	45.00
(119)	John B. Miller (Pittsburg)	220.00	75.00	45.00
(120)	Otto Miller (Brooklyn)	440.00	155.00	90.00
(121)	Roy Miller (Boston)	990.00	345.00	200.00
(122)	Ward Miller (Chicago)	8,000	4,000	2,000
(123)	Mike Mitchell (Cleveland, picture is Willie Mitchell.)	220.00	75.00	45.00
(124)	Mike Mitchell (Cincinnati)	330.00	110.00	65.00
(125)	Geo. Mogridge	1,500	750.00	375.00
(126)	Earl Moore	1,250	625.00	300.00
(127)	Patrick J. Moran	220.00	75.00	45.00
(128)	Cy Morgan (Philadelphia)	220.00	75.00	45.00
(129)	Ray Morgan (Washington)	220.00	75.00	45.00
(130)	George Moriarty	1,250	625.00	300.00
(131a)	George Mullin ("D" on cap.)	250.00	90.00	50.00
(131b)	George Mullin (No "D" on cap.)	745.00	260.00	150.00
(132)	Thomas Needham	330.00	110.00	65.00
(133)	Red Nelson	1,250	625.00	300.00
(134)	Herbert Northen (Hubbard)	310.00	110.00	60.00
(135)	Leslie Nunamaker	220.00	75.00	45.00
(136)	Rebel Oakes	220.00	75.00	45.00
(137)	Buck O'Brien	330.00	110.00	65.00
(138)	Rube Oldring	220.00	75.00	45.00
(139)	Ivan Olson	220.00	75.00	45.00
(140)	Martin J. O'Toole	220.00	75.00	45.00
(141)	George Paskart (Paskert)	220.00	75.00	45.00
(142)	Barney Pelty	2,000	1,250	500.00
(143)	Herbert Perdue	310.00	110.00	60.00
(144)	O.C. Peters	1,250	625.00	300.00
(145)	Arthur Phelan	1,250	625.00	300.00
(146)	Jack Quinn	440.00	155.00	90.00
(147)	Don Carlos Ragan	1,500	750.00	400.00
(148)	Arthur Rasmussen	1,500	750.00	400.00
(149)	Morris Rath	1,500	750.00	400.00
(150)	Edward Reulbach	330.00	115.00	65.00
(151)	Napoleon Rucker	440.00	155.00	90.00
(152)	J.B. Ryan	1,250	625.00	300.00
(153)	Victor Saier	2,300	810.00	470.00
(154)	William Scanlon	220.00	75.00	45.00
(155)	Germany Schaefer	220.00	75.00	45.00
(156)	Wilbur Schardt	220.00	75.00	45.00

		NM	EX	VG
(157)	Frank Schulte	220.00	75.00	45.00
(158)	Jim Scott	495.00	170.00	100.00
(159)	Henry Severoid (Severeid)	220.00	75.00	45.00
(160)	Mike Simon	220.00	75.00	45.00
(161)	Frank E. Smith (Cincinnati)	220.00	75.00	45.00
(162)	Wallace Smith (St. Louis)	220.00	75.00	45.00
(163)	Fred Snodgrass	220.00	75.00	45.00
(164)	Tristam Speaker	4,000	2,000	750.00
(165)	Harry Lee Spratt	220.00	75.00	45.00
(166)	Edward Stack	550.00	195.00	110.00
(167)	Oscar Stanage	220.00	75.00	45.00
(168)	William Steele	660.00	230.00	135.00
(169)	Harry Steinfeldt	440.00	155.00	90.00
(170)	George Stovall	220.00	75.00	45.00
(171)	Charles (Gabby) Street	250.00	90.00	50.00
(172)	Amos Strunk	220.00	75.00	45.00
(173)	William Sullivan	310.00	110.00	60.00
(174)	William J. Sweeney	1,250	625.00	300.00
(175)	Leeford Tannehill	220.00	75.00	45.00
(176)	C.D. Thomas	715.00	250.00	145.00
(177)	Joseph Tinker	880.00	310.00	175.00
(178)	Bert Tooley	220.00	75.00	45.00
(179)	Terence Turner (Terrence)	220.00	75.00	45.00
(180)	George Tyler	2,000	1,000	500.00
(181)	Jim Vaughn	385.00	135.00	75.00
(182)	Chas. (Heinie) Wagner	220.00	75.00	45.00
(183)	Ed (Dixie) Walker	220.00	75.00	45.00
(184)	Robert Wallace	1,250	625.00	300.00
(185)	John Warhop	220.00	75.00	45.00
(186)	George Weaver	5,225	1,815	1,045
(187)	Zach Wheat	880.00	310.00	175.00
(188)	G. Harris White	310.00	110.00	60.00
(189)	Ernest Wilie	275.00	95.00	55.00
(190)	Bob Williams	220.00	75.00	45.00
(191)	Arthur Wilson (New York)	250.00	90.00	50.00
(192)	Owen Wilson (Pittsburg)	1,250	625.00	300.00
(193)	George Wiltse	220.00	75.00	45.00
(194)	Ivey Wingo	385.00	135.00	75.00
(195)	Harry Wolverton	220.00	75.00	45.00
(196)	Joe Wood	2,640	925.00	530.00
(197)	Eugene Woodburn	880.00	310.00	175.00
(198)	Ralph Works	1,250	625.00	300.00
(199)	Stanley Yerkes	220.00	75.00	45.00
(200)	Rollie Zeider	330.00	110.00	65.00

1912 T227 Series Of Champions

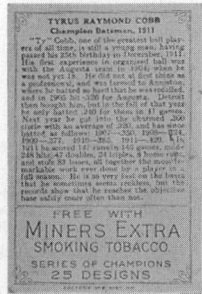

The 1912 "Series of Champions" card set issued by the "Honest Long Cut" and "Miners Extra" tobacco brands features several baseball stars among its 25 famous athletes of the day. Larger than a standard-size tobacco issue, each card in the "Champions" series measures 3-3/8" x 2-5/16". The back includes a relatively lengthy player biography, while the front features a lithograph of the player in action. Although the set includes only four baseball players, these attractive cards are popular among collectors because of the stature of the four players selected. The "Champions" series holds additional significance because it includes the only known baseball cards issued under the "Miners Extra" brand name. The set carries the American Card Catalog designation of T227.

		NM	EX	VG
Complete Set (4):		22,500	10,000	5,500
Common Player:		3,600	1,620	900.00
(1)	"Home Run" Baker	3,600	1,620	900.00
(2)	"Chief" Bender	3,600	1,620	900.00
(3)	Ty Cobb	16,200	7,200	4,200
(4)	Rube Marquard	3,600	1,620	900.00

U

1906 Ullman Postcards

The designation of Giants' players as "World's Champions" dates this issue to 1906. The 3-1/2" x 5-1/2" cards have a black-and-white photo surrounded by a greenish or reddish-brown tone wooden-look frame with a plaque printed in the bottom border. Backs are printed in brown with typical postcard markings and include mention of "Ullman's 'Art Frame' Series." This checklist is likely not complete. The card of "Harry" (name actually Henry) Mathewson is the only known baseball card appearance of Christy's kid brother.

		NM	EX	VG
Common Player:		750.00	375.00	225.00
(1)	Leon Ames	750.00	375.00	225.00
(2)	Mike Donlin	750.00	375.00	225.00
(3)	George Ferguson	750.00	375.00	225.00
(4)	Matty Fitzgerald	750.00	375.00	225.00
(5)	Billy Gilbert	750.00	375.00	225.00
(6)	Christy Matthewson (Mathewson)	3,500	1,750	1,000
(7)	Harry (Henry) Mathewson	1,200	600.00	360.00
(8)	Dan McGann (McGann on 1st Base.)	750.00	375.00	225.00
(9)	"Iron Arm" McGinnity	1,000	500.00	300.00
(10)	Manager McGraw	1,500	750.00	450.00
(11)	Strang and Bowerman (Sammy Strang, Frank Bowerman)	900.00	450.00	250.00
(12)	Hooks Wiltse	750.00	375.00	225.00
(13)	1906 National League Champion Chicago, Cubs			

1933 Uncle Jacks Candy

One of the lesser-known candy issues of the early 1930s was this New England regional set from Uncle Jacks, Inc., of Springfield, Mass., and Newport, R.I. The 1-7/8" x 2-7/8" blank-backed cards can be found printed in blue, red, purple or green duotone, and were sold in a see-through wax paper wrapper with a piece of candy and a coupon which could be redeemed (in quantities of 100) for a "league baseball" and a chance at a trip to the 1933 World Series. The set is among those listed in the American Card Catalog under the catchall number R317. The unnumbered cards are checklisted here alphabetically.

		NM	EX	VG
Complete Set (30):		25,000	12,500	7,500
Common Player:		400.00	200.00	120.00
(1)	Earl Averill	1,000	500.00	300.00
(2)	James L. Bottomley	1,000	500.00	300.00
(3)	Ed Brandt	400.00	200.00	120.00
(4)	Ben Chapman	400.00	200.00	120.00
(5)	Gordon Cochrane	1,000	500.00	300.00
(6)	Joe Cronin	1,000	500.00	300.00
(7)	Hazen Cuyler	400.00	200.00	120.00
(8)	George Earnshaw	400.00	200.00	120.00
(9)	Wesley Ferrell	400.00	200.00	120.00
(10)	Jimmie Foxx	1,500	750.00	450.00
(11)	Frank Frisch	1,000	500.00	300.00
(12)	Burleigh Grimes	1,000	500.00	300.00
(13)	"Lefty" Grove	1,250	625.00	375.00
(14)	"Wild Bill" Hallahan	400.00	200.00	120.00
(15)	Leo Hartnett	1,000	500.00	300.00
(16)	"Babe" Herman	400.00	200.00	120.00
(17)	Rogers Hornsby	1,200	600.00	360.00
(18)	Charles Klein	1,000	500.00	300.00
(19)	Tony Lazzeri	1,000	500.00	300.00
(20)	Fred Lindstrom	1,000	500.00	300.00
(21)	Ted Lyons	1,000	500.00	300.00
(22)	"Pepper" Martin	650.00	325.00	200.00
(23)	Herb Pennock	1,000	500.00	300.00
(24)	"Babe" Ruth ("King of Swat")	4,000	2,000	1,200
(25)	Al Simmons	1,000	500.00	300.00
(26)	"Bill" Terry	1,000	500.00	300.00
(27)	"Dazzy" Vance	1,000	500.00	300.00
(28)	Lloyd Waner	1,000	500.00	300.00
(29)	Paul Waner	1,000	500.00	300.00
(30)	Hack Wilson	1,000	500.00	300.00

1958 Union 76 Sports Club Booklets

This series of sports instructional booklets was issued by Union Oil in conjunction with its Sports Club television program for youngsters. Besides seven baseball players, the series featured football, track, bowling, skiing, and other stars. The booklets are 12 pages and measure about 4" x 5-1/2". Fronts have a drawing of the player and are printed in Union Oil logo colors of orange and blue. The sports tips inside are well illustrated. Books are numbered on front.

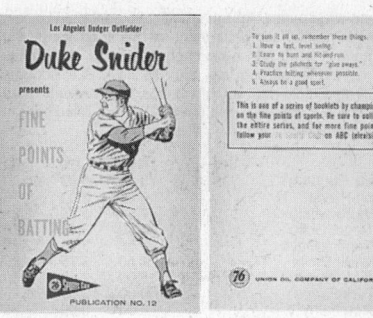

		NM	EX	VG
Complete (Baseball) Set (7):		160.00	80.00	45.00
Common Player:		15.00	7.50	4.50
12	Duke Snider	35.00	17.50	10.50
14	Bob Lemon	20.00	10.00	6.00
15	Red Schoendienst	20.00	10.00	6.00
20	Bill Rigney	15.00	7.50	4.50
38	Jackie Jensen	15.00	7.50	4.50
39	Warren Spahn	25.00	12.50	7.50
41	Ernie Banks	35.00	17.50	10.50

1960 Union Oil Dodger Family Booklets

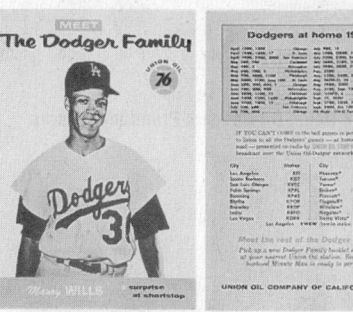

For its first major issue of Dodgers memorabilia, Union 76 gas stations in Southern California distributed a series of booklets profiling players and staff. Each 5-1/2" x 7-1/2" booklet has 16 black-and-white pages highlighted with red graphics. The covers have action poses with many other photos on the inside pages, along with a biography, personal information, career highlights, playing tips, etc. On back is a Dodgers schedule and Union 76 ad. The booklets were distributed on a one-per-week basis. They are listed here in alphabetical order.

		NM	EX	VG
Complete Set (23):		150.00	75.00	45.00
Common Player:		6.00	3.00	1.75
(1)	Walter Alston	7.50	3.75	2.25
(2)	Roger Craig	6.00	3.00	1.75
(3)	Tom Davis	7.50	3.75	2.25
(4)	Don Demeter	6.00	3.00	1.75
(5)	Don Drysdale	15.00	7.50	4.50
(6)	Chuck Essegian	6.00	3.00	1.75
(7)	Jim Gilliam	7.50	3.75	2.25
(8)	Gil Hodges	12.00	6.00	3.50
(9)	Frank Howard	7.50	3.75	2.25
(10)	Sandy Koufax	40.00	20.00	12.00
(11)	Norm Larker	6.00	3.00	1.75
(12)	Wally Moon	6.00	3.00	1.75
(13)	Charlie Neal	6.00	3.00	1.75
(14)	Johnny Podres	6.00	3.00	1.75
(15)	Ed Roebuck	6.00	3.00	1.75
(16)	John Roseboro	6.00	3.00	1.75
(17)	Larry Sherry	6.00	3.00	1.75
(18)	Norm Sherry	6.00	3.00	1.75
(19)	Duke Snider	15.00	7.50	4.50
(20)	Stan Williams	6.00	3.00	1.75
(21)	Maury Wills	7.50	3.75	2.25
(22)	Coaches (Joe Becker, Bobby Bragan, Greg Mulleavy, Pete Reiser)	6.00	3.00	1.75
(23)	Jerry Doggett, Vin Scully (Announcers)	6.00	3.00	1.75

1961 Union Oil Dodger Family Booklets

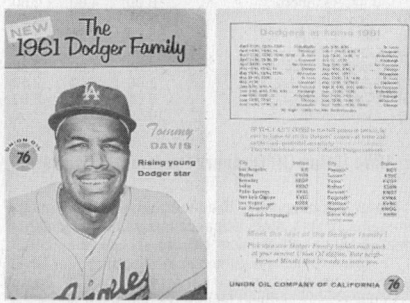

For a second consecutive year, Union 76 gas stations in Southern California distributed a series of booklets profiling team members and staff. The 5-1/2" x 7-1/2" booklets have 16

black-and-white pages highlighted with red graphics. The covers have large portraits while there are many photos on the inside pages, along with a biography, personal information, career highlights, playing tips, etc. On back is a Dodgers schedule and radio network information. The booklets were distributed on a one-per-week basis. They are listed here in alphabetical order.

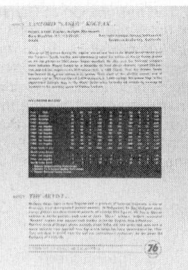

	NM	EX	VG
Complete Set (24):	175.00	85.00	50.00
Common Player:	6.00	3.00	1.75
(1) Walter Alston	7.50	3.75	2.25
(2) Roger Craig	6.00	3.00	1.75
(3) Tommy Davis	7.50	3.75	2.25
(4) Willie Davis	7.50	3.75	2.25
(5) Don Drysdale	15.00	7.50	4.50
(6) Dick Farrell	6.00	3.00	1.75
(7) Ron Fairly	6.00	3.00	1.75
(8) Jim Gilliam	7.50	3.75	2.25
(9) Gil Hodges	10.00	5.00	3.00
(10) Frank Howard	7.50	3.75	2.25
(11) Sandy Koufax	30.00	15.00	9.00
(12) Norm Larker	6.00	3.00	1.75
(13) Wally Moon	6.00	3.00	1.75
(14) Charlie Neal	6.00	3.00	1.75
(15) Ron Perranoski	6.00	3.00	1.75
(16) Johnny Podres	6.00	3.00	1.75
(17) John Roseboro	6.00	3.00	1.75
(18) Larry Sherry	6.00	3.00	1.75
(19) Norm Sherry	6.00	3.00	1.75
(20) Duke Snider	15.00	7.50	4.50
(21) Daryl Spencer	6.00	3.00	1.75
(22) Stan Williams	6.00	3.00	1.75
(23) Maury Wills	7.50	3.75	2.25
(24) Jerry Doggett, Vin Scully (Announcers)	6.00	3.00	1.75

1962 Union Oil Dodgers Premium Pictures

One of many premiums issued by Union Oil during the Dodgers' early years in Los Angeles, this set of player pictures is the most popular with collectors. The 8-1/2" x 11" pictures feature a large color pastel portrait of the player on front, along with a smaller action picture. The player's name is printed in the white border below. The artist's signature and a 1962 copyright are printed below the portrait. Backs are printed in black-and-white and include a career summary and complete minor and major league stats, a profile of sports artist Nicholas Volpe and an ad at bottom for Union Oil and its Union 76 brand of gasoline. The unnumbered pictures are checklisted here alphabetically. It was reported that 200,000 of each picture were produced.

	NM	EX	VG
Complete Set (24):	225.00	115.00	70.00
Common Player:	8.00	4.00	2.50
(1) Larry Burright	8.00	4.00	2.50
(2) Doug Camilli	8.00	4.00	2.50
(3) Andy Carey	8.00	4.00	2.50
(4) Tom Davis	10.00	5.00	3.00
(5) Willie Davis	10.00	5.00	3.00
(6) Don Drysdale	20.00	10.00	6.00
(7) Ron Fairly	8.00	4.00	2.50
(8) Jim Gilliam	10.00	5.00	3.00
(9) Tim Harkness	8.00	4.00	2.50
(10) Frank Howard	10.00	5.00	3.00
(11) Sandy Koufax	40.00	20.00	12.00
(12) Joe Moeller	8.00	4.00	2.50
(13) Wally Moon	8.00	4.00	2.50
(14) Ron Perranoski	8.00	4.00	2.50
(15) Johnny Podres	8.00	4.00	2.50
(16) Ed Roebuck	8.00	4.00	2.50
(17) John Roseboro	8.00	4.00	2.50
(18) Larry Sherry	8.00	4.00	2.50
(19) Norm Sherry	8.00	4.00	2.50
(20) Duke Snider	25.00	12.50	7.50
(21) Daryl Spencer	8.00	4.00	2.50
(22) Lee Walls	8.00	4.00	2.50
(23) Stan Williams	8.00	4.00	2.50
(24) Maury Wills	10.00	5.00	3.00

1964 Union Oil Dodgers Premium Pictures

Paired pastel portraits, one in uniform and one in mufti, from sports artist Nicholas Volpe are featured on these large-format (8-1/2" x 11") premium pictures sponsored by Union Oil. The player's name is printed in the bottom border while the artist's signature is printed beneath the portraits. Backs are in black-and-white and feature personal data about the player and artist, complete minor and major league stats and Union Oil/Union 76 logos. The unnumbered pictures are checklisted here alphabetically.

	NM	EX	VG
Complete Set (18):	165.00	80.00	50.00
Common Player:	8.00	4.00	2.50
(1) Tommy Davis	10.00	5.00	3.00
(2) Willie Davis	10.00	5.00	3.00
(3) Don Drysdale	20.00	10.00	6.00
(4) Ron Fairly	8.00	4.00	2.50
(5) Jim Gilliam	10.00	5.00	3.00
(6) Frank Howard	10.00	5.00	3.00
(7) Sandy Koufax	35.00	17.50	10.00
(8) Bob Miller	8.00	4.00	2.50
(9) Joe Moeller	8.00	4.00	2.50
(10) Wally Moon	8.00	4.00	2.50
(11) Phil Ortega	8.00	4.00	2.50
(12) Wes Parker	8.00	4.00	2.50
(13) Ron Perranoski	8.00	4.00	2.50
(14) John Podres	8.00	4.00	2.50
(15) John Roseboro	8.00	4.00	2.50
(16) Dick Tracewski	8.00	4.00	2.50
(17) Lee Walls	8.00	4.00	2.50
(18) Maury Wills	10.00	5.00	3.00

1969 Union Oil Dodgers Premium Pictures

These 8-1/2" x 11" cards were given to fans attending week night "Player Portrait Night" promotional games. The premiums are similar in format to earlier and later sets sponsored by Union Oil and created by sports artist Nicholas Volpe. Fronts have pastel player portraits and action drawings against a black background. Backs are in black-and-white and have player biographies, stats and a career summary, along with a word about the artist and an ad for Union Oil/Union 76. The unnumbered pictures are checklisted here alphabetically.

	NM	EX	VG
Complete Set (13):	120.00	60.00	35.00
Common Player:	8.00	4.00	2.50
(1) Walt Alston	10.00	5.00	3.00
(2) Jim Brewer	8.00	4.00	2.50
(3) Willie Davis	10.00	5.00	3.00
(4) Don Drysdale	20.00	10.00	6.00
(5) Ron Fairly	8.00	4.00	2.50
(6) Tom Haller	8.00	4.00	2.50
(7) Jim Lefebvre	8.00	4.00	2.50
(8) Claude Osteen	8.00	4.00	2.50
(9) Wes Parker	8.00	4.00	2.50
(10) Paul Popovich	8.00	4.00	2.50
(11) Bill Singer	8.00	4.00	2.50
(12) Bill Sudakis	8.00	4.00	2.50
(13) Don Sutton	13.50	6.75	4.00

1968 Uniroyal Keds Cincinnati Reds

These 2-1/2" x 3-1/4" cards are printed in blue duotone on thin paper. Blank backed, they were intended to be put into an accompanying album. It is unknown whether this checklist is complete.

	NM	EX	VG
Common Player:	20.00	10.00	6.00

(1) Dave Bristol	20.00	10.00	6.00
(2) Bob Johnson	20.00	10.00	6.00
(3) Bob Lee	20.00	10.00	6.00
(4) Jim Maloney	20.00	10.00	6.00
(5) Lee May	20.00	10.00	6.00
(6) Vada Pinson	25.00	12.50	7.50
(7) Pete Rose	150.00	75.00	45.00

1979 United Press International

Not widely circulated, and perhaps issued only as a prototype, these cards feature a tiny (2" x 2-1/4" clear vinyl record attached to the back. Overall, the card is 2-3/4" x 5" and has on front a black-and-white or color photo with a UPI credit line in the very wide white border at bottom. The back is headed either "Sports Nostalgia" or "Great Moments in Sports." Player identification and career highlights are printed on back. The vinyl mini-record could be played on an ancient electronic entertainment device known as a turntable. Similar card/records were produced for other sports and historical highlights.

	NM	EX	VG
Complete Set (9):	150.00	75.00	45.00
Common Player:	10.00	5.00	3.00
(1) Hank Aaron (715th HR)	15.00	7.50	4.50
(2) Joe DiMaggio (Hitting Streak Ends)	20.00	10.00	6.00
(3) Lou Gehrig (Gehrig Day 7/4/39)	20.00	10.00	6.00
(4) Mickey Mantle (Record HR)	25.00	12.50	7.50
(5) Stan Musial (3,000th Hit)	15.00	7.50	4.50
(6) Babe Ruth (Famous Home Run)	20.00	10.00	6.00
(7) Gene Tenace (Record HR)	10.00	5.00	3.00
(8) Bobby Thomson (Famous HR)	12.00	6.00	3.50
(9) Ted Williams (Last At-Bat)	15.00	7.50	4.50

1932 Universal Pictures Babe Ruth Premium

This 8" x 10" black-and-white photo was issued to promote what was advertised as a series of Babe Ruth shorts. The front pictures the movie star in a generic uniform with a facsimile autograph. On back is advertising for the theater bill. It is likely the pictures were distributed blank-backed, allowing local theaters to have their advertising added.

	NM	EX	VG
Babe Ruth	750.00	375.00	225.00

1925 Universal Toy & Novelty Brooklyn Dodgers (W504)

Printed on cheap paper in blue ink and intended to be cut apart into a team photo and 16 individual player cards, this set was originally issued on a 5-1/2" x 13" sheet. Single cut cards measure about 1-3/8" x 2-3/8", with the team picture about 5-1/2" x 3-1/2". Cards are blank-back. Cards are numbered in roughly alphabetical order beneath the photo, where the name, team, position and birth year are also printed.

		NM	EX	VG
Complete Sheet:		1,800	900.00	540.00
Complete Set, Singles (17):		1,200	600.00	360.00
Common Player:		50.00	25.00	15.00
101	Edward W. Brown	50.00	25.00	15.00
102	John H. De Berry	50.00	25.00	15.00
103	William L. Doak	50.00	25.00	15.00
104	Wm. C. Ehrhardt (First name Welton.)	50.00	25.00	15.00
105	J.F. Fournier	50.00	25.00	15.00
106	T.H. Griffith	50.00	25.00	15.00
107	Burleigh A. Grimes	100.00	50.00	30.00
108	C.P. Hargreaves	50.00	25.00	15.00
109	Andrew A. High	50.00	25.00	15.00
110	Andy. H. Johnston (First name Jimmy.)	50.00	25.00	15.00
111	John Mitchell	50.00	25.00	15.00
112	"Tiny" Osborne	50.00	25.00	15.00
113	Milton Stock	50.00	25.00	15.00
114	James W. Taylor	50.00	25.00	15.00
115	"Dazzy" Vance	100.00	50.00	30.00
116	Zack D. Wheat	100.00	50.00	30.00
---	Brooklyn National League Team Photo	550.00	275.00	165.00

1925 Universal Toy & Novelty New York Giants (W504)

Printed on thick cardboard and intended to be cut apart into a team photo and 16 individual player cards, this set was originally issued on a 5-1/2" x 13" sheet. Single cut cards measure about 1-3/8" x 2-3/8", with the team picture about 5" x 3-1/2". Cards are blank-back. Player cards are numbered beneath the photo, where the name, team, position and birth year are also printed.

		NM	EX	VG
Complete Sheet:		3,500	1,750	1,000
Complete Set (17):		3,000	1,500	900.00
Common Player:		125.00	60.00	35.00
133	Virgil Barnes	125.00	60.00	35.00
134	John N. Bentley	125.00	60.00	35.00
135	Frank Frisch	225.00	110.00	65.00
136	Harry Gowdy	125.00	60.00	35.00
137	Henry Groh	125.00	60.00	35.00
138	Travis Jackson	200.00	100.00	60.00
139	George Kelly	200.00	100.00	60.00
140	Emil Meusel	125.00	60.00	35.00
141	Hugh McQuillan	125.00	60.00	35.00
142	Arthur Nehf	125.00	60.00	35.00
143	Wilfred D. Ryan	125.00	60.00	35.00
144	Frank Snyder	125.00	60.00	35.00
145	Lewis R. Wilson	225.00	110.00	65.00
146	Ross Youngs	200.00	100.00	60.00
147	Hugh Jennings	200.00	100.00	60.00
148	John J. McGraw	200.00	100.00	60.00
---	New York National League Team Photo	400.00	200.00	120.00

1925 Universal Toy & Novelty N.Y. Yankees (W504)

Printed on thick cardboard and intended to be cut apart into a team photo and 16 individual player cards, this set was originally issued on a 5-1/2" x 13" sheet. Single cut cards measure about 1-3/8" x 2-3/8," with the team picture about 5" x 3-1/2". Cards are blank-back. Player cards are numbered in alphabetical order beneath the photo, where the name, team, position and birth year are also printed.

		NM	EX	VG
Complete Sheet:		4,000	2,000	1,200
Complete Set (17):		3,500	1,750	1,000
Common Player:		125.00	60.00	35.00
117	Bernard Bengough	125.00	60.00	35.00
118	Joseph Dugan	125.00	60.00	35.00
119	Waite Hoyt	200.00	100.00	60.00
120	Sam Jones	125.00	60.00	35.00
121	Robert Meusel	125.00	60.00	35.00
122	Walter C. Pipp	125.00	60.00	35.00
123	G.H. "Babe" Ruth	1,200	600.00	360.00
124	Wal. H. Schang	125.00	60.00	35.00
125	Robert J. Shawkey	125.00	60.00	35.00
126	Everett Scott	125.00	60.00	35.00
127	Urban Shocker	125.00	60.00	35.00
128	Aaron L. Ward	125.00	60.00	35.00
129	Lawton Witt	125.00	60.00	35.00
130	Carl Mays	140.00	70.00	42.00
131	Miller Huggins	200.00	100.00	60.00
132	Benj. Paschal	125.00	60.00	35.00
---	New York American League Team Photo	800.00	400.00	240.00

1925 Universal Toy & Novelty Washington Senators (W504)

Printed on thick cardboard and intended to be cut apart into a team photo and 16 individual player cards, this set was originally issued on a 5-1/2" x 13" sheet. Single cut cards measure about 1-3/8" x 2-3/8," with the team picture about 5" x 3-1/2". Cards are blank-back. Player cards are numbered beneath the photo, where the name, team, position and birth year are also printed.

		NM	EX	VG
Complete Sheet:				
Complete Set (17):				
Common Player:		50.00	25.00	15.00
149	Joe Judge	50.00	25.00	15.00
150	Wm. Hargrave	50.00	25.00	15.00
151	R. Peckinpaugh	50.00	25.00	15.00
152	O.L. Bluege	50.00	25.00	15.00
153	M.J. McNally	50.00	25.00	15.00
154	Sam Rice	200.00	100.00	60.00
155				
156				
157				
158				
159	Wm. Hargrave	50.00	25.00	15.00
160				
161				
162	Harold (Herold) Ruel	50.00	25.00	15.00
163				
164	George Mogridge	50.00	25.00	15.00
---	Washinton American League Team Photo	400.00	200.00	120.00

1933 U.S. Caramel (R328)

Produced by a Boston confectioner, this set is not limited to baseball, but is a set of 32 "Famous Athletes," of which 27 are baseball players. The 2-1/2" x 3" cards have a black-and-white picture on front with a red background and a white border. Backs feature the player's name, position, team and league as well as a redemption ad and card number. The issue was among the last of the caramel card sets. The cards could be redeemed for a baseball and glove and were returned punch-cancelled and stamped. Card #16, short-printed to limit the number of prizes claimed, was first discovered in the late 1980s; only two examples are currently known.

		NM	EX	VG
Common Player:		600.00	275.00	150.00
1	Edward T. (Eddie) Collins	1,000	450.00	250.00
2	Paul (Big Poison) Waner	1,000	450.00	250.00
3	Robert T. (Bobby) Jones (golfer)			
4	William (Bill) Terry	1,000	450.00	250.00
5	Earl B. Combs (Earle)	1,000	450.00	250.00
6	William (Bill) Dickey	1,000	450.00	250.00
7	Joseph (Joe) Cronin	1,000	450.00	250.00
8	Charles (Chick) Hafey	1,000	450.00	250.00
9	Gene Sarazen (golfer)			
10	Walter (Rabbit) Maranville	1,000	450.00	250.00
11	Rogers (Rajah) Hornsby	1,750	785.00	435.00
12	Gordon (Mickey) Cochrane	1,000	450.00	250.00
13	Lloyd (Little Poison) Waner	1,000	450.00	250.00
14	Tyrus (Ty) Cobb	3,000	1,350	750.00
15	Eugene (Gene) Tunney (boxer)			
16	Charles (Lindy) Lindstrom (2 known)			80,000
17	Al. Simmons	1,000	450.00	250.00
18	Anthony (Tony) Lazzeri	1,000	450.00	250.00
19	Walter (Wally) Berger	600.00	275.00	150.00
20	Charles (Large Charlie) Ruffing	1,000	450.00	250.00
21	Charles (Chuck) Klein	1,000	450.00	250.00
22	John (Jack) Dempsey (boxer)			
23	James (Jimmy) Foxx	1,750	785.00	435.00
24	Frank J. (Lefty) O'Doul	750.00	335.00	185.00
25	Jack (Sailor Jack) Sharkey (boxer)			
26	Henry (Lou) Gehrig	6,000	2,700	1,500
27	Robert (Lefty) Grove	1,200	540.00	300.00
28	Edward Brant (Brandt)	600.00	275.00	150.00
29	George Earnshaw	600.00	275.00	150.00
30	Frank (Frankie) Frisch	1,000	450.00	250.00
31	Vernon (Lefty) Gomez	1,000	450.00	250.00
32	George (Babe) Ruth	7,500	3,250	1,900

1973 U.S. Playing Card Ruth/Gehrig

These decks of playing cards were produced for sale by the Smithsonian Institution in Washington, D.C. The 2-1/4" x 3-1/2" cards were sold as a pair. Backs have colorized pictures of the Yankees greats; Ruth on an orange background and Gehrig on red.

	NM	EX	VG
Complete Set, Ruth (54):	25.00	12.50	7.50
Single Card, Ruth:	1.50	.75	.45
Complete Set, Gehrig (54):	15.00	7.50	4.50
Single Card, Gehrig:	.75	.40	.25

(A 50 percent premium attaches to a complete boxed pair of decks.)

1909-11 Uzit Cigarettes

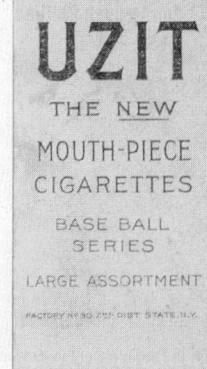

Uzit is generally accepted as the second scarcest back advertiser (after Drum) found on T206. The typographic back is printed in light blue ink.

PREMIUMS
Commons: 35-45X
Hall of Famers: 6-8X
(See T206 for checklist.)

V

1938-39 Val Decker Packing Co. Cincinnati Reds Postcards

(See 1937-39 Orcajo Cincinnati Reds postcards for checklist and values.)

1950s-70s Van Heusen Advisory Staff Photos

Not a great deal is known about the distribution of these 8" x 10" black-and-white player photos. It is likely the checklist here is not complete. The photos are bordered in white with the player name at bottom. In one of the lower corners is the logo of the clothing manufacturer. This issue is differentiated from the Phillies photos because of the action poses and multi-team composition of the known examples.

		NM	EX	VG
	Common Player:	20.00	10.00	6.00
(1)	Paul Blair	20.00	10.00	6.00
(2)	Curt Blefary	20.00	10.00	6.00
(3)	Jerry Coleman (Yankees, throwing.)	25.00	12.50	7.50
(4)	Tommy Davis (Dodgers, batting.)	20.00	10.00	6.00
(5)	Dick Hall (Phillies, portrait.)	20.00	10.00	6.00
(6)	Bob Hendley (Braves, follow-through.)	20.00	10.00	6.00
(7)	Chuck Hinton	20.00	10.00	6.00
(8)	Don Lock (Phillies, upper body.)	20.00	10.00	6.00
(9)	Jim Piersall	25.00	12.50	7.50
(10)	Cookie Rojas (Phillies, bat on shoulder.)	20.00	10.00	6.00
(11)	Bill Skowron (Dodgers, full-length.)	25.00	12.50	7.50
(12)	Maury Wills (Dodgers, batting.)	25.00	12.50	7.50

1967 Van Heusen Phillies

Not a great deal is known about the distribution of these 8" x 10" black-and-white player portraits. It is possible the checklist here is not complete. The photos are bordered in white with the player name at bottom. At lower-right is the logo of the clothing manufacturer. This issue is differentiated from the Advisory Staff Photos because of the similitude of the portrait photos of the teammates.

		NM	EX	VG
	Common Player:	20.00	10.00	6.00
(1)	Bo Belinsky	20.00	10.00	6.00

(2)	Jim Bunning	35.00	17.50	10.50
(3)	Wes Covington	20.00	10.00	6.00
(4)	Dick Ellsworth	20.00	10.00	6.00
(5)	Dick Groat	20.00	10.00	6.00
(6)	Chris Short	20.00	10.00	6.00
(7)	Bill White	20.00	10.00	6.00

1912 Vassar Sweaters

TY COBB

Star players of the day are pictured wearing the sponsor's product over their uniforms in this issue of 4" x 6-3/4" black-and-white cards. Player names are in the white border at bottom. It is not known whether this checklist is complete.

		NM	EX	VG
	Common Player:	1,250	625.00	375.00
(1)	Ty Cobb	5,000	2,500	1,500
(2)	Sam Crawford	1,750	875.00	525.00
(3)	Walter Johnson	2,750	1,375	825.00
(4)	Napoleon Lajoie	1,750	875.00	525.00
(5)	Smokey Joe Wood	1,250	625.00	375.00

1959 Venezuelan Topps

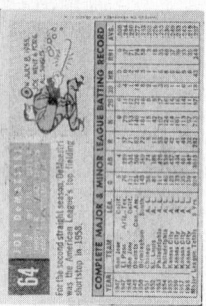

Beginning in 1959, Topps began marketing baseball cards in Venezuela, always a hotbed of baseball fandom. In most years, such as the debut set in 1959, the cards destined for the South American market represented a parallel of the first couple of series of Topps' regular U.S. issue. Print quality (usually lack of gloss on front) is the major difference between the two issues. Backs of some of the 1959 Venezuelan cards carry the credit line: "Impreso en Venezuela por Benco C.A." A reality of the Venezuelan cards is that they tend to survive in low-grade condition due to the local custom of gluing cards into albums and scrapbooks. After its 1959 issue, Topps produced Venezuelan cards only in the even-numbered years, except for 1967, until the last of the sets was issued in 1968.

		NM	EX	VG
	Complete Set (196):	10,000	4,000	2,400
	Common Player:	45.00	18.00	11.00
1	Ford Frick	60.00	24.00	14.50
2	Eddie Yost	45.00	18.00	11.00
3	Don McMahon	45.00	18.00	11.00
4	Albie Pearson	45.00	18.00	11.00
5	Dick Donovan	45.00	18.00	11.00
6	Alex Grammas	45.00	18.00	11.00
7	Al Pilarcik	45.00	18.00	11.00
8	Phillies Team	75.00	30.00	18.00
9	Paul Giel	45.00	18.00	11.00
10	Mickey Mantle	2,000	550.00	350.00
11	Billy Hunter	45.00	18.00	11.00
12	Vern Law	45.00	18.00	11.00
13	Dick Gernert	45.00	18.00	11.00
14	Pete Whisenant	45.00	18.00	11.00
15	Dick Drott	45.00	18.00	11.00
16	Joe Pignatano	45.00	18.00	11.00
17	Danny's All-Stars (Ted Kluszewski, Danny Murtaugh, Frank Thomas)	50.00	20.00	12.00
18	Jack Urban	45.00	18.00	11.00
19	Ed Bressoud	45.00	18.00	11.00
20	Duke Snider	200.00	80.00	48.00
21	Connie Johnson	45.00	18.00	11.00
22	Al Smith	45.00	18.00	11.00
23	Murry Dickson	45.00	18.00	11.00
24	Red Wilson	45.00	18.00	11.00
25	Don Hoak	45.00	18.00	11.00
26	Chuck Stobbs	45.00	18.00	11.00
27	Andy Pafko	45.00	18.00	11.00

28	Red Worthington	45.00	18.00	11.00
29	Jim Bolger	45.00	18.00	11.00
30	Nellie Fox	100.00	40.00	24.00
31	Ken Lehman	45.00	18.00	11.00
32	Don Buddin	45.00	18.00	11.00
33	Ed Fitz Gerald	45.00	18.00	11.00
34	Pitchers Beware (Al Kaline, Charlie Maxwell)	90.00	36.00	22.00
35	Ted Kluszewski	60.00	24.00	14.50
36	Hank Aguirre	45.00	18.00	11.00
37	Gene Green	45.00	18.00	11.00
38	Morrie Martin	45.00	18.00	11.00
39	Ed Bouchee	45.00	18.00	11.00
40	Warren Spahn	125.00	50.00	30.00
41	Bob Martyn	45.00	18.00	11.00
42	Murray Wall	45.00	18.00	11.00
43	Steve Bilko	45.00	18.00	11.00
44	Vito Valentinetti	45.00	18.00	11.00
45	Andy Carey	45.00	18.00	11.00
46	Bill Henry	45.00	18.00	11.00
47	Jim Finigan	45.00	18.00	11.00
48	Orioles Team/Checklist 1-88	75.00	30.00	18.00
49	Bill Hall	45.00	18.00	11.00
50	Willie Mays	450.00	180.00	108.00
51	Rip Coleman	45.00	18.00	11.00
52	Coot Veal	45.00	18.00	11.00
53	Stan Williams	45.00	18.00	11.00
54	Mel Roach	45.00	18.00	11.00
55	Tom Brewer	45.00	18.00	11.00
56	Carl Sawatski	45.00	18.00	11.00
57	Al Cicotte	45.00	18.00	11.00
58	Eddie Miksis	45.00	18.00	11.00
59	Irv Noren	45.00	18.00	11.00
60	Bob Turley	45.00	18.00	11.00
61	Dick Brown	45.00	18.00	11.00
62	Tony Taylor	45.00	18.00	11.00
63	Jim Hearn	45.00	18.00	11.00
64	Joe DeMaestri	45.00	18.00	11.00
65	Frank Torre	45.00	18.00	11.00
66	Joe Ginsberg	45.00	18.00	11.00
67	Brooks Lawrence	45.00	18.00	11.00
68	Dick Schofield	45.00	18.00	11.00
69	Giants Team/Checklist 89-176	75.00	30.00	18.00
70	Harvey Kuenn	50.00	20.00	12.00
71	Don Bessent	45.00	18.00	11.00
72	Bill Renna	45.00	18.00	11.00
73	Ron Jackson	45.00	18.00	11.00
74	Directing the Power (Cookie Lavagetto, Jim Lemon, Roy Sievers)	45.00	18.00	11.00
75	Sam Jones	45.00	18.00	11.00
76	Bobby Richardson	50.00	20.00	12.00
77	John Goryl	45.00	18.00	11.00
78	Pedro Ramos	45.00	18.00	11.00
79	Harry Chiti	45.00	18.00	11.00
80	Minnie Minoso	55.00	22.00	13.00
81	Hal Jeffcoat	45.00	18.00	11.00
82	Bob Boyd	45.00	18.00	11.00
83	Bob Smith	45.00	18.00	11.00
84	Reno Bertoia	45.00	18.00	11.00
85	Harry Anderson	45.00	18.00	11.00
86	Bob Keegan	45.00	18.00	11.00
87	Danny O'Connell	45.00	18.00	11.00
88	Herb Score	45.00	18.00	11.00
89	Billy Gardner	45.00	18.00	11.00
90	Bill Skowron	55.00	22.00	13.00
91	Herb Moford	45.00	18.00	11.00
92	Dave Philley	45.00	18.00	11.00
93	Julio Becquer	45.00	18.00	11.00
94	White Sox Team	100.00	40.00	24.00
95	Carl Willey	45.00	18.00	11.00
96	Lou Berberet	45.00	18.00	11.00
97	Jerry Lynch	45.00	18.00	11.00
98	Arnie Portocarrero	45.00	18.00	11.00
99	Ted Kazanski	45.00	18.00	11.00
100	Bob Cerv	45.00	18.00	11.00
101	Alex Kellner	45.00	18.00	11.00
102	Felipe Alou	60.00	24.00	14.50
103	Billy Goodman	45.00	18.00	11.00
104	Del Rice	45.00	18.00	11.00
105	Lee Walls	45.00	18.00	11.00
106	Hal Woodeshick	45.00	18.00	11.00
107	Norm Larker	45.00	18.00	11.00
108	Zack Monroe	45.00	18.00	11.00
109	Bob Schmidt	45.00	18.00	11.00
110	George Witt	45.00	18.00	11.00
111	Redlegs Team/Checklist 89-176	75.00	30.00	18.00
112	Billy Consolo	45.00	18.00	11.00
113	Taylor Phillips	45.00	18.00	11.00
114	Earl Battey	45.00	18.00	11.00
115	Mickey Vernon	45.00	18.00	11.00
116	Bob Allison	45.00	18.00	11.00
117	John Blanchard	45.00	18.00	11.00
118	John Buzhardt	45.00	18.00	11.00
119	John Callison	45.00	18.00	11.00
120	Chuck Coles	45.00	18.00	11.00
121	Bob Conley	45.00	18.00	11.00
122	Bennie Daniels	45.00	18.00	11.00
123	Don Dillard	45.00	18.00	11.00
124	Dan Dobbek	45.00	18.00	11.00
125	Ron Fairly	45.00	18.00	11.00
126	Eddie Haas	45.00	18.00	11.00
127	Kent Hadley	45.00	18.00	11.00
128	Bob Hartman	45.00	18.00	11.00
129	Frank Herrera	45.00	18.00	11.00
130	Lou Jackson	45.00	18.00	11.00
131	Deron Johnson	50.00	20.00	12.00
132	Don Lee	45.00	18.00	11.00
133	Bob Lillis	45.00	18.00	11.00
134	Jim McDaniel	45.00	18.00	11.00
135	Gene Oliver	45.00	18.00	11.00
136	Jim O'Toole	45.00	18.00	11.00
137	Dick Ricketts	45.00	18.00	11.00
138	John Romano	45.00	18.00	11.00
139	Ed Sadowski	45.00	18.00	11.00
140	Charlie Secrest	45.00	18.00	11.00
141	Joe Shipley	45.00	18.00	11.00

		NM	EX	VG
142	Dick Stigman	45.00	18.00	11.00
143	Willie Tasby	45.00	18.00	11.00
144	Jerry Walker	45.00	18.00	11.00
145	Dom Zanni	45.00	18.00	11.00
146	Jerry Zimmerman	45.00	18.00	11.00
147	Cubs' Clubbers (Ernie Banks, Dale Long, Walt Moryn)	90.00	36.00	22.00
148	Mike McCormick	45.00	18.00	11.00
149	Jim Bunning	100.00	40.00	24.00
150	Stan Musial	400.00	160.00	100.00
151	Bob Malkmus	45.00	18.00	11.00
152	Johnny Klippstein	45.00	18.00	11.00
153	Jim Marshall	45.00	18.00	11.00
154	Ray Herbert	45.00	18.00	11.00
155	Enos Slaughter	90.00	36.00	22.00
156	Ace Hurlers (Billy Pierce, Robin Roberts)	65.00	26.00	15.50
157	Felix Mantilla	45.00	18.00	11.00
158	Walt Dropo	45.00	18.00	11.00
159	Bob Shaw	45.00	18.00	11.00
160	Dick Groat	45.00	18.00	11.00
161	Frank Baumann	45.00	18.00	11.00
162	Bobby G. Smith	45.00	18.00	11.00
163	Sandy Koufax	450.00	180.00	110.00
164	Johnny Groth	45.00	18.00	11.00
165	Bill Bruton	45.00	18.00	11.00
166	Destruction Crew (Rocky Colavito, Larry Doby, Minnie Minoso)	125.00	50.00	30.00
167	Duke Maas	45.00	18.00	11.00
168	Carroll Hardy	45.00	18.00	11.00
169	Ted Abernathy	45.00	18.00	11.00
170	Gene Woodling	45.00	18.00	11.00
171	Willard Schmidt	45.00	18.00	11.00
172	A's Team/Checklist 177-242	75.00	30.00	18.00
173	Bill Monbouquette	45.00	18.00	11.00
174	Jim Pendleton	45.00	18.00	11.00
175	Dick Farrell	45.00	18.00	11.00
176	Preston Ward	45.00	18.00	11.00
177	Johnny Briggs	45.00	18.00	11.00
178	Ruben Amaro	45.00	18.00	11.00
179	Don Rudolph	45.00	18.00	11.00
180	Yogi Berra	200.00	80.00	48.00
181	Bob Porterfield	45.00	18.00	11.00
182	Milt Graff	45.00	18.00	11.00
183	Stu Miller	45.00	18.00	11.00
184	Harvey Haddix	45.00	18.00	11.00
185	Jim Busby	45.00	18.00	11.00
186	Mudcat Grant	45.00	18.00	11.00
187	Bubba Phillips	45.00	18.00	11.00
188	Juan Pizarro	45.00	18.00	11.00
189	Neil Chrisley	45.00	18.00	11.00
190	Bill Virdon	45.00	18.00	11.00
191	Russ Kemmerer	45.00	18.00	11.00
192	Charley Beamon	45.00	18.00	11.00
193	Sammy Taylor	45.00	18.00	11.00
194	Jim Brosnan	45.00	18.00	11.00
195	Rip Repulski	45.00	18.00	11.00
196	Billy Moran	45.00	18.00	11.00

1960 Venezuelan Topps

Unlike its 1959 issue, which had a printed-in-Venezuela notice on the backs, Topps' 1960 issue for that South American market is virtually identical, front and back, to the company's U.S. product. The Venezuelan cards have less gloss on the front and the black ink on their backs is lighter. The Latin American version is a parallel of the first 198 cards from Topps' set. As usual with Latin American cards, low-grade examples are the norm due to the local collecting custom of pasting cards into albums and scrapbooks.

		NM	EX	VG
	Complete Set (198):	7,900	3,150	1,900
	Common Player:	40.00	16.00	9.50
1	Early Wynn	95.00	30.00	20.00
2	Roman Mejias	40.00	16.00	9.50
3	Joe Adcock	40.00	16.00	9.50
4	Bob Purkey	40.00	16.00	9.50
5	Wally Moon	40.00	16.00	9.50
6	Lou Berberet	40.00	16.00	9.50
7	Master and Mentor (Willie Mays, Bill Rigney)	125.00	50.00	30.00
8	Bud Daley	40.00	16.00	9.50
9	Faye Throneberry	40.00	16.00	9.50
10	Ernie Banks	150.00	60.00	36.00
11	Norm Siebern	40.00	16.00	9.50
12	Milt Pappas	40.00	16.00	9.50
13	Wally Post	40.00	16.00	9.50
14	Jim Grant	40.00	16.00	9.50
15	Pete Runnels	40.00	16.00	9.50
16	Ernie Broglio	40.00	16.00	9.50
17	Johnny Callison	40.00	16.00	9.50
18	Dodgers Team/Checklist 1-88	100.00	40.00	24.00
19	Felix Mantilla	40.00	16.00	9.50
20	Roy Face	40.00	16.00	9.50
21	Dutch Dotterer	40.00	16.00	9.50
22	Rocky Bridges	40.00	16.00	9.50
23	Eddie Fisher	40.00	16.00	9.50
24	Dick Gray	40.00	16.00	9.50
25	Roy Sievers	40.00	16.00	9.50
26	Wayne Terwilliger	40.00	16.00	9.50
27	Dick Drott	40.00	16.00	9.50
28	Brooks Robinson	150.00	60.00	36.00
29	Clem Labine	40.00	16.00	9.50
30	Tito Francona	40.00	16.00	9.50
31	Sammy Esposito	40.00	16.00	9.50
32	Sophomore Stalwarts (Jim O'Toole, Vada Pinson)	40.00	16.00	9.50
33	Tom Morgan	40.00	16.00	9.50
34	Sparky Anderson	90.00	45.00	27.00
35	Whitey Ford	150.00	60.00	36.00
36	Russ Nixon	40.00	16.00	9.50
37	Bill Bruton	40.00	16.00	9.50
38	Jerry Casale	40.00	16.00	9.50
39	Earl Averill	40.00	16.00	9.50
40	Joe Cunningham	40.00	16.00	9.50
41	Barry Latman	40.00	16.00	9.50
42	Hobie Landrith	40.00	16.00	9.50
43	Senators Team/Checklist 1-88	75.00	30.00	18.00
44	Bobby Locke	40.00	16.00	9.50
45	Roy McMillan	40.00	16.00	9.50
46	Jack Fisher	40.00	16.00	9.50
47	Don Zimmer	40.00	16.00	9.50
48	Hal Smith	40.00	16.00	9.50
49	Curt Raydon	40.00	16.00	9.50
50	Al Kaline	150.00	60.00	36.00
51	Jim Coates	40.00	16.00	9.50
52	Dave Philley	40.00	16.00	9.50
53	Jackie Brandt	40.00	16.00	9.50
54	Mike Fornieles	40.00	16.00	9.50
55	Bill Mazeroski	90.00	45.00	27.00
56	Steve Korcheck	40.00	16.00	9.50
57	Win-Savers (Turk Lown, Gerry Staley)	40.00	16.00	9.50
58	Gino Cimoli	40.00	16.00	9.50
59	Juan Pizarro	40.00	16.00	9.50
60	Gus Triandos	40.00	16.00	9.50
61	Eddie Kasko	40.00	16.00	9.50
62	Roger Craig	40.00	16.00	9.50
63	George Strickland	40.00	16.00	9.50
64	Jack Meyer	40.00	16.00	9.50
65	Elston Howard	45.00	18.00	11.00
66	Bob Trowbridge	40.00	16.00	9.50
67	Jose Pagan	40.00	16.00	9.50
68	Dave Hillman	40.00	16.00	9.50
69	Billy Goodman	40.00	16.00	9.50
70	Lou Burdette	40.00	16.00	9.50
71	Marty Keough	40.00	16.00	9.50
72	Tigers Team/Checklist 89-176	75.00	30.00	18.00
73	Bob Gibson	100.00	40.00	24.00
74	Walt Moryn	40.00	16.00	9.50
75	Vic Power	40.00	16.00	9.50
76	Bill Fischer	40.00	16.00	9.50
77	Hank Foiles	40.00	16.00	9.50
78	Bob Grim	40.00	16.00	9.50
79	Walt Dropo	40.00	16.00	9.50
80	Johnny Antonelli	40.00	16.00	9.50
81	Russ Snyder	40.00	16.00	9.50
82	Ruben Gomez	40.00	16.00	9.50
83	Tony Kubek	40.00	16.00	9.50
84	Hal Smith	40.00	16.00	9.50
85	Frank Lary	40.00	16.00	9.50
86	Dick Gernert	40.00	16.00	9.50
87	John Romonosky	40.00	16.00	9.50
88	John Roseboro	40.00	16.00	9.50
89	Hal Brown	40.00	16.00	9.50
90	Bobby Avila	40.00	16.00	9.50
91	Bennie Daniels	40.00	16.00	9.50
92	Whitey Herzog	45.00	18.00	11.00
93	Art Schult	40.00	16.00	9.50
94	Leo Kiely	40.00	16.00	9.50
95	Frank Thomas	40.00	16.00	9.50
96	Ralph Terry	40.00	16.00	9.50
97	Ted Lepcio	40.00	16.00	9.50
98	Gordon Jones	40.00	16.00	9.50
99	Lenny Green	40.00	16.00	9.50
100	Nellie Fox	90.00	36.00	22.00
101	Bob Miller	40.00	16.00	9.50
102	Kent Hadley	40.00	16.00	9.50
103	Dick Farrell	40.00	16.00	9.50
104	Dick Schofield	40.00	16.00	9.50
105	Larry Sherry	40.00	16.00	9.50
106	Billy Gardner	40.00	16.00	9.50
107	Carl Willey	40.00	16.00	9.50
108	Pete Daley	40.00	16.00	9.50
109	Cletis Boyer	40.00	16.00	9.50
110	Cal McLish	40.00	16.00	9.50
111	Vic Wertz	40.00	16.00	9.50
112	Jack Harshman	40.00	16.00	9.50
113	Bob Skinner	40.00	16.00	9.50
114	Ken Aspromonte	40.00	16.00	9.50
115	Fork and Knuckler (Roy Face, Hoyt Wilhelm)	45.00	18.00	11.00
116	Jim Rivera	40.00	16.00	9.50
117	Tom Borland	40.00	16.00	9.50
118	Bob Bruce	40.00	16.00	9.50
119	Chico Cardenas	40.00	16.00	9.50
120	Duke Carmel	40.00	16.00	9.50
121	Camilo Carreon	40.00	16.00	9.50
122	Don Dillard	40.00	16.00	9.50
123	Dan Dobbek	40.00	16.00	9.50
124	Jim Donohue	40.00	16.00	9.50
125	Dick Ellsworth	40.00	16.00	9.50
126	Chuck Estrada	40.00	16.00	9.50
127	Ronnie Hansen	40.00	16.00	9.50
128	Bill Harris	40.00	16.00	9.50
129	Bob Hartman	40.00	16.00	9.50
130	Frank Herrera	40.00	16.00	9.50
131	Ed Hobaugh	40.00	16.00	9.50
132	Frank Howard	50.00	20.00	12.00
133	Manuel Javier	40.00	16.00	9.50
134	Deron Johnson	45.00	18.00	11.00
135	Ken Johnson	40.00	16.00	9.50
136	Jim Kaat	60.00	24.00	14.50
137	Lou Klimchock	40.00	16.00	9.50
138	Art Mahaffey	40.00	16.00	9.50
139	Carl Mathias	40.00	16.00	9.50
140	Julio Navarro	40.00	16.00	9.50
141	Jim Proctor	40.00	16.00	9.50
142	Bill Short	40.00	16.00	9.50
143	Al Spangler	40.00	16.00	9.50
144	Al Stieglitz	40.00	16.00	9.50
145	Jim Umbricht	40.00	16.00	9.50
146	Ted Wieand	40.00	16.00	9.50
147	Bob Will	40.00	16.00	9.50
148	Carl Yastrzemski	550.00	275.00	165.00
149	Bob Nieman	40.00	16.00	9.50
150	Billy Pierce	40.00	16.00	9.50
151	Giants Team/Checklist 177-264	75.00	30.00	18.00
152	Gail Harris	40.00	16.00	9.50
153	Bobby Thomson	40.00	16.00	9.50
154	Jim Davenport	40.00	16.00	9.50
155	Charlie Neal	40.00	16.00	9.50
156	Art Ceccarelli	40.00	16.00	9.50
157	Rocky Nelson	40.00	16.00	9.50
158	Wes Covington	40.00	16.00	9.50
159	Jim Piersall	45.00	18.00	11.00
160	Rival All-Stars (Ken Boyer, Mickey Mantle)	600.00	250.00	150.00
161	Ray Narleski	40.00	16.00	9.50
162	Sammy Taylor	40.00	16.00	9.50
163	Hector Lopez	40.00	16.00	9.50
164	Reds Team/Checklist 89-176	75.00	30.00	18.00
165	Jack Sanford	40.00	16.00	9.50
166	Chuck Essegian	40.00	16.00	9.50
167	Valmy Thomas	40.00	16.00	9.50
168	Alex Grammas	40.00	16.00	9.50
169	Jake Striker	40.00	16.00	9.50
170	Del Crandall	40.00	16.00	9.50
171	Johnny Groth	40.00	16.00	9.50
172	Willie Kirkland	40.00	16.00	9.50
173	Billy Martin	45.00	18.00	11.00
174	Indians Team/Checklist 89-176	75.00	30.00	18.00
175	Pedro Ramos	40.00	16.00	9.50
176	Vada Pinson	45.00	18.00	11.00
177	Johnny Kucks	40.00	16.00	9.50
178	Woody Held	40.00	16.00	9.50
179	Rip Coleman	40.00	16.00	9.50
180	Harry Simpson	40.00	16.00	9.50
181	Billy Loes	40.00	16.00	9.50
182	Glen Hobbie	40.00	16.00	9.50
183	Eli Grba	40.00	16.00	9.50
184	Gary Geiger	40.00	16.00	9.50
185	Jim Owens	40.00	16.00	9.50
186	Dave Sisler	40.00	16.00	9.50
187	Jay Hook	40.00	16.00	9.50
188	Dick Williams	40.00	16.00	9.50
189	Don McMahon	40.00	16.00	9.50
190	Gene Woodling	40.00	16.00	9.50
191	Johnny Klippstein	40.00	16.00	9.50
192	Danny O'Connell	40.00	16.00	9.50
193	Dick Hyde	40.00	16.00	9.50
194	Bobby Gene Smith	40.00	16.00	9.50
195	Lindy McDaniel	40.00	16.00	9.50
196	Andy Carey	40.00	16.00	9.50
197	Ron Kline	40.00	16.00	9.50
198	Jerry Lynch	40.00	16.00	9.50

1962 Venezuelan Topps

For the first time in its short history of producing baseball cards for the Venezuelan market, Topps in 1962 reprinted virtually the entire back of each card in Spanish (except the League Leaders cards #51-60). The player personal data, career summary and even the cartoon are En Espanol; only the stats are in English. There is no Topps credit or copyright line on the backs. Otherwise identical in format to the 1962 Topps North American issue, the Venezuelan set comprises the first 198 cards of the Topps issue, though cards #197 (Daryl Spencer) and 198 (Johnny Keane) have been replaced with two local Major Leaguers. Survivors of this issue tend to be in lower grades due to the common practice of gluing cards into albums or scrapbooks.

		NM	EX	VG
	Complete Set (198):	8,000	3,200	2,000
	Common Player:	30.00	12.00	7.50
1	Roger Maris	750.00	300.00	185.00
2	Jim Brosnan	30.00	12.00	7.50
3	Pete Runnels	30.00	12.00	7.50
4	John DeMerit	30.00	12.00	7.50
5	Sandy Koufax	400.00	160.00	100.00
6	Marv Breeding	30.00	12.00	7.50
7	Frank Thomas	30.00	12.00	7.50
8	Ray Herbert	30.00	12.00	7.50
9	Jim Davenport	30.00	12.00	7.50
10	Roberto Clemente	550.00	220.00	135.00
11	Tom Morgan	30.00	12.00	7.50
12	Harry Craft	30.00	12.00	7.50
13	Dick Howser	30.00	12.00	7.50
14	Bill White	30.00	12.00	7.50
15	Dick Donovan	30.00	12.00	7.50
16	Darrell Johnson	30.00	12.00	7.50
17	Johnny Callison	30.00	12.00	7.50
18	Managers' Dream (Mickey Mantle, Willie Mays)	1,500	600.00	375.00
19	Ray Washburn	30.00	12.00	7.50
20	Rocky Colavito	60.00	24.00	15.00
21	Jim Kaat	30.00	12.00	7.50
22	Checklist 1-88	30.00	12.00	7.50
23	Norm Larker	30.00	12.00	7.50
24	Tigers team	90.00	36.00	22.00
25	Ernie Banks	175.00	70.00	45.00
26	Chris Cannizzaro	30.00	12.00	7.50
27	Chuck Cottier	30.00	12.00	7.50
28	Minnie Minoso	45.00	18.00	11.00
29	Casey Stengel	125.00	50.00	30.00
30	Eddie Mathews	125.00	50.00	30.00
31	Tom Tresh	40.00	16.00	10.00

32	John Roseboro	30.00	12.00	7.50
33	Don Larsen	30.00	12.00	7.50
34	Johnny Temple	30.00	12.00	7.50
35	Don Schwall	30.00	12.00	7.50
36	Don Leppert	30.00	12.00	7.50
37	Tribe Hill Trio (Barry Latman, Jim Perry, Dick Stigman)	30.00	12.00	7.50
38	Gene Stephens	30.00	12.00	7.50
39	Joe Koppe	30.00	12.00	7.50
40	Orlando Cepeda	65.00	25.00	15.00
41	Cliff Cook	30.00	12.00	7.50
42	Jim King	30.00	12.00	7.50
43	Dodgers team	125.00	50.00	30.00
44	Don Taussig	30.00	12.00	7.50
45	Brooks Robinson	200.00	80.00	50.00
46	Jack Baldschun	30.00	12.00	7.50
47	Bob Will	30.00	12.00	7.50
48	Ralph Terry	30.00	12.00	7.50
49	Hal Jones	30.00	12.00	7.50
50	Stan Musial	250.00	100.00	60.00
51	A.L. Batting Leaders (Norm Cash, Elston Howard, Al Kaline, Jim Piersall)	80.00	32.00	20.00
52	N.L. Batting Leaders (Ken Boyer, Roberto Clemente, Wally Moon, Vada Pinson)	225.00	90.00	55.00
53	A.L. Home Run Leaders (Jim Gentile, Harmon Killebrew, Mickey Mantle, Roger Maris)	400.00	160.00	100.00
54	N.L. Home Run Leaders (Orlando Cepeda, Willie Mays, Frank Robinson)	125.00	50.00	30.00
55	A.L. E.R.A. Leaders (Dick Donovan, Don Mossi, Milt Pappas, Bill Stafford)	30.00	12.00	7.50
56	N.L. E.R.A. Leaders (Mike McCormick, Jim O'Toole, Curt Simmons, Warren Spahn)	35.00	14.00	8.75
57	A.L. Win Leaders (Steve Barber, Jim Bunning, Whitey Ford, Frank Lary)	45.00	18.00	11.00
58	N.L. Win Leaders (Joe Jay, Jim O'Toole, Warren Spahn)	35.00	14.00	8.75
59	A.L. Strikeout Leaders (Jim Bunning, Whitey Ford, Camilo Pascual, Juan Pizarro)	45.00	18.00	11.00
60	N.L. Strikeout Leaders (Don Drysdale, Sandy Koufax, Jim O'Toole, Stan Williams)	100.00	40.00	25.00
61	Cardinals Team	90.00	36.00	22.00
62	Steve Boros	30.00	12.00	7.50
63	Tony Cloninger	30.00	12.00	7.50
64	Russ Snyder	30.00	12.00	7.50
65	Bobby Richardson	40.00	16.00	10.00
66	Cuno Barragon (Barragan)	30.00	12.00	7.50
67	Harvey Haddix	30.00	12.00	7.50
68	Ken Hunt	30.00	12.00	7.50
69	Phil Ortega	30.00	12.00	7.50
70	Harmon Killebrew	125.00	50.00	30.00
71	Dick LeMay	30.00	12.00	7.50
72	Bob's Pupils (Steve Boros, Bob Scheffing, Jake Wood)	30.00	12.00	7.50
73	Nellie Fox	125.00	50.00	30.00
74	Bob Lillis	30.00	12.00	7.50
75	Milt Pappas	30.00	12.00	7.50
76	Howie Bedell	30.00	12.00	7.50
77	Tony Taylor	30.00	12.00	7.50
78	Gene Green	30.00	12.00	7.50
79	Ed Hobaugh	30.00	12.00	7.50
80	Vada Pinson	35.00	14.00	8.75
81	Jim Pagliaroni	30.00	12.00	7.50
82	Deron Johnson	30.00	12.00	7.50
83	Larry Jackson	30.00	12.00	7.50
84	Lenny Green	30.00	12.00	7.50
85	Gil Hodges	80.00	32.00	20.00
86	Donn Clendenon	30.00	12.00	7.50
87	Mike Roarke	30.00	12.00	7.50
88	Ralph Houk	30.00	12.00	7.50
89	Barney Schultz	30.00	12.00	7.50
90	Jim Piersall	30.00	12.00	7.50
91	J.C. Martin	30.00	12.00	7.50
92	Sam Jones	30.00	12.00	7.50
93	John Blanchard	30.00	12.00	7.50
94	Jay Hook	30.00	12.00	7.50
95	Don Hoak	30.00	12.00	7.50
96	Eli Grba	30.00	12.00	7.50
97	Tito Francona	30.00	12.00	7.50
98	Checklist 89-176	30.00	12.00	7.50
99	Boog Powell	75.00	30.00	18.50
100	Warren Spahn	125.00	50.00	30.00
101	Carroll Hardy	30.00	12.00	7.50
102	Al Schroll	30.00	12.00	7.50
103	Don Blasingame	30.00	12.00	7.50
104	Ted Savage	30.00	12.00	7.50
105	Don Mossi	30.00	12.00	7.50
106	Carl Sawatski	30.00	12.00	7.50
107	Mike McCormick	30.00	12.00	7.50
108	Willie Davis	30.00	12.00	7.50
109	Bob Shaw	30.00	12.00	7.50
110	Bill Skowron	35.00	14.00	8.75
111	Dallas Green	30.00	12.00	7.50
112	Hank Foiles	30.00	12.00	7.50
113	White Sox team	90.00	36.00	22.00
114	Howie Koplitz	30.00	12.00	7.50
115	Bob Skinner	30.00	12.00	7.50
116	Herb Score	30.00	12.00	7.50
117	Gary Geiger	30.00	12.00	7.50
118	Julian Javier	30.00	12.00	7.50
119	Danny Murphy	30.00	12.00	7.50
120	Bob Purkey	30.00	12.00	7.50
121	Billy Hitchcock	30.00	12.00	7.50
122	Norm Bass	30.00	12.00	7.50
123	Mike de la Hoz	30.00	12.00	7.50
124	Bill Pleis	30.00	12.00	7.50
125	Gene Woodling	30.00	12.00	7.50
126	Al Cicotte	30.00	12.00	7.50

127	Pride of the A's (Hank Bauer, Jerry Lumpe, Norm Siebern)	30.00	12.00	7.50
128	Art Fowler	30.00	12.00	7.50
129	Lee Walls	30.00	12.00	7.50
130	Frank Bolling	30.00	12.00	7.50
131	Pete Richert	30.00	12.00	7.50
132	Angels Team	90.00	36.00	22.00
133	Felipe Alou	45.00	18.00	11.00
134	Billy Hoeft	30.00	12.00	7.50
135	Babe as a Boy (Babe Ruth)	165.00	65.00	40.00
136	Babe Joins Yanks (Babe Ruth)	200.00	80.00	50.00
137	Babe and Mgr. Huggins (Babe Ruth)	165.00	65.00	40.00
138	The Famous Slugger (Babe Ruth)	200.00	80.00	50.00
139	Babe Hits 60 (Babe Ruth)	300.00	120.00	75.00
140	Gehrig and Ruth (Babe Ruth)	225.00	90.00	55.00
141	Twilight Years (Babe Ruth)	165.00	65.00	40.00
142	Coaching for the Dodgers (Babe Ruth)	165.00	65.00	40.00
143	Greatest Sports Hero (Babe Ruth)	165.00	65.00	40.00
144	Farewell Speech (Babe Ruth)	165.00	65.00	40.00
145	Barry Latman	30.00	12.00	7.50
146	Don Demeter	30.00	12.00	7.50
147	Bill Kunkel	30.00	12.00	7.50
148	Wally Post	30.00	12.00	7.50
149	Bob Duliba	30.00	12.00	7.50
150	Al Kaline	135.00	55.00	35.00
151	Johnny Klippstein	30.00	12.00	7.50
152	Mickey Vernon	30.00	12.00	7.50
153	Pumpsie Green	30.00	12.00	7.50
154	Lee Thomas	30.00	12.00	7.50
155	Stu Miller	30.00	12.00	7.50
156	Merritt Ranew	30.00	12.00	7.50
157	Wes Covington	30.00	12.00	7.50
158	Braves Team	90.00	36.00	22.00
159	Hal Reniff	30.00	12.00	7.50
160	Dick Stuart	30.00	12.00	7.50
161	Frank Baumann	30.00	12.00	7.50
162	Sammy Drake	30.00	12.00	7.50
163	Hot Corner Guardians (Cletis Boyer, Billy Gardner)	30.00	12.00	7.50
164	Hal Naragon	30.00	12.00	7.50
165	Jackie Brandt	30.00	12.00	7.50
166	Don Lee	30.00	12.00	7.50
167	Tim McCarver	125.00	50.00	30.00
168	Leo Posada	30.00	12.00	7.50
169	Bob Cerv	30.00	12.00	7.50
170	Ron Santo	40.00	16.00	10.00
171	Dave Sisler	30.00	12.00	7.50
172	Fred Hutchinson	30.00	12.00	7.50
173	Chico Fernandez	30.00	12.00	7.50
174	Carl Willey	30.00	12.00	7.50
175	Frank Howard	30.00	12.00	7.50
176	Eddie Yost	30.00	12.00	7.50
177	Bobby Shantz	30.00	12.00	7.50
178	Camilo Carreon	30.00	12.00	7.50
179	Tom Sturdivant	30.00	12.00	7.50
180	Bob Allison	30.00	12.00	7.50
181	Paul Brown	30.00	12.00	7.50
182	Bob Nieman	30.00	12.00	7.50
183	Roger Craig	30.00	12.00	7.50
184	Haywood Sullivan	30.00	12.00	7.50
185	Roland Sheldon	30.00	12.00	7.50
186	Mack Jones	30.00	12.00	7.50
187	Gene Conley	30.00	12.00	7.50
188	Chuck Hiller	30.00	12.00	7.50
189	Dick Hall	30.00	12.00	7.50
190	Wally Moon	30.00	12.00	7.50
191	Jim Brewer	30.00	12.00	7.50
192	Checklist 177-264	30.00	12.00	7.50
193	Eddie Kasko	30.00	12.00	7.50
194	Dean Chance	30.00	12.00	7.50
195	Joe Cunningham	30.00	12.00	7.50
196	Terry Fox	30.00	12.00	7.50
199	Elio Chacon	60.00	24.00	15.00
200	Luis Aparicio	250.00	100.00	62.00

1964 Venezuelan Topps

HANK AARON outfield

The first 370 cards of Topps' baseball set were issued in a parallel version for sale in Venezuela. Printed on thin cardboard with no front gloss, the cards are differentiated from the U.S. version by the use of a black border on back. Survivors of the issue are usually in low grade because of the common Latin American practice of collectors gluing the cards into the album that was available. Venezuelan Topps cards were often cut up to 1/8" smaller than their U.S. counterparts.

		NM	EX	VG
Complete Set (370):		9,500	3,800	2,400
Common Player:		30.00	12.00	7.50
Album:		300.00	125.00	75.00
1	N.L. E.R.A. Leaders (Dick Ellsworth, Bob Friend, Sandy Koufax)	90.00	36.00	22.00

2	A.L. E.R.A. Leaders (Camilo Pascual, Gary Peters, Juan Pizarro)	30.00	12.00	7.50
3	N.L. Pitching Leaders (Sandy Koufax, Jim Maloney, Juan Marichal, Warren Spahn)	60.00	24.00	15.00
4	A.L. Pitching Leaders (Jim Bouton, Whitey Ford, Camilo Pascual)	45.00	18.00	11.00
5	N.L. Strikeout Leaders (Don Drysdale, Sandy Koufax, Jim Maloney)	60.00	24.00	15.00
6	A.L. Strikeout Leaders (Jim Bunning, Camilo Pascual, Dick Stigman)	35.00	14.00	8.75
7	N.L. Batting Leaders (Hank Aaron, Roberto Clemente, Tommy Davis, Dick Groat)	100.00	40.00	25.00
8	A.L. Batting Leaders (Al Kaline, Rich Rollins, Carl Yastrzemski)	50.00	20.00	12.50
9	N.L. Home Run Leaders (Hank Aaron, Orlando Cepeda, Willie Mays, Willie McCovey)	75.00	30.00	18.50
10	A.L. Home Run Leaders (Bob Allison, Harmon Killebrew, Dick Stuart)	45.00	18.00	11.00
11	N.L. R.B.I. Leaders (Hank Aaron, Ken Boyer, Bill White)	50.00	20.00	12.50
12	A.L. R.B.I. Leaders (Al Kaline, Harmon Killebrew, Dick Stuart)	45.00	18.00	11.00
13	Hoyt Wilhelm	50.00	20.00	12.50
14	Dodgers Rookies (Dick Nen, Nick Willhite)	30.00	12.00	7.50
15	Zoilo Versalles	30.00	12.00	7.50
16	John Boozer	30.00	12.00	7.50
17	Willie Kirkland	30.00	12.00	7.50
18	Billy O'Dell	30.00	12.00	7.50
19	Don Wart	30.00	12.00	7.50
20	Bob Friend	30.00	12.00	7.50
21	Yogi Berra	100.00	40.00	25.00
22	Jerry Adair	30.00	12.00	7.50
23	Chris Zachary	30.00	12.00	7.50
24	Carl Sawatski	30.00	12.00	7.50
25	Bill Monbouquette	30.00	12.00	7.50
26	Gino Cimoli	30.00	12.00	7.50
27	Mets Team	65.00	26.00	16.00
28	Claude Osteen	30.00	12.00	7.50
29	Lou Brock	75.00	30.00	18.50
30	Ron Perranoski	30.00	12.00	7.50
31	Dave Nicholson	30.00	12.00	7.50
32	Dean Chance	30.00	12.00	7.50
33	Reds Rookies (Sammy Ellis, Mel Queen)	30.00	12.00	7.50
34	Jim Perry	30.00	12.00	7.50
35	Eddie Mathews	75.00	30.00	18.50
36	Hal Reniff	30.00	12.00	7.50
37	Smoky Burgess	30.00	12.00	7.50
38	Jim Wynn	30.00	12.00	7.50
39	Hank Aguirre	30.00	12.00	7.50
40	Dick Groat	30.00	12.00	7.50
41	Friendly Foes (Willie McCovey, Leon Wagner)	35.00	14.00	8.75
42	Moe Drabowsky	30.00	12.00	7.50
43	Roy Sievers	30.00	12.00	7.50
44	Duke Carmel	30.00	12.00	7.50
45	Milt Pappas	30.00	12.00	7.50
46	Ed Brinkman	30.00	12.00	7.50
47	Giants Rookies (Jesus Alou, Ron Herbel)	30.00	12.00	7.50
48	Bob Perry	30.00	12.00	7.50
49	Bill Henry	30.00	12.00	7.50
50	Mickey Mantle	1,800	720.00	450.00
51	Pete Richert	30.00	12.00	7.50
52	Chuck Hinton	30.00	12.00	7.50
53	Denis Menke	30.00	12.00	7.50
54	Sam Mele	30.00	12.00	7.50
55	Ernie Banks	75.00	30.00	18.50
56	Hal Brown	30.00	12.00	7.50
57	Tim Harkness	30.00	12.00	7.50
58	Don Demeter	30.00	12.00	7.50
59	Ernie Broglio	30.00	12.00	7.50
60	Frank Malzone	30.00	12.00	7.50
61	Angel Backstops (Bob Rodgers, Ed Sadowski)	30.00	12.00	7.50
62	Ted Savage	30.00	12.00	7.50
63	Johnny Orsino	30.00	12.00	7.50
64	Ted Abernathy	30.00	12.00	7.50
65	Felipe Alou	35.00	14.00	8.75
66	Eddie Fisher	30.00	12.00	7.50
67	Tigers Team	50.00	20.00	12.50
68	Willie Davis	30.00	12.00	7.50
69	Clete Boyer	35.00	14.00	8.75
70	Joe Torre	45.00	18.00	11.00
71	Jack Spring	30.00	12.00	7.50
72	Chico Cardenas	30.00	12.00	7.50
73	Jimmie Hall	30.00	12.00	7.50
74	Pirates Rookies (Tom Butters, Bob Priddy)	30.00	12.00	7.50
75	Wayne Causey	30.00	12.00	7.50
76	Checklist 1-88	30.00	12.00	7.50
77	Jerry Walker	30.00	12.00	7.50
78	Merritt Ranew	30.00	12.00	7.50
79	Bob Heffner	30.00	12.00	7.50
80	Vada Pinson	45.00	18.00	11.00
81	All-Star Vets (Nellie Fox, Harmon Killebrew)	50.00	20.00	12.50
82	Jim Davenport	30.00	12.00	7.50
83	Gus Triandos	30.00	12.00	7.50
84	Carl Willey	30.00	12.00	7.50
85	Pete Ward	30.00	12.00	7.50
86	Al Downing	30.00	12.00	7.50
87	Cardinals Team	100.00	40.00	25.00
88	John Roseboro	30.00	12.00	7.50
89	Boog Powell	35.00	14.00	8.75
90	Earl Battey	30.00	12.00	7.50
91	Bob Bailey	30.00	12.00	7.50

#	Player	NM	EX	VG
92	Steve Ridzik	30.00	12.00	7.50
93	Gary Geiger	30.00	12.00	7.50
94	Braves Rookies (Jim Britton, Larry Maxie)	30.00	12.00	7.50
95	George Altman	30.00	12.00	7.50
96	Bob Buhl	30.00	12.00	7.50
97	Jim Fregosi	30.00	12.00	7.50
98	Bill Bruton	30.00	12.00	7.50
99	Al Stanek	30.00	12.00	7.50
100	Elston Howard	35.00	14.00	8.75
101	Walt Alston	50.00	20.00	12.50
102	Checklist 89-176	30.00	12.00	7.50
103	Curt Flood	35.00	14.00	8.75
104	Art Mahaffey	30.00	12.00	7.50
105	Woody Held	30.00	12.00	7.50
106	Joe Nuxhall	30.00	12.00	7.50
107	White Sox Rookies (Bruce Howard, Frank Kreutzer)	30.00	12.00	7.50
108	John Wyatt	30.00	12.00	7.50
109	Rusty Staub	35.00	14.00	8.75
110	Albie Pearson	30.00	12.00	7.50
111	Don Elston	30.00	12.00	7.50
112	Bob Tillman	30.00	12.00	7.50
113	Grover Powell	30.00	12.00	7.50
114	Don Lock	30.00	12.00	7.50
115	Frank Bolling	30.00	12.00	7.50
116	Twins Rookies (Tony Oliva, Jay Ward)	45.00	18.00	11.00
117	Earl Francis	30.00	12.00	7.50
118	John Blanchard	30.00	12.00	7.50
119	Gary Kolb	30.00	12.00	7.50
120	Don Drysdale	75.00	30.00	18.50
121	Pete Runnels	30.00	12.00	7.50
122	Don McMahon	30.00	12.00	7.50
123	Jose Pagan	30.00	12.00	7.50
124	Orlando Pena	30.00	12.00	7.50
125	Pete Rose	450.00	180.00	110.00
126	Russ Snyder	30.00	12.00	7.50
127	Angels Rookies (Aubrey Gatewood, Dick Simpson)	30.00	12.00	7.50
128	Mickey Lolich	35.00	14.00	8.75
129	Amado Samuel	30.00	12.00	7.50
130	Gary Peters	30.00	12.00	7.50
131	Steve Boros	30.00	12.00	7.50
132	Braves Team	50.00	20.00	12.50
133	Jim Grant	30.00	12.00	7.50
134	Don Zimmer	30.00	12.00	7.50
135	Johnny Callison	30.00	12.00	7.50
136	World Series Game 1 (Koufax Strikes Out 15)	30.00	12.00	7.50
137	World Series Game 2 (Davis Sparks Rally)	30.00	12.00	7.50
138	World Series Game 3 (L.A. Takes 3rd Straight)	30.00	12.00	7.50
139	World Series Game 4 (Sealing Yanks' Doom)	30.00	12.00	7.50
140	World Series Summary (The Dodgers Celebrate)	30.00	12.00	7.50
141	Danny Murtaugh	30.00	12.00	7.50
142	John Bateman	30.00	12.00	7.50
143	Bubba Phillips	30.00	12.00	7.50
144	Al Worthington	30.00	12.00	7.50
145	Norm Siebern	30.00	12.00	7.50
146	Indians Rookies (Bob Chance, Tommy John)	50.00	20.00	12.50
147	Ray Sadecki	30.00	12.00	7.50
148	J.C. Martin	30.00	12.00	7.50
149	Paul Foytack	30.00	12.00	7.50
150	Willie Mays	375.00	150.00	94.00
151	Athletics Team	50.00	20.00	12.50
152	Denver Lemaster	30.00	12.00	7.50
153	Dick Williams	30.00	12.00	7.50
154	Dick Tracewski	30.00	12.00	7.50
155	Duke Snider	100.00	40.00	25.00
156	Bill Dailey	30.00	12.00	7.50
157	Gene Mauch	30.00	12.00	7.50
158	Ken Johnson	30.00	12.00	7.50
159	Charlie Dees	30.00	12.00	7.50
160	Ken Boyer	35.00	14.00	8.75
161	Dave McNally	30.00	12.00	7.50
162	Hitting Area (Vada Pinson, Dick Sisler)	30.00	12.00	7.50
163	Donn Clendenon	30.00	12.00	7.50
164	Bud Daley	30.00	12.00	7.50
165	Jerry Lumpe	30.00	12.00	7.50
166	Marty Keough	30.00	12.00	7.50
167	Senators Rookies (Mike Brumley, Lou Piniella)	60.00	24.00	15.00
168	Al Weis	30.00	12.00	7.50
169	Del Crandall	30.00	12.00	7.50
170	Dick Radatz	30.00	12.00	7.50
171	Ty Cline	30.00	12.00	7.50
172	Indians Team	50.00	20.00	12.50
173	Ryne Duren	30.00	12.00	7.50
174	Doc Edwards	30.00	12.00	7.50
175	Billy Williams	50.00	20.00	12.50
176	Tracy Stallard	30.00	12.00	7.50
177	Harmon Killebrew	75.00	30.00	18.50
178	Hank Bauer	30.00	12.00	7.50
179	Carl Warwick	30.00	12.00	7.50
180	Tommy Davis	30.00	12.00	7.50
181	Dave Wickersham	30.00	12.00	7.50
182	Sox Sockers (Chuck Schilling, Carl Yastrzemski)	50.00	20.00	12.50
183	Ron Taylor	30.00	12.00	7.50
184	Al Luplow	30.00	12.00	7.50
185	Jim O'Toole	30.00	12.00	7.50
186	Roman Mejias	30.00	12.00	7.50
187	Ed Roebuck	30.00	12.00	7.50
188	Checklist 177-264	30.00	12.00	7.50
189	Bob Hendley	30.00	12.00	7.50
190	Bobby Richardson	35.00	14.00	8.75
191	Clay Dalrymple	30.00	12.00	7.50
192	Cubs Rookies (John Boccabella, Billy Cowan)	30.00	12.00	7.50
193	Jerry Lynch	30.00	12.00	7.50
194	John Goryl	30.00	12.00	7.50
195	Floyd Robinson	30.00	12.00	7.50
196	Jim Gentile	30.00	12.00	7.50
197	Frank Lary	30.00	12.00	7.50
198	Len Gabrielson	30.00	12.00	7.50
199	Joe Azcue	30.00	12.00	7.50
200	Sandy Koufax	300.00	120.00	75.00
201	Orioles Rookies (Sam Bowens, Wally Bunker)	30.00	12.00	7.50
202	Galen Cisco	30.00	12.00	7.50
203	John Kennedy	30.00	12.00	7.50
204	Matty Alou	30.00	12.00	7.50
205	Nellie Fox	65.00	26.00	16.00
206	Steve Hamilton	30.00	12.00	7.50
207	Fred Hutchinson	30.00	12.00	7.50
208	Wes Covington	30.00	12.00	7.50
209	Bob Allen	30.00	12.00	7.50
210	Carl Yastrzemski	100.00	40.00	25.00
211	Jim Coker	30.00	12.00	7.50
212	Pete Lovrich	30.00	12.00	7.50
213	Angels Team	50.00	20.00	12.50
214	Ken McMullen	30.00	12.00	7.50
215	Ray Herbert	30.00	12.00	7.50
216	Mike de la Hoz	30.00	12.00	7.50
217	Jim King	30.00	12.00	7.50
218	Hank Fischer	30.00	12.00	7.50
219	Young Aces (Jim Bouton, Al Downing)	35.00	14.00	8.75
220	Dick Ellsworth	30.00	12.00	7.50
221	Bob Saverine	30.00	12.00	7.50
222	Bill Pierce	30.00	12.00	7.50
223	George Banks	30.00	12.00	7.50
224	Tommie Sisk	30.00	12.00	7.50
225	Roger Maris	300.00	120.00	75.00
226	Colts Rookies (Gerald Grote, Larry Yellen)	30.00	12.00	7.50
227	Barry Latman	30.00	12.00	7.50
228	Felix Mantilla	30.00	12.00	7.50
229	Charley Lau	30.00	12.00	7.50
230	Brooks Robinson	110.00	45.00	25.00
231	Dick Calmus	30.00	12.00	7.50
232	Al Lopez	50.00	20.00	12.50
233	Hal Smith	30.00	12.00	7.50
234	Gary Bell	30.00	12.00	7.50
235	Ron Hunt	30.00	12.00	7.50
236	Bill Faul	30.00	12.00	7.50
237	Cubs Team	50.00	20.00	12.50
238	Roy McMillan	30.00	12.00	7.50
239	Herm Starrette	30.00	12.00	7.50
240	Bill White	30.00	12.00	7.50
241	Jim Owens	30.00	12.00	7.50
242	Harvey Kuenn	30.00	12.00	7.50
243	Phillies Rookies (Richie Allen, John Herrnstein)	50.00	20.00	12.50
244	Tony LaRussa	35.00	14.00	8.75
245	Dick Stigman	30.00	12.00	7.50
246	Manny Mota	30.00	12.00	7.50
247	Dave DeBusschere	30.00	12.00	7.50
248	Johnny Pesky	30.00	12.00	7.50
249	Doug Camilli	30.00	12.00	7.50
250	Al Kaline	110.00	45.00	25.00
251	Choo Choo Coleman	30.00	12.00	7.50
252	Ken Aspromonte	30.00	12.00	7.50
253	Wally Post	30.00	12.00	7.50
254	Don Hoak	30.00	12.00	7.50
255	Lee Thomas	30.00	12.00	7.50
256	Johnny Weekly	30.00	12.00	7.50
257	Giants Team	50.00	20.00	12.50
258	Garry Roggenburk	30.00	12.00	7.50
259	Harry Bright	30.00	12.00	7.50
260	Frank Robinson	100.00	40.00	25.00
261	Jim Hannan	30.00	12.00	7.50
262	Cardinals Rookies (Harry Fanok, Mike Shannon)	35.00	14.00	8.75
263	Chuck Estrada	30.00	12.00	7.50
264	Jim Landis	30.00	12.00	7.50
265	Jim Bunning	50.00	20.00	12.50
266	Gene Freese	30.00	12.00	7.50
267	Wilbur Wood	30.00	12.00	7.50
268	Bill's Got It (Danny Murtaugh, Bill Virdon)	30.00	12.00	7.50
269	Ellis Burton	30.00	12.00	7.50
270	Rich Rollins	30.00	12.00	7.50
271	Bob Sadowski	30.00	12.00	7.50
272	Jake Wood	30.00	12.00	7.50
273	Mel Nelson	30.00	12.00	7.50
274	Checklist 265-352	30.00	12.00	7.50
275	John Tsitouris	30.00	12.00	7.50
276	Jose Tartabull	30.00	12.00	7.50
277	Ken Retzer	30.00	12.00	7.50
278	Bobby Shantz	30.00	12.00	7.50
279	Joe Koppe	30.00	12.00	7.50
280	Juan Marichal	65.00	26.00	16.00
281	Yankees Rookies (Jake Gibbs, Tom Metcalf)	30.00	12.00	7.50
282	Bob Bruce	30.00	12.00	7.50
283	Tommy McCraw	30.00	12.00	7.50
284	Dick Schofield	30.00	12.00	7.50
285	Robin Roberts	65.00	26.00	16.00
286	Don Landrum	30.00	12.00	7.50
287	Red Sox Rookies (Tony Conigliaro, Bill Spanswick)	35.00	14.00	8.75
288	Al Moran	30.00	12.00	7.50
289	Frank Funk	30.00	12.00	7.50
290	Bob Allison	30.00	12.00	7.50
291	Phil Ortega	30.00	12.00	7.50
292	Mike Roarke	30.00	12.00	7.50
293	Phillies Team	50.00	20.00	12.50
294	Ken Hunt	30.00	12.00	7.50
295	Roger Craig	30.00	12.00	7.50
296	Ed Kirkpatrick	30.00	12.00	7.50
297	Ken MacKenzie	30.00	12.00	7.50
298	Harry Craft	30.00	12.00	7.50
299	Bill Stafford	30.00	12.00	7.50
300	Hank Aaron	375.00	150.00	94.00
301	Larry Brown	30.00	12.00	7.50
302	Dan Pfister	30.00	12.00	7.50
303	Jim Campbell	30.00	12.00	7.50
304	Bob Johnson	30.00	12.00	7.50
305	Jack Lamabe	30.00	12.00	7.50
306	Giant Gunners (Orlando Cepeda, Willie Mays)	50.00	20.00	12.50
307	Joe Gibbon	30.00	12.00	7.50
308	Gene Stephens	30.00	12.00	7.50
309	Paul Toth	30.00	12.00	7.50
310	Jim Gilliam	30.00	12.00	7.50
311	Tom Brown	30.00	12.00	7.50
312	Tigers Rookies (Fritz Fisher, Fred Gladding)	30.00	12.00	7.50
313	Chuck Hiller	30.00	12.00	7.50
314	Jerry Buchek	30.00	12.00	7.50
315	Bo Belinsky	30.00	12.00	7.50
316	Gene Oliver	30.00	12.00	7.50
317	Al Smith	30.00	12.00	7.50
318	Twins Team	50.00	20.00	12.50
319	Paul Brown	30.00	12.00	7.50
320	Rocky Colavito	50.00	20.00	12.50
321	Bob Lillis	30.00	12.00	7.50
322	George Brunet	30.00	12.00	7.50
323	John Buzhardt	30.00	12.00	7.50
324	Casey Stengel	50.00	20.00	12.50
325	Hector Lopez	30.00	12.00	7.50
326	Ron Brand	30.00	12.00	7.50
327	Don Blasingame	30.00	12.00	7.50
328	Bob Shaw	30.00	12.00	7.50
329	Russ Nixon	30.00	12.00	7.50
330	Tommy Harper	30.00	12.00	7.50
331	A.L. Bombers (Norm Cash, Al Kaline, Mickey Mantle, Roger Maris)	600.00	240.00	150.00
332	Ray Washburn	30.00	12.00	7.50
333	Billy Moran	30.00	12.00	7.50
334	Lew Krausse	30.00	12.00	7.50
335	Don Mossi	30.00	12.00	7.50
336	Andre Rodgers	30.00	12.00	7.50
337	Dodgers Rookies (Al Ferrara, Jeff Torborg)	30.00	12.00	7.50
338	Jack Kralick	30.00	12.00	7.50
339	Walt Bond	30.00	12.00	7.50
340	Joe Cunningham	30.00	12.00	7.50
341	Jim Roland	30.00	12.00	7.50
342	Willie Stargell	65.00	26.00	16.00
343	Senators Team	50.00	20.00	12.50
344	Phil Linz	30.00	12.00	7.50
345	Frank Thomas	30.00	12.00	7.50
346	Joe Jay	30.00	12.00	7.50
347	Bobby Wine	30.00	12.00	7.50
348	Ed Lopat	30.00	12.00	7.50
349	Art Fowler	30.00	12.00	7.50
350	Willie McCovey	75.00	30.00	18.50
351	Dan Schneider	30.00	12.00	7.50
352	Eddie Bressoud	30.00	12.00	7.50
353	Wally Moon	30.00	12.00	7.50
354	Dave Giusti	30.00	12.00	7.50
355	Vic Power	30.00	12.00	7.50
356	Reds Rookies (Bill McCool, Chico Ruiz)	30.00	12.00	7.50
357	Charley James	30.00	12.00	7.50
358	Ron Kline	30.00	12.00	7.50
359	Jim Schaffer	30.00	12.00	7.50
360	Joe Pepitone	30.00	12.00	7.50
361	Jay Hook	30.00	12.00	7.50
362	Checklist 353-429	30.00	12.00	7.50
363	Dick McAuliffe	30.00	12.00	7.50
364	Joe Gaines	30.00	12.00	7.50
365	Cal McLish	30.00	12.00	7.50
366	Nelson Mathews	30.00	12.00	7.50
367	Fred Whitfield	30.00	12.00	7.50
368	White Sox Rookies (Fritz Ackley, Don Buford)	30.00	12.00	7.50
369	Jerry Zimmerman	30.00	12.00	7.50
370	Hal Woodeshick	30.00	12.00	7.50

1966 Venezuelan Topps

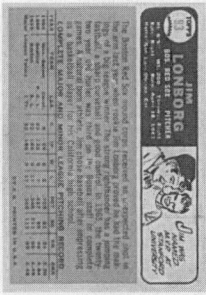

The first 370 cards on Topps' 1966 baseball set were reprinted for sale in the Venezuelan market. Identical in design to the Topps cards, they have no Spanish on them. The South American version is printed on darker cardboard that has virtually no gloss on front and bright orange-pink highlights on back. Low-grade cards are the norm for this and other Venezuelan issues as it is common collector practice south of the border to mount cards in scrapbooks and albums. The Venezuelan cards are often found up to 1/8" smaller than their U.S. counterparts.

		NM	EX	VG
Complete Set (370):		8,000	3,250	2,000
Common Player:		30.00	12.00	7.50
1	Willie Mays	400.00	160.00	100.00
2	Ted Abernathy	30.00	12.00	7.50
3	Sam Mele	30.00	12.00	7.50
4	Ray Culp	30.00	12.00	7.50
5	Jim Fregosi	30.00	12.00	7.50
6	Chuck Schilling	30.00	12.00	7.50
7	Tracy Stallard	30.00	12.00	7.50
8	Floyd Robinson	30.00	12.00	7.50

#	Player			
9	Clete Boyer	35.00	14.00	8.75
10	Tony Cloninger	30.00	12.00	7.50
11	Senators Rookies (Brant Alyea, Pete Craig)	30.00	12.00	7.50
12	John Tsitouris	30.00	12.00	7.50
13	Lou Johnson	30.00	12.00	7.50
14	Norm Siebern	30.00	12.00	7.50
15	Vern Law	30.00	12.00	7.50
16	Larry Brown	30.00	12.00	7.50
17	Johnny Stephenson	30.00	12.00	7.50
18	Roland Sheldon	30.00	12.00	7.50
19	Giants Team	75.00	30.00	18.50
20	Willie Horton	30.00	12.00	7.50
21	Don Nottebart	30.00	12.00	7.50
22	Joe Nossek	30.00	12.00	7.50
23	Jack Sanford	30.00	12.00	7.50
24	Don Kessinger	30.00	12.00	7.50
25	Pete Ward	30.00	12.00	7.50
26	Ray Sadecki	30.00	12.00	7.50
27	Orioles Rookies (Andy Etchebarren, Darold Knowles)	30.00	12.00	7.50
28	Phil Niekro	100.00	40.00	25.00
29	Mike Brumley	30.00	12.00	7.50
30	Pete Rose	375.00	150.00	94.00
31	Jack Cullen	30.00	12.00	7.50
32	Adolfo Phillips	30.00	12.00	7.50
33	Jim Pagliaroni	30.00	12.00	7.50
34	Checklist 1-88	30.00	12.00	7.50
35	Ron Swoboda	30.00	12.00	7.50
36	Catfish Hunter	100.00	40.00	25.00
37	Billy Herman	90.00	36.00	22.00
38	Ron Nischwitz	30.00	12.00	7.50
39	Ken Henderson	30.00	12.00	7.50
40	Jim Grant	30.00	12.00	7.50
41	Don LeJohn	30.00	12.00	7.50
42	Aubrey Gatewood	30.00	12.00	7.50
43	Don Landrum	30.00	12.00	7.50
44	Indians Rookies (Bill Davis, Tom Kelley)	30.00	12.00	7.50
45	Jim Gentile	30.00	12.00	7.50
46	Howie Koplitz	30.00	12.00	7.50
47	J.C. Martin	30.00	12.00	7.50
48	Paul Blair	30.00	12.00	7.50
49	Woody Woodward	30.00	12.00	7.50
50	Mickey Mantle	1,500	600.00	375.00
51	Gordon Richardson	30.00	12.00	7.50
52	Power Plus (Johnny Callison, Wes Covington)	30.00	12.00	7.50
53	Bob Duliba	30.00	12.00	7.50
54	Jose Pagan	30.00	12.00	7.50
55	Ken Harrelson	30.00	12.00	7.50
56	Sandy Valdespino	30.00	12.00	7.50
57	Jim Lefebvre	30.00	12.00	7.50
58	Dave Wickersham	30.00	12.00	7.50
59	Reds Team	75.00	30.00	18.50
60	Curt Flood	35.00	14.00	8.75
61	Bob Bolin	30.00	12.00	7.50
62	Merritt Ranew	30.00	12.00	7.50
63	Jim Stewart	30.00	12.00	7.50
64	Bob Bruce	30.00	12.00	7.50
65	Leon Wagner	30.00	12.00	7.50
66	Al Weis	30.00	12.00	7.50
67	Mets Rookies (Cleon Jones, Dick Selma)	35.00	14.00	8.75
68	Hal Reniff	30.00	12.00	7.50
69	Ken Hamlin	30.00	12.00	7.50
70	Carl Yastrzemski	150.00	60.00	37.00
71	Frank Carpin	30.00	12.00	7.50
72	Tony Perez	150.00	60.00	37.00
73	Jerry Zimmerman	30.00	12.00	7.50
74	Don Mossi	30.00	12.00	7.50
75	Tommy Davis	30.00	12.00	7.50
76	Red Schoendienst	90.00	36.00	22.00
77	Johnny Orsino	30.00	12.00	7.50
78	Frank Linzy	30.00	12.00	7.50
79	Joe Pepitone	30.00	12.00	7.50
80	Richie Allen	45.00	18.00	11.00
81	Ray Oyler	30.00	12.00	7.50
82	Bob Hendley	30.00	12.00	7.50
83	Albie Pearson	30.00	12.00	7.50
84	Braves Rookies (Jim Beauchamp, Dick Kelley)	30.00	12.00	7.50
85	Eddie Fisher	30.00	12.00	7.50
86	John Bateman	30.00	12.00	7.50
87	Dan Napoleon	30.00	12.00	7.50
88	Fred Whitfield	30.00	12.00	7.50
89	Ted Davidson	30.00	12.00	7.50
90	Luis Aparicio	250.00	100.00	62.00
91	Bob Uecker	45.00	18.00	11.00
92	Yankees Team	125.00	50.00	30.00
93	Jim Lonborg	30.00	12.00	7.50
94	Matty Alou	30.00	12.00	7.50
95	Pete Richert	30.00	12.00	7.50
96	Felipe Alou	45.00	18.00	11.00
97	Jim Merritt	30.00	12.00	7.50
98	Don Demeter	30.00	12.00	7.50
99	Buc Belters (Donn Clendenon, Willie Stargell)	60.00	24.00	15.00
100	Sandy Koufax	300.00	120.00	75.00
101	Checklist 89-176	30.00	12.00	7.50
102	Ed Kirkpatrick	30.00	12.00	7.50
103	Dick Groat	30.00	12.00	7.50
104	Alex Johnson	30.00	12.00	7.50
105	Milt Pappas	30.00	12.00	7.50
106	Rusty Staub	35.00	14.00	8.75
107	Athletics Rookies (Larry Stahl, Ron Tompkins)	30.00	12.00	7.50
108	Bobby Klaus	30.00	12.00	7.50
109	Ralph Terry	30.00	12.00	7.50
110	Ernie Banks	200.00	80.00	50.00
111	Gary Peters	30.00	12.00	7.50
112	Manny Mota	30.00	12.00	7.50
113	Hank Aguirre	30.00	12.00	7.50
114	Jim Gosger	30.00	12.00	7.50
115	Bill Henry	30.00	12.00	7.50
116	Walt Alston	90.00	36.00	22.00
117	Jake Gibbs	30.00	12.00	7.50
118	Mike McCormick	30.00	12.00	7.50
119	Art Shamsky	30.00	12.00	7.50
120	Harmon Killebrew	150.00	60.00	37.00
121	Ray Herbert	30.00	12.00	7.50
122	Joe Gaines	30.00	12.00	7.50
123	Pirates Rookies (Frank Bork, Jerry May)	30.00	12.00	7.50
124	Tug McGraw	30.00	12.00	7.50
125	Lou Brock	125.00	50.00	30.00
126	Jim Palmer	200.00	80.00	50.00
127	Ken Berry	30.00	12.00	7.50
128	Jim Landis	30.00	12.00	7.50
129	Jack Kralick	30.00	12.00	7.50
130	Joe Torre	45.00	18.00	11.00
131	Angels Team	75.00	30.00	18.50
132	Orlando Cepeda	100.00	40.00	25.00
133	Don McMahon	30.00	12.00	7.50
134	Wes Parker	30.00	12.00	7.50
135	Dave Morehead	30.00	12.00	7.50
136	Woody Held	30.00	12.00	7.50
137	Pat Corrales	30.00	12.00	7.50
138	Roger Repoz	30.00	12.00	7.50
139	Cubs Rookies (Byron Browne, Don Young)	30.00	12.00	7.50
140	Jim Maloney	30.00	12.00	7.50
141	Tom McCraw	30.00	12.00	7.50
142	Don Dennis	30.00	12.00	7.50
143	Jose Tartabull	30.00	12.00	7.50
144	Don Schwall	30.00	12.00	7.50
145	Bill Freehan	30.00	12.00	7.50
146	George Altman	30.00	12.00	7.50
147	Lum Harris	30.00	12.00	7.50
148	Bob Johnson	30.00	12.00	7.50
149	Dick Nen	30.00	12.00	7.50
150	Rocky Colavito	75.00	30.00	18.50
151	Gary Wagner	30.00	12.00	7.50
152	Frank Malzone	30.00	12.00	7.50
153	Rico Carty	30.00	12.00	7.50
154	Chuck Hiller	30.00	12.00	7.50
155	Marcelino Lopez	30.00	12.00	7.50
156	D P Combo (Hal Lanier, Dick Schofield)	30.00	12.00	7.50
157	Rene Lachemann	30.00	12.00	7.50
158	Jim Brewer	30.00	12.00	7.50
159	Chico Ruiz	30.00	12.00	7.50
160	Whitey Ford	150.00	60.00	37.00
161	Jerry Lumpe	30.00	12.00	7.50
162	Lee Maye	30.00	12.00	7.50
163	Tito Francona	30.00	12.00	7.50
164	White Sox Rookies (Tommie Agee, Marv Staehle)	30.00	12.00	7.50
165	Don Lock	30.00	12.00	7.50
166	Chris Krug	30.00	12.00	7.50
167	Boog Powell	45.00	18.00	11.00
168	Dan Osinski	30.00	12.00	7.50
169	Duke Sims	30.00	12.00	7.50
170	Cookie Rojas	30.00	12.00	7.50
171	Nick Willhite	30.00	12.00	7.50
172	Mets Team	150.00	60.00	37.00
173	Al Spangler	30.00	12.00	7.50
174	Ron Taylor	30.00	12.00	7.50
175	Bert Campaneris	45.00	18.00	11.00
176	Jim Davenport	30.00	12.00	7.50
177	Hector Lopez	30.00	12.00	7.50
178	Bob Tillman	30.00	12.00	7.50
179	Cardinals Rookies (Dennis Aust, Bob Tolan)	30.00	12.00	7.50
180	Vada Pinson	35.00	14.00	8.75
181	Al Worthington	30.00	12.00	7.50
182	Jerry Lynch	30.00	12.00	7.50
183	Checklist 177-264	30.00	12.00	7.50
184	Denis Menke	30.00	12.00	7.50
185	Bob Buhl	30.00	12.00	7.50
186	Ruben Amaro	30.00	12.00	7.50
187	Chuck Dressen	30.00	12.00	7.50
188	Al Luplow	30.00	12.00	7.50
189	John Roseboro	30.00	12.00	7.50
190	Jimmie Hall	30.00	12.00	7.50
191	Darrell Sutherland	30.00	12.00	7.50
192	Vic Power	30.00	12.00	7.50
193	Dave McNally	30.00	12.00	7.50
194	Senators Team	75.00	30.00	18.50
195	Joe Morgan	125.00	50.00	30.00
196	Don Pavletich	30.00	12.00	7.50
197	Sonny Siebert	30.00	12.00	7.50
198	Mickey Stanley	30.00	12.00	7.50
199	Chisox Clubbers (Floyd Robinson, Johnny Romano, Bill Skowron)	30.00	12.00	7.50
200	Eddie Mathews	125.00	50.00	30.00
201	Jim Dickson	30.00	12.00	7.50
202	Clay Dalrymple	30.00	12.00	7.50
203	Jose Santiago	30.00	12.00	7.50
204	Cubs Team	90.00	36.00	22.00
205	Tom Tresh	30.00	12.00	7.50
206	Alvin Jackson	30.00	12.00	7.50
207	Frank Quilici	30.00	12.00	7.50
208	Bob Miller	30.00	12.00	7.50
209	Tigers Rookies (Fritz Fisher, John Hiller)	30.00	12.00	7.50
210	Bill Mazeroski	75.00	30.00	18.50
211	Frank Kreutzer	30.00	12.00	7.50
212	Ed Kranepool	30.00	12.00	7.50
213	Fred Newman	30.00	12.00	7.50
214	Tommy Harper	30.00	12.00	7.50
215	N.L. Batting Leaders (Hank Aaron, Roberto Clemente, Willie Mays)	300.00	120.00	75.00
216	A.L. Batting Leaders (Vic Davalillo, Tony Oliva, Carl Yastrzemski)	150.00	60.00	37.00
217	N.L. Home Run Leaders (Willie Mays, Willie McCovey, Billy Williams)	150.00	60.00	37.00
218	A.L. Home Run Leaders (Norm Cash, Tony Conigliaro, Willie Horton)	60.00	24.00	15.00
219	N.L. RBI Leaders (Deron Johnson, Willie Mays, Frank Robinson)	90.00	36.00	22.00
220	A.L. RBI Leaders (Rocky Colavito, Willie Horton, Tony Oliva)	60.00	24.00	15.00
221	N.L. ERA Leaders (Sandy Koufax, Vern Law, Juan Marichal)	90.00	36.00	22.00
222	A.L. ERA Leaders (Eddie Fisher, Sam McDowell, Sonny Siebert)	35.00	14.00	8.75
223	N.L. Pitching Leaders (Tony Cloninger, Don Drysdale, Sandy Koufax)	90.00	36.00	22.00
224	A.L. Pitching Leaders (Jim Grant, Jim Kaat, Mel Stottlemyre)	30.00	12.00	7.50
225	N.L. Strikeout Leaders (Bob Gibson, Sandy Koufax, Bob Veale)	90.00	36.00	22.00
226	A.L. Strikeout Leaders (Mickey Lolich, Sam McDowell, Denny McLain, Sonny Siebert)	45.00	18.00	11.00
227	Russ Nixon	30.00	12.00	7.50
228	Larry Dierker	30.00	12.00	7.50
229	Hank Bauer	30.00	12.00	7.50
230	Johnny Callison	30.00	12.00	7.50
231	Floyd Weaver	30.00	12.00	7.50
232	Glenn Beckert	30.00	12.00	7.50
233	Dom Zanni	30.00	12.00	7.50
234	Yankees Rookies (Rich Beck, Roy White)	35.00	14.00	8.75
235	Don Cardwell	30.00	12.00	7.50
236	Mike Hershberger	30.00	12.00	7.50
237	Billy O'Dell	30.00	12.00	7.50
238	Dodgers Team	100.00	40.00	25.00
239	Orlando Pena	30.00	12.00	7.50
240	Earl Battey	30.00	12.00	7.50
241	Dennis Ribant	30.00	12.00	7.50
242	Jesus Alou	30.00	12.00	7.50
243	Nelson Briles	30.00	12.00	7.50
244	Astros Rookies (Chuck Harrison, Sonny Jackson)	30.00	12.00	7.50
245	John Buzhardt	30.00	12.00	7.50
246	Ed Bailey	30.00	12.00	7.50
247	Carl Warwick	30.00	12.00	7.50
248	Pete Mikkelsen	30.00	12.00	7.50
249	Bill Rigney	30.00	12.00	7.50
250	Sam Ellis	30.00	12.00	7.50
251	Ed Brinkman	30.00	12.00	7.50
252	Denver Lemaster	30.00	12.00	7.50
253	Don Wert	30.00	12.00	7.50
254	Phillies Rookies (Fergie Jenkins, Bill Sorrell)	100.00	40.00	25.00
255	Willie Stargell	125.00	50.00	30.00
256	Lew Krausse	30.00	12.00	7.50
257	Jeff Torborg	30.00	12.00	7.50
258	Dave Giusti	30.00	12.00	7.50
259	Red Sox Team	75.00	30.00	18.50
260	Bob Shaw	30.00	12.00	7.50
261	Ron Hansen	30.00	12.00	7.50
262	Jack Hamilton	30.00	12.00	7.50
263	Tom Egan	30.00	12.00	7.50
264	Twins Rookies (Andy Kosco, Ted Uhlaender)	30.00	12.00	7.50
265	Stu Miller	30.00	12.00	7.50
266	Pedro Gonzalez	30.00	12.00	7.50
267	Joe Sparma	30.00	12.00	7.50
268	John Blanchard	30.00	12.00	7.50
269	Don Heffner	30.00	12.00	7.50
270	Claude Osteen	30.00	12.00	7.50
271	Hal Lanier	30.00	12.00	7.50
272	Jack Baldschun	30.00	12.00	7.50
273	Astro Aces (Bob Aspromonte, Rusty Staub)	30.00	12.00	7.50
274	Buster Narum	30.00	12.00	7.50
275	Tim McCarver	35.00	14.00	8.75
276	Jim Bouton	35.00	14.00	8.75
277	George Thomas	30.00	12.00	7.50
278	Calvin Koonce	30.00	12.00	7.50
279	Checklist 265-352	30.00	12.00	7.50
280	Bobby Knoop	30.00	12.00	7.50
281	Bruce Howard	30.00	12.00	7.50
282	Johnny Lewis	30.00	12.00	7.50
283	Jim Perry	30.00	12.00	7.50
284	Bobby Wine	30.00	12.00	7.50
285	Luis Tiant	45.00	18.00	11.00
286	Gary Geiger	30.00	12.00	7.50
287	Jack Aker	30.00	12.00	7.50
288	Dodgers Rookies (Bill Singer, Don Sutton)	125.00	50.00	30.00
289	Larry Sherry	30.00	12.00	7.50
290	Ron Santo	45.00	18.00	11.00
291	Moe Drabowsky	30.00	12.00	7.50
292	Jim Coker	30.00	12.00	7.50
293	Mike Shannon	30.00	12.00	7.50
294	Steve Ridzik	30.00	12.00	7.50
295	Jim Hart	30.00	12.00	7.50
296	Johnny Keane	30.00	12.00	7.50
297	Jim Owens	30.00	12.00	7.50
298	Rico Petrocelli	30.00	12.00	7.50
299	Lou Burdette	30.00	12.00	7.50
300	Roberto Clemente	650.00	260.00	160.00
301	Greg Bollo	30.00	12.00	7.50
302	Ernie Bowman	30.00	12.00	7.50
303	Indians Team	75.00	30.00	18.50
304	John Herrnstein	30.00	12.00	7.50
305	Camilo Pascual	30.00	12.00	7.50
306	Ty Cline	30.00	12.00	7.50
307	Clay Carroll	30.00	12.00	7.50
308	Tom Haller	30.00	12.00	7.50
309	Diego Segui	30.00	12.00	7.50
310	Frank Robinson	125.00	50.00	30.00
311	Reds Rookies (Tommy Helms, Dick Simpson)	30.00	12.00	7.50
312	Bob Saverine	30.00	12.00	7.50

313	Chris Zachary	30.00	12.00	7.50
314	Hector Valle	30.00	12.00	7.50
315	Norm Cash	30.00	12.00	7.50
316	Jack Fisher	30.00	12.00	7.50
317	Dalton Jones	30.00	12.00	7.50
318	Harry Walker	30.00	12.00	7.50
319	Gene Freese	30.00	12.00	7.50
320	Bob Gibson	125.00	50.00	30.00
321	Rick Reichardt	30.00	12.00	7.50
322	Bill Faul	30.00	12.00	7.50
323	Ray Barker	30.00	12.00	7.50
324	John Boozer	30.00	12.00	7.50
325	Vic Davalillo	100.00	40.00	25.00
326	Braves Team	75.00	30.00	18.50
327	Bernie Allen	30.00	12.00	7.50
328	Jerry Grote	30.00	12.00	7.50
329	Pete Charton	30.00	12.00	7.50
330	Ron Fairly	30.00	12.00	7.50
331	Ron Herbel	30.00	12.00	7.50
332	Billy Bryan	30.00	12.00	7.50
333	Senators Rookies (Joe Coleman, Jim French)	30.00	12.00	7.50
334	Marty Keough	30.00	12.00	7.50
335	Juan Pizarro	30.00	12.00	7.50
336	Gene Alley	30.00	12.00	7.50
337	Fred Gladding	30.00	12.00	7.50
338	Dal Maxvill	30.00	12.00	7.50
339	Del Crandall	30.00	12.00	7.50
340	Dean Chance	30.00	12.00	7.50
341	Wes Westrum	30.00	12.00	7.50
342	Bob Humphreys	30.00	12.00	7.50
343	Joe Christopher	30.00	12.00	7.50
344	Steve Blass	30.00	12.00	7.50
345	Bob Allison	30.00	12.00	7.50
346	Mike de la Hoz	30.00	12.00	7.50
347	Phil Regan	30.00	12.00	7.50
348	Orioles Team	125.00	50.00	30.00
349	Cap Peterson	30.00	12.00	7.50
350	Mel Stottlemyre	30.00	12.00	7.50
351	Fred Valentine	30.00	12.00	7.50
352	Bob Aspromonte	30.00	12.00	7.50
353	Al McBean	30.00	12.00	7.50
354	Smoky Burgess	30.00	12.00	7.50
355	Wade Blasingame	30.00	12.00	7.50
356	Red Sox Rookies (Owen Johnson, Ken Sanders)	30.00	12.00	7.50
357	Gerry Arrigo	30.00	12.00	7.50
358	Charlie Smith	30.00	12.00	7.50
359	Johnny Briggs	30.00	12.00	7.50
360	Ron Hunt	30.00	12.00	7.50
361	Tom Satriano	30.00	12.00	7.50
362	Gates Brown	30.00	12.00	7.50
363	Checklist 353-429	30.00	12.00	7.50
364	Nate Oliver	30.00	12.00	7.50
365	Roger Maris	200.00	80.00	50.00
366	Wayne Causey	30.00	12.00	7.50
367	Mel Nelson	30.00	12.00	7.50
368	Charlie Lau	30.00	12.00	7.50
369	Jim King	30.00	12.00	7.50
370	Chico Cardenas	30.00	12.00	7.50

1967 Venezuelan League

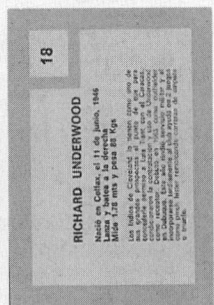

Three distinct series of baseball cards were issued in 1967 for sale in Venezuela, contiguously numbered. Cards #1-138 are players (including many future big leaguers) active in the country's Winter League. Cards are irregularly cut and somewhat smaller than the standard 2-1/2" x 3-1/2". Fronts have posed photos and a thin white border. The player name and position are at top in black, the team name is in large colored letters at bottom. Backs are printed horizontally in black on magenta with a few biographical bits and a one paragraph career summary. Like most of the Venezuelan cards of the era, these are crudely printed on cheap cardboard. Also like most Venezuelan cards, they are virtually impossible to find in any condition above Ex. Many are found with back damage due to having been glued into an album or scrapbook.

		NM	EX	VG
Complete Set (138):		3,500	1,750	1,000
Common Player:		20.00	10.00	6.00
1	Regino Otero	40.00	20.00	12.00
2	Alejandro Carrasquel	20.00	10.00	6.00
3	Pompeyo Davilillo	25.00	12.50	7.50
4	Gonzalo Marquez	20.00	10.00	6.00
5	Octavio (Cookie) Rojas	35.00	17.50	10.50
6	Teodoro Obregon	20.00	10.00	6.00
7	Paul Schaal	25.00	12.50	7.50
8	Juan Francia	20.00	10.00	6.00
9	Luis Tiant	60.00	30.00	18.00
10	Jose Tartabull	30.00	15.00	9.00
11	Vic Davalillo	25.00	12.50	7.50
12	Cesar Tovar	25.00	12.50	7.50
13	Ron Klimkowski	20.00	10.00	6.00
14	Diego Segui	35.00	17.50	10.50
15	Luis Penalver	20.00	10.00	6.00

16	Urbano Lugo	20.00	10.00	6.00
17	Aurelio Monteagudo	20.00	10.00	6.00
18	Richard Underwood	25.00	12.50	7.50
19	Nelson Castellanos	20.00	10.00	6.00
20	Manuel Mendible	20.00	10.00	6.00
21	Fidel Garcia	40.00	20.00	12.00
22	Luis Cordoba	20.00	10.00	6.00
23	Jesus Padron	20.00	10.00	6.00
24	Lorenzo Fernandez	20.00	10.00	6.00
25	Leopoldo Tovar	20.00	10.00	6.00
26	Carlos Loreto	20.00	10.00	6.00
27	Oswaldo Blanco	20.00	10.00	6.00
28	Sid (Syd) O'Brien	20.00	10.00	6.00
29	Cesar Gutierrez	20.00	10.00	6.00
30	Luis Garcia	20.00	10.00	6.00
31	Fred Klages	20.00	10.00	6.00
32	Isaias Chavez	20.00	10.00	6.00
33	Walter Williams	25.00	12.50	7.50
34	Jim Hicks	20.00	10.00	6.00
35	Gustavo Sposito	20.00	10.00	6.00
36	Cisco Carlos	20.00	10.00	6.00
37	Jim Mooring	20.00	10.00	6.00
38	Alonso Olivares	20.00	10.00	6.00
39	Graciliano Parra	20.00	10.00	6.00
40	Merritt Ranew	20.00	10.00	6.00
41	Everest Contramaestre	20.00	10.00	6.00
42	Orlando Reyes	20.00	10.00	6.00
43	Edicto Arteaga	20.00	10.00	6.00
44	Francisco Diaz	20.00	10.00	6.00
45	Victor Colina	20.00	10.00	6.00
46a	Ramon Diaz	20.00	10.00	6.00
46b	Francisco Diaz (Blue back.)	20.00	10.00	6.00
47	Luis E. Aparicio	185.00	90.00	55.00
48	Reynaldo Cordeiro	60.00	30.00	18.00
49	Luis Aparicio, Sr.	25.00	12.50	7.50
50	Ramon Webster	20.00	10.00	6.00
51	Remigio Hermoso	20.00	10.00	6.00
52	Miguel de la Hoz	20.00	10.00	6.00
53	Enzo Hernandez	20.00	10.00	6.00
54	Ed Watt	20.00	10.00	6.00
55	Angel Bravo	20.00	10.00	6.00
56	Marv (Merv) Rettenmund	25.00	12.50	7.50
57	Jose Herrera	20.00	10.00	6.00
58	Tom Fisher	20.00	10.00	6.00
59	Jim Weaver	20.00	10.00	6.00
60a	Juan Quintana	20.00	10.00	6.00
60b	Frank Fernandez (Blue back.)	20.00	10.00	6.00
61	Hector Urbano	20.00	10.00	6.00
62	Hector Brito (Blue back.)	20.00	10.00	6.00
63	Jesus Romero	20.00	10.00	6.00
64	Carlos A. Moreno	20.00	10.00	6.00
65	Nestor Mendible	20.00	10.00	6.00
66	Armando Ortiz	20.00	10.00	6.00
67	Graciano Ravelo	20.00	10.00	6.00
68	Paul Knechtges	20.00	10.00	6.00
69	Marcelino Lopez	25.00	12.50	7.50
70	Wilfredo Calvino	25.00	12.50	7.50
71	Jesus Avila	20.00	10.00	6.00
72	Carlos Pascual	45.00	22.00	13.50
73	Bob Burda	20.00	10.00	6.00
74	Elio Chacon	20.00	10.00	6.00
75	Jacinto Hernandez	20.00	10.00	6.00
76	Jose M. Tovar	20.00	10.00	6.00
77	Bill Whitby	20.00	10.00	6.00
78	Enrique Izquierdo	20.00	10.00	6.00
79	Hilario Valdespino	30.00	15.00	9.00
80	John Lewis	20.00	10.00	6.00
81	Hector Martinez	40.00	20.00	12.00
82	Rene Paredes	20.00	10.00	6.00
83	Danny Morris	20.00	10.00	6.00
84	Pedro Ramos	25.00	12.50	7.50
85	Jose Ramon Lopez	20.00	10.00	6.00
86	Jesus Rizales	20.00	10.00	6.00
87	Winston Acosta	20.00	10.00	6.00
88	Pablo Bello	20.00	10.00	6.00
89	David Concepcion	200.00	100.00	60.00
90	Manuel Garcia	20.00	10.00	6.00
91	Anibal Longa	20.00	10.00	6.00
92	Francisco Moscoso	20.00	10.00	6.00
93	Mel McGaha	20.00	10.00	6.00
94	Aquiles Gomez	20.00	10.00	6.00
95	Alfonso Carrasquel (Blue back.)	40.00	20.00	12.00
96	Tom Murray	20.00	10.00	6.00
97	Gustavo Gil	20.00	10.00	6.00
98	Damaso Blanco	20.00	10.00	6.00
99	Alberto Cambero	20.00	10.00	6.00
100	Don Bryant	20.00	10.00	6.00
101	George Culver	20.00	10.00	6.00
102	Teolindo Acosta	20.00	10.00	6.00
103	Aaron Pointer	20.00	10.00	6.00
104	Ed Kirkpatrick	20.00	10.00	6.00
105	Luis Rodriguez	20.00	10.00	6.00
106	Mike Daniel	20.00	10.00	6.00
107	Cecilio Prieto (Blue back.)	20.00	10.00	6.00
108	Juan Quiroz	20.00	10.00	6.00
108				
109	Juan Campos	20.00	10.00	6.00
110	Freddy Rivero	20.00	10.00	6.00
111	Dick LeMay	20.00	10.00	6.00
112	Raul Ortega	20.00	10.00	6.00
113	Bruno Estaba	20.00	10.00	6.00
114	Evangelista Nunez	20.00	10.00	6.00
115a	Robert Munoz	20.00	10.00	6.00
115b	Alfonso Carrasquel (Red back.)	40.00	20.00	12.00
116	Tony Castanos	20.00	10.00	6.00
117	Domingo Barboza	20.00	10.00	6.00
118	Lucio Celis	20.00	10.00	6.00
119	Carlos Santeliz	20.00	10.00	6.00
120	Barton Shirley	25.00	12.50	7.50
121	Neudo Morales	20.00	10.00	6.00
122	Robert Cox	100.00	50.00	30.00
123	Cruz Amaya (Blue back.)	20.00	10.00	6.00
124	Jim Campanis	75.00	37.50	22.00
125	Dave Roberts	20.00	10.00	6.00
126	Gerry Crider	20.00	10.00	6.00
127	Domingo Carrasquel	20.00	10.00	6.00

128	Leo Marentette	20.00	10.00	6.00
129	Frank Kreutzer	20.00	10.00	6.00
130	Jim Dickson	20.00	10.00	6.00
131	Bob Oliver	20.00	10.00	6.00
132	Jose Bracho	20.00	10.00	6.00
133a	Pablo Torrealba	20.00	10.00	6.00
133b	Pablo Torrealba (Different picture.)	20.00	10.00	6.00
134	Iran Paz	20.00	10.00	6.00
135	Eliecer Bueno	20.00	10.00	6.00
136	Claudio Urdaneta	20.00	10.00	6.00
137	Faustino Zabala	20.00	10.00	6.00
138	Dario Chirinos	20.00	10.00	6.00

1967 Venezuelan Retirado

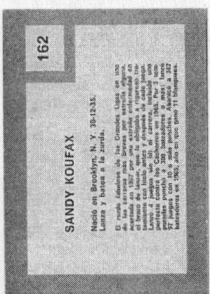

Three distinct series of baseball cards were issued in 1967 for sale in Venezuela, contiguously numbered. Cards #139-188 are former big league stars. The fronts of the roughly 2-1/2" x 3-1/2" Retirado cards have a blue background with the player's name in black at top and "RETIRADO" in red block letters at bottom. Player photos on the Retirado cards are sepia. Horizontal backs are printed in black on green with a bit of personal data and a career summary. Like most of the Venezuelan cards of the era, these are crudely printed on cheap cardboard. Also like most Venezuelan cards, they are virtually impossible to find in any condition above Ex. Many are found with back damage due to having been glued into an album or scrapbook.

		NM	EX	VG
Complete Set (50):		12,000	4,800	1,800
Common Player:		250.00	100.00	37.00
139	Walter Johnson	750.00	300.00	110.00
140	Bill Dickey	300.00	120.00	45.00
141	Lou Gehrig	1,750	700.00	260.00
142	Rogers Hornsby	300.00	120.00	45.00
143	Honus Wagner	650.00	260.00	100.00
144	Pie Traynor	250.00	100.00	35.00
145	Joe DiMaggio	1,850	740.00	275.00
146	Ty Cobb	1,350	540.00	200.00
147	Babe Ruth	2,400	960.00	360.00
148	Ted Williams	1,000	400.00	150.00
149	Mel Ott	250.00	100.00	35.00
150	Cy Young	370.00	150.00	55.00
151	Christy Mathewson	750.00	300.00	110.00
152	Warren Spahn	300.00	120.00	45.00
153	Mickey Cochrane	250.00	100.00	35.00
154	George Sisler	250.00	100.00	35.00
155	Jimmy Collins	250.00	100.00	35.00
156	Tris Speaker	300.00	120.00	45.00
157	Stan Musial	700.00	280.00	100.00
158	Luke Appling	250.00	100.00	35.00
159	Nap Lajoie	250.00	100.00	35.00
160	Bill Terry	250.00	100.00	35.00
161	Bob Feller	370.00	150.00	55.00
162	Sandy Koufax	800.00	320.00	120.00
163	Jimmie Foxx	300.00	120.00	45.00
164	Joe Cronin	250.00	100.00	35.00
165	Frankie Frisch	250.00	100.00	35.00
166	Paul Waner	250.00	100.00	35.00
167	Lloyd Waner	250.00	100.00	35.00
168	Lefty Grove	250.00	100.00	35.00
169	Bobby Doerr	250.00	100.00	35.00
170	Al Simmons	250.00	100.00	35.00
171	Grover Alexander	350.00	140.00	50.00
172	Carl Hubbell	250.00	100.00	35.00
173	Mordecai Brown	250.00	100.00	35.00
174	Ted Lyons	250.00	100.00	35.00
175	Johnny Vander Meer	250.00	100.00	35.00
176	Alex Carrasquel	300.00	120.00	45.00
177	Satchel Paige	600.00	240.00	90.00
178	Whitey Ford	500.00	200.00	75.00
179	Yogi Berra	500.00	200.00	75.00
180	Roy Campanella	450.00	180.00	65.00
181	Alfonso Carrasquel	370.00	150.00	55.00
182	Johnny Mize	250.00	100.00	35.00
183	Ted Kluszewski (Photo actually Gene Bearden.)	300.00	120.00	45.00
184	Jackie Robinson	750.00	300.00	110.00
185	Bobby Avila	250.00	100.00	35.00
186	Phil Rizzuto	300.00	120.00	45.00
187	Minnie Minoso	300.00	120.00	45.00
188	Connie Marrero	250.00	100.00	35.00

1967 Venezuelan Topps

Cards numbered #189-338 in the 1967 Venezuelan issue feature then-current major leaguers. Card fronts are taken from Topps' 1967 baseball series, but are borderless, making them somewhat smaller than 2-1/2" x 3-1/2". Backs of the South American cards are horizontal and printed in black on blue and offer a few bits of personal data and a one-paragraph career summary. Like most Venezuelan cards of the era,

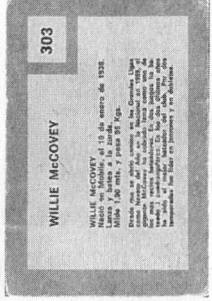

these are crudely printed on cheap cardboard and seldom found in condition better than Ex. Many will show evidence on back of having been glued into an album or scrapbook.

		NM	EX	VG
	Complete Set (150):	8,000	2,000	750.00
	Common Player:	35.00	14.00	5.25
189	Luis Aparicio	150.00	60.00	22.00
190	Vic Davalillo	35.00	14.00	5.25
191	Cesar Tovar	35.00	14.00	5.25
192	Mickey Mantle	1,500	600.00	225.00
193	Carl Yastrzemski	100.00	40.00	15.00
194	Frank Robinson	100.00	40.00	15.00
195	Willie Horton	35.00	14.00	5.25
196	Gary Peters	35.00	14.00	5.25
197	Bert Campaneris	40.00	16.00	6.00
198	Norm Cash	35.00	14.00	5.25
199	Boog Powell	35.00	14.00	5.25
200	George Scott	35.00	14.00	5.25
201	Frank Howard	35.00	14.00	5.25
202	Rick Reichardt	35.00	14.00	5.25
203	Jose Cardenal	35.00	14.00	5.25
204	Rico Petrocelli	35.00	14.00	5.25
205	Lew Krausse	35.00	14.00	5.25
206	Harmon Killebrew	100.00	40.00	15.00
207	Leon Wagner	35.00	14.00	5.25
208	Joe Foy	35.00	14.00	5.25
209	Joe Pepitone	40.00	16.00	6.00
210	Al Kaline	100.00	40.00	15.00
211	Brooks Robinson	100.00	40.00	15.00
212	Bill Freehan	35.00	14.00	5.25
213	Jim Lonborg	35.00	14.00	5.25
214a	Ed Mathews	100.00	40.00	15.00
214b	Jim Bunning (Should be #174.)	90.00	36.00	13.50
215	Dick Green	35.00	14.00	5.25
216	Tom Tresh	40.00	16.00	6.00
217	Dean Chance	35.00	14.00	5.25
218	Paul Blair	35.00	14.00	5.25
219	Larry Brown	35.00	14.00	5.25
220	Fred Valentine	35.00	14.00	5.25
221	Al Downing	35.00	14.00	5.25
222	Earl Battey	35.00	14.00	5.25
223	Don Mincher	35.00	14.00	5.25
224	Tommie Agee	35.00	14.00	5.25
225	Jim McGlothlin	35.00	14.00	5.25
226	Zoilo Versalles	35.00	14.00	5.25
227	Curt Blefary	35.00	14.00	5.25
228	Joel Horlen	35.00	14.00	5.25
229	Stu Miller	35.00	14.00	5.25
230	Tony Oliva	40.00	16.00	6.00
231	Paul Casanova	35.00	14.00	5.25
232	Orlando Pena	35.00	14.00	5.25
233	Ron Hansen	35.00	14.00	5.25
234	Earl Wilson	35.00	14.00	5.25
235	Ken Boyer	40.00	16.00	6.00
236	Jim Kaat	35.00	14.00	5.25
237	Dalton Jones	35.00	14.00	5.25
238	Pete Ward	35.00	14.00	5.25
239	Mickey Lolich	35.00	14.00	5.25
240	Jose Santiago	35.00	14.00	5.25
241	Dick McAuliffe	35.00	14.00	5.25
242	Mel Stottlemyre	35.00	14.00	5.25
243	Camilo Pascual	35.00	14.00	5.25
244	Jim Fregosi	35.00	14.00	5.25
245	Tony Conigliaro	40.00	16.00	6.00
246	Sonny Siebert	35.00	14.00	5.25
247	Jim Perry	35.00	14.00	5.25
248	Dave McNally	35.00	14.00	5.25
249	Fred Whitfield	35.00	14.00	5.25
250	Ken Berry	35.00	14.00	5.25
251	Jim Grant	35.00	14.00	5.25
252	Hank Aguirre	35.00	14.00	5.25
253	Don Wert	35.00	14.00	5.25
254	Wally Bunker	35.00	14.00	5.25
255	Elston Howard	40.00	16.00	6.00
256	Dave Johnson	35.00	14.00	5.25
257	Hoyt Wilhelm	75.00	30.00	11.00
258	Don Buford	35.00	14.00	5.25
259	Sam McDowell	35.00	14.00	5.25
260	Bobby Knoop	35.00	14.00	5.25
261	Denny McLain	35.00	14.00	5.25
262	Steve Hargan	35.00	14.00	5.25
263	Jim Nash	35.00	14.00	5.25
264	Jerry Adair	35.00	14.00	5.25
265	Tony Gonzalez	35.00	14.00	5.25
266	Mike Shannon	35.00	14.00	5.25
267	Bob Gibson	90.00	36.00	13.50
268	John Roseboro	35.00	14.00	5.25
269	Bob Aspromonte	35.00	14.00	5.25
270	Pete Rose	250.00	100.00	37.00
271	Rico Carty	40.00	16.00	6.00
272	Juan Pizarro	35.00	14.00	5.25
273	Willie Mays	250.00	100.00	37.00
274	Jim Bunning	90.00	36.00	13.50
275	Ernie Banks	100.00	40.00	15.00
276	Curt Flood	40.00	16.00	6.00
277	Mack Jones	35.00	14.00	5.25
278	Roberto Clemente	450.00	180.00	67.00

279	Sammy Ellis	35.00	14.00	5.25
280	Willie Stargell	90.00	36.00	13.50
281	Felipe Alou	40.00	16.00	6.00
282	Ed Kranepool	35.00	14.00	5.25
283	Nelson Briles	35.00	14.00	5.25
284	Hank Aaron	250.00	100.00	37.00
285	Vada Pinson	40.00	16.00	6.00
286	Jim LeFebvre	35.00	14.00	5.25
287	Hal Lanier	35.00	14.00	5.25
288	Ron Swoboda	35.00	14.00	5.25
289	Mike McCormick	35.00	14.00	5.25
290	Lou Johnson	35.00	14.00	5.25
291	Orlando Cepeda	90.00	36.00	13.50
292	Rusty Staub	40.00	16.00	6.00
293	Manny Mota	35.00	14.00	5.25
294	Tommy Harper	35.00	14.00	5.25
295	Don Drysdale	90.00	36.00	13.50
296	Mel Queen	35.00	14.00	5.25
297	Red Schoendienst	75.00	30.00	11.00
298	Matty Alou	35.00	14.00	5.25
299	Johnny Callison	35.00	14.00	5.25
300	Juan Marichal	90.00	36.00	13.50
301	Al McBean	35.00	14.00	5.25
302	Claude Osteen	35.00	14.00	5.25
303	Willie McCovey	90.00	36.00	13.50
304	Jim Owens	35.00	14.00	5.25
305	Chico Ruiz	35.00	14.00	5.25
306	Ferguson Jenkins	90.00	36.00	13.50
307	Lou Brock	90.00	36.00	13.50
308	Joe Morgan	90.00	36.00	13.50
309	Ron Santo	50.00	20.00	7.50
310	Chico Cardenas	35.00	14.00	5.25
311	Richie Allen	45.00	18.00	6.75
312	Gaylord Perry	75.00	30.00	11.00
313	Bill Mazeroski	75.00	30.00	11.00
314	Tony Taylor	35.00	14.00	5.25
315	Tommy Helms	35.00	14.00	5.25
316	Jim Wynn	35.00	14.00	5.25
317	Don Sutton	75.00	30.00	11.00
318	Mike Cuellar	45.00	18.00	6.75
319	Willie Davis	35.00	14.00	5.25
320	Julian Javier	35.00	14.00	5.25
321	Maury Wills	35.00	14.00	5.25
322	Gene Alley	35.00	14.00	5.25
323	Ray Sadecki	35.00	14.00	5.25
324	Joe Torre	45.00	18.00	6.75
325	Jim Maloney	35.00	14.00	5.25
326	Jim Davenport	35.00	14.00	5.25
327	Tony Perez	90.00	36.00	13.50
328	Roger Maris	100.00	40.00	15.00
329	Chris Short	35.00	14.00	5.25
330	Jesus Alou	35.00	14.00	5.25
331	Darron Johnson	35.00	14.00	5.25
332	Tommy Davis	35.00	14.00	5.25
333	Bob Veale	35.00	14.00	5.25
334	Bill McCool	35.00	14.00	5.25
335	Jim Hart	35.00	14.00	5.25
336	Roy Face	35.00	14.00	5.25
337	Billy Williams	75.00	30.00	11.00
338	Dick Groat	35.00	14.00	5.25

1968 Venezuelan Topps

The first 370 cards of Topps' 1968 baseball card set were reproduced in South America for sale in Venezuela. Besides being rather crudely printed on cheaper, non-gloss cardboard, the cards are virtually identical to the Topps U.S. version. The only difference is a tiny line of yellow type on back which reads: "Hecho en Venezuela - C.A. Litoven." Like most 1960s Venezuelan issues, these cards are seldom found in condition better than Excellent, and often with evidence on back of having been glued into an album or scrapbook. Venezuelan Topps cards are often found cut slightly smaller than the U.S. version, up to 1/8".

		NM	EX	VG
	Complete Set (370):	25,000	10,000	6,250
	Common Player:	30.00	12.00	7.50
1	N.L. Batting Leaders (Matty Alou, Roberto Clemente, Tony Gonzalez)	80.00	32.00	20.00
2	A.L. Batting Leaders (Al Kaline, Frank Robinson, Carl Yastrzemski)	50.00	20.00	12.50
3	N.L. RBI Leaders (Hank Aaron, Orlando Cepeda, Roberto Clemente)	80.00	32.00	20.00
4	A.L. RBI Leaders (Harmon Killebrew, Frank Robinson, Carl Yastrzemski)	50.00	20.00	12.50
5	N.L. Home Run Leaders (Hank Aaron, Willie McCovey, Ron Santo, Jim Wynn)	60.00	24.00	15.00
6	A.L. Home Run Leaders (Frank Howard, Harmon Killebrew, Carl Yastrzemski)	50.00	20.00	12.50

7	N.L. ERA Leaders (Jim Bunning, Phil Niekro, Chris Short)	30.00	12.00	7.50
8	A.L. ERA Leaders (Joe Horlen, Gary Peters, Sonny Siebert)	30.00	12.00	7.50
9	N.L. Pitching Leaders (Jim Bunning, Fergie Jenkins, Mike McCormick, Claude Osteen)	30.00	12.00	7.50
10	A.L. Pitching Leaders (Dean Chance, Jim Lonborg, Earl Wilson)	30.00	12.00	7.50
11	N.L. Strikeout Leaders (Jim Bunning, Fergie Jenkins, Gaylord Perry)	30.00	12.00	7.50
12	A.L. Strikeout Leaders (Dean Chance, Jim Lonborg, Sam McDowell)	30.00	12.00	7.50
13	Chuck Hartenstein	30.00	12.00	7.50
14	Jerry McNertney	30.00	12.00	7.50
15	Ron Hunt	30.00	12.00	7.50
16	Indians Rookies (Lou Piniella, Richie Scheinblum)	40.00	16.00	10.00
17	Dick Hall	30.00	12.00	7.50
18	Mike Hershberger	30.00	12.00	7.50
19	Juan Pizarro	30.00	12.00	7.50
20	Brooks Robinson	120.00	48.00	30.00
21	Ron Davis	30.00	12.00	7.50
22	Pat Dobson	30.00	12.00	7.50
23	Chico Cardenas	30.00	12.00	7.50
24	Bobby Locke	30.00	12.00	7.50
25	Julian Javier	30.00	12.00	7.50
26	Darrell Brandon	30.00	12.00	7.50
27	Gil Hodges	50.00	20.00	12.50
28	Ted Uhlaender	30.00	12.00	7.50
29	Joe Verbanic	30.00	12.00	7.50
30	Joe Torre	40.00	16.00	10.00
31	Ed Stroud	30.00	12.00	7.50
32	Joe Gibbon	30.00	12.00	7.50
33	Pete Ward	30.00	12.00	7.50
34	Al Ferrara	30.00	12.00	7.50
35	Steve Hargan	30.00	12.00	7.50
36	Pirates Rookies (Bob Moose, Bob Robertson)	30.00	12.00	7.50
37	Billy Williams	80.00	32.00	20.00
38	Tony Pierce	30.00	12.00	7.50
39	Cookie Rojas	30.00	12.00	7.50
40	Denny McLain	40.00	16.00	10.00
41	Julio Gotay	30.00	12.00	7.50
42	Larry Haney	30.00	12.00	7.50
43	Gary Bell	30.00	12.00	7.50
44	Frank Kostro	30.00	12.00	7.50
45	Tom Seaver	120.00	48.00	30.00
46	Dave Ricketts	30.00	12.00	7.50
47	Ralph Houk	30.00	12.00	7.50
48	Ted Davidson	30.00	12.00	7.50
49	Ed Brinkman	30.00	12.00	7.50
50	Willie Mays	350.00	140.00	90.00
51	Bob Locker	30.00	12.00	7.50
52	Hawk Taylor	30.00	12.00	7.50
53	Gene Alley	30.00	12.00	7.50
54	Stan Williams	30.00	12.00	7.50
55	Felipe Alou	40.00	16.00	10.00
56	Orioles Rookies (Dave Leonhard, Dave May)	30.00	12.00	7.50
57	Dan Schneider	30.00	12.00	7.50
58	Eddie Mathews	120.00	48.00	30.00
59	Don Lock	30.00	12.00	7.50
60	Ken Holtzman	30.00	12.00	7.50
61	Reggie Smith	30.00	12.00	7.50
62	Chuck Dobson	30.00	12.00	7.50
63	Dick Kenworthy	30.00	12.00	7.50
64	Jim Merritt	30.00	12.00	7.50
65	John Roseboro	30.00	12.00	7.50
66	Casey Cox	30.00	12.00	7.50
67	Checklist 1-109 (Jim Kaat)	30.00	12.00	7.50
68	Ron Willis	30.00	12.00	7.50
69	Tom Tresh	30.00	12.00	7.50
70	Bob Veale	30.00	12.00	7.50
71	Vern Fuller	30.00	12.00	7.50
72	Tommy John	30.00	12.00	7.50
73	Jim Hart	30.00	12.00	7.50
74	Milt Pappas	30.00	12.00	7.50
75	Don Mincher	30.00	12.00	7.50
76	Braves Rookies (Jim Britton, Ron Reed)	30.00	12.00	7.50
77	Don Wilson	30.00	12.00	7.50
78	Jim Northrup	30.00	12.00	7.50
79	Ted Kubiak	30.00	12.00	7.50
80	Rod Carew	120.00	48.00	30.00
81	Larry Jackson	30.00	12.00	7.50
82	Sam Bowens	30.00	12.00	7.50
83	John Stephenson	30.00	12.00	7.50
84	Bob Tolan	30.00	12.00	7.50
85	Gaylord Perry	80.00	32.00	20.00
86	Willie Stargell	100.00	40.00	25.00
87	Dick Williams	30.00	12.00	7.50
88	Phil Regan	30.00	12.00	7.50
89	Jake Gibbs	30.00	12.00	7.50
90	Vada Pinson	40.00	16.00	10.00
91	Jim Ollom	30.00	12.00	7.50
92	Ed Kranepool	30.00	12.00	7.50
93	Tony Cloninger	30.00	12.00	7.50
94	Lee Maye	30.00	12.00	7.50
95	Bob Aspromonte	30.00	12.00	7.50
96	Senators Rookies (Frank Coggins, Dick Nold)	30.00	12.00	7.50
97	Tom Phoebus	30.00	12.00	7.50
98	Gary Sutherland	30.00	12.00	7.50
99	Rocky Colavito	50.00	20.00	12.50
100	Bob Gibson	90.00	36.00	22.00
101	Glenn Beckert	30.00	12.00	7.50
102	Jose Cardenal	30.00	12.00	7.50
103	Don Sutton	80.00	32.00	20.00
104	Dick Dietz	30.00	12.00	7.50
105	Al Downing	30.00	12.00	7.50
106	Dalton Jones	30.00	12.00	7.50

No.	Player	NM	EX	VG
107	Checklist 110-196 (Juan Marichal)	30.00	12.00	7.50
108	Don Pavletich	30.00	12.00	7.50
109	Bert Campaneris	40.00	16.00	10.00
110	Hank Aaron	350.00	140.00	90.00
111	Rich Reese	30.00	12.00	7.50
112	Woody Fryman	30.00	12.00	7.50
113	Tigers Rookies (Tom Matchick, Daryl Patterson)	30.00	12.00	7.50
114	Ron Swoboda	30.00	12.00	7.50
115	Sam McDowell	30.00	12.00	7.50
116	Ken McMullen	30.00	12.00	7.50
117	Larry Jaster	30.00	12.00	7.50
118	Mark Belanger	30.00	12.00	7.50
119	Ted Savage	30.00	12.00	7.50
120	Mel Stottlemyre	30.00	12.00	7.50
121	Jimmie Hall	30.00	12.00	7.50
122	Gene Mauch	30.00	12.00	7.50
123	Jose Santiago	30.00	12.00	7.50
124	Nate Oliver	30.00	12.00	7.50
125	Joe Horlen	30.00	12.00	7.50
126	Bobby Etheridge	30.00	12.00	7.50
127	Paul Lindblad	30.00	12.00	7.50
128	Astros Rookies (Tom Dukes, Alonzo Harris)	30.00	12.00	7.50
129	Mickey Stanley	30.00	12.00	7.50
130	Tony Perez	90.00	36.00	22.00
131	Frank Bertaina	30.00	12.00	7.50
132	Bud Harrelson	30.00	12.00	7.50
133	Fred Whitfield	30.00	12.00	7.50
134	Pat Jarvis	30.00	12.00	7.50
135	Paul Blair	30.00	12.00	7.50
136	Randy Hundley	30.00	12.00	7.50
137	Twins Team	40.00	16.00	10.00
138	Ruben Amaro	30.00	12.00	7.50
139	Chris Short	30.00	12.00	7.50
140	Tony Conigliaro	40.00	16.00	10.00
141	Dal Maxvill	30.00	12.00	7.50
142	White Sox Rookies (Buddy Bradford, Bill Voss)	30.00	12.00	7.50
143	Pete Cimino	30.00	12.00	7.50
144	Joe Morgan	100.00	40.00	25.00
145	Don Drysdale	100.00	40.00	25.00
146	Sal Bando	30.00	12.00	7.50
147	Frank Linzy	30.00	12.00	7.50
148	Dave Bristol	30.00	12.00	7.50
149	Bob Saverine	30.00	12.00	7.50
150	Roberto Clemente	600.00	240.00	150.00
151	World Series Game 1 (Brock Socks 4 Hits in Opener)	30.00	12.00	7.50
152	World Series Game 2 (Yaz Smashes Two Homers)	40.00	16.00	10.00
153	World Series Game 3 (Briles Cools Off Boston)	30.00	12.00	7.50
154	World Series Game 4 (Gibson Hurls Shutout)	30.00	12.00	7.50
155	World Series Game 5 (Lonborg Wins Again)	30.00	12.00	7.50
156	World Series Game 6 (Petrocelli Socks Two Homers)	30.00	12.00	7.50
157	World Series Game 7 (St. Louis Wins It)	30.00	12.00	7.50
158	World Series Summary (The Cardinals Celebrate)	30.00	12.00	7.50
159	Don Kessinger	30.00	12.00	7.50
160	Earl Wilson	30.00	12.00	7.50
161	Norm Miller	30.00	12.00	7.50
162	Cardinals Rookies (Hal Gilson, Mike Torrez)	30.00	12.00	7.50
163	Gene Brabender	30.00	12.00	7.50
164	Ramon Webster	30.00	12.00	7.50
165	Tony Oliva	40.00	16.00	10.00
166	Claude Raymond	30.00	12.00	7.50
167	Elston Howard	30.00	12.00	7.50
168	Dodgers Team	50.00	20.00	12.50
169	Bob Bolin	30.00	12.00	7.50
170	Jim Fregosi	30.00	12.00	7.50
171	Don Nottebart	30.00	12.00	7.50
172	Walt Williams	30.00	12.00	7.50
173	John Boozer	30.00	12.00	7.50
174	Bob Tillman	30.00	12.00	7.50
175	Maury Wills	30.00	12.00	7.50
176	Bob Allen	30.00	12.00	7.50
177	Mets Rookies (*Jerry Koosman, Nolan Ryan*)	12,000	4,800	3,000
178	Don Wert	30.00	12.00	7.50
179	Bill Stoneman	30.00	12.00	7.50
180	Curt Flood	30.00	12.00	7.50
181	Jerry Zimmerman	30.00	12.00	7.50
182	Dave Giusti	30.00	12.00	7.50
183	Bob Kennedy	30.00	12.00	7.50
184	Lou Johnson	30.00	12.00	7.50
185	Tom Haller	30.00	12.00	7.50
186	Eddie Watt	30.00	12.00	7.50
187	Sonny Jackson	30.00	12.00	7.50
188	Cap Peterson	30.00	12.00	7.50
189	Bill Landis	30.00	12.00	7.50
190	Bill White	30.00	12.00	7.50
191	Dan Frisella	30.00	12.00	7.50
192	Checklist 197-283 (Carl Yastrzemski)	40.00	16.00	10.00
193	Jack Hamilton	30.00	12.00	7.50
194	Don Buford	30.00	12.00	7.50
195	Joe Pepitone	30.00	12.00	7.50
196	Gary Nolan	30.00	12.00	7.50
197	Larry Brown	30.00	12.00	7.50
198	Roy Face	30.00	12.00	7.50
199	A's Rookies (Darrell Osteen, Roberto Rodriguez)	30.00	12.00	7.50
200	Orlando Cepeda	80.00	32.00	20.00
201	Mike Marshall	30.00	12.00	7.50
202	Adolfo Phillips	30.00	12.00	7.50
203	Dick Kelley	30.00	12.00	7.50
204	Andy Etchebarren	30.00	12.00	7.50
205	Juan Marichal	90.00	36.00	22.00
206	Cal Ermer	30.00	12.00	7.50
207	Carroll Sembera	30.00	12.00	7.50
208	Willie Davis	30.00	12.00	7.50
209	Tim Cullen	30.00	12.00	7.50
210	Gary Peters	30.00	12.00	7.50
211	J.C. Martin	30.00	12.00	7.50
212	Dave Morehead	30.00	12.00	7.50
213	Chico Ruiz	30.00	12.00	7.50
214	Yankees Rookies (Stan Bahnsen, Frank Fernandez)	30.00	12.00	7.50
215	Jim Bunning	90.00	36.00	22.00
216	Bubba Morton	30.00	12.00	7.50
217	Turk Farrell	30.00	12.00	7.50
218	Ken Suarez	30.00	12.00	7.50
219	Rob Gardner	30.00	12.00	7.50
220	Harmon Killebrew	120.00	48.00	30.00
221	Braves Team	40.00	16.00	10.00
222	Jim Hardin	30.00	12.00	7.50
223	Ollie Brown	30.00	12.00	7.50
224	Jack Aker	30.00	12.00	7.50
225	Richie Allen	40.00	16.00	10.00
226	Jimmie Price	30.00	12.00	7.50
227	Joe Hoerner	30.00	12.00	7.50
228	Dodgers Rookies (Jack Billingham, Jim Fairey)	30.00	12.00	7.50
229	Fred Klages	30.00	12.00	7.50
230	Pete Rose	350.00	140.00	90.00
231	Dave Baldwin	30.00	12.00	7.50
232	Denis Menke	30.00	12.00	7.50
233	George Scott	30.00	12.00	7.50
234	Bill Monbouquette	30.00	12.00	7.50
235	Ron Santo	50.00	20.00	12.50
236	Tug McGraw	30.00	12.00	7.50
237	Alvin Dark	30.00	12.00	7.50
238	Tom Satriano	30.00	12.00	7.50
239	Bill Henry	30.00	12.00	7.50
240	Al Kaline	120.00	48.00	30.00
241	Felix Millan	30.00	12.00	7.50
242	Moe Drabowsky	30.00	12.00	7.50
243	Rich Rollins	30.00	12.00	7.50
244	John Donaldson	30.00	12.00	7.50
245	Tony Gonzalez	30.00	12.00	7.50
246	Fritz Peterson	30.00	12.00	7.50
247	Reds Rookies (Johnny Bench, Ron Tompkins)	400.00	160.00	100.00
248	Fred Valentine	30.00	12.00	7.50
249	Bill Singer	30.00	12.00	7.50
250	Carl Yastrzemski	130.00	52.00	32.00
251	Manny Sanguillen	40.00	16.00	10.00
252	Angels Team	40.00	16.00	10.00
253	Dick Hughes	30.00	12.00	7.50
254	Cleon Jones	30.00	12.00	7.50
255	Dean Chance	30.00	12.00	7.50
256	Norm Cash	40.00	16.00	10.00
257	Phil Niekro	80.00	32.00	20.00
258	Cubs Rookies (Jose Arcia, Bill Schlesinger)	30.00	12.00	7.50
259	Ken Boyer	30.00	12.00	7.50
260	Jim Wynn	30.00	12.00	7.50
261	Dave Duncan	30.00	12.00	7.50
262	Rick Wise	30.00	12.00	7.50
263	Horace Clarke	30.00	12.00	7.50
264	Ted Abernathy	30.00	12.00	7.50
265	Tommy Davis	30.00	12.00	7.50
266	Paul Popovich	30.00	12.00	7.50
267	Herman Franks	30.00	12.00	7.50
268	Bob Humphreys	30.00	12.00	7.50
269	Bob Tiefenauer	30.00	12.00	7.50
270	Matty Alou	30.00	12.00	7.50
271	Bobby Knoop	30.00	12.00	7.50
272	Ray Culp	30.00	12.00	7.50
273	Dave Johnson	30.00	12.00	7.50
274	Mike Cuellar	30.00	12.00	7.50
275	Tim McCarver	30.00	12.00	7.50
276	Jim Roland	30.00	12.00	7.50
277	Jerry Buchek	30.00	12.00	7.50
278	Checklist 284-370 (Orlando Cepeda)	30.00	12.00	7.50
279	Bill Hands	30.00	12.00	7.50
280	Mickey Mantle	1,900	760.00	475.00
281	Jim Campanis	30.00	12.00	7.50
282	Rick Monday	30.00	12.00	7.50
283	Mel Queen	30.00	12.00	7.50
284	John Briggs	30.00	12.00	7.50
285	Dick McAuliffe	30.00	12.00	7.50
286	Cecil Upshaw	30.00	12.00	7.50
287	White Sox Rookies (Mickey Abarbanel, Cisco Carlos)	30.00	12.00	7.50
288	Dave Wickersham	30.00	12.00	7.50
289	Woody Held	30.00	12.00	7.50
290	Willie McCovey	120.00	48.00	30.00
291	Dick Lines	30.00	12.00	7.50
292	Art Shamsky	30.00	12.00	7.50
293	Bruce Howard	30.00	12.00	7.50
294	Red Schoendienst	80.00	32.00	20.00
295	Sonny Siebert	30.00	12.00	7.50
296	Byron Browne	30.00	12.00	7.50
297	Russ Gibson	30.00	12.00	7.50
298	Jim Brewer	30.00	12.00	7.50
299	Gene Michael	30.00	12.00	7.50
300	Rusty Staub	40.00	16.00	10.00
301	Twins Rookies (George Mitterwald, Rick Renick)	30.00	12.00	7.50
302	Gerry Arrigo	30.00	12.00	7.50
303	Dick Green	30.00	12.00	7.50
304	Sandy Valdespino	30.00	12.00	7.50
305	Minnie Rojas	30.00	12.00	7.50
306	Mike Ryan	30.00	12.00	7.50
307	John Hiller	30.00	12.00	7.50
308	Pirates Team	50.00	20.00	12.50
309	Ken Henderson	30.00	12.00	7.50
310	Luis Aparicio	150.00	60.00	37.00
311	Jack Lamabe	30.00	12.00	7.50
312	Curt Blefary	30.00	12.00	7.50
313	Al Weis	30.00	12.00	7.50
314	Red Sox Rookies (Bill Rohr, George Spriggs)	30.00	12.00	7.50
315	Zoilo Versalles	30.00	12.00	7.50
316	Steve Barber	30.00	12.00	7.50
317	Ron Brand	30.00	12.00	7.50
318	Chico Salmon	30.00	12.00	7.50
319	George Culver	30.00	12.00	7.50
320	Frank Howard	40.00	16.00	10.00
321	Leo Durocher	50.00	20.00	12.50
322	Dave Boswell	30.00	12.00	7.50
323	Deron Johnson	30.00	12.00	7.50
324	Jim Nash	30.00	12.00	7.50
325	Manny Mota	30.00	12.00	7.50
326	Dennis Ribant	30.00	12.00	7.50
327	Tony Taylor	30.00	12.00	7.50
328	Angels Rookies (Chuck Vinson, Jim Weaver)	30.00	12.00	7.50
329	Duane Josephson	30.00	12.00	7.50
330	Roger Maris	120.00	48.00	30.00
331	Dan Osinski	30.00	12.00	7.50
332	Doug Rader	30.00	12.00	7.50
333	Ron Herbel	30.00	12.00	7.50
334	Orioles Team	50.00	20.00	12.50
335	Bob Allison	30.00	12.00	7.50
336	John Purdin	30.00	12.00	7.50
337	Bill Robinson	30.00	12.00	7.50
338	Bob Johnson	30.00	12.00	7.50
339	Rich Nye	30.00	12.00	7.50
340	Max Alvis	30.00	12.00	7.50
341	Jim Lemon	30.00	12.00	7.50
342	Ken Johnson	30.00	12.00	7.50
343	Jim Gosger	30.00	12.00	7.50
344	Donn Clendenon	30.00	12.00	7.50
345	Bob Hendley	30.00	12.00	7.50
346	Jerry Adair	30.00	12.00	7.50
347	George Brunet	30.00	12.00	7.50
348	Phillies Rookies (Larry Colton, Dick Thoenen)	30.00	12.00	7.50
349	Ed Spiezio	30.00	12.00	7.50
350	Hoyt Wilhelm	80.00	32.00	20.00
351	Bob Barton	30.00	12.00	7.50
352	Jackie Hernandez	30.00	12.00	7.50
353	Mack Jones	30.00	12.00	7.50
354	Pete Richert	30.00	12.00	7.50
355	Ernie Banks	130.00	55.00	35.00
356	Checklist 371-457 (Ken Holtzman)	30.00	12.00	7.50
357	Len Gabrielson	30.00	12.00	7.50
358	Mike Epstein	30.00	12.00	7.50
359	Joe Moeller	30.00	12.00	7.50
360	Willie Horton	30.00	12.00	7.50
361	Harmon Killebrew (All-Star)	50.00	20.00	12.50
362	Orlando Cepeda (All-Star)	40.00	16.00	10.00
363	Rod Carew (All-Star)	50.00	20.00	12.50
364	Joe Morgan (All-Star)	40.00	16.00	10.00
365	Brooks Robinson (All-Star)	50.00	20.00	12.50
366	Ron Santo (All-Star)	40.00	16.00	10.00
367	Jim Fregosi (All-Star)	30.00	12.00	7.50
368	Gene Alley (All-Star)	30.00	12.00	7.50
369	Carl Yastrzemski (All-Star)	50.00	20.00	12.50
370	Hank Aaron (All-Star)	250.00	100.00	62.00

1970 Ovenca Venezuelan League

JOE FOY
Norteamericano - Lanza y batea a la derecha.

Estuvo anteriormente con los Medias Rojas de Boston de la Liga Americana. Los Metropolitanos de Nueva York, con serios problemas en la tercera base, adquirieron sus servicios a partir de la recién finalizada campaña de Grandes Ligas.

Foy no rindió todo lo que de él se esperaba y el manager Hodges lo tuvo que alternar en la esquina caliente con Wayne Garret. Totalizó 239 a la ofensiva, producto de 76 imparables en 318 turnos, intervino en 98 juegos, anotó 39 carreras y remolcó 36, conectó 6 cuadrangulares y fue el factor mejor estabilizador de su equipo. Esta 23. Debido a su escaso rendimiento, fue enviado a las Menores al concluir la temporada. El próximo año deberá reportarse al club Triple "A".

After partial parallels of Topps cards were produced off and on between 1959 and 1968, Venezuelan collectors and fans were offered a completely home-brewed baseball card issue for the 1970-71 winter league season. Similar in quality (i.e., less substantial card stock) to earlier sets, these were printed by Sport Grafico for Ovenca, though neither entity is mentioned on the cards. Slightly larger than 2-1/2" x 3-1/2", cards have large color photos with color stripes above and below bearing player and team name and card number. Backs are printed in black on blue with lengthy comments about the player and his career. Gaps in this checklist will be filled as information comes to light.

		NM	EX	VG
Complete Set (300):		2,250	1,100	650.00
Common Player:		20.00	10.00	6.00
Album:		200.00	100.00	60.00
1	Cesar Gutierrez	20.00	10.00	6.00
2	Elio Chacon	20.00	10.00	6.00
3	Luis Rodriguez	20.00	10.00	6.00
4	David Concepcion	75.00	37.50	22.00
5	Roberto Munoz	20.00	10.00	6.00
6	Jesus Rizales	20.00	10.00	6.00
7	Virgilio Mata	20.00	10.00	6.00
8	Manuel Garcia	30.00	15.00	9.00
9	Cesar Garrido	20.00	10.00	6.00
10	Alejandro Tovar	20.00	10.00	6.00
11	William Salazar	20.00	10.00	6.00
12	Jose Lopez	20.00	10.00	6.00
13	Romulo Castillo	20.00	10.00	6.00
14	Victor Jimenez	20.00	10.00	6.00
15	Jose Saiz	20.00	10.00	6.00
16	Wilfredo Calvino	20.00	10.00	6.00
17	Jesus Avila	20.00	10.00	6.00
18	Cruz Rodriguez	20.00	10.00	6.00
19	Julio Bracho	20.00	10.00	6.00
20	David Concepcion, Cesar Gutierrez	25.00	12.50	7.50

#	Name	NM	EX	VG
21	Double Play (David Concepcion)	25.00	12.50	7.50
22	Tigres de Aragua Logo	10.00	5.00	3.00
23	Orlando Tavares	20.00	10.00	6.00
24	David Concepcion (In Action)	30.00	15.00	9.00
25	Aragua Action	10.00	5.00	3.00
26	Aragua Action	10.00	5.00	3.00
27	Cesar Gutierrez	20.00	10.00	6.00
28	Play at Home	10.00	5.00	3.00
29	Joe Foy	20.00	10.00	6.00
30	Dennis Paepke	20.00	10.00	6.00
31	Fred Norman	20.00	10.00	6.00
32	John Purdin	20.00	10.00	6.00
33	Steve Huntz	20.00	10.00	6.00
34	Claide (Clyde) Mashore	20.00	10.00	6.00
35	Steve Mingori	20.00	10.00	6.00
36	Jim Breazeale	20.00	10.00	6.00
37	Charles Day	20.00	10.00	6.00
38	Bob Stinson	20.00	10.00	6.00
39	Phil Hennigan	20.00	10.00	6.00
40	Aragua Checklist (Wilfredo Calvino)	25.00	12.50	7.50
41	Faustino Zabala	20.00	10.00	6.00
42	Pablo Torrealba	20.00	10.00	6.00
43	Erasmo Diaz	20.00	10.00	6.00
44	Sebastian Martinez	20.00	10.00	6.00
45	Neudo Morales	20.00	10.00	6.00
46	Iran Paz	20.00	10.00	6.00
47	Franklyn Moreno	20.00	10.00	6.00
48	Claudio Urdaneta	20.00	10.00	6.00
49	Dario Chirinos	20.00	10.00	6.00
50	Domingo Carrasquel	20.00	10.00	6.00
51	Enrique Gonzalez	20.00	10.00	6.00
52	Ednio Gonzalez	20.00	10.00	6.00
53	Humberto Donquis	20.00	10.00	6.00
54	Antonio Ruiz	20.00	10.00	6.00
55	Efrain Urquiola	20.00	10.00	6.00
56	Tony Pacheco	20.00	10.00	6.00
57	Lucio Celis	20.00	10.00	6.00
58	Domingo Barboza	20.00	10.00	6.00
59	Faustino Zabala, Neudo Morales	15.00	7.50	4.50
60	Lara Action	10.00	5.00	3.00
61	Tony Pacheco, Lucio Celis, Domingo Barboza	15.00	7.50	4.50
62	Lara Team Logo	10.00	5.00	3.00
63	Alexis Corro	20.00	10.00	6.00
64	Lara Rookies in Action	10.00	5.00	3.00
65	Lara Play at First	10.00	5.00	3.00
66	Lara Play at Home	10.00	5.00	3.00
67	Lara Action	10.00	5.00	3.00
68	Jim Shellenback	20.00	10.00	6.00
69	Scipio Spinks	20.00	10.00	6.00
70	Ken Forsch	20.00	10.00	6.00
71	Oscar Zamora	20.00	10.00	6.00
72	Ronald Cook	20.00	10.00	6.00
73	Jackie Brown	20.00	10.00	6.00
74	Orlando Martinez	20.00	10.00	6.00
75	Bobby Watson	25.00	12.50	7.50
76	Jose Martinez	20.00	10.00	6.00
77	Roger Metzger	20.00	10.00	6.00
78	Tommy Reynolds	20.00	10.00	6.00
79	Cleo James	20.00	10.00	6.00
80	Lara Checklist (Tony Pacheco)	10.00	5.00	3.00
81	Gustavo Gil	20.00	10.00	6.00
82	Jesus Aristimuno	20.00	10.00	6.00
83	Armando Ortiz	20.00	10.00	6.00
84	Orlando Reyes	20.00	10.00	6.00
85	Damaso Blanco	20.00	10.00	6.00
86				
87	Victor Colina	20.00	10.00	6.00
88	Nelson Cana	20.00	10.00	6.00
89	Francisco Diaz	20.00	10.00	6.00
90	Edito Arteaga	20.00	10.00	6.00
91	Concepcion Escalona	20.00	10.00	6.00
92	Gilberto Marcano	20.00	10.00	6.00
93	Luis A. Serrano	20.00	10.00	6.00
94				
95	Raul Ortega	20.00	10.00	6.00
96	Carlos Patato Pascual	20.00	10.00	6.00
97	Leopold Tovar	20.00	10.00	6.00
98	Manuel Gonzalez	20.00	10.00	6.00
99	Magallanes Action	10.00	5.00	3.00
100	Comienza el Partido	20.00	10.00	6.00
101	Magallanes Rookies	15.00	7.50	4.50
102				
103	Marcano en la Lomita	15.00	7.50	4.50
104	Magallanes Fans	10.00	5.00	3.00
105	Magallanes Action	10.00	5.00	3.00
106				
107	Hal King, Jim Holt, Clarence Gaston, Herman Hill	15.00	7.50	4.50
108	Magallanes Caribbean Champions	10.00	5.00	3.00
109				
110	Herman Hill	20.00	10.00	6.00
111	Jim Holt	20.00	10.00	6.00
112	Orlando Pena	20.00	10.00	6.00
113	Magallanes Action	10.00	5.00	3.00
114	Hal King	20.00	10.00	6.00
115	Jorge Lauzerique	20.00	10.00	6.00
116	Rigoberto Mendoza	20.00	10.00	6.00
117	Allan (Alan) Closter	20.00	10.00	6.00
118	Clarence Gaston	25.00	12.50	7.50
119	John Morris	20.00	10.00	6.00
120	Patato Pascual, Unknown	15.00	7.50	4.50
121	Victor Davalillo	20.00	10.00	6.00
122	Cesar Tovar	20.00	10.00	6.00
123	Gonzalo Marquez	20.00	10.00	6.00
124	Luis Penalver	20.00	10.00	6.00
125	Alberto Cambero	20.00	10.00	6.00
126	Urbano Lugo	20.00	10.00	6.00
127	Juan Campos	20.00	10.00	6.00
128	William Castillo	20.00	10.00	6.00
129	Nelson Garcia	20.00	10.00	6.00
130	Ramon Guanchez	20.00	10.00	6.00
131	Jesus Marcano Trillo	40.00	20.00	12.00
132	Manuel Mendible	20.00	10.00	6.00
133	Teodoro Obregon	20.00	10.00	6.00
134	Jesus Padron	20.00	10.00	6.00
135	Ulises Urrieta	20.00	10.00	6.00
136	Antonio "Loco" Torres	20.00	10.00	6.00
137	Leopoldo Posada	20.00	10.00	6.00
138	Pompeyo Davilillo	20.00	10.00	6.00
139	Alonso Olivares	20.00	10.00	6.00
140	Cesar Tovar (In Action)	15.00	7.50	4.50
141	Caracas Rookies in Action	15.00	7.50	4.50
142				
143	Andres Barrios	20.00	10.00	6.00
144	Heriberto Morillo	20.00	10.00	6.00
145	Angel Cordova	20.00	10.00	6.00
146	Freddy Rivero	20.00	10.00	6.00
147	Rafael Velasquez	20.00	10.00	6.00
148	Camilo Pascual	30.00	15.00	9.00
149	Cesar Tovar, Vic Davalillo	20.00	10.00	6.00
150	Luis Tiant	30.00	15.00	9.00
151	Roberto Musulungo Hernandez	20.00	10.00	6.00
152	Kurt Devecqua (Bevacqua)	30.00	15.00	9.00
153	Cookie Rojas	30.00	15.00	9.00
154	Larry Howard	20.00	10.00	6.00
155	Rick Scheinblum	20.00	10.00	6.00
156	Diego Segui	25.00	12.50	7.50
157	Gregory Conger	20.00	10.00	6.00
158	Richard Falker (Falkner)	20.00	10.00	6.00
159	Ed Sprague	20.00	10.00	6.00
160	Zulia Checklist (Pompeyo Davilillo)	15.00	7.50	4.50
161	Luis Aparicio	75.00	37.00	22.00
162	Teolindo Acosta	20.00	10.00	6.00
163	Gustavo Sposito	20.00	10.00	6.00
164	Juan Francia	20.00	10.00	6.00
165	Graciliano Parra	20.00	10.00	6.00
166	Simon Salaya	20.00	10.00	6.00
167	Nelson Castellanos	20.00	10.00	6.00
168	Edgar Urbina	20.00	10.00	6.00
169	Luis Gonzalez	20.00	10.00	6.00
170	Orlin Rojas	20.00	10.00	6.00
171	Everest Contramaestre	20.00	10.00	6.00
172	Juan Quiroz	20.00	10.00	6.00
173	Juan Quintana	20.00	10.00	6.00
174	Hugo Bello	20.00	10.00	6.00
175	Jesus Llamozas	20.00	10.00	6.00
176	Luis Aparicio (Manager)	45.00	22.00	13.50
177	Luis Aparicio, Sr.	25.00	12.50	7.50
178	Antonio Brinez	20.00	10.00	6.00
179	Carlos Dickson Bell	20.00	10.00	6.00
180	Alfonso Carrasquel	30.00	15.00	9.00
181	Zulia Action	10.00	5.00	3.00
182	Zulia Eagles Team Logo	20.00	10.00	6.00
183	Nidio Sirit	20.00	10.00	6.00
184	Zulia Action	10.00	5.00	3.00
185	Zulia Eagles Team Photo	10.00	5.00	3.00
186	Bobby Cox (In Action)	20.00	10.00	6.00
187	Zulia Play at Home	10.00	5.00	3.00
188	Alfonso Carrasquel, Luis Aparicio	25.00	12.50	7.50
189	Teolindo Acosta, Gustavo Sposito	15.00	7.50	4.50
190	Leonardo Cardenas	20.00	10.00	6.00
191	Bart Johnson	20.00	10.00	6.00
192	Jerry Crider	20.00	10.00	6.00
193	Getty Janesky (Gerry Janeski)	20.00	10.00	6.00
194	John Matias	20.00	10.00	6.00
195	Walter Williams	25.00	12.50	7.50
196	Steve Hovley	20.00	10.00	6.00
197	Frank Fernandez	20.00	10.00	6.00
198	John Donaldson	20.00	10.00	6.00
199	Donald Eddy	20.00	10.00	6.00
200	Zulia Checklist (Luis Aparicio)	30.00	15.00	9.00
201	Jose Herrera	20.00	10.00	6.00
202	Aurelio Monteagudo	20.00	10.00	6.00
203	Remigio Hermoso	20.00	10.00	6.00
204	Angel Bravo	20.00	10.00	6.00
205	Enzo Hernandez	20.00	10.00	6.00
206	Oswaldo Blanco	20.00	10.00	6.00
207	Carlos Moreno	20.00	10.00	6.00
208	Adolfo Philips (Phillips)	20.00	10.00	6.00
209	Roberto Romero	20.00	10.00	6.00
210	Euclides Camejo	20.00	10.00	6.00
211	Oswaldo Troconis	20.00	10.00	6.00
212	Roberto Marcano	20.00	10.00	6.00
213	Victor Patino	20.00	10.00	6.00
214	Hector Urbano	20.00	10.00	6.00
215	Antonio Pipo Correa	20.00	10.00	6.00
216	Dave Garcia	25.00	12.50	7.50
217	Graciano Ravelo	20.00	10.00	6.00
218	Reinaldo Cordeiro	20.00	10.00	6.00
219	La Guaira Action	10.00	5.00	3.00
220	La Tropa Completa	20.00	10.00	6.00
221	Tomas Liscano Arias	20.00	10.00	6.00
222				
223	Jesus Romero	20.00	10.00	6.00
224	Julian Yanez	20.00	10.00	6.00
225	Enrique Gutierrez	20.00	10.00	6.00
226	Dionel Durand	20.00	10.00	6.00
227	Jose Gregorio Salas	20.00	10.00	6.00
228	Luis Camaleon Garcia	20.00	10.00	6.00
229	Alfredo Ortiz	20.00	10.00	6.00
230	Luis Contreras	20.00	10.00	6.00
231	Ed Spiezio	20.00	10.00	6.00
232	Paul Casanova	25.00	12.50	7.50
233	Mike Epstein	25.00	12.50	7.50
234	Casey Cox	20.00	10.00	6.00
235	Marcelino Lopez	20.00	10.00	6.00
236	Jerry Cram	20.00	10.00	6.00
237	Danny Coombs	20.00	10.00	6.00
238	Del Unser	20.00	10.00	6.00
239	Hector Brito	20.00	10.00	6.00
240	La Guaira Checklist	10.00	5.00	3.00
241	Larry Howard, Richie Scheinblum (In Action)	15.00	7.50	4.50
242	Ed Spiezio (In Action)	15.00	7.50	4.50
243	Clarence Gaston, Cesar Tovar (In Action)	15.00	7.50	4.50
244	Paul Casanova, Unknown	15.00	7.50	4.50
245	Vitico, Cesar Tovar	15.00	7.50	4.50
246	Pasion en el Juego	10.00	5.00	3.00
247	Luis Aparicio (In Action)	35.00	17.50	10.50
248	Angel Bravo (In Action)	15.00	7.50	4.50
249	Bobby Watson (In Action)	20.00	10.00	6.00
250	Alejandro "Palon" Carrasquel (Immortal)	25.00	12.50	7.50
251	Enrique Fonseca (Veteran)	20.00	10.00	6.00
252	Manuel Pollo Malpica (Immortal)	20.00	10.00	6.00
253	Emilio Cueche	20.00	10.00	6.00
254				
255	Felix "Tirahuequito" Machado (Veteran)			
256	Herberto Leal (Veteran)	20.00	10.00	6.00
257	Chucho Ramos (Veteran)	20.00	10.00	6.00
258	Julian Ladera (Veteran)	20.00	10.00	6.00
259	Carlos Ascanio (Veteran)	20.00	10.00	6.00
260	Jose Perez Colmenare (Immortal)	20.00	10.00	6.00
261	Isaias "Latigo" Chaves (Immortal)	20.00	10.00	6.00
262	Victor Garcia (Veteran)	20.00	10.00	6.00
263	Valentin Arevalo (Immortal)	20.00	10.00	6.00
264	Adolfredo Gonzalez (Veteran)	20.00	10.00	6.00
265	Hector Benitez Redondo (Veteran)	20.00	10.00	6.00
266	Ramon Fernandez (Veteran)	20.00	10.00	6.00
267	Guillermo Vento (Veteran)	20.00	10.00	6.00
268	Rafael Garcia Cedeno (Veteran)	20.00	10.00	6.00
269	Luis Oliveros (Veteran)	20.00	10.00	6.00
270	Luis Mono Zuloaga (Veteran)	20.00	10.00	6.00
271	Carlos Santeliz (Veteran)	20.00	10.00	6.00
272	Aureliano Patino	20.00	10.00	6.00
273	Rafael Olivares (Veteran)	20.00	10.00	6.00
274	Tarzan Contreras (Veteran)	20.00	10.00	6.00
275	Daniel Canonico	20.00	10.00	6.00
276	Babbino Fuenmayor (Veteran)	20.00	10.00	6.00
277	Rafael Galiz Tello (Veteran)	20.00	10.00	6.00
278	Pantaleon Espinoza	20.00	10.00	6.00
279	Miguel Sanabria (Veteran)	20.00	10.00	6.00
280				
281	Alfonso Carrasquel (Veteran)	40.00	20.00	12.00
282	Luis "Camaleon" Garcia (Veteran)	20.00	10.00	6.00
283	Balbino Inojosa (Veteran)	20.00	10.00	6.00
284	Humberto Popita Leal (Veteran)	20.00	10.00	6.00
285	Manuel Carrasquel (Veteran)	20.00	10.00	6.00
286	Ignacio Florez (Veteran)	20.00	10.00	6.00
287	Oscar Buzo Solorzino (Veteran)	20.00	10.00	6.00
288	Pelayo Chacon (Veteran)	20.00	10.00	6.00
289				
290	Micolas Berbesia (Veteran)	20.00	10.00	6.00
291	Julio Bracho (Veteran)	20.00	10.00	6.00
292	Dionisio Acosta (Veteran)	20.00	10.00	6.00
293	Gualberto Acosta (Veteran)	20.00	10.00	6.00
294	Winston Acosta (Veteran)	20.00	10.00	6.00
295	Jose Manuel Tovar (Veteran)	20.00	10.00	6.00
296	Carrao Bracho (Veteran)	20.00	10.00	6.00
297	Luis Romero Petit (Veteran)	20.00	10.00	6.00
298	Dalmiro Finol (Veteran)	20.00	10.00	6.00
299	Cerveceria Caracas Team Photo	20.00	10.00	6.00
300	Magallanes Campeones Nacionales Team	20.00	10.00	6.00

1972 Venezuelan Baseball Stamps

Utilizing most of the same photos as the 1972 Topps baseball cards, the 242 player stamps in this set feature only Major Leaguers, though with an overrepresentation of Hispanics, rather than the usual mix of U.S. and local talent. Stamps measure 2" x 2-9/16" and feature tombstone-shaped color photos at center, surrounded by a green background. The only printing is the player name, team name (in Spanish) and stamp number, all in black. A white border surrounds the whole. Backs are blank as the stamps were meant to be mounted in an album. Because stamps are seldom seen in higher grade, only a VG price is presented here. Stamps in Good should be valued at 50 percent of the price shown, and stamps grading Fair at 25 percent.

		NM	EX	VG
Complete Set (242):		4,900	1,950	980.00
Common Player:		15.00	6.00	3.00
Album:		150.00	75.00	45.00
1	Vic Davalillo	50.00	20.00	10.00
2	Doug Griffin	15.00	6.00	3.00
3	Rod Carew	150.00	60.00	30.00
4	Joel Horlen	15.00	6.00	3.00
5	Jim Fregosi	15.00	6.00	3.00

		NM	EX	VG
6	Rod Carew	100.00	40.00	20.00
	("en acion" - In Action)			
7	Billy Champion	15.00	6.00	3.00
8	Ron Hansen	15.00	6.00	3.00
9	Bobby Murcer	15.00	6.00	3.00
10	Nellie Briles	15.00	6.00	3.00
11	Fred Patek	15.00	6.00	3.00
12	Mike Epstein	15.00	6.00	3.00
13	Dave Marshall	15.00	6.00	3.00
14	Steve Hargan	15.00	6.00	3.00
15	Duane Josephson	15.00	6.00	3.00
16	Steve Garvey	22.50	9.00	4.50
17	Eddie Fisher	15.00	6.00	3.00
18	Jack Aker	15.00	6.00	3.00
19	Ron Brand	15.00	6.00	3.00
20	Del Rice	15.00	6.00	3.00
21	Ollie Brown	15.00	6.00	3.00
22	Jamie McAndrew	15.00	6.00	3.00
23	Willie Horton	15.00	6.00	3.00
24	Eddie Leon	15.00	6.00	3.00
25	Steve Hovley	15.00	6.00	3.00
26	Moe Drabowsky	15.00	6.00	3.00
27	Dick Selma	15.00	6.00	3.00
28	Jim Lyttle	15.00	6.00	3.00
29	Sal Bando	15.00	6.00	3.00
30	Bill Lee	15.00	6.00	3.00
31	Al Kaline	150.00	60.00	30.00
32	Mike Lum	15.00	6.00	3.00
33	Les Cain	15.00	6.00	3.00
34	Richie Hebner	15.00	6.00	3.00
35	Donn Clendenon	15.00	6.00	3.00
36	Ralph Houk	15.00	6.00	3.00
37	Luis Melendez	15.00	6.00	3.00
38	Jim Hickman	15.00	6.00	3.00
39	Manny Mota	15.00	6.00	3.00
40	Bob Locker	15.00	6.00	3.00
41	Ron Santo	20.00	8.00	4.00
42	Tony Cloninger	15.00	6.00	3.00
43	Joe Ferguson	15.00	6.00	3.00
44	Mike McCormick	15.00	6.00	3.00
45	Bobby Wine	15.00	6.00	3.00
46	Preston Gomez	15.00	6.00	3.00
47	Pat Corrales (In Action)	15.00	6.00	3.00
48	Hector Torres	15.00	6.00	3.00
49	Fritz Peterson	15.00	6.00	3.00
50	Jim Rooker	15.00	6.00	3.00
51	Chris Short	15.00	6.00	3.00
52	Juan Marichal (In Action)	22.50	9.00	4.50
53	Teddy Martinez	15.00	6.00	3.00
54	Ken Aspromonte	15.00	6.00	3.00
55	Bobby Bonds	15.00	6.00	3.00
56	Rich Robertson	15.00	6.00	3.00
57	Nate Colbert (In Action)	15.00	6.00	3.00
58	Jose Pagan (In Action)	15.00	6.00	3.00
59	Curt Blefary (In Action)	15.00	6.00	3.00
60	Bill Mazeroski	100.00	40.00	20.00
61	John Odom	15.00	6.00	3.00
62	George Stone	15.00	6.00	3.00
63	Lew Krausse	15.00	6.00	3.00
64	Bobby Knoop	15.00	6.00	3.00
65	Pete Rose (In Action)	225.00	90.00	45.00
66	Steve Luebber	15.00	6.00	3.00
67	Bill Voss	15.00	6.00	3.00
68	Chico Salmon	15.00	6.00	3.00
69	Ivan Murrell	15.00	6.00	3.00
70	Gil Garrido	15.00	6.00	3.00
71	Terry Crowley	15.00	6.00	3.00
72	Bill Russell	15.00	6.00	3.00
73	Steve Dunning	15.00	6.00	3.00
74	Ray Sadecki (In Action)	15.00	6.00	3.00
75	Al Gallagher (In Action)	15.00	6.00	3.00
76	Cesar Gutierrez	15.00	6.00	3.00
77	John Kennedy	15.00	6.00	3.00
78	Joe Hague	15.00	6.00	3.00
79	Bruce Del Canton	15.00	6.00	3.00
80	Ken Holtzman	15.00	6.00	3.00
81	Rico Carty	15.00	6.00	3.00
82	Roger Repoz	15.00	6.00	3.00
83	Fran Healy	15.00	6.00	3.00
84	Al Gallagher	15.00	6.00	3.00
85	Rich McKinney	15.00	6.00	3.00
86	Lowell Palmer	15.00	6.00	3.00
87	Jose Cardenal	15.00	6.00	3.00
88	Ed Kirkpatrick (In Action)	15.00	6.00	3.00
89	Steve Carlton	150.00	60.00	30.00
90	Gail Hopkins	15.00	6.00	3.00
91	Reggie Smith	15.00	6.00	3.00
92	Denny Riddleberger	15.00	6.00	3.00
93	Don Sutton	60.00	24.00	12.00
94	Bob Moose	15.00	6.00	3.00
95	Joe Decker	15.00	6.00	3.00
96	Bill Wilson	15.00	6.00	3.00
97	Mike Ferraro	15.00	6.00	3.00
98	Jack Hiatt	15.00	6.00	3.00
99	Bill Grabarkewitz	15.00	6.00	3.00
100	Larry Stahl	15.00	6.00	3.00
101	Jim Slaton	15.00	6.00	3.00
102	Jim Wynn	15.00	6.00	3.00
103	Phil Niekro	60.00	24.00	12.00
104	Danny Cater	15.00	6.00	3.00
105	Ray Sadecki	15.00	6.00	3.00
106	Jack Billingham	15.00	6.00	3.00
107	Dave Nelson	15.00	6.00	3.00
108	Rudy May	15.00	6.00	3.00
109	Don Money	15.00	6.00	3.00
110	Diego Segui	15.00	6.00	3.00
111	Jose Pagan	15.00	6.00	3.00
112	John Strohmayer	15.00	6.00	3.00
113	Wade Blasingame	15.00	6.00	3.00
114	Ken Wright	15.00	6.00	3.00
115	Ken Tatum	15.00	6.00	3.00
116	Mike Paul	15.00	6.00	3.00
117	Tom McCraw	15.00	6.00	3.00
118	Bob Gibson	125.00	50.00	25.00
119	Al Santorini	15.00	6.00	3.00
120	Leo Cardenas	15.00	6.00	3.00
121	Jimmy Stewart	15.00	6.00	3.00
122	Willie Crawford	15.00	6.00	3.00

123	Bob Aspromonte	15.00	6.00	3.00
124	Frank Duffy	15.00	6.00	3.00
125	Hal Lanier	15.00	6.00	3.00
126	Nate Colbert	15.00	6.00	3.00
127	Russ Gibson	15.00	6.00	3.00
128	Cesar Geronimo	15.00	6.00	3.00
129	Pat Kelly	15.00	6.00	3.00
130	Horacio Pina	15.00	6.00	3.00
131	Charlie Brinkman	15.00	6.00	3.00
132	Bill Virdon	15.00	6.00	3.00
133	Hal McRae	15.00	6.00	3.00
134	Tony Oliva (In Action)	25.00	10.00	5.00
135	Gonzalo Marquez	15.00	6.00	3.00
136	Willie Montanez	15.00	6.00	3.00
137	Dick Green	15.00	6.00	3.00
138	Jim Ray	15.00	6.00	3.00
139	Denis Menke	15.00	6.00	3.00
140	Fred Kendall	15.00	6.00	3.00
141	Vida Blue	15.00	6.00	3.00
142	Tom Grieve	15.00	6.00	3.00
143	Ed Kirkpatrick (In Action)	15.00	6.00	3.00
144	George Scott	15.00	6.00	3.00
145	Hal Breeden	15.00	6.00	3.00
146	Ken McMullen	15.00	6.00	3.00
147	Jim Perry (In Action)	15.00	6.00	3.00
148	Wayne Granger	15.00	6.00	3.00
149	Mike Hegan	15.00	6.00	3.00
150	Al Oliver	20.00	8.00	4.00
151	Frank Robinson (In Action)	100.00	40.00	20.00
152	Paul Blair	15.00	6.00	3.00
153	Phil Hennigan	15.00	6.00	3.00
154	Ron Stone	15.00	6.00	3.00
155	Gene Michael	15.00	6.00	3.00
156	Jerry McNertney	15.00	6.00	3.00
157	Marcelino Lopez	15.00	6.00	3.00
158	Dave May	15.00	6.00	3.00
159	Jim Hart	15.00	6.00	3.00
160	Joe Coleman	15.00	6.00	3.00
161	Rick Reichardt	15.00	6.00	3.00
162	Ed Brinkman	15.00	6.00	3.00
163	Dick McAuliffe	15.00	6.00	3.00
164	Paul Doyle	15.00	6.00	3.00
165	Terry Forster	15.00	6.00	3.00
166	Steve Hamilton	15.00	6.00	3.00
167	Mike Corkins	15.00	6.00	3.00
168	Dave Concepcion	75.00	30.00	15.00
169	Bill Sudakis	15.00	6.00	3.00
170	Juan Marichal	100.00	40.00	20.00
171	Harmon Killebrew	150.00	60.00	30.00
172	Luis Tiant	20.00	8.00	4.00
173	Ted Uhlaender	15.00	6.00	3.00
174	Tim Foli	15.00	6.00	3.00
175	Luis Aparicio (In Action)	200.00	80.00	40.00
176	Bert Campaneris	15.00	6.00	3.00
177	Charlie Sands	15.00	6.00	3.00
178	Darold Knowles	15.00	6.00	3.00
179	Jerry Koosman	15.00	6.00	3.00
180	Leo Cardenas (In Action)	15.00	6.00	3.00
181	Luis Alvarado	15.00	6.00	3.00
182	Graig Nettles	17.50	7.00	3.50
183	Walter Alston	20.00	8.00	4.00
184	Nolan Ryan	550.00	220.00	110.00
185	Ed Sprague	15.00	6.00	3.00
186	Rich Reese	15.00	6.00	3.00
187	Pete Rose	300.00	120.00	60.00
188	Bernie Allen	15.00	6.00	3.00
189	Lou Piniella	17.50	7.00	3.50
190	Jerry Reuss	15.00	6.00	3.00
191	Bob Pfeil	15.00	6.00	3.00
192	Bob Burda	15.00	6.00	3.00
193	Walt Williams	15.00	6.00	3.00
194	Dusty Baker	17.50	7.00	3.50
195	Rich Morales	15.00	6.00	3.00
196	Bill Stoneman	15.00	6.00	3.00
197	Hal King	15.00	6.00	3.00
198	Julian Javier	15.00	6.00	3.00
199	Dave Mason	15.00	6.00	3.00
200	Bob Veale	15.00	6.00	3.00
201	Jim Beauchamp	15.00	6.00	3.00
202	Ron Santo (In Action)	17.50	7.00	3.50
203	Tom Seaver	150.00	60.00	30.00
204	Jim Merritt	15.00	6.00	3.00
205	Jerry Koosman (In Action)	15.00	6.00	3.00
206	Dick Woodson	15.00	6.00	3.00
207	Wayne Simpson	15.00	6.00	3.00
208	Jose Laboy	15.00	6.00	3.00
209	Sam McDowell	15.00	6.00	3.00
210	Bob Bailey	15.00	6.00	3.00
211	Jim Fairey	15.00	6.00	3.00
212	Felipe Alou	25.00	10.00	5.00
213	Dave Concepcion (In Action)	50.00	20.00	10.00
214	Wilbur Wood (In Action)	15.00	6.00	3.00
215	Enzo Hernandez	15.00	6.00	3.00
216	Ron Reed	15.00	6.00	3.00
217	Stan Bahnsen	15.00	6.00	3.00
218	Ollie Brown (In Action)	15.00	6.00	3.00
219	Pat Jarvis	15.00	6.00	3.00
220	Tim Foli (In Action)	15.00	6.00	3.00
221	Denny McLain	15.00	6.00	3.00
222	Jerry Grote	15.00	6.00	3.00
223	Davey Johnson	15.00	6.00	3.00
224	John Odom (In Action)	15.00	6.00	3.00
225	Paul Casanova	15.00	6.00	3.00
226	George Culver	15.00	6.00	3.00
227	Pat Corrales	15.00	6.00	3.00
228	Jim Kaat	15.00	6.00	3.00
229	Archie Reynolds	15.00	6.00	3.00
230	Frank Reberger	15.00	6.00	3.00
231	Carl Yastrzemski	150.00	60.00	30.00
232	Jim Holt	15.00	6.00	3.00
233	Lenny Randle	15.00	6.00	3.00
234	Doug Griffin (In Action)	15.00	6.00	3.00
235	Doug Rader	15.00	6.00	3.00
236	Jesus Alou	15.00	6.00	3.00
237	Wilbur Wood (In Action)	15.00	6.00	3.00
238	Jim Kaat (In Action)	15.00	6.00	3.00
239	Fritz Peterson (In Action)	15.00	6.00	3.00
240	Dennis Leonard	15.00	6.00	3.00

241	Brooks Robinson	150.00	60.00	30.00
242	Felix Millan	15.00	6.00	3.00

1972 Venezuelan League Stickers

Issued in the winter league season of 1972-73, the Venezuelan League sticker set bears more than a passing similitude to the 1972 Topps baseball cards. The 2-1/2" x 3-1/2" stickers have tombstone-shaped photos framed in multi-colored borders with the team name at top and the player name in an oval cartouche at bottom. The sticker number is in a circle at top-right. Because they were intended to be mounted in an accompanying album, the backs are blank. Because so many of the stickers were once pasted into albums, and due to unfavorable climactic conditions, high-grade examples of Venezuelan stickers from the era are particularly scarce.

		NM	EX	VG
Complete Set (249):		1,500	750.00	450.00
Common Player:		20.00	10.00	6.00
Album:		75.00	40.00	20.00
1	Dave Concepcion	30.00	15.00	9.00
2	Luis Rodriguez	25.00	12.50	7.50
3	Roberto Munoz	25.00	12.50	7.50
4	William Castillo	25.00	12.50	7.50
5	Jose Lopez	25.00	12.50	7.50
6	Armando Chacon	25.00	12.50	7.50
7	Juan Francia	25.00	12.50	7.50
8	Roric Harrison	25.00	12.50	7.50
9	Dave Concepcion, Escalona	30.00	15.00	9.00
10	Enrique Gutierrez	25.00	12.50	7.50
11	Luis Gonzalez	25.00	12.50	7.50
12	Jose Torres	25.00	12.50	7.50
13	William Salazar	25.00	12.50	7.50
14	Everest Contramaestre	25.00	12.50	7.50
15	Jesus Rizales	25.00	12.50	7.50
16	Ramon Velasquez	25.00	12.50	7.50
17	Rafael J. Velasquez	25.00	12.50	7.50
18	Jesus Loreto	25.00	12.50	7.50
19	Orlando Galindo	25.00	12.50	7.50
20	Jose Torres	25.00	12.50	7.50
21	Victor Jimenez	25.00	12.50	7.50
22	Hernan Silva	25.00	12.50	7.50
23	Leroy Stanton	25.00	12.50	7.50
24	Jesus Yanez	25.00	12.50	7.50
25	Orlando Tavares	25.00	12.50	7.50
26	Eddie Baez	25.00	12.50	7.50
27	Jim Frey	30.00	15.00	9.00
28	Eddie Watt	25.00	12.50	7.50
29	Aragua Team Logo	10.00	5.00	3.00
30	Carlos Orea	25.00	12.50	7.50
31	Rod Carew	75.00	37.00	22.00
32	Rod Carew, Enos Cabell	35.00	17.50	10.50
33	George Mitterwald	25.00	12.50	7.50
34	Enos Cabell	25.00	12.50	7.50
35	Eddy Baez	25.00	12.50	7.50
36	Teolindo Acosta	25.00	12.50	7.50
37	Ron Theobald	25.00	12.50	7.50
38	Milt Wilcox	30.00	15.00	9.00
39	Cesar Gutierrez	25.00	12.50	7.50
40	Ed Farmer	25.00	12.50	7.50
41	Dario Chirinos	25.00	12.50	7.50
42	Alberto Cambero	25.00	12.50	7.50
43	Eddy Diaz	25.00	12.50	7.50
44	Graciliano Parra	25.00	12.50	7.50
45	Bob Lee	25.00	12.50	7.50
46	Joe Keough	25.00	12.50	7.50
47	Dario Chirinos, Pablo Torrealba	25.00	12.50	7.50
48	Rafael Alvarez	25.00	12.50	7.50
49	Lucio Celis	25.00	12.50	7.50
50	Jose Martinez	25.00	12.50	7.50
51	Faustino Zabala	25.00	12.50	7.50
52	Jose Herrera	25.00	12.50	7.50
53	Monty Montgomery	25.00	12.50	7.50
54	Al Cowens	25.00	12.50	7.50
55	Lara Team	10.00	5.00	3.00
56	Luis Aparicio	60.00	30.00	18.00
57	Virgilio Mata	25.00	12.50	7.50
58	Franklin Moreno	25.00	12.50	7.50
59	Fidel Garcia	25.00	12.50	7.50
60	Victor Montilla	25.00	12.50	7.50
61	Bobby Mitchell	25.00	12.50	7.50
62	Pablo Torrealba	25.00	12.50	7.50
63	Joe Keough	25.00	12.50	7.50
64	Al Cowens	25.00	12.50	7.50
65	Dwight Evans	35.00	17.50	10.50
66	Rick Henninger	25.00	12.50	7.50
67	Lew Krausse	25.00	12.50	7.50
68	George Manz	25.00	12.50	7.50
69	John Lowenstein	25.00	12.50	7.50
70	Juan Quiroz	25.00	12.50	7.50
71	Sebastian Martinez	25.00	12.50	7.50
72	Claudio Urdaneta	25.00	12.50	7.50

		NM	EX	VG
73	Barry Raziano	25.00	12.50	7.50
74	Luis Aparicio	60.00	30.00	18.00
75	Lara Team Logo	10.00	5.00	3.00
76	Bobby Mitchell	25.00	12.50	7.50
77	Harold Hunter	25.00	12.50	7.50
78	Dick Pole	25.00	12.50	7.50
79	Carlos Davila	25.00	12.50	7.50
80	Enrique Gonzalez	25.00	12.50	7.50
81	Carlos Pascual	25.00	12.50	7.50
82	Edito Arteaga	25.00	12.50	7.50
83	William Fahey	25.00	12.50	7.50
84	Tomas Gonzalez	25.00	12.50	7.50
85	Rigoberto Mendoza	25.00	12.50	7.50
86	Rafael Jimenez	25.00	12.50	7.50
87	Jesus Aristimuno	25.00	12.50	7.50
88	Armando Ortiz	25.00	12.50	7.50
89	Bill Butler	25.00	12.50	7.50
90	Charles Day	25.00	12.50	7.50
91	Miguel Motolongo	25.00	12.50	7.50
92	Kurt Bavacqua (Bevacqua)	25.00	12.50	7.50
93	Esteban Padron	25.00	12.50	7.50
94	Angel Baez	25.00	12.50	7.50
95	Oscar Zamora	25.00	12.50	7.50
96	Manny Sarmiento	25.00	12.50	7.50
97	Nelson Canas	25.00	12.50	7.50
98	Victor Colina	25.00	12.50	7.50
99	Jerry Pirtle	25.00	12.50	7.50
100	Charles Day	25.00	12.50	7.50
101	Miguel Motolongo	25.00	12.50	7.50
102	Magallanes Group Photo	10.00	5.00	3.00
103	Jim Holt	25.00	12.50	7.50
104	Bob Darwin	25.00	12.50	7.50
105	Magallanes Team Logo	10.00	5.00	3.00
106	Oscar Del Busto	25.00	12.50	7.50
107	Jerry Jones	25.00	12.50	7.50
108	Eddie Leon	25.00	12.50	7.50
109	Armando Ortiz	25.00	12.50	7.50
110	Magallanes Team Photo	10.00	5.00	3.00
111	Magallanes Team Photo	10.00	5.00	3.00
112	Bob Darwin (Puzzle)	10.00	5.00	3.00
113	Bob Darwin	25.00	12.50	7.50
114	Rafael Cariel	25.00	12.50	7.50
115	Bob Darwin (Puzzle)	10.00	5.00	3.00
116	Bob Darwin (Puzzle)	10.00	5.00	3.00
117	Orlando Reyes	25.00	12.50	7.50
118	Edito Arteaga	25.00	12.50	7.50
119	Magallanes Roster (Carlos Pascual)	10.00	5.00	3.00
120	National Anthem	10.00	5.00	3.00
121	Barry Lersch	25.00	12.50	7.50
122	Elias Lugo	25.00	12.50	7.50
123	Simon Barreto	25.00	12.50	7.50
124	Manny Trillo	25.00	12.50	7.50
125	Joe Ferguson	25.00	12.50	7.50
126	Wilibaldo Quintana	25.00	12.50	7.50
127	Edgar Urbina	25.00	12.50	7.50
128	Nelson Garcia	25.00	12.50	7.50
129	Arguilio Freites	25.00	12.50	7.50
130	Carlos Rodriguez	25.00	12.50	7.50
131	Ozzie Virgil	25.00	12.50	7.50
132	Caracas Lions Team Logo	10.00	5.00	3.00
133	Virgilio Velasquez	25.00	12.50	7.50
134	Ed Sprague	25.00	12.50	7.50
135	Nelson Garcia	25.00	12.50	7.50
136	Jose Caldera	25.00	12.50	7.50
137	Antonio Armas	30.00	15.00	9.00
138	Dick Lange	25.00	12.50	7.50
139	Luis Sanz	25.00	12.50	7.50
140	Dave Lopez	25.00	12.50	7.50
141	Ulises Urrieta	25.00	12.50	7.50
142	Urbano Lugo	25.00	12.50	7.50
143	Bo Diaz	25.00	12.50	7.50
144	Andres Barrios	25.00	12.50	7.50
145	Victor Boll	25.00	12.50	7.50
146	Antonio Torres	25.00	12.50	7.50
147	Bert Campaneris	30.00	15.00	9.00
148	Carlos Alfonzo	25.00	12.50	7.50
149	Teodoro Obregon	25.00	12.50	7.50
150	Luis Penalver	25.00	12.50	7.50
151	Jose Ramon Jimenez	25.00	12.50	7.50
152	Cesar Tovar	25.00	12.50	7.50
153	Gonzalo Marquez	25.00	12.50	7.50
154	Dick Baney	25.00	12.50	7.50
155	Ed Armbrister	25.00	12.50	7.50
156	Ramon Webster	25.00	12.50	7.50
157	Francisco Navas	25.00	12.50	7.50
158	Hal McRae	25.00	12.50	7.50
159	Victor Davilillo	25.00	12.50	7.50
160	Geoff Zahn	25.00	12.50	7.50
161	Jesus Camacaro	25.00	12.50	7.50
162	Ruiz, Parra	25.00	12.50	7.50
163	Posada, Dick Billings	25.00	12.50	7.50
164	Tom Grieve	25.00	12.50	7.50
165	Tom Grieve	25.00	12.50	7.50
166	Dick Billings	25.00	12.50	7.50
167	Peter Broberg	25.00	12.50	7.50
168	Victor Fainette	25.00	12.50	7.50
169	Cruz Rodriguez	25.00	12.50	7.50
170	Oscar Gamble	25.00	12.50	7.50
171	Olinto Rojas	25.00	12.50	7.50
172	Nelson Paiva	25.00	12.50	7.50
173	Jackie Brown	25.00	12.50	7.50
174	Gustavo Sposito	25.00	12.50	7.50
175	Levy Ochoa	25.00	12.50	7.50
176	Larry Bittner (Biittner)	25.00	12.50	7.50
177	William Kirkpatrick	25.00	12.50	7.50
178	Nevil Romero	25.00	12.50	7.50
179	Eduardo Benitez	25.00	12.50	7.50
180	Heriberto Lemus	25.00	12.50	7.50
181	Toby Harrah	25.00	12.50	7.50
182	Alfonzo Collazo	25.00	12.50	7.50
183	Jesus Reyes	25.00	12.50	7.50
184	Hely Boscan	25.00	12.50	7.50
185	Mike (Mickey) Scott	25.00	12.50	7.50
186	Roberto Bracho	25.00	12.50	7.50
187	Walter William (Williams)	25.00	12.50	7.50
188	Nevil Romero	25.00	12.50	7.50
189	Jose Alfaro	25.00	12.50	7.50
190	Leonel Carrion	25.00	12.50	7.50
191	Jesus Padron	25.00	12.50	7.50
192	Posada, Chico Carrasquel	25.00	12.50	7.50
193	Domingo Barboza	25.00	12.50	7.50
194	Eduardo Benitez	25.00	12.50	7.50
195	Nidio Sirit	25.00	12.50	7.50
196	Jose Carrao Bracho	25.00	12.50	7.50
197	Levi Ochoa	25.00	12.50	7.50
198	Hely Boscan	25.00	12.50	7.50
199	Victor Fainette, Leonel Carrion	25.00	12.50	7.50
200	Luis Rivas	25.00	12.50	7.50
201	Luis Tiant	25.00	12.50	7.50
202	Graciano Ravelo	25.00	12.50	7.50
203	Hector Artiles	25.00	12.50	7.50
204	Enzo Hernandez	25.00	12.50	7.50
205	Remigio Hermoso	25.00	12.50	7.50
206	Hector Brito	25.00	12.50	7.50
207	Victor Patino	25.00	12.50	7.50
208	Romualdo Blanco	25.00	12.50	7.50
209	Antonio Carrera	25.00	12.50	7.50
210	Euclides Camejo	25.00	12.50	7.50
211	Carlos Moreno	25.00	12.50	7.50
212	Oswaldo Blanco	25.00	12.50	7.50
213	Jorge Padron	25.00	12.50	7.50
214	Manuel Garcia	25.00	12.50	7.50
215	La Guaira Group Photo	10.00	5.00	3.00
216	La Guaira Group Photo	10.00	5.00	3.00
217	Jose Salas	25.00	12.50	7.50
218	Luis Sanchez	25.00	12.50	7.50
219	Raul Velarde	25.00	12.50	7.50
220	Al Bumbry	25.00	12.50	7.50
221	Group Photo	10.00	5.00	3.00
222	Ivan Murrell	25.00	12.50	7.50
223	Jose Cardenal	25.00	12.50	7.50
224	Group Photo	10.00	5.00	3.00
225	Group Photo	10.00	5.00	3.00
226	Angel Bravo	25.00	12.50	7.50
227	Tom Murphy	25.00	12.50	7.50
228	Hector Urbano	25.00	12.50	7.50
229	Camilo Pascual	25.00	12.50	7.50
230	Pat Kelly	25.00	12.50	7.50
231	Robert Marcano	25.00	12.50	7.50
232	Paul Casanova	25.00	12.50	7.50
233	Preston Gomez	25.00	12.50	7.50
234	La Guaira Team Logo	10.00	5.00	3.00
235	Ken Forsch	25.00	12.50	7.50
236	Luis Tiant (Puzzle)	10.00	5.00	3.00
237	Luis Tiant (Puzzle)	10.00	5.00	3.00
238	Dionel Durand	25.00	12.50	7.50
239	Luis Tiant (Puzzle)	10.00	5.00	3.00
240	Luis Tiant (Puzzle)	10.00	5.00	3.00
241	Jim Rooker (Puzzle)	10.00	5.00	3.00
242	Jim Rooker (Puzzle)	10.00	5.00	3.00
243	William Parker	25.00	12.50	7.50
244	Jim Rooker (Puzzle)	10.00	5.00	3.00
245	Jim Rooker (Puzzle)	10.00	5.00	3.00
246	Jose Herrera	25.00	12.50	7.50
247	Aurelio Monteagudo	25.00	12.50	7.50
248	Ivan Murrell	25.00	12.50	7.50
249	Roster (Preston Gomez)	10.00	5.00	3.00

1973 Venezuelan League Stickers

Milt Wilcox

These stickers were made for collection in an album and as such are typically found in low grade and/or with evidence of once having been so mounted. Several gaps in the reported checklist require further research. Many former and future Major Leaguers are included in the issue. The basic player stickers have color photos surrounded by a multi-color border with the team name at top and the player name at bottom. Stickers are about 2-1/2" x 3-1/2" and numbered on front. A colorful album to house the set was also issued.

		NM	EX	VG
Common Player:		20.00	10.00	6.00
Album:		75.00	40.00	25.00
1	Orlando Galindo	20.00	10.00	6.00
2	William Castillo	20.00	10.00	6.00
3	Everest Contramaestre	20.00	10.00	6.00
4	Luis Gonzalez	20.00	10.00	6.00
5	Jose Lopez	20.00	10.00	6.00
6	Cesar Orea	20.00	10.00	6.00
7	Luis H. Silva	20.00	10.00	6.00
8	Victor Jimenez	20.00	10.00	6.00
9	David Torres	20.00	10.00	6.00
10	Jose Torres	20.00	10.00	6.00
11	Ramon Velasquez	20.00	10.00	6.00
12	Jesus Avila	20.00	10.00	6.00
13	Carlos Loreto	20.00	10.00	6.00
14	Jesus Padron	20.00	10.00	6.00
15	Don Osborne	20.00	10.00	6.00
16	John Glass	20.00	10.00	6.00
17	Teolindo Acosta	20.00	10.00	6.00
18	Jim Todd	20.00	10.00	6.00
19	Roberto Munoz	20.00	10.00	6.00
20	Pete Lakock (LaCock)	20.00	10.00	6.00
21	Francisco Leandro	20.00	10.00	6.00
22	Jesus Rizales	20.00	10.00	6.00
23	Enos Cabell	25.00	12.50	7.50
24	Adrian Garret (Garrett)	20.00	10.00	6.00
25	Kurt Bavaqua (Bevacqua)	20.00	10.00	6.00
26	Jerry Moses	20.00	10.00	6.00
27	Jim Wiloughby (Willoughby)	20.00	10.00	6.00
28	Joel Youngblood	20.00	10.00	6.00
29	Milt Wilcox	25.00	12.50	7.50
30	Cesar Gutierrez	20.00	10.00	6.00
31	Efrain Urquiola	20.00	10.00	6.00
32	Carlos Pascual	20.00	10.00	6.00
33	Julio Bracho	20.00	10.00	6.00
34	Rafael Velasquez	20.00	10.00	6.00
35	Eddy Baez	20.00	10.00	6.00
36	Daniel Dubuc	20.00	10.00	6.00
37	Angel Leon	20.00	10.00	6.00
38	Angel Vargas	20.00	10.00	6.00
39	Motis Romero	20.00	10.00	6.00
40	Graciliano Parra	20.00	10.00	6.00
41	John Lowenstein	20.00	10.00	6.00
42	Nelson Garcia	20.00	10.00	6.00
43	Richard Burleson	25.00	12.50	7.50
44	Doug DeCinces	35.00	17.50	10.50
45	Eugene Martin	20.00	10.00	6.00
46	Jim Cox	20.00	10.00	6.00
47	Mike Adams	20.00	10.00	6.00
48	Richard Henninger	20.00	10.00	6.00
49	Sebastian Martinez	20.00	10.00	6.00
50	Lucio Celis	20.00	10.00	6.00
51	Alberto Cambero	20.00	10.00	6.00
52	Claudio Urdaneta	20.00	10.00	6.00
53	Victor Montilla	20.00	10.00	6.00
54	Pastor Perez	20.00	10.00	6.00
55	Enrique Gonzalez	20.00	10.00	6.00
56	Andres Barrios	20.00	10.00	6.00
57	Diego Herrera	20.00	10.00	6.00
58	Luis Aparicio	60.00	30.00	18.00
59	Teodoro Obregon	20.00	10.00	6.00
60	Dave Johnson	25.00	12.50	7.50
61	Roger Polanco	20.00	10.00	6.00
62	Ray Miller	20.00	10.00	6.00
63	Craig Caskey	20.00	10.00	6.00
64	David Wallace	20.00	10.00	6.00
65	Lara Team Logo	10.00	5.00	3.00
66	Herbert Hutson	20.00	10.00	6.00
67	Edgar Carusi	20.00	10.00	6.00
68	Luis Aponte	20.00	10.00	6.00
69	Joel Alcala	20.00	10.00	6.00
70	Dario Chirinos	20.00	10.00	6.00
71	Arnaldo Alvarado	20.00	10.00	6.00
72	Jose Bekis	20.00	10.00	6.00
73	Bill Moran	20.00	10.00	6.00
74	Steve McCartney	20.00	10.00	6.00
75	Lara Action	10.00	5.00	3.00
76	Rafael Alvarez	20.00	10.00	6.00
77	Juan Quiroz	20.00	10.00	6.00
78	Jim Rice	125.00	62.00	37.00
79	Ivan Murrel (Murrell)	20.00	10.00	6.00
80	James McKee	20.00	10.00	6.00
81	Rafael Cariel	20.00	10.00	6.00
82	George Theodore	20.00	10.00	6.00
83	Esteban Padron	20.00	10.00	6.00
84	Manuel Gonzalez	20.00	10.00	6.00
85	Edito Arteaga	20.00	10.00	6.00
86	Gus Gil	20.00	10.00	6.00
87	Oswaldo Olivares	20.00	10.00	6.00
88	Nelson Canas	20.00	10.00	6.00
89	Jesus Aristimuno	20.00	10.00	6.00
90	Orlando Reyes	20.00	10.00	6.00
91	Armando Ortiz	20.00	10.00	6.00
92	Gregorio Machado	20.00	10.00	6.00
93	Victor Colina	20.00	10.00	6.00
94	Alexis Ramirez	20.00	10.00	6.00
95	Jose Rios-Chiripa	20.00	10.00	6.00
96	Ed Napoleon	20.00	10.00	6.00
97	Bob Bailor	25.00	12.50	7.50
98	Dave Agustine (Augustine)	20.00	10.00	6.00
99	Bob Darwin	20.00	10.00	6.00
100	Gilberto Marcano	20.00	10.00	6.00
101	Jim Frey	25.00	12.50	7.50
102	Steve Braun	20.00	10.00	6.00
103	Don Hood	20.00	10.00	6.00
104	Mike Reinbach	20.00	10.00	6.00
105	Thomas Dettore	20.00	10.00	6.00
106	Wayne Garland	20.00	10.00	6.00
107	Mark Weens	20.00	10.00	6.00
108	Nelson Paiva	20.00	10.00	6.00
109	Manuel Sarmiento	20.00	10.00	6.00
110	Miguel Motolongo	20.00	10.00	6.00
111	Miguel Navas	20.00	10.00	6.00
112	Angel Baez	20.00	10.00	6.00
113	Raul Ortega	20.00	10.00	6.00
114	Humberto Montero	20.00	10.00	6.00
115	Tomas Gonzalez	20.00	10.00	6.00
116	Ruben Cabrera	20.00	10.00	6.00
117	Flores Bolivar	20.00	10.00	6.00
118	Felix Rodriguez	20.00	10.00	6.00
119	Ali Arape	20.00	10.00	6.00
120	Alexis Heredia	20.00	10.00	6.00
121	Arguilio Freites	20.00	10.00	6.00
122	Alfredo Ortiz	20.00	10.00	6.00
123	Simon Barreto	20.00	10.00	6.00
124	Urbano Lugo	20.00	10.00	6.00
125	Bo Diaz	20.00	10.00	6.00
126	Victor Boll	20.00	10.00	6.00
127	Jose Vinay Caldera	20.00	10.00	6.00
128	Leopoldo Tovar	20.00	10.00	6.00
129	Wilibaldo Quintana	20.00	10.00	6.00
130	Edgar Urbina	20.00	10.00	6.00
131	Ulises Urrieta	20.00	10.00	6.00
132	Antonio Torres	20.00	10.00	6.00
133	Luis Penalver	20.00	10.00	6.00
134	Heriberto Morillo	20.00	10.00	6.00
135	Tony Pacheco	20.00	10.00	6.00
136	Victor Davilillo	20.00	10.00	6.00
137	Jose Martinez	20.00	10.00	6.00

		NM	EX	VG
138	Jacinto Betancourt	20.00	10.00	6.00
139	Antonio Armas	40.00	20.00	12.00
140	Cesar Tovar	20.00	10.00	6.00
141	Jerry Johnson	20.00	10.00	6.00
142	Mike Anderson	20.00	10.00	6.00
143	Gonzalo Marquez	20.00	10.00	6.00
144	Peter Koegel	20.00	10.00	6.00
145	Pat Dobson	20.00	10.00	6.00
146	Craig Robinson	20.00	10.00	6.00
147	Luis Saez	20.00	10.00	6.00
148	Francisco Navas	20.00	10.00	6.00
149	Elias Lugo	20.00	10.00	6.00
150	Pablo Torrealba	20.00	10.00	6.00
151	Tom Grieve	20.00	10.00	6.00
152	Manny Trillo	40.00	20.00	12.00
153	Ed Sprague	20.00	10.00	6.00
154	Virgilio Velasquez	20.00	10.00	6.00
155	Dave Hamilton	20.00	10.00	6.00
156	Rafael Jimenez	20.00	10.00	6.00
157	Ubaldo Heredia	20.00	10.00	6.00
158	Rich Dempsey	30.00	15.00	9.00
159	Bill Parson (Parsons)	20.00	10.00	6.00
160	Caracas Leones	10.00	5.00	3.00
161	Gene Garber	25.00	12.50	7.50
162	Frank White	35.00	17.50	10.50
163	John Buck Martinez	20.00	10.00	6.00
164	Manuel Garcia	20.00	10.00	6.00
165	Jesus Padron	20.00	10.00	6.00
166	Oscar Gamble	25.00	12.50	7.50
167	Nelson Castellanos	20.00	10.00	6.00
168	Leo Posada	20.00	10.00	6.00
169	Eduardo Benitez	20.00	10.00	6.00
170	Luis Rivas	20.00	10.00	6.00
171	Alfonso Collazo	20.00	10.00	6.00
172	Levy Ochoa	20.00	10.00	6.00
173	Heriberto Lemus	20.00	10.00	6.00
174	Domingo Barboza	20.00	10.00	6.00
175	Jesus Reyes Barrios	20.00	10.00	6.00
176	Inal Fainete	20.00	10.00	6.00
177	Nidio Sirit	20.00	10.00	6.00
178	Nelson Paiva	20.00	10.00	6.00
179	Alfonso Carrasquel	35.00	17.50	10.50
180	Heli Boscan	20.00	10.00	6.00
181	Leonel Carrion	20.00	10.00	6.00
182	Jose Bracho	20.00	10.00	6.00
183	Gustavo Sposito	20.00	10.00	6.00
184	Iran Paz	20.00	10.00	6.00
185	Rich Reese	20.00	10.00	6.00
186	Al Cowans (Cowens)	25.00	12.50	7.50
187	Zulio Group Photo	10.00	5.00	3.00
188	Leo Posada, Alfonso Carrasquel	15.00	7.50	4.50
189	Octavio Rojas	20.00	10.00	6.00
190	Orlando Reyes	20.00	10.00	6.00
191	Mickey Scott	20.00	10.00	6.00
192	Harold King	20.00	10.00	6.00
193	Eduardo Acosta	20.00	10.00	6.00
194	Carlos Alfonso	20.00	10.00	6.00
195	Jose Lopez	20.00	10.00	6.00
196	Jerry Martin	20.00	10.00	6.00
197	Craig Kusick	20.00	10.00	6.00
198	Charles Murray	20.00	10.00	6.00
199	Alexis Corro	20.00	10.00	6.00
200	Jose Luis Alfaro	20.00	10.00	6.00
201	Juan Fco. Monasterio	20.00	10.00	6.00
202	Oscar Zamora	20.00	10.00	6.00
203	Ramon Moreno	20.00	10.00	6.00
204	Carlos Castillo	20.00	10.00	6.00
205	Ken Forsch	20.00	10.00	6.00
206	Leroy Stanton	20.00	10.00	6.00
207	Nevil Romero	20.00	10.00	6.00
208	Romualdo Blanco	20.00	10.00	6.00
209	Remigio Hermoso	20.00	10.00	6.00
210	Paul Casanova	20.00	10.00	6.00
211	Oswaldo Blanco	20.00	10.00	6.00
212	Oswaldo Troconis	20.00	10.00	6.00
213	Antonio Pipo Correa	20.00	10.00	6.00
214	Euclides Camejo	20.00	10.00	6.00
215	Dionel Duran	20.00	10.00	6.00
216	Hector Brito	20.00	10.00	6.00
217	Reinaldo Cordeiro	20.00	10.00	6.00
218	Jose Herrera	20.00	10.00	6.00
219	Hector Urbano	20.00	10.00	6.00
220	Jose Salas	20.00	10.00	6.00
221	Robert Marcano	20.00	10.00	6.00
222	Enzo Hernandez	20.00	10.00	6.00
223	Angel Bravo	20.00	10.00	6.00
224	Tomas Liscano	20.00	10.00	6.00
225	James Granford	20.00	10.00	6.00
226	Luis Salazar	20.00	10.00	6.00
227	Carlos Moreno	20.00	10.00	6.00
228	Manuel Malave	20.00	10.00	6.00
229	Al Bumbry	25.00	12.50	7.50
230	Luis Sanchez	20.00	10.00	6.00
231	Graziano Ravelo	20.00	10.00	6.00
232	La Guaira Tiburones Logo	10.00	5.00	3.00
233	John Jetter (Jeter)	20.00	10.00	6.00
234	Unknown			
235	Orlando Martinez	20.00	10.00	6.00
236	Tom Griffin	20.00	10.00	6.00
237	Lee Pitlock	20.00	10.00	6.00
238	Ray Burry	20.00	10.00	6.00
239	Preston Gomez	20.00	10.00	6.00
240	Aurelio Monteagudo	20.00	10.00	6.00
241	Carvajal/Bat Boy	20.00	10.00	6.00
242-249	Unknown			
250	Eduardo Benitez (a-t)	20.00	10.00	6.00
251	Ted (Tom) Heintzelman (b-t)	20.00	10.00	6.00
252	Ossie Virgil (c-t)	25.00	12.50	7.50
253	Alan Closter (d-t)	20.00	10.00	6.00
254	Carlos Avila (e-t)	20.00	10.00	6.00
255	David Concepcion (g-t)	40.00	20.00	12.00
256	Enrique Colina (h-t)	20.00	10.00	6.00
257	Damaso Blanco (a-n)	20.00	10.00	6.00
258	George Manz (a-c)	20.00	10.00	6.00
259	Peter MacKanin (b-c)	20.00	10.00	6.00
260	Neldy Castillo (c-c)	20.00	10.00	6.00
261	Leovanny Baez (a-z)	20.00	10.00	6.00
262	Mike Easler (b-z)	25.00	12.50	7.50
263	Peter Broberg (c-z)	20.00	10.00	6.00
264	Reggie Cleveland (d-z)	20.00	10.00	6.00
265	Stan Perzanowsky (Perzanowski) (e-z)	20.00	10.00	6.00
266	Jerry Terrel (Terrell) (f-z)	20.00	10.00	6.00
267	Toby Harrah (h-z)	30.00	15.00	9.00
268	Franklyn Moreno (y-z)	20.00	10.00	6.00
269-275	Unknown			

1974 Venezuelan League Stickers

JOEL YOUNGBLOOD — OUTFIELD TIGRES

The 1974-75 winter league set of Venezuelan League stickers is a dead ringer for the 1968 Topps baseball cards. About 2-3/8" x 3-3/16", the stickers have photos framed in orange-mottled borders. The team name and position are in a circle at bottom, along with the player name in two colors. Because they were intended to be mounted in an accompanying album, the backs are blank. Because so many of the stickers were once pasted into albums, and due to unfavorable climactic conditions, high-grade examples of Venezuelan stickers from the era are particularly scarce.

		NM	EX	VG
Complete Set (275):		1,500	750.00	450.00
Common Player:		20.00	10.00	6.00
Album:		75.00	40.00	25.00
1	Arague Team Photo	10.00	5.00	3.00
2	Aragua Team Photo	10.00	5.00	3.00
3	Aragua Team Logo	10.00	5.00	3.00
4	Dave Concepcion	40.00	20.00	12.00
5	Ramon Velazquez	20.00	10.00	6.00
6	Carlos Orea	20.00	10.00	6.00
7	Francisco Leandro	20.00	10.00	6.00
8	Angel Hernandez	20.00	10.00	6.00
9	Armando Ortiz	20.00	10.00	6.00
10	Carlos Pascual	20.00	10.00	6.00
11	Argua Action	10.00	5.00	3.00
12	Milton Wilcox	25.00	12.50	7.50
13	Don Hood	20.00	10.00	6.00
14	Timothy Hosley	20.00	10.00	6.00
15	Teolindo Acosta	20.00	10.00	6.00
16	William Castillo	20.00	10.00	6.00
17	Aragua Action	10.00	5.00	3.00
18	Jesus Padron	20.00	10.00	6.00
19	Enos Cabell	25.00	12.50	7.50
20	Luis Silva	20.00	10.00	6.00
21	Aragua Action	10.00	5.00	3.00
22	Aragua Action	10.00	5.00	3.00
23	Joel Youngblood	25.00	12.50	7.50
24	Angel Vargas	20.00	10.00	6.00
25	Carlos Avila	20.00	10.00	6.00
26	Phil Gardner (Garner)	25.00	12.50	7.50
27	James Willoughby	20.00	10.00	6.00
28	Daniel Dubuc	20.00	10.00	6.00
29	Pancho	20.00	10.00	6.00
30	Aragua Action	10.00	5.00	3.00
31	Eastwick Rawlings (Rawly Eastwick)	25.00	12.50	7.50
32	David Torres	20.00	10.00	6.00
33	Robert Flynn	20.00	10.00	6.00
34	Duane Kuiper	25.00	12.50	7.50
35	Jesus Avila	20.00	10.00	6.00
36	Aragua Action	10.00	5.00	3.00
37	Aragua Action	10.00	5.00	3.00
38	Roberto Munoz	20.00	10.00	6.00
39	Eduardo Benitez	20.00	10.00	6.00
40	Aragua Action	10.00	5.00	3.00
41	Adrian Garret (Garrett)	20.00	10.00	6.00
42	Julio Bracho	20.00	10.00	6.00
43	Juan Quiroz	20.00	10.00	6.00
44	Angel Leon	20.00	10.00	6.00
45	Ossie Virgil	30.00	15.00	9.00
46	Lara Team Photo	10.00	5.00	3.00
47	Lara Team Photo	10.00	5.00	3.00
48	Lara Team Logo	10.00	5.00	3.00
49	Andres Barrios	20.00	10.00	6.00
50	Pastor Perez	20.00	10.00	6.00
51	Peter Koegel	20.00	10.00	6.00
52	Lara Action	10.00	5.00	3.00
53	Lowell Palmer	20.00	10.00	6.00
54	Alberto Cambero	20.00	10.00	6.00
55	Frank Snook	20.00	10.00	6.00
56	Steve McCartney	20.00	10.00	6.00
57	Lara Action	10.00	5.00	3.00
58	Dario Chirinos	20.00	10.00	6.00
59	Lara Action	10.00	5.00	3.00
60	Jim Cox	20.00	10.00	6.00
61	Terry Whitfield	20.00	10.00	6.00
62	Nelson Garcia	20.00	10.00	6.00
63	Lara Action	10.00	5.00	3.00
64	Sebastian Martinez	20.00	10.00	6.00
65	Lara Action	10.00	5.00	3.00
66	Rick Sawyer	20.00	10.00	6.00
67	Enrique Gonzalez	20.00	10.00	6.00
68	Tippy Martinez	30.00	15.00	9.00
69	Rafael Jimenez	20.00	10.00	6.00
70	Lara Action	10.00	5.00	3.00
71	Larvell Blanks	20.00	10.00	6.00
72	Franklin Tua	20.00	10.00	6.00
73	Craig Skok	20.00	10.00	6.00
74	Basilio Alvarado	20.00	10.00	6.00
75	Blas Arriechi	20.00	10.00	6.00
76	Dave Pagan	20.00	10.00	6.00
77	Roger Polanco	20.00	10.00	6.00
78	John Lowenstein	20.00	10.00	6.00
79	Francisco Leandro	20.00	10.00	6.00
80	Lucio Celis	20.00	10.00	6.00
81	Lara Action	10.00	5.00	3.00
82	Teodoro Obregon	20.00	10.00	6.00
83	Luis Aponte	20.00	10.00	6.00
84	Roberto Cox	40.00	20.00	12.00
85	Magallanes Team Photo	10.00	5.00	3.00
86	Magallanes Team Photo	10.00	5.00	3.00
87	Magallanes Team Logo	10.00	5.00	3.00
88	Oswaldo Olivares	20.00	10.00	6.00
89	Bob Bailor	25.00	12.50	7.50
90	Ali Arape	20.00	10.00	6.00
91	Jesus Aristimuno	20.00	10.00	6.00
92	Bob Andrews	20.00	10.00	6.00
93	Magallanes Action	10.00	5.00	3.00
94	Rick Stelmaszek	20.00	10.00	6.00
95	Damaso Blanco	20.00	10.00	6.00
96	Graciliano Parra	20.00	10.00	6.00
97	Merv Rettemund (Rettenmund)	25.00	12.50	7.50
98	Don Baylor	45.00	22.00	13.50
99	William Lister	20.00	10.00	6.00
100	Magallanes Action	10.00	5.00	3.00
101	Gregorio Machado	20.00	10.00	6.00
102	Doug Bair	20.00	10.00	6.00
103	Gilberto Marcano	20.00	10.00	6.00
104	Magallanes Action	10.00	5.00	3.00
105	Jim Sadowski	20.00	10.00	6.00
106	Miguel Nava	20.00	10.00	6.00
107	Ken (Kent) Tekulve	40.00	20.00	12.00
108	Wayne Garland	20.00	10.00	6.00
109	Magallanes Action	10.00	5.00	3.00
110	Alexis Ramirez	20.00	10.00	6.00
111	Dave Parker	60.00	30.00	18.00
112	Bob Veale	20.00	10.00	6.00
113	Manuel Sarmiento	20.00	10.00	6.00
114	Alberto Pedroza	20.00	10.00	6.00
115	Ruben Cabrera	20.00	10.00	6.00
116	Felix Rodriguez	20.00	10.00	6.00
117	Magallanes Action	10.00	5.00	3.00
118	Humberto Montero	20.00	10.00	6.00
119	Manuel Gonzalez	20.00	10.00	6.00
120	D. Flores	20.00	10.00	6.00
121	Jim Holt	20.00	10.00	6.00
122	Rafael Cariel	20.00	10.00	6.00
123	Magallanes Action	10.00	5.00	3.00
124	Deisi Bolivar	20.00	10.00	6.00
125	Edito Arteaga	20.00	10.00	6.00
126	Gustavo Gil	20.00	10.00	6.00
127	Larry Demeris (Demery)	20.00	10.00	6.00
128	Nelson Paiva	20.00	10.00	6.00
129	Steve Demeter	20.00	10.00	6.00
130	Caracas Leones Team Photo	10.00	5.00	3.00
131	Caracas Leones Team Photo	10.00	5.00	3.00
132	Caracas Leones Team Logo	10.00	5.00	3.00
133	Antonio Armas	40.00	20.00	12.00
134	Richard Dempsey	40.00	20.00	12.00
135	Toribio Garboza	20.00	10.00	6.00
136	Neldy Castillo	20.00	10.00	6.00
137	Ubaldo Heredia	20.00	10.00	6.00
138	Caracas Action	10.00	5.00	3.00
139	Jesus Marcano Trillo	40.00	20.00	12.00
140	Victor Albury	20.00	10.00	6.00
141	Uknown			
142	Peter Broberg	20.00	10.00	6.00
143	Alfredo Ortiz	20.00	10.00	6.00
144	Leopoldo Tovar	20.00	10.00	6.00
145	Caracas Action	10.00	5.00	3.00
146	Tom Buskey	20.00	10.00	6.00
147	Virgilio Velasquez	20.00	10.00	6.00
148	Cesar Tovar	20.00	10.00	6.00
149	Caracas Stadium	10.00	5.00	3.00
150	Don Stanhouse	20.00	10.00	6.00
151	Edgar Urbina	20.00	10.00	6.00
152	Pablo Torrealba	20.00	10.00	6.00
153	Jack Heidemann	20.00	10.00	6.00
154	Caracas Action	10.00	5.00	3.00
155	Luis Sanz	20.00	10.00	6.00
156	Gonzalo Marquez	20.00	10.00	6.00
157	Victor Davililllo	20.00	10.00	6.00
158	Bo Diaz	20.00	10.00	6.00
159	Caracas Action	10.00	5.00	3.00
160	Bill Butler	20.00	10.00	6.00
161	Elias Lugo	20.00	10.00	6.00
162	Tom Grieve	20.00	10.00	6.00
163	Caracas Action	10.00	5.00	3.00
164	Antonio Torres	20.00	10.00	6.00
165	Luis Penalver	20.00	10.00	6.00
166	Lenny Randle	20.00	10.00	6.00
167	Juan Gonzalez	20.00	10.00	6.00
168	Chuck Dobson	20.00	10.00	6.00
169	Urbano Lugo	20.00	10.00	6.00
170	Francisco Navas	20.00	10.00	6.00
171	Caracas Action	10.00	5.00	3.00
172	Jacinto Betancourt	20.00	10.00	6.00
173	Camilo Pascual	30.00	15.00	9.00
174	Frank White	30.00	15.00	9.00
175	Urbano Quintana	20.00	10.00	6.00
176	Jose Caldera	20.00	10.00	6.00
177	Caracas Action	10.00	5.00	3.00
178	Ulises Urrieta	20.00	10.00	6.00
179	Tomas Pacheco	20.00	10.00	6.00
180	La Guaira Tiburones Team Photo	10.00	5.00	3.00

		NM	EX	VG
181	La Guaira Tiburones Team Photo	10.00	5.00	3.00
182	La Guaira Tiburones Team Photo	10.00	5.00	3.00
183	Angel Bravo	20.00	10.00	6.00
184	Al Bumbry	25.00	12.50	7.50
185	Aurelio Monteagudo	20.00	10.00	6.00
186	Carlos Moreno	20.00	10.00	6.00
187	La Guaira Action	10.00	5.00	3.00
188	Hector Brito	20.00	10.00	6.00
189	Leroy Stanton	20.00	10.00	6.00
190	Romo Blanco	20.00	10.00	6.00
191	Marquina para Gorrias	10.00	5.00	3.00
192	Luis M. Sanchez	20.00	10.00	6.00
193	La Guaira Action	10.00	5.00	3.00
194	Jose Herrera	20.00	10.00	6.00
195	Victor Colina	20.00	10.00	6.00
196	Tiburones Team Bus	10.00	5.00	3.00
197	Jose Salas	20.00	10.00	6.00
198	La Guaira Action	10.00	5.00	3.00
199	Enzo Hernandez	20.00	10.00	6.00
200	Tomas Liscano	20.00	10.00	6.00
201	Paul Casanova	20.00	10.00	6.00
202	Machine	10.00	5.00	3.00
203	Graziano Ravelo	20.00	10.00	6.00
204	Ice Maker	10.00	5.00	3.00
205	Roland (Rowland) Office	20.00	10.00	6.00
206	Clubhouse	10.00	5.00	3.00
207	La Guaira Action	10.00	5.00	3.00
208	Dusty Baker	45.00	22.00	13.50
209	Replacements	10.00	5.00	3.00
210	Roric Harrison	20.00	10.00	6.00
211	Tom House	20.00	10.00	6.00
212	Jesus Aquino	20.00	10.00	6.00
213	Machine	10.00	5.00	3.00
214	La Guaira Action	10.00	5.00	3.00
215	Juan Monasterios	20.00	10.00	6.00
216	Angel Remigio Hermoso	20.00	10.00	6.00
217	Machine	10.00	5.00	3.00
218	Oswaldo Blanco	20.00	10.00	6.00
219	Infrared Light	10.00	5.00	3.00
220	Roberto Marcano	20.00	10.00	6.00
221	La Guaira Action	10.00	5.00	3.00
222	Jose Carvajal	20.00	10.00	6.00
223	Victor Patino	20.00	10.00	6.00
224	James Bird	20.00	10.00	6.00
225	La Guaira Action	10.00	5.00	3.00
226	Roland Sonny Jackson	25.00	12.50	7.50
227	Oscar Zamora	20.00	10.00	6.00
228	Antonio Pipo Correa	20.00	10.00	6.00
229	Manuel Malave	20.00	10.00	6.00
230	Nap Reyes	20.00	10.00	6.00
231	Zulia Aguilas Team Photo	10.00	5.00	3.00
232	Zluia Aguilas Team Photo	10.00	5.00	3.00
233	Zulia Aguilas Team Logo	10.00	5.00	3.00
234	Levy Ochoa	20.00	10.00	6.00
235	Billy Moran	20.00	10.00	6.00
236	Iran Paz	20.00	10.00	6.00
237	Alexis Corro	20.00	10.00	6.00
238	Zulia Action	10.00	5.00	3.00
239	Gus Sposito	20.00	10.00	6.00
240	Orlando Reyes	20.00	10.00	6.00
241	Carlos Alonso	20.00	10.00	6.00
242	Craig Kusick	20.00	10.00	6.00
243	Zulia Action	10.00	5.00	3.00
244	Domingo Barboza	20.00	10.00	6.00
245	Leonel Carrion	20.00	10.00	6.00
246	Jose Lopez	20.00	10.00	6.00
247	Bill Kirkpatrick	20.00	10.00	6.00
248	Alfonso Carrasquel	20.00	10.00	6.00
249	Richard Billings	20.00	10.00	6.00
250	Alfonzo Collazo	20.00	10.00	6.00
251	Orlando Ramirez	20.00	10.00	6.00
252	Ralph (Mickey) Scott	20.00	10.00	6.00
253	Luis Aparicio	60.00	30.00	18.00
254	Julio Bracho	20.00	10.00	6.00
255	Zulia Action	10.00	5.00	3.00
256	B. Jones	20.00	10.00	6.00
257	Heli Ramon Boscan	20.00	10.00	6.00
258	David Clyde	20.00	10.00	6.00
259	Cesar Gutierrez	20.00	10.00	6.00
260	Bob Randall	20.00	10.00	6.00
261	Jesus Reyes Barrios	20.00	10.00	6.00
262	Jose L. Alfaro	20.00	10.00	6.00
263	Claudio Urdaneta	20.00	10.00	6.00
264	Zulia Action	10.00	5.00	3.00
265	James Sundberg	30.00	15.00	9.00
266	Simon Barreto	20.00	10.00	6.00
267	Anthony Scott	20.00	10.00	6.00
268	Nidio Sirit	20.00	10.00	6.00
269	Zulia Action	10.00	5.00	3.00
270	Zulia Action	10.00	5.00	3.00
271	Leovanni Baez	20.00	10.00	6.00
272	Jefrey (Jeffrey) Terpko	20.00	10.00	6.00
273	Stan Perzanowski	20.00	10.00	6.00
274	Mike Easler	25.00	12.50	7.50
275	Jackie Moore	20.00	10.00	6.00

1976 Venezuelan League Stickers

TIGRES
34 TERRY WHITFIELD
Outfielder

The basic player stickers utilize a design very similar to Topps' 1975 baseball cards, with player photos surrounded by a colorful border with the team name in large outline letters at top and the position is a baseball at bottom. Stickers are 2-3/8" x 3-3/16" and numbered on front. Like other Latin issues of the era, they are seldom available in high grade due to their intended useage and climactic conditions. Most of the stickers after #217 are specialty pieces with action photos, non-player subjects, multiple players, etc. A colorful album to house the set was also issued.

		NM	EX	VG
Complete Set (330):		2,000	1,000	600.00
Common Player:		20.00	10.00	6.00
Album:		75.00	40.00	25.00
1	Ossie Virgil	30.00	15.00	9.00
2	Patato Pascual	20.00	10.00	6.00
3	Jesus Avila	20.00	10.00	6.00
4	Raul Ortega	20.00	10.00	6.00
5	Dave Concepcion	40.00	20.00	12.00
6	Jesus Araujo	20.00	10.00	6.00
7	Preston Hanna	20.00	10.00	6.00
8	Victor Davilillo	20.00	10.00	6.00
9	Jesus Padron	20.00	10.00	6.00
10	Joseph Sdeb (Zdeb)	20.00	10.00	6.00
11	Alfredo Ortiz	20.00	10.00	6.00
12	Teolindo Acosta	20.00	10.00	6.00
13	Cesar Tovar	20.00	10.00	6.00
14	Craig Kusick	20.00	10.00	6.00
15	Angel Hernandez	20.00	10.00	6.00
16	Roberto Munoz	20.00	10.00	6.00
17	Fred Andrews	20.00	10.00	6.00
18	Rafael Alvarez	20.00	10.00	6.00
19	Luis Aparicio	50.00	25.00	15.00
20	Jeffrey Newman	20.00	10.00	6.00
21	Tommy Sant (Sandt)	20.00	10.00	6.00
22	Simon Barreto	20.00	10.00	6.00
23	Willie Norwood	20.00	10.00	6.00
24	Juan Quiroz	20.00	10.00	6.00
25	Douglas Capilla	20.00	10.00	6.00
26	William Butler	20.00	10.00	6.00
27	William Castillo	20.00	10.00	6.00
28	Robert Maneely	20.00	10.00	6.00
29	Peter Bromberg (Broberg)	20.00	10.00	6.00
30	Jesse Jefferson	20.00	10.00	6.00
31	Carlos Avila	20.00	10.00	6.00
32	Aragua Action	10.00	5.00	3.00
33	Aragua Action	10.00	5.00	3.00
34	Terry Whitfield	20.00	10.00	6.00
35	Aragua Action	10.00	5.00	3.00
36	Gary Lance	20.00	10.00	6.00
37	Robert Cox	40.00	20.00	12.00
38	Leo Posada	20.00	10.00	6.00
39	Lucio Celis	20.00	10.00	6.00
40	Enrique Gonzalez	20.00	10.00	6.00
41	Jose Musiu Lopez	20.00	10.00	6.00
42	Jose Sandoval	20.00	10.00	6.00
43	Victor Correll	20.00	10.00	6.00
44	Pedro Lobaton	20.00	10.00	6.00
45	Jim Norris	20.00	10.00	6.00
46	Luis Aponte	20.00	10.00	6.00
47	Orlando Gonzalez	20.00	10.00	6.00
48	Edguardo Benitez	20.00	10.00	6.00
49	George Zeber	20.00	10.00	6.00
50	Carlos Rodriguez	20.00	10.00	6.00
51	Graig (Craig) Robinson	20.00	10.00	6.00
52	Hernan Silva	20.00	10.00	6.00
53	Bob Oliver	20.00	10.00	6.00
54	Jose Herrera	20.00	10.00	6.00
55	Pete Mackanin	20.00	10.00	6.00
56	Roger Polanco	20.00	10.00	6.00
57	Lara Stadium	10.00	5.00	3.00
58	Arnaldo Alvarado	20.00	10.00	6.00
59	Ron Selak	20.00	10.00	6.00
60	Nelson Canas	20.00	10.00	6.00
61	John Sutton	20.00	10.00	6.00
62	Nelson Garcia	20.00	10.00	6.00
63	Victor Patino	20.00	10.00	6.00
64	Francisco Navas	20.00	10.00	6.00
65	Robert Polinsky	20.00	10.00	6.00
66	Franklin Tua	20.00	10.00	6.00
67	Oscar Zamora	20.00	10.00	6.00
68	David Torres	20.00	10.00	6.00
69	Eddie Baez	20.00	10.00	6.00
70	Walter Williams	25.00	12.50	7.50
71	Cloyd Boyer	25.00	12.50	7.50
72	Carl (Garth?) lorg	20.00	10.00	6.00
73	Pat Corrales	20.00	10.00	6.00
74	Alfonso Carrasquel	20.00	10.00	6.00
75	Antonio Torres	20.00	10.00	6.00
76	Camilo Pascual	30.00	15.00	9.00
77	Antonio Armas	40.00	20.00	12.00
78	Baudilio Diaz	20.00	10.00	6.00
79	Gary Beare	20.00	10.00	6.00
80	Steve Barr	20.00	10.00	6.00
81	Toribio Garboza	20.00	10.00	6.00
82	Mike Bassik (Bacsik)	20.00	10.00	6.00
83	Diego Segui	20.00	10.00	6.00
84	Jack Bastable	20.00	10.00	6.00
85	Ubaldo Heredia	20.00	10.00	6.00
86	Warren Cromartie	25.00	12.50	7.50
87	Elias Lugo	20.00	10.00	6.00
88	Mike (Mick) Kelleher	20.00	10.00	6.00
89	Marcano Trillo	40.00	20.00	12.00
90	Lenny Randle	20.00	10.00	6.00
91	Gonzalo Marquez	20.00	10.00	6.00
92	Jim Sadowski	20.00	10.00	6.00
93	Len Barker	25.00	12.50	7.50
94	Willi Quintana	20.00	10.00	6.00
95	Pablo Torrealba	20.00	10.00	6.00
96	Jim Hughes	20.00	10.00	6.00
97	Jose V. Caldera	20.00	10.00	6.00
98	Angel Vargas	20.00	10.00	6.00
99	Juan Gonzalez	20.00	10.00	6.00
100	Ulises Urrieta	20.00	10.00	6.00
101	Flores Bolivar	20.00	10.00	6.00

		NM	EX	VG
102	Robert Bowling	20.00	10.00	6.00
103	Rick Bladt	20.00	10.00	6.00
104	Luis Turner	20.00	10.00	6.00
105	Neldy Castillo	20.00	10.00	6.00
106	Adrian Garret (Garrett)	20.00	10.00	6.00
107	Bob Davis	20.00	10.00	6.00
108	La Guaira Action	10.00	5.00	3.00
109	Pompeyo Davalillo	20.00	10.00	6.00
110	Graciano Ravelo	20.00	10.00	6.00
111	Luis Lunar	20.00	10.00	6.00
112	Lester Morales	20.00	10.00	6.00
113	Enzo Hernandez	20.00	10.00	6.00
114	Aurelio Monteagudo	20.00	10.00	6.00
115	Angel Bravo	20.00	10.00	6.00
116	Carlos Moreno	20.00	10.00	6.00
117	Jose Cardenal	25.00	12.50	7.50
118	Rupert (Ruppert) Jones	20.00	10.00	6.00
119	Romo Blanco	20.00	10.00	6.00
120	Milton Ramirez	20.00	10.00	6.00
121	Antonio Correa	20.00	10.00	6.00
122	Clarence Gaston	25.00	12.50	7.50
123	Steve Lubber (Luebber)	20.00	10.00	6.00
124	Edwin Verhelst	20.00	10.00	6.00
125	Robert Johnson	20.00	10.00	6.00
126	Earl Bass	20.00	10.00	6.00
127	Jose Salas	20.00	10.00	6.00
128	Oswaldo Blanco	20.00	10.00	6.00
129	Steve Staag (Staggs)	20.00	10.00	6.00
130	Steve Patchin	20.00	10.00	6.00
131	Mike Kekish (Kekich)	20.00	10.00	6.00
132	Oswaldo Troconis	20.00	10.00	6.00
133	Dave May	20.00	10.00	6.00
134	Luis Salazar	20.00	10.00	6.00
135	Larry Gura	20.00	10.00	6.00
136	Rich Dauer	20.00	10.00	6.00
137	Pastor Perez	20.00	10.00	6.00
138	Paul Siebert	20.00	10.00	6.00
139	Luis M. Sanchez	20.00	10.00	6.00
140	Victor Colina	20.00	10.00	6.00
141	Adrian Devine	20.00	10.00	6.00
142	Robert Marcano	20.00	10.00	6.00
143	Juan Berenger (Berenguer)	25.00	12.50	7.50
144	Juan Monasterio	20.00	10.00	6.00
145	Donald Leppert	20.00	10.00	6.00
146	Gregorio Machado	20.00	10.00	6.00
147	Manuel Gonzalez	20.00	10.00	6.00
148	Wayne Granger	20.00	10.00	6.00
149	Remigio Hermoso	20.00	10.00	6.00
150	Rafael Cariel	20.00	10.00	6.00
151	Steve Dillard	20.00	10.00	6.00
152	Mitchell Page	20.00	10.00	6.00
153	Alexis Ramirez, Felix Rodriguez	15.00	7.50	4.50
154	Gary Wood	20.00	10.00	6.00
155	Ali Arape	20.00	10.00	6.00
156	Chris Batton	20.00	10.00	6.00
157	Gustavo Gil	20.00	10.00	6.00
158	Craig Reynolds	20.00	10.00	6.00
159	Jesus Aristimuno	20.00	10.00	6.00
160	Miguel Barreto	20.00	10.00	6.00
161	Alfonso Collazo	20.00	10.00	6.00
162	Steve Nicosia	20.00	10.00	6.00
163	Oswaldo Olivares	20.00	10.00	6.00
164	Robert Galasso	20.00	10.00	6.00
165	Alexis Ramirez	20.00	10.00	6.00
166	Craig Mitchell	20.00	10.00	6.00
167	Nelson Paiva	20.00	10.00	6.00
168	Ken Macha	20.00	10.00	6.00
169	Ruben Cabrera	20.00	10.00	6.00
170	Paul Reuschell (Reuschel)	20.00	10.00	6.00
171	Edito Arteaga	20.00	10.00	6.00
172	Olinto Rojas	20.00	10.00	6.00
173	Magallanes Action	10.00	5.00	3.00
174	Manny Sarmiento	20.00	10.00	6.00
175	Billy Moran	20.00	10.00	6.00
176	Eddie Watt	20.00	10.00	6.00
177	Michael Willis	20.00	10.00	6.00
178	Felix Rodriguez	20.00	10.00	6.00
179	James Easterly	20.00	10.00	6.00
180	Dave Parker	40.00	20.00	12.00
181	Luis Aparicio	50.00	25.00	15.00
182	Teodoro Obregon	20.00	10.00	6.00
183	Domingo Barboza	20.00	10.00	6.00
184	Not Issued, See #190			
185	Gilberto Marcano	20.00	10.00	6.00
186	Jose Alfaro	20.00	10.00	6.00
187	Jesus Reyes	20.00	10.00	6.00
188	Mike (Mickey) Scott	20.00	10.00	6.00
189	Carl Frost	20.00	10.00	6.00
190a	Norman Shiera	20.00	10.00	6.00
190b	Orlando Pena (See #184.)	20.00	10.00	6.00
191	Orlando Reyes	20.00	10.00	6.00
192	Milt Wilcox	25.00	12.50	7.50
193	Andrew Dyes	20.00	10.00	6.00
194	J. Hernandez	20.00	10.00	6.00
195	Dario Chirinos	20.00	10.00	6.00
196	Greg Shanahan	20.00	10.00	6.00
197	Gustavo Sposito	20.00	10.00	6.00
198	Sebastian Martinez	20.00	10.00	6.00
199	Leonel Carrion	20.00	10.00	6.00
200	Dennis Lawallyn (Lewallyn)	20.00	10.00	6.00
201	Charky (Charlie) Moore	20.00	10.00	6.00
202	Steve Mallory	20.00	10.00	6.00
203	Gary Martz	20.00	10.00	6.00
204	Lamar Johnson	20.00	10.00	6.00
205	Tim Johnson	20.00	10.00	6.00
206	Levy Ochoa	20.00	10.00	6.00
207	Bill Dancy	20.00	10.00	6.00
208	Antonio Garcia	20.00	10.00	6.00
209	Nidio Sirit	20.00	10.00	6.00
210	Norman Shiera	20.00	10.00	6.00
211	Not Issued, See #221			
212	Jesus Alfaro	20.00	10.00	6.00
213	Bobby Darwin	20.00	10.00	6.00
214	Zulia Action	10.00	5.00	3.00
215	Mike Seoane	20.00	10.00	6.00
216	Jim Gatner (Gantner)	20.00	10.00	6.00
217	Caracas Action	10.00	5.00	3.00

218	Caracas Action	10.00	5.00	3.00
219	Caracas Action	10.00	5.00	3.00
220	Caracas Action	10.00	5.00	3.00
221a	Caracas Action	10.00	5.00	3.00
221b	Joe Chourio (See #211.)	20.00	10.00	6.00
222	Lara Action	10.00	5.00	3.00
223	Ulises Urrieta, Antonio Armas, Manny Trillo	20.00	10.00	6.00
224	Magallanes Dugout	10.00	5.00	3.00
225	Remigio Hermoso, Gustavo Gil	15.00	7.50	4.50
226	Caracas Action	10.00	5.00	3.00
227	Manny Trillo, Dave Concepcion	20.00	10.00	6.00
228	Zulia Action	10.00	5.00	3.00
229	Caracas Pizarra Scoreboard	10.00	5.00	3.00
230	La Guaira Action	10.00	5.00	3.00
231	Caracas Action	10.00	5.00	3.00
232	La Guaira Action	10.00	5.00	3.00
233	Zulia Action	10.00	5.00	3.00
234	Caracas Publico	10.00	5.00	3.00
235	Magallanes Action	10.00	5.00	3.00
236	Aragua Action	10.00	5.00	3.00
237	La Guaira Action	10.00	5.00	3.00
238	La Guaira Action	10.00	5.00	3.00
239	La Guaira Action	10.00	5.00	3.00
240	La Guaira Action	10.00	5.00	3.00
241	Manny Trillo, Jose Cardenal	20.00	10.00	6.00
242	Pompeyo Davalillo, Lacheman	15.00	7.50	4.50
243	La Guaira Action	10.00	5.00	3.00
244	La Guaira Action	10.00	5.00	3.00
245	Action	10.00	5.00	3.00
246	Zulia Action	10.00	5.00	3.00
247	Zulia Action	10.00	5.00	3.00
248	Tim Johnson	20.00	10.00	6.00
249	La Guaira Action	10.00	5.00	3.00
250	La Guaira Action	10.00	5.00	3.00
251	La Guaira Action	10.00	5.00	3.00
252	La Guaira Action	10.00	5.00	3.00
253	La Guaira Action	10.00	5.00	3.00
254	La Guaira Action	10.00	5.00	3.00
255	La Guaira Action	10.00	5.00	3.00
256	La Guaira Action	10.00	5.00	3.00
257	Caracas Action	10.00	5.00	3.00
258	La Guaira Action	10.00	5.00	3.00
259	Zulia Action	10.00	5.00	3.00
260	Caracas Action	10.00	5.00	3.00
261	Caracas Action	10.00	5.00	3.00
262	La Guaira Clubhouse	10.00	5.00	3.00
263	La Guaira Clubhouse	10.00	5.00	3.00
264	La Guaira Clubhouse	10.00	5.00	3.00
265	La Guaira Clubhouse	10.00	5.00	3.00
266	La Guaira Action	10.00	5.00	3.00
267	La Guaira Action	10.00	5.00	3.00
268	La Guaira Action	10.00	5.00	3.00
269	Panoramica	10.00	5.00	3.00
270	Zulia Action	10.00	5.00	3.00
271	Aragua Puzzle	10.00	5.00	3.00
272	Aragua Puzzle	10.00	5.00	3.00
273	Aragua Puzzle	10.00	5.00	3.00
274	Aragua Puzzle	10.00	5.00	3.00
275	Aragua Puzzle	10.00	5.00	3.00
276	Aragua Puzzle	10.00	5.00	3.00
277	Aragua Puzzle	10.00	5.00	3.00
278	Aragua Puzzle	10.00	5.00	3.00
279	Aragua Puzzle	10.00	5.00	3.00
280	Lara Puzzle	10.00	5.00	3.00
281	Lara Puzzle	10.00	5.00	3.00
282	Lara Puzzle	10.00	5.00	3.00
283	Lara Puzzle	10.00	5.00	3.00
284	Lara Puzzle	10.00	5.00	3.00
285	Lara Puzzle	10.00	5.00	3.00
286	Lara Puzzle	10.00	5.00	3.00
287	Lara Puzzle	10.00	5.00	3.00
288	Lara Puzzle	10.00	5.00	3.00
289	Caracas Puzzle	10.00	5.00	3.00
290	Caracas Puzzle	10.00	5.00	3.00
291	Caracas Puzzle	10.00	5.00	3.00
292	Caracas Puzzle	10.00	5.00	3.00
293	Caracas Puzzle	10.00	5.00	3.00
294	Caracas Puzzle	10.00	5.00	3.00
295	Caracas Puzzle	10.00	5.00	3.00
296	Caracas Puzzle	10.00	5.00	3.00
297	Caracas Puzzle	10.00	5.00	3.00
298	La Guaira Puzzle	10.00	5.00	3.00
299	La Guaira Puzzle	10.00	5.00	3.00
300	La Guaira Puzzle	10.00	5.00	3.00
301	La Guaira Puzzle	10.00	5.00	3.00
302	La Guaira Puzzle	10.00	5.00	3.00
303	La Guaira Puzzle	10.00	5.00	3.00
304	La Guaira Puzzle	10.00	5.00	3.00
305	La Guaira Puzzle	10.00	5.00	3.00
306	La Guaira Puzzle	10.00	5.00	3.00
307	Magallanes Puzzle	10.00	5.00	3.00
308	Magallanes Puzzle	10.00	5.00	3.00
309	Magallanes Puzzle	10.00	5.00	3.00
310	Magallanes Puzzle	10.00	5.00	3.00
311	Magallanes Puzzle	10.00	5.00	3.00
312	Magallanes Puzzle	10.00	5.00	3.00
313	Magallanes Puzzle	10.00	5.00	3.00
314	Magallanes Puzzle	10.00	5.00	3.00
315	Magallanes Puzzle	10.00	5.00	3.00
316	Zulia Puzzle	10.00	5.00	3.00
317	Zulia Puzzle	10.00	5.00	3.00
318	Zulia Puzzle	10.00	5.00	3.00
319	Zulia Puzzle	10.00	5.00	3.00
320	Zulia Puzzle	10.00	5.00	3.00
321	Zulia Puzzle	10.00	5.00	3.00
322	Zulia Puzzle	10.00	5.00	3.00
323	Zulia Puzzle	10.00	5.00	3.00
324	Zulia Puzzle	10.00	5.00	3.00
325	Magallanes Navagantes Logo	10.00	5.00	3.00
326	Aragua Tigres Logo	10.00	5.00	3.00
327	Caracas Leones Logo	10.00	5.00	3.00
328	Zulia Aguilas Logo	10.00	5.00	3.00
329	Lara Cardenales Logo	10.00	5.00	3.00
330	La Guaira Tiburones Logo	10.00	5.00	3.00

1977 Venezuelan Baseball Stickers

More than 400 pieces comprise this set of 2-3/8" x 3-1/8" blank-back stickers. The majority have color photos of winter league players with the team name, logo and position printed above, and the sticker number and name beneath the picture. There are many former and future Major League players in this group. A subset of some 50 stickers of American Major Leaguers is printed in reproduction of their 1977 Topps cards. Other stickers include group pictures, action photos, puzzle pieces, etc. The album issued to house the stickers has a player write-up in each space. Printed on very thin paper, and often removed from albums, these stickers are generally not found in condition above Very Good. For Good condition pieces, figure value at 50 percent of the prices shown here; stickers in Fair condition should be valued at 25 percent. Many of the stickers have player names misspelled.

		NM	EX	VG
	Complete Set (402):	4,000	1,600	800.00
	Common Player:	15.00	6.00	3.00
	Album:	125.00	50.00	25.00
1	Aragua Tigers Logo	15.00	6.00	3.00
2	Ozzie Virgil Sr.	20.00	8.00	4.00
3	Jesus Avila	15.00	6.00	3.00
4	Raul Ortega	15.00	6.00	3.00
5	Simon Barreto	15.00	6.00	3.00
6	Gustavo Quiroz	15.00	6.00	3.00
7	Jerry Cram	15.00	6.00	3.00
8	Pat Cristelli	15.00	6.00	3.00
9	Preston Hanna	15.00	6.00	3.00
10	Angel Hernandez	15.00	6.00	3.00
11	John M'Callen	15.00	6.00	3.00
12	Randy Miller	15.00	6.00	3.00
13	Dale Murray	15.00	6.00	3.00
14	Mike Nagy	15.00	6.00	3.00
15	Stan Perzanowski	15.00	6.00	3.00
16	Juan Quiroz	15.00	6.00	3.00
17	Graciano Parra	15.00	6.00	3.00
18	Larry Cox	15.00	6.00	3.00
19	Lenn Sakata	15.00	6.00	3.00
20	Lester Straker	15.00	6.00	3.00
21	Nelson Torres	15.00	6.00	3.00
22	Carlos Avila	15.00	6.00	3.00
23	Orlando Galindo	15.00	6.00	3.00
24	Dave Wagner	15.00	6.00	3.00
25	Dave Concepcion	60.00	24.00	12.00
26	Alfredo Ortiz	15.00	6.00	3.00
27	Mike Lum, Dave Concepcion, Larry Parrish	15.00	6.00	3.00
28	Jesus Padron	15.00	6.00	3.00
29	Larry Parrish	15.00	6.00	3.00
30	Rob Picciolo	15.00	6.00	3.00
31	Luis Rivas	15.00	6.00	3.00
32	Bob Slater	15.00	6.00	3.00
33	Larry Murray	15.00	6.00	3.00
34	Dave Soderholm	15.00	6.00	3.00
35	Luis Benitez	15.00	6.00	3.00
36	Cesar Tovar, Victor Davalillo	20.00	8.00	4.00
37	Luis Bravo	15.00	6.00	3.00
38	William Castillo	15.00	6.00	3.00
39	Terry Whitfield	15.00	6.00	3.00
40	Victor Davalillo	30.00	12.00	6.00
41	Mike Lum	15.00	6.00	3.00
42	Willie Norwood	15.00	6.00	3.00
43	Cesar Tovar	15.00	6.00	3.00
44	Joe Zdeb	15.00	6.00	3.00
45	Focion, Ozzie Virgil Sr.	15.00	6.00	3.00
46	Caracas Lions Logo	15.00	6.00	3.00
47	Felipe Alou	20.00	8.00	4.00
48	Alfonso Carrasquel (Chico)	35.00	14.00	7.00
49	Antonio Torres	15.00	6.00	3.00
50	Len Barker	15.00	6.00	3.00
51	Gary Beare	15.00	6.00	3.00
52	Cardell Camper	15.00	6.00	3.00
53	Juan Gonzalez	15.00	6.00	3.00
54	Paul Mirabella	15.00	6.00	3.00
55	Carney Lansford	15.00	6.00	3.00
56	Ubaldo Heredia	15.00	6.00	3.00
57	Elias Lugo	15.00	6.00	3.00
58	Oswaldo Troconis	15.00	6.00	3.00
59	Diego Segui	15.00	6.00	3.00
60	Lary Sorensen	15.00	6.00	3.00
61	Pablo Torrealba	15.00	6.00	3.00
62	Gustavo Bastardo	15.00	6.00	3.00
63	Luis Sanz	15.00	6.00	3.00
64	Steve Bowling	15.00	6.00	3.00
65	Tim Corcoran	15.00	6.00	3.00
66	Antonio Armas (Tony)	35.00	14.00	7.00
67	Toribio Garboza	15.00	6.00	3.00
68	Bob Molinaro	15.00	6.00	3.00
69	Willibaldo Quintana	15.00	6.00	3.00
70	Luis Turnes	15.00	6.00	3.00
71	Chuck Baker	15.00	6.00	3.00
72	Rob Belloir	15.00	6.00	3.00

73	Tom Brookens	15.00	6.00	3.00
74	Ron Hassey	15.00	6.00	3.00
75	Gonzalo Marquez	15.00	6.00	3.00
76	Bob Clark	15.00	6.00	3.00
77	Marcano Trillo (Manny)	30.00	12.00	6.00
78	Angel Vargas	15.00	6.00	3.00
79	Flores Bolivar	15.00	6.00	3.00
80	Baudilo Diaz (Bo)	15.00	6.00	3.00
81	Camilo Pascual	15.00	6.00	3.00
82	La Guaira Sharks Logo	15.00	6.00	3.00
83	Pompeyo Davalillo	17.50	7.00	3.50
84	Jose Martinez	15.00	6.00	3.00
85	Jim Willoughby	15.00	6.00	3.00
86	Romo Blanco	15.00	6.00	3.00
87	Mark Daly	15.00	6.00	3.00
88	Tom House	15.00	6.00	3.00
89	Danny Osborne	15.00	6.00	3.00
90	David Clyde	15.00	6.00	3.00
91	Luis Lunar	15.00	6.00	3.00
92	Randy McGilberry	15.00	6.00	3.00
93	Greg Minton	15.00	6.00	3.00
94	Aurelio Monteagudo	15.00	6.00	3.00
95	Carlos Moreno	15.00	6.00	3.00
96	Luis M. Sanchez	15.00	6.00	3.00
97	George Throop	15.00	6.00	3.00
98	Victor Colina	15.00	6.00	3.00
99	Edwin Verheist	15.00	6.00	3.00
100	John Wathan	15.00	6.00	3.00
101	Ruben Alcala	15.00	6.00	3.00
102	Ossie Blanco	15.00	6.00	3.00
103	Dave Cripe	15.00	6.00	3.00
104	Bob Marcano	15.00	6.00	3.00
105	Rudy Meoli	15.00	6.00	3.00
106	Pastor Perez	15.00	6.00	3.00
107	Milton Ramirez	15.00	6.00	3.00
108	Luis Salazar	15.00	6.00	3.00
109	Angel Bravo	15.00	6.00	3.00
110	Gene Clines	15.00	6.00	3.00
111	Jose Cardenal	15.00	6.00	3.00
112	Gabriel Ferrerc	15.00	6.00	3.00
113	Clint Hurdle	15.00	6.00	3.00
114	Juan Monasterio	15.00	6.00	3.00
115	Lester Morales	15.00	6.00	3.00
116	Carlos Hernandez	15.00	6.00	3.00
117	Nelo Lira	15.00	6.00	3.00
118	Raul Perez	15.00	6.00	3.00
119	Marcos Lunar	15.00	6.00	3.00
120	Franklin Moreno	15.00	6.00	3.00
121	Jerry Manuel	15.00	6.00	3.00
122	Ossie Blanco, Raul Perez	15.00	6.00	3.00
123	Tom McMillan	15.00	6.00	3.00
124	Roric Harrison	15.00	6.00	3.00
125	Tom Griffin	15.00	6.00	3.00
126	Juan Berenguer	15.00	6.00	3.00
127	Puzzle Piece (Reggie Jackson)	15.00	6.00	3,00
128	Puzzle Piece (Reggie Jackson)	15.00	6.00	3.00
129	Puzzle Piece (Reggie Jackson)	15.00	6.00	3.00
130	Puzzle Piece (Reggie Jackson)	15.00	6.00	3.00
131	Puzzle Piece (Reggie Jackson)	15.00	6.00	3.00
132	Puzzle Piece (Reggie Jackson)	15.00	6.00	3.00
133	Puzzle Piece (Reggie Jackson)	15.00	6.00	3.00
134	Puzzle Piece (Reggie Jackson)	15.00	6.00	3.00
135	Puzzle Piece (Reggie Jackson)	15.00	6.00	3.00
136	Reggie Jackson	325.00	130.00	65.00
137	Rod Carew	175.00	70.00	35.00
138	Dave Concepcion	90.00	36.00	18.00
139	Joe Morgan	125.00	50.00	25.00
140	Dave Parker	15.00	6.00	3.00
141	Carlton Fisk	125.00	50.00	25.00
142	Garry Maddox	15.00	6.00	3.00
143	George Foster	15.00	6.00	3.00
144	Fred Lynn	15.00	6.00	3.00
145	Lou Piniella	17.50	7.00	3.50
146	Mark Fidrych	15.00	6.00	3.00
147	Lou Brock	125.00	50.00	25.00
148	Mitchell Page	15.00	6.00	3.00
149	Sparky Lyle	15.00	6.00	3.00
150	Manny Sanguillen	15.00	6.00	3.00
151	Steve Carlton	125.00	50.00	25.00
152	Al Oliver	17.50	7.00	3.50
153	Davey Lopes	15.00	6.00	3.00
154	Johnny Bench	175.00	70.00	35.00
155	Richie Hebner	15.00	6.00	3.00
156	Cesar Cedeno	15.00	6.00	3.00
157	Manny Trillo	15.00	6.00	3.00
158	Nolan Ryan	1,500	600.00	300.00
159	Tom Seaver	175.00	70.00	35.00
160	Jim Palmer	125.00	50.00	25.00
161	Randy Jones	15.00	6.00	3.00
162	George Brett	325.00	130.00	65.00
163	Bill Madlock	15.00	6.00	3.00
164	Cesar Geronimo	15.00	6.00	3.00
165	Vida Blue	15.00	6.00	3.00
166	Tony Armas	35.00	14.00	7.00
167	Bill Campbell	15.00	6.00	3.00
168	Graig Nettles	15.00	6.00	3.00
169	Mike Schmidt	325.00	130.00	65.00
170	Willie Stargell	125.00	50.00	25.00
171	Ron Cey	15.00	6.00	3.00
172	Victor Davalillo	25.00	10.00	5.00
173	Pete Rose	375.00	150.00	75.00
174	Steve Yeager	15.00	6.00	3.00
175	Frank Tanana	15.00	6.00	3.00
176	Carl Yastrzemski	175.00	70.00	35.00
177	Willie McCovey	125.00	50.00	25.00
178	Thurman Munson	125.00	50.00	25.00
179	Chris Chambliss	15.00	6.00	3.00
180	Bill Russell	15.00	6.00	3.00
181	Lara Cardinals Logo	15.00	6.00	3.00

182	Leo Posada	15.00	6.00	3.00
183	Lucio Celis	15.00	6.00	3.00
184	Enrique Gonzalez	15.00	6.00	3.00
185	Brian Abraham	15.00	6.00	3.00
186	Luis Aponte	15.00	6.00	3.00
187	Jose Lopez	15.00	6.00	3.00
188	Bobby Ramos	15.00	6.00	3.00
189	Tom Dixon	15.00	6.00	3.00
190	Gary Melson	15.00	6.00	3.00
191	Mark Budaska	15.00	6.00	3.00
192	Mark Fischlin	15.00	6.00	3.00
193	Garth Iorg	15.00	6.00	3.00
194	Mike Rowland	15.00	6.00	3.00
195	Dennis DeBarr	15.00	6.00	3.00
196	Gary Wilson	15.00	6.00	3.00
197	Dave McKay	15.00	6.00	3.00
198	Roberto Munoz	15.00	6.00	3.00
199	Roger Polanco	15.00	6.00	3.00
200	Pat Kelly	15.00	6.00	3.00
201	Hernan Silva	15.00	6.00	3.00
202	Francisco Navas	15.00	6.00	3.00
203	Pedro Lobaton	15.00	6.00	3.00
204	Pete Mackanin	15.00	6.00	3.00
205	Jose Caldera	15.00	6.00	3.00
206	Carlos Rodriguez (In Action)	15.00	6.00	3.00
207	Eddy Baez	15.00	6.00	3.00
208	Gary Metzeger	15.00	6.00	3.00
209	Rafael Sandoval	15.00	6.00	3.00
210	Arturo Sanchez	15.00	6.00	3.00
211	Franklin Tua	15.00	6.00	3.00
212	Teolindo Acosta	15.00	6.00	3.00
213	Arnaldo Alvarado	15.00	6.00	3.00
214	Orlando Gonzalez	15.00	6.00	3.00
215	Nelson Garcia	15.00	6.00	3.00
216	Terry Puhl	15.00	6.00	3.00
217	David Torres	15.00	6.00	3.00
218	Teolindo Acosta, Roberto Munoz	15.00	6.00	3.00
219	Terry Puhl, Mark Budaska	15.00	6.00	3.00
220	Gary Gray	15.00	6.00	3.00
221	Gustavo Gil	15.00	6.00	3.00
222	Epi Guerrero	15.00	6.00	3.00
223	Bobby Ramos, Enrique Gonzalez	15.00	6.00	3.00
224	Rick Sawyer	15.00	6.00	3.00
225	S. Byre	15.00	6.00	3.00
226	Magallanes Navigators Logo	15.00	6.00	3.00
227	Alex Monchak	15.00	6.00	3.00
228	Manuel Gonzalez	15.00	6.00	3.00
229	Olinto Rojas	15.00	6.00	3.00
230	Gregorio Machado	15.00	6.00	3.00
231	Ali Arape	15.00	6.00	3.00
232	Miguel Barreto	15.00	6.00	3.00
233	Manny Sarmiento	15.00	6.00	3.00
234	Jesus Aristimuno, Alexis Ramirez, Felix Rodriguez	15.00	6.00	3.00
235	Ed Glynn	15.00	6.00	3.00
236	Luis Jiminez	15.00	6.00	3.00
237	Bob Adams	15.00	6.00	3.00
238	Edito Arteaga	15.00	6.00	3.00
239	Rafael Cariel	15.00	6.00	3.00
240	Eddie Solomon	15.00	6.00	3.00
241	Rick Williams	15.00	6.00	3.00
242	Miguel Nava	15.00	6.00	3.00
243	Rod Scurry	15.00	6.00	3.00
244	Mike Eduards (Edwards)	15.00	6.00	3.00
245	Earl Stephenson	15.00	6.00	3.00
246	Alfonso Collazo	15.00	6.00	3.00
247	Ruben Cabrera	15.00	6.00	3.00
248	Alfredo Torres	15.00	6.00	3.00
249	John Valle	15.00	6.00	3.00
250	Jesus Aristimuno	15.00	6.00	3.00
251	Joe Cannon	15.00	6.00	3.00
252	John Pacella	15.00	6.00	3.00
253	Oswaldo Olivares	15.00	6.00	3.00
254	Gary Hargis	15.00	6.00	3.00
255	Nelson Paiva	15.00	6.00	3.00
256	Bob Oliver	15.00	6.00	3.00
257	Alexis Ramirez	15.00	6.00	3.00
258	Larry Wolfe	15.00	6.00	3.00
259	Don Boyland (Doe)	15.00	6.00	3.00
260	Mark Wagner	15.00	6.00	3.00
261	Jim Wright	15.00	6.00	3.00
262	Mitchell Page	15.00	6.00	3.00
263	Felix Rodriguez	15.00	6.00	3.00
264	Willie Aaron	15.00	6.00	3.00
265	Justo Massaro	15.00	6.00	3.00
266	Norm Angelini	15.00	6.00	3.00
267	Fred Breining	15.00	6.00	3.00
268	Bill Sample	15.00	6.00	3.00
269	Than Smith	15.00	6.00	3.00
270	Harry Doris (Dorish)	15.00	6.00	3.00
271	Zulia Eagles Logo	15.00	6.00	3.00
272	Luis Aparicio	35.00	14.00	7.00
273	Toni Taylor (Tony)	15.00	6.00	3.00
274	Teodoro Obregon	15.00	6.00	3.00
275	Gilberto Marcano	15.00	6.00	3.00
276	Jose Alfaro	15.00	6.00	3.00
277	Danny Boitano	15.00	6.00	3.00
278	Jesus Reyes	15.00	6.00	3.00
279	Johel Chourio	15.00	6.00	3.00
280	Scott Sanderson	15.00	6.00	3.00
281	Charles Kiffin	15.00	6.00	3.00
282	Bill Dancy	15.00	6.00	3.00
283	Tim Johnson	15.00	6.00	3.00
284	Norman Shiera	15.00	6.00	3.00
285	Lonnie Smith	15.00	6.00	3.00
286	Manny Seoane	15.00	6.00	3.00
287	David Wallace	15.00	6.00	3.00
288	Lareu Whashington (LaRue Washington)	15.00	6.00	3.00
289	Danny Warthen	15.00	6.00	3.00
290	Sebastian Martinez	15.00	6.00	3.00
291	Warren Brusstar	15.00	6.00	3.00
292	Steven Waterburry (Waterbury)	15.00	6.00	3.00
293	Gustavo Sposito	15.00	6.00	3.00
294	Billy Connors	15.00	6.00	3.00

295	Bod Reece (Bob)	15.00	6.00	3.00
296	Al Velasquez	15.00	6.00	3.00
297	Jesus Alfaro	15.00	6.00	3.00
298	Todd Cruz	15.00	6.00	3.00
299	Efren Chourio	15.00	6.00	3.00
300	Tim Norrid	15.00	6.00	3.00
301	Leonel Carrion	15.00	6.00	3.00
302	Dario Chirinos	15.00	6.00	3.00
303	Bobby Darwin	15.00	6.00	3.00
304	Levy Ochoa	15.00	6.00	3.00
305	Orlando Reyez (Reyes)	15.00	6.00	3.00
306	Antonio Garcia	15.00	6.00	3.00
307	Fred Andrews	15.00	6.00	3.00
308	Domingo Barboza	15.00	6.00	3.00
309	Emilio Rodriguez	15.00	6.00	3.00
310	Roger Brown (Rogers "Bobby")	15.00	6.00	3.00
311	Nelson Munoz	15.00	6.00	3.00
312	Unknown	15.00	6.00	3.00
313	Greg Pryor	15.00	6.00	3.00
314	Early Espina	15.00	6.00	3.00
315	Leonel Carrion, Dario Chirinos	15.00	6.00	3.00
316	Luis Aparicio	25.00	10.00	5.00
317	Alfonso Carrasquel (Chico)	20.00	8.00	4.00
318	Dave Concepcion	20.00	8.00	4.00
319	Antonio Armas (Tony)	20.00	8.00	4.00
320	Marcano Trillo (Manny)	20.00	8.00	4.00
321	Pablo Torrealba	15.00	6.00	3.00
322	Manny Sarmiento	15.00	6.00	3.00
323	Baudilo Diaz (Bo)	15.00	6.00	3.00
324	Victor Davalillo	15.00	6.00	3.00
325	Puzzle Piece (Dave Parker)	15.00	6.00	3.00
326	Puzzle Piece (Dave Parker)	15.00	6.00	3.00
327	Puzzle Piece (Dave Parker)	15.00	6.00	3.00
328	Puzzle Piece (Dave Parker)	15.00	6.00	3.00
329	Puzzle Piece (Dave Parker)	15.00	6.00	3.00
330	Puzzle Piece (Dave Parker)	15.00	6.00	3.00
331	Puzzle Piece (Dave Parker)	15.00	6.00	3.00
332	Puzzle Piece (Dave Parker)	15.00	6.00	3.00
333	Puzzle Piece (Dave Parker)	15.00	6.00	3.00
334	Dave Parker	15.00	6.00	3.00
335	Steve Bowling	15.00	6.00	3.00
336	Jose Herrera	15.00	6.00	3.00
337	Mitchell Page	15.00	6.00	3.00
338	Enos Cabell	15.00	6.00	3.00
339	Orlando Reyes	15.00	6.00	3.00
340	Felix Rodriguez	15.00	6.00	3.00
341	Baudilo Diaz (Bo)	15.00	6.00	3.00
342	Gonzalo Marquez	15.00	6.00	3.00
343	Mike Kelleher	15.00	6.00	3.00
344	Juan Monasterio	15.00	6.00	3.00
345	Diego Segui	15.00	6.00	3.00
346	Steve Lueber (Luebber)	15.00	6.00	3.00
347	Mike Scott	15.00	6.00	3.00
348	Angel Bravo	15.00	6.00	3.00
349	Terry Whitfield	15.00	6.00	3.00
350	Bob Oliver	15.00	6.00	3.00
351	Tim Jonhson (Johnson)	15.00	6.00	3.00
352	Gustavo Sposito	15.00	6.00	3.00
353	Jim Norris	15.00	6.00	3.00
354	Marcano Trillo (Manny)	20.00	8.00	4.00
355	Gary Woods	15.00	6.00	3.00
356	Felix Rodriguez	15.00	6.00	3.00
357	Dave May	15.00	6.00	3.00
358	Don Lepper (Leppert)	15.00	6.00	3.00
359	Magallanes Team Photo	15.00	6.00	3.00
360	Magallanes Team Photo	15.00	6.00	3.00
361	Action Photo	15.00	6.00	3.00
362	Action Photo	15.00	6.00	3.00
363	Antonio Torres, Leo Posada	15.00	6.00	3.00
364	Action Photo	15.00	6.00	3.00
365	Action Photo	15.00	6.00	3.00
366	Action Photo	15.00	6.00	3.00
367	Action Photo	15.00	6.00	3.00
368	Action Photo	15.00	6.00	3.00
369	Action Photo	15.00	6.00	3.00
370	Action Photo	15.00	6.00	3.00
371	Action Photo	15.00	6.00	3.00
372	Action Photo	15.00	6.00	3.00
373	Action Photo	15.00	6.00	3.00
374	Action Photo	15.00	6.00	3.00
375	Action Photo	15.00	6.00	3.00
376	Action Photo	15.00	6.00	3.00
377	Action Photo	15.00	6.00	3.00
378	Action Photo	15.00	6.00	3.00
399	Action Photo (Misnumbered)	15.00	6.00	3.00
380	Action Photo	15.00	6.00	3.00
381	Action Photo	15.00	6.00	3.00
382	Action Photo	15.00	6.00	3.00
383	Action Photo	15.00	6.00	3.00
384	Action Photo	15.00	6.00	3.00
385	Action Photo	15.00	6.00	3.00
386	Action Photo	15.00	6.00	3.00
387	Action Photo	15.00	6.00	3.00
388	Action Photo	15.00	6.00	3.00
389	Antonio Torres, Franklin Parra	15.00	6.00	3.00
390	Action Photo	15.00	6.00	3.00
391	Angel Bravo, Luis Aparicio	20.00	8.00	4.00
392	Action Photo	15.00	6.00	3.00
393	Action Photo	15.00	6.00	3.00
394	Action Photo	15.00	6.00	3.00
395	Action Photo	15.00	6.00	3.00
396	Action Photo	15.00	6.00	3.00
397	Action Photo	15.00	6.00	3.00
398	Action Photo	15.00	6.00	3.00
399	Action Photo	15.00	6.00	3.00
400	Action Photo	15.00	6.00	3.00
401	Action Photo	15.00	6.00	3.00
402	Tony Armas, Manny Trillo, Gonzalo Marquez	15.00	6.00	3.00

1952 Victoria

Produced during the 1952-53 Winter League season, these paper cards were formatted in the popular Latin American manner to be pasted into a colorful accompanying album. It is possible a principal venue for the set was the ballpark at

Havana, since each card urges attendance at games there. The cards are printed on paper in a 2-1/8" x 3-1/8" size. Fronts have colorized photos with white borders, but no player identification. Backs are, of course, in Spanish and include a card number player personal data, career summary and a copyright notice. Besides local players, and former, current and future major league players, the set includes league umpires and broadcasters, etc. Names as presented in this checklist may not correspond exactly with those printed on card backs and may not be correct spellings of player names.

		NM	EX	VG
	Complete Set (168):	6,500	3,000	1,500
	Common Player:	45.00	20.00	10.00
	Album:	350.00	160.00	90.00
1	Amado Maestri (Umpire)	45.00	20.00	10.00
2	John Mullen (Umpire)	45.00	20.00	10.00
3	Havana Stadium	45.00	20.00	10.00
4	Bernardino Rodriguez (Umpire)	45.00	20.00	10.00
5	Raul Atan (Umpire)	45.00	20.00	10.00
6	Cuco Conde (Broadcaster)	45.00	20.00	10.00
7	Manolo de la Reguera (Broadcaster)	45.00	20.00	10.00
8	Rafael (Felo) Ramirez (Broadcaster)	60.00	30.00	20.00
9	Rafael Rubi (Broadcaster)	45.00	20.00	10.00
10	Gabino Delgado (Broadcaster)	45.00	20.00	10.00
11	Fernando Menendez (Broadcaster)	45.00	20.00	10.00
12	Buck Canel (Broadcaster)	50.00	25.00	15.00
13	Orlando Sanchez Diago (Broadcaster)	45.00	20.00	10.00
14	Pedro Galiana (Broadcaster)	45.00	20.00	10.00
15	Jess Losada (Broadcaster)	45.00	20.00	10.00
16	Juan Ealo (Broadcaster)	45.00	20.00	10.00
17	Rene Molina (Broadcaster)	45.00	20.00	10.00
18	Miguel A. Ruiz (Broadcaster)	45.00	20.00	10.00
19	Ruben Rodriguez (Broadcaster)	45.00	20.00	10.00
20	Havana Lions Pennant	30.00	15.00	9.00
21	Miguel Gonzalez	60.00	30.00	20.00
22	Tomas (Pipo) de la Noval	45.00	20.00	10.00
23	Salvador Hernandez	45.00	20.00	10.00
24	Manuel Garcia	45.00	20.00	10.00
25	Edilio Alfaro	45.00	20.00	10.00
26	Julio Navarro	45.00	20.00	10.00
27	Richard Rand	45.00	20.00	10.00
28	Andres Fleitas	45.00	20.00	10.00
29	Isaac Seoane	45.00	20.00	10.00
30	Jimmie Kerrigan	45.00	20.00	10.00
31	Robert Alexander	45.00	20.00	10.00
32	Charles Sipples	45.00	20.00	10.00
33	Adrian Zabala	45.00	20.00	10.00
34	Rogelio Martinez	45.00	20.00	10.00
35	Carlos Pascual	60.00	30.00	20.00
36	Mario Picone	45.00	20.00	10.00
37	Eusebio Perez (Silverio)	45.00	20.00	10.00
38	Julio Moreno	45.00	20.00	10.00
39	Gilberto Torres	45.00	20.00	10.00
40	Bert Haas	45.00	20.00	10.00
41	Johnny Jorgensen	45.00	20.00	10.00
42	Lou Klein	45.00	20.00	10.00
43	Damon Phillips	45.00	20.00	10.00
44	Orlando Varona	45.00	20.00	10.00
45	Jorge Lopez	45.00	20.00	10.00
46	Pedro Formenthal	60.00	30.00	20.00
47	Robert Usher	45.00	20.00	10.00
48	Edmundo (Sandy) Amoros	60.00	30.00	20.00
49	Alejandro Crespo	50.00	25.00	15.00
50	Oscar Sardinas	45.00	20.00	10.00
51	Almendares Pennant	30.00	15.00	9.00
52	Robert Bragan	50.00	25.00	15.00
53	Clemente (Sungo) Carreras	45.00	20.00	10.00
54	Rodolfo Fernandez	45.00	20.00	10.00
55	Manuel Fernandez	45.00	20.00	10.00
56	Orlando Echevarria	45.00	20.00	10.00
57	Charles Thompson	45.00	20.00	10.00
58	Oscar Fernandez	45.00	20.00	10.00
59	Hal Erickson	45.00	20.00	10.00
60	Conrado Marrero	50.00	25.00	15.00
61	Agapito Mayor	45.00	20.00	10.00
62	Octavio Rubert	45.00	20.00	10.00
63	Edward Roebuck	50.00	25.00	15.00
64	Duke Markell	50.00	20.00	10.00
65	Rene Massip	45.00	20.00	10.00
66	Pedro Naranjo	45.00	20.00	10.00
67	Roque Contreras	45.00	20.00	10.00
68	Wayne McLeland	45.00	20.00	10.00
69	Frank Kellert	45.00	20.00	10.00
70	Forrest Jacobs	50.00	25.00	15.00
71	Hector Rodriguez	50.00	25.00	15.00
72	Willy Miranda	50.00	25.00	15.00
73	Roberto Ortiz	50.00	25.00	15.00
74	Frank Carswell	45.00	20.00	10.00
75	Asdrubal Baro	45.00	20.00	10.00

#	Name	NM	EX	VG
76	Paul Smith	45.00	20.00	10.00
77	Antonio Napoles	45.00	20.00	10.00
78	Francisco Campos	45.00	20.00	10.00
79	Angel Scull	45.00	20.00	10.00
80	Raymond Coleman	45.00	20.00	10.00
81	Gino Cimolli (Cimoli)	50.00	25.00	15.00
82	Amado Ibanez	45.00	20.00	10.00
83	Avelino Canizarez	45.00	20.00	10.00
84	Conrado Perez	45.00	20.00	10.00
85	Marianao Pennant	30.00	15.00	9.00
86	Fermin Guerra	50.00	25.00	15.00
87	Jose Maria Fernandez	50.00	25.00	15.00
88	Jose (Joe) Olivares	45.00	20.00	10.00
89	Ramon Carneado	45.00	20.00	10.00
90	Alejandro (Baby) Fernandez	45.00	20.00	10.00
91	Emilio Cabrera	45.00	20.00	10.00
92	Sandalio Consuegra	50.00	25.00	15.00
93	Tomas Fine	45.00	20.00	10.00
94	Miguel Fornieles	50.00	25.00	15.00
95	Camilo Pascual	60.00	30.00	18.00
96	Miguel Lopez	45.00	20.00	10.00
97	Clarence Iott	50.00	25.00	15.00
98	Dale Matthewson	45.00	20.00	10.00
99	Hampton Coleman	50.00	25.00	15.00
100	Terris McDuffie	60.00	30.00	18.00
101	Raul Sanchez	45.00	20.00	10.00
102	Lorenzo Cabrera	45.00	20.00	10.00
103	Ray Dandridge	800.00	400.00	240.00
104	Silvio Garcia	45.00	20.00	10.00
105	Carlos De Souza	45.00	20.00	10.00
106	Oreste (Minnie) Minoso	100.00	50.00	30.00
107	Sebastian Basso	45.00	20.00	10.00
108	William Wilson	45.00	20.00	10.00
109	Hank Workman	50.00	25.00	15.00
110	Fernando Pedroso	45.00	20.00	10.00
111	Juan Antonio Vistuer	45.00	20.00	10.00
112	Hiram Gonzalez	45.00	20.00	10.00
113	Julio Becquer	45.00	20.00	10.00
114	Stan Rojek	45.00	20.00	10.00
115	Ramiro (Cuco) Vasquez	45.00	20.00	10.00
116	Juan Izaguirre	45.00	20.00	10.00
117	Cienfuegos Pennant	30.00	15.00	9.00
118	Billy Herman	110.00	55.00	35.00
119	Oscar Rodriguez	45.00	20.00	10.00
120	Julio Rojo	45.00	20.00	10.00
121	Pedro Pages	45.00	20.00	10.00
122	Felix Masud	45.00	20.00	10.00
123	Rafael Noble	50.00	25.00	15.00
124	Mario Diaz	45.00	20.00	10.00
125	Luis Aloma	45.00	20.00	10.00
126	Santiago Ulrich	45.00	20.00	10.00
127	Armando Roche	45.00	20.00	10.00
128	Raul Lopez	45.00	20.00	10.00
129	Armando Suarez	45.00	20.00	10.00
130	Vincente Lopez	45.00	20.00	10.00
131	Ernesto Morillas	45.00	20.00	10.00
132	Alfredo Ibanez	45.00	20.00	10.00
133	Allen J. Gettel	45.00	20.00	10.00
134	Ken Lehman	45.00	20.00	10.00
135	Pat Mc Clothin (McGlothin)	50.00	25.00	15.00
136	Rogenio Otero	45.00	20.00	10.00
137	Felipe Montemayor	45.00	20.00	10.00
138	Jack Cassini	50.00	25.00	15.00
139	Donald Zimmer	75.00	37.00	22.00
140	Robert Wilson	45.00	20.00	10.00
141	Humberto Fernandez	45.00	20.00	10.00
142	Pedro Ballester	45.00	20.00	10.00
143	Walt Morin (Moryn)	50.00	25.00	15.00
144	Roberto Fernandez	45.00	20.00	10.00
145	Claro Duany	60.00	30.00	18.00
146	Pablo Garcia	45.00	20.00	10.00
147	James Pendleton	50.00	25.00	15.00
148	Oscar Sierra	45.00	20.00	10.00
149	Adolfo Luque	80.00	40.00	25.00
150	Cando Lopez	45.00	20.00	10.00
151	Joe Black	100.00	50.00	30.00
152	Napoleon Reyes	60.00	30.00	18.00
153	Rafael (Villa) Cabrera	45.00	20.00	10.00
154	Charles (Red) Barrett	50.00	25.00	15.00
155	Fred Martin	45.00	20.00	10.00
156	Isidoro Leon	45.00	20.00	10.00
157	John Rutherford	50.00	25.00	15.00
158	Max Lanier	50.00	25.00	15.00
159	Julio Ramos	45.00	20.00	10.00
160	Manuel Hidalgo	45.00	20.00	10.00
161	Wilfredo Calvino	45.00	20.00	10.00
162	Joe Nakamura	60.00	30.00	20.00
163	Martiniano Garay	45.00	20.00	10.00
164	Fernando Rodriguez	45.00	20.00	10.00
165	Anibal Navarrette	45.00	20.00	10.00
166	Rafael Rivas	45.00	20.00	10.00
167	Wilfredo Salas	45.00	20.00	10.00
168	Jocko Thompson	45.00	20.00	10.00

1908 Victor Publishing Cy Young

Eschewing booze, women and gambling made Cy Young famous, according to this postcard issued by an Ohio company near the end of the pitcher's career. The 3-1/2" x 5-1/2" card has a large black-and-white photographic portrait at center with maroon and black illustrations emblematic of typical ballplayers' vices in the corners. The divided-back is printed in black with typical postcard markings.

	NM	EX	VG
Cy Young	450.00	225.00	135.00

1915 Victory Tobacco (T214)

 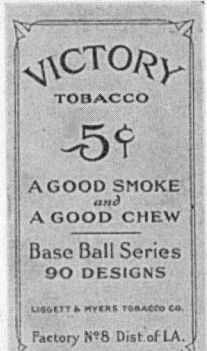

The T214 Victory set of 1915 is an obscure series of tobacco cards that is sometimes mistaken for the better-known T206 "White Border" set. The confusion is understandable because identical player poses were used for both sets. The Victory set can be easily identified, however, by the advertising for the Victory brand on the back of the cards. The set features players from the Federal League, both major leagues and at least one minor leaguer. While card backs advertise "90 Designs," fewer than 60 subjects have surfaced to date. The set had such limited distribution - apparently restricted to just the Louisiana area - and the cards are so rare that it may never be completely checklisted. Except for the advertising on the backs, the Victory cards are almost identical to the "Type 2" Coupon cards (T213), another obscure Louisiana tobacco set issued during the same period. Of the several tobacco sets issued in Louisana in the early part of the 20th Century, the T214 Victory cards are considered the most difficult to find. Gaps have been left in the numbering sequence to accommodate future additions.

		NM	EX	VG
	Common Player:	3,600	1,620	750.00
(1)	Red Ames	7,200	2,880	1,440
(2)	Chief Bender	14,400	5,760	2,880
(3)	Roger Bresnahan	14,400	5,760	2,880
(4)	Al Bridwell	7,200	2,880	1,440
(5)	Howie Camnitz	7,200	2,880	1,440
(6)	Hal Chase (Portrait)	10,200	4,080	2,040
(7)	Hal Chase (Throwing)	10,200	4,080	2,040
(8)	Ty Cobb (Portrait, red background.)	30,000	12,000	6,000
(9)	Doc Crandall	7,200	2,880	1,440
(10)	Birdie Cree	7,200	2,880	1,440
(11)	Josh Devore	7,200	2,880	1,440
(12)	Ray Demmitt	7,200	2,880	1,440
(13)	Mickey Doolan	7,200	2,880	1,440
(14)	Mike Donlin	7,200	2,880	1,440
(15)	Tom Downey	7,200	2,880	1,440
(16)	Larry Doyle	7,200	2,880	1,440
(17)	Kid Elberfeld	7,200	2,880	1,440
(18)	Johnny Evers	14,400	5,760	2,880
(19)	Russ Ford	7,200	2,880	1,440
(20)	Art Fromme	7,200	2,880	1,440
(21)	Chick Gandil	14,400	5,760	2,880
(22)	Rube Geyer	7,200	2,880	1,440
(23)	Clark Griffith	14,400	5,760	2,880
(24)	Bob Groom	7,200	2,880	1,440
(25)	Buck Herzog	7,200	2,880	1,440
(26)	Hughie Jennings	14,400	5,760	2,880
(27)	Walter Johnson (Hands at chest.)	18,000	7,200	3,600
(28)	Joe Kelley	14,400	5,760	2,880
(29)	Ed Konetchy	7,200	2,880	1,440
(30)	Nap Lajoie	14,400	5,760	2,880
(31)	Ed Lennox	7,200	2,880	1,440
(32)	Sherry Magee	7,200	2,880	1,440
(33)	Rube Marquard	14,400	5,760	2,880
(34)	John McGraw	14,400	5,760	2,880
(35)	George McQuillan	7,200	2,880	1,440
(36)	Chief Meyers (Catching)	7,200	2,880	1,440
(37)	Chief Meyers (Portrait)	7,200	2,880	1,440
(38)	George Mullin	7,200	2,880	1,440
(41)	Red Murray	7,200	2,880	1,440
(42)	Tom Needham	7,200	2,880	1,440
(43)	Rebel Oakes	7,200	2,880	1,440
(44)	Dode Paskert	7,200	2,880	1,440
(45)	Jack Quinn	7,200	2,880	1,440
(46)	Nap Rucker	7,200	2,880	1,440
(47)	Germany Schaefer	7,200	2,880	1,440
(48)	Wildfire Schulte	7,200	2,880	1,440
(49)	Frank Smith	7,200	2,880	1,440
(51)	Tris Speaker	16,200	6,480	3,240
(52)	George Stovall	7,200	2,880	1,440
(53)	Ed Summers	7,200	2,880	1,440
(54)	Bill Sweeney	7,200	2,880	1,440
(55)	Jeff Sweeney	7,200	2,880	1,440
(56)	Ira Thomas	7,200	2,880	1,440
(57)	Joe Tinker	14,400	5,760	2,880
(58)	Heinie Wagner	7,200	2,880	1,440
(59)	Zack Wheat	14,400	5,760	2,880
(60)	Kaiser Wilhelm	7,200	2,880	1,440
(61)	Hooks Wiltse	7,200	2,880	1,440

1886 Virginia Brights Black Stocking Nine (N48)

Issued during the late 1880s, though the attributed date is speculative, this series of cabinet-size (about 5" x 7-1/2") blank-back cards was available by sending in coupons found in Allen & Ginter's Virginia Brights brand cigarettes. Fronts have a sepia photo of Rubenesque women in baseball uniforms posed before a painted ballpark backdrop. In the bottom border is "BLACK STOCKING NINE. ALLEN & GINTER'S / Virginia Brights Cigarettes. / Crop of 1884 / HAND MADE CROP OF 1884." The beveled edges of the cabinet mount were originally gilt-trimmed.

	NM	EX	VG
Common Card:	1,200	600.00	350.00

1887 Virginia Brights Polka Dot Nine

Issued during the late 1880s, though the attributed date is speculative, this series of cabinet-size (about 5" x 7-1/2") blank-back cards was available by sending in coupons found in Allen & Ginter's Virginia Brights brand cigarettes. Fronts have a sepia photo of women in baseball uniforms and polka-dot bandanas posed before a backdrop. In the top border of the yellow cardboard mount, printed in gold leaf, is "Virginia Brights / Cigarettes / CROP OF 1884". In a cartouche beneath the photo is "POLKA DOT NINE". Below that is "THE FULL SET OF THIS SERIES COMPRISES NINE DIFFERENT SUBJECTS. / REPRESENTING THE VARIOUS POSITIONS IN BASE BALL."

	NM	EX	VG
Common Card:	1,100	540.00	330.00

1888 Virginia Brights Girl Baseball Players

(See 1888 Allen & Ginter Girl Baseball Players.)

1888 Virginia Brights Black Stocking Nine

Issued during the late 1880s, this series of cabinet-size (about 5" x 7-1/2") blank-back cards was available by sending in coupons found in Allen & Ginter's Virginia Brights brand cigarettes. Fronts have a sepia photo of Rubenesque women in a baseball uniform posed before a painted ballpark backdrop. The picture is framed by a fancy design. In the border above is "Virginia Brights / Cigarettes / Crop of 1884". Below the photo is the series title "Black Stocking Nine" and "The Full Set of this Series Comprises Nine Different / Subjects Representing the Various Positions in Base-Ball."

	NM	EX	VG
Common Card:	2,400	1,200	725.00

1911-16 Virginia Extra Cigarettes (T216)

The T216 baseball card set, issued by several brands of the Peoples Tobacco Co., is the last of the Louisana cigarette sets and the most confusing. Apparently issued over a period of several years between 1911 and 1916, the set employs the same pictures as several contemporary caramel and bakery sets. Cards measure a nominal 1-1/2" x 2-5/8", thought reasonable allowance must be made in consideration of original cutting methodology. Positive identification can be made by the back of the cards. The Peoples Tobacco cards carry advertising for one of three brands of cigarettes: Kotton, Mino or Virginia Extra. The Kotton brand is the most common, while the Virginia Extra and Mino backs command a premium. T216 cards are found in two types: one has a glossy front finish, while a second scarcer type is printed on a thin paper. The thin paper cards command an additional 15 percent premium. The cards represent players from the American, National and Federal Leagues.

		NM	EX	VG
Common Player:		3,300	1,320	660.00
(1)	Jack Barry (Batting)	3,300	1,320	660.00
(2)	Jack Barry (Fielding)	3,300	1,320	660.00
(3)	Harry Bemis	3,300	1,320	660.00
(4a)	Chief Bender (Philadelphia, striped cap.)	8,800	3,520	1,760
(4b)	Chief Bender (Baltimore, striped cap.)	8,800	3,520	1,760
(5a)	Chief Bender (Philadelphia, white cap.)	8,800	3,520	1,760
(5b)	Chief Bender (Baltimore, white cap.)	8,800	3,520	1,760
(6)	Bill Bergen	3,300	1,320	660.00
(7a)	Bob Bescher (Cincinnati)	3,300	1,320	660.00
(7b)	Bob Bescher (St. Louis)	3,300	1,320	660.00
(8)	Roger Bresnahan	8,800	3,520	1,760
(9)	Al Bridwell (Batting)	3,300	1,320	660.00
(10a)	Al Bridwell (New York, sliding.)	3,300	1,320	660.00
(10b)	Al Bridwell (St. Louis, sliding.)	3,300	1,320	660.00
(11)	Donie Bush	3,300	1,320	660.00
(12)	Doc Casey	3,300	1,320	660.00
(13)	Frank Chance	8,800	3,520	1,760
(14a)	Hal Chase (New York, fielding.)	3,300	1,320	660.00
(14b)	Hal Chase (Buffalo, fielding.)	3,300	1,320	660.00
(15)	Hal Chase (Portrait)	3,300	1,320	660.00
(16a)	Ty Cobb (Detroit Am., standing.)	35,750	14,300	7,150
(16b)	Ty Cobb (Detroit Americans, standing.)	33,000	13,200	6,600
(17)	Ty Cobb (Detroit Americans, batting.)	33,000	13,200	6,600
(18a)	Eddie Collins (Phila. Am.)	8,800	3,520	1,760
(18b)	Eddie Collins (Phila. Amer.)	8,800	3,520	1,760
(19)	Eddie Collins (Chicago)	8,800	3,520	1,760
(20a)	Sam Crawford (Small print.)	8,800	3,520	1,760
(20b)	Sam Crawford (Large print.)	8,800	3,520	1,760
(21)	Harry Davis	3,300	1,320	660.00
(22)	Ray Demmitt	3,300	1,320	660.00
(23)	Art Devlin	3,300	1,320	660.00
(24a)	Wild Bill Donovan (Detroit)	3,300	1,320	660.00
(24b)	Wild Bill Donovan (New York)	3,300	1,320	660.00
(25a)	Red Dooin (Philadelphia)	3,300	1,320	660.00
(25b)	Red Dooin (Cincinnati)	3,300	1,320	660.00
(26a)	Mickey Doolan (Philadelphia)	3,300	1,320	660.00
(26b)	Mickey Doolan (Baltimore)	3,300	1,320	660.00
(27)	Patsy Dougherty	3,300	1,320	660.00
(28a)	Larry Doyle (N.Y. Nat'l, batting.)	3,300	1,320	660.00
(28b)	Larry Doyle (New York Nat'l, batting.)	3,300	1,320	660.00
(29)	Larry Doyle (Throwing)	3,300	1,320	660.00
(30)	Clyde Engle	3,300	1,320	660.00
(31a)	Johnny Evers (Chicago)	8,800	3,520	1,760
(31b)	Johnny Evers (Boston)	8,800	3,520	1,760

		NM	EX	VG
(32)	Art Fromme	3,300	1,320	660.00
(33a)	George Gibson (Pittsburg Nat'l, back view.)	3,300	1,320	660.00
(33b)	George Gibson (Pittsburg Nat'l., back view.)	3,300	1,320	660.00
(34a)	George Gibson (Pittsburg Nat'l, front view.)	3,300	1,320	660.00
(34b)	George Gibson (Pittsburg Nat'l., front view.)	3,300	1,320	660.00
(35a)	Topsy Hartsel (Phila. Am.)	3,300	1,320	660.00
(35b)	Topsy Hartsel (Phila. Amer.)	3,300	1,320	660.00
(36)	Roy Hartzell (Batting)	3,300	1,320	660.00
(37)	Roy Hartzell (Catching)	3,300	1,320	660.00
(38a)	Fred Jacklitsch (Philadelphia)	3,300	1,320	660.00
(38b)	Fred Jacklitsch (Baltimore)	3,300	1,320	660.00
(39a)	Hughie Jennings (Orange background.)	8,800	3,520	1,760
(39b)	Hughie Jennings (Red background.)	8,800	3,520	1,760
(40)	Red Kleinow	3,300	1,320	660.00
(41a)	Otto Knabe (Philadelphia)	3,300	1,320	660.00
(41b)	Otto Knabe (Baltimore)	3,300	1,320	660.00
(42)	Jack Knight	3,300	1,320	660.00
(43a)	Nap Lajoie (Philadelphia, fielding.)	13,750	5,500	2,750
(43b)	Nap Lajoie (Cleveland, fielding.)	13,750	5,500	2,750
(44)	Nap Lajoie (Portrait)	13,750	5,500	2,750
(45a)	Hans Lobert (Cincinnati)	3,300	1,320	660.00
(45b)	Hans Lobert (New York)	3,300	1,320	660.00
(46)	Sherry Magee	3,300	1,320	660.00
(47)	Rube Marquard	8,800	3,520	1,760
(48a)	Christy Matthewson (Mathewson) (Large print.)	33,000	13,200	6,600
(48b)	Christy Matthewson (Mathewson) (Small print.)	33,000	13,200	6,600
(49a)	John McGraw (Large print.)	8,800	3,520	1,760
(49b)	John McGraw (Small print.)	8,800	3,520	1,760
(50)	Larry McLean	3,300	1,320	660.00
(51)	George McQuillan	3,300	1,320	660.00
(52)	Dots Miller (Batting)	3,300	1,320	660.00
(53a)	Dots Miller (Pittsburg, fielding.)	3,300	1,320	660.00
(53b)	Dots Miller (St. Louis, fielding.)	3,300	1,320	660.00
(54a)	Danny Murphy (Philadelphia)	3,300	1,320	660.00
(54b)	Danny Murphy (Brooklyn)	3,300	1,320	660.00
(55)	Rebel Oakes	3,300	1,320	660.00
(56)	Bill O'Hara	3,300	1,320	660.00
(57)	Eddie Plank	8,800	3,520	1,760
(58a)	Germany Schaefer (Washington)	3,300	1,320	660.00
(58b)	Germany Schaefer (Newark)	3,300	1,320	660.00
(59)	Admiral Schlei	3,300	1,320	660.00
(60)	Boss Schmidt	3,300	1,320	660.00
(61)	Johnny Seigle	3,300	1,320	660.00
(62)	Dave Shean	3,300	1,320	660.00
(63)	Boss Smith (Schmidt)	3,300	1,320	660.00
(64)	Tris Speaker	16,500	6,600	3,300
(65)	Oscar Stanage	3,300	1,320	660.00
(66)	George Stovall	3,300	1,320	660.00
(67)	Jeff Sweeney	3,300	1,320	660.00
(68a)	Joe Tinker (Chicago Nat'l, batting.)	8,800	3,520	1,760
(68b)	Joe Tinker (Chicago Feds, batting.)	8,800	3,520	1,760
(69)	Joe Tinker (Portrait)	8,800	3,520	1,760
(70a)	Honus Wagner (Batting, S.S.)	33,000	13,200	6,600
(70b)	Honus Wagner (Batting, 2b.)	33,000	13,200	6,600
(71a)	Honus Wagner (Throwing, S.S.)	33,000	13,200	6,600
(71b)	Honus Wagner (Throwing, 2b.)	33,000	13,200	6,600
(72)	Hooks Wiltse	3,300	1,320	660.00
(73)	Cy Young	22,000	8,800	4,400
(74a)	Heinie Zimmerman (2b.)	3,300	1,320	660.00
(74b)	Heinie Zimmerman (3b.)	3,300	1,320	660.00

1949 Vis-Ed Cleveland Indian Slide-cards

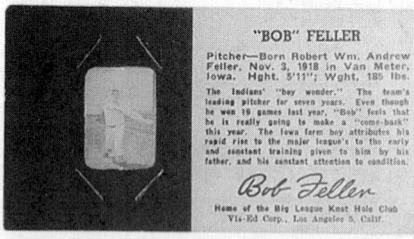

These unique novelties feature the members of the World Champion 1948 Cleveland Indians. The players are pictured on a single frame of 16mm film which has been inserted into slits cut on one end of the cardboard. The cardboard holders are dark blue and yellow, with blue printing. Fronts have player personal data, career highlights, the player's name in script and identification of the issuer. Backs have a list of "Magic Slides" which could be ordered for 33 cents each. It is likely that a slide-card exists for each of the players on that list, but only those which have been confirmed to date are checklisted here, in alphabetical order. Complete slide-cards measure 3-3/4" x 2". A plastic baseball-shaped viewer was sold with the slides.

		NM	EX	VG
Common Player:		75.00	37.00	22.00
(1)	Lou Boudreau	90.00	45.00	27.00
(2)	Larry Doby	100.00	50.00	30.00
(3)	Bob Feller	125.00	62.00	37.00
(4)	Joe Gordon	75.00	37.00	22.00
(5)	Jim Hegan	75.00	37.00	22.00
(6)	Ken Keltner	75.00	37.00	22.00

1949 Vis-Ed Cleveland Indian Magic Dials

Similar in concept to a Viewmaster, these hand-held "Magic Dial Big League Viewers" feature the members of the World Champion 1948 Cleveland Indians, plus Mickey Vernon, who joined the team in 1949, and, inexplicably, Pittsburgh Pirate Ralph Kiner. Each of the players is pictured on six single frames of 8 mm movie film (once in color, but now usually faded to sepia tones) mounted on a 2" cardboard circle within a red, white and blue 2-1/4" x 2" rectangular frame; the whole is held together by a metal rivet. The pictures can be viewed by turning the round cardboard dial. The dials came with a playing tips instructional pamphlet. Original price was 29 cents apiece.

		NM	EX	VG
Complete Set (15):		1,200	600.00	350.00
Common Player:		75.00	37.00	22.00
(1)	Gene Bearden	75.00	37.00	22.00
(2)	Lou Boudreau (Batting)	125.00	62.00	37.00
(3)	Lou Boudreau (Double play.)	125.00	62.00	37.00
(4)	Lou Boudreau (Shortstop)	125.00	62.00	37.00
(5)	Larry Doby	125.00	62.00	37.00
(6)	Bob Feller	150.00	75.00	45.00
(7)	Joe Gordon (Double play.)	75.00	37.00	22.00
(8)	Joe Gordon (Second base.)	75.00	37.00	22.00
(9)	Jim Hegan	75.00	37.00	22.00
(10)	Ken Keltner	75.00	37.00	22.00
(11)	Ralph Kiner	125.00	62.00	37.00
(12)	Bob Lemon	125.00	62.00	37.00
(13)	Dale Mitchell	75.00	37.00	22.00
(14)	Satchel Paige	200.00	100.00	60.00
(15)	Mickey Vernon	75.00	37.00	22.00

1966 Volpe Tumblers

A number of teams co-operated in the production of baseball player 12-oz. thermal tumblers which were distributed at local gas stations for a small sum and/or a minimum fuel purchase. The plastic tumblers have artwork portraits and smaller action pictures by Nicholas Volpe and facsimile autographs on colorful backgrounds. The glasses are 5-1/4" tall and 3" in diameter at the rim.

		NM	EX	VG
Common Player:		20.00	10.00	6.00
CINCINNATI REDS				
(1)	Chico Cardenas	20.00	10.00	6.00
(2)	Gordy Coleman	20.00	10.00	6.00
(3)	John Edwards	20.00	10.00	6.00
(4)	Sammy Ellis	20.00	10.00	6.00
(5)	Tommy Harper	20.00	10.00	6.00
(6)	Deron Johnson	20.00	10.00	6.00
(7)	Jim Maloney	20.00	10.00	6.00
(8)	Billy McCool	20.00	10.00	6.00
(9)	Joe Nuxhall	20.00	10.00	6.00
(10)	Jim O'Toole	20.00	10.00	6.00
(11)	Vada Pinson	30.00	15.00	9.00
(12)	Pete Rose	75.00	37.00	22.00
CLEVELAND INDIANS				
(1)	Max Alvis	20.00	10.00	6.00
(2)	Joe Azcue	20.00	10.00	6.00
(3)	Larry Brown	20.00	10.00	6.00
(4)	Rocky Colavito	50.00	25.00	15.00
(5)	Vic Davalillo	20.00	10.00	6.00
(6)	Chuck Hinton	20.00	10.00	6.00
(7)	Dick Howser	20.00	10.00	6.00
(8)	Sam McDowell	20.00	10.00	6.00
(9)	Don McMahon	20.00	10.00	6.00

		NM	EX	VG
(10)	Sonny Siebert	20.00	10.00	6.00
(11)	Leon Wagner	20.00	10.00	6.00
(12)	Fred Whitfield	20.00	10.00	6.00

NEW YORK METS

		NM	EX	VG
(1)	Larry Bearnarth	20.00	10.00	6.00
(2)	Yogi Berra	50.00	25.00	15.00
(3)	Jack Fisher	20.00	10.00	6.00
(4)	Rob Gardner	20.00	10.00	6.00
(5)	Jim Hickman	20.00	10.00	6.00
(6)	Ron Hunt	20.00	10.00	6.00
(7)	Ed Kranepool	20.00	10.00	6.00
(8)	Johnny Lewis	20.00	10.00	6.00
(9)	Tug McGraw	20.00	10.00	6.00
(10)	Roy McMillan	20.00	10.00	6.00
(11)	Dick Stuart	20.00	10.00	6.00
(12)	Ron Swoboda	20.00	10.00	6.00

DETROIT TIGERS

		NM	EX	VG
(1)	Hank Aguirre	20.00	10.00	6.00
(2)	Norm Cash	30.00	15.00	9.00
(3)	Don Demeter	20.00	10.00	6.00
(4)	Bill Freehan	20.00	10.00	6.00
(5)	Willie Horton	20.00	10.00	6.00
(6)	Al Kaline	50.00	25.00	15.00
(7)	Mickey Lolich	20.00	10.00	6.00
(8)	Dick McAuliffe	20.00	10.00	6.00
(9)	Denny McLain	20.00	10.00	6.00
(10)	Joe Sparma	20.00	10.00	6.00
(11)	Don Wert	20.00	10.00	6.00
(12)	Dave Wickersham	20.00	10.00	6.00

LOS ANGELES DODGERS

		NM	EX	VG
(1)	Tommy Davis	20.00	10.00	6.00
(2)	Willie Davis	20.00	10.00	6.00
(3)	Don Drysdale	40.00	20.00	12.00
(4)	Ron Fairly	20.00	10.00	6.00
(5)	John Kennedy	20.00	10.00	6.00
(6)	Jim Lefebvre	20.00	10.00	6.00
(7)	Sandy Koufax	60.00	30.00	18.00
(8)	Claude Osteen	20.00	10.00	6.00
(9)	Wes Parker	20.00	10.00	6.00
(10)	Ron Perranoski	20.00	10.00	6.00
(11)	Johnny Roseboro	20.00	10.00	6.00
(12)	Maury Wills	20.00	10.00	6.00

1913 Voskamp's Coffee Pittsburgh Pirates

The 1913 Pittsburgh Pirates are featured in this set of cards given away in packages of coffee and tea and redeemable for seats at Pirates games. The 2-1/4" x 3-5/8" cards have black-and-white player photos on a plain white background, along with ID and a "Photo by Johnston" credit line. The black-and-white back has a checklist of the set and details of the ticket redemption program. Pose variations of the Hofman and O'Toole cards are reported to exist. The checklist for the unnumbered cards is presented here alphabetically. Because the set was issued just after the great tobacco card era, several of the Pirates in this set are not found on any other cards.

		NM	EX	VG
Complete Set (20):		60,000	30,000	18,000
Common Player:		2,025	1,015	600.00
(1)	Babe Adams	2,025	1,015	600.00
(2)	Everitt Booe	2,025	1,015	600.00
(3)	Bobby Byrne	2,025	1,015	600.00
(4)	Howie Camnitz	2,025	1,015	600.00
(5)	Max Carey	3,000	1,500	900.00
(6)	Joe Conzelman	2,025	1,015	600.00
(7)	Jack Ferry	2,025	1,015	600.00
(8)	George Gibson	2,025	1,015	600.00
(9)	Claude Hendrix	2,025	1,015	600.00
(10)	Solly Hofman	2,025	1,015	600.00
(11)	Ham Hyatt	2,025	1,015	600.00
(12)	Bill Kelly	2,025	1,015	600.00
(13)	Ed Mensor	2,025	1,015	600.00
(14)	Dots Miller	2,025	1,015	600.00
(15)	Marty O'Toole	2,025	1,015	600.00
(16)	Hank Robinson	2,025	1,015	600.00
(17)	Mike Simon	2,025	1,015	600.00
(18)	Jim Viox	2,025	1,015	600.00
(19)	Honus Wagner	22,500	11,250	6,750
(20)	Owen Wilson	2,025	1,015	600.00

1910 Hans Wagner Cigars

Circa 1910 the Freeman Cigar Co. apparently envisioned marketing a product named for the Pirates star shortstop. While it appears the cigar was never actually produced, various pack-

aging elements have survived in proof examples. Most pieces are embossed and have a color lithograph which features a portrait of Wagner against a ballgame background. "HANS WAGNER" is in red and gold above. Usually found in the bottom border is "Title & Design Registered by Freeman Cigar Co." Collectors must be aware that various modern fantasy pieces purporting to be of the same genre exist in the market.

	NM	EX	VG
Hans Wagner (7-1/4" x 6-1/2" box label)	15,000	7,500	4,500
Hans Wagner (4-1/2" octagonal label)	12,000	6,000	3,500
Hans Wagner (4-1/4" oval label)	15,000	7,500	4,500
Hans Wagner (3" cigar band)	1,600	800.00	480.00
Hans Wagner (Typographic box-side label.)	1,500	750.00	450.00
Hans Wagner (Typographic box-top label.)	7,500	3,750	2,250

1880s John M. Ward Fan

The specific date of production for this ornate hand fan is unknown. Some examples show on their back an advertisement for "C. Philpot" of Springfield, Maine. The central portion of the fan is a round piece of heavy cardboard, about 7-3/4" in diameter, that features a color lithographic portrait of Ward on a baseball background. Around the picture is a peach-colored ribbon. A wooden handle is attached on back.

	NM	EX	VG
John M. Ward	7,800	4,200	2,700

1934 Ward's Sporties Pins

The date of issue can only be approximated for this issue pf 1-1/4" diameter celluloid pin-back buttons. Ward's Sporties was evidently some kind of food product; at the center of each button is a black-and-white or blue-and-white portrait photo of a player with his name above and "Eats" below the picture. Printed around the photo portion in white on a red background is: "Good Sports Enjoy / WARD'S SPORTIES." Ward's bakeries issue several type of baseball cards and collectibles over the years, such as the 1947 Tip-Top bread cards. The checklist is in alphabetical order, and may not yet be complete.

		NM	EX	VG
Complete Set (8):		4,500	2,250	1,350
Common Player:		325.00	160.00	100.00
(1)	Dizzy Dean	1,000	500.00	300.00
(2)	Jimmy Dykes	325.00	160.00	100.00
(3)	Jimmie Foxx	1,000	500.00	300.00
(4)	Frank Frisch	650.00	325.00	195.00

		NM	EX	VG
(5)	Charlie Gehringer	650.00	325.00	195.00
(6)	Charlie Grimm	325.00	160.00	100.00
(7)	Schoolboy Rowe	325.00	160.00	100.00
(8)	Jimmie Wilson	325.00	160.00	100.00

1916 Ware's

One of several regional advertisers to use this 200-card set as a promotional medium was this New Rochelle, N.Y., store's sporting goods department. The checklist and relative value information are listed under 1916 M101-4 Blank Backs. Collectors can expect to pay a significant premium for individual cards to enhance a type card or superstar card collection. The American Card Catalog listed these 1-5/8" x 3" black-and-white cards as H801-9.

PREMIUMS:
Common Players: 2-4X
Hall of Famers: 1.5-2.5X
(See 1916 Sporting News M101-4 for checklist and price guide.)

1872 Warren Studio Boston Red Stockings Cabinets

 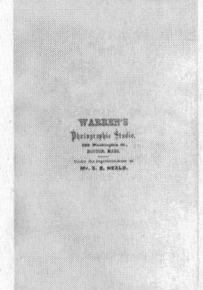

The champions from the premiere season of baseball's first professional league (some wearing their championship pins), are pictured on these cabinet cards. Members of the Boston Red Stockings were photographed in uniform at a local studio. The cards measure about 4-1/4" x 6-1/2" with sepia photos. In the bottom border is the name and address of the studio; information that is repeated on the otherwise blank back. Player identification is not found on the cards but can be deduced by studying contemporary team pictures.

		NM	EX	VG
Common Player:		6,500	3,000	2,000
(1)	Ross Barnes	9,000	4,000	2,500
(2)	Dave Birdsall	6,500	3,000	2,000
(3)	Charles Gould	6,500	3,000	2,000
(4)	Andy Leonard	6,500	3,000	2,000
(5)	Cal McVey	9,000	4,000	2,500
(6)	Fraley Rogers	6,500	3,000	2,000
(7)	John Ryan	6,500	3,000	2,000
(8)	Harry Schafer	6,500	3,000	2,000
(9)	Albert Spalding	42,000	9,000	5,400
(10)	George Wright	30,000	9,000	5,400
(11)	Harry Wright	30,000	9,000	5,400

1872 Warren Studio Boston Red Stockings CDVs

The champions from the premiere season of baseball's first professional league (some wearing their championship pins), are pictured on these cartes de visites depict. Members of the Boston Red Stockings were photographed at a local studio, most of them being pictured in coat-and-tie with only Harry Wright in uniform. The cards measure about 2-1/2" x 4-1/4" with sepia photos bordered in white. In the bottom border is the name and address of the studio; information which is repeated on the otherwise blank back. Player identification is not found on the cards but can be deduced by studying contemporary team pictures.

		NM	EX	VG
Common Player:		4,500	3,000	2,000
(1)	Ross Barnes	4,500	3,000	2,000
(2)	Dave Birdsall	4,500	3,000	2,000
(3)	Charlie Gould	4,500	3,000	2,000
(4)	Andy Leonard	4,500	3,000	2,000
(5)	Cal McVey	4,500	3,000	2,000
(6)	Fraley Rogers	4,500	3,000	2,000
(7)	John Ryan	4,500	3,000	2,000
(8)	Harry Schafer	4,500	3,000	2,000
(9)	Albert Spalding	15,000	7,500	3,750
(10)	George Wright	10,000	5,000	3,000
(11)	Harry Wright (Street clothes.)	10,000	5,000	3,000
(12)	Harry Wright (Uniform)	10,000	5,000	3,000

1874 Warren Studio Boston Red Stockings Cabinets

The champions from the National Association Boston Red Stockings were photographed in uniform at a local studio. The cards measure about 4-1/4" x 6-1/2" with sepia photos. In the bottom border is the name and address of the studio. Player identification is not found on the cards but can be deduced by studying contemporary team pictures.

		NM	EX	VG
Common Player:		5,500	2,750	1,650
(1)	Ross Barnes	8,250	2,750	1,650
(2)	Tommy Beals	6,600	2,750	1,650
(3)	George Hall	6,600	2,750	1,650
(4)	Andy Leonard	5,500	2,750	1,650
(5)	Cal McVey	8,250	2,750	1,650
(6)	Harry Schafer	6,600	2,750	1,650

1931 Washington Senators Picture Pack

This set of souvenir pictures offers player photos in a black-and-white, blank-back format of about 6-1/8" x 9-1/2". Each picture has a white border and a facsimile player autograph.

		NM	EX	VG
Complete Set (30):		800.00	400.00	240.00
Common Player:		25.00	12.50	7.50
(1)	Nick Altrock	35.00	17.50	10.50
(2)	Oswald Bluege	25.00	12.50	7.50
(3)	Cliff Bolton	25.00	12.50	7.50
(4)	Lloyd Brown	25.00	12.50	7.50
(5)	Robert Burke	25.00	12.50	7.50
(6)	Joe Cronin	50.00	25.00	15.00
(7)	Alvin Crowder	25.00	12.50	7.50
(8)	E.B. Eynon, Jr. (Secretary-Treasurer)	25.00	12.50	7.50
(9)	Charles Fischer	25.00	12.50	7.50
(10)	Edward Gharrity	25.00	12.50	7.50
(11)	Clark Griffith	45.00	22.00	13.50
(12)	Irving Hadley	25.00	12.50	7.50
(13)	William Hargrave	25.00	12.50	7.50
(14)	David Harris	25.00	12.50	7.50
(15)	Jack Hayes	25.00	12.50	7.50
(16)	Walter Johnson	125.00	62.00	37.00
(17)	Sam Jones	25.00	12.50	7.50
(18)	Baxter Jordan	25.00	12.50	7.50
(19)	Joe Judge	25.00	12.50	7.50
(20)	Joe Kuhel	25.00	12.50	7.50
(21)	Henry Manush	50.00	25.00	15.00
(22)	Fred Marberry	25.00	12.50	7.50
(23)	Mike Martin	25.00	12.50	7.50
(24)	Walter Masters	25.00	12.50	7.50
(25)	Charles Myer	25.00	12.50	7.50
(26)	Harry Rice	25.00	12.50	7.50
(27)	Sam Rice	25.00	12.50	7.50
(28)	Al Schacht	35.00	17.50	10.50
(29)	Roy Spencer	25.00	12.50	7.50
(30)	Sam West	25.00	12.50	7.50

1970 Washington Senators Traffic Safety

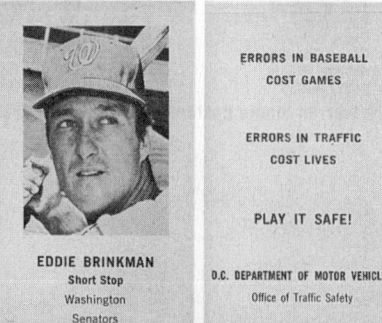

EDDIE BRINKMAN
Short Stop
Washington Senators

ERRORS IN BASEBALL COST GAMES

ERRORS IN TRAFFIC COST LIVES

PLAY IT SAFE!

D.C. DEPARTMENT OF MOTOR VEHICLES
Office of Traffic Safety

Distributed in 1970 by the Washington, D.C. Department of Motor Vehicles, this issue promoting traffic safety was one of the first police sets. Featuring black-and-white player photos, the cards measure 2-1/2" x 3-7/8" and have large borders surrounding the pictures. The player's name and position are below; the team name appears in smaller type at the bottom. The set can be found on either pink card stock, used for the

original print run, or on bright yellow stock, used for two subsequent printings. Aurelio Rodriguez, who joined the team after the season began, is known only in yellow; all other players can be found in both yellow and pink. The pink varieties carry a higher value. The backs of the cards offer traffic safety tips.

		NM	EX	VG
Complete Set, Pink (10):		150.00	75.00	45.00
Common Player, Pink:		3.50	1.75	1.00
Complete Set, Yellow (11):		25.00	12.50	7.50
Common Player, Yellow:		2.50	1.25	.70
(1a)	Dick Bosman (Pink)	3.50	1.75	1.00
(1b)	Dick Bosman (Yellow)	2.50	1.25	.70
(2a)	Eddie Brinkman (Pink)	3.50	1.75	1.00
(2b)	Eddie Brinkman (Yellow)	2.50	1.25	.70
(3a)	Paul Casanova (Pink)	3.50	1.75	1.00
(3b)	Paul Casanova (Yellow)	2.50	1.25	.70
(4a)	Mike Epstein (Pink)	3.50	1.75	1.00
(4b)	Mike Epstein (Yellow)	2.50	1.25	.70
(5a)	Frank Howard (Pink)	10.00	5.00	3.00
(5b)	Frank Howard (Yellow)	7.50	3.75	2.25
(6a)	Darold Knowles (Pink)	3.50	1.75	1.00
(6b)	Darold Knowles (Yellow)	2.50	1.25	.70
(7a)	Lee Maye (Pink)	3.50	1.75	1.00
(7b)	Lee Maye (Yellow)	2.50	1.25	.70
(8a)	Dave Nelson (Pink)(SP)	125.00	62.00	37.00
(8b)	Dave Nelson (Yellow)	2.50	1.25	.70
(9)	Aurelio Rodriguez (Yellow) (SP)	5.00	2.50	1.50
(10a)	John Roseboro (Pink)	3.50	1.75	1.00
(10b)	John Roseboro (Yellow)	2.50	1.25	.70
(11a)	Ed Stroud (Pink)	3.50	1.75	1.00
(11b)	Ed Stroud (Yellow)	2.50	1.25	.70

1971 Washington Senators Traffic Safety

DENNY McLAIN
Pitcher
Washington Senators

A FAST BALL CAN GET YOU "OUT" OF TROUBLE

A FAST CAR CAN GET YOU "INTO" TROUBLE

PLAY IT SAFE!

D.C. DEPARTMENT OF MOTOR VEHICLES
Office of Traffic Safety

The 1971 Senators safety set was again issued by the Washington, D.C., Department of Motor Vehicles and was similar in design and size (2-1/2" x 3-7/8") to the previous year, except that it was printed on a pale yellow stock. The set, which features several new players, contains no scarce cards. The backs contain traffic safety messages.

		NM	EX	VG
Complete Set (10):		12.50	6.25	3.75
Uncut Sheet:		12.50	6.25	3.75
Common Player:		1.00	.50	.30
(1)	Dick Bosman	1.00	.50	.30
(2)	Paul Casanova	1.00	.50	.30
(3)	Tim Cullen	1.00	.50	.30
(4)	Joe Foy	1.00	.50	.30
(5)	Toby Harrah	1.00	.50	.30
(6)	Frank Howard	2.50	1.25	.70
(7)	Elliott Maddox	1.00	.50	.30
(8)	Tom McCraw	1.00	.50	.30
(9)	Denny McLain	3.00	1.50	.90
(10)	Don Wert	.60	.30	.20

1910 Washington Times

WALKER
WASHINGTON

WASHINGTON TIMES
SERIES

Only American League players have so far been found in this issue by the Washington Times newspaper. The 2-9/16" x 3-9/16" cards have portrait or action photos of the players within a wide border. A white panel at bottom has the player name and team at left and "Washington Times Series" at right. All printing is in dark red. Backs are blank. The manner in which these cards were distributed is unknown, as is the extent of the checklist. The unnumbered cards are checklisted here in alphabetical order.

		NM	EX	VG
Common Player:		2,500	1,250	750.00
(1)	Ty Cobb	20,000	10,000	6,000

(2)	Eddie Collins	7,500	3,750	2,250
(3)	Wid Conroy	2,500	1,250	750.00
(4)	Sam Crawford	7,500	3,750	2,250
(5)	Harry Davis	2,500	1,250	750.00
(6)	Bob Groom	2,500	1,250	750.00
(7)	Nap Lajoie	7,500	3,750	2,250
(8)	George McBride	2,500	1,250	750.00
(9)	Clyde Milan	2,500	1,250	750.00
(10)	Frank Oberlin	2,500	1,250	750.00
(11)	Rube Oldring	2,500	1,250	750.00
(12)	Freddie Parent (Freddy)	2,500	1,250	750.00
(13)	Doc Reisling	2,500	1,250	750.00
(14)	Gabby Street	2,500	1,250	750.00
(15)	Lee Tannehill	2,500	1,250	750.00
(16)	Bob Unglaub	2,500	1,250	750.00
(17)	Dixie Walker	2,500	1,250	750.00
(18)	Ed. Walsh	7,500	3,750	2,250
(19)	Joe Wood	2,000	1,000	600.00
(20)	Cy Young	12,500	6,250	3,750

1951 WBKB "Lucky Fan" Chicago Cubs

This series of black-and-white player glossies appears to have been a promotional giveaway from WBKB radio or television station in conjunction with Ben Bey's "Lucky Fan" club or contest. The 8-1/8" x 10" photos have a facsimile autograph on front. On back is a three-line rubber-stamped "COURTESY OF / BEN BEY "LUCKY FAN" / WBKB - CHICAGO." The checklist is arranged alphabetically.

		NM	EX	VG
Complete Set (28):		900.00	450.00	270.00
Common Player:		40.00	20.00	12.00
(1)	Frank Baumholtz	40.00	20.00	12.00
(2)	Bob Borkowski	40.00	20.00	12.00
(3)	Smoky Burgess	50.00	25.00	15.00
(4)	Phil Cavarretta	40.00	20.00	12.00
(5)	Chuck Connors	100.00	50.00	30.00
(6)	Jack Cusick	40.00	20.00	12.00
(7)	Bruce Edwards	40.00	20.00	12.00
(8)	Dee Fondy	40.00	20.00	12.00
(9)	Joe Hatten	40.00	20.00	12.00
(10)	Gene Hermanski	40.00	20.00	12.00
(11)	Frank Hiller	40.00	20.00	12.00
(12)	Ransom Jackson	40.00	20.00	12.00
(13)	Hal Jeffcoat	40.00	20.00	12.00
(14)	Bob Kelly	40.00	20.00	12.00
(15)	Johnny Klippstein	40.00	20.00	12.00
(16)	Dutch Leonard	40.00	20.00	12.00
(17)	Turk Lown	40.00	20.00	12.00
(18)	Cal McLish	40.00	20.00	12.00
(19)	Eddie Miksis	40.00	20.00	12.00
(20)	Paul Minner	40.00	20.00	12.00
(21)	Mickey Owen	40.00	20.00	12.00
(22)	Andy Pafko	50.00	25.00	15.00
(23)	Bob Ramazotti	40.00	20.00	12.00
(24)	Bob Rush	40.00	20.00	12.00
(25)	Hank Sauer	40.00	20.00	12.00
(26)	Bob Schultz	40.00	20.00	12.00
(27)	Bill Serena	40.00	20.00	12.00
(28)	Roy Smalley	45.00	22.00	13.50

1911-14 Weber Bakery (D304)

 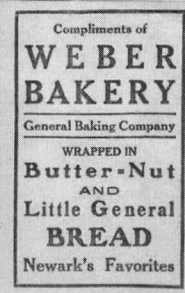

Compliments of
WEBER BAKERY
General Baking Company
WRAPPED IN
Butter-Nut
AND
Little General
BREAD
Newark's Favorites

RUBE MARQUARD, N.Y. NAT'L.

(See 1911-14 General Baking Co. for checklist and price information.)

1916 Weil Baking Co. (D329)

One of several issues by the New Orleans bakery, this 1-3/8" x 3" black-and-white set of 200 shares a checklist and relative values with the 1916 M101-4 Blank Backs set. Collectors can expect to pay a premium for a card with the Weil Baking ad on back to add to a type collection or superstar collection. The American Card Catalog lists this issue as D329.

JOE JACKSON
L. F.—Chicago White Sox
87

		NM	EX	VG
	Complete Set (200):	77,000	38,500	23,100
	Common Player:	195.00	100.00	50.00
1	Babe Adams	195.00	100.00	50.00
2	Sam Agnew	195.00	100.00	50.00
3	Eddie Ainsmith	195.00	100.00	50.00
4	Grover Alexander	880.00	455.00	230.00
5	Leon Ames	195.00	100.00	50.00
6	Jimmy Archer	195.00	100.00	50.00
7	Jimmy Austin	195.00	100.00	50.00
8	H.D. Baird	195.00	100.00	50.00
9	J. Franklin Baker	715.00	375.00	190.00
10	Dave Bancroft	715.00	375.00	190.00
11	Jack Barry	195.00	100.00	50.00
12	Zinn Beck	195.00	100.00	50.00
13	"Chief" Bender	715.00	375.00	190.00
14	Joe Benz	195.00	100.00	50.00
15	Bob Bescher	195.00	100.00	50.00
16	Al Betzel	195.00	100.00	50.00
17	Mordecai Brown	715.00	375.00	190.00
18	Eddie Burns	195.00	100.00	50.00
19	George Burns	195.00	100.00	50.00
20	Geo. J. Burns	195.00	100.00	50.00
21	Joe Bush	195.00	100.00	50.00
22	"Donie" Bush	195.00	100.00	50.00
23	Art Butler	195.00	100.00	50.00
24	Bobbie Byrne	195.00	100.00	50.00
25	Forrest Cady	195.00	100.00	50.00
26	Jimmy Callahan	195.00	100.00	50.00
27	Ray Caldwell	195.00	100.00	50.00
28	Max Carey	715.00	375.00	190.00
29	George Chalmers	195.00	100.00	50.00
30	Ray Chapman	195.00	100.00	50.00
31	Larry Cheney	195.00	100.00	50.00
32	Eddie Cicotte	1,000	375.00	190.00
33	Tom Clarke	195.00	100.00	50.00
34	Eddie Collins	715.00	375.00	190.00
35	"Shauno" Collins	195.00	100.00	50.00
36	Charles Comiskey	715.00	375.00	190.00
37	Joe Connolly	195.00	100.00	50.00
38	Ty Cobb	5,500	2,860	1,430
39	Harry Coveleskie (Coveleski)	195.00	100.00	50.00
40	Gavvy Cravath	195.00	100.00	50.00
41	Sam Crawford	715.00	375.00	190.00
42	Jean Dale	195.00	100.00	50.00
43	Jake Daubert	195.00	100.00	50.00
44	Charles Deal	195.00	100.00	50.00
45	Al Demaree	195.00	100.00	50.00
46	Josh Devore	195.00	100.00	50.00
47	William Doak	195.00	100.00	50.00
48	Bill Donovan	195.00	100.00	50.00
49	Charles Dooin	195.00	100.00	50.00
50	Mike Doolan	195.00	100.00	50.00
51	Larry Doyle	195.00	100.00	50.00
52	Jean Dubuc	195.00	100.00	50.00
53	Oscar Dugey	195.00	100.00	50.00
54	Johnny Evers	715.00	375.00	190.00
55	Urban Faber	715.00	375.00	190.00
56	"Hap" Felsch	2,000	860.00	430.00
57	Bill Fischer	195.00	100.00	50.00
58	Ray Fisher	195.00	100.00	50.00
59	Max Flack	195.00	100.00	50.00
60	Art Fletcher	195.00	100.00	50.00
61	Eddie Foster	195.00	100.00	50.00
62	Jacques Fournier	195.00	100.00	50.00
63	Del Gainer (Gainor)	195.00	100.00	50.00
64	"Chic" Gandil	715.00	375.00	190.00
65	Larry Gardner	195.00	100.00	50.00
66	Joe Gedeon	195.00	100.00	50.00
67	Gus Getz	195.00	100.00	50.00
68	Geo. Gibson	195.00	100.00	50.00
69	Wilbur Good	195.00	100.00	50.00
70	Hank Gowdy	195.00	100.00	50.00
71	John Graney	195.00	100.00	50.00
72	Clark Griffith	715.00	375.00	190.00
73	Tom Griffith	195.00	100.00	50.00
74	Heinie Groh	195.00	100.00	50.00
75	Earl Hamilton	195.00	100.00	50.00
76	Bob Harmon	195.00	100.00	50.00
77	Roy Hartzell	195.00	100.00	50.00
78	Claude Hendrix	195.00	100.00	50.00
79	Olaf Henriksen	195.00	100.00	50.00
80	John Henry	195.00	100.00	50.00
81	"Buck" Herzog	195.00	100.00	50.00
82	Hugh High	195.00	100.00	50.00
83	Dick Hoblitzell	195.00	100.00	50.00
84	Harry Hooper	715.00	375.00	190.00
85	Ivan Howard	195.00	100.00	50.00
86	Miller Huggins	715.00	375.00	190.00
87	Joe Jackson	20,000	7,150	3,575
88	William James	195.00	100.00	50.00
89	Harold Janvrin	195.00	100.00	50.00

90	Hugh Jennings	715.00	375.00	190.00
91	Walter Johnson	1,760	835.00	470.00
92	Fielder Jones	195.00	100.00	50.00
93	Joe Judge	195.00	100.00	50.00
94	Bennie Kauff	195.00	100.00	50.00
95	Wm. Killefer Jr.	195.00	100.00	50.00
96	Ed. Konetchy	195.00	100.00	50.00
97	Napoleon Lajoie	715.00	375.00	190.00
98	Jack Lapp	195.00	100.00	50.00
99	John Lavan	195.00	100.00	50.00
100	Jimmy Lavender	195.00	100.00	50.00
101	"Nemo" Leibold	195.00	100.00	50.00
102	H.B. Leonard	195.00	100.00	50.00
103	Duffy Lewis	175.00	100.00	50.00
104	Hans Lobert	195.00	100.00	50.00
105	Tom Long	195.00	100.00	50.00
106	Fred Luderus	195.00	100.00	50.00
107	Connie Mack	715.00	375.00	190.00
108	Lee Magee	195.00	100.00	50.00
109	Sherwood Magee	195.00	100.00	50.00
110	Al. Mamaux	195.00	100.00	50.00
111	Leslie Mann	195.00	100.00	50.00
112	"Rabbit" Maranville	715.00	375.00	190.00
113	Rube Marquard	715.00	375.00	190.00
114	J. Erskine Mayer	195.00	100.00	50.00
115	George McBride	195.00	100.00	50.00
116	John J. McGraw	715.00	375.00	190.00
117	Jack McInnis	195.00	100.00	50.00
118	Fred Merkle	195.00	100.00	50.00
119	Chief Meyers	195.00	100.00	50.00
120	Clyde Milan	195.00	100.00	50.00
121	John Miller	195.00	100.00	50.00
122	Otto Miller	195.00	100.00	50.00
123	Willie Mitchell	195.00	100.00	50.00
124	Fred Mollwitz	195.00	100.00	50.00
125	Pat Moran	195.00	100.00	50.00
126	Ray Morgan	195.00	100.00	50.00
127	Geo. Moriarty	195.00	100.00	50.00
128	Guy Morton	195.00	100.00	50.00
129	Mike Mowrey	195.00	100.00	50.00
130	Ed. Murphy	195.00	100.00	50.00
131	"Hy" Myers	195.00	100.00	50.00
132	J.A. Niehoff	195.00	100.00	50.00
133	Rube Oldring	195.00	100.00	50.00
134	Oliver O'Mara	195.00	100.00	50.00
135	Steve O'Neill	195.00	100.00	50.00
136	"Dode" Paskert	195.00	100.00	50.00
137	Roger Peckinpaugh	195.00	100.00	50.00
138	Walter Pipp	195.00	100.00	50.00
139	Derril Pratt (Derrill)	195.00	100.00	50.00
140	Pat Ragan	195.00	100.00	50.00
141	Bill Rariden	195.00	100.00	50.00
142	Eppa Rixey	715.00	375.00	190.00
143	Davey Robertson	195.00	100.00	50.00
144	Wilbert Robinson	715.00	375.00	190.00
145	Bob Roth	195.00	100.00	50.00
146	Ed. Roush	715.00	375.00	190.00
147	Clarence Rowland	195.00	100.00	50.00
148	"Nap" Rucker	195.00	100.00	50.00
149	Dick Rudolph	195.00	100.00	50.00
150	Reb Russell	195.00	100.00	50.00
151	Babe Ruth	27,500	14,300	7,150
152	Vic Saier	195.00	100.00	50.00
153	"Slim" Sallee	195.00	100.00	50.00
154	Ray Schalk	715.00	375.00	190.00
155	Walter Schang	195.00	100.00	50.00
156	Frank Schulte	195.00	100.00	50.00
157	Everett Scott	195.00	100.00	50.00
158	Jim Scott	195.00	100.00	50.00
159	Tom Seaton	195.00	100.00	50.00
160	Howard Shanks	195.00	100.00	50.00
161	Bob Shawkey	195.00	100.00	50.00
162	Ernie Shore	195.00	100.00	50.00
163	Burt Shotton	195.00	100.00	50.00
164	Geo. Sisler	715.00	375.00	190.00
165	J. Carlisle Smith	195.00	100.00	50.00
166	Fred Snodgrass	195.00	100.00	50.00
167	Geo. Stallings	195.00	100.00	50.00
168	Oscar Stanage	195.00	100.00	50.00
169	Charles Stengel	715.00	375.00	190.00
170	Milton Stock	195.00	100.00	50.00
171	Amos Strunk	195.00	100.00	50.00
172	Billy Sullivan	195.00	100.00	50.00
173	"Jeff" Tesreau	195.00	100.00	50.00
174	Joe Tinker	715.00	375.00	190.00
175	Fred Toney	195.00	100.00	50.00
176	Terry Turner	195.00	100.00	50.00
177	George Tyler	195.00	100.00	50.00
178	Jim Vaughn	195.00	100.00	50.00
179	Bob Veach	195.00	100.00	50.00
180	James Viox	195.00	100.00	50.00
181	Oscar Vitt	195.00	100.00	50.00
182	Hans Wagner	5,000	1,375	690.00
183	Clarence Walker	195.00	100.00	50.00
184	Ed. Walsh	715.00	375.00	190.00
185	W. Wambsganss (Photo actually Fritz Coumbe.)	195.00	100.00	50.00
186	Buck Weaver	1,320	690.00	340.00
187	Carl Weilman	195.00	100.00	50.00
188	Zach Wheat	715.00	375.00	190.00
189	Geo. Whitted	195.00	100.00	50.00
190	Fred Williams	195.00	100.00	50.00
191	Art Wilson	195.00	100.00	50.00
192	J. Owen Wilson	195.00	100.00	50.00
193	Ivy Wingo	195.00	100.00	50.00
194	"Mel" Wolfgang	195.00	100.00	50.00
195	Joe Wood	195.00	100.00	50.00
196	Steve Yerkes	195.00	100.00	50.00
197	"Pep" Young	195.00	100.00	50.00
198	Rollie Zeider	195.00	100.00	50.00
199	Heiny Zimmerman	195.00	100.00	50.00
200	Ed. Zwilling	195.00	100.00	50.00

1917 Weil Baking Co. (D328)

This set comprises one of several regional advertisers' use of the 200-card issue for promotional purposes. These cards are most often seen with the advertising of the Collins-McCar-

RAY CHAPMAN
S. S.—Cleveland Americans
30

thy Candy Co. of San Francisco. Cards measure 2" x 3-1/4" and are printed in black-and-white. This set was listed as D328 in the American Card Catalog.

		NM	EX	VG
	Complete Set (200):	140,000	70,000	42,500
	Common Player:	330.00	165.00	100.00
1	Sam Agnew	330.00	165.00	100.00
2	Grover Alexander	1,320	660.00	395.00
3	W.S. Alexander (W.E.)	330.00	165.00	100.00
4	Leon Ames	330.00	165.00	100.00
5	Fred Anderson	330.00	165.00	100.00
6	Ed Appleton	330.00	165.00	100.00
7	Jimmy Archer	330.00	165.00	100.00
8	Jimmy Austin	330.00	165.00	100.00
9	Jim Bagby	330.00	165.00	100.00
10	H.D. Baird	330.00	165.00	100.00
11	J. Franklin Baker	770.00	385.00	230.00
12	Dave Bancroft	770.00	385.00	230.00
13	Jack Barry	330.00	165.00	100.00
14	Joe Benz	330.00	165.00	100.00
15	Al Betzel	330.00	165.00	100.00
16	Ping Bodie	330.00	165.00	100.00
17	Joe Boehling	330.00	165.00	100.00
18	Eddie Burns	330.00	165.00	100.00
19	George Burns	330.00	165.00	100.00
20	Geo. J. Burns	330.00	165.00	100.00
21	Joe Bush	330.00	165.00	100.00
22	Owen Bush	330.00	165.00	100.00
23	Bobby Byrne	330.00	165.00	100.00
24	Forrest Cady	330.00	165.00	100.00
25	Max Carey	770.00	385.00	230.00
26	Ray Chapman	385.00	195.00	115.00
27	Larry Cheney	330.00	165.00	100.00
28	Eddie Cicotte	770.00	385.00	230.00
29	Tom Clarke	330.00	165.00	100.00
30	Ty Cobb	9,900	4,950	3,000
31	Eddie Collins	770.00	385.00	230.00
32	"Shauno" Collins (Shano)	330.00	165.00	100.00
33	Fred Coumbe	330.00	165.00	100.00
34	Harry Coveleskie (Coveleski)	330.00	165.00	100.00
35	Gavvy Cravath	330.00	165.00	100.00
36	Sam Crawford	770.00	385.00	230.00
37	Geo. Cutshaw	330.00	165.00	100.00
38	Jake Daubert	330.00	165.00	100.00
39	Geo. Dauss	330.00	165.00	100.00
40	Charles Deal	330.00	165.00	100.00
41	"Wheezer" Dell	330.00	165.00	100.00
42	William Doak	330.00	165.00	100.00
43	Bill Donovan	330.00	165.00	100.00
44	Larry Doyle	330.00	165.00	100.00
45	Johnny Evers	770.00	385.00	230.00
46	Urban Faber	770.00	385.00	230.00
47	"Hap" Felsch	1,650	825.00	495.00
48	Bill Fischer	330.00	165.00	100.00
49	Ray Fisher	330.00	165.00	100.00
50	Art Fletcher	330.00	165.00	100.00
51	Eddie Foster	330.00	165.00	100.00
52	Jacques Fournier	330.00	165.00	100.00
53	Del Gainer (Gainor)	330.00	165.00	100.00
54	Bert Gallia	330.00	165.00	100.00
55	"Chic" Gandil (Chick)	990.00	495.00	300.00
56	Larry Gardner	330.00	165.00	100.00
57	Joe Gedeon	330.00	165.00	100.00
58	Gus Getz	330.00	165.00	100.00
59	Frank Gilhooley	330.00	165.00	100.00
60	Wm. Gleason	330.00	165.00	100.00
61	M.A. Gonzales (Gonzalez)	330.00	165.00	100.00
62	Hank Gowdy	330.00	165.00	100.00
63	John Graney	330.00	165.00	100.00
64	Tom Griffith	330.00	165.00	100.00
65	Heinie Groh	330.00	165.00	100.00
66	Bob Groom	330.00	165.00	100.00
67	Louis Guisto	330.00	165.00	100.00
68	Earl Hamilton	330.00	165.00	100.00
69	Harry Harper	330.00	165.00	100.00
70	Grover Hartley	330.00	165.00	100.00
71	Harry Heilmann	770.00	385.00	230.00
72	Claude Hendrix	330.00	165.00	100.00
73	Olaf Henriksen	330.00	165.00	100.00
74	John Henry	330.00	165.00	100.00
75	"Buck" Herzog	330.00	165.00	100.00
76	Hugh High	330.00	165.00	100.00
77	Dick Hoblitzell	330.00	165.00	100.00
78	Walter Holke	330.00	165.00	100.00
79	Harry Hooper	770.00	385.00	230.00
80	Rogers Hornsby	1,320	660.00	395.00
81	Ivan Howard	330.00	165.00	100.00
82	Joe Jackson	27,500	13,750	8,250
83	Harold Janvrin	330.00	165.00	100.00
84	William James	330.00	165.00	100.00
85	C. Jamieson	330.00	165.00	100.00
86	Hugh Jennings	770.00	385.00	230.00
87	Walter Johnson	1,650	825.00	495.00
88	James Johnston	330.00	165.00	100.00

89	Fielder Jones	330.00	165.00	100.00
90	Joe Judge	330.00	165.00	100.00
91	Hans Lobert	330.00	165.00	100.00
92	Benny Kauff	330.00	165.00	100.00
93	Wm. Killefer Jr.	330.00	165.00	100.00
94	Ed. Konetchy	330.00	165.00	100.00
95	John Lavan	330.00	165.00	100.00
96	Jimmy Lavender	330.00	165.00	100.00
97	"Nemo" Leibold	330.00	165.00	100.00
98	H.B. Leonard	330.00	165.00	100.00
99	Duffy Lewis	330.00	165.00	100.00
100	Tom Long	330.00	165.00	100.00
101	Wm. Louden	330.00	165.00	100.00
102	Fred Luderus	330.00	165.00	100.00
103	Lee Magee	330.00	165.00	100.00
104	Sherwood Magee	330.00	165.00	100.00
105	Al Mamaux	330.00	165.00	100.00
106	Leslie Mann	330.00	165.00	100.00
107	"Rabbit" Maranville	770.00	385.00	230.00
108	Rube Marquard	770.00	385.00	230.00
109	Armando Marsans	330.00	165.00	100.00
110	J. Erskine Mayer	330.00	165.00	100.00
111	George McBride	330.00	165.00	100.00
112	Lew McCarty	330.00	165.00	100.00
113	John J. McGraw	770.00	385.00	230.00
114	Jack McInnis	330.00	165.00	100.00
115	Lee Meadows	330.00	165.00	100.00
116	Fred Merkle	330.00	165.00	100.00
117	"Chief" Meyers	330.00	165.00	100.00
118	Clyde Milan	330.00	165.00	100.00
119	Otto Miller	330.00	165.00	100.00
120	Clarence Mitchell	330.00	165.00	100.00
121	Ray Morgan	330.00	165.00	100.00
122	Guy Morton	330.00	165.00	100.00
123	"Mike" Mowrey	330.00	165.00	100.00
124	Elmer Myers	330.00	165.00	100.00
125	"Hy" Myers	330.00	165.00	100.00
126	A.E. Neale	385.00	195.00	115.00
127	Arthur Nehf	330.00	165.00	100.00
128	J.A. Niehoff	330.00	165.00	100.00
129	Steve O'Neill	330.00	165.00	100.00
130	"Dode" Paskert	330.00	165.00	100.00
131	Roger Peckinpaugh	330.00	165.00	100.00
132	"Pol" Perritt	330.00	165.00	100.00
133	"Jeff" Pfeffer	330.00	165.00	100.00
134	Walter Pipp	330.00	165.00	100.00
135	Derril Pratt (Derrill)	330.00	165.00	100.00
136	Bill Rariden	330.00	165.00	100.00
137	E.C. Rice	770.00	385.00	230.00
138	Wm. A. Ritter (Wm. H.)	330.00	165.00	100.00
139	Eppa Rixey	770.00	385.00	230.00
140	Davey Robertson	330.00	165.00	100.00
141	"Bob" Roth	330.00	165.00	100.00
142	Ed. Roush	770.00	385.00	230.00
143	Clarence Rowland	330.00	165.00	100.00
144	Dick Rudolph	330.00	165.00	100.00
145	William Rumler	330.00	165.00	100.00
146	Reb Russell	330.00	165.00	100.00
147	"Babe" Ruth	22,000	11,000	6,600
148	Vic Saier	330.00	165.00	100.00
149	"Slim" Sallee	330.00	165.00	100.00
150	Ray Schalk	770.00	385.00	230.00
151	Walter Schang	330.00	165.00	100.00
152	Frank Schulte	330.00	165.00	100.00
153	Ferd Schupp	330.00	165.00	100.00
154	Everett Scott	330.00	165.00	100.00
155	Hank Severeid	330.00	165.00	100.00
156	Howard Shanks	330.00	165.00	100.00
157	Bob Shawkey	330.00	165.00	100.00
158	Jas. Sheckard	330.00	165.00	100.00
159	Ernie Shore	330.00	165.00	100.00
160	C.H. Shorten	330.00	165.00	100.00
161	Burt Shotton	330.00	165.00	100.00
162	Geo. Sisler	770.00	385.00	230.00
163	Elmer Smith	330.00	165.00	100.00
164	J. Carlisle Smith	330.00	165.00	100.00
165	Fred Snodgrass	330.00	165.00	100.00
166	Tris Speaker	1,320	660.00	395.00
167	Oscar Stanage	330.00	165.00	100.00
168	Charles Stengel	770.00	385.00	230.00
169	Milton Stock	330.00	165.00	100.00
170	Amos Strunk	330.00	165.00	100.00
171	"Zeb" Terry	330.00	165.00	100.00
172	"Jeff" Tesreau	330.00	165.00	100.00
173	Chester Thomas	330.00	165.00	100.00
174	Fred Toney	330.00	165.00	100.00
175	Terry Turner	330.00	165.00	100.00
176	George Tyler	330.00	165.00	100.00
177	Jim Vaughn	330.00	165.00	100.00
178	Bob Veach	330.00	165.00	100.00
179	Oscar Vitt	330.00	165.00	100.00
180	Hans Wagner	7,700	3,850	2,300
181	Clarence Walker	330.00	165.00	100.00
182	Jim Walsh	330.00	165.00	100.00
183	Al Walters	330.00	165.00	100.00
184	W. Wambsganss	330.00	165.00	100.00
185	Buck Weaver	2,200	1,100	660.00
186	Carl Weilman	330.00	165.00	100.00
187	Zack Wheat	770.00	385.00	230.00
188	Geo. Whitted	330.00	165.00	100.00
189	Joe Wilhoit	330.00	165.00	100.00
190	Claude Williams	1,650	825.00	495.00
191	Fred Williams	330.00	165.00	100.00
192	Art Wilson	330.00	165.00	100.00
193	Lawton Witt	330.00	165.00	100.00
194	Joe Wood	495.00	250.00	150.00
195	William Wortman	330.00	165.00	100.00
196	Steve Yerkes	330.00	165.00	100.00
197	Earl Yingling	330.00	165.00	100.00
198	"Pep" (Ralph) Young	330.00	165.00	100.00
199	Rollie Zeider	330.00	165.00	100.00
200	Henry Zimmerman	330.00	165.00	100.00

1886 Welton Cigars N.Y. Giants (H812)

(See "1886 New York Base Ball Club" for checklist and values.)

1977 Wendy's Discs

Virtually identical in format to the several locally sponsored disc sets of the previous year, these 3-3/8" diameter player discs were given away at participating stores in the fast-food hamburger chain. Discs once again feature black-and-white player portrait photos in the center of a baseball design. The left and right panels are in one of several bright colors. Licensed by the Players Association through Mike Schechter Associates, the player photos carry no uniform logos. Backs are printed in green. The unnumbered discs are checklisted here alphabetically.

		NM	EX	VG
Complete Set (70):		325.00	165.00	100.00
Common Player:		3.00	1.50	.90
(1)	Sal Bando	3.00	1.50	.90
(2)	Buddy Bell	3.00	1.50	.90
(3)	Johnny Bench	20.00	10.00	6.00
(4)	Larry Bowa	3.00	1.50	.90
(5)	Steve Braun	3.00	1.50	.90
(6)	George Brett	50.00	25.00	15.00
(7)	Lou Brock	12.50	6.25	3.75
(8)	Jeff Burroughs	3.00	1.50	.90
(9)	Bert Campaneris	3.00	1.50	.90
(10)	John Candelaria	3.00	1.50	.90
(11)	Jose Cardenal	3.00	1.50	.90
(12)	Rod Carew	12.50	6.25	3.75
(13)	Steve Carlton	12.50	6.25	3.75
(14)	Dave Cash	3.00	1.50	.90
(15)	Cesar Cedeno	3.00	1.50	.90
(16)	Ron Cey	3.00	1.50	.90
(17)	Dave Concepcion	3.00	1.50	.90
(18)	Dennis Eckersley	12.50	6.25	3.75
(19)	Mark Fidrych	6.00	3.00	1.75
q20)	Rollie Fingers	12.50	6.25	3.75
(21)	Carlton Fisk	12.50	6.25	3.75
(22)	George Foster	3.00	1.50	.90
(23)	Wayne Garland	3.00	1.50	.90
(24)	Ralph Garr	3.00	1.50	.90
(25)	Steve Garvey	4.50	2.25	1.25
(26)	Cesar Geronimo	3.00	1.50	.90
(27)	Bobby Grich	3.00	1.50	.90
(28)	Ken Griffey Sr.	3.00	1.50	.90
(29)	Don Gullett	3.00	1.50	.90
(30)	Mike Hargrove	3.00	1.50	.90
(31)	Al Hrabosky	3.00	1.50	.90
(32)	Jim Hunter	12.50	6.25	3.75
(33)	Reggie Jackson	45.00	22.50	13.50
(34)	Randy Jones	3.00	1.50	.90
(35)	Dave Kingman	3.00	1.50	.90
(36)	Jerry Koosman	3.00	1.50	.90
(37)	Dave LaRoche	3.00	1.50	.90
(38)	Greg Luzinski	3.00	1.50	.90
(39)	Fred Lynn	3.00	1.50	.90
(40)	Bill Madlock	3.00	1.50	.90
(41)	Rick Manning	3.00	1.50	.90
(42)	Jon Matlock	3.00	1.50	.90
(43)	John Mayberry	3.00	1.50	.90
(44)	Hal McRae	3.00	1.50	.90
(45)	Andy Messersmith	3.00	1.50	.90
(46)	Rick Monday	3.00	1.50	.90
(47)	John Montefusco	3.00	1.50	.90
(48)	Joe Morgan	12.50	6.25	3.75
(49)	Thurman Munson	12.50	6.25	3.75
(50)	Bobby Murcer	3.00	1.50	.90
(51)	Bill North	3.00	1.50	.90
(52)	Jim Palmer	12.50	6.25	3.75
(53)	Tony Perez	12.50	6.25	3.75
(54)	Jerry Reuss	3.00	1.50	.90
(55)	Brooks Robinson	15.00	7.50	4.50
(56)	Pete Rose	55.00	27.50	16.50
(57)	Joe Rudi	3.00	1.50	.90
(58)	Nolan Ryan	65.00	32.50	20.00
(59)	Manny Sanguillen	3.00	1.50	.90
(60)	Mike Schmidt	50.00	25.00	15.00
(61)	Tom Seaver	20.00	10.00	6.00
(62)	Bill Singer	3.00	1.50	.90
(63)	Willie Stargell	12.50	6.25	3.75
(64)	Rusty Staub	4.00	2.00	1.25
(65)	Luis Tiant	3.00	1.50	.90
(66)	Bob Watson	3.00	1.50	.90
(67)	Butch Wynegar	3.00	1.50	.90
(68)	Carl Yastrzemski	20.00	10.00	6.00
(69)	Robin Yount	12.50	6.25	3.75
(70)	Richie Zisk	3.00	1.50	.90

1963 Western Oil Minnesota Twins

Issued by Mileage and DS gas stations, these 8-1/2" x 11" heavy paper portraits are the work of sports/entertainment artist Nicholas Volpe, who had done a similar series earlier for the Los Angeles Dodgers, and would do several more in the future for other baseball and NFL teams. The 1963 Twins issue features pastel portrait and action renderings against a black background on front. The player's name appears as a facsimile autograph in white on the painting and is printed in black in the white bottom border. Backs have biographical data and a career summary of the player at top. At center is a black box with complete major and minor league stats. At lower center is a biography of the artist, and, on most pictures, his portrait. The DS and Mileage logos of the Western Oil and Fuel Co. appear at bottom.

		NM	EX	VG
Complete Set (24):		150.00	75.00	45.00
Common Player:		10.00	5.00	3.00
(1)	Bernie Allen	10.00	5.00	3.00
(2)	Bob Allison	15.00	7.50	4.50
(3)	George Banks	10.00	5.00	3.00
(4)	Earl Battey	12.50	6.25	3.75
(5)	Bill Dailey	10.00	5.00	3.00
(6)	John Goryl	10.00	5.00	3.00
(7)	Lenny Green	10.00	5.00	3.00
(8)	Jimmie Hall	10.00	5.00	3.00
(9)	Jim Kaat	15.00	7.50	4.50
(10)	Harmon Killebrew	30.00	15.00	9.00
(11)	Sam Mele	10.00	5.00	3.00
(12)	Don Mincher	10.00	5.00	3.00
(13)	Ray Moore	10.00	5.00	3.00
(14)	Camilo Pascual	12.50	6.25	3.75
(15)	Jim Perry	10.00	5.00	3.00
(16)	Bill Pleis	10.00	5.00	3.00
(17)	Vic Power	12.00	6.00	3.50
(18)	Garry Roggenburk	10.00	5.00	3.00
(19)	Jim Roland	10.00	5.00	3.00
(20)	Rich Rollins	10.00	5.00	3.00
(21)	Lee Stange	10.00	5.00	3.00
(22)	Dick Stigman	10.00	5.00	3.00
(23)	Zoilo Versalles	12.50	6.25	3.75
(24)	Jerry Zimmerman	10.00	5.00	3.00

1964 Western Oil Minnesota Twins

Identical in format to the previous year's issue, the 1964 set of Twins pictures features the use of a second portrait of the player in civilian dress rather than an action picture. The 1964 issue also has background of pastel colors, rather than all-black, and, on back, an oval/arrow logo for Western brand gas, along with the Mileage and DS logos.

		NM	EX	VG
Complete Set (15):		120.00	60.00	35.00
Common Player:		10.00	5.00	3.00
(1)	Bernie Allen	10.00	5.00	3.00
(2)	Bob Allison	12.50	6.25	3.75
(3)	Earl Battey	12.50	6.25	3.75
(4)	Bill Dailey	10.00	5.00	3.00
(5)	Jimmie Hall	10.00	5.00	3.00
(6)	Jim Kaat	15.00	7.50	4.50
(7)	Harmon Killebrew	30.00	15.00	9.00

(8)	Don Mincher	10.00	5.00	3.00
(9)	Tony Oliva	25.00	12.50	7.50
(10)	Camilo Pascual	12.50	6.25	3.75
(11)	Bill Pleis	10.00	5.00	3.00
(12)	Jim Roland	10.00	5.00	3.00
(13)	Rich Rollins	10.00	5.00	3.00
(14)	Dick Stigman	10.00	5.00	3.00
(15)	Zoilo Versalles	12.50	6.25	3.75

1974 Weston Expos

This 10-card set features members of the Montreal Expos. Each full-color card measures 3-1/2" x 5-1/2" and includes a facsimile autograph in black ink with the player's name printed along the bottom. The backs are distinct because they are divided in half. The top of the card lists player data and 1973 statistics in English, while the bottom carries the same information in French. The cards are numbered according to the player's uniform number.

		NM	EX	VG
Complete Set (10):		10.00	5.00	3.00
Common Player:		1.50	.75	.45
3	Bob Bailey	1.50	.75	.45
8	Boots Day	1.50	.75	.45
12	John Boccabella	1.50	.75	.45
16	Mike Jorgensen	1.50	.75	.45
18	Steve Renko	1.50	.75	.45
19	Tim Foli	1.50	.75	.45
21	Ernie McAnally	1.50	.75	.45
26	Bill Stoneman	1.50	.75	.45
29	Ken Singleton	1.50	.75	.45
33	Ron Hunt	1.50	.75	.45

1888 WG1 Base Ball Playing Cards

This little-known set of playing cards featuring drawings of real baseball players in action poses was issued in 1888 and includes members of the eight National League teams of the day. Each club is represented by nine players - one at each position - making the set complete at 72 cards. The cards measure 2-1/2" x 3-1/2" and have a blue-on-blue lathework pattern on back. The cards were sold as a boxed set. They were designed to resemble a deck of regular playing cards, and the various positions were all assigned the same denomination (for example, all of the pitchers were kings, catchers were aces, etc.). There are no cards numbered either two, three, four or five; and rather than the typical hearts, clubs, diamonds and spades, each team represents a different "suit." The American Card Catalog designation is WG1.

		NM	EX	VG
Complete Set (72):		90,000	35,000	17,500
Common Player:		900.00	360.00	180.00
Box:		5,000	2,500	1,500
(1)	Ed Andrews	900.00	360.00	180.00
(2)	Cap Anson	6,250	2,500	1,250
(3)	Charles Bassett	900.00	360.00	180.00
(4)	Charles Bastian	900.00	360.00	180.00
(5)	Charles Bennett	900.00	360.00	180.00
(6)	Henry Boyle	900.00	360.00	180.00
(7)	Dan Brouthers	3,000	1,200	600.00
(8)	Tom Brown	900.00	360.00	180.00
(9)	Tom Burns	900.00	360.00	180.00
(10)	Fred Carroll	900.00	360.00	180.00
(11)	Dan Casey	900.00	360.00	180.00
(12)	John Clarkson	3,000	1,200	600.00
(13)	Jack Clements	900.00	360.00	180.00
(14)	John Coleman	900.00	360.00	180.00
(15)	Roger Connor	3,000	1,200	600.00
(16)	Abner Dalrymple	900.00	360.00	180.00
(17)	Jerry Denny	900.00	360.00	180.00
(18)	Jim Donelly	900.00	360.00	180.00
(19)	Fred Dunlap	900.00	360.00	180.00
(20)	Dude Esterbrook	900.00	360.00	180.00
(21)	Buck Ewing	3,000	1,200	600.00
(22)	Sid Farrar	900.00	360.00	180.00
(23)	Silver Flint	900.00	360.00	180.00
(24)	Jim Fogarty	900.00	360.00	180.00
(25)	Elmer Foster	900.00	360.00	180.00
(26)	Pud Galvin	3,000	1,200	600.00
(27)	Charlie Getzein (Getzien)	900.00	360.00	180.00
(28)	Jack Glasscock	900.00	360.00	180.00
(29)	George Gore	900.00	360.00	180.00
(30)	Ned Hanlon	3,000	1,200	600.00
(31)	Paul Hines	900.00	360.00	180.00
(32)	Joe Hornung	900.00	360.00	180.00
(33)	Dummy Hoy	1,350	550.00	275.00
(34)	Arthur Irwin (Philadelphia)	900.00	360.00	180.00
(35)	John Irwin (Washington)	900.00	360.00	180.00
(36)	Dick Johnston	900.00	360.00	180.00
(37)	Tim Keefe	3,000	1,200	600.00
(38)	King Kelly	4,250	1,700	850.00
(39)	Willie Kuehne	900.00	360.00	180.00
(40)	Connie Mack	3,250	1,300	650.00

(41)	Al Maul	900.00	360.00	180.00
(42)	Al Meyers (Myers) (Washington)	900.00	360.00	180.00
(43)	George Meyers (Myers) (Indianapolis)	900.00	360.00	180.00
(44)	John Morrill	900.00	360.00	180.00
(45)	Joseph Mulvey	900.00	360.00	180.00
(46)	Billy Nash	900.00	360.00	180.00
(47)	Billy O'Brien	900.00	360.00	180.00
(48)	Orator Jim O'Rourke	3,000	1,200	600.00
(49)	Bob Pettit	900.00	360.00	180.00
(50)	Fred Pfeffer	900.00	360.00	180.00
(51)	Danny Richardson (New York)	900.00	360.00	180.00
(52)	Hardy Richardson (Detroit)	900.00	360.00	180.00
(53)	Jack Rowe	900.00	360.00	180.00
(54)	Jimmy Ryan	900.00	360.00	180.00
(55)	Emmett Seery	900.00	360.00	180.00
(56)	George Shoch	900.00	360.00	180.00
(57)	Otto Shomberg (Schomberg)	900.00	360.00	180.00
(58)	Pap Smith	900.00	360.00	180.00
(59)	Marty Sullivan	900.00	360.00	180.00
(60)	Billy Sunday	3,000	1,200	600.00
(61)	Ezra Sutton	900.00	360.00	180.00
(62)	Sam Thompson	3,000	1,200	600.00
(63)	Mike Tiernan	900.00	360.00	180.00
(64)	Larry Twitchell	900.00	360.00	180.00
(65)	Rip Van Haltren	900.00	360.00	180.00
(66)	John Ward	3,000	1,200	600.00
(67)	Deacon White	900.00	360.00	180.00
(68)	Jim Whitney	900.00	360.00	180.00
(69)	Ned Williamson	900.00	360.00	180.00
(70)	Walt Wilmot	900.00	360.00	180.00
(71)	Medoc Wise	900.00	360.00	180.00
(72)	George Wood	900.00	360.00	180.00

1932 Wheaties Babe Ruth Flip Book

This novelty item measures about 1-3/4" x 2-1/2" and is stapled at the bottom. When properly thumbed, the individual black-and-white pages inside present a simulated moving picture, "Babe Ruth Shows You How to Hit a Home Run". The covers feature orange and blue artwork.

	NM	EX	VG
Babe Ruth	750.00	375.00	225.00

1933-1934 Wheaties

Sponsored by Wheaties via mail-in offers heard on baseball games on half a dozen radio stations, these black-and-white cards are blank-backed and feature posed action photo with facsimile autographs bordered in white. In a 3-1/4" x 5-3/8" format, they are similar in design to the later 1936 National Chicle "Fine Pens" (R313) and the Gold Medal Foods World Series (R313A) issue of 1934, though each of the photos found in this set are unique. To date, this likely incomplete checklist comprises on players from the Browns, Cardinals, Cubs, White Sox, Indians and the Des Moines Demons of the Western League.

		NM	EX	VG
Common Player:				
(1)	Earl Averill	275.00	135.00	80.00
(2)	Geo. E. Blaeholder	45.00	22.50	13.50
(3)	Irving "Jack" Burns	45.00	22.50	13.50
(4)	Bruce Campbell	45.00	22.50	13.50
(5)	"Tex" Carleton	45.00	22.50	13.50
(6)	George Earnshaw	45.00	22.50	13.50
(7)	Red Faber	80.00	40.00	24.00
(8)	Fabian Gaffke	45.00	22.50	13.50
(9)	Odell Hale	180.00	90.00	55.00
(10)	Mel Harder	45.00	22.50	13.50
(11)	Roy Hudson	45.00	22.50	13.50
(12)	Chuck Klein	80.00	40.00	24.00
(13)	Jack Knott	45.00	22.50	13.50
(14)	Al Marchand	45.00	22.50	13.50
(15)	Ossie Orwoll	45.00	22.50	13.50
(16)	Al Simmons	80.00	40.00	24.00
(17)	Hal Trosky	45.00	22.50	13.50
(18)	Joe Vosmik	45.00	22.50	13.50
(19)	Bill Walker	45.00	22.50	13.50

1935 Wheaties - Series 1

This set of major leaguers (plus fictional sports hero Jack Armstrong) was issued on the back of Wheaties cereal boxes in 1935 and because of its design, is known as "Fancy Frame with Script Signature." The unnumbered cards measure 6" x 6-1/4" with frame, and 5" x 5-1/2" without the frame. The player photo is tinted blue, while the background is blue and orange. A facsimile autograph appears at the bottom of the photo. Illinois high school track star Herman "Jack" Waddlington posed for the photos of fictional Jack Armstrong "All-American Boy."

		NM	EX	VG
Complete Set (27):		3,000	1,500	900.00
Common Player:		50.00	25.00	15.50
(1)	Jack Armstrong (Batting)	50.00	25.00	15.50
(2)	Jack Armstrong (Throwing)	50.00	25.00	15.00
(3)	Wally Berger	50.00	25.00	15.00
(4)	Tommy Bridges	50.00	25.00	15.00
(5)	Mickey Cochrane (Black hat)	90.00	45.00	27.00
(6)	Michey Cochrane (White hat)	425.00	210.00	125.00
(7)	James "Rip" Collins	50.00	25.00	15.00
(8)	Dizzy Dean	325.00	160.00	97.00
(9)	Dizzy Dean, Paul Dean	250.00	125.00	75.00
(10)	Paul Dean	55.00	27.50	16.50
(11)	William Delancey	50.00	25.00	15.00
(12)	"Jimmie" Foxx	190.00	95.00	60.00
(13)	Frank Frisch	75.00	37.50	22.00
(14)	Lou Gehrig	475.00	235.00	140.00
(15)	Goose Goslin	75.00	37.50	22.00
(16)	Lefty Grove	125.00	65.00	35.00
(17)	Carl Hubbell	85.00	40.00	25.00
(18)	Travis C. Jackson	75.00	37.50	22.00
(19)	"Chuck" Klein	75.00	37.50	22.00
(20)	Gus Mancuso	50.00	25.00	15.00
(21)	Pepper Martin (Batting)	55.00	27.00	16.50
(22)	Pepper Martin (Portrait)	55.00	27.00	16.50
(23)	Joe Medwick	75.00	37.50	22.00
(24)	Melvin Ott	90.00	45.00	27.00
(25)	Harold Schumacher	50.00	25.00	15.00
(26)	Al Simmons	75.00	37.50	22.00
(27)	"Jo Jo" White	50.00	25.00	15.00

1936 Wheaties - Series 3

Consisting of 12 unnumbered cards, this set is similar in size (6" x 6-1/4" with frame) and design to the Wheaties of the previous year, but is known as "Fancy Frame with Printed Name and Data" because the cards also include a few printed words describing the player.

		NM	EX	VG
Complete Set (12):		1,600	800.00	475.00
Common Player:		45.00	22.00	13.50
(1)	Earl Averill	60.00	30.00	18.00
(2)	Mickey Cochrane	60.00	30.00	18.00
(3)	Jimmy Foxx	200.00	100.00	60.00
(4)	Lou Gehrig	750.00	375.00	225.00
(5)	Hank Greenberg	175.00	90.00	50.00
(6)	"Gabby" Hartnett	60.00	30.00	18.00
(7)	Carl Hubbell	65.00	32.50	20.00
(8)	"Pepper" Martin	50.00	25.00	15.00
(9)	Van L. Mungo	45.00	22.50	13.50
(10)	"Buck" Newsom	45.00	22.50	13.50
(11)	"Arky" Vaughan	60.00	30.00	18.00
(12)	Jimmy Wilson	45.00	22.50	13.50

1936 Wheaties - Series 4

This larger size (8-1/2" x 6") card also made up the back of a Wheaties box, and because of its distinctive border which featured drawings of small athletic figures, it is referred to as "Thin Orange Border/Figures in Border." Twelve major leaguers are pictured in the unnumbered set. The photos are enclosed in a 4" x 6-1/2" box. Below the photo is an endorsement for Wheaties, the "Breakfast of Champions," and a facsimile autograph.

		NM	EX	VG
	Complete Set (12):	1,200	600.00	350.00
	Common Player:	45.00	22.00	13.50
(1)	Curt Davis	45.00	22.50	13.50
(2)	Lou Gehrig	500.00	250.00	150.00
(3)	Charley Gehringer	75.00	37.50	22.00
(4)	Lefty Grove	165.00	85.00	50.00
(5)	Rollie Hemsley	45.00	22.50	13.50
(6)	Billy Herman	75.00	37.50	22.00
(7)	Joe Medwick	75.00	37.50	22.00
(8)	Mel Ott	80.00	40.00	25.00
(9)	Schoolboy Rowe	45.00	22.50	13.50
(10)	Arky Vaughan	75.00	37.50	22.00
(11)	Joe Vosmik	45.00	22.50	13.50
(12)	Lon Warneke	45.00	22.50	13.50

1936 Wheaties - Series 5

Often referred to as "How to Play Winning Baseball," this 12-card set features a large player photo surrounded by blue and white drawings that illustrate various playing tips. Different major leaguers offer advice on different aspects of the game. The cards again made up the back panel of a Wheaties box and measure 8-1/2" x 6-1/2". The cards are numbered from 1 through 12, and it is now believed that each can be found with or without a small number "28" followed by a letter from "A" through "L."

		NM	EX	VG
	Complete Set (12):	1,000	500.00	300.00
	Common Player:	45.00	22.50	13.50
1	Lefty Gomez	85.00	45.00	25.00
2	Billy Herman	75.00	37.50	22.00
3	Luke Appling	75.00	37.50	22.00
4	Jimmie Foxx	90.00	45.00	27.00
5	Joe Medwick	75.00	37.50	22.00
6	Charles Gehringer	75.00	37.50	22.00
7a	Mel Ott (Tips in vertical sequence.)	95.00	45.00	25.00
7b	Mel Ott (Tips in two horizontal rows.)	95.00	45.00	25.00
8	Odell Hale	45.00	22.50	13.50
9	Bill Dickey	85.00	45.00	25.00
10	"Lefty" Grove	85.00	45.00	25.00
11	Carl Hubbell	80.00	40.00	25.00
12	Earl Averill	75.00	37.50	22.00

1937 Wheaties - Series 6

Similar to the Series 5 set, this numbered, 12-card series is known as "How to Star in Baseball" and again includes a large player photo with small instructional drawings to illustrate playing tips. The cards measure 8-1/4" x 6" and include a facsimile autograph.

		NM	EX	VG
	Complete Set (12):	1,000	500.00	300.00
	Common Player:	35.00	17.50	10.00
1	Bill Dickey	75.00	37.50	22.00
2	Red Ruffing	60.00	30.00	18.00
3	Zeke Bonura	35.00	17.50	10.00
4	Charlie Gehringer	60.00	30.00	18.00

5	"Arky" Vaughn (Vaughan)	60.00	30.00	18.00
6	Carl Hubbell	60.00	30.00	18.00
7	John Lewis	35.00	17.50	10.00
8	Heinie Manush	60.00	30.00	18.00
9	"Lefty" Grove	75.00	37.50	22.00
10	Billy Herman	60.00	30.00	18.00
11	Joe DiMaggio	400.00	200.00	120.00
12	Joe Medwick	60.00	30.00	18.00

1937 Wheaties - Series 7

This set of 6" x 8-1/4" panels contains several different card designs. One style (picturing Lombardi, Travis and Mungo) has a white background with an orange border and a large orange circle behind the player. Another design (showing Bonura, DiMaggio and Bridges) has the player outlined against a bright orange background with a Wheaties endorsement along the bottom. A third format (picturing Moore, Radcliff and Martin) has a distinctive red, white and blue border. And a fourth design (featuring Trosky, Demaree and Vaughan) has a tilted picture against an orange background framed in blue and white. The set also includes four Pacific Coast League Players (#29M-29P). The cards are numbered with a small "29" followed by a letter from "A" through "P."

		NM	EX	VG
	Complete Set (16):	1,200	600.00	350.00
	Common Player:	45.00	22.50	13.50
29A	"Zeke" Bonura	45.00	22.50	13.50
29B	Cecil Travis	45.00	22.50	13.50
29C	Frank Demaree	45.00	22.50	13.50
29D	Joe Moore	45.00	22.50	13.50
29E	Ernie Lombardi	60.00	30.00	18.00
29F	John L. "Pepper" Martin	50.00	25.00	15.00
29G	Harold Trosky	45.00	22.50	13.50
29H	Raymond Radcliff	45.00	22.50	13.50
29I	Joe DiMaggio	300.00	150.00	90.00
29J	Tom Bridges	45.00	22.50	13.50
29K	Van L. Mungo	45.00	22.50	13.50
29L	"Arky" Vaughn (Vaughan)	60.00	30.00	18.00
29M	Arnold Statz	100.00	50.00	30.00
29N	Wes Schulmerich	100.00	50.00	30.00
29O	Fred Mueller	100.00	50.00	30.00
29P	Gene Lillard	100.00	50.00	30.00

1937 Wheaties - Series 8

Another series printed on the back of Wheaties boxes in 1937, the eight cards in this set are unnumbered and measure 8-1/2" x 6". There are several different designs, but in all of them the player photo is surrounded by speckles of color, causing this series to be known as the "Speckled Orange, White and Blue" series. A facsimile autograph is included, along with brief printed 1936 season statistics.

		NM	EX	VG
	Complete Set (8):	1,300	650.00	400.00
	Common Player:	120.00	60.00	36.00
(1)	Luke Appling	100.00	50.00	30.00
(2)	Earl Averill	100.00	50.00	30.00
(3)	Joe DiMaggio	450.00	225.00	135.00
(4)	Robert Feller	225.00	110.00	65.00
(5)	Chas. Gehringer	100.00	50.00	30.00
(6)	Lefty Grove	125.00	65.00	35.00
(7)	Carl Hubbell	125.00	65.00	35.00
(8)	Joe Medwick	100.00	50.00	30.00

1937 Wheaties - Series 9

This unnumbered set includes one player from each of the 16 major league teams and is generally referred to as the "Color Series." The cards measure 8-1/2" x 6" and were the back panels of Wheaties boxes. The player photos are shown inside or

against large stars, circles, "V" shapes, rectangles and other geometric designs. A facsimile autograph and team designation are printed near the photo, while a Wheaties endorsement and a line of player stats appear along the bottom.

		NM	EX	VG
	Complete Set (16):	1,600	800.00	480.00
	Common Player:	50.00	25.00	15.00
(1)	Zeke Bonura	50.00	25.00	15.00
(2)	Tom Bridges	50.00	25.00	15.00
(3)	Harland Clift (Harlond)	50.00	25.00	15.00
(4)	Kiki Cuyler	75.00	37.50	22.50
(5)	Joe DiMaggio	600.00	300.00	180.00
(6)	Robert Feller	175.00	85.00	50.00
(7)	Lefty Grove	100.00	50.00	30.00
(8)	Billy Herman	75.00	37.50	22.50
(9)	Carl Hubbell	90.00	45.00	27.50
(10)	Buck Jordan	50.00	25.00	15.00
(11)	"Pepper" Martin	60.00	30.00	18.00
(12)	John Moore	50.00	25.00	15.00
(13)	Wally Moses	50.00	25.00	15.00
(14)	Van L. Mungo	50.00	25.00	15.00
(15)	Cecil Travis	50.00	25.00	15.00
(16)	Arky Vaughan	75.00	37.50	22.50

1937 Wheaties - Series 14

Much reduced in size (2-5/8" x 3-7/8"), these unnumbered cards made up the back panels of single-serving size Wheaties boxes. The player photo (which is sometimes identical to the photos used in the larger series) is set against an orange or white background. The player's name appears in large capital letters with his position and team in smaller capitals. A facsimile autograph and Wheaties endorsement are also included. Some cards are also found with the number "29" followed by a letter.

		NM	EX	VG
	Complete Set (16):	5,000	2,500	1,500
	Common Player:	200.00	100.00	60.00
(1)	"Zeke" Bonura	200.00	100.00	60.00
(2)	Tom Bridges	200.00	100.00	60.00
(3)	Dolph Camilli	200.00	100.00	60.00
(4)	Frank Demaree	200.00	100.00	60.00
(5)	Joe DiMaggio	1,300	650.00	390.00
(6)	Billy Herman	300.00	150.00	90.00
(7)	Carl Hubbell	350.00	175.00	105.00
(8)	Ernie Lombardi	300.00	150.00	90.00
(9)	"Pepper" Martin	250.00	125.00	75.00
(10)	Joe Moore	200.00	100.00	60.00
(11)	Van Mungo	200.00	100.00	60.00
(12)	Mel Ott	350.00	175.00	105.00
(13)	Raymond Radcliff	200.00	100.00	60.00
(14)	Cecil Travis	200.00	100.00	60.00
(15)	Harold Trosky	200.00	100.00	60.00
(16a)	"Arky" Vaughan (29L on card)	350.00	175.00	105.00
(16b)	"Arky" Vaughan (No 29L on card.)	350.00	175.00	105.00

1938 Wheaties - Series 10

One player from each major league team is included in this 16-card set, referred to as the "Biggest Thrills in Baseball" series. Measuring 8-1/2" x 6", each numbered card was the back panel of a Wheaties box and pictures a player along with a printed description of his biggest thrill in baseball and facsimile autograph. All 16 cards in this series have also been found on paper stock.

		NM	EX	VG
	Complete Set (16):	1,700	850.00	500.00
	Common Player:	45.00	22.50	13.50
1	Bob Feller	160.00	80.00	45.00
2	Cecil Travis	45.00	22.50	13.50
3	Joe Medwick	65.00	32.50	20.00
4	Gerald Walker	45.00	22.50	13.50
5	Carl Hubbell	65.00	32.50	20.00
6	Bob Johnson	45.00	22.50	13.50
7	Beau Bell	45.00	22.50	13.50
8	Ernie Lombardi	65.00	32.50	20.00
9	Lefty Grove	80.00	40.00	24.00
10	Lou Fette	45.00	22.50	13.50
11	Joe DiMaggio	600.00	300.00	180.00
12	Pinky Whitney	45.00	22.50	13.50
13	Dizzy Dean	175.00	85.00	55.00
14	Charley Gehringer	65.00	32.50	20.00
15	Paul Waner	65.00	32.50	20.00
16	Dolf Camilli	45.00	22.50	13.50

1938 Wheaties - Series 11

Cards in this unnumbered, eight-card series measure 8-1/2" x 6" and show the players in street clothes either eating or getting ready to enjoy a bowl of Wheaties. Sometimes a waitress or other person also appears in the photo. The set is sometimes called the "Dress Clothes" or "Civies" series.

		NM	EX	VG
	Complete Set (8):	750.00	375.00	225.00
	Common Player:	60.00	30.00	18.00
(1)	Lou Fette	60.00	30.00	18.00
(2)	Jimmie Foxx	145.00	75.00	45.00
(3)	Charlie Gehringer	115.00	55.00	35.00
(4)	Lefty Grove	115.00	55.00	35.00
(5)	Hank Greenberg, Roxie Lawson	115.00	55.00	35.00
(6)	Lee Grissom, Ernie Lombardi	85.00	40.00	25.00
(7)	Joe Medwick	85.00	40.00	25.00
(8)	Lon Warneke	60.00	30.00	18.00

1938 Wheaties - Series 15

Another set of small (2-5/8" x 3-7/8") cards, the photos in this unnumbered series made up the back panels of single-serving size Wheaties boxes. The panels have orange, blue and white backgrounds. Some of the photos are the same as those used in the larger Wheaties panels.

	NM	EX	VG
Complete Set (11):	4,500	2,250	1,350
Common Player:	160.00	80.00	45.00

		NM	EX	VG
(1)	"Zeke" Bonura	160.00	80.00	45.00
(2)	Joe DiMaggio	1,300	650.00	390.00
(3)	Charles Gehringer (Batting)	400.00	200.00	120.00
(4)	Chas. Gehringer (Leaping)	400.00	200.00	120.00
(5)	Hank Greenberg	500.00	250.00	150.00
(6)	Lefty Grove	400.00	200.00	120.00
(7)	Carl Hubbell	325.00	160.00	97.00
(8)	John (Buddy) Lewis	160.00	80.00	45.00
(9)	Heinie Manush	300.00	150.00	90.00
(10)	Joe Medwick	300.00	150.00	90.00
(11)	Arky Vaughan	300.00	150.00	90.00

1939 Wheaties - Series 12

The nine cards in this numbered series, known as the "Personal Pointers" series, measure 8-1/4" x 6" and feature an instructional format similar to earlier Wheaties issues. The cards feature a player photo along with printed tips on various aspects of hitting and pitching.

		NM	EX	VG
	Complete Set (9):	1,500	750.00	450.00
	Common Player:	100.00	50.00	30.00
1	Ernie Lombardi	160.00	80.00	45.00
2	Johnny Allen	100.00	50.00	30.00
3	Lefty Gomez	185.00	90.00	55.00
4	Bill Lee	100.00	50.00	30.00
5	Jimmie Foxx	250.00	125.00	75.00
6	Joe Medwick	160.00	80.00	45.00
7	Hank Greenberg	250.00	125.00	75.00
8	Mel Ott	185.00	90.00	55.00
9	Arky Vaughn (Vaughan)	160.00	80.00	45.00

1939 Wheaties - Series 13

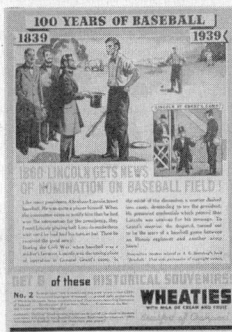

Issued in baseball's centennial year of 1939, this set of eight 6" x 6-3/4" cards commemorates "100 Years of Baseball." Each of the numbered panels illustrates a significant event in baseball history.

		NM	EX	VG
	Complete Set (8):	650.00	325.00	200.00
	Common Panel:	75.00	37.50	22.50
1	Design of First Diamond - 1838 (Abner Doubleday)	75.00	37.50	22.50
2	Gets News of Nomination on Field - 1860 (Abraham Lincoln)	125.00	62.50	37.50
3	Crowd Boos First Baseball Glove - 1869	75.00	37.50	22.50
4	Curve Ball Just an Illusion - 1877	75.00	37.50	22.50
5	Fencer's Mask is Pattern - 1877	75.00	37.50	22.50
6	Baseball Gets "All Dressed Up" - 1895	75.00	37.50	22.50
7	Modern Bludgeon Enters Game - 1895	75.00	37.50	22.50
8	"Casey at the Bat"	100.00	50.00	30.00

1940 Wheaties Champs of the USA

This set consists of 13 numbered panels (plus seven variations). Each pictures three athletes, including one, two or three baseball players; the others include football stars, golfers, skaters, racers, etc. The entire panel measures approximately 8-1/4" x 6", while the actual card measures approximately 6" square. Each athlete is pictured in what looks like a postage stamp with a serrated edge. A brief biography appears alongside the "stamp." Some variations are known to exist among the first nine panels. The cards are numbered in the upper right corner.

		NM	EX	VG
	Complete Set (20):	1,400	700.00	425.00
	Common Panel:	50.00	25.00	15.00
1A	Bob Feller, Lynn Patrick, Charles "Red" Ruffing	135.00	67.00	40.00
1B	Leo Durocher, Lynn Patrick, Charles "Red" Ruffing	90.00	45.00	27.00
2A	Joe DiMaggio, Don Budge, Hank Greenberg	300.00	150.00	90.00
2B	Joe DiMaggio, Mel Ott, Ellsworth Vines	200.00	100.00	60.00
3	Bernie Bierman, Bill Dickey, Jimmie Foxx	125.00	62.00	37.00
4	Morris Arhovich, Capt R.K. Baker, Earl "Dutch" Clark	50.00	25.00	15.00
5	Madison (Matty) Bell, Ab Jenkins, Joe Medwick	50.00	25.00	15.00
6A	Ralph Guldahl, John Mize, Davey O'Brien	50.00	25.00	15.00
6B	Bob Feller, John Mize, Rudy York	90.00	45.00	27.00
6C	Ralph Guldahl, Gabby Hartnett, Davey O'Brien	50.00	25.00	15.00
7A	Joe Cronin, Cecil Isbell, Byron Nelson	50.00	25.00	15.00
7B	Joe Cronin, Hank Greenberg, Byron Nelson	75.00	37.00	22.00
7C	Paul Derringer, Cecil Isbell, Byron Nelson	50.00	25.00	15.00
8A	Ernie Lombardi, Jack Manders, George I. Myers	50.00	25.00	15.00
8B	Paul Derringer, Ernie Lombardi, George I. Myers	50.00	25.00	15.00
9	Bob Bartlett, Captain R.C. Hanson, Terrell Jacobs	50.00	25.00	15.00
10	Lowell "Red" Dawson, Billy Herman, Adele Inge	50.00	25.00	15.00
11	Dolph Camilli, Antoinette Concello, Wallace Wade	50.00	25.00	15.00
12	Luke Appling, Stanley Hack, Hugh McManus	50.00	25.00	15.00
13	Felix Adler, Hal Trosky, Mabel Vinson	50.00	25.00	15.00

1941 Wheaties Champs of the USA

This eight-card series is actually a continuation of the previous year's Wheaties set, and the format is identical. The set begins with number 14, starting where the 1940 set ended.

		NM	EX	VG
	Complete Set (8):	800.00	400.00	240.00
	Common Panel:	50.00	25.00	15.00
14	Felix Adler, Jimmie Foxx, Capt. R.G. Hanson	90.00	45.00	27.00
15	Bernie Bierman, Bob Feller, Jessie McLeod	90.00	45.00	27.00
16	Lowell "Red" Dawson, Hank Greenberg, J.W. Stoker	80.00	40.00	24.00
17	Antoniette Concello, Joe DiMaggio, Byron Nelson	300.00	150.00	90.00
18	Capt. R.L. Baker, Frank "Buck" McCormick, Harold "Pee Wee" Reese	90.00	45.00	27.00
19	William W. Robbins, Gene Sarazen, Gerald "Gee" Walker	50.00	25.00	15.00
20	Harry Danning, Barney McCosky, Bucky Walters	50.00	25.00	15.00
21	Joe "Flash" Gordon, Stan Hack, George I. Myers	50.00	25.00	15.00

1951 Wheaties

Printed as the backs of single-serving size boxes of Wheaties, the six-card 1951 set includes three baseball players and one football player, basketball player and golfer. Welltrimmed cards measure 2-1/2" x 3-1/4". The cards feature blue line drawings of the athletes with a facsimile autograph and descriptive title below. There is a wide white border. A small hoard of complete sets of unused boxes made its way into the hobby in the early 1990s. Complete boxes should be priced at 1.5X the values shown here.

		NM	EX	VG
Complete Set (6):		650.00	325.00	195.00
Common Player:		85.00	42.00	25.00
(1)	Bob Feller (Baseball)	100.00	50.00	30.00
(2)	John Lujack (Football)	55.00	27.50	16.50
(3)	George Mikan (Basketball)	110.00	55.00	35.00
(4)	Stan Musial (Baseball)	150.00	75.00	45.00
(5)	Sam Snead (Golfer)	65.00	32.50	20.00
(6)	Ted Williams (Baseball)	200.00	100.00	60.00

1951 Wheaties Premium Photos

LARRY (YOGI) BERRA

Whether or not these 5" x 7" black-and-white, blank-back photos were ever issued at all, or only on a test basis is unknown. Despite being unmarked, they are reliably attributed to General Mills, possibly intended for use as a Wheaties premium. The photos found on several of the pictures are the same pictures used on the box-back Wheaties cards of 1952. The pictures appear in most cases to be re-uses of team-issued images from photo packs and the like. Player names are in the bottom border in capital letters. Each picture has a small alpha-numeric identifier in the lower-right corner. The scope of the issue is unknown as several letters from the sequence are missing. The letter shown in this checklist is preceded in each case by "A8491."

		NM	EX	VG
Complete Baseball Set (8):		2,600	1,300	775.00
Common Player:		66.00	33.00	20.00
A	Stan Musial	325.00	160.00	95.00
C	Richie Ashburn	120.00	60.00	36.00
D	Bob Feller	120.00	60.00	36.00
E	Al Rosen	65.00	32.50	20.00
F	Larry (Yogi) Berra	175.00	85.00	50.00
G	Mickey Mantle	1,600	800.00	480.00
H	Betty Schalow (Ice skater.)	15.00	7.50	4.50
J	Bob Lemon	65.00	32.50	20.00
K	Roy Campanella	150.00	75.00	45.00

1952 Wheaties

BOB FELLER
PITCHER, CLEVELAND INDIANS

These 2" x 2-3/4" cards appeared on the back of the popular cereal boxes. Actually, sports figures had been appearing on the backs of the boxes for many years, but in 1952, of the

30 athletes depicted, 10 were baseball players. That means there are 20 baseball cards, as each player appears in both a portrait and an action drawing. The cards have a blue line drawing on an orange background with a white border. The player's name, team, and position appear at the bottom. The cards have rounded corners, but are often found poorly cut from the boxes. This set was extensively counterfeited circa 2002, which had a chilling effect on values of cards not professionally graded by a major certification company.

		NM	EX	VG
Complete (Baseball) Set (20):		650.00	325.00	195.00
Common Player:		20.00	10.00	6.00
(1)	Larry "Yogi" Berra (Portrait)	50.00	25.00	15.00
(2)	Larry "Yogi" Berra (Action)	50.00	25.00	15.00
(3)	Roy Campanella (Portrait)	50.00	25.00	15.00
(4)	Roy Campanella (Action)	50.00	25.00	15.00
(5)	Bob Feller (Portrait)	30.00	15.00	9.00
(6)	Bob Feller (Action)	30.00	15.00	9.00
(7)	George Kell (Portrait)	25.00	12.50	7.50
(8)	George Kell (Action)	25.00	12.50	7.50
(9)	Ralph Kiner (Portrait)	25.00	12.50	7.50
(10)	Ralph Kiner (Action)	25.00	12.50	7.50
(11)	Bob Lemon (Portrait)	25.00	12.50	7.50
(12)	Bob Lemon (Action)	25.00	12.50	7.50
(13)	Stan Musial (Portrait)	60.00	30.00	18.00
(14)	Stan Musial (Action)	60.00	30.00	18.00
(15)	Phil Rizzuto (Portrait)	30.00	15.00	9.00
(16)	Phil Rizzuto (Action)	30.00	15.00	9.00
(17)	Elwin "Preacher" Roe (Portrait)	20.00	10.00	6.00
(18)	Elwin "Preacher" Roe (Action)	20.00	10.00	6.00
(19)	Ted Williams (Portrait)	100.00	50.00	30.00
(20)	Ted Williams (Action)	100.00	50.00	30.00

1952 Wheaties Tin Trays

This unique cereal box premium took the shape of a 4-7/8" x 5-1/8" tin tray which was glued to the back of Wheaties boxes. A cream-colored border surrounded the 3" x 4" color photo debossed at center. A black facsimile autograph appears across the photo. At top a small hole was punched for hanging the plaque. Backs were blank, and are often found with glue and paper residue on the gold-tone metal. Most of the plates have acquired numerous scratches and dings over the years, making true Near Mint examples very scarce. The unnumbered trays are checklisted alphabetically. A George Kell tray was long believed to exist but has never been verified.

		NM	EX	VG
Complete Set (4):		1,200	600.00	350.00
Common Player:		50.00	25.00	15.00
(1)	Ralph Kiner	50.00	25.00	15.00
(2)	Stan Musial	125.00	65.00	35.00
(3)	Phil Rizzuto	60.00	30.00	18.00
(4)	Jackie Robinson	1,100	550.00	330.00

1964 Wheaties Stamps

This General Mills' promotion included 50 player stamps and a 48-page orange album called "Wheaties Major League All-Star Baseball Player Stamp Album." The 2-1/2" x 2-3/4" stamps have a color player photo at center with a facsimile autograph and surrounded by a white border. Backs are blank. The unnumbered set is checklisted here in alphabetical order.

		NM	EX	VG
Complete Set (50):		325.00	160.00	95.00
Complete Set, In Album:		125.00	65.00	35.00
Common Player:		4.00	2.00	1.25
Album:		40.00	20.00	12.00
(1)	Hank Aaron	30.00	15.00	9.00
(2)	Bob Allison	4.00	2.00	1.25
(3)	Luis Aparicio	7.50	3.75	2.25
(4)	Ed Bailey	4.00	2.00	1.25
(5)	Steve Barber	4.00	2.00	1.25
(6)	Earl Battey	4.00	2.00	1.25
(7)	Jim Bouton	5.00	2.50	1.50
(8)	Ken Boyer	5.00	2.50	1.50
(9)	Jim Bunning	7.50	3.75	2.25

(10)	Orlando Cepeda	10.00	5.00	3.00
(11)	Roberto Clemente	45.00	22.50	13.50
(12)	Ray Culp	4.00	2.00	1.25
(13)	Tommy Davis	4.00	2.00	1.25
(14)	John Edwards	4.00	2.00	1.25
(15)	Whitey Ford	20.00	10.00	6.00
(16)	Nellie Fox	10.00	5.00	3.00
(17)	Bob Friend	4.00	2.00	1.25
(18)	Jim Gilliam	5.00	2.50	1.50
(19)	Jim Grant	4.00	2.00	1.25
(20)	Dick Groat	4.00	2.00	1.25
(21)	Elston Howard	5.00	2.50	1.50
(22)	Larry Jackson	4.00	2.00	1.25
(23)	Julian Javier	4.00	2.00	1.25
(24)	Al Kaline	12.50	6.25	3.75
(25)	Harmon Killebrew	12.50	6.25	3.75
(26)	Don Leppert	4.00	2.00	1.25
(27)	Frank Malzone	4.00	2.00	1.25
(28)	Juan Marichal	7.50	3.75	2.25
(29)	Willie Mays	30.00	15.00	9.00
(30)	Ken McBride	4.00	2.00	1.25
(31)	Willie McCovey	10.00	5.00	3.00
(32)	Jim O'Toole	4.00	2.00	1.25
(33)	Albie Pearson	4.00	2.00	1.25
(34)	Joe Pepitone	5.00	2.50	1.50
(35)	Ron Perranoski	4.00	2.00	1.25
(36)	Juan Pizzaro	4.00	2.00	1.25
(37)	Dick Radatz	4.00	2.00	1.25
(38)	Bobby Richardson	6.00	3.00	1.75
(39)	Brooks Robinson	12.50	6.25	3.75
(40)	Ron Santo	6.00	3.00	1.75
(41)	Norm Siebern	4.00	2.00	1.25
(42)	Duke Snider	20.00	10.00	6.00
(43)	Warren Spahn	12.50	6.25	3.75
(44)	Joe Torre	6.00	3.00	1.75
(45)	Tom Tresh	5.00	2.50	1.50
(46)	Zoilo Versailles (Versalles)	4.00	2.00	1.25
(47)	Leon Wagner	4.00	2.00	1.25
(48)	Bill White	4.00	2.00	1.25
(49)	Hal Woodeshick	4.00	2.00	1.25
(50)	Carl Yastrzemski	20.00	10.00	6.00

1937 WHIO-Sy Burick Cincinnati Reds postcards

(See 1937-39 Orcajo Cincinnati Reds postcards for checklist, values.)

1889 C.S. White & Co. Boston N.L.

(See 1889 Number 7 Cigars for checklist and value information.)

1977 Wiffle Insert Discs

Similar in concept and format to the many contemporary MSA baseball player disc sets, the pieces inserted within Wiffle brand baseball, softball and bat boxes differ in that they are smaller, at 2-3/8" diameter, and feature a larger checklist. The discs feature black-and-white player portrait photos in the center of a baseball design. The left and right panels are in one of several bright colors. Licensed by the players' association through Mike Schechter Associates, the player photos carry no uniform logos. Backs are printed in black and orange. The unnumbered discs are checklisted here alphabetically.

		NM	EX	VG
Complete Set (80):		325.00	160.00	100.00
Common Player:		2.50	1.25	.70
(1)	Sal Bando	2.50	1.25	.70
(2)	Buddy Bell	2.50	1.25	.70
(3)	Johnny Bench	7.50	3.75	2.25
(4)	Vida Blue	2.50	1.25	.70
(5)	Bert Blyleven	3.00	1.50	.90
(6)	Bobby Bonds	2.50	1.25	.70
(7)	George Brett	12.00	6.00	3.50
(8)	Lou Brock	6.00	3.00	1.75
(9)	Bill Buckner	2.50	1.25	.70
(10)	Ray Burris	2.50	1.25	.70
(11)	Jeff Burroughs	2.50	1.25	.70
(12)	Bert Campaneris	2.50	1.25	.70
(13)	Rod Carew	6.00	3.00	1.75
(14)	Steve Carlton	6.00	3.00	1.75
(15)	Dave Cash	2.50	1.25	.70
(16)	Cesar Cedeno	2.50	1.25	.70
(17)	Ron Cey	2.50	1.25	.70
(18)	Chris Chambliss	2.50	1.25	.70
(19)	Dave Concepcion	2.50	1.25	.70
(20)	Dennis Eckersley	6.00	3.00	1.75
(21)	Mark Fidrych	3.50	1.75	1.00
(22)	Rollie Fingers	6.00	3.00	1.75
(23)	Carlton Fisk	6.00	3.00	1.75
(24)	George Foster	2.50	1.25	.70
(25)	Wayne Garland	2.50	1.25	.70
(26)	Ralph Garr	2.50	1.25	.70
(27)	Steve Garvey	5.00	2.50	1.50
(28)	Don Gullett	2.50	1.25	.70
(29)	Larry Hisle	2.50	1.25	.70
(30)	Al Hrabosky	2.50	1.25	.70
(31)	Catfish Hunter	6.00	3.00	1.75
(32)	Reggie Jackson	12.00	6.00	3.50
(33)	Randy Jones	2.50	1.25	.70
(34)	Dave Kingman	2.50	1.25	.70
(35)	Jerry Koosman	2.50	1.25	.70
(36)	Ed Kranepool	2.50	1.25	.70
(37)	Ron LeFlore	2.50	1.25	.70
(38)	Sixto Lezcano	2.50	1.25	.70
(39)	Davey Lopes	2.50	1.25	.70
(40)	Greg Luzinski	2.50	1.25	.70
(41)	Fred Lynn	2.50	1.25	.70
(42)	Garry Maddox	2.50	1.25	.70
(43)	Jon Matlock	2.50	1.25	.70
(44)	Gary Matthews	2.50	1.25	.70
(45)	Lee May	2.50	1.25	.70
(46)	John Mayberry	2.50	1.25	.70
(47)	Bake McBride	2.50	1.25	.70
(48)	Tug McGraw	2.50	1.25	.70
(49)	Hal McRae	2.50	1.25	.70
(50)	Andy Messersmith	2.50	1.25	.70
(51)	Randy Moffitt	2.50	1.25	.70
(52)	John Montefusco	2.50	1.25	.70
(53)	Joe Morgan	6.00	3.00	1.75
(54)	Thurman Munson	6.00	3.00	1.75
(55)	Graig Nettles	2.50	1.25	.70
(56)	Al Oliver	2.50	1.25	.70
(57)	Jorge Orta	2.50	1.25	.70
(58)	Jim Palmer	6.00	3.00	1.75
(59)	Dave Parker	2.50	1.25	.70
(60)	Tony Perez	6.00	3.00	1.75
(61)	Gaylord Perry	6.00	3.00	1.75
(62)	Jim Rice	3.00	1.50	.90
(63)	Steve Rogers	2.50	1.25	.70
(64)	Pete Rose	15.00	7.50	4.50
(65)	Joe Rudi	2.50	1.25	.70
(66)	Nolan Ryan	30.00	15.00	9.00
(67)	Manny Sanguillen	2.50	1.25	.70
(68)	Mike Schmidt	12.00	6.00	3.50
(69)	Tom Seaver	7.50	3.75	2.25
(70)	Ted Simmons	2.50	1.25	.70
(71)	Reggie Smith	2.50	1.25	.70
(72)	Willie Stargell	6.00	3.00	1.75
(73)	Rusty Staub	2.50	1.25	.70
(74)	Frank Tanana	2.50	1.25	.70
(75)	Gene Tenace	2.50	1.25	.70
(76)	Luis Tiant	2.50	1.25	.70
(77)	Manny Trillo	2.50	1.25	.70
(78)	Bob Watson	2.50	1.25	.70
(79)	Carl Yastrzemski	7.50	3.75	2.25
(80)	Richie Zisk	2.50	1.25	.70

1978 Wiffle Box-Side Discs

Similar in concept and format to the many contemporary MSA baseball player disc sets, the pieces printed on the sides of Wiffle-brand baseball boxes differ in that they are smaller, at 2-3/8" diameter, and feature a larger checklist. The discs feature black-and-white player portrait photos in the center of a baseball design. The left and right panels are in one of sev-

eral bright colors. Licensed by the players' association through Mike Schechter Associates, the player photos carry no uniform logos. Backs are printed in black and orange. The unnumbered discs are checklisted here alphabetically.

		NM	EX	VG
Complete Set (88):		325.00	160.00	100.00
Common Player:		2.50	1.25	.70
(1)	Sal Bando	2.50	1.25	.70
(2)	Buddy Bell	2.50	1.25	.70
(3)	Johnny Bench	7.50	3.75	2.25
(4)	Vida Blue	2.50	1.25	.70
(5)	Bert Blyleven	3.00	1.50	.90
(6)	Bobby Bonds	2.50	1.25	.70
(7)	George Brett	12.00	6.00	3.50
(8)	Lou Brock	6.00	3.00	1.75
(9)	Bill Buckner	2.50	1.25	.70
(10)	Ray Burris	2.50	1.25	.70
(11)	Jeff Burroughs	2.50	1.25	.70
(12)	Bert Campaneris	2.50	1.25	.70
(13)	John Candelaria	2.50	1.25	.70
(14)	Jose Cardenal	2.50	1.25	.70
(15)	Rod Carew	6.00	3.00	1.75
(16)	Steve Carlton	6.00	3.00	1.75
(17)	Dave Cash	2.50	1.25	.70
(18)	Cesar Cedeno	2.50	1.25	.70
(19)	Ron Cey	2.50	1.25	.70
(20)	Chris Chambliss	2.50	1.25	.70
(21)	Dave Concepcion	2.50	1.25	.70
(22)	Dennis Eckersley	6.00	3.00	1.75
(23)	Mark Fidrych	3.50	1.75	1.00
(24)	Rollie Fingers	6.00	3.00	1.75
(25)	Carlton Fisk	6.00	3.00	1.75
(26)	George Foster	2.50	1.25	.70
(27)	Wayne Garland	2.50	1.25	.70
(28)	Ralph Garr	2.50	1.25	.70
(29)	Steve Garvey	5.00	2.50	1.50
(30)	Don Gullett	2.50	1.25	.70
(31)	Larry Hisle	2.50	1.25	.70
(32)	Al Hrabosky	2.50	1.25	.70
(33)	Catfish Hunter	6.00	3.00	1.75
(34)	Reggie Jackson	12.00	6.00	3.50
(35)	Randy Jones	2.50	1.25	.70
(36)	Von Joshua	2.50	1.25	.70
(37)	Dave Kingman	2.50	1.25	.70
(38)	Jerry Koosman	2.50	1.25	.70
(39)	Ed Kranepool	2.50	1.25	.70
(40)	Ron LeFlore	2.50	1.25	.70
(41)	Sixto Lezcano	2.50	1.25	.70
(42)	Davey Lopes	2.50	1.25	.70
(43)	Greg Luzinski	2.50	1.25	.70
(44)	Fred Lynn	2.50	1.25	.70
(45)	Garry Maddox	2.50	1.25	.70
(46)	Jon Matlock	2.50	1.25	.70
(47)	Gary Matthews	2.50	1.25	.70
(48)	Lee May	2.50	1.25	.70
(49)	John Mayberry	2.50	1.25	.70
(50)	Bake McBride	2.50	1.25	.70
(51)	Tug McGraw	2.50	1.25	.70
(52)	Hal McRae	2.50	1.25	.70
(53)	Andy Messersmith	2.50	1.25	.70
(54)	Randy Moffitt	2.50	1.25	.70
(55)	John Montefusco	2.50	1.25	.70
(56)	Joe Morgan	6.00	3.00	1.75
(57)	Thurman Munson	6.00	3.00	1.75
(58)	Graig Nettles	2.50	1.25	.70
(59)	Bill North	2.50	1.25	.70
(60)	Al Oliver	2.50	1.25	.70
(61)	Jorge Orta	2.50	1.25	.70
(62)	Jim Palmer	6.00	3.00	1.75
(63)	Dave Parker	2.50	1.25	.70
(64)	Tony Perez	6.00	3.00	1.75
(65)	Gaylord Perry	6.00	3.00	1.75
(66)	Jim Rice	3.00	1.50	.90
(67)	Ellie Rodriguez	2.50	1.25	.70
(68)	Steve Rogers	2.50	1.25	.70
(69)	Pete Rose	15.00	7.50	4.50
(70)	Joe Rudi	2.50	1.25	.70
(71)	Nolan Ryan	30.00	15.00	9.00
(72)	Manny Sanguillen	2.50	1.25	.70
(73)	Mike Schmidt	12.00	6.00	3.50
(74)	Tom Seaver	7.50	3.75	2.25
(75)	Ted Simmons	2.50	1.25	.70
(76)	Reggie Smith	2.50	1.25	.70
(77)	Jim Spencer	2.50	1.25	.70
(78)	Willie Stargell	6.00	3.00	1.75
(79)	Rusty Staub	2.50	1.25	.70
(80)	Rennie Stennett	2.50	1.25	.70
(81)	Frank Tanana	2.50	1.25	.70
(82)	Gene Tenace	2.50	1.25	.70
(83)	Luis Tiant	2.50	1.25	.70
(84)	Manny Trillo	2.50	1.25	.70
(85)	Bob Watson	2.50	1.25	.70
(86)	Butch Wynegar	2.50	1.25	.70
(87)	Carl Yastrzemski	7.50	3.75	2.25
(88)	Richie Zisk	2.50	1.25	.70

1922 Willard's Chocolates Premium

Details on distribution of this 7-1/8" x 11-1/4" premium are unclear, likely involving some sort of wrapper or coupon redemption. The blank-back piece has a central photo of Babe Ruth in action. A facsimile autograph appears in a panel at bottom.

	NM	EX	VG
Babe Ruth	4,000	2,000	1,200

1923 Willard's Chocolate (V100)

Issued circa 1923, this set was produced by the Willard Chocolate Co. of Canada and features sepia-toned photographs on cards measuring about 2" x 3-1/4". The cards are blank-backed and feature the player's name in script on the front, along with a tiny credit line: "Photo by International." The set is complete at 180 cards and nearly one-fourth of the photos used in the set are identical to the better known E120 American Caramel set. The Willard set is identified as V100 in the American Card Catalog.

		NM	EX	VG
Complete Set (180):		30,000	15,000	9,000
Common Player:		100.00	50.00	30.00
(1)	Chas. B. Adams	100.00	50.00	30.00
(2)	Grover C. Alexander	400.00	200.00	125.00
(3)	J.P. Austin	100.00	50.00	30.00
(4)	J.C. Bagby	100.00	50.00	30.00
(5)	J. Franklin Baker	300.00	150.00	90.00
(6)	David J. Bancroft	300.00	150.00	90.00
(7)	Turner Barber	100.00	50.00	30.00
(8)	Jesse L. Barnes	100.00	50.00	30.00
(9)	J.C. Bassler	100.00	50.00	30.00
(10)	L.A. Blue	100.00	50.00	30.00
(11)	Norman D. Boeckel	100.00	50.00	30.00
(12)	F.L. Brazil (Brazill)	100.00	50.00	30.00
(13)	G.H. Burns	100.00	50.00	30.00
(14)	Geo. J. Burns	100.00	50.00	30.00
(15)	Leon Cadore	100.00	50.00	30.00
(16)	Max G. Carey	300.00	150.00	90.00
(17)	Harold G. Carlson	100.00	50.00	30.00
(18)	Lloyd R Christenberry (Christenbury)	100.00	50.00	30.00
(19)	Vernon J. Clemons	100.00	50.00	30.00
(20)	T.R. Cobb	2,400	1,200	750.00
(21)	Bert Cole	100.00	50.00	30.00
(22)	John F. Collins	100.00	50.00	30.00
(23)	S. Coveleskie (Coveleski)	300.00	150.00	90.00
(24)	Walton E. Cruise	100.00	50.00	30.00
(25)	G.W. Cutshaw	100.00	50.00	30.00
(26)	Jacob E. Daubert	100.00	50.00	30.00
(27)	Geo. Dauss	100.00	50.00	30.00
(28)	F.T. Davis	100.00	50.00	30.00
(29)	Chas. A. Deal	100.00	50.00	30.00
(30)	William L. Doak	100.00	50.00	30.00
(31)	William E. Donovan	100.00	50.00	30.00
(32)	Hugh Duffy	300.00	150.00	90.00
(33)	J.A. Dugan	100.00	50.00	30.00
(34)	Louis B. Duncan	100.00	50.00	30.00
(35)	James Dykes	100.00	50.00	30.00
(36)	H.J. Ehmke	100.00	50.00	30.00
(37)	F.R. Ellerbe	100.00	50.00	30.00
(38)	E.G. Erickson	100.00	50.00	30.00
(39)	John J. Evers	300.00	150.00	90.00
(40)	U.C. Faber	300.00	150.00	90.00
(41)	B.A. Falk	100.00	50.00	30.00
(42)	Max Flack	100.00	50.00	30.00
(43)	Lee Fohl	100.00	50.00	30.00
(44)	Jacques F. Fournier	100.00	50.00	30.00
(45)	Frank F. Frisch	300.00	150.00	90.00
(46)	C.E. Galloway	100.00	50.00	30.00
(47)	W.C. Gardner	100.00	50.00	30.00
(48)	E.P. Gharrity	100.00	50.00	30.00
(49)	Geo. Gibson	100.00	50.00	30.00
(50)	Wm. Gleason	100.00	50.00	30.00
(51)	William Gleason	100.00	50.00	30.00
(52)	Henry M. Gowdy	100.00	50.00	30.00
(53)	I.M. Griffin	100.00	50.00	30.00
(54)	Tom Griffith	100.00	50.00	30.00
(55)	Burleigh A. Grimes	300.00	150.00	90.00
(56)	Charles J. Grimm	100.00	50.00	30.00
(57)	Jesse J. Haines	300.00	150.00	90.00
(58)	S.R. Harris	100.00	50.00	30.00
(59)	W.B. Harris	100.00	50.00	30.00
(60)	R.K. Hasty	100.00	50.00	30.00
(61)	H.E. Heilman (Heilmann)	300.00	150.00	90.00
(62)	Walter J. Henline	100.00	50.00	30.00
(63)	Walter L. Holke	100.00	50.00	30.00
(64)	Charles J. Hollocher	100.00	50.00	30.00
(65)	H.B. Hooper	300.00	150.00	90.00
(66)	Rogers Hornsby	400.00	200.00	125.00
(67)	W.C. Hoyt	300.00	150.00	90.00
(68)	Miller Huggins	300.00	150.00	90.00

		NM	EX	VG
(69)	W.C. Jacobsen (Jacobson)	100.00	50.00	30.00
(70)	C.D. Jamieson	100.00	50.00	30.00
(71)	Ernest Johnson	100.00	50.00	30.00
(72)	W.P. Johnson	750.00	375.00	225.00
(73)	James H. Johnston	100.00	50.00	30.00
(74)	R.W. Jones	100.00	50.00	30.00
(75)	Samuel Pond Jones	100.00	50.00	30.00
(76)	J.I. Judge	100.00	50.00	30.00
(77)	James W. Keenan	100.00	50.00	30.00
(78)	Geo. L. Kelly	300.00	150.00	90.00
(79)	Peter J. Kilduff	100.00	50.00	30.00
(80)	William Killefer	100.00	50.00	30.00
(81)	Lee King	100.00	50.00	30.00
(82)	Ray Kolp	100.00	50.00	30.00
(83)	John Lavan	100.00	50.00	30.00
(84)	H.L. Leibold	100.00	50.00	30.00
(85)	Connie Mack	300.00	150.00	90.00
(86)	J.W. Mails	100.00	50.00	30.00
(87)	Walter J. Maranville	300.00	150.00	90.00
(88)	Richard W. Marquard	300.00	150.00	90.00
(89)	C.W. Mays	100.00	50.00	30.00
(90)	Geo. F. McBride	100.00	50.00	30.00
(91)	H.M. McClellan	100.00	50.00	30.00
(92)	John J. McGraw	300.00	150.00	90.00
(93)	Austin B. McHenry	100.00	50.00	30.00
(94)	J. McInnis	100.00	50.00	30.00
(95)	Douglas McWeeney (McWeeny)	100.00	50.00	30.00
(96)	M. Menosky	100.00	50.00	30.00
(97)	Emil F. Meusel	100.00	50.00	30.00
(98)	R. Meusel	100.00	50.00	30.00
(99)	Henry W. Meyers	100.00	50.00	30.00
(100)	J.C. Milan	100.00	50.00	30.00
(101)	John K. Miljus	100.00	50.00	30.00
(102)	Edmund J. Miller	100.00	50.00	30.00
(103)	Elmer Miller	100.00	50.00	30.00
(104)	Otto L. Miller	100.00	50.00	30.00
(105)	Fred Mitchell	100.00	50.00	30.00
(106)	Geo. Mogridge	100.00	50.00	30.00
(107)	Patrick J. Moran	100.00	50.00	30.00
(108)	John D. Morrison	100.00	50.00	30.00
(109)	J.A. Mostil	100.00	50.00	30.00
(110)	Clarence F. Mueller	100.00	50.00	30.00
(111)	A. Earle Neale	100.00	50.00	30.00
(112)	Joseph Oeschger	100.00	50.00	30.00
(113)	Robert J. O'Farrell	100.00	50.00	30.00
(114)	J.C. Oldham	100.00	50.00	30.00
(115)	I.M. Olson	100.00	50.00	30.00
(116)	Geo. M. O'Neil	100.00	50.00	30.00
(117)	S.F. O'Neill	100.00	50.00	30.00
(118)	Frank J. Parkinson	100.00	50.00	30.00
(119)	Geo. H. Paskert	100.00	50.00	30.00
(120)	R.T. Peckinpaugh	100.00	50.00	30.00
(121)	H.J. Pennock	300.00	150.00	90.00
(122)	Ralph Perkins	100.00	50.00	30.00
(123)	Edw. J. Pfeffer	100.00	50.00	30.00
(124)	W.C. Pipp	100.00	50.00	30.00
(125)	Charles Elmer Ponder	100.00	50.00	30.00
(126)	Raymond R. Powell	100.00	50.00	30.00
(127)	D.B. Pratt	100.00	50.00	30.00
(128)	Joseph Rapp	100.00	50.00	30.00
(129)	John H. Rawlings	100.00	50.00	30.00
(130)	E.S. Rice (Should be E.C.)	300.00	150.00	90.00
(131)	Branch Rickey	350.00	175.00	110.00
(132)	James J. Ring	100.00	50.00	30.00
(133)	Eppa J. Rixey	300.00	150.00	90.00
(134)	Davis A. Robertson	100.00	50.00	30.00
(135)	Edwin Rommel	100.00	50.00	30.00
(136)	Edd J. Roush	300.00	150.00	90.00
(137)	Harold Ruel (Herold)	100.00	50.00	30.00
(138)	Allen Russell	100.00	50.00	30.00
(139)	G.H. Ruth	4,500	2,250	1,400
(140)	Wilfred D. Ryan	100.00	50.00	30.00
(141)	Henry F. Sallee	100.00	50.00	30.00
(142)	W.H. Schang	100.00	50.00	30.00
(143)	Raymond H. Schmandt	100.00	50.00	30.00
(144)	Everett Scott	100.00	50.00	30.00
(145)	Henry Severeid	100.00	50.00	30.00
(146)	Jos. W. Sewell	300.00	150.00	90.00
(147)	Howard S. Shanks	100.00	50.00	30.00
(148)	E.H. Sheely	100.00	50.00	30.00
(149)	Ralph Shinners	100.00	50.00	30.00
(150)	U.J. Shocker	100.00	50.00	30.00
(151)	G.H. Sisler	300.00	150.00	90.00
(152)	Earl L. Smith	100.00	50.00	30.00
(153)	Earl S. Smith	100.00	50.00	30.00
(154)	Geo. A. Smith	100.00	50.00	30.00
(155)	J.W. Smith	100.00	50.00	30.00
(156)	Tris E. Speaker	400.00	200.00	125.00
(157)	Arnold Staatz (Statz)	100.00	50.00	30.00
(158)	J.R. Stephenson	100.00	50.00	30.00
(159)	Milton J. Stock	100.00	50.00	30.00
(160)	John L. Sullivan	100.00	50.00	30.00
(161)	H.F. Tormahlen	100.00	50.00	30.00
(162)	Jas. A. Tierney	100.00	50.00	30.00
(163)	J.T. Tobin	100.00	50.00	30.00
(164)	Jas. L. Vaughn	100.00	50.00	30.00
(165)	R.H. Veach	100.00	50.00	30.00
(166)	C.W. Walker	100.00	50.00	30.00
(167)	A.L. Ward	100.00	50.00	30.00
(168)	Zack D. Wheat	300.00	150.00	90.00
(169)	George B. Whitted	100.00	50.00	30.00
(170)	Irvin K. Wilhelm	100.00	50.00	30.00
(171)	Roy H. Wilkinson	100.00	50.00	30.00
(172)	Fred C. Williams	100.00	50.00	30.00
(173)	K.R. Williams	100.00	50.00	30.00
(174)	Sam'l W. Wilson	100.00	50.00	30.00
(175)	Ivy B. Wingo	100.00	50.00	30.00
(176)	L.W. Witt	100.00	50.00	30.00
(177)	Joseph Wood	200.00	100.00	60.00
(178)	E. Yaryan	100.00	50.00	30.00
(179)	R.S. Young	100.00	50.00	30.00
(180)	Ross Young (Youngs)	300.00	150.00	90.00

1924 Willard's Chocolate Sports Champions (V122)

Three baseball players are featured among this 56-card Canadian set. The black-and-white cards are printed on thin

BABE RUTH HOME RUN CHAMPION

paper measuring 1-3/8" x 3-3/8". Backs are blank. The set features male and female athletes from many different sports, with a distinct Canadian flavor. The candy company was headquartered in Toronto.

		NM	EX	VG
2	Eddie Collins	600.00	300.00	180.00
5	Babe Ruth	3,250	1,625	975.00
39	Ty Cobb	2,250	1,125	675.00

1911 Williams Baking Philadelphia A's (D359)

GET A FULL SET OF 18 World's Champions For 1910 TO BE HAD ONLY WITH WILLIAMS' Wrapped Bread ADMIRAL AND POTATOE BRANDS GEIGER BROS., NEWARK, N. J.

This Philadelphia Athletics team set is among the scarcest early 20th Century baking company issues. It commemorates the A's 1910 Championship season, and, except for pitcher Jack Coombs, the checklist includes nearly all key members of the club, including manager Connie Mack. The cards are the standard size for the era, 1-1/2" x 2-5/8". Fronts feature a player portrait set against a colored background. The player's name and the word "Athletics" appear at the bottom, while "World's Champions 1910" is printed along the top. Backs of the cards advertise the set as the "Athletics Series." Collectors should be aware that the same checklist was used for a similar Athletics set issued by Rochester Baking and Cullivan's Fireside tobacco (T208) and also that blank-backed versions are also known to exist, cataloged as E104 in the American Card Catalog.

		NM	EX	VG
Complete Set (18):		85,000	35,000	17,000
Common Player:		3,200	1,600	800.00
(1)	Home Run Baker	7,000	3,500	1,750
(2)	Jack Barry	3,200	1,600	800.00
(3)	Chief Bender	7,000	3,500	1,750
(4)	Eddie Collins	7,000	3,500	1,750
(5)	Harry Davis	6,000	3,000	1,500
(6)	Jimmy Dygert	3,200	1,600	800.00
(7)	Topsy Hartsel	3,200	1,600	800.00
(8)	Harry Krause	3,200	1,600	800.00
(9)	Jack Lapp	3,200	1,600	800.00
(10)	Paddy Livingston	3,200	1,600	800.00
(11)	Bris Lord	3,200	1,600	800.00
(12)	Connie Mack	14,000	7,900	4,575
(13)	Cy Morgan	3,200	1,600	800.00
(14)	Danny Murphy	6,000	3,000	1,500
(15)	Rube Oldring	3,200	1,600	800.00
(16)	Eddie Plank	14,000	7,900	4,575
(17)	Amos Strunk	3,200	1,600	800.00
(18a)	Ira Thomas (1910 at top)	3,200	1,600	800.00
(18b)	Ira Thomas (1910 at right)	3,200	1,600	800.00

1910 Williams Caramels (E103)

This 30-card set issued by the Williams Caramel Co. of Oxford, Pa., in 1910 can be differentiated from other similar sets because it was printed on a thin paper stock rather than cardboard. Measuring approximately 1-3/4" x 2-5/8", each card features a player portrait set against a red background. The bottom of the card lists the player's last name, position

N. LAJOIE, 2d B., Cleveland
The Williams Caramel Co. Oxford, Pa.

and team; beneath that is the line, "The Williams Caramel Co. Oxford Pa." Nearly all of the photos in the set, which is designated E103 by the ACC, are identical to those in the M116 Sporting Life set.

		NM	EX	VG
Complete Set (30):		156,000	60,000	30,000
Common Player:		1,175	475.00	225.00
(1)	Chas. Bender	5,400	2,150	1,100
(2)	Roger Bresnahan	5,400	2,150	1,100
(3)	Mordecai Brown	5,400	2,150	1,100
(4)	Frank Chance	5,400	2,150	1,100
(5)	Hal Chase	3,600	1,450	700.00
(6)	Ty Cobb	45,000	18,000	9,000
(7)	Edward Collins	5,400	2,150	1,100
(8)	Sam Crawford	5,400	2,150	1,100
(9)	Harry Davis	1,175	475.00	225.00
(10)	Arthur Devlin	1,175	475.00	225.00
(11)	William Donovan	1,175	475.00	225.00
(12)	Chas. Dooin	1,175	475.00	225.00
(13)	L. Doyle	1,175	475.00	225.00
(14)	John Ewing	1,175	475.00	225.00
(15)	George Gibson	1,175	475.00	225.00
(16)	Hugh Jennings	5,400	2,150	1,100
(17)	David Jones	1,175	475.00	225.00
(18)	Tim Jordan	1,175	475.00	225.00
(19)	N. Lajoie	5,400	2,150	1,100
(20)	Thomas Leach	1,175	475.00	225.00
(21)	Harry Lord	1,175	475.00	225.00
(22)	Chris. Mathewson	18,000	7,200	3,600
(23)	John McLean	1,175	475.00	225.00
(24)	Geo. W. McQuillan	1,175	475.00	225.00
(25)	Pastorius	1,175	475.00	225.00
(26)	N. Rucker	1,175	475.00	225.00
(27)	Fred Tenny (Tenney)	1,175	475.00	225.00
(28)	Ira Thomas	1,175	475.00	225.00
(29)	Hans Wagner	36,000	14,400	7,200
(30)	Robert Wood	1,175	475.00	225.00

1889 E.R. Williams Card Game

This set of 52 playing cards came packed in its own box that advertised the set as the "Egerton R. Williams Popular Indoor Base Ball Game." Designed to look like a conventional deck of playing cards, the set included various players from the National League and the American Association. Although the set contains 52 cards (like a typical deck of playing cards) only 19 actually feature color drawings of players. Each of these cards pictures two different players (one at the top and a second at the bottom, separated by sepia-colored crossed bats in the middle), resulting in 38 different players. The remaining 33 cards in the deck are strictly game cards showing a specific baseball play (such as "Batter Out on Fly" or "Two Base Hit", etc.). The cards have green-tinted backs and measure 2-7/16" x 3-1/2". Each one carries an 1889 copyright line by E.R. Williams.

		NM	EX	VG
Complete Boxed Set:		24,000	12,000	7,250
Common Player Card:		600.00	300.00	225.00
Common Game Action Card:		110.00	55.00	30.00
(1)	Cap Anson, Buck Ewing	2,400	1,200	720.00
(2)	Dan Brouthers, Arlie Latham	900.00	450.00	275.00
(3)	Charles Buffinton, Bob Carruthers	600.00	300.00	225.00
(4)	Hick Carpenter, Cliff Carroll	600.00	300.00	225.00
(5)	Charles Comiskey, Roger Connor	1,200	600.00	360.00
(6)	Pop Corkhill, Jim Fogarty	600.00	300.00	225.00
(7)	John Clarkson, Tim Keefe	1,200	600.00	360.00

		NM	EX	VG
(8)	Jerry Denny, Mike Tiernan	600.00	300.00	225.00
(9)	Dave Foutz, King Kelly	2,200	1,100	660.00
(10)	Pud Galvin, Dave Orr	900.00	450.00	275.00
(11)	Jack Glasscock, Tommy Tucker	600.00	300.00	225.00
(12)	Mike Griffin, Ed McKean	600.00	300.00	225.00
(13)	Dummy Hoy, Long John Reilley (Reilly)	900.00	450.00	275.00
(14)	Arthur Irwin, Ned Williamson	600.00	300.00	225.00
(15)	Silver King, John Tener	900.00	450.00	275.00
(16)	Al Myers, Cub Stricker	600.00	300.00	225.00
(17)	Fred Pfeffer, Chicken Wolf	600.00	300.00	225.00
(18)	Tom Ramsey, Gus Weyhing	600.00	300.00	225.00
(19)	John Ward, Curt Welch	1,000	500.00	300.00

1961 J.B. Williams Co. Roger Maris Lithograph

The maker of Lectric Shave and Aqua Velva offered fans a lithograph of Roger Maris hitting his 59th home run at Baltimore, Sept. 20, 1961. The 16" x 11" black-and-white print on parchment paper was available by mail for 25 cents and a box top from either of the shaving products. The artwork is by Robert Riger.

	NM	EX	VG
Roger Maris	200.00	100.00	60.00

1908 R.C. Williams Cy Young Postcard

A mature Cy Young, about age 42, is pictured on this postcard bearing the imprint of R.C. Williams. No other contemporary cards with this imprint have been reported.

	NM	EX	VG
Cy Young	800.00	400.00	240.00

1954 Wilson Franks

 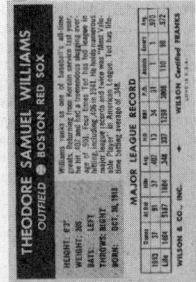

The 2-5/8" x 3-3/4" cards are among the most popular and scarcest baseball card sets issued with hot dogs during the 1950s. The cards feature color-added photos on the front along with a facsimile autograph and a package of frankfurters. Backs feature personal information, a career summary and 1953 and career statistics. Cards were packaged in direct contact with the meat, resulting in many exhibiting grease stains. Survival rates of the various players differ widely, probably based on the geography of initial distribution. A small hoard of roughly half the players was discovered in unissued condition in the late 1990s, temporarily influencing the market.

		NM	EX	VG
Complete Set (20):		30,000	12,000	6,000
Common Player:		650.00	260.00	130.00
Advertising Poster:		7,500	3,500	2,000
(1)	Roy Campanella	1,800	725.00	350.00

		NM	EX	VG
(2)	Del Ennis	650.00	260.00	130.00
(3)	Carl Erskine	675.00	275.00	135.00
(4)	Ferris Fain	650.00	260.00	130.00
(5)	Bob Feller	1,250	500.00	250.00
(6)	Nelson Fox	1,250	500.00	250.00
(7)	Johnny Groth	750.00	300.00	150.00
(8)	Stan Hack	1,100	440.00	220.00
(9)	Gil Hodges	2,750	1,100	550.00
(10)	Ray Jablonski	1,250	500.00	250.00
(11)	Harvey Kuenn	1,350	550.00	275.00
(12)	Roy McMillan	650.00	260.00	130.00
(13)	Andy Pafko	650.00	260.00	130.00
(14)	Paul Richards	900.00	360.00	180.00
(15)	Hank Sauer	900.00	360.00	180.00
(16)	Red Schoendienst	1,000	400.00	200.00
(17)	Enos Slaughter	800.00	320.00	160.00
(18)	Vern Stephens	650.00	260.00	130.00
(19)	Sammy White	650.00	260.00	130.00
(20)	Ted Williams	13,500	6,500	3,500

1961 Wilson Meats L.A. Dodgers/Angels

It is likely these 5-1/2" x 8-1/2" photos were prepared for promotional appearances by players on behalf of the meat company. The player name appears at the bottom of the photo and the sponsor's message appears at bottom, "Courtesy of WILSON & CO., Inc., Fine Meat Products." Backs are blank. The pictures are often found with player autographs, another indicator of their use at personal appearances.

		NM	EX	VG
(1)	Ron Fairly	50.00	25.00	15.00
(2)	Gil Hodges	75.00	37.00	22.00
(3)	Frank Howard	50.00	25.00	15.00
(4)	Ted Kluszewski	60.00	30.00	18.00

1950s-70s Wilson Advisory Staff Photos

Advisory staff photos were a promotional item which debuted in the early 1950s, flourished in the 1960s and died in the early 1970s. Generally 8" x 10" (sometimes a little larger), these black-and-white (a few later were color) glossy photos picture players who had contracted with a major baseball equipment company to endorse and use their product. Usually the product - most often a glove - was prominently displayed in the photo. The pictures were often displayed in the windows of sporting goods stores or the walls of sports departments and were sometimes made available to customers. Because the companies tended to stick with players over the years, some photos were reissued, sometimes with and sometimes without a change of team, pose or style. The photos are checklisted here in alphabetical order. A pose description is given where known. It is unlikely this list is complete. Gaps have been left in the assigned numbering to accommodate future additions. In general, Wilson advisory staff photos feature the player name and a line of type indicating the player's status as an advisory staffer in the bottom border.

		NM	EX	VG
Common Player:		14.00	7.00	4.00
(1)	Bob Allison (Twins, full-length.)	20.00	10.00	6.00
(2)	Felipe Alou (Braves, neck-to-cap.)	25.00	12.50	7.50
(3)	Felipe Alou (Braves, upper body.)	25.00	12.50	7.50
(4)	Max Alvis (Indians, hands on knees.)	20.00	10.00	6.00
(5)	Max Alvis (Indians, upper body.)	20.00	10.00	6.00
(6)	Luis Aparicio (White Sox, horizontal, fielding.)	50.00	25.00	15.00
(7)	Luis Aparicio (White Sox, fielding, full-length.)	40.00	20.00	12.00
(8)	Luis Aparicio (Orioles, full-length.)	50.00	25.00	15.00
(9)	Gerry Arrigo (Reds, full-length pitching.)	20.00	10.00	6.00
(10)	Ernie Banks (Batting)	75.00	37.00	22.00
(11)	Ernie Banks (Horizontal, fielding.)	60.00	30.00	18.00
(12)	Glenn Beckert (Cubs, fielding, ball in hand.)	25.00	12.50	7.50
(13)	Glenn Beckert (Cubs, fielding, no ball.)	25.00	12.50	7.50
(14)	Paul Blair (Orioles, full-length.)	25.00	12.50	7.50
(15)	Don Blasingame (Cardinals, belt-up.)	20.00	10.00	6.00
(16)	Bob Bolin (Giants, pitching follow-through.)	20.00	10.00	6.00
(17)	Dave Boswell (Twins, full-length.)	20.00	10.00	6.00
(18)	Dave Boswell (Twins, waist-up, stretch position.)	20.00	10.00	6.00
(19)	Jackie Brandt (Orioles, full-length.)	20.00	10.00	6.00
(20)	Smoky Burgess (Pirates, sitting on step w/ three bats.)	20.00	10.00	6.00
(21)	Rico Carty (Milwaukee Braves, batting.)	20.00	10.00	6.00
(22)	Rico Carty (Milwaukee Braves, dugout step.)	20.00	10.00	6.00
(23)	Rico Carty (Atlanta Braves, batting.)	20.00	10.00	6.00
(24)	Paul Casanova (Senators, catching crouch.)	20.00	10.00	6.00
(25)	Norm Cash (Tigers, batting, waist-up.)	25.00	12.50	7.50
(26)	Orlando Cepeda (Braves, batting.)	30.00	15.00	9.00
(27)	Orlando Cepeda (Cardinals, dugout step.)	25.00	12.50	7.50
(28)	Orlando Cepeda (Cardinals, fielding.)	25.00	12.50	7.50
(29)	Jim Davenport (Giants, fielding.)	20.00	10.00	6.00
(30)	Vic Davalillo (Indians, upper body.)	20.00	10.00	6.00
(31)	Willie Davis (Dodgers, full-length.)	20.00	10.00	6.00
(32)	Chuck Dobson (A's, full-length.)	20.00	10.00	6.00
(35)	"Moe" Drabowsky (Cubs, thighs-up.)	20.00	10.00	6.00
(36)	Don Drysdale (L.A. Dodgers, follow-through.)	25.00	12.50	7.50
(37)	Dick Ellsworth (Cubs, pitching follow-through.)	20.00	10.00	6.00
(38)	Dick Ellsworth (Phillies, full-length.)	20.00	10.00	6.00
(39)	Del Ennis (Cardinals, kneeling.)	20.00	10.00	6.00
(40)	Bob Feller (Seated, glove on knee.)	120.00	60.00	36.00
(41)	Nellie Fox (White Sox, chest-up.)	35.00	17.50	10.50
(42)	Nellie Fox (White Sox, fielding grounder.)	50.00	25.00	15.00
(43)	Nelson Fox (White Sox, seated.)	50.00	25.00	15.00
(44)	Nelson Fox (Colt .45s, batting.)	50.00	25.00	15.00
(45)	Bill Freehan (Catching crouch.)	20.00	10.00	6.00
(46)	Bill Freehan (Two pictures.)	20.00	10.00	6.00
(47)	Phil Gagliano (Cardinals, fielding, photo actually Ed Spiezio.)	25.00	12.50	7.50
(48)	Jim Gentile (Orioles, batting, chest-up.)	20.00	10.00	6.00
(49)	Vernon "Lefty" Gomez (w/ glasses.)	25.00	12.50	7.50
(50)	Lefty Gomez (No glasses.)	25.00	12.50	7.50
(51)	Jim Hall (Angels, fielding.)	25.00	12.50	7.50
(52a)	Don Hoak (Pirates, full-length, waist up.)	20.00	10.00	6.00
(52b)	Don Hoak (Pirates, waist up.)	20.00	10.00	6.00
(53)	Gil Hodges (L.A. Dodgers, belt-up batting.)	50.00	25.00	15.00
(54)	Willie Horton (Tigers, full-length.)	20.00	10.00	6.00
(55)	Bruce Howard (White Sox, pitching follow-through.)	20.00	10.00	6.00
(56)	Jim Hunter (K.C. A's, beginning wind-up.)	25.00	12.50	7.50
(57)	Jim Hunter (Oakland A's, full-length, photo actually Chuck Dobson.)	25.00	12.50	7.50
(58)	Mack Jones (Reds, full-length.)	20.00	10.00	6.00
(59)	Duane Josephson (White Sox, catching crouch.)	20.00	10.00	6.00
(61)	Jim Kaat (Twins, upper body.)	25.00	12.50	7.50
(62)	Al Kaline (Full-length, batting.)	75.00	37.00	22.00
(63)	Al Kaline (Upper body, batting.)	75.00	37.00	22.00
(64)	Al Kaline (Upper body, hands on knees.)	75.00	37.00	22.00
(65)	Al Kaline (Upper body.)	75.00	37.00	22.00
(66)	Al Kaline (Upper body, looking right.)	75.00	37.00	22.00
(67)	Harmon Killebrew (Twins, upper body, batting.)	50.00	25.00	15.00
(68)	Harmon Killebrew (Twins, batting, looking front.)	50.00	25.00	15.00

		NM	EX	VG
(69)	Harmon Killebrew (Twins, kneeling.)	50.00	25.00	15.00
(70)	Cal Koonce (Cubs, pitching follow-through.)	20.00	10.00	6.00
(71)	Harvey Kuenn (Tigers, batting.)	25.00	12.50	7.50
(72)	Harvey Kuenn (Tigers, upper body.)	25.00	12.50	7.50
(73)	Hal Lanier (Giants, throwing.)	20.00	10.00	6.00
(74)	Juan Marichal (Giants, upper body.)	25.00	12.50	7.50
(75)	Willie McCovey (Giants, batting.)	25.00	12.50	7.50
(76)	Sam McDowell (Indians, seated, no cap.)	25.00	12.50	7.50
(77)	Dennis McLain (Tigers, hands at chest.)	25.00	12.50	7.50
(78)	Roy McMillan (Braves, batting.)	20.00	10.00	6.00
(79)	Roy McMillan (Reds, belt-up.)	20.00	10.00	6.00
(81)	Denis Menke (Braves, fielding.)	20.00	10.00	6.00
(82)	Denis Menke (Braves, upper body.)	20.00	10.00	6.00
(83)	Don Mincher (Angels, full-length.)	20.00	10.00	6.00
(84)	Joe Morgan (Astros, batting.)	40.00	20.00	12.00
(85)	Joe Morgan (Astros, fielding.)	40.00	20.00	12.00
(86)	Jim Nash (A's, pitching.)	20.00	10.00	6.00
(87)	Rich Nye (Cubs, pitching.)	20.00	10.00	6.00
(88)	John Odom (Kansas City A's, pitching.)	20.00	10.00	6.00
(89)	John Odom (Oakland A's, belt-up pose.)	20.00	10.00	6.00
(90)	John Orsino (Orioles, kneeling.)	20.00	10.00	6.00
(91)	Jim O'Toole (Reds, upper body, warm-up jacket.)	20.00	10.00	6.00
(92)	Jim O'Toole (White Sox, upper body.)	20.00	10.00	6.00
(93)	Ray Oyler (Tigers, fielding.)	20.00	10.00	6.00
(94)	Milt Pappas (Orioles, pitching, full-length.)	20.00	10.00	6.00
(95)	Milt Pappas (Orioles, pitching, knees-up.)	20.00	10.00	6.00
(96)	Don Pavletich (Reds, full-length.)	20.00	10.00	6.00
(97)	Don Pavletich (Reds, squatting.)	20.00	10.00	6.00
(98)	Albie Pearson (Angels, glove under left arm.)	20.00	10.00	6.00
(99)	Ron Perranoski (Dodgers, upper body.)	20.00	10.00	6.00
(100)	Ron Perranoski (Twins, belt-up from side.)	25.00	12.50	7.50
(101)	Ron Perranoski (Twins, pitching.)	20.00	10.00	6.00
(102)	Gaylord Perry (Giants, pitching.)	25.00	12.50	7.50
(103)	Billy Pierce (White Sox, knees-up.)	25.00	12.50	7.50
(104)	Bob Purkey (Reds, waist-up.)	20.00	10.00	6.00
(105)	Doug Rader (Astros, fielding.)	20.00	10.00	6.00
(106)	Dick Rodatz (Radatz) (Red Sox, upper body.)	20.00	10.00	6.00
(107)	Dick Radatz (Red Sox, upper body.)	20.00	10.00	6.00
(108)	Pete Runnels (Red Sox, kneeling on deck.)	25.00	12.50	7.50
(109)	Ron Santo (Cubs, fielding.)	25.00	12.50	7.50
(110)	George Scott (Red Sox, upper body.)	20.00	10.00	6.00
(111)	Larry Sherry (Dodgers, full-length.)	20.00	10.00	6.00
(112)	Chris Short (Phillies, upper body.)	20.00	10.00	6.00
(113)	Hal Smith (Pirates, batting.)	25.00	12.50	7.50
(114)	Mickey Stanley (Tigers, full-length.)	20.00	10.00	6.00
(115)	Tony Taylor (Phillies, bat on shoulder.)	20.00	10.00	6.00
(116)	Frank Thomas (Pirates, waist-up.)	20.00	10.00	6.00
(117)	Frank Thomas" (Cubs, batting.)	20.00	10.00	6.00
(119)	Jeff Torborg (Dodgers, holding mask.)	20.00	10.00	6.00
(121)	Al Weis (White Sox, ready to throw.)	20.00	10.00	6.00
(122)	Al Weis (Mets, fielding.)	20.00	10.00	6.00
(123)	Ted Williams (Batting.)	125.00	62.00	37.00
(125)	Bobby Wine (Phillies, ready to throw.)	20.00	10.00	6.00
(126)	Rick Wise (Phillies, upper body.)	20.00	10.00	6.00
(128)	Woody Woodward (Reds, belt-to-cap.)	25.00	12.50	7.50
(130)	Early Wynn (White Sox, full-length.)	25.00	12.50	7.50
(131)	Jim Wynn (Colt .45s, batting, upper body.)	20.00	10.00	6.00
(132)	Jim Wynn (Astros, batting, full-length.)	20.00	10.00	6.00
(133)	Don Zimmer (Cubs, waist-up batting.)	20.00	10.00	6.00

1961 Wilson Advisory Staff Cards

Similar in format to the contemporary 8" x 10" photos, these 2-3/4" x 4" cards have black-and-white player poses on front, prominently displaying a Wilson glove. In the white bottom border is: "Member-Advisory Staff, Wilson Sporting Goods Co." A blue facsimile autograph is printed across the picture. Backs are blank. The checklist, presented here alphabetically, may not be complete.

		NM	EX	VG
Common Player:		10.00	5.00	3.00
(1)	Dick Ellsworth	10.00	5.00	3.00
(2)	Don Hoak	12.00	6.00	3.50
(3)	Harvey Kuenn	12.00	6.00	3.50
(4)	Roy McMillan	10.00	5.00	3.00
(5)	Jim Piersall	12.00	6.00	3.50
(6)	Ron Santo	16.00	8.00	4.75

1977 Wilson Sporting Goods Mini-Posters

Though unmarked as such, these 6" x 9" cards are a promotion from Wilson. The blank-back cards have a color action photo with white borders and a facsimile autograph.

		NM	EX	VG
Complete Set (10):		200.00	100.00	60.00
Common Player:		10.00	5.00	3.00
(1)	Johnny Bench	35.00	17.50	10.50
(2)	George Brett	50.00	25.00	15.00
(3)	Rod Carew	30.00	15.00	9.00
(4)	Dave Concepcion	10.00	5.00	3.00
(5)	Steve Garvey	15.00	7.50	4.50
(6)	Reggie Jackson	40.00	20.00	12.00
(7)	Greg Luzinski	10.00	5.00	3.00
(8)	Pete Rose	75.00	37.00	22.00
(9)	Mike Schmidt	40.00	20.00	12.00
(10)	Tom Seaver	40.00	17.50	10.50

1955-1958 Don Wingfield Washington Nationals Postcards

This series of 3-1/2" x 5-1/2" black-and-white glossy postcards provided Nationals' players with a vehicle for accommodating fan requests. Player portraits or action poses are bordered in white with three (or in the case of Valdivielso, five) lines of type at bottom identifying the player, team and copyright. Most have "Photo Post Card" at top on back and "Devolite Peerless" in the stamp box. The unnumbered cards are checklisted here in alphabetical order.

		NM	EX	VG
Complete Set (12):		1,800	900.00	550.00
Common Player:		150.00	75.00	45.00
(1)	Jim Busby	150.00	75.00	45.00
(2)	Chuck Dressen	150.00	75.00	45.00
(3)	Ed Fitz Gerald	150.00	75.00	45.00
(4)	Jim Lemon	175.00	85.00	55.00
(5)	Bob Porterfield	150.00	75.00	45.00
(6)	Pete Runnels	150.00	75.00	45.00
(7)	Roy Sievers	175.00	85.00	55.00
(8)	Chuck Stobbs	150.00	75.00	45.00
(9)	Dean Stone	150.00	75.00	45.00
(10)	Jose Valdivelso (Valdivielso)	175.00	85.00	55.00
(11)	Mickey Vernon	175.00	85.00	55.00
(12)	Ed Yost	150.00	75.00	45.00

1957-1959 Don Wingfield Photocards

These black-and-white glossy photocards are usually blank-back, evidently for use as in-person handouts, rather than by mail. In 3-1/2" x 5-1/2" size, the player photos are bordered in white with an especially wide white bottom border for affixing an autograph. Other than the autograph which may appear, the player is not identified on the card. Wingfield's name may appear in white letters in the lower-right corner of the photo, may be on a credit line on back or may not appear at all.

		NM	EX	VG
Common Player:		50.00	25.00	15.00
(1)	Ted Abernathy	50.00	25.00	15.00
(2)	Bobby Allison	50.00	25.00	15.00
(3)	Tex Clevenger	50.00	25.00	15.00
(4)	Russ Kemmerer	50.00	25.00	15.00
(5)	Harmon Killebrew	100.00	50.00	30.00
(6)	Bob Usher	50.00	25.00	15.00
(7)	Hal Woodeshick	50.00	25.00	15.00

1960s Don Wingfield Postcards - B/W

A second type of player photo postcards was produced by Alexandria, Va., photographer Don Wingfield beginning around 1960. Also black-and-white, the 3-1/2" x 5-1/2" cards have (usually) borderless poses on front with no extraneous graphics. Backs have standard postcard indicia plus (on most cards) the player name and team and a copyright line with Wingfield's name and address. At top on back is "Post Card," with "Place Stamp Here" in the postage box. Washington Senators players dominate the checklist which also includes stars of other teams. The autograph on the pictured card was added by the player after printing and is not part of the design. The currently known checklist is presented here alphabetically.

		NM	EX	VG
Common Player:		50.00	25.00	15.00
(1)	Bob Allison	55.00	27.50	16.50
(2)	Ernie Banks	100.00	50.00	30.00
(3)	Earl Battey (Batting, chest to cap.)	50.00	25.00	15.00
(4)	Earl Battey (Kneeling w/bat.)	50.00	25.00	15.00
(5)	Norm Cash	60.00	30.00	18.00
(6)	Jim Coates	50.00	25.00	15.00
(7)	Rocky Colavito	60.00	30.00	18.00
(8)	Chuck Cottier	50.00	25.00	15.00
(9)	Bennie Daniels	50.00	25.00	15.00
(10)	Dan Dobbek	50.00	25.00	15.00
(11)	Nellie Fox	60.00	30.00	18.00
(12)	Jim Gentile	50.00	25.00	15.00
(13)	Gene Green	50.00	25.00	15.00
(14)	Steve Hamilton	50.00	25.00	15.00
(15)	Ken Hamlin	50.00	25.00	15.00
(16a)	Rudy Hernandez (Postcard back.)	50.00	25.00	15.00
(16b)	Rudy Hernandez (Restuarant ad on back.)	60.00	30.00	18.00
(17)	Ed Hobaugh	50.00	25.00	15.00
(18)	Elston Howard	60.00	30.00	18.00
(19)	Bob Johnson	50.00	25.00	15.00

(20)	Russ Kemmerer	50.00	25.00	15.00
(21)	Harmon Killebrew	100.00	50.00	30.00
(22)	Dale Long	50.00	25.00	15.00
(23)	Mickey Mantle	325.00	160.00	100.00
(24)	Roger Maris	200.00	100.00	60.00
(25)	Willie Mays	250.00	125.00	75.00
(26)	Stan Musial	200.00	100.00	60.00
(27)	Claude Osteen	50.00	25.00	15.00
(28)	Ken Retzer	50.00	25.00	15.00
(29)	Brooks Robinson	100.00	50.00	30.00
(30)	Don Rudolph	50.00	25.00	15.00
(31)	Bill Skowron	60.00	30.00	18.00
(32)	Dave Stenhouse	50.00	25.00	15.00
(33)	Jose Valdivielso	50.00	25.00	15.00
(34)	Gene Woodling	50.00	25.00	15.00
(35)	Bud Zipfel	50.00	25.00	15.00

1960s Don Wingfield Postcards - Color

Similar in format to the contemporary series of black-and-white player photo postcards, only a single player is known to have been issued in color by Alexandria, Va., photographer Don Wingfield. The card is 3-1/2" x 5-1/2" with standard postcard indicia on back.

		NM	EX	VG
C14711	Harmon Killebrew	110.00	55.00	33.00

1951-53 Wisconsin's Athletic Hall of Fame Postcards

This set of black-and-white postcards reproduces the plaques of athletes in the state's Hall of Fame, as displayed in Milwaukee's Arena during the 1950s. Backs have typical postcard markings.

		NM	EX	VG
Complete Set (12):		150.00	75.00	45.00
Common Player:		10.00	5.00	3.00
(1)	Addie Joss	20.00	10.00	6.00
(2)	Alvin Kraenzlein (Track)	10.00	5.00	3.00
(3)	"Strangler" Lewis (Wrestling)	12.50	6.25	3.75
(4)	George McBride	10.00	5.00	3.00
(5)	Ralph Metcalfe (Track)	10.00	5.00	3.00
(6)	Ernie Nevers	20.00	10.00	6.00
(7)	"Kid" Nichols	20.00	10.00	6.00
(8)	"Pa" O'Dea (Football)	10.00	5.00	3.00
(9)	Dave Schreiner (Football)	10.00	5.00	3.00
(10)	Al Simmons	20.00	10.00	6.00
(11)	Billy Sullivan	12.50	6.25	3.75
(12)	Bob Zuppke (Basketball)	10.00	5.00	3.00

1922 Witmor Candy Co.

Two types of Witmor issues are known, both of which utilize the format of the 1921-22 W575-1 blank-back strip cards. Printed in black-and-white and measuring about 2" x 3-1/4" the two types of Witmor issues are differentiated by the ads on back for the San Francisco candy company. One type has the advertising in a horizontal format, the other has the advertising in a vertical design. Values of Witmor Candy cards carry a premium over the more common blank-back versions. The extent to which the Witmors and W575-1 share a checklist, particularly the latter's variations, is unknown.

WALTER JOHNSON
P.—Washington Americans

PREMIUMS:
Common Players: 3-4X
Hall of Famers: 3-4X
(See 1921-22 W575-1 for checklist and value information.)

1907 Wolverine News Co. Detroit Tigers

This series of postcards depicts members of the A.L. champ Tigers. The 3-5/16" x 5-5/16" black-and-white cards have poses or posed action photos on front, with a narrow white border at bottom carrying player identification. Backs are standard postcard format with a credit line to Wolverine News Co.

		NM	EX	VG
Complete Set (20):		9,000	4,500	2,700
Common Player:		100.00	50.00	30.00
(1)	Ty Cobb (Batting)	3,000	1,500	900.00
(2)	Ty Cobb (Portrait)	3,500	1,750	1,000
(3)	Bill Coughlin	100.00	50.00	30.00
(4)	Sam Crawford (Bunting)	250.00	125.00	75.00
(5)	Sam Crawford (Chest-to-cap portrait.)	250.00	125.00	75.00
(6)	"Wild Bill" Donovan (Pitching)	100.00	50.00	30.00
(7)	"Wild Bill" Donovan ("at the Water Wagon")	150.00	75.00	45.00
(8)	Jerry Downs	100.00	50.00	30.00
(9)	Hughie Jennings (Manager)	250.00	125.00	75.00
(10)	Hughie Jennings (On the Coaching line.)	300.00	150.00	90.00
(11)	Davy Jones	100.00	50.00	30.00
(12)	Ed Killian	100.00	50.00	30.00
(13)	George Mullin	100.00	50.00	30.00
(14)	Charlie O'Leary	100.00	50.00	30.00
(15)	Fred Payne	100.00	50.00	30.00
(16)	Claude Rossman	100.00	50.00	30.00
(17)	Herman Schaefer	100.00	50.00	30.00
(18)	Herman Schaefer, Charley O'Leary	100.00	50.00	30.00
(19)	Charlie Schmidt	100.00	50.00	30.00
(20)	Eddie Siever	100.00	50.00	30.00

1886 J. Wood Studio N.Y. Giants Cabinets

Members of the 1886 N.Y. Giants were immortalized in this series of 4-1/4" x 6-7/8" studio cabinets. The sepia portraits are bordered in gold. The photos were likely available singly from the studio or as a complete set, with an advertising frontpiece and a 6-9/16" x 4-3/16" composite photo. It is interesting to note that on one version of the composite card, baseball caps were artificially added to the portraits. The photos became the basis for the same players' cards in several late 1880s card series.

		NM	EX	VG
Common Player:		10,000	5,000	3,000
(1)	Roger Connor	25,000	7,500	4,500
(2)	Larry Corcoran	10,000	5,000	3,000
(3)	Pat Deasley	10,000	5,000	3,000
(4)	Mike Dorgan	10,000	5,000	3,000
(5)	Dude Esterbrook	10,000	5,000	3,000
(6)	Buck Ewing	35,000	7,500	4,500
(7)	Joe Gerhardt	10,000	5,000	3,000
(8)	Pete Gillespie	10,000	5,000	3,000
(9)	Tim Keefe	25,000	7,500	4,500
(10)	Jim Mutrie	10,000	5,000	3,000
(11)	Jim O'Rourke	30,000	7,500	4,500
(12)	Danny Richardson	10,000	5,000	3,000
(13)	John Ward	30,000	7,500	4,500
(14)	Mickey Welch	25,000	7,500	4,500
(15)	N.Y. Giants Team Composite (No caps.)	25,000	10,000	6,000
(16)	N.Y. Giants Team Composite (With caps.)	25,000	10,000	6,000

1886 J. Wood Studio N.Y. Metropolitans Cabinets

Nattily attired in dress shirts and sporty dotted ties, members of the 1886 N.Y. Metropolitans of the American Association were immortalized in this series of 4-1/2" x 6-1/2" studio cabinets. The vignetted sepia portraits are framed in gold. The photos became the basis for the same players' cards in the "dotted tie" subset of the 1887 Old Judge cigarette card issue, indicating that more of the cabinet-size photos may yet be added to this checklist.

	NM	EX	VG
Common Player:	12,500	6,250	3,750
Jos. Crotty	12,500	6,250	3,750
E.L. Cushman	12,500	6,250	3,750
E.E. Foster	12,500	6,250	3,750
Al. Mays	12,500	6,250	3,750
Jas. Roseman	12,500	6,250	3,750

1921 Wool's American-Maid Bread

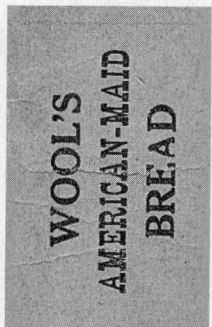

This seldom-seen variation of the W551 strip-card set appears to have been locally overprinted at an unknown location for use as a bread purchase premium. It is presumed the same checklist for W551 can be found with the Wool's back advertising. If ideally cut from the strip, the cards would measure 1-3/8" x 2-1/4". They feature color drawings and are unnumbered.

		NM	EX	VG
Complete Set (10):		6,000	3,000	1,800
Common Player:		160.00	80.00	48.00
(1)	Frank Baker	400.00	200.00	120.00
(2)	Dave Bancroft	400.00	200.00	120.00
(3)	Jess Barnes	250.00	125.00	75.00
(4)	Ty Cobb	2,000	1,000	600.00
(5)	Walter Johnson	750.00	375.00	225.00
(6)	Wally Pipp	300.00	150.00	90.00
(7)	Babe Ruth	2,500	1,250	750.00
(8)	George Sisler	400.00	200.00	120.00
(9)	Tris Speaker	600.00	300.00	180.00
(10)	Casey Stengel	450.00	225.00	135.00

1933 Worch Cigar

This set of unnumbered postcard-size (3-7/16" x 5-7/16") cards, utilizing photos from the Minneapolis Star and St. Paul Dispatch newspapers, was used as a promotion by Worch Cigar Co. of St. Paul, Minn. Although there is no advertising for Worch Cigars on the cards themselves, the cards were mailed in envelopes bearing the Worch name. The cards feature portrait or posed action photos. Player identification, which may be full name or last name, with or without team, may be found in several different styles, either printed on the background, or in a white or black box. Sometimes a photo credit is also present. Many pictures have the top of the background whited out.

		NM	EX	VG
Common Player:		90.00	40.00	25.00
(1)	Sparky Adams	90.00	40.00	25.00
(2)	Dale Alexander	90.00	40.00	25.00
(3)	Ivy Paul Andrews	90.00	40.00	25.00
(4a)	Earl Averill (Cleveland)	400.00	180.00	100.00
(4b)	Earl Averill (No team designation.)	400.00	180.00	100.00
(5)	Richard Bartell	90.00	40.00	25.00
(6)	Herman Bell	90.00	40.00	25.00
(7)	Walter Berger	90.00	40.00	25.00
(8)	Huck Betts	90.00	40.00	25.00
(9)	Max Bishop	90.00	40.00	25.00
(10)	Jim Bottomley	400.00	180.00	100.00
(11a)	Tom Bridges (Name and team in box.)	90.00	40.00	25.00
(11b)	Tom Bridges (No box.)	90.00	40.00	25.00
(12)	Clint Brown	90.00	40.00	25.00
(13a)	Donie Bush	90.00	40.00	25.00
(13b)	Donie Bush	90.00	40.00	25.00
(14a)	Max Carey (Brooklyn)	400.00	180.00	100.00
(14b)	Max Carey (No team designation.)	400.00	180.00	100.00
(15)	Tex Carlton	90.00	40.00	25.00
(16)	Ben Chapman	90.00	40.00	25.00
(17)	Chalmer Cissell	90.00	40.00	25.00
(18)	Mickey Cochrane	400.00	180.00	100.00
(19)	Ripper Collins	90.00	40.00	25.00
(20)	Earle Combs	400.00	180.00	100.00
(21)	Adam Comorosky	90.00	40.00	25.00
(22)	Estel Crabtree	90.00	40.00	25.00
(23)	Rodger Cramer (Roger)	90.00	40.00	25.00
(24)	Pat Crawford	90.00	40.00	25.00
(25)	Hugh Critz	90.00	40.00	25.00
(26a)	Joe Cronin (Name and team in box.)	400.00	180.00	100.00
(26b)	Joe Cronin (No box.)	400.00	180.00	100.00
(27)	Frank Crosetti	150.00	67.00	37.00
(28)	Alvin Crowder	90.00	40.00	25.00
(29a)	Tony Cuccinello (Photo background.)	90.00	40.00	25.00
(29b)	Tony Cuccinello (Blank background.)	90.00	40.00	25.00
(30)	KiKi Cuyler	400.00	180.00	100.00
(31)	Geo. Davis	90.00	40.00	25.00
(32)	Dizzy Dean	750.00	335.00	185.00
(33)	Wm. Dickey	450.00	200.00	110.00
(34)	Leo Durocher	400.00	180.00	100.00
(35)	James Dykes	90.00	40.00	25.00
(36)	George Earnshaw	90.00	40.00	25.00
(37)	Woody English	90.00	40.00	25.00
(38a)	Richard Ferrell (Name and team in box.)	400.00	180.00	100.00
(38b)	Richard Ferrell (No box.)	400.00	180.00	100.00
(39a)	Wesley Ferrell (Name and team in box.)	90.00	40.00	25.00
(39b)	Wesley Ferrell (No box.)	90.00	40.00	25.00
(40)	Fred Fitzsimmons	90.00	40.00	25.00
(41)	Lew Fonseca	90.00	40.00	25.00
(42)	Bob Fothergill	90.00	40.00	25.00
(43)	James Foxx	750.00	335.00	185.00
(44)	Fred Frankhouse	90.00	40.00	25.00
(45)	Frank Frisch	400.00	180.00	100.00
(46a)	Leon Gaslin (Name incorrect.)	400.00	180.00	100.00
(46b)	Leon Goslin (Name correct.)	400.00	180.00	100.00
(47)	Lou Gehrig	1,500	675.00	375.00
(48)	Charles Gehringer	400.00	180.00	100.00
(49)	George Gibson	90.00	40.00	25.00
(50)	Vernon Gomez	400.00	180.00	100.00
(51)	George Grantham	90.00	40.00	25.00
(52)	Grimes The Lord Of Burleigh (Burleigh Grimes)	400.00	180.00	100.00
(53)	Charlie Grimm	90.00	40.00	25.00
(54)	Robt. Grove	600.00	270.00	150.00
(55)	Frank Grube	90.00	40.00	25.00
(56)	Chic Hafey (Chick)	400.00	180.00	100.00
(57)	Jess Haines	400.00	180.00	100.00
(58)	Bill Hallahan	90.00	40.00	25.00
(59)	Mel Harder	90.00	40.00	25.00
(60)	Dave Harris	90.00	40.00	25.00
(61a)	Gabby Hartnett (Small projection.)	400.00	180.00	100.00
(61b)	Gabby Hartnett (Large projection.)	400.00	180.00	100.00
(62)	George Hass (Haas)	90.00	40.00	25.00
(63)	Ray Hayworth	90.00	40.00	25.00
(64)	Harvey Hendrick	90.00	40.00	25.00
(65)	Dutch Henry	90.00	40.00	25.00
(66)	"Babe" Herman	150.00	67.00	37.00
(67)	Bill Herman	400.00	180.00	100.00
(68)	Frank Higgins	90.00	40.00	25.00
(69)	Oral Hildebrand	90.00	40.00	25.00
(70)	"Shanty" Hogan	90.00	40.00	25.00
(71)	Roger Hornsby (Rogers)	600.00	270.00	150.00
(72)	Carl Hubbell	450.00	200.00	110.00
(73)	Travis Jackson	400.00	180.00	100.00
(74)	Hank Johnson	90.00	40.00	25.00
(75)	Syl Johnson	90.00	40.00	25.00
(76)	Smead Jolley	90.00	40.00	25.00
(77)	Wm. Kamm	90.00	40.00	25.00
(78)	Wes Kingdon	90.00	40.00	25.00
(79a)	Charles Klein (Philadelphia, N.L.)	400.00	180.00	100.00
(79b)	Charles Klein (Chicago, N.L.)	400.00	180.00	100.00
(80)	Jos. Kuhel	90.00	40.00	25.00
(81a)	Tony Lazzeri (Name and team in box.)	400.00	180.00	100.00
(81b)	Tony Lazzeri (No box.)	400.00	180.00	100.00
(82)	Sam Leslie	90.00	40.00	25.00

(83)	Ernie Lombardi	400.00	180.00	100.00
(84)	Al Lopez	400.00	180.00	100.00
(85)	Red Lucas	90.00	40.00	25.00
(86)	Adolfo Luque	90.00	40.00	22.00
(87)	Ted Lyons	400.00	180.00	100.00
(88)	Connie Mack	400.00	180.00	100.00
(89)	Gus Mancuso	90.00	40.00	25.00
(90)	Henry Manush	400.00	180.00	100.00
(91)	Fred Marberry	90.00	40.00	25.00
(92)	Pepper Martin	200.00	90.00	50.00
(93)	Wm. McKechnie	400.00	180.00	100.00
(94)	Joe Medwick	400.00	180.00	100.00
(95)	Jim Mooney	90.00	40.00	25.00
(96)	Joe Moore	90.00	40.00	25.00
(97)	Joe Mowry	90.00	40.00	25.00
(98)	Van Mungo	90.00	40.00	25.00
(99)	Buddy Myer	90.00	40.00	25.00
(100)	"Lefty" O'Doul	200.00	90.00	50.00
(101)	Bob O'Farrell	90.00	40.00	25.00
(102)	Ernie Orsatti	90.00	40.00	25.00
(103)	Melvin Ott	450.00	200.00	110.00
(104)	Roy Parmelee	90.00	40.00	25.00
(105)	Homer Peel	90.00	40.00	25.00
(106)	George Pipgras	90.00	40.00	25.00
(107)	Harry Rice	90.00	40.00	25.00
(108)	Paul Richards	90.00	40.00	25.00
(109)	Eppa Rixey	400.00	180.00	100.00
(110)	Charles Ruffing	400.00	180.00	100.00
(111)	Jack Russell	90.00	40.00	25.00
(112)	Babe Ruth	2,000	900.00	500.00
(113)	"Blondy" Ryan	90.00	40.00	25.00
(114)	Wilfred Ryan	90.00	40.00	25.00
(115)	Fred Schulte	90.00	40.00	25.00
(116)	Hal Schumacher	90.00	40.00	25.00
(117a)	Luke Sewel (Sewell) (Name and team in box.)	90.00	40.00	25.00
(117b)	Luke Sewel (Sewell) (No box.)	90.00	40.00	25.00
(118)	Al Simmons	400.00	180.00	100.00
(119)	Ray Spencer	90.00	40.00	25.00
(120)	Casey Stengel	400.00	180.00	100.00
(121)	Riggs Stephenson	90.00	40.00	25.00
(122)	Walter Stewart	90.00	40.00	25.00
(123)	John Stone	90.00	40.00	25.00
(124)	Gabby Street	90.00	40.00	25.00
(125)	Gus Suhr	90.00	40.00	25.00
(126)	Evar Swanson	90.00	40.00	25.00
(127)	Dan Taylor	90.00	40.00	25.00
(128)	Bill Terry	400.00	180.00	100.00
(129)	Al Todd	90.00	40.00	25.00
(130)	Pie Traynor	400.00	180.00	100.00
(131)	William Urbanski	90.00	40.00	25.00
(132)	Dazzy Vance	400.00	180.00	100.00
(133)	Lloyd (Floyd) Vaughan	400.00	180.00	100.00
(134)	Johnny Vergez	90.00	40.00	25.00
(135)	George Walberg	90.00	40.00	25.00
(136)	Bill Walker	90.00	40.00	25.00
(137)	Gerald Walker	90.00	40.00	25.00
(138a)	Lloyd Waner (Photo background.)	400.00	180.00	100.00
(138b)	Lloyd Waner (Blank background.)	400.00	180.00	100.00
(139a)	Paul Waner (Photo background.)	400.00	180.00	100.00
(139b)	Paul Waner (Blank background, small projection.)	400.00	180.00	100.00
(139c)	Lloyd Waner (Blank background, large projection.)	400.00	180.00	100.00
(140)	Lon Warneke	90.00	40.00	25.00
(141)	George Watkins	90.00	40.00	25.00
(142)	Monte Weaver	90.00	40.00	25.00
(143)	Sam West	90.00	40.00	25.00
(144)	Earl Whitehill	90.00	40.00	25.00
(145)	Hack Wilson	400.00	180.00	100.00
(146)	Jimmy Wilson	90.00	40.00	25.00

1933 World Wide Gum (Canadian Goudey, V353)

Also known as "Canadian Goudeys," this 94-card set drew heavily on its U.S. contemporary. Card fronts are identical to the '33 Goudeys and the backs are nearly so. The first 52 cards in the set carry the same card numbers as their American counterparts, while cards #53-94 have different numbers than the U.S. version. Card backs can be found printed entirely in English, or in English and French; the former being somewhat scarcer. Cards measure approximately 2-3/8" x 2-7/8".

		NM	EX	VG
Complete Set (94):		20,000	10,000	6,000
Common Player:		60.00	30.00	18.00
1	Benny Bengough	60.00	30.00	18.00
2	Arthur (Dazzy) Vance	250.00	110.00	60.00
3	Hugh Critz	60.00	30.00	18.00
4	Henry (Heinie) Schuble	60.00	30.00	18.00
5	Floyd (Babe) Herman	110.00	50.00	25.00
6	Jimmy Dykes	60.00	30.00	18.00
7	Ted Lyons	250.00	110.00	60.00
8	Roy Johnson	60.00	30.00	18.00
9	Dave Harris	60.00	30.00	18.00
10	Glenn Myatt	60.00	30.00	18.00
11	Billy Rogell	60.00	30.00	18.00

12	George Pipgras	60.00	30.00	18.00
13	Lafayette Thompson	60.00	30.00	18.00
14	Henry Johnson	60.00	30.00	18.00
15	Victor Sorrell	60.00	30.00	18.00
16	George Blaeholder	60.00	30.00	18.00
17	Watson Clark	60.00	30.00	18.00
18	Herold (Muddy) Ruel	60.00	30.00	18.00
19	Bill Dickey	275.00	125.00	70.00
20	Bill Terry	250.00	110.00	60.00
21	Phil Collins	60.00	30.00	18.00
22	Harold (Pie) Traynor	250.00	110.00	60.00
23	Hazen (Ki-Ki) Cuyler	250.00	110.00	60.00
24	Horace Ford	60.00	30.00	18.00
25	Paul Waner	250.00	110.00	60.00
26	Chalmer Cissell	60.00	30.00	18.00
27	George Connally	60.00	30.00	18.00
28	Dick Bartell	60.00	30.00	18.00
29	Jimmy Foxx	350.00	155.00	85.00
30	Frank Hogan	60.00	30.00	18.00
31	Tony Lazzeri	250.00	110.00	60.00
32	John (Bud) Clancy	60.00	30.00	18.00
33	Ralph Kress	60.00	30.00	18.00
34	Bob O'Farrell	60.00	30.00	18.00
35	Al Simmons	250.00	110.00	60.00
36	Tommy Thevenow	60.00	30.00	18.00
37	Jimmy Wilson	60.00	30.00	18.00
38	Fred Brickell	60.00	30.00	18.00
39	Mark Koenig	60.00	30.00	18.00
40	Taylor Douthit	60.00	30.00	18.00
41	Gus Mancuso	60.00	30.00	18.00
42	Eddie Collins	250.00	110.00	60.00
43	Lew Fonseca	60.00	30.00	18.00
44	Jim Bottomley	250.00	110.00	60.00
45	Larry Benton	60.00	30.00	18.00
46	Ethan Allen	60.00	30.00	18.00
47	Henry "Heinie" Manush	250.00	110.00	60.00
48	Marty McManus	60.00	30.00	18.00
49	Frank Frisch	250.00	110.00	60.00
50	Ed Brandt	60.00	30.00	18.00
51	Charlie Grimm	60.00	30.00	18.00
52	Andy Cohen	60.00	30.00	18.00
53	Jack Quinn	60.00	30.00	18.00
54	Urban (Red) Faber	250.00	110.00	60.00
55	Lou Gehrig	2,100	950.00	525.00
56	John Welch	60.00	30.00	18.00
57	Bill Walker	60.00	30.00	18.00
58	Frank (Lefty) O'Doul	90.00	40.00	22.50
59	Edmund (Bing) Miller	60.00	30.00	18.00
60	Waite Hoyt	250.00	110.00	60.00
61	Max Bishop	60.00	30.00	18.00
62	"Pepper" Martin	90.00	40.00	22.50
63	Joe Cronin	250.00	110.00	60.00
64	Burleigh Grimes	250.00	110.00	60.00
65	Milton Gaston	60.00	30.00	18.00
66	George Grantham	60.00	30.00	18.00
67	Guy Bush	60.00	30.00	18.00
68	Willie Kamm	60.00	30.00	18.00
69	Gordon (Mickey) Cochrane	250.00	110.00	60.00
70	Adam Comorosky	60.00	30.00	18.00
71	Alvin Crowder	60.00	30.00	18.00
72	Willis Hudlin	60.00	30.00	18.00
73	Eddie Farrell	60.00	30.00	18.00
74	Leo Durocher	250.00	110.00	60.00
75	Walter Stewart	60.00	30.00	18.00
76	George Walberg	60.00	30.00	18.00
77	Glenn Wright	60.00	30.00	18.00
78	Charles (Buddy) Myer	60.00	30.00	18.00
79	James (Zack) Taylor	60.00	30.00	18.00
80	George Herman (Babe) Ruth	4,000	1,800	1,000
81	D'Arcy (Jake) Flowers	60.00	30.00	18.00
82	Ray Kolp	60.00	30.00	18.00
83	Oswald Bluege	60.00	30.00	18.00
84	Morris (Moe) Berg	600.00	275.00	150.00
85	Jimmy Foxx	400.00	180.00	100.00
86	Sam Byrd	60.00	30.00	11.00
87	Danny Mcfayden (McFayden)	60.00	30.00	18.00
88	Joe Judge	60.00	30.00	18.00
89	Joe Sewell	250.00	110.00	60.00
90	Lloyd Waner	250.00	110.00	60.00
91	Luke Sewell	60.00	30.00	18.00
92	Leo Mangum	60.00	30.00	18.00
93	George Herman (Babe) Ruth	3,600	1,625	900.00
94	Al Spohrer	60.00	30.00	18.00

1934 World Wide Gum (Canadian Goudey, V354)

Again a near-clone of the American issue, the '34 "Canadian Goudeys" feature the same number (96) and size (2-3/8" x 2-7/8") of cards. Player selection is considerably different, however. Cards #1-48 feature the same front design as the '33 Wide/Goudey sets. Cards #49-96 have the "Lou Gehrig says..." graphic on the front. Unlike the 1933 cards, backs are only found with bi-lingual text.

		NM	EX	VG
Complete Set (96):		19,000	8,500	4,500
Common Player:		75.00	35.00	20.00
1	Rogers Hornsby	900.00	400.00	250.00
2	Eddie Morgan	75.00	35.00	20.00
3	Valentine J. (Val) Picinich	75.00	35.00	20.00

4	Rabbit Maranville	250.00	120.00	75.00
5	Flint Rhem	75.00	35.00	20.00
6	Jim Elliott	75.00	35.00	20.00
7	Fred (Red) Lucas	75.00	35.00	20.00
8	Fred Marberry	75.00	35.00	20.00
9	Clifton Heathcote	75.00	35.00	20.00
10	Bernie Friberg	75.00	35.00	20.00
11	Elwood (Woody) English	75.00	35.00	20.00
12	Carl Reynolds	75.00	35.00	20.00
13	Ray Benge	75.00	35.00	20.00
14	Ben Cantwell	75.00	35.00	20.00
15	Irvin (Bump) Hadley	75.00	35.00	20.00
16	Herb Pennock	250.00	120.00	75.00
17	Fred Lindstrom	250.00	120.00	75.00
18	Edgar (Sam) Rice	250.00	120.00	75.00
19	Fred Frankhouse	75.00	35.00	20.00
20	Fred Fitzsimmons	75.00	35.00	20.00
21	Earl Coombs (Earle Combs)	250.00	120.00	75.00
22	George Uhle	75.00	35.00	20.00
23	Richard Coffman	75.00	35.00	20.00
24	Travis C. Jackson	250.00	120.00	75.00
25	Robert J. Burke	75.00	35.00	20.00
26	Randy Moore	75.00	35.00	20.00
27	John Henry (Heinie) Sand	75.00	35.00	20.00
28	George Herman (Babe) Ruth	4,200	2,000	1,600
29	Tris Speaker	300.00	145.00	90.00
30	Perce (Pat) Malone	75.00	35.00	20.00
31	Sam Jones	75.00	35.00	20.00
32	Eppa Rixey	250.00	120.00	75.00
33	Floyd (Pete) Scott	75.00	35.00	20.00
34	Pete Jablonowski	75.00	35.00	20.00
35	Clyde Manion	75.00	35.00	20.00
36	Dibrell Williams	75.00	35.00	20.00
37	Glenn Spencer	75.00	35.00	20.00
38	Ray Kremer	75.00	35.00	20.00
39	Phil Todt	75.00	35.00	20.00
40	Russell Rollings	75.00	35.00	20.00
41	Earl Clark	75.00	35.00	20.00
42	Jess Petty	75.00	35.00	20.00
43	Frank O'Rourke	75.00	35.00	20.00
44	Jesse Haines	250.00	120.00	75.00
45	Horace Lisenbee	75.00	35.00	20.00
46	Owen Carroll	75.00	35.00	20.00
47	Tom Zachary	75.00	35.00	20.00
48	Charlie Ruffing	250.00	120.00	75.00
49	Ray Benge	75.00	35.00	20.00
50	Elwood (Woody) English	75.00	35.00	20.00
51	Ben Chapman	75.00	35.00	20.00
52	Joe Kuhel	75.00	35.00	20.00
53	Bill Terry	250.00	120.00	75.00
54	Robert (Lefty) Grove	300.00	145.00	90.00
55	Jerome (Dizzy) Dean	450.00	220.00	140.00
56	Charles (Chuck) Klein	250.00	120.00	75.00
57	Charley Gehringer	250.00	120.00	75.00
58	Jimmy Foxx	400.00	195.00	125.00
59	Gordon (Mickey) Cochrane	250.00	120.00	75.00
60	Willie Kamm	75.00	35.00	20.00
61	Charlie Grimm	75.00	35.00	20.00
62	Ed Brandt	75.00	35.00	20.00
63	Tony Piet	75.00	35.00	20.00
64	Frank Frisch	250.00	120.00	75.00
65	Alvin Crowder	75.00	35.00	20.00
66	Frank Hogan	75.00	35.00	20.00
67	Paul Waner	250.00	120.00	75.00
68	Henry (Heinie) Manush	250.00	120.00	75.00
69	Leo Durocher	250.00	120.00	75.00
70	Floyd Vaughan	250.00	120.00	75.00
71	Carl Hubbell	275.00	135.00	85.00
72	Hugh Critz	75.00	35.00	20.00
73	John (Blondy) Ryan	75.00	35.00	20.00
74	Roger Cramer	75.00	35.00	20.00
75	Baxter Jordan	75.00	35.00	20.00
76	Ed Coleman	75.00	35.00	20.00
77	Julius Solters	75.00	35.00	20.00
78	Charles (Chick) Hafey	250.00	120.00	75.00
79	Larry French	75.00	35.00	20.00
80	Frank (Don) Hurst	75.00	35.00	20.00
81	Gerald Walker	75.00	35.00	20.00
82	Ernie Lombardi	250.00	120.00	75.00
83	Walter (Huck) Betts	75.00	35.00	20.00
84	Luke Appling	250.00	120.00	75.00
85	John Frederick	75.00	35.00	20.00
86	Fred Walker	75.00	35.00	20.00
87	Tom Bridges	75.00	35.00	20.00
88	Dick Porter	75.00	35.00	20.00
89	John Stone	75.00	35.00	20.00
90	James (Tex) Carleton	75.00	35.00	20.00
91	Joe Stripp	75.00	35.00	20.00
92	Lou Gehrig	2,500	1,225	775.00
93	George Earnshaw	75.00	35.00	20.00
94	Oscar Melillo	75.00	35.00	20.00
95	Oral Hildebrand	75.00	35.00	20.00
96	John Allen	75.00	35.00	20.00

1936 World Wide Gum (Canadian Goudey, V355)

No. 119
THOMAS N. OLIVER,
Outfielder — Toronto Leafs — Voltigeur

Born at Montgomery, Ala., January 12, 1904. Bats and throws right. 6 feet. Fast, covers much ground. With Boston Red Sox and Phils in majors. With Baltimore in International one season. Can play third base as well as outfield.

Né à Montgomery, Ala., le 12 janvier, 1904. Droitier, 6 pieds. Rapide, couvre beaucoup de terrain. Avec Boston Red Sox et Phils dans les Majeures. Avec Baltimore une saison dans l'Internationale. Quelque voltigeur peut jouer au troisième but aussi.

BIG LEAGUE CHEWING GUM

World Wide Gum Co. Ltd. Granby, Que.
Printed in Canada.

No. 119 TOM OLIVER

This black and white Canadian set was issued by World Wide Gum in 1936. The cards measure approximately 2-1/2" x 2-7/8", and the set includes both portrait and action photos. The card number and player's name (appearing in all capital letters) are printed inside a white box below the photo.

		NM	EX	VG
	Complete Set (135):	40,000	20,000	12,000
	Common Player:	125.00	55.00	30.00
1	Jimmy Dykes	300.00	75.00	30.00
2	Paul Waner	250.00	125.00	75.00
3	Cy Blanton	125.00	55.00	30.00
4	Sam Leslie	125.00	55.00	30.00
5	Johnny Louis Vergez	125.00	55.00	30.00
6	Arky Vaughan	250.00	125.00	75.00
7	Bill Terry	250.00	125.00	75.00
8	Joe Moore	125.00	55.00	30.00
9	Gus Mancuso	125.00	55.00	30.00
10	Fred Marberry	125.00	55.00	30.00
11	George Selkirk	125.00	55.00	30.00
12	Spud Davis	125.00	55.00	30.00
13	Chuck Klein	250.00	125.00	75.00
14	Fred Fitzsimmons	125.00	55.00	30.00
15	Bill Delancey	125.00	55.00	30.00
16	Billy Herman	250.00	125.00	75.00
17	George Davis	125.00	55.00	30.00
18	Rip Collins	125.00	55.00	30.00
19	Dizzy Dean	400.00	200.00	120.00
20	Roy Parmelee	125.00	55.00	30.00
21	Vic Sorrell	125.00	55.00	30.00
22	Harry Danning	125.00	55.00	30.00
23	Hal Schumacher	125.00	55.00	30.00
24	Cy Perkins	125.00	55.00	30.00
25	Speedy Durocher	250.00	125.00	75.00
26	Glenn Myatt	125.00	55.00	30.00
27	Bob Seeds	125.00	55.00	30.00
28	Jimmy Ripple	125.00	55.00	30.00
29	Al Schacht	125.00	55.00	30.00
30	Pete Fox	125.00	55.00	30.00
31	Del Baker	125.00	55.00	30.00
32	Flea Clifton	125.00	55.00	30.00
33	Tommy Bridges	125.00	55.00	30.00
34	Bill Dickey	250.00	115.00	65.00
35	Wally Berger	125.00	55.00	30.00
36	Slick Castleman	125.00	55.00	30.00
37	Dick Bartell	125.00	55.00	30.00
38	Red Rolfe	125.00	55.00	30.00
39	Waite Hoyt	250.00	125.00	75.00
40	Wes Ferrell	125.00	55.00	30.00
41	Hank Greenberg	400.00	190.00	105.00
42	Charlie Gehringer	250.00	125.00	75.00
43	Goose Goslin	250.00	125.00	75.00
44	Schoolboy Rowe	125.00	55.00	30.00
45	Mickey Cochrane	250.00	125.00	75.00
46	Joe Cronin	250.00	125.00	75.00
47	Jimmie Foxx	475.00	225.00	125.00
48	Jerry Walker	125.00	55.00	30.00
49	Charlie Gelbert	125.00	55.00	30.00
50	Roy Hayworth (Ray)	125.00	55.00	30.00
51	Joe DiMaggio	15,000	7,000	4,000
52	Billy Rogell	125.00	55.00	30.00
53	Joe McCarthy	250.00	125.00	75.00
54	Phil Cavaretta (Cavarretta)	125.00	55.00	30.00
55	Kiki Cuyler	250.00	125.00	75.00
56	Lefty Gomez	250.00	125.00	75.00
57	Gabby Hartnett	250.00	125.00	75.00
58	Johnny Marcum	125.00	55.00	30.00
59	Burgess Whitehead	125.00	55.00	30.00
60	Whitey Whitehill	125.00	55.00	30.00
61	Buckey Walters	125.00	55.00	30.00
62	Luke Sewell	125.00	55.00	30.00
63	Joey Kuhel	125.00	55.00	30.00
64	Lou Finney	125.00	55.00	30.00
65	Fred Lindstrom	250.00	125.00	75.00
66	Paul Derringer	125.00	55.00	30.00
67	Steve O'Neil (O'Neill)	125.00	55.00	30.00
68	Mule Haas	125.00	55.00	30.00
69	Freck Owen	125.00	55.00	30.00
70	Wild Bill Hallahan	125.00	55.00	30.00
71	Bill Urbanski	125.00	55.00	30.00
72	Dan Taylor	125.00	55.00	30.00
73	Heinie Manush	250.00	125.00	75.00
74	Jo-Jo White	125.00	55.00	30.00
75	Mickey Medwick (Ducky)	250.00	125.00	75.00
76	Joe Vosmik	125.00	55.00	30.00
77	Al Simmons	250.00	125.00	75.00
78	Shag Shaughnessy	125.00	55.00	30.00
79	Harry Smythe	125.00	55.00	30.00
80	Benny Tate	125.00	55.00	30.00
81	Billy Rhiel	125.00	55.00	30.00
82	Lauri Myllykangas	125.00	55.00	30.00
83	Ben Sankey	125.00	55.00	30.00
84	Crip Polli	125.00	55.00	30.00
85	Jim Bottomley	250.00	125.00	75.00
86	William Clark	125.00	55.00	30.00
87	Ossie Bluege	125.00	55.00	30.00
88	Lefty Grove	250.00	115.00	65.00
89	Charlie Grimm	125.00	55.00	30.00
90	Ben Chapman	125.00	55.00	30.00
91	Frank Crosetti	125.00	60.00	30.00
92	John Pomorski	125.00	55.00	30.00
93	Jesse Haines	250.00	125.00	75.00
94	Chick Hafey	250.00	125.00	75.00
95	Tony Piet	125.00	55.00	30.00
96	Lou Gehrig	4,000	2,000	1,400
97	Bill Jurges	125.00	55.00	30.00
98	Smead Jolley	125.00	55.00	30.00
99	Jimmy Wilson	125.00	55.00	30.00
100	Lonnie Warneke	125.00	55.00	30.00
101	Lefty Tamulis	125.00	55.00	30.00
102	Charlie Ruffing	250.00	125.00	75.00
103	Earl Grace	125.00	55.00	30.00
104	Rox Lawson	125.00	55.00	30.00
105	Stan Hack	125.00	55.00	30.00
106	August Galan	125.00	55.00	30.00
107	Frank Frisch	250.00	125.00	75.00
108	Bill McKechnie	250.00	125.00	75.00
109	Bill Lee	125.00	55.00	30.00
110	Connie Mack	250.00	125.00	75.00
111	Frank Reiber	125.00	55.00	30.00
112	Zeke Bonura	125.00	55.00	30.00
113	Luke Appling	250.00	125.00	75.00
114	Monte Pearson	125.00	55.00	30.00
115	Bob O'Farrell	125.00	55.00	30.00
116	Marvin Duke	125.00	55.00	30.00
117	Paul Florence	125.00	55.00	30.00
118	John Berley	125.00	55.00	30.00
119	Tom Oliver	125.00	55.00	30.00
120	Norman Kies	125.00	55.00	30.00
121	Hal King	125.00	55.00	30.00
122	Tom Abernathy	125.00	55.00	30.00
123	Phil Hensick	125.00	55.00	30.00
124	Roy Schalk (Ray)	250.00	125.00	75.00
125	Paul Dunlap	125.00	55.00	30.00
126	Benny Bates	125.00	55.00	30.00
127	George Puccinelli	125.00	55.00	30.00
128	Stevie Stevenson	125.00	55.00	30.00
129	Rabbit Maranville	250.00	125.00	75.00
130	Bucky Harris	250.00	125.00	75.00
131	Al Lopez	250.00	125.00	75.00
132	Buddy Myer	125.00	55.00	30.00
133	Cliff Bolton	125.00	55.00	30.00
134	Estel Crabtree	125.00	55.00	30.00
135	Phil Weintraub	3,000	1,500	900.00

1939 World Wide Gum (Canadian Goudey, V351)

These premium pictures are analogous to the R303-A issue in the U.S. The 4" x 5-3/4" pictures were given away with the purchase of World Wide gum. The pictures are printed in sepia on cream-colored paper. Fronts have a bordered photo with facsimile autograph. Backs have a "How to . . ." baseball playing tip illustrated with drawings. Backs of the Canadian version differ from the U.S. pieces in the absence of a border line around the playing tip, and the use of a "Lithographed in Canada" notice at lower-right. The unnumbered pictures are checklisted here in alphabetical order.

		NM	EX	VG
	Complete Set (25):	5,500	2,750	1,650
	Common Player:	100.00	50.00	30.00
(1)	Morris Arnovich	100.00	50.00	30.00
(2)	Sam Bell	130.00	65.00	40.00
(3)	Zeke Bonura	100.00	50.00	30.00
(4)	Earl Caldwell	100.00	50.00	30.00
(5)	Flea Clifton	100.00	50.00	30.00
(6)	Frank Crosetti	140.00	70.00	40.00
(7)	Harry Danning	100.00	50.00	30.00
(8)	Dizzy Dean	250.00	125.00	75.00
(9)	Emile De Jonghe	130.00	65.00	40.00
(10)	Paul Derringer	100.00	50.00	30.00
(11)	Joe DiMaggio	1,500	750.00	450.00
(12)	Vince DiMaggio	100.00	50.00	30.00
(13)	Charlie Gehringer	225.00	110.00	67.00
(14)	Gene Hasson	130.00	65.00	40.00
(15)	Tommy Henrich	150.00	75.00	45.00
(16)	Fred Hutchinson	100.00	50.00	30.00
(17)	Phil Marchildon	100.00	50.00	30.00
(18)	Mike Meola	100.00	50.00	30.00
(19)	Arnold Moser	130.00	65.00	40.00
(20)	Frank Pytlak	100.00	50.00	30.00
(21)	Frank Reiber	100.00	50.00	30.00
(22)	Lee Rogers	100.00	50.00	30.00
(23)	Cecil Travis	100.00	50.00	30.00
(24)	Hal Trosky	100.00	50.00	30.00
(25)	Ted Williams	1,500	750.00	450.00

1975 WTMJ Milwaukee Brewers Broadcasters

To promote its schedule of radio and television broadcasts of Brewers baseball, WTMJ issued this set of broadcaster and schedule cards to potential sponsors. The standard 2-1/2" x 3-1/2" cards are printed in team colors of blue and gold. The on-air talent cards have portraits and facsimile autographs on front, with career summaries on back. The schedule cards have game-action photos on front along with the slogan, "Brewers 75: It's Gonna' Be A Whole New Ballgame!" The cards were distributed in a wax pack with gum.

		NM	EX	VG
	Complete Set (7):	25.00	12.50	7.50
	Common Card:	2.50	1.25	.70
1	Jim Irwin	4.00	2.00	1.25
2	Gary Bender	4.00	2.00	1.25
3	Bob Uecker	12.50	6.25	3.75
4	Merle Harmon	4.00	2.00	1.25
(5)	TV Schedule	2.50	1.25	.70
(6)	Radio Schedule, Part 1	2.50	1.25	.70
(7)	Radio Schedule, Part 2	2.50	1.25	.70

1910 W-UNC Strip Cards

Considerably earlier than most known strip cards, these pieces were cut from a notebook cover. The known players point to a 1910 issue date. Crudely printed on flimsy stock, the cards feature familiar colorized portraits of players on brightly colored backgrounds. The format is about 1-3/8" x 2-3/8" and some cards have evidence of a 1-16th" yellow strip around the outside of the black border. Player name and city are printed

MATHEWSON, N.Y.

in the white border at bottom. Backs are blank. The unnumbered cards are listed here in alphabetical order, though the checklist may or may not be complete.

		NM	EX	VG
Common Player:		300.00	120.00	60.00
(1)	Babe Adams	300.00	120.00	60.00
(2)	Chief Bender	600.00	240.00	120.00
(3)	Roger Bresnahan	600.00	240.00	120.00
(4)	Donie Bush	300.00	120.00	60.00
(5)	Bobby Byrne	300.00	120.00	60.00
(6)	Bill Carrigan	300.00	120.00	60.00
(7)	Frank Chance	600.00	240.00	120.00
(8)	Hal Chase	450.00	180.00	90.00
(9)	Ty Cobb	2,750	1,100	550.00
(10)	Willis Cole	300.00	120.00	60.00
(11)	Eddie Collins	600.00	240.00	120.00
(12)	Jack Coombs	300.00	120.00	60.00
(13)	Sam Crawford	600.00	240.00	120.00
(14)	Johnny Evers	600.00	240.00	120.00
(15)	Solly Hoffman	300.00	120.00	60.00
(16)	Hughie Jennings	600.00	240.00	120.00
(17)	Walter Johnston (Johnson)	1,500	600.00	300.00
(18)	Johnny Kling	300.00	120.00	60.00
(19)	Ed Konetchy	300.00	120.00	60.00
(20)	Harry Lord	300.00	120.00	60.00
(21)	Sherry Magee	300.00	120.00	60.00
(22)	Christy Mathewson	1,600	650.00	325.00
(23)	Mike Mitchell	300.00	120.00	60.00
(24)	Tris Speaker	750.00	300.00	150.00
(25)	Oscar Stanage	300.00	120.00	60.00
(26)	Honus Wagner	2,000	800.00	400.00

1912 W-UNC Strip Cards

The attributed issue date is speculative, based on the limited known roster. In much the same size and format as W555, these small (photo image area is 1-3/8" x 1-1/2") blank-back cards appear to have been cut off a box or other packaging and may actually be candy cards. Black-and-white photos are framed in dark green with the player's last name in white capital letters below.

		NM	EX	VG
Common Player:		2,000	800.00	400.00
(1)	Bill Carrigan	2,000	800.00	400.00
(2)	Tommy Leach	2,000	800.00	400.00
(3)	Oscar Stanage	2,000	800.00	400.00
(4)	Honus Wagner	7,500	3,000	1,500
(5)	Cy Young	6,500	2,600	1,300

1915 W-UNC Strip Cards

Walter Johnson, Wash. Amer.

Utilizing many photos familiar to collectors from contemporary card sets, including pictures that were several years old at the time of issue, this appears to be a strip-card issue whose scarcity has caused it to elude cataloging efforts heretofore. Cards are printed in black-and-white, blank-backed and are nominally 1-3/4" x 2-3/4". Player or photo identification appears in the bottom border, or at right on horizontally formatted cards.

		NM	EX	VG
Common Player:		500.00	250.00	150.00
(1)	Ty Cobb	6,500	2,600	1,300
(2)	Larry Doyle	500.00	200.00	100.00
(3)	Johnny Evers	1,500	600.00	300.00
(4)	Joe Jackson	16,000	6,400	3,200
(5)	Walter Johnson	2,500	1,000	500.00
(6)	Sherwood Magee	500.00	200.00	100.00
(7)	Fred Maisel	500.00	200.00	100.00
(8)	Walter (Rabbit) Maranville	1,500	600.00	300.00
(9)	Rube Marquard	1,500	600.00	300.00
(10)	Christy Mathewson	2,750	1,100	550.00
(11)	Phila. Athletics, Champ.	750.00	300.00	150.00
(12)	Ready for the Wallop (Honus Wagner, Roger Bresnahan)	1,500	600.00	300.00
(13)	Nap Rucker	500.00	200.00	100.00
(14)	Hans Wagner	3,500	1,400	700.00
(15)	Joe Wood	600.00	240.00	120.00

1916-20 W-UNC "Big Head" Strip Cards

Given the known player content (perhaps not complete as listed here) and the fact that no team designations are printed on the cards, it is impossible to more accurately date this blank-back strip card issue. The 1-3/8" x 2-1/2" cards have color artwork of the players in full-body poses. The pictures are unusual in that the players' heads are out of proportion to the rest of the body. Whether the portraits were meant to be accurate portrayals is conjecture. Player names given here are as printed on the cards.

		NM	EX	VG
Complete Set (20):		16,000	6,400	3,200
Common Player:		500.00	350.00	150.00
(1)	Jim Bagby	500.00	350.00	150.00
(2)	Home Run Baker	800.00	475.00	300.00
(3)	Dave Bancroft	800.00	475.00	300.00
(4)	Ping Bodie	500.00	350.00	150.00
(5)	Geo. Burns	500.00	350.00	150.00
(6)	Leon Cadore	500.00	350.00	150.00
(7)	Ty Cobb	4,000	2,500	1,250
(8)	Larry Doyle	500.00	350.00	150.00
(9)	Hinie Groh	500.00	350.00	150.00
(10)	R. Hornsby	2,000	1,000	750.00
(11)	Johnston (Walter Johnson)	1,500	850.00	500.00
(12)	Joe Judge	500.00	350.00	150.00
(13)	Eddy Konetchy	500.00	350.00	150.00
(14)	Carl Mays	500.00	350.00	150.00
(15)	Zeb Milan	500.00	350.00	150.00
(16)	Sam Rice	800.00	475.00	300.00
(17)	Babe Ruth	14,000	8,000	3,000
(18)	Ray Schalk	800.00	475.00	300.00
(19)	Wally Schang	500.00	350.00	150.00
(20)	Geo. Sisler	1,500	850.00	500.00

1921 W-UNC Self-Developing Strip Cards

"BABE" RUTH

N.Y. AM.

The technology of a self-developing photographic baseball card was popularized in the early 1930s by Ray-O-Print and again in the late late 1940s and early 1950s by Topps, but appears to have been pioneered circa 1921 by an unknown company which produced this series. Individual cards measure between 1-1/16" and 1-3/16" in width and 1-13/16" in depth. In black-and-white, they feature action poses on a dark background with the player name and team in white. A white border surrounds the picture. Backs are blank. The unnumbered cards are checklisted here alphabetically, though the list is probably incomplete.

		NM	EX	VG
Common Player:		100.00	40.00	20.00
(1)	Grover Alexander	450.00	180.00	90.00
(2)	Ty Cobb	2,000	800.00	400.00
(3)	Eddie Collins	300.00	120.00	60.00
(4)	Jake Daubert	100.00	40.00	20.00
(5)	Red Faber	250.00	100.00	50.00
(6)	Max Flack	100.00	40.00	20.00
(7)	"Roger (Rogers) Hornsby"	350.00	140.00	70.00
(8)	Doc Johnston	100.00	40.00	20.00
(9)	Walter Johnston (Johnson)	900.00	360.00	180.00
(10)	Bill Killifer (Killefer)	100.00	40.00	20.00
(11)	Steve O'Neill	100.00	40.00	20.00
(12)	Derrill Pratt	100.00	40.00	20.00
(13)	"Babe" Ruth	3,500	1,400	700.00
(14)	Wallie Schang	100.00	40.00	20.00

1929 W-UNC Playing Strip Cards (1)

Recent discoveries indicate that this issue was produced by Universal Toy & Novelty circa 1929. Likely printed on a sheet similar to other playing card/strip card sets of the era, the individual cards are about 1-1/2" x 2-1/2". The front has a crude black-and-white drawing of the player inside a suit-shaped design on a red background. Back is blank.

		NM	EX	VG
6C	Shanty Hogan	150.00	75.00	45.00
7S	Doug McWeeny	150.00	75.00	45.00

1920s W-UNC Playing Strip Cards (2)

Because only three players have thus far been checklisted from this set, it is not possible to more precisely date this issue. Likely printed on a sheet similar to other playing card/strip card sets of the era, the individual cards are about 1-1/2" x 2-1/2", printed in either red (hearts, diamonds) or black (clubs, spades), with a player photo at center. Backs are blank.

Values Undetermined
6C   Bob Meusel
9S   Tris Speaker
AD   Babe Ruth

1926 W-UNC Strip Cards

Ruth is the only baseball player known in this set of athletic, cinematic and historical subjects. The approximately 1-1/2" x 2-1/2" black-and-white, blue-and-white, or maroon-and-white blank-backed card identifies the player, position and team typographically within the photo and has the card number and name in the bottom border. The card has been seen with numbers 1, 52 and 71, as well as unnumbered.

		NM	EX	VG
1	Babe Ruth (Black-and-white.)	800.00	400.00	240.00
52	Babe Ruth (Blue duotone.)	800.00	400.00	240.00
71	Babe Ruth (Blue duotone.)	800.00	400.00	240.00
71	Babe Ruth (Maroon duotone.)	800.00	400.00	240.00
---	Babe Ruth (Unnumbered, maroon.)	1,100	550.00	330.00

1931 W-UNC Strip Cards

This issue is virtually identical in format to the various 1928-1931 issues cataloged as W502, York Caramel, Yuengling Ice Cream, etc. The black-and-white, cards measure about 1-3/8" (give or take a 1/16") x 2-1/2". Player photos are bordered in white with the name printed in capital letters at bottom. At bottom-left is a card number in parentheses. This issue's checklist is identical to the 1931 W502. the only difference being these cards have blank backs.

(14) ROBERT GROVE

		NM	EX	VG
Complete Set (60):		12,500	5,000	2,500
Common Player:		75.00	30.00	15.00
1	Muddy Ruel	75.00	30.00	15.00
2	John Grabowski	75.00	30.00	15.00
3	Mickey Cochrane	150.00	60.00	30.00
4	Bill Cissell	75.00	30.00	15.00
5	Carl Reynolds	75.00	30.00	15.00
6	Luke Sewell	75.00	30.00	15.00
7	Ted Lyons	150.00	60.00	30.00
8	Harvey Walker	75.00	30.00	15.00
9	Gerald Walker	75.00	30.00	15.00
10	Sam Byrd	75.00	30.00	15.00
11	Joe Vosmik	75.00	30.00	15.00
12	Dan MacFayden	75.00	30.00	15.00
13	William Dickey	150.00	60.00	30.00
14	Robert Grove	300.00	120.00	60.00
15	Al Simmons	150.00	60.00	30.00
16	Jimmy Foxx	300.00	120.00	60.00
17	Nick Altrock	75.00	30.00	15.00
18	Charlie Grimm	75.00	30.00	15.00
19	Bill Terry	150.00	60.00	30.00
20	Clifton Heathcote	75.00	30.00	15.00
21	Burleigh Grimes	150.00	60.00	30.00
22	Red Faber	150.00	60.00	30.00
23	Gabby Hartnett	150.00	60.00	30.00
24	Earl (Earle) Combs	150.00	60.00	30.00
25	Hack Wilson	150.00	60.00	30.00
26	Stanley Harris	150.00	60.00	30.00
27	John J. McGraw	150.00	60.00	30.00
28	Paul Waner	150.00	60.00	30.00
29	Babe Ruth	4,000	1,600	800.00
30	Herb Pennock	150.00	60.00	30.00
31	Joe Sewell	150.00	60.00	30.00
32	Lou Gehrig	2,000	800.00	400.00
33	Tony Lazzeri	150.00	60.00	30.00
34	Waite Hoyt	150.00	60.00	30.00
35	Glenn Wright	75.00	30.00	15.00
36	Leon (Goose) Goslin	150.00	60.00	30.00
37	Frank Frisch	150.00	60.00	30.00
38	George Uhle	75.00	30.00	15.00
39	Bob O'Farrell	75.00	30.00	15.00
40	Rogers Hornsby	200.00	80.00	40.00
41	"Pie" Traynor	150.00	60.00	30.00
42	Clarence Mitchell	75.00	30.00	15.00
43	Sherwood Smith	75.00	30.00	15.00
44	Miguel A. Gonzalez	75.00	30.00	15.00
45	Joe Judge	75.00	30.00	15.00
46	Eppa Rixey	150.00	60.00	30.00
47	Adolfo Luque	75.00	30.00	15.00
48	E.C. (Sam) Rice	150.00	60.00	30.00
49	Earl Sheely	75.00	30.00	15.00
50	Sam Jones	75.00	30.00	15.00
51	Bib A. Falk	75.00	30.00	15.00
52	Willie Kamm	75.00	30.00	15.00
53	Roger Peckinpaugh	75.00	30.00	15.00
54	Lester Bell	75.00	30.00	15.00
55	L. Waner	150.00	60.00	30.00
56	Eugene Hargrave	75.00	30.00	15.00
57	Harry Heilmann	150.00	60.00	30.00
58	Earl Smith	75.00	30.00	15.00
59	Dave Bancroft	150.00	60.00	30.00
60	George Kelly	150.00	60.00	30.00

1922 W501

G-4-22 8

TY COBB
Mgr.—Detroit Americans

This "strip card" set, known as W501 in the American Card Catalog, is closely connected to the more popular E121 American Caramel set of 1921 and 1922. Because they were handcut from strips, measurements are relative, with well-cut cards typically about 1-7/8" to 2" by about 3-3/8". The W501 cards are numbered in the upper-right corner and have the notation "G-4-22" in the upper-left corner, apparently indicating the cards were issued in April of 1922.

		NM	EX	VG
Complete Set (122):		30,000	12,000	6,000
Common Player:		100.00	40.00	20.00
1	Ed Rounnel (Rommel)	100.00	40.00	20.00
2	Urban Shocker	100.00	40.00	20.00
3	Dixie Davis	100.00	40.00	20.00
4	George Sisler	350.00	140.00	70.00
5	Bob Veach	100.00	40.00	20.00
6	Harry Heilman (Heilmann)	350.00	140.00	70.00
7a	Ira Falgstead (Name incorrect.)	100.00	40.00	20.00
7b	Ira Flagstead (Name correct.)	100.00	40.00	20.00
8	Ty Cobb	3,750	1,500	750.00
9	Oscar Vitt	100.00	40.00	20.00
10	Muddy Ruel	100.00	40.00	20.00
11	Derrill Pratt	100.00	40.00	20.00
12	Ed Gharrity	100.00	40.00	20.00
13	Joe Judge	100.00	40.00	20.00
14	Sam Rice	350.00	140.00	70.00
15	Clyde Milan	100.00	40.00	20.00
16	Joe Sewell	350.00	140.00	70.00
17	Walter Johnson	900.00	360.00	180.00
18	Jack McInnis	100.00	40.00	20.00
19	Tris Speaker	450.00	180.00	90.00
20	Jim Bagby	100.00	40.00	20.00
21	Stanley Coveleskie (Coveleski)	350.00	140.00	70.00
22	Bill Wambsganss	100.00	40.00	20.00
23	Walter Mails	100.00	40.00	20.00
24	Larry Gardner	100.00	40.00	20.00
25	Aaron Ward	100.00	40.00	20.00
26	Miller Huggins	350.00	140.00	70.00
27	Wally Schang	100.00	40.00	20.00
28	Tom Rogers	100.00	40.00	20.00
29	Carl Mays	125.00	50.00	25.00
30	Everett Scott	100.00	40.00	20.00
31	Robert Shawkey	100.00	40.00	20.00
32	Waite Hoyt	350.00	140.00	70.00
33	Mike McNally	100.00	40.00	20.00
34	Joe Bush	100.00	40.00	20.00
35	Bob Meusel	100.00	40.00	20.00
36	Elmer Miller	100.00	40.00	20.00
37	Dick Kerr	100.00	40.00	20.00
38	Eddie Collins	350.00	140.00	70.00
39	Kid Gleason	100.00	40.00	20.00
40	Johnny Mostil	100.00	40.00	20.00
41	Bib Falk (Bibb)	100.00	40.00	20.00
42	Clarence Hodge	100.00	40.00	20.00
43	Ray Schalk	350.00	140.00	70.00
44	Amos Strunk	100.00	40.00	20.00
45	Eddie Mulligan	100.00	40.00	20.00
46	Earl Sheely	100.00	40.00	20.00
47	Harry Hooper	350.00	140.00	70.00
48	Urban Faber	350.00	140.00	70.00
49	Babe Ruth	6,000	2,400	1,200
50	Ivy B. Wingo	100.00	40.00	20.00
51	Earle Neale	125.00	50.00	25.00
52	Jake Daubert	100.00	40.00	20.00
53	Ed Roush	350.00	140.00	70.00
54	Eppa J. Rixey	350.00	140.00	70.00
55	Elwood Martin	100.00	40.00	20.00
56	Bill Killifer (Killefer)	100.00	40.00	20.00
57	Charles Hollocher	100.00	40.00	20.00
58	Zeb Terry	100.00	40.00	20.00
59	G.C. Alexander (Arms above head.)	600.00	240.00	120.00
60	Turner Barber	100.00	40.00	20.00
61	John Rawlings	100.00	40.00	20.00
62	Frank Frisch	350.00	140.00	70.00
63	Pat Shea	100.00	40.00	20.00
64	Dave Bancroft	350.00	140.00	70.00
65	Cecil Causey	100.00	40.00	20.00
66	Frank Snyder	100.00	40.00	20.00
67	Heinie Groh	100.00	40.00	20.00
68	Ross Young (Youngs)	350.00	140.00	70.00
69	Fred Toney	100.00	40.00	20.00
70	Arthur Nehf	100.00	40.00	20.00
71	Earl Smith	100.00	40.00	20.00
72	George Kelly	350.00	140.00	70.00
73	John J. McGraw	350.00	140.00	70.00
74	Phil Douglas	100.00	40.00	20.00
75	Bill Ryan	100.00	40.00	20.00
76	Jess Haines	350.00	140.00	70.00
77	Milt Stock	100.00	40.00	20.00
78	William Doak	100.00	40.00	20.00
79	George Toporcer	100.00	40.00	20.00
80	Wilbur Cooper	100.00	40.00	20.00
81	George Whitted	100.00	40.00	20.00
82	Chas. Grimm	100.00	40.00	20.00
83	Rabbit Maranville	350.00	140.00	70.00
84	Babe Adams	100.00	40.00	20.00
85	Carson Bigbee	100.00	40.00	20.00
86	Max Carey	350.00	140.00	70.00
87	Whitey Glazner	100.00	40.00	20.00
88	George Gibson	100.00	40.00	20.00
89	Bill Southworth	100.00	40.00	20.00
90	Hank Gowdy	100.00	40.00	20.00
91	Walter Holke	100.00	40.00	20.00
92	Joe Oeschger	100.00	40.00	20.00
93	Pete Kilduff	100.00	40.00	20.00
94	Hy Myers	100.00	40.00	20.00
95	Otto Miller	100.00	40.00	20.00
96	Wilbert Robinson	350.00	140.00	70.00
97	Zach Wheat	350.00	140.00	70.00
98	Walter Ruether	100.00	40.00	20.00
99	Curtis Walker	100.00	40.00	20.00
100	Fred Williams	100.00	40.00	20.00
101	Dave Danforth	100.00	40.00	20.00
102	Ed Rounnel (Rommel)	100.00	40.00	20.00
103	Carl Mays	125.00	50.00	25.00
104	Frank Frisch	350.00	140.00	70.00
105	Lou DeVormer	100.00	40.00	20.00
106	Tom Griffith	100.00	40.00	20.00
107	Harry Harper	100.00	40.00	20.00
108a	John Lavan	100.00	40.00	20.00
108b	John J. McGraw	350.00	140.00	70.00
109	Elmer Smith	100.00	40.00	20.00
110	George Dauss	100.00	40.00	20.00
111	Alexander Gaston	100.00	40.00	20.00
112	John Graney	100.00	40.00	20.00
113	Emil Muesel	100.00	40.00	20.00
114	Rogers Hornsby	450.00	180.00	90.00
115	Leslie Nunamaker	100.00	40.00	20.00
116	Steve O'Neill	100.00	40.00	20.00
117	Max Flack	100.00	40.00	20.00
118	Bill Southworth	100.00	40.00	20.00
119	Arthur Nehf	100.00	40.00	20.00
120	Chick Fewster	100.00	40.00	20.00

1928 W502

 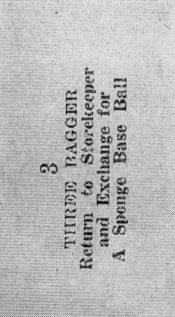

(6) BABE RUTH

3 THREE BAGGER
Return to Storekeeper
and Exchange for
A Sponge Base Ball

Issued in 1928, the manner of distribution for this set is unknown. Because some of the cards' backs indicate they were redeemable for prizes, they were most likely issued inside of a package of candy or similar product, or perhaps in an opaque envelope. The black-and-white cards measure about 1-3/8" x 2-1/2" and display the player's name at the bottom in capital letters preceded by a number in parentheses. The backs of the cards read either "One Bagger," "Three Bagger" or "Home Run." The listings here show two cards known to exist for numbers 38 and 40, which do not correspond to those numbers in 1931 W502. This raises the possibility there may have been a similar set issued in 1929 and/or 1930. The set carries the American Card Catalog designation W502.

		NM	EX	VG
Complete Set (62):		13,500	5,400	2,700
Common Player:		75.00	30.00	15.00
1	Burleigh Grimes	150.00	60.00	30.00
2	Walter Reuther (Ruether)	75.00	30.00	15.00
3	Joe Dugan	75.00	30.00	15.00
4	Red Faber	150.00	60.00	30.00
5	Gabby Hartnett	150.00	60.00	30.00
6	Babe Ruth	4,500	1,800	900.00
7	Bob Meusel	75.00	30.00	15.00
8	Herb Pennock	150.00	60.00	30.00
9	George Burns (Photo is George J., not George H. Burns.)	75.00	30.00	15.00
10	Joe Sewell	150.00	60.00	30.00
11	George Uhle	75.00	30.00	15.00
12	Bob O'Farrell	75.00	30.00	15.00
13	Rogers Hornsby	200.00	80.00	40.00
14	"Pie" Traynor	150.00	60.00	30.00
15	Clarence Mitchell	75.00	30.00	15.00
16	Eppa Jepha Rixey	150.00	60.00	30.00
17	Carl Mays	90.00	35.00	17.50
18	Adolfo Luque	75.00	30.00	15.00
19	Dave Bancroft	150.00	60.00	30.00
20	George Kelly	150.00	60.00	30.00
21	Earl Combs (Earle)	150.00	60.00	30.00
22	Harry Heilmann	150.00	60.00	30.00
23	Ray W. Schalk	150.00	60.00	30.00
24	Johnny Mostil	75.00	30.00	15.00
25	Hack Wilson (Photo actually Art Wilson.)	150.00	60.00	30.00
26	Lou Gehrig	1,750	700.00	350.00
27	Ty Cobb	1,750	700.00	350.00
28	Tris Speaker	200.00	80.00	40.00
29	Tony Lazzeri	150.00	60.00	30.00
30	Waite Hoyt	150.00	60.00	30.00
31	Sherwood Smith	75.00	30.00	15.00
32	Max Carey	150.00	60.00	30.00
33	Eugene Hargrave	75.00	30.00	15.00
34	Miguel L. Gonzales (Miguel A. Gonzalez)	75.00	30.00	15.00
35	Joe Judge	75.00	30.00	15.00
36	E.C. (Sam) Rice	150.00	60.00	30.00
37	Earl Sheely	75.00	30.00	15.00
38a	Sam Jones	75.00	30.00	15.00
38b	Emory E. Rigney	75.00	30.00	15.00
39	Bib A. Falk (Bibb)	75.00	30.00	15.00
40a	Nick Altrock	75.00	30.00	15.00
40b	Willie Kamm	75.00	30.00	15.00
41	Stanley Harris	150.00	60.00	30.00
42	John J. McGraw	150.00	60.00	30.00
43	Artie Nehf	75.00	30.00	15.00
44	Grover Alexander	250.00	100.00	50.00
45	Paul Waner	150.00	60.00	30.00
46	William H. Terry	150.00	60.00	30.00

		NM	EX	VG
47	Glenn Wright	75.00	30.00	15.00
48	Earl Smith	75.00	30.00	15.00
49	Leon (Goose) Goslin	150.00	60.00	30.00
50	Frank Frisch	150.00	60.00	30.00
51	Joe Harris	75.00	30.00	15.00
52	Fred (Cy) Williams	75.00	30.00	15.00
53	Eddie Roush	150.00	60.00	30.00
54	George Sisler	150.00	60.00	30.00
55	Ed Rommel	75.00	30.00	15.00
56	Rogers Peckinpaugh (Roger)	75.00	30.00	15.00
57	Stanley Coveleskie (Coveleski)	150.00	60.00	30.00
58	Lester Bell	75.00	30.00	15.00
59	Dave Bancroft	150.00	60.00	30.00
60	John P. McInnis	75.00	30.00	15.00

1931 W502

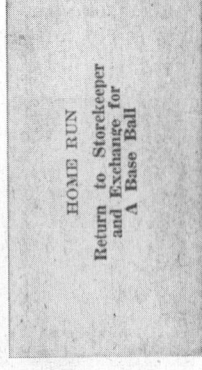

(46) EPPA RIXEY

HOME RUN
Return to Storekeeper and Exchange for A Base Ball

Issued in 1931, the manner of distribution for this set is unknown. Because some of the cards' backs indicate they were redeemable for prizes, they were most likely issued inside of a package of candy or similar product, or perhaps in an opaque envelope. The black-and-white cards measure about 1-3/8" x 2-1/2" and display the player's name at the bottom in capital letters preceded by a number in parentheses. The backs of the cards read either "One Bagger," "Three Bagger" or "Home Run." The set carries the American Card Catalog designation W502.

		NM	EX	VG
Complete Set (60):		12,500	5,500	2,750
Common Player:		90.00	35.00	17.50
1	Muddy Ruel	90.00	35.00	17.50
2	John Grabowski	90.00	35.00	17.50
3	Mickey Cochrane	150.00	60.00	30.00
4	Bill Cissell	90.00	35.00	17.50
5	Carl Reynolds	90.00	35.00	17.50
6	Luke Sewell	90.00	35.00	17.50
7	Ted Lyons	150.00	60.00	30.00
8	Harvey Walker	90.00	35.00	17.50
9	Gerald Walker	90.00	35.00	17.50
10	Sam Byrd	90.00	35.00	17.50
11	Joe Vosmik	90.00	35.00	17.50
12	Dan MacFayden	90.00	35.00	17.50
13	William Dickey	150.00	60.00	30.00
14	Robert Grove	250.00	100.00	50.00
15	Al Simmons	150.00	60.00	30.00
16	Jimmy Foxx	300.00	120.00	60.00
17	Nick Altrock	90.00	35.00	17.50
18	Charlie Grimm	90.00	35.00	17.50
19	Bill Terry	150.00	60.00	30.00
20	Clifton Heathcote	90.00	35.00	17.50
21	Burleigh Grimes	150.00	60.00	30.00
22	Red Faber	150.00	60.00	30.00
23	Gabby Hartnett	150.00	60.00	30.00
24	Earl (Earle) Combs	150.00	60.00	30.00
25	Hack Wilson	150.00	60.00	30.00
26	Stanley Harris	150.00	60.00	30.00
27	John J. McGraw	150.00	60.00	30.00
28	Paul Waner	150.00	60.00	30.00
29	Babe Ruth	4,500	1,800	900.00
30	Herb Pennock	150.00	60.00	30.00
31	Joe Sewell	150.00	60.00	30.00
32	Lou Gehrig	2,000	800.00	400.00
33	Tony Lazzeri	150.00	60.00	30.00
34	Waite Hoyt	150.00	60.00	30.00
35	Glenn Wright	90.00	35.00	17.50
36	Leon (Goose) Goslin	150.00	60.00	30.00
37	Frank Frisch	150.00	60.00	30.00
38	George Uhle	90.00	35.00	17.50
39	Bob O'Farrell	90.00	35.00	17.50
40	Rogers Hornsby	200.00	80.00	40.00
41	"Pie" Traynor	150.00	60.00	30.00
42	Clarence Mitchell	90.00	35.00	17.50
43	Sherwood Smith	90.00	35.00	17.50
44	Miguel A. Gonzalez	90.00	35.00	17.50
45	Joe Judge	90.00	35.00	17.50
46	Eppa Rixey	150.00	60.00	30.00
47	Adolfo Luque	90.00	35.00	17.50
48	E.C. (Sam) Rice	150.00	60.00	30.00
49	Earl Sheely	90.00	35.00	17.50
50	Sam Jones	90.00	35.00	17.50
51	Bib A. Falk	90.00	35.00	17.50
52	Willie Kamm	90.00	35.00	17.50
53	Roger Peckinpaugh	90.00	35.00	17.50
54	Lester Bell	90.00	35.00	17.50
55	L. Waner	150.00	60.00	30.00
56	Eugene Hargrave	90.00	35.00	17.50
57	Harry Heilmann	150.00	60.00	30.00
58	Earl Smith	90.00	35.00	17.50
59	Dave Bancroft	150.00	60.00	30.00
60	George Kelly	150.00	60.00	30.00

1922 W503

"IRISH" MEUSEL
GIANTS
N.Y.
18

Issued circa 1923, this 64-card set of blank-backed cards, measuring 1-3/4" x 2-3/4", feature black and white player photos surrounded by a white border. The player's name and team appear on the card, along with a card number in either the left or right bottom corner. There is no indication of the set's producer, although it is believed the cards were issued with candy or gum. The set carries a W503 American Card Catalog designation.

		NM	EX	VG
Complete Set (64):		40,000	16,000	8,000
Common Player:		350.00	140.00	70.00
1	Joe Bush	350.00	140.00	70.00
2	Wally Schang	350.00	140.00	70.00
3	Dave Robertson	350.00	140.00	70.00
4	Wally Pipp	375.00	150.00	75.00
5	Bill Ryan	350.00	140.00	70.00
6	George Kelly	900.00	360.00	180.00
7	Frank Snyder	350.00	140.00	70.00
8	Jimmy O'Connell	350.00	140.00	70.00
9	Bill Cunningham	350.00	140.00	70.00
10	Norman McMillan	350.00	140.00	70.00
11	Waite Hoyt	900.00	360.00	180.00
12	Art Nehf	350.00	140.00	70.00
13	George Sisler	900.00	360.00	180.00
14	Al DeVormer	350.00	140.00	70.00
15	Casey Stengel	900.00	360.00	180.00
16	Ken Williams	350.00	140.00	70.00
17	Joe Dugan	350.00	140.00	70.00
18	"Irish" Meusel	350.00	140.00	70.00
19	Bob Meusel	350.00	140.00	70.00
20	Carl Mays	375.00	150.00	75.00
21	Frank Frisch	900.00	360.00	180.00
22	Jess Barnes	350.00	140.00	70.00
23	Walter Johnson	1,500	600.00	300.00
24	Claude Jonnard	350.00	140.00	70.00
25	Dave Bancroft	900.00	360.00	180.00
26	Johnny Rawlings	350.00	140.00	70.00
27	"Pep" Young	350.00	140.00	70.00
28	Earl Smith	350.00	140.00	70.00
29	Willie Kamm	350.00	140.00	70.00
30	Art Fletcher	350.00	140.00	70.00
31	"Kid" Gleason	350.00	140.00	70.00
32	"Babe" Ruth	12,000	4,800	2,400
33	Guy Morton	350.00	140.00	70.00
34	Heinie Groh	350.00	140.00	70.00
35	Leon Cadore	350.00	140.00	70.00
36	Joe Tobin	350.00	140.00	70.00
37	"Rube" Marquard	900.00	360.00	180.00
38	Grover Alexander	1,200	480.00	240.00
39	George Burns	350.00	140.00	70.00
40	Joe Oeschger	350.00	140.00	70.00
41	"Chick" Shorten	350.00	140.00	70.00
42	Roger Hornsby (Rogers)	1,100	440.00	220.00
43	Adolfo Luque	350.00	140.00	70.00
44	Zack Wheat	900.00	360.00	180.00
45	Herb Pruett (Hub)	350.00	140.00	70.00
46	Rabbit Maranville	900.00	360.00	180.00
47	Jimmy Ring	350.00	140.00	70.00
48	Sherrod Smith	350.00	140.00	70.00
49	Lea Meadows (Lee)	350.00	140.00	70.00
50	Aaron Ward	350.00	140.00	70.00
51	Herb Pennock	900.00	360.00	180.00
52	Carlson Bigbee (Carson)	350.00	140.00	70.00
53	Max Carey	900.00	360.00	180.00
54	Charles Robertson	350.00	140.00	70.00
55	Urban Shocker	350.00	140.00	70.00
56	Dutch Ruether	350.00	140.00	70.00
57	Jake Daubert	350.00	140.00	70.00
58	Louis Guisto	350.00	140.00	70.00
59	Ivy Wingo	350.00	140.00	70.00
60	Bill Pertica	350.00	140.00	70.00
61	Luke Sewell	350.00	140.00	70.00
62	Hank Gowdy	350.00	140.00	70.00
63	Jack Scott	350.00	140.00	70.00
64	Stan Coveleskie (Coveleski)	900.00	360.00	180.00

1926 W511

Ruth is the only baseball player known in this set of athletic, cinematic and historical subjects. The approximately 1-1/2" x 2-1/2" black-and-white, blue-and-white, or maroon-and-white blank-backed card identifies the player, position and team typographically within the photo and has the card number and name in the bottom border. The card has been seen with numbers 1, 52 and 71, as well as unnumbered.

1. BABE RUTH

		NM	EX	VG
1	Babe Ruth (Black-and-white.)	800.00	400.00	240.00
52	Babe Ruth (Blue duotone.)	800.00	400.00	240.00
71	Babe Ruth (Blue duotone.)	800.00	400.00	240.00
71	Babe Ruth (Maroon duotone.)	800.00	400.00	240.00
---	Babe Ruth (Unnumbered, maroon.)	1,100	550.00	330.00

1926-27 W512

3 "TY" COBB
Ex-Mgr. Detroit A.L.

One of the many "strip card" sets of the period, the W512 set was initially issued in 1926 and includes 10 baseball players among its 50 cards. Also featured are boxers, golfers, tennis players, aviators, movie stars and other celebrities. The 1-3/8" x 2-1/4" cards feature crude color drawings of the subjects with their names below. A card number appears in the lower-left corner. Baseball players lead off the set and are numbered from 1 to 10. Like most strip cards, they have blank backs. At least four of the baseball player cards have been found in a second type, on which the team name is presented in a typewriter style font on the second line; these changes reflect player status as of 1927. Reprints of Ruth, Cobb, Johnson and Speaker are known.

		NM	EX	VG
Common Player:		55.00	22.50	10.00
1	Dave Bancroft	75.00	30.00	15.00
2a	Grover Alexander (Cubs)	190.00	75.00	35.00
2b	Grover Alexander (Cardinals)	95.00	40.00	20.00
3a	"Ty" Cobb	325.00	130.00	65.00
3b	"Ty" Cobb (Ex-Mgr. Detroit A.L.)	350.00	140.00	70.00
4a	Tris Speaker	95.00	40.00	20.00
4b	Tris Speaker (Ex-Mgr. Cleveland A.L.)	95.00	40.00	20.00
5	Glen Wright (Glenn)	55.00	22.50	10.00
6	"Babe" Ruth	360.00	145.00	70.00
7a	Everett Scott (Yankees)	75.00	30.00	15.00
7b	Everett Scott (White Sox)	55.00	22.50	10.00
8a	Frank Frisch (Giants)	75.00	30.00	15.00
8b	Frank Frisch (Cardinals)	75.00	30.00	15.00
9a	Rogers Hornsby (Cardinals)	95.00	40.00	20.00
9b	Rogers Hornsby (Giants)	95.00	40.00	20.00
10	Dazzy Vance	75.00	30.00	15.00

1928 W513

Rube Benton
Giants Pitcher
New York National
69

This "strip card" set, issued in 1928 was actually a continuation of the W512 set issued two years earlier and is numbered starting with number 61 where the W512 set ended. The blank-backed cards measure 1-3/8" x 2-1/4" and display color drawings of the athletes, which include 14 boxers and the 26 baseball players listed here. The cards are numbered in the lower-left corner.

		NM	EX	VG
Complete (Baseball) Set (26):		1,600	650.00	325.00
Common Player:		50.00	20.00	10.00
61	Eddie Roush	75.00	30.00	15.00
62	Waite Hoyt	75.00	30.00	15.00
63	"Gink" Hendrick	50.00	20.00	10.00
64	"Jumbo" Elliott	50.00	20.00	10.00
65	John Miljus	50.00	20.00	10.00
66	Jumping Joe Dugan	50.00	20.00	10.00
67	Smiling Bill Terry	75.00	30.00	15.00
68	Herb Pennock	75.00	30.00	15.00
69	Rube Benton	50.00	20.00	10.00
70	Paul Waner	75.00	30.00	15.00
71	Adolfo Luque	50.00	20.00	10.00
72	Burleigh Grimes	75.00	30.00	15.00
73	Lloyd Waner	75.00	30.00	15.00
74	Hack Wilson	75.00	30.00	15.00
75	Hal Carlson	50.00	20.00	10.00
76	L. Grantham	50.00	20.00	10.00
77	Wilcey Moore (Wilcy)	50.00	20.00	10.00
78	Jess Haines	75.00	30.00	15.00
79	Tony Lazzeri	75.00	30.00	15.00
80	Al DeVormer	50.00	20.00	10.00
81	Joe Harris	50.00	20.00	10.00
82	Pie Traynor	75.00	30.00	15.00
83	Mark Koenig	50.00	20.00	10.00
84	Babe Herman	60.00	24.00	12.00
85	George Harper	50.00	20.00	10.00
86	Earl Coombs (Earle Combs)	75.00	30.00	15.00

1919-21 W514

LEFTY WILLIAMS
PITCHER
CHICAGO "WHITE SOX" A. L.

Consisting of 120 cards, the W514 set is the largest of the various "strip card" issues of its era. Issued between 1919-1921, it is also one of the earliest and most widely-collected. The 1-3/8" x 2-1/2" cards feature color drawings of the players and display the card number in the lower-left corner. The player's name, position and team appear in the bottom border of the blank-backed cards. The set holds special interest for baseball historians because it includes seven of the eight Chicago "Black Sox" who were banned from baseball for their alleged role in throwing the 1919 World Series. The most famous of them, "Shoeless" Joe Jackson, makes his only strip card appearance in this set.

		NM	EX	VG
Complete Set (124):		30,000	12,000	6,000
Common Player:		75.00	30.00	15.00
1	Ira Flagstead	75.00	30.00	15.00
2	Babe Ruth (HOME RUN KING)	1,900	750.00	375.00
3	Happy Felsch	1,200	475.00	250.00
4	Doc Lavan	75.00	30.00	15.00
5	Phil Douglas	75.00	30.00	15.00
6	Earle Neale	75.00	30.00	15.00
7	Leslie Nunamaker	75.00	30.00	15.00
8	Sam Jones	75.00	30.00	15.00
9	Claude Hendrix	75.00	30.00	15.00
10	Frank Schulte	75.00	30.00	15.00
11	Cactus Cravath	75.00	30.00	15.00
12	Pat Moran	75.00	30.00	15.00
13	Dick Rudolph	75.00	30.00	15.00
14	Arthur Fletcher	75.00	30.00	15.00
15	Joe Jackson	5,000	2,000	1,000
16	Bill Southworth	75.00	30.00	15.00
17	Ad Luque	75.00	30.00	15.00
18	Charlie Deal	75.00	30.00	15.00
19	Al Mamaux	75.00	30.00	15.00
20	Stuffy McInness (McInnis)	75.00	30.00	15.00
21a	Rabbit Maranville (Braves)	200.00	80.00	40.00
21b	Rabbit Maranville (Pirates)	200.00	80.00	40.00
22	Max Carey	200.00	80.00	40.00
23	Dick Kerr	75.00	30.00	15.00
24	George Burns	75.00	30.00	15.00
25	Eddie Collins	200.00	80.00	40.00
26	Steve O'Neil (O'Neill)	75.00	30.00	15.00
27	Bill Fisher	75.00	30.00	15.00
28	Rube Bressler	75.00	30.00	15.00
29	Bob Shawkey	75.00	30.00	15.00
30	Donie Bush	75.00	30.00	15.00
31	Chick Gandil	700.00	280.00	140.00
32	Ollie Zeider	75.00	30.00	15.00

33	Vean Gregg	75.00	30.00	15.00
34	Miller Huggins	200.00	80.00	40.00
35	Lefty Williams	800.00	325.00	160.00
36	Tub Spencer	75.00	30.00	15.00
37	Lew McCarty	75.00	30.00	15.00
38	Hod Eller	75.00	30.00	15.00
39	Joe Gedeon	75.00	30.00	15.00
40a	Dave Bancroft (Quakers)	200.00	80.00	40.00
40b	Dave Bancroft (Giants)	200.00	80.00	40.00
41	Clark Griffith	200.00	80.00	40.00
42	Wilbur Cooper	75.00	30.00	15.00
43	Ty Cobb	1,750	700.00	350.00
44	Roger Peckinpaugh	75.00	30.00	15.00
45	Nic Carter (Nick)	75.00	30.00	15.00
46	Heinie Groh	75.00	30.00	15.00
47a	Bob Roth (Indians)	75.00	30.00	15.00
47b	Bob Roth (Yankees)	75.00	30.00	15.00
48	Frank Davis	75.00	30.00	15.00
49	Leslie Mann	75.00	30.00	15.00
50	Fielder Jones	75.00	30.00	15.00
51	Bill Doak	75.00	30.00	15.00
52	John J. McGraw	200.00	80.00	40.00
53	Charles Hollocher	75.00	30.00	15.00
54	Babe Adams	75.00	30.00	15.00
55	Dode Paskert	75.00	30.00	15.00
56	Roger Hornsby (Rogers)	250.00	100.00	50.00
57	Max Rath	75.00	30.00	15.00
58	Jeff Pfeffer	75.00	30.00	15.00
59	Nick Cullop	75.00	30.00	15.00
60	Ray Schalk	200.00	80.00	40.00
61	Bill Jacobson	75.00	30.00	15.00
62	Nap Lajoie	225.00	90.00	45.00
63	George Gibson	75.00	30.00	15.00
64	Harry Hooper	200.00	80.00	40.00
65	Grover Alexander	300.00	120.00	60.00
66	Ping Bodie	75.00	30.00	15.00
67	Hank Gowdy	75.00	30.00	15.00
68	Jake Daubert	75.00	30.00	15.00
69	Red Faber	200.00	80.00	40.00
70	Ivan Olson	75.00	30.00	15.00
71	Pickles Dilhoefer	75.00	30.00	15.00
72	Christy Mathewson	900.00	350.00	175.00
73	Ira Wingo (Ivy)	75.00	30.00	15.00
74	Fred Merkle	75.00	30.00	15.00
75	Bert Baker	200.00	80.00	40.00
76	Bert Gallia	75.00	30.00	15.00
77	Milton Watson	75.00	30.00	15.00
78	Bert Shotten (Shotton)	75.00	30.00	15.00
79	Sam Rice	200.00	80.00	40.00
80	Dan Greiner	75.00	30.00	15.00
81	Larry Doyle	75.00	30.00	15.00
82	Eddie Cicotte	750.00	300.00	150.00
83	Hugo Bezdek	75.00	30.00	15.00
84	Wally Pipp	90.00	35.00	17.50
85	Eddie Rousch (Roush)	200.00	80.00	40.00
86	Slim Sallee	75.00	30.00	15.00
87	Bill Killifer (Killefer)	75.00	30.00	15.00
88	Bob Veach	75.00	30.00	15.00
89	Jim Burke	75.00	30.00	15.00
90	Everett Scott	75.00	30.00	15.00
91	Buck Weaver	1,100	450.00	225.00
92	George Whitted	75.00	30.00	15.00
93	Ed Konetchy	75.00	30.00	15.00
94	Walter Johnson	600.00	240.00	120.00
95	Sam Crawford	200.00	80.00	40.00
96	Fred Mitchell	75.00	30.00	15.00
97	Ira Thomas	75.00	30.00	15.00
98	Jimmy Ring	75.00	30.00	15.00
99	Wally Shange (Schang)	75.00	30.00	15.00
100	Benny Kauff	75.00	30.00	15.00
101	George Sisler	200.00	80.00	40.00
102	Tris Speaker	250.00	100.00	50.00
103	Carl Mays	90.00	35.00	17.50
104	Buck Herzog	75.00	30.00	15.00
105	Swede Risberg	2,750	1,100	550.00
106a	Hugh Jennings (Tigers)	200.00	80.00	40.00
106b	Hughie Jennings (Giants)	200.00	80.00	40.00
107	Pep Young	75.00	30.00	15.00
108	Walter Reuther (Ruether)	75.00	30.00	15.00
109	Joe Gharrity (Ed)	75.00	30.00	15.00
110	Zach Wheat	200.00	80.00	40.00
111	Jim Vaughn	75.00	30.00	15.00
112	Kid Gleason	75.00	30.00	15.00
113	Casey Stengel	200.00	80.00	40.00
114	Hal Chase	150.00	60.00	30.00
115	Oscar Stange (Stanage)	75.00	30.00	15.00
116	Larry Shean	75.00	30.00	15.00
117	Steve Pendergast	75.00	30.00	15.00
118	Larry Kopf	75.00	30.00	15.00
119	Charles Whiteman	75.00	30.00	15.00
120	Jess Barnes	75.00	30.00	15.00

1923 W515-1

11. GEORGE SISLER
First Base
St. Louis Browns, A. L.

Cards in the 60-card "strip set" measure about 1-3/8" x 2-1/4" and feature color drawings. Backs are blank. The card number along with the player's name, position and team appear in the bottom border. Most cards also display a "U&U" copyright line, indicating that the photos on which the drawings were based were provided by Underwood & Underwood, a major news photo service of the day. The set has a heavy emphasis on New York players with 39 of the 60 cards depicting members of the Yankees, Dodgers or Giants. Babe Ruth appears on two cards and two other cards picture two players each.

		NM	EX	VG
Complete Set (60):		8,000	3,200	1,600
Common Player:		50.00	20.00	10.00
1	Bill Cunningham	50.00	20.00	10.00
2	Al Mamaux	50.00	20.00	10.00
3	"Babe" Ruth	1,600	650.00	325.00
4	Dave Bancroft	100.00	40.00	20.00
5	Ed Rommel	50.00	20.00	10.00
6	"Babe" Adams	50.00	20.00	10.00
7	Clarence Walker	50.00	20.00	10.00
8	Waite Hoyt	100.00	40.00	20.00
9	Bob Shawkey	50.00	20.00	10.00
10	"Ty" Cobb	750.00	300.00	150.00
11	George Sisler	100.00	40.00	20.00
12	Jack Bentley	50.00	20.00	10.00
13	Jim O'Connell	50.00	20.00	10.00
14	Frank Frisch	100.00	40.00	20.00
15	Frank Baker	100.00	40.00	20.00
16	Burleigh Grimes	100.00	40.00	20.00
17	Wally Schang	50.00	20.00	10.00
18	Harry Heilman (Heilmann)	100.00	40.00	20.00
19	Aaron Ward	50.00	20.00	10.00
20	Carl Mays	60.00	24.00	12.00
21	The Meusel Bros. (Bob Meusel, Irish Meusel)	60.00	24.00	12.00
22	Arthur Nehf	50.00	20.00	10.00
23	Lee Meadows	50.00	20.00	10.00
24	"Casey" Stengel	100.00	40.00	20.00
25	Jack Scott	50.00	20.00	10.00
26	Kenneth Williams	50.00	20.00	10.00
27	Joe Bush	50.00	20.00	10.00
28	Tris Speaker	150.00	60.00	30.00
29	Ross Young (Youngs)	100.00	40.00	20.00
30	Joe Dugan	50.00	20.00	10.00
31	The Barnes Bros. (Jesse Barnes, Virgil Barnes)	60.00	24.00	12.00
32	George Kelly	100.00	40.00	20.00
33	Hugh McQuillen (McQuillan)	50.00	20.00	10.00
34	Hugh Jennings	100.00	40.00	20.00
35	Tom Griffith	50.00	20.00	10.00
36	Miller Huggins	100.00	40.00	20.00
37	"Whitey" Witt	50.00	20.00	10.00
38	Walter Johnson	400.00	160.00	80.00
39	"Wally" Pipp	50.00	20.00	10.00
40	"Dutch" Reuther (Ruether)	50.00	20.00	10.00
41	Jim Johnston	50.00	20.00	10.00
42	Willie Kamm	50.00	20.00	10.00
43	Sam Jones	50.00	20.00	10.00
44	Frank Snyder	50.00	20.00	10.00
45	John McGraw	100.00	40.00	20.00
46	Everett Scott	50.00	20.00	10.00
47	"Babe" Ruth	1,600	650.00	325.00
48	Urban Shocker	50.00	20.00	10.00
49	Grover Alexander	150.00	60.00	30.00
50	"Rabbit" Maranville	100.00	40.00	20.00
51	Ray Schalk	100.00	40.00	20.00
52	"Heinie" Groh	50.00	20.00	10.00
53	Wilbert Robinson	100.00	40.00	20.00
54	George Burns	50.00	20.00	10.00
55	Rogers Hornsby	150.00	60.00	30.00
56	Zack Wheat	100.00	40.00	20.00
57	Eddie Roush	100.00	40.00	20.00
58	Eddie Collins	100.00	40.00	20.00
59	Charlie Hollocher	50.00	20.00	10.00
60	Red Faber	100.00	40.00	20.00

1923 W515-2

A near duplicate of the W515-1 set in every respect except size, the W515-2 strip cards are larger in format, at about 1-1/2" x 2-1/2". Placement of the U&U copyright also differs between some players' cards in each set. Cards may be found with letters in the top border from the title, "THE LITTLE WONDER PICTURE SERIES."

		NM	EX	VG
Complete Set (60):		8,000	3,200	1,600
Common Player:		50.00	25.00	15.00
1	Bill Cunningham	50.00	25.00	15.00

2	Al Mamaux	50.00	25.00	15.00
3	"Babe" Ruth	1,600	800.00	480.00
4	Dave Bancroft	100.00	50.00	30.00
5	Ed Rommel	50.00	25.00	15.00
6	"Babe" Adams	50.00	25.00	15.00
7	Clarence Walker	50.00	25.00	15.00
8	Waite Hoyt	100.00	50.00	30.00
9	Bob Shawkey	50.00	25.00	15.00
10	"Ty" Cobb	750.00	375.00	225.00
11	George Sisler	100.00	50.00	30.00
12	Jack Bentley	50.00	25.00	15.00
13	Jim O'Connell	50.00	25.00	15.00
14	Frank Frisch	100.00	50.00	30.00
15	Frank Baker	100.00	50.00	30.00
16	Burleigh Grimes	100.00	50.00	30.00
17	Wally Schang	50.00	25.00	15.00
18	Harry Heilman (Heilmann)	100.00	50.00	30.00
19	Aaron Ward	50.00	25.00	15.00
20	Carl Mays	60.00	30.00	18.00
21	The Meusel Bros. (Bob Meusel, Irish Meusel)	60.00	30.00	18.00
22	Arthur Nehf	50.00	25.00	15.00
23	Lee Meadows	50.00	25.00	15.00
24	"Casey" Stengel	100.00	50.00	30.00
25	Jack Scott	50.00	25.00	15.00
26	Kenneth Williams	50.00	25.00	15.00
27	Joe Bush	50.00	25.00	15.00
28	Tris Speaker	150.00	75.00	45.00
29	Ross Young (Youngs)	100.00	50.00	30.00
30	Joe Dugan	50.00	25.00	15.00
31	The Barnes Bros. (Jesse Barnes, Virgil Barnes)	60.00	30.00	18.00
32	George Kelly	100.00	50.00	30.00
33	Hugh McQuillen (McQuillan)	50.00	25.00	15.00
34	Hugh Jennings	100.00	50.00	30.00
35	Tom Griffith	50.00	25.00	15.00
36	Miller Huggins	100.00	50.00	30.00
37	"Whitey" Witt	50.00	25.00	15.00
38	Walter Johnson	400.00	200.00	120.00
39	"Wally" Pipp	50.00	25.00	15.00
40	"Dutch" Reuther (Ruether)	50.00	25.00	15.00
41	Jim Johnston	50.00	25.00	15.00
42	Willie Kamm	50.00	25.00	15.00
43	Sam Jones	50.00	25.00	15.00
44	Frank Snyder	50.00	25.00	15.00
45	John McGraw	100.00	50.00	30.00
46	Everett Scott	50.00	25.00	15.00
47	"Babe" Ruth	1,600	800.00	480.00
48	Urban Shocker	50.00	25.00	15.00
49	Grover Alexander	150.00	75.00	45.00
50	"Rabbit" Maranville	100.00	50.00	30.00
51	Ray Schalk	100.00	50.00	30.00
52	"Heinie" Groh	50.00	25.00	15.00
53	Wilbert Robinson	100.00	50.00	30.00
54	George Burns	50.00	25.00	15.00
55	Rogers Hornsby	150.00	75.00	45.00
56	Zack Wheat	100.00	50.00	30.00
57	Eddie Roush	100.00	50.00	30.00
58	Eddie Collins	100.00	50.00	30.00
59	Charlie Hollocher	50.00	25.00	15.00
60	Red Faber	100.00	50.00	30.00

1920 W516-1

LARRY DOYLE.
2ND B.   GIANTS

This "strip card" set consists of 30 cards featuring colored drawings - either portraits or full-length action poses. The blank-backed cards measure 1-1/2" x 2-1/2". The player's name, position and team appear beneath the picture in hand-printed style. To the right of the name is the card number. The set can be identified by an "IFS" copyright symbol. representing International Feature Service.

		NM	EX	VG
Complete Set (30):		5,250	2,000	1,000
Common Player:		50.00	25.00	10.00
1	Babe Ruth	2,000	800.00	400.00
2	Heinie Groh	50.00	25.00	10.00
3	Ping Bodie	50.00	25.00	10.00
4	Ray Shalk (Schalk)	100.00	40.00	20.00
5	Tris Speaker	150.00	60.00	30.00
6	Ty Cobb	750.00	300.00	150.00
7	Roger Hornsby (Rogers)	150.00	60.00	30.00
8	Walter Johnson	300.00	120.00	60.00
9	Grover Alexander	150.00	60.00	30.00
10	George Burns	50.00	25.00	10.00
11	Jimmy Ring	50.00	25.00	10.00
12	Jess Barnes	50.00	25.00	10.00
13	Larry Doyle	50.00	25.00	10.00
14	Arty Fletcher	50.00	25.00	10.00
15	Dick Rudolph	50.00	25.00	10.00

16	Benny Kauf (Kauff)	50.00	25.00	10.00
17	Art Nehf	50.00	25.00	10.00
18	Babe Adams	50.00	25.00	10.00
19	Will Cooper	50.00	25.00	10.00
20	R. Peckinpaugh	50.00	25.00	10.00
21	Eddie Cicotte	100.00	40.00	20.00
22	Hank Gowdy	50.00	25.00	10.00
23	Eddie Collins	100.00	40.00	20.00
24	Christy Mathewson	400.00	160.00	80.00
25	Clyde Milan	50.00	25.00	10.00
26	M. Kelley (Should be G. Kelly)	100.00	40.00	20.00
27	Ed Hooper (Harry)	100.00	40.00	20.00
28	Pep. Young	50.00	25.00	10.00
29	Eddie Rousch (Roush)	100.00	40.00	20.00
30	Geo. Bancroft (Dave)	100.00	40.00	20.00

1920 W516-1-2

TY COBB.
DETROIT   OUTFIELD

This set is a re-issue of the W516-1-1 set, with several changes: The pictures are reverse images of W516-1-1, and are printed only in black, red and yellow. Well cut, the blank-back cards measure a nominal 1-1/2" x 2-3/8". The cards display a backwards "IFC" copyright symbol.

		NM	EX	VG
Complete Set (30):		5,250	2,000	1,000
Common Player:		50.00	25.00	10.00
1	Babe Ruth	2,000	1,000	600.00
2	Heinie Groh	50.00	25.00	10.00
3	Ping Bodie	50.00	25.00	10.00
4	Ray Shalk (Schalk)	100.00	40.00	20.00
5	Tris Speaker	150.00	60.00	30.00
6	Ty Cobb	750.00	300.00	150.00
7	Roger Hornsby (Rogers)	150.00	75.00	45.00
8	Walter Johnson	300.00	150.00	90.00
9	Grover Alexander	150.00	60.00	30.00
10	George Burns	50.00	25.00	10.00
11	Jimmy Ring	50.00	25.00	10.00
12	Jess Barnes	50.00	25.00	10.00
13	Larry Doyle	50.00	25.00	10.00
14	Arty Fletcher	50.00	25.00	10.00
15	Dick Rudolph	50.00	25.00	10.00
16	Benny Kauf (Kauff)	50.00	25.00	10.00
17	Art Nehf	50.00	25.00	10.00
18	Babe Adams	50.00	25.00	10.00
19	Will Cooper	50.00	25.00	10.00
20	R. Peckinpaugh	50.00	25.00	10.00
21	Eddie Cicotte	100.00	50.00	30.00
22	Hank Gowdy	50.00	25.00	10.00
23	Eddie Collins	100.00	40.00	20.00
24	Christy Mathewson	400.00	200.00	120.00
25	Clyde Milan	50.00	25.00	10.00
26	M. Kelley (Should be G. Kelly)	100.00	40.00	20.00
27	Ed Hooper (Harry)	100.00	40.00	20.00
28	Pep. Young	50.00	25.00	10.00
29	Eddie Rousch (Roush)	100.00	40.00	20.00
30	Geo. Bancroft (Dave)	100.00	40.00	20.00

1921 W516-2-1

PING BODIE   HEINIE GROH   BABE RUTH
Outfielder   Third Base   Outfielder

This set is essentially a re-issue of the W516-1 set, with several changes: The pictures are reverse images of W516-1, and are printed only in red and blue. Cards have been renumbered and have player identification in typeset serifed style. The blank-backed cards measure about 1-1/2" x 2-3/8". The cards display a backwards "IFC" copyright symbol.

		NM	EX	VG
Complete Set (30):		4,500	1,800	900.00
Common Player:		50.00	25.00	10.00
1	George Burns	50.00	25.00	10.00
2	Grover Alexander	150.00	60.00	30.00
3	Walter Johnson	250.00	100.00	50.00
4	Roger Hornsby (Rogers)	125.00	50.00	25.00

5	Ty Cobb	750.00	300.00	150.00
6	Tris Speaker	125.00	50.00	25.00
7	Ray Shalk (Schalk)	75.00	30.00	15.00
8	Ping Bodie	50.00	25.00	10.00
9	Heinie Groh	50.00	25.00	10.00
10	Babe Ruth	1,500	600.00	300.00
11	R. Peckinpaugh	50.00	25.00	10.00
12	Will. Cooper	50.00	25.00	10.00
13	Babe Adams	50.00	25.00	10.00
14	Art Nehf	50.00	25.00	10.00
15	Benny Kauf (Kauff)	50.00	25.00	10.00
16	Dick Rudolph	50.00	25.00	10.00
17	Arty. Fletcher	50.00	25.00	10.00
18	Larry Doyle	50.00	25.00	10.00
19	Jess Barnes	50.00	25.00	10.00
20	Jimmy Ring	50.00	25.00	10.00
21	George Bancroft (Dave)	75.00	30.00	15.00
22	Eddie Rousch (Roush)	75.00	30.00	15.00
23	Pep Young	50.00	25.00	10.00
24	Ed Hooper (Harry)	75.00	30.00	15.00
25	M. Kelley (Should be G. Kelly.)	75.00	30.00	15.00
26	Clyde Milan	50.00	25.00	10.00
27	Christy Mathewson	350.00	140.00	70.00
28	Eddie Collins	75.00	30.00	15.00
29	Hank Gowdy	50.00	25.00	10.00
30	Eddie Cicotte	125.00	50.00	25.00

1921 W516-2-2

BABE RUTH
YANKS   PITCHER

This set is yet another variation in the W516 "family." In numbering it parallels W516-2-1, though the typography is in the same sans-serif font as W516-1. Like W516-2-1, the player pictures have been reversed. Well cut, the blank-backed cards measure a nominal 1-1/2" x 2-1/4". The cards display a backwards "IFC" copyright symbol in the picture portion.

		NM	EX	VG
Complete Set (30):		5,000	2,500	1,500
Common Player:		50.00	25.00	10.00
1	George Burns	50.00	25.00	10.00
2	Grover Alexander	150.00	75.00	45.00
3	Walter Johnson	300.00	150.00	90.00
4	Roger Hornsby (Rogers)	125.00	62.00	37.00
5	Ty Cobb	750.00	375.00	225.00
6	Tris Speaker	125.00	62.00	37.00
7	Ray Shalk (Schalk)	75.00	37.50	22.50
8	Ping Bodie	50.00	25.00	10.00
9	Heinie Groh	50.00	25.00	10.00
10	Babe Ruth	2,000	1,000	600.00
11	R. Peckinpaugh	50.00	25.00	10.00
12	Will. Cooper	50.00	25.00	10.00
13	Babe Adams	50.00	25.00	10.00
14	Art Nehf	50.00	25.00	10.00
15	Benny Kauf (Kauff)	50.00	25.00	10.00
16	Dick Rudolph	50.00	25.00	10.00
17	Arty. Fletcher	50.00	25.00	10.00
18	Larry Doyle	50.00	25.00	10.00
19	Jess Barnes	50.00	25.00	10.00
20	Jimmy Ring	50.00	25.00	10.00
21	George Bancroft (Dave)	75.00	37.50	22.50
22	Eddie Rousch (Roush)	75.00	37.50	22.50
23	Pep Young	75.00	37.50	22.50
24	Ed Hooper (Harry)	75.00	37.50	22.50
25	M. Kelley (Should be G. Kelly.)	75.00	37.50	22.50
26	Clyde Milan	50.00	25.00	10.00
27	Christy Mathewson	400.00	200.00	120.00
28	Eddie Collins	75.00	37.50	22.50
29	Hank Gowdy	50.00	25.00	10.00
30	Eddie Cicotte	100.00	50.00	30.00

1921 W516-2-3

JESS BARNES
Pitcher

This issue shares a checklist with W516-2-1, and is likewise printed only in red and blue, with typography in a serifed typeface. Unlike W516-2-1, however, the images on these cards are not reversed, as can easily be ascertained by looking at the copyright symbol and letters.

		NM	EX	VG
	Complete Set (30):	5,000	2,500	1,500
	Common Player:			
1	George Burns	50.00	25.00	10.00
2	Grover Alexander	150.00	75.00	45.00
3	Walter Johnson	300.00	150.00	90.00
4	Roger Hornsby (Rogers)	125.00	62.00	37.00
5	Ty Cobb	750.00	375.00	225.00
6	Tris Speaker	125.00	62.00	37.00
7	Ray Shalk (Schalk)	75.00	30.00	15.00
8	Ping Bodie	50.00	25.00	10.00
9	Heinie Groh	50.00	25.00	10.00
10	Babe Ruth	2,000	1,000	600.00
11	R. Peckinpaugh	50.00	25.00	10.00
12	Will. Cooper	50.00	25.00	10.00
13	Babe Adams	50.00	25.00	10.00
14	Art Nehf	50.00	25.00	10.00
15	Benny Kauf (Kauff)	50.00	25.00	10.00
16	Dick Rudolph	50.00	25.00	10.00
17	Arty. Fletcher	50.00	25.00	10.00
18	Larry Doyle	50.00	25.00	10.00
19	Jess Barnes	50.00	25.00	10.00
20	Jimmy Ring	50.00	25.00	10.00
21	George Bancroft (Dave)	75.00	30.00	15.00
22	Eddie Rousch (Roush)	75.00	30.00	15.00
23	Pep Young	50.00	25.00	10.00
24	Ed Hooper (Harry)	75.00	30.00	15.00
25	M. Kelley (Should be G. Kelly.)	75.00	30.00	15.00
26	Clyde Milan	50.00	25.00	10.00
27	Christy Mathewson	400.00	200.00	120.00
28	Eddie Collins	75.00	30.00	15.00
29	Hank Gowdy	50.00	25.00	10.00
30	Eddie Cicotte	100.00	50.00	30.00

1931 W517

The 54-player W517 set is an issue of 3" x 4" cards generally found in a sepia color, though other colors are known. The cards feature a player photo as well as his name and team. The card number appears in a small circle on the front, while the backs are blank. The set is heavy in stars of the period including two Babe Ruths (#4 and 20). The cards were sold in vertical strips of three cards; some cards are found with baseball plays in a line at top. Complete set prices do not include variations. The set was reprinted in three-card-strip format in 1997, with "W-517" printed in the lower-left corner of the reprints.

		NM	EX	VG
	Complete Set (59):	11,000	4,400	2,200
	Common Player:	75.00	35.00	20.00
1	Earl Combs (Earle)	160.00	70.00	40.00
2	Pie Traynor	160.00	70.00	40.00
3	Eddie Rausch (Roush)	160.00	70.00	40.00
4	Babe Ruth (Throwing)	1,500	675.00	375.00
5a	Chalmer Cissell (Chicago)	75.00	35.00	20.00
5b	Chalmer Cissell (Cleveland)	75.00	35.00	20.00
6	Bill Sherdel	75.00	35.00	20.00
7	Bill Shore	75.00	35.00	20.00
8	Geo. Earnshaw	75.00	35.00	20.00
9	Bucky Harris	160.00	70.00	40.00
10	Charlie Klein	160.00	70.00	40.00
11a	Geo. Kelly (Reds)	75.00	35.00	20.00
11b	Geo. Kelly (Brooklyn)	75.00	35.00	20.00
12	Travis Jackson	160.00	70.00	40.00
13	Willie Kamm	75.00	35.00	20.00
14	Harry Heilman (Heilmann)	160.00	70.00	40.00
15	Grover Alexander	250.00	110.00	60.00
16	Frank Frisch	160.00	70.00	40.00
17	Jack Quinn	75.00	35.00	20.00
18	Cy Williams	75.00	35.00	20.00
19	Kiki Cuyler	160.00	70.00	40.00
20	Babe Ruth (Portrait)	1,750	785.00	435.00
21	Jimmie Foxx	350.00	155.00	85.00
22	Jimmy Dykes	75.00	35.00	20.00
23	Bill Terry	160.00	70.00	40.00
24	Freddy Lindstrom	160.00	72.00	40.00
25	Hughey Critz	75.00	35.00	20.00
26	Pete Donahue	75.00	35.00	20.00
27	Tony Lazzeri	160.00	70.00	40.00
28	Heine Manush (Heinie)	160.00	70.00	40.00
29a	Chick Hafey (Cardinals)	160.00	70.00	40.00
29b	Chick Hafey (Cincinnati)	160.00	70.00	40.00
30	Melvin Ott	200.00	90.00	50.00
31	Bing Miller	75.00	35.00	20.00
32	Geo. Haas	75.00	35.00	20.00
33a	Lefty O'Doul (Phillies)	95.00	45.00	25.00
33b	Lefty O'Doul (Brooklyn)	95.00	45.00	25.00
(34)	Paul Waner (No card number.)	160.00	70.00	40.00
34	Paul Waner (W/card number.)	160.00	70.00	40.00

		NM	EX	VG
35	Lou Gehrig	900.00	400.00	225.00
36	Dazzy Vance	160.00	70.00	40.00
37	Mickey Cochrane	160.00	70.00	40.00
38	Rogers Hornsby	225.00	100.00	55.00
39	Lefty Grove	200.00	90.00	50.00
40	Al Simmons	160.00	70.00	40.00
41	Rube Walberg	75.00	35.00	20.00
42	Hack Wilson	160.00	70.00	40.00
43	Art Shires	75.00	35.00	20.00
44	Sammy Hale	75.00	35.00	20.00
45	Ted Lyons	160.00	70.00	40.00
46	Joe Sewell	160.00	70.00	40.00
47	Goose Goslin	160.00	70.00	40.00
48	Lou Fonseca (Lew)	75.00	35.00	20.00
49	Bob Muesel (Meusel)	75.00	35.00	20.00
50	Lu Blue	75.00	35.00	20.00
51	Earl Averill	160.00	70.00	40.00
52	Eddy Collins (Eddie)	160.00	70.00	40.00
53	Joe Judge	75.00	35.00	20.00
54	Mickey Cochrane	160.00	70.00	40.00

1931 W517 Mini

Little is known about these smaller-format (1-3/4" x 2-3/4") versions of the W517 strip cards. They are identical in design to the more common 3" x 4" cards, although some, if not all, do not have the card number-in-circle found on regular W517s. It is presumed, though not confirmed, that all 54 of the regular versions can be found in the mini size, as well as several color variations.

PREMIUM: 2-3X
(See W517 for checklist and base card values.)

1920 W519 - Numbered 1

Cards in this 20-card "strip set" measure 1-1/2" x 2-1/2" and feature player drawings set against a brightly colored background. A card number appears in the lower-left corner followed by the player's name, printed in capital letters. The player drawings are all posed portraits, except for Joe Murphy and Ernie Kreuger, who are shown catching. Like all strip cards, the cards were sold in strips and have blank backs. The date of issue may be approximate.

		NM	EX	VG
	Complete Set (20):	5,500	2,200	1,100
	Common Player:	100.00	40.00	20.00
1	Guy Morton	100.00	40.00	20.00
2	Rube Marquard	300.00	120.00	60.00
3	Gabby Cravath (Gavvy)	100.00	40.00	20.00
4	Ernie Krueger	100.00	40.00	20.00
5	Babe Ruth	2,400	960.00	480.00
6	George Sisler	300.00	120.00	60.00
7	Rube Benton	100.00	40.00	20.00
8	Jimmie Johnston	100.00	40.00	20.00
9	Wilbur Robinson (Wilbert)	300.00	120.00	60.00
10	Johnny Griffith	100.00	40.00	20.00
11	Frank Baker	300.00	120.00	60.00
12	Bob Veach	100.00	40.00	20.00
13	Jesse Barnes	100.00	40.00	20.00
14	Leon Cadore	100.00	40.00	20.00
15	Ray Schalk	300.00	120.00	60.00
16	Kid Gleasen (Gleason)	300.00	120.00	60.00
17	Joe Murphy	100.00	40.00	20.00
18	Frank Frisch	300.00	120.00	60.00
19	Eddie Collins	300.00	120.00	60.00
20	Wallie (Wally) Schang	100.00	40.00	20.00

1920 W519 - Numbered 2

A second type of numbered version of W519 exists on which the style of the card numbers differs as does, apparently, the numbering of the players. On Type 1 cards, the card number to the left of the player name is printed in the same heavy sans-serif style as the name. Type 2 cards have the number in a lighter typewriter-style font. While 10 Type 2 cards are currently confirmed to exist, it is expected the other 10 players from W519 were also issued.

		NM	EX	VG
12	Joe Murphy	100.00	40.00	20.00
12	Bobby Veach	100.00	40.00	20.00
13	Jesse Barnes	100.00	40.00	20.00
13	Frank Frisch	300.00	120.00	60.00
14	Eddie Collins	300.00	120.00	60.00
16	Guy Morton	100.00	40.00	20.00
17	Rube Marquard	300.00	120.00	60.00
19	Ernie Kreuger	100.00	40.00	20.00
20a	Babe Ruth	2,400	960.00	480.00
20b	Wallie Schange (Wally Schang)	100.00	40.00	20.00

1920 W519 - Unnumbered

Cards in this 10-card set are identical in design and size (1-1/2" x 2-1/2") to the W519 Numbered set, except the player drawings are all set against a blue background and the cards are not numbered. With the lone exception of Eddie Ciotte, all of the subjects in the unnumbered set also appear in the numbered set.

		NM	EX	VG
	Complete Set (10):	3,600	1,450	725.00
	Common Player:	90.00	40.00	20.00
(1)	Eddie Cicotte	350.00	140.00	70.00
(2)	Eddie Collins	275.00	110.00	55.00
(3)	Gabby Cravath (Gavvy)	90.00	40.00	20.00
(4)	Frank Frisch	275.00	110.00	55.00
(5)	Kid Gleasen (Gleason)	90.00	40.00	20.00
(6)	Ernie Kreuger	90.00	40.00	20.00
(7)	Rube Marquard	275.00	110.00	55.00
(8)	Guy Morton	90.00	40.00	20.00
(9)	Joe Murphy	90.00	40.00	20.00
(10)	Babe Ruth	2,000	800.00	400.00

1920 W520

Another "strip card" set issued circa 1920, cards in this set measure 1-3/8" x 2-1/4" and are numbered in the lower-right corner. The first nine cards in the set display portrait poses, while the rest are full-length action poses. Some of the poses in this set are the same as those in the W516 issue with the pictures reversed. The player's last name appears in the border beneath the picture. The cards are blank-backed.

		NM	EX	VG
	Complete Set (20):	4,000	1,600	800.00
	Common Player:	50.00	20.00	10.00
1	Dave Bancroft	150.00	60.00	30.00
2	Christy Mathewson	400.00	160.00	80.00
3	Larry Doyle	50.00	20.00	10.00
4	Jess Barnes	50.00	20.00	10.00
5	Art Fletcher	50.00	20.00	10.00
6	Wilbur Cooper	50.00	20.00	10.00
7	Mike Gonzales (Gonzalez)	50.00	20.00	10.00
8	Zach Wheat	150.00	60.00	30.00
9	Tris Speaker	200.00	80.00	40.00
10	Benny Kauff	50.00	20.00	10.00
11	Zach Wheat	150.00	60.00	30.00
12	Phil Douglas	50.00	20.00	10.00
13	Babe Ruth	2,000	800.00	400.00
14	Stan Koveleski (Coveleski)	150.00	60.00	30.00
15	Goldie Rapp	50.00	20.00	10.00
16	Pol Perritt	50.00	20.00	10.00
17	Otto Miller	50.00	20.00	10.00
18	George Kelly	150.00	60.00	30.00
19	Mike Gonzales (Gonzalez)	50.00	20.00	10.00
20	Les Nunamaker	50.00	20.00	10.00

1921 W521

10 JOHNNY GRIFFITH

This issue is closely related to the W519 Numbered set. In fact, it uses the same color drawings as that set with the pictures reversed, resulting in a mirror-image of the W519 cards. The player poses and the numbering system are identical, as are the various background colors. The W521 cards are blank-backed and were sold in strips.

		NM	EX	VG
	Complete Set (20):	3,000	1,200	600.00
	Common Player:	50.00	20.00	10.00
1	Guy Morton	50.00	20.00	10.00
2	Rube Marquard	150.00	60.00	30.00
3	Gabby Cravath (Gavvy)	50.00	20.00	10.00
4	Ernie Krueger	50.00	20.00	10.00
5	Babe Ruth	1,500	600.00	300.00
6	George Sisler	150.00	60.00	30.00
7	Rube Benton	50.00	20.00	10.00
8	Jimmie Johnston	50.00	20.00	10.00
9	Wilbur Robinson (Wilbert)	150.00	60.00	30.00
10	Johnny Griffith	50.00	20.00	10.00
11	Frank Baker	150.00	60.00	30.00
12	Bob Veach	50.00	20.00	10.00
13	Jesse Barnes	50.00	20.00	10.00
14	Leon Cadore	50.00	20.00	10.00
15	Ray Schalk	150.00	60.00	30.00
16	Kid Gleason (Gleason)	50.00	20.00	10.00
17	Joe Murphy	50.00	20.00	10.00
18	Frank Frisch	150.00	60.00	30.00
19	Eddie Collins	150.00	60.00	30.00
20	Wallie (Wally) Schang	50.00	20.00	10.00

1920 W522

42 MIKE GONZALES

The 20 cards in this "strip card" set, issued circa 1920, are numbered from 31-50 and use the same players and drawings as the W520 set, issued about the same time. The cards measure 1-3/8" x 2-1/4" and are numbered in the lower left corner followed by the player's name. The cards have blank backs.

		NM	EX	VG
	Complete Set (20):	5,000	2,000	1,000
	Common Player:	75.00	30.00	15.00
31	Benny Kauf (Kauff)	75.00	30.00	15.00
32	Tris Speaker	300.00	120.00	60.00
33	Zach Wheat	225.00	90.00	45.00
34	Mike Gonzales (Gonzalez)	75.00	30.00	15.00
35	Wilbur Cooper	75.00	30.00	15.00
36	Art Fletcher	75.00	30.00	15.00
37	Jess Barnes	75.00	30.00	15.00
38	Larry Doyle	75.00	30.00	15.00
39	Christy Mathewson	900.00	360.00	180.00
40	Dave Bancroft	225.00	90.00	45.00
41	Les Nunamaker	75.00	30.00	15.00
42	Mike Gonzales (Gonzalez)	75.00	30.00	15.00
43	George Kelly	225.00	90.00	45.00
44	Otto Miller	75.00	30.00	15.00
45	Pol Perritt	75.00	30.00	15.00
46	Goldie Rapp	75.00	30.00	15.00
47	Stan Koveleski (Coveleski)	225.00	90.00	45.00
48	Babe Ruth	2,250	900.00	450.00
49	Phil Douglas	75.00	30.00	15.00
50	Zach Wheat	225.00	90.00	45.00

1921 W551

JESS BARNES
"GIANTS" N. L.

Another "strip set" issued circa 1920, these ten cards measure 1-3/8" x 2-1/4" and feature color drawings. The cards are unnumbered and blank-backed.

		NM	EX	VG
	Complete Set (10):	2,000	800.00	400.00
	Complete Set, Uncut Strip:	2,500	1,000	500.00
	Common Player:	50.00	20.00	10.00
(1)	Frank Baker	125.00	50.00	25.00
(2)	Dave Bancroft	125.00	50.00	25.00
(3)	Jess Barnes	50.00	20.00	10.00
(4)	Ty Cobb	400.00	160.00	80.00
(5)	Walter Johnson	175.00	70.00	35.00
(6)	Wally Pipp	50.00	20.00	10.00
(7)	Babe Ruth	1,100	450.00	225.00
(8)	George Sisler	125.00	50.00	25.00
(9)	Tris Speaker	150.00	60.00	30.00
(10)	Casey Stengel	125.00	50.00	25.00

1929 W553

One of the more obscure strip card sets, and one of the last of the genre, this issue also is one of the most attractive. Player photos - the same pictures used in the contemporary Kashin Publications (R316) boxed set and anonymous W554 strip cards - are printed in either black on white or as duotones (blue, green and magenta seen thus far), with an ornate frame. Cards measure 1-3/4" x 2-3/4". There is a facsimile autograph on front and the player's team and league are also spelled out. Backs are blank. This checklist is probably incomplete. Gaps have been left in the assigned numbering for future additions.

	NM	EX	VG
Common Player:	100.00	50.00	30.00

		NM	EX	VG
(1)	Lu Blue	100.00	50.00	30.00
(2)	Mickey Cochrane	200.00	100.00	60.00
(4)	Jimmie Foxx	300.00	150.00	90.00
(5)	Frank Frisch	200.00	100.00	60.00
(6)	Lou Gehrig	750.00	375.00	225.00
(7)	Goose Goslin	200.00	100.00	60.00
(8)	Burleigh Grimes	200.00	100.00	60.00
(9)	Lefty Grove	250.00	125.00	75.00
(11)	Rogers Hornsby	250.00	125.00	75.00
(13)	Rabbit Maranville	200.00	100.00	60.00
(14)	Bing Miller	100.00	50.00	30.00
(15)	Lefty O'Doul	150.00	75.00	45.00
(16)	Babe Ruth	1,200	600.00	360.00
(17)	Al Simmons	200.00	100.00	60.00
(18)	Pie Traynor	200.00	100.00	60.00

1930 W554

EDDIE ROMMEL—Pitcher—PHILADELPHIA ATHLETICS

This unidentified set of black-and-white cards features most of the era's stars in action poses. A facsimile autograph appears on the front of each of the blank-back 5" x 7" pictures. Cards can be found either with and/or without player name and, sometimes, team spelled out in all-capital letters in the bottom white border, with the position in upper- and lower-case between. The unnumbered pictures are checklisted here in alphabetical order. A version of the issue has been seen with advertising for "Big Prize" on the back, printed in red. Another known back stamp is a round black ad for "A. Bonemery / ICE CREAM / CONFECTIONERY."

		NM	EX	VG
	Complete Set (18):	3,500	1,400	700.00
	Common Player:	60.00	25.00	12.50
(1)	Gordon S. (Mickey) Cochrane	100.00	40.00	20.00
(2)	Lewis A. Fonseca	60.00	25.00	12.50
(3)	Jimmy Foxx	200.00	80.00	40.00
(4)	Lou Gehrig	950.00	380.00	190.00
(5)	Burleigh Grimes	100.00	40.00	20.00
(6)	Robert M. Grove	125.00	50.00	25.00
(7)	Waite Hoyt	100.00	40.00	20.00
(8)	Joe Judge	60.00	25.00	12.50
(9)	Charles (Chuck) Klein	100.00	40.00	20.00
(10)	Douglas McWeeny	60.00	25.00	12.50
(11)	Frank O'Doul	75.00	30.00	15.00
(12)	Melvin Ott	125.00	50.00	25.00
(13)	Herbert Pennock	100.00	40.00	20.00
(14)	Eddie Rommel	60.00	25.00	12.50
(15)	Babe Ruth	1,200	480.00	240.00
(16)	Al Simmons	100.00	40.00	20.00
(17)	Lloyd Waner	100.00	40.00	20.00
(18)	Hack Wilson	125.00	50.00	25.00

1909-1910 W555

COBB, DETROIT AMER.

Designated as W555 in the American Card Catalog, the nearly square cards measure only 1-1/8" x 1-3-16" and feature a sepia-colored player photo. Sixty-six different cards have been discovered to date, but others may exist. A recent discovery indicates these cards were produced by Jay S. Meyer confectioners of Philly. The sets appear to be related to a series of contemporary candy cards (E93, E94, E97, and E98) because, with only two exceptions, the players and poses are the same. Recent discoveries also indicate the cards were issued four per box of Base Ball Snap Shots candy.

		NM	EX	VG
	Complete Set (67):	25,000	10,000	5,000
	Common Player:	125.00	50.00	25.00
(1)	Red Ames	125.00	50.00	25.00
(2)	Jimmy Austin	125.00	50.00	25.00
(3)	Johnny Bates	125.00	50.00	25.00
(4)	Chief Bender	375.00	150.00	75.00
(5)	Bob Bescher	125.00	50.00	25.00
(6)	Joe Birmingham	125.00	50.00	25.00
(7)	Bill Bradley	125.00	50.00	25.00
(8)	Kitty Bransfield	125.00	50.00	25.00
(9)	Mordecai Brown	375.00	150.00	75.00

(10)	Bobby Byrne	125.00	50.00	25.00
(11)	Frank Chance	375.00	150.00	75.00
(12)	Hal Chase	375.00	150.00	75.00
(13)	Ed Cicotte	375.00	150.00	75.00
(14)	Fred Clarke	375.00	150.00	75.00
(15)	Ty Cobb	4,500	1,800	900.00
(16)	Eddie Collins (Dark uniform.)	375.00	150.00	75.00
(17)	Eddie Collins (Light uniform.)	375.00	150.00	75.00
(18)	Harry Coveleskie (Coveleski)	125.00	50.00	25.00
(19)	Sam Crawford	375.00	150.00	75.00
(20)	Harry Davis	125.00	50.00	25.00
(21)	Jim Delehanty (Delahanty)	125.00	50.00	25.00
(22)	Art Devlin	125.00	50.00	25.00
(23)	Josh Devore	125.00	50.00	25.00
(24)	Wild Bill Donovan	125.00	50.00	25.00
(25)	Red Dooin	125.00	50.00	25.00
(26)	Mickey Doolan	125.00	50.00	25.00
(27)	Bull Durham	125.00	50.00	25.00
(28)	Jimmy Dygert	125.00	50.00	25.00
(29)	Johnny Evers	375.00	150.00	75.00
(30)	Russ Ford	125.00	50.00	25.00
(31)	George Gibson	125.00	50.00	25.00
(32)	Clark Griffith	375.00	150.00	75.00
(33)	Topsy Hartsell (Hartsel)	125.00	50.00	25.00
(34)	Bill Heinchman (Hinchman)	125.00	50.00	25.00
(35)	Ira Hemphill	125.00	50.00	25.00
(36)	Hughie Jennings	375.00	150.00	75.00
(37)	Davy Jones	125.00	50.00	25.00
(38)	Addie Joss	500.00	200.00	100.00
(39)	Wee Willie Keeler	375.00	150.00	75.00
(40)	Red Kleinow	125.00	50.00	25.00
(41)	Nap Lajoie	375.00	150.00	75.00
(42)	Joe Lake	125.00	50.00	25.00
(43)	Tommy Leach	125.00	50.00	25.00
(44)	Harry Lord	125.00	50.00	25.00
(45)	Sherry Magee	125.00	50.00	25.00
(46)	Christy Mathewson	2,000	800.00	400.00
(47)	Amby McConnell	125.00	50.00	25.00
(48)	John McGraw	375.00	150.00	75.00
(49)	Chief Meyers	125.00	50.00	25.00
(50)	Earl Moore	125.00	50.00	25.00
(51)	Mike Mowery	125.00	50.00	25.00
(52)	George Mullin	125.00	50.00	25.00
(53)	Red Murray	125.00	50.00	25.00
(54)	Nichols	125.00	50.00	25.00
(55)	Jim Pastorious (Pastorius)	125.00	50.00	25.00
(56)	Deacon Phillippi (Phillippe)	125.00	50.00	25.00
(57)	Eddie Plank	375.00	150.00	75.00
(58)	Fred Snodgrass	125.00	50.00	25.00
(59)	Harry Steinfeldt	125.00	50.00	25.00
(60)	Joe Tinker	375.00	150.00	75.00
(61)	Hippo Vaughn	125.00	50.00	25.00
(62)	Honus Wagner	2,500	1,000	500.00
(63)	Rube Waddell	375.00	150.00	75.00
(64)	Hooks Wiltse	125.00	50.00	25.00
(65)	Cy Young (Standing, full name on front.)	1,500	600.00	300.00
(66)	Cy Young (Standing, last name on front.)	1,500	600.00	300.00
(67)	Cy Young (Portrait)	1,650	660.00	330.00

1927 W560

AL SIMMONS
Philadelphia Athletics

Although assigned a "W" number by the American Card Catalog, this is not a "strip card" issue in the same sense as most other "W" sets, although W560 cards are frequently found in uncut sheets of 16 cards. Cards measure a nominal 1-3/4" x 2-3/4" and are designed like a deck of playing cards, with the pictures on the various suits. The set includes aviators and other athletes in addition to baseball players. Cards can be found with designs printed in red or black, or less commonly with both and red and black on each card. Some players will also be found with different suit/value combinations.

		NM	EX	VG
Complete Set, Sheets (64):		3,250	1,625	975.00
Complete (Baseball) Set (49):		2,400	1,200	725.00
Common Player:		25.00	12.50	7.50
(1)	Vic Aldridge	25.00	12.50	7.50
(2)	Lester Bell	25.00	12.50	7.50
(3)	Larry Benton	25.00	12.50	7.50
(4)	Max Bishop	25.00	12.50	7.50
(5)	Del Bissonette	25.00	12.50	7.50
(6)	Jim Bottomley	45.00	22.50	13.50
(7)	Guy Bush	25.00	12.50	7.50
(8)	W. Clark	25.00	12.50	7.50
(9)	Andy Cohen	25.00	12.50	7.50
(10)	Mickey Cochrane	45.00	22.50	13.50
(11)	Hugh Critz	25.00	12.50	7.50
(12)	Kiki Cuyler	45.00	22.50	13.50
(13)	Taylor Douthit	25.00	12.50	7.50
(14)	Fred Fitzsimmons	25.00	12.50	7.50

(15)	Jim Foxx	110.00	55.00	35.00
(16)	Lou Gehrig	325.00	160.00	100.00
(17)	Goose Goslin	45.00	22.50	13.50
(18)	Sam Gray	25.00	12.50	7.50
(19)	Lefty Grove	60.00	30.00	18.00
(20)	Jesse Haines	45.00	22.50	13.50
(21)	Babe Herman	30.00	15.00	9.00
(22)	Roger Hornsby (Rogers)	60.00	30.00	18.00
(23)	Waite Hoyt	45.00	22.50	13.50
(24)	Henry Johnson	25.00	12.50	7.50
(25)	Walter Johnson	150.00	75.00	45.00
(26)	Willie Kamm	25.00	12.50	7.50
(27)	Remy Kremer	25.00	12.50	7.50
(28)	Fred Lindstrom	45.00	22.50	13.50
(29)	Fred Maguire	25.00	12.50	7.50
(30)	Fred Marberry	25.00	12.50	7.50
(31)	Johnny Mostil	25.00	12.50	7.50
(32)	Buddy Myer	25.00	12.50	7.50
(33)	Herb Pennock	45.00	22.50	13.50
(34)	George Pipgras	25.00	12.50	7.50
(35)	Flint Rhem	25.00	12.50	7.50
(36)	Babe Ruth	400.00	200.00	120.00
(37)	Luke Sewell	25.00	12.50	7.50
(38)	Willie Sherdel	25.00	12.50	7.50
(39)	Al Simmons	45.00	22.50	13.50
(40)	Thomas Thevenow	25.00	12.50	7.50
(41)	Fresco Thompson	25.00	12.50	7.50
(42)	George Uhle	25.00	12.50	7.50
(43)	Dazzy Vance	45.00	22.50	13.50
(44)	Rube Walberg	25.00	12.50	7.50
(45)	Lloyd Waner	45.00	22.50	13.50
(46)	Paul Waner	45.00	22.50	13.50
(47)	Fred "Cy" Williams	25.00	12.50	7.50
(48)	Jim Wilson	25.00	12.50	7.50
(49)	Glen Wright (Glenn)	25.00	12.50	7.50

1928 W565

LOU GEHRIG
N.Y. YANKEES

Similar in concept to W560, the 50 cards comprising this set were printed on two 7" x 10-1/2" sheets of cheap cardboard, one in black-and-white and one in red-and-white, each with navy blue backs. Most of the cards in the issue are of movie stars, with a few boxers, ballplayers and other notables included. While most of the cards depict the person in the center of a playing card format, it is interesting to note that a full deck of cards cannot be made up by cutting the sheets. Individual cards are 1-1/4" x 2-1/8". Only the baseball players are listed here.

		NM	EX	VG
Complete Set, Sheets (50):		450.00	225.00	135.00
Common Player:		75.00	37.50	22.50
(1)	Lou Gehrig	300.00	150.00	90.00
(2)	Harry Heilmann	75.00	37.50	22.50
(3)	Tony Lazzeri	75.00	37.50	22.50
(4)	Al Simmons	75.00	37.50	22.50

1947 W571

(See 1947 Bond Bread.)

1923 W572

Jack Quinn
BOSTON A.L.

These cards, designated as W572 by the American Card Catalog, measure 1-5/16" x 2-1/2" and are blank-backed. Fronts feature black-and-white or sepia player photos. The set is closely related to the popular E120 American Caramel set issued in 1922 and, with the exception of Ty Cobb, it uses the same photos. The cards were originally issued as strips of 10, with baseball players and boxers often mixed. They are found on either a white, slick stock or a dark, coarser cardboard. The player's name on the front of the cards appears in script. All cards have on front a copyright symbol and one of several alphabetical combinations indicating the source of the photo. The baseball players from the set are checklisted here in alphabetical order.

		NM	EX	VG
Complete (Baseball) Set (121):		12,500	6,250	3,750
Common Player:		50.00	25.00	15.00
(1)	Eddie Ainsmith	50.00	25.00	15.00
(2)	Vic Aldridge	50.00	25.00	15.00
(3)	Grover Alexander	250.00	125.00	75.00
(4)	Dave Bancroft	150.00	75.00	45.00
(5)	Walt Barbare	50.00	25.00	15.00
(6)	Jess Barnes	50.00	25.00	15.00
(7)	John Bassler	50.00	25.00	15.00
(8)	Lu Blue	50.00	25.00	15.00
(9)	Norman Boeckel	50.00	25.00	15.00
(10)	George Burns	50.00	25.00	15.00
(11)	Joe Bush	50.00	25.00	15.00
(12)	Leon Cadore	50.00	25.00	15.00
(13)	Virgil Cheevers (Cheeves)	50.00	25.00	15.00
(14)	Ty Cobb	1,350	675.00	400.00
(15)	Eddie Collins	150.00	75.00	45.00
(16)	John Collins	50.00	25.00	15.00
(17)	Wilbur Cooper	50.00	25.00	15.00
(18)	Stanley Coveleski	150.00	75.00	45.00
(19)	Walton Cruise	50.00	25.00	15.00
(20)	Dave Danforth	50.00	25.00	15.00
(21)	Jake Daubert	50.00	25.00	15.00
(22)	Hank DeBerry	50.00	25.00	15.00
(23)	Lou DeVormer	50.00	25.00	15.00
(24)	Bill Doak	50.00	25.00	15.00
(25)	Pete Donohue	50.00	25.00	15.00
(26)	Pat Duncan	50.00	25.00	15.00
(27)	Jimmy Dykes	50.00	25.00	15.00
(28)	Urban Faber	150.00	75.00	45.00
(29)	Bib Falk (Bibb)	50.00	25.00	15.00
(30)	Frank Frisch	150.00	75.00	45.00
(31)	C. Galloway	50.00	25.00	15.00
(32)	Ed Gharrity	50.00	25.00	15.00
(33)	Chas. Glazner	50.00	25.00	15.00
(34)	Hank Gowdy	50.00	25.00	15.00
(35)	Tom Griffith	50.00	25.00	15.00
(36)	Burleigh Grimes	150.00	75.00	45.00
(37)	Ray Grimes	50.00	25.00	15.00
(38)	Heinie Groh	50.00	25.00	15.00
(39)	Joe Harris	50.00	25.00	15.00
(40)	Stanley Harris	150.00	75.00	45.00
(41)	Joe Hauser	50.00	25.00	15.00
(42)	Harry Heilmann	150.00	75.00	45.00
(43)	Walter Henline	50.00	25.00	15.00
(44)	Chas. Hollocher	50.00	25.00	15.00
(45)	Harry Hooper	150.00	75.00	45.00
(46)	Rogers Hornsby	150.00	75.00	45.00
(47)	Waite Hoyt	150.00	75.00	45.00
(48)	Wilbur Hubbell	50.00	25.00	15.00
(49)	Wm. Jacobson	50.00	25.00	15.00
(50)	Chas. Jamieson	50.00	25.00	15.00
(51)	S. Johnson	50.00	25.00	15.00
(52)	Walter Johnson	500.00	250.00	150.00
(53)	Jimmy Johnston	50.00	25.00	15.00
(54)	Joe Judge	50.00	25.00	15.00
(55)	Geo. Kelly	150.00	75.00	45.00
(56)	Lee King	50.00	25.00	15.00
(57)	Larry Kopff (Kopf)	50.00	25.00	15.00
(58)	Geo. Leverette	50.00	25.00	15.00
(59)	Al Mamaux	50.00	25.00	15.00
(60)	"Rabbit" Maranville	150.00	75.00	45.00
(61)	"Rube" Marquard	150.00	75.00	45.00
(62)	Martin McManus	50.00	25.00	15.00
(63)	Lee Meadows	50.00	25.00	15.00
(64)	Mike Menosky	50.00	25.00	15.00
(65)	Bob Meusel	50.00	25.00	15.00
(66)	Emil Meusel	50.00	25.00	15.00
(67)	Geo. Mogridge	50.00	25.00	15.00
(68)	John Morrison	50.00	25.00	15.00
(69)	Johnny Mostil	50.00	25.00	15.00
(70)	Roliene Naylor	50.00	25.00	15.00
(71)	Art Nehf	50.00	25.00	15.00
(72)	Joe Oeschger	50.00	25.00	15.00
(73)	Bob O'Farrell	50.00	25.00	15.00
(74)	Steve O'Neill	50.00	25.00	15.00
(75)	Frank Parkinson	50.00	25.00	15.00
(76)	Ralph Perkins	50.00	25.00	15.00
(77)	H. Pillette	50.00	25.00	15.00
(78)	Ralph Pinelli	50.00	25.00	15.00
(79)	Wallie Pipp (Wally)	60.00	30.00	18.00
(80)	Ray Powell	50.00	25.00	15.00
(81)	Jack Quinn	50.00	25.00	15.00
(82)	Goldie Rapp	50.00	25.00	15.00
(83)	Walter Reuther (Ruether)	50.00	25.00	15.00
(84)	Sam Rice	150.00	75.00	45.00
(85)	Emory Rigney	50.00	25.00	15.00
(86)	Eppa Rixey	150.00	75.00	45.00
(87)	Ed Rommel	50.00	25.00	15.00
(88)	Eddie Roush	150.00	75.00	45.00
(89)	Babe Ruth	3,500	1,750	1,000
(90)	Ray Schalk	150.00	75.00	45.00
(91)	Wallie Schang (Wally)	50.00	25.00	15.00
(92)	Walter Schmidt	50.00	25.00	15.00
(93)	Joe Schultz	50.00	25.00	15.00
(94)	Hank Severeid	50.00	25.00	15.00
(95)	Joe Sewell	150.00	75.00	45.00
(96)	Bob Shawkey	50.00	25.00	15.00
(97)	Earl Sheely	50.00	25.00	15.00
(98)	Will Sherdel	50.00	25.00	15.00
(99)	Urban Shocker	50.00	25.00	15.00

#	Player	NM	EX	VG
(100)	George Sisler	150.00	75.00	45.00
(101)	Earl Smith	50.00	25.00	15.00
(102)	Elmer Smith	50.00	25.00	15.00
(103)	Jack Smith	50.00	25.00	15.00
(104)	Bill Southworth	50.00	25.00	15.00
(105)	Tris Speaker	150.00	75.00	45.00
(106)	Arnold Statz	50.00	25.00	15.00
(107)	Milton Stock	50.00	25.00	15.00
(108)	Jim Tierney	50.00	25.00	15.00
(109)	Harold Traynor	150.00	75.00	45.00
(110)	Geo. Uhle	50.00	25.00	15.00
(111)	Bob Veach	50.00	25.00	15.00
(112)	Clarence Walker	50.00	25.00	15.00
(113)	Curtis Walker	50.00	25.00	15.00
(114)	Bill Wambsganss	50.00	25.00	15.00
(115)	Aaron Ward	50.00	25.00	15.00
(116)	Zach Wheat	150.00	75.00	45.00
(117)	Fred Williams	50.00	25.00	15.00
(118)	Ken Williams	50.00	25.00	15.00
(119)	Ivy Wingo	50.00	25.00	15.00
(120)	Joe Wood	75.00	37.50	22.50
(121)	J.T. Zachary	50.00	25.00	15.00

1922 W573

DAVE (BEAUTY) BANCROFT
SHORT STOP, NEW YORK NATIONALS

These cards, identified as W573 in the American Card Catalog, are blank-backed, black-and-white versions of the popular E120 American Caramel set. These "strip cards," were sold in strips of 10 for a penny. The cards measure about 2-1/16" x 3-3/8", but allowances in width must be made because the cards were hand-cut from a horizontal strip. Some cards have been found with the advertising of various firms on back.

#	Player	NM	EX	VG
	Complete Set (240):	22,500	11,250	6,750
	Common Player:	75.00	37.50	22.50
(1)	Charles (Babe) Adams	75.00	37.50	22.50
(2)	Eddie Ainsmith	75.00	37.50	22.50
(3)	Vic Aldridge	75.00	37.50	22.50
(4)	Grover C. Alexander	300.00	150.00	90.00
(5)	Jim Bagby	75.00	37.50	22.50
(6)	Frank (Home Run) Baker	200.00	100.00	60.00
(7)	Dave (Beauty) Bancroft	200.00	100.00	60.00
(8)	Walt Barbare	75.00	37.50	22.50
(9)	Turner Barber	75.00	37.50	22.50
(10)	Jess Barnes	75.00	37.50	22.50
(11)	Clyde Barnhart	75.00	37.50	22.50
(12)	John Bassler	75.00	37.50	22.50
(13)	Will Bayne	75.00	37.50	22.50
(14)	Walter (Huck) Betts	75.00	37.50	22.50
(15)	Carson Bigbee	75.00	37.50	22.50
(16)	Lu Blue	75.00	37.50	22.50
(17)	Norman Boeckel	75.00	37.50	22.50
(18)	Sammy Bohne	75.00	37.50	22.50
(19)	George Burns	75.00	37.50	22.50
(20)	George Burns	75.00	37.50	22.50
(21)	"Bullet Joe" Bush	75.00	37.50	22.50
(22)	Leon Cadore	75.00	37.50	22.50
(23)	Marty Callaghan	75.00	37.50	22.50
(24)	Frank Calloway (Callaway)	75.00	37.50	22.50
(25)	Max Carey	200.00	100.00	60.00
(26)	Jimmy Caveney	75.00	37.50	22.50
(27)	Virgil Cheeves	75.00	37.50	22.50
(28)	Vern Clemons	75.00	37.50	22.50
(29)	Ty Cob (Cobb)	1,350	675.00	400.00
(30)	Bert Cole	75.00	37.50	22.50
(31)	Eddie Collins	200.00	100.00	60.00
(32)	John (Shano) Collins	75.00	37.50	22.50
(33)	T.P. (Pat) Collins	75.00	37.50	22.50
(34)	Wilbur Cooper	75.00	37.50	22.50
(35)	Harry Courtney	75.00	37.50	22.50
(36)	Stanley Coveleskie (Coveleski)	200.00	100.00	60.00
(37)	Elmer Cox	75.00	37.50	22.50
(38)	Sam Crane	75.00	37.50	22.50
(39)	Walton Cruise	75.00	37.50	22.50
(40)	Bill Cunningham	75.00	37.50	22.50
(41)	George Cutshaw	75.00	37.50	22.50
(42)	Dave Danforth	75.00	37.50	22.50
(43)	Jake Daubert	75.00	37.50	22.50
(44)	George Dauss	75.00	37.50	22.50
(45)	Frank (Dixie) Davis	75.00	37.50	22.50
(46)	Hank DeBerry	75.00	37.50	22.50
(47)	Albert Devormer (Lou DeVormer)	75.00	37.50	22.50
(48)	Bill Doak	75.00	37.50	22.50
(49)	Pete Donohue	75.00	37.50	22.50
(50)	"Shufflin" Phil Douglas	75.00	37.50	22.50
(51)	Joe Dugan	75.00	37.50	22.50
(52)	Louis (Pat) Duncan	75.00	37.50	22.50
(53)	Jimmy Dykes	75.00	37.50	22.50
(54)	Howard Ehmke	75.00	37.50	22.50
(55)	Frank Ellerbe	75.00	37.50	22.50
(56)	Urban (Red) Faber	200.00	100.00	60.00
(57)	Bib Falk (Bibb)	75.00	37.50	22.50
(58)	Dana Fillingim	75.00	37.50	22.50
(59)	Max Flack	75.00	37.50	22.50
(60)	Ira Flagstead	75.00	37.50	22.50
(61)	Art Fletcher	75.00	37.50	22.50
(62)	Horace Ford	75.00	37.50	22.50
(63)	Jack Fournier	75.00	37.50	22.50
(64)	Frank Frisch	200.00	100.00	60.00
(65)	Ollie Fuhrman	75.00	37.50	22.50
(66)	Clarence Galloway	75.00	37.50	22.50
(67)	Larry Gardner	75.00	37.50	22.50
(68)	Walter Gerber	75.00	37.50	22.50
(69)	Ed Gharrity	75.00	37.50	22.50
(70)	John Gillespie	75.00	37.50	22.50
(71)	Chas. (Whitey) Glazner	75.00	37.50	22.50
(72)	Johnny Gooch	75.00	37.50	22.50
(73)	Leon Goslin	200.00	100.00	60.00
(74)	Hank Gowdy	75.00	37.50	22.50
(75)	John Graney	75.00	37.50	22.50
(76)	Tom Griffith	75.00	37.50	22.50
(77)	Burleigh Grimes	200.00	100.00	60.00
(78)	Oscar Ray Grimes	75.00	37.50	22.50
(79)	Charlie Grimm	75.00	37.50	22.50
(80)	Heinie Groh	75.00	37.50	22.50
(81)	Jesse Haines	200.00	100.00	60.00
(82)	Earl Hamilton	75.00	37.50	22.50
(83)	Gene (Bubbles) Hargrave	75.00	37.50	22.50
(84)	Bryan Harris (Harriss)	75.00	37.50	22.50
(85)	Joe Harris	75.00	37.50	22.50
(86)	Stanley Harris	200.00	100.00	60.00
(87)	Chas. (Dowdy) Hartnett	200.00	100.00	60.00
(88)	Bob Hasty	75.00	37.50	22.50
(89)	Joe Hauser	100.00	50.00	30.00
(90)	Clif Heathcote	75.00	37.50	22.50
(91)	Harry Heilmann	200.00	100.00	60.00
(92)	Walter (Butch) Henline	75.00	37.50	22.50
(93)	Clarence (Shovel) Hodge	75.00	37.50	22.50
(94)	Walter Holke	75.00	37.50	22.50
(95)	Charles Hollocher	75.00	37.50	22.50
(96)	Harry Hooper	200.00	100.00	60.00
(97)	Rogers Hornsby	250.00	125.00	75.00
(98)	Waite Hoyt	200.00	100.00	60.00
(99)	Wilbur Hubbell (Wilbert)	75.00	37.50	22.50
(100)	Bernard (Bud) Hungling	75.00	37.50	22.50
(101)	Will Jacobson	75.00	37.50	22.50
(102)	Charlie Jamieson	75.00	37.50	22.50
(103)	Ernie Johnson	75.00	37.50	22.50
(104)	Sylvester Johnson	75.00	37.50	22.50
(105)	Walter Johnson	750.00	375.00	225.00
(106)	Jimmy Johnston	75.00	37.50	22.50
(107)	W.R. (Doc) Johnston	75.00	37.50	22.50
(108)	"Deacon" Sam Jones	75.00	37.50	22.50
(109)	Bob Jones	75.00	37.50	22.50
(110)	Percy Jones	75.00	37.50	22.50
(111)	Joe Judge	75.00	37.50	22.50
(112)	Ben Karr	75.00	37.50	22.50
(113)	Johnny Kelleher	75.00	37.50	22.50
(114)	George Kelly	200.00	100.00	60.00
(115)	Lee King	75.00	37.50	22.50
(116)	Wm (Larry) Kopff (Kopf)	75.00	37.50	22.50
(117)	Marty Krug	75.00	37.50	22.50
(118)	Johnny Lavan	75.00	37.50	22.50
(119)	Nemo Leibold	75.00	37.50	22.50
(120)	Roy Leslie	75.00	37.50	22.50
(121)	George Leverette (Leverett)	75.00	37.50	22.50
(122)	Adolfo Luque	75.00	37.00	22.00
(123)	Walter Mails	75.00	37.50	22.50
(124)	Al Mamaux	75.00	37.50	22.50
(125)	"Rabbit" Maranville	200.00	100.00	60.00
(126)	Cliff Markle	75.00	37.50	22.50
(127)	Richard (Rube) Marquard	200.00	100.00	60.00
(128)	Carl Mays	75.00	37.50	22.50
(129)	Hervey McClellan (Harvey)	75.00	37.50	22.50
(130)	Austin McHenry	75.00	37.50	22.50
(131)	"Stuffy" McInnis	75.00	37.50	22.50
(132)	Martin McManus	75.00	37.50	22.50
(133)	Mike McNally	75.00	37.50	22.50
(134)	Hugh McQuillan	75.00	37.50	22.50
(135)	Lee Meadows	75.00	37.50	22.50
(136)	Mike Menosky	75.00	37.50	22.50
(137)	Bob (Dutch) Meusel	75.00	37.50	22.50
(138)	Emil (Irish) Meusel	75.00	37.50	22.50
(139)	Clyde Milan	75.00	37.50	22.50
(140)	Edmund (Bing) Miller	75.00	37.50	22.50
(141)	Elmer Miller	75.00	37.50	22.50
(142)	Lawrence (Hack) Miller	75.00	37.50	22.50
(143)	Clarence Mitchell	75.00	37.50	22.50
(144)	George Mogridge	75.00	37.50	22.50
(145)	Roy Moore	75.00	37.50	22.50
(146)	John L. Mokan	75.00	37.50	22.50
(147)	John Morrison	75.00	37.50	22.50
(148)	Johnny Mostil	75.00	37.50	22.50
(149)	Elmer Myers	75.00	37.50	22.50
(150)	Hy Myers	75.00	37.50	22.50
(151)	Roliene Naylor (Roleine)	75.00	37.50	22.50
(152)	Earl "Greasy" Neale	75.00	37.50	22.50
(153)	Art Nehf	75.00	37.50	22.50
(154)	Les Nunamaker	75.00	37.50	22.50
(155)	Joe Oeschger	75.00	37.50	22.50
(156)	Bob O'Farrell	75.00	37.50	22.50
(157)	Ivan Olson	75.00	37.50	22.50
(158)	Steve O'Neil	75.00	37.50	22.50
(159)	Steve O'Neill	75.00	37.50	22.50
(160)	Frank Parkinson	75.00	37.50	22.50
(161)	Roger Peckinpaugh	75.00	37.50	22.50
(162)	Herb Pennock	200.00	100.00	60.00
(163)	Ralph (Cy) Perkins	75.00	37.50	22.50
(164)	Will Pertica	75.00	37.50	22.50
(165)	Jack Peters	75.00	37.50	22.50
(166)	Tom Phillips	75.00	37.50	22.50
(167)	Val Picinich	75.00	37.50	22.50
(168)	Herman Pillette	75.00	37.50	22.50
(169)	Ralph Pinelli	75.00	37.50	22.50
(170)	Wallie Pipp	75.00	37.50	22.50
(171)	Clark Pittenger (Clarke)	75.00	37.50	22.50
(172)	Raymond Powell	75.00	37.50	22.50
(173)	Derrill Pratt	75.00	37.50	22.50
(174)	Jack Quinn	75.00	37.50	22.50
(175)	Joe (Goldie) Rapp	75.00	37.50	22.50
(176)	John Rawlings	75.00	37.50	22.50
(177)	Walter (Dutch) Reuther (Ruether)	75.00	37.50	22.50
(178)	Sam Rice	200.00	100.00	60.00
(179)	Emory Rigney	75.00	37.50	22.50
(180)	Jimmy Ring	75.00	37.50	22.50
(181)	Eppa Rixey	200.00	100.00	60.00
(182)	Charles Robertson	75.00	37.50	22.50
(183)	Ed Rommel	75.00	37.50	22.50
(184)	Eddie Roush	200.00	100.00	60.00
(185)	Harold (Muddy) Ruel (Herold)	75.00	37.50	22.50
(186)	Babe Ruth	2,750	1,375	825.00
(187)	Ray Schalk	200.00	100.00	60.00
(188)	Wallie Schang	75.00	37.50	22.50
(189)	Ray Schmandt	75.00	37.50	22.50
(190)	Walter Schmidt	75.00	37.50	22.50
(191)	Joe Schultz	75.00	37.50	22.50
(192)	Everett Scott	75.00	37.50	22.50
(193)	Henry Severeid	75.00	37.50	22.50
(194)	Joe Sewell	200.00	100.00	60.00
(195)	Howard Shanks	75.00	37.50	22.50
(196)	Bob Shawkey	75.00	37.50	22.50
(197)	Earl Sheely	75.00	37.50	22.50
(198)	Will Sherdel	75.00	37.50	22.50
(199)	Ralph Shinners	75.00	37.50	22.50
(200)	Urban Shocker	75.00	37.50	22.50
(201)	Charles (Chick) Shorten	75.00	37.50	22.50
(202)	George Sisler	200.00	100.00	60.00
(203)	Earl Smith	75.00	37.50	22.50
(204)	Earl Smith	75.00	37.50	22.50
(205)	Elmer Smith	75.00	37.50	22.50
(206)	Jack Smith	75.00	37.50	22.50
(207)	Sherrod Smith	75.00	37.50	22.50
(208)	Colonel Snover	75.00	37.50	22.50
(209)	Frank Snyder	75.00	37.50	22.50
(210)	Al Sothoron	75.00	37.50	22.50
(211)	Bill Southworth	75.00	37.50	22.50
(212)	Tris Speaker	250.00	125.00	75.00
(213)	Arnold Statz	75.00	37.50	22.50
(214)	Milton Stock	75.00	37.50	22.50
(215)	Amos Strunk	75.00	37.50	22.50
(216)	Jim Tierney	75.00	37.50	22.50
(217)	John Tobin	75.00	37.50	22.50
(218)	Fred Toney	75.00	37.50	22.50
(219)	George Toporcer	75.00	37.50	22.50
(220)	Harold (Pie) Traynor	200.00	100.00	60.00
(221)	George Uhle	75.00	37.50	22.50
(222)	Elam Vangilder	75.00	37.50	22.50
(223)	Bob Veach	75.00	37.50	22.50
(224)	Clarence (Tillie) Walker	75.00	37.50	22.50
(225)	Curtis Walker	75.00	37.50	22.50
(226)	Al Walters	75.00	37.50	22.50
(227)	Bill Wambsganss	75.00	37.50	22.50
(228)	Aaron Ward	75.00	37.50	22.50
(229)	John Watson	75.00	37.50	22.50
(230)	Frank Welch	75.00	37.50	22.50
(231)	Zach Wheat	200.00	100.00	60.00
(232)	Fred (Cy) Williams	75.00	37.50	22.50
(233)	Kenneth Williams	75.00	37.50	22.50
(234)	Ivy Wingo	75.00	37.50	22.50
(235)	Joe Wood	75.00	37.50	22.50
(236)	Lawrence Woodall	75.00	37.50	22.50
(237)	Russell Wrightstone	75.00	37.50	22.50
(238)	Everett Yaryan	75.00	37.50	22.50
(239)	Ross Young (Youngs)	200.00	100.00	60.00
(240)	J.T. Zachary	75.00	37.50	22.50

1933 W574

WHITE SOX

Cards in this set measure an unusual 2-1/4" x 2-7/8". They are unnumbered and are listed here in alphabetical order. The black-and-white photos have a facsimile autograph and team name at bottom.

#	Player	NM	EX	VG
	Complete Set (29):	3,000	1,500	900.00
	Common Player:	60.00	30.00	18.00
(1)	Dale Alexander	60.00	30.00	18.00
(2)	Ivy Paul Andrews	60.00	30.00	18.00
(3)	Luke Appling	250.00	100.00	50.00
(4)	Earl Averill	250.00	100.00	50.00
(5)	George Blaeholder	60.00	30.00	18.00
(6)	Irving Burns	60.00	30.00	18.00
(7)	Pat Caraway	60.00	30.00	18.00
(8)	Chalmer Cissell	60.00	30.00	18.00
(9)	Harry Davis	60.00	30.00	18.00
(10)	Jimmy Dykes	60.00	30.00	18.00
(11)	George Earnshaw	60.00	30.00	18.00
(12)	Urban Faber	250.00	100.00	50.00
(13)	Lewis Fonseca	60.00	30.00	18.00
(14)	Jimmy Foxx	450.00	180.00	90.00

		NM	EX	VG
(15)	Victor Frasier	60.00	30.00	18.00
(16)	Robert Grove	350.00	140.00	70.00
(17)	Frank Grube	60.00	30.00	18.00
(18)	Irving Hadley	60.00	30.00	18.00
(19)	Willie Kamm	60.00	30.00	18.00
(20)	Bill Killefer	60.00	30.00	18.00
(21)	Ralph Kress	60.00	30.00	18.00
(22)	Fred Marberry	60.00	30.00	18.00
(23)	Roger Peckinpaugh	60.00	30.00	18.00
(24)	Frank Reiber	60.00	30.00	18.00
(25)	Carl Reynolds	60.00	30.00	18.00
(26)	Al Simmons	250.00	100.00	50.00
(27)	Joe Vosmik	60.00	30.00	18.00
(28)	Gerald Walker	60.00	30.00	18.00
(29)	Whitlow Wyatt	60.00	30.00	18.00

1921-1922 W575-1

The known variations indicate this set was issued over a period of time, likely encompassing more than one calendar year or baseball season. Designated as W575 in the American Card Catalog, these "strip cards" are essentially blank-backed versions of the contemporary American Caramel E121 set, though the checklists do not exactly correspond. Ideally cut cards in W575-1 measure 2" x 3-1/4" and are printed in black-and-white. It is almost impossible to distinguish W575-1 cards from the blank-backed Koester's Bread Yankees and Giants cards issued to commemorate the 1921 "Subway" World Series. This checklist may not be complete. Gaps have been left among the assigned numbers to accommodate future additions.

		NM	EX	VG
	Common Player:	40.00	20.00	12.00
(1)	Chas. "Babe" Adams	40.00	20.00	12.00
(2)	G.C. Alexander	350.00	175.00	100.00
(3)	Grover Alexander	350.00	175.00	100.00
(4)	Jim Bagby	40.00	20.00	12.00
(5)	J. Franklin Baker	175.00	85.00	50.00
(6)	Frank Baker	175.00	85.00	50.00
(7)	Dave Bancroft (Batting)	175.00	85.00	50.00
(8)	Dave Bancroft (Fielding)	175.00	85.00	50.00
(9)	Turner Barber	40.00	20.00	12.00
(10)	Jesse Barnes	40.00	20.00	12.00
(11)	Howard Berry	40.00	20.00	12.00
(12)	L. Bigbee (Should be C.)	40.00	20.00	12.00
(13)	Ping Bodie	40.00	20.00	12.00
(14)	"Ed" Brown	40.00	20.00	12.00
(15)	George Burns	40.00	20.00	12.00
(16)	Geo. J. Burns	40.00	20.00	12.00
(17)	"Bullet Joe" Bush	40.00	20.00	12.00
(18)	Owen Bush	40.00	20.00	12.00
(19)	Max Carey (Batting)	175.00	85.00	50.00
(20)	Max Carey (Hands on hips.)	175.00	85.00	50.00
(21)	Ty Cobb	2,000	1,000	600.00
(22)	Eddie Collins	175.00	85.00	50.00
(23)	"Rip" Collins	40.00	20.00	12.00
(24)	Stanley Coveleskie (Coveleski)	175.00	85.00	50.00
(25)	Bill Cunningham	40.00	20.00	12.00
(26a)	Jake Daubert (1B.)	40.00	20.00	12.00
(26b)	Jake Daubert (1st B.)	40.00	20.00	12.00
(28)	George Dauss	40.00	20.00	12.00
(29)	Dixie Davis	40.00	20.00	12.00
(30)	Charles Deal (Dark uniform.)	40.00	20.00	12.00
(31)	Charles Deal (Light uniform.)	40.00	20.00	12.00
(32)	Lou DeVormer (Photo actually Emil "Irish" Meusel.)	40.00	20.00	12.00
(33)	William Doak	40.00	20.00	12.00
(34)	Bill Donovan (Pitching)	40.00	20.00	12.00
(35)	Bill Donovan (Portrait)	40.00	20.00	12.00
(36)	Phil Douglas	40.00	20.00	12.00
(37a)	Johnny Evers (Mgr.)	175.00	85.00	50.00
(37b)	Johnny Evers (Manager)	175.00	85.00	50.00
(39)	Urban Faber (Dark uniform.)	175.00	85.00	50.00
(40)	Urban Faber (White uniform.)	175.00	85.00	50.00
(42)	Bib Falk (Bibb)	40.00	20.00	12.00
(43)	Alex Ferguson	40.00	20.00	12.00
(44)	Wm. Fewster	40.00	20.00	12.00
(45)	Ira Flagstead	40.00	20.00	12.00
(46)	Art Fletcher	40.00	20.00	12.00
(47)	Eddie Foster	40.00	20.00	12.00
(48)	Frank Frisch	175.00	85.00	50.00
(49)	W.L. Gardner	40.00	20.00	12.00
(50)	Alexander Gaston	40.00	20.00	12.00
(51)	E.P. Gharrity	40.00	20.00	12.00
(52)	Chas. "Whitey" Glazner	40.00	20.00	12.00
(53)	"Kid" Gleason	40.00	20.00	12.00
(54)	"Mike" Gonzalez	40.00	20.00	12.00
(55)	Hank Gowdy	40.00	20.00	12.00
(56a)	John Graney (Util. o.f.)	40.00	20.00	12.00
(56b)	John Graney (O.F.)	40.00	20.00	12.00
(57)	Tom Griffith	40.00	20.00	12.00
(58)	Chas. Grimm	40.00	20.00	12.00
(59a)	Heinie Groh (Cincinnati)	40.00	20.00	12.00
(59b)	Heinie Groh (New York)	40.00	20.00	12.00
(62)	Jess Haines	175.00	85.00	50.00
(63)	Harry Harper	40.00	20.00	12.00
(64)	"Chicken" Hawks	40.00	20.00	12.00
(65)	Harry Heilman (Heilmann) (Holding bat.)	175.00	85.00	50.00
(66)	Harry Heilman (Heilmann) (Running)	175.00	85.00	50.00
(67)	John Henry	40.00	20.00	12.00
(68)	Clarence Hodge	40.00	20.00	12.00
(69)	Fred Hoffman	40.00	20.00	12.00
(70a)	Walter Holke (1st B., portrait)	40.00	20.00	12.00
(70b)	Walter Holke (1B, portrait)	40.00	20.00	12.00
(71)	Walter Holke (Throwing)	40.00	20.00	12.00
(72a)	Charles Hollacher (Name incorrect.)	40.00	20.00	12.00
(72b)	Charles Hollocher (Name correct.)	40.00	20.00	12.00
(73)	Harry Hooper	175.00	85.00	50.00
(74a)	Rogers Hornsby (2nd B.)	250.00	125.00	75.00

		NM	EX	VG
(74b)	Rogers Hornsby (O.F.)	250.00	125.00	75.00
(75)	Waite Hoyt	175.00	85.00	50.00
(76)	Miller Huggins	175.00	85.00	50.00
(78)	Wm. C. Jacobson	40.00	20.00	12.00
(79)	Hugh Jennings	175.00	85.00	50.00
(80)	Walter Johnson (Arms at chest.)	500.00	250.00	150.00
(81)	Walter Johnson (Throwing)	500.00	250.00	150.00
(82)	James Johnston	40.00	20.00	12.00
(84)	Joe Judge (Batting)	40.00	20.00	12.00
(85)	Joe Judge (Fielding)	40.00	20.00	12.00
(86a)	George Kelly (1st B.)	175.00	85.00	50.00
(86b)	George Kelly (1B.)	175.00	85.00	50.00
(88)	Dick Kerr	40.00	20.00	12.00
(89)	P.J. Kilduff	40.00	20.00	12.00
(90a)	Bill Killefer	40.00	20.00	12.00
(90b)	Bill Killifer (Killefer)	40.00	20.00	12.00
(92)	John Lavan	40.00	20.00	12.00
(93)	"Nemo" Leibold	40.00	20.00	12.00
(94)	Duffy Lewis	40.00	20.00	12.00
(95)	Walter Mails	40.00	20.00	12.00
(96)	Al. Mamaux	40.00	20.00	12.00
(97)	"Rabbit" Maranville	175.00	85.00	50.00
(98)	Elwood Martin	40.00	20.00	12.00
(99a)	Carl Mays (Name correct.)	40.00	20.00	12.00
(99b)	Carl May (Mays)	40.00	20.00	12.00
(100)	John McGraw (Mgr.)	175.00	85.00	50.00
(101)	John McGraw (Manager)	175.00	85.00	50.00
(102)	Jack McInnis	40.00	20.00	12.00
(103a)	M.J. McNally (3B.)	40.00	20.00	12.00
(103b)	M.J. McNally (3rd B.)	40.00	20.00	12.00
(104)	Lee Meadows	40.00	20.00	12.00
(105)	Emil Meusel	40.00	20.00	12.00
(106)	R. Meusel	40.00	20.00	12.00
(107)	Clyde Milan	40.00	20.00	12.00
(108)	Elmer Miller	40.00	20.00	12.00
(109)	Otto Miller	40.00	20.00	12.00
(110)	John Mitchell (S.S.)	40.00	20.00	12.00
(111)	John Mitchell (3rd B.)	40.00	20.00	12.00
(112)	Guy Morton	40.00	20.00	12.00
(113)	Johnny Mostil	40.00	20.00	12.00
(114)	Eddie Mulligan	40.00	20.00	12.00
(115)	Eddie Murphy	40.00	20.00	12.00
(116a)	"Hy" Myers (C.F./O.F.)	40.00	20.00	12.00
(116b)	Hy Myers (O.F.)	40.00	20.00	12.00
(117a)	A.E. Neale	75.00	37.50	22.50
(117b)	Earl Neale	75.00	37.00	22.00
(119)	Arthur Nehf	40.00	20.00	12.00
(120)	Joe Oeschger	40.00	20.00	12.00
(122)	Chas. O'Leary	40.00	20.00	12.00
(123)	Steve O'Neill	40.00	20.00	12.00
(124a)	Roger Peckinbaugh (Name incorrect.)	40.00	20.00	12.00
(124b)	Roger Peckinpaugh (Name correct.)	40.00	20.00	12.00
(125a)	Jeff Pfeffer (Brooklyn)	40.00	20.00	12.00
(125b)	Jeff Pfeffer (St. Louis)	40.00	20.00	12.00
(127)	William Piercy	40.00	20.00	12.00
(128)	Walter Pipp	40.00	20.00	12.00
(129)	D.B. Pratt	40.00	20.00	12.00
(130)	Jack Quinn	40.00	20.00	12.00
(131a)	John Rawlings (2nd B.)	40.00	20.00	12.00
(131b)	John Rawlings (2B.)	40.00	20.00	12.00
(133a)	E.S. Rice (Name incorrect.)	175.00	85.00	50.00
(133b)	E.C. Rice (Name correct.)	175.00	85.00	50.00
(134a)	Eppa Rixey	175.00	85.00	50.00
(134b)	Eppa Rixey, Jr.	175.00	85.00	50.00
(136)	Wilbert Robinson	175.00	85.00	50.00
(137)	Tom Rogers	40.00	20.00	12.00
(139)	Ed Rounnel (Rommel)	40.00	20.00	12.00
(140)	Robert Roth	40.00	20.00	12.00
(142a)	Ed Roush (O.F.)	175.00	85.00	50.00
(142b)	Ed Roush (C.F.)	175.00	85.00	50.00
(144)	"Muddy" Ruel	40.00	20.00	12.00
(145)	Walter Ruether	40.00	20.00	12.00
(146a)	"Babe" Ruth (R.F.)	3,500	1,750	1,000
(146b)	Babe Ruth (L.F.)	3,500	1,750	1,000
(147)	"Babe" Ruth (W/man, bird.)	3,500	1,750	1,000
(148a)	Bill Ryan	40.00	20.00	12.00
(148b)	"Bill" Ryan	40.00	20.00	12.00
(149a)	"Slim" Sallee (Ball in hand.)	40.00	20.00	12.00
(149b)	"Slim" Sallee (No ball in hand.)	40.00	20.00	12.00
(151)	Ray Schalk (Bunting)	175.00	85.00	50.00
(152)	Ray Schalk (Catching)	175.00	85.00	50.00
(153a)	Walter Schang	40.00	20.00	12.00
(153b)	Wally Schang	40.00	20.00	12.00
(154a)	Fred Schupp (Name incorrect.)	40.00	20.00	12.00
(154b)	Ferd Schupp (Name correct.)	40.00	20.00	12.00
(155a)	Everett Scott (Boston)	40.00	20.00	12.00
(155b)	Everett Scott (New York)	40.00	20.00	12.00
(157)	Hank Severeid	40.00	20.00	12.00
(159)	Robert Shawkey	40.00	20.00	12.00
(160a)	"Pat" Shea	40.00	20.00	12.00
(160b)	Pat Shea	40.00	20.00	12.00
(161)	Earl Sheely	40.00	20.00	12.00
(163)	Urban Shocker	40.00	20.00	12.00
(165)	George Sisler (Batting)	175.00	85.00	50.00
(166)	George Sisler (Throwing)	175.00	85.00	50.00
(168)	Earl Smith	40.00	20.00	12.00
(169)	Elmer Smith	40.00	20.00	12.00
(170)	J. Carlisle Smith	40.00	20.00	12.00
(171)	Frank Snyder	40.00	20.00	12.00
(172)	Bill Southworth	40.00	20.00	12.00
(173a)	Tris Speaker (Large projection.)	250.00	125.00	75.00
(173b)	Tris Speaker (Small projection.)	250.00	125.00	75.00
(175a)	Charles Stengel (Batting)	175.00	85.00	50.00
(175b)	Charles Stengel (Portrait)	175.00	85.00	50.00
(177)	Milton Stock	40.00	20.00	12.00
(178a)	Amos Strunk (C.F.)	40.00	20.00	12.00
(178b)	Amos Strunk (O.F.)	40.00	20.00	12.00
(180a)	Zeb Terry (Dark uniform, 2nd B.)	40.00	20.00	12.00
(180b)	Zeb Terry (Dark uniform, 2B.)	40.00	20.00	12.00
(181)	Zeb Terry (White uniform.)	40.00	20.00	12.00
(182)	Chester Thomas	40.00	20.00	12.00

		NM	EX	VG
(183)	Fred Toney (Both feet on ground.)	40.00	20.00	12.00
(184)	Fred Toney (One foot in air.)	40.00	20.00	12.00
(185)	George Toporcer	40.00	20.00	12.00
(186)	George Tyler	40.00	20.00	12.00
(187)	Jim Vaughn (Plain uniform.)	40.00	20.00	12.00
(188)	Jim Vaughn (Striped uniform.)	40.00	20.00	12.00
(189)	Bob Veach (Arm raised.)	40.00	20.00	12.00
(190)	Bob Veach (Arms folded.)	40.00	20.00	12.00
(191a)	Oscar Vitt (3rd B.)	40.00	20.00	12.00
(191b)	Oscar Vitt (3B.)	40.00	20.00	12.00
(192)	Curtis Walker	40.00	20.00	12.00
(193)	W. Wambsganss	40.00	20.00	12.00
(194)	Carl Weilman	40.00	20.00	12.00
(195)	Zach Wheat	175.00	85.00	50.00
(196)	George Whitted	40.00	20.00	12.00
(197)	Fred Williams	40.00	20.00	12.00
(198)	Ivy B. Wingo	40.00	20.00	12.00
(199)	Lawton Witt	40.00	20.00	12.00
(200)	Joe Wood	100.00	50.00	30.00
(202)	Pep Young	40.00	20.00	12.00
(203)	Ross Young (Youngs)	175.00	85.00	50.00

1922 W575-2

The blank-back, black-and-white cards in this set measure a nominal 2-1/8" x 3-3/8". Because of the design of the cards the set is sometimes called the "autograph on shoulder" series. Some cards have the player's position and team added to the name inscription. The cards were produced by Kromo Gravure Photo Co., Detroit, Mich.

		NM	EX	VG
	Complete Set (40):	10,000	5,000	3,000
	Common Player:	75.00	37.50	22.50
(1)	Dave Bancroft	200.00	100.00	60.00
(2)	Johnnie Bassler	75.00	37.50	22.50
(3)	Joe Bush	75.00	37.50	22.50
(4)	Ty Cobb	2,000	1,000	600.00
(5)	Eddie Collins	200.00	100.00	60.00
(6)	Stan Coveleskie (Coveleski)	200.00	100.00	60.00
(7)	Jake Daubert	75.00	37.50	22.50
(8)	Joe Dugan	75.00	37.50	22.50
(9)	Red Faber	200.00	100.00	60.00
(10)	Frank Frisch	200.00	100.00	60.00
(11)	Walter H. Gerber	75.00	37.50	22.50
(12)	Harry Heilmann	200.00	100.00	60.00
(13)	Harry Hooper	200.00	100.00	60.00
(14)	Rogers Hornsby	300.00	150.00	90.00
(15)	Waite Hoyt	200.00	100.00	60.00
(16)	Joe Judge	75.00	37.50	22.50
(17)	Geo. Kelly	200.00	100.00	60.00
(18)	Rabbit Maranville	200.00	100.00	60.00
(19)	Rube Marquard	200.00	100.00	60.00
(20)	Guy Morton	75.00	37.50	22.50
(21)	Art Nehf	75.00	37.50	22.50
(22)	Derrill B. Pratt	75.00	37.50	22.50
(23)	Jimmy Ring	75.00	37.50	22.50
(24)	Eppa Rixey	200.00	100.00	60.00
(25)	Gene Robertson	75.00	37.50	22.50
(26)	Ed Rommel (Rommel)	75.00	37.50	22.50
(27)	Babe Ruth	3,500	1,750	1,050
(28)	Wally Schang	75.00	37.50	22.50
(29)	Everett Scott	75.00	37.50	22.50
(30)	Henry Severeid	75.00	37.50	22.50
(31)	Joe Sewell	200.00	100.00	60.00
(32)	Geo. Sisler	200.00	100.00	60.00
(33)	Tris Speaker	300.00	150.00	90.00
(34)	(Riggs) Stephenson	75.00	37.50	22.50
(35)	Zeb Terry	75.00	37.50	22.50
(36)	Bobbie Veach	75.00	37.50	22.50
(37)	Clarence Walker	75.00	37.50	22.50
(38)	Johnnie Walker	75.00	37.50	22.50
(39)	Zach Wheat	200.00	100.00	60.00
(40)	Kenneth Williams	75.00	37.50	22.50

1925-31 W590

Originally unlisted in the American Card Catalog, this strip-card set was given the number W590 in later editions. It is part of a larger set cataloged as W580 which includes movie stars, boxers and other athletes. These cards measure approximately 1-3/8" x 2-1/2". Fronts have black-and-white player photos with a white border. In the bottom border is the player name, position, city and league or team nickname. Some cards can be found with a "Former" designation before the position. Several variations are known in team designations, indicating the set was probably reissued at least once between 1927-31. Backs are blank. Only the baseball players are listed here, in alphabetical order.

		NM	EX	VG
Common Player:		75.00	37.00	22.00
(1a)	Grover C. Alexander (Chicago N.L.)	300.00	150.00	90.00
(1b)	Grover C. Alexander (House of David)	600.00	300.00	180.00
(2a)	Dave Bancroft (Boston N.L.)	150.00	75.00	45.00
(2b)	Dave Bancroft (New York N.L.)	150.00	75.00	45.00
(3a)	Jess Barnes ("Pitcher" Boston N.L.)	75.00	37.50	22.50
(3b)	Jess Barnes ("Former Pitcher" Boston N.L.)	75.00	37.50	22.50
(4)	Ray Blades (St. Louis Cardinals)	75.00	37.50	22.50
(5)	Pictbred Bluege (Ossie)(Third Baseman)	75.00	37.50	22.50
(6a)	George Burns (New York N.L.)	75.00	37.50	22.50
(6b)	George Burns (Philadelphia N.L.)	75.00	37.50	22.50
(7a)	George Burns (Cleveland A.L. - 1st Baseman)	75.00	37.50	22.50
(7b)	George Burns (Cleveland A.L. - Former 1st Baseman)	75.00	37.50	22.50
(8)	Max Carey (Pittsburg N.L.)	150.00	75.00	45.00
(9a)	Caveney (Jimmy)(Short Stop)	75.00	37.50	22.50
(9b)	Caveney (Jimmy) (Former Short Stop)	75.00	37.50	22.50
(10)	"Ty" Cobb	1,300	650.00	390.00
(11a)	Eddie Collins (Chicago White Sox)	175.00	85.00	50.00
(11b)	Eddie Collins (Philadelphia A.L.)	175.00	85.00	50.00
(12)	George Dauss (Former Pitcher - Detroit)	75.00	37.50	22.50
(13)	"Red" Faber	150.00	75.00	45.00
(14a)	Frankie Frisch (New York N.L.)	175.00	85.00	50.00
(14b)	Frank Frisch (St. Louis N.L.)	175.00	85.00	50.00
(15)	Lou Gehrig (1st Baseman)	1,125	560.00	335.00
(17a)	Hank Gowdy (Catcher)	75.00	37.50	22.50
(17b)	Hank Gowdy (Former Catcher)	75.00	37.50	22.50
(18)	Sam Gray	75.00	37.50	22.50
(19)	Charley Grimm (Chicago N.L.)	75.00	37.50	22.50
(20)	"Buckey" Harris (Manager, Washington A.L.)	150.00	75.00	45.00
(21a)	Rogers Hornsby (St. Louis N.L.)	200.00	100.00	60.00
(21b)	Rogers Hornsby (Boston N.L.)	200.00	100.00	60.00
(22)	Travis Jackson (Short Stop, New York N.L.)	150.00	75.00	45.00
(23)	Walter Johnson (Pitcher)	600.00	300.00	180.00
(24a)	George Kelly (New York N.L.)	150.00	75.00	45.00
(24b)	George Kelly (Chicago N.L.)	150.00	75.00	45.00
(25)	Fred Lindstrom	150.00	75.00	45.00
(26a)	Rabbit Maranville (Chicago N.L.)	150.00	75.00	45.00
(26b)	Rabbit Maranville (Boston N.L.)	150.00	75.00	45.00
(27)	Bob Meusel (Fielder, New York A.L.)	75.00	37.50	22.50
(28)	Jack Quinn	75.00	37.50	22.50
(29)	Eppa Rixey (Cincinnati N.L.)	150.00	75.00	45.00
(31)	Eddie Rommel	75.00	37.50	22.50
(32)	"Babe" Ruth (King of the Bat)	2,250	1,125	675.00
(33)	Heinie Sand	75.00	37.50	22.50
(34)	Geo. Sissler (Sisler)	150.00	75.00	45.00
(35)	Earl Smith	75.00	37.50	22.50
(36a)	Tris Speaker (Cleveland A.L.)	200.00	100.00	60.00
(36b)	Tris Speaker (Manager, Newark)	200.00	100.00	60.00
(37)	Roy Spencer	75.00	37.50	22.50
(38)	Milton Stock	75.00	37.50	22.50
(39a)	Phil Todt (Boston A.L.)	75.00	37.50	22.50
(39b)	Phil Todt (Philadelphia A.L.)	75.00	37.50	22.50
(40)	Dazzy Vance	150.00	75.00	45.00
(41)	Zach Wheat (Brooklyn N.L.)	150.00	75.00	45.00
(42a)	Kenneth Williams (St. Louis A.L.)	75.00	37.50	22.50
(42b)	Kenneth Williams (Boston A.L.)	75.00	37.50	22.50
(43a)	Ross Young (Youngs) (Right Fielder)	150.00	75.00	45.00
(43b)	Ross Young (Youngs) (Former Right Fielder)	150.00	75.00	45.00

1921 W9316

As crude as many of the strip cards of the era were, this issue is the worst. In the same blank-back format and size (about 1-1/2" x 2-1/2") as many contemporary strip cards, the set features 10 of the players from W519/W521. The artwork on these cards is very crudely done, almost child-like. The most striking feature about the pictures is the ruby red lips on the players. Unlisted in the American Card Catalog, this set was given the designation W9316 in John Stirling's Sports Card Catalog.

		NM	EX	VG
Complete Set (10):		2,000	800.00	400.00
Common Player:		175.00	70.00	35.00
1	Bob Veach	175.00	70.00	35.00
2	Frank Baker	275.00	110.00	55.00
3	Wilbur (Wilbert) Robinson	275.00	110.00	55.00
4	Johnny Griffith	175.00	70.00	35.00
5	Jimmie Johnston	175.00	70.00	35.00
6	Wallie Schange (Wally Schang)	175.00	70.00	35.00
7	Leon Cadore	175.00	70.00	35.00
8	George Sisler	275.00	110.00	55.00
9	Ray Schalk	275.00	110.00	55.00
10	Jesse Barnes	175.00	70.00	35.00

Y

1972 The Yawkey Red Sox

Boston Red Sox players of the 1930s are featured in this collectors' issue. The issue date given is only a guess. The 2-1/2" x 3-1/2" cards have black-and-white player photos with brown borders and black graphics. Backs are in black-and-white with personal data, a career summary and a promotion for the Red Sox long-time charity, The Jimmy Fund. The unnumbered cards are listed here alphabetically.

		NM	EX	VG
Complete Set (45):		45.00	22.50	13.50
Common Player:		3.00	1.50	.90
(1)	Mel Almada	4.50	2.25	1.25
(2)	Morris "Moe" Berg	9.00	4.50	2.75
(3)	Max Bishop	3.00	1.50	.90
(4)	Doc Bowers	3.00	1.50	.90
(5)	Joe Cascarella	3.00	1.50	.90
(6)	Ben Chapman	3.00	1.50	.90
(7)	Bill Cissell	3.00	1.50	.90
(8)	Dusty Cooke	3.00	1.50	.90
(9)	Doc Cramer	3.00	1.50	.90
(10)	Joe Cronin	4.50	2.25	1.25
(11)	George Dickey	3.00	1.50	.90
(12)	Emerson Dickman	3.00	1.50	.90
(13)	Bobby Doerr	4.50	2.25	1.25
(14)	Rick Ferrell	4.50	2.25	1.25
(15)	Wes Ferrell	3.00	1.50	.90
(16)	Jimmie Foxx	7.50	3.75	2.25
(17)	Joe Gonzales	3.00	1.50	.90
(18)	Lefty Grove	6.00	3.00	1.75
(19)	Bucky Harris	4.50	2.25	1.25
(20)	Jim Henry	3.00	1.50	.90
(21)	Pinky Higgins	3.00	1.50	.90
(22)	Lefty Hockette	3.00	1.50	.90
(23)	Roy Johnson	3.00	1.50	.90
(24)	John Kroner	3.00	1.50	.90
(25)	Heinie Manush	4.50	2.25	1.25
(26)	Archie McKain	3.00	1.50	.90
(27)	Eric McNair	3.00	1.50	.90
(28)	Oscar Melillo	3.00	1.50	.90
(29)	Bing Miller	3.00	1.50	.90
(30)	Joe Mulligan	3.00	1.50	.90
(31)	Bobo Newsom	3.00	1.50	.90
(32)	Ted Olson	3.00	1.50	.90
(33)	Fritz Ostermueller	3.00	1.50	.90
(34)	George Pipgras	3.00	1.50	.90
(35)	Dusty Rhodes	3.00	1.50	.90
(36)	Walt Ripley	3.00	1.50	.90
(37)	Buck Rogers	3.00	1.50	.90
(38)	Jack Russell	3.00	1.50	.90
(39)	Tommy Thomas	3.00	1.50	.90
(40)	Hy Vandenberg	3.00	1.50	.90
(41)	Rube Walberg	3.00	1.50	.90
(42)	Johnny Welch	3.00	1.50	.90
(43)	Bill Werber	3.00	1.50	.90
(44)	Dib Williams	3.00	1.50	.90
(45)	Black Jack Wilson	3.00	1.50	.90

1959 Yoo-Hoo

Issued as a promotion for Yoo-Hoo chocolate flavored soft drink (it's a New York thing), this issue features five New York Yankees players. The black-and-white blank-backed cards measure 2-7/16" x 5-1/8", including a tab at the bottom which could be redeemed for various prizes. The top of the card features a posed spring training photo and includes a fac-simile autograph and "Me for Yoo-Hoo" slogan. Prices shown here are for complete sets; cards without tabs would be valued at one-half of these figures. A Mickey Mantle advertising piece in larger size is often collected as an adjunct to the set, but no card of Mantle was issued. The Berra card is considerably scarcer than the others.

		NM	EX	VG
Complete Set, W/Tabs (5):		4,500	2,250	1,350
Complete Set, No Tabs (5):		1,350	675.00	415.00
Common Player, W/Tab:		800.00	400.00	240.00
Common Player, No Tab:				
WITH TAB				
(1)	Yogi Berra	1,200	600.00	360.00
(2)	Whitey Ford	1,200	600.00	360.00
(3)	Tony Kubek	800.00	400.00	240.00
(4)	Gil McDougald	800.00	400.00	240.00
(5)	Bill Skowron	800.00	400.00	240.00
NO TAB				
(1)	Yogi Berra	300.00	150.00	90.00
(2)	Whitey Ford	300.00	150.00	90.00
(3)	Tony Kubek	250.00	125.00	75.00
(4)	Gil McDougald	250.00	125.00	75.00
(5)	Bill Skowron	250.00	125.00	75.00

1959 Yoo-Hoo Mickey Mantle

In a different format than the other contemporary Yoo-Hoo Yankees cards, the manner of original distribution of this card is unclear. The 2-5/8" x 3-5/8" black-and-white card has a portrait photo and endorsement for the product on front. Back is blank.

	NM	EX	VG
Mickey Mantle	1,600	800.00	480.00

1959 Yoo-Hoo Bottle Caps

These lids for the chocolate soft drink feature black-and-white player portraits with the player name across the chest and "ME FOR" above with "YOO-HOO" below. Caps come in two styles, the older pry-off style and a later screw-top.

		NM	EX	VG
Complete Set (6):		2,000	1,000	450.00
Common Player:		200.00	100.00	60.00
Screw-Tops: +25 Percent				
(1)	Yogi Berra	400.00	200.00	90.00
(2)	Whitey Ford	400.00	200.00	90.00
(3)	Tony Kubek	225.00	110.00	50.00
(4)	Mickey Mantle	800.00	400.00	175.00
(5)	Gil McDougald	200.00	100.00	45.00
(6)	Moose Skowron	225.00	110.00	50.00

1964 Yoo-Hoo Counter Sign

Seven N.Y. Yankees and Bill Skowron in a Senators' cap are pictured on this 11" x 14" easel-back counter display for the chocolate soft drink. Printed in brown, yellow and white, the sign has a hand holding a bottle in front of each player's portrait.

	NM	EX	VG
Yogi Berra, Whitey Ford, Elston Howard, Mickey Mantle, Joe Pepitone, Bobby Richardson, Moose Skowron, Tom Tresh	2,000	1,000	600.00

1927 York Caramels Type 1 (E210)

Issued in 1927 by the York Caramel Co. of York, Pa., these black-and-white cards are among the last of the caramel issues. Measuring 1-3/8" x 2-1/2", they are similar in appearance to earlier candy and tobacco cards. Fronts have the player's name in capital letters beneath the photo preceded by a number in parentheses. The back also lists the player's name in capital letters, along with a brief phrase describing him and the line, "This is one of a series of sixty of the most prominent stars in baseball." The bottom of the cards reads "York Caramel Co. York, Pa." The set includes several variations and is designated in the ACC as E210. It is closely related to the W502 set of the same year. Cards can be found on white or gray card stock. Type 1 cards can be differentiated from Type 2s by the orientation of the back printing. On Type 1 cards, the player name on back is at right when a normally-viewed front is turned over.

		NM	EX	VG
Complete Set (60):		40,000	16,000	8,000
Common Player:		250.00	100.00	50.00
1	Burleigh Grimes	500.00	200.00	100.00
2	Walter Reuther (Ruether)	500.00	200.00	100.00
3	Joe Duggan (Dugan)	250.00	100.00	50.00
4	Red Faber	500.00	200.00	100.00
5	Gabby Hartnett	500.00	200.00	100.00
6	Babe Ruth	15,000	4,800	2,400
7	Bob Meusel	250.00	100.00	50.00
8a	Herb Pennock (Team name on jersey.)	500.00	200.00	100.00
8b	Herb Pennock (No team name.)	500.00	200.00	100.00
9	George Burns	250.00	100.00	50.00
10	Joe Sewell	500.00	200.00	100.00
11	George Uhle	250.00	100.00	50.00
12a	Bob O'Farrel (O'Farrell) (Team name on jersey.)	250.00	100.00	50.00
12b	Bob O'Farrel (O'Farrell) (No team name.)	250.00	100.00	50.00
13	Rogers Hornsby	600.00	240.00	120.00
14	Pie Traynor	500.00	200.00	100.00
15	Clarence Mitchell	250.00	100.00	50.00
16	Eppa Jepha Rixey (Jeptha)	500.00	200.00	100.00
17	Carl Mays	250.00	100.00	50.00
18	Adolph Luque (Adolfo)	250.00	100.00	50.00
19	Dave Bancroft	500.00	200.00	100.00
20	George Kelly	500.00	200.00	100.00
21	Ira Flagstead	250.00	100.00	50.00
22	Harry Heilmann	500.00	200.00	100.00
23	Raymond W. Shalk (Schalk)	500.00	200.00	100.00
24	Johnny Mostil	250.00	100.00	50.00
25	Hack Wilson (Photo actually Art Wilson.)	500.00	200.00	100.00
26	Tom Zachary	250.00	100.00	50.00
27	Ty Cobb	6,500	2,600	1,300
28	Tris Speaker	600.00	240.00	120.00
29	Ralph Perkins	250.00	100.00	50.00
30	Jess Haines	500.00	200.00	100.00
31	Sherwood Smith (Photo actually Jack Coombs.)	250.00	100.00	50.00
32	Max Carey	500.00	200.00	100.00
33	Eugene Hargraves (Hargrave)	250.00	100.00	50.00
34	Miguel L. Gonzales (Miguel A. Gonzalez)	250.00	100.00	50.00
35a	Clifton Heathcot (Heathcote) (Team name on jersey.)	250.00	100.00	50.00
35b	Clifton Heathcot (Heathcote) (No team name.)	250.00	100.00	50.00
35c	Clifton Heathcote (Correct spelling.) (Team Name on jersey.)	250.00	100.00	50.00
36	E.C. (Sam) Rice	500.00	200.00	100.00
37	Earl Sheely	250.00	100.00	50.00

		NM	EX	VG
38a	Emory E. Rigney	250.00	100.00	50.00
	(Team name on jersey.)			
38b	Emory E. Rigney	250.00	100.00	50.00
	(No team name.)			
39	Bib A. Falk (Bibb)	250.00	100.00	50.00
40	Nick Altrock	250.00	100.00	50.00
41	Stanley Harris	500.00	200.00	100.00
42	John J. McGraw	500.00	200.00	100.00
43	Wilbert Robinson	500.00	200.00	100.00
44	Grover Alexander	750.00	300.00	150.00
45	Walter Johnson	1,000	400.00	200.00
46	William H. Terry	500.00	200.00	100.00
	(Photo actually Zeb Terry.)			
47	Edward Collins	500.00	200.00	100.00
48	Marty McManus	250.00	100.00	50.00
49	Leon (Goose) Goslin	500.00	200.00	100.00
50	Frank Frisch	500.00	200.00	100.00
51	Jimmie Dykes	250.00	100.00	50.00
52	Fred (Cy) Williams	250.00	100.00	50.00
53	Eddie Roush	500.00	200.00	100.00
54	George Sisler	500.00	200.00	100.00
55	Ed Rommel	250.00	100.00	50.00
56a	Rogers Peckinpaugh (Roger)	250.00	100.00	50.00
	(Card number upside-down.)			
56b	Rogers Peckinpaugh (Roger)	250.00	100.00	50.00
	(Card number corrected.)			
57	Stanley Coveleskie	500.00	200.00	100.00
	(Coveleski)			
58	Clarence Gallaway	250.00	100.00	50.00
	(Galloway)			
59	Bob Shawkey	250.00	100.00	50.00
60	John P. McInnis	250.00	100.00	50.00

1927 York Caramels Type 2 (E210)

Type 2 York Caramels are in the same size and format as the Type 1 cards. They can be differentiated from Type 1 cards by the orientation of the back printing. On Type 2 cards, the player name appears at left when a normally-held card is turned over. Type 2 cards are all printed on white stock. Some players and photos were changed, and the descriptive lines about the players were changed on most cards.

		NM	EX	VG
Complete Set (60):		45,000	18,000	9,000
Common Player:		250.00	100.00	50.00
1	Burleigh Grimes	500.00	200.00	100.00
2	Walter Reuther (Ruether)	250.00	100.00	50.00
3	Joe Dugan	250.00	100.00	50.00
4	Red Faber	500.00	200.00	100.00
5	Gabby Hartnett	500.00	200.00	100.00
6	Babe Ruth	12,000	4,800	2,400
7	Bob Meusel	250.00	100.00	50.00
8	Herb Pennock (Profile)	500.00	200.00	100.00
9	George Burns	250.00	100.00	50.00
10	Joe Sewell	500.00	200.00	100.00
11	George Uhle	250.00	100.00	50.00
12	Bob O'Farrell	250.00	100.00	50.00
13	Rogers Hornsby	600.00	240.00	120.00
14	Pie Traynor	500.00	200.00	100.00
15	Clarence Mitchell	250.00	100.00	50.00
16	Eppa Rixey	500.00	200.00	100.00
17	Carl Mays	250.00	100.00	50.00
18	Adolfo Luque	250.00	100.00	50.00
19	Dave Bancroft	500.00	200.00	100.00
20	George Kelly	500.00	200.00	100.00
21	Earle Combs	500.00	200.00	100.00
22	Harry Heilmann	500.00	200.00	100.00
23	Ray W. Schalk	500.00	200.00	100.00
24	Johnny Mostil	250.00	100.00	50.00
25	Hack Wilson	500.00	200.00	100.00
26	Lou Gehrig	10,000	2,600	1,300
27	Ty Cobb	6,500	2,600	1,300
28	Tris Speaker	600.00	240.00	120.00
29	Tony Lazzeri	500.00	200.00	100.00
30	Waite Hoyt	500.00	200.00	100.00
31	Sherwood Smith (Photo actually Jack Coombs.)	250.00	100.00	50.00
32	Max Carey	500.00	200.00	100.00
33	Eugene Hargrave (Hargraves)	250.00	100.00	50.00
34	Miguel L. Gonzales (Miguel A. Gonzalez)	250.00	100.00	50.00
35	Joe Judge	250.00	100.00	50.00
36	E.C. (Sam) Rice	500.00	200.00	100.00
37	Earl Sheely	250.00	100.00	50.00
38	Sam Jones	250.00	100.00	50.00
39	Bib (Bibb) A. Falk	250.00	100.00	50.00
40	Willie Kamm	250.00	100.00	50.00
41	Stanley Harris	500.00	200.00	100.00
42	John J. McGraw	500.00	200.00	100.00
43	Artie Nehf	250.00	100.00	50.00
44	Grover Alexander	750.00	300.00	150.00
45	Paul Waner	500.00	200.00	100.00
46	William H. Terry (Photo actually Zeb Terry.)	500.00	200.00	100.00
47	Glenn Wright	250.00	100.00	50.00
48	Earl Smith	250.00	100.00	50.00
49	Leon (Goose) Goslin	500.00	200.00	100.00
50	Frank Frisch	500.00	200.00	100.00
51	Joe Harris	250.00	100.00	50.00
52	Fred (Cy) Williams	250.00	100.00	50.00
53	Eddie Roush	500.00	200.00	100.00
54	George Sisler	500.00	200.00	100.00
55	Ed Rommel	250.00	100.00	50.00
56	Rogers Peckinpaugh (Roger)	250.00	100.00	50.00
57	Stanley Coveleskie (Coveleski)	500.00	200.00	100.00
58	Lester Bell	250.00	100.00	50.00
59	L. Waner	500.00	200.00	100.00
60	John P. McInnis	250.00	100.00	50.00

1917 Youth's Companion Stamps

The date attributed is speculative. This set of poster-stamps was issued to promote a Boston-based weekly magazine. Although he is not named, the left-handed pitcher depicted in very Red Sox-like uniform on one of the color litho

stamps evidently looks enough like Babe Ruth that collectors have been willing to pay hundreds of dollars for examples of this scarce issue. The 1-7/8" x 2-1/2" stamp is, of course, blank-backed and is part of a set which featured other sporting activities, hobbys and topics suitable for young readers.

	NM	EX	VG
(Babe Ruth?)	600.00	300.00	180.00

1928 Yuengling's Ice Cream (F50)

Issued in 1928, the Yuengling's Ice Cream issue consists of 60 black-and-white cards measuring 1-3/8" x 2-1/2". The photos are similar to those used in the E210 and W502 sets. Other ice cream companies such as Harrington's and Tharp's produced nearly identical cards. Two types of cards are seen, though whether either or both can be found for all players is unknown. Besides typographical placement differences on front, the back of one type mentions a "$5.00 skooter" as a redemption, while the other type has no mention of the toy. Collectors could redeem an entire set of Yuengling's cards for a gallon of ice cream.

		NM	EX	VG
Complete Set (60):		45,000	18,000	9,000
Common Player:		250.00	100.00	50.00
1	Burleigh Grimes	500.00	200.00	100.00
2	Walter Reuther (Ruether)	250.00	100.00	50.00
3	Joe Dugan	250.00	100.00	50.00
4	Red Faber	500.00	200.00	100.00
5	Gabby Hartnett	500.00	200.00	100.00
6	Babe Ruth	12,000	4,800	2,400
7	Bob Meusel	250.00	100.00	50.00
8	Herb Pennock	500.00	200.00	100.00
9	George Burns	250.00	100.00	50.00
10	Joe Sewell	500.00	200.00	100.00
11	George Uhle	250.00	100.00	50.00
12	Bob O'Farrell	250.00	100.00	50.00
13	Rogers Hornsby	600.00	240.00	120.00
14	"Pie" Traynor	500.00	200.00	100.00
15	Clarence Mitchell	250.00	100.00	50.00
16	Eppa Jepha Rixey	500.00	200.00	100.00
17	Carl Mays	250.00	100.00	50.00
18	Adolfo Luque	250.00	100.00	50.00
19	Dave Bancroft	500.00	200.00	100.00
20	George Kelly	500.00	200.00	100.00
21	Earl (Earle) Combs	500.00	200.00	100.00
22	Harry Heilmann	500.00	200.00	100.00
23	Ray W. Schalk	500.00	200.00	100.00
24	Johnny Mostil	250.00	100.00	50.00
25	Hack Wilson	500.00	200.00	100.00
26	Lou Gehrig	6,500	2,600	1,300
27	Ty Cobb	6,500	2,600	1,300
28	Tris Speaker	600.00	240.00	120.00
29	Tony Lazzeri	500.00	200.00	100.00
30	Waite Hoyt	500.00	200.00	100.00
31	Sherwood Smith	250.00	100.00	50.00
32	Max Carey	500.00	200.00	100.00
33	Eugene Hargrave	250.00	100.00	50.00
34	Miguel L. Gonzales (Miguel A. Gonzalez)	250.00	100.00	50.00
35	Joe Judge	250.00	100.00	50.00
36	E.C. (Sam) Rice	500.00	200.00	100.00
37	Earl Sheely	250.00	100.00	50.00
38	Sam Jones	250.00	100.00	50.00
39	Bib (Bibb) A. Falk	250.00	100.00	50.00

1888 Yum Yum Tobacco (N403)

An extremely rare series of tobacco cards, this set was issued in 1888 by August Beck & Co., Chicago. The cards vary slightly in size but average 1-3/8" x 2-3/4". They were distributed in packages of the company's Yum Yum smoking and chewing tobacco and are found in two distinct types: photographic portraits and full-length action drawings copied from photos used in the Old Judge sets of the same period. In both types, the player's name and position appear in capital letters below the photo, while the very bottom of the card states: "Smoke and Chew "Yum Yum" Tobacco. A. Beck & Co. Chicago, Ill." Players from all eight National League clubs, plus Brooklyn of the American Association, are included in the set. The checklist here has gaps left to accommodate future additions.

		NM	EX	VG
Common Player:		9,000	5,000	3,500
(3)	Cap Anson (Portrait)	45,000	22,500	13,500
(4)	Cap Anson (Batting)	23,750	11,250	6,750
(7)	Lady Baldwin	9,750	4,875	2,925
	(Left arm extended.)			
(11)	Dan Brouthers (Batting)	18,000	9,000	5,400
(13)	Willard "California" Brown	9,750	4,875	2,925
(15)	Charles Buffington (Buffinton)	9,750	4,875	2,925
(17)	Tom Burns (Portrait)	16,500	8,250	4,950
(18)	Tom Burns (With bat.)	9,750	4,875	2,925
(21)	John Clarkson (Portrait)	30,000	15,000	9,000
(22)	John Clarkson (Throwing, arm back.)	18,000	9,000	5,400
(25)	John Coleman (Portrait)	16,500	8,250	4,950
(27)	Roger Connor (Batting)	18,000	9,000	5,400
(28)	Roger Connor (Portrait)	30,000	15,000	9,000
(30)	Larry Corcoran (Portrait)	16,500	8,250	4,950
(34)	Tom Daily (Daly) (Portrait) (Photo actually Billy Sunday.)	17,250	8,625	5,175
(36)	Tom Deasley (Portrait)	16,500	8,250	4,950
(39)	Mike Dorgan (Portrait)	16,500	8,250	4,950
(40)	Dude Esterbrook (Portrait)	16,500	8,250	4,950
(41)	Buck Ewing (Portrait)	30,000	15,000	9,000
(42)	Buck Ewing (With bat.)	18,000	9,000	5,400
(45)	Silver Flint (Portrait)	16,500	8,250	4,950
(47)	Jim Fogarty (Throwing)	9,750	4,875	2,925
(49)	Pud Galvin (Ball in hands at chest.)	18,000	9,000	5,400
(51)	Joe Gerhardt	16,500	8,250	4,950
(53)	Charlie Getzein (Getzien)(Holding ball.)	9,750	4,875	2,925
(55)	Pete Gillespie (Portrait)	16,500	8,250	4,950
(57)	Jack Glasscock	9,750	4,875	2,925
(59)	George Gore (Leaning on bat.)	9,750	4,875	2,925
(61)	Ed Greer (Portrait)	16,500	8,250	4,950
(65)	Tim Keefe (Pitching)	18,000	9,000	5,400
(66)	Tim Keefe (Portrait)	30,000	15,000	9,000
(67)	King Kelly (Batting)	18,000	9,000	5,400
(68)	King Kelly (Photo, standing by urn.)	45,000	22,500	13,500
(70)	Gus Krock (Portrait)	16,500	8,250	4,950
(72)	Connie Mack	18,000	9,000	5,400
(74)	Kid Madden (Ball in raised right hand.)	9,750	4,875	2,925
(76)	Doggie Miller (Leaning on bat.)	9,750	4,875	2,925
(78)	John Morrill (Leaning on bat.)	9,750	4,875	2,925
(80)	James Mutrie (Portrait)	16,500	8,250	4,950
(82)	Billy Nash (Holding bat.)	9,750	4,875	2,925
(84)	Jim O'Rourke (Portrait)	30,000	15,000	9,000
(85)	Jim O'Rourke (With bat.)	18,000	9,000	5,400
(87)	Fred Pfeffer (Bat on shoulder.)	9,750	4,875	2,925
(90)	Danny Richardson (Portrait)	16,500	8,250	4,950
(92)	Chief Roseman (Portrait)	16,500	8,250	4,950
(94)	Jimmy Ryan (Portrait)	16,500	8,250	4,950
(95)	Jimmy Ryan (Throwing)	9,750	4,875	2,925
(97)	Bill Sowders (Ball in hands at chest.)	9,750	4,875	2,925
(100)	Marty Sullivan (Portrait)	16,500	8,250	4,950
(102)	Billy Sunday (Fielding)	18,000	9,000	5,400
(103)	Billy Sunday (Portrait)(Photo actually Mark Baldwin.)	18,000	9,000	5,400
(105)	Ezra Sutton (Batting)	9,750	4,875	2,925
(110)	Mike Tiernan (Portrait)	16,500	8,250	4,950
(111)	Mike Tiernan (With bat.)	9,750	4,875	2,925
(115)	Rip Van Haltren (Photo not Van Haltren.)	16,500	8,250	4,950
(119)	John Ward (Portrait)	30,000	15,000	9,000
(123)	Mickey Welch (Ball in hands at chest.)	18,000	9,000	5,400
(124)	Mickey Welch (Portrait)	30,000	15,000	9,000
(125)	Mickey Welch (Right arm extended.)	18,000	9,000	5,400
(129)	Jim Whitney (Throwing)	9,750	4,875	2,925
(133)	George Wood (Throwing, arm behind head.)	9,750	4,875	2,925

Z

1954-1955 Zipcards Baltimore Orioles

BALTIMORE

55-04   Tom Gastall
Zipcards

Given the homemade appearance of these cards, it must be surmised that they were an early collectors' issue. It is possible they date from as early as 1956, only a few years after the Orioles joined the American League. Cards are found in three formats. One type measures about 2" x 2-5/8" (all measurements are approximate due to the hand-cut nature of the cards) and is printed on thin yellow cardboard. They feature a chest-to-cap black-and-white circular player photo at center. A second type is about 2-3/4" x 3-5/8", black-and-white, with square portrait or posed action photos and "BALTIMORE" at top in what appears to be a picture of an embossed plastic Dymo label maker strip. The third type is also about 2-3/4" x 3-5/8" and is similar in design to the Dymo-lable format, except "Baltimore" is printed at top in a serifed italic typeface. All cards are blank-backed. Where known, the type of each card is indicated on this checklist by "RP" (round photo), "DL" (Dymo-label) or "SI" (serifed italic). It is possible this checklist is incomplete.

	NM	EX	VG
Common Player:	30.00	15.00	9.00
54-01 Jimmie Dykes	30.00	15.00	9.00
54-02 Tom Oliver	30.00	15.00	9.00
54-03 Frank Skaff	30.00	15.00	9.00
54-04 Eddie Waitkuss (Waitkus) (DL)	30.00	15.00	9.00
54-05 Chuck Diering (DL)	30.00	15.00	9.00
54-06 Chick Chakales (RP)	30.00	15.00	9.00
54-07 Marlin Stuart (RP)	30.00	15.00	9.00
54-08 Jim Brideweser (RP)	30.00	15.00	9.00
54-09 Chico Garcia (RP)	30.00	15.00	9.00
54-10 Jim Fridley (RP)	30.00	15.00	9.00
54-11 Billy O'Dell (DL)	30.00	15.00	9.00
54-12 Unknown			
54-13 Joe Durham (DL)	30.00	15.00	9.00
55-01 Wayne Causey (RP)	30.00	15.00	9.00
55-02 Jim Dyck	30.00	15.00	9.00
55-03 Hoot Evers (SI)	30.00	15.00	9.00
55-04 Tom Gastall (RP)	30.00	15.00	9.00
55-05 Bob Hale (RP)	30.00	15.00	9.00
55-06 Bob Kennedy (SI)	30.00	15.00	9.00
55-07 Don Leppert (SI)	30.00	15.00	9.00
55-08 Les Moss (SI)	30.00	15.00	9.00
55-09 Bob Nelson (RP)	30.00	15.00	9.00
55-10 Dave Philley (RP)	30.00	15.00	9.00

	NM	EX	VG
55-11 Unknown			
55-12 Unknown			
55-13 Art Schallock (RP)	30.00	15.00	9.00
55-14 Bobby Young (SI)	30.00	15.00	9.00
55-15 Unknown			
55-16 Lum Harris	30.00	15.00	9.00

1977 Zip'z Discs

Virtually identical in format to the several locally sponsored disc sets of the previous year, these 3-3/8" diameter player discs were given away at the sponsor's sundae bars around the cvountry. Some are found with a black rubber-stamp on back of the specific Zip's location. Discs once again feature black-and-white player portrait photos in the center of a baseball design. The left and right panels are in one of several bright colors. Licensed by the players' association through Mike Schechter Associates, the player photos carry no uniform logos. Backs are printed in reddish-orange. The unnumbered discs are checklisted here alphabetically.

	NM	EX	VG
Complete Set (70):	120.00	60.00	35.00
Common Player:	2.00	1.00	.60
(1) Sal Bando	2.00	1.00	.60
(2) Buddy Bell	2.00	1.00	.60
(3) Johnny Bench	7.50	3.75	2.25
(4) Larry Bowa	2.00	1.00	.60
(5) Steve Braun	2.00	1.00	.60
(6) George Brett	20.00	10.00	6.00
(7) Lou Brock	6.00	3.00	1.75
(8) Jeff Burroughs	2.00	1.00	.60
(9) Bert Campaneris	2.00	1.00	.60
(10) John Candelaria	2.00	1.00	.60
(11) Jose Cardenal	2.00	1.00	.60
(12) Rod Carew	6.00	3.00	1.75
(13) Steve Carlton	6.00	3.00	1.75
(14) Dave Cash	2.00	1.00	.60
(15) Cesar Cedeno	2.00	1.00	.60
(16) Ron Cey	2.00	1.00	.60
(17) Dave Concepcion	2.00	1.00	.60
(18) Dennis Eckersley	6.00	3.00	1.75
(19) Mark Fidrych	3.00	1.50	.90
(20) Rollie Fingers	6.00	3.00	1.75
(21) Carlton Fisk	6.00	3.00	1.75
(22) George Foster	2.00	1.00	.60
(23) Wayne Garland	2.00	1.00	.60
(24) Ralph Garr	2.00	1.00	.60
(25) Steve Garvey	5.00	2.50	1.50
(26) Cesar Geronimo	2.00	1.00	.60
(27) Bobby Grich	2.00	1.00	.60
(28) Ken Griffey Sr.	2.00	1.00	.60
(29) Don Gullett	2.00	1.00	.60
(30) Mike Hargrove	2.00	1.00	.60
(31) Al Hrabosky	2.00	1.00	.60
(32) Jim Hunter	6.00	3.00	1.75
(33) Reggie Jackson	15.00	7.50	4.50
(34) Randy Jones	2.00	1.00	.60
(35) Dave Kingman	2.00	1.00	.60
(36) Jerry Koosman	2.00	1.00	.60
(37) Dave LaRoche	2.00	1.00	.60
(38) Greg Luzinski	2.00	1.00	.60
(39) Fred Lynn	2.00	1.00	.60
(40) Bill Madlock	2.00	1.00	.60
(41) Rick Manning	2.00	1.00	.60
(42) Jon Matlock	2.00	1.00	.60
(43) John Mayberry	2.00	1.00	.60
(44) Hal McRae	2.00	1.00	.60
(45) Andy Messersmith	2.00	1.00	.60
(46) Rick Monday	2.00	1.00	.60
(47) John Montefusco	2.00	1.00	.60
(48) Joe Morgan	6.00	3.00	1.75
(49) Thurman Munson	5.00	2.50	1.50
(50) Bobby Murcer	2.00	1.00	.60
(51) Bill North	2.00	1.00	.60
(52) Jim Palmer	6.00	3.00	1.75
(53) Tony Perez	6.00	3.00	1.75
(54) Jerry Reuss	2.00	1.00	.60
(55) Brooks Robinson	7.50	3.75	2.25
(56) Pete Rose	25.00	12.50	7.50
(57) Joe Rudi	2.00	1.00	.60
(58) Nolan Ryan	35.00	17.50	10.00
(59) Manny Sanguillen	2.00	1.00	.60
(60) Mike Schmidt	15.00	7.50	4.50
(61) Tom Seaver	7.50	3.75	2.25
(62) Bill Singer	2.00	1.00	.60
(63) Willie Stargell	6.00	3.00	1.75
(64) Rusty Staub	2.00	1.00	.60
(65) Luis Tiant	2.00	1.00	.60
(66) Bob Watson	2.00	1.00	.60
(67) Butch Wynegar	2.00	1.00	.60
(68) Carl Yastrzemski	10.00	5.00	3.00
(69) Robin Yount	6.00	3.00	1.75
(70) Richie Zisk	2.00	1.00	.60

1950s Bill Zuber's Restaurant

 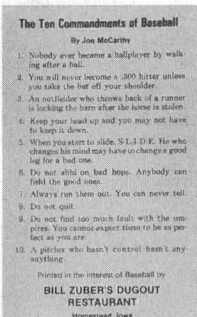

These 3-1/2" x 5-1/2" black-and-white cards were produced as a promotional item for an Iowa restaurant owned by the former big league pitcher (1936-47). The semi-gloss front has a portrait and facsimile autograph. One type has an advertising message at left and the inscription, "Good Hitting." On back are printed Joe McCarthy's "Ten Commandments of Baseball." A second type has the inscription, "Sincerest Wishes," with a postcard-style back featuring an advertising message in the top-left corner.

	NM	EX	VG
(1) Bill Zuber (Ten Commandments back.)	8.00	4.00	2.50
(2) Bill Zuber (Postcard back.)	8.00	4.00	2.50

MODERN MAJOR LEAGUE (1981-2009)

The vast majority of cards and collectibles listed in this section were issued between 1981 and May 2009 and feature only major league players.

Because modern cards are generally not collected in lower grades, cards in this section carry only a Near Mint-to-Mint (NM/M) value quote. In general, post-1980 cards that grade Near Mint will retail at about 75 percent of the NM/M price, while Excellent condition cards bring about 40 percent. Cards in lesser condition are generally not considered collectible.

Values shown are for "raw" cards, that is, cards not authenticated, graded and encapsulated by an independent certification firm. Many cards that have been graded Mint, Gem Mint or Pristine by recognized major grading companies (SCD, SGC, BGS, GAI or PSA) will sell at a premium over the values quoted here. Because the standards and reputations of these companies vary widely, prices listed here cannot be correlated to values for "slabbed" cards

A

1991 Acme Reproductions Ryan-Seaver

This collectors' issue was produced in an edition of 10,000 in an over-size (4-1/4" x 3") format and style approximating a 1967 Topps card. The future Hall of Famers are pictured in their early days with the Mets. Facsimile autographs appear at the bottom of each photo. A total of 420 of the cards was authentically autographed by both players. Backs have a cartoon and biographical data on each player, plus a career summary up to 1967. Original issue price was $29, or $109 for the autographed card. Each came in a lucite holder with numbered certificate of authenticity. A 17-1/2" x 12-1/2" lithograph was produced in an edition of 3,000, with the first 1,000 autographed by each player. The litho sold for $219 autographed and $109 unsigned.

	NM/M
Nolan Ryan, Tom Seaver	10.00
Nolan Ryan, Tom Seaver/Auto.	200.00

1988 Action Packed

Action Packed released this test set in an effort to receive a license from Major League Baseball. The cards are styled like the Action Packed football issues on the card fronts. The flip sides are styled like Score baseball cards. The Ozzie Smith card is considered scarcer than the other five cards in the test set, while a hoard of Mattingly cards revealed in 1998 drove down the price of his card. Action Packed did not receive a license to produce baseball cards.

		NM/M
Complete Set (6):		45.00
Common Player:		6.00
(1)	Wade Boggs	12.50
(2)	Andre Dawson	7.50
(3)	Dwight Gooden	6.00
(4)	Carney Lansford	6.00
(5)	Don Mattingly	6.00
(6)	Ozzie Smith	30.00

1992 Action Packed Promos

This set was produced to preview Action Packed's All-Star Gallery card issue. The promo cards are identical in format to the regularly issued cards and use the same player photos. The only differences in the promos are found on the back, where the card number is missing from the lower-left corner and where a white "1992 Prototype" is overprinted on the gray background beneath the black career highlights. The promos were widely distributed at trade shows and to Action Packed's dealer network. The unnumbered promo cards are checklisted here alphabetically.

		NM/M
Complete Set (5):		6.00
Common Player:		1.00
(1)	Yogi Berra	1.50
(2)	Bob Gibson	1.00
(3)	Willie Mays	3.00
(4)	Warren Spahn	1.00
(5)	Willie Stargell	1.00

1992 Action Packed All-Star Gallery Series 1

Action Packed, makers of a high quality, embossed style football card for several years, entered the baseball card field in 1992 with its 84-card All-Star Gallery Series 1. The cards feature former baseball greats, with 72 of the 84 cards in color and the remaining in sepia tone. Each foil pack of seven cards reportedly contained at least one Hall of Famer, and the company also made special 24K gold leaf stamped cards of all of the HOFers that were randomly inserted in the packs.

	NM/M
Complete Set (84):	15.00
Common Player:	.10
Wax Pack (7):	.75
Wax Box (24):	12.50

1	Yogi Berra	.50
2	Lou Brock	.25
3	Bob Gibson	.25
4	Ferguson Jenkins	.25
5	Ralph Kiner	.25
6	Al Kaline	.40
7	Lou Boudreau	.25
8	Bobby Doerr	.25
9	Billy Herman	.25
10	Monte Irvin	.25
11	George Kell	.25
12	Robin Roberts	.25
13	Johnny Mize	.25
14	Willie Mays	1.00
15	Enos Slaughter	.25
16	Warren Spahn	.25
17	Willie Stargell	.25
18	Billy Williams	.25
19	Vernon Law	.10
20	Virgil Trucks	.10
21	Mel Parnell	.10
22	Wally Moon	.10
23	Gene Woodling	.10
24	Richie Ashburn	.25
25	Mark Fidrych	.10
26	Elroy Face	.10
27	Larry Doby	.25
28	Dick Groat	.10
29	Cesar Cedeno	.10
30	Bob Horner	.10
31	Bobby Richardson	.25
32	Bobby Murcer	.10
33	Gil McDougald	.10
34	Roy White	.10
35	Bill Skowron	.25
36	Mickey Lolich	.10
37	Minnie Minoso	.10
38	Billy Pierce	.10
39	Ron Santo	.25
40	Sal Bando	.10
41	Ralph Branca	.10
42	Bert Campaneris	.10
43	Joe Garagiola	.25
44	Vida Blue	.10
45	Frank Crosetti	.10
46	Luis Tiant	.10
47	Maury Wills	.10
48	Sam McDowell	.10
49	Jimmy Piersall	.10
50	Jim Lonborg	.10
51	Don Newcombe	.15
52	Bobby Thomson	.10
53	Wilbur Wood	.10
54	Carl Erskine	.10
55	Chris Chambliss	.10
56	Dave Kingman	.10
57	Ken Holtzman	.10
58	Bud Harrelson	.10
59	Clem Labine	.10
60	Tony Oliva	.10
61	George Foster	.10
62	Bobby Bonds	.10
63	Harvey Haddix	.10
64	Steve Garvey	.10
65	Rocky Colavito	.15
66	Orlando Cepeda	.25
67	Ed Lopat	.10
68	Al Oliver	.10
69	Bill Mazeroski	.25
70	Al Rosen	.10
71	Bob Grich	.10
72	Curt Flood	.10
73	Willie Horton	.10
74	Rico Carty	.10
75	Davey Johnson	.10
76	Don Kessinger	.10
77	Frank Thomas	.10
78	Bobby Shantz	.10
79	Herb Score	.10
80	Boog Powell	.15
81	Rusty Staub	.15
82	Bill Madlock	.10
83	Manny Mota	.10
84	Bill White	.10

1993 Action Packed All-Star Gallery Series 2

The Second Series of Action Packed All-Star Gallery was released in 1993, with cards numbered from 85 to 168. In a similar fashion to the First Series, Series Two features 52 cards in color, 31 in sepia tone and one as a colorized black and white. The series also includes two tongue-in-cheek cards - "Who's on First?" duo Bud Abbot and Lou Costello, and a card highlighting the TV and radio career of Bob Uecker.

	NM/M
Complete Set (84):	10.00
Common Player:	.10
Wax Pack (7):	1.00
Wax Box (24):	17.50

85	Cy Young	.15
86	Honus Wagner	.25
87	Christy Mathewson	.15
88	Ty Cobb	1.00
89	Eddie Collins	.10
90	Walter Johnson	.15
91	Tris Speaker	.15
92	Grover Alexander	.10
93	Edd Roush	.10
94	Babe Ruth	2.00
95	Rogers Hornsby	.15
96	Pie Traynor	.10
97	Lou Gehrig	1.00
98	Mickey Cochrane	.10
99	Lefty Grove	.10
100	Jimmie Foxx	.15
101	Tony Lazzeri	.10
102	Mel Ott	.10
103	Carl Hubbell	.10
104	Al Lopez	.10
105	Lefty Gomez	.10
106	Dizzy Dean	.10
107	Hank Greenberg	.10
108	Joe Medwick	.10
109	Arky Vaughan	.10
110	Bob Feller	.15
111	Hal Newhouser	.10
112	Early Wynn	.10
113	Bob Lemon	.10
114	Red Schoendienst	.10
115	Satchel Paige	.25
116	Whitey Ford	.15
117	Eddie Mathews	.15
118	Harmon Killebrew	.15
119	Roberto Clemente	1.50
120	Brooks Robinson	.15
121	Don Drysdale	.15
122	Luis Aparicio	.15
123	Willie McCovey	.15
124	Juan Marichal	.10
125	Gaylord Perry	.10
126	Catfish Hunter	.10
127	Jim Palmer	.15
128	Rod Carew	.15
129	Tom Seaver	.15
130	Rollie Fingers	.15
131	Joe Jackson	2.00
132	Pepper Martin	.10
133	Joe Gordon	.10
134	Marty Marion	.10
135	Allie Reynolds	.10
136	Johnny Sain	.10
137	Gil Hodges	.15
138	Ted Kluszewski	.15
139	Nellie Fox	.15
140	Billy Martin	.10
141	Smoky Burgess	.10
142	Lew Burdette	.10
143	Joe Black	.10
144	Don Larsen	.10
145	Ken Boyer	.10
146	Johnny Callison	.10
147	Norm Cash	.10
148	Keith Hernandez	.10
149	Jim Kaat	.10
150	Bill Freehan	.10
151	Joe Torre	.10
152	Bob Uecker	.15
153	Dave McNally	.10
154	Denny McLain	.10
155	Dick Allen	.10
156	Jimmy Wynn	.10
157	Tommy John	.10
158	Paul Blair	.10
159	Reggie Smith	.10
160	Jerry Koosman	.10
161	Thurman Munson	.15
162	Graig Nettles	.10
163	Ron Cey	.10
164	Cecil Cooper	.10
165	Dave Parker	.10
166	Jim Rice	.10
167	Kent Tekulve	.10
168	Who's on First? (Bud Abbott, Lou Costello)	.75

1992 Action Packed Diamond Stars

The first 18 cards from Series 1 Action Packed ASG were produced in a gold-enhanced boxed-set version which included a diamond chip in 14-Karat gold setting. Each card was serially numbered from an edition of 500.

		NM/M
Complete Set (18):		80.00
Common Player:		4.00
1G	Yogi Berra	7.50
2G	Lou Brock	4.00
3G	Bob Gibson	4.00
4G	Ferguson Jenkins	4.00
5G	Ralph Kiner	4.00
6G	Al Kaline	5.00
7G	Lou Boudreau	4.00
8G	Bobby Doerr	4.00
9G	Billy Herman	4.00
10G	Monte Irvin	4.00
11G	George Kell	4.00
12G	Robin Roberts	4.00
13G	Johnny Mize	4.00
14G	Willie Mays	12.50
15G	Enos Slaughter	4.00
16G	Warren Spahn	4.00
17G	Willie Stargell	4.00
18G	Billy Williams	4.00

1992-93 Action Packed Gold

Essentially identical to the regular-issue Action Packed All-Star Gallery cards, these premium inserts are specially numbered with a "G" prefix and highlighted with 24-Karat gold detailing.

		NM/M
Complete Set (65):		175.00
Common Player:		2.50
Series 1		
1	Yogi Berra	4.00
2	Lou Brock	2.50
3	Bob Gibson	2.50
4	Ferguson Jenkins	2.50
5	Ralph Kiner	2.50
6	Al Kaline	3.50
7	Lou Boudreau	2.50
8	Bobby Doerr	2.50
9	Billy Herman	2.50
10	Monte Irvin	2.50
11	George Kell	2.50
12	Robin Roberts	2.50
13	Johnny Mize	2.50
14	Willie Mays	7.50
15	Enos Slaughter	2.50
16	Warren Spahn	2.50
17	Willie Stargell	2.50
18	Billy Williams	2.50
Series 2		
19	Cy Young	3.50
20	Honus Wagner	5.00
21	Christy Mathewson	3.50
22	Ty Cobb	6.00
23	Eddie Collins	2.50
24	Walter Johnson	3.50
25	Tris Speaker	3.50
26	Grover Alexander	3.25
27	Edd Roush	2.50
28	Babe Ruth	12.50
29	Rogers Hornsby	3.50
30	Pie Traynor	2.50
31	Lou Gehrig	10.00
32	Mickey Cochrane	3.25
33	Lefty Grove	3.25
34	Jimmie Foxx	3.50
35	Tony Lazzeri	2.50
36	Mel Ott	2.50
37	Carl Hubbell	2.50
38	Al Lopez	2.50
39	Lefty Gomez	3.50
40	Dizzy Dean	3.50
41	Hank Greenberg	3.50
42	Joe Medwick	2.50
43	Arky Vaughan	2.50
44	Bob Feller	3.50
45	Hal Newhouser	2.50
46	Early Wynn	2.50
47	Bob Lemon	2.50
48	Red Schoendienst	2.50
49	Satchel Paige	6.00
50	Whitey Ford	3.25
51	Eddie Mathews	3.25
52	Harmon Killebrew	3.25
53	Roberto Clemente	15.00
54	Brooks Robinson	3.25
55	Don Drysdale	3.25
56	Luis Aparicio	2.50
57	Willie McCovey	3.25
58	Juan Marichal	2.50
59	Gaylord Perry	2.50
60	Catfish Hunter	2.50
61	Jim Palmer	3.25
62	Rod Carew	3.25
63	Tom Seaver	3.25
64	Rollie Fingers	2.50

65	Who's on First? (Bud Abbott, Lou Costello)	3.50

1992 Action Packed 24-Kt. Gold

At least the first 18 cards in 1992 AP All-Star Gallery Series 1 were also issued in a full-coverage gold-foil version (as opposed to the gold-highlighted parallels). The cards are embossed front and back in gold-foil and numbered identically to the regular-issue cards. Each has a "24-Kt. Gold" imprint on front and is ink-jet serially numbered on back within an edition of 1,000.

		NM/M
	Complete Set (18):	35.00
	Common Player:	2.00
1	Yogi Berra	3.50
2	Lou Brock	2.50
3	Bob Gibson	2.50
4	Ferguson Jenkins	2.50
5	Ralph Kiner	2.50
6	Al Kaline	2.50
7	Lou Boudreau	2.00
8	Bobby Doerr	2.00
9	Billy Herman	2.00
10	Monte Irvin	2.00
11	George Kell	2.00
12	Robin Roberts	2.50
13	Johnny Mize	2.50
14	Willie Mays	7.50
15	Enos Slaughter	2.50
16	Warren Spahn	2.50
17	Willie Stargell	2.50
18	Billy Williams	2.50

1993 Action Packed Amoco/Coke

A special version of 18 of its All-Star Gallery cards was created by Action Packed for use as a premium by Amoco gas stations and Coca-Cola. Card fronts feature the same embossed color or sepia player photos with a heavily lacquered finish and gold-foil and black borders. Gray backs have biographical and career data, a few stats and sponsors' logos. Complete sets were available via a mail-in offer from Coke products. Most of these cards share card numbers and photos with AP's Series I ASG cards.

		NM/M
	Complete Set (18):	4.00
	Common Player:	.50
1	Yogi Berra	1.00
2	Lou Brock	.50
3	Bob Gibson	.50
4	Red Schoendienst	.50
5	Ralph Kiner	.50
6	Al Kaline	.75
7	Lou Boudreau	.50
8	Bobby Doerr	.50
9	Gaylord Perry	.50
10	Monte Irvin	.50
11	George Kell	.50
12	Robin Roberts	.60
13	Johnny Mize	.60
14	Willie Mays	2.00
15	Enos Slaughter	.50

16	Warren Spahn	.60
17	Willie Stargell	.60
18	Billy Williams	.50

1993 Action Packed 24-Kt. Gold

The first 46 cards of AP's All-Star Gallery Series II, along with the special Abbott & Costello card were produced in a limited gold edition as random pack inserts. Labeled "24-Kt. Gold" on front, the cards have the same format and design as the regular-issue, except the embossed front photo and incuse stats on back are on solid-gold foil. Each gold card carries a black ink-jetted serial number on back from within an edition of either 500 or 1,000.

		NM/M
	Complete Set (47):	80.00
	Common Player:	2.00
85	Cy Young	3.00
86	Honus Wagner	4.00
87	Christy Mathewson	4.00
88	Ty Cobb	6.00
89	Eddie Collins	2.00
90	Walter Johnson	4.00
91	Tris Speaker	2.00
92	Grover Alexander	2.00
93	Edd Roush	2.00
94	Babe Ruth	16.00
95	Rogers Hornsby	2.00
96	Pie Traynor	2.00
97	Lou Gehrig	10.00
98	Mickey Cochrane	2.00
99	Lefty Grove	2.00
100	Jimmie Foxx	3.00
101	Tony Lazzeri	2.00
102	Mel Ott	2.00
103	Carl Hubbell	2.00
104	Al Lopez	2.00
105	Lefty Gomez	2.00
106	Dizzy Dean	3.00
107	Hank Greenberg	3.00
108	Joe Medwick	2.00
109	Arky Vaughan	2.00
110	Bob Feller	3.00
111	Hal Newhouser	2.00
112	Early Wynn	2.00
113	Bob Lemon	2.00
114	Red Schoendienst	2.00
115	Satchel Paige	4.00
116	Whitey Ford	4.00
117	Eddie Mathews	2.00
118	Harmon Killebrew	2.00
119	Roberto Clemente	12.00
120	Brooks Robinson	2.00
121	Don Drysdale	2.00
122	Luis Aparicio	2.00
123	Willie McCovey	2.00
124	Juan Marichal	2.00
125	Gaylord Perry	2.00
126	Catfish Hunter	2.00
127	Jim Palmer	2.00
128	Rod Carew	2.00
129	Tom Seaver	2.00
130	Rollie Fingers	2.00
168	Who's on First? (Lou Costello, Bud Abbott)	3.00

1993 Action Packed Tom Seaver Prototypes

Tom Seaver's career was highlighted in this five-card promo set. Each card has an embossed front color photo surrounded by three gold pinstripes and a red border. Seaver's name is in red in a gold bar at bottom. Backs are printed in black and gold with a white undertype reading "1993 Prototype." Backs have biographical and career data, lifetime stats and a few sentences of career highlights. Cards have a "TS" prefix to the card number.

		NM/M
	Complete Set (5):	8.00
	Common Card:	2.00
1	The Franchise	2.00
2	Amazin' Mets	3.25
3	A Tearful Goodbye	2.00
4	Tom Terrific	2.00
5	Dazzling the Windy City	2.00

1983 Affiliated Food Rangers

This set, featuring the Texas Rangers, was issued as a promotion by the Affiliated Food Stores chain of Arlington, Texas. Complete sets were given to youngsters 13 and under at the September 3 Rangers game. Cards measure 2-3/8" x 3-1/2" and feature a full-color photo on the front. Also on the front, located inside a blue box, is the player's name, uniform number, and "1983 Rangers." Backs have a small player photo plus biographical and statistical information, along with the Affiliated logo and a brief promotional message. A total of 10,000 sets was reportedly printed. Cards are numbered by the players' uniform numbers in the checklist that follows.

		NM/M
	Complete Set (28):	6.00
	Common Player:	.25
1	Bill Stein	.25
2	Mike Richardt	.25
3	Wayne Tolleson	.25
5	Billy Sample	.25
6	Bobby Jones	.25
7	Bucky Dent	.35
8	Bobby Johnson	.25
9	Pete O'Brien	.25
10	Jim Sundberg	.25
11	Doug Rader	.25
12	Dave Hostetler	.25
14	Larry Biittner	.25
15	Larry Parrish	.25
17	Mickey Rivers	.30
21	Odell Jones	.25
24	Dave Schmidt	.25
25	Buddy Bell	.35
26	George Wright	.25
28	Frank Tanana	.25
29	John Butcher	.25
32	Jon Matlack	.25
40	Rick Honeycutt	.25
41	Dave Tobik	.25
44	Danny Darwin	.25
46	Jim Anderson	.25
48	Mike Smithson	.25
49	Charlie Hough	.30
---	Coaching Staff (Rich Donnelly, Glenn Ezell, Merv Rettenmund, Dick Such, Wayne Terwilliger)	.25

1990 Agfa Film

This "old-timers" set was distributed in three-card packs with the purchase of Agfa film. Produced by Michael Schecter Associates, whose logo appears on the back, the cards were not licensed by Major League Baseball, so team logos had to be eliminated from the photos. Cards have a white background with the film company's logos in the upper corners. Backs are in black-and-white and have full major league regular season and post-season stats.

		NM/M
	Complete Set (22):	7.50
	Common Player:	.50
1	Willie Mays	2.00
2	Carl Yastrzemski	1.00
3	Harmon Killebrew	1.00
4	Joe Torre	.50
5	Al Kaline	1.00
6	Hank Aaron	2.00
7	Rod Carew	.75
8	Roberto Clemente	2.50
9	Luis Aparicio	.75
10	Roger Maris	1.00
11	Joe Morgan	.75
12	Maury Wills	.50
13	Brooks Robinson	1.00
14	Tom Seaver	.75
15	Steve Carlton	.75
16	Whitey Ford	.75
17	Jim Palmer	.75
18	Rollie Fingers	.75
19	Bruce Sutter	.75
20	Willie McCovey	.75
21	Mike Schmidt	1.50
22	Yogi Berra	1.00

1990 All American Baseball Team

Produced by Mike Schecter Associates, this 24-card set includes many of the top players in the game. Team logos are airbrushed from the color photo on front, which is surrounded by a red, white and blue border and the MLB Players' Association logo. The backs are printed in blue on white stock, with a facsimile autograph appearing above the statistics.

		NM/M
	Complete Set (24):	20.00
	Common Player:	.50
1	George Brett	1.50
2	Mark McGwire	3.00
3	Wade Boggs	1.25
4	Cal Ripken, Jr.	4.00
5	Rickey Henderson	1.00
6	Dwight Gooden	.50
7	Bo Jackson	1.25
8	Roger Clemens	1.50
9	Orel Hershiser	.50
10	Ozzie Smith	1.25
11	Don Mattingly	2.00
12	Kirby Puckett	1.25
13	Robin Yount	1.25
14	Tony Gwynn	1.25
15	Jose Canseco	.60

LIFE GRAND SLAM

16	Nolan Ryan	4.00
17	Ken Griffey Jr.	2.50
18	Will Clark	.50
19	Ryne Sandberg	1.25
20	Kent Hrbek	.50
21	Carlton Fisk	1.00
22	Paul Molitor	1.00
23	Dave Winfield	1.00
24	Andre Dawson	.60

1987 Allstate Insurance

This six-card set was the second promotional series of baseball cards created by Allstate Insurance graphic artist Ray Lending for internal use by the company. Modeled after the famous "Diamond Stars" from the 1930s, this set features full-color player portraits of legendary sluggers. "Life Grand Slam" (the promotion theme) is printed beneath the player portrait and the player's name appears in an upper corner. Black and white backs provide personal information, player profiles and career highlights; 15,000 sets of the cards were distributed, although only a few filtered into the collecting hobby. Cards measure 2-3/4" x 3-5/8" in size. Full-color 22" x 28" reproductions of the cards in this set were produced in poster format.

		NM/M
	Complete Set (6):	75.00
	Common Player:	10.00
(1)	Hank Aaron	12.00
(2)	Joe DiMaggio	15.00
(3)	Jimmie Foxx	10.00
(4)	Lou Gehrig	15.00
(5)	Babe Ruth	20.00
(6)	Ted Williams	15.00

1994 AMC Theaters S.F. Giants

This series of large-format (about 4-1/4" x 11"), blank-back photocards was sponsored by a Bay Area movie house chain. Cards have black-and-white action photos at center with player identification below. At top is a team logo, at bottom is a sponsor's logo. The unnumbered cards are checklisted here in alphabetical order.

		NM/M
	Complete Set (33):	30.00
	Common Player:	1.00
(1)	Dusty Baker	1.25
(2)	Rod Beck (Ready to pitch.)	1.00
(3)	Rod Beck (Piching follow through.)	1.00
(4)	Mike Benjamin	1.00
(5)	Todd Benzinger	1.00
(6)	Barry Bonds ('93 jersey)	9.00
(7)	Barry Bonds ('94 jersey)	9.00
(8)	Dave Burba	1.00
(9)	John Burkett	1.00
(10)	Mark Carreon	1.00
(11)	Royce Clayton	1.00
(12)	Steve Frey	1.00
(13)	Bryan Hickerson	1.00
(14)	Mike Jackson	1.00
(15)	Darren Lewis	1.00
(16)	Kirt Manwaring	1.00
(17)	Dave Martinez ('93 jersey)	1.00
(18)	Dave Martinez ('94 jersey)	1.00
(19)	Willie McGee	1.00
(20)	Rich Monteleone	1.00
(21)	John Patterson	1.00
(22)	Mark Portugal (Negative reversed, pitching lefty.)	1.00
(23)	Mark Portugal (Correct, pitching righty.)	1.00
(24)	Jeff Reed	1.00
(25)	Kevin Rogers/Standing	1.00
(26)	Kevin Rogers/Pitching	1.00
(27)	Steve Scarsone	1.00

ORIGINS OF BASEBALL
BID McPHEE

(28)	Bill Swift	1.00
(29)	Robby Thompson ('93 jersey)	1.00
(30)	Robby Thompson ('94 jersey)	1.00
(31)	Salomon Torres	1.00
(32)	Matt Williams/Btg	1.50
(33)	Matt Williams/Fldg	1.50

1994 American Archives Origins of Baseball

This collectors' issue presents the history of baseball in America from 1744-1899. Sold in box-set form only, the cards are in standard 2-1/2" x 3-1/2" format. Fronts feature sepia-toned photos and line-art on a black background. Backs have a lengthy narrative, also printed in sepia on black. Both sides are UV coated. Individual cards feature early players, team photos, game action scenes or other historical vignettes. The set was produced by American Archives.

		NM/M
	Complete Set (101):	6.00
	Common Card:	.10
1	Abner Doubleday	.10
2	Doubleday Field	.10
3	Rounders 1744	.10
4	Early Baseball 700 A.D.	.10
5	The Knickerbockers	.10
6	Alex Cartwright	.10
7	Baseball in the 1850s	.10
8	Social Clubs	.10
9	Brooklyn Eckfords	.10
10	New England Baseball	.10
11	Henry Chadwick	.10
12	Brooklyn Excelsiors	.10
13	Abraham Lincoln	.10
14	Andrew Johnson	.10
15	First Enclosed Park	.10
16	Brooklyn Atlantics	.10
17	James Creighton	.10
18	Baseball in the 1860s	.10
19	1869 Red Stockings	.10
20	Cincinnati Celebration	.10
21	Harry Wright	.10
22	Boston Ball Club 1872	.10
23	Arthur Cummings	.10
24	William Hulbert	.10
25	George Wright	.10
26	Albert Spalding	.10
27	Albert Bushong	.10
28	Bid McPhee	.10
29	James O'Rourke	.10
30	Pud Galvin	.10
31	Edwin Bligh	.10
32	William Purcell	.10
33	Roger Connor	.10
34	Cincinnati Ball Club 1882	.10
35	Peter Browning	.10
36	William Gleason	.10
37	Paul Hines	.10
38	Baseball in the 1880s	.10
39	Robert Carruthers	.10
40	New York Metropolitans	.10
41	St. George's Field	.10
42	Charles Radbourne	.10
43	George Andrews	.10
44	William Hoy	.10
45	Chicago Ball Club 1886	.10
46	Cap Anson	.10
47	John Clarkson	.10
48	Mike Kelly	.10
49	Buffalo Bisons 1887	.10
50	Moses Walker	.10
51	Detroit Ball Club 1887	.10
52	Little League	.10
53	Louisville Ball Club 1888	.10
54	John Farrell	.10
55	Walter Latham	.10
56	Fred Dunlap	.10
57	Tim Keefe	.10
58	Cincinnati Ball Club 1888	.10
59	1889 World Tour	.10
60	Dan Brouthers	.10
61	John M. Ward	.10
62	Albert Spalding	.10
63	The Baseball Cap	.10
64	Tom Esterbrook	.10
65	Mark Baldwin	.10
66	Tony Mullane	.10
67	John Glasscock	.10

68	Amos Rusie	.10
69	Jake Beckley	.10
70	Jimmy Collins	.10
71	Charles Comiskey	.10
72	Tom Connolly	.10
73	Mickey Welch	.10
74	Ed Delahanty	.10
75	Hugh Duffy	.10
76	Buck Ewing	.10
77	Clark Griffith	.10
78	Kid Nichols	.10
79	Billy Hamilton	.10
80	Ban Johnson	.10
81	Willie Keeler	.10
82	Bobby Wallace	.10
83	Napoleon Lajoie	.10
84	Connie Mack	.10
85	Fred Clarke	.10
86	Tommy McCarthy	.10
87	John McGraw	.10
88	Jesse Burkett	.10
89	Frank Chance	.10
90	Mordecai Brown	.10
91	New York Nationals	.10
92	Jack Chesbro	.10
93	Sam Thompson	.10
94	Boston v. New York 1891	.10
95	Rube Waddell	.10
96	Joel Kelley	.10
97	Addie Joss	.10
98	The Boston Beaneaters	.10
99	Baltimore Baseball Club	.10
100	The Game in 1899	.10
----	Bibliography	.10

1989 Ames 20/20 Club

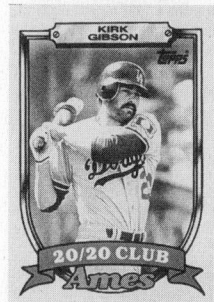

This 33-card set was produced by Topps for the Ames toy store chain. As its name implies, the special boxed set highlights players who have recorded 20 home runs and 20 stolen bases in the same season. The glossy cards feature action or posed photos on the front with the player's name at the top and "Ames 20/20 Club" along the bottom. The Topps logo appears in the upper-right corner. Backs have lifetime stats, biographical data and career highlights.

		NM/M
Complete Set (33):		4.00
Common Player:		.10
1	Jesse Barfield	.10
2	Kevin Bass	.10
3	Don Baylor	.10
4	George Bell	.10
5	Barry Bonds	2.00
6	Phil Bradley	.10
7	Ellis Burks	.10
8	Jose Canseco	.25
9	Joe Carter	.10
10	Kal Daniels	.10
11	Eric Davis	.10
12	Mike Davis	.10
13	Andre Dawson	.25
14	Kirk Gibson	.10
15	Pedro Guerrero	.10
16	Rickey Henderson	.45
17	Bo Jackson	.25
18	Howard Johnson	.10
19	Jeffrey Leonard	.10
20	Kevin McReynolds	.10
21	Dale Murphy	.25
22	Dwayne Murphy	.10
23	Dave Parker	.10
24	Kirby Puckett	.60
25	Juan Samuel	.10
26	Ryne Sandberg	.60
27	Mike Schmidt	.75
28	Darryl Strawberry	.10
29	Alan Trammell	.10
30	Andy Van Slyke	.10
31	Devon White	.10
32	Dave Winfield	.45
33	Robin Yount	.45

1990 Ames All-Stars

This 33-card boxed set was the second annual issue produced by Topps for the Ames toy store chain. The cards measure 2-1/2" x 3-1/2" and have a high-gloss finish on front. The set's checklist comprises the active career leaders in runs produced per game. Backs have a green striped background and present player personal data and seasonal major league stats. Issue price for the set was $2.

		NM/M
Complete Set (33):		4.00
Common Player:		.10
1	Dave Winfield	.50
2	George Brett	.75
3	Jim Rice	.25
4	Dwight Evans	.10
5	Robin Yount	.50
6	Dave Parker	.10
7	Eddie Murray	.50
8	Keith Hernandez	.10
9	Andre Dawson	.25
10	Fred Lynn	.10
11	Dale Murphy	.35
12	Jack Clark	.10
13	Rickey Henderson	.50
14	Paul Molitor	.50
15	Cal Ripken	1.50
16	Wade Boggs	.60
17	Tim Raines	.10
18	Don Mattingly	.75
19	Kent Hrbek	.10
20	Kirk Gibson	.10
21	Julio Franco	.10
22	George Bell	.10
23	Darryl Strawberry	.10
24	Kirby Puckett	.60
25	Juan Samuel	.10
26	Alvin Davis	.10
27	Joe Carter	.10
28	Eric Davis	.10
29	Jose Canseco	.40
30	Wally Joyner	.10
31	Will Clark	.10
32	Ruben Sierra	.10
33	Danny Tartabull	.10

1999 Anaheim Angels Police

Sponsored by the Santa Ana district of the California Highway Patrol, five of the cards in this set feature players photographed with police officers. The 2-1/2" x 3-1/2" cards have borderless photos on two sides, with dark blue and gold stripes bearing player identification. The team and CHP logos are in opposite corners. Backs have a smaller version of the front photo along with player data, career information and a safety message.

		NM/M
Complete Set (10):		12.50
Common Player:		.50
1	Chuck Finley	.50
2	Shigetosi Hasegawa	.50
3	Gary DiSarcina	.50
4	Darin Erstad	2.00
5	Mo Vaughn	.50
6	Tim Salmon (W/officers)	1.00
7	Troy Percival (W/officers)	.50
8	Jim Edmonds (W/officers)	3.00
9	Troy Glaus (W/officers)	5.00
10	Santa Ana CHPs	.25

2000 Anaheim Angels Police

The California Highway Patrol sponsored this promotional set given away at an Angels game. Standard-size cards have color game-action photos which are borderless on top and right. At left and bottom are dark blue and gold stripes. A CHP badge logo appears in the lower-right. Backs have a monochrome version of the front photo, player personal data and career information and a CHP Designated Driver logo at bottom. The back photos on Jim Edmonds' and Troy Percival's cards were switched.

		NM/M
Complete Set (33):		4.00
Common Player:		.10
1	Chuck Finley	1.00
2	Shigetosi Hasegawa	1.00
3	Gary Disarcina	1.00
4	Darin Erstad	2.00
5	Mo Vaughn	1.00
6	Tim Salmon	2.00
7	Troy Percival	1.00
8	Jim Edmonds	2.00
9	Troy Glaus	4.00
10	CHP San Ana Area Police Officers	1.00

2000 APBA Super Stars Baseball

In the premiere edition of its board game for children, APBA included six player-image game pieces and 30 player cards, one from each team. The irregularly shaped game pieces are 1-11/16" at their widest point and 2-5/16" tall. The same player action picture appears on each side on a brightly colored background. The player cards are round-cornered, 2-1/2" x 3-1/2", with a game-action photo and green borders. The game's APBA Andy logo appears at lower-left. Backs have a few personal data and dice-throw results chart used to play the game. Player cards are unnumbered and listed here in alphabetical order. Retail price at time of issue was $19.95.

		NM/M
Complete Game:		10.00
Common Game Piece:		.50
Common Player Card:		.25
(1)	Barry Bonds	.75
(2)	Nomar Garciaparra	.45
(3)	Ken Griffey Jr.	.50
(4)	Mark McGwire	.60
(5)	Mike Piazza	.50
(6)	Alex Rodriguez	.60
(1)	Roberto Alomar	.30
(2)	Jeff Bagwell	.40
(3)	Barry Bonds	.75
(4)	Jeromy Burnitz	.25
(5)	Carlos Delgado	.35
(6)	Jermaine Dye	.25
(7)	Cliff Floyd	.25
(8)	Jason Giambi	.35
(9)	Juan Gonzalez	.30
(10)	Shawn Green	.30
(11)	Ken Griffey Jr.	.50
(12)	Vladimir Guerrero	.40
(13)	Tony Gwynn	.45
(14)	Todd Helton	.30
(15)	Derek Jeter	.75
(16)	Randy Johnson	.40
(17)	Chipper Jones	.45
(18)	Jason Kendall	.25
(19)	Matt Lawton	.25
(20)	Pedro Martinez	.40
(21)	Mark McGwire	.60
(22)	Mike Piazza	.50
(23)	Cal Ripken Jr.	.75
(24)	Alex Rodriguez	.60
(25)	Ivan Rodriguez	.30
(26)	Scott Rolen	.30
(27)	Sammy Sosa	.45
(28)	Frank Thomas	.35
(29)	Greg Vaughn	.25
(30)	Mo Vaughn	.25

1996 Arby's Cleveland Indians

These cards honor, according to the logo on front, "1995 Tribe Milestones." Fronts are bordered in black with the action photo vignetted in black. The player's milestone is printed in white on a red strip at bottom. Backs have a large baseball, bat and glove in the background with a color portrait at top. A diamond shaped area at center has stats. Cello-wrapped cards were available one per week with a purchase.

		NM/M
Complete Set (8):		10.00
Common Player:		1.00
1	Eddie Murray (3,000th Hit)	3.00
2	Orel Hershiser (L.C.S. MVP in Both Leagues)	1.00
3	Manny Ramirez (Silver Slugger)	1.00
4	Jose Mesa (Saves Record)	1.00
5	Kenny Lofton (Gold Glove/Most Steals)	1.00
6	Omar Vizquel (3rd Straight Gold Glove)	1.00
7	Albert Belle (50/50 Season)	1.00
8	Carlos Baerga (.310+ Ave. Four Straight Years)	1.00

1997 AT&T Ambassadors of Baseball

Al Hrabosky

Taking over for the tour previously sponsored by MCI, AT&T brought a visiting team of former major league ballplayers to overseas military bases in 1997, where they played base teams in exhibition games. Card fronts feature photos (with uniform logos airbrushed away) from the players' major league days, with AT&T and Ambassadors Tour logos. Backs have typical player data.

		NM/M
Complete Set (4):		30.00
Common Player:		6.00
(1)	Jesse Barfield	6.00
(2)	Darrell Evans	12.00
(3)	Al Hrabosky	6.00
(4)	Jerry Koosman	12.00

1981 Atlanta Braves Police

Hank Aaron
Outfield
6-0—189

The first Atlanta Braves police set was a cooperative effort of the team, Hostess, Coca-Cola and the Atlanta Police Department. Card fronts feature full-color photos of 27 different Braves and manager Bobby Cox. Police and team logos are on the card backs. Card backs offer capsule biographies of the players, along with a tip for youngsters. The 2-5/8" x 4-1/8" cards are numbered by uniform number. Terry Harper (#19) appears to be somewhat scarcer than the other cards in the set. Reportedly, 33,000 sets were printed.

		NM/M
Complete Set (27):		10.00
Common Player:		.25
1	Jerry Royster	.25
3	Dale Murphy	3.00
5	Biff Pocoroba	.25
6	Bob Horner	.75
8	Bob Cox	.35
9	Luis Gomez	.25
10	Chris Chambliss	.25
15	Bill Nahorodny	.25
16	Rafael Ramirez	.25
17	Glenn Hubbard	.25
18	Claudell Washington	.25
19	Terry Harper (SP)	.75
23	Bruce Benedict	.25
24	John Montefusco	.25
25	Rufino Linares	.25
26	Gene Garber	.25
30	Brian Asselstine	.25
34	Larry Bradford	.25
35	Phil Niekro	1.50
37	Rick Camp	.25
39	Al Hrabosky	.25
40	Tommy Boggs	.25
42	Rick Mahler	.25
45	Ed Miller	.25
46	Gaylord Perry	1.50
49	Preston Hanna	.25
---	Hank Aaron	5.00

1982 Atlanta Braves Police

Dale Murphy (3)
Outfield

After their successful debut in 1981, the Atlanta Braves, the Atlanta Police Department, Coca-Cola and Hostess issued another card set in '82. This 30-card set is extremely close in format to the 1981 set and again measures 2-5/8" x 4-1/8". The full-color player photos are outstanding, and each card front also bears a statement marking the 1982 Braves' record-breaking 13-game win streak at the season's beginning. Card backs offer short biographies and "Tips from the Braves."

Brett Butler (22)
Outfielder

Sponsors logos are also included. Reportedly, only 8,000 of these sets were printed.

		NM/M
Complete Set (30):		10.00
Common Player:		.25
1	Jerry Royster	.25
3	Dale Murphy	4.00
5	Biff Pocoroba	.25
6	Bob Horner	.50
8	Randy Johnson	.25
9	Bob Watson	.25
10	Joe Torre	1.00
15	Chris Chambliss	.25
16	Claudell Washington	.25
17	Rafael Ramirez	.25
20	Glenn Hubbard	.25
22	Bruce Benedict	.25
23	Brett Butler	.50
24	Tommie Aaron	.50
25	Rufino Linares	.25
26	Gene Garber	.25
27	Larry McWilliams	.25
28	Larry Whisenton	.25
32	Steve Bedrosian	.25
35	Phil Niekro	1.50
37	Rick Camp	.25
38	Joe Cowley	.25
39	Al Hrabosky	.25
42	Rick Mahler	.25
43	Bob Walk	.25
45	Bob Gibson	3.00
49	Preston Hanna	.25
52	Joe Pignatano	.25
53	Dal Maxvill	.25
54	Rube Walker	.25

1983 Atlanta Braves Police

An almost exact replica of their 1982 set, the 1983 Atlanta Braves police set includes 30 cards numbered by uniform. Sponsors Hostess, Coca-Cola and the Atlanta Police Department returned for the third year. The cards are again 2-5/8" x 4-1/8", with full-color photos and police and team logos on the card fronts. A statement noting the team's 1982 National League Western Division title is the key difference on the card fronts. As in 1982, 8,000 sets were reportedly printed.

		NM/M
Complete Set (30):		6.00
Common Player:		.15
1	Jerry Royster	.15
3	Dale Murphy	3.00
5	Biff Pocoroba	.15
6	Bob Horner	.25
8	Randy G. Johnson	.15
9	Bob Watson	.15
10	Joe Torre	.50
15	Chris Chambliss	.15
16	Ken Smith	.15
17	Claudell Washington	.15
18	Rafael Ramirez	.15
19	Glenn Hubbard	.15
20	Terry Harper	.15
22	Bruce Benedict	.15
23	Brett Butler	.15
24	Larry Owen	.15
26	Gene Garber	.15
27	Pascual Perez	.15
29	Craig McMurtry	.15
32	Steve Bedrosian	.15
33	Pete Falcone	.15
35	Phil Niekro	1.00
36	Sonny Jackson	.15
37	Terry Forster	.15
42	Bob Gibson	2.00
46	Rick Camp	.15
48	Rick Behenna	.15
51	Terry Forster	.15
52	Joe Pignatano	.15
53	Dal Maxvill	.15
54	Rube Walker	.15

1984 Atlanta Braves Police

Bob Gibson (45)
Coach

A fourth annual effort by the Braves, the Atlanta Police Department, Coca-Cola and Hostess, this 30-card set continued to be printed in a 2-5/8" x 4-1/8" format, with full-color photos plus team and police logos on the card fronts. For the first time, the cards also have a large logo and date in the upper right corner. Hostess and Coke logos again are on the card backs, with brief player information and a safety tip. Two cards in the set (Pascual Perez and Rafael Ramirez) were issued in Spanish. Cards were distributed two per week by Atlanta police officers. As in 1982 and 1983, a reported 8,000 sets were printed.

		NM/M
Complete Set (30):		8.00
Common Player:		.25
1	Jerry Royster	.25
3	Dale Murphy	3.00
5	Bob Horner	.40
6	Randy Johnson	.25
8	Bob Watson	.25
9	Joe Torre	.75
10	Chris Chambliss	.25
11	Mike Jorgensen	.25
15	Claudell Washington	.25
16	Rafael Ramirez	.25
17	Glenn Hubbard	.25
19	Terry Harper	.25
20	Bruce Benedict	.25
25	Alex Trevino	.25
26	Gene Garber	.25
27	Pascual Perez	.25
28	Gerald Perry	.25
29	Craig McMurtry	.25
31	Donnie Moore	.25
32	Steve Bedrosian	.25
33	Pete Falcone	.25
37	Rick Camp	.25
39	Len Barker	.25
42	Rick Mahler	.25
45	Bob Gibson	2.50
51	Terry Forster	.25
52	Joe Pignatano	.25
53	Dal Maxvill	.25
54	Rube Walker	.25
55	Luke Appling	2.00

1985 Atlanta Braves Police

Dale Murphy (3)
Outfielder

There are again 30 full-color cards in this fifth annual set. Hostess, Coca-Cola and the Atlanta Police Department joined the team as sponsors again for the 2-5/8" x 4-1/8" set. Card backs are similar to previous years, with the only difference on the fronts being a swap in position for the year and team logo. The cards are checklisted by uniform number.

	NM/M
Complete Set (30):	4.00
Common Player:	.25

1986 Atlanta Braves Police

Glenn Hubbard (17)
Second Base

2	Albert Hall	.25
3	Dale Murphy	3.00
5	Rick Cerone	.25
7	Bobby Wine	.25
10	Chris Chambliss	.25
11	Bob Horner	.45
12	Paul Runge	.25
15	Claudell Washington	.25
16	Rafael Ramirez	.25
17	Glenn Hubbard	.25
18	Paul Zuvella	.25
19	Terry Harper	.25
20	Bruce Benedict	.25
22	Eddie Haas	.25
24	Ken Oberkfell	.25
26	Gene Garber	.25
27	Pascual Perez	.25
28	Gerald Perry	.25
29	Craig McMurtry	.25
32	Steve Bedrosian	.25
33	Johnny Sain	.30
34	Zane Smith	.25
36	Brad Komminsk	.25
37	Rick Camp	.25
39	Len Barker	.25
40	Bruce Sutter	1.50
42	Rick Mahler	.25
51	Terry Forster	.25
52	Leo Mazzone	.25
53	Bobby Dews	.25

1986 Atlanta Braves Police

The Police Athletic League of Atlanta issued a 30-card full-color set featuring Braves players and personnel. Cards measure 2-5/8" x 4-1/8". Fronts include player photos with name, uniform number and position below the photo. Backs offer the 100th Anniversary Coca-Cola logo, player information, statistics and a safety related tip. This was the sixth consecutive year that the Braves issued a safety set available from police officers in Atlanta.

	NM/M
Complete Set (30):	4.00
Common Player:	.25
2	Russ Nixon	.25
3	Dale Murphy	3.00
4	Bob Skinner	.25
5	Billy Sample	.25
7	Chuck Tanner	.25
8	Willie Stargell	1.50
9	Ozzie Virgil	.25
10	Chris Chambliss	.25
11	Bob Horner	.25
14	Andres Thomas	.25
15	Claudell Washington	.25
16	Rafael Ramirez	.25
17	Glenn Hubbard	.25
18	Omar Moreno	.25
19	Terry Harper	.25
20	Bruce Benedict	.25
23	Ted Simmons	.25
24	Ken Oberkfell	.25
26	Gene Garber	.25
29	Craig McMurtry	.25
30	Paul Assenmacher	.25
33	Johnny Sain	.25
34	Zane Smith	.25
38	Joe Johnson	.25
40	Bruce Sutter	2.00
42	Rick Mahler	.25
44	David Palmer	.25
48	Duane Ward	.25
49	Jeff Dedmon	.25
52	Al Monchak	.25

1987 Atlanta Braves Fire Safety

Wildfire Prevention

These fire safety cards were given out at several different Atlanta games, with about 25,000 sets in all being distributed. The 4" x 6" cards feature Braves players in an oval frame, bordered in red, white and blue. Only the player's last name is shown on front. Backs contain the player's name, position and personal data plus a Smokey Bear cartoon fire safety message.

		NM/M
Complete Set (27):		4.00
Common Player:		.25
1	Zane Smith	.25
2	Charlie Puleo	.25
3	Randy O'Neal	.25
4	David Palmer	.25
5	Rick Mahler	.25
6	Ed Olwine	.25
7	Jeff Dedmon	.25
8	Paul Assenmacher	.25
9	Gene Garber	.25
10	Jim Acker	.25
11	Bruce Benedict	.25
12	Ozzie Virgil	.25
13	Ted Simmons	.25
14	Dale Murphy	3.00
15	Graig Nettles	.35
16	Ken Oberkfell	.25
17	Gerald Perry	.25
18	Rafael Ramirez	.25
19	Ken Griffey	.25
20	Andres Thomas	.25
21	Glenn Hubbard	.25
22	Damaso Garcia	.25
23	Gary Roenicke	.25
24	Dion James	.25
25	Albert Hall	.25
26	Chuck Tanner	.25
---	Smokey Bear Logo	
	Card/Checklist	.10

1986 Ault Foods Blue Jays Stickers

BELL

The Ault Foods Blue Jays set is comprised of 24 full-color stickers. Designed to be placed in a special album, the stickers measure 2" x 3" in size. The attractive album measures 9" x 12" and is printed on glossy stock. While the stickers carry no information except for the player's last name and uniform number, the 20-page album contains extensive personal and statistical information about each of the 24 players.

		NM/M
Complete Set (24):		12.50
Common Player:		.50
Album:		4.00
1	Tony Fernandez	1.00
5	Rance Mulliniks	.50
6	Damaso Garcia	.50
11	George Bell	1.50
12	Ernie Whitt	.50
13	Buck Martinez	.50
15	Lloyd Moseby	.50

16	Garth Iorg	.50
17	Kelly Gruber	.50
18	Jim Clancy	.50
22	Jimmy Key	1.00
23	Cecil Fielder	5.00
25	Steve Davis	.50
26	Willie Upshaw	.50
29	Jesse Barfield	.50
31	Jim Acker	.50
33	Doyle Alexander	.50
36	Bill Caudill	.50
37	Dave Stieb	1.00
39	Don Gordon	.50
44	Cliff Johnson	.50
46	Gary Lavelle	.50
52	Tom Henke	.50
53	Dennis Lamp	.50

1982 Authentic Sports Autographs Mickey Mantle Story

1968-Hits HR No. 529

This 72-card set chronicles the life of Mickey Mantle in contemporary photos, many from Mantle's own collection and many picturing him with such stars of the era as Maris, DiMaggio, Ted Williams, Mays, etc. A total of 20,000 sets was produced; 5,000 of them feature a genuine Mantle autograph on card #1 and 15,000 sets have no autograph. Backs of cards from the autographed sets are printed in blue while the unautographed sets have backs printed in red. Issue price was $25 for the autographed set, $13 for the unsigned version.

		NM/M
Comp. Set, #1 Auto. (72):		200.00
Comp. Set, Unauto. (72):		45.00
Common Card:		1.00
1	Header card	1.00
2	Mickey & Merlyn 12/23/51	1.00
3	Spring Training 1951	1.50
4	Spring Training 1951	1.50
5	Mickey's Mom, Mickey & Merlyn	1.00
6	4/15/51 1st Homer in NY	1.00
7	1951 - DiMaggio, Mantle, Williams	1.50
8	1951- Mickey signs for 1952	1.00
9	Martin & Mickey Jr. 4/12/52	1.00
10	Brothers Roy and Ray	1.00
11	Spring Training 1952	1.00
12	1952- Bauer, Hopp, Mantle	1.50
13	1952 Season	1.00
14	Mantle & Martin 1952 Series	1.50
15	Billy & Mickey 1953	1.50
16	Knee Injury 1953	1.00
17	1953 - Before knee surgery	1.00
18	New business 1953	1.00
19	1953 World Series Power	1.00
20	1953 The long Home Run	1.50
21	1955 Hall of Fame Game	1.50
22	1955	1.00
23	1955 - Skowron, Rizzuto, Mantle	1.50
24	1954 - Jackie Robinson at 1st	1.00
25	1956 - Mickey with Ted Williams	1.00
26	1955 - Skowron, Berra, Mantle	1.50
27	1956 - Mickey safe at first	1.00
28	1956 World Series	1.00
29	1957 - Yogi, Whitey, Mickey	1.00
30	1957 - Roy Sievers with Mickey	1.00
31	1957 World Series	1.00
32	1957 Hitchcock Award	1.50
33	1957 - Mickey with Cardinal Spellman	1.00
34	1957 - Singing with Teresa Brewer	1.00

1964 with the Giants

35	1957 - Brooks Robinson & Mickey	1.50
36	1958 World Series	1.00
37	1958 All Star Game with Banks	1.50
38	With Stengel 1959	1.50
39	1960 - With Roger Maris	1.50
40	1960 World Series	1.00
41	1961 All Star Game with Maris & Mays	1.00
42	Blanchard	1.50
43	1961 - with Maris & Mrs. Babe Ruth	1.50
44	1961 - Mickey Congratulates Maris	1.00
45	1961 - Maris & Mantle	1.00
46	400th Career HR 9/11/62	1.00
47	1962 World Series	1.50
48	1963 season	1.50
49	1963 World Series	1.50
50	1964 World Series	1.50
51	1964 - Pepitone, Ford, Mantle	1.00
52	1964 season	1.50
53	1965 Mickey's Day	1.50
54	1965 season	1.50
55	1966 - with Joe DiMaggio	1.50
56	Mantle family	1.00
57	1967 season	1.00
58	1968 - hits HR No. 529	1.00
59	1968 - Retirement	1.00
60	1968 - His farewell	1.50
61	Mickey's trophy room	1.00
62	1970 - Welcome back Coach	1.00
63	1973 - TV commercial	1.00
64	1974 visit	1.00
65	1974 visit	1.00
66	1974 Hall of Fame inductees	1.00
67	1979 Old Timers Game	1.00
68	1981 Old Timers Game	1.00
69	Family Day	1.00
70	The Mantle Swing	1.00
71	The Mantle Swing	1.00
72	The Mantle Swing	1.00

1983 Authentic Sports Autographs

These collectors' issue sets of a dozen cards each present the careers of 11 Hall of Famers in pictures and words. Each card measures 2-1/2" x 3-1/2" and has a black-and-white or color photo on front with a card title and red or green border graphics. Backs present a narrative of the player's career and some include a small portrait photo. Each set was made available in both an unautographed version and a version in which the No. 1 card was authentically autographed.

		NM/M
(1)	Hank Aaron Story	15.00
(1a)	Hank Aaron Story/Auto.	50.00
(2)	Yogi Berra Story	6.00
(2a)	Yogi Berra Story/Auto.	20.00
(3)	Joe DiMaggio Story	15.00
(3a)	Joe DiMaggio Story/ Auto.	150.00
(4)	Bob Feller Story	7.50
(4a)	Bob Feller Story/Auto.	15.00
(5)	Juan Marichal Story	7.50
(5a)	Juan Marichal Story/ Auto.	20.00
(6)	Willie Mays Story	10.00
(6a)	Willie Mays Story/Auto.	20.00
(7)	Johnny Mize Story	6.00
(7a)	Johnny Mize Story/ Auto.	15.00
(8)	Brooks Robinson Story	6.00
(8a)	Brooks Robinson Story/ Auto.	15.00
(9)	Frank Robinson Story	6.00
(9a)	Frank Robinson Story/ Auto.	20.00
(10)	Duke Snider Story	6.00
(10a)	Duke Snider Story/Auto.	20.00
(11)	Warren Spahn Story	6.00
(11a)	Warren Spahn Story/ Auto.	20.00

B

1998 Ball Park Detroit Tigers

Fans in attendance at the August 9 game at Tiger Stadium received this team set sponsored by Ball Park franks, the stadium hot dog concessionairre. Cards are standard 2-1/2" x 3-1/2" format printed on light cardboard. Fronts have color posed or action photos with white borders. Player identification is in a strip at left. Backs have a light blue background, overprinted in dark blue with the player's personal data, stats and a 1997 season highlight, along with the sponsor's logo and a picture of a moving baseball.

		NM/M
Complete Set (26):		9.00
Common Player:		.50
01	Gabe Alvarez	.50
02	Matt Anderson	.50
03	Paul Bako	.50
04	Trey Beamon	.50
05	Buddy Bell	.50
06	Geronimo Berroa	.50
07	Doug Bochtler	.50
08	Doug Brocail	.50
09	Raul Casanova	.50
10	Frank Castillo	.50
11	Frank Catalanotto	.50
12	Tony Clark	.50
13	Dean Crow	.50
14	Deivi Cruz	.50
15	Damion Easley	.50
16	Bryce Florie	.50
17	Luis Gonzalez	2.50
18	Seth Greisinger	.50
19	Bobby Higginson	.75
20	Brian Hunter	.50
21	Todd Jones	.50
22	Brian Moehler	.50
23	Brian Powell	.50
24	Joe Randa	.50
25	Sean Runyan	.50
26	Justin Thompson	.50

1994 Baltimore Orioles Program Cards

Virtually the entire O's organization, major and minor leaguers, was included in this season-long promotion. One of 12 nine-card sheets was inserted into the team's programs, which sold for $3. A reported 17,000 sets were produced. The sheets are unperforated and measure 7-1/2" x 10-1/2". Fronts have color game-action or posed photos within an orange border. A team logo is at top-right. At bottom is a black strip with the player's number (if a major leaguer), name and position in white. Backs are printed in black and orange on white with biographical details and complete major and minor league stats. The unnumbered cards are checklisted here alphabetically.

		NM/M
Complete Set, Sheets (12):		25.00
Complete Set, Singles (108):		25.00
Common Player:		.25
(1)	Manny Alexander	.25
(2)	Brady Anderson	.25
(3)	Matt Anderson	.25
(4)	Harold Baines	.25
(5)	Myles Barnden	.25
(6)	Kimera Bartee	.25
(7)	Juan Bautista	.25
(8)	Armando Benitez	.25
(9)	Joe Borowski	.25
(10)	Brian Brewer	.25
(11)	Brandon Bridgers	.25
(12)	Cory Brown	.25
(13)	Damon Buford	.25
(14)	Philip Byrne	.25
(15)	Rocco Cafaro	.25
(16)	Paul Carey	.25
(17)	Carlos Chavez	.25
(18)	Eric Chavez	.25
(19)	Steve Chitren	.25
(20)	Mike Cook	.25
(21)	Shawn Curran	.25
(22)	Kevin Curtis	.25
(23)	Joey Dawley	.25
(24)	Jim Dedrick	.25
(25)	Cesar Devarez	.25
(26)	Mike Devereaux	.25
(27)	Brian DuBois	.25
(28)	Keith Eaddy	.25
(29)	Mark Eichhorn	.25
(30)	Scott Emerson	.25
(31)	Vaughn Eshelman	.25
(32)	Craig Faulkner	.25
(33)	Sid Fernandez	.25
(34)	Rick Forney	.25
(35)	Jim Foster	.25
(36)	Jesse Garcia	.25
(37)	Mike Garguilo	.25
(38)	Rich Gedman	.25
(39)	Leo Gomez	.25
(40)	Rene Gonzalez	.25
(41)	Curtis Goodwin	.25
(42)	Kris Gresham	.25
(43)	Shane Hale	.25
(44)	Jeffrey Hammonds	.25
(45)	Jimmy Haynes	.25
(46)	Chris Hoiles	.25
(47)	Tim Hullett	.25
(48)	Matt Jarvis	.25
(49)	Scott Klingenbeck	.25
(50)	Rick Krivda	.25
(51)	David Lamb	.25
(52)	Chris Lemp	.25
(53)	T.R. Lewis	.25
(54)	Brian Link	.25
(55)	John Lombardi	.25
(56)	Rob Lukachyk	.25
(57)	Calvin Maduro	.25
(58)	Barry Manuel	.25
(59)	Lincoln Martin	.25
(60)	Scott McClain	.25
(61)	Ben McDonald	.25
(62)	Kevin McGehee	.25
(63)	Mark McLemore	.25
(64)	Miguel Mejia	.25
(65)	Feliciano Mercedes	.25
(66)	Jose Millares	.25
(67)	Brent Miller	.25
(68)	Alan Mills	.25
(69)	Jamie Moyer	.25
(70)	Mike Mussina	1.50
(71)	Sherman Obando	.25
(72)	Alex Ochoa	.25
(73)	John O'Donoghue	.25
(74)	Mike Oquist	.25
(75)	Bo Ortiz	.25
(76)	Billy Owens	.25
(77)	Rafael Palmeiro	2.00
(78)	Dave Paveloff	.25
(79)	Brad Pennington	.25
(80)	Bill Percibel	.25
(81)	Jim Poole	.25
(82)	Jay Powell	.25
(83)	Arthur Rhodes	.25
(84)	Matt Riemer	.25
(85)	Cal Ripken Jr.	5.00
(86)	Kevin Ryan	.25
(87)	Chris Sabo	.25
(88)	Brian Sackinsky	.25
(89)	Francisco Saneaux	.25
(90)	Jason Satre	.25
(91)	David Segui	.25
(92)	Jose Serra	.25
(93)	Larry Shenk	.25
(94)	Lee Smith	.25
(95)	Lonnie Smith	.25
(96)	Mark Smith	.25
(97)	Garrett Stephenson	.25
(98)	Jeff Tackett	.25
(99)	Brad Tyler	.25
(100)	Pedro Ulises	.25
(101)	Jack Voight	.25
(102)	Jim Walker	.25
(103)	B.J. Waszgis	.25
(104)	Jim Wawruck	.25
(105)	Mel Wearing	.25
(106)	Mark Williamson	.25
(107)	Brian Wood	.25
(108)	Gregg Zaun	.25

1984 Baseball Cards Magazine Repli-Cards

DALE MURPHY
outfielder   ATLANTA BRAVES

With its August 1984 issue, Baseball Cards Magazine pioneered the use of "repli-cards" to enhance feature articles and increase sales. The cards were printed on cardboard stock and stapled into the magazines. Most of the cards were done in the style of earlier popular card issues. though some featured original designs and others were reproductions of actual cards. Some of baseball's best artists' and photographers' work appears on the cards. The inclusion of repli-cards ceased after 1993 when abuses by other "publishers" caused baseball's licensors to threaten legal action. Values quoted are for single cards cut from the panel; complete panels or magazines command a premium. Cards are grouped by magazine issue and numbered with a month-designation.

		NM/M
Complete Set (3):		10.00
Aug.	Ted Williams (1953 Topps style)	4.50
Aug.	Dale Murphy (1953 Topps style)	3.50
Oct.	Mickey Mantle (1949 Bowman style)	6.00

1985 Baseball Cards Magazine Repli-Cards

CHUCK CONNORS

In three of its 1985 issues, Baseball Cards Magazine offered "repli-cards" to enhance feature articles and increase sales. The cards were printed on cardboard stock and stapled into the magazines. Original designs and reproductions of earlier cards were used. Values quoted are for single cards cut from the panel; complete panels or magazines command a premium. Cards are grouped by magazine issue and numbered with a month-designation.

		NM/M
Complete Set (6):		12.00
Common Player:		2.00
April	Chuck Connors (Original design.)	2.00
April	Chuck Connors (1952 Topps style)	2.00
June	Pete Rose (Reproduction 1965 Topps.)	3.00
June	Fritz Ackley, Steve Carlton (Reproduction 1965 Topps.)	2.00
Oct.	Mickey Mantle (Reproduction 1955 Bowman #202.)	4.00
Oct.	Ernie Banks (Reproduction 1955 Bowman #242.)	2.00

1986 Baseball Cards Magazine Repli-Cards

No. 1 IN A SERIES OF 2

© 1986 BBC MAGAZINE

In three of its 1986 issues, Baseball Cards Magazine offered "repli-cards" to enhance feature articles and increase sales. The cards were printed on cardboard stock and stapled into the magazines. Reproductions of existing cards and modern player cards done in the style of vintage issues were used. Values quoted are for single cards cut from the panel; complete panels or magazines command a premium. Cards are grouped by magazine issue and numbered with a month-designation.

		NM/M
Complete Set (12):		12.00
Common Player:		.50
April	Vince Coleman (Kondritz Trading Cards sample.)	.50
April	Vince Coleman (Kondritz Trading Cards sample.)	.50
June	Stan Musial (Reproduction 1953 Bowman)	2.00
June	Roy Campanella (Reproduction 1953 Bowman.)	1.00
June	Yogi Berra (Reproduction 1953 Bowman.)	1.50
Dec.	Don Mattingly (1951 Topps Red Back style)	3.00
Dec.	Wally Joyner (1951 Topps Red Back style)	.50
Dec.	Wade Boggs (1951 Topps All-Stars style)	.50
Dec.	Dwight Gooden (1951 Topps All-Stars style)	.50
Dec.	George Brett (Reproduction 1981 Donruss proof.)	3.00
Dec.	Reggie Jackson (Reproduction 1981 Donruss proof.)	2.50
Dec.	Lou Piniella (Reproduction 1982 Fleer proof.)	.75

1987 Baseball Cards Magazine Repli-Cards

DOUBLE TROUBLE
McGWIRE AND DAVIS

In four of its 1987 issues, Baseball Cards Magazine offered "repli-cards" to enhance feature articles and increase sales. The cards were printed on cardboard stock and stapled into the magazines. Original designs and modern player cards done in the style of vintage issues were used. Values quoted are for single cards cut from the panel; complete panels or magazines command a premium. Cards are grouped by magazine issue and numbered with a month-designation.

		NM/M
Complete Set (10):		14.00
Common Player:		.40
April	Don Mattingly (1983 Donruss style)	5.00
April	Don Mattingly (1983 Topps style)	5.00
Sept.	Ozzie Canseco (Original "Future Stars" design.)	.40
Sept.	Patrick Lennon (Original "Future Stars" design.)	.40

		NM/M
Oct.	Eric Davis (1951 Bowman style)	.75
Oct.	Bo Jackson (1951 Bowman style)	.75
Oct.	Stan Musial (1951 Bowman style)	1.50
Dec.	Dale Murphy (1981 Fleer style)	1.50
Dec.	Tim Raines (1981 Fleer style)	.50
Dec.	Double Trouble (Eric Davis, Mark McGwire) (1981 Fleer style)	2.50

1988 Baseball Cards Magazine Repli-Cards

Mickey Mantle
OUTFIELD, NEW YORK YANKEES

In six of its 1988 issues, Baseball Cards Magazine offered "repli-cards" to enhance feature articles and increase sales. The cards were printed on cardboard stock and stapled into the magazines. Original designs, reproductions and modern player cards done in the style of vintage issues were used. Values quoted are for single cards cut from the panel; complete panels or magazines command a premium. Cards are grouped by magazine issue and numbered with a month-designation.

		NM/M
Complete Set (16):		27.50
Common Player:		.40
Feb.	Babe Ruth (1936 Diamond Stars style)	1.50
Feb.	Wade Boggs (1936 Diamond Stars style)	1.50
Feb.	Mark McGwire (1936 Diamond Stars style; available only via mail-in offer)	4.00
April	Ted Williams (1952 Topps style)	1.50
April	Ted Williams (Reproduction 1954 Bowman #66.)	2.50
June	Joey Meyer (Original design.)	.40
June	Sam Horn (Original design.)	.40
Aug.	Roger "Rocket" Clemens (1941 Play Ball style)	2.50
Aug.	Kirk Gibson (1941 Play Ball style)	.40
Aug.	Jack Clark (1941 Play Ball style)	.40
Oct.	Mickey Mantle (1956 Bowman proof style)	7.50
Oct.	Jackie Robinson (1952 Bowman style)	1.50
Oct.	Dave Winfield (1974 Topps "Washington" style)	1.25
Dec.	Mickey Mantle (Reproduction 1952 Bowman.)	2.50
Dec.	Mickey Mantle (Reproduction 1951 Bowman.)	4.50
Dec.	Mickey Mantle (Reproduction 1952 Topps.)	6.00

1989 Baseball Cards Magazine Repli-Cards

kirby puckett

MINNESOTA TWINS
OUTFIELD

Beginning with its January 1989 issue, Baseball Cards Magazine began issuing its repli-cards in panels of six cards per month, creating an annual set of 72 insert cards. Con-

temporary players were presented in the designs of classic Topps sets of the 1950s-1970s. In 1989 the magazine's cards were in the style of 1959 Topps. Besides the individual player's cards, specialty cards included "Rookie Stars of 1989" and multi-player feature cards.

		NM/M
Complete Set (72):		20.00
Common Player:		.15
1	Keith Hernandez	.15
2	Will Clark	.15
3	Andres Galarraga	.15
4	Mark McGwire	1.50
5	Don Mattingly	1.00
6	Ricky Jordan (Rookie Stars)	.15
7	Juan Samuel	.15
8	Julio Franco	.15
9	Harold Reynolds	.15
10	Gregg Jefferies (Rookie Stars)	.15
11	Ryne Sandberg	.75
12	Lou Whitaker	.15
13	Ozzie Smith	.75
14	Gary Sheffield (Rookie Stars)	.25
15	Alan Trammell	.15
16	Cal Ripken Jr.	2.00
17	Barry Larkin	.15
18	Tony Fernandez	.15
19	Mike Schmidt	1.00
20	Wade Boggs	.75
21	Gary Gaetti	.15
22	Chris Sabo (Rookie Stars)	.15
23	Paul Molitor	.60
24	Carney Lansford	.15
25	Dave Winfield	.60
26	Darryl Strawberry	.15
27	Tony Gwynn	.75
28	Darryl Hamilton	.15
29	Jose Canseco	.45
30	Andre Dawson	.25
31	Kirby Puckett	.75
32	Cameron Drew (Rookie Stars)	.15
33	Robin Yount	.60
34	Ellis Burks	.15
35	Eric Davis	.15
36	Joe Carter	.15
37	George Bell	.15
38	Kevin McReynolds	.15
39	Tim Raines	.15
40	Luis Medina (Rookie Stars)	.15
41	Mike Greenwell	.15
42	Kal Daniels	.15
43	Dwight Gooden	.15
44	Roger Clemens	1.00
45	Nolan Ryan	2.00
46	Erik Hanson	.15
47	Orel Hershiser	.15
48	Bret Saberhagen	.15
49	Jimmy Key	.15
50	Frank Viola	.15
51	Bruce Hurst	.15
52	Norm Charlton (Rookie Stars)	.15
53	Ted Higuera	.15
54	Mark Langston	.15
55	Damon Berryhill	.15
56	Carlton Fisk	.60
57	Terry Steinbach	.15
58	Sandy Alomar (Rookie Stars)	.15
59	Benito Santiago	.15
60	Bob Boone	.15
61	Jerome Walton (Rookie Stars)	.15
62	Jaime Navarro (Rookie Stars)	.15
63	Ken Griffey Jr. (Rookie Stars)	1.50
64	Jim Abbott (Rookie Stars)	.15
65	Junior Felix (Rookie Stars)	.15
66	Tom Gordon	.15
67	Power Plus (Kirby Puckett, Don Mattingly)	.65
68	Fence Busters (Julio Franco, Eric Davis, Ruben Sierra)	.15
69	N.L. Hitting Kings (Will Clark, Tony Gwynn)	.25
70	Keystone Combo (Ozzie Smith, Ryne Sandberg)	.15
71	Dinger Duo (Howard Johnson, Kevin Mitchell)	.15
72	Texas Heat (Nolan Ryan, Mike Scott)	.75

1990 Baseball Cards Magazine Repli-Cards

PAUL MOLITOR
2B-3B

BREWERS

Beginning with its January 1989 issue, Baseball Cards Magazine began issuing its repli-cards in panels of six cards per month, creating an annual set of 72 insert cards. Contemporary players were presented in the designs of classic Topps sets of the 1950s-1970s. In 1990 the magazine's cards were in the style of 1969 Topps. Besides the individual player's cards, there were a number of multi-player "Rookie Stars" cards.

		NM/M
Complete Set (72):		25.00
Common Player:		.15
1	Craig Biggio	.15
2	Kevin Mitchell	.15
3	Orel Hershiser	.15
4	Will Clark	.15
5	Eric Davis	.15
6	Tony Gwynn	.75
7	Mike Scott	.15
8	Barry Larkin	.15
9	John Smoltz	.15
10	Glenn Davis	.15
11	Roberto Alomar	.25
12	Rick Reuschel	.15
13	N.L. West Rookie Stars (Eric Anthony, Ed Whited)	.15
14	N.L. West Rookie Stars (Andy Benes, Steve Avery)	.15
15	N.L. West Rookie Stars (John Wetteland, Joe Oliver)	.15
16	Giants Rookie Stars (Randy McCament, Greg Litton)	.15
17	Dodgers Rookie Stars (Jose Offerman, Jose Vizcaino)	.15
18	Reds Rookie Stars (Scott Scudder, Rosario Rodriguez)	.15
19	Darryl Strawberry	.15
20	Von Hayes	.15
21	Dwight Smith	.15
22	Howard Johnson	.15
23	Pedro Guerrero	.15
24	Tim Raines	.15
25	Ozzie Smith	.75
26	Barry Bonds	2.00
27	Jerome Walton	.15
28	Ryne Sandberg	.75
29	Bobby Bonilla	.15
30	Mark Grace	.15
31	Cards Rookie Stars (Todd Zeile, Alex Cole)	.15
32	N.L. East Rookie Stars (Pat Combs, Dean Wilkins)	.15
33	N.L. East Rookie Stars (Steve Carter, Jeff Huson)	.15
34	Cubs Rookie Stars (Greg Smith, Derrick May)	.15
35	Expos Rookie Stars (Marquis Grissom, Larry Walker)	.45
36	Mets Rookie Stars (Wally Whitehurst, Blaine Beatty)	.15
37	Ken Griffey Jr.	1.50
38	Kirby Puckett	.75
39	Julio Franco	.15
40	Ruben Sierra	.15
41	Bo Jackson	.25
42	Jose Canseco	.35
43	Dennis Eckersley	.50
44	Bret Saberhagen	.15
45	Wally Joyner	.15
46	Carlton Fisk	.60
47	Nolan Ryan	2.00
48	Rickey Henderson	.60
49	White Sox Rookie Stars (Robin Ventura, Sammy Sosa)	7.50
50	A.L. West Rookie Stars (John Orton, Scott Radinsky)	.15
51	A.L. West Rookie Stars (Bobby Rose, Bob Hamelin)	.15

52	Rangers Rookie Stars (Monty Fariss, Juan Gonzalez)	.50
53	Mariners Rookie Stars (Tino Martinez, Roger Salkeld)	.15
54	Twins Rookie Stars (Terry Jorgensen, Paul Sorrento)	.15
55	Don Mattingly	1.00
56	Roger Clemens	1.00
57	Cal Ripken	2.00
58	Robin Yount	.60
59	Wade Boggs	.75
60	Fred McGriff	.15
61	Cecil Fielder	.15
62	Ellis Burks	.15
63	Sandy Alomar	.15
64	Alan Trammell	.15
65	Steve Sax	.15
66	Paul Molitor	.60
67	Brewers Rookie Stars (Bert Heffernan, Matias Carillo)	.15
68	A.L. East Rookie Stars (Ben McDonald, John Olerud)	.25
69	A.L. East Rookie Stars (Mark Whiten, Phil Clark)	.15
70	Yankees Rookie Stars (Jim Leyritz, Kevin Maas)	.15
71	Indians Rookie Stars (Mark Lewis, Carlos Baerga)	.15
72	Orioles Rookie Stars (David Segui, Chris Hoiles)	.15

WHITE SOX
Frank Thomas   1st BASE

1991 Baseball Cards Magazine Repli-Cards

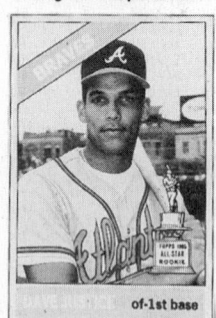

of-1st base

For the third year in 1991, Baseball Cards Magazine issued its repli-cards in panels of six cards per month, creating an annual set of 72 insert cards. Contemporary players were presented in the classic Topps design of 1966. Besides the individual players' cards, there are a number of multi-player feature cards and "Rookie Stars of 1991" multi-player cards, plus a 1952 Topps style card of Don Mattingly.

		NM/M
Complete Set (72):		18.00
Common Player:		.15
1	Eric Davis	.15
2	Cubs Rookie Stars (Lance Dickson, Hector Villanueva)	.15
3	Bobby Bonilla	.15
4	Len Dykstra	.15
5	John Franco	.15
6	Matt Williams	.15
7	Barry Bonds	2.00
8	Cards Rookie Stars (Geronimo Pena, Ray Lankford, Bernard Gilkey)	.15
9	Andre Dawson	.25
10	Dave Justice	.15
11	Triple Expos-ure (Larry Walker, Marquis Grissom, Delino DeShields)	.20
12	Howard Johnson	.15
13	Darryl Strawberry	.15
14	Astros Rookie Stars (Karl Rhodes, Andujar Cedeno, Mike Simms)	.15
15	Will Clark	.15
16	Barry Larkin	.15
17	Ramon Martinez	.15
18	Ron Gant	.15
19	Gregg Jefferies	.15
20	Giants Rookie Stars (Steve Decker, Steve Hosey, Mark Leonard)	.15
21	Todd Zeile	.15
22	Benito Santiago	.15
23	Eddie Murray	.60
24	Randy Myers	.15
25	Greg Maddux	.75

26	Phillies Rookie Stars (Mickey Morandini, Wes Chamberlain)	.15
27	Tim Wallach	.15
28	Dale Murphy	.25
29	Doug Drabek	.15
30	Kevin Mitchell	.15
31	Frank Viola	.15
32	Padres Rookie Stars (Rafael Valdez, Paul Faries)	.15
33	Hal Morris	.15
34	Pedro Guerrero	.15
35	Dwight Gooden	.15
36	Shawon Dunston	.15
37	Ken Griffey Jr.	1.00
38	Royals Rookie Stars (Sean Berry, Brian McRae)	.15
39	Roger Clemens	.85
40	Ellis Burks	.15
41	Robin Yount	.60
42	Frank Thomas	.60
43	Ruben Sierra	.15
44	Red Sox Rookie Stars (Mo Vaughn, Phil Plantier, Tim Naehring)	.15
45	Tim Raines	.15
46	Dave Parker	.15
47	Jose Canseco	.35
48	Glenn Davis	.15
49	Dave Winfield	.60
50	Chuck Knoblauch, Scott Leius, Willie Banks (Twins Rookie Stars)	.15
51	Joe Carter	.15
52	Cal Ripken	2.00
53	Carlton Fisk	.60
54	Julio Franco	.15
55	Don Mattingly	.85
56	Blue Jays Rookie Stars (Eddie Zosky, William Suero, Derek Bell)	.15
57	Sandy Alomar	.15
58	Juan Gonzalez	.30
59	Don Mattingly (1952 Topps style)	1.50
60	Mike Greenwell	.15
61	Chuck Finley	.15
62	Rangers Rookie Stars (Dean Palmer, Ivan Rodriguez, Gerald Alexander)	1.00
63	Scott Erickson	.15
64	Paul Molitor	.15
65	Triple Terrors (Cecil Fielder, Jose Canseco, Mark McGwire)	.60
66	Dennis Eckersley	.50
67	Brian Harper	.15
68	A.L. Rookie Stars (Bernie Williams, Wilson Alvarez) (No designation on front banner.)	.25
69	Robin Ventura	.15
70	Kirby Puckett	.75
71	Rafael Palmeiro	.50
72	Roberto Alomar	.15

1992 Baseball Cards Magazine Repli-Cards

The annual repli-card series inserted in Baseball Cards Magazine began in January with six-card panels each month. In May, panels were increased to eight cards and a UV coating was added to the front. Contemporary players were presented in the designs of classic Topps sets of the 1950s-1970s. In 1992 the magazine's cards were in the style of 1970 Topps. Besides the individual player's cards, specialty cards included "1992 Rookie Stars" multi-player and Team USA cards.

		NM/M
Complete Set (88):		20.00
Common Player:		.15
1	Eddie Murray	.50
2	Braves Rookie Stars (Ryan Klesko, Mark Wohlers)	.15
3	Barry Bonds	1.50
4	Will Clark	.15
5	Jose Canseco	.35

6	Ron Gant	.15
7	Ruben Sierra	.15
8	Reds Rookie Stars (Reggie Sanders, Mo Sanford)	.15
9	Terry Pendleton	.15
10	Hal Morris	.15
11	Kirby Puckett	.60
12	Paul Molitor	.50
13	Jack McDowell	.15
14	Dodgers Rookie Stars (Eric Karros, Tom Goodwin)	.15
15	Ramon Martinez	.15
16	Steve Avery	.15
17	Roger Clemens	.75
18	Jim Abbott	.15
19	Phil Plantier	.15
20	Giants Rookie Stars (Royce Clayton, Ted Wood)	.15
21	Frank Thomas	.50
22	Juan Gonzalez	.25
23	Felix Jose	.15
24	Chuck Knoblauch	.15
25	Tony Gwynn	.60
26	Julio Franco	.15
27	Greg Blosser, Frankie Rodriguez	.15
28	Wade Boggs	.60
29	Robin Ventura	.15
30	Shane Mack	.15
31	Roberto Alomar	.25
32	Don Mattingly	.75
33	Astros Rookie Stars (Ryan Bowen, Jeff Juden)	.15
34	Cal Ripken Jr.	1.50
35	Ozzie Smith	.60
36	Ken Griffey Jr.	1.00
37	Ivan Rodriguez	.40
38	Matt Williams	.15
39	Craig Biggio	.15
40	John Kruk	.15
41	George Brett	.75
42	Carlton Fisk	.50
43	Indians Rookie Stars (Kenny Lofton, Jim Thome)	.50
44	Andre Dawson	.25
45	Nolan Ryan	1.50
46	Robin Yount	.50
47	Ryne Sandberg	.60
48	Rickey Henderson	.50
49	Bobby Thigpen	.15
50	Dennis Eckersley	.40
51	Cards Rookie Stars (Brian Jordan, Dmitri Young)	.15
52	Jeff Reardon	.15
53	Bryan Harvey	.15
54	Tom Henke	.15
55	Lee Smith	.15
56	John Franco	.15
57	Cecil Fielder	.15
58	Darryl Strawberry	.15
59	Twins Rookie Stars (David McCarty, Scott Stahoviak)	.15
60	Mark McGwire	1.00
61	George Bell	.15
62	Fred McGriff	.15
63	Danny Tartabull	.15
64	Joe Carter	.15
65	Deion Sanders	.15
66	Roberto Alomar	.25
67	A.L. Rookie Stars (Eduardo Perez, Joe Vitiello, Bret Boone)	.15
68	Bip Roberts	.15
69	Ray Lankford	.15
70	Brady Anderson	.15
71	Tim Raines	.15
72	Marquis Grissom	.15
73	Dave Fleming	.15
74	Andy Benes	.15
75	Yankees Rookie Stars (Bob Wickman, Mark Hutton)	.15
76	Bill Swift	.15
77	Mike Mussina	.25
78	Donovan Osborne	.15
79	Juan Guzman	.15
80	Kevin Brown	.15
81	Charles Johnson (USA)	.15
82	Jeffrey Hammonds (USA)	.15
83	Rick Helling (USA)	.15
84	Chris Wimmer (USA)	.15
85	Darren Dreifort (USA)	.15
86	Calvin Murray (USA)	.15
87	Phil Nevin (USA)	.15
88	B.J. Wallace (USA)	.15

1993 Baseball Cards/Sports Cards Magazine Repli-Cards

SHORTSTOP
ORIOLES
CAL

The annual repli-card series began in Baseball Cards Magazine in 1989 continued in 1993 with eight-card panels of UV-coated repli-cards stapled into each monthly issue. (Only seven cards were included in July; there are two #32 and no #40.) Contemporary players were presented in the design of the classic 1968 Topps set. Backs are printed in black, white and yellow and include an investment advisory about the player's cards. Besides the individual player's repli-cards, there is a group of "1993 Rookie Stars" multi-player cards. Effective with its May issue, the magazine's title was changed to Sports Cards, the copyright line on back reflecting that change.

		NM/M
Complete Set (95):		25.00
Common Player:		.15
1	Andy Van Slyke	.15
2	Ruben Sierra	.15
3	Carlos Baerga	.15
4	Gary Sheffield	.30
5	Chuck Knoblauch	.15
6	Danny Tartabull	.15
7	Angels Rookie Stars (Chad Curtis, Tim Salmon)	.45
8	Darren Daulton	.15
9	Deion Sanders	.20
10	Pat Listach	.15
11	Albert Belle	.15
12	Frank Thomas	.60
13	Dave Hollins	.15
14	Braves Rookie Stars (Javy Lopez, Mike Kelly)	.15
15	Travis Fryman	.15
16	Edgar Martinez	.15
17	Barry Bonds	1.50
18	Dennis Eckersley	.50
19	Brady Anderson	.15
20	Fred McGriff	.15
21	Paul Molitor	.60
22	Juan Gonzalez	.30
23	Dodgers Rookie Stars (Bill Ashley, Mike Piazza)	1.50
24	Larry Walker	.15
25	Dave Winfield	.60
26	Robin Yount	.60
27	George Brett	.85
28	Jack Morris	.15
29	Eddie Murray	.50
30	Nolan Ryan	1.50
31	Carlton Fisk	.60
32a	Dale Murphy	.30
32b	Jeff Bagwell	.60
33	Eric Karros	.15
34	Roberto Alomar	.15
35	Robin Ventura	.15
36	Delino DeShields	.15
37	Ken Griffey Jr.	1.00
38	Eric Anthony	.15
39	Marquis Grissom	.15
41	Cecil Fielder	.15
42	Mark McGwire	1.25
43	Ryne Sandberg	.75
44	Kirby Puckett	.75
45	Cal Ripken Jr.	1.50
46	David McCarty	.15
47	Joe Carter	.15
48	Dean Palmer	.15
49	Jack McDowell	.15
50	Roger Clemens	.85
51	Cal Eldred	.15
52	Tom Glavine	.15
53	Steve Avery	.15
54	Mike Mussina	.15
55	Brien Taylor	.15
56	Mark Grace	.15
57	Ray Lankford	.15
58	Shane Mack	.15
59	Terry Pendleton	.15
60	Tony Gwynn	.75
61	Rafael Palmeiro	.15
62	Will Clark	.15
63	Wil Cordero	.15
64	Cliff Floyd	.15
65	Aaron Sele	.15

66	Chipper Jones	.75
67	Frank Rodriguez	.15
68	Ryan Klesko	.15
69	Manny Ramirez	.15
70	Carlos Delgado	.30
71	Paul Shuey	.15
72	Barry Bonds	1.50
73	Andre Dawson	.30
74	Paul Molitor	.60
75	Greg Maddux	.75
76	Wade Boggs	.75
77	Bryan Harvey	.15
78	Andres Galarraga	.15
79	Gregg Jefferies	.15
80	Mike Piazza	1.00
81	J.T. Snow	.15
82	Ivan Rodriguez	.50
83	Derrick May	.15
84	Tim Salmon	.15
85	Greg Vaughn	.15
86	Kenny Lofton	.15
87	John Olerud	.15
88	Sammy Sosa	.75
89	Lee Smith	.15
90	Matt Williams	.15
91	Don Mattingly	.85
92	Willie Greene	.15
93	Jim Abbott	.15
94	Mo Vaughn	.15
95	Randy Johnson	.15

1990-92 Baseball Cards Presents Repli-Cards

JON
JOHN OLERUD
John Olerud

Taking advantage of the boom in sports card collecting, Baseball Cards Magazine began a series of special newsstand magazine titles. Beginning with "Baseball Card Boom," dated February 1990, the series, officially known as "Baseball Cards Presents . . ." included baseball (and other sports) repli-cards in most of its issues through August 1992. Cards are listed here by issue in which they were inserted.

		NM/M
Complete Set (61):		27.50
Common Player:		.25
1	Don Mattingly	1.25
2	Dwight Gooden	.25
3	Jose Canseco	.35
4	Bo Jackson	.35
5	Ken Griffey Jr.	1.50
1	John Olerud	.50
2	Eric Anthony	.25
3	Greg Vaughn	.25
4	Todd Zeile	.25
5	Ben McDonald	.25
6	Deion Sanders (Mail-in offer only.)	.75
1	Mark Davis	.15
2	Bret Saberhagen	.25
3	Kirby Puckett	.65
4	Rickey Henderson	.50
5	Kevin Mitchell	.25
1	Cecil Fielder	.25
2	Rickey Henderson	.50
3	Barry Bonds	2.00
4	Ryne Sandberg	.65
5	Roger Clemens	1.00
1	Nolan Ryan	2.00
2	Eric Davis	.25
3	Ryne Sandberg	.75
4	Rickey Henderson	.50
5	Kevin Maas	.15
6	Dave Justice	.25
7	Jose Canseco	.35
8	Bo Jackson	.35
9	Roger Clemens	1.00
10	Ken Griffey Jr.	1.50
1	Babe Ruth (1936 Diamond Stars style)	1.00
1	Ted Williams (1952 Topps style)	.75
2	Rickey Henderson (1933 Goudey style)	.50
5	Roger Clemens (1941 Play Ball style)	1.00
325	Stan Musial (1951 Bowman style)	.65
11	Frank Thomas	.50
12	Dwight Gooden	.25
13	Robin Robinson/Basketball	.25
14	Will Clark	.50
15	Darryl Strawberry	.25

1992 The Baseball Enquirer

This set of "Mystery Interview" cards parodies baseball players and baseball cards. The 2-1/2" x 3-1/2" cards have caricatures of well-known players on front, surrounded by a gray border and a blank white name box. A blue "Fun Stuff" trademark is at bottom-right. Backs are printed in blue and black on white with a card number, another blank name box, issuer's trademarks and a mock interview with the player. Actual player names are not seen anywhere on the cards. Issued in 10-card polypacks at 49 cents, complete sets - 184,000 of them - were also issued at $5.

		NM/M
Complete Set (64):		7.50
Common Player:		.50
Pack (10):		.25
Box (36):		7.50
1	Bo Jackson	.65
2	Jose Canseco	.60
3	Mark Langston	.50
4	Billy Ripken	.60
5	David Justice	.50
6	Rob Deer	.50
7	Jack McDowell	.50
8	Cecil Fielder	.50
9	John Smoltz	.50
10	Will Clark	.50
11	Ken Caminiti	.50
12	Kent Hrbek	.50
13	Gregg Jefferies	.50
14	Bob Uecker	.75
15	Mike Greenwell	.50
16	No player	.05
17	Ken Griffey Jr.	.69
18	Robin Yount	.75
19	Joe DiMaggio	2.00
20	Mackey Sasser	.50
21	Dave Stewart	.50
22	Barry Bonds	3.00
23	Don Zimmer	.50
24	Jack Morris	.50
25	George Brett	1.50
26	Tommy Lasorda	.50
27	Whitey Ford	.50
28	Bill Buckner	.50
29	Ozzie Smith	1.00
30	Stump Merrill	.50
31	Randy Johnson	.75
32	George Bell	.50
33	Johnny Bench	1.00
34	Rickey Henderson	.75
35	Jack Clark	.50
36	Jim Palmer	.50
37	Lenny Dykstra	.50
38	George Steinbrenner	.50
39	Dave Stieb	.50
40	Nolan Ryan	3.00
41	Chris Sabo	.50
42	Unidentified player	.50
43	Kirby Puckett	1.00
44	Lou Piniella	.50
45	Wade Boggs	1.00
46	Andre Dawson	.50
47	Roger Clemens	1.25
48	Pete Rose	2.00
49	David Cone	.50
50	Warren Cromartie	.50
51	Unidentified Umpire	.50

16	Kevin Mitchell	.25
17	Tony Gwynn	.65
18	Cal Ripken Jr.	2.00
19	Michael Jordan	1.50
20	Don Mattingly	1.25
1	Frank Thomas	.50
2	Scott Erickson	.25
3	Terry Pendleton	.25
4	Cal Ripken	2.00
5	Barry Bonds	2.00
1	Frank Thomas	.50
2	Jeff Bagwell	.50
3	Cecil Fielder	.50
4	Ken Griffey Jr.	1.50
2	Juan Gonzalez	.35
1	Ryne Sandberg	.65
2	Phil Plantier	.25
3	Barry Larkin	.25
4	Cecil Fielder	.25
5	Dave Justice	.25

52	Phil Rizzuto	.50
53	Dan Gladden	.50
54	Mark Lemke	.50
55	Buck Rodgers	.50
56	Darryl Strawberry	.50
57	Rob Dibble	.50
58	Deion Sanders	.50
59	Tony Gwynn	1.00
60	Dale Murphy	.60
61	Albert Belle	.50
62	Don Mattingly	1.50
63	Andres Galarraga	.50
64	Babe Ruth	2.00

1980-88 Baseball Immortals

One of the most popular of the "collectors' issues," this set is produced with the permission of Major League Baseball by Renata Galasso Inc. and TCMA. The set features players in the Baseball Hall of Fame and was first issued in 1980. For several years thereafter the set was updated to include new inductees. The cards measure 2-1/2" x 3-1/2" and have colorful borders. The card fronts include the player's name, position and year of induction. The backs feature a short biography and a trivia question. The photos used are color; most players who were active before 1950 have colored black-and-white photos. The designation "first printing" appears on all cards issued in 1981 and after.

		NM/M
Complete 1980 Set (173):		15.00
Complete (199):		30.00
Common Player:		.10
1	Babe Ruth	2.00
2	Ty Cobb	1.00
3	Walter Johnson	.20
4	Christy Mathewson	.20
5	Honus Wagner	.20
6	Morgan Bulkeley	.10
7	Ban Johnson	.10
8	Larry Lajoie	.10
9	Connie Mack	.10
10	John McGraw	.10
11	Tris Speaker	.10
12	George Wright	.10
13	Cy Young	.10
14	Grover Alexander	.10
15	Alexander Cartwright	.10
16	Henry Chadwick	.10
17	Cap Anson	.10
18	Eddie Collins	.10
19	Charles Comiskey	.10
20	Candy Cummings	.10
21	Buck Ewing	.10
22	Lou Gehrig	1.50
23	Willie Keeler	.10
24	Hoss Radbourne	.10
25	George Sisler	.10
26	Albert Spalding	.10
27	Rogers Hornsby	.10
28	Judge Landis	.10
29	Roger Bresnahan	.10
30	Dan Brouthers	.10
31	Fred Clarke	.10
32	James Collins	.10
33	Ed Delahanty	.10
34	Hugh Duffy	.10
35	Hughie Jennings	.10
36	Mike "King" Kelly	.10
37	James O'Rourke	.10
38	Wilbert Robinson	.10
39	Jesse Burkett	.10
40	Frank Chance	.10
41	Jack Chesbro	.10
42	John Evers	.10
43	Clark Griffith	.10
44	Thomas McCarthy	.10
45	Joe McGinnity	.10
46	Eddie Plank	.10
47	Joe Tinker	.10
48	Rube Waddell	.10
49	Ed Walsh	.10
50	Mickey Cochrane	.10
51	Frankie Frisch	.10
52	Lefty Grove	.10
53	Carl Hubbell	.10
54	Herb Pennock	.10
55	Pie Traynor	.10
56	Three Finger Brown	.10
57	Charlie Gehringer	.10
58	Kid Nichols	.10
59	Jimmie Foxx	.10
60	Mel Ott	.10
61	Harry Heilmann	.10
62	Paul Waner	.10
63	Ed Barrow	.10
64	Chief Bender	.10
65	Tom Connolly	.10
66	Dizzy Dean	.10
67	Bill Klem	.10
68	Al Simmons	.10
69	Bobby Wallace	.10
70	Harry Wright	.10
71	Bill Dickey	.10
72	Rabbit Maranville	.10
73	Bill Terry	.10
74	Home Run Baker	.10
75	Joe DiMaggio	2.00
76	Gabby Hartnett	.10
77	Ted Lyons	.10
78	Ray Schalk	.10
79	Dazzy Vance	.10
80	Joe Cronin	.10
81	Hank Greenberg	.10
82	Sam Crawford	.10
83	Joe McCarthy	.10
84	Zack Wheat	.10
85	Max Carey	.10
86	Billy Hamilton	.10
87	Bob Feller	.10
88	Bill McKechnie	.10
89	Jackie Robinson	1.00
90	Edd Roush	.10
91	John Clarkson	.10
92	Elmer Flick	.10
93	Sam Rice	.10
94	Eppa Rixey	.10
95	Luke Appling	.10
96	Red Faber	.10
97	Burleigh Grimes	.10
98	Miller Huggins	.10
99	Tim Keefe	.10
100	Heinie Manush	.10
101	John Ward	.10
102	Pud Galvin	.10
103	Casey Stengel	.10
104	Ted Williams	1.00
105	Branch Rickey	.10
106	Red Ruffing	.10
107	Lloyd Waner	.10
108	Kiki Cuyler	.10
109	Goose Goslin	.10
110	Joe (Ducky) Medwick	.10
111	Roy Campanella	.20
112	Stan Coveleski	.10
113	Waite Hoyt	.10
114	Stan Musial	.50
115	Lou Boudreau	.10
116	Earle Combs	.10
117	Ford Frick	.10
118	Jesse Haines	.10
119	Dave Bancroft	.10
120	Jake Beckley	.10
121	Chick Hafey	.10
122	Harry Hooper	.10
123	Joe Kelley	.10
124	Rube Marquard	.10
125	Satchel Paige	.50
126	George Weiss	.10
127	Yogi Berra	.20
128	Josh Gibson	.10
129	Lefty Gomez	.10
130	Will Harridge	.10
131	Sandy Koufax	1.00
132	Buck Leonard	.10
133	Early Wynn	.10
134	Ross Youngs	.10
135	Roberto Clemente	2.00
136	Billy Evans	.10
137	Monte Irvin	.10
138	George Kelly	.10
139	Warren Spahn	.10
140	Mickey Welch	.10
141	Cool Papa Bell	.10
142	Jim Bottomley	.10
143	Jocko Conlan	.10
144	Whitey Ford	.10
145	Mickey Mantle	5.00
146	Sam Thompson	.10
147	Earl Averill	.10
148	Bucky Harris	.10
149	Billy Herman	.10
150	Judy Johnson	.10
151	Ralph Kiner	.10
152	Oscar Charleston	.10
153	Roger Connor	.10
154	Cal Hubbard	.10
155	Bob Lemon	.10
156	Fred Lindstrom	.10
157	Robin Roberts	.10
158	Ernie Banks	.25
159	Martin Dihigo	.10
160	Pop Lloyd	.10
161	Al Lopez	.10
162	Amos Rusie	.10
163	Joe Sewell	.10
164	Addie Joss	.10
165	Larry MacPhail	.10
166	Eddie Mathews	.10
167	Warren Giles	.10
168	Willie Mays	1.00
169	Hack Wilson	.10
170	Duke Snider	.20
171	Al Kaline	.10
172	Chuck Klein	.10
173	Tom Yawkey	.10
174	Bob Gibson	.10
175	Rube Foster	.10
176	Johnny Mize	.10
177	Hank Aaron	1.00
178	Frank Robinson	.10
179	Happy Chandler	.10
180	Travis Jackson	.10
181	Brooks Robinson	.10
182	Juan Marichal	.10
183	George Kell	.10
184	Walter Alston	.10
185	Harmon Killebrew	.10
186	Luis Aparicio	.10
187	Don Drysdale	.10
188	Pee Wee Reese	.10
189	Rick Ferrell	.10
190	Willie McCovey	.10
191	Ernie Lombardi	.10
192	Bobby Doerr	.10
193	Arky Vaughan	.10
194	Enos Slaughter	.10
195	Lou Brock	.10
196	Hoyt Wilhelm	.10
197	Billy Williams	.10
198	"Catfish" Hunter	.10
199	Ray Dandridge	.10

1990 Baseball Wit

This 108-card set was released in two printings. The first printing featured unnumbered cards and several errors. The second printing featured corrections and numbered cards. The set was available at several retail chains and feature trivia questions on the card backs. The set was dedicated to Little League baseball.

		NM/M
Complete Set (108):		12.50
Common Player:		.10
1	Orel Hershiser	.10
2	Tony Gwynn	.60
3	Mickey Mantle	2.50
4	Willie Stargell	.10
5	Don Baylor	.10
6	Hank Aaron	1.00
7	Don Larsen	.10
8	Lee Mazzilli	.10
9	Boog Powell	.10
10	Little League World Series	.10
11	Jose Canseco	.30
12	Mike Scott	.10
13	Bob Feller	.10
14	Ron Santo	.10
15	Mel Stottlemyre	.10
16	Shea Stadium	.10
17	Brooks Robinson	.25
18	Willie Mays	1.00
19	Ernie Banks	.30
20	Keith Hernandez	.10
21	Bret Saberhagen	.10
22	Hall of Fame	.10
23	Luis Aparicio	.10
24	Yogi Berra	.30
25	Manny Mota	.10
26	Steve Garvey	.10
27	Bill Shea	.10
28	Fred Lynn	.10
29	Todd Worrell	.10
30	Roy Campanella	.30
31	Bob Gibson	.10
32	Gary Carter	.10
33	Jim Palmer	.25
34	Carl Yastrzemski	.25
35	Dwight Gooden	.10
36	Stan Musial	.50
37	Rickey Henderson	.25
38	Dale Murphy	.25
39	Mike Schmidt	.75
40	Gaylord Perry	.10
41	Ozzie Smith	.60
42	Reggie Jackson	.75
43	Steve Carlton	.25
44	Jim Perry	.10
45	Vince Coleman	.10
46	Tom Seaver	.25
47	Marty Marion	.10
48	Frank Robinson	.25
49	Joe DiMaggio	1.50
50	Ted Williams	1.00
51	Rollie Fingers	.10
52	Jackie Robinson	1.00
53	Victor Raschi	.10
54	Johnny Bench	.25
55	Nolan Ryan	1.50
56	Ty Cobb	1.00
57	Harry Steinfeldt	.10
58	James O'Rourke	.10
59	John McGraw	.10
60	Candy Cummings	.10
61	Jimmie Foxx	.10
62	Walter Johnson	.25
63	1903 World Series	.10
64	Satchel Paige	.40
65	Bobby Wallace	.10
66	Cap Anson	.10
67	Hugh Duffy	.10
68	Buck Ewing	.10
69	Bobo Holloman	.10
70	Ed Delehanty (Delahanty)	.10
71	Dizzy Dean	.25
72	Tris Speaker	.10
73	Lou Gehrig	1.50
74	Wee Willie Keeler	.10
75	Cal Hubbard	.10
76	Eddie Collins	.10
77	Chris Von Der Ahe	.10
78	Sam Crawford	.10
79	Cy Young	.25
80	Johnny Vander Meer	.10
81	Joey Jay	.10
82	Zack Wheat	.10
83	Jim Bottomley	.10
84	Honus Wagner	.30
85	Casey Stengel	.10
86	Babe Ruth	1.50
87	John Lindemuth	.10
88	Max Carey	.10
89	Mordecai Brown	.10
90	1869 Red Stockings	.10
91	Rube Marquard	.10
92	Horse Radbourne	.10
93	Hack Wilson	.10
94	Lefty Grove	.10
95	Carl Hubbell	.10
96	A.J. Cartwright	.10
97	Rogers Hornsby	.10
98	Ernest Thayer	.10
99	Connie Mack	.10
100	1939 Centennial Celebration	.10
101	Branch Rickey	.10
102	Dan Brouthers	.10
103	First Baseball Uniform	.10
104	Christy Mathewson	.25
105	Joe Nuxhall	.10
106	1939 Centennial Celebration	.10
107	President Taft	.10
108	Abner Doubleday	.10

1987 Baseball's All-Time Greats

Though the producer is not identified anywhere on the cards, this collectors' issue was created primarily for insertion in beginner's baseball card kits. One series of 50 cards was produced about 1987, a second series some years later. All cards have bright green or orange borders with a "window" at center in which players are pictured in either color or black-and-white photos, or artwork. The player's major league career span is in a tan oval towards bottom. Horizontal backs have a red strip at top with personal data and also include a career summary. The unnumbered cards are checklisted here in alphabetical order. Variations in photos and the presence or absence of team logos have been observed on some cards. Gaps have been left in the checklist to accommodate additions; "g" for green or "o" for orange borders is shown in parentheses where verified.

		NM/M
Common Player:		.10
(1)	Henry Aaron	1.00
(2)	Joe Adcock	.10
(3)	Richie Allen	.10
(4)	Grover C. Alexander	.10
(5)	Luis Aparicio	.10
(6)	Luke Appling	.10
(7)	Ernie Banks	.25
(8)	Hank Bauer	.10
(9)	Johnny Bench	.15
(10)	"Yogi" Berra	.15
(11)	Lou Boudreau	.10
(12)	Lou Brock	.10
(13)	"Three Finger" Brown	.10
(14)	Jim Bunning	.10
(15)	Roy Campanella	.25
(16)	Rod Carew	.10
(18)	Orlando Cepeda	.10
(18)	Roberto Clemente	1.00
(19a)	Ty Cobb (g)	1.00
(19b)	Ty Cobb (o)	1.00
(20)	Mickey Cochrane	.10
(21)	Rocky Colavito	.10
(22)	Eddie Collins	.10
(23)	Sam Crawford	.10
(24)	Joe Cronin	.10
(25)	Alvin Dark	.10
(26)	Dizzy Dean	.10
(27)	Bill Dickey	.10
(28)	Joe DiMaggio	1.00
(29)	Larry Doby	.10
(30)	Don Drysdale	.10
(32)	Leo Durocher	.10
(32)	Carl Erskine	.10
(33)	Bob Feller	.10
(34)	Curt Flood	.10
(35a)	Whitey Ford (g) (Chest, cap logos.)	.10
(36)	Jimmie Foxx	.10
(37a)	Frankie Frisch (g) (Jersey logo.)	.10
(38)	Carl Furillo	.10
(39a)	Lou Gehrig (g)	1.25
(39b)	Lou Gehrig (o)	1.25
(40)	Charlie Gehringer	.10
(41)	Bob Gibson (g)	.25
(42)	Hank Greenberg	.10
(43)	"Lefty" Grove	.10
(44)	"Gabby" Hartnett	.10
(45)	Gil Hodges	.10
(46)	Rogers Hornsby	.10
(47)	Carl Hubbell	.10
(48)	Jim Hunter	.10
(49)	Monte Irvin	.10
(50)	Ferguson Jenkins	.10
(51)	Walter Johnson	.10
(52)	Jim Kaat	.10
(54)	George Kell	.10
(54)	Ralph Kiner	.10
(55)	Ted Kluszewski	.10
(57)	Don Larsen	.10
(58)	Bob Lemon	.10
(59)	Ernie Lombardi	.10
(61)	Eddie Lopat	.10
(62a)	Mickey Mantle (o) (Chest-up portrait.)	2.00
(63)	Juan Marichal	.10
(64)	Roger Maris	.50
(65)	Billy Martin	.10
(66)	Eddie Mathews	.10
(67)	Christy Mathewson	.25
(68)	Willie Mays	1.00
(69)	Bill Mazeroski	.10
(70)	Joe Morgan	.10
(71)	Thurman Munson	.10
(72)	Stan Musial	.50
(73)	Tony Oliva	.10
(74)	Mel Ott	.10
(75)	Jim Palmer	.10
(76)	Gaylord Perry	.10
(77)	Boog Powell	.10
(78)	Pee Wee Reese	.10
(79)	Robin Roberts	.10
(80a)	Brooks Robinson (g)(Baltimore jersey.)	.25
(81)	Frank Robinson (g)	.25
(82a)	Jackie Robinson (g)	1.00
(82b)	Jackie Robinson (o)	1.00
(83a)	Babe Ruth (g)	1.50
(83b)	Babe Ruth (o)	1.50
(84)	Tom Seaver	.10
(85)	Bobby Shantz	.10
(86)	Al Simmons	.10
(87)	George Sisler	.10
(88)	Enos Slaughter	.10
(89)	Duke Snider	.10
(91)	Warren Spahn (g)	.25
(92)	Tris Speaker	.10
(93)	Willie Stargell	.10
(94)	Bill Terry	.10
(95)	Bobby Thomson	.10
(96)	Pie Traynor	.10
(97)	Honus Wagner	.25
(98)	Ed Walsh	.10
(99)	Paul Waner	.10
(100)	Hoyt Wilhelm	.10
(101)	Billy Williams	.10
(102)	Ted Williams	1.00
(103)	Maury Wills	.10
(104)	Early Wynn	.10
(105)	Carl Yastrzemski	.25
(106)	Cy Young (o)	.25
(107)	Ross Youngs	.10

1988 Bazooka

This 22-card set from Topps marks the first Bazooka issue since 1971. Full-color player photos are bordered in white, with the player name printed on a red, white and blue bubble gum box in the lower right corner. Flip sides are also red, white and blue, printed vertically. A large, but faint, Bazooka logo backs the Topps baseball logo team name, card number, player's name and position, followed by batting records, personal information and brief career highlights. Cards were sold inside specially marked 59¢ and 79¢ Bazooka gum and candy boxes, one card per box.

		NM/M
Complete Set (22):		3.00
Common Player:		.10
1	George Bell	.10
2	Wade Boggs	.50
3	Jose Canseco	.25
4	Roger Clemens	.60
5	Vince Coleman	.10
6	Eric Davis	.10
7	Tony Fernandez	.10
8	Dwight Gooden	.10
9	Tony Gwynn	.50
10	Wally Joyner	.10
11	Don Mattingly	.60
12	Willie McGee	.10
13	Mark McGwire	.75
14	Kirby Puckett	.50
15	Tim Raines	.10
16	Dave Righetti	.10
17	Cal Ripken, Jr.	1.00
18	Juan Samuel	.10
19	Ryne Sandberg	.50
20	Benny Santiago	.10
21	Darryl Strawberry	.10
22	Todd Worrell	.10

1989 Bazooka

Topps produced this 22-card set in 1989 to be included (one card per box) in specially-marked boxes of its Bazooka brand bubblegum. The player photos have the words "Shining Star" along the top, while the player's name appears along the bottom of the card, along with the Topps Bazooka logo in the lower right corner. The cards are numbered alphabetically.

		NM/M
Complete Set (22):		3.00
Common Player:		.10
1	Tim Belcher	.10
2	Damon Berryhill	.10
3	Wade Boggs	.75
4	Jay Buhner	.10
5	Jose Canseco	.25
6	Vince Coleman	.10
7	Cecil Espy	.10
8	Dave Gallagher	.10
9	Ron Gant	.10
10	Kirk Gibson	.10
11	Paul Gibson	.10
12	Mark Grace	.10
13	Tony Gwynn	.75
14	Rickey Henderson	.50

15	Orel Hershiser	.10
16	Gregg Jefferies	.10
17	Ricky Jordan	.10
18	Chris Sabo	.10
19	Gary Sheffield	.40
20	Darryl Strawberry	.10
21	Frank Viola	.10
22	Walt Weiss	.10

1990 Bazooka

For the second consecutive year, Bazooka entitled its set "Shining Stars." Full-color action and posed player shots are featured on the card fronts. The flip sides feature player statistics in a style much like the cards from the previous two Bazooka issues. Unlike the past two releases, the cards are not numbered alphabetically. The cards measure 2-1/2" x 3-1/2" in size and 22 cards complete the set.

		NM/M
Complete Set (22):		3.00
Common Player:		.10
1	Kevin Mitchell	.10
2	Robin Yount	.40
3	Mark Davis	.10
4	Bret Saberhagen	.10
5	Fred McGriff	.10
6	Tony Gwynn	.50
7	Kirby Puckett	.50
8	Vince Coleman	.10
9	Rickey Henderson	.40
10	Ben McDonald	.10
11	Gregg Olson	.10
12	Todd Zeile	.10
13	Carlos Martinez	.10
14	Gregg Jefferies	.10
15	Craig Worthington	.10
16	Gary Sheffield	.25
17	Greg Briley	.10
18	Ken Griffey Jr.	1.50
19	Jerome Walton	.10
20	Bob Geren	.10
21	Tom Gordon	.10
22	Jim Abbott	.10

1991 Bazooka

For the third consecutive year Bazooka entitled its set "Shining Stars." The cards are styled like the 1990 issue, but include the Topps "40th Anniversary" logo. The 1991 issue is considered much scarcer than the previous releases. The cards measure 2-1/2" x 3-1/2" in size and 22 cards complete the set.

		NM/M
Complete Set (22):		5.00
Common Player:		.10
1	Barry Bonds	3.50
2	Rickey Henderson	.50
3	Bob Welch	.10
4	Doug Drabek	.10
5	Alex Fernandez	.10
6	Jose Offerman	.10
7	Frank Thomas	.50
8	Cecil Fielder	.10
9	Ryne Sandberg	.75
10	George Brett	1.00
11	Willie McGee	.10
12	Vince Coleman	.10
13	Hal Morris	.10
14	Delino DeShields	.10

15	Robin Ventura	.10
16	Jeff Huson	.10
17	Felix Jose	.10
18	Dave Justice	.10
19	Larry Walker	.10
20	Sandy Alomar, Jr.	.10
21	Kevin Appier	.10
22	Scott Radinsky	.10

1992 Bazooka

This set of 22 cards features miniature versions of the 1953 Topps Archives issue. The minicards are set against a blue background on front and back. Besides reproductions of issued 1953 Topps cards, these "Quadracards" include miniature versions of many of the special cards created for the Archives set. Cards feature the Bazooka logo on back, and were distributed in boxes of that bubble gum.

		NM/M
Complete Tin-Box Set (22):		16.00
Complete Set (22):		8.00
Common Player:		.25
1	Joe Adcock, Bob Lemon, Willie Mays, Vic Wertz	1.50
2	Carl Furillo, Don Newcombe, Phil Rizzuto, Hank Sauer	.25
3	Ferris Fain, John Logan, Ed Mathews, Bobby Shantz	.25
4	Yogi Berra, Del Crandall, Howie Pollett, Gene Woodling	.25
5	Richie Ashburn, Leo Durocher, Allie Reynolds, Early Wynn	.25
6	Hank Aaron, Ray Boone, Luke Easter, Dick Williams	1.50
7	Ralph Branca, Bob Feller, Rogers Hornsby, Bobby Thomson	.25
8	Jim Gilliam, Billy Martin, Orestes Minoso, Hal Newhouser	.25
9	Smoky Burgess, John Mize, Preacher Roe, Warren Spahn	.25
10	Monte Irvin, Bobo Newsom, Duke Snider, Wes Westrum	.25
11	Carl Erskine, Jackie Jensen, George Kell, Al Schoendienst	.25
12	Bill Bruton, Whitey Ford, Ed Lopat, Mickey Vernon	.25
13	Joe Black, Lew Burdette, Johnny Pesky, Enos Slaughter	.25
14	Gus Bell, Mike Garcia, Mel Parnell, Jackie Robinson	1.25
15	Alvin Dark, Dick Groat, Pee Wee Reese, John Sain	.25
16	Gil Hodges, Sal Maglie, Wilmer Mizell, Billy Pierce	.45
17	Nellie Fox, Ralph Kiner, Ted Kluszewski, Eddie Stanky	.25
18	Ewell Blackwell, Vern Law, Satchell Paige, Jim Wilson	.45
19	Lou Boudreau, Roy Face, Harvey Haddix, Bill Rigney	.25
20	Roy Campanella, Walt Dropo, Harvey Kuenn, Al Rosen	.45
21	Joe Garagiola, Robin Roberts, Casey Stengel, Hoyt Wilhelm	.25
22	John Antonelli, Bob Friend, Dixie Walker, Ted Williams	1.00

1993 Bazooka Team USA

The members of Team USA are featured on this boxed set. The 2-1/2" x 3-1/2" cards feature the same basic design as 1993 Topps baseball, except for a Bazooka gum logo in one of the upper corners. Both front and back feature posed player photos. Backs have a design simulating the U.S. flag and include amateur stats, biographical details and career highlights. The cards are virtually identical to the same players' cards in the 1993 Topps Traded set, with the addition of the Bazooka logo on front and the differences in card numbers. A special tin-boxed edition with 50 pieces of gum was produced in an edition reported as 750.

		NM/M
Complete Set (22):		100.00
Complete Tin Set (22):		150.00
Common Player:		.50
1	Terry Harvey	.50
2	Dante Powell	.50
3	Andy Barkett	.50
4	Steve Nesch	.50
5	Charlie Nelson	.50
6	Todd Walker	1.00
7	Dustin Hermanson	1.00
8	Pat Clougherty	.50
9	Danny Graves	.50
10	Paul Wilson	.75
11	Todd Helton	90.00
12	Russ Johnson	.50
13	Darren Grass	.50
14	A.J. Hinch	.50
15	Mark Merila	.50
16	John Powell	.50
17	Bob Scafa	.50
18	Matt Beaumont	.50
19	Todd Dunn	.50
20	Mike Martin	.50
21	Carlton Loewer	.50
22	Bret Wagner	.50

1995 Bazooka

Topps returned to the beginner's level baseball card niche in 1995 by resurrecting its Bazooka brand name. The set was unabashedly aimed at the younger collector, offering five cards and a Bazooka Joe cartoon-wrapped chunk of bubblegum for 50 cents. Cards feature on their backs a "roulette" wheel design based on the player's 1994 stats, to be used to play a game of spinner baseball. A game instruction card and cardboard spinner was included in each pack. Limiting the set to 132 cards allowed for a concentration of established stars and hot youngsters. A 22-card Red Hot insert set is found at the rate of one card per six packs, on average. The complete set offering the 132 base cards, five Red Hot inserts and 10 pieces of bubblegum were produced.

		NM/M
Complete Set (132):		3.00
Factory Set (132+5):		5.00
Common Player:		.05
Pack (5):		.30
Wax Box (36):		7.00
1	Greg Maddux	.50
2	Cal Ripken Jr.	1.00
3	Lee Smith	.05
4	Sammy Sosa	.50
5	Jason Bere	.05
6	Dave Justice	.05
7	Kevin Mitchell	.05
8	Ozzie Guillen	.05
9	Roger Clemens	.60
10	Mike Mussina	.30
11	Sandy Alomar	.05
12	Cecil Fielder	.05
13	Dennis Martinez	.05
14	Randy Myers	.05
15	Jay Buhner	.05
16	Ivan Rodriguez	.35
17	Mo Vaughn	.05
18	Ryan Klesko	.05
19	Chuck Finley	.05
20	Barry Bonds	1.00
21	Dennis Eckersley	.35
22	Kenny Lofton	.05
23	Rafael Palmeiro	.35
24	Mike Stanley	.05
25	Gregg Jefferies	.05
26	Robin Ventura	.05
27	Mark McGwire	.75
28	Ozzie Smith	.50
29	Troy Neel	.05
30	Tony Gwynn	.50
31	Ken Griffey Jr.	.65
32	Will Clark	.05
33	Craig Biggio	.05
34	Shawon Dunston	.05
35	Wilson Alvarez	.05
36	Bobby Bonilla	.05
37	Marquis Grissom	.05
38	Ben McDonald	.05
39	Delino DeShields	.05
40	Barry Larkin	.05
41	John Olerud	.05
42	Jose Canseco	.30
43	Greg Vaughn	.05
44	Gary Sheffield	.20
45	Paul O'Neill	.05
46	Bob Hamelin	.05
47	Don Mattingly	.60
48	John Franco	.05
49	Bret Boone	.05
50	Rick Aguilera	.05
51	Tim Wallach	.05
52	Roberto Kelly	.05
53	Danny Tartabull	.05
54	Randy Johnson	.40
55	Greg McMichael	.05
56	Bip Roberts	.05
57	David Cone	.05
58	Raul Mondesi	.05
59	Travis Fryman	.05
60	Jeff Conine	.05
61	Jeff Bagwell	.40
62	Rickey Henderson	.40
63	Fred McGriff	.05
64	Matt Williams	.05
65	Rick Wilkins	.05
66	Eric Karros	.05
67	Mel Rojas	.05
68	Juan Gonzalez	.20
69	Chuck Carr	.05
70	Moises Alou	.05
71	Mark Grace	.05
72	Alex Fernandez	.05
73	Rod Beck	.05
74	Ray Lankford	.05
75	Dean Palmer	.05
76	Joe Carter	.05
77	Mike Piazza	.65
78	Eddie Murray	.40
79	Dave Nilsson	.05
80	Brett Butler	.05
81	Roberto Alomar	.05
82	Jeff Kent	.05
83	Andres Galarraga	.05
84	Brady Anderson	.05
85	Jimmy Key	.05
86	Bret Saberhagen	.05
87	Chili Davis	.05
88	Jose Rijo	.05
89	Wade Boggs	.50
90	Len Dykstra	.05
91	Steve Howe	.05
92	Hal Morris	.05
93	Larry Walker	.05
94	Jeff Montgomery	.05
95	Wil Cordero	.05
96	Jay Bell	.05
97	Tom Glavine	.15
98	Chris Hoiles	.05
99	Steve Avery	.05
100	Ruben Sierra	.05
101	Mickey Tettleton	.05
102	Paul Molitor	.40
103	Carlos Baerga	.05
104	Walt Weiss	.05
105	Darren Daulton	.05
106	Jack McDowell	.05
107	Doug Drabek	.05
108	Mark Langston	.05
109	Manny Ramirez	.40
110	Kevin Appier	.05
111	Andy Benes	.05
112	Chuck Knoblauch	.05
113	Kirby Puckett	.50
114	Dante Bichette	.05
115	Deion Sanders	.10
116	Albert Belle	.05
117	Todd Zeile	.05
118	Devon White	.05
119	Tim Salmon	.05
120	Frank Thomas	.40
121	John Wetteland	.05
122	James Mouton	.05
123	Javy Lopez	.05
124	Carlos Delgado	.25
125	Cliff Floyd	.05
126	Alex Gonzalez	.05
127	Billy Ashley	.05
128	Rondell White	.05
129	Rico Brogna	.05
130	Melvin Nieves	.05
131	Jose Oliva	.05
132	J.R. Phillips	.05

Red Hot Inserts

Twenty-two of the game's biggest stars were chosen for inclusion in 1995 Bazooka's only insert set - Red Hots. The chase cards are found at an average rate of one per six packs. Red Hots are identical to the players' cards in the regular set except that the background has been rendered in shades of red, and the player name printed in gold foil. Card numbers have an "RH" prefix.

		NM/M
Complete Set (22):		7.00
Common Player:		.15
1	Greg Maddux	1.00
2	Cal Ripken Jr.	2.00
3	Barry Bonds	2.00
4	Kenny Lofton	.15
5	Mike Stanley	.15
6	Tony Gwynn	1.00
7	Ken Griffey Jr.	1.50
8	Barry Larkin	.15
9	Jose Canseco	.35
10	Paul O'Neill	.15
11	Randy Johnson	.75
12	David Cone	.15
13	Jeff Bagwell	.75
14	Matt Williams	.15
15	Mike Piazza	1.50
16	Roberto Alomar	.25
17	Jimmy Key	.15
18	Wade Boggs	1.00
19	Paul Molitor	.75
20	Carlos Baerga	.15
21	Albert Belle	.15
22	Frank Thomas	.75

1996 Bazooka

Topps' 1996 Bazooka set offers collectors interactive fun with its cards geared to a flipping game. Each front has an action photo of the player. The back contains one of five different Bazooka Joe characters, along with the Bazooka Ball game, the player's biographical data, and 1995 and career stats. Cards were available five per pack for 50 cents. The complete set was also offered in a factory set, packaged in an attractive gift box. As an exclusive bo-

nus, one 1959 Bazooka Mickey Mantle reprint card is found in every factory set, along with 10 pieces of bubble gum.

		NM/M
Unopened Fact. Set (133):		9.00
Complete Set (132):		6.00
Common Player:		.05
Pack (5):		.40
Wax Box (36):		9.00
1	Ken Griffey Jr.	.75
2	J.T. Snow	.05
3	Rondell White	.05
4	Reggie Sanders	.05
5	Jeff Montgomery	.05
6	Mike Stanley	.05
7	Bernie Williams	.05
8	Mike Piazza	.75
9	Brian Hunter	.05
10	Len Dykstra	.05
11	Ray Lankford	.05
12	Kenny Lofton	.05
13	Robin Ventura	.05
14	Devon White	.05
15	Cal Ripken Jr.	1.50
16	Heathcliff Slocumb	.05
17	Ryan Klesko	.05
18	Terry Steinbach	.05
19	Travis Fryman	.05
20	Sammy Sosa	.35
21	Jim Thome	.35
22	Kenny Rogers	.05
23	Don Mattingly	.60
24	Kirby Puckett	.50
25	Matt Williams	.05
26	Larry Walker	.05
27	Tim Wakefield	.05
28	Greg Vaughn	.05
29	Denny Neagle	.05
30	Ken Caminiti	.05
31	Garret Anderson	.05
32	Brady Anderson	.05
33	Carlos Baerga	.05
34	Wade Boggs	.50
35	Roberto Alomar	.15
36	Eric Karros	.05
37	Jay Buhner	.05
38	Dante Bichette	.05
39	Darren Daulton	.05
40	Jeff Bagwell	.40
41	Jay Bell	.05
42	Dennis Eckersley	.35
43	Will Clark	.05
44	Tom Glavine	.20
45	Rick Aguilera	.05
46	Kevin Seitzer	.05
47	Bret Boone	.05
48	Mark Grace	.05
49	Ray Durham	.05
50	Rico Brogna	.05
51	Kevin Appier	.05
52	Moises Alou	.05
53	Jeff Conine	.05
54	Marty Cordova	.05
55	Jose Mesa	.05
56	Rod Beck	.05
57	Marquis Grissom	.05
58	David Cone	.05
59	Albert Belle	.05
60	Lee Smith	.05
61	Frank Thomas	.40
62	Roger Clemens	.60
63	Bobby Bonilla	.05
64	Paul Molitor	.40
65	Chuck Knoblauch	.05
66	Steve Finley	.05
67	Craig Biggio	.05
68	Ramon Martinez	.05
69	Jason Isringhausen	.05
70	Mark Wohlers	.05
71	Vinny Castilla	.05
72	Ron Gant	.05
73	Juan Gonzalez	.20
74	Mark McGwire	1.00
75	Jeff King	.05
76	Pedro Martinez	.40
77	Chad Curtis	.05
78	John Olerud	.05
79	Greg Maddux	.50
80	Derek Jeter	1.50
81	Mike Mussina	.25
82	Gregg Jefferies	.05
83	Jim Edmonds	.05
84	Carlos Perez	.05
85	Mo Vaughn	.05
86	Todd Hundley	.05
87	Roberto Hernandez	.05
88	Derek Bell	.05
89	Andres Galarraga	.05
90	Brian McRae	.05
91	Joe Carter	.05
92	Orlando Merced	.05
93	Cecil Fielder	.05
94	Dean Palmer	.05
95	Randy Johnson	.40
96	Chipper Jones	.50
97	Barry Larkin	.05
98	Hideo Nomo	.25
99	Gary Gaetti	.05
100	Edgar Martinez	.05
101	John Wetteland	.05
102	Rafael Palmeiro	.05
103	Chuck Finley	.05
104	Ivan Rodriguez	.35
105	Shawn Green	.05
106	Manny Ramirez	.40

107	Lance Johnson	.05
108	Jose Canseco	.20
109	Fred McGriff	.05
110	David Segui	.05
111	Tim Salmon	.05
112	Hal Morris	.05
113	Tino Martinez	.05
114	Bret Saberhagen	.05
115	Brian Jordan	.05
116	David Justice	.05
117	Jack McDowell	.05
118	Barry Bonds	1.50
119	Mark Langston	.05
120	John Valentin	.05
121	Raul Mondesi	.05
122	Quilvio Veras	.05
123	Randy Myers	.05
124	Tony Gwynn	.50
125	Johnny Damon	.05
126	Doug Drabek	.05
127	Bill Pulsipher	.05
128	Paul O'Neill	.05
129	Rickey Henderson	.40
130	Deion Sanders	.10
131	Orel Hershiser	.05
132	Gary Sheffield	.20

Mickey Mantle 1959 Reprint

Continuing its tribute to the late Mickey Mantle across all of its product lines, Topps produced a special reprint of the 1959 Bazooka Mantle card exclusively for inclusion in factory sets of its 1996 Bazooka cards. While the original '59 Mantle was printed in nearly 3" x 5" size on the bottom of gum boxes, the reprint is in the current 2-1/2" x 3-1/2" size.

	NM/M
Mickey Mantle	7.50

1992 Ben's Bakery Super Hitters Discs

Ben's Bakery, a small, eastern Canadian bakery, inserted promotional discs in its hot dog and hamburger buns in 1992. As in the case of 1991, which was the company's first year in the promotion, the 1992 set contained 20 different players, including many of the top stars in the country. Twenty of the game's top hitters, with a special emphasis on Blue Jays players, are featured in this regional issue by a small Eastern Canada bakery. The 2-3/4" diameter discs were packaged in the company's hot dog and hamburger buns. Fronts feature a color photo on which team logos have been airbrushed away. The bakery logo is flanked by a red "Super Hitters" in the white border at top. The player's name appears in white in an orange banner beneath the photo, with his team and position in blue at bottom. Backs are printed in black and include a few biographical details and 1991 stats, along with a card number and appropriate logos and copyright notices.

	NM/M
Complete Set (20):	15.00
Common Player:	.75
1 Cecil Fielder	.75
2 Joe Carter	.75

3	Roberto Alomar	1.00
4	Devon White	.75
5	Kelly Gruber	.75
6	Cal Ripken, Jr.	3.50
7	Kirby Puckett	2.00
8	Paul Molitor	1.50
9	Julio Franco	.75
10	Ken Griffey Jr.	3.00
11	Frank Thomas	1.50
12	Jose Canseco	1.25
13	Danny Tartabull	.75
14	Terry Pendleton	.75
15	Tony Gwynn	2.00
16	Howard Johnson	.75
17	Will Clark	.75
18	Barry Bonds	3.50
19	Ryne Sandberg	2.00
20	Bobby Bonilla	.75

1993 Ben's Bakery Super Pitchers Discs

An emphasis on Toronto's pitchers is noted in the checklist for this regional bakery issue. The 2-3/4" diameter discs were packed with hot dog and hamburger buns and follow a 1991 issue by the company featuring super hitters. A color player portrait at center has had the uniform logos airbrushed away. "Super Pitchers" in red flanks the bakery logo in the white border above the photo. The player's name appears in white in an orange banner beneath the photo, with his team and position in blue at bottom. Backs are printed in black and include minimal biographical data, a card number, 1992 stats and copyright information.

	NM/M
Complete Set (20):	10.00
Common Player:	.45
1 Dennis Eckersley	1.50
2 Chris Bosio	.45
3 Jack Morris	.45
4 Greg Maddux	2.50
5 Dennis Martinez	.45
6 Tom Glavine	.75
7 Doug Drabek	.45
8 John Smoltz	.45
9 Randy Myers	.45
10 Jack McDowell	.45
11 John Wetteland	.45
12 Roger Clemens	3.00
13 Mike Mussina	.75
14 Juan Guzman	.45
15 Jose Rijo	.45
16 Tom Henke	.45
17 Gregg Olson	.45
18 Jim Abbott	.45
19 Jimmy Key	.45
20 Rheal Cormier	.45

1987 David Berg Hot Dogs Cubs

Changing sponsors from Gatorade to David Berg Pure Beef Hot Dogs, the Chicago Cubs handed out a 26-card set of baseball cards to fans attending the July 29th game at Wrigley Field. The cards are printed in full-color on white stock and measure 2-7/8" x 4-1/4" in size. The set is numbered by the players' uniform numbers. The card backs contain player personal and statistical information, plus a full-color

picture of a David Berg hot dog in a bun with all the garnishings. The set marked the sixth consecutive year the Cubs held a baseball card giveaway promotion.

	NM/M
Complete Set (26):	10.00
Common Player:	.40
1 Dave Martinez	.40
4 Gene Michael	.40
6 Keith Moreland	.40
7 Jody Davis	.40
8 Andre Dawson	1.00
10 Leon Durham	.40
12 Jim Sundberg	.40
12 Shawon Dunston	.40
19 Manny Trillo	.40
20 Bob Dernier	.40
21 Scott Sanderson	.40
22 Jerry Mumphrey	.40
23 Ryne Sandberg	5.00
24 Brian Dayett	.40
29 Chico Walker	.40
31 Greg Maddux	5.00
33 Frank DiPino	.40
34 Steve Trout	.40
36 Gary Matthews	.40
37 Ed Lynch	.40
39 Ron Davis	.40
40 Rick Sutcliffe	.40
46 Lee Smith	.40
47 Dickie Noles	.40
49 Jamie Moyer	.40
--- The Coaching Staff (Johnny Oates, Jim Snyder, Herm Starrette, John Vukovich, Billy Williams)	.40

1988 David Berg Hot Dogs Cubs

(17) MARK GRACE, IF

This oversized (2-7/8" x 4-1/2") set of 26 cards was distributed to fans at Wrigley Field on August 24th. The set includes cards for the manager and coaching staff, as well as players. Full-color action photos are framed in red and blue on a white background. The backs feature small black and white player close-ups, colorful team logos, statistics and sponsor logos (David Berg Hot Dogs and Venture Store Restaurants). The numbers in the following checklist refer to players' uniforms.

	NM/M
Complete Set (27):	17.50
Common Player:	.40
2 Vance Law	.40
4 Don Zimmer	.40
7 Jody Davis	.40
8 Andre Dawson	1.00
9 Damon Berryhill	.40
12 Shawon Dunston	.40
17 Mark Grace	1.00
18 Angel Salazar	.40
19 Manny Trillo	.40
21 Scott Sanderson	.40
22 Jerry Mumphrey	.40
23 Ryne Sandberg	4.00
24 Gary Varsho	.40
25 Rafael Palmeiro	2.50
28 Mitch Webster	.40
30 Darrin Jackson	.40
31 Greg Maddux	4.00
32 Calvin Schiraldi	.40
33 Frank DiPino	.40
37 Pat Perry	.40
40 Rick Sutcliffe	.40
44 Jeff Pico	.40
45 Al Nipper	.40
49 Jamie Moyer	.40
54 Les Lancaster	.40
54 Rich Gossage	.40
--- The Coaching Staff (Joe Altobelli, Chuck Cottier, Larry Cox, Jose Martinez, Dick Pole)	.40

1994 Big Apple 1969 Mets Discs

Big Apple Collector, Inc. released the "1969 World Champion Miracle Mets Commemorative Cap Sheet," which has likenesses of each of the 31 members of the squad captured in oil paintings by sports artist Ron Lewis. The player's likeness is centered in a 1-5/8" diameter round commemorative cap which is die cut but remains in place on the sheet. Each cap is gold foil accented, and each 11" x 14" sheet is produced in full color on 48-point card stock. The sheet has a suggested retail price of $39.95.

	NM/M
Complete Set (31):	12.00
Common Player:	.25
(1) Gil Hodges	1.50
(2) Rube Walker	.25
(3) Yogi Berra	1.50
(4) Joe Pignatano	.25
(5) Ed Yost	.25
(6) Tommie Agee	.25
(7) Ken Boswell	.25
(8) Don Cardwell	.25
(9) Ed Charles	.25
(10) Donn Clendenon	.25
(11) Jack DiLauro	.25
(12) Duffy Dyer	.25
(13) Wayne Garrett	.25
(14) Rod Gaspar	.25
(15) Gary Gentry	.25
(16) Jerry Grote	.25
(17) Bud Harrelson	.30
(18) Cleon Jones	.25
(19) Cal Koonce	.25
(20) Jerry Koosman	.30
(21) Ed Kranepool	.25
(22) J.C. Martin	.25
(23) Jim McAndrew	.25
(24) Tug McGraw	.40
(25) Bob Pfeil	.25
(26) Nolan Ryan	4.00
(27) Tom Seaver	2.00
(28) Art Shamsky	.25
(29) Ron Swoboda	.25
(30) Ron Taylor	.25
(31) Al Weis	.25

1980s Big League Cards

BOBBY LOANE OUTFIELDER 1939-1940

Former major league pitcher and author Jim Bouton was a principal in the most successful of many "vanity" card manufacturers which sprang up in the 1980s and 1990s. For a price, anybody could send a picture to the New Jersey company and have it placed on a run of baseball cards. Persons could, and did, also send photos of ballplayers to create fantasy cards and at least several ballplayers who never appeared on cards contemporary with their careers had cards made up for themselves retroactively. Fronts have black, blue and red graphics. Backs are printed in blue on white with personal data, stats and other information provided by person ordering the cards. Unlike most other contemporary vanity cards, the Big League Cards are printed on thick quality similar

to vintage baseball cards. There is no way to document the individual issue of these cards.

1986 Big League Chew

HOME RUN LEGENDS

1945

MEL OTT

OUTFIELDER

The 1986 Big League Chew set consists of 12 cards featuring the players who have hit 500 or more career home runs. The cards, which measure 2-1/2" x 3-1/2", were inserted in specially marked packages of Big League Chew, the shredded bubble gum developed by former major leaguer Jim Bouton. The set is entitled "Home Run Legends" and was available through a write-in offer on the package. Recent-day players in the set are shown in color photos, while the older sluggers are pictured in black and white.

	NM/M
Complete Set (12):	10.00
Common Player:	1.00
1 Hank Aaron	2.00
2 Babe Ruth	3.00
3 Willie Mays	2.00
4 Frank Robinson	1.00
5 Harmon Killebrew	1.00
6 Mickey Mantle	4.00
7 Jimmie Foxx	1.00
8 Ted Williams	2.00
9 Ernie Banks	1.00
10 Eddie Mathews	1.00
11 Mel Ott	1.00
12 500-HR Group Card	.50

1997 Big League Chew Alumni

BIG LEAGUE Alumni

JUAN MARICHAL

Autographed cards of three Hall of Famers were available through a mail-in offer by Big League Chew shredded bubble gum. Cards could be obtained by sending in proofs of purchase from pouches with the players' photos on them. Each card comes with a certificate of authenticity from Major League Baseball Players Alumni, which licensed the issue. Because the cards are not licensed by Major League Baseball, uniform logos have been removed from the color photos. Cards have a green, orange and white color scheme on front and back and are standard 2-1/2" x 3-1/2". Backs include career highlights and lifetime stats.

	NM/M
Complete Set (3):	20.00
Common Player:	7.50
(1) Juan Marichal	7.50
(2) Brooks Robinson	7.50
(3) Billy Williams	7.50

1982 Big League Collectibles Diamond Classics, Series 1

Attempting to recapture the flavor of vintage baseball cards, this collectors set presents former stars in a 2-1/2" x 3-3/4" format on

thick white cardboard stock. Fronts have a painted player portrait in color with no other graphic elements. Backs are in black and blue and include in-depth biographical sketches and career stats. The edition was limited to 10,000 sets.

	NM/M
Complete Set (56):	30.00
Common Player:	.60
1 Joe DiMaggio	5.00
2 Enos Slaughter	.60
3 Smokey Joe Wood (Smoky)	.60
4 Roy Campanella	1.25
5 Charlie Gehringer	.60
6 Carl Hubbell	.60
7 Rogers Hornsby	.60
8 Arky Vaughan	.60
9 Al Simmons	.60
10 Wally Berger	.60
11 Sam Rice	.60
12 Dizzy Dean	.60
13 Babe Ruth	5.00
14 Frankie Frisch	.60
15 George Kell	.60
16 Pee Wee Reese	.60
17 Earl Averill	.60
18 Willie Mays	2.50
19 Frank Baker	.60
20 Hack Wilson	.60
21 Ted Williams	3.00
22 Chuck Klein	.60
23 Bill Dickey	.60
24 Johnny Mize	.60
25 Luke Appling	.60
26 Duke Snider	.60
27 Wahoo Sam Crawford	.60
28 Waite Hoyt	.60
29 Eddie Collins	.60
30 Warren Spahn	.60
31 Satchel Paige	1.25
32 Ernie Lombardi	.60
33 Dom DiMaggio	.60
34 Joe Garagiola	.60
35 Lou Gehrig	2.50
36 Burleigh Grimes	.60
37 Walter Johnson	.60
38 Bill Terry	.60
39 Ty Cobb	2.50
40 Pie Traynor	.60
41 Ted Lyons	.60
42 Richie Ashburn	.60
43 Lefty Grove	.60
44 Edd Roush	.60
45 Phil Rizzuto	.60
46 Stan Musial	2.00
47 Bob Feller	.60
48 Jackie Robinson	2.50
49 Hank Greenberg	1.25
50 Mel Ott	.60
51 Joe Cronin	.60
52 Lefty O'Doul	.60
53 Indian Bob Johnson	.60
54 Kiki Cuyler	.60
55 Mickey Mantle	7.50
--- Checklist	.10

1983 Big League Collectibles Diamond Classics, Series 2

NEW YORK

A second series of cards featuring past greats was issued by Big League Collectibles in 1983. Again at

55 cards, the set featured painted portraits of the players on front, devoid of any other graphics. Backs are in red and black and include a lengthy career summary along with innovative stats and a few biographical bits. The 2-1/2" x 3-3/4" cards are printed on a heavy white cardboard stock. The series was produced in an edition of 10,000 sets.

		NM/M
Complete Set (56):		20.00
Common Player:		.60
56	Ernie Banks	1.50
57	Stan Coveleski	.60
58	Vince DiMaggio	.60
59	Sunny Jim Bottomley	.60
60	Sandy Koufax	4.00
61	Doc Cramer	.60
62	Ted Kluszewski	.60
63	Zeke Bonura	.60
64	Spud Davis	.60
65	Jackie Jensen	.60
66	Honus Wagner	.75
67	Brooks Robinson	1.25
68	Dazzy Vance	.60
69	George Uhle	.60
70	Juan Marichal	.60
71	Bobo Newsom	.60
72	Billy Herman	.60
73	Al Rosen	.60
74	Roberto Clemente	4.00
75	George Case	.60
76	Bill Nicholson	.60
77	Tommy Bridges	.60
78	Rabbit Maranville	.60
79	Bob Lemon	.60
80	Heinie Groh	.60
81	Tris Speaker	.60
82	Hank Aaron	4.00
83	Whitey Ford	1.25
84a	Guy Bush (Ernie Banks back.)	.60
84b	Guy Bush (Correct back.)	.60
85	Jimmie Foxx	.60
86	Marty Marion	.60
87a	Hal Newhouser (Charlie Grimm back.)	.60
87b	Hal Newhouser (Correct back.)	.60
88	George Kelley (Kelly)	.60
89	Harmon Killebrew	.60
90	Willie McCovey	.60
91	Mel Harder	.60
92	Vada Pinson	.60
93	Luis Aparicio	.60
94	Grover Alexander	.60
95	Joe Kuhel	.60
96	Casey Stengel	.60
97	Joe Sewell	.60
98	Red Lucas	.60
99	Luke Sewell	.60
100	Charlie Grimm	.60
101	Cecil Travis	.60
102	Travis Jackson	.60
103	Lou Boudreau	.60
104	Nap Rucker	.60
105	Chief Bender	.60
106	Riggs Stephenson	.60
107	Red Ruffing	.60
108	Robin Roberts	.60
109	Harland Clift (Harland)	.60
110	Ralph Kiner	.60
---	Checklist	.10

1983 Big League Collectibles Original All-Stars

Players in the first modern All-Star Game, staged in conjunction with the Chicago World's Fair in 1933, are featured in this collectors issue. The 2-1/2" x 3-3/4" cards feature pastel paintings of the players on front. A circled baseball at lower-left has player and set identification. Backs are printed in blue and black and include All-Star Game and overall 1933 season performance.

		NM/M
Complete Set (38):		20.00
Common Player:		.50
2	Connie Mack	.50

3	Alvin Crowder	.50
4	Lefty Gomez	.50
5	Jimmy Dykes	.50
6	Earl Averill	.50
7	Charlie Gehringer	.50
8	Lefty Grove	.50
9	Lou Gehrig	2.00
10	Al Simmons	.50
11	Ben Chapman	.50
12	Jimmie Foxx	.75
13	Oral Hildebrand	.50
14	Joe Cronin	.50
15	Bill Dickey	.50
16	Sam West	.50
17	Rick Ferrell	.50
18	Tony Lazzeri	.50
19	Wes Ferrell	.50
20	Babe Ruth	2.50
22	John McGraw	.50
23	Pepper Martin	.50
24	Woody English	.50
25	Paul Waner	.50
26	Lefty O'Doul	.50
27	Chuck Klein	.50
28	Tony Cuccinello	.50
29	Frankie Frisch	.50
30	Gabby Hartnett	.50
31	Carl Hubbell	.50
32	Chick Hafey	.50
33	Dick Bartell	.50
34	Bill Hallahan	.50
35	Hal Schumacher	.50
36	Lon Warneke	.50
37	Wally Berger	.50
38	Bill Terry	.50
39	Jimmy Wilson	.50
40	Pie Traynor	.50

1985 Big League Collectibles National Pastime 1930-1939

SYLVESTER W. JOHNSON *Phi-N P*

Major league baseball in the 1930s is chronicled in this boxed collectors set. In 2-1/8" x 3-1/8" format (the same size as the 1951-52 Bowmans), the cards feature painted player portraits on front with identification in the white border at bottom. Backs are in black and red and feature in-depth career summaries and unique stats. The edition was limited to 5,000 sets, with a serially numbered header card.

		NM/M
Complete Set (90):		45.00
Common Player:		.60
1	Header card	.10
2	William H. Walters	.60
3	Montgomery M. Pearson	.60
4	Stanley C. Hack	.60
5	Joseph E. Cronin	.60
6	Leo E. Durocher	.60
7	Max F. Bishop	.60
8	Frank O'Donnell Hurst	.60
9	W. Barney McCosky	.60
10	Remy P. Kremer	.60
11	Julius J. Solters	.60
12	Daniel K. MacFayden	.60
13	Gordon S. Cochrane	.60
14	Ethan N. Allen	.60
15	Luzerne A. Blue	.60
16	John R. Mize	.60
17	Joseph P. DiMaggio	3.50
18	George F. Grantham	.60
19	William E. Kamm	.60
20	Charles A. Root	.60
21	Morris Berg	2.00
22	Floyd C. Herman	.60
23	Henry E. Manush	.60
24	Adolf L. Camilli	.60
25	Rudolph P. York	.60
26	Truett B. Sewell	.60
27	Richard B. Ferrell	.60
28	Arthur C. Whitney	.60
29	Edmund J. Miller	.60
30	August R. Mancuso	.60
31	John B. Conlan	.60
32	Joseph M. Medwick	.60
33	John T. Allen	.60
34	John W. Vander Meer	.60
35	H. Earl Averill	.60
36	Taylor L. Douthit	.60
37	Charles S. Myer	.60

38	Van Lingle Mungo	.60
39	Smead P. Jolley	.60
40	C. Flint Rhem	.60
41	Leon A. Goslin	.60
42	Adam A. Comorosky	.60
43	Jack I. Burns	.60
44	Edward A. Brandt	.60
45	Robert L. Johnson	.60
46	Melvin T. Ott	.60
47	Monty F.P. Stratton	.60
48	Paul D. Dean	.60
49	H. Louis Gehrig	3.50
50	Frank A. McCormick	.60
51	J. Geoffrey Heath	.60
52	Charles L. Hartnett	.60
53	Oswald L. Bluege	.60
54	George H. Ruth	6.00
55	Robert P. Doerr	.60
56	Virgil L. Davis	.60
57	D. Dale Alexander	.60
58	James A. Tobin	.60
59	Joseph F. Vosmik	.60
60	Alfonso R. Lopez	.60
61	James E. Foxx	.60
62	Frederick L. Fitzsimmons	.60
63	Robert R. Fothergill	.60
64	Morton C. Cooper	.60
65	George A. Selkirk	.60
66	Burton E. Shotton	.60
67	Robert W.A. Feller	.60
68	Lawrence H. French	.60
69	Joseph I. Judge	.60
70	Clyde L. Sukeforth	.60
71	James R. Tabor	.60
72	Silas K. Johnson	.60
73	W. Earl Webb	.60
74	Charles F. Lucas	.60
75	Ralph Kress	.60
76	Charles D. Stengel	.60
77	George W. Haas	.60
78	Joe G. Moore	.60
79	Carl N. Reynolds	.60
80	James O. Carleton	.60
81	John J. Murphy	.60
82	Paul Derringer	.60
83	Harold A. Trosky, Sr.	.60
84	Fred C. Lindstrom	.60
85	Jack E. Russell	.60
86	Stanley G. Bordagaray	.60
87	Roy C. Johnson	.60
88	Sylvester W. Johnson	.60
89	Michael F. Higgins	.60
90	J. Floyd Vaughan	.60

1989 Bimbo Cookies Super Stars Discs

ROBERTO ALOMAR

A dozen Hispanic players are featured in this set of 2-3/4" diameter discs distributed in Puerto Rico in boxes of cookies. Color portrait photos at center have cap logos removed because the discs are licensed only by the players' union, not MLB; typical for issues from Michael Schechter Associates. The Bimbo bear logo is at top-center, with the player name in a yellow strip at bottom; team and position are in blue in the white border beneath that. Yellow stars, blue baseballs and red words "SUPER STARS" flank the player photo. Backs are printed in blue and have a few biographical details, 1988 and career stats, card number and appropriate logos.

		NM/M
Complete Set (12):		15.00
Common Player:		1.50
1	Carmelo Martinez	1.50
2	Candy Maldonado	1.50
3	Benito Santiago	1.50
4	Rey Quinones	1.50
5	Jose Oquendo	1.50
6	Ruben Sierra	1.50
7	Jose Lind	1.50
8	Juan Beniquez	1.50
9	Willie Hernandez	1.50
10	Juan Nieves	1.50
11	Jose Guzman	1.50
12	Roberto Alomar (Photo actually Sandy Alomar Jr.)	3.50

1991-1992 Bleachers Promos

To introduce its 1992 line-up of single-player 23-Karat gold trimmed card sets, Bleachers produced a series of promo cards.

Fronts have color portraits of the players. Backs have another picture of the player and information about ordering and coming releases. The Nolan Ryan card, showing him winding up in a tuxedo, is known in several variations with different card show names stamped on front in gold, representing venues at which sample cards were given away.

		NM/M
Complete Set (3):		3.00
(1)	Ken Griffey Jr.	1.00
(2)	David Justice	.50
(3)	Nolan Ryan	2.00

1991 Bleachers Frank Thomas

This limited edition three-card set features 23-Karat gold cards. The photos feature Frank Thomas at different stages of his baseball career before the big leagues. Production was limited to 10,000 sets and 1,500 uncut strips. All are numbered and feature a gold facsimile autograph on the back.

		NM/M
Complete Set (3):		4.00
Common Card:		2.00
1	Frank Thomas (Auburn Tigers)	2.00
2	Frank Thomas (Sarasota White Sox)	2.00
3	Frank Thomas (Birmingham Barons)	2.00

1992 Bleachers Ken Griffey, Jr.

KEN GRIFFEY, JR. MOELLER HIGH SCHOOL - OF

Young superstar Ken Griffey, Jr. is honored in this three-card set featuring him at different stages of his baseball career. The 23-Karat gold cards feature full-color photos and a facsimile autograph on the back. Production was limited to 10,000 cut sets and 1,500 uncut strips.

		NM/M
Complete Set (3):		10.00
Common Card:		3.00
1	Ken Griffey Jr. (Moeller High School)	4.00
2	Ken Griffey Jr. (Bellingham Mariners)	4.00
3	Ken Griffey Jr. (San Bernadino Spirit)	4.00

1992 Bleachers David Justice

Atlanta Brave slugger David Justice is the subject of this three card 23-Karat gold set. The cards depict Justice at different stages of his baseball career. Like the other Bleachers issues, production was limited to 10,000 cut card sets and 1,500 uncut strips.

		NM/M
Complete Set (3):		6.00
Common Card:		2.50
1	David Justice (Durham Bulls)	2.50
2	David Justice (Greenville Braves)	2.50
3	David Justice (Richmond Braves)	2.50

1992 Bleachers Nolan Ryan

Three stops along Ryan's minor league trail are recalled in this collectors issue. The 2-1/2" x 3-1/2" cards have photos of Ryan at center with different colored borders and trim on each card. "23KT," his name and team are gold-foil stamped on front. Backs have career information and highlights, along with a serial number from within an edition of 10,000. Cards with silver prismatic foil on front rather than gold were random inserts in sets. Three-card uncut strips were made available in an edition of 1,500.

		NM/M
Complete Set (3):		6.00
Common Card:		2.00
Silver-Foil:		2X
1	Nolan Ryan (Marion Mets)	2.00
2	Nolan Ryan (Greenville Mets)	2.00
3	Nolan Ryan (Jacksonville Suns)	2.00

1993 Bleachers Promos

Original 23Kt Genuine Gold Border Cards & Holographic Prism Cards

To introduce its 1993 issues, Bleachers distributed large quantities of promo cards within the hobby to dealers and to the public at several large card shows. Most of the '93

promos can be found with several different show logos overprinted in gold foil on the front. All cards carry a 1993 copyright date on back, except the plain Ryan/tuxedo card, which has a 1992 date on back, but 1993 card-show indicia on front.

		NM/M
Common Card:		1.00
(1)	Barry Bonds (Arizona State)	2.00
(2)	Ken Griffey Jr. (Moeller High School uniform.)	2.00
(3)	Nolan Ryan (Triple-exposure pitching.)	2.00
(4)	Nolan Ryan (Tuxedo, '92 copyright.)	2.00
(5)	Nolan Ryan (Tuxedo, gold background.)	2.00
(6)	Nolan Ryan (Tuxedo, silver speckled background.)	2.00
(7)	Nolan Ryan (Tuxedo, wavy silver background.)	2.00
(8)	Nolan Ryan (Western clothing.)	2.00
(9)	Nolan Ryan (W/glove and ball in Bleachers cap.)	2.00
(10)	Nolan Ryan (With Yellow Lab puppy.)	2.00
(11)	Ryne Sandberg (Three-sport high school photos.)	1.00

1993 Bleachers Barry Bonds

The pre-major league career of Barry Bonds is featured on this trio of collectors cards. Fronts have color photos of Bonds within a gold border. His name, team and the notation "23KT" are printed in gold foil. Backs have career data and highlights, along with a serial number. It was reported that 10,000 sets and 1,500 three-card strips were issued. Cards found with silver prismatic borders on front are random inserts in sets.

		NM/M
Complete Set (3):		9.00
Common Card:		4.00
Silver:		2X
1	Barry Bonds (Arizona State University)	4.00
2	Barry Bonds (Price Williams Pirates)	4.00
3	Barry Bonds (Hawaii Islanders)	4.00

1993 Bleachers Nolan Ryan

Nolan Ryan's career is recapped in this set of collectors issues. Fronts have prismatic foil borders around color and colorized photos. Information on front is stamped in gold foil. Backs have a photo of a young Ryan along with career data and stats, and a serial number from within an announced edition of 10,000 sets and 1,500 three-card uncut strips.

		NM/M
Complete Set (6):		15.00
Common Card:		3.00

1	Nolan Ryan (Little League)	3.00
2	Nolan Ryan (High school.)	3.00
3	Nolan Ryan (Minor league highlights.)	3.00
4	Nolan Ryan (Minor league stats.)	3.00
5	Nolan Ryan (Strikeout record.)	3.00
6	Nolan Ryan (Career highlights.)	3.00

1993 Bleachers Nolan Ryan 23KT

"The Express" is pictured with each of his four major league teams in this collectors issue. Each 2-1/2" x 3-1/2" card has a color photo of Ryan at center with variously colored borders and gold-foil graphic highlights. Backs have his stats with that team, a facsimile autograph and a serial number from within an edition of 10,000 sets. Uncut strips were also issued, numbered to 1,500.

		NM/M
Complete Set (4):		15.00
Uncut Strip:		20.00
Common Card:		4.00
1	Nolan Ryan (Mets)	4.00
2	Nolan Ryan (Angels)	4.00
3	Nolan Ryan (Astros)	4.00
4	Nolan Ryan (Rangers)	15.00

1993 Bleachers Ryne Sandberg

Ryno's pre-major league career is featured on this trio of collectors cards. Fronts have color photos of Sandberg within a gold border. His name, team and the notation "23KT" are printed in gold foil. Backs have career data and stats, along with a serial number. It was reported that 10,000 sets and 1,500 three-card, gold highlighted strips were issued. Cards found with silver prismatic borders on front are random inserts in sets.

		NM/M
Complete Set (3):		9.00
Common Card:		3.00
Gold Strip:		12.00
Silver:		3X
1	Ryne Sandberg (North Central H.S.)	3.00
2	Ryne Sandberg (Helena Phillies)	3.00
3	Ryne Sandberg (Reading Phillies)	3.00

1992 Blockbuster Video Pin/Cards

Given away at special promotional games, these combination collectibles feature a 2-3/4" x 4" card, beneath which is a perforated tab of 2-3/4" x 1-9/16". The card has a borderless photo with the player name and his uniform number. The tab has a sponsor's logo. Attached to the tab is an enameled pin, about 1-1/4" square, which has a representation of the player's jersey. The black-and-white back has a portrait photo, player biographical details and career highlights. On back of the tab is a list of the Blockbuster locations participating in the promotion.

		NM/M
Common Player:		3.00
3	Jay Bell	3.00
6	Orlando Merced	3.00
15	Doug Drabek	3.00
24	Barry Bonds	15.00

1988 Blue Cross/Blue Shield Bob Uecker Reprint

Issued as a fund-raiser and sold for $3 to benefit Bob Uecker's Ride for the Arts bicycling event in 1988, this 2-1/2" x 3-1/2" card features on its front a reprint of Uecker's card from the 1963 Topps set. Back has history and details of the fund-raiser and the logos of Blue Cross and Blue Shield.

		NM/M
(1)	Bob Uecker	6.00

1987 Bluegrass State Games

Athletes with ties to Kentucky and public figures from the state are featured on this set issued in conjunction with the 1987 Bluegrass State Games. Fronts have color photos on a blue background with white borders. Beneath the photo are the logos of Champions Against Drugs and sponsors Coke and Valvoline. Backs have an anti-drug message from the pictured celebrity. Cards were handed out over the period May 25-October 19 by law enforcement officers. Only the baseball-related cards are listed here.

		NM/M
Complete Set (24):		50.00
Common Player:		.50
5	Doug Flynn	1.00
13	Pee Wee Reese	5.00
22	A.B. (Happy) Chandler	1.00

1987 Boardwalk and Baseball All Time Record Holders

This boxed set was a repackaging of the cards produced by Topps for Woolworth stores in 1985. Fronts have "framed" black-and-white or color photos with player identification in a "plaque" at bottom. Blue-on-orange backs

have brief biographical data, a listing of the player's record and career highlights, and lifetime stats.

1987 Boardwalk and Baseball Top Run Makers

Created by Topps for distribution at the Boardwalk and Baseball theme park near Orlando, Fla., the cards are standard size with a thin, pink border around a color action photo. The backs are printed in black and light red, with the Topps and B/B logos at the bottom. There are 33-cards in the "Top Run Makers" boxed set, all hitters. A checklist appears on the back panel of the box. A much scarcer version of each card can be found with no slash between the "B's" on front.

		NM/M
Complete Set (33):		4.00
Common Player:		.10
No Slash:		3X
1	Mike Schmidt	1.00
2	Eddie Murray	.45
3	Dale Murphy	.25
4	Dave Winfield	.45
5	Jim Rice	.25
6	Cecil Cooper	.10
7	Dwight Evans	.10
8	Rickey Henderson	.45
9	Robin Yount	.45
10	Andre Dawson	.25
11	Gary Carter	.45
12	Keith Hernandez	.10
13	George Brett	1.00
14	Bill Buckner	.10
15	Tony Armas	.10
16	Harold Baines	.10
17	Don Baylor	.10
18	Steve Garvey	.10
19	Lance Parrish	.10
20	Dave Parker	.10
21	Buddy Bell	.10
22	Cal Ripken, Jr.	1.50
23	Bob Horner	.10
24	Tim Raines	.10
25	Jack Clark	.10
26	Leon Durham	.10
27	Pedro Guerrero	.10
28	Kent Hrbek	.10
29	Kirk Gibson	.10
30	Ryne Sandberg	.60
31	Wade Boggs	.60
32	Don Mattingly	.75
33	Darryl Strawberry	.10

1987 Bohemian Hearth Bread Padres

Bohemian Hearth Bread of San Diego issued this Padres team set. Produced in conjunction with Mike Schechter Associates, the cards are 2-1/2" x 3-1/2". Fronts have a color portrait photo encompassed by a yellow border. The Bohemian Hearth logo is located in the upper-left corner. Card backs are printed in light brown on a cream

stock and carry player personal and statistical information, along with a facsimile autograph.

		NM/M
Complete Set (22):		20.00
Common Player:		.50
1	Garry Templeton	.50
4	Jose Cora	.50
5	Randy Ready	.50
6	Steve Garvey	3.00
7	Kevin Mitchell	.50
8	John Kruk	.65
9	Benito Santiago	.75
10	Larry Bowa	.50
11	Tim Flannery	.50
14	Carmelo Martinez	.50
16	Marvell Wynne	.50
19	Tony Gwynn	15.00
21	James Steels	.50
22	Stan Jefferson	.50
30	Eric Show	.50
31	Ed Whitson	.50
34	Storm Davis	.50
37	Craig Lefferts	.50
40	Andy Hawkins	.50
41	Lance McCullers	.50
43	Dave Dravecky	.50
54	Rich Gossage	.50

1984 Borden's Reds Stickers

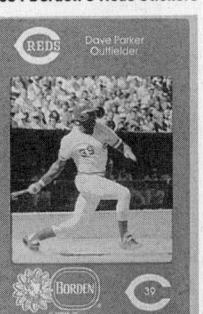

This regional set of eight Reds stickers was issued by Borden Dairy in the Cincinnati area in 1984. Originally issued in two perforated sheets of four stickers each, the individual stickers measure 2-1/2" x 3-7/8", while a full sheet measures 5-1/2" x 8". The colorful stickers feature a player photo surrounded by a bright red border with the Reds logo and the Borden logo in the corners. The backs display coupons for Borden dairy products. The set is numbered according to the players' uniform numbers.

		NM/M
Complete Panel Set (2):		8.00
Complete Singles Set (8):		8.00
Common Player:		.50
PANEL (1)		5.00
2	Gary Redus	.50
20	Eddie Milner	.50
32	Tony Perez	3.00
46	Jeff Russell	.50
PANEL (2)		3.00
16	Ron Oester	.50
36	Mario Soto	.50
39	Dave Parker	.60
44	Eric Davis	1.00

1983 Boston Herald SoxStamps

Current and former Red Sox stars are featured in this set of stamps issued by one of Boston's daily newspapers. Coupons in the paper could be redeemed for packets of stamps which could be mounted on a large (34" x 22") colorful wallchart. Persons completing the set could enter a contest for various prizes. Stamps #1-26 and 39-42 are in color and feature

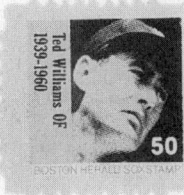

portrait photos of the '83 team. They measure 1" x 1-3/4". Stamps #27-38 and 43-50 are 1" x 1-1/8" and may have either color or black-and-white photos of current and former players. Values shown are for unused stamps.

		NM/M
Complete Set (50):		30.00
Common Player:		.50
Wallchart:		15.00
1	Jerry Remy	.50
2	Glenn Hoffman	.50
3	Luis Aponte	.50
4	Jim Rice	1.00
5	Mark Clear	.50
6	Reid Nichols	.50
7	Wade Boggs	5.00
8	Dennis Eckersley	2.00
9	Jeff Newman	.50
10	Bob Ojeda	.50
11	Ed Jurak	.50
12	Rick Miller	.50
13	Carl Yastrzemski	7.50
14	Mike Brown	.50
15	Bob Stanley	.50
16	John Tudor	.50
17	Gary Allenson	.50
18	Rich Gedman	.50
19	Tony Armas	.75
20	Doug Bird	.50
21	Bruce Hurst	.50
22	Dave Stapleton	.50
23	Dwight Evans	1.00
24	Julio Valdez	.50
25	John Henry Johnson	.50
26	Ralph Houk	.50
27	George Scott	.75
28	Bobby Doerr	.60
29	Frank Malzone	.50
30	Rico Petrocelli	.75
31	Carl Yastrzemski	5.00
32	Ted Williams	7.50
33	Dwight Evans	.75
34	Carlton Fisk	4.00
35	Dick Radatz	.50
36	Luis Tiant	.75
37	Mel Parnell	.50
38	Jim Rice	.75
39	Dennis Boyd	.60
40	Marty Barrett	.50
41	Brian Denman	.50
42	Steve Crawford	.50
43	Cy Young	.75
44	Jimmy Collins	.50
45	Tris Speaker	.75
46	Harry Hooper	.50
47	Lefty Grove	.60
48	Joe Cronin	.50
49	Jimmie Foxx	.50
50	Ted Williams	7.50

1982 Boston Red Sox Favorites

No issuer is identified on this collectors set, though some attribute it to the Boston Globe newspaper. The 2-1/2" x 3-1/2" cards are black-and-white with rather wide white borders on front. There is no player identification on front. Backs are roughly in the style of 1955 Bowmans and have player identification, personal data, stats, career highlights and a trivia question.

		NM/M
Complete Set (128):		35.00
Common Player:		.25
1	Harry Agganis	2.00
2	Ken Aspromonte	.25
3	Bobby Avila	.25
4	Frank Baumann	.25
5	Lou Berberet	.25
6	Milt Bolling	.25
7	Lou Boudreau	.50
8	Ted Bowsfield	.25
9	Tom Brewer	.25
10	Don Buddin	.25
11	Jerry Casale	.25
12	Billy Consolo	.25
13	Pete Daley	.25
14	Ike Delock	.25
15	Dom DiMaggio	1.00
16	Bobby Doerr	.50
17	Walt Dropo	.25
18	Arnold Earley	.25
19	Hoot Evers	.25
20	Mike Fornieles	.25
21	Gary Geiger	.25
22	Don Gile	.25
23	Joe Ginsberg	.25
24	Billy Goodman	.25
25	Pumpsie Green	.35
26	Grady Hatten	.25
27	Mike Higgins	.25
28	Jackie Jensen	.50
29	George Kell	.50
30	Marty Keough	.25
31	Leo Kiely	.25
32	Ellis Kinder	.25
33	Billy Klaus	.25
34	Don Lenhardt	.25
35	Ted Lepcio	.25
36	Frank Malzone	.35
37	Gene Mauch	.25
38	Maury McDermott	.25
39	Bill Monbouquette	.25
40	Chet Nichols	.25
41	Willard Nixon	.25
42	Jim Pagliaroni	.25
43	Mel Parnell	.25
44	Johnny Pesky	.25
45	Jimmy Piersall	.50
46	Bob Porterfield	.25
47	Pete Runnels	.25
48	Dave Sisler	.25
49	Riverboat Smith	.25
50	Gene Stephens	.25
51	Vern Stephens	.25
52	Chuck Stobbs	.25
53	Dean Stone	.25
54	Frank Sullivan	.25
55	Haywood Sullivan	.25
56	Birdie Tebbetts	.25
57	Mickey Vernon	.35
58	Vic Wertz	.25
59	Sammy White	.25
60	Ted Williams	6.00
61	Ted Wills	.25
62	Earl Wilson	.25
63	Al Zarilla	.25
64	Norm Zauchin	.25
65	Ted Williams, Carl Yastrzemski	4.00
66	Jim Lonborg, George Scott, Dick Williams, Carl Yastrzemski	2.00
67	Billy Conigliaro, Tony Conigliaro	.75
68	Jerry Adair	.25
69	Mike Andrews	.25
70	Gary Bell	.25
71	Dennis Bennett	.25
72	Ed Bressoud	.25
73	Ken Brett	.25
74	Lu Clinton	.25
75	Tony Conigliaro	1.00
76	Billy Conigliaro	.25
77	Gene Conley	.25
78	Ray Culp	.25
79	Dick Ellsworth	.25
80	Joe Foy	.25
81	Russ Gibson	.25
82	Jim Gosger	.25
83	Lennie Green	.25
84	Ken Harrelson	.25
85	Tony Horton	.35
86	Elston Howard	.35
87	Dalton Jones	.25
88	Eddie Kasko	.25
89	Joe Lahoud	.25
90	Jack Lamabe	.25
91	Jim Lonborg	.25
92	Sparky Lyle	.50
93	Felix Mantilla	.25
94	Roman Mejias	.25
95	Don McMahon	.25
96	Dave Morehead	.25
97	Gerry Moses	.25
98	Mike Nagy	.25
99	Russ Nixon	.25
100	Gene Oliver	.25
101	Dan Osinski	.25
102	Rico Petrocelli	.25
103	Juan Pizzaro	.25
104	Dick Radatz	.35
105	Vicente Romo	.25
106	Mike Ryan	.25
107	Jose Santiago	.25
108	Chuck Schilling	.35
109	Dick Schofield	.25
110	Don Schwall	.25
111	George Scott	.35
112	Norm Siebern	.25
113	Sonny Siebert	.25
114	Reggie Smith	.35
115	Bill Spanswick	.25
116	Tracy Stallard	.25
117	Lee Stange	.25

118	Jerry Stephenson	.25
119	Dick Stuart	.25
120	Tom Sturdivant	.25
121	Jose Tartabull	.25
122	George Thomas	.25
123	Lee Thomas	.25
124	Bob Tillman	.25
125	Gary Waslewski	.25
126	Dick Williams	.25
127	John Wyatt	.25
128	Carl Yastrzemski	4.00

1993 Boston Red Sox Police

This police set was issued by the police department and local sponsors around the Red Sox spring training base in Florida. Card fronts have studio poses of the players. The Winter Haven P.D. and Police Athletic League logos are at top, while the Red Sox logo, player ID and uniform number are beneath the portrait. Backs have a little personal data, some stats, a safety message and the names of sponsoring businesses.

		NM/M
	Complete Set (28):	10.00
	Common Player:	.50
1	Checklist	.10
2	Scott Bankhead	.50
3	Danny Darwin	.50
4	Andre Dawson	.75
5	Scott Fletcher	.50
6	Billy Hatcher	.50
7	Jack Clark	.50
8	Roger Clemens	5.00
9	Scott Cooper	.50
10	John Dopson	.50
11	Paul Quantrill	.50
12	Mike Greenwell	.50
13	Greg A. Harris	.50
14	Joe Hesketh	.50
15	Peter Hoy	.50
16	Daryl Irvine	.50
17	John Marzano	.50
18	Jeff McNeeley	.50
19	Tim Naehring	.50
20	Matt Young	.50
21	Jeff Plympton	.50
22	Bob Melvin	.50
23	Tony Pena	.50
24	Luis Rivera	.50
25	Scott Taylor	.50
26	John Valentin	.50
27	Mo Vaughn	.50
28	Frank Viola	.50

1987 Bowery Bank Joe DiMaggio

These cards were issued to promote the New York City bank's relationship with spokesman Joe DiMaggio. The 2-1/2" x 3-1/2" cards have a posed color photo on front. The back has biographical data, career highlights and stats printed in black and red.

	NM/M
Joe DiMaggio	17.50

1989 Bowman

Topps, which purchased Bowman in 1955, revived the brand name in 1989, issuing a 484-card set. The

2-1/2" x 3-3/4" cards are slightly taller than current standard. Fronts contain a full-color player photo, with facsimile autograph and the Bowman logo in an upper corner. Backs include a breakdown of the player's stats against each team in his league. A series of "Hot Rookie Stars" highlights the set. The cards were distributed in both wax packs and rack packs. Each pack included a special reproduction of a classic Bowman card with a sweepstakes on the back.

		NM/M
	Unopened Fact. Set (484):	20.00
	Complete Set (484):	15.00
	Common Player:	.05
	Wax Pack (12+1):	.75
	Wax Box (36):	15.00
	Rack Pack (40):	1.00
	Rack Box (24):	20.00
1	Oswald Peraza	.05
2	Brian Holton	.05
3	Jose Bautista	.05
4	Pete Harnisch RC	.10
5	Dave Schmidt	.05
6	Gregg Olson	.05
7	Jeff Ballard	.05
8	Bob Melvin	.05
9	Cal Ripken, Jr.	.75
10	Randy Milligan	.05
11	Juan Bell RC	.05
12	Billy Ripken	.05
13	Jim Trabor	.05
14	Pete Stanicek	.05
15	Steve Finley RC	.25
16	Larry Sheets	.05
17	Phil Bradley	.05
18	Brady Anderson	.05
19	Lee Smith	.05
20	Tim Fischer	.05
21	Mike Boddicker	.05
22	Rob Murphy	.05
23	Wes Gardner	.05
24	John Dopson	.05
25	Bob Stanley	.05
26	Roger Clemens	.60
27	Rich Gedman	.05
28	Marty Barrett	.05
29	Luis Rivera	.05
30	Jody Reed	.05
31	Nick Esasky	.05
32	Wade Boggs	.50
33	Jim Rice	.20
34	Mike Greenwell	.05
35	Dwight Evans	.05
36	Ellis Burks	.05
37	Chuck Finley	.05
38	Kirk McCaskill	.05
39	Jim Abbott	.05
40	Bryan Harvey RC	.05
41	Bert Blyleven	.05
42	Mike Witt	.05
43	Bob McClure	.05
44	Bill Schroeder	.05
45	Lance Parrish	.05
46	Dick Schofield	.05
47	Wally Joyner	.05
48	Jack Howell	.05
49	Johnny Ray	.05
50	Chili Davis	.05
51	Tony Armas	.05
52	Claudell Washington	.05
53	Brian Downing	.05
54	Devon White	.05
55	Bobby Thigpen	.05
56	Bill Long	.05
57	Jerry Reuss	.05
58	Shawn Hillegas	.05
59	Melido Perez	.05
60	Jeff Bittiger	.05
61	Jack McDowell	.05
62	Carlton Fisk	.40
63	Steve Lyons	.05
64	Ozzie Guillen	.05
65	Robin Ventura	.05
66	Fred Manrique	.05
67	Dan Pasqua	.05
68	Ivan Calderon	.05
69	Ron Kittle	.05
70	Daryl Boston	.05
71	Dave Gallagher	.05
72	Harold Baines	.05
73	Charles Nagy RC	.15
74	John Farrell	.05
75	Kevin Wickander	.05
76	Greg Swindell	.05
77	Mike Walker	.05
78	Doug Jones	.05
79	Rich Yett	.05
80	Tom Candiotti	.05
81	Jesse Orosco	.05
82	Bud Black	.05
83	Andy Allanson	.05
84	Pete O'Brien	.05
85	Jerry Browne	.05
86	Brook Jacoby	.05
87	Mark Lewis RC	.05
88	Luis Aguayo	.05
89	Cory Snyder	.05
90	Oddibe McDowell	.05
91	Joe Carter	.05
92	Frank Tanana	.05
93	Jack Morris	.05
94	Doyle Alexander	.05
95	Steve Searcy	.05
96	Randy Bockus	.05
97	Jeff Robinson	.05
98	Mike Henneman	.05
99	Paul Gibson	.05
100	Frank Williams	.05
101	Matt Nokes	.05
102	Rico Brogna	.05
103	Lou Whitaker	.05
104	Al Pedrique	.05
105	Alan Trammell	.05
106	Chris Brown	.05
107	Pat Sheridan	.05
108	Gary Pettis	.05
109	Keith Moreland	.05
110	Mel Stottlemyre, Jr.	.05
111	Bret Saberhagen	.05
112	Floyd Bannister	.05
113	Jeff Montgomery	.05
114	Steve Farr	.05
115	Tom Gordon	.05
116	Charlie Leibrandt	.05
117	Mark Gubicza	.05
118	Mike MacFarlane	.05
119	Bob Boone	.05
120	Kurt Stillwell	.05
121	George Brett	.60
122	Frank White	.05
123	Kevin Seitzer	.05
124	Willie Wilson	.05
125	Pat Tabler	.05
126	Bo Jackson	.10
127	Hugh Walker	.05
128	Danny Tartabull	.05
129	Teddy Higuera	.05
130	Don August	.05
131	Juan Nieves	.05
132	Mike Birkbeck	.05
133	Dan Plesac	.05
134	Chris Bosio	.05
135	Bill Wegman	.05
136	Chuck Crim	.05
137	B.J. Surhoff	.05
138	Joey Meyer	.05
139	Dale Sveum	.05
140	Paul Molitor	.40
141	Jim Gantner	.05
142	Gary Sheffield RC	.75
143	Greg Brock	.05
144	Robin Yount	.40
145	Glenn Braggs	.05
146	Rob Deer	.05
147	Fred Toliver	.05
148	Jeff Reardon	.05
149	Allan Anderson	.05
150	Frank Viola	.05
151	Shane Rawley	.05
152	Juan Berenguer	.05
153	Johnny Ard	.05
154	Tim Laudner	.05
155	Brian Harper	.05
156	Al Newman	.05
157	Kent Hrbek	.05
158	Gary Gaetti	.05
159	Wally Backman	.05
160	Gene Larkin	.05
161	Greg Gagne	.05
162	Kirby Puckett	.50
163	Danny Gladden	.05
164	Randy Bush	.05
165	Dave LaPoint	.05
166	Andy Hawkins	.05
167	Dave Righetti	.05
168	Lance McCullers	.05
169	Jimmy Jones	.05
170	Al Leiter	.05
171	John Candelaria	.05
172	Don Slaught	.05
173	Jamie Quirk	.05
174	Rafael Santana	.05
175	Mike Pagliarulo	.05
176	Don Mattingly	.60
177	Ken Phelps	.05
178	Steve Sax	.05
179	Dave Winfield	.40
180	Stan Jefferson	.05
181	Rickey Henderson	.25
182	Bob Brower	.05
183	Roberto Kelly	.05
184	Curt Young	.05
185	Gene Nelson	.05
186	Bob Welch	.05
187	Rick Honeycutt	.05
188	Dave Stewart	.05
189	Mike Moore	.05
190	Dennis Eckersley	.35
191	Eric Plunk	.05
192	Storm Davis	.05
193	Terry Steinbach	.05
194	Ron Hassey	.05
195	Stan Royer	.05
196	Walt Weiss	.05
197	Mark McGwire	.65
198	Carney Lansford	.05
199	Glenn Hubbard	.05
200	Dave Henderson	.05
201	Jose Canseco	.30
202	Dave Parker	.05
203	Scott Bankhead	.05
204	Tom Niedenfuer	.05
205	Mark Langston	.05
206	Erik Hanson RC	.05
207	Mike Jackson	.05
208	Dave Valle	.05
209	Scott Bradley	.05
210	Harold Reynolds	.05
211	Tino Martinez	.05
212	Rich Renteria	.05
213	Rey Quinones	.05
214	Jim Presley	.05
215	Alvin Davis	.05
216	Edgar Martinez	.05
217	Darnell Coles	.05
218	Jeffrey Leonard	.05
219	Jay Buhner	.05
220	Ken Griffey Jr. RC	6.00
221	Drew Hall	.05
222	Bobby Witt	.05
223	Jamie Moyer	.05
224	Charlie Hough	.05
225	Nolan Ryan	.75
226	Jeff Russell	.05
227	Jim Sundberg	.05
228	Julio Franco	.05
229	Buddy Bell	.05
230	Scott Fletcher	.05
231	Jeff Kunkel	.05
232	Steve Buechele	.05
233	Monty Fariss	.05
234	Rick Leach	.05
235	Ruben Sierra	.05
236	Cecil Espy	.05
237	Rafael Palmeiro	.35
238	Pete Incaviglia	.05
239	Dave Steib	.05
240	Jeff Musselman	.05
241	Mike Flanagan	.05
242	Todd Stottlemyre	.05
243	Jimmy Key	.05
244	Tony Castillo	.05
245	Alex Sanchez	.05
246	Tom Henke	.05
247	John Cerutti	.05
248	Ernie Whitt	.05
249	Bob Brenly	.05
250	Rance Mulliniks	.05
251	Kelly Gruber	.05
252	Ed Sprague	.05
253	Fred McGriff	.05
254	Tony Fernandez	.05
255	Tom Lawless	.05
256	George Bell	.05
257	Jesse Barfield	.05
258	Sandy Alomar, Sr.	.05
259	Ken Griffey (With Ken Griffey Jr.)	.30
260	Cal Ripken, Sr.	.05
261	Mel Stottlemyre, Sr.	.05
262	Zane Smith	.05
263	Charlie Puleo	.05
264	Derek Lilliquist	.05
265	Paul Assenmacher	.05
266	John Smoltz	.05
267	Tom Glavine	.25
268	Steve Avery RC	.05
269	Pete Smith RC	.05
270	Jody Davis	.05
271	Bruce Benedict	.05
272	Andres Thomas	.05
273	Gerald Perry	.05
274	Ron Gant	.05
275	Darrell Evans	.05
276	Dale Murphy	.25
277	Dion James	.05
278	Lonnie Smith	.05
279	Geronimo Berroa	.05
280	Steve Wilson	.05
281	Rick Sutcliffe	.05
282	Kevin Coffman	.05
283	Mitch Williams	.05
284	Greg Maddux	.50
285	Paul Kilgus	.05
286	Mike Harkey	.05
287	Lloyd McClendon	.05
288	Damon Berryhill	.05
289	Ty Griffin	.05
290	Ryne Sandberg	.50
291	Mark Grace	.05
292	Curt Wilkerson	.05
293	Vance Law	.05
294	Shawon Dunston	.05
295	Jerome Walton	.05
296	Mitch Webster	.05
297	Dwight Smith	.05
298	Andre Dawson	.25
299	Jeff Sellers	.05
300	Jose Rijo	.05
301	John Franco	.05
302	Rick Mahler	.05
303	Ron Robinson	.05
304	Danny Jackson	.05
305	Rob Dibble	.05
306	Tom Browning	.05
307	Bo Diaz	.05
308	Manny Trillo	.05
309	Chris Sabo RC	.05
310	Ron Oester	.05
311	Barry Larkin	.05
312	Todd Benzinger	.05
313	Paul O'Neill	.05
314	Kal Daniels	.05
315	Joel Youngblood	.05
316	Eric Davis	.05
317	Dave Smith	.05
318	Mark Portugal	.05
319	Brian Meyer	.05
320	Jim Deshaies	.05
321	Juan Agosto	.05
322	Mike Scott	.05
323	Rick Rhoden	.05
324	Jim Clancy	.05
325	Larry Andersen	.05
326	Alex Trevino	.05
327	Alan Ashby	.05
328	Craig Reynolds	.05
329	Bill Doran	.05
330	Rafael Ramirez	.05
331	Glenn Davis	.05
332	Willie Ansley RC	.05
333	Gerald Young	.05
334	Cameron Drew	.05
335	Jay Howell	.05
336	Tim Belcher	.05
337	Fernando Valenzuela	.05
338	Ricky Horton	.05
339	Tim Leary	.05
340	Bill Bene	.05
341	Orel Hershiser	.05
342	Mike Scioscia	.05
343	Rick Dempsey	.05
344	Willie Randolph	.05
345	Alfredo Griffin	.05
346	Eddie Murray	.40
347	Mickey Hatcher	.05
348	Mike Sharperson	.05
349	John Shelby	.05
350	Mike Marshall	.05
351	Kirk Gibson	.05
352	Mike Davis	.05
353	Bryn Smith	.05
354	Pascual Perez	.05
355	Kevin Gross	.05
356	Andy McGaffigan	.05
357	Brian Holman	.05
358	Dave Wainhouse	.05
359	Denny Martinez	.05
360	Tim Burke	.05
361	Nelson Santovenia	.05
362	Tim Wallach	.05
363	Spike Owen	.05
364	Rex Hudler	.05
365	Andres Galarraga	.05
366	Otis Nixon	.05
367	Hubie Brooks	.05
368	Mike Aldrete	.05
369	Rock Raines	.05
370	Dave Martinez	.05
371	Bob Ojeda	.05
372	Ron Darling	.05
373	Wally Whitehurst	.05
374	Randy Myers	.05
375	David Cone	.05
376	Dwight Gooden	.05
377	Sid Fernandez	.05
378	Dave Proctor	.05
379	Gary Carter	.40
380	Keith Miller	.05
381	Gregg Jefferies	.05
382	Tim Teufel	.05
383	Kevin Elster	.05
384	Dave Magadan	.05
385	Keith Hernandez	.05
386	Mookie Wilson	.05
387	Darryl Strawberry	.05
388	Kevin McReynolds	.05
389	Mark Carreon	.05
390	Jeff Parrett	.05
391	Mike Maddux	.05
392	Don Carman	.05
393	Bruce Ruffin	.05
394	Ken Howell	.05
395	Steve Bedrosian	.05
396	Floyd Youmans	.05
397	Larry McWilliams	.05
398	Pat Combs	.05
399	Steve Lake	.05
400	Dickie Thon	.05
401	Ricky Jordan	.05
402	Mike Schmidt	.60
403	Tom Herr	.05
404	Chris James	.05
405	Juan Samuel	.05
406	Von Hayes	.05
407	Ron Jones	.05
408	Curt Ford	.05
409	Bob Walk	.05
410	Jeff Robinson	.05
411	Jim Gott	.05
412	Scott Medvin	.05
413	John Smiley	.05
414	Bob Kipper	.05
415	Brian Fisher	.05
416	Doug Drabek	.05
417	Mike Lavalliere	.05
418	Ken Oberkfell	.05
419	Sid Bream	.05
420	Austin Manahan	.05
421	Jose Lind	.05
422	Bobby Bonilla	.05
423	Glenn Wilson	.05
424	Andy Van Slyke	.05
425	Gary Redus	.05
426	Barry Bonds	.75
427	Don Heinkel	.05
428	Ken Dayley	.05
429	Todd Worrell	.05
430	Brad DuVall	.05
431	Jose DeLeon	.05
432	Joe Magrane	.05
433	John Ericks	.05
434	Frank DiPino	.05
435	Tony Pena	.05
436	Ozzie Smith	.50
437	Terry Pendleton	.05
438	Jose Oquendo	.05
439	Tim Jones	.05
440	Pedro Guerrero	.05
441	Milt Thompson	.05
442	Willie McGee	.05
443	Vince Coleman	.05
444	Tom Brunansky	.05
445	Walt Terrell	.05
446	Eric Show	.05
447	Mark Davis	.05
448	Andy Benes RC	.10
449	Eddie Whitson	.05
450	Dennis Rasmussen	.05
451	Bruce Hurst	.05
452	Pat Clements	.05
453	Benito Santiago	.05
454	Sandy Alomar, Jr.	.05
455	Garry Templeton	.05
456	Jack Clark	.05
457	Tim Flannery	.05
458	Roberto Alomar	.25
459	Camelo Martinez	.05
460	John Kruk	.05
461	Tony Gwynn	.50
462	Jerald Clark	.05
463	Don Robinson	.05
464	Craig Lefferts	.05
465	Kelly Downs	.05
466	Rick Rueschel	.05
467	Scott Garrelts	.05
468	Wil Tejada	.05
469	Kirt Manwaring	.05
470	Terry Kennedy	.05
471	Jose Uribe	.05
472	Royce Clayton RC	.10
473	Robby Thompson	.05
474	Kevin Mitchell	.05
475	Ernie Riles	.05
476	Will Clark	.05
477	Donnell Nixon	.05
478	Candy Maldonado	.05
479	Tracy Jones	.05
480	Brett Butler	.05
481	Checklist 1-121	.05
482	Checklist 122-242	.05
483	Checklist 243-363	.05
484	Checklist 364-484	.05

Tiffany

A special collectors' version of the revitalized Bowman cards was produced in 1989, differing from the regular-issue cards in the application of a high-gloss finish to the front and the use of a white cardboard stock. The "Tiffany" version (as the glossies are known to collectors), was sold only in complete boxed sets, with an estimated production of 6,000 sets.

	NM/M
Unopened Set (495):	165.00
Complete Set (495):	100.00
Common Player:	.25

Inserts

Bowman inserted sweepstakes cards in its 1989 packs. Each sweepstakes card reproduces a classic Bowman card on the front, with a prominent "REPRINT" notice. With one card in each pack, they are by no means scarce. A "Tiffany" version of the reprints was produced for inclusion in the factory set of 1989 Bowman cards. The glossy-front inserts are valued at 10X the standard version.

	NM/M
Complete Set (11):	3.50
Common Player:	.10

No.	Player	Price
(1)	Richie Ashburn	.10
(2)	Yogi Berra	.10
(3)	Whitey Ford	.10
(4)	Gil Hodges	.10
(5)	Mickey Mantle/1951	2.00
(6)	Mickey Mantle/1953	1.50
(7)	Willie Mays	.50
(8)	Satchel Paige	.25
(9)	Jackie Robinson	1.00
(10)	Duke Snider	.10
(11)	Ted Williams	1.00

1990 Bowman

Bowman followed its 1989 re-birth with a 528-card set in 1990. The 1990 cards follow the classic Bowman style featuring a full-color photo bordered in white. The Bowman logo appears in the upper-left corner. The player's team nickname and name appear on the bottom border of the card photo. Unlike the 1989 set, the 1990 cards are standard 2-1/2" x 3-1/2". Backs are horizontal and display the player's statistics against the teams in his league.

	NM/M
Unopened Factory Set (528):	20.00
Complete Set (528):	15.00
Common Player:	.05
Wax Pack (15):	.75
Wax Box (36):	15.00
Jumbo Pack (31):	1.00
Jumbo Box (24):	15.00
Rack Pack (39):	1.50
Rack Box (24):	20.00

No.	Player	Price
1	Tommy Greene RC	.05
2	Tom Glavine	.30
3	Andy Nezelek	.05
4	Mike Stanton	.05
5	Rick Lueken	.05
6	Kent Mercker	.05
7	Derek Lilliquist	.05
8	Charlie Liebrandt	.05
9	Steve Avery	.05
10	John Smoltz	.05
11	Mark Lemke	.05
12	Lonnie Smith	.05
13	Oddibe McDowell	.05
14	Tyler Houston RC	.05
15	Jeff Blauser	.05
16	Ernie Whitt	.05
17	Alexis Infante	.05
18	Jim Presley	.05
19	Dale Murphy	.25
20	Nick Esasky	.05
21	Rick Sutcliffe	.05
22	Mike Bielecki	.05
23	Steve Wilson	.05
24	Kevin Blankenship	.05
25	Mitch Williams	.05
26	Dean Wilkins	.05
27	Greg Maddux	.50
28	Mike Harkey	.05
29	Mark Grace	.05
30	Ryne Sandberg	.50
31	Greg Smith	.05
32	Dwight Smith	.05
33	Damon Berryhill	.05
34	Earl Cunningham	.05
35	Jerome Walton	.05
36	Lloyd McClendon	.05
37	Ty Griffin	.05
38	Shawon Dunston	.05
39	Andre Dawson	.25
40	Luis Salazar	.05
41	Tim Layana	.05
42	Rob Dibble	.05
43	Tom Browning	.05
44	Danny Jackson	.05
45	Jose Rijo	.05
46	Scott Scudder	.05
47	Randy Myers	.05
48	Brian Lane	.05
49	Paul O'Neill	.05
50	Barry Larkin	.05
51	Reggie Jefferson	.05
52	Jeff Branson	.05
53	Chris Sabo	.05
54	Joe Oliver	.05
55	Todd Benzinger	.05
56	Rolando Roomes	.05
57	Hal Morris	.05
58	Eric Davis	.05
59	Scott Bryant	.05
60	Ken Griffey	.05
61	Darryl Kile RC	.05
62	Dave Smith	.05
63	Mark Portugal	.05
64	Jeff Juden RC	.05
65	Bill Gullickson	.05
66	Danny Darwin	.05
67	Larry Andersen	.05
68	Jose Cano	.05
69	Dan Schatzeder	.05
70	Jim Deshaies	.05
71	Mike Scott	.05
72	Gerald Young	.05
73	Ken Caminiti	.05
74	Ken Oberkfell	.05
75	Dave Rhode	.05
76	Bill Doran	.05
77	Andujar Cedeno	.05
78	Craig Biggio	.05
79	Karl Rhodes	.05
80	Glenn Davis	.05
81	Eric Anthony RC	.05
82	John Wetteland	.05
83	Jay Howell	.05
84	Orel Hershiser	.05
85	Tim Belcher	.05
86	Kiki Jones	.05
87	Mike Hartley	.05
88	Ramon Martinez	.05
89	Mike Scioscia	.05
90	Willie Randolph	.05
91	Juan Samuel	.05
92	Jose Offerman RC	.05
93	Dave Hansen	.05
94	Jeff Hamilton	.05
95	Alfredo Griffin	.05
96	Tom Goodwin	.05
97	Kirk Gibson	.05
98	Jose Vizcaino	.05
99	Kal Daniels	.05
100	Hubie Brooks	.05
101	Eddie Murray	.40
102	Dennis Boyd	.05
103	Tim Burke	.05
104	Bill Sampen	.05
105	Brett Gideon	.05
106	Mark Gardner	.05
107	Howard Farmer	.05
108	Mel Rojas	.05
109	Kevin Gross	.05
110	Dave Schmidt	.05
111	Denny Martinez	.05
112	Jerry Goff	.05
113	Andres Galarraga	.05
114	Tim Welch	.05
115	Marquis Grissom RC	.25
116	Spike Owen	.05
117	Larry Walker RC	1.00
118	Rock Raines	.05
119	Delino DeShields RC	.10
120	Tom Foley	.05
121	Dave Martinez	.05
122	Frank Viola	.05
123	Julio Valera	.05
124	Alejandro Pena	.05
125	David Cone	.05
126	Dwight Gooden	.05
127	Kevin Brown	.05
128	John Franco	.05
129	Terry Bross	.05
130	Blaine Beatty	.05
131	Sid Fernandez	.05
132	Mike Marshall	.05
133	Howard Johnson	.05
134	Jaime Roseboro	.05
135	Alan Zinter	.05
136	Keith Miller	.05
137	Kevin Elster	.05
138	Kevin McReynolds	.05
139	Barry Lyons	.05
140	Gregg Jefferies	.05
141	Darryl Strawberry	.05
142	Todd Hundley RC	.10
143	Scott Service	.05
144	Chuck Malone	.05
145	Steve Ontiveros	.05
146	Roger McDowell	.05
147	Ken Howell	.05
148	Pat Combs	.05
149	Jeff Parrett	.05
150	Chuck McElroy	.05
151	Jason Grimsley	.05
152	Len Dykstra	.05
153	Mickey Morandini	.05
154	John Kruk	.05
155	Dickie Thon	.05
156	Ricky Jordan	.05
157	Jeff Jackson	.05
158	Darren Daulton	.05
159	Tom Herr	.05
160	Von Hayes	.05
161	Dave Hollins RC	.05
162	Carmelo Martinez	.05
163	Bob Walk	.05
164	Doug Drabek	.05
165	Walt Terrell	.05
166	Bill Landrum	.05
167	Scott Ruskin	.05
168	Bob Patterson	.05
169	Bobby Bonilla	.05
170	Jose Lind	.05
171	Andy Van Slyke	.05
172	Mike LaValliere	.05
173	Willie Greene RC	.05
174	Jay Bell	.05
175	Sid Bream	.05
176	Tom Prince	.05
177	Wally Backman	.05
178	Moises Alou RC	.25
179	Steve Carter	.05
180	Gary Redus	.05
181	Barry Bonds	1.00
182	Don Slaught	.05
183	Joe Magrane	.05
184	Bryn Smith	.05
185	Todd Worrell	.05
186	Jose Deleon	.05
187	Frank DiPino	.05
188	John Tudor	.05
189	Howard Hilton	.05
190	John Ericks	.05
191	Ken Dayley	.05
192	Ray Lankford RC	.10
193	Todd Zeile	.05
194	Willie McGee	.05
195	Ozzie Smith	.50
196	Milt Thompson	.05
197	Terry Pendleton	.05
198	Vince Coleman	.05
199	Paul Coleman	.05
200	Jose Oquendo	.05
201	Pedro Guerrero	.05
202	Tom Brunansky	.05
203	Roger Smithberg	.05
204	Eddie Whitson	.05
205	Dennis Rasmussen	.05
206	Craig Lefferts	.05
207	Andy Benes	.05
208	Bruce Hurst	.05
209	Eric Show	.05
210	Rafael Valdez	.05
211	Joey Cora	.05
212	Thomas Howard	.05
213	Rob Nelson	.05
214	Jack Clark	.05
215	Garry Templeton	.05
216	Fred Lynn	.05
217	Tony Gwynn	.50
218	Benny Santiago	.05
219	Mike Pagliarulo	.05
220	Joe Carter	.05
221	Roberto Alomar	.25
222	Bip Roberts	.05
223	Rick Reuschel	.05
224	Russ Swan	.05
225	Eric Gunderson	.05
226	Steve Bedrosian	.05
227	Mike Remlinger	.05
228	Scott Garrelts	.05
229	Ernie Camacho	.05
230	Andres Santana	.05
231	Will Clark	.05
232	Kevin Mitchell	.05
233	Robby Thompson	.05
234	Bill Bathe	.05
235	Tony Perezchica	.05
236	Gary Carter	.40
237	Brett Butler	.05
238	Matt Williams	.05
239	Ernie Riles	.05
240	Kevin Bass	.05
241	Terry Kennedy	.05
242	Steve Hosey RC	.05
243	Ben McDonald RC	.15
244	Jeff Ballard	.05
245	Joe Price	.05
246	Curt Schilling	.30
247	Pete Harnisch	.05
248	Mark Williamson	.05
249	Gregg Olson	.05
250	Chris Myers	.05
251a	David Segui (No bio. data on back.)	3.50
251b	David Segui (Bio. data on back.)	.05
252	Joe Orsulak	.05
253	Craig Worthington	.05
254	Mickey Tettleton	.05
255	Cal Ripken, Jr.	1.00
256	Billy Ripken	.05
257	Randy Milligan	.05
258	Brady Anderson	.05
259	Chris Hoiles	.05
260	Mike Devereaux	.05
261	Phil Bradley	.05
262	Leo Gomez RC	.05
263	Lee Smith	.05
264	Mike Rochford	.05
265	Jeff Reardon	.05
266	Wes Gardner	.05
267	Mike Boddicker	.05
268	Roger Clemens	.60
269	Rob Murphy	.05
270	Mickey Pina	.05
271	Tony Pena	.05
272	Jody Reed	.05
273	Kevin Romine	.05
274	Mike Greenwell	.05
275	Mo Vaughn RC	.60
276	Danny Heep	.05
277	Scott Cooper	.05
278	Greg Blosser RC	.05
279	Dwight Evans	.05
280	Ellis Burks	.05
281	Wade Boggs	.50
282	Marty Barrett	.05
283	Kirk McCaskill	.05
284	Mark Langston	.05
285	Bert Blyleven	.05
286	Mike Fetters	.05
287	Kyle Abbott	.05
288	Jim Abbott	.05
289	Chuck Finley	.05
290	Gary DiSarcina	.05
291	Dick Schofield	.05
292	Devon White	.05
293	Bobby Rose	.05
294	Brian Downing	.05
295	Lance Parrish	.05
296	Jack Howell	.05
297	Claudell Washington	.05
298	John Orton	.05
299	Wally Joyner	.05
300	Lee Stevens	.05
301	Chili Davis	.05
302	Johnny Ray	.05
303	Greg Hibbard	.05
304	Eric King	.05
305	Jack McDowell	.05
306	Bobby Thigpen	.05
307	Adam Peterson	.05
308	Scott Radinsky RC	.05
309	Wayne Edwards	.05
310	Melido Perez	.05
311	Robin Ventura	.05
312	Sammy Sosa RC	2.00
313	Dan Pasqua	.05
314	Carlton Fisk	.40
315	Ozzie Guillen	.05
316	Ivan Calderon	.05
317	Daryl Boston	.05
318	Craig Grebeck	.05
319	Scott Fletcher	.05
320	Frank Thomas RC	3.00
321	Steve Lyons	.05
322	Carlos Martinez	.05
323	Joe Skalski	.05
324	Tom Candiotti	.05
325	Greg Swindell	.05
326	Steve Olin	.05
327	Kevin Wickander	.05
328	Doug Jones	.05
329	Jeff Shaw	.05
330	Kevin Bearse	.05
331	Dion James	.05
332	Jerry Browne	.05
333	Albert Belle	.05
334	Felix Fermin	.05
335	Candy Maldonado	.05
336	Cory Snyder	.05
337	Sandy Alomar	.05
338	Mark Lewis	.05
339	Carlos Baerga RC	.10
340	Chris James	.05
341	Brook Jacoby	.05
342	Keith Hernandez	.05
343	Frank Tanana	.05
344	Scott Aldred	.05
345	Mike Henneman	.05
346	Steve Wapnick	.05
347	Greg Gohr	.05
348	Eric Stone	.05
349	Brian DuBois	.05
350	Kevin Ritz	.05
351	Rico Brogna	.05
352	Mike Heath	.05
353	Alan Trammell	.05
354	Chet Lemon	.05
355	Dave Bergman	.05
356	Lou Whitaker	.05
357	Cecil Fielder	.05
358	Milt Cuyler	.05
359	Tony Phillips	.05
360	Travis Fryman RC	.10
361	Ed Romero	.05
362	Lloyd Moseby	.05
363	Mark Gubicza	.05
364	Bret Saberhagen	.05
365	Tom Gordon	.05
366	Steve Farr	.05
367	Kevin Appier	.05
368	Storm Davis	.05
369	Mark Davis	.05
370	Jeff Montgomery	.05
371	Frank White	.05
372	Brent Mayne	.05
373	Bob Boone	.05
374	Jim Eisenreich	.05
375	Danny Tartabull	.05
376	Kurt Stillwell	.05
377	Bill Pecota	.05
378	Bo Jackson	.10
379	Bob Hamelin RC	.05
380	Kevin Seitzer	.05
381	Rey Palacios	.05
382	George Brett	.60
383	Gerald Perry	.05
384	Teddy Higuera	.05
385	Tom Filer	.05
386	Dan Plesac	.05
387	Cal Eldred RC	.05
388	Jaime Navarro	.05
389	Chris Bosio	.05
390	Randy Veres	.05
391	Gary Sheffield	.25
392	George Canale	.05
393	B.J. Surhoff	.05
394	Tim McIntosh	.05
395	Greg Brock	.05
396	Greg Vaughn	.05
397	Darryl Hamilton	.05
398	Dave Parker	.05
399	Paul Molitor	.40
400	Jim Gantner	.05
401	Rob Deer	.05
402	Billy Spiers	.05
403	Glenn Braggs	.05
404	Robin Yount	.40
405	Rick Aguilera	.05
406	Johnny Ard	.05
407	Kevin Tapani RC	.10
408	Park Pittman	.05
409	Allan Anderson	.05
410	Juan Berenguer	.05
411	Willie Banks	.05
412	Rich Yett	.05
413	Dave West	.05
414	Greg Gagne	.05
415	Chuck Knoblauch RC	.50
416	Randy Bush	.05
417	Gary Gaetti	.05
418	Kent Hrbek	.05
419	Al Newman	.05
420	Danny Gladden	.05
421	Paul Sorrento	.05
422	Derek Parks	.05
423	Scott Leius	.05
424	Kirby Puckett	.50
425	Willie Smith	.05
426	Dave Righetti	.05
427	Jeff Robinson	.05
428	Alan Mills	.05
429	Tim Leary	.05
430	Pascual Perez	.05
431	Alvaro Espinoza	.05
432	Dave Winfield	.40
433	Jesse Barfield	.05
434	Randy Velarde	.05
435	Rick Cerone	.05
436	Steve Balboni	.05
437	Mel Hall	.05
438	Bob Geren	.05
439	Bernie Williams RC	1.00
440	Kevin Maas RC	.05
441	Mike Blowers	.05
442	Steve Sax	.05
443	Don Mattingly	.60
444	Roberto Kelly	.05
445	Mike Moore	.05
446	Reggie Harris	.05
447	Scott Sanderson	.05
448	Dave Otto	.05
449	Dave Stewart	.05
450	Rick Honeycutt	.05
451	Dennis Eckersley	.35
452	Carney Lansford	.05
453	Scott Hemond	.05
454	Mark McGwire	.75
455	Felix Jose	.05
456	Terry Steinbach	.05
457	Rickey Henderson	.40
458	Dave Henderson	.05
459	Mike Gallego	.05
460	Jose Canseco	.30
461	Walt Weiss	.05
462	Ken Phelps	.05
463	Darren Lewis RC	.05
464	Ron Hassey	.05
465	Roger Salkeld RC	.05
466	Scott Bankhead	.05
467	Keith Comstock	.05
468	Randy Johnson	.40
469	Erik Hanson	.05
470	Mike Schooler	.05
471	Gary Eave	.05
472	Jeffrey Leonard	.05
473	Dave Valle	.05
474	Omar Vizquel	.05
475	Pete O'Brien	.05
476	Henry Cotto	.05
477	Jay Buhner	.05
478	Harold Reynolds	.05
479	Alvin Davis	.05
480	Darnell Coles	.05
481	Ken Griffey Jr.	.65
482	Greg Briley	.05
483	Scott Bradley	.05
484	Tino Martinez	.05
485	Jeff Russell	.05
486	Nolan Ryan	1.00
487	Robb Nen	.05
488	Kevin Brown	.05
489	Brian Bohanon	.05
490	Ruben Sierra	.05
491	Pete Incaviglia	.05
492	Juan Gonzalez RC	1.00
493	Steve Buechele	.05
494	Scott Coolbaugh	.05
495	Geno Petralli	.05
496	Rafael Palmeiro	.35
497	Julio Franco	.05
498	Gary Pettis	.05
499	Donald Harris	.05
500	Monty Fariss	.05
501	Harold Baines	.05
502	Cecil Espy	.05
503	Jack Daugherty	.05
504	Willie Blair	.05
505	Dave Steib	.05
506	Tom Henke	.05
507	John Cerutti	.05
508	Paul Kilgus	.05
509	Jimmy Key	.05
510	John Olerud RC	.75
511	Ed Sprague	.05
512	Manny Lee	.05
513	Fred McGriff	.05
514	Glenallen Hill	.05
515	George Bell	.05
516	Mookie Wilson	.05
517	Luis Sojo	.05
518	Nelson Liriano	.05
519	Kelly Gruber	.05
520	Greg Myers	.05
521	Pat Borders	.05
522	Junior Felix	.05
523	Eddie Zosky	.05
524	Tony Fernandez	.05
525	Checklist	.05
526	Checklist	.05
527	Checklist	.05
528	Checklist	.05

Tiffany

Reported production of fewer than 10,000 sets has created a significant premium for these glossy "Tiffany" versions of Bowman's 1990 baseball card set. The use of white cardboard stock and high-gloss front finish distinguishes these cards from regular-issue Bowmans.

	NM/M
Unopened Set (539):	200.00
Complete Set (539):	60.00
Common Player:	.25

Inserts

Bowman inserted sweepstakes cards in its 1990 packs, much like in 1989. This 11-card set features current players displayed in drawings by Craig Pursley.

	NM/M
Complete Set (11):	1.00
Common Player:	.05
(1) Will Clark	.05
(2) Mark Davis	.05
(3) Dwight Gooden	.05
(4) Bo Jackson	.10
(5) Don Mattingly	.40
(6) Kevin Mitchell	.05
(7) Gregg Olson	.05
(8) Nolan Ryan	.50
(9) Bret Saberhagen	.05
(10) Jerome Walton	.05
(11) Robin Yount	.25

1990 Bowman Lithographs

The paintings which were the basis for the sweepstakes insert cards in 1990 Bowman were also used in the creation of a set of 11" x 14" lithographs. The lithographs were offered as a prize in the sweepstakes or could be purchased from hobby dealers for a retail price in the $400-450 range.

	NM/M
Complete Set (11):	250.00
Common Player:	10.00
(1) Will Clark	10.00
(2) Mark Davis	10.00
(3) Dwight Gooden	10.00
(4) Bo Jackson	20.00
(5) Don Mattingly	50.00
(6) Kevin Mitchell	10.00
(7) Gregg Olson	10.00
(8) Nolan Ryan	100.00
(9) Bret Saberhagen	10.00
(10) Jerome Walton	10.00
(11) Robin Yount	25.00

1991 Bowman

The 1991 Bowman set features 704 cards compared to 528 cards in the 1990 issue. The cards imitate the 1953 Bowman style. Special Rod Carew cards and gold foil-stamped cards are included. The set is numbered by teams. Like the 1989 and 1990 issues, the card backs feature a breakdown of performance against each other's team in the league.

	NM/M
Unopened Factory Set (704):	30.00
Complete Set (704):	20.00
Common Player:	.05
Wax Pack (14):	.75
Wax Box (36):	17.50
Cello Pack (29):	1.50
Cello Box (24):	25.00

1 Rod Carew-I .10
2 Rod Carew-II .10
3 Rod Carew-III .10
4 Rod Carew-IV .10
5 Rod Carew-V .10
6 Willie Fraser .05
7 John Olerud .05
8 William Suero .05
9 Roberto Alomar .20
10 Todd Stottlemyre .05
11 Joe Carter .05
12 Steve Karsay RC .10
13 Mark Whiten .05
14 Pat Borders .05
15 Mike Timlin .05
16 Tom Henke .05
17 Eddie Zosky .05
18 Kelly Gruber .05
19 Jimmy Key .05
20 Jerry Schunk .05
21 Manny Lee .05
22 Dave Steib .05
23 Pat Hentgen .05
24 Glenallen Hill .05
25 Rene Gonzales .05
26 Ed Sprague .05
27 Ken Dayley .05
28 Pat Tabler .05
29 Denis Boucher RC .05
30 Devon White .05
31 Dante Bichette .05
32 Paul Molitor .40
33 Greg Vaughn .05
34 Dan Plesac .05
35 Chris George .05
36 Tim McIntosh .05
37 Franklin Stubbs .05
38 Bo Dodson .05
39 Ron Robinson .05
40 Ed Nunez .05
41 Greg Brock .05
42 Jaime Navarro .05
43 Chris Bosio .05
44 B.J. Surhoff .05
45 Chris Johnson .05
46 Willie Randolph .05
47 Narciso Elvira .05
48 Jim Gantner .05
49 Kevin Brown .05
50 Julio Machado .05
51 Chuck Crim .05
52 Gary Sheffield .30
53 Angel Miranda .05
54 Teddy Higuera .05
55 Robin Yount .40
56 Cal Eldred .05
57 Sandy Alomar .05
58 Greg Swindell .05
59 Brook Jacoby .05
60 Efrain Valdez .05
61 Ever Magallanes .05
62 Tom Candiotti .05
63 Eric King .05
64 Alex Cole .05
65 Charles Nagy .05
66 Mitch Webster .05
67 Chris James .05
68 Jim Thome RC 3.00
69 Carlos Baerga .05
70 Mark Lewis .05
71 Jerry Browne .05
72 Jesse Orosco .05
73 Mike Huff .05
74 Jose Escobar .05
75 Jeff Manto .05
76 Turner Ward RC .05
77 Doug Jones .05
78 Bruce Egloff RC .05
79 Tim Costo .05
80 Beau Allred .05
81 Albert Belle .05
82 John Farrell .05
83 Glenn Davis .05
84 Joe Orsulak .05
85 Mark Williamson .05
86 Ben McDonald .05

87 Billy Ripken .05
88 Leo Gomez .05
89 Bob Melvin .05
90 Jeff Robinson .05
91 Jose Mesa .05
92 Gregg Olson .05
93 Mike Devereaux .05
94 Luis Mercedes .05
95 Arthur Rhodes RC .10
96 Juan Bell .05
97 Mike Mussina RC 3.00
98 Jeff Ballard .05
99 Chris Hoiles .05
100 Brady Anderson .05
101 Bob Milacki .05
102 David Segui .05
103 Dwight Evans .05
104 Cal Ripken, Jr. 1.00
105 Mike Linskey .05
106 Jeff Tackett RC .05
107 Jeff Reardon .05
108 Dana Kiecker .05
109 Ellis Burks .05
110 Dave Owen .05
111 Danny Darwin .05
112 Mo Vaughn .05
113 Jeff McNeely .05
114 Tom Bolton .05
115 Greg Blosser .05
116 Mike Greenwell .05
117 Phil Plantier RC .05
118 Roger Clemens .60
119 John Marzano .05
120 Jody Reed .05
121 Scott Taylor .05
122 Jack Clark .05
123 Derek Livernois .05
124 Tony Pena .05
125 Tom Brunansky .05
126 Carlos Quintana .05
127 Tim Naehring .05
128 Matt Young .05
129 Wade Boggs .50
130 Kevin Morton .05
131 Pete Incaviglia .05
132 Rob Deer .05
133 Bill Gullickson .05
134 Rico Brogna .05
135 Lloyd Moseby .05
136 Cecil Fielder .05
137 Tony Phillips .05
138 Mark Leiter .05
139 John Cerutti .05
140 Mickey Tettleton .05
141 Milt Cuyler .05
142 Greg Gohr .05
143 Tony Bernazard .05
144 Dan Gakeler .05
145 Travis Fryman .05
146 Dan Petry .05
147 Scott Aldred .05
148 John DeSilva .05
149 Rusty Meacham .05
150 Lou Whitaker .05
151 Dave Haas .05
152 Luis de los Santos .05
153 Ivan Cruz .05
154 Alan Trammell .05
155 Pat Kelly .05
156 Carl Everett RC .25
157 Greg Cadaret .05
158 Kevin Maas .05
159 Jeff Johnson .05
160 Willie Smith .05
161 Gerald Williams .05
162 Mike Humphreys .05
163 Alvaro Espinoza .05
164 Matt Nokes .05
165 Wade Taylor .05
166 Roberto Kelly .05
167 John Habyan .05
168 Steve Farr .05
169 Jesse Barfield .05
170 Steve Sax .05
171 Jim Leyritz .05
172 Robert Eenhoorn .05
173 Bernie Williams .05
174 Scott Lusader .05
175 Torey Lovullo .05
176 Chuck Cary .05
177 Scott Sanderson .05
178 Don Mattingly .60
179 Mel Hall .05
180 Juan Gonzalez .30
181 Hensley Meulens .05
182 Jose Offerman .05
183 Jeff Bagwell RC 2.50
184 Jeff Conine RC .25
185 Henry Rodriguez RC .05
186 Jimmie Reese .05
187 Kyle Abbott .05
188 Lance Parrish .05
189 Rafael Montalvo .05
190 Floyd Bannister .05
191 Dick Schofield .05
192 Scott Lewis .05
193 Jeff Robinson .05
194 Kent Anderson .05
195 Wally Joyner .05
196 Chuck Finley .05
197 Luis Sojo .05
198 Jeff Richardson .05
199 Dave Parker .05
200 Jim Abbott .05
201 Junior Felix .05
202 Mark Langston .05
203 Tim Salmon RC 1.00
204 Cliff Young .05

205 Scott Bailes .05
206 Bobby Rose .05
207 Gary Gaetti .05
208 Ruben Amaro .05
209 Luis Polonia .05
210 Dave Winfield .40
211 Bryan Harvey .05
212 Mike Moore .05
213 Rickey Henderson .40
214 Steve Chitren .05
215 Bob Welch .05
216 Terry Steinbach .05
217 Ernie Riles .05
218 Todd Van Poppel RC .10
219 Mike Gallego .05
220 Curt Young .05
221 Todd Burns .05
222 Vance Law .05
223 Eric Show .05
224 Don Peters RC .05
225 Dave Stewart .05
226 Dave Henderson .05
227 Jose Canseco .30
228 Walt Weiss .05
229 Dann Howitt .05
230 Willie Wilson .05
231 Harold Baines .05
232 Scott Hemond .05
233 Joe Slusarski .05
234 Mark McGwire .75
235 Kirk Dressendorfer RC .05
236 Craig Paquette RC .05
237 Dennis Eckersley .35
238 Dana Allison .05
239 Scott Bradley .05
240 Brian Holman .05
241 Mike Schooler .05
242 Rich Delucia .05
243 Edgar Martinez .05
244 Henry Cotto .05
245 Omar Vizquel .05
246a Ken Griffey Jr. .65
246b Ken Griffey Sr. (Should be #255.) .10
247 Jay Buhner .05
248 Bill Krueger .05
249 Dave Fleming RC .05
250 Patrick Lennon RC .05
251 Dave Valle .05
252 Harold Reynolds .05
253 Randy Johnson .40
254 Scott Bankhead .05
256 Greg Briley .05
257 Tino Martinez .05
258 Alvin Davis .05
259 Pete O'Brien .05
260 Erik Hanson .05
261 Bret Boone RC .50
262 Roger Salkeld .05
263 Dave Burba .05
264 Kerry Woodson RC .05
265 Julio Franco .05
266 Dan Peltier .05
267 Jeff Russell .05
268 Steve Buechele .05
269 Donald Harris .05
270 Robb Nen .05
271 Rich Gossage .05
272 Ivan Rodriguez RC 3.00
273 Jeff Huson .05
274 Kevin Brown .05
275 Dan Smith RC .05
276 Gary Pettis .05
277 Jack Daugherty .05
278 Mike Jeffcoat .05
279 Brad Arnsberg .05
280 Nolan Ryan 1.00
281 Eric McCray .05
282 Scott Chiamparino .05
283 Ruben Sierra .05
284 Geno Petralli .05
285 Monty Fariss .05
286 Rafael Palmeiro .35
287 Bobby Witt .05
288 Dean Palmer .05
289 Tony Scruggs .05
290 Kenny Rogers .05
291 Bret Saberhagen .05
292 Brian McRae RC .05
293 Storm Davis .05
294 Danny Tartabull .05
295 David Howard .05
296 Mike Boddicker .05
297 Joel Johnston .05
298 Tim Spehr .05
299 Hector Wagner .05
300 George Brett .60
301 Mike Macfarlane .05
302 Kirk Gibson .05
303 Harvey Pulliam .05
304 Jim Eisenreich .05
305 Kevin Seitzer .05
306 Mark Davis .05
307 Kurt Stillwell .05
308 Jeff Montgomery .05
309 Kevin Appier .05
310 Bob Hamelin .05
311 Tom Gordon .05
312 Kerwin Moore RC .05
313 Hugh Walker .05
314 Terry Shumpert .05
315 Warren Cromartie .05
316 Gary Thurman .05
317 Steve Bedrosian .05
318 Danny Gladden .05
319 Jack Morris .05
320 Kirby Puckett .50
321 Kent Hrbek .05

322 Kevin Tapani .05
323 Denny Neagle .05
324 Rich Garces .05
325 Larry Casian .05
326 Shane Mack .05
327 Allan Anderson .05
328 Junior Ortiz .05
329 Paul Abbott RC .05
330 Chuck Knoblauch .05
331 Chili Davis .05
332 Todd Ritchie RC .05
333 Brian Harper .05
334 Rick Aguilera .05
335 Scott Erickson .05
336 Pedro Munoz .05
337 Scott Leius .05
338 Greg Gagne .05
339 Mike Pagliarulo .05
340 Terry Leach .05
341 Willie Banks .05
342 Bobby Thigpen .05
343 Roberto Hernandez RC .10
344 Melido Perez .05
345 Carlton Fisk .40
346 Norberto Martin RC .05
347 Johnny Ruffin RC .05
348 Jeff Carter RC .05
349 Lance Johnson .05
350 Sammy Sosa .50
351 Alex Fernandez .05
352 Jack McDowell .05
353 Bob Wickman .05
354 Wilson Alvarez .05
355 Charlie Hough .05
356 Ozzie Guillen .05
357 Cory Snyder .05
358 Robin Ventura .05
359 Scott Fletcher .05
360 Cesar Bernhardt .05
361 Dan Pasqua .05
362 Tim Raines .05
363 Brian Drahman .05
364 Wayne Edwards .05
365 Scott Radinsky .05
366 Frank Thomas .40
367 Cecil Fielder .05
368 Julio Franco .05
369 Kelly Gruber .05
370 Alan Trammell .05
371 Rickey Henderson .30
372 Jose Canseco .15
373 Ellis Burks .05
374 Lance Parrish .05
375 Dave Parker .05
376 Eddie Murray .30
377 Ryne Sandberg .35
378 Matt Williams .05
379 Barry Larkin .05
380 Barry Bonds .75
381 Bobby Bonilla .05
382 Darryl Strawberry .05
383 Benny Santiago .05
384 Don Mattingly .05
385 Paul Coleman .05
386 Milt Thompson .05
387 Lee Smith .05
388 Ray Lankford .05
389 Tom Pagnozzi .05
390 Ken Hill .05
391 Jamie Moyer .05
392 Greg Carmona RC .05
393 John Ericks .05
394 Bob Tewksbury .05
395 Jose Oquendo .05
396 Rheal Cormier .05
397 Mike Milchin RC .05
398 Ozzie Smith .50
399 Aaron Holbert RC .05
400 Jose DeLeon .05
401 Felix Jose .05
402 Juan Agosto .05
403 Pedro Guerrero .05
404 Todd Zeile .05
405 Gerald Perry .05
406 Bryn Smith .05
407 Bernard Gilkey .05
408 Rex Hudler .05
410a Ralph Branca, Bobby Thomson .10
410b Donovan Osborne .05
411 Lance Dickson .05
412 Danny Jackson .05
413 Jerome Walton .05
414 Sean Cheetham .05
415 Joe Girardi .05
416 Ryne Sandberg .50
417 Mike Harkey .05
418 George Bell .05
419 Rick Wilkins RC .05
420 Earl Cunningham .05
421 Heathcliff Slocumb .05
422 Mike Bielecki .05
423 Jessie Hollins RC .05
424 Shawon Dunston .05
425 Dave Smith .05
426 Greg Maddux .50
427 Jose Vizcaino .05
428 Luis Salazar .05
429 Andre Dawson .25
430 Rick Sutcliffe .05
431 Paul Assenmacher .05
432 Erik Pappas .05
433 Mark Grace .05
434 Denny Martinez .05
435 Marquis Grissom .05
436 Wil Cordero RC .05
437 Tim Wallach .05
438 Brian Barnes RC .05

439 Barry Jones .05
440 Ivan Calderon .05
441 Stan Spencer RC .05
442 Larry Walker .05
443 Chris Haney RC .05
444 Hector Rivera .05
445 Delino DeShields .05
446 Andres Galarraga .05
447 Gilberto Reyes .05
448 Willie Greene .05
449 Greg Colbrunn .05
450 Rondell White RC .25
451 Steve Frey .05
452 Shane Andrews RC .10
453 Mike Fitzgerald .05
454 Spike Owen .05
455 Dave Martinez .05
456 Dennis Boyd .05
457 Eric Bullock .05
458 Reid Cornelius RC .05
459 Chris Nabholz .05
460 David Cone .05
461 Hubie Brooks .05
462 Sid Fernandez .05
463 Doug Simons RC .05
464 Howard Johnson .05
465 Chris Donnels .05
466 Anthony Young .05
467 Todd Hundley .05
468 Rick Cerone .05
469 Kevin Elster .05
470 Wally Whitehurst .05
471 Vince Coleman .05
472 Dwight Gooden .05
473 Charlie O'Brien .05
474 Jeromy Burnitz RC .50
475 John Franco .05
476 Daryl Boston .05
477 Frank Viola .05
478 D.J. Dozier .05
479 Kevin McReynolds .05
480 Tom Herr .05
481 Gregg Jefferies .05
482 Pete Schourek .05
483 Ron Darling .05
484 Dave Magadan .05
485 Andy Ashby RC .05
486 Dale Murphy .20
487 Von Hayes .05
488 Kim Batiste RC .05
489 Tony Longmire RC .05
490 Wally Backman .05
491 Jeff Jackson .05
492 Mickey Morandini .05
493 Darrel Akerfelds .05
494 Ricky Jordan .05
495 Randy Ready .05
496 Darrin Fletcher .05
497 Chuck Malone .05
498 Pat Combs .05
499 Dickie Thon .05
500 Roger McDowell .05
501 Len Dykstra .05
502 Joe Boever .05
503 John Kruk .05
504 Terry Mulholland .05
505 Wes Chamberlain RC .05
506 Mike Lieberthal RC .75
507 Darren Daulton .05
508 Charlie Hayes .05
509 John Smiley .05
510 Gary Varsho .05
511 Curt Wilkerson .05
512 Orlando Merced RC .05
513 Barry Bonds 1.00
514 Mike Lavalliere .05
515 Doug Drabek .05
516 Gary Redus .05
517 William Pennyfeather RC .05
518 Randy Tomlin .05
519 Mike Zimmerman RC .05
520 Jeff King .05
521 Kurt Miller RC .05
522 Jay Bell .05
523 Bill Landrum .05
524 Zane Smith .05
525 Bobby Bonilla .05
526 Bob Walk .05
527 Austin Manahan .05
528 Joe Ausanio RC .05
529 Andy Van Slyke .05
530 Jose Lind .05
531 Carlos Garcia RC .05
532 Don Slaught .05
533 Colin Powell .25
534 Frank Bolick RC .05
535 Gary Scott RC .05
536 Nikco Riesgo .05
537 Reggie Sanders RC .25
538 Tim Howard RC .05
539 Ryan Bowen RC .05
540 Eric Anthony .05
541 Jim Deshaies .05
542 Tom Nevers .05
543 Ken Caminiti .05
544 Karl Rhodes .05
545 Xavier Hernandez .05
546 Mike Scott .05
547 Jeff Juden .05
548 Darryl Kile .05
549 Willie Ansley .05
550 Luis Gonzalez RC 1.00
551 Mike Simms RC .05
552 Mark Portugal .05
553 Jimmy Jones .05
554 Jim Clancy .05
555 Pete Harnisch .05
556 Craig Biggio .05

557 Eric Yelding .05
558 Dave Rohde .05
559 Casey Candaele .05
560 Curt Schilling .25
561 Steve Finley .05
562 Javier Ortiz .05
563 Andujar Cedeno .05
564 Rafael Ramirez .05
565 Kenny Lofton RC .50
566 Steve Avery .05
567 Lonnie Smith .05
568 Kent Mercker .05
569 Chipper Jones RC 6.00
570 Terry Pendleton .05
571 Otis Nixon .05
572 Juan Berenguer .05
573 Charlie Leibrandt .05
574 Dave Justice .05
575 Keith Mitchell .05
576 Tom Glavine .25
577 Greg Olson .05
578 Rafael Belliard .05
579 Ben Rivera .05
580 John Smoltz .05
581 Tyler Houston .05
582 Mark Wohlers RC .05
583 Ron Gant .05
584 Ramon Caraballo .05
585 Sid Bream .05
586 Jeff Treadway .05
587 Javier Lopez RC .75
588 Deion Sanders .10
589 Mike Heath .05
590 Ryan Klesko RC .20
591 Bob Ojeda .05
592 Alfredo Griffin .05
593 Raul Mondesi RC .25
594 Greg Smith .05
595 Orel Hershiser .05
596 Juan Samuel .05
597 Brett Butler .05
598 Gary Carter .40
599 Stan Javier .05
600 Kal Daniels .05
601 Jamie McAndrew RC .05
602 Mike Sharperson .05
603 Jay Howell .05
604 Eric Karros RC .25
605 Tim Belcher .05
606 Dan Opperman .05
607 Lenny Harris .05
608 Tom Goodwin .05
609 Darryl Strawberry .05
610 Ramon Martinez .05
611 Kevin Gross .05
612 Zakary Shinall .05
613 Mike Scioscia .05
614 Eddie Murray .40
615 Ronnie Walden .05
616 Will Clark .05
617 Adam Hyzdu .05
618 Matt Williams .05
619 Don Robinson .05
620 Jeff Brantley .05
621 Greg Litton .05
622 Steve Decker .05
623 Robby Thompson .05
624 Mark Leonard RC .05
625 Kevin Bass .05
626 Scott Garrelts .05
627 Jose Uribe .05
628 Eric Gunderson .05
629 Steve Hosey .05
630 Trevor Wilson .05
631 Terry Kennedy .05
632 Dave Righetti .05
633 Kelly Downs .05
634 Johnny Ard .05
635 Eric Christopherson RC .05
636 Kevin Mitchell .05
637 John Burkett .05
638 Kevin Rogers RC .05
639 Bud Black .05
640 Willie McGee .05
641 Royce Clayton .05
642 Tony Fernandez .05
643 Ricky Bones .05
644 Thomas Howard .05
645 Dave Staton .05
646 Jim Presley .05
647 Tony Gwynn .05
648 Marty Barrett .05
649 Scott Coolbaugh .05
650 Craig Lefferts .05
651 Eddie Whitson .05
652 Oscar Azocar .05
653 Wes Gardner .05
654 Bip Roberts .05
655 Robbie Beckett RC .05
656 Benny Santiago .05
657 Greg W. Harris .05
658 Jerald Clark .05
659 Fred McGriff .05
660 Larry Andersen .05
661 Bruce Hurst .05
662 Steve Martin .05
663 Rafael Valdez .05
664 Paul Faries RC .05
665 Andy Benes .05
666 Randy Myers .05
667 Rob Dibble .05
668 Glenn Sutko .05
669 Glenn Braggs .05
670 Billy Hatcher .05
671 Joe Oliver .05
672 Freddie Benavides .05
673 Barry Larkin .05
674 Chris Sabo .05

#	Player	Price
675	Mariano Duncan	.05
676	Chris Jones RC	.05
677	Gino Minutelli RC	.05
678	Reggie Jefferson	.05
679	Jack Armstrong	.05
680	Chris Hammond	.05
681	Jose Rijo	.05
682	Bill Doran	.05
683	Terry Lee	.05
684	Tom Browning	.05
685	Paul O'Neill	.05
686	Eric Davis	.05
687	Dan Wilson RC	.05
688	Ted Power	.05
689	Tim Layana	.05
690	Norm Charlton	.05
691	Hal Morris	.05
692	Rickey Henderson	.35
693	Sam Militello RC	.05
694	Matt Mieske RC	.05
695	Paul Russo RC	.05
696	Domingo Mota RC	.05
697	Todd Guggiana RC	.05
698	Marc Newfield	.05
699	Checklist	.05
700	Checklist	.05
701	Checklist	.05
702	Checklist	.05
703	Checklist	.05
704	Checklist	.05

1992 Bowman

Topps introduced several changes with the release of its 1992 Bowman set. The 705-card set features 45 special insert cards stamped with gold foil. The cards are printed with a premium UV coated glossy card stock. Several players without major league experience are featured in the set. Included in this group are 1991 MVP's of the minor leagues and first round draft choices. Eighteen of the gold-foil enchanced cards have been identified as short-prints (designated SP in the listings), printed in quantities one-half the other foils.

	NM/M
Complete Set (705):	120.00
Common Player:	.10
Pack (15):	6.00
Wax Box (36):	160.00
Jumbo Pack (25):	8.00
Jumbo Box (36):	220.00

#	Player	Price
1	Ivan Rodriguez	1.25
2	Kirk McCaskill	.10
3	Scott Livingstone	.10
4	Salomon Torres RC	.50
5	Carlos Hernandez	.10
6	Dave Hollins	.10
7	Scott Fletcher	.10
8	Jorge Fabregas	.10
9	Andujar Cedeno	.10
10	Howard Johnson	.10
11	Trevor Hoffman RC	3.00
12	Roberto Kelly	.10
13	Gregg Jefferies	.10
14	Marquis Grissom	.10
15	Mike Ignasiak	.10
16	Jack Morris	.10
17	William Pennyfeather	.10
18	Todd Stottlemyre	.10
19	Chito Martinez	.10
20	Roberto Alomar	.40
21	Sam Militello	.10
22	Hector Fajardo	.10
23	Paul Quantrill RC	.10
24	Chuck Knoblauch	.10
25	Reggie Jefferson	.10
26	Jeremy McGarity	.10
27	Jerome Walton	.10
28	Chipper Jones	15.00
29	Brian Barber RC	.10
30	Ron Darling	.10
31	Roberto Petagine RC	.10
32	Chuck Finley	.10
33	Edgar Martinez	.10
34	Napoleon Robinson	.10
35	Andy Van Slyke	.10
36	Bobby Thigpen	.10
37	Travis Fryman	.10
38	Eric Christopherson	.10
39	Terry Mulholland	.10
40	Darryl Strawberry	.10
41	Manny Alexander RC	.10
42	Tracey Sanders RC	.10
43	Pete Incaviglia	.10
44	Kim Batiste	.10
45	Frank Rodriguez	.10
46	Greg Swindell	.10
47	Delino DeShields	.10
48	John Ericks	.10
49	Franklin Stubbs	.10
50	Tony Gwynn	2.00
51	Clifton Garrett RC	.10
52	Mike Gardella	.10
53	Scott Erickson	.10
54	Gary Caballo	.10
55	Jose Oliva RC	.10
56	Brook Fordyce	.10
57	Mark Whiten	.10
58	Joe Slusarski	.10
59	J.R. Phillips RC	.10
60	Barry Bonds	4.00
61	Bob Milacki	.10
62	Keith Mitchell	.10
63	Angel Miranda	.10
64	Raul Mondesi	.75
65	Brian Koelling	.10
66	Brian McRae	.10
67	John Patterson	.10
68	John Wetteland	.10
69	Wilson Alvarez	.10
70	Wade Boggs	2.00
71	Darryl Ratliff	.10
72	Jeff Jackson	.10
73	Jeremy Hernandez	.10
74	Darryl Hamilton	.10
75	Rafael Belliard	.10
76	Ricky Trilcek	.10
77	Felipe Crespo RC	.10
78	Carney Lansford	.10
79	Ryan Long	.10
80	Kirby Puckett	2.00
81	Earl Cunningham	.10
82	Pedro Martinez	1.50
83	Scott Hatteberg	.10
84	Juan Gonzalez	.75
85	Robert Nutting	.10
86	Calvin Reese RC	.50
87	Dave Silvestri	.10
88	Scott Ruffcorn RC	.10
89	Rick Aguilera	.10
90	Cecil Fielder	.10
91	Kirk Dressendorfer	.10
92	Jerry DiPoto	.10
93	Mike Felder	.10
94	Craig Paquette	.10
95	Elvin Paulino	.10
96	Donovan Osborne	.10
97	Hubie Brooks	.10
98	Derek Lowe RC	4.00
99	David Zancanaro	.10
100	Ken Griffey Jr.	2.75
101	Todd Hundley	.10
102	Mike Trombley	.10
103	Ricky Gutierrez RC	.10
104	Braulio Castillo	.10
105	Craig Lefferts	.10
106	Rick Sutcliffe	.10
107	Dean Palmer	.10
108	Henry Rodriguez	.10
109	Mark Clark RC	.10
110	Kenny Lofton	.10
111	Mark Carreon	.10
112	J.T. Bruett RC	.10
113	Gerald Williams	.10
114	Frank Thomas	1.50
115	Kevin Reimer	.10
116	Sammy Sosa	2.00
117	Mickey Tettleton	.10
118	Reggie Sanders	.10
119	Trevor Wilson	.10
120	Cliff Brantley	.10
121	Spike Owen	.10
122	Jeff Montgomery	.10
123	Alex Sutherland	.10
124	Brien Taylor RC	.10
125	Brian Williams	.10
126	Kevin Seitzer	.10
127	Carlos Delgado RC	15.00
128	Gary Scott	.10
129	Scott Cooper	.10
130	Domingo Jean RC	.10
131	Pat Mahomes RC	.10
132	Mike Boddicker	.10
133	Roberto Hernandez	.10
134	Dave Valle	.10
135	Kurt Stillwell	.10
136	Brad Pennington RC	.10
137	Jermaine Swifton	.10
138	Ryan Hawblitzel	.10
139	Tito Navarro	.10
140	Sandy Alomar	.10
141	Todd Benzinger	.10
142	Danny Jackson	.10
143	Melvin Nieves RC	.25
144	Jim Campanis	.10
145	Luis Gonzalez	.10
146	Dave Doorneweerd	.10
147	Charlie Hayes	.10
148	Greg Maddux	2.00
149	Brian Harper	.10
150	Brent Miller	.10
151	Shawn Estes RC	.75
152	Mike Williams	.10
153	Charlie Hough	.10
154	Randy Myers	.10
155	Kevin Young RC	.10
156	Rick Wilkins	.10
157	Terry Schumpert	.10
158	Steve Karsay	.10
159	Gary DiSarcina	.10
160	Deion Sanders	.10
161	Tom Browning	.10
162	Dickie Thon	.10
163	Luis Mercedes	.10
164	Ricardo Ingram	.10
165	Tavo Alavarez RC	.10
166	Rickey Henderson	1.50
167	Jaime Navarro	.10
168	Billy Ashley RC	.10
169	Phil Dauphin	.10
170	Ivan Cruz	.10
171	Harold Baines	.10
172	Bryan Harvey	.10
173	Alex Cole	.10
174	Curtis Shaw	.10
175	Matt Williams	.10
176	Felix Jose	.10
177	Sam Horn	.10
178	Randy Johnson	1.50
179	Ivan Calderon	.10
180	Steve Avery	.10
181	William Suero	.10
182	Bill Swift	.10
183	Howard Battle RC	.10
184	Ruben Amaro	.10
185	Jim Abbott	.10
186	Mike Fitzgerald	.10
187	Bruce Hurst	.10
188	Jeff Juden	.10
189	Jeromy Burnitz	.10
190	Dave Burba	.10
191	Kevin Brown	.10
192	Patrick Lennon	.10
193	Jeffrey McNeely	.10
194	Wil Cordero	.10
195	Chili Davis	.10
196	Milt Cuyler	.10
197	Von Hayes	.10
198	Todd Revening RC	.10
199	Joel Johnson	.10
200	Jeff Bagwell	1.50
201	Alex Fernandez	.10
202	Todd Jones	.10
203	Charles Nagy	.10
204	Tim Raines	.10
205	Kevin Maas	.10
206	Julio Franco	.10
207	Randy Velarde	.10
208	Lance Johnson	.10
209	Scott Leius	.10
210	Derek Lee	.10
211	Joe Sondrini	.10
212	Royce Clayton	.10
213	Chris George	.10
214	Gary Sheffield	.75
215	Mark Gubicza	.10
216	Mike Moore	.10
217	Rick Huisman	.10
218	Jeff Russell	.10
219	D.J. Dozier	.10
220	Dave Martinez	.10
221	Al Newman	.10
222	Nolan Ryan	4.00
223	Teddy Higuera	.10
224	Damon Buford RC	.10
225	Ruben Sierra	.10
226	Tom Nevers	.10
227	Tommy Greene	.10
228	Nigel Wilson RC	.10
229	John DeSilva	.10
230	Bobby Witt	.10
231	Greg Cadaret	.10
232	John VanderWal	.10
233	Jack Clark	.10
234	Bill Doran	.10
235	Bobby Bonilla	.10
236	Steve Olin	.10
237	Derek Bell	.10
238	David Cone	.10
239	Victor Cole	.10
240	Rod Bolton	.10
241	Tom Pagnozzi	.10
242	Rob Dibble	.10
243	Michael Carter	.10
244	Don Peters	.10
245	Mike LaValliere	.10
246	Joe Perona	.10
247	Mitch Williams	.10
248	Jay Buhner	.10
249	Andy Benes	.10
250	Alex Ochoa RC	.10
251	Greg Blosser	.10
252	Jack Armstrong	.10
253	Juan Samuel	.10
254	Terry Pendleton	.10
255	Ramon Martinez	.10
256	Rico Brogna	.10
257	John Smiley	.10
258	Carl Everett	.10
259	Tim Salmon	.10
260	Will Clark	.10
261	Ugueth Urbina RC	.40
262	Jason Wood	.10
263	Dave Magadan	.10
264	Dante Bichette	.10
265	Jose DeLeon	.10
266	Mike Neill RC	.10
267	Paul O'Neill	.10
268	Anthony Young	.10
269	Greg Harris	.10
270	Todd Van Poppel	.10
271	Pete Castellano	.10
272	Tony Phillips	.10
273	Mike Gallego	.10
274	Steve Cooke RC	.10
275	Robin Ventura	.10
276	Kevin Mitchell	.10
277	Doug Linton	.10
278	Robert Eenhorn	.10
279	Gabe White RC	.10
280	Dave Stewart	.10
281	Mo Sanford	.10
282	Greg Perschke	.10
283	Kevin Flora	.10
284	Jeff Williams	.10
285	Keith Miller	.10
286	Andy Ashby	.10
287	Doug Dascenzo	.10
288	Eric Karros	.10
289	Glenn Murray RC	.10
290	Troy Percival RC	1.00
291	Orlando Merced	.10
292	Peter Hoy	.10
293	Tony Fernandez	.10
294	Juan Guzman	.10
295	Jesse Barfield	.10
296	Sid Fernandez	.10
297	Scott Cepicky	.10
298	Garret Anderson RC	6.00
299	Cal Eldred	.10
300	Ryne Sandberg	2.00
301	Jim Gantner	.10
302	Mariano Rivera RC	25.00
303	Ron Lockett	.10
304	Jose Offerman	.10
305	Denny Martinez	.10
306	Luis Ortiz RC	.10
307	David Howard	.10
308	Russ Springer	.10
309	Chris Howard	.10
310	Kyle Abbott	.10
311	Aaron Sele RC	1.00
312	Dave Justice	.10
313	Pete O'Brien	.10
314	Greg Hansell	.10
315	Dave Winfield	1.50
316	Lance Dickson	.10
317	Eric King	.10
318	Vaughn Eshelman	.10
319	Tim Belcher	.10
320	Andres Galarraga	.10
321	Scott Bullett	.10
322	Doug Strange	.10
323	Jerald Clark	.10
324	Dave Righetti	.10
325	Greg Hibbard	.10
326	Eric Dillman	.10
327	Shane Reynolds RC	.25
328	Chris Hammond	.10
329	Albert Belle	.10
330	Rich Becker RC	.10
331	Eddie Williams	.10
332	Donald Harris	.10
333	Dave Smith	.10
334	Steve Fireovid	.10
335	Steve Buechele	.10
336	Mike Schooler	.10
337	Kevin McReynolds	.10
338	Hensley Meulens	.10
339	Benji Gil RC	.10
340	Don Mattingly	2.50
341	Alvin Davis	.10
342	Alan Mills	.10
343	Kelly Downs	.10
344	Leo Gomez	.10
345	Tarrik Brock RC	.10
346	Ryan Turner	.10
347	John Smoltz	.10
348	Bill Sampen	.10
349	Paul Byrd	.10
350	Mike Bordick	.10
351	Jose Lind	.10
352	David Wells	.10
353	Barry Larkin	.10
354	Bruce Ruffin	.10
355	Luis Rivera	.10
356	Sid Bream	.10
357	Julian Vasquez	.10
358	Jason Bere RC	.10
359	Ben McDonald	.10
360	Scott Stahoviak	.10
361	Kirt Manwaring	.10
362	Jeff Johnson	.10
363	Rob Deer	.10
364	Tony Pena	.10
365	Melido Perez	.10
366	Clay Parker	.10
367	Dale Sveum	.10
368	Mike Scioscia	.10
369	Roger Salkeld	.10
370	Mike Stanley	.10
371	Jack McDowell	.10
372	Tim Wallach	.10
373	Billy Ripken	.10
374	Mike Christopher	.10
375	Paul Molitor	1.50
376	Dave Stieb	.10
377	Pedro Guerrero	.10
378	Russ Swan	.10
379	Bob Ojeda	.10
380	Don Pall	.10
381	Eddie Zosky	.10
382	Darnell Coles	.10
383	Tom Smith	.10
384	Mark McGwire	3.00
385	Gary Carter	1.50
386	Rich Amaral	.10
387	Alan Embree	.10
388	Jonathan Hurst	.10
389	Bobby Jones RC	.10
390	Rico Rossy	.10
391	Dan Smith	.10
392	Terry Steinbach	.10
393	Jon Farrell	.10
394	Dave Anderson	.10
395	Benito Santiago	.10
396	Mark Wohlers	.10
397	Mo Vaughn	.10
398	Randy Kramer	.10
399	John Jaha RC	.10
400	Cal Ripken, Jr.	4.00
401	Ryan Bowen	.10
402	Tim McIntosh	.10
403	Bernard Gilkey	.10
404	Junior Felix	.10
405	Cris Colon	.10
406	Marc Newfield	.10
407	Bernie Williams	.10
408	Jay Howell	.10
409	Zane Smith	.10
410	Jeff Shaw	.10
411	Kerry Woodson	.10
412	Wes Chamberlain	.10
413	Dave Mlicki	.10
414	Benny Distefano	.10
415	Kevin Rogers	.10
416	Tim Naehring	.10
417	Clemente Nunez	.10
418	Luis Sojo	.10
419	Kevin Ritz	.10
420	Omar Oliveras	.10
421	Manuel Lee	.10
422	Julio Valera	.10
423	Omar Vizquel	.10
424	Darren Burton	.10
425	Mel Hall	.10
426	Dennis Powell	.10
427	Lee Stevens	.10
428	Glenn Davis	.10
429	Willie Greene	.10
430	Kevin Wickander	.10
431	Dennis Eckersley	1.25
432	Joe Orsulak	.10
433	Eddie Murray	1.50
434	Matt Stairs RC	.10
435	Wally Joyner	.10
436	Rondell White	.10
437	Rob Mauer	.10
438	Joe Redfield	.10
439	Mark Lewis	.10
440	Darren Daulton	.10
441	Mike Henneman	.10
442	John Cangelosi	.10
443	Vince Moore RC	.10
444	John Wehner	.10
445	Kent Hrbek	.10
446	Mark McLemore	.10
447	Bill Wegman	.10
448	Robby Thompson	.10
449	Mark Anthony	.10
450	Archi Cianfrocco	.10
451	Johnny Ruffin	.10
452	Javier Lopez	.10
453	Greg Gohr	.10
454	Tim Scott	.10
455	Stan Belinda	.10
456	Darrin Jackson	.10
457	Chris Gardner	.10
458	Esteban Beltre	.10
459	Phil Plantier	.10
460	Jim Thome	1.25
461	Mike Piazza RC	25.00
462	Matt Sinatro	.10
463	Scott Servais	.10
464	Brian Jordan RC	.75
465	Doug Drabek	.10
466	Carl Willis	.10
467	Bret Barbarie	.10
468	Hal Morris	.10
469	Steve Sax	.10
470	Jerry Willard	.10
471	Dan Wilson	.10
472	Chris Hoiles	.10
473	Rheal Cormier	.10
474	John Morris	.10
475	Jeff Reardon	.10
476	Mark Leiter	.10
477	Tom Gordon	.10
478	Kent Bottenfield RC	.10
479	Gene Larkin	.10
480	Dwight Gooden	.10
481	B.J. Surhoff	.10
482	Andy Stankiewicz	.10
483	Tino Martinez	.10
484	Craig Biggio	.10
485	Denny Neagle	.10
486	Rusty Meacham	.10
487	Kal Daniels	.10
488	Dave Henderson	.10
489	Tim Costo	.10
490	Doug Davis	.10
491	Frank Viola	.10
492	Cory Snyder	.10
493	Chris Martin	.10
494	Dion James	.10
495	Randy Tomlin	.10
496	Greg Vaughan	.10
497	Dennis Cook	.10
498	Rosario Rodriguez	.10
499	Dave Staton	.10
500	George Brett	2.50
501	Brian Barnes	.10
502	Butch Henry	.10
503	Harold Reynolds	.10
504	David Nied RC	.10
505	Lee Smith	.10
506	Steve Chitren	.10
507	Ken Hill	.10
508	Robbie Beckett	.10
509	Troy Afenir	.10
510	Terry Steinbach	.10
511	Bret Boone	.10
512	Jeff Branson	.10
513	Mike Jackson	.10
514	Pete Harnisch	.10
515	Chad Kreuter	.10
516	Joe Vitko	.10
517	Orel Hershiser	.10
518	John Doherty RC	.10
519	Jay Bell	.10
520	Mark Langston	.10
521	Dann Howitt	.10
522	Bobby Reed	.10
523	Roberto Munoz	.10
524	Todd Ritchie	.10
525	Bip Roberts	.10
526	Pat Listach RC	.10
527	Scott Brosius RC	.10
528	John Roper RC	.10
529	Phil Hiatt	.10
530	Denny Walling	.10
531	Carlos Baerga	.10
532	Manny Ramirez RC	25.00
533	Pat Clements	.10
534	Ron Gant	.10
535	Pat Kelly	.10
536	Billy Spiers	.10
537	Darren Reed	.10
538	Ken Caminiti	.10
539	Butch Huskey RC	.10
540	Matt Nokes	.10
541	John Kruk	.10
542	John Jaha/SP (Foil)	.40
543	Justin Thompson RC	.10
544	Steve Hosey	.10
545	Joe Kmak	.10
546	John Franco	.10
547	Devon White	.10
548	Elston Hansen/SP (Foil)	.40
549	Ryan Klesko	.10
550	Danny Tartabull	.10
551	Frank Thomas/SP (Foil)	1.50
552	Kevin Tapani	.10
553a	Willie Banks	.10
553b	Pat Clements	.10
554	B.J. Wallace RC/SP (Foil)	.40
555	Orlando Miller RC	.10
556	Mark Smith RC	.10
557	Tim Wallach (Foil)	.10
558	Bill Gullickson	.10
559	Derek Bell (Foil)	.10
560	Joe Randa (Foil)	.10
561	Frank Seminara	.10
562	Mark Gardner	.10
563	Rick Greene (Foil)	.10
564	Gary Gaetti	.10
565	Ozzie Guillen	.10
566	Charles Nagy (Foil)	.10
567	Mike Milchin	.10
568	Ben Shelton (Foil)	.10
569	Chris Roberts (Foil)	.10
570	Ellis Burks	.10
571	Scott Scudder	.10
572	Jim Abbott (Foil)	.10
573	Joe Carter	.10
574	Steve Finley	.10
575	Jim Olander (Foil)	.10
576	Carlos Garcia	.10
577	Greg Olson	.10
578	Greg Swindell (Foil)	.10
579	Matt Williams (Foil)	.10
580	Mark Grace	.10
581	Howard House (Foil)	.10
582	Luis Polonia	.10
583	Erik Hanson	.10
584	Salomon Torres (Foil)	.10
585	Carlton Fisk	1.50
586	Bret Saberhagen	.10
587	Chad McDonnell RC (Foil)	.10
588	Jimmy Key	.10
589	Mike MacFarlane	.10
590	Barry Bonds (Foil)	3.50
591	Jamie McAndrew	.10
592	Shane Mack	.10
593	Kerwin Moore	.10
594	Joe Oliver	.10
595	Chris Sabo	.10
596	Alex Gonzalez RC	.50
597	Brett Butler	.10
598	Mark Hutton	.10
599	Andy Benes (Foil)	.10
600	Jose Canseco	.75
601	Darryl Kile	.10
602	Matt Stairs/SP (Foil)	.40
603	Rob Butler (Foil)	.10
604	Willie McGee	.10
605	Jack McDowell	.10
606	Tom Candiotti	.10
607	Ed Martel	.10
608	Matt Mieske (Foil)	.10
609	Darrin Fletcher	.10
610	Rafael Palmeiro	1.25
611	Bill Swift (Foil)	.10
612	Mike Mussina	.75
613	Vince Coleman	.10
614	Scott Cepicky (Foil)	.10
615	Mike Greenwell	.10
616	Kevin McGehee	.10
617	Jeffrey Hammonds (Foil)	.10
618	Scott Taylor	.10
619	Dave Otto	.10
620	Mark McGwire (Foil)	3.00
621	Kevin Tatar	.10
622	Steve Farr	.10
623	Ryan Klesko (Foil)	.10
625	Andre Dawson	.40
626	Tino Martinez/SP (Foil)	.50
627	Chad Curtis RC	.50
628	Mickey Morandini	.10
629	Gregg Olson/SP (Foil)	.40
630	Lou Whitaker	.10
631	Arthur Rhodes	.10

#	Player	Price
632	Brandon Wilson	.10
633	Lance Jennings RC	.10
634	Allen Watson RC	.10
635	Len Dykstra	.10
636	Joe Girardi	.10
637	Kiki Hernandez/SP (Foil)	.40
638	Mike Hampton RC	1.00
639	Al Osuna	.10
640	Kevin Appier	.10
641	Rick Helling/SP (Foil)	.40
642	Jody Reed	.10
643	Ray Lankford	.10
644	John Olerud	.10
645	Paul Molitor/SP (Foil)	1.50
646	Pat Borders	.10
647	Mike Morgan	.10
648	Larry Walker	.10
649	Pete Castellano/SP (Foil)	.40
650	Fred McGriff	.10
651	Walt Weiss	.10
652	Calvin Murray RC/SP (Foil)	.40
653	Dave Nilsson	.10
654	Greg Pirkl	.10
655	Robin Ventura/SP (Foil)	.10
656	Mark Portugal	.10
657	Roger McDowell	.10
658	Rick Hirtensteiner/SP (Foil)	.40
659	Glenallen Hill	.10
660	Greg Gagne	.10
661	Charles Johnson/SP (Foil)	.40
662	Brian Hunter	.10
663	Mark Lemke	.10
664	Tim Belcher/SP (Foil)	.40
665	Rich DeLucia	.10
666	Bob Walk	.10
667	Joe Carter/SP (Foil)	.40
668	Jose Guzman	.10
669	Otis Nixon	.10
670	Phil Nevin (Foil)	.10
671	Eric Davis	.10
672	Damion Easley RC	.25
673	Will Clark (Foil)	.10
674	Mark Kiefer	.10
675	Ozzie Smith	2.00
676	Manny Ramirez RC	15.00
677	Gregg Olson	.10
678	Cliff Floyd RC	1.00
679	Duane Singleton	.10
680	Jose Rijo	.10
681	Willie Randolph	.10
682	Michael Tucker RC (Foil)	.25
683	Darren Lewis	.10
684	Dale Murphy	.50
685	Mike Pagliarulo	.10
686	Paul Miller	.10
687	Mike Robertson	.10
688	Mike Devereaux	.10
689	Pedro Astacio	.10
690	Alan Trammell	.10
691	Roger Clemens	2.50
692	Bud Black	.10
693	Turk Wendell	.10
694	Barry Larkin/SP (Foil)	.75
695	Todd Zeile	.10
696	Pat Hentgen	.10
697	Eddie Taubensee RC	.10
698	Guillermo Vasquez	.10
699	Tom Glavine	.75
700	Robin Yount	1.50
701	Checklist	.10
702	Checklist	.10
703	Checklist	.10
704	Checklist	.10
705	Checklist	.10

1993 Bowman

Bowman's 708-card 1993 set once again features a premium UV-coated glossy stock. There are also 48 special insert cards, with gold foil stamping, randomly inserted one per pack or two per jumbo pack. The foil cards, numbered 339-374 and 693-704, feature top prospects and rookie-of-the-year candidates, as do several regular cards in the set. Cards are standard size.

	NM/M
Complete Set (708):	35.00
Common Player:	.10
Pack (15):	.10
Wax Box (24):	35.00
Jumbo Pack (22):	2.50
Jumbo Box (20):	40.00

#	Player	Price
1	Glenn Davis	.10
2	Hector Roa RC	.10
3	Ken Ryan RC	.10
4	Derek Wallace RC	.10
5	Jorge Fabregas	.10
6	Joe Oliver	.10
7	Brandon Wilson	.10
8	Mark Thompson RC	.10
9	Tracy Sanders	.10
10	Rich Renteria	.10
11	Lou Whitaker	.10
12	Brian Hunter RC	.10
13	Joe Vitiello	.10
14	Eric Karros	.10
15	Joe Kmak	.10
16	Tavo Alvarez	.10
17	Steve Dunn RC	.10
18	Tony Fernandez	.10
19	Melido Perez	.10
20	Mike Lieberthal	.10
21	Terry Steinbach	.10
22	Stan Belinda	.10
23	Jay Buhner	.10
24	Allen Watson	.10
25	Daryl Henderson RC	.10
26	Ray McDavid RC	.10
27	Shawn Green	.30
28	Bud Black	.10
29	Sherman Obando RC	.10
30	Mike Hostetler	.10
31	Nate Hinchey RC	.10
32	Randy Myers	.10
33	Brian Grebeck	.10
34	John Roper	.10
35	Larry Thomas	.10
36	Alex Cole	.10
37	Tom Kramer RC	.10
38	Matt Whisenant RC	.10
39	Chris Gomez RC	.10
40	Luis Gonzalez	.10
41	Kevin Appier	.10
42	Omar Daal RC	.10
43	Duane Singleton	.10
44	Bill Risley	.10
45	Pat Meares RC	.10
46	Butch Huskey	.10
47	Bobby Munoz	.10
48	Juan Bell	.10
49	Scott Lydy RC	.10
50	Dennis Moeller	.10
51	Marc Newfield	.10
52	Tripp Cromer RC	.10
53	Kurt Miller	.10
54	Jim Pena	.10
55	Juan Guzman	.10
56	Matt Williams	.10
57	Harold Reynolds	.10
58	Donnie Elliott RC	.10
59	Jon Shave RC	.10
60	Kevin Roberson RC	.10
61	Hilly Hathaway RC	.10
62	Jose Rijo	.10
63	Kerry Taylor RC	.10
64	Ryan Hawblitzel RC	.10
65	Glenallen Hill	.10
66	Ramon D. Martinez RC	.10
67	Travis Fryman	.10
68	Tom Nevers	.10
69	Phil Hiatt	.10
70	Tim Wallach	.10
71	B.J. Surhoff	.10
72	Rondell White	.10
73	Denny Hocking RC	.10
74	Mike Oquist RC	.10
75	Paul O'Neill	.10
76	Willie Banks	.10
77	Bob Welch	.10
78	Jose Sandoval RC	.10
79	Bill Haselman	.10
80	Rheal Cormier	.10
81	Dean Palmer	.10
82	Pat Gomez RC	.10
83	Steve Karsay	.10
84	Carl Hanselman RC	.10
85	T.R. Lewis RC	.10
86	Chipper Jones	2.00
87	Scott Hatteberg	.10
88	Greg Hibbard	.10
89	Lance Painter RC	.10
90	Chad Mottola RC	.10
91	Jason Bere	.10
92	Dante Bichette	.10
93	Sandy Alomar	.10
94	Carl Everett	.10
95	Danny Bautista RC	.10
96	Steve Finley	.10
97	David Cone	.10
98	Todd Hollandsworth RC	.10
99	Matt Mieske	.10
100	Larry Walker	.10
101	Shane Mack	.10
102	Aaron Ledesma RC	.10
103	Andy Pettitte RC	4.00
104	Kevin Stocker	.10
105	Mike Mobler	.10
106	Tony Menedez	.10
107	Derek Lowe RC	.10
108	Basil Shabazz	.10
109	Dan Smith	.10
110	Scott Sanders RC	.10
111	Todd Stottlemyre	.10
112	Benji Sikonton RC	.10
113	Rick Sutcliffe	.10
114	Lee Heath RC	.10
115	Jeff Russell	.10
116	Dave Stevens RC	.10
117	Mark Holzemer RC	.10
118	Tim Belcher	.10
119	Bobby Thigpen	.10
120	Roger Bailey RC	.10
121	Tony Mitchell RC	.10
122	Junior Felix	.10
123	Rich Robertson RC	.10
124	Andy Cook RC	.10
125	Brian Bevil RC	.10
126	Darryl Strawberry	.10
127	Cal Eldred	.10
128	Cliff Floyd	.10
129	Alan Newman	.10
130	Howard Johnson	.10
131	Jim Abbott	.10
132	Chad McConnell	.10
133	Miguel Jimenez RC	.10
134	Brett Backlund RC	.10
135	John Cummings RC	.10
136	Brian Barber	.10
137	Rafael Palmeiro	1.25
138	Tim Worrell RC	.10
139	Jose Pett RC	.10
140	Barry Bonds	4.00
141	Damon Buford	.10
142	Jeff Blauser	.10
143	Frankie Rodriguez	.10
144	Mike Morgan	.10
145	Gary DeSarcina	.10
146	Calvin Reese	.10
147	Johnny Ruffin RC	.10
148	David Nied	.10
149	Charles Nagy	.10
150	Mike Myers RC	.10
151	Kenny Carlyle RC	.10
152	Eric Anthony	.10
153	Jose Lind	.10
154	Pedro Martinez	1.50
155	Mark Kiefer	.10
156	Tim Laker RC	.10
157	Pat Mahomes	.10
158	Bobby Bonilla	.10
159	Domingo Jean	.10
160	Darren Daulton	.10
161	Mark McGwire	3.50
162	Jason Kendall RC	1.00
163	Desi Relaford	.10
164	Ozzie Canseco	.10
165	Rick Helling	.10
166	Steve Pegues RC	.10
167	Paul Molitor	1.50
168	Larry Carter RC	.10
169	Arthur Rhodes	.10
170	Damon Hollins RC	.10
171	Frank Viola	.10
172	Steve Trachsel RC	.25
173	J.T. Snow RC	.50
174	Keith Gordon RC	.10
175	Carlton Fisk	1.50
176	Jason Bates RC	.10
177	Mike Crosby RC	.10
178	Benny Santiago	.10
179	Mike Moore	.10
180	Jeff Juden	.10
181	Darren Burton	.10
182	Todd Williams RC	.10
183	John Jaha	.10
184	Mike Lansing RC	.50
185	Pedro Grifol RC	.10
186	Vince Coleman	.10
187	Pat Kelly	.10
188	Clemente Alvarez RC	.10
189	Ron Darling	.10
190	Orlando Merced	.10
191	Chris Bosio	.10
192	Steve Dixon RC	.10
193	Doug Dascenzo	.10
194	Ray Holbert RC	.10
195	Willie Battle RC	.10
196	Willie McGee	.10
197	John O'Donoghue RC	.10
198	Steve Avery	.10
199	Greg Blosser	.10
200	Ryne Sandberg	2.00
201	Joe Grahe	.10
202	Dan Wilson	.10
203	Domingo Martinez RC	.10
204	Andres Galarraga	.10
205	Jamie Taylor RC	.10
206	Darrell Whitmore RC	.10
207	Ben Blomdahl RC	.10
208	Doug Drabek	.10
209	Keith Miller	.10
210	Billy Ashley	.10
211	Mike Farrell RC	.10
212	John Wetteland	.10
213	Randy Tomlin	.10
214	Sid Fernandez	.10
215	Quilvio Veras RC	.10
216	Dave Hollins	.10
217	Mike Neill	.10
218	Andy Van Slyke	.10
219	Bret Boone	.10
220	Tom Pagnozzi	.10
221	Mike Welch RC	.10
222	Frank Seminara	.10
223	Ron Villone	.10
224	D.J. Thielen RC	.10
225	Cal Ripken, Jr.	4.00
226	Pedro Borbon RC	.10
227	Carlos Quintana	.10
228	Tommy Shields RC	.10
229	Tim Salmon	.10
230	John Smiley	.10
231	Ellis Burks	.10
232	Pedro Castellano	.10
233	Paul Byrd	.10
234	Bryan Harvey	.10
235	Scott Livingstone	.10
236	James Mouton RC	.10
237	Joe Randa	.10
238	Pedro Astacio	.10
239	Darryl Hamilton	.10
240	Joey Eischen RC	.10
241	Edgar Herrera RC	.10
242	Dwight Gooden	.10
243	Sam Militello	.10
244	Ron Blazier RC	.10
245	Ruben Sierra	.10
246	Al Martin	.10
247	Mike Felder	.10
248	Bob Tewksbury	.10
249	Craig Lefferts	.10
250	Luis Lopez	.10
251	Devon White	.10
252	Will Clark	.10
253	Mark Smith	.10
254	Terry Pendleton	.10
255	Aaron Sele	.10
256	Jose Viera RC	.10
257	Damion Easley	.10
258	Rod Lofton RC	.10
259	Chris Snopek RC	.10
260	Quinton McCracken RC	.10
261	Mike Matthews RC	.10
262	Hector Carrasco RC	.10
263	Rick Greene	.10
264	Chris Bolt RC	.10
265	George Brett	2.50
266	Rick Gorecki RC	.10
267	Francisco Gamez RC	.10
268	Marquis Grissom	.10
269	Kevin Tapani	.10
270	Ryan Thompson	.10
271	Gerald Williams	.10
272	Paul Fletcher RC	.10
273	Lance Blankenship	.10
274	Marty Heff RC	.10
275	Shawn Estes	.10
276	Rene Arocha RC	.10
277	Scott Evre RC	.10
278	Phil Plantier	.10
279	Paul Spoljaric RC	.10
280	Chris Gahbs	.10
281	Harold Baines	.10
282	Jose Oliva RC	.10
283	Matt Whiteside	.10
284	Brant Brown RC	.10
285	Russ Springer	.10
286	Chris Sabo	.10
287	Ozzie Guillen	.10
288	Marcus Moore RC	.10
289	Chad Ogea	.10
290	Walt Weiss	.10
291	Brian Edmondson	.10
292	Jimmy Gonzalez	.10
293	Danny Miceli RC	.10
294	Jose Offerman	.10
295	Greg Vaughn	.10
296	Frank Bolick	.10
297	Mike Maksudian RC	.10
298	John Franco	.10
299	Danny Tartabull	.10
300	Len Dykstra	.10
301	Bobby Witt	.10
302	Trey Beamon RC	.10
303	Tino Martinez	.10
304	Aaron Holbert	.10
305	Juan Gonzalez	.75
306	Billy Hall RC	.10
307	Duane Ward	.10
308	Rod Beck	.10
309	Jose Mercedes RC	.10
310	Otis Nixon	.10
311	Gettys Glaze RC	.10
312	Candy Maldonado	.10
313	Chad Curtis	.10
314	Tim Costo	.10
315	Mike Robertson	.10
316	Nigel Wilson	.10
317	Greg McMichael RC	.10
318	Scott Pose RC	.10
319	Juan Cruz	.10
320	Greg Swindell	.10
321	Kevin McReynolds	.10
322	Tom Candiotti	.10
323	Bob Wishnevski RC	.10
324	Ken Hill	.10
325	Kirby Puckett	2.00
326	Tim Bogar RC	.10
327	Mariano Rivera	.30
328	Mitch Williams	.10
329	Craig Paquette	.10
330	Jay Bell	.10
331	Jose Martinez RC	.10
332	Rob Deer	.10
333	Brook Fordyce	.10
334	Matt Nokes	.10
335	Derek Lee	.10
336	Paul Ellis RC	.10
337	Desi Wilson RC	.10
338	Roberto Alomar	.30
339	Jim Tatum (Foil)	.10
340	J.T. Snow (Foil)	.10
341	Tim Salmon (Foil)	.10
342	Russ Davis RC (Foil)	.25
343	Javier Lopez (Foil)	.10
344	Troy O'Leary RC (Foil)	.10
345	Marty Cordova RC (Foil)	.60
346	Bubba Smith RC (Foil)	.10
347	Chipper Jones (Foil)	1.50
348	Jessie Hollins (Foil)	.10
349	Willie Greene (Foil)	.10
350	Mark Thompson (Foil)	.10
351	Nigel Wilson (Foil)	.10
352	Todd Jones (Foil)	.10
353	Raul Mondesi (Foil)	.10
354	Cliff Floyd (Foil)	.10
355	Bobby Jones (Foil)	.10
356	Kevin Stocker (Foil)	.10
357	Midre Cummings (Foil)	.10
358	Allen Watson (Foil)	.10
359	Ray McDavid (Foil)	.10
360	Steve Hosey (Foil)	.10
361	Brad Pennington (Foil)	.10
362	Frankie Rodriguez (Foil)	.10
363	Troy Percival (Foil)	.10
364	Jason Bere (Foil)	.10
365	Manny Ramirez (Foil)	.75
366	Justin Thompson (Foil)	.10
367	Joe Vitello (Foil)	.10
368	Tyrone Hill (Foil)	.10
369	David McCarty (Foil)	.10
370	Brien Taylor (Foil)	.10
371	Todd Van Poppel (Foil)	.10
372	Marc Newfield (Foil)	.10
373	Terrell Lowery RC (Foil)	.10
374	Alex Gonzalez (Foil)	.10
375	Ken Griffey Jr.	3.00
376	Donovan Osborne	.10
377	Ritchie Moody RC	.10
378	Shane Andrews	.10
379	Carlos Delgado	.65
380	Bill Swift	.10
381	Leo Gomez	.10
382	Ron Gant	.10
383	Scott Fletcher	.10
384	Matt Walbeck RC	.10
385	Chuck Finley	.10
386	Kevin Mitchell	.10
387	Wilson Alvarez	.10
388	John Burke RC	.10
389	Alan Embree	.10
390	Trevor Hoffman	.10
391	Alan Trammell	.10
392	Todd Jones	.10
393	Felix Jose	.10
394	Orel Hershiser	.10
395	Pat Listach	.10
396	Gabe White	.10
397	Dan Serafini RC	.10
398	Todd Hundley	.10
399	Wade Boggs	2.00
400	Tyler Green	.10
401	Mike Bordick	.10
402	Scott Bullett	.10
403	Lagrange Russell RC	.10
404	Ray Lankford	.10
405	Nolan Ryan	4.00
406	Robbie Beckett	.10
407	Brent Bowers RC	.10
408	Adell Davenport RC	.10
409	Brady Anderson	.10
410	Tom Glavine	.35
411	Doug Hecker RC	.10
412	Jose Guzman	.10
413	Luis Polonia	.10
414	Brian Williams	.10
415	Bo Jackson	.15
416	Eric Young	.10
417	Kenny Lofton	.10
418	Orestes Destrade	.10
419	Tony Phillips	.10
420	Jeff Bagwell	1.50
421	Hark Gardner	.10
422	Brett Butler	.10
423	Graeme Lloyd RC	.10
424	Delino DeShields	.10
425	Scott Erickson	.10
426	Jeff Kent	.10
427	Jimmy Key	.10
428	Mickey Morandini	.10
429	Marcos Arkas RC	.10
430	Don Slaught	.10
431	Randy Johnson	1.50
432	Omar Olivares	.10
433	Charlie Leibrandt	.10
434	Kurt Stillwell	.10
435	Scott Brow RC	.10
436	Robby Thompson	.10
437	Ben McDonald	.10
438	Deion Sanders	.10
439	Tony Pena	.10
440	Mark Grace	.10
441	Eduardo Perez	.10
442	Tim Pugh RC	.10
443	Scott Ruffcorn	.10
444	Jay Gainer RC	.10
445	Albert Belle	.10
446	Bret Barberie	.10
447	Justin Mashore RC	.10
448	Pete Harnisch	.10
449	Greg Gagne	.10
450	Eric Davis	.10
451	Dave Mlicki	.10
452	Moises Alou	.10
453	Rick Aguilera	.10
454	Eddie Murray	1.50
455	Bob Wickman	.10
456	Wes Chamberlain	.10
457	Brent Gates	.10
458	Paul Weber	.10
459	Mike Hampton	.10
460	Ozzie Smith	2.00
461	Tom Henke	.10
462	Ricky Gutierrez	.10
463	Jack Morris	.10
464	Joel Chimelis RC	.10
465	Gregg Olson	.10
466	Javier Lopez	.10
467	Scott Cooper	.10
468	Willie Wilson	.10
469	Mark Langston	.10
470	Barry Larkin	.10
471	Rod Bolton	.10
472	Freddie Benavides	.10
473	Ken Ramos RC	.10
474	Chuck Carr	.10
475	Cecil Fielder	.10
476	Eddie Taubensee	.10
477	Chris Eddy RC	.10
478	Greg Hansell	.10
479	Kevin Reimer	.10
480	Denny Martinez	.10
481	Chuck Knoblauch	.10
482	Mike Draper	.10
483	Spike Owen	.10
484	Terry Mulholland	.10
485	Dennis Eckersley	1.25
486	Blas Minor	.10
487	Dave Fleming	.10
488	Dan Cholonsky	.10
489	Ivan Rodriguez	1.25
490	Gary Sheffield	.45
491	Ed Sprague	.10
492	Steve Hosey	.10
493	Jimmy Haynes RC	.10
494	John Smoltz	.10
495	Andre Dawson	.35
496	Rey Sanchez	.10
497	Ty Van Burkleo RC	.10
498	Bobby Ayala RC	.10
499	Tim Raines	.10
500	Charlie Hayes	.10
501	Paul Sorrento	.10
502	Richie Lewis RC	.10
503	Jason Pfaff RC	.10
504	Ken Caminiti	.10
505	Mike Macfarlane	.10
506	Jody Reed	.10
507	Bobby Hughes RC	.10
508	Wil Cordero	.10
509	George Tsanis RC	.10
510	Bret Saberhagen	.10
511	Derek Jeter RC	20.00
512	Gene Schall	.10
513	Curtis Shaw	.10
514	Steve Cooke	.10
515	Edgar Martinez	.10
516	Mike Milchin	.10
517	Billy Ripken	.10
518	Andy Benes	.10
519	Juan de la Rosa RC	.10
520	John Burkett	.10
521	Alex Ochoa	.10
522	Tony Tarasco RC	.10
523	Luis Ortiz	.10
524	Rick Williams	.10
525	Chris Turner RC	.10
526	Rob Dibble	.10
527	Jack McDowell	.10
528	Daryl Boston	.10
529	Bill Wertz RC	.10
530	Charlie Hough	.10
531	Sean Bergman	.10
532	Doug Jones	.10
533	Jeff Montgomery	.10
534	Roger Cedeno RC	.25
535	Robin Yount	1.50
536	Mo Vaughn	.10
537	Brian Harper	.10
538	Juan Castillo	.10
539	Steve Farr	.10
540	John Kruk	.10
541	Troy Neel	.10
542	Danny Clyburn RC	.10
543	Jim Converse RC	.10
544	Gregg Jefferies	.10
545	Jose Canseco	.40
546	Julio Bruno RC	.10
547	Rob Butler	.10
548	Royce Clayton	.10
549	Chris Hoiles	.10
550	Greg Maddux	2.00
551	Joe Ciccarella RC	.10
552	Ozzie Timmons	.10
553	Chili Davis	.10
554	Brian Koelling	.10
555	Frank Thomas	1.50
556	Vinny Castilla	.10
557	Reggie Jefferson	.10
558	Rob Natal	.10
559	Mike Henneman	.10
560	Craig Biggio	.10
561	Billy Brewer RC	.10
562	Dan Melendez	.10
563	Kenny Felder RC	.10
564	Miguel Batista RC	.10
565	Dave Winfield	1.50
566	Al Shirley	.10
567	Robert Eenhoorn	.10
568	Mike Williams	.10
569	Tanyon Sturtze RC	.10
570	Tim Wakefield	.10
571	Greg Pirkl	.10
572	Sean Lowe RC	.25
573	Terry Burows RC	.10
574	Kevin Higgins RC	.10
575	Joe Carter	.10
576	Kevin Rogers	.10
577	Manny Alexander	.10
578	Dave Justice	.10
579	Brian Conroy RC	.10
580	Jessie Hollins RC	.10
581	Ron Watson RC	.10
582	Bip Roberts	.10
583	Tom Urbani RC	.10
584	Jason Hutchins RC	.10
585	Carlos Baerga	.10
586	Jeff Mutis	.10
587	Justin Thompson	.10
588	Orlando Miller	.10
589	Brian McRae	.10
590	Ramon Martinez	.10

#	Player	Price
591	Dave Nilsson	.10
592	Jose Vidro RC	1.50
593	Rich Becker	.10
594	Preston Wilson RC	1.50
595	Don Mattingly	2.50
596	Tony Longmire	.10
597	Kevin Seitzer	.10
598	Midre Cummings RC	.10
599	Omar Vizquel	.10
600	Lee Smith	.10
601	David Hulse RC	.10
602	Darrell Sherman RC	.10
603	Alex Gonzalez	.10
604	Geronimo Pena	.10
605	Mike Devereaux	.10
606	Sterling Hitchcock RC	.25
607	Mike Greenwell	.10
608	Steve Buechele	.10
609	Troy Percival	.10
610	Bobby Kelly	.10
611	James Baldwin RC	.10
612	Jerald Clark	.10
613	Albie Lopez RC	.10
614	Dave Magadan	.10
615	Mickey Tettleton	.10
616	Sean Runyan RC	.10
617	Bob Hamelin	.10
618	Raul Mondesi	.10
619	Tyrone Hill	.10
620	Darrin Fletcher	.10
621	Mike Trombley	.10
622	Jeromy Burnitz	.10
623	Bernie Williams	.10
624	Mike Farmer RC	.10
625	Rickey Henderson	1.50
626	Carlos Garcia	.10
627	Jeff Darwin RC	.10
628	Todd Zeile	.10
629	Benji Gil	.10
630	Tony Gwynn	2.00
631	Aaron Small RC	.10
632	Joe Rosselli RC	.10
633	Mike Mussina	1.00
634	Ryan Klesko	.10
635	Roger Clemens	2.50
636	Sammy Sosa	2.00
637	Orlando Palmeiro RC	.10
638	Willie Greene	.10
639	George Bell	.10
640	Garvin Alston RC	.10
641	Pete Janicki RC	.10
642	Chris Sheff RC	.10
643	Felipe Lira RC	.10
644	Roberto Petagine	.10
645	Wally Joyner	.10
646	Mike Piazza	3.00
647	Jaime Navarro	.10
648	Jeff Hartsock RC	.10
649	David McCarty	.10
650	Bobby Jones	.10
651	Mark Hutton	.10
652	Kyle Abbott	.10
653	Steve Cox RC	.10
654	Jeff King	.10
655	Norm Charlton	.10
656	Mike Gulan RC	.10
657	Julio Franco	.10
658	Cameron Cairncross RC	.10
659	John Olerud	.10
660	Salomon Torres	.10
661	Brad Pennington	.10
662	Melvin Nieves	.10
663	Ivan Calderon	.10
664	Turk Wendell	.10
665	Chris Pritchett	.10
666	Reggie Sanders	.10
667	Robin Ventura	.10
668	Joe Girardi	.10
669	Manny Ramirez	1.50
670	Jeff Conine	.10
671	Greg Gohr	.10
672	Andujar Cedeno	.10
673	Les Norman RC	.10
674	Mike James RC	.10
675	Marshall Boze RC	.10
676	B.J. Wallace	.10
677	Kent Hrbek	.10
678	Jack Voight	.10
679	Brien Taylor	.10
680	Curt Schilling	.35
681	Todd Van Poppel	.10
682	Kevin Young	.10
683	Tommy Adams	.10
684	Bernard Gilkey	.10
685	Kevin Brown	.10
686	Fred McGriff	.10
687	Pat Borders	.10
688	Kirt Manwaring	.10
689	Sid Bream	.10
690	John Valentin	.10
691	Steve Olsen RC	.10
692	Roberto Mejia RC	.10
693	Carlos Delgado (Foil)	.50
694	Steve Gibralter RC (Foil)	.10
695	Gary Mota (Foil)	.10
696	Jose Malave RC (Foil)	.10
697	Larry Sutton RC (Foil)	.10
698	Dan Frye RC (Foil)	.10
699	Tim Clark RC (Foil)	.10
700	Brian Rupp RC (Foil)	.10
701	Felipe Alou, Moises Alou (Foil)	.10
702	Bobby Bonds, Barry Bonds (Foil)	1.00
703	Ken Griffey Sr., Ken Griffey Jr. (Foil)	1.00
704	Hal McRae, Brian McRae (Foil)	.10
705	Checklist 1	.10
706	Checklist 2	.10
707	Checklist 3	.10
708	Checklist 4	.10

1994 Bowman Previews

Bowman Preview cards were randomly inserted into Stadium Club 1994 Baseball Series II at a rate of one every 24 packs. This 10-card set featured several proven major league stars, as well as minor league players. Card number 10, James Mouton, is designed as a special MVP foil card.

		NM/M
Complete Set (10):		7.00
Common Player:		.50
1	Frank Thomas	1.50
2	Mike Piazza	3.00
3	Albert Belle	.50
4	Javier Lopez	.50
5	Cliff Floyd	.50
6	Alex Gonzalez	.50
7	Ricky Bottalico	.50
8	Tony Clark	.50
9	Mac Suzuki	.50
10	James Mouton (Foil)	.50

1994 Bowman

Bowman baseball for 1994 was a 682-card set issued all in one series, including a 52-card sub-set. There were 11 regular cards plus one foil card in each pack, with a suggested retail price of $2. The cards have a full-bleed design, with gold-foil stamping on every card. As in the past, the set includes numerous rookies and prospects, along with the game's biggest stars. The 52-card foil subset features 28 Top Prospects, with the player's team logo in the background; 17 Minor League MVPs, with a stadium in the background; and seven Diamonds in the Rough, with, you guessed it, a diamond as a backdrop.

		NM/M
Complete Set (682):		40.00
Common Player:		.10
Pack (12):		1.50
Wax Box (24):		30.00
1	Joe Carter	.10
2	Marcus Moore	.10
3	Doug Creek RC	.10
4	Pedro Martinez	1.50
5	Ken Griffey Jr.	3.00
6	Greg Swindell	.10
7	J.J. Johnson	.10
8	Homer Bush RC	.10
9	Arquimedez Pozo RC	.10
10	Bryan Harvey	.10
11	J.T. Snow	.10
12	Alan Benes RC	.10
13	Chad Kreuter	.10
14	Eric Karros	.10
15	Frank Thomas	1.50
16	Bret Saberhagen	.10
17	Terrell Lowery	.10
18	Rod Bolton	.10
19	Harold Baines	.10
20	Matt Walbeck	.10
21	Tom Glavine	.30
22	Todd Jones	.10
23	Alberto Castillo	.10
24	Ruben Sierra	.10
25	Don Mattingly	2.50
26	Mike Morgan	.10
27	Jim Musselwhite RC	.10
28	Matt Brunson RC	.10
29	Adam Meinershagen RC	.10
30	Joe Girardi	.10
31	Shane Halter RC	.10
32	Jose Paniagua RC	.10
33	Paul Perkins	.10
34	John Hudek RC	.10
35	Frank Viola	.10
36	David Lamb RC	.10
37	Marshall Boze	.10
38	Jorge Posada RC	6.00
39	Brian Anderson RC	.25
40	Mark Whiten	.10
41	Sean Bergman	.10
42	Jose Parra RC	.10
43	Mike Robertson	.10
44	Pete Walker RC	.10
45	Juan Gonzalez	.75
46	Cleveland Ladell RC	.10
47	Mark Smith	.10
48	Kevin Jarvis RC	.10
49	Amaury Telemaco RC	.10
50	Andy Van Slyke	.10
51	Rikkert Faneyte RC	.10
52	Curtis Shaw	.10
53	Matt Beres RC	.10
54	Wilson Alvarez	.10
55	Manny Ramirez	1.50
56	Bobby Munoz	.10
57	Ed Sprague	.10
58	Jamey Wright RC	.10
59	Jeff Montgomery	.10
60	Kirk Rueter	.10
61	Edgar Martinez	.10
62	Luis Gonzalez	.10
63	Tim Vanegmond RC	.10
64	Bip Roberts	.10
65	John Jaha	.10
66	Chuck Carr	.10
67	Chuck Finley	.10
68	Aaron Holbert	.10
69	Cecil Fielder	.10
70	Tom Engle RC	.10
71	Ron Karkovice	.10
72	Joe Orsulak	.10
73	Duff Brumley RC	.10
74	Craig Clayton RC	.10
75	Cal Ripken, Jr.	4.00
76	Brad Fullmer RC	.50
77	Tony Tarasco	.10
78	Terry Farrar RC	.10
79	Matt Williams	.10
80	Rickey Henderson	1.50
81	Terry Mulholland	.10
82	Sammy Sosa	2.00
83	Paul Sorrento	.10
84	Pete Incaviglia	.10
85	Darren Hall RC	.10
86	Scott Klingenbeck	.10
87	Dario Perez RC	.10
88	Ugueth Urbina RC	.10
89	Dave Vanhof RC	.10
90	Domingo Jean	.10
91	Otis Nixon	.10
92	Andres Berumen	.10
93	Jose Valentin	.10
94	Edgar Renteria RC	5.00
95	Chris Turner	.10
96	Ray Lankford	.10
97	Danny Bautista	.10
98	Chan Ho Park RC	1.00
99	Glenn DiSarcina RC	.10
100	Butch Huskey	.10
101	Ivan Rodriguez	1.00
102	Johnny Ruffin	.10
103	Alex Ochoa	.10
104	Torii Hunter RC	6.00
105	Ryan Klesko	.10
106	Jay Bell	.10
107	Kurt Peltzer RC	.10
108	Miguel Jimenez	.10
109	Russ Davis	.10
110	Derek Wallace	.10
111	Keith Lockhart RC	.10
112	Mike Lieberthal	.10
113	Dave Stewart	.10
114	Tom Schmidt	.10
115	Brian McRae	.10
116	Moises Alou	.10
117	Dave Fleming	.10
118	Jeff Bagwell	1.50
119	Luis Ortiz	.10
120	Tony Gwynn	2.00
121	Jaime Navarro	.10
122	Benny Santiago	.10
123	Darrel Whitmore	.10
124	John Mabry RC	.15
125	Mickey Tettleton	.10
126	Tom Candiotti	.10
127	Tim Raines	.10
128	Bobby Bonilla	.10
129	John Dettmer	.10
130	Hector Carrasco	.10
131	Chris Hoiles	.10
132	Rick Aguilera	.10
133	Esteban Loaiza RC	1.50
134	Dave Justice	.10
135	Barry Bonds	4.00
136	Bob Welch	.10
137	Mike Stanley	.10
138	Roberto Hernandez	.10
139	Sandy Alomar	.10
140	Darren Daulton	.10
141	Angel Martinez RC	.10
142	Howard Johnson	.10
143	Bob Hamelin	.10
144	J.J. Thobe RC	.10
145	Roger Salkeld	.10
146	Orlando Miller	.10
147	Dmitri Young	.10
148	Tim Hyers RC	.10
149	Mark Loretta RC	3.00
150	Chris Hammond	.10
151	Joel Moore RC	.10
152	Todd Zeile	.10
153	Wil Cordero	.10
154	Chris Smith	.10
155	James Baldwin	.10
156	Edgardo Alfonzo RC	1.00
157	Kym Ashworth RC	.10
158	Paul Bako RC	.10
159	Rick Krivda RC	.10
160	Pat Mahomes	.10
161	Damon Hollins	.10
162	Felix Martinez RC	.10
163	Jason Myers RC	.10
164	Izzy Molina RC	.10
165	Brien Taylor	.10
166	Kevin Orie RC	.10
167	Casey Whitten RC	.10
168	Tony Longmire	.10
169	John Olerud	.10
170	Mark Thompson	.10
171	Jorge Fabregas	.10
172	John Wetteland	.10
173	Dan Wilson	.10
174	Doug Drabek	.10
175	Jeffrey McNeely	.10
176	Melvin Nieves	.10
177	Doug Glanville RC	.10
178	Javier De La Hoya RC	.10
179	Chad Curtis	.10
180	Brian Barber	.10
181	Mike Henneman	.10
182	Jose Offerman	.10
183	Robert Ellis RC	.10
184	John Franco	.10
185	Benji Gil	.10
186	Hal Morris	.10
187	Chris Sabo	.10
188	Blaise Ilsley RC	.10
189	Steve Avery	.10
190	Rick White RC	.10
191	Rod Beck	.10
(192)	Mark McGwire (No card number.)	3.00
193	Jim Abbott	.10
194	Randy Myers	.10
195	Kenny Lofton	.10
196	Mariano Duncan	.10
197	Lee Daniels RC	.10
198	Armando Reynoso	.10
199	Joe Randa	.10
200	Cliff Floyd	.10
201	Tim Harkrider RC	.10
202	Kevin Gallaher RC	.10
203	Scott Cooper	.10
204	Phil Stidham RC	.10
205	Jeff D'Amico RC	.25
206	Matt Whisenant	.10
207	De Shawn Warren	.10
208	Rene Arocha	.10
209	Tony Clark RC	.50
210	Jason Jacome RC	.10
211	Scott Christman RC	.10
212	Bill Pulsipher	.10
213	Dean Palmer	.10
214	Chad Mottola	.10
215	Manny Alexander	.10
216	Rich Becker	.10
217	Andre King RC	.10
218	Carlos Garcia	.10
219	Ron Pezzoni RC	.10
220	Steve Karsay	.10
221	Jose Musset RC	.10
222	Karl Rhodes	.10
223	Frank Cimorelli RC	.10
224	Kevin Jordan RC	.10
225	Duane Ward	.10
226	John Burke	.10
227	Mike MacFarlane	.10
228	Mike Lansing	.10
229	Chuck Knoblauch	.10
230	Ken Caminiti	.10
231	Gar Finnvold RC	.10
232	Derrek Lee RC	12.00
233	Brady Anderson	.10
234	Vic Darensbourg RC	.10
235	Mark Langston	.10
236	T.J. Mathews RC	.10
237	Lou Whitaker	.10
238	Roger Cedeno	.10
239	Alex Fernandez	.10
240	Ryan Thompson	.10
241	Kerry Lacy RC	.10
242	Reggie Sanders	.10
243	Brad Pennington	.10
244	Bryan Eversgerd RC	.10
245	Greg Maddux	2.00
246	Jason Kendall	.10
247	J.R. Phillips	.10
248	Bobby Witt	.10
249	Paul O'Neill	.10
250	Ryne Sandberg	2.00
251	Charles Nagy	.10
252	Kevin Stocker	.10
253	Shawn Green	.30
254	Charlie Hayes	.10
255	Donnie Elliott	.10
256	Rob Fitzpatrick RC	.10
257	Tim Davis	.10
258	James Mouton	.10
259	Mike Greenwell	.10
260	Ray McDavid	.10
261	Mike Kelly	.10
262	Andy Larkin RC	.10
(263)	Marquis Riley (No card number.)	.10
264	Bob Tewksbury	.10
265	Brian Edmondson	.10
266	Eduardo Lantigua RC	.10
267	Brandon Wilson	.10
268	Mike Welch	.10
269	Tom Henke	.10
270	Calvin Reese	.10
271	Gregg Zaun RC	.10
272	Todd Ritchie	.10
273	Javier Lopez	.10
274	Kevin Young	.10
275	Kirt Manwaring	.10
276	Bill Taylor RC	.10
277	Robert Eenhoorn	.10
278	Jessie Hollins	.10
279	Julian Tavarez RC	.10
280	Gene Schall	.10
281	Paul Molitor	1.50
282	Neifi Perez RC	.10
283	Greg Gagne	.10
284	Marquis Grissom	.10
285	Randy Johnson	1.50
286	Pete Harnisch	.10
287	Joel Bennett RC	.10
288	Derek Bell	.10
289	Darryl Hamilton	.10
290	Gary Sheffield	.40
291	Eduardo Perez	.10
292	Basil Shabazz	.10
293	Eric Davis	.10
294	Pedro Astacio	.10
295	Robin Ventura	.10
296	Jeff Kent	.10
297	Rick Helling	.10
298	Joe Oliver	.10
299	Lee Smith	.10
300	Dave Winfield	1.50
301	Deion Sanders	.10
302	Ravelo Manzanillo RC	.10
303	Mark Portugal	.10
304	Brent Gates	.10
305	Wade Boggs	2.00
306	Rick Wilkins	.10
307	Carlos Baerga	.10
308	Curt Schilling	.35
309	Shannon Stewart	.10
310	Darren Holmes	.10
311	Robert Toth RC	.10
312	Gabe White	.10
313	Mac Suzuki RC	.10
314	Alvin Morman RC	.10
315	Mo Vaughn	.10
316	Bryce Florie RC	.10
317	Gabby Martinez RC	.10
318	Carl Everett	.10
319	Kerwin Moore	.10
320	Tom Pagnozzi	.10
321	Chris Gomez	.10
322	Todd Williams	.10
323	Pat Hentgen	.10
324	Kirk Presley RC	.10
325	Kevin Brown	.10
326	Jason Isringhausen RC	1.50
327	Rick Forney RC	.10
328	Carlos Pulido RC	.10
329	Terrell Wade RC	.10
330	Al Martin	.10
331	Dan Carlson RC	.10
332	Mark Acre RC	.10
333	Sterling Hitchcock	.10
334	Jon Ratliff RC	.10
335	Alex Ramirez RC	.10
336	Phil Geisler RC	.10
337	Eddie Zambrano RC (Foil)	.10
338	Jim Thome (Foil)	.60
339	James Mouton (Foil)	.10
340	Cliff Floyd (Foil)	.10
341	Carlos Delgado (Foil)	.40
342	Roberto Petagine (Foil)	.10
343	Tim Clark (Foil)	.10
344	Bubba Smith (Foil)	.10
345	Randy Curtis RC (Foil)	.10
346	Joe Biasucci RC (Foil)	.10
347	D.J. Boston RC (Foil)	.10
348	Ruben Rivera RC (Foil)	.75
349	Bryan Link RC (Foil)	.10
350	Mike Bell RC (Foil)	.25
351	Marty Watson RC (Foil)	.10
352	Jason Myers RC (Foil)	.10
353	Chipper Jones (Foil)	1.25
354	Brooks Kieschnick (Foil)	.10
355	Calvin Reese (Foil)	.10
356	John Burke (Foil)	.10
357	Kurt Miller (Foil)	.10
358	Orlando Miller (Foil)	.10
359	Todd Hollandsworth (Foil)	.10
360	Rondell White (Foil)	.10
361	Bill Pulsipher (Foil)	.10
362	Tyler Green (Foil)	.10
363	Midre Cummings (Foil)	.10
364	Brian Barber (Foil)	.10
365	Melvin Nieves (Foil)	.10
366	Salomon Torres (Foil)	.10
367	Alex Ochoa (Foil)	.10
368	Frank Rodriguez (Foil)	.10
369	Brian Anderson (Foil)	.10
370	James Baldwin (Foil)	.10
371	Manny Ramirez (Foil)	.75
372	Justin Thompson (Foil)	.10
373	Johnny Damon (Foil)	.50
374	Jeff D'Amico (Foil)	.10
375	Rich Becker (Foil)	.10
376	Derek Jeter (Foil)	3.00
377	Steve Karsay (Foil)	.10
378	Mac Suzuki (Foil)	.10
379	Benji Gil (Foil)	.10
380	Alex Gonzalez (Foil)	.10
381	Jason Bere (Foil)	.10
382	Brett Butler (Foil)	.10
383	Jeff Conine (Foil)	.10
384	Darren Daulton (Foil)	.10
385	Jeff Kent (Foil)	.10
386	Don Mattingly (Foil)	1.50
387	Mike Piazza (Foil)	2.00
388	Ryne Sandberg (Foil)	1.25
389	Rich Amaral	.10
390	Craig Biggio	.10
391	Jeff Suppan RC	.35
392	Andy Benes	.10
393	Cal Eldred	.10
394	Jeff Conine	.10
395	Tim Salmon	.10
396	Ray Suplee RC	.10
397	Tony Phillips	.10
398	Ramon Martinez	.10
399	Julio Franco	.10
400	Dwight Gooden	.10
401	Kevin Lomon RC	.10
402	Jose Rijo	.10
403	Mike Devereaux	.10
404	Mike Zolecki RC	.10
405	Fred McGriff	.10
406	Danny Clyburn	.10
407	Robby Thompson	.10
408	Terry Steinbach	.10
409	Luis Polonia	.10
410	Mark Grace	.10
411	Albert Belle	.10
412	John Kruk	.10
413	Scott Spiezio RC	.25
414	Ellis Burks	.10
415	Joe Vitiello	.10
416	Tim Costo	.10
417	Marc Newfield	.10
418	Oscar Henriquez RC	.10
419	Matt Perisho RC	.10
420	Julio Bruno	.10
421	Kenny Felder	.10
422	Tyler Green	.10
423	Jim Edmonds	.10
424	Ozzie Smith	2.00
425	Rick Greene	.10
426	Todd Hollandsworth	.10
427	Eddie Pearson RC	.10
428	Quilvio Veras	.10
429	Kenny Rogers	.10
430	Willie Greene	.10
431	Vaughn Eshelman	.10
432	Pat Meares	.10
433	Jermaine Dye RC	8.00
434	Steve Cooke	.10
435	Bill Swift	.10
436	Fausto Cruz RC	.10
437	Mark Hutton	.10
438	Brooks Kieschnick RC	.10
439	Yorkis Perez	.10
440	Len Dykstra	.10
441	Pat Borders	.10
442	Doug Walls RC	.10
443	Wally Joyner	.10
444	Ken Hill	.10
445	Eric Anthony	.10
446	Mitch Williams	.10
447	Cory Bailey RC	.10
448	Dave Staton	.10
449	Greg Vaughn	.10
450	Dave Magadan	.10
451	Chili Davis	.10
452	Gerald Santos RC	.10
453	Joe Perona	.10
454	Deline DeShields	.10
455	Jack McDowell	.10
456	Todd Hundley	.10
457	Ritchie Moody	.10
458	Bret Boone	.10
459	Ben McDonald	.10
460	Kirby Puckett	2.00
461	Gregg Olson	.10
462	Rich Aude RC	.10
463	John Burkett	.10
464	Troy Neel	.10
465	Jimmy Key	.10
466	Ozzie Timmons	.10
467	Eddie Murray	1.50
468	Mark Tranberg RC	.10
469	Alex Gonzalez	.10
470	David Nied	.10
471	Barry Larkin	.10
472	Brian Looney RC	.10
473	Shawn Estes	.10
474	A.J. Sager RC	.10
475	Roger Clemens	2.50
476	Vince Moore	.10
477	Scott Karl RC	.10
478	Kurt Miller	.10
479	Garret Anderson	.10
480	Allen Watson	.10
481	Jose Lima RC	.10
482	Rick Gorecki	.10
483	Jimmy Hurst RC	.10
484	Preston Wilson	.10
485	Will Clark	.10
486	Mike Ferry RC	.10
487	Curtis Goodwin RC	.10
488	Mike Myers	.10
489	Chipper Jones	2.00
490	Jeff King	.10

#	Player	Price
491	Bill Van Landingham RC	.10
492	Carlos Reyes RC	.10
493	Andy Pettitte	.30
494	Brant Brown	.10
495	Daron Kirkreit RC	.10
496	Ricky Bottalico RC	.25
497	Devon White	.10
498	Jason Johnson RC	.10
499	Vince Coleman	.10
500	Larry Walker	.10
501	Bobby Ayala	.10
502	Steve Finley	.10
503	Scott Fletcher	.10
504	Brad Ausmus	.10
505	Scott Talanoa RC	.10
506	Orestes Destrade	.10
507	Gary DiSarcina	.10
508	Willie Smith RC	.10
509	Alan Trammell	.10
510	Mike Piazza	3.00
511	Ozzie Guillen	.10
512	Jeromy Burnitz	.10
513	Darren Oliver	.10
514	Kevin Mitchell	.10
515	Rafael Palmeiro	1.00
516	David McCarty	.10
517	Jeff Blauser	.10
518	Trey Beamon	.10
519	Royce Clayton	.10
520	Dennis Eckersley	1.00
521	Bernie Williams	.10
522	Steve Buechele	.10
523	Denny Martinez	.10
524	Dave Hollins	.10
525	Joey Hamilton	.10
526	Andres Galarraga	.10
527	Jeff Granger	.10
528	Joey Eischen	.10
529	Desi Relaford	.10
530	Roberto Petagine	.10
531	Andre Dawson	.30
532	Ray Holbert	.10
533	Duane Singleton	.10
534	Kurt Abbott RC	.20
535	Bo Jackson	.20
536	Gregg Jefferies	.10
537	David Mysel	.10
538	Raul Mondesi	.10
539	Chris Snopek	.10
540	Brook Fordyce	.10
541	Ron Frazier RC	.10
542	Brian Koelling	.10
543	Jimmy Haynes	.10
544	Marty Cordova	.10
545	Jason Green RC	.10
546	Orlando Merced	.10
547	Lou Pote RC	.10
548	Todd Van Poppel	.10
549	Pat Kelly	.10
550	Turk Wendell	.10
551	Herb Perry RC	.10
552	Ryan Karp RC	.10
553	Juan Guzman	.10
554	Bryan Rekar RC	.10
555	Kevin Appier	.10
556	Chris Schwab RC	.10
557	Jay Buhner	.10
558	Andujar Cedeno	.10
559	Ryan McGuire RC	.10
560	Ricky Gutierrez	.10
561	Keith Kimsey RC	.10
562	Tim Clark RC	.10
563	Damion Easley	.10
564	Clint Davis RC	.10
565	Mike Moore	.10
566	Orel Hershiser	.10
567	Jason Bere	.10
568	Kevin McReynolds	.10
569	Leland Macon RC	.10
570	John Courtright RC	.10
571	Sid Fernandez	.10
572	Chad Roper	.10
573	Terry Pendleton	.10
574	Danny Miceli	.10
575	Joe Rosselli	.10
576	Mike Bordick	.10
577	Danny Tartabull	.10
578	Jose Guzman	.10
579	Omar Vizquel	.10
580	Tommy Greene	.10
581	Paul Spoljaric	.10
582	Walt Weiss	.10
583	Oscar Jimenez RC	.10
584	Rod Henderson	.10
585	Derek Lowe RC	.10
586	Richard Hidalgo RC	1.00
587	Shayne Bennett RC	.10
588	Tim Belk RC	.10
589	Matt Mieske	.10
590	Nigel Wilson	.10
591	Jeff Knox RC	.10
592	Bernard Gilkey	.10
593	David Cone	.10
594	Paul LoDuca RC	5.00
595	Scott Ruffcorn	.10
596	Chris Roberts	.10
597	Oscar Munoz RC	.10
598	Scott Sullivan RC	.10
599	Matt Jarvis RC	.10
600	Jose Canseco	.35
601	Tony Graffanino RC	.10
602	Don Slaught	.10
603	Brett King RC	.10
604	Jose Herrera RC	.10
605	Melido Perez	.10
606	Mike Hubbard RC	.10
607	Chad Ogea RC	.10
608	Wayne Gomes RC	.10
609	Roberto Alomar	.25
610	Angel Echevarria RC	.10
611	Jose Lind	.10
612	Darrin Fletcher	.10
613	Chris Bosio	.10
614	Darryl Kile	.10
615	Frank Rodriguez	.10
616	Phil Plantier	.10
617	Pat Listach	.10
618	Charlie Hough	.10
619	Ryan Hancock RC	.10
620	Darrel Deak RC	.10
621	Travis Fryman	.10
622	Brett Butler	.10
623	Lance Johnson	.10
624	Pete Smith	.10
625	James Hurst	.10
626	Roberto Kelly	.10
627	Mike Mussina	.50
628	Kevin Tapani	.10
629	John Smoltz	.10
630	Midre Cummings	.10
631	Salomon Torres	.10
632	Willie Adams	.10
633	Derek Jeter	4.00
634	Steve Trachsel	.10
635	Albie Lopez	.10
636	Jason Moler	.10
637	Carlos Delgado	.50
638	Roberto Mejia	.10
639	Darren Burton	.10
640	B.J. Wallace	.10
641	Brad Clontz RC	.10
642	Billy Wagner RC	1.00
643	Aaron Sele	.10
644	Cameron Cairncross	.10
645	Brian Harper	.10
(646)	Marc Valdes (No card number.)	.10
647	Mark Ratekin	.10
648	Terry Bradshaw RC	.10
649	Justin Thompson	.10
650	Mike Busch RC	.10
651	Joe Hall RC	.10
652	Bobby Jones	.10
653	Kelly Stinnett RC	.10
654	Rod Steph RC	.10
655	Jay Powell RC	.10
(656)	Keith Garagozzo RC (No card number.)	.10
657	Todd Dunn	.10
658	Charles Peterson RC	.10
659	Darren Lewis	.10
660	John Wasdin RC	.10
661	Tate Seefried RC	.10
662	Hector Trinidad RC	.10
663	John Carter RC	.10
664	Larry Mitchell	.10
665	David Catlett RC	.10
666	Dante Bichette	.10
667	Felix Jose	.10
668	Rondell White	.10
669	Tino Martinez	.10
670	Brian Hunter	.10
671	Jose Malave	.10
672	Archi Cianfrocco	.10
673	Mike Matheny RC	.15
674	Bret Barberie	.10
675	Andrew Lorraine RC	.10
676	Brian Jordan	.10
677	Tim Belcher	.10
678	Antonio Osuna RC	.10
679	Checklist I	.10
680	Checklist II	.10
681	Checklist III	.10
682	Checklist IIII	.10

1994 Bowman Superstar Sampler

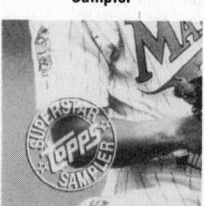

As an insert in 1994 Topps retail factory sets, three-card cello packs of "Superstar Sampler" cards were included. The packs contained special versions of the same player's 1994 Bowman, Finest and Stadium Club cards. Forty-five of the game's top stars are represented in the issue. The Bowman cards in this issue are identical to the cards in the regular set except for the appearance of a round "Topps Superstar Sampler" logo on back.

		NM/M
	Complete Set (45):	275.00
	Common Player:	2.00
1	Joe Carter	2.00
5	Ken Griffey Jr.	20.00
9	Frank Thomas	10.00
21	Tom Glavine	3.00
25	Don Mattingly	17.50
45	Juan Gonzalez	6.00
50	Andy Van Slyke	2.00
55	Manny Ramirez	10.00
69	Cecil Fielder	2.00
75	Cal Ripken Jr.	35.00
79	Matt Williams	2.00
118	Jeff Bagwell	10.00
120	Tony Gwynn	15.00
128	Bobby Bonilla	2.00
133	Dave Justice	2.00
135	Barry Bonds	35.00
169	Darren Daulton	2.00
200	John Olerud	2.00
201	Cliff Floyd	2.00
245	Greg Maddux	15.00
250	Ryne Sandberg	15.00
281	Paul Molitor	10.00
284	Marquis Grissom	2.00
286	Randy Johnson	10.00
290	Gary Sheffield	4.00
307	Carlos Baerga	2.00
315	Mo Vaughn	2.00
395	Tim Salmon	2.00
405	Fred McGriff	2.00
410	Mark Grace	2.00
411	Albert Belle	2.00
440	Len Dykstra	2.00
455	Jack McDowell	2.00
460	Kirby Puckett	15.00
465	Barry Larkin	2.00
475	Roger Clemens	17.50
485	Will Clark	2.00
500	Larry Walker	2.00
510	Mike Piazza	20.00
515	Rafael Palmeiro	9.00
526	Andres Galarraga	2.00
536	Gregg Jefferies	2.00
538	Raul Mondesi	2.00
600	Jose Canseco	6.00
609	Roberto Alomar	4.00

1994 Bowman's Best

The debut Bowman's Best consists of 90 red cards (largely veterans), 90 blue cards (rookies and young players) and 20 Mirror Images combining veteran and young stars by position. Utilizing Topps Finest technology, cards are full-color front and back with high-gloss surfaces. Cards were sold in eight-card foil packs with one Mirror Image card in each pack. A 200-card parallel version officially called "Special Effects," uses Topps refractor technology. Red and Blue sets each contain cards numbered 1-90, while the Mirror Image cards are numbered 91-110.

		NM/M
	Complete Set (200):	30.00
	Red Set (90):	10.00
	Blue Set (90):	20.00
	Common Player:	.15
	Pack (8):	1.50
	Wax Box (24):	30.00
1	Paul Molitor	1.50
2	Eddie Murray	1.50
3	Ozzie Smith	2.00
4	Rickey Henderson	1.50
5	Lee Smith	.15
6	Dave Winfield	1.50
7	Roberto Alomar	.30
8	Matt Williams	.15
9	Mark Grace	.15
10	Lance Johnson	.15
11	Darren Daulton	.15
12	Tom Glavine	.35
13	Gary Sheffield	.40
14	Rod Beck	.15
15	Fred McGriff	.15
16	Joe Carter	.15
17	Dante Bichette	.15
18	Danny Tartabull	.15
19	Juan Gonzalez	.75
20	Steve Avery	.15
21	John Wetteland	.15
22	Ben McDonald	.15
23	Jack McDowell	.15
24	Jose Canseco	.65
25	Tim Salmon	.15
26	Wilson Alvarez	.15
27	Gregg Jefferies	.15
28	John Burkett	.15
29	Greg Vaughn	.15
30	Robin Ventura	.15
31	Paul O'Neill	.15
32	Cecil Fielder	.15
33	Kevin Mitchell	.15
34	Jeff Conine	.15
35	Carlos Baerga	.15
36	Greg Maddux	2.00
37	Roger Clemens	2.25
38	Deion Sanders	.25
39	Delino DeShields	.15
40	Ken Griffey Jr.	2.50
41	Albert Belle	1.50
42	Wade Boggs	2.00
43	Andres Galarraga	.15
44	Aaron Sele	.15
45	Don Mattingly	2.25
46	David Cone	.15
47	Lenny Dykstra	.15
48	Brett Butler	.15
49	Bill Swift	.15
50	Bobby Bonilla	.15
51	Rafael Palmeiro	1.25
52	Moises Alou	.15
53	Jeff Bagwell	1.50
54	Mike Mussina	.50
55	Frank Thomas	1.50
56	Jose Rijo	.15
57	Ruben Sierra	.15
58	Randy Myers	.15
59	Barry Bonds	4.00
60	Jimmy Key	.15
61	Travis Fryman	.15
62	John Olerud	.15
63	David Justice	.15
64	Ray Lankford	.15
65	Bob Tewksbury	.15
66	Chuck Carr	.15
67	Jay Buhner	.15
68	Kenny Lofton	.15
69	Marquis Grissom	.15
70	Sammy Sosa	2.00
71	Cal Ripken Jr.	4.00
72	Ellis Burks	.15
73	Jeff Montgomery	.15
74	Julio Franco	.15
75	Kirby Puckett	2.00
76	Larry Walker	.15
77	Andy Van Slyke	.15
78	Tony Gwynn	2.00
79	Will Clark	.15
80	Mo Vaughn	.15
81	Mike Piazza	2.50
82	James Mouton	.15
83	Carlos Delgado	.60
84	Ryan Klesko	.15
85	Javy Lopez	.15
86	Raul Mondesi	.15
87	Cliff Floyd	.15
88	Manny Ramirez	1.50
89	Hector Carrasco	.15
90	Jeff Granger	.15
1	Chipper Jones	2.00
2	Derek Jeter	4.00
3	Bill Pulsipher	.15
4	James Baldwin	.15
5	Brooks Kieschnick RC	.50
6	Justin Thompson	.15
7	Midre Cummings	.15
8	Joey Hamilton	.15
9	Calvin Reese	.15
10	Brian Barber	.15
11	John Burke	.15
12	De Shawn Warren	.15
13	Edgardo Alfonzo RC	.75
14	Eddie Pearson RC	.15
15	Jimmy Haynes	.15
16	Danny Bautista	.15
17	Roger Cedeno	.15
18	Jon Lieber	.15
19	Billy Wagner RC	.75
20	Tate Seefried RC	.15
21	Chad Mottola	.15
22	Jose Malave	.15
23	Terrell Wade RC	.15
24	Shane Andrews	.15
25	Chan Ho Park RC	.75
26	Kirk Presley RC	.15
27	Robbie Beckett	.15
28	Orlando Miller	.15
29	Jorge Posada RC	8.00
30	Frank Rodriguez	.15
31	Brian Hunter	.15
32	Billy Ashley	.15
33	Rondell White	.15
34	John Roper	.15
35	Marc Valdes	.15
36	Scott Ruffcorn	.15
37	Rod Henderson	.15
38	Curt Goodwin	.15
39	Russ Davis	.15
40	Rick Gorecki	.15
41	Johnny Damon	.60
42	Roberto Petagine	.15
43	Chris Snopek	.15
44	Mark Acre	.15
45	Todd Hollandsworth	.15
46	Shawn Green	.35
47	John Carter	.15
48	Jim Pittsley	.15
49	John Wasdin RC	.15
50	D.J. Boston	.15
51	Tim Clark	.15
52	Alex Ochoa	.15
53	Chad Roper	.15
54	Mike Kelly	.15
55	Brad Fullmer RC	.50
56	Carl Everett	.15
57	Tim Belk RC	.15
58	Jimmy Hurst RC	.15
59	Mac Suzuki RC	.15
60	Michael Moore	.15
61	Alan Benes RC	.15
62	Tony Clark RC	1.00
63	Edgar Renteria RC	8.00
64	Trey Beamon	.15
65	LaTroy Hawkins RC	.15
66	Wayne Gomes RC	.15
67	Ray McDavid	.15
68	John Dettmer	.15
69	Willie Greene	.15
70	Dave Stevens	.15
71	Kevin Orie RC	.15
72	Chad Ogea	.15
73	Ben Van Ryn	.15
74	Kym Ashworth	.15
75	Dmitri Young	.15
76	Herb Perry	.15
77	Joey Eischen	.15
78	Arquimedez Pozo RC	.15
79	Ugueth Urbina	.15
80	Keith Williams	.15
81	John Frascatore RC	.15
82	Garey Ingram	.15
83	Aaron Small	.15
84	Olmedo Saenz RC	.15
85	Jesus Tavarez	.15
86	Jose Silva RC	.15
87	Gerald Witasick Jr. RC	.15
88	Jay Maldonado	.15
89	Keith Heberling	.15
90	Rusty Greer RC	.50
91	Frank Thomas, Kevin Young	.60
92	Fred McGriff, Brooks Kieschnick RC	.15
93	Matt Williams, Shane Andrews	.15
94	Cal Ripken Jr., Kevin Orie RC	1.50
95	Barry Larkin, Derek Jeter	1.50
96	Ken Griffey Jr., Johnny Damon	1.50
97	Barry Bonds, Rondell White	1.50
98	Albert Belle, Jimmy Hurst RC	.15
99	Raul Mondesi, Ruben Rivera RC	.15
100	Roger Clemens, Scott Ruffcorn	1.00
101	Greg Maddux, John Wasdin RC	.75
102	Tim Salmon, Chad Mottola	.15
103	Carlos Baerga, Arquimedez Pozo RC	.15
104	Mike Piazza, Bobby Hughes	1.00
105	Carlos Delgado, Melvin Nieves	.50
106	Javy Lopez, Jorge Posada RC	2.00
107	Manny Ramirez, Jose Malave	.65
108	Travis Fryman, Chipper Jones	.75
109	Steve Avery, Bill Pulsipher	.15
110	John Olerud, Shawn Green	.50

Refractors

This 200-card parallel set, officially titled "Special Effects," uses Topps' refractor technology. The refractors were packed at the rate of three per wax box of Bowman's Best, but are very difficult to differentiate from the regular high-tech cards.

Superstars:	8-10X
Stars:	4-8X

1995 Bowman

Large numbers of rookie cards and a lengthy run of etched-foil cards distinguishes the 1995 Bowman set. The set's basic cards share a design with a large color photo flanked at left by a severely horizontally compressed mirror image in green, and at bottom by a similar version in brown. Most of the bottom image is covered by the player's last name printed in silver (cards #1-220, rookies) or gold (cards #275-439, veterans) foil. A color team logo is in the lower-left corner of all cards, and the Bowman logo is in red foil at top. In between are the foil-etched subsets of "Minor League MVPs," "1st Impressions," and "Prime Prospects." Each of these cards, seeded one per regular pack and two per jumbo, has the player photo set against a background of textured color foil, with a prismatic silver border. Each of the foil cards can also be found in a gold-toned version, in a ratio of six silver to one gold. Backs of the rookies' cards have a portrait photo at right and a scouting report at left. Veterans' cards have either a scouting report for younger players, or a chart of stats versus each team played in 1994. Backs of all the foil cards have a scouting report.

		NM/M
	Complete Set (439):	150.00
	Common Player:	.10
	Pack (10):	6.00
	Wax Box (24):	125.00
	Rack Pack (15):	5.00
	Rack Box (24):	125.00
1	Billy Wagner	.10
2	Chris Widger	.10
3	Brent Bowers	.10
4	Bob Abreu	10.00
5	Lou Collier RC	.10
6	Juan Acevedo RC	.25
7	Jason Kelley RC	.10
8	Brian Sackinsky RC	.10
9	Scott Christman	.10
10	Damon Hollins	.10
11	Willis Otanez RC	.10
12	Jason Ryan RC	.10
13	Jason Giambi	.75
14	Andy Taulbee RC	.10
15	Mark Thompson	.10
16	Hugo Pivaral RC	.10
17	Brien Taylor	.10
18	Antonio Osuna	.10
19	Edgardo Alfonzo	.10
20	Carl Everett	.10
21	Matt Drews	.10
22	Bartolo Colon RC	4.00
23	Andruw Jones RC	8.00
24	Robert Person RC	.40
25	Derek Lee	.75
26	John Ambrose RC	.10
27	Eric Knowles RC	.10
28	Chris Roberts	.10
29	Don Wengert	.10
30	Marcus Jensen RC	.10
31	Brian Barber	.10
32	Kevin Brown	.10
33	Benji Gil	.10
34	Mike Hubbard	.10
35	Bart Evans RC	.10
36	Enrique Wilson RC	.50
37	Brian Buchanan RC	.10
38	Ken Ray RC	.10
39	Micah Franklin RC	.10
40	Ricky Otero RC	.10
41	Jason Kendall RC	.10
42	Jimmy Hurst	.10
43	Jerry Wolak RC	.10
44	Jayson Peterson RC	.10
45	Allen Battle RC	.10
46	Scott Stahoviak	.10
47	Steve Schrenk RC	.10
48	Travis Miller RC	.25
49	Eddie Rios RC	.10
50	Mike Hampton	.10
51	Chad Frontera RC	.10
52	Tom Evans RC	.10
53	C.J. Nitkowski RC	.10
54	Clay Caruthers RC	.10
55	Shannon Stewart	.10
56	Jorge Posada	.50
57	Aaron Holbert	.10
58	Harry Berrios RC	.10
59	Steve Rodriguez	.10
60	Shane Andrews	.10
61	Will Cunnane RC	.10
62	Richard Hidalgo	.10
63	Bill Selby RC	.10
64	Jay Cranford RC	.10
65	Jeff Suppan RC	.10
66	Curtis Goodwin	.10
67	John Thomson RC	.10

#	Player	Price
68	Justin Thompson	.10
69	Troy Percival	.10
70	Matt Wagner RC	.10
71	Terry Bradshaw	.10
72	Greg Hansell	.10
73	John Burke	.10
74	Jeff D'Amico	.10
75	Ernie Young	.10
76	Jason Bates	.10
77	Chris Stynes	.10
78	Cade Gaspar RC	.10
79	Melvin Nieves	.10
80	Rick Gorecki	.10
81	Felix Rodriguez RC	.50
82	Ryan Hancock	.10
83	Chris Carpenter RC	6.00
84	Ray McDavid	.10
85	Chris Wimmer	.10
86	Doug Glanville	.10
87	DeShawn Warren	.10
88	Damian Moss	.50
89	Rafael Orellano RC	.10
90	Vladimir Guerrero RC	50.00
91	Raul Casanova	.40
92	Karim Garcia RC	.75
93	Bryce Florie	.10
94	Kevin Orie	.10
95	Ryan Nye RC	.10
96	Matt Sachse RC	.10
97	Ivan Arteaga RC	.10
98	Glenn Murray	.10
99	Stacy Hollins RC	.10
100	Jim Pittsley	.10
101	Craig Mattson RC	.10
102	Neifi Perez	.10
103	Keith Williams	.10
104	Roger Cedeno	.10
105	Tony Terry RC	.10
106	Jose Malave	.10
107	Joe Rosselli	.10
108	Kevin Jordan	.10
109	Sid Roberson RC	.10
110	Alan Embree	.10
111	Terrell Wade	.10
112	Bob Wolcott	.10
113	Carlos Perez RC	.10
114	Mike Bovee RC	.10
115	Tommy Davis RC	.10
116	Jeremey Kendall RC	.10
117	Rich Aude	.10
118	Rick Huisman	.10
119	Tim Belk	.10
120	Edgar Renteria	.25
121	Calvin Maduro RC	.10
122	Jerry Martin RC	.10
123	Ramon Fermin RC	.10
124	Kimera Bartee RC	.10
125	Mark Farris	.10
126	Frank Rodriguez	.10
127	Bobby Higginson RC	.50
128	Bret Wagner	.10
129	Edwin Diaz RC	.10
130	Jimmy Haynes	.10
131	Chris Weinke	.75
132	Damian Jackson RC	.10
133	Felix Martinez	.10
134	Edwin Hurtado RC	.25
135	Matt Raleigh RC	.10
136	Paul Wilson	.10
137	Ron Villone	.10
138	Eric Stuckenschneider RC	.10
139	Tate Seefried	.10
140	Rey Ordonez RC	.75
141	Eddie Pearson	.10
142	Kevin Gallaher	.10
143	Torii Hunter	.25
144	Daron Kirkreit	.10
145	Craig Wilson	.10
146	Ugueth Urbina	.10
147	Chris Snopek	.10
148	Kym Ashworth	.10
149	Wayne Gomes	.10
150	Mark Loretta	.10
151	Ramon Morel	.10
152	Trot Nixon	.20
153	Desi Relaford	.10
154	Scott Sullivan	.10
155	Marc Barcelo	.10
156	Willie Adams	.10
157	Derrick Gibson RC	.10
158	Brian Meadows RC	.10
159	Julian Tavarez	.10
160	Bryan Rekar	.10
161	Steve Gibralter	.10
162	Esteban Loaiza	.10
163	John Wasdin	.10
164	Kirk Presley	.10
165	Mariano Rivera	.50
166	Andy Larkin	.10
167	Sean Whiteside RC	.10
168	Matt Apana RC	.10
169	Shawn Senior RC	.10
170	Scott Gentile	.10
171	Quilvio Veras	.10
172	Eliezer Marrero RC	1.00
173	Mendy Lopez RC	.10
174	Homer Bush	.10
175	Brian Stephenson RC	.10
176	Jon Nunnally	.10
177	Jose Herrera	.10
178	Corey Avrard RC	.10
179	David Bell	.10
180	Jason Isringhausen	.10
181	Jamey Wright	.10
182	Lonell Roberts RC	.10
183	Marty Cordova	.10
184	Amaury Telemaco	.10
185	John Mabry	.10
186	Andrew Vessel RC	.10
187	Jim Cole RC	.10
188	Marquis Riley	.10
189	Todd Dunn	.10
190	John Carter	.10
191	Donnie Sadler RC	.25
192	Mike Bell	.10
193	Chris Cumberland RC	.10
194	Jason Schmidt	.25
195	Matt Brunson	.10
196	James Baldwin	.10
197	Bill Simas RC	.10
198	Gus Gandarillas	.10
199	Mac Suzuki	.10
200	Rick Holifield RC	.10
201	Fernando Lunar RC	.10
202	Kevin Jarvis	.10
203	Everett Stull RC	.10
204	Steve Wojciechowski	.10
205	Shawn Estes	.10
206	Jermaine Dye	.10
207	Marc Kroon	.10
208	Peter Munro RC	.10
209	Pat Watkins	.10
210	Matt Smith	.10
211	Joe Vitiello	.10
212	Gerald Witasick Jr.	.10
213	Freddy Garcia RC	.10
214	Glenn Dishman RC	.10
215	Jay Canizaro RC	.10
216	Angel Martinez	.10
217	Yamil Benitez RC	.10
218	Fausto Macey RC	.10
219	Eric Owens	.10
220	Checklist	.10
221	Dwayne Hosey RC (Minor League MVPs)	.10
222	Brad Woodall RC (Minor League MVPs)	.25
223	Billy Ashley (Minor League MVPs)	.10
224	Mark Grudzielanek RC (Minor League MVPs)	2.00
225	Mark Johnson RC (Minor League MVPs)	.10
226	Tim Unroe RC (Minor League MVPs)	.10
227	Todd Greene (Minor League MVPs)	.10
228	Larry Sutton (Minor League MVPs)	.10
229	Derek Jeter (Minor League MVPs)	3.00
230	Sal Fasano RC (Minor League MVPs)	.10
231	Ruben Rivera (Minor League MVPs)	.10
232	Chris Truby RC (Minor League MVPs)	.10
233	John Donati (Minor League MVPs)	.10
234	Decomba Conner RC (Minor League MVPs)	.10
235	Sergio Nunez RC (Minor League MVPs)	.10
236	Ray Brown RC (Minor League MVPs)	.10
237	Juan Melo RC (Minor League MVPs)	.10
238	Hideo Nomo RC (First Impressions)	4.00
239	Jaime Bluma RC (First Impressions)	.10
240	Jay Payton RC (First Impressions)	1.50
241	Paul Konerko (First Impressions)	.75
242	Scott Elarton RC (First Impressions)	.50
243	Jeff Abbott RC (First Impressions)	.25
244	Jim Brower RC (First Impressions)	.10
245	Geoff Blum RC (First Impressions)	.10
246	Aaron Boone RC (First Impressions)	1.00
247	J.R. Phillips (Top Prospects)	.10
248	Alex Ochoa (Top Prospects)	.10
249	Nomar Garciaparra (Top Prospects)	5.00
250	Garret Anderson (Top Prospects)	.25
251	Ray Durham (Top Prospects)	.10
252	Paul Shuey (Top Prospects)	.10
253	Tony Clark (Top Prospects)	.10
254	Johnny Damon (Top Prospects)	1.00
255	Duane Singleton (Top Prospects)	.10
256	LaTroy Hawkins (Top Prospects)	.10
257	Andy Pettitte (Top Prospects)	.40
258	Ben Grieve (Top Prospects)	.10
259	Marc Newfield (Top Prospects)	.10
260	Terrell Lowery (Top Prospects)	.10
261	Shawn Green (Top Prospects)	.40
262	Chipper Jones (Top Prospects)	1.50
263	Brooks Kieschnick (Top Prospects)	.10
264	Calvin Reese (Top Prospects)	.10
265	Doug Million (Top Prospects)	.10
266	Marc Valdes (Top Prospects)	.10
267	Brian Hunter (Top Prospects)	.10
268	Todd Hollandsworth (Top Prospects)	.10
269	Rod Henderson (Top Prospects)	.10
270	Bill Pulsipher (Top Prospects)	.10
271	Scott Rolen RC (Top Prospects)	15.00
272	Trey Beamon (Top Prospects)	.10
273	Alan Benes (Top Prospects)	.10
274	Dustin Hermanson (Top Prospects)	.10
275	Ricky Bottalico	.10
276	Albert Belle	.10
277	Deion Sanders	.25
278	Matt Williams	.10
279	Jeff Bagwell	.75
280	Kirby Puckett	1.50
281	Dave Hollins	.10
282	Don Mattingly	1.50
283	Joey Hamilton	.10
284	Bobby Bonilla	.10
285	Moises Alou	.25
286	Tom Glavine	.10
287	Brett Butler	.10
288	Chris Hoiles	.10
289	Kenny Rogers	.10
290	Larry Walker	.25
291	Tim Raines	.10
292	Kevin Appier	.10
293	Roger Clemens	2.00
294a	Chuck Carr	.10
294b	Cliff Floyd (Should be #394.)	.10
295	Randy Myers	.10
296	Dave Nilsson	.10
297	Joe Carter	.10
298	Chuck Finley	.10
299	Ray Lankford	.10
300	Roberto Kelly	.10
301	Jon Lieber	.10
302	Travis Fryman	.10
303	Mark McGwire	1.50
304	Tony Gwynn	1.00
305	Kenny Lofton	.10
306	Mark Whiten	.10
307	Doug Drabek	.10
308	Terry Steinbach	.10
309	Ryan Klesko	.10
310	Mike Piazza	1.50
311	Ben McDonald	.10
312	Reggie Sanders	.10
313	Alex Fernandez	.10
314	Aaron Sele	.10
315	Gregg Jefferies	.10
316	Rickey Henderson	.75
317	Brian Anderson	.10
318	Jose Valentin	.10
319	Rod Beck	.10
320	Marquis Grissom	.10
321	Ken Griffey Jr.	2.00
322	Bret Saberhagen	.10
323	Juan Gonzalez	.50
324	Paul Molitor	.75
325	Gary Sheffield	.40
326	Darren Daulton	.10
327	Bill Swift	.10
328	Brian McRae	.10
329	Robin Ventura	.10
330	Lee Smith	.10
331	Fred McGriff	.20
332	Delino DeShields	.10
333	Edgar Martinez	.10
334	Mike Mussina	.50
335	Orlando Merced	.10
336	Carlos Baerga	.10
337	Wil Cordero	.10
338	Tom Pagnozzi	.10
339	Pat Hentgen	.10
340	Chad Curtis	.10
341	Darren Lewis	.10
342	Jeff Kent	.20
343	Bip Roberts	.10
344	Ivan Rodriguez	.50
345	Jeff Montgomery	.10
346	Hal Morris	.10
347	Danny Tartabull	.10
348	Raul Mondesi	.10
349	Ken Hill	.10
350	Pedro Martinez	1.00
351	Frank Thomas	.75
352	Manny Ramirez	1.00
353	Tim Salmon	.10
354	William Van Landingham	.10
355	Andres Galarraga	.10
356	Paul O'Neill	.10
357	Brady Anderson	.10
358	Ramon Martinez	.10
359	John Olerud	.10
360	Ruben Sierra	.10
361	Cal Eldred	.10
362	Jay Buhner	.10
363	Jay Bell	.10
364	Wally Joyner	.10
365	Chuck Knoblauch	.10
366	Len Dykstra	.10
367	John Wetteland	.25
368	Roberto Alomar	.25
369	Craig Biggio	.25
370	Ozzie Smith	1.50
371	Terry Pendleton	.10
372	Sammy Sosa	1.00
373	Carlos Garcia	.10
374	Jose Rijo	.10
375	Chris Gomez	.10
376	Barry Bonds	2.00
377	Steve Avery	.10
378	Rick Wilkins	.10
379	Pete Harnisch	.10
380	Dean Palmer	.10
381	Bob Hamelin	.10
382	Jason Bere	.10
383	Jimmy Key	.10
384	Dante Bichette	.10
385	Rafael Palmeiro	.50
386	David Justice	.10
387	Chili Davis	.10
388	Mike Greenwell	.10
389	Todd Zeile	.10
390	Jeff Conine	.10
391	Rick Aguilera	.10
392	Eddie Murray	.50
393	Mike Stanley	.10
394	Randy Johnson	1.00
395	David Nied	.10
396	Devon White	.10
397	Royce Clayton	.10
398	Andy Benes	.10
399	John Hudek	.10
400	Bobby Jones	.10
401	Eric Karros	.10
402	Will Clark	.25
403	Mark Langston	.10
404	Kevin Brown	.10
405	Greg Maddux	1.50
406	David Cone	.10
407	Wade Boggs	.75
408	Steve Trachsel	.10
409	Greg Vaughn	.10
410	Mo Vaughn	.10
411	Wilson Alvarez	.10
412	Cal Ripken Jr.	3.00
413	Rico Brogna	.10
414	Barry Larkin	.40
415	Cecil Fielder	.10
416	Jose Canseco	.50
417	Jack McDowell	.10
418	Mike Lieberthal	.10
419	Andrew Lorraine	.10
420	Rich Becker	.10
421	Tony Phillips	.10
422	Scott Ruffcorn	.10
423	Jeff Granger	.10
424	Greg Pirkl	.10
425	Dennis Eckersley	.50
426	Jose Lima	.10
427	Russ Davis	.10
428	Armando Benitez	.10
429	Alex Gonzalez	.10
430	Carlos Delgado	.25
431	Chan Ho Park	.10
432	Mickey Tettleton	.10
433	Dave Winfield	.75
434	John Burkett	.10
435	Orlando Miller	.10
436	Rondell White	.10
437	Jose Oliva	.10
438	Checklist	.10

cards have a similar stripe in tones of blue. All of those cards are printed in Topps' Finest technology. The 15 Mirror Image cards are in horizontal format, printed more conventionally on metallic foil, and have a rookie and veteran sharing the card. Backs of each card continue the color theme, have '94 and career stats and a highlight or two. Standard packaging was seven-card foil packs with inserts consisting of higher-tech parallel sets of the regular issue.

	NM/M
Complete Set (195):	200.00
Common Player:	.25
Pack (7):	12.00
Wax Box (24):	275.00
Complete Set Red (90):	45.00

#	Player	Price
1	Randy Johnson	1.50
2	Joe Carter	.25
3	Chili Davis	.25
4	Moises Alou	.25
5	Gary Sheffield	.40
6	Kevin Appier	.25
7	Denny Neagle	.25
8	Ruben Sierra	.25
9	Darren Daulton	.25
10	Cal Ripken Jr.	4.00
11	Bobby Bonilla	.25
12	Manny Ramirez	1.50
13	Barry Bonds	4.00
14	Eric Karros	.25
15	Greg Maddux	2.00
16	Jeff Bagwell	1.50
17	Paul Molitor	1.50
18	Ray Lankford	.25
19	Mark Grace	.25
20	Kenny Lofton	.25
21	Tony Gwynn	2.00
22	Will Clark	.25
23	Roger Clemens	2.25
24	Dante Bichette	.25
25	Barry Larkin	.25
26	Wade Boggs	2.00
27	Kirby Puckett	2.00
28	Cecil Fielder	.25
29	Jose Canseco	.50
30	Juan Gonzalez	.75
31	David Cone	.25
32	Craig Biggio	.25
33	Tim Salmon	.25
34	David Justice	.25
35	Sammy Sosa	2.00
36	Mike Piazza	2.50
37	Carlos Baerga	.25
38	Jeff Conine	.25
39	Rafael Palmeiro	1.25
40	Bret Saberhagen	.25
41	Len Dykstra	.25
42	Mo Vaughn	.25
43	Wally Joyner	.25
44	Chuck Knoblauch	.25
45	Robin Ventura	.25
46	Don Mattingly	2.25
47	Dave Hollins	.25
48	Andy Benes	.25
49	Ken Griffey Jr.	2.50
50	Albert Belle	.25
51	Matt Williams	.25
52	Rondell White	.25
53	Raul Mondesi	.25
54	Brian Jordan	.25
55	Greg Vaughn	.25
56	Fred McGriff	.25
57	Roberto Alomar	.40
58	Dennis Eckersley	1.25
59	Lee Smith	.25
60	Eddie Murray	1.50
61	Kenny Rogers	.25
62	Ron Gant	.25
63	Larry Walker	.25
64	Chad Curtis	.25
65	Frank Thomas	1.50
66	Paul O'Neill	.25
67	Kevin Seitzer	.25
68	Marquis Grissom	.25
69	Mark McGwire	3.00
70	Travis Fryman	.25
71	Andres Galarraga	.25
72	Carlos Perez RC	.25
73	Tyler Green	.25
74	Marty Cordova	.25
75	Shawn Green	.40
76	Vaughn Eshelman	.25
77	John Mabry	.25
78	Jason Bates	.25
79	Jon Nunnally	.25
80	Ray Durham	.25
81	Edgardo Alfonzo	.25
82	Esteban Loaiza	.25
83	Hideo Nomo	10.00
84	Orlando Miller	.25
85	Alex Gonzalez	.25
86	Mark Grudzielanek RC	.65
87	Julian Tavarez	.25
88	Benji Gil	.25
89	Quilvio Veras	.25
90	Ricky Bottalico	.25

Complete Set Blue (90):	150.00

#	Player	Price
1	Derek Jeter	3.00
2	Vladimir Guerrero RC	80.00
3	Bob Abreu RC	25.00
4	Chan Ho Park	.25
5	Paul Wilson	.25
6	Chad Ogea	.25
7	Andruw Jones RC	10.00
8	Brian Barber	.25
9	Andy Larkin	.25
10	Richie Sexson RC	6.00
11	Everett Stull RC	.25
12	Brooks Kieschnick	.25
13	Matt Murray	.25
14	John Wasdin	.25
15	Shannon Stewart	.25
16	Luis Ortiz	.25
17	Marc Kroon	.25
18	Todd Greene	.25
19	Juan Acevedo	.25
20	Tony Clark	.25
21	Jermaine Dye	.25
22	Derek Lee	1.00
23	Pat Watkins	.25
24	Calvin Reese	.25
25	Ben Grieve	.25
26	Julio Santana RC	.25
27	Felix Rodriguez RC	.50
28	Paul Konerko	.25
29	Nomar Garciaparra	2.00
30	Pat Ahearne	.25
31	Jason Schmidt	.25
32	Billy Wagner	.25
33	Rey Ordonez RC	1.00
34	Curtis Goodwin	.25
35	Sergio Nunez RC	.25
36	Tim Belk	.25
37	Scott Elarton RC	1.00
38	Jason Isringhausen	.25
39	Trot Nixon	.35
40	Sid Roberson	.25
41	Ron Villone	.25
42	Ruben Rivera	.25
43	Rick Huisman	.25
44	Todd Hollandsworth	.25
45	Johnny Damon	1.00
46	Garret Anderson	.25
47	Jeff D'Amico	.25
48	Dustin Hermanson	.25
49	Juan Encarnacion RC	3.00
50	Andy Pettitte	.50
51	Chris Stynes	.25
52	Troy Percival	.25
53	LaTroy Hawkins	.25
54	Roger Cedeno	.25
55	Alan Benes	.25
56	Karim Garcia RC	1.50
57	Andrew Lorraine	.25
58	Gary Rath RC	.25
59	Bret Wagner	.25
60	Jeff Suppan	.25
61	Bill Pulsipher	.25
62	Jay Payton RC	3.00
63	Alex Ochoa	.25
64	Ugueth Urbina	.25
65	Armando Benitez	.25
66	George Arias	.25
67	Raul Casanova RC	.50
68	Matt Drews	.25
69	Jimmy Haynes	.25
70	Jimmy Hurst	.25
71	C.J. Nitkowski	.25
72	Tommy Davis RC	.25
73	Bartolo Colon RC	5.00
74	Chris Carpenter RC	10.00
75	Trey Beamon	.25
76	Bryan Rekar	.25
77	James Baldwin	.25
78	Marc Valdes	.25
79	Tom Fordham RC	.25
80	Marc Newfield	.25
81	Angel Martinez	.25
82	Brian Hunter	.25
83	Jose Herrera	.25
84	Glenn Dishman RC	.25
85	Jacob Cruz RC	.25
86	Paul Shuey	.25
87	Scott Rolen RC	25.00
88	Doug Million	.25
89	Desi Relaford	.25
90	Michael Tucker	.50

Mirror Image:

#	Player	Price
1	Ben Davis RC, Ivan Rodriguez	1.00
2	Mark Redman RC, Manny Ramirez	1.50
3	Reggie Taylor RC, Deion Sanders	.50
4	Ryan Jaroncyk, Shawn Green	.50
5	Juan LeBron, Juan Gonzalez	1.00
6	Toby McKnight, Craig Biggio	.50

Gold

The only chase cards in the '95 Bowman set are gold versions of the foil-etched "Minor League MVPs," "1st Impressions" and "Prime Prospects." The gold cards are found in every 6th (regular) or 12th (jumbo) pack, on average, in place of the silver versions.

	NM/M
Complete Set (54):	100.00
Common Player:	.50
Stars/RCs:	2.5X

1995 Bowman's Best

Actually made up of three subsets, all cards feature a player photo set against a silver foil background. The 90 veterans' cards have a broad red-foil stripe in the background beneath the team logo; the 90 rookies'

7 Michael Barrett RC, Travis Fryman — 1.00
8 Corey Jenkins, Mo Vaughn — .50
9 Ruben Rivera, Frank Thomas — 1.50
10 Curtis Goodwin, Kenny Lofton — .50
11 Brian Hunter, Tony Gwynn — 1.75
12 Todd Greene, Ken Griffey Jr. — 2.50
13 Karim Garcia, Matt Williams — .75
14 Billy Wagner, Randy Johnson — 1.50
15 Pat Watkins, Jeff Bagwell — 1.50

Refractors

The large volume of silver foil in the background of the red and blue subsets in '95 Best make the Refractor technology much easier to see than in past issues. The chase cards, found one per six packs on average, also have a small "REFRACTOR" printed near the lower-left corner on back. The 15-card Mirror Image subset was not paralleled in Refractor technology, but in a process Topps calls "diffraction-foil" which creates a strong vertical-stripe rainbow effect in the background. Cards #72 (Carlos Perez) and 84 (Orlando Miller) can be found both with and without the "REFRACTOR" notice on back; neither version commands a premium.

NM/M
Common Player: 1.00
Stars: 3-6X
Rookies: 2-3X

Refractors - Jumbo

These super-size versions of Bowman's Best Refractors were produced exclusively for inclusion as a one-per-box insert in retail boxes of the product distributed by ANCO to large retail chains. The 4-1/4" x 5-3/4" cards are identical in all ways except size to the regular refractors. The jumbo inserts were not produced in equal quantities, with the most popular players being printed in greater numbers.

NM/M
Complete Set (10): 35.00
Common Player: 2.00
10 Cal Ripken Jr. 10.00
15 Greg Maddux 4.00
21 Tony Gwynn 4.00
35 Sammy Sosa 5.00
36 Mike Piazza 6.00
42 Mo Vaughn 6.00
49 Ken Griffey Jr. 6.00
50 Albert Belle 2.00
65 Frank Thomas 3.50
83 Hideo Nomo 3.00

1996 Bowman

In a "Guaranteed Value Program," Topps stated it would pay

KATSUHIRO MAEDA

$100 for this set in 1999, if collectors mail in a request form (one per three packs), a $5 fee and the complete set in numerical order (only one per person). Every set redeemed was destroyed. The 385-card set has 110 veteran stars and 275 prospects. Backs of the prospects' cards provide a detailed scouting report. A "1st Bowman Card" gold-foil stamped logo was included on the card front for 156 players making their first appearance in a Bowman set. Insert sets include Bowman's Best Previews (along with Refractor and Atomic Refractor versions), a 1952 Mickey Mantle Bowman reprint (1 in 48 packs) and Minor League Player of the Year candidates. A 385-card parallel version of the entire base set was also produced on 18-point foil-board; seeded one per pack.

NM/M
Complete Set (385): 50.00
Common Player: .10
Foils: 1.5X
Pack (11): 2.00
Wax Box (24): 40.00
1 Cal Ripken Jr. 2.00
2 Ray Durham .10
3 Ivan Rodriguez .50
4 Fred McGriff .20
5 Hideo Nomo .50
6 Troy Percival .10
7 Moises Alou .20
8 Mike Stanley .10
9 Jay Buhner .10
10 Shawn Green .25
11 Ryan Klesko .10
12 Andres Galarraga .10
13 Dean Palmer .10
14 Jeff Conine .10
15 Brian Hunter .10
16 J.T. Snow .10
17 Larry Walker .25
18 Barry Larkin .40
19 Alex Gonzalez .10
20 Edgar Martinez .10
21 Mo Vaughn .10
22 Mark McGwire 1.50
23 Jose Canseco .50
24 Jack McDowell .10
25 Dante Bichette .10
26 Wade Boggs .25
27 Mike Piazza 1.00
28 Ray Lankford .10
29 Craig Biggio .25
30 Rafael Palmeiro .50
31 Ron Gant .10
32 Javy Lopez .10
33 Brian Jordan .10
34 Paul O'Neill .20
35 Mark Grace .25
36 Matt Williams .20
37 Pedro Martinez .75
38 Rickey Henderson .25
39 Bobby Bonilla .10
40 Todd Hollandsworth .10
41 Jim Thome .75
42 Gary Sheffield .40
43 Tim Salmon .10
44 Gregg Jefferies .10
45 Roberto Alomar .25
45p Roberto Alomar (Unmarked promo card, fielding photo on front.) 3.00
46 Carlos Baerga .10
47 Mark Grudzielanek .10
48 Randy Johnson .75
49 Tino Martinez .10
50 Robin Ventura .10
51 Ryne Sandberg 1.50
52 Jay Bell .10
53 Jason Schmidt .10
54 Frank Thomas .75
55 Kenny Lofton .10
56 Ariel Prieto .10
57 David Cone .10
58 Reggie Sanders .10
59 Michael Tucker .10
60 Vinny Castilla .10
61 Lenny Dykstra .10
62 Todd Hundley .10
63 Brian McRae .10

64 Dennis Eckersley .40
65 Rondell White .10
66 Eric Karros .10
67 Greg Maddux 1.50
68 Kevin Appier .10
69 Eddie Murray .50
70 John Olerud .10
71 Tony Gwynn .75
72 David Justice .10
73 Ken Caminiti .10
74 Terry Steinbach .10
75 Alan Benes .10
76 Chipper Jones 1.00
77 Jeff Bagwell .50
77p Jeff Bagwell (Unmarked promo card, name in gold.) 6.00
78 Barry Bonds 2.00
79 Ken Griffey Jr. 1.50
80 Roger Cedeno .10
81 Joe Carter .10
82 Henry Rodriguez .10
83 Jason Isringhausen .10
84 Chuck Knoblauch .10
85 Manny Ramirez .75
86 Tom Glavine .30
87 Jeffrey Hammonds .10
88 Paul Molitor .75
89 Roger Clemens 2.00
90 Greg Vaughn .10
91 Marty Cordova .10
92 Albert Belle .25
93 Mike Mussina .40
94 Garret Anderson .10
95 Juan Gonzalez .40
96 John Valentin .10
97 Jason Giambi .50
98 Kirby Puckett 1.50
99 Jim Edmonds .25
100 Cecil Fielder .10
101 Mike Aldrete .10
102 Marquis Grissom .10
103 Derek Bell .10
104 Raul Mondesi .10
105 Sammy Sosa 1.00
106 Travis Fryman .10
107 Rico Brogna .10
108 Will Clark .25
109 Bernie Williams .40
110 Brady Anderson .10
111 Torii Hunter .10
112 Derek Jeter 2.00
113 Mike Kusiewicz RC .10
114 Scott Rolen 1.00
115 Ramon Castro .10
116 Jose Guillen RC .10
117 Wade Walker RC .10
118 Shawn Senior RC .10
119 Onan Masaoka RC .10
120 Marlon Anderson RC .75
121 Katsuhiro Maeda RC .25
122 Garrett Stephenson .25
123 Butch Huskey .10
124 D'Angelo Jimenez RC .50
125 Tony Mounce RC .20
126 Jay Canizaro .10
127 Juan Melo .10
128 Steve Gibralter .10
129 Freddy Garcia .10
130 Julio Santana .10
131 Richard Hidalgo .10
132 Jermaine Dye .10
133 Willie Adams .10
134 Everett Stull .10
135 Ramon Morel .10
136 Chan Ho Park .10
137 Jamey Wright .10
138 Luis Garcia RC .10
139 Dan Serafini .10
140 Ryan Dempster RC .50
141 Tate Seefried .10
142 Jimmy Hurst .10
143 Travis Miller .10
144 Curtis Goodwin .10
145 Rocky Coppinger RC .10
146 Enrique Wilson .10
147 Jaime Bluma .10
148 Andrew Vessel .10
149 Damian Moss .10
150 Shawn Gallagher RC .10
151 Pat Watkins .10
152 Jose Paniagua .10
153 Danny Graves RC .10
154 Bryon Gainey RC .10
155 Steve Soderstrom .10
156 Cliff Brumbaugh RC .10
157 Eugene Kingsale RC .10
158 Lou Collier .10
159 Todd Walker .10
160 Kris Detmers RC .10
161 Josh Booty RC .25
162 Greg Whiteman RC .10
163 Damian Jackson .10
164 Tony Clark .10
165 Jeff D'Amico .10
166 Johnny Damon .50
167 Rafael Orellano .10
168 Ruben Rivera .10
169 Alex Ochoa .10
170 Jay Powell .10
171 Tom Evans .10
172 Ron Villone .10
173 Shawn Estes .10
174 John Wasdin .10
175 Bill Simas .10
176 Kevin Brown .10
177 Shannon Stewart .10
178 Todd Greene .10

179 Bob Wolcott .10
180 Chris Snopek .10
181 Nomar Garciaparra .10
182 Cameron Smith RC .10
183 Matt Drews .10
184 Jimmy Haynes .10
185 Chris Carpenter .25
186 Desi Relaford .10
187 Ben Grieve .10
188 Mike Bell .10
189 Luis Castillo RC .75
190 Ugueth Urbina .10
191 Paul Wilson .10
191p Paul Wilson (Unmarked promo card, name in gold.) 1.00
192 Andruw Jones .75
193 Wayne Gomes .10
194 Craig Counsell RC .75
195 Jim Cole .10
196 Brooks Kieshnick .10
197 Trey Beamon .10
198 Marino Santana RC .10
199 Bob Abreu .25
200 Calvin Reese .10
201 Dante Powell .10
202 George Arias .10
202p George Arias (Unmarked promo card, name in gold.) 1.00
203 Jorge Velandia RC .10
204 George Lombard RC .10
205 Byron Browne RC .10
206 John Frascatore .10
207 Terry Adams .10
208 Wilson Delgado RC .10
209 Billy McMillon .10
210 Jeff Abbott .10
211 Trot Nixon .10
212 Amaury Telemaco .10
213 Scott Sullivan .10
214 Justin Thompson .10
215 Decomba Conner .10
216 Ryan McGuire .10
217 Matt Luke RC .10
218 Doug Million .10
219 Jason Dickson RC .10
220 Ramon Hernandez RC .50
221 Mark Redman RC .25
222 Eric Ludwick RC .10
223 Luke Wilcox RC .10
224 Marty Malloy RC .10
225 Gary Coffee RC .10
226 Wendell Magee RC .10
227 Brett Tomko RC .25
228 Derek Lowe .10
229 Jose Rosado RC .10
230 Steve Bourgeois RC .10
231 Neil Weber RC .10
232 Jeff Ware .10
233 Edwin Diaz .10
234 Greg Norton .10
235 Aaron Boone .10
236 Jeff Suppan .10
237 Bret Wagner .10
238 Elieser Marrero .10
239 Will Cunnane .10
240 Brian Barkley RC .10
241 Jay Payton .10
242 Marcus Jensen .10
243 Ryan Nye .10
244 Chad Mottola .10
245 Scott McClain RC .10
246 Jesse Ibarra RC .10
247 Mike Darr RC .10
248 Bobby Estalella RC .50
249 Michael Barrett .10
250 Jamie Lopiccolo RC .10
251 Shane Spencer RC .40
252 Ben Petrick RC .50
253 Jason Bell RC .10
254 Arnold Gooch RC .10
255 T.J. Mathews .10
256 Jason Ryan .10
257 Pat Cline RC .10
258 Rafael Carmona RC .10
259 Carl Pavano RC 1.00
260 Ben Davis .10
261 Matt Lawton RC 1.00
262 Kevin Sefcik RC .10
263 Chris Fussell RC .10
264 Mike Cameron RC 1.50
265 Marty Janzen RC .10
266 Livan Hernandez RC 1.00
267 Raul Ibanez RC 1.50
268 Juan Encarnacion .10
269 David Yocum RC .10
270 Jonathan Johnson RC .10
271 Reggie Taylor .10
272 Danny Buxbaum RC .10
273 Jacob Cruz .10
274 Bobby Morris RC .10
275 Andy Fox RC .10
276 Greg Keagle .10
277 Charles Peterson .10
278 Derrek Lee .50
279 Bryant Nelson RC .10
280 Antone Williamson .10
281 Scott Elarton .10
282 Shad Williams RC .10
283 Rich Hunter RC .10
284 Chris Sheff .10
285 Derrick Gibson .10
286 Felix Rodriguez .10
287 Brian Banks RC .10
288 Jason McDonald .10
289 Glendon Rusch RC .50
290 Gary Rath .10

291 Peter Munro .10
292 Tom Fordham .10
293 Jason Kendall .10
294 Russ Johnson .10
295 Joe Long RC .10
296 Robert Smith RC .10
297 Jarrod Washburn RC .75
298 Dave Coggin RC .10
299 Jeff Yoder RC .10
300 Jed Hansen RC .10
301 Matt Morris RC 1.00
302 Josh Bishop RC .10
303 Dustin Hermanson .10
304 Mike Gulan .10
305 Felipe Crespo .10
306 Quinton McCracken .10
307 Jim Bonnici RC .10
308 Sal Fasano .10
309 Gabe Alvarez RC .10
310 Heath Murray RC .10
311 Jose Valentin RC .10
312 Bartolo Colon .10
313 Olmedo Saenz .10
314 Norm Hutchins RC .10
315 Chris Holt RC .10
316 David Doster RC .10
317 Robert Person .10
318 Donne Wall RC .10
319 Adam Riggs RC .10
320 Homer Bush .10
321 Brad Rigby RC .10
322 Lou Merloni RC .25
323 Neifi Perez .10
324 Chris Cumberland .10
325 Alvie Shepherd RC .10
326 Jarrod Patterson RC .10
327 Ray Ricken RC .10
328 Danny Klassen RC .10
329 David Miller RC .10
330 Chad Alexander RC .10
331 Matt Beaumont .10
332 Damon Hollins .10
333 Todd Dunn .10
334 Mike Sweeney RC 1.50
335 Richie Sexson .40
336 Billy Wagner .10
337 Ron Wright RC .10
338 Paul Konerko .25
339 Tommy Phelps RC .10
340 Karim Garcia .10
341 Mike Grace RC .10
342 Russell Branyan RC .40
343 Randy Winn RC .50
344 A.J. Pierzynski RC 1.50
345 Mike Busby RC .10
346 Matt Beech RC .10
347 Jose Cepeda RC .10
348 Brian Stephenson .10
349 Rey Ordonez .10
350 Rich Aurilia RC 1.00
351 Edgard Velazquez RC .25
352 Raul Casanova .10
353 Carlos Guillen RC 1.00
354 Bruce Aven RC .10
355 Ryan Jones RC .10
356 Derek Aucoin RC .10
357 Brian Rose RC .10
358 Richard Almanzar RC .10
359 Fletcher Bates RC .10
360 Russ Ortiz RC .75
361 Wilton Guerrero RC .10
362 Geoff Jenkins RC 1.00
363 Pete Janicki .10
364 Yamil Benitez .10
365 Aaron Holbert .10
366 Tim Belk .10
367 Terrell Wade .10
368 Terrence Long .10
369 Brad Fullmer .10
370 Matt Wagner .10
371 Craig Wilson .10
372 Mark Loretta .10
373 Eric Owens .10
374 Vladimir Guerrero 1.00
375 Tommy Davis .10
376 Donnie Sadler .10
377 Edgar Renteria .25
378 Todd Helton .50
379 Ralph Milliard RC .10
380 Darin Blood RC .10
381 Shayne Bennett .10
382 Mark Redman .10
383 Felix Martinez .10
384 Sean Watkins RC .10
385 Oscar Henriquez .10

Minor League Player of the Year

Fifteen prospects who were candidates for Minor League Player of the Year are featured in this 1996 Bowman baseball insert set. Cards were seeded one per every 12 packs.

NM/M
Complete Set (15): 12.50
Common Player: .50
1 Andruw Jones 4.00
2 Derrick Gibson .50
3 Bob Abreu .75
4 Todd Walker .50
5 Jamey Wright .50
6 Wes Helms .50
7 Karim Garcia .75
8 Bartolo Colon 2.00
9 Alex Ochoa .50
10 Mike Sweeney 2.00
11 Ruben Rivera .50
12 Gabe Alvarez .50
13 Billy Wagner .50
14 Vladimir Guerrero 4.00
15 Edgard Velazquez .50

1952 Mickey Mantle Reprints

Reprints of Mickey Mantle's 1952 Bowman baseball card were created for insertion in Bowman and Bowman's Best products for 1996. The 2-1/2" x 3-1/2" card can be found in regular (gold seal on front), Finest, Finest Refractor and Atomic Refractor versions.

NM/M
Complete Set (4): 20.00
Common Card: 2.50
20 Mickey Mantle/Reprint 2.50
20 Mickey Mantle/Finest 2.50
20 Mickey Mantle/Refractor 7.50
20 Mickey Mantle/ Atomic Refractor 10.00

1996 Bowman's Best Preview

NOMAR GARCIAPARRA

These cards use Topps' Finest technology. The cards were seeded one per every 12 packs of 1996 Bowman baseball. Fifteen veterans and 15 prospects are featured in the set. Refractor versions are found one per 24 packs, with Atomic Refractors at 1:48 pick.

NM/M
Complete Set (30): 18.50
Common Player: .25
Refractors: 1.5X
Atomic Refractors: 2X
1 Chipper Jones 1.50
2 Alan Benes .25
3 Brooks Kieshnick .25
4 Barry Bonds 3.00
5 Rey Ordonez .25
6 Tim Salmon .25
7 Mike Piazza 2.00
8 Billy Wagner .25
9 Andruw Jones 1.00
10 Tony Gwynn 1.50
11 Paul Wilson .25
12 Calvin Reese .25
13 Frank Thomas 3.00
14 Greg Maddux 1.50
15 Derek Jeter 3.00
16 Jeff Bagwell 1.00
17 Barry Larkin .25

#	Player	Price
18	Todd Greene	.25
19	Ruben Rivera	.25
20	Richard Hidalgo	.25
21	Larry Walker	.25
22	Carlos Baerga	.25
23	Derrick Gibson	.25
24	Richie Sexson	.25
25	Mo Vaughn	.25
26	Hideo Nomo	.50
27	Nomar Garciaparra	1.50
28	Cal Ripken Jr.	3.00
29	Karim Garcia	.25
30	Ken Griffey Jr.	2.00

1996 Bowman's Best

Bowman's Best returns in its traditional format of 180 cards: 90 established stars and 90 up-and-coming prospects and rookies. Three types of insert sets are found in Bowman's Best: Mirror Image, Bowman's Best Cuts and the 1952 Bowman Mickey Mantle reprints. There are also parallel sets of Refractors and Atomic Refractors randomly seeded in packs. Refractors are found on average of one per 12 packs; Atomic Refractors are seeded one per 48 packs. Mirror Image Refractors are found one per 96 packs, while Mirror Image Atomic Refractors are seeded one per 192 packs. Refractor versions of the Mantle reprint are seeded one per every 96 packs; Atomic Refractor Mantle reprints are seeded in every 192nd pack.

		NM/M
Complete Set (180):		30.00
Common Player:		.25
Refractors:		2X
Atomics:		15X
1952 Mickey Mantle:		2.50
1952 Mantle Finest:		5.00
1952 Mantle Refractor:		7.50
1952 Mantle Atomic:		10.00
Pack (6):		2.50
Wax Box (24):		40.00
1	Hideo Nomo	.75
2	Edgar Martinez	.25
3	Cal Ripken Jr.	4.00
4	Wade Boggs	1.00
5	Cecil Fielder	.25
6	Albert Belle	.25
7	Chipper Jones	1.50
8	Ryne Sandberg	2.00
9	Tim Salmon	.25
10	Barry Bonds	3.00
11	Ken Caminiti	.25
12	Ron Gant	.25
13	Frank Thomas	1:00
14	Dante Bichette	.25
15	Jason Kendall	.25
16	Mo Vaughn	.25
17	Rey Ordonez	.25
18	Henry Rodriguez	.25
19	Ryan Klesko	1.00
20	Jeff Bagwell	1.00
21	Randy Johnson	1.50
22	Jim Edmonds	.50
23	Kenny Lofton	.50
24	Andy Pettitte	.50
25	Brady Anderson	.25
26	Mike Piazza	2.50
27	Greg Vaughn	.25
28	Joe Carter	.25
29	Jason Giambi	1.00
30	Ivan Rodriguez	1.00
31	Jeff Conine	.25
32	Rafael Palmeiro	.75
33	Roger Clemens	3.00
34	Chuck Knoblauch	.25
35	Reggie Sanders	.25
36	Andres Galarraga	.25
37	Paul O'Neill	.50
38	Tony Gwynn	2.00
39	Paul Wilson	.25
40	Garret Anderson	.25
41	David Justice	.25
42	Eddie Murray	1.00
43	Mike Grace RC	.25
44	Marty Cordova	.25
45	Kevin Appier	.25
46	Raul Mondesi	.25
47	Jim Thome	1.00
48	Sammy Sosa	2.00
49	Craig Biggio	.50
50	Marquis Grissom	.25
51	Alan Benes	.25
52	Manny Ramirez	1.50
53	Gary Sheffield	.75
54	Mike Mussina	.50
55	Robin Ventura	.25
56	Johnny Damon	1.00
57	Jose Canseco	.75
58	Juan Gonzalez	.75
59	Tino Martinez	.25
60	Brian Hunter	.25
61	Fred McGriff	.25
62	Jay Buhner	.25
63	Carlos Delgado	.75
64	Moises Alou	.50
65	Roberto Alomar	.50
66	Barry Larkin	.50
67	Vinny Castilla	.25
68	Ray Durham	.25
69	Travis Fryman	.25
70	Jason Isringhausen	.25
71	Ken Griffey Jr.	2.50
72	John Smoltz	.50
73	Matt Williams	.25
74	Chan Ho Park	.25
75	Mark McGwire	2.50
76	Jeffrey Hammonds	.25
77	Will Clark	.50
78	Kirby Puckett	2.00
79	Derek Jeter	4.00
80	Derek Bell	.25
81	Eric Karros	.25
82	Lenny Dykstra	.25
83	Larry Walker	.50
84	Mark Grudzielanek	.25
85	Greg Maddux	2.50
86	Carlos Baerga	.25
87	Paul Molitor	1.00
88	John Valentin	.25
89	Mark Grace	.50
90	Ray Lankford	.25
91	Andruw Jones	1.50
92	Nomar Garciaparra	2.00
93	Alex Ochoa	.25
94	Derrick Gibson	.25
95	Jeff D'Amico	.25
96	Ruben Rivera	.25
97	Vladimir Guerrero	1.50
98	Calvin Reese	.25
99	Richard Hidalgo	.25
100	Bartolo Colon	.25
101	Karim Garcia	.25
102	Ben Davis	.25
103	Jay Powell	.25
104	Chris Snopek	.25
105	Glendon Rusch RC	1.00
106	Enrique Wilson	.25
107	Antonio Alfonseca RC	.75
108	Wilton Guerrero RC	.50
109	Jose Guillen RC	3.00
110	Miguel Mejia RC	.25
111	Jay Payton	.25
112	Scott Elarton	.25
113	Brooks Kieschnick	.25
114	Dustin Hermanson	.25
115	Roger Cedeno	.25
116	Matt Wagner	.25
117	Lee Daniels	.25
118	Ben Grieve	.25
119	Ugueth Urbina	.25
120	Danny Graves	.25
121	Dan Donato RC	.25
122	Matt Ruebel RC	.25
123	Mark Sievert RC	.25
124	Chris Stynes	.25
125	Jeff Abbott	.25
126	Rocky Coppinger RC	.25
127	Jermaine Dye	.25
128	Todd Greene	.15
129	Chris Carpenter	1.00
130	Edgar Renteria	.50
131	Matt Drews	.25
132	Edgard Velazquez RC	.50
133	Casey Whitten	.25
134	Ryan Jones	.25
135	Todd Walker	.25
136	Geoff Jenkins RC	2.00
137	Matt Morris RC	2.00
138	Richie Sexson	.75
139	Todd Dunwoody RC	.50
140	Gabe Alvarez RC	.25
141	J.J. Johnson	.25
142	Shannon Stewart	.25
143	Brad Fullmer	.25
144	Julio Santana	.25
145	Scott Rolen	1.00
146	Amaury Telemaco	.25
147	Trey Beamon	.25
148	Billy Wagner	.20
149	Todd Hollandsworth	.25
150	Doug Million	.25
151	Jose Valentin RC	.25
152	Wes Helms RC	.50
153	Jeff Suppan RC	.25
154	Luis Castillo RC	1.50
155	Bob Abreu	.50
156	Paul Konerko	.50
157	Jamey Wright	.25
158	Eddie Pearson	.25
159	Jimmy Haynes	.25
160	Derrek Lee	.75
161	Damian Moss	.15
162	Carlos Guillen RC	2.00
163	Chris Fussell RC	.25
164	Mike Sweeney RC	3.00
165	Donnie Sadler	.15
166	Desi Relaford	.25
167	Steve Gibralter	.25
168	Neifi Perez	.25
169	Antone Williamson	.25
170	Marty Janzen RC	.25
171	Todd Helton	1.00
172	Raul Ibanez RC	2.00
173	Bill Selby	.25
174	Shane Monahan RC	.35
175	Robin Jennings RC	.25
176	Bobby Chouinard RC	.25
177	Einar Diaz	.25
178	Jason Thompson	.15
179	Rafael Medina RC	.25
180	Kevin Orie	.25

Cuts

Bowman's Best Cuts gave collectors the first die-cut chromium cards in a 15-card set of top stars. The cards were seeded one per 24 packs. Refractor versions are inserted on average of one per 48 packs; Atomic Refractor versions are found one per 96 packs.

		NM/M
Complete Set (15):		15.00
Common Player:		.25
Refractors:		1.5X
Atomic Refractors:		2X
1	Ken Griffey Jr.	2.50
2	Jason Isringhausen	.25
3	Derek Jeter	4.00
4	Andruw Jones	1.00
5	Chipper Jones	2.00
6	Ryan Klesko	.25
7	Raul Mondesi	.25
8	Hideo Nomo	.50
9	Mike Piazza	2.50
10	Manny Ramirez	1.00
11	Cal Ripken Jr.	4.00
12	Ruben Rivera	.25
13	Tim Salmon	.25
14	Frank Thomas	1.00
15	Jim Thome	.75

Mirror Image

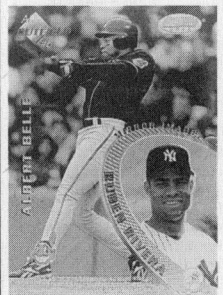

Mirror Image inserts feature four top players at 10 different positions, pairing an American League veteran and a prospect on one side and a National League veteran and prospect on the other. These cards are seeded one per every 48 packs. Mirror Image Refractors (one in every 96 packs) and Mirror Image Atomic Refractors (one in every 192 packs) were also produced.

		NM/M
Complete Set (10):		24.00
Common Card:		1.50
Refractors:		1.5X
Atomics:		2X
1	Jeff Bagwell, Todd Helton, Frank Thomas, Richie Sexson	3.00
2	Craig Biggio, Luis Castillo, Roberto Alomar, Desi Relaford	1.50
3	Chipper Jones, Scott Rolen, Wade Boggs, George Arias	3.50
4	Barry Larkin, Neifi Perez, Cal Ripken Jr., Mark Bellhorn	6.00
5	Larry Walker, Karim Garcia, Albert Belle, Ruben Rivera	1.50
6	Barry Bonds, Andruw Jones, Kenny Lofton, Donnie Sadler	6.00
7	Tony Gwynn, Vladimir Guerrero, Ken Griffey Jr., Ben Grieve	4.50
8	Mike Piazza, Ben Davis, Ivan Rodriguez, Jose Valentin	4.50
9	Greg Maddux, Jamey Wright, Mike Mussina, Bartolo Colon	3.50
10	Tom Glavine, Billy Wagner, Randy Johnson, Jarrod Washburn	1.50

1997 Bowman Pre-Production

The format for 1997 Bowman's base set was previewed in this sample issue distributed to card dealers and the hobby press. The samples are virtually identical to the issued versions of the same players' cards, except they carry a "PP" prefix to the number on back.

		NM/M
Complete Set (4):		9.00
Common Player:		1.50
PP1	Jose Cruz, Jr.	1.50
PP2	Andruw Jones	2.00
PP3	Derek Jeter	4.50
PP4	Sammy Sosa	3.00

1997 Bowman

The 1997 Bowman set consists of 440 base cards, an increase of 55 cards from the '96 set. Fronts have a player photo within a red or blue frame with black borders. Backs feature another color photo, along with 1996 statistics broken down by opponent. Players making their first appearance in a Bowman set have a "1st Bowman Card" designation on the card. Prospects' cards have red foil on front; veterans have blue. Inserts include International parallels, Certified Autographs, Scout's Honor Roll and Bowman's Best Previews. Cards were sold in 10-card packs with a suggested retail price of $2.50. Topps offered collectors a $125 guarantee on the value of the set through the year 2000.

		NM/M
Complete Set (440):		50.00
Complete Series 1 (221):		25.00
Complete Series 2 (219):		25.00
Common Player:		.10
Series 1 Pack (10):		2.00
Series 1 Wax Box (24):		35.00
Series 2 Pack (10):		2.00
Series 2 Wax Box (24):		35.00
1	Derek Jeter	2.00
2	Edgar Renteria	.10
3	Chipper Jones	1.00
4	Hideo Nomo	.40
5	Tim Salmon	.10
6	Jason Giambi	.50
7	Robin Ventura	.10
8	Tony Clark	.25
9	Barry Larkin	.25
10	Paul Molitor	.75
11	Bernard Gilkey	.10
12	Jack McDowell	.10
13	Andy Benes	.10
14	Ryan Klesko	.10
15	Mark McGwire	1.50
16	Ken Griffey Jr.	1.50
17	Robb Nen	.10
18	Cal Ripken Jr.	2.00
19	John Valentin	.10
20	Ricky Bottalico	.10
21	Mike Lansing	.10
22	Ryne Sandberg	1.00
23	Carlos Delgado	.50
24	Craig Biggio	.25
25	Eric Karros	.10
26	Kevin Appier	.10
27	Mariano Rivera	.50
28	Vinny Castilla	.10
29	Juan Gonzalez	.40
30	Al Martin	.10
31	Jeff Cirillo	.10
32	Eddie Murray	.75
33	Ray Lankford	.10
34	Manny Ramirez	.75
35	Roberto Alomar	.25
36	Will Clark	.25
37	Chuck Knoblauch	.25
38	Harold Baines	.10
39	Trevor Hoffman	.10
40	Edgar Martinez	.10
41	Geronimo Berroa	.10
42	Rey Ordonez	.10
43	Mike Stanley	.10
44	Mike Mussina	.40
45	Kevin Brown	.10
46	Dennis Eckersley	.50
47	Henry Rodriguez	.10
48	Tino Martinez	.10
49	Eric Young	.10
50	Bret Boone	.10
51	Raul Mondesi	.10
52	Sammy Sosa	1.00
53	John Smoltz	.25
54	Billy Wagner	.10
55	Jeff D'Amico	.10
56	Ken Caminiti	.10
57	Jason Kendall	.10
58	Wade Boggs	.75
59	Andres Galarraga	.25
60	Jeff Brantley	.10
61	Mel Rojas	.10
62	Brian Hunter	.10
63	Bobby Bonilla	.10
64	Roger Clemens	1.50
65	Jeff Kent	.20
66	Matt Williams	.10
67	Albert Belle	.25
68	Jeff King	.10
69	John Wetteland	.10
70	Deion Sanders	.25
71	Bubba Trammell RC	.25
72	Felix Heredia RC	.25
73	Billy Koch RC	.25
74	Sidney Ponson RC	.25
75	Ricky Ledee RC	.25
76	Brett Tomko	.10
77	Braden Looper RC	.25
78	Damian Jackson	.10
79	Jason Dickson	.10
80	Chad Green RC	.10
81	R.A. Dickey RC	.10
82	Jeff Liefer	.10
83	Matt Wagner	.10
84	Richard Hidalgo	.10
85	Adam Riggs	.10
86	Robert Smith	.10
87	Chad Hermansen RC	.25
88	Felix Martinez	.10
89	J.J. Johnson	.10
90	Todd Dunwoody	.10
91	Katsuhiro Maeda	.10
92	Darin Erstad	.25
93	Elieser Marrero	.10
94	Bartolo Colon	.10
95	Chris Fussell	.10
96	Ugueth Urbina	.10
97	Josh Paul RC	.10
98	Jaime Bluma	.10
99	Seth Greisinger RC	.10
100	Jose Cruz Jr.	.25
101	Todd Dunn	.10
102	Joe Yong RC	.10
103	Jonathan Johnson	.10
104	Justin Towle RC	.10
105	Brian Rose	.10
106	Jose Guillen	.10
107	Andruw Jones	.50
108	Mark Kotsay RC	1.00
109	Wilton Guerrero	.10
110	Jacob Cruz	.10
111	Mike Sweeney	.10
112	Julio Mosquera	.10
113	Matt Morris	.10
114	Wendell Magee	.10
115	John Thomson	.10
116	Javier Valentin RC	.10
117	Tom Fordham	.10
118	Ruben Rivera	.10
119	Mike Drumright RC	.10
120	Chris Holt	.10
121	Sean Maloney RC	.10
122	Michael Barrett	.10
123	Tony Saunders RC	.10
124	Kevin Brown	.10
125	Richard Almanzar	.10
126	Mark Redman	.10
127	Anthony Sanders RC	.10
128	Jeff Abbott	.10
129	Eugene Kingsale	.10
130	Paul Konerko	.40
131	Randall Simon RC	.25
132	Andy Larkin	.10
133	Rafael Medina	.10
134	Mendy Lopez	.10
135	Freddy Garcia	.15
136	Karim Garcia	.15
137	Larry Rodriguez RC	.10
138	Carlos Guillen	.10
139	Aaron Boone	.10
140	Donnie Sadler	.10
141	Brooks Kieschnick	.10
142	Scott Spiezio	.10
143	Everett Stull	.10
144	Enrique Wilson	.10
145	Milton Bradley RC	1.50
146	Kevin Orie	.10
147	Derek Wallace	.10
148	Russ Johnson	.10
149	Joe Lagarde RC	.10
150	Luis Castillo	.10
151	Jay Payton	.10
152	Joe Long	.10
153	Livan Hernandez	.10
154	Vladimir Nunez RC	.15
156a	George Arias	.10
156b	Calvin Reese (Should be #155.)	.10
157	Homer Bush	.10
159a	Eric Milton RC	.50
159b	Chris Carpenter (Should be #158.)	.50
160	Richie Sexson	.40
161	Carl Pavano	.10
162	Chris Gissell RC	.10
163	Mac Suzuki	.10
164	Pat Cline	.10
165	Ron Wright	.10
166	Dante Powell	.10
167	Mark Bellhorn	.10
168	George Lombard	.10
169	Pee Wee Lopez RC	.10
170	Paul Wilder RC	.10
171	Brad Fullmer	.10
172	Willie Martinez RC	.10
173	Dario Veras RC	.10
174	Dave Coggin	.10
175	Kris Benson RC	1.00
176	Torii Hunter	.25
177	D.T. Cromer RC	.10
178	Nelson Figueroa	.10
179	Hiram Bocachica RC	.15
180	Shane Monahan	.10
181	Jimmy Anderson RC	.10
182	Juan Melo	.10
183	Pablo Ortega RC	.10
184	Calvin Pickering RC	.50
185	Reggie Taylor	.10
186	Jeff Farnsworth RC	.10
187	Terrence Long	.10
188	Geoff Jenkins	.10
189	Steve Rain RC	.10
190	Nerio Rodriguez RC	.10
191	Derrick Gibson	.10
192	Darin Blood	.10
193	Ben Davis	.10
194	Adrian Beltre RC	2.00
195	Damian Sapp RC	.10
196	Kerry Wood RC	3.00
197	Nate Rolison RC	.10
198	Fernando Tatis RC	.25
199	Brad Penny RC	2.00
200	Jake Westbrook RC	.15
201	Edwin Diaz	.10
202	Joe Fontenot RC	.10
203	Matt Halloran RC	.10
204	Blake Stein RC	.10
205	Onan Masaoka	.10
206	Ben Petrick	.10
207	Matt Clement RC	1.00
208	Todd Greene	.10
209	Ray Ricken	.10
210	Eric Chavez RC	3.00
211	Edgard Velazquez	.10
212	Bruce Chen RC	.10
213	Danny Patterson RC	.10
214	Jeff Yoder	.10
215	Luis Ordaz RC	.10
216	Chris Widger	.10
217	Jason Brester	.10
218	Carlton Loewer	.10
219	Chris Reitsma RC	.10
220	Neifi Perez	.10
221	Hideki Irabu RC	.25
222	Ellis Burks	.10
223	Pedro Martinez	.75
224	Kenny Lofton	.75
225	Randy Johnson	.75
226	Terry Steinbach	.25
227	Bernie Williams	.25
228	Dean Palmer	.10
229	Alan Benes	.10
230	Marquis Grissom	.10
231	Gary Sheffield	.40
232	Curt Schilling	.10
233	Reggie Sanders	.10
234	Bobby Higginson	.10
235	Moises Alou	.20
236	Tom Glavine	.25
237	Mark Grace	.25
238	Ramon Martinez	.10
239	Rafael Palmeiro	.50
240	John Olerud	.10
241	Dante Bichette	.10
242	Greg Vaughn	.10
243	Jeff Bagwell	.50
244	Barry Bonds	2.00
245	Pat Hentgen	.10

#	Player	Price
246	Jim Thome	.50
247	Jermaine Allensworth	.10
248	Andy Pettitte	.25
249	Jay Bell	.10
250	John Jaha	.10
251	Jim Edmonds	.25
252	Ron Gant	.10
253	David Cone	.10
254	Jose Canseco	.40
255	Jay Buhner	.10
256	Greg Maddux	1.50
257	Brian McRae	.10
258	Lance Johnson	.10
259	Travis Fryman	.10
260	Paul O'Neill	.20
261	Ivan Rodriguez	.50
262	Gregg Jefferies	.10
263	Fred McGriff	.20
264	Derek Bell	.10
265	Jeff Conine	.10
266	Mike Piazza	1.50
267	Mark Grudzielanek	.10
268	Brady Anderson	.10
269	Marty Cordova	.10
270	Ray Durham	.10
271	Joe Carter	.10
272	Brian Jordan	.10
273	David Justice	.10
274	Tony Gwynn	1.00
275	Larry Walker	.20
276	Cecil Fielder	.10
277	Mo Vaughn	.10
278	Alex Fernandez	.10
279	Michael Tucker	.10
280	Jose Valentin	.10
281	Sandy Alomar	.10
282	Todd Hollandsworth	.10
283	Rico Brogna	.10
284	Rusty Greer	.10
285	Roberto Hernandez	.10
286	Hal Morris	.10
287	Johnny Damon	.75
288	Todd Hundley	.10
289	Rondell White	.10
290	Frank Thomas	.75
291	Don Denbow RC	.10
292	Derek Lee	.50
293	Todd Walker	.10
294	Scott Rolen	.50
295	Wes Helms	.10
296	Bob Abreu	.25
297	John Patterson RC	1.50
298	Alex Gonzalez RC	.25
299	Grant Roberts RC	.25
300	Jeff Suppan	.10
301	Luke Wilcox	.10
302	Marlon Anderson	.10
303	Ray Brown	.10
304	Mike Caruso RC	.25
305	Sam Marsonek RC	.10
306	Brady Raggio RC	.10
307	Kevin McGlinchy RC	.25
308	Roy Halladay RC	3.00
309	Jeremi Gonzalez RC	.10
310	Aramis Ramirez RC	4.00
311	Dermal Brown RC	.10
312	Justin Thompson	.10
313	Jay Tessmer RC	.10
314	Mike Johnson	.10
315	Danny Clyburn	.10
316	Bruce Aven	.10
317	Keith Foulke RC	1.50
318	Jimmy Osting RC	.10
319	Valerio De Los Santos RC	.25
320	Shannon Stewart	.10
321	Willie Adams	.10
322	Larry Barnes	.10
323	Mark Johnson	.10
324	Chris Stowers RC	.10
325	Brandon Reed	.10
326	Randy Winn	.10
327	Steven Chavez	.10
328	Nomar Garciaparra	1.00
329	Jacque Jones RC	1.00
330	Chris Clemons	.10
331	Todd Helton	.50
332	Ryan Brannan RC	.10
333	Alex Sanchez RC	.25
334	Arnold Gooch	.10
335	Russell Branyan	.10
336	Daryle Ward	.10
337	John LeRoy RC	.10
338	Steve Cox	.10
339	Kevin Witt	.10
340	Norm Hutchins	.10
341	Gabby Martinez	.10
342	Kris Detmers	.10
343	Mike Villano RC	.10
344	Preston Wilson	.10
345	Jim Manias RC	.10
346	Deivi Cruz RC	.25
347	Donzell McDonald RC	.10
348	Rod Myers RC	.10
349	Shawn Chacon RC	.25
350	Elvin Hernandez RC	.10
351	Orlando Cabrera RC	1.00
352	Brian Banks	.10
353	Robbie Bell	.10
354	Brad Rigby	.10
355	Scott Elarton	.10
356	Kevin Sweeney RC	.10
357	Steve Soderstrom	.10
358	Ryan Nye	.10
359	Marlon Allen RC	.10
360	Donny Leon RC	.10
361	Garrett Neubart RC	.10
362	Abraham Nunez	.25
363	Adam Eaton RC	.50

#	Player	Price
364	Octavio Dotel RC	.40
365	Dean Crow RC	.10
366	Jason Baker RC	.10
367	Sean Casey	.10
368	Joe Lawrence RC	.10
369	Adam Johnson RC	.10
370	Scott Schoeneweis RC	.25
371	Gerald Witasick Jr.	.10
372	Ronnie Belliard RC	.25
373	Russ Ortiz	.10
374	Robert Stratton RC	.10
375	Bobby Estalella	.10
376	Corey Lee RC	.10
377	Carlos Beltran RC	.50
378	Mike Cameron	.10
379	Scott Randall RC	.10
380	Corey Erickson RC	.10
381	Jay Canizaro	.10
382	Kerry Robinson RC	.10
383	Todd Noel RC	.10
384	A.J. Zapp RC	.10
385	Jarrod Washburn	.10
386	Ben Grieve	.10
387	Javier Vazquez RC	1.50
388	Tony Graffanino	.10
389	Travis Lee RC	.50
390	DaRond Stovall	.10
391	Dennis Reyes RC	.25
392	Danny Buxbaum	.10
393	Marc Lewis RC	.10
394	Kelvim Escobar RC	.25
395	Danny Klassen	.10
396	Ken Cloude RC	.25
397	Gabe Alvarez	.10
398	Jaret Wright RC	.50
399	Raul Casanova	.10
400	Clayton Brunner RC	.10
401	Jason Marquis RC	.50
402	Marc Kroon	.10
403	Jamey Wright	.10
404	Matt Snyder RC	.10
405	Josh Garrett RC	.10
406	Juan Encarnacion	.10
407	Heath Murray	.10
408	Brett Herbison RC	.10
409	Brent Butler RC	.25
410	Danny Peoples RC	.25
411	Miguel Tejada RC	10.00
412	Damian Moss	.10
413	Jim Pittsley	.10
414	Dmitri Young	.10
415	Glendon Rusch	.10
416	Vladimir Guerrero	.75
417	Cole Liniak RC	.10
418	Ramon Hernandez	.10
419	Cliff Politte RC	.25
420	Mel Rosario RC	.10
421	Jorge Carrion RC	.10
422	John Barnes RC	.10
423	Chris Stowe RC	.10
424	Vernon Wells RC	4.00
425	Brett Caradonna RC	.10
426	Scott Hodges RC	.10
427	Jon Garland RC	1.50
428	Nathan Haynes RC	.25
429	Geoff Goetz RC	.10
430	Adam Kennedy RC	.50
431	T.J. Tucker RC	.10
432	Aaron Akin RC	.10
433	Jayson Werth RC	.50
434	Glenn Davis RC	.10
435	Mark Mangum RC	.10
436	Troy Cameron RC	.10
437	J.J. Davis RC	.10
438	Lance Berkman RC	8.00
439	Jason Standridge RC	.25
440	Jason Dellaero RC	.25
441	Hideki Irabu RC	.75

Certified Autographs

Ninety players signed autographs for inclusion in Series 1 and 2 packs. Each autograph card features a gold-foil Certified Autograph stamp on front and can be found in one of three versions: Blue, 1:96 packs; black, 1:503 packs and gold, 1:1,509 packs. Derek Jeter's card can also be found in a green-ink autographed version, inserted one per 1,928 packs. Card numbers have a "CA" prefix.

	NM/M
Common Blue:	2.00
Black:	1.5X
Gold:	4X

#	Player	Price
	Derek Jeter Green:	1.5X
1	Jeff Abbott	2.00
2	Bob Abreu	40.00
3	Willie Adams	2.00
4	Brian Banks	2.00
5	Kris Benson	15.00
6	Darin Blood	2.00
7	Jaime Bluma	2.00
8	Kevin Brown	5.00
9	Ray Brown	2.00
10	Homer Bush	4.00
11	Mike Cameron	8.00
12	Jay Canizaro	3.00
13	Luis Castillo	5.00
14	Dave Coggin	5.00
15	Bartolo Colon	15.00
16	Rocky Coppinger	3.00
17	Jacob Cruz	5.00
18	Jose Cruz	8.00
19	Jeff D'Amico	5.00
20	Ben Davis	5.00
21	Mike Drumbright	5.00
22	Scott Elarton	5.00
23	Darin Erstad	10.00
24	Bobby Estalella	5.00
25	Joe Fontenot	4.00
26	Tom Fordham	5.00
27	Brad Fullmer	5.00
28	Chris Fussell	2.00
29	Karim Garcia	5.00
30	Kris Detmers	4.00
31	Todd Greene	2.00
32	Ben Grieve	20.00
33	Vladimir Guerrero	75.00
34	Jose Guillen	15.00
35	Roy Halladay	65.00
36	Wes Helms	5.00
37	Chad Hermansen	3.00
38	Richard Hidalgo	3.00
39	Todd Hollandsworth	3.00
40	Damian Jackson	3.00
41	Derek Jeter	120.00
42	Andruw Jones	20.00
43	Brooks Kieschnick	3.00
44	Eugene Kingsale	5.00
45	Paul Konerko	15.00
46	Marc Kroon	2.00
47	Derek Lee	40.00
48	Travis Lee	5.00
49	Terrence Long	4.00
50	Curt Lyons	2.00
51	Elieser Marrero	3.00
52	Rafael Medina	5.00
53	Juan Melo	3.00
54	Shane Monahan	2.00
55	Julio Mosquera	2.00
56	Heath Murray	2.00
57	Ryan Nye	2.00
58	Kevin Orie	4.00
59	Russ Ortiz	5.00
60	Carl Pavano	30.00
61	Jay Payton	5.00
62	Neifi Perez	3.00
63	Sidney Ponson	10.00
64	Calvin Reese	8.00
65	Ray Ricken	3.00
66	Brad Rigby	3.00
67	Adam Riggs	3.00
68	Ruben Rivera	5.00
69	J.J. Johnson	2.00
70	Scott Rolen	40.00
71	Tony Saunders	3.00
72	Donnie Sadler	5.00
73	Richie Sexson	15.00
74	Scott Spiezio	6.00
75	Everett Stull	2.00
76	Mike Sweeney	15.00
77	Fernando Tatis	4.00
78	Miguel Tejada	80.00
79	Justin Thompson	5.00
80	Justin Towle	6.00
81	Billy Wagner	20.00
82	Todd Walker	5.00
83	Luke Wilcox	2.00
84	Paul Wilder	4.00
85	Enrique Wilson	5.00
86	Kerry Wood	60.00
87	Jamey Wright	5.00
88	Ron Wright	5.00
89	Dmitri Young	10.00
90	Nelson Figueroa	2.00

International

Inserted at the rate of one per pack, the International parallel set replaces the regular photo background on front and back with the flag of the player's native land. Card #441 from the regular-issue version does not exist as an International parallel.

	NM/M
Complete Set (440):	75.00
Complete Series 1 (221):	40.00
Complete Series 2 (219):	40.00
Common Player:	.25
Stars and Rookies:	1.5X

International Best

This Series 2 insert set features a flag design in the background of each card front depicting the player's country of origin. On back is another color photo, player personal data, a record of his best season and

colored flags representing 14 nations which have sent players to the major leagues. One International Best card was inserted in every second series pack. Card numbers carry a "BBI" prefix. Refractor versions are a 1:48 parallel with Atomic Refractors found 1:96.

	NM/M
Complete Set (20):	20.00
Common Player:	.60
Refractors:	1.5X
Atomic Refractors:	2X
1	Frank Thomas	1.50
2	Ken Griffey Jr.	2.50
3	Juan Gonzalez	1.50
4	Bernie Williams	.60
5	Hideo Nomo	1.50
6	Sammy Sosa	3.50
7	Larry Walker	.60
8	Vinny Castilla	.60
9	Mariano Rivera	.75
10	Rafael Palmeiro	1.00
11	Nomar Garciaparra	3.50
12	Todd Walker	.60
13	Andruw Jones	1.50
14	Vladimir Guerrero	1.50
15	Ruben Rivera	.60
16	Bob Abreu	.75
17	Karim Garcia	.75
18	Katsuhiro Maeda	.60
19	Jose Cruz Jr.	1.00
20	Damian Moss	.60

Rookie of the Year Candidates

This 15-card insert was inserted in one per 12 packs of Bowman Series 2. Fronts feature a color shot of the player over a textured foil background, with the player's name across the bottom and the words "Rookie of the Year Favorites" across the top with the word "Rookie" in large script letters. Card numbers have a "ROY" prefix.

	NM/M
Complete Set (15):	9.00
Common Player:	.50
1	Jeff Abbott	.50
2	Karim Garcia	.50
3	Todd Helton	2.50
4	Richard Hidalgo	.50
5	Geoff Jenkins	.50
6	Russ Johnson	.50
7	Paul Konerko	.75
8	Mark Kotsay	.50
9	Ricky Ledee	.50
10	Travis Lee	.75
11	Derek Lee	.50
12	Elieser Marrero	.50
13	Juan Melo	.50
14	Brian Rose	.50
15	Fernando Tatis	.50

Scout's Honor Roll

This insert features 15 prospects deemed to have the most potential by Topps' scouts. Each card features a double-etched foil design and is inserted 1:12 packs.

1997 Bowman's Best Preview

This 20-card set, featuring 10 veterans and 10 prospects, is a preview of the format used in the Bowman's Best product. Three different versions of the Preview cards were available: Regular (1:12 packs), Refractors (1:48) and Atomic Refractors (1:96).

	NM/M
Complete Set (20):	30.00
Common Player:	.75
Refractors:	1.5X
Atomic Refractors:	2X
1	Frank Thomas	1.50
2	Ken Griffey Jr.	3.00
3	Barry Bonds	5.00
4	Derek Jeter	5.00
5	Chipper Jones	2.00
6	Mark McGwire	4.00
7	Cal Ripken Jr.	4.00
8	Kenny Lofton	.75
9	Gary Sheffield	.75
10	Jeff Bagwell	1.50
11	Wilton Guerrero	.75
12	Scott Rolen	.75
13	Todd Walker	.75
14	Ruben Rivera	.75
15	Andruw Jones	1.50
16	Nomar Garciaparra	2.00
17	Vladimir Guerrero	1.50
18	Miguel Tejada	1.00
19	Bartolo Colon	.75
20	Katsuhiro Maeda	.75

1997 Bowman Chrome

Bowman Chrome was released in one 300-card series following the conclusion of the 1997 season. Four-card foil packs carried an SRP of $3. Each card reprints one of the regular Bowman set, utilizing chromium technology on front. Inserts include: International parallels, Rookie of the Year Favorites and Scout's Honor Roll.

	NM/M
Complete Set (300):	150.00
Common Player:	.25
Pack (3):	5.00
Wax Box (24):	100.00
1	Derek Jeter	4.00
2	Chipper Jones	2.00
3	Hideo Nomo	.75
4	Tim Salmon	.25
5	Robin Ventura	.25
6	Tony Clark	.25
7	Barry Larkin	.50
8	Paul Molitor	1.00
9	Andy Benes	.25
10	Ryan Klesko	.25
11	Mark McGwire	3.00
12	Ken Griffey Jr.	2.50
13	Robb Nen	.25
14	Cal Ripken Jr.	4.00
15	John Valentin	.25
16	Ricky Bottalico	.25
17	Mike Lansing	.25
18	Ryne Sandberg	2.00
19	Carlos Delgado	1.00
20	Craig Biggio	.50
21	Eric Karros	.25
22	Kevin Appier	.25
23	Mariano Rivera	.75
24	Vinny Castilla	.25
25	Juan Gonzalez	.50
26	Al Martin	.25
27	Jeff Cirillo	.25
28	Ray Lankford	.25
29	Manny Ramirez	1.50
30	Roberto Alomar	.40
31	Will Clark	.50
32	Chuck Knoblauch	.25
33	Harold Baines	.25
34	Edgar Martinez	.50
35	Mike Mussina	.50
36	Kevin Brown	.25
37	Dennis Eckersley	.75
38	Tino Martinez	.25
39	Raul Mondesi	.25
40	Sammy Sosa	1.50
41	John Smoltz	.75
42	Billy Wagner	.25
43	Ken Caminiti	.25
44	Wade Boggs	1.50
45	Andres Galarraga	.25
46	Roger Clemens	3.00
47	Matt Williams	.25
48	Albert Belle	.25
49	Jeff King	.25
50	John Wetteland	.25
51	Deion Sanders	.50
52	Ellis Burks	.25
53	Pedro Martinez	1.50
54	Kenny Lofton	.50
55	Randy Johnson	1.50
56	Bernie Williams	.50
57	Marquis Grissom	.25
58	Gary Sheffield	.50
59	Curt Schilling	1.00
60	Reggie Sanders	.25
61	Bobby Higginson	.25
62	Moises Alou	.50
63	Tom Glavine	.50
64	Mark Grace	.50
65	Rafael Palmeiro	1.00
66	John Olerud	.25
67	Dante Bichette	.25
68	Jeff Bagwell	1.00
69	Barry Bonds	3.00
70	Pat Hentgen	.25
71	Jim Thome	1.00
72	Andy Pettitte	.50
73	Jay Bell	.25
74	Jim Edmonds	.50
75	Ron Gant	.25
76	David Cone	.25
77	Jose Canseco	.75
78	Jay Buhner	.25
79	Greg Maddux	2.50
80	Lance Johnson	.25
81	Travis Fryman	.25
82	Paul O'Neill	.50
83	Ivan Rodriguez	1.00
84	Fred McGriff	.25
85	Mike Piazza	2.50
86	Brady Anderson	.25
87	Marty Cordova	.25
88	Joe Carter	.25
89	Brian Jordan	.25
90	David Justice	.25
91	Tony Gwynn	2.00
92	Larry Walker	.40
93	Mo Vaughn	.25
94	Sandy Alomar	.25
95	Rusty Greer	.25
96	Roberto Hernandez	.25
97	Hal Morris	.25
98	Todd Hundley	.25
99	Rondell White	.25
100	Frank Thomas	1.50

101	Bubba Trammell RC	.75
102	Sidney Ponson RC	1.50
103	Ricky Ledee RC	.50
104	Brett Tomko RC	.25
105	Braden Looper RC	.50
106	Jason Dickson	.25
107	Chad Green RC	.25
108	R.A. Dickey RC	.25
109	Jeff Liefer	.25
110	Richard Hidalgo	.25
111	Chad Hermansen RC	.50
112	Felix Martinez	.25
113	J.J. Johnson	.25
114	Todd Dunwoody	.25
115	Katsuhiro Maeda	.25
116	Darin Erstad	.50
117	Elieser Marrero	.25
118	Bartolo Colon	.25
119	Ugueth Urbina	.25
120	Jaime Bluma	.25
121	Seth Greisinger RC	.50
122	Jose Cruz Jr. RC	1.50
123	Todd Dunn	.25
124	Justin Towle RC	.25
125	Brian Rose	.25
126	Jose Guillen	.25
127	Andruw Jones	1.50
128	Mark Kotsay RC	2.50
129	Wilton Guerrero	.25
130	Jacob Cruz	.25
131	Mike Sweeney	.25
132	Matt Morris	.25
133	John Thomson	.25
134	Javier Valentin RC	.25
135	Mike Drumright RC	.25
136	Michael Barrett	.25
137	Tony Saunders RC	.25
138	Kevin Brown	.25
139	Anthony Sanders RC	.25
140	Jeff Abbott	.25
141	Eugene Kingsale	.25
142	Paul Konerko	.50
143	Randall Simon RC	.25
144	Freddy Garcia	.25
145	Karim Garcia	.25
146	Carlos Guillen	.25
147	Aaron Boone	.25
148	Donnie Sadler	.25
149	Brooks Kieschnick	.25
150	Scott Elarton	.25
151	Kevin Orie	.25
152	Russ Johnson	.25
153	Livan Hernandez	.25
154	Vladimir Nunez RC	.75
155	Calvin Reese	.25
156	Chris Carpenter	.75
157	Eric Milton RC	1.50
158	Richie Sexson	.50
159	Carl Pavano	.25
160	Pat Cline	.25
161	Ron Wright	.25
162	Dante Powell	.25
163	Mark Bellhorn	.25
164	George Lombard	.25
165	Paul Wilder RC	.25
166	Brad Fullmer	.25
167	Kris Benson RC	2.00
168	Torii Hunter	.50
169	D.T. Cromer	.25
170	Nelson Figueroa RC	.50
171	Hiram Bocachica RC	.50
172	Shane Monahan	.25
173	Juan Melo	.25
174	Calvin Pickering RC	1.50
175	Reggie Taylor	.25
176	Geoff Jenkins	.25
177	Steve Rain RC	.25
178	Nerio Rodriguez	.25
179	Derrick Gibson	.25
180	Darin Blood	.25
181	Ben Davis	.25
182	Adrian Beltre RC	8.00
183	Kerry Wood RC	8.00
184	Nate Rolison	.25
185	Fernando Tatis RC	.25
186	Jake Westbrook RC	2.00
187	Edwin Diaz	.25
188	Joe Fontenot RC	.50
189	Matt Halloran RC	.25
190	Matt Clement RC	3.00
191	Todd Greene	.25
192	Eric Chavez RC	10.00
193	Edgard Velazquez	.25
194	Bruce Chen RC	.25
195	Jason Brester	.25
196	Chris Reitsma RC	.50
197	Neifi Perez	.25
198	Hideki Irabu RC	.50
199	Don Denbow RC	.25
200	Derrek Lee	.75
201	Todd Walker	.25
202	Scott Rolen	1.00
203	Wes Helms	.25
204	Bob Abreu	.50
205	John Patterson RC	2.00
206	Alex Gonzalez RC	1.00
207	Grant Roberts RC	.50
208	Jeff Suppan	.25
209	Luke Wilcox	.25
210	Marlon Anderson	.25
211	Mike Caruso RC	.75
212	Roy Halladay RC	8.00
213	Jeremi Gonzalez RC	.25
214	Aramis Ramirez RC	10.00
215	Dermal Brown RC	.25
216	Justin Thompson	.25
217	Danny Clyburn	.25
218	Bruce Aven	.25
219	Keith Foulke RC	2.00
220	Shannon Stewart	.25
221	Larry Barnes	.25
222	Mark Johnson RC	.25
223	Randy Winn	.25
224	Nomar Garciaparra	2.00
225	Jacque Jones RC	4.00
226	Chris Clemons	.25
227	Todd Helton	1.00
228	Ryan Brannan RC	.25
229	Alex Sanchez RC	.50
230	Russell Branyan	.25
231	Daryle Ward	.25
232	Kevin Witt	.25
233	Gabby Martinez	.25
234	Preston Wilson	.25
235	Donzell McDonald RC	.25
236	Orlando Cabrera RC	5.00
237	Brian Banks	.25
238	Robbie Bell	.25
239	Brad Rigby	.25
240	Scott Elarton	.25
241	Donny Leon RC	.25
242	Abraham Nunez RC	1.00
243	Adam Eaton RC	2.00
244	Octavio Dotel RC	1.00
245	Sean Casey	.35
246	Joe Lawrence RC	.25
247	Adam Johnson RC	.25
248	Ronnie Belliard RC	1.00
249	Bobby Estalella	.25
250	Corey Lee RC	.25
251	Mike Cameron	.25
252	Kerry Robinson RC	.25
253	A.J. Zapp RC	.25
254	Jarrod Washburn	.25
255	Ben Grieve	.25
256	Javier Vazquez RC	3.00
257	Travis Lee RC	1.00
258	Dennis Reyes RC	.50
259	Danny Buxbaum	.25
260	Kelvim Escobar RC	1.00
261	Danny Klassen	.25
262	Ken Cloude RC	.25
263	Gabe Alvarez	.25
264	Clayton Brunner RC	.25
265	Jason Marquis RC	1.50
266	Jamey Wright	.25
267	Matt Snyder RC	.25
268	Josh Garrett RC	.25
269	Juan Encarnacion	.25
270	Heath Murray	.25
271	Brent Butler RC	1.00
272	Danny Peoples RC	.50
273	Miguel Tejada RC	20.00
274	Jim Pittsley	.25
275	Dmitri Young	.25
276	Vladimir Guerrero	1.50
277	Cole Liniak RC	.50
278	Ramon Hernandez	.25
279	Cliff Politte RC	.50
280	Mel Rosario RC	.25
281	Jorge Carrion RC	.25
282	John Barnes RC	.25
283	Chris Stowe RC	.25
284	Vernon Wells RC	15.00
285	Brett Caradonna RC	.25
286	Scott Hodges RC	.25
287	Jon Garland RC	4.00
288	Nathan Haynes RC	.50
289	Geoff Goetz RC	.50
290	Adam Kennedy RC	1.00
291	T.J. Tucker RC	.25
292	Aaron Akin RC	.25
293	Jayson Werth RC	2.50
294	Glenn Davis RC	.25
295	Mark Mangum RC	.25
296	Troy Cameron RC	.25
297	J.J. Davis RC	.25
298	Lance Berkman RC	30.00
299	Jason Standridge RC	.75
300	Jason Dellaero RC	.25

Refractors

All 300 cards in Bowman Chrome were reprinted in Refractor versions and inserted one per 12 packs. The cards are very similar to the base cards, but feature a refractive foil finish on front.

	NM/M
Common Player:	1.00
Stars:	4X

International

Internationals paralleled all 300 cards in the base set with a flag from the player's native country in the background. These inserts were seeded one per four packs.

	NM/M
Common Player:	1.00
Stars:	3X
Inserted 1:4	

International Refractors

Each International parallel card was also reprinted in a Refractor version. International Refractors were seeded one per 24 packs.

	NM/M
Common Player:	2.00
Stars:	6X

ROY Candidates

This 15-card insert set features color action photos of 1998 Rookie of the Year candidates printed on chromium finish cards. Card backs are numbered with a "ROY" prefix and were inserted one per 24 packs of Bowman Chrome. Refractor versions are seeded one per 72 packs.

		NM/M
Complete Set (15):		9.00
Common Player:		.50
Refractors:		1.5X
1	Jeff Abbott	.50
2	Karim Garcia	.75
3	Todd Helton	2.50
4	Richard Hidalgo	.50
5	Geoff Jenkins	.50
6	Russ Johnson	.50
7	Paul Konerko	1.00
8	Mark Kotsay	.50
9	Ricky Ledee	.50
10	Travis Lee	.75
11	Derrek Lee	1.50
12	Elieser Marrero	.50
13	Juan Melo	.50
14	Brian Rose	.50
15	Fernando Tatis	.50

Scout's Honor Roll

This 15-card set features top prospects and rookies as selected by the Topps' scouts. These chromium cards are numbered with a "SHR" prefix and are inserted one per 12 packs, while Refractor versions are seeded one per 36 packs.

		NM/M
Complete Set (15):		12.00
Common Player:		.50
Refractors:		1.5X
1	Dmitri Young	.50
2	Bob Abreu	.75
3	Vladimir Guerrero	2.00
4	Paul Konerko	.75
5	Kevin Orie	.50
6	Todd Walker	.50
7	Ben Grieve	.50
8	Darin Erstad	1.00
9	Derrek Lee	1.00
10	Jose Cruz, Jr.	.50
11	Scott Rolen	.50
12	Travis Lee	.50
13	Andruw Jones	2.00
14	Wilton Guerrero	.50
15	Nomar Garciaparra	2.50

1997 Bowman's Best

The 200-card base set is divided into a 100-card subset featuring current stars on a gold-chromium stock, and 100 cards of top prospects in silver chromium. Packs contain six cards and were issued with a suggested retail price of $5. Autographed cards of 10 different players were randomly inserted into packs, with each player signing regular, Refractor and Atomic Refractor versions of their cards. Bowman's Best Laser Cuts

DEION SANDERS

and Mirror Image are the two other inserts, each with Refractor and Atomic Refractor editions.

		NM/M
Complete Set (200):		25.00
Common Player:		.25
Star Refractors:		4X
Star Atomics:		6X
Pack (6):		2.00
Wax Box (24):		40.00
1	Ken Griffey Jr.	1.50
2	Cecil Fielder	.25
3	Albert Belle	.25
4	Todd Hundley	.25
5	Mike Piazza	1.00
6	Matt Williams	.25
7	Mo Vaughn	.25
8	Ryne Sandberg	1.50
9	Chipper Jones	1.00
10	Edgar Martinez	.25
11	Kenny Lofton	.25
12	Ron Gant	.25
13	Moises Alou	.25
14	Pat Hentgen	.25
15	Steve Finley	.25
16	Mark Grace	.25
17	Jay Buhner	.25
18	Jeff Conine	.25
19	Jim Edmonds	.25
20	Todd Hollandsworth	.25
21	Andy Petitte	.50
22	Jim Thome	.75
23	Eric Young	.25
24	Ray Lankford	.25
25	Marquis Grissom	.25
26	Tony Clark	.25
27	Jermaine Allensworth	.25
28	Ellis Burks	.25
29	Tony Gwynn	1.50
30	Barry Larkin	.25
31	John Olerud	.25
32	Mariano Rivera	.40
33	Paul Molitor	1.00
34	Ken Caminiti	.25
35	Gary Sheffield	.45
36	Al Martin	.25
37	John Valentin	.25
38	Frank Thomas	.75
39	John Jaha	.25
40	Greg Maddux	1.50
41	Alex Fernandez	.25
42	Dean Palmer	.25
43	Bernie Williams	.25
44	Deion Sanders	.25
45	Mark McGwire	2.00
46	Brian Jordan	.25
47	Bernard Gilkey	.25
48	Will Clark	.25
49	Kevin Appier	.25
50	Tom Glavine	.40
51	Chuck Knoblauch	.25
52	Rondell White	.25
53	Greg Vaughn	.25
54	Mike Mussina	.50
55	Brian McRae	.25
56	Chili Davis	.25
57	Wade Boggs	1.50
58	Jeff Bagwell	.75
59	Roberto Alomar	.35
60	Dennis Eckersley	.50
61	Ryan Klesko	.25
62	Manny Ramirez	1.00
63	John Wetteland	.25
64	Cal Ripken Jr.	2.00
65	Edgar Renteria	.25
66	Tino Martinez	.25
67	Larry Walker	.25
68	Gregg Jefferies	.25
69	Lance Johnson	.25
70	Carlos Delgado	.50
71	Craig Biggio	.25
72	Jose Canseco	.50
73	Barry Bonds	2.00
74	Juan Gonzalez	.50
75	Eric Karros	.25
76	Reggie Sanders	.25
77	Robin Ventura	.25
78	Hideo Nomo	.50
79	David Justice	.25
80	Vinny Castilla	.25
81	Travis Fryman	.25
82	Derek Jeter	2.00
83	Sammy Sosa	1.50
84	Ivan Rodriguez	.75
85	Rafael Palmeiro	.25
86	Roger Clemens	2.00
87	Jason Giambi	.50
88	Andres Galarraga	.25
89	Jermaine Dye	.25
90	Joe Carter	.25
91	Brady Anderson	.25
92	Derek Bell	.25
93	Randy Johnson	1.00
94	Fred McGriff	.25
95	John Smoltz	.25
96	Harold Baines	.25
97	Raul Mondesi	.25
98	Tim Salmon	.25
99	Carlos Baerga	.25
100	Dante Bichette	.25
101	Vladimir Guerrero	1.00
102	Richard Hidalgo	.25
103	Paul Konerko	.25
104	Alex Gonzalez RC	.25
105	Jason Dickson	.25
106	Jose Rosado	.25
107	Todd Walker	.25
108	Seth Greisinger RC	.40
109	Todd Helton	.75
110	Ben Davis	.25
111	Bartolo Colon	.25
112	Elieser Marrero	.25
113	Jeff D'Amico	.25
114	Miguel Tejada RC	8.00
115	Darin Erstad	.50
116	Kris Benson RC	.25
117	Adrian Beltre RC	2.00
118	Neifi Perez	.25
119	Calvin Reese	.25
120	Carl Pavano	.25
121	Juan Melo	.25
122	Kevin McGlinchy RC	.25
123	Pat Cline	.25
124	Felix Heredia RC	.40
125	Aaron Boone	.25
126	Glendon Rusch	.25
127	Mike Cameron	.25
128	Justin Thompson	.25
129	Chad Hermansen RC	.25
130	Sidney Ponson RC	1.00
131	Willie Martinez RC	.25
132	Paul Wilder RC	.25
133	Geoff Jenkins	.25
134	Roy Halladay RC	2.00
135	Carlos Guillen	.25
136	Tony Batista	.25
137	Todd Greene	.25
138	Luis Castillo	.25
139	Jimmy Anderson RC	.25
140	Edgard Velazquez	.25
141	Chris Snopek	.25
142	Ruben Rivera	.25
143	Javier Valentin RC	.25
144	Brian Rose	.25
145	Fernando Tatis RC	.50
146	Dean Crow RC	.25
147	Karim Garcia	.25
148	Dante Powell	.25
149	Hideki Irabu RC	.40
150	Matt Morris	.25
151	Wes Helms	.25
152	Russ Johnson	.25
153	Jarrod Washburn	.25
154	Kerry Wood RC	4.00
155	Joe Fontenot RC	.25
156	Eugene Kingsale	.25
157	Terrence Long	.25
158	Calvin Maduro	.25
159	Jeff Suppan	.25
160	DaRond Stovall	.25
161	Mark Redman	.25
162	Ken Cloude RC	.25
163	Bobby Estalella	.25
164	Abraham Nunez RC	.75
165	Derrick Gibson	.25
166	Mike Drumright RC	.25
167	Katsuhiro Maeda	.25
168	Jeff Liefer	.25
169	Ben Grieve	.25
170	Bob Abreu	.25
171	Shannon Stewart	.25
172	Braden Looper RC	.40
173	Brant Brown	.25
174	Marlon Anderson	.25
175	Brad Fullmer	.25
176	Carlos Beltran	.25
177	Nomar Garciaparra	1.50
178	Derrek Lee	.75
179	Valerio De Los Santos RC	.25
180	Dmitri Young	.25
181	Jamey Wright	.25
182	Hiram Bocachica RC	.25
183	Wilton Guerrero	.25
184	Chris Carpenter	.25
185	Scott Spiezio	.25
186	Andruw Jones	1.00
187	Travis Lee RC	.75
188	Jose Cruz Jr. RC	1.00
189	Jose Guillen	.25
190	Jeff Abbott	.25
191	Ricky Ledee RC	.40
192	Mike Sweeney	.25
193	Donnie Sadler	.25
194	Scott Rolen	.75
195	Kevin Orie	.25
196	Jason Conti RC	.25
197	Mark Kotsay	.75
198	Eric Milton RC	1.00
199	Russell Branyan	.25
200	Alex Sanchez RC	.50

Autographs

Ten different players each signed 10 regular versions of their

SCOTT SPIEZIO

respective Bowman's Best cards (1:170 packs), 10 of their Bowman's Best Refractors (1:2,036 packs) and 10 of their Bowman's Best Atomic Refractors (1:6,107 packs). Each autograph card features a special Certified Autograph stamp on the front.

		NM/M
Complete Set (10):		150.00
Common Player:		5.00
Refractors:		1.5X
Atomics:		2X
29	Tony Gwynn	30.00
33	Paul Molitor	20.00
82	Derek Jeter	100.00
91	Brady Anderson	7.50
98	Tim Salmon	10.00
107	Todd Walker	5.00
183	Wilton Guerrero	5.00
185	Scott Spiezio	5.00
188	Jose Cruz Jr.	6.00
194	Scott Rolen	20.00

Cuts

MARK McGWIRE

Each of these 20-card inserts features a laser-cut pattern in the chromium stock. Backs have another color photo and list several of the player's career "Bests." Three different versions of each card are available: Regular (1:24 packs), Refractor (1:48) and Atomic Refractor (1:96). Cards are numbered with a "BC" prefix.

		NM/M
Complete Set (20):		20.00
Common Player:		.35
Refractors:		1.5X
Atomic Refractors:		2X
1	Derek Jeter	4.00
2	Chipper Jones	1.50
3	Frank Thomas	1.00
4	Cal Ripken Jr.	4.00
5	Mark McGwire	3.00
6	Ken Griffey Jr.	2.00
7	Jeff Bagwell	1.00
8	Mike Piazza	2.00
9	Ken Caminiti	.35
10	Albert Belle	.35
11	Jose Cruz Jr.	.35
12	Wilton Guerrero	.35
13	Darin Erstad	.50
14	Andruw Jones	1.00
15	Scott Rolen	.75
16	Jose Guillen	.35
17	Bob Abreu	.35
18	Vladimir Guerrero	1.00
19	Todd Walker	.35
20	Nomar Garciaparra	1.50

Mirror Image

This 10-card insert features four players on each double-sided card - two veterans and two rookies - utilizing Finest technology. Regular Mirror Image cards are found 1:48 packs, while Refractor versions are seeded 1:96 packs and Atomic Refractors are found 1:192 packs. Cards are numbered with an "MI" prefix.

NM/M

Complete Set (10):	35.00
Common Card:	2.00
Refractors:	1.5X
Atomic Refractors:	2X
1 Nomar Garciaparra, Derek Jeter, Hiram Bocachica, Barry Larkin	7.50
2 Travis Lee, Frank Thomas, Derrek Lee, Jeff Bagwell	3.50
3 Kerry Wood, Greg Maddux, Kris Benson, John Smoltz	3.50
4 Kevin Brown, Ivan Rodriguez, Elieser Marrero, Mike Piazza	5.00
5 Jose Cruz Jr., Ken Griffey Jr., Andruw Jones, Barry Bonds	7.50
6 Jose Guillen, Juan Gonzalez, Richard Hidalgo, Gary Sheffield	7.00
7 Paul Konerko, Mark McGwire, Todd Helton, Rafael Palmeiro	6.00
8 Wilton Guerrero, Craig Biggio, Donnie Sadler, Chuck Knoblauch	2.00
9 Russell Branyan, Matt Williams, Adrian Beltre, Chipper Jones	3.50
10 Bob Abreu, Kenny Lofton, Vladimir Guerrero, Albert Belle	3.00

1997 Bowman's Best Jumbos

This large-format (4" x 5-5/8") version of 1997 Bowman's Best features 16 of the season's top stars and hottest rookies. Utilizing chromium, Refractor and Atomic Refractor technologies, the cards are identical in every way except size to the regular-issue Bowman's Best. The jumbos were sold only through Topps Stadium Club. Each of the sets consists of 12 chromium cards, plus three randomly packaged Refractors and one Atomic Refractor. About 900 sets were produced according to Topps sales literature, which breaks down to 700 regular cards, 170 Refractors and 60 Atomic Refractors of each player.

NM/M

Complete Set (16):	90.00
Common Player:	4.50
Refractor:	1.5X
Atomic Refractor:	2X
1 Ken Griffey Jr.	7.50
5 Mike Piazza	7.50
9 Chipper Jones	6.00
11 Kenny Lofton	4.50
29 Tony Gwynn	6.00
33 Paul Molitor	5.00
38 Frank Thomas	5.00
45 Mark McGwire	9.00
64 Cal Ripken Jr.	12.00
73 Barry Bonds	12.00
74 Juan Gonzalez	4.50
82 Derek Jeter	12.00
101 Vladimir Guerrero	6.00
177 Nomar Garciaparra	6.00
186 Andruw Jones	5.00
188 Jose Cruz, Jr.	4.50

1998 Bowman

Bowman was a 441-card set released in a pair of 220-card series in 1998 (Orlando Hernandez, #221, was a late Series 1 addition.) Within each series are 150 prospects printed in a silver and blue design and 70 veterans printed in silver and red. Cards feature a Bowman seal, and in cases of a player's first Bowman card, a "Bowman Rookie Card" stamp is applied. The player's facsimile signature from his first contract runs down the side. The entire set was paralleled twice in Bowman International (one per pack) and Golden Anniversary (serially numbered to 50). Inserts in Series 1 include Autographs, Scout's Choice, and Japanese Rookies. Inserts in Series 2 include Autographs, 1999 Rookie of the Year Favorites, Minor League MVPs and Japanese Rookies.

NM/M

Complete Set (441):	40.00
Series 1 (221):	20.00
Series 2 (220):	20.00
Common Player:	.10
Internationals:	1.5X
Inserted 1:1	
Series 1 Pack (10):	2.00
Series 1 Wax Box (24):	30.00
Series 2 Pack (10):	1.50
Series 2 Wax Box (24):	25.00

#	Player	
1	Nomar Garciaparra	1.50
2	Scott Rolen	.75
3	Andy Pettitte	.30
4	Ivan Rodriguez	.65
5	Mark McGwire	2.50
6	Jason Dickson	.10
7	Jose Cruz Jr.	.10
8	Jeff Kent	.10
9	Mike Mussina	.30
10	Jason Kendall	.10
11	Brett Tomko	.10
12	Jeff King	.10
13	Brad Radke	.10
14	Robin Ventura	.10
15	Jeff Bagwell	1.00
16	Greg Maddux	1.50
17	John Jaha	.10
18	Mike Piazza	2.00
19	Edgar Martinez	.10
20	David Justice	.10
21	Todd Hundley	.10
22	Tony Gwynn	1.50
23	Larry Walker	.10
24	Bernie Williams	.10
25	Edgar Renteria	.10
26	Rafael Palmeiro	.75
27	Tim Salmon	.10
28	Matt Morris	.10
29	Shawn Estes	.10
30	Vladimir Guerrero	1.00
31	Fernando Tatis	.10
32	Justin Thompson	.10
33	Ken Griffey Jr.	2.00
34	Edgardo Alfonzo	.10
35	Mo Vaughn	.10
36	Marty Cordova	.10
37	Craig Biggio	.10
38	Roger Clemens	1.75
39	Mark Grace	.10
40	Ken Caminiti	.10
41	Tony Womack	.10
42	Albert Belle	.10
43	Tino Martinez	.10
44	Sandy Alomar	.10
45	Jeff Cirillo	.10
46	Jason Giambi	.50
47	Darin Erstad	.25
48	Livan Hernandez	.10
49	Mark Grudzielanek	.10
50	Sammy Sosa	1.50
51	Curt Schilling	.30
52	Brian Hunter	.10
53	Neifi Perez	.10
54	Todd Walker	.10
55	Jose Guillen	.10
56	Jim Thome	.30
57	Tom Glavine	.30
58	Todd Greene	.10
59	Rondell White	.10
60	Roberto Alomar	.25
61	Tony Clark	.10
62	Vinny Castilla	.10
63	Barry Larkin	.10
64	Hideki Irabu	.10
65	Johnny Damon	.35
66	Juan Gonzalez	.50
67	John Olerud	.10
68	Gary Sheffield	.25
69	Raul Mondesi	.10
70	Chipper Jones	1.50
71	David Ortiz	.50
72	Warren Morris RC	.50
73	Alex Gonzalez	.10
74	Nick Bierbrodt	.10
75	Roy Halladay	.10
76	Danny Buxbaum	.10
77	Adam Kennedy	.10
78	Jared Sandberg RC	.75
79	Michael Barrett	.10
80	Gil Meche	.10
81	Jayson Werth	.10
82	Abraham Nunez	.10
83	Ben Petrick	.10
84	Brett Caradonna	.10
85	Mike Lowell RC	3.00
86	Clay Bruner RC	.10
87	John Curtice RC	.10
88	Bobby Estalella	.10
89	Juan Melo	.10
90	Arnold Gooch	.10
91	Kevin Millwood RC	1.00
92	Richie Sexson	.10
93	Orlando Cabrera	.10
94	Pat Cline	.10
95	Anthony Sanders	.10
96	Russ Johnson	.10
97	Ben Grieve	.10
98	Kevin McGlinchy	.10
99	Paul Wilder	.10
100	Russ Ortiz	.10
101	Ryan Jackson RC	.10
102	Heath Murray	.10
103	Brian Rose	.10
104	Ryan Radmanovich RC	.10
105	Ricky Ledee	.10
106	Jeff Wallace RC	.10
107	Ryan Minor RC	.10
108	Dennis Reyes	.10
109	James Manias RC	.10
110	Chris Carpenter	.10
111	Daryle Ward	.10
112	Vernon Wells	.10
113	Chad Green	.10
114	Mike Stoner RC	.10
115	Brad Fullmer	.10
116	Adam Eaton	.10
117	Jeff Liefer	.10
118	Corey Koskie RC	1.00
119	Todd Helton	.75
120	Jaime Jones RC	.10
121	Mel Rosario	.10
122	Geoff Goetz	.10
123	Adrian Beltre	.40
124	Jason Dellaero	.10
125	Gabe Kapler RC	.50
126	Scott Schoeneweis	.10
127	Ryan Brannan	.10
128	Aaron Akin	.10
129	Ryan Anderson RC	.25
130	Brad Penny	.10
131	Bruce Chen	.10
132	Eli Marrero	.10
133	Eric Chavez	.30
134	Troy Glaus RC	3.00
135	Troy Cameron	.10
136	Brian Sikorski RC	.10
137	Mike Kinkade RC	.25
138	Braden Looper	.10
139	Mark Mangum	.10
140	Danny Peoples	.10
141	J.J. Davis	.10
142	Ben Davis	.10
143	Jacque Jones	.10
144	Derrick Gibson	.10
145	Bronson Arroyo	.10
146	Cristian Guzman RC	.50
147	Jeff Abbott	.10
148	Mike Cuddyer RC	1.00
149	Jason Romano	.10
150	Shane Monahan	.10
151	Ntema Ndungidi RC	.10
152	Alex Sanchez	.10
153	Jack Cust RC	1.50
154	Brent Butler	.10
155	Ramon Hernandez	.10
156	Norm Hutchins	.10
157	Jason Marquis	.10
158	Jacob Cruz	.10
159	Rob Burger RC	.10
160	Eric Milton	.10
161	Preston Wilson	.10
162	Jason Fitzgerald RC	.10
163	Dan Serafini	.10
164	Peter Munro	.10
165	Trot Nixon	.10
166	Homer Bush	.10
167	Dermal Brown	.10
168	Chad Hermansen	.10
169	Julio Moreno RC	.10
170	John Roskos RC	.10
171	Grant Roberts	.10
172	Ken Cloude	.10
173	Jason Brester	.10
174	Jason Conti	.10
175	Jon Garland	.10
176	Robbie Bell	.10
177	Nathan Haynes	.10
178	Ramon Ortiz RC	.50
179	Shannon Stewart	.10
180	Pablo Ortega	.10
181	Jimmy Rollins RC	4.00
182	Sean Casey	.30
183	Ted Lilly RC	.25
184	Chris Enochs RC	.10
185	Magglio Ordonez RC	3.00
186	Mike Drumright	.10
187	Aaron Boone	.10
188	Matt Clement	.10
189	Todd Dunwoody	.10
190	Larry Rodriguez	.10
191	Todd Noel	.10
192	Geoff Jenkins	.10
193	George Lombard	.10
194	Lance Berkman	.10
195	Marcus McCain RC	.10
196	Ryan McGuire	.10
197	Jhensy Sandoval RC	.10
198	Corey Lee	.10
199	Mario Valdez	.10
200	Robert Fick RC	.20
201	Donnie Sadler	.10
202	Marc Kroon	.10
203	David Miller	.10
204	Jarrod Washburn	.10
205	Miguel Tejada	.30
206	Raul Ibanez	.10
207	John Patterson	.10
208	Calvin Pickering	.10
209	Felix Martinez	.10
210	Mark Redman	.10
211	Scott Elarton	.10
212	Jose Amado RC	.10
213	Kerry Wood	.40
214	Dante Powell	.10
215	Aramis Ramirez	.10
216	A.J. Hinch	.10
217	Dustin Carr RC	.10
218	Mark Kotsay	.10
219	Jason Standridge	.10
220	Luis Ordaz	.10
221	Orlando Hernandez RC	.10
222	Cal Ripken Jr.	3.00
223	Paul Molitor	1.00
224	Derek Jeter	3.00
225	Barry Bonds	3.00
226	Jim Edmonds	.10
227	John Smoltz	.10
228	Eric Karros	.10
229	Ray Lankford	.10
230	Rey Ordonez	.10
231	Kenny Lofton	.10
232	Alex Rodriguez	2.50
233	Dante Bichette	.10
234	Pedro Martinez	1.00
235	Carlos Delgado	.45
236	Rod Beck	.10
237	Matt Williams	.10
238	Charles Johnson	.10
239	Rico Brogna	.10
240	Frank Thomas	1.00
241	Paul O'Neill	.10
242	Jaret Wright	.10
243	Brant Brown	.10
244	Ryan Klesko	.10
245	Chuck Finley	.10
246	Derek Bell	.10
247	Delino DeShields	.10
248	Chan Ho Park	.10
249	Wade Boggs	1.50
250	Jay Buhner	.10
251	Butch Huskey	.10
252	Steve Finley	.10
253	Will Clark	.10
254	John Valentin	.10
255	Bobby Higginson	.10
256	Darryl Strawberry	.10
257	Randy Johnson	1.00
258	Al Martin	.10
259	Travis Fryman	.10
260	Fred McGriff	.10
261	Jose Valentin	.10
262	Andruw Jones	1.00
263	Kenny Rogers	.10
264	Moises Alou	.10
265	Denny Neagle	.10
266	Ugueth Urbina	.10
267	Derrek Lee	.45
268	Ellis Burks	.10
269	Mariano Rivera	.30
270	Dean Palmer	.10
271	Eddie Taubensee	.10
272	Brady Anderson	.10
273	Brian Giles	.10
274	Quinton McCracken	.10
275	Henry Rodriguez	.10
276	Andres Galarraga	.10
277	Jose Canseco	.45
278	David Segui	.10
279	Bret Saberhagen	.10
280	Kevin Brown	.10
281	Chuck Knoblauch	.10
282	Jeromy Burnitz	.10
283	Jay Bell	.10
284	Manny Ramirez	1.00
285	Rick Helling	.10
286	Francisco Cordova	.10
287	Bob Abreu	.20
288	J.T. Snow Jr.	.10
289	Hideo Nomo	.50
290	Brian Jordan	.10
291	Javy Lopez	.10
292	Travis Lee	.10
293	Russell Branyan	.10
294	Paul Konerko	.10
295	Masato Yoshii RC	.50
296	Kris Benson	.10
297	Juan Encarnacion	.10
298	Eric Milton	.10
299	Mike Caruso	.10
300	Ricardo Aramboles RC	.10
301	Bobby Smith	.10
302	Billy Koch	.10
303	Richard Hidalgo	.10
304	Justin Baughman RC	.10
305	Chris Gissell	.10
306	Donnie Bridges RC	.10
307	Nelson Lara RC	.10
308	Randy Wolf RC	1.00
309	Jason LaRue RC	.25
310	Jason Gooding RC	.10
311	Edgar Clemente RC	.10
312	Andrew Vessel	.10
313	Chris Reitsma	.10
314	Jesus Sanchez RC	.10
315	Buddy Carlyle RC	.10
316	Randy Winn	.10
317	Luis Rivera	.10
318	Marcus Thames RC	1.50
319	A.J. Pierzynski	.10
320	Scott Randall	.10
321	Damian Sapp	.10
322	Eddie Yarnell RC	.10
323	Luke Allen RC	.10
324	J.D. Smart	.10
325	Willie Martinez	.10
326	Alex Ramirez	.10
327	Eric DuBose RC	.10
328	Kevin Witt	.10
329	Dan McKinley RC	.10
330	Cliff Politte	.10
331	Vladimir Nunez	.10
332	John Halama RC	.25
333	Nerio Rodriguez	.10
334	Desi Relaford	.10
335	Robinson Checo	.10
336	John Nicholson	.10
337	Tom LaRosa RC	.10
338	Kevin Nicholson RC	.10
339	Javier Vazquez	.10
340	A.J. Zapp	.10
341	Tom Evans	.10
342	Kerry Robinson	.10
343	Gabe Gonzalez RC	.10
344	Ralph Milliard	.10
345	Enrique Wilson	.10
346	Elvin Hernandez	.10
347	Mike Lincoln RC	.10
348	Cesar King RC	.10
349	Cristian Guzman RC	1.00
350	Donzell McDonald	.10
351	Jim Parque RC	.25
352	Mike Saipe RC	.10
353	Carlos Febles RC	.40
354	Dernell Stenson RC	.10
355	Mark Osborne RC	.10
356	Odalis Perez RC	.10
357	Jason Dewey RC	.10
358	Joe Fontenot	.10
359	Jason Grilli RC	.40
360	Kevin Haverbusch RC	.25
361	Jay Yennaco RC	.10
362	Brian Buchanan	.10
363	John Barnes	.10
364	Chris Fussell	.10
365	Kevin Gibbs RC	.10
366	Joe Lawrence	.10
367	DaRond Stovall	.10
368	Brian Fuentes RC	.10
369	Jimmy Anderson	.10
370	Laril Gonzalez RC	.40
371	Scott Williamson RC	.10
372	Milton Bradley	.10
373	Jason Halper RC	.10
374	Brent Billingsley RC	.10
375	Joe DePastino RC	.10
376	Jake Westbrook	.10
377	Octavio Dotel	.10
378	Jason Williams RC	.10
379	Julio Ramirez RC	.10
380	Seth Greisinger	.10
381	Mike Judd RC	.10
382	Ben Ford RC	.10
383	Tom Bennett	.10
384	Adam Butler RC	.10
385	Wade Miller RC	.75
386	Kyle Peterson RC	.10
387	Tommy Peterman RC	.10
388	Onan Masaoka	.10
389	Jason Rakers RC	.10
390	Rafael Medina	.10
391	Luis Lopez	.10
392	Jeff Yoder	.10
393	Vance Wilson RC	.10
394	Fernando Seguignol RC	.25
395	Ron Wright	.10
396	Ruben Mateo RC	.40
397	Steve Lomasney RC	.25
398	Damian Jackson	.10
399	Mike Jerzembeck RC	.10
400	Luis Rivas RC	.25
401	Kevin Burford RC	.10
402	Glenn Davis	.10
403	Robert Luce RC	.10
404	Cole Liniak	.10
405	Matthew LeCroy RC	.20
406	Jeremy Giambi RC	.40
407	Shawn Chacon	.10
408	Dewayne Wise RC	.10
409	Steve Woodard RC	.10
410	Francisco Cordero RC	.25
411	Damon Minor RC	.20
412	Lou Collier	.10
413	Justin Towle	.10
414	Juan LeBron	.10
415	Michael Coleman	.10
416	Felix Rodriguez	.10
417	Paul Ah Yat RC	.10
418	Kevin Barker RC	.25
419	Brian Meadows	.10
420	Darnell McDonald RC	.20
421	Matt Kinney RC	.25
422	Mike Vavrek RC	.10
423	Courtney Duncan RC	.10
424	Kevin Millar RC	.50
425	Ruben Rivera	.10
426	Steve Shoemaker RC	.10
427	Dan Reichert RC	.10
428	Carlos Lee RC	2.00
429	Rod Barajas	.10
430	Pablo Ozuna RC	.20
431	Todd Belitz RC	.10
432	Sidney Ponson	.10
433	Steve Carver RC	.10
434	Esteban Yan	.10
435	Cedrick Bowers RC	.10
436	Marlon Anderson	.10
437	Carl Pavano	.10
438	Jae Weong Seo RC	.50
439	Jose Taveras RC	.10
440	Matt Anderson RC	.25
441	Darron Ingram RC	.10

Golden Anniversary

This 441-card parallel set celebrates Bowman's 50th anniversary with a gold, rather than black, facsimile autograph on each card. Golden Anniversary cards were inserted in both Series 1 (1:237) and Series 2 (1:194) packs and are sequentially numbered to 50.

NM/M

Common Player:	4.00
Veteran Stars:	15-30X
Young Stars:	5-10X
Rookie Cards:	5-10X

International

All 441 cards in Bowman Series 1 and 2 are paralleled in an International version, with the player's native country highlighted. Background map designs and vital information were translated into the player's native language on these one per pack parallel cards.

NM/M

Common Player:	.25
Stars:	1.5X
Inserted 1:1	

Autographs

Rookies and prospects are featured on the certified autograph cards found as '98 Bowman inserts. Each player signed cards in blue, silver and gold ink. The front of each autographed card bears a certification seal. Relative values in the current market come nowhere near reflecting those scarcities.

	NM/M
Common Player:	3.00
Inserted 1:149	
Silvers (1:992):	1.5-2.5X
Golds (1:2,976):	2-4X
1 Adrian Beltre	15.00
2 Brad Fullmer	5.00
3 Ricky Ledee	5.00
4 David Ortiz	35.00
5 Fernando Tatis	3.00
6 Kerry Wood	20.00
7 Mel Rosario	3.00
8 Cole Liniak	5.00
9 A.J. Hinch	5.00
10 Jhensy Sandoval	3.00
11 Jose Cruz Jr.	5.00
12 Richard Hidalgo	6.00
13 Geoff Jenkins	8.00
14 Carl Pavano	10.00
15 Richie Sexson	12.00
16 Tony Womack	5.00
17 Scott Rolen	20.00
18 Ryan Minor	5.00
19 Elieser Marrero	5.00
20 Jason Marquis	5.00
21 Mike Lowell	30.00
22 Todd Helton	20.00
23 Chad Green	3.00
24 Scott Elarton	5.00
25 Russell Branyan	5.00
26 Mike Drumright	3.00
27 Ben Grieve	5.00
28 Jacque Jones	8.00
29 Jared Sandberg	5.00
30 Grant Roberts	5.00
31 Mike Stoner	3.00
32 Brian Rose	5.00
33 Randy Winn	5.00
34 Justin Towle	3.00
35 Anthony Sanders	3.00
36 Rafael Medina	3.00
37 Corey Lee	3.00
38 Mike Kinkade	5.00
39 Norm Hutchins	3.00
40 Jason Brester	3.00
41 Ben Davis	5.00
42 Nomar Garciaparra	40.00
43 Jeff Liefer	3.00
44 Eric Milton	6.00
45 Preston Wilson	8.00
46 Miguel Tejada	30.00
47 Luis Ordaz	3.00
48 Travis Lee	5.00
49 Kris Benson	6.00
50 Jacob Cruz	5.00
51 Dermal Brown	3.00
52 Marc Kroon	3.00
53 Chad Hermansen	5.00
54 Roy Halladay	15.00
55 Eric Chavez	10.00
56 Jason Conti	3.00
57 Juan Encarnacion	5.00
58 Paul Wilder	3.00
59 Aramis Ramirez	15.00
60 Cliff Politte	3.00
61 Todd Dunwoody	3.00
62 Paul Konerko	10.00
63 Shane Monahan	3.00
64 Alex Sanchez	3.00
65 Jeff Abbott	3.00
66 John Patterson	3.00
67 Peter Munro	3.00
68 Jarrod Washburn	5.00
69 Derrek Lee	20.00
70 Ramon Hernandez	5.00

Japanese Rookies

Bowman offered collectors a chance to receive original 1991 BBM-brand Japanese rookie cards of three players. Series 1 had rookie cards of Hideo Nomo and Shigetoshi Hasegawa inserted in one per 2,685 packs, while Series 2 offered Hideki Irabu seeded one per 4,411 packs. Card numbers have a "BBM" prefix.

	NM/M
Complete Set (3):	15.00
Common Player:	3.00
11 Hideo Nomo	10.00
17 Shigetoshi Hasegawa	5.00
Hideki Irabu	5.00

Minor League MVP

This 11-card insert set features players who are former Minor League MVPs who had graduated to the majors. Minor League MVPs are seeded one per 12 packs of Series 2 and are numbered with a "MVP" prefix.

	NM/M
Complete Set (11):	9.00
Common Player:	.50
1 Jeff Bagwell	1.00
2 Andres Galarraga	.50
3 Juan Gonzalez	.60
4 Tony Gwynn	1.50
5 Vladimir Guerrero	1.00
6 Derek Jeter	3.00
7 Andruw Jones	1.00
8 Tino Martinez	.50
9 Manny Ramirez	1.00
10 Gary Sheffield	.60
11 Jim Thome	.65

Rookie of the Year Favorites

Rookie of the Year Favorites displays 10 players who had a legitimate shot at the 1999 ROY award in the opinion of the Bowman scouts. The insert was seeded one per 12 packs of Series 2 and numbered with an "ROY" prefix.

	NM/M
Complete Set (10):	6.00
Common Player:	.50
1 Adrian Beltre	.75
2 Troy Glaus	3.00
3 Chad Hermansen	.50
4 Matt Clement	.50
5 Eric Chavez	.75
6 Kris Benson	.50
7 Richie Sexson	.50
8 Randy Wolf	.50
9 Ryan Minor	.50
10 Alex Gonzalez	.50

Scout's Choice

This Series 1 insert has players with potential for Major League stardom. Fronts have action photos with gold-foil highlights. Backs have a portrait photo and an assessment of the player's skills in the traditional five areas of raw talent. Cards are numbered with an "SC" prefix.

	NM/M
Complete Set (21):	8.00
Common Player:	.25
Inserted 1:12	
1 Paul Konerko	.50
2 Richard Hidalgo	.25
3 Mark Kotsay	.25
4 Ben Grieve	.25
5 Chad Hermansen	.25
6 Matt Clement	.25
7 Brad Fullmer	.25
8 Eli Marrero	.25
9 Kerry Wood	1.50
10 Adrian Beltre	1.50
11 Ricky Ledee	.25
12 Travis Lee	.25
13 Abraham Nunez	.25
14 Ryan Anderson	.25
15 Dermal Brown	.25
16 Juan Encarnacion	.25
17 Aramis Ramirez	.25
18 Todd Helton	2.50
19 Kris Benson	.25
20 Russell Branyan	.25
21 Mike Stoner	.25

1998 Bowman Chrome

All 441 cards in Bowman 1 and 2 were reprinted with a chromium finish for Bowman Chrome. Chrome contains International and Golden Anniversary parallels, like Bowman. Internationals are seeded one per four packs, with Refractor versions every 24 packs. Golden Anniversary parallels are exclusive to hobby packs and inserted one per 164 packs and sequentially numbered to 50 sets. Refractor versions are seeded one per 1,279 packs and numbered to just five sets. In addition, 50 Bowman Chrome Reprints were inserted with 25 in each series.

	NM/M
Complete Set (441):	100.00
Complete Series 1 (221):	60.00
Complete Series 2 (220):	50.00
Common Player:	.20
Series 1 Pack (4):	2.50
Series 2 Pack (4):	2.00
Series 1 Box (24):	45.00
Series 2 Box (24):	35.00
1 Nomar Garciaparra	1.00
2 Scott Rolen	.75
3 Andy Pettitte	.40
4 Ivan Rodriguez	.75
5 Mark McGwire	2.50
6 Jason Dickson	.20
7 Jose Cruz Jr.	.20
8 Jeff Kent	.20
9 Mike Mussina	.50
10 Jason Kendall	.20
11 Brett Tomko	.20
12 Jeff King	.20
13 Brad Radke	.20
14 Robin Ventura	.20
15 Jeff Bagwell	1.00
16 Greg Maddux	1.50
17 John Jaha	.20
18 Mike Piazza	2.00
19 Edgar Martinez	.20
20 David Justice	.20
21 Todd Hundley	.20
22 Tony Gwynn	1.50
23 Larry Walker	.20
24 Bernie Williams	.20
25 Edgar Renteria	.20
26 Rafael Palmeiro	.75
27 Tim Salmon	.20
28 Matt Morris	.20
29 Shawn Estes	.20
30 Vladimir Guerrero	1.00
31 Fernando Tatis	.20
32 Justin Thompson	.20
33 Ken Griffey Jr.	2.00
34 Edgardo Alfonzo	.20
35 Mo Vaughn	.20
36 Marty Cordova	.20
37 Craig Biggio	.20
38 Roger Clemens	2.00
39 Mark Grace	.20
40 Ken Caminiti	.20
41 Tony Womack	.20
42 Albert Belle	.20
43 Tino Martinez	.20
44 Sandy Alomar	.20
45 Jeff Cirillo	.20
46 Jason Giambi	.50
47 Darin Erstad	.45
48 Livan Hernandez	.20
49 Mark Grudzielanek	.20
50 Sammy Sosa	1.50
51 Curt Schilling	.50
52 Brian Hunter	.20
53 Neifi Perez	.20
54 Todd Walker	.20
55 Jose Guillen	.20
56 Jim Thome	.20
57 Tom Glavine	.40
58 Todd Greene	.20
59 Rondell White	.20
60 Roberto Alomar	.35
61 Tony Clark	.20
62 Vinny Castilla	.20
63 Barry Larkin	.20
64 Hideki Irabu	.20
65 Johnny Damon	.60
66 Juan Gonzalez	.50
67 John Olerud	.20
68 Gary Sheffield	.45
69 Raul Mondesi	.20
70 Chipper Jones	1.50
71 David Ortiz	.75
72 Warren Morris RC	.50
73 Alex Gonzalez	.20
74 Nick Bierbrodt	.20
75 Roy Halladay	.20
76 Danny Buxbaum	.20
77 Adam Kennedy	.20
78 Jared Sandberg RC	.50
79 Michael Barrett	.20
80 Gil Meche	.20
81 Jayson Werth	.20
82 Abraham Nunez	.20
83 Ben Petrick	.20
84 Brett Caradonna	.20
85 Mike Lowell RC	6.00
86 Clay Bruner RC	.20
87 John Curtice RC	.20
88 Bobby Estalella	.20
89 Juan Melo	.20
90 Arnold Gooch	.20
91 Kevin Millwood RC	4.00
92 Richie Sexson	.20
93 Orlando Cabrera	.20
94 Pat Cline	.20
95 Anthony Sanders	.20
96 Russ Johnson	.20
97 Ben Grieve	.20
98 Kevin McGlinchy	.20
99 Paul Wilder	.20
100 Russ Ortiz	.20
101 Ryan Jackson RC	.50
102 Heath Murray	.20
103 Brian Rose	.20
104 Ryan Radmanovich RC	.20
105 Ricky Ledee	.20
106 Jeff Wallace RC	.20
107 Ryan Minor RC	.45
108 Dennis Reyes	.20
109 James Manias RC	.20
110 Chris Carpenter	.20
111 Daryle Ward	.20
112 Vernon Wells	.20
113 Chad Green	.20
114 Mike Stoner RC	.20
115 Brad Fullmer	.20
116 Adam Eaton	.20
117 Jeff Liefer	.20
118 Corey Koskie RC	1.50
119 Todd Helton	.75
120 Jaime Jones RC	.20
121 Mel Rosario	.20
122 Geoff Goetz	.20
123 Adrian Beltre	.40
124 Jason Dellaero	.20
125 Gabe Kapler RC	1.00
126 Scott Schoeneweis	.20
127 Ryan Brannan	.20
128 Aaron Akin	.20
129 Ryan Anderson RC	.50
130 Brad Penny	.20
131 Bruce Chen	.20
132 Eli Marrero	.20
133 Eric Chavez	.35
134 Troy Glaus RC	10.00
135 Troy Cameron	.20
136 Brian Sikorski RC	.20
137 Mike Kinkade RC	.50
138 Braden Looper	.20
139 Mark Mangum	.20
140 Danny Peoples	.20
141 J.J. Davis	.20
142 Ben Davis	.20
143 Jacque Jones	.20
144 Derrick Gibson	.20
145 Bronson Arroyo	.20
146 Luis De Los Santos RC	.20
147 Jeff Abbott	.20
148 Mike Cuddyer RC	1.50
149 Jason Romano	.20
150 Shane Monahan	.20
151 Ntema Ndungidi RC	.20
152 Alex Sanchez	.20
153 Jack Cust RC	5.00
154 Brent Butler	.20
155 Ramon Hernandez	.20
156 Norm Hutchins	.20
157 Jason Marquis	.20
158 Jacob Cruz	.20
159 Rob Burger RC	.20
160 Eric Milton	.20
161 Preston Wilson	.20
162 Jason Fitzgerald RC	.20
163 Dan Serafini	.20
164 Peter Munro	.20
165 Trot Nixon	.40
166 Homer Bush	.20
167 Dermal Brown	.20
168 Chad Hermansen	.20
169 Julio Moreno RC	.20
170 John Roskos RC	.20
171 Grant Roberts	.20
172 Ken Cloude	.20
173 Jason Brester	.20
174 Jason Conti	.20
175 Jon Garland	.20
176 Robbie Bell	.20
177 Nathan Haynes	.20
178 Ramon Ortiz RC	.50
179 Shannon Stewart	.20
180 Pablo Ortega	.20
181 Jimmy Rollins RC	10.00
182 Sean Casey	.45
183 Ted Lilly RC	.20
184 Chris Enochs RC	.20
185 Magglio Ordonez RC	3.00
186 Mike Drumright	.20
187 Aaron Boone	.20
188 Todd Dunwoody	.20
189 Larry Rodriguez	.20
190 Todd Noel	.20
191 Geoff Jenkins	.20
192 George Lombard	.20
193 Lance Berkman	.20
194 Marcus McCain RC	.20
195 Ryan McGuire	.20
196 Jhensy Sandoval RC	.20
197 Corey Lee	.20
198 Mario Valdez	.20
199 Robert Fick RC	.20
200 Donnie Sadler	.20
201 Marc Kroon	.20
202 David Miller	.20
203 Jarrod Washburn	.20
204 Miguel Tejada	.40
205 Raul Ibanez	.20
206 John Patterson	.20
207 Calvin Pickering	.20
208 Felix Martinez	.20
209 Mark Redman	.20
210 Scott Elarton	.20
211 Jose Amado RC	.20
212 Kerry Wood	.50
213 Dante Powell	.20
214 Aramis Ramirez	.20
215 A.J. Hinch	.20
216 Dustin Carr RC	.20
217 Mark Kotsay	.20
218 Jason Standridge	.20
219 Luis Ordaz	.20
220 Orlando Hernandez RC	3.00
221 Cal Ripken Jr.	3.00
222 Paul Molitor	1.00
223 Derek Jeter	3.00
224 Barry Bonds	3.00
225 Jim Edmonds	.20
226 John Smoltz	.20
227 Eric Karros	.20
228 Ray Lankford	.20
229 Rey Ordonez	.20
230 Kenny Lofton	.20
231 Alex Rodriguez	2.50
232 Dante Bichette	.20
233 Pedro Martinez	1.00
234 Carlos Delgado	.50
235 Rod Beck	.20
236 Matt Williams	.20
237 Charles Johnson	.20
238 Rico Brogna	.20
239 Frank Thomas	1.00
240 Paul O'Neill	.20
241 Jaret Wright	.20
242 Brant Brown	.20
243 Ryan Klesko	.20
244 Chuck Finley	.20
245 Derek Bell	.20
246 Delino DeShields	.20
247 Chan Ho Park	.20
248 Wade Boggs	1.50
249 Jay Buhner	.20
250 Butch Huskey	.20
251 Steve Finley	.20
252 Will Clark	.20
253 John Valentin	.20
254 Bobby Higginson	.20
255 Darryl Strawberry	.20
256 Randy Johnson	1.00
257 Al Martin	.20
258 Travis Fryman	.20
259 Fred McGriff	.20
260 Jose Valentin	.20
261 Andruw Jones	1.00
262 Kenny Rogers	.20
263 Moises Alou	.20
264 Denny Neagle	.20
265 Ugueth Urbina	.20
266 Derrek Lee	.50
267 Ellis Burks	.20
268 Mariano Rivera	.40
269 Dean Palmer	.20
270 Eddie Taubensee	.20
271 Brady Anderson	.20
272 Brian Giles	.20
273 Quinton McCracken	.20
275 Henry Rodriguez	.20
276 Andres Galarraga	.20
277 Jose Canseco	.40
278 David Segui	.20
279 Bret Saberhagen	.20
280 Kevin Brown	.20
281 Chuck Knoblauch	.20
282 Jeromy Burnitz	.20
283 Jay Bell	.20
284 Manny Ramirez	1.00
285 Rick Helling	.20
286 Francisco Cordova	.20
287 Bob Abreu	.30
288 J.T. Snow Jr.	.20
289 Hideo Nomo	.50
290 Brian Jordan	.20
291 Javy Lopez	.20
292 Aaron Akin RC	.20
293 Russell Branyan	.20
294 Paul Konerko	.20
295 Masato Yoshii RC	1.00
296 Kris Benson	.20
297 Juan Encarnacion	.20
298 Eric Milton	.20
299 Mike Caruso	.20
300 Ricardo Aramboles RC	.20
301 Bobby Smith	.20
302 Billy Koch	.20
303 Richard Hidalgo	.20
304 Justin Baughman RC	.20
305 Chris Gissell	.20
306 Donnie Bridges RC	.20
307 Nelson Lara RC	.20
308 Randy Wolf RC	1.00
309 Jason LaRue RC	.50
310 Jason Gooding RC	.20
311 Edgar Clemente RC	.20
312 Andrew Vessel	.20
313 Chris Reitsma	.20
314 Jesus Sanchez RC	.20
315 Buddy Carlyle RC	.20
316 Randy Winn	.20
317 Luis Rivera	.20
318 Marcus Thames RC	5.00
319 A.J. Pierzynski	.20
320 Scott Randall	.20
321 Damian Sapp	.20
322 Eddie Yarnell RC	.20
323 Luke Allen RC	.20
324 J.D. Smart	.20
325 Willie Martinez	.20
326 Alex Ramirez	.20
327 Eric DuBose RC	.20
328 Kevin Witt	.20
329 Dan McKinley RC	.20
330 Cliff Politte	.20
331 Vladimir Nunez	.20
332 John Halama RC	.50
333 Nerio Rodriguez	.20
334 Desi Relaford	.20
335 Robinson Checo	.20
336 John Nicholson RC	.20
337 Tom LaRosa RC	.20
338 Kevin Nicholson RC	.20
339 Javier Vazquez	.20
340 A.J. Zapp	.20
341 Tom Evans	.20
342 Kerry Robinson	.20
343 Gabe Gonzalez RC	.20
344 Ralph Milliard	.20
345 Enrique Wilson	.20
346 Elvin Hernandez	.20
347 Mike Lincoln RC	.35
348 Cesar King RC	.20
349 Cristian Guzman RC	.50
350 Donzell McDonald	.20
351 Jim Parque RC	.20
352 Mike Saipe RC	.20
353 Carlos Febles RC	.50
354 Dernell Stenson RC	.20
355 Mark Osborne RC	.20
356 Odalis Perez RC	2.00
357 Jason Dewey RC	.20
358 Joe Fontenot	.20
359 Jason Grilli RC	.40
360 Kevin Haverbusch RC	.20
361 Jay Yennaco RC	.20
362 Brian Buchanan	.20
363 John Barnes	.20
364 Chris Fussell	.20
365 Kevin Gibbs RC	.20
366 Joe Lawrence	.20
367 DaRond Stovall	.20
368 Brian Fuentes RC	.20
369 Jimmy Anderson	.20
370 Laril Gonzalez RC	.20
371 Scott Williamson RC	1.00
372 Milton Bradley	.20
373 Jason Halper RC	.20
374 Brent Billingsley RC	.20
375 Joe DePastino RC	.20
376 Jake Westbrook	.20
377 Octavio Dotel	.20
378 Jason Williams RC	.20
379 Julio Ramirez RC	.20
380 Seth Greisinger	.20
381 Mike Judd RC	.20
382 Ben Ford RC	.20
383 Tom Bennett RC	.20
384 Adam Butler RC	.20
385 Mike Miller RC	1.50
386 Kyle Peterson RC	.20
387 Tommy Peterman RC	.20
388 Onan Masaoka	.20
389 Jason Rakers RC	.20
390 Rafael Medina	.20
391 Luis Lopez	.20
392 Jeff Yoder	.20

393	Vance Wilson **RC**	.20
394	Fernando Seguignol **RC**	.35
395	Ron Wright	.20
396	Ruben Mateo **RC**	1.00
397	Steve Lomasney **RC**	.50
398	Damian Jackson	.20
399	Mike Jerzembeck **RC**	.20
400	Luis Rivas **RC**	.50
401	Kevin Burford **RC**	.20
402	Glenn Davis	.20
403	Robert Luce **RC**	.20
404	Cole Liniak	.20
405	Matthew LeCroy **RC**	.50
406	Jeremy Giambi **RC**	.50
407	Shawn Chacon **RC**	.20
408	Dewayne Wise **RC**	.20
409	Steve Woodard **RC**	.50
410	Francisco Cordero **RC**	.20
411	Damon Minor **RC**	.20
412	Lou Collier	.20
413	Justin Towle	.20
414	Juan LeBron	.20
415	Michael Coleman	.20
416	Felix Rodriguez	.20
417	Paul Ah Yat **RC**	.20
418	Kevin Barker **RC**	.20
419	Brian Meadows	.20
420	Darnell McDonald **RC**	.40
421	Matt Kinney **RC**	.40
422	Mike Vavrek **RC**	.20
423	Courtney Duncan **RC**	.20
424	Kevin Millar **RC**	1.50
425	Ruben Rivera	.20
426	Steve Shoemaker **RC**	.20
427	Dan Reichert **RC**	.20
428	Carlos Lee **RC**	6.00
429	Rod Barajas **RC**	.20
430	Pablo Ozuna **RC**	.50
431	Todd Belitz **RC**	.20
432	Sidney Ponson **RC**	.20
433	Steve Carver **RC**	.20
434	Esteban Yan **RC**	.20
435	Cedrick Bowers **RC**	.20
436	Marlon Anderson	.20
437	Carl Pavano	.20
438	Jae Weong Seo **RC**	1.00
439	Jose Taveras **RC**	.20
440	Matt Anderson **RC**	.50
441	Darron Ingram **RC**	.20

Refractors

Refractor versions for all 441 cards in Bowman Chrome Series 1 and 2 were created. The cards contained the word "Refractor" on the back in black letters directly under the card number.

	NM/M
Common Player:	2.00
Stars:	3X
Inserted 1:12	
Int'l Refractors:	6X
Inserted 1:24	

Golden Anniversary

JAVY LOPEZ

Golden Anniversary parallels were printed for all 441 cards in Bowman Chrome. They are exclusive to hobby packs, seeded one per 164 packs and sequentially numbered to 50 sets. Refractor versions were also available, numbered to just five sets and inserted one per 1,279 packs.

	NM/M
Common Player:	5.00
Stars:	20X
Common Refractor:	20.00

International

All 441 cards throughout Bowman Chrome Series 1 and 2 were paralleled in International versions. Cards fronts have the regular background replaced by a map denoting the player's birthplace. Backs are written in the player's native language.

	NM/M
Common Player:	.50
Stars and Rookies:	1.5X
Inserted 1:4	

Reprints

Bowman Chrome Reprints showcase 50 of the most popular

1ST IMPRESSIONS

rookie cards to appear in the brand since 1948. The 25 odd-numbered cards are found in Series 1; the evens in Series 2. The Reprints are numbered with a "BC" prefix.

		NM/M
Complete Set (50):		20.00
Common Player:		.25
Inserted 1:12		
Refractors:		1.5X
Inserted 1:36		
1	Yogi Berra	.75
2	Jackie Robinson	2.00
3	Don Newcombe	.50
4	Satchel Paige	.50
5	Willie Mays	2.00
6	Gil McDougald	.25
7	Don Larsen	.50
8	Elston Howard	.25
9	Robin Ventura	.25
10	Brady Anderson	.25
11	Gary Sheffield	.50
12	Tino Martinez	.25
13	Ken Griffey Jr.	1.50
14	John Smoltz	.50
15	Sandy Alomar Jr.	.25
16	Larry Walker	.25
17	Todd Hundley	.25
18	Mo Vaughn	.25
19	Sammy Sosa	1.00
20	Frank Thomas	.50
21	Chuck Knoblauch	.25
22	Bernie Williams	.25
23	Juan Gonzalez	.50
24	Mike Mussina	.50
25	Jeff Bagwell	.50
26	Tim Salmon	.25
27	Ivan Rodriguez	.50
28	Kenny Lofton	.25
29	Chipper Jones	1.00
30	Javier Lopez	.25
31	Ryan Klesko	.25
32	Raul Mondesi	.25
33	Jim Thome	.50
34	Carlos Delgado	.25
35	Mike Piazza	1.00
36	Manny Ramirez	.50
37	Andy Pettitte	.50
38	Derek Jeter	2.00
39	Brad Fullmer	.25
40	Richard Hidalgo	.25
41	Tony Clark	.25
42	Andruw Jones	.50
43	Vladimir Guerrero	.75
44	Nomar Garciaparra	.75
45	Paul Konerko	.50
46	Ben Grieve	.25
47	Hideo Nomo	.25
48	Scott Rolen	.50
49	Jose Guillen	.25
50	Livan Hernandez	.25

1998 Bowman's Best

CHUCK KNOBLAUCH

Bowman's Best was issued in a single 200-card series comprised of 100 prospects and 100 veterans. Prospects are shown on a silver background, while the veterans are showcased on gold. The set was paralleled twice: A Refractor version is seeded one per 20 packs and sequentially numbered to 400, while an Atomic Refractor is a 1:82 find and numbered to 100 sets. Inserts include regular, Re-

fractor and Atomic Refractor versions of: Autographs, Mirror Image and Performers.

	NM/M
Complete Set (200):	30.00
Common Player:	.25
Refractors:	8X
Production 400 Sets	
Atomic Refractors:	12X
Production 100 Sets	
Pack (6):	2.50
Wax Box (24):	35.00

1	Mark McGwire	2.00
2	Hideo Nomo	.50
3	Barry Bonds	3.00
4	Dante Bichette	.25
5	Chipper Jones	1.50
6	Frank Thomas	1.00
7	Kevin Brown	.25
8	Juan Gonzalez	.50
9	Jay Buhner	.25
10	Chuck Knoblauch	.25
11	Cal Ripken Jr.	3.00
12	Matt Williams	.25
13	Jim Edmonds	.25
14	Manny Ramirez	1.00
15	Tony Clark	.25
16	Mo Vaughn	.25
17	Bernie Williams	.25
18	Scott Rolen	.75
19	Gary Sheffield	.40
20	Albert Belle	.25
21	Mike Piazza	2.00
22	John Olerud	.25
23	Tony Gwynn	1.50
24	Jay Bell	.25
25	Jose Cruz Jr.	.25
26	Justin Thompson	.25
27	Ken Griffey Jr.	2.00
28	Sandy Alomar	.25
29	Mark Grudzielanek	.25
30	Mark Grace	.25
31	Ron Gant	.25
32	Javy Lopez	.25
33	Jeff Bagwell	1.00
34	Fred McGriff	.25
35	Rafael Palmeiro	.75
36	Vinny Castilla	.25
37	Andy Benes	.25
38	Pedro Martinez	1.00
39	Andy Pettitte	.40
40	Marty Cordova	.25
41	Rusty Greer	.25
42	Kevin Orie	.25
43	Chan Ho Park	.25
44	Ryan Klesko	.25
45	Alex Rodriguez	2.50
46	Travis Fryman	.25
47	Jeff King	.25
48	Roger Clemens	2.00
49	Darin Erstad	.50
50	Brady Anderson	.25
51	Jason Kendall	.25
52	John Valentin	.25
53	Ellis Burks	.25
54	Brian Hunter	.25
55	Paul O'Neill	.25
56	Ken Caminiti	.25
57	David Justice	.25
58	Eric Karros	.25
59	Pat Hentgen	.25
60	Greg Maddux	1.50
61	Craig Biggio	.25
62	Edgar Martinez	.25
63	Mike Mussina	.50
64	Larry Walker	.25
65	Tino Martinez	.25
66	Jim Thome	.60
67	Tom Glavine	.40
68	Raul Mondesi	.25
69	Marquis Grissom	.25
70	Randy Johnson	1.00
71	Steve Finley	.25
72	Jose Guillen	.25
73	Nomar Garciaparra	1.50
74	Wade Boggs	1.50
75	Bobby Higginson	.25
76	Robin Ventura	.25
77	Derek Jeter	3.00
78	Andruw Jones	1.00
79	Ray Lankford	.25
80	Vladimir Guerrero	1.00
81	Kenny Lofton	.25
82	Ivan Rodriguez	.75
83	Neifi Perez	.25
84	John Smoltz	.25
85	Tim Salmon	.25
86	Carlos Delgado	.50
87	Sammy Sosa	1.50
88	Jaret Wright	.25
89	Roberto Alomar	.40
90	Paul Molitor	1.00
91	Dean Palmer	.25
92	Barry Larkin	.25
93	Jason Giambi	.50
94	Curt Schilling	.40
95	Eric Young	.25
96	Denny Neagle	.25
97	Moises Alou	.25
98	Livan Hernandez	.25
99	Todd Hundley	.25
100	Andres Galarraga	.25
101	Travis Lee	.50
102	Lance Berkman	.25
103	Orlando Cabrera	.25
104	Mike Lowell **RC**	2.00
105	Ben Grieve	.25
106	Jae Weong Seo **RC**	.50
107	Richie Sexson	.25
108	Eli Marrero	.25
109	Aramis Ramirez	.25
110	Paul Konerko	.25
111	Carl Pavano	.25
112	Brad Fullmer	.25
113	Matt Clement	.25
114	Donzell McDonald	.25
115	Todd Helton	.25
116	Mike Caruso	.25
117	Donnie Sadler	.25
118	Bruce Chen	.25
119	Jarrod Washburn	.25
120	Adrian Beltre	.40
121	Ryan Jackson **RC**	.50
122	Kevin Millar	1.50
123	Corey Koskie **RC**	1.00
124	Dermal Brown	.25
125	Kerry Wood	.50
126	Juan Melo	.25
127	Ramon Hernandez	.25
128	Roy Halladay	.25
129	Ron Wright	.25
130	Darnell McDonald **RC**	.50
131	Odalis Perez **RC**	.75
132	Alex Cora **RC**	.25
133	Justin Towle	.25
134	Juan Encarnacion	.25
135	Brian Rose	.25
136	Russell Branyan	.25
137	Cesar King **RC**	.25
138	Ruben Rivera	.25
139	Ricky Ledee	.25
140	Vernon Wells	.25
141	Luis Rivas **RC**	.25
142	Brent Butler	.25
143	Karim Garcia	.25
144	George Lombard	.25
145	Masato Yoshii **RC**	.50
146	Braden Looper	.25
147	Alex Sanchez	.25
148	Kris Benson	.25
149	Mark Kotsay	.25
150	Richard Hidalgo	.25
151	Scott Elarton	.25
152	Ryan Minor **RC**	.25
153	Troy Glaus **RC**	5.00
154	Carlos Lee **RC**	2.00
155	Michael Coleman	.25
156	Jason Grilli **RC**	.50
157	Julio Ramirez **RC**	.50
158	Randy Wolf **RC**	.75
159	Ryan Brannan	.25
160	Edgar Clemente **RC**	.50
161	Miguel Tejada	.40
162	Chad Hermansen	.25
163	Ryan Anderson **RC**	.50
164	Ben Petrick	.25
165	Alex Gonzalez	.25
166	Ben Davis	.25
167	John Patterson	.25
168	Cliff Politte	.25
169	Randall Simon	.25
170	Javier Vazquez	.25
171	Kevin Witt	.25
172	Geoff Jenkins	.25
173	David Ortiz	.60
174	Derrick Gibson	.25
175	Abraham Nunez	.25
176	A.J. Hinch	.25
177	Ruben Mateo **RC**	.75
178	Magglio Ordonez **RC**	2.50
179	Todd Dunwoody	.25
180	Daryle Ward	.25
181	Mike Kinkade **RC**	.50
182	Willie Martinez	.25
183	Orlando Hernandez **RC**	1.50
184	Eric Milton	.25
185	Eric Chavez	.50
186	Damian Jackson	.25
187	Jim Parque **RC**	.50
188	Dan Reichert **RC**	.25
189	Mike Drumright	.25
190	Todd Walker	.25
191	Shane Monahan	.25
192	Derrek Lee	.65
193	Jeremy Giambi **RC**	.50
194	Dan McKinley **RC**	.25
195	Tony Armas **RC**	.75
196	Matt Anderson **RC**	.50
197	Jim Chamblee **RC**	.25
198	Francisco Cordero **RC**	.25
199	Calvin Pickering	.25
200	Reggie Taylor	.25

1998 Bowman's Best Refractors

Refractor versions for all 200 cards in Bowman's Best were available. Fronts featured a reflective finish, while backs were numbered to 400 and inserted one per 20 packs.

	NM/M
Common Player:	4.00
Stars:	8X
Production 400 Sets	

1998 Bowman's Best Atomic Refractors

Atomic Refractor versions were available for all 200 cards in Bowman's Best. The cards were printed in a prismatic foil on the

front, sequentially numbered to 100 sets on the back and inserted one per 82 packs.

	NM/M
Common Player:	6.00
Stars:	12X
Production 100 Sets	

Autographs

This 10-card set offers autographs from five prospects and five veteran stars. Each card has on front the Topps "Certified Autograph Issue" logo for authentication.

		NM/M
Complete Set (10):		65.00
Common Player:		5.00
Inserted 1:180		
Refractors:		1.5X
Inserted 1:2,158		
Atomics:		2X
Inserted 1:6,437		
5	Chipper Jones	35.00
10	Chuck Knoblauch	5.00
15	Tony Clark	5.00
20	Albert Belle	8.00
25	Jose Cruz Jr.	5.00
105	Ben Grieve	5.00
110	Paul Konerko	15.00
115	Todd Helton	15.00
120	Adrian Beltre	15.00
125	Kerry Wood	20.00

Mirror Image Fusion

This 20-card die-cut insert features a veteran star on one side and a young player at the same position on the other. Regular versions are seeded one per 12 packs, while Refractors are found 1:809 packs and numbered within an edition of 100, and Atomic Refractors are a 1:3,237 find numbered to 25. All have a "MI" prefix to the card number.

		NM/M
Complete Set (20):		35.00
Common Player (1:12):		.50
Refractor (1:809):		6X
Atomic Refractor (1:3,237):		12X
1	Frank Thomas, David Ortiz	2.00
2	Chuck Knoblauch, Enrique Wilson	.50
3	Nomar Garciaparra, Miguel Tejada	2.50
4	Alex Rodriguez, Mike Caruso	3.50
5	Cal Ripken Jr., Ryan Minor	4.50
6	Ken Griffey Jr., Ben Grieve	3.00
7	Juan Gonzalez, Juan Encarnacion	.75
8	Jose Cruz Jr., Ruben Mateo	.50
9	Randy Johnson, Ryan Anderson	1.50
10	Ivan Rodriguez, A.J. Hinch	1.25
11	Jeff Bagwell, Paul Konerko	1.50
12	Mark McGwire, Travis Lee	3.50
13	Craig Biggio, Chad Hermanson	.50
14	Mark Grudzielanek, Alex Gonzalez	.50
15	Chipper Jones, Adrian Beltre	2.50
16	Larry Walker, Mark Kotsay	.50
17	Tony Gwynn, Preston Wilson	2.50
18	Barry Bonds, Richard Hidalgo	4.50
19	Greg Maddux, Kerry Wood	2.50
20	Mike Piazza, Ben Petrick	3.00

Performers

Performers are 10 players who had the best minor league seasons in 1997. Regular versions were in-

RYAN MINOR

serted one per six packs, while Refractors are seeded 1:809 and serially numbered to 200, and Atomic Refractors are 1:3,237 and numbered to 50 sets. All versions have card numbers with a "BP" prefix.

		NM/M
Complete Set (10):		4.00
Common Player:		.35
Refractor (1:309):		3X
Atomic Refractor (1:3,237):		5X
1	Ben Grieve	.35
2	Travis Lee	.35
3	Ryan Minor	.35
4	Todd Helton	2.00
5	Brad Fullmer	.35
6	Paul Konerko	.50
7	Adrian Beltre	.75
8	Richie Sexson	.35
9	Aramis Ramirez	.35
10	Russell Branyan	.35

1999 Bowman Pre-Production

DERNELL STENSON

Bowman's 1999 issue was introduced with this group of sample cards. Format is nearly identical to the issued cards, except for the use of a "PP" prefix to the card number on back.

		NM/M
Complete Set (6):		4.00
Common Player:		.60
1	Andres Galarraga	.60
2	Raul Mondesi	.60
3	Vinny Castilla	.60
4	Corey Koskie	2.00
5	Octavio Dotel	.60
6	Dernell Stenson	.60

1999 Bowman

ALEX RAMIREZ

The set was issued in two 220-card series, each comprised of 70 veterans and 150 rookies and prospects. Rookie/prospect cards have blue metallic foil highlights; veteran cards are highlighted with red foil. On each card is the player's facsimile autograph, reproduced from their initial Topps contract.

	NM/M
Complete Set (440):	60.00
Complete Series 1 (220):	30.00
Complete Series 2 (220):	35.00
Common Player:	.10

Series 1 Pack (10):	2.00	
Series 1 Box (24):	35.00	
Series 2 Pack (10):	3.00	
Series 2 Box (24):	50.00	

No.	Player	Price
1	Ben Grieve	.10
2	Kerry Wood	.40
3	Ruben Rivera	.10
4	Sandy Alomar	.10
5	Cal Ripken Jr.	2.00
6	Mark McGwire	1.75
7	Vladimir Guerrero	.75
8	Moises Alou	.10
9	Jim Edmonds	.10
10	Greg Maddux	1.00
11	Gary Sheffield	.40
12	John Valentin	.10
13	Chuck Knoblauch	.10
14	Tony Clark	.10
15	Rusty Greer	.10
16	Al Leiter	.10
17	Travis Lee	.10
18	Jose Cruz Jr.	.10
19	Pedro Martinez	.75
20	Paul O'Neill	.10
21	Todd Walker	.10
22	Vinny Castilla	.10
23	Barry Larkin	.10
24	Curt Schilling	.40
25	Jason Kendall	.10
26	Scott Erickson	.10
27	Andres Galarraga	.10
28	Jeff Shaw	.10
29	John Olerud	.10
30	Orlando Hernandez	.10
31	Larry Walker	.10
32	Andruw Jones	.75
33	Jeff Cirillo	.10
34	Barry Bonds	2.00
35	Manny Ramirez	.75
36	Mark Kotsay	.10
37	Ivan Rodriguez	.60
38	Jeff King	.10
39	Brian Hunter	.10
40	Ray Durham	.10
41	Bernie Williams	.10
42	Darin Erstad	.30
43	Chipper Jones	1.00
44	Pat Hentgen	.10
45	Eric Young	.10
46	Jaret Wright	.10
47	Juan Guzman	.10
48	Jorge Posada	.10
49	Bobby Higginson	.10
50	Jose Guillen	.10
51	Trevor Hoffman	.10
52	Ken Griffey Jr.	1.50
53	David Justice	.10
54	Matt Williams	.10
55	Eric Karros	.10
56	Derek Bell	.10
57	Ray Lankford	.10
58	Mariano Rivera	.25
59	Brett Tomko	.10
60	Mike Mussina	.40
61	Kenny Lofton	.10
62	Chuck Finley	.10
63	Alex Gonzalez	.10
64	Mark Grace	.10
65	Raul Mondesi	.10
66	David Cone	.10
67	Brad Fullmer	.10
68	Andy Benes	.10
69	John Smoltz	.10
70	Shane Reynolds	.10
71	Bruce Chen	.10
72	Adam Kennedy	.10
73	Jack Cust	.10
74	Matt Clement	.10
75	Derrick Gibson	.10
76	Darnell McDonald	.10
77	Adam Everett RC	.50
78	Ricardo Aramboles	.10
79	Mark Quinn	.25
80	Jason Rakers	.10
81	Seth Etherton RC	.35
82	Jeff Urban RC	.25
83	Manny Aybar	.10
84	Mike Nannini RC	.25
85	Onan Masaoka	.10
86	Rod Barajas	.10
87	Mike Frank	.10
88	Scott Randall	.10
89	Justin Bowles RC	.25
90	Chris Haas	.10
91	Arturo McDowell RC	.25
92	Matt Belisle RC	.35
93	Scott Elarton	.10
94	Vernon Wells	.10
95	Pat Cline	.10
96	Ryan Anderson	.10
97	Kevin Barker	.10
98	Ruben Mateo	.10
99	Robert Fick	.10
100	Corey Koskie	.10
101	Ricky Ledee	.10
102	Rick Elder RC	.25
103	Jack Cressend RC	.25
104	Joe Lawrence	.10
105	Mike Lincoln	.10
106	Kit Pellow RC	.35
107	Matt Burch RC	.25
108	Brent Butler	.10
109	Jason Dewey	.10
110	Cesar King	.10
111	Julio Ramirez	.10
112	Jake Westbrook	.10
113	Eric Valent RC	.35
114	Roosevelt Brown RC	.35
115	Choo Freeman RC	.50
116	Juan Melo	.10
117	Jason Grilli	.10
118	Jared Sandberg RC	.10
119	Glenn Davis	.10
120	David Riske RC	.25
121	Jacque Jones	.10
122	Corey Lee	.10
123	Michael Barrett	.10
124	Lariel Gonzalez	.10
125	Mitch Meluskey	.10
126	Freddy Garcia	.10
127	Tony Torcato RC	.25
128	Jeff Liefer	.10
129	Ntema Ndungidi	.10
130	Andy Brown RC	.35
131	Ryan Mills RC	.25
132	Andy Abad RC	.25
133	Carlos Febles	.10
134	Jason Tyner RC	.25
135	Mark Osborne	.10
136	Phil Norton RC	.25
137	Nathan Haynes	.10
138	Roy Halladay	.10
139	Juan Encarnacion	.10
140	Brad Penny	.10
141	Grant Roberts	.10
142	Aramis Ramirez	.10
143	Cristian Guzman	.10
144	Mamon Tucker RC	.25
145	Ryan Bradley	.10
146	Brian Simmons	.10
147	Dan Reichert	.10
148	Russ Branyon	.10
149	Victor Valencia RC	.25
150	Scott Schoeneweis	.10
151	Sean Spencer RC	.25
152	Odalis Perez	.10
153	Joe Fontenot	.10
154	Milton Bradley	.10
155	Josh McKinley RC	.25
156	Terrence Long	.10
157	Danny Klassen	.10
158	Paul Hoover RC	.25
159	Ron Belliard	.10
160	Armando Rios	.10
161	Ramon Hernandez	.10
162	Jason Conti	.10
163	Chad Hermansen	.10
164	Jason Standridge	.10
165	Jason Dellaero	.10
166	John Curtice	.10
167	Clayton Andrews RC	.25
168	Jeremy Giambi	.10
169	Alex Ramirez	.10
170	Gabe Molina RC	.10
171	Mario Encarnacion RC	.25
172	Mike Zywica RC	.25
173	Chip Ambres RC	.25
174	Trot Nixon	.10
175	Pat Burrell RC	2.00
176	Jeff Yoder	.10
177	Chris Jones RC	.25
178	Kevin Witt	.10
179	Keith Luuloa RC	.25
180	Billy Koch	.10
181	Damaso Marte RC	.25
182	Ryan Glynn RC	.25
183	Calvin Pickering	.10
184	Michael Cuddyer	.10
185	Nick Johnson	.75
186	Doug Mientkiewicz RC	1.00
187	Nate Cornejo RC	.35
188	Octavio Dotel	.10
189	Wes Helms	.10
190	Nelson Lara	.10
191	Chuck Abbott RC	.25
192	Tony Armas Jr.	.10
193	Gil Meche	.10
194	Ben Petrick	.10
195	Chris George RC	.25
196	Scott Hunter RC	.25
197	Ryan Brannan	.10
198	Amaury Garcia RC	.25
199	Chris Gissell	.10
200	Austin Kearns RC	1.50
201	Marcus Knox	.10
202	Wade Miller	.10
203	Scott Williamson	.10
204	Chris Enochs	.10
205	Peter Seguignol	.10
206	Marlon Anderson	.10
207	Todd Sears RC	.25
208	Nate Bump RC	.25
209	J.M. Gold RC	.25
210	Matt LeCroy	.10
211	Alex Hernandez	.10
212	Luis Rivera	.10
213	Troy Cameron	.10
214	Alex Escobar RC	.50
215	Jason LaRue	.10
216	Kyle Peterson	.10
217	Brett Butler	.10
218	Dernell Stenson	.10
219	Adrian Beltre	.10
220	Daryle Ward	.10
----	Series 1 Checklist Folder	
221	Jim Thome	.60
222	Cliff Floyd	.10
223	Rickey Henderson	.75
224	Garret Anderson	.10
225	Ken Caminiti	.10
226	Bret Boone	.10
227	Jeromy Burnitz	.10
228	Steve Finley	.10
229	Miguel Tejada	.40
230	Greg Vaughn	.10
231	Jose Offerman	.10
232	Andy Ashby	.10
233	Albert Belle	.10
234	Fernando Tatis	.10
235	Todd Helton	.65
236	Sean Casey	.25
237	Brian Giles	.10
238	Andy Pettitte	.25
239	Fred McGriff	.10
240	Roberto Alomar	.30
241	Edgar Martinez	.10
242	Lee Stevens	.10
243	Shawn Green	.25
244	Ryan Klesko	.10
245	Sammy Sosa	1.00
246	Todd Hundley	.10
247	Shannon Stewart	.10
248	Randy Johnson	.75
249	Rondell White	.10
250	Mike Piazza	1.50
251	Craig Biggio	.25
252	David Wells	.10
253	Brian Jordan	.10
254	Edgar Renteria	.10
255	Bartolo Colon	.10
256	Frank Thomas	.75
257	Will Clark	.10
258	Dean Palmer	.10
259	Dmitri Young	.10
260	Scott Rolen	.60
261	Jeff Kent	.10
262	Dante Bichette	.10
263	Nomar Garciaparra	1.00
264	Tony Gwynn	1.00
265	Alex Rodriguez	1.75
266	Jose Canseco	.45
267	Jason Giambi	.40
268	Jeff Bagwell	.75
269	Carlos Delgado	.40
270	Tom Glavine	.40
271	Eric Davis	.10
272	Edgardo Alfonzo	.10
273	Tim Salmon	.10
274	Johnny Damon	.35
275	Rafael Palmeiro	.65
276	Denny Neagle	.10
277	Neifi Perez	.10
278	Roger Clemens	1.25
279	Brant Brown	.10
280	Kevin Brown	.10
281	Jay Bell	.10
282	Jay Buhner	.10
283	Matt Lawton	.10
284	Robin Ventura	.10
285	Juan Gonzalez	.35
286	Mo Vaughn	.10
287	Kevin Millwood	.10
288	Tino Martinez	.10
289	Justin Thompson	.10
290	Derek Jeter	2.00
291	Ben Davis	.10
292	Mike Lowell	.10
293	Joe Crede RC	.75
294	Micah Bowie RC	.25
295	Lance Berkman	.10
296	Jason Marquis	.10
297	Chad Green	.10
298	Dee Brown	.10
299	Jerry Hairston Jr.	.10
300	Gabe Kapler	.10
301	Brent Stentz RC	.25
302	Scott Mullen RC	.10
303	Brandon Reed	.10
304	Shea Hillenbrand RC	.50
305	J.D. Closser RC	.25
306	Gary Matthews Jr.	.10
307	Toby Hall RC	.25
308	Jason Phillips RC	.25
309	Jose Macias RC	.25
310	Jung Bong RC	.25
311	Ramon Soler RC	.25
312	Kelly Dransfeldt RC	.25
313	Carlos Hernandez RC	.25
314	Kevin Haverbusch	.10
315	Aaron Myette RC	.25
316	Chad Harville RC	.35
317	Kyle Farnsworth RC	.50
318	Travis Dawkins RC	.50
319	Willie Martinez	.10
320	Carlos Lee	.10
321	Carlos Pena RC	1.00
322	Peter Bergeron RC	.25
323	A.J. Burnett RC	.50
324	Bucky Jacobsen RC	.25
325	Mo Bruce RC	.25
326	Reggie Taylor	.10
327	Jackie Rexrode	.10
328	Alvin Morrow RC	.25
329	Carlos Beltran	.40
330	Eric Chavez	.10
331	John Patterson	.10
332	Jayson Werth	.10
333	Richie Sexson	.10
334	Randy Wolf	.10
335	Eli Marrero	.10
336	Paul LoDuca	.10
337	J.D. Smart	.10
338	Ryan Minor	.10
339	Kris Benson	.10
340	George Lombard	.10
341	Troy Glaus	.10
342	Eddie Yarnell	.10
343	Kip Wells RC	.25
344	C.C. Sabathia RC	2.00
345	Sean Burroughs RC	.75
346	Felipe Lopez RC	1.50
347	Ryan Rupe RC	.25
348	Orber Moreno RC	.25
349	Rafael Roque RC	.10
350	Alfonso Soriano RC	5.00
351	Pablo Ozuna	.10
352	Corey Patterson RC	1.00
353	Braden Looper	.10
354	Robbie Bell	.10
355	Mark Mulder RC	2.00
356	Angel Pena	.10
357	Kevin McGlinchy	.10
358	Michael Restovich RC	.35
359	Eric DuBose	.10
360	Geoff Jenkins	.10
361	Mark Harriger RC	.25
362	Junior Herndon RC	.25
363	Tim Raines Jr. RC	.25
364	Rafael Furcal RC	.75
365	Marcus Giles RC	1.00
366	Ted Lilly	.10
367	Jorge Toca RC	.25
368	David Kelton RC	.35
369	Adam Dunn RC	5.00
370	Guillermo Mota RC	.35
371	Brett Laxton RC	.25
372	Travis Harper RC	.25
373	Tom Davey RC	.25
374	Darren Blakely RC	.25
375	Tim Hudson RC	3.00
376	Jason Romano	.10
377	Dan Reichert	.10
378	Julio Lugo RC	.75
379	Jose Garcia RC	.25
380	Erubiel Durazo RC	.25
381	Jose Jimenez	.10
382	Chris Fussell	.10
383	Steve Lomasney	.10
384	Juan Pena RC	.25
385	Allen Levrault RC	.25
386	Juan Rivera RC	.25
387	Steve Colyer RC	.25
388	Joe Nathan RC	.25
389	Ron Walker RC	.25
390	Nick Bierbrodt	.10
391	Luke Prokopec RC	.25
392	Dave Roberts RC	.40
393	Mike Darr	.10
394	Abraham Nunez RC	.35
395	Giuseppe Chiaramonte RC	.25
396	Jermaine Van Buren RC	.25
397	Mike Kusiewicz	.10
398	Matt Wise RC	.25
399	Joe McEwing RC	.40
400	Matt Holliday RC	5.00
401	Willi Mo Pena RC	1.50
402	Ruben Quevedo RC	.25
403	Rob Ryan RC	.25
404	Freddy Garcia RC	1.00
405	Kevin Eberwein RC	.25
406	Jesus Colome RC	.25
407	Chris Singleton RC	.25
408	Bubba Crosby RC	.50
409	Jesus Cordero RC	.25
410	Donny Leon	.10
411	Goefrey Tomlinson RC	.25
412	Jeff Winchester RC	.25
413	Adam Piatt RC	.50
414	Robert Stratton	.10
415	T.J. Tucker	.10
416	Ryan Langerhans RC	.25
417	Anthony Shumaker RC	.25
418	Matt Miller RC	.25
419	Doug Clark RC	.25
420	Kory DeHaan RC	.25
421	David Eckstein RC	.75
422	Brian Cooper RC	.25
423	Brady Clark RC	.25
424	Chris Magruder RC	.25
425	Bobby Seay RC	.25
426	Aubrey Huff RC	1.00
427	Mike Jerzembeck	.10
428	Matt Blank RC	.25
429	Benny Agbayani RC	.25
430	Kevin Beirne RC	.25
431	Josh Hamilton RC	6.00
432	Josh Girdley RC	.25
433	Kyle Snyder RC	.25
434	Mike Paradis RC	.25
435	Jason Jennings RC	.25
436	David Walling RC	.25
437	Omar Ortiz RC	.25
438	Jay Gehrke RC	.25
439	Casey Burns RC	.25
440	Carl Crawford RC	2.50

an edition of 99, designate these parallels. Stated odds of finding the Gold cards were one per 111 packs of Series 1, and 1:59 in Series 2.

	NM/M
Common Player:	3.00
Gold Stars:	10X

International

International parallels are a one-per-pack insert. Fronts are printed in metallic silver on which the photo's background has been replaced with a scenic picture supposed to be indicative of the player's native land. That location is spelled out at the lower-left corner of the photo. Backs of the Internationals are printed in the player's native language.

	NM/M
Common Player:	.25
Int'l Stars:	1.5X

Autographs

Autographs were randomly seeded in Series 1 and 2 packs, with each card bearing a Topps Certified Autograph seal on the front and numbered with a "BA" prefix on back. Levels of scarcity are color coded by the metallic-foil highlights on front: Golds are the most difficult to find at 1:1,941 Series 1 packs and 1:1,024 Series 2. Silvers are seeded 1:485 in Series 1, 1:256 Series 2. Blues are found at an average rate of 1:162 in first series and 1:85 in second series.

	NM/M
Common Player:	3.00
Blues inserted 1:162 or 1:85	
Silvers inserted 1:485 or 1:256	
Golds inserted 1:1,954 or 1:1,024	

No.	Player	Price
1	Ruben Mateo/B	5.00
2	Troy Glaus/G	40.00
3	Ben Davis/B	8.00
4	Jayson Werth/B	5.00
5	Jerry Hairston Jr./B	6.00
6	Darnell McDonald/B	4.00
7	Calvin Pickering/S	8.00
8	Ryan Minor/B	5.00
9	Alex Escobar/B	6.00
10	Grant Roberts/B	5.00
11	Carlos Guillen/B	10.00
12	Ryan Anderson/B	6.00
13	Gil Meche/S	5.00
14	Russell Branyan/S	5.00
15	Alex Ramirez/S	5.00
16	Jason Rakers/S	5.00
17	Eddie Yarnell/B	5.00
18	Freddy Garcia/S	15.00
19	Jason Conti/B	3.00
20	Corey Koskie/B	5.00
21	Roosevelt Brown/B	5.00
22	Willie Martinez/B	3.00
23	Mike Jerzembeck/S	3.00
24	Lariel Gonzalez/B	3.00
25	Fernando Seguignol/B	3.00
26	Robert Fick/S	5.00
27	J.D. Smart/B	3.00
28	Ryan Mills/B	3.00
29	Chad Hermansen/G	6.00
30	Jason Grilli/B	5.00
31	Michael Cuddyer/S	5.00
32	Jacque Jones/S	10.00
33	Reggie Taylor/B	3.00
34	Richie Sexson/B	15.00
35	Michael Barrett/B	8.00
36	Paul LoDuca/B	8.00
37	Adrian Beltre/G	30.00
38	Peter Bergeron/B	4.00
39	Joe Fontenot/B	3.00
40	Randy Wolf/B	6.00
41	Nick Johnson/B	12.00
42	Ryan Bradley/B	4.00
43	Mike Lowell/S	15.00
44	Ricky Ledee/B	5.00
45	Mike Lincoln/S	4.00
46	Jeremy Giambi/B	5.00
47	Dermal Brown/S	3.00
48	Derrick Gibson/S	3.00
49	Scott Randall/B	5.00
50	Ben Petrick/S	5.00
51	Jason LaRue/B	3.00
52	Cole Liniak/B	3.00
53	John Curtice/B	3.00
54	Jackie Rexrode/B	3.00
55	John Patterson/B	4.00
56	Brad Penny/S	6.00
57	Jared Sandberg/B	6.00
58	Kerry Wood/G	25.00
59	Eli Marrero/B	5.00
60	Jason Marquis/B	8.00
61	George Lombard/S	5.00
62	Bruce Chen/S	3.00
63	Kevin Witt/S	4.00
64	Vernon Wells/B	15.00
65	Billy Koch/B	3.00
66	Roy Halladay/B	20.00
67	Nathan Haynes/B	3.00
68	Ben Grieve/G	8.00
69	Eric Chavez/G	10.00
70	Lance Berkman/B	50.00

Gold

Gold, rather than black, ink for the facsimile autograph, Bowman logo and player name on front, and a serial number on back from within

1999 Bowman Early Risers

This insert set features 11 current baseball superstars who have already won a Rookie of the Year award and who continue to excel. Cards have an "ER" prefix to the number on back.

	NM/M
Complete Set (11):	8.00
Common Player:	.25
Inserted 1:12	

No.	Player	Price
1	Mike Piazza	1.00
2	Cal Ripken Jr.	2.00
3	Jeff Bagwell	.50
4	Ben Grieve	.25
5	Kerry Wood	.40
6	Mark McGwire	1.50
7	Nomar Garciaparra	.75
8	Derek Jeter	.50
9	Scott Rolen	.50
10	Jose Canseco	.45
11	Raul Mondesi	.25

Late Bloomers

This 10-card set features late-round picks from previous drafts who have emerged as bona fide stars. These inserts are numbered with an "LB" prefix.

	NM/M
Complete Set (10):	4.00
Common Player:	.25
Inserted 1:12	

LB1	Mike Piazza	2.00
LB2	Jim Thome	.75
LB3	Larry Walker	.25
LB4	Vinny Castilla	.25
LB5	Andy Pettitte	.50
LB6	Jim Edmonds	.25
LB7	Kenny Lofton	.25
LB8	John Smoltz	.25
LB9	Mark Grace	.25
LB10	Trevor Hoffman	.25

Scout's Choice

Scout's Choice inserts were randomly inserted in Series 1 packs and feature a borderless, double-etched design. The 21-card set focuses on prospects who have potential to win a future Rookie of the Year award.

		NM/M
Complete Set (21):		12.00
Common Player:		.40
Inserted 1:12		
SC1	Ruben Mateo	.40
SC2	Ryan Anderson	.40
SC3	Pat Burrell	3.00
SC4	Troy Glaus	4.00
SC5	Eric Chavez	1.00
SC6	Adrian Beltre	.40
SC7	Bruce Chen	.40
SC8	Carlos Beltran	1.00
SC9	Alex Gonzalez	.40
SC10	Carlos Lee	.50
SC11	George Lombard	.40
SC12	Matt Clement	.40
SC13	Calvin Pickering	.40
SC14	Marlon Anderson	.40
SC15	Chad Hermansen	.40
SC16	Russell Branyan	.40
SC17	Jeremy Giambi	.40
SC18	Ricky Ledee	.40
SC19	John Patterson	.40
SC20	Roy Halladay	.75
SC21	Michael Barrett	.40

2000 Rookie of the Year

Randomly inserted in Series 2 packs, these cards have a borderless, double-etched foil design. The 10-card set focuses on players that have potential to win the 2000 Rookie of the Year award.

		NM/M
Complete Set (10):		7.00
Common Player:		.50
Inserted 1:12		
1	Ryan Anderson	.50
2	Pat Burrell	2.50
3	A.J. Burnett	.50
4	Ruben Mateo	.50
5	Alex Escobar	.50
6	Pablo Ozuna	.50
7	Mark Mulder	1.00
8	Corey Patterson	.50
9	George Lombard	.50
10	Nick Johnson	.50

1999 Bowman Chrome

Bowman Chrome was released in two 220-card series as an upscale chromium parallel version of Bowman Baseball. Like Bowman, each series has 150 prospect cards with

JUAN GONZALEZ

blue foil, while 70 veteran cards have red foil. Packs contain four cards with an original SRP of $3.

		NM/M
Complete Set (440):		175.00
Complete Series 1 (220):		65.00
Complete Series 2 (220):		125.00
Common Player:		.25
Series 1 Pack (4):		3.00
Series 1 Wax Box (24):		50.00
Series 2 Pack (4):		5.00
Series 2 Wax Box (24):		100.00
1	Ben Grieve	.25
2	Kerry Wood	.45
3	Ruben Rivera	.25
4	Sandy Alomar	.25
5	Cal Ripken Jr.	3.00
6	Mark McGwire	1.50
7	Vladimir Guerrero	1.00
8	Moises Alou	.25
9	Jim Edmonds	.25
10	Greg Maddux	1.50
11	Gary Sheffield	.50
12	John Valentin	.25
13	Chuck Knoblauch	.25
14	Tony Clark	.25
15	Rusty Greer	.25
16	Al Leiter	.25
17	Travis Lee	.25
18	Jose Cruz Jr.	.25
19	Pedro Martinez	1.00
20	Paul O'Neill	.25
21	Todd Walker	.25
22	Vinny Castilla	.25
23	Barry Larkin	.25
24	Curt Schilling	.40
25	Jason Kendall	.25
26	Scott Erickson	.25
27	Andres Galarraga	.25
28	Jeff Shaw	.25
29	John Olerud	.25
30	Orlando Hernandez	.40
31	Larry Walker	.40
32	Andruw Jones	.40
33	Jeff Cirillo	.25
34	Barry Bonds	3.00
35	Manny Ramirez	1.00
36	Mark Kotsay	.25
37	Ivan Rodriguez	.50
38	Jeff King	.25
39	Brian Hunter	.25
40	Ray Durham	.40
41	Bernie Williams	.25
42	Darin Erstad	.50
43	Chipper Jones	1.50
44	Pat Hentgen	.25
45	Eric Young	.25
46	Jaret Wright	.25
47	Juan Guzman	.25
48	Jorge Posada	.25
49	Bobby Higginson	.25
50	Jose Guillen	.25
51	Trevor Hoffman	.25
52	Ken Griffey Jr.	2.00
53	David Justice	.25
54	Matt Williams	.25
55	Eric Karros	.25
56	Derek Bell	.25
57	Ray Lankford	.25
58	Mariano Rivera	.40
59	Brett Tomko	.25
60	Mike Mussina	.50
61	Kenny Lofton	.25
62	Chuck Finley	.25
63	Alex Gonzalez	.25
64	Mark Grace	.25
65	Raul Mondesi	.25
66	David Cone	.25
67	Brad Fullmer	.25
68	Andy Benes	.25
69	John Smoltz	.25
70	Shane Reynolds	.25
71	Bruce Chen	.25
72	Adam Kennedy	.25
73	Jack Cust	.25
74	Matt Clement	.25
75	Derrick Gibson	.25
76	Darnell McDonald	.25
77	Adam Everett RC	.75
78	Ricardo Aramboles RC	.25
79	Mark Quinn RC	.50
80	Jason Rakers	.25
81	Seth Etherton RC	.50
82	Jeff Urban RC	.25
83	Manny Aybar	.25
84	Mike Nannini RC	.35
85	Onan Masaoka	.25
86	Rod Barajas	.25
87	Mike Frank	.25
88	Scott Randall	.25
89	Justin Bowles RC	.35
90	Chris Haas	.25
91	Arturo McDowell RC	.35
92	Matt Belisle RC	.50
93	Scott Elarton	.25
94	Vernon Wells	.25
95	Pat Cline	.25
96	Ryan Anderson	.25
97	Kevin Barker	.25
98	Ruben Mateo	.25
99	Robert Fick	.25
100	Corey Koskie	.25
101	Ricky Ledee	.25
102	Rick Elder RC	.25
103	Jack Cressend RC	.35
104	Joe Lawrence	.25
105	Mike Lincoln	.25
106	Kit Pellow RC	.50
107	Matt Burch RC	.25
108	Brent Butler	.25
109	Jason Dewey	.25
110	Cesar King	.25
111	Julio Ramirez	.25
112	Jake Westbrook	.25
113	Eric Valent RC	1.00
114	Roosevelt Brown RC	.50
115	Choo Freeman RC	1.50
116	Juan Melo	.25
117	Jason Grilli	.25
118	Jared Sandberg	.25
119	Glenn Davis	.25
120	David Riske RC	.35
121	Jacque Jones	.25
122	Corey Lee	.25
123	Michael Barrett	.25
124	Lariel Gonzalez	.25
125	Mitch Meluskey	.25
126	Freddy Garcia RC	.35
127	Tony Torcato RC	.35
128	Jeff Liefer	.25
129	Ntema Ndungidi	.25
130	Andy Brown RC	.50
131	Ryan Mills RC	.35
132	Andy Abad RC	.50
133	Carlos Febles	.25
134	Jason Tyner RC	.50
135	Mark Osborne	.25
136	Phil Norton RC	.35
137	Nathan Haynes	.25
138	Roy Halladay	.25
139	Juan Encarnacion	.25
140	Brad Penny	.25
141	Grant Roberts	.25
142	Aramis Ramirez	.25
143	Cristian Guzman	.25
144	Mamon Tucker RC	.35
145	Ryan Bradley	.25
146	Brian Simmons	.25
147	Dan Reichert	.25
148	Russ Branyon	.25
149	Victor Valencia RC	.35
150	Scott Schoeneweis	.25
151	Sean Spencer RC	.35
152	Odalis Perez	.25
153	Joe Fontenot	.25
154	Milton Bradley	.25
155	Josh McKinley RC	.35
156	Terrence Long	.25
157	Danny Klassen	.25
158	Paul Hoover RC	.35
159	Ron Belliard	.25
160	Armando Rios	.25
161	Ramon Hernandez	.25
162	Jason Conti	.25
163	Chad Hermansen	.25
164	Jason Standridge	.25
165	Jason Dellaero	.25
166	John Curtice	.25
167	Clayton Andrews RC	.35
168	Jeremy Giambi	.25
169	Alex Ramirez	.25
170	Gabe Molina RC	.35
171	Mario Encarnacion RC	.35
172	Mike Zywica RC	.35
173	Chip Ambres RC	.35
174	Trot Nixon	.25
175	Pat Burrell RC	10.00
176	Jeff Yoder	.25
177	Chris Jones RC	.25
178	Kevin Witt	.25
179	Keith Luuloa RC	.35
180	Billy Koch	.25
181	Damaso Marte RC	.35
182	Ryan Glynn RC	.35
183	Calvin Pickering	.25
184	Michael Cuddyer	.25
185	Nick Johnson RC	2.00
186	Doug Mientkiewicz RC	.35
187	Nate Cornejo RC	1.00
188	Octavio Dotel	.25
189	Wes Helms	.25
190	Nelson Lara	.25
191	Chuck Abbott RC	.35
192	Tony Armas Jr.	.25
193	Gil Meche	.25
194	Ben Petrick	.25
195	Chris George RC	.25
196	Scott Hunter RC	.25
197	Ryan Brannan	.25
198	Amaury Garcia RC	.35
199	Chris Gissell	.25
200	Austin Kearns RC	2.00
201	Alex Gonzalez	.25
202	Wade Miller	.25
203	Scott Williamson	.25
204	Chris Enochs	.25
205	Fernando Seguignol	.25
206	Marlon Anderson	.25
207	Todd Sears RC	.35
208	Nate Bump RC	.35
209	J.M. Gold RC	.50
210	Matt LeCroy RC	.35
211	Alex Hernandez	.25
212	Luis Rivera	.25
213	Troy Cameron	.25
214	Alex Escobar RC	1.00
215	Jason LaRue	.25
216	Kyle Peterson	.25
217	Brent Butler	.25
218	Dernell Stenson	.25
219	Adrian Beltre	.40
220	Daryle Ward	.25
221	Jim Thome	.50
222	Cliff Floyd	.25
223	Rickey Henderson	1.00
224	Garret Anderson	.25
225	Ken Caminiti	.25
226	Bret Boone	.25
227	Jeromy Burnitz	.25
228	Steve Finley	.25
229	Miguel Tejada	.40
230	Greg Vaughn	.25
231	Jose Offerman	.25
232	Andy Ashby	.25
233	Albert Belle	.25
234	Fernando Tatis	.25
235	Todd Helton	.25
236	Sean Casey	.40
237	Brian Giles	.25
238	Andy Pettitte	.40
239	Fred McGriff	.25
240	Roberto Alomar	.40
241	Edgar Martinez	.25
242	Lee Stevens	.25
243	Shawn Green	.40
244	Ryan Klesko	.25
245	Sammy Sosa	1.00
246	Todd Hundley	.25
247	Shannon Stewart	.25
248	Randy Johnson	1.00
249	Rondell White	.25
250	Mike Piazza	2.00
251	Craig Biggio	.25
252	David Wells	.25
253	Brian Jordan	.25
254	Edgar Renteria	.25
255	Bartolo Colon	.25
256	Frank Thomas	1.00
257	Will Clark	.25
258	Dean Palmer	.25
259	Dmitri Young	.25
260	Scott Rolen	.50
261	Jeff Kent	.25
262	Dante Bichette	.25
263	Nomar Garciaparra	.50
264	Tony Gwynn	1.00
265	Alex Rodriguez	.25
266	Jose Canseco	.50
267	Jason Giambi	.25
268	Jeff Bagwell	.50
269	Carlos Delgado	.25
270	Tom Glavine	.25
271	Eric Davis	.25
272	Edgardo Alfonzo	.25
273	Tim Salmon	.25
274	Johnny Damon	.25
275	Rafael Palmeiro	.50
276	Denny Neagle	.25
277	Neifi Perez	.25
278	Roger Clemens	1.50
279	Brant Brown	.25
280	Kevin Brown	.25
281	Jay Bell	.25
282	Jay Buhner	.25
283	Matt Lawton	.25
284	Robin Ventura	.25
285	Juan Gonzalez	.50
286	Mo Vaughn	.25
287	Kevin Millwood	.25
288	Tino Martinez	.25
289	Justin Thompson	.25
290	Derek Jeter	3.00
291	Ben Davis	.25
292	Mike Lowell	.25
293	Joe Crede	3.00
294	Micah Bowie RC	.50
295	Lance Berkman	.50
296	Jason Marquis	.25
297	Chad Green	.25
298	Dee Brown	.25
299	Jerry Hairston Jr.	.25
300	Gabe Kapler	.25
301	Brent Stentz RC	.35
302	Scott Mullen RC	.35
303	Brandon Reed	.25
304	Shea Hillenbrand RC	1.50
305	J.D. Closser RC	.35
306	Gary Matthews Jr.	.25
307	Toby Hall RC	.50
308	Jason Phillips RC	.35
309	Jose Macias RC	.35
310	Jung Bong RC	.35
311	Ramon Soler RC	.35
312	Kelly Dransfeldt RC	.50
313	Carlos Hernandez RC	.50
314	Kevin Haverbusch	.25
315	Aaron Myette RC	.35
316	Chad Harville RC	.35
317	Kyle Farnsworth RC	1.00
318	Travis Dawkins RC	.35
319	Willie Martinez	.25
320	Carlos Lee	.25
321	Carlos Pena RC	4.00
322	Peter Bergeron RC	.50
323	A.J. Burnett RC	4.00
324	Bucky Jacobsen RC	.50
325	Mo Bruce RC	.35
326	Reggie Taylor	.25
327	Jackie Rexrode	.25
328	Alvin Morrow RC	.35
329	Carlos Beltran	.50
330	Eric Chavez	.50
331	John Patterson	.25
332	Jayson Werth RC	.25
333	Richie Sexson	.25
334	Randy Wolf	.25
335	Eli Marrero	.25
336	Paul LoDuca	.25
337	J.D. Smart	.25
338	Ryan Minor	.25
339	Kris Benson	.25
340	George Lombard	.25
341	Troy Glaus	.50
342	Eddie Yarnell	.25
343	Kip Wells RC	1.00
344	C.C. Sabathia RC	8.00
345	Sean Burroughs RC	1.00
346	Felipe Lopez RC	4.00
347	Ryan Rupe RC	.50
348	Orber Moreno RC	.35
349	Rafael Roque RC	.35
350	Alfonso Soriano RC	20.00
351	Pablo Ozuna	.25
352	Corey Patterson RC	2.00
353	Braden Looper	.25
354	Robbie Bell	.25
355	Mark Mulder RC	2.00
356	Angel Pena	.25
357	Kevin McGlinchy RC	.25
358	Michael Restovich RC	1.00
359	Eric DuBose	.25
360	Geoff Jenkins	.25
361	Mark Harriger RC	.35
362	Junior Herndon RC	.35
363	Tim Raines Jr. RC	.35
364	Rafael Furcal RC	3.00
365	Marcus Giles RC	1.50
366	Ted Lilly	.25
367	Jorge Toca RC	.35
368	David Kelton RC	1.00
369	Adam Dunn RC	25.00
370	Guillermo Mota RC	.35
371	Brett Laxton RC	.35
372	Travis Harper RC	.35
373	Tom Davey RC	.35
374	Darren Blakely RC	.35
375	Tim Hudson RC	10.00
376	Jason Romano	.25
377	Dan Reichert	.25
378	Julio Lugo RC	.35
379	Jose Garcia RC	.35
380	Erubiel Durazo RC	1.00
381	Jose Jimenez	.25
382	Chris Fussell	.25
383	Steve Lomasney	.25
384	Juan Pena RC	.50
385	Allen Levrault RC	.35
386	Juan Rivera RC	.35
387	Steve Colyer RC	.35
388	Joe Nathan RC	1.50
389	Ron Walker RC	.35
390	Nick Bierbrodt	.25
391	Luke Prokopec RC	.35
392	Dave Roberts RC	.50
393	Mike Darr	.25
394	Abraham Nunez RC	1.00
395	Giuseppe Chiaramonte RC	.35
396	Jermaine Van Buren RC	.35
397	Mike Kusiewicz	.25
398	Matt Wise RC	.35
399	Joe McEwing RC	.50
400	Matt Holliday RC	20.00
401	Willi Mo Pena RC	4.00
402	Ruben Quevedo RC	.35
403	Rob Ryan RC	.35
404	Freddy Garcia RC	2.00
405	Kevin Eberwein RC	.35
406	Jesus Colome RC	.35
407	Chris Singleton RC	.35
408	Bubba Crosby RC	1.00
409	Jesus Cordero RC	.35
410	Donny Leon	.25
411	Goefrey Tomlinson RC	.25
412	Jeff Winchester RC	.35
413	Adam Piatt RC	.50
414	Robert Stratton	.25
415	T.J. Tucker	.25
416	Ryan Langerhans RC	1.00
417	Chris Wakeland RC	.35
418	Matt Miller RC	.35
419	Doug Clark RC	.35
420	Kory DeHaan RC	.35
421	David Eckstein RC	2.00
422	Brian Cooper RC	.25
423	Brady Clark RC	1.00
424	Chris Magruder RC	.35
425	Bobby Seay RC	.25
426	Aubrey Huff RC	5.00
427	Mike Jerzembeck	.25
428	Matt Blank RC	.35
429	Benny Agbayani RC	.35
430	Kevin Beirne RC	.35
431	Josh Hamilton RC	30.00
432	Josh Girdley RC	.35
433	Kyle Snyder RC	.35
434	Mike Paradis RC	.35
435	Jason Jennings RC	.75
436	David Walling RC	.35
437	Omar Ortiz RC	.35
438	Jay Gehrke RC	.35
439	Casey Burns RC	.35
440	Carl Crawford RC	12.00

Refractors

PAT BERGERON

Refractor versions of all Bowman Chrome base cards and inserts were also created. Base card Refractors are found at the average rate of one per 12 packs. Scout's Choice Refractors are a 1:48 find; International Refractors (serially numbered within an edition of 100 each) are 1:76 and Diamond Aces Refractors are 1:84.

	NM/M
Common Player:	1.00
Refractor Stars:	5X

Gold

JOSH McKINLEY

A gold, rather than black, facsimile signature differentiates this parallel from the base-card issue. At an average insertion rate of 1:12, the Series 1 Golds are twice as easy as the Series 2 (1:24). Conversely, a Refractor version which is limited to 25 serially numbered sets, is an easier pull in Series 2 (1:200) than in Series 1 (1:305).

	NM/M
Common Player, Series 1:	1.50
Common Player, Series 2:	2.00
Stars:	3X
Gold Refractors:	30X

International

BRUCE CHEN

Replacing the regular-card background with a scene from the player's native land gives this parallel issue an international flavor. For the geographically challenged, the place of birth is spelled out in the lower-left corner of the photo. In addition, the card backs are printed in the player's native language. Series 1 Internationals are found on the average of one per four packs, while the scarcer Series 2 Internationals are a 1:12 pick. Conversely, the Refractor version, individually numbered within an edition of 100 each is scarcer in Series 1 (1:76) than in Series 2 (1:50).

	NM/M
Common Player, Series 1:	.25
Common Player, Series 2:	.50
Stars:	1.5X
Common Refractor:	5.00
Refractors:	12X

Diamond Aces

This 18-card set features nine emerging stars along with nine proven veterans. The cards have a prismatic look with "Diamond Aces" across the top. They are inserted in Series 1 packs. A parallel Refractor version is also randomly inserted.

		NM/M
Complete Set (18):		24.00
Common Player:		.50
Inserted 1:21		
Refractors:		1.5X
Inserted 1:84		
DA1	Troy Glaus	1.50
DA2	Eric Chavez	.75
DA3	Fernando Seguignol	.50
DA4	Ryan Anderson	.50
DA5	Ruben Mateo	.50
DA6	Carlos Beltran	1.00
DA7	Adrian Beltre	.75
DA8	Bruce Chen	.50
DA9	Pat Burrell	2.00
DA10	Mike Piazza	3.00
DA11	Ken Griffey Jr.	3.00
DA12	Chipper Jones	2.00
DA13	Derek Jeter	4.00
DA14	Mark McGwire	3.50
DA15	Nomar Garciaparra	2.00
DA16	Sammy Sosa	2.00
DA17	Juan Gonzalez	.75
DA18	Alex Rodriguez	3.50

Early Impact

The checklist of this Series 2 insert mixes a dozen youngsters - labeled "Early Impact" on front - who are already making a mark in the majors with eight veteran stars, whose cards are labeled "Lasting Impact." A Refractor version is a parallel.

		NM/M
Complete Set (20):		35.00
Common Player:		.75
Inserted 1:15		
Refractor:		1.5X
Inserted 1:75		
1	Alfonso Soriano	2.00
2	Pat Burrell	2.00
3	Ruben Mateo	.75
4	A.J. Burnett	.75
5	Corey Patterson	1.00
6	Daryle Ward	.75
7	Eric Chavez	1.00
8	Troy Glaus	2.00
9	Sean Casey	1.00
10	Joe McEwing	.75
11	Gabe Kapler	.75
12	Michael Barrett	.75
13	Sammy Sosa	2.50
14	Alex Rodriguez	4.00
15	Mark McGwire	4.00
16	Derek Jeter	5.00
17	Nomar Garciaparra	4.00
18	Mike Piazza	3.00
19	Chipper Jones	2.50
20	Ken Griffey Jr.	3.00

Scout's Choice

This is a chromium parallel of the inserts found in Series 1 Bowman. The 21-card set showcases prospects that have potential to win a future Rookie of the Year award. Refractor parallels are also randomly inserted.

		NM/M
Complete Set (21):		20.00
Common Player:		.75
Inserted 1:12		
Refractors:		1.5X
Inserted 1:48		
SC1	Ruben Mateo	.75
SC2	Ryan Anderson	.75
SC3	Pat Burrell	3.00
SC4	Troy Glaus	4.00
SC5	Eric Chavez	2.00
SC6	Adrian Beltre	1.50
SC7	Bruce Chen	.75
SC8	Carlos Beltran	2.50
SC9	Alex Gonzalez	.75
SC10	Carlos Lee	1.00
SC11	George Lombard	.75
SC12	Matt Clement	.75
SC13	Calvin Pickering	.75
SC14	Marlon Anderson	.75
SC15	Chad Hermansen	.75
SC16	Russell Branyan	.75
SC17	Jeremy Giambi	.75
SC18	Ricky Ledee	.75
SC19	John Patterson	.75
SC20	Roy Halladay	1.00
SC21	Michael Barrett	.75

2000 Rookie of the Year

This is a chromium parallel of the inserts found in Series 2 Bowman. The 10-card set is inserted in Series 2 Chrome packs and showcases prospects that have potential to win the 2000 Rookie of the Year award. Refractor parallels are also randomly inserted.

		NM/M
Complete Set (10):		12.00
Common Player:		1.00
Inserted 1:20		
Refractors:		1.5-3X
Inserted 1:100		
1	Ryan Anderson	1.00
2	Pat Burrell	4.00
3	A.J. Burnett	1.00
4	Ruben Mateo	1.00
5	Alex Escobar	1.00
6	Pablo Ozuna	1.00
7	Mark Mulder	1.50
8	Corey Patterson	2.00
9	George Lombard	1.00
10	Nick Johnson	2.00

1999 Bowman's Best Pre-Production

These cards were issued to draw interest to the '99 Bowman's Best issue. The promos are virtually identical to the issued version of each player's card except for the card number which is preceeded by a "PP" prefix.

		NM/M
Complete Set (3):		3.00
Common Player:		2.00
PP1	Javy Lopez	1.00
PP2	Marlon Anderson	1.00
PP3	J.M. Gold	1.00

1999 Bowman's Best

Bowman's Best consists of 200 cards printed on thick 27-point stock. Within the base set are 85 veteran stars printed on gold foil, 15 Best Performers on bronze foil, 50 Prospects on silver foil and 50 rookies on blue foil. The rookies are seeded one per pack. There are also two parallel versions: Refractors and Atomic Refractors. Refractors are inserted 1:15 packs and are sequentially numbered to 400, while Atomic Refractors are found 1:62 packs and are sequentially numbered to 100.

		NM/M
Complete Set (200):		30.00
Common Player:		.25
Pack (6):		2.00
Wax Box (24):		40.00
1	Chipper Jones	1.50
2	Brian Jordan	.25
3	David Justice	.25
4	Jason Kendall	.25
5	Mo Vaughn	.25
6	Jim Edmonds	.25
7	Wade Boggs	1.50
8	Jeromy Burnitz	.25
9	Todd Hundley	.25
10	Rondell White	.25
11	Cliff Floyd	.25
12	Sean Casey	.40
13	Bernie Williams	.25
14	Dante Bichette	.25
15	Greg Vaughn	.25
16	Andres Galarraga	.25
17	Ray Durham	.25
18	Jim Thome	.60
19	Gary Sheffield	.45
20	Frank Thomas	1.00
21	Orlando Hernandez	.35
22	Ivan Rodriguez	.75
23	Jose Cruz Jr.	.25
24	Jason Giambi	.50
25	Craig Biggio	.25
26	Kerry Wood	.45
27	Manny Ramirez	1.00
28	Curt Schilling	.45
29	Mike Mussina	.45
30	Tim Salmon	.25
31	Mike Piazza	2.00
32	Roberto Alomar	.40
33	Larry Walker	.25
34	Barry Larkin	.25
35	Nomar Garciaparra	1.50
36	Paul O'Neill	.25
37	Todd Walker	.25
38	Eric Karros	.25
39	Brad Fullmer	.25
40	John Olerud	.25
41	Todd Helton	.75
42	Raul Mondesi	.25
43	Jose Canseco	.50
44	Matt Williams	.25
45	Ray Lankford	.25
46	Carlos Delgado	.50
47	Darin Erstad	.25
48	Vladimir Guerrero	1.00
49	Robin Ventura	.25
50	Alex Rodriguez	2.50
51	Vinny Castilla	.25
52	Tony Clark	.25
53	Pedro Martinez	1.00
54	Rafael Palmeiro	.65
55	Scott Rolen	.65
56	Tino Martinez	.25
57	Tony Gwynn	1.50
58	Barry Bonds	3.00
59	Kenny Lofton	.25
60	Javy Lopez	.25
61	Mark Grace	.25
62	Travis Lee	.25
63	Kevin Brown	.25
64	Al Leiter	.25
65	Albert Belle	.25
66	Sammy Sosa	1.50
67	Greg Maddux	1.50
68	Mark Kotsay	.25
69	Dmitri Young	.25
70	Mark McGwire	2.50
71	Juan Gonzalez	.50
72	Andruw Jones	1.00
73	Derek Jeter	3.00
74	Randy Johnson	1.00
75	Cal Ripken Jr.	3.00
76	Shawn Green	.25
77	Moises Alou	.25
78	Tom Glavine	.25
79	Sandy Alomar	.25
80	Ken Griffey Jr.	2.00
81	Ryan Klesko	.25
82	Jeff Bagwell	1.00
83	Ben Grieve	.25
84	John Smoltz	.25
85	Roger Clemens	1.75
86	Ken Griffey Jr.	1.00
87	Roger Clemens	.85
88	Derek Jeter	1.50

Refractors

Inserted at an average rate of about one per 15 packs, Best Refractor's are so marked on the back in the card-number box at upper-right. Also found on back is a serial numbered stamped in gold-foil from within an edition of 400.

89	Nomar Garciaparra	.75
90	Mark McGwire	1.25
91	Sammy Sosa	.75
92	Alex Rodriguez	1.25
93	Greg Maddux	.75
94	Vladimir Guerrero	1.00
95	Chipper Jones	.75
96	Kerry Wood	.30
97	Ben Grieve	.25
98	Tony Gwynn	.75
99	Juan Gonzalez	.30
100	Mike Piazza	1.00
101	Eric Chavez	.40
102	Billy Koch	.25
103	Dernell Stenson	.25
104	Marlon Anderson	.25
105	Ron Belliard	.25
106	Bruce Chen	.25
107	Carlos Beltran	.40
108	Chad Hermansen	.25
109	Ryan Anderson	.25
110	Michael Barrett	.25
111	Matt Clement	.25
112	Ben Davis	.25
113	Calvin Pickering	.25
114	Brad Penny	.25
115	Paul Konerko	.35
116	Alex Gonzalez	.25
117	George Lombard	.35
118	John Patterson	.25
119	Rob Bell	.25
120	Ruben Mateo	.35
121	Troy Glaus	.35
122	Ryan Bradley	.25
123	Carlos Lee	.35
124	Gabe Kapler	.35
125	Ramon Hernandez	.25
126	Carlos Febles	.25
127	Mitch Meluskey	.25
128	Michael Cuddyer	.25
129	Pablo Ozuna	.25
130	Jayson Werth	.25
131	Ricky Ledee	.25
132	Jeremy Giambi	.25
133	Danny Klassen	.25
134	Mark DeRosa	.25
135	Randy Wolf	.25
136	Roy Halladay	.35
137	Derrick Gibson	.25
138	Ben Petrick	.25
139	Warren Morris	.25
140	Lance Berkman	.25
141	Russell Branyan	.25
142	Adrian Beltre	.40
143	Juan Encarnacion	.25
144	Fernando Seguignol	.25
145	Corey Koskie	.25
146	Preston Wilson	.25
147	Homer Bush	.25
148	Daryle Ward	.25
149	Joe McEwing RC	.50
150	Peter Bergeron RC	.50
151	Pat Burrell RC	3.00
152	Choo Freeman RC	.50
153	Matt Belisle RC	.50
154	Carlos Pena RC	1.00
155	A.J. Burnett RC	.75
156	Doug Mientkiewicz RC	.75
157	Sean Burroughs RC	.50
158	Mike Zywica RC	.35
159	Corey Patterson RC	1.50
160	Austin Kearns RC	2.00
161	Chip Ambres RC	.35
162	Kelly Dransfeldt RC	.35
163	Mike Nannini RC	.35
164	Mark Mulder RC	2.00
165	Jason Tyner RC	.35
166	Bobby Seay RC	.50
167	Alex Escobar RC	.75
168	Nick Johnson RC	1.00
169	Alfonso Soriano RC	4.00
170	Clayton Andrews RC	.35
171	C.C. Sabathia RC	2.00
172	Matt Holliday RC	5.00
173	Brad Lidge RC	1.00
174	Kit Pellow RC	.50
175	J.M. Gold RC	.50
176	Roosevelt Brown RC	.50
177	Eric Valent RC	.50
178	Adam Everett RC	.75
179	Jorge Toca RC	.50
180	Matt Roney RC	.35
181	Andy Brown RC	.35
182	Phil Norton RC	.35
183	Mickey Lopez RC	.35
184	Chris George RC	.35
185	Arturo McDowell RC	.35
186	Jose Fernandez RC	.35
187	Seth Etherton RC	.50
188	Josh McKinley RC	.50
189	Nate Cornejo RC	.35
190	Giuseppe Chiaramonte RC	.35
191	Mamon Tucker RC	.35
192	Ryan Mills RC	.50
193	Chad Moeller RC	.35
194	Tony Torcato RC	.35
195	Jeff Winchester RC	.35
196	Rick Elder RC	.35
197	Matt Burch RC	.35
198	Jeff Urban RC	.35
199	Chris Jones RC	.35
200	Masao Kida RC	.50

	NM/M
Complete Set (200):	250.00
Common Player:	1.00
Stars:	6X
Production 400 Sets	

Atomic Refractors

The vibrant refractive background on front announces these parallels which are found on average of about once per 62 packs. Backs identify the variation in the card-number box at upper-right and with a serial number from within an edition of 100 per card.

	NM/M
Common Player:	3.00
Stars:	12X
Production 100 Sets	

Franchise Best

Ten league leaders are featured in this insert set on three different technologies: Mach I, Mach II and Mach III. Mach I features die-cut Serillusion stock and is numbered to 3,000. Mach II features die-cut refractive styrene stock, numbered to 1,000; and, Mach III features die-cut polycarbonate stock and is limited to 500 numbered sets. All cards number have an "FB" prefix.

		NM/M
Complete Set (10):		15.00
Common Player:		.75
Production 3,000 Sets		
Mach II (1,000):		1.5X
Mach III (500):		2.5X
1	Mark McGwire	2.50
2	Ken Griffey Jr.	1.50
3	Sammy Sosa	1.25
4	Alex Rodriguez	2.50
5	Derek Jeter	3.50
6	Mike Piazza	1.50
7	Frank Thomas	1.00
8	Chipper Jones	1.25
9	Juan Gonzalez	.75

Franchise Favorites

This six-card set features retired legends and current stars in

three versions. Version A features a current star, Version B features a retired player and Version C pairs the current star with the retired player. Cards have an "FR" prefix to the number on back.

		NM/M
Complete Set (6):		12.00
Common Player:		.50
Inserted 1:75		
1A	Derek Jeter	5.00
1B	Don Mattingly	2.00
1C	Derek Jeter, Don Mattingly	5.00
2A	Scott Rolen	.50
2B	Mike Schmidt	1.50
2C	Scott Rolen, Mike Schmidt	1.00

Franchise Favorites Autographs

This is a parallel autographed version of the regular Franchise Favorites inserts.

		NM/M
Common Player:		15.00
Version A & B 1:1,548		
Version C 1:6,191		
1A	Derek Jeter	100.00
1B	Don Mattingly	60.00
1C	Derek Jeter, Don Mattingly	300.00
2A	Scott Rolen	20.00
2B	Mike Schmidt	50.00
2C	Scott Rolen, Mike Schmidt	100.00

Future Foundations

Ten up-and-coming players are featured in this set that has the same technologies as the Franchise Best inserts and broken down the same way. The insert rates are 1:41 packs for Mach I, 1:124 for Mach II and 1:248 for Mach III.

		NM/M
Complete Set (10):		16.00
Common Player:		.75
Production 3,000 Sets		
Mach II (1,000):		1.5X
Mach III (500):		2.5X
1	Ruben Mateo	.75
2	Troy Glaus	4.00
3	Eric Chavez	1.50
4	Pat Burrell	4.00
5	Adrian Beltre	1.50
6	Ryan Anderson	.75
7	Alfonso Soriano	3.00
8	Brad Penny	.75
9	Derrick Gibson	.75
10	Bruce Chen	.75

Mirror Image

These inserts feature a veteran player on one side and a prospect on the other side for a total of 10 double-sided cards featuring 20 players. There are also parallel Refractor and Atomic Refractor versions.

NM/M

Complete Set (10):		20.00
Common Player:		1.50
Inserted 1:24		
Refractors (1:96):		1.5X
Atomic Refractors (1:192):		2X
1	Alex Rodriguez,	
	Alex Gonzalez	2.50
2	Ken Griffey Jr.,	
	Ruben Mateo	2.00
3	Derek Jeter,	
	Alfonso Soriano	4.00
4	Sammy Sosa,	
	Corey Patterson	1.50
5	Greg Maddux,	
	Bruce Chen	1.50
6	Chipper Jones,	
	Eric Chavez	1.50
7	Vladimir Guerrero,	
	Carlos Beltran	1.50
8	Frank Thomas,	
	Nick Johnson	1.50
9	Nomar Garciaparra,	
	Pablo Ozuna	1.50
10	Mark McGwire, Pat Burrell	3.00

Rookie Locker Room Autographs

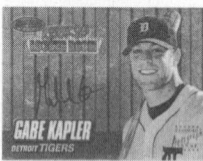

This five-card set features autographs of baseball's current hot prospects. Each card is branded with a "Topps Certified Autograph Issue" stamp.

NM/M

Common Player:		4.00
Inserted 1:248		
1	Pat Burrell	15.00
2	Michael Barrett	4.00
3	Troy Glaus	10.00
4	Gabe Kapler	4.00
5	Eric Chavez	7.50

Rookie Locker Room Game-Worn Jerseys

This four-card set spotlights hot prospects and has a swatch of game-used jersey from the featured player embedded into the card.

NM/M

Common Player:		3.00
Inserted 1:270		
1	Richie Sexson	5.00
2	Michael Barrett	3.00
3	Troy Glaus	8.00
4	Eric Chavez	5.00

Rookie Locker Room Game-Used Lumber

This six-card set features actual pieces of each player's game-used bat embedded into the cards.

NM/M

Complete Set (6):		35.00
Common Player:		4.00
Inserted 1:258		
1	Pat Burrell	10.00
2	Michael Barrett	4.00
3	Troy Glaus	10.00
4	Gabe Kapler	4.00
5	Eric Chavez	7.50
6	Richie Sexson	5.00

Rookie of the Year

This set salutes 1998 AL and NL Rookie of Year award winners Kerry Wood and Ben Grieve. They are inserted 1:95 packs and are numbered with a ROY prefix. Ben Grieve also autographed some of the inserts which feature a "Topps Certified Autograph Issue" stamp. Autographs are seeded 1:1,241 packs.

NM/M

Complete Set (2):		4.00
1	Ben Grieve	2.00
2	Kerry Wood	2.00
A1	Ben Grieve/Auto.	6.00

2000 Bowman

Released in one 440-card series. The card fronts are foil stamped to differentiate Veterans (gold foil) from Rookies and Prospects (silver). All card fronts feature facsimile signatures from the players' original Topps contracts. All bona fide rookie cards also exhibit the "Bowman Rookie Card" stamped under the 2000 Bowman logo.

NM/M

Complete Set (440):		65.00
Common Player:		.15
Common Rookie:		.25
Pack (10):		2.50
Box (24):		40.00
1	Vladimir Guerrero	.75
2	Chipper Jones	.75
3	Todd Walker	.15
4	Barry Larkin	.25
5	Bernie Williams	.40
6	Todd Helton	.75
7	Jermaine Dye	.15
8	Brian Giles	.15
9	Freddy Garcia	.15
10	Greg Vaughn	.15
11	Alex Gonzalez	.15
12	Luis Gonzalez	.25
13	Ron Belliard	.15
14	Ben Grieve	.15
15	Carlos Delgado	.50
16	Brian Jordan	.15
17	Fernando Tatis	.15
18	Ryan Rupe	.15
19	Miguel Tejada	.50
20	Mark Grace	.30
21	Kenny Lofton	.25
22	Eric Karros	.15
23	Cliff Floyd	.15
24	John Halama	.15
25	Cristian Guzman	.15
26	Scott Williamson	.15
27	Mike Lieberthal	.15
28	Tim Hudson	.40
29	Warren Morris	.15
30	Pedro Martinez	1.00
31	John Smoltz	.15
32	Ray Durham	.15
33	Chad Allen	.15
34	Tony Clark	.15
35	Tino Martinez	.25
36	J.T. Snow Jr.	.15
37	Kevin Brown	.25
38	Bartolo Colon	.15
39	Rey Ordonez	.15
40	Jeff Bagwell	.50
41	Ivan Rodriguez RC	.50
42	Eric Chavez	.25
43	Eric Milton	.15
44	Jose Canseco	.50
45	Shawn Green	.25
46	Rich Aurilia	.15
47	Roberto Alomar	.40
48	Brian Daubach	.15
49	Magglio Ordonez	.25
50	Derek Jeter	2.00
51	Kris Benson	.15
52	Albert Belle	.15
53	Rondell White	.15
54	Justin Thompson	.15
55	Nomar Garciaparra	.75
56	Chuck Finley	.15
57	Omar Vizquel	.15
58	Luis Castillo	.15
59	Richard Hidalgo	.15
60	Barry Bonds	2.00
61	Craig Biggio	.15
62	Doug Glanville	.15
63	Gabe Kapler	.15
64	Johnny Damon	.15
65	Pokey Reese	.15
66	Andy Pettitte	.25
67	B.J. Surhoff	.15
68	Richie Sexson	.40
69	Javy Lopez	.15
70	Raul Mondesi	.15
71	Darin Erstad	.25
72	Kevin Millwood	.15
73	Ricky Ledee	.15
74	John Olerud	.15
75	Sean Casey	.25
76	Carlos Febles	.15
77	Paul O'Neill	.15
78	Bob Abreu	.15
79	Neifi Perez	.15
80	Tony Gwynn	.75
81	Russ Ortiz	.15
82	Matt Williams	.15
83	Chris Carpenter	.15
84	Roger Cedeno	.15
85	Tim Salmon	.30
86	Billy Koch	.15
87	Jeromy Burnitz	.15
88	Edgardo Alfonzo	.15
89	Jay Bell	.15
90	Manny Ramirez	.75
91	Frank Thomas	.75
92	Mike Mussina	.50
93	J.D. Drew	.25
94	Adrian Beltre	.25
95	Alex Rodriguez	2.00
96	Larry Walker	.15
97	Juan Encarnacion	.15
98	Mike Sweeney	.15
99	Rusty Greer	.15
100	Randy Johnson	.75
101	Jose Vidro	.15
102	Preston Wilson	.15
103	Greg Maddux	1.50
104	Jason Giambi	.50
105	Cal Ripken Jr.	2.00
106	Carlos Beltran	.50
107	Vinny Castilla	.15
108	Mariano Rivera	.25
109	Mo Vaughn	.15
110	Rafael Palmeiro	.50
111	Shannon Stewart	.15
112	Mike Hampton	.15
113	Joe Nathan	.15
114	Ben Davis	.15
115	Andruw Jones	.50
116	Robin Ventura	.15
117	Damion Easley	.15
118	Jeff Cirillo	.15
119	Kerry Wood	.25
120	Scott Rolen	.75
121	Sammy Sosa	.75
122	Ken Griffey Jr.	1.50
123	Shane Reynolds	.15
124	Troy Glaus	.40
125	Tom Glavine	.35
126	Michael Barrett	.15
127	Al Leiter	.15
128	Jason Kendall	.15
129	Roger Clemens	2.00
130	Juan Gonzalez	.40
131	Corey Koskie	.15
132	Curt Schilling	.50
133	Mike Piazza	1.00
134	Gary Sheffield	.40
135	Jim Thome	.40
136	Orlando Hernandez	.25
137	Ray Lankford	.15
138	Geoff Jenkins	.15
139	Jose Lima	.15
140	Mark McGwire	1.50
141	Adam Piatt	.15
142	Pat Manning RC	.25
143	Marcos Castillo RC	.25
144	Lesli Brea RC	.25
145	Humberto Cota RC	.25
146	Ben Petrick RC	.25
147	Kip Wells RC	.25
148	Willi Mo Pena RC	.25
149	Chris Wakeland RC	.15
150	Brad Baker RC	.25
151	Robbie Morrison RC	.25
152	Reggie Taylor RC	.15
153	Brian Cole RC	.15
154	Peter Bergeron RC	.25
155	Roosevelt Brown RC	.15
156	Matt Cepicky RC	.25
157	Ramon Castro	.15
158	Brad Baisley RC	.25
159	Jeff Goldbach RC	.25
160	Mitch Meluskey	.15
161	Chad Harville	.15
162	Brian Cooper	.15
163	Marcus Giles	.15
164	Jim Morris	.50
165	Geoff Goetz	.15
166	Bobby Bradley RC	.25
167	Rob Bell	.15
168	Joe Crede	.25
169	Michael Restovich	.15
170	Quincy Foster RC	.25
171	Enrique Cruz RC	.25
172	Mark Quinn	.15
173	Nick Johnson	.15
174	Jeff Liefer	.15
175	Kevin Mench RC	.75
176	Steve Lomasney	.15
177	Jayson Werth	.15
178	Tim Drew	.15
179	Chip Ambres	.15
180	Ryan Anderson	.15
181	Matt Blank	.15
182	Giuseppe Chiaramonte	.15
183	Corey Myers RC	.25
184	Jeff Yoder	.15
185	Craig Dingman RC	.15
186	Jon Hamilton RC	.25
187	Toby Hall	.15
188	Russell Branyan	.15
189	Brian Falkenborg RC	.25
190	Aaron Harang RC	.75
191	Juan Pena	.15
192	Travis Thompson RC	.25
193	Alfonso Soriano	.50
194	Alejandro Diaz RC	.25
195	Carlos Pena	.15
196	Kevin Nicholson	.15
197	Mo Bruce	.15
198	C.C. Sabathia	.15
199	Carl Crawford	.15
200	Rafael Furcal	.15
201	Andrew Beinbrink RC	.25
202	Jimmy Osting	.15
203	Aaron McNeal RC	.25
204	Brett Laxton	.15
205	Chris George	.15
206	Felipe Lopez	.15
207	Ben Sheets RC	1.50
208	Mike Meyers RC	.40
209	Jason Conti	.15
210	Milton Bradley	.15
211	Chris Mears RC	.15
212	Carlos Hernandez RC	.50
213	Jason Romano	.15
214	Goefrey Tomlinson	.15
215	Jimmy Rollins	.40
216	Pablo Ozuna	.15
217	Steve Cox	.15
218	Terrence Long	.25
219	Jeff DaVanon RC	.40
220	Rick Ankiel	.25
221	Jason Standridge	.15
222	Tony Armas	.15
223	Jason Tyner	.15
224	Ramon Ortiz	.15
225	Daryle Ward	.15
226	Enger Veras RC	.25
227	Chris Jones RC	.25
228	Eric Cammack RC	.25
229	Ruben Mateo	.15
230	Ken Harvey RC	.50
231	Jake Westbrook	.15
232	Rob Purvis RC	.15
233	Choo Freeman	.15
234	Aramis Ramirez	.15
235	A.J. Burnett	.15
236	Kevin Barker	.15
237	Chance Caple RC	.25
238	Jarrod Washburn	.15
239	Lance Berkman	.15
240	Michael Wenner RC	.25
241	Alex Sanchez	.15
242	Jake Esteves RC	.25
243	Grant Roberts	.15
244	Mark Ellis RC	.50
245	Donny Leon	.15
246	David Eckstein	.15
247	Dicky Gonzalez RC	.25
248	John Patterson	.15
249	Chad Green	.15
250	Scot Shields RC	.25
251	Troy Cameron	.15
252	Jose Molina	.15
253	Rob Pugmire RC	.15
254	Rick Elder	.15
255	Sean Burroughs	.25
256	Josh Kalinowski RC	.25
257	Matt LeCroy	.15
258	Alex Graman RC	.50
259	Tomokazu Ohka RC	.50
260	Brady Clark	.15
261	Rico Washington RC	.25
262	Gary Matthews Jr.	.15
263	Matt Wise	.15
264	Keith Reed RC	.25
265	Santiago Ramirez RC	.25
266	Ben Broussard RC	.50
267	Ryan Langerhans	.15
268	Juan Rivera	.25
269	Shawn Gallagher	.15
270	Jorge Toca	.15
271	Brad Lidge	.15
272	Leo Estrella RC	.25
273	Ruben Quevedo	.15
274	Jack Cust	.15
275	T.J. Tucker	.15
276	Mike Colangelo	.15
277	Brian Schneider	.15
278	Calvin Murray	.15
279	Josh Girdley	.15
280	Mike Paradis	.15
281	Chad Hermansen	.15
282	Ty Howington RC	.50
283	Aaron Myette	.15
284	D'Angelo Jimenez	.15
285	Dernell Stenson	.15
286	Jerry Hairston Jr.	.15
287	Gary Majewski RC	.25
288	Derrin Ebert RC	.15
289	Steve Fish RC	.25
290	Carlos Hernandez	.15
291	Allen Levrault	.15
292	Sean McNally RC	.25
293	Randey Dorame RC	.25
294	Wes Anderson RC	.50
295	B.J. Ryan	.15
296	Alan Webb RC	.25
297	Brandon Inge RC	.75
298	David Walling	.15
299	Sun-Woo Kim RC	.40
300	Pat Burrell	.15
301	Rick Guttormson RC	.15
302	Gil Meche	.15
303	Carlos Zambrano RC	3.00
304	Eric Byrnes RC (Photo actually Bo Porter.)	1.00
305	Robb Quinlan RC	.15
306	Jackie Rexrode	.15
307	Nate Bump	.15
308	Sean DePaula RC	.25
309	Matt Riley	.15
310	Ryan Minor	.15
311	J.J. Davis	.15
312	Randy Wolf	.15
313	Jason Jennings	.15
314	Scott Seabol RC	.25
315	Doug Davis	.15
316	Todd Moser RC	.25
317	Rob Ortiz	.15
318	Bubba Crosby	.15
319	Lyle Overbay RC	1.00
320	Mario Encarnacion	.15
321	Francisco Rodriguez RC	2.00
322	Michael Cuddyer	.15
323	Eddie Yarnall	.15
324	Cesar Saba RC	.15
325	Travis Dawkins	.15
326	Alex Escobar	.15
327	Julio Zuleta RC	.40
328	Josh Hamilton	1.00
329	Nick Neugebauer RC	.15
330	Matt Belisle	.15
331	Kurt Ainsworth RC	.50
332	Tim Raines Jr.	.15
333	Eric Munson	.15
334	Donzell McDonald	.15
335	Larry Bigbie RC	.25
336	Matt Watson	.15
337	Aubrey Huff	.15
338	Julio Ramirez	.15
339	Jason Grabowski RC	.25
340	Jon Garland	.15
341	Austin Kearns	.15
342	Josh Pressley	.15
343	Miguel Olivo RC	.25
344	Julio Lugo	.15
345	Roberto Vaz	.15
346	Ramon Soler	.15
347	Brandon Phillips RC	2.00
348	Vince Faison RC	.25
349	Mike Venafro	.15
350	Rick Asadoorian RC	.25
351	B.J. Garbe RC	.25
352	Dan Reichert	.15
353	Jason Stumm RC	.25
354	Ruben Salazar RC	.15
355	Francisco Cordero	.15
356	Juan Guzman RC	.25
357	Mike Bacsik RC	.25
358	Jared Sandberg	.15
359	Rod Barajas	.15
360	Junior Brignac RC	.25
361	J.M. Gold	.15
362	Octavio Dotel	.15
363	David Kelton	.15
364	Scott Morgan RC	.15
365	Wascar Serrano RC	.25
366	Wilton Veras	.15
367	Eugene Kingsale	.15
368	Ted Lilly	.15
369	George Lombard	.15
370	Chris Haas	.15
371	Wilton Pena RC	.50
372	Vernon Wells	.15
373	Jason Royer RC	.25
374	Jeff Heaverlo RC	.25
375	Calvin Pickering	.15
376	Mike Lamb RC	.40
377	Kyle Snyder	.15
378	Javier Cardona RC	.25
379	Aaron Rowand RC	.25
380	Dee Brown	.15
381	Brett Myers RC	1.00
382	Abraham Nunez	.15
383	Eric Valent	.15
384	Jody Gerut RC	.25
385	Adam Dunn	.50
386	Jay Gehrke	.15
387	Omar Ortiz	.15
388	Darnell McDonald	.15
389	Chad Alexander	.15
390	J.D. Closser	.15
391	Ben Christensen RC	.25
392	Adam Kennedy	.15
393	Nick Green RC	.25
394	Ramon Hernandez	.15
395	Roy Oswalt RC	4.00
396	Andy Tracy RC	.50
397	Eric Gagne	.15
398	Michael Tejera RC	.25
399	Adam Everett	.15
400	Corey Patterson	.75
401	Gary Knotts RC	.25
402	Ryan Christianson RC	.50
403	Eric Ireland RC	.25
404	Andrew Good RC	.25
405	Brad Penny	.15
406	Jason LaRue	.25
407	Kit Pellow	.15
408	Kevin Beirne	.15
409	Kelly Dransfeldt	.15
410	Jason Grilli	.15
411	Scott Downs RC	.25
412	Jesus Colome	.15
413	John Sneed RC	.25
414	Tony McKnight RC	.25
415	Luis Rivera	.15
416	Adam Eaton	.15
417	Mike MacDougal RC	.50
418	Mike Nannini	.15
419	Barry Zito RC	1.50
420	Dewayne Wise	.15
421	Jason Dellaero	.15
422	Chad Moeller	.15
423	Jason Marquis	.25
424	Tim Redding RC	.50
425	Mark Mulder	.25
426	Josh Paul	.15
427	Chris Enochs	.15
428	Wilfredo Rodriguez RC	.50
429	Kevin Witt	.15
430	Scott Sobkowiak RC	.25
431	McKay Christensen	.15
432	Jung Bong	.15
433	Keith Evans RC	.25
434	Garry Maddox Jr.	.15
435	Ramon Santiago RC	.50
436	Alex Cora	.15
437	Carlos Lee	.15
438	Jason Repko RC	.25
439	Matt Burch	.15
440	Shawn Sonnier RC	.25

Gold

Golds are a 440-card parallel to the base set and are highlighted by gold-stamped facsimile autographs on the card front. Golds are limited to 99 serial numbered sets.

Stars:	10-20X
Rookies:	4-8X
Production 99 Sets	

Retro/Future

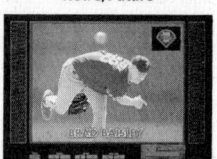

These inserts are a parallel to the 440-card base set. The foiled card fronts have a horizontal format and a design reminiscent of the 1955 Bowman "television set" design. They were seeded one per pack.

NM/M

Common Player:	.25
Stars:	2-3X
Rookies:	.75-2X
Inserted 1:1	

Autographs

This set consists of 40 players with card rarity differentiated by either a Blue, Silver or Gold foil Topps "Certified Autograph Issue" stamp. Card backs are numbered using the player initials and have a Topps serial numbered foil hologram to ensure the authenticity of the autograph.

NM/M

Common Autograph:	5.00
Blue Inserted 1:144	
Silver 1:312	
Gold 1:1,604	

CA	Chip Ambres/B	5.00
RA	Rick Ankiel/G	25.00
CB	Carlos Beltran/G	40.00
LB	Lance Berkman/S	20.00
DB	Dee Brown/S	8.00
SB	Sean Burroughs/S	8.00
JDC	J.D. Closser/B	5.00
SC	Steve Cox/B	5.00
MC	Mike Cuddyer/S	10.00
JC	Jack Cust/S	15.00
SD	Scott Downs/S	10.00
JDD	J.D. Drew/G	25.00
AD	Adam Dunn/B	25.00
CF	Choo Freeman/B	5.00
RF	Rafael Furcal/S	15.00
AH	Aubrey Huff/B	8.00
JJ	Jason Jennings/B	8.00
NJ	Nick Johnson/S	10.00
AK	Austin Kearns/S	15.00
DK	David Kelton/B	5.00
RM	Ruben Mateo/G	15.00
MM	Mike Meyers/B	5.00
CP	Corey Patterson/S	15.00
BWP	Brad Penny/S	8.00
BP	Ben Petrick/G	10.00
AP	Adam Piatt/S	8.00
MQ	Mark Quinn/B	8.00
MR	Mike Restovich/B	5.00
MR	Matt Riley/S	8.00
JR	Jason Romano/B	5.00
BS	Ben Sheets/B	25.00
AS	Alfonso Soriano/S	40.00
EV	Eric Valent/B	5.00
JV	Jose Vidro/B	10.00
VW	Vernon Wells/G	20.00
SW	Scott Williamson/S	10.00
KJW	Kevin Witt/S	10.00
KLW	Kerry Wood/S	25.00
EY	Eddie Yarnall/S	10.00
JZ	Julio Zuleta/S	5.00

Bowman's Best Previews

This 10-card insert set is identical in design to 2000 Bowman's Best. The card fronts have a Refractor like sheen and the card backs are numbered with a "BBP" prefix.

		NM/M
Complete Set (10):		15.00
Common Player:		.50
Inserted 1:18		
1	Derek Jeter	4.00
2	Ken Griffey Jr.	3.00
3	Nomar Garciaparra	2.00
4	Mike Piazza	2.00
5	Alex Rodriguez	3.00
6	Sammy Sosa	2.00
7	Mark McGwire	3.00
8	Pat Burrell	1.00
9	Josh Hamilton	1.00
10	Adam Piatt	.50

Early Indications

This 10-card set has a blue foiled card front with red foil stamping. Card backs are numbered with an "E" prefix.

		NM/M
Complete Set (10):		18.00
Common Player:		1.00
Inserted 1:24		
1	Nomar Garciaparra	4.00
2	Cal Ripken Jr.	4.00
3	Derek Jeter	4.00
4	Mark McGwire	2.50
5	Alex Rodriguez	3.00

6	Chipper Jones	1.50
7	Todd Helton	1.00
8	Vladimir Guerrero	1.50
9	Mike Piazza	1.50
10	Jose Canseco	1.00

Major Power

This 10-card set spotlights the top home run hitters. Card fronts have a red border on a full foiled card front. These are numbered with an "MP" prefix on the card back.

		NM/M
Complete Set (10):		15.00
Common Player:		1.00
Inserted 1:24		
1	Mark McGwire	3.00
2	Chipper Jones	2.50
3	Alex Rodriguez	4.00
4	Sammy Sosa	2.50
5	Rafael Palmeiro	1.00
6	Ken Griffey Jr.	3.00
7	Nomar Garciaparra	1.50
8	Barry Bonds	2.00
9	Derek Jeter	5.00
10	Jeff Bagwell	1.00

Tool Time

This 20-card set focuses on the top minor league Prospects in five different categories: batting, power, speed, arm strength and defense. These are seeded 1:8 packs. Backs are numbered with a "TT" prefix.

		NM/M
Complete Set (20):		8.00
Common Player:		.40
Inserted 1:8		
1	Pat Burrell	1.00
2	Aaron Rowand	.40
3	Chris Wakeland	.40
4	Ruben Mateo	.40
5	Pat Burrell	1.00
6	Adam Piatt	.50
7	Nick Johnson	1.00
8	Jack Cust	.40
9	Rafael Furcal	.40
10	Julio Ramirez	.40
11	Travis Dawkins	.40
12	Corey Patterson	1.00
13	Ruben Mateo	.40
14	Jason Dellaero	.40
15	Sean Burroughs	.40
16	Ryan Langerhans	.40
17	D'Angelo Jimenez	.40
18	Corey Patterson	1.00
19	Troy Cameron	.40
20	Michael Cuddyer	.50

2000 Bowman Chrome

Released as a single series 440-card set, Bowman Chrome is identical in design to 2000 Bowman besides the Chromium finish on all cards. Foil highlights differentiate rookies and prospects (blue) from veterans (red). Three parallels to the base set are randomly included: Refractors, Retro/Future and Retro/Future Refractors.

		NM/M
Complete Set (440):		120.00
Common Player:		.25
Common Rookie:		.50
Pack (4):		2.50
Box (24):		50.00
1	Vladimir Guerrero	.75
2	Chipper Jones	1.00
3	Todd Walker	.25
4	Barry Larkin	.25
5	Bernie Williams	.50
6	Todd Helton	.75
7	Jermaine Dye	.25
8	Brian Giles	.25
9	Freddy Garcia	.25
10	Greg Vaughn	.25
11	Alex Gonzalez	.25
12	Luis Gonzalez	.25
13	Ron Belliard	.25
14	Ben Grieve	.25
15	Carlos Delgado	.75
16	Brian Jordan	.25
17	Fernando Tatis	.25
18	Ryan Rupe	.25
19	Miguel Tejada	.40
20	Mark Grace	.35
21	Kenny Lofton	.25
22	Eric Karros	.25
23	Cliff Floyd	.25
24	John Halama	.25
25	Cristian Guzman	.25
26	Scott Williamson	.25
27	Mike Lieberthal	.25
28	Tim Hudson	.40
29	Warren Morris	.25
30	Pedro Martinez	.75
31	John Smoltz	.25
32	Ray Durham	.25
33	Chad Allen	.25
34	Tony Clark	.25
35	Tino Martinez	.25
36	J.T. Snow Jr.	.25
37	Kevin Brown	.40
38	Bartolo Colon	.25
39	Rey Ordonez	.25
40	Jeff Bagwell	.50
41	Ivan Rodriguez	.50
42	Eric Chavez	.25
43	Eric Milton	.25
44	Jose Canseco	.50
45	Shawn Green	.40
46	Rich Aurilia	.25
47	Roberto Alomar	.50
48	Brian Daubach	.25
49	Magglio Ordonez	.50
50	Derek Jeter	2.00
51	Kris Benson	.25
52	Albert Belle	.25
53	Rondell White	.25
54	Justin Thompson	.25
55	Nomar Garciaparra	.50
56	Chuck Finley	.25
57	Omar Vizquel	.25
58	Luis Castillo	.25
59	Richard Hidalgo	.25
60	Barry Bonds	2.00
61	Craig Biggio	.25
62	Doug Glanville	.25
63	Gabe Kapler	.25
64	Johnny Damon	.40
65	Pokey Reese	.25
66	Andy Pettitte	.50
67	B.J. Surhoff	.25
68	Richie Sexson	.25
69	Javy Lopez	.25
70	Raul Mondesi	.25
71	Darin Erstad	.40
72	Kevin Millwood	.40
73	Ricky Ledee	.25
74	John Olerud	.25
75	Sean Casey	.25
76	Carlos Febles	.25
77	Paul O'Neill	.25
78	Bob Abreu	.25
79	Neifi Perez	.25
80	Tony Gwynn	1.00
81	Russ Ortiz	.25
82	Matt Williams	.25
83	Chris Carpenter	.25
84	Roger Cedeno	.25
85	Tim Salmon	.35
86	Billy Koch	.25
87	Jeromy Burnitz	.25
88	Edgardo Alfonzo	.25
89	Jay Bell	.15
90	Manny Ramirez	.75
91	Frank Thomas	.75
92	Mike Mussina	.50

93	J.D. Drew	.40
94	Adrian Beltre	.40
95	Alex Rodriguez	2.00
96	Larry Walker	.25
97	Juan Encarnacion	.25
98	Mike Sweeney	.25
99	Rusty Greer	.25
100	Randy Johnson	.75
101	Jose Vidro	.25
102	Preston Wilson	.25
103	Greg Maddux	1.50
104	Jason Giambi	.50
105	Cal Ripken Jr.	3.00
106	Carlos Beltran	.25
107	Vinny Castilla	.25
108	Mariano Rivera	.35
109	Mo Vaughn	.25
110	Rafael Palmeiro	.50
111	Shannon Stewart	.25
112	Mike Hampton	.25
113	Joe Nathan	.25
114	Ben Davis	.25
115	Andruw Jones	.40
116	Robin Ventura	.25
117	Damion Easley	.25
118	Jeff Cirillo	.25
119	Kerry Wood	.40
120	Scott Rolen	.50
121	Sammy Sosa	1.00
122	Ken Griffey Jr.	2.00
123	Shane Reynolds	.25
124	Troy Glaus	.50
125	Tom Glavine	.40
126	Michael Barrett	.25
127	Al Leiter	.25
128	Jason Kendall	.25
129	Roger Clemens	1.50
130	Juan Gonzalez	.50
131	Corey Koskie	.25
132	Curt Schilling	.75
133	Mike Piazza	1.00
134	Gary Sheffield	.50
135	Jim Thome	.50
136	Orlando Hernandez	.40
137	Ray Lankford	.25
138	Geoff Jenkins	.25
139	Jose Lima	.25
140	Mark McGwire	1.50
141	Adam Piatt	.25
142	Pat Manning RC	.50
143	Marcos Castillo RC	.50
144	Lesli Brea RC	.50
145	Humberto Cota RC	.50
146	Ben Petrick	.25
147	Kip Wells	.25
148	Willi Mo Pena	.40
149	Chris Wakeland	.25
150	Brad Baker RC	.50
151	Robbie Morrison RC	.50
152	Reggie Taylor	.25
153	Matt Ginter RC	.50
154	Peter Bergeron	.25
155	Roosevelt Brown	.25
156	Matt Cepicky RC	.50
157	Ramon Castro	.25
158	Brad Baisley RC	.50
159	Jason Hart RC	1.00
160	Mitch Meluskey	.25
161	Chad Harville	.25
162	Brian Cooper	.25
163	Marcus Giles	.25
164	Jim Morris	.50
165	Geoff Goetz	.25
166	Bobby Bradley RC	.50
167	Rob Bell	.25
168	Joe Crede	.25
169	Michael Restovich	.25
170	Quincy Foster RC	.50
171	Enrique Cruz RC	.50
172	Mark Quinn	.25
173	Nick Johnson	.40
174	Jeff Liefer	.25
175	Kevin Mench RC	1.00
176	Steve Lomasney	.25
177	Jayson Werth	.25
178	Tim Drew	.25
179	Chip Ambres	.25
180	Ryan Anderson	.25
181	Matt Blank	.25
182	Giuseppe Chiaramonte	.25
183	Corey Myers RC	.50
184	Jeff Yoder	.25
185	Craig Dingman RC	.50
186	Jon Hamilton RC	.50
187	Toby Hall	.25
188	Russell Branyan	.25
189	Brian Falkenborg RC	.50
190	Aaron Harang RC	3.00
191	Juan Pena	.25
192	Chin-Hui Tsao RC	1.00
193	Alfonso Soriano	.75
194	Alejandro Diaz RC	.50
195	Carlos Pena RC	.25
196	Kevin Nicholson	.25
197	Mo Bruce	.25
198	C.C. Sabathia	.25
199	Carl Crawford	.25
200	Rafael Furcal	.25
201	Andrew Beinbrink RC	.25
202	Jimmy Osting	.25
203	Aaron McNeal RC	.25
204	Brett Laxton	.25
205	Chris George	.25
206	Felipe Lopez	.25
207	Ben Sheets	3.00
208	Mike Meyers RC	.50
209	Jason Conti	.25
210	Milton Bradley	.25

211	Chris Mears RC	.50
212	Carlos Hernandez RC	.50
213	Jason Romano	.25
214	Goefrey Tomlinson	.25
215	Jimmy Rollins	.75
216	Pablo Ozuna	.25
217	Steve Cox	.25
218	Terrence Long	.25
219	Jeff DaVanon RC	.50
220	Rick Ankiel	.75
221	Jason Standridge	.25
222	Tony Armas	.25
223	Jason Tyner	.25
224	Ramon Ortiz	.25
225	Daryle Ward	.25
226	Enger Veras RC	.50
227	Chris Jones RC	.50
228	Eric Cammack RC	.50
229	Ruben Mateo	.25
230	Ken Harvey RC	1.00
231	Jake Westbrook	.25
232	Rob Purvis RC	.50
233	Choo Freeman	.25
234	Aramis Ramirez	.25
235	A.J. Burnett	.25
236	Kevin Barker	.25
237	Chance Caple RC	.50
238	Jarrod Washburn	.25
239	Lance Berkman	.25
240	Michael Wenner RC	.50
241	Alex Sanchez	.25
242	Jake Esteves RC	.50
243	Grant Roberts	.25
244	Mark Ellis RC	.50
245	Donny Leon	.25
246	David Eckstein	.25
247	Dicky Gonzalez RC	.50
248	John Patterson	.25
249	Chad Green	.25
250	Scot Shields RC	.50
251	Troy Cameron	.25
252	Jose Molina	.25
253	Rob Pugmire RC	.50
254	Rick Elder	.25
255	Sean Burroughs	.25
256	Josh Kalinowski RC	.50
257	Matt LeCroy	.25
258	Alex Graman RC	.50
259	Juan Silvestre RC	.50
260	Brady Clark	.25
261	Rico Washington RC	.50
262	Gary Matthews Jr.	.25
263	Matt Wise	.25
264	Keith Reed RC	.50
265	Santiago Ramirez RC	.50
266	Ben Broussard RC	.50
267	Ryan Langerhans	.25
268	Juan Rivera	.25
269	Shawn Gallagher	.25
270	Jorge Toca	.25
271	Brad Lidge	.25
272	Leo Estrella RC	.50
273	Ruben Quevedo	.25
274	Jack Cust	.25
275	T.J. Tucker	.25
276	Mike Colangelo	.25
277	Brian Schneider	.25
278	Calvin Murray	.25
279	Josh Girdley	.25
280	Mike Paradis	.25
281	Chad Hermansen	.25
282	Ty Howington RC	.50
283	Aaron Myette	.25
284	D'Angelo Jimenez	.25
285	Dernell Stenson	.25
286	Jerry Hairston Jr.	.25
287	Gary Majewski RC	.50
288	Derrin Ebert RC	.50
289	Steve Fish RC	.50
290	Carlos Hernandez	.25
291	Allen Levrault	.25
292	Sean McNally RC	.50
293	Randey Dorame RC	.50
294	Wes Anderson RC	.50
295	B.J. Ryan	.25
296	Alan Webb RC	.50
297	Brandon Inge RC	2.00
298	David Walling	.25
299	Sun-Woo Kim RC	1.00
300	Pat Burrell	.50
301	Rick Guttormson RC	.50
302	Gil Meche	.25
303	Carlos Zambrano RC	10.00
304	Eric Byrnes RC (Photo actually Bo Porter.)	3.00
305	Robb Quinlan RC	.50
306	Jackie Rexrode	.25
307	Nate Bump	.25
308	Sean DePaula RC	.50
309	Matt Riley	.25
310	Ryan Minor	.25
311	J.J. Davis	.25
312	Randy Wolf	.25
313	Jason Jennings	.25
314	Scott Seabol RC	.50
315	Doug Davis	.25
316	Todd Moser RC	.50
317	Rob Ryan	.25
318	Bubba Crosby	.25
319	Lyle Overbay RC	1.50
320	Mario Encarnacion	.25
321	Francisco Rodriguez RC	6.00
322	Michael Cuddyer	.25
323	Eddie Yarnall	.25
324	Cesar Saba RC	.50
325	Travis Dawkins	.25
326	Alex Escobar	.25
327	Julio Zuleta RC	.50

328	Josh Hamilton	1.50
329	Carlos Urquiola RC	.50
330	Matt Belisle	.25
331	Kurt Ainsworth RC	1.00
332	Tim Raines Jr.	.25
333	Eric Munson	.25
334	Donzell McDonald	.25
335	Larry Bigbie RC	.50
336	Matt Watson	.25
337	Aubrey Huff	.25
338	Julio Ramirez	.25
339	Jason Grabowski RC	.50
340	Jon Garland	.50
341	Austin Kearns	.50
342	Josh Pressley	.25
343	Miguel Olivo RC	.50
344	Julio Lugo	.25
345	Roberto Vaz	.25
346	Ramon Soler	.25
347	Brandon Phillips RC	5.00
348	Vince Faison RC	.50
349	Mike Venafro	.25
350	Rick Asadoorian RC	.50
351	B.J. Garbe RC	.50
352	Dan Reichert	.25
353	Jason Stumm RC	.50
354	Ruben Salazar RC	.25
355	Francisco Cordero	.25
356	Juan Guzman RC	.50
357	Mike Bacsik RC	.50
358	Jared Sandberg	.25
359	Rod Barajas	.25
360	Junior Brignac RC	.50
361	J.M. Gold	.25
362	Octavio Dotel	.25
363	David Kelton	.25
364	Scott Morgan RC	.50
365	Wascar Serrano RC	.50
366	Wilton Veras	.25
367	Eugene Kingsale	.25
368	Ted Lilly	.25
369	George Lombard	.25
370	Chris Haas	.25
371	Wilton Pena RC	.50
372	Vernon Wells	.25
373	Keith Ginter RC	.50
374	Jeff Heaverlo RC	.50
375	Calvin Pickering	.25
376	Mike Lamb RC	.50
377	Kyle Snyder	.25
378	Javier Cardona RC	.50
379	Aaron Rowand RC	3.00
380	Dee Brown	.25
381	Brett Myers RC	2.00
382	Abraham Nunez	.25
383	Eric Valent	.25
384	Jody Gerut RC	.50
385	Adam Dunn	.50
386	Jay Gehrke	.25
387	Omar Ortiz	.25
388	Darnell McDonald	.25
389	Chad Alexander	.25
390	J.D. Closser	.25
391	Ben Christensen RC	.50
392	Adam Kennedy	.25
393	Nick Green RC	.50
394	Ramon Hernandez	.25
395	Roy Oswalt RC	15.00
396	Andy Tracy RC	1.00
397	Eric Gagne	.25
398	Michael Tejera RC	.50
399	Adam Everett	.25
400	Corey Patterson	.50
401	Gary Knotts RC	.50
402	Ryan Christianson RC	.50
403	Eric Ireland RC	.50
404	Andrew Good RC	.50
405	Brad Penny	.25
406	Jason LaRue	.25
407	Kit Pellow	.25
408	Kevin Beirne	.25
409	Kelly Dransfeldt	.25
410	Jason Grilli	.25
411	Scott Downs RC	.50
412	Jesus Colome	.25
413	John Sneed RC	.50
414	Tony McKnight RC	.50
415	Luis Rivera	.25
416	Adam Eaton	.25
417	Mike MacDougal RC	1.00
418	Mike Nannini	.25
419	Barry Zito RC	3.00
420	Dewayne Wise	.25
421	Jason Dellaero	.25
422	Chad Moeller	.25
423	Jason Marquis	.25
424	Tim Redding RC	.50
425	Mark Mulder	.25
426	Josh Paul	.25
427	Chris Enochs	.25
428	Wilfredo Rodriguez RC	.50
429	Kevin Witt	.25
430	Scott Sobkowiak RC	.50
431	McKay Christensen	.25
432	Jung Bong	.25
433	Keith Evans RC	.50
434	Garry Maddox Jr.	.25
435	Ramon Santiago RC	.50
436	Alex Cora	.25
437	Carlos Lee	.25
438	Jason Repko RC	.50
439	Matt Burch	.25
440	Shawn Sonnier	1.00

Refractors

A parallel to the 440-card base set, these inserts have a mirror like sheen to them on the card front and are listed Refractor underneath the card number on the back. These were seeded 1:12 packs.

Stars: 4-8X
Rookies: 2-4X
Inserted 1:12

Retro/Future

This 440-card parallel to the base set is modeled after the 1955 Bowman "television set" design and are seeded 1:6 packs, with Refractors seeded 1:60 packs.

Stars: 1.5-3X
Rookies: .75X
Inserted 1:6
Refractors: 6-8X
Rookies: 1-30X
Inserted 1:60

Bidding for the Call

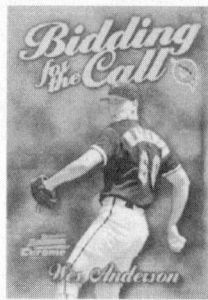

Top minor league prospects are highlighted on a design with gold foil background on an all chromium finish. Card backs are numbered with a "BC" prefix. A Refractor parallel version was also produced.

		NM/M
Complete Set (15):		8.00
Common Player:		.50
Inserted 1:16		
Refractors:		2-4X
Inserted 1:160		
1	Adam Piatt	.50
2	Pat Burrell	1.00
3	Mark Mulder	.50
4	Nick Johnson	.50
5	Alfonso Soriano	2.00
6	Chin-Feng Chen	.50
7	Scott Sobkowiak	.50
8	Corey Patterson	.50
9	Jack Cust	.75
10	Sean Burroughs	.50
11	Josh Hamilton	2.00
12	Corey Myers	.50
13	Eric Munson	.50
14	Wes Anderson	.50
15	Lyle Overbay	.50

Meteoric Rise

This 10-card set spotlights players who all made their first All-Star team within their first two years. Card fronts have a futuristic background, with the player in an intergalactic setting. Card backs are numbered with a "MR" prefix. A Refractor parallel version also exists.

		NM/M
Complete Set (10):		15.00
Common Player:		1.00
Inserted 1:24		
Refractors:		2-4X
Inserted 1:240		
1	Nomar Garciaparra	1.50
2	Mark McGwire	3.00
3	Ken Griffey Jr.	3.00
4	Chipper Jones	2.50
5	Manny Ramirez	2.00
6	Mike Piazza	3.00
7	Cal Ripken Jr.	5.00
8	Ivan Rodriguez	1.00
9	Greg Maddux	3.00
10	Randy Johnson	2.00

Oversize

		NM/M
Complete Set (8):		8.00
Common Player:		.75
Inserted 1:Box		
1	Pat Burrell	2.00
2	Josh Hamilton	2.00
3	Rafael Furcal	1.00
4	Corey Patterson	1.50
5	A.J. Burnett	.75
6	Eric Munson	.75
7	Nick Johnson	1.00
8	Alfonso Soriano	2.00

Rookie Class 2000

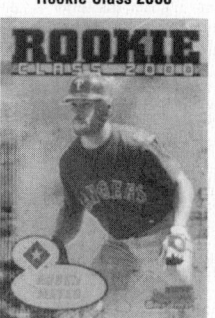

This set highlighted 10 prospects who were thought to contend for the 2000 Rookie of the Year awards. Backs are numbered with a "RC" prefix. A Refractor parallel version was also issued.

		NM/M
Complete Set (10):		6.00
Common Player:		.75
Inserted 1:24		
Refractors:		2-4X
Inserted 1:240		
1	Pat Burrell	2.00
2	Rick Ankiel	1.50
3	Ruben Mateo	.50
4	Vernon Wells	1.50
5	Mark Mulder	.50
6	A.J. Burnett	.75
7	Chad Hermansen	.50
8	Corey Patterson	.50
9	Rafael Furcal	1.00
10	Mike Lamb	.50

Teen Idols

This 15-card set highlights top teenagers who are predicted to emerge as major league standouts.

		NM/M
Complete Set (15):		10.00
Common Player:		.75
Inserted 1:16		
Refractors:		2-4X
Inserted 1:160		
1	Alex Rodriguez	5.00
2	Andruw Jones	.75
3	Juan Gonzalez	1.00
4	Ivan Rodriguez	1.00
5	Ken Griffey Jr.	3.00
6	Bobby Bradley	.50
7	Brett Myers	.75
8	C.C. Sabathia	1.50
9	Ty Howington	.50
10	Brandon Phillips	1.00
11	Rick Asadoorian	.50
12	Wily Pena	.50
13	Sean Burroughs	.50
14	Josh Hamilton	3.00
15	Rafael Furcal	.50

2000 Bowman Draft Picks and Prospects

		NM/M
Complete Set (110):		40.00
Common Player:		.15
1	Pat Burrell	.25
2	Rafael Furcal	.25
3	Grant Roberts	.15
4	Barry Zito	.50
5	Julio Zuleta	.15
6	Mark Mulder	.25
7	Rob Bell	.15
8	Adam Piatt	.15
9	Mike Lamb	.15
10	Pablo Ozuna	.15
11	Jason Tyner	.15
12	Jason Marquis	.15
13	Eric Munson	.15
14	Seth Etherton	.15
15	Milton Bradley	.15
16	Nick Green	.15
17	Chin-Feng Chen RC	1.00
18	Matt Boone RC	.25
19	Kevin Gregg RC	.25
20	Eddy Garabito RC	.25
21	Aaron Capista RC	.25
22	Esteban German RC	.25
23	Derek Thompson RC	.25
24	Phil Merrell RC	.25
25	Brian O'Connor RC	.25
26	Yamid Haad	.15
27	Hector Mercado RC	.25
28	Jason Woolf RC	.25
29	Eddie Furniss RC	.25
30	Cha Sueng Baek RC	.25
31	Colby Lewis RC	.25
32	Pasqual Coco RC	.25
33	Jorge Cantu RC	1.50
34	Erasmo Ramirez RC	.25
35	Bobby Kielty RC	.50
36	Joaquin Benoit RC	.25
37	Brian Esposito RC	.25
38	Michael Wenner	.15
39	Juan Rincon RC	.25
40	Yorvit Torrealba RC	.25
41	Chad Durham RC	.25
42	Jim Mann RC	.25
43	Shane Loux RC	.25
44	Luis Rivas	.15
45	Ken Chenard RC	.25
46	Mike Lockwood RC	.25
47	Yovanny Lara RC	.25
48	Bubba Carpenter RC	.25
49	Jeremy Griffiths RC	.25
50	John Stephens RC	.25
51	Pedro Feliz RC	.75
52	Kenny Kelly RC	.25
53	Neil Jenkins RC	.25
54	Mike Glendenning RC	.25
55	Bo Porter	.15
56	Eric Byrnes RC	.25
57	Tony Alvarez RC	.25
58	Kazuhiro Sasaki RC	.50
59	Chad Durbin RC	.25
60	Mike Bynum RC	.25
61	Travis Wilson RC	.25
62	Jose Leon RC	.25
63	Bill Ortega RC	.25
64	Geraldo Guzman RC	.25
65	Craig Anderson RC	.25
66	Carlos Silva RC	.50
67	Brad Thomas RC	.25
68	Chin-Hui Tsao RC	.75
69	Mark Buehrle RC	2.00
70	Juan Salas RC	.25
71	Denny Abreu RC	.25
72	Keith McDonald RC	.25
73	Chris Richard RC	.25
74	Tomas de la Rosa RC	.25
75	Vicente Padilla	.50
76	Justin Brunette RC	.25
77	Scott Linebrink RC	.25
78	Jeff Sparks RC	.25
79	Tike Redman RC	.25
80	John Lackey RC	1.50
81	Joe Strong RC	.25
82	Brian Tollberg RC	.25
83	Steve Sisco RC	.25
84	Chris Clapinski	.15
85	Augie Ojeda RC	.25
86	Adrian Gonzalez RC (Draft Picks)	3.00
87	Mike Stodolka RC (Draft Picks)	.25
88	Adam Johnson RC (Draft Picks)	.25
89	Matt Wheatland RC (Draft Picks)	.25
90	Corey Smith RC (Draft Picks)	.25
91	Rocco Baldelli RC (Draft Picks)	1.50
92	Keith Bucktrot RC (Draft Picks)	.25
93	Adam Wainwright RC (Draft Picks)	1.50
94	Blaine Boyer RC (Draft Picks)	.25
95	Aaron Herr RC (Draft Picks)	.25
96	Scott Thorman RC (Draft Picks)	1.00
97	Brian Digby RC (Draft Picks)	.25
98	Josh Shortslef RC (Draft Picks)	.25
99	Sean Smith RC (Draft Picks)	.25
100	Alex Cruz RC (Draft Picks)	.25
101	Marc Love RC (Draft Picks)	.25
102	Kevin Lee RC (Draft Picks)	.25
103	Victor Ramos RC (Draft Picks)	.25
104	Jason Kanoi RC (Draft Picks)	.25
105	Luis Escobar RC (Draft Picks)	.25
106	Tripper Johnson RC (Draft Picks)	.25
107	Phil Dumatrait RC (Draft Picks)	.25
108	Bryan Edwards RC (Draft Picks)	.25
109	Grady Sizemore RC (Draft Picks)	20.00
110	Thomas Mitchell RC (Draft Picks)	.25

Autograph

Pat Burrell

		NM/M
Common Autograph:		5.00
Inserted 1:Set		
1	Pat Burrell	20.00
2	Rafael Furcal	20.00
3	Grant Roberts	5.00
4	Barry Zito	20.00
5	Julio Zuleta	5.00
6	Mark Mulder	10.00
7	Bob Bell	5.00
8	Adam Piatt	5.00
9	Mike Lamb	10.00
10	Pablo Ozuna	5.00
11	Jason Tyner	5.00
12	Jason Marquis	10.00
13	Eric Munson	6.00
14	Seth Etherton	5.00
15	Milton Bradley	15.00
16	Michael Wenner	5.00
17	Mike Glendenning	5.00
18	Mike Glendenning	5.00
19	Tony Alvarez	5.00
20	Adrian Gonzalez	70.00
21	Corey Smith	10.00
22	Matt Wheatland	5.00
23	Adam Johnson	5.00
24	Mike Stodolka	5.00
25	Rocco Baldelli	20.00
26	Juan Rincon	5.00
27	Chad Durbin	5.00
28	Yorvit Torrealba	5.00
29	Nick Green	10.00
30	Derek Thompson	5.00
31	John Lackey	50.00

2000 Bowman Chrome Draft Picks and Prospects

		NM/M
33	Kevin Gregg	8.00
35	Denny Abreu	5.00
36	Brian Tollberg	5.00
37	Yamid Haad	5.00
38	Grady Sizemore	225.00
39	Carlos Silva	10.00
41	Jorge Cantu	30.00
42	Bobby Kielty	5.00
43	Scott Thorman	10.00
45	Juan Salas	10.00
46	Phil Dumatrait	5.00
47	Mike Lockwood	5.00
48	Yovanny Lara	5.00
49	Tripper Johnson	5.00
50	Colby Lewis	5.00
51	Neil Jenkins	5.00
52	Keith Bucktrot	5.00
53	Eric Byrnes	20.00
54	Aaron Herr	5.00
56	Erasmo Ramirez	5.00
57	Chris Richard	5.00
58	Mike Bynum	5.00
59	Brian Esposito	5.00
60	Chris Clapinski	5.00
	Augie Ojeda	5.00

Jon Rauch

		NM/M
Complete Set (110):		50.00
Common Player:		.25
1	Pat Burrell	.50
2	Rafael Furcal	.50
3	Grant Roberts	.25
4	Barry Zito	2.00
5	Julio Zuleta	.50
6	Mark Mulder	.25
7	Rob Bell	.25
8	Adam Piatt	.50
9	Mike Lamb	.25
10	Pablo Ozuna	.25
11	Jason Tyner	.25
12	Jason Marquis	.25
13	Eric Munson	.25
14	Seth Etherton	.25
15	Milton Bradley	.25
16	Nick Green	.25
17	Chin-Feng Chen RC	1.00
18	Matt Boone RC	.50
19	Kevin Gregg RC	.50
20	Eddy Garabito RC	.50
21	Aaron Capista RC	.50
22	Esteban German RC	.50
23	Derek Thompson RC	.50
24	Phil Merrell RC	.50
25	Brian O'Connor RC	.50
26	Yamid Haad	.25
27	Hector Mercado RC	.50
28	Jason Woolf RC	.50
29	Eddie Furniss RC	.50
30	Cha Sueng Baek RC	.50
31	Colby Lewis RC	.50
32	Pasqual Coco RC	.50
33	Jorge Cantu RC	3.00
34	Erasmo Ramirez RC	.50
35	Bobby Kielty RC	.50
36	Joaquin Benoit RC	.50
37	Brian Esposito RC	.50
38	Michael Wenner	.25
39	Juan Rincon RC	.50
40	Yorvit Torrealba RC	.50
41	Chad Durham RC	.50
42	Jim Mann RC	.50
43	Shane Loux RC	.50
44	Luis Rivas	.25
45	Ken Chenard RC	.50
46	Mike Lockwood RC	.50
47	Giovanni Lara RC	.50
48	Bubba Carpenter RC	.50
49	Ryan Dittfurth RC	.50
50	John Stephens RC	.50
51	Pedro Feliz RC	2.00
52	Kenny Kelly RC	.50
53	Neil Jenkins RC	.50
54	Mike Glendenning RC	.50
55	Bo Porter	.25
56	Eric Byrnes RC	.50
57	Tony Alvarez RC	.50
58	Kazuhiro Sasaki RC	.50
59	Chad Durbin RC	.50
60	Mike Bynum RC	.50
61	Travis Wilson RC	.50
62	Jose Leon RC	.50
63	Ryan Vogelsong RC	.50
64	Geraldo Guzman RC	.50
65	Craig Anderson RC	.50
66	Carlos Silva RC	.50
67	Brad Thomas RC	.50
68	Chin-Hui Tsao RC	1.50
69	Mark Buehrle RC	5.00
70	Juan Salas RC	.50
71	Denny Abreu RC	.50
72	Keith McDonald RC	.50
73	Chris Richard RC	.50
74	Tomas de la Rosa RC	.50
75	Vicente Padilla	.50
76	Justin Brunette RC	.50
77	Scott Linebrink RC	.50
78	Jeff Sparks RC	.50
79	Tike Redman RC	.50
80	John Lackey RC	3.00
81	Joe Strong RC	.50
82	Brian Tollberg RC	.50
83	Steve Sisco RC	.50
84	Chris Clapinski	.25
85	Augie Ojeda RC	.50
86	Adrian Gonzalez RC (Draft Picks)	6.00
87	Mike Stodolka RC (Draft Picks)	.50
88	Adam Johnson RC (Draft Picks)	.50
89	Matt Wheatland RC (Draft Picks)	.50
90	Corey Smith RC (Draft Picks)	.50
91	Rocco Baldelli RC (Draft Picks)	2.00
92	Keith Bucktrot RC (Draft Picks)	.50
93	Adam Wainwright RC (Draft Picks)	3.00
94	Blaine Boyer RC (Draft Picks)	.50
95	Aaron Herr RC (Draft Picks)	.50
96	Scott Thorman RC (Draft Picks)	1.50
97	Brian Digby RC (Draft Picks)	.50
98	Josh Shortslef RC (Draft Picks)	.50
99	Sean Smith RC (Draft Picks)	.50
100	Alex Cruz RC (Draft Picks)	.50
101	Marc Love RC (Draft Picks)	.50
102	Kevin Lee RC (Draft Picks)	.50
103	Timoniel Perez RC (Draft Picks)	.50
104	Alex Cabrera RC (Draft Picks)	.50
105	Shane Heams RC (Draft Picks)	.50
106	Tripper Johnson RC (Draft Picks)	.50
107	Brent Abernathy RC (Draft Picks)	.50
108	John Cotton RC (Draft Picks)	.50
109	Brad Wilkerson RC (Draft Picks)	1.50
110	Jon Rauch RC (Draft Picks)	.50

2000 Bowman's Best Pre-Production

BRETT MYERS

Three-card cello packs of promotional cards introduced the Bowman's Best issue for 2000. The cards are virtually identical to the regularly issued version except for the numbering on the back which includes a "PP" prefix.

		NM/M
Complete Set (3):		6.00
Common Player:		2.00
PP1	Larry Walker	2.00
PP2	Adam Dunn	2.00
PP3	Brett Myers	2.00

2000 Bowman's Best

The base set consists of 200-cards on a mirror like sheen, reminiscent of Refractors. Veteran cards have gold highlights while rookies and prospects have blue highlights. There are three subsets: Best Performers (86-100), Prospects (101-150) and Rookies (151-200). Rookies are serially numbered to 2,999 on the card back and are randomly inserted on the average of 1:7 packs.

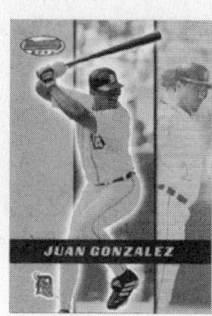

JUAN GONZALEZ

		NM/M
Complete Set (200):		275.00
Common Player:		.20
Common Rookie (151-200):		5.00
Production 2,999 Sets		
Pack (4):		4.00
Box (24):		75.00
1	Nomar Garciaparra	1.00
2	Chipper Jones	1.50
3	Damion Easley	.20
4	Bernie Williams	.40
5	Barry Bonds	3.00
6	Jermaine Dye	.20
7	John Olerud	.20
8	Mike Hampton	.20
9	Cal Ripken Jr.	3.00
10	Jeff Bagwell	.75
11	Troy Glaus	.50
12	J.D. Drew	.40
13	Jeromy Burnitz	.20
14	Carlos Delgado	.75
15	Shawn Green	.40
16	Kevin Millwood	.40
17	Rondell White	.20
18	Scott Rolen	.75
19	Jeff Cirillo	.20
20	Barry Larkin	.40
21	Brian Giles	.20
22	Roger Clemens	1.50
23	Manny Ramirez	1.00
24	Alex Gonzalez	.20
25	Mark Grace	.40
26	Fernando Tatis	.20
27	Randy Johnson	1.00
28	Roger Cedeno	.20
29	Brian Jordan	.20
30	Kevin Brown	.40
31	Greg Vaughn	.20
32	Roberto Alomar	.50
33	Larry Walker	.20
34	Rafael Palmeiro	.50
35	Curt Schilling	.50
36	Orlando Hernandez	.20
37	Todd Walker	.20
38	Juan Gonzalez	.50
39	Sean Casey	.25
40	Tony Gwynn	1.00
41	Albert Belle	.20
42	Gary Sheffield	.40
43	Michael Barrett	.20
44	Preston Wilson	.20
45	Jim Thome	.40
46	Shannon Stewart	.20
47	Mo Vaughn	.20
48	Ben Grieve	.20
49	Adrian Beltre	.40
50	Sammy Sosa	1.50
51	Bob Abreu	.40
52	Edgardo Alfonzo	.20
53	Carlos Febles	.20
54	Frank Thomas	1.00
55	Alex Rodriguez	2.50
56	Cliff Floyd	.20
57	Jose Canseco	.40
58	Erubiel Durazo	.20
59	Tim Hudson	.50
60	Craig Biggio	.20
61	Eric Karros	.20
62	Mike Mussina	.50
63	Robin Ventura	.20
64	Carlos Beltran	.75
65	Pedro Martinez	1.00
66	Gabe Kapler	.20
67	Jason Kendall	.20
68	Derek Jeter	3.00
69	Magglio Ordonez	.50
70	Mike Piazza	2.00
71	Mike Lieberthal	.20
72	Andres Galarraga	.20
73	Raul Mondesi	.20
74	Eric Chavez	.40
75	Greg Maddux	2.00
76	Matt Williams	.25
77	Kris Benson	.20
78	Ivan Rodriguez	.50
79	Pokey Reese	.20
80	Vladimir Guerrero	1.00
81	Mark McGwire	2.00
82	Vinny Castilla	.20
83	Todd Helton	1.00
84	Andruw Jones	.50
85	Ken Griffey Jr.	2.00
86	Mark McGwire	
	(Best Performers)	1.00
87	Derek Jeter	
	(Best Performers)	1.50
88	Chipper Jones	
	(Best Performers)	.75
89	Nomar Garciaparra	
	(Best Performers)	.50

90	Sammy Sosa	
	(Best Performers)	.75
91	Cal Ripken Jr.	
	(Best Performers)	1.50
92	Juan Gonzalez	
	(Best Performers)	.50
93	Alex Rodriguez	
	(Best Performers)	1.25
94	Barry Bonds	
	(Best Performers)	1.50
95	Sean Casey	
	(Best Performers)	.25
96	Vladimir Guerrero	
	(Best Performers)	.50
97	Mike Piazza	
	(Best Performers)	1.00
98	Shawn Green	
	(Best Performers)	.25
99	Jeff Bagwell	
	(Best Performers)	.50
100	Ken Griffey Jr.	
	(Best Performers)	1.00
101	Rick Ankiel (Prospects)	.75
102	John Patterson	
	(Prospects)	.20
103	David Walling (Prospects)	.20
104	Michael Restovich	
	(Prospects)	.20
105	A.J. Burnett (Prospects)	.20
106	Matt Riley (Prospects)	.20
107	Chad Hermansen	
	(Prospects)	.20
108	Choo Freeman (Prospects)	.20
109	Mark Quinn (Prospects)	.20
110	Corey Patterson	
	(Prospects)	.40
111	Ramon Ortiz (Prospects)	.40
112	Vernon Wells (Prospects)	.40
113	Milton Bradley (Prospects)	.50
114	Travis Dawkins	
	(Prospects)	.20
115	Sean Burroughs	
	(Prospects)	.25
116	Willi Mo Pena (Prospects)	.40
117	Dee Brown (Prospects)	.20
118	C.C. Sabathia	
	(Prospects)	1.00
119	Larry Bigbie	
	(Prospects)	.20
120	Octavio Dotel (Prospects)	.20
121	Kip Wells (Prospects)	.20
122	Ben Petrick (Prospects)	.20
123	Mark Mulder (Prospects)	.40
124	Jason Standridge	
	(Prospects)	.20
125	Adam Piatt (Prospects)	.20
126	Steve Lomasney	
	(Prospects)	.20
127	Jayson Werth (Prospects)	.20
128	Alex Escobar (Prospects)	.20
129	Ryan Anderson	
	(Prospects)	.20
130	Adam Dunn (Prospects)	.50
131	Omar Ortiz (Prospects)	.20
132	Brad Penny (Prospects)	.20
133	Daryle Ward (Prospects)	.20
134	Eric Munson (Prospects)	.20
135	Nick Johnson (Prospects)	.50
136	Jason Jennings	
	(Prospects)	.20
137	Tim Raines Jr. (Prospects)	.20
138	Ruben Mateo (Prospects)	.20
139	Jack Cust (Prospects)	.40
140	Rafael Furcal (Prospects)	.50
141	Eric Gagne (Prospects)	.20
142	Tony Armas (Prospects)	.20
143	Mike Paradis (Prospects)	.20
144	Chris George (Prospects)	.20
145	Alfonso Soriano	
	(Prospects)	.75
146	Josh Hamilton	
	(Prospects)	1.50
147	Michael Cuddyer	
	(Prospects)	.40
148	Jay Gehrke (Prospects)	.20
149	Josh Girdley (Prospects)	.20
150	Pat Burrell (Prospects)	.75
151	Brett Myers RC	10.00
152	Scott Seabol RC	5.00
153	Keith Reed RC	5.00
154	Francisco Rodriguez RC	20.00
155	Barry Zito RC	20.00
156	Pat Manning RC	5.00
157	Ben Christensen RC	5.00
158	Corey Myers RC	5.00
159	Wascar Serrano RC	5.00
160	Wes Anderson RC	5.00
161	Andy Tracy RC	5.00
162	Cesar Saba RC	5.00
163	Mike Lamb RC	5.00
164	Bobby Bradley RC	5.00
165	Vince Faison RC	5.00
166	Ty Howington RC	8.00
167	Ken Harvey RC	8.00
168	Josh Kalinowski RC	5.00
169	Ruben Salazar RC	5.00
170	Aaron Rowand RC	10.00
171	Ramon Santiago RC	5.00
172	Scott Sobkowiak RC	5.00
173	Lyle Overbay RC	10.00
174	Rico Washington RC	5.00
175	Rick Asadoorian RC	5.00
176	Matt Ginter RC	5.00
177	Jason Stumm RC	5.00
178	B.J. Garbe RC	5.00
179	Mike MacDougal RC	5.00
180	Ryan Christianson RC	5.00
181	Kurt Ainsworth RC	5.00

182	Brad Baisley RC	5.00
183	Ben Broussard RC	5.00
184	Aaron McNeal RC	5.00
185	John Sneed RC	5.00
186	Junior Brignac RC	5.00
187	Chance Caple RC	5.00
188	Scott Downs RC	5.00
189	Matt Cepicky RC	5.00
190	Chin-Feng Chen RC	10.00
191	Johan Santana RC	100.00
192	Brad Baker RC	5.00
193	Jason Repko RC	5.00
194	Craig Dingman RC	5.00
195	Chris Wakeland RC	5.00
196	Rogelio Arias RC	5.00
197	Luis Matos RC	8.00
198	Robert Ramsay RC	5.00
199	Willie Bloomquist RC	10.00
200	Tony Pena Jr. RC	5.00

Bets

RUBEN MATEO

This 10-card set highlighted prospects who had the best chance of making the big league. The upper left corner and bottom right corner are die-cut. A small action photo is superimposed over a larger background shot of the featured player. Backs are numbered with a "BBB" prefix.

		NM/M
Complete Set (10):		10.00
Common Player:		.75
Inserted 1:15		
1	Pat Burrell	2.00
2	Alfonso Soriano	2.00
3	Corey Patterson	1.50
4	Eric Munson	.75
5	Sean Burroughs	1.00
6	Rafael Furcal	.75
7	Rick Ankiel	1.00
8	Nick Johnson	1.50
9	Ruben Mateo	.75
10	Josh Hamilton	1.00

Franchise Favorites

Two current players and two retired stars are featured in this six-card set. Card backs are numbered with a "FR" prefix.

		NM/M
Complete Set (6):		15.00
Common Player:		1.00
Inserted 1:17		
1A	Sean Casey	1.00
1B	Johnny Bench	3.00
1C	Sean Casey,	
	Johnny Bench	3.00
2A	Cal Ripken Jr.	5.00
2B	Brooks Robinson	2.00
2C	Cal Ripken Jr.,	
	Brooks Robinson	5.00

Franchise Favorites Autograph

BROOKS ROBINSON

182			

These autographs are seeded 1:1,291 packs, while the two dual autographed versions are inserted 1:5,153 packs.

		NM/M
Common Player:		20.00
Version A & B 1:1,291		
Version C 1:5,153		
1A	Sean Casey	20.00
1B	Johnny Bench	50.00
1C	Sean Casey,	
	Johnny Bench	100.00
2A	Cal Ripken Jr.	125.00
2B	Brooks Robinson	50.00
2C	Cal Ripken Jr.,	
	Brooks Robinson	250.00

Franchise 2000

Each of the 25-cards in this set have rounded corners on a holographic silver design. Backs are numbered with a "F" prefix.

		NM/M
Complete Set (25):		60.00
Common Player:		1.00
Inserted 1:18		
1	Cal Ripken Jr.	8.00
2	Nomar Garciaparra	6.00
3	Frank Thomas	2.00
4	Manny Ramirez	2.00
5	Juan Gonzalez	1.50
6	Carlos Beltran	2.00
7	Derek Jeter	8.00
8	Alex Rodriguez	6.00
9	Ben Grieve	1.00
10	Jose Canseco	1.50
11	Ivan Rodriguez	1.50
12	Mo Vaughn	1.00
13	Randy Johnson	3.00
14	Chipper Jones	4.00
15	Sammy Sosa	5.00
16	Ken Griffey Jr.	5.00
17	Larry Walker	1.00
18	Preston Wilson	1.00
19	Jeff Bagwell	2.00
20	Shawn Green	1.00
21	Vladimir Guerrero	2.00
22	Mike Piazza	5.00
23	Scott Rolen	2.00
24	Tony Gwynn	3.50
25	Barry Bonds	8.00

Locker Room Collection Autographs

ADAM PIATT

Part of the Locker Room Collection, these autographs feature 19 players. Backs are numbered with a "LRCA" prefix.

		NM/M
Common Player:		8.00
Inserted 1:57		
1	Carlos Beltran	25.00
2	Rick Ankiel	20.00
3	Vernon Wells	12.00
4	Ruben Mateo	8.00
5	Ben Petrick	8.00
6	Adam Piatt	8.00
7	Eric Munson	8.00
8	Alfonso Soriano	40.00
9	Kerry Wood	25.00
10	Jack Cust	8.00
11	Rafael Furcal	15.00
12	Josh Hamilton	50.00
13	Brad Penny	8.00
14	Dee Brown	8.00
15	Milton Bradley	12.00
16	Ryan Anderson	8.00
17	John Patterson	8.00
18	Nick Johnson	10.00
19	Peter Bergeron	8.00

Locker Room Collection Jerseys

CARLOS BELTRAN

These inserts have a piece of game-worn jersey embedded into them and are numbered with a "LRCJ" prefix.

		NM/M
Common Player:		4.00
Inserted 1:206		
1	Carlos Beltran	12.00
2	Rick Ankiel	5.00
3	Adam Kennedy	4.00
4	Ben Petrick	4.00
5	Adam Piatt	4.00

Locker Room Collection Lumber

These inserts have a piece of game-used bat embedded into them. They are numbered with a "LRCL" prefix on the back.

		NM/M
Common Player:		5.00
Inserted 1:376		
1	Carlos Beltran	15.00
2	Rick Ankiel	5.00
3	Vernon Wells	5.00
4	Adam Kennedy	5.00
5	Ben Petrick	5.00
6	Adam Piatt	5.00
7	Eric Munson	5.00
8	Rafael Furcal	8.00
9	J.D. Drew	8.00
10	Pat Burrell	10.00

Rookie Signed Baseballs

Redemption inserts, redeemable for Rookie Signed Baseballs, were randomly inserted. Signed baseball displays the Bowman "Rookie Autograph" logo and the Topps "Genuine Issue" sticker.

		NM/M
Complete Set (5):		75.00
Common Player:		15.00
Inserted 1:688		
1	Josh Hamilton	40.00
2	Rick Ankiel	20.00
3	Alfonso Soriano	50.00
4	Nick Johnson	30.00
5	Corey Patterson	20.00

Selections

PAT BURRELL
PHILADELPHIA PHILLIES

This 15-card set is printed on a luminescent, die-cut design. The set features former Rookies of the Year and former No. 1 overall Draft Picks. These are seeded 1:30 packs. Backs are numbered with a "BBS" prefix.

		NM/M
Complete Set (15):		50.00
Common Player:		1.00
Inserted 1:30		
1	Alex Rodriguez	7.50
2	Ken Griffey Jr.	6.00
3	Pat Burrell	2.00
4	Mark McGwire	6.00
5	Derek Jeter	10.00
6	Nomar Garciaparra	3.00
7	Mike Piazza	6.00
8	Josh Hamilton	5.00
9	Cal Ripken Jr.	8.00
10	Jeff Bagwell	2.00
11	Chipper Jones	3.00
12	Jose Canseco	1.50
13	Carlos Beltran	3.00
14	Kerry Wood	3.00
15	Ben Grieve	1.00

Year By Year

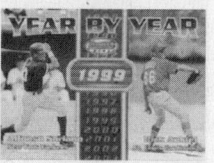

This 10-card set highlights 10 duos who began their careers in the same year. They have a horizontal format on a mirror foiled card front. Backs are numbered with a "YY" prefix.

		NM/M
Complete Set (10):		25.00
Common Card:		1.50
Inserted 1:23		
1	Sammy Sosa,	
	Ken Griffey Jr.	4.00
2	Nomar Garciaparra,	
	Vladimir Guerrero	4.00
3	Alex Rodriguez,	
	Jeff Cirillo	5.00
4	Mike Piazza,	
	Pedro Martinez	4.00
5	Derek Jeter,	
	Edgardo Alfonzo	6.00
6	Alfonso Soriano,	
	Rick Ankiel	2.00
7	Mark McGwire,	
	Barry Bonds	6.00
8	Juan Gonzalez,	
	Larry Walker	1.50
9	Ivan Rodriguez,	
	Jeff Bagwell	1.50
10	Shawn Green,	
	Manny Ramirez	1.50

1992-2004 Boy Scouts of America Atlanta Braves

COLLECTOR'S EDITION
Official B.S.A. Baseball Card

JEFF TREADWAY

In 1992 the Atlanta-area Boy Scouts of America began a "Collector's Edition" series of commemorative baseball cards featuring Braves players. The 2-1/2" x 3-1/2" cards have a variety of designs with color photos, usually game-action. Red, white and blue backs have player information and stats and logos of the team, sponsor(s), and/or BSA.

		NM/M
Complete Set (13):		50.00
Common Player:		2.00
(1)	Jeff Treadway/1992	3.00
(2)	Dale Murphy/1993	15.00
(3)	Deion Sanders/1994	8.00
(4)	Gregory McMichael/	
	1995	3.00
(5)	Ryan Klesko/1996	5.00
(6)	Jeff Blauser/1997	3.00
(7)	Greg Maddux/1998	12.00
(8)	John Rocker/1999	5.00
(9)	John Smoltz/2000	3.00
(10)	Tom Glavine/2001	3.00
(11)	Kevin Millwood/2002	2.00
(12)	Marcus Giles/2003	2.00
(13)	Russ Ortiz/2004	2.00

1998 Bryan Braves Photo Set

After a one-year absence and a change of stadium hot dog vendors, the Braves again distributed a team photo foldout in 1998. The 10-5/8" x 31-3/8" three-panel perforated sheet has a large team photo and individual 2-1/8" x 3-1/8" cards of 35 players and staff. The player cards have a portrait photo on a background of brown baseballs and faded red "A"s. The player name is in gold at the bottom; his position vertically in a blue strip at left. A red Bryan logo is at top-left. Backs are in red, white and blue with biographical and career notes and stats. The unnumbered cards are checklisted here alpabetically.

		NM/M
Complete Foldout Set:		8.00
Common Player:		.10
(1)	Danny Bautista	.10
(2)	Jim Beauchamp	.10
(3)	Rafael Belliard	.10
(4)	Adam Butler	.10
(5)	Norm Charlton	.10
(6)	Greg Colbrunn	.10
(7)	Pat Corrales	.10
(8)	Bobby Cox	.10
(9)	Bobby Dews	.10
(10)	Frank Fultz	.10
(11)	Andres Galarraga	.10
(12)	Tom Glavine	1.00
(13)	Tony Graffanino	.10
(14)	Ozzie Guillen	.10
(15)	Andruw Jones	1.50
(16)	Chipper Jones	3.00
(17)	Clarence Jones	.10
(18)	Ryan Klesko	.10
(19)	Kerry Ligtenberg	.10
(20)	Keith Lockhart	.10
(21)	Javy Lopez	.10
(22)	Greg Maddux	2.00
(23)	Dennis Martinez	.10
(24)	Leo Mazzone	.10
(25)	Kevin Millwood	.50
(26)	Denny Neagle	.10
(27)	Eddie Perez	.10
(28)	John Rocker	.10
(29)	Rudy Seanez	.10
(30)	John Smoltz	1.00
(31)	Russ Springer	.10
(32)	Michael Tucker	.10
(33)	Walt Weiss	.10
(34)	Gerald Williams	.10
(35)	Ned Yost	.10
(36)	Team Photo	.50

1999 Bryan Braves

These Tuesday-night homestand give-away cards were sponsored by the team's hot dog vendor and given away three players at a time to children only. Completion of a set is thus a challenge. The cards of Hernandez, Mulholland and Myers were late-season additions and differ from the rest of the set in that the player names in gold vertically at left are in upper- and lower-case type, while most cards have the name in all-caps. The 2-1/2" x 3-1/2" cards have player portraits bordered in blue at left and bottom. The position is in gold at bottom; the uniform number in gold at top. A red Bryan logo is at lower-left. Black, white and blue backs have minimal player vitae and full professional stats. The unnumbered cards are checklisted here in alphabetical order.

		NM/M
Complete Set (30):		32.50
Common Player:		1.00
(1)	Don Baylor	1.00
(2)	Bret Boone	1.00
(3)	Pat Corrales	1.00

(4)	Bobby Cox	1.00
(5)	Bobby Dews	1.00
(6)	Tom Glavine	1.50
(7)	Ozzie Guillen	1.00
(8)	Jose Hernandez	1.00
(9)	Glenn Hubbard	1.00
(10)	Brian Hunter	1.00
(11)	Andruw Jones	2.50
(12)	Chipper Jones	4.00
(13)	Brian Jordan	1.00
(14)	Ryan Klesko	1.00
(15)	Keith Lockhart	1.00
(16)	Javy Lopez	1.00
(17)	Greg Maddux	3.00
(18)	Leo Mazzone	1.00
(19)	Kevin Millwood	1.00
(20)	Terry Mulholland	1.00
(21)	Greg Myers	1.00
(22)	Otis Nixon	1.00
(23)	Eddie Perez	1.00
(24)	Odalis Perez	1.00
(25)	Mike Remlinger	1.00
(26)	John Rocker	1.00
(27)	Rudy Seanez	1.00
(28)	John Smoltz	1.50
(29)	Walt Weiss	1.00
(30)	Ned Yost	1.00

1999 Bryan Braves Team Photo Set

Children visiting Turner Field for a late-season game received this foldout sponsored by the team's hot dog vendor. The 10-5/8" x 31-3/8" three-panel perforated sheet has a large team photo and individual 2-1/8" x 3-1/8" cards of 35 players and staff. The player cards have a portrait photo on a baseball background. The player name and position are at left. A large red Bryan logo is at top-right. Backs are in red, white and black with biographical and career notes and stats. The unnumbered cards are checklisted here alpabetically.

		NM/M
Complete Foldout Set:		8.00
Common Player:		.10
(1)	Don Baylor	.10
(2)	Bret Boone	.25
(3)	Bruce Chen	.10
(4)	Pat Corrales	.10
(5)	Bobby Cox	.10
(6)	Bobby Dews	.10
(7)	Frank Fultz	.10
(8)	Tom Glavine	1.00
(9)	Ozzie Guillen	.10
(10)	Jose Hernandez	.10
(11)	Glenn Hubbard	.10
(12)	Brian Hunter	.10
(13)	Andruw Jones	1.50
(14)	Chipper Jones	3.00
(15)	Brian Jordan	.10
(16)	Ryan Klesko	.10
(17)	Keith Lockhart	.10
(18)	Javy Lopez	.10
(19)	Greg Maddux	2.00
(20)	Leo Mazzone	.10
(21)	Kevin McGlinchy	.10
(22)	Kevin Millwood	.50
(23)	Terry Mulholland	.10
(24)	Greg Myers	.10
(25)	Otis Nixon	.10
(26)	Eddie Perez	.10
(27)	Mike Remlinger	.10
(28)	John Rocker	.10
(29)	Rudy Seanez	.10
(30)	Randall Simon	.10
(31)	John Smoltz	1.00
(32)	Russ Springer	.10
(33)	Walt Weiss	.10
(34)	Gerald Williams	.10
(35)	Ned Yost	.10
(36)	Team Photo	.50

2000 Bryan Braves Team Photo Set

Children visiting Turner Field for a late-season game received this foldout sponsored by the team's hot dog vendor. The 10-5/8" x 31-3/8" three-panel perforated sheet has a large team photo and individual 2-1/8" x 3-1/8" cards of 35 players and staff. The staff cards have a portrait photo on a blue

be issued in more than one variation to allow for three cards to be given away each date. The 2-1/2" x 3-1/2" cards have game-action photos vignetted with blue borders. The player's full name and position are in red at left, and his last name in white at right. His uniform number is at top. A red Bryan logo is at bottom. Black, white and blue backs have a few bits of personal data and complete minor and major league stats. The unnumbered cards are checklisted here alphabetically.

		NM/M
Complete Set (39):		45.00
Common Player:		1.00
(1)	Andy Ashby	1.00
(2)	Bobby Bonilla	1.00
(3)	John Burkett	1.00
(4)	Pat Corrales	1.00
(5)	Bobby Cox	1.00
(6)	Bobby Dews	1.00
(7)	Rafael Furcal	1.50
(8)	Andres Galarraga/Btg	1.00
(9)	Andres Galarraga/Fldg	1.00
(10)	Tom Glavine	2.00
(11)	Glenn Hubbard	1.00
(12)	Andruw Jones (Batting stance.)	2.50
(13)	Andruw Jones (Follow-through.)	2.50
(14)	Chipper Jones (Back turned.)	4.00
(15)	Chipper Jones/Fldg	4.00
(16)	Brian Jordan/Btg	1.00
(17)	Brian Jordan/Portrait	1.00
(18)	Wally Joyner	1.00
(19)	Kerry Ligtenberg	1.00
(20)	Keith Lockhart	1.00
(21)	Javy Lopez/Btg	1.00
(22)	Javy Lopez/Catching	1.00
(23)	Greg Maddux	3.00
(24)	Leo Mazzone	1.00
(25)	Kevin McGlinchy	1.00
(26)	Kevin Millwood	1.00
(27)	Terry Mulholland	1.00
(28)	Eddie Perez	1.00
(29)	Odalis Perez	1.00
(30)	Mike Remlinger	1.00
(31)	Merv Rettenmund	1.00
(32)	John Rocker	1.00
(33)	Reggie Sanders	1.00
(34)	Rudy Seanez	1.00
(35)	John Smoltz	2.00
(36)	B.J. Surhoff	1.00
(37)	Quilvio Veras	1.00
(38)	Walt Weiss	1.00
(39)	Ned Yost	1.00

2000 Bryan Braves Team Photo Set

For the first time since the Braves hot dog concessionaires began issuing annual stadium give-away card sets in 1989, the number of Tuesday home games in 2000 dictated that some players

background. The player cards have game-action photos. All cards are bordered in brown with a nameplate design at bottom with identification and a Bryan logo. Backs are in red, white and black with biographical and career notes and stats. The unnumbered cards are checklisted here alpabetically.

		NM/M
Complete Foldout Set:		8.00
Common Player:		.10
(1)	Andy Ashby	.10
(2)	Bobby Bonilla	.10
(3)	John Burkett	.10
(4)	Bobby Cox	.10
(5)	Pat Corrales	.10
(6)	Bobby Dews	.10
(7)	Frank Fultz	.10
(8)	Rafael Furcal	.75
(9)	Andres Galarraga	.10
(10)	Tom Glavine	1.00
(11)	Glenn Hubbard	.10
(12)	Andruw Jones	1.00
(13)	Chipper Jones	3.00
(14)	Brian Jordan	.10
(15)	Wally Joyner	.10
(16)	Kerry Ligtenberg	.10
(17)	Keith Lockhart	.10
(18)	Javy Lopez	.10
(19)	Greg Maddux	1.50
(20)	Leo Mazzone	.10
(21)	Kevin McGlinchy	.10
(22)	Kevin Millwood	.10
(23)	Terry Mulholland	.10
(24)	Eddie Perez	.10
(25)	Odalis Perez	.10
(26)	Mike Remlinger	.10
(27)	Merv Rettenmund	.10
(28)	John Rocker	.10
(29)	Reggie Sanders	.10
(30)	Rudy Seanez	.10
(31)	John Smoltz	1.00
(32)	B.J. Surhoff	.10
(33)	Quilvio Veras	.10
(34)	Walt Weiss	.10
(35)	Ned Yost	.10

1982 Builders Emporium Los Angeles Dodgers

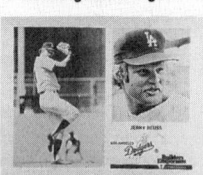

Shoppers at this chain of building supply stores in Southern California were able to receive one of this seven-card set with each visit. Cards are printed in black-and-white in 11" x 8-1/2" format with blank backs. Fronts of the player cards have both portrait and action photos, the manager's card has only a portrait. Team and sponsors' logos are at bottom-right. The unnumbered cards are checklisted here in alphabetical order.

		NM/M
Complete Set (7):		35.00
Common Player:		6.00
(1)	Dusty Baker	6.00
(2)	Ron Cey	6.00
(3)	Steve Garvey	9.00
(4)	Pedro Guerrero	6.00
(5)	Tommy Lasorda	6.00
(6)	Jerry Reuss	6.00
(7)	Steve Sax	6.00

1982 Burger King Braves

A set consisting of 27 "Collector Lids" featuring the Atlanta Braves was issued by Burger King restaurants in 1982. The plastic lids, 3-5/8" in diameter, were placed on a special Coca-Cola cup which listed the scores of the Braves' season-opening 13-game win streak. A black-and-white photo plus the player's name, position, height,

weight, and 1981 statistics are found on the lid front. The unnumbered, blank-backed lids also contain logos for Burger King, Coca-Cola, and the Major League Baseball Players Association.

		NM/M
Complete Set (27):		20.00
Common Player:		1.00
(1)	Steve Bedrosian	1.00
(2)	Bruce Benedict	1.00
(3)	Tommy Boggs	1.00
(4)	Brett Butler	1.50
(5)	Rick Camp	1.00
(6)	Chris Chambliss	1.00
(7)	Ken Dayley	1.00
(8)	Gene Garber	1.00
(9)	Preston Hanna	1.00
(10)	Terry Harper	1.00
(11)	Bob Horner	1.50
(12)	Al Hrabosky	1.00
(13)	Glenn Hubbard	1.00
(14)	Randy Johnson	1.00
(15)	Rufino Linares	1.00
(16)	Rick Mahler	1.00
(17)	Larry McWilliams	1.00
(18)	Dale Murphy	12.50
(19)	Phil Niekro	3.00
(20)	Biff Pocoroba	1.00
(21)	Rafael Ramirez	1.00
(22)	Jerry Royster	1.00
(23)	Ken Smith	1.00
(24)	Bob Walk	1.00
(25)	Claudell Washington	1.00
(26)	Bob Watson	1.00
(27)	Larry Whisenton	1.00

1982 Burger King Indians

Dave Garcia
MANAGER

SPORTSMANSHIP

It's always important to win a ball game. What makes it even more important is the way you conduct yourself on the field. Try to treat your opposition the way you expect them to treat you.

TIPS FROM THE DUGOUT

This set was sponsored by WUAB-TV and Burger Kings in the Cleveland vicinity. The cards' green borders encompass a large yellow area which contains a black-and-white photo plus a baseball tip. Manager Dave Garcia and his coaches provide the baseball hints. The cards, which measure 3" x 5", are unnumbered and blank-backed.

		NM/M
Complete Set (12):		7.00
Common Player:		.75
(1)	Dave Garcia (Be In The Game)	.75
(2)	Dave Garcia (Sportsmanship)	.75
(3)	Johnny Goryl (Rounding The Bases)	.75
(4)	Johnny Goryl (3rd Base Running)	.75
(5)	Tom McCraw (Follow Thru)	.75
(6)	Tom McCraw (Selecting A Bat)	.75
(7)	Tom McCraw (Watch The Ball)	.75
(8)	Mel Queen (Master One Pitch)	.75
(9)	Mel Queen (Warm Up)	.75
(10)	Dennis Sommers (Get Down On A Ground Ball)	.75
(11)	Dennis Sommers (Protect Your Fingers)	.75
(12)	Dennis Sommers (Tagging First Base)	.75

1986 Burger King

Burger King restaurants in the Pennsylvania and New Jersey areas issued a set entitled "All-Pro Series." Cards were issued with the purchase of a Whopper sandwich and came in folded panels of two cards each, along with a coupon card. Fronts feature a color photo and identification plus the Burger King logo. Due to a lack of MLB licensing, team insignias on the players' uniforms were airbrushed

away. Backs are in black-and-white and contain brief biographical and statistical information.

		NM/M
Complete Panel Set (10):		3.00
Complete Singles Set (20):		3.00
Common Panel:		.25
Common Single Player:		.05
PANEL (1)		.40
1	Tony Pena	.05
2	Dave Winfield	.20
PANEL (2)		1.00
3	Fernando Valenzuela	.05
4	Pete Rose	.45
PANEL (3)		1.00
5	Mike Schmidt	.40
6	Steve Carlton	.20
PANEL (4)		.25
7	Glenn Wilson	.05
8	Jim Rice	.15
PANEL (5)		.50
9	Wade Boggs	.25
10	Juan Samuel	.05
PANEL (6)		.50
11	Dale Murphy	.10
12	Reggie Jackson	.35
PANEL (7)		.40
13	Kirk Gibson	.05
14	Eddie Murray	.20
PANEL (8)		1.00
15	Cal Ripken Jr.	.50
16	Willie McGee	.05
PANEL (9)		.40
17	Dwight Gooden	.05
18	Steve Garvey	.10
PANEL (10)		1.00
19	Don Mattingly	.40
20	George Brett	.40

1987 Burger King

The 1987 "All-Pro 2nd Edition Series" set was part of a giveaway promotion at participating Burger King restaurants. The set is comprised of 20 players on ten different panels. Cards measure 2-1/2" x 3-1/2" each with a three-card panel (includes a coupon card) measuring 7-5/8" x 3-1/2". Fronts feature a full-color photo and Burger King logo surrounded by a blue stars-and-stripes border. Backs are black-and-white with a brief biography and 1986/Career statistics. The set was produced by Mike Schecter Associates and, as with many MSA issues, all team insignias were airbrushed away.

		NM/M
Complete Panel Set (10):		3.00
Complete Singles Set (20):		3.00
Common Panel:		.30
Common Single Player:		.05
PANEL (1)		.75
1	Wade Boggs	.40
2	Gary Carter	.30
PANEL (2)		.75
3	Will Clark	.05
4	Roger Clemens	.40
PANEL (3)		.40
5	Steve Garvey	.20
6	Ron Darling	.05
PANEL (4)		.30
7	Pedro Guerrero	.05
8	Von Hayes	.05

PANEL (5)		.40
9	Rickey Henderson	.30
10	Keith Hernandez	.05
PANEL (6)		.30
11	Wally Joyner	.05
12	Mike Krukow	.05
PANEL (7)		1.00
13	Don Mattingly	.50
14	Ozzie Smith	.40
PANEL (8)		.30
15	Tony Pena	.05
16	Jim Rice	.20
PANEL (9)		1.00
17	Ryne Sandberg	.40
18	Mike Schmidt	.50
PANEL (10)		.30
19	Darryl Strawberry	.05
20	Fernando Valenzuela	.05

1994 Burger King Cal Ripken Jr.

Although the cards themselves do not indicate it, this issue was co-sponsored by Burger King and Coke, and distributed in BK restaurants in the Baltimore-Washington area. Cards were available in three-card packs for 25 cents with the purchase of a Coke product. Each pack contains two regular cards and a gold card. Each of the nine cards could be found in a regular and gold version. Cards feature color photos with a semi-circular black border at top or left. "Score '94" appears in orange in one of the upper corners, along with an Orioles logo. Cal Ripken, Jr.'s name appears at the bottom. On the gold premium version, there is a gold-foil circle around the Orioles logo and Ripken's name appears in gold, rather than white. Backs have a smaller color photo, again meeting at a semi-circular edge with the black border at left and bottom. In the black are another Score logo, a card number, an Orioles logo, a headline and a few career details and/or stats. Cards are UV coated on each side. Several hundred of the cards were personally autographed by Ripken and distributed in a drawing.

		NM/M
Complete Set (9):		5.00
Complete Set, Gold (9):		9.00
Common Card:		.75
Common Card, Gold:		1.25
Autographed Card:		185.00
1	Double Honors	.75
1a	Double Honors/Gold	1.25
2	Perennial All-Star	.75
2a	Perennial All-Star/Gold	1.25
3	Peerless Power	.75
3a	Peerless Power/Gold	1.25
4	Fitness Fan	.75
4a	Fitness Fan/Gold	1.25
5	Prime Concerns	.75
5a	Prime Concerns/Gold	1.25
6	Home Run Club	.75
6a	Home Run Club/Gold	1.25
7	The Iron Man	.75
7a	The Iron Man/Gold	1.25
8	Heavy Hitter	.75
8a	Heavy Hitter/Gold	1.25
9	Gold Glover	.75
9a	Gold Glover/Gold	1.25

1997 Burger King Cal Ripken Jr.

Three years after its 1994 tribute, Burger King in 1997 created an eight-card set honoring the future Hall of Famer. Participating BK outlets in Maryland, the District of Columbia, Delaware, Pennsylvania, Virginia and West Virginia offered the cards for 99¢ with a meal purchase or $1.15 without. Each card

CAL RIPKEN, JR. # 8
1 of 10,000

was produced in two forms: with and without a gold holographic foil facsimile autograph and "1 of 10,000" notation. The 2-1/2" x 3-1/2" cards have action photos of Ripken on front with muted backgrounds. His name, uniform number and team logo also appear. Backs, numbered "X/8" have another color photo with ghosted background and a paragraph of a career highlight. Autographed cards were part of a prize structure explained on information cards accompanying the Ripken card in each pack.

		NM/M
Complete Set (8):		5.00
Complete Gold Set (8):		10.00
Common Card:		1.00
Common Gold Card:		2.00
Autographed Card:		185.00
1-8	Cal Ripken Jr.	1.00
	Autograph Information Card	.25

1999 Burger King N.Y. Yankees

Members of the World Champion 1998 N.Y. Yankees are featured on this three-sheet set of cards sold by metropolitan New York Burger King restaurants in April-May, 1999. The 12-1/2" x 10-1/2" perforated sheets each include nine standard-size cards. Fronts feature action photos with the Yankees and Fleer logos. Backs have the same photo along with season and career stats and highlights, printed on a ghosted background of a Yankees pinstriped jersey. The Fleer and team logos appear on back, as do those of the players' union and the restaurant chain. On the sheet along with the player cards are a checklist, team schedule, mention of the BK Cancer Foundation of New York and a kids' club offer.

		NM/M
Complete Sheet Set (3):		7.50
Complete Singles Set (27):		7.50
Common Player:		.25
SHEET 1		6.00
1	Derek Jeter	4.00
2	Paul O'Neill	.25
3	Scott Brosius	.25
4	Mariano Rivera	.50
5	Chuck Knoblauch	.25
6	Graeme Lloyd	.25
7	Joe Girardi	.25
8	Orlando Hernandez	.25
9	Tim Raines	.25
SHEET 2		3.50
10	Bernie Williams	.45
11	Tino Martinez	.25
12	Andy Pettitte	.40
13	Hideki Irabu	.25
14	Ramiro Mendoza	.25
15	Jeff Nelson	.25
16	Homer Bush	.25
17	Darren Holmes	.25
18	Yankees Championship History	.25
SHEET 3		3.50
19	David Cone	.25
20	David Wells	.25
21	Chili Davis	.25
22	Darryl Strawberry	.25
23	Ricky Ledee	.25
24	Jorge Posada	.25
25	Luis Sojo	.25
26	Chad Curtis	.25
27	Mike Stanton	.25

C

1989 Cadaco All-Star Baseball Discs

This set of player discs was sold with and intended for use in a board game. Fronts of the 3-1/2" diameter position players' discs have a yellow border sectioned with numbers from 1 to 14, indicating that player's likelihood of performing a specific baseball result based on career stats. At center is a color player photo from which the uniform details have been airbrushed. Logos of the game's producer and the Major League Players Association flank the portrait. The player's name, team and position are below the photo. Backs have up to five years of recent stats and lifetime totals, along with a few biographical data. Several of the discs have player names misspelled. Each disc can be found either with or without the team name and league on back. Four error discs from the initial print run (with team, league on back) were corrected. The unnumbered discs are checklisted alphabetically.

		NM/M
Complete Set (63):		20.00
Common Player:		.25
(1)	Harold Baines	.25
(2)	Wade Boggs	2.00
(3)	Bobby Bonilla	.25
(4)	George Brett	2.50
(5)	Jose Canseco	1.00
(6)	Gary Carter	1.50
(7)	Joe Carter	.25
(8)	Will Clark	.25
(9a)	Rodger Clemens (First name misspelled.)	3.00
(9b)	Roger Clemens (Corrected)	3.00
(10)	Vince Coleman	.25
(11)	David Cone	.25
(12)	Alvin Davis	.25
(13)	Eric Davis	.25
(14)	Glenn Davis	.25
(15)	Andre Dawson	.65
(16)	Shawon Dunston	.25
(17)	Dennis Eckersley	.60
(18)	Carlton Fisk	1.50
(19)	Scott Fletcher	.25
(20a)	John Frannko (Last name misspelled.)	.35
(20b)	John Franco (Corrected)	.35
(21)	Julio Franco (Franco)	.25
(22)	Gary Gaetti	.25
(23)	Andres Galarraga	.25
(24)	Kirk Gibson	.25
(25)	Mike Greenwell	.25
(26)	Mark Gubicza	.25
(27)	Pedro Guerrero	.25
(28)	Tony Gwynn	2.00
(29)	Rickey Henderson	1.50
(30)	Orel Hershiser	.25
(31)	Kent Hrbek	.25
(32)	Danny Jackson	.25
(33a)	Barry Larkin (Wrong photo.)	.65
(33b)	Barry Larkin (Corrected)	.65
(34)	Greg Maddux	2.00
(35)	Don Mattingly	2.50
(36a)	Mark McGuire (Last name misspelled.)	4.50
(36b)	Mark McGwire (Corrected)	4.50
(37)	Fred McGriff	.25
(38)	Paul Molitor	1.50
(39)	Tony Pena	.25
(40)	Gerald Perry	.25
(41)	Dan Plesac	.25
(42)	Kirby Puckett	2.00
(43)	Johnny Ray	.25
(44)	Jeff Reardon	.25
(45)	Cal Ripken, Jr.	4.50
(46)	Babe Ruth	3.50
(47)	Nolan Ryan	4.50
(48)	Juan Samuel	.25
(49)	Ryne Sandberg	2.00
(50)	Benito Santiago	.25
(51)	Steve Sax	.25
(52)	Mike Schmidt	2.25
(53)	Kevin Seitzer	.25
(54)	Ozzie Smith	2.00
(55)	Terry Steinbach	.25
(56)	Dave Stewart	.25
(57)	Darryl Strawberry	.25
(58)	Andres Thomas	.25
(59)	Alan Trammell (Trammell)	.25
(60)	Andy Van Slyke	.25
(61)	Frank Viola	.25
(62)	Dave Winfield	1.50
(63)	Todd Worrell	.25

1990 Cadaco All-Star Baseball Discs

This set of player discs was sold with and intended for use in a board game. Fronts of the 3-1/2" diameter position players' discs have a border sectioned with numbers from 1 to 14, indicating that player's likelihood of performing a specific baseball result based on career stats. At center is a color player photo from which the uniform details have been airbrushed. Logos of the game's producer and the Major League Players Association flank the portrait. The player's name, team and position are below the photo. Backs have up to five years of recent stats and lifetime totals, along with brief biographical data. A handful of the game's past greats were included among the contemporary players which make up the bulk of the disc set. The unnumbered discs are checklisted alphabetically.

		NM/M
Complete Set (63):		20.00
Common Player:		.25
(1)	Harold Baines	.25
(2)	Damon Berryhill	.25
(3)	Craig Biggio	.25
(4)	Wade Boggs	2.00
(5)	Bobby Bonilla	.25
(6)	Jose Canseco	1.00
(7)	Will Clark	.25
(8)	Roger Clemens	2.50
(9)	Roberto Clemente	4.00
(10)	Ty Cobb	2.50
(11)	Vince Coleman	.25
(12)	Eric Davis	.25
(13)	Glenn Davis	.25
(14)	Andre Dawson	.65
(15)	Shawon Dunston	.25
(16)	Tony Fernandez	.25
(17)	Carlton Fisk	1.50
(18)	Julio Franco	.25
(19)	Gary Gaetti	.25
(20)	Lou Gehrig	4.00
(21)	Kirk Gibson	.25
(22)	Mark Grace	.25
(23)	Ken Griffey Jr.	3.00
(24)	Pedro Guerrero	.25
(25)	Tony Gwynn	2.00
(26)	Rickey Henderson	1.50
(27)	Orel Hershiser	.25
(28)	Bo Jackson	.60
(29)	Howard Johnson	.25
(30)	Carney Lansford	.25
(31)	Barry Larkin	.25
(32)	Greg Maddux	2.00
(33)	Don Mattingly	2.50
(34)	Fred McGriff	.25
(35)	Mark McGwire	3.50
(36)	Kevin Mitchell	.25
(37)	Tony Pena	.25
(38)	Kirby Puckett	2.00
(39)	Willie Randolph	.25
(40)	Cal Ripken Jr.	4.50
(41)	Babe Ruth	4.00
(42)	Nolan Ryan	4.50
(43)	Bret Saberhagen	.25
(44)	Chris Sabo	.25
(45)	Ryne Sandberg	2.00
(46)	Benito Santiago	.25
(47)	Steve Sax	.25
(48)	Mike Scott	.25
(49)	Kevin Seitzer	.25
(50)	Ruben Sierra	.25
(51)	Ozzie Smith	2.00
(52)	Terry Steinbach	.25
(53)	Dave Stewart	.25
(54)	Mickey Tettleton	.25
(55)	Robby Thompson	.25
(56)	Alan Trammell	.25
(57)	Jose Uribe	.25
(58)	Andy Van Slyke	.25
(59)	Honus Wagner	1.50
(60)	Jerome Walton	.25
(61)	Lou Whitaker	.25
(62)	Matt Williams	.25
(63)	Robin Yount	1.50

1991 Cadaco All-Star Baseball Discs

This set of player discs was sold with and intended for use in a board game. Fronts of the 3-1/2" diameter discs have a yellow border sectioned with numbers from 1 to 14, indicating that player's likelihood of performing a specific baseball result based on career stats. At center is a color player photo from which the uniform details have been airbrushed. Logos of the game's producer and the Major League Players Association flank the portrait. The player's name, team and position are below the photo. Backs have up to five years of recent stats and lifetime totals, along with a few biographical data. The unnumbered discs are checklisted alphabetically.

		NM/M
Complete Set (62):		20.00
Common Player:		.25
(1)	Roberto Alomar	.35
(2)	Harold Baines	.25
(3)	Craig Biggio	.25
(4)	Wade Boggs	2.00
(5)	Barry Bonds	4.50
(6)	Bobby Bonilla	.25
(7)	Jose Canseco	.75
(8)	Will Clark	.25
(9)	Roger Clemens	2.50
(10)	Roberto Clemente	4.00
(11)	Ty Cobb	2.50
(12)	Vince Coleman	.25
(13)	Eric Davis	.25
(14)	Glenn Davis	.25
(15)	Andre Dawson	.65
(16)	Delino DeShields	.25
(17)	Shawon Dunston	.25
(18)	Tony Fernandez	.25
(19)	Cecil Fielder	.25
(20)	Carlton Fisk	1.50
(21)	Julio Franco	.25
(22)	Gary Gaetti	.25
(23)	Lou Gehrig	3.00
(24)	Kirk Gibson	.25
(25)	Mark Grace	.25
(26)	Ken Griffey Jr.	3.00
(27)	Kelly Gruber	.25
(28)	Tony Gwynn	2.00
(29)	Rickey Henderson	1.50
(30)	Orel Hershiser	.25
(31)	David Justice	.25
(32)	Bo Jackson	.50
(33)	Howard Johnson	.25
(34)	Barry Larkin	.25
(35)	Ramon Martinez	.25
(36)	Don Mattingly	2.50
(37)	Fred McGriff	.25
(38)	Mark McGwire	3.50
(39)	Kevin Mitchell	.25
(40)	Lance Parrish	.25
(41)	Tony Pena	.25
(42)	Kirby Puckett	2.00
(43)	Cal Ripken Jr.	4.00
(44)	Babe Ruth	4.00
(45)	Nolan Ryan	4.50
(46)	Bret Saberhagen	.25
(47)	Chris Sabo	.25
(48)	Ryne Sandberg	2.00
(49)	Benito Santiago	.25
(50)	Steve Sax	.25
(51)	Gary Sheffield	.75
(52)	Ruben Sierra	.25
(53)	Ozzie Smith	2.00
(54)	Terry Steinbach	.25
(55)	Benito Santiago	.25
(56)	Mickey Tettleton	.25
(57)	Alan Trammell	.25
(58)	Jose Uribe	.25
(59)	Honus Wagner	1.50
(60)	Lou Whitaker	.25
(61)	Matt Williams	.25
(62)	Robin Yount	1.50

1993 Cadaco All-Star Baseball Discs

This set of player discs was sold with and intended for use in a board game. Fronts of the 3-1/2" diameter discs have a yellow border sectioned with numbers from 1 to 14, indicating that player's likelihood of performing a specific baseball result based on career stats. At center is a color player photo from which the uniform details have been airbrushed. Logos of the game's producer and the Major League Players Association flank the portrait. The player's name, team and position are below the photo. Backs have up to five years of recent stats and lifetime totals, along with a few biographical data. The unnumbered discs are checklisted alphabetically.

		NM/M
Complete Set (62):		20.00
Common Player:		.25
(1)	Kevin Appier	.25
(2)	Carlos Baerga	.25
(3)	Harold Baines	.25
(4)	Derek Bell	.25
(5)	George Bell	.25
(6)	Jay Bell	.25
(7)	Mike Boddicker	.25
(8)	Wade Boggs	2.00
(9)	Hubie Brooks	.25
(10)	Jose Canseco	.75
(11)	Roger Clemens	2.50
(12)	Roberto Clemente	4.00
(13)	Ty Cobb	2.50
(14)	Alex Cole	.25
(15)	Jeff Conine	.25
(16)	Andre Dawson	.65
(17)	Shawon Dunston	.25
(18)	Lenny Dykstra	.25
(19)	Carlton Fisk	1.50
(20)	Darrin Fletcher	.25
(21)	Gary Gaetti	.25
(22)	Greg Gagne	.25
(23)	Mike Gallego	.25
(24)	Lou Gehrig	4.00
(25)	Kirk Gibson	.25
(26)	Tom Glavine	.50
(27)	Mark Grace	.25
(28)	Ken Griffey Jr.	3.00
(29)	Tony Gwynn	2.00
(30)	Charlie Hayes	.25
(31)	Rickey Henderson	1.50
(32)	Orel Hershiser	.25
(33)	Bo Jackson	.50
(34)	Howard Johnson	.25
(35)	Randy Johnson	1.50
(36)	Ricky Jordan	.25
(37)	David Justice	.25
(38)	Ray Lankford	.25
(39)	Ramon Martinez	.25
(40)	Don Mattingly	2.50
(41)	Mark McGwire	3.50
(42)	Brian McRae	.25
(43)	Joe Oliver	.25
(44)	Tony Pena	.25
(45)	Kirby Puckett	2.00
(46)	Cal Ripken Jr.	4.50
(47)	Babe Ruth	4.00
(48)	Nolan Ryan	4.50
(49)	Bret Saberhagen	.25
(50)	Chris Sabo	.25
(51)	Ryne Sandberg	2.00
(52)	Benito Santiago	.25
(53)	Steve Sax	.25
(54)	Gary Sheffield	.25
(55)	Ozzie Smith	2.00
(56)	Dave Stewart	.25
(57)	Darryl Strawberry	.25
(58)	Frank Thomas	1.50
(59)	Robin Ventura	.25
(60)	Hector Villanueva	.25
(61)	Honus Wagner	1.50
(62)	Lou Whitaker	.25

1985 Cain's Potato Chips Tigers

This set commemorating the 1984 World Champion Tigers was issued in bags of Cain's Potato Chips in the Michigan area in 1985. The yellow-bordered, unnumbered cards measure 2-3/4" in diameter and feature full-color oval photos inside a diamond. The word "Cain's" appears in the upper left corner, while the player's name appears in the lower left with his position directly below the photo. The words "1984 World Champions" are printed in the upper right corner. Backs include 1984 statistics.

		NM/M
Complete Set (20):		10.00
Common Player:		.50
(1)	Doug Bair	.50
(2)	Juan Berenguer	.50
(3)	Dave Bergman	.50
(4)	Tom Brookens	.50
(5)	Marty Castillo	.50
(6)	Darrell Evans	1.00
(7)	Barbaro Garbey	.50
(8)	Kirk Gibson	1.00
(9)	John Grubb	.50
(10)	Willie Hernandez	.50
(11)	Larry Herndon	.50
(12)	Chet Lemon	.50
(13)	Aurelio Lopez	.50
(14)	Jack Morris	1.00
(15)	Lance Parrish	1.00
(16)	Dan Petry	.50
(17)	Bill Scherrer	.50
(18)	Alan Trammell	2.50
(19)	Lou Whitaker	1.50
(20)	Milt Wilcox	.50

1986 Cain's Potato Chips Tigers

For the second year in a row, player discs of the Detroit Tigers were found in boxes of Cain's Potato Chips sold in the Detroit area. Twenty discs make up the set which is branded as a "1986 Annual Collectors' Edition." Discs, measuring 2-3/4" in diameter, have fronts which contain a color photo plus the player's name, team and position. The Cain's logo and the Major League Baseball Players Association's logo also appear. The backs, which display black print on white stock, contain player information plus the card number.

		NM/M
Complete Set (20):		7.50
Common Player:		.50
1	Tom Brookens	.50
2	Willie Hernandez	.50
3	Dave Bergman	.50
4	Lou Whitaker	1.25
5	Dave LaPoint	.50
6	Lance Parrish	.75
7	Randy O'Neal	.50
8	Nelson Simmons	.50
9	Larry Herndon	.50
10	Doug Flynn	.50
11	Jack Morris	.75
12	Dan Petry	.50
13	Walt Terrell	.50
14	Chet Lemon	.50
15	Frank Tanana	.50
16	Kirk Gibson	.75
17	Darrell Evans	.75
18	Dave Collins	.50
19	John Grubb	.50
20	Alan Trammell	2.00

1987 Cain's Potato Chips Tigers

Player discs of the Detroit Tigers were inserted in boxes of Cain's Potato Chips for the third consecutive year. The 1987 edition is made up of cards each measuring 2-3/4" in diameter. The discs, which were packaged in a cellophane wrapper, feature a full-color photo surrounded by an orange border. Backs are printed in red on white stock. The set was produced by Mike Schechter and Associates.

		NM/M
Complete Set (20):		12.50
Common Player:		.60
1	Tom Brookens	.60
2	Darnell Coles	.60
3	Mike Heath	.60
4	Dave Bergman	.60
5	Dwight Lowry	.60
6	Darrell Evans	1.00
7	Alan Trammell	2.50
8	Lou Whitaker	1.75
9	Kirk Gibson	1.00
10	Chet Lemon	.60
11	Larry Herndon	.60
12	John Grubb	.60
13	Willie Hernandez	.60
14	Jack Morris	1.00
15	Dan Petry	.60
16	Walt Terrell	.60
17	Mark Thurmond	.60
18	Pat Sheridan	.60
19	Eric King	.60
20	Frank Tanana	.60

1984 California Angels Fire Safety

This 32-card set was distributed at a June home game to fans 14 and under. Cards measure 2-1/2" x 3-1/2". Fronts have full-color action photos along a portrait of Smokey the Bear and U.S. and California Forest Service logos commemorating Smokey's 40th birthday. Black-and-white backs have minimal player data and stats and a tip for preventing forest fires.

		NM/M
Complete Set (32):		4.00
Common Player:		.25
(1)	Don Aase	.25
(2)	Juan Beniquez	.25
(3)	Bob Boone	.45
(4)	Rick Burleson	.25
(5)	Rod Carew	1.50
(6)	John Curtis	.25
(7)	Doug DeCinces	.25
(8)	Brian Downing	.25
(9)	Ken Forsch	.25
(10)	Bobby Grich	.25
(11)	Reggie Jackson	2.00
(12)	Ron Jackson	.25
(13)	Tommy John	.50
(14)	Curt Kaufman	.25
(15)	Bruce Kison	.25
(16)	Frank LaCorte	.25
(17)	Fred Lynn	.45
(18)	John McNamara	.25
(19)	Jerry Narron	.25
(20)	Gary Pettis	.25
(21)	Robert Picciolo	.25
(22)	Ron Romanick	.25
(23)	Luis Sanchez	.25
(24)	Dick Schofield	.25
(25)	Daryl Sconiers	.25
(26)	Jim Slaton	.25
(27)	Ellis Valentine	.25
(28)	Robert Wilfong	.25
(29)	Mike Witt	.25
(30)	Geoff Zahn	.25
---	Forestry Dept. Logo Card	.10
---	Smokey Logo Card	.10

1985 California Angels Fire Safety

This full-color set of large-format cards was given to fans attending the July 14 game at Anaheim Stadium. Fronts feature player photos with their last name at the top above the picture. In the bottom border are a portrait of Smokey the Bear, and logos of the Angels, California Forestry Service and U.S. Forestry Service. Cards measure 4-1/4" x 6". On back, printed in black-and-white, are personal data, a few stats and a wildfire safety tip.

		NM/M
Complete Set (24):		5.00
Common Player:		.25
1	Mike Witt	.25
2	Reggie Jackson	1.50
3	Bob Boone	.45
4	Mike Brown	.25
5	Rod Carew	1.00
6	Doug DeCinces	.25
7	Brian Downing	.25
8	Ken Forsch	.25
9	Gary Pettis	.25
10	Jerry Narron	.25
11	Ron Romanick	.25
12	Bobby Grich	.25
13	Dick Schofield	.25
14	Juan Beniquez	.25
15	Geoff Zahn	.25
16	Luis Sanchez	.25
17	Jim Slaton	.25
18	Doug Corbett	.25
19	Ruppert Jones	.25
20	Rob Wilfong	.25
21	Donnie Moore	.25
22	Pat Clements	.25
23	Tommy John	.50
24	Gene Mauch	.25

1986 California Angels Fire Safety

The Angels, in conjuction with the U.S. and California Forestry Services, issued this set promoting Wildfire Prevention. Cards measure 4-1/4" x 6" and offer a full-color front with the player's picture in an oval frame. Backs have player stats with a drawing and a fire safety tip. The sets were given out August 9 at the game in Anaheim Stadium.

		NM/M
Complete Set (24):		5.00
Common Player:		.25
1	Mike Witt	.25
2	Reggie Jackson	1.50
3	Bob Boone	.40
4	Don Sutton	1.00

1985 California Angels Fire Safety (continued)

		NM/M
5	Kirk McCaskill	.25
6	Doug DeCinces	.25
7	Brian Downing	.25
8	Doug Corbett	.25
9	Gary Pettis	.25
10	Jerry Narron	.25
11	Ron Romanick	.25
12	Bobby Grich	.25
13	Dick Schofield	.25
14	George Hendrick	.25
15	Rick Burleson	.25
16	John Candelaria	.25
17	Jim Slaton	.25
18	Darrell Miller	.25
19	Ruppert Jones	.25
20	Rob Wilfong	.25
21	Donnie Moore	.25
22	Wally Joyner	1.00
23	Terry Forster	.25
24	Gene Mauch	.25

1987 California Angels Fire Safety

The U.S. Forestry Service distributed this set to 25,000 fans in attendance at Anaheim Stadium on August 1. The full-color cards measure 4" x 6". Fronts carry a design of baseballs and bats framing the player photo. Only the player's last name is given. At bottom is a Smokey Bear portrait and team logo. Backs contain the player's name, position and personal data along with a Smokey Bear cartoon fire prevention tip and sponsors' logos.

		NM/M
Complete Set (24):		5.00
Common Player:		.25
1	John Candelaria	.25
2	Don Sutton	1.00
3	Mike Witt	.25
4	Gary Lucas	.25
5	Kirk McCaskill	.25
6	Chuck Finley	.25
7	Willie Fraser	.25
8	Donnie Moore	.25
9	Urbano Lugo	.25
10	Butch Wynegar	.25
11	Darrell Miller	.25
12	Wally Joyner	.75
13	Mark McLemore	.25
14	Mark Ryal	.25
15	Dick Schofield	.25
16	Jack Howell	.25
17	Doug DeCinces	.25
18	Gus Polidor	.25
19	Brian Downing	.25
20	Gary Pettis	.25
21	Ruppert Jones	.25
22	George Hendrick	.25
23	Devon White	.25
---	Smokey Bear Logo Card/Checklist	.10

1988 California Angels Fire Safety

These borderless full-color cards (2-1/2" x 3-1/2") are highlighted by a thin white outline on front. The player name, team logo and a Smokey Bear picture logo appear in the photo's lower-right cor-

ner. Backs are black-and-white and include personal information and a large cartoon fire prevention tip. Part of the U.S. Forest Service fire prevention campaign, the cards were distributed in three separate in-stadium giveaways during August and September games.

		NM/M
Complete Set (25):		4.50
Common Player:		.25
1	Cookie Rojas	.25
2	Johnny Ray	.25
3	Jack Howell	.25
4	Mike Witt	.25
5	Tony Armas	.25
6	Gus Polidor	.25
7	DeWayne Buice	.25
8	Dan Petry	.25
9	Bob Boone	.50
10	Chili Davis	.25
11	Greg Minton	.25
12	Kirk McCaskill	.25
13	Devon White	.25
14	Willie Fraser	.25
15	Chuck Finley	.25
16	Dick Schofield	.25
17	Wally Joyner	.50
18	Brian Downing	.25
19	Stewart Cliburn	.25
20	Donnie Moore	.25
21	Bryan Harvey	.25
22	Mark McLemore	.25
23	Butch Wynegar	.25
24	George Hendrick	.25
---	Team Logo/Checklist	.10

1989 California Angels All-Stars Fire Safety

The U.S. Forest Service, in conjunction with the California Angels, issued this all-time team set. The 2-1/2" x 3-1/2" cards have a silver border with the player photo outlined in red. Beneath the photo a banner across homeplate reads "Angels All-Stars," along with the player's name and position, which are flanked by Smokey Bear on the left and the Angels 1989 All-Star Game logo on the right. Card backs highlight the player's career with the Angels and include an illustrated fire prevention tip.

		NM/M
Complete Set (20):		6.00
Common Player:		.25
1	Bill Rigney	.25
2	Dean Chance	.40
3	Jim Fregosi	.25
4	Bobby Knoop	.25
5	Don Mincher	.25
6	Clyde Wright	.25
7	Nolan Ryan	4.00
8	Frank Robinson	1.00
9	Frank Tanana	.25
10	Rod Carew	1.00
11	Bobby Grich	.25
12	Brian Downing	.25
13	Don Baylor	.25
14	Fred Lynn	.35
15	Reggie Jackson	1.50
16	Doug DeCinces	.25
17	Bob Boone	.35
18	Wally Joyner	.50
19	Mike Witt	.25
20	Johnny Ray	.25

1990 California Angels Fire Safety

This set was released by the U.S. Forestry Service in conjunction with the California Angels. The sets were distributed at the May 27 home game. The 2-1/2" x 3-1/2" cards feature full-color action photos surrounded by metallic silver borders. Team and Smokey Bear logos appear on front. Backs con-

tain player data and a cartoon Smokey Bear message urging the prevention of forest fires.

		NM/M
Complete Set (20):		5.00
Common Player:		.25
1	Jim Abbott	.50
2	Bert Blyleven	.50
3	Chili Davis	.25
4	Brian Downing	.25
5	Chuck Finley	.25
6	Willie Fraser	.25
7	Bryan Harvey	.25
8	Jack Howell	.25
9	Wally Joyner	.50
10	Mark Langston	.25
11	Kirk McCaskill	.25
12	Mark McLemore	.25
13	Lance Parrish	.25
14	Johnny Ray	.25
15	Dick Schofield	.25
16	Mike Witt	.25
17	Claudell Washington	.25
18	Devon White	.25
19	Scott Bailes	.25
20	Bob McClure	.25

1991 California Angels Fire Safety

This set was sponsored by the California Department of Forestry. Front of the 2-1/2" x 3-1/2" cards features gray borders surrounding full-color action photos. The flip sides feature a fire safety cartoon and biographical information, along with sponsor logos, printed in blue and red on white.

		NM/M
Complete Set (20):		6.00
Common Player:		.25
1	Luis Polonia	.25
2	Junior Felix	.25
3	Dave Winfield	2.00
4	Dave Parker	.25
5	Lance Parrish	.25
6	Wally Joyner	.35
7	Jim Abbott	.45
8	Mark Langston	.25
9	Dick Schofield	.25
10	Kirk McCaskill	.25
11	Jack Howell	.25
12	Donnie Hill	.25
13	Gary Gaetti	.25
14	Chuck Finley	.25
15	Luis Sojo	.25
16	Mark Eichhorn	.25
17	Bryan Harvey	.25
18	Jeff Robinson	.25
19	Scott Lewis	.25
20	John Orton	.25

1992 California Angels Police

This safety set was sponsored by Carl's Jr. fast food restaurants and distributed by the Orange County Sheriff's Dept. Single cards were distributed to children over the course of the season and complete sets were handed out at the Angels' September 19 game. Fronts have color player action photos on a star-studded red, white and blue border.

Backs have a small black-and-white portrait photo, stats, career highlights, an anti-drug message and sponsors' logos.

		NM/M
Complete Set (18):		8.00
Common Player:		.50
1	Jim Abbott	.60
2	Gene Autry	1.00
3	Bert Blyleven	.75
4	Hubie Brooks	.50
5	Chad Curtis	.50
6	Alvin Davis	.50
7	Gary DiSarcina	.50
8	Junior Felix	.50
9	Chuck Finley	.50
10	Gary Gaetti	.50
11	Rene Gonzalez	.50
12	Von Hayes	.50
13	Carl Karcher	.50
14	Mark Langston	.50
15	Luis Polonia	.50
16	Bobby Rose	.50
17	Lee Stevens	.50
18	Happy Star (Mascot)	.50

1993 California Angels Police

J.T. Snow
First Base

Sponsored by the Carl's Jr. hamburger restaurant chain and distributed through the California Chiefs & Sheriffs Assn., it was reported that 20,000-25,000 sets were produced. The 2-1/2" x 3-1/2" cards have a player action photo on front. Backs are printed in blue and black and include a portrait photo, career highlights, stats and an anti-drug message.

		NM/M
Complete Set (21):		16.00
Common Player:		.50
1	Gene Autry	1.00
2	Carl Karcher	.50
3	Buck Rodgers	.50
4	Rod Carew	3.50
5	Kelly Gruber	.50
6	Chili Davis	.50
7	Chad Curtis	.50
8	Mark Langston	.50
9	Scott Sanderson	.50
10	J.T. Snow	2.00
11	Rene Gonzalez	.50
12	Jimmie Reese	.50
13	Damion Easley	.50
14	Julio Valera	.50
15	Luis Polonia	.50
16	John Orton	.50
17	Gary DiSarcina	.50
18	Greg Myers	.50
19	Chuck Finley	.50
20	Tim Salmon	2.50
21	Happy Star (Mascot)	.50

1995 California Angels Police

The California Highway Patrol sponsored this safety set to coincide with the Angels 35th anniversary. Cards have action photos bordered in gray and dark blue. The team's anniversary logo and CHP logo appear in opposite corners. Black-and-white backs have a few bit of player data and a safety tip.

		NM/M
Complete Set (16):		20.00
Common Player:		1.00
1	Tim Salmon	2.00
2	Chuck Finley	1.00
3	Mark Langston	1.00
4	Gary Disarcina	1.00
5	Damion Easley	1.00
6	Spike Owen	1.00
7	Troy Percival	1.00
8	Chili Davis	1.00
9	Jim Edmonds	2.00
10	Rex Hudler	1.00
11	Greg Myers	1.00
12	Brian Anderson	1.00
13	J.T. Snow	1.50
14	Tony Phillips	1.00
15	Lee Smith	1.50
16	Marcel Lachemann, Don Watkins (Chief, CHP)	1.00

1992-93 Canadian Card News Repli-Cards

3   Roberto Alomar

Krause Publications short-lived attempt to service the Canadian card collecting market with a newsstand magazine included the use of repli-card panels of five in each of the magazine's five issues. The cards feature a mix of hockey players, CFL stars and Blue Jays and Expos. Only the baseball players are listed here.

		NM/M
Complete (Baseball) Set (12):		6.50
Common Player:		.50
2	Kelly Gruber	.50
3	Roberto Alomar	.75
5	Larry Walker, Marquis Grissom, Delino DeShields	.50
8	Dave Winfield	2.00
14	Ken Hill	.50
17	Jimmy Key	.50
17	Pat Borders	.50
21	Joe Carter	.50
22	Larry Walker	.75
23	Delino DeShields	.50
24	Derek Bell	.50
25	Wil Cordero	.50

1996 Canadian Club Classic Stars of the Game

A promotion for Canadian Club's Classic 12 whisky offered a series of autographed Hall of Famer cards. One card was included in a special folder attached to bottles. An offer sheet inside gave details for ordering other cards for $5 each plus proof of purchase. Also in the bottle-hanger was a certificate of authenticity for the enclosed signed card. In standard 2-1/2" x 3-1/2" format, cards feature vintage color player photos on which uniform logos have been deleted. Cards have a black border, are highlighted in gold foil and have an authentic autograph on front. Backs have ca-

reer stats and summary. Cards #1-4 were labeled as Series I, cards #5-6 are Series II.

		NM/M
Complete Set (6):		60.00
Common Player:		6.00
1	Brooks Robinson	12.00
2	Billy Williams	6.00
3	Willie Stargell	13.50
4	Ernie Banks	17.50
5	Frank Robinson	15.00
6	Rollie Fingers	6.00

2000 CaP Cure Home Run Challenge

JASON GIAMBI

As part of its fund-raising "Home Run Challenge" promotion June 15-20, 2000, the Association for the Cure of Cancer of the Prostate issued a nine-card perforated sheet of 2-1/2" x 3-1/2" cards. Fronts have an action photo with black borders. At top-left is the CaP Cure logo, at lower-right is the MLBPA logo. Backs have messages promoting the cause, along with contact information for the organization.

		NM/M
Complete Sheet:		20.00
Complete Set (9):		20.00
Common Player:		2.00
(1)	Jason Giambi	2.00
(2)	Ken Griffey Jr.	3.00
(3)	Tony Gwynn	2.50
(4)	Derek Jeter	5.00
(5)	Mark McGwire	4.00
(6)	Alex Rodriguez	4.00
(7)	Sammy Sosa	2.50
(8)	Robin Ventura	1.00
(9)	Header Card	.25

1994 Capital Cards 1969 Mets Postcards

Nolan Ryan

Capital Cards, produced a 32-card postcard set of members of the 1969 World Champion New York Mets from Ron Lewis paintings, limited to 25,000 sets. Capital Cards also produced 5,000 uncut sheets that are individually numbered and carried a suggested retail price of $99.95. The boxed postcard set retailed for $39.95. The cards could also be purchased with autographs.

		NM/M
Complete Set (32):		15.00
Common Player:		.35
Uncut Sheet:		15.00
1	Logo Card	.35
2	Gil Hodges	2.00
3	Rube Walker	.35
4	Yogi Berra	.35
5	Joe Pignatano	.35
6	Ed Yost	.35
7	Tommie Agee	.35
8	Ken Boswell	.35
9	Don Cardwell	.35
10	Ed Charles	.35
11	Donn Clendenon	.35
12	Jack DiLauro	.35
13	Duffy Dyer	.35
14	Wayne Garrett	.35
15	Rod Gaspar	.35
16	Gary Gentry	.35
17	Jerry Grote	.35
18	Bud Harrelson	.50
19	Cleon Jones	.50
20	Cal Koonce	.35
21	Jerry Koosman	.50
22	Ed Kranepool	.35
23	J.C. Martin	.35
24	Jim McAndrew	.35
25	Tug McGraw	.50
26	Bob Pfeil	.35
27	Nolan Ryan	6.00
28	Tom Seaver	3.00
29	Art Shamsky	.35
30	Ron Swoboda	.35
31	Ron Taylor	.35
32	Al Weis	.35

1989 Cap'n Crunch

ERIC DAVIS
Outfield   Cincinnati Reds

This 22-card set was produced by Topps for Cap'n Crunch cereal boxes. Two cards and a stick of gum were included in each cereal box while the offer was active. The fronts of these 2-1/2" x 3-1/2" cards feature red, white and blue borders. The card backs are horizontal and feature lifetime statistics. The set was not offered in any complete set deal.

		NM/M
Complete Set (22):		5.00
Common Player:		.10
1	Jose Canseco	.40
2	Kirk Gibson	.10
3	Orel Hershiser	.10
4	Frank Viola	.10
5	Tony Gwynn	.65
6	Cal Ripken	1.50
7	Darryl Strawberry	.10
8	Don Mattingly	.75
9	George Brett	.75
10	Andre Dawson	.25
11	Dale Murphy	.25
12	Alan Trammell	.10
13	Eric Davis	.10
14	Jack Clark	.10
15	Eddie Murray	.50
16	Mike Schmidt	.75
17	Dwight Gooden	.10
18	Roger Clemens	.75
19	Will Clark	.10
20	Kirby Puckett	.65
21	Robin Yount	.50
22	Mark McGwire	1.00

1995 Cardtoons

Just about everything related to baseball comes in for the jab in this set of parody cards. Players, teams, attitudes, owners, mascots, Hall of Famers, announcers and the business of baseball are all panned. Besides a base set of 95 cards, there are several insert issues and send-away prizes. Cards are standard 2-1/2" x 3-1/2" with easily identifiable caricatures on front and sophomoric humor on the back. The cards make a point of stating they are parodies and not licensed either by the players or Major League Baseball. While they carry a 1993 copyright date, the cards were not issued until 1995.

		NM/M
Complete Set (95):		10.00
Common Card:		.25
1	Hey Abbott	.25
2	Robin Adventura	.25
3	Roberto Alamode	.30
4	Don Battingly	1.25
5	Cow Belle	.25
6	Jay Bellhop	.25
7	Fowl Boggs	1.00
8	Treasury Bonds	2.50
9	True Brett	1.25
10	Wild Pitch Mitch	.25
11	Balou's Brothers (Felipe Balou, Moises Balou)	.25
12	Charlie Bustle	2.00
13	Brett Butter	.25
14	Rambo Canseco	.40
15	Roberto Cementie	2.50
16	Roger Clemency	1.25
17	Will Clock	.25
18	David Clone	.25
19	Tom Clowning	.25
20	Mr. Club	1.00
21	Joe Crater	.25
22	Doolin' Daulton	.25
23	Chili Dog Davis	.25
24	Doug Drawback	.25
25	Dennis Excellency	.65
26	Silly Fanatic	.25
27	Wand Gonzalez	.40
28	Amazing Grace	.25
29	Tom Grapevine	.25
30	Marquis Gruesome	.25
31	Homerin' Hank	2.00
32	Kevin Happier	.25
33	Pete Harness	.25
34	Charlie Haze	.25
35	Egotisticky Henderson	.75
36	Sayanora Infielder	.25
37	Snoozin' Ted & Tarzan Jane	.25
38	Cloud Johnson	.75
39	Sandy K-Fax	2.00
40	The Say What Kid	2.00
41	Tommy Lasagna	.25
42	Greg Maddogs	1.00
43	Stamp the Man	1.00
44	Mark McBash	2.00
45	Fred McGruff	.25
46	Mount Mick	3.00
47	Pat Moustache	.25
48	Ozzie Myth	1.00
49	Bob Nukesbury	.25
50	Reggie October	1.00
51	Doctor OK	.25
52	Rafael Palmist	.65
53	Lose Piniella	.25
54	Vince Poleman	.25
55	Charlie Puff	.25
56	Rob Quibble	.25
57	Darryl Razzberry	.25
58	Cal Ripkenwinkle	2.50
59	Budge Rodriguez	.65
60	Ryne Sandbox	1.00
61	Steve Saxophone	.25
62	Harry Scary	.25
63	Scary Sheffield	.45
64	Ruben Siesta	.25
65	Dennis Smartinez	.25
66	Lee Smite	.25
67	Ken Spiffey Jr.	1.50
68	Nails Spikestra	.25
69	The Splendid Spinner	2.00
70	Toad Stottlemyre	.25
71	Raging Tartabull	.25
72	Robbery Thompson	.25
73	Alan Trampoline	.25
74	Monster Truk	.25
75	Shawon Tungsten	.25
76	Tony Twynn	1.00
77	Andy Van Tyke	.25
78	Derrick Ventriloquist	.25
79	Frank Violin	.25
80	Rap Winfielder	.75
81	Robinhood Yount	.75
82	Swift Justice	.25
83	Brat Saberhagen	.25
84	Mike Pizazz	1.50
85	Andres Colorado	.25
86	Money Bagswell	.75
87	Video Nomo	.40
88	Out of the Park	.25
89	Tim Wallet	.25
90	Checklist	.10
91	Greenback Jack	.25
92	Mighty Matt Power Hitter	.25
93	Frankenthomas	.75
94	Neon Peon Slanders	.25
95	Just Air Jordan	2.50
---	Replacement Card No. 1 (Redeemable for "Cardtoons Annual Awards" set with payment of $26.95.)	.10
---	Replacement Card No. 2 (Redeemable for Cardtoons binder and plastic sheets with payment of $18.95.)	.13
---	Replacement card No. 3 (Redeemable for Cardtoons phone card set of four with payment of $39.95.)	.13

1995 Cardtoons Awards Replacement Set

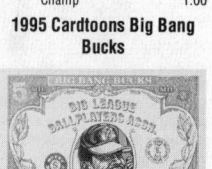

This set was available via a mail-in offer for $26.95.

		NM/M
Complete Set (8):		6.25
Common Card:		1.00
R1	No Ball Peace Prize	1.00
R2	Forrest Grump	1.00
R3	Most Virtous Player	1.00
R4	Golden Glove Award	1.00
R5	Comdown Player of the Year	1.00
R6	Corkville Slugger	1.00
R7	Can't Get No Relief	1.00
R8	1994 World Series Champ	1.00

1995 Cardtoons Big Bang Bucks

This insert set lampoons baseball's top 20 salaried players. Fronts resemble U.S. currency overprinted with gold foil in denominations of five, six and seven million. A player caricature portrait is in color at center of the 3-1/2" x 2-1/2" card. Backs give the player's salary history and rationale for his being overpaid. A statement on back says the cards are intended to be a parody and that they are not licensed by MLB or the Players Union. The cards are numbered with the "BB" prefix.

		NM/M
Complete Set (20):		20.00
Common Card:		1.00
1	Treasury Bonds	4.00
2	Sayanora Infielder	1.00
3	Cal Ripkenwinkle	4.00
4	Bobby Bonus	1.00
5	Joe Crater	1.00
6	Kirby Plunkit	2.00
7	David Clone	1.00
8	Ken Spiffey Jr.	3.00
9	Ruben Siesta	1.00
10	Greg Maddogs	2.00
11	Mark McBash	3.50
12	Rafael Palmist	1.50
13	Roberto Alamode	1.00
14	Greenback Jack	1.00
15	Raging Tartabull	1.00
16	Jimmy Kiwi	1.00
17	Roger Clemency	2.25
18	Rambo Canseco	1.25
19	Tom Grapevine	1.00
20	John Smileyface	1.00

1995 Cardtoons Field of Greed Puzzle Set

These nine-cards are inserts which form a "Field of Greed" picture when the individual cards are aligned. Fronts have 1/9th of the cartoon puzzle, backs have a history of baseball's recent labor problems. Cards have an "FOG" prefix to their number.

		NM/M
Complete Set (9):		1.50
Common Card:		.25
1	1972 Strike	.25
2	1973 Lockout	.25
3	1976 Lockout	.25

4	1980 Strike	.25
5	1981 Strike	.25
6	1985 Strike	.25
7	1990 Lockout	.25
8	1994 Strike	.25
9	Future Problems	.25

1995 Cardtoons Grand Slam Foils

This insert set utilizes foil printing technology to give a high-tech look to the caricatures of major leaguers. Fronts have cartoon parodies of the players, backs attempt to be humorous. A note on back says the cards are not licensed by either the players or Major League Baseball. Cards are numbered with a "F" prefix.

		NM/M
Complete Set (10):		12.00
Common Player:		1.00
1	Bo Action	1.50
2	Andre Awesome	1.25
3	Bobby Bonus	1.00
4	Steve Bravery	1.00
5	Carlton Fist	2.00
6	E.T. McGee	1.00
7	Kirby Plunkit	4.00
8	Jose Rheostat	1.00
9	Sir Noble Ryan	6.00
10	Day-Glo Sabo	1.00

1995 Cardtoons Politics in Baseball

This insert set takes a poke at the perceived problems of baseball during the 1994-95 strike. Fronts have cartoons, backs have pointed commentary. Cards are numbered with the "S" prefix.

		NM/M
Complete Set (11):		3.00
Common Card:		.15
1	Pledge of Allegiance	.15
2	The Wave	.15
3	Slick Willie	1.50
4	Umpires Convention	.15
5	The Slide	.15
6	SH-H-H-H-H-H	.15
7	Throwing Out the First Contract	.15
8	Babe Rush	1.00
9	Hot Prospect	.15

| 10 | Let's Play Ball | .15 |
| 11 | Role Model | .15 |

1992 Carl's Jr. Padres

For the fifth consecutive year the San Diego Padres issued a card set in conjunction with the Jr. Padres program. Carl's Jr., a fast food chain, began sponsoring the set in 1991. The set contains 25 cards and was available in either nine-card perforated sheets or precut. At 2-9/16" x 3-9/16" the cards are slightly larger than current standard. Player photos feature an All-Star Game logo in the lower-right corner. On the white border, the player's name and position are printed in dark blue beneath the photo. The team name is in light brown above the photo. On back, the player's stats, career highlights and biographical data are printed in dark blue. The unnumbered cards are checklisted here in alphabetical order.

		NM/M
Complete Set (25):		6.00
Common Player:		.25
(1)	Larry Anderson	.25
(2)	Oscar Azocar	.25
(3)	Andy Benes	.25
(4)	Dann Bilardello	.25
(5)	Jerald Clark	.25
(6)	Tony Fernandez	.25
(7)	Tony Gwynn	4.00
(8)	Greg Harris	.25
(9)	Bruce Hurst	.25
(10)	Darrin Jackson	.25
(11)	Craig Lefferts	.25
(12)	Mike Maddux	.25
(13)	Fred McGriff	.25
(14)	Jose Melendez	.25
(15)	Randy Myers	.25
(16)	Greg Riddoch	.25
(17)	Rich Rodriguez	.25
(18)	Benito Santiago	.25
(19)	Gary Sheffield	.50
(20)	Craig Shipley	.25
(21)	Kurt Stillwell	.25
(22)	Tim Teufel	.25
(23)	Kevin Ward	.25
(24)	Ed Whitson	.25
(25)	All-Star Logo	.25

1992 Carlson Travel 1982 Brewers

The team's American League Championship season of 1982 was commemorated a decade later with this card set given away at a Brewers promotional date. The cards were sponsored by Carlson Travel and United Airlines, whose logos appear on the front of the cards, along with Channel 6 television, whose logo is on the back. Fronts feature game-action photos of the '82 Brewers, borderless at top and sides. Beneath the photo is a thin gold stripe, then a blue stripe with the player's name and

position in white. A red, white and blue 1982 World Series logo appears in the lower-left corner. Backs are printed in blue, and include 1982 stats and a summary of the player's season. Player cards are numbered by uniform number in the upper-left.

		NM/M
Complete Set (31):		12.00
Common Player:		.25
4	Paul Molitor	5.00
5	Ned Yost	.25
7	Don Money	.25
10	Bob McClure	.25
11	Ed Romero	.25
14	Roy Howell	.25
15	Cecil Cooper	.25
16	Marshall Edwards	.25
17	Jim Gantner	.25
19	Robin Yount	5.00
20	Gorman Thomas	.25
21	Don Sutton	1.00
22	Charlie Moore	.25
23	Ted Simmons	.25
24	Ben Oglivie	.25
27	Pete Ladd	.25
29	Mark Brouhard	.25
30	Moose Haas	.25
32	Harvey Kuenn	.25
33	Doc Medich	.25
34	Rollie Fingers	1.00
41	Jim Slaton	.25
44	Jerry Augustine	.25
47	Dwight Bernard	.25
48	Mike Caldwell	.25
50	Pete Vuckovich	.25
---	Coaches (Pat Dobson, Larry Haney, Ron Hansen, Cal McLish, Harry Warner)	.25
---	Team Card	.25
---	Bernie Brewer (Mascot)	.25
---	Post-season Rally	.25
---	$50 Travel Coupon	.25

1985 CBS Radio Game of the Week

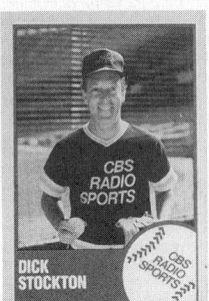

To promote its Game of the Week radio broadcasts, CBS issued a six-card set picturing network announcers, including Hall of Famer Johnny Bench. The cards, standard 2-1/2" x 3-1/2" format, were sent to CBS affiliate stations only. Fronts of the full-color cards picture the announcers in CBS Radio Sports baseball-style uniforms.

		NM/M
Complete Set (6):		55.00
Common Player:		3.00
(1)	Johnny Bench	35.00
(2)	Brent Musburger	15.00
(3)	Lindsey Nelson	7.50
(4)	John Rooney	3.00
(5)	Dick Stockton	4.50
(6)	Bill White	7.50

1986 CBS Radio Game of the Week

For the second consecutive year, CBS Radio Sports issued a five-card set featuring announcers used by the network for the Game

of the Week and post-season broadcasts. The cards, packaged in a custom-designed wax wrapper, were sent to CBS radio affiliates as a promotion. The color cards measure 2-1/2" x 3-1/2".

		NM/M
Complete Set (5):		35.00
Common Player:		3.00
(1)	Sparky Anderson	15.00
(2)	Jack Buck	10.00
(3)	Howard David	3.00
(4)	Ernie Harwell	10.00
(5)	Ted Robinson	3.00

1987 Champion Phillies

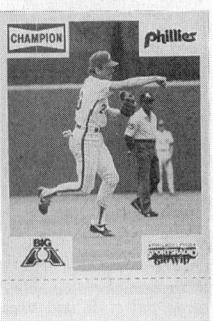

This four card set is interesting in that the players are not identified on the card fronts or backs. The full-color cards, which measure 2-3/4" x 4-5/16", were produced by the Champion Spark Plug Co. as part of a contest held at participating Big A, Car Quest and Pep Boys auto parts stores. Entrants were advised to return the scratch-off coupon portion of the card for a chance to win a Blackbird Racer. Each card contains a scratch-off portion which may have contained an instant prize. Each card can be found with either a Big A, Car Quest or Pep Boys logo in the lower left corner on the card front. The contest was also sponsored in part by the Philadelphia Phillies and radio station WIP.

		NM/M
Complete Set (4):		15.00
Common Player:		1.00
(1)	Von Hayes (Glove on knee.)	1.00
(2)	Steve Jeltz (#30 on uniform)	1.00
(3)	Juan Samuel (Laying on base.)	1.00
(4)	Mike Schmidt (Making throw.)	12.00

1981 Champions of American Sport

From June 1981, through June 1982, Phillip Morris and Miller Beer sponsored a traveling exhibition of sporting art and artifacts from The National Portrait Gallery and the Smithsonian Institution. In conjunction with the exhibitions in Washington, D.C., Chicago, Los Angeles and New York, an 18-card souvenir set was issued featuring many of the top athletes featured in the exhibits. The set was released in the form of an 8" x 11" eight-page booklet. Inside were two sheets of nine cards each. The perforated cards could

be separated into individual cards of 2-1/2" x 3-3/4" dimensions. Fronts featured colored photos or artwork, backs had quotes about the athlete and stats. The unnumbered cards are checklisted here alphabetically.

		NM/M
Complete Set, Booklet:		60.00
Complete Set, Singles (18):		40.00
Common Player:		2.00
(1)	Muhammad Ali	6.00
(2)	Arthur Ashe	2.00
(3)	Peggy Fleming	2.00
(4)	A.J. Foyt	2.00
(5)	Eric Heiden	2.00
(6)	Bobby Hull	4.00
(7)	Sandy Koufax	6.00
(8)	Joe Louis	3.00
(9)	Bob Mathias	2.00
(10)	Willie Mays	6.00
(11)	Joe Namath	5.00
(12)	Jack Nicklaus	5.00
(13)	Knute Rockne	2.00
(14)	Bill Russell	5.00
(15)	Jim Ryun	2.00
(16)	Willie Shoemaker	2.00
(17)	Casey Stengel	2.00
(18)	Johnny Unitas	2.00

1988 Chef Boyardee

This uncut sheet features 12 each American and National League players. Color player portraits are printed beneath a red, white and blue "1988 1st Annual Collector's Edition" header. The player name, team and position appear beneath his photo. Card backs are printed in blue on red and include biographical information, stats and career highlights. The set was produced by American Home Food Products for distribution via a mail-in offer involving proofs of purchase from the company's Chef Boyardee products. Photos, licensed only by the Players Union, have had uniform logos airbrushed off.

		NM/M
Complete Set, Sheet:		6.00
Complete Set, Singles (24):		6.00
Common Player:		.10
1	Mark McGwire	1.00
2	Eric Davis	.10
3	Jack Morris	.10
4	George Bell	.10
5	Ozzie Smith	.50
6	Tony Gwynn	.60
7	Cal Ripken, Jr.	1.50
8	Todd Worrell	.10
9	Larry Parrish	.10
10	Gary Carter	.50
11	Ryne Sandberg	.60
12	Keith Hernandez	.10
13	Kirby Puckett	.60
14	Mike Schmidt	.75
15	Frank Viola	.10
16	Don Mattingly	.75
17	Dale Murphy	.25
18a	Andre Dawson (1987 team is Expos)	.25
18b	Andre Dawson (1987 team is Cubs)	.25
19	Mike Scott	.10
20	Rickey Henderson	.50
21	Jim Rice	.25
22	Wade Boggs	.60
23	Roger Clemens	.75
24	Fernando Valenzuela	.10

1996 Chevrolet/Geo Pirates Team Sheet

Western Pennsylvania Chevy/Geo dealers sponsored this issue of a team card set given away at the May 12 game vs. the Giants. The individual 2-1/4" x 3-1/4" cards are perforated for removal from the sheet. Individual cards have a color player photo at center with team

name and '96 logo at top in a red stripe and the player name and Chev logo at bottom in an orange stripe. Backs are in black-and-white. The cards are checklisted here in alphabetical order.

		NM/M
Complete Set, Uncut Sheet:		9.00
Complete Set, Singles (30):		7.00
Common Player:		.25
(1)	Jay Bell	.25
(2)	Cam Bonifay	.25
(3)	Jacob Brumfield	.25
(4)	Jason Christiansen	.25
(5)	Dave Clark	.25
(6)	Steve Cooke	.25
(7)	Francisco Cordova	.25
(8)	Danny Darwin	.25
(9)	John Ericks	.25
(10)	Carlos Garcia	.25
(11)	Lee Hancock	.25
(12)	Charlie Hayes	.25
(13)	Mark Johnson	.25
(14)	Jason Kendall	.75
(15)	Jim Leyland	.25
(16)	Jeff King	.25
(17)	Mike Kingery	.25
(18)	Nelson Liriano	.25
(19)	Jon Lieber	.25
(20)	Al Martin	.25
(21)	Orlando Merced	.25
(22)	Dan Miceli	.25
(23)	Denny Neagle	.25
(24)	Keith Osik	.25
(25)	Steve Parris	.25
(26)	Dan Plesac	.25
(27)	Zane Smith	.25
(28)	Paul Wagner	.25
(29)	John Wehner	.25
(30)	Pirate Parrot (Mascot)	.25

1992 Chevron Giants Hall of Fame Pins

This series of card/pin combinations was distributed by Chevron gas stations honoring San Francisco Giants enshrined in baseball's Hall of Fame. Fronts of the 2-1/2" x 5" cards have a color player photo in an oval frame with an orange border. The player name and team logo are in a large white strip at bottom. Black-and-white backs have a small player portrait photo, some personal data, career highlights and pictures of the pins in the set. An enameled pin, about 1-1/8" x 1-1/4", with a representation of the player in action, is attached at the bottom of the card.

		NM/M
Complete Set (3):		15.00
Common Player:		4.00
24	Willie Mays	7.50

36	Gaylord Perry	4.00
44	Willie McCovey	4.00

1985 Chicago Cubs Playing Cards

A regular 52-card deck plus two jokers comprise this set produced by long-time Cubs broadcaster Jack Brickhouse, whose photo and trademark phrase "Hey Hey!" are featured on the back of each card. Card fronts have a black-and-white photo with player(s) names and a date beneath. Traditional suit and value marking of a playing card deck are included in the corners of the 2-1/2" x 3-1/2" round-cornered cards. The cards are arranged in roughly chronological order.

		NM/M
	Complete Set (54):	10.00
	Common Player:	.25
AH	Jack Brickhouse	.25
2H	1876 Champions (Team composite photo.)	.25
3H	Cap Anson	.25
4H	Joe Tinker, Johnny Evers, Frank Chance, Harry Steinfeldt	2.00
5H	Ed Reulbach	.25
6H	Mordecai Brown	.25
7H	Jim Vaughn	.25
8H	Joe McCarthy	.25
9H	Jimmy Cooney	.25
10H	Rogers Hornsby	.50
JH	Hack Wilson	.25
QH	"Homers Row" (Hack Wilson, Babe Ruth, Lou Gehrig)	.50
KH	Babe Ruth ("Called the Shot")	4.00
AC	Lon Warneke	.25
2C	Augie Galan	.25
3C	1935 Pennant Winning Cubs (Team photo.)	.25
4C	Dizzy Dean	.50
5C	Gabby Hartnett	.25
6C	Billy Herman	.25
7C	Charlie Root	.25
8C	Charlie Grimm	.25
9C	Andy Pafko	.25
10C	Stan Hack	.25
JC	Phil Cavarretta	.25
QC	National League Champs 1945 (Team photo.)	.25
KC	Bill Nicholson	.25
KD	Hank Sauer	.25
QD	Ernie Banks	4.00
JD	Sam Jones	.25
10D	Dale Long	.25
9D	Lou Boudreau	.30
8D	Don Cardwell	.25
7D	Ken Hubbs	.50
6D	Billy Williams	.30
5D	1969 Cubs - The Team That Almost Made It (Composite photo.)	.25
4D	Ken Holtzman	.25
3D	Ron Santo	.30
2D	Fergie Jenkins	.40
AD	Burt Hooten (Hooton)	.25
KS	Milt Pappas	.25
QS	Rick Reuschel	.25
JS	Bill Madlock	.25
10S	Dallas Green	.25
9S	Jody Davis	.25
8S	Rick Sutcliffe	.25
7S	Jim Frey	.25
6S	Ryne Sandberg	4.00
5S	Eastern Division Champs 1984 (Team photo.)	.25
4S	Bob Dernier	.25
3S	Gary Matthews	.25
2S	Keith Moreland	.25
AS	Leon Durham	.25
Joker	Ron Cey	.25
Joker	Hey Hey! and Holy Cow! (Jack Brickhouse, Harry Caray)	.25

1988 Chicago Cubs Fire Safety

This set of four oversize (approximately 3-7/8" x 5-1/2") cards was produced on a single perforated sheet for distribution to fans as part of a U.S. Forest Service fire prevention campaign. Card fronts feature color player photos framed with vertical blue and pink borders and the player's name in light blue at bottom. Team and Smokey logos flank the name while the team name is printed in red above the photo. Backs have a bit of player biography and a large cartoon fire safety message.

		NM/M
	Complete Set (4):	7.00
	Common Card:	1.00
1	Vance Law (With Smokey.)	2.00
2	Vance Law/Fldg	2.00
3	Vance Law/Btg	2.00
4	Smokey Bear	1.00

1992 Chicago White Sox 1917 Team Issue Reprints

Card dealer Greg Manning, who purchased the unique original set of 1917 White Sox team-issue cards in 1991 issued a collectors' reprint set a year later. The reprints are in 2" x 3" format, slightly larger than the originals. The cards of the banned "Black Sox" have had a black frame added around the picture and have career information and 1919 stats on back. The other cards have blank backs. A second, colorized card of Joe Jackson was added to the reprint set. The unnumbered cards are checklisted here in alphabetical order.

		NM/M
	Complete Set (26):	9.00
	Common Player:	.25
(1)	Joe Benz	.25
(2)	Eddie Cicotte	1.00
(3)	Eddie Collins	.25
(4)	Shano Collins	.25
(5)	Charles Comiskey	.25
(6)	Dave Danforth	.25
(7)	Red Faber	.25
(8)	Happy Felsch	.50
(9)	Chick Gandil	1.00
(10)	Kid Gleason	.25
(11)	Joe Jackson (Black-and-white.)	3.00
(12)	Joe Jackson (Colorized)	3.00
(13)	Joe Jenkins	.25
(13)	Ted Jourdan	.25
(14)	Nemo Leibold	.25
(15)	Byrd Lynn	.25
(16)	Fred McMullen	.50
(17)	Eddie Murphy	.25
(18)	Swede Risberg	.50
(19)	Pants Rowland	.25
(20)	Reb Russell	.25
(21)	Ray Schalk	.25
(22)	James Scott	.25
(23)	Buck Weaver	1.00
(24)	Lefty Williams	.50
(25)	Mellie Wolfgang	.25

1994 Churchs Chicken Hometown Stars

Produced by Pinnacle Brands for distribution in the fried chicken restaurant chain, the cards were distributed in packs of four with the purchase of a nine-piece family meal or were sold separately for 69 cents. Each foil pack contained three regular cards and one card with gold foil instead of regular printing on the player's name and "Hometown Stars." Every fourth pack contains one of 10 "Show Stoppers" Dufex-process chase cards. In standard 2-1/2" x 3-1/2", the cards featured full-bleed front action photos with the Churchs logo at lower-left and the player's name at lower-right. "Hometown Stars" is printed vertically at top-left. Backs have a portrait photo at left, a career summary and 1993 and career stats. Because the cards were licensed by the Major League Baseball Players Association, but not Major League Baseball, both the front and the back photos on each card have had the uniform logos airbrushed away.

		NM/M
	Complete Set (28):	7.00
	Complete Set (Gold) (28):	15.00
	Common Player:	.10
	Common Player (Gold):	.25
1	Brian McRae	.10
1a	Brian McRae/Gold	.25
2	Dwight Gooden	.10
2a	Dwight Gooden/Gold	.25
3	Ruben Sierra	.10
3a	Ruben Sierra/Gold	.25
4	Greg Maddux	1.00
4a	Greg Maddux/Gold	1.50
5	Kirby Puckett	1.00
5a	Kirby Puckett/Gold	1.50
6	Jeff Bagwell	.75
6a	Jeff Bagwell/Gold	1.00
7	Cal Ripken, Jr.	1.50
7a	Cal Ripken, Jr./Gold	2.50
8	Lenny Dykstra	.10
8a	Lenny Dykstra/Gold	.25
9	Tim Salmon	.10
9a	Tim Salmon/Gold	.25
10	Matt Williams	.10
10a	Matt Williams/Gold	.25
11	Roberto Alomar	.30
11a	Roberto Alomar/Gold	.45
12	Barry Larkin	.10
12a	Barry Larkin/Gold	.25
13	Roger Clemens	1.00
13a	Roger Clemens/Gold	1.75
14	Mike Piazza	1.25
14a	Mike Piazza/Gold	2.00
15	Travis Fryman	.10
15a	Travis Fryman/Gold	.25
16	Ryne Sandberg	1.00
16a	Ryne Sandberg/Gold	1.50
17	Robin Ventura	.10
17a	Robin Ventura/Gold	.25
18	Gary Sheffield	.35
18a	Gary Sheffield/Gold	.50
19	Carlos Baerga	.10
19a	Carlos Baerga/Gold	.25
20	Jay Bell	.10
20a	Jay Bell (Gold)	.25
21	Edgar Martinez	.10
21a	Edgar Martinez/Gold	.25
22	Phil Plantier	.10
22a	Phil Plantier/Gold	.25
23	Danny Tartabull	.10
23a	Danny Tartabull/Gold	.25
24	Marquis Grissom	.10
24a	Marquis Grissom/Gold	.25
25	Robin Yount	.75
25a	Robin Yount/Gold	1.00
26	Ozzie Smith	1.00
26a	Ozzie Smith/Gold	1.50
27	Ivan Rodriguez	.60
27a	Ivan Rodriguez/Gold	.75
28	Dante Bichette	.10
28a	Dante Bichette/Gold	.25

1994 Churchs Chicken Show Stoppers

Ten of baseball's top home-run hitters are featured in this insert set. Found approximately once every four packs in the four-card packs distributed by the fried chicken chain, the cards were produced by Pinnacle Brands using its foil-printing Dufex process. A player action photo is depicted inside a home-plate shaped frame at right. "Show Stoppers" is printed vertically at left in red and yellow tones. The background merges from green at left to purple at right, with the player's name in black in a yellow-to-red rainbow effect box beneath the photo. The Churchs logo is at bottom-left. On back is a portrait photo in a light blue box. There is a description of the player's home run prowess along with gold boxes showing his 1993 homers, slugging percentage and at bat/home run ratio. The border mirrors the front's green-to-purple effect. Because the cards are not licensed by Major League Baseball, the uniform logos have been removed from both the front and back photos.

		NM/M
	Complete Set (10):	7.50
	Common Player:	.50
1	Juan Gonzalez	.75
2	Barry Bonds	2.50
3	Ken Griffey Jr.	2.00
4	David Justice	.50
5	Frank Thomas	1.50
6	Fred McGriff	.50
7	Albert Belle	.50
8	Joe Carter	.50
9	Cecil Fielder	.50
10	Mickey Tettleton	.50

1998 CHW San Francisco Giants

At four special Senior Citizens Days at 3Com Park Giants home games, cards of four Hall of Famers were given away. The promotion was sponsored by Catholic Healthcare West, whose logo and name appear at top-left on the cards' fronts. Fronts combine vintage action photos with recent portrait shots and include a facsimile autograph. Backs provide a tip for healthy living and the phone numbers of various health care providers.

		NM/M
	Complete Set (4):	20.00
	Common Player:	4.00
(1)	Orlando Cepeda	4.00
(2)	Juan Marichal	4.00
(3)	Willie Mays	12.00
(4)	Willie McCovey	4.00

1982 Cincinnati Reds Yearbook Cards

In 1982 the Reds began a series of yearbook inserts consisting of two nine-card sheets. The 16-3/4" x 10-7/8" sheet contains 18 perforated 2-5/8" x 3-3/4" cards. Fronts have color photos with red graphics and a white border. Backs are in black-and-white and include complete major and minor league stats. The cards are checklisted here by uniform number.

		NM/M
	Complete Set, Sheet:	7.50
	Complete Set, Singles (18):	6.00
	Common Player:	.25
3	John McNamara	.25
5	Johnny Bench	3.00
16	Dave Concepcion	.25
16	Ron Oester	.25
21	Paul Householder	.25
22	Dan Driessen	.25
28	Cesar Cedeno	.25
29	Alex Trevino	.25
30	Clint Hurdle	.25
36	Frank Pastore	.25
36	Mario Soto	.25
38	Bruce Berenyi	.25
41	Tom Seaver	2.00
47	Tom Hume	.25
49	Joe Price	.25
51	Mike LaCoss	.25
---	Best in Baseball	.25
---	Riverfront Stadium	.25

1983 Cincinnati Reds Yearbook Cards

This 16-3/4" x 10-7/8" cardboard sheet was stapled into the Reds 1983 yearbook. The sheet contains 18 2-5/8" x 3-3/4" cards perforated for removal. Fronts have color game-action photos with red graphics. Backs are in black-and-white and include complete career stats. Cards are checklisted here by uniform number.

		NM/M
	Complete Set, Sheet:	6.00
	Complete Set, Singles (18):	5.00
	Common Player:	.25
2	Gary Redus	.25
5	Johnny Bench	3.00
7	Russ Nixon	.25
13	Dave Concepcion	.25
16	Ron Oester	.25
20	Eddie Milner	.25
21	Paul Householder	.25
22	Dan Driessen	.25
28	Charlie Puleo	.25
28	Cesar Cedeno	.25
29	Alex Trevino	.25
32	Rich Gale	.25
35	Frank Pastore	.25
36	Mario Soto	.25
38	Bruce Berenyi	.25
47	Tom Hume	.25
49	Joe Price	.25
---	Riverfront Stadium	.25

1984 Cincinnati Reds Yearbook Cards

Once again in 1984 the Reds inserted a 16-3/4" x 11" cardboard panel into their yearbook. The sheet contains 18 cards, 2-5/8" x 3-3/4", perforated for removal. Fronts have color photos with a large red frame and white borders. Backs are in black-and-white and include complete major and minor league stats. Cards are checklisted here by uniform number.

		NM/M
	Complete Set, Sheet:	5.00
	Complete Set, Singles (18):	3.00
	Common Player:	.25
2	Gary Redus	.25
9	Vern Rapp	.25
11	Dann Bilardello	.25
12	Nick Esasky	.25
13	Dave Concepcion	.25
16	Ron Oester	.25
20	Eddie Milner	.25
22	Dan Driessen	.25
24	Tony Perez	1.00
26	Duane Walker	.25
34	Bill Scherrer	.25
35	Frank Pastore	.25
36	Mario Soto	.25
38	Bruce Berenyi	.25
39	Dave Parker	.35
47	Tom Hume	.25
49	Joe Price	.25
---	Bob Howsam (President)	.25

1985 Cincinnati Reds Yearbook Cards

Once again in 1985 the Reds inserted a 16-3/4" x 11" cardboard panel into their yearbook. The sheet contains 18 cards, 2-5/8" x 3-3/4", perforated for removal. Fronts have color photos with red and white graphics. Backs are in black-and-white with complete major and minor league stats. Cards are checklisted here alphabetically.

		NM/M
	Complete Sheet:	6.00
	Complete Set (18):	5.00
	Common Player:	.25
(1)	Cesar Cedeno	.25
(2)	Dave Concepcion	.25
(3)	Eric Davis	.75
(4)	Nick Esasky	.25
(5)	Tom Foley	.25
(6)	John Franco	.25
(7)	Brad Gulden	.25
(8)	Wayne Krenchicki	.25
(9)	Eddie Milner	.25
(10)	Ron Oester	.25
(11)	Dave Parker	.25
(12)	Ted Power	.25
(13)	Joe Price	.25
(14)	Pete Rose	3.00
(15)	Jeff Russell	.25
(16)	Mario Soto	.25
(17)	Jay Tibbs	.25
(18)	Duane Walker	.25

1996 Circa

This hobby-exclusive product was limited to 2,000 sequentially numbered cases. The regular-issue set has 196 player cards, including 18 top prospects and four prospects. Circa also has a 200-card parallel set called Rave which is limited to 150 sets. Each Rave card is sequentially numbered from 1-150. Two other insert sets were also produced - Access and Boss.

		NM/M
Complete Set (200):		15.00
Common Player:		.10
Raves:		30X
Pack (8):		1.50
Wax Box (24):		25.00
1	Roberto Alomar	.25
2	Brady Anderson	.10
3	Rocky Coppinger RC	.10
4	Eddie Murray	.75
5	Mike Mussina	.35
6	Randy Myers	.10
7	Rafael Palmeiro	.65
8	Cal Ripken Jr.	2.00
9	Jose Canseco	.50
10	Roger Clemens	1.00
11	Mike Greenwell	.10
12	Tim Naehring	.10
13	John Valentin	.10
14	Mo Vaughn	.10
15	Tim Wakefield	.10
16	Jim Abbott	.10
17	Garret Anderson	.10
18	Jim Edmonds	.10
19	Darin Erstad RC	2.00
20	Chuck Finley	.10
21	Troy Percival	.10
22	Tim Salmon	.10
23	J.T. Snow	.10
24	Wilson Alvarez	.10
25	Harold Baines	.10
26	Ray Durham	.10
27	Alex Fernandez	.10
28	Tony Phillips	.10
29	Frank Thomas	.75
30	Robin Ventura	.10
31	Sandy Alomar Jr.	.10
32	Albert Belle	.10
33	Kenny Lofton	.10
34	Dennis Martinez	.10
35	Jose Mesa	.10
36	Charles Nagy	.10
37	Manny Ramirez	.75
37p	Manny Ramirez/OPS	2.00
38	Jim Thome	.60
39	Travis Fryman	.10
40	Bob Higginson	.10
41	Melvin Nieves	.10
42	Alan Trammell	.10
43	Kevin Appier	.10
44	Johnny Damon	.30
45	Keith Lockhart	.10
46	Jeff Montgomery	.10
47	Joe Randa	.10
48	Bip Roberts	.10
49	Ricky Bones	.10
50	Jeff Cirillo	.10
51	Marc Newfield	.10
52	Dave Nilsson	.10
53	Kevin Seitzer	.10
54	Ron Coomer	.10
55	Marty Cordova	.10
56	Roberto Kelly	.10
57	Chuck Knoblauch	.10
58	Paul Molitor	.75
59	Kirby Puckett	1.00
60	Scott Stahoviak	.10
61	Wade Boggs	1.00
62	David Cone	.10
63	Cecil Fielder	.10
64	Dwight Gooden	.10
65	Derek Jeter	2.00
66	Tino Martinez	.10
67	Paul O'Neill	.10
68	Andy Pettitte	.35
69	Ruben Rivera	.10
70	Bernie Williams	.10
71	Geronimo Berroa	.10
72	Jason Giambi	.45
73	Mark McGwire	1.50
74	Terry Steinbach	.10
75	Todd Van Poppel	.10
76	Jay Buhner	.10
77	Norm Charlton	.10
78	Ken Griffey Jr.	1.25
79	Randy Johnson	.75
80	Edgar Martinez	.10
81	Alex Rodriguez	1.50
82	Paul Sorrento	.10
83	Dan Wilson	.10
84	Will Clark	.10
85	Kevin Elster	.10
86	Juan Gonzalez	.40
87	Rusty Greer	.10
88	Ken Hill	.10
89	Mark McLemore	.10
90	Dean Palmer	.10
91	Roger Pavlik	.10
92	Ivan Rodriguez	.65
93	Joe Carter	.10
94	Carlos Delgado	.35
95	Juan Guzman	.10
96	John Olerud	.10

97	Ed Sprague	.10
98	Jermaine Dye	.10
99	Tom Glavine	.30
100	Marquis Grissom	.10
101	Andruw Jones	.75
102	Chipper Jones	1.00
103	David Justice	.10
104	Ryan Klesko	.10
105	Greg Maddux	1.00
106	Fred McGriff	.10
107	John Smoltz	.10
108	Brant Brown	.10
109	Mark Grace	.10
110	Brian McRae	.10
111	Ryne Sandberg	1.00
112	Sammy Sosa	1.00
113	Steve Trachsel	.10
114	Bret Boone	.10
115	Eric Davis	.10
116	Steve Gibralter	.10
117	Barry Larkin	.10
118	Reggie Sanders	.10
119	John Smiley	.10
120	Dante Bichette	.10
121	Ellis Burks	.10
122	Vinny Castilla	.10
123	Andres Galarraga	.10
124	Larry Walker	.10
125	Eric Young	.10
126	Kevin Brown	.10
127	Greg Colbrunn	.10
128	Jeff Conine	.10
129	Charles Johnson	.10
130	Al Leiter	.10
131	Gary Sheffield	.50
132	Devon White	.10
133	Jeff Bagwell	.75
134	Derek Bell	.10
135	Craig Biggio	.10
136	Doug Drabek	.10
137	Brian Hunter	.10
138	Darryl Kile	.10
139	Shane Reynolds	.10
140	Brett Butler	.10
141	Eric Karros	.10
142	Ramon Martinez	.10
143	Raul Mondesi	.10
144	Hideo Nomo	.40
145	Chan Ho Park	.10
146	Mike Piazza	1.25
147	Moises Alou	.10
148	Yamil Benitez	.10
149	Mark Grudzielanek	.10
150	Pedro Martinez	.75
151	Henry Rodriguez	.10
152	David Segui	.10
153	Rondell White	.10
154	Carlos Baerga	.10
155	John Franco	.10
156	Bernard Gilkey	.10
157	Todd Hundley	.10
158	Jason Isringhausen	.10
159	Lance Johnson	.10
160	Alex Ochoa	.10
161	Rey Ordonez	.10
162	Paul Wilson	.10
163	Ron Blazier	.10
164	Ricky Bottalico	.10
165	Jim Eisenreich	.10
166	Pete Incaviglia	.10
167	Mickey Morandini	.10
168	Ricky Otero	.10
169	Curt Schilling	.25
170	Jay Bell	.10
171	Charlie Hayes	.10
172	Jason Kendall	.10
173	Jeff King	.10
174	Al Martin	.10
175	Alan Benes	.10
176	Royce Clayton	.10
177	Brian Jordan	.10
178	Ray Lankford	.10
179	John Mabry	.10
180	Willie McGee	.10
181	Ozzie Smith	1.00
182	Todd Stottlemyre	.10
183	Andy Ashby	.10
184	Ken Caminiti	.10
185	Steve Finley	.10
186	Tony Gwynn	1.00
187	Rickey Henderson	.75
188	Wally Joyner	.10
189	Fernando Valenzuela	.10
190	Greg Vaughn	.10
191	Rod Beck	.10
192	Barry Bonds	2.00
193	Shawon Dunston	.10
194	Chris Singleton	.10
195	Robby Thompson	.10
196	Matt Williams	.10
197	Checklist (Barry Bonds)	.10
198	Checklist (Ken Griffey Jr.)	.65
199	Checklist (Cal Ripken Jr.)	.75
200	Checklist (Frank Thomas)	.40

Rave

Rainbow metallic foil highlights on front and a serial number on back from within an edition of 150 of each card differentiate this parallel issue from the Circa base cards. Announced insertion rate for Raves was one per 60 packs.

		NM/M
Common Player:		2.00
Stars:		30X

Access

This 1996 Fleer Circa insert set highlights 30 players on a three-panel foldout design that includes multiple photographs, personal information and statistics. The cards were seeded about one every 12 packs.

		NM/M
Complete Set (30):		50.00
Common Player:		.60
1	Cal Ripken Jr.	6.00
2	Mo Vaughn	.60
3	Tim Salmon	.75
4	Frank Thomas	2.00
5	Albert Belle	.75
6	Kenny Lofton	.60
7	Manny Ramirez	1.00
8	Paul Molitor	2.00
9	Kirby Puckett	3.00
10	Paul O'Neill	.60
11	Mark McGwire	5.00
12	Ken Griffey Jr.	4.00
13	Randy Johnson	2.00
14	Greg Maddux	3.00
15	John Smoltz	.60
16	Sammy Sosa	4.00
17	Barry Larkin	.60
18	Gary Sheffield	1.00
19	Jeff Bagwell	2.00
20	Hideo Nomo	2.00
21	Mike Piazza	4.00
22	Moises Alou	.60
23	Henry Rodriguez	.60
24	Rey Ordonez	.60
25	Jay Bell	.60
26	Ozzie Smith	3.00
27	Tony Gwynn	3.00
28	Rickey Henderson	1.00
29	Barry Bonds	6.00
30	Matt Williams	.60
30p	Matt Williams/OPS	1.00

Boss

This insert set showcases the game's top stars on an embossed design. Cards were seeded one per six packs.

		NM/M
Complete Set (50):		50.00
Common Player:		.45

1	Roberto Alomar	1.00
2	Cal Ripken Jr.	5.00
2p	Cal Ripken Jr./OPS	
3	Jose Canseco	1.50
4	Mo Vaughn	.45
5	Tim Salmon	.60
6	Frank Thomas	2.00
7	Robin Ventura	.45
8	Albert Belle	.60
9	Kenny Lofton	.45
10	Manny Ramirez	2.00
11	Dave Nilsson	.45
12	Chuck Knoblauch	.45
13	Paul Molitor	2.00
14	Kirby Puckett	3.00
15	Wade Boggs	3.00
16	Dwight Gooden	.45
17	Paul O'Neill	.45
18	Mark McGwire	4.00
19	Jay Buhner	.45
20	Ken Griffey Jr.	3.50
21	Randy Johnson	2.00
22	Will Clark	.60
23	Juan Gonzalez	2.00
24	Joe Carter	.45
25	Tom Glavine	.45
26	Ryan Klesko	.45
27	Greg Maddux	3.00
28	John Smoltz	.45
29	Ryne Sandberg	3.00
30	Sammy Sosa	3.50
31	Barry Larkin	.45
32	Reggie Sanders	.45
33	Dante Bichette	.45
34	Andres Galarraga	.45
35	Charles Johnson	.45
36	Gary Sheffield	1.50
37	Jeff Bagwell	2.00
38	Hideo Nomo	2.00
39	Mike Piazza	3.50
40	Moises Alou	.45
41	Henry Rodriguez	.45
42	Rey Ordonez	.45
43	Ricky Otero	.45
44	Jay Bell	.45
45	Royce Clayton	.45
46	Ozzie Smith	3.00
47	Tony Gwynn	3.00
48	Rickey Henderson	2.00
49	Barry Bonds	5.00
50	Matt Williams	.45

1997 Circa

Circa baseball returned for the second year in 1997, with a 400-card set, including 393 player cards and seven checklists. Cards feature action photos on a dynamic graphic arts background, and arrived in eight-card packs. The set was paralleled in a Rave insert and was accompanied by five inserts: Boss, Fast Track, Icons, Limited Access and Rave Reviews.

		NM/M
Complete Set (400):		15.00
Common Player:		.10
Pack (8):		1.00
Retail Wax Box (18):		15.00
Hobby Wax Box (36):		30.00
1	Kenny Lofton	.10
2	Ray Durham	.10
3	Mariano Rivera	.20
4	Jon Lieber	.10
5	Tim Salmon	.10
6	Mark Grudzielanek	.10
7	Neifi Perez	.10
8	Cal Ripken Jr.	3.00
9	John Olerud	.10
10	Edgar Renteria	.10
11	Jose Rosado	.10
12	Mickey Morandini	.10
13	Orlando Miller	.10
14	Ben McDonald	.10
15	Hideo Nomo	.40
16	Fred McGriff	.10
17	Sean Berry	.10
18	Roger Pavlik	.10
19	Aaron Sele	.10
20	Joey Hamilton	.10
21	Roger Clemens	1.25
22	Jose Herrera	.10
23	Ryne Sandberg	.50
24	Ken Griffey Jr.	1.50
25	Barry Bonds	3.00
26	Dan Naulty	.10

27	Wade Boggs	1.00
28	Ray Lankford	.10
29	Rico Brogna	.10
30	Wally Joyner	.10
31	F.P. Santangelo	.10
32	Vinny Castilla	.10
33	Eddie Murray	.75
34	Kevin Elster	.10
35	Mike Macfarlane	.10
36	Jeff Kent	.10
37	Orlando Merced	.10
38	Jason Isringhausen	.10
39	Chad Ogea	.10
40	Greg Gagne	.10
41	Curt Lyons	.10
42	Mo Vaughn	.10
43	Rusty Greer	.10
44	Shane Reynolds	.10
45	Frank Thomas	.75
46	Chris Hoiles	.10
47	Scott Sanders	.10
48	Mark Lemke	.10
49	Fernando Vina	.10
50	Mark McGwire	2.00
51	Bernie Williams	.10
52	Bobby Higginson	.10
53	Kevin Tapani	.10
54	Rich Becker	.10
55	Felix Heredia RC	.30
56	Delino DeShields	.10
57	Rick Wilkins	.10
58	Edgardo Alfonzo	.10
59	Brett Butler	.10
60	Ed Sprague	.10
61	Joe Randa	.10
62	Ugueth Urbina	.10
63	Todd Greene	.10
64	Devon White	.10
65	Bruce Ruffin	.10
66	Mark Gardner	.10
67	Omar Vizquel	.10
68	Luis Gonzalez	.10
69	Tom Glavine	.25
70	Cal Eldred	.10
71	William Van Landingham	.10
72	Jay Buhner	.10
73	James Baldwin	.10
74	Robin Jennings	.10
75	Terry Steinbach	.10
76	Billy Taylor	.10
77	Armando Benitez	.10
78	Joe Girardi	.10
79	Jay Bell	.10
80	Damon Buford	.10
81	Deion Sanders	.15
82	Bill Haselman	.10
83	John Flaherty	.10
84	Todd Stottlemyre	.10
85	J.T. Snow	.10
86	Felipe Lira	.10
87	Steve Avery	.10
88	Trey Beamon	.10
89	Alex Gonzalez	.10
90	Mark Clark	.10
91	Shane Andrews	.10
92	Randy Myers	.10
93	Gary Gaetti	.10
94	Jeff Blauser	.10
95	Tony Batista	.10
96	Todd Worrell	.10
97	Jim Edmonds	.10
98	Eric Young	.10
99	Roberto Kelly	.10
100	Alex Rodriguez	2.00
100p	Alex Rodriguez/OPS	2.00
101	Julio Franco	.10
102	Jeff Bagwell	.75
103	Bobby Witt	.10
104	Tino Martinez	.10
105	Shannon Stewart	.10
106	Brian Banks	.10
107	Eddie Taubensee	.10
108	Terry Mulholland	.10
109	Lyle Mouton	.10
110	Jeff Conine	.10
111	Johnny Damon	.30
112	Quilvio Veras	.10
113	Wilton Guerrero	.10
114	Dmitri Young	.10
115	Garret Anderson	.10
116	Bill Pulsipher	.10
117	Jacob Brumfield	.10
118	Mike Lansing	.10
119	Jose Canseco	.50
120	Mike Bordick	.10
121	Kevin Stocker	.10
122	Frank Rodriguez	.10
123	Mike Cameron	.10
124	Tony Womack RC	.25
125	Bret Boone	.10
126	Moises Alou	.10
127	Tim Naehring	.10
128	Brant Brown	.10
129	Todd Zeile	.10
130	Dave Nilsson	.10
131	Donne Wall	.10
132	Jose Mesa	.10
133	Mark McLemore	.10
134	Mike Stanton	.10
135	Dan Wilson	.10
136	Jose Offerman	.10
137	David Justice	.10
138	Kirt Manwaring	.10
139	Raul Casanova	.10
140	Ron Coomer	.10
141	Dave Hollins	.10
142	Shawn Estes	.10
143	Darren Daulton	.10

144	Turk Wendell	.10
145	Darrin Fletcher	.10
146	Marquis Grissom	.10
147	Andy Benes	.10
148	Nomar Garciaparra	1.00
149	Andy Pettitte	.30
150	Tony Gwynn	1.00
151	Robb Nen	.10
152	Kevin Seitzer	.10
153	Ariel Prieto	.10
154	Scott Karl	.10
155	Carlos Baerga	.10
156	Wilson Alvarez	.10
157	Thomas Howard	.10
158	Kevin Appier	.10
159	Russ Davis	.10
160	Justin Thompson	.10
161	Pete Schourek	.10
162	John Burkett	.10
163	Roberto Alomar	.25
164	Darren Holmes	.10
165	Travis Miller	.10
166	Mark Langston	.10
167	Juan Guzman	.10
168	Pedro Astacio	.10
169	Mark Johnson	.10
170	Mark Leiter	.10
171	Heathcliff Slocumb	.10
172	Dante Bichette	.10
173	Brian Giles RC	1.00
174	Paul Wilson	.10
175	Eric Davis	.10
176	Charles Johnson	.10
177	Willie Greene	.10
178	Geronimo Berroa	.10
179	Mariano Duncan	.10
180	Robert Person	.10
181	David Segui	.10
182	Ozzie Guillen	.10
183	Osvaldo Fernandez	.10
184	Dean Palmer	.10
185	Bob Wickman	.10
186	Eric Karros	.10
187	Travis Fryman	.10
188	Andy Ashby	.10
189	Scott Stahoviak	.10
190	Norm Charlton	.10
191	Craig Paquette	.10
192	John Smoltz	.10
193	Orel Hershiser	.10
194	Glenallen Hill	.10
195	George Arias	.10
196	Brian Jordan	.10
197	Greg Vaughn	.10
198	Rafael Palmeiro	.60
199	Darryl Kile	.10
200	Derek Jeter	3.00
201	Jose Vizcaino	.10
202	Rick Aguilera	.10
203	Jason Schmidt	.10
204	Trot Nixon	.10
205	Tom Pagnozzi	.10
206	Mark Wohlers	.10
207	Lance Johnson	.10
208	Carlos Delgado	.40
209	Cliff Floyd	.10
210	Kent Mercker	.10
211	Matt Mieske	.10
212	Ismael Valdes	.10
213	Shawon Dunston	.10
214	Melvin Nieves	.10
215	Tony Phillips	.10
216	Scott Spiezio	.10
217	Michael Tucker	.10
218	Matt Williams	.10
219	Ricky Otero	.10
220	Kevin Ritz	.10
221	Darryl Strawberry	.10
222	Troy Percival	.10
223	Eugene Kingsale	.10
224	Julian Tavarez	.10
225	Jermaine Dye	.10
226	Jason Kendall	.10
227	Sterling Hitchcock	.10
228	Jeff Cirillo	.10
229	Roberto Hernandez	.10
230	Ricky Bottalico	.10
231	Bobby Bonilla	.10
232	Edgar Martinez	.10
233	John Valentin	.10
234	Ellis Burks	.10
235	Benito Santiago	.10
236	Terrell Wade	.10
237	Armando Reynoso	.10
238	Danny Graves	.10
239	Ken Hill	.10
240	Dennis Eckersley	.65
241	Darin Erstad	.25
242	Lee Smith	.10
243	Cecil Fielder	.10
244	Tony Clark	.10
245	Scott Erickson	.10
246	Bob Abreu	.10
247	Ruben Sierra	.10
248	Chili Davis	.10
249	Darryl Hamilton	.10
250	Albert Belle	.10
251	Todd Hollandsworth	.10
252	Terry Adams	.10
253	Rey Ordonez	.10
254	Steve Finley	.10
255	Jose Valentin	.10
256	Royce Clayton	.10
257	Sandy Alomar	.10
258	Mike Lieberthal	.10
259	Ivan Rodriguez	.65
260	Rod Beck	.10
261	Ron Karkovice	.10

#	Player	Price
262	Mark Gubicza	.10
263	Chris Holt	.10
264	Jaime Bluma	.10
265	Francisco Cordova	.10
266	Javy Lopez	.10
267	Reggie Jefferson	.10
268	Kevin Brown	.10
269	Scott Brosius	.10
270	Dwight Gooden	.10
271	Marty Cordova	.10
272	Jeff Brantley	.10
273	Joe Carter	.10
274	Todd Jones	.10
275	Sammy Sosa	1.00
276	Randy Johnson	.75
277	B.J. Surhoff	.10
278	Chan Ho Park	.10
279	Jamey Wright	.10
280	Manny Ramirez	.75
281	John Franco	.10
282	Tim Worrell	.10
283	Scott Rolen	.60
284	Reggie Sanders	.10
285	Mike Fetters	.10
286	Tim Wakefield	.10
287	Trevor Hoffman	.10
288	Donovan Osborne	.10
289	Phil Nevin	.10
290	Jermaine Allensworth	.10
291	Rocky Coppinger	.10
292	Tim Raines	.10
293	Henry Rodriguez	.10
294	Paul Sorrento	.10
295	Tom Goodwin	.10
296	Raul Mondesi	.10
297	Allen Watson	.10
298	Derek Bell	.10
299	Gary Sheffield	.45
300	Paul Molitor	.75
301	Shawn Green	.15
302	Darren Oliver	.10
303	Jack McDowell	.10
304	Denny Neagle	.10
305	Doug Drabek	.10
306	Mel Rojas	.10
307	Andres Galarraga	.10
308	Alex Ochoa	.10
309	Gary DiSarcina	.10
310	Ron Gant	.10
311	Gregg Jefferies	.10
312	Ruben Rivera	.10
313	Vladimir Guerrero	.75
314	Willie Adams	.10
315	Bip Roberts	.10
326	Mark Grace	.10
317	Bernard Gilkey	.10
318	Marc Newfield	.10
319	Al Leiter	.10
320	Otis Nixon	.10
321	Tom Candiotti	.10
322	Mike Stanley	.10
323	Jeff Fassero	.10
324	Billy Wagner	.10
325	Todd Walker	.10
326	Chad Curtis	.10
327	Quinton McCracken	.10
328	Will Clark	.10
329	Andruw Jones	.75
330	Robin Ventura	.10
331	Curtis Pride	.10
332	Barry Larkin	.10
333	Jimmy Key	.10
334	David Wells	.10
335	Mike Holtz	.10
336	Paul Wagner	.10
337	Greg Maddux	1.00
338	Curt Schilling	.35
339	Steve Trachsel	.10
340	John Wetteland	.10
341	Rickey Henderson	.75
342	Ernie Young	.10
343	Harold Baines	.10
344	Bobby Jones	.10
345	Jeff D'Amico	.10
346	John Mabry	.10
347	Pedro Martinez	.75
348	Mark Lewis	.10
349	Dan Miceli	.10
350	Chuck Knoblauch	.10
351	John Smiley	.10
352	Brady Anderson	.10
353	Jim Leyritz	.10
354	Al Martin	.10
355	Pat Hentgen	.10
356	Mike Piazza	1.50
357	Charles Nagy	.10
358	Luis Castillo	.10
359	Paul O'Neill	.10
360	Steve Reed	.10
361	Tom Gordon	.10
362	Craig Biggio	.10
363	Jeff Montgomery	.10
364	Jamie Moyer	.10
365	Ryan Klesko	.10
366	Todd Hundley	.10
367	Bobby Estalella	.10
368	Jason Giambi	.50
369	Brian Hunter	.10
370	Ramon Martinez	.10
371	Carlos Garcia	.10
372	Hal Morris	.10
373	Juan Gonzalez	.40
374	Brian McRae	.10
375	Mike Mussina	.40
376	John Ericks	.10
377	Larry Walker	.10
378	Chris Gomez	.10
379	John Jaha	.10

#	Player	Price
380	Rondell White	.10
381	Chipper Jones	1.00
382	David Cone	.10
383	Alan Benes	.10
384	Troy O'Leary	.10
385	Ken Caminiti	.10
386	Jeff King	.10
387	Mike Hampton	.10
388	Jaime Navarro	.10
389	Brad Radke	.10
390	Joey Cora	.10
391	Jim Thome	.60
392	Alex Fernandez	.10
393	Chuck Finley	.10
394	Andruw Jones Checklist	.35
395	Ken Griffey Jr. Checklist	.60
396	Frank Thomas Checklist	.35
397	Alex Rodriguez Checklist	.75
398	Cal Ripken Jr. Checklist	1.00
399	Mike Piazza Checklist	.60
400	Greg Maddux Checklist	.45

Rave

In its second year, Circa Rave parallel inserts were limited to inclusion only in hobby packs at the stated. rate of one card per "30 to 40" packs. Raves are distinguished from regular-edition Circa cards by the use of purple metallic foil for the brand name and player identification on front. Rave backs carry a silver-foil serial number detailing its position within a production of 150 for each card.

	NM/M
Common Player:	3.00
Stars/Rookies:	10-15X

Boss

Boss was Circa's most common insert series. Twenty embossed cards were seeded one per six packs, displaying some of baseball's best players. A Super Boss parallel insert features metallic-foil background and graphics on front, and is inserted at a rate of one per 36 packs.

		NM/M
Complete Set (20):		10.00
Common Player:		.15
Super Boss:		2X
1	Jeff Bagwell	.60
2	Albert Belle	.15
3	Barry Bonds	2.00
4	Ken Caminiti	.15
5	Juan Gonzalez	.30
6	Ken Griffey Jr.	1.00
7	Tony Gwynn	.75
8	Derek Jeter	2.00
9	Andruw Jones	.60
10	Chipper Jones	.75
11	Greg Maddux	.75
12	Mark McGwire	1.50
13	Mike Piazza	1.00
14	Manny Ramirez	.60
15	Cal Ripken Jr.	2.00
16	Alex Rodriguez	1.50
17	John Smoltz	.15
18	Frank Thomas	.60
19	Mo Vaughn	.15
20	Bernie Williams	.15

Emerald Autograph Redemption Cards

These box-topper cards were a hobby exclusive redeemable until May 31, 1998, for autographed special cards of six young stars. Fronts have a green-foil enhanced player action photo. Backs provide details of the redemption program.

		NM/M
Complete Set (6):		6.50
Common Player:		.50
(1)	Darin Erstad	1.25
(2)	Todd Hollandsworth	.50
(3)	Alex Ochoa	.50
(4)	Alex Rodriguez	6.00
(5)	Scott Rolen	1.50
(6)	Todd Walker	.50

Emerald Autographs

Special green-foil enhanced cards of six top young stars were available via a mail-in redemption. The cards feature authentic player signatures on front and an embossed authentication seal. Backs are identical to the regular card of each featured player.

		NM/M
Complete Set (6):		100.00
Common Player:		6.00
100	Alex Rodriguez	75.00
241	Darin Erstad	9.00
251	Todd Hollandsworth	6.00
283	Scott Rolen	12.00
308	Alex Ochoa	6.00
325	Todd Walker	6.00

Fast Track

Fast Track highlights 10 top rookies and young stars on a flocked background simulating grass. Cards were inserted every 24 packs.

		NM/M
Complete Set (10):		12.00
Common Player:		1.00
1	Vladimir Guerrero	1.50
2	Todd Hollandsworth	.50
3	Derek Jeter	4.00
4	Andruw Jones	1.50
5	Chipper Jones	2.50
6	Andy Pettitte	1.00
7	Mariano Rivera	.75

#	Player	Price
8	Alex Rodriguez	3.00
9	Scott Rolen	1.25
10	Todd Walker	.50

Icons

Twelve of baseball's top sluggers were displayed on 100-percent holofoil cards in Icons. Icons were found at a rate of one per 36 packs.

		NM/M
Complete Set (12):		25.00
Common Player:		.50
1	Juan Gonzalez	.75
2	Ken Griffey Jr.	3.00
3	Tony Gwynn	2.00
4	Derek Jeter	5.00
5	Chipper Jones	2.00
6	Greg Maddux	2.00
7	Mark McGwire	4.00
8	Mike Piazza	3.00
9	Cal Ripken Jr.	5.00
10	Alex Rodriguez	4.00
11	Frank Thomas	1.50
12	Matt Williams	.50

Limited Access

Limited Access was a retail-only insert found every 18 packs. Cards feature an in-depth, statistical analysis including the player's favorite pitcher to hit and each pitcher's least favorite hitter to face. Limited Access is formatted as a die-cut, bi-fold design resembling a book.

		NM/M
Complete Set (15):		30.00
Common Player:		1.25
1	Jeff Bagwell	2.00
2	Albert Belle	1.25
3	Barry Bonds	5.00
4	Juan Gonzalez	1.50
5	Ken Griffey Jr.	3.25
6	Tony Gwynn	2.50
7	Derek Jeter	5.00
8	Chipper Jones	2.50
9	Greg Maddux	2.50
10	Mark McGwire	4.00
11	Mike Piazza	3.50
12	Cal Ripken Jr.	5.00
13	Alex Rodriguez	3.00
14	Frank Thomas	2.00
15	Mo Vaughn	1.25

Rave Reviews

Hitters that continually put up great numbers were selected for Rave Reviews. The insert was found every 288 packs and was printed on 100-percent holofoil.

		NM/M
Complete Set (12):		75.00
Common Player:		3.00
1	Albert Belle	3.00
2	Barry Bonds	12.00
3	Juan Gonzalez	3.00
4	Ken Griffey Jr.	7.50
5	Tony Gwynn	6.00
6	Greg Maddux	6.00
7	Mark McGwire	9.00
8	Eddie Murray	4.00
9	Mike Piazza	7.50
10	Cal Ripken Jr.	12.00
11	Alex Rodriguez	9.00
12	Frank Thomas	4.50

1998 Circa Thunder

Circa Thunder was issued as one series of 300 cards, sold in packs of eight for $1.59. The set marked SkyBox's brand transition from Circa to Thunder so the cards are labeled with both names. Inserts include: Rave and Super Rave parallels, Boss, Fast Track, Quick Strike, Limited Access, Rave Review and Thunder Boomers.

		NM/M
Complete Set (300):		10.00
Common Player:		.10
Pack (8):		1.00
Wax Box (36):		20.00
1	Ben Grieve	.10
2	Derek Jeter	2.50
3	Alex Rodriguez	2.00
4	Paul Molitor	.75
5	Nomar Garciaparra	1.00
6	Fred McGriff	.10
7	Kenny Lofton	.10
8a	Cal Ripken Jr.	2.50
8b	Marquis Grissom (Should be #280.)	.10
8s	Cal Ripken Jr. ("PROMOTIONAL SAMPLE" on back.)	2.50
9	Matt Williams	.10
10	Chipper Jones	1.00
11	Barry Larkin	.10
12	Steve Finley	.10
13	Billy Wagner	.10
14	Rico Brogna	.10
15	Tim Salmon	.10
16	Hideo Nomo	.40
17	Tony Clark	.10
18	Jason Kendall	.10
19	Juan Gonzalez	.40
20	Jeromy Burnitz	.10
21	Roger Clemens	1.25
22	Mark Grace	.10
23	Robin Ventura	.10
24	Manny Ramirez	.75
25	Mark McGwire	2.00
26	Gary Sheffield	.50
27	Vladimir Guerrero	.75
28	Butch Huskey	.10
29	Cecil Fielder	.10
30	Roderick Myers	.10
31	Greg Maddux	1.00
32	Bill Mueller	.10
33	Larry Walker	.10
34	Henry Rodriguez	.10
35	Mike Mussina	.35
36	Ricky Ledee	.10
37	Bobby Bonilla	.10
38	Curt Schilling	.35
39	Luis Gonzalez	.10
40	Troy Percival	.10
41	Eric Milton	.10
42	Mo Vaughn	.10
43	Raul Mondesi	.10
44	Kenny Rogers	.10
45	Frank Thomas	.75
46	Jose Canseco	.50
47	Tom Glavine	.35
48	Rich Butler RC	.10
49	Jay Buhner	.10
50	Jose Cruz Jr.	.10
51	Bernie Williams	.10
52	Doug Glanville	.10

#	Player	Price
53	Travis Fryman	.10
54	Rey Ordonez	.10
55	Jeff Conine	.10
56	Trevor Hoffman	.10
57	Kirk Rueter	.10
58	Ron Gant	.10
59	Carl Everett	.10
60	Joe Carter	.10
61	Livan Hernandez	.10
62	John Jaha	.10
63	Ivan Rodriguez	.65
64	Willie Blair	.10
65	Todd Helton	.65
66	Kevin Young	.10
67	Mike Caruso	.10
68	Steve Trachsel	.10
69	Marty Cordova	.10
70	Alex Fernandez	.10
71	Eric Karros	.10
72	Reggie Sanders	.10
73	Russ Davis	.10
74	Roberto Hernandez	.10
75	Barry Bonds	2.50
76	Alex Gonzalez	.10
77	Roberto Alomar	.25
78	Troy O'Leary	.10
79	Bernard Gilkey	.10
80	Ismael Valdes	.10
81	Travis Lee	.10
82	Brant Brown	.10
83	Gary DiSarcina	.10
84	Joe Randa	.10
85	Jaret Wright	.10
86	Quilvio Veras	.10
87	Rickey Henderson	.75
88	Randall Simon	.10
89	Mariano Rivera	.25
90	Ugueth Urbina	.10
91	Fernando Vina	.10
92	Alan Benes	.10
93	Dante Bichette	.10
94	Karim Garcia	.10
95	A.J. Hinch	.10
96	Shane Reynolds	.10
97	Kevin Stocker	.10
98	John Wetteland	.10
99	Terry Steinbach	.10
100	Ken Griffey Jr.	1.50
101	Mike Cameron	.10
102	Damion Easley	.10
103	Randy Myers	.10
104	Jason Schmidt	.10
105	Jeff King	.10
106	Gregg Jefferies	.10
107	Sean Casey	.10
108	Mark Kotsay	.10
109	Brad Fullmer	.10
110	Wilson Alvarez	.10
111	Sandy Alomar Jr.	.10
112	Walt Weiss	.10
113	Doug Jones	.10
114	Andy Benes	.10
115	Paul O'Neill	.10
116	Dennis Eckersley	.65
117	Todd Greene	.10
118	Bobby Jones	.10
119	Darrin Fletcher	.10
120	Eric Young	.10
121	Jeffrey Hammonds	.10
122	Mickey Morandini	.10
123	Chuck Knoblauch	.10
124	Moises Alou	.10
125	Miguel Tejada	.15
126	Brian Anderson	.10
127	Edgar Renteria	.10
128	Mike Lansing	.10
129	Quinton McCracken	.10
130	Ray Lankford	.10
131	Andy Ashby	.10
132	Kelvim Escobar	.10
133	Mike Lowell RC	.10
134	Randy Johnson	.75
135	Andres Galarraga	.10
136	Armando Benitez	.10
137	Rusty Greer	.10
138	Jose Guillen	.15
139	Paul Konerko	.10
140	Edgardo Alfonzo	.10
141	Jim Leyritz	.10
142	Mark Clark	.10
143	Brian Johnson	.10
144	Scott Rolen	.60
145	David Cone	.10
146	Jeff Shaw	.10
147	Shannon Stewart	.10
148	Brian Hunter	.10
149	Garret Anderson	.10
150	Jeff Bagwell	.75
151	James Baldwin	.10
152	Devon White	.10
153	Jim Thome	.60
154	Wally Joyner	.10
155	Mark Wohlers	.10
156	Jeff Cirillo	.10
157	Jason Giambi	.60
158	Royce Clayton	.10
159	Dennis Reyes	.10
160	Raul Casanova	.10
161	Pedro Astacio	.10
162	Todd Dunwoody	.10
163	Sammy Sosa	1.00
164	Todd Hundley	.10
165	Wade Boggs	1.00
166	Robb Nen	.10
167	Dan Wilson	.10
168	Hideki Irabu	.10
169	B.J. Surhoff	.10
170	Carlos Delgado	.40

171	Fernando Tatis	.10
172	Bob Abreu	.15
173	David Ortiz	.50
174	Tony Womack	.10
175	Magglio Ordonez RC	1.00
176	Aaron Boone	.10
177	Brian Giles	.10
178	Kevin Appier	.10
179	Chuck Finley	.10
180	Brian Rose	.10
181	Ryan Klesko	.10
182	Mike Stanley	.10
183	Dave Nilsson	.10
184	Carlos Perez	.10
185	Jeff Blauser	.10
186	Richard Hidalgo	.10
187	Charles Johnson	.10
188	Vinny Castilla	.10
189	Joey Hamilton	.10
190	Bubba Trammell	.10
191	Eli Marrero	.10
192	Scott Erickson	.10
193	Pat Hentgen	.10
194	Jorge Fabregas	.10
195	Tino Martinez	.10
196	Bobby Higginson	.10
197	Dave Hollins	.10
198	Rolando Arrojo RC	.25
199	Joey Cora	.10
200	Mike Piazza	1.50
201	Reggie Jefferson	.10
202	John Smoltz	.10
203	Bobby Smith	.10
204	Tom Goodwin	.10
205	Omar Vizquel	.10
206	John Olerud	.10
207	Matt Stairs	.10
208	Bobby Estalella	.10
209	Miguel Cairo	.10
210	Shawn Green	.20
211	Jon Nunnally	.10
212	Al Leiter	.10
213	Matt Lawton	.10
214	Brady Anderson	.10
215	Jeff Kent	.10
216	Ray Durham	.10
217	Al Martin	.10
218	Jeff D'Amico	.10
219	Kevin Tapani	.10
220	Jim Edmonds	.10
221	Jose Vizcaino	.10
222	Jay Bell	.10
223	Ken Caminiti	.10
224	Craig Biggio	.10
225	Bartolo Colon	.10
226	Neifi Perez	.10
227	Delino DeShields	.10
228	Javier Lopez	.10
229	David Wells	.10
230	Brad Rigby	.10
231	John Franco	.10
232	Michael Coleman	.10
233	Edgar Martinez	.10
234	Francisco Cordova	.10
235	Johnny Damon	.30
236	Deivi Cruz	.10
237	J.T. Snow	.10
238	Enrique Wilson	.10
239	Rondell White	.10
240	Aaron Sele	.10
241	Tony Saunders	.10
242	Ricky Bottalico	.10
243	Cliff Floyd	.10
244	Chili Davis	.10
245	Brian McRae	.10
246	Brad Radke	.10
247	Chan Ho Park	.10
248	Lance Johnson	.10
249	Rafael Palmeiro	.65
250	Tony Gwynn	1.00
251	Denny Neagle	.10
252	Dean Palmer	.10
253	Jose Valentin	.10
254	Matt Morris	.10
255	Ellis Burks	.10
256	Jeff Suppan	.10
257	Jimmy Key	.10
258	Justin Thompson	.10
259	Brett Tomko	.10
260	Mark Grudzielanek	.10
261	Mike Hampton	.10
262	Jeff Fassero	.10
263	Charles Nagy	.10
264	Pedro Martinez	.75
265	Todd Zeile	.10
266	Will Clark	.10
267	Abraham Nunez	.10
268	Dave Martinez	.10
269	Jason Dickson	.10
270	Eric Davis	.10
271	Kevin Orie	.10
272	Derrek Lee	.50
273	Andruw Jones	.75
274	Juan Encarnacion	.10
275	Carlos Baerga	.10
276	Andy Pettitte	.35
277	Brent Brede	.10
278	Paul Sorrento	.10
279	Mike Lieberthal	.10
280	(Not issued, see #8)	
281	Darin Erstad	.25
282	Willie Greene	.10
283	Derek Bell	.10
284	Scott Spiezio	.10
285	David Segui	.10
286	Albert Belle	.10
287	Ramon Martinez	.10
288	Jeremi Gonzalez	.10

289	Shawn Estes	.10
290	Ron Coomer	.10
291	John Valentin	.10
292	Kevin Brown	.10
293	Michael Tucker	.10
294	Brian Jordan	.10
295	Darryl Kile	.10
296	David Justice	.10
297	Jose Cruz Jr. Checklist	.10
298	Alex Rodriguez Checklist	1.00
299	Ken Griffey Jr. Checklist	.75
300	Frank Thomas Checklist	.65

Rave

Rave parallels each card in Circa Thunder except for the four checklist cards. A special silver sparkling foil is used on the player's name and the Thunder logo on front. This 296-card set was inserted approximately one per 36 packs and sequentially numbered to 150 sets on the back.

	NM/M
Common Player:	2.00
Stars:	15X

Super Rave

Only '25 Super Rave parallel sets were printed and they were inserted approximately one per 216 packs. The set contains 296 player cards (no checklist cards). Fronts are identified by sparkling gold foil on the left and the Thunder logo, with sequential numbering on the back to 25.

	NM/M
Common Player:	6.00
Stars:	40X

Boss

This insert set has cards embossed with the player's last name in large letters across the top.

		NM/M
Complete Set (20):		10.00
Common Player:		.25
Inserted 1:6		
1B	Jeff Bagwell	.75
2B	Barry Bonds	2.00
3B	Roger Clemens	1.00
4B	Jose Cruz Jr.	.25
5B	Nomar Garciaparra	1.00
6B	Juan Gonzalez	.40
7B	Ken Griffey Jr.	1.25
8B	Tony Gwynn	1.00
9B	Derek Jeter	2.00
10B	Chipper Jones	1.00
11B	Travis Lee	.25
12B	Greg Maddux	1.50
13B	Pedro Martinez	.75
14B	Mark McGwire	1.50
15B	Mike Piazza	1.25
16B	Cal Ripken Jr.	2.00
17B	Alex Rodriguez	1.50
18B	Scott Rolen	.65
19B	Frank Thomas	.75
20B	Larry Walker	.25

Fast Track

This 10-card insert showcases some of the top young stars in baseball. Fronts picture the player

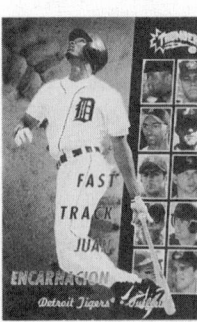

over a closeup of a gold foil baseball on the left. The right side has smaller head shots of all 10 players with the featured player's head in gold foil.

		NM/M
Complete Set (10):		8.00
Common Player:		.25
Inserted 1:24		
1FT	Jose Cruz Jr.	.25
2FT	Juan Encarnacion	.25
3FT	Brad Fullmer	.25
4FT	Nomar Garciaparra	4.00
5FT	Todd Helton	2.50
6FT	Livan Hernandez	.25
7FT	Travis Lee	.25
8FT	Neifi Perez	.25
9FT	Scott Rolen	1.50
10FT	Jaret Wright	.25

Limited Access

These retail-exclusive insert cards are bi-fold and die-cut with foil stamping on front. The theme of the insert was to provide an in-depth statistical scouting analysis of each player.

		NM/M
Complete Set (15):		17.50
Common Player:		.50
Inserted 1:18		
1LA	Jeff Bagwell	1.25
2LA	Roger Clemens	1.75
3LA	Jose Cruz Jr.	.50
4LA	Nomar Garciaparra	1.50
5LA	Juan Gonzalez	1.00
6LA	Ken Griffey Jr.	2.00
7LA	Tony Gwynn	1.50
8LA	Derek Jeter	3.00
9LA	Greg Maddux	1.50
10LA	Pedro Martinez	1.25
11LA	Mark McGwire	2.50
12LA	Mike Piazza	2.00
13LA	Alex Rodriguez	2.50
14LA	Frank Thomas	1.25
15LA	Larry Walker	.50

Quick Strike

This insert pictures players over a colorful die-cut foil-board front.

		NM/M
Complete Set (12):		20.00
Common Player:		.50
Inserted 1:36		
1QS	Jeff Bagwell	2.00

2QS	Roger Clemens	2.75
3QS	Jose Cruz Jr.	.50
4QS	Nomar Garciaparra	2.50
5QS	Ken Griffey Jr.	3.00
6QS	Greg Maddux	2.50
7QS	Pedro Martinez	2.00
8QS	Mark McGwire	4.00
9QS	Mike Piazza	3.00
10QS	Alex Rodriguez	4.00
11QS	Frank Thomas	2.00
12QS	Larry Walker	.50

Rave Reviews

Rave Reviews cards are die-cut in a horizontal design with bronze foil etching and the image of a ballfield in the background.

		NM/M
Complete Set (15):		100.00
Common Player:		2.00
Inserted 1:288		
1RR	Jeff Bagwell	5.00
2RR	Barry Bonds	15.00
3RR	Roger Clemens	7.50
4RR	Jose Cruz Jr.	2.00
5RR	Nomar Garciaparra	6.00
6RR	Juan Gonzalez	3.50
7RR	Ken Griffey Jr.	10.00
8RR	Tony Gwynn	6.00
9RR	Derek Jeter	15.00
10RR	Greg Maddux	6.00
11RR	Mark McGwire	12.50
12RR	Mike Piazza	10.00
13RR	Alex Rodriguez	12.50
14RR	Frank Thomas	5.00
15RR	Larry Walker	2.00

Thunder Boomers

Thunder Boomers feature top power hitters imposed over a see-through cloud-like plastic center with the imagery of a wooden fence with a large hole blasted through the middle of it.

		NM/M
Complete Set (12):		50.00
Common Player:		1.50
Inserted 1:96		
1TB	Jeff Bagwell	6.00
2TB	Barry Bonds	10.00
3TB	Jay Buhner	1.50
4TB	Andres Galarraga	1.50
5TB	Juan Gonzalez	3.00
6TB	Ken Griffey Jr.	7.50
7TB	Tino Martinez	1.50
8TB	Mark McGwire	9.00
9TB	Mike Piazza	7.50
10TB	Frank Thomas	6.00
11TB	Jim Thome	4.50
12TB	Larry Walker	1.50

1985 Circle K

Produced by Topps for Circle K stores, this set is titled "Baseball All Time Home Run Kings." The 2-1/2" x

3-1/2" cards are numbered on the back according to the player's position on the all-time career home run list. Joe DiMaggio, who ranked 31st, was not included in the set. Glossy card fronts generally feature a color photo, although black-and-whites were utilized for a few of the homer kings who played before 1960. Backs have blue and red print on white stock and contain the player's career batting statistics. The set was issued in a specially designed box.

		NM/M
Complete Set (33):		5.00
Common Player:		.10
1	Hank Aaron	1.25
2	Babe Ruth	2.00
3	Willie Mays	1.25
4	Frank Robinson	.15
5	Harmon Killebrew	.15
6	Mickey Mantle	2.50
7	Jimmie Foxx	.15
8	Willie McCovey	.15
9	Ted Williams	1.25
10	Ernie Banks	.30
11	Eddie Mathews	.15
12	Mel Ott	.15
13	Reggie Jackson	.60
14	Lou Gehrig	1.25
15	Stan Musial	.75
16	Willie Stargell	.25
17	Carl Yastrzemski	.25
18	Billy Williams	.15
19	Mike Schmidt	.60
20	Duke Snider	.15
21	Al Kaline	.25
22	Johnny Bench	.25
23	Frank Howard	.15
24	Orlando Cepeda	.15
25	Norm Cash	.15
26	Dave Kingman	.15
27	Rocky Colavito	.15
28	Tony Perez	.15
29	Gil Hodges	.30
30	Ralph Kiner	.15
31	Johnny Mize	.15
32	Yogi Berra	.30
33	Hank Greenberg	.15
34	Lee May	.10

1993 City Pride Roberto Clemente

To assist in the building of the statue of Roberto Clemente which was unveiled at Three Rivers Stadium during All-Star festivities in 1994, Pittsburgh's City Pride bakery contributed a portion of sales proceeds from a special run of bread loaves featuring Roberto Clemente cards. The cards came in a special plastic pouch within the bread wrapper to protect them from stains. The wrapper itself included a portrait of Clemente and details of the statue project. The 2-1/2" x 3-1/2" cards featured sepia-toned or color photos of Clemente inside black and gold borders. A color team logo appears in the lower-right corner with his name in an orange stripe at the bottom of the photo. Backs are in black-and-white and contain a narrative of Clemente's career, with one card containing his lifetime stats. The unnumbered cards are checklisted here in chronological order.

		NM/M
Complete Set (6):		6.00
Common Card:		1.50
(1)	Roberto Clemente/Btg (1934-1958, sepia photo)	1.50
(2)	Roberto Clemente/Btg (1960-1966, color photo)	1.50
(3)	Roberto Clemente (1971-1972, running to first base)	1.50
(4)	Roberto Clemente/Portrait (1972-1973)	1.50

(5)	Roberto Clemente (Fielding records, kneeling with one bat.)	1.50
(6)	Roberto Clemente (Batting record, kneeling with five bats.)	1.50

1993 Clark Candy Reggie Jackson

The reintroduction of the "Reggie" candy bar by the Clark company was accompanied by a three-card set highlighting his career produced by Upper Deck. One card was found in each candy bar. Cards have a color photo of Jackson on front, on which uniform logos have been removed. Backs have an equipment montage and a paragraph about the slugger. Clark and UD logos appear on front, with an UD hologram on back. A limited number (200) of autographed cards were randomly inserted.

		NM/M
Complete Set (3):		3.00
Common Player:		1.00
Autographed Card:		75.00
C1	Reggie Jackson (Hall of Fame, 1993)	1.00
C2	Reggie Jackson (Mr. October, 1977)	1.00
C3	Reggie Jackson (A.L. MVP, 1973)	1.00

1987 Classic Major League Baseball Game

The "Classic Major League Baseball Board Game" set consists of 100 full-color cards used to play the game in which participants answer trivia questions found on the card backs. Cards measure 2-1/2" x 3-1/2" and are printed on semi-gloss stock. Backs carry the player's career stats besides the trivia questions. The game was produced by Game Time, Ltd. of Marietta, Ga., and sold for $19.95 in most retail outlets. In 1991-92 the set was selling for $200 or more, with the Bo Jackson card advertised as high as $80.

		NM/M
Complete Boxed Set:		25.00
Complete Set (100):		20.00
Common Player:		.05
1	Pete Rose	2.00
2	Len Dykstra	.05
3	Darryl Strawberry	.05
4	Keith Hernandez	.05
5	Gary Carter	.65
6	Wally Joyner	.05
7	Andres Thomas	.05
8	Pat Dodson	.05
9	Kirk Gibson	.05
10	Don Mattingly	1.00
11	Dave Winfield	.65
12	Rickey Henderson	.65
13	Dan Pasqua	.05
14	Don Baylor	.05
15	Bo Jackson	2.50
16	Pete Incaviglia	.05

17	Kevin Bass	.05
18	Barry Larkin	.05
19	Dave Magadan	.05
20	Steve Sax	.05
21	Eric Davis	.05
22	Mike Pagliarulo	.05
23	Fred Lynn	.05
24	Reggie Jackson	1.00
25	Larry Parrish	.05
26	Tony Gwynn	.75
27	Steve Garvey	.20
28	Glenn Davis	.05
29	Tim Raines	.05
30	Vince Coleman	.05
31	Willie McGee	.05
32	Ozzie Smith	.75
33	Dave Parker	.05
34	Tony Pena	.05
35	Ryne Sandberg	.75
36	Brett Butler	.05
37	Dale Murphy	.25
38	Bob Horner	.05
39	Pedro Guerrero	.05
40	Brook Jacoby	.05
41	Carlton Fisk	.65
42	Harold Baines	.05
43	Rob Deer	.05
44	Robin Yount	.65
45	Paul Molitor	.65
46	Jose Canseco	.50
47	George Brett	1.00
48	Jim Presley	.05
49	Rich Gedman	.05
50	Lance Parrish	.05
51	Eddie Murray	.65
52	Cal Ripken, Jr.	3.00
53	Kent Hrbek	.05
54	Gary Gaetti	.05
55	Kirby Puckett	.75
56	George Bell	.05
57	Tony Fernandez	.05
58	Jesse Barfield	.05
59	Jim Rice	.25
60	Wade Boggs	.75
61	Marty Barrett	.05
62	Mike Schmidt	1.00
63	Von Hayes	.05
64	Jeff Leonard	.05
65	Chris Brown	.05
66	Dave Smith	.05
67	Mike Krukow	.05
68	Ron Guidry	.05
69	Rob Woodward (Photo actually Pat Dodson.)	.05
70	Rob Murphy	.05
71	Andres Galarraga	.05
72	Dwight Gooden	.05
73	Bob Ojeda	.05
74	Sid Fernandez	.05
75	Jesse Orosco	.05
76	Roger McDowell	.05
77	John Tutor (Tudor)	.05
78	Tom Browning	.05
79	Rick Aguilera	.05
80	Lance McCullers	.05
81	Mike Scott	.05
82	Nolan Ryan	3.00
83	Bruce Hurst	.05
84	Roger Clemens	1.00
85	Oil Can Boyd	.05
86	Dave Righetti	.05
87	Dennis Rasmussen	.05
88	Bret Saberhagan (Saberhagen)	.05
89	Mark Langston	.05
90	Jack Morris	.05
91	Fernando Valenzuela	.05
92	Orel Hershiser	.05
93	Rick Honeycutt	.05
94	Jeff Reardon	.05
95	John Habyan	.05
96	Goose Gossage	.05
97	Todd Worrell	.05
98	Floyd Youmans	.05
99	Don Aase	.05
100	John Franco	.05

1987 Classic Travel Update (Yellow)

B.J. Surhoff

Game Time, Ltd. of Marietta, Ga., issued as an update to its Classic Baseball Board Game a 50-card set entitled "Travel Edition." Cards measure 2-1/2" x 3-1/2" in the same format as the first release, though with yellow, rather than green, borders. Numbered from 101 to 150, the "Travel Edition," besides updating player trades and showcasing rookies, offers several highlights from the 1987 season. All new trivia questions are found on the card backs. It was reported that about 50,000 of the set's 150,000 press run was mistakenly printed with green, rather than yellow backs; the green-back errors sell for a premium.

		NM/M
Complete Set (50):		15.00
Common Player:		.05
Green-backs:		1.5X
101	Mike Schmidt	.75
102	Eric Davis	.05
103	Pete Rose	1.50
104	Don Mattingly	.75
105	Wade Boggs	.60
106	Dale Murphy	.20
107	Glenn Davis	.05
108	Wally Joyner	.05
109	Bo Jackson	.15
110	Cory Snyder	.05
111	Jim Lindeman	.05
112	Kirby Puckett	.60
113	Barry Bonds	10.00
114	Roger Clemens	.75
115	Oddibe McDowell	.05
116	Bret Saberhagen	.05
117	Joe Magrane	.05
118	Scott Fletcher	.05
119	Mark McLemore	.05
120	Who Me? (Joe Niekro)	.25
121	Mark McGwire	2.00
122	Darryl Strawberry	.05
123	Mike Scott	.05
124	Andre Dawson	.20
125	Jose Canseco	.50
126	Kevin McReynolds	.05
127	Joe Carter	.05
128	Casey Candaele	.05
129	Matt Nokes	.05
130	Kal Daniels	.05
131	Pete Incaviglia	.05
132	Benito Santiago	.05
133	Barry Larkin	.05
134	Gary Pettis	.05
135	B.J. Surhoff	.05
136	Juan Nieves	.05
137	Jim Deshaies	.05
138	Pete O'Brien	.05
139	Kevin Seitzer	.05
140	Devon White	.05
141	Rob Deer	.05
142	Kurt Stillwell	.05
143	Edwin Correa	.05
144	Dion James	.05
145	Danny Tartabull	.05
146	Jerry Browne	.05
147	Ted Higuera	.05
148	Jack Clark	.05
149	Ruben Sierra	.05
150	Mark McGwire, Eric Davis	.60

1988 Classic Travel Update 1 (Red)

Phil Niekro

This set was produced for use with the travel edition of Game Time's Classic Baseball Board Game. Special cards in the set include a McGwire/Mattingly, an instruction card with McGwire/Canseco and three different cards featuring Phil Niekro (in different uniforms). Update I card fronts have red borders, a yellow Classic logo in the upper-left corner and a black and beige name banner beneath the photo. Backs are printed in red and pink on white and include the player name, personal info, major league records, a baseball question and space for the player autograph. Classic card series sold via hobby dealers and retail toy stores nationwide. Game Time Ltd., the set's producer, was purchased by Scoreboard of Cherry Hill, N.J. in 1988.

		NM/M
Complete Set (50):		4.00
Common Player:		.05
151	Don Mattingly, Mark McGwire	.45
152	Don Mattingly	.65
153	Mark McGwire	1.00
154	Eric Davis	.05
155	Wade Boggs	.50
156	Dale Murphy	.15
157	Andre Dawson	.15
158	Roger Clemens	.65
159	Kevin Seitzer	.05
160	Benito Santiago	.05
161	Kal Daniels	.05
162	John Kruk	.05
163	Bill Ripken	.05
164	Kirby Puckett	.50
165	Jose Canseco	.30
166	Matt Nokes	.05
167	Mike Schmidt	.60
168	Tim Raines	.05
169	Ryne Sandberg	.50
170	Dave Winfield	.40
171	Dwight Gooden	.05
172	Bret Saberhagen	.05
173	Willie McGee	.05
174	Jack Morris	.05
175	Jeff Leonard	.05
176	Cal Ripken, Jr.	1.50
177	Pete Incaviglia	.05
178	Devon White	.05
179	Nolan Ryan	1.50
180	Ruben Sierra	.05
181	Todd Worrell	.05
182	Glenn Davis	.05
183	Frank Viola	.05
184	Cory Snyder	.05
185	Tracy Jones	.05
186	Terry Steinbach	.05
187	Julio Franco	.05
188	Larry Sheets	.05
189	John Marzano	.05
190	Kevin Elster	.05
191	Vincente Palacios	.05
192	Kent Hrbek	.05
193	Eric Bell	.05
194	Kelly Downs	.05
195	Jose Lind	.05
196	Dave Stewart	.05
197	Jose Canseco, Mark McGwire	.45
198	Phil Niekro	.10
199	Phil Niekro	.10
200	Phil Niekro	.10

1988 Classic Travel Update 2 (Blue)

Darryl Strawberry

This set was produced for use with the travel edition of Game Time's Classic Baseball Board Game. Fronts have blue borders, a yellow Classic logo in the upper-left corner and a black and beige name banner beneath the photo. Backs are printed in blue on white and include the player name, personal info, major league records, a baseball question and space for the player autograph. Classic card series are sold via hobby dealers and retail toy stores nationwide. Game Time Ltd., the set's producer, was purchased by Scoreboard of Cherry Hill, N.J. in 1988.

		NM/M
Complete Set (50):		4.00
Common Player:		.05
201	Dale Murphy, Eric Davis	.10
202	B.J. Surhoff	.05
203	John Kruk	.05
204	Sam Horn	.05
205	Jack Clark	.05
206	Wally Joyner	.05
207	Matt Nokes	.05
208	Bo Jackson	.10
209	Darryl Strawberry	.05
210	Ozzie Smith	.60
211	Don Mattingly	.75
212	Mark McGwire	1.50
213	Eric Davis	.05
214	Wade Boggs	.60
215	Dale Murphy	.25
216	Andre Dawson	.25
217	Roger Clemens	.75
218	Kevin Seitzer	.05
219	Benito Santiago	.05
220	Tony Gwynn	.60
221	Mike Scott	.05
222	Steve Bedrosian	.05
223	Vince Coleman	.05
224	Rick Sutcliffe	.05
225	Will Clark	.05
226	Pete Rose	1.00
227	Mike Greenwell	.05
228	Ken Caminiti	.05
229	Ellis Burks	.05
230	Dave Magadan	.05
231	Alan Trammell	.05
232	Paul Molitor	.50
233	Gary Gaetti	.05
234	Rickey Henderson	.50
235	Danny Tartabull	.05
236	Bobby Bonilla	.05
237	Mike Dunne	.05
238	Al Leiter	.05
239	John Farrell	.05
240	Joe Magrane	.05
241	Mike Henneman	.05
242	George Bell	.05
243	Gregg Jefferies	.10
244	Jay Buhner	.05
245	Todd Benzinger	.05
246	Matt Williams	.05
(247)	Don Mattingly, Mark McGwire (No card number on back.)	.50
248	George Brett	.75
249	Jimmy Key	.05
250	Mark Langston	.05

1989 Classic

David Cone

This 100-card set was released by The Score Board to accompany trivia board games. Fronts have a wide border which graduates from pink at the top to blue at the bottom. Card backs are printed in blue. The flip side includes personal information, and major league record in a boxed area. Another boxed area below the record presents five trivia questions. The lower border on back provides an autograph space. The Classic card series was sold by retail stores and hobby dealers nationwide.

		NM/M
Complete Set (100):		6.00
Common Player:		.05
1	Orel Hershiser	.05
2	Wade Boggs	.50
3	Jose Canseco	.30
4	Mark McGwire	1.00
5	Don Mattingly	.60
6	Gregg Jefferies	.05
7	Dwight Gooden	.05
8	Darryl Strawberry	.05
9	Eric Davis	.05
10	Joey Meyer	.05
11	Joe Carter	.05
12	Paul Molitor	.40
13	Mark Grace	.05
14	Kurt Stillwell	.05
15	Kirby Puckett	.50
16	Keith Miller	.05
17	Glenn Davis	.05
18	Will Clark	.05
19	Cory Snyder	.05
20	Jose Lind	.05
21	Andres Thomas	.05
22	Dave Smith	.05
23	Mike Scott	.05
24	Kevin McReynolds	.05
25	B.J. Surhoff	.05
26	Mackey Sasser	.05
27	Chad Kreuter	.05
28	Hal Morris	.05
29	Wally Joyner	.05
30	Tony Gwynn	.50
31	Kevin Mitchell	.05
32	Dave Winfield	.40
33	Billy Bean	.05
34	Steve Bedrosian	.05
35	Ron Gant	.05
36	Len Dykstra	.05
37	Andre Dawson	.25
38	Brett Butler	.05
39	Rob Deer	.05
40	Tommy John	.05
41	Gary Gaetti	.05
42	Tim Raines	.05
43	George Bell	.05
44	Dwight Evans	.05
45	Denny Martinez	.05
46	Andres Galarraga	.05
47	George Brett	.60
48	Mike Schmidt	.60
49	Dave Steib	.05
50	Rickey Henderson	.40
51	Craig Biggio	.05
52	Mark Lemke	.05
53	Chris Sabo	.05
54	Jeff Treadway	.05
55	Kent Hrbek	.05
56	Cal Ripken, Jr.	1.50
57	Tim Belcher	.05
58	Ozzie Smith	.50
59	Keith Hernandez	.05
60	Pedro Guerrero	.05
61	Greg Swindell	.05
62	Bret Saberhagen	.05
63	John Tudor	.05
64	Gary Carter	.40
65	Kevin Seitzer	.05
66	Jesse Barfield	.05
67	Luis Medina	.05
68	Walt Weiss	.05
69	Terry Steinbach	.05
70	Barry Larkin	.05
71	Pete Rose	.75
72	Luis Salazar	.05
73	Benito Santiago	.05
74	Kal Daniels	.05
75	Kevin Elster	.05
76	Rob Dibble	.05
77	Bobby Witt	.05
78	Steve Searcy	.05
79	Sandy Alomar (Photo is Roberto Alomar.)	.05
80	Chili Davis	.05
81	Alvin Davis	.05
82	Charlie Leibrandt	.05
83	Robin Yount	.40
84	Mark Carreon	.05
85	Pascual Perez	.05
86	Dennis Rasmussen	.05
87	Ernie Riles	.05
88	Melido Perez	.05
89	Doug Jones	.05
90	Dennis Eckersley	.35
91	Bob Welch	.05
92	Bob Milacki	.05
93	Jeff Robinson	.05
94	Mike Henneman	.05
95	Randy Johnson	1.00
96	Ron Jones	.05
97	Jack Armstrong	.05
98	Willie McGee	.05
99	Ryne Sandberg	.50
100	David Cone, Danny Jackson	.05

1989 Classic Travel Update 1 (Orange)

Roberto Alomar

Sold only as a 50-card complete set under the official name of "Travel Update I," these cards are identical in format to the 1989 Classic 100-card set with the exception that the borders are orange at the top, graduating to maroon at the bottom. Backs are maroon.

		NM/M
Complete Set (50):		5.00
Common Player:		.05
101	Gary Sheffield	.25
102	Wade Boggs	.50
103	Jose Canseco	.30
104	Mark McGwire	1.00
105	Orel Hershiser	.05
106	Don Mattingly	.60
107	Dwight Gooden	.05
108	Darryl Strawberry	.05
109	Eric Davis	.05
110	Bam Bam Meulens	.05
111	Andy Van Slyke	.05
112	Al Leiter	.05
113	Matt Nokes	.05
114	Mike Krukow	.05
115	Tony Fernandez	.05
116	Fred McGriff	.05
117	Barry Bonds	1.50
118	Gerald Perry	.05
119	Roger Clemens	.60
120	Kirk Gibson	.05
121	Greg Maddux	.50
122	Bo Jackson	.10
123	Danny Jackson	.05
124	Dale Murphy	.20
125	David Cone	.05
126	Tom Browning	.05
127	Roberto Alomar	.25
128	Alan Trammell	.05
129	Ricky Jordan	.05
130	Ramon Martinez	.05
131	Ken Griffey Jr.	3.00
132	Gregg Olson	.05
133	Carlos Quintana	.05
134	Dave West	.05
135	Cameron Drew	.05
136	Ted Higuera	.05
137	Sil Campusano	.05
138	Mark Gubicza	.05
139	Mike Boddicker	.05
140	Paul Gibson	.05
141	Jose Rijo	.05
142	John Costello	.05
143	Cecil Espy	.05
144	Frank Viola	.05
145	Erik Hanson	.05
146	Juan Samuel	.05
147	Harold Reynolds	.05
148	Joe Magrane	.05
149	Mike Greenwell	.05
150	Darryl Strawberry, Will Clark	.05

1989 Classic Travel Update 2 (Purple)

Jerome Walton

Numbered from 151-200, this set features rookies and traded players with their new teams. The cards are purple and gray and were sold as part of a board game with baseball trivia questions.

		NM/M
Complete Set (50):		5.00
Common Player:		.05
151	Jim Abbott	.05
152	Ellis Burks	.05
153	Mike Schmidt	.75
154	Gregg Jefferies	.05
155	Mark Grace	.05
156	Jerome Walton	.05
157	Bo Jackson	.10
158	Jack Clark	.05
159	Tom Glavine	.20
160	Eddie Murray	.45
161	John Dopson	.05
162	Ruben Sierra	.05
163	Rafael Palmeiro	.40
164	Nolan Ryan	1.50
165	Barry Larkin	.05
166	Tommy Herr	.05
167	Roberto Kelly	.05
168	Glenn Davis	.05
169	Glenn Braggs	.05
170	Juan Bell	.05
171	Todd Burns	.05
172	Derek Lilliquist	.05
173	Orel Hershiser	.05
174	John Smoltz	.05
175	Ozzie Guillen, Ellis Burks	.05
176	Kirby Puckett	.60
177	Robin Ventura	.05
178	Allan Anderson	.05
179	Steve Sax	.05
180	Will Clark	.05
181	Mike Devereaux	.05
182	Tom Gordon	.05
183	Rob Murphy	.05
184	Pete O'Brien	.05
185	Cris Carpenter	.05
186	Tom Brunansky	.05
187	Bob Boone	.05
188	Lou Whitaker	.05
189	Dwight Gooden	.05
190	Mark McGwire	1.00
191	John Smiley	.05
192	Tommy Gregg	.05
193	Ken Griffey Jr.	3.00
194	Bruce Hurst	.05
195	Greg Swindell	.05
196	Nelson Liriano	.05
197	Randy Myers	.05
198	Kevin Mitchell	.05
199	Dante Bichette	.05
200	Deion Sanders	.10

1990 Classic

Classic baseball returned in 1990 with a 150-card set. Cards have a blue border on front, with splashes

Ozzie Smith

of pink. The cards were again sold as part of a baseball trivia game.

		NM/M
Complete Set (150):		4.00
Common Player:		.05
1	Nolan Ryan	1.00
2	Bo Jackson	.10
3	Gregg Olson	.05
4	Tom Gordon	.05
5	Robin Ventura	.05
6	Will Clark	.05
7	Ruben Sierra	.05
8	Mark Grace	.05
9	Luis de los Santos	.05
10	Bernie Williams	.05
11	Eric Davis	.05
12	Carney Lansford	.05
13	John Smoltz	.05
14	Gary Sheffield	.20
15	Kent Merker	.05
16	Don Mattingly	.60
17	Tony Gwynn	.50
18	Ozzie Smith	.05
19	Fred McGriff	.05
20	Ken Griffey Jr.	.65
21a	Deion Sanders ("Prime Time")	.30
21b	Deion Sanders (Deion "Prime Time" Sanders)	.15
22	Jose Canseco	.25
23	Mitch Williams	.05
24	Cal Ripken, Jr.	1.00
25	Bob Geren	.05
26	Wade Boggs	.50
27	Ryne Sandberg	.50
28	Kirby Puckett	.50
29	Mike Scott	.05
30	Dwight Smith	.05
31	Craig Worthington	.05
32	Ricky Jordan	.05
33	Darryl Strawberry	.05
34	Jerome Walton	.05
35	John Olerud	.05
36	Tom Glavine	.15
37	Rickey Henderson	.30
38	Rolando Roomes	.05
39	Mickey Tettleton	.05
40	Jim Abbott	.05
41	Dave Righetti	.05
42	Mike LaValliere	.05
43	Rob Dibble	.05
44	Pete Harnisch	.05
45	Jose Offerman	.05
46	Walt Weiss	.05
47	Mike Greenwell	.05
48	Barry Larkin	.05
49	Dave Gallagher	.05
50	Junior Felix	.05
51	Roger Clemens	.60
52	Lonnie Smith	.05
53	Jerry Browne	.05
54	Greg Briley	.05
55	Delino DeShields	.05
56	Carmelo Martinez	.05
57	Craig Biggio	.05
58	Dwight Gooden	.05
59a	Bo, Ruben, Mark (Bo Jackson, Ruben Sierra, Mark McGwire)	.25
59b	A.L. Fence Busters (Bo Jackson, Ruben Sierra, Mark McGwire)	.15
60	Greg Vaughn	.05
61	Roberto Alomar	.20
62	Steve Bedrosian	.05
63	Devon White	.05
64	Kevin Mitchell	.05
65	Marquis Grissom	.05
66	Brian Holman	.05
67	Julio Franco	.05
68	Dave West	.05
69	Harold Baines	.05
70	Eric Anthony	.05
71	Glenn Davis	.05
72	Mark Langston	.05
73	Matt Williams	.05
74	Rafael Palmeiro	.25
75	Pete Rose, Jr.	.05
76	Ramon Martinez	.05
77	Dwight Evans	.05
78	Mackey Sasser	.05
79	Mike Schooler	.05
80	Dennis Cook	.05
81	Orel Hershiser	.05
82	Barry Bonds	1.00
83	Geronimo Berroa	.05
84	George Bell	.05
85	Andre Dawson	.25
86	John Franco	.05
87a	Clark/Gwynn (Will Clark, Tony Gwynn)	.25
87b	N.L. Hit Kings (Will Clark, Tony Gwynn)	.15
88	Glenallen Hill	.05
89	Jeff Ballard	.05
90	Todd Zeile	.05
91	Frank Viola	.05
92	Ozzie Guillen	.05
93	Jeff Leonard	.05
94	Dave Smith	.05
95	Dave Parker	.05
96	Jose Gonzalez	.05
97	Dave Steib	.05
98	Charlie Hayes	.05
99	Jesse Barfield	.05
100	Joey Belle	.15
101	Jeff Reardon	.05
102	Bruce Hurst	.05
103	Luis Medina	.05
104	Mike Moore	.05
105	Vince Coleman	.05
106	Alan Trammell	.05
107	Randy Myers	.05
108	Frank Tanana	.05
109	Craig Lefferts	.05
110	John Wetteland	.05
111	Chris Gwynn	.05
112	Mark Carreon	.05
113	Von Hayes	.05
114	Doug Jones	.05
115	Andres Galarraga	.05
116	Carlton Fisk	.30
117	Paul O'Neill	.05
118	Tim Raines	.05
119	Tom Brunansky	.05
120	Andy Benes	.05
121	Mark Portugal	.05
122	Willie Randolph	.05
123	Jeff Blauser	.05
124	Don August	.05
125	Chuck Cary	.05
126	John Smiley	.05
127	Terry Mulholland	.05
128	Harold Reynolds	.05
129	Hubie Brooks	.05
130	Ben McDonald	.05
131	Kevin Ritz	.05
132	Luis Quinones	.05
133a	Bam Bam Muelens (Last name incorrect.)	.25
133b	Bam Bam Meulens (Last name correct.)	.05
134	Bill Spiers	.05
135	Andy Hawkins	.05
136	Alvin Davis	.05
137	Lee Smith	.05
138	Joe Carter	.05
139	Bret Saberhagen	.05
140	Sammy Sosa	1.00
141	Matt Nokes	.05
142	Bert Blyleven	.05
143	Bobby Bonilla	.05
144	Howard Johnson	.05
145	Joe Magrane	.05
146	Pedro Guerrero	.05
147	Robin Yount	.30
148	Dan Gladden	.05
149	Steve Sax	.05
150a	Clark/Mitchell (Will Clark, Kevin Mitchell)	.25
150b	Bay Bombers (Will Clark, Kevin Mitchell)	.25

1990 Classic Series 2

Juan Gonzalez

As in previous years, Classic released a 50-card second series set for use with its trivia board game. Unlike earlier update sets, the 1990 Series II set is numbered 1-50 with a "T" designation accompanying the card number. Cards measure 2-1/2" x 3-1/2" and share the format of the original 1990 Classic cards; Series II cards have pink borders with blue highlights. The cards were issued only in complete set form.

		NM/M
Complete Set (50):		3.00
Common Player:		.05
1	Gregg Jefferies	.05
2	Steve Adkins	.05
3	Sandy Alomar, Jr.	.05
4	Steve Avery	.05
5	Mike Blowers	.05
6	George Brett	.75
7	Tom Browning	.05
8	Ellis Burks	.05
9	Joe Carter	.05
10	Jerald Clark	.05
11	"Hot Corners" (Matt Williams, Will Clark)	.10
12	Pat Combs	.05
13	Scott Cooper	.05
14	Mark Davis	.05
15	Storm Davis	.05
16	Larry Walker	.05
17	Brian DuBois	.05
18	Len Dykstra	.05
19	John Franco	.05
20	Kirk Gibson	.05
21	Juan Gonzalez	.20
22	Tommy Greene	.05
23	Kent Hrbek	.05
24	Mike Huff	.05
25	Bo Jackson	.10
26	Nolan Knows Bo (Bo Jackson, Nolan Ryan)	1.50
27	Roberto Kelly	.05
28	Mark Langston	.05
29	Ray Lankford	.05
30	Kevin Maas	.05
31	Julio Machado	.05
32	Greg Maddux	.60
33	Mark McGwire	1.00
34	Paul Molitor	.40
35	Hal Morris	.05
36	Dale Murphy	.20
37	Eddie Murray	.40
38	Jaime Navarro	.05
39	Dean Palmer	.05
40	Derek Parks	.05
41	Bobby Rose	.05
42	Wally Joyner	.05
43	Chris Sabo	.05
44	Benito Santiago	.05
45	Mike Stanton	.05
46	Terry Steinbach	.05
47	Dave Stewart	.05
48	Greg Swindell	.05
49	Jose Vizcaino	.05
---	"Royal Flush" (Bret Saberhagen, Mark Davis)	.05

1990 Classic Series 3

Scott Coolbaugh

Classic's third series of 1990 features the same format as the previous two releases. Series 3 borders are yellow with blue accents. The cards have trivia questions on back and are numbered 1T-100T. No card 51T or 57T exists. Two cards in the set are unnumbered. Like other Classic issues, the cards are designed for use with the trivia board game and were sold only as complete sets.

		NM/M
Complete Set (100):		4.00
Common Player:		.05
1	Ken Griffey Jr.	.75
2	John Tudor	.05
3	John Kruk	.05
4	Mark Gardner	.05
5	Scott Radinsky	.05
6	John Burkett	.05
7	Will Clark	.05
8	Gary Carter	.40
9	Ted Higuera	.05
10	Dave Parker	.05
11	Dante Bichette	.05
12	Don Mattingly	.60
13	Greg Harris	.05
14	David Hollins	.05
15	Matt Nokes	.05
16	Kevin Tapani	.05
17	Shane Mack	.05
18	Randy Myers	.05
19	Greg Olson	.05
20	Shawn Abner	.05
21	Jim Presley	.05
22	Randy Johnson	.40
23	Edgar Martinez	.05
24	Scott Coolbaugh	.05
25	Jeff Treadway	.05
26	Joe Klink	.05
27	Rickey Henderson	.40
28	Sam Horn	.05
29	Kurt Stillwell	.05
30	Andy Van Slyke	.05
31	Willie Banks	.05
32	Jose Canseco	.35
33	Felix Jose	.05
34	Candy Maldonado	.05
35	Carlos Baerga	.05
36	Keith Hernandez	.05
37	Frank Viola	.05
38	Pete O'Brien	.05
39	Pat Borders	.05
40	Mike Heath	.05
41	Kevin Brown	.05
42	Chris Bosio	.05
43	Shawn Boskie	.05
44	Carlos Quintana	.05
45	Juan Samuel	.05
46	Tim Layana	.05
47	Mike Harkey	.05
48	Gerald Perry	.05
49	Mike Witt	.05
50	Joe Orsulak	.05
52	Willie Blair	.05
53	Gene Larkin	.05
54	Jody Reed	.05
55	Jeff Reardon	.05
56	Kevin McReynolds	.05
58	Eric Yelding	.05
59	Fred Lynn	.05
60	Jim Leyritz	.05
61	John Orton	.05
62	Mike Lieberthal	.05
63	Mike Hartley	.05
64	Kal Daniels	.05
65	Terry Shumpert	.05
66	Sil Campusano	.05
67	Tony Pena	.05
68	Barry Bonds	1.00
69	Oddibe McDowell	.05
70	Kelly Gruber	.05
71	Willie Randolph	.05
72	Rick Parker	.05
73	Bobby Bonilla	.05
74	Jack Armstrong	.05
75	Hubie Brooks	.05
76	Sandy Alomar, Jr.	.05
77	Ruben Sierra	.05
78	Erik Hanson	.05
79	Tony Phillips	.05
80	Rondell White	.05
81	Bobby Thigpen	.05
82	Ron Walden	.05
83	Don Peters	.05
84	#6 (Nolan Ryan)	1.00
85	Lance Dickson	.05
86	Ryne Sandberg	.60
87	Eric Christopherson	.05
88	Shane Andrews	.05
89	Marc Newfield	.05
90	Adam Hyzdu	.05
91	"Texas Heat" (Nolan Ryan, Reid Ryan)	1.00
92	Chipper Jones	.75
93	Frank Thomas	.75
94	Cecil Fielder	.05
95	Delino DeShields	.05
96	John Olerud	.05
97	Dave Justice	.05
98	Joe Oliver	.05
99	Alex Fernandez	.05
100	Todd Hundley	.05
---	Mike Marshall (Game instructions on back.)	.05
---	4 in 1 (Frank Viola, Nolan/Reid Ryan, Chipper Jones, Don Mattingly)	.50

1991 Classic

Kirby Puckett

Top rookies and draft picks highlight this set from Classic. The cards come with a trivia board game and accessories. Fronts have fading blue borders with a touch of red. A blank-back "4-in-1" micro-player card is included with each game set.

		NM/M
Complete Set (99):		4.00
Common Player:		.05
1	John Olerud	.05
2	Tino Martinez	.05
3	Ken Griffey Jr.	.65
4	Jeromy Burnitz	.05
5	Ron Gant	.05
6	Mike Benjamin	.05
7	Steve Decker	.05
8	Matt Williams	.05
9	Rafael Novoa	.05
10	Kevin Mitchell	.05
11	Dave Justice	.05
12	Leo Gomez	.05
13	Chris Hoiles	.05
14	Ben McDonald	.05
15	David Segui	.05
16	Anthony Telford	.05
17	Mike Mussina	.30
18	Roger Clemens	.50
19	Wade Boggs	.50
20	Tim Naehring	.05
21	Joe Carter	.05
22	Phil Plantier	.05
23	Rob Dibble	.05
24	Mo Vaughn	.05
25	Lee Stevens	.05
26	Chris Sabo	.05
27	Mark Grace	.05
28	Derrick May	.05
29	Ryne Sandberg	.50
30	Matt Stark	.05
31	Bobby Thigpen	.05
32	Frank Thomas	.60
33	Don Mattingly	.60
34	Eric Davis	.05
35	Reggie Jefferson	.05
36	Alex Cole	.05
37	Mark Lewis	.05
38	Tim Costo	.05
39	Sandy Alomar, Jr.	.05
40	Travis Fryman	.05
41	Cecil Fielder	.05
42	Milt Cuyler	.05
43	Andujar Cedeno	.05
44	Danny Darwin	.05
45	Randy Henis	.05
46	George Brett	.60
47	Jeff Conine	.05
48	Bo Jackson	.10
49	Brian McRae	.05
50	Brent Mayne	.05
51	Eddie Murray	.40
52	Ramon Martinez	.05
53	Jim Neidlinger	.05
54	Jim Poole	.05
55	Tim McIntosh	.05
56	Randy Veres	.05
57	Kirby Puckett	.50
58	Todd Ritchie	.05
59	Rich Garces	.05
60	Moises Alou	.05
61	Delino DeShields	.05
62	Oscar Azocar	.05
63	Kevin Maas	.05
64	Alan Mills	.05
65	John Franco	.05
66	Chris Jelic	.05
67	Dave Magadan	.05
68	Darryl Strawberry	.05
69	Hensley Meulens	.05
70	Juan Gonzalez	.20
71	Reggie Harris	.05
72	Rickey Henderson	.40
73	Mark McGwire	.75
74	Willie McGee	.05
75	Todd Van Poppel	.05
76	Bob Welch	.05
77	"Future Aces" (Todd Van Poppel, Don Peters, David Zancanaro, Kirk Dressendorfer)	.05
78	Lenny Dykstra	.05
79	Mickey Morandini	.05
80	Wes Chamberlain	.05
81	Barry Bonds	1.00
82	Doug Drabek	.05
83	Randy Tomlin	.05
84	Scott Chiamparino	.05
85	Rafael Palmeiro	.35
86	Nolan Ryan	1.00
87	Bobby Witt	.05
88	Fred McGriff	.05
89	Dave Steib	.05
90	Ed Sprague	.05
91	Vince Coleman	.05
92	Rod Brewer	.05
93	Bernard Gilkey	.05
94	Roberto Alomar	.20
95	Chuck Finley	.05
96	Dale Murphy	.20
97	Jose Rijo	.05
98	Hal Morris	.05
99	"Friendly Foes" (Dwight Gooden, Darryl Strawberry)	.05
---	John Olerud, Dwight Gooden, Jose Canseco, Darryl Strawberry	.10

1991 Classic Series 2

Classic released a 100-card second series in 1991. Cards feature the same format as the first series, with the exception of border color; Series II features maroon borders. The cards are designed for trivia game use. Series II includes several players with new teams and top rookies. Special Four-In-One, 300 Game Winner and Strikeout Kings cards are included with each set.

Tim Raines

		NM/M
Complete Set (100):		4.50
Common Player:		.05
1	Ken Griffey Jr.	.75
2	Wilfredo Cordero	.05
3	Cal Ripken, Jr.	1.00
4	D.J. Dozier	.05
5	Darrin Fletcher	.05
6	Glenn Davis	.05
7	Alex Fernandez	.05
8	Cory Snyder	.05
9	Tim Raines	.05
10	Greg Swindell	.05
11	Mark Lewis	.05
12	Rico Brogna	.05
13	Gary Sheffield	.30
14	Paul Molitor	.50
15	Kent Hrbek	.05
16	Scott Erickson	.05
17	Steve Sax	.05
18	Dennis Eckersley	.40
19	Jose Canseco	.30
20	Kirk Dressendorfer	.05
21	Ken Griffey Sr.	.05
22	Erik Hanson	.05
23	Dan Peltier	.05
24	John Olerud	.05
25	Eddie Zosky	.05
26	Steve Avery	.05
27	John Smoltz	.05
28	Frank Thomas	.50
29	Jerome Walton	.05
30	George Bell	.05
31	Jose Rijo	.05
32	Randy Myers	.05
33	Barry Larkin	.05
34	Eric Anthony	.05
35	Dave Hansen	.05
36	Eric Karros	.05
37	Jose Offerman	.05
38	Marquis Grissom	.05
39	Dwight Gooden	.05
40	Gregg Jefferies	.05
41	Pat Combs	.05
42	Todd Zeile	.05
43	Benito Santiago	.05
44	Dave Staton	.05
45	Tony Fernandez	.05
46	Fred McGriff	.05
47	Jeff Brantley	.05
48	Junior Felix	.05
49	Jack Morris	.05
50	Chris George	.05
51	Henry Rodriguez	.05
52	Paul Marak	.05
53	Ryan Klesko	.05
54	Darren Lewis	.05
55	Lance Dickson	.05
56	Anthony Young	.05
57	Willie Banks	.05
58	Mike Bordick	.05
59	Roger Salkeld	.05
60	Steve Karsay	.05
61	Bernie Williams	.05
62	Mickey Tettleton	.05
63	Dave Justice	.05
64	Steve Decker	.05
65	Roger Clemens	.65
66	Phil Plantier	.05
67	Ryne Sandberg	.60
68	Sandy Alomar, Jr.	.05
69	Cecil Fielder	.05
70	George Brett	.65
71	Delino DeShields	.05
72	Dave Magadan	.05
73	Darryl Strawberry	.05
74	Juan Gonzalez	.25
75	Rickey Henderson	.50
76	Willie McGee	.05
77	Todd Van Poppel	.05
78	Barry Bonds	1.00
79	Doug Drabek	.05
80	Nolan Ryan (300 games)	1.00
81	Roberto Alomar	.20
82	Ivan Rodriguez	.50
83	Dan Opperman	.05
84	Jeff Bagwell	.50
85	Braulio Castillo	.05
86	Doug Simons	.05
87	Wade Taylor	.05
88	Gary Scott	.05
89	Dave Stewart	.05
90	Mike Simms	.05
91	Luis Gonzalez	.05
92	Bobby Bonilla	.05
93	Tony Gwynn	.60
94	Will Clark	.05
95	Rich Rowland	.05

96	Alan Trammell	.05
97	"Strikeout Kings" (Nolan Ryan, Roger Clemens)	.50
98	Joe Carter	.05
99	Jack Clark	.05
100	Four-In-One	.20

1991 Classic Series 3

Green borders highlight Classic's third series of cards for 1991. The set includes a gameboard and player cards featuring trivia questions on the back. Statistics and biographical information are also found on back.

NM/M
Complete Set (100):		4.50
Common Player:		.05
1	Jim Abbott	.05
2	Craig Biggio	.05
3	Wade Boggs	.45
4	Bobby Bonilla	.05
5	Ivan Calderon	.05
6	Jose Canseco	.25
7	Andy Benes	.05
8	Wes Chamberlain	.05
9	Will Clark	.05
10	Royce Clayton	.05
11	Gerald Alexander	.05
12	Chili Davis	.05
13	Eric Davis	.05
14	Andre Dawson	.25
15	Rob Dibble	.05
16	Chris Donnels	.05
17	Scott Erickson	.05
18	Monty Fariss	.05
19	Ruben Amaro Jr.	.05
20	Chuck Finley	.05
21	Carlton Fisk	.35
22	Carlos Baerga	.05
23	Ron Gant	.05
24	Dave Justice, Ron Gant	.05
25	Mike Gardiner	.05
26	Tom Glavine	.15
27	Joe Grahe	.05
28	Derek Bell	.05
29	Mike Greenwell	.05
30	Ken Griffey Jr.	.75
31	Leo Gomez	.05
32	Tom Goodwin	.05
33	Tony Gwynn	.45
34	Mel Hall	.05
35	Brian Harper	.05
36	Dave Henderson	.05
37	Albert Belle	.05
38	Orel Hershiser	.05
39	Brian Hunter	.05
40	Howard Johnson	.05
41	Felix Jose	.05
42	Wally Joyner	.05
43	Jeff Juden	.05
44	Pat Kelly	.05
45	Jimmy Key	.05
46	Chuck Knoblauch	.05
47	John Kruk	.05
48	Ray Lankford	.05
49	Ced Landrum	.05
50	Scott Livingstone	.05
51	Kevin Maas	.05
52	Greg Maddux	.45
53	Dennis Martinez	.05
54	Edgar Martinez	.05
55	Pedro Martinez	.05
56	Don Mattingly	.50
57	Orlando Merced	.05
58	Keith Mitchell	.05
59	Kevin Mitchell	.05
60	Paul Molitor	.35
61	Jack Morris	.05
62	Hal Morris	.05
63	Kevin Morton	.05
64	Pedro Munoz	.05
65	Eddie Murray	.35
66	Jack McDowell	.05
67	Jeff McNeely	.05
68	Brian McRae	.05
69	Kevin McReynolds	.05
70	Gregg Olson	.05
71	Rafael Palmeiro	.30
72	Dean Palmer	.05
73	Tony Phillips	.05
74	Kirby Puckett	.45
75	Carlos Quintana	.05
76	Pat Rice	.05
77	Cal Ripken, Jr.	1.00
78	Ivan Rodriguez	.30
79	Nolan Ryan	1.00
80	Bret Saberhagen	.05
81	Tim Salmon	.05
82	Juan Samuel	.05
83	Ruben Sierra	.05
84	Heathcliff Slocumb	.05
85	Joe Slusarski	.05
86	John Smiley	.05
87	Dave Smith	.05
88	Ed Sprague	.05
89	Todd Stottlemyre	.05
90	Mike Timlin	.05
91	Greg Vaughn	.05
92	Frank Viola	.05
93	John Wehner	.05
94	Devon White	.05
95	Matt Williams	.05
96	Rick Wilkins	.05
97	Bernie Williams	.05
98	Starter & Stopper (Goose Gossage, Nolan Ryan)	.20
99	Gerald Williams	.05
----	4-in-1 (Bobby Bonilla, Will Clark, Cal Ripken Jr., Scott Erickson)	.25

1991 Classic Collector's Edition

The Classic Collector's edition made its debut in 1991. This package includes a board game, trivia baseball player cards, a baseball tips booklet and a certificate of authenticity, all packaged in a collector's edition box. Each box is individually and sequentially numbered on the outside, with a reported 100,000 available.

NM/M
Complete Set (200):		7.50
Common Player:		.05
1	Frank Viola	.05
2	Tim Wallach	.05
3	Lou Whitaker	.05
4	Brett Butler	.05
5	Jim Abbott	.05
6	Jack Armstrong	.05
7	Craig Biggio	.05
8	Brian Barnes	.05
9	Dennis "Oil Can" Boyd	.05
10	Tom Browning	.05
11	Tom Brunansky	.05
12	Ellis Burks	.05
13	Harold Baines	.05
14	Kal Daniels	.05
15	Mark Davis	.05
16	Storm Davis	.05
17	Tom Glavine	.25
18	Mike Greenwell	.05
19	Kelly Gruber	.05
20	Mark Gubicza	.05
21	Pedro Guerrero	.05
22	Mike Harkey	.05
23	Orel Hershiser	.05
24	Ted Higuera	.05
25	Von Hayes	.05
26	Andre Dawson	.25
27	Shawon Dunston	.05
28	Roberto Kelly	.05
29	Joe Magrane	.05
30	Dennis Martinez	.05
31	Kevin McReynolds	.05
32	Matt Nokes	.05
33	Dan Plesac	.05
34	Dave Parker	.05
35	Randy Johnson	.40
36	Bret Saberhagen	.05
37	Mackey Sasser	.05
38	Mike Scott	.05
39	Ozzie Smith	.50
40	Kevin Seitzer	.05
41	Ruben Sierra	.05
42	Kevin Tapani	.05
43	Danny Tartabull	.05
44	Robby Thompson	.05
45	Andy Van Slyke	.05
46	Greg Vaughn	.05
47	Harold Reynolds	.05
48	Will Clark	.05
49	Gary Gaetti	.05
50	Joe Grahe	.05
51	Carlton Fisk	.40
52	Robin Ventura	.05
53	Ozzie Guillen	.05
54	Tom Candiotti	.05
55	Doug Jones	.05
56	Eric King	.05
57	Kirk Gibson	.05
58	Tim Costo	.05
59	Robin Yount	.40
60	Sammy Sosa	.50
61	Jesse Barfield	.05
62	Marc Newfield	.05
63	Jimmy Key	.05
64	Felix Jose	.05
65	Mark Whiten	.05
66	Tommy Greene	.05
67	Kent Mercker	.05
68	Greg Maddux	.50
69	Danny Jackson	.05
70	Reggie Sanders	.05
71	Eric Yelding	.05
72	Karl Rhodes	.05
73	Fernando Valenzuela	.05
74	Chris Nabholz	.05
75	Andres Galarraga	.05
76	Howard Johnson	.05
77	Hubie Brooks	.05
78	Terry Mulholland	.05
79	Paul Molitor	.40
80	Roger McDowell	.05
81	Darren Daulton	.05
82	Zane Smith	.05
83	Ray Lankford	.05
84	Bruce Hurst	.05
85	Andy Benes	.05
86	John Burkett	.05
87	Dave Righetti	.05
88	Steve Karsay	.05
89	D.J. Dozier	.05
90	Jeff Bagwell	.40
91	Joe Carter	.05
92	Wes Chamberlain	.05
93	Vince Coleman	.05
94	Pat Combs	.05
95	Jerome Walton	.05
96	Jeff Conine	.05
97	Alan Trammell	.05
98	Don Mattingly	.55
99	Ramon Martinez	.05
100	Dave Magadan	.05
101	Greg Swindell	.05
102	Dave Stewart	.05
103	Gary Sheffield	.30
104	George Bell	.05
105	Mark Grace	.05
106	Steve Sax	.05
107	Ryne Sandberg	.50
108	Chris Sabo	.05
109	Jose Rijo	.05
110	Cal Ripken, Jr.	1.00
111	Kirby Puckett	.50
112	Eddie Murray	.40
113	Roberto Alomar	.20
114	Randy Myers	.05
115	Rafael Palmeiro	.35
116	John Olerud	.05
117	Gregg Jefferies	.05
118	Kent Hrbek	.05
119	Marquis Grissom	.05
120	Ken Griffey Jr.	.60
121	Dwight Gooden	.05
122	Juan Gonzalez	.20
123	Ron Gant	.05
124	Travis Fryman	.05
125	John Franco	.05
126	Dennis Eckersley	.35
127	Cecil Fielder	.05
128	Phil Plantier	.05
129	Kevin Mitchell	.05
130	Kevin Maas	.05
131	Mark McGwire	.75
132	Ben McDonald	.05
133	Lenny Dykstra	.05
134	Delino DeShields	.05
135	Jose Canseco	.30
136	Eric Davis	.05
137	George Brett	.55
138	Steve Avery	.05
139	Eric Anthony	.05
140	Bobby Thigpen	.05
141	Ken Griffey Sr.	.05
142	Barry Larkin	.05
143	Jeff Brantley	.05
144	Bobby Bonilla	.05
145	Jose Offerman	.05
146	Mike Mussina	.30
147	Erik Hanson	.05
148	Dale Murphy	.15
149	Roger Clemens	.55
150	Tino Martinez	.05
151	Todd Van Poppel	.05
152	Mo Vaughn	.05
153	Derrick May	.05
154	Jack Clark	.05
155	Dave Hansen	.05
156	Tony Gwynn	.50
157	Brian McRae	.05
158	Matt Williams	.05
159	Kirk Dressendorfer	.05
160	Scott Erickson	.05
161	Tony Fernandez	.05
162	Willie McGee	.05
163	Fred McGriff	.05
164	Leo Gomez	.05
165	Bernard Gilkey	.05
166	Bobby Witt	.05
167	Doug Drabek	.05
168	Rob Dibble	.05
169	Glenn Davis	.05
170	Danny Darwin	.05
171	Eric Karros	.05
172	Eddie Zosky	.05
173	Todd Zeile	.05
174	Tim Raines	.05
175	Benito Santiago	.05
176	Dan Peltier	.05
177	Darryl Strawberry	.05
178	Hal Morris	.05
179	Hensley Meulens	.05
180	John Smoltz	.05
181	Frank Thomas	.40
182	Dave Staton	.05
183	Scott Chiamparino	.05
184	Alex Fernandez	.05
185	Mark Lewis	.05
186	Bo Jackson	.10
187	Mickey Morandini (Photo actually Darren Daulton.)	.05
188	Cory Snyder	.05
189	Rickey Henderson	.40
190	Junior Felix	.05
191	Milt Cuyler	.05
192	Wade Boggs	.50
193	"Justice Prevails" (David Justice)	.05
194	Sandy Alomar, Jr.	.05
195	Barry Bonds	1.00
196	Nolan Ryan	1.00
197	Rico Brogna	.05
198	Steve Decker	.05
199	Bob Welch	.05
200	Andujar Cedeno	.05

1991 Classic/American Collectables Nolan Ryan

This set of Nolan Ryan highlights was produced by Classic for American Collectables and sold as a limited-edition issue. The cards feature color photos of Ryan bordered in a garish green and yellow design. Backs have personal data and stats printed in black on green, along with a color MLB logo.

NM/M
Complete Set (10):		7.50
Common Card:		1.00
1	Nolan Ryan (Mets '66-'71)	1.00
2	Nolan Ryan (Angels '72-'79)	1.00
3	Nolan Ryan (Astros '80-'88)	1.00
4	Nolan Ryan (Rangers '89-'90)	1.00
5	Nolan Ryan (5000 K's)	1.00
6	Nolan Ryan (6th No-No)	1.00
7	Nolan Ryan (Angels '72-'79)	1.00
8	Nolan Ryan (Astros '80-'88)	1.00
9	Nolan Ryan (Rangers '89-'90)	1.00
10	Nolan Ryan (300 Wins)	1.00

1992 Classic Series 1

CHITO MARTINEZ

Classic introduced an innovative design with the release of its 1992 set. Fronts feature full-color photos bordered in white, while backs feature statistics, biographical information and trivia questions accented by a fading stadium shot.

The cards were released with a gameboard and are numbered on back with a "T" prefix.

NM/M
Complete Set (100):		4.50
Common Player:		.05
1	Jim Abbott	.05
2	Kyle Abbott	.05
3	Scott Aldred	.05
4	Roberto Alomar	.20
5	Wilson Alvarez	.05
6	Andy Ashby	.05
7	Steve Avery	.05
8	Jeff Bagwell	.40
9	Bret Barberie	.05
10	Kim Batiste	.05
11	Derek Bell	.05
12	Jay Bell	.05
13	Albert Belle	.05
14	Andy Benes	.05
15	Sean Berry	.05
16	Barry Bonds	1.00
17	Ryan Bowen	.05
18	Trifecta (Alejandro Pena, Mark Wohlers, Kent Mercker)	.05
19	Scott Brosius	.05
20	Jay Buhner	.05
21	David Burba	.05
22	Jose Canseco	.35
23	Andujar Cedeno	.05
24	Will Clark	.05
25	Royce Clayton	.05
26	Roger Clemens	.50
27	David Cone	.05
28	Scott Cooper	.05
29	Chris Cron	.05
30	Len Dykstra	.05
31	Cal Eldred	.05
32	Hector Fajardo	.05
33	Cecil Fielder	.05
34	Dave Fleming	.05
35	Steve Foster	.05
36	Julio Franco	.05
37	Carlos Garcia	.05
38	Tom Glavine	.15
39	Tom Goodwin	.05
40	Ken Griffey Jr.	.65
41	Chris Haney	.05
42	Bryan Harvey	.05
43	Rickey Henderson	.40
44	Carlos Hernandez	.05
45	Roberto Hernandez	.05
46	Brook Jacoby	.05
47	Howard Johnson	.05
48	Pat Kelly	.05
49	Darryl Kile	.05
50	Chuck Knoblauch	.05
51	Ray Lankford	.05
52	Mark Leiter	.05
53	Darren Lewis	.05
54	Scott Livingstone	.05
55	Shane Mack	.05
56	Chito Martinez	.05
57	Dennis Martinez	.05
58	Don Mattingly	.50
59	Paul McClellan	.05
60	Chuck McElroy	.05
61	Fred McGriff	.05
62	Orlando Merced	.05
63	Luis Mercedes	.05
64	Kevin Mitchell	.05
65	Hal Morris	.05
66	Jack Morris	.05
67	Mike Mussina	.30
68	Denny Neagle	.05
69	Tom Pagnozzi	.05
70	Terry Pendleton	.05
71	Phil Plantier	.05
72	Kirby Puckett	.45
73	Carlos Quintana	.05
74	Willie Randolph	.05
75	Arthur Rhodes	.05
76	Cal Ripken	1.00
77	Ivan Rodriguez	.35
78	Nolan Ryan	1.00
79	Ryne Sandberg	.45
80	Deion Sanders	.10
81	Reggie Sanders	.05
82	Mo Sanford	.05
83	Terry Shumpert	.05
84	Tim Spehr	.05
85	Lee Stevens	.05
86	Darryl Strawberry	.05
87	Kevin Tapani	.05
88	Danny Tartabull	.05
89	Frank Thomas	.40
90	Jim Thome	.30
91	Todd Van Poppel	.05
92	Andy Van Slyke	.05
93	John Wehner	.05
94	John Wetteland	.05
95	Devon White	.05
96	Brian Williams	.05
97	Mark Wohlers	.05
98	Robin Yount	.40
99	Eddie Zosky	.05
----	4-in-1 (Barry Bonds, Roger Clemens, Steve Avery, Nolan Ryan)	.50

1992 Classic Series 2

The 100-cards in Classic's 1992 Series II came packaged with a gameboard and spinner. In a completely different format from

Classic's other '92 issues, Series II features player photos bordered at left and right with red or blue color bars which fade toward top and bottom. Backs have biographical data, previous-year and career statistics and five trivia questions, along with a color representation of the team's uniform. Cards, except the 4-In-1, are numbered with a "T" prefix.

NM/M
Complete Set (100):		4.50
Common Player:		.05
1	Jim Abbott	.05
2	Jeff Bagwell	.40
3	Jose Canseco	.30
4	Julio Valera	.05
5	Scott Brosius	.05
6	Mark Langston	.05
7	Andy Stankiewicz	.05
8	Gary DiSarcina	.05
9	Pete Harnisch	.05
10	Mark McGwire	.75
11	Ricky Bones	.05
12	Steve Avery	.05
13	Deion Sanders	.10
14	Mike Mussina	.25
15	Dave Justice	.45
16	Pat Hentgen	.05
17	Tom Glavine	.20
18	Juan Guzman	.05
19	Ron Gant	.05
20	Kelly Gruber	.05
21	Eric Karros	.05
22	Derrick May	.05
23	Dave Hansen	.05
24	Andre Dawson	.25
25	Eric Davis	.05
26	Ozzie Smith	.45
27	Sammy Sosa	.05
28	Lee Smith	.05
29	Ryne Sandberg	.45
30	Robin Yount	.40
31	Matt Williams	.05
32	John Vander Wal	.05
33	Bill Swift	.05
34	Delino DeShields	.05
35	Royce Clayton	.05
36	Moises Alou	.05
37	Will Clark	.05
38	Darryl Strawberry	.05
39	Larry Walker	.05
40	Ramon Martinez	.05
41	Howard Johnson	.05
42	Tino Martinez	.05
43	Dwight Gooden	.05
44	Ken Griffey Jr.	.60
45	David Cone	.05
46	Kenny Lofton	.05
47	Bobby Bonilla	.05
48	Carlos Baerga	.05
49	Don Mattingly	.50
50	Sandy Alomar, Jr.	.05
51	Lenny Dykstra	.05
52	Tony Gwynn	.45
53	Felix Jose	.05
54	Rick Sutcliffe	.05
55	Wes Chamberlain	.05
56	Cal Ripken, Jr.	1.00
57	Kyle Abbott	.05
58	Leo Gomez	.05
59	Gary Sheffield	.20
60	Anthony Young	.05
61	Roger Clemens	.50
62	Rafael Palmeiro	.35
63	Wade Boggs	.45
64	Andy Van Slyke	.05
65	Ruben Sierra	.05
66	Denny Neagle	.05
67	Nolan Ryan	1.00
68	Doug Drabek	.05
69	Ivan Rodriguez	.35
70	Barry Bonds	1.00
71	Chuck Knoblauch	.05
72	Reggie Sanders	.05
73	Cecil Fielder	.05
74	Barry Larkin	.05
75	Scott Aldred	.05
76	Rob Dibble	.05
77	Brian McRae	.05
78	Tim Belcher	.05
79	George Brett	.50
80	Frank Viola	.05
81	Roberto Kelly	.05
82	Jack McDowell	.05

83	Mel Hall	.05
84	Esteban Beltre	.05
85	Robin Ventura	.05
86	George Bell	.05
87	Frank Thomas	.40
88	John Smiley	.05
89	Bobby Thigpen	.05
90	Kirby Puckett	.45
91	Kevin Mitchell	.05
92	Peter Hoy	.05
93	Russ Springer	.05
94	Donovan Osborne	.05
95	Dave Silvestri	.05
96	Chad Curtis	.05
97	Pat Mahomes	.05
98	Danny Tartabull	.05
99	John Doherty	.05
---	4-in-1 (Ryne Sandberg, Mike Mussina, Reggie Sanders, Jose Canseco)	.25

1992 Classic Collector's Edition

TIM RAINES

The second annual 200-card "Collector's Edition" set was packaged with a gameboard, spinner, generic player pieces, a mechanical scoreboard and a book of tips from star players. The UV-coated card fronts feature color player photos against a deep purple border. Backs have a few biographical details, previous season and career stats, plus five trivia questions in case anyone actually wanted to play the game.

		NM/M
Complete Set (200):		9.00
Common Player:		.05
1	Chuck Finley	.05
2	Craig Biggio	.05
3	Luis Gonzalez	.05
4	Pete Harnisch	.05
5	Jeff Juden	.05
6	Harold Baines	.05
7	Kirk Dressendorfer	.05
8	Dennis Eckersley	.35
9	Dave Henderson	.05
10	Dave Stewart	.05
11	Joe Carter	.05
12	Juan Guzman	.05
13	Dave Stieb	.05
14	Todd Stottlemyre	.05
15	Ron Gant	.05
16	Brian Hunter	.05
17	Dave Justice	.05
18	John Smoltz	.05
19	Mike Stanton	.05
20	Chris George	.05
21	Paul Molitor	.40
22	Omar Olivares	.05
23	Lee Smith	.05
24	Ozzie Smith	.50
25	Todd Zeile	.05
26	George Bell	.05
27	Andre Dawson	.25
28	Shawon Dunston	.05
29	Mark Grace	.05
30	Greg Maddux	.50
31	Dave Smith	.05
32	Brett Butler	.05
33	Orel Hershiser	.05
34	Eric Karros	.05
35	Ramon Martinez	.05
36	Jose Offerman	.05
37	Juan Samuel	.05
38	Delino DeShields	.05
39	Marquis Grissom	.05
40	Tim Wallach	.05
41	Eric Gunderson	.05
42	Willie McGee	.05
43	Dave Righetti	.05
44	Robby Thompson	.05
45	Matt Williams	.05
46	Sandy Alomar, Jr.	.05
47	Reggie Jefferson	.05
48	Mark Lewis	.05
49	Robin Ventura	.05
50	Tino Martinez	.05
51	Roberto Kelly	.05
52	Vince Coleman	.05
53	Dwight Gooden	.05
54	Todd Hundley	.05
55	Kevin Maas	.05
56	Wade Taylor	.05
57	Bryan Harvey	.05
58	Leo Gomez	.05
59	Ben McDonald	.05
60	Ricky Bones	.05
61	Tony Gwynn	.50
62	Benito Santiago	.05
63	Wes Chamberlain	.05
64	Tommy Greene	.05
65	Dale Murphy	.15
66	Steve Buechele	.05
67	Doug Drabek	.05
68	Joe Grahe	.05
69	Rafael Palmeiro	.35
70	Wade Boggs	.50
71	Ellis Burks	.05
72	Mike Greenwell	.05
73	Mo Vaughn	.05
74	Derek Bell	.05
75	Rob Dibble	.05
76	Barry Larkin	.05
77	Jose Rijo	.05
78	Doug Henry	.05
79	Chris Sabo	.05
80	Pedro Guerrero	.05
81	George Brett	.60
82	Tom Gordon	.05
83	Mark Gubicza	.05
84	Mark Whiten	.05
85	Brian McRae	.05
86	Danny Jackson	.05
87	Milt Cuyler	.05
88	Travis Fryman	.05
89	Mickey Tettleton	.05
90	Alan Trammell	.05
91	Lou Whitaker	.05
92	Chili Davis	.05
93	Scott Erickson	.05
94	Kent Hrbek	.05
95	Alex Fernandez	.05
96	Carlton Fisk	.40
97	Ramon Garcia	.05
98	Ozzie Guillen	.05
99	Tim Raines	.05
100	Bobby Thigpen	.05
101	Kirby Puckett	.50
102	Bernie Williams	.05
103	Dave Hansen	.05
104	Kevin Tapani	.05
105	Don Mattingly	.60
106	Frank Thomas	.40
107	Monty Fariss	.05
108	Bo Jackson	.10
109	Jim Abbott	.05
110	Jose Canseco	.25
111	Phil Plantier	.05
112	Brian Williams	.05
113	Mark Langston	.05
114	Wilson Alvarez	.05
115	Roberto Hernandez	.05
116	Darryl Kile	.05
117	Ryan Bowen	.05
118	Rickey Henderson	.40
119	Mark McGwire	1.00
120	Devon White	.05
121	Roberto Alomar	.20
122	Kelly Gruber	.05
123	Eddie Zosky	.05
124	Tom Glavine	.25
125	Kal Daniels	.05
126	Cal Eldred	.05
127	Deion Sanders	.10
128	Robin Yount	.40
129	Cecil Fielder	.05
130	Ray Lankford	.05
131	Ryne Sandberg	.50
132	Darryl Strawberry	.05
133	Chris Haney	.05
134	Dennis Martinez	.05
135	Bryan Hickerson	.05
136	Will Clark	.05
137	Hal Morris	.05
138	Charles Nagy	.05
139	Jim Thome	.35
140	Albert Belle	.05
141	Reggie Sanders	.05
142	Scott Cooper	.05
143	David Cone	.05
144	Anthony Young	.05
145	Howard Johnson	.05
146	Arthur Rhodes	.05
147	Scott Aldred	.05
148	Mike Mussina	.25
149	Fred McGriff	.05
150	Andy Benes	.05
151	Ruben Sierra	.05
152	Len Dykstra	.05
153	Andy Van Slyke	.05
154	Orlando Merced	.05
155	Barry Bonds	1.50
156	John Smiley	.05
157	Julio Franco	.05
158	Juan Gonzalez	.20
159	Ivan Rodriguez	.35
160	Willie Banks	.05
161	Eric Davis	.05
162	Eddie Murray	.40
163	Dave Fleming	.05
164	Wally Joyner	.05
165	Kevin Mitchell	.05
166	Ed Taubensee	.05
167	Danny Tartabull	.05
168	Ken Hill	.05
169	Willie Randolph	.05
170	Kevin McReynolds	.05
171	Gregg Jefferies	.05
172	Patrick Lennon	.05
173	Luis Mercedes	.05
174	Glenn Davis	.05
175	Bret Saberhagen	.05
176	Bobby Bonilla	.05
177	Kenny Lofton	.05
178	Jose Lind	.05
179	Royce Clayton	.05
180	Scott Scudder	.05
181	Chuck Knoblauch	.05
182	Terry Pendleton	.05
183	Nolan Ryan	1.50
184	Rob Maurer	.05
185	Brian Bohanon	.05
186	Ken Griffey Jr.	.75
187	Jeff Bagwell	.40
188	Steve Avery	.05
189	Roger Clemens	.60
190	Cal Ripken, Jr.	1.50
191	Kim Batiste	.05
192	Bip Roberts	.05
193	Greg Swindell	.05
194	Dave Winfield	.40
195	Steve Sax	.05
196	Frank Viola	.05
197	Mo Sanford	.05
198	Kyle Abbott	.05
199	Jack Morris	.05
200	Andy Ashby	.05

1993 Classic

DAVID JUSTICE OF

A 100-card travel edition of Classic's baseball trivia cards was produced for 1993. Cards feature game-action player photos with dark blue borders. Backs have previous season and career stats along with five trivia questions. Card numbers have a "T" prefix.

		NM/M
Complete Set (100):		4.00
Common Player:		.05
1	Jim Abbott	.05
2	Roberto Alomar	.20
3	Moises Alou	.05
4	Brady Anderson	.05
5	Eric Anthony	.05
6	Alex Arias	.05
7	Pedro Astacio	.05
8	Steve Avery	.05
9	Carlos Baerga	.05
10	Jeff Bagwell	.40
11	George Bell	.05
12	Albert Belle	.05
13	Craig Biggio	.05
14	Barry Bonds	1.00
15	Bobby Bonilla	.05
16	Mike Bordick	.05
17	George Brett	.55
18	Jose Canseco	.30
19	Joe Carter	.05
20	Royce Clayton	.05
21	Roger Clemens	.55
22	Greg Colbrunn	.05
23	David Cone	.05
24	Darren Daulton	.05
25	Delino DeShields	.05
26	Rob Dibble	.05
27	Dennis Eckersley	.35
28	Cal Eldred	.05
29	Scott Erickson	.05
30	Junior Felix	.05
31	Tony Fernandez	.05
32	Cecil Fielder	.05
33	Steve Finley	.05
34	Dave Fleming	.05
35	Travis Fryman	.05
36	Tom Glavine	.25
37	Juan Gonzalez	.20
38	Ken Griffey Jr.	.60
39	Marquis Grissom	.05
40	Juan Guzman	.05
41	Tony Gwynn	.50
42	Rickey Henderson	.40
43	Felix Jose	.05
44	Wally Joyner	.05
45	David Justice	.05
46	Eric Karros	.05
47	Roberto Kelly	.05
48	Ryan Klesko	.05
49	Chuck Knoblauch	.05
50	John Kruk	.05
51	Ray Lankford	.05
52	Barry Larkin	.05
53	Pat Listach	.05
54	Kenny Lofton	.05
55	Shane Mack	.05
56	Greg Maddux	.50
57	Dave Magadan	.05
58	Edgar Martinez	.05
59	Don Mattingly	.55
60	Ben McDonald	.05
61	Jack McDowell	.05
62	Fred McGriff	.05
63	Mark McGwire	.75
64	Kevin McReynolds	.05
65	Sam Militello	.05
66	Paul Molitor	.40
67	Jeff Montgomery	.05
68	Jack Morris	.05
69	Eddie Murray	.40
70	Mike Mussina	.30
71	Otis Nixon	.05
72	Donovan Osborne	.05
73	Terry Pendleton	.05
74	Mike Piazza	.60
75	Kirby Puckett	.50
76	Cal Ripken, Jr.	1.00
77	Bip Roberts	.05
78	Ivan Rodriguez	.35
79	Nolan Ryan	1.00
80	Ryne Sandberg	.50
81	Deion Sanders	.10
82	Reggie Sanders	.05
83	Frank Seminara	.05
84	Gary Sheffield	.30
85	Ruben Sierra	.05
86	John Smiley	.05
87	Lee Smith	.05
88	Ozzie Smith	.50
89	John Smoltz	.05
90	Danny Tartabull	.05
91	Bob Tewksbury	.05
92	Frank Thomas	.40
93	Andy Van Slyke	.05
94	Mo Vaughn	.05
95	Robin Ventura	.05
96	Tim Wakefield	.05
97	Larry Walker	.05
98	Dave Winfield	.40
99	Robin Yount	.40
---	4-in-1 (Mark McGwire, Sam Militello, Ryan Klesko, Greg Maddux)	.50

1996 Classic/Metallic Impressions Nolan Ryan

Nolan Ryan's career is traced in this set of 2-5/8" x 3-5/8" embossed metal cards produced for Classic by Metallic Impressions. The center of each card's front is a raised color photo which continues in muted tones of yellow and orange to the edges. The Classic and The Metal Edge logos are embossed, as well. Horizontal backs are identical in design with a color portrait of Ryan at left and a paragraph describing a highlight or milestone at right. Classic and Cooperstown Collection logos are in opposite corners. Each of 14,950 sets was sold with a numbered certificate of authenticity in an embossed lithographed metal box.

		NM/M
Complete Boxed Set (10):		7.50
Single Card:		1.00
1	Nolan Ryan (Career ends with Rangers.)	1.00
2	Nolan Ryan (1970s, California Angels.)	1.00
3	Nolan Ryan (Major League debut.)	1.00
4	Nolan Ryan (Over-40 no-hitters.)	1.00
5	Nolan Ryan (Rangers no-hitters.)	1.00
6	Nolan Ryan (Mets trade Ryan.)	1.00
7	Nolan Ryan (Joins Astros.)	1.00
8	Nolan Ryan (Career records.)	1.00
9	Nolan Ryan (Lean years in Houston.)	1.00
10	Nolan Ryan ("Ryan Express" returns to A.L.)	1.00

1989 Cleveland Indians Team Issue

(28) Cory Snyder, OF

The Cleveland Indians released this oversized (2-3/4" x 4-1/2") set in 1989. Cards feature a full-color player photo on front with the "Tribe" logo in the upper left corner. Card backs include major and minor league statistics and a facsimile autograph.

		NM/M
Complete Set (28):		6.00
Common Player:		.25
(1)	Doc Edwards	.25
(2)	Joel Skinner	.25
(3)	Andy Allanson	.25
(4)	Tom Candiotti	.25
(5)	Doug Jones	.25
(6)	Keith Atherton	.25
(7)	Rich Yett	.25
(8)	John Farrell	.25
(9)	Rod Nichols	.25
(10)	Joe Skalski	.25
(11)	Pete O'Brien	.25
(12)	Jerry Browne	.25
(13)	Brook Jacoby	.25
(14)	Felix Fermin	.25
(15)	Bud Black	.25
(16)	Brad Havens	.25
(17)	Greg Swindell	.25
(18)	Scott Bailes	.25
(19)	Jesse Orosco	.25
(20)	Oddibe McDowell	.25
(21)	Joe Carter	.50
(22)	Cory Snyder	.25
(23)	Louie Medina	.25
(24)	Dave Clark	.25
(25)	Brad Komminsk	.25
(26)	Luis Aguayo	.25
(27)	Pat Keedy	.25
(28)	Tribe Coaches	.25

1990 Cleveland Indians Team Issue

(17) Keith Hernandez, 1B

The Cleveland Indians released this oversized (2-7/8" x 4-1/4") set in 1990. Cards feature a full-color portrait photo on front with the "Tribe" logo in the top-left corner. Player name, uniform number and position are in the bottom border. Backs are blank.

		NM/M
Complete Set (46):		12.00
Common Player:		.25
(1)	Beau Allred	.25
(2)	Sandy Alomar Jr.	.50
(3)	Carlos Baerga	.25
(4)	Kevin Bearse	.25
(5)	Joey (Albert) Belle	2.00
(6)	Bud Black	.25
(7)	Tom Brookens	.25
(8)	Jerry Browne	.25
(9)	Tom Candiotti	.25
(10)	Colin Charland	.25
(11)	Rich Dauer	.25
(12)	John Farrell	.25
(13)	Felix Fermin	.25
(14)	Cecilio Guante	.25
(15)	Mike Hargrove	.35
(16)	Keith Hernandez	.40
(17)	Luis Isaac	.25
(18)	Brook Jacoby	.25
(19)	Chris James	.25
(20)	Dion James	.25
(21)	Doug Jones	.25
(22)	Carl Kelipuleole	.25
(23)	Tom Lampkin	.25
(24)	Tom Magrann	.25
(25)	Candy Maldonado	.25
(26)	Jeff Manto	.25
(27)	John McNamara	.25
(28)	Jose Morales	.25
(29)	Rod Nichols	.25
(30)	Al Nipper	.25
(31)	Steve Olin	.25
(32)	Jesse Orosco	.25
(33)	Doug Robertson	.25
(34)	Rudy Seanez	.25
(35)	Jeff Shaw	.25
(36)	Doug Sisk	.25
(37)	Joe Skalski	.25
(38)	Joel Skinner	.25
(39)	Cory Snyder	.25
(40)	Greg Swindell	.25
(41)	Sergio Valdez	.25
(42)	Mike Walker	.25
(43)	Mitch Webster	.25
(44)	Kevin Wickander	.25
(45)	Mark Wiley	.25
(46)	Billy Williams	.25

1993 Cleveland Indians Team Issue

ALBERT BELLE

Only the mascot's card carries the logo of the television station which sponsored this team set. In 2-1/2" x 3-1/2" format printed on thin cardboard, the fronts feature color game-action photos with borders of red, white and blue. The player's uniform number appears in the lower-left corner. Backs are in black-and-white with major league career stats and a log commemorating the team's 61 years at Municipal Stadium. The set is checklisted here alphabetically.

		NM/M
Complete Set (34):		12.00
Common Player:		.25
(1)	Sandy Alomar Jr.	.50
(2)	Carlos Baerga	.25
(3)	Albert Belle	1.00
(4)	Mike Bielecki	.25
(5)	Mike Christopher	.25
(6)	Mark Clark	.25
(7)	Dennis Cook	.25
(8)	Alvaro Espinoza	.25
(9)	Felix Fermin	.25
(10)	Mike Hargrove	.25
(11)	Glenallen Hill	.25
(12)	Thomas Howard	.25
(13)	Reggie Jefferson	.25
(14)	Wayne Kirby	.25
(15)	Tom Kramer	.25
(16)	Mark Lewis	.25
(17)	Derek Lilliquist	.25
(18)	Kenny Lofton	.35
(19)	Carlos Martinez	.25
(20)	Jose Mesa	.25
(21)	Jeff Mutis	.25
(22)	Charles Nagy	.25
(23)	Bob Ojeda	.25
(24)	Junior Ortiz	.25
(25)	Eric Plunk	.25
(26)	Ted Power	.25
(27)	Scott Scudder	.25
(28)	Joel Skinner	.25
(29)	Paul Sorrento	.25
(30)	Jim Thome	2.00
(31)	Jeff Treadway	.25
(32)	Kevin Wickander	.25
(33)	Indians Coaches (Rick Adair, Ken Bolke, Dom Chiti, Ron Clark, Jose Morales, Dave Nelson, Jeff Newman)	.25
(34)	Slider (Mascot)	.25

1992 Clovis Police Department Mark's Moments

Highlights of Mark McGwire's career to that point are shown and/or described in this set of police cards from the Clovis, Calif., P.D.

MARK McGWIRE

Cards have color photos framed in gold with green borders. The city seal is at upper-left, the Oakland description of a "Moment," a safety tip, the description of the "Moment" on front, a safety tip, the logo of the Clovis P.D., another team logo and sponsors' credits.

	NM/M
Complete Set (24):	35.00
Common Card:	1.50

1981 Coca-Cola

JOHNNY BENCH

In 1981 Topps produced for Coca-Cola 12-card sets for 11 American and National League teams. The sets include 11 player cards and one unnumbered header card. The 2-1/2" x 3-1/2" cards are identical in format to the 1981 Topps regular issue with an added Coca-Cola logo. Backs differ from the '81 Topps regular set in that they are numbered 1-11 and carry the Coca-Cola trademark and copyright line. The header cards contain an offer for 132-card uncut sheets of 1981 Topps baseball cards. Some New York Yankees' cards were prepared, but never issued; to date, only three of the players are known.

	NM/M
Complete Set (No Yankees) (132):	20.00
Common Player:	.10

Boston Red Sox Team Set 3.00
1	Tom Burgmeier	.10
2	Dennis Eckersley	.35
3	Dwight Evans	.20
4	Bob Stanley	.10
5	Glenn Hoffman	.10
6	Carney Lansford	.10
7	Frank Tanana	.75
8	Tony Perez	.75
9	Jim Rice	.50
10	Dave Stapleton	.10
11	Carl Yastrzemski	2.00
----	Red Sox Header Card	.05

Chicago Cubs Team Set 1.25
1	Tim Blackwell	.10
2	Bill Buckner	.35
3	Ivan DeJesus	.10
4	Leon Durham	.10
5	Steve Henderson	.10
6	Mike Krukow	.10
7	Ken Reitz	.10
8	Rick Reuschel	.10
9	Scot Thompson	.10
10	Dick Tidrow	.10
11	Mike Tyson	.10
----	Cubs Header Card	.05

Chicago White Sox Team Set 1.00
1	Britt Burns	.10
2	Todd Cruz	.10
3	Rich Dotson	.10
4	Jim Essian	.10
5	Ed Farmer	.10
6	Lamar Johnson	.10
7	Ron LeFlore	.10
8	Chet Lemon	.10
9	Bob Molinaro	.10
10	Jim Morrison	.10

| 11 | Wayne Nordhagen | .10 |
| ---- | White Sox Header Card | .05 |

Cincinnati Reds Team Set 3.50
1	Johnny Bench	2.75
2	Dave Collins	.10
3	Dave Concepcion	.20
4	Dan Driessen	.10
5	George Foster	.20
6	Ken Griffey	.20
7	Tom Hume	.10
8	Ray Knight	.20
9	Ron Oester	.10
10	Tom Seaver	1.75
11	Mario Soto	.10
----	Reds Header Card	.05

Detroit Tigers Team Set 2.25
1	Champ Summers	.10
2	Al Cowens	.10
3	Rich Hebner	.10
4	Steve Kemp	.10
5	Aurelio Lopez	.10
6	Jack Morris	.35
7	Lance Parrish	.35
8	Johnny Wockenfuss	.10
9	Alan Trammell	.75
10	Lou Whitaker	.35
11	Kirk Gibson	.35
----	Tigers Header Card	.05

Houston Astros Team Set 5.00
1a	Alan Ashby	.10
1b	Nolan Ryan	25.00
2	Cesar Cedeno	.10
3	Jose Cruz	.10
4	Art Howe	.10
5	Rafael Landestoy	.10
6	Joe Niekro	.20
7	Terry Puhl	.10
8	J.R. Richard	.20
9	Nolan Ryan	4.00
10	Joe Sambito	.10
11	Don Sutton	.75
----	Astros Header Card	.10

Kansas City Royals Team Set 3.00
1	Willie Aikens	.10
2	George Brett	1.00
3	Larry Gura	.10
4	Dennis Leonard	.10
5	Hal McRae	.20
6	Amos Otis	.10
7	Dan Quisenberry	.10
8	U.L. Washington	.10
9	John Wathan	.10
10	Frank White	.10
11	Willie Wilson	.20
----	Royals Header Card	.05

New York Mets Team Set 1.25
1	Neil Allen	.10
2	Doug Flynn	.10
3	Dave Kingman	.35
4	Randy Jones	.10
5	Pat Zachry	.10
6	Lee Mazzilli	.10
7	Rusty Staub	.20
8	Craig Swan	.10
9	Frank Taveras	.10
10	Alex Trevino	.10
11	Joel Youngblood	.10
----	Mets Header Card	.05

New York Yankees Team Set 75.00
1	Rich Gossage	15.00
2	Reggie Jackson	60.00
3	Rick Cerone	12.50
----	Yankees Header Card	4.00

Philadelphia Phillies Team Set 6.00
1	Bob Boone	.35
2	Larry Bowa	.20
3	Steve Carlton	1.25
4	Greg Luzinski	.10
5	Garry Maddox	.10
6	Bake McBride	.10
7	Tug McGraw	.20
8	Pete Rose	2.75
9	Mike Schmidt	2.75
10	Lonnie Smith	.10
11	Manny Trillo	.10
----	Phillies Header Card	.05

Pittsburgh Pirates Team Set 3.00
1	Jim Bibby	.10
2	John Candelaria	.10
3	Mike Easler	.10
4	Tim Foli	.10
5	Phil Garner	.10
6	Bill Madlock	.20
7	Omar Moreno	.10
8	Ed Ott	.10
9	Dave Parker	.30
10	Willie Stargell	1.00
11	Kent Tekulve	.10
----	Pirates Header Card	.05

St. Louis Cardinals Team Set 1.25
1	Bob Forsch	.10
2	George Hendrick	.10
3	Keith Hernandez	.20
4	Tom Herr	.10
5	Sixto Lezcano	.10
6	Ken Oberkfell	.10
7	Darrell Porter	.10
8	Tony Scott	.10
9	Lary Sorensen	.10
10	Bruce Sutter	.10
11	Garry Templeton	.10
----	Cardinals Header Card	.05

1981 Coca-Cola Brigham's Red Sox Ad Signs

These 6" x 17-1/2" blank-back cardboard ad pieces were designed to be folded into a countertop tent card, identical on each side. The color player photos on the ad pieces are different than those found on the issued cards.

	NM/M
Complete Set (11):	35.00
Common Player:	2.00
(1)	Tom Burgmeier	2.00
(2)	Dennis Eckersley	4.00
(3)	Dwight Evans	3.00
(4)	Bob Stanley	2.00
(5)	Glenn Hoffman	2.00
(6)	Carney Lansford	2.00
(7)	Frank Tanana	2.00
(8)	Tony Perez	6.00
(9)	Jim Rice	8.00
(10)	Dave Stapleton	2.00
(11)	Carl Yastrzemski	15.00

1982 Coca-Cola Brigham's Red Sox

CARL YASTRZEMSKI

Coca-Cola, in conjunction with Brigham's Ice Cream stores, issued a 23-card set in the Boston area featuring Red Sox players. The Topps-produced cards, 2-1/2" x 3-1/2", are identical in format to the regular 1982 Topps set but contain the Coca-Cola and Brigham's logos in the corners. The cards were distributed in three-card cello packs, including an unnumbered header card.

	NM/M
Complete Set (23):	5.00
Common Player:	.25
1	Gary Allenson	.25
2	Tom Burgmeier	.25
3	Mark Clear	.25
4	Steve Crawford	.25
5	Dennis Eckersley	1.50
6	Dwight Evans	.35
7	Rich Gedman	.25
8	Garry Hancock	.25
9	Glen Hoffman (Glenn)	.25
10	Carney Lansford	.25
11	Rick Miller	.25
12	Reid Nichols	.25
13	Bob Ojeda	.25
14	Tony Perez	1.50
15	Chuck Rainey	.25
16	Jerry Remy	.25
17	Jim Rice	1.00
18	Bob Stanley	.25
19	Dave Stapleton	.25
20	Mike Torrez	.25
21	Jim Tudor	.25
22	Carl Yastrzemski	3.00
----	Header Card	.10

1982 Coca-Cola Reds

JOHNNY BENCH

Produced by Topps for Coca-Cola, the set consists of 23 cards featuring the Cincinnati Reds and was distributed in the Cincinnati area. The cards, which are 2-1/2" x 3-1/2" in size, are identical in design to the regular 1982 Topps set but have a Coca-Cola logo on the front and red backs. An unnumbered header card is included in the set.

	NM/M
Complete Set (23):	3.00
Common Player:	.25
1	Johnny Bench	2.00
2	Bruce Berenyi	.25
3	Larry Biittner	.25
4	Cesar Cedeno	.35
5	Dave Concepcion	.25
6	Dan Driessen	.25
7	Greg Harris	.25
8	Paul Householder	.25
9	Tom Hume	.25
10	Clint Hurdle	.25
11	Jim Kern	.25
12	Wayne Krenchicki	.25
13	Rafael Landestoy	.25
14	Charlie Leibrandt	.25
15	Mike O'Berry	.25
16	Ron Oester	.25
17	Frank Pastore	.25
18	Joe Price	.25
19	Tom Seaver	1.00
20	Mario Soto	.25
21	Alex Trevino	.25
22	Mike Vail	.25
----	Header Card	.05

1985 Coca-Cola Dodgers Photocards

Mariano Duncan

©1986 L.A. Dodgers   All Rights Reserved

The first of two annual player photocard sets sponsored by Coke, these 3-1/2" x 5-1/2" cards feature color player action photos on front, surrounded by a white border. Below the photo is a 1985 copyright notice; the player's name is at bottom. Backs have a Coca-Cola logo in the lower-right corner, and may be found both with and without a printed message. The unnumbered cards are checklisted here in alphabetical order.

	NM/M
Complete Set (34):	15.00
Common Player:	.50
(1)	Joe Amalfitano	.50
(2)	Dave Anderson	.50
(3)	Bob Bailor	.50
(4)	Monty Basgall	.50
(5)	Tom Brennan	.50
(6)	Greg Brock	.50
(7)	Bobby Castillo	.50
(8)	Mark Cresse	.50
(9)	Carlos Diaz	.50
(10)	Mariano Duncan	.50
(11)	Pedro Guerrero	.50
(12)	Orel Hershiser	2.00
(13)	Rick Honeycutt	.50
(14)	Steve Howe	.50
(15)	Ken Howell	.50

(16)	Jay Johnstone	.50
(17)	Ken Landreaux	.50
(18)	Tommy Lasorda	.75
(19)	Candy Maldonado	.50
(20)	Mike Marshall	.50
(21)	Manny Mota	.50
(22)	Tom Niedenfuer	.50
(23)	Al Oliver	.60
(24)	Alejandro Pena	.50
(25)	Ron Perranoski	.50
(26)	Jerry Reuss	.50
(27)	R.J. Reynolds	.50
(28)	Bill Russell	.50
(29)	Steve Sax	.50
(30)	Mike Scioscia	.50
(31)	Fernando Valenzuela	.75
(32)	Bob Welch	.50
(33)	Terry Whitfield	.50
(34)	Steve Yeager	.50

1985 Coca-Cola Pirates

PITTSBURGH PIRATES

13 Steve Kemp OF

A companion set to the cards issued in the 1985 Pirates yearbook, this set was given away to the first 10,000 youngsters attending May 18 and July 13 home games. The card of Kent Tekulve was withdrawn after his trade to the Phillies, making it quite scarce. The 2-1/2" x 3-1/2" cards have a color photo at center, surrounded by black and gold borders. A white panel at bottom has the player's name, position and uniform number. Backs are in black-and-white and feature complete major and minor league stats, plus the Cameron/Coca-Cola sponsors' logos.

	NM/M
Complete Set (29) (No Tekulve.):	12.00
Complete Set (30) (W/Tekulve.):	20.00
Common Player:	.50
2	Jim Morrison	.50
3	Johnny Ray	.50
5	Bill Madlock	1.00
6	Tony Pena	.60
7	Chuck Tanner	.50
10	Tim Foli	.50
11	Joe Orsulak	.50
12	Bill Almon	.50
13	Steve Kemp	.50
15	George Hendrick	.50
16	Lee Mazzilli	.50
17	Jerry Dybzinski	.50
19	Rod Scurry	.50
25	Lee Tunnell	.50
25	Jose DeLeon	.50
27	Kent Tekulve	7.50
28	Sixto Lezcano	.50
29	Rick Rhoden	.50
30	Jason Thompson	.50
34	Mike Bielecki	.50
35	Al Holland	.50
36	Marvell Wynne	.50
37	Rafael Belliard	.50
43	Don Robinson	.50
45	John Candelaria	.50
47	Cecilio Guante	.50
49	Larry McWilliams	.50
51	Doug Frobel	.50
----	Pirates Coaches	.50

1985 Coca-Cola White Sox

Featuring past and present White Sox players, the cards in this set were given out on Tuesday night home games. The 2-5/8" x 4-1/8" cards contain a color photo of a current Sox member. A red box at the bottom of the card carries the team logo, player name, uniform number and position, plus a small oval portrait of a past Sox player. Backs contain the Coca-Cola logo and lifetime stats for the current and past player. The set is listed here by the player's uniform number with the last three cards being unnumbered. Complete sets were available through a fan club offer found in White Sox programs.

Outfielder 42 RON KITTLE

	NM/M
Complete Set (30):	7.50
Common Player:	.25
0	Oscar Gamble, Zeke Bonura	.25
1	Scott Fletcher, Luke Appling	.60
3	Harold Baines, Bill Melton	.75
4	Luis Salazar, Chico Carrasquel	.25
7	Marc Hill, Sherman Lollar	.25
8	Daryl Boston, Jim Landis	.25
10	Tony LaRussa, Al Lopez	.75
12	Julio Cruz, Nellie Fox	1.50
13	Ozzie Guillen, Luis Aparicio	2.00
17	Jerry Hairston Sr., Smoky Burgess	.50
20	Joe DeSa, Carlos May	.25
22	Joel Skinner, J.C. Martin	.25
23	Rudy Law, Bill Skowron	.50
29	Floyd Bannister, Red Faber	.25
29	Greg Walker, Dick Allen	1.00
30	Gene Nelson, Early Wynn	.50
32	Tim Hulett, Pete Ward	.25
34	Richard Dotson, Ed Walsh	.25
37	Dan Spillner, Thornton Lee	.25
40	Britt Burns, Gary Peters	.25
41	Tom Seaver, Ted Lyons	2.00
42	Ron Kittle, Minnie Minoso	1.00
43	Bob James, Hoyt Wilhelm	.25
44	Tom Paciorek, Eddie Collins	.25
46	Tim Lollar, Billy Pierce	.25
50	Juan Agosto, Wilbur Wood	.25
72	Carlton Fisk, Ray Schalk	1.50
---	Comiskey Park	.50
---	Ribbie and Roobarb (Mascots)	.25
---	Nancy Faust (Organist)	.25

1986 Coca-Cola Dodgers Photocards

Dave Anderson

©1986 L.A. Dodgers   All Rights Reserved

For a second year Coke sponsored this set of 3-1/2" x 5-1/2" color cards. Fronts feature an action photo with white borders. Beneath the photo is a 1986 copyright line; the player's name is at bottom. Backs have a red Coca-Cola logo in the lower-right corner, and can be found either with a message to fans from the pictured player, along with a facsimile autograph. The unnumbered cards are checklisted here alphabetically.

	NM/M
Complete Set (34):	15.00
Common Player:	.50
(1)	Joe Amalfitano	.50
(2)	Dave Anderson	.50
(3)	Monty Basgall	.50
(4)	Greg Brock	.50
(5)	Enos Cabell	.50
(6)	Cesar Cedeno	.50
(7)	Mark Cresse	.50
(8)	Carlos Diaz	.50

(9)	Mariano Duncan	.50
(10)	Pedro Guerrero	.50
(11)	Orel Hershiser	1.00
(12)	Ben Hines	.50
(13)	Rick Honeycutt	.50
(14)	Ken Howell	.50
(15)	Ken Landreaux	.50
(16)	Tom Lasorda	.75
(17)	Bill Madlock	.50
(18)	Mike Marshall	.50
(19)	Len Matuszek	.50
(20)	Manny Mota	.50
(21)	Tom Niedenfuer	.50
(22)	Alejandro Pena	.50
(23)	Ron Perranoski	.50
(24)	Dennis Powell	.50
(25)	Jerry Reuss	.50
(26)	Bill Russell	.50
(27)	Steve Sax	.50
(28)	Mike Scioscia	.50
(29)	Franklin Stubbs	.50
(30)	Alex Trevino	.50
(31)	Fernando Valenzuela	.75
(32)	Ed Vande Berg	.50
(33)	Bob Welch	.50
(34)	Terry Whitfield	.50

1986 Coca-Cola White Sox

For the second year in a row, Coca-Cola, in conjunction with the Chicago White Sox, issued a 30-card set. As in 1985, cards were given out at the park on Tuesday night games. Full sets were available through a fan club offer found in the White Sox program. The 2-5/8" x 4-1/8" cards feature 25 players plus other team personnel. Fronts have a color photo (a game-action shot in most instances) and a white bar at the bottom. A black and white bat with "SOX" shown on the barrel is located within the white bar, along with the player's name, position and uniform number. The white and gray backs with black print include the Coca-Cola trademark. Lifetime statistics are shown on all player cards, but there is no personal information such as height, weight or age. The non-player cards are blank-backed save for the name and logo at the top. The cards in the checklist that follows are numbered by the players' uniform numbers, with the last five cards of the set being unnumbered.

		NM/M
Complete Set (30):		12.00
Common Player:		.25
1	Wayne Tolleson	.25
3	Harold Baines	.75
7	Marc Hill	.25
8	Daryl Boston	.25
12	Julio Cruz	.25
13	Ozzie Guillen	.50
17	Jerry Hairston Sr.	.25
19	Floyd Bannister	.25
20	Reid Nichols	.25
22	Joel Skinner	.25
24	Dave Schmidt	.25
26	Bobby Bonilla	1.00
29	Greg Walker	.25
30	Gene Nelson	.25
32	Tim Hulett	.25
33	Neil Allen	.25
34	Richard Dotson	.25
40	Joe Cowley	.25
41	Tom Seaver	3.00
42	Ron Kittle	.35
43	Bob James	.25
44	John Cangelosi	.25
50	Juan Agosto	.25
52	Joel Davis	.25
72	Carlton Fisk	3.00
---	Ribbie & Roobarb (Mascots)	.25
---	Nancy Faust (Organist)	.25
---	Ken "Hawk" Harrelson	.35
---	Tony LaRussa	.60
---	Minnie Minoso	1.50

1987 Coca-Cola Tigers

Pat Sheridan
DETROIT TIGERS   OUTFIELD

Coca-Cola and S. Abraham & Sons, Inc. issued a set of 18 baseball cards featuring members of the Detroit Tigers. The set is comprised of six four-part folding panels. Each panel includes three player cards (each 2-1/2" x 3-1/2") and one team logo card. A bright yellow border surrounds the full-color photo. The backs are designed on a vertical format and contain personal data and career statistics. The set was produced by Mike Schecter and Associates.

		NM/M
Complete Panel Set (6):		4.00
Complete Singles Set (18):		2.00
Common Panel:		.50
Common Player:		.05
Panel		.85
1	Kirk Gibson	.30
2	Larry Herndon	.05
3	Walt Terrell	.05
Panel		1.50
4	Alan Trammell	.50
5	Frank Tanana	.05
6	Pat Sheridan	.05
Panel		.85
7	Jack Morris	.30
8	Mike Heath	.05
9	Dave Bergman	.05
Panel		.50
10	Chet Lemon	.05
11	Dwight Lowry	.05
12	Dan Petry	.05
Panel		.85
13	Darrell Evans	.25
14	Darnell Coles	.05
15	Willie Hernandez	.05
Panel		1.00
16	Lou Whitaker	.25
17	Tom Brookens	.05
18	John Grubb	.05

1987 Coca-Cola White Sox

3 Harold Baines, OF

The Chicago White Sox Fan Club, in conjunction with Coca-Cola, offered members a set of 30 trading cards. For the $10 membership fee, fans received the set plus additional fan club gifts and privileges. The cards, 2-5/8" x 4", feature full-color photos inside a blue and red border. Backs include the player's name, position, uniform number and statistics, plus the Coca-Cola logo. Cards are checklisted here by uniform number.

		NM/M
Complete Set (30):		7.50
Common Player:		.25
3	Jerry Royster	.25
3	Harold Baines	.50
6	Ron Karkovice	.25
8	Daryl Boston	.25
10	Fred Manrique	.25
12	Steve Lyons	.25
13	Ozzie Guillen	.50
14	Russ Morman	.25

15	Donnie Hill	.25
16	Jim Fregosi	.25
17	Jerry Hairston Sr.	.25
19	Floyd Bannister	.25
21	Gary Redus	.25
22	Ivan Calderon	.25
25	Ron Hassey	.25
26	Jose DeLeon	.25
29	Greg Walker	.25
32	Tim Hulett	.25
33	Neil Allen	.25
34	Rich Dotson	.25
36	Ray Searage	.25
37	Bobby Thigpen	.25
40	Jim Winn	.25
43	Bob James	.25
50	Joel McKeon	.25
52	Joel Davis	.25
72	Carlton Fisk	3.00
---	Ribbie & Roobarb (Mascots)	.25
---	Nancy Faust (Organist)	.25
---	Minnie Minoso	.75

1988 Coca-Cola Padres

LARRY BOWA
#10 Manager

A 20-card set sponsored by Coca-Cola was designed as part of the San Diego Padres Junior Fan Club promotion for 1988. This set was distributed as a nine-card starter sheet, with 11 additional single cards handed out during various home games. The standard-size cards feature full-color player photos framed by a black and orange border. The player's name is printed above the photo; uniform number and position appear at lower-right. A large Padres logo curves upward from the lower-left corner. Backs are brown on white and include the Padres logo at upper-left opposite the player's name and personal information. Career highlights and 1987 stats appear in the center of the card back above the Coca-Cola and Junior Padres Fan Club logos.

		NM/M
Complete Set (21):		20.00
Common Player:		.50
Panel		
1	Garry Templeton	.60
5	Randy Ready	.50
10	Larry Bowa	.60
17	Tim Flannery	.50
35	Chris Brown	.50
45	Jimmy Jones	.50
48	Mark Davis	.50
55	Mark Grant	.50
----	20th Anniversary Logo Card	.10
Singles		
7	Keith Moreland	1.00
8	John Kruk	2.00
14	Benito Santiago	2.00
19	Carmelo Martinez	1.00
15	Jack McKeon	1.00
19	Tony Gwynn	6.00
22	Stan Jefferson	1.00
27	Mark Parent	1.00
30	Eric Show	1.00
31	Ed Whitson	1.00
41	Lance McCullers	1.00
51	Greg Booker	1.00

1988 Coca-Cola White Sox

Part of a fan club membership package, this unnumbered 30-card set features full-color photos of 27 players, the team mascot, team organist and Comiskey Park. Cards have a bright red border, with team logo in the photo's lower-left corner. The player name fills the bottom border. Backs are printed in black on gray and white and include player name, personal info and career summary. The set was included in

JERRY REUSS

the $10 membership package, with a portion of the cost going to the ChiSox Kids Charity.

		NM/M
Complete Set (30):		5.00
Common Player:		.25
(1)	Harold Baines	.50
(2)	Daryl Boston	.25
(3)	Ivan Calderon	.25
(4)	John Davis	.25
(5)	Jim Fregosi	.25
(6)	Carlton Fisk	2.50
(7)	Ozzie Guillen	.50
(8)	Donnie Hill	.25
(9)	Rick Horton	.25
(10)	Lance Johnson	.25
(11)	Dave LaPoint	.25
(12)	Bill Long	.25
(13)	Steve Lyons	.25
(14)	Jack McDowell	.30
(15)	Fred Manrique	.25
(16)	Minnie Minoso	.75
(17)	Dan Pasqua	.25
(18)	John Pawlowski	.25
(19)	Melido Perez	.25
(20)	Billy Pierce	.25
(21)	Gary Redus	.25
(22)	Jerry Reuss	.25
(23)	Mark Salas	.25
(24)	Jose Segura	.25
(25)	Bobby Thigpen	.25
(26)	Greg Walker	.25
(27)	Kenny Williams	.25
(28)	Nancy Faust (Organist)	.25
(29)	Ribbie & Roobarb (Mascots)	.25
(30)	Comiskey Park	.40

1989 Coca-Cola Padres

#25 First Base
JACK CLARK

This 20-card set is part of the Junior Padres Fan Club membership package. Members receive a nine-card starter set printed on one large perforated sheet. Additional cards are distributed to kids at specially designated games (free admission for kids). Fronts feature an orange-and-brown double border, with a bright orange Padres logo printed at lower-left. Uniform number and position are printed diagonally across the upper-left corner, with the player's name in large block letters along the bottom border.

		NM/M
Complete Set (21):		26.00
Common Player:		.50
Panel		
1	Garry Templeton	.60
5	Randy Ready	.50
12	Roberto Alomar	4.50
14	Carmelo Martinez	.50
15	Jack McKeon	.50
30	Eric Show	.50
31	Ed Whitson	.50
43	Dennis Rasmussen	.50
----	Logo Card	.10
Singles		
6	Luis Salazar	1.00
8	Benito Santiago	1.00
10	Leon Roberts	1.00
17	Tim Flannery	1.00
18	Chris James	1.00
19	Tony Gwynn	8.00

25	Jack Clark	1.00
27	Mark Parent	1.00
35	Walt Terrell	1.00
47	Bruce Hurst	1.00
48	Mark Davis	1.00
55	Mark Grant	1.00

1989 Coca-Cola White Sox

White Sox
Chicago's American Pastime
Steve Lyons • 28

For the fifth straight year, Coca-Cola sponsored a set of cards featuring the Chicago White Sox. The 30-card set was distributed to fans attending a special promotional game at Comiskey Park and was also available by mail to members of the ChiSox fan club. Card fronts feature blue borders with red and white graphics and a pair of crossed bats. Horizontal backs include player biographies, personal data and the Coca-Cola logo. Cards measure 2-5/8" x 3-1/2".

		NM/M
Complete Set (30):		5.00
Common Player:		.20
1	New Comiskey Park/1991	.40
2	Comiskey Park	.40
3	Jeff Torborg	.20
4	Coaching staff (Dave LaRoche, Terry Bevington, Walt Hriniak, Sammy Ellis, Glenn Rosenbaum, Ron Clark)	.20
5	Harold Baines	.45
6	Daryl Boston	.20
7	Ivan Calderon	.20
8	Carlton Fisk	2.50
9	Dave Gallagher	.20
10	Ozzie Guillen	.50
11	Shawn Hillegas	.20
12	Barry Jones	.20
13	Ron Karkovice	.20
14	Eric King	.20
15	Ron Kittle	.20
16	Bill Long	.20
17	Steve Lyons	.20
18	Donn Pall	.20
19	Dan Pasqua	.20
20	Ken Patterson	.20
21	Melido Perez	.20
22	Jerry Reuss	.20
23	Billy Jo Robidoux	.20
24	Steve Rosenberg	.20
25	Jeff Schaefer	.20
26	Bobby Thigpen	.20
27	Greg Walker	.20
28	Eddie Williams	.20
29	Nancy Faust (Organist)	.20
30	Minnie Minoso	.75

1990 Coca-Cola Padres

PADRES
TONY GWYNN

This set was designed for members of the Junior Padres Club sponsored by Coca-Cola. Each member received an eight-card panel and then received two different single cards at every Junior Padres Club game attended. Card fronts feature full-color photos with the Padres logo in the upper-right corner of the card. Backs feature statistics, career

highlights and a red Coca-Cola logo. The cards are numbered by the player's uniform number.

		NM/M
Complete Set (21):		16.00
Common Player:		.35
Panel		
10	Bip Roberts	.35
15	Jack McKeon	.35
30	Eric Show	.35
31	Ed Whitson	.35
40	Andy Benes	.75
43	Dennis Rasmussen	.35
55	Mark Grant	.35
----	Logo Card	.35
Singles		
1	Garry Templeton	.50
8	Fred Lynn	.75
9	Benito Santiago	1.00
11	Craig Lefferts	.50
12	Roberto Alomar	4.00
13	Mike Pagliarulo	.50
19	Joe Carter	1.00
19	Tony Gwynn	6.00
25	Jack Clark	.50
27	Mark Parent	.50
38	Calvin Schiraldi	.50
46	Greg Harris	.50
47	Bruce Hurst	.50

1990 Coca-Cola Garry Templeton

MOST GAMES PLAYED
THE CAPTAIN
PADRES
TEMPLETON

Coca-Cola, Vons stores and the Padres joined forces to release this special pin/baseball card collectible in honor of Garry Templeton becoming the club's all-time leader in games played. The card front features a full-color photo of Templeton and displays "Most Games Played" and "The Captain" in orange at the top of the photo. "Templeton" appears vertically in white along the left border. The Coca-Cola and Padre logos also appear on the card front. The bottom of the card features a perforated edge where the pin is attached as an extension of the card. The card back is printed in black and white and displays biographical information, career highlights and career statistics.

		NM/M
Card/Pin Combination:		1.50
(1)	Most Games Played Card (Garry Templeton)	.50
(2)	Most Games Played Pin (Garry Templeton)	1.00

1990 Coca-Cola Tigers

Detroit Tigers
(9) LARRY SHEETS
Outfielder

Once again utilizing the larger 2-7/8" x 4-1/4" format, this set was jointly sponsored by Coke and Kroger grocery stores and distributed at the July 14 game. Cards feature color action photos on front, surrounded by green borders. Backs have a black-and-white portrait photo, the appropriate logos and complete minor and major league stats. The player's uniform number appears in the upper-left corner.

		NM/M
Complete Set (28):		6.00
Common Player:		.15
(1)	Sparky Anderson	.50
(2)	Dave Bergman	.15
(3)	Brian DuBois	.15
(4)	Cecil Fielder	.25
(5)	Paul Gibson	.15
(6)	Jerry D. Gleaton	.15
(7)	Mike Heath	.15
(8)	Mike Henneman	.15
(9)	Tracy Jones	.15
(10)	Chet Lemon	.15
(11)	Urbano Lugo	.15
(12)	Jack Morris	.20
(13)	Lloyd Moseby	.15
(14)	Matt Nokes	.15
(15)	Edwin Nunez	.15
(16)	Dan Petry	.15
(17)	Tony Phillips	.25
(18)	Kevin Ritz	.15
(19)	Jeff Robinson	.15
(20)	Ed Romero	.15
(21)	Mark Salas	.15
(22)	Larry Sheets	.15
(23)	Frank Tanana	.15
(24)	Alan Trammell	.75
(25)	Gary Ward	.15
(26)	Lou Whitaker	.40
(27)	Ken Williams	.15
(28)	Coaches (Billy Consolo, Alex Grammas, Billy Muffett, Vada Pinson, Dick Tracewski)	.15

1990 Coca-Cola White Sox

An attractive "Comiskey Park 1910-1990" logo is featured on the front of each card in this set. Fronts also feature full-color photos with a thin white inner border. The cards are numbered according to uniform number, with the exception of four special cards including Top Prospect Frank Thomas. Horizontal card backs feature black print on white and gray stock; 1989 statistics and career highlights are provided. The 1990 set marks the sixth straight year that Coca-Cola sponsored a White Sox set.

		NM/M
Complete Set (30):		80.00
Common Player:		.25
1	Lance Johnson	.25
7	Scott Fletcher	.25
10	Jeff Torborg	.25
12	Steve Lyons	.25
13	Ozzie Guillen	.50
14	Craig Grebeck	.25
17	Dave Gallagher	.25
20	Ron Karkovice	.25
22	Ivan Calderon	.25
23	Robin Ventura	1.00
24	Carlos Martinez	.25
25	Sammy Sosa	65.00
27	Greg Hibbard	.25
29	Jack McDowell	.25
30	Donn Pall	.25
31	Scott Radinsky	.25
33	Melido Perez	.25
34	Ken Patterson	.25
36	Eric King	.25
37	Bobby Thigpen	.25
42	Ron Kittle	.25
44	Dan Pasqua	.25
45	Wayne Edwards	.25
50	Barry Jones	.25
52	Jerry Kutzler	.25
72	Carlton Fisk	5.00
---	Top Prospect (Frank Thomas)	15.00
---	White Sox Manager, Coaches (Jeff Torborg)	.25

| --- | Captains (Ozzie Guillen, Carlton Fisk) | 1.00 |
| --- | Rookies (Wayne Edwards, Craig Greback, Jerry Kutzler, Scott Radinsky, Robin Ventura) | .35 |

1991 Coca-Cola Don Mattingly

Though sponsored by Coca-Cola, the manner of distribution of this issue is unclear. The "Mattingly's 23" logo on each side of the card suggests a connection to his Evansville, Ind., restaurant. Fronts of the 2-1/2" x 3-1/2" cards have photos in black-and-white or color, or artwork. The border is white with blue pinstripes. The year of the picture is at top of the photo and there is a Coke logo at bottom. Backs are printed in red and blue and contain career highlights and stats, along with a card number and logos.

		NM/M
Complete Set (15):		10.00
Common Card:		1.00
1	Don Mattingly/1978	1.00
2	Don Mattingly/1979	1.00
3	Don Mattingly/1980	1.00
4	Don Mattingly/1981	1.00
5	Don Mattingly/1982	1.00
6	Don Mattingly/1983	1.00
7	Don Mattingly/'83-'84	1.00
8	Don Mattingly/1984	1.00
9	Don Mattingly/1985	1.00
10	Don Mattingly/1986	1.00
11	Don Mattingly/1987	1.00
12	Don Mattingly/1990	1.00
13	Don Mattingly/1991 (Photo)	1.00
14	Don Mattingly/1991 (Artwork)	1.00
15	Don Mattingly/1991 (Coca-Cola logo.)	1.00

1991 Coca-Cola Tigers

This set was sponsored by Coca-Cola and Kroger, whose logos appear on the red, white and blue backs. The oversize (2-7/8" x 4-1/4") cards feature game-action or portrait color photos on front along with the player's name vertically printed on the right border and the Tigers logo in the lower-left corner. Backs are printed horizontally and feature complete minor and major league statistics. The set is numbered according to uniform number, which appears in an orange triangle on front.

		NM/M
Complete Set (28):		7.00
Common Player:		.35
1	Lou Whitaker	.75
3	Alan Trammell	1.00
4	Tony Phillips	.35
10	Andy Allanson	.35
14	Sparky Anderson	.75
20	Dave Bergman	.35
23	Lloyd Moseby	.35

19	Jerry Don Gleaton	.35
20	Mickey Tettleton	.35
22	Milt Cuyler	.35
23	Mark Leiter	.35
24	Travis Fryman	.35
25	John Shelby	.35
26	Frank Tanana	.35
27	Mark Salas	.35
31	Pete Incaviglia	.35
31	Kevin Ritz	.35
36	Walt Terrell	.35
36	Bill Gullickson	.35
39	Mike Henneman	.35
42	Mike Dalton	.35
44	Rob Deer	.35
45	Cecil Fielder	.50
46	Dan Petry	.35
48	Paul Gibson	.35
49	Steve Searcy	.35
55	John Cerutti	.35
---	Tigers Coaches (Billy Consolo, Jim Davenport, Alex Grammas, Billy Muffett, Vada Pinson, Dick Tracewski)	

1992 Coca-Cola Nolan Ryan Career Series

This 26-card set was produced by Donruss in conjunction with Coca-Cola to honor Nolan Ryan's 26 major league seasons. One Nolan Ryan card was packaged with three regular 1992 Donruss cards in special 12-packs of Coke. Complete sets, in a black, red and gold box, were available through a mail-in offer. The 2-1/2" x 3-1/2" cards have a full-color photo on front, framed by a gold border. Ryan's name is printed in gold toward the bottom, above a blue bar which presents a team and year. The Coke logo is at upper right. On back there are details of Ryan's performance in the indicated year, the card number, and team and Coke logos. An 18" x 12" color poster picturing the cards and a photo of a Ryan-autographed ball was issued as a point-of-purchase display.

		NM/M
Complete Set (26):		7.50
Common Card:		.50
Display Poster:		15.00
1	1966 Breaking In	.50
2	1968 Record-Setting Rookie	.50
3	1969 World Champions	.50
4	1970 Growing Pains	.50
5	1971 Traded	.50
6	1972 Fitted for a Halo	.50
7	1973 Two No-Nos and a Record	.50
8	1974 No-Hitter No. 3/ Another K Record	.50
9	1975 Tying Koufax	.50
10	1976 Back on Track	.50
11	1977 Carrying the Load	.50
12	1978 A Year of Injuries	.50
13	1979 California Farewell	.50
14	1980 Coming Home	.50
15	1981 A Gusher in Houston	.50
16	1982 Mounting 'Em Up	.50
17	1983 Passing the Big Train	.50
18	1984 Misleading Signs of Age	.50
19	1985 Another Milestone/ A New Contract	.50
20	1986 The Elbow Flares Up Again	.50
21	1987 Another ERA/ Strikeout Crown at 40	.50
22	1988 Leaving Home Again	.50
23	1989 5,000 Strikeouts	.50
24	1990 Win No. 300, No-Hitter No. 6	.50
25	1991 No-Hitter No. 7	.50
26	1992 Man of Records	.50

1992 Coca-Cola Tigers

This set of large-format (2-7/8" x 4-1/4") cards features central photos of the Bengals in action. Dark blue stripes at top and bottom have the team name in white, while the player name, uniform number and position are printed in black on an orange stripe directly beneath the photo. A color team logo in the upper-right completes the front design. Backs have complete major and minor league stats, a few personal data and color logos of Coke and the Kroger grocery chain.

		NM/M
Complete Set (28):		5.00
Common Player:		.15
1	Lou Whitaker	.35
3	Alan Trammell	.75
4	Tony Phillips	.15
7	Scott Livingstone	.15
9	Skeeter Barnes	.15
11	Sparky Anderson	.15
14	Dave Bergman	.15
15	Mark Carreon	.15
18	Gary Pettis	.15
19	Chad Kreuter	.15
20	Mickey Tettleton	.15
22	Milt Cuyler	.15
23	Mark Leiter	.15
24	Travis Fryman	.25
26	Frank Tanana	.15
27	Kurt Knudsen	.15
28	Rob Deer	.15
31	Kevin Ritz	.15
32	Dan Gladden	.15
35	Walt Terrell	.15
36	Bill Gullickson	.15
39	Mike Henneman	.15
44	Mike Munoz	.15
44	John Doherty	.15
45	Cecil Fielder	.25
46	John Kiely	.15
48	Les Lancaster	.15
---	Tigers Coaches (Billy Consolo, Gene Roof, Larry Herndon, Dick Tracewksi, Billy Muffett, Dan Whitmer)	

1992 Coca-Cola/Hardees Major League Line-Up Discs

This set of 3" diameter "Major League Line-Up" cardboard discs was a regional give-away sponsored by Coca-Cola and distributed by Hardee's restaurants. The glossy discs have player photos at center with position and uniform numbers at the sides. Backs are in black-and-white with a few stats and career highlights and various logos. A checklist disc was also distributed.

		NM/M
Complete Set (24):		12.00
Common Player:		.50
1	Roger Clemens	2.50
2	Sandy Alomar Jr.	.50
3	Rafael Palmeiro	.50
4	Roberto Alomar	.75
5	Kelly Gruber	.50
6	Ozzie Guillen	.50
8	Devon White	.50
9	Robin Yount	1.50
10	Chili Davis	.50

11	Chuck Knoblauch	.50
12	Paul Molitor	1.50
13	Tom Glavine	.75
14	Benito Santiago	.50
15	Hal Morris	.50
16	Delino DeShields	.50
17	Matt Williams	.50
18	Ozzie Smith	2.00
19	Andy Van Slyke	.50
20	Andre Dawson	.75
21	Ron Gant	.50
22	Jeff Bagwell	1.50
23	Terry Pendleton	.50
24	Brett Butler	.50

1993 Coca-Cola Commanders of the Hill

Coca-Cola and Topps teamed up to print a 30-card Commanders of the Hill set in 1993. The cards were available in five-card packages with soft-drink purchases on military bases at base exchange food court concessions. The set was divided into three areas: Cy Young Winners, Strikeout Leaders and Team ERA Leaders, with the National League player's names in yellow on a red background and the American League in red on yellow.

		NM/M
Complete Set (30):		5.00
Common Player:		.10
1	Dennis Eckersley	.50
2	Mike Mussina	.40
3	Roger Clemens	1.00
4	Jim Abbott	.10
5	Jack McDowell	.10
6	Charles Nagy	.10
7	Bill Gullickson	.10
8	Kevin Appier	.10
9	Bill Wegman	.10
10	John Smiley	.10
11	Melido Perez	.10
12	Dave Stewart	.10
13	Dave Fleming	.10
14	Kevin Brown	.10
15	Juan Guzman	.10
16	Randy Johnson	.60
17	Greg Maddux	.75
18	Tom Glavine	.35
19	Greg Maddux	.75
20	Jose Rijo	.10
21	Pete Harnisch	.10
22	Tom Candiotti	.10
23	Denny Martinez	.10
24	Sid Fernandez	.10
25	Curt Schilling	.35
26	Doug Drabek	.10
27	Bob Tewksbury	.10
28	Andy Benes	.10
29	Bill Swift	.10
30	John Smoltz	.10

1995 Coca-Cola Minnesota Twins POGs

Over the course of three games in July 1995, the Twins issued a three-sheet series of POGs, 15,000 at each game. The souvenir measures about 10-1/4" x 9-1/2" and features a large color game photo, around and above which are POGs, about 1-1/8" diameter, of players, coaches and sponsors. The POGs are die-cut for removal from the sheets. Each sheet has 11 players or coaches, and each has the same four sponsors' POGs.

Fronts have player portrait photos while backs have a repeating Coca-Cola logo. The POGs are unnumbered and listed here alphabetically by sheet. The players are not identified on the POGs themselves.

		NM/M
Complete Set, Sheets (3):		12.00
Complete Set, Singles (33):		9.00
Common Player:		.25
Series 1, July 1		4.00
(1)	Rick Aguilera	.25
(2)	Rich Becker	.25
(3)	Marty Cordova	.25
(4)	Terry Crowley	.25
(5)	Eddie Guardado	.25
(6)	Jeff Reboulet	.25
(7)	Rich Robertson	.25
(8)	Scott Stahoviak	.25
(9)	Dick Such	.25
(10)	Kevin Tapani	.25
(11)	Matt Walbeck	.25
Series 2, July 17		3.00
(12)	Alex Cole	.25
(13)	Scott Erickson	.25
(14)	Ron Gardenhire	.25
(15)	Chip Hale	.25
(16)	Chuck Knoblauch	.25
(17)	Scott Leius	.25
(18)	Pat Mahomes	.25
(19)	Pedro Munoz	.25
(20)	Erik Schullstrom	.25
(21)	Dave Stevens	.25
(22)	Scott Ullger	.25
Series 3, July 28		5.00
(23)	Jerald Clark	.25
(24)	Mark Guthrie	.25
(25)	Tom Kelly	.25
(26)	Kevin Maas	.25
(27)	Pat Meares	.25
(28)	Matt Merullo	.25
(29)	Kirby Puckett	3.50
(30)	Brad Radke	.25
(31)	Rick Stelmaszek	.25
(32)	Mike Trombley	.25
(33)	Jerry White	.25
---	Coca-Cola	.05
---	Fox 29 TV	.05
---	Minnesota Twins Logo	.10
---	Nestle	.05

1995 Coca-Cola Pittsburgh Pirates POGs

To celebrate the 25th anniversary of Three Rivers Stadium, Coca-Cola and the Pirates issued a set of POGs marking the 25 greatest baseball moments at the stadium. The POGs were issued nine apiece on heavy 6" x 8" cardboard panels. Individual POGs measure about 1-3/4" diameter and are perforated at the edge so they can be removed from the panel. Most fronts have a border of team-color orange and black, with central photos in black-and-white or color. Backs of #1-8 have a green Fruitopia ad; backs of #10-18 have an ad for Sprite in green, while #9, 19-25 have a red Coca-Cola ad on back.

		NM/M
Complete Set Panels (3):		15.00
Complete Set Singles (27):		9.00
Common POG:		.25
1	1994 All-Star Game (All-Star logo)	.25
2	Roberto Clemente (3,000th Hit)	2.00
3	Roberto Clemente (Uniform #21 retired.)	2.00
4	Pirates Win 1979 N.L. Pennant (We Are Family logo)	.25
5	John Candelaria (No-Hits Dodgers)	.25
6	Willie Stargell (Uniform #8 retired.)	.50
7	Mike Schmidt (500th Home Run)	.75
8	Kent Tekulve (First Game, 7/16/70)	.25
---	Coke/Fruitopia Logos	.05
9	First World Series Night Game	.25
10	Nellie Briles (1971 World Series 2-Hitter)	.25

11	Pirates Win 1971 N.L. Pennant	.25
12	Pirates Clinch N.L. East, 1979	.25
13	Pirates Clinch N.L. East, 1992 (Jim Leyland)	.25
14	Bob Gibson (No-Hits Pirates 8/14/71)	.40
15	1979 World Series Game 5 (Jim Rooker)	.25
16	Pirates Clinch N.L. East, 1971	.25
17	Beat Braves in NLCS Game 5, 1992	.25
18	John Milner (Grand Slam Beats Phillis 8/5/79)	.25
19	Barry Bonds (11th Inning HR Beats St. Louis 8/12/91)	.75
20	Jeff King (5 Runs in 9th to Beat Dodgers, 5/28/90)	.25
21	Danny Murtaugh (Murtaugh, Joe L. Brown Retire)	.25
22	"Gunner" Returns to Broadcast Booth	.25
23	Sweep Phillies in 9/29/78 Doubleheader	.25
24	Jim Leyland (Makes Pittsburgh Debut)	.25
25	1974 All-Star Game (Program)	.25
---	Coke Logos	.05

1995 Coca-Cola/Publix Florida Marlins

Coca-Cola and the Publix grocery store chain sponsored this team set issue. Fronts of the standard-size (2-1/2" x 3-1/2") cards have color player action photos on a large background of the team logo. Backs have a color portrait photo and stats. Cards are checklisted here by uniform number.

		NM/M
	Complete Set (27):	7.50
	Common Player:	.50
3	Quilvio Veras	.50
4	Greg Colbrunn	.50
6	Tommy Gregg	.50
7	Kurt Abbott	.50
8	Andre Dawson	2.50
9	Terry Pendleton	.50
10	Gary Sheffield	2.50
11	Chris Hammond	.50
14	Jerry Browne	.50
15	Marcel Lachman	.50
17	Darrell Whitmore	.50
21	Chuck Carr	.50
23	Charles Johnson	.50
26	Alex Arias	.50
28	Mark Gardner	.50
29	Mario Diaz	.50
31	Robb Nen	.50
33	John Burkett	.50
34	Bryan Harvey	.50
35	David Weathers	.50
42	Jeremy Hernandez	.50
48	Pat Rapp	.50
51	Terry Mathews	.50
52	Randy Veres	.50
58	Yorkis Perez	.50
---	Coaches	.50
---	Billy the Marlin (Mascot)	.50

1996 Coca-Cola/Kroger Nolan Ryan Card/Pin

Culminating activities during Nolan Ryan Appreciation Week at Arlington, September 12-15, fans attending the September 15 game, during which Ryan's uniform number was retired by the Rangers, received a baseball card/pin combination sponsored by Coca-Cola and Kroger grocers. The giveaway is a 2-1/2" x 5-1/2" cardboard panel. At top is a 2-1/2" x 3-7/8" card separated by perforations from the bottom panel on which the 1-1/8" x 1-1/2" enameled jersey pin is affixed. The front has a spring training game-action color photo of Ryan. The back is in black-and-white with a career summary, sponsor' logos and a picture of the pin.

	NM/M
Card/Pin Combination:	7.00

1998 Coca-Cola Chipper Jones

This 2-1/2" x 3-1/2" card was an Atlanta-area exclusive. The front shows the Braves' star enjoying a Coke. On back is a coupon for a free 20-oz. Coca-Cola.

	NM/M
Chipper Jones	10.00

1989 Barry Colla Postcards

In 1989 California baseball photographer Barry Colla began a series of player postcard sets. Each set contains eight postcards of the player and was sold in a white paper envelope with the team logo. The postcards are identical in format, measuring 3-1/2" x 5-1/2". Fronts feature borderless color photos on high-gloss stock. Backs are printed in black-and-white and feature a team logo at center. The player's name, uniform number, team and position are printed in the upper-left. A card number appears at top-center.

		NM/M
1-8	Will Clark	3.00
1-8	Jose Canseco	4.00
1-8	Andre Dawson	4.00
1-8	Mike Greenwell	3.00
1-8	Don Mattingly	5.00
1-8	Mark McGwire	6.00

| 1-8 | Kevin Mitchell | 3.00 |
| 1-8 | Ozzie Smith | 4.50 |

1990 Barry Colla Promos

Each of the 12-card single-player sets produced by photographer Barry Colla in 1990 was preceded by a promo card. The promos feature the same borderless color photography as the issued cards. Backs have information on date and size of the limited-edition issues and ordering information printed in black and white. Checklist of the unnumbered cards is presented here in alphabetical order.

		NM/M
	Complete Set (4):	6.00
	Common Player:	1.00
(1)	Jose Canseco	2.00
(2)	Will Clark	1.00
(3)	Kevin Maas	1.00
(4)	Don Mattingly	3.00

1990 Barry Colla

In 1990 baseball photographer Barry Colla began production of a series of single-player card sets. In standard 2-1/2" x 3-1/2" size, the cards featured high-gloss borderless photos on front, with no extraneous graphics. Backs feature stats, career notes, personal data and team logos. The 12-card sets were sold in small decorative cardboard boxes. Production figures are noted in parentheses.

		NM/M
1-12	Jose Canseco (20,000)	3.00
1-12	Will Clark (15,000)	2.00
1-12	Kevin Maas (7,500)	2.00
1-12	Don Mattingly (15,000)	7.50

1990 Barry Colla Postcards

Barry Colla continued his series of single-player postcard sets 1990. The basic format continued unchanged, like the 1989-90 issues, features full-color game-action and posed photos on high-gloss stock. Black-and-white

backs feature a team logo at center, a card number at top and, in the upper-left, the player's name, uniform number, team and position. Sets were sold in white paper envelopes with color team logos on the front.

		NM/M
1-8	Mark Grace	3.00

1991 Barry Colla Promos

Each of the eight 12-card single-player sets produced by California photographer Barry Colla in 1991 was preceded by the issue of a promo card. Identical in format, the promos feature high quality borderless photos on glossy stock. Backs are printed in black-and-white and include information on the size and release date of the limited-edition set, along with ordering information and appropriate logos. The checklist of the unnumbered promo cards is presented here alphabetically.

		NM/M
	Complete Set (10):	12.00
	Common Player:	1.00
(1a)	Roberto Alomar	1.25
(1b)	Roberto Alomar (French)	1.50
(2)	Barry Bonds	4.00
(3a)	Joe Carter	1.00
(3b)	Joe Carter (French)	1.00
(4)	Dwight Gooden	1.00
(5)	Ken Griffey Jr.	3.00
(6)	Dave Justice	1.00
(7)	Ryne Sandberg	2.50
(8)	Darryl Strawberry	1.00

1991 Barry Colla

In 1991 baseball photographer Barry Colla continued production of a series of single-player card sets. In standard 2-1/2" x 3-1/2" size, the cards featured high-gloss borderless photos on front, with no extraneous graphics. Backs feature stats, career notes, personal data and team logos. The 12-card sets were sold in small decorative cardboard boxes. Production figures are noted in parentheses.

		NM/M
1-12	Roberto Alomar/7,500	2.00
1-12	Barry Bonds/7,500	12.00
1-12	Joe Carter/7,500	1.50
1-12	Dwight Gooden/15,000	1.50
1-12	Ken Griffey Jr./15,000	6.00
1-12	David Justice/15,000	1.50
1-12	Ryne Sandberg/15,000	4.00
1-12	Darryl Strawberry/15,000	1.50

1991 Barry Colla Postcards

Only one single-player postcard set was produced by Barry Colla in 1991: Ryne Sandberg. The eight-card set, like the 1989-90 issues, features full-color game-action and posed photos presented on a borderless, high-gloss 3-1/2"

x 5-1/2" format. Back design was changed for the 1991 issue. The team logo now appears in the upper-left corner with the player's name at top and his uniform number, team and position beneath. Sets were sold in a white paper envelope featuring a color Cubs logo.

		NM/M
1-8	Ryne Sandberg	5.00

1992 Barry Colla Promos

Each of the seven card sets produced by California photographer Barry Colla in 1992 was preceded by a promo card. In standard 2-1/2" x 3-1/2" size, the promos follow the format of the regular-issue cards with a borderless color photo on high-gloss stock. All of the card backs are printed in black-and-white and feature ordering information about the sets, expected release date and issue size and appropriate logos. Some promo cards feature checklists of all existing Colla Collection card sets. The unnumbered promo cards are checklisted here alphabetically.

		NM/M
	Complete Set (7):	7.50
	Common Player:	1.00
(1)	All-Star Set (Juan Guzman)	1.00
(2)	Steve Avery	1.00
(3)	Jeff Bagwell	1.50
(4)	Tony Gwynn	1.50
(5)	Mark McGwire	2.00
(6)	Frank Thomas	1.50
(7)	Nolan Ryan	2.50

1992 Barry Colla

In 1992 photographer Barry Colla continued production of a series of single-player card sets. In standard 2-1/2" x 3-1/2" size, the cards featured high-gloss borderless photos on front, with no extraneous graphics. Backs feature stats, career notes, personal data, team logos and/or a cartoon. Card #1 in each set was serially numbered on the back. The 12-card sets were sold in small decorative cardboard boxes. Production figures are noted in parentheses. One in every 125 Mark McGwire sets

contained an autographed card numbered from an edition of 200, but since the cards are not otherwise marked, caution should be exercised in paying a significant premium for such a set.

		NM/M
1-12	Steve Avery/7,500	2.00
1-12	Jeff Bagwell/25,000	4.00
1-12	Tony Gwynn/7,500	6.00
1-12	Mark McGwire/15,000	6.00
1-12	Mark McGwire (Autographed edition.)	300.00
1-12	Nolan Ryan/25,000	6.00
1-12	Frank Thomas/25,000	4.00

1992 Barry Colla All-Stars

The 1992 Colla All-Star set consists of 24 players from the All-Star game in San Diego that year, packaged in a collector's box. Limited to 25,000 sets, the first card in each set is numbered and collectors had the opportunity to win numbered and autographed Roberto Alomar cards. Two hundred autographed Frank Thomas cards were also created for use as a premium, but he did not play in the 1992 All-Star Game due to injury.

		NM/M
	Complete Set (24):	7.00
	Common Player:	.25
1	Mark McGwire	1.50
2	Will Clark	.25
3	Roberto Alomar	.35
3a	Roberto Alomar (Autographed)	10.00
4	Ryne Sandberg	1.00
5	Cal Ripken, Jr.	2.00
6	Ozzie Smith	1.00
7	Wade Boggs	1.00
8	Terry Pendleton	.25
9	Kirby Puckett	1.00
10	Chuck Knoblauch	.25
11	Ken Griffey Jr.	1.25
12	Joe Carter	.25
13	Sandy Alomar, Jr.	.25
14	Benito Santiago	.25
15	Mike Mussina	.35
16	Fred McGriff	.25
17	Dennis Eckersley	.75
18	Tony Gwynn	1.00
19	Roger Clemens	1.00
20	Gary Sheffield	.35
21	Jose Canseco	.35
22	Barry Bonds	2.00
23	Ivan Rodriguez	.75
24	Tony Fernandez	.25
---	Frank Thomas/Auto.	25.00

1992 Barry Colla Postcards

KEN GRIFFEY, JR.

Only one single-player postcard set was produced by Barry Colla in 1992: Ivan Rodriguez. The four-card set, like the 1989-91 issues, features full-color game-action and posed photos presented on a borderless, high-gloss 3-1/2" x 5-1/2" format. Besides the I-Rod set, Colla also produced at least one one-card "set," apparently on special order. These cards are in the same format as his other issues and are individually serially numbered on back from within an edition of 4,000.

		NM/M
1-4	Ivan Rodriguez	4.00
6492	Ken Griffey Jr.	6.00

1993 Barry Colla All-Stars

For the second year in 1993 California photographer Barry Colla produced a 24-card All-Star set commemorating the game played in Baltimore on July 13. The specially boxed collector's edition includes an unnumbered All-Star logo/checklist card. Cards feature black borders on the UV-coated front, featuring game-action or posed photos. Team logos are centered beneath the photo, with the player's name and position in white at bottom. Backs are also bordered in black and include another player color photo, league and All-Star logos and information and stats on prior All-Star Game appearances.

		NM/M
Complete Set (25):		4.00
Common Player:		.15
1	Roberto Alomar	.30
2	Barry Bonds	.75
3	Ken Griffey Jr.	.50
4	John Kruk	.15
5	Kirby Puckett	.45
6	Darren Daulton	.15
7	Wade Boggs	.45
8	Matt Williams	.15
9	Cal Ripken, Jr.	.75
10	Ryne Sandberg	.45
11	Ivan Rodriguez	.30
12	Andy Van Slyke	.15
13	John Olerud	.15
14	Tom Glavine	.25
15	Juan Gonzalez	.30
16	David Justice	.15
17	Mike Mussina	.25
18	Tony Gwynn	.45
19	Joe Carter	.15
20	Barry Larkin	.15
21	Brian Harper	.15
22	Ozzie Smith	.45
23	Mark McGwire	.60
24	Mike Piazza	.50
	Checklist	.05

1993 Barry Colla Postcards

Following a one-year layoff, Barry Colla continued his single-player, eight-card postcard series in 1993 with a pair of sets. Like the earlier issues, the cards are 3-1/2" x 5-1/2" and feature high-gloss fronts with borderless game-action and posed photos. Black-and-white backs have a more traditional postcard format than earlier issues.

The sets were sold in white paper envelopes with color team logos on front. A version of each set was made with an embossed gold-foil team logo on front; they are valued about 5X the regular issue.

		NM/M
1-8	Mike Piazza	3.50
1-8	Cal Ripken Jr.	6.00

1994 Collector's Choice Promos

Upper Deck used a pair of promo cards to preview its new 1994 Collector's Choice brand. Ken Griffey Jr. was featured on the promos, though the photos differ from those which appear on his regular-issue card, as does the card number. "For Promotional Use Only" is printed diagonally in black on the front and back of the regular-size card. The 5" x 7-3/8" promo card uses the same front photo as the smaller promo and has advertising on the back describing the Collector's Choice issue.

		NM/M
50	Ken Griffey Jr.	5.00
---	Ken Griffey Jr. (Jumbo)	5.00

1994 Collector's Choice

This base-brand set, released in two series, was more widely available than the regular 1994 Upper Deck issue. Cards feature UD production staples such as UV coating and hologram and have large photos with a narrow pinstripe border. Backs have stats and a color photo. Series 1 has 320 cards and subsets titled Rookie Class, Draft Picks and Top Performers. Series 2 subsets are Up Close and Personal, Future Foundation and Rookie Class. Each of the set's player cards can also be found with either a gold- (1 in 36 packs) or silver-foil replica-autograph card; one silver-signature card appears in every pack. Factory sets include five randomly selected gold-signature cards.

		NM/M
Unopened Fact. Set (675):		25.00
Complete Set (670):		20.00
Common Player:		.05
Silver Signature:		2.5X
Gold Signature:		15X
Series 1 Pack (12):		.35
Series 1 Box (36):		8.00
Series 2 Pack (12):		.75
Series 2 Box (36):		17.50
1	Rich Becker RC	.05
2	Greg Blosser	.05
3	Midre Cummings	.05
4	Carlos Delgado	.30
5	Steve Dreyer RC	.05
6	Carl Everett RC	.50
7	Cliff Floyd	.05

8	Alex Gonzalez	.05
9	Shawn Green	.10
10	Butch Huskey	.05
11	Mark Hutton	.05
12	Miguel Jimenez	.05
13	Steve Karsay	.05
14	Marc Newfield	.05
15	Luis Ortiz	.05
16	Manny Ramirez	.60
17	Johnny Ruffin	.05
18	Scott Stahoviak RC	.05
19	Salomon Torres	.05
20	Gabe White RC	.10
21	Brian Anderson RC	.05
22	Wayne Gomes RC	.05
23	Jeff Granger	.05
24	Steve Soderstrom RC	.05
25	Trot Nixon RC	.50
26	Kirk Presley RC	.05
27	Matt Brunson RC	.05
28	Brooks Kieschnick RC	.05
29	Billy Wagner RC	.50
30	Matt Drews RC	.05
31	Kurt Abbott RC	.05
32	Luis Alicea	.05
33	Roberto Alomar	.20
34	Sandy Alomar Jr.	.05
35	Moises Alou	.05
36	Wilson Alvarez	.05
37	Rich Amaral	.05
38	Eric Anthony	.05
39	Luis Aquino	.05
40	Jack Armstrong	.05
41	Rene Arocha	.05
42	Rich Aude RC	.05
43	Brad Ausmus	.05
44	Steve Avery	.05
45	Bob Ayrault	.05
46	Willie Banks	.05
47	Bret Barberie	.05
48	Kim Batiste	.05
49	Rod Beck	.05
50	Jason Bere	.05
51	Sean Berry	.05
52	Dante Bichette	.05
53	Jeff Blauser	.05
54	Mike Blowers	.05
55	Tim Bogar	.05
56	Tom Bolton	.05
57	Ricky Bones	.05
58	Bobby Bonilla	.05
59	Bret Boone	.05
60	Pat Borders	.05
61	Mike Bordick	.05
62	Daryl Boston	.05
63	Ryan Bowen	.05
64	Jeff Branson	.05
65	George Brett	.85
66	Steve Buechele	.05
67	Dave Burba	.05
68	John Burkett	.05
69	Jeromy Burnitz	.05
70	Brett Butler	.05
71	Rob Butler	.05
72	Ken Caminiti	.05
73	Cris Carpenter	.05
74	Vinny Castilla	.05
75	Andujar Cedeno	.05
76	Wes Chamberlain	.05
77	Archi Cianfrocco	.05
78	Dave Clark	.05
79	Jerald Clark	.05
80	Royce Clayton	.05
81	David Cone	.05
82	Jeff Conine	.05
83	Steve Cooke	.05
84	Scott Cooper	.05
85	Joey Cora	.05
86	Tim Costa	.05
87	Chad Curtis	.05
88	Ron Darling	.05
89	Danny Darwin	.05
90	Rob Deer	.05
91	Jim Deshaies	.05
92	Delino DeShields	.05
93	Rob Dibble	.05
94	Gary DiSarcina	.05
95	Doug Drabek	.05
96	Scott Erickson	.05
97	Rikkert Faneyte RC	.05
98	Jeff Fassero	.05
99	Alex Fernandez	.05
100	Cecil Fielder	.05
101	Dave Fleming	.05
102	Darrin Fletcher	.05
103	Scott Fletcher	.05
104	Mike Gallego	.05
105	Carlos Garcia	.05
106	Jeff Gardner	.05
107	Brent Gates	.05
108	Benji Gil	.05
109	Bernard Gilkey	.05
110	Chris Gomez	.05
111	Luis Gonzalez	.05
112	Tom Gordon	.05
113	Jim Gott	.05
114	Mark Grace	.05
115	Tommy Greene	.05
116	Willie Greene	.05
117	Ken Griffey Jr.	1.00
118	Bill Gullickson	.05
119	Ricky Gutierrez	.05
120	Juan Guzman	.05
121	Chris Gwynn	.05
122	Tony Gwynn	.75
123	Jeffrey Hammonds	.05
124	Erik Hanson	.05
125	Gene Harris	.05

126	Greg Harris	.05
127	Bryan Harvey	.05
128	Billy Hatcher	.05
129	Hilly Hathaway	.05
130	Charlie Hayes	.05
131	Rickey Henderson	.60
132	Mike Henneman	.05
133	Pat Hentgen	.05
134	Roberto Hernandez	.05
135	Orel Hershiser	.05
136	Phil Hiatt	.05
137	Glenallen Hill	.05
138	Ken Hill	.05
139	Eric Hillman	.05
140	Chris Hoiles	.05
141	Dave Hollins	.05
142	David Hulse	.05
143	Todd Hundley	.05
144	Pete Incaviglia	.05
145	Danny Jackson	.05
146	John Jaha	.05
147	Domingo Jean	.05
148	Gregg Jefferies	.05
149	Reggie Jefferson	.05
150	Lance Johnson	.05
151	Bobby Jones	.05
152	Chipper Jones	.75
153	Todd Jones	.05
154	Brian Jordan	.05
155	Wally Joyner	.05
156	Dave Justice	.05
157	Ron Karkovice	.05
158	Eric Karros	.05
159	Jeff Kent	.05
160	Jimmy Key	.05
161	Mark Kiefer	.05
162	Darryl Kile	.05
163	Jeff King	.05
164	Wayne Kirby	.05
165	Ryan Klesko	.05
166	Chuck Knoblauch	.05
167	Chad Kreuter	.05
168	John Kruk	.05
169	Mark Langston	.05
170	Mike Lansing	.05
171	Barry Larkin	.05
172	Manuel Lee	.05
173	Phil Leftwich RC	.05
174	Darren Lewis	.05
175	Derek Lilliquist	.05
176	Jose Lind	.05
177	Albie Lopez	.05
178	Javier Lopez	.05
179	Torey Lovullo	.05
180	Scott Lydy	.05
181	Mike Macfarlane	.05
182	Shane Mack	.05
183	Greg Maddux	.75
184	Dave Magadan	.05
185	Joe Magrane	.05
186	Kirt Manwaring	.05
187	Al Martin	.05
188	Pedro A. Martinez RC	.05
189	Pedro Martinez	.60
190	Ramon Martinez	.05
191	Tino Martinez	.05
192	Don Mattingly	.85
193	Derrick May	.05
194	David McCarty	.05
195	Ben McDonald	.05
196	Roger McDowell	.05
197	Fred McGriff	.05
198	Mark McLemore	.05
199	Greg McMichael	.05
200	Jeff McNeely	.05
201	Brian McRae	.05
202	Pat Meares	.05
203	Roberto Mejia	.05
204	Orlando Merced	.05
205	Jose Mesa	.05
206	Blas Minor	.05
207	Angel Miranda	.05
208	Paul Molitor	.60
209	Raul Mondesi	.05
210	Jeff Montgomery	.05
211	Mickey Morandini	.05
212	Mike Morgan	.05
213	Jamie Moyer	.05
214	Bobby Munoz	.05
215	Troy Neel	.05
216	Dave Nilsson	.05
217	John O'Donoghue	.05
218	Paul O'Neill	.05
219	Jose Offerman	.05
220	Joe Oliver	.05
221	Greg Olson	.05
222	Donovan Osborne	.05
223	Jayhawk Owens	.05
224	Mike Pagliarulo	.05
225	Craig Paquette	.05
226	Roger Pavlik	.05
227	Brad Pennington	.05
228	Eduardo Perez	.05
229	Mike Perez	.05
230	Tony Phillips	.05
231	Hipolito Pichardo	.05
232	Phil Plantier	.05
233	Curtis Pride RC	.05
234	Tim Pugh	.05
235	Scott Radinsky	.05
236	Pat Rapp	.05
237	Kevin Reimer	.05
238	Armando Reynoso	.05
239	Jose Rijo	.05
240	Cal Ripken, Jr.	2.00
241	Kevin Roberson	.05
242	Kenny Rogers	.05
243	Kevin Rogers	.05

244	Mel Rojas	.05
245	John Roper	.05
246	Kirk Rueter	.05
247	Scott Ruffcorn	.05
248	Ken Ryan	.05
249	Nolan Ryan	2.00
250	Bret Saberhagen	.05
251	Tim Salmon	.05
252	Reggie Sanders	.05
253	Curt Schilling	.20
254	David Segui	.05
255	Aaron Sele	.05
256	Scott Servais	.05
257	Gary Sheffield	.30
258	Ruben Sierra	.05
259	Don Slaught	.05
260	Lee Smith	.05
261	Cory Snyder	.05
262	Paul Sorrento	.05
263	Sammy Sosa	.75
264	Bill Spiers	.05
265	Mike Stanley	.05
266	Dave Staton	.05
267	Terry Steinbach	.05
268	Kevin Stocker	.05
269	Todd Stottlemyre	.05
270	Doug Strange	.05
271	Bill Swift	.05
272	Kevin Tapani	.05
273	Tony Tarasco	.05
274	Julian Tavarez RC	.05
275	Mickey Tettleton	.05
276	Ryan Thompson	.05
277	Chris Turner	.05
278	John Valentin	.05
279	Todd Van Poppel	.05
280	Andy Van Slyke	.05
281	Mo Vaughn	.05
282	Robin Ventura	.05
283	Frank Viola	.05
284	Jose Vizcaino	.05
285	Omar Vizquel	.05
286	Larry Walker	.05
287	Duane Ware	.05
288	Allen Watson	.05
289	Bill Wegman	.05
290	Turk Wendell	.05
291	Lou Whitaker	.05
292	Devon White	.05
293	Rondell White	.05
294	Mark Whiten	.05
295	Darrell Whitmore	.05
296	Bob Wickman	.05
297	Rick Wilkins	.05
298	Bernie Williams	.05
299	Matt Williams	.05
300	Woody Williams	.05
301	Nigel Wilson	.05
302	Dave Winfield	.60
303	Anthony Young	.05
304	Eric Young	.05
305	Todd Zeile	.05
306	Jack McDowell, John Burkett, Tom Glavine/TP	.05
307	Randy Johnson/TP	.25
308	Randy Myers/TP	.05
309	Jack McDowell/TP	.05
310	Mike Piazza/TP	.40
311	Barry Bonds/TP	.60
312	Andres Galarraga/TP	.05
313	Juan Gonzalez, Barry Bonds/TP	.45
314	Albert Belle/TP	.05
315	Kenny Lofton/TP	.05
316	Checklist 1-64 (Barry Bonds)	.50
317	Checklist 65-128 (Ken Griffey Jr.)	.35
318	Checklist 129-192 (Mike Piazza)	.35
319	Checklist 193-256 (Kirby Puckett)	.25
320	Checklist 257-320 (Nolan Ryan)	.05
321	Checklist 321-370 (Roberto Alomar)	.10
322	Checklist 371-420 (Roger Clemens)	.30
323	Checklist 421-470 (Juan Gonzalez)	.10
324	Checklist 471-520 (Ken Griffey Jr.)	.35
325	Checklist 521-570 (David Justice)	.05
326	Checklist 571-620 (John Kruk)	.05
327	Checklist 621-670 (Frank Thomas)	.20
328	Angels Checklist (Tim Salmon)	.05
329	Astros Checklist (Jeff Bagwell)	.20
330	Athletics Checklist (Mark McGwire)	.45
331	Blue Jays Checklist (Roberto Alomar)	.10
332	Braves Checklist (David Justice)	.05
333	Brewers Checklist (Pat Listach)	.05
334	Cardinals Checklist (Ozzie Smith)	.05
335	Cubs Checklist (Ryne Sandberg)	.25
336	Dodgers Checklist (Mike Piazza)	.35
337	Expos Checklist (Cliff Floyd)	.05

338	Giants Checklist (Barry Bonds)	.50
339	Indians Checklist (Albert Belle)	.05
340	Mariners Checklist (Ken Griffey Jr.)	.35
341	Marlins Checklist (Gary Sheffield)	.10
342	Mets Checklist (Dwight Gooden)	.05
343	Orioles Checklist (Cal Ripken, Jr.)	.50
344	Padres Checklist (Tony Gwynn)	.25
345	Phillies Checklist (Lenny Dykstra)	.05
346	Pirates Checklists (Andy Van Slyke)	.05
347	Rangers Checklist (Juan Gonzalez)	.10
348	Red Sox Checklist (Roger Clemens)	.30
349	Reds Checklist (Barry Larkin)	.05
350	Rockies Checklist (Andres Galarraga)	.05
351	Royals Checklist (Kevin Appier)	.05
352	Tigers Checklist (Cecil Fielder)	.05
353	Twins Checklist (Kirby Puckett)	.25
354	White Sox Checklist (Frank Thomas)	.20
355	Yankees Checklist (Don Mattingly)	.30
356	Bo Jackson	.10
357	Randy Johnson	.60
358	Darren Daulton	.05
359	Charlie Hough	.05
360	Andres Galarraga	.05
361	Mike Felder	.05
362	Chris Hammond	.05
363	Shawon Dunston	.05
364	Junior Felix	.05
365	Ray Lankford	.05
366	Darryl Strawberry	.05
367	Dave Magadan	.05
368	Gregg Olson	.05
369	Len Dykstra	.05
370	Darrin Jackson	.05
371	Dave Stewart	.05
372	Terry Pendleton	.05
373	Arthur Rhodes	.05
374	Benito Santiago	.05
375	Travis Fryman	.05
376	Scott Brosius	.05
377	Stan Belinda	.05
378	Derek Parks	.05
379	Kevin Seitzer	.05
380	Wade Boggs	.75
381	Wally Whitehurst	.05
382	Scott Leius	.05
383	Danny Tartabull	.05
384	Harold Reynolds	.05
385	Tim Raines	.05
386	Darryl Hamilton	.05
387	Felix Fermin	.05
388	Jim Eisenreich	.05
389	Kurt Abbott	.05
390	Kevin Appier	.05
391	Chris Bosio	.05
392	Randy Tomlin	.05
393	Bob Hamelin	.05
394	Kevin Gross	.05
395	Wil Cordero	.05
396	Joe Girardi	.05
397	Orestes Destrade	.05
398	Chris Haney	.05
399	Xavier Hernandez	.05
400	Mike Piazza	1.00
401	Alex Arias	.05
402	Tom Candiotti	.05
403	Kirk Gibson	.05
404	Chuck Carr	.05
405	Brady Anderson	.05
406	Greg Gagne	.05
407	Bruce Ruffin	.05
408	Scott Hemond	.05
409	Keith Miller	.05
410	John Wetteland	.05
411	Eric Anthony	.05
412	Andre Dawson	.25
413	Doug Henry	.05
414	John Franco	.05
415	Julio Franco	.05
416	Dave Hansen	.05
417	Mike Harkey	.05
418	Jack Armstrong	.05
419	Joe Orsulak	.05
420	John Smoltz	.05
421	Scott Livingstone	.05
422	Darren Holmes	.05
423	Ed Sprague	.05
424	Jay Buhner	.05
425	Kirby Puckett	.75
426	Phil Clark	.05
427	Anthony Young	.05
428	Reggie Jefferson	.05
429	Mariano Duncan	.05
430	Tom Glavine	.20
431	Dave Henderson	.05
432	Melido Perez	.05
433	Paul Wagner	.05
434	Tim Worrell	.05
435	Ozzie Guillen	.05
436	Mike Butcher	.05
437	Jim Deshaies	.05

438 Kevin Young .05
439 Tom Browning .05
440 Mike Greenwell .05
441 Mike Stanton .05
442 John Doherty .05
443 John Dopson .05
444 Carlos Baerga .05
445 Jack McDowell .05
446 Kent Mercker .05
447 Ricky Jordan .05
448 Jerry Browne .05
449 Fernando Vina .05
450 Jim Abbott .05
451 Teddy Higuera .05
452 Tim Naehring .05
453 Jim Leyritz .05
454 Frank Castillo .05
455 Joe Carter .05
456 Craig Biggio .05
457 Geronimo Pena .05
458 Alejandro Pena .05
459 Mike Moore .05
460 Randy Myers .05
461 Greg Myers .05
462 Greg Hibbard .05
463 Jose Guzman .05
464 Tom Pagnozzi .05
465 Marquis Grissom .05
466 Tim Wallach .05
467 Joe Grahe .05
468 Bob Tewksbury .05
469 B.J. Surhoff .05
470 Kevin Mitchell .05
471 Bobby Witt .05
472 Milt Thompson .05
473 John Smiley .05
474 Alan Trammell .05
475 Mike Mussina .30
476 Rick Aguilera .05
477 Jose Valentin .05
478 Harold Baines .05
479 Bip Roberts .05
480 Edgar Martinez .05
481 Rheal Cormier .05
482 Hal Morris .05
483 Pat Kelly .05
484 Roberto Kelly .05
485 Chris Sabo .05
486 Kent Hrbek .05
487 Scott Kamieniecki .05
488 Walt Weiss .05
489 Karl Rhodes .05
490 Derek Bell .05
491 Chili Davis .05
492 Brian Harper .05
493 Felix Jose .05
494 Trevor Hoffman .05
495 Dennis Eckersley .50
496 Pedro Astacio .05
497 Jay Bell .05
498 Randy Velarde .05
499 David Wells .05
500 Frank Thomas .60
501 Mark Lemke .05
502 Mike Devereaux .05
503 Chuck McElroy .05
504 Luis Polonia .05
505 Damion Easley .05
506 Greg A. Harris .05
507 Chris James .05
508 Terry Mulholland .05
509 Pete Smith .05
510 Rickey Henderson .60
511 Sid Fernandez .05
512 Al Leiter .05
513 Doug Jones .05
514 Steve Farr .05
515 Chuck Finley .05
516 Bobby Thigpen .05
517 Jim Edmonds .05
518 Graeme Lloyd .05
519 Dwight Gooden .05
520 Pat Listach .05
521 Kevin Bass .05
522 Willie Banks .05
523 Steve Finley .05
524 Delino DeShields .05
525 Mark McGwire 1.50
526 Greg Swindell .05
527 Chris Nabholz .05
528 Scott Sanders .05
529 David Segui .05
530 Howard Johnson .05
531 Jaime Navarro .05
532 Jose Vizcaino .05
533 Mark Lewis .05
534 Pete Harnisch .05
535 Robby Thompson .05
536 Marcus Moore .05
537 Kevin Brown .05
538 Mark Clark .05
539 Sterling Hitchcock .05
540 Will Clark .05
541 Denis Boucher .05
542 Jack Morris .05
543 Pedro Munoz .05
544 Bret Boone .05
545 Ozzie Smith .75
546 Dennis Martinez .05
547 Dan Wilson .05
548 Rick Sutcliffe .05
549 Kevin McReynolds .05
550 Roger Clemens .85
551 Todd Benzinger .05
552 Bill Haselman .05
553 Bobby Munoz .05
554 Ellis Burks .05
555 Ryne Sandberg .75

556 Lee Smith .05
557 Danny Bautista .05
558 Rey Sanchez .05
559 Norm Charlton .05
560 Jose Canseco .35
561 Tim Belcher .05
562 Denny Neagle .05
563 Eric Davis .05
564 Jody Reed .05
565 Kenny Lofton .05
566 Gary Gaetti .05
567 Todd Worrell .05
568 Mark Portugal .05
569 Dick Schofield .05
570 Andy Benes .05
571 Zane Smith .05
572 Bobby Ayala .05
573 Chip Hale .05
574 Bob Welch .05
575 Deion Sanders .10
576 Dave Nied .05
577 Pat Mahomes .05
578 Charles Nagy .05
579 Otis Nixon .05
580 Dean Palmer .05
581 Roberto Petagine .05
582 Dwight Smith .05
583 Jeff Russell .05
584 Mark Dewey .05
585 Greg Vaughn .05
586 Brian Hunter .05
587 Willie McGee .05
588 Pedro J. Martinez .60
589 Roger Salkeld .05
590 Jeff Bagwell .60
591 Spike Owen .05
592 Jeff Reardon .05
593 Erik Pappas .05
594 Brian Williams .05
595 Eddie Murray .60
596 Henry Rodriguez .05
597 Erik Hanson .05
598 Stan Javier .05
599 Mitch Williams .05
600 John Olerud .05
601 Vince Coleman .05
602 Damon Berryhill .05
603 Tom Brunansky .05
604 Robb Nen .05
605 Rafael Palmeiro .50
606 Cal Eldred .05
607 Jeff Brantley .05
608 Alan Mills .05
609 Jeff Nelson .05
610 Barry Bonds 2.00
611 Carlos Pulido RC .05
612 Tim Hyers RC .05
613 Steve Howe .05
614 Brian Turang RC .05
615 Leo Gomez .05
616 Jesse Orosco .05
617 Dan Pasqua .05
618 Marvin Freeman .05
619 Tony Fernandez .05
620 Albert Belle .60
621 Eddie Taubensee .05
622 Mike Jackson .05
623 Jose Bautista .05
624 Jim Thome .40
625 Ivan Rodriguez .50
626 Ben Rivera .05
627 Dave Valle .05
628 Tom Henke .05
629 Omar Vizquel .05
630 Juan Gonzalez .30
631 Roberto Alomar (Up Close) .10
632 Barry Bonds (Up Close) .60
633 Juan Gonzalez (Up Close) .15
634 Ken Griffey Jr. (Up Close) .50
635 Michael Jordan (Up Close) 1.50
636 Dave Justice (Up Close) .05
637 Mike Piazza (Up Close) .50
638 Kirby Puckett (Up Close) .25
639 Tim Salmon (Up Close) .05
640 Frank Thomas (Up Close) .35
641 Alan Benes RC/FF .05
642 Johnny Damon/FF .35
643 Brad Fullmer RC/FF .05
644 Derek Jeter/FF 2.00
645 Derrek Lee RC/FF .75
646 Alex Ochoa/FF .05
647 Alex Rodriguez RC/FF 6.00
648 Jose Silva RC/FF .05
649 Terrell Wade RC/FF .05
650 Preston Wilson/FF .05
651 Shane Andrews (Rookie Class) .05
652 James Baldwin (Rookie Class) .05
653 Ricky Bottalico RC (Rookie Class) .10
654 Tavo Alvarez (Rookie Class) .05
655 Donnie Elliott (Rookie Class) .05
656 Joey Eischen (Rookie Class) .05
657 Jason Giambi (Rookie Class) .50
658 Todd Hollandsworth (Rookie Class) .05
659 Brian Hunter (Rookie Class) .05
660 Charles Johnson (Rookie Class) .05

661 Michael Jordan RC (Rookie Class) 3.00
662 Jeff Juden (Rookie Class) .05
663 Mike Kelly (Rookie Class) .05
664 James Mouton (Rookie Class) .05
665 Ray Holbert (Rookie Class) .05
666 Pokey Reese (Rookie Class) .05
667 Ruben Santana RC (Rookie Class) .05
668 Paul Spoljaric (Rookie Class) .05
669 Luis Lopez (Rookie Class) .05
670 Matt Walbeck (Rookie Class) .05

1994 Collector's Choice Silver Signature

Each of the cards in the debut edition of Upper Deck's Collector's Choice brand was also issued in a parallel edition bearing a facsimile silver-foil signature on front. The silver-signature cards were inserted at a one-per-pack rate in the set's foil packs, and proportionately in other types of packaging.

	NM/M
Common Player:	.15

647 Alex Rodriguez (White Letters. Some A-Rod Silver Signature parallels were mistakenly printed on base cards with his name and other details on front and back printed in white, rather than gray.) 100.00

1994 Collector's Choice Gold Signature

A super-scarce parallel set of the premiere-issue Collector's Choice in 1994 was the gold-signature version found on average of only once per 36 foil packs. In addition to a gold-foil facsimile signature on the card front, this edition features gold-colored borders on the regular player cards.

	NM/M
Common Player:	2.00
Stars:	15X

Home Run All-Stars

Among the most attractive of the 1994 chase cards, the perceived high production (over a million sets according to stated odds of winning) of this set keeps it affordable. Sets were available by a mail-in offer to persons who found a winner card in Series 1 foil packs (about one per box). Cards feature a combination of brick-bordered hologram and color player photo on front, along with a gold-foil facsimile autograph. On back the brick border is repeated, as is the photo on the hologram, though this time in full color. There is a stadium photo in the background, over which is printed a description of the player's home run prowess. A numbering error resulted in two cards numbered HA4 and no card with the HA5 number.

	NM/M
Complete Set (8):	4.00
Common Player:	.25
1HA Juan Gonzalez	.50
2HA Ken Griffey Jr.	1.50
3HA Barry Bonds	2.50
4HAa Bobby Bonilla	.25
4HAb Cecil Fielder	.25
6HA Albert Belle	.25
7HA David Justice	.25
8HA Mike Piazza	1.50

1994 Collector's Choice Team vs. Team Scratchoff

Team vs. Team scratch-offs are a 15-card set, with one game card being inserted into every pack of Collector's Choice 1994 baseball. Each card allowed two persons to play a nine-inning baseball game. Game cards also double as a prize card in the "You Crash The Deck" contest.

	NM/M
Complete Set (15):	4.50
Common Card:	.25

1 Blue Jays-White Sox (Roberto Alomar, Frank Thomas) .30
2 Phillies-Braves (Lenny Dykstra, David Justice) .25
3 Mariners-Rangers (Ken Griffey Jr., Juan Gonzalez) .50
4 Dodgers-Giants (Mike Piazza, Barry Bonds) .75
5 Red Sox-Yankees (Roger Clemens, Don Mattingly) .45
6 Reds-Astros (Barry Larkin, Jeff Bagwell) .25
7 Orioles-Tigers (Cal Ripken Jr., Cecil Fielder) .25
8 Cubs-Cardinals (Ryne Sandberg, Ozzie Smith) .35
9 Athletics-Angels (Mark McGwire, Tim Salmon) .60
10 Pirates-Expos (Andy Van Slyke, Cliff Floyd) .25
11 Brewers-Indians (Pat Listach, Albert Belle) .25
12 Rockies-Padres (Andres Galarraga, Tony Gwynn) .35
13 Twins-Royals (Kirby Puckett, Brian McRae) .35
14 Mets-Marlins (Dwight Gooden, Gary Sheffield) .25
15 N.L. All-Stars-A.L. All-Stars (Barry Bonds, Ken Griffey Jr.) .75

1995 Collector's Choice

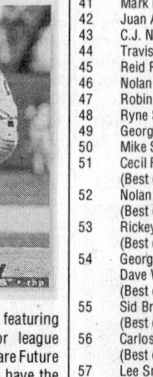

Issued in a single series, Upper Deck's base-brand baseball series features a number of subsets within the main body of the issue, as well as several insert sets. Basic cards feature large photos on front and back, with the back having full major league stats. The set opens with a 27-card Rookie Class subset featuring front photos on which the background has been rendered in hot pink tones. Backs have a lime-green box with a scouting report on the player and a box featuring 1994 minor and major league stats. The next 18 cards are Future Foundation cards which have the prospects pictured with a posterized background on front, with backs similar to the Rookie Class cards. Career finale cards of five retired superstars follow, then a run of Best of the '90s cards honoring record-setting achievements, followed by cards depicting major award winners of the previous season. Each of the last three named subsets features borderless color photos on front, with backs similar to the regular cards. Immediately preceding the regular cards, which are arranged in team-set order, is a five-card What's the Call? subset featuring cartoon representations of the players. A set of five checklist cards marking career highlights ends the set.

	NM/M
Unopened Fact. Set (545):	17.50
Complete Set (530):	12.50
Common Player:	.05
Silver Stars:	2X
Gold Stars:	6X
Pack (12):	1.00
Wax Box (36):	20.00

1 Charles Johnson (Rookie Class) .05
2 Scott Ruffcorn (Rookie Class) .05
3 Ray Durham (Rookie Class) .15
4 Armando Benitez (Rookie Class) .05
5 Alex Rodriguez (Rookie Class) 1.25
6 Julian Tavarez (Rookie Class) .05
7 Chad Ogea (Rookie Class) .05
8 Quilvio Veras (Rookie Class) .05
9 Phil Nevin (Rookie Class) .05
10 Michael Tucker (Rookie Class) .05
11 Mark Thompson (Rookie Class) .05
12 Rod Henderson (Rookie Class) .05
13 Andrew Lorraine (Rookie Class) .05
14 Joe Randa (Rookie Class) .05
15 Derek Jeter (Rookie Class) 1.50
16 Tony Clark (Rookie Class) .05
17 Juan Castillo (Rookie Class) .05
18 Mark Acre (Rookie Class) .05
19 Orlando Miller (Rookie Class) .05
20 Paul Wilson (Rookie Class) .05
21 John Mabry (Rookie Class) .05
22 Garey Ingram (Rookie Class) .05
23 Garret Anderson (Rookie Class) .05
24 Dave Stevens (Rookie Class) .05
25 Dustin Hermanson (Rookie Class) .05
26 Paul Shuey (Rookie Class) .05
27 J.R. Phillips .05
28 Ruben Rivera/FF .05
29 Nomar Garciaparra/FF .75
30 John Wasdin/FF .05
31 Jim Pittsley/FF .05
32 Scott Elarton RC/FF .15
33 Raul Casanova RC/FF .05
34 Todd Greene/FF .05
35 Bill Pulsipher/FF .05
36 Trey Beamon/FF .05
37 Curtis Goodwin/FF .05
38 Doug Million/FF .05
39 Karim Garcia RC/FF 1.00
40 Ben Grieve/FF .05

41 Mark Farris/FF .05
42 Juan Acevedo RC/FF .05
43 C.J. Nitkowski/FF .05
44 Travis Miller RC/FF .10
45 Reid Ryan/FF .10
46 Nolan Ryan 1.50
47 Robin Yount .50
48 Ryne Sandberg .75
49 George Brett .85
50 Mike Schmidt .85
51 Cecil Fielder (Best of the 90's) .05
52 Nolan Ryan (Best of the 90's) .75
53 Rickey Henderson (Best of the 90's) .20
54 George Brett, Robin Yount, Dave Winfield (Best of the 90's) .25
55 Sid Bream (Best of the 90's) .05
56 Carlos Baerga (Best of the 90's) .05
57 Lee Smith (Best of the 90's) .05
58 Mark Whiten (Best of the 90's) .05
59 Joe Carter (Best of the 90's) .05
60 Barry Bonds (Best of the 90's) .75
61 Tony Gwynn (Best of the 90's) .40
62 Ken Griffey Jr. (Best of the 90's) .50
63 Greg Maddux (Best of the 90's) .40
64 Frank Thomas (Best of the 90's) .35
65 Dennis Martinez, Kenny Rogers (Best of the 90's) .05
66 David Cone (Cy Young) .05
67 Greg Maddux (Cy Young) .75
68 Jimmy Key (Most Victories) .05
69 Fred McGriff (All-Star MVP) .05
70 Ken Griffey Jr. (HR Champ) 1.00
71 Matt Williams (HR Champ) .05
72 Paul O'Neill (Batting Title) .05
73 Tony Gwynn (Batting Title) .40
74 Randy Johnson (Ks Leader) .60
75 Frank Thomas (MVP) .60
76 Jeff Bagwell (MVP) .60
77 Kirby Puckett (RBI leader) .75
78 Bob Hamelin (ROY) .05
79 Raul Mondesi (ROY) .05
80 Mike Piazza (All-Star) 1.00
81 Kenny Lofton (SB Leader) .05
82 Barry Bonds (Gold Glove) 1.50
83 Albert Belle/AS .05
84 Juan Gonzalez (HR Champ) .30
85 Cal Ripken Jr. (2,000 Straight Games) 1.50
86 Barry Bonds (What's the Call?) .75
87 Mike Piazza (What's the Call?) .60
88 Ken Griffey Jr. (What's the Call?) .50
89 Frank Thomas (What's the Call?) .35
90 Juan Gonzalez (What's the Call?) .10
91 Jorge Fabregas .05
92 J.T. Snow .05
93 Spike Owen .05
94 Eduardo Perez .05
95 Bo Jackson .10
96 Damion Easley .05
97 Gary DiSarcina .05
98 Jim Edmonds .05
99 Chad Curtis .05
100 Tim Salmon .05
101 Chili Davis .05
102 Chuck Finley .05
103 Mark Langston .05
104 Brian Anderson .05
105 Lee Smith .05
106 Phil Leftwich .05
107 Chris Donnels .05
108 John Hudek .05
109 Craig Biggio .05
110 Luis Gonzalez .05
111 Brian L. Hunter .05
112 James Mouton .05
113 Scott Servais .05
114 Tony Eusebio .05
115 Derek Bell .05
116 Doug Drabek .05
117 Shane Reynolds .05
118 Darryl Kile .05
119 Greg Swindell .05
120 Phil Plantier .05
121 Todd Jones .05
122 Steve Ontiveros .05
123 Bobby Witt .05
124 Brent Gates .05
125 Rickey Henderson .60
126 Scott Brosius .05
127 Mike Bordick .05
128 Fausto Cruz .05

No.	Player	Price
129	Stan Javier	.05
130	Mark McGwire	1.25
131	Geronimo Berroa	.05
132	Terry Steinbach	.05
133	Steve Karsay	.05
134	Dennis Eckersley	.50
135	Ruben Sierra	.05
136	Ron Darling	.05
137	Todd Van Poppel	.05
138	Alex Gonzalez	.05
139	John Olerud	.05
140	Roberto Alomar	.20
141	Darren Hall	.05
142	Ed Sprague	.05
143	Devon White	.05
144	Shawn Green	.20
145	Paul Molitor	.60
146	Pat Borders	.05
147	Carlos Delgado	.35
148	Juan Guzman	.05
149	Pat Hentgen	.05
150	Joe Carter	.05
151	Dave Stewart	.05
152	Todd Stottlemyre	.05
153	Dick Schofield	.05
154	Chipper Jones	.75
155	Ryan Klesko	.05
156	Dave Justice	.05
157	Mike Kelly	.05
158	Roberto Kelly	.05
159	Tony Tarasco	.05
160	Javier Lopez	.05
161	Steve Avery	.05
162	Greg McMichael	.05
163	Kent Mercker	.05
164	Mark Lemke	.05
165	Tom Glavine	.20
166	Jose Oliva	.05
167	John Smoltz	.05
168	Jeff Blauser	.05
169	Troy O'Leary	.05
170	Greg Vaughn	.05
171	Jody Reed	.05
172	Kevin Seitzer	.05
173	Jeff Cirillo	.05
174	B.J. Surhoff	.05
175	Cal Eldred	.05
176	Jose Valentin	.05
177	Turner Ward	.05
178	Darryl Hamilton	.05
179	Pat Listach	.05
180	Matt Mieske	.05
181	Brian Harper	.05
182	Dave Nilsson	.05
183	Mike Fetters	.05
184	John Jaha	.05
185	Ricky Bones	.05
186	Geronimo Pena	.05
187	Bob Tewksbury	.05
188	Todd Zeile	.05
189	Danny Jackson	.05
190	Ray Lankford	.05
191	Bernard Gilkey	.05
192	Brian Jordan	.05
193	Tom Pagnozzi	.05
194	Rick Sutcliffe	.05
195	Mark Whiten	.05
196	Tom Henke	.05
197	Rene Arocha	.05
198	Allen Watson	.05
199	Mike Perez	.05
200	Ozzie Smith	.75
201	Anthony Young	.05
202	Rey Sanchez	.05
203	Steve Buechele	.05
204	Shawon Dunston	.05
205	Mark Grace	.05
206	Glenallen Hill	.05
207	Eddie Zambrano	.05
208	Rick Wilkins	.05
209	Derrick May	.05
210	Sammy Sosa	.75
211	Kevin Roberson	.05
212	Steve Trachsel	.05
213	Willie Banks	.05
214	Kevin Foster	.05
215	Randy Myers	.05
216	Mike Morgan	.05
217	Rafael Bournigal	.05
218	Delino DeShields	.05
219	Tim Wallach	.05
220	Eric Karros	.05
221	Jose Offerman	.05
222	Tom Candiotti	.05
223	Ismael Valdes	.05
224	Henry Rodriguez	.05
225	Billy Ashley	.05
226	Darren Dreifort	.05
227	Ramon Martinez	.05
228	Pedro Astacio	.05
229	Orel Hershiser	.05
230	Brett Butler	.05
231	Todd Hollandsworth	.05
232	Chan Ho Park	.05
233	Mike Lansing	.05
234	Sean Berry	.05
235	Rondell White	.05
236	Ken Hill	.05
237	Marquis Grissom	.05
238	Larry Walker	.05
239	John Wetteland	.05
240	Cliff Floyd	.05
241	Joey Eischen	.05
242	Lou Frazier	.05
243	Darrin Fletcher	.05
244	Pedro J. Martinez	.60
245	Wil Cordero	.05
246	Jeff Fassero	.05

No.	Player	Price
247	Butch Henry	.05
248	Mel Rojas	.05
249	Kirk Rueter	.05
250	Moises Alou	.05
251	Rod Beck	.05
252	John Patterson	.05
253	Robby Thompson	.05
254	Royce Clayton	.05
255	William Van Landingham	.05
256	Darren Lewis	.05
257	Kirt Manwaring	.05
258	Mark Portugal	.05
259	Bill Swift	.05
260	Rikkert Faneyte	.05
261	Mike Jackson	.05
262	Todd Benzinger	.05
263	Bud Black	.05
264	Salomon Torres	.05
265	Eddie Murray	.60
266	Mark Clark	.05
267	Paul Sorrento	.05
268	Jim Thome	.45
269	Omar Vizquel	.05
270	Carlos Baerga	.05
271	Jeff Russell	.05
272	Herbert Perry	.05
273	Sandy Alomar Jr.	.05
274	Dennis Martinez	.05
275	Manny Ramirez	.60
276	Wayne Kirby	.05
277	Charles Nagy	.05
278	Albie Lopez	.05
279	Jeromy Burnitz	.05
280	Dave Winfield	.60
281	Tim Davis	.05
282	Marc Newfield	.05
283	Tino Martinez	.05
284	Mike Blowers	.05
285	Goose Gossage	.05
286	Luis Sojo	.05
287	Edgar Martinez	.05
288	Rich Amaral	.05
289	Felix Fermin	.05
290	Jay Buhner	.05
291	Dan Wilson	.05
292	Bobby Ayala	.05
293	Dave Fleming	.05
294	Greg Pirkl	.05
295	Reggie Jefferson	.05
296	Greg Hibbard	.05
297	Yorkis Perez	.05
298	Kurt Miller	.05
299	Chuck Carr	.05
300	Gary Sheffield	.30
301	Jerry Browne	.05
302	Dave Magadan	.05
303	Kurt Abbott	.05
304	Pat Rapp	.05
305	Jeff Conine	.05
306	Benito Santiago	.05
307	Dave Weathers	.05
308	Robb Nen	.05
309	Chris Hammond	.05
310	Bryan Harvey	.05
311	Charlie Hough	.05
312	Greg Colbrunn	.05
313	David Segui	.05
314	Rico Brogna	.05
315	Jeff Kent	.05
316	Jose Vizcaino	.05
317	Jim Lindeman	.05
318	Carl Everett	.05
319	Ryan Thompson	.05
320	Bobby Bonilla	.05
321	Joe Orsulak	.05
322	Pete Harnisch	.05
323	Doug Linton	.05
324	Todd Hundley	.05
325	Bret Saberhagen	.05
326	Kelly Stinnett	.05
327	Jason Jacome	.05
328	Bobby Jones	.05
329	John Franco	.05
330	Rafael Palmeiro	.50
331	Chris Hoiles	.05
332	Leo Gomez	.05
333	Chris Sabo	.05
334	Brady Anderson	.05
335	Jeffrey Hammonds	.05
336	Dwight Smith	.05
337	Jack Voigt	.05
338	Harold Baines	.05
339	Ben McDonald	.05
340	Mike Mussina	.30
341	Bret Barberie	.05
342	Jamie Moyer	.05
343	Mike Oquist	.05
344	Sid Fernandez	.05
345	Eddie Williams	.05
346	Joey Hamilton	.05
347	Brian Williams	.05
348	Luis Lopez	.05
349	Steve Finley	.05
350	Andy Benes	.05
351	Andujar Cedeno	.05
352	Bip Roberts	.05
353	Ray McDavid	.05
354	Ken Caminiti	.05
355	Trevor Hoffman	.05
356	Mel Nieves	.05
357	Brad Ausmus	.05
358	Andy Ashby	.05
359	Scott Sanders	.05
360	Gregg Jefferies	.05
361	Mariano Duncan	.05
362	Dave Hollins	.05
363	Kevin Stocker	.05
364	Fernando Valenzuela	.05

No.	Player	Price
365	Lenny Dykstra	.05
366	Jim Eisenreich	.05
367	Ricky Bottalico	.05
368	Doug Jones	.05
369	Ricky Jordan	.05
370	Darren Daulton	.05
371	Mike Lieberthal	.05
372	Bobby Munoz	.05
373	John Kruk	.05
374	Curt Schilling	.20
375	Orlando Merced	.05
376	Carlos Garcia	.05
377	Lance Parrish	.05
378	Steve Cooke	.05
379	Jeff King	.05
380	Jay Bell	.05
381	Al Martin	.05
382	Paul Wagner	.05
383	Rick White	.05
384	Midre Cummings	.05
385	Jon Lieber	.05
386	Dave Clark	.05
387	Don Slaught	.05
388	Denny Neagle	.05
389	Zane Smith	.05
390	Andy Van Slyke	.05
391	Ivan Rodriguez	.50
392	David Hulse	.05
393	John Burkett	.05
394	Kevin Brown	.05
395	Dean Palmer	.05
396	Otis Nixon	.05
397	Rick Helling	.05
398	Kenny Rogers	.05
399	Darren Oliver	.05
400	Will Clark	.05
401	Jeff Frye	.05
402	Kevin Gross	.05
403	John Dettmer	.05
404	Manny Lee	.05
405	Rusty Greer	.05
406	Aaron Sele	.05
407	Carlos Rodriguez	.05
408	Scott Cooper	.05
409	John Valentin	.05
410	Roger Clemens	.85
411	Mike Greenwell	.05
412	Tim Vanegmond	.05
413	Tom Brunansky	.05
414	Steve Farr	.05
415	Jose Canseco	.35
416	Joe Hesketh	.05
417	Ken Ryan	.05
418	Tim Naehring	.05
419	Frank Viola	.05
420	Andre Dawson	.25
421	Mo Vaughn	.05
422	Jeff Brantley	.05
423	Pete Schourek	.05
424	Hal Morris	.05
425	Deion Sanders	.10
426	Brian L. Hunter	.05
427	Bret Boone	.05
428	Willie Greene	.05
429	Ron Gant	.05
430	Barry Larkin	.05
431	Reggie Sanders	.05
432	Eddie Taubensee	.05
433	Jack Morris	.05
434	Jose Rijo	.05
435	Johnny Ruffin	.05
436	John Smiley	.05
437	John Roper	.05
438	David Nied	.05
439	Roberto Mejia	.05
440	Andres Galarraga	.05
441	Mike Kingery	.05
442	Curt Leskanic	.05
443	Walt Weiss	.05
444	Marvin Freeman	.05
445	Charlie Hayes	.05
446	Eric Young	.05
447	Ellis Burks	.05
448	Joe Girardi	.05
449	Lance Painter	.05
450	Dante Bichette	.05
451	Bruce Ruffin	.05
452	Jeff Granger	.05
453	Wally Joyner	.05
454	Jose Lind	.05
455	Jeff Montgomery	.05
456	Gary Gaetti	.05
457	Greg Gagne	.05
458	Vince Coleman	.05
459	Mike Macfarlane	.05
460	Brian McRae	.05
461	Tom Gordon	.05
462	Kevin Appier	.05
463	Billy Brewer	.05
464	Mark Gubicza	.05
465	Travis Fryman	.05
466	Danny Bautista	.05
467	Sean Bergman	.05
468	Mike Henneman	.05
469	Mike Moore	.05
470	Cecil Fielder	.05
471	Alan Trammell	.05
472	Kirk Gibson	.05
473	Tony Phillips	.05
474	Mickey Tettleton	.05
475	Lou Whitaker	.05
476	Chris Gomez	.05
477	John Doherty	.05
478	Greg Gohr	.05
479	Bill Gullickson	.05
480	Rick Aguilera	.05
481	Matt Walbeck	.05
482	Kevin Tapani	.05

No.	Player	Price
483	Scott Erickson	.05
484	Steve Dunn	.05
485	David McCarty	.05
486	Scott Leius	.05
487	Pat Meares	.05
488	Jeff Reboulet	.05
489	Pedro Munoz	.05
490	Chuck Knoblauch	.05
491	Rich Becker	.05
492	Alex Cole	.05
493	Pat Mahomes	.05
494	Ozzie Guillen	.05
495	Tim Raines	.05
496	Kirk McCaskill	.05
497	Olmedo Saenz	.05
498	Scott Sanderson	.05
499	Lance Johnson	.05
500	Michael Jordan	1.50
501	Warren Newson	.05
502	Ron Karkovice	.05
503	Wilson Alvarez	.05
504	Jason Bere	.05
505	Robin Ventura	.05
506	Alex Fernandez	.05
507	Roberto Hernandez	.05
508	Norberto Martin	.05
509	Bob Wickman	.05
510	Don Mattingly	.85
511	Melido Perez	.05
512	Pat Kelly	.05
513	Randy Velarde	.05
514	Tony Fernandez	.05
515	Jack McDowell	.05
516	Luis Polonia	.05
517	Bernie Williams	.05
518	Danny Tartabull	.05
519	Mike Stanley	.05
520	Wade Boggs	.75
521	Jim Leyritz	.05
522	Steve Howe	.05
523	Scott Kamieniecki	.05
524	Russ Davis	.05
525	Jim Abbott	.05
526	Checklist 1-106 (Eddie Murray)	.20
527	Checklist 107-212 (Alex Rodriguez)	.40
528	Checklist 213-318 (Jeff Bagwell)	.20
529	Checklist 319-424 (Joe Carter)	.05
530	Checklist 425-530 (Fred McGriff)	.05
---	National Packtime Offer Card	.05

Silver Signature

A silver-foil facsimile autograph added to the card front is the only difference between these chase cards and regular-issue Collector's Choice cards. The silver-signature inserts are found one per pack in regular foil packs, and two per pack in retail jumbo packs.

	NM/M
Common Player:	.10
Stars:	2X

Gold Signature

The top-of-the-line chase card in 1995 Collector's Choice is the Gold Signature parallel set. Each of the 530 cards in the set was created in a special gold version that was found on average

only one per box of foil packs. Other than the addition of a gold-foil facsimile autograph on front, the cards are identical to regular-issue Collector's Choice.

	NM/M
Common Player:	.50
Stars:	6X

1995 Collector's Choice Trade Cards

A series of five mail-in redemption cards was included as inserts into UD Collector's Choice, at the rate of approximately one per 11 packs. The cards could be sent in with $2 to receive 11 Collector's Choice Update cards, as specified on the front of the card. The trade offer expired on Feb. 1, 1996. Cards are numbered with the "TC" prefix.

		NM/M
Complete Set (5):		1.00
Common Player:		.25
1	Larry Walker (#531-541)	.25
2	David Cone (#542-552)	.25
3	Marquis Grissom (#553-563)	.25
4	Terry Pendleton (#564-574)	.25
5	Fernando Valenzuela (#575-585)	.25

1995 Collector's Choice Redemption Cards

These update cards were available only via a mail-in offer involving trade cards found in foil packs. Each trade card was redeemable for a specific 11-card set of players shown in their new uniforms as a result of rookie call-ups, trades and free agent signings. The cards are in the same format as the regular 1995 Collector's Choice issue. The update redemption cards are numbered by team nickname from Angels through Yankees, the numbers running contiguously from the body of the CC set.

		NM/M
Complete Set (55):		2.50
Common Player:		.10
531	Tony Phillips	.10
532	Dave Magadan	.10
533	Mike Gallego	.10
534	Dave Stewart	.10
535	Todd Stottlemyre	.10
536	David Cone	.10
537	Marquis Grissom	.10
538	Derrick May	.10
539	Joe Oliver	.10
540	Scott Cooper	.10
541	Ken Hill	.10
542	Howard Johnson	.10
543	Brian McRae	.10
544	Jaime Navarro	.10
545	Ozzie Timmons	.10
546	Roberto Kelly	.10
547	Hideo Nomo	1.50

No.	Player	Price
548	Shane Andrews	.10
549	Mark Grudzielanek	.10
550	Carlos Perez	.10
551	Henry Rodriguez	.10
552	Tony Tarasco	.10
553	Glenallen Hill	.10
554	Terry Mulholland	.10
555	Orel Hershiser	.10
556	Darren Bragg	.10
557	John Burkett	.10
558	Bobby Witt	.10
559	Terry Pendleton	.10
560	Andre Dawson	.50
561	Brett Butler	.10
562	Kevin Brown	.10
563	Doug Jones	.10
564	Andy Van Slyke	.10
565	Jody Reed	.10
566	Fernando Valenzuela	.10
567	Charlie Hayes	.10
568	Benji Gil	.10
569	Mark McLemore	.10
570	Mickey Tettleton	.10
571	Bob Tewksbury	.10
572	Rheal Cormier	.10
573	Vaughn Eshelman	.10
574	Mike Macfarlane	.10
575	Mark Whiten	.10
576	Benito Santiago	.10
577	Jason Bates	.10
578	Bill Swift	.10
579	Larry Walker	.10
580	Chad Curtis	.10
581	Bobby Higginson	.10
582	Marty Cordova	.10
583	Mike Devereaux	.10
584	John Kruk	.10
585	John Wetteland	.10

1995 Collector's Choice Crash the Game

These insert cards gave collectors a reason to follow box scores around the major leagues between June 18-October 1. Each of 20 noted home run hitters can be found with three different dates foil-stamped on the card front. If the player hit a home run on that day, the card could be redeemed for a set of 20 special prize cards. Stated odds of finding a You Crash the Game card were one in five packs. Most of the inserts are silver-foil enhanced, with about one in eight being found with gold foil. Winning cards are much scarcer than the others since they had to be mailed in for redemption.

		NM/M
Complete Set, Silver (20):		5.00
Common Player, Silver:		.15
Complete Set, Gold (20):		12.00
Common Player, Gold:		.35
CG1	Jeff Bagwell (July 30)	.25
CG1	Jeff Bagwell (Aug. 13)	.25
CG1	Jeff Bagwell (Sept. 28)	.25
CG2	Albert Belle (June 18)	.15
CG2	Albert Belle (Aug. 26)	.15
CG2	Albert Belle (Sept. 20)	.15
CG3	Barry Bonds (June 28)	1.00
CG3	Barry Bonds (July 9)	1.00
CG3	Barry Bonds (Sept. 6)	1.00
CG4	Jose Canseco (June 30)(Winner)	1.00
CG4	Jose Canseco (July 30)(Winner)	1.00
CG4	Jose Canseco (Sept. 3)	.35
CG5	Joe Carter (July 14)	.15
CG5	Joe Carter (Aug. 9)	.15
CG5	Joe Carter (Sept. 23)	.15
CG6	Cecil Fielder (Aug. 2)	.15
CG6	Cecil Fielder (Sept. 4)	.15
CG6	Cecil Fielder (Oct. 1)	.15
CG7	Juan Gonzalez (June 29)	.30
CG7	Juan Gonzalez (Aug. 13)	.30
CG7	Juan Gonzalez (Sept. 3)(Winner)	1.00
CG8	Ken Griffey Jr. (July 2)	.60
CG8	Ken Griffey Jr. (Sept. 15)	.60
CG8	Ken Griffey Jr. (Aug. 24)(Winner)	2.50
CG9	Bob Hamelin (July 23)	.15
CG9	Bob Hamelin (Aug. 1)	.15

CG9	Bob Hamelin (Sept. 29)	.15
CG10	David Justice (June 24)	.15
CG10	David Justice (July 25)	.15
CG10	David Justice (Sept. 17)	.15
CG11	Ryan Klesko (July 13)	.15
CG11	Ryan Klesko (Aug. 20)	.15
CG11	Ryan Klesko (Sept. 10)	.15
CG12	Fred McGriff (Aug. 25)	.15
CG12	Fred McGriff (Sept. 8)	.15
CG12	Fred McGriff (Sept. 24)	.15
CG13	Mark McGwire (July 23)	.75
CG13	Mark McGwire (Aug. 3)(Winner)	3.00
CG13	Mark McGwire (Sept. 27)	.75
CG14	Raul Mondesi (July 27)(Winner)	.75
CG14	Raul Mondesi (Aug. 13)	.15
CG14	Raul Mondesi (Sept. 15)(Winner)	.75
CG15	Mike Piazza (July 23)(Winner)	2.00
CG15	Mike Piazza (Aug. 27)(Winner)	2.00
CG15	Mike Piazza (Sept. 19)	.60
CG16	Manny Ramirez (June 21)	.35
CG16	Manny Ramirez (Aug. 13)	.35
CG16	Manny Ramirez (Sept. 26)	.35
CG17	Alex Rodriguez (Sept. 10)	.75
CG17	Alex Rodriguez (Sept. 18)	.75
CG17	Alex Rodriguez (Sept. 24)	.75
CG18	Gary Sheffield (July 5)	.30
CG18	Gary Sheffield (Aug. 13)	.30
CG18	Gary Sheffield (Sept. 4)(Winner)	1.00
CG19	Frank Thomas (July 26)	.50
CG19	Frank Thomas (Aug. 17)	.50
CG19	Frank Thomas (Sept. 23)	.50
CG20	Matt Williams (July 29)	.15
CG20	Matt Williams (Aug. 12)	.15
CG20	Matt Williams (Sept. 19)	.15

1995 Collector's Choice Crash Winners

These 20-card sets were awarded to collectors who redeemed "You Crash the Game" winners cards. A silver-foil enhanced set was sent to winners with silver redemption cards, a gold version was sent to gold winners. A $3 redemption fee was required. Fronts are similar to the game cards, except for the foil printing down the left side in the place of the game date. Instead of redemption rules on the back of award cards there are career highlights at left and a panel at right with the names of the players in the set.

		NM/M
Complete Set, Silver (20):		6.00
Complete Set, Gold (20):		25.00
Common Player, Silver:		.25
Common Player, Gold:		1.00
CR1	Jeff Bagwell	.60
CR2	Albert Belle	.25
CR3	Barry Bonds	2.50
CR4	Jose Canseco	.50
CR5	Joe Carter	.25
CR6	Cecil Fielder	.25
CR7	Juan Gonzalez	.50
CR8	Ken Griffey Jr.	1.50
CR9	Bob Hamelin	.25
CR10	Dave Justice	.25
CR11	Ryan Klesko	.25
CR12	Fred McGriff	.25
CR13	Mark McGwire	2.00
CR14	Raul Mondesi	.25
CR15	Mike Piazza	1.50
CR16	Manny Ramirez	.60
CR17	Alex Rodriguez	2.00
CR18	Gary Sheffield	.50
CR19	Frank Thomas	.60
CR20	Matt Williams	.25

1995 Collector's Choice Michael Jordan Jumbo

A limited edition of 10,000 of these 3" x 5" cards was produced for direct sales to consumers. The card is in the format of the 1995 Collector's Choice Rookie Class subset and includes a silver foil facsimile of Jordan's autograph on front. Back includes a serial number in the lower-right corner.

		NM/M
661	Michael Jordan	15.00

1995 Collector's Choice Ichiro Suzuki

This card was part of a set produced by Upper Deck's Collector's Choice brand in conjunction with a series of NBA games held in Japan. The cards were made for various members of the media, sports dignitaries, etc., to be used as personal business cards. Cards are in standard 2-1/2" x 3-1/2" format.

		NM/M
59	Ichiro Suzuki	1,000

1995 Collector's Choice/SE

The first Upper Deck baseball card issue for 1995 was this 265-card set which uses blue borders and a blue foil "Special Edition" trapezoidal logo to impart a premium look. The set opens with a Rookie Class subset of 25 cards on which the background has been rendered in orange hues. A series of six Record Pace cards, horizontal with blue and yellow backgrounds, immediately precedes the regular cards. Base cards in the set are arranged in team-alpha order. Front and back have large color photos, while backs offer complete major league stats. Interspersed within the teams are special cards with borderless front designs honoring players who won significant awards in the 1994 season. Another subset, Stat Leaders, pictures various players in a silver dollar-sized circle at the center of the card and lists the 1994 leaders in that category on the back. A dozen-card Fantasy Team subset near the end of the set lists on back the top-rated players at each position, picturing one of them on front, with a giant blue baseball. The set closes with five checklists honoring career highlights from the '94 season.

		NM/M
Complete Set (265):		17.50
Common Player:		.05
Silver Stars:		1.5X
Gold Stars:		8X
Pack (12):		1.25
Wax Box (36):		25.00
1	Alex Rodriguez	1.50
2	Derek Jeter	2.00
3	Dustin Hermanson	.05
4	Bill Pulsipher	.05
5	Terrell Wade	.05
6	Darren Dreifort	.05
7	LaTroy Hawkins	.05
8	Alex Ochoa	.05
9	Paul Wilson	.05
10	Ernie Young	.05
11	Alan Benes	.05
12	Garret Anderson	.05
13	Armando Benitez	.05
14	Robert Perez	.05
15	Herbert Perry	.05
16	Jose Silva	.05
17	Orlando Miller	.05
18	Russ Davis	.05
19	Jason Isringhausen	.05
20	Ray McDavid	.05
21	Duane Singleton	.05
22	Paul Shuey	.05
23	Steve Dunn	.05
24	Mike Lieberthal	.05
25	Chan Ho Park	.05
26	Ken Griffey Jr. (Record Pace)	.65
27	Tony Gwynn (Record Pace)	.40
28	Chuck Knoblauch (Record Pace)	.05
29	Frank Thomas (Record Pace)	.35
30	Matt Williams (Record Pace)	.05
31	Chili Davis	.05
32	Chad Curtis	.05
33	Brian Anderson	.05
34	Chuck Finley	.05
35	Tim Salmon	.05
36	Bo Jackson	.10
37	Doug Drabek	.05
38	Craig Biggio	.05
39	Ken Caminiti	.05
40	Jeff Bagwell	.65
41	Darryl Kile	.05
42	John Hudek	.05
43	Brian L. Hunter	.05
44	Dennis Eckersley	.60
45	Mark McGwire	1.50
46	Brent Gates	.05
47	Steve Karsay	.05
48	Rickey Henderson	.65
49	Terry Steinbach	.05
50	Ruben Sierra	.05
51	Roberto Alomar	.25
52	Carlos Delgado	.05
53	Alex Gonzalez	.05
54	Joe Carter	.05
55	Paul Molitor	.65
56	Juan Guzman	.05
57	John Olerud	.05
58	Shawn Green	.25
59	Tom Glavine	.05
60	Greg Maddux	.75
61	Roberto Kelly	.05
62	Ryan Klesko	.05
63	Javier Lopez	.05
64	Jose Oliva	.05
65	Fred McGriff	.05
66	Steve Avery	.05
67	Dave Justice	.05
68	Ricky Bones	.05
69	Cal Eldred	.05
70	Greg Vaughn	.05
71	Dave Nilsson	.05
72	Jose Valentin	.05
73	Matt Mieske	.05
74	Todd Zeile	.05
75	Ozzie Smith	.75
76	Bernard Gilkey	.05
77	Ray Lankford	.05
78	Bob Tewksbury	.05
79	Mark Whiten	.05
80	Gregg Jefferies	.05
81	Randy Myers	.05
82	Shawon Dunston	.05
83	Mark Grace	.05
84	Derrick May	.05
85	Sammy Sosa	.75
86	Steve Trachsel	.05
87	Brett Butler	.05
88	Delino DeShields	.05
89	Orel Hershiser	.05
90	Mike Piazza	1.00
91	Todd Hollandsworth	.05
92	Eric Karros	.05
93	Ramon Martinez	.05
94	Tim Wallach	.05
95	Raul Mondesi	.05
96	Larry Walker	.05
97	Wil Cordero	.05
98	Marquis Grissom	.05
99	Ken Hill	.05
100	Cliff Floyd	.05
101	Pedro J. Martinez	.65
102	John Wetteland	.05
103	Rondell White	.05
104	Moises Alou	.05
105	Barry Bonds	2.00
106	Darren Lewis	.05
107	Mark Portugal	.05
108	Matt Williams	.05
109	William Van Landingham	.05
110	Bill Swift	.05
111	Robby Thompson	.05
112	Rod Beck	.05
113	Darryl Strawberry	.05
114	Jim Thome	.50
115	Dave Winfield	.65
116	Eddie Murray	.65
117	Manny Ramirez	.75
118	Carlos Baerga	.05
119	Kenny Lofton	.05
120	Albert Belle	.05
121	Mark Clark	.05
122	Dennis Martinez	.05
123	Randy Johnson	.65
124	Jay Buhner	.05
125	Ken Griffey Jr.	1.00
125a	Ken Griffey Jr./OPS	1.50
126	Rich Gossage	.05
127	Tino Martinez	.05
128	Reggie Jefferson	.05
129	Edgar Martinez	.05
130	Gary Sheffield	.30
131	Pat Rapp	.05
132	Bret Barberie	.05
133	Chuck Carr	.05
134	Jeff Conine	.05
135	Charles Johnson	.05
136	Benito Santiago	.05
137	Matt Williams (Stat Leaders)	.05
138	Jeff Bagwell (Stat Leaders)	.35
139	Kenny Lofton (Stat Leaders)	.05
140	Tony Gwynn (Stat Leaders)	.40
141	Jimmy Key (Stat Leaders)	.05
142	Greg Maddux (Stat Leaders)	.40
143	Randy Johnson (Stat Leaders)	.25
144	Lee Smith (Stat Leaders)	.05
145	Bobby Bonilla	.05
146	Jason Jacome	.05
147	Jeff Kent	.05
148	Ryan Thompson	.05
149	Bobby Jones	.05
150	Bret Saberhagen	.05
151	John Franco	.05
152	Lee Smith	.05
153	Rafael Palmeiro	.60
154	Brady Anderson	.05
155	Cal Ripken Jr.	2.00
156	Jeffrey Hammonds	.05
157	Mike Mussina	.35
158	Chris Hoiles	.05
159	Ben McDonald	.05
160	Tony Gwynn	.75
161	Joey Hamilton	.05
162	Andy Benes	.05
163	Trevor Hoffman	.05
164	Phil Plantier	.05
165	Derek Bell	.05
166	Bip Roberts	.05
167	Eddie Williams	.05
168	Fernando Valenzuela	.05
169	Mariano Duncan	.05
170	Lenny Dykstra	.05
171	Darren Daulton	.05
172	Danny Jackson	.05
173	Bobby Munoz	.05
174	Doug Jones	.05
175	Jay Bell	.05
176	Zane Smith	.05
177	Jon Lieber	.05
178	Carlos Garcia	.05
179	Orlando Merced	.05
180	Andy Van Slyke	.05
181	Rick Helling	.05
182	Rusty Greer	.05
183	Kenny Rogers	.05
184	Will Clark	.05
185	Jose Canseco	.40
186	Juan Gonzalez	.35
187	Dean Palmer	.05
188	Ivan Rodriguez	.60
189	John Valentin	.05
190	Roger Clemens	.85
191	Aaron Sele	.05
192	Scott Cooper	.05
193	Mike Greenwell	.05
194	Mo Vaughn	.05
195	Andre Dawson	.25
196	Ron Gant	.05
197	Jose Rijo	.05
198	Bret Boone	.05
199	Deion Sanders	.10
200	Barry Larkin	.05
201	Hal Morris	.05
202	Reggie Sanders	.05
203	Kevin Mitchell	.05
204	Marvin Freeman	.05
205	Andres Galarraga	.05
206	Walt Weiss	.05
207	Charlie Hayes	.05
208	David Nied	.05
209	Dante Bichette	.05
210	David Cone	.05
211	Jeff Montgomery	.05
212	Felix Jose	.05
213	Mike Macfarlane	.05
214	Wally Joyner	.05
215	Bob Hamelin	.05
216	Brian McRae	.05
217	Kirk Gibson	.05
218	Lou Whitaker	.05
219	Chris Gomez	.05
220	Cecil Fielder	.05
221	Mickey Tettleton	.05
222	Travis Fryman	.05
223	Tony Phillips	.05
224	Rick Aguilera	.05
225	Scott Erickson	.05
226	Chuck Knoblauch	.05
227	Kent Hrbek	.05
228	Shane Mack	.05
229	Kevin Tapani	.05
230	Kirby Puckett	.75
231	Julio Franco	.05
232	Jack McDowell	.05
233	Jason Bere	.05
234	Alex Fernandez	.05
235	Frank Thomas	.65
236	Ozzie Guillen	.05
237	Robin Ventura	.05
238	Michael Jordan	2.00
239	Wilson Alvarez	.05
240	Don Mattingly	.85
241	Jim Abbott	.05
242	Jim Leyritz	.05
243	Paul O'Neill	.05
244	Melido Perez	.05
245	Wade Boggs	.75
246	Mike Stanley	.05
247	Danny Tartabull	.05
248	Jimmy Key	.05
249	Greg Maddux (Fantasy Team)	.40
250	Randy Johnson (Fantasy Team)	.20
251	Bret Saberhagen (Fantasy Team)	.05
252	John Wetteland (Fantasy Team)	.05
253	Mike Piazza (Fantasy Team)	.50
254	Jeff Bagwell (Fantasy Team)	.50
255	Craig Biggio (Fantasy Team)	.05
256	Matt Williams (Fantasy Team)	.05
257	Wil Cordero (Fantasy Team)	.05
258	Kenny Lofton (Fantasy Team)	.05
259	Barry Bonds (Fantasy Team)	.75
260	Dante Bichette (Fantasy Team)	.05
261	Checklist 1-53 (Ken Griffey Jr.)	.35
262	Checklist 54-106 (Goose Gossage)	.05
263	Checklist 107-159 (Cal Ripken Jr.)	.45
264	Checklist 160-212 (Kenny Rogers)	.05
265	Checklist 213-265 (John Valentin)	.05

Silver

The cards in this parallel edition feature the addition of a silver-foil facsimile autograph on the card front. Also, the blue SE logo and card borders have been replaced with silver on the chase cards, which are found on average of one per pack.

	NM/M
Common Player:	.15
Stars:	1.5X

Gold

Each of the cards in the SE issue can be found in a premium chase card version which replaces the blue border and SE logo with gold, and adds a gold-foil facsimile autograph to the front of the card. The gold-version SE inserts are found on average of one per 36 packs.

	NM/M
Common Player:	1.00
Stars:	8X

1996 Collector's Choice Promo

To introduce its base-brand set, Upper Deck issued a promotional sample card of Ken Griffey, Jr. Numbered 100 (he's #310 in the issued set), the back is overprinted "For Promotional Use Only".

		NM/M
100	Ken Griffey Jr.	4.00

1996 Collector's Choice

The third year for Collector's Choice includes 730 cards in two series with packs formatted in retail and hobby versions. The 280 regular player cards are joined by subsets of Rookie Class, International Flavor, Traditional Threads, Fantasy Team, Stat Leaders, Season Highlights, First Class, Arizona Fall League, Awards and Checklists. Packs feature a number of different insert sets including silver and gold signature parallel sets, interactive "You Make the Play" cards, four cards from the cross-brand Cal Ripken Collection and three postseason trade cards redeemable for 10-card sets recalling the League Championships and World Series. An additional 30 cards (#761-790) featuring traded players in their new uniforms was issued only in factory sets.

	NM/M
Unopened Fact. Set (790):	17.50
Complete Set: (760):	12.50
Traded Set (366T-395T):	3.00
Common Player:	.05
Series 1 Pack (12):	.75
Series 1 Wax Box (36):	22.50
Series 2 Pack (14):	1.00
Series 2 Wax Box (40):	25.00

#	Player	Price
1	Cal Ripken Jr.	2.00
2	Edgar Martinez, Tony Gwynn (1995 Stat Leaders)	.05
3	Albert Belle, Dante Bichette (1995 Stat Leaders)	.05
4	Albert Belle, Mo Vaughn, Dante Bichette (1995 Stat Leaders)	.05
5	Kenny Lofton, Quilvio Veras (1995 Stat Leaders)	.05
6	Mike Mussina, Greg Maddux (1995 Stat Leaders)	.40
7	Randy Johnson, Hideo Nomo (1995 Stat Leaders)	.25
8	Randy Johnson, Greg Maddux (1995 Stat Leaders)	.40
9	Jose Mesa, Randy Myers (1995 Stat Leaders)	.05
10	Johnny Damon (Rookie Class)	.35
11	Rick Krivda (Rookie Class)	.05
12	Roger Cedeno (Rookie Class)	.05
13	Angel Martinez (Rookie Class)	.05
14	Ariel Prieto (Rookie Class)	.05
15	John Wasdin (Rookie Class)	.05
16	Edwin Hurtado (Rookie Class)	.05
17	Lyle Mouton (Rookie Class)	.05
18	Chris Snopek (Rookie Class)	.05
19	Mariano Rivera (Rookie Class)	.15
20	Ruben Rivera (Rookie Class)	.05
21	Juan Castro RC (Rookie Class)	.05
22	Jimmy Haynes (Rookie Class)	.05
23	Bob Wolcott (Rookie Class)	.05
24	Brian Barber (Rookie Class)	.05
25	Frank Rodriguez (Rookie Class)	.05
26	Jesus Tavarez (Rookie Class)	.05
27	Glenn Dishman (Rookie Class)	.05
28	Jose Herrera (Rookie Class)	.05
29	Chan Ho Park (Rookie Class)	.05
30	Jason Isringhausen (Rookie Class)	.05
31	Doug Johns (Rookie Class)	.05
32	Gene Schall (Rookie Class)	.05
33	Kevin Jordan (Rookie Class)	.05
34	Matt Lawton RC (Rookie Class)	.10
35	Karim Garcia (Rookie Class)	.05
36	George Williams (Rookie Class)	.05
37	Orlando Palmeiro (Rookie Class)	.05
38	Jamie Brewington (Rookie Class)	.05
39	Robert Person (Rookie Class)	.05
40	Greg Maddux	.75
41	Marquis Grissom	.05
42	Chipper Jones	.75
43	David Justice	.05
44	Mark Lemke	.05
45	Fred McGriff	.05
46	Javy Lopez	.05
47	Mark Wohlers	.05
48	Jason Schmidt	.05
49	John Smoltz	.05
50	Curtis Goodwin	.05
51	Gregg Zaun	.05
52	Armando Benitez	.05
53	Manny Alexander	.05
54	Chris Hoiles	.05
55	Harold Baines	.05
56	Ben McDonald	.05
57	Scott Erickson	.05
58	Jeff Manto	.05
59	Luis Alicea	.05
60	Roger Clemens	.85
61	Rheal Cormier	.05
62	Vaughn Eshelman	.05
63	Zane Smith	.05
64	Mike Macfarlane	.05
65	Erik Hanson	.05
66	Tim Naehring	.05
67	Lee Tinsley	.05
68	Troy O'Leary	.05
69	Garret Anderson	.05
70	Chili Davis	.05
71	Jim Edmonds	.05
72	Troy Percival	.05
73	Mark Langston	.05
74	Spike Owen	.05
75	Tim Salmon	.05
76	Brian Anderson	.05
77	Lee Smith	.05
78	Jim Abbott	.05
79	Jim Bullinger	.05
80	Mark Grace	.05
81	Todd Zeile	.05
82	Kevin Foster	.05
83	Howard Johnson	.05
84	Brian McRae	.05
85	Randy Myers	.05
86	Jaime Navarro	.05
87	Luis Gonzalez	.05
88	Ozzie Timmons	.05
89	Wilson Alvarez	.05
90	Frank Thomas	.60
91	James Baldwin	.05
92	Ray Durham	.05
93	Alex Fernandez	.05
94	Ozzie Guillen	.05
95	Tim Raines	.05
96	Roberto Hernandez	.05
97	Lance Johnson	.05
98	John Kruk	.05
99	Mark Portugal	.05
100	Don Mattingly (Traditional Threads)	.65
101	Jose Canseco (Traditional Threads)	.15
102	Raul Mondesi (Traditional Threads)	.05
103	Cecil Fielder (Traditional Threads)	.05
104	Ozzie Smith (Traditional Threads)	.40
105	Frank Thomas (Traditional Threads)	.45
106	Sammy Sosa (Traditional Threads)	.50
107	Fred McGriff (Traditional Threads)	.05
108	Barry Bonds (Traditional Threads)	1.00
109	Thomas Howard	.05
110	Ron Gant	.05
111	Eddie Taubensee	.05
112	Hal Morris	.05
113	Jose Rijo	.05
114	Pete Schourek	.05
115	Reggie Sanders	.05
116	Benito Santiago	.05
117	Jeff Brantley	.05
118	Julian Tavarez	.05
119	Carlos Baerga	.05
120	Jim Thome	.40
121	Jose Mesa	.05
122	Dennis Martinez	.05
123	Dave Winfield	.60
124	Eddie Murray	.60
125	Manny Ramirez	.60
126	Paul Sorrento	.05
127	Kenny Lofton	.60
128	Eric Young	.05
129	Jason Bates	.05
130	Bret Saberhagen	.05
131	Andres Galarraga	.05
132	Joe Girardi	.05
133	John Vander Wal	.05
134	David Nied	.05
135	Dante Bichette	.05
136	Vinny Castilla	.05
137	Kevin Ritz	.05
138	Felipe Lira	.05
139	Joe Boever	.05
140	Cecil Fielder	.05
141	John Flaherty	.05
142	Kirk Gibson	.05
143	Brian Maxcy	.05
144	Lou Whitaker	.05
145	Alan Trammell	.05
146	Bobby Higginson	.05
147	Chad Curtis	.05
148	Quilvio Veras	.05
149	Jerry Browne	.05
150	Andre Dawson	.25
151	Robb Nen	.05
152	Greg Colbrunn	.05
153	Chris Hammond	.05
154	Kurt Abbott	.05
155	Charles Johnson	.05
156	Terry Pendleton	.05
157	Dave Weathers	.05
158	Mike Hampton	.05
159	Craig Biggio	.05
160	Jeff Bagwell	.60
161	Brian L. Hunter	.05
162	Mike Henneman	.05
163	Dave Magadan	.05
164	Shane Reynolds	.05
165	Derek Bell	.05
166	Orlando Miller	.05
167	James Mouton	.05
168	Melvin Bunch	.05
169	Tom Gordon	.05
170	Kevin Appier	.05
171	Tom Goodwin	.05
172	Greg Gagne	.05
173	Gary Gaetti	.05
174	Jeff Montgomery	.05
175	Jon Nunnally	.05
176	Michael Tucker	.05
177	Joe Vitiello	.05
178	Billy Ashley	.05
179	Tom Candiotti	.05
180	Hideo Nomo	.30
181	Chad Fonville	.05
182	Todd Hollandsworth	.05
183	Eric Karros	.05
184	Roberto Kelly	.05
185	Mike Piazza	1.00
186	Ramon Martinez	.05
187	Tim Wallach	.05
188	Jeff Cirillo	.05
189	Sid Roberson	.05
190	Kevin Seitzer	.05
191	Mike Fetters	.05
192	Steve Sparks	.05
193	Matt Mieske	.05
194	Joe Oliver	.05
195	B.J. Surhoff	.05
196	Alberto Reyes	.05
197	Fernando Vina	.05
198	LaTroy Hawkins	.05
199	Marty Cordova	.05
200	Kirby Puckett	.75
201	Brad Radke	.05
202	Pedro Munoz	.05
203	Scott Klingenbeck	.05
204	Pat Meares	.05
205	Scott Stahoviak	.05
206	Dave Stevens	.05
207	Shane Andrews	.05
208	Moises Alou	.05
209	David Segui	.05
210	Cliff Floyd	.05
211	Carlos Perez	.05
212	Mark Grudzielanek	.05
213	Butch Henry	.05
214	Rondell White	.05
215	Mel Rojas	.05
216	Mel Rojas	.05
217	Ugueth Urbina	.05
218	Edgardo Alfonzo	.05
219	Carl Everett	.05
220	John Franco	.05
221	Todd Hundley	.05
222	Bobby Jones	.05
223	Bill Pulsipher	.05
224	Rico Brogna	.05
225	Jeff Kent	.05
226	Chris Jones	.05
227	Butch Huskey	.05
228	Robert Eenhoorn	.05
229	Sterling Hitchcock	.05
230	Wade Boggs	.75
231	Derek Jeter	2.00
232	Tony Fernandez	.05
233	Jack McDowell	.05
234	Andy Pettitte	.35
235	David Cone	.05
236	Mike Stanley	.05
237	Don Mattingly	.85
238	Geronimo Berroa	.05
239	Scott Brosius	.05
240	Rickey Henderson	.60
241	Terry Steinbach	.05
242	Mike Gallego	.05
243	Jason Giambi	.40
244	Steve Ontiveros	.05
245	Dennis Eckersley	.50
246	Dave Stewart	.05
247	Don Wengert	.05
248	Paul Quantrill	.05
249	Ricky Bottalico	.05
250	Kevin Stocker	.05
251	Lenny Dykstra	.05
252	Tony Longmire	.05
253	Tyler Green	.05
254	Mike Mimbs	.05
255	Charlie Hayes	.05
256	Mickey Morandini	.05
257	Heathcliff Slocumb	.05
258	Jeff King	.05
259	Midre Cummings	.05
260	Mark Johnson	.05
261	Freddy Garcia	.05
262	Jon Lieber	.05
263	Esteban Loaiza	.05
264	Danny Miceli	.05
265	Orlando Merced	.05
266	Denny Neagle	.05
267	Steve Parris	.05
268	Fantasy Team '95 (Greg Maddux)	.35
269	Fantasy Team '95 (Randy Johnson)	.20
270	Fantasy Team '95 (Hideo Nomo)	.15
271	Fantasy Team '95 (Jose Mesa)	.05
272	Fantasy Team '95 (Mike Piazza)	.60
273	Fantasy Team '95 (Mo Vaughn)	.05
274	Fantasy Team '95 (Craig Biggio)	.05
275	Fantasy Team '95 (Edgar Martinez)	.05
276	Fantasy Team '95 (Barry Larkin)	.05
277	Fantasy Team '95 (Sammy Sosa)	.50
278	Fantasy Team '95 (Dante Bichette)	.05
279	Fantasy Team '95 (Albert Belle)	.05
280	Ozzie Smith	.75
281	Mark Sweeney	.05
282	Terry Bradshaw	.05
283	Allen Battle	.05
284	Danny Jackson	.05
285	Tom Henke	.05
286	Scott Cooper	.05
287	Tripp Cromer	.05
288	Bernard Gilkey	.05
289	Brian Jordan	.05
290	Tony Gwynn	.75
291	Brad Ausmus	.05
292	Bryce Florie	.05
293	Andres Berumen	.05
294	Ken Caminiti	.05
295	Bip Roberts	.05
296	Trevor Hoffman	.05
297	Roberto Petagine	.05
298	Jody Reed	.05
299	Fernando Valenzuela	.05
300	Barry Bonds	2.00
301	Mark Leiter	.05
302	Mark Carreon	.05
303	Royce Clayton	.05
304	Kirt Manwaring	.05
305	Glenallen Hill	.05
306	Deion Sanders	.10
307	Joe Rosselli	.05
308	Robby Thompson	.05
309	William Van Landingham	.05
310	Ken Griffey Jr.	1.00
311	Bobby Ayala	.05
312	Joey Cora	.05
313	Mike Blowers	.05
314	Darren Bragg	.05
315	Randy Johnson	.60
316	Alex Rodriguez	1.50
317	Andy Benes	.05
318	Tino Martinez	.05
319	Dan Wilson	.05
320	Will Clark	.05
321	Jeff Frye	.05
322	Benji Gil	.05
323	Rick Helling	.05
324	Mark McLemore	.05
325	Dave Nilsson	.05
326	Larry Walker (International Flavor)	.05
327	Jose Canseco (International Flavor)	.15
328	Raul Mondesi (International Flavor)	.05
329	Manny Ramirez (International Flavor)	.30
330	Robert Eenhoorn (International Flavor)	.05
331	Chili Davis (International Flavor)	.05
332	Hideo Nomo (International Flavor)	.15
333	Benji Gil (International Flavor)	.05
334	Fernando Valenzuela (International Flavor)	.05
335	Dennis Martinez (International Flavor)	.05
336	Roberto Kelly (International Flavor)	.05
337	Carlos Baerga (International Flavor)	.05
338	Juan Gonzalez (International Flavor)	.15
339	Roberto Alomar (International Flavor)	.10
340	Chan Ho Park (International Flavor)	.05
341	Andres Galarraga (International Flavor)	.05
342	Midre Cummings (International Flavor)	.05
343	Otis Nixon	.05
344	Jeff Russell	.05
345	Ivan Rodriguez	.50
346	Mickey Tettleton	.05
347	Bob Tewksbury	.05
348	Domingo Cedeno	.05
349	Lance Parrish	.05
350	Joe Carter	.05
351	Devon White	.05
352	Carlos Delgado	.35
353	Alex Gonzalez	.05
354	Darren Hall	.05
355	Paul Molitor	.60
356	Al Leiter	.05
357	Randy Knorr	.05
358	Checklist 1-46 (12-player Astros-Padres trade)	.05
359	Checklist 47-92 (Hideo Nomo)	.15
360	Checklist 93-138 (Ramon Martinez)	.05
361	Checklist 139-184 (Robin Ventura)	.05
362	Checklist 185-230 (Cal Ripken Jr.)	.30
363	Checklist 231-275 (Ken Caminiti)	.05
364	Checklist 276-320 (Eddie Murray)	.20
365	Checklist 321-365 (Randy Johnson)	.15
366	A.L. Divisional Series (Tony Pena)	.10
367	A.L. Divisional Series (Jim Thome)	.25
368	A.L. Divisional Series (Don Mattingly)	.60
369	A.L. Divisional Series (Jim Leyritz)	.10
370	A.L. Divisional Series (Ken Griffey Jr.)	.60
371	A.L. Divisional Series (Edgar Martinez)	.10
372	N.L. Divisional Series (Pete Schourek)	.10
373	N.L. Divisional Series (Mark Lewis)	.10
374	N.L. Divisional Series (Chipper Jones)	.50
375	N.L. Divisional Series (Fred McGriff)	.10
376	N.L. Championship Series (Javy Lopez)	.10
377	N.L. Championship Series (Fred McGriff)	.10
378	N.L. Championship Series (Charlie O'Brien)	.10
379	N.L. Championship Series (Mike Devereaux)	.10
380	N.L. Championship Series (Mark Wohlers)	.10
381	A.L. Championship Series (Bob Wolcott)	.10
382	A.L. Championship Series (Manny Ramirez)	.25
383	A.L. Championship Series (Jay Buhner)	.10
384	A.L. Championship Series (Orel Hershiser)	.10
385	A.L. Championship Series (Kenny Lofton)	.10
386	World Series (Greg Maddux)	.50
387	World Series (Javy Lopez)	.10
388	World Series (Kenny Lofton)	.10
389	World Series (Eddie Murray)	.10
390	World Series (Luis Polonia)	.10
391	World Series (Pedro Borbon)	.10
392	World Series (Jim Thome)	.25
393	World Series (Orel Hershiser)	.10
394	World Series (David Justice)	.10
395	World Series (Tom Glavine)	.10
396	Braves Team Checklist (Greg Maddux)	.25
397	Mets Team Checklist (Brett Butler)	.05
398	Phillies Team Checklist (Darren Daulton)	.05
399	Marlins Team Checklist (Gary Sheffield)	.05
400	Expos Team Checklist (Moises Alou)	.05
401	Reds Team Checklist (Barry Larkin)	.05
402	Astros Team Checklist (Jeff Bagwell)	.20
403	Cubs Team Checklist (Sammy Sosa)	.35
404	Cardinals Team Checklist (Ozzie Smith)	.25
405	Pirates Team Checklist (Jeff King)	.05
406	Dodgers Team Checklist (Mike Piazza)	.50
407	Rockies Team Checklist (Dante Bichette)	.05
408	Padres Team Checklist (Tony Gwynn)	.25
409	Giants Team Checklist (Barry Bonds)	.45
410	Indians Team Checklist (Kenny Lofton)	.05
411	Royals Team Checklist (Jon Nunnally)	.05
412	White Sox Team Checklist (Frank Thomas)	.20
413	Brewers Team Checklist (Greg Vaughn)	.05
414	Twins Team Checklist (Paul Molitor)	.20
415	Mariners Team Checklist (Ken Griffey Jr.)	.35
416	Angels Team Checklist (Jim Edmonds)	.05
417	Rangers Team Checklist (Juan Gonzalez)	.15
418	Athletics Team Checklist (Mark McGwire)	.75
419	Red Sox Team Checklist (Roger Clemens)	.30
420	Yankees Team Checklist (Wade Boggs)	.35
421	Orioles Team Checklist (Cal Ripken Jr.)	.40
422	Tigers Team Checklist (Cecil Fielder)	.05
423	Blue Jays Team Checklist (Joe Carter)	.05
424	Osvaldo Fernandez RC (Rookie Class)	.15
425	Billy Wagner (Rookie Class)	.05
426	George Arias (Rookie Class)	.05
427	Mendy Lopez (Rookie Class)	.05
428	Jeff Suppan (Rookie Class)	.05
429	Rey Ordonez (Rookie Class)	.05
430	Brooks Kieschnick (Rookie Class)	.05
431	Raul Ibanez RC (Rookie Class)	.05
432	Livan Hernandez RC (Rookie Class)	.20
433	Shannon Stewart (Rookie Class)	.05
434	Steve Cox (Rookie Class)	.05
435	Trey Beamon (Rookie Class)	.05
436	Sergio Nunez (Rookie Class)	.05
437	Jermaine Dye (Rookie Class)	.05
438	Mike Sweeney RC (Rookie Class)	.45
439	Richard Hidalgo (Rookie Class)	.05
440	Todd Greene (Rookie Class)	.05
441	Robert Smith RC (Rookie Class)	.05
442	Rafael Orellano (Rookie Class)	.05
443	Wilton Guerrero RC (Rookie Class)	.05
444	David Doster RC (Rookie Class)	.05
445	Jason Kendall (Rookie Class)	.05
446	Edgar Renteria (Rookie Class)	.05
447	Scott Spiezio (Rookie Class)	.05
448	Jay Canizaro (Rookie Class)	.05
449	Enrique Wilson (Rookie Class)	.05
450	Bob Abreu (Rookie Class)	.10
451	Dwight Smith	.05

No.	Player	Price
452	Jeff Blauser	.05
453	Steve Avery	.05
454	Brad Clontz	.05
455	Tom Glavine	.20
456	Mike Mordecai	.05
457	Rafael Belliard	.05
458	Greg McMichael	.05
459	Pedro Borbon	.05
460	Ryan Klesko	.05
461	Terrell Wade	.05
462	Brady Anderson	.05
463	Roberto Alomar	.20
464	Bobby Bonilla	.05
465	Mike Mussina	.40
466	Cesar Devarez RC	.05
467	Jeffrey Hammonds	.05
468	Mike Devereaux	.05
469	B.J. Surhoff	.05
470	Rafael Palmeiro	.50
471	John Valentin	.05
472	Mike Greenwell	.05
473	Dwayne Hosey	.05
474	Tim Wakefield	.05
475	Jose Canseco	.35
476	Aaron Sele	.05
477	Stan Belinda	.05
478	Mike Stanley	.05
479	Jamie Moyer	.05
480	Mo Vaughn	.05
481	Randy Velarde	.05
482	Gary DiSarcina	.05
483	Jorge Fabregas	.05
484	Rex Hudler	.05
485	Chuck Finley	.05
486	Tim Wallach	.05
487	Eduardo Perez	.05
488	Scott Sanderson	.05
489	J.T. Snow	.05
490	Sammy Sosa	.75
491	Terry Adams	.05
492	Matt Franco	.05
493	Scott Servais	.05
494	Frank Castillo	.05
495	Ryne Sandberg	.75
496	Rey Sanchez	.05
497	Steve Trachsel	.05
498	Jose Hernandez	.05
499	Dave Martinez	.05
500	Babe Ruth (First Class)	1.00
501	Ty Cobb (First Class)	.50
502	Walter Johnson (First Class)	.10
503	Christy Mathewson (First Class)	.10
504	Honus Wagner (First Class)	.25
505	Robin Ventura	.05
506	Jason Bere	.05
507	Mike Cameron RC	.25
508	Ron Karkovice	.05
509	Matt Karchner	.05
510	Harold Baines	.05
511	Kirk McCaskill	.05
512	Larry Thomas	.05
513	Danny Tartabull	.05
514	Steve Gibralter	.05
515	Bret Boone	.05
516	Jeff Branson	.05
517	Kevin Jarvis	.05
518	Xavier Hernandez	.05
519	Eric Owens	.05
520	Barry Larkin	.05
521	Dave Burba	.05
522	John Smiley	.05
523	Paul Assenmacher	.05
524	Chad Ogea	.05
525	Orel Hershiser	.05
526	Alan Embree	.05
527	Tony Pena	.05
528	Omar Vizquel	.05
529	Mark Clark	.05
530	Albert Belle	.05
531	Charles Nagy	.05
532	Herbert Perry	.05
533	Darren Holmes	.05
534	Ellis Burks	.05
535	Bill Swift	.05
536	Armando Reynoso	.05
537	Curtis Leskanic	.05
538	Quinton McCracken	.05
539	Steve Reed	.05
540	Larry Walker	.05
541	Walt Weiss	.05
542	Bryan Rekar	.05
543	Tony Clark	.05
544	Steve Rodriguez	.05
545	C.J. Nitkowski	.05
546	Todd Steverson	.05
547	Jose Lima	.05
548	Phil Nevin	.05
549	Chris Gomez	.05
550	Travis Fryman	.05
551	Mark Lewis	.05
552	Alex Arias	.05
553	Marc Valdes	.05
554	Kevin Brown	.05
555	Jeff Conine	.05
556	John Burkett	.05
557	Devon White	.05
558	Pat Rapp	.05
559	Jay Powell	.05
560	Gary Sheffield	.30
561	Jim Dougherty	.05
562	Todd Jones	.05
563	Tony Eusebio	.05
564	Darryl Kile	.05
565	Doug Drabek	.05
566	Mike Simms	.05

No.	Player	Price
567	Derrick May	.05
568	Donne Wall RC	.05
569	Greg Swindell	.05
570	Jim Pittsley	.05
571	Bob Hamelin	.05
572	Mark Gubicza	.05
573	Chris Haney	.05
574	Keith Lockhart	.05
575	Mike Macfarlane	.05
576	Les Norman	.05
577	Joe Randa	.05
578	Chris Stynes	.05
579	Greg Gagne	.05
580	Raul Mondesi	.05
581	Delino DeShields	.05
582	Pedro Astacio	.05
583	Antonio Osuna	.05
584	Brett Butler	.05
585	Todd Worrell	.05
586	Mike Blowers	.05
587	Felix Rodriguez	.05
588	Ismael Valdes	.05
589	Ricky Bones	.05
590	Greg Vaughn	.05
591	Mark Loretta	.05
592	Cal Eldred	.05
593	Chuck Carr	.05
594	Dave Nilsson	.05
595	John Jaha	.05
596	Scott Karl	.05
597	Pat Listach	.05
598	Jose Valentin RC	.05
599	Mike Trombley	.05
600	Paul Molitor	.60
601	Dave Hollins	.05
602	Ron Coomer	.05
603	Matt Walbeck	.05
604	Roberto Kelly	.05
605	Rick Aguilera	.05
606	Pat Mahomes	.05
607	Jeff Reboulet	.05
608	Rich Becker	.05
609	Tim Scott	.05
610	Pedro J. Martinez	.60
611	Kirk Rueter	.05
612	Tavo Alvarez	.05
613	Yamil Benitez	.05
614	Darrin Fletcher	.05
615	Mike Lansing	.05
616	Henry Rodriguez	.05
617	Tony Tarasco	.05
618	Alex Ochoa	.05
619	Tim Bogar	.05
620	Bernard Gilkey	.05
621	Dave Mlicki	.05
622	Brent Mayne	.05
623	Ryan Thompson	.05
624	Pete Harnisch	.05
625	Lance Johnson	.05
626	Jose Vizcaino	.05
627	Doug Henry	.05
628	Scott Kamieniecki	.05
629	Jim Leyritz	.05
630	Ruben Sierra	.05
631	Pat Kelly	.05
632	Joe Girardi	.05
633	John Wetteland	.05
634	Melido Perez	.05
635	Paul O'Neill	.05
636	Jorge Posada	.05
637	Bernie Williams	.05
638	Mark Acre	.05
639	Mike Bordick	.05
640	Mark McGwire	1.50
641	Fausto Cruz	.05
642	Ernie Young	.05
643	Todd Van Poppel	.05
644	Craig Paquette	.05
645	Brent Gates	.05
646	Pedro Munoz	.05
647	Andrew Lorraine	.05
648	Sid Fernandez	.05
649	Jim Eisenreich	.05
650	Johnny Damon (Arizona Fall League)	.30
651	Dustin Hermanson (Arizona Fall League)	.05
652	Joe Randa (Arizona Fall League)	.05
653	Michael Tucker (Arizona Fall League)	.05
654	Alan Benes (Arizona Fall League)	.05
655	Chad Fonville (Arizona Fall League)	.05
656	David Bell (Arizona Fall League)	.05
657	Jon Nunnally (Arizona Fall League)	.05
658	Chan Ho Park (Arizona Fall League)	.05
659	LaTroy Hawkins (Arizona Fall League)	.05
660	Jamie Brewington (Arizona Fall League)	.05
661	Quinton McCracken (Arizona Fall League)	.05
662	Tim Unroe (Arizona Fall League)	.05
663	Jeff Ware (Arizona Fall League)	.05
664	Todd Greene (Arizona Fall League)	.05
665	Andrew Lorraine (Arizona Fall League)	.05
666	Ernie Young (Arizona Fall League)	.05
667	Toby Borland	.05
668	Lenny Webster	.05
669	Benito Santiago	.05
670	Gregg Jefferies	.05

No.	Player	Price
671	Darren Daulton	.05
672	Curt Schilling	.25
673	Mark Whiten	.05
674	Todd Zeile	.05
675	Jay Bell	.05
676	Paul Wagner	.05
677	Dave Clark	.05
678	Nelson Liriano	.05
679	Ramon Morel	.05
680	Charlie Hayes	.05
681	Angelo Encarnacion	.05
682	Al Martin	.05
683	Jacob Brumfield	.05
684	Mike Kingery	.05
685	Carlos Garcia	.05
686	Tom Pagnozzi	.05
687	David Bell	.05
688	Todd Stottlemyre	.05
689	Jose Oliva	.05
690	Ray Lankford	.05
691	Mike Morgan	.05
692	John Frascatore	.05
693	John Mabry	.05
694	Mark Petkovsek	.05
695	Alan Benes	.05
696	Steve Finley	.05
697	Marc Newfield	.05
698	Andy Ashby	.05
699	Marc Kroon	.05
700	Wally Joyner	.05
701	Joey Hamilton	.05
702	Dustin Hermanson	.05
703	Scott Sanders	.05
704	Marty Cordova (Award Win.-ROY)	.05
705	Hideo Nomo (Award Win.-ROY)	.15
706	Mo Vaughn (Award Win.-MVP)	.05
707	Barry Larkin (Award Win.-MVP)	.05
708	Randy Johnson (Award Win.-CY)	.20
709	Greg Maddux (Award Win.-CY)	.35
710	Mark McGwire (Award-Comeback)	.75
711	Ron Gant (Award-Comeback)	.05
712	Andujar Cedeno	.05
713	Brian Johnson	.05
714	J.R. Phillips	.05
715	Rod Beck	.05
716	Sergio Valdez	.05
717	Marvin Benard RC	.25
718	Steve Scarsone	.05
719	Rich Aurilia RC	.10
720	Matt Williams	.05
721	John Patterson	.05
722	Shawn Estes	.05
723	Russ Davis	.05
724	Rich Amaral	.05
725	Edgar Martinez	.05
726	Norm Charlton	.05
727	Paul Sorrento	.05
728	Luis Sojo	.05
729	Arquimedez Pozo	.05
730	Jay Buhner	.05
731	Chris Bosio	.05
732	Chris Widger	.05
733	Kevin Gross	.05
734	Darren Oliver	.05
735	Dean Palmer	.05
736	Matt Whiteside	.05
737	Luis Ortiz	.05
738	Roger Pavlik	.05
739	Damon Buford	.05
740	Juan Gonzalez	.30
741	Rusty Greer	.05
742	Lou Frazier	.05
743	Pat Hentgen	.05
744	Tomas Perez	.05
745	Juan Guzman	.05
746	Otis Nixon	.05
747	Robert Perez	.05
748	Ed Sprague	.05
749	Tony Castillo	.05
750	John Olerud	.10
751	Shawn Green	.05
752	Jeff Ware	.05
753	Checklist 396-441/Blake St. Bombers (Dante Bichette, Larry Walker, Andres Galarraga, Vinny Castilla)	.05
754	Checklist 442-487 (Greg Maddux)	.25
755	Checklist 488-533 (Marty Cordova)	.05
756	Checklist 534-579 (Ozzie Smith)	.35
757	Checklist 580-625 (John Vander Wal)	.05
758	Checklist 626-670 (Andres Galarraga)	.05
759	Checklist 671-715 (Frank Thomas)	.25
760	Checklist 716-760 (Tony Gwynn)	.25
761	Randy Myers	.10
762	Kent Mercker	.10
763	David Wells	.10
764	Tom Gordon	.10
765	Wil Cordero	.10
766	Dave Magadan	.10
767	Doug Jones	.10
768	Kevin Tapani	.10
769	Curtis Goodwin	.10
770	Julio Franco	.10
771	Jack McDowell	.10
772	Al Leiter	.10

No.	Player	Price
773	Sean Berry	.10
774	Bip Roberts	.10
775	Jose Offerman	.10
776	Ben McDonald	.10
777	Dan Serafini	.10
778	Ryan McGuire	.10
779	Tim Raines	.10
780	Tino Martinez	.10
781	Kenny Rogers	.10
782	Bob Tewksbury	.10
783	Rickey Henderson	.60
784	Ron Gant	.10
785	Gary Gaetti	.10
786	Andy Benes	.10
787	Royce Clayton	.10
788	Darryl Hamilton	.10
789	Ken Hill	.10
790	Erik Hanson	.10

Silver Signature

A silver border instead of white, and a facsimile autograph in silver ink on the card front differentiate these parallel insert cards from the regular-issue Collector's Choice. The inserts are seeded at the rate of one per pack.

	NM/M
Common Player:	.10
Stars:	1.5X

Gold Signature

This insert set parallels each card in the regular Collector's Choice set. Found on average of one per 35 packs, the cards are nearly identical to the regular version except for the presence of a facsimile autograph in gold ink on the front and gold, instead of white, borders.

	NM/M
Common Player:	1.00
Stars:	10X

1996 Collector's Choice A Cut Above

This 10-card set highlights the career of Ken Griffey Jr. The front has a color photo with "The Griffey Years" printed in the left border and a title in the right border. Die-cut gold-foil tops have "A CUT ABOVE" in black. Backs have a portrait photo on a marbled border and a narrative. This set was inserted one per six-card Wal-Mart exclusive pack.

	NM/M
Complete Set (10):	8.00
Common Card:	1.00
CA1	Ken Griffey Jr. (Teenage Rookie)	1.00
CA2	Ken Griffey Jr. (Great Defense)	1.00
CA3	Ken Griffey Jr. (Fun-Loving)	1.00
CA4	Ken Griffey Jr. (All-Star Games)	1.00
CA5	Ken Griffey Jr. ('93 Season)	1.00
CA7	Ken Griffey Jr. ('94 Season)	1.00
CA8	Ken Griffey Jr. ('95 Season)	1.00
CA9	Ken Griffey Jr. ('95 Postseason)	1.00
CA10	Ken Griffey Jr. ('96: A Look Ahead)	1.00

Crash the Game

For a second season, UD continued its interactive chase card series, "You Crash the Game." At a ratio of about one per five packs for a silver version and one per 49 packs for a gold version, cards of the game's top sluggers can be found bearing one of three date ranges representing a three- or four-game series in which that player was scheduled to play during the 1996 season. If the player hit a home run during the series shown on the card, the card could be redeemed (for $1.75) by mail for a "Super Premium" wood-and-plastic card of the player. Both silver and gold Crash cards feature silver and red prismatic foil behind the player action photo. Silver versions have the Crash logo, series dates and player ID in silver foil on front; those details are in gold foil on the gold cards. Backs have contest rules printed on a gray (silver) or yellow (gold) background. Card numbers are preceded by a "CG" prefix. Cards were redeemable only until Nov. 25, 1996. Winning cards are indicated with an asterisk; they would be in shorter supply than those which could not be redeemed.

	NM/M
Complete Set (90):	75.00
Common Silver Player:	.50
Golds:	2X
1a	Chipper Jones (July 11-14*)	2.50
1b	Chipper Jones (Aug. 27-29*)	2.50
1c	Chipper Jones (Sept. 19-23)	1.50
2a	Fred McGriff (July 1-3)	.50
2b	Fred McGriff (Aug. 30-Sept. 1)	.50
2c	Fred McGriff (Sept. 10-12*)	1.00
3a	Rafael Palmeiro (July 4-7*)	1.75
3b	Rafael Palmeiro (Aug. 29-Sept. 1)	.75
3c	Rafael Palmeiro (Sept. 26-29)	.75
4a	Cal Ripken Jr. (June 27-30)	2.50
4b	Cal Ripken Jr. (July 25-28*)	5.00
4c	Cal Ripken Jr. (Sept. 2-4)	2.50
5a	Jose Canseco (June 27-30)	.65
5b	Jose Canseco (July 11-14*)	1.50
5c	Jose Canseco (Aug. 23-25)	.65
6a	Mo Vaughn (June 21-23*)	1.00
6b	Mo Vaughn (July 18-21*)	1.00
6c	Mo Vaughn (Sept. 20-22)	.50
7a	Jim Edmonds (July 18-21*)	1.00
7b	Jim Edmonds (Aug. 16-18*)	1.00

7c	Jim Edmonds (Sept. 20-22)	.50
8a	Tim Salmon (June 20-23)	.50
8b	Tim Salmon (July 30-Aug. 1)	.50
8c	Tim Salmon (Sept. 9-12)	.50
9a	Sammy Sosa (July 4-7*)	2.50
9b	Sammy Sosa (Aug. 1-4*)	2.50
9c	Sammy Sosa (Sept. 2-4)	1.50
10a	Frank Thomas (June 27-30)	1.00
10b	Frank Thomas (July 4-7)	1.00
10c	Frank Thomas (Sept. 2-4*)	2.00
11a	Albert Belle (June 25-26)	.50
11b	Albert Belle (Aug. 2-5*)	1.00
11c	Albert Belle (Sept. 6-8)	.50
12a	Manny Ramirez (July 18-21*)	2.00
12b	Manny Ramirez (Aug. 26-28)	1.00
12c	Manny Ramirez (Sept. 9-12*)	2.00
13a	Jim Thome (June 27-30)	.75
13b	Jim Thome (July 4-7*)	.75
13c	Jim Thome (Sept. 23-25)	.75
14a	Dante Bichette (July 11-14*)	1.00
14b	Dante Bichette (Aug. 9-11)	.50
14c	Dante Bichette (Sept. 9-12)	.50
15a	Vinny Castilla (July 1-3)	.50
15b	Vinny Castilla (Aug. 23-25*)	1.00
15c	Vinny Castilla (Sept. 13-15*)	1.00
16a	Larry Walker (June 24-26)	.50
16b	Larry Walker (July 18-21)	.50
16c	Larry Walker (Sept. 27-29)	.50
17a	Cecil Fielder (June 27-30)	.50
17b	Cecil Fielder (July 30-Aug. 1*)	1.00
17c	Cecil Fielder (Sept. 17-19*)	1.00
18a	Gary Sheffield (July 4-7)	.65
18b	Gary Sheffield (Aug. 2-4)	.65
18c	Gary Sheffield (Sept. 5-8*)	1.50
19a	Jeff Bagwell (July 4-7*)	2.00
19b	Jeff Bagwell (Aug. 16-18)	1.00
19c	Jeff Bagwell (Sept. 13-15)	1.00
20a	Eric Karros (July 4-7*)	1.00
20b	Eric Karros (Aug. 13-15*)	1.00
20c	Eric Karros (Sept. 16-18)	.50
21a	Mike Piazza (June 27-30*)	3.00
21b	Mike Piazza (July 26-28)	1.75
21c	Mike Piazza (Sept. 12-15*)	3.00
22a	Ken Caminiti (July 11-14*)	1.00
22b	Ken Caminiti (Aug. 16-18*)	1.00
22c	Ken Caminiti (Sept. 19-22*)	1.00
23a	Barry Bonds (June 27-30*)	5.00
23b	Barry Bonds (July 22-24)	2.50
23c	Barry Bonds (Sept. 24-26)	2.50
24a	Matt Williams (July 11-14*)	1.00
24b	Matt Williams (Aug. 19-21)	.50
24c	Matt Williams (Sept. 27-29)	.50
25a	Jay Buhner (June 20-23)	.50
25b	Jay Buhner (July 25-28)	.50
25c	Jay Buhner (Aug. 29-Sept. 1*)	1.00
26a	Ken Griffey Jr. (July 18-21*)	3.00
26b	Ken Griffey Jr. (Aug. 16-18*)	3.00
26c	Ken Griffey Jr. (Sept. 20-22*)	3.00
27a	Ron Gant (June 24-27*)	1.00
27b	Ron Gant (July 11-14*)	1.00
27c	Ron Gant (Sept. 27-29*)	1.00
28a	Juan Gonzalez (June 28-30*)	1.25
28b	Juan Gonzalez (July 15-17*)	1.25
28c	Juan Gonzalez (Aug. 6-8)	.60
29a	Mickey Tettleton (July 4-7*)	1.00
29b	Mickey Tettleton (Aug. 6-8)	.50
29c	Mickey Tettleton (Sept. 6-8*)	1.00
30a	Joe Carter (June 25-27)	.50
30b	Joe Carter (Aug. 5-8)	.50
30c	Joe Carter (Sept. 23-25)	.50

1996 Collector's Choice Crash Winners

Collectors who held "You Crash The Game" insert cards with date ranges on which the pictured player hit a home run could redeem them (for $1.75 per card) for a premium card of that player. The redemption cards have a layer of clear plastic bonded to a wood-laminate front. Within a starburst cutout at center is the player photo with a red background. Cards have a Crash/Game logo in the lower-right corner, in either silver or gold, depending on which winning card was submitted for exchange. Backs have 1995 and career stats along with licensing and copyright data. There are no winning cards of Tim Salmon, Larry Walker or Joe Carter.

	NM/M
Complete Set (27):	35.00
Common Player:	1.00
Golds:	2X
CR1 Chipper Jones	2.50
CR2 Fred McGriff	1.00
CR3 Rafael Palmeiro	1.75
CR4 Cal Ripken Jr.	4.00
CR5 Jose Canseco	1.50
CR6 Mo Vaughn	1.00
CR7 Jim Edmonds	1.00
CR8 Sammy Sosa	2.50
CR9 Frank Thomas	2.00
CR10 Albert Belle	1.00
CR11 Manny Ramirez	2.00
CR12 Jim Thome	1.50
CR13 Dante Bichette	1.00
CR14 Vinny Castilla	1.00
CR15 Cecil Fielder	1.00
CR16 Gary Sheffield	1.50
CR17 Jeff Bagwell	2.00
CR18 Eric Karros	1.00
CR19 Mike Piazza	3.00
CR20 Ken Caminiti	1.00
CR21 Barry Bonds	4.00
CR22 Matt Williams	1.00
CR23 Jay Buhner	1.00
CR24 Ken Griffey Jr.	3.00
CR25 Ron Gant	1.00
CR26 Juan Gonzalez	1.50
CR27 Mickey Tettleton	1.00

Nomo Scrapbook

The five-card, regular-sized set was randomly inserted in 1996 Collector's Choice baseball. Fronts depict the Dodgers pitcher in action with his name in atypical lower-case type up the right border. Backs feature in-depth text below Nomo's name. A version featuring Japanese text was issued in Japan.

	NM/M
Complete Set (5):	10.00
Common Card:	2.00
Japanese:	3X
1-5 Hideo Nomo	2.00

Ripken Collection

The 23-card, regular-sized Cal Ripken Collection was randomly inserted in various Upper Deck baseball releases in 1996. Cards #1-4 were found in Series 1 Collector's Choice; cards 5-8 were found in Upper Deck Series 1; cards 9-12 in Collector's Choice Series 2; cards 13-17 in Upper Deck Series 2; cards 18-22 in SP baseball and the header card in Collector's Choice.

	NM/M
Complete Set (1-4, 9-12):	15.00
Common Card:	2.50
Header Card:	2.00

1996 Collector's Choice Cal Ripken Jr. Jumbo

This 5" x 3-1/2" card is a virtual parallel to the #1 card in the multi-brand Ripken set which was issued to mark his career to the point of his 2,131st consecutive game. This version, however, was sold only through a television shopping program. The front has a silver facsimile autograph. On back is a "Limited Edition" seal and a serial number within an edition of 21,310.

	NM/M
1 Cal Ripken Jr.	5.00

1996 Collector's Choice You Make the Play

This insert series of interactive game cards was packaged with Series 1 Collector's Choice. Each player's card can be found with one of two play outcomes printed thereon, which are then used to play a baseball card game utilizing a playing field and scorecard found on box bottoms. Regular versions of the cards are seeded one per pack, while gold-signature versions are found one per 36 packs.

	NM/M
Complete Set (45):	60.00
Common Player:	.50
Gold:	4X
1a Kevin Appier (Strike out.)	.50
1b Kevin Appier (Pick off.)	.50
2a Carlos Baerga (Home run.)	.50
2b Carlos Baerga (Ground out.)	.50
3a Jeff Bagwell (Walk)	1.00
3b Jeff Bagwell (Strike out.)	1.00
4a Jay Bell (Sacrifice)	.50
4b Jay Bell (Walk)	.50
5a Albert Belle (Fly out.)	.50
5b Albert Belle (Home run.)	.50
6a Craig Biggio (Single)	.50
6b Craig Biggio (Strike out.)	.50
7a Wade Boggs (Single)	1.50
7b Wade Boggs (Ground out.)	1.50
8a Barry Bonds (Strike out.)	3.00
8b Barry Bonds (Reach on error.)	3.00
9a Bobby Bonilla (Walk)	.50
9b Bobby Bonilla (Strike out.)	.50
10a Jose Canseco (Strike out.)	.75
10b Jose Canseco (Double)	.75
11a Joe Carter (Double)	.50

11b Joe Carter (Fly out.)	.50
12a Darren Daulton (Ground out.)	.50
12b Darren Daulton (Catcher's interference.)	.50
13a Cecil Fielder (Stolen base.)	.50
13b Cecil Fielder (Home run.)	.50
14a Ron Gant (Home run.)	.50
14b Ron Gant (Fly out.)	.50
15a Juan Gonzalez (Double)	.65
15b Juan Gonzalez (Fly out.)	.65
16a Ken Griffey Jr. (Home run.)	2.00
16b Ken Griffey Jr. (Hit by pitch.)	2.00
17a Tony Gwynn (Single)	1.50
17b Tony Gwynn (Ground out.)	1.50
18a Randy Johnson (Strike out.)	1.00
18b Randy Johnson (K-Reach on wild pitch.)	1.00
19a Chipper Jones (Walk)	1.50
19b Chipper Jones (Strike out.)	1.50
20a Barry Larkin (Ground out.)	.50
20b Barry Larkin (Stolen base.)	.50
21a Kenny Lofton (Triple)	.50
21b Kenny Lofton (Stolen base.)	.50
22a Greg Maddux (Single)	1.50
22b Greg Maddux (Strike out.)	1.50
23a Don Mattingly (Fly out.)	1.75
23b Don Mattingly (Double)	1.75
24a Fred McGriff (Double)	.50
24b Fred McGriff (Home run.)	.50
25a Mark McGwire (Strike out.)	2.50
25b Mark McGwire (Home run.)	2.50
26a Paul Molitor (Ground out.)	1.00
26b Paul Molitor (Single)	1.00
27a Raul Mondesi (Single)	.50
27b Raul Mondesi (Fly out.)	.50
28a Eddie Murray (Sacrifice fly.)	1.00
28b Eddie Murray (Ground out.)	1.00
29a Hideo Nomo (Strike out.)	.65
29b Hideo Nomo (Balk)	.65
30a Jon Nunnally (Single)	.50
30b Jon Nunnally (Error)	.50
31a Mike Piazza (Strike out.)	2.00
31b Mike Piazza (Single)	2.00
32a Kirby Puckett (Walk)	1.50
32b Kirby Puckett (Ground out.)	1.50
33a Cal Ripken Jr. (Home run.)	3.00
33b Cal Ripken Jr. (Double)	3.00
34a Alex Rodriguez (Strike out.)	2.50
34b Alex Rodriguez (Triple)	2.50
35a Tim Salmon (Sacrifice fly.)	.50
35b Tim Salmon (Strike out.)	.50
36a Gary Sheffield (Fly out.)	.65
36b Gary Sheffield (Single)	.65
37a Lee Smith (Strike out.)	.50
37b Lee Smith (Pick off of lead runner.)	.50
38a Ozzie Smith (Ground out.)	1.50
38b Ozzie Smith (Single)	1.50
39a Sammy Sosa (Stolen base.)	1.50
39b Sammy Sosa (Single)	1.50
40a Frank Thomas (Walk)	1.00
40b Frank Thomas (Home run.)	1.00
41a Greg Vaughn (Sacrifice fly.)	.50
41b Greg Vaughn (Strike out.)	.50
42a Mo Vaughn (Hit by pitch.)	.50
42b Mo Vaughn (Stolen base.)	.50
43a Larry Walker (Strike out.)	.50
43b Larry Walker (Walk)	.50
44a Rondell White (Triple)	.50
44b Rondell White (Fly out.)	.50
45a Matt Williams (Home run.)	.50
45b Matt Williams (Single)	.50

1997 Collector's Choice

The 506-card, standard-size set contains five subsets: Rookie Class (1-27), Leaders (56-63), Postseason

(218-224), Ken Griffey Jr. Checklists (244-249) and Griffey Hot List (325-334). Insert sets are: All-Star Connection, Big Shots, Stick'Ums, Premier Power, Clearly Dominant, The Big Show, Toast of the Town and New Frontier. Basic card fronts feature a color action shot with the player's name appearing on the bottom edge. The team logo is located in the lower-left corner and each card features a white border. Backs contain another action shot on the upper half with biography, and career/season stats. The cards were issued in 12-card packs retailing for 99 cents. A factory set was issued that includes 10 Premier Power jumbo cards.

	NM/M
Factory Set (516):	16.00
Complete Set (506):	12.00
Common Player:	.05
Pack (12):	1.00
Wax Box (36):	20.00
1 Andruw Jones (Rookie Class)	1.00
2 Rocky Coppinger (Rookie Class)	.05
3 Jeff D'Amico (Rookie Class)	.05
4 Dmitri Young (Rookie Class)	.05
5 Darin Erstad (Rookie Class)	.75
6 Jermaine Allensworth (Rookie Class)	.05
7 Damian Jackson (Rookie Class)	.05
8 Bill Mueller (Rookie Class)	.05
9 Jacob Cruz (Rookie Class)	.05
10 Vladimir Guerrero (Rookie Class)	1.00
11 Marty Janzen (Rookie Class)	.05
12 Kevin L. Brown (Rookie Class)	.05
13 Willie Adams (Rookie Class)	.05
14 Wendell Magee (Rookie Class)	.05
15 Scott Rolen (Rookie Class)	.65
16 Matt Beech (Rookie Class)	.05
17 Neifi Perez (Rookie Class)	.05
18 Jamey Wright (Rookie Class)	.05
19 Jose Paniagua (Rookie Class)	.05
20 Todd Walker (Rookie Class)	.05
21 Justin Thompson (Rookie Class)	.05
22 Robin Jennings (Rookie Class)	.05
23 Dario Veras RC (Rookie Class)	.05
24 Brian Lesher (Rookie Class)	.05
25 Nomar Garciaparra (Rookie Class)	1.25
26 Luis Castillo (Rookie Class)	.05
27 Brian Giles RC (Rookie Class)	.75
28 Jermaine Dye	.05
29 Terrell Wade	.05
30 Fred McGriff	.05
31 Marquis Grissom	.05
32 Ryan Klesko	.05
33 Javier Lopez	.05
34 Mark Wohlers	.05
35 Tom Glavine	.25
36 Denny Neagle	.05
37 Scott Erickson	.05
38 Chris Hoiles	.05
39 Roberto Alomar	.25
40 Eddie Murray	.75
41 Cal Ripken Jr.	2.00
42 Randy Myers	.05
43 B.J. Surhoff	.05
44 Rick Krivda	.05
45 Jose Canseco	.50
46 Heathcliff Slocumb	.05
47 Jeff Suppan	.05
48 Tom Gordon	.05
49 Aaron Sele	.05
50 Mo Vaughn	.50
51 Darren Bragg	.05
52 Wil Cordero	.05
53 Scott Bullett	.05
54 Terry Adams	.05
55 Jackie Robinson	.35
56 Tony Gwynn, Alex Rodriguez (Batting Leaders)	.50
57 Andres Galarraga, Mark McGwire (Homer Leaders)	.50
58 Andres Galarraga, Albert Belle (RBI Leaders)	.25
59 Eric Young, Kenny Lofton (SB Leaders)	.05
60 John Smoltz, Andy Pettitte (Victory Leaders)	.05

61 John Smoltz, Roger Clemens (Strikeout Leaders)	.20
62 Kevin Brown, Juan Guzman (ERA Leaders)	.05
63 John Wetteland, Todd Worrell, Jeff Brantley (Save Leaders)	.05
64 Scott Servais	.05
65 Sammy Sosa	1.00
66 Ryne Sandberg	1.00
67 Frank Castillo	.05
68 Rey Sanchez	.05
69 Steve Trachsel	.05
70 Robin Ventura	.05
71 Wilson Alvarez	.05
72 Tony Phillips	.05
73 Lyle Mouton	.05
74 Mike Cameron	.05
75 Harold Baines	.05
76 Albert Belle	.05
77 Chris Snopek	.05
78 Reggie Sanders	.05
79 Jeff Brantley	.05
80 Barry Larkin	.05
81 Kevin Jarvis	.05
82 John Smiley	.05
83 Pete Schourek	.05
84 Thomas Howard	.05
85 Lee Smith	.05
86 Omar Vizquel	.05
87 Julio Franco	.05
88 Orel Hershiser	.05
89 Charles Nagy	.05
90 Matt Williams	.05
91 Dennis Martinez	.05
92 Jose Mesa	.05
93 Sandy Alomar Jr.	.05
94 Jim Thome	.50
95 Vinny Castilla	.05
96 Armando Reynoso	.05
97 Kevin Ritz	.05
98 Larry Walker	.05
99 Eric Young	.05
100 Dante Bichette	.05
101 Quinton McCracken	.05
102 John Vander Wal	.05
103 Phil Nevin	.05
104 Tony Clark	.05
105 Alan Trammell	.05
106 Felipe Lira	.05
107 Curtis Pride	.05
108 Bobby Higginson	.05
109 Mark Lewis	.05
110 Travis Fryman	.05
111 Al Leiter	.05
112 Devon White	.05
113 Jeff Conine	.05
114 Charles Johnson	.05
115 Andre Dawson	.25
116 Edgar Renteria	.05
117 Robb Nen	.05
118 Kevin Brown	.05
119 Derek Bell	.05
120 Bob Abreu	.10
121 Mike Hampton	.05
122 Todd Jones	.05
123 Billy Wagner	.05
124 Shane Reynolds	.05
125 Jeff Bagwell	.75
126 Brian L. Hunter	.05
127 Jeff Montgomery	.05
128 Rod Myers RC	.05
129 Tim Belcher	.05
130 Kevin Appier	.05
131 Mike Sweeney	.05
132 Craig Paquette	.05
133 Joe Randa	.05
134 Michael Tucker	.05
135 Raul Mondesi	.05
136 Tim Wallach	.05
137 Brett Butler	.05
138 Karim Garcia	.10
139 Todd Hollandsworth	.05
140 Eric Karros	.05
141 Hideo Nomo	.40
142 Ismael Valdes	.05
143 Cal Eldred	.05
144 Scott Karl	.05
145 Matt Mieske	.05
146 Mike Fetters	.05
147 Mark Loretta	.05
148 Fernando Vina	.05
149 Jeff Cirillo	.05
150 Dave Nilsson	.05
151 Kirby Puckett	1.00
152 Rich Becker	.05
153 Chuck Knoblauch	.05
154 Marty Cordova	.05
155 Paul Molitor	.75
156 Rick Aguilera	.05
157 Pat Meares	.05
158 Frank Rodriguez	.05
159 David Segui	.05
160 Henry Rodriguez	.05
161 Shane Andrews	.05
162 Pedro J. Martinez	.75
163 Mark Grudzielanek	.05
164 Mike Lansing	.05
165 Rondell White	.05
166 Ugueth Urbina	.05
167 Rey Ordonez	.05
168 Robert Person	.05
169 Carlos Baerga	.05
170 Bernard Gilkey	.05
171 John Franco	.05
172 Pete Harnisch	.05
173 Butch Huskey	.05
174 Paul Wilson	.05

175 Bernie Williams	.05
176 Dwight Gooden	.05
177 Wade Boggs	1.00
178 Ruben Rivera	.05
179 Jim Leyritz	.05
180 Derek Jeter	2.00
181 Tino Martinez	.05
182 Tim Raines	.05
183 Scott Brosius	.05
184 Jason Giambi	.60
185 Geronimo Berroa	.05
186 Ariel Prieto	.05
187 Scott Spiezio	.05
188 John Wasdin	.05
189 Ernie Young	.05
190 Mark McGwire	1.50
191 Jim Eisenreich	.05
192 Ricky Bottalico	.05
193 Darren Daulton	.05
194 David Doster	.05
195 Gregg Jefferies	.05
196 Lenny Dykstra	.05
197 Curt Schilling	.20
198 Todd Stottlemyre	.05
199 Willie McGee	.05
200 Ozzie Smith	1.00
201 Dennis Eckersley	.65
202 Ray Lankford	.05
203 John Mabry	.05
204 Alan Benes	.05
205 Ron Gant	.05
206 Archi Cianfrocco	.05
207 Fernando Valenzuela	.05
208 Greg Vaughn	.05
209 Steve Finley	.05
210 Tony Gwynn	1.00
211 Rickey Henderson	.75
212 Trevor Hoffman	.05
213 Jason Thompson	.05
214 Osvaldo Fernandez	.05
215 Glenallen Hill	.05
216 William Van Landingham	.05
217 Marvin Benard	.05
218 Juan Gonzalez (Postseason)	.10
219 Roberto Alomar (Postseason)	.05
220 Brian Jordan (Postseason)	.05
221 John Smoltz (Postseason)	.05
222 Javy Lopez (Postseason)	.05
223 Bernie Williams (Postseason)	.05
224 Jim Leyritz, John Wetteland (Postseason)	.05
225 Barry Bonds	2.00
226 Rich Aurilia	.05
227 Jay Canizaro	.05
228 Dan Wilson	.05
229 Bob Wolcott	.05
230 Ken Griffey Jr.	1.25
231 Sterling Hitchcock	.05
232 Edgar Martinez	.05
233 Joey Cora	.05
234 Norm Charlton	.05
235 Alex Rodriguez	1.50
236 Bobby Witt	.05
237 Darren Oliver	.05
238 Kevin Elster	.05
239 Rusty Greer	.05
240 Juan Gonzalez	.40
241 Will Clark	.05
242 Dean Palmer	.05
243 Ivan Rodriguez	.65
244 Checklist (Ken Griffey Jr.)	.25
245 Checklist (Ken Griffey Jr.)	.25
246 Checklist (Ken Griffey Jr.)	.25
247 Checklist (Ken Griffey Jr.)	.25
248 Checklist (Ken Griffey Jr.)	.25
249 Checklist (Ken Griffey Jr.)	.25
250 Eddie Murray	.75
251 Troy Percival	.05
252 Garret Anderson	.05
253 Allen Watson	.05
254 Jason Dickson	.05
255 Jim Edmonds	.05
256 Chuck Finley	.05
257 Randy Velarde	.05
258 Shigetosi Hasegawa	.05
259 Todd Greene	.05
260 Tim Salmon	.05
261 Mark Langston	.05
262 Dave Hollins	.05
263 Gary DiSarcina	.05
264 Kenny Lofton	.05
265 John Smoltz	.05
266 Greg Maddux	1.00
267 Jeff Blauser	.05
268 Alan Embree	.05
269 Mark Lemke	.05
270 Chipper Jones	1.00
271 Mike Mussina	.65
272 Rafael Palmeiro	.65
273 Jimmy Key	.05
274 Mike Bordick	.05
275 Brady Anderson	.05
276 Eric Davis	.05
277 Jeffrey Hammonds	.05
278 Reggie Jefferson	.05
279 Tim Naehring	.05
280 John Valentin	.05
281 Troy O'Leary	.05
282 Shane Mack	.05
283 Mike Stanley	.05
284 Tim Wakefield	.05
285 Brian McRae	.05
286 Brooks Kieschnick	.05
287 Shawon Dunston	.05
288 Kevin Foster	.05

289	Mel Rojas	.05
290	Mark Grace	.05
291	Brant Brown	.05
292	Amaury Telemaco	.05
293	Dave Martinez	.05
294	Jaime Navarro	.05
295	Ray Durham	.05
296	Ozzie Guillen	.05
297	Roberto Hernandez	.05
298	Ron Karkovice	.05
299	James Baldwin	.05
300	Frank Thomas	.75
301	Eddie Taubensee	.05
302	Bret Boone	.05
303	Willie Greene	.05
304	Dave Burba	.05
305	Deion Sanders	.10
306	Reggie Sanders	.05
307	Hal Morris	.05
308	Pokey Reese	.05
309	Tony Fernandez	.05
310	Manny Ramirez	.75
311	Chad Ogea	.05
312	Jack McDowell	.05
313	Kevin Mitchell	.05
314	Chad Curtis	.05
315	Steve Kline	.05
316	Kevin Seitzer	.05
317	Kirt Manwaring	.05
318	Bill Swift	.05
319	Ellis Burks	.05
320	Andres Galarraga	.05
321	Bruce Ruffin	.05
322	Mark Thompson	.05
323	Walt Weiss	.05
324	Todd Jones	.05
325	Andruw Jones (Griffey Hot List)	.50
326	Chipper Jones (Griffey Hot List)	.75
327	Mo Vaughn (Griffey Hot List)	.05
328	Frank Thomas (Griffey Hot List)	.50
329	Albert Belle (Griffey Hot List)	.10
330	Mark McGwire (Griffey Hot List)	1.00
331	Derek Jeter (Griffey Hot List)	1.50
332	Alex Rodriguez (Griffey Hot List)	.05
333	Jay Buhner (Griffey Hot List)	.05
334	Ken Griffey Jr. (Griffey Hot List)	.75
335	Brian L. Hunter	.05
336	Brian Johnson	.05
337	Omar Olivares	.05
338	Deivi Cruz RC	.05
339	Damion Easley	.05
340	Melvin Nieves	.05
341	Moises Alou	.05
342	Jim Eisenreich	.05
343	Mark Hutton	.05
344	Alex Fernandez	.05
345	Gary Sheffield	.35
346	Pat Rapp	.05
347	Brad Ausmus	.05
348	Sean Berry	.05
349	Darryl Kile	.05
350	Craig Biggio	.05
351	Chris Holt	.05
352	Luis Gonzalez	.05
353	Pat Listach	.05
354	Jose Rosado	.05
355	Mike Macfarlane	.05
356	Tom Goodwin	.05
357	Chris Haney	.05
358	Chili Davis	.05
359	Jose Offerman	.05
360	Johnny Damon	.30
361	Bip Roberts	.05
362	Ramon Martinez	.05
363	Pedro Astacio	.05
364	Todd Zeile	.05
365	Mike Piazza	1.25
366	Greg Gagne	.05
367	Chan Ho Park	.05
368	Wilton Guerrero	.05
369	Todd Worrell	.05
370	John Jaha	.05
371	Steve Sparks	.05
372	Mike Matheny	.05
373	Marc Newfield	.05
374	Jeromy Burnitz	.05
375	Jose Valentin	.05
376	Ben McDonald	.05
377	Roberto Kelly	.05
378	Bob Tewksbury	.05
379	Ron Coomer	.05
380	Brad Radke	.05
381	Matt Lawton	.05
382	Dan Naulty	.05
383	Scott Stahoviak	.05
384	Matt Wagner	.05
385	Jim Bullinger	.05
386	Carlos Perez	.05
387	Darrin Fletcher	.05
388	Chris Widger	.05
389	F.P. Santangelo	.05
390	Lee Smith	.05
391	Bobby Jones	.05
392	John Olerud	.05
393	Mark Clark	.05
394	Jason Isringhausen	.05
395	Todd Hundley	.05
396	Lance Johnson	.05
397	Edgardo Alfonzo	.05
398	Alex Ochoa	.05
399	Darryl Strawberry	.05
400	David Cone	.05
401	Paul O'Neill	.05
402	Joe Girardi	.05
403	Charlie Hayes	.05
404	Andy Pettitte	.25
405	Mariano Rivera	.25
406	Mariano Duncan	.05
407	Kenny Rogers	.05
408	Cecil Fielder	.05
409	George Williams	.05
410	Jose Canseco	.35
411	Tony Batista	.05
412	Steve Karsay	.05
413	Dave Telgheder	.05
414	Billy Taylor	.05
415	Mickey Morandini	.05
416	Calvin Maduro	.05
417	Mark Leiter	.05
418	Kevin Stocker	.05
419	Mike Lieberthal	.05
420	Rico Brogna	.05
421	Mark Portugal	.05
422	Rex Hudler	.05
423	Mark Johnson	.05
424	Esteban Loiaza	.05
425	Lou Collier	.05
426	Kevin Elster	.05
427	Francisco Cordova	.05
428	Marc Wilkins	.05
429	Joe Randa	.05
430	Jason Kendall	.05
431	Jon Lieber	.05
432	Steve Cooke	.05
433	Emil Brown RC	.05
434	Tony Womack RC	.25
435	Al Martin	.05
436	Jason Schmidt	.05
437	Andy Benes	.05
438	Delino DeShields	.05
439	Royce Clayton	.05
440	Brian Jordan	.05
441	Donovan Osborne	.05
442	Gary Gaetti	.05
443	Tom Pagnozzi	.05
444	Joey Hamilton	.05
445	Wally Joyner	.05
446	John Flaherty	.05
447	Chris Gomez	.05
448	Sterling Hitchcock	.05
449	Andy Ashby	.05
450	Ken Caminiti	.05
451	Tim Worrell	.05
452	Jose Vizcaino	.05
453	Rod Beck	.05
454	Wilson Delgado	.05
455	Darryl Hamilton	.05
456	Mark Lewis	.05
457	Mark Gardner	.05
458	Rick Wilkins	.05
459	Scott Sanders	.05
460	Kevin Orie	.05
461	Glendon Rusch	.05
462	Juan Melo	.05
463	Richie Sexson	.05
464	Bartolo Colon	.05
465	Jose Guillen	.05
466	Heath Murray	.05
467	Aaron Boone	.05
468	Bubba Trammell RC	.05
469	Jeff Abbott	.05
470	Derrick Gibson	.05
471	Matt Morris	.05
472	Ryan Jones	.05
473	Pat Cline	.05
474	Adam Riggs	.05
475	Jay Payton	.05
476	Derrek Lee	.50
477	Elieser Marrero	.05
478	Lee Tinsley	.05
479	Jamie Moyer	.05
480	Jay Buhner	.05
481	Bob Wells	.05
482	Jeff Fassero	.05
483	Paul Sorrento	.05
484	Russ Davis	.05
485	Randy Johnson	.75
486	Roger Pavlik	.05
487	Damon Buford	.05
488	Julio Santana	.05
489	Mark McLemore	.05
490	Mickey Tettleton	.05
491	Ken Hill	.05
492	Benji Gil	.05
493	Ed Sprague	.05
494	Mike Timlin	.05
495	Pat Hentgen	.05
496	Orlando Merced	.05
497	Carlos Garcia	.05
498	Carlos Delgado	.35
499	Juan Guzman	.05
500	Roger Clemens	1.00
501	Erik Hanson	.05
502	Otis Nixon	.05
503	Shawn Green	.10
504	Charlie O'Brien	.05
505	Joe Carter	.05
506	Alex Gonzalez	.05

All-Star Connection

This 45-card insert from Series 2 highlights All-Star caliber players. Cards feature a large starburst pat-

tern on a metallic-foil background behind the player's photo. They were inserted one per pack.

		NM/M
	Complete Set (45):	10.00
	Common Player:	.10
1	Mark McGwire*	1.00
2	Chuck Knoblauch	.10
3	Jim Thome	.35
4	Alex Rodriguez	1.00
5	Ken Griffey Jr.	.75
6	Brady Anderson	.10
7	Albert Belle	.40
8	Ivan Rodriguez	.40
9	Pat Hentgen	.10
10	Frank Thomas	.50
11	Roberto Alomar	.25
12	Robin Ventura	.10
13	Cal Ripken Jr.	1.50
14	Juan Gonzalez	.25
15	Manny Ramirez	.50
16	Bernie Williams	.10
17	Terry Steinbach	.10
18	Andy Pettitte	.25
19	Jeff Bagwell	.50
20	Craig Biggio	.10
21	Ken Caminiti	.10
22	Barry Larkin	.10
23	Tony Gwynn	.60
24	Barry Bonds	1.50
25	Kenny Lofton	.10
26	Mike Piazza	.75
27	John Smoltz	.10
28	Andres Galarraga	.10
29	Ryne Sandberg	.60
30	Chipper Jones	.75
31	Mark Grudzielanek	.10
32	Sammy Sosa	.60
33	Steve Finley	.10
34	Gary Sheffield	.25
35	Todd Hundley	.10
36	Greg Maddux	.60
37	Mo Vaughn	.10
38	Eric Young	.10
39	Vinny Castilla	.10
40	Derek Jeter	1.50
41	Lance Johnson	.10
42	Ellis Burks	.10
43	Dante Bichette	.10
44	Javy Lopez	.10
45	Hideo Nomo	.25

Big Shots

This 20-card insert depicts the game's top stars in unique photos. Cards were inserted 1:12 packs. Gold Signature Editions, featuring a gold foil-stamped facsimile autograph, were inserted 1:144 packs. Fronts are highlighted in silver foil. Backs repeat a portion of the front photo, have a picture of the photographer and his comments about the picture.

		NM/M
	Complete Set (19):	15.00
	Common Player:	.25
	Gold Signature Edition:	2X
1	Ken Griffey Jr.	2.00
2	Nomar Garciaparra	.75
3	Brian Jordan	.25
4	Scott Rolen	.75
5	Alex Rodriguez	2.50
6	Larry Walker	.25
7	Mariano Rivera	.35
8	Cal Ripken Jr.	3.00
9	Deion Sanders	.25
10	Frank Thomas	1.00
11	Dean Palmer	.25
12	Ken Caminiti	.25
13	Derek Jeter	3.00
14	Barry Bonds	3.00
15	Chipper Jones	1.50
16	Mo Vaughn	.25
17	Jay Buhner	.25
18	Mike Piazza	2.00
19	Tony Gwynn	1.50

Big Show

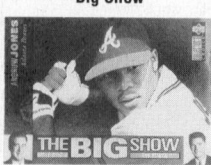

The 45-card, regular-sized set was inserted one per pack of Series 1. Backs feature player comments written by ESPN SportsCenter hosts Keith Olbermann and Dan Patrick, whose portraits appear both front and back. On front, printed on metallic foil, is an action shot of the player, with his name printed along the left border of the horizontal cards. The cards are numbered "X/45." A parallel set to this chase-card series carries a gold-foil "World Headquarters Edition" seal at lower-right and was a 1:35 insert.

		NM/M
	Complete Set (45):	7.00
	Common Player:	.10
	World Headquarters:	8X
1	Greg Maddux	.50
2	Chipper Jones	.50
3	Andruw Jones	.40
4	John Smoltz	.10
5	Cal Ripken Jr.	1.00
6	Roberto Alomar	.25
7	Rafael Palmeiro	.35
8	Eddie Murray	.40
9	Jose Canseco	.30
10	Roger Clemens	.55
11	Mo Vaughn	.10
12	Jim Edmonds	.10
13	Tim Salmon	.10
14	Sammy Sosa	.40
15	Albert Belle	.10
16	Frank Thomas	.40
17	Barry Larkin	.10
18	Kenny Lofton	.10
19	Manny Ramirez	.40
20	Matt Williams	.10
21	Dante Bichette	.10
22	Gary Sheffield	.30
23	Craig Biggio	.10
24	Jeff Bagwell	.40
25	Todd Hollandsworth	.10
26	Raul Mondesi	.10
27	Hideo Nomo	.25
28	Mike Piazza	.60
29	Paul Molitor	.40
30	Kirby Puckett	.50
31	Rondell White	.10
32	Rey Ordonez	.10
33	Paul Wilson	.10
34	Derek Jeter	1.00
35	Andy Pettitte	.25
36	Mark McGwire	.75
37	Jason Kendall	.10
38	Ozzie Smith	.50
39	Tony Gwynn	.50
40	Barry Bonds	1.00
41	Alex Rodriguez	.75
42	Jay Buhner	.10
43	Ken Griffey Jr.	.40
44	Randy Johnson	.40
45	Juan Gonzalez	.25

1997 Collector's Choice Big Show World Headquarters

This 45-card chase set in Series 2 is also found in a special parallel version which carries a "World Headquarters Edition" gold-foil seal on front at the lower-right.

		NM/M
	Complete Set (45):	50.00
	Common Player:	1.50
	Stars:	8X

Clearly Dominant

The five-card, regular-sized set features Seattle outfielder Ken Griffey Jr. on each card and was

inserted every 144 packs of 1997 Collector's Choice baseball.

		NM/M
	Complete Set (5):	16.00
	Common Card:	4.00
CD1-CD5	Ken Griffey Jr.	4.00

1997 Collector's Choice Clearly Dominant Jumbos

Each of the five Ken Griffey Jr. cards from the Collector's Choice insert set was also produced in a special retail-only 5" x 3-1/2" jumbo version. The super-size Clearly Dominant cards were packaged in a special collectors' kit which also included a Griffey stand-up figure and eight packs of CC cards, retailing for about $15. The cards could also be purchased as a complete set for $10. Cards are numbered with a "CD" prefix.

		NM/M
	Complete Set (5):	10.00
	Common Card:	2.00
1-5	Ken Griffey Jr.	2.00

1997 Collector's Choice Hot List Jumbos

These 5" x 7" versions of the "Ken Griffey Jr.'s Hot List" subset from Series 2 are an exclusive box-topper in certain retail packaging of Collector's Choice. Other than size, the jumbos are identical to the regular Hot List cards, including foil background printing on front.

		NM/M
	Complete Set (10):	15.00
	Common Player:	.50
325	Andruw Jones	1.50
326	Chipper Jones	2.00
327	Mo Vaughn	.50
328	Frank Thomas	1.50
329	Albert Belle	.50
330	Mark McGwire	3.00
331	Derek Jeter	4.00
332	Alex Rodriguez	3.00
333	Jay Buhner	.50
334	Ken Griffey Jr.	2.50

New Frontier

This is a 40-card Series 2 insert highlighting anticipated interleague matchups. Cards were designed with each player's action photo superimposed on a metallic-foil background depicting half of a ballfield. Pairs could then be displayed side-by-side. Cards were inserted 1:69 packs. They are numbered and carry a "NF" prefix.

		NM/M
	Complete Set (40):	75.00
	Common Player:	1.00
1	Alex Rodriguez	5.00
2	Tony Gwynn	3.00
3	Jose Canseco	1.25
4	Hideo Nomo	1.25
5	Mark McGwire	5.00
6	Barry Bonds	6.00
7	Juan Gonzalez	1.25
8	Ken Caminiti	1.00
9	Tim Salmon	1.00
10	Mike Piazza	4.00
11	Ken Griffey Jr.	4.00
12	Andres Galarraga	1.00
13	Jay Buhner	1.00
14	Dante Bichette	1.00
15	Frank Thomas	2.00
16	Ryne Sandberg	3.00
17	Roger Clemens	3.50
18	Andruw Jones	2.00
19	Jim Thome	1.50
20	Sammy Sosa	3.00
21	David Justice	1.00
22	Deion Sanders	1.00
23	Todd Walker	1.00
24	Kevin Orie	1.00
25	Albert Belle	1.00
26	Jeff Bagwell	2.00
27	Manny Ramirez	2.00
28	Brian Jordan	1.00
29	Derek Jeter	6.00
30	Chipper Jones	3.00
31	Mo Vaughn	1.00
32	Gary Sheffield	1.50
33	Carlos Delgado	1.50
34	Vladimir Guerrero	2.00
35	Cal Ripken Jr.	6.00
36	Greg Maddux	3.00
37	Cecil Fielder	1.00
38	Todd Hundley	1.00
39	Mike Mussina	1.25
40	Scott Rolen	1.50

Premier Power

The 20-card, regular-sized set was included one per 15 packs of Series 1. Fronts feature an action photo with the "Premier Power" logo in silver foil in the lower half and "spotlights" aiming out toward the sides. The bottom portion of the card is transparent red. Backs are bordered in red with the same card front shot appearing in black-and-white above a brief description and "Power Facts." The cards are numbered with a "PP" prefix. A parallel gold-foil version was available every 69 packs.

		NM/M
	Complete Set (20):	20.00
	Common Player:	.40
	Gold:	2X
1	Mark McGwire	3.00
2	Brady Anderson	.40
3	Ken Griffey Jr.	2.50
4	Albert Belle	.40
5	Juan Gonzalez	.60
6	Andres Galarraga	.40
7	Jay Buhner	.40
8	Mo Vaughn	.40
9	Barry Bonds	3.50
10	Gary Sheffield	.75
11	Todd Hundley	.40
12	Frank Thomas	1.50
13	Sammy Sosa	2.00
14	Ken Caminiti	.40
15	Vinny Castilla	.40
16	Ellis Burks	.40
17	Rafael Palmeiro	1.00
18	Alex Rodriguez	3.00
19	Mike Piazza	2.50
20	Eddie Murray	1.50

1997 Collector's Choice Premier Power Jumbo

Each factory set of 1997 Collector's Choice included 10 super-size (3" x 5") versions of the Premier Power inserts. Besides the size, the jumbos differ from the insert version in the addition of a metallic facsimile autograph on front.

		NM/M
Complete Set (20):		15.00
Common Player:		.50
1	Mark McGwire	2.50
2	Brady Anderson	.50
3	Ken Griffey Jr.	2.00
4	Albert Belle	.50
5	Juan Gonzalez	.75
6	Andres Galarraga	.50
7	Jay Buhner	.50
8	Mo Vaughn	.50
9	Barry Bonds	3.00
10	Gary Sheffield	.65
11	Todd Hundley	.50
12	Frank Thomas	1.00
13	Sammy Sosa	1.50
14	Ken Caminiti	.50
15	Vinny Castilla	.50
16	Ellis Burks	.50
17	Rafael Palmeiro	.75
18	Alex Rodriguez	2.50
19	Mike Piazza	2.00
20	Eddie Murray	1.00

Stick'Ums

The 30-piece 2-1/2" x 3-1/2" sticker set was inserted one per three packs of Series 1 Collector's Choice. Fronts feature a bright background color and include five different peel-off stickers: An action shot of the player, a pennant in team colors featuring the player's name, a team logo, an Upper Deck Collector's Choice logo and a "Super Action Stick'Ums" decal. Backs feature the player checklist in black ink over a gray background. An unnumbered version of the stickers (without Smith and Puckett) was sold in a special retail-only package.

		NM/M
Complete Set (30):		5.00
Common Player:		.05
1	Ozzie Smith	.50
2	Andruw Jones	.40
3	Alex Rodriguez	.75
4	Paul Molitor	.40
5	Jeff Bagwell	.40
6	Manny Ramirez	.40
7	Kenny Lofton	.05
8	Albert Belle	.05
9	Jay Buhner	.05
10	Chipper Jones	.50
11	Barry Larkin	.05
12	Dante Bichette	.05
13	Mike Piazza	.60
14	Andres Galarraga	.05
15	Barry Bonds	1.00
16	Brady Anderson	.05
17	Gary Sheffield	.20
18	Jim Thome	.35
19	Tony Gwynn	.50
20	Cal Ripken Jr.	1.00
21	Sammy Sosa	.50
22	Juan Gonzalez	.50
23	Greg Maddux	.50
24	Ken Griffey Jr.	.60
25	Mark McGwire	.50
26	Kirby Puckett	.50
27	Mo Vaughn	.25
28	Vladimir Guerrero	.40
29	Ken Caminiti	.05
30	Frank Thomas	.40

Toast of the Town

This 30-card Series 2 insert features top stars on foil-enhanced cards. Odds of finding one are 1:35 packs. Cards are numbered with a "T" prefix.

		NM/M
Complete Set (30):		40.00
Common Player:		.30
1	Andruw Jones	2.00
2	Chipper Jones	2.50
3	Greg Maddux	2.50
4	John Smoltz	.30
5	Kenny Lofton	.30
6	Brady Anderson	.30
7	Cal Ripken Jr.	6.00
8	Mo Vaughn	.30
9	Sammy Sosa	2.50
10	Albert Belle	.30
11	Frank Thomas	2.00
12	Barry Larkin	.30
13	Manny Ramirez	2.00
14	Jeff Bagwell	2.00
15	Mike Piazza	4.00
16	Paul Molitor	2.00
17	Vladimir Guerrero	2.00
18	Todd Hundley	.30
19	Derek Jeter	6.00
20	Andy Pettitte	.45
21	Bernie Williams	.30
22	Mark McGwire	5.00
23	Scott Rolen	1.00
24	Ken Caminiti	.30
25	Tony Gwynn	2.50
26	Barry Bonds	6.00
27	Ken Griffey Jr.	4.00
28	Alex Rodriguez	5.00
29	Juan Gonzalez	.75
30	Roger Clemens	3.00

1997 Collector's Choice Update

This update set was offered via a mail-in redemption offer. Traded players in their new uniforms and 1997 rookies are the focus of the set. Fronts are color photos which are borderless at top and sides. Beneath each photo the player's name and team logo appear in a red (A.L.) or blue (N.L.) baseball design. Backs have another photo, major and minor league career stats and a trivia question. Cards are numbered with a "U" prefix.

		NM/M
Complete Set (30):		2.00
Common Player:		.10
1	Jim Leyritz	.10
2	Matt Perisho	.10
3	Michael Tucker	.10
4	Mike Johnson	.10
5	Jaime Navarro	.10
6	Doug Drabek	.10
7	Terry Mulholland	.10
8	Brett Tomko	.10
9	Marquis Grissom	.10
10	David Justice	.10
11	Brian Moehler	.10
12	Bobby Bonilla	.10
13	Todd Dunwoody	.10
14	Tony Saunders	.10
15	Jay Bell	.10
16	Jeff King	.10
17	Terry Steinbach	.10
18	Steve Bieser	.10
19	Takashi Kashiwada RC	.10
20	Hideki Irabu	.10
21	Damon Mashore	.10
22	Quilvio Veras	.10
23	Will Cunnane	.10
24	Jeff Kent	.50
25	J.T. Snow	.10
26	Dante Powell	.10
27	Jose Cruz Jr.	.10
28	John Burkett	.10
29	John Wetteland	.10
30	Benito Santiago	.10

You Crash the Game

A 30-player interactive set found in Series 2 packs features the game's top home run hitters. Cards were inserted 1:5 packs. Fronts feature a red-foil Crash logo and a range of game dates. Those holding cards of players who homered in that span could (for $2 per card handling fee) redeem them for high-tech versions. Instant winner cards (seeded 1:721) were redeemable for complete 30-card upgrade sets. Winning cards are marked with an asterisk; theoretically they would be scarcer than losing cards because many were redeemed. The contest cards expired on Sept. 8, 1997. Cards are numbered with a "CG" prefix.

	NM/M
Complete Set (90):	65.00
Common Player:	.25
July 28-30	.25
August 8-11	.25
Sept. 19-21	.25
August 15-17	1.00
August 29-31	1.00
Sept. 12-14	1.00
August 22-24*	1.50
Sept. 1-3	.75
Sept. 19-22	.75
July 31-Aug. 3*	.50
Sept. 4-7	.25
Sept. 19-22	.25
July 29-30	.60
Aug. 29-31	.60
Sept. 26-28	.60
August 8-10*	4.00
Sept. 1-3*	4.00
Sept. 11-14	2.00
August 14-17	.25
August 29-31*	.50
Sept. 23-25*	.50
August 1-3*	2.00
August 29-31	1.00
Sept. 19-21*	2.00
August 7-10	.25
Sept. 11-14	.25
Sept. 19-21*	.50
August 29-31	.50
Sept. 1-3	.75
Sept. 23-25*	1.50
August 12-14*	1.50
August 29-31	.75
Sept. 11-14*	1.50
July 28-30	.50
August 15-18*	1.00
Sept. 19-22	.50
August 4-5	.25
Sept. 1-3*	.50
Sept. 23-25	.25
July 24-27*	.75
August 28-29	.25
Sept. 26-28*	.25
August 12-13	.25
Sept. 4-7*	.50
Sept. 19-21	.25
August 8-10*	.50
August 30-31	.25
Sept. 12-14	.25
August 1-3*	.75
Sept. 1-3*	.75
Sept. 12-14*	.75
Sept. 9-10	.75
Sept. 19-22*	1.50
Sept. 23-25*	1.50
August 1-3	.25
August 15-17	.25
Sept. 25-28*	.50
August 11-12	1.25
Sept. 5-8*	2.50
Sept. 19-21*	2.50
August 22-24	.75
August 29-31	.75
Sept. 19-22	.25
August 29-31	.25
Sept. 4-7	.25
Sept. 26-28*	.50
August 22-24	.25
Sept. 12-14	.35
Sept. 26-28	.35
July 31-Aug. 3	1.50
August 30-31	1.50
Sept. 19-22*	3.00
August 8-10	.25
Sept. 4-7	.25
Sept. 17-18*	.50
August 5-7	2.00
Sept. 4-7*	4.00
Sept. 23-24*	4.00
August 7-10	.25
August 28-29	.25
Sept. 1-3	.25
August 22-24*	2.50
August 28-29	1.25
Sept. 19-22*	2.50
July 29-31	1.50
August 30-31	1.50
Sept. 12-15	1.50
August 11-13*	.75
August 30-31	.40
Sept. 19-21*	.75

You Crash the Game Winners

These are the prize cards from CC's interactive "You Crash the Game" cards in Series 2. Persons who redeemed a Crash card with the correct date(s) on which the pictured player homered received (for a $2 handling fee) this high-end version of the Crash card. The redemption cards have the same basic design as the contest cards, but use different player photos with fronts printed on metallic-foil stock, and a team logo in place of the Crash foil logo. Where the contest cards have game rules on back, the redemption cards have another photo of the player and career highlights. Complete redemption sets were available upon redeeming an instant winner card, found on average of one per 721 packs. Because some cards were only available in complete redemption sets (marked with an "SP" here), and others might have been available for more than one date range, some cards will be scarcer than others.

		NM/M
Complete Set (30):		55.00
Common Player:		.50
CG1	Ryan Klesko/SP	1.25
CG2	Chipper Jones/SP	12.00
CG3	Andruw Jones	.75
CG4	Brady Anderson	.50
CG5	Rafael Palmeiro/SP	2.50
CG6	Cal Ripken Jr.	10.00
CG7	Mo Vaughn	.50
CG8	Sammy Sosa	3.00
CG9	Albert Belle	1.00
CG10	Frank Thomas	1.00
CG11	Manny Ramirez	.75
CG12	Jim Thome	.65
CG13	Matt Williams	.50
CG14	Dante Bichette	.50
CG15	Vinny Castilla	.50
CG16	Andres Galarraga	.50
CG17	Gary Sheffield	.65
CG18	Jeff Bagwell	.75
CG19	Eric Karros	.50
CG20	Mike Piazza	2.50
CG21	Vladimir Guerrero/SP	3.00
CG22	Cecil Fielder/SP	1.25
CG23	Jose Canseco/SP	1.25
CG24	Mark McGwire	7.50
CG25	Ken Caminiti	.50
CG26	Barry Bonds	10.00
CG27	Jay Buhner/SP	1.25
CG28	Ken Griffey Jr.	2.50
CG29	Alex Rodriguez/SP	9.00
CG30	Juan Gonzalez	.60

You Crash/Game Instant Winner

Found on average of one per 721 packs, these Instant Winner cards could be redeemed (with a $2 handling fee) for a complete set of You Crash the Game exchange cards - the only way eight of the Crash winner cards could be ob-

tained. These special cards have a red foil "instant winner!" logo on front and a congratulatory message on back, along with instructions for redemption prior to the Dec. 8, 1997, deadline.

	NM/M
Complete Set (30):	300.00
Common Player:	2.00

1997 Collector's Choice Team Sets

A special version of Collector's Choice cards for several popular major league teams was produced in two retail packages by Upper Deck. In one version, blister packs containing 13 player cards and a metallic-foil team logo/checklist card was sold for a suggested retail price of $1.99. The second version, exclusive to Wal-Mart, is a hard plastic blister pack containing two cello-wrapped packages. One holds a random assortment of 15 Series 1 Collector's Choice cards. The other has 13 player cards and a foil logo/checklist card for a specific team. The team-set cards are identical to the regular-issue cards, from either Series 1 or Series 2, except each of the team-set cards has a number on back which differs from the regular edition. Packaged with the Wal-Mart version is a 3-1/2" x 5" "Home Team Heroes" card, listed seperately.

		NM/M
Common Player:		.10
Atlanta Braves Team Set:		3.00
AB	Team Logo/Checklist	.10
AB1	Andruw Jones	.60
AB2	Kenny Lofton	.10
AB3	Fred McGriff	.10
AB4	Michael Tucker	.10
AB5	Ryan Klesko	.10
AB6	Javy Lopez	.10
AB7	Mark Wohlers	.10
AB8	Tom Glavine	.25
AB9	Denny Neagle	.10
AB10	Chipper Jones	.75
AB11	Jeff Blauser	.10
AB12	Greg Maddux	.75
AB13	John Smoltz	.10
Baltimore Orioles Team Set:		2.00
BO	Team Logo/Checklist	.10
BO1	Rocky Coppinger	.10
BO2	Scott Erickson	.10
BO3	Chris Hoiles	.10
BO4	Roberto Alomar	.30
BO5	Cal Ripken Jr.	1.50
BO6	Randy Myers	.10
BO7	B.J. Surhoff	.10
BO8	Mike Mussina	.40
BO9	Rafael Palmeiro	.10
BO10	Jimmy Key	.10
BO11	Mike Bordick	.10
BO12	Brady Anderson	.10
BO13	Eric Davis	.10
Chicago White Sox Team Set:		2.50
CW	Team Logo/Checklist	.10
CW1	Robin Ventura	.10
CW2	Wilson Alvarez	.10
CW3	Tony Phillips	.10
CW4	Lyle Mouton	.10
CW5	James Baldwin	.10
CW6	Harold Baines	.10
CW7	Albert Belle	.10
CW8	Chris Snopek	.10
CW9	Ray Durham	.10
CW10	Frank Thomas	.60
CW11	Ozzie Guillen	.10
CW12	Roberto Hernandez	.10
CW13	Jaime Navarro	.10
Cleveland Indians Team Set:		1.50
CI	Team Logo/Checklist	.10
CI1	Brian Giles	.10
CI2	Omar Vizquel	.10
CI3	Julio Franco	.10
CI4	Orel Hershiser	.10
CI5	Charles Nagy	.10
CI6	Matt Williams	.10
CI7	Jose Mesa	.10
CI8	Sandy Alomar	.10
CI9	Jim Thome	.50
CI10	David Justice	.10
CI11	Marquis Grissom	.10
CI12	Chad Ogea	.10
CI13	Manny Ramirez	.60
Colorado Rockies Team Set:		1.25
CR	Team Logo/Checklist	.10
CR1	Dante Bichette	.10
CR2	Vinny Castilla	.10
CR3	Kevin Ritz	.10
CR4	Larry Walker	.10
CR5	Eric Young	.10
CR6	Quinton McCracken	.10
CR7	John Vander Wal	.10
CR8	Jamey Wright	.10
CR9	Mark Thompson	.10
CR10	Andres Galarraga	.10
CR11	Ellis Burks	.10
CR12	Kirt Manwaring	.10
CR13	Walt Weiss	.10
Florida Marlins Team Set:		2.00
FM	Team Logo/Checklist	.10
FM1	Luis Castillo	.10
FM2	Al Leiter	.10
FM3	Devon White	.10
FM4	Jeff Conine	.10
FM5	Charles Johnson	.10
FM6	Edgar Renteria	.10
FM7	Robb Nen	.10
FM8	Kevin Brown	.10
FM9	Gary Sheffield	.45
FM10	Alex Fernandez	.10
FM11	Pat Rapp	.10
FM12	Moises Alou	.10
FM13	Bobby Bonilla	.10
L.A. Dodgers Team Set:		3.00
LA	Team Logo/Checklist	.10
LA1	Raul Mondesi	.10
LA2	Brett Butler	.10
LA3	Todd Hollandsworth	.10
LA4	Eric Karros	.10
LA5	Hideo Nomo	.30
LA6	Ismael Valdes	.10
LA7	Wilton Guerrero	.10
LA8	Ramon Martinez	.10
LA9	Greg Gagne	.10
LA10	Mike Piazza	1.00
LA11	Chan Ho Park	.10
LA12	Todd Worrell	.10
LA13	Todd Zeile	.10
New York Yankees Team Set:		3.00
NY	Team Logo/Checklist	.10
NY1	Bernie Williams	.10
NY2	Dwight Gooden	.10
NY3	Wade Boggs	.75
NY4	Ruben Rivera	.10
NY5	Derek Jeter	1.50
NY6	Tino Martinez	.10
NY7	Tim Raines	.10
NY8	Joe Girardi	.10
NY9	Charlie Hayes	.10
NY10	Andy Pettitte	.30
NY11	Cecil Fielder	.10
NY12	Paul O'Neil	.10
NY13	David Cone	.10
Seattle Mariners Team Set:		3.00
SM	Team Logo/Checklist	.10
SM1	Dan Wilson	.10
SM2	Ken Griffey Jr.	1.00
SM3	Edgar Martinez	.10
SM4	Joey Cora	.10
SM5	Norm Charlton	.10
SM6	Alex Rodriguez	1.25
SM7	Randy Johnson	.60
SM8	Paul Sorrento	.10
SM9	Jamie Moyer	.10
SM10	Jay Buhner	.10
SM11	Russ Davis	.10
SM12	Jeff Fassero	.10
SM13	Bob Wells	.10
Texas Rangers Team Set:		3.00
TR	Team Logo/Checklist	.10
TR1	Bobby Witt	.10
TR2	Darren Oliver	.10
TR3	Rusty Greer	.10
TR4	Juan Gonzalez	.30
TR5	Will Clark	.10
TR6	Dean Palmer	.10
TR7	Ivan Rodriguez	.50
TR8	John Wetteland	.10
TR9	Mark McLemore	.10
TR10	John Burkett	.10
TR11	Benji Gil	.10
TR12	Ken Hill	.10
TR13	Mickey Tettleton	.10

1998 Collector's Choice

The 530-card Collectors Choice set was issued in two 265-card series. Series 1 features 197 regular cards, five checklists and four subsets: Cover Story features 18 of the leagues' top stars, Rookie Class has 27 young players, the nine-card Top of the Charts subset honors 1997's statistical leaders and Masked Marauders is a nine-card subset. Inserts in Series 1 are Super Action Stick-Ums, Evolution Revolution and StarQuest. Series 2 has 233 regular cards, five checklist cards, an 18-card Rookie Class subset and the nine-card Golden Jubilee subset. Inserts in Series 2 include Mini Bobbing Head Cards, You Crash the Game and StarQuest. Factory sets include a random assortment of 10 StarQuest cards.

		NM/M
Unopened Fact. Set (540):		15.00
Complete Set (530):		10.00
Common Player:		.05
Pack (14):		1.00
Wax Box (36):		15.00
1	Nomar Garciaparra (Cover Glory)	.50
2	Roger Clemens (Cover Glory)	.50
3	Larry Walker (Cover Glory)	
4	Mike Piazza (Cover Glory)	.60
5	Mark McGwire (Cover Glory)	.75
6	Tony Gwynn (Cover Glory)	.45
7	Jose Cruz Jr. (Cover Glory)	.05
8	Frank Thomas (Cover Glory)	.40
9	Tino Martinez (Cover Glory)	.05
10	Ken Griffey Jr. (Cover Glory)	.60
11	Barry Bonds (Cover Glory)	.85
12	Scott Rolen (Cover Glory)	.30
13	Randy Johnson (Cover Glory)	.15
14	Ryne Sandberg (Cover Glory)	.35
15	Eddie Murray (Cover Glory)	.15
16	Kevin Brown (Cover Glory)	.05
17	Greg Maddux (Cover Glory)	.35
18	Sandy Alomar Jr. (Cover Glory)	.05
19	Checklist (Ken Griffey Jr., Adam Riggs)	.40
20	Checklist (Nomar Garciaparra, Charlie O'Brien)	.10
21	Checklist (Ben Grieve, Ken Griffey Jr., Larry Walker, Mark McGwire)	.50
22	Checklist (Mark McGwire, Cal Ripken Jr.)	.50
23	Checklist (Tino Martinez)	.05
24	Jason Dickson	.05
25	Darin Erstad	.25
26	Todd Greene	.05
27	Chuck Finley	.05
28	Garret Anderson	.05
29	Dave Hollins	.05
30	Rickey Henderson	.60
31	John Smoltz	.05
32	Michael Tucker	.05
33	Jeff Blauser	.05
34	Javier Lopez	.05
35	Andruw Jones	.60
36	Denny Neagle	.05
37	Randall Simon	.05
38	Mark Wohlers	.05
39	Harold Baines	.05
40	Cal Ripken Jr.	1.50
41	Mike Bordick	.05
42	Jimmy Key	.05
43	Armando Benitez	.05
44	Scott Erickson	.05
45	Eric Davis	.05
46	Bret Saberhagen	.05
47	Darren Bragg	.05
48	Steve Avery	.05
49	Jeff Frye	.05
50	Aaron Sele	.05
51	Scott Hatteberg	.05
52	Tom Gordon	.05
53	Kevin Orie	.05
54	Kevin Foster	.05
55	Ryne Sandberg	.75
56	Doug Glanville	.05
57	Tyler Houston	.05
58	Steve Trachsel	.05
59	Mark Grace	.05
60	Frank Thomas	.60
61	Scott Eyre RC	.05
62	Jeff Abbott	.05
63	Chris Clemons	.05
64	Jorge Fabregas	.05

65	Robin Ventura	.05
66	Matt Karchner	.05
67	Jon Nunnally	.05
68	Aaron Boone	.05
69	Pokey Reese	.05
70	Deion Sanders	.10
71	Jeff Shaw	.05
72	Eduardo Perez	.05
73	Brett Tomko	.05
74	Bartolo Colon	.05
75	Manny Ramirez	.60
76	Jose Mesa	.05
77	Brian Giles	.05
78	Richie Sexson	.05
79	Orel Hershiser	.05
80	Matt Williams	.05
81	Walt Weiss	.05
82	Jerry DiPoto	.05
83	Quinton McCracken	.05
84	Neifi Perez	.05
85	Vinny Castilla	.05
86	Ellis Burks	.05
87	John Thomson	.05
88	Willie Blair	.05
89	Bob Hamelin	.05
90	Tony Clark	.05
91	Todd Jones	.05
92	Deivi Cruz	.05
93	Frank Catalanotto RC	.15
94	Justin Thompson	.05
95	Gary Sheffield	.25
96	Kevin Brown	.05
97	Charles Johnson	.05
98	Bobby Bonilla	.05
99	Livan Hernandez	.05
100	Paul Konerko (Rookie Class)	.10
101	Craig Counsell (Rookie Class)	.05
102	Magglio Ordonez RC (Rookie Class)	1.00
103	Garrett Stephenson (Rookie Class)	.05
104	Ken Cloude (Rookie Class)	.05
105	Miguel Tejada (Rookie Class)	.25
106	Juan Encarnacion (Rookie Class)	.05
107	Dennis Reyes (Rookie Class)	.05
108	Orlando Cabrera (Rookie Class)	.05
109	Kelvim Escobar (Rookie Class)	.05
110	Ben Grieve (Rookie Class)	.05
111	Brian Rose (Rookie Class)	.05
112	Fernando Tatis (Rookie Class)	.05
113	Tom Evans (Rookie Class)	.05
114	Tom Fordham (Rookie Class)	.05
115	Mark Kotsay (Rookie Class)	.05
116	Mario Valdez (Rookie Class)	.05
117	Jeremi Gonzalez (Rookie Class)	.05
118	Todd Dunwoody (Rookie Class)	.05
119	Javier Valentin (Rookie Class)	.05
120	Todd Helton (Rookie Class)	.50
121	Jason Varitek (Rookie Class)	.10
122	Chris Carpenter (Rookie Class)	.05
123	Kevin Millwood RC (Rookie Class)	.75
124	Brad Fullmer (Rookie Class)	.05
125	Jaret Wright (Rookie Class)	.05
126	Brad Rigby (Rookie Class)	.05
127	Edgar Renteria	.05
128	Robb Nen	.05
129	Tony Pena	.05
130	Craig Biggio	.05
131	Brad Ausmus	.05
132	Shane Reynolds	.05
133	Mike Hampton	.05
134	Billy Wagner	.05
135	Richard Hidalgo	.05
136	Jose Rosado	.05
137	Yamil Benitez	.05
138	Felix Martinez	.05
139	Jeff King	.05
140	Jose Offerman	.05
141	Joe Vitiello	.05
142	Tim Belcher	.05
143	Brett Butler	.05
144	Greg Gagne	.05
145	Mike Piazza	1.00
146	Ramon Martinez	.05
147	Raul Mondesi	.05
148	Adam Riggs	.05
149	Eddie Murray	.50
150	Jeff Cirillo	.05
151	Scott Karl	.05
152	Mike Fetters	.05
153	Dave Nilsson	.05
154	Antone Williamson	.05
155	Jeff D'Amico	.05
156	Jose Valentin	.05
157	Brad Radke	.05
158	Torii Hunter	.05
159	Chuck Knoblauch	.05
160	Paul Molitor	.60

161	Travis Miller	.05
162	Rich Robertson	.05
163	Ron Coomer	.05
164	Mark Grudzielanek	.05
165	Lee Smith	.05
166	Vladimir Guerrero	.60
167	Dustin Hermanson	.05
168	Ugueth Urbina	.05
169	F.P. Santangelo	.05
170	Rondell White	.05
171	Bobby Jones	.05
172	Edgardo Alfonzo	.05
173	John Franco	.05
174	Carlos Baerga	.05
175	Butch Huskey	.05
176	Rey Ordonez	.05
177	Matt Franco	.05
178	Dwight Gooden	.05
179	Chad Curtis	.05
180	Tino Martinez	.05
181	Charlie O'Brien (Masked Marauders)	.05
182	Sandy Alomar Jr. (Masked Marauders)	.25
183	Raul Casanova (Masked Marauders)	.05
184	Jim Leyritz (Masked Marauders)	.05
185	Mike Piazza (Masked Marauders)	.60
186	Ivan Rodriguez (Masked Marauders)	.25
187	Charles Johnson (Masked Marauders)	.05
188	Brad Ausmus (Masked Marauders)	.05
189	Brian Johnson (Masked Marauders)	.05
190	Wade Boggs	.75
191	David Wells	.05
192	Tim Raines	.05
193	Ramiro Mendoza	.05
194	Willie Adams	.05
195	Matt Stairs	.05
196	Jason McDonald	.05
197	Dave Magadan	.05
198	Mark Bellhorn	.05
199	Ariel Prieto	.05
200	Jose Canseco	.35
201	Bobby Estalella	.05
202	Tony Barron RC	.05
203	Midre Cummings	.05
204	Ricky Bottalico	.05
205	Mike Grace	.05
206	Rico Brogna	.05
207	Mickey Morandini	.05
208	Lou Collier	.05
209	Kevin Polcovich RC	.05
210	Kevin Young	.05
211	Jose Guillen	.05
212	Esteban Loaiza	.05
213	Marc Wilkins	.05
214	Jason Schmidt	.05
215	Gary Gaetti	.05
216	Fernando Valenzuela	.05
217	Willie McGee	.05
218	Alan Benes	.05
219	Eli Marrero	.05
220	Mark McGwire	1.25
221	Matt Morris	.05
222	Trevor Hoffman	.05
223	Will Cunnane	.05
224	Joey Hamilton	.05
225	Ken Caminiti	.05
226	Derrek Lee	.35
227	Mark Sweeney	.05
228	Carlos Hernandez	.05
229	Brian Johnson	.05
230	Jeff Kent	.05
231	Kirk Rueter	.05
232	Bill Mueller	.05
233	Dante Powell	.05
234	J.T. Snow	.05
235	Shawn Estes	.05
236	Dennis Martinez	.05
237	Jamie Moyer	.05
238	Dan Wilson	.05
239	Joey Cora	.05
240	Ken Griffey Jr.	1.00
241	Paul Sorrento	.05
242	Jay Buhner	.05
243	Hanley Frias RC	.05
244	John Burkett	.05
245	Jon Gonzalez	.30
246	Rick Helling	.05
247	Darren Oliver	.05
248	Mickey Tettleton	.05
249	Ivan Rodriguez	.45
250	Joe Carter	.05
251	Pat Hentgen	.05
252	Marty Janzen	.05
253	Frank Thomas, Tony Gwynn (Top of the Charts)	.25
254	Mark McGwire, Ken Griffey Jr., Larry Walker (Top of the Charts)	.50
255	Ken Griffey Jr., Andres Galarraga (Top of the Charts)	.40
256	Brian Hunter, Tony Womack (Top of the Charts)	.05
257	Roger Clemens, Denny Neagle (Top of the Charts)	.10
258	Roger Clemens, Curt Schilling (Top of the Charts)	.30

259	Roger Clemens, Pedro J. Martinez (Top of the Charts)	.25
260	Randy Myers, Jeff Shaw (Top of the Charts)	.05
261	Nomar Garciaparra, Scott Rolen (Top of the Charts)	.25
262	Charlie O'Brien	.05
263	Shannon Stewart	.05
264	Robert Person	.05
265	Carlos Delgado	.25
266	Checklist (Matt Williams, Travis Lee)	.05
267	Checklist (Nomar Garciaparra, Cal Ripken Jr.)	.50
268	Checklist (Mark McGwire, Mike Piazza)	.05
269	Checklist (Tony Gwynn, Ken Griffey Jr.)	.40
270	Checklist (Fred McGriff, Jose Cruz Jr.)	.05
271	Andruw Jones (Golden Jubilee)	.25
272	Alex Rodriguez (Golden Jubilee)	.65
273	Juan Gonzalez (Golden Jubilee)	.15
274	Nomar Garciaparra (Golden Jubilee)	.50
275	Ken Griffey Jr. (Golden Jubilee)	.60
276	Tino Martinez (Golden Jubilee)	.05
277	Roger Clemens (Golden Jubilee)	.40
278	Barry Bonds (Golden Jubilee)	.85
279	Mike Piazza (Golden Jubilee)	.60
280	Tim Salmon (Golden Jubilee)	.05
281	Gary DiSarcina	.05
282	Cecil Fielder	.05
283	Ken Hill	.05
284	Troy Percival	.05
285	Jim Edmonds	.05
286	Allen Watson	.05
287	Brian Anderson	.05
288	Jay Bell	.05
289	Jorge Fabregas	.05
290	Devon White	.05
291	Yamil Benitez	.05
292	Jeff Suppan	.05
293	Tony Batista	.05
294	Brent Brede	.05
295	Andy Benes	.05
296	Felix Rodriguez	.05
297	Karim Garcia	.05
298	Omar Daal	.05
299	Andy Stankiewicz	.05
300	Matt Williams	.05
301	Willie Blair	.05
302	Ryan Klesko	.05
303	Tom Glavine	.25
304	Walt Weiss	.05
305	Greg Maddux	.75
306	Chipper Jones	.75
307	Keith Lockhart	.05
308	Andres Galarraga	.05
309	Chris Hoiles	.05
310	Roberto Alomar	.25
311	Joe Carter	.05
312	Doug Drabek	.05
313	Jeffrey Hammonds	.05
314	Rafael Palmeiro	.40
315	Mike Mussina	.40
316	Brady Anderson	.05
317	B.J. Surhoff	.05
318	Dennis Eckersley	.45
319	Jim Leyritz	.05
320	Mo Vaughn	.05
321	Nomar Garciaparra	.75
322	Reggie Jefferson	.05
323	Tim Naehring	.05
324	Troy O'Leary	.05
325	Pedro J. Martinez	.50
326	John Valentin	.05
327	Mark Clark	.05
328	Rod Beck	.05
329	Mickey Morandini	.05
330	Sammy Sosa	.75
331	Jeff Blauser	.05
332	Lance Johnson	.05
333	Scott Servais	.05
334	Kevin Tapani	.05
335	Henry Rodriguez	.05
336	Jaime Navarro	.05
337	Benji Gil	.05
338	James Baldwin	.05
339	Mike Cameron	.05
340	Ray Durham	.05
341	Chris Snopek	.05
342	Eddie Taubensee	.05
343	Bret Boone	.05
344	Willie Greene	.05
345	Barry Larkin	.05
346	Chris Stynes	.05
347	Pete Harnisch	.05
348	Dave Burba	.05
349	Sandy Alomar Jr.	.05
350	Kenny Lofton	.05
351	Geronimo Berroa	.05
352	Omar Vizquel	.05
353	Travis Fryman	.05
354	Dwight Gooden	.05
355	Jim Thome	.40
356	David Justice	.05

357	Charles Nagy	.05
358	Chad Ogea	.05
359	Pedro Astacio	.05
360	Larry Walker	.05
361	Mike Lansing	.05
362	Kirt Manwaring	.05
363	Dante Bichette	.05
364	Jamey Wright	.05
365	Darryl Kile	.05
366	Luis Gonzalez	.05
367	Joe Randa	.05
368	Raul Casanova	.05
369	Damion Easley	.05
370	Brian L. Hunter	.05
371	Bobby Higginson	.05
372	Brian Moehler	.05
373	Scott Sanders	.05
374	Jim Eisenreich	.05
375	Derrek Lee	.35
376	Jay Powell	.05
377	Cliff Floyd	.05
378	Alex Fernandez	.05
379	Felix Heredia	.05
380	Jeff Bagwell	.60
381	Bill Spiers	.05
382	Chris Holt	.05
383	Carl Everett	.05
384	Derek Bell	.05
385	Moises Alou	.05
386	Ramon Garcia	.05
387	Mike Sweeney	.05
388	Glendon Rusch	.05
389	Kevin Appier	.05
390	Dean Palmer	.05
391	Jeff Conine	.05
392	Johnny Damon	.25
393	Jose Vizcaino	.05
394	Todd Hollandsworth	.05
395	Eric Karros	.05
396	Todd Zeile	.05
397	Chan Ho Park	.05
398	Ismael Valdes	.05
399	Eric Young	.05
400	Hideo Nomo	.25
401	Mark Loretta	.05
402	Doug Jones	.05
403	Jeromy Burnitz	.05
404	John Jaha	.05
405	Marquis Grissom	.05
406	Mike Matheny	.05
407	Todd Walker	.05
408	Marty Cordova	.05
409	Matt Lawton	.05
410	Terry Steinbach	.05
411	Pat Meares	.05
412	Rick Aguilera	.05
413	Otis Nixon	.05
414	Derrick May	.05
415	Carl Pavano (Rookie Class)	.05
416	A.J. Hinch (Rookie Class)	.05
417	David Dellucci RC (Rookie Class)	.10
418	Bruce Chen (Rookie Class)	.05
419	Darron Ingram RC (Rookie Class)	.05
420	Sean Casey (Rookie Class)	.20
421	Mark L. Johnson (Rookie Class)	.05
422	Gabe Alvarez (Rookie Class)	.05
423	Alex Gonzalez (Rookie Class)	.05
424	Daryle Ward (Rookie Class)	.05
425	Russell Branyan (Rookie Class)	.05
426	Mike Caruso (Rookie Class)	.20
427	Mike Kinkade RC (Rookie Class)	.05
428	Ramon Hernandez (Rookie Class)	.05
429	Matt Clement (Rookie Class)	.05
430	Travis Lee (Rookie Class)	.05
431	Shane Monahan (Rookie Class)	.05
432	Rich Butler RC (Rookie Class)	.05
433	Chris Widger	.05
434	Jose Vidro	.05
435	Carlos Perez	.05
436	Ryan McGuire	.05
437	Brian McRae	.05
438	Al Leiter	.05
439	Rich Becker	.05
440	Todd Hundley	.05
441	Dave Mlicki	.05
442	Bernard Gilkey	.05
443	John Olerud	.05
444	Paul O'Neill	.05
445	Andy Pettitte	.30
446	David Cone	.05
447	Chili Davis	.05
448	Bernie Williams	.05
449	Joe Girardi	.05
450	Derek Jeter	1.50
451	Mariano Rivera	.20
452	George Williams	.05
453	Kenny Rogers	.05
454	Tom Candiotti	.05
455	Rickey Henderson	.60
456	Jason Giambi	.40
457	Scott Spiezio	.05
458	Doug Glanville	.05
459	Desi Relaford	.05

460	Curt Schilling	.20
461	Bob Abreu	.10
462	Gregg Jefferies	.05
463	Scott Rolen	.40
464	Mike Lieberthal	.05
465	Tony Womack	.05
466	Jermaine Allensworth	.05
467	Francisco Cordova	.05
468	Jon Lieber	.05
469	Al Martin	.05
470	Jason Kendall	.05
471	Todd Stottlemyre	.05
472	Royce Clayton	.05
473	Brian Jordan	.05
474	John Mabry	.05
475	Ray Lankford	.05
476	Delino DeShields	.05
477	Ron Gant	.05
478	Mark Langston	.05
479	Steve Finley	.05
480	Tony Gwynn	.75
481	Andy Ashby	.05
482	Wally Joyner	.05
483	Greg Vaughn	.05
484	Sterling Hitchcock	.05
485	J. Kevin Brown	.05
486	Orel Hershiser	.05
487	Charlie Hayes	.05
488	Darryl Hamilton	.05
489	Mark Gardner	.05
490	Barry Bonds	1.50
491	Robb Nen	.05
492	Kirk Rueter	.05
493	Randy Johnson	.50
494	Jeff Fassero	.05
495	Alex Rodriguez	1.25
496	David Segui	.05
497	Rich Amaral	.05
498	Russ Davis	.05
499	Bubba Trammell	.05
500	Wade Boggs	.75
501	Roberto Hernandez	.05
502	Dave Martinez	.05
503	Dennis Springer	.05
504	Paul Sorrento	.05
505	Wilson Alvarez	.05
506	Mike Kelly	.05
507	Albie Lopez	.05
508	Tony Saunders	.05
509	John Flaherty	.05
510	Fred McGriff	.05
511	Quinton McCracken	.05
512	Terrell Wade	.05
513	Kevin Stocker	.05
514	Kevin Elster	.05
515	Will Clark	.05
516	Bobby Witt	.05
517	Tom Goodwin	.05
518	Aaron Sele	.05
519	Lee Stevens	.05
520	Rusty Greer	.05
521	John Wetteland	.05
522	Darrin Fletcher	.05
523	Jose Canseco	.35
524	Randy Myers	.05
525	Jose Cruz Jr.	.05
526	Shawn Green	.15
527	Tony Fernandez	.05
528	Alex Gonzalez	.05
529	Ed Sprague	.05
530	Roger Clemens	.85

1998 Collector's Choice Cover Glory 5x7

		NM/M
Complete Set (10):		10.00
Common Player:		1.00
1	Nomar Garciaparra	1.50
2	Roger Clemens	2.00
3	Larry Walker	1.00
4	Mike Piazza	2.50
5	Mark McGwire	3.00
6	Tony Gwynn	1.50
7	Jose Cruz Jr.	1.00
8	Frank Thomas	1.25
9	Tino Martinez	1.00
10	Ken Griffey Jr.	2.50

Evolution Revolution

This 28-card insert features one player from each Major League team. The fronts picture the team jersey and open to reveal the player's top 1997 accomplishment. Evolution Revolution was inserted in Series 1 packs. Cards are numbered with an "ER" prefix.

		NM/M
Complete Set (28):		36.00
Common Player:		.40
Inserted 1:13		
1	Tim Salmon	.40
2	Greg Maddux	2.50
3	Cal Ripken Jr.	6.00
4	Mo Vaughn	.40
5	Sammy Sosa	2.50
6	Frank Thomas	1.50
7	Barry Larkin	.40
8	Jim Thome	.65
9	Larry Walker	.40
10	Travis Fryman	.40
11	Gary Sheffield	.65
12	Jeff Bagwell	1.50
13	Johnny Damon	.65
14	Mike Piazza	4.00
15	Jeff Cirillo	.40
16	Paul Molitor	1.50
17	Vladimir Guerrero	1.50
18	Todd Hundley	.40
19	Tino Martinez	.40
20	Jose Canseco	.65
21	Scott Rolen	.75
22	Al Martin	.40
23	Mark McGwire	5.00
24	Tony Gwynn	2.50
25	Barry Bonds	6.00
26	Ken Griffey Jr.	4.00
27	Juan Gonzalez	.75
28	Roger Clemens	3.00

1998 Collector's Choice Golden Jubilee Jumbos

The Golden Jubilee subset cards from Series 2 C.C. were reproduced in 4X (5" x 7") size as one-per-box inserts in special versions of retail packaging.

		NM/M
Complete Set (9):		17.50
Common Player:		1.00
271	Andruw Jones	1.50
272	Alex Rodriguez	4.00
273	Juan Gonzalez	1.00
274	Nomar Garciaparra	2.00
275	Ken Griffey Jr.	3.00
276	Tino Martinez	1.00
277	Roger Clemens	2.00
278	Barry Bonds	5.00
279	Mike Piazza	3.00

1998 Collector's Choice Jumbos (3.5x5)

These double-size versions of various Series 1 cards were available one per special blister pack of Collector's Choice sold in retail chains.

		NM/M
Complete Set (15):		17.50
Common Player:		1.00
35	Andruw Jones	1.50
40	Cal Ripken Jr.	3.00
55	Ryne Sandberg	1.75
60	Frank Thomas	1.50
95	Gary Sheffield	1.25
97	Charles Johnson	1.00
145	Mike Piazza	3.00
160	Paul Molitor	1.50

180	Tino Martinez	1.00
220	Mark McGwire	2.50
225	Ken Caminiti	1.00
240	Ken Griffey Jr.	2.00
242	Jay Buhner	1.00
245	Juan Gonzalez	1.25
249	Ivan Rodriguez	1.25

1998 Collector's Choice Jumbos (5x7)

These super-size (5" x 7") cards were one-per-box inserts in Series 2 retail packaging. Besides being four times the size of a normal card, the 5x7s are identical to the regular versions.

		NM/M
Complete Set (10):		15.00
Common Player:		1.00
306	Chipper Jones	2.00
321	Nomar Garciaparra	2.00
360	Larry Walker	1.00
450	Derek Jeter	4.00
463	Scott Rolen	1.25
480	Tony Gwynn	2.00
490	Barry Bonds	4.00
495	Alex Rodriguez	3.00
525	Jose Cruz Jr.	1.00
530	Roger Clemens	2.50

Mini Bobbing Heads

The cards in this 30-card insert series can be punched out and assembled into a stand-up figure with a removable bobbing head. They are a Series 2 insert.

		NM/M
Complete Set (30):		20.00
Common Player:		.25
Inserted 1:3		
1	Tim Salmon	.25
2	Travis Lee	.25
3	Matt Williams	.25
4	Chipper Jones	1.00
5	Greg Maddux	1.00
6	Cal Ripken Jr.	2.50
7	Nomar Garciaparra	1.00
8	Mo Vaughn	.25
9	Sammy Sosa	1.00
10	Frank Thomas	.75
11	Kenny Lofton	.25
12	Jaret Wright	.25
13	Larry Walker	.25
14	Tony Clark	.25
15	Edgar Renteria	.25
16	Jeff Bagwell	.75
17	Mike Piazza	1.50
18	Vladimir Guerrero	.75
19	Derek Jeter	2.00
20	Ben Grieve	.25
21	Scott Rolen	.50
22	Mark McGwire	1.50
23	Tony Gwynn	1.00
24	Barry Bonds	2.50
25	Ken Griffey Jr.	1.50

26	Alex Rodriguez	2.00
27	Fred McGriff	.25
28	Juan Gonzalez	.40
29	Roger Clemens	1.25
30	Jose Cruz Jr.	.25

Rookie Class: Prime Choice

This 18-card set is a parallel of the Rookie Class subset. Each card is foil-stamped with the words "Prime Choice Reserve." This hobby-only set is sequentially numbered to 500 and was inserted in Series 2 packs.

		NM/M
Complete Set (18):		30.00
Common Player:		2.00
415	Carl Pavano	2.00
416	A.J. Hinch	2.00
417	David Dellucci	2.00
418	Bruce Chen	2.00
419	Darron Ingram	2.00
420	Sean Casey	5.00
421	Mark L. Johnson	2.00
422	Gabe Alvarez	2.00
423	Alex Gonzalez	2.00
424	Daryle Ward	2.00
425	Russell Branyan	2.00
426	Mike Caruso	2.00
427	Mike Kinkade	2.00
428	Ramon Hernandez	2.00
429	Matt Clement	2.00
430	Travis Lee	2.50
431	Shane Monahan	2.00
432	Rich Butler	2.00

StarQuest - Series 1

The StarQuest insert in Series 1 consists of 90 cards within four tiers. The tiers are designated by the number of stars found on front, the more the better: Special Delivery (#1-45, one star), Students of the Game (two stars, #46-65), Super Powers (three stars, #66-80) and Super Star Domain (four stars, #81-90). All cards are numbered with a "SQ" prefix.

		NM/M
Complete Set (90):		185.00
Common Special Delivery (1-45):		.25
Inserted 1:1		
Common Student of the Game (46-65):		.75
Inserted 1:21		
Common Super Power (66-80):		2.00
Inserted 1:71		
Common Superstar Domain (81-90):		3.00
Inserted 1:145		
1	Nomar Garciaparra	1.50
2	Scott Rolen	.75
3	Jason Dickson	.25
4	Jaret Wright	.25
5	Kevin Orie	.25
6	Jose Guillen	.25
7	Matt Morris	.25
8	Mike Cameron	.25
9	Kevin Polcovich	.25
10	Jose Cruz Jr.	.25
11	Miguel Tejada	.40
12	Fernando Tatis	.25
13	Todd Helton	.65
14	Ken Cloude	.25

15	Ben Grieve	.25
16	Dante Powell	.25
17	Bubba Trammell	.25
18	Juan Encarnacion	.25
19	Derek Lee	.50
20	Paul Konerko	.35
21	Richard Hidalgo	.25
22	Denny Neagle	.25
23	David Justice	.25
24	Pedro J. Martinez	1.00
25	Greg Maddux	1.50
26	Edgar Martinez	.25
27	Cal Ripken Jr.	2.50
28	Tim Salmon	.25
29	Shawn Estes	.25
30	Ken Griffey Jr.	2.00
31	Brad Radke	.25
32	Andy Pettitte	.40
33	Curt Schilling	.50
34	Raul Mondesi	.25
35	Alex Rodriguez	2.25
36	Jeff Kent	.25
37	Jeff Bagwell	1.00
38	Juan Gonzalez	.50
39	Barry Bonds	2.50
40	Mark McGwire	2.00
41	Frank Thomas	1.00
42	Ray Lankford	.25
43	Tony Gwynn	1.50
44	Mike Piazza	1.75
45	Tino Martinez	.25
46	Nomar Garciaparra	3.00
47	Paul Molitor	1.50
48	Chuck Knoblauch	.75
49	Rusty Greer	.75
50	Cal Ripken Jr.	6.00
51	Roberto Alomar	1.00
52	Scott Rolen	1.00
53	Derek Jeter	6.00
54	Mark Grace	.75
55	Randy Johnson	1.50
56	Craig Biggio	.75
57	Kenny Lofton	.75
58	Eddie Murray	1.50
59	Ryne Sandberg	2.00
60	Rickey Henderson	1.50
61	Darin Erstad	1.00
62	Jim Edmonds	.75
63	Ken Caminiti	.75
64	Ivan Rodriguez	1.25
65	Tony Gwynn	2.00
66	Tony Clark	2.00
67	Andres Galarraga	2.00
68	Rafael Palmeiro	3.00
69	Manny Ramirez	6.00
70	Albert Belle	2.00
71	Jay Buhner	2.00
72	Mo Vaughn	2.00
73	Barry Bonds	15.00
74	Chipper Jones	7.50
75	Jeff Bagwell	6.00
76	Jim Thome	3.00
77	Sammy Sosa	7.50
78	Todd Hundley	2.00
79	Matt Williams	2.00
80	Vinny Castilla	2.00
81	Jose Cruz Jr.	3.00
82	Frank Thomas	7.50
83	Juan Gonzalez	4.00
84	Mike Piazza	15.00
85	Alex Rodriguez	20.00
86	Larry Walker	3.00
87	Tino Martinez	3.00
88	Greg Maddux	12.50
89	Mark McGwire	20.00
90	Ken Griffey Jr.	15.00

StarQuest - Series 2

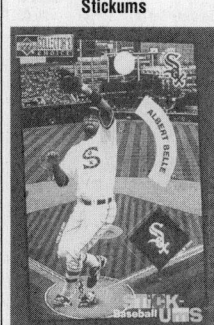

The 30-card StarQuest insert was included in Series 2 packs. The insert has four parallel tiers - Single, Double, Triple and Home Run - designated by the number of baseball diamond icons on the card front. Single cards were inserted 1:1, Doubles 1:21, Triples 1:71 and Home Runs are sequentially numbered to 100. The second series SQ cards feature a front design with the letters "QSUTEASRT" in color blocks vertically at left.

		NM/M
Complete Set (30):		17.50
Common Player:		.25
Singles 1:1		

Doubles 1:21		2X
Triples 1:71		6X
Home Runs		15X
1	Ken Griffey Jr.	4.00
2	Jose Cruz Jr.	.25
3	Cal Ripken Jr.	2.00
4	Roger Clemens	1.00
5	Frank Thomas	.75
6	Derek Jeter	2.00
7	Alex Rodriguez	1.50
8	Andruw Jones	.75
9	Vladimir Guerrero	.75
10	Mark McGwire	1.50
11	Kenny Lofton	.25
12	Pedro J. Martinez	.75
13	Greg Maddux	1.00
14	Larry Walker	.25
15	Barry Bonds	2.00
16	Chipper Jones	1.00
17	Jeff Bagwell	.75
18	Juan Gonzalez	.50
19	Tony Gwynn	1.00
20	Mike Piazza	1.25
21	Tino Martinez	.25
22	Mo Vaughn	.20
23	Ben Grieve	.25
24	Scott Rolen	.60
25	Nomar Garciaparra	1.00
26	Paul Konerko	.35
27	Jaret Wright	.25
28	Gary Sheffield	.50
29	Travis Lee	.25
30	Todd Helton	.65

1998 Collector's Choice StarQuest Super Powers Jumbos

This enlarged (3-1/2" x 5") version of the StarQuest Super Powers cards from Series 1 were a retail-only variation found one per blister pack of specially marked Collector's Choice product.

		NM/M
Complete Set (10):		17.50
Common Player:		1.00
SQ67	Andres Galarraga	1.00
SQ68	Rafael Palmeiro	2.00
SQ69	Manny Ramirez	2.50
SQ70	Albert Belle	1.00
SQ71	Jay Buhner	1.00
SQ72	Mo Vaughn	1.00
SQ73	Barry Bonds	5.00
SQ74	Chipper Jones	3.00
SQ75	Jeff Bagwell	2.50
SQ76	Jim Thome	1.50

Stickums

This 30-card insert was seeded 1:3 Series 1 packs. The stickers can be peeled off the card and reused.

		NM/M
Complete Set (30):		7.00
Common Player:		.10
Inserted 1:3		
1	Andruw Jones	.35
2	Chipper Jones	.50
3	Cal Ripken Jr.	1.00
4	Nomar Garciaparra	.45
5	Mo Vaughn	.20
6	Ryne Sandberg	.45
7	Sammy Sosa	.45
8	Frank Thomas	.35
9	Albert Belle	.20

10	Jim Thome	.30
11	Manny Ramirez	.35
12	Larry Walker	.10
13	Gary Sheffield	.20
14	Jeff Bagwell	.35
15	Mike Piazza	.60
16	Paul Molitor	.35
17	Pedro J. Martinez	.35
18	Todd Hundley	.10
19	Derek Jeter	1.00
20	Tino Martinez	.10
21	Curt Schilling	.25
22	Mark McGwire	.75
23	Tony Gwynn	.45
24	Barry Bonds	1.00
25	Ken Griffey Jr.	.60
26	Alex Rodriguez	.75
27	Juan Gonzalez	.20
28	Ivan Rodriguez	.30
29	Roger Clemens	.50
30	Jose Cruz Jr.	.10

You Crash the Game

These 90 game cards were inserted one per five Series 2 packs. Each card features a player and a list of dates. If the pictured player hit a home run on one of those days, collectors with the card could mail it in for a graphically enhanced prize version. Instant Winner cards of each player were also inserted at the rate of 1:721 and could be exchanged for the complete 30-card prize set. Deadline for exchange of all winning cards was Dec. 1, 1998. Winning cards are designated here with an asterisk and can be expected to be somewhat scarcer than non-winning dates.

		NM/M
Complete Set (90):		75.00
Common Player:		.50
Instant Winner:		8X
Inserted 1:5		
CG1	Ken Griffey Jr. (June 26-28*)	3.00
CG1	Ken Griffey Jr. (July 7)	1.25
CG1	Ken Griffey Jr. (Sept. 21-24*)	3.00
CG2	Travis Lee (July 27-30)	.50
CG2	Travis Lee (Aug. 27-30)	.50
CG2	Travis Lee (Sept. 17-20)	.50
CG3	Larry Walker (July 17-19)	.50
CG3	Larry Walker (Aug. 27-30*)	1.00
CG3	Larry Walker (Sept. 25-27*)	1.00
CG4	Tony Clark (July 9-12*)	1.00
CG4	Tony Clark (June 30-July 2)	.50
CG4	Tony Clark (Sept. 4-6)	.50
CG5	Cal Ripken Jr. (June 22-25*)	4.00
CG5	Cal Ripken Jr. (July 7)	2.00
CG5	Cal Ripken Jr. (Sept. 4-6)	2.00
CG6	Tim Salmon (June 22-25)	.50
CG6	Tim Salmon (Aug. 28-30)	.50
CG6	Tim Salmon (Sept. 14-15)	.50
CG7	Vinny Castilla (June 30-July 2*)	1.00
CG7	Vinny Castilla (Aug. 27-30*)	1.00
CG7	Vinny Castilla (Sept. 7-10*)	1.00
CG8	Fred McGriff (June 22-25)	.50
CG8	Fred McGriff (July 3-5)	.50
CG8	Fred McGriff (Sept. 18-20*)	.50
CG9	Matt Williams (July 17-29)	.50
CG9	Matt Williams (Sept. 14-16*)	1.00
CG9	Matt Williams (Sept. 18-20)	.50
CG10	Mark McGwire (July 7)	1.50
CG10	Mark McGwire (July 24-26*)	3.50
CG10	Mark McGwire (Aug. 18-19*)	3.50
CG11	Albert Belle (July 3-5)	.50
CG11	Albert Belle (Aug. 21-23*)	1.00
CG11	Albert Belle (Sept. 11-13)	.50
CG12	Jay Buhner (July 9-12*)	1.00
CG12	Jay Buhner (Aug. 6-9)	.50
CG12	Jay Buhner (Sept. 25-27)	.50
CG13	Vladimir Guerrero (June 22-25)	.75
CG13	Vladimir Guerrero (Aug. 10-12*)	1.50
CG13	Vladimir Guerrero (Sept. 14-16*)	1.50
CG14	Andruw Jones (July 16-19*)	1.50

		NM/M
CG14	Andruw Jones (Aug. 27-30*)	1.50
CG14	Andruw Jones (Sept. 17-20)	.75
CG15	Nomar Garciaparra (July 9-12*)	1.00
CG15	Nomar Garciaparra (Aug. 13-16*)	2.50
CG15	Nomar Garciaparra (Sept. 24-27)	1.00
CG16	Ken Caminiti (June 26-28*)	1.00
CG16	Ken Caminiti (July 13-15*)	1.00
CG16	Ken Caminiti (Sept. 10-13)	.50
CG17	Sammy Sosa (July 9-12*)	2.50
CG17	Sammy Sosa (Aug. 27-30*)	2.50
CG17	Sammy Sosa (Sept. 18-20)	1.00
CG18	Ben Grieve (June 30-July 2*)	1.00
CG18	Ben Grieve (Aug. 14-16)	.50
CG18	Ben Grieve (Sept. 24-27)	.50
CG19	Mo Vaughn (July 7)	.50
CG19	Mo Vaughn (Sept. 7-9)	.50
CG19	Mo Vaughn (Sept. 24-27*)	1.00
CG20	Frank Thomas (July 7)	.75
CG20	Frank Thomas (July 17-19*)	1.50
CG20	Frank Thomas (Sept. 4-6)	.75
CG21	Manny Ramirez (July 9-12)	.75
CG21	Manny Ramirez (Aug. 13-16*)	1.50
CG21	Manny Ramirez (Sept. 18-20*)	1.50
CG22	Jeff Bagwell (July 7)	.75
CG22	Jeff Bagwell (Aug. 28-30*)	1.50
CG22	Jeff Bagwell (Sept. 4-6*)	1.50
CG23	Jose Cruz Jr. (July 9-12)	.50
CG23	Jose Cruz Jr. (Aug. 13-16)	.50
CG23	Jose Cruz Jr. (Sept. 18-20)	.50
CG24	Alex Rodriguez (July 7*)	3.50
CG24	Alex Rodriguez (Aug. 6-9*)	3.50
CG24	Alex Rodriguez (Sept. 21-23*)	3.50
CG25	Mike Piazza (June 22-25*)	3.00
CG25	Mike Piazza (July 7)	1.25
CG25	Mike Piazza (Sept. 10-13*)	3.00
CG26	Tino Martinez (June 26-28*)	1.00
CG26	Tino Martinez (July 9-12)	.50
CG26	Tino Martinez (Aug. 13-16)	.50
CG27	Chipper Jones (July 3-5)	1.00
CG27	Chipper Jones (Aug. 27-30)	1.00
CG27	Chipper Jones (Sept. 17-20)	1.00
CG28	Juan Gonzalez (July 7)	.60
CG28	Juan Gonzalez (Aug. 6-9*)	1.25
CG28	Juan Gonzalez (Sept. 11-13*)	1.25
CG29	Jim Thome (June 22-23)	.60
CG29	Jim Thome (July 23-26*)	1.25
CG29	Jim Thome (Sept. 24-27)	.60
CG30	Barry Bonds (July 7*)	4.00
CG30	Barry Bonds (Sept. 4-6)	2.00
CG30	Barry Bonds (Sept. 18-20*)	4.00

1998 Collector's Choice You Crash the Game Winners

Collectors who redeemed winning "Crash" cards prior to the Dec. 1, 1998 deadline received an upgraded version of that player's card. Similar in format, the winners' cards have an action photo on front (different than the game card), with a metallic foil background. Instead of dates in the three circles at bottom are the letters "W I N." Backs have a career summary and stats, instead of the redemption instructions found on the game cards. The cards are numbered with a "CG" prefix. Cards of players who didn't homer during their designated dates were available only by redeeming a scarce (1:721 packs) Instant Win card. They are indicated here by "SP."

	NM/M
Complete Set (30):	9.00
Common Player:	.25
CG1	Ken Griffey Jr.	1.00
CG2	Travis Lee (SP)	.75
CG3	Larry Walker	.25
CG4	Tony Clark	.25
CG5	Cal Ripken Jr.	1.50
CG6	Tim Salmon/SP	.60
CG7	Vinny Castilla	.25
CG8	Fred McGriff	.25
CG9	Matt Williams	.25
CG10	Mark McGwire	1.25
CG11	Albert Belle	.25
CG12	Jay Buhner	.25
CG13	Vladimir Guerrero	.50
CG14	Andruw Jones	.50
CG15	Nomar Garciaparra	.75
CG16	Ken Caminiti	.25
CG17	Sammy Sosa	.75
CG18	Ben Grieve	.25
CG19	Mo Vaughn	.25
CG20	Frank Thomas	.50
CG21	Manny Ramirez	.50
CG22	Jeff Bagwell	.50
CG23	Jose Cruz Jr./SP	.60
CG24	Alex Rodriguez	1.25
CG25	Mike Piazza	1.00
CG26	Tino Martinez	.25
CG27	Chipper Jones/SP	1.50
CG28	Juan Gonzalez	.35
CG29	Jim Thome	.35
CG30	Barry Bonds	1.50

You Crash/Game Instant Winner

Found on average of one per 721 packs, these Instant Winner cards could be redeemed (with a $2 handling fee) for a complete set of You Crash the Game exchange cards - the only way Crash winner cards of Travis Lee, Jose Cruz Jr. and Chipper Jones could be obtained. These special cards have an instant winner logo on front in place of game dates, and a congratulatory message on back along with instructions for redemption prior to the Dec. 1, 1998 deadline.

	NM/M
Complete Set (30):	250.00
Common Player:	4.00

1995 Collector's Edge Ball Park Franks Baseball Legends

"Baseball Legends" Yogi Berra and Brooks Robinson are featured in this hot dog promotional set. Sunday newspapers on March 5 featured a coupon used to obtain the pair of autographed cards for eight proofs-of-purchase, or $2.50 with four UPCs or $5 with two UPCs. Cards have color photos, with uniform logos removed, and marbled borders. An authentic autograph is across the front of the card. Backs have a portrait photo and career summary. Each card was accompanied by a card-like certificate of authenticity.

	NM/M
Complete Set (2):	20.00
(1)	Yogi Berra	16.00
(2)	Frank Robinson	8.00

1993 Colorado Fever Rockies

In its inaugural issue, a fan magazine titled "Colorado Fever" issued a sheet of nine baseball cards in both its "Regional" and "Metro" editions. Stapled into the center of the magazine is an 8-3/8" x 11" cardboard insert. One panel has nine Rockies cards which are not perforated and would measure about 2-5/8" x 3-5/8" if cut from the sheet. Cards from the Metro

edition feature players in uniform; most of the cards from the Regional edition show the players in street clothes. It is not known whether future editions of the announced twice-annual magazine were ever published or if they contained baseball card inserts.

	NM/M
Complete Set (18):	8.00
Common Player:	.50
1M	David Nied	.50
2M	Charlie Hayes	.50
3M	Andy Ashby	.50
4M	Joe Girardi	.50
5M	Don Baylor	.60
6M	Andres Galarraga	.50
7M	Jim Tatum	.50
8M	Eric Young	.50
9M	Dante Bichette	.50
1R	Alex Cole	.50
2R	Don Baylor	.60
3R	Dante Bichette	.50
4R	Jeff Parrett	.50
5R	David Nied	.50
6R	Butch Henry	.50
7R	Andres Galarraga	.50
8R	Daryl Boston	.50
9R	Joe Girardi	.50

1994 Colorado Rockies Police

Howard Johnson
Outfield

The Rockies' premiere police set is an oversized (2-5/8" x 4") effort with posed and action player photos on a yellow and purple background on front. Team logo and name are above the photo, while ID and uniform number are beneath the photo. Backs are printed in purple with a few bits of personal data and stats, a safety message and sponsors' logos. The cards are checklisted here in alphabetical order.

	NM/M
Complete Set (27):	6.00
Common Player:	.50
(1)	Don Baylor	.75
(2)	Dante Bichette	.75
(3)	Willie Blair	.50
(4)	Kent Bottenfield	.50
(5)	Ellis Burks	.50
(6)	Vinny Castilla	.50
(7)	Marvin Freeman	.50
(8)	Andres Galarraga	.75
(9)	Andres Galarraga (Batting champion.)	.75
(10)	Joe Girardi	.50
(11)	Mike Harkey	.50
(12)	Greg Harris	.50
(13)	Charlie Hayes	.50
(14)	Darren Holmes	.50
(15)	Howard Johnson	.50
(16)	Nelson Liriano	.50
(17)	Roberto Mejia	.50
(18)	Mike Munoz	.50
(19)	David Nied	.50
(20)	Steve Reed	.50
(21)	Armando Reynoso	.50
(22)	Bruce Ruffin	.50
(23)	Danny Sheaffer	.50
(24)	Darrell Sherman	.50
(25)	Walt Weiss	.50
(26)	Eric Young	.50
(27)	Rockies Coaches (Larry Bearnarth, Dwight Evans, Gene Glynn, Ron Hassey, Bill Plummer, Don Zimmer)	.50

1995 Colorado Rockies Police

With only a dozen players included, this is one of the smallest safety sets of the genre. The 2-5/8" x 4" cards have color player action photos on front, bordered in black with the team logo in the lower-right corner. The player's last name and year appear in orange in the

upper-right. Backs are in black-and-white and include a safety message or cartoon, and a few biographical data and stats. Cards are checklisted by uniform number.

	NM/M
Complete Set (12):	5.00
Common Player:	.50
6	Jason Bates	.50
7	Joe Girardi	.50
9	Vinny Castilla	.50
10	Dante Bichette	.50
12	Mike Kingery	.50
14	Andres Galarraga	.75
20	Bill Swift	.50
21	Eric Young	.50
22	Walt Weiss	.50
25	Don Baylor	.75
26	Ellis Burks	.50
33	Larry Walker	1.50

1996 Colorado Rockies Police

Painter • 28

The Rockies third annual safety set is the team's largest, at 27 cards. The set's format is 2-5/8" x 4" and is sponsored by Kansas City Life Insurance. Fronts have game-action photos, with the team logo, player last name and uniform number at bottom. Backs are printed in purple and feature a safety-message cartoon. The set was initially distributed to fans attending an April game. The set is checklisted here by uniform number. A Spanish-language version of the set was also issued.

	NM/M
Complete Set (27):	5.00
Common Player:	.25
Spanish:	2X
1	Trenidad Hubbard	.25
3	Quinton McCracken	.25
9	Jason Bates	.25
10	Vinny Castilla	.25
10	Dante Bichette	.25
14	Andres Galarraga	.50
16	Curtis Leskanic	.25
18	Bruce Ruffin	.25
20	Bill Swift	.25
21	Eric Young	.25
22	Walt Weiss	.25
23	Bryan Rekar	.25
25	Don Baylor	.35
26	Ellis Burks	.25
28	Lance Painter	.25
31	Kevin Ritz	.25
31	Bret Saberhagen	.35
32	Mark Thompson	.25
33	Larry Walker	1.00
34	Jayhawk Owens	.25
35	John Vander Wal	.25
38	Roger Bailey	.25
39	Steve Reed	.25
40	Darren Holmes	.25
41	Armando Reynoso	.25
43	Mike Munoz	.25
44	Marvin Freeman	.25

1997 Colorado Rockies Police

In conjunction with the Colorado Association of Chiefs of Police, the Rockies handed out this safety set at a designated home game early in the season. It is the team's fourth annual safety set. The 2-1/2" x 3-1/2" cards feature game-action photos on front surrounded by a white border. The team logo is at upper-left; player identification is in purple and gray stripes diagonally at bottom. Backs are in black-and-white and have some player personal data, a career-best stat lines and a safety message. Cards are numbered by uniform number in a baseball at upper-right.

	NM/M
Complete Set (12):	5.00
Common Player:	.60
3	Quinton McCracken	.60
8	Kirt Manwaring	.60
9	Vinny Castilla	.60
10	Dante Bichette	.60
14	Andres Galarraga	.75
20	Bill Swift	.60
21	Eric Young	.60
22	Walt Weiss	.60
25	Don Baylor	.75
26	Ellis Burks	.60
33	Larry Walker	1.50
00	Dinger (Mascot)	.60

1998 Colorado Rockies Police

Children attending a May 31 promotional game at Coors Field received this set of Rockies cards. Game-action color photos are featured on front, borderless at top, bottom and left. At right is a vertical gray stripe with the player's name and position; team logo and name are at bottom. On back is a player portrait photo, identification, biographical details, an inspirational message and logos of the sponsoring organizations.

	NM/M
Complete Set (12):	6.00
Common Player:	.35
3	Mike Lansing	.50
5	Neifi Perez	.50
8	Kirt Manwaring	.50
9	Vinny Castilla	.50
10	Dante Bichette	.50
17	Todd Helton	4.00
25	Don Baylor	.60
26	Ellis Burks	.50
33	Larry Walker	1.00
34	Pedro Astacio	.50
57	Darryl Kile	.50
00	Dinger (Mascot)	.50

1999 Colorado Rockies Police

Children attending a promotional game at Coors Field received this set of Rockies cards. Borderless game-action color photos are featured on front. At right is a vertical strip with the team name; the

player name and position are at bottom. On back is a player portrait photo, identification, biographical details, a safety message and logos of the sponsoring organizations.

	NM/M
Complete Set (12):	6.00
Common Player:	1.00
(1)	Dante Bichette	1.00
(2)	Vinny Castilla	1.00
(3)	Dinger (Mascot)	1.00
(4)	Jerry DiPoto	1.00
(5)	Darryl Hamilton	1.00
(6)	Todd Helton	2.50
(7)	Darryl Kile	1.00
(8)	Mike Lansing	1.00
(9)	Jim Leyland	1.00
(10)	Kirt Manwaring	1.00
(11)	Neifi Perez	1.00
(12)	Larry Walker	1.50

2000 Colorado Rockies Police

Children attending a May 28 promotional game at Coors Field received this set of Rockies cards. Borderless game-action color photos are featured on front. On back is a player portrait photo, identification, biographical details, an inspirational message and a credit line for the Colorado Association of Chiefs of Police.

	NM/M
Complete Set (12):	6.00
Common Player:	.75
3	Mike Lansing	.75
6	Jeffrey Hammonds	.75
5	Neifi Perez	.75
7	Jeff Cirillo	.75
8	Brent Mayne	.75
17	Todd Helton	3.00
24	Tom Goodwin	.75
25	Buddy Bell	.75
30	Rolando Arrojo	.75
33	Larry Walker	1.50
00	Dinger (Mascot)	.75
---	Coors Field	.75

1995 Comic Images National Pastime Promo

This unnumbered card was issued to promote Comic Images' set of baseball history cards. The 2-1/2" x 3-1/2" card has a familiar

Castilla • 1995

Colorado ROCKIES

color photo of company spokesman Phil Rizzuto on front, done up in chromium technology and with the Yankees team logos removed from the uniform. The back advertises the forthcoming card set.

	NM/M
Phil Rizzuto	3.00

1995 Comic Images The National Pastime

This set is principally made up of 19th Century baseball images done up in 20th Century chromium card technology to detail the history of baseball from the 1860s through the 1950s. As might be expected, there was little positive reaction from collectors. Photos of old baseball collectibles, including a few vintage baseball cards are scattered throughout the set as are a few actual player photos. Hall of Famer Phil Rizzuto was tapped to promote the issue, but his name was misspelled on the cards' box. A number of special inserts including Rizzuto autographed cards were part of the issue.

	NM/M
Complete Set (90):	8.00
Common Card:	.10
Autographed Rizzuto Card:	35.00
MagnaChrome	
Career Card (6):	2.00
MagnaChrome Diamond	
Cover (3):	1.00
Medallion Card:	2.00
Six-card Case-Topper Sheet:	6.00
1 Sportsman's Park	.10
2 Harper's Weekly, August, 1913	.10
3 Shibe Park	.10
4 Polo Grounds Print	.10
5 Forbes Field	.10
6 Hall of Fame (Phil Rizzuto)	.25
7 League Park	.10
8 Highlander Park	.10
9 South Side Park	.10
10 Catchers' Mitt	.10
11 Baseball Trophy	.10
12 Baseball Plate	.10
13 Bisque Figure	.10
14 Beanbag	.10
15 Tobacco Carved Figure	.10
16 Sunday Magazine	.10
17 Street & Smith Sport	.10
18 Collier's	.10
19 Bluebook	.10
20 Chadwick's	.10
21 Harper's Weekly	.10
22 American Magazine	.10
23 Crazy Baseball Stories	.10
24 New York Giants, 1892	.10
25 Cincinnati American Association, 1882	.10
26 Chicago White Stockings, 1885	.10
27 Baltimore Blues, 1890	.10
28 Chicago & All-Americans, 1889	.10
29 Philadelphia Baseball Team, 1910	.10
30 1887 Goodwin & Co. Champions	.25
31 John McGraw	.15
32 Home Run (1885 trade card)	.10
33 Lorillard Chicago BBC	.10
34 Boston BBC	.10
35 Out at First (Trade card.)	.10
36 "Coffee Cards"	.10
37 Uncut Sheet - Detail	.10
38 Tobin Lithographers	.10
39 Uncut Sheet - Die Cut	.10
40 Patsy Dougherty (T207)	.10
41 A Regular Corker (1885 trade card)	.10
42 Barker's Advertising Book	.10
43 Toledo BBC Tobacco Poster	.10
44 Shredded Wheat Advertisement	.10

45	BVD Advertisement	.10
46	Police Gazette Poster	.10
47	Japanese Poster	.10
48	Safe Hit Vegetable Crate Label	.10
49	Slide, Kelly, Slide Poster	.10
50	Peck & Snyder Hat Advertisement	.10
51	Reach Gloves Catalog	.10
52	New York Giants Scorecard	.10
53	Game Card	.10
54	Wright & Ditson Guide	.10
55	1933 All-Star Game Program	.10
56	Stadium Scene	.10
57	Currier & Ives Print	.10
58	Scorecard Artwork	.10
59	Folk Art	.10
60	Batter (Wrong front, belongs to #73.)	.10
61	Cartoon	.10
62	Teddy Roosevelt Cartoon	.10
63	Uncle Sam Cartoon	.10
64	Casey at the Bat	.15
65	Seymour Church Print	.10
66	Valentine Card	.10
67	Pinup Book	.10
68	Uncle Sam WWI Sheet Music	.10
69	Baseball Sheet Music	.10
70	Saturday Globe	.10
71	Ft. Wayne Woman Player	.15
72	Spalding Baseball Guide	.10
73	Rally Day Postcard (Wrong front, belongs to #60.)	.10
74	Spalding Advertisement Die Cut	.10
75	Our Baseball Club Cover	.10
76	Jake Beckley	.15
77	Cap Anson (Allen & Ginter album page)	.25
78	St. Louis Player	.10
79	Sam Thompson (Scrap's Die Cut)	.15
80	Bobby Wallace (Turkey Red cabinet)	.15
81	Fogarty & McGuire (Jim Fogarty, Deacon McGuire (1887 Kalamazoo Bats detail)	.15
82	Yank Robinson (1887 die-cut game card)	.15
83	Charles Comiskey (1887 Scrap's tobacco die-cut)	.15
84	Picked Off! (Action photo.)	.10
85	Error (Action photo.)	.10
86	Third Base (Action photo.)	.10
87	Safe at Home (Action photo.)	.10
88	Baseball Action (Action photo.)	.10
89	Great Fielding (Action photo.)	.10
90	Checklist	.10

1991 Conlon Collection Prototypes

BABE RUTH BOSTON RED SOX - PITCHER   1916

The cards which previewed the debut set of Conlon Collection cards in the 1990s can generally be identified by the lack of Major League Baseball logo and Curtis Management copyright information on back. Except for the colorized Babe Ruth card, they are not otherwise marked as prototypes. While most of the 1991 Conlon prototypes were distributed in relatively small quantities, reportedly 2,940, the colorized Ty Cobbs was an edition of 60,000 and the colorized Babe Ruth card was produced for the 12th National Sports Collectors Convention in Anaheim, Calif., to the tune of 225,000 cards.

	NM/M
Complete Set (6):	9.00
Common Player:	2.00
13 Ty Cobb (Colorized edition of 60,000.)	4.50
34 Dizzy Dean	2.00
111 Lou Gehrig	3.50
145 Babe Ruth	4.50

145	Babe Ruth (Colorized, edition of 225,000.)	3.00
250	Ty Cobb	3.00

1991 Conlon Collection

JOE DUGAN NEW YORK YANKEES - 3RD BASE   1927

This 330-card set features the photography of Charles Martin Conlon, who was active from before 1910 through the early 1940s. Black-and-white photos are set against black borders on the UV-coated card fronts. Megacards worked with The Sporting News (owners of the Conlon photos) to release the set. Several subsets are featured such as Hall of Famers, 1927 New York Yankees, MVPs and more. The backs feature statistics and career highlights and can be found either with or without the MLB logo.

	NM/M
Complete Factory Set (330):	13.50
Factory Set w/Auto. Feller:	16.00
Complete Set (330):	9.00
Common Player:	.10
Wax Pack (18):	.50
Wax Box (36):	15.00
1 Rogers Hornsby	.25
2 James E. Foxx	.25
3 Jay H. Dean	.25
4 Walter J.V. Maranville	.10
5 Paul G. Waner	.10
6 Lloyd J. Waner	.10
7 Melvin T. Ott	.15
8 John P. Wagner	.30
9 Walter P. Johnson	.25
10 Carl O. Hubbell	.15
11 Frank F. Frisch	.15
12 Hazen S. Cuyler	.10
13 Charles H. Ruffing	.10
14 Henry B. Greenberg	.15
15 John J. Evers	.10
16 Hugh A. Jennings	.10
17 David J. Bancroft	.10
18 Joseph M. Medwick	.10
19 Theodore A. Lyons	.10
20 Charles A. Bender	.10
21 Edward T. Collins	.10
22 James L. Bottomley	.10
23 Robert M. Grove	.15
24 Max Carey	.10
25 Burleigh A. Grimes	.10
26 Ross M. Youngs	.10
27 Ernest N. Lombardi	.10
28 Joseph V. McCarthy	.10
29 Lewis R, Wilson	.10
30 Charles H. Klein	.10
31 Howard E. Averill Sr.	.10
32 Grover C. Alexander	.15
33 Charles J. Hafey	.10
34 William B. McKechnie	.10
35 Robert W.A. Feller	.15
36 Harold J. Traynor	.10
37 Charles D. Stengel	.15
38 Joseph F. Vaughan	.10
39 Eppa Rixey	.10
40 Joseph W. Sewell	.10
41 Urban C. Faber	.10
42 Travis C. Jackson	.10
43 Jesse J. Haines	.10
44 Tristram E. Speaker	.25
45 Cornelius Mack	.10
46 Cornelius Mack	.10
47 Cornelius Mack	.10
48 Raymond W. Schalk	.10
49 Aloysius H. Simmons	.10
50 Joseph E. Cronin	.10
51 Gordon S. Cochrane	.10
52 Harry E. Heilmann	.10
53 John R. Mize	.15
54 Edgar C. Rice	.10
55 Edd J. Roush	.10
56 Enos B. Slaughter	.10
57 Christopher Mathewson	.25
58 Fred C. Lindstrom	.10
59 Charles L. Hartnett	.10
60 George L. Kelly	.10
61 Stanley R. Harris	.10
62 Leon A. Goslin	.10
63 Henry E. Manush	.10
64 William H. Terry	.10
65 John J. McGraw	.10
66 George H. Sisler	.10
67 Vernon L. Gomez	.10

68	Joseph I. Judge	.10
69	Thomas J. Thevenow	.10
70	Charles M. Gelbert	.10
71	Minter C. Hayes	.10
72	Robert R. Fothergill	.10
73	Adam A. Comorosky	.10
74	Earl S. Smith	.10
75	Samuel D. Gray	.10
76	Peter W. Appleton	.10
77	Eugene Moore Jr.	.10
78	Arndt L. Jorgens	.10
79	William H. Knickerbocker	.10
80	Carl N. Reynolds	.10
81	Oscar D. Melillo	.10
82	John H. Burnett	.10
83	Alvin J. Powell	.10
84	John J. Murphy	.10
85	Leroy E. Parmelee	.10
86	James A. Ripple	.10
87	Gerald H. Walker	.10
88	George L. Earnshaw	.10
89	William H. Southworth	.10
90	Wallace Moses	.10
91	George E. Walberg	.10
92	James J. Dykes	.10
93	Charles H. Root	.10
94	John W. Cooney	.10
95	Charles J. Grimm	.10
96	Robert L. Johnson	.10
97	John W. Scott	.10
98	Raymond A. Radcliff	.10
99	Frederick R. Ostermueller	.10
100	Julian V. Wera	.10
101	Miller J. Huggins	.10
102	Raymond A. Morehart	.10
103	Bernard O. Bengough	.10
104	Walter H. Ruether	.10
105	Earle B. Combs	.10
106	Myles L. Thomas	.10
107	Benjamin E. Paschal	.10
108	Cedric M. Durst	.10
109	William W. Moore	.10
110	George H. Ruth	1.00
111	Louis H. Gehrig	.50
112	Joseph A. Dugan	.10
113	Anthony M. Lazzeri	.10
114	Urban J. Shocker	.10
115	Waite C. Hoyt	.10
116	Charles T. O'Leary	.10
117	Arthur Fletcher	.10
118	Tharon L. Collins	.10
119	Joseph O. Giard	.10
120	Herbert J. Pennock	.10
121	Michael Gazella	.10
122	Robert W. Meusel	.10
123	George W. Pipgras	.10
124	John P. Grabowski	.10
125	Mark A. Koenig	.10
126	Stanley C. Hack	.10
127	Earl O. Whitehill	.10
128	William C. Lee	.10
129	Frank O. Mancuso	.10
130	Francis R. Blades	.10
131	John I. Burns	.10
132	Clinton H. Brown	.10
133	William J. Dietrich	.10
134	Darrell E. Blanton	.10
135	Harry B. Hooper	.10
136	Charles H. Shorten	.10
137	Clarence W. Walker	.10
138	George Foster	.10
139	John J. Barry	.10
140	Samuel P. Jones	.10
141	Ernest G. Shore	.10
142	Hubert B. Leonard	.10
143	Herbert J. Pennock	.10
144	Harold C. Janvrin	.10
145	George H. Ruth	1.00
146	George E. Lewis	.10
147	William L. Gardner	.10
148	Richard C. Hoblitzel	.10
149	Lewis E. Scott	.10
150	Carl W. Mays	.10
151	John A. Niehoff	.10
152	Burton E. Shotton	.10
153	Leon K. Ames	.10
154	Fred Williams	.10
155	William W. Hinchman	.10
156	James R. Shawkey	.10
157	Walter C. Pipp	.10
158	George J. Burns	.10
159	Robert H. Veach	.10
160	Harold H. Chase	.10
161	Thomas L. Hughes	.10
162	Derrill B. Pratt	.10
163	Henry K. Groh	.10
164	Zachariah D. Wheat	.10
165	Francis J. O'Doul	.10
166	William E. Kamm	.10
167	Paul G. Waner	.10
168	Fred C. Snodgrass	.10
169	Floyd C. Herman	.10
170	Albert H. Bridwell	.10
171	John T. Meyers	.10
172	John B. Lobert	.10
173	Raymond B. Bressler	.10
174	Samuel P. Jones	.10
175	Robert A. O'Farrell	.10
176	George Toporcer	.10
177	George E. McNeely	.10
178	John H. Knott	.10
179	Clarence F. Mueller	.10
180	Thomas J.D. Bridges	.10
181	Lloyd A. Brown	.10
182	Lawrence J. Benton	.10
183	Max F. Bishop	.10
184	Morris Berg	.20
185	Ralph F. Perkins	.10

186	Stephen F. O'Neill	.10
187	Glenn C. Myatt	.10
188	Joseph A. Kuhel	.10
189	Martin J. McManus	.10
190	Charles F. Lucas	.10
191	John P. McInnis	.10
192	Edmund J. Miller	.10
193	James L. Sewell	.10
194	William H. Sherdel	.10
195	Harold J. Rhyne	.10
196	Guy T. Bush	.10
197	Ervin Fox	.10
198	Wesley C. Ferrell	.10
199	Roy C. Johnson	.10
200	William Wambsganss	.10
201	George H. Burns	.10
202	Clarence E. Mitchell	.10
203	Cornelius Ball	.10
204	John H. Neun	.10
205	Homer W. Summa	.10
206	Ernest K. Padgett	.10
207	Walter H. Holke	.10
208	Forrest G. Wright	.10
209	Henry M. Gowdy	.10
210	James W. Taylor	.10
211	Benjamin C. Cantwell	.10
212	Joseph F. Demaree	.10
213	Samuel P. Derringer	.10
214	William A. Hallahan	.10
215	Daniel K. MacFayden	.10
216	Harry F. Rice	.10
217	Robert Eldridge Smith	.10
218	Jackson R. Stephenson	.10
219	Perce L. Malone	.10
220	Henry B. Tate	.10
221	Joseph F. Vosmik	.10
222	George A. Watkins	.10
223	James Wilson	.10
224	George E. Uhle	.10
225	Melvin T. Ott	.15
226	Nicholas Altrock	.10
227	Charles H. Ruffing	.10
228	Joseph V.L. Krakauskas	.10
229	Walter A. Berger	.10
230	Norman L. Newsom	.10
231	Lonnie Warneke	.10
232	Frank E. Snyder	.10
233	Myril O. Hoag	.10
234	Baldomero M. Almada	.10
235	Ivy B. Wingo	.10
236	James P. Austin	.10
237	Henry J. Bonura	.10
238	Russell G. Wrightstone	.10
239	Alfred C. Todd	.10
240	Harold B. Warstler	.10
241	Samuel F. West	.10
242	Arthur C. Reinhart	.10
243	Walter C. Stewart	.10
244	John B. Gooch	.10
245	Eugene F. Hargrave	.10
246	George W. Harper	.10
247	George W. Connally	.10
248	Edgar G. Braxton	.10
249	Walter H. Schang	.10
250	Tyrus S. Cobb	.50
251	Rogers Hornsby	.15
252	Richard M. Marquard	.10
253	Carl O. Hubbell	.15
254	Joe Wood	.10
255	Robert M. Grove	.15
256	Lynwood T. Rowe	.10
257	Alvin F. Crowder	.10
258	Walter P. Johnson	.15
259	Charles J. Hafey	.10
260	Frederick L. Fitzsimmons	.10
261	William E. Webb	.10
262	Earle B. Combs	.10
263	Edward J. Konetchy	.10
264	Taylor L. Douthit	.10
265	Lloyd J. Waner	.10
266	Gordon S. Cochrane	.10
267	John O. Wilson	.10
268	Harold J. Traynor	.10
269	Virgil L. Davis	.10
270	Henry E. Manush	.10
271	Michael F. Higgins	.10
272	Adrian Joss	.10
273	Edward Augustine Walsh	.10
274	Johnny L.R. Martin	.10
275	Joseph W. Sewell	.10
276	Hubert B. Leonard	.10
277	Clifford C. Cravath	.10
278	Oral C. Hildebrand	.10
279	Remy P. Kremer	.10
280	Frank A. Pytlak	.10
281	Samuel D. Byrd	.10
282	Curtis B. Davis	.10
283	Lewis A. Fonseca	.10
284	Herold D. Ruel	.10
285	Julius J. Solters	.10
286	Fred W. Schulte	.10
287	John P. Quinn	.10
288	Arthur C. Whitney	.10
289	Jonathon T. Stone	.10
290	Hugh M. Critz	.10
291	Ira J. Flagstead	.10
292	George F. Grantham	.10
293	Samuel D. Hale	.10
294	James F. Hogan	.10
295	Oswald L. Bluege	.10
296	Debs Garms	.10
297	Augustaf B. Friberg	.10
298	Edward A. Brandt	.10
299	Ralston B. Hemsley	.10
300	Charles H. Klein	.10
301	Morton C. Cooper	.10
302	James L. Bottomley	.10
303	James E. Foxx	.15

304	Frank Schulte	.10
305	Frank F. Frisch	.15
306	Frank A. McCormick	.10
307	Jacob E. Daubert	.10
308	Roger T. Peckinpaugh	.10
309	George H. Burns	.10
310	Louis H. Gehrig	.50
311	Aloysius H. Simmons	.10
312	Edward T. Collins	.10
313	Charles L. Hartnett	.10
314	Joseph E. Cronin	.10
315	Paul G. Waner	.10
316	Robert A. O'Farrell	.10
317	Lawrence J. Doyle	.10
318	Lynford H. Lary	.10
319	Frank S. May	.10
320	Roy H. Spencer	.10
321	Samuel R. Coffman	.10
322	Peter J. Donohue	.10
323	George W. Haas	.10
324	Edward S. Farrell	.10
325	Charles F. Rhem	.10
326	Frederick Marberry	.10
327	Charles Martin Conlon	.10
328	Checklist 1-110	.10
329	Checklist 111-220	.10
330	Checklist 221-330	.10

1992 Conlon Collection Prototypes

JOE JACKSON CLEVELAND INDIANS - OUTFIELD   1913

Along with the 1991 Babe Ruth prototype card, these five cards were distributed at the Anaheim National Sports Collectors Convention in 1991. The announced distribution was 20,000 of each card except the Joe Jackson, which had a press run of 67,000. Except for card 331, all the prototypes have different numbers than the same card in the regular-issue Conlon set. Each of the 1992 cards has a gray "PROTOTYPE" overprinted diagonally on the back.

	NM/M
Complete Set (6):	9.00
Common Player:	.50
14 Joe Jackson (Colorized, edition of 60,000.)	3.00
331 Christy Mathewson	1.50
400 Joe Jackson	2.50
450 Hughie Jennings	.50
500 Ty Cobb	2.00
520 Goose Goslin	.50

1992 Conlon Collection

ALLEN SOTHORON ST. LOUIS BROWNS - PITCHER   1917

In their second season, the 330 cards of the Conlon Collection were numbered consecutively where the 1991 premiere issue ended. Cards 331-660 also maintained the high-gloss black-and-white format of the previous year. Many subsets within the issue carry special designations on the card fronts. Subsets included no-hitters, Triple Crown winners, "Great Stories," nicknames and more.

	NM/M
Factory Set (330):	25.00
Complete Set (330):	15.00
Common Player:	.10
Wax Pack:	.50
Wax Box (36):	15.00

#	Player	Price
331	Christopher Mathewson	.15
332	George L. Wiltse	.10
333	George N. Rucker	.10
334	Leon K. Ames	.10
335	Charles A. Bender	.10
336	Joe Wood	.10
337	Edward Augustine Walsh	.10
338	George J. Mullin	.10
339	Earl A. Hamilton	.10
340	Charles M Tesreau	.10
341	James Scott	.10
342	Richard W. Marquard	.10
343	Claude R. Hendrix	.15
344	James S. Lavender	.10
345	Leslie A. Bush	.10
346	Hubert B. Leonard	.10
347	Fred A. Toney	.10
348	James L. Vaughn	.10
349	Ernest G. Koob	.10
350	Robert Groom	.10
351	Ernest G. Shore	.10
352	Horace O. Eller	.10
353	Walter P. Johnson	.15
354	Charles C. Robertson	.10
355	Jesse L. Barnes	.10
356	Samuel P. Jones	.10
357	Howard J. Ehmke	.10
358	Jesse J. Haines	.10
359	Theodore A. Lyons	.10
360	Carl O. Hubbell	.15
361	Wesley C. Ferrell	.10
362	Robert J. Burke	.10
363	Paul D. Dean	.10
364	Norman L. Newsom	.10
365	Lloyd V. Kennedy	.10
366	William J. Dietrich	.10
367	John S. Vander Meer	.10
368	John S. Vander Meer	.10
369	Montgomery M. Pearson	.10
370	Robert W.A. Feller	.15
371	Lonnie Warneke	.10
372	James A. Tobin	.10
373	Earl A. Moore	.10
374	William H. Dineen	.10
375	Malcolm W. Eason	.10
376	George A. Mogridge	.10
377	Clarence A. Vance	.10
378	James O. Carleton	.10
379	Clyde M. Shoun	.10
380	Franklin W. Hayes	.10
381	Benjamin R. Frey	.10
382	Henry W. Johnson	.10
383	Ralph Kress	.10
384	John T. Allen	.10
385	Harold A. Trosky Sr.	.10
386	Eugene E. Robertson	.10
387	Lemuel F. Young	.10
388	George A. Selkirk	.10
389	Edwin L. Wells	.10
390	James D. Weaver	.10
391	George H. McQuinn	.10
392	John B. Lobert	.10
393	Ernest E. Swanson	.10
394	Ernest A. Nevers	.10
395	James J. Levey	.10
396	Hugo F. Bezdek	.10
397	Walter E. French	.10
398	Charles F. Berry	.10
399	Franklin T. Grube	.10
400	Charles W. Dressen	.10
401	Alfred E. Neale	.10
402	Henry A. Vick	.10
403	James F. Thorpe	.50
404	Walter J. Gilbert	.10
405	John L. Urban	.10
406	Everett V. Purdy	.10
407	Albert O. Wright	.10
408	William M. Urbanski	.10
409	Charles W. Fischer	.10
410	John R. Warner	.10
411	Chalmer W. Cissell	.10
412	Mervin D.J. Shea	.10
413	Adolfo Luque	.10
414	John L. Bassler	.10
415	Arvel O. Hale	.10
416	Lawrence R. French	.10
417	William C. Walker	.10
418	Allen L. Cooke	.10
419	Philip J. Todt	.10
420	Ivy P. Andrews	.10
421	William J. Herman	.10
422	Tristram E. Speaker	.15
423	Aloysius H. Simmons	.10
424	Lewis R. Wilson	.10
425	Tyrus R. Cobb	.40
426	George H. Ruth	.50
427	Ernest N. Lombardi	.10
428	Jay H. Dean	.15
429	Lloyd J. Waner	.10
430	Henry B. Greenberg	.15
431	Robert M. Grove	.10
432	Gordon S. Cochrane	.10
433	Burleigh A. Grimes	.10
434	Harold J. Traynor	.10
435	John R. Mize	.15
436	Edgar C. Rice	.10
437	Leon A. Goslin	.10
438	Charles H. Klein	.10
439	Cornelius Mack	.10
440	James L. Bottomley	.10
441	Jackson R. Stephenson	.10
442	Kenneth Williams	.10
443	Charles B. Adams	.10
444	Joseph J. Jackson	.50
445	Harold Newhouser	.10
446	Wesley C. Ferrell	.10
447	Francis J. O'Doul	.10
448	Walter H. Schang	.10
449	Sherwood R. Magee	.10
450	Michael J. Donlin	.10
451	Roger M. Cramer	.10
452	Richard W. Bartell	.10
453	Earle T. Mack	.10
454	Walter G. Brown	.10
455	John A. Heving	.10
456	Percy L. Jones	.10
457	Theodore Blankenship	.10
458	Absalom H. Wingo	.10
459	Roger P. Bresnahan	.10
460	William J. Klem	.10
461	Charles L. Gehringer	.10
462	Stanley A. Coveleski	.10
463	Edward S. Plank	.10
464	Clark C.F. Griffith	.10
465	Herbert J. Pennock	.10
466	Earle B. Combs	.10
467	Robert P. Doerr	.10
468	Waite C. Hoyt	.10
469	Thomas H. Connolly	.10
470	Harry B. Hooper	.10
471	Richard B. Ferrell	.10
472	William G. Evans	.10
473	William J. Herman	.10
474	William M. Dickey	.15
475	Lucius B. Appling	.15
476	Ralph A. Pinelli	.10
477	Donald E. McNair	.10
478	John F. Blake	.10
479	Valentine J. Picinich	.10
480	Fred A. Heimach	.10
481	John G. Graney	.10
482	Ewell A. Russell	.10
483	Urban C. Faber	.10
484	Benjamin M. Kauff	.10
485	Clarence L. Rowland	.10
486	Robert H. Veach	.10
487	James C. Bagby	.10
488	William D. Perritt	.10
489	Charles L. Herzog	.10
490	Arthur Fletcher	.10
491	Walter H. Holke	.10
492	Arthur N. Nehf	.10
493	Lafayette F. Thompson	.10
494	James D. Welsh	.10
495	Oscar J. Vitt	.10
496	Owen T. Carroll	.10
497	James K. O'Dea	.10
498	Fredrick M. Frankhouse	.10
499	Jewel W. Ens	.10
500	Morris Arnovich	.10
501	Walter Gerber	.10
502	George W. Davis	.10
503	Charles S. Myer	.10
504	Samuel A. Leslie	.10
505	William C. Bolton	.10
506	Fred Walker	.10
507	John W. Smith	.10
508	Irving D. Hadley	.10
509	Clyde E. Crouse	.10
510	Joseph C. Glenn	.10
511	Clyde E. Kimsey	.10
512	Louis K. Finney	.10
513	Alfred V. Lawson	.10
514	Charles P. Fullis	.10
515	Earl H. Sheely	.10
516	George Gibson	.10
517	John J. Broaca	.10
518	Bibb A. Falk	.10
519	Frank O. Hurst	.10
520	Grover A. Hartley	.10
521	Donald H. Heffner	.10
522	Harvey L. Hendrick	.10
523	Allen S. Sothoron	.10
524	Anthony F. Piet	.10
525	Tyrus R. Cobb	.40
526	James E. Foxx	.15
527	Rogers Hornsby	.15
528	Napoleon LaJoie	.15
529	Louis H. Gehrig	.40
530	Henry Zimmerman	.10
531	Charles H. Klein	.10
532	Hugh Duffy	.10
533	Robert M. Grove	.15
534	Grover C. Alexander	.10
535	Amos W. Rusie	.10
536	Vernon L. Gomez	.10
537	Walter H. Walters	.10
538	Urban J. Hodapp	.10
539	Bruce D. Campbell	.10
540	Horace M. Lisenbee	.10
541	John F. Fournier	.10
542	James R. Tabor	.10
543	John H. Burnett	.10
544	Roy A. Hartzell	.10
545	Walter P. Gautreau	.10
546	Emil O. Yde	.10
547	Robert L. Johnson	.10
548	Joseph J. Hauser	.10
549	Edward M. Reulbach	.10
550	Baldomero M. Almada	.10
551	Gordon S. Cochrane	.10
552	Carl O. Hubbell	.15
553	Charles L. Gehringer	.10
554	Aloysius H. Simmons	.10
555	Mordecai P.C. Brown	.10
556	Hugh A. Jennings	.10
557	Norman A. Elberfeld	.10
558	Charles D. Stengel	.10
559	Alexander Schacht	.10
560	James E. Foxx	.15
561	George L. Kelly	.10
562	Lloyd J. Waner	.10
563	Paul W. Waner	.15
564	Walter P. Johnson	.15
565	John Franklin Baker	.10
566	Roy J. Hughes	.10
567	Lewis S. Riggs	.10
568	John H. Whitehead	.10
569	Elam R. Vangilder	.10
570	William A. Zitzmann	.10
571	Walter J. Schmidt	.10
572	John A. Tavener	.10
573	Joseph E. Genewich	.10
574	John A. Marcum	.10
575	Fred Hofmann	.10
576	Robert A. Rolfe	.10
577	Victor G. Sorrell	.10
578	Floyd J. Scott	.10
579	Alphonse Thomas	.10
580	Alfred J. Smith	.10
581	Walter J. Henline	.10
582	Edward T. Collins	.10
583	Earle B. Combs	.10
584	John J. McGraw	.10
585	Lewis R. Wilson	.10
586	Charles L. Hartnett	.10
587	Hazen S. Cuyler	.10
588	William H. Terry	.10
589	Joseph V. McCarthy	.10
590	Henry B. Greenberg	.15
591	Tristram E. Speaker	.10
592	William B. McKechnie	.10
593	Stanley R. Harris	.10
594	Herbert J. Pennock	.10
595	George H. Sisler	.10
596	Fred C. Lindstrom	.10
597	Howard E. Averill Sr.	.10
598	David J. Bancroft	.10
599	Cornelius Mack	.10
600	Joseph E. Cronin	.10
601	Kenneth L. Ash	.10
602	Alfred R. Spohrer	.10
603	Lee R. Mahaffey	.10
604	James F. O'Rourke	.10
605	Ulysses S.G. Stoner	.10
606	Frank H. Gabler	.10
607	Thomas F. Padden	.10
608	Charles A. Shires	.10
609	Sherrod M. Smith	.10
610	Philip Weintraub	.10
611	Russell Van Atta	.10
612	Joyner C. White	.10
613	Clifford G. Melton	.10
614	James J. Ring	.10
615	John H. Sand	.10
616	David D. Alexander	.10
617	Kent Greenfield	.10
618	Edwin H. Dyer	.10
619	William H. Sherdel	.10
620	Hubert M. Lanier	.10
621	Robert A. O'Farrell	.10
622	Rogers Hornsby	.15
623	William A. Beckman	.10
624	Morton C. Cooper	.10
625	William P. Delancey	.10
626	Martin W. Marion	.10
627	William H. Southworth	.10
628	John R. Mize	.15
629	Joseph M. Medwick	.15
630	Grover C. Alexander	.15
631	Paul D. Dean	.10
632	Herman S. Bell	.10
633	William W. Cooper	.10
634	Frank F. Frisch	.10
635	Jay H. Dean	.15
636	Donald J. Gutteridge	.10
637	Johnny L.R. Martin	.10
638	Edward J. Konetchy	.10
639	William A. Hallahan	.10
640	Lonnie Warneke	.10
641	Terry B. Moore	.10
642	Enos B. Slaughter	.10
643	Clarence F. Mueller	.10
644	George Toporcer	.10
645	James L. Bottomley	.10
646	Francis R. Blades	.10
647	Jesse J. Haines	.10
648	Andrew A. High	.10
649	Miller J. Huggins	.10
650	Ernesto P. Orsatti	.10
651	Lester R. Bell	.10
652	Charles E. Street	.10
653	Walter H. Roettger	.10
654	Sylvester W. Johnson	.10
655	Miguel A. Gonzalez	.10
656	James A. Collins	.10
657	Charles J. Hafey	.10
658	Checklist 331-440	.10
659	Checklist 441-550	.10
660	Checklist 551-660	.10

Four of the heroes of the inaugural All-Star Game of 1933 were featured in a pop-up ad in the program for the 1992 Game in San Diego. One card was inserted into each of the programs printed for distribution at the game and by mail order. Each card was reported printed in an edition of 34,000. Cards are similar in format to the regular Conlon Collection issues except for the gold-foil border around the player photo on front and the use of a "G" suffix to the card number. A banner at top front reads, "Game of the Century." On back is a summary of the player's 1933 All-Star performance and his stats. Gold editions of other Conlon cards were also issued in several different venues in 1993-94. Six cards (#665-880) were included in 1992 Conlon factory sets in editions of up to 90,000. The Johnson-Ryan gold card was available only in packaging sold in Eckerd stores, while the 1994 Cobb gold card was only available at Toys R Us. Cards are numbered with a "G" suffix.

		NM/M
Complete Set (12):		50.00
Common Player:		2.00
661	Bill Terry	2.00
662	Lefty Gomez	2.00
663	Babe Ruth	12.00
664	Frankie Frisch	2.00
665	Carl Hubbell	2.00
667	Charlie Gehringer (Edition of 20,000.)	4.00
730	Luke Appling (Edition of 20,000.)	4.00
770	Tommy Henrich	2.00
820	John McGraw	2.00
880	Gabby Hartnett	2.00
934	Walter Johnson, Nolan Ryan (Edition of 100,000.)	12.00
1000	Ty Cobb (Edition of 100,000.)	6.00

1992 Conlon Collection 13th National

These samples of the 1993 Conlon Collection series were distributed at the National Sports Collectors Convention in Atlanta in 1992. Other than the Joe Jackson card, they carry the same numbers as the regularly issued versions. Designs are also identical except for the overprint on back in outline letters, "13TH NATIONAL."

		NM/M
Complete Set (4):		4.00
Common Player:		.50
14	Joe Jackson	1.00
663	George H. Ruth	2.00
775	John T. Meyers	.50
800	James L. Vaughn	.50

1993 Conlon Collection Prototypes

RED FABER
CHICAGO WHITE SOX - PITCHER 1932

The cards in this issue were produced to preview the basic set and various subsets of the 1993 Conlon Collection issue. Cards are similar to the regular-issue set with the exception that the word "PROTOTYPE" is printed in gray diagonally on back. Production of most of the black-and-white photos was 60,000, though Gomez and Frisch were limited to 10,000 apiece. Three of the cards can be found with "All Star FanFest" notations on back, having been distributed as samples there.

1992-94 Conlon Collection Gold

FRANKIE FRISCH
NATIONAL LEAGUE - 2ND BASE 1933

		NM/M
Complete Set (8):		3.00
Common Player:		1.00
661	Bill Terry	1.00
661	Bill Terry (All Star FanFest)	2.00
662	Lefty Gomez	1.00
663	Babe Ruth	6.00
664	Frankie Frisch	1.00
710	Red Faber	1.00
710	Red Faber (All Star FanFest)	2.00
775	Chief Meyers	1.00
800	Hippo Vaughn	1.00
888	Babe Ruth (Colorized, edition of 52,000.)	5.00
905	Lena Blackburne	1.00
905	Lena Blackbourne (All Star FanFest)	2.00
934	Walter Johnson, Nolan Ryan (Colorized edition of 52,000.)	4.00

1993 Conlon Collection

GREAT STORIES
WALTER JOHNSON
HURLER OF THE UNSEEN FASTBALL 1927

The third annual Conlon Collection issue of 330 cards is numbered 661-990, a continuation of the series produced in 1991-92. The format of black-and-white photos produced 50-90 years ago by Charles Martin Conlon and surrounded by a wide black border and UV coating was continued. As with earlier issues, card backs contain brief biographical data, a few stats and well-written career highlights. The 1993 set also featured many subsets arranged by topic, such as spitballers, native Americans, players who overcame handicaps, etc. One subset compared Nolan Ryan with star pitchers in baseball history and included a fantasy photo of Ryan shaking hands in the dugout with Walter Johnson (card #934).

		NM/M
Complete Set in Commemorative Tin:		20.00
Complete Set (330):		15.00
Common Player:		.10
Wax Pack:		.50
Wax Box (36):		15.00
661	William H. Terry	.10
662	Vernon L. Gomez	.10
663	George H. Ruth	.50
664	Frank F. Frisch	.10
665	Carl O. Hubbell	.10
666	Aloysius H. Simmons	.15
667	Charles L. Gehringer	.15
668	Howard E. Averill Sr.	.10
669	Robert M. Grove	.15
670	Harold J. Traynor	.15
671	Charles H. Klein	.15
672	Paul G. Waner	.15
673	Louis H. Gehrig	.40
674	Richard B. Ferrell	.10
675	Charles L. Hartnett	.15
676	Joseph E. Cronin	.10
677	Charles J. Hafey	.10
678	James J. Dykes	.10
679	Samuel F. West	.10
680	Johnny L.R. Martin	.10
681	Francis J. O'Doul	.10
682	Alvin F. Crowder	.10
683	James Wilson	.10
684	Richard W. Bartell	.10
685	William A. Hallahan	.10
686	Walter A. Berger	.10
687	Lonnie Warneke	.10
688	William B. Chapman	.10
689	Elwood Q. English	.10
690	James H. Reese	.10
691	Roscoe A. Holm	.10
692	Charles D. Jamieson	.10
693	Jonathan T.W. Zachary	.10
694	John C. Ryan	.10
695	Earl J. Adams	.10
696	William E. Hunnefield	.10
697	Henry L. Meadows	.10
698	Thomas F. Carey	.10
699	John W. Rawlings	.10
700	Kenneth E. Holloway	.10
701	Lance C. Richbourg	.10
702	Raymond L. Fisher	.10
703	Edward Augustine Walsh	.10
704	Richard Rudolph	.10
705	Raymond B. Caldwell	.10
706	Burleigh A. Grimes	.10
707	Stanley A. Coveleski	.10
708	George A. Hildebrand	.10
709	John P. Quinn	.10
710	Urban C. Faber	.10
711	Urban J. Shocker	.10
712	Hubert B. Leonard	.10
713	Louis L. Koupal	.10
714	James C. Wasdell	.10
715	John H. Lindell	.10
716	Don W. Padgett	.10
717	Nelson T. Potter	.10
718	Lynwood T. Rowe	.10
719	David C. Danforth	.10
720	Claude W. Passeau	.10
721	Harry L. Kelley	.10
722	John T. Allen	.10
723	Thomas J.D. Bridges	.10
724	William C. Lee	.10
725	Fredrick M. Frankhouse	.10
726	John J. McCarthy	.10
727	Glen D. Russell	.10
728	Emory E. Rigney	.10
729	Howard S. Shanks	.10
730	Lucius B. Appling	.10
731	William J. Byron	.10
732	Earle B. Combs	.10
733	Henry B. Greenberg	.15
734	Walter W. Beck	.10
735	Hollis J. Thurston	.10
736	Lewis R. Wilson	.10
737	William A. McGowan	.10
738	Henry J. Bonura	.10
739	Thomas C. Baker	.10
740	William C. Jacobson	.10
741	Hazen S. Cuyler	.10
742	George F. Blaeholder	.10
743	Wilson D. Miles	.10
744	Lee E. Handley	.10
745	John F. Collins	.10
746	Wilfred P. Ryan	.10
747	Aaron L. Ward	.10
748	Montgomery M. Pearson	.10
749	Jacob W. Early	.10
750	William F. Atwood	.10
751	Mark A. Koenig	.10
752	John A. Hassett	.10
753	David J. Jones	.10
754	John P. Wagner	.25
755	William M. Dickey	.15
756	Albert M. Butcher	.10
757	Waite C. Hoyt	.10
758	Walter P. Johnson	.10
759	Howard J. Ehmke	.10
760	Norman L. Newsom	.10
761	Anthony M. Lazzeri	.10
762	Anthony M. Lazzeri	.10
763	Spurgeon F. Chandler	.10
764	Walter K. Higbe	.10
765	Paul R. Richards	.10
766	Rogers Hornsby	.15
767	Joseph F. Vosmik	.10
768	Jesse J. Haines	.10
769	William H. Walters	.10
770	Thomas D. Henrich	.10
771	James F. Thorpe	.40
772	Euel W. Moore	.10
773	Rudolph P. York	.10
774	Charles A. Bender	.10
775	John T. Meyers	.10
776	Robert L. Johnson	.10
777	Roy C. Johnson	.10
778	Richard T. Porter	.10
779	Ethan N. Allen	.10
780	Harry F. Sallee	.10
781	Roy C. Bell	.10
782	Arnold J. Statz	.10
783	Frank J. Henry	.10
784	Charles L. Woodall	.10
785	Philip E. Collins	.10
786	Joseph W. Sewell	.10
787	William J. Herman	.10
788	Rueben H. Oldring	.10
789	William H. Walker	.10
790	Joseph C. Schultz	.10
791	Fred E. Maguire	.10
792	Claude W. Willoughby	.10
793	James A. Ferguson	.10
794	John D. Morrison	.10
795	Tristram E. Speaker	.15
796	Tyrus R. Cobb	.40
797	Max Carey	.10
798	George H. Sisler	.10
799	Charles J. Hollocher	.10
800	James L. Vaughn	.10
801	Samuel P. Jones	.10
802	Harry B. Hooper	.10
803	Clifford C. Cravath	.10
804	Walter P. Johnson	.15
805	Jacob E. Daubert	.10
806	Jesse C. Milan	.10
807	Hugh A. McQuillan	.10
808	George F. Brickell	.10
809	Joseph V. Stripp	.10
810	Urban J. Hodapp	.10
811	John L. Vergez	.10
812	Linus R. Frey	.10
813	William W. Regan	.10
814	Norman R. Young	.10
815	Charles R. Robertson	.10
816	Walter F. Judnich	.10
817	Joseph B. Tinker	.15
818	John Evers	.15
819	Frank L. Chance	.15

820	John J. McGraw	.10
821	Charles J. Grimm	.10
822	Ted Lyons	.10
823	Joe McCarthy	.10
824	Connie Mack	.10
825	George Gibson	.10
826	Steve O'Neill	.10
827	Tristram E. Speaker	.15
828	William F. Carrigan	.10
829	Charles D. Stengel	.15
830	Miller J. Huggins	.10
831	William B. McKechnie	.10
832	Charles W. Dressen	.10
833	Charles E. Street	.10
834	Melvin T. Ott	.15
835	Frank F. Frisch	.10
836	George H. Sisler	.10
837	Napoleon LaJoie	.15
838	Tyrus R. Cobb	.40
839	William H. Southworth	.10
840	Clark C.F. Griffith	.10
841	William H. Terry	.10
842	Rogers Hornsby	.15
843	Joseph E. Cronin	.10
844	Alfonso R. Lopez	.10
845	Stanley R. Harris	.10
846	Wilbert Robinson	.10
847	Hugh A. Jennings	.10
848	James J. Dykes	.10
849	Roy J. Cullenbine	.10
850	Graham E. Moore	.10
851	John H. Rothrock	.10
852	William H. Lamar	.10
853	Monte Weaver	.10
854	Ival R. Goodman	.10
855	Henry L. Severeid	.10
856	Fred G. Haney	.10
857	Joseph B. Shaute	.10
858	Smead P. Jolley	.10
859	Edwin D. Williams	.10
860	Bernard O. Bengough	.10
861	Richard B. Ferrell	.10
862	Robert A. O'Farrell	.10
863	Virgil L. Davis	.10
864	Franklin W. Hayes	.10
865	Herold D. Ruel	.10
866	Gordon S. Cochrane	.10
867	John Kling	.10
868	Ivy B. Wingo	.10
869	William M. Dickey	.15
870	Frank E. Snyder	.10
871	Roger P. Bresnahan	.10
872	Walter H. Schang	.10
873	Alfonso R. Lopez	.10
874	James Wilson	.10
875	Valentine J. Picinich	.10
876	Stephen F. O'Neill	.10
877	Ernest N. Lombardi	.10
878	John L. Bassler	.10
879	Raymond W. Schalk	.10
880	Charles L. Hartnett	.10
881	Bruce D. Campbell	.10
882	Charles H. Ruffing	.10
883	Mordecai P.C. Brown	.10
884	Peter J. Archer	.10
885	David E. Keefe	.10
886	Herold M. Andrews	.10
887	Edgar C. Rice	.10
888	George H. Ruth	.50
889	Charles J. Hafey	.10
890	Oscar D. Melillo	.10
891	Joe Wood	.10
892	John J. Evers	.10
893	George Toporcer	.10
894	Myril O. Hoag	.10
895	Robert G. Weiland	.10
896	Joseph A. Marty	.10
897	Sherwood R. Magee	.10
898	Daniel T. Taylor	.10
899	William E. Kamm	.10
900	Samuel J.T. Sheckard	.10
901	Sylvester W. Johnson	.10
902	Stephen R. Sundra	.10
903	Roger M. Cramer	.10
904	Hubert S. Pruett	.10
905	Russell A. Blackburne	.10
906	Eppa Rixey	.10
907	Leon A. Goslin	.10
908	George L. Kelly	.10
909	James L. Bottomley	.10
910	Christopher Mathewson	.15
911	Anthony M. Lazzeri	.10
912	John A. Mostil	.10
913	Robert P. Doerr	.10
914	Walter J.V. Maranville	.10
915	Harry E. Heilmann	.10
916	Rodrick J. Wallace	.10
917	James E. Foxx	.15
918	John R. Mize	.10
919	John N. Bentley	.10
920	Alexander Schacht	.10
921	Parke E. Coleman	.10
922	George H. Paskert	.10
923	Horace H. Ford	.10
924	Randolph E. Moore	.10
925	Milburn S. Shoffner	.10
926	Richard W. Siebert	.10
927	Anthony C. Kaufmann	.10
928	Jay H. Dean, Nolan Ryan	.25
929	Clarence A. Vance, Nolan Ryan	.25
930	Robert M. Grove, Nolan Ryan	.25
931	George E. Waddell, Nolan Ryan	.25
932	Grover C. Alexander, Nolan Ryan	.25

933	Robert W.A. Feller, Nolan Ryan	.25
934	Walter P. Johnson, Nolan Ryan	.50
935	Theodore A. Lyons, Nolan Ryan	.25
936	James C. Bagby	.10
937	Joseph Sugden	.10
938	Robert E. Grace	.10
939	John G. Heath	.10
940	Kenneth Williams	.10
941	Marvin J. Owen	.10
942	Cyril R. Weatherly	.10
943	Edward C. Morgan	.10
944	John C. Rizzo	.10
945	Archie R. McKain	.10
946	Robert M. Garbark	.10
947	John B. Osborn	.10
948	John S. Podgajny	.10
949	Joseph P. Evans	.10
950	George A. Rensa	.10
951	John H. Humphries	.10
952	Merritt P. Cain	.10
953	Roy E. Hansen	.10
954	John A. Niggeling	.10
955	Harold J. Wiltse	.10
956	Alejandro A.A.E. Carrasquel	.10
957	George A. Grant	.10
958	Philip W. Weinert	.10
959	Ervin B. Brame	.10
960	Raymond J. Harrell	.10
961	Edward K. Linke	.10
962	Samuel B. Gibson	.10
963	John C. Watwood	.10
964	James T. Prothro	.10
965	Julio G. Bonetti	.10
966	Howard R. Mills	.10
967	Clarence E. Galloway	.10
968	Harold J. Kelleher	.10
969	Elon C. Hogsett	.10
970	Edward B. Heusser	.10
971	Edward J. Baecht	.10
972	Otto H. Saltzgaver	.10
973	Leroy G. Herrmann	.10
974	Beveric B. Bean	.10
975	Harry Seibold	.10
976	Howard V. Keen	.10
977	William J. Barrett	.10
978	Patrick H. McNulty	.10
979	George E. Turbeville	.10
980	Edward D. Phillips	.10
981	Garland M. Buckeye	.10
982	Victor P. Frasier	.10
983	John G. Rhodes	.10
984	Emile D. Barnes	.10
985	James C. Edwards	.10
986	Herschel E. Bennett	.10
987	Carmen P. Hill	.10
988	Checklist 661-770	.10
989	Checklist 771-880	.10
990	Checklist 881-990	.10

1993-95 Conlon Collection Color

BOB FELLER
CLEVELAND INDIANS • PITCHER 1938
HOF 1962

The cards in this set were previously released in black-and-white in regular 1991-94 Conlon sets. Cards 1-12 were issued as bonus cards in Megacards accessory items; 250,000 of each were produced. Cards 13-20 were randomly inserted in 1993 Conlon counter and blister packs; 100,000 of those were produced. Cards 21-22, in an edition of 75,000, were only available through a send-away offer. Card 23 was available exclusively as an insert in the 7th Edition SCD Baseball Card Price Guide, in an edition of 60,000. Cards 24-39 were issued in 1994. Numbers 24-28 were random inserts printed to the number of 84,000 apiece. Cards 29-30 were a send-away premium; #31-33 were hobby foil inserts. All were issued in quantities of 12,000. Cards 34-37 - 48,000 of each - were a Toys R Us exclusive insert. Cards 38-39 were special-offer premiums. A special printing of 24,000 of #28 were issued with a "Conlon

Collection Day" overprint on back and were distributed at the Sept. 11, 1994, St. Louis Cardinals game.

		NM/M
Complete Set (47):		100.00
Common Player:		2.00
1	Sunny Jim Bottomley	2.00
2	Lefty Grove	2.00
3	Lou Gehrig	10.00
4	Babe Ruth	10.00
5	Casey Stengel	3.00
6	Rube Marquard	2.00
7	Walter Johnson	3.00
8	Lou Gehrig	5.00
9	Christy Mathewson	3.00
10	Ty Cobb	5.00
11	Mel Ott	2.00
12	Carl Hubbell	2.00
13	Al Simmons	2.00
14	Connie Mack	2.00
15	Grover C. Alexander	2.00
16	Jimmie Foxx	3.00
17	Lloyd Waner	2.00
18	Tris Speaker	4.00
19	Dizzy Dean	5.00
20	Rogers Hornsby	5.00
21	Shoeless Joe Jackson	7.50
22	Jim Thorpe	7.50
23	Bob Feller	8.00
24	Hal Newhouser	2.00
25	Hughie Jennings	2.00
26	Red Faber	2.00
27	Enos Slaughter	2.00
28	Johnny Mize	2.00
28CCD	Johnny Mize	4.00
29	Pie Traynor	2.00
30	Walter Johnson, Nolan Ryan	4.00
31	Lou Gehrig	2.00
32	Benny Bengough	2.00
33	Babe Ruth	2.00
34	Charlie Gehringer	2.00
35	Babe Ruth	2.00
36	Bill Dickey	2.00
37	Mordecai Brown	2.00
38	Ray Schalk	4.00
39	Home Run Baker	5.00
40	Frank Frisch	2.00
41	Hack Wilson	2.00
42	Ty Cobb	6.00
43	Honus Wagner	6.00
44	John McGraw	2.00
45	Reds vs. Giants	2.00
46	Indians vs. Yanks	2.00
47	Babe Ruth	12.00

1993 Conlon Collection Master Series

"The Best There Was" was the subtitle on this portfolio of oversized (10" x 8") cards produced from the photos of Charles Martin Conlon. On the high-gloss card fronts, a wide black border surrounds the black-and-white photo, with a gold-foil pinstripe border between the two. The player's name appears in gold at the bottom. Backs are printed in black-and-white and feature a large player portrait, complete major league stats and a career summary. A serial numbered certificate placing the set within an edition of 25,000 was included with the set; a deluxe portfolio album to house the collection was available for $10.

		NM/M
Complete Set (9):		15.00
Common Card:		1.50
1	Title card	.50
2	Babe Ruth	6.00
3	Lou Gehrig, Walter Johnson	4.00
4	Honus Wagner	3.00
5	Mickey Cochrane	1.50
6	Tris Speaker	1.50
7	Ty Cobb	4.00
8	Rogers Hornsby	1.50
9	Pie Traynor	1.50

1993 Conlon Collection Color Masters

Some of the premier photography of Charles Martin Conlon was computer color-enhanced and placed on these oversized (10" x 8") cards in a special edition of 25,000. High-gloss fronts feature the col-

orized photos separated by a thin white pinstripe from the dark blue background. Backs are printed in black and blue on white and feature a career summary or other historical data, along with a description of the front photo. A serially numbered certificate of authenticity accompanied the set and could be redeemed, along with $10, for a deluxe portfolio to house the collection.

		NM/M
Complete Set (9):		15.00
Common Player:		1.50
1	Title Card	.50
2	Napoleon Lajoie	1.50
3	Walter Johnson, Nolan Ryan (Fantasy photo.)	6.00
4	Action at Hilltop Park	.50
5	Babe Ruth	6.00
6	Frank Baker	1.50
7	John McGraw	1.50
8	John McGraw, Wilbert Robinson, Christy Mathewson	1.50
9	Hughie Jennings	1.50

1994 Conlon Collection Prototypes

A large gray "PROTOTYPE" overprint on back identifies these cards as sample of the fourth annual edition of Conlon Collection cards by Megacards. Cards carry the same number as issued versions. It was reported that 26,000 prototypes were issued of Martin, Traynor, Hubbell, Klem and Koenig; while 52,000 each were issued of Jackson and the Deans.

		NM/M
Complete Set (8):		8.00
Common Player		1.00
991	Pepper Martin	1.00
1030	Joe Jackson	3.00
1050	Pie Traynor	1.00
1105	Carl Hubbell	1.00
1140	Lefty Grove	1.00
1170	Dizzy Dean, Paul Dean	1.50
1190	Bill Klem	1.00
1230	Mark Koenig	1.00

1994 Conlon Collection

DAFFY & DIZZY DEAN

The production of "old-timers" cards based on the baseball photography of Charles M. Conlon from the 1910s through the 1930s continued into a fourth year in 1994 with another 330-card series, numbered 991-1320. Once again the format of previous years was continued. Subsets included the 1919 Chicago White Sox, major league brothers and action photos.

		NM/M
Complete Set in Commemorative Tin:		40.00
Complete Set (330):		30.00
Common Player:		.10
Wax Box (36):		40.00
991	Johnny L.R. Martin	.10
992	Joseph W. Sewell	.10
993	Edd J. Roush	.10
994	Richard B. Ferrell	.10
995	John J. Broaca	.10
996	James L. Sewell	.10
997	Burleigh A. Grimes	.10
998	Lewis R. Wilson	.10
999	Robert M. Grove	.15

1000	Tyrus R. Cobb	.40
1001	John J. McGraw	.10
1002	Edward S. Plank	.10
1003	Samuel P. Jones	.10
1004	James L. Bottomley	.10
1005	Henry B. Greenberg	.15
1006	Lloyd J. Waner	.10
1007	William W. Moore	.10
1008	Lucius B. Appling	.10
1009	Harold Newhouser	.10
1010	Alfonso R. Lopez	.10
1011	Tyrus R. Cobb	.40
1012	Charles A. Nichols	.10
1013	Edward Augustine Walsh	.10
1014	Hugh Duffy	.10
1015	Richard W. Marquard	.10
1016	Adrian Joss	.10
1017	Rodrick J. Wallace	.10
1018	William H. Keeler	.10
1019	Jacob E. Daubert	.10
1020	Harry F. Sallee	.10
1021	Adolfo Luque	.10
1022	Ivy B. Wingo	.10
1023	Edd J. Roush	.10
1024	William A. Rariden	.10
1025	Sherwood R. Magee	.10
1026	Louis B. Duncan	.10
1027	Horace O. Eller	.10
1028	Alfred E. Neale	.10
1029	George D. Weaver	.10
1030	Joseph J. Jackson	.50
1031	Arnold Gandil	.10
1032	Charles A. Risberg	.10
1033	Raymond W. Schalk	.10
1034	Edward V. Cicotte	.10
1035	William H. James	.10
1036	Harry L. Leibold	.10
1037	Richard H. Kerr	.10
1038	William J. Gleason	.10
1039	Frederick W. McMullin (Middle initial actually "D.")	.10
1040	Edward T. Collins	.10
1041	Sox Pitchers (Lefty Williams, Bill James, Ed Cicotte, Dicky Kerr)	.10
1042	Sox Outfielders (Nemo Leibold, Happy Felsch, Shano Collins)	.10
1043	Kenneth F. Keltner	.10
1044	Charles F. Berry	.10
1045	Walter J. Lutzke	.10
1046	John C. Schulte	.10
1047	John V. Welch	.10
1048	Jack E. Russell	.10
1049	John J. Murray	.10
1050	Harold J. Traynor	.10
1051	Michael J. Donlin	.10
1052	Charles L. Hartnett	.10
1053	Anthony M. Lazzeri	.10
1054	Lawrence H. Miller	.10
1055	Clarence A. Vance	.10
1056	Williams F. Carrigan	.10
1057	John J. Murphy	.10
1058	Clifton E Heathcote	.10
1059	Joseph A. Dugan	.10
1060	Walter J.V. Maranville	.10
1061	Thomas D. Henrich	.10
1062	Leroy E. Parmelee	.10
1063	Vernon L. Gomez	.10
1064	Ernest N. Lombardi	.10
1065	David J. Bancroft	.10
1066	William B. McKechnie	.10
1067	John A. Hassett	.10
1068	Spurgeon F. Chandler	.10
1069	Roy J. Hughes	.10
1070	George A. Dauss	.10
1071	Joseph J. Hauser	.10
1072	Virgil L. Davis	.10
1073	Albert M. Butcher	.10
1074	Louis P. Chiozza	.10
1075	Center Field Bleachers	.10
1076	Charles L. Gehringer	.10
1077	Henry E. Manush	.10
1078	Charles H. Ruffing	.10
1079	Melvin L. Harder	.10
1080	George H. Ruth	.50
1081	William B. Chapman	.10
1082	Louis H. Gehrig	.40
1083	James E. Foxx	.15
1084	Aloysius H. Simmons	.10
1085	Joseph E. Cronin	.10
1086	William M. Dickey	.15
1087	Gordon S. Cochrane	.10
1088	Vernon L. Gomez	.10
1089	Howard E. Averill Sr.	.10
1090	Samuel F. West	.10
1091	Frank F. Frisch	.10
1092	William J. Herman	.10
1093	Harold J. Traynor	.10
1094	Joseph M. Medwick	.10
1095	Charles M. Klein	.10
1096	Hank S. Greenberg	.10
1097	Melvin T. Ott	.15
1098	Walter T. Berger	.10
1099	Paul G. Waner	.10
1100	William H. Terry	.10
1101	Travis C. Jackson	.10
1102	Joseph F. Vaughan	.10
1103	Charles L. Hartnett	.10
1104	Alfonso R. Lopez	.10
1105	Carl O. Hubbell	.10
1106	Lonnie Warneke	.10
1107	Van L. Mungo	.10
1108	Johnny J.R. Martin	.10
1109	Jay H. Dean	.15
1110	Fredrick M. Frankhouse	.10
1111	Giulladeau Spink Heydler	.10

1112	JG Taylor Spink/ Mrs. Spink	.10
1113	Hirchman, Keller	.10
1114	Victor E. Aldridge	.10
1115	Michael F. Higgins	.10
1116	Harold G. Carlson	.10
1117	Frederick L. Fitzsimmons	.10
1118	William H. Walters	.10
1119	Nicholas Altrock	.10
1120	Charles W. Dressen	.10
1121	Mark A. Koenig	.10
1122	Charles L. Gehringer	.10
1123	Lloyd V. Kennedy	.10
1124	Harlond B. Clift	.10
1125	Ernest G. Phelps	.10
1126	John R. Mize	.10
1127	Harold H. Schumacher	.10
1128	Ethan N. Allen	.10
1129	William A. Wambsganss	.10
1130	Frederick Leach	.10
1131	John W. Clancy	.10
1132	John F. Stewart	.10
1133	Wilbur L. Brubaker	.10
1134	Leslie Mann	.10
1135	Howard J. Ehmke	.10
1136	Aloysius H. Simmons	.10
1137	George L. Earnshaw	.10
1138	George W. Haas	.10
1139	Edmund J. Miller	.10
1140	Robert M. Grove	.15
1141	John P. Boley	.10
1142	Edward T. Collins Sr.	.10
1143	Walter E. French	.10
1144	Donald E. McNair	.10
1145	William D. Shores	.10
1146	Gordon S. Cochrane	.10
1147	Homer W. Summa	.10
1148	John P. Quinn	.10
1149	Max F. Bishop	.10
1150	James J. Dykes	.10
1151	George E. Walberg	.10
1152	James E. Foxx	.15
1153	George H. Burns	.10
1154	Roger M. Cramer	.10
1155	Samuel D. Hale	.10
1156	Edwin A. Rommel	.10
1157	Ralph F. Perkins	.10
1158	James J. Cronin	.10
1159	Cornelius Mack	.10
1160	Raymond C. Kolp	.10
1161	Clyde J. Manion	.10
1162	Franklin T. Grube	.10
1163	Stephen A. Swetonic	.10
1164	Joseph B. Tinker	.15
1165	John J. Evers	.15
1166	Frank L. Chance	.15
1167	Emerson Dickman	.10
1168	John T. Tobin	.10
1169	Wesley C. Ferrell	.10
1170	Jay H. Dean	.15
1171	Tony & Al Cuccinello (Tony Cuccinello, Al Cuccinello)	
1172	Harry Coveleski, Stan Coveleski	.10
1173	Bob Johnson, Roy Johnson	.10
1174	Andy & Hugh High	.10
1175	Joe Sewell, Luke Sewell	.10
1176	Joe Heving, John Heving	.10
1177	Ab & Ivy Wingo	.10
1178	Wade Killefer, Bill Killefer	.10
1179	Bubbles Hargrave, Pinky Hargrave	.10
1180	Paul Waner, Lloyd Waner	.10
1181	John S. Vander Meer	.10
1182	Joe G. Moore	.10
1183	Robert J. Burke	.10
1184	John F. Moore	.10
1185	John J. Egan	.10
1186	Thomas H. Connolly	.10
1187	Frank H. O'Loughlin	.10
1188	John E. Reardon	.10
1189	Charles B. Moran	.10
1190	William J. Klem	.10
1191	Albert D. Stark	.10
1192	Albert L. Orth	.10
1193	William E. Bransfield	.10
1194	Roy Van Graflan	.10
1195	Eugene F. Hart	.10
1196	John B. Conlan	.10
1197	Ralph A. Pinelli	.10
1198	John F. Sheridan	.10
1199	Richard F. Nallin	.10
1200	William H. Dineen	.10
1201	Henry F. O'Day	.10
1202	Charles Rigler	.10
1203	Robert D. Emslie	.10
1204	Charles H. Pfirman	.10
1205	Harry C. Geisel	.10
1206	Ernest C. Quigley	.10
1207	Emmett T. Ormsby	.10
1208	George A. Hildebrand	.10
1209	George J. Moriarty	.10
1210	William G. Evans	.10
1211	Clarence B. Owens	.10
1212	William A. McGowan	.10
1213	Walter K. Higbe	.10
1214	Taylor L. Douthit	.10
1215	Delmar D. Baker	.10
1216	Albert M. Demaree	.10
1217	Cornelius Mack	.10
1218	Napoleon Lajoie	.15
1219	John P. Wagner	.25
1220	Christopher Mathewson	.15
1221	Samuel E. Crawford	.10
1222	Tristram E. Speaker	.15
1223	Grover C. Alexander	.15

1224	Joseph E. Bowman	.10
1225	John D. Rigney	.10
1226	William E. Webb	.10
1227	Lloyd A. Moore	.10
1228	Bruce D. Campbell	.10
1229	Luzerne A. Blue	.10
1230	Mark A. Koenig	.10
1231	Walter H. Schang	.10
1232	Max Carey	.10
1233	Frank F. Frisch	.10
1234	Owen J. Bush	.10
1235	Goerge S. Davis	.10
1236	William G. Rogell	.10
1237	James A. Collins	.10
1238	Mauricel L. Burrus	.10
1239	Ernest E. Swanson	.10
1240	Elwood G. English	.10
1241	Joseph Harris	.10
1242	Harry H. McCurdy	.10
1243	Richard W. Bartell	.10
1244	Rupert L. Thompson	.10
1245	Charles B. Adams	.10
1246	Arthur N. Nehf	.10
1247	John G. Graney	.10
1248	Theodore A. Lyons	.10
1249	Louis E. Gehrig	.40
1250	Michael F. Welch	.10
1251	Urban C. Faber	.10
1252	Joseph J. McGinnity	.10
1253	Rogers Hornsby	.15
1254	Melvin T. Ott	.15
1255	Walter P. Johnson	.15
1256	Edgar C. Rice	.10
1257	James A. Tobin	.10
1258	Roger T. Peckinpaugh	.10
1259	George T. Stovall	.10
1260	Fredrick C. Merkle	.10
1261	Harry W. Collins	.10
1262	Henry C. Lind	.10
1263	George N. Rucker	.10
1264	Hollis J. Thurston	.10
1265	Alexander Metzler	.10
1266	Charles Martin Conlon	.10
1267	McCarty Gets Magee (Lew McCarty, Lee Magee)	.10
1268	Sliding Home	.10
1269	Kauff Safe at 3rd (Benny Kauff)	.10
1270	Groh Out at 3rd (Heine Groh)	.10
1271	Mollwitz Out at the Plate (Fred Mollwitz)	.10
1272	Burns Safe at Home	.10
1273	Lee Magee Out Stealing 3rd (Lee Magee)	.10
1274	Killefer Out at Plate (Bill Killefer)	.10
1275	John M. Warhop	.10
1276	Emil J. Leonard	.10
1277	Alvin F. Crowder	.10
1278	Chester P. Laabs	.10
1279	Leslie A. Bush	.10
1280	Raymond B. Bressler	.10
1281	Robret M. Brown	.10
1282	Bernard Deviveiros	.10
1283	Leslie W. Tietje	.10
1284	Charles Devens	.10
1285	Elliott A. Bigelow	.10
1286	John O. Dickshot	.10
1287	Charles L. Chatham	.10
1288	Walter E. Beall	.10
1289	Richard D. Attreau	.10
1290	Anthony V. Brief	.10
1291	James J. Gleason	.10
1292	Walter D. Shaner	.10
1293	Clifford R. Crawford	.10
1294	Manuel Salvo	.10
1295	Calvin L. Dorsett	.10
1296	Russell D. Peters	.10
1297	John D. Couch	.10
1298	Frank W. Ulrich	.10
1299	James M. Bivin	.10
1300	Paul E. Strand	.10
1301	John Y. Lanning	.10
1302	William R. Brenzel	.10
1303	Don Songer	.10
1304	Emil H. Levsen	.10
1305	Otto A. Bluege	.10
1306	Fabian S. Gaffke	.10
1307	Maurice J. Archdeacon	.10
1308	James B. Chaplin	.10
1309	Lawrence J. Rosenthal	.10
1310	William M. Bagwell	.10
1311	Ralph F. Dawson	.10
1312	John P.J. Sturm	.10
1313	Haskell C. Billings	.10
1314	Vernon S. Wilshere	.10
1315	Robert A. Asbjornson	.10
1316	Henry J. Steinbacher	.10
1317	Stanwood F. Baumgartner	.10
1318	Checklist 991-1100	.10
1319	Checklist 1101-1210	.10
1320	Checklist 1211-1320	.10

1994 Conlon Collection Burgundy

A parallel version of the 1994 Conlon series with burgundy, rather than black, borders was issued as a one-per-pack insert.

	NM/M
Complete Set (330):	30.00
Common Player:	.50

1995 Conlon Collection Prototypes

LOU GEHRIG
NEW YORK YANKEES - 1ST BASE 1935

Megacards issued this 10-card series of prototypes to introduce its basic series for 1995. Cards are similar to the issued versions except that they lack the gold-foil enhancements on front and have different card numbers on some of the card backs. Cards have "PROMOTIONAL" printed diagonally on the back. Prototypes are listed here alphabetically.

		NM/M
Complete Set (10):		12.00
Common Player:		2.00
(1)	Lou Boudreau	2.00
(2)	Ray Chapman	2.00
(3)	Charles Comiskey	2.00
(4)	Bill Dickey	2.00
(5)	Bob Feller	2.00
(6)	Lou Gehrig	3.00
(7)	Charles L. Hartnett	2.00
(8)	Walter J.V. Maranville	2.00
(9)	Babe Ruth	4.00
(10)	Tris Speaker	2.00

1995 Conlon Collection

ANDY COHEN
NEW YORK GIANTS - 2ND BASE 1926

Gold-foil enhanced printing was a first for the Conlon Collection in 1995. For the first time, each regular card in the issue featured gold frames around the black-and-white photos, and a gold Conlon Collection seal at lower-right. Background for the 1995 cards is in dark green, with typography in white. Backs are black-and-white and feature an indepth historical vignette. In its fifth year, numbers for Conlon Collection cards continued from previous years, beginning at #1321. The first series, cards 1321-1430, were issued in February, a second series, #1431-1540, was announced for August release but was never issued. A special Babe Ruth 100th birthday anniversary card was included with the issue, bearing a combined Topps/Conlon Collection logo and paralleling card #3 in the 1995 Topps issue. Conlon cards for 1995 were issued in plastic clam-shell packaging of 22, 55 or 110 cards. Once again, many of the cards in the set were grouped into themes such as "Baseball Goes to War," "Nicknames" and "Beating the Odds."

	NM/M
Complete Set, Commemorative Tin:	100.00
Complete Set (111):	80.00
Common Player:	1.00
1321	Grover Alexander	1.00
1322	Christy Mathewson	1.50
1323	Eddie Grant	1.00
1324	Gabby Street	1.00
1325	Hank Gowdy	1.00

1326	Jack Bentley	1.00
1327	Eppa Rixey	1.00
1328	Bob Meusel	1.00
1329	Rabbit Maranville	1.00
1330	Casey Stengel	1.00
1331	Herb Pennock	1.00
1332	Eddie Collins	1.00
1333	Buddy Hassett	1.00
1334	Andy Cohen	1.00
1335	Hank Greenberg	1.50
1336	Andy High	1.00
1337	Bob Feller	1.00
1338	George Earnshaw	1.00
1339	Jack Knott	1.00
1340	Larry French	1.00
1341	Skippy Roberge	1.00
1342	Boze Berger	1.00
1343	Bill Posedel	1.00
1344	Kirby Higbe	1.00
1345	Bob Neighbors	1.00
1346	Hugh Mulcahy	1.00
1347	Harry Walker	1.00
1348	Buddy Lewis	1.00
1349	Cecil Travis	1.00
1350	Moe Berg	2.00
1351	Nixey Callahan	1.00
1352	Heinie Peitz	1.00
1353	Doc White	1.00
1354	Smokey Joe Wood	1.00
1355	Larry Gardner	1.00
1356	Steve O'Neill	1.00
1357	Tris Speaker	1.00
1358	Bill Wambsganss	1.00
1359	Geo. H. Burns	1.00
1360	Charlie Jamieson	1.00
1361	Les Nunamaker	1.00
1362	Stan Coveleski	1.00
1363	Joe Sewell	1.00
1364	Jim Bagby	1.00
1365	Duster Mails	1.00
1366	Jack Graney	1.00
1367	Elmer Smith	1.00
1368	Tommy Leach	1.00
1369	Russ Ford	1.00
1370	Harry Wolter	1.00
1371	Dazzy Vance	1.00
1372	Germany Schaefer	1.00
1373	Elbie Fletcher	1.00
1374	Clark Griffith	1.00
1375	Al Simmons	1.00
1376	Billy Jurges	1.00
1377	Earl Averill	1.00
1378	Bill Klem	1.00
1379	Armando Marsans	1.00
1380	Mike Gonzalez	1.00
1381	Jacques Fournier	1.00
1382	Ol' Stubblebeard (Burleigh Grimes)	1.00
1383	Freshest Man on Earth (Arlie Latham)	1.00
1384	Cracker (Ray Schalk)	1.00
1385	Goose (Goose Goslin)	1.00
1386	Unser Choe (Joe Hauser)	1.00
1387	The People's Cherce (Dixie Walker)	1.00
1388	The Crab (Jesse Burkett)	1.00
1389	Mountain Music (Cliff Melton)	1.00
1390	Gee (Gee Walker)	1.00
1391	Tony Cuccinello	1.00
1392	Vern Kennedy	1.00
1393	Tuck Stainback	1.00
1394	Ed Barrow	1.00
1395	Ford Frick	1.00
1396	Ban Johnson	1.00
1397	Charles Comiskey	1.00
1398	Jacob Ruppert	1.00
1399	Branch Rickey	1.00
1400	Jack Kieran	1.00
1401	Mike Ryba	1.00
1402	Stan Spence	1.00
1403	Red Barrett	1.00
1404	Gabby Hartnett	1.00
1405	Babe Ruth	3.00
1406	Fred Merkle	1.00
1407	Claude Passeau	1.00
1408	Smokey Joe Wood	1.00
1409	Cliff Heathcote	1.00
1410	Walt Cruise	1.00
1411	Cookie Lavagetto	1.00
1412	Tony Lazzari	1.00
1413	Atley Donald	1.00
1414	Ken Raffensberger	1.00
1415	Dizzy Trout	1.00
1416	Augie Galan	1.00
1417	Monty Stratton	1.00
1418	Claude Passeau	1.00
1419	Oscar Grimes Jr.	1.00
1420	Rollie Hemsley	1.00
1421	Lou Gehrig	2.00
1422	Tom Sunkel	1.00
1423	Tris Speaker	1.00
1424	Chick Fewster	1.00
1425	Lou Boudreau	1.00
1426	Hank Leiber	1.00
1427	Eddie Mayo	1.00
1428	Charley Gelbert	1.00
1429	Jackie Hayes	1.00
1430	Checklist 1321-1430	1.00
3C	Babe Ruth (100th Birthday)	1.00

1995 Conlon Collection In the Zone

An eight-card set comparing Ken Griffey Jr. with superstars of the past was randomly inserted

KEN GRIFFEY JR.

WITH TY COBB

into 1995 Conlon Collection packs. Fronts feature a colorized background photo of the player with whom Griffey is being compared. A smaller color photo of Griffey is in the foreground. An "In the Zone" logo is at lower-left. Backs share a background photo of Griffey and have a black-and-white portrait of the comparison player in the upper-left. Narrative describes how the two players compare. A card number is at upper-right in the Zone logo. Megacard and Cooperstown Collection logos are at bottom. The first six cards of the series coould be found in Conlon Collection packs, cards 7 and 8 were available only through a mail-in offer for $2 plus five proofs-of-purchase. The print run was announced as no more than 50,000 sets.

		NM/M
Complete Set (8):		12.00
Common Card:		2.00
1	Ken Griffey Jr., Babe Ruth	3.50
2	Ken Griffey Jr., Lou Gehrig	3.00
3	Ken Griffey Jr., Ty Cobb	3.00
4	Ken Griffey Jr., Jimmie Foxx	2.00
5	Ken Griffey Jr., Mel Ott	2.00
6	Ken Griffey Jr., Joe Jackson	3.00
7	Ken Griffey Jr., Tris Speaker	2.00
8	Ken Griffey Jr., Jim Bottomley	2.00

1979-83 Coral-Lee Postcards

A number of baseball subjects were among a series of sports postcards published by Coral-Lee of California. Two formats are seen, standard postcard size of 3-1/2" x 5-1/2", and a larger 4" x 6" style seen on cards numbered 14 or higher. The standard-size cards have borderless color portrait photos on front, with no identification. Postcard style backs have the player's id, along with publisher, printer and copyright information in black-and-white. Most are dated. The larger cards have action photos on front, with backs similar to the smaller type. This list may not be complete as far as baseball-related cards within the series.

		NM/M
Common Player:		.25
1	Pete Rose	3.00
2	Davey Lopes	.25
3	Dave Winfield	1.50
4	Billy Martin	1.00

5	George Steinbrenner, Billy Martin, Reggie Jackson, Thurman Munson	1.50
6	Reggie Jackson	1.50
7	Bruce Kison	.25
8	Bobby Grich	.25
9	Rod Carew	.50
10	Tommy John	.25
11	Dick Howser	.25
12	George Brett	1.00
14-C	Cal Ripken Jr.	2.00
15-C	Carl Yastrzemski	1.00
16-C	Joe Morgan	.50
18-C	Graig Nettles	.25
69	Willie Mays, Ronald Reagan, Edward Stack	1.00
81	Fernando Valenzuela, Jose Lopez Portillo	1.00

1988-93 Costacos Brothers Ad Cards

KIRBY PUCKETT
PUCKETT WRECKING CO.
TIM WRECKING BALL

During the hey-day of sports hero personality posters in the late 1980s and early 1990s, one of the industry's major players, Costacos Brothers, issued a series of 4" x 6" cards to advertise their poster offerings. Card fronts duplicate the issued poster, while backs contain an ad for the poster company. Players in many sports were included in the series but only the baseball players are listed here.

		NM/M
Complete Set (31):		125.00
Common Player:		4.00
(1)	Barry Bonds (License to Thrill)	10.00
(2)	Bobby Bonilla (Bobby Bo)	4.00
(3)	Will Clark (Thriller)	4.00
(4)	Will Clark (Willpower)	4.00
(5)	Roger Clemens (The Rocket)	8.00
(6)	Darren Daulton (D-Day)	4.00
(7)	Glenn Davis (The Big Bopper)	4.00
(8)	Andre Dawson (Class for All Seasons) (w/Jordan, Payton)	4.00
(9)	Lenny Dykstra (Nails)	4.00
(10)	Dennis Eckersley (Cy of Relief)	5.00
(11)	Andres Galarraga (The Big Cat)	4.00
(12)	Kirk Gibson (Big Game Hunter)	4.00
(13)	Dwight Gooden (Doc)	4.00
(14)	Tom Gordon (Flash)	4.00
(15)	Mike Greenwell (Gator Tough)	4.00
(16)	Ken Griffey Sr., Ken Griffey Jr. (The Next Generation)	8.00
(17)	Ken Griffey Jr. (In Jr. We Trust)	9.00
(18)	Derek Jeter (Jeter Airways)	9.00
(19)	Howard Johnson (HoJo)	4.00
(20)	Eric Karros (The Artful Dodger)	4.00
(21)	Barry Larkin (Red Hot)	4.00
(22)	Don Mattingly (The Man With The Golden Glove)	7.50
(23)	Fred McGriff (Blue Thunder)	4.00
(24)	Kevin Mitchell (Bat Man)	4.00
(25)	Kirby Puckett (The Wrecking Ball)	7.50
(26)	Tim Raines (Steal Wheels)	4.00
(27)	Harold Reynolds (Turning Point)	4.00
(28)	Benito Santiago (Thou Shalt Not Steal!)	4.00
(29)	Steve Sax (Sax Appeal)	4.00
(30)	Darryl Strawberry (Straw-Some)	4.00
(31)	Greg Swindell, Pete Harnisch, Doug Drabek (Shooting Stars)	4.00

1991 Country Hearth Mariners

KEN GRIFFEY JR.
Outfield
Seattle Mariners

This 29-card set was inserted in loaves of bread and also given away at a Mariner home game. The card fronts feature full-color glossy photos, while the flip sides feature statistics.

		NM/M
Complete Set (29):		15.00
Common Player:		.50
1	Jim Lefebvre	.50
2	Jeff Schaefer	.50
3	Harold Reynolds	.75
4	Greg Briley	.50
5	Scott Bradley	.50
6	Dave Valle	.50
7	Edgar Martinez	1.00
8	Pete O'Brien	.50
9	Omar Vizquel	1.00
10	Tino Martinez	1.00
11	Scott Bankhead	.50
12	Bill Swift	.50
13	Jay Buhner	1.00
14	Alvin Davis	.50
15	Ken Griffey, Jr.	10.00
16	Tracy Jones	.50
17	Brent Knackert	.50
18	Henry Cotto	.50
19	Ken Griffey Sr.	.50
20	Keith Comstock	.50
21	Brian Holman	.50
22	Russ Swan	.50
23	Mike Jackson	.50
24	Erik Hanson	.50
25	Mike Schooler	.50
26	Randy Johnson	3.00
27	Rich DeLucia	.50
28	The Griffeys (Ken Griffey Jr., Ken Griffey Sr.)	2.00
29	Mascot	.50

1993 Country Time Brooks Robinson

COUNTRY TIME LEGENDS

Sponsored by Country Time drink mix, this set honors the career of the Orioles' Hall of Fame third baseman. The 2-1/2" x 3-5/8" cards feature color and colorized action photos with pale yellow frames, black diamond and textured green backgrounds and red and black borders. "Country Time Legends" and MLB logos appear in one of the bottom corners. Backs are printed in black, green and yellow and have a few sentences about some phase of Robinson's career. The cards are not numbered.

		NM/M
Complete Set (8):		7.00
Common Card:		1.00
(1)	Title Card	.25
(2)	Brooks Robinson/Btg (Back view.)	1.00
(3)	Brooks Robinson/Btg (Front view.)	1.00
(4)	Brooks Robinson/Btg (Horizontal)	1.00
(5)	Brooks Robinson/Fldg (Horizontal white jersey.)	1.00
(6)	Brooks Robinson/Fldg (Horizontal orange jersey.)	1.00
(7)	Brooks Robinson/Fldg (Vertical)	1.00
(8)	Brooks Robinson (Saluting view.)	1.00

1982 Cracker Jack

The Topps-produced 1982 Cracker Jack set was issued to promote the first "Old Timers Baseball

7	Don Mattingly	1.00
8	Pedro Guerrero	.25
9	Jose Rijo	.25
10	Jose Canseco	.40
11	Dave Parker	.25
12	Doug Drabek	.25
13	Cal Ripken	3.00
14	Dave Justice	.25
15	George Brett	1.00
16	Eric Davis	.25
17	Mark Langston	.25
18	Rickey Henderson	.60
19	Barry Bonds	3.00
20	Kevin Maas	.25
21	Len Dykstra	.25
22	Roger Clemens	1.00
23	Robin Yount	.60
24	Mark Grace	.25
25	Bo Jackson	.40
26	Tony Gwynn	.75
27	Mark McGwire	2.00
28	Dwight Gooden	.25
29	Wade Boggs	.75
30	Kevin Mitchell	.25
31	Cecil Fielder	.25
32	Bobby Thigpen	.25
33	Benito Santiago	.25
34	Kirby Puckett	.75
35	Will Clark	.25
36	Ken Griffey Jr.	1.50

Classic," held in Washington, D.C. The set was issued in two sheets of eight player cards, plus an advertising card located in the center. Individual cards are 2-1/2" x 3-1/2," with the complete sheets measuring 7-1/2" x 10-1/2". Cards #1-8 feature American League players with #9-16 being former National League stars. Fronts feature a full-color photo inside a Cracker Jack border. Backs contain the sponsor's logo plus a short player biography and his lifetime pitching or batting record. Complete sheets were available through a write-in offer.

		NM/M
Complete Panel Set (2):		12.00
Complete Singles Set (17):		10.00
Common Single Player:		.50
A.L. Panel		6.00
1	Larry Doby	.50
2	Bob Feller	.50
3	Whitey Ford	.50
4	Al Kaline	.50
5	Harmon Killebrew	.50
6	Mickey Mantle	5.00
7	Tony Oliva	.50
8	Brooks Robinson	.50
---	Advertising Card	.05
N.L. Panel		4.00
9	Hank Aaron	2.00
10	Ernie Banks	.50
11	Ralph Kiner	.50
12	Eddie Mathews	.50
13	Willie Mays	2.00
14	Robin Roberts	.50
15	Duke Snider	.50
16	Warren Spahn	.50
---	Advertising Card	.05

1991 Cracker Jack Topps 1st Series

In their first issue in almost 10 years, Cracker Jack inserted minia- ture cards (1-1/4" x 1-3/4") as the toy surprise in packages of the famous snack. The company produced two 36-card series, portraying many of the top stars in the game. Card fronts are identical to the corresponding regular-issue Topps cards, but the backs are significantly different be- cause of the small amount of space available for statistics. The Cracker Jack sailor logo appears on the bright red backs, along with copyright infor- mation listing Borden, Cracker Jack's parent company. These are some- times found on 2-1/2" x 3-1/2" cards bearing four different of the mini- cards; these were cut from sheets il- legally removed from the printer.

		NM/M
Complete Set (36):		10.00
Common Player:		.25
1	Nolan Ryan	3.00
2	Paul Molitor	.60
3	Tim Raines	.25
4	Frank Viola	.25
5	Sandy Alomar Jr.	.25
6	Ryne Sandberg	.75

1-3/4") was numbered 1-36 and features many top players. Card fronts are identical to the regular- issue '92 Donruss, but the backs have a different format and much less information because of the tiny space available. The backs have a blue border, with some spot red printing and the Cracker Jack sailor logo in the lower-left corner.

		NM/M
Complete Set (36):		20.00
Common Player:		.50
Album:		10.00
1	Dennis Eckersley	1.00
2	Jeff Bagwell	1.25
3	Jim Abbott	.50
4	Steve Avery	.50
5	Kelly Gruber	.50
6	Ozzie Smith	1.50
7	Lance Dickson	.50
8	Robin Yount	1.25
9	Brett Butler	.50
10	Sandy Alomar Jr.	.50
11	Travis Fryman	.50
12	Ken Griffey Jr.	2.00
13	Cal Ripken, Jr.	4.00
14	Will Clark	.50
15	Nolan Ryan	4.00
16	Tony Gwynn	1.00
17	Roger Clemens	1.75
18	Wes Chamberlain	.50
19	Barry Larkin	.50
20	Brian McRae	.50
21	Marquis Grissom	.50
22	Cecil Fielder	.50
23	Dwight Gooden	.50
24	Chuck Knoblauch	.50
25	Jose Canseco	.65
26	Terry Pendleton	.50
27	Ivan Rodriguez	1.00
28	Ryne Sandberg	1.50
29	Kent Hrbek	.50
30	Ramon Martinez	.50
31	Todd Zeile	.50
32	Hal Morris	.50
33	Robin Ventura	.50
34	Doug Drabek	.50
35	Frank Thomas	1.25
36	Don Mattingly	1.75

1992 Cracker Jack Donruss Series 2

The Second Series of the 1992 Crack Jack Donruss set is al- most identical to the first series, with the only change being differ- ent players and red border on the back instead of blue. The micro cards are numbered 1-36, just as in the first series.

		NM/M
Complete Set (36):		15.00
Common Player:		.50
1	Craig Biggio	.50
2	Tom Glavine	.65
3	David Justice	.50
4	Lee Smith	.50
5	Mark Grace	.50
6	George Bell	.50
7	Darryl Strawberry	.50
8	Eric Davis	.50
9	Ivan Calderon	.50
10	Royce Clayton	.50
11	Matt Williams	.50
12	Fred McGriff	.50
13	Len Dykstra	.50
14	Barry Bonds	3.00
15	Reggie Sanders	.50
16	Chris Sabo	.50
17	Howard Johnson	.50
18	Bobby Bonilla	.50
19	Rickey Henderson	.75
20	Mark Langston	.50
21	Joe Carter	.50
22	Paul Molitor	.75
23	Glenallen Hill	.50
24	Edgar Martinez	.50
25	Gregg Olson	.50
26	Ruben Sierra	.50
27	Julio Franco	.50
28	Phil Plantier	.50
29	Wade Boggs	1.00
30	George Brett	1.25

31	Alan Trammell	.50
32	Kirby Puckett	1.00
33	Scott Erickson	.50
34	Matt Nokes	.50
35	Danny Tartabull	.50
36	Jack McDowell	.50

1993 Cracker Jack Anniversary

In 1993, as part of the compa- ny's 100th anniversary celebration, Cracker Jack issued a 24-card set of mini replicas of its famous 1915 cards. The cards, 1-1/4" x 1-3/4", were included in specially-marked packages of the famous snack. The set features Hall of Famers such as Cobb, Mathewson, Walter Johnson and others, plus the Joe Jackson card. A red plastic album, with color pictures of the replicas inside, was also available.

		NM/M
Complete Set (24):		10.00
Common Player:		.50
Album:		5.00
1	Ty Cobb	1.50
2	Joe Jackson	3.00
3	Honus Wagner	1.00
4	Christy Mathewson	.75
5	Walter Johnson	.75
6	Tris Speaker	.50
7	Grover Alexander	.50
8	Nap Lajoie	.50
9	Rube Marquard	.50
10	Connie Mack	.50
11	Johnny Evers	.50
12	Branch Rickey	.50
13	Fred Clarke	.50
14	Harry Hooper	.50
15	Zack Wheat	.50
16	Joe Tinker	.50
17	Eddie Collins	.50
18	Mordecai Brown	.50
19	Eddie Plank	.50
20	Rabbit Maranville	.50
21	John McGraw	.50
22	Miller Huggins	.50
23	Ed Walsh	.50
24	Leslie Bush	.50

1997 Cracker Jack All Stars

After an hiatus of three years, Cracker Jack resumed the use of baseball cards as premiums in 1997 with a 20-card All Stars set. Like the other CJ issues of the 1990s, this set features miniature (1-5/16" x 1-3/4") cards. Cards fea- ture player action photos on front along with a Cracker Jack All Stars logo. Photos have uniform logos removed as the set is licensed only by the Players Association and not Major League Baseball. Backs are printed in red and blue with Crack- er Jack and MLBPA logos, a few stats and personal data. Cards were also distributed as prizes in various promotional contests con- ducted by American Sports Clas-

sics, which inserted a logo card within the regular Cracker Jack prize wrapping.

		NM/M
Complete Set (20):		15.00
Common Player:		.50
1	Jeff Bagwell	1.00
2	Chuck Knoblauch	.50
3	Cal Ripken Jr.	3.00
4	Chipper Jones	1.50
5	Derek Jeter	3.00
6	Barry Larkin	.50
7	Bernie Williams	.50
8	Barry Bonds	3.00
9	Kenny Lofton	.50
10	Gary Sheffield	.65
11	Sammy Sosa	1.50
12	Paul Molitor	1.00
13	Andres Galarraga	.50
14	Ivan Rodriguez	.75
15	Mike Piazza	2.00
16	Andy Pettitte	.65
17	Tom Glavine	.65
18	Albert Belle	.50
19	Mark McGwire	2.50
20	Mo Vaughn	.50
Album:		

1999 Cracker Jack Mac Stickers

In conjunction with its season- long promotion with Rawlings in which various Big Mac equipment items were given away, individual boxes of the snack could be found bearing one of 10 different McGwire stickers. The 1-1/2" x 2-1/8" stickers each include some type of interac- tive play element. Values shown are for opened, but complete, prize booklets. The color photos of McG- wire on the stickers have had uni- form logos removed.

		NM/M
Complete Set (10):		5.00
Common Sticker:		.50

1999 Cracker Jack Mark McGwire Home Run Record

One of several premiums which were part of a Rawlings pro- motion in boxes of Cracker Jack and related mail-in offers, this card marks McGwire's 70-HR season of 1998. The front is optical-variable, offering an image of McGwire in his home run-followthrough and, with a change in viewing angle, tipping his helmet to the crowd. Back has the date and distance of each of his 1998 homers, along with Rawling and Cracker Jack logos. The card is in standard 2-1/2" x 3-1/2" format.

	NM/M
Mark McGwire	10.00

1999 Cracker Jack Mark McGwire Spinners

"Home Run Around" is the name given to these spinner discs found as prizes in Cracker Jack

boxes. The 1-5/8" plastic discs have a "magic motion" picture of McG- wire on front with a large "70." Around the front rim are segments with other numbers. Instructions on back are to spin the disc and stop it to see if the player can hit more homers than McGwire. A raised spot at center allow the disc to be spun. While the Rawlings logo ap- pears on front and back, Cardinals uniform logos have been deleted from the photos.

		NM/M
Complete Set (5):		10.00
Common Disc:		2.00

1980-83 Cramer Baseball Legends

Consecutively numbered, this set was issued over a period of four years by Cramer Sports Promotions, the forerunner of to- day's Pacific card company. Sold in wax packs and measuring the standard 2-1/2" x 3-1/2", the cards have a sepia-toned photo on front with a black frame. In the back- ground is a weathered wooden slat design with the player's name on a hanging board beneath. The bor- ders are dull yellow. Backs are printed in brown and include a few personal data, career stats and a career summary. Cards 1-30 were issued in 1980; #31-60 in 1981; #61-90 in 1982 and #90-124 in 1983. Cards #121-124 were is- sued on the 1983 wax box.

		NM/M
Complete Set (124):		45.00
Complete Set (120):		
Common Player:		.25
1980		
1	Babe Ruth	3.00
2	Heinie Manush	.25
3	Rabbit Maranville	.25
4	Earl Averill	.25
5	Joe DiMaggio	2.00
6	Mickey Mantle	3.00
7	Hank Aaron	1.50
8	Stan Musial	1.25
9	Bill Terry	.25
10	Sandy Koufax	1.50
11	Ernie Lombardi	.25
12	Dizzy Dean	.50
13	Lou Gehrig	2.00
14	Walter Alston	.25
15a	Jackie Robinson/Portrait	4.00
15b	Jackie Robinson/Btg	1.00
16	Jimmie Foxx	.25
17	Billy Southworth	.25
18	Honus Wagner	.50
19	Duke Snider	.25
20	Rogers Hornsby	.25
21	Paul Waner	.25
22	Luke Appling	.25
23	Billy Herman	.25
24	Lloyd Waner	.25
25	Fred Hutchinson	.25
26	Eddie Collins	.25
27	Lefty Grove	.25
28	Chuck Connors	.25
29	Lefty O'Doul	.25
30	Hank Greenberg	.25
1981		
31	Ty Cobb	2.50

1991 Cracker Jack Topps 2nd Series

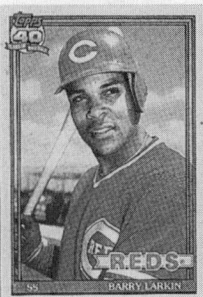

A second series of 36 micro cards was found in Cracker Jack boxes later in the 1991 season. Again numbered from 1-18, the 1- 1/4" x 1-3/4" cards carry a "2nd Se- ries" designation on the back above the card number. Like the first se- ries, these cards replicate the front of the 1991 Topps issue and have modified back design which in- cludes the "Sailor Jack" logo of the candy company. Four-card panels, believed to have been cut from sheets illegally removed from the printer, are known.

		NM/M
Complete Set (36):		5.00
Common Player:		.35
1	Eddie Murray	.75
2	Carlton Fisk	.75
3	Eric Anthony	.40
4	Kelly Gruber	.40
5	Von Hayes	.40
6	Ben McDonald	.40
7	Andre Dawson	.60
8	Ellis Burks	.40
9	Matt Williams	.40
10	Dave Stewart	.40
11	Barry Larkin	.40
12	Chuck Finley	.40
13	Shane Andrews	.40
14	Bret Saberhagen	.40
15	Bobby Bonilla	.40
16	Roberto Kelly	.40
17	Orel Hershiser	.40
18	Ruben Sierra	.40
19	Ron Gant	.40
20	Frank Thomas	1.00
21	Tim Wallach	.40
22	Gregg Olson	.40
23	Shawon Dunston	.40
24	Kent Hrbek	.40
25	Ramon Martinez	.40
26	Alan Trammell	.40
27	Ozzie Smith	2.00
28	Bob Welch	.40
29	Chris Sabo	.40
30	Steve Sax	.40
31	Bip Roberts	.40
32	Dave Steib	.40
33	Howard Johnson	.40
34	Mike Greenwell	.40
35	Delino DeShields	.40
36	Alex Fernandez	.40

1992 Cracker Jack Donruss Series 1

In 1992, Cracker Jack turned to Donruss to produce the cards for the surprise in their packages. The first series of micro cards (1-1/4" x

No.	Player	Price
32	Enos Slaughter	.25
33	Ernie Banks	.45
34	Christy Mathewson	.35
35	Mel Ott	.25
36	Pie Traynor	.25
37	Clark Griffith	.25
38	Mickey Cochrane	.25
39	Joe Cronin	.25
40	Leo Durocher	.25
41	Frank Baker	.25
42	Joe Tinker	.25
43	John McGraw	.25
44	Bill Dickey	.25
45	Walter Johnson	.35
46	Frankie Frisch	.25
47	Casey Stengel	.25
48	Willie Mays	2.00
49	Johnny Mize	.25
50	Roberto Clemente	4.00
51	Burleigh Grimes	.25
52	Pee Wee Reese	.25
53	Bob Feller	.25
54	Brooks Robinson	.25
55	Sam Crawford	.25
56	Robin Roberts	.25
57	Warren Spahn	.25
58	Joe McCarthy	.25
59	Jocko Conlan	.25
60	Satchel Paige	.75

1982

No.	Player	Price
61	Ted Williams	3.00
62	George Kelly	.25
63	Gil Hodges	.25
64	Jim Bottomley	.25
65	Al Kaline	.25
66	Harvey Kuenn	.25
67	Yogi Berra	.25
68	Nellie Fox	.25
69	Harmon Killebrew	.25
70	Edd Roush	.25
71	Mordecai Brown	.25
72	Gabby Hartnett	.25
73	Early Wynn	.25
74	Nap Lajoie	.25
75	Charlie Grimm	.25
76	Joe Garagiola	.25
77	Ted Lyons	.25
78	Mickey Vernon	.25
79	Lou Bourdreau	.25
80	Al Dark	.25
81	Ralph Kiner	.25
82	Phil Rizzuto	.25
83	Stan Hack	.25
84	Frank Chance	.25
85	Ray Schalk	.25
86	Bill McKechnie	.25
87	Travis Jackson	.25
88	Pete Reiser	.25
89	Carl Hubbell	.25
90	Roy Campanella	.25

1983

No.	Player	Price
91	Cy Young	.25
92	Kiki Cuyler	.25
93	Chief Bender	.25
94	Richie Ashburn	.25
95	Riggs Stephenson	.25
96	Minnie Minoso	.25
97	Hack Wilson	.25
98	Al Lopez	.25
99	Willie Keeler	.25
100	Fred Lindstrom	.25
101	Roger Maris	.25
102	Roger Bresnahan	.25
103	Monty Stratton	.25
104	Goose Goslin	.25
105	Earle Combs	.25
106	Pepper Martin	.25
107	Joe Jackson	3.00
108	George Sisler	.25
109	Red Ruffing	.25
110	Johnny Vander Meer	.25
111	Herb Pennock	.25
112	Chuck Klein	.25
113	Paul Derringer	.25
114	Addie Joss	.25
115	Bobby Thomson	.25
116	Chick Hafey	.25
117	Lefty Gomez	.25
118	George Kell	.25
119	Al Simmons	.25
120	Bob Lemon	.25
121	Hoyt Wilhelm	1.00
122	Arky Vaughan	1.00
123	Frank Robinson	1.50
124	Grover Alexander	1.50

1991 Crown/Coke Orioles

issued in four series. The first three series contain 120 cards each in a format of a dozen perforated cards on each of 10 sheets. Those series were given away at May 17, June 28 and August 11 home games. The fourth series, 12 sheets of 12 cards each, including three blank cards, was available only at participating Crown gas stations, which also sold the first three series following the give-away days at the ballpark. Cards measure 2-1/2" x 3-3/16" and are perforated on two, three or four sides, depending on their position on the sheet. All players are featured in sepia-toned head shots, virtually all in Orioles' uniform. Around the photos are borders of, successively, green, orange, black and white. The player's name and position appear in a black banner above the photo. In the lower-left corner is a 1954-1991 Memorial Stadium "Season to Remember" logo. That logo is repeated at bottom-center of the black-and-white backs, flanked by the logos of Coca-Cola and Crown. A card number appears in the lower-right. Most cards are numbered alphabetically. Backs include stats for the player's major league career and time with the Orioles.

No.	Player	NM/M
	Complete Set (501):	30.00
	Common Player:	.15
1	Don Aase	.15
2	Cal Abrams	.15
3	Jerry Adair	.15
4	Bobby Adams	.15
5	Mike Adamson	.15
6	Jay Aldrich	.15
7	Bob Alexander	.15
8	Doyle Alexander	.15
9	Brady Anderson	.40
10	John Anderson	.15
11	Mike Anderson	.15
12	Luis Aparicio	1.25
13	Tony Arnold	.15
14	Bobby Avila	.15
15	Benny Ayala	.15
16	Bob Bailor	.15
17	Frank Baker	.15
18	Jeff Ballard	.15
19	George Bamberger	.15
20	Steve Barber	.15
21	Ray "Buddy" Barker	.15
22	Ed Barnowski	.15
23	Jose Bautista	.15
24	Don Baylor	.40
25	Charlie Beamon	.15
26	Fred Beene	.15
27	Mark Belanger	.25
28	Eric Bell	.15
29	Juan Bell	.15
30	Juan Beniquez	.15
31	Neil Berry	.15
32	Frank Bertaina	.15
33	Fred Besana	.15
34	Vern Bickford	.15
35	Babe Birrer	.15
36	Paul Blair	.15
37	Curt Blefary	.15
38	Mike Blyzka	.15
39	Mike Boddicker	.15
40	Juan Bonilla	.15
41	Bob Bonner	.15
42	Dan Boone	.15
43	Rich Bordi	.15
44	Dave Boswell	.15
45	Sam Bowens	.15
46	Bob Boyd	.15
47	Gene Brabender	.15
48	Phil Bradley	.15
49	Jackie Brandt	.15
50	Marv Breeding	.15
51	Jim Brideweser	.15
52	Nellie Briles	.15
53	Dick Brown	.15
54	Hal Brown	.15
55	Larry Brown	.15
56	Mark Brown	.15
57	Marty Brown	.15
58	George Brunet	.15
59	Don Buford	.25
60	Al Bumbry	.15
61	Wally Bunker	.15
62	Leo Burke	.15
63	Rick Burleson	.15
64	Pete Burnside	.15
65	Jim Busby	.15
66	John Buzhardt	.15
67	Harry Byrd	.15
68	Enos Cabell	.15
69	Chico Carrasquel	.15
70	Camilo Carreon	.15
71	Foster Castleman	.15
72	Wayne Causey	.15
73	Art Ceccarelli	.15
74	Bob Chakales	.15
75	Tony Chevez	.15
76	Tom Chism	.15
77	Gino Cimoli	.15
78	Gil Coan	.15
79	Rich Coggins	.15
80	Joe Coleman	.15
81	Rip Coleman	.15
82	Fritz Connally	.15
83	Sandy Consuegra	.15
84	Doug Corbett	.15
85	Mark Corey	.15
86	Clint Courtney	.15
87	Billy Cox	.15
88	Dave Criscione	.15
89	Terry Crowley	.15
90	Todd Cruz	.15
91	Mike Cuellar	.30
92	Angie Dagres	.15
93	Clay Dalrymple	.15
94	Rich Dauer	.15
95	Jerry DaVanon	.15
96	Butch Davis	.15
97	Storm Davis	.15
98	Tommy Davis	.15
99	Doug DeCinces	.25
100	Luis DeLeon	.15
101	Ike Delock	.15
102	Rick Dempsey	.25
103	Mike Devereaux	.15
104	Chuck Diering	.15
105	Gordon Dillard	.15
106	Bill Dillman	.15
107	Mike Dimmel	.15
108	Ken Dixon	.15
109	Pat Dobson	.15
110	Tom Dodd	.15
111	Harry Dorish	.15
112	Moe Drabowsky	.15
113	Dick Drago	.15
114	Walt Dropo	.15
115	Tom Dukes	.15
116	Dave Duncan	.15
117	Ryne Duren	.15
118	Joe Durham	.15
119	Jim Dwyer	.15
120	Jim Dyck	.15
121	Mike Epstein	.15
122	Chuck Essegian	.15
123	Chuck Estrada	.15
124	Andy Etchebarren	.15
125	Hoot Evers	.15
126	Ed Farmer	.15
127	Chico Fernandez	.15
128	Don Ferrarese	.15
129	Jim Finigan	.15
130	Steve Finley	.15
131	Mike Fiore	.15
132	Eddie Fisher	.15
133	Jack Fisher	.15
134	Tom Fisher	.15
135	Mike Flanagan	.15
136	John Flinn	.15
137	Bobby Floyd	.15
138	Hank Foiles	.15
139	Dan Ford	.15
140	Dave Ford	.15
141	Mike Fornieles	.15
142	Howie Fox	.15
143	Tito Francona	.15
144	Joe Frazier	.15
145	Roger Freed	.15
146	Jim Fridley	.15
147	Jim Fuller	.15
148	Joe Gaines	.15
149	Vinicio "Chico" Garcia	.15
150	Kiko Garcia	.15
151	Billy Gardner	.15
152	Wayne Garland	.15
153	Tommy Gastall	.15
154	Jim Gentile	.25
155	Ken Gerhart	.15
156	Paul Gilliford	.15
157	Joe Ginsberg	.15
158	Leo Gomez	.15
159	Rene Gonzales	.15
160	Billy Goodman	.15
161	Dan Graham	.15
162	Ted Gray	.15
163	Gene Green	.15
164	Lenny Green	.15
165	Bobby Grich	.30
166	Mike Griffin	.15
167	Ross Grimsley	.15
168	Wayne Gross	.15
169	Glenn Gulliver	.15
170	Jackie Gutierrez	.15
171	John Habyan	.15
172	Harvey Haddix	.15
173	Bob Hale	.15
174	Dick Hall	.15
175	Bert Hamric	.15
176	Larry Haney	.15
177	Ron Hansen	.15
178	Jim Hardin	.15
179	Larry Harlow	.15
180	Pete Harnisch	.15
181	Tommy Harper	.15
182	Bob Harrison	.15
183	Roric Harrison	.15
184	Jack Harshman	.15
185	Mike Hart	.15
186	Paul Hartzell	.15
187	Grady Hatton	.15
188	Brad Havens	.15
189	Drungo Hazewood	.15
190	Jehosie Heard	.15
191	Mel Held	.15
192	Woodie Held	.15
193	Ellie Hendricks	.25
194	Leo Hernandez	.15
195	Whitey Herzog	.15
196	Kevin Hickey	.15
197	Billy Hoeft	.15
198	Chris Hoiles	.15
199	Fred Holdsworth	.15
200	Brian Holton	.15
201	Ken Holtzman	.15
202	Don Hood	.15
203	Sam Horn	.15
204	Art Houtteman	.15
205	Bruce Howard	.15
206	Rex Hudler	.15
207	Phil Huffman	.15
208	Keith Hughes	.15
209	Mark Huismann	.15
210	Tim Hulett	.15
211	Billy Hunter	.15
212	Dave Huppert	.15
213	Jim Hutto	.15
214	Dick Hyde	.15
215	Grant Jackson	.15
216	Lou Jackson	.15
217	Reggie Jackson	5.00
218	Ron Jackson	.15
219	Jesse Jefferson	.15
220	Stan Jefferson	.15
221	Bob Johnson	.15
222	Connie Johnson	.15
223	Darrell Johnson	.15
224	Dave Johnson	.15
225	Davey Johnson	.25
226	David Johnson	.15
227	Don Johnson	.15
228	Ernie Johnson	.15
229	Gordon Jones	.15
230	Ricky Jones	.15
231	O'Dell Jones	.15
232	Sam Jones	.15
233	George Kell	.75
234	Frank Kellert	.15
235	Pat Kelly	.15
236	Bob Kennedy	.15
237	Terry Kennedy	.15
238	Joe Kerrigan	.15
239	Mike Kinnunen	.15
240	Willie Kirkland	.15
241	Ron Kittle	.15
242	Billy Klaus	.15
243	Ray Knight	.25
244	Darold Knowles	.15
245	Dick Kokos	.15
246	Brad Komminsk	.15
247	Dave Koslo	.15
248	Wayne Krenchicki	.15
249	Lou Kretlow	.15
250	Dick Kryhoski	.15
251	Bob Kuzava	.15
252	Lee Lacy	.15
253	Hobie Landrith	.15
254	Tito Landrum	.15
255	Don Larsen	.25
256	Charlie Lau	.25
257	Jim Lehew	.15
258	Ken Lehman	.15
259	Don Lenhardt	.15
260	Dave Leonhard	.15
261	Don Leppert	.15
262	Dick Littlefield	.15
263	Charlie Locke	.15
264	Whitey Lockman	.15
265	Billy Loes	.15
266	Ed Lopat	.15
267	Carlos Lopez	.15
268	Marcelino Lopez	.15
269	John Lowenstein	.15
270	Steve Luebber	.15
271	Dick Luebke	.15
272	Fred Lynn	.45
273	Bobby Mabe	.15
274	Elliott Maddox	.15
275	Hank Majeski	.15
276	Roger Marquis	.15
277	Freddie Marsh	.15
278	Jim Marshall	.15
279	Morrie Martin	.15
280	Dennis Martinez	.25
281	Tippy Martinez	.25
282	Tom Matchick	.15
283	Charlie Maxwell	.15
284	Dave May	.15
285	Lee May	.15
286	Rudy May	.15
287	Mike McCormick	.15
288	Ben McDonald	.15
289	Jim McDonald	.15
290	Scott McGregor	.25
291	Mickey McGuire	.15
292	Jeff McKnight	.15
293	Dave McNally	.25
294	Sam Mele	.15
295	Francisco Melendez	.15
296	Bob Melvin	.15
297	Jose Mesa	.15
298	Eddie Miksis	.15
299	Bob Milacki	.15
300	Bill Miller	.15
301	Dyar Miller	.15
302	John Miller	.15
303	Randy Miller	.15
304	Stu Miller	.15
305	Randy Milligan	.15
306	Paul Mirabella	.15
307	Willy Miranda	.15
308	John Mitchell	.15
309	Paul Mitchell	.15
310	Ron Moeller	.15
311	Bob Molinaro	.15
312	Ray Moore	.15
313	Andres Mora	.15
314	Jose Morales	.15
315	Keith Moreland	.15
316	Mike Morgan	.15
317	Dan Morogiello	.15
318	John Morris	.15
319	Les Moss	.15
320	Curt Motton	.15
321	Eddie Murray	1.50
322	Ray Murray	.15
323	Tony Muser	.15
324	Buster Narum	.15
325	Bob Nelson	.15
326	Roger Nelson	.15
327	Carl Nichols	.15
328	Dave Nicholson	.15
329	Tom Niedenfuer	.15
330	Bob Nieman	.15
331	Donell Nixon	.15
332	Joe Nolan	.15
333	Dickie Noles	.15
334	Tim Nordbrook	.15
335	Jim Northrup	.15
336	Jack O'Connor	.15
337	Billy O'Dell	.15
338	John O'Donoghue	.15
339	Tom O'Malley	.15
340	Johnny Oates	.15
341	Claude Oertel	.15
342	Bob Oliver	.15
343	Gregg Olson	.15
344	John Orsino	.15
345	Joe Orsulak	.15
346	John Pacella	.15
347	Dave Pagan	.15
348	Erv Palica	.15
349	Jim Palmer	1.50
350	Joe Papa	.15
351	Milt Pappas	.15
352	Al Pardo	.15
353	Kelly Paris	.15
354	Mike Parrott	.15
355	Tom Patton	.15
356	Albie Pearson	.15
357	Orlando Pena	.15
358	Oswaldo Peraza	.15
359	Buddy Peterson	.15
360	Dave Philley	.15
361	Tom Phoebus	.15
362	Al Pilarcik	.15
363	Duane Pillette	.15
364	Lou Piniella	.25
365	Dave Pope	.15
366	Arnie Portocarrero	.15
367	Boog Powell	1.00
368	Johnny Powers	.15
369	Carl Powis	.15
370	Joe Price	.15
371	Jim Pyburn	.15
372	Art Quirk	.15
373	Jamie Quirk	.15
374	Allan Ramirez	.15
375	Floyd Rayford	.15
376	Mike Reinbach	.15
377	Merv Rettenmund	.15
378	Bob Reynolds	.15
379	Del Rice	.15
380	Pete Richert	.15
381	Jeff Rineer	.15
382	Bill Ripken	.15
383	Cal Ripken	9.00
384	Robin Roberts	1.25
385	Brooks Robinson	4.00
386	Earl Robinson	.15
387	Eddie Robinson	.15
388	Frank Robinson	3.00
389	Sergio Robles	.15
390	Aurelio Rodriguez	.15
391	Vic Rodriguez	.15
392	Gary Roenicke	.15
393	Saul Rogovin	.15
394	Wade Rowdon	.15
395	Ken Rowe	.15
396	Willie Royster	.15
397	Vic Roznovsky	.15
398	Ken Rudolph	.15
399	Lenn Sakata	.15
400	Chico Salmon	.15
401	Orlando Sanchez	.15
402	Bob Saverine	.15
403	Art Schallock	.15
404	Bill Scherrer	.15
405	Curt Schilling	.75
406	Dave Schmidt	.15
407	Johnny Schmitz	.15
408	Jeff Schneider	.15
409	Rick Schu	.15
410	Mickey Scott	.15
411	Kal Segrist	.15
412	David Segui	.15
413	Al Severinsen	.15
414	Larry Sheets	.15
415	John Shelby	.15
416	Barry Shetrone	.15
417	Tom Shopay	.15
418	Bill Short	.15
419	Norm Siebern	.15
420	Nelson Simmons	.15
421	Ken Singleton	.25
422	Doug Sisk	.15
423	Dave Skaggs	.15
424	Lou Sleater	.15
425	Al Smith	.15
426	Billy Smith	.15
427	Hal Smith	.15
428	"Texas" Mike Smith	.15
429	Nate Smith	.15
430	Nate Snell	.15
431	Russ Snyder	.15
432	Don Stanhouse	.15
433	Pete Stanicek	.15
434	Herm Starrette	.15
435	John Stefero	.15
436	Gene Stephens	.15
437	Vern Stephens	.15
438	Earl Stephenson	.15
439	Sammy Stewart	.15
440	Royle Stillman	.15
441	Wes Stock	.15
442	Tim Stoddard	.15
443	Dean Stone	.15
444	Jeff Stone	.15
445	Steve Stone	.25
446	Marlin Stuart	.15
447	Gordie Sundin	.15
448	Bill Swaggerty	.15
449	Willie Tasby	.15
450	Joe Taylor	.15
451	Dorn Taylor	.15
452	Anthony Telford	.15
453	Johnny Temple	.15
454	Mickey Tettleton	.15
455	Valmy Thomas	.15
456	Bobby Thomson	.25
457	Marv Thorneberry	.15
458	Mark Thurmond	.15
459	Jay Tibbs	.15
460	Mike Torrez	.15
461	Jim Traber	.15
462	Gus Triandos	.15
463	Paul "Dizzy" Trout	.15
464	Bob Turley	.15
465	Tom Underwood	.15
466	Fred Valentine	.15
467	Dave Van Gorder	.15
468	Dave Vineyard	.15
469	Ozzie Virgil	.15
470	Eddie Waitkus	.15
471	Greg Walker	.15
472	Jerry Walker	.15
473	Pete Ward	.15
474	Carl Warwick	.15
475	Ron Washington	.15
476	Eddie Watt	.15
477	Don Welchel	.15
478	George Werley	.15
479	Vic Wertz	.15
480	Wally Westlake	.15
481	Mickey Weston	.15
482	Alan Wiggins	.15
483	Bill Wight	.15
484	Hoyt Wilhelm	.50
485	Dallas Williams	.15
486	Dick Williams	.15
487	Earl Williams	.15
488	Mark Williamson	.15
489	Jim Wilson	.15
490	Gene Woodling	.15
491	Craig Worthington	.15
492	Bobby Young	.15
493	Mike Young	.15
494	Frank Zupo	.15
495	George Zuverink	.15
496	Glenn Davis	.15
497	Dwight Evans	.25
498	Dave Gallagher	.15
499	Paul Kilgus	.15
500	Jeff Robinson	.15
501	Ernie Whitt	.15

FRANK ZUPO - C

Claiming to include every player for the modern (1954-1991) Baltimore Orioles, this 501-card set was

1992 Crown Orioles Action Standups

Crown Petroleum released a set of standup cards in 1992 of 12 Oriole greats, most retired, that was sold at service stations in three series. The 4-1/4" x 9" cards have color photos on a white background on front; backs have black-and-white stats, logos, and career highlights. Cal Ripken, Jr. and Tippy Martinez were the only active players portrayed in the set. Suggested retail price at issue was $4 per series; about $2 with a gasoline purchase. A collector's album could also be purchased.

	NM/M
Complete Set (12):	20.00
Common Player:	1.00
SET 1	10.00
(1) Frank Robinson	3.00
(2) Brooks Robinson	4.00
(3) Jim Palmer	3.00
(4) Rick Dempsey	1.00
SET 2	12.00
(5) Cal Ripken Jr.	10.00
(6) Tippy Martinez	1.00
(7) Bobby Grich	1.00
(8) Earl Weaver	1.00
SET 3	4.00
(9) Boog Powell	1.50
(10) Paul Blair	1.00
(11) Terry Crowley	1.00
(12) Ken Singleton	1.00

1998 CyberAction

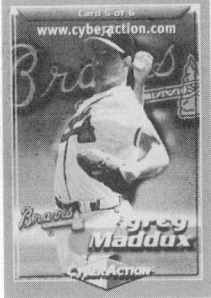

During the 1998 National Sports Collectors Convention in Chicago, CyberAction gave away samples of its product. The cards are printed on flimsy cardboard in standard 2-1/2" x 3-1/2" format. Fronts have a blue-bordered action photo at center. In the background is a large team logo. The firm's website address is at top; its logo at bottom. Backs have details on winning a World Series trip.

	NM/M
Complete Set (6):	11.00
Common Player:	1.50
1 Ken Griffey Jr.	2.25
2 Mark McGwire	2.50
3 Barry Bonds	3.00
4 Derek Jeter	3.00
5 Greg Maddux	2.00
6 Larry Walker	1.50

D

1992 Dairy Queen Team USA

In 1992, in conjunction with the Dairy Queen Team USA Sundae-in-a-Helmet promotion, customers received a four-card pack of Team USA cards, part of a 33-card set manufactured by Topps for the company. Included in the set are Team USA players from the 1984 and 1988 Olympics, many of whom have gone on to major league stardom. The set also has 15 Team USA Prospects, a 1988 Gold Medal team celebration card and a card of 1992 coach Ron Fraser. Fronts feature each player in their Team USA uniform and the backs include statistics from amateur, Team USA and professional competition.

	NM/M
Complete Set (33):	13.50
Common Player:	.25
1 Mark McGwire/1984	4.00
2 Will Clark/1984	1.00
3 John Marzano/1984	.25
4 Barry Larkin/1984	1.00
5 Bobby Witt/1984	.25
6 Scott Bankhead/1984	.25
7 B.J. Surhoff/1984	.25
8 Shane Mack/1984	.25
9 Jim Abbott/1988	.35
10 Ben McDonald/1988	.25
11 Robin Ventura/1988	.50
12 Charles Nagy/1988	.25
13 Andy Benes/1988	.25
14 Joe Slusarski/1988	.25
15 Ed Sprague/1988	.25
16 Bret Barberie/1988	.25
17 Gold Medal/1988	.25
18 Jeff Granger/1992	.25
19 John Dettmer/1992	.25
20 Todd Greene/1992	.25
21 Jeffrey Hammonds/1992	.25
22 Dan Melendez/1992	.25
23 Kennie Steenstra/1992	.25
24 Todd Johnson/1992	.25
25 Chris Roberts/1992	.25
26 Steve Rodriguez/1992	.25
27 Charles Johnson/1992	.25
28 Chris Wimmer/1992	.25
29 Tony Phillips/1992	.25
30 Craig Wilson/1992	.25
31 Jason Giambi/1992	6.00
32 Paul Shuey/1992	.25
33 Ron Fraser/1992 (Coach)	.25

1993 Dairy Queen Magic Mariner Moments Pin/Cards

	NM/M
Complete Set (4):	10.00
Common Player:	2.00
1 Randy Johnson ('92 AL K King)	3.25
2 Edgar Martinez ('92 AL Batting Champ)	2.00
3 Chris Bosio (No-Hitter)	2.00
4 Ken Griffey Jr. ('92 All-Star MVP)	4.00

1994 Dairy Queen Ken Griffey, Jr.

Distributed by Dairy Queen stores in the Pacific Northwest, this set was issued in two different versions, with green borders and with gold borders. All cards feature a "Ken Griffey Jr. Golden Moments" logo in the upper-left corner. His name and the DQ logo appear at the bottom. Backs have another photo of Griffey along with a description of the career highlight depicted on front, sponsors' logos and a card number. Values

shown here are for green-bordered cards; gold-bordered cards sell for about twice those figures.

	NM/M
Complete Set (10):	7.50
Common Player:	.75
Gold:	2X
1 Ken Griffey Jr. ("The Spider Man Catch")	.75
2 Ken Griffey Jr. ("Back to Back Homeruns")	.75
3 Ken Griffey Jr. (Hit .327 in 1991)	.75
4 Ken Griffey Jr. (1992 All-Star MVP)	.75
5 Ken Griffey Jr. ("Dialing Long Distance")	.75
6 Ken Griffey Jr. ("8 Straight Homeruns")	.75
7 Ken Griffey Jr. (4-Time Golden Glove Winner)	.75
8 Ken Griffey Jr. (45 Homeruns in 1993)	.75
9 Ken Griffey Jr. (Major League Career Hitting Record)	.75
10 Ken Griffey Jr. ("Looking to 1994")	.75

Danbury Mint 22 Kt. Gold Cooperstown Collection

A series of embossed 22kt. gold-foil cards was offered by the private mint beginning in 1996. Each month two cards were sent to subscribers. The standard-size cards have a player picture on front with team logo and player identification at bottom. Backs have career stats. Each card was sealed in acrylic. An album for the set has identification labels with name in both printed and facsimile autograph form. Only persons who completed Set 1 were allowed to purchase subsequent sets. While each card is numbered, they are checklisted here alphabetically within series. Because the Babe Ruth card was used as a free promotional give-away, it is more common than the others.

	NM/M
Complete Set (200):	750.00
Common Player (1-50):	5.00
Common Player (51-100):	6.00
Common Player (101-150):	7.50
Common Player (151-200):	7.50
(1) Richie Allen	4.00
(2) Paul Blair	3.00
(3) Vida Blue	3.00
(4) Bert Blyleven	3.00
(5) Roy Campanella	6.00
(6) Bert Campaneris	3.00
(7) Gary Carter	4.00
(8) Cesar Cedeno	4.00
(9) Orlando Cepeda	4.00
(10) Ty Cobb	7.50
(11) Mickey Cochrane	3.00
(12) Eddie Collins	3.00
(13) Dizzy Dean	5.00
(14) Bob Feller	4.00
(15) George Foster	3.00
(16) Steve Garvey	3.00
(17) Lou Gehrig	7.50
(18) Lefty Gomez	3.00
(19) Gil Hodges	4.00
(20) Carl Hubbell	3.00
(21) Walter Johnson	5.00
(22) Jim Kaat	3.00
(23) Don Kessinger	3.00
(24) Harmon Killebrew	4.00
(25) Jerry Koosman	3.00
(26) Mickey Lolich	3.00
(27) Sparky Lyle	3.00
(28) Fred Lynn	3.00
(29) Bill Mazeroski	4.00
(30) Minnie Minoso	3.00
(31) Johnny Mize	3.00
(32) Thurman Munson	5.00
(33) Graig Nettles	3.00
(34) Phil Niekro	3.00
(35) Tony Oliva	3.00
(36) Al Oliver	3.00

(37)	Satchel Paige	7.50
(38)	Jim Palmer	3.00
(39)	Herb Pennock	3.00
(40)	Tony Perez	3.00
(41)	Boog Powell	3.00
(42)	Brooks Robinson	4.00
(43)	Babe Ruth	2.50
(44)	Duke Snider	3.00
(45)	Tris Speaker	3.00
(46)	Willie Stargell	3.00
(47)	Luis Tiant	3.00
(48)	Honus Wagner	5.00
(49)	Maury Wills	3.00
(50)	Cy Young	5.00
(51)	Grover Alexander	6.00
(52)	Sandy Alomar Jr.	6.00
(53)	Jeff Bagwell	9.00
(54)	Dusty Baker	6.00
(55)	Albert Belle	6.00
(56)	Wade Boggs	10.00
(57)	Barry Bonds	17.50
(58)	Joe Carter	6.00
(59)	Will Clark	6.00
(60)	Roger Clemens	12.00
(61)	Dwight Evans	6.00
(62)	Jim Fregosi	6.00
(63)	Andres Galarraga	6.00
(64)	Bob Gibson	6.00
(65)	Ken Griffey Jr.	13.50
(66)	Tony Gwynn	10.00
(67)	Rogers Hornsby	6.00
(68)	Catfish Hunter	6.00
(69)	Joe Jackson	17.50
(70)	Ferguson Jenkins	6.00
(71)	Derek Jeter	17.50
(72)	Randy Johnson	9.00
(73)	Jimmy Key	6.00
(74)	Ralph Kiner	6.00
(75)	Don Larsen	6.00
(76)	Greg Maddux	10.00
(77)	Juan Marichal	6.00
(78)	Eddie Mathews	7.50
(79)	Christy Mathewson	9.00
(80)	Fred McGriff	6.00
(81)	Mark McGwire	15.00
(82)	Dave McNally	6.00
(83)	Bobby Murcer	6.00
(84)	Dale Murphy	7.50
(85)	Gaylord Perry	6.00
(86)	Rico Petrocelli	6.00
(87)	Andy Pettitte	7.50
(88)	Mike Piazza	13.50
(89)	Cal Ripken Jr.	17.50
(90)	Alex Rodriguez	15.00
(91)	Joe Rudi	6.00
(92)	Ron Santo	6.00
(93)	Gary Sheffield	6.00
(94)	John Smoltz	6.00
(95)	Sammy Sosa	10.00
(96)	Warren Spahn	6.00
(97)	Billy Williams	6.00
(98)	Bobby Thomson	6.00
(99)	Mo Vaughn	6.00
(100)	Hoyt Wilhelm	6.00
(101)	Brady Anderson	7.50
(102)	Luis Aparicio	7.50
(103)	Kevin Appier	7.50
(104)	Richie Ashburn	7.50
(105)	Lou Boudreau	9.00
(106)	Lou Brock	7.50
(107)	Kevin Brown	7.50
(108)	Jim Bunning	7.50
(109)	Jose Canseco	9.00
(110)	David Cone	7.50
(111)	Rollie Fingers	7.50
(112)	Chuck Finley	7.50
(113)	Curt Flood	7.50
(114)	Jimmie Foxx	10.00
(115)	Nomar Garciaparra	12.00
(116)	Tom Glavine	7.50
(117)	Juan Gonzalez	7.50
(118)	Luis Gonzalez	7.50
(119)	Mark Grace	7.50
(120)	Shawn Green	7.50
(121)	Burleigh Grimes	7.50
(122)	Lefty Grove	7.50
(123)	Al Hrabosky	7.50
(124)	Chipper Jones	12.00
(125)	Al Kaline	9.00
(126)	Tony Lazzeri	7.50
(127)	Bill Lee	7.50
(128)	Jose Lima	7.50
(129)	Bill Madlock	7.50
(130)	Roger Maris	9.00
(131)	Pedro Martinez	10.00
(132)	Tino Martinez	7.50
(133)	Tug McGraw	7.50
(134)	Kevin Millwood	7.50
(135)	Joe Morgan	7.50
(136)	Charles Nagy	7.50
(137)	Mel Ott	7.50
(138)	Rafael Palmeiro	7.50
(139)	Manny Ramirez	9.00
(140)	Jim Rice	7.50
(141)	Ivan Rodriguez	7.50
(142)	Edd Roush	7.50
(143)	Manny Sanguillen	7.50
(144)	Curt Schilling	7.50
(145)	Ron Swoboda	7.50
(146)	Greg Vaughn	7.50
(147)	Larry Walker	7.50
(148)	Zack Wheat	7.50
(149)	Bernie Williams	7.50
(150)	Jim Wynn	7.50
(151)	Bobby Abreu	7.50
(152)	Roberto Alomar	7.50
(153)	Moises Alou	7.50
(154)	Carlos Beltran	7.50

(155)	Armando Benitez	7.50
(156)	Lance Berkman	7.50
(157)	Bret Boone	7.50
(158)	Ellis Burks	7.50
(159)	Sean Casey	7.50
(160)	Carlos Delgado	10.00
(161)	J.D. Drew	10.00
(162)	Jim Edmonds	7.50
(163)	Cliff Floyd	7.50
(164)	Freddy Garcia	7.50
(165)	Jason Giambi	10.00
(166)	Brian Giles	7.50
(167)	Troy Glaus	10.00
(168)	Vladimir Guerrero	12.50
(169)	Mike Hampton	7.50
(170)	Todd Helton	10.00
(171)	Trevor Hoffman	7.50
(172)	Tim Hudson	10.00
(173)	Andruw Jones	12.50
(174)	Jeff Kent	7.50
(175)	Ryan Klesko	7.50
(176)	Al Leiter	7.50
(177)	Edgar Martinez	7.50
(178)	Raul Mondesi	7.50
(179)	Matt Morris	7.50
(180)	Jamie Moyer	7.50
(181)	Mark Mulder	7.50
(182)	Mike Mussina	9.00
(183)	Robb Nen	7.50
(184)	Phil Nevin	7.50
(185)	John Olerud	7.50
(186)	Magglio Ordonez	7.50
(187)	Roy Oswalt	7.50
(188)	Chan Ho Park	7.50
(189)	Troy Percival	7.50
(190)	Albert Pujols	15.00
(191)	Brad Radke	7.50
(192)	Mariano Rivera	7.50
(193)	Kazuhiro Sasaki	7.50
(194)	Jeff Shaw	7.50
(195)	Alfonso Soriano	9.00
(196)	Frank Thomas	12.50
(197)	Jim Thome	7.50
(198)	Billy Wagner	7.50
(199)	Kerry Wood	9.00
(200)	Barry Zito	9.00

1991 Jimmy Dean

SANDY ALOMAR JR.
Cleveland Indians • Catcher

Baseball cards were inserted into packages of Jimmy Dean sausages in 1991. The complete set consists of 25 star players' cards. Red and yellow borders surround color player photos on the card fronts. No team logos appear on the cards. The card backs feature statistics, biographical information and a facsimile autograph. The set is entitled the "Signature Edition." An uncut sheet was also available via special offer.

	NM/M
Complete Set (25):	5.00
Common Player:	.15
Uncut Sheet:	6.00
1 Will Clark	.15
2 Ken Griffey Jr.	.75
3 Dale Murphy	.15
4 Barry Bonds	1.00
5 Darryl Strawberry	.15
6 Ryne Sandberg	.50
7 Gary Sheffield	.25
8 Sandy Alomar, Jr.	.15
9 Frank Thomas	.45
10 Barry Larkin	.15
11 Kirby Puckett	.50
12 George Brett	.60
13 Kevin Mitchell	.15
14 Dave Justice	.15
15 Cal Ripken, Jr.	.60
16 Craig Biggio	.15
17 Rickey Henderson	.45
18 Roger Clemens	.60
19 Jose Canseco	.25
20 Ozzie Smith	.50
21 Cecil Fielder	.15
22 Dave Winfield	.45
23 Kevin Maas	.15
24 Nolan Ryan	1.00
25 Dwight Gooden	.15

1992 Jimmy Dean

For the second year in a row, baseball cards were inserted into packages of Jimmy Dean sausage in

JIM ABBOTT
CALIFORNIA ANGELS • PITCHER

1992. Featuring 18 star players, the set portrays the player's name on a vertical panel at the left of the card, along with his team name and position. The Jimmy Dean logo appears in the lower-right corner. Major League team logos have been eliminated from the photos.

	NM/M
Complete Set (18):	5.00
Common Player:	.15
1 Jim Abbott	.15
2 Barry Bonds	1.50
3 Jeff Bagwell	.45
4 Frank Thomas	.45
5 Steve Avery	.15
6 Chris Sabo	.15
7 Will Clark	.15
8 Don Mattingly	.60
9 Darryl Strawberry	.15
10 Roger Clemens	.60
11 Ken Griffey Jr.	1.00
12 Chuck Knoblauch	.15
13 Tony Gwynn	.50
14 Juan Gonzalez	.30
15 Cecil Fielder	.15
16 Bobby Bonilla	.15
17 Wes Chamberlain	.15
18 Ryne Sandberg	.50

1992 Jimmy Dean Living Legends

GEORGE BRETT
KANSAS CITY ROYALS • FIRST BASE

Approximately 100,000 of these six-card sets were made available via a mail-in offer for $1 and proofs of purchase from the company's breakfast meats. Color photos on front have had uniform logos removed and are overprinted with a gold-foil facsimile autograph. Other gold foil highlights the player, team and sponsor names on front. Backs are printed in black and yellow and include a few biographical details, career highlights and summary statistics.

	NM/M
Complete Set (6):	8.00
Common Player:	1.00
1 George Brett	2.00
2 Carlton Fisk	1.00
3 Ozzie Smith	1.50
4 Robin Yount	1.00
5 Cal Ripken, Jr.	3.00
6 Nolan Ryan	3.00

1992 Jimmy Dean Rookie Stars

Nine of 1992's hottest rookies were featured in this set issued as inserts into various Jimmy Dean meat products. Cards feature full-bleed photos on which uniform logos have been airbrushed away. A 1992 Rookie Star logo appears at upper-left, atop a black vertical strip containing the player's name, team and position. A white strip at bottom has the Jimmy Dean logo. On back, personal data and minor and major league stats are featured in a center panel, surrounded by a light blue border.

		NM/M
Complete Set (9):		3.00
Common Player:		.50
1	Andy Stankiewicz	.50
2	Pat Listach	.50
3	Brian Jordan	.50
4	Eric Karros	.50
5	Reggie Sanders	.50
6	Dave Fleming	.50
7	Donovan Osborne	.50
8	Kenny Lofton	.50
9	Moises Alou	.50

1993 Jimmy Dean

Issued in the company's meat products and via a mail-in offer, this set once again features player photos on which the uniform logos have been airbrushed away, due to lack of a license from Major League Baseball. A pair of horizontal color bars in one of the lower corners contains a Jimmy Dean logo and the player's name. Backs have a line drawing portrait of the player, along with stats, personal data and logos.

		NM/M
Complete Set (28):		6.00
Common Player:		.15
1	Frank Thomas	.50
2	Barry Larkin	.15
3	Cal Ripken, Jr.	1.25
4	Andy Van Slyke	.15
5	Darren Daulton	.15
6	Don Mattingly	.65
7	Roger Clemens	.65
8	Juan Gonzalez	.35
9	Mark Langston	.15
10	Barry Bonds	1.25
11	Ken Griffey Jr.	.75
12	Cecil Fielder	.15
13	Kirby Puckett	.60
14	Tom Glavine	.25
15	George Brett	.65
16	Nolan Ryan	1.50
17	Eddie Murray	.50
18	Gary Sheffield	.35
19	Doug Drabek	.15
20	Ray Lankford	.15
21	Benito Santiago	.15
22	Mark McGwire	1.00
23	Kenny Lofton	.15
24	Eric Karros	.15
25	Ryne Sandberg	.60
26	Charlie Hayes	.15
27	Mike Mussina	.25
28	Pat Listach	.15

1993 Jimmy Dean Rookie Cards

Jimmy Dean Foods issued a Rookie Stars baseball card set in 1993. The nine-card set features promising rookies, with players highlighted against a marblized background with color photos on both sides of the cards. The cards

were distributed randomly in three-card sets in specially-marked packages of Jimmy Dean products.

		NM/M
Complete Set (9):		3.00
Common Player:		.10
(1)	Rich Amaral	.10
(2)	Vinny Castilla	.15
(3)	Jeff Conine	.25
(4)	Brent Gates	.10
(5)	Wayne Kirby	.10
(6)	Mike Lansing	.25
(7)	David Nied	.10
(8)	Mike Piazza	2.00
(9)	Tim Salmon	.75

1995 Jimmy Dean All Time Greats

Six Hall of Famers are featured in this promotion for the country singer's breakfast meats. Besides inclusion of regular cards in food packages, a send-away deal offered autographed cards of three of the players for proofs of purchase and $7 apiece. Cards feature action photos on which team uniform logos have been removed; while the cards are licensed by the Major League Baseball Players Alumni, they are not sanctioned by MLB. A large "1995 All Time Greats Collectors Set" logo appears in the upper-right corner on front, while the Jimmy Dean logo and player name are in the lower-left. Full color backs offer a career summary and lifetime stats, along with a ghost image of the front photo.

		NM/M
Complete Set (6):		5.00
Common Player:		.50
1	Rod Carew	1.00
2	Jim "Catfish" Hunter	.50
2a	Jim "Catfish" Hunter/ Auto.	15.00
3	Al Kaline	1.50
3a	Al Kaline/Auto.	8.00
4	Mike Schmidt	1.50
5	Billy Williams	.50
5a	Billy Williams/Auto.	8.00
6	Carl Yastrzemski	1.50

1997 Jimmy Dean Great Moments

These two-card sets were available via a mail-in offer for $12.95 apiece plus proofs of purchase. Each set consists of an autographed "Great Moments in

Baseball" card with an action photo and a "Great Baseball Stadiums" card featuring a player photo set against the stadium background. All pictures are sepia toned with uniform logos removed. Cards have player or stadium information on the backs and came with a certificate of authenticity.

		NM/M
Complete Set (4):		35.00
(1)	Yogi Berra/Auto.	20.00
(2)	Yogi Berra (Yankee Stadium)	5.00
(3)	Brooks Robinson/Auto.	10.00
(4)	Brooks Robinson (Memorial Stadium)	3.00

1984 Decathlon Negro League Baseball Stars

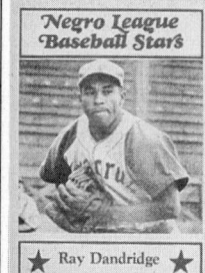

According to contemporary advertising, this set was produced in conjunction with the Negro Baseball Hall of History in Kentucky, to a total of 2,000 sets and 300 uncut sheets. The cards and checklist are identical to the 1986 issue by Larry Fritsch Cards, which purchased rights to the set, except for the copyright line at bottom on back.

	NM/M
Complete Set (119):	35.00
Common Player:	.30
Stars:	3X

1985 Decathlon Ultimate Baseball Card Set

Originally intended to be a six-series, 90-card issue, this collectors' set was cut short after the first series. The large-format (4" x 5-5/8") cards feature on front color artwork by former Topps artist Gerry Dvorak. The portraits are surrounded by a white border. Black-and-white backs have a career capsule. Announced as an edition of 10,000 sets, original issue price was about $11.

		NM/M
Complete Set (15):		20.00
Common Player:		1.00
1	Ty Cobb	3.00
2	Honus Wagner	3.00
3	Babe Ruth	5.00
4	Lou Gehrig	4.00
5	Frank Baker	1.00
6	Casey Stengel	1.00
7	Moses Walker	1.00
8	Cy Young	1.00
9	Joe DiMaggio	4.00
10	John McGraw	1.00
11	Josh Gibson	1.00
12	Johnny Mize	1.00
13	Walter Johnson	1.00
14	Walter Alston	1.00
15	Enos Slaughter	1.00

1993 Dempster's Blue Jays

One of several Canadian baseball card issues marking the 1992 World Series victory of the

Toronto Blue Jays, the Dempster's stores set is a 25-card issue in standard 2-1/2" x 3-1/2", UV-coatd on both sides. Fronts have a large dark blue border with white horizontal white pinstripes. An action photo is at center, with the player's name and position below. The Jays World Championship logo and Players Association logo are at top; the sponsor's logo at lower-right. A baseball at bottom center has the card number. Backs feature a large portrait photo at top, against a dark blue background. Color bars carry the player's '92 and career stats. A facsimile autograph appears beneath the team logo at right.

		NM/M
Complete Set (25):		6.50
Common Player:		.25
1	Juan Guzman	.25
2	Roberto Alomar	.75
3	Danny Cox	.25
4	Paul Molitor	4.00
5	Todd Stottlemyre	.25
6	Joe Carter	.50
7	Jack Morris	.35
8	Ed Sprague	.25
9	Turner Ward	.25
10	John Olerud	.75
11	Duane Ward	.25
12	Alfredo Griffin	.25
13	Cito Gaston	.25
14	Dave Stewart	.25
15	Mark Eichhorn	.25
16	Darnell Coles	.25
17	Randy Knorr	.25
18	Al Leiter	.25
19	Pat Hentgen	.25
20	Devon White	.25
21	Pat Borders	.25
22	Darrin Jackson	.25
23	Dick Schofield	.25
24	Luis Sojo	.25
25	Mike Timlin	.25

1991 Denny's Grand Slam

This 26-card set was produced by Upper Deck and features one player from each Major League team. One hologram card was distributed with the purchase of a Grand Slam meal. The cards are numbered on the front and are 3-D. The card backs describe grand slams hit by the featured player.

		NM/M
Complete Set (26):		12.50
Common Player:		.50
1	Ellis Burks	.50
2	Cecil Fielder	.50
3	Will Clark	.50
4	Eric Davis	.50
5	Dave Parker	.50
6	Kelly Gruber	.50
7	Kent Hrbek	.50
8	Don Mattingly	1.50
9	Brook Jacoby	.50
10	Mark McGwire	2.00
11	Howard Johnson	.50
12	Tim Wallach	.50

13	Ricky Jordan	.50
14	Andre Dawson	.75
15	Eddie Murray	1.00
16	Danny Tartabull	.50
17	Bobby Bonilla	.50
18	Benito Santiago	.50
19	Alvin Davis	.50
20	Cal Ripken	2.50
21	Ruben Sierra	.50
22	Pedro Guerrero	.50
23	Wally Joyner	.50
24	Craig Biggio	.50
25	Dave Justice	.50
26	Tim Raines	.50

1992 Denny's Grand Slam

The second year of the Denny's Gland Slam promotion featured one power hitter from each major league team, portrayed on a hologram in front of a scene from his team's city. As in the first year, the cards were produced by Upper Deck and given away, one at a time, with a Denny's purchase during the middle of the summer. An album with plastic pages holding four cards each was also available.

		NM/M
Complete Set (26):		7.50
Common Player:		.25
Album:		3.00
1	Marquis Grissom	.25
2	Ken Caminiti	.25
3	Fred McGriff	.25
4	Felix Jose	.25
5	Jack Clark	.25
6	Albert Belle	.25
7	Sid Bream	.25
8	Robin Ventura	.25
9	Cal Ripken, Jr.	2.00
10	Ryne Sandberg	1.00
11	Paul O'Neill	.25
12	Luis Polonia	.25
13	Cecil Fielder	.25
14	Kal Daniels	.25
15	Brian McRae	.25
16	Howard Johnson	.25
17	Greg Vaughn	.25
18	Dale Murphy	.60
19	Kent Hrbek	.25
20	Barry Bonds	2.00
21	Matt Nokes	.25
22	Jose Canseco	.50
23	Jay Buhner	.25
24	Will Clark	.25
25	Ruben Sierra	.25
26	Joe Carter	.25

1993 Denny's Grand Slam

The 1993 Denny's Grand Slam set expanded to 28 cards with the addition of the Florida and Colorado expansion teams. The featured color photos of one grand slam slugger for each team superimposed over a hologram background. The reverse of each card gives anecdotes about the player's grand slams along with his career total. The cards were distributed at participating Denny's restaurants during mid-summer.

		NM/M
Complete Set (28):		7.50
Common Player:		.25
1	Chili Davis	.25
2	Eric Anthony	.25
3	Rickey Henderson	.60
4	Joe Carter	.25
5	Terry Pendleton	.25
6	Robin Yount	.60
7	Ray Lankford	.25
8	Ryne Sandberg	.75
9	Darryl Strawberry	.25
10	Marquis Grissom	.25
11	Will Clark	.25
12	Albert Belle	.25
13	Edgar Martinez	.25
14	Benito Santiago	.25
15	Eddie Murray	.60
16	Cal Ripken, Jr.	2.00
17	Gary Sheffield	.45
18	Dave Hollins	.25
19	Andy Van Slyke	.25
20	Juan Gonzalez	.45
21	John Valentin	.25
22	Joe Oliver	.25
23	Dante Bichette	.25
24	Wally Joyner	.25
25	Cecil Fielder	.25
26	Kirby Puckett	.75
27	Robin Ventura	.25
28	Danny Tartabull	.25

1994 Denny's Grand Slam

For its fourth annual hologram card promotion, Denny's chose a horizontal format with portrait and action photos of one player from each major league team. Designated the "Anniversary Edition," the set features the 125th year logo at bottom center, with the player's name at left; Upper Deck and Denny's logos are at top. On back the same two photos are conventionally printed along with a brief player biography, appropriate logos and copyright notices. The cards are numbered alphabetically. Cards were available with certain menu items from July 1 through Aug. 31. Each restaurant received one special boxed set for use as a contest prize. These sets include a special Reggie Jackson "Route to Cooperstown" hologram card; the edition was limited to about 1,500.

		NM/M
Complete Set (28 / No Jackson):		7.50
Common Player:		.25
1	Jim Abbott	.25
2	Roberto Alomar	.35
3	Kevin Appier	.25
4	Jeff Bagwell	.60
5	Albert Belle	.25
6	Barry Bonds	2.00
7	Bobby Bonilla	.25
8	Lenny Dykstra	.25
9	Cal Eldred	.25
10	Cecil Fielder	.25
11	Andres Galarraga	.25
12	Juan Gonzalez	.40
13	Ken Griffey Jr.	1.00
14	Tony Gwynn	.75
15	Rickey Henderson	.60
16	Kent Hrbek	.25
17	David Justice	.25
18	Mike Piazza	1.50
19	Jose Rijo	.25
20	Cal Ripken, Jr.	2.00
21	Tim Salmon	.25
22	Ryne Sandberg	.75
23	Gary Sheffield	.35
24	Ozzie Smith	.75
25	Frank Thomas	.60
26	Andy Van Slyke	.25
27	Mo Vaughn	.25
28	Larry Walker	.25
---	Reggie Jackson	60.00

1995 Denny's Classic Hits

For the fifth consecutive year, this August 1-September 30 promotion offered a hologram baseball card with the purchase of selected items from the restaurant's "Classic Hits" menu. The cards were produced for Denny's by Upper Deck and combine photographic and holographic images of the player on the horizontal-format front. Backs have another color photo, career highlights, and past-season/lifetime stats. Each Major League team is represented in the set by one player card. According to advertisements for the promotion, a total of 8,000,000 cards was produced - about 286,000 of each player.

		NM/M
Complete Set (28):		6.00
Common Player:		.15
1	Roberto Alomar	.30
2	Moises Alou	.15
3	Jeff Bagwell	.35
4	Albert Belle	.15
5	Jason Bere	.15
6	Roger Clemens	.60
7	Darren Daulton	.15
8	Cecil Fielder	.15
9	Andres Galarraga	.15
10	Juan Gonzalez	.35
11	Ken Griffey Jr.	.75
12	Tony Gwynn	.50
13	Barry Larkin	.15
14	Greg Maddux	.50
15	Don Mattingly	.50
16	Mark McGwire	1.00
17	Orlando Merced	.15
18	Jeff Montgomery	.15
19	Rafael Palmeiro	.35
20	Mike Piazza	1.00
21	Kirby Puckett	.50
22	Bret Saberhagen	.15
23	Tim Salmon	.15
24	Gary Sheffield	.30
25	Ozzie Smith	.50
26	Sammy Sosa	.50
27	Greg Vaughn	.15
28	Matt Williams	.15

1996 Denny's Instant Replay Holograms

Pinnacle, in its first year as supplier for Denny's annual baseball card promotion, attempted breakthrough technology that didn't quite hit the mark. The hologram portion of the card front was supposed to show as much as four seconds of on-field action, but unless viewed at exactly the right distance and angle, and under exacting light requirements, the action is little more than a silver-foil streak. Card fronts also included a color player photo. Another color photo appears on the back, along with a description of the action on front for those who couldn't master the "Full Motion" hologram. Cards were sold in single-card foil packs for 49 cents (limit two) with a qualifying purchase. Besides the hologram card, each pack includes a card explaining "How To View a Full Motion Hologram." Besides the regular cards, two "Grand Slam" chase sets were issued along with instant winner cards for complete card sets or trips to the World Series. Stated odds on the chase cards would indicate about 750,000 of each regular card were produced. One player from each team is represented in the checklist.

		NM/M
Complete Set (28):		5.00
Common Player:		.15
1	Greg Maddux	.50
2	Cal Ripken Jr.	1.00
3	Frank Thomas	.45
4	Albert Belle	.15
5	Mo Vaughn	.15
6	Jeff Bagwell	.45
7	Jay Buhner	.15
8	Barry Bonds	1.00

9	Ryne Sandberg	.50
10	Hideo Nomo	.35
11	Kirby Puckett	.50
12	Gary Sheffield	.30
13	Barry Larkin	.15
14	Wade Boggs	.50
15	Tony Gwynn	.50
16	Tim Salmon	.15
17	Jason Isringhausen	.15
18	Cecil Fielder	.15
19	Dante Bichette	.15
20	Ozzie Smith	.50
21	Ivan Rodriguez	.35
22	Kevin Appier	.15
23	Joe Carter	.15
24	Moises Alou	.15
25	Mark McGwire	.75
26	Kevin Seitzer	.15
27	Darren Daulton	.15
28	Jay Bell	.15

1996 Denny's Grand Slam

Exploding fireworks in the background are an allegory for the firepower brought to the plate by the sluggers featured in this chase set from Denny's annual baseball card promotion. A Grand Slam card is randomly substituted for the standard hologram card about once every 56 packs.

		NM/M
Complete Set (10):		13.50
Common Player:		1.00
1	Cal Ripken Jr.	2.50
2	Frank Thomas	1.50
3	Mike Piazza	2.25
4	Tony Gwynn	2.00
5	Sammy Sosa	2.00
6	Barry Bonds	2.50
7	Jeff Bagwell	1.50
8	Albert Belle	1.00
9	Mo Vaughn	1.00
10	Kirby Puckett	2.00

1996 Denny's Grand Slam Artist's Proofs

A specially marked Artist's Proof version of the Grand Slam chase cards are substituted for the standard hologram card in about every 360 packs, according to stated odds.

		NM/M
Complete Set (10):		50.00
Common Player:		2.00
1	Cal Ripken Jr.	10.00
2	Frank Thomas	5.00
3	Mike Piazza	7.50
4	Tony Gwynn	6.00
5	Sammy Sosa	6.00
6	Barry Bonds	10.00
7	Jeff Bagwell	5.00
8	Albert Belle	2.00
9	Mo Vaughn	2.00
10	Kirby Puckett	6.00

1997 Denny's 3-D Holograms

Denny's seventh annual baseball card issue was produced by Pinnacle and showcases two popular card technologies. Fronts of the 3-1/2" x 2-1/2" horizontal cards feature a deep 3D look. Backs have a player portrait hologram at the right. A partial baseball at left is the background for player data and stats along with sponsor and licensor logos. Cards were distributed one per pack for 59 cents from June 26-September 3, with 10 cents from the sale of each card donated to children's charities. The set features one player from each major league team, plus a Jackie Robinson tribute card.

		NM/M
Complete Set (29):		8.00
Common Player:		.20
1	Tim Salmon	.20

2	Rafael Palmeiro	.45
3	Mo Vaughn	.20
4	Frank Thomas	.50
5	David Justice	.20
6	Travis Fryman	.20
7	Johnny Damon	.35
8	John Jaha	.20
9	Chuck Knoblauch	.20
10	Mark McGwire	1.00
11	Alex Rodriguez	1.00
12	Juan Gonzalez	.35
13	Roger Clemens	.65
14	Derek Jeter	1.50
15	Andruw Jones	.50
16	Sammy Sosa	.60
17	Barry Larkin	.20
18	Dante Bichette	.20
19	Jeff Bagwell	.50
20	Mike Piazza	.75
21	Gary Sheffield	.35
22	Vladimir Guerrero	.50
23	Todd Hundley	.20
24	Jason Kendall	.20
25	Ray Lankford	.20
26	Ken Caminiti	.20
27	Barry Bonds	1.50
28	Scott Rolen	.40
29	Jackie Robinson (50th Anniversary Commemorative)	1.50

1997 Denny's Larry Doby

In the same format as the restaurant chain's regular set of 1997, this card honors the first black player to appear in the American League. The card was available only at the All-Star FanFest and All-Star Game in Cleveland in early July. Fronts have a black-and-white 3-D image; backs have a color hologram at right and a 50th anniversary logo at upper-left. Personal data, career highlights and stats are included, as well as appropriate logos.

		NM/M
1	Larry Doby	6.00

1981 Detroit News Tigers Centennial

The 100th anniversary of professional baseball in Detroit was marked by "The Detroit News" with the issue of this set honoring "The Boys of Summer." The 2-1/2" x 3-1/2" cards have black-and-white photos on front, a mock sports page. Cards can be found either with or without a red border on front, though the relative scarcity of each version is not known. Black-and-white backs have player data, career summary and stats, or a description of the front photo/highlight.

		NM/M
Complete Set (135):		30.00
Common Player:		.25
1	Detroit Boys of Summer 100th Anniversary	.25
2	Charles W. Bennett	.25
3	Mickey Cochrane	.25
4	Harry Heilmann	.25
5	Walter O. Briggs	.25
6	Mark Fidrych	.75
7	1887 Tigers	.25
8	Tiger Stadium	.25
9	Rudy York	.25
10	George Kell	.25
11	Steve O'Neill	.25
12	John Hiller	.25

13	1934 Tigers	.25
14	Charlie Gehringer	.45
15	Denny McLain	.60
16	Billy Rogell	.25
17	Ty Cobb	5.00
18	Sparky Anderson	.60
19	Davy Jones	.25
20	Kirk Gibson	.45
21	Pat Mullin	.25
22	1972 Tigers	.25
23	What a Night	.25
24	"Doc" Cramer	.25
25	Mickey Stanley	.25
26	Johnny Lipon	.25
27	Jo Jo White	.25
28	Recreation Park	.25
29	Wild Bill Donovan	.25
30	Ray Oyler	.25
31	Earl Whitehill	.25
32	Billy Hoeft	.25
33	Johnny Groth	.25
34	Hughie Jennings	.25
35	Mayo Smith	.25
36	Bennett Park	.25
37	Tigers Win	.25
38	Donie Bush	.25
39	Harry Coveleski	.25
40	Paul Richards	.25
41	Johnston Stone	.25
42	Bill Swift	.25
43	Roy Cullenbine	.25
44	Hoot Evers	.25
45	Tigers Win Series	.25
46	Art Houtteman	.25
47	Aurelio Rodriguez	.25
48	Fred Hutchinson	.25
49	Don Mossi	.25
50	Gehrig's Streak Ends in Detroit (Lou Gehrig)	2.50
51	Earl Wilson	.25
52	Jim Northrup	.25
53	1907 Tigers	.25
54	Greenberg's Two Homers Tie Ruth (Hank Greenberg)	.45
55	Mickey Lolich	.45
56	Tommy Bridges	.25
57	Al Benton	.25
58	Del Baker	.25
59	Lou Whitaker	.45
60	Navin Field	.25
61	1945 Tigers	.25
62	Ernie Harwell	.25
63	League Champs	.25
64	Bobo Newsom	.25
65	Don Wert	.25
66	Ed Summers	.25
67	Billy Martin	.25
68	Alan Trammell	1.50
69	Dale Alexander	.25
70	Ed Brinkman	.25
71	Right Man in Right Place Wins (Ted Williams)	2.00
72	Bill Freehan	.25
73	Norm Cash	.60
74	George Dauss	.25
75	Aurelio Lopez	.25
76	Charlie Maxwell	.25
77	Ed Barrow	.25
78	Willie Horton	.25
79	Denny Sets Record (Denny McLain)	.45
80	Dan Brouthers	.25
81	John E. Fetzer	.25
82	Heinie Manush	.25
83	1935 Tigers	.25
84	Ray Boone	.25
85	Bob Fothergill	.25
86	Steve Kemp	.25
87	Ed Killian	.25
88	Giebell is Ineligible (Floyd Giebell)	.25
89	Pinky Higgins	.25
90	Lance Parrish	.25
91	Eldon Auker	.25
92	Birdie Tebbetts	.25
93	Schoolboy Rowe	.25
94	McLain Wins 30th (Denny McLain)	.45
95	1909 Tigers	.25
96	Harvey Kuenn	.40
97	Jim Bunning	.60
98	1940 Tigers	.25
99	Rocky Colavito	2.50
100	Kaline Enters Hall of Fame (Al Kaline)	1.00
101	Billy Bruton	.25
102	Germany Schaefer	.25
103	Frank Bolling	.25
104	Briggs Stadium	.25
105	Bucky Harris	.25
106	Gates Brown	.25
107	Martin Made the Difference (Billy Martin)	.25
108	1908 Tigers	.25
109	"Gee" Walker	.25
110	Pete Fox	.25
111	Virgil Trucks	.25
112	1968 Tigers	1.50
113	Dizzy Trout	.25
114	Barney McCosky	.25
115	Lu Blue	.25
116	Hal Newhouser	.45
117	Tigers are Home for Series	.25
118	Bobby Veach	.25
119	George Mullins (Mullin)	.25
120	Reggie's Super Homer (Reggie Jackson)	.60
121	Sam Crawford	.25

122	Hank Aguirre	.25
123	Vic Wertz	.25
124	Goose Goslin	.25
125	Frank Lary	.25
126	Joe Coleman	.25
127	Ed Katalinas	.25
128	Jack Morris	.25
129	3 Time AL Leaders	.25
130	James A. Campbell	.25
131	Ted Gray	.25
132	Al Kaline	5.00
133	Hank Greenberg	2.50
134	Dick McAuliffe	.25
135	Ozzie Virgil	.25

1988 Detroit Tigers Police

This unnumbered issue, sponsored by the Michigan State Police features 13 players and manager Sparky Anderson in full-color standard-size (2-1/2" x 3-1/2") cards. Player photos are framed by a blue border, with the Detroit logo upper left and a large name block that lists the player's name, position batting/throwing preference, height, weight and birthday beneath the photo. The backs carry an anti-drug or anti-crime message.

		NM/M
Complete Set (14):		7.00
Common Player:		.50
(1)	Doyle Alexander	.50
(2)	Sparky Anderson	1.00
(3)	Dave Bergman	.50
(4)	Tom Brookens	.50
(5)	Darrell Evans	.60
(6)	Larry Herndon	.50
(7)	Chet Lemon	.50
(8)	Jack Morris	.60
(9)	Matt Nokes	.50
(10)	Jeff Robinson	.50
(11)	Frank Tanana	.50
(12)	Walt Terrell	.50
(13)	Alan Trammell	1.00
(14)	Lou Whitaker	.75

1989 Detroit Tigers Police

This unnumbered issue, distributed and sponsored by the Michigan State Police Department features 14 full-color 2-1/2" x 3-1/2" cards. Player photos are framed by a blue and orange border, with the team logo in the upper left and biographical information below the photo. The card backs featue anti-drug or anti-crime messages.

		NM/M
Complete Set (14):		4.00
Common Player:		.25
(1)	Doyle Alexander	.25
(2)	Sparky Anderson	.75
(3)	Dave Bergman	.25
(4)	Mike Henneman	.25
(5)	Guillermo Hernandez	.25
(6)	Chet Lemon	.25
(7)	Fred Lynn	.25
(8)	Jack Morris	.35
(9)	Matt Nokes	.25
(10)	Jeff Robinson	.25
(11)	Pat Sheridan	.25
(12)	Frank Tanana	.25
(13)	Alan Trammell	.75
(14)	Lou Whitaker	.50

1991 Detroit Tigers Police

One of the scarcer safety issues is this Tigers team issue. Cards have a color player action photo on front with orange and blue team-color graphics. Backs have a safety message and the logos of sponsors HSP and Team Michigan, along with the Michigan State Police. The unnumbered cards are checklisted here alphabetically.

		NM/M
Complete Set (14):		7.00
Common Player:		.50
(1)	Sparky Anderson	.75
(2)	Dave Bergman	.50
(3)	Cecil Fielder	.75
(4)	Travis Fryman	.50
(5)	Paul Gibson	.50
(6)	Jerry Don Gleaton	.50
(7)	Lloyd Moseby	.50
(8)	Dan Petry	.50
(9)	Tony Phillips	.50
(10)	Mark Salas	.50
(11)	John Shelby	.50
(12)	Frank Tanana	.50
(13)	Alan Trammell	.75
(14)	Lou Whitaker	.75

1993 DiamondMarks Prototypes

In the same format as the regular-issue DiamondMark cards, these promos were produced to preview the concept for dealers and collectors. The promo cards feature different photos than those used on the issued version. The unnumbered cards are listed here alphabetically. On the back of the promos, the phrase "1993 PROTOTYPE" appears vertically at left.

		NM/M
Complete Set (8):		40.00
Common Player:		3.00
(1)	Roberto Alomar	4.00
(2)	Will Clark	3.00
(3)	Dennis Eckersley	5.00
(4)	Juan Gonzalez	4.00
(5)	Ken Griffey Jr.	10.00
(6)	Kirby Puckett	7.50
(7)	Ryne Sandberg	6.00
(8)	Frank Thomas	6.00

1993 DiamondMarks

While they look like baseball cards and were sold in foil packs like baseball cards, Daimond-Marks were licensed as book marks. Issued by Barry Colla Productions, the 2-1/2" x 5" cards feature Barry Colla's trademark high-quality player photos on front and back. The UV-coated fronts feature black borders with the player's name in white above the photo and a color team logo beneath. Backs, also bordered in black, feature two color player photos in an open book design. There is a portrait photo on the left and a head-and-shoulders reproduction of the front photo at right. A bookmark with team logo is incorporated in the design. The 120-card set is unnumbered and is arranged in the checklist below alphabetically within league and team.

	NM/M
Complete Set (120):	12.00
Common Player:	.15
Wax Box (48):	20.00

Atlanta Braves

(1)	Steve Avery	.15
(2)	Ron Gant	.15
(3)	Tom Glavine	.35
(4)	David Justice	.15
(5)	Terry Pendleton	.15
(6)	Deion Sanders	.25
(7)	John Smoltz	.15

Chicago Cubs

(8)	Mark Grace	.15
(9)	Randy Myers	.15
(10)	Ryne Sandberg	.75
(11)	Jose Vizcaino	.15

Cincinnati Reds

(12)	Bobby Kelly	.15
(13)	Barry Larkin	.15
(14)	Kevin Mitchell	.15
(15)	Jose Rijo	.15
(16)	Reggie Sanders	.15

Colorado Rockies

(17)	Dante Bichette	.15
(18)	Daryl Boston	.15
(19)	Andres Galarraga	.15
(20)	Charlie Hayes	.15

Florida Marlins

(21)	Orestes Destrade	.15
(22)	Benito Santiago	.15
(23)	Gary Sheffield	.35
(24)	Walt Weiss	.15

Houston Astros

(25)	Jeff Bagwell	.60
(26)	Craig Biggio	.15
(27)	Ken Caminiti	.15
(28)	Luis Gonzalez	.15

Los Angeles Dodgers

(29)	Brett Butler	.15
(30)	Eric Davis	.15
(31)	Orel Hershiser	.15
(32)	Eric Karros	.15
(33)	Ramon Martinez	.15
(34)	Mike Piazza	1.50
(35)	Darryl Strawberry	.15

Montreal Expos

(36)	Moises Alou	.15
(37)	Delino DeShields	.15
(38)	Marquis Grissom	.15
(39)	Dennis Martinez	.15
(40)	Larry Walker	.15

New York Mets

(41)	Bobby Bonilla	.15
(42)	Dwight Gooden	.15
(43)	Howard Johnson	.15
(44)	Eddie Murray	.60

Philadelphia Phillies

(45)	Darren Daulton	.15
(46)	Lenny Dykstra	.15
(47)	Dave Hollins	.15
(48)	John Kruk	.15

Pittsburgh Pirates

(49)	Jay Bell	.15
(50)	Al Martin	.15
(51)	Orlando Merced	.15
(52)	Andy Van Slyke	.15

St. Louis Cardinals

(53)	Gregg Jefferies	.15
(54)	Tom Pagnozzi	.15
(55)	Ozzie Smith	.75
(56)	Todd Zeile	.15

San Diego Padres

(57)	Derek Bell	.15
(58)	Tony Gwynn	.75
(59)	Fred McGriff	.60

San Francisco Giants

(60)	Barry Bonds	2.00
(61)	John Burkett	.15
(62)	Will Clark	.15
(63)	Matt Williams	.15

Baltimore Orioles

(64)	Brady Anderson	.15
(65)	Mike Mussina	.30
(66)	Cal Ripken, Jr.	2.00

Boston Red Sox

(67)	Roger Clemens	1.00
(68)	Andre Dawson	.30
(69)	Mike Greenwell	.15
(70)	Mo Vaughn	.15

Detroit Tigers

(71)	Cecil Fielder	.15
(72)	Tony Phillips	.15
(73)	Mickey Tettleton	.15
(74)	Alan Trammell	.15

Cleveland Indians

(75)	Sandy Alomar Jr.	.15
(76)	Carlos Baerga	.15
(77)	Albert Belle	.15
(78)	Kenny Lofton	.15

Chicago White Sox

(79)	Bo Jackson	.25
(80)	Frank Thomas	.15
(81)	Robin Ventura	.15

California Angels

(82)	Chad Curtis	.15
(83)	Gary DiSarcina	.15
(84)	Tim Salmon	.15
(85)	J.T. Snow	.15

Kansas City Royals

(86)	George Brett	1.00
(87)	Wally Joyner	.15
(88)	Mike MacFarlane	.15
(89)	Brian McRae	.15

Milwaukee Brewers

(90)	Darryl Hamilton	.15
(91)	Pat Listach	.15
(92)	B.J. Surhoff	.15
(93)	Robin Yount	.60

Minnesota Twins

(94)	Kent Hrbek	.15
(95)	Chuck Knoblauch	.15
(96)	Kirby Puckett	.75
(97)	Dave Winfield	.60

New York Yankees

(98)	Wade Boggs	.75
(99)	Don Mattingly	1.00
(100)	Danny Tartabull	.15

Oakland Athletics

(101)	Dennis Eckersley	.50
(102)	Rickey Henderson	.60
(103)	Mark McGwire	1.50
(104)	Ruben Sierra	.15
(105)	Terry Steinbach	.15

Seattle Mariners

(106)	Ken Griffey Jr.	1.50
(107)	Edgar Martinez	.15
(108)	Pete O'Brien	.15
(109)	David Valle	.15

Texas Rangers

(110)	Jose Canseco	.35
(111)	Juan Gonzalez	.35
(112)	Ivan Rodriguez	.50
(113)	Nolan Ryan	2.00

Toronto Blue Jays

(114)	Roberto Alomar	.30
(115)	Pat Borders	.15
(116)	Joe Carter	.15
(117)	Juan Guzman	.15
(118)	Paul Molitor	.60
(119)	John Olerud	.15
(120)	Dave Stewart	.15

1993 DiamondMarks Inserts

KEN GRIFFEY, JR.

Randomly inserted into packs of DiamondMarks cards at the rate of one per 48-pack carton was a series of eight cards featuring the baseball artwork of Terry Smith. The inserts are the same 2-1/2" x 5" size as the regular issue and carry on with the basic black bordered design, though the inserts are UV-coated both front and back. Beneath the fantasy-design player art on the front is the player's name. On back the open book design is seen again, with a short player profile on the left and a Barry Colla photo portrait on the right, along with the appropriate team logo.

	NM/M
Complete Set (8):	50.00
Common Player:	5.00
(1)	Roberto Alomar	6.00
(2)	Barry Bonds	15.00
(3)	Ken Griffey Jr.	10.00
(4)	David Justice	5.00
(5)	John Olerud	5.00
(6)	Nolan Ryan	15.00
(7)	Frank Thomas	7.50
(8)	Robin Yount	7.50

1981 Diamond Stars Extension Set

BENNY FREY

About 1980 an uncut sheet of artwork apparently intended for use in the original Diamond Stars series (1934-36) was discovered. The art was used to create a collectors' issue "extension" set by Den's Collectors Den of Maryland. The new cards were printed in the same 2-3/8" x 2-7/8" format as the 1930s issue with the player name on front. Backs are printed in blue with a career summary, biographical details and a 1981 copyright line. The set was sold in a heavy paper wrapper patterned after the original.

	NM/M
Complete Set (12):	5.00
Uncut Sheet:	25.00
Common Player:	.25
109	Benny Frey	.25
110	Pete Fox	.25
111	Phil Cavarretta	.25
112	Leon Goslin	.50
113	Mel Harder	.25
114	Roger Cramer	.35
115	Gene Moore	.25
116	Rip Collins	.25
117	Linus Frey	.25
118	Vernon Gomez	1.00
119	Jim Bottomley, Rogers Hornsby	1.50
120	Lon Warneke	.25

1993 Diamond Stars Extension Set

In the style of the 1934-36 Diamond Stars bubblegum cards from National Chicle Co., this collectors' issue features colorful painting of players from the mid-1930s. Cards measure about 2-3/8" x 2-7/8" with white borders on front with no player identification or other graphics. The artwork is by D'August Roth Martin. Backs have player id, personal data and a career summary purporting to have been written by Travis Lake in Aug., 1936, the man who wrote the backs for the original cards. A copyright line at bottom identifies the "Extended Edition" as a 1993 issue of "The Chicle Fantasy Co." According to the set's producer, 4,166 were printed with 1,936 cut into hand-numbered sets which were originally sold at $19.95. Promo versions of each card in the set have a red rubber-stamped ad on back.

	NM/M
Complete Set, Uncut Sheet:	15.00
Complete Set (36):	10.00
Common Player:	.25
121	Moe Berg	2.00
122	Harlond Clift	.25
123	Joe Cronin	.50
124	Dizzy Dean	1.00
125	Paul Dean	.50
126	Joe DiMaggio	3.00
127	Leo Durocher	.50
128	Bob Feller	1.00
129	Carl Fisher	.25
130	Lou Gehrig	2.00
131	Bump Hadley	.25
132	Jesse Haines	.25
133	Bad News Hale	.25
134	Gabby Hartnett	.25
135	Babe Herman	.25
136	Billy Herman	.25
137	Waite Hoyt	.25
138	Bob Johnson	.25
139	Chuck Klein	.50
140	Mike Kreevich	.25
141	Fred Lindstrom	.25
142	Connie Mack	.50
143	Joe McCarthy	.25
144	Bill McKechnie	.25
145	Johnny Mize	.60
146	Johnny Moore	.25
147	Hugh Mulcahy	.25
148	Buck Newsom	.25
149	Al Smith	.25
150	Casey Stengel	1.00
151	Arky Vaughan	.25
152	Gee Walker	.25
153	Kenesaw M. Landis	.25
	Cool Papa Bell	.25
	Josh Gibson	.50
	Satchel Paige	1.00
	Title Card	.10

1992 Diet Pepsi Collector Series

Dwight Gooden

This Canadian issue includes 30 top stars, with a slight emphasis on the two Canadian teams. Because the set is licensed only by the players' association, and not Major League Baseball, all photos had team logos eliminated. Fronts feature action photo with Diet Pepsi logos in a strip below. Backs have a portrait photo, recent stats and a facsimile autograph. Card number 5 of Tom Glavine can be found showing him pitching right-handed (error) or left-handed (right). Cards are UV coated on both sides. A poster picturing all 30 cards was also issued. Cards were issued in three-card packs.

	NM/M
Complete Set (30):	7.00
Poster:	7.50
Common Player:	.15
1	Roger Clemens	.60
2	Dwight Gooden	.15
3	Tom Henke	.15
4	Dennis Martinez	.15
5a	Tom Glavine (Pitching right-handed.)	.25
5b	Tom Glavine (Pitching left-handed.)	.75
6	Jack Morris	.15
7	Dennis Eckersley	.35
8	Jeff Reardon	.15
9	Bryan Harvey	.15
10	Sandy Alomar Jr.	.15
11	Carlton Fisk	.40
12	Gary Carter	.40
13	Cecil Fielder	.15
14	Will Clark	.15
15	Roberto Alomar	.30
16	Ryne Sandberg	.50
17	Cal Ripken Jr.	1.50
18	Barry Larkin	.15
19	Ozzie Smith	.50
20	Kelly Gruber	.15
21	Wade Boggs	.50
22	Tim Wallach	.15
23	Howard Johnson	.15
24	Jose Canseco	.30
25	Joe Carter	.15
26	Ken Griffey Jr.	.65
27	Kirby Puckett	.50
28	Rickey Henderson	.40
29	Barry Bonds	1.50
30	Dave Winfield	.40

1988 Domino's Pizza Tigers

Domino's Pizza produced a 28-card set commemorating the 20th anniversary of the 1968 World Champion Detroit Tigers. The cards were given away at an Old Timers Game at Tiger Stadium

Denny McLain

in 1988. The cards, which measure 2-1/2" x 3-1/2", feature black and white photos semi-surrounded by a two-stripe band. The stripes on the card's left side are the same color (red and light blue) as the Domino's Pizza logo in the upper corner. The stripes on the card's right side match the colors of the Tigers logo (red and dark blue). The backs of all the cards (except for Ernie Harwell) contain a brief summary of the Tigers' 1968 season. Located at the bottom on the card back are the players' major league records through 1968 plus their 1968 World Series statistics.

	NM/M
Complete Set (29):	8.00
Common Player:	.25
(1)	Gates Brown	.25
(2)	Norm Cash	1.00
(3)	Wayne Comer	.25
(4)	Pat Dobson	.25
(5)	Bill Freehan	.60
(6)	John Hiller	.25
(7)	Ernie Harwell (Announcer)	.30
(8)	Willie Horton	.40
(9a)	Al Kaline/Btg	3.00
(9b)	Al Kaline (In outfield.)	3.00
(10)	Fred Lasher	.25
(11)	Mickey Lolich	.75
(12)	Tom Matchick	.25
(13)	Ed Mathews	1.25
(14)	Dick McAuliff (McAuliffe)	.25
(15)	Denny McLain	.75
(16)	Don McMahon	.25
(17)	Jim Northrup	.25
(18)	Ray Oyler	.25
(19)	Daryl Patterson	.25
(20)	Jim Price	.25
(21)	Joe Sparma	.25
(22)	Mickey Stanley	.25
(23)	Dick Tracewski	.25
(24)	Jon Warden	.25
(25)	Don Wert	.25
(26)	Earl Wilson	.25
(27)	Header Card	.05
(28)	Coupon Card	.05

1980 Donruss Prototypes

REGGIE JACKSON

When it became apparent that Topps' monopoly on baseball card production was going to be ended by the courts, Memphis-based Donruss began work to produce a bubblegum card set for 1981. As part of its research, Donruss created a three-card prototype panel in three different sizes to test collector preference. Two of the prototypes have player pictures, the third does not. Backs are blank.

	NM/M
Small Panel	
(About 6" x 2-3/4".):	75.00
Regular Panel	
(About 7-1/2" x 3-1/2".):	75.00
Large Panel (About 10-1/2" x 4-3/4".):	75.00
George Brett (2" x 2-3/4")	35.00

George Brett (2-1/2" x 3-1/2") 35.00
George Brett (3-1/2" x 4-3/4") 30.00
Reggie Jackson (2" x 2-3/4") 35.00
Reggie Jackson (2-1/2" x 3-1/2") 35.00
Reggie Jackson (3-1/2" x 4-3/4") 30.00
No Player Pictured (2" x 2-3/4") 7.50
No Player Pictured (2-1/2" x 3-1/2") 5.00
No Player Pictured (3-1/2" x 4-3/4") 5.00

1981 Donruss Promo Sheet

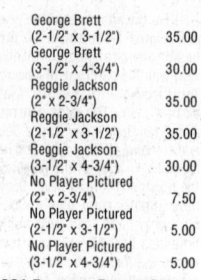

Rookie sensation Joe Charbonneau was the featured attraction when this sample sheet was issued to introduce Donruss' debut baseball card issue. The 10" x 7" sheet is comprised of eight of the cards which appeared in the set.

	NM/M
Complete Sheet:	35.00

1981 Donruss

TOM SEAVER PITCHER Reds

The Donruss Co. of Memphis, Tenn., produced its premiere baseball card issue in 1981 with a set that consisted of 600 numbered cards and five unnumbered checklists. The cards, which measure 2-1/2" x 3-1/2", are printed on thin stock. The card fronts contain the Donruss logo plus the year of issue. The card backs are designed on a vertical format and have black print on red and white. The set, entitled "First Edition Collector Series," contains nearly 40 variations, those being first-printing errors that were corrected in a subsequent print run. The cards were sold in wax packs with bubblegum. The complete set price does not include the higher priced variations.

	NM/M
Complete Set (605):	25.00
Uncut Sheet Set (5):	65.00
Common Player:	.10
Wax Pack (18):	2.00
Wax Box (36):	60.00
1	Ozzie Smith	2.00
2	Rollie Fingers	1.00
3	Rick Wise	.10
4	Gene Richards	.10
5	Alan Trammell	.10
6	Tom Brookens	.10
7a	Duffy Dyer (1980 Avg. .185)	.25
7b	Duffy Dyer (1980 Avg. .185)	.10
8	Mark Fidrych	.15
9	Dave Rozema	.10
10	Ricky Peters	.10
11	Mike Schmidt	3.00
12	Willie Stargell	1.25
13	Tim Foli	.10
14	Manny Sanguillen	.10
15	Grant Jackson	.10
16	Eddie Solomon	.10
17	Omar Moreno	.10
18	Joe Morgan	1.25
19	Rafael Landestoy	.10
20	Bruce Bochy	.10
21	Joe Sambito	.10
22	Manny Trillo	.10
23a	Dave Smith RC (Incomplete box around stats.)	.10

No.	Player	Price
23b	Dave Smith RC (Complete box around stats.)	.15
24	Terry Puhl	.10
25	Bump Wills	.10
26a	John Ellis (Danny Walton photo - with bat.)	.30
26b	John Ellis (John Ellis photo - with glove.)	
27	Jim Kern	.10
28	Richie Zisk	.10
29	John Mayberry	.10
30	Bob Davis	.10
31	Jackson Todd	.10
32	Al Woods	.10
33	Steve Carlton	1.50
34	Lee Mazzilli	.10
35	John Stearns	.10
36	Roy Jackson	.10
37	Mike Scott	.10
38	Lamar Johnson	.10
39	Kevin Bell	.10
40	Ed Farmer	.10
41	Ross Baumgarten	.10
42	Leo Sutherland	.10
43	Dan Meyer	.10
44	Ron Reed	.10
45	Mario Mendoza	.10
46	Rick Honeycutt	.10
47	Glenn Abbott	.10
48	Leon Roberts	.10
49	Rod Carew	1.50
50	Bert Campaneris	.10
51a	Tom Donahue (Incorrect spelling.)	.25
51b	Tom Donohue (Donohue on front.)	.10
52	Dave Frost	.10
53	Ed Halicki	.10
54	Dan Ford	.10
55	Garry Maddox	.10
56a	Steve Garvey (Surpassed 25 HR..)	1.25
56b	Steve Garvey (Surpassed 21 HR..)	.60
57	Bill Russell	.10
58	Don Sutton	1.00
59	Reggie Smith	.10
60	Rick Monday	.10
61	Ray Knight	.10
62	Johnny Bench	1.50
63	Mario Soto	.10
64	Doug Bair	.10
65	George Foster	.10
66	Jeff Burroughs	.10
67	Keith Hernandez	.10
68	Tom Herr	.10
69	Bob Forsch	.10
70	John Fulgham	.10
71a	Bobby Bonds (Lifetime HR 986.)	.35
71b	Bobby Bonds (Lifetime HR 326.)	.15
72a	Rennie Stennett ("...breaking broke leg..." on back)	.25
72b	Rennie Stennett ("...breaking leg..." on back)	
73	Joe Strain	.10
74	Ed Whitson	.10
75	Tom Griffin	.10
76	Bill North	.10
77	Gene Garber	.10
78	Mike Hargrove	.10
79	Dave Rosello	.10
80	Ron Hassey	.10
81	Sid Monge	.10
82a	Joe Charboneau RC ("For some reason, Phillies..." on back.)	2.00
82b	Joe Charboneau RC ("Phillies..." on back.)	.25
83	Cecil Cooper	.10
84	Sal Bando	.10
85	Moose Haas	.10
86	Mike Caldwell	.10
87a	Larry Hisle ("...Twins with 28 RBI." on back.)	
87b	Larry Hisle ("...Twins with 28 HR" on back.)	.10
88	Luis Gomez	.10
89	Larry Parrish	.10
90	Gary Carter	1.25
91	Bill Gullickson RC	.15
92	Fred Norman	.10
93	Tommy Hutton	.10
94	Carl Yastrzemski	1.50
95	Glenn Hoffman	.10
96	Dennis Eckersley	1.25
97a	Tom Burgmeier (Throws: Right)	.25
97b	Tom Burgmeier (Throws: Left)	.10
98	Win Remmerswaal	.10
99	Bob Horner	.10
100	George Brett	3.00
101	Dave Chalk	.10
102	Dennis Leonard	.10
103	Renie Martin	.10
104	Amos Otis	.10
105	Graig Nettles	.15
106	Eric Soderholm	.10
107	Tommy John	.10
108	Tom Underwood	.10
109	Lou Piniella	.15
110	Mickey Klutts	.10
111	Bobby Murcer	.10
112	Eddie Murray	1.50
113	Rick Dempsey	.10
114	Scott McGregor	.10
115	Ken Singleton	.10
116	Gary Roenicke	.10
117	Dave Revering	.10
118	Mike Norris	.10
119	Rickey Henderson	2.00
120	Mike Heath	.10
121	Dave Cash	.10
122	Randy Jones	.10
123	Eric Rasmussen	.10
124	Jerry Mumphrey	.10
125	Richie Hebner	.10
126	Mark Wagner	.10
127	Jack Morris	.10
128	Dan Petry	.10
129	Bruce Robbins	.10
130	Champ Summers	.10
131a	Pete Rose ("See card 251" on back.)	2.00
131b	Pete Rose ("See card 371" on back.)	2.00
132	Willie Stargell	1.25
133	Ed Ott	.10
134	Jim Bibby	.10
135	Bert Blyleven	.10
136	Dave Parker	.10
137	Bill Robinson	.10
138	Enos Cabell	.10
139	Dave Bergman	.10
140	J.R. Richard	.10
141	Ken Forsch	.10
142	Larry Bowa	.10
143	Frank LaCorte (Photo actually Randy Niemann.)	.10
144	Dennis Walling	.10
145	Buddy Bell	.10
146	Fergie Jenkins	1.00
147	Danny Darwin	.10
148	John Grubb	.10
149	Alfredo Griffin	.10
150	Jerry Garvin	.10
151	Paul Mirabella RC	.10
152	Rick Bosetti	.10
153	Dick Ruthven	.10
154	Frank Taveras	.10
155	Craig Swan	.10
156	Jeff Reardon RC	1.00
157	Steve Henderson	.10
158	Jim Morrison	.10
159	Glenn Borgmann	.10
160	Lamarr Hoyt (LaMarr) RC	.10
161	Rich Wortham	.10
162	Thad Bosley	.10
163	Julio Cruz	.10
164a	Del Unser (No 3B in stat heads.)	.25
164b	Del Unser (3B in stat heads.)	.10
165	Jim Anderson	.10
166	Jim Beattie	.10
167	Shane Rawley	.10
168	Joe Simpson	.10
169	Rod Carew	1.50
170	Fred Patek	.10
171	Frank Tanana	.10
172	Alfredo Martinez	.10
173	Chris Knapp	.10
174	Joe Rudi	.10
175	Greg Luzinski	.10
176	Steve Garvey	.60
177	Joe Ferguson	.10
178	Bob Welch	.10
179	Dusty Baker	.10
180	Rudy Law	.10
181	Dave Concepcion	.10
182	Johnny Bench	1.50
183	Mike LaCoss	.10
184	Ken Griffey	.10
185	Dave Collins	.10
186	Brian Asselstine	.10
187	Garry Templeton	.10
188	Mike Phillips	.10
189	Pete Vukovich	.10
190	John Urrea	.10
191	Tony Scott	.10
192	Darrell Evans	.10
193	Milt May	.10
194	Bob Knepper	.10
195	Randy Moffitt	.10
196	Larry Herndon	.10
197	Rick Camp	.10
198	Andre Thornton	.10
199	Tom Veryzer	.10
200	Gary Alexander	.10
201	Rick Waits	.10
202	Rick Manning	.10
203	Paul Molitor	1.25
204	Jim Gantner	.10
205	Paul Mitchell	.10
206	Reggie Cleveland	.10
207	Sixto Lezcano	.10
208	Bruce Benedict	.10
209	Rodney Scott	.10
210	John Tamargo	.10
211	Bill Lee	.10
212	Andre Dawson	.75
213	Rowland Office	.10
214	Carl Yastrzemski	1.50
215	Jerry Remy	.10
216	Mike Torrez	.10
217	Skip Lockwood	.10
218	Fred Lynn	.10
219	Chris Chambliss	.10
220	Willie Aikens	.10
221	John Wathan	.10
222	Dan Quisenberry	.10
223	Willie Wilson	.10
224	Clint Hurdle	.10
225	Bob Watson	.10
226	Jim Spencer	.10
227	Ron Guidry	.15
228	Reggie Jackson	2.00
229	Oscar Gamble	.10
230	Jeff Cox	.10
231	Luis Tiant	.10
232	Rich Dauer	.10
233	Dan Graham	.10
234	Mike Flanagan	.10
235	John Lowenstein	.10
236	Benny Ayala	.10
237	Wayne Gross	.10
238	Rick Langford	.10
239	Tony Armas	.10
240a	Bob Lacy (Incorrect spelling.)	.25
240b	Bob Lacey (Correct spelling.)	.10
241	Gene Tenace	.10
242	Bob Shirley	.10
243	Gary Lucas	.10
244	Jerry Turner	.10
245	John Wockenfuss	.10
246	Stan Papi	.10
247	Milt Wilcox	.10
248	Dan Schatzeder	.10
249	Steve Kemp	.10
250	Jim Lentine	.10
251	Pete Rose	2.00
252	Bill Madlock	.10
253	Dale Berra	.10
254	Kent Tekulve	.10
255	Enrique Romo	.10
256	Mike Easler	.10
257	Chuck Tanner	.10
258	Art Howe	.10
259	Alan Ashby	.10
260	Nolan Ryan	5.00
261a	Vern Ruhle (Ken Forsch photo - head shot.)	.25
261b	Vern Ruhle (Vern Ruhle photo - waist to head shot.)	.10
262	Bob Boone	.10
263	Cesar Cedeno	.10
264	Jeff Leonard	.10
265	Pat Putnam	.10
266	Jon Matlack	.10
267	Dave Rajsich	.10
268	Billy Sample	.10
269	Damaso Garcia RC	.10
270	Tom Buskey	.10
271	Joey McLaughlin	.10
272	Barry Bonnell	.10
273	Tug McGraw	.10
274	Mike Jorgensen	.10
275	Pat Zachry	.10
276	Neil Allen	.10
277	Joel Youngblood	.10
278	Greg Pryor	.10
279	Britt Burns RC	.10
280	Rich Dotson RC	.25
281	Chet Lemon	.10
282	Rusty Kuntz	.10
283	Ted Cox	.10
284	Sparky Lyle	.10
285	Larry Cox	.10
286	Floyd Bannister	.10
287	Byron McLaughlin	.10
288	Rodney Craig	.10
289	Bobby Grich	.10
290	Dickie Thon	.10
291	Mark Clear	.10
292	Dave Lemanczyk	.10
293	Jason Thompson	.10
294	Rick Miller	.10
295	Lonnie Smith	.10
296	Ron Cey	.10
297	Steve Yeager	.10
298	Bobby Castillo	.10
299	Manny Mota	.10
300	Jay Johnstone	.10
301	Dan Driessen	.10
302	Joe Nolan	.10
303	Paul Householder	.10
304	Harry Spilman	.10
305	Cesar Geronimo	.10
306a	Gary Mathews (Mathews on front.)	.35
306b	Gary Matthews (Matthews on front.)	.10
307	Ken Reitz	.10
308	Ted Simmons	.10
309	John Littlefield	.10
310	George Frazier	.10
311	Dane Iorg	.10
312	Mike Ivie	.10
313	Dennis Littlejohn	.10
314	Gary LaVelle (Lavelle)	.10
315	Jack Clark	.10
316	Jim Wohlford	.10
317	Rick Matula	.10
318	Toby Harrah	.10
319a	Dwane Kuiper (Dwane on front.)	.25
319b	Duane Kuiper (Duane on front.)	.10
320	Len Barker	.10
321	Victor Cruz	.10
322	Dell Alston	.10
323	Robin Yount	1.25
324	Charlie Moore	.10
325	Lary Sorensen	.10
326a	Gorman Thomas ("...30-HR mark 4th..." on back)	.10
326b	Gorman Thomas ("...30-HR mark 3rd..." on back)	.10
327	Bob Rodgers	.10
328	Phil Niekro	1.00
329	Chris Speier	.10
330a	Steve Rodgers (Rodgers on front.)	.25
330b	Steve Rogers (Rogers on front.)	.10
331	Woodie Fryman	.10
332	Warren Cromartie	.10
333	Jerry White	.10
334	Tony Perez	1.25
335	Carlton Fisk	1.25
336	Dick Drago	.10
337	Steve Renko	.10
338	Jim Rice	.75
339	Jerry Royster	.10
340	Frank White	.10
341	Jamie Quirk	.10
342a	Paul Spittorff (Spittorff on front.)	.25
342b	Paul Splittorff (Splittorff on front.)	.10
343	Marty Pattin	.10
344	Pete LaCock	.10
345	Willie Randolph	.10
346	Rick Cerone	.10
347	Rich Gossage	.10
348	Reggie Jackson	2.00
349	Ruppert Jones	.10
350	Dave McKay	.10
351	Yogi Berra	.50
352	Doug Decinces (DeCinces)	.10
353	Jim Palmer	1.25
354	Tippy Martinez	.10
355	Al Bumbry	.10
356	Earl Weaver	.50
357a	Bob Picciolo (Bob on front.)	.25
357b	Rob Picciolo (Rob on front.)	.10
358	Matt Keough	.10
359	Dwayne Murphy	.10
360	Brian Kingman	.10
361	Bill Fahey	.10
362	Steve Mura	.10
363	Dennis Kinney	.10
364	Dave Winfield	1.25
365	Lou Whitaker	.10
366	Lance Parrish	.10
367	Tim Corcoran	.10
368	Pat Underwood	.10
369	Al Cowens	.10
370	Sparky Anderson	.50
371	Pete Rose	3.00
372	Phil Garner	.10
373	Steve Nicosia	.10
374	John Candelaria	.10
375	Don Robinson	.10
376	Lee Lacy	.10
377	John Milner	.10
378	Craig Reynolds	.10
379a	Luis Pujols (Pujois on front.)	.25
379b	Luis Pujols (Pujols on front.)	.10
380	Joe Niekro	.10
381	Joaquin Andujar	.10
382	Keith Moreland RC	.15
383	Jose Cruz	.10
384	Bill Virdon	.10
385	Jim Sundberg	.10
386	Doc Medich	.10
387	Al Oliver	.10
388	Jim Norris	.10
389	Bob Bailor	.10
390	Ernie Whitt	.10
391	Otto Velez	.10
392	Roy Howell	.10
393	Bob Walk RC	.10
394	Doug Flynn	.10
395	Pete Falcone	.10
396	Tom Hausman	.10
397	Elliott Maddox	.10
398	Mike Squires	.10
399	Marvis Foley	.10
400	Steve Trout	.10
401	Wayne Nordhagen	.10
402	Tony Larussa (LaRussa)	.10
403	Bruce Bochte	.10
404	Bake McBride	.10
405	Jerry Narron	.10
406	Rob Dressler	.10
407	Dave Heaverlo	.10
408	Tom Paciorek	.10
409	Carney Lansford	.10
410	Brian Downing	.10
411	Don Aase	.10
412	Jim Barr	.10
413	Don Baylor	.10
414	Jim Fregosi	.10
415	Dallas Green	.10
416	Dave Lopes	.10
417	Jerry Reuss	.10
418	Rick Sutcliffe	.10
419	Derrel Thomas	.10
420	Tommy LaSorda	.10
421	Charlie Leibrandt RC	.25
422	Tom Seaver	1.50
423	Ron Oester	.10
424	Junior Kennedy	.10
425	Tom Seaver	1.50
426	Bobby Cox	.10
427	Leon Durham RC	.20
428	Terry Kennedy	.10
429	Silvio Martinez	.10
430	George Hendrick	.10
431	Red Schoendienst	.50
432	John LeMaster	.10
433	Vida Blue	.10
434	John Montefusco	.10
435	Terry Whitfield	.10
436	Dave Bristol	.10
437	Dale Murphy	.75
438	Jerry Dybzinski	.10
439	Jorge Orta	.10
440	Wayne Garland	.10
441	Miguel Dilone	.10
442	Dave Garcia	.10
443	Don Money	.10
444a	Buck Martinez (Photo reversed.)	.35
444b	Buck Martinez (Photo correct.)	.10
445	Jerry Augustine	.10
446	Ben Oglivie	.10
447	Jim Slaton	.10
448	Doyle Alexander	.10
449	Tony Bernazard	.10
450	Scott Sanderson	.10
451	Dave Palmer	.10
452	Stan Bahnsen	.10
453	Dick Williams	.10
454	Rick Burleson	.10
455	Gary Allenson	.10
456	Bob Stanley	.10
457a	John Tudor RC (Lifetime W/L 9.7.)	.40
457b	John Tudor RC (Lifetime W/L 9-7.)	.20
458	Dwight Evans	.10
459	Glenn Hubbard	.10
460	U L Washington	.10
461	Larry Gura	.10
462	Rich Gale	.10
463	Hal McRae	.10
464	Jim Frey	.10
465	Bucky Dent	.10
466	Dennis Werth	.10
467	Ron Davis	.10
468	Reggie Jackson	2.50
469	Bobby Brown	.10
470	Mike Davis RC	.10
471	Gaylord Perry	1.25
472	Mark Belanger	.10
473	Jim Palmer	1.25
474	Sammy Stewart	.10
475	Tim Stoddard	.10
476	Steve Stone	.10
477	Jeff Newman	.10
478	Steve McCatty	.10
479	Billy Martin	.10
480	Mitchell Page	.10
481	Steve Carlton (CY)	.40
482	Bill Buckner	.10
483a	Ivan DeJesus (Lifetime hits 702.)	.25
483b	Ivan DeJesus (Lifetime hits 642.)	.10
484	Cliff Johnson	.10
485	Lenny Randle	.10
486	Larry Milbourne	.10
487	Roy Smalley	.10
488	John Castino	.10
489	Ron Jackson	.10
490a	Dave Roberts (1980 highlights begins "Showed pop...")	.25
490b	Dave Roberts (1980 highlights begins "Declared himself...")	.10
491	George Brett (MVP)	1.50
492	Mike Cubbage	.10
493	Rob Wilfong	.10
494	Danny Goodwin	.10
495	Jose Morales	.10
496	Mickey Rivers	.10
497	Mike Edwards	.10
498	Mike Sadek	.10
499	Lenn Sakata	.10
500	Gene Michael	.10
501	Dave Roberts	.10
502	Steve Dillard	.10
503	Jim Essian	.10
504	Rance Mulliniks	.10
505	Darrell Porter	.10
506	Joe Torre	.50
507	Terry Crowley	.10
508	Bill Travers	.10
509	Nelson Norman	.10
510	Bob McClure	.10
511	Steve Howe RC	.15
512	Dave Rader	.10
513	Mick Kelleher	.10
514	Kiko Garcia	.10
515	Larry Biittner	.10
516a	Willie Norwood (1980 highlights begins "Spent most...")	.25
516b	Willie Norwood (1980 highlights begins "Traded to...")	.10
517	Bo Diaz	.10
518	Juan Beniquez	.10
519	Scot Thompson	.10
520	Jim Tracy	.10
521	Carlos Lezcano	.10
522	Joe Amalfitano	.10
523	Preston Hanna	.10
524a	Ray Burris (1980 highlights begins "Went on...")	.25
524b	Ray Burris (1980 highlights begins "Drafted by...")	.10
525	Broderick Perkins	.10
526	Mickey Hatcher	.10
527	John Goryl	.10
528	Dick Davis	.10
529	Butch Wynegar	.10
530	Sal Butera	.10
531	Jerry Koosman	.10
532a	Jeff (Geoff) Zahn (1980 highlights begins "Was 2nd in...")	.25
532b	Jeff (Geoff) Zahn (1980 highlights begins "Signed a 3 year ...")	.10
533	Dennis Martinez	.10
534	Gary Thomasson	.10
535	Steve Macko	.10
536	Jim Kaat	.15
537	Best Hitters (George Brett, Rod Carew)	1.50
538	Tim Raines RC	3.00
539	Keith Smith	.10
540	Ken Macha	.10
541	Burt Hooton	.10
542	Butch Hobson	.10
543	Bill Stein	.10
544	Dave Stapleton	.10
545	Bob Pate	.10
546	Doug Corbett	.10
547	Darrell Jackson	.10
548	Pete Redfern	.10
549	Roger Erickson	.10
550	Al Hrabosky	.10
551	Dick Tidrow	.10
552	Dave Ford	.10
553	Dave Kingman	.10
554a	Mike Vail (1980 highlights begins "After...")	.25
554b	Mike Vail (1980 highlights begins "Traded...")	.10
555a	Jerry Martin (1980 highlights begins "Overcame...")	.25
555b	Jerry Martin (1980 highlights begins "Traded...")	.10
556a	Jesus Figueroa (1980 highlights begins "Had...")	.25
556b	Jesus Figueroa (1980 highlights begins "Traded...")	.10
557	Don Stanhouse	.10
558	Barry Foote	.10
559	Tim Blackwell	.10
560	Bruce Sutter	1.25
561	Rick Reuschel	.10
562	Lynn McGlothen	.10
563a	Bob Owchinko (1980 highlights begins "Traded...")	.25
563b	Bob Owchinko (1980 highlights begins "Involved...")	.10
564	John Verhoeven	.10
565	Ken Landreaux	.10
566a	Glen Adams (Glen on front.)	.25
566b	Glenn Adams (Glenn on front.)	.10
567	Hosken Powell	.10
568	Dick Noles	.10
569	Danny Ainge RC	2.00
570	Bobby Mattick	.10
571	Joe LeFebvre (Lefebvre)	.10
572	Bobby Clark	.10
573	Dennis Lamp	.10
574	Randy Lerch	.10
575	Mookie Wilson RC	.30
576	Ron LeFlore	.10
577	Jim Dwyer	.10
578	Bill Castro	.10
579	Greg Minton	.10
580	Mark Littell	.10
581	Andy Hassler	.10
582	Dave Stieb	.10
583	Ken Oberkfell	.10
584	Larry Bradford	.10
585	Fred Stanley	.10
586	Bill Caudill	.10
587	Doug Capilla	.10
588	George Riley	.10
589	Willie Hernandez	.10
590	Mike Schmidt (MVP)	1.50
591	Steve Stone	.10
592	Rick Sofield	.10
593	Bombo Rivera	.10
594	Gary Ward	.10
595a	Dave Edwards (1980 highlights begins "Sidelined...")	.25
595b	Dave Edwards (1980 highlights begins "Traded...")	.10
596	Mike Proly	.10
597	Tommy Boggs	.10
598	Greg Gross	.10
599	Elias Sosa	.10
600	Pat Kelly	.10
----	Checklist 1-120 (51 Tom Donohue)	.25
----	Checklist 1-120 (51 Tom Donohue)	.25
----	Checklist 121-240	.25
----	Checklist 241-360 (306 Gary Mathews)	.25
----	Checklist 241-360 (306 Gary Matthews)	.10
----	Checklist 361-480 (379 Luis Pujois)	.25
----	Checklist 361-480 (379 Luis Pujols)	.25
----	Checklist 481-600 (566 Glen Adams)	.25
----	Checklist 481-600 (566 Glenn Adams)	.10

1982 Donruss

Using card stock thicker than the previous year, Donruss issued a 660-card set which includes 653 numbered cards and seven unnumbered checklists. The cards were sold with puzzle pieces rather than gum as a result of a lawsuit by Topps. The puzzle pieces (three pieces on one card per pack) feature Babe Ruth. The first 26 cards of the set, entitled Diamond Kings, showcase the artwork of Dick Perez. Card fronts display the Donruss logo and the year of issue. Backs have black and blue ink on white stock and include the player's career highlights. The complete set price does not include the higher priced variations.

	NM/M
Unopened Fact. Set (660):	50.00
Complete Set (660):	45.00
Complete Set, Uncut Sheets (5):	175.00
Common Player:	.10
Babe Ruth Puzzle:	1.00
Wax Pack (15):	2.50
Wax Box (36):	80.00

No.	Name	Price
1	Pete Rose (Diamond King)	4.00
2	Gary Carter (DK)	1.25
3	Steve Garvey (DK)	.45
4	Vida Blue (DK)	.10
5a	Alan Trammel (DK) (Last name incorrect.)	1.00
5b	Alan Trammell (DK)(Corrected)	.30
6	Len Barker (DK)	.10
7	Dwight Evans (DK)	.15
8	Rod Carew (DK)	1.25
9	George Hendrick (DK)	.10
10	Phil Niekro (DK)	1.00
11	Richie Zisk (DK)	.10
12	Dave Parker (DK)	.10
13	Nolan Ryan (DK)	5.00
14	Ivan DeJesus (DK)	.10
15	George Brett (DK)	2.00
16	Tom Seaver (DK)	1.25
17	Dave Kingman (DK)	.15
18	Dave Winfield (DK)	1.25
19	Mike Norris (DK)	.10
20	Carlton Fisk (DK)	1.25
21	Ozzie Smith (DK)	1.50
22	Roy Smalley (DK)	.10
23	Buddy Bell (DK)	.10
24	Ken Singleton (DK)	.10
25	John Mayberry (DK)	.10
26	Gorman Thomas (DK)	.10
27	Earl Weaver	.50
28	Rollie Fingers	1.00
29	Sparky Anderson	.50
30	Dennis Eckersley	1.25
31	Dave Winfield	1.25
32	Burt Hooton	.10
33	Rick Waits	.10
34	George Brett	2.00
35	Steve McCatty	.10
36	Steve Rogers	.10
37	Bill Stein	.10
38	Steve Renko	.10
39	Mike Squires	.10
40	George Hendrick	.10
41	Bob Knepper	.10
42	Steve Carlton	1.25
43	Larry Biittner	.10
44	Chris Welsh	.10
45	Steve Nicosia	.10
46	Jack Clark	.10
47	Chris Chambliss	.10
48	Ivan DeJesus	.10
49	Lee Mazzilli	.10
50	Julio Cruz	.10
51	Pete Redfern	.10
52	Dave Stieb	.10
53	Doug Corbett	.10
54	George Bell RC	.50
55	Joe Simpson	.10
56	Rusty Staub	.10
57	Hector Cruz	.10
58	Claudell Washington RC	.10
59	Enrique Romo	.10
60	Gary Lavelle	.10
61	Tim Flannery	.10
62	Joe Nolan	.10
63	Larry Bowa	.10
64	Sixto Lezcano	.10
65	Joe Sambito	.10
66	Bruce Kison	.10
67	Wayne Nordhagen	.10
68	Woodie Fryman	.10
69	Billy Sample	.10
70	Amos Otis	.10
71	Matt Keough	.10
72	Toby Harrah	.10
73	Dave Righetti RC	.30
74	Carl Yastrzemski	1.50
75	Bob Welch	.10
76a	Alan Trammel (Last name misspelled.)	1.00
76b	Alan Trammell (Corrected)	.10
77	Rick Dempsey	.10
78	Paul Molitor	1.25
79	Dennis Martinez	.10
80	Jim Slaton	.10
81	Champ Summers	.10
82	Carney Lansford	.10
83	Barry Foote	.10
84	Steve Garvey	.45
85	Rick Manning	.10
86	John Wathan	.10
87	Brian Kingman	.10
88	Andre Dawson	.50
89	Jim Kern	.10
90	Bobby Grich	.10
91	Bob Forsch	.10
92	Art Howe	.10
93	Marty Bystrom	.10
94	Ozzie Smith	1.50
95	Dave Parker	.10
96	Doyle Alexander	.10
97	Al Hrabosky	.10
98	Frank Taveras	.10
99	Tim Blackwell	.10
100	Floyd Bannister	.10
101	Alfredo Griffin	.10
102	Dave Engle	.10
103	Mario Soto	.10
104	Ross Baumgarten	.10
105	Ken Singleton	.10
106	Ted Simmons	.10
107	Jack Morris	.25
108	Bob Watson	.10
109	Dwight Evans	.10
110	Tom Lasorda	.50
111	Bert Blyleven	.10
112	Dan Quisenberry	.10
113	Rickey Henderson	1.25
114	Gary Carter	1.25
115	Brian Downing	.10
116	Al Oliver	.10
117	LaMarr Hoyt	.10
118	Cesar Cedeno	.10
119	Keith Moreland	.10
120	Bob Shirley	.10
121	Terry Kennedy	.10
122	Frank Pastore	.10
123	Gene Garber	.10
124	Tony Pena RC	.10
125	Allen Ripley	.10
126	Randy Martz	.10
127	Richie Zisk	.10
128	Mike Scott	.10
129	Lloyd Moseby	.10
130	Rob Wilfong	.10
131	Tim Stoddard	.10
132	Gorman Thomas	.10
133	Dan Petry	.10
134	Bob Stanley	.10
135	Lou Piniella	.15
136	Pedro Guerrero	.10
137	Len Barker	.10
138	Richard Gale	.10
139	Wayne Gross	.10
140	Tim Wallach RC	.50
141	Gene Mauch	.10
142	Doc Medich	.10
143	Tony Bernazard	.10
144	Bill Virdon	.10
145	John Littlefield	.10
146	Dave Bergman	.10
147	Dick Davis	.10
148	Tom Seaver	1.50
149	Matt Sinatro	.10
150	Chuck Tanner	.10
151	Leon Durham	.10
152	Gene Tenace	.10
153	Al Bumbry	.10
154	Mark Brouhard	.10
155	Rick Peters	.10
156	Jerry Remy	.10
157	Rick Reuschel	.10
158	Steve Howe	.10
159	Alan Bannister	.10
160	U L Washington	.10
161	Rick Langford	.10
162	Bill Gullickson	.10
163	Mark Wagner	.10
164	Geoff Zahn	.10
165	Ron LeFlore	.10
166	Dane Iorg	.10
167	Joe Niekro	.10
168	Pete Rose	3.00
169	Dave Collins	.10
170	Rick Wise	.10
171	Jim Bibby	.10
172	Larry Herndon	.10
173	Bob Horner	.10
174	Steve Dillard	.10
175	Mookie Wilson	.10
176	Dan Meyer	.10
177	Fernando Arroyo	.10
178	Jackson Todd	.10
179	Darrell Jackson	.10
180	Al Woods	.10
181	Jim Anderson	.10
182	Dave Kingman	.10
183	Steve Henderson	.10
184	Brian Asselstine	.10
185	Rod Scurry	.10
186	Fred Breining	.10
187	Danny Boone	.10
188	Junior Kennedy	.10
189	Sparky Lyle	.10
190	Whitey Herzog	.10
191	Dave Smith	.10
192	Ed Ott	.10
193	Greg Luzinski	.10
194	Bill Lee	.10
195	Don Zimmer	.10
196	Hal McRae	.10
197	Mike Norris	.10
198	Duane Kuiper	.10
199	Rick Cerone	.10
200	Jim Rice	.45
201	Steve Yeager	.10
202	Tom Brookens	.10
203	Jose Morales	.10
204	Roy Howell	.10
205	Tippy Martinez	.10
206	Moose Haas	.10
207	Al Cowens	.10
208	Dave Stapleton	.10
209	Bucky Dent	.10
210	Ron Cey	.10
211	Jorge Orta	.10
212	Jamie Quirk	.10
213	Jeff Jones	.10
214	Tim Raines	.25
215	Jon Matlack	.10
216	Rod Carew	1.50
217	Jim Kaat	.15
218	Joe Pittman	.10
219	Larry Christenson	.10
220	Juan Bonilla	.10
221	Mike Easler	.10
222	Vida Blue	.10
223	Rick Camp	.10
224	Mike Jorgensen	.10
225	Jody Davis RC	.15
226	Mike Parrott	.10
227	Jim Clancy	.10
228	Hosken Powell	.10
229	Tom Hume	.10
230	Britt Burns	.10
231	Jim Palmer	1.25
232	Bob Rodgers	.10
233	Milt Wilcox	.10
234	Dave Revering	.10
235	Mike Torrez	.10
236	Robert Castillo	.10
237	Von Hayes RC	.25
238	Renie Martin	.10
239	Dwayne Murphy	.10
240	Rodney Scott	.10
241	Fred Patek	.10
242	Mickey Rivers	.10
243	Steve Trout	.10
244	Jose Cruz	.10
245	Manny Trillo	.10
246	Lary Sorensen	.10
247	Dave Edwards	.10
248	Dan Driessen	.10
249	Tommy Boggs	.10
250	Dale Berra	.10
251	Ed Whitson	.10
252	Lee Smith RC	4.00
253	Tom Paciorek	.10
254	Pat Zachry	.10
255	Luis Leal	.10
256	John Castino	.10
257	Rich Dauer	.10
258	Cecil Cooper	.10
259	Dave Rozema	.10
260	John Tudor	.10
261	Jerry Mumphrey	.10
262	Jay Johnstone	.10
263	Bo Diaz	.10
264	Dennis Leonard	.10
265	Jim Spencer	.10
266	John Milner	.10
267	Don Aase	.10
268	Jim Sundberg	.10
269	Lamar Johnson	.10
270	Frank LaCorte	.10
271	Barry Evans	.10
272	Enos Cabell	.10
273	Del Unser	.10
274	George Foster	.10
275	Brett Butler RC	.50
276	Lee Lacy	.10
277	Ken Reitz	.10
278	Keith Hernandez	.10
279	Doug DeCinces	.10
280	Charlie Moore	.10
281	Lance Parrish	.10
282	Ralph Houk	.10
283	Rich Gossage	.10
284	Jerry Reuss	.10
285	Mike Stanton	.10
286	Frank White	.10
287	Bob Owchinko	.10
288	Scott Sanderson	.10
289	Bump Wills	.10
290	Dave Frost	.10
291	Chet Lemon	.10
292	Tito Landrum	.10
293	Vern Ruhle	.10
294	Mike Schmidt	2.00
295	Sam Mejias	.10
296	Gary Lucas	.10
297	John Candelaria	.10
298	Jerry Martin	.10
299	Dale Murphy	.50
300	Mike Lum	.10
301	Tom Hausman	.10
302	Glenn Abbott	.10
303	Roger Erickson	.10
304	Otto Velez	.10
305	Danny Goodwin	.10
306	John Mayberry	.10
307	Lenny Randle	.10
308	Bob Bailor	.10
309	Jerry Morales	.10
310	Rufino Linares	.10
311	Kent Tekulve	.10
312	Joe Morgan	1.25
313	John Urrea	.10
314	Paul Householder	.10
315	Garry Maddox	.10
316	Mike Ramsey	.10
317	Alan Ashby	.10
318	Bob Clark	.10
319	Tony LaRussa	.15
320	Charlie Lea	.10
321	Danny Darwin	.10
322	Cesar Geronimo	.10
323	Tom Underwood	.10
324	Andre Thornton	.10
325	Rudy May	.10
326	Frank Tanana	.10
327	Davey Lopes	.10
328	Richie Hebner	.10
329	Mike Flanagan	.10
330	Mike Caldwell	.10
331	Scott McGregor	.10
332	Jerry Augustine	.10
333	Stan Papi	.10
334	Rick Miller	.10
335	Graig Nettles	.15
336	Dusty Baker	.10
337	Dave Garcia	.10
338	Larry Gura	.10
339	Cliff Johnson	.10
340	Warren Cromartie	.10
341	Steve Comer	.10
342	Rick Burleson	.10
343	John Martin	.10
344	Craig Reynolds	.10
345	Mike Proly	.10
346	Ruppert Jones	.10
347	Omar Moreno	.10
348	Greg Minton	.10
349	Rick Mahler RC	.10
350	Alex Trevino	.10
351	Mike Krukow	.10
352a	Shane Rawley (Jim Anderson photo - shaking hands.)	.50
352b	Shane Rawley (Correct photo - kneeling.)	.15
353	Garth Iorg	.10
354	Pete Mackanin	.10
355	Paul Moskau	.10
356	Richard Dotson	.10
357	Steve Stone	.10
358	Larry Hisle	.10
359	Aurelio Lopez	.10
360	Oscar Gamble	.10
361	Tom Burgmeier	.10
362	Terry Forster	.10
363	Joe Charboneau	.25
364	Ken Brett	.10
365	Tony Armas	.10
366	Chris Speier	.10
367	Fred Lynn	.10
368	Buddy Bell	.10
369	Jim Essian	.10
370	Terry Puhl	.10
371	Greg Gross	.10
372	Bruce Sutter	1.25
373	Joe Lefebvre	.10
374	Ray Knight	.10
375	Bruce Benedict	.10
376	Tim Foli	.10
377	Al Holland	.10
378	Ken Kravec	.10
379	Jeff Burroughs	.10
380	Pete Falcone	.10
381	Ernie Whitt	.10
382	Brad Havens	.10
383	Terry Crowley	.10
384	Don Money	.10
385	Dan Schatzeder	.10
386	Gary Allenson	.10
387	Yogi Berra	.50
388	Ken Landreaux	.10
389	Mike Hargrove	.10
390	Darryl Motley	.10
391	Dave McKay	.10
392	Stan Bahnsen	.10
393	Ken Forsch	.10
394	Mario Mendoza	.10
395	Jim Morrison	.10
396	Mike Ivie	.10
397	Broderick Perkins	.10
398	Darrell Evans	.10
399	Ron Reed	.10
400	Johnny Bench	1.50
401	Steve Bedrosian RC	.20
402	Bill Robinson	.10
403	Bill Buckner	.10
404	Ken Oberkfell	.10
405	Cal Ripken, Jr. RC	40.00
406	Jim Gantner	.10
407	Kirk Gibson	.10
408	Tony Perez	1.00
409	Tommy John	.10
410	Dave Stewart RC	2.50
411	Dan Spillner	.10
412	Willie Aikens	.10
413	Mike Heath	.10
414	Ray Burris	.10
415	Leon Roberts	.10
416	Mike Witt RC	.15
417	Bobby Molinaro	.10
418	Steve Braun	.10
419	Nolan Ryan	4.00
420	Tug McGraw	.10
421	Dave Concepcion	.10
422a	Juan Eichelberger (Gary Lucas photo - white player.)	.50
422b	Juan Eichelberger (Correct photo - black player.)	.10
423	Rick Rhoden	.10
424	Frank Robinson	.50
425	Eddie Miller	.10
426	Bill Caudill	.10
427	Doug Flynn	.10
428	Larry Anderson (Andersen)	.10
429	Al Williams	.10
430	Jerry Garvin	.10
431	Glenn Adams	.10
432	Barry Bonnell	.10
433	Jerry Narron	.10
434	John Stearns	.10
435	Mike Tyson	.10
436	Glenn Hubbard	.10
437	Eddie Solomon	.10
438	Jeff Leonard	.10
439	Randy Bass	.10
440	Mike LaCoss	.10
441	Gary Matthews	.10
442	Mark Littell	.10
443	Don Sutton	1.00
444	John Harris	.10
445	Vada Pinson	.10
446	Elias Sosa	.10
447	Charlie Hough	.10
448	Willie Wilson	.10
449	Fred Stanley	.10
450	Tom Veryzer	.10
451	Ron Davis	.10
452	Mark Clear	.10
453	Bill Russell	.10
454	Lou Whitaker	.10
455	Dan Graham	.10
456	Reggie Cleveland	.10
457	Sammy Stewart	.10
458	Pete Vuckovich	.10
459	John Wockenfuss	.10
460	Glenn Hoffman	.10
461	Willie Randolph	.10
462	Fernando Valenzuela	.10
463	Ron Hassey	.10
464	Paul Splittorff	.10
465	Rob Picciolo	.10
466	Larry Parrish	.10
467	Johnny Grubb	.10
468	Dan Ford	.10
469	Silvio Martinez	.10
470	Kiko Garcia	.10
471	Bob Boone	.10
472	Luis Salazar	.10
473	Randy Niemann	.10
474	Tom Griffin	.10
475	Phil Niekro	1.00
476	Hubie Brooks RC	.10
477	Dick Tidrow	.10
478	Jim Beattie	.10
479	Damaso Garcia	.10
480	Mickey Hatcher	.10
481	Joe Price	.10
482	Ed Farmer	.10
483	Eddie Murray	1.25
484	Ben Oglivie	.10
485	Kevin Saucier	.10
486	Bobby Murcer	.10
487	Bill Campbell	.10
488	Reggie Smith	.10
489	Wayne Garland	.10
490	Jim Wright	.10
491	Billy Martin	.10
492	Jim Fanning	.10
493	Don Baylor	.10
494	Rick Honeycutt	.10
495	Carlton Fisk	1.25
496	Denny Walling	.10
497	Bake McBride	.10
498	Darrell Porter	.10
499	Gene Richards	.10
500	Ron Oester	.10
501	Ken Dayley RC	.10
502	Jason Thompson	.10
503	Milt May	.10
504	Doug Bird	.10
505	Bruce Bochte	.10
506	Neil Allen	.10
507	Joey McLaughlin	.10
508	Butch Wynegar	.10
509	Gary Roenicke	.10
510	Robin Yount	1.25
511	Dave Tobik	.10
512	Rich Gedman RC	.15
513	Gene Nelson RC	.10
514	Rick Monday	.10
515	Miguel Dilone	.10
516	Clint Hurdle	.10
517	Jeff Newman	.10
518	Grant Jackson	.10
519	Andy Hassler	.10
520	Pat Putnam	.10
521	Greg Pryor	.10
522	Tony Scott	.10
523	Steve Mura	.10
524	Johnnie LeMaster	.10
525	Dick Ruthven	.10
526	John McNamara	.10
527	Larry McWilliams	.10
528	Johnny Ray RC	.15
529	Pat Tabler RC	.15
530	Tom Herr	.10
531a	San Diego Chicken (W/trademark symbol.)	.75
531b	San Diego Chicken (No trademark symbol.)	.50
532	Sal Butera	.10
533	Mike Griffin	.10
534	Kelvin Moore	.10
535	Reggie Jackson	2.00
536	Ed Romero	.10
537	Derrel Thomas	.10
538	Mike O'Berry	.10
539	Jack O'Connor	.10
540	Bob Ojeda RC	.25
541	Roy Lee Jackson	.10
542	Lynn Jones	.10
543	Gaylord Perry	1.00
544a	Phil Garner (Photo reversed.)	.50
544b	Phil Garner (Photo correct.)	.10
545	Garry Templeton	.10
546	Rafael Ramirez	.10
547	Jeff Reardon	.10
548	Ron Guidry	.10
549	Tim Laudner RC	.10
550	John Henry Johnson	.10
551	Chris Bando	.10
552	Bobby Brown	.10
553	Larry Bradford	.10
554	Scott Fletcher RC	.20
555	Jerry Royster	.10
556	Shooty Babbitt	.10
557	Kent Hrbek RC	2.00
558	Yankee Winners (Ron Guidry, Tommy John)	.15
559	Mark Bomback	.10
560	Julio Valdez	.10
561	Buck Martinez	.10
562	Mike Marshall RC	.15
563	Rennie Stennett	.10
564	Steve Crawford	.10
565	Bob Babcock	.10
566	Johnny Podres	.10
567	Paul Serna	.10
568	Harold Baines	1.00
569	Dave LaRoche	.10
570	Lee May	.10
571	Gary Ward	.10
572	John Denny	.10
573	Roy Smalley	.10
574	Bob Brenly RC	.20
575	Bronx Bombers (Reggie Jackson, Dave Winfield)	1.50
576	Luis Pujols	.10
577	Butch Hobson	.10
578	Harvey Kuenn	.10
579	Cal Ripken, Sr.	.10
580	Juan Berenguer	.10
581	Benny Ayala	.10
582	Vance Law	.10
583	Rick Leach RC	.15
584	George Frazier	.10
585	Phillies Finest (Pete Rose, Mike Schmidt)	1.00
586	Joe Rudi	.10
587	Juan Beniquez	.10
588	Luis DeLeon RC	.10
589	Craig Swan	.10
590	Dave Chalk	.10
591	Billy Gardner	.10
592	Sal Bando	.10
593	Bert Campaneris	.10
594	Steve Kemp	.10
595a	Randy Lerch (Braves)	.25
595b	Randy Lerch (Brewers)	.10
596	Bryan Clark	.10
597	Dave Ford	.10
598	Mike Scioscia	.10
599	John Lowenstein	.10
600	Rene Lachmann (Lachemann)	.10
601	Mick Kelleher	.10
602	Ron Jackson	.10
603	Jerry Koosman	.10
604	Dave Goltz	.10
605	Ellis Valentine	.10
606	Lonnie Smith	.10
607	Joaquin Andujar	.10
608	Garry Hancock	.10
609	Jerry Turner	.10
610	Bob Bonner	.10
611	Jim Dwyer	.10
612	Terry Bulling	.10
613	Joel Youngblood	.10
614	Larry Milbourne	.10
615	Phil Roof (Photo actually Gene Roof.)	.10
616	Keith Drumright	.10
617	Dave Rosello	.10
618	Rickey Keeton	.10
619	Dennis Lamp	.10
620	Sid Monge	.10
621	Jerry White	.10
622	Luis Aguayo RC	.10
623	Jamie Easterly	.10
624	Steve Sax RC	.50
625	Dave Roberts	.10
626	Rick Bosetti	.10
627	Terry Francona RC	.50

628 Pride of the Reds (Johnny Bench, Tom Seaver) 1.00
629 Paul Mirabella .10
630 Rance Mulliniks .10
631 Kevin Hickey .10
632 Reid Nichols .10
633 Dave Geisel .10
634 Ken Griffey .10
635 Bob Lemon .15
636 Orlando Sanchez .10
637 Bill Almon .10
638 Danny Ainge 1.00
639 Willie Stargell 1.25
640 Bob Sykes .10
641 Ed Lynch .10
642 John Ellis .10
643 Fergie Jenkins 1.00
644 Lenn Sakata .10
645 Julio Gonzales .10
646 Jesse Orosco .10
647 Jerry Dybzinski .10
648 Tommy Davis .10
649 Ron Gardenhire .10
650 Felipe Alou .10
651 Harvey Haddix .10
652 Willie Upshaw .10
653 Bill Madlock .10
---- Checklist 1-26 DK (5 Trammel) .25
---- Checklist 1-26 DK (5 Trammell) .10
---- Checklist 27-130 .10
---- Checklist 131-234 .10
---- Checklist 235-338 .10
---- Checklist 339-442 .10
---- Checklist 443-544 .10
---- Checklist 545-653 .10

1982-89 Donruss Puzzle Promo Sheets

Part of the advertising materials which Donruss issued each year was a series of approximately 8" x 10-7/8" color glossy sheets picturing the Dick Perez art which appear on the Diamond Kings puzzle pieces inserted into card packs.

NM/M
Complete Set (10): 20.00
Common Player: 2.50
(1) Babe Ruth (1982) 2.50
(2) Ty Cobb (1983) 2.50
(3) Mickey Mantle (1983) 2.50
(4) Duke Snider (1984) 2.50
(5) Ted Williams (1984) 2.50
(6) Lou Gehrig (1985) 2.50
(7) Hank Aaron (1986) 2.50
(8) Roberto Clemente (1987) 2.50
(9) Stan Musial (1988) 2.50
(10) Warren Spahn (1989) 2.50

1983 Donruss Promo Sheet

To debut its 1983 card design for dealers, Donruss prepared this eight-card sheet, including one Diamond Stars card. Card fronts are identical to the issued versions. Backs of most cards differ in the Career Highlights write-up. The sheet measures 10" x 7".

NM/M
Uncut Sheet: 10.00

1983 Donruss

The 1983 Donruss set consists of 653 numbered cards plus seven unnumbered checklists. The 2-1/2" x 3-1/2" cards were issued with puzzle pieces (three pieces on one card per pack) that feature Ty Cobb. The first 26 cards in the set were once again the Diamond Kings series. The card fronts dis-

play the Donruss logo and the year of issue. The card backs have black print on yellow and white and include statistics, career highlights, and the player's contract status. (DK) in the checklist below indicates cards which belong to the Diamond Kings series.

NM/M
Unopened Fact. Set (660): 50.00
Complete Set (660): 40.00
Common Player: .10
Ty Cobb Puzzle: 2.50
Wax Pack (15): 2.50
Wax Box (36): 80.00
1 Fernando Valenzuela (DK) .15
2 Rollie Fingers (DK) .75
3 Reggie Jackson (DK) 2.50
4 Jim Palmer (DK) 1.00
5 Jack Morris (DK) .75
6 George Foster (DK) .15
7 Jim Sundberg (DK) .10
8 Willie Stargell (DK) 1.00
9 Dave Stieb (DK) .15
10 Joe Niekro (DK) .15
11 Rickey Henderson (DK) 1.25
12 Dale Murphy (DK) .50
13 Toby Harrah (DK) .10
14 Bill Buckner (DK) .15
15 Willie Wilson (DK) .10
16 Steve Carlton (DK) 1.25
17 Ron Guidry (DK) .15
18 Steve Rogers (DK) .10
19 Kent Hrbek (DK) .15
20 Keith Hernandez (DK) .10
21 Floyd Bannister (DK) .10
22 Johnny Bench (DK) 2.00
23 Britt Burns (DK) .10
24 Joe Morgan (DK) 1.25
25 Carl Yastrzemski (DK) 2.00
26 Terry Kennedy (DK) .10
27 Gary Roenicke .10
28 Dwight Bernard .10
29 Pat Underwood .10
30 Gary Allenson .10
31 Ron Guidry .10
32 Burt Hooton .10
33 Chris Bando .10
34 Vida Blue .10
35 Rickey Henderson 1.25
36 Ray Burris .10
37 John Butcher .10
38 Don Aase .10
39 Jerry Koosman .10
40 Bruce Sutter 1.00
41 Jose Cruz .10
42 Pete Rose 3.00
43 Cesar Cedeno .10
44 Floyd Chiffer .10
45 Larry McWilliams .10
46 Alan Fowlkes .10
47 Dale Murphy .50
48 Doug Bird .10
49 Hubie Brooks .10
50 Floyd Bannister .10
51 Jack O'Connor .10
52 Steve Senteney .10
53 Gary Gaetti RC 1.00
54 Damaso Garcia .10
55 Gene Nelson .10
56 Mookie Wilson .10
57 Allen Ripley .10
58 Bob Horner .10
59 Tony Pena .10
60 Gary Lavelle .10
61 Tim Lollar .10
62 Frank Pastore .10
63 Garry Maddox .10
64 Bob Forsch .10
65 Harry Spilman .10
66 Geoff Zahn .10
67 Salome Barojas .10
68 David Palmer .10
69 Charlie Hough .10
70 Dan Quisenberry .10
71 Tony Armas .10
72 Rick Sutcliffe .10
73 Steve Balboni .10
74 Jerry Remy .10
75 Mike Scioscia .10
76 John Wockenfuss .10
77 Jim Palmer 1.00
78 Rollie Fingers .75
79 Joe Nolan .10
80 Pete Vuckovich .10
81 Rick Leach .10

82 Rick Miller .10
83 Graig Nettles .15
84 Ron Cey .10
85 Miguel Dilone .10
86 John Wathan .10
87 Kelvin Moore .10
88a Byrn Smith (First name incorrect.) .35
88b Bryn Smith (First name correct.) .10
89 Dave Hostetler .10
90 Rod Carew 1.50
91 Lonnie Smith .10
92 Bob Knepper .10
93 Marty Bystrom .10
94 Chris Welsh .10
95 Jason Thompson .10
96 Tom O'Malley .10
97 Phil Niekro .75
98 Neil Allen .10
99 Bill Buckner .10
100 Ed Vande Berg RC .10
101 Jim Clancy .10
102 Robert Castillo .10
103 Bruce Berenyi .10
104 Carlton Fisk 1.25
105 Mike Flanagan .10
106 Cecil Cooper .10
107 Jack Morris .10
108 Mike Morgan .10
109 Luis Aponte .10
110 Pedro Guerrero .10
111 Len Barker .10
112 Willie Wilson .10
113 Dave Beard .10
114 Mike Gates .10
115 Reggie Jackson 2.50
116 George Wright .10
117 Vance Law .10
118 Nolan Ryan 4.00
119 Mike Krukow .10
120 Ozzie Smith 2.00
121 Broderick Perkins .10
122 Tom Seaver 1.50
123 Chris Chambliss .10
124 Chuck Tanner .10
125 Johnnie LeMaster .10
126 Mel Hall RC .15
127 Bruce Bochte .10
128 Charlie Puleo RC .10
129 Luis Leal .10
130 John Pacella .10
131 Glenn Gulliver .10
132 Don Money .10
133 Dave Rozema .10
134 Bruce Hurst .10
135 Rudy May .10
136 Tom LaSorda (Lasorda) .40
137 Dan Spillner (Photo actually Ed Whitson.) .10
138 Jerry Martin .10
139 Mike Norris .10
140 Al Oliver .10
141 Daryl Sconiers .10
142 Lamar Johnson .10
143 Harold Baines .10
144 Alan Ashby .10
145 Garry Templeton .10
146 Al Holland .10
147 Bo Diaz .10
148 Dave Concepcion .10
149 Rick Camp .10
150 Jim Morrison .10
151 Randy Martz .10
152 Keith Hernandez .10
153 John Lowenstein .10
154 Mike Caldwell .10
155 Milt Wilcox .10
156 Rich Gedman .10
157 Rich Gossage .20
158 Jerry Reuss .10
159 Ron Hassey .10
160 Larry Gura .10
161 Dwayne Murphy .10
162 Woodie Fryman .10
163 Steve Comer .10
164 Ken Forsch .10
165 Dennis Lamp .10
166 David Green .10
167 Terry Puhl .10
168 Mike Schmidt 2.50
169 Eddie Milner RC .10
170 John Curtis .10
171 Don Robinson .10
172 Richard Gale .10
173 Steve Bedrosian .10
174 Willie Hernandez .10
175 Ron Gardenhire .10
176 Jim Beattie .10
177 Tim Laudner .10
178 Buck Martinez .10
179 Kent Hrbek .10
180 Alfredo Griffin .10
181 Larry Andersen .10
182 Pete Falcone .10
183 Jody Davis .10
184 Glenn Hubbard .10
185 Dale Berra .10
186 Greg Minton .10
187 Gary Lucas .10
188 Dave Van Gorder .10
189 Bob Dernier .10
190 Willie McGee RC 1.50
191 Dickie Thon .10
192 Bob Boone .10
193 Britt Burns .10
194 Jeff Reardon .10
195 Jon Matlack .10

196 Don Slaught RC .15
197 Fred Stanley .10
198 Rick Manning .10
199 Dave Righetti .10
200 Dave Stapleton .10
201 Steve Yeager .10
202 Enos Cabell .10
203 Sammy Stewart .10
204 Moose Haas .10
205 Lenn Sakata .10
206 Charlie Moore .10
207 Alan Trammell .15
208 Jim Rice .40
209 Roy Smalley .10
210 Bill Russell .10
211 Andre Thornton .10
212 Willie Aikens .10
213 Dave McKay .10
214 Tim Blackwell .10
215 Buddy Bell .10
216 Doug DeCinces .10
217 Tom Herr .10
218 Frank LaCorte .10
219 Steve Carlton 1.25
220 Terry Kennedy .10
221 Mike Easler .10
222 Jack Clark .10
223 Gene Garber .10
224 Scott Holman .10
225 Mike Proly .10
226 Terry Bulling .10
227 Jerry Garvin .10
228 Ron Davis .10
229 Tom Hume .10
230 Marc Hill .10
231 Dennis Martinez .10
232 Jim Gantner .10
233 Larry Pashnick .10
234 Dave Collins .10
235 Tom Burgmeier .10
236 Ken Landreaux .10
237 John Denny .10
238 Hal McRae .10
239 Matt Keough .10
240 Doug Flynn .10
241 Fred Lynn .10
242 Billy Sample .10
243 Tom Paciorek .10
244 Joe Sambito .10
245 Sid Monge .10
246 Ken Oberkfell .10
247 Joe Pittman (Photo actually Juan Eichelberger.) .10
248 Mario Soto .10
249 Claudell Washington .10
250 Rick Rhoden .10
251 Darrell Evans .10
252 Steve Henderson .10
253 Manny Castillo .10
254 Craig Swan .10
255 Joey McLaughlin .10
256 Pete Redfern .10
257 Ken Singleton .10
258 Robin Yount 1.25
259 Elias Sosa .10
260 Bob Ojeda .10
261 Bobby Murcer .10
262 Candy Maldonado RC .10
263 Rick Waits .10
264 Greg Pryor .10
265 Bob Owchinko .10
266 Chris Speier .10
267 Bruce Kison .10
268 Mark Wagner .10
269 Steve Kemp .10
270 Phil Garner .10
271 Gene Richards .10
272 Renie Martin .10
273 Dave Roberts .10
274 Dan Driessen .10
275 Rufino Linares .10
276 Lee Lacy .10
277 Ryne Sandberg RC 12.00
278 Darrell Porter .10
279 Cal Ripken, Jr. 4.00
280 Jamie Easterly .10
281 Bill Fahey .10
282 Glenn Hoffman .10
283 Willie Randolph .10
284 Fernando Valenzuela .10
285 Alan Bannister .10
286 Paul Splittorff .10
287 Joe Rudi .10
288 Bill Gullickson .10
289 Danny Darwin .10
290 Andy Hassler .10
291 Ernesto Escarrega .10
292 Steve Mura .10
293 Tony Scott .10
294 Manny Trillo .10
295 Greg Harris .10
296 Luis DeLeon .10
297 Kent Tekulve .10
298 Atlee Hammaker .10
299 Bruce Benedict .10
300 Fergie Jenkins .75
301 Dave Kingman .10
302 Bill Caudill .10
303 John Castino .10
304 Ernie Whitt .10
305 Randy S. Johnson .10
306 Garth Iorg .10
307 Gaylord Perry .75
308 Ed Lynch .10
309 Keith Moreland .10
310 Rafael Ramirez .10
311 Bill Madlock .10
312 Milt May .10

313 John Montefusco .10
314 Wayne Krenchicki .10
315 George Vukovich .10
316 Joaquin Andujar .10
317 Craig Reynolds .10
318 Rick Burleson .10
319 Richard Dotson .10
320 Steve Rogers .10
321 Dave Schmidt .10
322 Bud Black RC .15
323 Jeff Burroughs .10
324 Von Hayes .10
325 Butch Wynegar .10
326 Carl Yastrzemski 1.50
327 Ron Roenicke .10
328 Howard Johnson RC 1.00
329 Rick Dempsey .10
330a Jim Slaton (One yellow box on back.) .25
330b Jim Slaton (Two yellow boxes on back.) .10
331 Benny Ayala .10
332 Ted Simmons .10
333 Lou Whitaker .10
334 Chuck Rainey .10
335 Lou Piniella .15
336 Steve Sax .10
337 Toby Harrah .10
338 George Brett 2.50
339 Davey Lopes .10
340 Gary Carter 1.25
341 John Grubb .10
342 Tim Foli .10
343 Jim Kaat .15
344 Mike LaCoss .10
345 Larry Christenson .10
346 Juan Bonilla .10
347 Omar Moreno .10
348 Chili Davis .10
349 Tommy Boggs .10
350 Rusty Staub .15
351 Bump Wills .10
352 Rick Sweet .10
353 Jim Gott RC .15
354 Terry Felton .10
355 Jim Kern .10
356 Bill Almon .10
357 Tippy Martinez .10
358 Roy Howell .10
359 Dan Petry .10
360 Jerry Mumphrey .10
361 Mark Clear .10
362 Mike Marshall .10
363 Lary Sorensen .10
364 Amos Otis .10
365 Rick Langford .10
366 Brad Mills .10
367 Brian Downing .10
368 Mike Richardt .10
369 Aurelio Rodriguez .10
370 Dave Smith .10
371 Tug McGraw .10
372 Doug Bair .10
373 Ruppert Jones .10
374 Alex Trevino .10
375 Ken Dayley .10
376 Rod Scurry .10
377 Bob Brenly .10
378 Scot Thompson .10
379 Julio Cruz .10
380 John Stearns .10
381 Dale Murray .10
382 Frank Viola RC 1.50
383 Al Bumbry .10
384 Ben Oglivie .10
385 Dave Tobik .10
386 Bob Stanley .10
387 Andre Robertson .10
388 Jorge Orta .10
389 Ed Whitson .10
390 Don Hood .10
391 Tom Underwood .10
392 Tim Wallach .10
393 Steve Renko .10
394 Mickey Rivers .10
395 Greg Luzinski .10
396 Art Howe .10
397 Alan Wiggins .10
398 Jim Barr .10
399 Ivan DeJesus .10
400 Tom Lawless RC .10
401 Bob Walk .10
402 Jimmy Smith .10
403 Lee Smith .20
404 George Hendrick .10
405 Eddie Murray 1.25
406 Marshall Edwards .10
407 Lance Parrish .10
408 Carney Lansford .10
409 Dave Winfield 1.25
410 Bob Welch .10
411 Larry Milbourne .10
412 Dennis Leonard .10
413 Dan Meyer .10
414 Charlie Lea .10
415 Rick Honeycutt .10
416 Mike Witt .10
417 Steve Trout .10
418 Glenn Brummer .10
419 Denny Walling .10
420 Gary Matthews .10
421 Charlie Liebrandt (Leibrandt) .10
422 Juan Eichelberger .10
423 Matt Guante (Cecilio) RC .10
424 Bill Laskey .10
425 Jerry Royster .10
426 Dickie Noles .10

427 George Foster .10
428 Mike Moore RC .25
429 Gary Ward .10
430 Barry Bonnell .10
431 Ron Washington .10
432 Rance Mulliniks .10
433 Mike Stanton .10
434 Jesse Orosco .10
435 Larry Bowa .10
436 Biff Pocoroba .10
437 Johnny Ray .10
438 Joe Morgan 1.25
439 Eric Show RC .15
440 Larry Biittner .10
441 Greg Gross .10
442 Gene Tenace .10
443 Danny Heep .10
444 Bobby Clark .10
445 Kevin Hickey .10
446 Scott Sanderson .10
447 Frank Tanana .10
448 Cesar Geronimo .10
449 Jimmy Sexton .10
450 Mike Hargrove .10
451 Doyle Alexander .10
452 Dwight Evans .10
453 Terry Forster .10
454 Tom Brookens .10
455 Rich Dauer .10
456 Rob Picciolo .10
457 Terry Crowley .10
458 Ned Yost .10
459 Kirk Gibson .10
460 Reid Nichols .10
461 Oscar Gamble .10
462 Dusty Baker .10
463 Jack Perconte .10
464 Frank White .10
465 Mickey Klutts .10
466 Warren Cromartie .10
467 Larry Parrish .10
468 Bobby Grich .10
469 Dane Iorg .10
470 Joe Niekro .10
471 Ed Farmer .10
472 Tim Flannery .10
473 Dave Parker .10
474 Jeff Leonard .10
475 Al Hrabosky .10
476 Ron Hodges .10
477 Leon Durham .10
478 Jim Essian .10
479 Roy Lee Jackson .10
480 Brad Havens .10
481 Joe Price .10
482 Tony Bernazard .10
483 Scott McGregor .10
484 Paul Molitor 1.25
485 Mike Ivie .10
486 Ken Griffey .10
487 Dennis Eckersley 1.00
488 Steve Garvey .40
489 Mike Fischlin .10
490 U.L. Washington .10
491 Steve McCatty .10
492 Roy Johnson .10
493 Don Baylor .10
494 Bobby Johnson .10
495 Mike Squires .10
496 Bert Roberge .10
497 Dick Ruthven .10
498 Tito Landrum .10
499 Sixto Lezcano .10
500 Johnny Bench 1.50
501 Larry Whisenton .10
502 Manny Sarmiento .10
503 Fred Breining .10
504 Bill Campbell .10
505 Todd Cruz .10
506 Bob Bailor .10
507 Dave Stieb .10
508 Al Williams .10
509 Dan Ford .10
510 Gorman Thomas .10
511 Chet Lemon .10
512 Mike Torrez .10
513 Shane Rawley .10
514 Mark Belanger .10
515 Rodney Craig .10
516 Onix Concepcion .10
517 Mike Heath .10
518 Andre Dawson .50
519 Luis Sanchez .10
520 Terry Bogener .10
521 Rudy Law .10
522 Ray Knight .10
523 Joe Lefebvre .10
524 Jim Wohlford .10
525 Julio Franco RC 2.00
526 Ron Oester .10
527 Rick Mahler .10
528 Steve Nicosia .10
529 Junior Kennedy .10
530a Whitey Herzog (One yellow box on back.) .25
530b Whitey Herzog (Two yellow boxes on back.) .10
531a Don Sutton (Blue frame.) .75
531b Don Sutton (Green frame.) .75
532 Mark Brouhard .10
533a Sparky Anderson (One yellow box on back.) .50
533b Sparky Anderson (Two yellow boxes on back.) .50
534 Roger LaFrancois .10
535 George Frazier .10
536 Tom Niedenfuer .10
537 Ed Glynn .10

538	Lee May	.10
539	Bob Kearney	.10
540	Tim Raines	.10
541	Paul Mirabella	.10
542	Luis Tiant	.10
543	Ron LeFlore	.10
544	Dave LaPoint RC	.15
545	Randy Moffitt	.10
546	Luis Aguayo	.10
547	Brad Lesley	.10
548	Luis Salazar	.10
549	John Candelaria	.10
550	Dave Bergman	.10
551	Bob Watson	.10
552	Pat Tabler	.10
553	Brent Gaff	.10
554	Al Cowens	.10
555	Tom Brunansky	.10
556	Lloyd Moseby	.10
557a	Pascual Perez (Twins)	.25
557b	Pascual Perez (Braves)	.10
558	Willie Upshaw	.10
559	Richie Zisk	.10
560	Pat Zachry	.10
561	Jay Johnstone	.10
562	Carlos Diaz	.10
563	John Tudor	.10
564	Frank Robinson	.50
565	Dave Edwards	.10
566	Paul Householder	.10
567	Ron Reed	.10
568	Mike Ramsey	.10
569	Kiko Garcia	.10
570	Tommy John	.10
571	Tony LaRussa	.10
572	Joel Youngblood	.10
573	Wayne Tolleson RC	.10
574	Keith Creel	.10
575	Billy Martin	.10
576	Jerry Dybzinski	.10
577	Rick Cerone	.10
578	Tony Perez	1.00
579	Greg Brock RC	.10
580	Glen Wilson (Glenn)	.10
581	Tim Stoddard	.10
582	Bob McClure	.10
583	Jim Dwyer	.10
584	Ed Romero	.10
585	Larry Herndon	.10
586	Wade Boggs RC	10.00
587	Jay Howell	.10
588	Dave Stewart	.10
589	Bert Blyleven	.10
590	Dick Howser	.10
591	Wayne Gross	.10
592	Terry Francona	.10
593	Don Werner	.10
594	Bill Stein	.10
595	Jesse Barfield	.10
596	Bobby Molinaro	.10
597	Mike Vail	.10
598	Tony Gwynn RC	12.00
599	Gary Rajsich	.10
600	Jerry Ujdur	.10
601	Cliff Johnson	.10
602	Jerry White	.10
603	Bryan Clark	.10
604	Joe Ferguson	.10
605	Guy Sularz	.10
606a	Ozzie Virgil (Green frame around photo.)	.25
606b	Ozzie Virgil (Orange frame around photo.)	.10
607	Terry Harper	.10
608	Harvey Kuenn	.10
609	Jim Sundberg	.10
610	Willie Stargell	1.25
611	Reggie Smith	.10
612	Rob Wilfong	.10
613	Niekro Brothers (Joe Niekro, Phil Niekro)	.25
614	Lee Elia	.10
615	Mickey Hatcher	.10
616	Jerry Hairston Sr.	.10
617	John Martin	.10
618	Wally Backman	.10
619	Storm Davis RC	.10
620	Alan Knicely	.10
621	John Stuper	.10
622	Matt Sinatro	.10
623	Gene Petralli RC	.10
624	Duane Walker	.10
625	Dick Williams	.10
626	Pat Corrales	.10
627	Vern Ruhle	.10
628	Joe Torre	.10
629	Anthony Johnson	.10
630	Steve Howe	.10
631	Gary Woods	.10
632	Lamarr Hoyt (LaMarr)	.10
633	Steve Swisher	.10
634	Terry Leach	.10
635	Jeff Newman	.10
636	Brett Butler	.10
637	Gary Gray	.10
638	Lee Mazzilli	.10
639a	Ron Jackson (A's)	2.50
639b	Ron Jackson (Angels - green frame around photo.)	.25
639c	Ron Jackson (Angels - red frame around photo.)	.15
640	Juan Beniquez	.10
641	Dave Rucker	.10
642	Luis Pujols	.10
643	Rick Monday	.10
644	Hosken Powell	.10
645	San Diego Chicken	.20
646	Dave Engle	.10

647	Dick Davis	.10
648	MVP's (Vida Blue, Joe Morgan, Frank Robinson)	.15
649	Al Chambers	.10
650	Jesus Vega	.10
651	Jeff Jones	.10
652	Marvis Foley	.10
653	Ty Cobb (puzzle)	.10
----	DK checklist (Dick Perez (No word "Checklist" on back.)	
----	DK Checklist (Dick Perez (Word "Checklist" on back.)	.25
----	Checklist 27-130	.10
----	Checklist 131-234	.10
----	Checklist 235-338	.10
----	Checklist 339-442	.10
----	Checklist 443-546	.10
----	Checklist 547-653	.10

1983 Donruss Action All-Stars Promo Sheet

To introduce its series of large-format star cards, Donruss issued this sample sheet with four players on a 10" x 7" format.

NM/M
Complete Sheet: 15.00

1983 Donruss Action All-Stars

Eddie Murray

The cards in this 60-card set are designed on a horizontal format and contain a large close-up photo of the player on the left and a smaller action photo on the right. The 5" x 3-1/2" cards have deep red borders and contain the Donruss logo and the year of issue. Backs are printed in black on red and white and contain statistical and biographical information. The cards were sold with puzzle pieces (three pieces on one card per pack) that feature Mickey Mantle.

NM/M
Complete Set (60): 6.00
Common Player: .05
Mickey Mantle Puzzle: 6.00
Cello Pack (3): .35
Cello Box (3): 8.00

1	Eddie Murray	.30
2	Dwight Evans	.05
3a	Reggie Jackson (Red covers part of statistics on back.)	.50
3b	Reggie Jackson (Red does not cover any statistics on back.)	.50
4	Greg Luzinski	.05
5	Larry Herndon	.05
6	Al Oliver	.05
7	Bill Buckner	.05
8	Jason Thompson	.05
9	Andre Dawson	.20
10	Greg Minton	.05
11	Terry Kennedy	.05
12	Phil Niekro	.25
13	Willie Wilson	.05
14	Johnny Bench	.45
15	Ron Guidry	.05
16	Hal McRae	.05
17	Damaso Garcia	.05
18	Gary Ward	.05
19	Cecil Cooper	.05
20	Keith Hernandez	.05
21	Ron Cey	.05
22	Rickey Henderson	.30
23	Nolan Ryan	2.00
24	Steve Carlton	.30
25	John Stearns	.05
26	Jim Sundberg	.05
27	Joaquin Andujar	.05
28	Gaylord Perry	.25
29	Jack Clark	.05
30	Bill Madlock	.05
31	Pete Rose	1.00
32	Mookie Wilson	.05
33	Rollie Fingers	.25
34	Lonnie Smith	.05
35	Tony Pena	.05
36	Dave's Winfield	.30
37	Tim Lollar	.05
38	Rod Carew	.30
39	Toby Harrah	.05
40	Buddy Bell	.05
41	Bruce Sutter	.25
42	George Brett	.75
43	Carlton Fisk	.30
44	Carl Yastrzemski	.45
45	Dale Murphy	.20
46	Bob Horner	.05
47	Dave Concepcion	.05
48	Dave Stieb	.05
49	Kent Hrbek	.05
50	Lance Parrish	.05
51	Joe Niekro	.05
52	Cal Ripken, Jr.	2.00
53	Fernando Valenzuela	.05
54	Rickie Zisk	.05
55	Leon Durham	.05
56	Robin Yount	.30
57	Mike Schmidt	.75
58	Gary Carter	.30
59	Fred Lynn	.05
60	Checklist	.05

1983 Donruss Hall of Fame Heroes Promo Sheet

To introduce its series of former star Perez-Steele art cards, Donruss issued this sample sheet which reproduces four of the cards in a 5" x 7" format.

NM/M
Complete Sheet: 10.00

1983 Donruss Hall of Fame Heroes

The artwork of Dick Perez is featured in the 44-card Hall of Fame Heroes set issued in 1983. The 2-1/2" x 3-1/2" cards were available in wax packs that contained eight cards plus a Mickey Mantle puzzle piece card (three pieces on one card). Backs display red and blue print on white stock and contain a short biographical sketch.

NM/M
Complete Set (44): 5.00
Common Player: .10
Mickey Mantle Puzzle: 6.00
Wax Pack (8): .75
Wax Box (36): 15.00

1	Ty Cobb	.75
2	Walter Johnson	.15
3	Christy Mathewson	.15
4	Josh Gibson	.35
5	Honus Wagner	.35
6	Jackie Robinson	.75
7	Mickey Mantle	2.00
8	Luke Appling	.15
9	Ted Williams	.75
10	Johnny Mize	.15
11	Satchel Paige	.35
12	Lou Boudreau	.10
13	Jimmie Foxx	.25
14	Duke Snider	.25
15	Monte Irvin	.15
16	Hank Greenberg	.25
17	Roberto Clemente	1.00
18	Al Kaline	.15
19	Frank Robinson	.15
20	Joe Cronin	.10
21	Burleigh Grimes	.10
22	The Waner Brothers (Lloyd Waner, Paul Waner)	.10
23	Grover Alexander	.10
24	Yogi Berra	.25
25	James Bell	.10
26	Bill Dickey	.10
27	Cy Young	.15
28	Charlie Gehringer	.10
29	Dizzy Dean	.15
30	Bob Lemon	.10
31	Red Ruffing	.10
32	Stan Musial	.60
33	Carl Hubbell	.10
34	Hank Aaron	.75
35	John McGraw	.10
36	Bob Feller	.15
37	Casey Stengel	.10
38	Ralph Kiner	.10
39	Roy Campanella	.25
40	Mel Ott	.15
41	Robin Roberts	.10
42	Early Wynn	.10
43	Mickey Mantle Puzzle Card	.25
----	Checklist	.05

1984 Donruss Promo Sheet

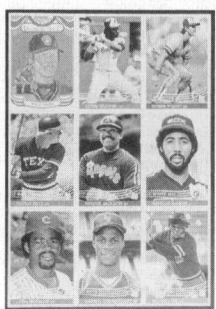

The front designs of nine 1984 Donruss baseball cards were printed on this glossy paper sheet to introduce the company's design for 1994. The 7-1/2" x 10-1/2" sheets are blank-backed. Players are listed here alphabetically.

NM/M
Complete Sheet: 15.00

1984 Donruss

JOE NIEKRO

The 1984 Donruss set consists of 651 numbered cards, seven unnumbered checklists and two "Living Legends" cards (designated A and B). The A and B cards were issued only in wax packs and were not available to hobby dealers purchasing factory sets. The card fronts differ in style from the previous years, however the Donruss logo and year of issue are still included. Backs have black print on green and white and are identical in format to the preceding year. The 2-1/2" x 3-1/2" cards were issued in packs with three pieces of a 63-piece puzzle of Duke Snider. The complete set price in the checklist that follows does not include the higher priced variations. Cards marked with (DK) or (RR) in the checklist refer to the Diamond Kings and Rated Rookies subsets. Each of the Diamond Kings cards and the DK checklist can be found in two varieties. The more common has Frank Steele's name misspelled "Steel" in the credit line at the bottom-right corner on the back. The error was later corrected.

NM/M
Unopened Fact. Set (658): 150.00
Complete Set (660): 75.00

	Common Player:	.15
	Duke Snider Puzzle:	2.00
	Wax Pack (15):	4.50
	Wax Box (36):	150.00
	Rack Pack (45):	15.00
A	Living Legends (Rollie Fingers, Gaylord Perry)	1.50
B	Living Legends (Johnny Bench, Carl Yastrzemski)	4.00
1a	Robin Yount (DK) (Steel)	2.50
1b	Robin Yount (DK) (Steele)	3.00
2a	Dave Concepcion (DK) (Steel)	.25
2b	Dave Concepcion (DK) (Steele)	.35
3a	Dwayne Murphy (DK) (Steel)	.25
3b	Dwayne Murphy (DK) (Steele)	.35
4a	John Castino (DK) (Steel)	.25
4b	John Castino (DK) (Steele)	.25
5a	Leon Durham (DK) (Steel)	.25
5b	Leon Durham (DK) (Steele)	.35
6a	Rusty Staub (DK) (Steel)	.30
6b	Rusty Staub (DK) (Steele)	.45
7a	Jack Clark (DK) (Steel)	.25
7b	Jack Clark (DK) (Steele)	.35
8a	Dave Dravecky (DK) (Steel)	.25
8b	Dave Dravecky (DK) (Steele)	.35
9a	Al Oliver (DK) (Steel)	.35
9b	Al Oliver (DK) (Steele)	.50
10a	Dave Righetti (DK) (Steel)	.25
10b	Dave Righetti (DK) (Steele)	.35
11a	Hal McRae (DK) (Steel)	.25
11b	Hal McRae (DK) (Steele)	.35
12a	Ray Knight (DK) (Steel)	.25
12b	Ray Knight (DK) (Steele)	.35
13a	Bruce Sutter (DK) (Steel)	2.50
13b	Bruce Sutter (DK) (Steele)	3.00
14a	Bob Horner (DK) (Steel)	.25
14b	Bob Horner (DK) (Steele)	.35
15a	Lance Parrish ((DK) (Steel)	.25
15b	Lance Parrish (DK) (Steele)	.35
16a	Matt Young (DK) (Steel)	.35
16b	Matt Young (DK) (Steele)	.35
17a	Fred Lynn (DK) (Steel)	.35
17b	Fred Lynn (DK) (Steele)	.50
18a	Ron Kittle (DK) (Steel)	.25
18b	Ron Kittle (DK) (Steele)	.35
19a	Jim Clancy (DK) (Steel)	.25
19b	Jim Clancy (DK) (Steele)	.35
20a	Bill Madlock (DK) (Steel)	.25
20b	Bill Madlock (DK) (Steele)	.35
21a	Larry Parrish (DK) (Steel)	.25
21b	Larry Parrish (DK) (Steele)	.35
22a	Eddie Murray (DK) (Steel)	2.50
22b	Eddie Murray (DK) (Steele)	3.00
23a	Mike Schmidt (DK) (Steel)	3.00
23b	Mike Schmidt (DK) (Steele)	4.00
24a	Pedro Guerrero (DK) (Steel)	.25
24b	Pedro Guerrero (DK) (Steele)	.25
25a	Andre Thornton (DK) (Steel)	.25
25b	Andre Thornton (DK) (Steele)	.35
26a	Wade Boggs (DK) (Steel)	3.00
26b	Wade Boggs (DK) (Steele)	3.00
27	Joel Skinner RC (RR)	.15
28	Tom Dunbar (RR)	.15
29a	Mike Stenhouse (RR) (no number on back)	.15
29b	Mike Stenhouse (RR) (29 on back)	1.00
30a	Ron Darling RC (RR) (no number on back)	1.50
30b	Ron Darling RC (RR) (30 on back)	2.50
31	Dion James RC (RR)	.15
32	Tony Fernandez RC (RR)	3.00
33	Angel Salazar (RR)	.15
34	Kevin McReynolds RC (RR)	1.50
35	Dick Schofield RC (RR)	.20
36	Brad Komminsk RC (RR)	.15
37	Tim Teufel RC (RR)	.25
38	Doug Frobel (RR)	.15
39	Greg Gagne RC (RR)	1.00
40	Mike Fuentes (RR)	.15
41	Joe Carter RC (RR)	8.00
42	Mike Brown (RR)	.15
43	Mike Jeffcoat (RR)	.15
44	Sid Fernandez RC (RR)	2.00
45	Brian Dayett (RR)	.15
46	Chris Smith (RR)	.15
47	Eddie Murray	3.00
48	Robin Yount	3.00
49	Lance Parrish	.15
50	Jim Rice	1.00
51	Dave Winfield	3.00
52	Fernando Valenzuela	.15
53	George Brett	5.00

54	Rickey Henderson	3.00
55	Gary Carter	3.00
56	Buddy Bell	.15
57	Reggie Jackson	5.00
58	Harold Baines	.15
59	Ozzie Smith	4.00
60	Nolan Ryan	8.00
61	Pete Rose	7.50
62	Ron Oester	.15
63	Steve Garvey	.75
64	Jason Thompson	.15
65	Jack Clark	.15
66	Dale Murphy	1.50
67	Leon Durham	.15
68	Darryl Strawberry	2.00
69	Richie Zisk	.15
70	Kent Hrbek	.15
71	Dave Stieb	.15
72	Ken Schrom	.15
73	George Bell	.15
74	John Moses	.15
75	Ed Lynch	.15
76	Chuck Rainey	.15
77	Biff Pocoroba	.15
78	Cecilio Guante	.15
79	Jim Barr	.15
80	Kurt Bevacqua	.15
81	Tom Foley	.15
82	Joe Lefebvre	.15
83	Andy Van Slyke RC	2.00
84	Bob Lillis	.15
85	Rick Adams	.15
86	Jerry Hairston Sr.	.15
87	Bob James	.15
88	Joe Altobelli	.15
89	Ed Romero	.15
90	John Grubb	.15
91	John Henry Johnson	.15
92	Juan Espino	.15
93	Candy Maldonado	.15
94	Andre Thornton	.15
95	Onix Concepcion	.15
96	Don Hill RC	.15
97	Andre Dawson	1.50
98	Frank Tanana	.15
99	Curt Wilkerson RC	.15
100	Larry Gura	.15
101	Dwayne Murphy	.15
102	Tom Brennan	.15
103	Dave Righetti	.15
104	Steve Sax	.15
105	Dan Petry	.15
106	Cal Ripken, Jr.	8.00
107	Paul Molitor	3.00
108	Fred Lynn	.15
109	Neil Allen	.15
110	Joe Niekro	.15
111	Steve Carlton	3.00
112	Terry Kennedy	.15
113	Bill Madlock	.15
114	Chili Davis	.15
115	Jim Gantner	.15
116	Tom Seaver	4.00
117	Bill Buckner	.15
118	Bill Caudill	.15
119	Jim Clancy	.15
120	John Castino	.15
121	Dave Concepcion	.15
122	Greg Luzinski	.15
123	Mike Boddicker	.15
124	Pete Ladd	.15
125	Juan Berenguer	.15
126	John Montefusco	.15
127	Ed Jurak	.15
128	Tom Niedenfuer	.15
129	Bert Blyleven	.25
130	Bud Black	.15
131	Gorman Heimueller	.15
132	Dan Schatzeder	.15
133	Ron Jackson	.15
134	Tom Henke RC	1.00
135	Kevin Hickey	.15
136	Mike Scott	.15
137	Bo Diaz	.15
138	Glenn Brummer	.15
139	Sid Monge	.15
140	Rich Gale	.15
141	Brett Butler	.15
142	Brian Harper	.15
143	John Rabb	.15
144	Gary Woods	.15
145	Pat Putnam	.15
146	Jim Acker RC	.15
147	Mickey Hatcher	.15
148	Todd Cruz	.15
149	Tom Tellmann	.15
150	John Wockenfuss	.15
151	Wade Boggs	5.00
152	Don Baylor	.15
153	Bob Welch	.15
154	Alan Bannister	.15
155	Willie Aikens	.15
156	Jeff Burroughs	.15
157	Bryan Little	.15
158	Bob Boone	.15
159	Dave Hostetler	.15
160	Jerry Dybzinski	.15
161	Mike Madden	.15
162	Luis DeLeon	.15
163	Willie Hernandez	.15
164	Frank Pastore	.15
165	Rick Camp	.15
166	Lee Mazzilli	.15
167	Scot Thompson	.15
168	Bob Forsch	.15
169	Mike Flanagan	.15
170	Rick Manning	.15
171	Chet Lemon	.15

No.	Player	Price
172	Jerry Remy	.15
173	Ron Guidry	.20
174	Pedro Guerrero	.15
175	Willie Wilson	.15
176	Carney Lansford	.15
177	Al Oliver	.15
178	Jim Sundberg	.15
179	Bobby Grich	.15
180	Richard Dotson	.15
181	Joaquin Andujar	.15
182	Jose Cruz	.15
183	Mike Schmidt	5.00
184	Gary Redus RC	.25
185	Garry Templeton	.15
186	Tony Pena	.15
187	Greg Minton	.15
188	Phil Niekro	1.50
189	Fergie Jenkins	1.50
190	Mookie Wilson	.15
191	Jim Beattie	.15
192	Gary Ward	.15
193	Jesse Barfield	.15
194	Pete Filson	.15
195	Roy Lee Jackson	.15
196	Rick Sweet	.15
197	Jesse Orosco	.15
198	Steve Lake RC	.15
199	Ken Dayley	.15
200	Manny Sarmiento	.15
201	Mark Davis	.15
202	Tim Flannery	.15
203	Bill Scherrer	.15
204	Al Holland	.15
205	David Von Ohlen	.15
206	Mike LaCoss	.15
207	Juan Beniquez	.15
208	Juan Agosto RC	.15
209	Bobby Ramos	.15
210	Al Bumbry	.15
211	Mark Brouhard	.15
212	Howard Bailey	.15
213	Bruce Hurst	.15
214	Bob Shirley	.15
215	Pat Zachry	.15
216	Julio Franco	.15
217	Mike Armstrong	.15
218	Dave Beard	.15
219	Steve Rogers	.15
220	John Butcher	.15
221	Mike Smithson RC	.15
222	Frank White	.15
223	Mike Heath	.15
224	Chris Bando	.15
225	Roy Smalley	.15
226	Dusty Baker	.15
227	Lou Whitaker	.15
228	John Lowenstein	.15
229	Ben Oglivie	.15
230	Doug DeCinces	.15
231	Lonnie Smith	.15
232	Ray Knight	.15
233	Gary Matthews	.15
234	Juan Bonilla	.15
235	Rod Scurry	.15
236	Atlee Hammaker	.15
237	Mike Caldwell	.15
238	Keith Hernandez	.15
239	Larry Bowa	.15
240	Tony Bernazard	.15
241	Damaso Garcia	.15
242	Tom Brunansky	.15
243	Dan Driessen	.15
244	Ron Kittle	.15
245	Tim Stoddard	.15
246	Bob L. Gibson	.15
247	Marty Castillo	.15
248	Don Mattingly RC	25.00
249	Jeff Newman	.15
250	Alejandro Pena RC	.15
251	Toby Harrah	.15
252	Cesar Geronimo	.15
253	Tom Underwood	.15
254	Doug Flynn	.15
255	Andy Hassler	.15
256	Odell Jones	.15
257	Rudy Law	.15
258	Harry Spilman	.15
259	Marty Bystrom	.15
260	Dave Rucker	.15
261	Ruppert Jones	.15
262	Jeff Jones	.15
263	Gerald Perry RC	.15
264	Gene Tenace	.15
265	Brad Wellman	.15
266	Dickie Noles	.15
267	Jamie Allen	.15
268	Jim Gott	.15
269	Ron Davis	.15
270	Benny Ayala	.15
271	Ned Yost	.15
272	Dave Rozema	.15
273	Dave Stapleton	.15
274	Lou Piniella	.25
275	Jose Morales	.15
276	Brod Perkins	.15
277	Butch Davis	.15
278	Tony Phillips RC	.15
279	Jeff Reardon	.15
280	Ken Forsch	.15
281	Pete O'Brien RC	.15
282	Tom Paciorek	.15
283	Frank LaCorte	.15
284	Tim Lollar	.15
285	Greg Gross	.15
286	Alex Trevino	.15
287	Gene Garber	.15
288	Dave Parker	.15
289	Lee Smith	.25
290	Dave LaPoint	.15
291	John Shelby RC	.15
292	Charlie Moore	.15
293	Alan Trammell	.15
294	Tony Armas	.15
295	Shane Rawley	.15
296	Greg Brock	.15
297	Hal McRae	.15
298	Mike Davis	.15
299	Tim Raines	.15
300	Bucky Dent	.15
301	Tommy John	.25
302	Carlton Fisk	3.00
303	Darrell Porter	.15
304	Dickie Thon	.15
305	Garry Maddox	.15
306	Cesar Cedeno	.15
307	Gary Lucas	.15
308	Johnny Ray	.15
309	Andy McGaffigan	.15
310	Claudell Washington	.15
311	Ryne Sandberg	5.00
312	George Foster	.15
313	Spike Owen RC	.25
314	Gary Gaetti	.15
315	Willie Upshaw	.15
316	Al Williams	.15
317	Jorge Orta	.15
318	Orlando Mercado	.15
319	Junior Ortiz RC	.15
320	Mike Proly	.15
321	Randy S. Johnson	.15
322	Jim Morrison	.15
323	Max Venable	.15
324	Tony Gwynn	5.00
325	Duane Walker	.15
326	Ozzie Virgil	.15
327	Jeff Lahti	.15
328	Bill Dawley RC	.15
329	Rob Wilfong	.15
330	Marc Hill	.15
331	Ray Burris	.15
332	Allan Ramirez	.15
333	Chuck Porter	.15
334	Wayne Krenchicki	.15
335	Gary Allenson	.15
336	Bob Meacham RC	.15
337	Joe Beckwith	.15
338	Rick Sutcliffe	.15
339	Mark Huismann RC	.15
340	Tim Conroy RC	.15
341	Scott Sanderson	.15
342	Larry Biittner	.15
343	Dave Stewart	.15
344	Darryl Motley	.15
345	Chris Codiroli RC	.15
346	Rick Behenna	.15
347	Andre Robertson	.15
348	Mike Marshall	.15
349	Larry Herndon	.15
350	Rich Dauer	.15
351	Cecil Cooper	.15
352	Rod Carew	3.00
353	Willie McGee	.15
354	Phil Garner	.15
355	Joe Morgan	3.00
356	Luis Salazar	.15
357	John Candelaria	.15
358	Bill Laskey	.15
359	Bob McClure	.15
360	Dave Kingman	.15
361	Ron Cey	.15
362	Matt Young RC	.15
363	Lloyd Moseby	.15
364	Frank Viola	.15
365	Eddie Milner	.15
366	Floyd Bannister	.15
367	Dan Ford	.15
368	Moose Haas	.15
369	Doug Bair	.15
370	Ray Fontenot RC	.15
371	Luis Aponte	.15
372	Jack Fimple	.15
373	Neal Heaton RC	.15
374	Greg Pryor	.15
375	Wayne Gross	.15
376	Charlie Lea	.15
377	Steve Lubratich	.15
378	Jon Matlack	.15
379	Julio Cruz	.15
380	John Mizerock	.15
381	Kevin Gross RC	.15
382	Mike Ramsey	.15
383	Doug Gwosdz	.15
384	Kelly Paris	.15
385	Pete Falcone	.15
386	Milt May	.15
387	Fred Breining	.15
388	Craig Lefferts RC	.25
389	Steve Henderson	.15
390	Randy Moffitt	.15
391	Ron Washington	.15
392	Gary Roenicke	.15
393	Tom Candiotti RC	.75
394	Larry Pashnick	.15
395	Dwight Evans	.15
396	Goose Gossage	.25
397	Derrel Thomas	.15
398	Juan Eichelberger	.15
399	Leon Roberts	.15
400	Davey Lopes	.15
401	Bill Gullickson	.15
402	Geoff Zahn	.15
403	Billy Sample	.15
404	Mike Squires	.15
405	Craig Reynolds	.15
406	Eric Show	.15
407	John Denny	.15
408	Dann Bilardello	.15
409	Bruce Benedict	.15
410	Kent Tekulve	.15
411	Mel Hall	.15
412	John Stuper	.15
413	Rick Dempsey	.15
414	Don Sutton	1.50
415	Jack Morris	.15
416	John Tudor	.15
417	Willie Randolph	.15
418	Jerry Reuss	.15
419	Don Slaught	.15
420	Steve McCatty	.15
421	Tim Wallach	.15
422	Larry Parrish	.15
423	Brian Downing	.15
424	Britt Burns	.15
425	David Green	.15
426	Jerry Mumphrey	.15
427	Ivan DeJesus	.15
428	Mario Soto	.15
429	Gene Richards	.15
430	Dale Berra	.15
431	Darrell Evans	.15
432	Glenn Hubbard	.15
433	Jody Davis	.15
434	Danny Heep	.15
435	Ed Nunez RC	.15
436	Bobby Castillo	.15
437	Ernie Whitt	.15
438	Scott Ullger	.15
439	Doyle Alexander	.15
440	Domingo Ramos	.15
441	Craig Swan	.15
442	Warren Brusstar	.15
443	Len Barker	.15
444	Mike Easler	.15
445	Renie Martin	.15
446	Dennis Rasmussen RC	.25
447	Ted Power	.15
448	Charlie Hudson RC	.15
449	Danny Cox RC	.15
450	Kevin Bass	.15
451	Daryl Sconiers	.15
452	Scott Fletcher	.15
453	Bryn Smith	.15
454	Jim Dwyer	.15
455	Rob Picciolo	.15
456	Enos Cabell	.15
457	Dennis Boyd	.20
458	Butch Wynegar	.15
459	Burt Hooton	.15
460	Ron Hassey	.15
461	Danny Jackson RC	.15
462	Bob Kearney	.15
463	Terry Francona	.15
464	Wayne Tolleson	.15
465	Mickey Rivers	.15
466	John Wathan	.15
467	Bill Almon	.15
468	George Vukovich	.15
469	Steve Kemp	.15
470	Ken Landreaux	.15
471	Milt Wilcox	.15
472	Tippy Martinez	.15
473	Ted Simmons	.15
474	Tim Foli	.15
475	George Hendrick	.15
476	Terry Puhl	.15
477	Von Hayes	.15
478	Bobby Brown	.15
479	Lee Lacy	.15
480	Joel Youngblood	.15
481	Jim Slaton	.15
482	Mike Fitzgerald RC	.15
483	Keith Moreland	.15
484	Ron Roenicke	.15
485	Luis Leal	.15
486	Bryan Oelkers	.15
487	Bruce Berenyi	.15
488	LaMarr Hoyt	.15
489	Joe Nolan	.15
490	Marshall Edwards	.15
491	Mike Laga RC	.15
492	Rick Cerone	.15
493	Mike Miller (Rick)	.15
494	Rick Honeycutt	.15
495	Mike Hargrove	.15
496	Joe Simpson	.15
497	Keith Atherton RC	.15
498	Chris Welsh	.15
499	Bruce Kison	.15
500	Bob Johnson	.15
501	Jerry Koosman	.15
502	Frank DiPino	.15
503	Tony Perez	2.00
504	Ken Oberkfell	.15
505	Mark Thurmond RC	.15
506	Joe Price	.15
507	Pascual Perez	.15
508	Marvell Wynne RC	.15
509	Mike Krukow	.15
510	Dick Ruthven	.15
511	Al Cowens	.15
512	Cliff Johnson	.15
513	Randy Bush RC	.15
514	Sammy Stewart	.15
515	Bill Schroeder RC	.15
516	Aurelio Lopez	.15
517	Mike Brown	.15
518	Graig Nettles	.25
519	Dave Sax	.15
520	Gerry Willard	.15
521	Paul Splittorff	.15
522	Tom Burgmeier	.15
523	Chris Speier	.15
524	Bobby Clark	.15
525	George Wright	.15
526	Dennis Lamp	.15
527	Tony Scott	.15
528	Ed Whitson	.15
529	Ron Reed	.15
530	Charlie Puleo	.15
531	Jerry Royster	.15
532	Don Robinson	.15
533	Steve Trout	.15
534	Bruce Sutter	2.50
535	Bob Horner	.15
536	Pat Tabler	.15
537	Chris Chambliss	.15
538	Bob Ojeda	.15
539	Alan Ashby	.15
540	Jay Johnstone	.15
541	Bob Dernier	.15
542	Brook Jacoby RC	.15
543	U.L. Washington	.15
544	Danny Darwin	.15
545	Kiko Garcia	.15
546	Vance Law	.15
547	Tug McGraw	.15
548	Dave Smith	.15
549	Len Matuszek	.15
550	Tom Hume	.15
551	Dave Dravecky	.15
552	Rick Rhoden	.15
553	Duane Kuiper	.15
554	Rusty Staub	.20
555	Bill Campbell	.15
556	Mike Torrez	.15
557	Dave Henderson	.15
558	Len Whitehouse	.15
559	Barry Bonnell	.15
560	Rick Lysander	.15
561	Garth Iorg	.15
562	Bryan Clark	.15
563	Brian Giles	.15
564	Vern Ruhle	.15
565	Steve Bedrosian	.15
566	Larry McWilliams	.15
567	Jeff Leonard	.15
568	Alan Wiggins	.15
569	Jeff Russell RC	.15
570	Salome Barojas	.15
571	Dane Iorg	.15
572	Bob Knepper	.15
573	Gary Lavelle	.15
574	Gorman Thomas	.15
575	Manny Trillo	.15
576	Jim Palmer	3.00
577	Dale Murray	.15
578	Tom Brookens	.15
579	Rich Gedman	.15
580	Bill Doran RC	.25
581	Steve Yeager	.15
582	Dan Spillner	.15
583	Dan Quisenberry	.15
584	Rance Mulliniks	.15
585	Storm Davis	.15
586	Dave Schmidt	.15
587	Bill Russell	.15
588	Pat Sheridan RC	.15
589	Rafael Ramirez	.15
590	Bud Anderson	.15
591	George Frazier	.15
592	Lee Tunnell RC	.15
593	Kirk Gibson	.15
594	Scott McGregor	.15
595	Bob Bailor	.15
596	Tom Herr	.15
597	Luis Sanchez	.15
598	Dave Engle	.15
599	Craig McMurtry RC	.15
600	Carlos Diaz	.15
601	Tom O'Malley	.15
602	Nick Esasky RC	.15
603	Ron Hodges	.15
604	Ed Vande Berg	.15
605	Alfredo Griffin	.15
606	Glenn Hoffman	.15
607	Hubie Brooks	.15
608	Richard Barnes (Photo actually Neal Heaton.)	.15
609	Greg Walker RC	.15
610	Ken Singleton	.20
611	Mark Clear	.15
612	Buck Martinez	.15
613	Ken Griffey	.20
614	Reid Nichols	.15
615	Doug Sisk RC	.15
616	Bob Brenly	.15
617	Joey McLaughlin	.15
618	Glenn Wilson	.15
619	Bob Stoddard	.15
620	Len Sakata (Lenn)	.15
621	Mike Young RC	.15
622	John Stefero	.15
623	Carmelo Martinez RC	.15
624	Dave Bergman	.15
625	Runnin' Reds (David Green, Willie McGee, Lonnie Smith, Ozzie Smith)	.75
626	Rudy May	.15
627	Matt Keough	.15
628	Jose DeLeon RC	.15
629	Jim Essian	.15
630	Darnell Coles RC	.15
631	Mike Warren	.15
632	Del Crandall	.15
633	Dennis Martinez	.15
634	Mike Moore	.15
635	Lary Sorensen	.15
636	Ricky Nelson	.15
637	Omar Moreno	.15
638	Charlie Hough	.15
639	Dennis Eckersley	2.50
640	Walt Terrell RC	.15
641	Denny Walling	.15
642	Dave Anderson RC	.15
643	Jose Oquendo RC	.15
644	Bob Stanley	.15
645	Dave Geisel	.15
646	Scott Garrelts RC	.15
647	Gary Pettis RC	.15
648	Duke Snider Puzzle Card	.15
----	Johnnie LeMaster	.15
650	Dave Collins	.15
651	San Diego Chicken	.25
----	Checklist 1-26 DK (Perez-Steel on back.)	.15
----	Checklist 1-26 DK (Perez-Steele on back.)	.15
----	Checklist 27-130	.15
----	Checklist 131-234	.15
----	Checklist 235-338	.15
----	Checklist 339-442	.15
----	Checklist 443-546	.15
----	Checklist 547-651	.15

1984 Donruss Action All-Stars

Full-color photos on the card fronts and backs make the 1984 Donruss Action All-Stars set somewhat unusual. Fronts contain a large action photo plus the Donruss logo and year of issue inside a deep red border. The top half of the backs features a close-up photo with the bottom portion containing biographical and statistical information. The 3-1/2" x 5" cards were sold with Ted Williams puzzle pieces.

	NM/M
Complete Set (60):	4.00
Common Player:	.05
Ted Williams Puzzle:	2.50
Cello Pack (5):	.75
Cello Box (36):	12.50
1 Gary Lavelle	.05
2 Willie McGee	.05
3 Tony Pena	.05
4 Lou Whitaker	.05
5 Robin Yount	.40
6 Doug DeCinces	.05
7 John Castino	.05
8 Terry Kennedy	.05
9 Rickey Henderson	.40
10 Bob Horner	.05
11 Harold Baines	.05
12 Buddy Bell	.05
13 Fernando Valenzuela	.05
14 Nolan Ryan	1.00
15 Andre Thornton	.05
16 Gary Redus	.05
17 Pedro Guerrero	.05
18 Andre Dawson	.05
19 Dave Stieb	.05
20 Cal Ripken, Jr.	1.00
21 Ken Griffey	.05
22 Wade Boggs	.50
23 Keith Hernandez	.05
24 Steve Carlton	.40
25 Hal McRae	.05
26 John Lowenstein	.05
27 Fred Lynn	.05
28 Bill Buckner	.05
29 Chris Chambliss	.05
30 Richie Zisk	.05
31 Jack Clark	.05
32 George Hendrick	.05
33 Bill Madlock	.05
34 Lance Parrish	.05
35 Paul Molitor	.40
36 Reggie Jackson	.60
37 Kent Hrbek	.05
38 Steve Garvey	.15
39 Carney Lansford	.05
40 Dale Murphy	.15
41 Greg Luzinski	.05
42 Larry Parrish	.05
43 Ryne Sandberg	.50
44 Dickie Thon	.05
45 Bert Blyleven	.05
46 Ron Oester	.05
47 Dusty Baker	.05
48 Steve Rogers	.05
49 Jim Clancy	.05
50 Eddie Murray	.35
51 Ron Guidry	.05
52 Jim Rice	.20
53 Tom Seaver	.40
54 Pete Rose	.75
55 George Brett	.60
56 Dan Quisenberry	.05
57 Mike Schmidt	.60
58 Ted Simmons	.05
59 Dave Righetti	.05
60 Checklist	.05

1984 Donruss Champions

The Champions set includes ten Hall of Famers, 49 current players and a numbered checklist. Hall of Famers' cards (called Grand Champions) feature the artwork of Dick Perez, while cards of the current players (called Champions) are color photos. All cards measure 3-1/2" x 5". The Grand Champions represent hallmarks of excellence in various statistical categories, while the Champions are the leaders among then-active players in each category. The cards were issued with Duke Snider puzzle pieces.

	NM/M
Complete Set (60):	4.00
Common Player:	.10
Duke Snider Puzzle:	2.00
Pack (5):	.75
Box (36):	12.50
1 Babe Ruth	1.25
2 George Foster	.10
3 Dave Kingman	.10
4 Jim Rice	.25
5 Gorman Thomas	.10
6 Ben Oglivie	.10
7 Jeff Burroughs	.10
8 Hank Aaron	.75
9 Reggie Jackson	.60
10 Carl Yastrzemski	.50
11 Mike Schmidt	.60
12 Graig Nettles	.10
13 Greg Luzinski	.10
14 Ted Williams	.75
15 George Brett	.60
16 Wade Boggs	.50
17 Hal McRae	.10
18 Bill Buckner	.10
19 Eddie Murray	.35
20 Rogers Hornsby	.10
21 Rod Carew	.35
22 Bill Madlock	.10
23 Lonnie Smith	.10
24 Cecil Cooper	.10
25 Ken Griffey	.10
26 Ty Cobb	.60
27 Pete Rose	.75
28 Rusty Staub	.10
29 Tony Perez	.10
30 Al Oliver	.10
31 Cy Young	.25
32 Gaylord Perry	.15
33 Ferguson Jenkins	.15
34 Phil Niekro	.15
35 Jim Palmer	.15
36 Tommy John	.15
37 Walter Johnson	.25
38 Steve Carlton	.15
39 Nolan Ryan	1.25
40 Tom Seaver	.35
41 Don Sutton	.15
42 Bert Blyleven	.15
43 Frank Robinson	.35
44 Joe Morgan	.35
45 Rollie Fingers	.15
46 Keith Hernandez	.15
47 Robin Yount	.35
48 Cal Ripken, Jr.	1.25
49 Dale Murphy	.15
50 Mickey Mantle	1.50
51 Johnny Bench	.35
52 Carlton Fisk	.35
53 Tug McGraw	.15
54 Paul Molitor	.35
55 Carl Hubbell	.10
56 Steve Garvey	.15
57 Dave Parker	.10
58 Gary Carter	.35
59 Fred Lynn	.10
60 Checklist	.05

1985 Donruss Promo Sheet

To introduce its design for 1985, Donruss distributed this 8-1/2" x 11" paper sample sheet to dealers. The blank-back sheet has examples of nine Donruss cards from the '85 set. Players are listed here in alphabetical order.

	NM/M
Complete Sheet:	8.00

1985 Donruss

The black-bordered 1985 Donruss set includes 653 numbered cards and seven unnumbered checklists. Displaying the artwork of Dick Perez for the fourth consecutive year, cards #1-26 feature the Diamond Kings series. Donruss, reacting to the hobby craze over rookie cards, included a Rated Rookies subset (cards #27-46). The cards, in standard 2-1/2" x3-1/2", were issued with a Lou Gehrig puzzle. Backs repeat the format of previous years with black print on yellow and white. The complete set price does not include the higher priced variations. (DK) and (RR) refer to the Diamond Kings and Rated Rookies subsets.

	NM/M
Unopened Fact. Set (660):	75.00
Complete Set (660):	50.00
Common Player:	.10
Lou Gehrig Puzzle:	3.00
Wax Pack (15):	4.00
Wax Box (36):	120.00
Rack Pack (45):	7.00
1 Ryne Sandberg (DK)	2.50
2 Doug DeCinces (DK)	.10
3 Rich Dotson (DK)	.10
4 Bert Blyleven (DK)	.25
5 Lou Whitaker (DK)	.10
6 Dan Quisenberry (DK)	.10
7 Don Mattingly (DK)	4.00
8 Carney Lansford (DK)	.10
9 Frank Tanana (DK)	.10
10 Willie Upshaw (DK)	.10
11 Claudell Washington (DK)	.10
12 Mike Marshall (DK)	.10
13 Joaquin Andujar (DK)	.10
14 Cal Ripken, Jr. (DK)	6.00
15 Jim Rice (DK)	.75
16 Don Sutton (DK)	1.00
17 Frank Viola (DK)	.10
18 Alvin Davis (DK)	.10
19 Mario Soto (DK)	.10
20 Jose Cruz (DK)	.10
21 Charlie Lea (DK)	.10
22 Jesse Orosco (DK)	.10
23 Juan Samuel (DK)	.10
24 Tony Pena (DK)	.10
25 Tony Gwynn (DK)	2.50
26 Bob Brenly (DK)	.10
27 Danny Tartabull RC (RR)	1.50
28 Mike Bielecki RC (RR)	.10
29 Steve Lyons RC (RR)	.25
30 Jeff Reed RC (RR)	.10
31 Tony Brewer (RR)	.10
32 John Morris RC (RR)	.10
33 Daryl Boston RC (RR)	.15
34 Alfonso Pulido (RR)	.10
35 Steve Kiefer RC (RR)	.10

36 Larry Sheets RC (RR)	.10
37 Scott Bradley RC (RR)	.10
38 Calvin Schiraldi RC (RR)	.10
39 Shawon Dunston RC (RR)	1.50
40 Charlie Mitchell (RR)	.10
41 Billy Hatcher RC (RR)	.15
42 Russ Stephans (RR)	.10
43 Alejandro Sanchez (RR)	.10
44 Steve Jeltz RC (RR)	.10
45 Jim Traber RC (RR)	.10
46 Doug Loman (RR)	.10
47 Eddie Murray	2.00
48 Robin Yount	2.00
49 Lance Parrish	.10
50 Jim Rice	.75
51 Dave Winfield	2.00
52 Fernando Valenzuela	.10
53 George Brett	3.00
54 Dave Kingman	.10
55 Gary Carter	2.00
56 Buddy Bell	.10
57 Reggie Jackson	3.00
58 Harold Baines	.10
59 Ozzie Smith	2.00
60 Nolan Ryan	6.00
61 Mike Schmidt	3.00
62 Dave Parker	.10
63 Tony Gwynn	2.50
64 Tony Pena	.10
65 Jack Clark	.10
66 Dale Murphy	.60
67 Ryne Sandberg	2.50
68 Keith Hernandez	.10
69 Alvin Davis	.10
70 Kent Hrbek	.10
71 Willie Upshaw	.10
72 Dave Engle	.10
73 Alfredo Griffin	.10
74a Jack Perconte (Last line of highlights begins "Batted .346...")	.10
74b Jack Perconte (Last line of highlights begins "Led the ...")	.15
75 Jesse Orosco	.10
76 Jody Davis	.10
77 Bob Horner	.10
78 Larry McWilliams	.10
79 Joel Youngblood	.10
80 Alan Wiggins	.10
81 Ron Oester	.10
82 Ozzie Virgil	.10
83 Ricky Horton RC	.10
84 Bill Doran	.10
85 Rod Carew	2.00
86 LaMarr Hoyt	.10
87 Tim Wallach	.10
88 Mike Flanagan	.10
89 Jim Sundberg	.10
90 Chet Lemon	.10
91 Bob Stanley	.10
92 Willie Randolph	.10
93 Bill Russell	.10
94 Julio Franco	.10
95 Dan Quisenberry	.10
96 Bill Caudill	.10
97 Bill Gullickson	.10
98 Danny Darwin	.10
99 Curtis Wilkerson	.10
100 Bud Black	.10
101 Tony Phillips	.10
102 Tony Bernazard	.10
103 Jay Howell	.10
104 Burt Hooton	.10
105 Milt Wilcox	.10
106 Rich Dauer	.10
107 Don Sutton	1.00
108 Mike Witt	.10
109 Bruce Sutter	1.50
110 Enos Cabell	.10
111 John Denny	.10
112 Dave Dravecky	.10
113 Marvell Wynne	.10
114 Johnnie LeMaster	.10
115 Chuck Porter	.10
116 John Gibbons	.10
117 Keith Moreland	.10
118 Darnell Coles	.10
119 Dennis Lamp	.10
120 Ron Davis	.10
121 Nick Esasky	.10
122 Vance Law	.10
123 Gary Roenicke	.10
124 Bill Schroeder	.10
125 Dave Rozema	.10
126 Bobby Meacham	.10
127 Marty Barrett	.10
128 R.J. Reynolds RC	.15
129 Ernie Camacho	.10
130 Jorge Orta	.10
131 Lary Sorensen	.10
132 Terry Francona	.10
133 Fred Lynn	.10
134 Bobby Jones	.10
135 Jerry Hairston Sr.	.10
136 Kevin Bass	.10
137 Garry Maddox	.10
138 Dave LaPoint	.10
139 Kevin McReynolds	.10
140 Wayne Krenchicki	.10
141 Rafael Ramirez	.10
142 Rod Scurry	.10
143 Greg Minton	.10
144 Tim Stoddard	.10
145 Steve Henderson	.10
146 George Bell	.10
147 Dave Meier	.10

148 Sammy Stewart	.10
149 Mark Brouhard	.10
150 Larry Herndon	.10
151 Oil Can Boyd	.10
152 Brian Dayett	.10
153 Tom Niedenfuer	.10
154 Brook Jacoby	.10
155 Onix Concepcion	.10
156 Tim Conroy	.10
157 Joe Hesketh RC	.15
158 Brian Downing	.10
159 Tommy Dunbar	.10
160 Marc Hill	.10
161 Phil Garner	.10
162 Jerry Davis	.10
163 Bill Campbell	.10
164 John Franco RC	1.50
165 Len Barker	.10
166 Benny Distefano RC	.10
167 George Frazier	.10
168 Tito Landrum	.10
169 Cal Ripken, Jr.	6.00
170 Cecil Cooper	.10
171 Alan Trammell	.10
172 Wade Boggs	2.50
173 Don Baylor	.10
174 Pedro Guerrero	.10
175 Frank White	.10
176 Rickey Henderson	2.00
177 Charlie Lea	.10
178 Pete O'Brien	.10
179 Doug DeCinces	.10
180 Ron Kittle	.10
181 George Hendrick	.10
182 Joe Niekro	.10
183 Juan Samuel	.10
184 Mario Soto	.10
185 Goose Gossage	.15
186 Johnny Ray	.10
187 Bob Brenly	.10
188 Craig McMurtry	.10
189 Leon Durham	.10
190 Dwight Gooden	.25
191 Barry Bonnell	.10
192 Tim Teufel	.10
193 Dave Stieb	.10
194 Mickey Hatcher	.10
195 Jesse Barfield	.10
196 Al Cowens	.10
197 Hubie Brooks	.10
198 Steve Trout	.10
199 Glenn Hubbard	.10
200 Bill Madlock	.10
201 Jeff Robinson RC	.10
202 Eric Show	.10
203 Dave Concepcion	.10
204 Ivan DeJesus	.10
205 Neil Allen	.10
206 Jerry Mumphrey	.10
207 Mike Brown	.10
208 Carlton Fisk	2.00
209 Bryn Smith	.10
210 Tippy Martinez	.10
211 Dion James	.10
212 Willie Hernandez	.10
213 Mike Easler	.10
214 Ron Guidry	.10
215 Rick Honeycutt	.10
216 Brett Butler	.10
217 Larry Gura	.10
218 Ray Burris	.10
219 Steve Rogers	.10
220 Frank Tanana	.10
221 Ned Yost	.10
222 Bret Saberhagen	.25
223 Mike Davis	.10
224 Bert Blyleven	.15
225 Steve Kemp	.10
226 Jerry Reuss	.10
227 Darrell Evans	.10
228 Wayne Gross	.10
229 Jim Gantner	.10
230 Bob Boone	.10
231 Lonnie Smith	.10
232 Frank DiPino	.10
233 Jerry Koosman	.10
234 Graig Nettles	.15
235 John Tudor	.10
236 John Rabb	.10
237 Rick Manning	.10
238 Mike Fitzgerald	.10
239 Gary Matthews	.10
240 Jim Presley RC	.10
241 Dave Collins	.10
242 Gary Gaetti	.10
243 Dann Bilardello	.10
244 Rudy Law	.10
245 John Lowenstein	.10
246 Tom Tellmann	.10
247 Howard Johnson	.10
248 Ray Fontenot	.10
249 Tony Armas	.10
250 Candy Maldonado	.10
251 Mike Jeffcoat RC	.10
252 Dane Iorg	.10
253 Bruce Bochte	.10
254 Pete Rose	5.00
255 Don Aase	.10
256 George Wright	.10
257 Britt Burns	.10
258 Mike Scott	.10
259 Len Matuszek	.10
260 Dave Rucker	.10
261 Craig Lefferts	.10
262 Jay Tibbs RC	.10
263 Bruce Benedict	.10
264 Don Robinson	.10
265 Gary Lavelle	.10

266 Scott Sanderson	.10
267 Matt Young	.10
268 Ernie Whitt	.10
269 Houston Jimenez	.10
270 Ken Dixon RC	.10
271 Peter Ladd	.10
272 Juan Berenguer	.10
273 Roger Clemens	25.00
274 Rick Cerone	.10
275 Dave Anderson	.10
276 George Vukovich	.10
277 Greg Pryor	.10
278 Mike Warren	.10
279 Bob James	.10
280 Bobby Grich	.10
281 Mike Mason RC	.10
282 Ron Reed	.10
283 Alan Ashby	.10
284 Mark Thurmond	.10
285 Joe Lefebvre	.10
286 Ted Power	.10
287 Chris Chambliss	.10
288 Lee Tunnell	.10
289 Rich Bordi	.10
290 Glenn Brummer	.10
291 Mike Boddicker	.10
292 Rollie Fingers	1.00
293 Lou Whitaker	.10
294 Dwight Evans	.10
295 Don Mattingly	5.00
296 Mike Marshall	.10
297 Willie Wilson	.10
298 Mike Heath	.10
299 Tim Raines	.10
300 Larry Parrish	.10
301 Geoff Zahn	.10
302 Rich Dotson	.10
303 David Green	.10
304 Jose Cruz	.10
305 Steve Carlton	2.00
306 Gary Redus	.10
307 Steve Garvey	.40
308 Jose DeLeon	.10
309 Randy Lerch	.10
310 Claudell Washington	.10
311 Lee Smith	.25
312 Darryl Strawberry	.10
313 Jim Beattie	.10
314 John Butcher	.10
315 Damaso Garcia	.10
316 Mike Smithson	.10
317 Luis Leal	.10
318 Ken Phelps	.10
319 Wally Backman	.10
320 Ron Cey	.10
321 Brad Komminsk	.10
322 Jason Thompson	.10
323 Frank Williams RC	.10
324 Tim Lollar	.10
325 Eric Davis RC	1.50
326 Von Hayes	.10
327 Andy Van Slyke	.10
328 Craig Reynolds	.10
329 Dick Schofield	.10
330 Scott Fletcher	.10
331 Jeff Reardon	.10
332 Rick Dempsey	.10
333 Ben Oglivie	.10
334 Dan Petry	.10
335 Jackie Gutierrez	.10
336 Dave Righetti	.10
337 Alejandro Pena	.10
338 Mel Hall	.10
339 Pat Sheridan	.10
340 Keith Atherton	.10
341 David Palmer	.10
342 Gary Ward	.10
343 Dave Stewart	.10
344 Mark Gubicza RC	.50
345 Carney Lansford	.10
346 Jerry Willard	.10
347 Ken Griffey	.10
348 Franklin Stubbs RC	.10
349 Aurelio Lopez	.10
350 Al Bumbry	.10
351 Charlie Moore	.10
352 Luis Sanchez	.10
353 Darrell Porter	.10
354 Bill Dawley	.10
355 Charlie Hudson	.10
356 Garry Templeton	.10
357 Cecilio Guante	.10
358 Jeff Leonard	.10
359 Paul Molitor	2.00
360 Ron Gardenhire	.10
361 Larry Bowa	.10
362 Bob Kearney	.10
363 Garth Iorg	.10
364 Tom Brunansky	.10
365 Brad Gulden	.10
366 Greg Walker	.10
367 Mike Young	.10
368 Rick Waits	.10
369 Doug Bair	.10
370 Bob Shirley	.10
371 Bob Ojeda	.10
372 Bob Welch	.10
373 Neal Heaton	.10
374 Danny Jackson (Photo actually Steve Farr.)	.10
375 Donnie Hill	.10
376 Mike Stenhouse	.10
377 Bruce Kison	.10
378 Wayne Tolleson	.10
379 Floyd Bannister	.10
380 Vern Ruhle	.10
381 Tim Corcoran	.10
382 Kurt Kepshire	.10

383 Bobby Brown	.10
384 Dave Van Gorder	.10
385 Rick Mahler	.10
386 Lee Mazzilli	.10
387 Bill Laskey	.10
388 Thad Bosley	.10
389 Al Chambers	.10
390 Tony Fernandez	.10
391 Ron Washington	.10
392 Bill Swaggerty	.10
393 Bob L. Gibson	.10
394 Marty Castillo	.10
395 Steve Crawford	.10
396 Clay Christiansen	.10
397 Bob Bailor	.10
398 Mike Hargrove	.10
399 Charlie Leibrandt	.10
400 Tom Burgmeier	.10
401 Razor Shines	.10
402 Rob Wilfong	.10
403 Tom Henke	.10
404 Al Jones	.10
405 Mike LaCoss	.10
406 Luis DeLeon	.10
407 Greg Gross	.10
408 Tom Hume	.10
409 Rick Camp	.10
410 Milt May	.10
411 Henry Cotto RC	.10
412 Dave Von Ohlen	.10
413 Scott McGregor	.10
414 Ted Simmons	.10
415 Jack Morris	.10
416 Bill Buckner	.10
417 Butch Wynegar	.10
418 Steve Sax	.10
419 Steve Balboni	.10
420 Dwayne Murphy	.10
421 Andre Dawson	.65
422 Charlie Hough	.10
423 Tommy John	.15
424a Tom Seaver (Floyd Bannister photo, left-hander.)	2.00
424b Tom Seaver (Correct photo.)	7.50
425 Tom Herr	.10
426 Terry Puhl	.10
427 Al Holland	.10
428 Eddie Milner	.10
429 Terry Kennedy	.10
430 John Candelaria	.10
431 Manny Trillo	.10
432 Ken Oberkfell	.10
433 Rick Sutcliffe	.10
434 Ron Darling	.10
435 Spike Owen	.10
436 Frank Viola	.10
437 Lloyd Moseby	.10
438 Kirby Puckett	8.00
439 Jim Clancy	.10
440 Mike Moore	.10
441 Doug Sisk	.10
442 Dennis Eckersley	1.50
443 Gerald Perry	.10
444 Dale Berra	.10
445 Dusty Baker	.10
446 Ed Whitson	.10
447 Cesar Cedeno	.10
448 Rick Schu RC	.10
449 Joaquin Andujar	.10
450 Mark Bailey RC	.10
451 Ron Romanick RC	.10
452 Julio Cruz	.10
453 Miguel Dilone	.10
454 Storm Davis	.10
455 Jaime Cocanower	.10
456 Barbaro Garbey	.10
457 Rich Gedman	.10
458 Phil Niekro	1.00
459 Mike Scioscia	.10
460 Pat Tabler	.10
461 Darryl Motley	.10
462 Chris Codoroli (Codiroli)	.10
463 Doug Flynn	.10
464 Billy Sample	.10
465 Mickey Rivers	.10
466 John Wathan	.10
467 Bill Krueger	.10
468 Andre Thornton	.10
469 Rex Hudler	.10
470 Sid Bream RC	.25
471 Kirk Gibson	.10
472 John Shelby	.10
473 Moose Haas	.10
474 Doug Corbett	.10
475 Willie McGee	.10
476 Bob Knepper	.10
477 Kevin Gross	.10
478 Carmelo Martinez	.10
479 Kent Tekulve	.10
480 Chili Davis	.10
481 Bobby Clark	.10
482 Mookie Wilson	.10
483 Dave Owen	.10
484 Ed Nunez	.10
485 Rance Mulliniks	.10
486 Ken Schrom	.10
487 Jeff Russell	.10
488 Tom Paciorek	.10
489 Dan Ford	.10
490 Mike Caldwell	.10
491 Scottie Earl	.10
492 Jose Rijo	.10
493 Bruce Hurst	.10
494 Ken Landreaux	.10
495 Mike Fischlin	.10
496 Don Slaught	.10
497 Steve McCatty	.10

498 Gary Lucas	.10
499 Gary Pettis	.10
500 Marvis Foley	.10
501 Mike Squires	.10
502 Jim Pankovitz RC	.10
503 Luis Aguayo	.10
504 Ralph Citarella	.10
505 Bruce Bochy	.10
506 Bob Owchinko	.10
507 Pascual Perez	.10
508 Lee Lacy	.10
509 Atlee Hammaker	.10
510 Bob Dernier	.10
511 Ed Vande Berg	.10
512 Cliff Johnson	.10
513 Len Whitehouse	.10
514 Dennis Martinez	.10
515 Ed Romero	.10
516 Rusty Kuntz	.10
517 Rick Miller	.10
518 Dennis Rasmussen	.10
519 Steve Yeager	.10
520 Chris Bando	.10
521 U.L. Washington	.10
522 Curt Young RC	.10
523 Angel Salazar	.10
524 Curt Kaufman	.10
525 Odell Jones	.10
526 Juan Agosto	.10
527 Denny Walling	.10
528 Andy Hawkins	.10
529 Sixto Lezcano	.10
530 Skeeter Barnes	.10
531 Randy S. Johnson	.10
532 Jim Morrison	.10
533 Warren Brusstar	.10
534a Jeff Pendleton RC (Error)	1.00
534b Terry Pendleton (Correct)	4.50
535 Vic Rodriguez	.10
536 Bob McClure	.10
537 Dave Bergman	.10
538 Mark Clear	.10
539 Mike Pagliarulo RC	.25
540 Terry Whitfield	.10
541 Joe Beckwith	.10
542 Jeff Burroughs	.10
543 Dan Schatzeder	.10
544 Donnie Scott	.10
545 Jim Slaton	.10
546 Greg Luzinski	.10
547 Mark Salas RC	.10
548 Dave Smith	.10
549 John Wockenfuss	.10
550 Frank Pastore	.10
551 Tim Flannery	.10
552 Rick Rhoden	.10
553 Mark Davis	.10
554 Jeff Dedmon RC	.15
555 Gary Woods	.10
556 Danny Heep	.10
557 Mark Langston	.10
558 Darrell Brown	.10
559 Jimmy Key	.10
560 Rick Lysander	.10
561 Doyle Alexander	.10
562 Mike Stanton	.10
563 Sid Fernandez	.10
564 Richie Hebner	.10
565 Alex Trevino	.10
566 Brian Harper	.10
567 Dan Gladden RC	.25
568 Luis Salazar	.10
569 Tom Foley	.10
570 Larry Andersen	.10
571 Danny Cox	.10
572 Joe Sambito	.10
573 Juan Beniquez	.10
574 Joel Skinner	.10
575 Randy St. Claire RC	.10
576 Floyd Rayford	.10
577 Roy Howell	.10
578 John Grubb	.10
579 Ed Jurak	.10
580 John Montefusco	.10
581 Orel Hershiser RC	3.00
582 Tom Waddell RC	.10
583 Mark Huismann	.10
584 Joe Morgan	2.00
585 Jim Wohlford	.10
586 Dave Schmidt	.10
587 Jeff Kunkel RC	.10
588 Hal McRae	.10
589 Bill Almon	.10
590 Carmen Castillo	.10
591 Omar Moreno	.10
592 Ken Howell RC	.10
593 Tom Brookens	.10
594 Joe Nolan	.10
595 Willie Lozado	.10
596 Tom Nieto RC	.10
597 Walt Terrell	.10
598 Al Oliver	.10
599 Shane Rawley	.10
600 Denny Gonzalez RC	.10
601 Mark Grant RC	.10
602 Mike Armstrong	.10
603 George Foster	.10
604 Davey Lopes	.10
605 Salome Barojas	.10
606 Roy Lee Jackson	.10
607 Pete Filson	.10
608 Duane Walker	.10
609 Glenn Wilson	.10
610 Rafael Santana	.10
611 Roy Smith	.10
612 Ruppert Jones	.10
613 Joe Cowley	.10

614	Al Nipper RC (Photo actually Mike Brown.)	.15
615	Gene Nelson	.10
616	Joe Carter	.10
617	Ray Knight	.10
618	Chuck Rainey	.10
619	Dan Driessen	.10
620	Daryl Sconiers	.10
621	Bill Stein	.10
622	Roy Smalley	.10
623	Ed Lynch	.10
624	Jeff Stone RC	.10
625	Bruce Berenyi	.10
626	Kelvin Chapman	.10
627	Joe Price	.10
628	Steve Bedrosian	.10
629	Vic Mata	.10
630	Mike Krukow	.10
631	Phil Bradley RC	.15
632	Jim Gott	.10
633	Randy Bush	.10
634	Tom Browning RC	.25
635	Lou Gehrig Puzzle Card	.10
636	Reid Nichols	.10
637	Dan Pasqua RC	.25
638	German Rivera	.10
639	Don Schulze RC	.10
640a	Mike Jones (Last line of highlights begins "Was 11- 7...")	.10
640b	Mike Jones (Last line of highlights begins "Spent some ...")	.15
641	Pete Rose	4.00
642	Wade Rowdon RC	.10
643	Jerry Narron	.10
644	Darrell Miller RC	.10
645	Tim Hulett RC	.10
646	Andy McGaffigan	.10
647	Kurt Bevacqua	.10
648	John Russell RC	.10
649	Ron Robinson RC	.10
650	Donnie Moore	.10
651a	Two for the Title (Don Mattingly, Dave Winfield) (Yellow letters.)	3.00
651b	Two for the Title (Don Mattingly, Dave Winfield) (White letters.)	4.50
652	Tim Laudner	.10
653	Steve Farr RC	.10
----	Checklist 1-26 DK	.10
----	Checklist 27-130	.10
----	Checklist 131-234	.10
----	Checklist 235-338	.10
----	Checklist 339-442	.10
----	Checklist 443-546	.10
----	Checklist 547-653	.10

1985 Donruss Box Panels

In 1985, Donruss placed on the bottoms of its wax pack boxes a four-card panel which included three player cards and a Lou Gehrig puzzle card. The player cards, numbered PC1 through PC3, have backs identical to the regular 1985 Donruss issue. The card fronts are identical in design to the regular issue, but carry different photos.

		NM/M
Complete Panel:		2.50
Complete Singles Set (4):		2.50
Common Player:		.10
PC1	Dwight Gooden	.25
PC2	Ryne Sandberg	2.50
PC3	Ron Kittle	.10
----	Lou Gehrig (Puzzle card.)	.10

1985 Donruss Action All-Stars

In 1985, Donruss issued an Action All-Stars set for the third consecutive year. Card fronts feature an action photo with an inset portrait of the player inside a black border with grey boxes through it. The card backs have black print on blue and white and include statistical and biographical information. The cards were issued with a Lou Gehrig puzzle.

	NM/M
Complete Set (60):	4.00
Common Player:	.05

Lou Gehrig Puzzle:		3.00
Cello Pack (3):		.50
Cello Box (36):		9.00
1	Tim Raines	.05
2	Jim Gantner	.05
3	Mario Soto	.05
4	Spike Owen	.05
5	Lloyd Moseby	.05
6	Damaso Garcia	.05
7	Cal Ripken, Jr.	1.00
8	Dan Quisenberry	.05
9	Eddie Murray	.50
10	Tony Pena	.05
11	Buddy Bell	.05
12	Dave Winfield	.50
13	Ron Kittle	.05
14	Rich Gossage	.05
15	Dwight Evans	.05
16	Al Davis	.05
17	Mike Schmidt	.75
18	Pascual Perez	.05
19	Tony Gwynn	.60
20	Nolan Ryan	1.00
21	Robin Yount	.50
22	Mike Marshall	.05
23	Brett Butler	.05
24	Ryne Sandberg	.60
25	Dale Murphy	.20
26	George Brett	.75
27	Jim Rice	.25
28	Ozzie Smith	.60
29	Larry Parrish	.05
30	Jack Clark	.05
31	Manny Trillo	.05
32	Dave Kingman	.05
33	Geoff Zahn	.05
34	Pedro Guerrero	.05
35	Dave Parker	.05
36	Rollie Fingers	.35
37	Fernando Valenzuela	.05
38	Wade Boggs	.60
39	Reggie Jackson	.75
40	Kent Hrbek	.05
41	Keith Hernandez	.05
42	Lou Whitaker	.05
43	Tom Herr	.05
44	Alan Trammell	.05
45	Butch Wynegar	.05
46	Leon Durham	.05
47	Dwight Gooden	.20
48	Don Mattingly	.75
49	Phil Niekro	.25
50	Johnny Ray	.05
51	Doug DeCinces	.05
52	Willie Upshaw	.05
53	Lance Parrish	.05
54	Jody Davis	.05
55	Steve Carlton	.50
56	Juan Samuel	.05
57	Gary Carter	.50
58	Harold Baines	.05
59	Eric Show	.05
60	Checklist	.04

1985 Donruss Diamond Kings Supers

The 1985 Donruss Diamond Kings Supers are enlarged versions of the Diamond Kings cards in the regular 1985 Donruss set. The cards measure 4-15/16" x 6-3/4". The Diamond Kings series features the artwork of Dick Perez. Twenty-eight cards make up the Super set - 26 DK cards, an unnumbered checklist, and an unnumbered Dick Perez card. The back of the Perez card contains a brief history of Dick Perez and the Perez-Steele Galleries. The set could be obtained through a mail-in offer found on wax pack wrappers.

		NM/M
Complete Set (28):		5.00
Common Player:		.10
1	Ryne Sandberg	1.00
2	Doug DeCinces	.10
3	Richard Dotson	.10
4	Bert Blyleven	.10
5	Lou Whitaker	.10
6	Dan Quisenberry	.10
7	Don Mattingly	1.50
8	Carney Lansford	.10
9	Frank Tanana	.10
10	Willie Upshaw	.10
11	Claudell Washington	.10
12	Mike Marshall	.10
13	Joaquin Andujar	.10
14	Cal Ripken, Jr.	2.00
15	Jim Rice	.25
16	Don Sutton	.50
17	Frank Viola	.10
18	Alvin Davis	.10
19	Mario Soto	.10
20	Jose Cruz	.10
21	Charlie Lea	.10
22	Jesse Orosco	.10
23	Juan Samuel	.10
24	Tony Pena	.10
25	Tony Gwynn	1.00
26	Bob Brenly	.10
----	Checklist	.03
----	Dick Perez (DK artist)	.10

1985 Donruss Highlights

Designed in the style of the regular 1985 Donruss set, this issue features the Player of the Month in the major leagues plus highlight cards of special baseball events and milestones of the 1985 season. Fifty-six cards, including an unnumbered checklist, comprise the set which was available only through hobby dealers. The cards measure 2-1/2" x 3-1/2" and have glossy fronts. The last two cards in the set feature Donruss' picks for the A.L. and N.L. Rookies of the Year. The set was issued in a specially designed box.

		NM/M
Complete Set (56):		3.00
Common Player:		.05
1	Sets Opening Day Record (Tom Seaver)	.10
2	Establishes A.L. Save Mark (Rollie Fingers)	.05
3	A.L. Player of the Month - April (Mike Davis)	.05
4	A.L. Pitcher of the Month - April (Charlie Leibrandt)	.05
5	N.L. Player of the Month - April (Dale Murphy)	.05
6	N.L. Pitcher of the Month - April (Fernando Valenzuela)	.05
7	N.L. Shortstop Record (Larry Bowa)	.05
8	Joins Reds 2000 Hit Club (Dave Concepcion)	.05
9	Eldest Grand Slammer (Tony Perez)	.05
10	N.L. Career Run Leader (Pete Rose)	.50
11	A.L. Player of the Month - May (George Brett)	.25
12	A.L. Pitcher of the Month - May (Dave Stieb)	.05
13	N.L. Player of the Month - May (Dave Parker)	.05
14	N.L. Pitcher of the Month - May (Andy Hawkins)	.05
15	Records 11th Straight Win (Andy Hawkins)	.05
16	Two Homers In First Inning (Von Hayes)	.05
17	A.L. Player of the Month - June (Rickey Henderson)	.15
18	A.L. Pitcher of the Month - June (Jay Howell)	.05
19	N.L. Player of the Month - June (Pedro Guerrero)	.05
20	N.L. Pitcher of the Month - June (John Tudor)	.05
21	Marathon Game Iron Men (Gary Carter, Keith Hernandez)	.05
22	Records 4000th K (Nolan Ryan)	.50
23	All-Star Game MVP (LaMarr Hoyt)	.05
24	1st Ranger To Hit For Cycle (Oddibe McDowell)	.05
25	A.L. Player of the Month - July (George Brett)	.25
26	A.L. Pitcher of the Month - July (Bret Saberhagen)	.05
27	N.L. Player of the Month - July (Keith Hernandez)	.05
28	N.L. Pitcher of the Month - July (Fernando Valenzuela)	.05
29	Record Setting Base Stealers (Vince Coleman, Willie McGee)	.05
30	Notches 300th Career Win (Tom Seaver)	.10
31	Strokes 3000th Hit (Rod Carew)	.10
32	Establishes Met Record (Dwight Gooden)	.05
33	Achieves Strikeout Milestone (Dwight Gooden)	.05
34	Explodes For 9 RBI (Eddie Murray)	.10
35	A.L. Career Hbp Leader (Don Baylor)	.05
36	A.L. Player of the Month - August (Don Mattingly)	.50
37	A.L. Pitcher of the Month - August (Dave Righetti)	.05
38	N.L. Player of the Month (Willie McGee)	.05
39	N.L. Pitcher of the Month - August (Shane Rawley)	.05
40	Ty-Breaking Hit (Pete Rose)	.50
41	Hits 3 HRs, Drives In 8 Runs (Andre Dawson)	.05
42	Sets Yankee Theft Mark (Rickey Henderson)	.15
43	20 Wins In Rookie Season (Tom Browning)	.05
44	Yankee Milestone For Hits (Don Mattingly)	.50
45	A.L. Player of the Month - September (Don Mattingly)	.50
46	A.L. Pitcher of the Month - September (Charlie Leibrandt)	.05
47	N.L. Player of the Month - September (Gary Carter)	.05
48	N.L. Pitcher of the Month - September (Dwight Gooden)	.05
49	Major League Record Setter (Wade Boggs)	.25
50	Hurls Shutout For 300th Win (Phil Niekro)	.05
51	Venerable HR King (Darrell Evans)	.05
52	N.L. Switch-hitting Record (Willie McGee)	.05
53	Equals DiMaggio Feat (Dave Winfield)	.10
54	Donruss N.L. Rookie of the Year (Vince Coleman)	.10
55	Donruss A.L. Rookie of the Year (Ozzie Guillen)	.10
----	Checklist	.05

1985 Donruss Sluggers of The Hall of Fame

In much the same manner as the 1959-71 Bazooka cards were issued, this eight-player set consists of cards printed on the bottom panel of a box of bubble gum. When cut off the box, cards measure 3-1/2" x 6-1/2", with blank backs. Players are pictured on the cards in paintings done by Dick Perez. Cards were issued on blue Color Bubbles brand boxes and on red Super Bubble boxes, each numbered on a tab at top or bottom; this checklist is arranged by the number on the card front.

		NM/M
Complete Set (8):		6.00
Common Player:		.30
1	Babe Ruth	2.00
2	Ted Williams	1.00
3	Lou Gehrig	1.00
4	Johnny Mize	.30
5	Stan Musial	.60
6	Mickey Mantle	2.50
7	Hank Aaron	.75
8	Frank Robinson	.45

1986 Donruss

In 1986, Donruss issued a 660-card set which included 653 numbered cards and seven un-numbered checklists. The 2-1/2" x 3-1/2" cards have fronts that feature blue borders and backs that have black print on blue and white. For the fifth year in a row, the first 26 cards in the set are Diamond Kings. The Rated Rookies subset (#27-46) appears once again. The cards were distributed with a Hank Aaron puzzle. The complete set price does not include the higher priced variations. In the checklist that follows, (DK) and (RR) refer to the Diamond Kings and Rated Rookies series.

		NM/M
Unopened Factory Set (660):		35.00
Complete Set (660):		30.00
Common Player:		.05
Hank Aaron Puzzle:		3.00
Wax Pack (15):		1.25
Wax Box (36):		35.00
Rack Pack (45):		2.50
1	Kirk Gibson (DK)	.15
2	Goose Gossage (DK)	.15
3	Willie McGee (DK)	.10
4	George Bell (DK)	.05
5	Tony Armas (DK)	.05
6	Chili Davis (DK)	.05
7	Cecil Cooper (DK)	.05
8	Mike Boddicker (DK)	.05
9	Davey Lopes (DK)	.05
10	Bill Doran (DK)	.05
11	Bret Saberhagen (DK)	.10
12	Brett Butler (DK)	.10
13	Harold Baines (DK)	.15
14	Mike Davis (DK)	.05
15	Tony Perez (DK)	1.00
16	Willie Randolph (DK)	.05
17	Bob Boone (DK)	.10
18	Orel Hershiser (DK)	.10
19	Johnny Ray (DK)	.05
20	Gary Ward (DK)	.05
21	Rick Mahler (DK)	.05
22	Phil Bradley (DK)	.05
23	Jerry Koosman (DK)	.10
24	Tom Brunansky (DK)	.05
25	Andre Dawson (DK)	.50
26	Dwight Gooden (DK)	.10
27	Kal Daniels RC (RR)	.10
28	Fred McGriff RC (RR)	4.00
29	Cory Snyder RC (RR)	.10
30	Jose Guzman RC (RR)	.05
31	Ty Gainey RC (RR)	.05
32	Johnny Abrego RC (RR)	.05
33a	Andres Galarraga RC (RR)(Accent mark over e of Andres on back.)	2.00
33b	Andres Galarraga RC (RR) (No accent mark.)	2.00
34	Dave Shipanoff RC (RR)	.05
35	Mark McLemore RC (RR)	.50
36	Marty Clary RC (RR)	.05
37	Paul O'Neill RC (RR)	2.00
38	Danny Tartabull (RR)	.05
39	Jose Canseco RC (RR)	6.00
40	Juan Nieves RC (RR)	.05
41	Lance McCullers RC (RR)	.05
42	Rick Surhoff RC (RR)	.05
43	Todd Worrell RC (RR)	.25
44	Bob Kipper (RR)	.05
45	John Habyan RC (RR)	.05
46	Mike Woodard RC (RR)	.05
47	Mike Boddicker	.05
48	Robin Yount	1.50
49	Lou Whitaker	.05
50	Dennis Boyd	.05
51	Rickey Henderson	1.50
52	Mike Marshall	.05
53	George Brett	2.50
54	Dave Kingman	.05
55	Hubie Brooks	.05
56	Oddibe McDowell RC	.15
57	Doug DeCinces	.05
58	Britt Burns	.05
59	Ozzie Smith	2.00
60	Jose Cruz	.05
61	Mike Schmidt	2.50
62	Pete Rose	3.00
63	Steve Garvey	.40
64	Tony Pena	.05
65	Chili Davis	.05
66	Dale Murphy	.40
67	Ryne Sandberg	2.00
68	Gary Carter	1.50
69	Alvin Davis	.05
70	Kent Hrbek	.05
71	George Bell	.05
72	Kirby Puckett	2.00
73	Lloyd Moseby	.05
74	Bob Kearney	.05
75	Dwight Gooden	.05
76	Gary Matthews	.05
77	Rick Mahler	.05
78	Benny Distefano	.05
79	Jeff Leonard	.05
80	Kevin McReynolds	.05
81	Ron Oester	.05
82	John Russell	.05
83	Tommy Herr	.05
84	Jerry Mumphrey	.05
85	Ron Romanick	.05
86	Daryl Boston	.05
87	Andre Dawson	.50
88	Eddie Murray	1.50
89	Dion James	.05
90	Chet Lemon	.05
91	Bob Stanley	.05
92	Willie Randolph	.05
93	Mike Scioscia	.05
94	Tom Waddell	.05
95	Danny Jackson	.05
96	Mike Davis	.05
97	Mike Fitzgerald	.05
98	Gary Ward	.05
99	Pete O'Brien	.05
100	Bret Saberhagen	.05
101	Alfredo Griffin	.05
102	Brett Butler	.05
103	Ron Guidry	.15
104	Jerry Reuss	.05
105	Jack Morris	.05
106	Rick Dempsey	.05
107	Ray Burris	.05
108	Brian Downing	.05
109	Willie McGee	.05
110	Bill Doran	.05
111	Kent Tekulve	.05
112	Tony Gwynn	2.00
113	Marvell Wynne	.05
114	David Green	.05
115	Jim Gantner	.05
116	George Foster	.05
117	Steve Trout	.05
118	Mark Langston	.05
119	Tony Fernandez	.05
120	John Butcher	.05
121	Ron Robinson	.05
122	Dan Spillner	.05
123	Mike Young	.05
124	Paul Molitor	1.50
125	Kirk Gibson	.05
126	Ken Griffey	.05
127	Tony Armas	.05
128	Mariano Duncan RC	.15
129	Pat Tabler (Mr. Clutch)	.05
130	Frank White	.05
131	Carney Lansford	.05
132	Vance Law	.05
133	Dick Schofield	.05
134	Wayne Tolleson	.05
135	Greg Walker	.05
136	Denny Walling	.05
137	Ozzie Virgil	.05
138	Ricky Horton	.05
139	LaMarr Hoyt	.05
140	Wayne Krenchicki	.05
141	Glenn Hubbard	.05
142	Cecilio Guante	.05
143	Mike Krukow	.05
144	Lee Smith	.15
145	Edwin Nunez	.05
146	Dave Stieb	.05
147	Mike Smithson	.05
148	Ken Dixon	.05
149	Danny Darwin	.05
150	Chris Pittaro	.05
151	Bill Buckner	.05
152	Mike Pagliarulo	.05
153	Bill Russell	.05
154	Brook Jacoby	.05
155	Pat Sheridan	.05
156	Mike Gallego RC	.05
157	Jim Wohlford	.05
158	Gary Pettis	.05
159	Toby Harrah	.05
160	Richard Dotson	.05
161	Bob Knepper	.05
162	Dave Dravecky	.05
163	Greg Gross	.05
164	Eric Davis	.05
165	Gerald Perry	.05
166	Rick Rhoden	.05
167	Keith Moreland	.05
168	Jack Clark	.05
169	Storm Davis	.05
170	Cecil Cooper	.05
171	Alan Trammell	.05
172	Roger Clemens	2.50
173	Don Mattingly	2.50
174	Pedro Guerrero	.05
175	Willie Wilson	.05
176	Dwayne Murphy	.05
177	Tim Raines	.05
178	Larry Parrish	.05
179	Mike Witt	.05
180	Harold Baines	.05
181	Vince Coleman RC	.35

No.	Player	Price
182	Jeff Heathcock RC	.05
183	Steve Carlton	1.50
184	Mario Soto	.05
185	Goose Gossage	.10
186	Johnny Ray	.05
187	Dan Gladden	.05
188	Bob Horner	.05
189	Rick Sutcliffe	.05
190	Keith Hernandez	.05
191	Phil Bradley	.05
192	Tom Brunansky	.05
193	Jesse Barfield	.05
194	Frank Viola	.05
195	Willie Upshaw	.05
196	Jim Beattie	.05
197	Darryl Strawberry	.05
198	Ron Cey	.05
199	Steve Bedrosian	.05
200	Steve Kemp	.05
201	Manny Trillo	.05
202	Garry Templeton	.05
203	Dave Parker	.05
204	John Denny	.05
205	Terry Pendleton	.05
206	Terry Puhl	.05
207	Bobby Grich	.05
208	Ozzie Guillen RC	2.00
209	Jeff Reardon	.05
210	Cal Ripken, Jr.	3.00
211	Bill Schroeder	.05
212	Dan Petry	.05
213	Jim Rice	.50
214	Dave Righetti	.05
215	Fernando Valenzuela	.05
216	Julio Franco	.05
217	Darryl Motley	.05
218	Dave Collins	.05
219	Tim Wallach	.05
220	George Wright	.05
221	Tommy Dunbar	.05
222	Steve Balboni	.05
223	Jay Howell	.05
224	Joe Carter	.05
225	Ed Whitson	.05
226	Orel Hershiser	.05
227	Willie Hernandez	.05
228	Lee Lacy	.05
229	Rollie Fingers	1.00
230	Bob Boone	.05
231	Joaquin Andujar	.05
232	Craig Reynolds	.05
233	Shane Rawley	.05
234	Eric Show	.05
235	Jose DeLeon	.05
236	Jose Uribe RC	.05
237	Moose Haas	.05
238	Wally Backman	.05
239	Dennis Eckersley	1.25
240	Mike Moore	.05
241	Damaso Garcia	.05
242	Tim Teufel	.05
243	Dave Concepcion	.05
244	Floyd Bannister	.05
245	Fred Lynn	.05
246	Charlie Moore	.05
247	Walt Terrell	.05
248	Dave Winfield	1.50
249	Dwight Evans	.05
250	Dennis Powell RC	.05
251	Andre Thornton	.05
252	Onix Concepcion	.05
253	Mike Heath	.05
254a	David Palmer (2B on front)	.05
254b	David Palmer (P on front)	.15
255	Donnie Moore	.05
256	Curtis Wilkerson	.05
257	Julio Cruz	.05
258	Nolan Ryan	3.00
259	Jeff Stone	.05
260a	John Tudor (1981 Games is .18)	.05
260b	John Tudor (1981 Games is 18)	.15
261	Mark Thurmond	.05
262	Jay Tibbs	.05
263	Rafael Ramirez	.05
264	Larry McWilliams	.05
265	Mark Davis	.05
266	Bob Dernier	.05
267	Matt Young	.05
268	Jim Clancy	.05
269	Mickey Hatcher	.05
270	Sammy Stewart	.05
271	Bob L. Gibson	.05
272	Nelson Simmons	.05
273	Rich Gedman	.05
274	Butch Wynegar	.05
275	Ken Howell	.05
276	Mel Hall	.05
277	Jim Sundberg	.05
278	Chris Codiroli	.05
279	Herman Winningham RC	.05
280	Rod Carew	1.50
281	Don Slaught	.05
282	Scott Fletcher	.05
283	Bill Dawley	.05
284	Andy Hawkins	.05
285	Glenn Wilson	.05
286	Nick Esasky	.05
287	Claudell Washington	.05
288	Lee Mazzilli	.05
289	Jody Davis	.05
290	Darrell Porter	.05
291	Scott McGregor	.05
292	Ted Simmons	.05
293	Aurelio Lopez	.05
294	Marty Barrett	.05
295	Dale Berra	.05
296	Greg Brock	.05
297	Charlie Leibrandt	.05
298	Bill Krueger	.05
299	Bryn Smith	.05
300	Burt Hooton	.05
301	Stu Cliburn RC	.05
302	Luis Salazar	.05
303	Ken Dayley	.05
304	Frank DiPino	.05
305	Von Hayes	.05
306a	Gary Redus (1983 2B is .20)	.05
306b	Gary Redus (1983 2B is 20)	.15
307	Craig Lefferts	.05
308	Sam Khalifa	.05
309	Scott Garrelts	.05
310	Rick Cerone	.05
311	Shawon Dunston	.05
312	Howard Johnson	.05
313	Jim Presley	.05
314	Gary Gaetti	.05
315	Luis Leal	.05
316	Mark Salas	.05
317	Bill Caudill	.05
318	Dave Henderson	.05
319	Rafael Santana	.05
320	Leon Durham	.05
321	Bruce Sutter	1.25
322	Jason Thompson	.05
323	Bob Brenly	.05
324	Carmelo Martinez	.05
325	Eddie Milner	.05
326	Juan Samuel	.05
327	Tom Nieto	.05
328	Dave Smith	.05
329	Urbano Lugo RC	.05
330	Joel Skinner	.05
331	Bill Gullickson	.05
332	Floyd Rayford	.05
333	Ben Oglivie	.05
334	Lance Parrish	.05
335	Jackie Gutierrez	.05
336	Dennis Rasmussen	.05
337	Terry Whitfield	.05
338	Neal Heaton	.05
339	Jorge Orta	.05
340	Donnie Hill	.05
341	Joe Hesketh	.05
342	Charlie Hough	.05
343	Dave Rozema	.05
344	Greg Pryor	.05
345	Mickey Tettleton	.05
346	George Vukovich	.05
347	Don Baylor	.05
348	Carlos Diaz	.05
349	Barbaro Garbey	.05
350	Larry Sheets	.05
351	Ted Higuera RC	.10
352	Juan Beniquez	.05
353	Bob Forsch	.05
354	Mark Bailey	.05
355	Larry Andersen	.05
356	Terry Kennedy	.05
357	Don Robinson	.05
358	Jim Gott	.05
359	Earnest Riles RC	.05
360	John Christensen RC	.05
361	Ray Fontenot	.05
362	Spike Owen	.05
363	Jim Acker	.05
364a	Ron Davis (Last line in highlights ends with "...inMay.")	.05
364b	Ron Davis (Last line in highlights ends with "...relievers (9).")	.15
365	Tom Hume	.05
366	Carlton Fisk	1.50
367	Nate Snell	.05
368	Rick Manning	.05
369	Darrell Evans	.05
370	Ron Hassey	.05
371	Wade Boggs	2.00
372	Rick Honeycutt	.05
373	Chris Bando	.05
374	Bud Black	.05
375	Steve Henderson	.05
376	Charlie Lea	.05
377	Reggie Jackson	2.50
378	Dave Schmidt	.05
379	Bob James	.05
380	Glenn Davis	.05
381	Tim Corcoran	.05
382	Danny Cox	.05
383	Tim Flannery	.05
384	Tom Browning	.05
385	Rick Camp	.05
386	Jim Morrison	.05
387	Dave LaPoint	.05
388	Davey Lopes	.05
389	Al Cowens	.05
390	Doyle Alexander	.05
391	Tim Laudner	.05
392	Don Aase	.05
393	Jaime Cocanower	.05
394	Randy O'Neal	.05
395	Mike Easler	.05
396	Scott Bradley	.05
397	Tom Niedenfuer	.05
398	Jerry Willard	.05
399	Lonnie Smith	.05
400	Bruce Bochte	.05
401	Terry Francona	.05
402	Jim Slaton	.05
403	Bill Stein	.05
404	Tim Hulett	.05
405	Alan Ashby	.05
406	Tim Stoddard	.05
407	Garry Maddox	.05
408	Ted Power	.05
409	Len Barker	.05
410	Denny Gonzalez	.05
411	George Frazier	.05
412	Andy Van Slyke	.05
413	Jim Dwyer	.05
414	Paul Householder	.05
415	Alejandro Sanchez	.05
416	Steve Crawford	.05
417	Dan Pasqua	.05
418	Enos Cabell	.05
419	Mike Jones	.05
420	Steve Kiefer	.05
421	Tim Burke RC	.05
422	Mike Mason	.05
423	Ruppert Jones	.05
424	Jerry Hairston Sr.	.05
425	Tito Landrum	.05
426	Jeff Calhoun	.05
427	Don Carman RC	.05
428	Tony Perez	1.00
429	Jerry Davis	.05
430	Bob Walk	.05
431	Brad Wellman	.05
432	Terry Forster	.05
433	Billy Hatcher	.05
434	Clint Hurdle	.05
435	Ivan Calderon RC	.05
436	Pete Filson	.05
437	Tom Henke	.05
438	Dave Engle	.05
439	Tom Filer	.05
440	Gorman Thomas	.05
441	Rick Aguilera RC	.25
442	Scott Sanderson	.05
443	Jeff Dedmon	.05
444	Joe Orsulak RC	.10
445	Atlee Hammaker	.05
446	Jerry Royster	.05
447	Buddy Bell	.05
448	Dave Rucker	.05
449	Ivan DeJesus	.05
450	Jim Pankovits	.05
451	Jerry Narron	.05
452	Bryan Little	.05
453	Gary Lucas	.05
454	Dennis Martinez	.05
455	Ed Romero	.05
456	Bob Melvin RC	.05
457	Glenn Hoffman	.05
458	Bob Shirley	.05
459	Bob Welch	.05
460	Carmen Castillo	.05
461	Dave Leeper	.05
462	Tim Birtsas RC	.05
463	Randy St. Claire	.05
464	Chris Welsh	.05
465	Greg Harris	.05
466	Lynn Jones	.05
467	Dusty Baker	.05
468	Roy Smith	.05
469	Andre Robertson	.05
470	Ken Landreaux	.05
471	Dave Bergman	.05
472	Gary Roenicke	.05
473	Pete Vuckovich	.05
474	Kirk McCaskill RC	.10
475	Jeff Lahti	.05
476	Mike Scott	.05
477	Darren Daulton RC	1.50
478	Graig Nettles	.15
479	Bill Almon	.05
480	Greg Minton	.05
481	Randy Ready	.05
482	Len Dykstra RC	1.50
483	Thad Bosley	.05
484	Harold Reynolds RC	1.00
485	Al Oliver	.05
486	Roy Smalley	.05
487	John Franco	.05
488	Juan Agosto	.05
489	Al Pardo	.05
490	Bill Wegman RC	.05
491	Frank Tanana	.05
492	Brian Fisher RC	.05
493	Mark Clear	.05
494	Len Matuszek	.05
495	Ramon Romero	.05
496	John Wathan	.05
497	Rob Picciolo	.05
498	U.L. Washington	.05
499	John Candelaria	.05
500	Duane Walker	.05
501	Gene Nelson	.05
502	John Mizerock	.05
503	Luis Aguayo	.05
504	Kurt Kepshire	.05
505	Ed Wojna	.05
506	Joe Price	.05
507	Milt Thompson RC	.05
508	Junior Ortiz	.05
509	Vida Blue	.05
510	Steve Engel	.05
511	Karl Best	.05
512	Cecil Fielder RC	2.00
513	Frank Eufemia	.05
514	Tippy Martinez	.05
515	Billy Robidoux RC	.05
516	Bill Scherrer	.05
517	Bruce Hurst	.05
518	Rich Bordi	.05
519	Steve Yeager	.05
520	Tony Bernazard	.05
521	Hal McRae	.05
522	Jose Rijo	.05
523	Mitch Webster RC	.05
524	Jack Howell RC	.05
525	Alan Bannister	.05
526	Ron Kittle	.05
527	Phil Garner	.05
528	Kurt Bevacqua	.05
529	Kevin Gross	.05
530	Bo Diaz	.05
531	Ken Oberkfell	.05
532	Rick Reuschel	.05
533	Ron Meridith	.05
534	Steve Braun	.05
535	Wayne Gross	.05
536	Ray Searage	.05
537	Tom Brookens	.05
538	Al Nipper	.05
539	Billy Sample	.05
540	Steve Sax	.05
541	Dan Quisenberry	.05
542	Tony Phillips	.05
543	Floyd Youmans RC	.05
544	Steve Buechele RC	.05
545	Craig Gerber	.05
546	Joe DeSa	.05
547	Brian Harper	.05
548	Kevin Bass	.05
549	Tom Foley	.05
550	Dave Van Gorder	.05
551	Bruce Bochy	.05
552	R.J. Reynolds	.05
553	Chris Brown RC	.05
554	Bruce Benedict	.05
555	Warren Brusstar	.05
556	Danny Heep	.05
557	Darnell Coles	.05
558	Greg Gagne	.05
559	Ernie Whitt	.05
560	Ron Washington	.05
561	Jimmy Key	.05
562	Billy Swift	.05
563	Ron Darling	.05
564	Dick Ruthven	.05
565	Zane Smith	.05
566	Sid Bream	.05
567a	Joel Youngblood (P on front)	.05
567b	Joel Youngblood (IF on front)	.15
568	Mario Ramirez	.05
569	Tom Runnells	.05
570	Rick Schu	.05
571	Bill Campbell	.05
572	Dickie Thon	.05
573	Al Holland	.05
574	Reid Nichols	.05
575	Bert Roberge	.05
576	Mike Flanagan	.05
577	Tim Leary	.05
578	Mike Laga	.05
579	Steve Lyons	.05
580	Phil Niekro	1.00
581	Gilberto Reyes	.05
582	Jamie Easterly	.05
583	Mark Gubicza	.05
584	Stan Javier RC	.15
585	Bill Laskey	.05
586	Jeff Russell	.05
587	Dickie Noles	.05
588	Steve Farr	.05
589	Steve Ontiveros RC	.05
590	Mike Hargrove	.05
591	Marty Bystrom	.05
592	Franklin Stubbs	.05
593	Larry Herndon	.05
594	Bill Swaggerty	.05
595	Carlos Ponce	.05
596	Pat Perry RC	.05
597	Ray Knight	.05
598	Steve Lombardozzi RC	.05
599	Brad Havens	.05
600	Pat Clements RC	.05
601	Joe Niekro	.05
602	Hank Aaron Puzzle Card	.05
603	Dwayne Henry RC	.05
604	Mookie Wilson	.05
605	Buddy Biancalana	.05
606	Rance Mulliniks	.05
607	Alan Wiggins	.05
608	Joe Cowley	.05
609a	Tom Seaver (Green stripes around name.)	1.50
609b	Tom Seaver (Yellow stripes around name.)	2.00
610	Neil Allen	.05
611	Don Sutton	1.00
612	Fred Toliver RC	.05
613	Jay Baller	.05
614	Marc Sullivan	.05
615	John Grubb	.05
616	Bruce Kison	.05
617	Bill Madlock	.05
618	Chris Chambliss	.05
619	Dave Stewart	.05
620	Tim Lollar	.05
621	Gary Lavelle	.05
622	Charles Hudson	.05
623	Joel Davis RC	.05
624	Joe Johnson RC	.05
625	Sid Fernandez	.05
626	Dennis Lamp	.05
627	Terry Harper	.05
628	Jack Lazorko	.05
629	Roger McDowell RC	.25
630	Mark Funderburk	.05
631	Ed Lynch	.05
632	Rudy Law	.05
633	Roger Mason RC	.05
634	Mike Felder RC	.05
635	Ken Schrom	.05
636	Bob Ojeda	.05
637	Ed Vande Berg	.05
638	Bobby Meacham	.05
639	Cliff Johnson	.05
640	Garth Iorg	.05
641	Dan Driessen	.05
642	Mike Brown	.05
643	John Shelby	.05
644	Pete Rose (RB)	.50
645	Knuckle Brothers (Joe Niekro, Phil Niekro)	.25
646	Jesse Orosco	.05
647	Billy Beane RC	.05
648	Cesar Cedeno	.05
649	Bert Blyleven	.15
650	Max Venable	.05
651	Fleet Feet (Vince Coleman, Willie McGee)	.05
652	Calvin Schiraldi	.05
653	King of Kings (Pete Rose)	3.00
----	Checklist 1-26 DK	.05
----	Checklist 27-130 (45 is Beane)	.05
----	Checklist 27-130 (45 is Habyan)	.05
----	Checklist 131-234	.05
----	Checklist 235-338	.05
----	Checklist 339-442	.05
----	Checklist 443-546	.05
----	Checklist 547-653	.05

1986 Donruss Box Panels

For the second year in a row, Donruss placed baseball cards on the bottom of its wax and cello pack boxes. The cards, printed four to a panel, are standard 2-1/2" x 3-1/2". With numbering that begins where Donruss left off in 1985, cards PC4 through PC6 were found on boxes of regular Donruss issue wax packs. Cards PC7 through PC9 were found on boxes of the 1986 All-Star/Pop-up packs. An unnumbered Hank Aaron puzzle card was included on each box.

	NM/M
Complete Panel Set (2):	3.00
Complete Singles Set (8):	3.00
Common Single Player:	.05
Panel	.50
PC4 Kirk Gibson	.15
PC5 Willie Hernandez	.15
PC6 Doug DeCinces	.15
---- Aaron Puzzle Card	.05
Panel	2.00
PC7 Wade Boggs	1.50
PC8 Lee Smith	.20
PC9 Cecil Cooper	.15
---- Aaron Puzzle Card	.05

1986 Donruss All-Stars

Issued in conjunction with the 1986 Donruss Pop-Ups set, the All-Stars consist of 60 cards in 3-1/2" x 5" format. Fifty-nine players involved in the 1985 All-Star game plus an unnumbered checklist comprise the set. Card fronts have the same blue border found on the regular 1986 Donruss issue. Retail packs included one Pop-up card, three All-Star cards and one Hank Aaron puzzle-piece card.

	NM/M
Complete Set (60):	6.00
Common Player:	.05
Hank Aaron puzzle:	3.00
Cello Pack (3):	.50
Cello Box (36):	6.00
1 Tony Gwynn	.50
2 Tommy Herr	.05
3 Steve Garvey	.20
4 Dale Murphy	.20
5 Darryl Strawberry	.05
6 Graig Nettles	.05
7 Terry Kennedy	.05
8 Ozzie Smith	.50
9 LaMarr Hoyt	.05
10 Rickey Henderson	.35
11 Lou Whitaker	.05
12 George Brett	.75
13 Eddie Murray	.40
14 Cal Ripken, Jr.	1.50
15 Dave Winfield	.40
16 Jim Rice	.25
17 Carlton Fisk	.40
18 Jack Morris	.25
19 Jose Cruz	.05
20 Tim Raines	.05
21 Nolan Ryan	1.50
22 Tony Pena	.05
23 Jack Clark	.05
24 Dave Parker	.05
25 Tim Wallach	.05
26 Ozzie Virgil	.05
27 Fernando Valenzuela	.05
28 Dwight Gooden	.05
29 Glenn Wilson	.05
30 Garry Templeton	.05
31 Goose Gossage	.05
32 Ryne Sandberg	.50
33 Jeff Reardon	.05
34 Pete Rose	1.00
35 Scott Garrelts	.05
36 Willie McGee	.05
37 Ron Darling	.05
38 Dick Williams	.05
39 Paul Molitor	.40
40 Damaso Garcia	.05
41 Phil Bradley	.05
42 Dan Petry	.05
43 Willie Hernandez	.05
44 Tom Brunansky	.05
45 Alan Trammell	.05
46 Donnie Moore	.05
47 Wade Boggs	.50
48 Ernie Whitt	.05
49 Harold Baines	.05
50 Don Mattingly	.75
51 Gary Ward	.05
52 Bert Blyleven	.05
53 Jimmy Key	.05
54 Cecil Cooper	.05
55 Dave Stieb	.05
56 Rich Gedman	.05
57 Jay Howell	.05
58 Sparky Anderson	.05
59 Minneapolis Metrodome	.05
---- Checklist	.05

1986 Donruss Diamond Kings Supers

Donruss produced a set of large-format Diamond Kings in 1986 for the second year in a row. The 4-11/16" x 6-3/4" cards are enlarged versions of the 26 Diamond Kings cards found in the regular 1986 Donruss set, plus an unnumbered checklist and an unnumbered Pete Rose "King of Kings" card.

	NM/M
Complete Set (28):	6.00
Common Player:	.25
1 Kirk Gibson	.25
2 Goose Gossage	.25
3 Willie McGee	.25
4 George Bell	.25
5 Tony Armas	.25
6 Chili Davis	.25
7 Cecil Cooper	.25
8 Mike Boddicker	.25
9 Davey Lopes	.25
10 Bill Doran	.25
11 Bret Saberhagen	.25

12	Brett Butler	.25
13	Harold Baines	.25
14	Mike Davis	.25
15	Tony Perez	.75
16	Willie Randolph	.25
18	Orel Hershiser	.25
19	Johnny Ray	.25
20	Gary Ward	.25
21	Rick Mahler	.25
22	Phil Bradley	.25
23	Jerry Koosman	.25
24	Tom Brunansky	.25
25	Andre Dawson	.50
26	Dwight Gooden	.25
	Checklist	.05
	King of Kings (Pete Rose)	4.00

1986 Donruss Highlights

Donruss, for the second year in a row, issued a 56-card highlights set featuring cards of each league's Player of the Month plus significant events of the 1986 season. The cards, 2-1/2" x 3-1/2", are similar in design to the regular 1986 Donruss set but have a gold border instead of blue. A yellow "Highlights" logo appears in the lower-left corner of each card front. Backs are designed on a vertical format and feature black print on a yellow background. As in 1985, the set includes Donruss' picks for the Rookies of the Year. A new feature was three cards honoring the 1986 Hall of Fame inductees. The set, available only through hobby dealers, was issued in a specially designed box. Each card can also be found with the word "Highlights" in the logo in white, a much scarcer variation that sometimes attracts significant premiums from single-player specialist collectors.

		NM/M
Complete Set (56):		3.00
Common Player:		.05
White "Highlights":		20X
1	Homers In First At-Bat (Will Clark)	.05
2	Oakland Milestone For Strikeouts (Jose Rijo)	.05
3	Royals' All-Time Hit Man (George Brett)	.50
4	Phillies RBI Leader (Mike Schmidt)	.50
5	KKKKKKKKKKKKKKKKKK (Roger Clemens)	.50
6	A.L. Pitcher of the Month-April (Roger Clemens)	.50
7	A.L. Player of the Month-April (Kirby Puckett)	.25
8	N.L. Pitcher of the Month-April (Dwight Gooden)	.05
9	N.L. Player of the Month-April (Johnny Ray)	.05
10	Eclipses Mantle HR Record (Reggie Jackson)	.50
11	First Five Hit Game of Career (Wade Boggs)	.25
12	A.L. Pitcher of the Month-May (Don Aase)	.05
13	A.L. Player of the Month-May (Wade Boggs)	.25
14	N.L. Pitcher of the Month-May (Jeff Reardon)	.05
15	N.L. Pitcher of the Month-May (Hubie Brooks)	.05
16	Notches 300th Career Win (Don Sutton)	.05
17	Starts Season 14-0 (Roger Clemens)	.50
18	A.L. Pitcher of the Month-June (Roger Clemens)	.50
19	A.L. Player of the Month-June (Kent Hrbek)	.05
20	N.L. Pitcher of the Month-June (Rick Rhoden)	.05
21	N.L. Player of the Month-June (Kevin Bass)	.05
22	Blasts 4 HRS in 1 Game (Bob Horner)	.05
23	Starting All Star Rookie (Wally Joyner)	.05
24	Starts 3rd Straight All Star Game (Darryl Strawberry)	.05
25	Ties All Star Game Record (Fernando Valenzuela)	.05
26	All Star Game MVP (Roger Clemens)	.50
27	A.L. Pitcher of the Month-July (Jack Morris)	.05
28	A.L. Player of the Month-July (Scott Fletcher)	.05
29	N.L. Pitcher of the Month-July (Todd Worrell)	.05
30	N.L. PLayer of the Month-July (Eric Davis)	.05
31	Records 3000th Strikeout (Bert Blyleven)	.05
32	1986 Hall of Fame Inductee (Bobby Doerr)	.05
33	1986 Hall of Fame Inductee (Ernie Lombardi)	.05
34	1986 Hall of Fame Inductee (Willie McCovey)	.25
35	Notches 4000th K (Steve Carlton)	.25
36	Surpasses DiMaggio Record (Mike Schmidt)	.50
37	Records 3rd "Quadruple Double" (Juan Samuel)	.05
38	A.L. Pitcher of the Month-August (Mike Witt)	.05
39	A.L. Player of the Month-August (Doug DeCinces)	.05
40	N.L. Pitcher of the Month-August (Bill Gullickson)	.05
41	N.L. Player of the Month-August (Dale Murphy)	.15
42	Sets Tribe Offensive Record (Joe Carter)	.05
43	Longest HR In Royals Stadium (George Brett)	.15
44	Majors 1st No-Hitter In 2 Years (Joe Cowley)	.05
45	Sets M.L. Strikeout Record (Jim Deshaies)	.05
46	No Hitter Clinches Division (Mike Scott)	.05
47	A.L. Pitcher of the Month-September (Bruce Hurst)	.05
48	A.L. Player of the Month-September (Don Mattingly)	.50
49	N.L. Pitcher of the Month-September (Mike Krukow)	.05
50	N.L. Player of the Month-September (Steve Sax)	.05
51	A.L. Record For Steals By A Rookie (John Cangelosi)	.05
52	Shatters M.L. Save Mark (Dave Righetti)	.05
53	Yankee Record For Hits & Doubles (Don Mattingly)	.50
54	Donruss N.L. Rookie of the Year (Todd Worrell)	.05
55	Donruss A.L. Rookie of the Year (Jose Canseco)	.50
56	Highlight Checklist	.05

1986 Donruss Pop-Ups

Issued in conjunction with the 1986 Donruss All-Stars set, the Pop-Ups (18 unnumbered cards) feature the 1985 All-Star Game starting lineups. The cards, 2-1/2" x 5", are die-cut and fold out to form a three-dimensional stand-up card. The background for the cards is the Minneapolis Metrodome, site of the 1985 All-Star Game. Retail packs included one Pop-Up card, three All-Star cards and one Hank Aaron puzzle card.

	NM/M
Complete Set (18):	4.00
Common Player:	.05

Hank Aaron Puzzle:		
Cello Pack (3):		.50
Cello Box (36):		6.00
(1)	George Brett	.75
(2)	Carlton Fisk	.40
(3)	Steve Garvey	.20
(4)	Tony Gwynn	.50
(5)	Rickey Henderson	.40
(6)	Tommy Herr	.05
(7)	LaMarr Hoyt	.05
(8)	Terry Kennedy	.05
(9)	Jack Morris	.05
(10)	Dale Murphy	.25
(11)	Eddie Murray	.40
(12)	Graig Nettles	.05
(13)	Jim Rice	.25
(14)	Cal Ripken, Jr.	1.00
(15)	Ozzie Smith	.50
(16)	Darryl Strawberry	.05
(17)	Lou Whitaker	.05
(18)	Dave Winfield	.40

Rookies

Entitled "The Rookies," this 56-card set includes the top 55 rookies of 1986 plus an unnumbered checklist. The cards are similar in format to the 1986 Donruss regular issue, except that the borders are green rather than blue. Several of the rookies who had cards in the regular 1986 Donruss set appear again in "The Rookies" set. The sets, which were only available through hobby dealers, came in a specially designed box.

		NM/M
Unopened Set (56):		35.00
Opened Set (56):		30.00
Common Player:		.05
1	Wally Joyner RC	.50
2	Tracy Jones	.05
3	Allan Anderson	.05
4	Ed Correa	.05
5	Reggie Williams	.05
6	Charlie Kerfeld	.05
7	Andres Galarraga	.15
8	Bob Tewksbury	.05
9	Al Newman	.05
10	Andres Thomas	.05
11	Barry Bonds RC	25.00
12	Juan Nieves	.05
13	Mark Eichhorn	.05
14	Dan Plesac	.05
15	Cory Snyder	.05
16	Kelly Gruber	.05
17	Kevin Mitchell RC	.25
18	Steve Lombardozzi	.05
19	Mitch Williams	.05
20	John Cerutti	.05
21	Todd Worrell	.05
22	Jose Canseco	2.00
23	Pete Incaviglia RC	.15
24	Jose Guzman	.05
25	Scott Bailes	.05
26	Greg Mathews	.05
27	Eric King	.05
28	Paul Assenmacher	.05
29	Jeff Sellers	.05
30	Bobby Bonilla RC	.25
31	Doug Drabek RC	.05
32	Will Clark RC	1.00
33	Bip Roberts	.05
34	Jim Deshaies	.05
35	Mike LaValliere	.05
36	Scott Bankhead	.05
37	Dale Sveum	.05
38	Bo Jackson RC	2.00
39	Rob Thompson	.05
40	Eric Plunk	.05
41	Bill Bathe	.05
42	John Kruk RC	.25
43	Andy Allanson	.05
44	Mark Portugal	.05
45	Danny Tartabull	.05
46	Bob Kipper	.05
47	Gene Walter	.05
48	Rey Quinonez	.05
49	Bobby Witt	.05
50	Bill Mooneyham	.05
51	John Cangelosi	.05
52	Ruben Sierra RC	.25
53	Rob Woodward	.05
54	Ed Hearn	.05
55	Joel McKeon	.05
56	Checklist 1-56	.05

1987 Donruss

LANCE McCULLERS P

The 1987 Donruss set consists of 660 numbered cards, each measuring 2-1/2" x 3-1/2". Color photos are surrounded by a bold black border separated by two narrow bands of yellow which enclose a brown area filled with baseballs. The player's name, team and team logo appear on the card fronts along with the words "Donruss '87." The card backs are designed on a horizontal format and contain black print on a yellow and white background. The backs are very similar to those in previous years' sets. Backs of cards issued in wax and rack packs face to the left when turned over, while those issued in factory sets face to the right. Cards were sold with Roberto Clemente puzzle pieces in each pack. Cards checklisted with a (DK) suffix are Diamond Kings; cards with an (RR) suffix are Rated Rookies.

		NM/M
Unopened Fact. Set (660):		40.00
Complete Set (660):		30.00
Common Player:		.05
Roberto Clemente Puzzle:		2.50
Wax Pack (15):		1.25
Wax Box (36):		35.00
Rack Pack (45):		3.00
Jumbo Rack (75):		4.00
1	Wally Joyner (DK)	.25
2	Roger Clemens (DK)	1.00
3	Dale Murphy (DK)	.25
4	Darryl Strawberry (DK)	.10
5	Ozzie Smith (DK)	.75
6	Jose Canseco (DK)	.40
7	Charlie Hough (DK)	.05
8	Brook Jacoby (DK)	.05
9	Fred Lynn (DK)	.10
10	Rick Rhoden (DK)	.05
11	Chris Brown (DK)	.05
12	Von Hayes (DK)	.05
13	Jack Morris (DK)	.05
14a	Kevin McReynolds (DK) (No yellow stripe on back.)	.25
14b	Kevin McReynolds (DK) (Yellow stripe on back.)	.25
15	George Brett (DK)	1.00
16	Ted Higuera (DK)	.05
17	Hubie Brooks (DK)	.05
18	Mike Scott (DK)	.05
19	Kirby Puckett (DK)	.75
20	Dave Winfield (DK)	.60
21	Lloyd Moseby (DK)	.05
22a	Eric Davis (DK) (No yellow stripe on back.)	.25
22b	Eric Davis (DK) (Yellow stripe on back.)	.15
23	Jim Presley (DK)	.05
24	Keith Moreland (DK)	.05
25a	Greg Walker (DK) (No yellow stripe on back.)	.25
25b	Greg Walker (DK) (Yellow stripe on back.)	.10
26	Steve Sax (DK)	.10
27	Checklist 1-27	.05
28	B.J. Surhoff (RR)	.30
29	Randy Myers RC (RR)	.50
30	Ken Gerhart RC (RR)	.05
31	Benito Santiago (RR)	.15
32	Greg Swindell RC (RR)	.15
33	Mike Birkbeck RC (RR)	.05
34	Terry Steinbach RC (RR)	.15
35	Bo Jackson (RR)	1.50
36	Greg Maddux RC (RR)	8.00
37	Jim Lindeman RC (RR)	.05
38	Devon White RC (RR)	.75
39	Eric Bell RC (RR)	.05
40	Will Fraser RC (RR)	.05
41	Jerry Browne RC (RR)	.05
42	Chris James RC (RR)	.05
43	Rafael Palmeiro RC (RR)	4.00
44	Pat Dodson RC (RR)	.05
45	Duane Ward RC (RR)	.10
46	Mark McGwire RC (RR)	6.00
47	Bruce Fields RC (RR) (Photo actually Darnell Coles.)	.10
48	Eddie Murray	.60
49	Ted Higuera	.05
50	Kirk Gibson	.05
51	Oil Can Boyd	.05
52	Don Mattingly	1.00
53	Pedro Guerrero	.05
54	George Brett	1.00
55	Jose Rijo	.05
56	Tim Raines	.05
57	Ed Correa RC	.05
58	Mike Witt	.05
59	Greg Walker	.05
60	Ozzie Smith	.75
61	Glenn Davis	.05
62	Glenn Wilson	.05
63	Tom Browning	.05
64	Tony Gwynn	.75
65	R.J. Reynolds	.05
66	Will Clark	.25
67	Ozzie Virgil	.05
68	Rick Sutcliffe	.05
69	Gary Carter	.60
70	Mike Moore	.05
71	Bert Blyleven	.10
72	Tony Fernandez	.05
73	Kent Hrbek	.05
74	Lloyd Moseby	.05
75	Alvin Davis	.05
76	Keith Hernandez	.05
77	Ryne Sandberg	.60
78	Dale Murphy	.40
79	Sid Bream	.05
80	Chris Brown	.05
81	Steve Garvey	.25
82	Mario Soto	.05
83	Shane Rawley	.05
84	Willie McGee	.05
85	Jose Cruz	.05
86	Brian Downing	.05
87	Ozzie Guillen	.05
88	Hubie Brooks	.05
89	Cal Ripken, Jr.	2.50
90	Juan Nieves	.05
91	Lance Parrish	.05
92	Jim Rice	.25
93	Ron Guidry	.10
94	Fernando Valenzuela	.05
95	Andy Allanson RC	.05
96	Willie Wilson	.05
97	Jose Canseco	.40
98	Jeff Reardon	.05
99	Bobby Witt RC	.20
100	Checklist 28-133	.05
101	Jose Guzman	.05
102	Steve Balboni	.05
103	Tony Phillips	.05
104	Brook Jacoby	.05
105	Dave Winfield	.60
106	Orel Hershiser	.05
107	Lou Whitaker	.05
108	Fred Lynn	.05
109	Bill Wegman	.05
110	Donnie Moore	.05
111	Jack Clark	.05
112	Bob Knepper	.05
113	Von Hayes	.05
114	Bip Roberts RC	.25
115	Tony Pena	.05
116	Scott Garrelts	.05
117	Paul Molitor	.60
118	Darryl Strawberry	.05
119	Shawon Dunston	.05
120	Jim Presley	.05
121	Jesse Barfield	.05
122	Gary Gaetti	.05
123	Kurt Stillwell RC	.10
124	Joel Davis	.05
125	Mike Boddicker	.05
126	Robin Yount	.60
127	Alan Trammell	.05
128	Dave Righetti	.05
129	Dwight Evans	.05
130	Mike Scioscia	.05
131	Julio Franco	.05
132	Bret Saberhagen	.05
133	Mike Davis	.05
134	Joe Hesketh	.05
135	Wally Joyner	.05
136	Don Slaught	.05
137	Daryl Boston	.05
138	Nolan Ryan	2.50
139	Mike Schmidt	1.00
140	Tommy Herr	.05
141	Garry Templeton	.05
142	Kal Daniels	.05
143	Billy Sample	.05
144	Johnny Ray	.05
145	Rob Thompson RC	.10
146	Bob Dernier	.05
147	Danny Tartabull	.05
148	Ernie Whitt	.05
149	Kirby Puckett	.75
150	Mike Young	.05
151	Ernest Riles	.05
152	Frank Tanana	.05
153	Rich Gedman	.05
154	Willie Randolph	.05
155a	Bill Madlock (Name in brown band.)	.10
155b	Bill Madlock (Name in red band.)	.25
156a	Joe Carter (Name in brown band.)	.10
156b	Joe Carter (Name in red band.)	.25
157	Danny Jackson	.05
158	Carney Lansford	.05
159	Bryn Smith	.05
160	Gary Pettis	.05
161	Oddibe McDowell	.05
162	John Cangelosi RC	.10
163	Mike Scott	.05
164	Eric Show	.05
165	Juan Samuel	.05
166	Nick Esasky	.05
167	Zane Smith	.05
168	Mike Brown	.05
169	Keith Moreland	.05
170	John Tudor	.05
171	Ken Dixon	.05
172	Jim Gantner	.05
173	Jack Morris	.05
174	Bruce Hurst	.05
175	Dennis Rasmussen	.05
176	Mike Marshall	.05
177	Dan Quisenberry	.05
178	Eric Plunk	.05
179	Tim Wallach	.05
180	Steve Buechele	.05
181	Don Sutton	.50
182	Dave Schmidt	.05
183	Terry Pendleton	.05
184	Jim Deshaies RC	.05
185	Steve Bedrosian	.05
186	Pete Rose	2.00
187	Dave Dravecky	.05
188	Rick Reuschel	.05
189	Dan Gladden	.05
190	Rick Mahler	.05
191	Thad Bosley	.05
192	Ron Darling	.05
193	Matt Young	.05
194	Tom Brunansky	.05
195	Dave Stieb	.05
196	Frank Viola	.05
197	Tom Henke	.05
198	Karl Best	.05
199	Dwight Gooden	.05
200	Checklist 134-239	.05
201	Steve Trout	.05
202	Rafael Ramirez	.05
203	Bob Walk	.05
204	Roger Mason	.05
205	Terry Kennedy	.05
206	Ron Oester	.05
207	John Russell	.05
208	Greg Mathews RC	.05
209	Charlie Kerfeld	.05
210	Reggie Jackson	1.00
211	Floyd Bannister	.05
212	Vance Law	.05
213	Rich Bordi	.05
214	Dan Plesac RC	.10
215	Dave Collins	.05
216	Bob Stanley	.05
217	Joe Niekro	.05
218	Tom Niedenfuer	.05
219	Brett Butler	.05
220	Charlie Leibrandt	.05
221	Steve Ontiveros	.05
222	Tim Burke	.05
223	Curtis Wilkerson	.05
224	Pete Incaviglia RC	.10
225	Lonnie Smith	.05
226	Chris Codiroli	.05
227	Scott Bailes RC	.05
228	Rickey Henderson	.60
229	Ken Howell	.05
230	Darnell Coles	.05
231	Don Aase	.05
232	Tim Leary	.05
233	Bob Boone	.05
234	Ricky Horton	.05
235	Mark Bailey	.05
236	Kevin Gross	.05
237	Lance McCullers	.05
238	Cecilio Guante	.05
239	Bob Melvin	.05
240	Billy Jo Robidoux	.05
241	Roger McDowell	.05
242	Leon Durham	.05
243	Ed Nunez	.05
244	Jimmy Key	.05
245	Mike Smithson	.05
246	Bo Diaz	.05
247	Carlton Fisk	.60
248	Larry Sheets	.05
249	Juan Castillo RC	.05
250	Eric King RC	.05
251	Doug Drabek	.05
252	Wade Boggs	.75
253	Mariano Duncan	.05
254	Pat Tabler	.05
255	Frank White	.05
256	Alfredo Griffin	.05
257	Floyd Youmans	.05
258	Rob Wilfong	.05
259	Pete O'Brien	.05
260	Tim Hulett	.05
261	Dickie Thon	.05
262	Darren Daulton	.05
263	Vince Coleman	.05
264	Andy Hawkins	.05
265	Eric Davis	.05
266	Andres Thomas RC	.05
267	Mike Diaz RC	.05
268	Chili Davis	.05
269	Jody Davis	.05
270	Phil Bradley	.05
271	George Bell	.05
272	Keith Atherton	.05
273	Storm Davis	.05
274	Rob Deer	.05
275	Walt Terrell	.05
276	Roger Clemens	1.00
277	Mike Easler	.05
278	Steve Sax	.05
279	Andre Thornton	.05

#	Player	Price
280	Jim Sundberg	.05
281	Bill Bathe	.05
282	Jay Tibbs	.05
283	Dick Schofield	.05
284	Mike Mason	.05
285	Jerry Hairston Sr.	.05
286	Bill Doran	.05
287	Tim Flannery	.05
288	Gary Redus	.05
289	John Franco	.05
290	Paul Assenmacher RC	.10
291	Joe Orsulak	.05
292	Lee Smith	.10
293	Mike Laga	.05
294	Rick Dempsey	.05
295	Mike Felder	.05
296	Tom Brookens	.05
297	Al Nipper	.05
298	Mike Pagliarulo	.05
299	Franklin Stubbs	.05
300	Checklist 240-345	.05
301	Steve Farr	.05
302	Bill Mooneyham RC	.05
303	Andres Galarraga	.05
304	Scott Fletcher	.05
305	Jack Howell	.05
306	Russ Morman RC	.05
307	Todd Worrell	.05
308	Dave Smith	.05
309	Jeff Stone	.05
310	Ron Robinson	.05
311	Bruce Bochy	.05
312	Jim Winn	.05
313	Mark Davis	.05
314	Jeff Dedmon	.05
315	Jamie Moyer RC	.10
316	Wally Backman	.05
317	Ken Phelps	.05
318	Steve Lombardozzi	.05
319	Rance Mulliniks	.05
320	Tim Laudner	.05
321	Mark Eichhorn RC	.10
322	Lee Guetterman RC	.05
323	Sid Fernandez	.05
324	Jerry Mumphrey	.05
325	David Palmer	.05
326	Bill Almon	.05
327	Candy Maldonado	.05
328	John Kruk	.05
329	John Denny	.05
330	Milt Thompson	.05
331	Mike LaValliere RC	.10
332	Alan Ashby	.05
333	Doug Corbett	.05
334	Ron Karkovice RC	.05
335	Mitch Webster	.05
336	Lee Lacy	.05
337	Glenn Braggs RC	.05
338	Dwight Lowry	.05
339	Don Baylor	.05
340	Brian Fisher	.05
341	Reggie Williams RC	.05
342	Tom Candiotti	.05
343	Rudy Law	.05
344	Curt Young	.05
345	Mike Fitzgerald	.05
346	Ruben Sierra	.25
347	Mitch Williams RC	.25
348	Jorge Orta	.05
349	Mickey Tettleton	.05
350	Ernie Camacho	.05
351	Ron Kittle	.05
352	Ken Landreaux	.05
353	Chet Lemon	.05
354	John Shelby	.05
355	Mark Clear	.05
356	Doug DeCinces	.05
357	Ken Dayley	.05
358	Phil Garner	.05
359	Steve Jeltz	.05
360	Ed Whitson	.05
361	Barry Bonds	10.00
362	Vida Blue	.05
363	Cecil Cooper	.05
364	Bob Ojeda	.05
365	Dennis Eckersley	.50
366	Mike Morgan	.05
367	Willie Upshaw	.05
368	Allan Anderson RC	.05
369	Bill Gullickson	.05
370	Bobby Thigpen RC	.10
371	Juan Beniquez	.05
372	Charlie Moore	.05
373	Dan Petry	.05
374	Rod Scurry	.05
375	Tom Seaver	.75
376	Ed Vande Berg	.05
377	Tony Bernazard	.05
378	Greg Pryor	.05
379	Dwayne Murphy	.05
380	Andy McGaffigan	.05
381	Kirk McCaskill	.05
382	Greg Harris	.05
383	Rich Dotson	.05
384	Craig Reynolds	.05
385	Greg Gross	.05
386	Tito Landrum	.05
387	Craig Lefferts	.05
388	Dave Parker	.05
389	Bob Horner	.05
390	Pat Clements	.05
391	Jeff Leonard	.05
392	Chris Speier	.05
393	John Moses	.05
394	Garth Iorg	.05
395	Greg Gagne	.05
396	Nate Snell	.05
397	Bryan Clutterbuck RC	.05
398	Darrell Evans	.05
399	Steve Crawford	.05
400	Checklist 346-451	.05
401	Phil Lombardi RC	.05
402	Rick Honeycutt	.05
403	Ken Schrom	.05
404	Bud Black	.05
405	Donnie Hill	.05
406	Wayne Krenchicki	.05
407	Chuck Finley RC	.35
408	Toby Harrah	.05
409	Steve Lyons	.05
410	Kevin Bass	.05
411	Marvell Wynne	.05
412	Ron Roenicke	.05
413	Tracy Jones RC	.05
414	Gene Garber	.05
415	Mike Bielecki	.05
416	Frank DiPino	.05
417	Andy Van Slyke	.05
418	Jim Dwyer	.05
419	Ben Oglivie	.05
420	Dave Bergman	.05
421	Joe Sambito	.05
422	Bob Tewksbury RC	.30
423	Len Matuszek	.05
424	Mike Kingery RC	.05
425	Dave Kingman	.05
426	Al Newman RC	.05
427	Gary Ward	.05
428	Ruppert Jones	.05
429	Harold Baines	.05
430	Pat Perry	.05
431	Terry Puhl	.05
432	Don Carman	.05
433	Eddie Milner	.05
434	LaMarr Hoyt	.05
435	Rick Rhoden	.05
436	Jose Uribe	.05
437	Ken Oberkfell	.05
438	Ron Davis	.05
439	Jesse Orosco	.05
440	Scott Bradley	.05
441	Randy Bush	.05
442	John Cerutti RC	.05
443	Roy Smalley	.05
444	Kelly Gruber	.05
445	Bob Kearney	.05
446	Ed Hearn RC	.05
447	Scott Sanderson	.05
448	Bruce Benedict	.05
449	Junior Ortiz	.05
450	Mike Aldrete RC	.05
451	Kevin McReynolds	.05
452	Rob Murphy RC	.05
453	Kent Tekulve	.05
454	Curt Ford	.05
455	Davey Lopes	.05
456	Bobby Grich	.05
457	Jose DeLeon	.05
458	Andre Dawson	.35
459	Mike Flanagan	.05
460	Joey Meyer RC	.05
461	Chuck Cary RC	.05
462	Bill Buckner	.05
463	Bob Shirley	.05
464	Jeff Hamilton RC	.05
465	Phil Niekro	.50
466	Mark Gubicza	.05
467	Jerry Willard	.05
468	Bob Sebra RC	.05
469	Larry Parrish	.05
470	Charlie Hough	.05
471	Hal McRae	.05
472	Dave Leiper RC	.05
473	Mel Hall	.05
474	Dan Pasqua	.05
475	Bob Welch	.05
476	Johnny Grubb	.05
477	Jim Traber	.05
478	Chris Bosio RC	.05
479	Mark McLemore	.05
480	John Morris	.05
481	Billy Hatcher	.05
482	Dan Schatzeder	.05
483	Rich Gossage	.10
484	Jim Morrison	.05
485	Bob Brenly	.05
486	Bill Schroeder	.05
487	Mookie Wilson	.05
488	Dave Martinez RC	.10
489	Harold Reynolds	.05
490	Jeff Hearron	.05
491	Mickey Hatcher	.05
492	Barry Larkin RC	2.00
493	Bob James	.05
494	John Habyan	.05
495	Jim Adduci RC	.05
496	Mike Heath	.05
497	Tim Stoddard	.05
498	Tony Armas	.05
499	Dennis Powell	.05
500	Checklist 452-557	.05
501	Chris Bando	.05
502	David Cone RC	2.00
503	Jay Howell	.05
504	Tom Foley	.05
505	Ray Chadwick RC	.05
506	Mike Loynd RC	.05
507	Neil Allen	.05
508	Danny Darwin	.05
509	Rick Schu	.05
510	Jose Oquendo	.05
511	Gene Walter	.05
512	Terry McGriff RC	.05
513	Ken Griffey	.05
514	Benny Distefano	.05
515	Terry Mulholland RC	.25
516	Ed Lynch	.05
517	Bill Swift	.05
518	Manny Lee	.05
519	Andre David	.05
520	Scott McGregor	.05
521	Rick Manning	.05
522	Willie Hernandez	.05
523	Marty Barrett	.05
524	Wayne Tolleson	.05
525	Jose Gonzalez RC	.05
526	Cory Snyder	.05
527	Buddy Biancalana	.05
528	Moose Haas	.05
529	Wilfredo Tejada RC	.05
530	Stu Cliburn	.05
531	Dale Mohorcic RC	.05
532	Ron Hassey	.05
533	Ty Gainey	.05
534	Jerry Royster	.05
535	Mike Maddux RC	.05
536	Ted Power	.05
537	Ted Simmons	.05
538	Rafael Belliard RC	.05
539	Chico Walker	.05
540	Bob Forsch	.05
541	John Stefero	.05
542	Dale Sveum RC	.05
543	Mark Thurmond	.05
544	Jeff Sellers RC	.05
545	Joel Skinner	.05
546	Alex Trevino	.05
547	Randy Kutcher RC	.05
548	Joaquin Andujar	.05
549	Casey Candaele RC	.10
550	Jeff Russell	.05
551	John Candelaria	.05
552	Joe Cowley	.05
553	Danny Cox	.05
554	Denny Walling	.05
555	Bruce Ruffin RC	.10
556	Buddy Bell	.05
557	Jimmy Jones RC	.05
558	Bobby Bonilla	.05
559	Jeff Robinson	.05
560	Ed Olwine	.05
561	Glenallen Hill RC	.25
562	Lee Mazzilli	.05
563	Mike Brown	.05
564	George Frazier	.05
565	Mike Sharperson RC	.10
566	Mark Portugal RC	.05
567	Rick Leach	.05
568	Mark Langston	.05
569	Rafael Santana	.05
570	Manny Trillo	.05
571	Cliff Speck	.05
572	Bob Kipper	.05
573	Kelly Downs RC	.05
574	Randy Asadoor RC	.05
575	Dave Magadan RC	.25
576	Marvin Freeman RC	.05
577	Jeff Lahti	.05
578	Jeff Calhoun	.05
579	Gus Polidor	.05
580	Gene Nelson	.05
581	Tim Teufel	.05
582	Odell Jones	.05
583	Mark Ryal	.05
584	Randy O'Neal	.05
585	Mike Greenwell RC	.50
586	Ray Knight	.05
587	Ralph Bryant RC	.15
588	Carmen Castillo	.05
589	Ed Wojna	.05
590	Stan Javier	.05
591	Jeff Musselman RC	.05
592	Mike Stanley RC	.05
593	Darrell Porter	.05
594	Drew Hall RC	.05
595	Rob Nelson RC	.05
596	Bryan Oelkers	.05
597	Scott Nielsen RC	.05
598	Brian Holton RC	.05
599	Kevin Mitchell RC	.05
600	Checklist 558-660	.05
601	Jackie Gutierrez	.05
602	Barry Jones RC	.05
603	Jerry Narron	.05
604	Steve Lake	.05
605	Jim Pankovits	.05
606	Ed Romero	.05
607	Dave LaPoint	.05
608	Don Robinson	.05
609	Mike Krukow	.05
610	Dave Valle RC	.05
611	Len Dykstra	.05
612	Roberto Clemente Puzzle Card	.25
613	Mike Trujillo	.05
614	Damaso Garcia	.05
615	Neal Heaton	.05
616	Juan Berenguer	.05
617	Steve Carlton	.75
618	Gary Lucas	.05
619	Geno Petralli	.05
620	Rick Aguilera	.05
621	Fred McGriff	.05
622	Dave Henderson	.05
623	Dave Clark RC	.05
624	Angel Salazar	.05
625	Randy Hunt	.05
626	John Gibbons	.05
627	Kevin Brown RC	2.00
628	Bill Dawley	.05
629	Aurelio Lopez	.05
630	Charlie Hudson	.05
631	Ray Soff	.05
632	Ray Hayward RC	.05
633	Spike Owen	.05
634	Glenn Hubbard	.05
635	Kevin Elster RC	.10
636	Mike LaCoss	.05
637	Dwayne Henry	.05
638	Rey Quinones RC	.05
639	Jim Clancy	.05
640	Larry Andersen	.05
641	Calvin Schiraldi	.05
642	Stan Jefferson RC	.05
643	Marc Sullivan	.05
644	Mark Grant	.05
645	Cliff Johnson	.05
646	Howard Johnson	.05
647	Dave Sax	.05
648	Dave Stewart	.05
649	Danny Heep	.05
650	Joe Johnson	.05
651	Bob Brower RC	.05
652	Rob Woodward	.05
653	John Mizerock	.05
654	Tim Pyznarski RC	.05
655	Luis Aquino RC	.05
656	Mickey Brantley	.05
657	Doyle Alexander	.05
658	Sammy Stewart	.05
659	Jim Acker	.05
660	Pete Ladd	.05

1987 Donruss Box Panels

Continuing with an idea they initiated in 1985, Donruss once again placed baseball cards on the bottoms of their retail boxes. The cards, which are 2-1/2" x 3-1/2" in size, come four to a panel with each panel containing an unnumbered Roberto Clemente puzzle card. With numbering that begins where Donruss left off in 1986, cards PC 10 through PC 12 were found on boxes of Donruss regular issue wax packs. Cards PC 13 through PC 15 were located on boxes of the 1987 All-Star/Pop-Up packs.

		NM/M
Complete Panel Set (2):		4.00
Complete Singles Set (8):		4.00
Common Single Player:		.15
Panel		1.50
10	Dale Murphy	.40
11	Jeff Reardon	.15
12	Jose Canseco	.60
----	Roberto Clemente Puzzle Card	.15
Panel		3.00
13	Mike Scott	.15
14	Roger Clemens	2.00
15	Mike Krukow	.15
----	Roberto Clemente Puzzle Card	.15

1987 Donruss All-Stars

Issued in conjunction with the Donruss Pop-Ups set for the second consecutive year, the 1987 Donruss All-Stars consist of 59 players (plus a checklist) who were selected to the 1986 All-Star Game. Measuring 3-1/2" x 5" in size, the card fronts feature black borders and American or National League logos. Included on back are the player's career highlights and All-Star Game statistics. Retail packs included one Pop-Up card, three All-Star cards and one Roberto Clemente puzzle card.

		NM/M
Complete Set (60):		4.00
Common Player:		.05
Roberto Clemente Puzzle:		2.50
Wax Pack:		.35
Wax Box (48):		5.00
1	Wally Joyner	.05
2	Dave Winfield	.40
3	Lou Whitaker	.05
4	Kirby Puckett	.50
5	Cal Ripken, Jr.	1.00
6	Rickey Henderson	.40
7	Wade Boggs	.50
8	Roger Clemens	.65
9	Lance Parrish	.05
10	Dick Howser	.05
11	Keith Hernandez	.05
12	Darryl Strawberry	.05
13	Ryne Sandberg	.50
14	Dale Murphy	.25
15	Ozzie Smith	.50
16	Tony Gwynn	.50
17	Mike Schmidt	.65
18	Dwight Gooden	.05
19	Gary Carter	.40
20	Whitey Herzog	.05
21	Jose Canseco	.25
22	John Franco	.05
23	Jesse Barfield	.05
24	Rick Rhoden	.05
25	Harold Baines	.05
26	Sid Fernandez	.05
27	George Brett	.65
28	Steve Sax	.05
29	Jim Presley	.05
30	Dave Smith	.05
31	Eddie Murray	.40
32	Mike Scott	.05
33	Don Mattingly	.65
34	Dave Parker	.05
35	Tony Fernandez	.05
36	Tim Raines	.05
37	Brook Jacoby	.05
38	Chili Davis	.05
39	Rich Gedman	.05
40	Kevin Bass	.05
41	Frank White	.05
42	Glenn Davis	.05
43	Willie Hernandez	.05
44	Chris Brown	.05
45	Jim Rice	.25
46	Tony Pena	.05
47	Don Aase	.05
48	Hubie Brooks	.05
49	Charlie Hough	.05
50	Jody Davis	.05
51	Mike Witt	.05
52	Jeff Reardon	.05
53	Ken Schrom	.05
54	Fernando Valenzuela	.05
55	Dave Righetti	.05
56	Shane Rawley	.05
57	Ted Higuera	.05
58	Mike Krukow	.05
59	Lloyd Moseby	.05
60	Checklist	.05

1987 Donruss Diamond Kings Supers

For a third season, Donruss produced a set of enlarged Diamond Kings, measuring 4-11/16" x 6-3/4". The 28-cards feature the artwork of Dick Perez, and contain 26 player cards, a checklist and a Roberto Clemente puzzle card. The set was available through a mail-in offer for $9.50 plus three wrappers.

		NM/M
Complete Set (28):		5.00
Common Player:		.15
1	Wally Joyner	.15
2	Roger Clemens	1.50
3	Dale Murphy	.30
4	Darryl Strawberry	.15
5	Ozzie Smith	1.00
6	Jose Canseco	.30
7	Charlie Hough	.15
8	Brook Jacoby	.15
9	Fred Lynn	.15
10	Rick Rhoden	.15
11	Chris Brown	.15
12	Von Hayes	.15
13	Jack Morris	.15
14	Kevin McReynolds	.15
15	George Brett	1.50
16	Ted Higuera	.15
17	Hubie Brooks	.15
18	Mike Scott	.15
19	Kirby Puckett	1.00
20	Dave Winfield	.60
21	Lloyd Moseby	.15
22	Eric Davis	.15
23	Jim Presley	.15
24	Keith Moreland	.15
25	Greg Walker	.15
26	Steve Sax	.15
27	Checklist	.05
---	Roberto Clemente Puzzle Card	.50

1987 Donruss Highlights

For a third consecutive year, Donruss produced a 56-card set which highlighted the special events of the 1987 baseball season. The 2-1/2" x 3-1/2" cards feature a front design similar to the regular 1987 Donruss set. A blue border and the "Highlights" logo are the significant differences. The backs feature black print on a white background and include the date the event took place plus the particulars. As in the past, the set includes Donruss' picks for the A.L. and N.L. Rookies of the Year. The set was issued in a specially designed box and was available only through hobby dealers.

		NM/M
Complete Set (56):		3.00
Common Player:		.05
1	First No-Hitter For Brewers (Juan Nieves)	.05
2	Hits 500th Homer (Mike Schmidt)	.35
3	N.L. Player of the Month - April (Eric Davis)	
4	N.L. Pitcher of the Month - April (Sid Fernandez)	.05
5	A.L. Player of the Month - April (Brian Downing)	.05
6	A.L. Pitcher of the Month - April (Bret Saberhagen)	.05
7	Free Agent Holdout Returns (Tim Raines)	.05
8	N.L. Player of the Month - May (Eric Davis)	.05
9	N.L. Pitcher of the Month - May (Steve Bedrosian)	.05
10	A.L. Player of the Month - May (Larry Parrish)	.05
11	A.L. Pitcher of the Month - May (Jim Clancy)	.05
12	N.L. Player of the Month - June (Tony Gwynn)	.25
13	N.L. Pitcher of the Month - June (Orel Hershiser)	.05
14	A.L. Player of the Month - June (Wade Boggs)	.25
15	A.L. Pitcher of the Month - June (Steve Ontiveros)	.05
16	All Star Game Hero (Tim Raines)	
17	Consecutive Game Homer Streak (Don Mattingly)	.35
18	1987 Hall of Fame Inductee (Jim "Catfish" Hunter)	.10
19	1987 Hall of Fame Inductee (Ray Dandridge)	.10
20	1987 Hall of Fame Inductee (Billy Williams)	.10
21	N.L. Player of the Month - July (Bo Diaz)	
22	N.L. Pitcher of the Month - July (Floyd Youmans)	
23	A.L. Player of the Month - July (Don Mattingly)	.05
24	A.L. Pitcher of the Month - July (Frank Viola)	.05
25	Strikes Out 4 Batters In 1 Inning (Bobby Witt)	.05

26	Ties A.L. 9-Inning Game Hit Mark (Kevin Seitzer)	.05
27	Sets Rookie Home Run Record (Mark McGwire)	.50
28	Sets Cubs' 1st Year Homer Mark (Andre Dawson)	.05
29	Hits In 39 Straight Games (Paul Molitor)	.15
30	Record Weekend (Kirby Puckett)	.25
31	N.L. Player of the Month - August (Andre Dawson)	.05
32	N.L. Pitcher of the Month - August (Doug Drabek)	.05
33	A.L. Player of the Month - August (Dwight Evans)	.05
34	A.L. Pitcher of the Month - August (Mark Langston)	.05
35	100 RBI In 1st 2 Major League Seasons (Wally Joyner)	.05
36	100 SB In 1st 3 Major League Seasons (Vince Coleman)	.05
37	Orioles' All Time Homer King (Eddie Murray)	.15
38	Ends Consecutive Innings Streak (Cal Ripken)	.50
39	Blue Jays Hit Record 10 Homers In 1 Game (Rob Ducey, Fred McGriff, Ernie Whitt)	.05
40	Equal A's RBI Marks (Jose Canseco, Mark McGwire)	.35
41	Sets All-Time Catching Record (Bob Boone)	.05
42	Sets Mets' One-Season HR Mark (Darryl Strawberry)	.05
43	N.L.'s All-Time Switch Hit HR King (Howard Johnson)	.05
44	Five Straight 200-Hit Seasons (Wade Boggs)	.25
45	Eclipses Rookie Game Hitting Streak (Benito Santiago)	.05
46	Eclipses Jackson's A's HR Record (Mark McGwire)	.45
47	13th Rookie To Collect 200 Hits (Kevin Seitzer)	.05
48	Sets Slam Record (Don Mattingly)	.35
49	N.L. Player of the Month - September (Darryl Strawberry)	.05
50	N.L. Pitcher of the Month - September (Pascual Perez)	.05
51	A.L. Player of the Month - September (Alan Trammell)	.05
52	A.L. Pitcher of the Month - September (Doyle Alexander)	.05
53	Strikeout King - Again (Nolan Ryan)	.15
54	Donruss A.L. Rookie of the Year (Mark McGwire)	.50
55	Donruss N.L. Rookie of the Year (Benito Santiago)	.05
56	Highlight Checklist	.05

1987 Donruss Opening Day

The Donruss Opening Day set includes all players in major league baseball's starting lineups on the opening day of the 1987 baseball season. Cards in the 272-piece set measure 2-1/2" x 3-1/2" and have a glossy coating. The fronts are identical in design to the regular Donruss set, but new photos were utilized along with maroon borders as opposed to black. The backs carry black printing on white and yellow and offer a brief player biography plus the player's career statistics. The set was packaged in a sturdy 15" by 5" by 2" box with a clear acetate lid.

		NM/M
Unopened Fact. Set (272):		25.00
Complete Set (272):		12.00
Common Player:		.10
1	Doug DeCinces	.10
2	Mike Witt	.10
3	George Hendrick	.10
4	Dick Schofield	.10

5	Devon White	.10
6	Butch Wynegar	.10
7	Wally Joyner	.10
8	Mark McLemore	.10
9	Brian Downing	.10
10	Gary Pettis	.10
11	Bill Doran	.10
12	Phil Garner	.10
13	Jose Cruz	.10
14	Kevin Bass	.10
15	Mike Scott	.10
16	Glenn Davis	.10
17	Alan Ashby	.10
18	Billy Hatcher	.10
19	Craig Reynolds	.10
20	Carney Lansford	.10
21	Mike Davis	.10
22	Reggie Jackson	.75
23	Mickey Tettleton	.10
24	Jose Canseco	.35
25	Rob Nelson	.10
26	Tony Phillips	.10
27	Dwayne Murphy	.10
28	Alfredo Griffin	.10
29	Curt Young	.10
30	Willie Upshaw	.10
31	Mike Sharperson	.10
32	Rance Mulliniks	.10
33	Ernie Whitt	.10
34	Jesse Barfield	.10
35	Tony Fernandez	.10
36	Lloyd Moseby	.10
37	Jimmy Key	.10
38	Fred McGriff	.10
39	George Bell	.10
40	Dale Murphy	.25
41	Rick Mahler	.10
42	Ken Griffey	.10
43	Andres Thomas	.10
44	Dion James	.10
45	Ozzie Virgil	.10
46	Ken Oberkfell	.10
47	Gary Roenicke	.10
48	Glenn Hubbard	.10
49	Bill Schroeder	.10
50	Greg Brock	.10
51	Billy Jo Robidoux	.10
52	Glenn Braggs	.10
53	Jim Gantner	.10
54	Paul Molitor	.50
55	Dale Sveum	.10
56	Ted Higuera	.10
57	Rob Deer	.10
58	Robin Yount	.50
59	Jim Lindeman	.10
60	Vince Coleman	.10
61	Tommy Herr	.10
62	Terry Pendleton	.10
63	John Tudor	.10
64	Tony Pena	.10
65	Ozzie Smith	.60
66	Tito Landrum	.10
67	Jack Clark	.10
68	Bob Dernier	.10
69	Rick Sutcliffe	.10
70	Andre Dawson	.30
71	Keith Moreland	.10
72	Jody Davis	.10
73	Brian Dayett	.10
74	Leon Durham	.10
75	Ryne Sandberg	.60
76	Shawon Dunston	.10
77	Mike Marshall	.10
78	Bill Madlock	.10
79	Orel Hershiser	.10
80	Mike Ramsey	.10
81	Ken Landreaux	.10
82	Mike Scioscia	.10
83	Franklin Stubbs	.10
84	Mariano Duncan	.10
85	Steve Sax	.10
86	Mitch Webster	.10
87	Reid Nichols	.10
88	Tim Wallach	.10
89	Floyd Youmans	.10
90	Andres Galarraga	.10
91	Hubie Brooks	.10
92	Jeff Reed	.10
93	Alonzo Powell	.10
94	Vance Law	.10
95	Bob Brenly	.10
96	Will Clark	.75
97	Chili Davis	.10
98	Mike Krukow	.10
99	Jose Uribe	.10
100	Chris Brown	.10
101	Rob Thompson	.10
102	Candy Maldonado	.10
103	Jeff Leonard	.10
104	Tom Candiotti	.10
105	Chris Bando	.10
106	Cory Snyder	.10
107	Pat Tabler	.10
108	Andre Thornton	.10
109	Joe Carter	.10
110	Tony Bernazard	.10
111	Julio Franco	.10
112	Brook Jacoby	.10
113	Brett Butler	.10
114	Donnell Nixon	.10
115	Alvin Davis	.10
116	Mark Langston	.10
117	Harold Reynolds	.10
118	Ken Phelps	.10
119	Mike Kingery	.10
120	Dave Valle	.10
121	Rey Quinones	.10
122	Phil Bradley	.10

123	Jim Presley	.10
124	Keith Hernandez	.10
125	Kevin McReynolds	.10
126	Rafael Santana	.10
127	Bob Ojeda	.10
128	Darryl Strawberry	.10
129	Mookie Wilson	.10
130	Gary Carter	.50
131	Tim Teufel	.10
132	Howard Johnson	.10
133	Cal Ripken, Jr.	2.00
134	Rick Burleson	.10
135	Fred Lynn	.10
136	Eddie Murray	.50
137	Ray Knight	.10
138	Alan Wiggins	.10
139	John Shelby	.10
140	Mike Boddicker	.10
141	Ken Gerhart	.10
142	Terry Kennedy	.10
143	Steve Garvey	.25
144	Marvell Wynne	.10
145	Kevin Mitchell	.10
146	Tony Gwynn	.60
147	Joey Cora	.10
148	Benito Santiago	.10
149	Eric Show	.10
150	Garry Templeton	.10
151	Carmelo Martinez	.10
152	Von Hayes	.10
153	Lance Parrish	.10
154	Milt Thompson	.10
155	Mike Easler	.10
156	Juan Samuel	.10
157	Steve Jeltz	.10
158	Glenn Wilson	.10
159	Shane Rawley	.10
160	Mike Schmidt	.75
161	Andy Van Slyke	.10
162	Johnny Ray	.10
163a	Barry Bonds (Dark jersey, photo actually Johnny Ray.)	600.00
163b	Barry Bonds (White jersey, correct photo.)	9.00
164	Junior Ortiz	.10
165	Rafael Belliard	.10
166	Bob Patterson	.10
167	Bobby Bonilla	.10
168	Sid Bream	.10
169	Jim Morrison	.10
170	Jerry Browne	.10
171	Scott Fletcher	.10
172	Ruben Sierra	.10
173	Larry Parrish	.10
174	Pete O'Brien	.10
175	Pete Incaviglia	.10
176	Don Slaught	.10
177	Oddibe McDowell	.10
178	Charlie Hough	.10
179	Steve Buechele	.10
180	Bob Stanley	.10
181	Wade Boggs	.60
182	Jim Rice	.30
183	Bill Buckner	.10
184	Dwight Evans	.10
185	Spike Owen	.10
186	Don Baylor	.10
187	Marc Sullivan	.10
188	Marty Barrett	.10
189	Dave Henderson	.10
190	Bo Diaz	.10
191	Barry Larkin	.10
192	Kal Daniels	.10
193	Terry Francona	.10
194	Tom Browning	.10
195	Ron Oester	.10
196	Buddy Bell	.10
197	Eric Davis	.10
198	Dave Parker	.10
199	Steve Balboni	.10
200	Danny Tartabull	.10
201	Ed Hearn	.10
202	Buddy Biancalana	.10
203	Danny Jackson	.10
204	Frank White	.10
205	Bo Jackson	.25
206	George Brett	.75
207	Kevin Seitzer	.10
208	Willie Wilson	.10
209	Orlando Mercado	.10
210	Darrell Evans	.10
211	Larry Herndon	.10
212	Jack Morris	.10
213	Chet Lemon	.10
214	Mike Heath	.10
215	Darnell Coles	.10
216	Alan Trammell	.10
217	Terry Harper	.10
218	Lou Whitaker	.10
219	Gary Gaetti	.10
220	Tom Nieto	.10
221	Kirby Puckett	.60
222	Tom Brunansky	.10
223	Greg Gagne	.10
224	Dan Gladden	.10
225	Mark Davidson	.10
226	Bert Blyleven	.10
227	Steve Lombardozzi	.10
228	Kent Hrbek	.10
229	Gary Redus	.10
230	Ivan Calderon	.10
231	Tim Hulett	.10
232	Carlton Fisk	.50
233	Greg Walker	.10
234	Ron Karkovice	.10
235	Ozzie Guillen	.10
236	Harold Baines	.10

237	Donnie Hill	.10
238	Rich Dotson	.10
239	Mike Pagliarulo	.10
240	Joel Skinner	.10
241	Don Mattingly	.75
242	Gary Ward	.10
243	Dave Winfield	.50
244	Dan Pasqua	.10
245	Wayne Tolleson	.10
246	Willie Randolph	.10
247	Dennis Rasmussen	.10
248	Rickey Henderson	.50
249	Angels Checklist	.05
250	Astros Checklist	.05
251	Athletics Checklist	.05
252	Blue Jays Checklist	.05
253	Braves Checklist	.05
254	Brewers Checklist	.05
255	Cardinals Checklist	.05
256	Dodgers Checklist	.05
257	Expos Checklist	.05
258	Giants Checklist	.05
259	Indians Checklist	.05
260	Mariners Checklist	.05
261	Orioles Checklist	.05
262	Padres Checklist	.05
263	Phillies Checklist	.05
264	Pirates Checklist	.05
265	Rangers Checklist	.05
266	Red Sox Checklist	.05
267	Reds Checklist	.05
268	Royals Checklist	.05
269	Tigers Checklist	.05
270	Twins Checklist	.05
271	White Sox/Cubs Checklist	.05
272	Yankees/Mets Checklist	.05

1987 Donruss Pop-Ups

For the second straight year, Donruss released in conjunction with its All-Stars issue a set of cards designed to fold out to form a three-dimensional stand-up card. Consisting of 20 cards, as opposed to the previous year's 18, the 1987 Donruss Pop-Ups set contains players selected to the 1986 All-Star Game. Background for the 2-1/2" x 5" cards is the Houston Astrodome, site of the 1986 mid-summer classic. Retail packs included one Pop-Up card, three All-Star cards and one Roberto Clemente puzzle card.

		NM/M
Complete Set (20):		3.00
Common Player:		.10
Roberto Clemente Puzzle:		2.50
Wax Pack:		.35
Wax Box (48):		5.00
(1)	Wade Boggs	.50
(2)	Gary Carter	.40
(3)	Roger Clemens	.60
(4)	Dwight Gooden	.50
(5)	Tony Gwynn	.50
(6)	Rickey Henderson	.40
(7)	Keith Hernandez	.10
(8)	Whitey Herzog	.10
(9)	Dick Howser	.10
(10)	Wally Joyner	.10
(11)	Dale Murphy	.25
(12)	Lance Parrish	.10
(13)	Kirby Puckett	.50
(14)	Cal Ripken, Jr.	.75
(15)	Ryne Sandberg	.50
(16)	Mike Schmidt	.50
(17)	Ozzie Smith	.50
(18)	Darryl Strawberry	.50
(19)	Lou Whitaker	.10
(20)	Dave Winfield	.40

Rookies

As they did in 1986, Donruss issued a 56-card set highlighting the major leagues' most promising rookies. The cards are standard 2-1/2" x

3-1/2" and are identical in design to the regular Donruss issue. The card fronts have green borders as opposed to the black found in the regular issue and carry the words "The Rookies" in the lower-left portion of the card. The set came housed in a specially designed box and was available only through hobby dealers.

		NM/M
Unopened Fact. Set (56):		15.00
Complete Set (56):		10.00
Common Player:		.05
1	Mark McGwire	6.00
2	Eric Bell	.05
3	Mark Williamson	.05
4	Mike Greenwell	.25
5	Ellis Burks	.25
6	DeWayne Buice	.05
7	Mark McLemore (McLemore)	.05
8	Devon White	.05
9	Willie Fraser	.05
10	Lester Lancaster	.05
11	Ken Williams	.05
12	Matt Nokes	.05
13	Jeff Robinson	.05
14	Bo Jackson	.25
15	Kevin Seitzer	.05
16	Billy Ripken	.05
17	B.J. Surhoff	.05
18	Chuck Crim	.05
19	Mike Birbeck	.05
20	Chris Bosio	.05
21	Les Straker	.05
22	Mark Davidson	.05
23	Gene Larkin	.05
24	Ken Gerhart	.05
25	Luis Polonia	.05
26	Terry Steinbach	.05
27	Mickey Brantley	.05
28	Mike Stanley	.05
29	Jerry Browne	.05
30	Todd Benzinger	.05
31	Fred McGriff	.25
32	Mike Henneman	.05
33	Casey Candaele	.05
34	Dave Magadan	.05
35	David Cone	.25
36	Mike Jackson	.05
37	John Mitchell	.05
38	Mike Dunne	.05
39	John Smiley	.05
40	Joe Magrane	.05
41	Jim Lindeman	.05
42	Shane Mack	.05
43	Stan Jefferson	.05
44	Benito Santiago	.05
45	Matt Williams **RC**	1.50
46	Dave Meads	.05
47	Rafael Palmeiro	4.00
48	Bill Long	.05
49	Bob Brower	.05
50	James Steels	.05
51	Paul Noce	.05
52	Greg Maddux	5.00
53	Jeff Musselman	.05
54	Brian Holton	.05
55	Chuck Jackson	.05
56	Checklist 1-56	.03

1988 Donruss Promo Sheet

The full effect of the 1988 Donruss border design of black, blue and red geometric patterns was previewed on this promo sheet. Printed on glossy paper with blank-back, eight regular cards (all pitchers!) and a Diamond King are showcased on the 7-1/2" x 10-1/2" sheet.

	NM/M
Uncut Sheet:	7.50

1988 Donruss

The 1988 Donruss set consists of 660 cards, each measuring 2-1/2" x 3-1/2". Fronts feature a full-color photo surrounded by a colorful border - alternating stripes of black, red, black, blue, black, blue, black, red and black (in that order) - separated by soft-focus edges and airbrushed fades. The player's name and position appear in a red band at the bottom of the card. The Donruss logo is situated in the upper-left corner, while the team logo is located in the lower-right. For the seventh consecutive season, Donruss included a subset of "Diamond Kings" cards (#1-27) in the issue. And for the fifth straight year, Donruss incorporated the popular "Rated Rookies" (card #28-47) with the set. Twenty-six of the cards between #603-660 were short-printed to accommodate the printing of the 26 MVP insert cards.

		NM/M
Unopened Fact. Set (660):		10.00
Complete Set (660):		8.00
Common Player:		.05
Stan Musial Puzzle:		1.00
Wax Pack (15):		.40
Wax Box (36):		10.00
Cello Pack (36):		.75
Cello Box (24):		12.00
Rack Pack (45):		.75
1	Mark McGwire (DK)	.75
2	Tim Raines (DK)	.05
3	Benito Santiago (DK)	.05
4	Alan Trammell (DK)	.05
5	Danny Tartabull (DK)	.05
6	Ron Darling (DK)	.05
7	Paul Molitor (DK)	.40
8	Devon White (DK)	.05
9	Andre Dawson (DK)	.25
10	Julio Franco (DK)	.05
11	Scott Fletcher (DK)	.05
12	Tony Fernandez (DK)	.05
13	Shane Rawley (DK)	.05
14	Kal Daniels (DK)	.05
15	Jack Clark (DK)	.05
16	Dwight Evans (DK)	.05
17	Tommy John (DK)	.05
18	Andy Van Slyke (DK)	.05
19	Gary Gaetti (DK)	.05
20	Mark Langston (DK)	.05
21	Will Clark (DK)	.05
22	Glenn Hubbard (DK)	.05
23	Billy Hatcher (DK)	.05
24	Bob Welch (DK)	.05
25	Ivan Calderon (DK)	.05
26	Cal Ripken, Jr. (DK)	1.00
27	Checklist 1-27	.05
28	Mackey Sasser **RC** (RR)	.05
29	Jeff Treadway **RC** (RR)	.05
30	Mike Campbell **RC** (RR)	.05
31	Lance Johnson **RC** (RR)	.15
32	Nelson Liriano **RC** (RR)	.05
33	Shawn Abner (RR)	.05
34	Roberto Alomar **RC** (RR)	1.00
35	Shawn Hillegas **RC** (RR)	.05
36	Joey Meyer (RR)	.05
37	Kevin Elster (RR)	.05
38	Jose Lind **RC** (RR)	.05
39	Kirt Manwaring **RC** (RR)	.05
40	Mark Grace **RC** (RR)	1.00
41	Jody Reed **RC** (RR)	.10
42	John Farrell **RC** (RR)	.05
43	Al Leiter **RC** (RR)	.20
44	Gary Thurman **RC** (RR)	.05
45	Vicente Palacios **RC** (RR)	.05
46	Eddie Williams **RC** (RR)	.05
47	Jack McDowell **RC** (RR)	.20
48	Ken Dixon	.05
49	Mike Birbeck	.05
50	Eric King	.05

No.	Player	Val	No.	Player	Val
51	Roger Clemens	.60	168	Junior Ortiz	.05
52	Pat Clements	.05	169	Jamie Moyer	.05
53	Fernando Valenzuela	.05	170	Tony Pena	.05
54	Mark Gubicza	.05	171	Cal Ripken, Jr.	1.00
55	Jay Howell	.05	172	B.J. Surhoff	.05
56	Floyd Youmans	.05	173	Lou Whitaker	.05
57	Ed Correa	.05	174	Ellis Burks RC	.20
58	DeWayne Buice RC	.05	175	Ron Guidry	.10
59	Jose DeLeon	.05	176	Steve Sax	.05
60	Danny Cox	.05	177	Danny Tartabull	.05
61	Nolan Ryan	1.00	178	Carney Lansford	.05
62	Steve Bedrosian	.05	179	Casey Candaele	.05
63	Tom Browning	.05	180	Scott Fletcher	.05
64	Mark Davis	.05	181	Mark McLemore	.05
65	R.J. Reynolds	.05	182	Ivan Calderon	.05
66	Kevin Mitchell	.05	183	Jack Clark	.05
67	Ken Oberkfell	.05	184	Glenn Davis	.05
68	Rick Sutcliffe	.05	185	Luis Aguayo	.05
69	Dwight Gooden	.05	186	Bo Diaz	.05
70	Scott Bankhead	.05	187	Stan Jefferson	.05
71	Bert Blyleven	.10	188	Sid Bream	.05
72	Jimmy Key	.05	189	Bob Brenly	.05
73	Les Straker RC	.05	190	Dion James	.05
74	Jim Clancy	.05	191	Leon Durham	.05
75	Mike Moore	.05	192	Jesse Orosco	.05
76	Ron Darling	.05	193	Alvin Davis	.05
77	Ed Lynch	.05	194	Gary Gaetti	.05
78	Dale Murphy	.20	195	Fred McGriff	.05
79	Doug Drabek	.05	196	Steve Lombardozzi	.05
80	Scott Garrelts	.05	197	Rance Mulliniks	.05
81	Ed Whitson	.05	198	Rey Quinones	.05
82	Rob Murphy	.05	199	Gary Carter	.40
83	Shane Rawley	.05	200a	Checklist 138-247	.05
84	Greg Mathews	.05	200b	Checklist 134-239	.05
85	Jim Deshaies	.05	201	Keith Moreland	.05
86	Mike Witt	.05	202	Ken Griffey	.05
87	Donnie Hill	.05	203	Tommy Gregg RC	.05
88	Jeff Reed	.05	204	Will Clark	.05
89	Mike Boddicker	.05	205	John Kruk	.05
90	Ted Higuera	.05	206	Buddy Bell	.05
91	Walt Terrell	.05	207	Von Hayes	.05
92	Bob Stanley	.05	208	Tommy Herr	.05
93	Dave Righetti	.05	209	Craig Reynolds	.05
94	Orel Hershiser	.05	210	Gary Pettis	.05
95	Chris Bando	.05	211	Harold Baines	.05
96	Bret Saberhagen	.05	212	Vance Law	.05
97	Curt Young	.05	213	Ken Gerhart	.05
98	Tim Burke	.05	214	Jim Gantner	.05
99	Charlie Hough	.05	215	Chet Lemon	.05
100a	Checklist 28-137	.05	216	Dwight Evans	.05
100b	Checklist 28-133	.05	217	Don Mattingly	.60
101	Bobby Witt	.05	218	Franklin Stubbs	.05
102	George Brett	.60	219	Pat Tabler	.05
103	Mickey Tettleton	.05	220	Bo Jackson	.10
104	Scott Bailes	.05	221	Tony Phillips	.05
105	Mike Pagliarulo	.05	222	Tim Wallach	.05
106	Mike Scioscia	.05	223	Ruben Sierra	.05
107	Tom Brookens	.05	224	Steve Buechele	.05
108	Ray Knight	.05	225	Frank White	.05
109	Dan Plesac	.05	226	Alfredo Griffin	.05
110	Wally Joyner	.05	227	Greg Swindell	.05
111	Bob Forsch	.05	228	Willie Randolph	.05
112	Mike Scott	.05	229	Mike Marshall	.05
113	Kevin Gross	.05	230	Alan Trammell	.05
114	Benito Santiago	.05	231	Eddie Murray	.40
115	Bob Kipper	.05	232	Dale Sveum	.05
116	Mike Krukow	.05	233	Dick Schofield	.05
117	Chris Bosio	.05	234	Jose Oquendo	.05
118	Sid Fernandez	.05	235	Bill Doran	.05
119	Jody Davis	.05	236	Milt Thompson	.05
120	Mike Morgan	.05	237	Marvell Wynne	.05
121	Mark Eichhorn	.05	238	Bobby Bonilla	.05
122	Jeff Reardon	.05	239	Chris Speier	.05
123	John Franco	.05	240	Glenn Braggs	.05
124	Richard Dotson	.05	241	Wally Backman	.05
125	Eric Bell	.05	242	Ryne Sandberg	.50
126	Juan Nieves	.05	243	Phil Bradley	.05
127	Jack Morris	.05	244	Kelly Gruber	.05
128	Rick Rhoden	.05	245	Tom Brunansky	.05
129	Rich Gedman	.05	246	Ron Oester	.05
130	Ken Howell	.05	247	Bobby Thigpen	.05
131	Brook Jacoby	.05	248	Fred Lynn	.05
132	Danny Jackson	.05	249	Paul Molitor	.40
133	Gene Nelson	.05	250	Darrell Evans	.05
134	Neal Heaton	.05	251	Gary Ward	.05
135	Willie Fraser	.05	252	Bruce Hurst	.05
136	Jose Guzman	.05	253	Bob Welch	.05
137	Ozzie Guillen	.05	254	Joe Carter	.05
138	Bob Knepper	.05	255	Willie Wilson	.05
139	Mike Jackson RC	.05	256	Mark McGwire	.75
140	Joe Magrane RC	.05	257	Mitch Webster	.05
141	Jimmy Jones	.05	258	Brian Downing	.05
142	Ted Power	.05	259	Mike Stanley	.05
143	Ozzie Virgil	.05	260	Carlton Fisk	.40
144	Felix Fermin RC	.05	261	Billy Hatcher	.05
145	Kelly Downs	.05	262	Glenn Wilson	.05
146	Shawon Dunston	.05	263	Ozzie Smith	.50
147	Scott Bradley	.05	264	Randy Ready	.05
148	Dave Stieb	.05	265	Kurt Stillwell	.05
149	Frank Viola	.05	266	David Palmer	.05
150	Terry Kennedy	.05	267	Mike Diaz	.05
151	Bill Wegman	.05	268	Rob Thompson	.05
152	Matt Nokes RC	.10	269	Andre Dawson	.25
153	Wade Boggs	.50	270	Lee Guetterman	.05
154	Wayne Tolleson	.05	271	Willie Upshaw	.05
155	Mariano Duncan	.05	272	Randy Bush	.05
156	Julio Franco	.05	273	Larry Sheets	.05
157	Charlie Leibrandt	.05	274	Rob Deer	.05
158	Terry Steinbach	.05	275	Kirk Gibson	.05
159	Mike Fitzgerald	.05	276	Marty Barrett	.05
160	Jack Lazorko	.05	277	Rickey Henderson	.40
161	Mitch Williams	.05	278	Pedro Guerrero	.05
162	Greg Walker	.05	279	Brett Butler	.05
163	Alan Ashby	.05	280	Kevin Seitzer	.05
164	Tony Gwynn	.50	281	Mike Davis	.05
165	Bruce Ruffin	.05	282	Andres Galarraga	.05
166	Ron Robinson	.05	283	Devon White	.05
167	Zane Smith	.05	284	Pete O'Brien	.05

No.	Player	Val	No.	Player	Val
285	Jerry Hairston Sr.	.05	401	Tommy John	.10
286	Kevin Bass	.05	402	Brian Holton	.05
287	Carmelo Martinez	.05	403	Carmen Castillo	.05
288	Juan Samuel	.05	404	Jamie Quirk	.05
289	Kal Daniels	.05	405	Dwayne Murphy	.05
290	Albert Hall	.05	406	Jeff Parrett RC	.05
291	Andy Van Slyke	.05	407	Don Sutton	.05
292	Lee Smith	.10	408	Jerry Browne	.05
293	Vince Coleman	.05	409	Jim Winn	.05
294	Tom Niedenfuer	.05	410	Dave Smith	.05
295	Robin Yount	.40	411	Shane Mack RC	.05
296	Jeff Robinson RC	.05	412	Greg Gross	.05
297	Todd Benzinger RC	.10	413	Nick Esasky	.05
298	Dave Winfield	.40	414	Damaso Garcia	.05
299	Mickey Hatcher	.05	415	Brian Fisher	.05
300a	Checklist 248-357	.05	416	Brian Dayett	.05
300b	Checklist 240-345	.05	417	Curt Ford	.05
301	Bud Black	.05	418	Mark Williamson RC	.05
302	Jose Canseco	.25	419	Bill Schroeder	.05
303	Tom Foley	.05	420	Mike Henneman RC	.10
304	Pete Incaviglia	.05	421	John Marzano RC	.05
305	Bob Boone	.05	422	Ron Kittle	.05
306	Bill Long RC	.05	423	Matt Young	.05
307	Willie McGee	.05	424	Steve Balboni	.05
308	Ken Caminiti RC	.20	425	Luis Polonia RC	.05
309	Darren Daulton	.05	426	Randy St. Claire	.05
310	Tracy Jones	.05	427	Greg Harris	.05
311	Greg Booker	.05	428	Johnny Ray	.05
312	Mike LaValliere	.05	429	Ray Searage	.05
313	Chili Davis	.05	430	Ricky Horton	.05
314	Glenn Hubbard	.05	431	Gerald Young RC	.05
315	Paul Noce RC	.05	432	Rick Schu	.05
316	Keith Hernandez	.05	433	Paul O'Neill	.05
317	Mark Langston	.05	434	Rich Gossage	.10
318	Keith Atherton	.05	435	John Cangelosi	.05
319	Tony Fernandez	.05	436	Mike LaCoss	.05
320	Kent Hrbek	.05	437	Gerald Perry	.05
321	John Cerutti	.05	438	Dave Martinez	.05
322	Mike Kingery	.05	439	Darryl Strawberry	.05
323	Dave Magadan	.05	440	John Moses	.05
324	Rafael Palmeiro	.35	441	Greg Gagne	.05
325	Jeff Dedmon	.05	442	Jesse Barfield	.05
326	Barry Bonds	1.00	443	George Frazier	.05
327	Jeffrey Leonard	.05	444	Garth Iorg	.05
328	Tim Flannery	.05	445	Ed Nunez	.05
329	Dave Concepcion	.05	446	Rick Aguilera	.05
330	Mike Schmidt	.60	447	Jerry Mumphrey	.05
331	Bill Dawley	.05	448	Rafael Ramirez	.05
332	Larry Andersen	.05	449	John Smiley RC	.10
333	Jack Howell	.05	450	Atlee Hammaker	.05
334	Ken Williams RC	.05	451	Lance McCullers	.05
335	Bryn Smith	.05	452	Guy Hoffman	.05
336	Billy Ripken RC	.10	453	Chris James	.05
337	Greg Brock	.05	454	Terry Pendleton	.05
338	Mike Heath	.05	455	Dave Meads RC	.05
339	Mike Greenwell	.05	456	Bill Buckner	.05
340	Claudell Washington	.05	457	John Pawlowski RC	.05
341	Jose Gonzalez	.05	458	Bob Sebra	.05
342	Mel Hall	.05	459	Jim Dwyer	.05
343	Jim Eisenreich	.05	460	Jay Aldrich RC	.05
344	Tony Bernazard	.05	461	Frank Tanana	.05
345	Tim Raines	.05	462	Oil Can Boyd	.05
346	Bob Brower	.05	463	Dan Pasqua	.05
347	Larry Parrish	.05	464	Tim Crews RC	.10
348	Thad Bosley	.05	465	Andy Allanson	.05
349	Dennis Eckersley	.35	466	Bill Pecota RC	.05
350	Cory Snyder	.05	467	Steve Ontiveros	.05
351	Rick Cerone	.05	468	Hubie Brooks	.05
352	John Shelby	.05	469	Paul Kilgus RC	.05
353	Larry Herndon	.05	470	Dale Mohorcic	.05
354	John Habyan	.05	471	Dan Quisenberry	.05
355	Chuck Crim RC	.05	472	Dave Stewart	.05
356	Gus Polidor	.05	473	Dave Clark	.05
357	Ken Dayley	.05	474	Joel Skinner	.05
358	Danny Darwin	.05	475	Dave Anderson	.05
359	Lance Parrish	.05	476	Dan Petry	.05
360	James Steels RC	.05	477	Carl Nichols RC	.05
361	Al Pedrique RC	.05	478	Ernest Riles	.05
362	Mike Aldrete	.05	479	George Hendrick	.05
363	Juan Castillo	.05	480	John Morris	.05
364	Len Dykstra	.05	481	Manny Hernandez RC	.05
365	Luis Quinones	.05	482	Jeff Stone	.05
366	Jim Presley	.05	483	Chris Brown	.05
367	Lloyd Moseby	.05	484	Mike Bielecki	.05
368	Kirby Puckett	.50	485	Dave Dravecky	.05
369	Eric Davis	.05	486	Rick Manning	.05
370	Gary Redus	.05	487	Bill Almon	.05
371	Dave Schmidt	.05	488	Jim Sundberg	.05
372	Mark Clear	.05	489	Ken Phelps	.05
373	Dave Bergman	.05	490	Tom Henke	.05
374	Charles Hudson	.05	491	Dan Gladden	.05
375	Calvin Schiraldi	.05	492	Barry Larkin	.05
376	Alex Trevino	.05	493	Fred Manrique RC	.05
377	Tom Candiotti	.05	494	Mike Griffin	.05
378	Steve Farr	.05	495	Mark Knudson RC	.05
379	Mike Gallego	.05	496	Bill Madlock	.05
380	Andy McGaffigan	.05	497	Tim Stoddard	.05
381	Kirk McCaskill	.05	498	Sam Horn RC	.05
382	Oddibe McDowell	.05	499	Tracy Woodson RC	.05
383	Floyd Bannister	.05	500a	Checklist 468-577	.05
384	Denny Walling	.05	500b	Checklist 452-557	.05
385	Don Carman	.05	501	Ken Schrom	.05
386	Todd Worrell	.05	502	Angel Salazar	.05
387	Eric Show	.05	503	Eric Plunk	.05
388	Dave Parker	.05	504	Joe Hesketh	.05
389	Rick Mahler	.05	505	Greg Minton	.05
390	Mike Dunne RC	.10	506	Geno Petralli	.05
391	Candy Maldonado	.05	507	Bob James	.05
392	Bob Dernier	.05	508	Robbie Wine RC	.05
393	Dave Valle	.05	509	Jeff Calhoun	.05
394	Ernie Whitt	.05	510	Steve Lake	.05
395	Juan Berenguer	.05	511	Mark Grant	.05
396	Mike Young	.05	512	Frank Williams	.05
397	Mike Felder	.05	513	Jeff Blauser RC	.10
398	Willie Hernandez	.05	514	Bob Walk	.05
399	Jim Rice	.25	515	Craig Lefferts	.05
400a	Checklist 358-467	.05	516	Manny Trillo	.05
400b	Checklist 346-451	.05	517	Jerry Reed	.05

No.	Player	Val	No.	Player	Val
518	Rick Leach	.05	632	Bob Ojeda/SP	.10
519	Mark Davidson RC	.05	633	Rafael Santana	.05
520	Jeff Ballard RC	.05	634	Wes Gardner RC	.05
521	Dave Stapleton RC	.05	635	Roberto Kelly RC/SP	.15
522	Pat Sheridan	.05	636	Mike Flanagan/SP	.10
523	Al Nipper	.05	637	Jay Bell RC	.35
524	Steve Trout	.05	638	Bob Melvin	.05
525	Jeff Hamilton	.05	639	Damon Berryhill RC	.05
526	Tommy Hinzo RC	.05	640	David Wells RC/SP	.40
527	Lonnie Smith	.05	641	Stan Musial Puzzle Card	.05
528	Greg Cadaret RC	.05	642	Doug Sisk	.05
529	Rob McClure (Bob)	.05	643	Keith Hughes RC	.05
530	Chuck Finley	.05	644	Tom Glavine RC	1.00
531	Jeff Russell	.05	645	Al Newman	.05
532	Steve Lyons	.05	646	Scott Sanderson	.05
533	Terry Puhl	.05	647	Scott Terry	.05
534	Eric Nolte RC	.05	648	Tim Teufel/SP	.10
535	Kent Tekulve	.05	649	Garry Templeton/SP	.10
536	Pat Pacillo RC	.05	650	Manny Lee/SP	.10
537	Charlie Puleo	.05	651	Roger McDowell/SP	.10
538	Tom Prince RC	.05	652	Mookie Wilson/SP	.10
539	Greg Maddux	.50	653	David Cone/SP	.10
540	Jim Lindeman	.05	654	Ron Gant RC/SP	.20
541	Pete Stanicek RC	.05	655	Joe Price/SP	.10
542	Steve Kiefer	.05	656	George Bell/SP	.10
543	Jim Morrison	.05	657	Gregg Jefferies RC/SP	.25
544	Spike Owen	.05	658	Todd Stottlemyre RC/SP	.25
545	Jay Buhner RC	.50	659	Geronimo Berroa RC/SP	.20
546	Mike Devereaux RC	.10	660	Jerry Royster/SP	.05
547	Jerry Don Gleaton	.05			
548	Jose Rijo	.05			
549	Dennis Martinez	.05			
550	Mike Loynd	.05			
551	Darrell Miller	.05			
552	Dave LaPoint	.05			
553	John Tudor	.05			
554	Rocky Childress RC	.05			
555	Wally Ritchie RC	.05			
556	Terry McGriff	.05			
557	Dave Leiper	.05			
558	Jeff Robinson	.05			
559	Jose Uribe	.05			
560	Ted Simmons	.05			
561	Lester Lancaster RC	.10			
562	Keith Miller RC	.05			
563	Harold Reynolds	.05			
564	Gene Larkin RC	.05			
565	Cecil Fielder	.05			
566	Roy Smalley	.05			
567	Duane Ward	.05			
568	Bill Wilkinson RC	.05			
569	Howard Johnson	.05			
570	Frank DiPino	.05			
571	Pete Smith RC	.05			
572	Darnell Coles	.05			
573	Don Robinson	.05			
574	Rob Nelson	.05			
575	Dennis Rasmussen	.05			
576	Steve Jeltz (Photo actually Juan Samuel.)	.05			
577	Tom Pagnozzi RC	.05			
578	Ty Gainey	.05			
579	Gary Lucas	.05			
580	Ron Hassey	.05			
581	Herm Winningham	.05			
582	Rene Gonzales RC	.05			
583	Brad Komminsk	.05			
584	Doyle Alexander	.05			
585	Jeff Sellers	.05			
586	Bill Gullickson	.05			
587	Tim Belcher	.05			
588	Doug Jones RC	.05			
589	Melido Perez RC	.05			
590	Rick Honeycutt	.05			
591	Pascual Perez	.05			
592	Curt Wilkerson	.05			
593	Steve Howe	.05			
594	John Davis RC	.05			
595	Storm Davis	.05			
596	Sammy Stewart	.05			
597	Neil Allen	.05			
598	Alejandro Pena	.05			
599	Mark Thurmond	.05			
600a	Checklist 578-BC26	.05			
600b	Checklist 558-660	.05			
601	Jose Mesa RC	.10			
602	Don August RC	.05			
603	Terry Leach/SP	.10			
604	Tom Newell RC	.05			
605	Randall Byers RC/SP	.10			
606	Jim Gott	.05			
607	Harry Spilman	.05			
608	John Candelaria	.05			
609	Mike Brumley RC	.05			
610	Mickey Brantley	.05			
611	Jose Nunez RC/SP	.10			
612	Tom Nieto	.05			
613	Rick Reuschel	.05			
614	Lee Mazzilli/SP	.05			
615	Scott Lusader RC	.05			
616	Bobby Meacham	.05			
617	Kevin McReynolds/SP	.10			
618	Gene Garber	.05			
619	Barry Lyons RC/SP	.10			
620	Randy Myers	.05			
621	Donnie Moore	.05			
622	Domingo Ramos	.05			
623	Ed Romero	.05			
624	Greg Myers RC	.10			
625	Ripken Baseball Family (Billy Ripken, Cal Ripken, Jr., Cal Ripken, Sr.)	.40			
626	Pat Perry	.05			
627	Andres Thomas/SP	.05			
628	Matt Williams/SP	.10			
629	Dave Hengel/SP	.05			
630	Jeff Musselman/SP	.05			
631	Tim Laudner	.05			

1988 Donruss MVP

Dale Murphy OF

This 26-card set of standard-size player cards replaced the Donruss box-bottom cards in 1988. The bonus cards (numbered BC1 - BC26) were randomly inserted in Donruss wax or rack packs. Cards feature the company's choice of Most Valuable Player for each major league team and are titled "Donruss MVP." The MVP cards were not included in the factory-collated sets. Fronts carry the same basic red-blue-black border design as the 1988 Donruss basic issue. Backs are the same as the regular issue, except for the numbering system.

		NM/M
Complete Set (26):		3.00
Common Player:		.10
1	Cal Ripken, Jr.	1.00
2	Eric Davis	.10
3	Paul Molitor	.40
4	Mike Schmidt	.60
5	Ivan Calderon	.10
6	Tony Gwynn	.50
7	Wade Boggs	.50
8	Andy Van Slyke	.10
9	Joe Carter	.10
10	Andre Dawson	.25
11	Alan Trammell	.10
12	Mike Scott	.10
13	Wally Joyner	.10
14	Dale Murphy	.20
15	Kirby Puckett	.50
16	Pedro Guerrero	.10
17	Kevin Seitzer	.10
18	Tim Raines	.10
19	George Bell	.10
20	Darryl Strawberry	.10
21	Don Mattingly	.60
22	Ozzie Smith	.50
23	Mark McGwire	.75
24	Will Clark	.10
25	Alvin Davis	.10
26	Ruben Sierra	.10

1988 Donruss All-Stars

For the third consecutive year, this set of 64 cards was marketed in conjunction with Donruss Pop-Ups. The 1988 issue included a major change - the cards were reduced in size from 3-1/2" x 5" to a standard 2-1/2" x 3-1/2". The set features players from the 1987 All-Star Game starting lineup. Card fronts feature full-color photos, framed in blue, black and white, with a Donruss logo at upper-left. Player name and position appear in a red banner below the photo, along with the appropriate Nation-

Keith Hernandez 1B

Don Mattingly 1B

al or American League logo. Backs include player stats and All-Star Game record. In 1988, All-Stars cards were distributed in individual packages containing three All-Stars, one Pop-Up and three Stan Musial puzzle pieces.

	NM/M
Complete Set (64):	5.00
Common Player:	.05
Stan Musial Puzzle:	1.00
Wax Pack:	.50
Wax Box (48):	10.00
1 Don Mattingly	.60
2 Dave Winfield	.40
3 Willie Randolph	.05
4 Rickey Henderson	.40
5 Cal Ripken, Jr.	1.00
6 George Bell	.05
7 Wade Boggs	.50
8 Bret Saberhagen	.05
9 Terry Kennedy	.05
10 John McNamara	.05
11 Jay Howell	.05
12 Harold Baines	.05
13 Harold Reynolds	.05
14 Bruce Hurst	.05
15 Kirby Puckett	.50
16 Matt Nokes	.05
17 Pat Tabler	.05
18 Dan Plesac	.05
19 Mark McGwire	.75
20 Mike Witt	.05
21 Larry Parrish	.05
22 Alan Trammell	.05
23 Dwight Evans	.05
24 Jack Morris	.05
25 Tony Fernandez	.05
26 Mark Langston	.05
27 Kevin Seitzer	.05
28 Tom Henke	.05
29 Dave Righetti	.05
30 Oakland Coliseum	.05
31 Wade Boggs (Top Vote Getter)	.25
32 Checklist 1-32	.05
33 Jack Clark	.05
34 Darryl Strawberry	.05
35 Ryne Sandberg	.50
36 Andre Dawson	.05
37 Ozzie Smith	.05
38 Eric Davis	.05
39 Mike Schmidt	.60
40 Mike Scott	.05
41 Gary Carter	.40
42 Davey Johnson	.05
43 Rick Sutcliffe	.05
44 Willie McGee	.05
45 Hubie Brooks	.05
46 Dale Murphy	.20
47 Bo Diaz	.05
48 Pedro Guerrero	.05
49 Keith Hernandez	.05
50 Ozzie Virgil	.05
51 Tony Gwynn	.50
52 Rick Reuschel	.05
53 John Franco	.05
54 Jeffrey Leonard	.05
55 Juan Samuel	.05
56 Orel Hershiser	.05
57 Tim Raines	.05
58 Sid Fernandez	.05
59 Tim Wallach	.05
60 Lee Smith	.05
61 Steve Bedrosian	.05
62 Tim Raines (MVP)	.05
63 Ozzie Smith (Top Vote Getter)	.25
64 Checklist 33-64	.05

1988 Donruss Baseball's Best

The design of this 336-card set is similar to the regular 1988 Donruss issue with the exception of the borders which are orange, instead of blue. Player photos on the glossy front are framed by the Donruss logo upper-left, team logo lower-right and a bright red and white player name that spans the bottom margin. Backs are black and white, framed by a yellow border, and include personal information, year-by-year stats and major league totals. This set was packaged in a bright red cardboard box containing six individually shrink-wrapped packs of 56 cards. Donruss marketed the set via retail chain outlets with a suggested retail price of $21.95.

	NM/M
Complete Set (336):	10.00
Common Player:	.05
1 Don Mattingly	.75
2 Ron Gant	.05
3 Bob Boone	.05
4 Mark Grace	.15
5 Andy Allanson	.05
6 Kal Daniels	.05
7 Floyd Bannister	.05
8 Alan Ashby	.05
9 Marty Barrett	.05
10 Tim Belcher	.05
11 Harold Baines	.05
12 Hubie Brooks	.05
13 Doyle Alexander	.05
14 Gary Carter	.50
15 Glenn Braggs	.05
16 Steve Bedrosian	.05
17 Barry Bonds	1.50
18 Bert Blyleven	.10
19 Tom Brunansky	.05
20 John Candelaria	.05
21 Shawn Abner	.05
22 Jose Canseco	.30
23 Brett Butler	.05
24 Scott Bradley	.05
25 Ivan Calderon	.05
26 Rich Gossage	.05
27 Brian Downing	.05
28 Jim Rice	.25
29 Dion James	.05
30 Terry Kennedy	.05
31 George Bell	.05
32 Scott Fletcher	.05
33 Bobby Bonilla	.05
34 Tim Burke	.05
35 Darrell Evans	.05
36 Mike Davis	.05
37 Shawon Dunston	.05
38 Kevin Bass	.05
39 George Brett	.75
40 David Cone	.05
41 Ron Darling	.05
42 Roberto Alomar	.60
43 Dennis Eckersley	.40
44 Vince Coleman	.05
45 Sid Bream	.05
46 Gary Gaetti	.05
47 Phil Bradley	.05
48 Jim Clancy	.05
49 Jack Clark	.05
50 Mike Krukow	.05
51 Henry Cotto	.05
52 Rich Dotson	.05
53 Jim Gantner	.05
54 John Franco	.05
55 Pete Incaviglia	.05
56 Joe Carter	.60
57 Roger Clemens	.75
58 Gerald Perry	.05
59 Jack Howell	.05
60 Vance Law	.05
61 Jay Bell	.05
62 Eric Davis	.05
63 Gene Garber	.05
64 Glenn Davis	.05
65 Wade Boggs	.60
66 Kirk Gibson	.05
67 Carlton Fisk	.50
68 Casey Candaele	.05
69 Mike Heath	.05
70 Kevin Elster	.05
71 Greg Brock	.05
72 Don Carman	.05
73 Doug Drabek	.05
74 Greg Gagne	.05
75 Danny Cox	.05
76 Rickey Henderson	.50
77 Chris Brown	.05
78 Terry Steinbach	.05
79 Will Clark	.05
80 Mickey Brantley	.05
81 Ozzie Guillen	.05
82 Greg Maddux	.60
83 Kirk McCaskill	.05
84 Dwight Evans	.05
85 Ozzie Virgil	.05
86 Mike Morgan	.05
87 Tony Fernandez	.05
88 Jose Guzman	.05
89 Mike Dunne	.05
90 Andres Galarraga	.05
91 Mike Henneman	.05
92 Alfredo Griffin	.05
93 Rafael Palmeiro	.40
94 Jim Deshaies	.05
95 Mark Gubicza	.05
96 Dwight Gooden	.05
97 Howard Johnson	.05
98 Mark Davis	.05
99 Dave Stewart	.05
100 Joe Magrane	.05
101 Brian Fisher	.05
102 Kent Hrbek	.05
103 Kevin Gross	.05
104 Tom Henke	.05
105 Mike Pagliarulo	.05
106 Kelly Downs	.05
107 Alvin Davis	.05
108 Willie Randolph	.05
109 Rob Deer	.05
110 Bo Diaz	.05
111 Paul Kilgus	.05
112 Tom Candiotti	.05
113 Dale Murphy	.20
114 Rick Mahler	.05
115 Wally Joyner	.05
116 Ryne Sandberg	.60
117 John Farrell	.05
118 Nick Esasky	.05
119 Bo Jackson	.10
120 Bill Doran	.05
121 Ellis Burks	.05
122 Pedro Guerrero	.05
123 Dave LaPoint	.05
124 Neal Heaton	.05
125 Willie Hernandez	.05
126 Roger McDowell	.05
127 Ted Higuera	.05
128 Von Hayes	.05
129 Mike LaValliere	.05
130 Dan Gladden	.05
131 Willie McGee	.05
132 Al Leiter	.05
133 Mark Grant	.05
134 Bob Welch	.05
135 Dave Dravecky	.05
136 Mark Langston	.05
137 Dan Pasqua	.05
138 Rick Sutcliffe	.05
139 Dan Petry	.05
140 Rich Gedman	.05
141 Ken Griffey	.05
142 Eddie Murray	.50
143 Jimmy Key	.05
144 Dale Mohorcic	.05
145 Jose Lind	.05
146 Dennis Martinez	.05
147 Chet Lemon	.05
148 Orel Hershiser	.05
149 Dave Martinez	.05
150 Billy Hatcher	.05
151 Charlie Leibrandt	.05
152 Keith Hernandez	.05
153 Kevin McReynolds	.05
154 Tony Gwynn	.60
155 Stan Javier	.05
156 Tony Pena	.05
157 Andy Van Slyke	.05
158 Gene Larkin	.05
159 Chris James	.05
160 Fred McGriff	.05
161 Rick Rhoden	.05
162 Scott Garrelts	.05
163 Mike Campbell	.05
164 Dave Righetti	.05
165 Paul Molitor	.50
166 Danny Jackson	.05
167 Pete O'Brien	.05
168 Julio Franco	.05
169 Mark McGwire	1.00
170 Zane Smith	.05
171 Johnny Ray	.05
172 Lester Lancaster	.05
173 Mel Hall	.05
174 Tracy Jones	.05
175 Kevin Seitzer	.05
176 Bob Knepper	.05
177 Mike Greenwell	.05
178 Mike Marshall	.05
179 Melido Perez	.05
180 Tim Raines	.05
181 Jack Morris	.05
182 Darryl Strawberry	.05
183 Robin Yount	.50
184 Lance Parrish	.05
185 Darnell Coles	.05
186 Kirby Puckett	.60
187 Terry Pendleton	.05
188 Don Slaught	.05
189 Jimmy Jones	.05
190 Dave Parker	.05
191 Mike Aldrete	.05
192 Mike Moore	.05
193 Greg Walker	.05
194 Calvin Schiraldi	.05
195 Dick Schofield	.05
196 Jody Reed	.05
197 Pete Smith	.05
198 Cal Ripken, Jr.	1.50
199 Lloyd Moseby	.05
200 Ruben Sierra	.05
201 R.J. Reynolds	.05
202 Bryn Smith	.05
203 Gary Pettis	.05
204 Steve Sax	.05
205 Frank DiPino	.05
206 Mike Scott	.05
207 Kurt Stillwell	.05
208 Mookie Wilson	.05
209 Lee Mazzilli	.05
210 Lance McCullers	.05
211 Rick Honeycutt	.05
212 John Tudor	.05
213 Jim Gott	.05
214 Frank Viola	.05
215 Juan Samuel	.05
216 Jesse Barfield	.05
217 Claudell Washington	.05
218 Rick Reuschel	.05
219 Jim Presley	.05
220 Tommy John	.05
221 Dan Plesac	.05
222 Barry Larkin	.05
223 Mike Stanley	.05
224 Cory Snyder	.05
225 Andre Dawson	.25
226 Ken Oberkfell	.05
227 Devon White	.05
228 Jamie Moyer	.05
229 Brook Jacoby	.05
230 Rob Murphy	.05
231 Bret Saberhagen	.05
232 Nolan Ryan	1.50
233 Bruce Hurst	.05
234 Jesse Orosco	.05
235 Bobby Thigpen	.05
236 Pascual Perez	.05
237 Matt Nokes	.05
238 Bob Ojeda	.05
239 Joey Meyer	.05
240 Shane Rawley	.05
241 Jeff Robinson	.05
242 Jeff Reardon	.05
243 Ozzie Smith	.60
244 Dave Winfield	.50
245 John Kruk	.05
246 Carney Lansford	.05
247 Candy Maldonado	.05
248 Ken Phelps	.05
249 Ken Williams	.05
250 Al Nipper	.05
251 Mark McLemore	.05
252 Lee Smith	.05
253 Albert Hall	.05
254 Billy Ripken	.05
255 Kelly Gruber	.05
256 Charlie Hough	.05
257 John Smiley	.05
258 Tim Wallach	.05
259 Frank Tanana	.05
260 Mike Scioscia	.05
261 Damon Berryhill	.05
262 Dave Smith	.05
263 Willie Wilson	.05
264 Len Dykstra	.05
265 Randy Myers	.05
266 Keith Moreland	.05
267 Eric Plunk	.05
268 Todd Worrell	.05
269 Bob Walk	.05
270 Keith Atherton	.05
271 Mike Schmidt	.75
272 Mike Flanagan	.05
273 Rafael Santana	.05
274 Rob Thompson	.05
275 Rey Quinones	.05
276 Cecilio Guante	.05
277 B.J. Surhoff	.05
278 Chris Sabo	.05
279 Mitch Williams	.05
280 Greg Swindell	.05
281 Alan Trammell	.05
282 Storm Davis	.05
283 Chuck Finley	.05
284 Dave Stieb	.05
285 Scott Bailes	.05
286 Larry Sheets	.05
287 Danny Tartabull	.05
288 Checklist	.05
289 Todd Benzinger	.05
290 John Shelby	.05
291 Steve Lyons	.05
292 Mitch Webster	.05
293 Walt Terrell	.05
294 Pete Stanicek	.05
295 Chris Bosio	.05
296 Milt Thompson	.05
297 Fred Lynn	.05
298 Juan Berenguer	.05
299 Ken Dayley	.05
300 Joel Skinner	.05
301 Benito Santiago	.05
302 Ron Hassey	.05
303 Jose Uribe	.05
304 Harold Reynolds	.05
305 Dale Sveum	.05
306 Glenn Wilson	.05
307 Mike Witt	.05
308 Ron Robinson	.05
309 Denny Walling	.05
310 Joe Orsulak	.05
311 David Wells	.05
312 Steve Buechele	.05
313 Jose Oquendo	.05
314 Floyd Youmans	.05
315 Lou Whitaker	.05
316 Fernando Valenzuela	.05
317 Mike Boddicker	.05
318 Gerald Young	.05
319 Frank White	.05
320 Bill Wegman	.05
321 Tom Niedenfuer	.05
322 Ed Whitson	.05
323 Curt Young	.05
324 Greg Mathews	.05
325 Doug Jones	.05
326 Tommy Herr	.05
327 Kent Tekulve	.05
328 Rance Mulliniks	.05
329 Checklist	.05
330 Craig Lefferts	.05
331 Franklin Stubbs	.05
332 Rick Cerone	.05
333 Dave Schmidt	.05
334 Larry Parrish	.05
335 Tom Browning	.05
336 Checklist	.05

1988 Donruss Diamond Kings Supers

TOMMY JOHN

This 28-card set (including the checklist) marks the fourth edition of Donruss' super-size (5" x 7") set. These cards are exact duplicates of the 1988 Diamond Kings that feature player portraits by Dick Perez. A 12-piece Stan Musial puzzle was also included with the purchase of the super-size set which was marketed via a mail-in offer printed on Donruss wrappers.

	NM/M
Complete Set (28):	5.00
Common Player:	.10
1 Mark McGwire	2.00
2 Tim Raines	.10
3 Benito Santiago	.10
4 Alan Trammell	.10
5 Danny Tartabull	.10
6 Ron Darling	.10
7 Paul Molitor	1.00
8 Devon White	.10
9 Andre Dawson	.25
10 Julio Franco	.10
11 Scott Fletcher	.10
12 Tony Fernandez	.10
13 Shane Rawley	.10
14 Kal Daniels	.10
15 Jack Clark	.10
16 Dwight Evans	.10
17 Tommy John	.15
18 Andy Van Slyke	.10
19 Gary Gaetti	.10
20 Mark Langston	.10
21 Will Clark	.10
22 Glenn Hubbard	.10
23 Billy Hatcher	.10
24 Bob Welch	.10
25 Ivan Calderon	.10
26 Cal Ripken, Jr.	3.00
27 Checklist	.05
641 Stan Musial Puzzle Card	.10

1988 Donruss Pop-Ups

WADE BOGGS RED SOX - 3B

Donruss' 1988 Pop-Up cards were reduced to the standard 2-1/2" x 3-1/2". The set includes 20 cards that fold out so that the upper portion of the player stands upright, giving a three-dimensional effect. Pop-Ups feature players from the All-Star Game starting lineup. Fronts have the player's name, team and position printed in black on a yellow banner near the bottom. As in previous issues, backs contain only the player's name, league and position and a Leaf copyright. Pop-Ups were distributed in individual packages containing one Pop-Up, five Stan Musial puzzle pieces and three All-Star cards.

	NM/M
Complete Set (20):	4.00
Common Player:	.05
Stan Musial Puzzle:	1.00
Wax Pack:	.50
Wax Box (48):	10.00
(1) George Bell	.05
(2) Wade Boggs	.50
(3) Gary Carter	.40
(4) Jack Clark	.05
(5) Eric Davis	.05
(6) Andre Dawson	.25
(7) Rickey Henderson	.40
(8) Davey Johnson	.05
(9) Don Mattingly	.65
(10) Terry Kennedy	.05
(11) John McNamara	.05
(12) Willie Randolph	.05
(13) Cal Ripken, Jr.	1.00
(14) Bret Saberhagen	.05
(15) Ryne Sandberg	.50
(16) Mike Schmidt	.65
(17) Mike Scott	.05
(18) Ozzie Smith	.50
(19) Darryl Strawberry	.05
(20) Dave Winfield	.40

Rookies

Mark Grace 1B

For the third consecutive year, Donruss issued a 56-card boxed set highlighting current rookies. The complete set includes a checklist and a 15-piece Stan Musial Diamond Kings puzzle. As in previous years, the set is similar to the company's basic issue, with the exception of the logo and border color. Card fronts feature red, green and black-striped borders, with a red-and-white player name printed in the lower-left corner beneath the photo. "The Rookies" logo is printed in red, white and black in the lower-right corner. Backs are printed in black on bright aqua and include personal data, recent performance stats and major league totals, as well as 1984-88 minor league stats. The cards are the standard 2-1/2" x 3-1/2".

	NM/M
Complete Set (56):	4.00
Common Player:	.05
1 Mark Grace	.25
2 Mike Campbell	.05
3 Todd Frowirth RC	.05
4 Dave Stapleton	.05
5 Shawn Abner	.05
6 Jose Cecena RC	.05
7 Dave Gallagher RC	.05
8 Mark Parent RC	.05
9 Cecil Espy RC	.05
10 Pete Smith	.05
11 Jay Buhner	.25
12 Pat Borders RC	.05
13 Doug Jennings RC	.05
14 Brady Anderson RC	1.00
15 Pete Stanicek	.05
16 Roberto Kelly	.05
17 Jeff Treadway	.05
18 Walt Weiss RC	.05
19 Paul Gibson RC	.05
20 Tim Crews	.05
21 Melido Perez	.05
22 Steve Peters RC	.05
23 Craig Worthington RC	.05
24 John Trautwein RC	.05
25 DeWayne Vaughn RC	.05
26 David Wells	.15
27 Al Leiter	.05
28 Tim Belcher	.05
29 Johnny Paredes RC	.05
30 Chris Sabo RC	.05
31 Damon Berryhill	.05
32 Randy Milligan	.05
33 Gary Thurman	.05
34 Kevin Elster	.05
35 Roberto Alomar	1.50

#	Player	Price
36	Edgar Martinez RC (Photo actually Edwin Nunez.)	1.50
37	Todd Stottlemyre	.15
38	Joey Meyer	.05
39	Carl Nichols	.05
40	Jack McDowell	.05
41	Jose Bautista RC	.05
42	Sil Campusano RC	.05
43	John Dopson RC	.05
44	Jody Reed	.05
45	Darrin Jackson RC	.05
46	Mike Capel RC	.05
47	Ron Gant	.05
48	John Davis	.05
49	Kevin Coffman RC	.05
50	Cris Carpenter RC	.05
51	Mackey Sasser	.05
52	Luis Alicea RC	.05
53	Bryan Harvey RC	.05
54	Steve Ellsworth RC	.05
55	Mike Macfarlane RC	.05
56	Checklist 1-56	.05

1988 Donruss Team Books

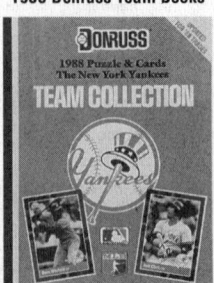

Three pages of nine cards each and a Stan Musial puzzle highlight these special team collection books. The cards feature the same design as the regular 1988 Donruss cards, but contain a 1988 copyright date instead of 1987 like the regular set. The cards are numbered with the exception of new cards of traded players and rookies produced especially for the team collection books. Books are commonly found complete with the cards and puzzle. The puzzle pieces are perforated for removal, but the card sheets are not.

		NM/M
Complete Set, Books (5):		12.00
Common Player:		.05
Boston Red Sox Team Book		3.00
NEW	Brady Anderson	.50
NEW	Rick Cerone	.05
NEW	Steve Ellsworth	.05
NEW	Dennis Lamp	.05
NEW	Kevin Romine	.05
NEW	Lee Smith	.25
NEW	Mike Smithson	.05
NEW	John Trautwein	.05
41	Jody Reed	.05
51	Roger Clemens	.75
92	Bob Stanley	.05
129	Rich Gedman	.05
153	Wade Boggs	.65
174	Ellis Burks	.05
216	Dwight Evans	.05
252	Bruce Hurst	.05
276	Marty Barrett	.05
297	Todd Benzinger	.05
339	Mike Greenwell	.05
399	Jim Rice	.25
421	John Marzano	.05
462	Oil Can Boyd	.05
498	Sam Horn	.05
544	Spike Owen	.05
585	Jeff Sellers	.05
623	Ed Romero	.05
634	Wes Gardner	.05
Chicago Cubs Team Book:		3.00
NEW	Mike Bielecki	.05
NEW	Rich Gossage	.25
NEW	Drew Hall	.05
NEW	Darrin Jackson	.05
NEW	Vance Law	.05
NEW	Al Nipper	.05
NEW	Angel Salazar	.05
NEW	Calvin Schiraldi	.05
40	Mark Grace	.50
68	Rick Sutcliffe	.05
119	Jody Davis	.05
146	Shawon Dunston	.05
169	Jamie Moyer	.05
191	Leon Durham	.05
242	Ryne Sandberg	.25
269	Andre Dawson	.25
315	Paul Noce	.05
324	Rafael Palmeiro	.40
438	Dave Martinez	.05
447	Jerry Mumphrey	.05
488	Jim Sundberg	.05
516	Manny Trillo	.05
539	Greg Maddux	.65

561	Les Lancaster	.05
570	Frank DiPino	.05
639	Damon Berryhill	.05
646	Scott Sanderson	.05
N.Y. Mets Team Book:		3.00
NEW	Jeff Innis	.05
NEW	Mackey Sasser	.05
NEW	Gene Walter	.05
37	Kevin Elster	.05
69	Dwight Gooden	.05
76	Ron Darling	.05
118	Sid Fernandez	.05
199	Gary Carter	.50
241	Wally Backman	.05
316	Keith Hernandez	.05
323	Dave Magadan	.05
364	Len Dykstra	.05
439	Darryl Strawberry	.05
446	Rick Aguilera	.05
562	Keith Miller	.05
569	Howard Johnson	.05
603	Terry Leach	.05
614	Lee Mazzilli	.05
617	Kevin McReynolds	.05
619	Barry Lyons	.05
620	Randy Myers	.05
632	Bob Ojeda	.05
648	Tim Teufel	.05
651	Roger McDowell	.05
652	Mookie Wilson	.05
653	David Cone	.05
657	Gregg Jefferies	.35
N.Y. Yankees Team Book:		3.00
NEW	John Candelaria	.05
NEW	Jack Clark	.05
NEW	Jose Cruz	.05
NEW	Richard Dotson	.05
NEW	Cecilio Guante	.05
NEW	Lee Guetterman	.05
NEW	Rafael Santana	.05
NEW	Steve Shields	.05
NEW	Don Slaught	.15
43	Al Leiter	.05
93	Dave Righetti	.05
105	Mike Pagliarulo	.05
128	Rick Rhoden	.05
175	Ron Guidry	.10
217	Don Mattingly	.75
228	Willie Randolph	.05
251	Gary Ward	.05
277	Rickey Henderson	.50
278	Dave Winfield	.50
340	Claudell Washington	.05
374	Charles Hudson	.05
401	Tommy John	.10
474	Joel Skinner	.05
497	Tim Stoddard	.05
545	Jay Buhner	.10
616	Bobby Meacham	.05
635	Roberto Kelly	.05
Oakland A's Team Book:		3.00
NEW	Don Baylor	.25
NEW	Ron Hassey	.05
NEW	Dave Henderson	.05
NEW	Glenn Hubbard	.05
NEW	Stan Javier	.05
NEW	Doug Jennings	.05
NEW	Ed Jurak	.05
NEW	Dave Parker	.15
NEW	Walt Weiss	.15
NEW	Bob Welch	.05
NEW	Matt Young	.05
97	Curt Young	.05
133	Gene Nelson	.05
158	Terry Steinbach	.05
178	Carney Lansford	.05
221	Tony Phillips	.05
256	Mark McGwire	1.00
302	Jose Canseco	.30
349	Dennis Eckersley	.40
425	Luis Polonia	.05
467	Steve Ontiveros	.05
472	Dave Stewart	.05
503	Eric Plunk	.05
528	Greg Cadaret	.05
590	Rick Honeycutt	.05
595	Storm Davis	.05

1989 Donruss Promo Sheet

To introduce its card design for 1989, Donruss produced this sheet. Printed on semi-gloss paper, the 7-1/2" x 10-1/2" blank-back sheet has images of seven regular cards, a Diamond King and an MVP.

	NM/M
Complete Sheet:	10.00

1989 Donruss

Fred McGriff 1B

This basic annual issue consists of 660 2-1/2" x 3-1/2" cards, including 26 Diamond Kings (DK) portrait cards and 20 Rated Rookies (RR) cards. Top and bottom borders of the cards are printed in a variety of colors that fade from dark to light. A white-lettered player name is printed across the top margin. The team logo appears upper-right and the Donruss logo lower-left. A black outer stripe varnish gives faintly visible filmstrip texture to the border. Backs are in orange and black, similar to the 1988 design, with personal info, recent stats and major league totals. Team logo sticker cards (22 total) and Warren Spahn puzzle cards (63 total) are included in individual wax packs of cards. Each regular player card can be found with a back variation in the header line across the stats: i.e., "*De-notes" or "*Denotes*." Neither version carries a premium.

	NM/M
Unopened Fact. Set (660):	17.50
Complete Set (660):	15.00
Common Player:	.05
Warren Spahn Puzzle:	.50
Wax Pack (15):	.75
Wax Box (36):	15.00
Cello Pack (32):	1.00
Cello Box (24):	15.00
Rack Pack (45):	.75

#	Player	Price
1	Mike Greenwell (DK)	.05
2	Bobby Bonilla (DK)	.05
3	Pete Incaviglia (DK)	.05
4	Chris Sabo (DK)	.05
5	Robin Yount (DK)	.40
6	Tony Gwynn (DK)	.50
7	Carlton Fisk (DK)	.40
8	Cory Snyder (DK)	.05
9	David Cone (DK)	.05
10	Kevin Seitzer (DK)	.05
11	Rick Reuschel (DK)	.05
12	Johnny Ray (DK)	.05
13	Dave Schmidt (DK)	.05
14	Andres Galarraga (DK)	.05
15	Kirk Gibson (DK)	.05
16	Fred McGriff (DK)	.05
17	Mark Grace (DK)	.15
18	Jeff Robinson (DK)	.05
19	Vince Coleman (DK)	.05
20	Dave Henderson (DK)	.05
21	Harold Reynolds (DK)	.05
22	Gerald Perry (DK)	.05
23	Frank Viola (DK)	.05
24	Steve Bedrosian (DK)	.05
25	Glenn Davis (DK)	.05
26	Don Mattingly (DK)	.60
27	Checklist 1-27	.05
28	Sandy Alomar, Jr. RC (RR)	.35
29	Steve Searcy RC (RR)	.05
30	Cameron Drew RC (RR)	.05
31	Gary Sheffield RC (RR)	1.00
32	Erik Hanson RC (RR)	.05
33	Ken Griffey Jr. RC (RR)	6.00
34	Greg Harris RC (RR)	.05
35	Gregg Jefferies RC (RR)	.05
36	Luis Medina RC (RR)	.05
37	Carlos Quintana RC (RR)	.05
38	Felix Jose RC (RR)	.05
39	Cris Carpenter RC (RR)	.05
40	Ron Jones RC (RR)	.05
41	Dave West RC (RR)	.05
42	Randy Johnson RC (RR)	3.00
43	Mike Harkey RC (RR)	.05
44	Pete Harnisch RC (RR)	.10
45	Tom Gordon RC (RR)	.05
46	Gregg Olson RC (RR)	.10
47	Alex Sanchez RC (RR)	.05
48	Ruben Sierra	.05
49	Rafael Palmeiro	.05
50	Ron Gant	.05
51	Cal Ripken, Jr.	1.00
52	Wally Joyner	.05
53	Gary Carter	.40
54	Andy Van Slyke	.05
55	Robin Yount	.40
56	Pete Incaviglia	.05
57	Greg Brock	.05
58	Melido Perez	.05
59	Craig Lefferts	.05
60	Gary Pettis	.05
61	Danny Tartabull	.05
62	Guillermo Hernandez	.05
63	Ozzie Smith	.50
64	Gary Gaetti	.05
65	Mark Davis	.05
66	Lee Smith	.05
67	Dennis Eckersley	.35
68	Wade Boggs	.50
69	Mike Scott	.05
70	Fred McGriff	.05
71	Tom Browning	.05
72	Claudell Washington	.05
73	Mel Hall	.05
74	Don Mattingly	.60
75	Steve Bedrosian	.05
76	Juan Samuel	.05
77	Mike Scioscia	.05
78	Dave Righetti	.05
79	Alfredo Griffin	.05
80	Eric Davis	.05
81	Juan Berenguer	.05
82	Todd Worrell	.05
83	Joe Carter	.05
84	Steve Sax	.05
85	Frank White	.05
86	John Kruk	.05
87	Rance Mulliniks	.05
88	Alan Ashby	.05
89	Charlie Leibrandt	.05
90	Frank Tanana	.05
91	Jose Canseco	.25
92	Barry Bonds	1.00
93	Harold Reynolds	.05
94	Mark McLemore	.05
95	Mark McGwire	.75
96	Eddie Murray	.40
97	Tim Raines	.05
98	Rob Thompson	.05
99	Kevin McReynolds	.05
100	Checklist 28-137	.05
101	Carlton Fisk	.40
102	Dave Martinez	.05
103	Glenn Braggs	.05
104	Dale Murphy	.15
105	Ryne Sandberg	.50
106	Dennis Martinez	.05
107	Pete O'Brien	.05
108	Dick Schofield	.05
109	Henry Cotto	.05
110	Mike Marshall	.05
111	Keith Moreland	.05
112	Tom Brunansky	.05
113	Kelly Gruber	.05
114	Brook Jacoby	.05
115	Keith Brown RC	.05
116	Matt Nokes	.05
117	Keith Hernandez	.05
118	Bob Forsch	.05
119	Bert Blyleven	.10
120	Willie Wilson	.05
121	Tommy Gregg	.05
122	Jim Rice	.25
123	Bob Knepper	.05
124	Danny Jackson	.05
125	Eric Plunk	.05
126	Brian Fisher	.05
127	Mike Pagliarulo	.05
128	Tony Gwynn	.50
129	Lance McCullers	.05
130	Andres Galarraga	.05
131	Jose Uribe	.05
132	Kirk Gibson	.05
133	David Palmer	.05
134	R.J. Reynolds	.05
135	Greg Walker	.05
136	Kirk McCaskill	.05
137	Shawon Dunston	.05
138	Andy Allanson	.05
139	Rob Murphy	.05
140	Mike Aldrete	.05
141	Terry Kennedy	.05
142	Scott Fletcher	.05
143	Steve Balboni	.05
144	Bret Saberhagen	.05
145	Ozzie Virgil	.05
146	Dale Sveum	.05
147	Darryl Strawberry	.05
148	Harold Baines	.10
149	George Bell	.05
150	Dave Parker	.05
151	Bobby Bonilla	.05
152	Mookie Wilson	.05
153	Ted Power	.05
154	Nolan Ryan	1.00
155	Jeff Reardon	.05
156	Tim Wallach	.05
157	Jamie Moyer	.05
158	Rich Gossage	.05
159	Dave Winfield	.40
160	Von Hayes	.05
161	Willie McGee	.05
162	Rich Gedman	.05
163	Tony Pena	.05
164	Mike Morgan	.05
165	Charlie Hough	.05
166	Mike Stanley	.05
167	Andre Dawson	.20
168	Joe Boever	.05
169	Pete Stanicek	.05
170	Bob Boone	.05
171	Ron Darling	.05
172	Bob Walk	.05
173	Rob Deer	.05
174	Steve Buechele	.05
175	Ted Higuera	.05
176	Ozzie Guillen	.05
177	Candy Maldonado	.05
178	Doyle Alexander	.05
179	Mark Gubicza	.05
180	Alan Trammell	.05
181	Vince Coleman	.05
182	Kirby Puckett	.50
183	Chris Brown	.05
184	Marty Barrett	.05
185	Stan Javier	.05
186	Mike Greenwell	.05
187	Billy Hatcher	.05
188	Jimmy Key	.05
189	Nick Esasky	.05
190	Don Slaught	.05
191	Cory Snyder	.05
192	John Candelaria	.05
193	Mike Schmidt	.60
194	Kevin Gross	.05
195	John Tudor	.05
196	Neil Allen	.05
197	Orel Hershiser	.05
198	Kal Daniels	.05
199	Kent Hrbek	.05
200	Checklist 138-247	.05
201	Joe Magrane	.05
202	Scott Bailes	.05
203	Tim Belcher	.05
204	George Brett	.60
205	Benito Santiago	.05
206	Tony Fernandez	.05
207	Gerald Young	.05
208	Bo Jackson	.10
209	Chet Lemon	.05
210	Storm Davis	.05
211	Doug Drabek	.05
212	Mickey Brantley (Photo actually Nelson Simmons.)	.05
213	Devon White	.05
214	Dave Stewart	.05
215	Dave Schmidt	.05
216	Bryn Smith	.05
217	Brett Butler	.05
218	Bob Ojeda	.05
219	Steve Rosenberg RC	.05
220	Hubie Brooks	.05
221	B.J. Surhoff	.05
222	Rick Mahler	.05
223	Rick Sutcliffe	.05
224	Neal Heaton	.05
225	Mitch Williams	.05
226	Chuck Finley	.05
227	Mark Langston	.05
228	Jesse Orosco	.05
229	Ed Whitson	.05
230	Terry Pendleton	.05
231	Lloyd Moseby	.05
232	Greg Swindell	.05
233	John Franco	.05
234	Jack Morris	.05
235	Howard Johnson	.05
236	Glenn Davis	.05
237	Frank Viola	.05
238	Kevin Seitzer	.05
239	Gerald Perry	.05
240	Dwight Evans	.05
241	Jim Deshaies	.05
242	Bo Diaz	.05
243	Carney Lansford	.05
244	Mike LaValliere	.05
245	Rickey Henderson	.40
246	Roberto Alomar	.20
247	Jimmy Jones	.05
248	Pascual Perez	.05
249	Will Clark	.05
250	Fernando Valenzuela	.05
251	Shane Rawley	.05
252	Sid Bream	.05
253	Steve Lyons	.05
254	Brian Downing	.05
255	Mark Grace	.05
256	Tom Candiotti	.05
257	Barry Larkin	.05
258	Mike Krukow	.05
259	Billy Ripken	.05
260	Cecilio Guante	.05
261	Scott Bradley	.05
262	Floyd Bannister	.05
263	Pete Smith	.05
264	Jim Gantner	.05
265	Roger McDowell	.05
266	Bobby Thigpen	.05
267	Jim Clancy	.05
268	Terry Steinbach	.05
269	Mike Dunne	.05
270	Dwight Gooden	.05
271	Mike Heath	.05
272	Dave Smith	.05
273	Keith Atherton	.05
274	Tim Burke	.05
275	Damon Berryhill	.05
276	Vance Law	.05
277	Rich Dotson	.05
278	Lance Parrish	.05
279	Dennis Walling	.05
280	Roger Clemens	.60
281	Greg Mathews	.05
282	Tom Niedenfuer	.05
283	Paul Kilgus	.05
284	Jose Guzman	.05
285	Calvin Schiraldi	.05
286	Charlie Puleo	.05
287	Joe Orsulak	.05
288	Jack Howell	.05
289	Kevin Elster	.05
290	Jose Lind	.05
291	Paul Molitor	.40
292	Cecil Espy	.05
293	Bill Wegman	.05
294	Dan Pasqua	.05
295	Scott Garrelts	.05
296	Walt Terrell	.05
297	Ed Hearn	.05
298	Lou Whitaker	.05
299	Ken Dayley	.05
300	Checklist 248-357	.05
301	Tommy Herr	.05
302	Mike Brumley	.05
303	Ellis Burks	.05
304	Curt Young	.05
305	Jody Reed	.05
306	Bill Doran	.05
307	David Wells	.05
308	Ron Robinson	.05
309	Rafael Santana	.05
310	Julio Franco	.05
311	Jack Clark	.05
312	Chris James	.05
313	Milt Thompson	.05
314	John Shelby	.05
315	Al Leiter	.05
316	Mike Davis	.05
317	Chris Sabo RC	.15
318	Greg Gagne	.05
319	Jose Oquendo	.05
320	John Farrell	.05
321	Franklin Stubbs	.05
322	Kurt Stillwell	.05
323	Shawn Abner	.05
324	Mike Flanagan	.05
325	Kevin Bass	.05
326	Pat Tabler	.05
327	Mike Henneman	.05
328	Rick Honeycutt	.05
329	John Smiley	.05
330	Rey Quinones	.05
331	Johnny Ray	.05
332	Bob Welch	.05
333	Larry Sheets	.05
334	Jeff Parrett	.05
335	Rick Reuschel	.05
336	Randy Myers	.05
337	Ken Williams	.05
338	Andy McGaffigan	.05
339	Joey Meyer	.05
340	Dion James	.05
341	Les Lancaster	.05
342	Tom Foley	.05
343	Geno Petralli	.05
344	Dan Petry	.05
345	Alvin Davis	.05
346	Mickey Hatcher	.05
347	Marvell Wynne	.05
348	Danny Cox	.05
349	Dave Stieb	.05
350	Jay Bell	.05
351	Jeff Treadway	.05
352	Luis Salazar	.05
353	Len Dykstra	.05
354	Juan Agosto	.05
355	Gene Larkin	.05
356	Steve Farr	.05
357	Paul Assenmacher	.05
358	Todd Benzinger	.05
359	Larry Andersen	.05
360	Paul O'Neill	.05
361	Ron Hassey	.05
362	Jim Gott	.05
363	Ken Phelps	.05
364	Tim Flannery	.05
365	Randy Ready	.05
366	Nelson Santovenia RC	.05
367	Kelly Downs	.05
368	Danny Heep	.05
369	Phil Bradley	.05
370	Jeff Robinson	.05
371	Ivan Calderon	.05
372	Mike Witt	.05
373	Greg Maddux	.50
374	Carmen Castillo	.05
375	Jose Rijo	.05
376	Joe Price	.05
377	R.C. Gonzalez	.05
378	Oddibe McDowell	.05
379	Jim Presley	.05
380	Brad Wellman	.05
381	Tom Glavine	.20
382	Dan Plesac	.05
383	Wally Backman	.05
384	Dave Gallagher RC	.05
385	Tom Henke	.05
386	Luis Polonia	.05
387	Junior Ortiz	.05
388	David Cone	.05
389	Dave Bergman	.05
390	Danny Darwin	.05
391	Dan Gladden	.05
392	John Dopson RC	.05
393	Frank DiPino	.05
394	Al Nipper	.05
395	Willie Randolph	.05
396	Don Carman	.05
397	Scott Terry	.05
398	Rick Cerone	.05
399	Tom Pagnozzi	.05
400	Checklist 358-467	.05
401	Mickey Tettleton	.05
402	Curtis Wilkerson	.05
403	Jeff Russell	.05
404	Pat Perry	.05
405	Jose Alvarez RC	.05
406	Rick Schu	.05
407	Sherman Corbett RC	.05

#	Player	Price		#	Player	Price		#	Player	Price
408	Dave Magadan	.05		526	Rick Aguilera	.05		641	Brian Harper	.05
409	Bob Kipper	.05		527	Tom Prince	.05		642	John Smoltz	.05
410	Don August	.05		528	Mark Clear	.05		643	Jose Bautista (40/40)	.15
411	Bob Brower	.05		529	Jerry Browne	.05		644	Bill Schroeder	.05
412	Chris Bosio	.05		530	Juan Castillo	.05		645	Edgar Martinez	.10
413	Jerry Reuss	.05		531	Jack McDowell	.05		646	Dennis Cook RC	.05
414	Atlee Hammaker	.05		532	Chris Speier	.05		647	Barry Jones	.05
415	Jim Walewander	.05		533	Darrell Evans	.05		648	Orel Hershiser (59 and Counting)	.05
416	Mike Macfarlane RC	.10		534	Luis Aquino	.05		649	Rod Nichols RC	.05
417	Pat Sheridan	.05		535	Eric King	.05		650	Jody Davis	.05
418	Pedro Guerrero	.05		536	Ken Hill RC	.05		651	Bob Milacki RC	.05
419	Allan Anderson	.05		537	Randy Bush	.05		652	Mike Jackson	.05
420	Mark Parent RC	.05		538	Shane Mack	.05		653	Derek Lilliquist RC	.05
421	Bob Stanley	.05		539	Tom Bolton	.05		654	Paul Mirabella	.05
422	Mike Gallego	.05		540	Gene Nelson	.05		655	Mike Diaz	.05
423	Bruce Hurst	.05		541	Wes Gardner	.05		656	Jeff Musselman	.05
424	Dave Meads	.05		542	Ken Caminiti	.05		657	Jerry Reed	.05
425	Jesse Barfield	.05		543	Duane Ward	.05		658	Kevin Blankenship RC	.05
426	Rob Dibble RC	.15		544	Norm Charlton RC	.10		659	Wayne Tolleson	.05
427	Joel Skinner	.05		545	Hal Morris RC	.25		660	Eric Hetzel RC	.05
428	Ron Kittle	.05		546	Rich Yett	.05				
429	Rick Rhoden	.05		547	Hensley Meulens RC	.10				
430	Bob Dernier	.05		548	Greg Harris	.05				
431	Steve Jeltz	.05		549	Darren Daulton	.05				
432	Rick Dempsey	.05		550	Jeff Hamilton	.05				
433	Roberto Kelly	.05		551	Luis Aguayo	.05				
434	Dave Anderson	.05		552	Tim Leary	.05				
435	Herm Winningham	.05		553	Ron Oester	.05				
436	Al Newman	.05		554	Steve Lombardozzi	.05				
437	Jose DeLeon	.05		555	Tim Jones RC	.05				
438	Doug Jones	.05		556	Bud Black	.05				
439	Brian Holton	.05		557	Alejandro Pena	.05				
440	Jeff Montgomery	.05		558	Jose DeJesus RC	.05				
441	Dickie Thon	.05		559	Dennis Rasmussen	.05				
442	Cecil Fielder	.05		560	Pat Borders RC	.25				
443	John Fishel RC	.05		561	Craig Biggio RC	.05				
444	Jerry Don Gleaton	.05		562	Luis de los Santos RC	.05				
445	Paul Gibson RC	.05		563	Fred Lynn	.05				
446	Walt Weiss	.05		564	Todd Burns RC	.05				
447	Glenn Wilson	.05		565	Felix Fermin	.05				
448	Mike Moore	.05		566	Darnell Coles	.05				
449	Chili Davis	.05		567	Willie Fraser	.05				
450	Dave Henderson	.05		568	Glenn Hubbard	.05				
451	Jose Bautista RC	.05		569	Craig Worthington RC	.05				
452	Rex Hudler	.05		570	Johnny Paredes RC	.05				
453	Bob Brenly	.05		571	Don Robinson	.05				
454	Mackey Sasser	.05		572	Barry Lyons	.05				
455	Daryl Boston	.05		573	Bill Long	.05				
456	Mike Fitzgerald	.05		574	Tracy Jones	.05				
457	Jeffery Leonard	.05		575	Juan Nieves	.05				
458	Bruce Sutter	.35		576	Andres Thomas	.05				
459	Mitch Webster	.05		577	Rolando Roomes RC	.05				
460	Joe Hesketh	.05		578	Luis Rivera	.05				
461	Bobby Witt	.05		579	Chad Kreuter RC	.10				
462	Stew Cliburn	.05		580	Tony Armas	.05				
463	Scott Bankhead	.05		581	Jay Buhner	.05				
464	Ramon Martinez RC	.25		582	Ricky Horton	.05				
465	Dave Leiper	.05		583	Andy Hawkins	.05				
466	Luis Alicea RC	.05		584	Sil Campusano RC	.05				
467	John Cerutti	.05		585	Dave Clark	.05				
468	Ron Washington	.05		586	Van Snider RC	.05				
469	Jeff Reed	.05		587	Todd Frohwirth	.05				
470	Jeff Robinson	.05		588	Warren Spahn Puzzle Card	.05				
471	Sid Fernandez	.05		589	William Brennan RC	.05				
472	Terry Puhl	.05		590	German Gonzalez RC	.05				
473	Charlie Lea	.05		591	Ernie Whitt	.05				
474	Israel Sanchez RC	.05		592	Jeff Blauser	.05				
475	Bruce Benedict	.05		593	Spike Owen	.05				
476	Oil Can Boyd	.05		594	Matt Williams	.05				
477	Craig Reynolds	.05		595	Lloyd McClendon	.05				
478	Frank Williams	.05		596	Steve Ontiveros	.05				
479	Greg Cadaret	.05		597	Scott Medvin RC	.05				
480	Randy Kramer RC	.05		598	Hipolito Pena RC	.05				
481	Dave Eiland RC	.05		599	Jerald Clark RC	.05				
482	Eric Show	.05		600a	Checklist 578-BC26 (#635 is Kurt Schilling)	.10				
483	Garry Templeton	.05		600b	Checklist 578-BC26 (#635 is Curt Schilling)	.05				
484	Wallace Johnson	.05		601	Carmelo Martinez	.05				
485	Kevin Mitchell	.05		602	Mike LaCoss	.05				
486	Tim Crews	.05		603	Mike Devereaux	.05				
487	Mike Maddux	.05		604	Alex Madrid RC	.05				
488	Dave LaPoint	.05		605	Gary Redus	.05				
489	Fred Manrique	.05		606	Lance Johnson	.05				
490	Greg Minton	.05		607	Terry Clark RC	.05				
491	Doug Dascenzo RC	.05		608	Manny Trillo	.05				
492	Willie Upshaw	.05		609	Scott Jordan RC	.05				
493	Jack Armstrong RC	.05		610	Jay Howell	.05				
494	Kirt Manwaring	.05		611	Francisco Melendez RC	.05				
495	Jeff Ballard	.05		612	Mike Boddicker	.05				
496	Jeff Kunkel	.05		613	Kevin Brown	.05				
497	Mike Campbell	.05		614	Dave Valle	.05				
498	Gary Thurman	.05		615	Tim Laudner	.05				
499	Zane Smith	.05		616	Andy Nezelek RC	.05				
500	Checklist 468-577	.05		617	Chuck Crim	.05				
501	Mike Birkbeck	.05		618	Jack Savage	.05				
502	Terry Leach	.05		619	Adam Peterson	.05				
503	Shawn Hillegas	.05		620	Todd Stottlemyre	.05				
504	Manny Lee	.05		621	Lance Blankenship RC	.05				
505	Doug Jennings RC	.05		622	Miguel Garcia RC	.05				
506	Ken Oberkfell	.05		623	Keith Miller	.05				
507	Tim Teufel	.05		624	Ricky Jordan RC	.05				
508	Tom Brookens	.05		625	Ernest Riles	.05				
509	Rafael Ramirez	.05		626	John Moses	.05				
510	Fred Toliver	.05		627	Nelson Liriano	.05				
511	Brian Holman RC	.05		628	Mike Smithson	.05				
512	Mike Bielecki	.05		629	Scott Sanderson	.05				
513	Jeff Pico RC	.05		630	Dale Mohorcic	.05				
514	Charles Hudson	.05		631	Marvin Freeman	.05				
515	Bruce Ruffin	.05		632	Mike Young	.05				
516	Larry McWilliams	.05		633	Dennis Lamp	.05				
517	Jeff Sellers	.05		634	Dante Bichette RC	.05				
518	John Costello RC	.05		635	Curt Schilling RC	3.00				
519	Brady Anderson	.05		636	Scott May RC	.05				
520	Craig McMurtry	.05		637	Mike Schooler RC	.05				
521	Ray Hayward	.05		638	Rick Leach	.05				
522	Drew Hall	.05		639	Tom Lampkin RC	.05				
523	Mark Lemke RC	.05		640	Brian Meyer RC	.05				
524	Oswald Peraza RC	.05								
525	Bryan Harvey RC	.05								

1989 Donruss Grand Slammers

One card from this 12-card set was included in each Donruss cello pack. The complete insert set was included in factory sets. The featured players all hit grand slams in 1988. The 2-1/2" x 3-1/2" cards feature full color action photos. Backs tell the story of the player's grand slam. As many as five border-color variations on the front of each card have been discovered, but the prices are not affected.

		NM/M
Complete Set (12):		2.00
Common Player:		.25
1	Jose Canseco	.35
2	Mike Marshall	.25
3	Walt Weiss	.25
4	Kevin McReynolds	.25
5	Mike Greenwell	.25
6	Dave Winfield	.50
7	Mark McGwire	1.50
8	Keith Hernandez	.25
9	Franklin Stubbs	.25
10	Danny Tartabull	.25
11	Jesse Barfield	.25
12	Ellis Burks	.25

1989 Donruss Blue Chip Cards

		NM/M
Complete Set (12):		1,200
Common Player:		60.00
1	Jose Canseco	125.00
2	Mike Marshall	60.00
3	Walt Weiss	60.00
4	Kevin McReynolds	60.00
5	Mike Greenwell	60.00
6	Dave Winfield	150.00
7	Mark McGwire	400.00
8	Keith Hernandez	75.00
9	Franklin Stubbs	60.00
10	Danny Tartabull	60.00
11	Jesse Barfield	60.00
12	Ellis Burks	60.00

1989 Donruss MVP

This set, numbered BC1-BC26, was randomly inserted in Donruss wax packs, but not included in factory sets or other card packs. Players highlighted were selected by Donruss, one player per team. MVP cards feature a variation of the design in the basic Donruss issue, with multi-color upper and lower borders and black side borders. The "MVP" designation in large, bright letters serves as a backdrop for the full-color player photo. The cards measure 2-1/2" x 3-1/2".

		NM/M
Complete Set (26):		2.00
Common Player:		.05
1	Kirby Puckett	.40
2	Mike Scott	.05
3	Joe Carter	.05
4	Orel Hershiser	.05
5	Jose Canseco	.25
6	Darryl Strawberry	.05
7	George Brett	.50
8	Andre Dawson	.20
9	Paul Molitor	.30
10	Andy Van Slyke	.05
11	Dave Winfield	.30
12	Kevin Gross	.05
13	Mike Greenwell	.05
14	Ozzie Smith	.40
15	Cal Ripken	1.00
16	Andres Galarraga	.05
17	Alan Trammell	.05
18	Kal Daniels	.05
19	Fred McGriff	.05
20	Tony Gwynn	.40
21	Wally Joyner	.05
22	Will Clark	.05
23	Ozzie Guillen	.05
24	Gerald Perry	.05
25	Alvin Davis	.05
26	Ruben Sierra	.05

1989 Donruss All-Stars

For the fourth consecutive year Donruss featured a 64-card set with players from the 1988 All-Star Game. The card fronts include a red-to-gold fade or gold-to-red fade border and blue vertical side borders. The top border features the player's name and position along with the "Donruss 89" logo. Each full-color player photo is highlighted by a thin white line and includes a league logo in the lower right corner. Card backs reveal an orange-gold border and black and white printing. The player's ID and personal information is displayed with a gold star on both sides. The star in the left corner includes the card number. 1988 All-Star game statistics and run totals follow along with a career highlights feature surrounded by the team, All-Star Game MLB, MLBPA, and Leaf Inc. logos. The All-Stars were distributed in wax packages containing five All-Stars, one Pop-Up, and one three-piece Warren Spahn puzzle card.

		NM/M
Complete Set (64):		4.00
Common Player:		.10
Warren Spahn Puzzle:		.50
Wax Pack (5+1):		.30
Wax Box (48):		10.00
1	Mark McGwire	.75
2	Jose Canseco	.25
3	Paul Molitor	.25
4	Rickey Henderson	.40
5	Cal Ripken, Jr.	1.00
6	Dave Winfield	.40
7	Wade Boggs	.50
8	Frank Viola	.10
9	Terry Steinbach	.10
10	Tom Kelly	.10
11	George Brett	.65
12	Doyle Alexander	.10
13	Gary Gaetti	.10
14	Roger Clemens	.65
15	Mike Greenwell	.10
16	Dennis Eckersley	.40
17	Carney Lansford	.10
18	Mark Gubicza	.10
19	Tim Laudner	.10
20	Doug Jones	.10
21	Don Mattingly	.65
22	Dan Plesac	.10
23	Kirby Puckett	.50
24	Jeff Reardon	.10
25	Johnny Ray	.10
26	Jeff Russell	.10
27	Harold Reynolds	.10
28	Dave Stieb	.10
29	Kurt Stillwell	.10
30	Jose Canseco	.25
31	Terry Steinbach	.10
32	A.L. Checklist	.05
33	Will Clark	.10
34	Darryl Strawberry	.10
35	Ryne Sandberg	.50
36	Andre Dawson	.25
37	Ozzie Smith	.50
38	Vince Coleman	.10
39	Bobby Bonilla	.10
40	Dwight Gooden	.10
41	Gary Carter	.40
42	Whitey Herzog	.10
43	Shawon Dunston	.10
44	David Cone	.10
45	Andres Galarraga	.10
46	Mark Davis	.10
47	Barry Larkin	.10
48	Kevin Gross	.10
49	Vance Law	.10
50	Orel Hershiser	.10
51	Willie McGee	.10
52	Danny Jackson	.10
53	Rafael Palmeiro	.35
54	Bob Knepper	.10
55	Lance Parrish	.10
56	Greg Maddux	.50
57	Gerald Perry	.10
58	Bob Walk	.10
59	Chris Sabo	.10
60	Todd Worrell	.10
61	Andy Van Slyke	.10
62	Ozzie Smith	.50
63	Riverfront Stadium	.05
64	N.L. Checklist	.05

1989 Donruss Baseball's Best

For the second consecutive year, Donruss issued a "Baseball's Best" set in 1989 to highlight the game's top players. The special 336-card set was packaged in a special box and was sold at various retail chains nationwide following the conclusion of the 1989 baseball season. The cards are styled after the regular 1989 Donruss set with green borders and a glossy finish. The set included a Warren Spahn puzzle.

		NM/M		#	Player	Price
Unopened Set (336):		30.00		31	Kelly Gruber	.05
Complete Set (336):		25.00		32	Julio Franco	.05
Common Player:		.05		33	Bobby Bonilla	.05
1	Don Mattingly	.75		34	Tim Wallach	.05
2	Tom Glavine	.25		35	Lou Whitaker	.05
3	Bert Blyleven	.10		36	Jay Howell	.05
4	Andre Dawson	.05		37	Greg Maddux	.60
5	Pete O'Brien	.05		38	Bill Doran	.05
6	Eric Davis	.05		39	Danny Tartabull	.05
7	George Brett	.75		40	Darryl Strawberry	.05
8	Glenn Davis	.05		41	Ron Darling	.05
9	Ellis Burks	.05		42	Tony Gwynn	.60
10	Kirk Gibson	.05		43	Mark McGwire	1.00
11	Carlton Fisk	.50		44	Ozzie Smith	.60
12	Andres Galarraga	.05		45	Andy Van Slyke	.05
13	Alan Trammell	.05		46	Juan Berenguer	.05
14	Dwight Gooden	.05		47	Von Hayes	.05
15	Paul Molitor	.50		48	Tony Fernandez	.05
16	Roger McDowell	.05		49	Eric Plunk	.05
17	Doug Drabek	.05		50	Ernest Riles	.05
18	Kent Hrbek	.05		51	Harold Reynolds	.05
19	Vince Coleman	.05		52	Andy Hawkins	.05
20	Steve Sax	.05		53	Robin Yount	.50
21	Roberto Alomar	.20		54	Danny Jackson	.05
22	Carney Lansford	.05		55	Nolan Ryan	1.50
23	Will Clark	.05		56	Joe Carter	.05
24	Alvin Davis	.05		57	Jose Canseco	.35
25	Bobby Thigpen	.05		58	Jody Davis	.05
26	Ryne Sandberg	.60		59	Lance Parrish	.05
27	Devon White	.05		60	Mitch Williams	.05
28	Mike Greenwell	.05		61	Brook Jacoby	.05
29	Dale Murphy	.20		62	Tom Browning	.05
30	Jeff Ballard	.05		63	Kurt Stillwell	.05
				64	Rafael Ramirez	.05
				65	Roger Clemens	.75
				66	Mike Scioscia	.05
				67	Dave Gallagher	.05
				68	Mark Langston	.05
				69	Chet Lemon	.05
				70	Kevin McReynolds	.05
				71	Rob Deer	.05
				72	Tommy Herr	.05
				73	Barry Bonds	1.50
				74	Frank Viola	.05
				75	Pedro Guerrero	.05
				76	Dave Righetti	.05
				77	Bruce Hurst	.05
				78	Rickey Henderson	.50
				79	Robby Thompson	.05
				80	Randy Johnson	6.00
				81	Harold Baines	.05
				82	Calvin Schiraldi	.05
				83	Kirk McCaskill	.05
				84	Lee Smith	.05
				85	John Smoltz	1.00
				86	Mickey Tettleton	.05
				87	Jimmy Key	.05
				88	Rafael Palmeiro	.45
				89	Sid Bream	.05
				90	Dennis Martinez	.05
				91	Frank Tanana	.05
				92	Eddie Murray	.50
				93	Shawon Dunston	.05
				94	Mike Scott	.05
				95	Bret Saberhagen	.05
				96	David Cone	.05
				97	Kevin Elster	.05
				98	Jack Clark	.05
				99	Dave Stewart	.05
				100	Jose Oquendo	.05
				101	Jose Lind	.05
				102	Gary Gaetti	.05
				103	Ricky Jordan	.05
				104	Fred McGriff	.05
				105	Don Slaught	.05
				106	Jose Uribe	.05
				107	Jeffrey Leonard	.05
				108	Lee Guetterman	.05
				109	Chris Bosio	.05
				110	Barry Larkin	.05
				111	Ruben Sierra	.05
				112	Greg Swindell	.05
				113	Gary Sheffield	1.00
				114	Lonnie Smith	.05
				115	Chili Davis	.05
				116	Damon Berryhill	.05
				117	Tom Candiotti	.05
				118	Kal Daniels	.05
				119	Mark Gubicza	.05
				120	Jim Deshaies	.05
				121	Dwight Evans	.05
				122	Mike Morgan	.05
				123	Dan Pasqua	.05
				124	Bryn Smith	.05
				125	Doyle Alexander	.05
				126	Howard Johnson	.05
				127	Chuck Crim	.05
				128	Darren Daulton	.05
				129	Jeff Robinson	.05
				130	Kirby Puckett	.60
				131	Joe Magrane	.05
				132	Jesse Barfield	.05
				133	Mark Davis (Photo actually Dave Leiper.)	.05
				134	Dennis Eckersley	.45
				135	Mike Krukow	.05
				136	Jay Buhner	.05
				137	Ozzie Guillen	.05
				138	Rick Sutcliffe	.05
				139	Wally Joyner	.05
				140	Wade Boggs	.60
				141	Jeff Treadway	.05
				142	Cal Ripken	1.50
				143	Dave Stieb	.05
				144	Pete Incaviglia	.05
				145	Bob Walk	.05
				146	Nelson Santovenia	.05
				147	Mike Heath	.05

148	Willie Randolph	.05
149	Paul Kilgus	.05
150	Billy Hatcher	.05
151	Steve Farr	.05
152	Gregg Jefferies	.05
153	Randy Myers	.05
154	Garry Templeton	.05
155	Walt Weiss	.05
156	Terry Pendleton	.05
157	John Smiley	.05
158	Greg Gagne	.05
159	Lenny Dykstra	.05
160	Nelson Liriano	.05
161	Alvaro Espinoza	.05
162	Rick Reuschel	.05
163	Omar Vizquel	.05
164	Clay Parker	.05
165	Dan Plesac	.05
166	John Franco	.05
167	Scott Fletcher	.05
168	Cory Snyder	.05
169	Bo Jackson	.10
170	Tommy Gregg	.05
171	Jim Abbott	.05
172	Jerome Walton	.05
173	Doug Jones	.05
174	Todd Benzinger	.05
175	Frank White	.05
176	Craig Biggio	.50
177	John Dopson	.05
178	Alfredo Griffin	.05
179	Melido Perez	.05
180	Tim Burke	.05
181	Matt Nokes	.05
182	Gary Carter	.50
183	Ted Higuera	.05
184	Ken Howell	.05
185	Rey Quinones	.05
186	Wally Backman	.05
187	Tom Brunansky	.05
188	Steve Balboni	.05
189	Marvell Wynne	.05
190	Dave Henderson	.05
191	Don Robinson	.05
192	Ken Griffey Jr.	9.00
193	Ivan Calderon	.05
194	Mike Bielecki	.05
195	Johnny Ray	.05
196	Rob Murphy	.05
197	Andres Thomas	.05
198	Phil Bradley	.05
199	Junior Felix	.05
200	Jeff Russell	.05
201	Mike LaValliere	.05
202	Kevin Gross	.05
203	Keith Moreland	.05
204	Mike Marshall	.05
205	Dwight Smith	.05
206	Jim Clancy	.05
207	Kevin Seitzer	.05
208	Keith Hernandez	.05
209	Bob Ojeda	.05
210	Ed Whitson	.05
211	Tony Phillips	.05
212	Milt Thompson	.05
213	Randy Kramer	.05
214	Randy Bush	.05
215	Randy Ready	.05
216	Duane Ward	.05
217	Jimmy Jones	.05
218	Scott Garrelts	.05
219	Scott Bankhead	.05
220	Lance McCullers	.05
221	B.J. Surhoff	.05
222	Chris Sabo	.05
223	Steve Buechele	.05
224	Joel Skinner	.05
225	Orel Hershiser	.05
226	Derek Lilliquist	.05
227	Claudell Washington	.05
228	Lloyd McClendon	.05
229	Felix Fermin	.05
230	Paul O'Neill	.05
231	Charlie Leibrandt	.05
232	Dave Smith	.05
233	Bob Stanley	.05
234	Tim Belcher	.05
235	Eric King	.05
236	Spike Owen	.05
237	Mike Henneman	.05
238	Juan Samuel	.05
239	Greg Brock	.05
240	John Kruk	.05
241	Glenn Wilson	.05
242	Jeff Reardon	.05
243	Todd Worrell	.05
244	Dave LaPoint	.05
245	Walt Terrell	.05
246	Mike Moore	.05
247	Kelly Downs	.05
248	Dave Valle	.05
249	Ron Kittle	.05
250	Steve Wilson	.05
251	Dick Schofield	.05
252	Marty Barrett	.05
253	Dion James	.05
254	Bob Milacki	.05
255	Ernie Whitt	.05
256	Kevin Brown	.05
257	R.J. Reynolds	.05
258	Tim Raines	.05
259	Frank Williams	.05
260	Jose Gonzalez	.05
261	Mitch Webster	.05
262	Ken Caminiti	.05
263	Bob Boone	.05
264	Dave Magadan	.05
265	Rick Aguilera	.05

266	Chris James	.05
267	Bob Welch	.05
268	Ken Dayley	.05
269	Junior Ortiz	.05
270	Allan Anderson	.05
271	Steve Jeltz	.05
272	George Bell	.05
273	Roberto Kelly	.05
274	Brett Butler	.05
275	Mike Schooler	.05
276	Ken Phelps	.05
277	Glenn Braggs	.05
278	Jose Rijo	.05
279	Bobby Witt	.05
280	Jerry Browne	.05
281	Kevin Mitchell	.05
282	Craig Worthington	.05
283	Greg Minton	.05
284	Nick Esasky	.05
285	John Farrell	.05
286	Rick Mahler	.05
287	Tom Gordon	.05
288	Gerald Young	.05
289	Jody Reed	.05
290	Jeff Hamilton	.05
291	Gerald Perry	.05
292	Hubie Brooks	.05
293	Bo Diaz	.05
294	Terry Puhl	.05
295	Jim Gantner	.05
296	Jeff Parrett	.05
297	Mike Boddicker	.05
298	Dan Gladden	.05
299	Tony Pena	.05
300	Checklist	.05
301	Tom Henke	.05
302	Pascual Perez	.05
303	Steve Bedrosian	.05
304	Ken Hill	.05
305	Jerry Reuss	.05
306	Jim Eisenreich	.05
307	Jack Howell	.05
308	Rick Cerone	.05
309	Tim Leary	.05
310	Joe Orsulak	.05
311	Jim Dwyer	.05
312	Geno Petralli	.05
313	Rick Honeycutt	.05
314	Tom Foley	.05
315	Kenny Rogers	.05
316	Mike Flanagan	.05
317	Bryan Harvey	.05
318	Billy Ripken	.05
319	Jeff Montgomery	.05
320	Erik Hanson	.05
321	Brian Downing	.05
322	Gregg Olson	.05
323	Terry Steinbach	.05
324	Sammy Sosa	12.00
325	Gene Harris	.05
326	Mike Devereaux	.05
327	Dennis Cook	.05
328	David Wells	.05
329	Checklist	.05
330	Kirt Manwaring	.05
331	Jim Presley	.05
332	Checklist	.05
333	Chuck Finley	.05
334	Rob Dibble	.05
335	Cecil Espy	.05
336	Dave Parker	.05

1989 Donruss Diamond King Supers

Once again for 1989, collectors could acquire a 4-3/4" x 6-3/4" version of the Diamond King subset via a wrapper mail-in offer. Other than size, cards are identical to the DKs in the regular issue.

		NM/M
Complete Set (27):		5.00
Common Player:		.25
1	Mike Greenwell	.25
2	Bobby Bonilla	.25
3	Pete Incaviglia	.25
4	Chris Sabo	.25
5	Robin Yount	1.00
6	Tony Gwynn	1.50
7	Carlton Fisk	1.00
8	Cory Snyder	.25
9	David Cone	.25
10	Kevin Seitzer	.25
11	Rick Reuschel	.25
12	Johnny Ray	.25
13	Dave Schmidt	.25
14	Andres Galarraga	.25
15	Kirk Gibson	.25
16	Fred McGriff	.25
17	Mark Grace	.25
18	Jeff Robinson	.25
19	Vince Coleman	.25
20	Dave Henderson	.25
21	Harold Reynolds	.25
22	Gerald Perry	.25
23	Frank Viola	.25
24	Steve Bedrosian	.25
25	Glenn Davis	.25
26	Don Mattingly	2.00
27		

1989 Donruss Pop-Ups

This set features the 18 starters from the 1988 Major League All-Star game. The cards are designed with a perforated outline so

DWIGHT GOODEN METS · P

each player can be popped up to stand upright. The flip side features a red, white, and blue "Cincinnati Reds All-Star Game" logo at the top, a league designation, and the player's name and position. The lower portion displays instructions for creating the base of the Pop-Up. The Pop-Ups were marketed in packs with five All-Star cards and Warren Spahn puzzle-piece cards.

	NM/M
Complete Set (20):	2.00
Common Player:	.10
Warren Spahn Puzzle:	.50
Wax Pack (5+1):	.30
Wax Box (48):	10.00
(1) Mark McGwire	.45
(2) Jose Canseco	.20
(3) Paul Molitor	.25
(4) Rickey Henderson	.25
(5) Cal Ripken, Jr.	.50
(6) Dave Winfield	.25
(7) Wade Boggs	.35
(8) Frank Viola	.10
(9) Terry Steinbach	.10
(10) Tom Kelly	.10
(11) Will Clark	.10
(12) Darryl Strawberry	.10
(13) Ryne Sandberg	.35
(14) Andre Dawson	.10
(15) Ozzie Smith	.35
(16) Vince Coleman	.10
(17) Bobby Bonilla	.10
(18) Dwight Gooden	.10
(19) Gary Carter	.25
(20) Whitey Herzog	.10

Rookies

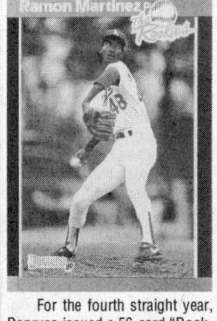

Ramon Martinez P

For the fourth straight year, Donruss issued a 56-card "Rookies" set in 1989. As in previous years, the set is similar in design to the regular Donruss set, except for a new "The Rookies" logo and a green and black border.

		NM/M
Complete Set (56):		8.00
Common Player:		.05
1	Gary Sheffield	.75
2	Gregg Jefferies	.25
3	Ken Griffey Jr.	5.00
4	Tom Gordon	.05
5	Billy Spiers	.05
6	Deion Sanders RC	.50
7	Donn Pall	.05
8	Steve Carter	.05
9	Francisco Oliveras	.05
10	Steve Wilson	.05
11	Bob Geren	.05
12	Tony Castillo	.05
13	Kenny Rogers	.05
14	Carlos Martinez	.05
15	Edgar Martinez	.05
16	Jim Abbott	.05
17	Torey Lovullo	.05
18	Mark Carreon	.05
19	Geronimo Berroa	.05
20	Luis Medina	.05
21	Sandy Alomar, Jr.	.05
22	Bob Milacki	.05
23	Joe Girardi RC	.10
24	German Gonzalez	.05

25	Craig Worthington	.05
26	Jerome Walton	.05
27	Gary Wayne	.05
28	Tim Jones	.05
29	Dante Bichette	.05
30	Alexis Infante	.05
31	Ken Hill	.05
32	Dwight Smith	.05
33	Luis de los Santos	.05
34	Eric Yelding	.05
35	Gregg Olson	.05
36	Phil Stephenson	.05
37	Ken Patterson	.05
38	Rick Wrona	.05
39	Mike Brumley	.05
40	Cris Carpenter	.05
41	Jeff Brantley	.05
42	Ron Jones	.05
43	Randy Johnson	2.00
44	Kevin Brown	.05
45	Ramon Martinez	.05
46	Greg Harris	.05
47	Steve Finley	.05
48	Randy Kramer	.05
49	Erik Hanson	.05
50	Matt Merullo	.05
51	Mike Devereaux	.05
52	Clay Parker	.05
53	Omar Vizquel	.05
54	Derek Lilliquist	.05
55	Junior Felix	.05
56	Checklist	.05

1989 Donruss Traded

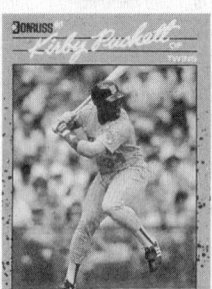

Rafael Palmeiro OF

Donruss issued its first "Traded" set in 1989, releasing a 56-card boxed set designed in the same style as the regular 1989 Donruss set. The set included a Stan Musial puzzle card and a checklist.

		NM/M
Complete Set (56):		2.00
Common Player:		.05
1	Jeffrey Leonard	.05
2	Jack Clark	.05
3	Kevin Gross	.05
4	Tommy Herr	.05
5	Bob Boone	.05
6	Rafael Palmeiro	.30
7	John Dopson	.05
8	Willie Randolph	.05
9	Chris Brown	.05
10	Wally Backman	.05
11	Steve Ontiveros	.05
12	Eddie Murray	.45
13	Lance McCullers	.05
14	Spike Owen	.05
15	Rob Murphy	.05
16	Pete O'Brien	.05
17	Ken Williams	.05
18	Nick Esasky	.05
19	Nolan Ryan	1.50
20	Brian Holton	.05
21	Mike Moore	.05
22	Joel Skinner	.05
23	Steve Sax	.05
24	Rick Mahler	.05
25	Mike Aldrete	.05
26	Jesse Orosco	.05
27	Dave LaPoint	.05
28	Walt Terrell	.05
29	Eddie Williams	.05
30	Mike Devereaux	.05
31	Julio Franco	.05
32	Jim Clancy	.05
33	Felix Fermin	.05
34	Curtis Wilkerson	.05
35	Bert Blyleven	.05
36	Mel Hall	.05
37	Eric King	.05
38	Mitch Williams	.05
39	Jamie Moyer	.05
40	Rick Rhoden	.05
41	Phil Bradley	.05
42	Paul Kilgus	.05
43	Milt Thompson	.05
44	Jerry Browne	.05
45	Bruce Hurst	.05
46	Claudell Washington	.05
47	Todd Benzinger	.05
48	Steve Balboni	.05
49	Oddibe McDowell	.05
50	Charles Hudson	.05
51	Ron Kittle	.05
52	Andy Hawkins	.05
53	Tom Brookens	.05

1990 Donruss Previews

1990 PREVIEW CARDS
No. 10 of 12
JEROME WALTON
OUTFIELDER
CAREER HIGHLIGHTS

To introduce its 1990 baseball issue, Donruss sent two preview cards from a set of 12 to each member of its dealers' network. Though the cards are different than those used on the issued versions, the front format was the same. Backs are printed in black on white and contain career highlights, but no stats. Issued at the dawn of the "promo card" craze, and succeeding the relatively valueless sample sheets used by most companies in earlier years, little value was attached to these preview cards initially. Today they are among the scarcest of the early-1990s promos.

		NM/M
Complete Set (12):		85.00
Common Player:		3.00
1	Todd Zeile	3.00
2	Ben McDonald	3.00
3	Bo Jackson	7.50
4	Will Clark	3.00
5	Dave Stewart	3.00
6	Kevin Mitchell	3.00
7	Nolan Ryan	50.00
8	Howard Johnson	3.00
9	Tony Gwynn	25.00
10	Jerome Walton	3.00
11	Wade Boggs	25.00
12	Kirby Puckett	25.00

1990 Donruss

DONRUSS
Kirby Puckett

Donruss marked its 10th anniversary in the baseball card hobby with a 715-card set in 1990, up from previous 660-card sets. The standard-size cards feature bright red borders with the player's name in script at the top. The set includes 26 "Diamond Kings" (DK) in the checklist, 20 "Rated Rookies" (RR) and a Carl Yastrzemski puzzle. Each All-Star card back has two variations. The more common has the stats box headed "All-Star Performance." Slightly scarcer versions say "Recent Major League Performance," and are worth about twice the value of the correct version.

		NM/M
Unopened Factory Set (716):		10.00
Complete Set (716):		7.50
Common Player:		.05
Carl Yastrzemski Puzzle:		1.00
Wax Pack (16):		.50
Wax Box (36):		10.00
Rack Pack (48):		1.00
Blister Rack (78):		1.50
1	Bo Jackson (Diamond King)	.15
2	Steve Sax (DK)	.05
3a	Ruben Sierra (DK) (No vertical black line at top-right on back.)	.25
3b	Ruben Sierra (DK) (Vertical line at top-right on back.)	.05
4	Ken Griffey Jr. (DK)	.65
5	Mickey Tettleton (DK)	.05
6	Dave Stewart (DK)	.05
7	Jim Deshaies (DK)	.05
8	John Smoltz (DK)	.05
9	Mike Bielecki (DK)	.05

10a	Brian Downing (DK) (Reversed negative.))	.25
10b	Brian Downing (DK) (Corrected))	.05
11	Kevin Mitchell (DK)	.05
12	Kelly Gruber (DK)	.05
13	Joe Magrane (DK)	.05
14	John Franco (DK)	.05
15	Ozzie Guillen (DK)	.05
16	Lou Whitaker (DK)	.05
17	John Smiley (DK)	.05
18	Howard Johnson (DK)	.05
19	Willie Randolph (DK)	.05
20	Chris Bosio (DK)	.05
21	Tommy Herr (DK)	.05
22	Dan Gladden (DK)	.05
23	Ellis Burks (DK)	.05
24	Pete O'Brien (DK)	.05
25	Bryn Smith (DK)	.05
26	Ed Whitson (DK)	.05
27	Checklist 1-27	.05
28	Robin Ventura (Rated Rookie)	.05
29	Todd Zeile RC	.15
30	Sandy Alomar, Jr. (RR)	.05
31	Kent Mercker RC (RR)	.10
32	Ben McDonald RC (RR)	.25
33a	Juan Gonzalez (Reversed negative.) RC (RR)	2.00
33b	Juan Gonzalez RC (Corrected)	1.50
34	Eric Anthony RC (RR)	.05
35	Mike Fetters RC (RR)	.05
36	Marquis Grissom RC (RR)	.50
37	Greg Vaughn RC (RR)	.25
38	Brian Dubois RC (RR)	.05
39	Steve Avery RC (RR)	.10
40	Mark Gardner RC (RR)	.05
41	Andy Benes (RR)	.05
42	Delino DeShields RC (RR)	.15
43	Scott Coolbaugh RC (RR)	.05
44	Pat Combs RC (RR)	.10
45	Alex Sanchez RC (RR)	.05
46	Kelly Mann RC (RR)	.05
47	Julio Machado RC (RR)	.05
48	Pete Incaviglia	.05
49	Shawon Dunston	.05
50	Jeff Treadway	.05
51	Jeff Ballard	.05
52	Claudell Washington	.05
53	Juan Samuel	.05
54	John Smiley	.05
55	Rob Deer	.05
56	Geno Petralli	.05
57	Chris Bosio	.05
58	Carlton Fisk	.40
59	Kirt Manwaring	.05
60	Chet Lemon	.05
61	Bo Jackson	.10
62	Doyle Alexander	.05
63	Pedro Guerrero	.05
64	Allan Anderson	.05
65	Greg Harris	.05
66	Mike Greenwell	.05
67	Walt Weiss	.05
68	Wade Boggs	.50
69	Jim Clancy	.05
70	Junior Felix RC	.05
71	Barry Larkin	.05
72	Dave LaPoint	.05
73	Joel Skinner	.05
74	Jesse Barfield	.05
75	Tommy Herr	.05
76	Ricky Jordan	.05
77	Eddie Murray	.40
78	Steve Sax	.05
79	Tim Belcher	.05
80	Danny Jackson	.05
81	Kent Hrbek	.05
82	Milt Thompson	.05
83	Brook Jacoby	.05
84	Mike Marshall	.05
85	Kevin Seitzer	.05
86	Tony Gwynn	.50
87	Dave Steib	.05
88	Dave Smith	.05
89	Bret Saberhagen	.05
90	Alan Trammell	.05
91	Tony Phillips	.05
92	Doug Drabek	.05
93	Jeffrey Leonard	.05
94	Wally Joyner	.05
95	Carney Lansford	.05
96	Cal Ripken, Jr.	1.00
97	Andres Galarraga	.05
98	Kevin Mitchell	.05
99	Howard Johnson	.05
100a	Checklist 28-129	.05
100b	Checklist 28-125	.05
101	Melido Perez	.05
102	Spike Owen	.05
103	Paul Molitor	.40
104	Geronimo Berroa	.05
105	Ryne Sandberg	.50
106	Bryn Smith	.05
107	Steve Buechele	.05
108	Jim Abbott	.05
109	Alvin Davis	.05
110	Lee Smith	.05
111	Roberto Alomar	.20
112	Rick Reuschel	.05
113a	Kelly Gruber (Born 2/22.)	.05
113b	Kelly Gruber (Born 2/26.)	.20
114	Joe Carter	.05
115	Jose Rijo	.05
116	Greg Minton	.05
117	Bob Ojeda	.05

No.	Player	NM/M
118	Glenn Davis	.05
119	Jeff Reardon	.05
120	Kurt Stillwell	.05
121	John Smoltz	.05
122	Dwight Evans	.05
123	Eric Yelding	.05
124	John Franco	.05
125	Jose Canseco	.20
126	Barry Bonds	1.00
127	Lee Guetterman	.05
128	Jack Clark	.05
129	Dave Valle	.05
130	Hubie Brooks	.05
131	Ernest Riles	.05
132	Mike Morgan	.05
133	Steve Jeltz	.05
134	Jeff Robinson	.05
135	Ozzie Guillen	.05
136	Chili Davis	.05
137	Mitch Webster	.05
138	Jerry Browne	.05
139	Bo Diaz	.05
140	Robby Thompson	.05
141	Craig Worthington	.05
142	Julio Franco	.05
143	Brian Holman	.05
144	George Brett	.60
145	Tom Glavine	.20
146	Robin Yount	.40
147	Gary Carter	.40
148	Ron Kittle	.05
149	Tony Fernandez	.05
150	Dave Stewart	.05
151	Gary Gaetti	.05
152	Kevin Elster	.05
153	Gerald Perry	.05
154	Jesse Orosco	.05
155	Wally Backman	.05
156	Dennis Martinez	.05
157	Rick Sutcliffe	.05
158	Greg Maddux	.50
159	Andy Hawkins	.05
160	John Kruk	.05
161	Jose Oquendo	.05
162	John Dopson	.05
163	Joe Magrane	.05
164	Billy Ripken	.05
165	Fred Manrique	.05
166	Nolan Ryan	1.00
167	Damon Berryhill	.05
168	Dale Murphy	.20
169	Mickey Tettleton	.05
170a	Kirk McCaskill (Born 4/19.)	.05
170b	Kirk McCaskill (Born 4/9.)	.10
171	Dwight Gooden	.05
172	Jose Lind	.05
173	B.J. Surhoff	.05
174	Ruben Sierra	.05
175	Dan Plesac	.05
176	Dan Pasqua	.05
177	Kelly Downs	.05
178	Matt Nokes	.05
179	Luis Aquino	.05
180	Frank Tanana	.05
181	Tony Pena	.05
182	Dan Gladden	.05
183	Bruce Hurst	.05
184	Roger Clemens	.60
185	Mark McGwire	.75
186	Rob Murphy	.05
187	Jim Deshaies	.05
188	Fred McGriff	.05
189	Rob Dibble	.05
190	Don Mattingly	.60
191	Felix Fermin	.05
192	Roberto Kelly	.05
193	Dennis Cook	.05
194	Darren Daulton	.05
195	Alfredo Griffin	.05
196	Eric Plunk	.05
197	Orel Hershiser	.05
198	Paul O'Neill	.05
199	Randy Bush	.05
200a	Checklist 130-231	.05
200b	Checklist 126-223	.05
201	Ozzie Smith	.50
202	Pete O'Brien	.05
203	Jay Howell	.05
204	Mark Gubicza	.05
205	Ed Whitson	.05
206	George Bell	.05
207	Mike Scott	.05
208	Charlie Leibrandt	.05
209	Mike Heath	.05
210	Dennis Eckersley	.35
211	Mike LaValliere	.05
212	Darnell Coles	.05
213	Lance Parrish	.05
214	Mike Moore	.05
215	Steve Finley RC	.20
216	Tim Raines	.05
217a	Scott Garrelts (Born 10/20.)	.05
217b	Scott Garrelts (Born 10/30.)	.10
218	Kevin McReynolds	.05
219	Dave Gallagher	.05
220	Tim Wallach	.05
221	Chuck Crim	.05
222	Lonnie Smith	.05
223	Andre Dawson	.20
224	Nelson Santovenia	.05
225	Rafael Palmeiro	.35
226	Devon White	.05
227	Harold Reynolds	.05
228	Ellis Burks	.05
229	Mark Parent	.05
230	Will Clark	.05
231	Jimmy Key	.05
232	John Farrell	.05
233	Eric Davis	.05
234	Johnny Ray	.05
235	Darryl Strawberry	.05
236	Bill Doran	.05
237	Greg Gagne	.05
238	Jim Eisenreich	.05
239	Tommy Gregg	.05
240	Marty Barrett	.05
241	Rafael Ramirez	.05
242	Chris Sabo	.05
243	Dave Henderson	.05
244	Andy Van Slyke	.05
245	Alvaro Espinoza	.05
246	Garry Templeton	.05
247	Gene Harris	.05
248	Kevin Gross	.05
249	Brett Butler	.05
250	Willie Randolph	.05
251	Roger McDowell	.05
252	Rafael Belliard	.05
253	Steve Rosenberg	.05
254	Jack Howell	.05
255	Marvell Wynne	.05
256	Tom Candiotti	.05
257	Todd Benzinger	.05
258	Don Robinson	.05
259	Phil Bradley	.05
260	Cecil Espy	.05
261	Scott Bankhead	.05
262	Frank White	.05
263	Andres Thomas	.05
264	Glenn Braggs	.05
265	David Cone	.05
266	Bobby Thigpen	.05
267	Nelson Liriano	.05
268	Terry Steinbach	.05
269	Kirby Puckett	.50
270	Gregg Jefferies	.05
271	Jeff Blauser	.05
272	Cory Snyder	.05
273	Roy Smith	.05
274	Tom Foley	.05
275	Mitch Williams	.05
276	Paul Kilgus	.05
277	Don Slaught	.05
278	Von Hayes	.05
279	Vince Coleman	.05
280	Mike Boddicker	.05
281	Ken Dayley	.05
282	Mike Devereaux	.05
283	Kenny Rogers RC	.05
284	Jeff Russell	.05
285	Jerome Walton RC	.10
286	Derek Lilliquist	.05
287	Joe Orsulak	.05
288	Dick Schofield	.05
289	Ron Darling	.05
290	Bobby Bonilla	.05
291	Jim Gantner	.05
292	Bobby Witt	.05
293	Greg Brock	.05
294	Ivan Calderon	.05
295	Steve Bedrosian	.05
296	Mike Henneman	.05
297	Tom Gordon	.05
298	Lou Whitaker	.05
299	Terry Pendleton	.05
300a	Checklist 232-333	.05
300b	Checklist 224-321	.05
301	Juan Berenguer	.05
302	Mark Davis	.05
303	Nick Esasky	.05
304	Rickey Henderson	.40
305	Rick Cerone	.05
306	Craig Biggio	.05
307	Duane Ward	.05
308	Tom Browning	.05
309	Walt Terrell	.05
310	Greg Swindell	.05
311	Dave Righetti	.05
312	Mike Maddux	.05
313	Len Dykstra	.05
314	Jose Gonzalez	.05
315	Steve Balboni	.05
316	Mike Scioscia	.05
317	Ron Oester	.05
318	Gary Wayne RC	.05
319	Todd Worrell	.05
320	Doug Jones	.05
321	Jeff Hamilton	.05
322	Danny Tartabull	.05
323	Chris James	.05
324	Mike Flanagan	.05
325	Gerald Young	.05
326	Bob Boone	.05
327	Frank Williams	.05
328	Dave Parker	.05
329	Sid Bream	.05
330	Mike Schooler	.05
331	Bert Blyleven	.10
332	Bob Welch	.05
333	Bob Milacki	.05
334	Tim Burke	.05
335	Jose Uribe	.05
336	Randy Myers	.05
337	Eric King	.05
338	Mark Langston	.05
339	Ted Higuera	.05
340	Oddibe McDowell	.05
341	Lloyd McClendon	.05
342	Pascual Perez	.05
343	Kevin Brown	.05
344	Chuck Finley	.05
345	Erik Hanson	.05
346	Rich Gedman	.05
347	Bip Roberts	.05
348	Matt Williams	.05
349	Tom Henke	.05
350	Brad Komminsk	.05
351	Jeff Reed	.05
352	Brian Downing	.05
353	Frank Viola	.05
354	Terry Puhl	.05
355	Brian Harper	.05
356	Steve Farr	.05
357	Joe Boever	.05
358	Danny Heep	.05
359	Larry Andersen	.05
360	Rolando Roomes	.05
361	Mike Gallego	.05
362	Bob Kipper	.05
363	Clay Parker	.05
364	Mike Pagliarulo	.05
365	Ken Griffey Jr.	.65
366	Rex Hudler	.05
367	Pat Sheridan	.05
368a	Kirk Gibson (May 25 birthdate.)	.05
368b	Kirk Gibson (May 28 birthdate.)	.05
369	Jeff Parrett	.05
370	Bob Walk	.05
371	Ken Patterson	.05
372	Bryan Harvey	.05
373	Mike Bielecki	.05
374	Tom Magrann RC	3.00
375	Rick Mahler	.05
376	Craig Lefferts	.05
377	Gregg Olson	.05
378	Jamie Moyer	.05
379	Randy Johnson	.40
380	Jeff Montgomery	.05
381	Marty Clary	.05
382	Bill Spiers RC	.05
383	Dave Magadan	.05
384	Greg Hibbard RC	.05
385	Ernie Whitt	.05
386	Rick Honeycutt	.05
387	Dave West	.05
388	Keith Hernandez	.05
389	Jose Alvarez	.05
390	Albert Belle	.05
391	Rick Aguilera	.05
392	Mike Fitzgerald	.05
393	Dwight Smith RC	.05
394	Steve Wilson RC	.05
395	Bob Geren RC	.05
396	Randy Ready	.05
397	Ken Hill	.05
398	Jody Reed	.05
399	Tom Brunansky	.05
400a	Checklist 334-435	.05
400b	Checklist 322-419	.05
401	Rene Gonzales	.05
402	Harold Baines	.05
403	Cecilio Guante	.05
404	Joe Girardi	.05
405a	Sergio Valdez RC (Black line crosses S in Sergio.)	.10
405b	Sergio Valdez (Corrected)	.05
406	Mark Williamson	.05
407	Glenn Hoffman	.05
408	Jeff Innis RC	.05
409	Randy Kramer	.05
410	Charlie O'Brien	.05
411	Charlie Hough	.05
412	Gus Polidor	.05
413	Ron Karkovice	.05
414	Trevor Wilson	.05
415	Kevin Ritz RC	.05
416	Gary Thurman	.05
417	Jeff Robinson	.05
418	Scott Terry	.05
419	Tim Laudner	.05
420	Dennis Rasmussen	.05
421	Luis Rivera	.05
422	Jim Corsi	.05
423	Dennis Lamp	.05
424	Ken Caminiti	.05
425	David Wells	.05
426	Norm Charlton	.05
427	Deion Sanders	.05
428	Dion James	.05
429	Chuck Cary	.05
430	Ken Howell	.05
431	Steve Lake	.05
432	Kal Daniels	.05
433	Lance McCullers	.05
434	Lenny Harris	.05
435	Scott Scudder RC	.05
436	Gene Larkin	.05
437	Dan Quisenberry	.05
438	Steve Olin RC	.05
439	Mickey Hatcher	.05
440	Willie Wilson	.05
441	Mark Grant	.05
442	Mookie Wilson	.05
443	Alex Trevino	.05
444	Pat Tabler	.05
445	Dave Bergman	.05
446	Todd Burns	.05
447	R.J. Reynolds	.05
448	Jay Buhner	.05
449	Lee Stevens RC	.05
450	Ron Hassey	.05
451	Bob Melvin	.05
452	Dave Martinez	.05
453	Greg Litton RC	.05
454	Mark Carreon	.05
455	Scott Fletcher	.05
456	Otis Nixon	.05
457	Tony Fossas RC	.05
458	John Russell	.05
459	Paul Assenmacher	.05
460	Zane Smith	.05
461	Jack Daugherty RC	.05
462	Rich Monteleone RC	.05
463	Greg Briley	.05
464	Mike Smithson	.05
465	Benito Santiago	.05
466	Jeff Brantley RC	.05
467	Jose Nunez	.05
468	Scott Bailes	.05
469	Ken Griffey	.05
470	Bob McClure	.05
471	Mackey Sasser	.05
472	Glenn Wilson	.05
473	Kevin Tapani RC	.10
474	Bill Buckner	.05
475	Ron Gant	.05
476	Kevin Romine	.05
477	Juan Agosto	.05
478	Herm Winningham	.05
479	Storm Davis	.05
480	Jeff King	.05
481	Kevin Mmahat RC	.05
482	Carmelo Martinez	.05
483	Omar Vizquel	.05
484	Jim Dwyer	.05
485	Bob Knepper	.05
486	Dave Anderson	.05
487	Ron Jones	.05
488	Jay Bell	.05
489	Sammy Sosa RC	3.00
490	Kent Anderson RC	.05
491	Domingo Ramos	.05
492	Dave Clark	.05
493	Tim Birtsas	.05
494	Ken Oberkfell	.05
495	Larry Sheets	.05
496	Jeff Kunkel	.05
497	Jim Presley	.05
498	Mike Macfarlane	.05
499	Pete Smith	.05
500a	Checklist 436-537	.05
500b	Checklist 420-517	.05
501	Gary Sheffield	.20
502	Terry Bross RC	.05
503	Jerry Kutzler RC	.05
504	Lloyd Moseby	.05
505	Curt Young	.05
506	Al Newman	.05
507	Keith Miller	.05
508	Mike Stanton RC	.20
509	Rich Yett	.05
510	Tim Drummond RC	.05
511	Joe Hesketh	.05
512	Rick Wrona RC	.05
513	Luis Salazar	.05
514	Hal Morris	.05
515	Terry Mullholland	.05
516	John Morris	.05
517	Carlos Quintana	.05
518	Frank DiPino	.05
519	Randy Milligan	.05
520	Chad Kreuter	.05
521	Mike Jeffcoat	.05
522	Mark Harkey	.05
523a	Andy Nezelek (Born 1985.)	.05
523b	Andy Nezelek (Born 1965.)	.05
524	Dave Schmidt	.05
525	Tony Armas	.05
526	Barry Lyons	.05
527	Rick Reed RC	.05
528	Jerry Reuss	.05
529	Dean Palmer RC	.10
530	Jeff Peterek RC	.05
531	Carlos Martinez RC	.05
532	Atlee Hammaker	.05
533	Mike Brumley	.05
534	Terry Leach	.05
535	Doug Strange RC	.05
536	Jose DeLeon	.05
537	Shane Rawley	.05
538	Joey Cora	.05
539	Eric Hetzel	.05
540	Gene Nelson	.05
541	Wes Gardner	.05
542	Mark Portugal	.05
543	Al Leiter	.05
544	Jack Armstrong	.05
545	Greg Cadaret	.05
546	Rod Nichols	.05
547	Luis Polonia	.05
548	Charlie Hayes	.05
549	Dickie Thon	.05
550	Tim Crews	.05
551	Dave Winfield	.40
552	Mike Davis	.05
553	Ron Robinson	.05
554	Carmen Castillo	.05
555	John Costello	.05
556	Bud Black	.05
557	Rick Dempsey	.05
558	Jim Acker	.05
559	Eric Show	.05
560	Pat Borders	.05
561	Danny Darwin	.05
562	Rick Luecken RC	.05
563	Edwin Nunez	.05
564	Felix Jose	.05
565	John Cangelosi	.05
566	Billy Swift	.05
567	Bill Schroeder	.05
568	Stan Javier	.05
569	Jim Traber	.05
570	Wallace Johnson	.05
571	Donell Nixon	.05
572	Sid Fernandez	.05
573	Lance Johnson	.05
574	Andy McGaffigan	.05
575	Mark Knudson	.05
576	Tommy Greene RC	.05
577	Mark Grace	.05
578	Larry Walker RC	1.00
579	Mike Stanley	.05
580	Mike Witt	.05
581	Scott Bradley	.05
582	Greg Harris	.05
583a	Kevin Hickey (Black stripe over top of "K" vertical stroke.)	.05
583b	Kevin Hickey (Black stripe under "K.")	.05
584	Lee Mazzilli	.05
585	Jeff Pico	.05
586	Joe Oliver RC	.05
587	Willie Fraser	.05
588	Puzzle card (Carl Yastrzemski)	.05
589	Kevin Bass	.05
590	John Moses	.05
591	Tom Pagnozzi	.05
592	Tony Castillo RC	.05
593	Jerald Clark	.05
594	Dan Schatzeder	.05
595	Luis Quinones	.05
596	Pete Harnisch	.05
597	Gary Redus	.05
598	Mel Hall	.05
599	Rick Schu	.05
600a	Checklist 538-639	.05
600b	Checklist 518-617	.05
601	Mike Kingery	.05
602	Terry Kennedy	.05
603	Mike Sharperson	.05
604	Don Carman	.05
605	Jim Gott	.05
606	Donn Pall	.05
607	Rance Mulliniks	.05
608	Curt Wilkerson	.05
609	Mike Felder	.05
610	Guillermo Hernandez	.05
611	Candy Maldonado	.05
612	Mark Thurmond	.05
613	Rick Leach	.05
614	Jerry Reed	.05
615	Franklin Stubbs	.05
616	Billy Hatcher	.05
617	Don August	.05
618	Tim Teufel	.05
619	Shawn Hillegas	.05
620	Manny Lee	.05
621	Gary Ward	.05
622	Mark Guthrie RC	.05
623	Jeff Musselman	.05
624	Mark Lemke	.05
625	Fernando Valenzuela	.05
626	Paul Sorrento RC	.05
627	Glenallen Hill	.05
628	Les Lancaster	.05
629	Vance Law	.05
630	Randy Velarde	.05
631	Todd Frohwirth	.05
632	Willie McGee	.05
633	Oil Can Boyd	.05
634	Cris Carpenter	.05
635	Brian Holton	.05
636	Tracy Jones	.05
637	Terry Steinbach/AS	.05
638	Brady Anderson	.05
639a	Jack Morris (Black line crosses J of Jack.)	.10
639b	Jack Morris (Corrected)	.05
640	Jaime Navarro RC	.05
641	Darrin Jackson	.05
642	Mike Dyer RC	.05
643	Mike Schmidt	.60
644	Henry Cotto	.05
645	John Cerutti	.05
646	Francisco Cabrera RC	.05
647	Scott Sanderson	.05
648	Brian Meyer	.05
649	Ray Searage	.05
650	Bo Jackson/AS	.25
651	Steve Lyons	.05
652	Mike LaCoss	.05
653	Ted Power	.05
654	Howard Johnson/AS	.05
655	Mauro Gozzo RC	.05
656	Mike Blowers RC	.05
657	Paul Gibson	.05
658	Neal Heaton	.05
659a	Nolan Ryan 5,000 K's (King of Kings (#665) back.)	1.50
659b	Nolan Ryan 5,000 K's (Correct back.)	.60
660a	Harold Baines/AS (Black line through star on front, Recent Major League Performance on back.)	.05
660b	Harold Baines/AS (Black line through star on front, All-Star Game Performance on back.)	.25
660c	Harold Baines/AS (Black line behind star on front, Recent Major League Performance on back.)	.25
660d	Harold Baines/AS (Black line behind star on front, All-Star Game Performance on back.)	.10
661	Gary Pettis	.05
662	Clint Zavaras RC	.05
663	Rick Reuschel/AS	.05
664	Alejandro Pena	.05
665a	Nolan Ryan (King of Kings) (5,000 K's (#659) back.)	1.50
665b	Nolan Ryan (King of Kings) (Correct back.)	1.00
665c	Nolan Ryan (King of Kings) (No number on back.)	1.00
666	Ricky Horton	.05
667	Curt Schilling	.05
668	Bill Landrum	.05
669	Todd Stottlemyre	.05
670	Tim Leary	.05
671	John Wetteland RC	.25
672	Calvin Schiraldi	.05
673	Ruben Sierra/AS	.05
674	Pedro Guerrero/AS	.05
675	Ken Phelps	.05
676	Cal Ripken/AS	.50
677	Denny Walling	.05
678	Goose Gossage	.05
679	Gary Mielke RC	.05
680	Bill Bathe	.05
681	Tom Lawless	.05
682	Xavier Hernandez RC	.05
683	Kirby Puckett/AS	.25
684	Mariano Duncan	.05
685	Ramon Martinez	.05
686	Tim Jones	.05
687	Tom Filer	.05
688	Steve Lombardozzi	.05
689	Bernie Williams RC	1.00
690	Chip Hale RC	.05
691	Beau Allred RC	.05
692	Ryne Sandberg/AS	.25
693	Jeff Huson RC	.05
694	Curt Ford	.05
695	Eric Davis (AS)	.05
696	Scott Lusader	.05
697	Mark McGwire (AS)	.40
698	Steve Cummings RC	.05
699	George Canale RC	.05
700a	Checklist 640-715/ BC1-BC26	.05
700b	Checklist 640-716/ BC1-BC26	.05
700c	Checklist 618-716	.05
701	Julio Franco/AS	.05
702	Dave Johnson RC	.05
703	Dave Stewart/AS	.05
704	Dave Justice RC	.50
705	Tony Gwynn/AS	.05
706	Greg Myers	.05
707	Will Clark/AS	.05
708	Benito Santiago/AS	.05
709	Larry McWilliams	.05
710	Ozzie Smith/AS	.05
711	John Olerud RC	.50
712	Wade Boggs/AS	.05
713	Gary Eave RC	.05
714	Bob Tewksbury	.05
715	Kevin Mitchell/AS	.05
716	A. Bartlett Giamatti	.25

1990 Donruss Grand Slammers

For the second consecutive year Donruss produced a set in honor of players who hit grand slams in the previous season. The cards are styled after the 1990 Donruss regular issue. The cards were inserted into 1990 Donruss factory sets, and one card per cello pack. Each card can be found with blue borders or with blue and green borders, and with or without the split black stripe near the right end on back.

	NM/M
Complete Set (12):	2.00
Common Player:	.10
1 Matt Williams	.10
2 Jeffrey Leonard	.10
3 Chris James	.10
4 Mark McGwire	1.50
5 Dwight Evans	.10
6 Will Clark	.10
7 Mike Scioscia	.10
8 Todd Benzinger	.10
9 Fred McGriff	.10
10 Kevin Bass	.10
11 Jack Clark	.10
12 Bo Jackson	.25

1990 Donruss MVP

This special 26-card set includes one player from each Major League team. Numbered BC-1 (the "BC" stands for "Bonus Card") through BC-26, the cards from this set were randomly packed in 1990 Donruss wax packs and were not available in factory sets or other types of packaging. The red-bordered cards are similar in design to the regular 1990 Donruss set, except the player photos are set against a special background made up of the "MVP" logo.

		NM/M
Complete Set (26):		1.25
Common Player:		.10
1	Bo Jackson	.20
2	Howard Johnson	.10
3	Dave Stewart	.10
4	Tony Gwynn	.35
5	Orel Hershiser	.10
6	Pedro Guerrero	.10
7	Tim Raines	.10
8	Kirby Puckett	.35
9	Alvin Davis	.10
10	Ryne Sandberg	.35
11	Kevin Mitchell	.10
12a	John Smoltz (Photo of Tom Glavine.)	1.50
12b	John Smoltz (Corrected)	.30
13	George Bell	.10
14	Julio Franco	.10
15	Paul Molitor	.25
16	Bobby Bonilla	.10
17	Mike Greenwell	.10
18	Cal Ripken	.50
19	Carlton Fisk	.25
20	Chili Davis	.10
21	Glenn Davis	.10
22	Steve Sax	.10
23	Eric Davis	.10
24	Greg Swindell	.10
25	Von Hayes	.10
26	Alan Trammell	.10

1990 Donruss Aqueous Test

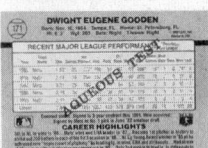

Little is known about this mystery issue which few hobbyists had ever heard of prior to 1999. The cards appear in all major respects to be regular 1990 Donruss cards, but on back have the words "AQUEOUS TEST" printed. The test cards also lack the period after "INC" in the copyright line in upper-right. Approximately 2,000-2,500 cards in total are known, with only part of the '90D checklist represented in the test issue. As few as one specimen each are known for some cards, while a half-dozen or more of others are recorded. Because of limited supply, prices can be volatile depending on the activity of single-player specialist collectors at any given time. It is possible the checklist here is not complete. The cards may have been produced to test a semi-gloss coating known in the printing trade as aqueous.

		NM/M
Common Player:		5.00
1	Bo Jackson/DK	17.50
3	Ruben Sierra/DK	5.00
6	Dave Stewart/DK	6.50
7	Mike Bielecki/DK	5.00
9	Mike Bielecki/DK	5.00
16	Lou Whitaker/DK	5.00

18	Howard Johnson/DK	5.00
22	Dan Gladden/DK	5.00
24	Pete O'Brien/DK	5.00
28	Robin Ventura (Rated Rookie)	15.00
29	Todd Zeile (Rated Rookie)	15.00
30	Sandy Alomar Jr. (Rated Rookie)	15.00
31	Kent Mercker (Rated Rookie)	5.00
32	Ben McDonald (Rated Rookie)	7.50
33	Juan Gonzalez (Rated Rookie) (Reversed negatives.)	75.00
34	Eric Anthony (Rated Rookie)	5.00
35	Mike Fetters (Rated Rookie)	5.00
48	Pete Incaviglia	5.00
51	Jeff Ballard	5.00
52	Claudell Washington	5.00
54	Rob Deer	5.00
56	Geno Petralli	5.00
57	Chris Bosio	5.00
60	Chet Lemon	5.00
61	Bo Jackson	25.00
63	Pedro Guerrero	5.00
64	Allan Anderson	5.00
66	Mike Greenwell	5.00
68	Wade Boggs	60.00
70	Junior Felix	5.00
71	Barry Larkin	5.00
72	Dave LaPoint	5.00
74	Jesse Barfield	5.00
77	Eddie Murray	45.00
78	Steve Sax	5.00
79	Tim Belcher	5.00
80	Danny Jackson	5.00
81	Kent Hrbek	5.00
83	Brook Jacoby	5.00
84	Mike Marshall	5.00
85	Kevin Seitzer	5.00
86	Tony Gwynn	60.00
87	Dave Steib	5.00
89	Bret Saberhagen	5.00
90	Alan Trammell	5.00
91	Tony Phillips	5.00
93	Jeff Leonard	5.00
94	Wally Joyner	5.00
95	Carney Lansford	5.00
96	Cal Ripken Jr.	100.00
97	Andres Galarraga	5.00
98	Kevin Mitchell	5.00
100	Checklist 28-129	2.50
102	Spike Owen	5.00
103	Paul Molitor	45.00
105	Ryne Sandberg	60.00
107	Steve Buechele	5.00
108	Jim Abbott	5.00
109	Alvin Davis	5.00
110	Lee Smith	5.00
111	Roberto Alomar	15.00
112	Rick Reuschel	5.00
113	Kelly Gruber	5.00
114	Joe Carter	5.00
115	Jose Rijo	5.00
117	Bobby Ojeda	5.00
118	Glenn Davis	5.00
119	Jeff Reardon	5.00
121	Kurt Stillwell	5.00
122	Dwight Evans	5.00
123	John Franco	5.00
125	Jose Canseco	35.00
126	Barry Bonds	100.00
127	Lee Guetterman	5.00
128	Jack Clark	5.00
129	Dave Valle	5.00
132	Mike Morgan	5.00
133	Steve Jeltz	5.00
134	Jeff Robinson	5.00
139	Bo Diaz	5.00
140	Robby Thompson	5.00
141	Craig Worthington	5.00
144	George Brett	75.00
145	Tom Glavine	15.00
146	Robin Yount	45.00
147	Gary Carter	45.00
148	Ron Kittle	5.00
149	Tony Fernandez	5.00
150	Dave Stewart	5.00
151	Gary Gaetti	5.00
154	Jesse Orosco	5.00
155	Wally Backman	5.00
156	Dennis Martinez	5.00
157	Rick Sutcliffe	6.50
158	Greg Maddux	60.00
160	John Kruk	5.00
162	John Dopson	5.00
164	Billy Ripken	5.00
165	Fred Manrique	5.00
166	Nolan Ryan	100.00
167	Damon Berryhill	5.00
168	Dale Murphy	35.00
169	Mickey Tettleton	5.00
170	Kirk McCaskill	5.00
171	Dwight Gooden	5.00
172	Jose Lind	5.00
173	B.J. Surhoff	5.00
174	Ruben Sierra	5.00
175	Dan Plesac	5.00
177	Dan Pasqua	5.00
177	Kelly Downs	5.00
178	Matt Nokes	5.00
179	Luis Aquino	5.00
180	Frank Tanana	5.00
181	Tony Pena	5.00
182	Dan Gladden	5.00
183	Bruce Hurst	5.00

184	Roger Clemens	75.00
185	Mark McGwire	85.00
186	Rob Murphy	5.00
187	Jim Deshaies	5.00
188	Fred McGriff	5.00
189	Rob Dibble	5.00
190	Don Mattingly	75.00
191	Felix Fermin	5.00
192	Roberto Kelly	5.00
193	Dennis Cook	5.00
194	Darren Daulton	5.00
195	Alfredo Griffin	5.00
196	Eric Plunk	5.00
197	Orel Hershiser	5.00
198	Paul O'Neill	5.00
199	Randy Bush	5.00
201	Ozzie Smith	60.00
202	Pete O'Brien	5.00
203	Jay Howell	5.00
204	Mark Gubicza	5.00
205	Ed Whitson	5.00
206	George Bell	5.00
207	Mike Scott	5.00
208	Charlie Leibrandt	5.00
209	Mike Heath	5.00
210	Dennis Eckersley	45.00
211	Mike LaValliere	5.00
212	Darnell Coles	5.00
213	Lance Parrish	5.00
214	Mike Moore	5.00
215	Steve Finley	5.00
216	Tim Raines	5.00
217	Scott Garrelts	5.00
218	Kevin McReynolds	5.00
219	Dave Gallagher	5.00
220	Tim Wallach	5.00
221	Chuck Crim	5.00
222	Lonnie Smith	5.00
223	Andre Dawson	15.00
224	Nelson Santovenia	5.00
225	Rafael Palmeiro	45.00
226	Devon White	5.00
227	Harold Reynolds	6.50
228	Ellis Burks	5.00
229	Mark Parent	5.00
230	Will Clark	6.50
231	Jimmy Key	5.00
232	John Farrell	5.00
233	Eric Davis	5.00
234	Johnny Ray	5.00
235	Darryl Strawberry	5.00
236	Bill Doran	5.00
237	Greg Gagne	5.00
238	Jim Eisenreich	5.00
239	Tommy Gregg	5.00
240	Marty Barrett	5.00
241	Rafael Ramirez	5.00
242	Chris Sabo	5.00
243	Dave Henderson	5.00
244	Andy Van Slyke	5.00
245	Alvaro Espinoza	5.00
246	Garry Templeton	5.00
247	Gene Harris	5.00
248	Kevin Gross	5.00
249	Brett Butler	5.00
250	Willie Randolph	5.00
251	Roger McDowell	5.00
252	Rafael Belliard	5.00
253	Steve Rosenberg	5.00
254	Jack Howell	5.00
255	Marvell Wynne	5.00
256	Tom Candiotti	5.00
257	Todd Benzinger	5.00
258	Don Robinson	5.00
259	Phil Bradley	5.00
260	Cecil Espy	5.00
261	Scott Bankhead	5.00
262	Frank White	5.00
263	Andre Thomas	5.00
264	Glenn Braggs	5.00
265	David Cone	5.00
266	Bobby Thigpen	5.00
267	Nelson Liriano	5.00
268	Terry Steinbach	5.00
269	Kirby Puckett	60.00
270	Gregg Jeffries	5.00
271	Jeff Blauser	5.00
272	Cory Snyder	5.00
273	Roy Smith	5.00
274	Tom Foley	5.00
275	Mitch Williams	5.00
276	Paul Kilgus	5.00
277	Don Slaught	5.00
279	Von Hayes	5.00
279	Vince Coleman	5.00
280	Mike Boddicker	5.00
281	Ken Dayley	5.00
282	Mike Devereaux	5.00
283	Kenny Rogers	5.00
BC-1	Bo Jackson (MVP)	15.00
BC-2	Howard Johnson (MVP)	5.00
BC-3	Dave Stewart (MVP)	5.00
BC-4	Tony Gwynn (MVP)	45.00
BC-5	Orel Hershiser (MVP)	5.00
BC-6	Pedro Guerrero (MVP)	5.00
BC-7	Tim Raines (MVP)	6.50
BC-8	Kirby Puckett (MVP)	45.00
BC-9	Alvin Davis	5.00

1990 Donruss Blue/White Test Issue

Relatively few examples of this test printing have found their way into the hobby. The cards are "two-headed" with the fronts of two different cards printed back-to-back. The cards use the same pho-

tos found on the issued versions and differ only in the border colors. Each card can be found with one side bordered in blue and the other bordered in white. The blue side of the card has a glossier finish than the white. The number of different players' cards which can be found in this version is unknown.

1990 Donruss Best A.L.

This 144-card set features the top players of the American League. The 2-1/2" x 3-1/2" cards feature the same front design as the regular Donruss set, exception with blue borders instead of red. Backs feature a yellow frame with complete statistics and biographical information provided. This marks the first year that Donruss divided its baseball-best issue into two sets designated by league.

		NM/M
Complete Set (144):		10.00
Common Player:		.05
1	Ken Griffey Jr.	1.00
2	Bob Milacki	.05
3	Mike Boddicker	.05
4	Bert Blyleven	.05
5	Carlton Fisk	.50
6	Greg Swindell	.05
7	Alan Trammell	.05
8	Mark Davis	.05
9	Chris Bosio	.05
10	Gary Gaetti	.05
11	Matt Nokes	.05
12	Dennis Eckersley	.45
13	Kevin Brown	.05
14	Tom Henke	.05
15	Mickey Tettleton	.05
16	Jody Reed	.05
17	Mark Langston	.05
18	Melido Perez	.05
19	John Farrell	.05
20	Tony Phillips	.05
21	Bret Saberhagen	.05
22	Robin Yount	.50
23	Kirby Puckett	.60
24	Steve Sax	.05
25	Dave Stewart	.05
26	Alvin Davis	.05
27	Geno Petralli	.05
28	Mookie Wilson	.05
29	Jeff Ballard	.05
30	Ellis Burks	.05
31	Wally Joyner	.05
32	Bobby Thigpen	.05
33	Keith Hernandez	.05
34	Jack Morris	.05
35	George Brett	.75
36	Dan Plesac	.05
37	Brian Harper	.05
38	Don Mattingly	.75
39	Dave Henderson	.05
40	Scott Bankhead	.05
41	Rafael Palmeiro	.45
42	Jimmy Key	.05
43	Gregg Olson	.05
44	Tony Pena	.05
45	Jack Howell	.05
46	Eric King	.05
47	Cory Snyder	.05
48	Frank Tanana	.05
49	Nolan Ryan	2.00

50	Bob Boone	.05
51	Dave Parker	.05
52	Allan Anderson	.05
53	Tim Leary	.05
54	Mark McGwire	1.50
55	Dave Valle	.05
56	Fred McGriff	.05
57	Cal Ripken	2.00
58	Roger Clemens	.75
59	Lance Parrish	.05
60	Robin Ventura	.05
61	Doug Jones	.05
62	Lloyd Moseby	.05
63	Bo Jackson	.15
64	Paul Molitor	.50
65	Kent Hrbek	.05
66	Mel Hall	.05
67	Bob Welch	.05
68	Erik Hanson	.05
69	Harold Baines	.05
70	Junior Felix	.05
71	Craig Worthington	.05
72	Jeff Reardon	.05
73	Johnny Ray	.05
74	Ozzie Guillen	.05
75	Brook Jacoby	.05
76	Chet Lemon	.05
77	Mark Gubicza	.05
78	B.J. Surhoff	.05
79	Rick Aguilera	.05
80	Pascual Perez	.05
81	Jose Canseco	.30
82	Mike Schooler	.05
83	Jeff Huson	.05
84	Kelly Gruber	.05
85	Randy Milligan	.05
86	Wade Boggs	.60
87	Dave Winfield	.50
88	Scott Fletcher	.05
89	Tom Candiotti	.05
90	Mike Heath	.05
91	Kevin Seitzer	.05
92	Ted Higuera	.05
93	Kevin Tapani	.05
94	Roberto Kelly	.05
95	Walt Weiss	.05
96	Checklist	.05
97	Sandy Alomar	.05
98	Pete O'Brien	.05
99	Jeff Russell	.05
100	John Olerud	.05
101	Pete Harnisch	.05
102	Dwight Evans	.05
103	Chuck Finley	.05
104	Sammy Sosa	6.00
105	Mike Henneman	.05
106	Kurt Stillwell	.05
107	Greg Vaughn	.05
108	Dan Gladden	.05
109	Jesse Barfield	.05
110	Willie Randolph	.05
111	Randy Johnson	.50
112	Julio Franco	.05
113	Tony Fernandez	.05
114	Ben McDonald	.05
115	Mike Greenwell	.05
116	Luis Polonia	.05
117	Carney Lansford	.05
118	Bud Black	.05
119	Lou Whitaker	.05
120	Jim Eisenreich	.05
121	Gary Sheffield	.20
122	Shane Mack	.05
123	Alvaro Espinoza	.05
124	Rickey Henderson	.50
125	Jeffrey Leonard	.05
126	Gary Pettis	.05
127	Dave Steib	.05
128	Danny Tartabull	.05
129	Joe Orsulak	.05
130	Tom Brunansky	.05
131	Dick Schofield	.05
132	Candy Maldonado	.05
133	Cecil Fielder	.05
134	Terry Shumpert	.05
135	Greg Gagne	.05
136	Dave Righetti	.05
137	Terry Steinbach	.05
138	Harold Reynolds	.05
139	George Bell	.05
140	Carlos Quintana	.05
141	Ivan Calderon	.05
142	Greg Brock	.05
143	Ruben Sierra	.05
144	Checklist	.05

1990 Donruss Best N.L.

This 144-card set features the top players in the National League for 1990. The 2-1/2" x 3-1/2" cards feature the same design as the regular 1990 Donruss cards, except they have blue, rather than red borders. Traded players are featured with their new teams. This set, along with the A.L. Best set, was available at select retail stores and within the hobby.

		NM/M
Complete Set (144):		7.50
Common Player:		.05
1	Eric Davis	.05
2	Tom Glavine	.20
3	Mike Bielecki	.05
4	Jim Deshaies	.05
5	Mike Scioscia	.05
6	Spike Owen	.05
7	Dwight Gooden	.05
8	Ricky Jordan	.05
9	Doug Drabek	.05
10	Bryn Smith	.05
11	Tony Gwynn	.75
12	John Burkett	.05
13	Nick Esasky	.05
14	Greg Maddux	.75
15	Joe Oliver	.05
16	Mike Scott	.05
17	Tim Belcher	.05
18	Kevin Gross	.05
19	Howard Johnson	.05
20	Darren Daulton	.05
21	John Smiley	.05
22	Ken Dayley	.05
23	Craig Lefferts	.05
24	Will Clark	.75
25	Greg Olson	.05
26	Ryne Sandberg	.75
27	Tom Browning	.05
28	Eric Anthony	.05
29	Juan Samuel	.05
30	Dennis Martinez	.05
31	Kevin Elster	.05
32	Tom Herr	.05
33	Sid Bream	.05
34	Terry Pendleton	.05
35	Roberto Alomar	.20
36	Kevin Bass	.05
37	Jim Presley	.05
38	Les Lancaster	.05
39	Paul O'Neill	.05
40	Dave Smith	.05
41	Kirk Gibson	.05
42	Tim Burke	.05
43	David Cone	.05
44	Ken Howell	.05
45	Barry Bonds	6.00
46	Joe Magrane	.05
47	Andy Benes	.05
48	Gary Carter	.50
49	Pat Combs	.05
50	John Smoltz	.05
51	Mark Grace	.05
52	Barry Larkin	.05
53	Danny Darwin	.05
54	Orel Hershiser	.05
55	Tim Wallach	.05
56	Dave Magadan	.05
57	Roger McDowell	.05
58	Bill Landrum	.05
59	Jose DeLeon	.05
60	Bip Roberts	.05
61	Matt Williams	.05
62	Dale Murphy	.20
63	Dwight Smith	.05
64	Chris Sabo	.05
65	Glenn Davis	.05
66	Jay Howell	.05
67	Andres Galarraga	.05
68	Frank Viola	.05
69	John Kruk	.05
70	Bobby Bonilla	.05
71	Todd Zeile	.05
72	Joe Carter	.05
73	Robby Thompson	.05
74	Jeff Blauser	.05
75	Mitch Williams	.05
76	Rob Dibble	.05
77	Rafael Ramirez	.05
78	Eddie Murray	.50
79	Dave Martinez	.05
80	Darryl Strawberry	.05
81	Dickie Thon	.05
82	Jose Lind	.05
83	Ozzie Smith	.75
84	Bruce Hurst	.05
85	Kevin Mitchell	.05
86	Lonnie Smith	.05
87	Joe Girardi	.05
88	Randy Myers	.05
89	Craig Biggio	.05
90	Fernando Valenzuela	.05
91	Larry Walker	.05
92	John Franco	.05
93	Dennis Cook	.05
94	Bob Walk	.05
95	Pedro Guerrero	.05
96	Checklist	.05
97	Andre Dawson	.25
98	Ed Whitson	.05
99	Steve Bedrosian	.05
100	Oddibe McDowell	.05
101	Todd Benzinger	.05

102	Bill Doran	.05
103	Alfredo Griffin	.05
104	Tim Raines	.05
105	Sid Fernandez	.05
106	Charlie Hayes	.05
107	Mike LaValliere	.05
108	Jose Oquendo	.05
109	Jack Clark	.05
110	Scott Garrelts	.05
111	Ron Gant	.05
112	Shawon Dunston	.05
113	Mariano Duncan	.05
114	Eric Yelding	.05
115	Hubie Brooks	.05
116	Delino DeShields	.05
117	Gregg Jefferies	.05
118	Len Dykstra	.05
119	Andy Van Slyke	.05
120	Lee Smith	.05
121	Benito Santiago	.05
122	Jose Uribe	.05
123	Jeff Treadway	.05
124	Jerome Walton	.05
125	Billy Hatcher	.05
126	Ken Caminiti	.05
127	Kal Daniels	.05
128	Marquis Grissom	.05
129	Kevin McReynolds	.05
130	Wally Backman	.05
131	Willie McGee	.05
132	Terry Kennedy	.05
133	Garry Templeton	.05
134	Lloyd McClendon	.05
135	Daryl Boston	.05
136	Jay Bell	.05
137	Mike Pagliarulo	.05
138	Vince Coleman	.05
139	Brett Butler	.05
140	Von Hayes	.05
141	Ramon Martinez	.05
142	Jack Armstrong	.05
143	Franklin Stubbs	.05
144	Checklist	.05

1990 Donruss Diamond Kings Supers

Donruss made this set available through a mail-in offer. Three wrappers, $10 and $2 for postage were necessary to obtain this set. The cards are exactly the same design as the regular Donruss Diamond Kings except they measure approximately 5" x 6-3/4" in size. The artwork of Dick Perez is featured.

		NM/M
	Complete Set (26):	5.00
	Common Player:	.10
1	Bo Jackson	.25
2	Steve Sax	.10
3	Ruben Sierra	.10
4	Ken Griffey Jr.	4.00
5	Mickey Tettleton	.10
6	Dave Stewart	.10
7	Jim Deshaies	.10
8	John Smoltz	.10
9	Mike Bielecki	.10
10	Brian Downing	.10
11	Kevin Mitchell	.10
12	Kelly Gruber	.10
13	Joe Magrane	.10
14	John Franco	.10
15	Ozzie Guillen	.10
16	Lou Whitaker	.10
17	John Smiley	.10
18	Howard Johnson	.10
19	Willie Randolph	.10
20	Chris Bosio	.10
21	Tommy Herr	.10
22	Dan Gladden	.10
23	Ellis Burks	.10
24	Pete O'Brien	.10
25	Bryn Smith	.10
26	Ed Whitson	.10

1990 Donruss Learning Series

Cards from this 55-card set were released as part of an educational package available to schools. The cards are styled like the regular-issue 1990 Donruss cards, but feature a special "learning series" logo on the front. The backs feature career highlights, statistics and card numbers. The cards were not released directly to the hobby.

		NM/M
	Complete Set (55):	25.00
	Common Player:	.10
1	George Brett (DK)	3.00
2	Kevin Mitchell	.10
3	Andy Van Slyke	.10
4	Benito Santiago	.10
5	Gary Carter	1.00
6	Jose Canseco	.50
7	Rickey Henderson	1.00
8	Ken Griffey Jr.	4.00
9	Ozzie Smith	2.00
10	Dwight Gooden	.10
11	Ryne Sandberg (DK)	2.00
12	Don Mattingly	2.50
13	Ozzie Guillen	.10
14	Dave Righetti	.10
15	Rick Dempsey	.10
16	Tom Herr	.10
17	Julio Franco	.10
18	Von Hayes	.10
19	Cal Ripken	6.00
20	Alan Trammell	.10
21	Wade Boggs	2.00
22	Glenn Davis	.10
23	Will Clark	.10
24	Nolan Ryan	6.00
25	George Bell	.10
26	Cecil Fielder	.10
27	Gregg Olson	.10
28	Tim Wallach	.10
29	Ron Darling	.10
30	Kelly Gruber	.10
31	Shawn Boskie	.10
32	Mike Greenwell	.10
33	Dave Parker	.10
34	Joe Magrane	.10
35	Dave Stewart	.10
36	Kent Hrbek	.10
37	Robin Yount	1.00
38	Bo Jackson	.15
39	Fernando Valenzuela	.10
40	Sandy Alomar, Jr.	.10
41	Lance Parrish	.10
42	Candy Maldonado	.10
43	Mike LaValliere	.10
44	Jim Abbott	.10
45	Edgar Martinez	.10
46	Kirby Puckett	2.00
47	Delino DeShields	.10
48	Tony Gwynn	2.00
49	Carlton Fisk	1.00
50	Mike Scott	.10
51	Barry Larkin	.10
52	Andre Dawson	.35
53	Tom Glavine	.10
54	Tom Browning	.10
55	Checklist	.05

Rookies

For the fifth straight year, Donruss issued a 56-card "Rookies" set in 1990. As in previous years, the set is similar in design to the regular Donruss set, except for a new "The Rookies" logo and green borders instead of red. The set is packaged in a special box and includes a Carl Yastrzemski puzzle card.

		NM/M
	Complete Set (56):	1.00
	Common Player:	.05
1	Sandy Alomar	.05
2	John Olerud	.40
3	Pat Combs	.05
4	Brian Dubois	.05
5	Felix Jose	.05
6	Delino DeShields	.05
7	Mike Stanton	.05
8	Mike Munoz	.05
9	Craig Grebeck	.05
10	Joe Kraemer	.05
11	Jeff Huson	.05
12	Bill Sampen	.05
13	Brian Bohanon	.05
14	Dave Justice	.40
15	Robin Ventura	.05
16	Greg Vaughn	.05
17	Wayne Edwards	.05

18	Shawn Boskie	.05
19	Carlos Baerga RC	.20
20	Mark Gardner	.05
21	Kevin Appier	.05
22	Mike Harkey	.05
23	Tim Layana	.05
24	Glenallen Hill	.05
25	Jerry Kutzler	.05
26	Mike Blowers	.05
27	Scott Ruskin	.05
28	Dana Kiecker	.05
29	Willie Blair	.05
30	Ben McDonald	.05
31	Todd Zeile	.05
32	Scott Coolbaugh	.05
33	Xavier Hernandez	.05
34	Mike Hartley	.05
35	Kevin Tapani	.05
36	Kevin Wickander	.05
37	Carlos Hernandez	.05
38	Brian Traxler	.05
39	Marty Brown	.05
40	Scott Radinsky	.05
41	Julio Machado	.05
42	Steve Avery	.05
43	Mark Lemke	.05
44	Alan Mills	.05
45	Marquis Grissom	.05
46	Greg Olson	.05
47	Dave Hollins	.05
48	Jerald Clark	.05
49	Eric Anthony	.05
50	Tim Drummond	.05
51	John Burkett	.05
52	Brent Knackert	.05
53	Jeff Shaw	.05
54	John Orton	.05
55	Terry Shumpert	.05
56	Checklist	.05

1991 Donruss Previews

Once again in late 1990 Donruss distributed individual cards from a 12-card preview issue to its dealer network as an introduction to its 1991 issue. Like the previous year's preview cards, the '91 samples utilized the format which would follow on the regular-issue cards, but the photos were different. This has helped create demand for these cards from superstar collectors. Backs are printed in black-and-white and have little more than a player name, card number and MLB logos.

		NM/M
	Complete Set (12):	135.00
	Common Player:	2.50
1	Dave Justice	2.50
2	Doug Drabek	2.50
3	Scott Chiamparino	2.50
4	Ken Griffey Jr.	35.00
5	Bob Welch	2.50
6	Tino Martinez	2.50
7	Nolan Ryan	45.00
8	Dwight Gooden	2.50
9	Ryne Sandberg	17.50
10	Barry Bonds	45.00
11	Jose Canseco	7.50
12	Eddie Murray	12.00

1991 Donruss

Donruss used a two-series format in 1991. The first series was released in December 1990, and the second in February 1991. The 1991 design is somewhat reminiscent of the 1986 set, with blue borders on Series I cards; green on Series II. Limited edition cards including an autographed Ryne Sandberg card (5,000) were randomly inserted in wax packs. Other features of the set include 40 Rated Rookies, (RR) in the checklist, Legends and Elite insert series, and another Diamond King (DK) subset. Cards were distributed in packs with Willie Stargell puzzle pieces.

		NM/M
	Factory Set w/Previews (788):	12.00
	Factory Collector's Set (792):	12.00
	Complete Set (770):	8.00
	Common Player:	.05
	Willie Stargell Puzzle:	.50
	Series 1 or 2 Pack (15):	.50
	Series 1 or 2 Wax Box (36):	12.50
1	Dave Steib/DK	.05
2	Craig Biggio/DK	.05
3	Cecil Fielder/DK	.05
4	Barry Bonds/DK	1.00
5	Barry Larkin/DK	.05
6	Dave Parker/DK	.05
7	Len Dykstra/DK	.05
8	Bobby Thigpen/DK	.05
9	Roger Clemens/DK	.60
10	Ron Gant/DK	.05
11	Delino DeShields/DK	.05
12	Roberto Alomar/DK	.20
13	Sandy Alomar/DK	.05
14	Ryne Sandberg/DK	.50
15	Ramon Martinez/DK	.05
16	Edgar Martinez/DK	.05
17	Dave Magadan/DK	.05
18	Matt Williams/DK	.05
19	Rafael Palmeiro/DK	.40
20	Bob Welch/DK	.05
21	Dave Righetti/DK	.05
22	Brian Harper/DK	.05
23	Gregg Olson/DK	.05
24	Kurt Stillwell/DK	.05
25	Pedro Guerrero/DK	.05
26	Chuck Finley/DK	.05
27	Diamond King checklist	.05
28	Tino Martinez (Rated Rookie)	.05
29	Mark Lewis (RR)	.05
30	Bernard Gilkey RC (RR)	.10
31	Hensley Meulens (RR)	.05
32	Derek Bell RC (RR)	.30
33	Jose Offerman (RR)	.05
34	Terry Bross (RR)	.05
35	Leo Gomez RC (RR)	.05
36	Derrick May (RR)	.05
37	Kevin Morton RC (RR)	.05
38	Moises Alou (RR)	.05
39	Julio Valera RC (RR)	.05
40	Milt Cuyler (RR)	.05
41	Phil Plantier RC (RR)	.15
42	Scott Chiamparino RC (RR)	.05
43	Ray Lankford RC (RR)	.20
44	Mickey Morandini RC (RR)	.10
45	Dave Hansen (RR)	.05
46	Kevin Belcher RC (RR)	.05
47	Darrin Fletcher (RR)	.05
48	Dave Sax/AS	.05
49	Ken Griffey Jr./AS	.30
50a	Jose Canseco/AS (A's in stat line on back.)	.10
50b	Jose Canseco/AS (AL in stat line on back.)	.25
51	Sandy Alomar /AS	.05
52	Cal Ripken, Jr./AS	.05
53	Rickey Henderson/AS	.20
54	Bob Welch/AS	.05
55	Wade Boggs/AS	.25
56	Mark McGwire/AS	.50
57a	Jack McDowell (Career Games 30)	.05
57b	Jack McDowell (Career Games 63)	.25
58	Jose Lind	.05
59	Alex Fernandez	.05
60	Pat Combs	.05
61	Mike Walker RC	.05
62	Juan Samuel	.05
63	Mike Blowers	.05
64	Mark Guthrie	.05
65	Mark Salas	.05
66	Tim Jones	.05
67	Tim Leary	.05
68	Andres Galarraga	.05
69	Bob Milacki	.05
70	Tim Belcher	.05
71	Todd Zeile	.05
72	Jerome Walton	.05
73	Kevin Seitzer	.05
74	Jerald Clark	.05
75	John Smoltz	.05
76	Mike Henneman	.05
77	Ken Griffey Jr.	.05
78	Jim Abbott	.05
79	Gregg Jefferies	.05
80	Kevin Reimer	.05

81	Roger Clemens	.60
82	Mike Fitzgerald	.05
83	Bruce Hurst	.05
84	Eric Davis	.05
85	Paul Molitor	.40
86	Will Clark	.05
87	Mike Bielecki	.05
88	Bret Saberhagen	.05
89	Nolan Ryan	1.00
90	Bobby Thigpen	.05
91	Dickie Thon	.05
92	Duane Ward	.05
93	Luis Polonia	.05
94	Terry Kennedy	.05
95	Kent Hrbek	.05
96	Danny Jackson	.05
97	Sid Fernandez	.05
98	Jimmy Key	.05
99	Franklin Stubbs	.05
100	Checklist 28-103	.05
101	R.J. Reynolds	.05
102	Dave Stewart	.05
103	Dan Pasqua	.05
104	Dan Plesac	.05
105	Mark McGwire	.75
106	John Farrell	.05
107	Don Mattingly	.60
108	Carlton Fisk	.40
109	Ken Oberkfell	.05
110	Darrel Akerfelds	.05
111	Gregg Olson	.05
112	Mike Scioscia	.05
113	Bryn Smith	.05
114	Bob Geren	.05
115	Tom Candiotti	.05
116	Kevin Tapani	.05
117	Jeff Treadway	.05
118	Alan Trammell	.05
119	Pete O'Brien	.05
120	Joel Skinner	.05
121	Mike LaValliere	.05
122	Dwight Evans	.05
123	Jody Reed	.05
124	Lee Guetterman	.05
125	Tim Burke	.05
126	Dave Johnson	.05
127	Fernando Valenzuela	.05
128	Jose DeLeon	.05
129	Andre Dawson	.20
130	Gerald Perry	.05
131	Greg Harris	.05
132	Tom Glavine	.25
133	Lance McCullers	.05
134	Randy Johnson	.40
135	Lance Parrish	.05
136	Mackey Sasser	.05
137	Geno Petralli	.05
138	Dennis Lamp	.05
139	Dennis Martinez	.05
140	Mike Pagliarulo	.05
141	Hal Morris	.05
142	Dave Parker	.05
143	Brett Butler	.05
144	Paul Assenmacher	.05
145	Mark Gubicza	.05
146	Charlie Hough	.05
147	Sammy Sosa	.50
148	Randy Ready	.05
149	Kelly Gruber	.05
150	Devon White	.05
151	Gary Carter	.40
152	Gene Larkin	.05
153	Chris Sabo	.05
154	David Cone	.05
155	Todd Stottlemyre	.05
156	Glenn Wilson	.05
157	Bob Walk	.05
158	Mike Gallego	.05
159	Greg Hibbard	.05
160	Chris Bosio	.05
161	Mike Moore	.05
162	Jerry Browne	.05
163	Steve Sax	.05
164	Melido Perez	.05
165	Danny Darwin	.05
166	Roger McDowell	.05
167	Bill Ripken	.05
168	Mike Sharperson	.05
169	Lee Smith	.05
170	Matt Nokes	.05
171	Jesse Orosco	.05
172	Rick Aguilera	.05
173	Jim Presley	.05
174	Lou Whitaker	.05
175	Harold Reynolds	.05
176	Brook Jacoby	.05
177	Wally Backman	.05
178	Wade Boggs	.50
179	Chuck Cary	.05
180	Tom Foley	.05
181	Pete Harnisch	.05
182	Mike Morgan	.05
183	Bob Tewksbury	.05
184	Joe Girardi	.05
185	Storm Davis	.05
186	Ed Whitson	.05
187	Steve Avery	.05
188	Lloyd Moseby	.05
189	Scott Bankhead	.05
190	Mark Langston	.05
191	Kevin McReynolds	.05
192	Julio Franco	.05
193	John Dopson	.05
194	Oil Can Boyd	.05
195	Bip Roberts	.05
196	Billy Hatcher	.05
197	Edgar Diaz	.05
198	Greg Litton	.05

199	Mark Grace	.05
200	Checklist 104-179	.05
201	George Brett	.60
202	Jeff Russell	.05
203	Ivan Calderon	.05
204	Ken Howell	.05
205	Tom Henke	.05
206	Bryan Harvey	.05
207	Steve Bedrosian	.05
208	Al Newman	.05
209	Randy Myers	.05
210	Daryl Boston	.05
211	Manny Lee	.05
212	Dave Smith	.05
213	Don Slaught	.05
214	Walt Weiss	.05
215	Donn Pall	.05
216	Jamie Navarro	.05
217	Willie Randolph	.05
218	Rudy Seanez	.05
219	Jim Leyritz RC	.15
220	Ron Karkovice	.05
221	Ken Caminiti	.05
222a	Von Hayes (Traded players' first names included in How Acquired on back.)	.05
222b	Von Hayes (No first names.)	.05
223	Cal Ripken, Jr.	1.00
224	Lenny Harris	.05
225	Milt Thompson	.05
226	Alvaro Espinoza	.05
227	Chris James	.05
228	Dan Gladden	.05
229	Jeff Blauser	.05
230	Mike Heath	.05
231	Omar Vizquel	.05
232	Doug Jones	.05
233	Jeff King	.05
234	Luis Rivera	.05
235	Ellis Burks	.05
236	Greg Cadaret	.05
237	Dave Martinez	.05
238	Mark Williamson	.05
239	Stan Javier	.05
240	Ozzie Smith	.50
241	Shawn Boskie RC	.05
242	Tom Gordon	.05
243	Tony Gwynn	.50
244	Tommy Gregg	.05
245	Jeff Robinson	.05
246	Keith Comstock	.05
247	Jack Howell	.05
248	Keith Miller	.05
249	Bobby Witt	.05
250	Rob Murphy	.05
251	Spike Owen	.05
252	Garry Templeton	.05
253	Glenn Braggs	.05
254	Ron Robinson	.05
255	Kevin Mitchell	.05
256	Les Lancaster	.05
257	Mel Stottlemyre RC	.10
258	Kenny Rogers	.05
259	Lance Johnson	.05
260	John Kruk	.05
261	Fred McGriff	.05
262	Dick Schofield	.05
263	Trevor Wilson	.05
264	David West	.05
265	Scott Scudder	.05
266	Dwight Gooden	.05
267	Willie Blair RC	.05
268	Mark Portugal	.05
269	Doug Drabek	.05
270	Dennis Eckersley	.35
271	Eric King	.05
272	Robin Yount	.40
273	Carney Lansford	.05
274	Carlos Baerga	.05
275	Dave Righetti	.05
276	Scott Fletcher	.05
277	Eric Yelding	.05
278	Charlie Hayes	.05
279	Jeff Ballard	.05
280	Orel Hershiser	.05
281	Jose Oquendo	.05
282	Mike Witt	.05
283	Mitch Webster	.05
284	Greg Gagne	.05
285	Greg Olson RC	.05
286	Tony Phillips	.05
287	Scott Bradley	.05
288	Cory Snyder	.05
289	Jay Bell	.05
290	Kevin Romine	.05
291	Jeff Robinson	.05
292	Steve Frey	.05
293	Craig Worthington	.05
294	Tim Crews	.05
295	Joe Magrane	.05
296	Hector Villanueva RC	.05
297	Terry Shumpert RC	.05
298	Joe Carter	.05
299	Kent Mercker	.05
300	Checklist 180-255	.05
301	Chet Lemon	.05
302	Mike Schooler	.05
303	Dante Bichette	.05
304	Kevin Elster	.05
305	Jeff Huson	.05
306	Greg Harris	.05
307	Marquis Grissom	.05
308	Calvin Schiraldi	.05
309	Mariano Duncan	.05
310	Bill Spiers	.05
311	Scott Garrelts	.05
312	Mitch Williams	.05

#	Player	Price
313	Mike Macfarlane	.05
314	Kevin Brown	.05
315	Robin Ventura	.05
316	Darren Daulton	.05
317	Pat Borders	.05
318	Mark Eichhorn	.05
319	Jeff Brantley	.05
320	Shane Mack	.05
321	Rob Dibble	.05
322	John Franco	.05
323	Junior Felix	.05
324	Casey Candaele	.05
325	Bobby Bonilla	.05
326	Dave Henderson	.05
327	Wayne Edwards	.05
328	Mark Knudson	.05
329	Terry Steinbach	.05
330	Colby Ward RC	.05
331	Oscar Azocar RC	.05
332	Scott Radinsky RC	.10
333	Eric Anthony	.05
334	Steve Lake	.05
335	Bob Melvin	.05
336	Kal Daniels	.05
337	Tom Pagnozzi	.05
338	Alan Mills RC	.05
339	Steve Olin	.05
340	Juan Berenguer	.05
341	Francisco Cabrera	.05
342	Dave Bergman	.05
343	Henry Cotto	.05
344	Sergio Valdez	.05
345	Bob Patterson	.05
346	John Marzano	.05
347	Dana Kiecker RC	.05
348	Dion James	.05
349	Hubie Brooks	.05
350	Bill Landrum	.05
351	Bill Sampen RC	.05
352	Greg Briley	.05
353	Paul Gibson	.05
354	Dave Eiland	.05
355	Steve Finley	.05
356	Bob Boone	.05
357	Steve Buechele	.05
358	Chris Hoiles	.05
359	Larry Walker	.05
360	Frank DiPino	.05
361	Mark Grant	.05
362	Dave Magadan	.05
363	Robby Thompson	.05
364	Lonnie Smith	.05
365	Steve Farr	.05
366	Dave Valle	.05
367	Tim Naehring RC	.05
368	Jim Acker	.05
369	Jeff Reardon	.05
370	Tim Teufel	.05
371	Juan Gonzalez	.20
372	Luis Salazar	.05
373	Rick Honeycutt	.05
374	Greg Maddux	.50
375	Jose Uribe	.05
376	Donnie Hill	.05
377	Don Carman	.05
378	Craig Grebeck RC	.05
379	Willie Fraser	.05
380	Glenallen Hill	.05
381	Joe Oliver	.05
382	Randy Bush	.05
383	Alex Cole	.05
384	Norm Charlton	.05
385	Gene Nelson	.05
386a	Checklist 256-331 (Blue Borders)	.05
386b	Checklist 256-331 (Green Borders)	.05
387	Rickey Henderson (MVP)	.20
388	Lance Parrish (MVP)	.05
389	Fred McGriff (MVP)	.05
390	Dave Parker (MVP)	.05
391	Candy Maldonado (MVP)	.05
392	Ken Griffey Jr. (MVP)	.50
393	Gregg Olson (MVP)	.05
394	Rafael Palmeiro (MVP)	.05
395	Roger Clemens (MVP)	.30
396	George Brett (MVP)	.30
397	Cecil Fielder (MVP)	.05
398	Brian Harper (MVP)	.05
399	Bobby Thigpen (MVP)	.05
400	Roberto Kelly (MVP)	.05
401	Danny Darwin (MVP)	.05
402	Dave Justice (MVP)	.05
403	Lee Smith (MVP)	.05
404	Ryne Sandberg (MVP)	.05
405	Eddie Murray (MVP)	.20
406	Tim Wallach (MVP)	.05
407	Kevin Mitchell (MVP)	.05
408	Darryl Strawberry (MVP)	.05
409	Joe Carter (MVP)	.05
410	Len Dykstra (MVP)	.05
411	Doug Drabek (MVP)	.05
412	Chris Sabo (MVP)	.05
413	Paul Marak RC (RR)	.05
414	Tim McIntosh (RR)	.05
415	Brian Barnes RC (RR)	.05
416	Eric Gunderson RC (RR)	.05
417	Mike Gardiner RC (RR)	.05
418	Steve Carter (RR)	.05
419	Gerald Alexander RC (RR)	.05
420	Rich Garces RC (RR)	.05
421	Chuck Knoblauch RC (RR)	.50
422	Scott Aldred RC (RR)	.05
423	Wes Chamberlain RC (RR)	.05
424	Lance Dickson RC (RR)	.05
425	Greg Colbrunn RC (RR)	.10
426	Rich Delucia RC (RR)	.05
427	Jeff Conine RC (RR)	.50
428	Steve Decker RC (RR)	.05
429	Turner Ward RC (RR)	.05
430	Mo Vaughn (RR)	.05
431	Steve Chitren RC (RR)	.05
432	Mike Benjamin (RR)	.05
433	Ryne Sandberg/AS	.25
434	Len Dykstra/AS	.05
435	Andre Dawson/AS	.15
436	Mike Scioscia/AS	.05
437	Ozzie Smith/AS	.25
438	Kevin Mitchell/AS	.05
439	Jack Armstrong/AS	.05
440	Chris Sabo/AS	.05
441	Will Clark/AS	.25
442	Mel Hall	.05
443	Mark Gardner	.05
444	Mike Devereaux	.05
445	Kirk Gibson	.05
446	Terry Pendleton	.05
447	Mike Harkey	.05
448	Jim Eisenreich	.05
449	Benito Santiago	.05
450	Oddibe McDowell	.05
451	Cecil Fielder	.05
452	Ken Griffey Sr.	.05
453	Bert Blyleven	.10
454	Howard Johnson	.05
455	Monty Farris	.05
456	Tony Pena	.05
457	Tim Raines	.05
458	Dennis Rasmussen	.05
459	Luis Quinones	.05
460	B.J. Surhoff	.05
461	Ernest Riles	.05
462	Rick Sutcliffe	.05
463	Danny Tartabull	.05
464	Pete Incaviglia	.05
465	Carlos Martinez	.05
466	Ricky Jordan	.05
467	John Cerutti	.05
468	Dave Winfield	.40
469	Francisco Oliveras	.05
470	Roy Smith	.05
471	Barry Larkin	.05
472	Ron Darling	.05
473	David Wells	.05
474	Glenn Davis	.05
475	Neal Heaton	.05
476	Ron Hassey	.05
477	Frank Thomas	.40
478	Greg Vaughn	.05
479	Todd Burns	.05
480	Candy Maldonado	.05
481	Dave LaPoint	.05
482	Alvin Davis	.05
483	Mike Scott	.05
484	Dale Murphy	.20
485	Ben McDonald	.05
486	Jay Howell	.05
487	Vince Coleman	.05
488	Alfredo Griffin	.05
489	Sandy Alomar	.05
490	Kirby Puckett	.50
491	Andres Thomas	.05
492	Jack Morris	.05
493	Matt Young	.05
494	Greg Myers	.05
495	Barry Bonds	1.00
496	Scott Cooper	.05
497	Dan Schatzeder	.05
498	Jesse Barfield	.05
499	Jerry Goff	.05
500	Checklist 332-408	.05
501	Anthony Telford RC	.05
502	Eddie Murray	.40
503	Omar Olivares RC	.05
504	Ryne Sandberg	.50
505	Jeff Montgomery	.05
506	Mark Parent	.05
507	Ron Gant	.05
508	Frank Tanana	.05
509	Jay Buhner	.05
510	Max Venable	.05
511	Wally Whitehurst	.05
512	Gary Pettis	.05
513	Tom Brunansky	.05
514	Tim Wallach	.05
515	Craig Lefferts	.05
516	Tim Layana RC	.05
517	Darryl Hamilton	.05
518	Rick Reuschel	.05
519	Steve Wilson	.05
520	Kurt Stillwell	.05
521	Rafael Palmeiro	.30
522	Ken Patterson	.05
523	Len Dykstra	.05
524	Tony Fernandez	.05
525	Kent Anderson	.05
526	Mark Leonard RC	.05
527	Allan Anderson	.05
528	Tom Browning	.05
529	Frank Viola	.05
530	John Olerud	.05
531	Juan Agosto	.05
532	Zane Smith	.05
533	Scott Sanderson	.05
534	Barry Jones	.05
535	Mike Felder	.05
536	Jose Canseco	.20
537	Felix Fermin	.05
538	Roberto Kelly	.05
539	Brian Holman	.05
540	Mark Davidson	.05
541	Terry Mulholland	.05
542	Randy Milligan	.05
543	Jose Gonzalez	.05
544	Craig Wilson RC	.05
545	Mike Hartley	.05
546	Greg Swindell	.05
547	Gary Gaetti	.05
548	Dave Justice	.05
549	Steve Searcy	.05
550	Erik Hanson	.05
551	Dave Stieb	.05
552	Andy Van Slyke	.05
553	Mike Greenwell	.05
554	Kevin Maas	.05
555	Delino Deshields	.05
556	Curt Schilling	.20
557	Ramon Martinez	.05
558	Pedro Guerrero	.05
559	Dwight Smith	.05
560	Mark Davis	.05
561	Shawn Abner	.05
562	Charlie Leibrandt	.05
563	John Shelby	.05
564	Bill Swift	.05
565	Mike Fetters	.05
566	Alejandro Pena	.05
567	Ruben Sierra	.05
568	Carlos Quintana	.05
569	Kevin Gross	.05
570	Derek Lilliquist	.05
571	Jack Armstrong	.05
572	Greg Brock	.05
573	Mike Kingery	.05
574	Greg Smith	.05
575	Brian McRae RC	.10
576	Jack Daugherty	.05
577	Ozzie Guillen	.05
578	Joe Boever	.05
579	Luis Sojo	.05
580	Chili Davis	.05
581	Don Robinson	.05
582	Brian Harper	.05
583	Paul O'Neill	.05
584	Bob Ojeda	.05
585	Mookie Wilson	.05
586	Rafael Ramirez	.05
587	Gary Redus	.05
588	Jamie Quirk	.05
589	Shawn Hilligas	.05
590	Tom Edens RC	.05
591	Joe Klink	.05
592	Charles Nagy	.05
593	Eric Plunk	.05
594	Tracy Jones	.05
595	Craig Biggio	.05
596	Jose DeJesus	.05
597	Mickey Tettleton	.05
598	Chris Gwynn	.05
599	Rex Hudler	.05
600	Checklist 409-506	.05
601	Jim Gott	.05
602	Jeff Manto	.05
603	Nelson Liriano	.05
604	Mark Lemke	.05
605	Clay Parker	.05
606	Edgar Martinez	.05
607	Mark Whiten RC	.10
608	Ted Power	.05
609	Tom Bolton	.05
610	Tom Herr	.05
611	Andy Hawkins	.05
612	Scott Ruskin	.05
613	Ron Kittle	.05
614	John Wetteland	.05
615	Mike Perez RC	.05
616	Dave Clark	.05
617	Brent Mayne	.05
618	Jack Clark	.05
619	Marvin Freeman	.05
620	Edwin Nunez	.05
621	Russ Swan	.05
622	Johnny Ray	.05
623	Charlie O'Brien	.05
624	Joe Bitker RC	.05
625	Mike Marshall	.05
626	Otis Nixon	.05
627	Andy Benes	.05
628	Ron Oester	.05
629	Ted Higuera	.05
630	Kevin Bass	.05
631	Damon Berryhill	.05
632	Bo Jackson	.10
633	Brad Arnsberg	.05
634	Jerry Willard	.05
635	Tommy Greene	.05
636	Bob MacDonald RC	.05
637	Kirk McCaskill	.05
638	John Burkett	.05
639	Paul Abbott RC	.05
640	Todd Benzinger	.05
641	Todd Hundley	.05
642	George Bell	.05
643	Javier Ortiz RC	.05
644	Sid Bream	.05
645	Bob Welch	.05
646	Phil Bradley	.05
647	Bill Krueger	.05
648	Rickey Henderson	.40
649	Kevin Wickander	.05
650	Steve Balboni	.05
651	Gene Harris	.05
652	Jim Deshaies	.05
653	Jason Grimsley	.05
654	Joe Orsulak	.05
655	Jimmy Poole RC	.05
656	Felix Jose	.05
657	Dennis Cook	.05
658	Tom Brookens	.05
659	Junior Ortiz	.05
660	Jeff Parrett	.05
661	Jerry Don Gleaton	.05
662	Brent Knackert	.05
663	Rance Mulliniks	.05
664	John Smiley	.05
665	Larry Andersen	.05
666	Willie McGee	.05
667	Chris Nabholz RC	.05
668	Brady Anderson	.05
669	Darren Holmes RC	.10
670	Ken Hill	.05
671	Gary Varsho	.05
672	Bill Pecota	.05
673	Fred Lynn	.05
674	Kevin D. Brown	.05
675	Dan Petry	.05
676	Mike Jackson	.05
677	Wally Joyner	.05
678	Danny Jackson	.05
679	Bill Haselman RC	.05
680	Mike Boddicker	.05
681	Mel Rojas RC	.05
682	Roberto Alomar	.20
683	Dave Justice (R.O.Y.)	.05
684	Chuck Crim	.05
685a	Matt Williams (Last line of Career Highlights ends, "most DP's in.")	.10
685b	Matt Williams (Last line ends "8/24-27/87.")	.25
686	Shawon Dunston	.05
687	Jeff Schulz RC	.05
688	John Barfield RC	.05
689	Gerald Young	.05
690	Luis Gonzalez RC	.75
691	Frank Wills	.05
692	Chuck Finley	.05
693	Sandy Alomar (R.O.Y.)	.05
694	Tim Drummond	.05
695	Herm Winningham	.05
696	Darryl Strawberry	.05
697	Al Leiter	.05
698	Karl Rhodes RC	.05
699	Stan Belinda	.05
700	Checklist 507-604	.05
701	Lance Blankenship	.05
702	Willie Stargell (Puzzle Card)	.05
703	Jim Gantner	.05
704	Reggie Harris RC	.05
705	Rob Ducey	.05
706	Tim Hulett	.05
707	Atlee Hammaker	.05
708	Xavier Hernandez	.05
709	Chuck McElroy	.05
710	John Mitchell	.05
711	Carlos Hernandez	.05
712	Geronimo Pena	.05
713	Jim Neidlinger RC	.05
714	John Orton	.05
715	Terry Leach	.05
716	Mike Stanton	.05
717	Walt Terrell	.05
718	Luis Aquino	.05
719	Bud Black	.05
720	Bob Kipper	.05
721	Jeff Gray RC	.05
722	Jose Rijo	.05
723	Curt Young	.05
724	Jose Vizcaino	.05
725	Randy Tomlin RC	.05
726	Junior Noboa	.05
727	Bob Welch (Award Winner)	.05
728	Gary Ward	.05
729	Rob Deer	.05
730	David Segui RC	.05
731	Mark Carreon	.05
732	Vicente Palacios	.05
733	Sam Horn	.05
734	Howard Farmer RC	.05
735	Ken Dayley	.05
736	Kelly Mann	.05
737	Joe Grahe RC	.05
738	Kelly Downs	.05
739	Jimmy Kremers RC	.05
740	Kevin Appier	.05
741	Jeff Reed	.05
742	Jose Rijo (World Series)	.05
743	Dave Rohde RC	.05
744	Dr. Dirt/Mr. Clean (Len Dykstra, Dale Murphy)	.10
745	Paul Sorrento	.05
746	Thomas Howard	.05
747	Matt Stark RC	.05
748	Harold Baines	.05
749	Doug Dascenzo	.05
750	Doug Drabek (Award Winner)	.05
751	Gary Sheffield	.20
752	Terry Lee RC	.05
753	Jim Vatcher RC	.05
754	Lee Stevens	.05
755	Randy Veres	.05
756	Bill Doran	.05
757	Gary Wayne	.05
758	Pedro Munoz RC	.05
759	Chris Hammond	.05
760	Checklist 605-702	.05
761	Rickey Henderson (MVP)	.50
762	Barry Bonds (MVP)	.50
763	Billy Hatcher (World Series)	.05
764	Julio Machado	.05
765	Jose Mesa	.05
766	Willie Randolph (World Series)	.05
767	Scott Erickson RC	.10
768	Travis Fryman	.05
769	Rich Rodriguez RC	.05
770	Checklist 703-770; BC1-BC22	.05

Elite

THE ELITE SERIES
GEORGE BRETT

Donruss released a series of special inserts in 1991. Ten thousand of each Elite card was released, while 7,500 Legend cards and 5,000 Signature cards were issued. Cards were inserted in wax packs and feature marble borders. The Legend card features a Dick Perez drawing. Each card is designated with a serial number on the back.

		NM/M
Complete Set (10):		250.00
Common Player:		15.00
1	Barry Bonds	60.00
2	George Brett	40.00
3	Jose Canseco	25.00
4	Andre Dawson	15.00
5	Doug Drabek	7.50
6	Cecil Fielder	7.50
7	Rickey Henderson	25.00
8	Matt Williams	7.50
---	Nolan Ryan (Legend)	65.00
---	Ryne Sandberg (Signature)	100.00

1991 Donruss Grand Slammers

GRAND SLAMMER

This set features players who hit grand slams in 1990. The cards are styled after the 1991 Donruss regular-issue cards. The featured player is showcased with a star in the background. The set was included in factory sets and randomly in jumbo packs.

		NM/M
Complete Set (14):		2.00
Common Player:		.10
1	Joe Carter	.10
2	Bobby Bonilla	.10
3	Kal Daniels	.10
4	Jose Canseco	.30
5	Barry Bonds	1.00
6	Jay Buhner	.10
7	Cecil Fielder	.10
8	Matt Williams	.10
9	Andres Galarraga	.10
10	Luis Polonia	.10
11	Mark McGwire	.75
12	Ron Karkovice	.10
13	Darryl Strawberry	.10
14	Mike Greenwell	.10

1991 Donruss Highlights

These inserts feature highlights from the 1990 season. Cards have a "BC" (Bonus Card) prefix to the number and are styled after the 1991 regular-issue Donruss cards. Cards 1-10 feature blue borders due to their release with Series 1 cards. Cards 11-22 feature green borders and were released with Series 2 cards. A highlight logo appears on the front of the card. Each highlight is explained in depth on the card back.

		NM/M
Complete Set (22):		3.00
Common Player:		.10

1	Mark Langston, Mike Witt (No-Hit Mariners)	.10
2	Randy Johnson (No-Hits Tigers)	.25
3	Nolan Ryan (No-Hits A's)	.50
4	Dave Stewart (No-Hits Blue Jays)	.10
5	Cecil Fielder (50 Homer Club)	.10
6	Carlton Fisk (Record Home Run)	.20
7	Ryne Sandberg (Sets Fielding Records)	.25
8	Gary Carter (Breaks Catching Mark)	.20
9	Mark McGwire (Home Run Milestone)	.45
10	Bo Jackson (4 Consecutive HRs)	.15
11	Fernando Valenzuela (No-Hits Cardinals)	.10
12a	Andy Hawkins (PITCHER)	2.50
12b	Andy Hawkins (No-Hits White Sox)	.10
13	Melido Perez (No-Hits Yankees)	.10
14	Terry Mulholland (No-Hits Giants)	.10
15	Nolan Ryan (300th Win)	.50
16	Delino DeShields (4 Hits In Debut)	.10
17	Cal Ripken (Errorless Games)	.50
18	Eddie Murray (Switch Hit Homers)	.20
19	George Brett (3 Decade Champ)	.30
20	Bobby Thigpen (Shatters Save Mark)	.10
21	Dave Stieb (No-Hits Indians)	.10
22	Willie McGee (NL Batting Champ)	.10

1991 Donruss Diamond Kings Supers

Donruss made this set available through a mail-in offer. Three wrappers, $12 and postage were necessary to obtain this set. The cards are exactly the same design as the regular Donruss Diamond Kings except they measure approximately 5" x 6-3/4" in size. The artwork of Dick Perez is featured.

		NM/M
Complete Set (26):		8.00
Common Player:		.25
1	Dave Stieb	.25
2	Craig Biggio	.25
3	Cecil Fielder	.25
4	Barry Bonds	4.50
5	Barry Larkin	.25
6	Dave Parker	.25
7	Len Dykstra	.25
8	Bobby Thigpen	.25
9	Roger Clemens	2.50
10	Ron Gant	.25
11	Delino DeShields	.25
12	Roberto Alomar	.40
13	Sandy Alomar	.25
14	Ryne Sandberg	1.50
15	Ramon Martinez	.25
16	Edgar Martinez	.25
17	Dave Magadan	.25
18	Matt Williams	.25
19	Rafael Palmeiro	1.00
20	Bob Welch	.25
21	Dave Righetti	.25
22	Brian Harper	.25
23	Gregg Olson	.25
24	Kurt Stillwell	.25
25	Pedro Guerrero	.25
26	Chuck Finley	.25

Rookies

Red borders highlight the 1991 Donruss Rookies cards. This set marks the sixth year that Donruss produced such an issue. As in past years, "The Rookies" logo appears on the card fronts. The set is packaged in a special box and includes a Willie Stargell puzzle card.

		NM/M
Complete Set (56):		4.00
Common Player:		.05
1	Pat Kelly	.05
2	Rich DeLucia	.05
3	Wes Chamberlain	.05
4	Scott Leius	.05
5	Darryl Kile	.05
6	Milt Cuyler	.05
7	Todd Van Poppel	.05
8	Ray Lankford	.05
9	Brian Hunter	.05
10	Tony Perezchica	.05
11	Ced Landrum	.05
12	Dave Burba	.05
13	Ramon Garcia	.05
14	Ed Sprague	.05
15	Warren Newson	.05
16	Paul Faries	.05
17	Luis Gonzalez	.15
18	Charles Nagy	.05
19	Chris Hammond	.05
20	Frank Castillo	.05
21	Pedro Munoz	.05
22	Orlando Merced	.05
23	Jose Melendez	.05
24	Kirk Dressendorfer	.05
25	Heathcliff Slocumb	.05
26	Doug Simons	.05
27	Mike Timlin	.05
28	Jeff Fassero	.05
29	Mark Leiter	.05
30	Jeff Bagwell RC	2.50
31	Brian McRae	.05
32	Mark Whiten	.05
33	Ivan Rodriguez RC	1.50
34	Wade Taylor	.05
35	Darren Lewis	.05
36	Mo Vaughn	.25
37	Mike Remlinger	.05
38	Rick Wilkins	.05
39	Chuck Knoblauch	.05
40	Kevin Morton	.05
41	Carlos Rodriguez	.05
42	Mark Lewis	.05
43	Brent Mayne	.05
44	Chris Haney	.05
45	Denis Boucher	.05
46	Mike Gardiner	.05
47	Jeff Johnson	.05
48	Dean Palmer	.05
49	Chuck McElroy	.05
50	Chris Jones	.05
51	Scott Kamienicki	.05
52	Al Osuna	.05
53	Rusty Meacham	.05
54	Chito Martinez	.05
55	Reggie Jefferson	.05
56	Checklist	.05

1992 Donruss Previews

Four-card cello packs distributed to members of the Donruss dealers' network previewed the forthcoming 1992 baseball card issue. The preview cards have the same format, front and back photos as their counterparts in the regular set. Only the card number, the security underprinting, "Donruss Preview Card," and the stats, complete only through 1990, differ.

		NM/M
Complete Set (12):		25.00
Common Player:		.50
1	Wade Boggs	2.50

2	Barry Bonds	7.50
3	Will Clark	.50
4	Andre Dawson	.75
5	Dennis Eckersley	1.50
6	Robin Ventura	.50
7	Ken Griffey Jr.	4.00
8	Kelly Gruber	.50
9	Ryan Klesko	
	(Rated Rookie)	.50
10	Cal Ripken, Jr.	7.50
11	Nolan Ryan (Highlight)	7.50
12	Todd Van Poppel	.50

1992 Donruss

For the second consecutive year, Donruss released its card set in two series. The 1992 cards feature improved stock, an anti-counterfeit feature and include both front and back photos. Once again Rated Rookies and All-Stars are included in the set. Special highlight cards also can be found in the 1992 Donruss set. Production was reduced in 1992 compared to 1988-1991. Retail factory sets include four 1992 Leaf preview cards.

		NM/M
Unopened Retail Set (788):		15.00
Unopened Hobby Set (784):		12.50
Unopened "Coca-Cola" Set (784):		25.00
Complete Set (784):		12.00
Common Player:		.05
Rod Carew Puzzle:		.50
Series 1 or 2 Pack (15):		.50
Series 1 or 2 Wax Box (36):		15.00
Blister Rack (92):		1.50
1	Mark Wohlers/RR RC	.05
2	Wil Cordero/RR	.05
3	Kyle Abbott/RR	.05
4	Dave Nilsson/RR RC	.05
5	Kenny Lofton/RR	.15
6	Luis Mercedes/RR RC	.05
7	Roger Salkeld/RR RC	.05
8	Eddie Zosky/RR	.05
9	Todd Van Poppel/RR RC	.10
10	Frank Seminara/RR RC	.05
11	Andy Ashby/RR RC	.10
12	Reggie Jefferson/RR	.05
13	Ryan Klesko/RR	.05
14	Carlos Garcia/RR RC	.10
15	John Ramos/RR RC	.05
16	Eric Karros/RR	.05
17	Pat Lennon/RR RC	.05
18	Eddie Taubensee/RR RC	.05
19	Roberto Hernandez/RR RC	.05
20	D.J. Dozier/RR	.05
21	Dave Henderson/AS	.05
22	Cal Ripken, Jr./AS	.50
23	Wade Boggs/AS	.25
24	Ken Griffey Jr./AS	.35
25	Jack Morris/AS	.05
26	Danny Tartabull/AS	.05
27	Cecil Fielder/AS	.05
28	Roberto Alomar/AS	.10
29	Sandy Alomar/AS	.05
30	Rickey Henderson/AS	.25
31	Ken Hill	.05
32	John Habyan	.05
33	Otis Nixon (Highlight)	.05
34	Tim Wallach	.05
35	Cal Ripken, Jr.	1.00
36	Gary Carter	.35
37	Juan Agosto	.05
38	Doug Dascenzo	.05
39	Kirk Gibson	.05
40	Benito Santiago	.05
41	Otis Nixon	.05
42	Andy Allanson	.05
43	Brian Holman	.05
44	Dick Schofield	.05
45	Dave Magadan	.05
46	Rafael Palmeiro	.35
47	Jody Reed	.05
48	Ivan Calderon	.05
49	Greg Harris	.05
50	Chris Sabo	.05
51	Paul Molitor	.35
52	Robby Thompson	.05
53	Dave Smith	.05
54	Mark Davis	.05
55	Kevin Brown	.05
56	Donn Pall	.05
57	Len Dykstra	.05

58	Roberto Alomar	.15
59	Jeff Robinson	.05
60	Willie McGee	.05
61	Jay Buhner	.05
62	Mike Pagliarulo	.05
63	Paul O'Neill	.05
64	Hubie Brooks	.05
65	Kelly Gruber	.05
66	Ken Caminiti	.05
67	Gary Redus	.05
68	Harold Baines	.05
69	Charlie Hough	.05
70	B.J. Surhoff	.05
71	Walt Weiss	.05
72	Shawn Hillegas	.05
73	Roberto Kelly	.05
74	Jeff Ballard	.05
75	Craig Biggio	.05
76	Pat Combs	.05
77	Jeff Robinson	.05
78	Tim Belcher	.05
79	Cris Carpenter	.05
80	Checklist 1-79	.05
81	Steve Avery	.05
82	Chris James	.05
83	Brian Harper	.05
84	Charlie Leibrandt	.05
85	Mickey Tettleton	.05
86	Pete O'Brien	.05
87	Danny Darwin	.05
88	Bob Walk	.05
89	Jeff Reardon	.05
90	Bobby Rose	.05
91	Danny Jackson	.05
92	John Morris	.05
93	Bud Black	.05
94	Tommy Greene (Highlight)	.05
95	Rick Aguilera	.05
96	Gary Gaetti	.05
97	David Cone	.05
98	John Olerud	.05
99	Joel Skinner	.05
100	Jay Bell	.05
101	Bob Milacki	.05
102	Norm Charlton	.05
103	Chuck Crim	.05
104	Terry Steinbach	.05
105	Juan Samuel	.05
106	Steve Howe	.05
107	Rafael Belliard	.05
108	Joey Cora	.05
109	Tommy Greene	.05
110	Gregg Olson	.05
111	Frank Tanana	.05
112	Lee Smith	.05
113	Greg Harris	.05
114	Dwayne Henry	.05
115	Chili Davis	.05
116	Kent Mercker	.05
117	Brian Barnes	.05
118	Rich DeLucia	.05
119	Andre Dawson	.20
120	Carlos Baerga	.05
121	Mike LaValliere	.05
122	Jeff Gray	.05
123	Bruce Hurst	.05
124	Alvin Davis	.05
125	John Candelaria	.05
126	Matt Nokes	.05
127	George Bell	.05
128	Bret Saberhagen	.05
129	Jeff Russell	.05
130	Jim Abbott	.05
131	Bill Gullickson	.05
132	Todd Zeile	.05
133	Dave Winfield	.35
134	Wally Whitehurst	.05
135	Matt Williams	.05
136	Tom Browning	.05
137	Marquis Grissom	.05
138	Erik Hanson	.05
139	Rob Dibble	.05
140	Don August	.05
141	Tom Henke	.05
142	Dan Pasqua	.05
143	George Brett	.60
144	Jerald Clark	.05
145	Robin Ventura	.05
146	Dale Murphy	.05
147	Dennis Eckersley	.30
148	Eric Yelding	.05
149	Mario Diaz	.05
150	Casey Candaele	.05
151	Steve Olin	.05
152	Luis Salazar	.05
153	Kevin Maas	.05
154	Nolan Ryan (Highlight)	.50
155	Barry Jones	.05
156	Chris Hoiles	.05
157	Bobby Ojeda	.05
158	Pedro Guerrero	.05
159	Paul Assenmacher	.05
160	Checklist 80-157	.05
161	Mike Macfarlane	.05
162	Craig Lefferts	.05
163	Brian Hunter RC	.05
164	Alan Trammell	.05
165	Ken Griffey Jr.	.65
166	Lance Parrish	.05
167	Brian Downing	.05
168	John Barfield	.05
169	Jack Clark	.05
170	Chris Nabholz	.05
171	Tim Teufel	.05
172	Chris Hammond	.05
173	Robin Yount	.35
174	Dave Righetti	.05
175	Joe Girardi	.05

176	Mike Boddicker	.05
177	Dean Palmer	.05
178	Greg Hibbard	.05
179	Randy Ready	.05
180	Devon White	.05
181	Mark Eichhorn	.05
182	Mike Felder	.05
183	Joe Klink	.05
184	Steve Bedrosian	.05
185	Barry Larkin	.05
186	John Franco	.05
187	Ed Sprague RC	.05
188	Mark Portugal	.05
189	Jose Lind	.05
190	Bob Welch	.05
191	Alex Fernandez	.05
192	Gary Sheffield	.20
193	Rickey Henderson	.35
194	Rod Nichols	.05
195	Scott Kamieniecki RC	.05
196	Mike Flanagan	.05
197	Steve Finley	.05
198	Darren Daulton	.05
199	Leo Gomez	.05
200	Mike Morgan	.05
201	Bob Tewksbury	.05
202	Sid Bream	.05
203	Sandy Alomar	.05
204	Greg Gagne	.05
205	Juan Berenguer	.05
206	Cecil Fielder	.05
207	Randy Johnson	.35
208	Tony Pena	.05
209	Doug Drabek	.05
210	Wade Boggs	.45
211	Bryan Harvey	.05
212	Jose Vizcaino	.05
213	Alonzo Powell RC	.05
214	Will Clark	.05
215	Rickey Henderson (Highlight)	.20
216	Jack Morris	.05
217	Junior Felix	.05
218	Vince Coleman	.05
219	Jimmy Key	.05
220	Alex Cole	.05
221	Bill Landrum	.05
222	Randy Milligan	.05
223	Jose Rijo	.05
224	Greg Vaughn	.05
225	Dave Stewart	.05
226	Lenny Harris	.05
227	Scott Sanderson	.05
228	Jeff Blauser	.05
229	Ozzie Guillen	.05
230	John Kruk	.05
231	Bob Melvin	.05
232	Milt Cuyler	.05
233	Felix Jose	.05
234	Ellis Burks	.05
235	Pete Harnisch	.05
236	Kevin Tapani	.05
237	Terry Pendleton	.05
238	Mark Gardner	.05
239	Harold Reynolds	.05
240	Checklist 158-237	.05
241	Mike Harkey	.05
242	Felix Fermin	.05
243	Barry Bonds	1.00
244	Roger Clemens	.60
245	Dennis Rasmussen	.05
246	Jose DeLeon	.05
247	Orel Hershiser	.05
248	Mel Hall	.05
249	Rick Wilkins RC	.05
250	Tom Gordon	.05
251	Kevin Reimer	.05
252	Luis Polonia	.05
253	Mike Henneman	.05
254	Tom Pagnozzi	.05
255	Chuck Finley	.05
256	Mackey Sasser	.05
257	John Burkett	.05
258	Hal Morris	.05
259	Larry Walker	.05
260	Billy Swift	.05
261	Joe Oliver	.05
262	Julio Machado	.05
263	Todd Stottlemyre	.05
264	Matt Merullo	.05
265	Brent Mayne	.05
266	Thomas Howard	.05
267	Lance Johnson	.05
268	Terry Mulholland	.05
269	Rick Honeycutt	.05
270	Luis Gonzalez	.05
271	Jose Guzman	.05
272	Jimmy Jones	.05
273	Mark Lewis	.05
274	Rene Gonzales	.05
275	Jeff Johnson RC	.05
276	Dennis Martinez (Highlight)	.05
277	Delino DeShields	.05
278	Sam Horn	.05
279	Kevin Gross	.05
280	Jose Oquendo	.05
281	Mark Grace	.05
282	Mark Gubicza	.05
283	Fred McGriff	.05
284	Ron Gant	.05
285	Lou Whitaker	.05
286	Edgar Martinez	.05
287	Ron Tingley	.05
288	Kevin McReynolds	.05
289	Ivan Rodriguez	.30
290	Mike Gardiner	.05
291	Chris Haney RC	.05

292	Darrin Jackson	.05
293	Bill Doran	.05
294	Ted Higuera	.05
295	Jeff Brantley	.05
296	Les Lancaster	.05
297	Jim Eisenreich	.05
298	Ruben Sierra	.05
299	Scott Radinsky	.05
300	Jose DeJesus	.05
301	Mike Timlin RC	.05
302	Luis Sojo	.05
303	Kelly Downs	.05
304	Scott Bankhead	.05
305	Pedro Munoz	.05
306	Scott Scudder	.05
307	Kevin Elster	.05
308	Duane Ward	.05
309	Darryl Kile RC	.10
310	Orlando Merced	.05
311	Dave Henderson	.05
312	Tim Raines	.05
313	Mark Lee RC	.05
314	Mike Gallego	.05
315	Charles Nagy	.05
316	Jesse Barfield	.05
317	Todd Frohwirth	.05
318	Al Osuna	.05
319	Darrin Fletcher	.05
320	Checklist 238-316	.05
321	David Segui	.05
322	Stan Javier	.05
323	Bryn Smith	.05
324	Jeff Treadway	.05
325	Mark Whiten	.05
326	Kent Hrbek	.05
327	Dave Justice	.05
328	Tony Phillips	.05
329	Rob Murphy	.05
330	Kevin Morton	.05
331	John Smiley	.05
332	Luis Rivera	.05
333	Wally Joyner	.05
334	Heathcliff Slocumb RC	.05
335	Rick Cerone	.05
336	Mike Remlinger RC	.05
337	Mike Moore	.05
338	Lloyd McClendon	.05
339	Al Newman	.05
340	Kirk McCaskill	.05
341	Howard Johnson	.05
342	Greg Myers	.05
343	Kal Daniels	.05
344	Bernie Williams	.05
345	Shane Mack	.05
346	Gary Thurman	.05
347	Dante Bichette	.05
348	Mark McGwire	.75
349	Travis Fryman	.05
350	Ray Lankford	.05
351	Mike Jeffcoat	.05
352	Jack McDowell	.05
353	Mitch Williams	.05
354	Mike Devereaux	.05
355	Andres Galarraga	.05
356	Henry Cotto	.05
357	Scott Bailes	.05
358	Jeff Bagwell	.35
359	Scott Leius	.05
360	Zane Smith	.05
361	Bill Pecota	.05
362	Tony Fernandez	.05
363	Glenn Braggs	.05
364	Bill Spiers	.05
365	Vicente Palacios	.05
366	Tim Burke	.05
367	Randy Tomlin	.05
368	Kenny Rogers	.05
369	Brett Butler	.05
370	Pat Kelly	.05
371	Bip Roberts	.05
372	Gregg Jefferies	.05
373	Kevin Bass	.05
374	Ron Karkovice	.05
375	Paul Gibson	.05
376	Bernard Gilkey	.05
377	Dave Gallagher	.05
378	Bill Wegman	.05
379	Pat Borders	.05
380	Ed Whitson	.05
381	Gilberto Reyes	.05
382	Russ Swan	.05
383	Andy Van Slyke	.05
384	Wes Chamberlain	.05
385	Steve Chitren	.05
386	Greg Olson	.05
387	Brian McRae	.05
388	Rich Rodriguez	.05
389	Steve Decker	.05
390	Chuck Knoblauch	.05
391	Bobby Witt	.05
392	Eddie Murray	.35
393	Juan Gonzalez	.20
394	Scott Ruskin	.05
395	Jay Howell	.05
396	Checklist 317-396	.05
397	Royce Clayton/RR	.05
398	John Jaha/RR RC	.05
399	Dan Wilson/RR RC	.05
400	Archie Corbin/RR RC	.05
401	Barry Manuel/RR RC	.05
402	Kim Batiste/RR	.05
403	Pat Mahomes/RR RC	.05
404	Dave Fleming/RR	.05
405	Jeff Juden/RR	.05
406	Jim Thome/RR	.40
407	Sam Militello/RR	.05
408	Jeff Nelson/RR RC	.05
409	Anthony Young/RR	.05

410	Tino Martinez/RR	.05
411	Jeff Mutis/RR RC	.05
412	Rey Sanchez/RR RC	.05
413	Chris Gardner/RR RC	.05
414	John Vander Wal/RR RC	.10
415	Reggie Sanders/RR	.05
416	Brian Williams/RR RC	.05
417	Mo Sanford/RR	.05
418	David Weathers/RR RC	.05
419	Hector Fajardo/RR RC	.05
420	Steve Foster/RR RC	.05
421	Lance Dickson/RR	.05
422	Andre Dawson/AS	.15
423	Ozzie Smith/AS	.25
424	Chris Sabo/AS	.05
425	Tony Gwynn/AS	.25
426	Tom Glavine/AS	.05
427	Bobby Bonilla/AS	.05
428	Will Clark/AS	.05
429	Ryne Sandberg/AS	.25
430	Benito Santiago/AS	.05
431	Ivan Calderon/AS	.05
432	Ozzie Smith	.45
433	Tim Leary	.05
434	Bret Saberhagen (Highlight)	.05
435	Mel Rojas	.05
436	Ben McDonald	.05
437	Tim Crews	.05
438	Rex Hudler	.05
439	Chico Walker	.05
440	Kurt Stillwell	.05
441	Tony Gwynn	.45
442	John Smoltz	.05
443	Lloyd Moseby	.05
444	Mike Schooler	.05
445	Joe Grahe	.05
446	Dwight Gooden	.05
447	Oil Can Boyd	.05
448	John Marzano	.05
449	Bret Barberie	.05
450	Mike Maddux	.05
451	Jeff Reed	.05
452	Dale Sveum	.05
453	Jose Uribe	.05
454	Bob Scanlan	.05
455	Kevin Appier	.05
456	Jeff Huson	.05
457	Ken Patterson	.05
458	Ricky Jordan	.05
459	Tom Candiotti	.05
460	Lee Stevens	.05
461	Rod Beck RC	.10
462	Dave Valle	.05
463	Scott Erickson	.05
464	Chris Jones	.05
465	Mark Carreon	.05
466	Rob Ducey	.05
467	Jim Corsi	.05
468	Jeff King	.05
469	Curt Young	.05
470	Bo Jackson	.15
471	Chris Bosio	.05
472	Jamie Quirk	.05
473	Jesse Orosco	.05
474	Alvaro Espinoza	.05
475	Joe Orsulak	.05
476	Checklist 397-477	.05
477	Gerald Young	.05
478	Wally Backman	.05
479	Juan Bell	.05
480	Mike Scioscia	.05
481	Omar Olivares	.05
482	Francisco Cabrera	.05
483	Greg Swindell	.05
484	Terry Leach	.05
485	Tommy Gregg	.05
486	Scott Aldred	.05
487	Greg Briley	.05
488	Phil Plantier	.05
489	Curtis Wilkerson	.05
490	Tom Brunansky	.05
491	Mike Fetters	.05
492	Frank Castillo	.05
493	Joe Boever	.05
494	Kirt Manwaring	.05
495	Wilson Alvarez (Highlight)	.05
496	Gene Larkin	.05
497	Gary DiSarcina	.05
498	Frank Viola	.05
499	Manuel Lee	.05
500	Albert Belle	.05
501	Stan Belinda	.05
502	Dwight Evans	.05
503	Eric Davis	.05
504	Darren Holmes	.05
505	Mike Bordick	.05
506	Dave Hansen	.05
507	Lee Guetterman	.05
508	Keith Mitchell RC	.05
509	Melido Perez	.05
510	Dickie Thon	.05
511	Mark Williamson	.05
512	Mark Salas	.05
513	Milt Thompson	.05
514	Mo Vaughn	.05
515	Jim Deshaies	.05
516	Rich Garces	.05
517	Lonnie Smith	.05
518	Spike Owen	.05
519	Tracy Jones	.05
520	Greg Maddux	.45
521	Carlos Martinez	.05
522	Neal Heaton	.05
523	Mike Greenwell	.05
524	Andy Benes	.05
525	Jeff Schaefer	.05
526	Mike Sharperson	.05

No.	Player	Price
527	Wade Taylor	.05
528	Jerome Walton	.05
529	Storm Davis	.05
530	Jose Hernandez RC	.05
531	Mark Langston	.05
532	Rob Deer	.05
533	Geronimo Pena	.05
534	Juan Guzman RC	.10
535	Pete Schourek	.05
536	Todd Benzinger	.05
537	Billy Hatcher	.05
538	Tom Foley	.05
539	Dave Cochrane	.05
540	Mariano Duncan	.05
541	Edwin Nunez	.05
542	Rance Mulliniks	.05
543	Carlton Fisk	.35
544	Luis Aquino	.05
545	Ricky Bones	.05
546	Craig Grebeck	.05
547	Charlie Hayes	.05
548	Jose Canseco	.25
549	Andujar Cedeno	.05
550	Geno Petralli	.05
551	Javier Ortiz	.05
552	Rudy Seanez	.05
553	Rich Gedman	.05
554	Eric Plunk	.05
555	Nolan Ryan, Rich Gossage (Highlight)	.25
556	Checklist 478-555	.05
557	Greg Colbrunn	.05
558	Chito Martinez RC	.05
559	Darryl Strawberry	.05
560	Luis Alicea	.05
561	Dwight Smith	.05
562	Terry Shumpert	.05
563	Jim Vatcher	.05
564	Deion Sanders	.10
565	Walt Terrell	.05
566	Dave Burba	.05
567	Dave Howard	.05
568	Todd Hundley	.05
569	Jack Daugherty	.05
570	Scott Cooper	.05
571	Bill Sampen	.05
572	Jose Melendez	.05
573	Freddie Benavides	.05
574	Jim Gantner	.05
575	Trevor Wilson	.05
576	Ryne Sandberg	.45
577	Kevin Seitzer	.05
578	Gerald Alexander	.05
579	Mike Huff	.05
580	Von Hayes	.05
581	Derek Bell	.05
582	Mike Stanley	.05
583	Kevin Mitchell	.05
584	Mike Jackson	.05
585	Dan Gladden	.05
586	Ted Power	.05
587	Jeff Innis	.05
588	Bob MacDonald	.05
589	Jose Tolentino RC	.05
590	Bob Patterson	.05
591	Scott Brosius RC	.10
592	Frank Thomas	.35
593	Darryl Hamilton	.05
594	Kirk Dressendorfer	.05
595	Jeff Shaw	.05
596	Don Mattingly	.60
597	Glenn Davis	.05
598	Andy Mota	.05
599	Jason Grimsley	.05
600	Jimmy Poole	.05
601	Jim Gott	.05
602	Stan Royer	.05
603	Marvin Freeman	.05
604	Denis Boucher	.05
605	Denny Neagle	.05
606	Mark Lemke	.05
607	Jerry Don Gleaton	.05
608	Brent Knackert	.05
609	Carlos Quintana	.05
610	Bobby Bonilla	.05
611	Joe Hesketh	.05
612	Daryl Boston	.05
613	Shawon Dunston	.05
614	Danny Cox	.05
615	Darren Lewis	.05
616	Alejandro Pena, Kent Mercker, Mark Wohlers (Highlight)	.05
617	Kirby Puckett	.45
618	Franklin Stubbs	.05
619	Chris Donnels	.05
620	David Wells	.05
621	Mike Aldrete	.05
622	Bob Kipper	.05
623	Anthony Telford	.05
624	Randy Myers	.05
625	Willie Randolph	.05
626	Joe Slusarski	.05
627	John Wetteland	.05
628	Greg Cadaret	.05
629	Tom Glavine	.20
630	Wilson Alvarez	.05
631	Wally Ritchie	.05
632	Mike Mussina	.25
633	Mark Leiter	.05
634	Gerald Perry	.05
635	Matt Young	.05
636	Checklist 556-635	.05
637	Scott Hemond	.05
638	David West	.05
639	Jim Clancy	.05
640	Doug Piatt	.05
641	Omar Vizquel	.05
642	Rick Sutcliffe	.05
643	Glenallen Hill	.05
644	Gary Varsho	.05
645	Tony Fossas	.05
646	Jack Howell	.05
647	Jim Campanis RC	.05
648	Chris Gwynn	.05
649	Jim Leyritz	.05
650	Chuck McElroy	.05
651	Sean Berry	.05
652	Donald Harris	.05
653	Don Slaught	.05
654	Rusty Meacham RC	.05
655	Scott Terry	.05
656	Ramon Martinez	.05
657	Keith Miller	.05
658	Ramon Garcia	.05
659	Milt Hill RC	.05
660	Steve Frey	.05
661	Bob McClure	.05
662	Ced Landrum RC	.05
663	Doug Henry RC	.05
664	Candy Maldonado	.05
665	Carl Willis	.05
666	Jeff Montgomery	.05
667	Craig Shipley RC	.05
668	Warren Newson RC	.05
669	Mickey Morandini	.05
670	Brook Jacoby	.05
671	Ryan Bowen RC	.05
672	Bill Krueger	.05
673	Rob Mallicoat	.05
674	Doug Jones	.05
675	Scott Livingstone	.05
676	Danny Tartabull	.05
677	Joe Carter (Highlight)	.05
678	Cecil Espy	.05
679	Randy Velarde	.05
680	Bruce Ruffin	.05
681	Ted Wood RC	.05
682	Dan Plesac	.05
683	Eric Bullock	.05
684	Junior Ortiz	.05
685	Dave Hollins	.05
686	Dennis Martinez	.05
687	Larry Andersen	.05
688	Doug Simons	.05
689	Tim Spehr RC	.05
690	Calvin Jones RC	.05
691	Mark Guthrie	.05
692	Alfredo Griffin	.05
693	Joe Carter	.05
694	Terry Mathews RC	.05
695	Pascual Perez	.05
696	Gene Nelson	.05
697	Gerald Williams	.05
698	Chris Cron RC	.05
699	Steve Buechele	.05
700	Paul McClellan	.05
701	Jim Lindeman	.05
702	Francisco Oliveras	.05
703	Rob Maurer RC	.05
704	Pat Hentgen RC	.15
705	Jaime Navarro	.05
706	Mike Magnante RC	.05
707	Nolan Ryan	1.00
708	Bobby Thigpen	.05
709	John Cerutti	.05
710	Steve Wilson	.05
711	Hensley Meulens	.05
712	Rheal Cormier RC	.05
713	Scott Bradley	.05
714	Mitch Webster	.05
715	Roger Mason	.05
716	Checklist 636-716	.05
717	Jeff Fassero RC	.05
718	Cal Eldred	.05
719	Sid Fernandez	.05
720	Bob Zupcic RC	.05
721	Jose Offerman	.05
722	Cliff Brantley RC	.05
723	Ron Darling	.05
724	Dave Stieb	.05
725	Hector Villanueva	.05
726	Mike Hartley	.05
727	Arthur Rhodes RC	.05
728	Randy Bush	.05
729	Steve Sax	.05
730	Dave Otto	.05
731	John Wehner RC	.05
732	Dave Martinez	.05
733	Ruben Amaro RC	.05
734	Billy Ripken	.05
735	Steve Farr	.05
736	Shawn Abner	.05
737	Gil Heredia RC	.05
738	Ron Jones	.05
739	Tony Castillo	.05
740	Sammy Sosa	.45
741	Julio Franco	.05
742	Tim Naehring	.05
743	Steve Wapnick RC	.05
744	Craig Wilson	.05
745	Darrin Chapin RC	.05
746	Chris George RC	.05
747	Mike Simms	.05
748	Rosario Rodriguez	.05
749	Skeeter Barnes	.05
750	Roger McDowell	.05
751	Dann Howitt	.05
752	Paul Sorrento	.05
753	Braulio Castillo RC	.05
754	Yorkis Perez RC	.05
755	Willie Fraser	.05
756	Jeremy Hernandez RC	.05
757	Curt Schilling	.20
758	Steve Lyons	.05
759	Dave Anderson	.05
760	Willie Banks	.05
761	Mark Leonard	.05
762	Jack Armstrong	.05
763	Scott Servais	.05
764	Ray Stephens	.05
765	Junior Noboa	.05
766	Jim Olander RC	.05
767	Joe Magrane	.05
768	Lance Blankenship	.05
769	Mike Humphreys RC	.05
770	Jarvis Brown RC	.05
771	Damon Berryhill	.05
772	Alejandro Pena	.05
773	Jose Mesa	.05
774	Gary Cooper RC	.05
775	Carney Lansford	.05
776	Mike Bielecki	.05
777	Charlie O'Brien	.05
778	Carlos Hernandez	.05
779	Howard Farmer	.05
780	Mike Stanton	.05
781	Reggie Harris	.05
782	Xavier Hernandez	.05
783	Bryan Hickerson RC	.05
784	Checklist 717-BC8	.05

1992 Donruss Bonus Cards

The eight bonus cards were randomly inserted in 1992 foil packs and are numbered with a "BC" prefix. Both leagues' MVPs, Cy Young and Rookie of the Year award winners are featured, as are logo cards for the expansion Colorado Rockies and Florida Marlins. Cards are standard size in a format similar to the regular issue.

		NM/M
Complete Set (8):		5.00
Common Player:		.25
1	Cal Ripken, Jr. (MVP)	2.50
2	Terry Pendleton (MVP)	.25
3	Roger Clemens (Cy Young)	2.00
4	Tom Glavine (Cy Young)	.40
5	Chuck Knoblauch (Rookie of the Year)	.25
6	Jeff Bagwell (Rookie of the Year)	1.50
7	Colorado Rockies	.25
8	Florida Marlins	.25

Diamond Kings

Donruss changed its Diamond Kings style and distribution in 1992. The cards still feature the art of Dick Perez, but quality was improved from past years. The cards were randomly inserted in foil packs. One player from each team is featured. Card numbers have a "DK" prefix.

		NM/M
Complete Set (27):		17.50
Common Player:		.40
1	Paul Molitor	2.00
2	Will Clark	.50
3	Joe Carter	.50
4	Julio Franco	.50
5	Cal Ripken, Jr.	6.00
6	Dave Justice	.50
7	George Bell	.50
8	Frank Thomas	2.00
9	Wade Boggs	4.00
10	Scott Sanderson	.50
11	Jeff Bagwell	2.00
12	John Kruk	.50
13	Felix Jose	.50
14	Harold Baines	.50
15	Dwight Gooden	.50
16	Brian McRae	.50
17	Jay Bell	.50
18	Brett Butler	.50
19	Hal Morris	.50
20	Mark Langston	.50
21	Scott Erickson	.50
22	Randy Johnson	2.00
23	Greg Swindell	.50
24	Dennis Martinez	.50
25	Tony Phillips	.50
26	Fred McGriff	.50
27	Checklist	.10

1992 Donruss Diamond Kings Supers

Produced in very limited numbers, possibly as a prototype for use in a sales presentation to a major retail chain, these 4-7/8" x 6-3/4" cards are identical in virtually everything but size to the regular 1992 DK inserts. Both front and back feature a high-gloss finish.

		NM/M
Complete Set (27):		900.00
Common Player:		15.00
1	Paul Molitor	95.00
2	Will Clark	15.00
3	Joe Carter	15.00
4	Julio Franco	15.00
5	Cal Ripken, Jr.	335.00
6	Dave Justice	15.00
7	George Bell	15.00
8	Frank Thomas	100.00
9	Wade Boggs	125.00
10	Scott Sanderson	15.00
11	Jeff Bagwell	95.00
12	John Kruk	15.00
13	Felix Jose	15.00
14	Harold Baines	15.00
15	Dwight Gooden	15.00
16	Brian McRae	15.00
17	Jay Bell	15.00
18	Brett Butler	15.00
19	Hal Morris	15.00
20	Mark Langston	15.00
21	Scott Erickson	15.00
22	Randy Johnson	75.00
23	Greg Swindell	15.00
24	Dennis Martinez	15.00
25	Tony Phillips	15.00
26	Fred McGriff	15.00
27	Checklist (Dick Perez)	5.00

Elite

Donruss continued its Elite series in 1992 by inserting cards in foil packs. Each card was released in the same quantity as the 1991 inserts - 10,000 Elite, 7,500 Legend and 5,000 Signature. The Elite cards, now featuring a prismatic border, are numbered as a continuation of the 1991 issue.

		NM/M
Complete Set (12):		300.00
Common Player:		7.50
9	Wade Boggs	15.00
10	Joe Carter	7.50
11	Will Clark	7.50
12	Dwight Gooden	7.50
13	Ken Griffey Jr.	30.00
14	Tony Gwynn	15.00
15	Howard Johnson	7.50
16	Terry Pendleton	7.50
17	Kirby Puckett	15.00
18	Frank Thomas	15.00
---	Rickey Henderson (Legend)	20.00
---	Cal Ripken, Jr. (Signature)	250.00

Rookies

Donruss increased the size of its Rookies set in 1992 to include 132 cards. In the past the cards were released only in boxed set form, but the 1992 cards were available in packs. Special "Phenoms" cards were randomly inserted into Rookies packs. The Phenoms cards feature black borders, while the Rookies cards are styled after the regular 1992 Donruss issue. The cards are numbered alphabetically.

		NM/M
Complete Set (132):		6.00
Common Player:		.05
Pack (12):		.50
Wax Box (36):		10.00
1	Kyle Abbott	.05
2	Troy Afenir	.05
3	Rich Amaral	.05
4	Ruben Amaro	.05
5	Billy Ashley	.05
6	Pedro Astacio	.05
7	Jim Austin	.05
8	Robert Ayrault	.05
9	Kevin Baez	.05
10	Esteban Beltre	.05
11	Brian Bohanon	.05
12	Kent Bottenfield	.05
13	Jeff Branson	.05
14	Brad Brink	.05
15	John Briscoe	.05
16	Doug Brocail	.05
17	Rico Brogna	.05
18	J.T. Bruett	.05
19	Jacob Brumfield	.05
20	Jim Bullinger	.05
21	Kevin Campbell	.05
22	Pedro Castellano	.05
23	Mike Christopher	.05
24	Archi Cianfrocco	.05
25	Mark Clark	.05
26	Craig Colbert	.05
27	Victor Cole	.05
28	Steve Cooke	.05
29	Tim Costo	.05
30	Chad Curtis	.05
31	Doug Davis	.05
32	Gary DiSarcina	.05
33	John Doherty	.05
34	Mike Draper	.05
35	Monty Fariss	.05
36	Bien Figueroa	.05
37	John Flaherty	.05
38	Tim Fortugno	.05
39	Eric Fox	.05
40	Jeff Frye RC	.05
41	Ramon Garcia	.05
42	Brent Gates	.05
43	Tom Goodwin	.05
44	Buddy Groom	.05
45	Jeff Grotewold	.05
46	Juan Guerrero	.05
47	Johnny Guzman	.05
48	Shawn Hare	.05
49	Ryan Hawblitzel	.05
50	Bert Heffernan	.05
51	Butch Henry	.05
52	Cesar Hernandez	.05
53	Vince Horsman	.05
54	Steve Hosey	.05
55	Pat Howell	.05
56	Peter Hoy	.05
57	Jon Hurst	.05
58	Mark Hutton	.05
59	Shawn Jeter	.05
60	Joel Johnston	.05
61	Jeff Kent	1.00
62	Kurt Knudsen	.05
63	Kevin Koslofski	.05
64	Danny Leon	.05
65	Jesse Levis	.05
66	Tom Marsh	.05
67	Ed Martel	.05
68	Al Martin	.05
69	Pedro Martinez	2.00
70	Derrick May	.05
71	Matt Maysey	.05
72	Russ McGinnis	.05
73	Tim McIntosh	.05
74	Jim McNamara	.05
75	Jeff McNeely	.05
76	Rusty Meacham	.05
77	Tony Melendez	.05
78	Henry Mercedes	.05
79	Paul Miller	.05
80	Joe Millette	.05
81	Blas Minor	.05
82	Dennis Moeller	.05
83	Raul Mondesi	.25
84	Rob Natal	.05
85	Troy Neel	.05
86	David Nied	.05
87	Jerry Nielsen	.05
88	Donovan Osborne	.05
89	John Patterson	.05
90	Roger Pavlik	.05
91	Dan Peltier	.05
92	Jim Pena	.05
93	William Pennyweather	.05
94	Mike Perez	.05
95	Hipolito Pichardo	.05
96	Greg Pirkl	.05
97	Harvey Pulliam	.05
98	Manny Ramirez RC	3.00
99	Pat Rapp	.05
100	Jeff Reboulet	.05
101	Darren Reed	.05
102	Shane Reynolds	.05
103	Bill Risley	.05
104	Ben Rivera	.05
105	Henry Rodriguez	.05
106	Rico Rossy	.05
107	Johnny Ruffin	.05
108	Steve Scarsone	.05
109	Tim Scott	.05
110	Steve Shifflett	.05
111	Dave Silvestri	.05
112	Matt Stairs	.05
113	William Suero	.05
114	Jeff Tackett	.05
115	Eddie Taubensee	.05
116	Rick Trlicek	.05
117	Scooter Tucker	.05
118	Shane Turner	.05
119	Julio Valera	.05
120	Paul Wagner	.05
121	Tim Wakefield	.05
122	Mike Walker	.05
123	Bruce Walton	.05
124	Lenny Webster	.05
125	Bob Wickman	.05
126	Mike Williams	.05
127	Kerry Woodson	.05
128	Eric Young	.05
129	Kevin Young	.05
130	Pete Young	.05
131	Checklist	.05
132	Checklist	.05

Rookie Phenoms

The first 12 cards in this insert set were available in Donruss Rookies foil packs. Cards 13-20 were found randomly packed in jumbo packs. Predominantly black on both front and back, the borders are highlighted with gold. A gold-foil "Phenoms" appears at top front.

		NM/M
Complete Set (20):		12.50
Common Player:		.25
1	Moises Alou	.25
2	Bret Boone	.50
3	Jeff Conine	.25
4	Dave Fleming	.25
5	Tyler Green	.25
6	Eric Karros	.25
7	Pat Listach	.25
8	Kenny Lofton	.25
9	Mike Piazza	10.00
10	Tim Salmon	.50
11	Andy Stankiewicz	.25
12	Dan Walters	.25
13	Ramon Caraballo	.25
14	Brian Jordan	.25
15	Ryan Klesko	.25

16	Sam Militello	.25
17	Frank Seminara	.25
18	Salomon Torres	.25
19	John Valentin	.25
20	Wil Cordero	.25

Update

Each retail factory set of 1992 Donruss cards contained a cello-wrapped four-card selection from this 22-card Update set. The cards feature the same basic format as the regular '92 Donruss, except they carry a "U" prefix to the card number on back. The cards feature rookies, highlights and traded players from the 1992 season.

		NM/M
Complete Set (22):		15.00
Common Player:		.50
1	Pat Listach/RR	.50
2	Andy Stankiewicz/RR	.50
3	Brian Jordan/RR	.50
4	Dan Walters/RR	.50
5	Chad Curtis/RR	.50
6	Kenny Lofton/RR	1.50
7	Mark McGwire (Highlight)	8.00
8	Eddie Murray (Highlight)	1.00
9	Jeff Reardon (Highlight)	.50
10	Frank Viola	.50
11	Gary Sheffield	.75
12	George Bell	.50
13	Rick Sutcliffe	.50
14	Wally Joyner	.50
15	Kevin Seitzer	.50
16	Bill Krueger	.50
17	Danny Tartabull	.50
18	Dave Winfield	2.00
19	Gary Carter	1.50
20	Bobby Bonilla	.50
21	Cory Snyder	.50
22	Bill Swift	.50

1992 Donruss/Durivage Montreal Expos

Green borders and posed portrait photos are featured in this custom-published team set which Donruss produced for the Quebec bakery Durivage. Bilingual backs have personal data, recent major league stats and appropriate logos on a gray pinstriped background. Roster changes are reflected in the assignment of the same number to different players in several cases.

		NM/M
Complete Set (26):		50.00
Common Player:		2.00
Album:		5.00
1	Bret Barberie	2.00
2a	Chris Haney	2.00
2b	Brian Barnes	2.00
3a	Bill Sampen	2.00
3b	Phil Bradley	2.00
4	Ivan Calderon	2.00
5	Gary Carter	10.00
6	Delino DeShields	2.00
7	Jeff Fassero	2.00
8	Darrin Fletcher	2.00
9	Mark Gardner	2.00
10	Marquis Grissom	2.00
11	Ken Hill	2.00
12	Dennis Martinez	2.00
13	Chris Nabholz	2.00
14	Spike Owen	2.00
15	Tom Runnells	2.00
15b	Felipe Alou	3.00
16a	John Vander Wal	2.00
16b	Matt Stairs	2.00
17a	Bill Landrum	2.00
17b	Dave Wainhouse	2.00
18	Larry Walker	10.00
19	Tim Wallach	2.00
20	John Wetteland	2.00
---	Checklist	1.00

1993 Donruss Previews

Twenty-two of the game's biggest stars were selected for inclusion in the preview version of Donruss' 1993 baseball card set. The previews follow the same basic format of the regular-issue 1993 except for the addition of the word "PREVIEW" above the card number in the home plate on back. Front photos are different between the preview and issued versions.

		NM/M
Complete Set (22):		60.00
Common Player:		1.50
1	Tom Glavine	2.00
2	Ryne Sandberg	5.00
3	Barry Larkin	1.50
4	Jeff Bagwell	4.00
5	Eric Karros	1.50
6	Larry Walker	1.50
7	Eddie Murray	4.00
8	Darren Daulton	1.50
9	Andy Van Slyke	1.50
10	Gary Sheffield	2.00
11	Will Clark	1.50
12	Cal Ripken Jr.	9.00
13	Roger Clemens	6.00
14	Frank Thomas	4.00
15	Cecil Fielder	1.50
16	George Brett	6.00
17	Robin Yount	4.00
18	Don Mattingly	6.00
19	Dennis Eckersley	3.50
20	Ken Griffey Jr.	7.50
21	Jose Canseco	2.50
22	Roberto Alomar	2.00

1993 Donruss

Rated Rookies and a randomly inserted Diamond Kings subset once again are featured in the 1993 Donruss set. Series I of the set includes 396 cards. Card fronts feature white borders surrounding a full-color player photo. The flip sides feature an additional photo, biographical information and career statistics. The cards are numbered on the back and the card's series is given with the number. The cards are UV coated. Series II contains a subset of players labeled with an "Expansion Draft" headline over their Marlins or Rockies team logo on front, even though the player photos are in the uniform of their previous team.

		NM/M
Complete Set (792):		10.00
Common Player:		.05
Series 1 or 2 Pack (14):		.50
Series 1 or 2 Box (36):		10.00
1	Craig Lefferts	.05
2	Kent Mercker	.05
3	Phil Plantier	.05
4	Alex Arias RC	.05
5	Julio Valera	.05
6	Dan Wilson	.05
7	Frank Thomas	.50
8	Eric Anthony	.05
9	Derek Lilliquist	.05
10	Rafael Bournigal RC	.05
11	Manny Alexander RC (Rated Rookie)	.05
12	Bret Barberie	.05
13	Mickey Tettleton	.05
14	Anthony Young	.05
15	Tim Spehr	.05
16	Bob Ayrault RC	.05
17	Bill Wegman	.05
18	Jay Bell	.05
19	Rick Aguilera	.05
20	Todd Zeile	.05
21	Steve Farr	.05
22	Andy Benes	.05
23	Lance Blankenship	.05
24	Ted Wood	.05
25	Omar Vizquel	.05
26	Steve Avery	.05
27	Brian Bohanon	.05
28	Rick Wilkins	.05
29	Devon White	.05
30	Bobby Ayala RC	.05
31	Leo Gomez	.05
32	Mike Simms	.05
33	Ellis Burks	.05
34	Steve Wilson	.05
35	Jim Abbott	.05
36	Tim Wallach	.05
37	Wilson Alvarez	.05
38	Daryl Boston	.05
39	Sandy Alomar, Jr.	.05
40	Mitch Williams	.05
41	Rico Brogna	.05
42	Gary Varsho	.05
43	Kevin Appier	.05
44	Eric Wedge/RR	.05
45	Dante Bichette	.05
46	Jose Oquendo	.05
47	Mike Trombley RC	.05
48	Dan Walters	.05
49	Gerald Williams	.05
50	Bud Black	.05
51	Bobby Witt	.05
52	Mark Davis	.05
53	Shawn Barton RC	.05
54	Paul Assenmacher	.05
55	Kevin Reimer	.05
56	Billy Ashley/RR RC	.05
57	Eddie Zosky	.05
58	Chris Sabo	.05
59	Billy Ripken	.05
60	Scooter Tucker RC	.05
61	Tim Wakefield/RR RC	.10
62	Mitch Webster	.05
63	Jack Clark	.05
64	Mark Gardner	.05
65	Lee Stevens	.05
66	Todd Hundley	.05
67	Bobby Thigpen	.05
68	Dave Hollins	.05
69	Jack Armstrong	.05
70	Alex Cole	.05
71	Mark Carreon	.05
72	Todd Worrell	.05
73	Steve Shifflett RC	.05
74	Jerald Clark	.05
75	Paul Molitor	.50
76	Larry Carter RC	.05
77	Rich Rowland	.05
78	Damon Berryhill	.05
79	Willie Banks	.05
80	Hector Villanueva	.05
81	Mike Gallego	.05
82	Tim Belcher	.05
83	Mike Bordick	.05
84	Craig Biggio	.05
85	Lance Parrish	.05
86	Brett Butler	.05
87	Mike Timlin	.05
88	Brian Barnes	.05
89	Brady Anderson	.05
90	D.J. Dozier	.05
91	Frank Viola	.05
92	Darren Daulton	.05
93	Chad Curtis	.05
94	Zane Smith	.05
95	George Bell	.05
96	Rex Hudler	.05
97	Mark Whiten	.05
98	Tim Teufel	.05
99	Kevin Ritz	.05
100	Jeff Brantley	.05
101	Jeff Conine	.05
102	Vinny Castilla	.05
103	Greg Vaughn	.05
104	Steve Buechele	.05
105	Darren Reed	.05
106	Bip Roberts	.05
107	John Habyan	.05
108	Scott Servais	.05
109	Walt Weiss	.05
110	J.T. Snow/RR RC	.50
111	Jay Buhner	.05

		NM/M
112	Darryl Strawberry	.05
113	Roger Pavlik RC	.05
114	Chris Nabholz	.05
115	Pat Borders	.05
116	Pat Howell RC	.05
117	Gregg Olson	.05
118	Curt Schilling	.25
119	Roger Clemens	.65
120	Victor Cole RC	.05
121	Gary DiSarcina	.05
122	Checklist 1-80	.05
123	Steve Sax	.05
124	Chuck Carr	.05
125	Mark Lewis	.05
126	Tony Gwynn	.60
127	Travis Fryman	.05
128	Dave Burba	.05
129	Wally Joyner	.05
130	John Smoltz	.05
131	Cal Eldred	.05
132	Checklist 81-159	.05
133	Arthur Rhodes	.05
134	Jeff Blauser	.05
135	Scott Cooper	.05
136	Doug Strange	.05
137	Luis Sojo	.05
138	Jeff Branson RC	.05
139	Alex Fernandez	.05
140	Ken Caminiti	.05
141	Charles Nagy	.05
142	Tom Candiotti	.05
143	Willie Green/RR	.05
144	John Vander Wal	.05
145	Kurt Knudsen RC	.05
146	John Franco	.05
147	Eddie Pierce RC	.05
148	Kim Batiste	.05
149	Darren Holmes	.05
150	Steve Cooke RC	.05
151	Terry Jorgensen	.05
152	Mark Clark RC	.05
153	Randy Velarde	.05
154	Greg Harris	.05
155	Kevin Campbell RC	.05
156	John Burkett	.05
157	Kevin Mitchell	.05
158	Deion Sanders	.05
159	Jose Canseco	.25
160	Jeff Hartsock RC	.05
161	Tom Quinlan RC	.05
162	Tim Pugh RC	.05
163	Glenn Davis	.05
164	Shane Reynolds RC	.10
165	Jody Reed	.05
166	Mike Sharperson	.05
167	Scott Lewis	.05
168	Dennis Martinez	.05
169	Scott Radinsky	.05
170	Dave Gallagher	.05
171	Jim Thome	.45
172	Terry Mulholland	.05
173	Milt Cuyler	.05
174	Bob Patterson	.05
175	Jeff Montgomery	.05
176	Tim Salmon/RR	.25
177	Franklin Stubbs	.05
178	Donovan Osborne	.05
179	Jeff Reboulet RC	.05
180	Jeremy Hernandez	.05
181	Charlie Hayes	.05
182	Matt Williams	.05
183	Mike Raczka	.05
184	Francisco Cabrera	.05
185	Rich DeLucia	.05
186	Sammy Sosa	.60
187	Ivan Rodriguez	.45
188	Bret Boone/RR	.15
189	Juan Guzman	.05
190	Tom Browning	.05
191	Randy Milligan	.05
192	Steve Finley	.05
193	John Patterson/RR	.05
194	Kip Gross	.05
195	Tony Fossas	.05
196	Ivan Calderon	.05
197	Junior Felix	.05
198	Pete Schourek	.05
199	Craig Grebeck	.05
200	Juan Bell	.05
201	Glenallen Hill	.05
202	Danny Jackson	.05
203	John Kiely	.05
204	Bob Tewksbury	.05
205	Kevin Koslofski RC	.05
206	Craig Shipley	.05
207	John Jaha	.05
208	Royce Clayton	.05
209	Mike Piazza/RR	2.00
210	Ron Gant	.05
211	Scott Erickson	.05
212	Doug Dascenzo	.05
213	Andy Stankiewicz	.05
214	Geronimo Berroa	.05
215	Dennis Eckersley	.45
216	Al Osuna	.05
217	Tino Martinez	.05
218	Henry Rodriguez RC	.05
219	Ed Sprague	.05
220	Ken Hill	.05
221	Chito Martinez	.05
222	Bret Saberhagen	.05
223	Mike Greenwell	.05
224	Mickey Morandini	.05
225	Chuck Finley	.05
226	Denny Neagle	.05
227	Kirk McCaskill	.05
228	Rheal Cormier	.05
229	Paul Sorrento	.05

230	Darrin Jackson	.05
231	Rob Deer	.05
232	Bill Swift	.05
233	Kevin McReynolds	.05
234	Terry Pendleton	.05
235	Dave Nilsson	.05
236	Chuck McElroy	.05
237	Derek Parks	.05
238	Norm Charlton	.05
239	Matt Nokes	.05
240	Juan Guerrero RC	.05
241	Jeff Parrett	.05
242	Ryan Thompson/RR	.05
243	Dave Fleming	.05
244	Dave Hansen	.05
245	Monty Fariss	.05
246	Archi Cianfrocco RC	.05
247	Pat Hentgen	.05
248	Bill Pecota	.05
249	Ben McDonald	.05
250	Cliff Brantley	.05
251	John Valentin RC	.05
252	Jeff King	.05
253	Reggie Williams RC	.05
254	Checklist 160-238	.05
255	Ozzie Guillen	.05
256	Mike Perez	.05
257	Thomas Howard	.05
258	Kurt Stillwell	.05
259	Mike Henneman	.05
260	Steve Decker	.05
261	Brent Mayne	.05
262	Otis Nixon	.05
263	Mark Keifer RC	.05
264	Checklist 239-317	.05
265	Richie Lewis RC	.05
266	Pat Gomez RC	.05
267	Scott Taylor RC	.05
268	Shawon Dunston	.05
269	Greg Myers	.05
270	Tim Costo	.05
271	Greg Hibbard	.05
272	Pete Harnisch	.05
273	Dave Mlicki RC	.05
274	Orel Hershiser	.05
275	Sean Berry/RR	.05
276	Doug Simons	.05
277	John Doherty RC	.05
278	Eddie Murray	.50
279	Chris Haney	.05
280	Stan Javier	.05
281	Jaime Navarro	.05
282	Orlando Merced	.05
283	Kent Hrbek	.05
284	Bernard Gilkey	.05
285	Russ Springer	.05
286	Mike Maddux	.05
287	Eric Fox RC	.05
288	Mark Leonard	.05
289	Tim Leary	.05
290	Brian Hunter	.05
291	Donald Harris	.05
292	Bob Scanlan	.05
293	Turner Ward	.05
294	Hal Morris	.05
295	Jimmy Poole	.05
296	Doug Jones	.05
297	Tony Pena	.05
298	Ramon Martinez	.05
299	Tim Fortugno RC	.05
300	Marquis Grissom	.05
301	Lance Johnson	.05
302	Jeff Kent RC	1.00
303	Reggie Jefferson	.05
304	Wes Chamberlain	.05
305	Shawn Hare RC	.05
306	Mike LaValliere	.05
307	Greg Jefferies	.05
308	Troy Neel/RR RC	.05
309	Pat Listach	.05
310	Geronimo Pena	.05
311	Pedro Munoz	.05
312	Guillermo Velasquez RC	.05
313	Roberto Kelly	.05
314	Mike Jackson	.05
315	Rickey Henderson	.50
316	Mark Lemke	.05
317	Erik Hanson	.05
318	Derrick May	.05
319	Geno Petralli	.05
320	Melvin Nieves/RR	.05
321	Doug Linton RC	.05
322	Rob Dibble	.05
323	Chris Hoiles	.05
324	Jimmy Jones	.05
325	Dave Staton/RR	.05
326	Pedro Astacio	.05
327	Paul Quantrill RC	.05
328	Greg Colbrunn	.05
329	Hilly Hathaway RC	.05
330	Jeff Innis	.05
331	Ron Karkovice	.05
332	Keith Shepherd RC	.05
333	Alan Embree RC	.05
334	Paul Wagner RC	.05
335	Dave Haas RC	.05
336	Ozzie Canseco	.05
337	Bill Sampen	.05
338	Rich Rodriguez	.05
339	Dean Palmer	.05
340	Greg Litton	.05
341	Jim Tatum/RR RC	.05
342	Todd Haney RC	.05
343	Larry Casian	.05
344	Ryne Sandberg	.60
345	Sterling Hitchcock RC	.10
346	Chris Hammond	.05
347	Vince Horsman RC	.05

348	Butch Henry RC	.05
349	Dann Howitt	.05
350	Roger McDowell	.05
351	Jack Morris	.05
352	Bill Krueger	.05
353	Cris Colon RC	.05
354	Joe Vitko RC	.05
355	Willie McGee	.05
356	Jay Baller	.05
357	Pat Mahomes	.05
358	Roger Mason	.05
359	Jerry Nielsen RC	.05
360	Tom Pagnozzi	.05
361	Kevin Baez RC	.05
362	Tim Scott RC	.05
363	Domingo Martinez RC	.05
364	Kirt Manwaring	.05
365	Rafael Palmeiro	.45
366	Ray Lankford	.05
367	Tim McIntosh	.05
368	Jessie Hollins RC	.05
369	Scott Leius	.05
370	Bill Doran	.05
371	Sam Militello RC	.05
372	Ryan Bowen	.05
373	Dave Henderson	.05
374	Dan Smith/RR	.05
375	Steve Reed RC	.05
376	Jose Offerman	.05
377	Kevin Brown	.05
378	Darrin Fletcher	.05
379	Duane Ward	.05
380	Wayne Kirby/RR	.05
381	Steve Scarsone RC	.05
382	Mariano Duncan	.05
383	Ken Ryan RC	.05
384	Lloyd McClendon	.05
385	Brian Holman	.05
386	Braulio Castillo	.05
387	Danny Leon RC	.05
388	Omar Olivares	.05
389	Kevin Wickander	.05
390	Fred McGriff	.05
391	Phil Clark	.05
392	Darren Lewis	.05
393	Phil Hiatt RC	.10
394	Mike Morgan	.05
395	Shane Mack	.05
396	Checklist 318-396	.05
397	David Segui	.05
398	Rafael Belliard	.05
399	Tim Naehring	.05
400	Frank Castillo	.05
401	Joe Grahe	.05
402	Reggie Sanders	.05
403	Roberto Hernandez	.05
404	Luis Gonzalez	.05
405	Carlos Baerga	.05
406	Carlos Hernandez	.05
407	Pedro Astacio/RR	.05
408	Mel Rojas	.05
409	Scott Livingstone	.05
410	Chico Walker	.05
411	Brian McRae	.05
412	Ben Rivera	.05
413	Ricky Bones	.05
414	Andy Van Slyke	.05
415	Chuck Knoblauch	.05
416	Luis Alicea	.05
417	Bob Wickman	.05
418	Doug Brocail	.05
419	Scott Brosius	.05
420	Rod Beck	.05
421	Edgar Martinez	.05
422	Ryan Klesko	.05
423	Nolan Ryan	1.50
424	Rey Sanchez	.05
425	Roberto Alomar	.20
426	Barry Larkin	.05
427	Mike Mussina	.30
428	Jeff Bagwell	.50
429	Mo Vaughn	.05
430	Eric Karros	.05
431	John Orton	.05
432	Wil Cordero	.05
433	Jack McDowell	.05
434	Howard Johnson	.05
435	Albert Belle	.05
436	John Kruk	.05
437	Skeeter Barnes	.05
438	Don Slaught	.05
439	Rusty Meacham	.05
440	Tim Laker/RR	.05
441	Robin Yount	.50
442	Brian Jordan	.05
443	Kevin Tapani	.05
444	Gary Sheffield	.25
445	Rich Monteleone	.05
446	Will Clark	.05
447	Jerry Browne	.05
448	Jeff Treadway	.05
449	Mike Schooler	.05
450	Mike Harkey	.05
451	Julio Franco	.05
452	Kevin Young/RR	.05
453	Kelly Gruber	.05
454	Jose Rijo	.05
455	Mike Devereaux	.05
456	Andujar Cedeno	.05
457	Damion Easley/RR	.05
458	Kevin Gross	.05
459	Matt Young	.05
460	Matt Stairs	.05
461	Luis Polonia	.05
462	Dwight Gooden	.05
463	Warren Newson	.05
464	Jose DeLeon	.05
465	Jose Mesa	.05

No.	Player	Price
466	Danny Cox	.05
467	Dan Gladden	.05
468	Gerald Perry	.05
469	Mike Boddicker	.05
470	Jeff Gardner	.05
471	Doug Henry	.05
472	Mike Benajmin	.05
473	Dan Peltier/RR	.05
474	Mike Stanton	.05
475	John Smiley	.05
476	Dwight Smith	.05
477	Jim Leyritz	.05
478	Dwayne Henry	.05
479	Mark McGwire	1.00
480	Pete Incaviglia	.05
481	Dave Cochrane	.05
482	Eric Davis	.05
483	John Olerud	.05
484	Ken Bottenfield	.05
485	Mark McLemore	.05
486	Dave Magadan	.05
487	John Marzano	.05
488	Ruben Amaro	.05
489	Rob Ducey	.05
490	Stan Belinda	.05
491	Dan Pasqua	.05
492	Joe Magrane	.05
493	Brook Jacoby	.05
494	Gene Harris	.05
495	Mark Leiter	.05
496	Bryan Hickerson	.05
497	Tom Gordon	.05
498	Pete Smith	.05
499	Chris Bosio	.05
500	Shawn Boskie	.05
501	Dave West	.05
502	Milt Hill	.05
503	Pat Kelly	.05
504	Joe Boever	.05
505	Terry Steinbach	.05
506	Butch Huskey/RR	.05
507	David Valle	.05
508	Mike Scioscia	.05
509	Kenny Rogers	.05
510	Moises Alou	.05
511	David Wells	.05
512	Mackey Sasser	.05
513	Todd Frohwirth	.05
514	Ricky Jordan	.05
515	Mike Gardiner	.05
516	Gary Redus	.05
517	Gary Gaetti	.05
518	Checklist 397-476	.05
519	Carlton Fisk	.50
520	Ozzie Smith	.60
521	Rod Nichols	.05
522	Benito Santiago	.05
523	Bill Gullickson	.05
524	Robby Thompson	.05
525	Mike Macfarlane	.05
526	Sid Bream	.05
527	Darryl Hamilton	.05
528	Checklist 477-555	.05
529	Jeff Tackett	.05
530	Greg Olson	.05
531	Bob Zupcic	.05
532	Mark Grace	.05
533	Steve Frey	.05
534	Dave Martinez	.05
535	Robin Ventura	.05
536	Casey Candaele	.05
537	Kenny Lofton	.05
538	Jay Howell	.05
539	Fernando Ramsey/RR	.05
540	Larry Walker	.05
541	Cecil Fielder	.05
542	Lee Guetterman	.05
543	Keith Miller	.05
544	Len Dykstra	.05
545	B.J. Surhoff	.05
546	Bob Walk	.05
547	Brian Harper	.05
548	Lee Smith	.05
549	Danny Tartabull	.05
550	Frank Seminara	.05
551	Henry Mercedes	.05
552	Dave Righetti	.05
553	Ken Griffey Jr.	.75
554	Tom Glavine	.25
555	Juan Gonzalez	.25
556	Jim Bullinger	.05
557	Derek Bell	.05
558	Cesar Hernandez	.05
559	Cal Ripken, Jr.	1.50
560	Eddie Taubensee	.05
561	John Flaherty	.05
562	Todd Benzinger	.05
563	Hubie Brooks	.05
564	Delino DeShields	.05
565	Tim Raines	.05
566	Sid Fernandez	.05
567	Steve Olin	.05
568	Tommy Greene	.05
569	Buddy Groom	.05
570	Randy Tomlin	.05
571	Hipolito Pichardo	.05
572	Rene Arocha/RR	.05
573	Mike Fetters	.05
574	Felix Jose	.05
575	Gene Larkin	.05
576	Bruce Hurst	.05
577	Bernie Williams	.05
578	Trevor Wilson	.05
579	Bob Welch	.05
580	Dave Justice	.05
581	Randy Johnson	.50
582	Jose Vizcaino	.05
583	Jeff Huson	.05

No.	Player	Price
584	Rob Maurer/RR	.05
585	Todd Stottlemyre	.05
586	Joe Oliver	.05
587	Bob Milacki	.05
588	Rob Murphy	.05
589	Greg Pirkl/RR	.05
590	Lenny Harris	.05
591	Luis Rivera	.05
592	John Wetteland	.05
593	Mark Langston	.05
594	Bobby Bonilla	.05
595	Esteban Beltre	.05
596	Mike Hartley	.05
597	Felix Fermin	.05
598	Carlos Garcia	.05
599	Frank Tanana	.05
600	Pedro Guerrero	.05
601	Terry Shumpert	.05
602	Wally Whitehurst	.05
603	Kevin Seitzer	.05
604	Chris James	.05
605	Greg Gohr/RR	.05
606	Mark Wohlers	.05
607	Kirby Puckett	.60
608	Greg Maddux	.60
609	Don Mattingly	.65
610	Greg Cadaret	.05
611	Dave Stewart	.05
612	Mark Portugal	.05
613	Pete O'Brien	.05
614	Bobby Ojeda	.05
615	Joe Carter	.05
616	Pete Young	.05
617	Sam Horn	.05
618	Vince Coleman	.05
619	Wade Boggs	.60
620	Todd Pratt **RC**	.05
621	Ron Tingley	.05
622	Doug Drabek	.05
623	Scott Hemond	.05
624	Tim Jones	.05
625	Dennis Cook	.05
626	Jose Melendez	.05
627	Mike Munoz	.05
628	Jim Pena	.05
629	Gary Thurman	.05
630	Charlie Leibrandt	.05
631	Scott Fletcher	.05
632	Andre Dawson	.25
633	Greg Gagne	.05
634	Greg Swindell	.05
635	Kevin Maas	.05
636	Xavier Hernandez	.05
637	Ruben Sierra	.05
638	Dimitri Young/RR	.05
639	Harold Reynolds	.05
640	Tom Goodwin	.05
641	Todd Burns	.05
642	Jeff Fassero	.05
643	Dave Winfield	.50
644	Willie Randolph	.05
645	Luis Mercedes	.05
646	Dale Murphy	.20
647	Danny Darwin	.05
648	Dennis Moeller	.05
649	Chuck Crim	.05
650	Checklist 556-634	.05
651	Shawn Abner	.05
652	Tracy Woodson	.05
653	Scott Scudder	.05
654	Tom Lampkin	.05
655	Alan Trammell	.05
656	Cory Snyder	.05
657	Chris Gwynn	.05
658	Lonnie Smith	.05
659	Jim Austin	.05
660	Checklist 635-713	.05
661	Tim Hulett	.05
662	Marvin Freeman	.05
663	Greg Harris	.05
664	Heathcliff Slocumb	.05
665	Mike Butcher	.05
666	Steve Foster	.05
667	Donn Pall	.05
668	Darryl Kile	.05
669	Jesse Levis	.05
670	Jim Gott	.05
671	Mark Hutton **RC**	.05
672	Brian Drahman	.05
673	Chad Kreuter	.05
674	Tony Fernandez	.05
675	Jose Lind	.05
676	Kyle Abbott	.05
677	Dan Plesac	.05
678	Barry Bonds	1.50
679	Chili Davis	.05
680	Stan Royer	.05
681	Scott Kamieniecki	.05
682	Carlos Martinez	.05
683	Mike Moore	.05
684	Candy Maldanado	.05
685	Jeff Nelson	.05
686	Lou Whitaker	.05
687	Jose Guzman	.05
688	Manuel Lee	.05
689	Bob MacDonald	.05
690	Scott Bankhead	.05
691	Alan Mills	.05
692	Brian Williams	.05
693	Tom Brunansky	.05
694	Lenny Webster	.05
695	Greg Briley	.05
696	Paul O'Neill	.05
697	Joey Cora	.05
698	Charlie O'Brien	.05
699	Junior Ortiz	.05
700	Ron Darling	.05
701	Tony Phillips	.05

No.	Player	Price
702	William Pennyfeather	.05
703	Mark Gubicza	.05
704	Steve Hosey/RR	.05
705	Henry Cotto	.05
706	David Hulse **RC**	.05
707	Mike Pagliarulo	.05
708	Dave Stieb	.05
709	Melido Perez	.05
710	Jimmy Key	.05
711	Jeff Russell	.05
712	David Cone	.05
713	Russ Swan	.05
714	Mark Guthrie	.05
715	Checklist 714-792	.05
716	Al Martin/RR	.05
717	Randy Knorr	.05
718	Mike Stanley	.05
719	Rick Sutcliffe	.05
720	Terry Leach	.05
721	Chipper Jones/RR	1.00
722	Jim Eisenriech	.05
723	Tom Henke	.05
724	Jeff Frye	.05
725	Harold Baines	.05
726	Scott Sanderson	.05
727	Tom Foley	.05
728	Bryan Harvey/ED	.05
729	Tom Edens	.05
730	Eric Young/ED	.05
731	Dave Weathers/ED	.05
732	Spike Owen	.05
733	Scott Aldred/ED	.05
734	Cris Carpenter/ED	.05
735	Dion James	.05
736	Joe Girardi/ED	.05
737	Nigel Wilson/ED	.05
738	Scott Chiamparino/ED	.05
739	Jeff Reardon	.05
740	Willie Blair/ED	.05
741	Jim Corsi/ED	.05
742	Ken Patterson	.05
743	Andy Ashby/ED	.05
744	Rob Natal/ED	.05
745	Kevin Bass	.05
746	Freddie Benavides/ED	.05
747	Chris Donnels/ED	.05
748	Kerry Woodson **RC**	.05
749	Calvin Jones/ED	.05
750	Gary Scott	.05
751	Joe Orsulak	.05
752	Armando Reynoso/ED	.05
753	Monty Farriss/ED	.05
754	Billy Hatcher	.05
755	Denis Boucher/ED	.05
756	Walt Weiss	.05
757	Mike Fitzgerald	.05
758	Rudy Seanez	.05
759	Bret Barberie/ED	.05
760	Mo Sanford/ED	.05
761	Pedro Castellano/ED **RC**	.05
762	Chuck Carr/ED	.05
763	Steve Howe	.05
764	Andres Galarraga	.05
765	Jeff Conine/ED	.05
766	Ted Power	.05
767	Butch Henry/ED	.05
768	Steve Decker/ED	.05
769	Storm Davis	.05
770	Vinny Castilla/ED	.05
771	Junior Felix/ED	.05
772	Walt Terrell	.05
773	Brad Ausmus/ED	.05
774	Jamie McAndrew/ED	.05
775	Milt Thompson	.05
776	Charlie Hayes/ED	.05
777	Jack Armstrong/ED	.05
778	Dennis Rasmussen	.05
779	Darren Holmes/ED	.05
780	Alex Arias **RC**	.05
781	Randy Bush	.05
782	Javier Lopez/RR	.05
783	Dante Bichette	.05
784	John Johnstone/ED	.05
785	Rene Gonzales	.05
786	Alex Cole/ED	.05
787	Jeromy Burnitz/RR	.05
788	Michael Huff	.05
789	Anthony Telford	.05
790	Jerald Clark/ED	.05
791	Joel Johnston	.05
792	David Nied/RR	.05

cards were found in Series 1 packs, while cards 16-31 were available in the second series packs.

	NM/M
Complete Set (31):	17.50
Common Player:	.25
1 Ken Griffey Jr.	4.00
2 Ryne Sandberg	3.00
3 Roger Clemens	3.50
4 Kirby Puckett	3.00
5 Bill Swift	.25
6 Larry Walker	.25
7 Juan Gonzalez	.75
8 Wally Joyner	.25
9 Andy Van Slyke	.25
10 Robin Ventura	.25
11 Bip Roberts	.25
12 Roberto Kelly	.25
13 Carlos Baerga	.25
14 Orel Hershiser	.25
15 Cecil Fielder	.25
16 Robin Yount	1.50
17 Darren Daulton	.25
18 Mark McGwire	4.00
19 Tom Glavine	.75
20 Roberto Alomar	.50
21 Gary Sheffield	.75
22 Bob Tewksbury	.25
23 Brady Anderson	.25
24 Craig Biggio	.25
25 Eddie Murray	1.50
26 Luis Polonia	.25
27 Nigel Wilson	.25
28 David Nied	.25
29 Pat Listach	.25
30 Eric Karros	.25
31 Checklist	.05

Elite

Continuing the card numbering from the 1992 Elite set, the Elite '93 inserts utilized a silver-foil prismatic front border with blue back printing. Each card is serial numbered as one of 10,000; this identified production number helping to make the Elites among the more valuable of insert cards.

	NM/M
Complete Set (20):	150.00
Common Player:	10.00
19 Fred McGriff	10.00
20 Ryne Sandberg	20.00
21 Eddie Murray	15.00
22 Paul Molitor	15.00
23 Barry Larkin	10.00
24 Don Mattingly	25.00
25 Dennis Eckersley	15.00
26 Roberto Alomar	12.50
27 Edgar Martinez	10.00
28 Gary Sheffield	12.50
29 Darren Daulton	10.00
30 Larry Walker	10.00
31 Barry Bonds	30.00
32 Andy Van Slyke	10.00
33 Mark McGwire	25.00
34 Cecil Fielder	10.00
35 Dave Winfield	15.00
36 Juan Gonzalez	12.50
--- Robin Yount (Legend)	17.50
--- Will Clark (Signature)	40.00

Diamond Kings

The traditional Donruss Diamond Kings cards were again used as an insert in Series 2 and Series 2 foil packs in 1993. The first 15

1993 Donruss Elite Supers

This set was inserted in jumbo packs of both Series 1 and Series 2. Cards carry a MVP prefix to the card number.

A Wal-Mart exclusive, Donruss produced 3-1/2" x 5" versions of its 1993 Elite inserts, added Nolan Ryan and Frank Thomas and a new card of Barry Bonds in his Giants uniform and packaged them one per shrink-wrapped box with Series 1 Donruss left-overs. Each super-size card features a color player photo and silver-foil prismatic borders on front. Backs are printed in blue and include a serial number identifying each of the cards from an edition of 5,000.

	NM/M
Complete Set (20):	150.00
Common Player:	5.00
1 Fred McGriff	5.00
2 Ryne Sandberg	17.50
3 Eddie Murray	10.00
4 Paul Molitor	10.00
5 Barry Larkin	5.00
6 Don Mattingly	20.00
7 Dennis Eckersley	10.00
8 Roberto Alomar	6.50
9 Edgar Martinez	5.00
10 Gary Sheffield	6.50
11 Darren Daulton	5.00
12 Larry Walker	5.00
13 Barry Bonds	25.00
14 Andy Van Slyke	5.00
15 Mark McGwire	25.00
16 Cecil Fielder	5.00
17 Dave Winfield	10.00
18 Juan Gonzalez	7.50
19 Frank Thomas	15.00
20 Nolan Ryan	40.00

Long Ball Leaders

Carrying a prefix of "LL" before the card number, these inserts were released in Series 1 (#1-9) and Series 2 (#10-18) jumbo packs, detailing mammoth home runs of the previous season.

	NM/M
Complete Set (18):	5.00
Common Player:	.10
1 Rob Deer	.10
2 Fred McGriff	.10
3 Albert Belle	.10
4 Mark McGwire	2.00
5 Dave Justice	.10
6 Jose Canseco	.25
7 Kent Hrbek	.10
8 Roberto Alomar	.20
9 Ken Griffey Jr.	1.50
10 Frank Thomas	.75
11 Darryl Strawberry	.10
12 Felix Jose	.10
13 Cecil Fielder	.10
14 Juan Gonzalez	.25
15 Ryne Sandberg	.75
16 Gary Sheffield	.20
17 Jeff Bagwell	.50
18 Larry Walker	.10

MVPs

This set was inserted in jumbo packs of both Series 1 and Series 2. Cards carry a MVP prefix to the card number.

	NM/M
Complete Set (26):	10.00
Common Player:	.10
1 Luis Polonia	.10
2 Frank Thomas	.60
3 George Brett	.75
4 Paul Molitor	.60
5 Don Mattingly	.75
6 Roberto Alomar	.10
7 Terry Pendleton	.10
8 Eric Karros	.10
9 Larry Walker	.10
10 Eddie Murray	.60
11 Darren Daulton	.10
12 Ray Lankford	.10
13 Will Clark	.10
14 Cal Ripken, Jr.	2.00
15 Roger Clemens	.75
16 Carlos Baerga	.10
17 Cecil Fielder	.10
18 Kirby Puckett	.65
19 Mark McGwire	1.50
20 Ken Griffey Jr.	1.25
21 Juan Gonzalez	.30
22 Ryne Sandberg	.65
23 Bip Roberts	.10
24 Jeff Bagwell	.60
25 Barry Bonds	2.00
26 Gary Sheffield	.25

Spirit of the Game

Series 1 and Series 2 foil and jumbo packs could be found with these cards randomly inserted. Several multi-player cards are included in the set. Card numbers bear an SG prefix.

	NM/M
Complete Set (20):	5.00
Common Player:	.25
1 Turning Two (Dave Winfield, Mike Bordick)	.35
2 Play at the Plate (David Justice)	.25
3 In There (Roberto Alomar)	.30
4 Pumped (Dennis Eckersley)	.60
5 Dynamic Duo (Juan Gonzalez, Jose Canseco)	.50
6 Gone (Frank Thomas, George Bell)	.60
7 Safe or Out? (Wade Boggs)	.75
8 The Thrill (Will Clark)	.30
9 Safe at Home (Damon Berryhill, Bip Roberts, Glenn Braggs)	.25
10 Thirty X 31 (Cecil Fielder, Mickey Tettleton, Rob Deer)	.25
11 Bag Bandit (Kenny Lofton)	.25
12 Back to Back (Fred McGriff, Gary Sheffield)	.30
13 Range Rovers (Greg Gagne, Barry Larkin)	.25
14 The Ball Stops Here (Ryne Sandberg)	.25
15 Over the Top (Carlos Baerga, Gary Gaetti)	.25
16 At the Wall (Danny Tartabull)	.25
17 Head First (Brady Anderson)	.25
18 Big Hurt (Frank Thomas)	.65
19 No-Hitter (Kevin Gross)	.25
20 3,000 (Robin Yount)	.65

1993 Donruss Elite Dominators

Created as a premium to move left-over boxes of its 1993 product on a home shopping network at $100 apiece, this special edition was produced in standard 2-1/2" x 3-1/2" size in a format similar to the 1991-93 Donruss Elite chase cards. Cards feature green prismatic borders, liberal use of foil stamping, etc. Only 5,000 of each card were produced, and each card is serially numbered on the back. Half of the cards of Nolan

Ryan, Juan Gonzalez, Don Mattingly and Paul Molitor were personally autographed by the player.

		NM/M
Complete Set (20):		135.00
Common Player:		3.00
1	Ryne Sandberg	10.00
2	Fred McGriff	3.00
3	Greg Maddux	10.00
4	Ron Gant	3.00
5	Dave Justice	3.00
6	Don Mattingly	12.00
7	Tim Salmon	3.00
8	Mike Piazza	12.00
9	John Olerud	3.00
10	Nolan Ryan	20.00
11	Juan Gonzalez	5.00
12	Ken Griffey Jr.	12.00
13	Frank Thomas	7.50
14	Tom Glavine	4.50
15	George Brett	12.00
16	Barry Bonds	20.00
17	Albert Belle	3.00
18	Paul Molitor	7.50
19	Cal Ripken, Jr.	20.00
20	Roberto Alomar	5.00
Autographed Cards:		
6	Don Mattingly	35.00
10	Nolan Ryan	65.00
11	Juan Gonzalez	20.00
18	Paul Molitor	20.00

1993 Donruss Masters of the Game

Donruss issued a series of "Masters of the Game" art cards that were available only at Wal-Mart stores. The oversized cards (3-1/2" x 5") feature the artwork of Dick Perez, creator of the Diamond Kings cards for the same company. The cards came issued one to a pack, along with a foil pack of 1993 Donruss cards for a retail price of about $3.

		NM/M
Complete Set (16):		15.00
Common Player:		1.00
1	Frank Thomas	1.50
2	Nolan Ryan	3.00
3	Gary Sheffield	1.25
4	Fred McGriff	1.00
5	Ryne Sandberg	1.75
6	Cal Ripken, Jr.	2.50
7	Jose Canseco	1.25
8	Ken Griffey Jr.	2.50
9	Will Clark	1.00
10	Roberto Alomar	1.00
11	Juan Gonzalez	1.25
12	David Justice	1.00
13	Kirby Puckett	1.75
14	Barry Bonds	3.00
15	Robin Yount	1.50
16	Deion Sanders	1.00

1993 Donruss 1992 Blue Jays Commemorative Set

Issued only as a special gold-boxed set, this series commemorates the Toronto Blue Jays 1992 World Championship. Each player on the Jays '92 roster has a card. There are also special cards recall-

ing each game of the Series and a SkyDome card. The World Series highlights cards have a bunting design at top and a gold-foil World Series logo on front. Player cards feature borderless photos; a Blue Jays "Commemorative Set" logo is at lower-left. Backs have a player photo at top and a stat box at bottom with season, career and 1992 LCS and World Series numbers.

		NM/M
Complete Set (54):		5.00
Common Card:		.15
1	Checklist/Logo Card	.15
2	Roberto Alomar	.45
3	Derek Bell	.15
4	Pat Borders	.15
5	Joe Carter	.45
6	Alfredo Griffin	.15
7	Kelly Gruber	.15
8	Manuel Lee	.15
9	Candy Maldonado	.15
10	John Olerud	.45
11	Ed Sprague	.15
12	Pat Tabler	.15
13	Devon White	.15
14	Dave Winfield	1.00
15	David Cone	.25
16	Mark Eichhorn	.15
17	Juan Guzman	.15
18	Tom Henke	.15
19	Jimmy Key	.15
20	Jack Morris	.25
21	Todd Stottlemyre	.15
22	Mike Timlin	.15
23	Duane Ward	.15
24	David Wells	.40
25	Randy Knorr	.15
26	Rance Mulliniks	.15
27	Tom Quinlan	.15
28	Cito Gaston	.15
29	Dave Steib	.15
30	Ken Dayley	.15
31	Turner Ward	.15
32	Eddie Zosky	.15
33	Pat Hentgen	.15
34	Al Leiter	.15
35	Doug Linton	.15
36	Bob MacDonald	.15
37	Rick Trlicek	.15
38	Domingo Martinez	.15
39	Mike Maksudian	.15
40	Rob Ducey	.15
41	Jeff Kent	.60
42	Greg Myers	.15
43	Dave Weathers	.15
44	Skydome	.15
45	Trophy Presentation (Jim Kaat, Cito Gaston, Paul Beeston, Bobby Brown)	.15
World Series Highlights		.10
1WS	Series Opener (Blue Jays vs. Braves)	.10
2WS	Game 1 - Carter Homers in 4th	.25
3WS	Homer	.10
4WS	Game 3 - Maldonado Drives in Game-Winner	.10
5WS	Game 4 - Key's Win Puts Jays Up 3-1	.10
6WS	Game 5 - Olerud Scores Both Jays Runs	.10
7WS	Game 6 - Winfield's Double in 11th Wins	.25
8WS	Pat Border Series MVP	.10
9WS	World Champs Celebration	.10

1994 Donruss Promotional Samples

To introduce both its regular 1994 issue and the "Special Edition" gold cards, Donruss pro-

duced this 12-card promo set for distribution to its dealer network. The promos are virtually identical in format to the regular cards except for the large gray diagonal overprint "PROMOTIONAL SAMPLE" on both front and back. Card numbers also differ on the promos.

		NM/M
Complete Set (12):		10.00
Common Player:		.50
1	Barry Bonds	2.00
2	Darren Daulton	.50
3	John Olerud	.50
4	Frank Thomas	1.00
5	Mike Piazza	1.50
6	Tim Salmon	.50
7	Ken Griffey Jr.	1.50
8	Fred McGriff	.50
9	Don Mattingly	1.25
10	Gary Sheffield	.75
Special Edition Gold:		
1G	Barry Bonds (Special Edition Gold)	2.50
4G	Frank Thomas (Special Edition Gold)	1.00

1994 Donruss

Donruss released its 1994 set in two 330-card series. Each series also includes, 50 Special Edition gold cards and several insert sets. Regular cards have full-bleed photos and are UV coated and foil stamped. Special Edition cards are gold-foil stamped on both sides and are included in each pack. Insert sets titled Spirit of the Game and Decade Dominators were produced in regular and super (3-1/2" x 5") formats. Other inserts were MVPs and Long Ball Leaders in regular size and super-size Award Winners. An Elite series of cards, continuing from previous years with #37-48, was also issued as inserts. A 10th Anniversary insert set features 10 popular 1984 Donruss cards in gold-foil enhanced reprint versions.

		NM/M
Complete Set (660):		15.00
Common Player:		.05
Series 1 or 2 Pack (13):		.50
Series 1 or 2 Box (36):		12.50
1	Nolan Ryan (Career Salute 27 Years.)	2.00
2	Mike Piazza	1.00
3	Moises Alou	.05
4	Ken Griffey Jr.	1.00
5	Gary Sheffield	.25
6	Roberto Alomar	.20
7	John Kruk	.05
8	Gregg Olson	.05
9	Gregg Jefferies	.05
10	Tony Gwynn	.65
11	Chad Curtis	.05
12	Craig Biggio	.05
13	John Burkett	.05
14	Carlos Baerga	.05
15	Robin Yount	.60
16	Dennis Eckersley	.50
17	Dwight Gooden	.05
18	Ryne Sandberg	.65
19	Rickey Henderson	.60
20	Jack McDowell	.05
21	Jay Bell	.05
22	Kevin Brown	.05
23	Robin Ventura	.05
24	Paul Molitor	.60
25	Dave Justice	.05
26	Rafael Palmeiro	.50
27	Cecil Fielder	.05
28	Chuck Knoblauch	.05
29	Dave Hollins	.05
30	Jimmy Key	.05
31	Mark Langston	.05
32	Darryl Kile	.05
33	Ruben Sierra	.05
34	Ron Gant	.05
35	Ozzie Smith	.65
36	Wade Boggs	.65

37	Marquis Grissom	.05
38	Will Clark	.05
39	Kenny Lofton	.05
40	Cal Ripken, Jr.	2.00
41	Steve Avery	.05
42	Mo Vaughn	.05
43	Brian McRae	.05
44	Mickey Tettleton	.05
45	Barry Larkin	.05
46	Charlie Hayes	.05
47	Kevin Appier	.05
48	Robby Thompson	.05
49	Juan Gonzalez	.30
50	Paul O'Neill	.05
51	Marcos Armas	.05
52	Mike Butcher	.05
53	Ken Caminiti	.05
54	Pat Borders	.05
55	Pedro Munoz	.05
56	Tim Belcher	.05
57	Paul Assenmacher	.05
58	Damon Berryhill	.05
59	Ricky Bones	.05
60	Rene Arocha	.05
61	Shawn Boskie	.05
62	Pedro Astacio	.05
63	Frank Bolick	.05
64	Bud Black	.05
65	Sandy Alomar, Jr.	.05
66	Rich Amaral	.05
67	Luis Aquino	.05
68	Kevin Baez	.05
69	Mike Devereaux	.05
70	Andy Ashby	.05
71	Larry Andersen	.05
72	Steve Cooke	.05
73	Mario Diaz	.05
74	Rob Deer	.05
75	Bobby Ayala	.05
76	Freddie Benavides	.05
77	Stan Belinda	.05
78	John Doherty	.05
79	Willie Banks	.05
80	Spike Owen	.05
81	Mike Bordick	.05
82	Chili Davis	.05
83	Luis Gonzalez	.05
84	Ed Sprague	.05
85	Jeff Reboulet	.05
86	Jason Bere	.05
87	Mark Hutton	.05
88	Jeff Blauser	.05
89	Cal Eldred	.05
90	Bernard Gilkey	.05
91	Frank Castillo	.05
92	Jim Gott	.05
93	Greg Colbrunn	.05
94	Jeff Brantley	.05
95	Jeremy Hernandez	.05
96	Norm Charlton	.05
97	Alex Arias	.05
98	John Franco	.05
99	Chris Hoiles	.05
100	Brad Ausmus	.05
101	Wes Chamberlain	.05
102	Mark Dewey	.05
103	Benji Gil/RR	.05
104	John Dopson	.05
105	John Smiley	.05
106	David Nied	.05
107	George Brett (Career Salute 21 Years.)	.75
108	Kirk Gibson	.05
109	Larry Casian	.05
110	Checklist (Ryne Sandberg 2,000 Hits)	.25
111	Brent Gates	.05
112	Damion Easley	.05
113	Pete Harnisch	.05
114	Danny Cox	.05
115	Kevin Tapani	.05
116	Roberto Hernandez	.05
117	Domingo Jean	.05
118	Sid Bream	.05
119	Doug Henry	.05
120	Omar Olivares	.05
121	Mike Harkey	.05
122	Carlos Hernandez	.05
123	Jeff Fassero	.05
124	Dave Burba	.05
125	Wayne Kirby	.05
126	John Cummings	.05
127	Bret Barberie	.05
128	Todd Hundley	.05
129	Tim Hulett	.05
130	Phil Clark	.05
131	Danny Jackson	.05
132	Tom Foley	.05
133	Donald Harris	.05
134	Scott Fletcher	.05
135	Johnny Ruffin/RR	.05
136	Jerald Clark	.05
137	Billy Brewer	.05
138	Dan Gladden	.05
139	Eddie Guardado	.05
140	Checklist (Cal Ripken, Jr. 2,000 Hits)	.35
141	Scott Hemond	.05
142	Steve Frey	.05
143	Xavier Hernandez	.05
144	Mark Eichhorn	.05
145	Ellis Burks	.05
146	Jim Leyritz	.05
147	Mark Lemke	.05
148	Pat Listach	.05
149	Donovan Osborne	.05
150	Glenallen Hill	.05
151	Orel Hershiser	.05

152	Darrin Fletcher	.05
153	Royce Clayton	.05
154	Derek Lilliquist	.05
155	Mike Felder	.05
156	Jeff Conine	.05
157	Ryan Thompson	.05
158	Ben McDonald	.05
159	Ricky Gutierrez	.05
160	Terry Mulholland	.05
161	Carlos Garcia	.05
162	Tom Henke	.05
163	Mike Greenwell	.05
164	Thomas Howard	.05
165	Joe Girardi	.05
166	Hubie Brooks	.05
167	Greg Gohr	.05
168	Chip Hale	.05
169	Rick Honeycutt	.05
170	Hilly Hathaway	.05
171	Todd Jones	.05
172	Tony Fernandez	.05
173	Bo Jackson	.10
174	Bobby Munoz	.05
175	Greg McMichael	.05
176	Graeme Lloyd	.05
177	Tom Pagnozzi	.05
178	Derrick May	.05
179	Pedro Martinez	.60
180	Ken Hill	.05
181	Bryan Hickerson	.05
182	Jose Mesa	.05
183	Dave Fleming	.05
184	Henry Cotto	.05
185	Jeff Kent	.05
186	Mark McLemore	.05
187	Trevor Hoffman	.05
188	Todd Pratt	.05
189	Blas Minor	.05
190	Charlie Leibrandt	.05
191	Tony Pena	.05
192	Larry Luebbers RC	.05
193	Greg Harris	.05
194	David Cone	.05
195	Bill Gullickson	.05
196	Brian Harper	.05
197	Steve Karsay/RR	.05
198	Greg Myers	.05
199	Mark Portugal	.05
200	Pat Hentgen	.05
201	Mike La Valliere	.05
202	Mike Stanley	.05
203	Kent Mercker	.05
204	Dave Nilsson	.05
205	Erik Pappas	.05
206	Mike Morgan	.05
207	Roger McDowell	.05
208	Mike Lansing	.05
209	Kirt Manwaring	.05
210	Randy Milligan	.05
211	Erik Hanson	.05
212	Orestes Destrade	.05
213	Mike Maddux	.05
214	Alan Mills	.05
215	Tim Mauser	.05
216	Ben Rivera	.05
217	Don Slaught	.05
218	Bob Patterson	.05
219	Carlos Quintana	.05
220	Checklist (Tim Raines 2,000 Hits)	.05
221	Hal Morris	.05
222	Darren Holmes	.05
223	Chris Gwynn	.05
224	Chad Kreuter	.05
225	Mike Hartley	.05
226	Scott Lydy	.05
227	Eduardo Perez	.05
228	Greg Swindell	.05
229	Al Leiter	.05
230	Scott Radinsky	.05
231	Bob Wickman	.05
232	Otis Nixon	.05
233	Kevin Reimer	.05
234	Geronimo Pena	.05
235	Kevin Roberson/RR	.05
236	Jody Reed	.05
237	Kirk Rueter/RR	.05
238	Willie McGee	.05
239	Charles Nagy	.05
240	Tim Leary	.05
241	Carl Everett	.05
242	Charlie O'Brien	.05
243	Mike Pagliarulo	.05
244	Kerry Taylor	.05
245	Kevin Stocker	.05
246	Joel Johnston	.05
247	Geno Petralli	.05
248	Jeff Russell	.05
249	Joe Oliver	.05
250	Robert Mejia	.05
251	Chris Haney	.05
252	Bill Krueger	.05
253	Shane Mack	.05
254	Terry Steinbach	.05
255	Luis Polonia	.05
256	Eddie Taubensee	.05
257	Dave Stewart	.05
258	Tim Raines	.05
259	Bernie Williams	.05
260	John Smoltz	.05
261	Kevin Seitzer	.05
262	Bob Tewksbury	.05
263	Bob Scanlan	.05
264	Henry Rodriguez	.05
265	Tim Scott	.05
266	Scott Sanderson	.05
267	Eric Plunk	.05
268	Edgar Martinez	.05

269	Charlie Hough	.05
270	Joe Orsulak	.05
271	Harold Reynolds	.05
272	Tim Teufel	.05
273	Bobby Thigpen	.05
274	Randy Tomlin	.05
275	Gary Redus	.05
276	Ken Ryan	.05
277	Tim Pugh	.05
278	Jayhawk Owens	.05
279	Phil Hiatt/RR	.05
280	Alan Trammell	.05
281	Dave McCarty/RR	.05
282	Bob Welch	.05
283	J.T. Snow	.05
284	Brian Williams	.05
285	Devon White	.05
286	Steve Sax	.05
287	Tony Tarasco	.05
288	Bill Spiers	.05
289	Allen Watson	.05
290	Checklist (Rickey Henderson 2,000 Hits)	.05
291	Joe Vizcaino	.05
292	Darryl Strawberry	.05
293	John Wetteland	.05
294	Bill Swift	.05
295	Jeff Treadway	.05
296	Tino Martinez	.05
297	Richie Lewis	.05
298	Bret Saberhagen	.05
299	Arthur Rhodes	.05
300	Guillermo Velasquez	.05
301	Milt Thompson	.05
302	Doug Strange	.05
303	Aaron Sele	.05
304	Bip Roberts	.05
305	Bruce Ruffin	.05
306	Jose Lind	.05
307	David Wells	.05
308	Bobby Witt	.05
309	Mark Wohlers	.05
310	B.J. Surhoff	.05
311	Mark Whiten	.05
312	Turk Wendell	.05
313	Raul Mondesi	.05
314	Brian Turang RC	.05
315	Chris Hammond	.05
316	Tim Bogar	.05
317	Brad Pennington	.05
318	Tim Worrell	.05
319	Mitch Williams	.05
320	Rondell White/RR	.05
321	Frank Viola	.05
322	Manny Ramirez/RR	.75
323	Gary Wayne	.05
324	Mike Macfarlane	.05
325	Russ Springer	.05
326	Tim Wallach	.05
327	Salomon Torres/RR	.05
328	Omar Vizquel	.05
329	Andy Tomberlin RC	.05
330	Chris Sabo	.05
331	Mike Mussina	.30
332	Andy Benes	.05
333	Darren Daulton	.05
334	Orlando Merced	.05
335	Mark McGwire	1.50
336	Dave Winfield	.60
337	Sammy Sosa	.65
338	Eric Karros	.05
339	Greg Vaughn	.05
340	Don Mattingly	.75
341	Frank Thomas	.60
342	Fred McGriff	.60
343	Kirby Puckett	.65
344	Roberto Kelly	.05
345	Wally Joyner	.05
346	Andres Galarraga	.05
347	Bobby Bonilla	.05
348	Benito Santiago	.05
349	Barry Bonds	2.00
350	Delino DeShields	.05
351	Albert Belle	.05
352	Randy Johnson	.60
353	Tim Salmon	.05
354	John Olerud	.05
355	Dean Palmer	.05
356	Roger Clemens	.75
357	Jim Abbott	.05
358	Mark Grace	.05
359	Ozzie Guillen	.05
360	Lou Whitaker	.05
361	Jose Rijo	.05
362	Jeff Montgomery	.05
363	Chuck Finley	.05
364	Tom Glavine	.05
365	Jeff Bagwell	.60
366	Joe Carter	.05
367	Ray Lankford	.05
368	Ramon Martinez	.05
369	Jay Buhner	.05
370	Matt Williams	.05
371	Larry Walker	.05
372	Jose Canseco	.30
373	Len Dykstra	.05
374	Bryan Harvey	.05
375	Andy Van Slyke	.05
376	Ivan Rodriguez	.50
377	Kevin Mitchell	.05
378	Travis Fryman	.05
379	Duane Ward	.05
380	Greg Maddux	.65
381	Scott Servais	.05
382	Greg Olson	.05
383	Rey Sanchez	.05
384	Tom Kramer	.05
385	David Valle	.05

#	Player	
386	Eddie Murray	.60
387	Kevin Higgins	.05
388	Dan Wilson	.05
389	Todd Frohwirth	.05
390	Gerald Williams	.05
391	Hipolito Pichardo	.05
392	Pat Meares	.05
393	Luis Lopez	.05
394	Ricky Jordan	.05
395	Bob Walk	.05
396	Sid Fernandez	.05
397	Todd Worrell	.05
398	Darryl Hamilton	.05
399	Randy Myers	.05
400	Rod Brewer	.05
401	Lance Blankenship	.05
402	Steve Finley	.05
403	Phil Leftwich RC	.05
404	Juan Guzman	.05
405	Anthony Young	.05
406	Jeff Gardner	.05
407	Ryan Bowen	.05
408	Fernando Valenzuela	.05
409	David West	.05
410	Kenny Rogers	.05
411	Bob Zupcic	.05
412	Eric Young	.05
413	Bret Boone	.05
414	Danny Tartabull	.05
415	Bob MacDonald	.05
416	Ron Karkovice	.05
417	Scott Cooper	.05
418	Dante Bichette	.05
419	Tripp Cromer	.05
420	Billy Ashley	.05
421	Roger Smithberg	.05
422	Dennis Martinez	.05
423	Mike Blowers	.05
424	Darren Lewis	.05
425	Junior Ortiz	.05
426	Butch Huskey	.05
427	Jimmy Poole	.05
428	Walt Weiss	.05
429	Scott Bankhead	.05
430	Deion Sanders	.05
431	Scott Bullett	.05
432	Jeff Huson	.05
433	Tyler Green	.05
434	Billy Hatcher	.05
435	Bob Hamelin	.05
436	Reggie Sanders	.05
437	Scott Erickson	.05
438	Steve Reed	.05
439	Randy Velarde	.05
440	Checklist (Tony Gwynn 2,000 Hits)	.15
441	Terry Leach	.05
442	Danny Bautista	.05
443	Kent Hrbek	.05
444	Rick Wilkins	.05
445	Tony Phillips	.05
446	Dion James	.05
447	Joey Cora	.05
448	Andre Dawson	.15
449	Pedro Castellano	.05
450	Tom Gordon	.05
451	Rob Dibble	.05
452	Ron Darling	.05
453	Chipper Jones	.65
454	Joe Grahe	.05
455	Domingo Cedeno	.05
456	Tom Edens	.05
457	Mitch Webster	.05
458	Jose Bautista	.05
459	Troy O'Leary	.05
460	Todd Zeile	.05
461	Sean Berry	.05
462	Brad Holman RC	.05
463	Dave Martinez	.05
464	Mark Lewis	.05
465	Paul Carey	.05
466	Jack Armstrong	.05
467	David Telgheder	.05
468	Gene Harris	.05
469	Danny Darwin	.05
470	Kim Batiste	.05
471	Tim Wakefield	.05
472	Craig Lefferts	.05
473	Jacob Brumfield	.05
474	Lance Painter	.05
475	Milt Cuyler	.05
476	Melido Perez	.05
477	Derek Parks	.05
478	Gary DiSarcina	.05
479	Steve Bedrosian	.05
480	Eric Anthony	.05
481	Julio Franco	.05
482	Tommy Greene	.05
483	Pat Kelly	.05
484	Nate Minchey/RR	.05
485	William Pennyfeather	.05
486	Harold Baines	.05
487	Howard Johnson	.05
488	Angel Miranda	.05
489	Scott Sanders	.05
490	Shawon Dunston	.05
491	Mel Rojas	.05
492	Jeff Nelson	.05
493	Archi Cianfrocco	.05
494	Al Martin	.05
495	Mike Gallego	.05
496	Mike Henneman	.05
497	Armando Reynoso	.05
498	Mickey Morandini	.05
499	Rick Renteria	.05
500	Rick Sutcliffe	.05
501	Bobby Jones/RR	.05
502	Gary Gaetti	.05
503	Rick Aguilera	.05
504	Todd Stottlemyre	.05
505	Mike Mohler	.05
506	Mike Stanton	.05
507	Jose Guzman	.05
508	Kevin Rogers	.05
509	Chuck Carr	.05
510	Chris Jones	.05
511	Brent Mayne	.05
512	Greg Harris	.05
513	Dave Henderson	.05
514	Eric Hillman	.05
515	Dan Peltier	.05
516	Craig Shipley	.05
517	John Valentin	.05
518	Wilson Alvarez	.05
519	Andujar Cedeno	.05
520	Troy Neel	.05
521	Tom Candiotti	.05
522	Matt Mieske	.05
523	Jim Thome	.50
524	Lou Frazier	.05
525	Mike Jackson	.05
526	Pedro Martinez	.05
527	Roger Pavlik	.05
528	Kent Bottenfield	.05
529	Felix Jose	.05
530	Mark Guthrie	.05
531	Steve Farr	.05
532	Craig Paquette	.05
533	Doug Jones	.05
534	Luis Alicea	.05
535	Cory Snyder	.05
536	Paul Sorrento	.05
537	Nigel Wilson	.05
538	Jeff King	.05
539	Willie Green	.05
540	Kirk McCaskill	.05
541	Al Osuna	.05
542	Greg Hibbard	.05
543	Brett Butler	.05
544	Jose Valentin	.05
545	Wil Cordero	.05
546	Chris Bosio	.05
547	Jamie Moyer	.05
548	Jim Eisenreich	.05
549	Vinny Castilla	.05
550	Checklist (Dave Winfield 3,000 Hits)	.05
551	John Roper	.05
552	Lance Johnson	.05
553	Scott Kamienicki	.05
554	Mike Moore	.05
555	Steve Buechele	.05
556	Terry Pendleton	.05
557	Todd Van Poppel	.05
558	Rob Butler	.05
559	Zane Smith	.05
560	David Hulse	.05
561	Tim Costo	.05
562	John Habyan	.05
563	Terry Jorgensen	.05
564	Matt Nokes	.05
565	Kevin McReynolds	.05
566	Phil Plantier	.05
567	Chris Turner	.05
568	Carlos Delgado	.40
569	John Jaha	.05
570	Dwight Smith	.05
571	John Vander Wal	.05
572	Trevor Wilson	.05
573	Felix Fermin	.05
574	Marc Newfield/RR	.05
575	Jeromy Burnitz	.05
576	Leo Gomez	.05
577	Curt Schilling	.25
578	Kevin Young	.05
579	Jerry Spradlin RC	.05
580	Curt Leskanic	.05
581	Carl Willis	.05
582	Alex Fernandez	.05
583	Mark Holzemer	.05
584	Domingo Martinez	.05
585	Pete Smith	.05
586	Brian Jordan	.05
587	Kevin Gross	.05
588	J.R. Phillips/RR	.05
589	Chris Nabholz	.05
590	Bill Wertz	.05
591	Derek Bell	.05
592	Brady Anderson	.05
593	Matt Turner	.05
594	Pete Incaviglia	.05
595	Greg Gagne	.05
596	John Flaherty	.05
597	Scott Livingstone	.05
598	Rod Bolton	.05
599	Mike Perez	.05
600	Checklist (Roger Clemens 2,000 Strikeouts)	.25
601	Tony Castillo	.05
602	Henry Mercedes	.05
603	Mike Fetters	.05
604	Rod Beck	.05
605	Damon Buford	.05
606	Matt Whiteside	.05
607	Shawn Green	.25
608	Midre Cummings/RR	.05
609	Jeff McNeely	.05
610	Danny Sheaffer	.05
611	Paul Wagner	.05
612	Torey Lovullo	.05
613	Javier Lopez	.05
614	Mariano Duncan	.05
615	Doug Brocail	.05
616	Dave Hansen	.05
617	Ryan Klesko	.05
618	Eric Davis	.05
619	Scott Ruffcorn/RR	.05
620	Mike Trombley	.05
621	Jaime Navarro	.05
622	Rheal Cormier	.05
623	Jose Offerman	.05
624	David Segui	.05
625	Robb Nen/RR	.05
626	Dave Gallagher	.05
627	Julian Tavarez RC	.05
628	Chris Gomez	.05
629	Jeffrey Hammonds/RR	.05
630	Scott Brosius	.05
631	Willie Blair	.05
632	Doug Drabek	.05
633	Bill Wegman	.05
634	Jeff McKnight	.05
635	Rich Rodriguez	.05
636	Steve Trachsel	.05
637	Buddy Groom	.05
638	Sterling Hitchcock	.05
639	Chuck McElroy	.05
640	Rene Gonzales	.05
641	Dan Plesac	.05
642	Jeff Branson	.05
643	Darrell Whitmore	.05
644	Paul Quantrill	.05
645	Rich Rowland	.05
646	Curtis Pride RC	.05
647	Erik Plantenberg	.05
648	Albie Lopez	.05
649	Rich Batchelor RC	.05
650	Lee Smith	.05
651	Cliff Floyd	.05
652	Pete Schourek	.05
653	Reggie Jefferson	.05
654	Bill Haselman	.05
655	Steve Hosey	.05
656	Mark Clark	.05
657	Mark Davis	.05
658	Dave Magadan	.05
659	Candy Maldonado	.05
660	Checklist (Mark Langston 2,000 Strikeouts)	.05

Special Edition - Gold

In 1994 Donruss added a Special Edition subset of 100 of the game's top players. Fifty cards each were included one or two per pack in all types of Donruss' Series 1 and 2 packaging. The cards use the same photos and format as the regular-issue version, but have special gold-foil stamping on front in the area of the team logo and player name, and on back in a "Special Edition" number box in the upper-left corner.

		NM/M
Complete Set (100):		7.50
Common Player:		.10
1	Nolan Ryan	1.50
2	Mike Piazza	1.00
3	Moises Alou	.10
4	Ken Griffey Jr.	1.00
5	Gary Sheffield	.25
6	Roberto Alomar	.20
7	John Kruk	.10
8	Gregg Olson	.10
9	Gregg Jefferies	.10
10	Tony Gwynn	.65
11	Chad Curtis	.10
12	Craig Biggio	.10
13	John Burkett	.10
14	Carlos Baerga	.10
15	Robin Yount	.60
16	Dennis Eckersley	.50
17	Dwight Gooden	.10
18	Ryne Sandberg	.65
19	Rickey Henderson	.60
20	Jack McDowell	.10
21	Jay Bell	.10
22	Kevin Brown	.10
23	Robin Ventura	.10
24	Paul Molitor	.60
25	David Justice	.10
26	Rafael Palmeiro	.50
27	Cecil Fielder	.10
28	Chuck Knoblauch	.10
29	Dave Hollins	.10
30	Jimmy Key	.10
31	Mark Langston	.10
32	Darryl Kile	.10
33	Ruben Sierra	.10
34	Ron Gant	.10
35	Ozzie Smith	.65

#	Player	
36	Wade Boggs	.65
37	Marquis Grissom	.10
38	Will Clark	.10
39	Kenny Lofton	.10
40	Cal Ripken, Jr.	1.50
41	Steve Avery	.10
42	Mo Vaughn	.10
43	Brian McRae	.10
44	Mickey Tettleton	.10
45	Barry Larkin	.10
46	Charlie Hayes	.10
47	Kevin Appier	.10
48	Robby Thompson	.10
49	Juan Gonzalez	.30
50	Paul O'Neill	.10
51	Mike Mussina	.40
52	Andy Benes	.10
53	Darren Daulton	.10
54	Orlando Merced	.10
55	Mark McGwire	1.25
56	Dave Winfield	.60
57	Sammy Sosa	.65
58	Eric Karros	.10
59	Greg Vaughn	.10
60	Don Mattingly	.75
61	Frank Thomas	.60
62	Fred McGriff	.10
63	Kirby Puckett	.65
64	Roberto Kelly	.10
65	Wally Joyner	.10
66	Andres Galarraga	.10
67	Bobby Bonilla	.10
68	Benito Santiago	.10
69	Barry Bonds	1.50
70	Delino DeShields	.10
71	Albert Belle	.10
72	Randy Johnson	.60
73	Tim Salmon	.10
74	John Olerud	.10
75	Dean Palmer	.10
76	Roger Clemens	.75
77	Jim Abbott	.10
78	Mark Grace	.10
79	Ozzie Guillen	.10
80	Lou Whitaker	.10
81	Jose Rijo	.10
82	Jeff Montgomery	.10
83	Chuck Finley	.10
84	Tom Glavine	.25
85	Jeff Bagwell	.60
86	Joe Carter	.10
87	Ray Lankford	.10
88	Ramon Martinez	.10
89	Jay Buhner	.10
90	Matt Williams	.10
91	Larry Walker	.10
92	Jose Canseco	.25
93	Len Dykstra	.10
94	Bryan Harvey	.10
95	Andy Van Slyke	.10
96	Ivan Rodriguez	.50
97	Kevin Mitchell	.10
98	Travis Fryman	.10
99	Duane Ward	.10
100	Greg Maddux	.65

Anniversary-1984

This set commemorates and features 10 of the most popular cards from Donruss' 1984 set. The cards, inserted in Series I hobby foil packs only, are "holographically enhanced" with foil stamping and UV coating.

		NM/M
Complete Set (10):		20.00
Common Player:		1.00
1	Joe Carter	1.00
2	Robin Yount	1.50
3	George Brett	2.50
4	Rickey Henderson	1.50
5	Nolan Ryan	6.00
6	Cal Ripken, Jr.	6.00
7	Wade Boggs	2.00
8	Don Mattingly	2.50
9	Ryne Sandberg	2.00
10	Tony Gwynn	2.00

1994 Donruss Award Winners Supers

Major award winners of the 1993 season are honored in this super-size (3-1/2" x 5") insert set. One card was packaged in each box of U.S. jumbo packs and in each Ca-

nadian foil-pack box. On a gold-tone background, the card backs have another player photo, a description of his award winning performance and a white strip with a serial number identifying the card's place in an edition of 10,000.

		NM/M
Complete Set (10):		25.00
Common Player:		1.25
1	Barry Bonds (N.L. MVP)	5.00
2	Greg Maddux (N.L. Cy Young)	2.50
3	Mike Piazza (N.L. ROY)	3.50
4	Barry Bonds (N.L. HR Champ)	5.00
5	Kirby Puckett (All-Star MVP)	2.50
6	Frank Thomas (A.L. MVP)	2.00
7	Jack McDowell (A.L. Cy Young)	1.25
8	Tim Salmon (A.L. ROY)	1.25
9	Juan Gonzalez (A.L. HR Champ)	1.50
10	Paul Molitor (World Series MVP)	2.00

Decade Dominators

Donruss selected 10 top home run hitters (Series I) and 10 RBI leaders of the 1990s for this insert set. Cards were issued in all types of Series I and II packs. Full-bleed UV-coated cards were gold-foil enhanced on the front. Backs featured another full-color player photo and charted information on his 1990s home run or RBI output and ranking.

		NM/M
Complete Set (20):		15.00
Common Player:		.35
Series 1		
1	Cecil Fielder	.35
2	Barry Bonds	2.50
3	Fred McGriff	.35
4	Matt Williams	.35
5	Joe Carter	.35
6	Juan Gonzalez	.40
7	Jose Canseco	.50
8	Ron Gant	.35
9	Ken Griffey Jr.	1.50
10	Mark McGwire	2.00
Series 2		
1	Tony Gwynn	1.00
2	Frank Thomas	.75
3	Paul Molitor	.75
4	Edgar Martinez	.35
5	Kirby Puckett	1.00
6	Ken Griffey, Jr.	1.50
7	Barry Bonds	2.50
8	Willie McGee	.35
9	Len Dykstra	.35
10	John Kruk	.35

1994 Donruss Decade Dominators Supers

Super-size (3-1/2" x 5") versions of the 1994 Donruss Decade Dominators insert cards were produced as a premium, one card

being packaged in a paper checklist envelope in each hobby box of Donruss foil packs. The supers are identical in format to the regular-size cards with the exception of a white serial number strip on the back, identifying each card's position in an edition of 10,000.

		NM/M
Complete Set (20):		25.00
Common Player:		1.00
Series 1		
1	Cecil Fielder	1.00
2	Barry Bonds	2.50
3	Fred McGriff	1.00
4	Matt Williams	1.00
5	Joe Carter	1.00
6	Juan Gonzalez	1.00
7	Jose Canseco	1.25
8	Ron Gant	1.00
9	Ken Griffey Jr.	2.00
10	Mark McGwire	2.00
Series 2		
1	Tony Gwynn	2.00
2	Frank Thomas	1.50
3	Paul Molitor	1.50
4	Edgar Martinez	1.00
5	Kirby Puckett	2.00
6	Ken Griffey, Jr.	2.25
7	Barry Bonds	2.50
8	Willie McGee	1.00
9	Lenny Dykstra	2.00
10	John Kruk	1.00

Diamond Kings

The artwork of Dick Perez is again featured on this insert set included in foil packs. Player art is set against garish color backgrounds with a red-and-silver "Diamond Kings" foil logo above, and the player's name in script at bottom. Backs are printed in red on pale yellow and feature a 1993 season summary. Cards have a DK preface to the number. Cards #1-14 and #29, Dave Winfield, were included in Series 1 packs; cards #15-28 are found in Series 2, along with the checklist card (#30), featuring a Dick Perez self-portrait.

		NM/M
Complete Set (30):		12.00
Common Player:		.25
1	Barry Bonds	2.50
2	Mo Vaughn	.25
3	Steve Avery	.25
4	Tim Salmon	.50
5	Rick Wilkins	.25
6	Brian Harper	.25
7	Andres Galarraga	.25
8	Albert Belle	.50
9	John Kruk	.25
10	Ivan Rodriguez	.75
11	Tony Gwynn	1.25
12	Brian McRae	.25
13	Bobby Bonilla	.25
14	Ken Griffey Jr.	2.00
15	Mike Piazza	2.00
16	Don Mattingly	1.50
17	Barry Larkin	.25
18	Ruben Sierra	.25
19	Orlando Merced	.25

20	Greg Vaughn	.25
21	Gregg Jefferies	.25
22	Cecil Fielder	.25
23	Moises Alou	.25
24	John Olerud	.25
25	Gary Sheffield	.25
26	Mike Mussina	.60
27	Jeff Bagwell	1.00
28	Frank Thomas	1.00
29	Dave Winfield (King of Kings)	1.00
30	Dick Perez (Checklist)	.25

1994 Donruss Diamond Kings Supers

Each retail box of 1994 Donruss foil packs contains one super-size (4-7/8" x 6-13/16") version of the Diamond Kings inserts. Series 1 boxes offer cards #1-14, while #15-28 are found in Series 2 boxes. A 29th card, honoring Dave Winfield, was also produced. Super DKs are identical in format to the regular-size inserts, with the exception of a white serial number strip on the back which identifies the card within an edition of 10,000.

		NM/M
Complete Set (29):		70.00
Common Player:		2.00
1	Barry Bonds	7.50
2	Mo Vaughn	2.00
3	Steve Avery	2.00
4	Tim Salmon	2.00
5	Rick Wilkins	2.00
6	Brian Harper	2.00
7	Andres Galarraga	2.00
8	Albert Belle	2.00
9	John Kruk	2.00
10	Ivan Rodriguez	3.50
11	Tony Gwynn	5.00
12	Brian McRae	2.00
13	Bobby Bonilla	2.00
14	Ken Griffey Jr.	6.50
15	Mike Piazza	6.50
16	Don Mattingly	6.00
17	Barry Larkin	2.00
18	Ruben Sierra	2.00
19	Orlando Merced	2.00
20	Greg Vaughn	2.00
21	Gregg Jefferies	2.00
22	Cecil Fielder	2.00
23	Moises Alou	2.00
24	John Olerud	2.00
25	Gary Sheffield	3.00
26	Mike Mussina	3.00
27	Jeff Bagwell	4.00
28	Frank Thomas	4.00
29	Dave Winfield (King of Kings)	4.00

Elite

Donruss continued its popular Elite Series with 12 more players in 1994. The cards, numbered #37-48, were inserted in foil packs only. The cards feature the player in a diamond on the front; the back offers an opinion of why the player is considered an elite and is serially numbered to 10,000.

	NM/M
Complete Set (12):	50.00

Common Player:		4.00
37	Frank Thomas	6.00
38	Tony Gwynn	7.50
39	Tim Salmon	4.00
40	Albert Belle	4.00
41	John Kruk	4.00
42	Juan Gonzalez	5.00
43	John Olerud	4.00
44	Barry Bonds	12.00
45	Ken Griffey Jr.	9.00
46	Mike Piazza	9.00
47	Jack McDowell	4.00
48	Andres Galarraga	4.00

Long Ball Leaders

The "Tale of the Tape" for the 1993 season is chronicled in this Series 1 hobby-only foil-pack insert. Silver prismatic foil highlights the typography on the front of the card which includes the "Long Ball Leaders" logos (complete with embossed baseball), the player's last name and the distance of his blast. Cards backs have another player photo superimposed on the venue in which the home run was hit. The distance is repeated in silver over the ballpark photo. In a wide silver box at bottom is data about the home run.

		NM/M
Complete Set (10):		6.00
Common Player:		.30
1	Cecil Fielder	.30
2	Dean Palmer	.30
3	Andres Galarraga	.30
4	Bo Jackson	.40
5	Ken Griffey Jr.	1.50
6	Dave Justice	.30
7	Mike Piazza	1.50
8	Frank Thomas	1.00
9	Barry Bonds	3.00
10	Juan Gonzalez	.50

MVPs

These inserts were included in 1994 jumbo packs only. The fronts have a large metallic blue MVP logo, beneath which is a red stripe with the player's name and position in white. Backs have a portrait photo, stats for 1993 and a summary of why the player was selected as team MVP.

		NM/M
Complete Set (28):		20.00
Common Player:		.25
1	Dave Justice	.25
2	Mark Grace	.25
3	Jose Rijo	.25
4	Andres Galarraga	.25
5	Bryan Harvey	.25
6	Jeff Bagwell	1.00
7	Mike Piazza	2.50
8	Moises Alou	.25
9	Bobby Bonilla	.25
10	Len Dykstra	.25
11	Jeff King	.25
12	Gregg Jefferies	.25
13	Tony Gwynn	1.50
14	Barry Bonds	4.00
15	Cal Ripken, Jr.	4.00
16	Mo Vaughn	.25
17	Tim Salmon	.25
18	Frank Thomas	1.00
19	Albert Belle	.25
20	Cecil Fielder	.25
21	Wally Joyner	.25
22	Greg Vaughn	.25
23	Kirby Puckett	1.50
24	Don Mattingly	2.00
25	Ruben Sierra	.25
26	Ken Griffey Jr.	2.50
27	Juan Gonzalez	.50
28	John Olerud	.25

Spirit of the Game

Ten players are featured in this insert set, packaged exclusively in retail boxes. Horizontal in format, fronts feature a color player action photo set against a gold-tone background which has the appearance of a multiple-exposure photo. On back a player portrait photo is set against a backdrop of red, white and blue bunting. There is a short previous-season write-up at right. Cards #1-5 were included with Series I, cards 6-10 were in Series II only.

		NM/M
Complete Set (10):		10.00
Common Player:		.70
1	John Olerud	.50
2	Barry Bonds	2.50
3	Ken Griffey Jr.	2.00
4	Mike Piazza	2.00
5	Juan Gonzalez	.60
6	Frank Thomas	1.00
7	Tim Salmon	.50
8	Dave Justice	.50
9	Don Mattingly	.50
10	Len Dykstra	.50

1994 Donruss Spirit of the Game Supers

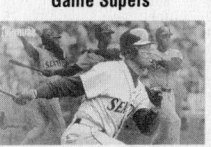

Virtually identical in format to the regular-size "Spirit of the Game" cards, these 3-1/2" x 5" versions have gold-foil, rather than holographic printing on the front, and have a serial number on back identifying it from an edition of 10,000. One super card was inserted in each specially designated retail box.

		NM/M
Complete Set (10):		20.00
Common Player:		1.50
1	John Olerud	1.50
2	Barry Bonds	4.00
3	Ken Griffey Jr.	3.50
4	Mike Piazza	3.50
5	Juan Gonzalez	2.00
6	Frank Thomas	2.50
7	Tim Salmon	1.50
8	Dave Justice	1.50
9	Don Mattingly	3.00
10	Len Dykstra	1.50

1995 Donruss Samples

The cards in this preview release of Donruss' 1995 baseball issue are virtually identical to the issued versions of the same players' cards except for slight picture cropping differences. They are unmarked as to sample status.

		NM/M
Complete Set (7):		10.00
Common Player:		1.00
5	Mike Piazza	2.00
8	Barry Bonds	3.00
20	Jeff Bagwell	1.50
42	Juan Gonzalez	1.00
55	Don Mattingly	1.00
275	Frank Thomas	1.50
331	Greg Maddux	1.50

1995 Donruss

A pair of player photos on the front of each card and silver-foil highlights are featured on the 1995 Donruss set. Besides the main ac-

tion photo on front, each card has a second photo in a home plate frame at lower-left. A silver-foil ribbon beneath has the player's team and name embossed. Above the small photo is the player's position, with a half-circle of stars over all; both elements in silver foil. Completing the silver-foil highlights is the Donruss logo at upper-left. Full-bleed backs have yet another action photo at center, with a large team logo at left and five years' worth of stats plus career numbers at bottom. Donruss was issued in retail and hobby 12-card packs, magazine distributor packs of 16 and jumbo packs of 20 cards. New to Donruss in 1995 were Super Packs. These were packs that contained complete insert sets and were seeded every 90 packs.

		NM/M
Complete Set (550):		20.00
Common Player:		.05
Press Proofs:		15X
Series 1 or 2 Pack (12):		.75
Series 1 or 2 Wax Box (36):		20.00
1	Dave Justice	.05
2	Rene Arocha	.05
3	Sandy Alomar Jr.	.05
4	Luis Lopez	.05
5	Mike Piazza	1.50
6	Bobby Jones	.05
7	Damion Easley	.05
8	Barry Bonds	2.50
9	Mike Mussina	.40
10	Kevin Seitzer	.05
11	John Smiley	.05
12	W. Van Landingham	.05
13	Ron Darling	.05
14	Walt Weiss	.05
15	Mike Lansing	.05
16	Allen Watson	.05
17	Aaron Sele	.05
18	Randy Johnson	.65
19	Dean Palmer	.05
20	Jeff Bagwell	.65
21	Curt Schilling	.25
22	Darrell Whitmore	.05
23	Steve Trachsel	.05
24	Dan Wilson	.05
25	Steve Finley	.05
26	Bret Boone	.05
27	Charles Johnson	.05
28	Mike Stanton	.05
29	Ismael Valdes	.05
30	Salomon Torres	.05
31	Eric Anthony	.05
32	Spike Owen	.05
33	Joey Cora	.05
34	Robert Eenhoorn	.05
35	Rick White	.05
36	Omar Vizquel	.05
37	Carlos Delgado	.45
38	Eddie Williams	.05
39	Shawon Dunston	.05
40	Darrin Fletcher	.05
41	Leo Gomez	.05
42	Juan Gonzalez	.40
43	Luis Alicea	.05
44	Ken Ryan	.05
45	Lou Whitaker	.05
46	Mike Blowers	.05
47	Willie Blair	.05
48	Todd Van Poppel	.05
49	Roberto Alomar	.25
50	Ozzie Smith	.75
51	Sterling Hitchcock	.05
52	Mo Vaughn	.50
53	Rick Aguilera	.05
54	Kent Mercker	.05
55	Don Mattingly	1.00
56	Bob Scanlan	.05
57	Wilson Alvarez	.05
58	Jose Mesa	.05
59	Scott Kamieniecki	.05
60	Todd Jones	.05
61	John Kruk	.05
62	Mike Stanley	.05
63	Tino Martinez	.05
64	Eddie Zambrano	.05
65	Todd Hundley	.05
66	Jamie Moyer	.05
67	Rich Amaral	.05
68	Jose Valentin	.05
69	Alex Gonzalez	.05
70	Kurt Abbott	.05
71	Delino DeShields	.05
72	Brian Anderson	.05
73	John Vander Wal	.05
74	Turner Ward	.05
75	Tim Raines	.05
76	Mark Acre	.05
77	Jose Offerman	.05
78	Jimmy Key	.05
79	Mark Whiten	.05
80	Mark Gubicza	.05
81	Darren Hall	.05
82	Travis Fryman	.05
83	Cal Ripken, Jr.	2.50
84	Geronimo Berroa	.05
85	Bret Barberie	.05
86	Andy Ashby	.05
87	Steve Avery	.05
88	Rich Becker	.05
89	John Valentin	.05
90	Glenallen Hill	.05
91	Carlos Garcia	.05
92	Dennis Martinez	.05
93	Pat Kelly	.05
q4	Orlando Miller	.05
95	Felix Jose	.05
96	Mike Kingery	.05
97	Jeff Kent	.05
98	Pete Incaviglia	.05
99	Chad Curtis	.05
100	Thomas Howard	.05
101	Hector Carrasco	.05
102	Tom Pagnozzi	.05
103	Danny Tartabull	.05
104	Donnie Elliott	.05
105	Danny Jackson	.05
106	Steve Dunn	.05
107	Roger Salkeld	.05
108	Jeff King	.05
109	Cecil Fielder	.05
110	Checklist	.05
111	Denny Neagle	.05
112	Troy Neel	.05
113	Rod Beck	.05
114	Alex Rodriguez	2.00
115	Joey Eischen	.05
116	Tom Candiotti	.05
117	Ray McDavid	.05
118	Vince Coleman	.05
119	Pete Harnisch	.05
120	David Nied	.05
121	Pat Rapp	.05
122	Sammy Sosa	.75
123	Steve Reed	.05
124	Jose Oliva	.05
125	Rick Bottalico	.05
126	Jose DeLeon	.05
127	Pat Hentgen	.05
128	Will Clark	.05
129	Mark Dewey	.05
130	Greg Vaughn	.05
131	Darren Dreifort	.05
132	Ed Sprague	.05
133	Lee Smith	.05
134	Charles Nagy	.05
135	Phil Plantier	.05
136	Jason Jacome	.05
137	Jose Lima	.05
138	J.R. Phillips	.05
139	J.T. Snow	.05
140	Mike Huff	.05
141	Billy Brewer	.05
142	Jeromy Burnitz	.05
143	Ricky Bones	.05
144	Carlos Rodriguez	.05
145	Luis Gonzalez	.05
146	Mark Lemke	.05
147	Al Martin	.05
148	Mike Bordick	.05
149	Robb Nen	.05
150	Wil Cordero	.05
151	Edgar Martinez	.05
152	Gerald Williams	.05
153	Esteban Beltre	.05
154	Mike Moore	.05
155	Mark Langston	.05
156	Mark Clark	.05
157	Bobby Ayala	.05
158	Rick Wilkins	.05
159	Bobby Munoz	.05
160	Checklist	.05
161	Scott Erickson	.05
162	Paul Molitor	.65
163	Jon Lieber	.05
164	Jason Grimsley	.05
165	Norberto Martin	.05
166	Javier Lopez	.05
167	Brian McRae	.05
168	Gary Sheffield	.40
169	Marcus Moore	.05
170	John Hudek	.05
171	Kelly Stinett	.05
172	Chris Gomez	.05
173	Rey Sanchez	.05
174	Juan Guzman	.05
175	Chan Ho Park	.05
176	Terry Shumpert	.05
177	Steve Ontiveros	.05
178	Brad Ausmus	.05
179	Tim Davis	.05
180	Billy Ashley	.05
181	Vinny Castilla	.05
182	Bill Spiers	.05
183	Randy Knorr	.05
184	Brian Hunter	.05
185	Pat Meares	.05
186	Steve Buechele	.05
187	Kirt Manwaring	.05
188	Tim Naehring	.05
189	Matt Mieske	.05
190	Josias Manzanillo	.05
191	Greg McMichael	.05
192	Chuck Carr	.05
193	Midre Cummings	.05
194	Darryl Strawberry	.05
195	Greg Gagne	.05
196	Steve Cooke	.05
197	Woody Williams	.05
198	Ron Karkovice	.05
199	Phil Leftwich	.05
200	Jim Thome	.50
201	Brady Anderson	.05
202	Pedro Martinez	.65
203	Steve Karsay	.05
204	Reggie Sanders	.05
205	Bill Risley	.05
206	Jay Bell	.05
207	Kevin Brown	.05
208	Tim Scott	.05
209	Len Dykstra	.05
210	Willie Greene	.05
211	Jim Eisenreich	.05
212	Cliff Floyd	.05
213	Otis Nixon	.05
214	Eduardo Perez	.05
215	Manuel Lee	.05
216	Armando Benitez RC	.10
217	Dave McCarty	.05
218	Scott Livingstone	.05
219	Chad Kreuter	.05
220	Checklist	.05
221	Brian Jordan	.05
222	Matt Whiteside	.05
223	Jim Edmonds	.05
224	Tony Gwynn	.75
225	Jose Lind	.05
226	Marvin Freeman	.05
227	Ken Hill	.05
228	David Hulse	.05
229	Joe Hesketh	.05
230	Roberto Petagine	.05
231	Jeffrey Hammonds	.05
232	John Jaha	.05
233	John Burkett	.05
234	Hal Morris	.05
235	Tony Castillo	.05
236	Ryan Bowen	.05
237	Wayne Kirby	.05
238	Brent Mayne	.05
239	Jim Bullinger	.05
240	Mike Lieberthal	.05
241	Barry Larkin	.05
242	David Segui	.05
243	Jose Bautista	.05
244	Hector Fajardo	.05
245	Orel Hershiser	.05
246	James Mouton	.05
247	Scott Leius	.05
248	Tom Glavine	.25
249	Danny Bautista	.05
250	Jose Mercedes	.05
251	Marquis Grissom	.05
252	Charlie Hayes	.05
253	Ryan Klesko	.05
254	Vicente Palacios	.05
255	Matias Carillo	.05
256	Gary DiSarcina	.05
257	Kirk Gibson	.05
258	Garey Ingram	.05
259	Alex Fernandez	.05
260	John Mabry	.05
261	Chris Howard	.05
262	Miguel Jimenez	.05
263	Heath Slocumb	.05
264	Albert Belle	.05
265	Dave Clark	.05
266	Joe Orsulak	.05
267	Joey Hamilton	.05
268	Mark Portugal	.05
269	Kevin Tapani	.05
270	Sid Fernandez	.05
271	Steve Dreyer	.05
272	Denny Hocking	.05
273	Troy O'Leary	.05
274	Milt Cuyler	.05
275	Frank Thomas	.05
276	Jorge Fabregas	.05
277	Mike Gallego	.05
278	Mickey Morandini	.05
279	Roberto Hernandez	.05
280	Henry Rodriguez	.05
281	Garret Anderson	.05
282	Bob Wickman	.05
283	Gar Finnvold	.05
284	Paul O'Neill	.05
285	Royce Clayton	.05
286	Chuck Knoblauch	.05
287	Johnny Ruffin	.05
288	Dave Nilsson	.05
289	David Cone	.05
290	Chuck McElroy	.05
291	Kevin Stocker	.05
292	Jose Rijo	.05
293	Sean Berry	.05
294	Ozzie Guillen	.05
295	Chris Hoiles	.05
296	Kevin Foster	.05
297	Jeff Frye	.05
298	Lance Johnson	.05
299	Mike Kelly	.05
300	Ellis Burks	.05
301	Roberto Kelly	.05
302	Dante Bichette	.05

303 Alvaro Espinoza	.05	421 Paul Wagner	.05
304 Alex Cole	.05	422 Geronimo Pena	.05
305 Rickey Henderson	.65	423 Ivan Rodriguez	.60
306 Dave Weathers	.05	424 Kevin Gross	.05
307 Shane Reynolds	.05	425 Kirk McCaskill	.05
308 Bobby Bonilla	.05	426 Greg Myers	.05
309 Junior Felix	.05	427 Roger Clemens	1.00
310 Jeff Fassero	.05	428 Chris Hammond	.05
311 Darren Lewis	.05	429 Randy Myers	.05
312 John Doherty	.05	430 Roger Mason	.05
313 Scott Servais	.05	431 Bret Saberhagen	.05
314 Rick Helling	.05	432 Jeff Reboulet	.05
315 Pedro Martinez	.65	433 John Olerud	.05
316 Wes Chamberlain	.05	434 Bill Gullickson	.05
317 Bryan Eversgerd	.05	435 Eddie Murray	.65
318 Trevor Hoffman	.05	436 Pedro Munoz	.05
319 John Patterson	.05	437 Charlie O'Brien	.05
320 Matt Walbeck	.05	438 Jeff Nelson	.05
321 Jeff Montgomery	.05	439 Mike Macfarlane	.05
322 Mel Rojas	.05	440 Checklist	.05
323 Eddie Taubensee	.05	441 Derrick May	.05
324 Ray Lankford	.05	442 John Roper	.05
325 Jose Vizcaino	.05	443 Darryl Hamilton	.05
326 Carlos Baerga	.05	444 Dan Miceli	.05
327 Jack Voigt	.05	445 Tony Eusebio	.05
328 Julio Franco	.05	446 Jerry Browne	.05
329 Brent Gates	.05	447 Wally Joyner	.05
330 Checklist	.05	448 Brian Harper	.05
331 Greg Maddux	.75	449 Scott Fletcher	.05
332 Jason Bere	.05	450 Bip Roberts	.05
333 Bill Wegman	.05	451 Pete Smith	.05
334 Tuffy Rhodes	.05	452 Chili Davis	.05
335 Kevin Young	.05	453 Dave Hollins	.05
336 Andy Benes	.05	454 Tony Pena	.05
337 Pedro Astacio	.05	455 Butch Henry	.05
338 Reggie Jefferson	.05	456 Craig Biggio	.05
339 Tim Belcher	.05	457 Zane Smith	.05
340 Ken Griffey Jr.	1.50	458 Ryan Thompson	.05
341 Mariano Duncan	.05	459 Mike Jackson	.05
342 Andres Galarraga	.05	460 Mark McGwire	2.00
343 Rondell White	.05	461 John Smoltz	.05
344 Cory Bailey	.05	462 Steve Scarsone	.05
345 Bryan Harvey	.05	463 Greg Colbrunn	.05
346 John Franco	.05	464 Shawn Green	.25
347 Greg Swindell	.05	465 David Wells	.05
348 David West	.05	466 Jose Hernandez	.05
349 Fred McGriff	.05	467 Chip Hale	.05
350 Jose Canseco	.35	468 Tony Tarasco	.05
351 Orlando Merced	.05	469 Kevin Mitchell	.05
352 Rheal Cormier	.05	470 Billy Hatcher	.05
353 Carlos Pulido	.05	471 Jay Buhner	.05
354 Terry Steinbach	.05	472 Ken Caminiti	.05
355 Wade Boggs	.75	473 Tom Henke	.05
356 B.J. Surhoff	.05	474 Todd Worrell	.05
357 Rafael Palmeiro	.60	475 Mark Eichhorn	.05
358 Anthony Young	.05	476 Bruce Ruffin	.05
359 Tom Brunansky	.05	477 Chuck Finley	.05
360 Todd Stottlemyre	.05	478 Marc Newfield	.05
361 Chris Turner	.05	479 Paul Shuey	.05
362 Joe Boever	.05	480 Bob Tewksbury	.05
363 Jeff Blauser	.05	481 Ramon Martinez	.05
364 Derek Bell	.05	482 Melvin Nieves	.05
365 Matt Williams	.05	483 Todd Zeile	.05
366 Jeremy Hernandez	.05	484 Benito Santiago	.05
367 Joe Girardi	.05	485 Stan Javier	.05
368 Mike Devereaux	.05	486 Kirk Rueter	.05
369 Jim Abbott	.05	487 Andre Dawson	.25
370 Manny Ramirez	.65	488 Eric Karros	.05
371 Kenny Lofton	.05	489 Dave Magadan	.05
372 Mark Smith	.05	490 Checklist	.05
373 Dave Fleming	.05	491 Randy Velarde	.05
374 Dave Stewart	.05	492 Larry Walker	.05
375 Roger Pavlik	.05	493 Cris Carpenter	.05
376 Hipolito Pichardo	.05	494 Tom Gordon	.05
377 Bill Taylor	.05	495 Dave Burba	.05
378 Robin Ventura	.05	496 Darren Bragg	.05
379 Bernard Gilkey	.05	497 Darren Daulton	.05
380 Kirby Puckett	.75	498 Don Slaught	.05
381 Steve Howe	.05	499 Pat Borders	.05
382 Devon White	.05	500 Lenny Harris	.05
383 Roberto Mejia	.05	501 Joe Ausanio	.05
384 Darrin Jackson	.05	502 Alan Trammell	.05
385 Mike Morgan	.05	503 Mike Fetters	.05
386 Rusty Meacham	.05	504 Scott Ruffcorn	.05
387 Bill Swift	.05	505 Rich Rowland	.05
388 Lou Frazier	.05	506 Juan Samuel	.05
389 Andy Van Slyke	.05	507 Bo Jackson	.10
390 Brett Butler	.05	508 Jeff Branson	.05
391 Bobby Witt	.05	509 Bernie Williams	.05
392 Jeff Conine	.05	510 Paul Sorrento	.05
393 Tim Hyers	.05	511 Dennis Eckersley	.60
394 Terry Pendleton	.05	512 Pat Mahomes	.05
395 Ricky Jordan	.05	513 Rusty Greer	.05
396 Eric Plunk	.05	514 Luis Polonia	.05
397 Melido Perez	.05	515 Willie Banks	.05
398 Darryl Kile	.05	516 John Wetteland	.05
399 Mark McLemore	.05	517 Mike LaValliere	.05
400 Greg Harris	.05	518 Tommy Greene	.05
401 Jim Leyritz	.05	519 Mark Grace	.05
402 Doug Strange	.05	520 Bob Hamelin	.05
403 Tim Salmon	.05	521 Scott Sanderson	.05
404 Terry Mulholland	.05	522 Joe Carter	.05
405 Robby Thompson	.05	523 Jeff Brantley	.05
406 Ruben Sierra	.05	524 Andrew Lorraine	.05
407 Tony Phillips	.05	525 Rico Brogna	.05
408 Moises Alou	.05	526 Shane Mack	.05
409 Felix Fermin	.05	527 Mark Wohlers	.05
410 Pat Listach	.05	528 Scott Sanders	.05
411 Kevin Bass	.05	529 Chris Bosio	.05
412 Ben McDonald	.05	530 Andujar Cedeno	.05
413 Scott Cooper	.05	531 Kenny Rogers	.05
414 Jody Reed	.05	532 Doug Drabek	.05
415 Deion Sanders	.05	533 Curt Leskanic	.05
416 Ricky Gutierrez	.05	534 Craig Shipley	.05
417 Gregg Jefferies	.05	535 Craig Grebeck	.05
418 Jack McDowell	.05	536 Cal Eldred	.05
419 Al Leiter	.05	537 Mickey Tettleton	.05
420 Tony Longmire	.05	538 Harold Baines	.05

539 Tim Wallach	.05
540 Damon Buford	.05
541 Lenny Webster	.05
542 Kevin Appier	.05
543 Raul Mondesi	.05
544 Eric Young	.05
545 Russ Davis	.05
546 Mike Benjamin	.05
547 Mike Greenwell	.05
548 Scott Brosius	.05
549 Brian Dorsett	.05
550 Checklist	.05

Press Proofs

Designated as Press Proofs, the first 2,000 cards of each player in the '95 Donruss set were enhanced with gold, rather than silver, foil and inserted into packs at an average rate of one per 20 packs.

	NM/M
Complete Set (550):	150.00
Common Player:	1.00
Stars:	15X

All-Stars

Exclusive to Wal-Mart jumbo packs were Donruss All-Stars. Nine cards featuring American Leaguers were inserted into Series 1, while nine National League All-Stars were inserted into Series 2 jumbos.

		NM/M
Complete Set (18):		26.00
Common Player:		.40
AL1	Jimmy Key	.40
AL2	Ivan Rodriguez	1.25
AL3	Frank Thomas	1.50
AL4	Roberto Alomar	.60
AL5	Wade Boggs	2.00
AL6	Cal Ripken, Jr.	4.50
AL7	Joe Carter	.40
AL8	Ken Griffey Jr.	3.00
AL9	Kirby Puckett	2.00
NL1	Greg Maddux	2.00
NL2	Mike Piazza	3.00
NL3	Gregg Jefferies	.40
NL4	Mariano Duncan	.40
NL5	Matt Williams	.40
NL6	Ozzie Smith	2.00
NL7	Barry Bonds	4.50
NL8	Tony Gwynn	2.00
NL9	Dave Justice	.40

Bomb Squad

Bomb Squad features the top six home run hitters in each league on double-sided cards. These cards were only inserted into Series I retail and magazine distributor packs at a rate of one per 24 retail packs and one per 16 magazine distributor packs.

	NM/M
Complete Set (6):	3.00
Common Player:	.50
1 Ken Griffey Jr., Matt Williams	1.00
2 Frank Thomas, Jeff Bagwell	.75
3 Albert Belle, Barry Bonds	1.50
4 Jose Canseco, Fred McGriff	.60
5 Cecil Fielder, Andres Galarraga	.50
6 Joe Carter, Kevin Mitchell	.50

Diamond Kings

Continuing a tradition begun in 1982, artist Dick Perez painted a series of 28 water colors to produce insert cards of the game's best; 14 in each series. A portrait of the player appears on a party-colored background, with Diamond Kings in gold across the top. DKs were inserted in Series 1 and 2 packs at a rate of one per 10.

		NM/M
Complete Set (29):		35.00
Common Player:		.75
1	Frank Thomas	3.00
2	Jeff Bagwell	3.00
3	Chili Davis	.75
4	Dante Bichette	.75
5	Ruben Sierra	.75
6	Jeff Conine	.75
7	Paul O'Neill	.75
8	Bobby Bonilla	.75
9	Joe Carter	.75
10	Moises Alou	.75
11	Kenny Lofton	.75
12	Matt Williams	.75
13	Kevin Seitzer	.75
14	Sammy Sosa	3.50
15	Scott Cooper	.75
16	Raul Mondesi	.75
17	Will Clark	.75
18	Lenny Dykstra	.75
19	Kirby Puckett	3.50
20	Hal Morris	.75
21	Travis Fryman	.75
22	Greg Maddux	3.50
23	Rafael Palmeiro	2.50
24	Tony Gwynn	3.50
25	David Cone	.75
26	Al Martin	.75
27	Ken Griffey Jr.	5.00
28	Gregg Jefferies	.75
29	Checklist	.10

Dominators

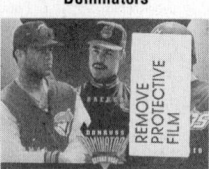

Dominators is a nine-card chase set inserted into hobby packs of Series II Donruss baseball at a rate of one per 24 packs. These acetate cards feature three of the top players at each position on a horizontal format.

	NM/M
Complete Set (9):	7.50
Common Player:	.50
1 David Cone, Mike Mussina, Greg Maddux	1.00
2 Ivan Rodriguez, Mike Piazza, Darren Daulton	.75
3 Fred McGriff, Frank Thomas, Jeff Bagwell	1.50
4 Roberto Alomar, Carlos Baerga, Craig Biggio	.75
5 Robin Ventura, Travis Fryman, Matt Williams	.50
6 Cal Ripken Jr., Barry Larkin, Wil Cordero	2.50

	NM/M
7 Albert Belle, Barry Bonds, Moises Alou	2.50
8 Ken Griffey Jr., Kenny Lofton, Marquis Grissom	2.00
9 Kirby Puckett, Paul O'Neill, Tony Gwynn	2.00

Elite

Another Donruss insert tradition continues with the fifth annual presentation of the Elite series. Each of the 12 cards (six each Series 1 and 2) is produced in a numbered edition of 10,000 and inserted into all types of packaging at the rate of one per 210 packs.

		NM/M
Complete Set (12):		100.00
Common Player:		6.00
49	Jeff Bagwell	12.00
50	Paul O'Neill	6.00
51	Greg Maddux	15.00
52	Mike Piazza	17.50
53	Matt Williams	6.00
54	Ken Griffey Jr.	17.50
55	Frank Thomas	12.00
56	Barry Bonds	20.00
57	Kirby Puckett	15.00
58	Fred McGriff	6.00
59	Jose Canseco	9.00
60	Albert Belle	6.00

Long Ball Leaders

Exclusive to Series 1 hobby packs, these cards feature the top long-distance home runs of 1994 in an eye-popping holographic foil presentation. Stated odds of picking one from a hobby pack are one in 24.

		NM/M
Complete Set (8):		7.50
Common Player:		.50
1	Frank Thomas	1.50
2	Fred McGriff	.50
3	Ken Griffey Jr.	2.00
4	Matt Williams	.50
5	Mike Piazza	2.00
6	Jose Canseco	.75
7	Barry Bonds	2.50
8	Jeff Bagwell	1.50

Mound Marvels

Mound Marvels is an eight-card insert set containing some of the best pitchers in baseball. Cards were inserted into one per 18 retail and magazine packs of Donruss Series II. Each card features a two-way mirror that allows collectors to see the players' face through the mirror.

	NM/M
Complete Set (8):	7.50
Common Player:	1.00

1	Greg Maddux	4.00
2	David Cone	1.00
3	Mike Mussina	2.00
4	Bret Saberhagen	1.00
5	Jimmy Key	1.00
6	Doug Drabek	1.00
7	Randy Johnson	3.00
8	Jason Bere	1.00

1995 Donruss/Top of the Order Card Game

In one of the earliest efforts to wed the play factor and collectibility that had made various fantasy card games so successful in 1994-95, Donruss created the interactive Top of the Order baseball card game. Printed on playing card stock with rounded corners and semi-gloss surface, the player cards feature color action photos and all manners of game-action indicators. Backs of each card are printed primarily in green with Donruss logos. Cards were sold in several types of packaging, including 80- and 160-card boxed sets, and 12-card foil "booster" packs. Stars' cards were printed in lesser quantities than those of journeyman players, resulting in values higher than would be the case based on player popularity alone if all cards were printed in equal quantities. The unnumbered cards are checklisted here in alphabetical order within team and league.

		NM/M
Complete Set (360):		125.00
Common Player:		.10
Starter Deck (80):		6.00
Starter Deck (160):		12.00
Wax Pack (12):		1.00
Wax Box (36):		20.00
(1)	Brady Anderson	.10
(2)	Harold Baines	.10
(3)	Bret Barberie	.10
(4)	Armando Benitez	.10
(5)	Bobby Bonilla	.10
(6)	Scott Erickson	.10
(7)	Leo Gomez	.10
(8)	Curtis Goodwin	.10
(9)	Jeffrey Hammonds	.10
(10)	Chris Hoiles	.10
(11)	Doug Jones	.10
(12)	Ben McDonald	.10
(13)	Mike Mussina	1.50
(14)	Rafael Palmeiro	2.50
(15)	Cal Ripken Jr.	10.00
(16)	Rick Aguilera	.10
(17)	Luis Alicea	.10
(18)	Jose Canseco	1.50
(19)	Roger Clemens	5.00
(20)	Mike Greenwell	.10
(21)	Erik Hanson	.10
(22)	Mike Macfarlane	.10
(23)	Tim Naehring	.10
(24)	Troy O'Leary	.10
(25)	Ken Ryan	.10
(26)	Aaron Sele	.10
(27)	Lee Tinsley	.10
(28)	John Valentin	.10
(29)	Mo Vaughn	.10
(30)	Jim Abbott	.10
(31)	Mike Butcher	.10
(32)	Chili Davis	.10
(33)	Gary DiSarcina	.10
(34)	Damion Easley	.10
(35)	Jim Edmonds	.10
(36)	Chuck Finley	.10
(37)	Mark Langston	.10
(38)	Greg Myers	.10
(39)	Spike Owen	.10
(40)	Troy Percival	.10
(41)	Tony Phillips	.10
(42)	Tim Salmon	.10
(43)	Lee Smith	.10
(44)	J.T. Snow	.10
(45)	Jason Bere	.10
(46)	Mike Devereaux	.10
(47)	Ray Durham	.10
(48)	Alex Fernandez	.10
(49)	Ozzie Guillen	.10

No.	Player	Price
(50)	Roberto Hernandez	.10
(51)	Lance Johnson	.10
(52)	Ron Karkovice	.10
(53)	Tim Raines	.10
(54)	Frank Thomas	3.00
(55)	Robin Ventura	.10
(56)	Sandy Alomar Jr.	.10
(57)	Carlos Baerga	.10
(58)	Albert Belle	.10
(59)	Kenny Lofton	.10
(60)	Dennis Martinez	.10
(61)	Jose Mesa	.10
(62)	Eddie Murray	3.00
(63)	Charles Nagy	.10
(64)	Tony Pena	.10
(65)	Eric Plunk	.10
(66)	Manny Ramirez	3.00
(67)	Paul Sorrento	.10
(68)	Jim Thome	2.00
(69)	Omar Vizquel	.10
(70)	Danny Bautista	.10
(71)	Joe Boever	.10
(72)	Chad Curtis	.10
(73)	Cecil Fielder	.10
(74)	John Flaherty	.10
(75)	Travis Fryman	.10
(76)	Kirk Gibson	.10
(77)	Chris Gomez	.10
(78)	Mike Henneman	.10
(79)	Bob Higginson	.10
(80)	Alan Trammell	.10
(81)	Lou Whitaker	.10
(82)	Kevin Appier	.10
(83)	Billy Brewer	.10
(84)	Vince Coleman	.10
(85)	Gary Gaetti	.10
(86)	Greg Gagne	.10
(87)	Tom Goodwin	.10
(88)	Tom Gordon	.10
(89)	Mark Gubicza	.10
(90)	Bob Hamelin	.10
(91)	Phil Hiatt	.10
(92)	Wally Joyner	.10
(93)	Brent Mayne	.10
(94)	Jeff Montgomery	.10
(95)	Ricky Bones	.10
(96)	Mike Fetters	.10
(97)	Darryl Hamilton	.10
(98)	Pat Listach	.10
(99)	Matt Mieske	.10
(100)	Dave Nilsson	.10
(101)	Joe Oliver	.10
(102)	Kevin Seitzer	.10
(103)	B.J. Surhoff	.10
(104)	Jose Valentin	.10
(105)	Greg Vaughn	.10
(106)	Bill Wegman	.10
(107)	Alex Cole	.10
(108)	Marty Cordova	.10
(109)	Chuck Knoblauch	.10
(110)	Scott Leius	.10
(111)	Pat Meares	.10
(112)	Pedro Munoz	.10
(113)	Kirby Puckett	4.00
(114)	Scott Stahoviak	.10
(115)	Mike Trombley	.10
(116)	Matt Walbeck	.10
(117)	Wade Boggs	4.00
(118)	David Cone	.10
(119)	Tony Fernandez	.10
(120)	Don Mattingly	5.00
(121)	Jack McDowell	.10
(122)	Paul O'Neill	.10
(123)	Melido Perez	.10
(124)	Luis Polonia	.10
(125)	Ruben Sierra	.10
(126)	Mike Stanley	.10
(127)	Randy Velarde	.10
(128)	John Wetteland	.10
(129)	Bob Wickman	.10
(130)	Bernie Williams	.10
(131)	Gerald Williams	.10
(132)	Geronimo Berroa	.10
(133)	Mike Bordick	.10
(134)	Scott Brosius	.10
(135)	Dennis Eckersley	.10
(136)	Brent Gates	.10
(137)	Rickey Henderson	3.00
(138)	Stan Javier	.10
(139)	Mark McGwire	8.00
(140)	Steve Ontiveros	.10
(141)	Terry Steinbach	.10
(142)	Todd Stottlemyre	.10
(143)	Danny Tartabull	.10
(144)	Bobby Ayala	.10
(145)	Andy Benes	.10
(146)	Mike Blowers	.10
(147)	Jay Buhner	.10
(148)	Joey Cora	.10
(149)	Alex Diaz	.10
(150)	Ken Griffey Jr.	6.00
(151)	Randy Johnson	3.00
(152)	Edgar Martinez	.10
(153)	Tino Martinez	.10
(154)	Bill Risley	.10
(155)	Alex Rodriguez	8.00
(156)	Dan Wilson	.10
(157)	Will Clark	.10
(158)	Jeff Frye	.10
(159)	Benji Gil	.10
(160)	Juan Gonzalez	1.50
(161)	Rusty Greer	.10
(162)	Mark McLemore	.10
(163)	Otis Nixon	.10
(164)	Dean Palmer	.10
(165)	Ivan Rodriguez	2.50
(166)	Kenny Rogers	.10
(167)	Jeff Russell	.10
(168)	Mickey Tettleton	.10
(169)	Bob Tewksbury	.10
(170)	Bobby Witt	.10
(171)	Roberto Alomar	.30
(172)	Joe Carter	.10
(173)	Alex Gonzalez	.10
(174)	Candy Maldonado	.10
(175)	Paul Molitor	3.00
(176)	John Olerud	.10
(177)	Lance Parrish	.10
(178)	Ed Sprague	.10
(179)	Devon White	.10
(180)	Woody Williams	.10
(181)	Steve Avery	.10
(182)	Jeff Blauser	.10
(183)	Tom Glavine	.50
(184)	Marquis Grissom	.10
(185)	Chipper Jones	4.00
(186)	Dave Justice	.10
(187)	Ryan Klesko	.10
(188)	Mark Lemke	.10
(189)	Javier Lopez	.10
(190)	Greg Maddux	4.00
(191)	Fred McGriff	.10
(192)	Greg McMichael	.10
(193)	John Smoltz	.10
(194)	Mark Wohlers	.10
(195)	Jim Bullinger	.10
(196)	Shawon Dunston	.10
(197)	Kevin Foster	.10
(198)	Luis Gonzalez	.10
(199)	Mark Grace	.10
(200)	Brian McRae	.10
(201)	Randy Myers	.10
(202)	Jaime Navarro	.10
(203)	Rey Sanchez	.10
(204)	Scott Servais	.10
(205)	Sammy Sosa	4.00
(206)	Steve Trachsel	.10
(207)	Todd Zeile	.10
(208)	Bret Boone	.10
(209)	Jeff Branson	.10
(210)	Jeff Brantley	.10
(211)	Hector Carrasco	.10
(212)	Ron Gant	.10
(213)	Lenny Harris	.10
(214)	Barry Larkin	.10
(215)	Darren Lewis	.10
(216)	Hal Morris	.10
(217)	Mark Portugal	.10
(218)	Jose Rijo	.10
(219)	Reggie Sanders	.10
(220)	Pete Schourek	.10
(221)	John Smiley	.10
(222)	Eddie Taubensee	.10
(223)	Dave Wells	.10
(224)	Jason Bates	.10
(225)	Dante Bichette	.10
(226)	Vinny Castilla	.10
(227)	Andres Galarraga	.10
(228)	Joe Girardi	.10
(229)	Mike Kingery	.10
(230)	Steve Reed	.10
(231)	Bruce Ruffin	.10
(232)	Bret Saberhagen	.10
(233)	Bill Swift	.10
(234)	Larry Walker	.10
(235)	Walt Weiss	.10
(236)	Eric Young	.10
(237)	Kurt Abbott	.10
(238)	John Burkett	.10
(239)	Chuck Carr	.10
(240)	Greg Colbrunn	.10
(241)	Jeff Conine	.10
(242)	Andre Dawson	.35
(243)	Chris Hammond	.10
(244)	Charles Johnson	.10
(245)	Robb Nen	.10
(246)	Terry Pendleton	.10
(247)	Gary Sheffield	.50
(248)	Quilvio Veras	.10
(249)	Jeff Bagwell	3.00
(250)	Derek Bell	.10
(251)	Craig Biggio	.10
(252)	Doug Drabek	.10
(253)	Tony Eusebio	.10
(254)	John Hudek	.10
(255)	Brian Hunter	.10
(256)	Todd Jones	.10
(257)	Dave Magadan	.10
(258)	Orlando Miller	.10
(259)	James Mouton	.10
(260)	Shane Reynolds	.10
(261)	Greg Swindell	.10
(262)	Billy Ashley	.10
(263)	Tom Candiotti	.10
(264)	Delino DeShields	.10
(265)	Eric Karros	.10
(266)	Roberto Kelly	.10
(267)	Ramon Martinez	.10
(268)	Raul Mondesi	.10
(269)	Hideo Nomo	1.50
(270)	Jose Offerman	.10
(271)	Mike Piazza	6.00
(272)	Kevin Tapani	.10
(273)	Ismael Valdes	.10
(274)	Tim Wallach	.10
(275)	Todd Worrell	.10
(276)	Moises Alou	.10
(277)	Sean Berry	.10
(278)	Wil Cordero	.10
(279)	Jeff Fassero	.10
(280)	Darrin Fletcher	.10
(281)	Mike Lansing	.10
(282)	Pedro J. Martinez	3.00
(283)	Carlos Perez	.10
(284)	Mel Rojas	.10
(285)	Tim Scott	.10
(286)	David Segui	.10
(287)	Tony Tarasco	.10
(288)	Rondell White	.10
(289)	Rico Brogna	.10
(290)	Brett Butler	.10
(291)	John Franco	.10
(292)	Pete Harnisch	.10
(293)	Todd Hundley	.10
(294)	Bobby Jones	.10
(295)	Jeff Kent	.10
(296)	Joe Orsulak	.10
(297)	Ryan Thompson	.10
(298)	Jose Vizcaino	.10
(299)	Ricky Bottalico	.10
(300)	Darren Daulton	.10
(301)	Mariano Duncan	.10
(302)	Lenny Dykstra	.10
(303)	Jim Eisenreich	.10
(304)	Tyler Green	.10
(305)	Charlie Hayes	.10
(306)	Dave Hollins	.10
(307)	Gregg Jefferies	.10
(308)	Mickey Morandini	.10
(309)	Curt Schilling	.50
(310)	Heathcliff Slocumb	.10
(311)	Kevin Stocker	.10
(312)	Jay Bell	.10
(313)	Jacob Brumfield	.10
(314)	Dave Clark	.10
(315)	Carlos Garcia	.10
(316)	Mark Johnson	.10
(317)	Jeff King	.10
(318)	Nelson Liriano	.10
(319)	Al Martin	.10
(320)	Orlando Merced	.10
(321)	Dan Miceli	.10
(322)	Denny Neagle	.10
(323)	Mark Parent	.10
(324)	Dan Plesac	.10
(325)	Scott Cooper	.10
(326)	Bernard Gilkey	.10
(327)	Tom Henke	.10
(328)	Ken Hill	.10
(329)	Danny Jackson	.10
(330)	Brian Jordan	.10
(331)	Ray Lankford	.10
(332)	John Mabry	.10
(333)	Jose Oquendo	.10
(334)	Tom Pagnozzi	.10
(335)	Ozzie Smith	4.00
(336)	Andy Ashby	.10
(337)	Brad Ausmus	.10
(338)	Ken Caminiti	.10
(339)	Andujar Cedeno	.10
(340)	Steve Finley	.10
(341)	Tony Gwynn	4.00
(342)	Joey Hamilton	.10
(343)	Trevor Hoffman	.10
(344)	Jody Reed	.10
(345)	Bip Roberts	.10
(346)	Eddie Williams	.10
(347)	Rod Beck	.10
(348)	Mike Benjamin	.10
(349)	Barry Bonds	10.00
(350)	Royce Clayton	.10
(351)	Glenallen Hill	.10
(352)	Kirt Manwaring	.10
(353)	Terry Mulholland	.10
(354)	John Patterson	.10
(355)	J.R. Phillips	.10
(356)	Deion Sanders	.25
(357)	Steve Scarsone	.10
(358)	Robby Thompson	.10
(359)	William VanLandingham	.10
(360)	Matt Williams	.10

1996 Donruss Samples

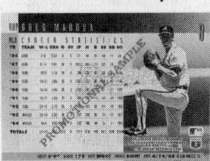

To introduce its 1996 series to dealers and the hobby press, Donruss issued an eight-card sample set. Identical in format to the issued version, the samples are numbered differently from the same players' cards in the regular issue (except #1, Frank Thomas). The samples also differ in that they lack 1995 stats on back, may have slightly different wording in the career highlights, and have printed on front and back a diagonal gray "PROMOTIONAL SAMPLE."

		NM/M
Complete Set (8):		9.00
Common Player:		1.00
1	Frank Thomas	1.00
2	Barry Bonds	2.50
3	Hideo Nomo	1.50
4	Ken Griffey Jr.	1.50
5	Cal Ripken Jr.	2.50
6	Manny Ramirez	1.00
7	Mike Piazza	1.50
8	Greg Maddux	1.25

1996 Donruss

DANTE BICHETTE

A clean, borderless look marks the 1996 Donruss regular-issue cards. Besides the player name in white inside a fading team-color stripe at top-right, the only graphic enhancement on front is a 7/8" square foil box at bottom-center with the company and team name, team logo, player position and uniform number. The foil box is enhanced with team colors, which are carried over to the horizontal backs. Backs also feature a color action photo, a large gray team logo, stats and career highlights. Basic packaging was 12-card foil packs with a suggested retail price of $1.79. Several types of insert cards were offered, each at a virtually unprecedented rate of scarcity. The set was issued in two series; Series 1 with 330 cards, Series 2 with 220 cards.

		NM/M
Complete Set (550):		20.00
Complete Series 1 (330):		12.00
Complete Series 2 (220):		10.00
Common Player:		.05
Press Proofs:		7X
Series 1 Pack (12):		1.00
Series 1 Wax Box (36):		20.00
Series 2 Pack (12):		1.00
Series 2 Wax Box (18):		12.50
1	Frank Thomas	1.00
2	Jason Bates	.05
3	Steve Sparks	.05
4	Scott Servais	.05
5	Angelo Encarnacion	.05
6	Scott Sanders	.05
7	Billy Ashley	.05
8	Alex Rodriguez	2.00
9	Sean Bergman	.05
10	Brad Radke	.05
11	Andy Van Slyke	.05
12	Joe Girardi	.05
13	Mark Grudzielanek	.05
14	Rick Aguilera	.05
15	Randy Veres	.05
16	Tim Bogar	.05
17	Dave Veres	.05
18	Kevin Stocker	.05
19	Marquis Grissom	.05
20	Will Clark	.05
21	Jay Bell	.05
22	Allen Battle	.05
23	Frank Rodriguez	.05
24	Terry Steinbach	.05
25	Gerald Williams	.05
26	Sid Roberson	.05
27	Gregg Zaun	.05
28	Ozzie Timmons	.05
29	Vaughn Eshelman	.05
30	Ed Sprague	.05
31	Gary DiSarcina	.05
32	Joe Boever	.05
33	Steve Avery	.05
34	Brad Ausmus	.05
35	Kirt Manwaring	.05
36	Gary Sheffield	.25
37	Jason Bere	.05
38	Jeff Manto	.05
39	David Cone	.05
40	Manny Ramirez	1.00
41	Sandy Alomar	.05
42	Curtis Goodwin/RR	.05
43	Tino Martinez	.05
44	Woody Williams	.05
45	Dean Palmer	.05
46	Hipolito Pichardo	.05
47	Jason Giambi	.60
48	Lance Johnson	.05
49	Bernard Gilkey	.05
50	Kirby Puckett	1.25
51	Tony Fernandez	.05
52	Alex Gonzalez	.05
53	Bret Saberhagen	.05
54	Lyle Mouton/RR	.05
55	Brian McRae	.05
56	Mark Gubicza	.05
57	Sergio Valdez	.05
58	Darrin Fletcher	.05
59	Steve Parris	.05
60	Johnny Damon/RR	.35
61	Rickey Henderson	1.00
62	Darrell Whitmore	.05
63	Roberto Petagine	.05
64	Trenidad Hubbard	.05
65	Heathcliff Slocumb	.05
66	Steve Finley	.05
67	Mariano Rivera	.25
68	Brian Hunter	.05
69	Jamie Moyer	.05
70	Ellis Burks	.05
71	Pat Kelly	.05
72	Mickey Tettleton	.05
73	Garret Anderson	.05
74	Andy Pettitte/RR	.75
75	Glenallen Hill	.05
76	Brent Gates	.05
77	Lou Whitaker	.05
78	David Segui	.05
79	Dan Wilson	.05
80	Pat Listach	.05
81	Jeff Bagwell	1.00
82	Ben McDonald	.05
83	John Valentin	.05
84	John Jaha	.05
85	Pete Schourek	.05
86	Bryce Florie	.05
87	Brian Jordan	.05
88	Ron Karkovice	.05
89	Al Leiter	.05
90	Tony Longmire	.05
91	Nelson Liriano	.05
92	David Bell	.05
93	Kevin Gross	.05
94	Tom Candiotti	.05
95	Dave Martinez	.05
96	Greg Myers	.05
97	Rheal Cormier	.05
98	Chris Hammond	.05
99	Randy Myers	.05
100	Bill Pulsipher/RR	.05
101	Jason Isringhausen/RR	.05
102	Dave Stevens	.05
103	Roberto Alomar	.20
104	Bob Higginson/RR	.05
105	Eddie Murray	1.00
106	Matt Walbeck	.05
107	Mark Wohlers	.05
108	Jeff Nelson	.05
109	Tom Goodwin	.05
110	Checklist 1-83	
	Cal Ripken Jr. (2,131 Consecutive Games)	1.25
111	Rey Sanchez	.05
112	Hector Carrasco	.05
113	B.J. Surhoff	.05
114	Dan Miceli	.05
115	Dean Hartgraves	.05
116	John Burkett	.05
117	Gary Gaetti	.05
118	Ricky Bones	.05
119	Mike Macfarlane	.05
120	Bip Roberts	.05
121	Dave Mlicki	.05
122	Chili Davis	.05
123	Mark Whiten	.05
124	Herbert Perry	.05
125	Butch Henry	.05
126	Derek Bell	.05
127	Al Martin	.05
128	John Franco	.05
129	William Van Landingham	.05
130	Mike Bordick	.05
131	Mike Mordecai	.05
132	Robby Thompson	.05
133	Greg Colbrunn	.05
134	Domingo Cedeno	.05
135	Chad Curtis	.05
136	Jose Hernandez	.05
137	Scott Klingenbeck	.05
138	Ryan Klesko	.05
139	John Smiley	.05
140	Charlie Hayes	.05
141	Jay Buhner	.05
142	Doug Drabek	.05
143	Roger Pavlik	.05
144	Todd Worrell	.05
145	Cal Ripken Jr.	2.50
146	Steve Reed	.05
147	Chuck Finley	.05
148	Mike Blowers	.05
149	Orel Hershiser	.05
150	Allen Watson	.05
151	Ramon Martinez	.05
152	Melvin Nieves	.05
153	Tripp Cromer	.05
154	Yorkis Perez	.05
155	Stan Javier	.05
156	Mel Rojas	.05
157	Aaron Sele	.05
158	Eric Karros	.05
159	Robb Nen	.05
160	Raul Mondesi	.05
161	John Wetteland	.05
162	Tim Scott	.05
163	Kenny Rogers	.05
164	Melvin Bunch	.05
165	Rod Beck	.05
166	Andy Benes	.05
167	Lenny Dykstra	.05
168	Orlando Merced	.05
169	Tomas Perez	.05
170	Xavier Hernandez	.05
171	Ruben Sierra	.05
172	Alan Trammell	.05
173	Mike Fetters	.05
174	Wilson Alvarez	.05
175	Erik Hanson	.05
176	Travis Fryman	.05
177	Jim Abbott	.05
178	Bret Boone	.05
179	Sterling Hitchcock	.05
180	Pat Mahomes	.05
181	Mark Acre	.05
182	Charles Nagy	.05
183	Rusty Greer	.05
184	Mike Stanley	.05
185	Jim Bullinger	.05
186	Shane Andrews	.05
187	Brian Keyser	.05
188	Tyler Green	.05
189	Mark Grace	.05
190	Bob Hamelin	.05
191	Luis Ortiz	.05
192	Joe Carter	.05
193	Eddie Taubensee	.05
194	Brian Anderson	.05
195	Edgardo Alfonzo	.05
196	Pedro Munoz	.05
197	David Justice	.05
198	Trevor Hoffman	.05
199	Bobby Ayala	.05
200	Tony Eusebio	.05
201	Jeff Russell	.05
202	Mike Hampton	.05
203	Walt Weiss	.05
204	Joey Hamilton	.05
205	Roberto Hernandez	.05
206	Greg Vaughn	.05
207	Felipe Lira	.05
208	Harold Baines	.05
209	Tim Wallach	.05
210	Manny Alexander	.05
211	Tim Laker	.05
212	Chris Haney	.05
213	Brian Maxcy	.05
214	Eric Young	.05
215	Darryl Strawberry	.05
216	Barry Bonds	2.50
217	Tim Naehring	.05
218	Scott Brosius	.05
219	Reggie Sanders	.05
220	Checklist 84-166	
	Eddie Murray (3,000 Career Hits)	.35
221	Luis Alicea	.05
222	Albert Belle	.05
223	Benji Gil	.05
224	Dante Bichette	.05
225	Bobby Bonilla	.05
226	Todd Stottlemyre	.05
227	Jim Edmonds	.05
228	Todd Jones	.05
229	Shawn Green	.25
230	Javy Lopez	.05
231	Ariel Prieto	.05
232	Tony Phillips	.05
233	James Mouton	.05
234	Jose Oquendo	.05
235	Royce Clayton	.05
236	Chuck Carr	.05
237	Doug Jones	.05
238	Mark Mclemore (McLemore)	.05
239	Bill Swift	.05
240	Scott Leius	.05
241	Russ Davis	.05
242	Ray Durham/RR	.05
243	Matt Mieske	.05
244	Brent Mayne	.05
245	Thomas Howard	.05
246	Troy O'Leary	.05
247	Jacob Brumfield	.05
248	Mickey Morandini	.05
249	Todd Hundley	.05
250	Chris Bosio	.05
251	Omar Vizquel	.05
252	Mike Lansing	.05
253	John Mabry	.05
254	Mike Perez	.05
255	Delino DeShields	.05
256	Wil Cordero	.05
257	Mike James	.05
258	Todd Van Poppel	.05
259	Joey Cora	.05
260	Andre Dawson	.25
261	Jerry DiPoto	.05
262	Rick Krivda	.05
263	Glenn Dishman	.05
264	Mike Mimbs	.05
265	John Ericks	.05
266	Jose Canseco	.35
267	Jeff Branson	.05
268	Curt Leskanic	.05
269	Jon Nunnally	.05
270	Scott Stahoviak	.05
271	Jeff Montgomery	.05
272	Hal Morris	.05
273	Esteban Loaiza	.05
274	Rico Brogna	.05
275	Dave Winfield	1.00
276	J.R. Phillips	.05
277	Todd Zeile	.05
278	Tom Pagnozzi	.05
279	Mark Lemke	.05
280	Dave Magadan	.05
281	Greg McMichael	.05
282	Mike Morgan	.05
283	Moises Alou	.05
284	Dennis Martinez	.05
285	Jeff Kent	.05
286	Mark Johnson	.05
287	Darren Lewis	.05
288	Brad Clontz	.05
289	Chad Fonville/RR	.05
290	Paul Sorrento	.05

#	Player	Price
291	Lee Smith	.05
292	Tom Glavine	.25
293	Antonio Osuna	.05
294	Kevin Foster	.05
295	Sandy Martinez RC	.05
296	Mark Leiter	.05
297	Julian Tavarez	.05
298	Mike Kelly	.05
299	Joe Oliver	.05
300	John Flaherty	.05
301	Don Mattingly	1.50
302	Pat Meares	.05
303	John Doherty	.05
304	Joe Vitiello	.05
305	Vinny Castilla	.05
306	Jeff Brantley	.05
307	Mike Greenwell	.05
308	Midre Cummings	.05
309	Curt Schilling	.25
310	Ken Caminiti	.05
311	Scott Erickson	.05
312	Carl Everett	.05
313	Charles Johnson	.05
314	Alex Diaz	.05
315	Jose Mesa	.05
316	Mark Carreon	.05
317	Carlos Perez/RR	.05
318	Ismael Valdes	.05
319	Frank Castillo	.05
320	Tom Henke	.05
321	Spike Owen	.05
322	Joe Orsulak	.05
323	Paul Menhart	.05
324	Pedro Borbon	.05
325	Checklist 167-249 Paul Molitor (1,000 Career RBI)	.35
326	Jeff Cirillo	.05
327	Edwin Hurtado	.05
328	Orlando Miller	.05
329	Steve Ontiveros	.05
330	Checklist 250-330 Kirby Puckett (1,000 Career RBI)	.75
331	Scott Bullett	.05
332	Andres Galarraga	.05
333	Cal Eldred	.05
334	Sammy Sosa	1.25
335	Don Slaught	.05
336	Jody Reed	.05
337	Roger Cedeno	.05
338	Ken Griffey Jr.	1.75
339	Todd Hollandsworth	.05
340	Mike Trombley	.05
341	Gregg Jefferies	.05
342	Larry Walker	.05
343	Pedro Martinez	.05
344	Dwayne Hosey	.05
345	Terry Pendleton	.05
346	Pete Harnisch	.05
347	Tony Castillo	.05
348	Paul Quantrill	.05
349	Fred McGriff	.05
350	Ivan Rodriguez	.65
351	Butch Huskey	.05
352	Ozzie Smith	1.25
353	Marty Cordova	.05
354	John Wasdin	.05
355	Wade Boggs	1.25
356	Dave Nilsson	.05
357	Rafael Palmeiro	.65
358	Luis Gonzalez	.05
359	Reggie Jefferson	.05
360	Carlos Delgado	.60
361	Orlando Palmeiro	.05
362	Chris Gomez	.05
363	John Smoltz	.05
364	Marc Newfield	.05
365	Matt Williams	.05
366	Jesus Tavarez	.05
367	Bruce Ruffin	.05
368	Sean Berry	.05
369	Randy Velarde	.05
370	Tony Pena	.05
371	Jim Thome	.60
372	Jeffrey Hammonds	.05
373	Bob Wolcott	.05
374	Juan Guzman	.05
375	Juan Gonzalez	.50
376	Michael Tucker	.05
377	Doug Johns	.05
378	Mike Cameron RC	.75
379	Ray Lankford	.05
380	Jose Parra	.05
381	Jimmy Key	.05
382	John Olerud	.05
383	Kevin Ritz	.05
384	Tim Raines	.05
385	Rich Amaral	.05
386	Keith Lockhart	.05
387	Steve Scarsone	.05
388	Cliff Floyd	.05
389	Rich Aude	.05
390	Hideo Nomo	.50
391	Geronimo Berroa	.05
392	Pat Rapp	.05
393	Dustin Hermanson	.05
394	Greg Maddux	1.25
395	Darren Daulton	.05
396	Kenny Lofton	.05
397	Ruben Rivera	.05
398	Billy Wagner	.05
399	Kevin Brown	.05
400	Mike Kingery	.05
401	Bernie Williams	.05
402	Otis Nixon	.05
403	Damion Easley	.05
404	Paul O'Neill	.05
405	Deion Sanders	.05
406	Dennis Eckersley	1.00
407	Tony Clark	.05
408	Rondell White	.05
409	Luis Sojo	.05
410	David Hulse	.05
411	Shane Reynolds	.05
412	Chris Hoiles	.05
413	Lee Tinsley	.05
414	Scott Karl	.05
415	Ron Gant	.05
416	Brian Johnson	.05
417	Jose Oliva	.05
418	Jack McDowell	.05
419	Paul Molitor	1.00
420	Ricky Bottalico	.05
421	Paul Wagner	.05
422	Terry Bradshaw	.05
423	Bob Tewksbury	.05
424	Mike Piazza	1.75
425	Luis Andujar RC	.05
426	Mark Langston	.05
427	Stan Belinda	.05
428	Kurt Abbott	.05
429	Shawon Dunston	.05
430	Bobby Jones	.05
431	Jose Vizcaino	.05
432	Matt Lawton RC	.05
433	Pat Hentgen	.05
434	Cecil Fielder	.05
435	Carlos Baerga	.05
436	Rich Becker	.05
437	Chipper Jones	1.25
438	Bill Risley	.05
439	Kevin Appier	.05
440	Checklist	
441	Jaime Navarro	.05
442	Barry Larkin	.05
443	Jose Valentin RC	.05
444	Bryan Rekar	.05
445	Rick Wilkins	.05
446	Quilvio Veras	.05
447	Greg Gagne	.05
448	Mark Kiefer	.05
449	Bobby Witt	.05
450	Andy Ashby	.05
451	Alex Ochoa	.05
452	Jorge Fabregas	.05
453	Gene Schall	.05
454	Ken Hill	.05
455	Tony Tarasco	.05
456	Donnie Wall	.05
457	Carlos Garcia	.05
458	Ryan Thompson	.05
459	Marvin Benard RC	.05
460	Jose Herrera	.05
461	Jeff Blauser	.05
462	Chris Hook	.05
463	Jeff Conine	.05
464	Devon White	.05
465	Danny Bautista	.05
466	Steve Trachsel	.05
467	C.J. Nitkowski	.05
468	Mike Devereaux	.05
469	David Wells	.05
470	Jim Eisenreich	.05
471	Edgar Martinez	.05
472	Craig Biggio	.05
473	Jeff Frye	.05
474	Karim Garcia	.05
475	Jimmy Haynes	.05
476	Darren Holmes	.05
477	Tim Salmon	.05
478	Randy Johnson	1.00
479	Eric Plunk	.05
480	Scott Cooper	.05
481	Chan Ho Park	.05
482	Ray McDavid	.05
483	Mark Petkovsek	.05
484	Greg Swindell	.05
485	George Williams	.05
486	Yamil Benitez	.05
487	Tim Wakefield	.05
488	Kevin Tapani	.05
489	Derrick May	.05
490	Checklist (Ken Griffey Jr.)	1.00
491	Derek Jeter	2.50
492	Jeff Fassero	.05
493	Benito Santiago	.05
494	Tom Gordon	.05
495	Jamie Brewington	.05
496	Vince Coleman	.05
497	Kevin Jordan	.05
498	Jeff King	.05
499	Mike Simms	.05
500	Jose Rijo	.05
501	Denny Neagle	.05
502	Jose Lima	.05
503	Kevin Seitzer	.05
504	Alex Fernandez	.05
505	Mo Vaughn	.05
506	Phil Nevin	.05
507	J.T. Snow	.05
508	Andujar Cedeno	.05
509	Ozzie Guillen	.05
510	Mark Clark	.05
511	Mark McGwire	2.00
512	Jeff Reboulet	.05
513	Armando Benitez	.05
514	LaTroy Hawkins	.05
515	Brett Butler	.05
516	Tavo Alvarez	.05
517	Chris Snopek	.05
518	Mike Mussina	.50
519	Darryl Kile	.05
520	Wally Joyner	.05
521	Willie McGee	.05
522	Kent Mercker	.05
523	Mike Jackson	.05
524	Troy Percival	.05
525	Tony Gwynn	1.25
526	Ron Coomer	.05
527	Darryl Hamilton	.05
528	Phil Plantier	.05
529	Norm Charlton	.05
530	Craig Paquette	.05
531	Dave Burba	.05
532	Mike Henneman	.05
533	Terrell Wade	.05
534	Eddie Williams	.05
535	Robin Ventura	.05
536	Chuck Knoblauch	.05
537	Les Norman	.05
538	Brady Anderson	.05
539	Roger Clemens	1.50
540	Mark Portugal	.05
541	Mike Matheny	.05
542	Jeff Parrett	.05
543	Roberto Kelly	.05
544	Damon Buford	.05
545	Chad Ogea	.05
546	Jose Offerman	.05
547	Brian Barber	.05
548	Danny Tartabull	.05
549	Duane Singleton	.05
550	Checklist (Tony Gwynn)	.75

1996 Donruss Press Proofs

The first 2,000 of each regular card issued in the 1996 Donruss set are distinguished by the addition of a gold-foil "PRESS PROOF" stamped along the right side. As opposed to regular-issue cards which have silver-and-black card numbers and personal data strip at bottom, the Press Proof cards have those elements printed in black-on-gold. Stated odds of finding a Press Proof are one per 12 packs in Series 1, one per 10 packs in Series 2, on average.

	NM/M
Complete Set (550):	150.00
Common Player:	.50

Diamond Kings

The most "common" of the '96 Donruss inserts are the popular Diamond Kings, featuring the portraits of Dick Perez on a black background within a mottled gold-foil frame. Once again, the DKs feature one player from each team, with 14 issued in each of Series 1 and 2. Like all '96 Donruss inserts, the DKs are numbered on back, within an edition of 10,000. Also on back are color action photos and career highlights. Diamond Kings are inserted at the rate of one per 60 foil packs (Series 1), and one per 30 packs (Series 2), on average.

	NM/M
Complete Set (31):	160.00
Common Player:	2.25
1 Frank Thomas	7.50
2 Mo Vaughn	2.50
3 Manny Ramirez	7.50
4 Mark McGwire	13.50
5 Juan Gonzalez	4.00
6 Roberto Alomar	3.00
7 Tim Salmon	2.50
8 Barry Bonds	15.00
9 Tony Gwynn	10.00
10 Reggie Sanders	2.50
11 Larry Walker	2.50
12 Pedro Martinez	7.50
13 Jeff King	2.50
14 Mark Grace	2.50
15 Greg Maddux	10.00
16 Don Mattingly	12.50
17 Gregg Jefferies	2.50
18 Chad Curtis	2.50
19 Jason Isringhausen	2.50
20 B.J. Surhoff	2.50
21 Jeff Conine	2.50
22 Kirby Puckett	10.00
23 Derek Bell	2.50
24 Wally Joyner	2.50
25 Brian Jordan	2.50
26 Edgar Martinez	2.50
27 Hideo Nomo	4.00
28 Mike Mussina	5.00
29 Eddie Murray	7.50
30 Cal Ripken Jr.	15.00
31 Checklist	.25

Elite

The Elite series continued as a Donruss insert in 1996, and they are the elite of the chase cards, being found on average only once per 140 packs (Series 1) or once per 75 packs (Series 2). The '96 Elite cards have a classic look bespeaking value. Player action photos at top center are framed in mottled silver foil and bordered in bright silver. Backs have another action photo, a few words about the player and a serial number from within an edition of 10,000 cards each. As usual, card numbering continues from the previous year.

	NM/M
Complete Set (12):	55.00
Complete Series 1 (61-66):	25.00
Complete Series 2 (67-72):	30.00
Common Player Series 1:	2.50
Common Player Series 2:	2.00
61 Cal Ripken Jr.	12.00
62 Hideo Nomo	3.00
63 Reggie Sanders	2.00
64 Mo Vaughn	2.00
65 Tim Salmon	2.50
66 Chipper Jones	8.00
67 Manny Ramirez	6.00
68 Greg Maddux	10.00
69 Frank Thomas	6.00
70 Ken Griffey Jr.	10.00
71 Dante Bichette	2.00
72 Tony Gwynn	8.00

Freeze Frame

One of two insert sets exclusive to Series 2 Donruss is the Freeze Frame insert. Printed on heavy, round-cornered cardboard stock, the inserts feature multiple photos of the player on both front and back. Fronts combine matte and glossy finish plus a gold-foil Donruss logo. Backs are conventionally printed, include 1995 season highlights and a serial number from within the edition of 5,000. Stated odds of pulling a Freeze Frame insert are one per 60 packs.

	NM/M
Complete Set (8):	16.00

Hit List

Printed on metallic foil with gold-foil graphic highlights, players who hit for high average with power or who collected milestone hits are featured in this insert set. Eight inserts were included in each of Series 1 and 2. Backs have a color action photo, a description of the player's batting prowess and a serial number from an edition of 10,000 cards each. Hit List inserts are found at an average rate of once per 106 foil packs in Series 1 and once per 60 packs in Series 2.

	NM/M
Complete Set (16):	30.00
Common Player:	.60
1 Tony Gwynn	3.00
2 Ken Griffey Jr.	5.00
3 Will Clark	.60
4 Mike Piazza	5.00
5 Carlos Baerga	.60
6 Mo Vaughn	.60
7 Mark Grace	.60
8 Kirby Puckett	3.00
9 Frank Thomas	2.00
10 Barry Bonds	6.00
11 Jeff Bagwell	2.00
12 Edgar Martinez	.60
13 Tim Salmon	.60
14 Wade Boggs	3.00
15 Don Mattingly	4.00
16 Eddie Murray	2.00

Long Ball Leaders

Once again the previous season's longest home runs are recalled in this retail-only insert set, found at an average rate of once per 96 packs in Series 1 only. Fronts are bordered and trimmed in bright silver foil and feature the player in his home run stroke against a black background. The date, location and distance of his tape-measure shot are in an arc across the card front. Backs feature another batting action photo, further details of the home run and a serial number within an edition of 5,000.

	NM/M
Complete Set (8):	45.00
Common Player:	1.50
1 Barry Bonds	15.00
2 Ryan Klesko	1.50
3 Mark McGwire	15.00
4 Raul Mondesi	1.50
5 Cecil Fielder	1.50
6 Ken Griffey Jr.	12.00
7 Larry Walker	1.50
8 Frank Thomas	6.00

Power Alley

Among the most visually dazzling of 1996's inserts is this hobby-only chase set featuring baseball's top sluggers. Action batting photos are found within several layers of prismatic foil in geometric patterns on front. Backs are horizontally formatted, feature portrait photos at left and power stats at right and bottom. In the lower-left corner is an individual serial number from within an edition of 5,000 cards each. The first 500 of each player's cards are specially die-cut at left- and right-center. Found only in Series 1 hobby foil packs, Power Alley inserts are a one per 92 pack pick.

	NM/M
Complete Set (10):	30.00
Common Player	2.00
Die-cuts	2X
1 Frank Thomas	4.00
2 Barry Bonds	7.50
3 Reggie Sanders	2.00
4 Albert Belle	2.00
5 Tim Salmon	2.00
6 Dante Bichette	2.00
7 Mo Vaughn	2.00
8 Jim Edmonds	2.00
9 Manny Ramirez	4.00
10 Ken Griffey Jr.	6.00

Pure Power

These cards were random inserts found only in Series 2 retail packs. Fronts are printed on foil backgrounds and at bottom have a die-cut hole giving the impression a baseball has been batted through the card. On back the inserts are individually serial numbered within an edition of 5,000.

	NM/M
Complete Set (8):	25.00
Common Player:	2.25
1 Raul Mondesi	2.25
2 Barry Bonds	10.00
3 Albert Belle	2.25
4 Frank Thomas	4.50
5 Mike Piazza	7.50
6 Dante Bichette	2.25
7 Manny Ramirez	4.50
8 Mo Vaughn	2.25

Round Trippers

An embossed white home plate design bearing the player's 1995 dinger output is featured on this Series 2 insert set. The entire background has been rendered in gold-flecked sepia tones. Typography on front is laid over the sepia background photo and include a month-by-month bar graph of the player's 1995 and career homers. Within the white home plate frame is the card's unique serial number from within an edition of 5,000. Odds of finding a Round Trippers card are stated at one per 55 packs, in hobby packs only.

		NM/M
Complete Set (10):		35.00
Common Player:		2.50
1	Albert Belle	2.50
2	Barry Bonds	7.50
3	Jeff Bagwell	4.00
4	Tim Salmon	2.50
5	Mo Vaughn	2.50
6	Ken Griffey Jr.	5.00
7	Mike Piazza	5.00
8	Cal Ripken Jr.	7.50
9	Frank Thomas	4.00
9p	Frank Thomas (Promo)	2.50
10	Dante Bichette	2.50

Showdown

Baseball's top hitters and pitchers are matched on a silver and black foil background in this insert set. Gold-foil graphic highlights complete the horizontal front design. Backs are printed on a black and gold background with color action photos and write-ups about each player. At top is a serial number from within an edition of 10,000 cards each. Showdown inserts are found at an average rate of one per Series 1 foil packs.

		NM/M
Complete Set (8):		22.50
Common Player:		.75
1	Frank Thomas, Hideo Nomo	3.00
2	Barry Bonds, Randy Johnson	6.00
3	Greg Maddux, Ken Griffey Jr.	5.00
4	Roger Clemens, Tony Gwynn	4.50
5	Mike Piazza, Mike Mussina	5.00
6	Cal Ripken Jr., Pedro Martinez	6.00
7	Tim Wakefield, Matt Williams	.75
8	Manny Ramirez, Carlos Perez	2.50

1997 Donruss

Donruss' 1997 Series 1 features 270 base cards with a full-bleed color action photo on the front. Horizontal backs have a photo, career statistics, a brief player profile and biographical tidbits. A Press Proofs parallel was made of the base cards in an edition of 2,000 each. Other Series 1 inserts include the annual Diamond Kings, Elites, Armed and Dangerous cards, Longball Leaders and Rocket Launchers. A 180-card Update set was released later as a follow-up to the regular '97 Donruss series. The Updates are numbered contiguously, #271-450, from the first series. Press Proofs and Gold Press Proof parallel inserts were available; other Update inserts include Dominators, Franchise Futures, Power Alley, Rookie Diamond Kings and a special Cal Ripken Jr. set.

	NM/M
Complete Set (450):	20.00
Series 1 Set (270):	10.00
Update Set (180):	10.00
Common Player:	.05
Common Press Proof:	.50
Press Proof Stars:	5X
Common Press Proof Gold:	2.00
Press Proof Gold Stars:	10X
Wax Pack (10):	1.50
Hobby Wax Box (18):	25.00
Retail Wax Box (36):	40.00
Magazine Pack (13):	1.50
Magazine Box (24):	20.00
Update Pack (10):	1.50
Update Wax Box (24):	30.00

#	Player	Price
1	Juan Gonzalez	.40
2	Jim Edmonds	.05
3	Tony Gwynn	1.00
4	Andres Galarraga	.05
5	Joe Carter	.05
6	Raul Mondesi	.05
7	Greg Maddux	1.00
8	Travis Fryman	.05
9	Brian Jordan	.05
10	Henry Rodriguez	.05
11	Manny Ramirez	.75
12	Mark McGwire	1.75
13	Marc Newfield	.05
14	Craig Biggio	.05
15	Sammy Sosa	1.00
16	Brady Anderson	.05
17	Wade Boggs	1.00
18	Charles Johnson	.05
19	Matt Williams	.05
20	Denny Neagle	.05
21	Ken Griffey Jr.	1.50
22	Robin Ventura	.05
23	Barry Larkin	.05
24	Todd Zeile	.05
25	Chuck Knoblauch	.05
26	Todd Hundley	.05
27	Roger Clemens	1.25
28	Michael Tucker	.05
29	Rondell White	.05
30	Osvaldo Fernandez	.05
31	Ivan Rodriguez	.65
32	Alex Fernandez	.05
33	Jason Isringhausen	.05
34	Chipper Jones	1.00
35	Paul O'Neill	.05
36	Hideo Nomo	.40
37	Roberto Alomar	.20
38	Derek Bell	.05
39	Paul Molitor	.75
40	Andy Benes	.05
41	Steve Trachsel	.05
42	J.T. Snow	.05
43	Jason Kendall	.05
44	Alex Rodriguez	1.75
45	Joey Hamilton	.05
46	Carlos Delgado	.50
47	Jason Giambi	.50
48	Larry Walker	.05
49	Derek Jeter	2.00
50	Kenny Lofton	.05
51	Devon White	.05
52	Matt Mieske	.05
53	Melvin Nieves	.05
54	Jose Canseco	.40
55	Tino Martinez	.05
56	Rafael Palmeiro	.65
57	Edgardo Alfonzo	.05
58	Jay Buhner	.05
59	Shane Reynolds	.05
60	Steve Finley	.05
61	Bobby Higginson	.05
62	Dean Palmer	.05
63	Terry Pendleton	.05
64	Marquis Grissom	.05
65	Mike Stanley	.05
66	Moises Alou	.05
67	Ray Lankford	.05
68	Marty Cordova	.05
69	John Olerud	.05
70	David Cone	.05
71	Benito Santiago	.05
72	Ryne Sandberg	1.00
73	Rickey Henderson	.75
74	Roger Cedeno	.05
75	Wilson Alvarez	.05
76	Tim Salmon	.05
77	Orlando Merced	.05
78	Vinny Castilla	.05
79	Ismael Valdes	.05
80	Dante Bichette	.05
81	Kevin Brown	.05
82	Andy Pettitte	.40
83	Scott Stahoviak	.05
84	Mickey Tettleton	.05
85	Jack McDowell	.05
86	Tom Glavine	.30
87	Gregg Jefferies	.05
88	Chili Davis	.05
89	Randy Johnson	.75
90	John Mabry	.05
91	Billy Wagner	.05
92	Jeff Cirillo	.05
93	Trevor Hoffman	.05
94	Juan Guzman	.05
95	Geronimo Berroa	.05
96	Bernard Gilkey	.05
97	Danny Tartabull	.05
98	Johnny Damon	.35
99	Charlie Hayes	.05
100	Reggie Sanders	.05
101	Robby Thompson	.05
102	Bobby Bonilla	.05
103	Reggie Jefferson	.05
104	John Smoltz	.05
105	Jim Thome	.60
106	Ruben Rivera	.05
107	Darren Oliver	.05
108	Mo Vaughn	.05
109	Roger Pavlik	.05
110	Terry Steinbach	.05
111	Jermaine Dye	.05
112	Mark Grudzielanek	.05
113	Rick Aguilera	.05
114	Jamey Wright	.05
115	Eddie Murray	.75
116	Brian Hunter	.05
117	Hal Morris	.05
118	Tom Pagnozzi	.05
119	Mike Mussina	.40
120	Mark Grace	.05
121	Cal Ripken Jr.	2.00
122	Tom Goodwin	.05
123	Paul Sorrento	.05
124	Jay Bell	.05
125	Todd Hollandsworth	.05
126	Edgar Martinez	.05
127	George Arias	.05
128	Greg Vaughn	.05
129	Roberto Hernandez	.05
130	Delino DeShields	.05
131	Bill Pulsipher	.05
132	Joey Cora	.05
133	Mariano Rivera	.15
134	Mike Piazza	1.50
135	Carlos Baerga	.05
136	Jose Mesa	.05
137	Will Clark	.05
138	Frank Thomas	.75
139	John Wetteland	.05
140	Shawn Estes	.05
141	Garret Anderson	.05
142	Andre Dawson	.25
143	Eddie Taubensee	.05
144	Ryan Klesko	.05
145	Rocky Coppinger	.05
146	Jeff Bagwell	.75
147	Donovan Osborne	.05
148	Greg Myers	.05
149	Brant Brown	.05
150	Kevin Elster	.05
151	Bob Wells	.05
152	Wally Joyner	.05
153	Rico Brogna	.05
154	Dwight Gooden	.05
155	Jermaine Allensworth	.05
156	Ray Durham	.05
157	Cecil Fielder	.05
158	Ryan Hancock	.05
159	Gary Sheffield	.30
160	Albert Belle	.05
161	Tomas Perez	.05
162	David Doster	.05
163	John Valentin	.05
164	Danny Graves	.05
165	Jose Paniagua	.05
166	Brian Giles RC	.50
167	Barry Bonds	2.00
168	Sterling Hitchcock	.05
169	Bernie Williams	.05
170	Fred McGriff	.05
171	George Williams	.05
172	Amaury Telemaco	.05
173	Ken Caminiti	.05
174	Ron Gant	.05
175	David Justice	.05
176	James Baldwin	.05
177	Pat Hentgen	.05
178	Ben McDonald	.05
179	Tim Naehring	.05
180	Jim Eisenreich	.05
181	Ken Hill	.05
182	Paul Wilson	.05
183	Marvin Benard	.05
184	Alan Benes	.05
185	Ellis Burks	.05
186	Scott Servais	.05
187	David Segui	.05
188	Scott Brosius	.05
189	Jose Offerman	.05
190	Eric Davis	.05
191	Brett Butler	.05
192	Curtis Pride	.05
193	Yamil Benitez	.05
194	Chan Ho Park	.05
195	Bret Boone	.05
196	Omar Vizquel	.05
197	Orlando Miller	.05
198	Ramon Martinez	.05
199	Harold Baines	.05
200	Eric Young	.05
201	Fernando Vina	.05
202	Alex Gonzalez	.05
203	Fernando Valenzuela	.05
204	Steve Avery	.05
205	Ernie Young	.05
206	Kevin Appier	.05
207	Randy Myers	.05
208	Jeff Suppan	.05
209	James Mouton	.05
210	Russ Davis	.05
211	Al Martin	.05
212	Troy Percival	.05
213	Al Leiter	.05
214	Dennis Eckersley	.65
215	Mark Johnson	.05
216	Eric Karros	.05
217	Royce Clayton	.05
218	Tony Phillips	.05
219	Tim Wakefield	.05
220	Alan Trammell	.05
221	Eduardo Perez	.05
222	Butch Huskey	.05
223	Tim Belcher	.05
224	Jamie Moyer	.05
225	F.P. Santangelo	.05
226	Rusty Greer	.05
227	Jeff Brantley	.05
228	Mark Langston	.05
229	Ray Montgomery	.05
230	Rich Becker	.05
231	Ozzie Smith	1.00
232	Rey Ordonez	.05
233	Ricky Otero	.05
234	Mike Cameron	.05
235	Mike Sweeney	.05
236	Mark Lewis	.05
237	Luis Gonzalez	.05
238	Marcus Jensen	.05
239	Ed Sprague	.05
240	Jose Valentin	.05
241	Jeff Frye	.05
242	Charles Nagy	.05
243	Carlos Garcia	.05
244	Mike Hampton	.05
245	B.J. Surhoff	.05
246	Wilton Guerrero	.05
247	Frank Rodriguez	.05
248	Gary Gaetti	.05
249	Lance Johnson	.05
250	Darren Bragg	.05
251	Darryl Hamilton	.05
252	John Jaha	.05
253	Craig Paquette	.05
254	Jaime Navarro	.05
255	Shawon Dunston	.05
256	Ron Wright	.05
257	Tim Belk	.05
258	Jeff Darwin	.05
259	Ruben Sierra	.05
260	Chuck Finley	.05
261	Darryl Strawberry	.05
262	Shannon Stewart	.05
263	Pedro Martinez	.05
264	Neifi Perez	.05
265	Jeff Conine	.05
266	Orel Hershiser	.05
267	Checklist 1-90 Eddie Murray (500 Career HR)	.05
268	Checklist 91-180 Paul Molitor (3,000 Career Hits)	.05
269	Checklist 181-270 Barry Bonds (300 Career HR)	.90
270	Checklist - inserts Mark McGwire (300 Career HR)	.75
271	Matt Williams	.05
272	Todd Zeile	.05
273	Roger Clemens	1.25
274	Michael Tucker	.05
275	J.T. Snow	.05
276	Kenny Lofton	.05
277	Jose Canseco	.40
278	Marquis Grissom	.05
279	Moises Alou	.05
280	Benito Santiago	.05
281	Willie McGee	.05
282	Chili Davis	.05
283	Ron Coomer	.05
284	Orlando Merced	.05
285	Delino DeShields	.05
286	John Wetteland	.05
287	Darren Daulton	.05
288	Lee Stevens	.05
289	Albert Belle	.05
290	Sterling Hitchcock	.05
291	David Justice	.05
292	Eric Davis	.05
293	Brian Hunter	.05
294	Darryl Hamilton	.05
295	Steve Avery	.05
296	Joe Vitiello	.05
297	Jaime Navarro	.05
298	Eddie Murray	.75
299	Randy Myers	.05
300	Francisco Cordova	.05
301	Javier Lopez	.05
302	Geronimo Berroa	.05
303	Jeffrey Hammonds	.05
304	Deion Sanders	.05
305	Jeff Fassero	.05
306	Curt Schilling	.25
307	Robb Nen	.05
308	Mark McLemore	.05
309	Jimmy Key	.05
310	Quilvio Veras	.05
311	Bip Roberts	.05
312	Esteban Loaiza	.05
313	Andy Ashby	.05
314	Sandy Alomar Jr.	.05
315	Shawn Green	.20
316	Luis Castillo	.05
317	Benji Gil	.05
318	Otis Nixon	.05
319	Aaron Sele	.05
320	Brad Ausmus	.05
321	Troy O'Leary	.05
322	Terrell Wade	.05
323	Jeff King	.05
324	Kevin Seitzer	.05
325	Mark Wohlers	.05
326	Edgar Renteria	.05
327	Dan Wilson	.05
328	Brian McRae	.05
329	Rod Beck	.05
330	Julio Franco	.05
331	Dave Nilsson	.05
332	Glenallen Hill	.05
333	Kevin Elster	.05
334	Joe Girardi	.05
335	David Wells	.05
336	Jeff Blauser	.05
337	Darryl Kile	.05
338	Jeff Kent	.05
339	Jim Leyritz	.05
340	Todd Stottlemyre	.05
341	Tony Clark	.05
342	Chris Hoiles	.05
343	Mike Lieberthal	.05
344	Matt Lawton	.05
345	Alex Ochoa	.05
346	Chris Snopek	.05
347	Rudy Pemberton	.05
348	Eric Owens	.05
349	Joe Randa	.05
350	John Olerud	.05
351	Steve Karsay	.05
352	Mark Whiten	.05
353	Bob Abreu	.10
354	Bartolo Colon	.05
355	Vladimir Guerrero	.75
356	Darin Erstad	.30
357	Scott Rolen	.60
358	Andruw Jones	.75
359	Scott Spiezio	.05
360	Karim Garcia	.05
361	Hideki Irabu RC	.25
362	Nomar Garciaparra	1.00
363	Dmitri Young	.05
364	Bubba Trammell RC	.25
365	Kevin Orie	.05
366	Jose Rosado	.05
367	Jose Guillen	.05
368	Brooks Kieschnick	.05
369	Pokey Reese	.05
370	Glendon Rusch	.05
371	Jason Dickson	.05
372	Todd Walker	.05
373	Justin Thompson	.05
374	Todd Greene	.05
375	Jeff Suppan	.05
376	Trey Beamon	.05
377	Damon Mashore	.05
378	Wendell Magee	.05
379	Shigetosi Hasegawa	.05
380	Bill Mueller	.05
381	Chris Widger	.05
382	Tony Grafannino	.05
383	Derrek Lee	.50
384	Brian Moehler	.05
385	Quinton McCracken	.05
386	Matt Morris	.05
387	Marvin Benard	.05
388	Deivi Cruz RC	.25
389	Javier Valentin RC	.05
390	Todd Dunwoody	.05
391	Derrick Gibson	.05
392	Raul Casanova	.05
393	George Arias	.05
394	Tony Womack RC	.25
395	Antone Williamson	.05
396	Jose Cruz Jr. RC	.50
397	Desi Relaford	.05
398	Frank Thomas/HL	.40
399	Ken Griffey Jr./HL	.65
400	Cal Ripken Jr./HL	1.00
401	Chipper Jones/HL	.50
402	Mike Piazza/HL	.65
403	Gary Sheffield/HL	.15
404	Alex Rodriguez/HL	.75
405	Wade Boggs/HL	.50
406	Juan Gonzalez/HL	.25
407	Tony Gwynn/HL	.50
408	Edgar Martinez/HL	.05
409	Jeff Bagwell/HL	.40
410	Larry Walker/HL	.05
411	Kenny Lofton/HL	.05
412	Manny Ramirez/HL	.40
413	Mark McGwire/HL	.75
414	Roberto Alomar/HL	.10
415	Derek Jeter/HL	1.00
416	Brady Anderson/HL	.05
417	Paul Molitor/HL	.35
418	Dante Bichette/HL	.05
419	Jim Edmonds/HL	.05
420	Mo Vaughn/HL	.05
421	Barry Bonds/HL	.90
422	Rusty Greer/HL	.05
423	Greg Maddux (King of the Hill)	.50
424	Andy Pettitte (King of the Hill)	.15
425	John Smoltz (King of the Hill)	.05
426	Randy Johnson (King of the Hill)	.40
427	Hideo Nomo (King of the Hill)	.20
428	Roger Clemens (King of the Hill)	.60
429	Tom Glavine (King of the Hill)	.15
430	Pat Hentgen (King of the Hill)	.05
431	Kevin Brown (King of the Hill)	.05
432	Mike Mussina (King of the Hill)	.20
433	Alex Fernandez (King of the Hill)	.05
434	Kevin Appier (King of the Hill)	.05
435	David Cone (King of the Hill)	.05
436	Jeff Fassero (King of the Hill)	.05
437	John Wetteland (King of the Hill)	.05
438	Barry Bonds, Ivan Rodriguez/IS	.90
439	Ken Griffey Jr., Andres Galarraga/IS	.65
440	Fred McGriff, Rafael Palmeiro/IS	.05
441	Barry Larkin, Jim Thome/IS	.05
442	Sammy Sosa, Albert Belle/IS	.50
443	Bernie Williams, Todd Hundley/IS	.05
444	Chuck Knoblauch, Brian Jordan/IS	.05
445	Mo Vaughn, Jeff Conine/IS	.05
446	Ken Caminiti, Jason Giambi/IS	.25
447	Raul Mondesi, Tim Salmon/IS	.05
448	Checklist (Cal Ripken Jr.)	.75
449	Checklist (Greg Maddux)	.60
450	Checklist (Ken Griffey Jr.)	.50

1997 Donruss Press Proofs

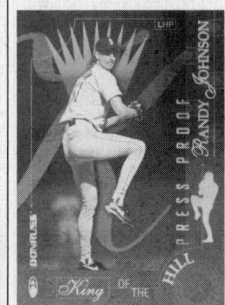

Each of the 450 cards in the Donruss base set was also produced in a Press Proof parallel edition of 2,000 cards. Virtually identical in design to the regular cards, the Press Proofs are printed on a metallic background with silver-foil highlights. Most Press Proof backs carry the notation "1 of 2000." Stated odds of finding a press proof are one per eight packs. A special "gold" press proof chase set features cards with gold-foil highlights, die-cut at top and bottom and the note "1 of 500" on back. Gold press proofs are found on average once per 32 packs.

	NM/M
Common Player:	.50
Stars/Rookies:	5X
Common Gold Player:	2.00
Gold Stars/Rookies:	10X

Armed and Dangerous

These 15 cards are numbered up to 5,000. They were inserted in 1997 Donruss Series 1 retail packs only.

	NM/M
Complete Set (15):	35.00

Common Player:		1.00
1	Ken Griffey Jr.	4.00
2	Raul Mondesi	1.00
3	Chipper Jones	3.00
4	Ivan Rodriguez	1.50
5	Randy Johnson	2.00
6	Alex Rodriguez	5.00
7	Larry Walker	1.00
8	Cal Ripken Jr.	6.00
9	Kenny Lofton	1.00
10	Barry Bonds	6.00
11	Derek Jeter	6.00
12	Charles Johnson	1.00
13	Greg Maddux	3.00
14	Roberto Alomar	1.00
15	Barry Larkin	1.00

Diamond Kings

Diamond Kings for 1997 are sequentially numbered from 1 to 10,000. To celebrate 15 years of this popular insert set, Donruss offered collectors a one-of-a-kind piece of artwork if they find one of the 10 cards with the serial number 1,982 (1982 was the first year of the Diamond Kings). Those who find these cards can redeem them for an original artwork provided by artist Dan Gardiner. In addition, Donruss printed the first 500 of each card on canvas stock.

		NM/M
Complete Set (10):		30.00
Common Player:		1.00
Canvas (1st 500):		2X
1	Ken Griffey Jr.	6.00
2	Cal Ripken Jr.	10.00
3	Mo Vaughn	1.00
4	Chuck Knoblauch	1.00
5	Jeff Bagwell	2.50
6	Henry Rodriguez	1.00
7	Mike Piazza	6.00
8	Ivan Rodriguez	2.50
9	Frank Thomas	3.00
10	Chipper Jones	5.00

Elite Inserts

There were 2,500 sets of these insert cards made. The cards were randomly included in 1997 Donruss Series I packs. Fronts have a white marbled border and are graphically enhanced with silver foil, including a large script "E." On back is another photo, a career summary and a serial number from within the edition limit of 2,500. A promo card version of each card also exists.

		NM/M
Complete Set (12):		100.00
Common Player:		3.00
Promos: 50 Percent		
1	Frank Thomas	7.50
2	Paul Molitor	7.50
3	Sammy Sosa	10.00
4	Barry Bonds	20.00
5	Chipper Jones	10.00
6	Alex Rodriguez	15.00
7	Ken Griffey Jr.	12.50
8	Jeff Bagwell	7.50
9	Cal Ripken Jr.	20.00
10	Mo Vaughn	3.00
11	Mike Piazza	12.50
12	Juan Gonzalez	4.50

Longball Leaders

These 1997 Donruss Series 1 inserts have an action photo printed on a metallic foil background. Printed on the gold-foil border is a gauge with the player's 1996 home run total indicated. Horizontal backs have a player photo and record of career HRs by season. Each card is serially numbered within an edition of 5,000. The set was seeded in retail packs only.

		NM/M
Complete Set (15):		20.00
Common Player:		.50
1	Frank Thomas	2.00
2	Albert Belle	.50
3	Mo Vaughn	.50
4	Brady Anderson	.50
5	Greg Vaughn	.50
6	Ken Griffey Jr.	3.00
7	Jay Buhner	.50
8	Juan Gonzalez	.75
9	Mike Piazza	3.00
10	Jeff Bagwell	2.00
11	Sammy Sosa	2.50
12	Mark McGwire	4.00
13	Cecil Fielder	.50
14	Ryan Klesko	.50
15	Jose Canseco	.85

Rated Rookies

Although numbered more like an insert set, Rated Rookies are part of the regular-issue set. Cards are numbered 1-30, with no ratio given on packs. The cards are differentiated by a large silver-foil strip on the top right side with the words Rated Rookie.

		NM/M
Complete Set (30):		10.00
Common Player:		.50
1	Jason Thompson	.50
2	LaTroy Hawkins	.50
3	Scott Rolen	1.50
4	Trey Beamon	.50
5	Kimera Bartee	.50
6	Nerio Rodriguez	.50
7	Jeff D'Amico	.50
8	Quinton McCracken	.50
9	John Wasdin	.50
10	Robin Jennings	.50
11	Steve Gibralter	.50
12	Tyler Houston	.50
13	Tony Clark	.50
14	Ugueth Urbina	.50
15	Billy McMillon	.50
16	Raul Casanova	.50
17	Brooks Kieschnick	.50
18	Luis Castillo	.50
19	Edgar Renteria	.50
20	Andruw Jones	2.00
21	Chad Mottola	.50
22	Makoto Suzuki	.50
23	Justin Thompson	.50
24	Darin Erstad	1.00
25	Todd Walker	.50
26	Todd Greene	.50
27	Vladimir Guerrero	2.00
28	Darren Dreifort	.50
29	John Burke	.50
30	Damon Mashore	.50

1997 Donruss Jackie Robinson Rookie Reprint

In conjunction with its program of special issues and giveaways honoring the 50th anniversary of Robinson's major league debut, Donruss issued this "Commemorative Rookie Card." Printed in the same size as the 1949 Leaf Robinson, and on heavier, coarser stock than modern cards, the card carries a reprint notice and is serially numbered on back in gold foil from within an edition of 1,948.

		NM/M
79	Jackie Robinson	10.00

Jackie Robinson Sweepstakes Scratch-Off

This pack insert features inside a scratch-off contest in which genuine vintage 1948-49 Leaf Jackie Robinson cards were awarded. The 2-3/8" x 2-7/8" folder has a color photo of the Leaf Robinson rookie card on front. On back is information on ordering numbered lithographs of the Robinson card; an edition of 1,000 selling for $199 apiece, an edition of 500 autographed by his widow selling for $299 apiece.

	NM/M
Jackie Robinson	.50

Rocket Launchers

These 1997 Donruss Series 1 inserts are limited to 5,000 each. They were only included in magazine packs.

		NM/M
Complete Set (15):		25.00
Common Player:		.75
1	Frank Thomas	2.50
2	Albert Belle	.75
3	Chipper Jones	3.00
4	Mike Piazza	4.00
5	Mo Vaughn	.75
6	Juan Gonzalez	1.00
7	Fred McGriff	.75
8	Jeff Bagwell	2.50
9	Matt Williams	.75
10	Gary Sheffield	1.00
11	Barry Bonds	5.00
12	Manny Ramirez	2.00
13	Henry Rodriguez	.75
14	Jason Giambi	1.50
15	Cal Ripken Jr.	5.00

Update Dominators

This 20-card insert highlights players known for being able to "take over a game." Each card features silver-foil highlights on front and stats on back.

		NM/M
Complete Set (20):		22.50
Common Player:		.50
1	Frank Thomas	1.25
2	Ken Griffey Jr.	2.25
3	Greg Maddux	1.50
4	Cal Ripken Jr.	3.00
5	Alex Rodriguez	2.50
6	Albert Belle	.50
7	Mark McGwire	2.50
8	Juan Gonzalez	.65
9	Chipper Jones	1.50
10	Hideo Nomo	.65
11	Roger Clemens	2.00
12	John Smoltz	.50
13	Mike Piazza	2.25
14	Sammy Sosa	1.50
15	Matt Williams	.50
16	Kenny Lofton	.50
17	Barry Larkin	.50
18	Rafael Palmeiro	1.00
19	Ken Caminiti	.50
20	Gary Sheffield	.75

Update Franchise Features

This hobby-exclusive insert consists of 15 cards designed with a movie poster theme. The double-front design highlights a top veteran player on one side with an up-and-coming rookie on the other. The side featuring the veteran has the designation "Now Playing," while the rookie side carries the banner "Coming Attraction." Each card is printed on an all-foil stock and numbered to 3,000.

		NM/M
Complete Set (15):		45.00
Common Player:		2.00
1	Ken Griffey Jr., Andruw Jones	4.00
2	Frank Thomas, Darin Erstad	2.50
3	Alex Rodriguez, Nomar Garciaparra	5.00
4	Chuck Knoblauch, Wilton Guerrero	2.00
5	Juan Gonzalez, Bubba Trammell	2.00
6	Chipper Jones, Todd Walker	3.00
7	Barry Bonds, Vladimir Guerrero	6.00
8	Mark McGwire, Dmitri Young	5.00
9	Mike Piazza, Mike Sweeney	4.00
10	Mo Vaughn, Tony Clark	2.00
11	Gary Sheffield, Jose Guillen	2.00
12	Kenny Lofton, Shannon Stewart	2.00
13	Cal Ripken Jr., Scott Rolen	6.00
14	Derek Jeter, Pokey Reese	6.00
15	Tony Gwynn, Bob Abreu	2.00

Update Power Alley

This 24-card insert is fractured into three different styles: Gold, Blue and Green. Each card is micro-etched and printed on holographic foil board. All cards are sequentially numbered, with the first 250 cards in each level being die-cut. Twelve players' cards feature a green finish and are numbered to 4,000. Eight players are printed on blue cards that are numbered to 2,000. Four players are found on gold cards numbered to 1,000.

		NM/M
Complete Set (24):		100.00
Common Gold:		7.50
Common Blue:		3.00
Common Green:		1.50
Die-Cuts:		3X
1	Frank Thomas (G)	7.50
2	Ken Griffey Jr. (G)	10.00
3	Cal Ripken Jr. (G)	15.00
4	Jeff Bagwell (B)	5.00
5	Mike Piazza (B)	7.50
6	Andruw Jones (GR)	3.50
7	Alex Rodriguez (G)	12.50
8	Albert Belle (GR)	1.50
9	Mo Vaughn (GR)	1.50
10	Chipper Jones (B)	6.00
11	Juan Gonzalez (B)	3.00
12	Ken Caminiti (GR)	1.50
13	Manny Ramirez (GR)	3.50
14	Mark McGwire (GR)	6.00
15	Kenny Lofton (B)	3.00
16	Barry Bonds (GR)	7.50
17	Gary Sheffield (GR)	1.50
18	Tony Gwynn (GR)	4.50
19	Vladimir Guerrero (B)	5.00
20	Ivan Rodriguez (B)	3.50
21	Paul Molitor (B)	5.00
22	Sammy Sosa (GR)	4.50
23	Matt Williams (GR)	1.50
24	Derek Jeter (GR)	7.50

1997 Donruss Update Press Proofs

This 180-card parallel set is printed on an all-foil stock with bright foil accents. Each card is numbered "1 of 2,000." Special die-cut gold versions are numbered as "1 of 500."

	NM/M
Common Player:	.50
Stars:	7X
Common Player, Gold:	.50
Gold Stars:	15X

Update Cal Ripken

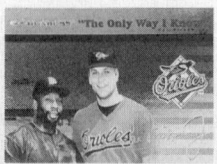

This 10-card set salutes Cal Ripken Jr. and is printed on an all-foil stock with foil highlights. Photos and text are taken from Ripken's autobiography, "The Only Way I Know." The first nine cards of the set were randomly inserted into packs. The 10th card was only available inside the book. Each card found within packs was numbered to 5,000.

		NM/M
Complete Set (10):		75.00
Common Card:		10.00
1-9	Cal Ripken Jr.	10.00
10	Cal Ripken Jr. (Book insert.)	10.00

Update Rookie Diamond Kings

This popular Donruss Update insert set features a new twist - all 10 cards feature promising rookies. Each card is sequentially numbered to 10,000, with the first 500 cards of each player printed on actual canvas.

		NM/M
Complete Set (10):		20.00
Common Player:		1.50
Canvas:		1.5X
1	Andruw Jones	4.00
2	Vladimir Guerrero	10.00
3	Scott Rolen	2.00
4	Todd Walker	1.50
5	Bartolo Colon	2.00
6	Jose Guillen	1.50
7	Nomar Garciaparra	6.00
8	Darin Erstad	2.00
9	Dmitri Young	1.50
10	Wilton Guerrero	1.50

1997 Donruss Team Sets

A total of 163 cards were part of the Donruss Team Set issue. Packs consisted solely of players from one of 11 different teams. In addition, a full 163-card parallel set called Pennant Edition was available, featuring red and gold foil and a special "Pennant Edition" logo. Cards were sold in five-card packs for $1.99 each. The Angels and Indians were sold only at their teams' souvenir outlets. Cards #131 Bernie Williams and #144 Russ Davis were never issued. The Team Set cards utilize team-color foil highlights and the numbers on back differ from the regular-issue version.

	NM/M
Comp. Angels Set (1-15):	1.25
Comp. Braves Set (16-30):	3.00
Comp. Orioles Set (31-45):	2.00
Comp. Red Sox Set (46-60):	1.50
Comp. White Sox Set (61-75):	2.00
Comp. Indians Set (76-90):	1.50
Comp. Rockies Set (91-105):	1.50
Comp. Dodgers Set (106-120):	2.25
Comp. Yankees Set (121-135):	4.50
Comp. Mariners Set (136-150):	4.50
Comp. Cardinals Set (151-165):	2.00
Common Player:	.05
Pennant Edition Stars:	3X

#	Player	Price
1	Jim Edmonds	.05
2	Tim Salmon	.05
3	Tony Phillips	.05
4	Garret Anderson	.05
5	Troy Percival	.05
6	Mark Langston	.05
7	Chuck Finley	.05
8	Eddie Murray	.75
9	Jim Leyritz	.05
10	Darin Erstad	.30
11	Jason Dickson	.05
12	Allen Watson	.05
13	Shigetoshi Hasegawa	.05
14	Dave Hollins	.05
15	Gary DiSarcina	.05
16	Greg Maddux	1.00
17	Denny Neagle	.05
18	Chipper Jones	1.00
19	Tom Glavine	.25
20	John Smoltz	.05
21	Ryan Klesko	.05
22	Fred McGriff	.05
23	Michael Tucker	.05
24	Kenny Lofton	.05
25	Javier Lopez	.05
26	Mark Wohlers	.05
27	Jeff Blauser	.05
28	Andruw Jones	.75
29	Tony Graffanino	.05
30	Terrell Wade	.05
31	Brady Anderson	.05
32	Roberto Alomar	.15
33	Rafael Palmeiro	.65
34	Mike Mussina	.35
35	Cal Ripken Jr.	2.00
36	Rocky Coppinger	.05
37	Randy Myers	.05
38	B.J. Surhoff	.05
39	Eric Davis	.05
40	Armando Benitez	.05
41	Jeffrey Hammonds	.05
42	Jimmy Key	.05
43	Chris Hoiles	.05
44	Mike Bordick	.05
45	Pete Incaviglia	.05
46	Mike Stanley	.05
47	Reggie Jefferson	.05
48	Mo Vaughn	.05
49	John Valentin	.05
50	Tim Naehring	.05
51	Jeff Suppan	.05
52	Tim Wakefield	.05
53	Jeff Frye	.05
54	Darren Bragg	.05
55	Steve Avery	.05
56	Shane Mack	.05
57	Aaron Sele	.05
58	Troy O'Leary	.05
59	Rudy Pemberton	.05
60	Nomar Garciaparra	1.00
61	Robin Ventura	.05
62	Wilson Alvarez	.05
63	Roberto Hernandez	.05
64	Frank Thomas	.75
65	Ray Durham	.05
66	James Baldwin	.05
67	Harold Baines	.05
68	Doug Drabek	.05
69	Mike Cameron	.05
70	Albert Belle	.05
71	Jaime Navarro	.05
72	Chris Snopek	.05
73	Lyle Mouton	.05
74	Dave Martinez	.05
75	Ozzie Guillen	.05
76	Manny Ramirez	.75
77	Jack McDowell	.05
78	Jim Thome	.50
79	Jose Mesa	.05
80	Brian Giles	.05
81	Omar Vizquel	.05
82	Charles Nagy	.05
83	Orel Hershiser	.05
84	Matt Williams	.05
85	Marquis Grissom	.05
86	David Justice	.05
87	Sandy Alomar	.05
88	Kevin Seitzer	.05
89	Julio Franco	.05
90	Bartolo Colon	.05
91	Andres Galarraga	.05
92	Larry Walker	.05
93	Vinny Castilla	.05
94	Dante Bichette	.05
95	Jamey Wright	.05
96	Ellis Burks	.05
97	Eric Young	.05
98	Neifi Perez	.05
99	Quinton McCracken	.05
100	Bruce Ruffin	.05
101	Walt Weiss	.05
102	Roger Bailey	.05
103	Jeff Reed	.05
104	Bill Swift	.05
105	Kirt Manwaring	.05
106	Raul Mondesi	.05
107	Hideo Nomo	.35
108	Roger Cedeno	.05
109	Ismael Valdes	.05
110	Todd Hollandsworth	.05
111	Mike Piazza	1.50
112	Brett Butler	.05
113	Chan Ho Park	.05
114	Ramon Martinez	.05
115	Eric Karros	.05
116	Wilton Guerrero	.05
117	Todd Zeile	.05
118	Karim Garcia	.05

#	Player	Price
119	Greg Gagne	.05
120	Darren Dreifort	.05
121	Wade Boggs	1.00
122	Paul O'Neill	.05
123	Derek Jeter	2.00
124	Tino Martinez	.05
125	David Cone	.05
126	Andy Pettitte	.25
127	Charlie Hayes	.05
128	Mariano Rivera	.15
129	Dwight Gooden	.05
130	Cecil Fielder	.05
131	Darryl Strawberry	.05
132	Joe Girardi	.05
133	David Wells	.05
134	David Wells	.05
135	Hideki Irabu	.05
136	Ken Griffey Jr.	1.25
137	Alex Rodriguez	1.50
138	Jay Buhner	.05
139	Randy Johnson	.75
140	Paul Sorrento	.05
141	Edgar Martinez	.05
142	Joey Cora	.05
143	Bob Wells	.05
145	Jamie Moyer	.05
146	Jeff Fassero	.05
147	Dan Wilson	.05
148	Jose Cruz, Jr.	.05
149	Scott Sanders	.05
150	Rich Amaral	.05
151	Brian Jordan	.05
152	Andy Benes	.05
153	Ray Lankford	.05
154	John Mabry	.05
155	Tom Pagnozzi	.05
156	Ron Gant	.05
157	Alan Benes	.05
158	Dennis Eckersley	.65
159	Royce Clayton	.05
160	Todd Stottlemyre	.05
161	Gary Gaetti	.05
162	Willie McGee	.05
163	Delino DeShields	.05
164	Dmitri Young	.05
165	Matt Morris	.05

1997 Donruss Team Sets MVP

The top players at each position were available in this 18-card insert set. Each card is sequentially numbered to 1,000. Fronts are printed with a textured foil background and holographic foil highlights. Backs have a portrait photo.

		NM/M
	Complete Set (18):	45.00
	Common Player:	.50
1	Ivan Rodriguez	1.50
2	Mike Piazza	5.50
3	Frank Thomas	2.50
4	Jeff Bagwell	2.50
5	Chuck Knoblauch	.50
6	Eric Young	.50
7	Alex Rodriguez	6.00
8	Barry Larkin	.50
9	Cal Ripken Jr.	7.50
10	Chipper Jones	4.00
11	Albert Belle	.50
12	Barry Bonds	7.50
13	Ken Griffey Jr.	5.50
14	Kenny Lofton	.50
15	Juan Gonzalez	1.00
16	Larry Walker	.50
17	Roger Clemens	5.00
18	Greg Maddux	4.00

1997 Donruss Elite

Donruss Elite Baseball is a 150-card, single-series set distributed as a hobby-only product. The regular-issue cards feature a silver border around the entire card, with a marblized frame around a color player photo at center. Backs feature a color player photo and minimal statistics and personal data. Elite was accompanied by an Elite Stars parallel set and three inserts: Leather and Lumber, Passing the Torch and Turn of the Century.

Vladimir Guerrero
Expos

		NM/M
	Complete Set (150):	10.00
	Common Player:	.10
	Common Elite Star:	.50
	Elite Stars Stars/RC's:	4X
	Pack (6):	2.50
	Wax Box (18):	35.00
1	Juan Gonzalez	.40
2	Alex Rodriguez	2.00
3	Frank Thomas	.75
4	Greg Maddux	.75
5	Ken Griffey Jr.	1.50
6	Cal Ripken Jr.	2.50
7	Mike Piazza	1.50
8	Chipper Jones	1.00
9	Albert Belle	.10
10	Andruw Jones	.75
11	Vladimir Guerrero	.75
12	Mo Vaughn	.75
13	Ivan Rodriguez	.65
14	Andy Pettitte	.40
15	Tony Gwynn	1.00
16	Barry Bonds	2.50
17	Jeff Bagwell	.75
18	Manny Ramirez	.75
19	Kenny Lofton	.75
20	Roberto Alomar	.20
21	Mark McGwire	2.00
22	Ryan Klesko	.10
23	Tim Salmon	.10
24	Derek Jeter	2.50
25	Eddie Murray	.75
26	Jermaine Dye	.10
27	Ruben Rivera	.10
28	Jim Edmonds	.10
29	Mike Mussina	.40
30	Randy Johnson	.75
31	Sammy Sosa	1.00
32	Hideo Nomo	.40
33	Chuck Knoblauch	.10
34	Paul Molitor	.75
35	Rafael Palmeiro	.75
36	Brady Anderson	.10
37	Will Clark	.10
38	Craig Biggio	.10
39	Jason Giambi	.50
40	Roger Clemens	1.25
41	Jay Buhner	.10
42	Edgar Martinez	.10
43	Gary Sheffield	.35
44	Fred McGriff	.10
45	Bobby Bonilla	.10
46	Tom Glavine	.25
47	Wade Boggs	1.00
48	Jeff Conine	.10
49	John Smoltz	.10
50	Jim Thome	.60
51	Billy Wagner	.10
52	Jose Canseco	.40
53	Javy Lopez	.10
54	Cecil Fielder	.10
55	Garret Anderson	.10
56	Alex Ochoa	.10
57	Scott Rolen	.60
58	Darin Erstad	.30
59	Rey Ordonez	.10
60	Dante Bichette	.10
61	Joe Carter	.10
62	Moises Alou	.10
63	Jason Isringhausen	.10
64	Karim Garcia	.10
65	Brian Jordan	.10
66	Ruben Sierra	.10
67	Todd Hollandsworth	.10
68	Paul Wilson	.10
69	Ernie Young	.10
70	Ryne Sandberg	1.00
71	Raul Mondesi	.10
72	George Arias	.10
73	Ray Durham	.10
74	Dean Palmer	.10
75	Shawn Green	.30
76	Eric Young	.10
77	Jason Kendall	.10
78	Greg Vaughn	.10
79	Terrell Wade	.10
80	Bill Pulsipher	.10
81	Bobby Higginson	.10
82	Mark Grudzielanek	.10
83	Ken Caminiti	.10
84	Todd Greene	.10
85	Carlos Delgado	.50
86	Mark Grace	.10
87	Rondell White	.10
88	Barry Larkin	.10
89	J.T. Snow	.10
90	Alex Gonzalez	.10
91	Raul Casanova	.10

#	Player	Price
92	Marc Newfield	.10
93	Jermaine Allensworth	.10
94	John Mabry	.10
95	Kirby Puckett	1.00
96	Travis Fryman	.10
97	Kevin Brown	.15
98	Andres Galarraga	.10
99	Marty Cordova	.10
100	Henry Rodriguez	.10
101	Sterling Hitchcock	.10
102	Trey Beamon	.10
103	Brett Butler	.10
104	Rickey Henderson	.75
105	Tino Martinez	.10
106	Kevin Appier	.10
107	Brian Hunter	.10
108	Eric Karros	.10
109	Andre Dawson	.10
110	Darryl Strawberry	.10
111	James Baldwin	.10
112	Chad Mottola	.10
113	Dave Nilsson	.10
114	Carlos Baerga	.10
115	Chan Ho Park	.10
116	John Jaha	.10
117	Alan Benes	.10
118	Mariano Rivera	.20
119	Ellis Burks	.10
120	Tony Clark	.10
121	Todd Walker	.10
122	Dwight Gooden	.10
123	Ugueth Urbina	.10
124	David Cone	.10
125	Ozzie Smith	1.00
126	Kimera Bartee	.10
127	Rusty Greer	.10
128	Pat Hentgen	.10
129	Charles Johnson	.10
130	Quinton McCracken	.10
131	Troy Percival	.10
132	Shane Reynolds	.10
133	Charles Nagy	.10
134	Tom Goodwin	.10
135	Ron Gant	.10
136	Dan Wilson	.10
137	Matt Williams	.10
138	LaTroy Hawkins	.10
139	Kevin Seitzer	.10
140	Michael Tucker	.10
141	Todd Hundley	.10
142	Alex Fernandez	.10
143	Marquis Grissom	.10
144	Steve Finley	.10
145	Curtis Pride	.10
146	Derek Bell	.10
147	Butch Huskey	.10
148	Dwight Gooden	.10
149	Al Leiter	.10
150	Hideo Nomo	.40

1997 Donruss Elite Stars

Ozzie Smith
Cardinals

Gold, rather than silver, foil differentiates the parallel set of Elite Stars from the regular-issue versions of each of the base cards in the Elite set. The parallels also have a small "Elite Stars" printed at top, flanking the position. Stated odds of finding a Stars insert are about one per five packs.

	NM/M
Common Player:	1.00

Leather & Lumber

Leather and Lumber is a 10-card insert set filled with veterans. Genuine leather is featured on one side of the card, while wood card stock is on the other. There were 500 sequentially numbered sets produced.

		NM/M
	Complete Set (10):	140.00
	Common Player:	4.00
1	Ken Griffey Jr.	20.00
2	Alex Rodriguez	25.00
3	Frank Thomas	9.00
4	Chipper Jones	12.50
5	Ivan Rodriguez	7.50
6	Cal Ripken Jr.	35.00
7	Barry Bonds	35.00
8	Chuck Knoblauch	4.00
9	Manny Ramirez	9.00
10	Mark McGwire	25.00

Passing the Torch

Frank Thomas
Chicago White Sox

Passing the Torch is a 12-card insert limited to 1,500 individually numbered sets. It features eight different stars, each with their own cards and then featured on a double-sided card with another player from the set.

		NM/M
	Complete Set (12):	110.00
	Common Player:	4.50
1	Cal Ripken Jr.	20.00
2	Alex Rodriguez	15.00
3	Cal Ripken Jr., Alex Rodriguez	17.50
4	Kirby Puckett	10.00
5	Andruw Jones	7.50
6	Kirby Puckett, Andruw Jones	7.50
7	Cecil Fielder	4.50
8	Frank Thomas	7.50
9	Cecil Fielder, Frank Thomas	6.00
10	Ozzie Smith	10.00
11	Derek Jeter	20.00
12	Ozzie Smith, Derek Jeter	12.00

Passing the Torch Autographs

The first 150 individually numbered sets of the Passing the Torch insert were autographed. This means that cards 3, 6, 9 and 12 are dual-autographed on their double-sided format.

		NM/M
	Common Card:	15.00
1	Cal Ripken Jr.	200.00
2	Alex Rodriguez	275.00
3	Cal Ripken Jr., Alex Rodriguez	750.00
4	Kirby Puckett	80.00
5	Andruw Jones	40.00
6	Kirby Puckett, Andruw Jones	140.00
7	Cecil Fielder	45.00
8	Frank Thomas	75.00
9	Cecil Fielder, Frank Thomas	125.00
10	Ozzie Smith	120.00
11	Derek Jeter	160.00
12	Ozzie Smith, Derek Jeter	325.00

Turn of the Century

Scott Rolen

Turn of the Century includes 20 potential year 2000 superstars on an insert set numbered to 3,500. The first 500 of these sets feature an external die-cut design. Cards feature the player over a framed background image on silver foil board, with black strips down each side. Backs have a color photo, a few words about the player and the serial number. Each card can also be found in an over-printed "SAMPLE" version.

		NM/M
	Complete Set (20):	55.00
	Common Player:	1.00
	Die-Cuts:	3X
	Samples:	1X
1	Alex Rodriguez	10.00
2	Andruw Jones	6.00
3	Chipper Jones	7.50
4	Todd Walker	1.00
5	Scott Rolen	4.00
6	Trey Beamon	1.00
7	Derek Jeter	12.50
8	Darin Erstad	3.00
9	Tony Clark	1.00
10	Todd Greene	1.00
11	Jason Giambi	3.00
12	Justin Thompson	1.00
13	Ernie Young	1.00
14	Jason Kendall	1.00
15	Alex Ochoa	1.00
16	Brooks Kieschnick	1.00
17	Bobby Higginson	1.00
18	Ruben Rivera	1.00
19	Chan Ho Park	1.00
20	Chad Mottola	1.00

1997 Donruss Limited

Each of the 200 base cards in this set features a double-front design showcasing an action photo on each side. The set is divided into four subsets. Counterparts (100 cards) highlights two different players from the same position; Double Team (40 cards) features some of the majors' top teammate duos; Star Factor (40 cards) consists of two photos of some of the hobby's favorite players; and Unlimited Potential/Talent (20 cards) combines a top veteran with a top prospect. The issue also includes a Limited Exposure parallel set and a multi-tiered insert called Fabric of the Game. Odds of finding any insert card were 1:5 packs. Less than 1,100 base sets were available. Cards were sold in five-card packs for $4.99.

		NM/M
	Complete Set (200):	450.00
	Common Counterpart:	.20
	Common Double Team:	.75
	Common Star Factor:	1.50
	Common Unlimited Potential:	1.25
	Pack (5):	2.00
	Wax Box (24):	45.00
1	Ken Griffey Jr., Rondell White (Counterparts)	1.00

2 Greg Maddux, David Cone (Counterparts) .75
3 Gary Sheffield, Moises Alou/DT 1.25
4 Frank Thomas/SF 10.00
5 Cal Ripken Jr., Kevin Orie (Counterparts) 2.00
6 Vladimir Guerrero, Barry Bonds (Unlimited Potential/Talent) 20.00
7 Eddie Murray, Reggie Jefferson (Counterparts) .60
8 Manny Ramirez, Marquis Grissom/DT 2.50
9 Mike Piazza/SF 15.00
10 Barry Larkin, Rey Ordonez (Counterparts) .20
11 Jeff Bagwell, Eric Karros (Counterparts) .60
12 Chuck Knoblauch, Ray Durham (Counterparts) .20
13 Alex Rodriguez, Edgar Renteria (Counterparts) 1.50
14 Matt Williams, Vinny Castilla (Counterparts) .20
15 Todd Hollandsworth, Bob Abreu (Counterparts) .20
16 John Smoltz, Pedro Martinez (Counterparts) .60
17 Jose Canseco, Chili Davis (Counterparts) .40
18 Jose Cruz, Jr., Ken Griffey Jr./UPT 15.00
19 Ken Griffey Jr./SF 15.00
20 Paul Molitor, John Olerud (Counterparts) .60
21 Roberto Alomar, Luis Castillo (Counterparts) .35
22 Derek Jeter, Lou Collier (Counterparts) .75
23 Chipper Jones, Robin Ventura (Counterparts) .75
24 Gary Sheffield, Ron Gant (Counterparts) .25
25 Ramon Martinez, Bobby Jones (Counterparts) .20
26 Mike Piazza, Raul Mondesi (Double Team) 7.50
27 Darin Erstad, Jeff Bagwell/UPT 7.50
28 Ivan Rodriguez/SF 7.50
29 J.T. Snow, Kevin Young (Counterparts) .20
30 Ryne Sandberg, Julio Franco (Counterparts) .75
31 Travis Fryman, Chris Snopek (Counterparts) .20
32 Wade Boggs, Russ Davis (Counterparts) .75
33 Brooks Kieschnick, Marty Cordova (Counterparts) .20
34 Andy Pettitte, Denny Neagle (Counterparts) .35
35 Paul Molitor, Matt Lawton (Double Team) 2.50
36 Scott Rolen, Cal Ripken Jr./UPT 20.00
37 Cal Ripken Jr./SF 20.00
38 Jim Thome, Dave Nilsson (Counterparts) .50
39 Tony Womack RC, Carlos Baerga (Counterparts) .20
40 Nomar Garciaparra, Mark Grudzielanek (Counterparts) .75
41 Todd Greene, Chris Widger (Counterparts) .20
42 Deion Sanders, Bernard Gilkey (Counterparts) .20
43 Hideo Nomo, Charles Nagy (Counterparts) .75
44 Ivan Rodriguez, Rusty Greer (Double Team) 2.00
45 Todd Walker, Chipper Jones/UPT 10.00
46 Greg Maddux/SF 12.00
47 Mo Vaughn, Cecil Fielder (Counterparts) .20
48 Craig Biggio, Scott Spiezio (Counterparts) .20
49 Pokey Reese, Jeff Blauser (Counterparts) .20
50 Ken Caminiti, Joe Randa (Counterparts) .20
51 Albert Belle, Shawn Green (Counterparts) .20
52 Randy Johnson, Jason Dickson (Counterparts) .60
53 Hideo Nomo, Chan Ho Park/DT 2.00
54 Scott Spiezio, Chuck Knoblauch/UPT 1.25
55 Chipper Jones/SF 12.00
56 Tino Martinez, Ryan McGuire (Counterparts) .20
57 Eric Young, Wilton Guerrero (Counterparts) .20
58 Ron Coomer, Dave Hollins (Counterparts) .20

59 Sammy Sosa, Angel Echevarria (Counterparts) .75
60 Dennis Reyes RC, Jimmy Key (Counterparts) .20
61 Barry Larkin, Deion Sanders (Double Team) .75
62 Wilton Guerrero, Roberto Alomar/UPT 2.00
63 Albert Belle/SF 1.50
64 Mark McGwire, Andres Galarraga (Counterparts) 1.50
65 Edgar Martinez, Todd Walker (Counterparts) .20
66 Steve Finley, Rich Becker (Counterparts) .20
67 Tom Glavine, Andy Ashby (Counterparts) .30
68 Sammy Sosa, Ryne Sandberg/DT 5.00
69 Nomar Garciaparra, Alex Rodriguez/UPT 15.00
70 Jeff Bagwell/SF 10.00
71 Darin Erstad, Mark Grace (Counterparts) .40
72 Scott Rolen, Edgardo Alfonzo (Counterparts) .50
73 Kenny Lofton, Lance Johnson (Counterparts) .20
74 Joey Hamilton, Brett Tomko (Counterparts) .20
75 Eddie Murray, Tim Salmon (Double Team) 2.50
76 Dmitri Young, Mo Vaughn/UPT 1.25
77 Juan Gonzalez/SF 3.00
78 Frank Thomas, Tony Clark (Counterparts) .60
79 Shannon Stewart, Bip Roberts (Counterparts) .20
80 Shawn Estes, Alex Fernandez (Counterparts) .20
81 John Smoltz, Javier Lopez (Double Team) .75
82 Todd Greene, Mike Piazza/UPT 15.00
83 Derek Jeter/SF 20.00
84 Dmitri Young, Antone Williamson (Counterparts) .20
85 Rickey Henderson, Darryl Hamilton (Counterparts) .20
86 Billy Wagner, Dennis Eckersley (Counterparts) .60
87 Larry Walker, Eric Young (Double Team) .75
88 Mark Kotsay, Juan Gonzalez/UPT 3.00
89 Barry Bonds/SF 20.00
90 Will Clark, Jeff Conine (Counterparts) .20
91 Tony Gwynn, Brett Butler (Counterparts) .75
92 John Wetteland, Rod Beck (Counterparts) .20
93 Bernie Williams, Tino Martinez/DT 1.25
94 Andruw Jones, Kenny Lofton/UPT 7.50
95 Mo Vaughn/SF 1.50
96 Joe Carter, Derrek Lee (Counterparts) .50
97 John Mabry, F.P. Santangelo (Counterparts) .20
98 Esteban Loaiza, Wilson Alvarez (Counterparts) .20
99 Matt Williams, David Justice/SF .75
100 Derrek Lee, Frank Thomas/UPT 7.50
101 Mark McGwire/SF 17.50
102 Fred McGriff, Paul Sorrento (Counterparts) .20
103 Jermaine Allensworth, Bernie Williams (Counterparts) .20
104 Ismael Valdes, Chris Holt (Counterparts) .20
105 Fred McGriff, Ryan Klesko/DT .75
106 Tony Clark, Mark McGwire/UPT 17.50
107 Tony Gwynn/SF 12.00
108 Jeffrey Hammonds, Ellis Burks (Counterparts) .20
109 Shane Reynolds, Andy Benes (Counterparts) .20
110 Roger Clemens, Carlos Delgado/DT 10.00
111 Karim Garcia, Albert Belle/UPT 1.25
112 Paul Molitor/SF 10.00
113 Trey Beamon, Eric Owens (Counterparts) .20
114 Curt Schilling, Darryl Kile (Counterparts) .30
115 Tom Glavine, Michael Tucker/DT .75
116 Pokey Reese, Derek Jeter/UPT 20.00
117 Manny Ramirez/SF 10.00
118 Juan Gonzalez, Brant Brown (Counterparts) .40

119 Juan Guzman, Francisco Cordova (Counterparts) .20
120 Randy Johnson, Edgar Martinez/DT 2.50
121 Hideki Irabu, Greg Maddux/UPT 10.00
122 Alex Rodriguez/SF 17.50
123 Barry Bonds, Quinton McCracken (Counterparts) 2.00
124 Roger Clemens, Alan Benes (Counterparts) .85
125 Wade Boggs, Paul O'Neill (Double Team) 1.75
126 Mike Cameron, Larry Walker/UPT 1.25
127 Gary Sheffield/SF 2.50
128 Andruw Jones, Raul Mondesi (Counterparts) .85
129 Brian Anderson, Terrell Wade (Counterparts) .20
130 Brady Anderson, Rafael Palmeiro/DT 2.00
131 Neifi Perez, Barry Larkin/UPT 1.25
132 Ken Caminiti/SF 1.50
133 Larry Walker, Rusty Greer (Counterparts) .20
134 Mariano Rivera, Mark Wohlers (Counterparts) .30
135 Hideki Irabu, Andy Pettitte/SF 1.50
136 Jose Guillen, Tony Gwynn/UPT 10.00
137 Hideo Nomo/SF 3.00
138 Vladimir Guerrero, Jim Edmonds (Counterparts) .60
139 Justin Thompson, Dwight Gooden (Counterparts) .20
140 Andres Galarraga, Dante Bichette/DT .75
141 Kenny Lofton/SF 1.50
142 Tim Salmon, Manny Ramirez (Counterparts) .60
143 Kevin Brown, Matt Morris (Counterparts) .20
144 Craig Biggio, Bob Abreu/DT .75
145 Roberto Alomar/SF 2.00
146 Jose Guillen, Brian Jordan (Counterparts) .20
147 Bartolo Colon, Kevin Appier (Counterparts) .20
148 Ray Lankford, Brian Jordan/DT .75
149 Chuck Knoblauch/SF 1.50
150 Henry Rodriguez, Ray Lankford (Counterparts) .20
151 Jaret Wright RC, Ben McDonald (Counterparts) .20
152 Bobby Bonilla, Kevin Brown/DT .75
153 Barry Larkin/SF 1.50
154 David Justice, Reggie Sanders (Counterparts) .20
155 Mike Mussina, Ken Hill (Counterparts) .40
156 Mark Grace, Brooks Kieschnick/DT .75
157 Jim Thome/SF 2.50
158 Michael Tucker, Curtis Goodwin (Counterparts) .20
159 Jeff Suppan, Jeff Fassero (Counterparts) .20
160 Mike Mussina, Jeffrey Hammonds/DT 1.00
161 John Smoltz/SF 1.50
162 Moises Alou, Eric Davis (Counterparts) .20
163 Sandy Alomar Jr., Dan Wilson (Counterparts) .20
164 Rondell White, Henry Rodriguez/DT .75
165 Roger Clemens/SF 12.50
166 Brady Anderson, Al Martin (Counterparts) .20
167 Jason Kendall, Charles Johnson (Counterparts) .20
168 Jason Giambi, Jose Canseco/DT 2.00
169 Larry Walker/SF 1.50
170 Jay Buhner, Geronimo Berroa (Counterparts) .20
171 Ivan Rodriguez, Mike Sweeney (Counterparts) .50
172 Kevin Appier, Jose Rosado/DT .75
173 Bernie Williams/SF 1.50
174 Todd Dunwoody, Brian Giles RC (Counterparts) .40
175 Javier Lopez, Scott Hatteberg (Counterparts) .20
176 John Jaha, Jeff Cirillo/DT .75
177 Andy Pettitte/SF 2.00
178 Dante Bichette, Butch Huskey (Counterparts) .20

179 Raul Casanova, Todd Hundley (Counterparts) .20
180 Jim Edmonds, Garret Anderson/DT .75
181 Deion Sanders/SF 1.50
182 Ryan Klesko, Paul O'Neill (Counterparts) .20
183 Joe Carter, Pat Hentgen/DT .75
184 Brady Anderson/SF 1.50
185 Carlos Delgado, Wally Joyner (Counterparts) .50
186 Jermaine Dye, Johnny Damon/DT 1.00
187 Randy Johnson/SF 7.50
188 Todd Hundley, Carlos Baerga/DT .75
189 Tom Glavine/SF 2.50
190 Damon Mashore, Jason McDonald/DT .75
191 Wade Boggs/SF 12.00
192 Al Martin, Jason Kendall/DT .75
193 Matt Williams/SF 1.50
194 Will Clark, Dean Palmer/DT .75
195 Sammy Sosa/SF 12.00
196 Jose Cruz, Jr., Jay Buhner/DT .75
197 Eddie Murray/SF 10.00
198 Darin Erstad, Jason Dickson/DT 1.00
199 Fred McGriff/SF 1.50
200 Bubba Trammell, Bobby Higginson/DT .75

Exposure

A complete 200-card parallel set printed with Holographic Poly-Chromium technology on both sides and featuring a special "Limited Exposure" stamp. Less than 40 sets of the Star Factor Limited Exposures are thought to exist.

	NM/M
Common Counterparts:	.75
Common Double Team:	3.00
Common Star Factor:	6.50
Common Unlimited:	4.50
Stars:	4X

Exposure Non-Glossy

In error, half (100 cards) of the Limited Exposure parallels were produced in regular technology (non-chrome) on regular (non-glossy) cardboard stock. These cards do carry the Limited Exposure identification in the card-number box on back, but do not carry the correct cards' higher values. No checklist of which 100 cards were involved in the error is available.

	NM/M
Common Non-Glossy:	.50
Stars: 25 Percent	

Fabric of the Game

This fractured insert set consists of 69 different cards highlighting three different technologies representing three statistical categories: Canvas (stolen bases), Leather (doubles) and Wood (home runs). Each of the 23 cards in each category are found in varying levels of scarcity: Legendary Material (one card per theme; numbered to 100), Hall of Fame Material (four cards numbered to 250), Superstar Material (five cards numbered to 500), Star Ma-

terial (six cards numbered to 750), and Major League Material (seven cards numbered to 1,000).

	NM/M
Complete Set: (69)	275.00
Common Player:	1.50
Complete Canvas Set (23):	80.00
Rickey Henderson/100	12.00
Barry Bonds/250	15.00
Kenny Lofton/250	2.50
Roberto Alomar/250	4.50
Ryne Sandberg/250	12.00
Tony Gwynn/500	7.50
Barry Larkin/500	2.00
Brady Anderson/500	2.00
Chuck Knoblauch/500	2.00
Craig Biggio/500	2.00
Sammy Sosa/750	7.50
Gary Sheffield/750	2.00
Eric Young/750	1.50
Larry Walker/750	1.50
Ken Griffey Jr./750	10.00
Deion Sanders/750	1.50
Raul Mondesi/1,000	1.50
Rondell White/1,000	1.50
Derek Jeter/1,000	10.00
Nomar Garciaparra/1,000	6.00
Wilton Guerrero/1,000	1.50
Pokey Reese/1,000	1.50
Darin Erstad/1,000	2.00
Complete Leather Set (23):	90.00
Paul Molitor/100	15.00
Wade Boggs/250	12.00
Cal Ripken Jr./250	20.00
Tony Gwynn/250	12.00
Joe Carter/250	2.50
Rafael Palmeiro/500	5.00
Mark Grace/500	1.50
Bobby Bonilla/500	1.50
Andres Galarraga/500	1.50
Edgar Martinez/500	1.50
Ken Caminiti/750	1.50
Ivan Rodriguez/750	4.50
Frank Thomas/750	6.00
Jeff Bagwell/750	6.00
Albert Belle/750	1.50
Bernie Williams/750	1.50
Chipper Jones/1,000	7.50
Rusty Greer/1,000	1.50
Todd Walker/1,000	1.50
Scott Rolen/1,000	3.00
Bob Abreu/1,000	1.50
Jose Guillen/1,000	1.50
Jose Cruz, Jr./1,000	1.50
Complete Wood Set (23):	110.00
Eddie Murray/100	12.00
Cal Ripken Jr./250	20.00
Barry Bonds/250	20.00
Mark McGwire/250	17.50
Fred McGriff/250	3.50
Ken Griffey Jr./500	7.50
Albert Belle/500	2.00
Frank Thomas/500	6.50
Juan Gonzalez/500	3.00
Matt Williams/500	2.00
Mike Piazza/500	7.50
Jeff Bagwell/750	6.00
Mo Vaughn/750	1.50
Gary Sheffield/750	2.00
Tim Salmon/750	1.50
David Justice/750	1.50
Manny Ramirez/1,000	5.00
Jim Thome/1,000	2.50
Tino Martinez/1,000	1.50
Andruw Jones/1,000	3.50
Vladimir Guerrero/1,000	5.00
Tony Clark/1,000	1.50
Dmitri Young/1,000	1.50

1997 Donruss Preferred

Each of the 200 base cards is printed on all-foil microetched stock. Conventional backs have a color player photo and a few stats. The set is fractured into four increasingly scarce levels: 100 Bronze cards, 70 Silver, 20 Gold and 10 Platinum. Instead of traditional packs, cards were sold in five-card collectible tins. Four different inserts were included with the product: Staremaster, X-Ponential Power, Cut To The Chase

(a die-cut parallel) and Precious Metals. Odds of finding any insert were 1:4 packs.

	NM/M
Complete Set (200):	225.00
Common Bronze:	.10
Common Silver:	.60
Common Gold:	1.25
Common Platinum:	6.00
Cut to the Chase:	1.5X
Tin Pack (5):	2.50
Tin Box (24):	40.00
1 Frank Thomas/P	7.50
2 Ken Griffey Jr./P	12.50
3 Cecil Fielder/B	.10
4 Chuck Knoblauch/G	1.25
5 Garret Anderson/B	.10
6 Greg Maddux/P	10.00
7 Matt Williams/S	.60
8 Marquis Grissom/S	.60
9 Jason Isringhausen/B	.10
10 Larry Walker/B	.60
11 Charles Nagy/B	.10
12 Dan Wilson/B	.10
13 Albert Belle/G	1.25
14 Javier Lopez/B	.10
15 David Cone/B	.10
16 Bernard Gilkey/B	.10
17 Andres Galarraga/S	.60
18 Bill Pulsipher/B	.10
19 Alex Fernandez/B	.10
20 Andy Pettitte/S	1.25
21 Mark Grudzielanek/B	.10
22 Juan Gonzalez/P	6.00
23 Reggie Sanders/B	.10
24 Kenny Lofton/B	1.25
25 Andy Ashby/B	.10
26 John Wetteland/B	.10
27 Bobby Bonilla/B	.10
28 Hideo Nomo/B	2.50
29 Joe Carter/B	.10
30 Jose Canseco/B	.40
31 Ellis Burks/B	.10
32 Edgar Martinez/S	.60
33 Chan Ho Park/B	.10
34 David Justice/B	.10
35 Carlos Delgado/S	.50
36 Jeff Cirillo/B	.60
37 Charles Johnson/B	.10
38 Manny Ramirez/G	4.50
39 Greg Vaughn/B	.10
40 Henry Rodriguez/B	.10
41 Darryl Strawberry/B	.10
42 Jim Thome/B	2.50
43 Ryan Klesko/S	.60
44 Jermaine Allensworth/B	.10
45 Brian Jordan/B	1.25
46 Tony Gwynn/P	10.00
47 Rafael Palmeiro/G	3.50
48 Dante Bichette/S	.60
49 Ivan Rodriguez/G	3.50
50 Mark McGwire/G	8.00
51 Tim Salmon/S	.60
52 Roger Clemens/S	1.50
53 Matt Lawton/B	.10
54 Wade Boggs/S	3.50
55 Travis Fryman/B	.10
56 Bobby Higginson/S	.60
57 John Jaha/B	.60
58 Rondell White/S	.60
59 Tom Glavine/S	1.25
60 Eddie Murray/S	2.50
61 Vinny Castilla/B	.10
62 Todd Hundley/B	.10
63 Jay Buhner/S	.60
64 Paul O'Neill/B	.10
65 Steve Finley/B	.10
66 Kevin Appier/B	.10
67 Ray Durham/B	.10
68 Dave Nilsson/B	.10
69 Jeff Bagwell/G	4.50
70 Al Martin/S	.60
71 Paul Molitor/G	4.50
72 Kevin Brown/B	.10
73 Ron Gant/B	.10
74 Dwight Gooden/B	.10
75 Quinton McCracken/B	.10
76 Rusty Greer/S	.60
77 Juan Guzman/B	.10
78 Fred McGriff/S	.60
79 Tino Martinez/B	.10
80 Ray Lankford/B	.10
81 Ken Caminiti/G	1.25
82 James Baldwin/B	.10
83 Jermaine Dye/G	1.25
84 Mark Grace/S	.60
85 Pat Hentgen/S	.60
86 Jason Giambi/S	1.50
87 Brian Hunter/B	.10
88 Andy Benes/B	.10
89 Jose Rosado/B	.10
90 Shawn Green/S	.25
91 Jason Kendall/B	.10
92 Alex Rodriguez/P	15.00
93 Chipper Jones/P	10.00
94 Barry Bonds/P	10.00
95 Brady Anderson/G	1.25
96 Ryne Sandberg/S	3.50
97 Lance Johnson/B	.10
98 Cal Ripken Jr./P	17.50
99 Craig Biggio/S	.60
100 Dean Palmer/B	.10
101 Gary Sheffield/S	1.50
102 Johnny Damon/S	.35
103 Mo Vaughn/S	1.25
104 Randy Johnson/S	2.50
105 Raul Mondesi/B	.60

106	Roberto Alomar/G	2.00
107	Mike Piazza/P	12.50
108	Rey Ordonez/B	.10
109	Barry Larkin/G	1.25
110	Tony Clark/S	.60
111	Bernie Williams/B	.60
112	John Smoltz/G	1.25
113	Moises Alou/B	.10
114	Will Clark/B	.10
115	Sammy Sosa/G	6.00
116	Jim Edmonds/S	.60
117	Jeff Conine/B	.10
118	Joey Hamilton/B	.10
119	Todd Hollandsworth/B	.10
120	Troy Percival/B	.10
121	Paul Wilson/B	.10
122	Ken Hill/B	.10
123	Mariano Rivera/S	.75
124	Eric Karros/B	.10
125	Derek Jeter/G	10.00
126	Eric Young/B	.10
127	John Mabry/B	.10
128	Gregg Jefferies/B	.10
129	Ismael Valdes/S	.60
130	Marty Cordova/B	.10
131	Omar Vizquel/B	.10
132	Mike Mussina/S	1.25
133	Darin Erstad/B	.30
134	Edgar Renteria/B	.10
135	Billy Wagner/B	.10
136	Alex Ochoa/B	.10
137	Luis Castillo/B	.10
138	Rocky Coppinger/B	.10
139	Mike Sweeney/B	.10
140	Michael Tucker/B	.10
141	Chris Snopek/B	.10
142	Dmitri Young/B	.60
143	Andruw Jones/P	7.50
144	Mike Cameron/S	.60
145	Brant Brown/B	.10
146	Todd Walker/G	1.25
147	Nomar Garciaparra/B	6.00
148	Glendon Rusch/B	.10
149	Karim Garcia/S	.60
150	Bubba Trammell/S RC	.60
151	Todd Greene/B	.10
152	Wilton Guerrero/G	1.25
153	Scott Spiezio/B	.10
154	Brooks Kieschnick/B	.10
155	Vladimir Guerrero/G	4.50
156	Brian Giles/S RC	1.50
157	Pokey Reese/B	.10
158	Jason Dickson/G	1.25
159	Kevin Orie/S	.60
160	Scott Rolen/G	3.00
161	Bartolo Colon/S	.60
162	Shannon Stewart/G	1.25
163	Wendell Magee/B	.10
164	Jose Guillen/S	.60
165	Bob Abreu/S	.60
166	Deivi Cruz/B RC	.25
167	Alex Rodriguez/B (National Treasures)	3.00
168	Frank Thomas/B (National Treasures)	.75
169	Cal Ripken Jr./B (National Treasures)	4.00
170	Chipper Jones/B (National Treasures)	1.50
171	Mike Piazza/B (National Treasures)	2.50
172	Tony Gwynn/S (National Treasures)	3.50
173	Juan Gonzalez/B (National Treasures)	.40
174	Kenny Lofton/S (National Treasures)	.60
175	Ken Griffey Jr./B (National Treasures)	2.50
176	Mark McGwire/B (National Treasures)	3.00
177	Jeff Bagwell/B (National Treasures)	.75
178	Paul Molitor/S (National Treasures)	2.50
179	Andruw Jones/B (National Treasures)	.75
180	Manny Ramirez/S (National Treasures)	2.50
181	Ken Caminiti/S (National Treasures)	.60
182	Barry Bonds/B (National Treasures)	4.00
183	Mo Vaughn/B (National Treasures)	.10
184	Derek Jeter/B (National Treasures)	4.00
185	Barry Larkin/S (National Treasures)	.60
186	Ivan Rodriguez/B (National Treasures)	.65
187	Albert Belle/S (National Treasures)	.60
188	John Smoltz/S (National Treasures)	.60
189	Chuck Knoblauch/S (National Treasures)	.60
190	Brian Jordan/S (National Treasures)	.60
191	Gary Sheffield/S (National Treasures)	1.00
192	Jim Thome/S (National Treasures)	2.00
193	Brady Anderson/S (National Treasures)	.60
194	Hideo Nomo/S (National Treasures)	1.50

195	Sammy Sosa/S (National Treasures)	3.50
196	Greg Maddux/B (National Treasures)	1.25
197	Checklist (Vladimir Guerrero/B)	.40
198	Checklist (Scott Rolen/B)	.15
199	Checklist (Todd Walker/B)	.10
200	Checklist (Nomar Garciaparra/B)	.60

Cut To The Chase

Each of the cards in the Donruss Preferred series can also be found in this parallel set with die-cut borders, in the same bronze, silver, gold and platinum finishes. Multiplier values of the die-cuts are inverse to that usually found, with platinum cards the lowest, followed by gold, silver and bronze. Besides die-cutting, the chase cards feature a "CUT TO THE CHASE" designation at bottom.

Typical Value: 1.5X

Precious Metals

This 25-card partial parallel set features cards printed on actual silver, gold and platinum stock. Only 100 of each card were produced.

		NM/M
	Common Player:	7.50
1	Frank Thomas/P	45.00
2	Ken Griffey Jr./P	75.00
3	Greg Maddux/P	60.00
4	Albert Belle/G	7.50
5	Juan Gonzalez/P	25.00
6	Kenny Lofton/G	7.50
7	Tony Gwynn/P	60.00
8	Ivan Rodriguez/G	30.00
9	Mark McGwire/G	90.00
10	Matt Williams/S	7.50
11	Wade Boggs/S	60.00
12	Eddie Murray/S	45.00
13	Jeff Bagwell/G	45.00
14	Ken Caminiti/G	7.50
15	Alex Rodriguez/P	90.00
16	Chipper Jones/P	60.00
17	Barry Bonds/P	125.00
18	Cal Ripken Jr./P	125.00
19	Mo Vaughn/G	7.50
20	Mike Piazza/P	75.00
21	Derek Jeter/P	125.00
22	Bernie Williams/S	7.50
23	Andruw Jones/P	45.00
24	Vladimir Guerrero/G	45.00
25	Jose Guillen/S	7.50

Staremasters

A 20-card insert printed on foil stock and accented with holographic foil, Staremasters is designed to show up-close "game-face" photography. Each card is sequentially numbered to 1,500. Each of the Staremasters inserts can also be found in a version overprinted with a large diagonal black "SAMPLE" on front and back. These were distributed to

dealers and the media. The sample cards have a "PROMO/1500" on back in place of a serial number.

		NM/M
	Complete Set (20):	55.00
	Common Player:	1.00
	Samples: 50 Percent	
1	Alex Rodriguez	6.00
2	Frank Thomas	3.00
3	Chipper Jones	4.00
4	Cal Ripken Jr.	7.50
5	Mike Piazza	4.50
6	Juan Gonzalez	2.25
7	Derek Jeter	7.50
8	Jeff Bagwell	3.00
9	Ken Griffey Jr.	4.50
10	Tony Gwynn	4.00
11	Barry Bonds	3.00
12	Albert Belle	1.00
13	Greg Maddux	.50
14	Mark McGwire	6.00
15	Ken Caminiti	1.00
16	Hideo Nomo	2.25
17	Gary Sheffield	1.50
18	Andruw Jones	3.00
19	Mo Vaughn	1.00
20	Ivan Rodriguez	2.25

X-Ponential Power

This 20-card die-cut insert contains two top hitters from 10 different teams. Placing the cards of teammates together forms an "X" shape. Cards are printed on thick plastic stock and gold holographic foil stamping and are sequentially numbered to 3,000.

		NM/M
	Complete Set (20):	50.00
	Common Player:	1.00
1A	Manny Ramirez	3.50
1B	Jim Thome	2.00
2A	Paul Molitor	3.50
2B	Chuck Knoblauch	1.00
3A	Ivan Rodriguez	2.50
3B	Juan Gonzalez	2.00
4A	Albert Belle	1.00
4B	Frank Thomas	3.50
5A	Roberto Alomar	1.25
5B	Cal Ripken Jr.	9.00
6A	Tim Salmon	1.00
6B	Jim Edmonds	1.00
7A	Ken Griffey Jr.	6.00
7B	Alex Rodriguez	7.50
8A	Chipper Jones	5.00
8B	Andruw Jones	3.50
9A	Mike Piazza	6.00
9B	Raul Mondesi	1.00
10A	Tony Gwynn	4.50
10B	Ken Caminiti	1.00

1997 Donruss Preferred Tins

Twenty-five different players are featured on the lithographed steel tins which were the "packs" of Donruss Preferred baseball. The 3" x 4-1/2" x 5/8" tins are hinged along the left side and were produced in two versions. Predominantly blue tins are the standard package. A premium parallel version is gold-colored and serially numbered within an edition of 1,200. Gold tins were packed one per 24-pack box of Preferred. Values

shown are for opened tins. Shrink-wrapped unopened tins are valued about 1.5-3X the figures shown.

		NM/M
	Complete Set, Blue (25):	10.00
	Common Tin:	.25
	Gold:	10X
1	Frank Thomas	.40
2	Ken Griffey Jr.	.60
3	Andruw Jones	.40
4	Cal Ripken Jr.	1.00
5	Mike Piazza	.60
6	Chipper Jones	.50
7	Alex Rodriguez	.75
8	Derek Jeter	1.00
9	Juan Gonzalez	.30
10	Albert Belle	.25
11	Tony Gwynn	.50
12	Greg Maddux	.50
13	Jeff Bagwell	.40
14	Roger Clemens	.55
15	Mark McGwire	.75
16	Gary Sheffield	.30
17	Manny Ramirez	.40
18	Hideo Nomo	.30
19	Kenny Lofton	.25
20	Mo Vaughn	.25
21	Ryne Sandberg	.50
22	Barry Bonds	1.00
23	Sammy Sosa	.50
24	John Smoltz	.25
25	Ivan Rodriguez	.35

1997 Donruss Preferred Tin Boxes

Twenty-five different players are featured on the lithographed steel boxes in which the "packs" of Donruss Preferred baseball were sold. Boxes measure about 5-1/4" x 9-1/4" x 5-3/8". Inside the removable lid is a serial number from within an edition of 1,200 (blue) or 299 (gold). The gold versions were a later, hobby-only release.

		NM/M
	Complete Set, Blue (25):	70.00
	Common Box:	2.00
	Gold:	4X
1	Frank Thomas	5.00
2	Ken Griffey Jr.	5.00
3	Andruw Jones	3.00
4	Cal Ripken Jr.	7.50
5	Mike Piazza	5.00
6	Chipper Jones	4.00
7	Alex Rodriguez	6.00
8	Derek Jeter	7.50
9	Juan Gonzalez	2.50
10	Albert Belle	2.00
11	Tony Gwynn	4.00
12	Greg Maddux	4.00
13	Jeff Bagwell	3.00
14	Roger Clemens	4.50
15	Mark McGwire	6.00
16	Gary Sheffield	2.50
17	Manny Ramirez	3.00
18	Hideo Nomo	2.50
19	Kenny Lofton	2.00
20	Mo Vaughn	2.00
21	Ryne Sandberg	4.00
22	Barry Bonds	7.50
23	Sammy Sosa	4.00
24	John Smoltz	2.00
25	Ivan Rodriguez	2.50

1997 Donruss Signature

Donruss ventured in the autograph-per-pack market with this series featuring 100 base cards (unsigned) and various types and

versions of authentically autographed cards. The suggested retail price for each five-card pack was $14.99. Base cards have textured silver-foil borders and highlights on front. Backs have a second photo and lengthy stats. A parallel insert edition of each base card was also issued, labeled "Platinum Press Proof," the parallels have blue metallic foil on front and are designated "1 of 150" on the back.

		NM/M
	Complete Set (100):	15.00
	Common Player:	.10
	Platinum Stars/RC's:	12X
	Pack (5):	7.50
	Wax Box (12):	80.00
1	Mark McGwire	1.25
2	Kenny Lofton	.10
3	Tony Gwynn	.75
4	Tony Clark	.10
5	Tim Salmon	.10
6	Ken Griffey Jr.	1.00
7	Mike Piazza	1.00
8	Greg Maddux	.75
9	Roberto Alomar	.20
10	Andres Galarraga	.10
11	Roger Clemens	.90
12	Bernie Williams	.10
13	Rondell White	.10
14	Kevin Appler	.10
15	Ray Lankford	.10
16	Frank Thomas	.65
17	Will Clark	.10
18	Chipper Jones	.75
19	Jeff Bagwell	.65
20	Manny Ramirez	.65
21	Ryne Sandberg	.75
22	Paul Molitor	.65
23	Gary Sheffield	.10
24	Jim Edmonds	.10
25	Barry Larkin	.10
26	Rafael Palmeiro	.60
27	Alan Benes	.10
28	David Justice	.10
29	Randy Johnson	.65
30	Barry Bonds	1.50
31	Mo Vaughn	.10
32	Michael Tucker	.10
33	Larry Walker	.10
34	Tino Martinez	.10
35	Jose Guillen	.10
36	Carlos Delgado	.40
37	Jason Dickson	.10
38	Tom Glavine	.25
39	Raul Mondesi	.10
40	Jose Cruz Jr. RC	.50
41	Johnny Damon	.10
42	Mark Grace	.10
43	Juan Gonzalez	.35
44	Vladimir Guerrero	.65
45	Kevin Brown	.10
46	Justin Thompson	.10
47	Eric Young	.10
48	Ron Coomer	.10
49	Mark Kotsay	.10
50	Scott Rolen	.60
51	Derek Jeter	1.50
52	Jim Thome	.50
53	Fred McGriff	.10
54	Albert Belle	.10
55	Garret Anderson	.10
56	Wilton Guerrero	.10
57	Jose Canseco	.40
58	Cal Ripken Jr.	1.50
59	Sammy Sosa	.75
60	Dmitri Young	.10
61	Alex Rodriguez	1.25
62	Javier Lopez	.10
63	Sandy Alomar Jr.	.10
64	Joe Carter	.10
65	Dante Bichette	.10
66	Al Martin	.10
67	Darin Erstad	.30
68	Pokey Reese	.10
69	Brady Anderson	.10
70	Andruw Jones	.65
71	Ivan Rodriguez	.50
72	Nomar Garciaparra	.75
73	Moises Alou	.10
74	Andy Pettitte	.35
75	Jay Buhner	.10
76	Craig Biggio	.10
77	Wade Boggs	.75

78	Shawn Estes	.10
79	Neifi Perez	.10
80	Rusty Greer	.10
81	Pedro Martinez	.60
82	Mike Mussina	.40
83	Jason Giambi	.40
84	Hideo Nomo	.35
85	Todd Hundley	.10
86	Deion Sanders	.10
87	Mike Cameron	.10
88	Bobby Bonilla	.10
89	Todd Greene	.10
90	Kevin Orie	.10
91	Ken Caminiti	.10
92	Chuck Knoblauch	.10
93	Matt Morris	.10
94	Matt Williams	.10
95	Pat Hentgen	.10
96	John Smoltz	.10
97	Edgar Martinez	.10
98	Jason Kendall	.10
99	Checklist (Ken Griffey Jr.)	.50
100	Checklist (Frank Thomas)	.30

1997 Donruss Signature Platinum Press Proofs

This parallel insert set features metallic blue borders and graphics on front and has a "1 of 150" notation on back.

	NM/M
Common Player:	2.00
Stars:	12X

1997 Donruss Signature Autographs Promo

The "autograph" on the front of this promo card is a facsimile signature, rather than hand-penned. The sample is identical in format to the common red base level autographs in the set, but Thomas does not appear in that format.

	NM/M
Frank Thomas	6.00

Autographs (Red)

The basic level of authentically autographed cards found one per ($15) pack in Donruss Signature is the unnumbered "red" version. Cards have the background of the front photo printed only in red. For most players, 3,900 cards of the red version were autographed for insertion. Some players, however, signed fewer reds. Exchange cards had to be issued for Raul Mondesi and Edgar Renteria, whose signed cards were not ready when the set was first issued. It has been reported that Mondesi never signed any of the red version autograph cards. Cards are checklisted here in alphabetical order, in concordance with the larger Millenium checklist. The reported number of red cards signed appears in parentheses. This list differs significantly from the original list announced by Donruss in November 1997 due to last minute editions and deletions. Players signed in black and/or blue ink. Some players also added personal touches to some or all of their signatures, such as Bible verse citations, uniform numbers, etc.

		NM/M
Complete Set (116):		700.00
Common Player:		2.00
(1)	Jeff Abbott/3,900	2.00
(2)	Bob Abreu/3,900	8.00
(3)	Edgardo Alfonzo/3,900	3.00
(4)	Roberto Alomar/150	50.00
(5)	Sandy Alomar Jr./1,400	6.00
(6)	Moises Alou	10.00
(7)	Garret Anderson/3,900	7.00
(8)	Andy Ashby/3,900	3.00
(10)	Trey Beamon/3,900	2.00
(12)	Alan Benes/3,900	2.00
(13)	Geronimo Berroa/3,900	2.00
(14)	Wade Boggs/150	175.00
(18)	Kevin L. Brown/3,900	2.00
(20)	Brett Butler/1,400	3.50
(21)	Mike Cameron/3,900	7.00
(22)	Giovanni Carrara/2,900	2.00
(23)	Luis Castillo/3,900	4.00
(24)	Tony Clark/3,900	3.00
(25)	Will Clark/1,400	12.00
(27)	Lou Collier/3,900	3.00
(28)	Bartolo Colon/3,900	12.50
(29)	Ron Coomer/3,900	3.00
(30)	Marty Cordova/3,900	3.00
(31)	Jacob Cruz/3,900	3.00
(32)	Jose Cruz Jr./3,900	8.00
(33)	Russ Davis/3,900	3.00
(34)	Jason Dickson/3,900	2.00
(35)	Todd Dunwoody/3,900	2.00
(36)	Jermaine Dye/3,900	3.00
(37)	Jim Edmonds/3,900	12.00
(38)	Darin Erstad/900	8.00
(39)	Bobby Estalella/3,900	3.00
(40)	Shawn Estes/3,900	3.00
(41)	Jeff Fassero/3,900	2.00
(42)	Andres Galarraga/3,900	6.00
(43)	Karim Garcia/3,900	3.00
(45)	Derrick Gibson/3,900	3.00
(46)	Brian Giles/3,900	8.00
(47)	Tom Glavine/150	50.00
(49)	Rick Gorecki/3,900	4.50
(50)	Shawn Green/1,900	15.00
(51)	Todd Greene/3,900	3.00
(52)	Rusty Greer/3,900	3.00
(53)	Ben Grieve/3,900	3.00
(54)	Mark Grudzielanek/3,900	3.00
(55)	Vladimir Guerrero/1,900	20.00
(56)	Wilton Guerrero/2,150	3.00
(57)	Jose Guillen/2,900	8.00
(59)	Jeffrey Hammonds/2,150	3.50
(60)	Todd Helton/1,400	16.00
(61)	Todd Hollandsworth/2,900	3.00
(62)	Trenidad Hubbard/900	4.00
(63)	Todd Hundley/1,400	3.00
(66)	Bobby Jones/3,900	2.00
(68)	Brian Jordan/1,400	4.00
(69)	David Justice/900	10.00
(70)	Eric Karros/650	4.50
(71)	Jason Kendall/3,900	6.00
(72)	Jimmy Key/3,900	5.00
(73)	Brooks Kieschnick/3,900	2.00
(74)	Ryan Klesko/225	10.00
(76)	Paul Konerko/900	10.00
(77)	Mark Kotsay/2,400	3.00
(78)	Ray Lankford/3,900	3.00
(79)	Barry Larkin/150	35.00
(80)	Derrek Lee/3,900	10.00
(81)	Esteban Loaiza/3,900	3.00
(82)	Javier Lopez/1,400	10.00
(84)	Edgar Martinez/150	50.00
(85)	Pedro Martinez/3,900	35.00
(87)	Rafael Medina/3,900	3.00
(88)	Raul Mondesi (Exchange Card)	3.00
(89)	Matt Morris/3,900	4.00
(92)	Paul O'Neill/900	15.00
(93)	Kevin Orie/3,900	2.00
(94)	David Ortiz/3,900	50.00
(95)	Rafael Palmeiro/900	30.00
(96)	Jay Payton/3,900	2.50
(97)	Neifi Perez/3,900	2.00
(99)	Manny Ramirez/900	40.00
(100)	Joe Randa/3,900	3.00
(101)	Calvin Reese/3,900	3.00
(102)	Edgar Renteria (?)	20.00
(102)	Edgar Renteria (Exchange Card)	3.00

(103)	Dennis Reyes/3,900	2.00
(106)	Henry Rodriguez/3,900	2.00
(108)	Scott Rolen (1,900)	25.00
(109)	Kirk Rueter/2,900	2.00
(110)	Ryne Sandberg (400)	60.00
(112)	Dwight Smith/2,900	3.00
(113)	J.T. Snow/900	4.00
(114)	Scott Spiezio/3,900	2.00
(115)	Shannon Stewart/2,900	3.00
(116)	Jeff Suppan/1,900	3.00
(117)	Mike Sweeney/3,900	6.00
(118)	Miguel Tejada/3,900	25.00
(121)	Justin Thompson/2,400	3.00
(122)	Brett Tomko/3,900	3.00
(123)	Bubba Trammell/3,900	2.50
(124)	Michael Tucker/3,900	2.00
(125)	Javier Valentin/3,900	2.00
(126)	Mo Vaughn/150	12.00
(127)	Robin Ventura/1,400	8.00
(128)	Terrell Wade/3,900	2.00
(129)	Billy Wagner/3,900	12.00
(130)	Larry Walker/900	25.00
(131)	Todd Walker/2,400	3.00
(132)	Rondell White/3,900	6.00
(133)	Kevin Wickander/900	4.00
(134)	Chris Widger/3,900	3.00
(136)	Matt Williams/150	25.00
(137)	Antone Williamson/3,900	2.00
(138)	Dan Wilson/3,900	3.00
(139)	Tony Womack/3,900	5.00
(140)	Jaret Wright/3,900	12.00
(141)	Dmitri Young/3,900	8.00
(142)	Eric Young/3,900	2.50
(143)	Kevin Young/3,900	2.50

Century Marks (Blue)

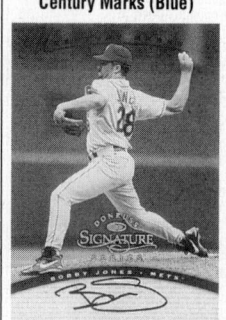

Virtually identical to the more common red and green (Millenium) versions, the Century Marks are identifiable at first glance by the use of blue ink in the background of the front photo and the "Century Marks" designation at top. On back, the cards are numbered from 0001 through 0100 in metallic foil at center. Several players initially had to be represented in the set by exchange cards. The unnumbered cards are checklisted here alphabetically.

		NM/M
Common Player:		20.00
(1)	Jeff Abbott	20.00
(2)	Bob Abreu	30.00
(3)	Edgardo Alfonzo	20.00
(4)	Roberto Alomar	75.00
(5)	Sandy Alomar Jr.	25.00
(6)	Moises Alou	35.00
(7)	Garret Anderson	60.00
(8)	Andy Ashby	20.00
(9)	Jeff Bagwell	80.00
(10)	Trey Beamon	20.00
(11)	Albert Belle	30.00
(12)	Alan Benes	20.00
(13)	Geronimo Berroa	20.00
(14)	Wade Boggs	100.00
(15)	Barry Bonds	300.00
(16)	Bobby Bonilla	20.00
(17)	Kevin Brown	75.00
(18)	Kevin L. Brown	20.00
(19)	Jay Buhner	30.00
(20)	Brett Butler	20.00
(21)	Mike Cameron	25.00
(22)	Giovanni Carrara	20.00
(23)	Luis Castillo	20.00
(24)	Tony Clark	20.00
(25)	Will Clark	100.00
(26)	Roger Clemens	200.00
(27)	Lou Collier	20.00
(28)	Bartolo Colon	30.00
(29)	Ron Coomer	20.00
(30)	Marty Cordova	20.00
(31)	Jacob Cruz	20.00
(32)	Jose Cruz Jr.	30.00
(33)	Russ Davis	20.00
(34)	Jason Dickson	25.00
(35)	Todd Dunwoody	20.00
(36)	Jermaine Dye	20.00
(37)	Jim Edmonds	60.00
(38)	Darin Erstad	40.00
(39)	Bobby Estalella	20.00
(40)	Shawn Estes	20.00
(41)	Jeff Fassero	20.00
(42)	Andres Galarraga	30.00
(43)	Karim Garcia	20.00

(44)	Nomar Garciaparra/ SP/62	225.00
(45)	Derrick Gibson	20.00
(46)	Brian Giles	30.00
(47)	Tom Glavine	100.00
(48)	Juan Gonzalez	55.00
(49)	Rick Gorecki	20.00
(50)	Shawn Green	90.00
(51)	Todd Greene	20.00
(52)	Rusty Greer	20.00
(53)	Ben Grieve	20.00
(54)	Mark Grudzielanek	20.00
(55)	Vladimir Guerrero	100.00
(56)	Wilton Guerrero	20.00
(57)	Jose Guillen	30.00
(58)	Tony Gwynn	95.00
(59)	Jeffrey Hammonds	20.00
(60)	Todd Helton	60.00
(61)	Todd Hollandsworth	20.00
(62)	Trenidad Hubbard	20.00
(63)	Todd Hundley	25.00
(64)	Derek Jeter	200.00
(65)	Andruw Jones	50.00
(66)	Bobby Jones	20.00
(67)	Chipper Jones	100.00
(68)	Brian Jordan	35.00
(69)	David Justice	30.00
(70)	Eric Karros	25.00
(71)	Jason Kendall	30.00
(72)	Jimmy Key	50.00
(73)	Brooks Kieschnick	20.00
(74)	Ryan Klesko	25.00
(75)	Chuck Knoblauch	20.00
(76)	Paul Konerko	25.00
(77)	Mark Kotsay	25.00
(78)	Ray Lankford	20.00
(79)	Barry Larkin	60.00
(80)	Derrek Lee	40.00
(81)	Esteban Loaiza	20.00
(82)	Javy Lopez	45.00
(83)	Greg Maddux	175.00
(84)	Edgar Martinez	50.00
(85)	Pedro Martinez	100.00
(86)	Tino Martinez	50.00
(87)	Rafael Medina	20.00
(88)	Raul Mondesi	35.00
(88)	Raul Mondesi (Exchange card.)	5.00
(89)	Matt Morris	40.00
(90)	Eddie Murray	75.00
(91)	Mike Mussina	80.00
(92)	Paul O'Neill	40.00
(93)	Kevin Orie	20.00
(94)	David Ortiz	100.00
(95)	Rafael Palmeiro	80.00
(96)	Jay Payton	20.00
(97)	Neifi Perez	20.00
(98)	Andy Petitte	50.00
(99)	Manny Ramirez	100.00
(100)	Joe Randa	20.00
(101)	Calvin Reese	20.00
(102)	Edgar Renteria	50.00
(102)	Edgar Renteria (Exchange card.)	5.00
(103)	Dennis Reyes	20.00
(104)	Cal Ripken Jr.	225.00
(105)	Alex Rodriguez	180.00
(106)	Henry Rodriguez	20.00
(107)	Ivan Rodriguez	75.00
(108)	Scott Rolen	75.00
(109)	Kirk Rueter	20.00
(110)	Ryne Sandberg	125.00
(111)	Gary Sheffield	50.00
(112)	Dwight Smith	20.00
(113)	J.T. Snow	25.00
(114)	Scott Spiezio	20.00
(115)	Shannon Stewart	20.00
(116)	Jeff Suppan	20.00
(117)	Mike Sweeney	25.00
(118)	Miguel Tejada	120.00
(119)	Frank Thomas	80.00
(120)	Jim Thome	75.00
(120)	Jim Thome (Exchange card.)	5.00
(121)	Justin Thompson	20.00
(122)	Brett Tomko	20.00
(123)	Bubba Trammell	20.00
(124)	Michael Tucker	20.00
(125)	Javier Valentin	20.00
(126)	Mo Vaughn	20.00
(127)	Robin Ventura	30.00
(128)	Terrell Wade	20.00
(129)	Billy Wagner	40.00
(130)	Larry Walker	80.00
(131)	Todd Walker	25.00
(132)	Rondell White	25.00
(133)	Kevin Wickander	20.00
(134)	Chris Widger	20.00
(135)	Bernie Williams	75.00
(136)	Matt Williams	50.00
(137)	Antone Williamson	20.00
(138)	Dan Wilson	20.00
(139)	Tony Womack	25.00
(140)	Jaret Wright	35.00
(141)	Dmitri Young	30.00
(142)	Eric Young	30.00
(143)	Kevin Young	20.00

Millennium Marks (Green)

One thousand cards of most of the players who signed Signature Autographs are found in an edition marked on front as "Millenium Marks." These cards are also distinguished by the use of green ink in the background of the front photo. On back, the cards have a silver-foil

serial number between (generally) 0101-1,000. Some cards as noted in the alphabetical checklist here were produced in lower numbers. The MM autographs were a random insert among the one-per-pack autographed cards found in $15 packs of Donruss Signature. Packs carried exchange cards redeemable for autographed cards of Raul Mondesi, Edgar Renteria and Jim Thome. This checklist differs significantly from that released in November 1997 by Donruss due to the last-minute addition, deletion and substitution of players. It is possible that cards exist of players not shown here.

		NM/M
Complete Set (143):		1,450
Common Player:		2.00
(1)	Jeff Abbott	2.00
(2)	Bob Abreu	8.00
(3)	Edgardo Alfonzo	5.00
(4)	Roberto Alomar	20.00
(5)	Sandy Alomar Jr.	5.00
(6)	Moises Alou	15.00
(7)	Garret Anderson	10.00
(8)	Andy Ashby	5.00
(9)	Jeff Bagwell/400	75.00
(10)	Trey Beamon	2.00
(11)	Albert Belle/400	12.50
(12)	Alan Benes	2.00
(13)	Geronimo Berroa	2.00
(14)	Wade Boggs	30.00
(15)	Barry Bonds/400	200.00
(16)	Bobby Bonilla/900	7.50
(17)	Kevin Brown/900	20.00
(18)	Kevin L. Brown	10.00
(19)	Jay Buhner/900	10.00
(20)	Brett Butler	6.00
(21)	Mike Cameron	4.00
(22)	Giovanni Carrara	2.00
(23)	Luis Castillo	5.00
(24)	Tony Clark	5.00
(25)	Will Clark	12.00
(26)	Roger Clemens/400	120.00
(27)	Lou Collier	2.00
(28)	Bartolo Colon	8.00
(29)	Ron Coomer	2.00
(30)	Marty Cordova	2.00
(31)	Jacob Cruz	2.00
(32)	Jose Cruz Jr.	6.00
(33)	Russ Davis	2.00
(34)	Jason Dickson	5.00
(35)	Todd Dunwoody	2.00
(36)	Jermaine Dye	2.00
(37)	Jim Edmonds	30.00
(38)	Darin Erstad	10.00
(39)	Bobby Estalella	3.00
(40)	Shawn Estes	2.00
(41)	Jeff Fassero	4.00
(42)	Andres Galarraga	10.00
(43)	Karim Garcia	2.00
(44)	Nomar Garciaparra/650	75.00
(45)	Derrick Gibson	4.00
(46)	Brian Giles	8.00
(47)	Tom Glavine	25.00
(48)	Juan Gonzalez/250	25.00
(49)	Rick Gorecki	2.00
(50)	Shawn Green	20.00
(51)	Todd Greene	7.50
(52)	Rusty Greer	7.50
(53)	Ben Grieve	5.00
(54)	Mark Grudzielanek	2.00
(55)	Vladimir Guerrero	25.00
(56)	Wilton Guerrero	2.00
(57)	Jose Guillen	6.00
(58)	Tony Gwynn/900	30.00
(59)	Jeffrey Hammonds	2.00
(60)	Todd Helton	30.00
(61)	Todd Hollandsworth	2.00
(62)	Trenidad Hubbard	2.00
(63)	Todd Hundley	6.00
(64)	Derek Jeter/400	100.00
(65)	Andruw Jones/900	15.00
(66)	Bobby Jones	2.00
(67)	Chipper Jones	30.00
(68)	Brian Jordan	7.50
(69)	David Justice	10.00
(70)	Eric Karros	6.00
(71)	Jason Kendall	8.00
(72)	Jimmy Key	5.00
(73)	Brooks Kieschnick	4.00
(74)	Ryan Klesko	5.00
(75)	Chuck Knoblauch/900	5.00
(76)	Paul Konerko	5.00
(77)	Mark Kotsay	6.00
(78)	Ray Lankford	2.00
(79)	Barry Larkin	30.00
(80)	Derrek Lee	20.00
(81)	Esteban Loaiza	2.00
(82)	Javy Lopez	8.00
(83)	Greg Maddux/400	80.00
(84)	Edgar Martinez	25.00
(85)	Pedro Martinez	40.00
(86)	Tino Martinez/900	15.00
(87)	Rafael Medina	2.00
(88)	Raul Mondesi	10.00
(88)	Raul Mondesi (Exchange card.)	2.00
(89)	Matt Morris	15.00
(90)	Eddie Murray/900	27.50
(91)	Mike Mussina/900	20.00
(92)	Paul O'Neill	12.50
(93)	Kevin Orie	2.00
(94)	David Ortiz	40.00
(95)	Rafael Palmeiro	30.00
(96)	Jay Payton	5.00
(97)	Neifi Perez	2.00
(98)	Andy Petitte/900	25.00
(99)	Manny Ramirez	30.00
(100)	Joe Randa	2.00
(101)	Calvin Reese	2.00
(102)	Edgar Renteria	30.00
(102)	Edgar Renteria (Exchange card.)	2.00
(103)	Dennis Reyes	3.00
(104)	Cal Ripken Jr./400	135.00
(105)	Alex Rodriguez	100.00
(106)	Henry Rodriguez	3.00
(107)	Ivan Rodriguez/900	20.00
(108)	Scott Rolen	25.00
(109)	Kirk Rueter	2.00
(110)	Ryne Sandberg	40.00
(111)	Gary Sheffield/400	25.00
(112)	Dwight Smith	2.00
(113)	J.T. Snow	7.50
(114)	Scott Spiezio	5.00
(115)	Shannon Stewart	2.00
(116)	Jeff Suppan	2.00
(117)	Mike Sweeney	5.00
(118)	Miguel Tejada	40.00
(119)	Frank Thomas/400	50.00
(120)	Jim Thome/900	30.00
(120)	Jim Thome (Exchange card.)	2.00
(121)	Justin Thompson	2.00
(122)	Brett Tomko	2.00
(123)	Bubba Trammell	4.00
(124)	Michael Tucker	2.00
(125)	Javier Valentin	2.00
(126)	Mo Vaughn	8.00
(127)	Robin Ventura	8.00
(128)	Terrell Wade	2.00
(129)	Billy Wagner	10.00
(130)	Larry Walker	20.00
(131)	Todd Walker	6.00
(132)	Rondell White	6.00
(133)	Kevin Wickander	2.00
(134)	Chris Widger	2.00
(135)	Bernie Williams/400	60.00
(136)	Matt Williams	10.00
(137)	Antone Williamson	2.00
(138)	Dan Wilson	2.00
(139)	Tony Womack	2.00
(140)	Jaret Wright	15.00
(141)	Dmitri Young	5.00
(142)	Eric Young	5.00
(143)	Kevin Young	2.00

Notable Nicknames

Current and former players whose nicknames are instantly recognized are featured in this Signature Series insert. The autographs are generally enhanced by the appearance of those nicknames, though Roger Clemens omitted "The Rocket" from many of his cards. Backs have a serial number from within an edition of 200 of each card.

		NM/M
Common Player:		20.00
(1)	Ernie Banks (Mr. Cub)	150.00
(2)	Tony Clark (The Tiger)	20.00
(3)	Roger Clemens (The Rocket)	300.00
(4)	Reggie Jackson (Mr. October)	125.00
(5)	Randy Johnson (Big Unit)	300.00
(6)	Stan Musial (The Man)	180.00
(7)	Ivan Rodriguez (Pudge)	100.00
(8)	Frank Thomas (The Big Hurt)	125.00
(9)	Mo Vaughn (Hit Dog)	20.00
(10)	Billy Wagner (The Kid)	40.00

Significant Signatures

Retired superstars from the early 1960s through the mid 1990s are featured in this insert series. Cards are horizontal in format with color photos on front and back. Generally autographed on front, each card is serially numbered on back from within an edition of 2,000. The unnumbered cards are listed here in alphabetical order.

		NM/M
Common Player:		15.00
(1)	Ernie Banks	25.00
(2)	Johnny Bench	30.00
(3)	Yogi Berra	30.00
(4)	George Brett	40.00
(5)	Lou Brock	25.00
(6)	Rod Carew	25.00
(7)	Steve Carlton	20.00
(8)	Larry Doby	35.00
(9)	Carlton Fisk	30.00
(10)	Bob Gibson	25.00
(11)	Reggie Jackson	25.00
(12)	Al Kaline	25.00
(13)	Harmon Killebrew	30.00
(14)	Don Mattingly	40.00
(15)	Stan Musial	45.00
(16)	Jim Palmer	15.00
(17)	Brooks Robinson	30.00
(18)	Frank Robinson	15.00
(19)	Mike Schmidt	35.00
(20)	Tom Seaver	30.00
(21)	Duke Snider	20.00
(22)	Carl Yastrzemski	40.00

1997 Donruss Frank Thomas The Big Heart

In one of several specialty card charitable endeavors, Thomas and Donruss teamed up to issue this set as a fund raiser for "The Big Hurt's" charitable foundation. Each of the cards was available in an edition limited to 2,500 for a $20 donation. Cards are standard 2-1/2" x 3-1/2" with posed photos on front and "THE BIG HEART," a play on his nickname. Backs have information on the foundation, a second photo and a gold-foil serial number.

		NM/M
Complete Set (4):		20.00
Common Card:		5.00
1	Frank Thomas, Rod Carew	5.00
2	Frank Thomas	5.00
3	Frank Thomas	5.00
4	Frank Thomas	5.00

1997 Donruss VXP 1.0

This set was issued to accompany the hobby's first major effort to bring baseball cards into the computer age. The standard-format cards have motion-variable portrait and action photos on front and another photo on back. Cards were sold in packs of 10 with one of six CD ROMs for about $10.

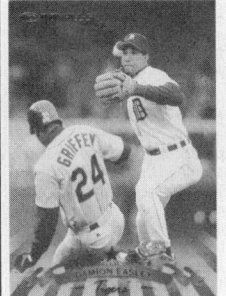

		NM/M
Complete Set (50):		17.50
Common Player:		.25
1	Darin Erstad	.40
2	Jim Thome	.50
3	Alex Rodriguez	1.50
4	Greg Maddux	1.00
5	Scott Rolen	.65
6	Roberto Alomar	.30
7	Tony Clark	.25
8	Randy Johnson	.75
9	Sammy Sosa	1.00
10	Jose Guillen	.25
11	Cal Ripken Jr.	2.00
12	Paul Molitor	.75
13	Jose Cruz Jr.	.25
14	Barry Larkin	.25
15	Ken Caminiti	.25
16	Rafael Palmeiro	.65
17	Chuck Knoblauch	.25
18	Juan Gonzalez	.40
19	Larry Walker	.25
20	Tony Gwynn	1.00
21	Brady Anderson	.25
22	Derek Jeter	2.00
23	Rusty Greer	.25
24	Gary Sheffield	.35
25	Barry Bonds	2.00
26	Mo Vaughn	.20
27	Tino Martinez	.25
28	Ivan Rodriguez	.65
29	Jeff Bagwell	.75
30	Tim Salmon	.25
31	Nomar Garciaparra	1.00
32	Bernie Williams	.25
33	Kenny Lofton	.25
34	Mike Piazza	1.25
35	Jim Edmonds	.25
36	Frank Thomas	.75
37	Andy Pettitte	.35
38	Andruw Jones	.75
39	Raul Mondesi	.25
40	John Smoltz	.25
41	Albert Belle	.25
42	Mark McGwire	1.50
43	Chipper Jones	1.00
44	Hideo Nomo	.40
45	David Justice	.25
46	Manny Ramirez	.75
47	Ken Griffey Jr.	1.25
48	Roger Clemens	1.00
49	Vladimir Guerrero	.75
50	Ryne Sandberg	1.00

1997 Donruss VXP 1.0 CDs

One of the earliest attempts to bring baseball cards into the computer age was Donruss "VXP 1.0 CD ROM" trading cards. Retailed, with 10 special-series player cards for about $10, the 4" x 2-3/4" "card" is a CD with player portrait and action photos on front. The CD was sold in a cardboard folder with the player's picture on front and instructions for use inside. CDs feature player stats, action footage and other interactive elements.

		NM/M
Complete Set (6):		12.00
Common Player:		2.00
(1)	Ken Griffey Jr.	2.25
(2)	Greg Maddux	2.00
(3)	Mike Piazza	2.25
(4)	Cal Ripken Jr.	3.00
(5)	Alex Rodriguez	2.50
(6)	Frank Thomas	2.00

1998 Donruss

This 170-card set includes 155 regular player cards, the 10-card Fan Club subset and five checklists. The cards have color photos and the player's name listed at the bottom. The backs have a horizontal layout

with stats and a biography on the left and another photo on the right. The base set is paralleled twice. Silver Press Proofs is a silver foil and die-cut parallel numbered "1 of 1,500." Gold Press Proofs is die-cut, has gold foil and is numbered "1 of 500." The inserts are Crusade, Diamond Kings, Longball Leaders, Production Line and Rated Rookies.

		NM/M
Complete Set (420):		30.00
Complete Series 1 (170):		10.00
Complete Update 2 (250):		15.00
Common Player:		.05
Silver Press Proofs:		3X
Production 1,500 Sets		
Gold Press Proofs:		8X
Production 500 Sets		
Pack (10):		1.00
Wax Box (24):		16.00
1	Paul Molitor	.75
2	Juan Gonzalez	.40
3	Darryl Kile	.05
4	Randy Johnson	.75
5	Tom Glavine	.25
6	Pat Hentgen	.05
7	David Justice	.05
8	Kevin Brown	.05
9	Mike Mussina	.45
10	Ken Caminiti	.05
11	Todd Hundley	.05
12	Frank Thomas	.75
13	Ray Lankford	.05
14	Justin Thompson	.05
15	Jason Dickson	.05
16	Kenny Lofton	.05
17	Ivan Rodriguez	.65
18	Pedro Martinez	.75
19	Brady Anderson	.05
20	Barry Larkin	.05
21	Chipper Jones	1.50
22	Tony Gwynn	1.50
23	Roger Clemens	1.50
24	Sandy Alomar Jr.	.05
25	Tino Martinez	.05
26	Jeff Bagwell	.75
27	Shawn Estes	.05
28	Ken Griffey Jr.	1.75
29	Javier Lopez	.05
30	Denny Neagle	.05
31	Mike Piazza	1.75
32	Andres Galarraga	.05
33	Larry Walker	.05
34	Alex Rodriguez	2.00
35	Greg Maddux	1.50
36	Albert Belle	.05
37	Barry Bonds	2.50
38	Mo Vaughn	.05
39	Kevin Appier	.05
40	Wade Boggs	1.50
41	Garret Anderson	.05
42	Jeffrey Hammonds	.05
43	Marquis Grissom	.05
44	Jim Edmonds	.05
45	Brian Jordan	.05
46	Raul Mondesi	.05
47	John Valentin	.05
48	Brad Radke	.05
49	Ismael Valdes	.05
50	Matt Stairs	.05
51	Matt Williams	.05
52	Reggie Jefferson	.05
53	Alan Benes	.05
54	Charles Johnson	.05
55	Chuck Knoblauch	.05
56	Edgar Martinez	.05
57	Nomar Garciaparra	1.50
58	Craig Biggio	.05
59	Bernie Williams	.05
60	David Cone	.05
61	Cal Ripken Jr.	2.50
62	Mark McGwire	2.00
63	Roberto Alomar	.20
64	Fred McGriff	.05
65	Eric Karros	.05
66	Robin Ventura	.05
67	Darin Erstad	.30
68	Michael Tucker	.05
69	Jim Thome	.60
70	Mark Grace	.05
71	Lou Collier	.05
72	Karim Garcia	.05
73	Alex Fernandez	.05
74	J.T. Snow	.05
75	Reggie Sanders	.05

76	John Smoltz	.05
77	Tim Salmon	.05
78	Paul O'Neill	.05
79	Vinny Castilla	.05
80	Rafael Palmeiro	.65
81	Jaret Wright	.05
82	Jay Buhner	.05
83	Brett Butler	.05
84	Todd Greene	.05
85	Scott Rolen	.65
86	Sammy Sosa	1.50
87	Jason Giambi	.50
88	Carlos Delgado	.50
89	Deion Sanders	.05
90	Wilton Guerrero	.05
91	Andy Pettitte	.30
92	Brian Giles	.05
93	Dmitri Young	.05
94	Ron Coomer	.05
95	Mike Cameron	.05
96	Edgardo Alfonzo	.05
97	Jimmy Key	.05
98	Ryan Klesko	.05
99	Andy Benes	.05
100	Derek Jeter	2.50
101	Jeff Fassero	.05
102	Neifi Perez	.05
103	Hideo Nomo	.40
104	Andruw Jones	.75
105	Todd Helton	.50
106	Livan Hernandez	.05
107	Brett Tomko	.05
108	Shannon Stewart	.05
109	Bartolo Colon	.05
110	Matt Morris	.05
111	Miguel Tejada	.20
112	Pokey Reese	.05
113	Fernando Tatis	.05
114	Todd Dunwoody	.05
115	Jose Cruz Jr.	.05
116	Chan Ho Park	.05
117	Kevin Young	.05
118	Rickey Henderson	.75
119	Hideki Irabu	.05
120	Francisco Cordova	.05
121	Al Martin	.05
122	Tony Clark	.05
123	Curt Schilling	.25
124	Rusty Greer	.05
125	Jose Canseco	.40
126	Edgar Renteria	.05
127	Todd Walker	.05
128	Wally Joyner	.05
129	Bill Mueller	.05
130	Jose Guillen	.05
131	Manny Ramirez	.75
132	Bobby Higginson	.05
133	Kevin Orie	.05
134	Will Clark	.05
135	Dave Nilsson	.05
136	Jason Kendall	.05
137	Ivan Cruz	.05
138	Gary Sheffield	.25
139	Bubba Trammell	.05
140	Vladimir Guerrero	.75
141	Dennis Reyes	.05
142	Bobby Bonilla	.05
143	Ruben Rivera	.05
144	Ben Grieve	.90
145	Moises Alou	.05
146	Tony Womack	.05
147	Eric Young	.05
148	Paul Konerko	.10
149	Dante Bichette	.05
150	Joe Carter	.05
151	Rondell White	.05
152	Chris Holt	.05
153	Shawn Green	.20
154	Mark Grudzielanek	.05
155	Jermaine Dye	.05
156	Ken Griffey Jr. (Fan Club)	.90
157	Frank Thomas (Fan Club)	.50
158	Chipper Jones (Fan Club)	.75
159	Mike Piazza (Fan Club)	.90
160	Cal Ripken Jr. (Fan Club)	1.25
161	Greg Maddux (Fan Club)	.75
162	Juan Gonzalez (Fan Club)	.20
163	Alex Rodriguez (Fan Club)	1.00
164	Mark McGwire (Fan Club)	1.00
165	Derek Jeter (Fan Club)	1.25
166	Checklist (Larry Walker)	.05
167	Checklist (Tony Gwynn)	.60
168	Checklist (Tino Martinez)	.05
169	Checklist (Scott Rolen)	.15
170	Checklist (Nomar Garciaparra)	.60
171	Mike Sweeney	.05
172	Dustin Hermanson	.05
173	Darren Dreifort	.05
174	Ron Gant	.05
175	Todd Hollandsworth	.05
176	John Jaha	.05
177	Kerry Wood	.30
178	Chris Stynes	.05
179	Kevin Elster	.05
180	Derek Bell	.05
181	Darryl Strawberry	.05
182	Damion Easley	.05
183	Jeff Cirillo	.05
184	John Thomson	.05
185	Dan Wilson	.05
186	Jay Bell	.05
187	Bernard Gilkey	.05
188	Marc Valdes	.05
189	Ramon Martinez	.05
190	Charles Nagy	.05

191	Derek Lowe	.05
192	Andy Benes	.05
193	Delino DeShields	.05
194	Ryan Jackson **RC**	.05
195	Kenny Lofton	.05
196	Chuck Knoblauch	.05
197	Andres Galarraga	.05
198	Jose Canseco	.50
199	John Olerud	.05
200	Lance Johnson	.05
201	Darryl Kile	.05
202	Luis Castillo	.05
203	Joe Carter	.05
204	Dennis Eckersley	.65
205	Steve Finley	.05
206	Esteban Loaiza	.05
207	Ryan Christenson **RC**	.05
208	Deivi Cruz	.05
209	Mariano Rivera	.15
210	Mike Judd **RC**	.05
211	Billy Wagner	.05
212	Scott Spiezio	.05
213	Russ Davis	.05
214	Jeff Suppan	.05
215	Doug Glanville	.05
216	Dmitri Young	.05
217	Rey Ordonez	.05
218	Cecil Fielder	.05
219	Masato Yoshii **RC**	.10
220	Raul Casanova	.05
221	Rolando Arrojo **RC**	.20
222	Ellis Burks	.05
223	Butch Huskey	.05
224	Brian Hunter	.05
225	Marquis Grissom	.05
226	Kevin Brown	.05
227	Joe Randa	.05
228	Henry Rodriguez	.05
229	Omar Vizquel	.05
230	Fred McGriff	.05
231	Matt Williams	.05
232	Moises Alou	.05
233	Travis Fryman	.05
234	Wade Boggs	1.50
235	Pedro Martinez	.75
236	Rickey Henderson	.75
237	Bubba Trammell	.05
238	Mike Caruso	.05
239	Wilson Alvarez	.05
240	Geronimo Berroa	.05
241	Eric Milton	.05
242	Scott Erickson	.05
243	Todd Erdos **RC**	.05
244	Bobby Hughes	.05
245	Dave Hollins	.05
246	Dean Palmer	.05
247	Carlos Baerga	.05
248	Jose Silva	.05
249	Jose Cabrera **RC**	.05
250	Tom Evans	.05
251	Marty Cordova	.05
252	Hanley Frias **RC**	.05
253	Javier Valentin	.05
254	Mario Valdez	.05
255	Joey Cora	.05
256	Mike Lansing	.05
257	Jeff Kent	.05
258	David Dellucci **RC**	.10
259	Curtis King **RC**	.05
260	David Segui	.05
261	Royce Clayton	.05
262	Jeff Blauser	.05
263	Manny Aybar **RC**	.05
264	Mike Cather **RC**	.05
265	Todd Zeile	.05
266	Richard Hidalgo	.05
267	Dante Powell	.05
268	Mike DeJean **RC**	.05
269	Ken Cloude	.05
270	Danny Klassen	.05
271	Sean Casey	.15
272	A.J. Hinch	.05
273	Rich Butler **RC**	.05
274	Ben Ford **RC**	.05
275	Billy McMillon	.05
276	Wilson Delgado	.05
277	Orlando Cabrera	.05
278	Geoff Jenkins	.05
279	Enrique Wilson	.05
280	Derrek Lee	.60
281	Marc Pisciotta **RC**	.05
282	Abraham Nunez	.05
283	Aaron Boone	.05
284	Brad Fullmer	.05
285	Rob Stanifer **RC**	.05
286	Preston Wilson	.05
287	Greg Norton	.05
288	Bobby Smith	.05
289	Josh Booty	.05
290	Russell Branyan	.05
291	Jeremi Gonzalez	.05
292	Michael Coleman	.05
293	Cliff Politte	.05
294	Eric Ludwick	.05
295	Rafael Medina	.05
296	Jason Varitek	.05
297	Ron Wright	.05
298	Mark Kotsay	.05
299	David Ortiz	.50
300	Frank Catalanotto **RC**	.20
301	Robinson Checo	.05
302	Kevin Millwood **RC**	.75
303	Jacob Cruz	.05
304	Javier Vazquez	.05
305	Magglio Ordonez **RC**	1.50
306	Kevin Witt	.05
307	Derrick Gibson	.05
308	Shane Monahan	.05

309	Brian Rose	.05
310	Bobby Estalella	.05
311	Felix Heredia	.05
312	Desi Relaford	.05
313	Esteban Yan **RC**	.05
314	Ricky Ledee	.05
315	Steve Woodard **RC**	.05
316	Pat Watkins	.05
317	Damian Moss	.05
318	Bob Abreu	.05
319	Jeff Abbott	.05
320	Miguel Cairo	.05
321	Rigo Beltran **RC**	.05
322	Tony Saunders	.05
323	Randall Simon	.05
324	Hiram Bocachica	.05
325	Richie Sexson	.05
326	Karim Garcia	.05
327	Mike Lowell **RC**	1.00
328	Pat Cline	.05
329	Matt Clement	.05
330	Scott Elarton	.05
331	Manuel Barrios **RC**	.05
332	Bruce Chen	.05
333	Juan Encarnacion	.05
334	Travis Lee	.05
335	Wes Helms	.05
336	Chad Fox **RC**	.05
337	Donnie Sadler	.05
338	Carlos Mendoza **RC**	.05
339	Damian Jackson	.05
340	Julio Ramirez **RC**	.05
341	John Halama **RC**	.05
342	Edwin Diaz	.05
343	Felix Martinez	.05
344	Eli Marrero	.05
345	Carl Pavano	.05
346	Vladimir Guerrero	.40
347	Barry Bonds/HL	1.25
348	Darin Erstad/HL	.10
349	Albert Belle/HL	.05
350	Kenny Lofton/HL	.05
351	Mo Vaughn/HL	.05
352	Jose Cruz Jr./HL	.05
353	Tony Clark/HL	.05
354	Roberto Alomar/HL	.10
355	Manny Ramirez/HL	.40
356	Paul Molitor/HL	.40
357	Jim Thome/HL	.05
358	Tino Martinez/HL	.05
359	Tim Salmon/HL	.05
360	David Justice/HL	.05
361	Raul Mondesi/HL	.05
362	Mark Grace/HL	.05
363	Craig Biggio/HL	.05
364	Larry Walker/HL	.05
365	Mark McGwire/HL	1.00
366	Juan Gonzalez/HL	.20
367	Derek Jeter/HL	1.25
368	Chipper Jones/HL	.75
369	Frank Thomas/HL	.50
370	Alex Rodriguez/HL	1.00
371	Mike Piazza/HL	.90
372	Tony Gwynn/HL	.75
373	Jeff Bagwell/HL	.40
374	Nomar Garciaparra/HL	.75
375	Ken Griffey Jr./HL	.90
376	Livan Hernandez (Untouchables)	
377	Chan Ho Park (Untouchables)	.05
378	Mike Mussina (Untouchables)	.20
379	Andy Pettitte (Untouchables)	.05
380	Greg Maddux (Untouchables)	.75
381	Hideo Nomo (Untouchables)	.20
382	Roger Clemens (Untouchables)	.80
383	Randy Johnson (Untouchables)	.40
384	Pedro Martinez (Untouchables)	.40
385	Jaret Wright (Untouchables)	.05
386	Ken Griffey Jr. (Spirit of the Game)	.90
387	Todd Helton (Spirit of the Game)	.05
388	Paul Konerko (Spirit of the Game)	.05
389	Cal Ripken Jr. (Spirit of the Game)	1.25
390	Larry Walker (Spirit of the Game)	.05
391	Ken Caminiti (Spirit of the Game)	.05
392	Jose Guillen (Spirit of the Game)	.05
393	Jim Edmonds (Spirit of the Game)	.05
394	Barry Larkin (Spirit of the Game)	.05
395	Bernie Williams (Spirit of the Game)	.05
396	Tony Clark (Spirit of the Game)	.05
397	Jose Cruz Jr. (Spirit of the Game)	.05
398	Ivan Rodriguez (Spirit of the Game)	.30
399	Darin Erstad (Spirit of the Game)	.10
400	Scott Rolen (Spirit of the Game)	.15

401	Mark McGwire (Spirit of the Game)	1.00
402	Andruw Jones (Spirit of the Game)	.40
403	Juan Gonzalez (Spirit of the Game)	.20
404	Derek Jeter (Spirit of the Game)	1.25
405	Chipper Jones (Spirit of the Game)	.75
406	Greg Maddux (Spirit of the Game)	.75
407	Frank Thomas (Spirit of the Game)	.50
408	Alex Rodriguez (Spirit of the Game)	1.00
409	Mike Piazza (Spirit of the Game)	.90
410	Tony Gwynn (Spirit of the Game)	.75
411	Jeff Bagwell (Spirit of the Game)	.40
412	Nomar Garciaparra (Spirit of the Game)	.75
413	Hideo Nomo (Spirit of the Game)	.20
414	Barry Bonds (Spirit of the Game)	1.25
415	Ben Grieve (Spirit of the Game)	.05
416	Checklist (Barry Bonds)	1.25
417	Checklist (Mark McGwire)	1.00
418	Checklist (Roger Clemens)	.65
419	Checklist (Livan Hernandez)	.05
420	Checklist (Ken Griffey Jr.)	.75

1998 Donruss Silver Press Proofs

Silver Press Proofs paralleled all 420 cards in the Donruss and Donruss Update Baseball. Cards featured silver foil stamping and a die-cut top right corner. Backs had a silver tint and were numbered "1 of 1500" in the bottom left corner.

	NM/M
Complete Set (420):	150.00
Common Player:	.50
Stars/RC's:	2X
Production 1,500 Sets	

1998 Donruss Gold Press Proofs

All 420 cards in Donruss and Donruss Update were also issued in Gold Press Proofs. These cards were die-cut on the top right corner and contained gold foil stamping. Backs featured a gold tint and "1 of 500" was printed in black in the bottom-left corner.

	NM/M
Common Player:	1.00
Stars/RC's:	6X
Production 500 Sets	

Crusade

This 100-card insert was included in 1998 Donruss (40 cards), Leaf (30) and Donruss Update (30). The cards use refractive technology and the background features heral-

PEDRO MARTINEZ

CRUSADE

MONTREAL EXPOS

dic-style lions. The cards are sequentially numbered to 250. Crusade Purple (numbered to 100) and Red (25) parallels were also inserted in the three products.

		NM/M
Common Player:		4.00
Production 250 Sets		
Purples (100 Sets):		1X
Reds (25 Sets):		4X
5	Jason Dickson	4.00
6	Todd Greene	4.00
7	Roberto Alomar	5.00
8	Cal Ripken Jr.	40.00
12	Mo Vaughn	4.00
13	Nomar Garciaparra	15.00
16	Mike Cameron	4.00
20	Sandy Alomar Jr.	4.00
21	David Justice	4.00
25	Justin Thompson	4.00
27	Kevin Appier	4.00
33	Tino Martinez	4.00
36	Hideki Irabu	4.00
37	Jose Canseco	4.00
39	Ken Griffey Jr.	30.00
42	Edgar Martinez	5.00
45	Will Clark	6.00
47	Rusty Greer	4.00
50	Shawn Green	5.00
51	Jose Cruz Jr.	4.00
52	Kenny Lofton	4.00
53	Chipper Jones	15.00
62	Kevin Orie	4.00
65	Deion Sanders	6.00
67	Larry Walker	6.00
68	Dante Bichette	4.00
71	Todd Helton	10.00
74	Bobby Bonilla	4.00
75	Kevin Brown	4.00
78	Craig Biggio	6.00
82	Wilton Guerrero	4.00
85	Pedro Martinez	15.00
86	Edgardo Alfonzo	4.00
88	Scott Rolen	10.00
89	Francisco Cordova	4.00
90	Jose Guillen	4.00
92	Ray Lankford	4.00
93	Mark McGwire	20.00
94	Matt Morris	4.00
100	Shawn Estes	4.00

1998 Donruss Days

Similar in design, but featuring heavier stock, a metallic foil background and gold-foil graphic highlights on front, these cards were part of a ballpark promotion conducted by Donruss during the 1998 baseball season. Fans were given exchange cards at selected ballparks which could be traded at specially designated card shops in those locales for one of these premium star cards. Production was reportedly fewer than 10,000 of each card. Backs are numbered "X of 14," but are otherwise identical to the regular-issue version.

		NM/M
Complete Set (14):		16.00
Common Player:		.50
1	Frank Thomas	1.00
2	Tony Clark	.50
3	Ivan Rodriguez	.65

4	David Justice	.50
5	Nomar Garciaparra	1.50
6	Mark McGwire	2.50
7	Travis Lee	.50
8	Cal Ripken Jr.	3.00
9	Jeff Bagwell	1.00
10	Barry Bonds	3.00
11	Ken Griffey Jr.	2.00
12	Derek Jeter	3.00
13	Raul Mondesi	.50
14	Greg Maddux	1.50

Diamond Kings

Diamond Kings is a 20-card insert featuring a painted portrait by Dan Gardiner. Backs have a ghosted image of the portrait with a player biography and the card's number overprinted. A total of 10,000 sets were produced with the first 500 of each card printed on canvas. A Frank Thomas sample card was also created.

		NM/M
Complete Set (20):		65.00
Common Player:		2.00
Production 9,500 Sets		
Canvas (1st 500 Sets):		2X
1	Cal Ripken Jr.	9.00
2	Greg Maddux	4.50
3	Ivan Rodriguez	2.50
4	Tony Gwynn	4.50
5	Paul Molitor	3.00
6	Kenny Lofton	2.00
7	Andy Pettitte	2.00
8	Darin Erstad	2.00
9	Randy Johnson	3.00
10	Derek Jeter	9.00
11	Hideo Nomo	2.50
12	David Justice	2.00
13	Bernie Williams	2.00
14	Roger Clemens	5.00
15	Barry Larkin	2.00
16	Andruw Jones	3.00
17	Mike Piazza	6.50
18	Frank Thomas	3.00
18s	Frank Thomas (Sample)	3.00
19	Alex Rodriguez	7.50
20	Ken Griffey Jr.	6.50

Longball Leaders

LONGBALL
LEADERS

Longball Leaders features 24 top home run hitters. The right border features a home run meter with zero at the bottom, 61 at the top and the player's 1997 home run total marked. Each card is sequentially numbered to 5,000.

		NM/M
Complete Set (24):		50.00
Common Player:		1.00
Production 5,000 Sets		
1	Ken Griffey Jr.	5.00
2	Mark McGwire	6.00
3	Tino Martinez	1.00
4	Barry Bonds	7.50
5	Frank Thomas	3.00
6	Albert Belle	1.00
7	Mike Piazza	5.00
8	Chipper Jones	4.00
9	Vladimir Guerrero	3.00
10	Matt Williams	1.00
11	Sammy Sosa	4.00
12	Tim Salmon	1.00
13	Raul Mondesi	1.00

Production Line-ob

PRODUCTION LINE

ON-BASE PERCENTAGE

This 20-card insert is printed on holographic foil board. Inserted in magazine packs, this insert features player's with a high on-base percentage in 1997. Each player's card is sequentially numbered to his on-base percentage from that season. The card back has a player photo and a list of the 20 players with their stat.

		NM/M
Complete Set (20):		85.00
Common Player:		1.50
1	Frank Thomas/456	6.00
2	Edgar Martinez/456	1.50
3	Roberto Alomar/390	2.00
4	Chuck Knoblauch/390	1.50
5	Mike Piazza/431	10.00
6	Barry Larkin/440	1.50
7	Kenny Lofton/409	1.50
8	Jeff Bagwell/425	6.00
9	Barry Bonds/446	15.00
10	Rusty Greer/405	1.50
11	Gary Sheffield/424	2.00
12	Mark McGwire/393	12.00
13	Chipper Jones/371	8.00
14	Tony Gwynn/409	8.00
15	Craig Biggio/415	1.50
16	Mo Vaughn/420	1.50
17	Bernie Williams/408	1.50
18	Ken Griffey Jr./382	10.00
19	Brady Anderson/393	1.50
20	Derek Jeter/370	15.00

Production Line-Pi

PRODUCTION LINE

POWER INDEX

This 20-card insert was printed on holographic board. The set features players with a high power index from 1997. Each card is sequentially numbered to that player's power index from that season.

		NM/M
Complete Set (20):		85.00
Common Player:		1.50
1	Frank Thomas/1,067	6.00
2	Mark McGwire/1,039	12.00
3	Barry Bonds/1,031	12.50
4	Jeff Bagwell/1,017	5.00
5	Ken Griffey Jr./1,028	10.00
6	Alex Rodriguez/846	12.00
7	Chipper Jones/850	7.00
8	Mike Piazza/1,070	10.00
9	Mo Vaughn/980	1.50
10	Brady Anderson/863	1.50
11	Manny Ramirez/953	5.00
12	Albert Belle/823	1.50
13	Jim Thome/1,001	2.50
14	Bernie Williams/952	1.50
15	Scott Rolen/846	2.00
16	Vladimir Guerrero/833	5.00
17	Larry Walker/1,172	1.50
18	David Justice/1,013	1.50

14	Jeff Bagwell	3.00
15	Mo Vaughn	1.00
16	Manny Ramirez	3.00
17	Jim Thome	2.00
18	Jim Edmonds	1.00
19	Tony Clark	1.00
20	Nomar Garciaparra	4.00
21	Juan Gonzalez	1.50
22	Scott Rolen	2.00
23	Larry Walker	1.00
24	Andres Galarraga	1.00

Production Line-Sg

SLUGGING PERCENTAGE

224/646

This 20-card insert was printed on holographic board. It featured players with high slugging percentages in 1997. Each card is sequentially numbered to the player's slugging percentage from that season.

		NM/M
Complete Set (20):		135.00
Common Player:		3.00
1	Mark McGwire/646	20.00
2	Ken Griffey Jr./646	12.50
3	Andres Galarraga/585	3.00
4	Barry Bonds/585	22.50
5	Juan Gonzalez/589	4.50
6	Mike Piazza/638	12.50
7	Jeff Bagwell/592	7.50
8	Manny Ramirez/538	7.50
9	Jim Thome/579	4.50
10	Mo Vaughn/560	3.00
11	Larry Walker/720	3.00
12	Tino Martinez/577	3.00
13	Frank Thomas/611	7.50
14	Tim Salmon/517	3.00
15	Raul Mondesi/541	3.00
16	Alex Rodriguez/496	15.00
17	Nomar Garciaparra/534	10.00
18	Jose Cruz Jr./499	3.00
19	Tony Clark/500	3.00
20	Cal Ripken Jr./402	25.00

Rated Rookies

RATED ROOKIES

This 30-card insert features top young players. The fronts have a color player photo in front of a stars and stripes background, with "Rated Rookies" and the player's name printed on the right. The backs have another photo, basic player information and career highlights. A rare (250 each) Medalist version is micro-etched on gold holographic foil.

		NM/M
Complete Set (30):		32.50
Common Player:		1.00
Medalists (250 Sets):		6X
1	Mark Kotsay	1.00
2	Neifi Perez	1.00
3	Paul Konerko	1.50
4	Jose Cruz Jr.	1.00
5	Hideki Irabu	1.00
6	Mike Cameron	1.00
7	Jeff Suppan	1.00
8	Kevin Orie	1.00
9	Pokey Reese	1.00
10	Todd Dunwoody	1.00
11	Miguel Tejada	1.50
12	Jose Guillen	1.00
13	Bartolo Colon	1.50
14	Derek Lee	2.50
15	Antone Williamson	1.00
16	Wilton Guerrero	1.00
17	Jaret Wright	1.00
18	Todd Helton	4.00
19	Shannon Stewart	1.00
20	Nomar Garciaparra	6.00
21	Brett Tomko	1.00
22	Fernando Tatis	1.00
23	Raul Ibanez	1.00
24	Dennis Reyes	1.00
25	Bobby Estalella	1.00

26	Lou Collier	1.00
27	Bubba Trammell	1.00
28	Ben Grieve	1.00
29	Ivan Cruz	1.00
30	Karim Garcia	1.00

Update Crusade

This 30-card insert is continued from 1998 Donruss and Leaf baseball sets. Each card features a color action photo in front of a Medieval background. The player's name and background are green and each card is serial numbered to 250. Purple (numbered to 100) and Red (25) parallel versions were also created. Crusade is a 130-card cross-brand insert with 40 cards included in 1998 Donruss and 30 each in 1998 Leaf and Leaf Rookies & Stars.

		NM/M
Complete Set, Green (30):		325.00
Common Player:		6.00
Production 250 Sets		
Purples (100 Sets):		3X
Reds (25 Sets):		10X
1	Tim Salmon	6.00
2	Garret Anderson	6.00
9	Rafael Palmeiro	15.00
10	Brady Anderson	6.00
14	Frank Thomas	15.00
17	Robin Ventura	6.00
22	Matt Williams	6.00
23	Tony Clark	6.00
29	Chuck Knoblauch	6.00
31	Bernie Williams	6.00
32	Derek Jeter	50.00
38	Jason Giambi	10.00
43	Jay Buhner	6.00
47	Juan Gonzalez	7.50
49	Carlos Delgado	9.00
53	Greg Maddux	20.00
57	Tom Glavine	9.00
60	Mark Grace	6.00
61	Sammy Sosa	20.00
63	Barry Larkin	6.00
69	Neifi Perez	6.00
72	Gary Sheffield	7.50
77	Jeff Bagwell	15.00
80	Raul Mondesi	6.00
81	Hideo Nomo	7.50
83	Rondell White	6.00
84	Vladimir Guerrero	15.00
87	Todd Hundley	6.00
96	Brian Jordan	6.00
99	Barry Bonds	50.00

Update Dominators

DOMINATORS

This 30-card insert features color player photos and holographic foil.

		NM/M
Complete Set (30):		25.00
Common Player:		.25
Approx: 1:12		
1	Roger Clemens	1.50
2	Tony Clark	.25
3	Darin Erstad	.50
4	Jeff Bagwell	1.00
5	Ken Griffey Jr.	1.75
6	Andruw Jones	1.00
7	Juan Gonzalez	.50
8	Ivan Rodriguez	.75
9	Randy Johnson	1.00
10	Tino Martinez	.25
11	Mark McGwire	2.00
12	Chuck Knoblauch	.25
13	Jim Thome	.65
14	Alex Rodriguez	2.00
15	Hideo Nomo	.50
16	Jose Cruz Jr.	.25
17	Chipper Jones	1.50
18	Tony Gwynn	1.50
19	Barry Bonds	2.50
20	Mo Vaughn	.25
21	Cal Ripken Jr.	2.50
22	Greg Maddux	1.50
23	Manny Ramirez	.50
24	Andres Galarraga	.25
25	Vladimir Guerrero	.25
26	Albert Belle	.25
27	Nomar Garciaparra	1.50
28	Kenny Lofton	.25

29	Mike Piazza	1.75
30	Frank Thomas	1.00

Update Elite

Elite
SERIES

ANDRUW JONES

This 20-card insert features color player photos in a diamond-shaped border at the top with the Elite Series logo and player's name at the bottom. The fronts have a cream-colored border.

		NM/M
Complete Set (20):		115.00
Common Player:		3.00
Production 2,500 Sets		
1	Jeff Bagwell	4.50
2	Andruw Jones	4.50
3	Ken Griffey Jr.	7.50
4	Derek Jeter	15.00
5	Juan Gonzalez	3.50
6	Mark McGwire	10.00
7	Ivan Rodriguez	3.50
8	Paul Molitor	4.50
9	Hideo Nomo	3.50
10	Mo Vaughn	3.00
11	Chipper Jones	6.00
12	Nomar Garciaparra	6.00
13	Mike Piazza	7.50
14	Frank Thomas	4.50
15	Greg Maddux	6.00
16	Cal Ripken Jr.	15.00
17	Alex Rodriguez	10.00
18	Scott Rolen	3.50
19	Barry Bonds	6.00
20	Tony Gwynn	15.00

Update FANtasy Team

This 20-card set features the top vote getters from the Donruss online Fan Club ballot box. The top 10 make up the 1st Team FANtasy Team and are sequentially numbered to 2,000. The other players are included in the 2nd Team FANtasy Team and are numbered to 4,000. The first 250 cards of each player are die-cut. The front of the cards feature a color photo inside a stars and stripes border.

		NM/M
Complete Set (20):		35.00
Common Player (1-10)		
	(1,750 Sets):	1.50
Common Player (11-20)		
	(3,750 Sets):	1.00
Die-Cuts (250 Each):		2X
1	Frank Thomas	2.00
2	Ken Griffey Jr.	3.50
3	Cal Ripken Jr.	3.00
4	Jose Cruz Jr.	1.00
5	Travis Lee	1.00
6	Greg Maddux	2.50
7	Alex Rodriguez	4.00
8	Mark McGwire	4.00
9	Chipper Jones	2.50
10	Andruw Jones	2.00
11	Mike Piazza	3.50
12	Tony Gwynn	2.50
13	Larry Walker	1.00
14	Nomar Garciaparra	3.00
15	Jaret Wright	1.00
16	Livan Hernandez	1.00
17	Roger Clemens	2.75
18	Derek Jeter	5.00
19	Scott Rolen	1.25
20	Jeff Bagwell	2.00

Update Rookie Diamond Kings

The Rookie Diamond Kings insert features color portraits by artist Dan Gardiner of young players inside a golden border. Player identification and Rookie Diamond Kings logo are at the bottom. Each card is sequentially numbered to 10,000 with the first 500 printed on canvas.

	NM/M
Complete Set (12):	20.00
Common Player:	2.00
Production 9,500 Sets	
Canvas (500 Sets):	2X
1 Travis Lee	2.00
2 Fernando Tatis	2.00
3 Livan Hernandez	2.00
4 Todd Helton	5.00
5 Derrek Lee	3.50
6 Jaret Wright	2.00
7 Ben Grieve	2.00
8 Paul Konerko	2.50
9 Jose Cruz Jr.	2.00
10 Mark Kotsay	2.00
11 Todd Greene	2.00
12 Brad Fullmer	2.00

Update Sony MLB 99

This 20-card set promotes the MLB '99 game for Sony PlayStation systems. The card front has a color player photo with a red border on two sides. The Donruss, PlayStation and MLB '99 logos appear on the front as well. The backs have a MLB '99 Tip and instructions on entering the PlayStation MLB '99 Sweepstakes.

	NM/M
Complete Set (20):	3.00
Common Player:	.05
1 Cal Ripken Jr.	.75
2 Nomar Garciaparra	.40
3 Barry Bonds	.75
4 Mike Mussina	.20
5 Pedro Martinez	.25
6 Derek Jeter	.75
7 Andruw Jones	.40
8 Kenny Lofton	.05
9 Gary Sheffield	.05
10 Raul Mondesi	.05
11 Jeff Bagwell	.40
12 Tim Salmon	.05
13 Tom Glavine	.15
14 Ben Grieve	.50
15 Matt Williams	.05
16 Juan Gonzalez	.15
17 Mark McGwire	.50
18 Bernie Williams	.05
19 Andres Galarraga	.05
20 Jose Cruz Jr.	.05

1998 Donruss Collections

Collections consists of a 750-card base set made up of cards from the Donruss (200 cards), Leaf (200), Donruss Elite (150) and Donruss Preferred (200) sets. The cards were reproduced with a chromium finish and have the

scripted word "Collections" vertically at left-front. The Collections logo is repeated on back and each card has a second number within the 750-piece set. The Donruss and Leaf cards were inserted two per pack, Elite was inserted one per pack and Preferred cards had a production run of less than 1,400, averaging one card per two packs. The 200 Collections versions of Donruss cards can be found with a large black "SAMPLE" overprint value on back.

	NM/M
Complete Donruss Set (200):	100.00
Complete Leaf Set (200):	125.00
Complete Elite Set (150):	125.00
Complete Preferred Set (200):	300.00
Prized Collections Parallel:	2X
Pack (5):	4.00
Wax Box (20):	75.00
Samples:	6X
1 Paul Molitor	2.00
2 Juan Gonzalez	1.00
3 Darryl Kile	.25
4 Randy Johnson	2.00
5 Tom Glavine	.50
6 Pat Hentgen	.25
7 David Justice	.25
8 Kevin Brown	.25
9 Mike Mussina	.50
10 Ken Caminiti	.25
11 Todd Hundley	.25
12 Frank Thomas	2.00
13 Ray Lankford	.25
14 Justin Thompson	.25
15 Jason Dickson	.25
16 Kenny Lofton	.25
17 Ivan Rodriguez	1.50
18 Pedro Martinez	2.00
19 Brady Anderson	.25
20 Barry Larkin	.25
21 Chipper Jones	3.00
22 Tony Gwynn	3.00
23 Roger Clemens	3.25
24 Sandy Alomar Jr.	.25
25 Tino Martinez	.25
26 Jeff Bagwell	2.00
27 Shawn Estes	.25
28 Ken Griffey Jr.	3.50
29 Javier Lopez	.25
30 Denny Neagle	.25
31 Mike Piazza	3.50
32 Andres Galarraga	.25
33 Larry Walker	.25
34 Alex Rodriguez	4.50
35 Greg Maddux	3.00
36 Albert Belle	.25
37 Barry Bonds	6.00
38 Mo Vaughn	.25
39 Kevin Appier	.25
40 Wade Boggs	3.00
41 Garret Anderson	.25
42 Jeffrey Hammonds	.25
43 Marquis Grissom	.25
44 Jim Edmonds	.25
45 Brian Jordan	.25
46 Raul Mondesi	.25
47 John Valentin	.25
48 Brad Radke	.25
49 Ismael Valdes	.25
50 Matt Stairs	.25
51 Matt Williams	.25
52 Reggie Jefferson	.25
53 Alan Benes	.25
54 Charles Johnson	.25
55 Chuck Knoblauch	.25
56 Edgar Martinez	.25
57 Nomar Garciaparra	3.00
58 Craig Biggio	.25
59 Bernie Williams	.50
60 Cal Ripken Jr.	6.00
61 Cal Ripken Jr.	6.00
62 Mark McGwire	4.50
63 Roberto Alomar	.25
64 Fred McGriff	.25
65 Eric Karros	.25
66 Robin Ventura	.25
67 Darin Erstad	.50
68 Michael Tucker	.25
69 Jim Thome	1.00
70 Mark Grace	.25
71 Lou Collier	.25
72 Karim Garcia	.25

73	Alex Fernandez	.25
74	J.T. Snow	.25
75	Reggie Sanders	.25
76	John Smoltz	.25
77	Tim Salmon	.25
78	Paul O'Neill	.25
79	Vinny Castilla	.25
80	Rafael Palmeiro	1.50
81	Jaret Wright	.25
82	Jay Buhner	.25
83	Brett Butler	.25
84	Todd Greene	.25
85	Scott Rolen	1.50
86	Sammy Sosa	3.00
87	Jason Giambi	1.00
88	Carlos Delgado	.75
89	Deion Sanders	.25
90	Wilton Guerrero	.25
91	Andy Pettitte	.45
92	Brian Giles	.25
93	Dmitri Young	.25
94	Ron Coomer	.25
95	Mike Cameron	.25
96	Edgardo Alfonzo	.25
97	Jimmy Key	.25
98	Ryan Klesko	.25
99	Andy Benes	.25
100	Derek Jeter	6.00
101	Jeff Fassero	.25
102	Neifi Perez	.25
103	Hideo Nomo	1.00
104	Andruw Jones	2.00
105	Todd Helton	1.50
106	Livan Hernandez	.25
107	Brett Tomko	.25
108	Shannon Stewart	.25
109	Bartolo Colon	.25
110	Matt Morris	.25
111	Miguel Tejada	.40
112	Pokey Reese	.25
113	Fernando Tatis	.25
114	Todd Dunwoody	.25
115	Jose Cruz Jr.	.25
116	Chan Ho Park	.25
117	Kevin Young	.25
118	Rickey Henderson	2.00
119	Hideki Irabu	.25
120	Francisco Cordova	.25
121	Al Martin	.25
122	Tony Clark	.25
123	Curt Schilling	.40
124	Rusty Greer	.25
125	Jose Canseco	.60
126	Edgar Renteria	.25
127	Todd Walker	.25
128	Wally Joyner	.25
129	Bill Mueller	.25
130	Jose Guillen	.25
131	Manny Ramirez	2.00
132	Bobby Higginson	.25
133	Kevin Orie	.25
134	Will Clark	.25
135	Dave Nilsson	.25
136	Jason Kendall	.25
137	Ivan Cruz	.25
138	Gary Sheffield	.40
139	Bubba Trammell	.25
140	Vladimir Guerrero	2.00
141	Dennis Reyes	.25
142	Bobby Bonilla	.25
143	Ruben Rivera	.25
144	Ben Grieve	.25
145	Moises Alou	.25
146	Tony Womack	.25
147	Eric Young	.25
148	Paul Konerko	.35
149	Dante Bichette	.25
150	Joe Carter	.25
151	Rondell White	.25
152	Chris Holt	.25
153	Shawn Green	.40
154	Mark Grudzielanek	.25
155	Jermaine Dye	.25
156	Ken Griffey Jr. (Fan Club)	1.75
157	Frank Thomas (Fan Club)	1.00
158	Chipper Jones (Fan Club)	1.50
159	Mike Piazza (Fan Club)	1.75
160	Cal Ripken Jr. (Fan Club)	3.00
161	Greg Maddux (Fan Club)	1.50
162	Juan Gonzalez (Fan Club)	.50
163	Alex Rodriguez (Fan Club)	2.25
164	Mark McGwire (Fan Club)	2.25
165	Derek Jeter (Fan Club)	3.00
166	Larry Walker (Checklist)	.25
167	Tony Gwynn (Checklist)	.75
168	Tino Martinez (Checklist)	.25
169	Scott Rolen (Checklist)	.40
170	Nomar Garciaparra (Checklist)	.75
1	Mark Kotsay	.50
2	Neifi Perez	.50
3	Paul Konerko	1.00
4	Jose Cruz Jr.	.50
5	Hideki Irabu	.50
6	Mike Cameron	.50
7	Jeff Suppan	.50
8	Kevin Orie	.50
9	Pokey Reese	.50
10	Todd Dunwoody	.50
11	Miguel Tejada	1.00
12	Jose Guillen	.50
13	Bartolo Colon	.50
14	Derek Lee	.75
15	Antone Williamson	.50
16	Wilton Guerrero	.50
17	Jaret Wright	.50

18	Todd Helton	2.00
19	Shannon Stewart	.50
20	Nomar Garciaparra	3.00
21	Brett Tomko	.50
22	Fernando Tatis	.50
23	Raul Ibanez	.50
24	Dennis Reyes	.50
25	Bobby Estalella	.50
26	Lou Collier	.50
27	Bubba Trammell	.50
28	Ben Grieve	.50
29	Ivan Cruz	.50
30	Karim Garcia	.50
1	Rusty Greer	.25
2	Tino Martinez	.25
3	Bobby Bonilla	.25
4	Jason Giambi	.65
5	Matt Morris	.25
6	Craig Counsell	.25
7	Reggie Jefferson	.25
8	Brian Rose	.25
9	Ruben Rivera	.25
10	Shawn Estes	.25
11	Tony Gwynn	3.00
12	Jeff Abbott	.25
13	Jose Cruz Jr.	.25
14	Francisco Cordova	.25
15	Ryan Klesko	.25
16	Tim Salmon	.25
17	Brett Tomko	.25
18	Matt Williams	.25
19	Joe Carter	.25
20	Harold Baines	.25
21	Gary Sheffield	.40
22	Charles Johnson	.25
23	Aaron Boone	.35
24	Eddie Murray	2.00
25	Matt Stairs	.25
26	David Cone	.25
27	Jon Nunnally	.25
28	Chris Stynes	.25
29	Enrique Wilson	.25
30	Randy Johnson	2.00
31	Garret Anderson	.25
32	Manny Ramirez	2.00
33	Jeff Suppan	.25
34	Rickey Henderson	2.00
35	Scott Spiezio	.25
36	Rondell White	.25
37	Todd Greene	.25
38	Delino DeShields	.25
39	Kevin Brown	.25
40	Chili Davis	.25
41	Jimmy Key	.25
42	Mike Mussina	1.00
43	Joe Randa	.25
44	Chan Ho Park	.25
45	Brad Radke	.25
46	Geronimo Berroa	.25
47	Wade Boggs	3.00
48	Kevin Appier	.25
49	Moises Alou	.25
50	David Justice	.25
51	Ivan Rodriguez	1.50
52	J.T. Snow	.25
53	Brian Giles	.25
54	Will Clark	.25
55	Justin Thompson	.25
56	Javier Lopez	.25
57	Hideki Irabu	.25
58	Mark Grudzielanek	.25
59	Abraham Nunez	.25
60	Todd Hollandsworth	.25
61	Jay Bell	.25
62	Nomar Garciaparra	3.00
63	Vinny Castilla	.25
64	Lou Collier	.25
65	Kevin Orie	.25
66	John Valentin	.25
67	Robin Ventura	.25
68	Denny Neagle	.25
69	Tony Womack	.25
70	Dennis Reyes	.25
71	Wally Joyner	.25
72	Kevin Brown	.35
73	Ray Durham	.25
74	Mike Cameron	.25
75	Dante Bichette	.25
76	Jose Guillen	.25
77	Carlos Delgado	.60
78	Paul Molitor	2.00
79	Jason Kendall	.25
80	Mark Belhorn	.25
81	Damian Jackson	.25
82	Bill Mueller	.25
83	Kevin Young	.25
84	Curt Schilling	.50
85	Jeffrey Hammonds	.25
86	Sandy Alomar Jr.	.25
87	Bartolo Colon	.25
88	Wilton Guerrero	.25
89	Bernie Williams	.25
90	Deion Sanders	.25
91	Mike Piazza	3.50
92	Butch Huskey	.25
93	Edgardo Alfonzo	.25
94	Alan Benes	.25
95	Craig Biggio	.25
96	Mark Grace	.40
97	Shawn Green	.25
98	Derek Lee	1.00
99	Ken Griffey Jr.	3.50
100	Tim Raines	.25
101	Pokey Reese	.25
102	Lee Stevens	.25
103	Shannon Stewart	.25
104	John Smoltz	.25
105	Frank Thomas	2.00

107	Jeff Fassero	.25
108	Jay Buhner	.25
109	Jose Canseco	.45
110	Omar Vizquel	.25
111	Travis Fryman	.25
112	Dave Nilsson	.25
113	John Olerud	.25
114	Larry Walker	.25
115	Jim Edmonds	.25
116	Bobby Higginson	.25
117	Todd Hundley	.25
118	Paul O'Neill	.25
119	Bip Roberts	.25
120	Ismael Valdes	.25
121	Pedro Martinez	2.00
122	Jeff Cirillo	.25
123	Andy Benes	.25
124	Bobby Jones	.25
125	Brian Hunter	.25
126	Darryl Kile	.25
127	Pat Hentgen	.25
128	Marquis Grissom	.25
129	Eric Davis	.25
130	Chipper Jones	3.00
131	Edgar Martinez	.25
132	Andy Pettitte	.50
133	Cal Ripken Jr.	6.00
134	Scott Rolen	1.50
135	Ron Coomer	.25
136	Luis Castillo	.25
137	Fred McGriff	.25
138	Neifi Perez	.25
139	Eric Karros	.25
140	Alex Fernandez	.25
141	Jason Dickson	.25
142	Lance Johnson	.25
143	Ray Lankford	.25
144	Sammy Sosa	3.00
145	Eric Young	.25
146	Bubba Trammell	.25
147	Todd Walker	.25
148	Mo Vaughn/CC	.25
149	Jeff Bagwell/CC	2.00
150	Kenny Lofton/CC	.25
151	Raul Mondesi/CC	.25
152	Mike Piazza/CC	3.50
153	Chipper Jones/CC	3.00
154	Larry Walker/CC	.25
155	Greg Maddux/CC	3.00
156	Ken Griffey Jr./CC	3.50
157	Frank Thomas/CC	.25
158	Darin Erstad/GLS	2.00
159	Roberto Alomar/GLS	1.50
160	Albert Belle/GLS	1.00
161	Jim Thome/GLS	1.00
162	Tony Clark/GLS	1.00
163	Chuck Knoblauch/GLS	1.00
164	Derek Jeter/GLS	12.00
165	Alex Rodriguez/GLS	8.00
166	Tony Gwynn/GLS	6.00
167	Roger Clemens/GLS	7.00
168	Barry Larkin/GLS	1.00
169	Andres Galarraga/GLS	1.00
170	Vladimir Guerrero/GLS	4.50
171	Mark McGwire/GLS	8.00
172	Barry Bonds/GLS	12.00
173	Juan Gonzalez/GLS	2.50
174	Andruw Jones/GLS	4.50
175	Paul Molitor/GLS	1.00
176	Hideo Nomo/GLS	2.50
177	Cal Ripken Jr./GLS	12.50
178	Brad Fullmer/GLR	1.00
179	Jaret Wright/GLR	1.00
180	Bobby Estalella/GLR	1.00
181	Ben Grieve/GLR	1.00
182	Paul Konerko/GLR	1.50
183	David Ortiz/GLR	3.00
184	Todd Helton/GLR	3.00
185	Juan Encarnacion/GLR	1.00
186	Miguel Tejada/GLR	1.50
187	Jacob Cruz/GLR	1.00
188	Mark Kotsay/GLR	1.00
189	Fernando Tatis/GLR	1.00
190	Ricky Ledee/GLR	1.00
191	Richard Hidalgo/GLR	1.00
192	Richie Sexson/GLR	1.00
193	Luis Ordaz/GLR	1.00
194	Eli Marrero/GLR	1.00
195	Livan Hernandez/GLR	1.00
196	Homer Bush/GLR	1.00
197	Raul Ibanez/GLR	1.00
198	Checklist (Nomar Garciaparra)	1.00
199	Checklist (Scott Rolen)	.75
200	Checklist (Jose Cruz Jr.)	.25
201	Al Martin	.25
1	Ken Griffey Jr.	4.00
2	Frank Thomas	2.50
3	Alex Rodriguez	6.00
4	Mike Piazza	4.00
5	Greg Maddux	3.00
6	Cal Ripken Jr.	7.00
7	Chipper Jones	3.00
8	Derek Jeter	7.00
9	Tony Gwynn	3.00
10	Andruw Jones	2.50
11	Juan Gonzalez	1.25
12	Jeff Bagwell	2.50
13	Mark McGwire	6.00
14	Roger Clemens	3.00
15	Albert Belle	.50
16	Barry Bonds	7.00
17	Kenny Lofton	.50
18	Ivan Rodriguez	2.00
19	Manny Ramirez	2.50
20	Jim Thome	1.50
21	Chuck Knoblauch	.50
22	Paul Molitor	2.50

23	Barry Larkin	.50
24	Andy Pettitte	1.00
25	John Smoltz	.50
26	Randy Johnson	2.50
27	Bernie Williams	.50
28	Larry Walker	.50
29	Mo Vaughn	.50
30	Bobby Higginson	.50
31	Edgardo Alfonzo	.50
32	Justin Thompson	.50
33	Jeff Suppan	.50
34	Roberto Alomar	1.00
35	Hideo Nomo	1.25
36	Rusty Greer	.50
37	Tim Salmon	.50
38	Jim Edmonds	.50
39	Gary Sheffield	.75
40	Ken Caminiti	.50
41	Sammy Sosa	3.00
42	Tony Womack	.50
43	Matt Williams	.50
44	Andres Galarraga	.50
45	Garret Anderson	.50
46	Rafael Palmeiro	2.00
47	Mike Mussina	1.00
48	Craig Biggio	.50
49	Wade Boggs	3.00
50	Tom Glavine	.75
51	Jason Giambi	1.00
52	Will Clark	.50
53	David Justice	.50
54	Sandy Alomar Jr.	.50
55	Edgar Martinez	.50
56	Brady Anderson	.50
57	Eric Young	.50
58	Ray Lankford	.50
59	Kevin Brown	.60
60	Raul Mondesi	.50
61	Bobby Bonilla	.50
62	Javier Lopez	.50
63	Fred McGriff	.50
64	Rondell White	.50
65	Todd Hundley	.50
66	Mark Grace	.50
67	Alan Benes	.50
68	Jeff Abbott	.50
69	Bob Abreu	.50
70	Deion Sanders	.50
71	Tino Martinez	.50
72	Shannon Stewart	.50
73	Homer Bush	.50
74	Carlos Delgado	1.50
75	Raul Ibanez	.50
76	Hideki Irabu	.50
77	Jose Cruz Jr.	.50
78	Tony Clark	.50
79	Wilton Guerrero	.50
80	Vladimir Guerrero	2.50
81	Scott Rolen	2.25
82	Nomar Garciaparra	3.00
83	Darin Erstad	1.00
84	Chan Ho Park	.50
85	Mike Cameron	.50
86	Todd Walker	.50
87	Todd Dunwoody	.50
88	Neifi Perez	.50
89	Brett Tomko	.50
90	Jose Guillen	.50
91	Matt Morris	.50
92	Bartolo Colon	.50
93	Jaret Wright	.50
94	Shawn Estes	.50
95	Livan Hernandez	.50
96	Bobby Estalella	.50
97	Ben Grieve	.50
98	Paul Konerko	.75
99	David Ortiz	.50
100	Todd Helton	2.00
101	Juan Encarnacion	.50
102	Bubba Trammell	.50
103	Miguel Tejada	1.00
104	Jacob Cruz	.50
105	Todd Greene	.50
106	Kevin Orie	.50
107	Mark Kotsay	.50
108	Fernando Tatis	.50
109	Jay Payton	.50
110	Pokey Reese	.50
111	Derrek Lee	1.50
112	Richard Hidalgo	.50
113	Ricky Ledee	.50
114	Lou Collier	.50
115	Ruben Rivera	.50
116	Shawn Green	1.00
117	Moises Alou	.50
118	Ken Griffey Jr. (Generations)	2.00
119	Frank Thomas (Generations)	1.25
120	Alex Rodriguez (Generations)	3.00
121	Mike Piazza (Generations)	2.00
122	Greg Maddux (Generations)	1.75
123	Cal Ripken Jr. (Generations)	3.50
124	Chipper Jones (Generations)	2.00
125	Derek Jeter (Generations)	3.50
126	Tony Gwynn (Generations)	1.75
127	Andruw Jones (Generations)	1.25
128	Juan Gonzalez (Generations)	.75

1	Mark Kotsay	.50
2	Neifi Perez	.50
3	Paul Konerko	1.00
4	Jose Cruz Jr.	.50
5	Hideki Irabu	.50
6	Mike Cameron	.50
7	Jeff Suppan	.50
8	Kevin Orie	.50
9	Pokey Reese	.50
10	Todd Dunwoody	.50
11	Miguel Tejada	1.00
12	Jose Guillen	.50
13	Bartolo Colon	.50
14	Derek Lee	.75
15	Antone Williamson	.50
16	Wilton Guerrero	.50
17	Jaret Wright	.50

129	Jeff Bagwell (Generations)	1.25
130	Mark McGwire (Generations)	3.00
131	Roger Clemens (Generations)	1.75
132	Albert Belle (Generations)	.50
133	Barry Bonds (Generations)	3.50
134	Kenny Lofton (Generations)	.50
135	Ivan Rodriguez (Generations)	1.00
136	Manny Ramirez (Generations)	1.25
137	Jim Thome (Generations)	1.00
138	Chuck Knoblauch (Generations)	.50
139	Paul Molitor (Generations)	1.25
140	Barry Larkin (Generations)	.50
141	Mo Vaughn (Generations)	.50
142	Hideki Irabu (Generations)	.50
143	Jose Cruz Jr. (Generations)	.50
144	Tony Clark (Generations)	.50
145	Vladimir Guerrero (Generations)	1.25
146	Scott Rolen (Generations)	1.00
147	Nomar Garciaparra (Generations)	2.00
148	Checklist (Nomar Garciaparra)	1.00
149	Checklist (Larry Walker)	.50
150	Checklist (Tino Martinez)	.50
1	Ken Griffey Jr./EX	12.00
2	Frank Thomas/EX	7.50
3	Cal Ripken Jr./EX	17.50
4	Alex Rodriguez/EX	15.00
5	Greg Maddux/EX	10.00
6	Mike Piazza/EX	12.00
7	Chipper Jones/EX	10.00
8	Tony Gwynn/FB	10.00
9	Derek Jeter/FB	17.50
10	Jeff Bagwell/EX	7.50
11	Juan Gonzalez/EX	4.00
12	Nomar Garciaparra/EX	10.00
13	Andruw Jones/FB	7.50
14	Hideo Nomo/FB	4.00
15	Roger Clemens/FB	13.50
16	Mark McGwire/FB	15.00
17	Scott Rolen/FB	6.00
18	Vladimir Guerrero/FB	7.50
19	Barry Bonds/FB	17.50
20	Darin Erstad/FB	4.00
21	Albert Belle/FB	2.00
22	Kenny Lofton/FB	2.00
23	Mo Vaughn/FB	2.00
24	Tony Clark/FB	2.00
25	Ivan Rodriguez/FB	6.00
26	Larry Walker/CL	2.00
27	Eddie Murray/CL	7.50
28	Andy Pettitte/CL	2.00
29	Roberto Alomar/CL	2.00
30	Randy Johnson/CL	7.50
31	Manny Ramirez/CL	7.50
32	Paul Molitor/FB	7.50
33	Mike Mussina/CL	4.00
34	Jim Thome/FB	2.00
35	Tino Martinez/CL	2.00
36	Gary Sheffield/CL	3.00
37	Chuck Knoblauch/CL	2.00
38	Bernie Williams/CL	2.00
39	Tim Salmon/CL	2.00
40	Sammy Sosa/CL	10.00
41	Wade Boggs/MZ	10.00
42	Will Clark/GS	2.00
43	Andres Galarraga/CL	2.00
44	Raul Mondesi/CL	2.00
45	Rickey Henderson/GS	6.50
46	Jose Canseco/GS	4.00
47	Pedro Martinez/GS	6.50
48	Jay Buhner/GS	2.00
49	Ryan Klesko/GS	2.00
50	Barry Larkin/CL	2.00
51	Charles Johnson/GS	2.00
52	Tom Glavine/GS	3.00
53	Edgar Martinez/CL	2.00
54	Fred McGriff/GS	2.00
55	Moises Alou/MZ	2.00
56	Dante Bichette/GS	2.00
57	Jim Edmonds/CL	2.00
58	Mark Grace/MZ	2.00
59	Chan Ho Park/MZ	2.00
60	Justin Thompson/MZ	2.00
61	John Smoltz/MZ	2.00
62	Craig Biggio/CL	2.00
63	Ken Caminiti/MZ	2.00
64	Deion Sanders/MZ	2.00
65	Carlos Delgado/GS	4.00
66	David Justice/CL	2.00
67	J.T. Snow/MZ	2.00
68	Jason Giambi/CL	4.00
69	Garret Anderson/MZ	2.00
70	Rondell White/MZ	2.00
71	Matt Williams/MZ	2.00
72	Brady Anderson/MZ	2.00
73	Eric Karros/GS	2.00
74	Javier Lopez/GS	2.00
75	Pat Hentgen/GS	2.00
76	Todd Hundley/GS	2.00
77	Ray Lankford/GS	2.00
78	Denny Neagle/GS	2.00
79	Henry Rodriguez/GS	2.00
80	Sandy Alomar Jr./MZ	2.00
81	Rafael Palmeiro/MZ	5.00
82	Robin Ventura/GS	2.00
83	John Olerud/GS	2.00
84	Omar Vizquel/GS	2.00
85	Joe Randa/GS	2.00
86	Lance Johnson/GS	2.00
87	Kevin Brown/GS	2.00
88	Curt Schilling/GS	4.00
89	Ismael Valdes/GS	2.00
90	Francisco Cordova/GS	2.00
91	David Cone/GS	2.00
92	Paul O'Neill/GS	2.00
93	Jimmy Key/GS	2.00
94	Brad Radke/GS	2.00
95	Kevin Appier/GS	2.00
96	Al Martin/GS	2.00
97	Rusty Greer/MZ	2.00
98	Reggie Jefferson/GS	2.00
99	Ron Coomer/GS	2.00
100	Vinny Castilla/GS	2.00
101	Bobby Bonilla/MZ	2.00
102	Eric Young/GS	2.00
103	Tony Womack/GS	2.00
104	Jason Kendall/GS	2.00
105	Jeff Suppan/GS	2.00
106	Shawn Estes/MZ	2.00
107	Shawn Green/GS	2.00
108	Edgardo Alfonso/MZ	2.00
109	Alan Benes/MZ	2.00
110	Bobby Higginson/GS	2.00
111	Mark Grudzielanek/GS	2.00
112	Wilton Guerrero/GS	2.00
113	Todd Greene/MZ	2.00
114	Pokey Reese/GS	2.00
115	Jose Guillen/CL	2.00
116	Neifi Perez/MZ	2.00
117	Luis Castillo/GS	2.00
118	Edgar Renteria/GS	2.00
119	Karim Garcia/GS	2.00
120	Butch Huskey/GS	2.00
121	Michael Tucker/GS	2.00
122	Jason Dickson/GS	2.00
123	Todd Walker/MZ	2.00
124	Brian Jordan/GS	2.00
125	Joe Carter/GS	2.00
126	Matt Morris/MZ	2.00
127	Brett Tomko/MZ	2.00
128	Mike Cameron/CL	2.00
129	Russ Davis/GS	2.00
130	Shannon Stewart/MZ	2.00
131	Kevin Orie/GS	2.00
132	Scott Spiezio/GS	2.00
133	Brian Giles/GS	2.00
134	Raul Casanova/GS	2.00
135	Jose Cruz Jr./CL	2.00
136	Hideki Irabu/GS	2.00
137	Bubba Trammell/GS	2.00
138	Richard Hidalgo/CL	2.00
139	Paul Konerko/GS	2.50
140	Todd Helton/FB	5.00
141	Miguel Tejada/MZ	3.00
142	Fernando Tatis/MZ	2.00
143	Ben Grieve/GS	2.00
144	Travis Lee/FB	2.00
145	Mark Kotsay/CL	2.00
146	Eli Marrero/MZ	2.00
147	David Ortiz/CL	4.00
148	Juan Encarnacion/MZ	2.00
149	Jaret Wright/MZ	2.00
150	Livan Hernandez/CL	2.00
151	Ruben Rivera/MZ	2.00
152	Brad Fullmer/MZ	2.00
153	Dennis Reyes/GS	2.00
154	Enrique Wilson/MZ	2.00
155	Todd Dunwoody/MZ	2.00
156	Derrick Gibson/MZ	2.00
157	Aaron Boone/MZ	2.00
158	Ron Wright/MZ	2.00
159	Preston Wilson/MZ	2.00
160	Abraham Nunez/GS	2.00
161	Shane Monahan/GS	2.00
162	Carl Pavano/GS	2.00
163	Derrek Lee/GS	4.00
164	Jeff Abbott/GS	2.00
165	Wes Helms/MZ	2.00
166	Brian Rose/GS	2.00
167	Bobby Estalella/MZ	2.00
168	Ken Griffey Jr./GS	9.00
169	Frank Thomas/GS	6.00
170	Cal Ripken Jr./GS	15.00
171	Alex Rodriguez/GS	12.00
172	Greg Maddux/GS	7.50
173	Mike Piazza/GS	9.00
174	Chipper Jones/GS	8.00
175	Tony Gwynn/GS	7.50
176	Derek Jeter/GS	15.00
177	Jeff Bagwell/GS	6.00
178	Juan Gonzalez/GS	3.00
179	Nomar Garciaparra/GS	7.50
180	Andruw Jones/GS	6.00
181	Hideo Nomo/GS	3.00
182	Roger Clemens/GS	8.00
183	Mark McGwire/GS	12.00
184	Scott Rolen/GS	3.00
185	Barry Bonds/GS	15.00
186	Darin Erstad/GS	3.00
187	Mo Vaughn/GS	2.00
188	Ivan Rodriguez/GS	5.00
189	Larry Walker/MZ	3.00
190	Andy Pettitte/GS	3.00
191	Randy Johnson/GS	6.00
192	Paul Molitor/GS	3.00
193	Jim Thome/GS	4.00
194	Tino Martinez/GS	3.00
195	Gary Sheffield/GS	3.00
196	Albert Belle/GS	3.00
197	Jose Cruz Jr./GS	4.00
198	Todd Helton/GS	5.00
199	Ben Grieve/GS	2.00
200	Paul Konerko/GS	2.50

1998 Donruss Elite

Donruss Elite consists of a 150-card base set with two parallels and five inserts. The base cards feature a foil background with player photo on front. Another photo is on the back with stats and basic player information. The Aspirations parallel is numbered to 750 and the Status parallel is numbered to 100. The base set also includes the 30-card Generations subset and three checklists. The inserts are Back to the Future, Back to the Future Autographs, Craftsmen, Prime Numbers and Prime Numbers Die-Cuts.

		NM/M
Complete Set (150):		15.00
Common Player:		.10
Aspirations (750 Sets):		2.5X
Status (100 Sets):		15X
Pack (5):		2.50
Wax Box (18):		40.00
1	Ken Griffey Jr.	1.50
2	Frank Thomas	.75
3	Alex Rodriguez	2.00
4	Mike Piazza	1.50
5	Greg Maddux	1.00
6	Cal Ripken Jr.	2.50
7	Chipper Jones	1.00
8	Derek Jeter	2.50
9	Tony Gwynn	1.00
10	Andruw Jones	.75
11	Juan Gonzalez	.40
12	Jeff Bagwell	.75
13	Mark McGwire	2.00
14	Roger Clemens	1.25
15	Albert Belle	.10
16	Barry Bonds	2.50
17	Kenny Lofton	.10
18	Ivan Rodriguez	.75
19	Manny Ramirez	.75
20	Jim Thome	.50
21	Chuck Knoblauch	.10
22	Paul Molitor	.75
23	Barry Larkin	.10
24	Andy Pettitte	.40
25	John Smoltz	.10
26	Randy Johnson	.75
27	Bernie Williams	.10
28	Larry Walker	.10
29	Mo Vaughn	.10
30	Bobby Higginson	.10
31	Edgardo Alfonso	.10
32	Justin Thompson	.10
33	Jeff Suppan	.10
34	Roberto Alomar	.30
35	Hideo Nomo	.40
36	Rusty Greer	.10
37	Tim Salmon	.10
38	Jim Edmonds	.10
39	Gary Sheffield	.25
40	Ken Caminiti	.10
41	Sammy Sosa	1.00
42	Tony Womack	.10
43	Matt Williams	.10
44	Andres Galarraga	.10
45	Garret Anderson	.10
46	Rafael Palmeiro	.65
47	Mike Mussina	.40
48	Craig Biggio	.40
49	Wade Boggs	1.00
50	Tom Glavine	.25
51	Jason Giambi	.50
52	Will Clark	.50
53	David Justice	.10
54	Sandy Alomar Jr.	.10
55	Edgar Martinez	.10
56	Brady Anderson	.10
57	Eric Young	.10
58	Ray Lankford	.10
59	Kevin Brown	.10
60	Raul Mondesi	.10
61	Bobby Bonilla	.10
62	Javier Lopez	.10
63	Fred McGriff	.10
64	Rondell White	.10
65	Todd Hundley	.10
66	Mark Grace	.10
67	Alan Benes	.10
68	Jeff Abbott	.10
69	Bob Abreu	.10
70	Deion Sanders	.10
71	Tino Martinez	.10
72	Shannon Stewart	.10
73	Homer Bush	.10
74	Carlos Delgado	.50
75	Raul Ibanez	.10
76	Hideki Irabu	.10
77	Jose Cruz Jr.	.10
78	Tony Clark	.10
79	Wilton Guerrero	.10
80	Vladimir Guerrero	.75
81	Scott Rolen	.60
82	Nomar Garciaparra	1.00
83	Darin Erstad	.30
84	Chan Ho Park	.10
85	Mike Cameron	.10
86	Todd Walker	.10
87	Todd Dunwoody	.10
88	Neifi Perez	.10
89	Brett Tomko	.10
90	Jose Guillen	.10
91	Matt Morris	.10
92	Bartolo Colon	.10
93	Jaret Wright	.10
94	Shawn Estes	.10
95	Livan Hernandez	.10
96	Bobby Estalella	.10
97	Ben Grieve	.10
98	Paul Konerko	.15
99	David Ortiz	.40
100	Todd Helton	.65
101	Juan Encarnacion	.10
102	Bubba Trammell	.10
103	Miguel Tejada	.25
104	Jacob Cruz	.10
105	Todd Greene	.10
106	Kevin Orie	.10
107	Mark Kotsay	.10
108	Fernando Tatis	.10
109	Jay Payton	.10
110	Pokey Reese	.10
111	Derrek Lee	.10
112	Richard Hidalgo	.10
113	Ricky Ledee	.10
114	Lou Collier	.10
115	Ruben Rivera	.10
116	Shawn Green	.20
117	Moises Alou	.10
118	Ken Griffey Jr. (Generations)	.65
119	Frank Thomas (Generations)	.40
120	Alex Rodriguez (Generations)	.75
121	Mike Piazza (Generations)	.65
122	Greg Maddux (Generations)	.50
123	Cal Ripken Jr. (Generations)	1.00
124	Chipper Jones (Generations)	.50
125	Derek Jeter (Generations)	1.00
126	Tony Gwynn (Generations)	.50
127	Andruw Jones (Generations)	.40
128	Juan Gonzalez (Generations)	.40
129	Jeff Bagwell (Generations)	.40
130	Mark McGwire (Generations)	.75
131	Roger Clemens (Generations)	.65
132	Albert Belle (Generations)	.10
133	Barry Bonds (Generations)	1.00
134	Kenny Lofton (Generations)	.10
135	Ivan Rodriguez (Generations)	.25
136	Manny Ramirez (Generations)	.40
137	Jim Thome (Generations)	.25
138	Chuck Knoblauch (Generations)	.10
139	Paul Molitor (Generations)	.40
140	Barry Larkin (Generations)	.10
141	Mo Vaughn (Generations)	.10
142	Hideki Irabu (Generations)	.10
143	Jose Cruz Jr. (Generations)	.10
144	Tony Clark (Generations)	.10
145	Vladimir Guerrero (Generations)	.40
146	Scott Rolen (Generations)	.20
147	Nomar Garciaparra (Generations)	.50
148	Checklist (Nomar Garciaparra Hit Streaks)	.40
149	Checklist Larry Walker (Long HR-Coors)	.10
150	Checklist Tino Martinez (3 HR in game)	.10

1998 Donruss Elite Aspirations

A parallel edition of 750 of each player are found in this die-cut set. Cards have a scalloped treatment cut into the top and sides and red, rather than silver metallic borders. The word "ASPIRATIONS" in printed on front at bottom-right. Backs have the notation "1 of 750."

	NM/M
Common Player:	.50
Stars/Rookies:	2.5X

1998 Donruss Elite Status

Just 100 serially numbered cards of each player are found in this die-cut parallel set. Cards have a scalloped treatment cut into the top and sides and red, rather than silver metallic borders.

	NM/M
Common Player:	1.50
Stars/Rookies:	15X

Back to the Future

These double-front cards feature a veteran or retired star on one side and a young player on the other. Each player's name, team and "Back to the Future" are printed in the border. The cards are numbered to 1,500, with the first 100 of each card signed by both players. Exceptions are cards #1 and #6. Ripken and Konerko did not sign the same cards and Frank Thomas did not sign his Back to the Future card. Thomas instead signed 100 copies of his Elite base set card which was specially marked.

		NM/M
Complete Set (8):		40.00
Common Player:		2.50
Production 1,400 Sets		
1	Cal Ripken Jr., Paul Konerko	9.00
2	Jeff Bagwell, Todd Helton	4.50
3	Eddie Mathews, Chipper Jones	5.00
4	Juan Gonzalez, Ben Grieve	2.50
5	Hank Aaron, Jose Cruz Jr.	10.00
6	Frank Thomas, David Ortiz	4.50
7	Nolan Ryan, Greg Maddux	9.00
8	Alex Rodriguez, Nomar Garciaparra	9.00

Back to the Future Autographs

The first 100 of each card in the Back to the Future insert was autographed by both players. Exceptions are cards #1 and #6. Ripken and Konerko did not sign the same cards and Frank Thomas did not sign his Back to the Future card. Thomas instead signed 100 specially marked copies of his Elite base-set card.

		NM/M
Production 100 Sets		
1a	Paul Konerko	30.00
1b	Cal Ripken Jr.	150.00
2	Jeff Bagwell, Todd Helton	120.00
3	Eddie Mathews, Chipper Jones	200.00
4	Juan Gonzalez, Ben Grieve	30.00
5	Hank Aaron, Jose Cruz Jr.	250.00
7	Nolan Ryan, Greg Maddux	850.00
8	Alex Rodriguez, Nomar Garciaparra	450.00
9	Frank Thomas (Specially autographed Elite)	45.00

Craftsmen

This 30-card insert has color player photos on the front and back. The set is sequentially numbered to 3,500. The Master Craftsmen parallel is numbered to 100.

		NM/M
Complete Set (30):		40.00
Common Player:		.50
Production 3,500 Sets		
Master Craftsman (100 Sets):		10X
1	Ken Griffey Jr.	3.00
2	Frank Thomas	1.50
3	Alex Rodriguez	4.00
4	Cal Ripken Jr.	5.00
5	Greg Maddux	2.00
6	Mike Piazza	3.00
7	Chipper Jones	2.00
8	Derek Jeter	5.00
9	Tony Gwynn	2.00
10	Nomar Garciaparra	2.00
11	Scott Rolen	1.25
12	Jose Cruz Jr.	.50
13	Tony Clark	.50
14	Vladimir Guerrero	1.50
15	Todd Helton	1.25
16	Ben Grieve	.50
17	Andruw Jones	1.50
18	Jeff Bagwell	1.50
19	Mark McGwire	4.00
20	Juan Gonzalez	.75
21	Roger Clemens	2.50
22	Albert Belle	.50
23	Barry Bonds	5.00
24	Kenny Lofton	.50
25	Ivan Rodriguez	1.25
26	Paul Molitor	1.50
27	Barry Larkin (Incorrect "CARDINALS" on front.)	.50
28	Mo Vaughn	.50
29	Larry Walker	.50
30	Tino Martinez	.50

Prime Numbers

This 36-card insert includes three cards for each of 12 players. Each card has a single number in the background. The three numbers for each player represent a key statistic for the player (ex. Mark McGwire's cards are 3-8-7; his career home run total at the time was 387). Each card in the set is sequentially numbered. The total is dependent upon the player's statistic. Promo versions with no serial number and a large "SAMPLE" on back exist for each card.

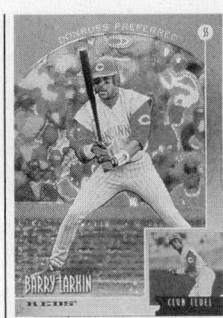

		NM/M
Common Card:		5.00
Samples: 50 Percent Player's Common		
1A	Ken Griffey Jr. 2/94	25.00
1B	Ken Griffey Jr. 9/204	20.00
1C	Ken Griffey Jr. 4/290	17.50
2A	Frank Thomas 4/56	7.50
2B	Frank Thomas 5/406	7.50
2C	Frank Thomas 6/450	7.50
3A	Mark McGwire 3/87	20.00
3B	Mark McGwire 8/307	20.00
3C	Mark McGwire 7/380	20.00
4A	Cal Ripken Jr. 5/17	135.00
4B	Cal Ripken Jr. 1/507	13.50
4C	Cal Ripken Jr. 7/510	13.50
5A	Mike Piazza 5/76	30.00
5B	Mike Piazza 7/506	12.00
5C	Mike Piazza 6/570	12.00
6A	Chipper Jones 4/89	25.00
6B	Chipper Jones 8/409	10.00
6C	Chipper Jones 9/480	10.00
7A	Tony Gwynn 3/72	25.00
7B	Tony Gwynn 7/302	9.00
7C	Tony Gwynn 2/370	9.00
8A	Barry Bonds 3/74	45.00
8B	Barry Bonds 7/304	12.00
8C	Barry Bonds 4/370	12.00
9A	Jeff Bagwell 4/25	25.00
9B	Jeff Bagwell 2/405	7.50
9C	Jeff Bagwell 5/420	7.50
10A	Juan Gonzalez 5/89	9.00
10B	Juan Gonzalez 8/509	6.00
10C	Juan Gonzalez 9/580	6.00
11A	Alex Rodriguez 5/34	55.00
11B	Alex Rodriguez 3/504	12.00
11C	Alex Rodriguez 4/530	12.00
12A	Kenny Lofton 3/54	15.00
12B	Kenny Lofton 5/304	5.00
12C	Kenny Lofton 4/350	5.00

Prime Numbers Die-Cuts

This set is a die-cut parallel of the Prime Numbers insert. Each card is sequentially numbered. The production run for each player is the number featured on his first card times 100, his second card times 10 and his third card is sequentially numbered to the number featured on the card.

		NM/M
Common Player:		4.00
1A	Ken Griffey Jr. 2/200	20.00
1B	Ken Griffey Jr. 9/90	35.00
1C	Ken Griffey Jr. 4/4	130.00
2A	Frank Thomas 4/400	6.00
2B	Frank Thomas 5/50	20.00
2C	Frank Thomas 6/6	60.00
3A	Mark McGwire 3/300	17.50
3B	Mark McGwire 8/80	50.00
3C	Mark McGwire 7/7	110.00
4A	Cal Ripken Jr. 5/500	12.50
4B	Cal Ripken Jr. 1/10	95.00
4C	Cal Ripken Jr. 7/7	120.00
5A	Mike Piazza 5/500	10.00
5B	Mike Piazza 7/70	30.00
5C	Mike Piazza 6/6	75.00
6A	Chipper Jones 4/400	7.50
6B	Chipper Jones 8/80	25.00
6C	Chipper Jones 9/9	55.00
7A	Tony Gwynn 3/300	9.00
7B	Tony Gwynn 7/70	25.00
7C	Tony Gwynn 2/2	75.00
8A	Barry Bonds 3/300	10.00
8B	Barry Bonds 7/70	35.00
8C	Barry Bonds 4/4	160.00
9A	Jeff Bagwell 4/400	4.00
9B	Jeff Bagwell 2/20	25.00
9C	Jeff Bagwell 5/5	55.00
10A	Juan Gonzalez 5/500	4.00
10B	Juan Gonzalez 8/80	15.00
10C	Juan Gonzalez 9/9	55.00
11A	Alex Rodriguez 5/500	6.00
11B	Alex Rodriguez 3/30	60.00
11C	Alex Rodriguez 4/4	160.00
12A	Kenny Lofton 3/300	4.00
12B	Kenny Lofton 5/50	7.00
12C	Kenny Lofton 4/4	30.00

1998 Donruss Preferred

The Donruss Preferred 200-card base set is broken down into five subsets: 100 Grand Stand cards (5:1), 40 Mezzanine (1:6), 30 Club Level (1:12), 20 Field Box (1:23) and 10 Executive Suite (1:65). The base set is paralleled in the Preferred Seating set. Each

subset has a different die-cut in the parallel. Inserts in this product include Great X-Pectations, Precious Metals and Title Waves.

		NM/M
Complete Set (200):		90.00
Common Grand Stand (5:1):		.10
Common Mezzanine (1:6):		.20
Common Club Level (1:12):		.30
Common Field Box: (1:23)		.40
Common Executive Suite (1:65):		1.50
Tin Pack (5):		3.00
Tin Box (24):		40.00
1	Ken Griffey Jr./EX	4.00
2	Frank Thomas/EX	2.50
3	Cal Ripken Jr./EX	7.50
4	Alex Rodriguez/EX	5.00
5	Greg Maddux/EX	3.00
6	Mike Piazza/EX	4.00
7	Chipper Jones/EX	3.00
8	Tony Gwynn/FB	2.50
9	Derek Jeter/FB	6.00
10	Jeff Bagwell/EX	2.00
11	Juan Gonzalez/EX	1.50
12	Nomar Garciaparra/EX	3.00
13	Andruw Jones/FB	2.00
14	Hideo Nomo/FB	.65
15	Roger Clemens/FB	3.00
16	Mark McGwire/FB	5.00
17	Scott Rolen/FB	.75
18	Vladimir Guerrero/FB	2.00
19	Barry Bonds/FB	4.00
20	Darin Erstad/FB	.60
21	Albert Belle/FB	.40
22	Kenny Lofton/FB	.40
23	Mo Vaughn/FB	.40
24	Tony Clark/FB	.40
25	Ivan Rodriguez/FB	1.50
26	Larry Walker/CL	.30
27	Eddie Murray/CL	1.00
28	Andy Pettitte/CL	.45
29	Roberto Alomar/CL	.40
30	Randy Johnson/CL	1.00
31	Manny Ramirez/CL	.50
32	Paul Molitor/FB	2.00
33	Mike Mussina/CL	.50
34	Jim Thome/FB	.75
35	Tino Martinez/CL	.30
36	Gary Sheffield/CL	.45
37	Chuck Knoblauch/CL	.30
38	Bernie Williams/CL	.30
39	Tim Salmon/CL	.30
40	Sammy Sosa/CL	1.50
41	Wade Boggs/MZ	.75
42	Will Clark/GS	.10
43	Andres Galarraga/CL	.50
44	Raul Mondesi/CL	.30
45	Rickey Henderson/GS	.35
46	Jose Canseco/GS	.35
47	Pedro Martinez/GS	.50
48	Jay Buhner/GS	.20
49	Ryan Klesko/GS	.10
50	Barry Larkin/GS	.20
51	Charles Johnson/GS	.10
52	Tom Glavine/GS	.25
53	Edgar Martinez/GS	.20
54	Fred McGriff/GS	.20
55	Moises Alou/MZ	.20
56	Dante Bichette/GS	.10
57	Jim Edmonds/CL	.30
58	Mark Grace/MZ	.20
59	Chan Ho Park/MZ	.20
60	Justin Thompson/MZ	.20
61	John Smoltz/MZ	.20
62	Craig Biggio/CL	.30
63	Ken Caminiti/MZ	.20
64	Deion Sanders/MZ	.20
65	Carlos Delgado/GS	.30
66	David Justice/CL	.30
67	J.T. Snow/GS	.10
68	Jason Giambi/CL	.20
69	Garret Anderson/MZ	.20
70	Rondell White/MZ	.20
71	Matt Williams/MZ	.20
72	Brady Anderson/MZ	.20
73	Eric Karros/MZ	.10
74	Javier Lopez/GS	.10
75	Pat Hentgen/GS	.10
76	Todd Hundley/GS	.10
77	Ray Lankford/GS	.10
78	Denny Neagle/GS	.10
79	Henry Rodriguez/MZ	.20
80	Sandy Alomar Jr./MZ	.20
81	Rafael Palmeiro/MZ	.50
82	Robin Ventura/MZ	.20
83	John Olerud/GS	.10
84	Omar Vizquel/GS	.10
85	Joe Randa/GS	.10
86	Lance Johnson/GS	.10
87	Kevin Brown/GS	.10
88	Curt Schilling/GS	.25
89	Ismael Valdes/GS	.10
90	Francisco Cordova/GS	.10
91	David Cone/GS	.10
92	Paul O'Neill/GS	.10
93	Jimmy Key/GS	.10
94	Brad Radke/GS	.10
95	Kevin Appier/GS	.10
96	Al Martin/GS	.10
97	Rusty Greer/MZ	.20
98	Reggie Jefferson/GS	.10
99	Ron Coomer/GS	.10
100	Vinny Castilla/GS	.20
101	Bobby Bonilla/MZ	.20
102	Eric Young/GS	.10
103	Tony Womack/GS	.20
104	Jason Kendall/GS	.10
105	Jeff Suppan/GS	.10
106	Shawn Estes/MZ	.20
107	Shawn Green/GS	.25
108	Edgardo Alfonzo/MZ	.20
109	Alan Benes/MZ	.20
110	Bobby Higginson/GS	.10
111	Mark Grudzielanek/GS	.10
112	Wilton Guerrero/GS	.10
113	Todd Greene/MZ	.20
114	Pokey Reese/GS	.10
115	Jose Guillen/CL	.30
116	Neifi Perez/MZ	.20
117	Luis Castillo/GS	.10
118	Edgar Renteria/GS	.10
119	Karim Garcia/GS	.10
120	Butch Huskey/GS	.10
121	Michael Tucker/GS	.10
122	Jason Dickson/GS	.10
123	Todd Walker/MZ	.20
124	Brian Jordan/GS	.10
125	Joe Carter/GS	.20
126	Matt Morris/MZ	.20
127	Brett Tomko/MZ	.20
128	Mike Cameron/CL	.30
129	Russ Davis/MZ	.20
130	Shannon Stewart/MZ	.20
131	Kevin Orie/GS	.10
132	Scott Spiezio/GS	.10
133	Brian Giles/GS	.10
134	Raul Casanova/GS	.10
135	Jose Cruz Jr./CL	.30
136	Hideki Irabu/GS	.10
137	Bubba Trammell/GS	.10
138	Richard Hidalgo/GS	.30
139	Paul Konerko/CL	.35
140	Todd Helton/FB	1.00
141	Miguel Tejada/CL	.40
142	Fernando Tatis/MZ	.20
143	Ben Grieve/FB	.40
144	Travis Lee/FB	.65
145	Mark Kotsay/CL	.30
146	Eli Marrero/GS	.20
147	David Ortiz/CL	.50
148	Juan Encarnacion/MZ	.20
149	Jaret Wright/MZ	.50
150	Livan Hernandez/CL	.30
151	Ruben Rivera/GS	.10
152	Brad Fullmer/MZ	.20
153	Dennis Reyes/GS	.10
154	Enrique Wilson/MZ	.20
155	Todd Dunwoody/MZ	.20
156	Derrick Gibson/MZ	.20
157	Aaron Boone/MZ	.20
158	Ron Wright/MZ	.20
159	Preston Wilson/MZ	.20
160	Abraham Nunez/GS	.10
161	Shane Monahan/GS	.10
162	Carl Pavano/GS	.10
163	Derek Lee/GS	.35
164	Jeff Abbott/GS	.10
165	Wes Helms/MZ	.20
166	Brian Rose/GS	.10
167	Bobby Estalella/GS	.10
168	Ken Griffey Jr./GS	.75
169	Frank Thomas/GS	.50
170	Cal Ripken Jr./GS	1.50
171	Alex Rodriguez/GS	1.00
172	Greg Maddux/GS	.60
173	Mike Piazza/GS	.75
174	Chipper Jones/GS	.60
175	Tony Gwynn/GS	.60
176	Derek Jeter/GS	1.50
177	Jeff Bagwell/GS	.50
178	Juan Gonzalez/GS	.30
179	Nomar Garciaparra/GS	.60
180	Andruw Jones/GS	.50
181	Hideo Nomo/GS	.30
182	Roger Clemens/GS	.65
183	Mark McGwire/GS	1.00
184	Scott Rolen/GS	.35
185	Barry Bonds/GS	1.50
186	Darin Erstad/GS	.25
187	Mo Vaughn/GS	.10
188	Ivan Rodriguez/GS	.40
189	Larry Walker/MZ	.20
190	Andy Pettitte/GS	.30
191	Randy Johnson/MZ	.60
192	Paul Molitor/GS	.20
193	Jim Thome/GS	.35
194	Tino Martinez/GS	.20
195	Gary Sheffield/GS	.20
196	Albert Belle/GS	.10
197	Jose Cruz Jr./GS	.40
198	Todd Helton/GS	.40
199	Ben Grieve/GS	.30
200	Paul Konerko/GS	.10

Seating

Preferred Seating is a die-cut parallel of the base set. Each section of the base set has a different die-cut.

	NM/M
Common Grand Stand:	.50
Stars and Rookies:	4X
Common Mezzanine:	.50
Stars and Rookies:	2X
Common Club Level:	.50
Stars and Rookies:	2X
Common Field Box:	1.00
Stars and Rookies:	1.5X
Common Executive Suite:	2.50
Stars and Rookies:	1X

Great X-pectations

This 26-card insert features a veteran player on one side and a young player on the other. A large "GX" appears in the background on each side. The cards are sequentially numbered to 2,700, with the first 300 of each die-cut around the "GX."

		NM/M
Complete Set (26):		35.00
Common Player:		.75
Die-Cuts:		3X
Samples:		1X
1	Jeff Bagwell, Travis Lee	1.25
2	Jose Cruz Jr.,	
	Ken Griffey Jr.	2.00
3	Larry Walker, Ben Grieve	.75
4	Frank Thomas,	
	Todd Helton	1.25
5	Jim Thome,	
	Paul Konerko	1.00
6	Alex Rodriguez,	
	Miguel Tejada	2.50
7	Greg Maddux,	
	Livan Hernandez	1.75
8	Roger Clemens,	
	Jaret Wright	1.75
9	Albert Belle,	
	Juan Encarnacion	.75
10	Mo Vaughn, David Ortiz	1.00
11	Manny Ramirez,	
	Mark Kotsay	1.00
12	Tim Salmon, Brad Fullmer	.75
13	Cal Ripken Jr.,	
	Fernando Tatis	3.50
14	Hideo Nomo,	
	Hideki Irabu	1.50
15	Mike Piazza,	
	Todd Greene	2.00
16	Gary Sheffield,	
	Richard Hidalgo	.75
17	Paul Molitor,	
	Darin Erstad	1.25
18	Ivan Rodriguez,	
	Eli Marrero	1.00
19	Ken Caminiti, Todd Walker	.75
20	Tony Gwynn,	
	Jose Guillen	1.75
21	Derek Jeter,	
	Nomar Garciaparra	3.50
22	Chipper Jones,	
	Scott Rolen	1.75
23	Juan Gonzalez,	
	Andruw Jones	1.25
24	Barry Bonds,	
	Vladimir Guerrero	3.50

25	Mark McGwire,	
	Tony Clark	2.50
26	Bernie Williams,	
	Mike Cameron	.75

Precious Metals

Precious Metals is a 30-card partial parallel of the Preferred base set. Each card was printed on stock using real silver, gold or platinum. Fifty complete sets were produced.

		NM/M
Complete Set (30):		850.00
Common Player:		7.50
1	Ken Griffey Jr.	50.00
2	Frank Thomas	35.00
3	Cal Ripken Jr.	75.00
4	Alex Rodriguez	60.00
5	Greg Maddux	45.00
6	Mike Piazza	50.00
7	Chipper Jones	45.00
8	Tony Gwynn	45.00
9	Derek Jeter	75.00
10	Jeff Bagwell	35.00
11	Juan Gonzalez	15.00
12	Nomar Garciaparra	45.00
13	Andruw Jones	35.00
14	Hideo Nomo	15.00
15	Roger Clemens	45.00
16	Mark McGwire	60.00
17	Scott Rolen	25.00
18	Barry Bonds	75.00
19	Darin Erstad	15.00
20	Kenny Lofton	7.50
21	Mo Vaughn	7.50
22	Ivan Rodriguez	25.00
23	Randy Johnson	35.00
24	Paul Molitor	35.00
25	Jose Cruz Jr.	7.50
26	Paul Konerko	7.50
27	Todd Helton	25.00
28	Ben Grieve	7.50
29	Travis Lee	7.50
30	Mark Kotsay	7.50

Title Waves

This 30-card set features players who won awards or titles between 1993-1997. Printed on plastic stock, each card is sequentially numbered to the year the player won the award. The card fronts feature the Title Waves logo, a color player photo in front of a background of fans and the name of the award the player won.

		NM/M
Complete Set (30):		100.00
Common Player:		1.00
1	Nomar Garciaparra	5.00
2	Scott Rolen	2.50
3	Roger Clemens	5.50
4	Gary Sheffield	1.50
5	Jeff Bagwell	3.50
6	Cal Ripken Jr.	10.00
7	Frank Thomas	3.50
8	Ken Griffey Jr.	6.00
9	Larry Walker	1.00
10	Derek Jeter	10.00
11	Juan Gonzalez	2.00
12	Bernie Williams	1.00
13	Andruw Jones	3.50
14	Andy Pettitte	1.50
15	Ivan Rodriguez	2.50
16	Alex Rodriguez	8.00

17	Mark McGwire	8.00
18	Andres Galarraga	1.00
19	Hideo Nomo	2.00
20	Mo Vaughn	1.00
21	Randy Johnson	3.50
22	Chipper Jones	5.00
23	Greg Maddux	5.00
24	Manny Ramirez	3.50
25	Tony Gwynn	5.00
26	Albert Belle	1.00
27	Kenny Lofton	1.00
28	Mike Piazza	6.00
29	Paul Molitor	3.50
30	Barry Bonds	10.00

Tins

Donruss Preferred was packaged in collectible tins. Each tin contained five cards and featured one of 24 players on the top. Silver (numbered to 999) and gold (199) parallel tins were also produced and included in hobby-only boxes. The values shown are for empty tins.

		NM/M
Complete Set (24):		17.50
Common Player:		.25
Gold Tins (199):		3X
Silver Tins (999):		1.5X
1	Todd Helton	.65
2	Ben Grieve	.25
3	Cal Ripken Jr.	2.50
4	Alex Rodriguez	2.00
5	Greg Maddux	1.00
6	Mike Piazza	1.50
7	Chipper Jones	1.00
8	Travis Lee	.25
9	Derek Jeter	2.50
10	Jeff Bagwell	.75
11	Juan Gonzalez	.50
12	Mark McGwire	2.00
13	Hideo Nomo	.50
14	Roger Clemens	1.25
15	Andruw Jones	.75
16	Paul Molitor	.75
17	Vladimir Guerrero	.75
18	Jose Cruz Jr.	.25
19	Nomar Garciaparra	1.00
20	Scott Rolen	.65
21	Ken Griffey Jr.	1.50
22	Larry Walker	.25
23	Frank Thomas	.75
24	Tony Gwynn	2.00

1998 Donruss Preferred Double-Wide Tins

Double-wide flip-top tins of Donruss Preferred cards were a reail exclusive with a price tag of about $6. The double-wide retail tins use the same player checklist and photo as the green hobby-version single tins, but have predominantly blue color. Values shown are for opened tins.

		NM/M
Complete Set (12):		12.00
Common Tin:		.65
1	Todd Helton, Ben Grieve	.65
2	Cal Ripken Jr.,	
	Alex Rodriguez	2.00
3	Greg Maddux,	
	Mike Piazza	1.25
4	Chipper Jones,	
	Travis Lee	1.00
5	Derek Jeter, Jeff Bagwell	2.00
6	Juan Gonzalez,	
	Mark McGwire	1.50
7	Hideo Nomo,	
	Roger Clemens	1.00
8	Andruw Jones,	
	Paul Molitor	.75
9	Vladimir Guerrero,	
	Jose Cruz Jr.	.75
10	Nomar Garciaparra,	
	Scott Rolen	1.00
11	Ken Griffey Jr.,	
	Larry Walker	1.25
12	Tony Gwynn,	
	Frank Thomas	

1998 Donruss Preferred Tin Boxes

The boxes for 1998 Donruss Preferred consisted of a lithographed steel lidded box which contained 24 tin packs. The basic tin box was green in color and individually serial numbered to 999. A parallel gold box issue was randomly inserted in Preferred cases and had boxes numbered to 199. Values shown are for empty boxes.

	NM/M
Complete Set (24):	85.00
Common Player:	1.00
Gold:	1.5X
1 Todd Helton	.2.50
2 Ben Grieve	1.00
3 Cal Ripken Jr.	10.00
4 Alex Rodriguez	7.50
5 Greg Maddux	5.00
6 Mike Piazza	6.00
7 Chipper Jones	5.00
8 Travis Lee	1.00
9 Derek Jeter	10.00
10 Jeff Bagwell	3.00
11 Juan Gonzalez	5.00
12 Mark McGwire	7.50
13 Hideo Nomo	1.50
14 Roger Clemens	5.50
15 Andruw Jones	3.00
16 Paul Molitor	3.00
17 Vladimir Guerrero	3.00
18 Jose Cruz Jr.	1.00
19 Nomar Garciaparra	5.00
20 Scott Rolen	2.00
21 Ken Griffey Jr.	6.00
22 Larry Walker	1.00
23 Frank Thomas	3.00
24 Tony Gwynn	5.00

Signature Series Preview Autographs

This insert was a surprise addition to Donruss Update. The set features autographs from top rookies and stars. The number of cards produced varies for each player. The card fronts have a color player photo in front of a gold checkered border with the signature in a white area near the bottom. Cards of a number of players (Alou, Casey, Jenkins, Wilson, etc.) were never officially released, having been returned too late by the players; specimens, have, however made their way into the hobby market in unknown numbers.

	NM/M
Common Player:	10.00
(1) Sandy Alomar Jr./96	30.00
(2) Moises Alou	10.00
(3) Andy Benes/135	15.00
(4) Russell Branyan/188	15.00
(5) Sean Casey	85.00
(6) Tony Clark/188	20.00
(7) Juan Encarnacion/193	15.00
(8) Brad Fullmer/396	10.00
(9) Juan Gonzalez/108	115.00
(10) Ben Grieve/100	35.00
(11) Todd Helton/101	50.00
(12) Richard Hidalgo/380	10.00
(13) A.J. Hinch/400	10.00
(14) Damian Jackson/15	65.00
(15) Geoff Jenkins	185.00
(16) Derek Jeter	1,225

(17) Chipper Jones/112	125.00
(18) Chuck Knoblauch/98	50.00
(19) Travis Lee/101	20.00
(20) Mike Lowell/450	15.00
(21) Greg Maddux/92	165.00
(22) Kevin Millwood/395	30.00
(23) Magglio Ordonez/420	50.00
(24) David Ortiz/393	75.00
(25) Rafael Palmeiro/107	50.00
(26) Cal Ripken Jr./22	850.00
(27) Alex Rodriguez/23	1,150
(28) Curt Schilling/100	100.00
(29) Randall Simon/380	10.00
(30) Fernando Tatis/400	10.00
(31) Miguel Tejada/375	40.00
(32) Robin Ventura/395	30.00
(33) Dan Wilson	85.00
(34) Kerry Wood/375	40.00

1998 Donruss Signature Series

The 140-card base set has a white border encasing the player photo with the logo stamped with silver foil. Card backs have a small photo and complete year-by-year statistics. Signature Proofs are a parallel to the base set utilizing holo-foil treatment and "Signature Proof" written down the left edge of the card front. Each card is numbered "1 of 150" on the card back.

	NM/M
Complete Set (140):	30.00
Common Player:	.10
Signature Proofs:	12X
Pack (5):	12.50
Wax Box (12):	150.00
1 David Justice	.10
2 Derek Jeter	2.50
3 Nomar Garciaparra	1.00
4 Ryan Klesko	.10
5 Jeff Bagwell	.75
6 Dante Bichette	.10
7 Ivan Rodriguez	.65
8 Albert Belle	.10
9 Cal Ripken Jr.	2.50
10 Craig Biggio	.10
11 Barry Larkin	.10
12 Jose Guillen	.10
13 Will Clark	.10
14 J.T. Snow	.10
15 Chuck Knoblauch	.10
16 Todd Walker	.10
17 Scott Rolen	.60
18 Rickey Henderson	.75
19 Juan Gonzalez	.40
20 Justin Thompson	.10
21 Roger Clemens	1.25
22 Ray Lankford	.10
23 Jose Cruz Jr.	.10
24 Ken Griffey Jr.	1.50
25 Andruw Jones	.75
26 Darin Erstad	.30
27 Jim Thome	.50
28 Wade Boggs	1.00
29 Ken Caminiti	.10
30 Todd Hundley	.10
31 Mike Piazza	1.50
32 Sammy Sosa	1.00
33 Larry Walker	.10
34 Matt Williams	.10
35 Frank Thomas	.75
36 Gary Sheffield	.30
37 Alex Rodriguez	2.00
38 Hideo Nomo	.40
39 Kenny Lofton	.10
40 John Smoltz	.10
41 Mo Vaughn	.10
42 Edgar Martinez	.10
43 Paul Molitor	.75
44 Rafael Palmeiro	.65
45 Barry Bonds	2.50
46 Vladimir Guerrero	.75
47 Carlos Delgado	.50
48 Bobby Higginson	.10
49 Greg Maddux	1.00
50 Jim Edmonds	.10
51 Randy Johnson	.75
52 Mark McGwire	2.00
53 Rondell White	.10
54 Raul Mondesi	.10
55 Manny Ramirez	.75
56 Pedro Martinez	.75
57 Tim Salmon	.10

58 Moises Alou	.10
59 Fred McGriff	.10
60 Garret Anderson	.10
61 Sandy Alomar Jr.	.10
62 Chan Ho Park	.10
63 Mark Kotsay	.10
64 Mike Mussina	.50
65 Tom Glavine	.25
66 Tony Clark	.10
67 Mark Grace	.10
68 Tony Gwynn	1.00
69 Tino Martinez	.10
70 Kevin Brown	.10
71 Todd Greene	.10
72 Andy Pettitte	.30
73 Livan Hernandez	.10
74 Curt Schilling	.25
75 Andres Galarraga	.10
76 Rusty Greer	.10
77 Jay Buhner	.10
78 Bobby Bonilla	.10
79 Chipper Jones	1.00
80 Eric Young	.10
81 Jason Giambi	.50
82 Javy Lopez	.10
83 Roberto Alomar	.25
84 Bernie Williams	.10
85 A.J. Hinch	.10
86 Kerry Wood	.40
87 Juan Encarnacion	.10
88 Brad Fullmer	.10
89 Ben Grieve	.10
90 Magglio Ordonez RC	2.00
91 Todd Helton	.65
92 Richard Hidalgo	.15
93 Paul Konerko	.15
94 Aramis Ramirez	.10
95 Ricky Ledee	.10
96 Derek Lee	.50
97 Travis Lee	.15
98 Matt Anderson RC	.25
99 Jaret Wright	.10
100 David Ortiz	.35
101 Carl Pavano	.10
102 Orlando Hernandez RC	.50
103 Fernando Tatis	.10
104 Miguel Tejada	.30
105 Rolando Arrojo RC	.10
106 Kevin Millwood RC	1.00
107 Ken Griffey Jr. (Checklist)	.50
108 Frank Thomas (Checklist)	.10
109 Cal Ripken Jr. (Checklist)	.75
110 Greg Maddux (Checklist)	.40
111 John Olerud	.10
112 David Cone	.10
113 Vinny Castilla	.10
114 Jason Kendall	.10
115 Brian Jordan	.10
116 Hideki Irabu	.10
117 Bartolo Colon	.10
118 Greg Vaughn	.10
119 David Segui	.10
120 Bruce Chen	.10
121 Julio Ramirez RC	.10
122 Troy Glaus RC	4.00
123 Jeremy Giambi RC	.50
124 Ryan Minor RC	.15
125 Richie Sexson	.10
126 Dermal Brown	.10
127 Adrian Beltre	.15
128 Eric Chavez	.30
129 J.D. Drew RC	4.00
130 Gabe Kapler RC	.30
131 Masato Yoshii RC	.25
132 Mike Lowell RC	2.00
133 Jim Parque RC	.25
134 Roy Halladay	.10
135 Carlos Lee RC	1.00
136 Jin Ho Cho RC	.25
137 Michael Barrett	.10
138 Fernando Seguignol RC	.40
139 Odalis Perez RC	.50
140 Mark McGwire (Checklist)	.65

Proofs

This parallel set differs from the regular issue Signature Series base cards in the presence at left-front of a vertical stack of gold refractive foil strips on which SIGNATURE PROOF is spelled out. Also, backs of the proofs have a gold, rather than white, background.

	NM/M
Complete Set (140):	450.00
Common Player:	1.00
Stars/Rookies:	12X

1998 Donruss Signature Series Autographs Samples

An unknown number of cards can be found with facsimile signatures on front and a "SAMPLE" overprint on back.

	NM/M
Adrian Beltre (Century)	12.50
Will Clark (Century)	12.50
Travis Lee (Red)	3.00

Autographs (Red)

Autographs were inserted one per pack and feature the player photo over a silver and red foil background. The featured player's autograph appears on the bottom portion on front with the Donruss logo stamped in gold foil. Autographs are un-numbered. The first 100 cards signed by each player are blue, sequentially numbered and designated as "Century Marks." The next 1,000 signed are green, sequentially numbered and designated as "Millennium Marks." Greg Maddux signed only 12 regular Donruss Signature Autographs.

	NM/M
Common Player:	2.50
(1) Roberto Alomar/150	35.00
(2) Sandy Alomar Jr./700	10.00
(3) Moises Alou/900	15.00
(4) Gabe Alvarez/2,900	2.50
(5) Wilson Alvarez/1,600	4.00
(6) Jay Bell/1,500	4.00
(7) Adrian Beltre/1,900	25.00
(8) Andy Benes/2,600	4.00
(9) Aaron Boone/3,400	8.00
(10) Russell Branyan/1,650	4.00
(11) Orlando Cabrera/3,100	8.00
(12) Mike Cameron/1,150	8.00
(13) Joe Carter/400	10.00
(14) Sean Casey/2,275	8.00
(15) Bruce Chen/150	5.00
(16) Tony Clark/2,275	5.00
(17) Will Clark/1,400	15.00
(18) Matt Clement/1,400	4.00
(19) Pat Cline/400	5.00
(20) Ken Cloude/3,400	2.50
(21) Michael Coleman/2,800	2.50
(22) David Cone/25	50.00
(23) Jeff Conine/1,400	5.00
(24) Jacob Cruz/3,200	2.50
(25) Russ Davis/3,500	2.50
(26) Jason Dickson/1,400	4.00
(27) Todd Dunwoody/3,500	2.50
(28) Juan Encarnacion/3,400	5.00
(29) Darin Erstad/700	8.00
(30) Bobby Estalella/3,400	2.50
(31) Jeff Fassero/3,400	2.50
(32) John Franco/1,800	2.50
(33) Brad Fullmer/3,100	5.00
(34) Jason Giambi/3,100	15.00
(35) Derrick Gibson/1,200	5.00
(36) Todd Greene/1,400	5.00
(37) Ben Grieve/1,400	5.00
(38) Mark Grudzielanek/3,100	2.50
(39) Vladimir Guerrero/2,100	25.00
(40) Wilton Guerrero/1,900	4.00
(41) Jose Guillen/2,400	5.00
(42) Todd Helton/1,300	20.00
(43) Richard Hidalgo/3,400	4.00

(44) A.J. Hinch/2,900	4.00
(45) Butch Huskey/1,900	4.00
(46) Raul Ibanez/3,300	2.50
(47) Damian Jackson/900	2.50
(48) Geoff Jenkins/3,100	6.00
(49) Eric Karros/650	8.00
(50) Ryan Klesko/400	8.00
(51) Mark Kotsay/3,600	5.00
(52) Ricky Ledee/2,200	5.00
(53) Derek Lee/3,400	15.00
(54) Travis Lee/150	10.00
(54s) Travis Lee (Facsimile autograph, "SAMPLE" on back.)	3.00
(55) Javier Lopez/650	8.00
(56) Mike Lowell/3,500	10.00
(57) Greg Maddux/12	625.00
(58) Eli Marrero/3,400	5.00
(59) Al Martin/1,300	4.00
(60) Rafael Medina/1,400	2.50
(61) Scott Morgan/900	4.50
(62) Abraham Nunez/3,500	2.50
(63) Paul O'Neill/1,900	20.00
(64) Luis Ordaz/2,700	2.50
(65) Magglio Ordonez/3,200	15.00
(66) Kevin Orie/1,350	4.00
(67) David Ortiz/3,400	25.00
(68) Rafael Palmeiro/1,000	25.00
(69) Carl Pavano/2,600	5.00
(70) Neifi Perez/3,300	2.50
(71) Dante Powell/3,050	2.50
(72) Aramis Ramirez/2,800	10.00
(73) Mariano Rivera/900	35.00
(74) Felix Rodriguez/1,400	3.00
(75) Henry Rodriguez/3,400	3.00
(76) Scott Rolen/1,900	30.00
(77) Brian Rose/1,400	3.00
(78) Curt Schilling/900	30.00
(79) Richie Sexson/3,500	8.00
(80) Randall Simon/3,500	3.00
(81) J.T. Snow/400	10.00
(82) Jeff Suppan/1,400	5.00
(83) Fernando Tatis/3,900	3.00
(84) Miguel Tejada/3,800	15.00
(85) Brett Tomko/3,400	2.50
(86) Bubba Trammell/3,900	2.50
(87) Ismael Valdez/1,900	5.00
(88) Robin Ventura/1,400	5.00
(89) Billy Wagner/3,900	10.00
(90) Todd Walker/1,900	5.00
(91) Daryle Ward/400	4.00
(92) Rondell White/3,400	4.00
(93) Antone Williamson/3,350	2.50
(94) Dan Wilson/2,400	4.00
(95) Enrique Wilson/3,400	2.50
(96) Preston Wilson/2,100	5.00
(97) Tony Womack/3,500	2.50
(98) Kerry Wood/3,400	10.00

Century Marks (Blue)

This 121-card set is a serially numbered, blue-foil parallel of the Autographs insert set and limited to 100 cards signed by each featured player (unless otherwise shown in the checklist). Jason Kendall's cards were never signed or returned to Donruss for packaging. A few have made their way into the hobby.

	NM/M
Common Player:	10.00
(1) Roberto Alomar	60.00
(2) Sandy Alomar Jr.	15.00
(3) Moises Alou	40.00
(4) Gabe Alvarez	10.00
(5) Wilson Alvarez	10.00
(6) Brady Anderson	15.00
(7) Jay Bell	15.00
(8) Albert Belle	20.00
(9) Adrian Beltre	25.00
(10) Andy Benes	10.00
(11) Wade Boggs	60.00
(12) Barry Bonds	250.00
(13) Aaron Boone	25.00
(14) Russell Branyan	10.00
(15) Jay Buhner	10.00
(16) Ellis Burks	10.00
(17) Orlando Cabrera	25.00
(18) Mike Cameron	10.00
(19) Ken Caminiti	25.00
(20) Joe Carter	20.00
(21) Sean Casey	15.00
(22) Bruce Chen	10.00
(23) Tony Clark	10.00
(24) Will Clark	40.00

(25) Roger Clemens	200.00
(26) Matt Clement	20.00
(27) Pat Cline	10.00
(28) Ken Cloude	10.00
(29) Michael Coleman	10.00
(30) David Cone	25.00
(31) Jeff Conine	10.00
(32) Jacob Cruz	10.00
(33) Jose Cruz Jr.	15.00
(34) Russ Davis	10.00
(35) Jason Dickson	10.00
(36) Todd Dunwoody	10.00
(37) Scott Elarton	10.00
(38) Darin Erstad	25.00
(39) Bobby Estalella	10.00
(40) Jeff Fassero	10.00
(41) John Franco	10.00
(42) Brad Fullmer	10.00
(43) Andres Galarraga	15.00
(44) Nomar Garciaparra	80.00
(45) Jason Giambi	10.00
(46) Derrick Gibson	10.00
(47) Tom Glavine	75.00
(48) Juan Gonzalez	50.00
(49) Todd Greene	10.00
(50) Ben Grieve	10.00
(51) Mark Grudzielanek	10.00
(52) Vladimir Guerrero	75.00
(53) Wilton Guerrero	10.00
(54) Jose Guillen	10.00
(55) Tony Gwynn	80.00
(56) Todd Helton	60.00
(57) Richard Hidalgo	10.00
(58) A.J. Hinch	10.00
(59) Butch Huskey	10.00
(60) Raul Ibanez	10.00
(61) Damian Jackson	10.00
(62) Geoff Jenkins	10.00
(63) Derek Jeter	200.00
(64) Randy Johnson	150.00
(65) Chipper Jones	120.00
(66) Eric Karros/50	15.00
(67) Jason Kendall (Unsigned)	20.00
(68) Ryan Klesko	10.00
(69) Chuck Knoblauch	10.00
(70) Mark Kotsay	10.00
(71) Ricky Ledee	10.00
(72) Derek Lee	25.00
(73) Travis Lee	15.00
(74) Javier Lopez	25.00
(75) Mike Lowell	30.00
(76) Greg Maddux	150.00
(77) Eli Marrero	10.00
(78) Al Martin	10.00
(79) Rafael Medina	10.00
(80) Paul Molitor	50.00
(81) Scott Morgan	10.00
(82) Mike Mussina	75.00
(83) Abraham Nunez	10.00
(84) Paul O'Neill	40.00
(85) Luis Ordaz	10.00
(86) Magglio Ordonez	30.00
(87) Kevin Orie	10.00
(88) David Ortiz	75.00
(89) Rafael Palmeiro	75.00
(90) Carl Pavano	25.00
(91) Neifi Perez	10.00
(92) Andy Pettitte	50.00
(93) Aramis Ramirez	25.00
(94) Cal Ripken Jr.	200.00
(95) Mariano Rivera	75.00
(96) Alex Rodriguez	200.00
(97) Felix Rodriguez	10.00
(98) Henry Rodriguez	10.00
(99) Scott Rolen	70.00
(100) Brian Rose	10.00
(101) Curt Schilling	50.00
(102) Richie Sexson	20.00
(103) Randall Simon	10.00
(104) J.T. Snow	10.00
(105) Darryl Strawberry	40.00
(106) Jeff Suppan	10.00
(107) Fernando Tatis	10.00
(108) Brett Tomko	10.00
(109) Bubba Trammell	10.00
(110) Ismael Valdez	10.00
(111) Robin Ventura	20.00
(112) Billy Wagner	40.00
(113) Todd Walker	15.00
(114) Daryle Ward	10.00
(115) Rondell White	20.00
(116) Matt Williams/80	35.00
(117) Antone Williamson	10.00
(118) Dan Wilson	15.00
(119) Enrique Wilson	15.00
(120) Preston Wilson	15.00
(121) Tony Womack	10.00
(122) Kerry Wood	40.00

Millennium Marks (Green)

This is a green-foil parallel version of the Autographs insert set and features 1,000 cards signed by the featured player (unless otherwise shown in the checklist). Cards are not numbered.

	NM/M
Common Player:	3.00
(1) Roberto Alomar	25.00
(2) Sandy Alomar Jr.	5.00
(3) Moises Alou	10.00
(4) Gabe Alvarez	3.00
(5) Wilson Alvarez	3.00
(6) Brady Anderson/800	8.00
(7) Jay Bell	3.00

(8)	Albert Belle/400	10.00
(9)	Adrian Beltre	15.00
(10)	Andy Benes	3.00
(11)	Wade Boggs/900	20.00
(12)	Barry Bonds/400	150.00
(13)	Aaron Boone	4.00
(14)	Russell Branyan	3.00
(15)	Jay Buhner/400	10.00
(16)	Ellis Burks/900	5.00
(17)	Orlando Cabrera	3.00
(18)	Mike Cameron	5.00
(19)	Ken Caminiti/900	20.00
(20)	Joe Carter	8.00
(21)	Sean Casey	8.00
(22)	Bruce Chen	3.00
(23)	Tony Clark	5.00
(24)	Will Clark	25.00
(25)	Roger Clemens/400	75.00
(26)	Matt Clement/900	8.00
(27)	Pat Cline	3.00
(28)	Ken Cloude	3.00
(29)	Michael Coleman	3.00
(30)	David Cone	10.00
(31)	Jeff Conine	3.00
(32)	Jacob Cruz	3.00
(33)	Jose Cruz Jr./850	5.00
(34)	Russ Davis/950	3.00
(35)	Jason Dickson/950	3.00
(36)	Todd Dunwoody	3.00
(37)	Scott Elarton/900	3.00
(38)	Juan Encarnacion	5.00
(39)	Darin Erstad	20.00
(40)	Bobby Estalella	3.00
(41)	Jeff Fassero	3.00
(42)	John Franco/950	5.00
(43)	Brad Fullmer	3.00
(44)	Andres Galarraga/900	10.00
(45)	Nomar Garciaparra/400	60.00
(46)	Jason Giambi	20.00
(47)	Derrick Gibson	3.00
(48)	Tom Glavine/700	25.00
(49)	Juan Gonzalez	20.00
(50)	Todd Greene	3.00
(51)	Ben Grieve	4.00
(52)	Mark Grudzielanek	3.00
(53)	Vladimir Guerrero	30.00
(54)	Wilton Guerrero	3.00
(55)	Jose Guillen	3.00
(56)	Tony Gwynn/900	30.00
(57)	Todd Helton	20.00
(58)	Richard Hidalgo	3.00
(59)	A.J. Hinch	3.00
(60)	Butch Huskey	3.00
(61)	Raul Ibanez	3.00
(62)	Damian Jackson	3.00
(63)	Geoff Jenkins	3.00
(64)	Derek Jeter/400)	100.00
(65)	Randy Johnson/800	50.00
(66)	Chipper Jones/900	30.00
(67)	Eric Karros	5.00
(68)	Ryan Klesko	5.00
(69)	Chuck Knoblauch/900	10.00
(70)	Mark Kotsay	5.00
(71)	Ricky Ledee	3.00
(72)	Derrek Lee	20.00
(73)	Travis Lee	5.00
(74)	Javier Lopez/800	3.00
(75)	Mike Lowell	10.00
(76)	Greg Maddux/400	85.00
(77)	Eli Marrero	3.00
(78)	Al Martin/950	3.00
(79)	Rafael Medina/850	3.00
(80)	Paul Molitor/900	20.00
(81)	Scott Morgan	3.00
(82)	Mike Mussina/900	15.00
(83)	Abraham Nunez	3.00
(84)	Paul O'Neill/900	20.00
(85)	Luis Ordaz	3.00
(86)	Magglio Ordonez	15.00
(87)	Kevin Orie	3.00
(88)	David Ortiz	40.00
(89)	Rafael Palmeiro/900	30.00
(90)	Carl Pavano	10.00
(91)	Neifi Perez	3.00
(92)	Andy Pettitte/900	20.00
(93)	Dante Powell/950	3.00
(94)	Aramis Ramirez	3.00
(95)	Cal Ripken Jr./375	100.00
(96)	Mariano Rivera	30.00
(97)	Alex Rodriguez/350	75.00
(98)	Felix Rodriguez	3.00
(99)	Henry Rodriguez	3.00
(100)	Scott Rolen	20.00
(101)	Brian Rose	3.00
(102)	Curt Schilling	20.00
(103)	Richie Sexson	8.00
(104)	Randall Simon	3.00
(105)	J.T. Snow	4.00

(106)	Darryl Strawberry/900	40.00
(107)	Jeff Suppan	3.00
(108)	Fernando Tatis	5.00
(109)	Miguel Tejada	40.00
(110)	Brett Tomko	3.00
(111)	Bubba Trammell	3.00
(112)	Ismael Valdes	3.00
(113)	Robin Ventura	5.00
(114)	Billy Wagner/900	10.00
(115)	Todd Walker	4.00
(116)	Daryle Ward	3.00
(117)	Rondell White	5.00
(118)	Matt Williams/820	8.00
(119)	Antone Williamson	3.00
(120)	Dan Wilson	3.00
(121)	Enrique Wilson	3.00
(122)	Preston Wilson/400	5.00
(123)	Tony Womack	3.00
(124)	Kerry Wood	20.00

Significant Signatures

This 18-card autographed set features some of baseball's all-time great players. Each card is sequentially numbered to 2,000. The Sandy Koufax autographs weren't received in time prior to release and was redeemable by sending in the Billy Williams autograph, the collector would then receive both the Williams and Koufax back. Exchange cards were also initially released for Nolan Ryan and Ozzie Smith. Early in the 2000s, a large quantity of the Koufax cards found its way into the hobby market.

		NM/M
Complete Set (18):		425.00
Common Player:		10.00
	Ernie Banks	25.00
	Yogi Berra	25.00
	George Brett	40.00
	Catfish Hunter	35.00
	Al Kaline	25.00
	Harmon Killebrew	25.00
	Ralph Kiner	10.00
	Sandy Koufax	100.00
	Eddie Mathews	25.00
	Don Mattingly	50.00
	Willie McCovey	25.00
	Stan Musial	40.00
	Phil Rizzuto	
	(Edition of 1,000.)	20.00
	Nolan Ryan	60.00
	Nolan Ryan	
	(Exchange card.)	
	Ozzie Smith	20.00
	Ozzie Smith	
	(Exchange card.)	5.00
	Duke Snider	25.00
	Don Sutton	12.00
	Billy Williams	12.00

Redemption Baseballs

Redemption cards for authentically autographed baseballs were randomly inserted in Donruss Signature Series packs. Baseballs are laser burned with a Donruss seal to ensure authenticity. Every ball, except Ben Grieve's, is serial numbered within the edition limit shown. Signing Bonus redemption cards, no longer valid, are valued about 10 percent of the corresponding ball.

		NM/M
Common Autographed Ball:		15.00
Redemption Card: 10 Percent		
(1)	Roberto Alomar/60	35.00
(2)	Sandy Alomar Jr./60	20.00
(3)	Ernie Banks/12	85.00
(4)	Ken Caminiti/60	20.00
(5)	Tony Clark/60	20.00
(6)	Jacob Cruz/12	20.00
(7)	Russ Davis/60	15.00
(8)	Juan Encarnacion/60	20.00
(9)	Bobby Estalella/60	15.00
(10)	Jeff Fassero/60	15.00
(11)	Mark Grudzielanek/60	15.00
(12)	Ben Grieve/30	20.00
(13)	Jose Guillen/120	20.00
(14)	Tony Gwynn/60	100.00

(15)	Al Kaline/12	75.00
(16)	Paul Konerko/100	15.00
(17)	Travis Lee/100	20.00
(18)	Mike Lowell/60	15.00
(19)	Eli Marrero/60	15.00
(20)	Eddie Mathews/12	80.00
(21)	Paul Molitor/60	65.00
(22)	Stan Musial/12	125.00
(23)	Abraham Nunez/12	20.00
(24)	Luis Ordaz/12	20.00
(25)	Magglio Ordonez/12	50.00
(26)	Scott Rolen/60	45.00
(27)	Bubba Trammell/24	25.00
(28)	Robin Ventura/60	20.00
(29)	Billy Wagner/60	20.00
(30)	Rondell White/60	20.00
(31)	Antone Williamson/12	15.00
(32)	Tony Womack/60	15.00

1986 Dorman's Cheese

Found in specially-marked packages of Dorman's American Cheese Singles, this set consists of 10 two-card panels of baseball superstars. Labeled "Super Star Limited Edition," the panels measure 2" x 1-1/2" and have a perforation line in the center. Fronts have a color photo along with the Dorman's logo and the player's name, team and position. Due to a lack of MLB licensing, all team insignias have been airbrushed from the players' caps. Backs contain brief player statistics. The unnumbered panels and cards are listed here alphabetically by the player on the left.

		NM/M
Complete Panel Set (10):		5.00
Complete Singles Set (20):		4.00
Common Panel:		.50
Common Player:		.20
Panel 1		1.00
(1)	George Brett	.75
(2)	Jack Morris	.20
Panel 2		1.50
(3)	Gary Carter	.40
(4)	Cal Ripken Jr.	1.00
Panel 3		.65
(5)	Dwight Gooden	.20
(6)	Kent Hrbek	.20
Panel 4		1.00
(7)	Rickey Henderson	.40
(8)	Mike Schmidt	.75
Panel 5		.75
(9)	Keith Hernandez	.20
(10)	Dale Murphy	.25
Panel 6		1.00
(11)	Reggie Jackson	.60
(12)	Eddie Murray	.40
Panel 7		1.25
(13)	Don Mattingly	.75
(14)	Ryne Sandberg	.60
Panel 8		1.00
(15)	Willie McGee	.20
(16)	Robin Yount	.40
Panel 9		1.00
(17)	Rick Sutcliff (Sutcliffe)	.20
(18)	Wade Boggs	.60
Panel 10		1.00
(19)	Dave Winfield	.40
(20)	Jim Rice	.25

1981 Drake's

Producing its first baseball card set since 1950, Drake Bakeries, in conjunction with Topps, issued a 33-card set entitled "Big Hitters." The cards, in standard 2-1/2" x 3-1/2" size, feature 19 American League and 14 National League sluggers. Full-color action photos, containing a facsimile autograph,

are positioned in red frames for A.L. players and blue frames for N.L. hitters. The player's name, team, position, and Drake's logo are also on front. Backs, which are similar to the regular 1981 Topps issue, contain the card number, statistical and biographical information, and the Drake's logo.

		NM/M
Complete Set (33):		6.00
Common Player:		.25
1	Carl Yastrzemski	1.50
2	Rod Carew	1.00
3	Pete Rose	3.00
4	Dave Parker	.25
5	George Brett	2.00
6	Eddie Murray	1.00
7	Mike Schmidt	2.00
8	Jim Rice	.50
9	Fred Lynn	.25
10	Reggie Jackson	1.50
11	Steve Garvey	.50
12	Ken Singleton	.25
13	Bill Buckner	.25
14	Dave Winfield	1.00
15	Jack Clark	.25
16	Cecil Cooper	.25
17	Bob Horner	.25
18	George Foster	.25
19	Dave Kingman	.25
20	Cesar Cedeno	.25
21	Joe Charboneau	.75
22	George Hendrick	.25
23	Gary Carter	1.00
24	Al Oliver	.25
25	Bruce Bochte	.25
26	Jerry Mumphrey	.25
27	Steve Kemp	.25
28	Bob Watson	.25
29	John Castino	.25
30	Tony Armas	.25
31	John Mayberry	.25
32	Carlton Fisk	1.00
33	Lee Mazzilli	.25

1982 Drake's

Drake Bakeries produced, in conjunction with Topps, a "2nd Annual Collectors' Edition" in 1982. Thirty-three standard-size cards (2-1/2" x 3-1/2") make up the set. Like the previous year, the set is entitled "Big Hitters" and is comprised of 19 American League players and 14 from the National League. Fronts have a mounted photo appearance and contain a facsimile autograph. The player's name, team, position, and the Drake's logo also are on front. Backs, other than being numbered 1-33 and containing a Drake's copyright line, are identical to the regular 1982 Topps.

		NM/M
Complete Set (33):		5.00
Common Player:		.25
1	Tony Armas	.25
2	Buddy Bell	.25
3	Johnny Bench	.50
4	George Brett	1.00
5	Bill Buckner	.25
6	Rod Carew	.50
7	Gary Carter	.50
8	Jack Clark	.25
9	Cecil Cooper	.25
10	Jose Cruz	.25
11	Dwight Evans	.25
12	Carlton Fisk	.50
13	George Foster	.25
14	Steve Garvey	.40
15	Kirk Gibson	.25
16	Mike Hargrove	.25
17	George Hendrick	.25
18	Bob Horner	.25
19	Reggie Jackson	.75
20	Terry Kennedy	.25
21	Dave Kingman	.25
22	Greg Luzinski	.25
23	Bill Madlock	.25
24	John Mayberry	.25

1983 Drake's

Seventeen American League and 16 National League "Big Hitters" make up the 33-card "3rd Annual Collectors' Edition" set issued by Drake Bakeries in 1983. The Topps-produced cards measure 2-1/2" x 3-1/2". Fronts are somewhat similar in design to the previous year's set. Backs are identical to the 1983 Topps regular issue except for being numbered 1-33 and containing a Drake's logo and copyright line.

		NM/M
Complete Set (33):		5.00
Common Player:		.25
1	Don Baylor	.25
2	Bill Buckner	.25
3	Rod Carew	.60
4	Gary Carter	.60
5	Jack Clark	.25
6	Cecil Cooper	.25
7	Dwight Evans	.25
8	George Foster	.25
9	Pedro Guerrero	.25
10	George Hendrick	.25
11	Bob Horner	.25
12	Reggie Jackson	.75
13	Steve Kemp	.25
14	Dave Kingman	.25
15	Bill Madlock	.25
16	Gary Matthews	.25
17	Hal McRae	.25
18	Dale Murphy	.40
19	Eddie Murray	.60
20	Ben Oglivie	.25
21	Al Oliver	.25
22	Jim Rice	.40
23	Cal Ripken, Jr.	3.00
24	Pete Rose	2.00
25	Mike Schmidt	1.50
26	Ken Singleton	.25
27	Gorman Thomas	.25
28	Jason Thompson	.25
29	Mookie Wilson	.25
30	Willie Wilson	.25
31	Dave Winfield	.60
32	Carl Yastrzemski	.75
33	Robin Yount	.60

1984 Drake's

For the fourth year in a row, Drake Bakeries issued a 33-card "Big Hitters" set. The 1984 edition, produced again by Topps, includes 17 National League players and 16 from the American League. As in all previous years, card fronts feature the player in a batting pose. Backs are identical to the 1984 Topps regular issue except for being numbered 1-33 and carrying the Drake's logo and copyright line. The cards are the standard 2-1/2" x 3-1/2".

		NM/M
25	Eddie Murray	.50
26	Graig Nettles	.25
27	Jim Rice	.40
28	Pete Rose	2.00
29	Mike Schmidt	1.00
30	Ken Singleton	.25
31	Dave Winfield	.50
32	Butch Wynegar	.25
33	Richie Zisk	.25

1985 Drake's

The "5th Annual Collectors' Edition" set produced by Topps for Drake Bakeries consists of 33 "Big Hitters" and 11 "Super Pitchers." The new "Super Pitchers" feature increased the set's size from the usual 33 cards to 44. The 2-1/2" x 3-1/2" cards show the player in a game-action photo. Backs differ from the regular 1985 Topps issue only in that they are numbered 1-44 and carry the Drake's logo.

		NM/M
Complete Set (33):		4.00
Common Player:		.25
1	Don Baylor	.25
2	Wade Boggs	.75
3	George Brett	1.00
4	Bill Buckner	.25
5	Rod Carew	.50
6	Gary Carter	.50
7	Ron Cey	.25
8	Cecil Cooper	.25
9	Andre Dawson	.35
10	Steve Garvey	.35
11	Pedro Guerrero	.25
12	George Hendrick	.25
13	Keith Hernandez	.25
14	Bob Horner	.25
15	Reggie Jackson	.75
16	Steve Kemp	.25
17	Ron Kittle	.25
18	Greg Luzinski	.25
19	Fred Lynn	.25
20	Bill Madlock	.25
21	Gary Matthews	.25
22	Dale Murphy	.35
23	Eddie Murray	.50
24	Al Oliver	.25
25	Jim Rice	.25
26	Cal Ripken, Jr.	2.00
27	Pete Rose	1.25
28	Mike Schmidt	1.00
29	Darryl Strawberry	.50
30	Alan Trammell	.25
31	Mookie Wilson	.25
32	Dave Winfield	.50
33	Robin Yount	.50

		NM/M
Complete Set (44):		3.00
Common Player:		.15
1	Tony Armas	.15
2	Harold Baines	.15
3	Don Baylor	.15
4	George Brett	.75
5	Gary Carter	.40
6	Ron Cey	.15
7	Jose Cruz	.15
8	Alvin Davis	.15
9	Chili Davis	.15
10	Dwight Evans	.15
11	Steve Garvey	.15
12	Kirk Gibson	.15
13	Pedro Guerrero	.15
14	Tony Gwynn	.50
15	Keith Hernandez	.15
16	Kent Hrbek	.15
17	Reggie Jackson	.50
18	Gary Matthews	.15
19	Don Mattingly	.75
20	Dale Murphy	.25
21	Eddie Murray	.40
22	Dave Parker	.15
23	Lance Parrish	.15
24	Tim Raines	.15
25	Jim Rice	.25
26	Cal Ripken, Jr.	1.50
27	Juan Samuel	.15
28	Ryne Sandberg	.50
29	Mike Schmidt	.75
30	Darryl Strawberry	.15
31	Alan Trammell	.15
32	Dave Winfield	.40
33	Robin Yount	.40
34	Mike Boddicker	.15
35	Steve Carlton	.40
36	Dwight Gooden	.15
37	Willie Hernandez	.15
38	Mark Langston	.15
39	Dan Quisenberry	.15
40	Dave Righetti	.15
41	Tom Seaver	.40
42	Bob Stanley	.15
43	Rick Sutcliff	.15
44	Bruce Sutter	.30

1986 Drake's

For the sixth consecutive year, Drake Bakeries issued a baseball card set. The 1986 set was the first in that sequence not produced by Topps. Cards were available only by buying the snack products on whose boxes the cards were printed. Cards, measuring 2-1/2" x 3-1/2", were issued in either two-, three-, or four-card panels. Fourteen panels, consisting of 37 different players, comprise the set. The players who make up the set are tabbed as either "Big Hitters" or "Super Pitchers." Logos of various Drake's products can be found on the panel backs. The value of the set is higher when collected in either panel or complete box form.

		NM/M
Complete Panel Set (14):		20.00
Complete Singles Set (37):		12.00
Common Panel:		1.00
Common Player:		.25
Panel (1)		.75
1	Gary Carter	.40
2	Dwight Evans	.25
Panel (2)		1.00
3	Reggie Jackson	.50
4	Dave Parker	.25
Panel (3)		1.50
5	Rickey Henderson	.40
6	Pedro Guerrero	.25
Panel (4)		3.00
7	Don Mattingly	.75
8	Mike Marshall	.25
9	Keith Moreland	.25
Panel (5)		4.00
10	Keith Hernandez	.25
11	Cal Ripken Jr.	2.50
Panel (6)		2.50
12	Dale Murphy	.35
13	Jim Rice	.35
Panel (7)		3.00
14	George Brett	.75
15	Tim Raines	.25
Panel (8)		1.50
16	Darryl Strawberry	.25
17	Bill Buckner	.25
Panel (9)		3.00
18	Dave Winfield	.40
19	Ryne Sandberg	.50
20	Steve Balboni	.25
21	Tommy Herr	.25
Panel (10)		3.00
22	Pete Rose	1.50
23	Willie McGee	.25
24	Harold Baines	.25
25	Eddie Murray	.40
Panel (11)		3.00
26	Mike Schmidt	.75
27	Wade Boggs	.50
28	Kirk Gibson	.25
Panel (12)		1.50
29	Bret Saberhagen	.25
30	John Tudor	.25
31	Orel Hershiser	.25
Panel (13)		4.00
32	Ron Guidry	.25
33	Nolan Ryan	2.50
34	Dave Steib	.25
Panel (14)		1.50
35	Dwight Gooden	.25
36	Fernando Valenzuela	.25
37	Tom Browning	.25

1987 Drake's

For the seventh consecutive season, Drake Bakeries produced a baseball card set. The 2-1/2" x 3-1/2" cards were printed in either two-, three-, or four-card panels on boxes of various snack products distributed in the eastern U.S. The set is comprised of 33 cards, with 25 players branded as "Big Hitters" and eight as "Super Pitchers." Fronts carry a game-action photo and the Drake's logo surrounded by a brown and yellow border. Backs have the player's complete major league record.

		NM/M
Complete Panel Set (12):		20.00
Complete Singles Set (33):		10.00
Common Panel:		1.50
Common Player:		.25
Panel (1)		2.00
1	Don Mattingly	1.00
2	Tim Raines	.25
Panel (2)		2.00
3	Darryl Strawberry	.25
4	Wade Boggs	.75
Panel (3)		6.00
5	Keith Hernandez	.25
6	Mark McGwire	1.50
Panel (4)		3.00
7	Rickey Henderson	.60

8	Mike Schmidt	1.00
9	Dwight Evans	.25
Panel (5)		2.00
10	Gary Carter	.60
11	Paul Molitor	.60
Panel (6)		3.50
12	Dave Winfield	.60
13	Alan Trammell	.25
14	Tony Gwynn	.75
Panel (7)		2.50
15	Dale Murphy	.35
16	Andre Dawson	.35
17	Von Hayes	.25
18	Willie Randolph	.25
Panel (8)		3.50
19	Kirby Puckett	.75
20	Juan Samuel	.25
21	Eddie Murray	.60
Panel (9)		1.00
22	George Bell	.25
23	Larry Sheets	.25
24	Eric Davis	.25
Panel (10)		5.00
25	Cal Ripken Jr.	2.00
26	Pedro Guerrero	.25
27	Will Clark	.25
Panel (11)		1.00
28	Dwight Gooden	.25
29	Frank Viola	.25
Panel (12)		3.00
30	Roger Clemens	1.00
31	Rick Sutcliffe	.25
32	Jack Morris	.25
33	John Tudor	.25

1989 Dubuque Braves

Given away at Sunday home games to correspond with player appearances at a stadium autograph booth, these 2-3/8" x 3-1/2" cards were sponsored by the Braves hot dog concessionaire, Dubuque Meats. Cards have player photos centered within a dark blue border. A Braves cap is at upper-left, the hot dog company's logo at lower-left. The player's name, team and position are white. Backs, printed in black on white, have the Braves logo, a few personal facts and figures and previous year/career stats. Because only 15,000 of each card were distributed over the course of the season, compilation of complete sets is extremely challenging. The checklist here is arranged in alphabetical order.

		NM/M
Complete Set (33):		40.00
Common Player:		.50
(1)	Paul Assenmacher	.50
(2)	Jim Acker	.50
(3)	Jose Alvarez	.50
(4)	Bruce Benedict	.50
(5)	Geronimo Berroa/SP	8.00
(6)	Jeff Blauser	.50
(7)	Joe Boever	.50
(8)	Marty Clary	.50
(9)	Bruce dal Canton	.50
(10)	Jody Davis	.50
(11)	Mark Eichhorn	.50
(12)	Ron Gant	1.50
(13)	Tom Glavine	5.00
(14)	Tommy Gregg	.50
(15)	Dion James/SP	4.00
(16)	Clarence Jones	.50
(17)	Derek Lilliquist	.50
(18)	Roy Majtyka	.50
(19)	Oddibe McDowell	.50
(20)	Dale Murphy	6.00
(21)	Russ Nixon	.50
(22)	Gerald Perry	.50
(23)	John Russell	.50
(24)	Lonnie Smith	.50
(25)	Pete Smith	.50
(26)	Zane Smith	.50
(27)	John Smoltz	4.00
(28)	Brian Snitker	.50
(29)	Andres Thomas	.50
(30)	Jeff Treadway	.50
(31)	Jeff Wetherby	.50
(32)	Ed Whited	.50
(33)	Bobby Wine	.50

1990 Dubuque Braves

For a second season, the Braves' hot dog vendor, Dubuque Meats, sponsored this season-long promotion. Up to four different player cards were given out at Sunday home games, corresponding with player appearances at an autograph booth. Some player cards were distributed more than once, while others, such as Dale Murphy, who was traded, were only given out one day. Players were added to the set right up through the final Sunday home game of the season. Complete sets are extremely difficult to assemble. The player photo on these 2-3/8" x 3-1/2" cards have a white border. A red banner beneath the photo has the player's name, uniform number and position printed in black. Backs are printed in dark blue and feature full minor and major league stats. The checklist here is arranged alphabetically.

		NM/M
Complete Set (35):		25.00
Common Player:		.50
(1)	Steve Avery	.50
(2)	Jeff Blauser	.50
(3)	Joe Boever	.50
(4)	Francisco Cabrera	.50
(5)	Pat Corrales	.50
(6)	Bobby Cox	.50
(7)	Nick Esasky	.50
(8)	Ron Gant	1.50
(9)	Tom Glavine	4.00
(10)	Mark Grant	.50
(11)	Tommy Gregg	.50
(12)	Dwayne Henry	.50
(13)	Alexis Infante	.50
(14)	Clarence Jones	.50
(15)	Dave Justice	4.50
(16)	Jimmy Kremers	.50
(17)	Charlie Leibrandt	.50
(18)	Mark Lemke	.50
(19)	Roy Majtyka	.50
(20)	Leo Mazzone	.50
(21)	Oddibe McDowell	.50
(22)	Dale Murphy	5.00
(23)	Phil Niekro	3.00
(24)	Greg Olson	.50
(25)	Jim Presley	.50
(26)	Lonnie Smith	.50
(27)	Pete Smith	.50
(28)	John Smoltz	1.50
(29)	Brian Snitker	.50
(30)	Andres Thomas	.50
(31)	Jeff Treadway	.50
(32)	Ernie Whitt	.50
(33)	Jimmy Williams	.50
(34)	Homer the Brave (Mascot)	.50
(35)	Rally (Mascot)	.50

1990 Dubuque Braves Team Photo Set

This three-panel team set was given away at an early-season game, commemorating the Braves

25th season in Atlanta. The sheet measures 11" x 28-1/2". The top panel is a team photo. The two lower panels contain 30 individual cards, 2-1/2" x 3-1/4", perforated to allow them to be separated. Backs are printed in red and blue. The perforated team set is much more common than the Dubuque cards given out a few at a time during Sunday home games. The checklist below is arranged according to uniform numbers which appear on the front of each card.

		NM/M
Complete Panel:		9.00
Common Player:		.25
1	Oddibe McDowell	.25
2	Russ Nixon	.25
3	Dale Murphy	3.00
4	Jeff Blauser	.25
5	Ron Gant	.50
10	Greg Olson	.25
12	Ernie Whitt	.25
14	Andres Thomas	.25
15	Jeff Treadway	.25
16	Tommy Gregg	.25
17	Nick Esasky	.25
18	Jim Presley	.25
19	Francisco Cabrera	.25
20	Mark Lemke	.25
23	Dave Justice	2.00
24	Derek Lilliquist	.25
25	Pete Smith	.25
26	Lonnie Smith	.25
29	John Smoltz	1.00
30	Mike Stanton	.25
36	Tony Castillo	.25
37	Joe Boever	.25
40	Charlie Kerfeld	.25
45	Charlie Leibrandt	.25
46	Dwayne Henry	.25
47	Tom Glavine	1.50
48	Marty Clary	.25
49	Rick Luecken	.25
58a	Joe Hesketh	.25
58b	Alexis Infante	.25

1991 Dubuque Braves

At each Sunday home game the Braves distributed some 15,000 of each of three to six player cards to kids under 14. The cards corresponded to appearances by those players at an autograph session. That method of distribution makes accumulation of complete sets very difficult. Sponsor of the set for the third straight year was the stadium's hot dog concessionaire, Dubuque Meats. Their logo appears in the upper-left corner of the player photo. At lower-right on the 2-1/4" x 3-1/2" cards is a baseball diamond figure with the team and player name and the year of issue. There is a white outer border on the card, with the photo framed in white-pinstriped dark blue. Backs are printed in dark blue, with logos, complete stats, biographical information and the player's uniform number. Cards are checklisted here in alphabetical order.

		NM/M
Complete Set (41):		25.00
Common Player:		.50
(1)	Steve Avery	.50
(2)	Jim Beauchamp	.50
(3)	Mike Bell	.50
(4)	Rafael Belliard	.50
(5)	Juan Berenguer	.50
(6)	Jeff Blauser	.50
(7)	Sid Bream	.50
(8)	Francisco Cabrera	.50
(9)	Jim Clancy	.50
(10)	Pat Corrales	.50
(11)	Bobby Cox	.50
(12)	Nick Esasky	.50
(13)	Marvin Freeman	.50

(14)	Ron Gant	1.00
(15)	Tom Glavine	3.00
(16)	Mark Grant	.50
(17)	Tommy Gregg	.50
(18)	Mike Heath	.50
(19)	Brian Hunter	.50
(20)	Clarence Jones	.50
(21)	David Justice	2.00
(22)	Charlie Leibrandt	.50
(23)	Mark Lemke	.50
(24)	Leo Mazzone	.50
(25)	Kent Mercker	.50
(26)	Keith Mitchell	.50
(27)	Otis Nixon	.50
(28)	Greg Olson	.50
(29)	Jeff Parrett	.50
(30)	Terry Pendleton	.50
(31)	Armando Reynoso	.50
(32)	Deion Sanders	3.00
(33)	Lonnie Smith	.50
(34)	Pete Smith	.50
(35)	John Smoltz	1.50
(36)	Mike Stanton	.50
(37)	Jeff Treadway	.50
(38)	Jimy Williams	.50
(39)	Ned Yost	.50
(40)	Homer the Brave (Mascot)	.50
(41)	Rally (Mascot)	.50

1991 Dubuque Braves Team Photo Set

This team photo/player card triptych was an early season giveaway. Each of the three fold-out panels measures about 9-1/2" x 10-1/2". The 30 individual player cards have perforated edges for easy removal from the sheet. The 2-1/8" x 3-1/8" cards have a player portrait photo at center, with blue diamond designs at the corners. A red box below the photo has the player's name and uniform number. Blue Braves and Dubuque logos appear at the lower corners of the white border. Backs are printed in red and blue and include full stats and a facsimile autograph, plus a few biographical details. The team sheet cards are considered much more common than the other Braves baseball card promotional giveaways, especially in complete sets. Cards are checklisted here alphabetically.

		NM/M
Complete Panel:		15.00
Common Player:		.50
(1)	Steve Avery	.50
(2)	Rafael Belliard	.50
(3)	Juan Berenguer	.50
(4)	Jeff Blauser	.50
(5)	Sid Bream	.50
(6)	Francisco Cabrera	.50
(7)	Bobby Cox	.50
(8)	Nick Esasky	.50
(9)	Marvin Freeman	.50
(10)	Ron Gant	.75
(11)	Tom Glavine	3.00
(12)	Mark Grant	.50
(13)	Tommy Gregg	.50
(14)	Mike Heath	.50
(15)	Danny Heep	.50
(16)	David Justice	2.00
(17)	Charlie Leibrandt	.50
(18)	Mark Lemke	.50
(19)	Kent Mercker	.50
(20)	Otis Nixon	.50
(21)	Greg Olson	.50
(22)	Jeff Parrett	.50
(23)	Terry Pendleton	.50
(24)	Deion Sanders	2.00
(25)	Doug Sisk	.50
(26)	Lonnie Smith	.50
(27)	Pete Smith	.50
(28)	John Smoltz	1.50
(29)	Mike Stanton	.50
(30)	Jeff Treadway	.50

1992 Dunkin' Donuts Red Sox

The 1992 Boston Red Sox were the subject of a set of 30 cards, including the manager and coaches.

#16 FRANK VIOLA — LHP — RED SOX — WVIT 30 — DUNKIN DONUTS

Co-sponsored by Dunkin Donuts and WVIT-TV and released in May in Connecticut, the set was sold as an uncut, perforated sheet of 30 cards, measuring about 9-1/2" x 10-3/4". Individual perforated cards could be removed from the sheet; they measure 2-1/8" x 3-1/8". Fronts have a player photo framed in black on a white background. In the border beneath the photo are the player's name, position, uniform number and sponsors' logos. Backs have complete major and minor league stats. The cards are checklisted here by uniform number, which appears on the card front.

		NM/M
	Complete Panel:	7.50
	Common Player:	.25
2	Luis Rivera	.25
3	Jody Reed	.25
6	Tony Pena	.25
7	Rick Burleson	.25
11	Tim Naehring	.25
12	Ellis Burks	.25
16	Frank Viola	.25
17	Butch Hobson	.25
18	Carlos Quintana	.25
20	John Marzano	.25
21	Roger Clemens	6.00
23	Tom Brunansky	.25
25	Jack Clark	.25
26	Wade Boggs	3.00
27	Greg Harris	.25
29	Phil Plantier	.25
30	Matt Young	.25
32	Gary Allenson	.25
34	Don Zimmer	.25
35	Rich Gale	.25
37	Al Bumbry	.25
39	Mike Greenwell	.25
41	Jeff Reardon	.25
42	Mo Vaughn	.35
43	Kevin Morton	.25
44	Danny Darwin	.25
47	Mike Gardiner	.25
48	Tony Fossas	.25
50	Tom Bolton	.25
55	Joe Hesketh	.25

1993 Duracell Power Players

The Duracell battery company issued a 48-card set in 1993 that was presented in two 24-card series. The cards were available through the mail with proofs of purchase from selected Duracell products. Cards feature a Duracell logo at top, with a black and orange border surrounding a color photo of the player. The player's name is printed in yellow with team and position in white on top of a green background. Because the set was not licensed to use major league uniform logos, they were airbrushed off the photos. Backs have a player portrait photo, a facsimile autograph, recent stats and a few biographical and career details printed over a ballpark scene. Series I cards are number "X of 24;" Series II cards are so indicated beneath the card number.

		NM/M
	Complete Set (48):	4.00
	Common Player:	.10
	Series 1	2.00
1	Roger Clemens	.60
2	Frank Thomas	.40
3	Andre Dawson	.25
4	Orel Hershiser	.10
5	Kirby Puckett	.50
6	Edgar Martinez	.10
7	Craig Biggio	.10
8	Terry Pendleton	.10
9	Mark McGwire	.75
10	Dave Stewart	.10
11	Ozzie Smith	.50
12	Doug Drabek	.10
13	Dwight Gooden	.10
14	Tony Gwynn	.50
15	Carlos Baerga	.10
16	Robin Yount	.40
17	Barry Bonds	1.00
18	Bip Roberts	.10
19	Don Mattingly	.60
20	Nolan Ryan	1.00
21	Tom Glavine	.25
22	Will Clark	.10
23	Cecil Fielder	.10
24	Dave Winfield	.40
	Series 2	2.00
1	Cal Ripken, Jr.	1.00
2	Melido Perez	.10
3	John Kruk	.10
4	Charlie Hayes	.10
5	George Brett	.60
6	Ruben Sierra	.10
7	Deion Sanders	.15
8	Andy Van Slyke	.10
9	Fred McGriff	.10
10	Benito Santiago	.10
11	Charles Nagy	.10
12	Greg Maddux	.50
13	Ryne Sandberg	.50
14	Dennis Martinez	.10
15	Ken Griffey Jr.	.75
16	Jim Abbott	.10
17	Barry Larkin	.10
18	Gary Sheffield	.30
19	Jose Canseco	.25
20	Jack McDowell	.10
21	Darryl Strawberry	.10
22	Delino DeShields	.10
23	Dennis Eckersley	.40
24	Paul Molitor	.40

E

1990 Eclipse Stars of the Negro Leagues

OSCAR CHARLESTON

Better known in the field of comic books than baseball cards, Eclipse of California produced this set of cards honoring stars of the defunct Negro Leagues. The 2-1/2" x 3-1/2" cards have water color paintings (by Mark Chiarello) of the players on front. Well-written (by Jack Morelli) career summaries on back give a real flavor for this brand of pro ball and its era. Copyright lines for all parties are at bottom back. The issue was sold only as a boxed set.

		NM/M
	Complete Set (36):	16.00
	Common Player:	.50
1	Header Card	.25
2a	Josh Gibson (Wrong picture, "H" on cap.)	4.00
2b	Josh Gibson (Correct picture, "G" on cap.)	4.00
3	Cannonball Redding	.50
4	Biz Mackey	2.00
5	Pop Lloyd	1.00
6	Bingo DeMoss	1.00
7	Willard Brown	2.00
8	John Donaldson	.50
9	Monte Irvin	1.50
10	Ben Taylor	2.00
11	Willie Wells	1.25
12	Dave Brown	.50
13	Leon Day	1.00
14	Ray Dandridge	1.00
15	Turkey Stearnes	1.00
16	Rube Foster	1.00
17	Oliver Marcelle	.50
18	Judy Johnson	1.00
19	Christobel Torrienti	2.00
20	Satchel Paige	4.00
21	Mule Suttles	2.00
22	John Beckwith	.50
23	Martin Dihigo	1.00
24	Willie Foster	.50
25	Dick Lundy	.50
26	Buck Leonard	1.00
27	Smokey Joe Williams	1.00
28	Cool Papa Bell	1.00
29	Bullet Rogan	1.00
30	Newt Allen	.75
31	Bruce Petway	.50
32	Jose Mendez	2.00
33	Louis Santop	2.00
34	Jud Wilson	2.00
35	Sammy Hughes	.50
36a	Oscar Charleston (Wrong picture, "G" on cap.)	1.00
36b	Oscar Charleston (Correct picture, "H" on cap.)	1.00

1992 Eclipse Negro League BPA - Paul Lee

RAY DANDRIDGE — THIRD BASE

Four Negro League baseball cards were handed out to the first 50,000 fans attending Negro League Baseball Players Association night at Shea Stadium on June 2. Cards feature the artwork of Paul Lee on front. Backs have a career summary and biographical details, along with the Mets and Eclipse logos.

		NM/M
	Complete Set (4):	4.00
	Common Player:	1.50
1	Monte Irvin	1.50
2	"Buck" Leonard	1.00
3	Josh Gibson	3.00
4	Ray Dandridge	1.00

1992 Eclipse Negro League BPA - John Clapp

MARTINEZ JACKSON — Second Base

Sponsored by Kraft, and produced by Eclipse, 15,000 sets of these cards were made for distribution at The Negro League Baseball Players Association night, August 9 at Lackawanna County Stadium, home of the Scranton Wilkes-Barre Red Barons. The 2-1/2" x 3-1/2" cards have watercolor player pictures on front, by artist John Clapp. Backs have career summaries, sponsor and issuer logos and copyright information.

		NM/M
	Complete Set (18):	6.00
	Common Player:	.50
1	Leon Day	1.50
2	Clinton (Casey) Jones	.50
3	Lester Lockett	.50
4	Monte Irvin	2.00
5	Armando Vazquez	.50
6	Jimmie Crutchfield	.50
7	Ted Radcliffe	.50
8	Albert Haywood	.50
9	Artie Wilson	1.50
10	Sam Jethroe	1.25
11	Edsall Walker	.50
12	Bill Wright	.50
13	Jim Cohen	.50
14	Andy Porter	.50
15	Tommy Sampson	.50
16	Buck Leonard	1.50
17	Josh Gibson	2.00
18	Martinez Jackson	1.50

1990 Elite Senior League

EARL WEAVER

This 126-card set features the players of the first Senior League season. Cards are printed on high quality stock with full-color photos. The card backs feature statistics. Earl Weaver and Mike Easler cards were distributed as promo cards. Original retail price was about $12 per boxed set, the only manner of distribution.

		NM/M
	Complete Set (126):	4.00
	Common Player:	.05
1	Curt Flood	.15
2	Bob Tolan	.05
3	Dick Bosman	.05
4	Ivan DeJesus	.05
5	Dock Ellis	.05
6	Roy Howell	.05
7	Lamar Johnson	.05
8	Steve Kemp	.05
9	Ken Landreaux	.05
10	Randy Lerch	.05
11	Jon Matlack	.05
12	Gary Rajsich	.05
13	Lenny Randle	.05
14	Elias Sosa	.05
15	Ozzie Virgil	.05
16	Milt Wilcox	.05
17	Steve Henderson	.05
18	Ray Burris	.05
19	Mike Easler	.05
20	Juan Eichelberger	.05
21	Rollie Fingers	.50
22	Toby Harrah	.05
23	Randy Johnson	.05
24	Dave Kingman	.15
25	Lee Lacy	.05
26	Tito Landrum	.05
27	Paul Mirabella	.05
28	Mickey Rivers	.10
29	Rodney Scott	.05
30	Tim Stoddard	.05
31	Ron Washington	.05
32	Jerry White	.05
33	Dick Williams	.05
34	Clete Boyer	.10
35	Steve Dillard	.05
36	Garth Iorg	.05
37	Bruce Kison	.05
38	Wayne Krenchicki	.05
39	Ron LeFlore	.10
40	Tippy Martinez	.05
41	Omar Moreno	.05
42	Jim Morrison	.05
43	Graig Nettles	.15
44	Jim Nettles	.05
45	Wayne Nordhagen	.05
46	Al Oliver	.15
47	Jerry Royster	.05
48	Sammy Stewart	.05
49	Randy Bass	.05
50	Vida Blue	.10
51	Bruce Bochy	.05
52	Doug Corbett	.05
53	Jose Cruz	.05
54	Jamie Easterly	.05
55	Pete Falcone	.05
56	Bob Galasso	.05
57	Johnny Grubb	.05
58	Bake McBride	.05
59	Dyar Miller	.05
60	Tom Paciorek	.05
61	Ken Reitz	.05
62	U.L. Washington	.05
63	Alan Ashby	.05
64	Pat Dobson	.05
65	Doug Bird	.05
66	Marty Castillo	.05
67	Dan Driessen	.05
68	Wayne Garland	.05
69	Tim Ireland	.05
70	Ron Jackson	.05
71	Bobby Jones	.05
72	Dennis Leonard	.05
73	Rick Manning	.05
74	Amos Otis	.05
75	Pat Putnam	.05
76	Eric Rasmussen	.05
77	Paul Blair	.05
78	Bert Campaneris	.05
79	Cesar Cedeno	.10
80	Ed Figueroa	.05
81	Ross Grimsley	.05
82	George Hendrick	.05
83	Cliff Johnson	.05
84	Mike Kekich	.05
85	Rafael Landestoy	.05
86	Larry Milbourne	.05
87	Bobby Molinaro	.05
88	Sid Monge	.05
89	Rennie Stennett	.05
90	Derrell Thomas	.05
91	Earl Weaver	.30
92	Gary Allenson	.05
93	Pedro Borbon	.05
94	Al Bumbry	.05
95	Bill Campbell	.05
96	Bernie Carbo	.05
97	Ferguson Jenkins	.50
98	Pete LaCock	.05
99	Bill Lee	.05
100	Tommy McMillan	.05
101	Joe Pittman	.05
102	Gene Richards	.05
103	Leon Roberts	.05
104	Tony Scott	.05
105	Doug Simunic	.05
106	Rick Wise	.05
107	Willie Aikens	.05
108	Juan Beniquez	.05
109	Bobby Bonds	.10
110	Sergio Ferrer	.05
111	Chuck Ficks	.05
112	George Foster	.10
113	Dave Hilton	.05
114	Al Holland	.05
115	Clint Hurdle	.05
116	Bill Madlock	.10
117	Steve Ontiveros	.05
118	Roy Thomas	.05
119	Luis Tiant	.10
120	Walt Williams	.05
121	Vida Blue	.10
122	Bobby Bonds	.10
123	Rollie Fingers	.50
124	George Foster	.10
125	Fergie Jenkins	.50
126	Dave Kingman	.10

1983 English's Chicken Baltimore Orioles Lids

English's Salutes — CAL RIPKEN, JR. — ★ SHORTSTOP ★ — BALTIMORE ORIOLES — 1983 Champions

The World Champion O's were featured on this set of fried chicken bucket lids. Printed on thick cardboard discs with the blank backs heavily waxed, the lids come in two sizes, 8-3/8" diameter and 7-1/4". The design is the same on each, with a black, white and orange player portrait at center, flanked by some personal data and '83 stats. His name is in orange below, with his position and team in black beneath that. In the wide orange border is "English's Salutes / 1983 Champions." The player's union logo is at right of the portrait, but cap logos are missing because the issue was not licensed through MLB. The lids are not numbered.

		NM/M
	Complete Set (13):	45.00
	Common Player:	2.00
(1)	Mike Boddicker	2.00
(2)	Rich Dauer	2.00
(3)	Storm Davis	2.00
(4)	Mike Flanagan	2.00
(5)	John Lowenstein	2.00
(6)	Tippy Martinez	2.00
(7)	Gary Roenicke	2.00
(8)	Ken Singleton	2.00
(9)	Rick Dempsey	2.00
(10)	Scott McGregor	2.00
(11)	Eddie Murray	6.00
(12)	Jim Palmer	6.00
(13)	Cal Ripken, Jr.	30.00

1991 Enor Kevin Maas Story

Kevin Maas

This 20-card set was produced by one of the hobby's leading manufacturers of plastic supplies. Not surprisingly, the set was housed in a 6" x 8-1/4" plastic album with eight four-card plastic sheets inside. Besides the cards and album, the set came with a biographical brochure on the 1990 A.L. Rookie of the Year runner-up. Each of the 2-1/2" x 3-1/2" cards features one or more color photos of the player on front. A series of red stripes at the top of the card features the player's name in the uppermost stripe. Backs have the same stripe motif at top and include career information or stats at center. The logos of MLB, the Yankees and Enor appear at the bottom.

	NM/M
Complete Set w/Album (20):	4.00
Single Card:	.10

F

1981 Family Fun Centers Padres

Six Padres players or staff are featured on these 13" x 10" coupon sheets. At the right end of each glossy paper sheet is a group of coupons and advertising for the recreation centers, printed in black, yellow and green. At left are six photos. Each of the 3" x 4" photos has a color player pose. At either top or bottom, depending on placement on the sheet, is the player name in black, "FAMILY FUN CENTER" in green and a red building logo. Backs are blank and the sheets are not perforated.

		NM/M
	Complete Set (5):	110.00
	Common Sheet:	10.00
(1)	Randy Bass, Frank Howard, Gary Lucas, Gene Richards, Ozzie Smith, Jerry Turner	60.00
(2)	Kurt Bevacqua, Dave Cash, Paul Dade, Rollie Fingers, Don Williams, Dave Winfield	25.00
(3)	Dan Boone, Chuck Estrada, Joe Lefebvre, Tim Lollar, Ed Stevens, Steve Swisher	10.00
(4)	John Curtis, Barry Evans, Tim Flannery, Terry Kennedy, Steve Mura, Bob Tolan	10.00
(5)	Von Joshua, Fred Kendall, Dennis Kinney, Jerry Mumphrey, Steve Mura, Dick Phillips	10.00

1994 FanFest Roberto Clemente Commemorative

In an unprecedented show of co-operation, the five Major League Baseball trading card licensees created this set of Roberto Clemente commemorative cards for distribution at the All-Star Fan Fest. Cards were available at participating manufacturers' booths, making complete sets somewhat difficult to assemble. Topps and Fleer based their commemorative cards on their companies' respective 1955 and 1963 Clemente cards. Donruss had artist Dick Perez create a Diamond King card of Clemente, while Upper Deck and Score Select created new designs. It is believed fewer than 10,000 of each card exist.

	NM/M
Complete Set (5):	30.00
Common Card:	6.00
1 Roberto Clemente (Donruss Diamond King)	6.00
2 Roberto Clemente (Fleer 1963 reprint)	6.00
3 Roberto Clemente (Score Select)	6.00
4 Roberto Clemente (Topps 1955 reprint)	10.00
5 Roberto Clemente (Upper Deck)	6.00

1995 FanFest Nolan Ryan Commemorative

At the July 7-11, 1995, FanFest, held in Dallas, Texas, site of the All-Star Game, five of Major League Baseball's principal licensees combined on a wrapper redemption program which offered Nolan Ryan Tribute cards. With 3,000 of the cards pegged as each day's maximum giveaway, only 15,000 total sets were available. Most of the companies opted for gold-leaf and/or foil-print extravaganzas, while Topps chose to recreate a single-player 1968-style Nolan Ryan rookie card with full career stats on back.

	NM/M
Complete Set (5):	16.00
Common Card:	4.00
1 Nolan Ryan (Upper Deck)	4.00
2 Nolan Ryan (Topps)	4.50
3 Nolan Ryan (Pinnacle)	4.00
4 Nolan Ryan (Fleer Ultra)	4.00
5 Nolan Ryan (Donruss)	4.00

1996 FanFest Steve Carlton Commemorative

Philadelphia's most famous Lefty (before Rocky Balboa) was chosen as the subject of the '96 All-Star FanFest multi-company card tribute. Each of the five largest baseball card

licensees produced a Carlton card for use in a wrapper redemption promotion at the annual show. Each of the cards featured the Liberty Bell All-Star Game logo along with such bells and whistles as embossing, metallic-foil highlights, etc.

	NM/M
Complete Set (5):	12.50
Common Card:	3.00
1 Steve Carlton (Donruss)	3.00
2 Steve Carlton (Fleer Ultra)	3.00
3 Steve Carlton (Pinnacle)	3.00
4 Steve Carlton (Topps)	4.00
5 Steve Carlton (Upper Deck)	3.00

1997 FanFest Jackie Robinson Commemorative

In conjunction with FanFest in Cleveland, July 4-8, preceding the All-Star Game, five of the major card companies combined to create a card set honoring Jackie Robinson. Each company made its card available at the show in a wrapper redemption exchange. In most cases the tribute cards showcased the respective companies' technical expertise. Production of each card was limited to 15,000.

	NM/M
Complete Set (5):	12.00
Common Card:	2.50
1 Jackie Robinson (Pinnacle Dufex)	2.50
2 Jackie Robinson (Topps Finest '52 reprint)	3.00
3 Jackie Robinson (Upper Deck)	2.50
4 Jackie Robinson (Donruss - 1948 Leaf reprint)	2.50
5 Jackie Robinson (Fleer)	2.50

1998 FanFest Lou Brock Commemorative

In the years before the Rockies joined the National League, Denver's "home team" was the St. Louis Cardinals. One of that team's greatest players of the 1960s and 1970s, Hall of Famer Lou Brock, was selected to be honored in the annual All-Star FanFest commemorative series used by the card companies as a wrapper redemption premium (five wrappers for each card). Card fronts include the All-Star Game logo, backs have the Cooperstown Collection logo. Topps' card is a chromium version reproduction of Brock's 1962 rookie card, which depicts him as a Cub.

	NM/M
Complete Set (5):	3.00
Common Card:	.50
1 Lou Brock (Topps)	2.00
2 Lou Brock (Pinnacle)	1.00
3 Lou Brock (Fleer)	.50
4 Lou Brock (Donruss DK)	1.00
5 Lou Brock (Upper Deck)	.50

1999 FanFest Carl Yastrzemski Commemorative

One of the modern Red Sox most popular players of the of the 1960s-1980s, Hall of Famer Carl Yastrzemski, was selected to be honored in the 1999 Boston All-Star FanFest commemorative series used by the card companies as a wrapper redemption premium (five wrappers for each card). Card fronts include the All-Star Game logo.

	NM/M
Complete Set (4):	7.50
Common Card:	2.00
1 Carl Yastrzemski (Topps)	2.75
2 Carl Yastrzemski (Ultra)	2.00
3 Carl Yastrzemski (Upper Deck)	2.00
4 Carl Yastrzemski (Pacific)	2.00

2000 FanFest Hank Aaron Commemorative

As in past years, each of Major League Baseball's major card licensees produced a special card in conjunction with FanFest in Atlanta prior to the All-Star Game. Visitors to the Collector's Showcase area of FanFest could obtain one card from each company's booth via a wrapper redemption.

	NM/M
Complete Set (4):	7.50
Common Card:	2.50
1 Hank Aaron (Topps)	2.50
2 Hank Aaron (Fleer)	2.50
3 Hank Aaron (Upper Deck)	2.50
4 Hank Aaron (Pacific)	2.50

2000 FanFest Hank Aaron Rookie Reprint

It has been reported that Topps originally intended to use this rookie reprint as its redemption card at FanFest, but later switched to a version of the Aaron card which appeared in 2000 Topps. It is said the rookie version was only distributed to a few of the vendors. Like

the other cards in the redemption program, the '54 Topps reprint has the event logo on front. It is numbered "1 of 4" on back.

	NM/M
1 Hank Aaron (1954 Topps reprint)	4.00

1988 Fantastic Sam's

This set of color player discs (2-1/2" diameter) was distributed during a Superstar Sweepstakes sponsored by Fantastic Sam's Family Haircutters' 1,800 stores nationwide. Each card consists of two connected discs (bright orange fronts, white backs) perforated for easy separation. One disc features the baseball player photo, the other carries the sweepstakes logo and a list of prizes. Player discs carry a Fantastic Sam's Baseball Superstars header curved above the photo, with player name, team and position printed in black. Backs are black-and-white and include personal info, card number and 1987 stats. Sweepstakes discs list contest prizes (Grand Prize was 4 tickets to a 1988 Championship game) on the front and an entry form on the flipside. Below the prize list is a silver scratch-off rectangle which may reveal an instant prize.

	NM/M
Complete Set (20):	4.00
Uncut Sheet:	10.00
Common Player:	.10
1 Kirby Puckett	.50
2 George Brett	.75
3 Mark McGwire	1.00
4 Wally Joyner	.10
5 Paul Molitor	.45
6 Alan Trammell	.10
7 George Bell	.10
8 Wade Boggs	.50
9 Don Mattingly	.75
10 Julio Franco	.10
11 Ozzie Smith	.50
12 Will Clark	.10
13 Dale Murphy	.15
14 Eric Davis	.10
15 Andre Dawson	.10
16 Tim Raines	.10
17 Darryl Strawberry	.10
18 Tony Gwynn	.50
19 Mike Schmidt	.75
20 Pedro Guerrero	.10

1984 Farmer Jack Detroit Tigers

Though there is no indication on the picutres themselves, this issue was a promotion by the Farmer Jack grocery store chain. Printed on semi-gloss paper, the color photos are bordered in white and measure 6" x 9". A facsimile autograph is printed on front. The unnumbered pictures are blank-backed and are checklisted here in alphabetical order.

	NM/M
Complete Set (16):	15.00
Common Player:	.50
(1) Dave Bergman	.50
(2) Darrell Evans	1.25
(3) Barbaro Garbey	.50
(4) Kirk Gibson	1.00
(5) John Grubb	.50
(6) Willie Hernandez	.50

(7) Larry Herndon	.50
(8) Howard Johnson	.90
(9) Chet Lemon	.75
(10) Jack Morris	.90
(11) Lance Parrish	1.00
(12) Dan Petry	.50
(13) Dave Rozema	.50
(14) Alan Trammell	4.00
(15) Lou Whitaker	2.50
(16) Milt Wilcox	.50

1987 Farmland Dairies Mets

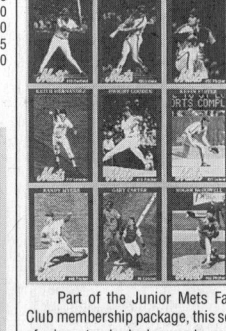

The New York Mets and Farmland Dairies produced a nine-card panel of baseball cards for members of the Junior Mets Club. Members of the club, kids 14 years of age and younger, received the perforated panel as part of a package featuring gifts and special privileges. The cards are the standard 2-1/2" x 3-1/2" with fronts containing a full-color photo encompassed by a blue border. The backs are designed on a vertical format and have player statistics and career highlights. The Farmland Dairies and Junior Mets Club logos are also carried on the card backs.

	NM/M
Complete Panel Set:	4.50
Complete Singles Set (9):	3.00
Common Single Player:	.25
1 Mookie Wilson	.35
4 Lenny Dykstra	.35
8 Gary Carter	1.50
12 Ron Darling	.25
18 Darryl Strawberry	.35
19 Bob Ojeda	.25
22 Kevin McReynolds	.25
42 Roger McDowell	.25
--- Team Card	.25

1988 Farmland Dairies Mets

Part of the Junior Mets Fan Club membership package, this set of nine standard size cards was printed on a single panel. Card fronts feature full-color action shots framed in orange and blue. A white player name runs across the top border, with a large team logo, uniform number and position printed below the photo. Card backs are blue on brown and include personal data, stats and 1987 season highlights. The set was offered to fans 14 years and younger for a $6 fan club membership fee, with a $1 discount for those who sent in two proofs of purchase from Farmland Dairies milk cartons.

	NM/M
Complete Panel Set:	4.50
Complete Singles Set (9):	2.50
Common Single Player:	.25
8 Gary Carter	1.50
16 Dwight Gooden	.25
17 Keith Hernandez	.40
18 Darryl Strawberry	.25
20 Howard Johnson	.25
21 Kevin Elster	.25
42 Roger McDowell	.25

48 Randy Myers	.25
50 Sid Fernandez	.25

1989 Farmland Dairies Mets

For the third consecutive year in 1989, Farmland Dairies sponsored the Junior Mets fan club. One of the club's membership benefits was a nine-card set issued on a 7-1/2" x 10-1/2" perforated sheet. Individual cards measure the standard 2-1/2" x 3-1/2" with team-color borders of blue and gold. Backs have the Junior Mets and Farmland logos along with 1988 highlights and stats, career stats and some biographical data. The checklist is by uniform number as shown on the cards' front.

	NM/M
Complete Set, Sheet	3.50
Complete Set, Singles (9):	3.00
Common Player:	.50
8 Gary Carter	1.50
9 Gregg Jefferies	.50
16 Dwight Gooden	.25
18 Darryl Strawberry	.25
22 Kevin McReynolds	.25
25 Keith Miller	.25
42 Roger McDowell	.25
44 David Cone	.50
--- 1988 Eastern Division Champs (Team Photo)	.25

1993 Fax Pax

Roger Clemens

Titled "Fax Pax World of Sports," this 40-card set was issued in Great Britain and features top athletes from many sports around the world. The 2-1/2" x 3-1/2" cards have borderless color action photos on front. A white strip near the bottom carries the player's name and the flag of his nation. Black, white and red backs have biographical data, stats and a career summary. Only the baseball players are listed here.

	NM/M
Common Player:	1.00
1 Roger Clemens	1.50
2 Ken Griffey Jr.	2.00
3 John Olerud	1.00
4 Nolan Ryan	3.00

1982 FBI Foods Discs

This set was issued in the form of a pair of 2-7/8" diameter discs printed on the bottoms of six-pack cartons of Canadian soft drinks. The discs have black-and-white player portrait photos at center, with cap logos airbrushed off. At top is a green and orange FBI logo. Player identification flanks the photo. The copyright and logo of the Players Association appear at right. The initials of the set's producer, Mike Schechter Associates, appear at lower-left. The unnumbered discs are checklisted here in alphabetical order. Because of their appearance on the bottom of a cardboard box, many cards suffer scuffing on the front, or show indentations from the soda cans. A premium of 25-50 percent attaches to intact boxes or panels.

		NM/M
Complete Set, Singles (30):		650.00
Common Player:		10.00
(1)	Vida Blue	10.00
(2)	George Brett	100.00
(3)	Rod Carew	25.00
(4)	Steve Carlton	30.00
(5)	Gary Carter	30.00
(6)	Warren Cromartie	10.00
(7)	Andre Dawson	15.00
(8)	Rollie Fingers	20.00
(9)	Carlton Fisk	30.00
(10)	Steve Garvey	15.00
(11)	Goose Gossage	10.00
(12)	Bill Gullickson	10.00
(13)	Steve Henderson	10.00
(14)	Keith Hernandez	10.00
(15)	John Mayberry	10.00
(16)	Al Oliver	10.00
(17)	Dave Parker	10.00
(18)	Tim Raines	10.00
(19)	Jim Rice	15.00
(20)	Steve Rogers	10.00
(21)	Pete Rose	150.00
(22)	Nolan Ryan	150.00
(23)	Mike Schmidt	100.00
(24)	Tom Seaver	30.00
(25)	Ken Singleton	10.00
(26)	Dave Steib	10.00
(27)	Bruce Sutter	20.00
(28)	Ellis Valentine	10.00
(29)	Fernando Valenzuela	10.00
(30)	Dave Winfield	30.00

1993 Finest Promos

Debuting at the 1993 National Convention in Chicago, this three-card set introduced the hobby to the Topps Finest baseball issue. While the promos are identical in high-tech format to the regular Finest cards issued later, including the same card numbers, there are differences in the promos; some subtle, some glaring. For instance, the Ryan and Alomar cards were issued in promo form in the "gray" style of the basic set. In the regularly issued set, those cards were in the green All-Star format. Each of the promos is overprinted in red on the back, "Promotional Sample 1 of 5000." Of considerably greater rarity are refractor versions of these promo cards, with production numbers unknown.

		NM/M
Complete Set (3):		25.00
Complete Set, Refractors (3):		1,500
88	Roberto Alomar	3.50
88r	Roberto Alomar (Refractor)	300.00
98	Don Mattingly	10.00
98r	Don Mattingly (Refractor)	500.00
107	Nolan Ryan	15.00
107r	Nolan Ryan (Refractor)	750.00

1993 Finest

This 199-card set uses a process of multi-color metallization; this chromium technology adds depth and dimension to the card. The set has a 33-card subset of All-Stars; a parallel version of these cards (Refractors) were also created with refracting foil using the metallization enhancement process. There is one refracting foil card in every nine packs. Packs have five cards. Each 18-count box contains a 5" x 7" version of one of the 33 All-Star players in the set.

		NM/M
Complete Set (199):		75.00
Common Player:		.50
Refractors:		40-50X
Pack (6):		15.00
Wax Box (18):		300.00
1	Dave Justice	.50
2	Lou Whitaker	.50
3	Bryan Harvey	.50
4	Carlos Garcia	.50
5	Sid Fernandez	.50
6	Brett Butler	.50
7	Scott Cooper	.50
8	B.J. Surhoff	.50
9	Steve Finley	.50
10	Curt Schilling	2.00
11	Jeff Bagwell	4.00
12	Alex Cole	.50
13	John Olerud	.50
14	John Smiley	.50
15	Bip Roberts	.50
16	Albert Belle	.50
17	Duane Ward	.50
18	Alan Trammell	.50
19	Andy Benes	.50
20	Reggie Sanders	.50
21	Todd Zeile	.50
22	Rick Aguilera	.50
23	Dave Hollins	.50
24	Jose Rijo	.50
25	Matt Williams	.50
26	Sandy Alomar	.50
27	Alex Fernandez	.50
28	Ozzie Smith	6.00
29	Ramon Martinez	.50
30	Bernie Williams	.50
31	Gary Sheffield	1.00
32	Eric Karros	.50
33	Frank Viola	.50
34	Kevin Young	.50
35	Ken Hill	.50
36	Tony Fernandez	.50
37	Tim Wakefield	.50
38	John Kruk	.50
39	Chris Sabo	.50
40	Marquis Grissom	.50
41	Glenn Davis	.50
42	Jeff Montgomery	.50
43	Kenny Lofton	.50
44	John Burkett	.50
45	Darryl Hamilton	.50
46	Jim Abbott	.50
47	Ivan Rodriguez	3.00
48	Eric Young	.50
49	Mitch Williams	.50
50	Harold Reynolds	.50
51	Brian Harper	.50
52	Rafael Palmeiro	3.00
53	Bret Saberhagen	.50
54	Jeff Conine	.50
55	Ivan Calderon	.50
56	Juan Guzman	.50
57	Carlos Baerga	.50
58	Charles Nagy	.50
59	Wally Joyner	.50
60	Charlie Hayes	.50
61	Shane Mack	.50
62	Pete Harnisch	.50
63	George Brett	8.00
64	Lance Johnson	.50
65	Ben McDonald	.50
66	Bobby Bonilla	.50
67	Terry Steinbach	.50
68	Ron Gant	.50
69	Doug Jones	.50
70	Paul Molitor	4.00
71	Brady Anderson	.50
72	Chuck Finley	.50
73	Mark Grace	.75
74	Mike Devereaux	.50
75	Tony Phillips	.50
76	Chuck Knoblauch	.50
77	Tony Gwynn	6.00
78	Kevin Appier	.50
79	Sammy Sosa	6.00
80	Mickey Tettleton	.50
81	Felix Jose	.50
82	Mark Langston	.50
83	Gregg Jefferies	.50
84	Andre Dawson/AS	1.00
85	Greg Maddux/AS	6.00
86	Rickey Henderson/AS	4.00
87	Tom Glavine/AS	2.50
88	Roberto Alomar/AS	1.00
89	Darryl Strawberry/AS	.50
90	Wade Boggs/AS	6.00
91	Bo Jackson/AS	1.00
92	Mark McGwire/AS	6.00
93	Robin Ventura/AS	.50
94	Joe Carter/AS	.50
95	Lee Smith/AS	.50
96	Cal Ripken, Jr./AS	10.00
97	Larry Walker/AS	.50
98	Don Mattingly/AS	8.00
99	Jose Canseco/AS	2.50
100	Dennis Eckersley/AS	3.00
101	Terry Pendleton/AS	.50
102	Frank Thomas/AS	4.00
103	Barry Bonds/AS	10.00
104	Roger Clemens/AS	8.00
105	Ryne Sandberg/AS	6.00
106	Fred McGriff/AS	.50
107	Nolan Ryan/AS	10.00
108	Will Clark/AS	.50
109	Pat Listach/AS	.50
110	Ken Griffey Jr./AS	6.00
111	Cecil Fielder/AS	.50
112	Kirby Puckett/AS	6.00
113	Dwight Gooden/AS	.50
114	Barry Larkin/AS	.50
115	David Cone/AS	.50
116	Juan Gonzalez/AS	2.50
117	Kent Hrbek	.50
118	Tim Wallach	.50
119	Craig Biggio	.50
120	Bobby Kelly	.50
121	Greg Olson	.50
122	Eddie Murray	4.00
123	Wil Cordero	.50
124	Jay Buhner	.50
125	Carlton Fisk	4.00
126	Eric Davis	.50
127	Doug Drabek	.50
128	Ozzie Guillen	.50
129	John Wetteland	.50
130	Andres Galarraga	.50
131	Ken Caminiti	.50
132	Tom Candiotti	.50
133	Pat Borders	.50
134	Kevin Brown	.50
135	Travis Fryman	.50
136	Kevin Mitchell	.50
137	Greg Swindell	.50
138	Benny Santiago	.50
139	Reggie Jefferson	.50
140	Chris Bosio	.50
141	Deion Sanders	.60
142	Scott Erickson	.50
143	Howard Johnson	.50
144	Orestes Destrade	.50
145	Jose Guzman	.50
146	Chad Curtis	.50
147	Cal Eldred	.50
148	Willie Greene	.50
149	Tommy Greene	.50
150	Erik Hanson	.50
151	Bob Welch	.50
152	John Jaha	.50
153	Harold Baines	.50
154	Randy Johnson	4.00
155	Al Martin	.50
156	J.T. Snow RC	1.50
157	Mike Mussina	2.50
158	Ruben Sierra	.50
159	Dean Palmer	.50
160	Steve Avery	.50
161	Julio Franco	.50
162	Dave Winfield	4.00
163	Tim Salmon	.50
164	Tom Henke	.50
165	Mo Vaughn	.50
166	John Smoltz	.50
167	Danny Tartabull	.50
168	Delino DeShields	.50
169	Charlie Hough	.50
170	Paul O'Neill	.50
171	Darren Daulton	.50
172	Jack McDowell	.50
173	Junior Felix	.50
174	Jimmy Key	.50
175	George Bell	.50
176	Mike Stanton	.50
177	Len Dykstra	.50
178	Norm Charlton	.50
179	Eric Anthony	.50
180	Bob Dibble	.50
181	Otis Nixon	.50
182	Randy Myers	.50
183	Tim Raines	.50
184	Orel Hershiser	.50
185	Andy Van Slyke	.50
186	Mike Lansing RC	1.00
187	Ray Lankford	.50
188	Mike Morgan	.50
189	Moises Alou	.50
190	Edgar Martinez	.50
191	John Franco	.50
192	Robin Yount	5.00
193	Bob Tewksbury	.50
194	Jay Bell	.50
195	Luis Gonzalez	.50
196	Dave Fleming	.50
197	Mike Greenwell	.50
198	David Nied	.50
199	Mike Piazza	10.00

Refractors

This parallel insert set comprises each of the 199 cards from the regular Topps Finest set recreated with refracting foil using the metallization enhancement process. One refractor card was inserted in every nine packs, on average. Estimated production was about 250 of each card, though short-prints are known. In the mid 2000s large quantities of the refractors began appearing in the market, fueling speculation that some form of unissued remainder inventory had been released from the printer.

		NM/M
Common Player:		15.00
1	Dave Justice	15.00
2	Lou Whitaker	15.00
3	Bryan Harvey/SP	45.00
4	Carlos Garcia	15.00
5	Sid Fernandez	15.00
6	Brett Butler	15.00
7	Scott Cooper	15.00
8	B.J. Surhoff	15.00
9	Steve Finley	15.00
10	Curt Schilling	50.00
11	Jeff Bagwell	100.00
12	Alex Cole	15.00
13	John Olerud	15.00
14	John Smiley	15.00
15	Bip Roberts	15.00
16	Albert Belle	15.00
17	Duane Ward	15.00
18	Alan Trammell	15.00
19	Andy Benes	15.00
20	Reggie Sanders	15.00
21	Todd Zeile	15.00
22	Rick Aguilera	15.00
23	Dave Hollins	15.00
24	Jose Rijo	15.00
25	Matt Williams	15.00
26	Sandy Alomar	15.00
27	Alex Fernandez	15.00
28	Ozzie Smith	100.00
29	Ramon Martinez	15.00
30	Bernie Williams	15.00
31	Gary Sheffield	40.00
32	Eric Karros	15.00
33	Frank Viola	15.00
34	Kevin Young	15.00
35	Ken Hill	15.00
36	Tony Fernandez	15.00
37	Tim Wakefield	15.00
38	John Kruk	15.00
39	Chris Sabo/SP	75.00
40	Marquis Grissom	15.00
41	Glenn Davis/SP	50.00
42	Jeff Montgomery	15.00
43	Kenny Lofton	15.00
44	John Burkett	15.00
45	Darryl Hamilton	15.00
46	Jim Abbott	15.00
47	Ivan Rodriguez	150.00
48	Eric Young	15.00
49	Mitch Williams	15.00
50	Harold Reynolds	15.00
51	Brian Harper	15.00
52	Rafael Palmeiro	75.00
53	Bret Saberhagen	15.00
54	Jeff Conine	15.00
55	Ivan Calderon	15.00
56	Juan Guzman	15.00
57	Carlos Baerga	15.00
58	Charles Nagy	15.00
59	Wally Joyner	15.00
60	Charlie Hayes	15.00
61	Shane Mack	15.00
62	Pete Harnisch	15.00
63	George Brett	125.00
64	Lance Johnson	15.00
65	Ben McDonald	15.00
66	Bobby Bonilla	15.00
67	Terry Steinbach	15.00
68	Ron Gant	15.00
69	Doug Jones	15.00
70	Paul Molitor	100.00
71	Brady Anderson	15.00
72	Chuck Finley	15.00
73	Mark Grace	15.00
74	Mike Devereaux	15.00
75	Tony Phillips	15.00
76	Chuck Knoblauch	15.00
77	Tony Gwynn	100.00
78	Kevin Appier	15.00
79	Sammy Sosa	150.00
80	Mickey Tettleton	15.00
81	Felix Jose	15.00
82	Mark Langston	15.00
83	Gregg Jefferies	15.00
84	Andre Dawson/AS	35.00
85	Greg Maddux/AS	150.00
86	Rickey Henderson/AS	125.00
87	Tom Glavine/AS	50.00
88	Roberto Alomar/AS	45.00
89	Darryl Strawberry/AS	15.00
90	Wade Boggs/AS	100.00
91	Bo Jackson/AS	60.00
92	Mark McGwire/AS	200.00
93	Robin Ventura/AS	15.00
94	Joe Carter/AS/SP	50.00
95	Lee Smith/AS	15.00
96	Cal Ripken, Jr./AS	500.00
97	Larry Walker/AS/SP	100.00
98	Don Mattingly/AS	100.00
99	Jose Canseco/AS	50.00
100	Dennis Eckersley/AS	75.00
101	Terry Pendleton/AS	15.00
102	Frank Thomas/AS/SP	200.00
103	Barry Bonds/AS	300.00
104	Roger Clemens/AS	200.00
105	Ryne Sandberg/AS	125.00
106	Fred McGriff/AS	15.00
107	Nolan Ryan/AS	500.00
108	Will Clark/AS/SP	75.00
109	Pat Listach/AS	15.00
110	Ken Griffey Jr./AS	450.00
111	Cecil Fielder/AS	15.00
112	Kirby Puckett/AS	100.00
113	Dwight Gooden/AS	15.00
114	Barry Larkin/AS	15.00
115	David Cone/AS	15.00
116	Juan Gonzalez/AS/SP	150.00
117	Kent Hrbek	15.00
118	Tim Wallach	15.00
119	Craig Biggio	15.00
120	Bobby Kelly	15.00
121	Greg Olson	15.00
122	Eddie Murray	100.00
123	Wil Cordero	15.00
124	Jay Buhner	15.00
125	Carlton Fisk	75.00
126	Eric Davis	15.00
127	Doug Drabek	15.00
128	Ozzie Guillen	15.00
129	John Wetteland	15.00
130	Andres Galarraga	15.00
131	Ken Caminiti	15.00
132	Tom Candiotti	15.00
133	Pat Borders	15.00
134	Kevin Brown	15.00
135	Travis Fryman	15.00
136	Kevin Mitchell	15.00
137	Greg Swindell	15.00
138	Benny Santiago	15.00
139	Reggie Jefferson	15.00
140	Chris Bosio	15.00
141	Deion Sanders	15.00
142	Scott Erickson	15.00
143	Howard Johnson	15.00
144	Orestes Destrade	15.00
145	Jose Guzman	15.00
146	Chad Curtis	15.00
147	Cal Eldred	15.00
148	Willie Greene/SP	75.00
149	Tommy Greene	15.00
150	Erik Hanson	15.00
151	Bob Welch	15.00
152	John Jaha	15.00
153	Harold Baines	15.00
154	Randy Johnson	100.00
155	Al Martin	15.00
156	J.T. Snow	15.00
157	Mike Mussina	45.00
158	Ruben Sierra	15.00
159	Dean Palmer	15.00
160	Steve Avery	15.00
161	Julio Franco	15.00
162	Dave Winfield	100.00
163	Tim Salmon/SP	50.00
164	Tom Henke	15.00
165	Mo Vaughn	15.00
166	John Smoltz	15.00
167	Danny Tartabull	15.00
168	Delino DeShields	15.00
169	Charlie Hough	15.00
170	Paul O'Neill	15.00
171	Darren Daulton	15.00
172	Jack McDowell	15.00
173	Junior Felix	15.00
174	Jimmy Key	15.00
175	George Bell	15.00
176	Mike Stanton	15.00
177	Len Dykstra	15.00
178	Norm Charlton	15.00
179	Eric Anthony	15.00
180	Bob Dibble	15.00
181	Otis Nixon	15.00
182	Randy Myers	15.00
183	Tim Raines	15.00
184	Orel Hershiser	15.00
185	Andy Van Slyke	15.00
186	Mike Lansing	15.00
187	Ray Lankford	15.00
188	Mike Morgan	15.00
189	Moises Alou	15.00
190	Edgar Martinez	15.00
191	John Franco	15.00
192	Robin Yount	90.00
193	Bob Tewksbury	15.00
194	Jay Bell	15.00
195	Luis Gonzalez	15.00
196	Dave Fleming	15.00
197	Mike Greenwell	15.00
198	David Nied	15.00
199	Mike Piazza	250.00

Jumbo All-Stars

These 4-1/2" x 6" cards were produced using the chromium metallization process. Each 18-pack Finest box contains one of the All-Star jumbo cards. Based on '93 Finest production, it is estimated fewer than 1,500 of each were issued.

		NM/M
Complete Set (33):		185.00
Common Player:		2.00
84	Andre Dawson	2.50
85	Greg Maddux	10.00
86	Rickey Henderson	7.50
87	Tom Glavine	3.00
88	Roberto Alomar	3.00
89	Darryl Strawberry	2.00
90	Wade Boggs	10.00
91	Bo Jackson	2.00
92	Mark McGwire	20.00
93	Robin Ventura	2.00
94	Joe Carter	2.00
95	Lee Smith	2.00
96	Cal Ripken, Jr.	30.00
97	Larry Walker	2.00
98	Don Mattingly	12.00
99	Jose Canseco	3.50
100	Dennis Eckersley	6.00
101	Terry Pendleton	2.00
102	Frank Thomas	7.50
103	Barry Bonds	30.00
104	Roger Clemens	12.00
105	Ryne Sandberg	10.00
106	Fred McGriff	2.00
107	Nolan Ryan	30.00
108	Will Clark	2.50
109	Pat Listach	2.00
110	Ken Griffey Jr.	15.00
111	Cecil Fielder	2.00
112	Kirby Puckett	10.00
113	Dwight Gooden	2.00
114	Barry Larkin	2.00
115	David Cone	2.00
116	Juan Gonzalez	7.50

1994 Finest Pre-Production

Forty cards premiering the upcoming 1994 Topps Finest set were issued as a random insert in packs of Topps Series 2 regular-issue cards. The promos are in the same format as the regular-issue Finest cards and share the same card numbers. On back there is a red "Pre-Production" notice printed diagonally over the statistics.

		NM/M
Complete Set (40):		35.00
Common Player:		1.00
22	Deion Sanders	1.00
23	Jose Offerman	1.00
26	Alex Fernandez	1.00
31	Steve Finley	1.00
34	Andres Galarraga	1.00
43	Reggie Sanders	1.00
45	Dave Hollins	1.00
52	David Cone	1.00
59	Dante Bichette	1.00

#	Player	Price
61	Orlando Merced	1.00
62	Brian McRae	1.00
66	Mike Mussina	2.50
76	Mike Stanley	1.00
78	Mark McGwire	6.00
79	Pat Listach	1.00
82	Dwight Gooden	1.00
84	Phil Plantier	1.00
90	Jeff Russell	1.00
92	Gregg Jefferies	1.00
93	Jose Guzman	1.00
100	John Smoltz	1.00
102	Jim Thome	3.00
121	Moises Alou	1.00
125	Devon White	1.00
126	Ivan Rodriguez	3.00
130	Dave Magadan	1.00
136	Ozzie Smith	4.00
141	Chris Hoiles	1.00
149	Jim Abbott	1.00
151	Bill Swift	1.00
154	Edgar Martinez	1.00
157	J.T. Snow	1.00
159	Alan Trammell	1.00
163	Roberto Kelly	1.00
166	Scott Erickson	1.00
168	Scott Cooper	1.00
169	Rod Beck	1.00
177	Dean Palmer	1.00
182	Todd Van Poppel	1.00
185	Paul Sorrento	1.00

1994 Finest

The 1994 Finest set comprises two series of 220 cards each; subsets of 20 superstars and 20 top rookies are featured in each series. Each card has a metallic look to it, using Topps Finest technology. Backs picture the player on the top half and statistics on the bottom. Baseball's Finest was limited to 4,000 cases and available to dealers through an allocation process, based on their sales the previous year. Along with the regular-issue set, there was a parallel set, called Refractors, of 440 cards and a 4 x 6-inch version of the 80 subset cards.

	NM/M
Complete Set (440):	40.00
Common Player:	.15
Refractors:	3X
Series 1 or 2 Pack (7):	1.50
Series 1 or 2 Box (24):	25.00

#	Player	Price
1	Mike Piazza	3.00
2	Kevin Stocker	.15
3	Greg McMichael	.15
4	Jeff Conine	.15
5	Rene Arocha	.15
6	Aaron Sele	.15
7	Brent Gates	.15
8	Chuck Carr	.15
9	Kirk Rueter	.15
10	Mike Lansing	.15
11	Al Martin	.15
12	Jason Bere	.15
13	Troy Neel	.15
14	Armando Reynoso	.15
15	Jeromy Burnitz	.15
16	Rich Amaral	.15
17	David McCarty	.15
18	Tim Salmon	.15
19	Steve Cooke	.15
20	Wil Cordero	.15
21	Kevin Tapani	.15
22	Deion Sanders	.15
23	Jose Offerman	.15
24	Mark Langston	.15
25	Ken Hill	.15
26	Alex Fernandez	.15
27	Jeff Blauser	.15
28	Royce Clayton	.15
29	Brad Ausmus	.15
30	Ryan Bowen	.15
31	Steve Finley	.15
32	Charlie Hayes	.15
33	Jeff Kent	.15
34	Mike Henneman	.15
35	Andres Galarraga	.15
36	Wayne Kirby	.15
37	Joe Oliver	.15
38	Terry Steinbach	.15
39	Ryan Thompson	.15
40	Luis Alicea	.15
41	Randy Velarde	.15
42	Bob Tewksbury	.15
43	Reggie Sanders	.15
44	Brian Williams	.15
45	Joe Orsulak	.15
46	Jose Lind	.15
47	Dave Hollins	.15
48	Graeme Lloyd	.15
49	Jim Gott	.15
50	Andre Dawson	.40
51	Steve Buechele	.15
52	David Cone	.15
53	Ricky Gutierrez	.15
54	Lance Johnson	.15
55	Tino Martinez	.15
56	Phil Hiatt	.15
57	Carlos Garcia	.15
58	Danny Darwin	.15
59	Dante Bichette	.15
60	Scott Kamieniecki	.15
61	Orlando Merced	.15
62	Brian McRae	.15
63	Pat Kelly	.15
64	Tom Henke	.15
65	Jeff King	.15
66	Mike Mussina	.75
67	Tim Pugh	.15
68	Robby Thompson	.15
69	Paul O'Neill	.15
70	Hal Morris	.15
71	Ron Karkovice	.15
72	Joe Girardi	.15
73	Eduardo Perez	.15
74	Raul Mondesi	.15
75	Mike Gallego	.15
76	Mike Stanley	.15
77	Kevin Roberson	.15
78	Mark McGwire	4.00
79	Pat Listach	.15
80	Eric Davis	.15
81	Mike Bordick	.15
82	Dwight Gooden	.15
83	Mike Moore	.15
84	Phil Plantier	.15
85	Darren Lewis	.15
86	Rick Wilkins	.15
87	Darryl Strawberry	.15
88	Rob Dibble	.15
89	Greg Vaughn	.15
90	Jeff Russell	.15
91	Mark Lewis	.15
92	Gregg Jefferies	.15
93	Jose Guzman	.15
94	Kenny Rogers	.15
95	Mark Lemke	.15
96	Mike Morgan	.15
97	Andujar Cedeno	.15
98	Orel Hershiser	.15
99	Greg Swindell	.15
100	John Smoltz	.15
101	Pedro Martinez	.15
102	Jim Thome	1.00
103	David Segui	.15
104	Charles Nagy	.15
105	Shane Mack	.15
106	John Jaha	.15
107	Tom Candiotti	.15
108	David Wells	.15
109	Bobby Jones	.15
110	Bob Hamelin	.15
111	Bernard Gilkey	.15
112	Chili Davis	.15
113	Todd Stottlemyre	.15
114	Derek Bell	.15
115	Mark McLemore	.15
116	Mark Whiten	.15
117	Mike Devereaux	.15
118	Terry Pendleton	.15
119	Pat Meares	.15
120	Pete Harnisch	.15
121	Moises Alou	.15
122	Jay Buhner	.15
123	Wes Chamberlain	.15
124	Mike Perez	.15
125	Devon White	.15
126	Ivan Rodriguez	1.25
127	Don Slaught	.15
128	John Valentin	.15
129	Jaime Navarro	.15
130	Dave Magadan	.15
131	Brady Anderson	.15
132	Juan Guzman	.15
133	John Wetteland	.15
134	Dave Stewart	.15
135	Scott Servais	.15
136	Ozzie Smith	2.50
137	Darrin Fletcher	.15
138	Jose Mesa	.15
139	Wilson Alvarez	.15
140	Pete Incaviglia	.15
141	Chris Hoiles	.15
142	Darryl Hamilton	.15
143	Chuck Finley	.15
144	Archi Cianfrocco	.15
145	Bill Wegman	.15
146	Joey Cora	.15
147	Darrell Whitmore	.15
148	David Hulse	.15
149	Jim Abbott	.15
150	Curt Schilling	.40
151	Bill Swift	.15
152	Tommy Greene	.15
153	Roberto Mejia	.15
154	Edgar Martinez	.15
155	Roger Pavlik	.15
156	Randy Tomlin	.15
157	J.T. Snow	.15
158	Bob Welch	.15
159	Alan Trammell	.15
160	Ed Sprague	.15
161	Ben McDonald	.15
162	Derrick May	.15
163	Roberto Kelly	.15
164	Bryan Harvey	.15
165	Ron Gant	.15
166	Scott Erickson	.15
167	Anthony Young	.15
168	Scott Cooper	.15
169	Rod Beck	.15
170	John Franco	.15
171	Gary DiSarcina	.15
172	Dave Fleming	.15
173	Wade Boggs	2.50
174	Kevin Appier	.15
175	Jose Bautista	.15
176	Wally Joyner	.15
177	Dean Palmer	.15
178	Tony Phillips	.15
179	John Smiley	.15
180	Charlie Hough	.15
181	Scott Fletcher	.15
182	Todd Van Poppel	.15
183	Mike Blowers	.15
184	Willie McGee	.15
185	Paul Sorrento	.15
186	Eric Young	.15
187	Bret Barberie	.15
188	Manuel Lee	.15
189	Jeff Branson	.15
190	Jim Deshaies	.15
191	Ken Caminiti	.15
192	Tim Raines	.15
193	Joe Grahe	.15
194	Hipolito Pichardo	.15
195	Denny Neagle	.15
196	Dave Staton	.15
197	Mike Benjamin	.15
198	Milt Thompson	.15
199	Bruce Ruffin	.15
200	Chris Hammond	.15
201	Tony Gwynn	2.50
202	Robin Ventura	.15
203	Frank Thomas	1.50
204	Kirby Puckett	2.50
205	Roberto Alomar	.30
206	Dennis Eckersley	1.25
207	Joe Carter	.15
208	Albert Belle	.15
209	Greg Maddux	2.50
210	Ryne Sandberg	2.50
211	Juan Gonzalez	.75
212	Jeff Bagwell	1.50
213	Randy Johnson	1.50
214	Matt Williams	.15
215	Dave Winfield	1.50
216	Larry Walker	.15
217	Roger Clemens	2.75
218	Kenny Lofton	.15
219	Cecil Fielder	.15
220	Darren Daulton	.15
221	John Olerud	.15
222	Jose Canseco	.75
223	Rickey Henderson	1.50
224	Fred McGriff	.15
225	Gary Sheffield	.50
226	Jack McDowell	.15
227	Rafael Palmeiro	1.25
228	Travis Fryman	.15
229	Marquis Grissom	.15
230	Barry Bonds	5.00
231	Carlos Baerga	.15
232	Ken Griffey Jr.	3.00
233	Dave Justice	.15
234	Bobby Bonilla	.15
235	Cal Ripken	5.00
236	Sammy Sosa	2.50
237	Len Dykstra	.15
238	Will Clark	.15
239	Paul Molitor	1.50
240	Barry Larkin	.15
241	Bo Jackson	.35
242	Mitch Williams	.15
243	Ron Darling	.15
244	Darryl Kile	.15
245	Geronimo Berroa	.15
246	Gregg Olson	.15
247	Brian Harper	.15
248	Rheal Cormier	.15
249	Rey Sanchez	.15
250	Jeff Fassero	.15
251	Sandy Alomar	.15
252	Chris Bosio	.15
253	Andy Stankiewicz	.15
254	Harold Baines	.15
255	Andy Ashby	.15
256	Tyler Green	.15
257	Kevin Brown	.15
258	Mo Vaughn	.15
259	Mike Harkey	.15
260	Dave Henderson	.15
261	Kent Hrbek	.15
262	Darrin Jackson	.15
263	Bob Wickman	.15
264	Spike Owen	.15
265	Todd Jones	.15
266	Pat Borders	.15
267	Tom Glavine	.45
268	Dave Nilsson	.15
269	Rich Batchelor	.15
270	Delino DeShields	.15
271	Felix Fermin	.15
272	Orestes Destrade	.15
273	Mickey Morandini	.15
274	Otis Nixon	.15
275	Ellis Burks	.15
276	Greg Gagne	.15
277	John Doherty	.15
278	Julio Franco	.15
279	Bernie Williams	.15
280	Rick Aguilera	.15
281	Mickey Tettleton	.15
282	David Nied	.15
283	Johnny Ruffin	.15
284	Dan Wilson	.15
285	Omar Vizquel	.15
286	Willie Banks	.15
287	Erik Pappas	.15
288	Cal Eldred	.15
289	Bobby Witt	.15
290	Luis Gonzalez	.15
291	Greg Pirkl	.15
292	Alex Cole	.15
293	Ricky Bones	.15
294	Denis Boucher	.15
295	John Burkett	.15
296	Steve Trachsel	.15
297	Ricky Jordan	.15
298	Mark Dewey	.15
299	Jimmy Key	.15
300	Mike MacFarlane	.15
301	Tim Belcher	.15
302	Carlos Reyes	.15
303	Greg Harris	.15
304	Brian Anderson **RC**	.15
305	Terry Mulholland	.15
306	Felix Jose	.15
307	Darren Holmes	.15
308	Jose Rijo	.15
309	Paul Wagner	.15
310	Bob Scanlan	.15
311	Mike Jackson	.15
312	Jose Vizcaino	.15
313	Rob Butler	.15
314	Kevin Seitzer	.15
315	Geronimo Pena	.15
316	Hector Carrasco	.15
317	Eddie Murray	1.50
318	Roger Salkeld	.15
319	Todd Hundley	.15
320	Danny Jackson	.15
321	Kevin Young	.15
322	Mike Greenwell	.15
323	Kevin Mitchell	.15
324	Chuck Knoblauch	.15
325	Danny Tartabull	.15
326	Vince Coleman	.15
327	Marvin Freeman	.15
328	Andy Benes	.15
329	Mike Kelly	.15
330	Karl Rhodes	.15
331	Allen Watson	.15
332	Damion Easley	.15
333	Reggie Jefferson	.15
334	Kevin McReynolds	.15
335	Arthur Rhodes	.15
336	Brian Hunter	.15
337	Tom Browning	.15
338	Pedro Munoz	.15
339	Billy Ripken	.15
340	Gene Harris	.15
341	Fernando Vina	.15
342	Sean Berry	.15
343	Pedro Astacio	.15
344	B.J. Surhoff	.15
345	Doug Drabek	.15
346	Jody Reed	.15
347	Ray Lankford	.15
348	Steve Farr	.15
349	Eric Anthony	.15
350	Pete Smith	.15
351	Lee Smith	.15
352	Mariano Duncan	.15
353	Doug Strange	.15
354	Tim Bogar	.15
355	Dave Weathers	.15
356	Eric Karros	.15
357	Randy Myers	.15
358	Chad Curtis	.15
359	Steve Avery	.15
360	Brian Jordan	.15
361	Tim Wallach	.15
362	Pedro Martinez	1.50
363	Bip Roberts	.15
364	Lou Whitaker	.15
365	Luis Polonia	.15
366	Benny Santiago	.15
367	Brett Butler	.15
368	Shawon Dunston	.15
369	Kelly Stinnett	.15
370	Chris Turner	.15
371	Ruben Sierra	.15
372	Greg Harris	.15
373	Xavier Hernandez	.15
374	Howard Johnson	.15
375	Duane Ward	.15
376	Roberto Hernandez	.15
377	Scott Leius	.15
378	Dave Valle	.15
379	Sid Fernandez	.15
380	Doug Jones	.15
381	Zane Smith	.15
382	Craig Biggio	.15
383	Rick White	.15
384	Tom Pagnozzi	.15
385	Chris James	.15
386	Bret Boone	.15
387	Jeff Montgomery	.15
388	Chad Kreuter	.15
389	Greg Hibbard	.15
390	Mark Grace	.15
391	Phil Leftwich	.15
392	Don Mattingly	2.75
393	Ozzie Guillen	.15
394	Gary Gaetti	.15
395	Erik Hanson	.15
396	Scott Brosius	.15
397	Tom Gordon	.15
398	Bill Gullickson	.15
399	Matt Mieske	.15
400	Pat Hentgen	.15
401	Walt Weiss	.15
402	Greg Blosser	.15
403	Stan Javier	.15
404	Greg Henry	.15
405	Ramon Martinez	.15
406	Frank Viola	.15
407	Mike Hampton	.15
408	Andy Van Slyke	.15
409	Bobby Ayala	.15
410	Todd Zeile	.15
411	Jay Bell	.15
412	Denny Martinez	.15
413	Mark Portugal	.15
414	Bobby Munoz	.15
415	Kirt Manwaring	.15
416	John Kruk	.15
417	Trevor Hoffman	.15
418	Chris Sabo	.15
419	Bret Saberhagen	.15
420	Chris Nabholz	.15
421	James Mouton	.15
422	Tony Tarasco	.15
423	Carlos Delgado	.75
424	Rondell White	.15
425	Javier Lopez	.15
426	Chan Ho Park **RC**	1.00
427	Cliff Floyd	.15
428	Dave Staton	.15
429	J.R. Phillips	.15
430	Manny Ramirez	1.50
431	Kurt Abbott	.15
432	Melvin Nieves	.15
433	Alex Gonzalez	.15
434	Rick Helling	.15
435	Danny Bautista	.15
436	Matt Walbeck	.15
437	Ryan Klesko	.15
438	Steve Karsay	.15
439	Salomon Torres	.15
440	Scott Ruffcorn	.15

Refractors

It takes an experienced eye and good light to detect a Refractor parallel card from a regular-issue Topps Finest. The Refractor utilizes a variation of the Finest metallic printing process to produce rainbow-effect highlights on the card front. The Refractors share the checklist with the regular-issue Finest and were inserted at a rate of about one per 10 packs.

	NM/M
Complete Set (440):	300.00
Common Player:	1.00
Stars/Rookies:	3X

Superstar Jumbos

Identical in format to the Superstars subset in the Finest issue, these cards measure about 4" x 5-1/2" and were distributed one per box in Finest foil packs. Backs carry a card number under the banner with the player's name and position. There were 20 rookies and 20 superstars from both Series 1 and Series 2.

	NM/M
Complete Set (80):	140.00
Common Player:	1.00

#	Player	Price
1	Mike Piazza	12.50
2	Kevin Stocker	1.00
3	Greg McMichael	1.00
4	Jeff Conine	1.00
5	Rene Arocha	1.00
6	Aaron Sele	1.00
7	Brent Gates	1.00
8	Chuck Carr	1.00
9	Kirk Rueter	1.00
10	Mike Lansing	1.00
11	Al Martin	1.00
12	Jason Bere	1.00
13	Troy Neel	1.00
14	Armando Reynoso	1.00
15	Jeromy Burnitz	1.00
16	Rich Amaral	1.00
17	David McCarty	1.00
18	Tim Salmon	1.00
19	Steve Cooke	1.00
20	Wil Cordero	1.00
201	Tony Gwynn	7.50
202	Robin Ventura	1.00
203	Frank Thomas	6.00
204	Kirby Puckett	7.50
205	Roberto Alomar	2.00
206	Dennis Eckersley	5.00
207	Joe Carter	1.00
208	Albert Belle	1.00
209	Greg Maddux	7.50
210	Ryne Sandberg	7.50
211	Juan Gonzalez	3.00
212	Jeff Bagwell	6.00
213	Randy Johnson	6.00
214	Matt Williams	1.00
215	Dave Winfield	6.00
216	Larry Walker	1.00
217	Roger Clemens	10.00
218	Kenny Lofton	1.00
219	Cecil Fielder	1.00
220	Darren Daulton	1.00
221	John Olerud	1.00
222	Jose Canseco	4.00
223	Rickey Henderson	6.00
224	Fred McGriff	1.00
225	Gary Sheffield	2.00
226	Jack McDowell	1.00
227	Rafael Palmeiro	5.00
228	Travis Fryman	1.00
229	Marquis Grissom	1.00
230	Barry Bonds	20.00
231	Carlos Baerga	1.00
232	Ken Griffey Jr.	12.50
233	Dave Justice	1.00
234	Bobby Bonilla	1.00
235	Cal Ripken	20.00
236	Sammy Sosa	7.50
237	Len Dykstra	1.00
238	Will Clark	1.00
239	Paul Molitor	6.00
240	Barry Larkin	1.00
421	James Mouton	1.00
422	Tony Tarasco	1.00
423	Carlos Delgado	3.00
424	Rondell White	1.00
425	Javier Lopez	1.00
426	Chan Ho Park	1.00
427	Cliff Floyd	1.00
428	Dave Staton	1.00
429	J.R. Phillips	1.00
430	Manny Ramirez	6.00
431	Kurt Abbott	1.00
432	Melvin Nieves	1.00
433	Alex Gonzalez	1.00
434	Rick Helling	1.00
435	Danny Bautista	1.00
436	Matt Walbeck	1.00
437	Ryan Klesko	1.00
438	Steve Karsay	1.00
439	Salomon Torres	1.00
440	Scott Ruffcorn	1.00

Superstar Sampler

This special version of 45 of the biggest-name stars from the 1994 Topps Finest set was issued in a three-card cello pack with the same player's '94 Bowman and Stadium Club cards. The packs were available only in 1994 Topps retail factory sets. Cards are identical to the regular-issue Finest cards except for a round, red "Topps Superstar Sampler" logo printed at bottom center on back.

	NM/M
Complete Set (45):	400.00
Common Player:	4.00
1 Mike Piazza	35.00
18 Tim Salmon	4.00

35	Andres Galarraga	4.00
74	Raul Mondesi	4.00
92	Gregg Jefferies	4.00
201	Tony Gwynn	20.00
203	Frank Thomas	15.00
204	Kirby Puckett	20.00
205	Roberto Alomar	6.00
207	Joe Carter	4.00
208	Albert Belle	4.00
209	Greg Maddux	20.00
210	Ryne Sandberg	20.00
211	Juan Gonzalez	7.50
212	Jeff Bagwell	15.00
213	Randy Johnson	15.00
214	Matt Williams	4.00
216	Larry Walker	4.00
217	Roger Clemens	30.00
219	Cecil Fielder	4.00
220	Darren Daulton	4.00
221	John Olerud	4.00
222	Jose Canseco	7.50
224	Fred McGriff	4.00
225	Gary Sheffield	6.00
226	Jack McDowell	4.00
227	Rafael Palmeiro	12.00
229	Marquis Grissom	4.00
230	Barry Bonds	65.00
231	Carlos Baerga	4.00
232	Ken Griffey Jr.	35.00
233	Dave Justice	4.00
234	Bobby Bonilla	4.00
235	Cal Ripken Jr.	65.00
237	Len Dykstra	4.00
238	Will Clark	4.00
239	Paul Molitor	15.00
240	Barry Larkin	4.00
258	Mo Vaughn	4.00
267	Tom Glavine	7.50
390	Mark Grace	4.00
392	Don Mattingly	30.00
408	Andy Van Slyke	4.00
427	Cliff Floyd	4.00
430	Manny Ramirez	15.00

Bronze

This three-card set was included as part of the purchase of a 1994 Topps Stadium Club Members Only set, but was also made available on a limited basis via newspaper ads. The cards feature a version of Topps' Finest technology with the multi-colored front design laminated to a bronze base by a heavy lucite overlay. Backs are engraved in black on bronze and contain complete major and minor league stats and a few personal data. The Finest bronze cards are slightly larger than current standard suze, measuring 2-3/4" x 3-3/4".

		NM/M
Complete Set (3):		40.00
Common Player:		10.00
1	Barry Bonds	20.00
2	Ken Griffey Jr.	15.00
3	Frank Thomas	10.00

1995 Finest

In its third year Finest baseball was reduced to a 220-card base set. All cards feature the chrome-printing technology associated with the Finest logo and include a peel-off plastic protector on the card front. Backgrounds are green with gold

pinstripes. Behind the action photo at center is a large diamond with each corner intersected by a silver semi-circle. On the Finest Rookies subset which makes up the first 30 cards of the issue, the diamond has a graduated pink to orange center, with flecks of red throughout. Veterans cards have a graduated blue to purple center of the diamond. On the rookies cards there is a teal brand name at top, while the vets show a gold "FINEST." Backs repeat the front background motif in shades of green. There is a player photo at right, with biographical data, 1994 and career stats, and a "Finest Moment" career highlight at left. Finest was sold in seven-card packs with a suggested retail price of $4.99.

		NM/M
Complete Set (220):		75.00
Common Player:		.25
Refractors:		5X
Series 1 or 2 Pack (7):		2.00
Series 1 or 2 Wax Box (24):		30.00
1	Raul Mondesi	
	(Rookie Theme)	.25
2	Kurt Abbott	
	(Rookie Theme)	.25
3	Chris Gomez	
	(Rookie Theme)	.25
4	Manny Ramirez	
	(Rookie Theme)	1.50
5	Rondell White	
	(Rookie Theme)	.25
6	William Van Landingham	
	(Rookie Theme)	.25
7	Jon Lieber	
	(Rookie Theme)	.25
8	Ryan Klesko	
	(Rookie Theme)	.25
9	John Hudek	
	(Rookie Theme)	.25
10	Joey Hamilton	
	(Rookie Theme)	.25
11	Bob Hamelin	
	(Rookie Theme)	.25
12	Brian Anderson	
	(Rookie Theme)	.25
13	Mike Lieberthal	
	(Rookie Theme)	.25
14	Rico Brogna	
	(Rookie Theme)	.25
15	Rusty Greer	
	(Rookie Theme)	.25
16	Carlos Delgado	
	(Rookie Theme)	1.00
17	Jim Edmonds	
	(Rookie Theme)	.65
18	Steve Trachsel	
	(Rookie Theme)	.25
19	Matt Walbeck	
	(Rookie Theme)	.25
20	Armando Benitez	
	(Rookie Theme)	.25
21	Steve Karsay	
	(Rookie Theme)	.25
22	Jose Oliva	
	(Rookie Theme)	.25
23	Cliff Floyd (Rookie Theme)	.25
24	Kevin Foster	
	(Rookie Theme)	.25
25	Javier Lopez	
	(Rookie Theme)	.25
26	Jose Valentin	
	(Rookie Theme)	.25
27	James Mouton	
	(Rookie Theme)	.25
28	Hector Carrasco	
	(Rookie Theme)	.25
29	Orlando Miller	
	(Rookie Theme)	.25
30	Garret Anderson	
	(Rookie Theme)	.25
31	Marvin Freeman	.25
32	Brett Butler	.25
33	Roberto Kelly	.25
34	Rod Beck	.25
35	Jose Rijo	.25
36	Edgar Martinez	.25
37	Jim Thome	.65
38	Rick Wilkins	.25
39	Wally Joyner	.25
40	Wil Cordero	.25
41	Tommy Greene	.25
42	Travis Fryman	.25
43	Don Slaught	.25
44	Brady Anderson	.25
45	Matt Williams	.25
46	Rene Arocha	.25
47	Rickey Henderson	1.50
48	Mike Mussina	.75
49	Greg McMichael	.25
50	Jody Reed	.25
51	Tino Martinez	.25
52	Dave Clark	.25
53	John Valentin	.25
54	Bret Boone	.25
55	Walt Weiss	.25
56	Kenny Lofton	.75
57	Scott Leius	.25
58	Eric Karros	.25

59	John Olerud	.25
60	Chris Hoiles	.25
61	Sandy Alomar	.25
62	Tim Wallach	.25
63	Cal Eldred	.25
64	Tom Glavine	.50
65	Mark Grace	.25
66	Rey Sanchez	.25
67	Bobby Ayala	.25
68	Dante Bichette	.25
69	Andres Galarraga	.25
70	Chuck Carr	.25
71	Bobby Witt	.25
72	Steve Avery	.25
73	Bobby Jones	.25
74	Delino DeShields	.25
75	Kevin Tapani	.25
76	Randy Johnson	1.50
77	David Nied	.25
78	Pat Hentgen	.25
79	Tim Salmon	.25
80	Todd Zeile	.25
81	John Wetteland	.25
82	Albert Belle	.25
83	Ben McDonald	.25
84	Bobby Munoz	.25
85	Bip Roberts	.25
86	Mo Vaughn	.25
87	Chuck Finley	.25
88	Chuck Knoblauch	.25
89	Frank Thomas	1.50
90	Danny Tartabull	.25
91	Dean Palmer	.25
92	Len Dykstra	.25
93	J.R. Phillips	.25
94	Tom Candiotti	.25
95	Marquis Grissom	.25
96	Barry Larkin	.25
97	Bryan Harvey	.25
98	Dave Justice	.25
99	David Cone	.25
100	Wade Boggs	2.50
101	Jason Bere	.25
102	Hal Morris	.25
103	Fred McGriff	.25
104	Bobby Bonilla	.25
105	Jay Buhner	.25
106	Allen Watson	.25
107	Mickey Tettleton	.25
108	Kevin Appier	.25
109	Ivan Rodriguez	1.00
110	Carlos Garcia	.25
111	Andy Benes	.25
112	Eddie Murray	1.50
113	Mike Piazza	3.50
114	Greg Vaughn	.25
115	Paul Molitor	1.50
116	Terry Steinbach	.25
117	Jeff Bagwell	1.50
118	Ken Griffey Jr.	3.50
119	Gary Sheffield	.75
120	Cal Ripken Jr.	5.00
121	Jeff Kent	.25
122	Jay Bell	.25
123	Will Clark	.25
124	Cecil Fielder	.25
125	Alex Fernandez	.25
126	Don Mattingly	3.00
127	Reggie Sanders	.25
128	Moises Alou	.25
129	Craig Biggio	.25
130	Eddie Williams	.25
131	John Franco	.25
132	John Kruk	.25
133	Jeff King	.25
134	Royce Clayton	.25
135	Doug Drabek	.25
136	Ray Lankford	.25
137	Roberto Alomar	.50
138	Todd Hundley	.25
139	Alex Cole	.25
140	Shawon Dunston	.25
141	John Roper	.25
142	Mark Langston	.25
143	Tom Pagnozzi	.25
144	Wilson Alvarez	.25
145	Scott Cooper	.25
146	Kevin Mitchell	.25
147	Mark Whiten	.25
148	Jeff Conine	.25
149	Chili Davis	.25
150	Luis Gonzalez	.25
151	Juan Guzman	.25
152	Mike Greenwell	.25
153	Mike Henneman	.25
154	Rick Aguilera	.25
155	Dennis Eckersley	1.00
156	Darrin Fletcher	.25
157	Darren Lewis	.25
158	Juan Gonzalez	.75
159	Dave Hollins	.25
160	Jimmy Key	.25
161	Roberto Hernandez	.25
162	Randy Myers	.25
163	Joe Carter	.25
164	Darren Daulton	.25
165	Mike MacFarlane	.25
166	Bret Saberhagen	.25
167	Kirby Puckett	2.50
168	Lance Johnson	.25
169	Mark McGwire	4.00
170	Jose Canseco	.75
171	Mike Stanley	.25
172	Lee Smith	.25
173	Robin Ventura	.25
174	Greg Gagne	.25
175	Brian McRae	.25
176	Mike Bordick	.25

177	Rafael Palmeiro	1.00
178	Kenny Rogers	.25
179	Chad Curtis	.25
180	Devon White	.25
181	Paul O'Neill	.25
182	Ken Caminiti	.25
183	Dave Nilsson	.25
184	Tim Naehring	.25
185	Roger Clemens	3.00
186	Otis Nixon	.25
187	Tim Raines	.25
188	Dennis Martinez	.25
189	Pedro Martinez	1.50
190	Jim Abbott	.25
191	Ryan Thompson	.25
192	Barry Bonds	5.00
193	Joe Girardi	.25
194	Steve Finley	.25
195	John Jaha	.25
196	Tony Gwynn	2.50
197	Sammy Sosa	2.50
198	John Burkett	.25
199	Carlos Baerga	.25
200	Ramon Martinez	.25
201	Aaron Sele	.25
202	Eduardo Perez	.25
203	Alan Trammell	.25
204	Orlando Merced	.25
205	Deion Sanders	.35
206	Robb Nen	.25
207	Jack McDowell	.25
208	Ruben Sierra	.25
209	Bernie Williams	.25
210	Kevin Seitzer	.25
211	Charles Nagy	.25
212	Tony Phillips	.25
213	Greg Maddux	2.50
214	Jeff Montgomery	.25
215	Larry Walker	.25
216	Andy Van Slyke	.25
217	Ozzie Smith	2.50
218	Geronimo Pena	.25
219	Gregg Jefferies	.25
220	Lou Whitaker	.25

Refractors

A parallel set with a counterpart to each of the 220 cards in the regular Finest emission, the Refractors are printed in a version of the Finest chrome technology that produces a rainbow effect when viewed at the proper angle. The relatively open spaces of the 1995 Finest design make the Refractors easier to spot than the previous years' versions, but just to assist the identification process, Topps placed a small black "REFRACTOR" in the dark green background on the cards' backs, as well. Advertised rate of insertion for the Refractors was about one per 12 packs.

	NM/M
Complete Set (220):	400.00
Common Player:	1.00
Stars:	5X

Flame Throwers

The scarcest of the Finest inserts is the nine-card set of baseball's hardest throwing pitchers. Flame Throwers cards are found at an average rate of one per 48 packs.

Fronts have a central photo of a pitcher bringing his best heat. Behind the photo is the Flame Throwers typographic logo in tones of red, yellow and orange. Backs have another photo and a bar graph rating the pitcher's skill levels.

		NM/M
Complete Set (9):		20.00
Common Player:		1.50
1	Jason Bere	1.50
2	Roger Clemens	8.00
3	Juan Guzman	1.50
4	John Hudek	1.50
5	Randy Johnson	5.00
6	Pedro Martinez	4.00
7	Jose Rijo	1.50
8	Bret Saberhagen	1.50
9	John Wetteland	1.50

Power Kings

The emphasis is on youth in this chase set of baseball's top distance threats. Found at a rate of one per 24 packs, on average, the Power Kings inserts have a central photo of the player in batting action. The background, in shades of blue, features lightning strokes. Backs feature another pair of player photos and a bar graph charting the hitter's power skills.

		NM/M
Complete Set (18):		35.00
Common Player:		.75
1	Bob Hamelin	.75
2	Raul Mondesi	.75
3	Ryan Klesko	.75
4	Carlos Delgado	1.50
5	Manny Ramirez	3.00
6	Mike Piazza	5.00
7	Jeff Bagwell	3.00
8	Mo Vaughn	.75
9	Frank Thomas	3.00
10	Ken Griffey Jr.	5.00
11	Albert Belle	.75
12	Sammy Sosa	4.00
13	Dante Bichette	.75
14	Gary Sheffield	.75
15	Matt Williams	.75
16	Fred McGriff	.75
17	Barry Bonds	7.50
18	Cecil Fielder	.75

Update

Players who changed teams through trades or free agent signings and more of the season's rookie player crop are included in the Finest Update series of 110 cards. The cards are numbered contiguously with the base Finest set and share the same design. Once again, Refractor cards were found on an average of once per 12 packs. Finest Update was sold in seven-card packs with a suggested retail price of $4.99.

	NM/M
Complete Set (110):	20.00
Common Player:	.25
Refractors:	5X
Wax Pack (7):	1.25

	Wax Box (24):	20.00
221	Chipper Jones	2.50
222	Benji Gil	.25
223	Tony Phillips	.25
224	Trevor Wilson	.25
225	Tony Tarasco	.25
226	Roberto Petagine	.25
227	Mike MacFarlane	.25
228	Hideo Nomo RC	3.00
229	Mark McLemore	.25
230	Ron Gant	.25
231	Andujar Cedeno	.25
232	Mike Mimbs RC	.25
233	Jim Abbott	.25
234	Ricky Bones	.25
235	Marty Cordova	.25
236	Mark Johnson	.25
237	Marquis Grissom	.25
238	Tom Henke	.25
239	Terry Pendleton	.25
240	John Wetteland	.25
241	Lee Smith	.25
242	Jaime Navarro	.25
243	Luis Alicea	.25
244	Scott Cooper	.25
245	Gary Gaetti	.25
246	Edgardo Alfonzo	.25
247	Brad Clontz	.25
248	Dave Mlicki	.25
249	Dave Winfield	1.50
250	Mark Grudzielanek RC	.50
251	Alex Gonzalez	.25
252	Kevin Brown	.25
253	Esteban Loaiza	.25
254	Vaughn Eshelman	.25
255	Bill Swift	.25
256	Brian McRae	.25
257	Bobby Higginson RC	.50
258	Jack McDowell	.25
259	Scott Stahoviak	.25
260	Jon Nunnally	.25
261	Charlie Hayes	.25
262	Jacob Brumfield	.25
263	Chad Curtis	.25
264	Heathcliff Slocumb	.25
265	Mark Whiten	.25
266	Mickey Tettleton	.25
267	Jose Mesa	.25
268	Doug Jones	.25
269	Trevor Hoffman	.25
270	Paul Sorrento	.25
271	Shane Andrews	.25
272	Brett Butler	.25
273	Curtis Goodwin	.25
274	Larry Walker	.25
275	Phil Plantier	.25
276	Ken Hill	.25
277	Vinny Castilla	.25
278	Billy Ashley	.25
279	Derek Jeter	6.00
280	Bob Tewksbury	.25
281	Jose Offerman	.25
282	Glenallen Hill	.25
283	Tony Fernandez	.25
284	Mike Devereaux	.25
285	John Burkett	.25
286	Geronimo Berroa	.25
287	Quivilo Veras	.25
288	Jason Bates	.25
289	Lee Tinsley	.25
290	Derek Bell	.25
291	Jeff Fassero	.25
292	Ray Durham	.25
293	Chad Ogea	.25
294	Bill Pulsipher	.25
295	Phil Nevin	.25
296	Carlos Perez RC	.25
297	Roberto Kelly	.25
298	Tim Wakefield	.25
299	Jeff Manto	.25
300	Brian Hunter	.25
301	C.J. Nitkowski	.25
302	Dustin Hermanson	.25
303	John Mabry	.25
304	Orel Hershiser	.25
305	Ron Villone	.25
306	Sean Bergman	.25
307	Tom Goodwin	.25
308	Al Reyes	.25
309	Todd Stottlemyre	.25
310	Rich Becker	.25
311	Joey Cora	.25
312	Ed Sprague	.25
313	John Smoltz	.25
314	Frank Castillo	.25
315	Chris Hammond	.25
316	Ismael Valdes	.25
317	Pete Harnisch	.25
318	Bernard Gilkey	.25
319	John Kruk	.25
320	Marc Newfield	.25
321	Brian Johnson	.25
322	Mark Portugal	.25
323	David Hulse	.25
324	Luis Ortiz	.25
325	Mike Benjamin	.25
326	Brian Jordan	.25
327	Shawn Green	.75
328	Joe Oliver	.25
329	Felipe Lira	.25
330	Andre Dawson	.75

Update Refractors

The special version of Topps' chromium printing process which creates a rainbow effect was applied to a limited number of each card in the Finest Update set to create a parallel Refractor edition. To assist in identification, a small black "REFRACTOR" is printed on the cards' backs, as well. Refractors are found on average once every 12 packs of Finest Update.

	NM/M
Complete Set (110):	100.00
Common Player:	1.00
Stars:	5X

Bronze League Leaders

Available only by mail directly from Topps, this set features N.L. and A.L. leaders in various batting categories for the 1994 season. Fronts employ Topps' Finest technology with a stained-glass effect in the background, overlaid with a heavy layer of resin. Backs are bronze and feature 1994 stats and highlights embossed in blue. The cards are oversized, measuring 2-3/4" x 3-3/4".

		NM/M
Complete Set (6):		20.00
Common Player:		2.50
1	Matt Williams	2.50
2	Tony Gwynn	6.50
3	Jeff Bagwell	5.00
4	Ken Griffey Jr.	9.00
5	Paul O'Neill	2.50
6	Frank Thomas	5.00

1996 Finest

Utilizing three levels of base-card scarcity, the 359-card Finest set comprises 220 Commons (Bronze), 91 Uncommons (Silver) and 49 Rares (Gold). Cards were somewhat randomly assigned a status. Uncommon cards are found one in four packs; Rare cards are seeded one per 24 packs. The set has eight themes. Series 1 themes are Phenoms, Intimidators, Gamers and Sterling, the latter of which consists of star players already included within the first three themes. Series 2 themes are Franchise, Additions, Prodigies and Sterling. Regular-issue cards are not only numbered from 1-359 in the set as a whole, but also numbered within each subset. Finest Refractor parallel cards were also made. Rare Refractor cards are found one every 288 packs (fewer than 150 of each produced), while Uncommon Refractors are found one per 48 packs. Common Refractors are seeded 1:12.

	NM/M
Complete Set (359):	300.00
Bronze Set (220):	60.00
Common Bronze:	.15
Silver Set (91):	90.00
Typical Silver:	.50
Gold Set (47):	200.00
Typical Gold:	2.00

		NM/M
Series 1 Pack (6):		1.50
Series 1 Wax Box (24):		30.00
Series 2 Pack (6):		1.50
Series 2 Wax Box (24):		30.00
1	Greg Maddux/S (Intimidators)	3.00
2	Bernie Williams/S (Gamers)	.50
3	Ivan Rodriguez/S (Intimidators)	1.50
4	Marty Cordova/G (Phenoms)	2.00
5	Roberto Hernandez (Intimidators)	.15
6	Tony Gwynn/G (Gamers)	7.50
7	Barry Larkin/S (Sterling)	.50
8	Terry Pendleton (Gamers)	.15
9	Albert Belle/G (Sterling)	2.00
10	Ray Lankford/S (Gamers)	.50
11	Mike Piazza/S (Sterling)	4.00
12	Ken Caminiti (Intimidators)	.15
13	Larry Walker/S (Intimidators)	.50
14	Matt Williams (Intimidators)	.50
15	Dan Miceli (Phenoms)	.15
16	Chipper Jones (Sterling)	2.00
17	John Wetteland (Intimidators)	.15
18	Kirby Puckett (Sterling)	7.50
19	Tim Naehring (Gamers)	.15
20	Karim Garcia (Phenoms)	2.00
21	Eddie Murray (Gamers)	1.25
22	Tim Salmon/S (Intimidators)	.50
23	Kevin Appier (Intimidators)	.15
24	Ken Griffey Jr. (Sterling)	3.00
25	Cal Ripken Jr./G (Gamers)	15.00
26	Brian McRae (Gamers)	.15
27	Pedro Martinez (Intimidators)	1.25
28	Brian Jordan (Gamers)	.15
29	Mike Fetters (Intimidators)	.15
30	Carlos Delgado (Phenoms)	.65
31	Shane Reynolds (Intimidators)	.15
32	Terry Steinbach (Gamers)	.15
33	Hideo Nomo/G (Sterling)	2.50
34	Mark Leiter (Gamers)	.15
35	Edgar Martinez/S (Intimidators)	.50
36	David Segui (Gamers)	.15
37	Gregg Jefferies/S (Gamers)	.50
38	Bill Pulsipher/S (Phenoms)	.50
39	Ryne Sandberg/G (Gamers)	7.50
40	Fred McGriff (Intimidators)	.15
41	Shawn Green/S (Phenoms)	.75
42	Jeff Bagwell/G (Sterling)	5.00
43	Jim Abbott/S (Gamers)	.50
44	Glenallen Hill (Intimidators)	.15
45	Brady Anderson (Gamers)	.15
46	Roger Clemens/S (Intimidators)	3.50
47	Jim Thome (Gamers)	.60
48	Frank Thomas (Sterling)	1.25
49	Chuck Knoblauch (Gamers)	.15
50	Lenny Dykstra (Gamers)	.15
51	Jason Isringhausen/G (Phenoms)	2.00
52	Rondell White/S (Phenoms)	.50
53	Tom Pagnozzi (Gamers)	.15
54	Dennis Eckersley/S (Intimidators)	1.50
55	Ricky Bones (Gamers)	.15
56	David Justice (Intimidators)	.15
57	Steve Avery (Gamers)	.15
58	Robby Thompson (Gamers)	.15
59	Hideo Nomo/S (Phenoms)	1.00
60	Gary Sheffield/S (Intimidators)	.75
61	Tony Gwynn (Sterling)	2.00
62	Will Clark/S (Gamers)	.50
63	Denny Neagle (Gamers)	.15
64	Mo Vaughn/G (Intimidators)	2.00
65	Bret Boone/S (Gamers)	.50
66	Dante Bichette/S (Sterling)	2.00
67	Robin Ventura (Intimidators)	.15
68	Rafael Palmeiro/S (Intimidators)	1.50
69	Carlos Baerga/S (Gamers)	.15
70	Kevin Seitzer (Gamers)	.15
71	Ramon Martinez (Intimidators)	.15
72	Tom Glavine/S (Gamers)	.50
73	Garret Anderson/S (Phenoms)	.50
74	Mark McGwire/G (Intimidators)	12.00
75	Brian Hunter (Phenoms)	.15
76	Alan Benes (Phenoms)	.15
77	Randy Johnson/S (Intimidators)	2.00
78	Jeff King/S (Gamers)	.50
79	Kirby Puckett/S (Intimidators)	3.00
80	Ozzie Guillen (Gamers)	.15
81	Kenny Lofton/S (Intimidators)	2.00
82	Benji Gil (Phenoms)	.15
83	Jim Edmonds/S (Gamers)	2.00
84	Cecil Fielder (Intimidators)	.50
85	Todd Hundley (Gamers)	.15
86	Reggie Sanders/S (Intimidators)	.50
87	Pat Hentgen (Gamers)	.15
88	Ryan Klesko/S (Intimidators)	.50
89	Chuck Finley (Gamers)	.15
90	Mike Mussina/G (Intimidators)	2.50
91	John Valentin/S (Intimidators)	.50
92	Derek Jeter (Phenoms)	4.00
93	Paul O'Neill (Intimidators)	.15
94	Darrin Fletcher (Gamers)	.15
95	Manny Ramirez/S (Phenoms)	2.00
96	Delino DeShields (Gamers)	.15
97	Tim Salmon (Sterling)	.15
98	John Olerud (Gamers)	.15
99	Vinny Castilla/S (Intimidators)	.50
100	Jeff Conine/G (Gamers)	2.00
101	Tim Wakefield (Gamers)	.15
102	Johnny Damon/G (Phenoms)	3.50
103	Dave Stevens (Gamers)	.15
104	Orlando Merced (Gamers)	.15
105	Barry Bonds/G (Sterling)	15.00
106	Jay Bell (Gamers)	.15
107	John Burkett (Gamers)	.15
108	Chris Hoiles (Gamers)	.15
109	Carlos Perez/S (Phenoms)	.50
110	Dave Nilsson (Gamers)	.15
111	Rod Beck (Intimidators)	.15
112	Craig Biggio/S (Gamers)	.50
113	Mike Piazza (Intimidators)	3.00
114	Mark Langston (Gamers)	.15
115	Juan Gonzalez/S (Intimidators)	1.00
116	Rico Brogna (Gamers)	.15
117	Jose Canseco/S (Intimidators)	3.00
118	Tom Goodwin (Gamers)	.15
119	Bryan Rekar (Phenoms)	.15
120	David Cone (Intimidators)	.15
121	Ray Durham/S (Phenoms)	.50
122	Andy Pettitte (Phenoms)	.40
123	Chili Davis (Intimidators)	.15
124	John Smoltz (Gamers)	.15
125	Heathcliff Slocumb (Intimidators)	.15
126	Dante Bichette (Intimidators)	.15
127	C.J. Nitkowski/S (Phenoms)	.50
128	Alex Gonzalez (Phenoms)	.15
129	Jeff Montgomery (Intimidators)	.15
130	Raul Mondesi/S (Intimidators)	.50
131	Denny Martinez (Gamers)	.15
132	Mel Rojas (Intimidators)	.15
133	Derek Bell (Gamers)	.15
134	Trevor Hoffman (Intimidators)	.15
135	Ken Griffey Jr./G (Intimidators)	9.00
136	Darren Daulton (Gamers)	.15
137	Pete Schourek (Gamers)	.15
138	Phil Nevin (Phenoms)	.15
139	Andres Galarraga (Intimidators)	.15
140	Chad Fonville (Phenoms)	.15
141	Chipper Jones/G (Phenoms)	8.00
142	Lee Smith/S (Intimidators)	.50
143	Joe Carter/S (Gamers)	.50
144	J.T. Snow (Gamers)	.15
145	Greg Maddux/S (Sterling)	7.50
146	Barry Bonds (Intimidators)	4.00
147	Orel Hershiser (Gamers)	.15
148	Quilvio Veras (Phenoms)	.15
149	Will Clark (Sterling)	.15
150	Jose Rijo (Gamers)	.15
151	Mo Vaughn/S (Sterling)	.50
152	Travis Fryman (Gamers)	.15
153	Frank Rodriguez/S (Phenoms)	.15
154	Alex Fernandez (Gamers)	.15
155	Wade Boggs (Gamers)	2.00
156	Troy Percival (Gamers)	.15
157	Moises Alou (Gamers)	.15
158	Javy Lopez (Gamers)	.15
159	Jason Giambi (Phenoms)	.50
160	Steve Finley/S (Gamers)	.50
161	Jeff Bagwell (Intimidators)	2.00
162	Mark McGwire (Sterling)	3.50
163	Eric Karros (Gamers)	.15
164	Jay Buhner/G (Intimidators)	2.00
165	Cal Ripken Jr./S (Sterling)	6.00
166	Mickey Tettleton (Intimidators)	.15
167	Barry Larkin (Intimidators)	.15
168	Lyle Mouton/S (Phenoms)	.50
169	Ruben Sierra (Intimidators)	.15
170	Bill Swift (Gamers)	.15
171	Sammy Sosa/S (Intimidators)	3.00
172	Chad Curtis (Gamers)	.15
173	Dean Palmer (Gamers)	.15
174	John Franco/S (Gamers)	.50
175	Bobby Bonilla (Intimidators)	.15
176	Greg Colbrunn (Gamers)	.15
177	Jose Mesa (Intimidators)	.15
178	Mike Greenwell (Gamers)	.15
179	Greg Vaughn/S (Intimidators)	.50
180	Mark Wohlers/S (Intimidators)	.50
181	Doug Drabek (Gamers)	.15
182	Paul O'Neill/S (Sterling)	.50
183	Wilson Alvarez (Gamers)	.15
184	Marty Cordova (Sterling)	.15
185	Hal Morris (Gamers)	.15
186	Frank Thomas/S (Intimidators)	6.00
187	Carlos Garcia (Gamers)	.15
188	Albert Belle/S (Intimidators)	.50
189	Mark Grace/S (Gamers)	.50
190	Marquis Grissom (Gamers)	.15
191	Checklist	.15
192	Chipper Jones/G	8.00
193	Will Clark	.15
194	Paul Molitor	1.25
195	Kenny Rogers	.15
196	Reggie Sanders	.15
197	Roberto Alomar/S	2.50
198	Dennis Eckersley/S	4.00
199	Raul Mondesi	.15
200	Lance Johnson	.15
201	Alvin Mormon	.15
202	George Arias/G	2.00
203	Jack McDowell	.15
204	Randy Myers	.15
205	Harold Baines	.15
206	Marty Cordova	.15
207	Rich Hunter RC	.15
208	Al Leiter	.15
209	Greg Gagne	.15
210	Ben McDonald	.15
211	Ernie Young/S	.50
212	Terry Adams	.15
213	Paul Sorrento	.15
214	Albert Belle	.15
215	Mike Blowers	.15
216	Jim Edmonds	.15
217	Felipe Crespo	.15
218	Fred McGriff/S	.15
219	Shawon Dunston	.15
220	Jimmy Haynes	.15
221	Jose Canseco	.50
222	Eric Davis	.15
223	Kimera Bartee/S	.15
224	Tim Raines	.15
225	Tony Phillips	.15
226	Charlie Hayes	.15
227	Eric Owens	.15
228	Roberto Alomar	.30
229	Rickey Henderson/S	2.00
230	Sterling Hitchcock/S	.50
231	Bernard Gilkey/S	.50
232	Hideo Nomo/G	2.50
233	Kenny Lofton	.15
234	Ryne Sandberg/S	3.00
235	Greg Maddux/S	3.00
236	Mark McGwire	3.50
237	Jay Buhner	.15
238	Craig Biggio	.15
239	Todd Stottlemyre/S	.15
240	Barry Bonds	4.00
241	Jason Kendall/S	.15
242	Paul O'Neill/S	.50
243	Chris Snopek/S	2.00
244	Ron Gant	.15
245	Paul Wilson	.15
246	Todd Hollandsworth	.15
247	Todd Zeile	.15
248	David Justice	.15
249	Tim Salmon/G	2.00
250	Moises Alou	.15
251	Bob Wolcott	.15
252	David Wells	.15
253	Juan Gonzalez	.65
254	Andres Galarraga	.15
255	Dave Hollins	.15
256	Devon White/S	.50
257	Sammy Sosa	.50
258	Ivan Rodriguez	.75
259	Bip Roberts	.15
260	Tino Martinez	.15
261	Chuck Knoblauch/S	.50
262	Mike Stanley	.15
263	Wally Joyner/S	.50
264	Butch Huskey	.15
265	Jeff Conine	.15
266	Matt Williams/G	2.00
267	Mark Grace	.15
268	Jason Schmidt	.15
269	Otis Nixon	.15
270	Randy Johnson/S	5.00
271	Kirby Puckett	2.00
272	Andy Fox/S RC	.50
273	Andy Benes	.15
274	Sean Berry/S	.15
275	Mike Piazza	3.00
276	Rey Ordonez	.50
277	Benito Santiago/S	.50
278	Gary Gaetti	.15
279	Paul Molitor/G	5.00
280	Robin Ventura	.15
281	Cal Ripken Jr.	4.00
282	Carlos Baerga	.15
283	Roger Cedeno	.15
284	Chad Mottola/G	.50
285	Terrell Wade	.15
286	Kevin Brown	.15
287	Rafael Palmeiro	1.00
288	Mo Vaughn	.50
289	Dante Bichette/S	.50
290	Cecil Fielder/G	2.00
291	Doc Gooden/S	.50
292	Bob Tewksbury	.15
293	Kevin Mitchell/S	.15
294	Livan Hernandez/G RC	2.00
295	Russ Davis/S	.50
296	Chan Ho Park/S	.50
297	T.J. Mathews	.15
298	Manny Ramirez	1.25
299	Jeff Bagwell	1.25
300	Marty Janzen/G RC	2.00
301	Wade Boggs	2.00
302	Larry Walker/S	.15
303	Steve Gibralter	.15
304	B.J. Surhoff	.15
305	Ken Griffey Jr./S	4.00
306	Royce Clayton	.15
307	Sal Fasano	.15
308	Ron Gant/S	2.00
309	Gary Sheffield	.40
310	Ken Hill	.15
311	Joe Girardi	.15
312	Matt Lawton RC	.15
313	Billy Wagner/S	.50
314	Julio Franco	.15
315	Joe Carter	.15
316	Brooks Kieschnick	.15
317	Mike Grace/S RC	.50
318	Heathcliff Slocumb	.15
319	Barry Larkin	.15
320	Tony Gwynn	2.00
321	Ryan Klesko/G	2.00
322	Frank Thomas	1.25
323	Edgar Martinez	.15
324	Jermaine Dye/G	2.00
325	Henry Rodriguez	.15
326	Marvin Benard RC	.50
327	Kenny Lofton/S	.50
328	Derek Bell/S	.15
329	Ugueth Urbina	.15
330	Jason Giambi/G	3.00
331	Roger Salkeld	.15
332	Edgar Renteria	.15
333	Ryan Klesko	.15
334	Ray Lankford	.15
335	Edgar Martinez/G	2.00
336	Justin Thompson	.15
337	Gary Sheffield/S	.75
338	Rey Ordonez/G	2.00
339	Mark Clark	.15
340	Ruben Rivera	.15
341	Mark Grace/S	.50
342	Matt Williams	.15
343	Francisco Cordova RC	.25
344	Cecil Fielder	.15
345	Andres Galarraga/S	.50
346	Brady Anderson/S	.50
347	Sammy Sosa/S	7.50
348	Mark Grudzielanek	.15
349	Ron Coomer	.15
350	Derek Jeter/S	6.00
351	Rich Aurilia	.15
352	Jose Herrera	.15
353	Jay Buhner/S	.50
354	Juan Gonzalez/G	2.50
355	Craig Biggio/G	2.00
356	Tony Clark	.50
357	Tino Martinez/S	.50
358	Dan Naulty RC	.15
359	Checklist	.15

Refractors

Finest Refractor cards were created as a parallel set to Topps' 1996 Finest set. Rare Refractor cards are found about one per 288 packs (less than 150 of these sets were produced), while Uncommon Refractors are found one every 48 packs. Common Refractors are seeded one every 12 packs.

	NM/M
Complete Set (359):	900.00
Bronze Set (220):	300.00
Common Bronze:	1.00
Bronze Stars:	4X
Silver Set (91):	250.00
Typical Silver:	2.00
Silver Stars:	2.5X
Gold Set (48):	600.00
Typical Gold:	6.00
Gold Stars:	2X

1997 Finest Samples

Many of the subsets included in the 1997 Finest issue were previewed with a cello-wrapped pack of five cards distributed to hobby dealers. Cards are virtually identical to the issued versions and are designated a Refractor on back. Overprinted on back is a red notice, "PROMOTIONAL SAMPLE / NOT FOR RESALE."

		NM/M
Complete Set (5):		15.00
Common Player:		2.50
1	Barry Bonds	3.50
15	Derek Jeter	3.50
30	Mark McGwire	3.00
143	Hideo Nomo	2.50
159	Jeff Bagwell	2.50

1997 Finest

Finest returned for 1997 in its three-tiered format from 1996, but added several new twists. Issued in two series of 175 cards each, cards numbered 1-100 and 176-275 are bronze; 101-150 and 276-325 are silver and 151-175 and 326-350 are gold. All cards are designated among one of five different subsets per series. In Series 1 they are: Warriors, Blue Chips, Power, Hurlers and Masters. Series 2 subsets are: Power, Masters, Blue Chips, Competitors and Acquisitions. The bronze cards are the "common" card, while silvers are found every four packs and golds every 24 packs. Each card has a parallel Refractor version: bronze (1:12), silver (1:48) and gold (1:288). In addition, silver and gold cards have an additional parallel set. Silvers are found in an embossed version (1:16) and embossed Refractor version (1:192), while golds are found in a die-cut embossed version (1:96) and a die-cut embossed Refractor (1:1152).

	NM/M
Complete Set (350):	200.00
Bronze Set (200):	15.00
Common Bronze:	.15
Silver Set (100):	75.00
Typical Silver:	.50
Embossed Silvers:	2X

Gold Set (50):	150.00		
Typical Gold:	2.00		
Embossed Die-Cut Golds:	1.5X		
Series 1 or 2 Pack (6):	1.50		
Series 1 or 2 Wax Box (24):	25.00		
1	Barry Bonds/B	2.00
2	Ryne Sandberg/B	.75
3	Brian Jordan/B	.15
4	Rocky Coppinger/B	.15
5	Dante Bichette/B	.15
6	Al Martin/B	.15
7	Charles Nagy/B	.15
8	Otis Nixon/B	.15
9	Mark Johnson/B	.15
10	Jeff Bagwell/B	.60
11	Ken Hill/B	.15
12	Willie Adams/B	.15
13	Raul Mondesi/B	.15
14	Reggie Sanders/B	.15
15	Derek Jeter/B	2.00
16	Jermaine Dye/B	.15
17	Edgar Renteria/B	.15
18	Travis Fryman/B	.15
19	Roberto Hernandez/B	.15
20	Sammy Sosa/B	.75
21	Garret Anderson/B	.15
22	Rey Ordonez/B	.15
23	Glenallen Hill/B	.15
24	Dave Nilsson/B	.15
25	Kevin Brown/B	.15
26	Brian McRae/B	.15
27	Joey Hamilton/B	.15
28	Jamey Wright/B	.15
29	Frank Thomas/B	.60
30	Mark McGwire/B	1.50
31	Ramon Martinez/B	.15
32	Jaime Bluma/B	.15
33	Frank Rodriguez/B	.15
34	Andy Benes/B	.15
35	Jay Buhner/B	.15
36	Justin Thompson/B	.15
37	Darin Erstad/B	.30
38	Gregg Jefferies/B	.15
39	Jeff D'Amico/B	.15
40	Pedro Martinez/B	.60
41	Nomar Garciaparra/B	.75
42	Jose Valentin/B	.15
43	Pat Hentgen/B	.15
44	Will Clark/B	.15
45	Bernie Williams/B	.15
46	Luis Castillo/B	.15
47	B.J. Surhoff/B	.15
48	Greg Gagne/B	.15
49	Pete Schourek/B	.15
50	Mike Piazza/B	1.00
51	Dwight Gooden/B	.15
52	Javy Lopez/B	.15
53	Chuck Finley/B	.15
54	James Baldwin/B	.15
55	Jack McDowell/B	.15
56	Royce Clayton/B	.15
57	Carlos Delgado/B	.35
58	Neifi Perez/B	.15
59	Eddie Taubensee/B	.15
60	Rafael Palmeiro/B	.50
61	Marty Cordova/B	.15
62	Wade Boggs/B	.75
63	Rickey Henderson/B	.60
64	Mike Hampton/B	.15
65	Troy Percival/B	.15
66	Barry Larkin/B	.15
67	Jermaine Allensworth/B	.15
68	Mark Clark/B	.15
69	Mike Lansing/B	.15
70	Mark Grudzielanek/B	.15
71	Todd Stottlemyre/B	.15
72	Juan Guzman/B	.15
73	John Burkett/B	.15
74	Wilson Alvarez/B	.15
75	Ellis Burks/B	.15
76	Bobby Higginson/B	.15
77	Ricky Bottalico/B	.15
78	Omar Vizquel/B	.15
79	Paul Sorrento/B	.15
80	Denny Neagle/B	.15
81	Roger Pavlik/B	.15
82	Mike Lieberthal/B	.15
83	Devon White/B	.15
84	John Olerud/B	.15
85	Kevin Appier/B	.15
86	Joe Girardi/ B	.15
87	Paul O'Neill/B	.15
88	Mike Sweeney/B	.15
89	John Smiley/B	.15
90	Ivan Rodriguez/B	.50
91	Randy Myers/B	.15
92	Bip Roberts/B	.15
93	Jose Mesa/B	.15
94	Paul Wilson/B	.15
95	Mike Mussina/B	.30
96	Ben McDonald/B	.15
97	John Mabry/B	.15
98	Tom Goodwin/B	.15
99	Edgar Martinez/B	.15
100	Andruw Jones/B	.60
101	Jose Canseco/S	.75
102	Billy Wagner/S	.50
103	Dante Bichette/S	.50
104	Curt Schilling/S	1.00
105	Dean Palmer/S	.50
106	Larry Walker/S	.50
107	Bernie Williams/S	.50
108	Chipper Jones/S	2.00
109	Gary Sheffield/S	1.00
110	Randy Johnson/S	1.50
111	Roberto Alomar/S	.75
112	Todd Walker/S	.50
113	Sandy Alomar/S	.50

114	John Jaha/S	.50
115	Ken Caminiti/S	.50
116	Ryan Klesko/S	.50
117	Mariano Rivera/S	.75
118	Jason Giambi/S	1.00
119	Lance Johnson/S	.50
120	Robin Ventura/S	.50
121	Todd Hollandsworth/S	.50
122	Johnny Damon/S	.75
123	William Van Landingham/S	.50
124	Jason Kendall/S	.50
125	Vinny Castilla/S	.50
126	Harold Baines/S	.50
127	Joe Carter/S	.50
128	Craig Biggio/S	.50
129	Tony Clark/S	.50
130	Ron Gant/S	.50
131	David Segui/S	.50
132	Steve Trachsel/S	.50
133	Scott Rolen/S	1.00
134	Mike Stanley/S	.50
135	Cal Ripken Jr./S	5.00
136	John Smoltz/S	.50
137	Bobby Jones/S	.50
138	Manny Ramirez/S	1.50
139	Ken Griffey Jr./S	3.00
140	Chuck Knoblauch/S	.50
141	Mark Grace/S	.50
142	Chris Snopek/S	.50
143	Hideo Nomo/S	.75
144	Tim Salmon/S	.50
145	David Cone/S	.50
146	Eric Young/S	.50
147	Jeff Brantley/S	.50
148	Jim Thome/S	1.00
149	Trevor Hoffman/S	.50
150	Juan Gonzalez/S	.75
151	Mike Piazza/G	8.00
152	Ivan Rodriguez/G	4.00
153	Mo Vaughn/G	2.00
154	Brady Anderson/G	2.00
155	Mark McGwire/G	8.00
156	Rafael Palmeiro/G	4.00
157	Barry Larkin/G	2.00
158	Greg Maddux/G	7.50
159	Jeff Bagwell/G	5.00
160	Frank Thomas/G	6.00
161	Ken Caminiti/G	2.00
162	Andruw Jones/G	4.00
163	Dennis Eckersley/G	2.00
164	Jeff Conine/G	2.00
165	Jim Edmonds/G	2.00
166	Derek Jeter/G	12.00
167	Vladimir Guerrero/G	6.00
168	Sammy Sosa/G	5.00
169	Tony Gwynn/G	6.00
170	Andres Galarraga/G	2.00
171	Todd Hundley/G	2.00
172	Jay Buhner/G	2.00
173	Paul Molitor/G	6.00
174	Kenny Lofton/G	2.00
175	Barry Bonds/G	12.00
176	Gary Sheffield/G	.35
177	Dmitri Young/B	.15
178	Jay Bell/B	.15
179	David Wells/B	.15
180	Walt Weiss/B	.15
181	Paul Molitor/B	.60
182	Jose Guillen/B	.15
183	Al Leiter/B	.15
184	Mike Fetters/B	.15
185	Mark Langston/B	.15
186	Fred McGriff/B	.15
187	Darrin Fletcher/B	.15
188	Brant Brown/B	.15
189	Geronimo Berroa/B	.15
190	Jim Thome/B	.15
191	Jose Vizcaino/B	.15
192	Andy Ashby/B	.15
193	Rusty Greer/B	.15
194	Brian Hunter/B	.15
195	Chris Hoiles/B	.15
196	Orlando Merced/B	.15
197	Brett Butler/B	.15
198	Derek Bell/B	.15
199	Bobby Bonilla/B	.15
200	Alex Ochoa/B	.15
201	Wally Joyner/B	.15
202	Mo Vaughn/B	.15
203	Doug Drabek/B	.15
204	Tino Martinez/B	.30
205	Roberto Alomar/B	.30
206	Brian Giles/B RC	.75
207	Todd Worrell/B	.15
208	Alan Benes/B	.15
209	Jim Leyritz/B	.15
210	Darryl Hamilton/B	.15
211	Jimmy Key/B	.15
212	Juan Gonzalez/B	.35
213	Vinny Castilla/B	.15
214	Chuck Knoblauch/B	.15
215	Tony Phillips/B	.15
216	Jeff Cirillo/B	.15
217	Carlos Garcia/B	.15
218	Brooks Kieschnick/B	.15
219	Marquis Grissom/B	.15
220	Dan Wilson/B	.15
221	Greg Vaughn/B	.15
222	John Wetteland/B	.15
223	Andres Galarraga/B	.15
224	Ozzie Guillen/B	.15
225	Kevin Elster/B	.15
226	Bernard Gilkey/B	.15
227	Mike MacFarlane/B	.15
228	Heathcliff Slocumb/B	.15
229	Wendell Magee Jr./B	.15
230	Carlos Baerga/B	.15

231	Kevin Seitzer/B	.15
232	Henry Rodriguez/B	.15
233	Roger Clemens/B	1.00
234	Mark Wohlers/B	.15
235	Eddie Murray/B	.60
236	Todd Zeile/B	.15
237	J.T. Snow/B	.15
238	Ken Griffey Jr./B	1.00
239	Sterling Hitchcock/B	.15
240	Albert Belle/B	.15
241	Terry Steinbach/B	.15
242	Robb Nen/B	.15
243	Mark McLemore/B	.15
244	Jeff King/B	.15
245	Tony Clark/B	.15
246	Tim Salmon/B	.15
247	Benito Santiago/B	.15
248	Robin Ventura/B	.15
249	Bubba Trammell/B RC	.15
250	Chili Davis/B	.15
251	John Valentin/B	.15
252	Cal Ripken Jr./B	2.00
253	Matt Williams/B	.15
254	Jeff Kent/B	.15
255	Eric Karros/B	.15
256	Ray Lankford/B	.15
257	Ed Sprague/B	.15
258	Shane Reynolds/B	.15
259	Jaime Navarro/B	.15
260	Eric Davis/B	.15
261	Orel Hershiser/B	.15
262	Mark Grace/B	.15
263	Rod Beck/B	.15
264	Ismael Valdes/B	.15
265	Manny Ramirez/B	.60
266	Ken Caminiti/B	.15
267	Tim Naehring/B	.15
268	Jose Rosado/B	.15
269	Greg Colbrunn/B	.15
270	Dean Palmer/B	.15
271	David Justice/B	.15
272	Scott Spiezio/B	.15
273	Chipper Jones/B	.75
274	Mel Rojas/B	.15
275	Bartolo Colon/B	.15
276	Darin Erstad/S	1.00
277	Sammy Sosa/S	2.00
278	Rafael Palmeiro/S	1.00
279	Frank Thomas/S	1.50
280	Ruben Rivera/S	.50
281	Hal Morris/S	.50
282	Jay Buhner/S	.50
283	Kenny Lofton/S	.50
284	Jose Canseco/S	.75
285	Alex Fernandez/S	.50
286	Todd Helton/S	1.25
287	Andy Pettitte/S	1.00
288	John Franco/S	.50
289	Ivan Rodriguez/S	1.25
290	Ellis Burks/S	.50
291	Julio Franco/S	.50
292	Mike Piazza/S	3.00
293	Brian Jordan/S	.50
294	Greg Maddux/S	2.00
295	Bob Abreu/S	.50
296	Rondell White/S	.50
297	Moises Alou/S	.50
298	Tony Gwynn/S	2.00
299	Deion Sanders/S	.50
300	Jeff Montgomery/S	.50
301	Ray Durham/S	.50
302	John Wasdin/S	.50
303	Ryne Sandberg/S	.75
304	Delino DeShields/S	.50
305	Mark McGwire/S	3.00
306	Andruw Jones/S	1.50
307	Kevin Orie/S	.50
308	Matt Williams/S	.50
309	Karim Garcia/S	.50
310	Derek Jeter/S	5.00
311	Mo Vaughn/S	1.00
312	Brady Anderson/S	.50
313	Barry Bonds/S	5.00
314	Steve Finley/S	.50
315	Vladimir Guerrero/S	1.50
316	Matt Morris/S	.50
317	Tom Glavine/S	1.00
318	Jeff Bagwell/S	1.50
319	Albert Belle/S	.50
320	Hideki Irabu/S RC	1.00
321	Andres Galarraga/S	.50
322	Cecil Fielder/S	.50
323	Barry Larkin/S	.50
324	Todd Hundley/S	.50
325	Fred McGriff/S	.50
326	Gary Sheffield/G	3.00
327	Craig Biggio/G	2.00
328	Raul Mondesi/G	2.00
329	Edgar Martinez/G	2.00
330	Chipper Jones/G	8.00
331	Bernie Williams/G	3.00
332	Juan Gonzalez/G	3.00
333	Ron Gant/G	2.00
334	Cal Ripken Jr./G	12.00
335	Larry Walker/G	2.00
336	Matt Williams/G	2.00
337	Jose Cruz Jr./G	2.00
338	Joe Carter/G	2.00
339	Wilton Guerrero/G	2.00
340	Cecil Fielder/G	2.00
341	Todd Walker/G	2.00
342	Ken Griffey Jr./G	10.00
343	Ryan Klesko/G	2.00
344	Roger Clemens/G	10.00
345	Hideo Nomo/G	3.00
346	Dante Bichette/G	2.00
347	Albert Belle/G	2.00
348	Randy Johnson/G	6.00

349	Manny Ramirez/G	6.00
350	John Smoltz/G	2.00

Embossed

Each Uncommon (silver) and Rare (gold) card in both Series 1 and 2 Finest was also issued in a parallel Embossed version. The Embossed Silver were a 1:16 find, while the die-cut Embossed Gold were found on average of just one per 96 packs.

	NM/M
Common Embossed Silver:	1.00
Embossed Silver Stars:	2X
Common Embossed Gold:	3.00
Embossed/Die-Cut Gold Stars:	1.5X

Refractors

Every card in '97 Finest - both regular and embossed parallel - has a Refractor version. The Uncommon parallel set of Refractors features a mosaic pattern in the background while the Rare embossed die-cut parallel set of Refractors are produced with a hyper-plaid foil design. The number of cards and the insertion ratios for each level of Refractors is as follows: Common (200 cards, 1:12 packs), Uncommon (100, 1:48), Rare (50, 1:288), Embossed Uncommon (100, 1:192), Embossed Die-cut Rare (50, 1:1152).

	NM/M
Common Bronze:	2.00
Bronze Stars:	6X
Typical Silver:	3.00
Silver Stars:	3X
Typical Gold:	8.00
Gold Stars:	2X
Typical Embossed Silver:	7.50
Embossed Silver Stars:	7X
Typical Embossed Gold:	20.00
Embossed Gold Stars:	5X

1998 Finest Pre-Production

Five-card cello packs of '98 Finest were distributed in the hobby market to preview the always-popular issue. The cards are virtually identical to the issued versions except for the card number, which bears a "PP" prefix.

		NM/M
Complete Set (5):		8.00
Common Player:		2.00
1	Nomar Garciaparra	2.25
2	Mark McGwire	3.00
3	Ivan Rodriguez	2.00
4	Ken Griffey Jr.	2.50
5	Roger Clemens	2.25

1998 Finest

Finest dropped its three-tiered format in 1998 and produced a 275-card set on a thicker 26-point stock, with 150 cards in Series 1 and 125 in Series 2. The catch in 1998 was that each card arrived in Protector, No-Protector, Protector

Refractor and No-Protector Refractor versions. Six-card packs sold for a suggested retail price of $5. Finest also included insert sets for the first time since 1995. Included in Series 1 packs were Centurions, Mystery Finest and Power Zone inserts. Series 2 had Mystery Finest, Stadium Stars and The Man. Throughout both series, Finest Protector cards are considered base cards, while No-Protector are inserted one per two packs (HTA odds 1:1), No-Protector Refractors are seeded 1:24 packs (HTA odds 1:10) and Finest Refractors are seeded 1:12 packs (HTA odds 1:5).

		NM/M
Complete Set (275):		30.00
Common Player:		.15
No-Protector:		2.5X
Refractors:		4X
No-Protector Refractor:		8X
Pack (6):		1.50
Wax Box (24):		25.00
Jumbo Pack (13):		2.50
Jumbo Box (12):		25.00
1	Larry Walker	.15
2	Andruw Jones	.75
3	Ramon Martinez	.15
4	Geronimo Berroa	.15
5	David Justice	.15
6	Rusty Greer	.15
7	Chad Ogea	.15
8	Tom Goodwin	.15
9	Tino Martinez	.15
10	Jose Guillen	.15
11	Jeffrey Hammonds	.15
12	Brian McRae	.15
13	Jeremi Gonzalez	.15
14	Craig Counsell	.15
15	Mike Piazza	1.50
16	Greg Maddux	1.00
17	Todd Greene	.15
18	Rondell White	.15
19	Kirk Rueter	.15
20	Tony Clark	.15
21	Brad Radke	.15
22	Jaret Wright	.15
23	Carlos Delgado	.50
24	Dustin Hermanson	.15
25	Gary Sheffield	.40
26	Jose Canseco	.35
27	Kevin Young	.15
28	David Wells	.15
29	Mariano Rivera	.25
30	Reggie Sanders	.15
31	Mike Cameron	.15
32	Bobby Witt	.15
33	Kevin Orie	.15
34	Royce Clayton	.15
35	Edgar Martinez	.15
36	Neifi Perez	.15
37	Kevin Appier	.15
38	Darryl Hamilton	.15
39	Michael Tucker	.15
40	Roger Clemens	1.25
41	Carl Everett	.15
42	Mike Sweeney	.15
43	Pat Meares	.15
44	Brian Giles	.15
45	Matt Morris	.15
46	Jason Dickson	.15
47	Rich Loiselle	.15
48	Joe Girardi	.15
49	Steve Trachsel	.15
50	Ben Grieve	.15
51	Jose Vizcaino	.15
52	Hideki Irabu	.15
53	J.T. Snow	.15
54	Mike Hampton	.15
55	Dave Nilsson	.15
56	Alex Fernandez	.15
57	Brett Tomko	.15
58	Wally Joyner	.15
59	Kelvim Escobar	.15
60	Roberto Alomar	.30
61	Todd Jones	.15
62	Paul O'Neill	.15
63	Jamie Moyer	.15
64	Mark Wohlers	.15
65	Jose Cruz Jr.	.15
66	Troy Percival	.15
67	Rick Reed	.15
68	Will Clark	.15

69	Jamey Wright	.15
70	Mike Mussina	.35
71	David Cone	.15
72	Ryan Klesko	.15
73	Scott Hatteberg	.15
74	James Baldwin	.15
75	Tony Womack	.15
76	Carlos Perez	.15
77	Charles Nagy	.15
78	Jeromy Burnitz	.15
79	Shane Reynolds	.15
80	Cliff Floyd	.15
81	Jason Kendall	.15
82	Chad Curtis	.15
83	Matt Karchner	.15
84	Ricky Bottalico	.15
85	Sammy Sosa	1.00
86	Javy Lopez	.15
87	Jeff Kent	.15
88	Shawn Green	.25
89	Devon White	.15
90	Tony Gwynn	1.00
91	Bob Tewksbury	.15
92	Derek Jeter	2.50
93	Eric Davis	.15
94	Jeff Fassero	.15
95	Denny Neagle	.15
96	Ismael Valdes	.15
97	Tim Salmon	.15
98	Mark Grudzielanek	.15
99	Curt Schilling	.35
100	Ken Griffey Jr.	1.50
101	Edgardo Alfonzo	.15
102	Vinny Castilla	.15
103	Jose Rosado	.15
104	Scott Erickson	.15
105	Alan Benes	.15
106	Shannon Stewart	.15
107	Delino DeShields	.15
108	Mark Loretta	.15
109	Todd Hundley	.15
110	Chuck Knoblauch	.15
111	Quinton McCracken	.15
112	F.P. Santangelo	.15
113	Gerald Williams	.15
114	Omar Vizquel	.15
115	John Valentin	.15
116	Damion Easley	.15
117	Matt Lawton	.15
118	Jim Thome	.60
119	Sandy Alomar	.15
120	Albert Belle	.15
121	Chris Stynes	.15
122	Butch Huskey	.15
123	Shawn Estes	.15
124	Terry Adams	.15
125	Ivan Rodriguez	.60
126	Ron Gant	.15
127	John Mabry	.15
128	Jeff Shaw	.15
129	Jeff Montgomery	.15
130	Justin Thompson	.15
131	Livan Hernandez	.15
132	Ugueth Urbina	.15
133	Doug Glanville	.15
134	Troy O'Leary	.15
135	Cal Ripken Jr.	2.50
136	Quilvio Veras	.15
137	Pedro Astacio	.15
138	Willie Greene	.15
139	Lance Johnson	.15
140	Nomar Garciaparra	1.00
141	Jose Offerman	.15
142	Scott Rolen	.60
143	Derek Bell	.15
144	Johnny Damon	.35
145	Mark McGwire	2.00
146	Chan Ho Park	.15
147	Edgar Renteria	.15
148	Eric Young	.15
149	Craig Biggio	.15
150	Checklist 1-150	.15
151	Frank Thomas	.75
152	John Wetteland	.15
153	Mike Lansing	.15
154	Pedro Martinez	.75
155	Rico Brogna	.15
156	Kevin Brown	.15
157	Alex Rodriguez	2.00
158	Wade Boggs	1.00
159	Richard Hidalgo	.15
160	Mark Grace	.15
161	Jose Mesa	.15
162	John Olerud	.15
163	Tim Belcher	.15
164	Chuck Finley	.15
165	Brian Hunter	.15
166	Joe Carter	.15
167	Stan Javier	.15
168	Jay Bell	.15
169	Ray Lankford	.15
170	John Smoltz	.15
171	Ed Sprague	.15
172	Jason Giambi	.50
173	Todd Walker	.15
174	Paul Konerko	.60
175	Rey Ordonez	.15
176	Dante Bichette	.15
177	Bernie Williams	.15
178	Jon Nunnally	.15
179	Rafael Palmeiro	.60
180	Jay Buhner	.15
181	Devon White	.15
182	Jeff D'Amico	.15
183	Walt Weiss	.15
184	Scott Spiezio	.15
185	Moises Alou	.15
186	Carlos Baerga	.15

187	Todd Zeile	.15
188	Gregg Jefferies	.15
189	Mo Vaughn	.15
190	Terry Steinbach	.15
191	Ray Durham	.15
192	Robin Ventura	.15
193	Jeff Reed	.15
194	Ken Caminiti	.15
195	Eric Karros	.15
196	Wilson Alvarez	.15
197	Gary Gaetti	.15
198	Andres Galarraga	.15
199	Alex Gonzalez	.15
200	Garret Anderson	.15
201	Andy Benes	.15
202	Harold Baines	.15
203	Ron Coomer	.15
204	Dean Palmer	.15
205	Reggie Jefferson	.15
206	John Burkett	.15
207	Jermaine Allensworth	.15
208	Bernard Gilkey	.15
209	Jeff Bagwell	.75
210	Kenny Lofton	.15
211	Bobby Jones	.15
212	Bartolo Colon	.15
213	Jim Edmonds	.15
214	Pat Hentgen	.15
215	Matt Williams	.15
216	Bob Abreu	.15
217	Jorge Posada	.15
218	Marty Cordova	.15
219	Ken Hill	.15
220	Steve Finley	.15
221	Jeff King	.15
222	Quinton McCracken	.15
223	Matt Stairs	.15
224	Darin Erstad	.35
225	Fred McGriff	.15
226	Marquis Grissom	.15
227	Doug Glanville	.15
228	Tom Glavine	.35
229	John Franco	.15
230	Darren Bragg	.15
231	Barry Larkin	.15
232	Trevor Hoffman	.15
233	Brady Anderson	.15
234	Al Martin	.15
235	B.J. Surhoff	.15
236	Ellis Burks	.15
237	Randy Johnson	.75
238	Mark Clark	.15
239	Tony Saunders	.15
240	Hideo Nomo	.40
241	Brad Fullmer	.15
242	Chipper Jones	1.00
243	Jose Valentin	.15
244	Manny Ramirez	.75
245	Derek Lee	.50
246	Jimmy Key	.15
247	Tim Naehring	.15
248	Bobby Higginson	.15
249	Charles Johnson	.15
250	Chili Davis	.15
251	Tom Gordon	.15
252	Mike Lieberthal	.15
253	Billy Wagner	.15
254	Juan Guzman	.15
255	Todd Stottlemyre	.15
256	Brian Jordan	.15
257	Barry Bonds	2.50
258	Dan Wilson	.15
259	Paul Molitor	.75
260	Juan Gonzalez	.40
261	Francisco Cordova	.15
262	Cecil Fielder	.15
263	Travis Lee	.15
264	Kevin Tapani	.15
265	Raul Mondesi	.15
266	Travis Fryman	.15
267	Armando Benitez	.15
268	Pokey Reese	.15
269	Rick Aguilera	.15
270	Andy Pettitte	.35
271	Jose Vizcaino	.15
272	Kerry Wood	.40
273	Vladimir Guerrero	.75
274	John Smiley	.15
275	Checklist 151-275	.15

Refractors

All 275 cards from Finest Series 1 and 2 are available in a Refractor version. seeded one per 12 packs. Besides the refractive qual-ity of the printing of front, Refractors are designated with an "R" suffix to the card number on back.

	NM/M
Complete Set (275):	200.00
Common Player:	1.00
Stars/Rookies:	4X

No-Protector

This parallel to the 275-card base set foregoes the peel-off front protector and adds Finest technology to the back of the card. Stated insertion rates were one per two packs or one per pack in Home Team Advantage (HTA) boxes.

	NM/M
Complete Set (275):	150.00
Common Player:	.50
Stars/Rookies:	2.5X

No-Protector Refractor

A Refractor parallel to the 275 No-Protector parallel cards was a 1:24 pack insert. In Series 1, only the refractive quality of the front and back printing reveals this insert. Series 2 No-Protector Refractors have an "R" suffix to the card number on back.

	NM/M
Complete Set (275):	400.00
Common Player:	2.00
Stars/Rookies:	8X

Centurions

Centurions is a 20-card insert found only Series 1 hobby (1:153) and Home Team Advantage packs (1:71). The theme of the insert to top players who will lead the game into the next century. Each card is sequentially numbered on the back to 500, while Refractor versions are numbered to 75.

	NM/M
Complete Set (20):	75.00
Common Player:	1.50
Production 500 Sets	
Refractors (75 Sets):	4X
C1	Andruw Jones	4.50
C2	Vladimir Guerrero	4.50
C3	Nomar Garciaparra	6.00
C4	Scott Rolen	3.50
C5	Ken Griffey Jr.	8.00
C6	Jose Cruz Jr.	1.50
C7	Barry Bonds	12.00
C8	Mark McGwire	10.00
C9	Juan Gonzalez	2.50
C10	Jeff Bagwell	4.50
C11	Frank Thomas	4.50
C12	Paul Konerko	2.00
C13	Alex Rodriguez	10.00
C14	Mike Piazza	8.00
C15	Travis Lee	1.50
C16	Chipper Jones	6.00
C17	Larry Walker	1.50
C18	Mo Vaughn	1.50
C19	Livan Hernandez	1.50
C20	Jaret Wright	1.50

Mystery Finest

This 50-card insert was seeded one per 36 Series 1 packs and one per 15 HTA packs. The set includes 20 top players, each matched on a double-sided card with three other players and once with himself. Each side of the card is printed on a chromium finish and arrives with a black opaque protector. Mystery Finest inserts are numbered with an "M" prefix. Refractor versions were seeded one per 64 packs (HTA odds 1:15).

		NM/M
Complete Set (50):		125.00
Common Player:		1.50
Refractors:		4X
M1	Frank Thomas, Ken Griffey Jr.	3.00
M2	Frank Thomas, Mike Piazza	3.00
M3	Frank Thomas, Mark McGwire	4.00
M4	Frank Thomas, Frank Thomas	2.00
M5	Ken Griffey Jr., Mike Piazza	3.00
M6	Ken Griffey Jr., Mark McGwire	4.00
M7	Ken Griffey Jr., Ken Griffey Jr.	4.00
M8	Mike Piazza, Mark McGwire	4.00
M9	Mike Piazza, Mike Piazza	4.00
M10	Mark McGwire, Mark McGwire	6.00
M11	Nomar Garciaparra, Jose Cruz Jr.	2.50
M12	Nomar Garciaparra, Derek Jeter	5.00
M13	Nomar Garciaparra, Andruw Jones	2.50
M14	Nomar Garciaparra, Nomar Garciaparra	3.00
M15	Jose Cruz Jr., Derek Jeter	5.00
M16	Jose Cruz Jr., Andruw Jones	1.50
M17	Jose Cruz Jr., Jose Cruz Jr.	1.50
M18	Derek Jeter, Andruw Jones	5.00
M19	Derek Jeter, Derek Jeter	7.50
M20	Andruw Jones, Andruw Jones	2.00
M21	Cal Ripken Jr., Tony Gwynn	5.00
M22	Cal Ripken Jr., Barry Bonds	5.00
M23	Cal Ripken Jr., Greg Maddux	5.00
M24	Cal Ripken Jr., Cal Ripken Jr.	7.50
M25	Tony Gwynn, Barry Bonds	5.00
M26	Tony Gwynn, Greg Maddux	2.50
M27	Tony Gwynn, Tony Gwynn	3.00
M28	Barry Bonds, Greg Maddux	5.00
M29	Barry Bonds, Barry Bonds	7.50
M30	Greg Maddux, Greg Maddux	3.00
M31	Juan Gonzalez, Larry Walker	1.50
M32	Juan Gonzalez, Andres Galarraga	1.50
M33	Juan Gonzalez, Chipper Jones	2.50
M34	Juan Gonzalez, Juan Gonzalez	1.50
M35	Larry Walker, Andres Galarraga	1.50
M36	Larry Walker, Chipper Jones	2.50
M37	Larry Walker, Larry Walker	1.50
M38	Andres Galarraga, Chipper Jones	2.50
M39	Andres Galarraga, Andres Galarraga	1.50
M40	Chipper Jones, Chipper Jones	3.00
M41	Gary Sheffield, Sammy Sosa	3.00
M42	Gary Sheffield, Jeff Bagwell	1.50
M43	Gary Sheffield, Tino Martinez	1.50
M44	Gary Sheffield, Gary Sheffield	2.00
M45	Sammy Sosa, Jeff Bagwell	3.00
M46	Sammy Sosa, Tino Martinez	3.00
M47	Sammy Sosa, Sammy Sosa	3.00
M48	Jeff Bagwell, Tino Martinez	1.50
M49	Jeff Bagwell, Jeff Bagwell	2.00
M50	Tino Martinez, Tino Martinez	1.50

Mystery Finest 2

Forty more Mystery Finest inserts were seeded in Series 2 packs at a rate of one per 36 packs (HTA odds 1:15), with Refrators every 1:144 packs (HTA odds 1:64). As with Series 1, 20 players are in the checklist; some players are found with another player on the back or by himself on each side. Each side is printed in Finest technology with an opaque black protector.

		NM/M
Complete Set (40):		100.00
Common Player:		1.50
Refractors:		4X
M1	Nomar Garciaparra, Frank Thomas	3.50
M2	Nomar Garciaparra, Albert Belle	3.50
M3	Nomar Garciaparra, Scott Rolen	3.50
M4	Frank Thomas, Albert Belle	2.50
M5	Frank Thomas, Scott Rolen	2.50
M6	Albert Belle, Scott Rolen	1.50
M7	Ken Griffey Jr., Jose Cruz	4.00
M8	Ken Griffey Jr., Alex Rodriguez	6.00
M9	Ken Griffey Jr., Roger Clemens	4.50
M10	Jose Cruz, Alex Rodriguez	6.00
M11	Jose Cruz, Roger Clemens	3.00
M12	Alex Rodriguez, Roger Clemens	6.00
M13	Mike Piazza, Barry Bonds	6.00
M14	Mike Piazza, Derek Jeter	6.00
M15	Mike Piazza, Bernie Williams	5.00
M16	Barry Bonds, Derek Jeter	6.50
M17	Barry Bonds, Bernie Williams	4.00
M18	Derek Jeter, Bernie Williams	6.00
M19	Mark McGwire, Jeff Bagwell	4.50
M20	Mark McGwire, Mo Vaughn	5.00
M21	Mark McGwire, Jim Thome	5.00
M22	Jeff Bagwell, Mo Vaughn	2.00
M23	Jeff Bagwell, Jim Thome	1.50
M24	Mo Vaughn, Jim Thome	1.50
M25	Juan Gonzalez, Travis Lee	1.50
M26	Juan Gonzalez, Ben Grieve	1.50
M27	Juan Gonzalez, Fred McGriff	1.50
M28	Travis Lee, Ben Grieve	1.50
M29	Travis Lee, Fred McGriff	1.50
M30	Ben Grieve, Fred McGriff	1.50
M31	Albert Belle, Albert Belle	1.50
M32	Scott Rolen, Scott Rolen	2.00
M33	Alex Rodriguez, Alex Rodriguez	6.00
M34	Roger Clemens, Roger Clemens	4.00
M35	Bernie Williams, Bernie Williams	1.50
M36	Mo Vaughn, Mo Vaughn	1.50
M37	Jim Thome, Jim Thome	1.50
M38	Travis Lee, Travis Lee	1.50
M39	Fred McGriff, Fred McGriff	1.50
M40	Ben Grieve, Ben Grieve	1.50

Mystery Finest Jumbo

Series 2 Home Team Advantage (HTA) boxes were the exclusive venue for these large-format (3" x 5") versions of Mystery Finest. Regular cards were found one per six boxes of HTA, while Refractor versions were a 1:12 seed.

		NM/M
Complete Set (3):		12.50
Common Card:		4.00
Refractor:		1.5X
1	Ken Griffey Jr., Alex Rodriguez	4.00
2	Derek Jeter, Bernie Williams	5.00
3	Mark McGwire, Jeff Bagwell	4.00

Power Zone

This Series 1 insert features Topps' new "Flop Inks" technology which changes the color of the card depending at what angle it is viewed. They are inserted one per 72 hobby packs (HTA odds 1:32). Cards are numbered with a "P" prefix.

		NM/M
Complete Set (20):		25.00
Common Player:		.50
1	Ken Griffey Jr.	3.00
2	Jeff Bagwell	2.00
3	Jose Cruz Jr.	.50
4	Barry Bonds	5.00
5	Mark McGwire	4.00
6	Jim Thome	1.50
7	Mo Vaughn	.50
8	Gary Sheffield	1.00
9	Andres Galarraga	.50
10	Nomar Garciaparra	2.50
11	Rafael Palmeiro	1.50
12	Sammy Sosa	2.50
13	Jay Buhner	.50
14	Tony Clark	.50
15	Mike Piazza	3.00
16	Larry Walker	.50
17	Albert Belle	.50
18	Tino Martinez	.50
19	Juan Gonzalez	1.25
20	Frank Thomas	2.00

Stadium Stars

Stadium Stars is a 24-card insert that features Topps' new lenticular holographic chromium technology. These are exclusive to Series 2 packs and carried an insertion rate of one per 72 packs (HTA odds 1:32).

		NM/M
Complete Set (24):		95.00
Common Player:		1.00
SS1	Ken Griffey Jr.	8.00
SS2	Alex Rodriguez	10.00
SS3	Mo Vaughn	1.00
SS4	Nomar Garciaparra	6.00
SS5	Frank Thomas	4.50
SS6	Albert Belle	1.00
SS7	Derek Jeter	12.00
SS8	Chipper Jones	6.00
SS9	Cal Ripken Jr.	12.00
SS10	Jim Thome	3.00
SS11	Mike Piazza	8.00
SS12	Juan Gonzalez	2.50
SS13	Jeff Bagwell	4.50
SS14	Sammy Sosa	6.00
SS15	Jose Cruz Jr.	1.00
SS16	Gary Sheffield	2.00
SS17	Larry Walker	1.00
SS18	Tony Gwynn	6.00
SS19	Mark McGwire	10.00
SS20	Barry Bonds	12.00
SS21	Tino Martinez	1.00
SS22	Manny Ramirez	4.50
SS23	Ken Caminiti	1.00
SS24	Andres Galarraga	1.00

The Man

This 20-card insert features the top players in baseball and was exclusively found in Series 2 packs. Regular versions are sequentially numbered to 500 and inserted one per 119 packs, while Refractor versions are numbered to 75 and inserted one per 793 packs.

		NM/M
Complete Set (20):		125.00
Common Player:		1.50
Refractors:		3X
TM1	Ken Griffey Jr.	10.00
TM2	Barry Bonds	15.00
TM3	Frank Thomas	6.00
TM4	Chipper Jones	7.50
TM5	Cal Ripken Jr.	15.00
TM6	Nomar Garciaparra	7.50
TM7	Mark McGwire	12.50
TM8	Mike Piazza	10.00
TM9	Derek Jeter	15.00
TM10	Alex Rodriguez	12.50
TM11	Jose Cruz Jr.	1.50
TM12	Larry Walker	1.50
TM13	Jeff Bagwell	6.00
TM14	Tony Gwynn	7.50
TM15	Travis Lee	2.00
TM16	Juan Gonzalez	6.00
TM17	Scott Rolen	4.50
TM18	Randy Johnson	6.00
TM19	Roger Clemens	9.00
TM20	Greg Maddux	7.50

Jumbo

Eight oversized cards were inserted into both Series 1 and Series 2 boxes as box toppers. The cards measure 3" x 5" and are inserted one per three boxes, with Refractor versions every six boxes. The oversized cards are similar to the regular-issue cards except for the numbering which designates each "X of 8."

	NM/M
Complete Set (16):	30.00
Common Player:	1.00
Refractors:	1.5X
1 Mark McGwire	4.00
2 Cal Ripken Jr.	5.00
3 Nomar Garciaparra	2.00
4 Mike Piazza	3.00
5 Greg Maddux	2.00
6 Jose Cruz Jr.	1.00
7 Roger Clemens	2.50
8 Ken Griffey Jr.	3.00
1 Frank Thomas	1.50
2 Bernie Williams	1.00
3 Randy Johnson	1.50
4 Chipper Jones	2.00
5 Manny Ramirez	1.50
6 Barry Bonds	5.00
7 Juan Gonzalez	1.25
8 Jeff Bagwell	1.50

1999 Finest

Released in two series, with each consisting of 100 regular and 50 subset cards divided into three categories: Gems, Sensations and Rookies in Series 1, and Sterling, Gamers and Rookies in the second series. The subset cards are short-printed, seeded one per pack. Cards are printed on 27-point stock utilizing chromium technology. There are two parallels: Refractors and die-cut Gold Refractors. Refractors are seeded 1:12 packs, while Gold Refractors are numbered to 100 sets. Six-cards packs carried an SRP of $4.99.

	NM/M
Complete Set (300):	80.00
Complete Series 1 (150):	30.00
Complete Series 2 (150):	50.00
Common Player:	.15
Common SP (101-150, 251-300):	.50
Star Refractors:	6X
SP Refractors:	3X
Star Gold Refractors:	15X
SP Gold Refractors:	10X
Pack (6):	1.50
Wax Box (24):	30.00
1 Darin Erstad	.35
2 Javy Lopez	.15
3 Vinny Castilla	.15
4 Jim Thome	.60
5 Tino Martinez	.15
6 Mark Grace	.15
7 Shawn Green	.40
8 Dustin Hermanson	.15
9 Kevin Young	.15
10 Tony Clark	.15
11 Scott Brosius	.15
12 Craig Biggio	.15
13 Brian McRae	.15
14 Chan Ho Park	.15
15 Manny Ramirez	1.00
16 Chipper Jones	1.50
17 Rico Brogna	.15
18 Quinton McCracken	.15
19 J.T. Snow Jr.	.15
20 Tony Gwynn	1.50
21 Juan Guzman	.15
22 John Valentin	.15
23 Rick Helling	.15
24 Sandy Alomar	.15
25 Frank Thomas	1.00
26 Jorge Posada	.15
27 Dmitri Young	.15
28 Rick Reed	.15
29 Kevin Tapani	.15
30 Troy Glaus	.75
31 Kenny Rogers	.15
32 Jeromy Burnitz	.15
33 Mark Grudzielanek	.15
34 Mike Mussina	.50
35 Scott Rolen	.75
36 Neifi Perez	.15
37 Brad Radke	.15
38 Darryl Strawberry	.15
39 Robb Nen	.15
40 Moises Alou	.15
41 Eric Young	.15
42 Livan Hernandez	.15
43 John Wetteland	.15
44 Matt Lawton	.15
45 Ben Grieve	.15
46 Fernando Tatis	.15
47 Travis Fryman	.15
48 David Segui	.15
49 Bob Abreu	.15
50 Nomar Garciaparra	1.50
51 Paul O'Neill	.15
52 Jeff King	.15
53 Francisco Cordova	.15
54 John Olerud	.15
55 Vladimir Guerrero	1.00
56 Fernando Vina	.15
57 Shane Reynolds	.15
58 Chuck Finley	.15
59 Rondell White	.15
60 Greg Vaughn	.15
61 Ryan Minor	.15
62 Tom Gordon	.15
63 Damion Easley	.15
64 Ray Durham	.15
65 Orlando Hernandez	.15
66 Bartolo Colon	.15
67 Jaret Wright	.15
68 Royce Clayton	.15
69 Tim Salmon	.15
70 Mark McGwire	2.50
71 Alex Gonzalez	.15
72 Tom Glavine	.40
73 David Justice	.15
74 Omar Vizquel	.15
75 Juan Gonzalez	.50
76 Bobby Higginson	.15
77 Todd Walker	.15
78 Dante Bichette	.15
79 Kevin Millwood	.15
80 Roger Clemens	1.75
81 Kerry Wood	.50
82 Cal Ripken Jr.	3.00
83 Jay Bell	.15
84 Barry Bonds	3.00
85 Alex Rodriguez	2.50
86 Doug Glanville	.15
87 Jason Kendall	.15
88 Sean Casey	.25
89 Aaron Sele	.15
90 Derek Jeter	3.00
91 Andy Ashby	.15
92 Rusty Greer	.15
93 Rod Beck	.15
94 Matt Williams	.15
95 Mike Piazza	2.00
96 Wally Joyner	.15
97 Barry Larkin	.15
98 Eric Milton	.15
99 Gary Sheffield	.50
100 Greg Maddux	1.50
101 Ken Griffey Jr. (Gem)	4.00
102 Frank Thomas (Gem)	2.00
103 Nomar Garciaparra (Gem)	3.00
104 Mark McGwire (Gem)	5.00
105 Alex Rodriguez (Gem)	5.00
106 Tony Gwynn (Gem)	3.00
107 Juan Gonzalez (Gem)	.75
108 Jeff Bagwell (Gem)	2.00
109 Sammy Sosa (Gem)	3.00
110 Vladimir Guerrero (Gem)	2.00
111 Roger Clemens (Gem)	3.50
112 Barry Bonds (Gem)	6.00
113 Darin Erstad (Gem)	.75
114 Mike Piazza (Gem)	4.00
115 Derek Jeter (Gem)	6.00
116 Chipper Jones (Gem)	3.00
117 Larry Walker (Gem)	.50
118 Scott Rolen (Sensations)	1.50
119 Cal Ripken Jr. (Gem)	6.00
120 Greg Maddux (Gem)	3.00
121 Troy Glaus (Sensations)	1.50
122 Ben Grieve (Sensations)	.50
123 Ryan Minor (Sensations)	.50
124 Kerry Wood (Sensations)	.50
125 Travis Lee (Sensations)	.50
126 Adrian Beltre (Sensations)	.50
127 Brad Fullmer (Sensations)	.50
128 Aramis Ramirez (Sensations)	.50
129 Eric Chavez (Sensations)	.50
130 Todd Helton (Sensations)	1.50
131 Pat Burrell RC (Finest Rookies)	4.00
132 Ryan Mills RC (Finest Rookies)	.15
133 Austin Kearns RC (Finest Rookies)	3.00
134 Josh McKinley RC (Finest Rookies)	.50
135 Adam Everett RC (Finest Rookies)	.75
136 Marlon Anderson	.50
137 Bruce Chen	.50
138 Matt Clement	.50
139 Alex Gonzalez	.50
140 Roy Halladay	.50
141 Calvin Pickering	.50
142 Randy Wolf	.50
143 Ryan Anderson	.50
144 Ruben Mateo	.50
145 Alex Escobar RC	.50
146 Jeremy Giambi	.50
147 Lance Berkman	.50
148 Michael Barrett	.50
149 Preston Wilson	.50
150 Gabe Kapler	.50
151 Roger Clemens	1.75
152 Jay Buhner	.15
153 Brad Fullmer	.15
154 Ray Lankford	.15
155 Jim Edmonds	.15
156 Jason Giambi	.60
157 Bret Boone	.15
158 Jeff Cirillo	.15
159 Rickey Henderson	1.00
160 Edgar Martinez	.15
161 Ron Gant	.15
162 Mark Kotsay	.15
163 Trevor Hoffman	.15
164 Jason Schmidt	.15
165 Brett Tomko	.15
166 David Ortiz	.50
167 Dean Palmer	.15
168 Hideki Irabu	.15
169 Mike Cameron	.15
170 Pedro Martinez	1.00
171 Tom Goodwin	.15
172 Brian Hunter	.15
173 Al Leiter	.15
174 Charles Johnson	.15
175 Curt Schilling	.50
176 Robin Ventura	.15
177 Travis Lee	.15
178 Jeff Shaw	.15
179 Ugueth Urbina	.15
180 Roberto Alomar	.30
181 Cliff Floyd	.15
182 Adrian Beltre	.25
183 Tony Womack	.15
184 Brian Jordan	.15
185 Randy Johnson	1.00
186 Mickey Morandini	.15
187 Todd Hundley	.15
188 Jose Valentin	.15
189 Eric Davis	.15
190 Ken Caminiti	.15
191 David Wells	.15
192 Ryan Klesko	.15
193 Garret Anderson	.15
194 Eric Karros	.15
195 Ivan Rodriguez	.75
196 Aramis Ramirez	.15
197 Mike Lieberthal	.15
198 Will Clark	.15
199 Rey Ordonez	.15
200 Ken Griffey Jr.	2.00
201 Jose Guillen	.15
202 Scott Erickson	.15
203 Paul Konerko	.15
204 Johnny Damon	.40
205 Larry Walker	.15
206 Denny Neagle	.15
207 Jose Offerman	.15
208 Andy Pettitte	.30
209 Bobby Jones	.15
210 Kevin Brown	.15
211 John Smoltz	.15
212 Henry Rodriguez	.15
213 Tim Belcher	.15
214 Carlos Delgado	.50
215 Andruw Jones	1.00
216 Andy Benes	.15
217 Fred McGriff	.15
218 Edgar Renteria	.15
219 Miguel Tejada	.25
220 Bernie Williams	.15
221 Justin Thompson	.15
222 Marty Cordova	.15
223 Delino DeShields	.15
224 Ellis Burks	.15
225 Kenny Lofton	.15
226 Steve Finley	.15
227 Eric Chavez	.25
228 Jose Cruz Jr.	.15
229 Marquis Grissom	.15
230 Jeff Bagwell	1.00
231 Jose Canseco	.50
232 Edgardo Alfonzo	.15
233 Richie Sexson	.15
234 Jeff Kent	.15
235 Rafael Palmeiro	.75
236 David Cone	.15
237 Gregg Jefferies	.15
238 Mike Lansing	.15
239 Mariano Rivera	.25
240 Albert Belle	.15
241 Chuck Knoblauch	.15
242 Derek Bell	.15
243 Pat Hentgen	.15
244 Andres Galarraga	.15
245 Mo Vaughn	.15
246 Wade Boggs	1.50
247 Devon White	.15
248 Todd Helton	.75
249 Raul Mondesi	.15
250 Sammy Sosa	1.50
251 Nomar Garciaparra (Sterling)	3.00
252 Mark McGwire (Sterling)	5.00
253 Alex Rodriguez (Sterling)	5.00
254 Juan Gonzalez (Sterling)	.75
255 Vladimir Guerrero (Sterling)	2.00
256 Ken Griffey Jr. (Sterling)	4.00
257 Mike Piazza (Sterling)	4.00
258 Derek Jeter (Sterling)	6.00
259 Albert Belle (Sterling)	.50
260 Greg Vaughn (Sterling)	.50
261 Sammy Sosa (Sterling)	3.00
262 Greg Maddux (Sterling)	3.00
263 Frank Thomas (Sterling)	2.00
264 Mark Grace (Sterling)	.50
265 Ivan Rodriguez (Sterling)	1.25
266 Roger Clemens (Gamers)	3.50
267 Mo Vaughn (Gamers)	.50
268 Jim Thome (Gamers)	.75
269 Darin Erstad (Gamers)	.65
270 Chipper Jones (Gamers)	2.50
271 Larry Walker (Gamers)	.50
272 Cal Ripken Jr. (Gamers)	6.00
273 Scott Rolen (Gamers)	1.25
274 Randy Johnson (Gamers)	2.00
275 Tony Gwynn (Gamers)	2.50
276 Barry Bonds (Gamers)	6.00
277 Sean Burroughs RC	1.50
278 J.M. Gold RC	.50
279 Carlos Lee	.50
280 George Lombard	.50
281 Carlos Beltran	1.50
282 Fernando Seguignol	.50
283 Eric Chavez	.65
284 Carlos Pena RC	3.00
285 Corey Patterson RC	2.00
286 Alfonso Soriano RC	12.00
287 Nick Johnson RC	2.00
288 Jorge Toca RC	.50
289 A.J. Burnett RC	1.00
290 Andy Brown RC	.50
291 Doug Mientkiewicz RC	1.00
292 Bobby Seay RC	.50
293 Chip Ambres RC	.50
294 C.C. Sabathia RC	3.00
295 Choo Freeman RC	1.00
296 Eric Valent RC	.50
297 Matt Belisle RC	.50
298 Jason Tyner RC	.50
299 Masao Kida RC	.50
300 Hank Aaron, Mark McGwire (Homerun Kings)	3.00

Complements

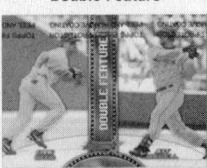

This Series 2 insert set pairs two players on a "split-screen" card front. There are three different versions for each card, Non-Refractor/Refractor (1:56), Refractor/Non-Refractor (1:56) and Refractor/Refractor (1:168). Each card is numbered with a "C" prefix. Values shown are for cards with either the left- or right-side player as Refractor; dual-refractor cards valued at 2X.

	NM/M
Complete Set (7):	25.00
Common Player:	2.50
Inserted 1:56	
Dual-Refractors:	2X
Inserted 1:168	
1 Mike Piazza, Ivan Rodriguez	4.00
2 Tony Gwynn, Wade Boggs	3.00
3 Kerry Wood, Roger Clemens	3.50
4 Juan Gonzalez, Sammy Sosa	3.00
5 Derek Jeter, Nomar Garciaparra	6.00
6 Mark McGwire, Frank Thomas	5.00
7 Vladimir Guerrero, Andruw Jones	2.50

Double Feature

Similar to Finest Complements, this Series 2 set utilizes split-screen fronts to accomodate two players on a horizontal format. Each card has three versions: Non-Refractor/Refractor (1:56), Refractor/Non-Refractor (1:56) and Refractor/Refractor (1:168). Card numbers have a "DF" prefix. Values shown are for cards with either left- or right-side Refractor; Dual-Refractor cards are valued at 2X.

	NM/M
Complete Set (7):	30.00
Common Player:	2.00
Dual-Refractors:	2X
1 Ken Griffey Jr., Alex Rodriguez	10.00
2 Chipper Jones, Andruw Jones	6.00
3 Darin Erstad, Mo Vaughn	2.00
4 Craig Biggio, Jeff Bagwell	4.00
5 Ben Grieve, Eric Chavez	2.00
6 Albert Belle, Cal Ripken Jr.	10.00
7 Scott Rolen, Pat Burrell	3.00

Franchise Records

This Series 2 insert set focuses on players who led their teams in various statistical categories. They are randomly seeded 1:129 packs, while a parallel Refractor version is inserted 1:378. Card numbers have a "FR" prefix.

	NM/M
Common Player:	3.00
Stars:	15X
SP's:	10X
Complete Set (10):	35.00

	NM/M
Common Player:	2.00
Refractors:	3X
1 Frank Thomas	2.50
2 Ken Griffey Jr.	5.00
3 Mark McGwire	6.00
4 Juan Gonzalez	2.00
5 Nomar Garciaparra	3.00
6 Mike Piazza	5.00
7 Cal Ripken Jr.	7.50
8 Sammy Sosa	3.00
9 Barry Bonds	7.50
10 Tony Gwynn	3.00

Future's Finest

This Series 2 insert focuses on up-and-coming players who are primed to emerge as superstars. These are seeded 1:171 packs and limited to 500 numbered sets. Card numbers have a "FF" prefix.

	NM/M
Complete Set (10):	35.00
Common Player:	2.00
1 Pat Burrell	10.00
2 Troy Glaus	12.50
3 Eric Chavez	3.00
4 Ryan Anderson	2.00
5 Ruben Mateo	2.00
6 Gabe Kapler	2.00
7 Alex Gonzalez	2.00
8 Michael Barrett	2.00
9 Lance Berkman	2.00
10 Fernando Seguignol	2.00

Hank Aaron Award Contenders

This insert set focuses on nine players who had the best chance to win baseball's newest award. Production varies from card to card, with nine times as many of card #9 as of card #1, and so on. Insertion odds thus vary greatly, from 1:12 to 1:216. Refractor versions are found at odds which vary from 1:96 to 1:1728. Card numbers have an "HA" prefix.

	NM/M
Complete Set (9):	20.00
Common Player:	2.00
Refractors:	3X
1 Juan Gonzalez	2.00
2 Vladimir Guerrero	2.50
3 Nomar Garciaparra	3.00
4 Albert Belle	2.00
5 Frank Thomas	2.50
6 Sammy Sosa	3.00
7 Alex Rodriguez	5.00
8 Ken Griffey Jr.	4.00
9 Mark McGwire	5.00

Leading Indicators

Utilizing a heat-sensitive, thermal ink technology, these cards highlight the 1998 home run totals of 10 players. Touching the left, right or center field portion of the card behind each player's image reveals his 1998 season home run total in that specific direction. These are seeded in Series 1 packs.

	NM/M
Complete Set (10):	20.00
Common Player:	.50

Refractors

Inserted at the rate of one card per 12 packs, Refractors use special technology to impart a more colorful sheen to the card fronts. To eliminate doubt, the backs have the word "REFRACTOR" printed to the right of the card number at top.

	NM/M
Complete Set (300):	750.00
Common Player:	1.00
Stars:	6X
SP's:	3X

Gold Refractors

At the top of Finest's chase-card line-up for 1999 are the Gold Refractors. Fronts have an overall gold tone in the background. Backs are individually serial numbered in gold foil with an edition of 100 each, and have the words "GOLD REFRACTOR" printed at top, to the right of the card number. The Gold Refractors are die-cut along the edges to create a deckled effect. Stated pack insertion rates were between 1:26 and 1:82 depending on series and type.

	NM/M
Common Player:	3.00
Stars:	15X
SP's:	10X

Inserted 1:24

L1	Mark McGwire	5.00
L2	Sammy Sosa	3.00
L3	Ken Griffey Jr.	4.00
L4	Greg Vaughn	.50
L5	Albert Belle	.50
L6	Juan Gonzalez	.75
L7	Andres Galarraga	.50
L8	Alex Rodriguez	5.00
L9	Barry Bonds	6.00
L10	Jeff Bagwell	1.50

Milestones

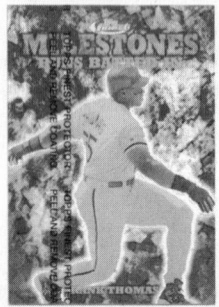

This Series 2 insert set is fractured into four subsets, each focusing on a statistical category: Hits, Home Runs, RBIs and Doubles. The Hits category is limited to 3,000 numbered sets. Home Runs are limited to 500 numbered sets. RBIs are limited to 1,400 numbered sets and Doubles is limited to 500 numbered sets. Each card number carries an "M" prefix.

		NM/M
Complete Set (40):		125.00
Common Hits (1-10):		.50
Common Homeruns (11-20):		2.00
Common RBI (21-30):		1.00
Common Doubles (31-40):		2.00
1	Tony Gwynn (Hits)	1.50
2	Cal Ripken Jr. (Hits)	3.00
3	Wade Boggs (Hits)	1.50
4	Ken Griffey Jr. (Hits)	2.00
5	Frank Thomas (Hits)	1.00
6	Barry Bonds (Hits)	3.00
7	Travis Lee (Hits)	.50
8	Alex Rodriguez (Hits)	2.50
9	Derek Jeter (Hits)	3.00
10	Vladimir Guerrero (Hits)	1.00
11	Mark McGwire (Home Runs)	8.00
12	Ken Griffey Jr. (Home Runs)	7.00
13	Vladimir Guerrero (Home Runs)	4.00
14	Alex Rodriguez (Home Runs)	8.00
15	Barry Bonds (Home Runs)	10.00
16	Sammy Sosa (Home Runs)	5.00
17	Albert Belle (Home Runs)	2.00
18	Frank Thomas (Home Runs)	4.00
19	Jose Canseco (Home Runs)	3.00
20	Mike Piazza (Home Runs)	7.00
21	Jeff Bagwell (RBI)	2.00
22	Barry Bonds (RBI)	6.00
23	Ken Griffey Jr. (RBI)	4.00
24	Albert Belle (RBI)	1.00
25	Juan Gonzalez (RBI)	1.50
26	Vinny Castilla (RBI)	1.00
27	Mark McGwire (RBI)	5.00
28	Alex Rodriguez (RBI)	5.00
29	Nomar Garciaparra (RBI)	3.00
30	Frank Thomas (RBI)	2.50
31	Barry Bonds (Doubles)	10.00
32	Albert Belle (Doubles)	2.00
33	Ben Grieve (Doubles)	2.00
34	Craig Biggio (Doubles)	2.00
35	Vladimir Guerrero (Doubles)	4.00
36	Nomar Garciaparra (Doubles)	5.00
37	Alex Rodriguez (Doubles)	7.00
38	Derek Jeter (Doubles)	10.00
39	Ken Griffey Jr. (Doubles)	7.00
40	Brad Fullmer (Doubles)	2.00

Peel & Reveal

This Series 1 insert offers 20 players produced in varying levels of scarcity designated by background design: Sparkle is common, Hyperplaid is uncommon and Stadium Stars is rare. Each card has a peel-off opaque protective coating on both front and back. Stated insertion odds are: Sparkle 1:30; Hyperplaid 1:60, and Stadium Stars 1:120. Home Team Advantage (HTA) boxes have odds which are twice as good.

		NM/M
Complete Set (20):		40.00
Common Player:		1.00
Hyperplaid:		1.5X
Stadium Stars:		2.5X
1	Kerry Wood	1.50
2	Mark McGwire	5.00
3	Sammy Sosa	3.00
4	Ken Griffey Jr.	4.00
5	Nomar Garciaparra	3.00
6	Greg Maddux	3.00
7	Derek Jeter	6.00
8	Andres Galarraga	1.00
9	Alex Rodriguez	5.00
10	Frank Thomas	2.00
11	Roger Clemens	3.50
12	Juan Gonzalez	1.50
13	Ben Grieve	1.00
14	Jeff Bagwell	2.00
15	Todd Helton	2.00
16	Chipper Jones	3.00
17	Barry Bonds	6.00
18	Travis Lee	1.00
19	Vladimir Guerrero	2.00
20	Pat Burrell	1.50

Prominent Figures

Fifty cards on Refractor technology highlight superstars chasing the all-time records in five different statistical categories: Home Runs, Slugging Percentage, Batting Average, RBIs and Total Bases. Ten players are featured in each category, each sequentially numbered to the all-time single season record statistic for that category. Home Run category is numbered to 70, Slugging Percentage to 847, Batting Average to 424, RBIs to 190 and Total Bases to 457.

		NM/M
Complete Set (50):		250.00
Common Home Runs (1-10):		
#'d to 70:		3.00
Common Slugging % (11-20):		
#'d to 847:		1.00
Common Batting Ave. (21-30):		
#'d to 424:		1.75
Common RBIs (31-40); #'d to 190:		
		2.00

Common Total Bases (41-50); #'d to 457:   1.75

1	Mark McGwire (HR)	25.00
2	Sammy Sosa (HR)	10.00
3	Ken Griffey Jr. (HR)	15.00
4	Mike Piazza (HR)	15.00
5	Juan Gonzalez (HR)	5.00
6	Greg Vaughn (HR)	3.00
7	Alex Rodriguez (HR)	25.00
8	Manny Ramirez (HR)	7.50
9	Jeff Bagwell (HR)	7.50
10	Andres Galarraga (HR)	3.00
11	Mark McGwire (S%)	6.00
12	Sammy Sosa (S%)	5.00
13	Juan Gonzalez (S%)	2.50
14	Ken Griffey Jr. (S%)	7.50
15	Barry Bonds (S%)	7.50
16	Greg Vaughn (S%)	1.00
17	Larry Walker (S%)	1.00
18	Andres Galarraga (S%)	1.00
19	Jeff Bagwell (S%)	2.50
20	Albert Belle (S%)	1.00
21	Tony Gwynn (BA)	5.00
22	Mike Piazza (BA)	6.00
23	Larry Walker (BA)	1.75
24	Alex Rodriguez (BA)	7.50
25	John Olerud (BA)	1.75
26	Frank Thomas (BA)	3.50
27	Bernie Williams (BA)	1.75
28	Chipper Jones (BA)	5.00
29	Jim Thome (BA)	2.50
30	Barry Bonds (BA)	9.00
31	Juan Gonzalez (RBI)	3.00
32	Sammy Sosa (RBI)	9.00
33	Mark McGwire (RBI)	20.00
34	Albert Belle (RBI)	2.00
35	Ken Griffey Jr. (RBI)	15.00
36	Jeff Bagwell (RBI)	6.00
37	Chipper Jones (RBI)	10.00
38	Vinny Castilla (RBI)	2.00
39	Alex Rodriguez (RBI)	20.00
40	Andres Galarraga (RBI)	2.00
41	Sammy Sosa (TB)	6.00
42	Mark McGwire (TB)	7.50
43	Albert Belle (TB)	1.75
44	Ken Griffey Jr. (TB)	6.00
45	Jeff Bagwell (TB)	3.50
46	Juan Gonzalez (TB)	3.50
47	Barry Bonds (TB)	9.00
48	Vladimir Guerrero (TB)	3.50
49	Larry Walker (TB)	1.75
50	Alex Rodriguez (TB)	7.50

Split Screen

Players who share a common bond are highlighted in this Series 1 insert set which includes 14 paired players. Each card is available in three variations: Non-Refractor/Refractor (1:28), Refractor/Non-Refractor (1:28) and Refractor/Refractor (1:84). Values shown are for a card with either left- or right-side Refractor; dual-Refractor cards are worth 2X.

		NM/M
Complete Set (14):		30.00
Common Card:		1.00
Dual-Refractor:		2X
1	Mark McGwire, Sammy Sosa	4.00
2	Ken Griffey Jr., Alex Rodriguez	4.00
3	Nomar Garciaparra, Derek Jeter	5.00
4	Barry Bonds, Albert Belle	4.00
5	Cal Ripken Jr., Tony Gwynn	4.00
6	Manny Ramirez, Juan Gonzalez	1.50
7	Frank Thomas, Andres Galarraga	1.50
8	Scott Rolen, Chipper Jones	2.00
9	Ivan Rodriguez, Mike Piazza	3.00
10	Kerry Wood, Roger Clemens	2.50
11	Greg Maddux, Tom Glavine	1.50
12	Troy Glaus, Eric Chavez	1.50
13	Ben Grieve, Todd Helton	1.50
14	Travis Lee, Pat Burrell	2.50

Team Finest

The first 10 cards are showcased in Series 1 while the last 10 cards showcased in Series 2. Team Finest are available in three colors: Blue, Red and Gold (Red and Gold are only available in Home Team Advantage packs). All Team Finest are serially numbered as follows: Blue, numbered to 1,500; Blue Re-

fractors to 150; Red to 500; Red Refractors to 50; Gold to 250 and Gold Refractors to 25. Cards have a TF prefix to the card number.

	NM/M
Complete Set (20):	25.00
Common Blue:	1.00
Production 1,500 Sets	
Blue Refractors:	3X
Production 150 Sets	
Reds:	1.5X
Production 500 Sets	
Red Refractors:	7X
Production 50 Sets	
Golds:	2X
Production 250 Sets	
Gold Refractors:	10X
Production 25 Sets	

1	Greg Maddux	2.50
2	Mark McGwire	4.50
3	Sammy Sosa	2.50
4	Juan Gonzalez	1.25
5	Alex Rodriguez	4.50
6	Travis Lee	1.00
7	Roger Clemens	2.75
8	Darin Erstad	1.25
9	Todd Helton	1.75
10	Mike Piazza	3.50
11	Kerry Wood	1.25
12	Ken Griffey Jr.	3.50
13	Frank Thomas	2.00
14	Jeff Bagwell	2.00
15	Nomar Garciaparra	2.50
16	Derek Jeter	6.00
17	Chipper Jones	2.50
18	Barry Bonds	6.00
19	Tony Gwynn	2.50
20	Ben Grieve	1.00

2000 Finest

The 286-card base set has the traditional chromium finish with the Topps Finest logo in the upper left portion on the front. Also in the upper left portion is a partial image of a baseball with seams in the background of the player photo. Card backs have a small photo with '99 stats and career totals. The rookies from Series 1 are serial numbered to 2,000 and in Series 2 to 3,000.

	NM/M
Complete Set (286):	250.00
Complete Series 1 (147):	175.00
Complete Series 2 (140):	125.00
Common Player:	.25
Common Rookie (101-120):	4.00
Production 2,000	
Common Rookie (247-266):	4.00
Production 3,000	
Common Counterpart (267-276):	.75
Inserted 1:8	
Common Gem (136-145):	1.50
Inserted 1:24	
Pack (6):	2.00
Series 1 & 2 Box (24):	40.00
1	Nomar Garciaparra	2.00
2	Chipper Jones	1.50
3	Erubiel Durazo	.25
4	Robin Ventura	.25
5	Garret Anderson	.25
6	Dean Palmer	.25
7	Mariano Rivera	.35
8	Rusty Greer	.25
9	Jim Thome	.25

10	Jeff Bagwell	1.00
11	Jason Giambi	.75
12	Jeromy Burnitz	.25
13	Mark Grace	.35
14	Russ Ortiz	.25
15	Kevin Brown	.25
16	Kevin Millwood	.25
17	Scott Williamson	.25
18	Orlando Hernandez	.25
19	Todd Walker	.25
20	Carlos Beltran	.50
21	Ruben Rivera	.25
22	Curt Schilling	.40
23	Brian Giles	.25
24	Eric Karros	.25
25	Preston Wilson	.25
26	Al Leiter	.25
27	Juan Encarnacion	.25
28	Tim Salmon	.40
29	B.J. Surhoff	.25
30	Bernie Williams	.45
31	Lee Stevens	.25
32	Pokey Reese	.25
33	Mike Sweeney	.25
34	Corey Koskie	.25
35	Roberto Alomar	.40
36	Tim Hudson	.40
37	Tom Glavine	.40
38	Jeff Kent	.25
39	Mike Lieberthal	.25
40	Barry Larkin	.25
41	Paul O'Neill	.25
42	Rico Brogna	.25
43	Brian Daubach	.25
44	Rich Aurilia	.25
45	Vladimir Guerrero	1.00
46	Luis Castillo	.25
47	Bartolo Colon	.25
48	Kevin Appier	.25
49	Mo Vaughn	.25
50	Alex Rodriguez	2.50
51	Randy Johnson	1.00
52	Kris Benson	.25
53	Tony Clark	.25
54	Chad Allen	.25
55	Larry Walker	.25
56	Freddy Garcia	.25
57	Paul Konerko	.35
58	Edgardo Alfonzo	.25
59	Brady Anderson	.25
60	Derek Jeter	3.00
61	Mike Hampton	.25
62	Jeff Cirillo	.25
63	Shannon Stewart	.25
64	Greg Maddux	1.50
65	Mark McGwire	2.50
66	Gary Sheffield	.50
67	Kevin Young	.25
68	Tony Gwynn	1.50
69	Rey Ordonez	.25
70	Cal Ripken Jr.	3.00
71	Todd Helton	1.00
72	Brian Jordan	.25
73	Jose Canseco	.50
74	Luis Gonzalez	.25
75	Barry Bonds	3.00
76	Jermaine Dye	.25
77	Jose Offerman	.25
78	Magglio Ordonez	.40
79	Fred McGriff	.25
80	Ivan Rodriguez	.60
81	Josh Hamilton (Prospects)	.50
82	Vernon Wells (Prospects)	.50
83	Mark Mulder (Prospects)	.35
84	John Patterson (Prospects)	.25
85	Nick Johnson (Prospects)	.50
86	Pablo Ozuna (Prospects)	.25
87	A.J. Burnett (Prospects)	.25
88	Jack Cust (Prospects)	.25
89	Adam Piatt (Prospects)	.25
90	Rob Ryan (Prospects)	.25
91	Sean Burroughs (Prospects)	.35
92	D'Angelo Jimenez (Prospects)	.25
93	Chad Hermansen (Prospects)	.25
94	Rob Fick (Prospects)	.25
95	Ruben Mateo (Prospects)	.25
96	Alex Escobar (Prospects)	.25
97	Willi Mo Pena (Prospects)	.25
98	Corey Patterson (Prospects)	.50
99	Eric Munson (Prospects)	.50
100	Pat Burrell (Prospects)	.75
101	Michael Tejera RC	4.00
102	Bobby Bradley RC	4.00
103	Larry Bigbie RC	6.00
104	B.J. Garbe RC	4.00
105	Josh Kalinowski RC	4.00
106	Brett Myers RC	15.00
107	Chris Mears RC	4.00
108	Aaron Rowand RC	10.00
109	Corey Myers RC	4.00
110	John Sneed RC	4.00
111	Ryan Christenson RC	4.00
112	Kyle Snyder RC	4.00
113	Mike Paradis RC	4.00
114	Chance Caple RC	4.00
115	Ben Christiansen RC	4.00
116	Brad Baker RC	4.00
117	Rob Purvis RC	4.00
118	Rick Asadoorian RC	4.00
119	Ruben Salazar RC	4.00
120	Julio Zuleta RC	4.00

121	Ken Griffey Jr., Alex Rodriguez (Features)	4.00
122	Nomar Garciaparra, Derek Jeter (Features)	4.00
123	Mark McGwire, Sammy Sosa (Features)	4.00
124	Randy Johnson, Pedro Martinez (Features)	2.00
125	Mike Piazza, Ivan Rodriguez (Features)	3.00
126	Manny Ramirez, Roberto Alomar (Features)	2.00
127	Chipper Jones, Andruw Jones (Features)	2.00
128	Cal Ripken Jr., Tony Gwynn (Features)	2.00
129	Jeff Bagwell, Craig Biggio (Features)	1.50
130	Vladimir Guerrero, Barry Bonds (Features)	5.00
131	Alfonso Soriano, Nick Johnson (Features)	2.00
132	Josh Hamilton, Pat Burrell (Features)	1.50
133	Corey Patterson, Ruben Mateo (Features)	.75
134	Larry Walker, Todd Helton (Features)	1.50
135	Edgardo Alfonzo, Rey Ordonez (Features)	.75
136	Derek Jeter (Gems)	10.00
137	Alex Rodriguez (Gems)	8.00
138	Chipper Jones (Gems)	5.00
139	Mike Piazza (Gems)	6.00
140	Mark McGwire (Gems)	8.00
141	Ivan Rodriguez (Gems)	2.00
142	Cal Ripken Jr. (Gems)	10.00
143	Vladimir Guerrero (Gems)	3.00
144	Randy Johnson (Gems)	3.00
145	Jeff Bagwell (Gems)	3.00
146	Ken Griffey Jr. field	1.50
146a	Ken Griffey Jr. press	1.50
147	Andruw Jones	1.00
148	Kerry Wood	.50
149	Jim Edmonds	.25
150	Pedro Martinez	1.00
151	Warren Morris	.25
152	Trevor Hoffman	.25
153	Eric Young	.25
154	Andy Pettitte	.40
155	Frank Thomas	1.00
156	Damion Easley	.25
157	Cliff Floyd	.25
158	Ben Davis	.25
159	John Valentin	.25
160	Rafael Palmeiro	.65
161	Andy Ashby	.25
162	J.D. Drew	.40
163	Jay Bell	.25
164	Adam Kennedy	.25
165	Manny Ramirez	1.00
166	John Halama	.25
167	Octavio Dotel	.25
168	Darin Erstad	.40
169	Jose Lima	.25
170	Andres Galarraga	.25
171	Scott Rolen	.75
172	Delino DeShields	.25
173	J.T. Snow Jr.	.25
174	Tony Womack	.25
175	John Olerud	.25
176	Jason Kendall	.25
177	Carlos Lee	.25
178	Eric Milton	.25
179	Jeff Cirillo	.25
180	Gabe Kapler	.25
181	Greg Vaughn	.25
182	Denny Neagle	.25
183	Tino Martinez	.25
184	Doug Mientkiewicz	.25
185	Juan Gonzalez	1.00
186	Ellis Burks	.25
187	Mike Hampton	.25
188	Royce Clayton	.25
189	Mike Mussina	.50
190	Carlos Delgado	.50
191	Ben Grieve	.25
192	Fernando Tatis	.25
193	Matt Williams	.25
194	Rondell White	.25
195	Shawn Green	.50
196	Justin Thompson	.25
197	Troy Glaus	1.00
198	Roger Cedeno	.25
199	Ray Lankford	.25
200	Sammy Sosa	2.00
201	Kenny Lofton	.25
202	Edgar Martinez	.25
203	Mark Kotsay	.25
204	David Wells	.25
205	Craig Biggio	.25
206	Ray Durham	.25
207	Troy O'Leary	.25
208	Rickey Henderson	.75
209	Bob Abreu	.25
210	Neifi Perez	.25
211	Carlos Febles	.25
212	Chuck Knoblauch	.25
213	Moises Alou	.25
214	Omar Vizquel	.25
215	Vinny Castilla	.25
216	Javy Lopez	.25
217	Johnny Damon	.40
218	Roger Clemens	1.75

219	Miguel Tejada	.40
220	Deion Sanders	.35
221	Matt Lawton	.25
222	Albert Belle	.25
223	Adrian Beltre	.50
224	Dante Bichette	.25
225	Raul Mondesi	.25
226	Mike Piazza	2.00
227	Brad Penny (Prospects)	.25
228	Kip Wells (Prospects)	.25
229	Adam Everett (Prospects)	.25
230	Eddie Yarnall (Prospects)	.25
231	Matt LeCroy (Prospects)	.25
232	Ryan Anderson (Prospects)	.25
233	Rick Ankiel (Prospects)	.25
234	Daryle Ward (Prospects)	.25
235	Rafael Furcal (Prospects)	.25
236	Dee Brown (Prospects)	.25
237	Travis Dawkins (Prospects)	.25
238	Eric Valent (Prospects)	.25
239	Peter Bergeron (Prospects)	.25
240	Alfonso Soriano (Prospects)	1.50
241	John Patterson (Prospects)	.25
242	Jorge Toca (Prospects)	.25
243	Ryan Anderson (Prospects)	.25
244	Jason Dallaero (Prospects)	.25
245	Jason Grilli (Prospects)	.25
246	Chad Hermansen (Prospects)	.25
247	Scott Downs RC	4.00
248	Keith Reed RC	4.00
249	Edgar Cruz RC	4.00
250	Wes Anderson RC	4.00
251	Lyle Overbay RC	10.00
252	Mike Lamb RC	4.00
253	Vince Faison RC	4.00
254	Chad Alexander RC	4.00
255	Chris Wakeland RC	4.00
256	Aaron McNeal RC	4.00
257	Tomokazu Ohka RC	4.00
258	Ty Howington RC	6.00
259	Javier Colina RC	4.00
260	Jason Jennings RC	4.00
261	Ramon Santiago RC	4.00
262	Johan Santana RC	150.00
263	Quincey Foster RC	4.00
264	Junior Brignac RC	4.00
265	Rico Washington RC	4.00
266	Scott Sobkowiak RC	4.00
267	Pedro Martinez, Rick Ankiel (Counterparts)	2.00
268	Manny Ramirez, Vladimir Guerrero (Counterparts)	2.00
269	A.J. Burnett, Mark Mulder (Counterparts)	.75
270	Mike Piazza, Eric Munson (Counterparts)	2.50
271	Josh Hamilton, Corey Patterson (Counterparts)	1.00
272	Ken Griffey Jr., Sammy Sosa (Counterparts)	3.00
273	Derek Jeter, Alfonso Soriano (Counterparts)	5.00
274	Mark McGwire, Pat Burrell (Counterparts)	5.00
275	Chipper Jones, Cal Ripken Jr. (Counterparts)	5.00
276	Nomar Garciaparra, Alex Rodriguez (Counterparts)	4.00
277	Pedro Martinez (Gems)	3.00
278	Tony Gwynn (Gems)	5.00
279	Barry Bonds (Gems)	10.00
280	Juan Gonzalez (Gems)	3.00
281	Larry Walker (Gems)	1.50
282	Nomar Garciaparra (Gems)	8.00
283	Ken Griffey Jr. (Gems)	6.00
284	Manny Ramirez (Gems)	3.00
285	Shawn Green (Gems)	2.00
286	Sammy Sosa (Gems)	6.00

Refractor

These are a parallel to the base set and have a mirror like sheen. Card backs have "refractor" written underneath the card number.

Stars (1-100): 5-10X

Inserted 1:24
Rookies (101-120,247-266): .5-1X
Production 500 Sets
Features (121-135): 2-3X
Inserted 1:96
Counterparts (267-276): 2-3X
Inserted 1:96
Gems (136-145,277-286): 2-3X
Inserted 1:288

Gold Refractor

A parallel to the base set, these have the usual mirror like appearance with a deckle edged border. Regular cards are seeded 1:240 packs, Rookies are limited to 100 serial numbered sets, Features and Counterparts subsets (1:960) and Gems (1:2,880).

Stars (1-100): 20-40X
Inserted 1:240
Rookies (101-120, 247-266): 1-2X
Production 100 Sets
Features: 4-8X
Inserted 1:960
Counterparts: 4-8X
Inserted 1:960
Gems: 5-10X
Inserted 1:2,880

Ballpark Bounties

Seeded across both Series 1 and 2 these inserts use Serigraph Fresnal technology and have a metallic looking image of a baseball in the background of the player photo. Card backs are numbered with a "BB" prefix.

		NM/M
Complete Set (30):		85.00
Complete Series 1 (15):		45.00
Complete Series 2 (15):		45.00
Common Player:		1.50
Inserted 1:24		
1	Chipper Jones	5.00
2	Mike Piazza	6.00
3	Vladimir Guerrero	3.00
4	Sammy Sosa	6.00
5	Nomar Garciaparra	6.00
6	Manny Ramirez	3.00
7	Jeff Bagwell	3.00
8	Scott Rolen	2.00
9	Carlos Beltran	2.50
10	Pedro Martinez	3.00
11	Greg Maddux	5.00
12	Josh Hamilton	2.00
13	Adam Piatt	1.50
14	Pat Burrell	2.00
15	Alfonso Soriano	3.00
16	Alex Rodriguez	8.00
17	Derek Jeter	10.00
18	Cal Ripken Jr.	10.00
19	Larry Walker	1.50
20	Barry Bonds	10.00
21	Ken Griffey Jr.	6.00
22	Mark McGwire	8.00
23	Ivan Rodriguez	2.00
24	Andruw Jones	2.50
25	Todd Helton	2.50
26	Randy Johnson	3.00
27	Ruben Mateo	1.50
28	Corey Patterson	1.50
29	Sean Burroughs	1.50
30	Eric Munson	1.50

Dream Cast

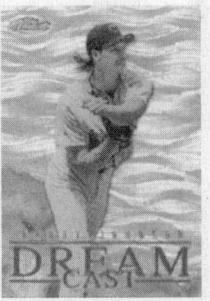

These inserts are found exclusively in Series 2 packs and utilize Duflex technology. The card fronts try to portray a "dream sequence" with sky and clouds in the background. They are numbered with a "DC" prefix on the card back.

		NM/M
Complete Set (10):		40.00
Common Player:		2.00
Inserted 1:36		
1	Mark McGwire	8.00
2	Roberto Alomar	2.00
3	Chipper Jones	5.00
4	Derek Jeter	10.00
5	Barry Bonds	10.00
6	Ken Griffey Jr.	6.00
7	Sammy Sosa	6.00
8	Mike Piazza	6.00
9	Pedro Martinez	3.00
10	Randy Johnson	3.00

Finest Moments

This four-card set pays tribute to milestone achievements accomplished during the 1999 season. They are numbered with a "FM" prefix. A Refractor parallel version is seeded 1:20 packs.

		NM/M
Complete Set (4):		6.00
Common Player:		1.00
Inserted 1:9		
Refractor:		1-2X
Inserted 1:20		
1	Chipper Jones	3.00
2	Ivan Rodriguez	1.50
3	Tony Gwynn	3.00
4	Wade Boggs	3.00

Moments Autographs

An autographed version of the four-card set, these were seeded 1:425 packs.

		NM/M
Common Autograph:		25.00
Inserted 1:425		
1	Chipper Jones	50.00
2	Ivan Rodriguez	25.00
3	Tony Gwynn	50.00
4	Wade Boggs	25.00

For The Record

Printed on Finest Clear Card technology, each of the 10 players featured has three cards. Each card sequentially numbered to the distance of the outfield wall in their home ballpark (left, center and right). Combining all three cards forms a panoramic view of the stadium.

		NM/M
Complete Set (30):		300.00
Common Player:		8.00
1A	Derek Jeter/318	20.00
1B	Derek Jeter/408	20.00
1C	Derek Jeter/314	20.00
2A	Mark McGwire/330	15.00
2B	Mark McGwire/402	15.00
2C	Mark McGwire/330	15.00
3A	Ken Griffey Jr./331	10.00
3B	Ken Griffey Jr./405	10.00
3C	Ken Griffey Jr./327	10.00
4A	Alex Rodriguez/331	15.00
4B	Alex Rodriguez/405	15.00
4C	Alex Rodriguez/327	15.00
5A	Nomar Garciaparra/310	10.00
5B	Nomar Garciaparra/390	10.00
5C	Nomar Garciaparra/302	10.00
6A	Cal Ripken Jr./333	20.00
6B	Cal Ripken Jr./410	20.00
6C	Cal Ripken Jr./318	20.00
7A	Sammy Sosa/355	10.00
7B	Sammy Sosa/400	10.00
7C	Sammy Sosa/353	10.00
8A	Manny Ramirez/325	8.00
8B	Manny Ramirez/410	8.00
8C	Manny Ramirez/325	8.00
9A	Mike Piazza/338	10.00
9B	Mike Piazza/410	10.00
9C	Mike Piazza/338	10.00
10A	Chipper Jones/335	9.00
10B	Chipper Jones/401	10.00
10C	Chipper Jones/330	10.00

Gems Oversized

Each of the 10 Gems subset cards in series 1 and 2 were also done on an oversized format. The oversized cards were added as a box topper to each box. Home Team Advantage stores received Refractor versions of the Gems Oversized cards as a box topper.

		NM/M
Complete Set (20):		50.00
Common Player:		1.00
Inserted 1:Box		
1	Derek Jeter	6.00
2	Alex Rodriguez	5.00
3	Chipper Jones	3.00
4	Mike Piazza	4.00
5	Mark McGwire	5.00
6	Ivan Rodriguez	1.25
7	Cal Ripken Jr.	6.00
8	Vladimir Guerrero	2.00
9	Randy Johnson	2.00
10	Jeff Bagwell	2.00
11	Nomar Garciaparra	4.00
12	Ken Griffey Jr.	4.00
13	Manny Ramirez	2.00
14	Shawn Green	1.50
15	Sammy Sosa	4.00
16	Pedro Martinez	2.00
17	Tony Gwynn	2.00
18	Barry Bonds	6.00
19	Juan Gonzalez	1.50
20	Larry Walker	1.00

Going the Distance

This 12-card set highlights the top hitters in baseball, utilizing Photopolymer hologram technology. Card backs are numbered with a "GTD" prefix.

		NM/M
Complete Set (12):		45.00
Common Player:		3.00
Inserted 1:24		
1	Tony Gwynn	3.50
2	Alex Rodriguez	6.00
3	Derek Jeter	8.00
4	Chipper Jones	4.00
5	Nomar Garciaparra	4.00
6	Sammy Sosa	4.00
7	Ken Griffey Jr.	4.00

8	Vladimir Guerrero	3.00
9	Mark McGwire	6.00
10	Mike Piazza	4.00
11	Manny Ramirez	3.00
12	Cal Ripken Jr.	8.00

1993 Flair Promos

Among the scarcest modern baseball promo cards are those produced to introduce Fleer's new premium product for 1993, Flair. Basically similar to the issued versions, the promo cards have "000" in place of the card number on back. The promos are checklisted here in alphabetical order.

		NM/M
Complete Set (8):		200.00
Common Player:		10.00
(1)	Will Clark	10.00
(2)	Darren Daulton	10.00
(3)	Andres Galarraga	10.00
(4)	Bryan Harvey	10.00
(5)	David Justice	10.00
(6)	Jody Reed	10.00
(7)	Nolan Ryan	100.00
(8)	Sammy Sosa	60.00

1993 Flair

Designed as Fleer's super-premium card brand, this 300-card set contains extra-thick cards which feature gold-foil highlights and UV coating front and back. Portrait and action photos are combined in a high-tech front picture and there is a muted photo on the back, as well.

		NM/M
Complete Set (300):		15.00
Common Player:		.10
Pack (10):		1.50
Wax Box (24):		20.00
1	Steve Avery	.10
2	Jeff Blauser	.10
3	Ron Gant	.10
4	Tom Glavine	.25
5	Dave Justice	.10
6	Mark Lemke	.10
7	Greg Maddux	1.00
8	Fred McGriff	.10
9	Terry Pendleton	.10
10	Deion Sanders	.15
11	John Smoltz	.10
12	Mike Stanton	.10
13	Steve Buechele	.10
14	Mark Grace	.10
15	Greg Hibbard	.10
16	Derrick May	.10
17	Chuck McElroy	.10
18	Mike Morgan	.10
19	Randy Myers	.10
20	Ryne Sandberg	1.00
21	Dwight Smith	.10
22	Sammy Sosa	1.00
23	Jose Vizcaino	.10
24	Tim Belcher	.10
25	Rob Dibble	.10
26	Roberto Kelly	.10
27	Barry Larkin	.10
28	Kevin Mitchell	.10
29	Hal Morris	.10
30	Joe Oliver	.10
31	Jose Rijo	.10
32	Bip Roberts	.10
33	Chris Sabo	.10
34	Reggie Sanders	.10
35	Dante Bichette	.10
36	Willie Blair	.10
37	Jerald Clark	.10
38	Alex Cole	.10
39	Andres Galarraga	.10
40	Joe Girardi	.10
41	Charlie Hayes	.10
42	Chris Jones	.10
43	David Nied	.10
44	Eric Young	.10
45	Alex Arias	.10
46	Jack Armstrong	.10
47	Bret Barberie	.10
48	Chuck Carr	.10
49	Jeff Conine	.10
50	Orestes Destrade	.10
51	Chris Hammond	.10
52	Bryan Harvey	.10
53	Benito Santiago	.10
54	Gary Sheffield	.35
55	Walt Weiss	.10
56	Eric Anthony	.10
57	Jeff Bagwell	.75
58	Craig Biggio	.10
59	Ken Caminiti	.10
60	Andujar Cedeno	.10
61	Doug Drabek	.10
62	Steve Finley	.10
63	Luis Gonzalez	.10
64	Pete Harnisch	.10
65	Doug Jones	.10
66	Darryl Kile	.10
67	Greg Swindell	.10
68	Brett Butler	.10
69	Jim Gott	.10
70	Orel Hershiser	.10
71	Eric Karros	.10
72	Pedro Martinez	.75
73	Ramon Martinez	.10
74	Roger McDowell	.10
75	Mike Piazza	1.50
76	Jody Reed	.10
77	Tim Wallach	.10
78	Moises Alou	.10
79	Greg Colbrunn	.10
80	Wil Cordero	.10
81	Delino DeShields	.10
82	Jeff Fassero	.10
83	Marquis Grissom	.10
84	Ken Hill	.10
85	Mike Lansing RC	.25
86	Dennis Martinez	.10
87	Larry Walker	.10
88	John Wetteland	.10
89	Bobby Bonilla	.10
90	Vince Coleman	.10
91	Dwight Gooden	.10
92	Todd Hundley	.10
93	Howard Johnson	.10
94	Eddie Murray	.75
95	Joe Orsulak	.10
96	Bret Saberhagen	.10
97	Darren Daulton	.10
98	Mariano Duncan	.10
99	Len Dykstra	.10
100	Jim Eisenreich	.10
101	Tommy Greene	.10
102	Dave Hollins	.10
103	Pete Incaviglia	.10
104	Danny Jackson	.10
105	John Kruk	.10
106	Terry Mulholland	.10
107	Curt Schilling	.25
108	Mitch Williams	.10
109	Stan Belinda	.10
110	Jay Bell	.10
111	Steve Cooke	.10
112	Carlos Garcia	.10
113	Jeff King	.10
114	Al Martin	.10
115	Orlando Merced	.10
116	Don Slaught	.10
117	Andy Van Slyke	.10
118	Tim Wakefield	.10
119	Rene Arocha RC	.10
120	Bernard Gilkey	.10
121	Gregg Jefferies	.10
122	Ray Lankford	.10
123	Donovan Osborne	.10
124	Tom Pagnozzi	.10
125	Erik Pappas	.10
126	Geronimo Pena	.10
127	Lee Smith	.10
128	Ozzie Smith	1.00
129	Bob Tewksbury	.10
130	Mark Whiten	.10

No.	Player	Price
131	Derek Bell	.10
132	Andy Benes	.10
133	Tony Gwynn	1.00
134	Gene Harris	.10
135	Trevor Hoffman	.10
136	Phil Plantier	.10
137	Rod Beck	.10
138	Barry Bonds	2.50
139	John Burkett	.10
140	Will Clark	.10
141	Royce Clayton	.10
142	Mike Jackson	.10
143	Darren Lewis	.10
144	Kirt Manwaring	.10
145	Willie McGee	.10
146	Bill Swift	.10
147	Robby Thompson	.10
148	Matt Williams	.10
149	Brady Anderson	.10
150	Mike Devereaux	.10
151	Chris Hoiles	.10
152	Ben McDonald	.10
153	Mark McLemore	.10
154	Mike Mussina	.40
155	Gregg Olson	.10
156	Harold Reynolds	.10
157	Cal Ripken, Jr.	2.50
158	Rick Sutcliffe	.10
159	Fernando Valenzuela	.10
160	Roger Clemens	1.25
161	Scott Cooper	.10
162	Andre Dawson	.30
163	Scott Fletcher	.10
164	Mike Greenwell	.10
165	Greg Harris	.10
166	Billy Hatcher	.10
167	Jeff Russell	.10
168	Mo Vaughn	.10
169	Frank Viola	.10
170	Chad Curtis	.10
171	Chili Davis	.10
172	Gary DiSarcina	.10
173	Damion Easley	.10
174	Chuck Finley	.10
175	Mark Langston	.10
176	Luis Polonia	.10
177	Tim Salmon	.10
178	Scott Sanderson	.10
179	J.T. Snow RC	.50
180	Wilson Alvarez	.10
181	Ellis Burks	.10
182	Joey Cora	.10
183	Alex Fernandez	.10
184	Ozzie Guillen	.10
185	Roberto Hernandez	.10
186	Bo Jackson	.20
187	Lance Johnson	.10
188	Jack McDowell	.10
189	Frank Thomas	.75
190	Robin Ventura	.10
191	Carlos Baerga	.10
192	Albert Belle	.10
193	Wayne Kirby	.10
194	Derek Lilliquist	.10
195	Kenny Lofton	.10
196	Carlos Martinez	.10
197	Jose Mesa	.10
198	Eric Plunk	.10
199	Paul Sorrento	.10
200	John Doherty	.10
201	Cecil Fielder	.10
202	Travis Fryman	.10
203	Kirk Gibson	.10
204	Mike Henneman	.10
205	Chad Kreuter	.10
206	Scott Livingstone	.10
207	Tony Phillips	.10
208	Mickey Tettleton	.10
209	Alan Trammell	.10
210	David Wells	.10
211	Lou Whitaker	.10
212	Kevin Appier	.10
213	George Brett	1.25
214	David Cone	.10
215	Tom Gordon	.10
216	Phil Hiatt	.10
217	Felix Jose	.10
218	Wally Joyner	.10
219	Jose Lind	.10
220	Mike Macfarlane	.10
221	Brian McRae	.10
222	Jeff Montgomery	.10
223	Cal Eldred	.10
224	Darryl Hamilton	.10
225	John Jaha	.10
226	Pat Listach	.10
227	Graeme Lloyd RC	.10
228	Kevin Reimer	.10
229	Bill Spiers	.10
230	B.J. Surhoff	.10
231	Greg Vaughn	.10
232	Robin Yount	.75
233	Rick Aguilera	.10
234	Jim Deshaies	.10
235	Brian Harper	.10
236	Kent Hrbek	.10
237	Chuck Knoblauch	.10
238	Shane Mack	.10
239	David McCarty	.10
240	Pedro Munoz	.10
241	Mike Pagliarulo	.10
242	Kirby Puckett	1.00
243	Dave Winfield	.75
244	Jim Abbott	.10
245	Wade Boggs	1.00
246	Pat Kelly	.10
247	Jimmy Key	.10
248	Jim Leyritz	.10
249	Don Mattingly	1.25
250	Matt Nokes	.10
251	Paul O'Neill	.10
252	Mike Stanley	.10
253	Danny Tartabull	.10
254	Bob Wickman	.10
255	Bernie Williams	.10
256	Mike Bordick	.10
257	Dennis Eckersley	.60
258	Brent Gates	.10
259	Goose Gossage	.10
260	Rickey Henderson	.75
261	Mark McGwire	2.00
262	Ruben Sierra	.10
263	Terry Steinbach	.10
264	Bob Welch	.10
265	Bobby Witt	.10
266	Rich Amaral	.10
267	Chris Bosio	.10
268	Jay Buhner	.10
269	Norm Charlton	.10
270	Ken Griffey Jr.	1.50
271	Erik Hanson	.10
272	Randy Johnson	.75
273	Edgar Martinez	.10
274	Tino Martinez	.10
275	Dave Valle	.10
276	Omar Vizquel	.10
277	Kevin Brown	.10
278	Jose Canseco	.45
279	Julio Franco	.10
280	Juan Gonzalez	.40
281	Tom Henke	.10
282	David Hulse	.10
283	Rafael Palmeiro	.65
284	Dean Palmer	.10
285	Ivan Rodriguez	.65
286	Nolan Ryan	2.50
287	Roberto Alomar	.25
288	Pat Borders	.10
289	Joe Carter	.10
290	Juan Guzman	.10
291	Pat Hentgen	.10
292	Paul Molitor	.75
293	John Olerud	.10
294	Ed Sprague	.10
295	Dave Stewart	.10
296	Duane Ward	.10
297	Devon White	.10
298	Checklist	.05
299	Checklist	.05
300	Checklist	.05

Wave of the Future

The game's top prospects are featured in this insert issue randomly packaged in Flair packs. Cards #19-20, Darrell Whitmore and Nigel Wilson, were printed with each other's back; no corrected version was made.

		NM/M
Complete Set (20):		6.00
Common Player:		.15
1	Jason Bere	.15
2	Jeremy Burnitz	.15
3	Russ Davis	.15
4	Jim Edmonds	.25
5	Cliff Floyd	.15
6	Jeffrey Hammonds	.15
7	Trevor Hoffman	.15
8	Domingo Jean	.15
9	David McCarty	.15
10	Bobby Munoz	.15
11	Brad Pennington	.15
12	Mike Piazza	3.00
13	Manny Ramirez	2.00
14	John Roper	.15
15	Tim Salmon	.25
16	Aaron Sele	.15
17	Allen Watson	.15
18	Rondell White	.15
19	Darell Whitmore	.15
20	Nigel Wilson	.15

1994 Flair

One of the success stories of 1993 returned with the release of Fleer Flair for 1994. At $4 per pack this was pricey stuff, but collectors apparently liked the look that includes an extremely thick card stock, full-bleed photos and gold-foil graphics on both sides with a protective polyester laminate described as "far be- yond mere UV coating." In addition to the 250 regular-issue cards, there are three 10-card, insert sets; Wave of the Future, Outfield Power and Hot Numbers in Series 1, the last with players' images printed on 100 percent etched foil. Series 2 has 200 base cards and Hot Glove, Infield Power and 10 more Wave of the Future insert cards.

		NM/M
Complete Set (450):		60.00
Common Player:		.10
Series 1 Pack (10):		1.50
Series 1 Box (24):		20.00
Series 2 Pack (10):		3.00
Series 2 Box (24):		50.00
1	Harold Baines	.10
2	Jeffrey Hammonds	.10
3	Chris Hoiles	.10
4	Ben McDonald	.10
5	Mark McLemore	.10
6	Jamie Moyer	.10
7	Jim Poole	.10
8	Cal Ripken, Jr.	3.00
9	Chris Sabo	.10
10	Scott Bankhead	.10
11	Scott Cooper	.10
12	Danny Darwin	.10
13	Andre Dawson	.30
14	Billy Hatcher	.10
15	Aaron Sele	.10
15a	Aaron Sele/OPS	2.00
16	John Valentin	.10
17	Dave Valle	.10
18	Mo Vaughn	.10
19	Brian Anderson RC	.50
20	Gary DiSarcina	.10
21	Jim Edmonds	.10
22	Chuck Finley	.10
23	Bo Jackson	.20
24	Mark Leiter	.10
25	Greg Myers	.10
26	Eduardo Perez	.10
27	Tim Salmon	.10
28	Wilson Alvarez	.10
29	Jason Bere	.10
30	Alex Fernandez	.10
31	Ozzie Guillen	.10
32	Joe Hall	.10
33	Darrin Jackson	.10
34	Kirk McCaskill	.10
35	Tim Raines	.10
36	Frank Thomas	1.00
37	Carlos Baerga	.15
38	Albert Belle	.15
39	Mark Clark	.10
40	Wayne Kirby	.10
41	Dennis Martinez	.10
42	Charles Nagy	.10
43	Manny Ramirez	1.00
44	Paul Sorrento	.10
45	Jim Thome	.65
46	Eric Davis	.10
47	John Doherty	.10
48	Junior Felix	.10
49	Cecil Fielder	.10
50	Kirk Gibson	.10
51	Mike Moore	.10
52	Tony Phillips	.10
53	Alan Trammell	.10
54	Kevin Appier	.10
55	Stan Belinda	.10
56	Vince Coleman	.10
57	Greg Gagne	.10
58	Bob Hamelin	.10
59	Dave Henderson	.10
60	Wally Joyner	.10
61	Mike Macfarlane	.10
62	Jeff Montgomery	.10
63	Ricky Bones	.10
64	Jeff Bronkey	.10
65	Alex Diaz	.10
66	Cal Eldred	.10
67	Darryl Hamilton	.10
68	John Jaha	.10
69	Mark Kiefer	.10
70	Kevin Seitzer	.10
71	Turner Ward	.10
72	Rich Becker	.10
73	Scott Erickson	.10
74	Keith Garagozzo	.10
75	Kent Hrbek	.10
76	Scott Leius	.10
77	Kirby Puckett	1.50
78	Matt Walkbeck	.10
79	Dave Winfield	1.00
80	Mike Gallego	.10
81	Xavier Hernandez	.10
82	Jimmy Key	.10
83	Jim Leyritz	.10
84	Don Mattingly	1.75
85	Matt Nokes	.10
86	Paul O'Neill	.10
87	Melido Perez	.10
88	Danny Tartabull	.10
89	Mike Bordick	.10
90	Ron Darling	.10
91	Dennis Eckersley	.75
92	Stan Javier	.10
93	Steve Karsay	.10
94	Mark McGwire	2.50
95	Troy Neel	.10
96	Terry Steinbach	.10
97	Bill Taylor	.10
98	Eric Anthony	.10
99	Chris Bosio	.10
100	Tim Davis	.10
101	Felix Fermin	.10
102	Dave Fleming	.10
103	Ken Griffey Jr.	2.00
104	Greg Hibbard	.10
105	Reggie Jefferson	.10
106	Tino Martinez	.10
107	Jack Armstrong	.10
108	Will Clark	.10
109	Juan Gonzalez	.50
110	Rick Helling	.10
111	Tom Henke	.10
112	David Hulse	.10
113	Manuel Lee	.10
114	Doug Strange	.10
115	Roberto Alomar	.25
116	Joe Carter	.10
117	Carlos Delgado	.50
118	Pat Hentgen	.10
119	Paul Molitor	1.00
120	John Olerud	.10
121	Dave Stewart	.10
122	Todd Stottlemyre	.10
123	Mike Timlin	.10
124	Jeff Blauser	.10
125	Tom Glavine	.30
126	Dave Justice	.10
127	Mike Kelly	.10
128	Ryan Klesko	.10
129	Javier Lopez	.10
130	Greg Maddux	1.50
131	Fred McGriff	.10
132	Kent Mercker	.10
133	Mark Wohlers	.10
134	Willie Banks	.10
135	Steve Buechele	.10
136	Shawon Dunston	.10
137	Jose Guzman	.10
138	Glenallen Hill	.10
139	Randy Myers	.10
140	Karl Rhodes	.10
141	Ryne Sandberg	1.50
142	Steve Trachsel	.10
143	Bret Boone	.10
144	Tom Browning	.10
145	Hector Carrasco	.10
146	Barry Larkin	.10
147	Hal Morris	.10
148	Jose Rijo	.10
149	Reggie Sanders	.10
150	John Smiley	.10
151	Dante Bichette	.10
152	Ellis Burks	.10
153	Joe Girardi	.10
154	Mike Harkey	.10
155	Roberto Mejia	.10
156	Marcus Moore	.10
157	Armando Reynoso	.10
158	Bruce Ruffin	.10
159	Eric Young	.10
160	Kurt Abbott RC	.10
161	Jeff Conine	.10
162	Orestes Destrade	.10
163	Chris Hammond	.10
164	Bryan Harvey	.10
165	Dave Magadan	.10
166	Gary Sheffield	.40
167	David Weathers	.10
168	Andujar Cedeno	.10
169	Tom Edens	.10
170	Luis Gonzalez	.10
171	Pete Harnisch	.10
172	Todd Jones	.10
173	Darryl Kile	.10
174	James Mouton	.10
175	Scott Servais	.10
176	Mitch Williams	.10
177	Pedro Astacio	.10
178	Orel Hershiser	.10
179	Raul Mondesi	.10
180	Jose Offerman	.10
181	Chan Ho Park RC	1.00
182	Mike Piazza	2.00
183	Cory Snyder	.10
184	Tim Wallach	.10
185	Todd Worrell	.10
186	Sean Berry	.10
187	Wil Cordero	.10
188	Darrin Fletcher	.10
189	Cliff Floyd	.10
190	Marquis Grissom	.10
191	Rod Henderson	.10
192	Ken Hill	.10
193	Pedro Martinez	1.00
194	Kirk Rueter	.10
195	Jeromy Burnitz	.10
196	John Franco	.10
197	Dwight Gooden	.10
198	Todd Hundley	.10
199	Bobby Jones	.10
200	Jeff Kent	.10
201	Mike Maddux	.10
202	Ryan Thompson	.10
203	Jose Vizcaino	.10
204	Darren Daulton	.10
205	Len Dykstra	.10
206	Jim Eisenreich	.10
207	Dave Hollins	.10
208	Danny Jackson	.10
209	Doug Jones	.10
210	Jeff Juden	.10
211	Ben Rivera	.10
212	Kevin Stocker	.10
213	Milt Thompson	.10
214	Jay Bell	.10
215	Steve Cooke	.10
216	Mark Dewey	.10
217	Al Martin	.10
218	Orlando Merced	.10
219	Don Slaught	.10
220	Zane Smith	.10
221	Rick White	.10
222	Kevin Young	.10
223	Rene Arocha	.10
224	Rheal Cormier	.10
225	Brian Jordan	.10
226	Ray Lankford	.10
227	Mike Perez	.10
228	Ozzie Smith	1.50
229	Mark Whiten	.10
230	Todd Zeile	.10
231	Derek Bell	.10
232	Archi Cianfrocco	.10
233	Ricky Gutierrez	.10
234	Trevor Hoffman	.10
235	Phil Plantier	.10
236	Dave Staton	.10
237	Wally Whitehurst	.10
238	Todd Benzinger	.10
239	Barry Bonds	3.00
240	John Burkett	.10
241	Royce Clayton	.10
242	Bryan Hickerson	.10
243	Mike Jackson	.10
244	Darren Lewis	.10
245	Kirt Manwaring	.10
246	Mark Portugal	.10
247	Salomon Torres	.10
248	Checklist	.10
249	Checklist	.10
250	Checklist	.10
251	Brady Anderson	.10
252	Mike Devereaux	.10
253	Sid Fernandez	.10
254	Leo Gomez	.10
255	Mike Mussina	.40
256	Mike Oquist	.10
257	Rafael Palmeiro	.75
258	Lee Smith	.10
259	Damon Berryhill	.10
260	Wes Chamberlain	.10
261	Roger Clemens	1.75
262	Gar Finnvold	.10
263	Mike Greenwell	.10
264	Tim Naehring	.10
265	Otis Nixon	.10
266	Ken Ryan	.10
267	Chad Curtis	.10
268	Chili Davis	.10
269	Damion Easley	.10
270	Jorge Fabregas	.10
271	Mark Langston	.10
272	Phil Leftwich	.10
273	Harold Reynolds	.10
274	J.T. Snow	.10
275	Joey Cora	.10
276	Julio Franco	.10
277	Roberto Hernandez	.10
278	Lance Johnson	.10
279	Ron Karkovice	.10
280	Jack McDowell	.10
281	Robin Ventura	.10
282	Sandy Alomar Jr.	.10
283	Kenny Lofton	.10
284	Jose Mesa	.10
285	Jack Morris	.10
286	Eddie Murray	1.00
287	Chad Ogea	.10
288	Eric Plunk	.10
289	Paul Shuey	.10
290	Omar Vizquel	.10
291	Danny Bautista	.10
292	Travis Fryman	.10
293	Greg Gohr	.10
294	Chris Gomez	.10
295	Mickey Tettleton	.10
296	Lou Whitaker	.10
297	David Cone	.10
298	Gary Gaetti	.10
299	Tom Gordon	.10
300	Felix Jose	.10
301	Jose Lind	.10
302	Brian McRae	.10
303	Mike Fetters	.10
304	Brian Harper	.10
305	Pat Listach	.10
306	Matt Mieske	.10
307	Dave Nilsson	.10
308	Jody Reed	.10
309	Greg Vaughn	.10
310	Bill Wegman	.10
311	Rick Aguilera	.10
312	Alex Cole	.10
313	Denny Hocking	.10
314	Chuck Knoblauch	.10
315	Shane Mack	.10
316	Pat Meares	.10
317	Kevin Tapani	.10
318	Jim Abbott	.10
319	Wade Boggs	1.00
320	Sterling Hitchcock	.10
321	Pat Kelly	.10
322	Terry Mulholland	.10
323	Luis Polonia	.10
324	Mike Stanley	.10
325	Bob Wickman	.10
326	Bernie Williams	.10
327	Mark Acre	.10
328	Geronimo Berroa	.10
329	Scott Brosius	.10
330	Brent Gates	.10
331	Rickey Henderson	1.00
332	Carlos Reyes	.10
333	Ruben Sierra	.10
334	Bobby Witt	.10
335	Bobby Ayala	.10
336	Jay Buhner	.10
337	Randy Johnson	1.00
338	Edgar Martinez	.10
339	Bill Risley	.10
340	Alex Rodriguez RC	40.00
341	Roger Salkeld	.10
342	Dan Wilson	.10
343	Kevin Brown	.10
344	Jose Canseco	.45
345	Dean Palmer	.10
346	Ivan Rodriguez	.75
347	Kenny Rogers	.10
348	Pat Borders	.10
349	Juan Guzman	.10
350	Ed Sprague	.10
351	Devon White	.10
352	Steve Avery	.10
353	Roberto Kelly	.10
354	Mark Lemke	.10
355	Greg McMichael	.10
356	Terry Pendleton	.10
357	John Smoltz	.10
358	Mike Stanton	.10
359	Tony Tarasco	.10
360	Mark Grace	.10
361	Derrick May	.10
362	Rey Sanchez	.10
363	Sammy Sosa	1.50
364	Rick Wilkins	.10
365	Jeff Brantley	.10
366	Tony Fernandez	.10
367	Chuck McElroy	.10
368	Kevin Mitchell	.10
369	John Roper	.10
370	Johnny Ruffin	.10
371	Deion Sanders	.15
372	Marvin Freeman	.10
373	Andres Galarraga	.10
374	Charlie Hayes	.10
375	Nelson Liriano	.10
376	David Nied	.10
377	Walt Weiss	.10
378	Bret Barberie	.10
379	Jerry Browne	.10
380	Chuck Carr	.10
381	Greg Colbrunn	.10
382	Charlie Hough	.10
383	Kurt Miller	.10
384	Benito Santiago	.10
385	Jeff Bagwell	1.00
386	Craig Biggio	.10
387	Ken Caminiti	.10
388	Doug Drabek	.10
389	Steve Finley	.10
390	John Hudek	.10
391	Orlando Miller	.10
392	Shane Reynolds	.10
393	Brett Butler	.10
394	Tom Candiotti	.10
395	Delino DeShields	.10
396	Kevin Gross	.10
397	Eric Karros	.10
398	Ramon Martinez	.10
399	Henry Rodriguez	.10
400	Moises Alou	.10
401	Jeff Fassero	.10
402	Mike Lansing	.10
403	Mel Rojas	.10
404	Larry Walker	.10
405	John Wetteland	.10
406	Gabe White	.10
407	Bobby Bonilla	.10
408	Josias Manzanillo	.10
409	Bret Saberhagen	.10
410	David Segui	.10
411	Mariano Duncan	.10
412	Tommy Greene	.10
413	Billy Hatcher	.10
414	Ricky Jordan	.10
415	John Kruk	.10
416	Bobby Munoz	.10
417	Curt Schilling	.30
418	Fernando Valenzuela	.10
419	David West	.10
420	Carlos Garcia	.10
421	Brian Hunter	.10
422	Jeff King	.10
423	Jon Lieber	.10
424	Ravelo Manzanillo	.10
425	Denny Neagle	.10
426	Andy Van Slyke	.10
427	Bryan Eversgerd	.10
428	Bernard Gilkey	.10
429	Gregg Jefferies	.10
430	Tom Pagnozzi	.10
431	Bob Tewksbury	.10
432	Allen Watson	.10

433	Andy Ashby	.10
434	Andy Benes	.10
435	Donnie Elliott	.10
436	Tony Gwynn	1.50
437	Joey Hamilton	.10
438	Tim Hyers	.10
439	Luis Lopez	.10
440	Bip Roberts	.10
441	Scott Sanders	.10
442	Rod Beck	.10
443	Dave Burba	.10
444	Darryl Strawberry	.10
445	Bill Swift	.10
446	Robby Thompson	.10
447	William Van Landingham RC	.10
448	Matt Williams	.10
449	Checklist	.10
450	Checklist	.10

Hot Gloves

Hot Glove is a 10-card Series 2 insert set. It focuses on players with outstanding defensive ability. Cards feature a die-cut design, with the player photo in front of a baseball glove. Player identification and a "Hot Glove" logo are in gold foil in the lower-left corner.

		NM/M
Complete Set (10):		40.00
Common Player:		2.00
1	Barry Bonds	10.00
2	Will Clark	2.00
3	Ken Griffey Jr.	7.50
4	Kenny Lofton	2.00
5	Greg Maddux	5.00
6	Don Mattingly	6.50
7	Kirby Puckett	5.00
8	Cal Ripken, Jr.	10.00
9	Tim Salmon	2.00
10	Matt Williams	2.00

Hot Numbers

Hot Numbers is an insert set found in Series 1 packs at an average rate of 1:24. Each card is printed on 100 percent etched foil and displays the player in the forefront with a background made up of floating numbers. The player's name is in gold foil across the bottom-right side and a large foil "Hot Numbers" and that player's uniform number are in a square at bottom-left.

		NM/M
Complete Set (10):		15.00
Common Player:		.50
1	Roberto Alomar	1.00
2	Carlos Baerga	.50
3	Will Clark	.50
4	Fred McGriff	.50
5	Paul Molitor	3.00
6	John Olerud	.50
7	Mike Piazza	4.50
8	Cal Ripken, Jr.	6.00
9	Ryne Sandberg	4.00
10	Frank Thomas	3.00

Infield Power

Infield Power is a horizontally formatted insert set. Cards show the player batting on one half and in the field on the other half of the card, di-

vided by a black, diagonal strip that reads "Infield Power" and the player's name. The set spotlights infielders that often hit the longball. Infield Power was inserted into Series 2 packs at an average rate of 1:5.

		NM/M
Complete Set (10):		5.00
Common Player:		.25
1	Jeff Bagwell	.75
2	Will Clark	.25
3	Darren Daulton	.25
4	Don Mattingly	1.25
5	Fred McGriff	.25
6	Rafael Palmeiro	.65
7	Mike Piazza	1.50
8	Cal Ripken, Jr.	2.50
9	Frank Thomas	.75
10	Matt Williams	.25

Outfield Power

Flair's Outfield Power was randomly inserted in Series 1 packs at a 1:5 rate. This vertically formatted card shows the player in the field on top, while the bottom half shows the player at the plate. The photos divided by a black strip with "Outfield Power" and the player's name on it.

		NM/M
Complete Set (10):		5.00
Common Player:		.30
1	Albert Belle	.30
2	Barry Bonds	2.00
3	Joe Carter	.30
4	Len Dykstra	.30
5	Juan Gonzalez	.45
6	Ken Griffey Jr.	1.50
7	Dave Justice	.30
8	Kirby Puckett	1.00
9	Tim Salmon	.30
10	Dave Winfield	.75

Wave of the Future 1

Series 1 Wave of the Future is horizontally formatted and depicts 10 outstanding 1994 rookies who have the potential to become superstars. Each player is featured on a colorful wavelike background. A Wave of the Future gold-foil stamp is placed in the bottom-right corner with the player name in gold foil starting in the opposite bottom corner and running across the bottom. Advertised insertion rate was 1:5.

		NM/M
Complete Set (10):		6.00
Common Player:		.25
1	Kurt Abbott	.25
2	Carlos Delgado	5.00
3	Steve Karsay	.25
4	Ryan Klesko	.25
5	Javier Lopez	.25
6	Raul Mondesi	.25
7	James Mouton	.25
8	Chan Ho Park	.25
9	Dave Staton	.25
10	Rick White	.25

Wave of the Future 2

Series 2 Flair also has a Wave of the Future insert set. Unlike the earlier series, this 10-card set is vertically formated. The Wave of the Future logo appears in the bottom-left with the player's name stretching across the rest of the bottom. The background has a swirling water effect, on which the player is superimposed. Insertion rate is one per five packs.

		NM/M
Complete Set (10):		22.50
Common Player:		.50
1	Mark Acre	.50
2	Chris Gomez	.50
3	Joey Hamilton	.50
4	John Hudek	.50
5	Jon Lieber	.50
6	Matt Mieske	.50
7	Orlando Miller	.50
8	Alex Rodriguez	20.00
9	Tony Tarasco	.50
10	Bill VanLandingham	.50

1995 Flair

There's no mistaking that 1995 Flair is Fleer's super-premium brand. Cards are printed on double-thick cardboard with a background of etched metallic foil: Gold for National Leaguers, silver for American. A portrait and an action photo are featured on the horizontal front design. Backs are vertically formatted with a borderless action photo, several years worth of stats and foil trim. The basic set was issued in two series of 216 basic cards each, along with several insert sets exclusive to each series. Cards were sold in a hard pack of nine with a suggested retail price of $5.

		NM/M
Complete Set (432):		30.00
Common Player:		.10
Series 1 or 2 Pack (9):		1.00
Series 1 or 2 Wax Box (24):		15.00
1	Brady Anderson	.10
2	Harold Baines	.10
3	Leo Gomez	.10
4	Alan Mills	.10
5	Jamie Moyer	.10
6	Mike Mussina	.40
7	Mike Oquist	.10
8	Arthur Rhodes	.10
9	Cal Ripken Jr.	3.00
10	Roger Clemens	1.75
11	Scott Cooper	.10
12	Mike Greenwell	.10
13	Aaron Sele	.10
14	John Valentin	.10
15	Mo Vaughn	.10
16	Chad Curtis	.10
17	Gary DiSarcina	.10
18	Chuck Finley	.10
19	Andrew Lorraine	.10
20	Spike Owen	.10
21	Tim Salmon	.10
22	J.T. Snow	.10
23	Wilson Alvarez	.10
24	Jason Bere	.10
25	Ozzie Guillen	.10
26	Mike LaValliere	.10
27	Frank Thomas	1.00
28	Robin Ventura	.10
29	Carlos Baerga	.25
30	Albert Belle	.10
31	Jason Grimsley	.10
32	Dennis Martinez	.10
33	Eddie Murray	1.00

34	Charles Nagy	.10
35	Manny Ramirez	1.00
36	Paul Sorrento	.10
37	John Doherty	.10
38	Cecil Fielder	.10
39	Travis Fryman	.10
40	Chris Gomez	.10
41	Tony Phillips	.10
42	Lou Whitaker	.10
43	David Cone	.10
44	Gary Gaetti	.10
45	Mark Gubicza	.10
46	Bob Hamelin	.10
47	Wally Joyner	.10
48	Rusty Meacham	.10
49	Jeff Montgomery	.10
50	Ricky Bones	.10
51	Cal Eldred	.10
52	Pat Listach	.10
53	Matt Mieske	.10
54	Dave Nilsson	.10
55	Greg Vaughn	.10
56	Bill Wegman	.10
57	Chuck Knoblauch	.10
58	Scott Leius	.10
59	Pat Mahomes	.10
60	Pat Meares	.10
61	Pedro Munoz	.10
62	Kirby Puckett	1.50
63	Wade Boggs	1.00
64	Jimmy Key	.10
65	Jim Leyritz	.10
66	Don Mattingly	1.75
67	Paul O'Neill	.10
68	Melido Perez	.10
69	Danny Tartabull	.10
70	John Briscoe	.10
71	Scott Brosius	.10
72	Ron Darling	.10
73	Brent Gates	.10
74	Rickey Henderson	1.00
75	Stan Javier	.10
76	Mark McGwire	2.50
77	Todd Van Poppel	.10
78	Bobby Ayala	.10
79	Mike Blowers	.10
80	Jay Buhner	.10
81	Ken Griffey Jr.	2.00
82	Randy Johnson	1.00
83	Tino Martinez	.10
84	Jeff Nelson	.10
85	Alex Rodriguez	2.50
86	Will Clark	.10
87	Jeff Frye	.10
88	Juan Gonzalez	.50
89	Rusty Greer	.10
90	Darren Oliver	.10
91	Dean Palmer	.10
92	Ivan Rodriguez	.75
93	Matt Whiteside	.10
94	Roberto Alomar	.25
95	Joe Carter	.10
96	Tony Castillo	.10
97	Juan Guzman	.10
98	Pat Hentgen	.10
99	Mike Huff	.10
100	John Olerud	.10
101	Woody Williams	.10
102	Roberto Kelly	.10
103	Ryan Klesko	.10
104	Javier Lopez	.10
105	Greg Maddux	1.50
106	Fred McGriff	.10
107	Jose Oliva	.10
108	John Smoltz	.10
109	Tony Tarasco	.10
110	Mark Wohlers	.10
111	Jim Bullinger	.10
112	Shawon Dunston	.10
113	Derrick May	.10
114	Randy Myers	.10
115	Karl Rhodes	.10
116	Rey Sanchez	.10
117	Steve Trachsel	.10
118	Eddie Zambrano	.10
119	Bret Boone	.10
120	Brian Dorsett	.10
121	Hal Morris	.10
122	Jose Rijo	.10
123	John Roper	.10
124	Reggie Sanders	.10
125	Pete Schourek	.10
126	John Smiley	.10
127	Ellis Burks	.10
128	Vinny Castilla	.10
129	Marvin Freeman	.10
130	Andres Galarraga	.10
131	Mike Munoz	.10
132	David Nied	.10
133	Bruce Ruffin	.10
134	Walt Weiss	.10
135	Eric Young	.10
136	Greg Colbrunn	.10
137	Jeff Conine	.10
138	Jeremy Hernandez	.10
139	Charles Johnson	.10
140	Robb Nen	.10
141	Gary Sheffield	.40
142	Dave Weathers	.10
143	Jeff Bagwell	1.00
144	Craig Biggio	.10
145	Tony Eusebio	.10
146	Luis Gonzalez	.10
147	John Hudek	.10
148	Darryl Kile	.10
149	Dave Veres	.10
150	Billy Ashley	.10
151	Pedro Astacio	.10

152	Rafael Bournigal	.10
153	Delino DeShields	.10
154	Raul Mondesi	.10
155	Mike Piazza	2.00
156	Rudy Seanez	.10
157	Ismael Valdes	.10
158	Tim Wallach	.10
159	Todd Worrell	.10
160	Moises Alou	.10
161	Cliff Floyd	.10
162	Gil Heredia	.10
163	Mike Lansing	.10
164	Pedro Martinez	1.00
165	Kirk Rueter	.10
166	Tim Scott	.10
167	Jeff Shaw	.10
168	Rondell White	.10
169	Bobby Bonilla	.10
170	Rico Brogna	.10
171	Todd Hundley	.10
172	Jeff Kent	.10
173	Jim Lindeman	.10
174	Joe Orsulak	.10
175	Bret Saberhagen	.10
176	Toby Borland	.10
177	Darren Daulton	.10
178	Lenny Dykstra	.10
179	Jim Eisenreich	.10
180	Tommy Greene	.10
181	Tony Longmire	.10
182	Bobby Munoz	.10
183	Kevin Stocker	.10
184	Jay Bell	.10
185	Steve Cooke	.10
186	Ravelo Manzanillo	.10
187	Al Martin	.10
188	Denny Neagle	.10
189	Don Slaught	.10
190	Paul Wagner	.10
191	Rene Arocha	.10
192	Bernard Gilkey	.10
193	Jose Oquendo	.10
194	Tom Pagnozzi	.10
195	Ozzie Smith	1.50
196	Allen Watson	.10
197	Mark Whiten	.10
198	Andy Ashby	.10
199	Donnie Elliott	.10
200	Bryce Florie	.10
201	Tony Gwynn	1.50
202	Trevor Hoffman	.10
203	Brian Johnson	.10
204	Tim Mauser	.10
205	Bip Roberts	.10
206	Rod Beck	.10
207	Barry Bonds	3.00
208	Royce Clayton	.10
209	Darren Lewis	.10
210	Mark Portugal	.10
211	Kevin Rogers	.10
212	William Van Landingham	.10
213	Matt Williams	.10
214	Checklist	.10
215	Checklist	.10
216	Checklist	.10
217	Bret Barberie	.10
218	Armando Benitez	.10
219	Kevin Brown	.10
220	Sid Fernandez	.10
221	Chris Hoiles	.10
222	Doug Jones	.10
223	Ben McDonald	.10
224	Rafael Palmeiro	.75
225	Andy Van Slyke	.10
226	Jose Canseco	.40
227	Vaughn Eshelman	.10
228	Mike Macfarlane	.10
229	Tim Naehring	.10
230	Frank Rodriguez	.10
231	Lee Tinsley	.10
232	Mark Whiten	.10
233	Garret Anderson	.10
234	Chili Davis	.10
235	Jim Edmonds	.10
236	Mark Langston	.10
237	Troy Percival	.10
238	Tony Phillips	.10
239	Lee Smith	.10
240	Jim Abbott	.10
241	James Baldwin	.10
242	Mike Devereaux	.10
243	Ray Durham	.10
244	Alex Fernandez	.10
245	Roberto Hernandez	.10
246	Lance Johnson	.10
247	Ron Karkovice	.10
248	Tim Raines	.10
249	Sandy Alomar Jr.	.10
250	Orel Hershiser	.10
251	Julian Tavarez	.10
252	Jim Thome	.65
253	Omar Vizquel	.10
254	Dave Winfield	1.00
255	Chad Curtis	.10
256	Kirk Gibson	.10
257	Mike Henneman	.10
258	Bob Higginson RC	.25
259	Felipe Lira	.10
260	Rudy Pemberton	.10
261	Alan Trammell	.10
262	Kevin Appier	.10
263	Pat Borders	.10
264	Tom Gordon	.10
265	Jose Lind	.10
266	Jon Nunnally	.10
267	Dilson Torres	.10
268	Michael Tucker	.10
269	Jeff Cirillo	.10

270	Darryl Hamilton	.10
271	David Hulse	.10
272	Mark Kiefer	.10
273	Graeme Lloyd	.10
274	Joe Oliver	.10
275	Al Reyes	.10
276	Kevin Seitzer	.10
277	Rick Aguilera	.10
278	Marty Cordova	.10
279	Scott Erickson	.10
280	LaTroy Hawkins	.10
281	Brad Radke	.10
282	Kevin Tapani	.10
283	Tony Fernandez	.10
284	Sterling Hitchcock	.10
285	Pat Kelly	.10
286	Jack McDowell	.10
287	Andy Pettitte	.30
288	Mike Stanley	.10
289	John Wetteland	.10
290	Bernie Williams	.10
291	Mark Acre	.10
292	Geronimo Berroa	.10
293	Dennis Eckersley	.75
294	Steve Ontiveros	.10
295	Ruben Sierra	.10
296	Terry Steinbach	.10
297	Dave Stewart	.10
298	Todd Stottlemyre	.10
299	Darren Bragg	.10
300	Joey Cora	.10
301	Edgar Martinez	.10
302	Bill Risley	.10
303	Ron Villone	.10
304	Dan Wilson	.10
305	Benji Gil	.10
306	Wilson Heredia	.10
307	Mark McLemore	.10
308	Otis Nixon	.10
309	Kenny Rogers	.10
310	Jeff Russell	.10
311	Mickey Tettleton	.10
312	Bob Tewksbury	.10
313	David Cone	.10
314	Carlos Delgado	.50
315	Alex Gonzalez	.10
316	Shawn Green	.40
317	Paul Molitor	1.00
318	Ed Sprague	.10
319	Devon White	.10
320	Steve Avery	.10
321	Jeff Blauser	.10
322	Brad Clontz	.10
323	Tom Glavine	.30
324	Marquis Grissom	.10
325	Chipper Jones	1.50
326	Dave Justice	.10
327	Mark Lemke	.10
328	Kent Mercker	.10
329	Jason Schmidt	.10
330	Steve Buechele	.10
331	Kevin Foster	.10
332	Mark Grace	.10
333	Brian McRae	.10
334	Sammy Sosa	1.50
335	Ozzie Timmons	.10
336	Rick Wilkins	.10
337	Hector Carrasco	.10
338	Ron Gant	.10
339	Barry Larkin	.10
340	Deion Sanders	.15
341	Benito Santiago	.10
342	Roger Bailey	.10
343	Jason Bates	.10
344	Dante Bichette	.10
345	Joe Girardi	.10
346	Bill Swift	.10
347	Mark Thompson	.10
348	Larry Walker	.10
349	Kurt Abbott	.10
350	John Burkett	.10
351	Chuck Carr	.10
352	Andre Dawson	.30
353	Chris Hammond	.10
354	Charles Johnson	.10
355	Terry Pendleton	.10
356	Quilvio Veras	.10
357	Derek Bell	.10
358	Jim Dougherty	.10
359	Doug Drabek	.10
360	Todd Jones	.10
361	Orlando Miller	.10
362	James Mouton	.10
363	Phil Plantier	.10
364	Shane Reynolds	.10
365	Todd Hollandsworth	.10
366	Eric Karros	.10
367	Ramon Martinez	.10
368	Hideo Nomo RC	3.00
369	Jose Offerman	.10
370	Antonio Osuna	.10
371	Todd Williams	.10
372	Shane Andrews	.10
373	Wil Cordero	.10
374	Jeff Fassero	.10
375	Darrin Fletcher	.10
376	Mark Grudzielanek RC	.50
377	Carlos Perez RC	.25
378	Mel Rojas	.10
379	Tony Tarasco	.10
380	Edgardo Alfonzo	.10
381	Brett Butler	.10
382	Carl Everett	.10
383	John Franco	.10
384	Pete Harnisch	.10
385	Bobby Jones	.10
386	Dave Mlicki	.10
387	Jose Vizcaino	.10

388	Ricky Bottalico	.10
389	Tyler Green	.10
390	Charlie Hayes	.10
391	Dave Hollins	.10
392	Gregg Jefferies	.10
393	Michael Mimbs RC	.10
394	Mickey Morandini	.10
395	Curt Schilling	.30
396	Heathcliff Slocumb	.10
397	Jason Christiansen	.10
398	Midre Cummings	.10
399	Carlos Garcia	.10
400	Mark Johnson	.10
401	Jeff King	.10
402	Jon Lieber	.10
403	Esteban Loaiza	.10
404	Orlando Merced	.10
405	Gary Wilson RC	.10
406	Scott Cooper	.10
407	Tom Henke	.10
408	Ken Hill	.10
409	Danny Jackson	.10
410	Brian Jordan	.10
411	Ray Lankford	.10
412	John Mabry	.10
413	Todd Zeile	.10
414	Andy Benes	.10
415	Andres Berumen	.10
416	Ken Caminiti	.10
417	Andujar Cedeno	.10
418	Steve Finley	.10
419	Joey Hamilton	.10
420	Dustin Hermanson	.10
421	Melvin Nieves	.10
422	Roberto Petagine	.10
423	Eddie Williams	.10
424	Glenallen Hill	.10
425	Kirt Manwaring	.10
426	Terry Mulholland	.10
427	J.R. Phillips	.10
428	Joe Rosselli	.10
429	Robby Thompson	.10
430	Checklist	.10
431	Checklist	.10
432	Checklist	.10

Cal Ripken, Jr. Enduring Flair

The career of Cal Ripken, Jr., is traced in this insert set found in Series 2 Flair at the average rate of once per dozen packs. Each card has a vintage photo on front, with a large silver-foil "ENDURING" logo toward bottom. Backs have another color photo, a quote and other information about the milestone. The series was extended by a special mail-in offer for five additional cards which chronicled Ripken's record-breaking 1995 season.

		NM/M
Complete Set (15):		40.00
Common Card:		4.00
1	Rookie Of The Year	4.00
2	1st MVP Season	4.00
3	World Series Highlight	4.00
4	Family Tradition	4.00
5	8,243 Consecutive Innings	4.00
6	95 Consecutive Errorless Games	4.00
7	All-Star MVP	4.00
8	1,000th RBI	4.00
9	287th Home Run	4.00
10	2,000th Consecutive Game	4.00
11	Record-tying Game	6.00
12	Record-breaking Game	6.00
13	Defensive Prowess	6.00
14	Literacy Work	6.00
15	2,153 and Counting	6.00

Hot Gloves

The cream of the crop among Series 2 Flair inserts is this set featuring fine fielders. Cards have a background of an embossed gold-foil glove, with a color player photo centered in front. Silver foil comprises the card title and player name at bottom and the Flair logo at top. Backs have a white background, a photo of a glove with a career summary overprinted and a

player portrait photo in a lower corner. These inserts are found at the average rate of once per 25 packs.

		NM/M
Complete Set (12):		35.00
Common Player:		1.25
1	Roberto Alomar	2.00
2	Barry Bonds	10.00
3	Ken Griffey Jr.	7.50
4	Marquis Grissom	1.25
5	Barry Larkin	1.25
6	Darren Lewis	1.25
7	Kenny Lofton	1.25
8	Don Mattingly	6.00
9	Cal Ripken Jr.	10.00
10	Ivan Rodriguez	2.50
11	Devon White	1.25
12	Matt Williams	1.25

Hot Numbers

These Series 1 inserts are a 1:9 find. Gold metallic-foil background with 1994 seasonal stat numbers are the background for a color action photo on front. Horizontal backs have a ghosted portrait photo at right and career highlights at left.

		NM/M
Complete Set (10):		10.00
Common Player:		.50
1	Jeff Bagwell	1.00
2	Albert Belle	.50
3	Barry Bonds	2.25
4	Ken Griffey Jr.	2.00
5	Kenny Lofton	.50
6	Greg Maddux	1.25
7	Mike Piazza	2.00
8	Cal Ripken Jr.	2.25
9	Frank Thomas	1.00
10	Matt Williams	.50

Infield Power

Power rays and waves emanating from the player's bat in an action photo are the front design of this Series 2 chase set. The card title, name and team at bottom, and the Flair logo at top are in silver foil. Backs repeat the wave theme with a player photo on one end and a career summary at the other. These inserts are seeded at the average rate of one per five packs.

		NM/M
Complete Set (12):		15.00
Common Player:		1.00
1	Jeff Bagwell	3.00
2	Jason Bere	1.00
3	Cliff Floyd	1.00
4	Chuck Knoblauch	1.00
5	Kenny Lofton	1.00
6	Javier Lopez	1.00
7	Raul Mondesi	1.00
8	Mike Mussina	1.00
9	Mike Piazza	5.00
10	Manny Ramirez	3.00
11	Tim Salmon	1.00
12	Frank Thomas	3.00

		NM/M
Complete Set (10):		4.00
Common Player:		.25
1	Jeff Bagwell	.75
2	Darren Daulton	.25
3	Cecil Fielder	.25
4	Andres Galarraga	.25
5	Fred McGriff	.25
6	Rafael Palmeiro	.65
7	Mike Piazza	1.50
8	Frank Thomas	1.00
9	Mo Vaughn	.25
10	Matt Williams	.25

Outfield Power

Laser-like colored rays are the background to the action photo on front and portrait on back of this series. The card title, player identification and Flair logo on front are in silver foil. Backs are horizontal, silver-foil enhanced and include a career summary. This chase set is seeded at the average rate of one card per six packs of Series 1 Flair.

		NM/M
Complete Set (10):		4.00
Common Player:		.25
1	Albert Belle	.25
2	Dante Bichette	.25
3	Barry Bonds	2.00
4	Jose Canseco	.50
5	Joe Carter	.25
6	Juan Gonzalez	.50
7	Ken Griffey Jr.	1.00
8	Kirby Puckett	.75
9	Gary Sheffield	.50
10	Ruben Sierra	.25

Today's Spotlight

The premier insert set in Flair Series I, found once every 30 packs or so, this die-cut issue has the player action photo spotlighted in a 2-3/8" bright spot, with the rest of the photo muted in gray and dark gray. The card title, Flair logo, player name and team are in silver foil. The horizontal backs have a portrait photo in the spotlight and career summary on the side.

Wave Of The Future

The cream of baseball's rookie crop is featured in this Series 2 insert set, found once per eight packs on average. Fronts have a graduated color background with a base-

ball/wave morph, which is repeated at the bottom in silver foil, along with the player name. A color action photo is at center. The player's name, team and "Wave of the Future" are repeated in horizontal rows behind the photo. Horizontal backs repeat the wave logo, have another player photo and a career summary.

		NM/M
Complete Set (10):		7.50
Common Player:		.35
1	Jason Bates	.25
2	Armando Benitez	.25
3	Marty Cordova	.25
4	Ray Durham	.25
5	Vaughn Eshelman	.25
6	Carl Everett	.25
7	Shawn Green	1.50
8	Dustin Hermanson	.25
9	Chipper Jones	4.00
10	Hideo Nomo	1.50

1996 Flair Promotional Sheet

Three samples of Flair's 1996 issue and an information card are included on this 5" x 7" promotional sheet. Sheets are found with either a gold or silver finish.

	NM/M
Complete Sheet:	5.00

1996 Flair

Fleer's 1996 Flair baseball set has 400 cards, a parallel set and four insert types. Regular card fronts have two photos of the featured player; backs have a photo and career statistics. All cards have a silver-foil version and a gold-foil version, with each version appearing in equal numbers. Seven-card packs carried an issue price of $4.99.

		NM/M
Complete Set (400):		50.00
Common Player:		.15
Pack (9):		3.00
Wax Box (18):		40.00
1	Roberto Alomar	.30
2	Brady Anderson	.15
3	Bobby Bonilla	.15
4	Scott Erickson	.15
5	Jeffrey Hammonds	.15
6	Jimmy Haynes	.15
7	Chris Hoiles	.15
8	Kent Mercker	.15
9	Mike Mussina	.50
10	Randy Myers	.15
11	Rafael Palmeiro	.75
12	Cal Ripken Jr.	3.00
(12p)	Cal Ripken Jr./OPS (No card #.)	3.00
13	B.J. Surhoff	.15
14	David Wells	.15
15	Jose Canseco	.30
16	Roger Clemens	1.75
17	Wil Cordero	.15
18	Tom Gordon	.15
19	Mike Greenwell	.15
20	Dwayne Hosey	.15
21	Jose Malave	.15
22	Tim Naehring	.15
23	Troy O'Leary	.15
24	Aaron Sele	.15
25	Heathcliff Slocumb	.15
26	Mike Stanley	.15
27	Jeff Suppan	.15
28	John Valentin	.15
29	Mo Vaughn	.30
30	Tim Wakefield	.15
31	Jim Abbott	.15
32	Garret Anderson	.15
33	George Arias	.15
34	Chili Davis	.15
35	Gary DiSarcina	.15
36	Jim Edmonds	.15
37	Chuck Finley	.15
38	Todd Greene	.15
39	Mark Langston	.15
40	Troy Percival	.15
41	Tim Salmon	.15
42	Lee Smith	.15
43	J.T. Snow	.15
44	Randy Velarde	.15
45	Tim Wallach	.15
46	Wilson Alvarez	.15
47	Harold Baines	.15
48	Jason Bere	.15
49	Ray Durham	.15
50	Alex Fernandez	.15
51	Ozzie Guillen	.15
52	Roberto Hernandez	.15
53	Ron Karkovice	.15
54	Darren Lewis	.15
55	Lyle Mouton	.15
56	Tony Phillips	.15
57	Chris Snopek	.15
58	Kevin Tapani	.15
59	Danny Tartabull	.15
60	Frank Thomas	1.00
61	Robin Ventura	.15
62	Sandy Alomar	.15
63	Carlos Baerga	.15
64	Albert Belle	.15
65	Julio Franco	.15
66	Orel Hershiser	.15
67	Kenny Lofton	.15
68	Dennis Martinez	.15
69	Jack McDowell	.15
70	Jose Mesa	.15
71	Eddie Murray	1.00
72	Charles Nagy	.15
73	Tony Pena	.15
74	Manny Ramirez	1.00
75	Julian Tavarez	.15
76	Jim Thome	.65
77	Omar Vizquel	.15
78	Chad Curtis	.15
79	Cecil Fielder	.15
80	Travis Fryman	.15
81	Chris Gomez	.15
82	Bob Higginson	.15
83	Mark Lewis	.15
84	Felipe Lira	.15
85	Alan Trammell	.15
86	Kevin Appier	.15
87	Johnny Damon	.50
88	Tom Goodwin	.15
89	Mark Gubicza	.15
90	Bob Hamelin	.15
91	Keith Lockhart	.15
92	Jeff Montgomery	.15
93	Jon Nunnally	.15
94	Bip Roberts	.15
95	Michael Tucker	.15
96	Joe Vitiello	.15
97	Ricky Bones	.15
98	Chuck Carr	.15
99	Jeff Cirillo	.15
100	Mike Fetters	.15
101	John Jaha	.15
102	Mike Matheny	.15
103	Ben McDonald	.15
104	Matt Mieske	.15
105	Dave Nilsson	.15
106	Kevin Seitzer	.15
107	Steve Sparks	.15
108	Jose Valentin	.15
109	Greg Vaughn	.15
110	Rick Aguilera	.15
111	Rich Becker	.15
112	Marty Cordova	.15
113	LaTroy Hawkins	.15
114	Dave Hollins	.15
115	Roberto Kelly	.15
116	Chuck Knoblauch	.15
117	Matt Lawton RC	.50
118	Pat Meares	.15
119	Paul Molitor	1.00
120	Kirby Puckett	1.50
121	Brad Radke	.15
122	Frank Rodriguez	.15
123	Scott Stahoviak	.15
124	Matt Walbeck	.15
125	Wade Boggs	1.00
126	David Cone	.15
127	Joe Girardi	.15
128	Dwight Gooden	.15
129	Derek Jeter	3.00
130	Jimmy Key	.15
131	Jim Leyritz	.15
132	Tino Martinez	.15
133	Paul O'Neill	.15
134	Andy Pettitte	.40
135	Tim Raines	.15
136	Ruben Rivera	.15
137	Kenny Rogers	.15
138	Ruben Sierra	.15
139	John Wetteland	.15
140	Bernie Williams	.15
141	Tony Batista RC	.50
142	Allen Battle	.15
143	Geronimo Berroa	.15
144	Mike Bordick	.15
145	Scott Brosius	.15
146	Steve Cox	.15
147	Brent Gates	.15
148	Jason Giambi	.65
149	Doug Johns	.15
150	Mark McGwire	2.50
151	Pedro Munoz	.15
152	Ariel Prieto	.15
153	Terry Steinbach	.15
154	Todd Van Poppel	.15
155	Bobby Ayala	.15
156	Chris Bosio	.15
157	Jay Buhner	.15
158	Joey Cora	.15
159	Russ Davis	.15
160	Ken Griffey Jr.	2.00
161	Sterling Hitchcock	.15
162	Randy Johnson	1.00
163	Edgar Martinez	.15
164	Alex Rodriguez	2.50
165	Paul Sorrento	.15
166	Dan Wilson	.15
167	Will Clark	.15
168	Benji Gil	.15
169	Juan Gonzalez	.50
170	Rusty Greer	.15
171	Kevin Gross	.15
172	Darryl Hamilton	.15
173	Mike Henneman	.15
174	Ken Hill	.15
175	Mark McLemore	.15
176	Dean Palmer	.15
177	Roger Pavlik	.15
178	Ivan Rodriguez	.75
179	Mickey Tettleton	.15
180	Bobby Witt	.15
181	Joe Carter	.15
182	Felipe Crespo	.15
183	Alex Gonzalez	.15
184	Shawn Green	.40
185	Juan Guzman	.15
186	Erik Hanson	.15
187	Pat Hentgen	.15
188	Sandy Martinez RC	.15
189	Otis Nixon	.15
190	John Olerud	.15
191	Paul Quantrill	.15
192	Bill Risley	.15
193	Ed Sprague	.15
194	Steve Avery	.15
195	Jeff Blauser	.15
196	Brad Clontz	.15
197	Jermaine Dye	.15
198	Tom Glavine	.40
199	Marquis Grissom	.15
200	Chipper Jones	1.50
201	David Justice	.15
202	Ryan Klesko	.15
203	Mark Lemke	.15
204	Javier Lopez	.15
205	Greg Maddux	1.50
206	Fred McGriff	.15
207	Greg McMichael	.15
208	Wonderful Monds	.15
209	Jason Schmidt	.15
210	John Smoltz	.15
211	Mark Wohlers	.15
212	Jim Bullinger	.15
213	Frank Castillo	.15
214	Kevin Foster	.15
215	Luis Gonzalez	.15
216	Mark Grace	.15
217	Robin Jennings RC	.15
218	Doug Jones	.15
219	Dave Magadan	.15
220	Brian McRae	.15
221	Jaime Navarro	.15
222	Rey Sanchez	.15
223	Ryne Sandberg	1.50
224	Scott Servais	.15
225	Sammy Sosa	1.50
226	Ozzie Timmons	.15
227	Bret Boone	.15
228	Jeff Branson	.15
229	Jeff Brantley	.15
230	Dave Burba	.15
231	Vince Coleman	.15
232	Steve Gibralter	.15
233	Mike Kelly	.15
234	Barry Larkin	.15
235	Hal Morris	.15
236	Mark Portugal	.15
237	Jose Rijo	.15
238	Reggie Sanders	.15
239	Pete Schourek	.15

No.	Player	Price
240	John Smiley	.15
241	Eddie Taubensee	.15
242	Jason Bates	.15
243	Dante Bichette	.15
244	Ellis Burks	.15
245	Vinny Castilla	.15
246	Andres Galarraga	.15
247	Darren Holmes	.15
248	Curt Leskanic	.15
249	Steve Reed	.15
250	Kevin Ritz	.15
251	Bret Saberhagen	.15
252	Bill Swift	.15
253	Larry Walker	.15
254	Walt Weiss	.15
255	Eric Young	.15
256	Kurt Abbott	.15
257	Kevin Brown	.15
258	John Burkett	.15
259	Greg Colbrunn	.15
260	Jeff Conine	.15
261	Andre Dawson	.40
262	Chris Hammond	.15
263	Charles Johnson	.15
264	Al Leiter	.15
265	Robb Nen	.15
266	Terry Pendleton	.15
267	Pat Rapp	.15
268	Gary Sheffield	.50
269	Quilvio Veras	.15
270	Devon White	.15
271	Bob Abreu	.15
272	Jeff Bagwell	1.00
273	Derek Bell	.15
274	Sean Berry	.15
275	Craig Biggio	.15
276	Doug Drabek	.15
277	Tony Eusebio	.15
278	Richard Hidalgo	.15
279	Brian Hunter	.15
280	Todd Jones	.15
281	Derrick May	.15
282	Orlando Miller	.15
283	James Mouton	.15
284	Shane Reynolds	.15
285	Greg Swindell	.15
286	Mike Blowers	.15
287	Brett Butler	.15
288	Tom Candiotti	.15
289	Roger Cedeno	.15
290	Delino DeShields	.15
291	Greg Gagne	.15
292	Karim Garcia	.15
293	Todd Hollandsworth	.15
294	Eric Karros	.15
295	Ramon Martinez	.15
296	Raul Mondesi	.15
297	Hideo Nomo	.50
298	Mike Piazza	2.00
299	Ismael Valdes	.15
300	Todd Worrell	.15
301	Moises Alou	.15
302	Shane Andrews	.15
303	Yamil Benitez	.15
304	Jeff Fassero	.15
305	Darrin Fletcher	.15
306	Cliff Floyd	.15
307	Mark Grudzielanek	.15
308	Mike Lansing	.15
309	Pedro Martinez	1.00
310	Ryan McGuire	.15
311	Carlos Perez	.15
312	Mel Rojas	.15
313	David Segui	.15
314	Rondell White	.15
315	Edgardo Alfonzo	.15
316	Rico Brogna	.15
317	Carl Everett	.15
318	John Franco	.15
319	Bernard Gilkey	.15
320	Todd Hundley	.15
321	Jason Isringhausen	.15
322	Lance Johnson	.15
323	Bobby Jones	.15
324	Jeff Kent	.15
325	Rey Ordonez	.15
326	Bill Pulsipher	.15
327	Jose Vizcaino	.15
328	Paul Wilson	.15
329	Ricky Bottalico	.15
330	Darren Daulton	.15
331	David Doster RC	.15
332	Lenny Dykstra	.15
333	Jim Eisenreich	.15
334	Sid Fernandez	.15
335	Gregg Jefferies	.15
336	Mickey Morandini	.15
337	Benito Santiago	.15
338	Curt Schilling	.40
339	Kevin Stocker	.15
340	David West	.15
341	Mark Whiten	.15
342	Todd Zeile	.15
343	Jay Bell	.15
344	John Ericks	.15
345	Carlos Garcia	.15
346	Charlie Hayes	.15
347	Jason Kendall	.15
348	Jeff King	.15
349	Mike Kingery	.15
350	Al Martin	.15
351	Orlando Merced	.15
352	Dan Miceli	.15
353	Denny Neagle	.15
354	Alan Benes	.15
355	Andy Benes	.15
356	Royce Clayton	.15
357	Dennis Eckersley	.75
358	Gary Gaetti	.15
359	Ron Gant	.15
360	Brian Jordan	.15
361	Ray Lankford	.15
362	John Mabry	.15
363	T.J. Mathews	.15
364	Mike Morgan	.15
365	Donovan Osborne	.15
366	Tom Pagnozzi	.15
367	Ozzie Smith	1.50
368	Todd Stottlemyre	.15
369	Andy Ashby	.15
370	Brad Ausmus	.15
371	Ken Caminiti	.15
372	Andujar Cedeno	.15
373	Steve Finley	.15
374	Tony Gwynn	1.50
375	Joey Hamilton	.15
376	Rickey Henderson	1.00
377	Trevor Hoffman	.15
378	Wally Joyner	.15
379	Marc Newfield	.15
380	Jody Reed	.15
381	Bob Tewksbury	.15
382	Fernando Valenzuela	.15
383	Rod Beck	.15
384	Barry Bonds	3.00
385	Mark Carreon	.15
386	Shawon Dunston	.15
387	Osvaldo Fernandez RC	.40
388	Glenallen Hill	.15
389	Stan Javier	.15
390	Mark Leiter	.15
391	Kirt Manwaring	.15
392	Robby Thompson	.15
393	William Van Landingham	.15
394	Allen Watson	.15
395	Matt Williams	.15
396	Checklist	.15
397	Checklist	.15
398	Checklist	.15
399	Checklist	.15
400	Checklist	.15

Diamond Cuts

Ten of the game's top stars are showcased on these 1996 Flair inserts. They are seeded one per 20 packs. Fronts have a textured background rainbow metallic foil and silver glitter.

		NM/M
Complete Set (12):		25.00
Common Player:		1.00
1	Jeff Bagwell	2.50
2	Albert Belle	1.00
3	Barry Bonds	6.00
4	Juan Gonzalez	1.25
5	Ken Griffey Jr.	4.00
6	Greg Maddux	3.00
7	Eddie Murray	2.50
8	Mike Piazza	4.00
9	Cal Ripken Jr.	6.00
10	Frank Thomas	2.50
11	Mo Vaughn	1.00
12	Matt Williams	1.00

Hot Gloves

Ten top defensive players are highlighted on these die-cut insert cards, a design first made popular in 1994. Hot Gloves can only be found in hobby packs, at a rate of one per every 90 packs.

		NM/M
Complete Set (10):		60.00
Common Player:		3.00
1	Roberto Alomar	4.00
2	Barry Bonds	15.00
3	Will Clark	3.00
4	Ken Griffey Jr.	10.00
5	Kenny Lofton	3.00
6	Greg Maddux	7.50
7	Mike Piazza	10.00
8	Cal Ripken Jr.	15.00
9	Ivan Rodriguez	6.00
10	Matt Williams	3.00

Powerline

Ten of baseball's top sluggers are featured on these Flair inserts. They are the easiest of the Flair inserts to obtain; seeded one per six packs. Fronts combine yellow-green artwork with the player photo. Backs have a vertical color photo and career information.

		NM/M
Complete Set (10):		6.00
Common Player:		.25
1	Albert Belle	.25
2	Barry Bonds	2.00
3	Juan Gonzalez	.35
4	Ken Griffey Jr.	.75
5	Mark McGwire	1.00
6	Mike Piazza	.75
7	Manny Ramirez	.50
8	Sammy Sosa	.65
9	Frank Thomas	.75
10	Matt Williams	.25

Wave of the Future

These inserts feature up-and-coming young talent in baseball. Twenty 1996 rookies and prospects are printed on lenticular cards. They are seeded one per every 72 packs.

		NM/M
Complete Set (20):		30.00
Common Player:		2.00
1	Bob Abreu	3.00
2	George Arias	2.00
3	Tony Batista	2.00
4	Alan Benes	2.00
5	Yamil Benitez	2.00
6	Steve Cox	2.00
7	David Doster	2.00
8	Jermaine Dye	2.00
9	Osvaldo Fernandez	2.00
10	Karim Garcia	3.00
11	Steve Gibralter	2.00
12	Todd Greene	2.00
13	Richard Hidalgo	2.00
14	Robin Jennings	2.00
15	Jason Kendall	2.00
16	Jose Malave	2.00
17	Wonderful Monds	2.00
18	Rey Ordonez	2.00
19	Ruben Rivera	2.00
20	Paul Wilson	2.00

1997 Flair Showcase Promo Strip

The concept of Flair Showcase's Style-Grace-Showcase set composition is debuted on this 7-1/2" x 3-1/2" strip featuring three cards of Alex Ro-

driguez. The cards are overprinted in gold on front and black on back with "PROMOTIONAL SAMPLE."

	NM/M
Complete Strip (3):	5.00

Row 2 (Style)

The 1997 Flair issue is actually three different versions of a 180-player set printed on a super-glossy thick stock. The most common version, Style, is designated Row 2 on back. Fronts have a color action photo with a black-and-white portrait image in the background, all printed on silver foil. Cards #1-60 are designated "Showtime" on back; #61-120 are "Showpiece" and #121-180 are labeled "Showstopper" and were inserted in varying ratios: Showtime - 1.5:1; Showpiece 1:1.5 and Showstopper 1:1. Cards were sold exclusively at hobby shops in five-card packs for $4.99.

		NM/M
Complete Set (180):		15.00
Common Showtime (1-60):		.15
Common Showpiece (61-120):		.25
Common Showstopper (121-180):		.20
A-Rod Glove Exchange:		125.00
Pack (5):		2.00
Wax Box (24):		35.00
1	Andruw Jones	1.25
2	Derek Jeter	3.00
3	Alex Rodriguez	2.25
4	Paul Molitor	1.25
5	Jeff Bagwell	1.25
6	Scott Rolen	1.00
7	Kenny Lofton	.15
8	Cal Ripken Jr.	3.00
9	Brady Anderson	.15
10	Chipper Jones	1.50
11	Todd Greene	.15
12	Todd Walker	.15
13	Billy Wagner	.15
14	Craig Biggio	.15
15	Kevin Orie	.15
16	Hideo Nomo	.65
17	Kevin Appier	.15
18	Bubba Trammell RC	.25
19	Juan Gonzalez	.65
20	Randy Johnson	1.25
21	Roger Clemens	1.75
22	Johnny Damon	.35
23	Ryne Sandberg	1.50
24	Ken Griffey Jr.	2.00
25	Barry Bonds	3.00
26	Nomar Garciaparra	1.50
27	Vladimir Guerrero	1.50
28	Ron Gant	.15
29	Joe Carter	.15
30	Tim Salmon	.35
31	Mike Piazza	2.00
32	Barry Larkin	.35
33	Manny Ramirez	1.25
34	Sammy Sosa	1.50
35	Frank Thomas	1.25
36	Melvin Nieves	.15
37	Tony Gwynn	1.50
38	Gary Sheffield	.35
39	Darin Erstad	.50
40	Ken Caminiti	.15
41	Jermaine Dye	.15
42	Mo Vaughn	.50
43	Raul Mondesi	.15
44	Greg Maddux	1.50
45	Chuck Knoblauch	.15
46	Andy Pettitte	.50
47	Deion Sanders	.25
48	Albert Belle	.35
49	Jamey Wright	.15
50	Rey Ordonez	.15
51	Bernie Williams	.15
52	Mark McGwire	2.25
53	Mike Mussina	.50
54	Bob Abreu	.20
55	Reggie Sanders	.15
56	Brian Jordan	.15
57	Ivan Rodriguez	1.00
58	Roberto Alomar	.30
59	Tim Naehring	.15
60	Edgar Renteria	.25
61	Dean Palmer	.25
62	Benito Santiago	.25
63	David Cone	.25
64	Carlos Delgado	.75
65	Brian Giles RC	.75
66	Alex Ochoa	.25
67	Rondell White	.25
68	Robin Ventura	.25
69	Eric Karros	.25
70	Jose Valentin	.25
71	Rafael Palmeiro	1.00
72	Chris Snopek	.25
73	David Justice	.25
74	Tom Glavine	.45
75	Rudy Pemberton	.25
76	Larry Walker	.25
77	Jim Thome	.75
78	Charles Johnson	.25
79	Dante Powell	.25
80	Derrek Lee	.75
81	Jason Kendall	.25
82	Todd Hollandsworth	.25
83	Bernard Gilkey	.25
84	Mel Rojas	.25
85	Dmitri Young	.25
86	Bret Boone	.25
87	Pat Hentgen	.25
88	Bobby Bonilla	.25
89	John Wetteland	.25
90	Todd Hundley	.25
91	Wilton Guerrero	.25
92	Geronimo Berroa	.25
93	Al Martin	.25
94	Danny Tartabull	.25
95	Brian McRae	.25
96	Steve Finley	.25
97	Todd Stottlemyre	.25
98	John Smoltz	.25
99	Matt Williams	.25
100	Eddie Murray	1.25
101	Henry Rodriguez	.25
102	Marty Cordova	.25
103	Juan Guzman	.25
104	Chili Davis	.25
105	Eric Young	.25
106	Jeff Abbott	.25
107	Shannon Stewart	.25
108	Rocky Coppinger	.25
109	Jose Canseco	.65
110	Dante Bichette	.25
111	Dwight Gooden	.25
112	Scott Brosius	.25
113	Steve Avery	.25
114	Andres Galarraga	.25
115	Sandy Alomar Jr.	.25
116	Ray Lankford	.25
117	Jorge Posada	.25
118	Ryan Klesko	.25
119	Jay Buhner	.25
120	Jose Guillen	.25
121	Paul O'Neill	.20
122	Jimmy Key	.20
123	Hal Morris	.20
124	Travis Fryman	.20
125	Jim Edmonds	.20
126	Jeff Cirillo	.20
127	Fred McGriff	.20
128	Alan Benes	.20
129	Derek Bell	.20
130	Tony Graffanino	.20
131	Shawn Green	.40
132	Denny Neagle	.20
133	Alex Fernandez	.20
134	Mickey Morandini	.20
135	Royce Clayton	.20
136	Jose Mesa	.20
137	Edgar Martinez	.20
138	Curt Schilling	.40
139	Lance Johnson	.20
140	Andy Benes	.20
141	Charles Nagy	.20
142	Mariano Rivera	.40
143	Mark Wohlers	.20
144	Ken Hill	.20
145	Jay Bell	.20
146	Bob Higginson	.20
147	Mark Grudzielanek	.20
148	Ray Durham	.20
149	John Olerud	.20
150	Joey Hamilton	.20
151	Trevor Hoffman	.20
152	Dan Wilson	.20
153	J.T. Snow	.20
154	Marquis Grissom	.20
155	Yamil Benitez	.20
156	Rusty Greer	.20
157	Darryl Kile	.20
158	Ismael Valdes	.20
159	Jeff Conine	.20
160	Darren Daulton	.20
161	Chan Ho Park	.20
162	Troy Percival	.20
163	Wade Boggs	1.50
164	Dave Nilsson	.20
165	Vinny Castilla	.20
166	Kevin Brown	.20
167	Dennis Eckersley	1.00
168	Wendell Magee Jr.	.20
169	John Jaha	.20
170	Garret Anderson	.20
171	Jason Giambi	.75
172	Mark Grace	.15
173	Tony Clark	.20
174	Moises Alou	.20
175	Brett Butler	.20
176	Cecil Fielder	.20
177	Chris Widger	.20
178	Doug Drabek	.20
179	Ellis Burks	.20
180	Shigetosi Hasegawa	.20

Row 1 (Grace)

The second level of '97 Flair scarcity is represented by the Row 1/Grace cards (so designated on back). These are visually differentiated on front by the use of a full background for the action photo, and the addition of a color portrait. Row 1/Grace cards are further broken down by their designation on back as: "Showstopper" (#1-60; seeded 1:2.5 packs), "Showtime" (#61-120; 1:2) and "Showpiece" (#121-180; 1:3) with varying insertion rates as shown.

	NM/M
Complete Set (180):	50.00
Common Showstopper (1-60):	.35
Stars:	1.5X
Common Showtime (#61-120):	.25
Stars:	1X
Common Showpiece (#121-180):	.60
Stars:	1.5X

Row 0 (Showcase)

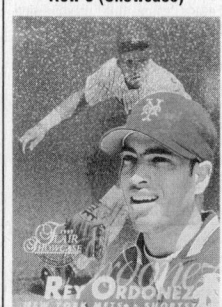

The scarcest level of '97 Flair is the Row 0/Showcase cards (so designated on front and back). These are identifiable on front by the use of a color portrait in the foreground, with a large action photo behind, printed on a gold-flecked metallic background. Row 0/Showcase cards are further broken down by their designation on back as: "Showpiece" (#1-60; seeded 1:24 packs), "Showstopper" (#61-120; 1:12) and "Showtime" (#121-180; 1:5) with varying insertion rates as shown.

	NM/M
Complete Set (180):	200.00
Common Showpiece (1-60):	1.50
Stars:	2X
Common Showstopper (61-120):	.75
Stars:	4X
Common Showtime (121-180):	.35
Stars:	3X

Legacy Collection

This 540-card parallel set is printed on matte-finish stock rather than the high-gloss of the regular cards. Front graphic highlights are in blue foil, as is the serial number on back from within each card's edition of just 100. Stated odds of insertion are one per 30 packs. Because all Legacies are printed in identical numbers, there is no premium for cards of different rows.

	NM/M
Common Player:	10.00
Stars:	25X

Legacy Masterpiece

The insert card chase reached its inevitable zenith with the creation of this series of one-of-a-kind inserts. Each of the 180 players' three cards (Row 2/Style, Row 1/Grace, Row 0/Showcase) in the '97 Flair Legacy Collection was also produced in an edition of one card and inserted at a rate of about one per 3,000 packs. Instead of the blue metallic foil highlights on front and back of the regular Legacy cards, the one-of-a-kind Masterpieces are highlighted in purple and carry a notation on back, "The Only 1 of 1 Masterpiece." Because of the unique nature of each card, value depends solely on demand, thus presentation of meaningful "catalog" values is not possible.

	NM/M
Common Player:	100.00

Diamond Cuts

This 20-card insert, found 1:20 packs, features a die-cut design with an action photo of the player appearing above a baseball diamond in the lower background.

		NM/M
Complete Set (20):		55.00
Common Player:		1.50
1	Jeff Bagwell	3.00
2	Albert Belle	1.50
3	Ken Caminiti	1.50
4	Juan Gonzalez	2.00
5	Ken Griffey Jr.	4.50
6	Tony Gwynn	4.00
7	Todd Hundley	1.50
8	Andruw Jones	3.00
9	Chipper Jones	4.00
10	Greg Maddux	5.00
11	Mark McGwire	5.00
12	Mike Piazza	4.50
13	Derek Jeter	6.00
14	Manny Ramirez	3.00
15	Cal Ripken Jr.	6.00
16	Alex Rodriguez	5.00
17	Frank Thomas	3.00
18	Mo Vaughn	1.50
19	Bernie Williams	1.50
20	Matt Williams	1.50

Hot Gloves

Inserted 1:90 packs, Hot Gloves features 15 cards with a die-cut "flaming glove" design printed in thermally active inks and saluting some of baseball's best defensive players.

		NM/M
Complete Set (15):		125.00
Common Player:		2.50
1	Roberto Alomar	3.00
2	Barry Bonds	20.00
3	Juan Gonzalez	6.00
4	Ken Griffey Jr.	15.00
5	Marquis Grissom	2.50
6	Derek Jeter	20.00

7	Chipper Jones	12.00
8	Barry Larkin	2.50
9	Kenny Lofton	2.50
10	Greg Maddux	12.00
11	Mike Piazza	15.00
12	Cal Ripken Jr.	20.00
13	Alex Rodriguez	17.50
14	Ivan Rodriguez	7.50
15	Frank Thomas	10.00

Wave of the Future

This insert focuses on some of the up-and-coming young stars in the game. Cards were seeded 1:4 packs. A large ocean wave makes up the background of each card front.

		NM/M
Complete Set (27):		10.00
Common Player:		.25
1	Todd Greene	.25
2	Andruw Jones	1.50
3	Randall Simon	.25
4	Wady Almonte	.25
5	Pat Cline	.25
6	Jeff Abbott	.25
7	Justin Towle	.25
8	Richie Sexson	.25
9	Bubba Trammell	.25
10	Bob Abreu	.35
11	David Arias (Last name actually Ortiz.)	9.00
12	Todd Walker	.25
13	Orlando Cabrera	.25
14	Vladimir Guerrero	1.50
15	Ricky Ledee	.25
16	Jorge Posada	.25
17	Ruben Rivera	.25
18	Scott Spiezio	.25
19	Scott Rolen	1.00
20	Emil Brown	.25
21	Jose Guillen	.25
22	T.J. Staton	.25
23	Elieser Marrero	.25
24	Fernando Tatis	.25
25	Ryan Jones	.25
WF1	Hideki Irabu	.25
WF2	Jose Cruz Jr.	.25

1998 Flair Showcase Promo Strip

Each of the Row 0, 1, 2 and 3 variations of Cal Ripken's cards are featured on this 10" x 3-1/2" promo strip. The front of each card has "PROMOTIONAL SAMPLE" printed diagonally in gold; on the back the notice is printed in black-and-white.

	NM/M
Complete Promo Strip:	5.00

1998 Flair Showcase Row 3

Row 3, or Flair, cards are considered the base cards of '98 Showcase. They feature a close-up black-and-white portrait photo in the background and an action shot in front, overprinted on a silver-foil background. Flair/Showtime (#1-30) cards are inserted 1:.9 packs,

Flair/Showstopper (#31-60) are found 1:1.1 packs, Flair/Showdown (#61-90) cards are inserted 1:1.5 packs and Flair/Showdown (#91-120) cards are inserted 1:2 packs.

		NM/M
Complete Set (120):		20.00
Common Player (1-30):		.25
Common Player (31-60):		.25
Common Player (61-90):		.35
Common Player (91-120):		.45
Pack (5):		2.50
Wax Box (24):		45.00
1	Ken Griffey Jr.	2.00
2	Travis Lee	.25
3	Frank Thomas	1.25
4	Ben Grieve	.25
5	Nomar Garciaparra	1.50
6	Jose Cruz Jr.	.25
7	Alex Rodriguez	2.50
8	Cal Ripken Jr.	3.00
9	Mark McGwire	2.50
10	Chipper Jones	1.50
11	Paul Konerko	.40
12	Todd Helton	1.00
13	Greg Maddux	1.50
14	Derek Jeter	3.00
15	Jaret Wright	.25
16	Livan Hernandez	.25
17	Mike Piazza	2.00
18	Juan Encarnacion	.25
19	Tony Gwynn	1.50
20	Scott Rolen	1.00
21	Roger Clemens	1.75
22	Tony Clark	.25
23	Albert Belle	.25
24	Mo Vaughn	.25
25	Andruw Jones	1.25
26	Jason Dickson	.25
27	Fernando Tatis	.25
28	Ivan Rodriguez	.75
29	Ricky Ledee	.50
30	Darin Erstad	.25
31	Brian Rose	.25
32	Magglio Ordonez RC	3.00
33	Larry Walker	.25
34	Bobby Higginson	.25
35	Chili Davis	.25
36	Barry Bonds	3.00
37	Vladimir Guerrero	1.25
38	Jeff Bagwell	1.25
39	Kenny Lofton	.25
40	Ryan Klesko	.25
41	Mike Cameron	.25
42	Charles Johnson	.25
43	Andy Pettitte	.40
44	Juan Gonzalez	1.25
45	Tim Salmon	.25
46	Hideki Irabu	.25
47	Paul Molitor	1.25
48	Edgar Renteria	.25
49	Manny Ramirez	1.25
50	Jim Edmonds	.25
51	Bernie Williams	.25
52	Roberto Alomar	.40
53	David Justice	.25
54	Rey Ordonez	.25
55	Ken Caminiti	.25
56	Jose Guillen	.25
57	Randy Johnson	1.25
58	Brady Anderson	.25
59	Hideo Nomo	.50
60	Tino Martinez	.50
61	John Smoltz	.35
62	Joe Carter	.35
63	Matt Williams	.35
64	Robin Ventura	.35
65	Barry Larkin	.35
66	Dante Bichette	.35
67	Travis Fryman	.35
68	Gary Sheffield	.60
69	Eric Karros	.35
70	Matt Stairs	.35
71	Al Martin	.35
72	Jay Buhner	.35
73	Ray Lankford	.35
74	Carlos Delgado	.65
75	Edgardo Alfonzo	.35
76	Rondell White	.35
77	Chuck Knoblauch	.35
78	Raul Mondesi	.35
79	Johnny Damon	.60
80	Matt Morris	.35
81	Tom Glavine	.60
82	Kevin Brown	.35
83	Garret Anderson	.35
84	Mike Mussina	.40
85	Pedro Martinez	1.25
86	Craig Biggio	.35
87	Darryl Kile	.35
88	Rafael Palmeiro	.75
89	Jim Thome	.60
90	Andres Galarraga	.35
91	Sammy Sosa	1.50
92	Willie Greene	.45
93	Vinny Castilla	.45
94	Justin Thompson	.45
95	Jeff King	.45
96	Jeff Cirillo	.45
97	Mark Grudzielanek	.45
98	Brad Radke	.45
99	John Olerud	.45
100	Curt Schilling	.65
101	Steve Finley	.45
102	J.T. Snow	.45
103	Edgar Martinez	.45
104	Wilson Alvarez	.45
105	Rusty Greer	.45
106	Pat Hentgen	.45
107	David Cone	.45
108	Fred McGriff	.45
109	Jason Giambi	.75
110	Tony Womack	.45
111	Bernard Gilkey	.45
112	Alan Benes	.45
113	Mark Grace	.45
114	Reggie Sanders	.45
115	Moises Alou	.45
116	John Jaha	.45
117	Henry Rodriguez	.45
118	Dean Palmer	.45
119	Mike Lieberthal	.45
120	Shawn Estes	.45

Row 2

Row 2, or Style (as they are designated on front) cards in Flair Showcase are the second easiest type of card to pull from packs. Fronts are similar to Row 3 base cards, but include the entire background of the action photo and have a color portrait photo. Cards #1-30 are inserted one per three packs, #31-60 are found 1:2.5 packs, #61-90 cards are 1:4 and #91-120 are inserted one per three packs.

	NM/M
Complete Set (120):	40.00
Common Player:	.50
Stars:	1.5-2X

Row 1

Row 1, also referred to as Grace, was the second most difficult type of card to pull from Flair Showcase. The front design has an action photo overprinted on a large portrait which is printed on a rainbow metallic-foil background. Cards #1-30 are seeded one per 16 packs, #31-60 are 1:24, #61-90 are 1:6 and #91-120 are 1:10.

	NM/M
Complete Set (1-120):	100.00
Commons (1-30):	1.00
Stars:	2X
Commons (31-60):	1.25
Stars:	3X
Commons (61-90):	.35
Stars:	1X
Commons (91-120):	.75
Stars:	1.5X

Row 0

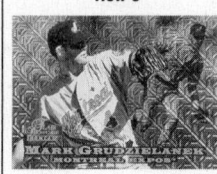

Row 0 is the most difficult of the four tiers to obtain from packs. Two action photos are combined on a horizontal format with one in a prismatic foil background. The first 30 cards are serially numbered to 250, cards #30-60 are numbered to 500, #61-90 are numbered to 1,000 and #91-120 are numbered within an edition of 2,000.

	NM/M
Complete Set (120):	350.00
Common Player (1-30):	5.00
Stars:	10X
Common Player (31-60):	3.00
Stars:	8X
Common Player (61-90):	2.00
Stars:	6X
Common Player (91-120):	1.00
Stars:	4X

Legacy Collection

Legacy Collection parallels all 480 cards in the Flair Showcase set. Each Legacy Collection card displays the player's name in black plate laminated on the back, with the card's sequential numbering to 100 in gold foil.

	NM/M
Common Player:	7.50
Stars:	25X

Legacy Masterpiece

Each of the 120 players' four cards (Rows 3, 2, 1 and 0) in the '98 Flair Legacy Collection was also produced in an edition of one card and inserted at a rate of about one per 3,000 packs. The one-of-a-kind cards carry a notation on back: "The Only 1 of 1 Masterpiece." With supply a fixed quantity, value depends on demand at any particular time, thus it is not possible to present meaningful "catalog" values.

	NM/M
Common Player:	50.00

Perfect 10

Perfect 10 features the game's most popular players on a silk-screen technology design. The cards were serial numbered to 10 on the back and were inserted into packs of Flair Showcase.

		NM/M
Complete Set (10):		1,600
Common Player:		100.00
1	Ken Griffey Jr.	200.00
2	Cal Ripken Jr.	300.00
3	Frank Thomas	125.00
4	Mike Piazza	200.00
5	Greg Maddux	150.00
6	Nomar Garciaparra	150.00
7	Mark McGwire	250.00
8	Scott Rolen	100.00
9	Alex Rodriguez	250.00
10	Roger Clemens	175.00

Wave of the Future

Twelve up-and-coming players with hot minor league stats and Major League potential are displayed in Wave of the Future. The cards contain a clear acetate card inside a plastic covering that is filled with vegetable oil and glitter. These were inserted one per 20 packs and are numbered with a "WF" prefix.

		NM/M
Complete Set (12):		10.00
Common Player:		.50
WF1	Travis Lee	.50
WF2	Todd Helton	5.00
WF3	Ben Grieve	.50
WF4	Juan Encarnacion	.50
WF5	Brad Fullmer	.50
WF6	Ruben Rivera	.50
WF7	Paul Konerko	.75
WF8	Derrek Lee	1.50
WF9	Mike Lowell	.50
WF10	Magglio Ordonez	2.00
WF11	Rich Butler	.50
WF12	Eli Marrero	.50

1999 Flair Showcase Row 3 (Power)

Power is one of three tiers in 1999 Showcase. The front on this base-level version is rainbow holo-foil including the large portrait photo in the background. In the foreground is a color action photo. Matte textured silver spot embossing is printed over the player's name and team at lower-right. All three Rows of Showcase can be found with three different back designs. Showtime presents traditional annual and career stats. Horizontally formatted Showpiece cards have a black-and-white player photo as a "Classic Matchup" of the player's stats to those of a past star. Showdown backs have a color action photo on a brightly-colored wave-pattern background. A stat box at center offers career numbers in four unique categories like day-night, grass-turf, etc. Each of these three back-design levels of scarcity has a different advertised insertion rate. Within Row 3/Power, these vary only between one card in .9 packs, and one card in 1.2 packs, thus there is no practical value differential. Five-card packs of Flair Showcase had a $4.99 SRP.

		NM/M
Complete Set (144):		25.00
Common Player:		.25
Pack (5):		3.00
Wax Box (24):		45.00
1	Mark McGwire	2.50
2	Sammy Sosa	1.50
3	Ken Griffey Jr.	2.00
4	Chipper Jones	1.50
5	Ben Grieve	.25
6	J.D. Drew	.75
7	Jeff Bagwell	1.00
8	Cal Ripken Jr.	3.00
9	Tony Gwynn	1.50
10	Nomar Garciaparra	1.50
11	Travis Lee	.35
12	Troy Glaus	.75
13	Mike Piazza	2.00
14	Alex Rodriguez	2.50
15	Kevin Brown	.25
16	Darin Erstad	.50
17	Scott Rolen	.50
18	Micah Bowie RC	.25
19	Juan Gonzalez	.50
20	Kerry Wood	.50
21	Roger Clemens	1.75
22	Derek Jeter	3.00
23	Pat Burrell RC	3.00
24	Tim Salmon	.25
25	Barry Bonds	3.00
26	Roosevelt Brown RC	.25
27	Vladimir Guerrero	1.00
28	Randy Johnson	1.00
29	Mo Vaughn	.25
30	Fernando Seguignol	.25
31	Greg Maddux	1.50
32	Tony Clark	.25
33	Eric Chavez	.40
34	Kris Benson	.25
35	Frank Thomas	1.00
36	Mario Encarnacion	.25
37	Gabe Kapler	.25
38	Jeremy Giambi	.25
39	Peter Tucci RC	.25
40	Manny Ramirez	1.00
41	Albert Belle	.25
42	Warren Morris	.25
43	Michael Barrett	.25
44	Andruw Jones	1.00
45	Carlos Delgado	.60
46	Jaret Wright	.25
47	Juan Encarnacion	.25
48	Scott Hunter	.25
49	Tino Martinez	.25
50	Craig Biggio	.25
51	Jim Thome	.60
52	Vinny Castilla	.25
53	Tom Glavine	.40
54	Bob Higginson	.25
55	Moises Alou	.25
56	Robin Ventura	.25
57	Bernie Williams	.25
58	Pedro J. Martinez	1.00
59	Greg Vaughn	.25
60	Ray Lankford	.25
61	Jose Canseco	.40
62	Ivan Rodriguez	1.00
63	Shawn Green	.40
64	Rafael Palmeiro	.75
65	Ellis Burks	.25
66	Jason Kendall	.25
67	David Wells	.25
68	Rondell White	.25
69	Gary Sheffield	.40
70	Ken Caminiti	.25
71	Cliff Floyd	.25
72	Larry Walker	.25
73	Bartolo Colon	.25
74	Barry Larkin	.25
75	Calvin Pickering	.25
76	Jim Edmonds	.25
77	Henry Rodriguez	.25
78	Roberto Alomar	.40
79	Andres Galarraga	.25
80	Richie Sexson	.25
81	Todd Helton	.75
82	Damion Easley	.25
83	Livan Hernandez	.25
84	Carlos Beltran	.60
85	Todd Hundley	.25
86	Todd Walker	.25
87	Scott Brosius	.25
88	Bob Abreu	.25
89	Corey Koskie	.25
90	Ruben Rivera	.25

91	Edgar Renteria	.25
92	Quinton McCracken	.25
93	Bernard Gilkey	.25
94	Shannon Stewart	.25
95	Dustin Hermanson	.25
96	Mike Caruso	.25
97	Alex Gonzalez	.25
98	Raul Mondesi	.25
99	David Cone	.25
100	Curt Schilling	.40
101	Brian Giles	.25
102	Edgar Martinez	.25
103	Rolando Arrojo	.25
104	Derek Bell	.25
105	Denny Neagle	.25
106	Marquis Grissom	.25
107	Bret Boone	.25
108	Mike Mussina	.50
109	John Smoltz	.25
110	Brett Tomko	.25
111	David Justice	.25
112	Andy Pettitte	.40
113	Eric Karros	.25
114	Dante Bichette	.25
115	Jeromy Burnitz	.25
116	Paul Konerko	.40
117	Steve Finley	.25
118	Ricky Ledee	.25
119	Edgardo Alfonzo	.25
120	Dean Palmer	.25
121	Rusty Greer	.25
122	Luis Gonzalez	.25
123	Randy Winn	.25
124	Jeff Kent	.25
125	Doug Glanville	.25
126	Justin Thompson	.25
127	Bret Saberhagen	.25
128	Wade Boggs	1.50
129	Al Leiter	.25
130	Paul O'Neill	.25
131	Chan Ho Park	.25
132	Johnny Damon	.60
133	Darryl Kile	.25
134	Reggie Sanders	.25
135	Kevin Millwood	.25
136	Charles Johnson	.25
137	Ray Durham	.25
138	Rico Brogna	.25
139	Matt Williams	.25
140	Sandy Alomar	.25
141	Jeff Cirillo	.25
142	Devon White	.25
143	Andy Benes	.25
144	Mike Stanley	.25
	Checklist Card	.05

FRow 2 (Passion)

The metallic-foil background in the second level of Flair Showcase - Row 2/Passion - has an action photo printed in front of large textured numerals representing the player's uniform number. In the foreground is another action shot. Backs have the same three designs as Row 3, but only vary in insertion rate from one card per 1.3 packs to one card per three packs.

		NM/M
Complete Set (144):		65.00
Common Player:		.25
Showdown (1-48):		2X
Showpiece (49-96):		1X
Showtime (97-144):		1X

Row 1 (Showcase)

Showcase level - Row 1 - presents two portraits and an action photo and the player's uniform number on a plastic laminate in a horizontal format. A gold-foil serial number is stamped into the upper-left corner in one of three levels of scarcity: Showpiece (#1-48) is lim-

ited to 1,500 numbered sets, Showtime (#49-96) is limited to 3,000 sets and Showdown (#97-144) is numbered to 6,000 sets.

		NM/M
Complete Set (144):		300.00
Common Showpiece (1-48):		2.00
Showpiece Stars:		5X
Common Showtime (49-96):		1.00
Showtime Stars:		3X
Common Showdown (97-144):		.50
Showdown Stars:		2X

Legacy / Masterpiece

Each of the 432 total cards in Flair Showcase was also produced in a pair of extremely limited parallels. The blue-foil enhanced Legacy Collection cards are serially numbered within an edition of just 99. The presence of purple foil on front signifies a Legacy Masterpiece card, which is identified on front by the notation, "The Only 1 of 1 Masterpiece." Because of their unique nature, determination of a "book value" for Masterpiece cards is not possible.

	NM/M
Common Legacy:	6.00
Legacy Stars:	20X
Common Masterpiece:	50.00

Measure of Greatness

This 15-card set captures baseball's top superstars who were closing in on milestones during the 1999 season. Each card is sequentially numbered to 500.

		NM/M
Complete Set (15):		100.00
Common Player:		3.00
Production 500 Sets		
1	Roger Clemens	7.50
2	Nomar Garciaparra	6.50
3	Juan Gonzalez	3.00
4	Ken Griffey Jr.	9.00
5	Vladimir Guerrero	5.00
6	Tony Gwynn	6.50
7	Derek Jeter	15.00
8	Chipper Jones	8.00
9	Mark McGwire	12.50
10	Mike Piazza	9.00
11	Manny Ramirez	5.00
12	Cal Ripken Jr.	15.00
13	Alex Rodriguez	12.50
14	Sammy Sosa	6.50
15	Frank Thomas	5.00

Wave of the Future

This insert set spotlights young stars on the rise and is limited to 1,000 serial numbered sets.

		NM/M
Complete Set (15):		40.00
Common Player:		1.50
Production 1,000 Sets		
1	Kerry Wood	4.00
2	Ben Grieve	1.50
3	J.D. Drew	4.00
4	Juan Encarnacion	1.50
5	Travis Lee	2.00
6	Todd Helton	7.50
7	Troy Glaus	7.50
8	Ricky Ledee	1.50
9	Eric Chavez	2.00
10	Ben Davis	1.50
11	George Lombard	1.50
12	Jeremy Giambi	1.50
13	Roosevelt Brown	1.50
14	Pat Burrell	6.00
15	Preston Wilson	1.50

1981 Fleer

For the first time in 18 years, Fleer issued a baseball card set featuring current players. The 660-card effort included numerous errors in the first print run which were subsequently corrected. The 2-1/2" x 3-1/2" cards are numbered by team in order of the previous season's finish. Card fronts feature a full-color photo inside a border which is color-coded by team. Backs are printed in black, gray and yellow on white stock and carry full player statistical information. The player's batting average or earned run average is located in a circle in the upper-right corner of the back. The complete set price in the checklist that follows does not include the higher priced variations.

		NM/M
Complete Set (660):		30.00
Common Player:		.05
Wax Pack (17):		1.75
Wax Box (38):		50.00
Vending Box (500):		20.00
1	Pete Rose	3.00
2	Larry Bowa	.05
3	Manny Trillo	.05
4	Bob Boone	.05
5a	Mike Schmidt/Portrait	2.50
5b	Mike Schmidt/Btg	2.00
6a	Steve Carlton	
	("Lefty" on front.)	1.00
6b	Steve Carlton	
	(Pitcher of the Year on front, date 1066 on back.)	2.00
6c	Steve Carlton	
	(Pitcher of the Year on front, date 1966 on back.)	2.50
7a	Tug McGraw	
	(Game Saver on front.)	.50
7b	Tug McGraw	
	(Pitcher on front.)	.05
8	Larry Christenson	.05
9	Bake McBride	.05
10	Greg Luzinski	.05
11	Ron Reed	.05
12	Dickie Noles	.05
13	Keith Moreland RC	.15
14	Bob Walk RC	.05
15	Lonnie Smith	.05
16	Dick Ruthven	.05
17	Sparky Lyle	.05
18	Greg Gross	.05
19	Garry Maddox	.05
20	Nino Espinosa	.05
21	George Vukovich	.05
22	John Vukovich	.05
23	Ramon Aviles	.05
24a	Kevin Saucier	
	(Ken Saucier on back.)	.10
24b	Kevin Saucier	
	(Kevin Saucier on back.)	.50
25	Randy Lerch	.05
26	Del Unser	.05
27	Tim McCarver	.15
28a	George Brett/Btg	2.00
28b	George Brett/Portait	2.00

29a	Willie Wilson/Portait	.50
29b	Willie Wilson/Btg	.15
30	Paul Splittorff	.05
31	Dan Quisenberry	.05
32a	Amos Otis/Btg	.50
32b	Amos Otis (Portrait)	.10
33	Steve Busby	.05
34	U.L. Washington	.05
35	Dave Chalk	.05
36	Darrell Porter	.05
37	Marty Pattin	.05
38	Larry Gura	.05
39	Renie Martin	.05
40	Rich Gale	.05
41a	Hal McRae (Dark blue "Royals" on front.)	.40
41b	Hal McRae (Light blue "Royals" on front.)	.10
42	Dennis Leonard	.05
43	Willie Aikens	.05
44	Frank White	.05
45	Clint Hurdle	.05
46	John Wathan	.05
47	Pete LaCock	.05
48	Rance Mulliniks	.05
49	Jeff Twitty	.05
50	Jamie Quirk	.05
51	Art Howe	.05
52	Ken Forsch	.05
53	Vern Ruhle	.05
54	Joe Niekro	.05
55	Frank LaCorte	.05
56	J.R. Richard	.05
57	Nolan Ryan	4.00
58	Enos Cabell	.05
59	Cesar Cedeno	.05
60	Jose Cruz	.05
61	Bill Virdon	.05
62	Terry Puhl	.05
63	Joaquin Andujar	.05
64	Alan Ashby	.05
65	Joe Sambito	.05
66	Denny Walling	.05
67	Jeff Leonard	.05
68	Luis Pujols	.05
69	Bruce Bochy	.05
70	Rafael Landestoy	.05
71	Dave Smith RC	.05
72	Danny Heep RC	.05
73	Julio Gonzalez	.05
74	Craig Reynolds	.05
75	Gary Woods	.05
76	Dave Bergman	.05
77	Randy Niemann	.05
78	Joe Morgan	1.00
79a	Reggie Jackson/Portrait	2.50
79b	Reggie Jackson/Btg	2.00
80	Bucky Dent	.10
81	Tommy John	.10
82	Luis Tiant	.05
83	Rick Cerone	.05
84	Dick Howser	.05
85	Lou Piniella	.10
86	Ron Davis	.05
87a	Graig Nettles (Craig on back.)	4.50
87b	Graig Nettles (Graig on back.)	.15
88	Ron Guidry	.10
89	Rich Gossage	.10
90	Rudy May	.05
91	Gaylord Perry	.75
92	Eric Soderholm	.05
93	Bob Watson	.05
94	Bobby Murcer	.10
95	Bobby Brown	.05
96	Jim Spencer	.05
97	Tom Underwood	.05
98	Oscar Gamble	.05
99	Johnny Oates	.05
100	Fred Stanley	.05
101	Ruppert Jones	.05
102	Dennis Werth	.05
103	Joe Lefebvre	.05
104	Brian Doyle	.05
105	Aurelio Rodriguez	.05
106	Doug Bird	.05
107	Mike Griffin	.05
108	Tim Lollar	.05
109	Willie Randolph	.05
110	Steve Garvey	.30
111	Reggie Smith	.05
112	Don Sutton	.75
113	Burt Hooton	.05
114a	Davy Lopes (Davey) (No finger on back.)	.05
114b	Davy Lopes (Davey) (Small finger on back.)	.50
115	Dusty Baker	.05
116	Tom Lasorda	.10
117	Bill Russell	.05
118	Jerry Reuss	.05
119	Terry Forster	.05
120a	Bob Welch (Bob on back.)	.10
120b	Bob Welch (Robert)	.50
121	Don Stanhouse	.05
122	Rick Monday	.05
123	Derrel Thomas	.05
124	Joe Ferguson	.05
125	Rick Sutcliffe	.10
126a	Ron Cey (No finger on back.)	
126b	Ron Cey (Small finger on back.)	.50
127	Dave Goltz	.05
128	Jay Johnstone	.05
129	Steve Yeager	.05
130	Gary Weiss	.05

131	Mike Scioscia RC	.50
132	Vic Davalillo	.05
133	Doug Rau	.05
134	Pepe Frias	.05
135	Mickey Hatcher	.05
136	Steve Howe RC	.10
137	Robert Castillo	.05
138	Gary Thomasson	.05
139	Rudy Law	.05
140	Fernando Valenzuela RC	1.50
141	Manny Mota	.05
142	Gary Carter	1.00
143	Steve Rogers	.05
144	Warren Cromartie	.05
145	Andre Dawson	.40
146	Larry Parrish	.05
147	Rowland Office	.05
148	Ellis Valentine	.05
149	Dick Williams	.05
150	Bill Gullickson RC	.15
151	Elias Sosa	.05
152	John Tamargo	.05
153	Chris Speier	.05
154	Ron LeFlore	.05
155	Rodney Scott	.05
156	Stan Bahnsen	.05
157	Bill Lee	.05
158	Fred Norman	.05
159	Woodie Fryman	.05
160	Dave Palmer	.05
161	Jerry White	.05
162	Roberto Ramos	.05
163	John D'Acquisto	.05
164	Tommy Hutton	.05
165	Charlie Lea RC	.15
166	Scott Sanderson	.05
167	Ken Macha	.05
168	Tony Bernazard	.05
169	Jim Palmer	1.00
170	Steve Stone	.10
171	Mike Flanagan	.05
172	Al Bumbry	.05
173	Doug DeCinces	.05
174	Scott McGregor	.05
175	Mark Belanger	.05
176	Tim Stoddard	.05
177a	Rick Dempsey (No finger on front.)	.05
177b	Rick Dempsey (Small finger on front.)	.50
178	Earl Weaver	.25
179	Tippy Martinez	.05
180	Dennis Martinez	.05
181	Sammy Stewart	.05
182	Rich Dauer	.05
183	Lee May	.05
184	Eddie Murray	1.00
185	Benny Ayala	.05
186	John Lowenstein	.05
187	Gary Roenicke	.05
188	Ken Singleton	.05
189	Dan Graham	.05
190	Terry Crowley	.05
191	Kiko Garcia	.05
192	Dave Ford	.05
193	Mark Corey	.05
194	Lenn Sakata	.05
195	Doug DeCinces	.05
196	Johnny Bench	1.00
197	Dave Concepcion	.05
198	Ray Knight	.05
199	Ken Griffey	.10
200	Tom Seaver	1.00
201	Dave Collins	.05
202	George Foster	.05
203	Junior Kennedy	.05
204	Frank Pastore	.05
205	Dan Driessen	.05
206	Hector Cruz	.05
207	Paul Moskau	.05
208	Charlie Leibrandt RC	.25
209	Harry Spilman	.05
210	Joe Price RC	.05
211	Tom Hume	.05
212	Joe Nolan	.05
213	Doug Bair	.05
214	Mario Soto	.05
215a	Bill Bonham (No finger on back.)	.05
215b	Bill Bonham (Small finger on back.)	.50
216a	George Foster (Slugger on front.)	.25
216b	George Foster (Outfield on front.)	.15
217	Paul Householder	.05
218	Ron Oester	.05
219	Sam Mejias	.05
220	Sheldon Burnside	.05
221	Carl Yastrzemski	1.00
222	Jim Rice	.40
223	Fred Lynn	.05
224	Carlton Fisk	1.00
225	Rick Burleson	.05
226	Dennis Eckersley	.75
227	Butch Hobson	.05
228	Tom Burgmeier	.05
229	Garry Hancock	.05
230	Don Zimmer	.05
231	Steve Renko	.05
232	Dwight Evans	.05
233	Mike Torrez	.05
234	Bob Stanley	.05
235	Jim Dwyer	.05
236	Dave Stapleton	.05
237	Glenn Hoffman	.05
238	Jerry Remy	.05
239	Dick Drago	.05

#	Player	Price
240	Bill Campbell	.05
241	Tony Perez	.75
242	Phil Niekro	.75
243	Dale Murphy	.30
244	Bob Horner	.05
245	Jeff Burroughs	.05
246	Rick Camp	.05
247	Bob Cox	.25
248	Bruce Benedict	.05
249	Gene Garber	.05
250	Jerry Royster	.05
251a	Gary Matthews (No finger on back.)	.05
251b	Gary Matthews (Small finger on back.)	.50
252	Chris Chambliss	.05
253	Luis Gomez	.05
254	Bill Nahorodny	.05
255	Doyle Alexander	.05
256	Brian Asselstine	.05
257	Biff Pocoroba	.05
258	Mike Lum	.05
259	Charlie Spikes	.05
260	Glenn Hubbard	.05
261	Tommy Boggs	.05
262	Al Hrabosky	.05
263	Rick Matula	.05
264	Preston Hanna	.05
265	Larry Bradford	.05
266	Rafael Ramirez RC	.05
267	Larry McWilliams	.05
268	Rod Carew	1.00
269	Bobby Grich	.05
270	Carney Lansford	.05
271	Don Baylor	.05
272	Joe Rudi	.05
273	Dan Ford	.05
274	Jim Fregosi	.05
275	Dave Frost	.05
276	Frank Tanana	.05
277	Dickie Thon	.05
278	Jason Thompson	.05
279	Rick Miller	.05
280	Bert Campaneris	.05
281	Tom Donohue	.05
282	Brian Downing	.05
283	Fred Patek	.05
284	Bruce Kison	.05
285	Dave LaRoche	.05
286	Don Aase	.05
287	Jim Barr	.05
288	Alfredo Martinez	.05
289	Larry Harlow	.05
290	Andy Hassler	.05
291	Dave Kingman	.05
292	Bill Buckner	.05
293	Rick Reuschel	.05
294	Bruce Sutter	.75
295	Jerry Martin	.05
296	Scot Thompson	.05
297	Ivan DeJesus	.05
298	Steve Dillard	.05
299	Dick Tidrow	.05
300	Randy Martz	.05
301	Lenny Randle	.05
302	Lynn McGlothen	.05
303	Cliff Johnson	.05
304	Tim Blackwell	.05
305	Dennis Lamp	.05
306	Bill Caudill	.05
307	Carlos Lezcano	.05
308	Jim Tracy	.05
309	Doug Capilla	.05
310	Willie Hernandez	.05
311	Mike Vail	.05
312	Mike Krukow	.05
313	Barry Foote	.05
314	Larry Biittner	.05
315	Mike Tyson	.05
316	Lee Mazzilli	.05
317	John Stearns	.05
318	Alex Trevino	.05
319	Craig Swan	.05
320	Frank Taveras	.05
321	Steve Henderson	.05
322	Neil Allen	.05
323	Mark Bomback	.05
324	Mike Jorgensen	.05
325	Joe Torre	.25
326	Elliott Maddox	.05
327	Pete Falcone	.05
328	Ray Burris	.05
329	Claudell Washington	.05
330	Doug Flynn	.05
331	Joel Youngblood	.05
332	Bill Almon	.05
333	Tom Hausman	.05
334	Pat Zachry	.05
335	Jeff Reardon RC	2.00
336	Wally Backman RC	.15
337	Dan Norman	.05
338	Jerry Morales	.05
339	Ed Farmer	.05
340	Bob Molinaro	.05
341	Todd Cruz	.05
342a	Britt Burns RC (No finger on front.)	.10
342b	Britt Burns RC (Small finger on front.)	.50
343	Kevin Bell	.05
344	Tony LaRussa	.25
345	Steve Trout	.05
346	Harold Baines RC	3.00
347	Richard Wortham	.05
348	Wayne Nordhagen	.05
349	Mike Squires	.05
350	Lamar Johnson	.05
351	Rickey Henderson	2.50

#	Player	Price
352	Francisco Barrios	.05
353	Thad Bosley	.05
354	Chet Lemon	.05
355	Bruce Kimm	.05
356	Richard Dotson RC	.05
357	Jim Morrison	.05
358	Mike Proly	.05
359	Greg Pryor	.05
360	Dave Parker	.05
361	Omar Moreno	.05
362a	Kent Tekulve (1071 Waterbury on back)	.15
362b	Kent Tekulve (1971 Waterbury on back)	.50
363	Willie Stargell	1.00
364	Phil Garner	.05
365	Ed Ott	.05
366	Don Robinson	.05
367	Chuck Tanner	.05
368	Jim Rooker	.05
369	Dale Berra	.05
370	Jim Bibby	.05
371	Steve Nicosia	.05
372	Mike Easler	.05
373	Bill Robinson	.05
374	Lee Lacy	.05
375	John Candelaria	.05
376	Manny Sanguillen	.05
377	Rick Rhoden	.05
378	Grant Jackson	.05
379	Tim Foli	.05
380	Rod Scurry RC	.05
381	Bill Madlock	.05
382a	Kurt Bevacqua (Photo reversed, backwards "P" on cap.)	.15
382b	Kurt Bevacqua (Correct photo.)	.50
383	Bert Blyleven	.10
384	Eddie Solomon	.05
385	Enrique Romo	.05
386	John Milner	.05
387	Mike Hargrove	.05
388	Jorge Orta	.05
389	Toby Harrah	.05
390	Tom Veryzer	.05
391	Miguel Dilone	.05
392	Dan Spillner	.05
393	Jack Brohamer	.05
394	Wayne Garland	.05
395	Sid Monge	.05
396	Rick Waits	.05
397	Joe Charboneau RC	.50
398	Gary Alexander	.05
399	Jerry Dybzinski	.05
400	Mike Stanton	.05
401	Mike Paxton	.05
402	Gary Gray	.05
403	Rick Manning	.05
404	Bo Diaz	.05
405	Ron Hassey	.05
406	Ross Grimsley	.05
407	Victor Cruz	.05
408	Len Barker	.05
409	Bob Bailor	.05
410	Otto Velez	.05
411	Ernie Whitt	.05
412	Jim Clancy	.05
413	Barry Bonnell	.05
414	Dave Stieb	.05
415	Damaso Garcia RC	.10
416	John Mayberry	.05
417	Roy Howell	.05
418	Dan Ainge RC	3.00
419a	Jesse Jefferson (Pirates on back.)	.10
419b	Jesse Jefferson (Blue Jays on back.)	.50
420	Joey McLaughlin	.05
421	Lloyd Moseby RC	.10
422	Al Woods	.05
423	Garth Iorg	.05
424	Doug Ault	.05
425	Ken Schrom RC	.05
426	Mike Willis	.05
427	Steve Braun	.05
428	Bob Davis	.05
429	Jerry Garvin	.05
430	Alfredo Griffin	.05
431	Bob Mattick	.05
432	Vida Blue	.05
433	Jack Clark	.05
434	Willie McCovey	1.00
435	Mike Ivie	.05
436a	Darrel Evans (Darrel on front.)	.15
436b	Darrell Evans (Darrell on front.)	.50
437	Terry Whitfield	.05
438	Rennie Stennett	.05
439	John Montefusco	.05
440	Jim Wohlford	.05
441	Bill North	.05
442	Milt May	.05
443	Max Venable	.05
444	Ed Whitson	.05
445	Al Holland RC	.05
446	Randy Moffitt	.05
447	Bob Knepper	.05
448	Gary Lavelle	.05
449	Greg Minton	.05
450	Johnnie LeMaster	.05
451	Larry Herndon	.05
452	Rich Murray	.05
453	Joe Pettini	.05
454	Allen Ripley	.05
455	Dennis Littlejohn	.05
456	Tom Griffin	.05

#	Player	Price
457	Alan Hargesheimer	.05
458	Joe Strain	.05
459	Steve Kemp	.05
460	Sparky Anderson	.25
461	Alan Trammell	.05
462	Mark Fidrych	.25
463	Lou Whitaker	.05
464	Dave Rozema	.05
465	Milt Wilcox	.05
466	Champ Summers	.05
467	Lance Parrish	.05
468	Dan Petry	.05
469	Pat Underwood	.05
470	Rick Peters	.05
471	Al Cowens	.05
472	John Wockenfuss	.05
473	Tom Brookens	.05
474	Richie Hebner	.05
475	Jack Morris	.05
476	Jim Lentine	.05
477	Bruce Robbins	.05
478	Mark Wagner	.05
479	Tim Corcoran	.05
480a	Stan Papi (Pitcher on front.)	.15
480b	Stan Papi (Shortstop on front.)	.50
481	Kirk Gibson RC	5.00
482	Dan Schatzeder	.05
483	Amos Otis	.05
484	Dave Winfield	1.00
485	Rollie Fingers	.75
486	Gene Richards	.05
487	Randy Jones	.05
488	Ozzie Smith	2.00
489	Gene Tenace	.05
490	Bill Fahey	.05
491	John Curtis	.05
492	Dave Cash	.05
493a	Tim Flannery (Photo reversed, batting righty.)	.15
493b	Tim Flannery (Photo correct, batting lefty.)	.50
494	Jerry Mumphrey	.05
495	Bob Shirley	.05
496	Steve Mura	.05
497	Eric Rasmussen	.05
498	Broderick Perkins	.05
499	Barry Evans	.05
500	Chuck Baker	.05
501	Luis Salazar RC	.05
502	Gary Lucas	.05
503	Mike Armstrong	.05
504	Jerry Turner	.05
505	Dennis Kinney	.05
506	Willy Montanez (Willie)	.05
507	Gorman Thomas	.05
508	Ben Oglivie	.05
509	Jim Kern	.05
510	Sal Bando	.05
511	Robin Yount	1.00
512	Mike Caldwell	.05
513	Sixto Lezcano	.05
514a	Charlie Moore (Billy Travers photo.)	.15
514b	Charlie Moore (Correct name with photo.)	.50
515	Paul Molitor	1.00
516	Moose Haas	.05
517	Bill Castro	.05
518	Jim Slaton	.05
519	Lary Sorensen	.05
520	Bob McClure	.05
521	Charlie Moore	.05
522	Jim Gantner	.05
523	Reggie Cleveland	.05
524	Don Money	.05
525	Billy Travers	.05
526	Buck Martinez	.05
527	Dick Davis	.05
528	Ted Simmons	.05
529	Garry Templeton	.05
530	Ken Reitz	.05
531	Tony Scott	.05
532	Ken Oberkfell	.05
533	Bob Sykes	.05
534	Keith Smith	.05
535	John Littlefield	.05
536	Jim Kaat	.05
537	Bob Forsch	.05
538	Mike Phillips	.05
539	Terry Landrum RC	.05
540	Leon Durham RC	.10
541	Terry Kennedy	.05
542	George Hendrick	.05
543	Dane Iorg	.05
544	Mark Littell (Photo actually Jeff Little.)	.05
545	Keith Hernandez	.05
546	Silvio Martinez	.05
547a	Pete Vuckovich (Photo actually Don Hood.)	.15
547b	Don Hood (Correct name with photo.)	.15
548	Bobby Bonds	.10
549	Mike Ramsey	.05
550	Tom Herr	.05
551	Roy Smalley	.05
552	Jerry Koosman	.05
553	Ken Landreaux	.05
554	John Castino	.05
555	Doug Corbett	.05
556	Bombo Rivera	.05
557	Ron Jackson	.05
558	Butch Wynegar	.05
559	Hosken Powell	.05
560	Pete Redfern	.05
561	Roger Erickson	.05

#	Player	Price
562	Glenn Adams	.05
563	Rick Sofield	.05
564	Geoff Zahn	.05
565	Pete Mackanin	.05
566	Mike Cubbage	.05
567	Darrell Jackson	.05
568	Dave Edwards	.05
569	Rob Wilfong	.05
570	Sal Butera	.05
571	Jose Morales	.05
572	Rick Langford	.05
573	Mike Norris	.05
574	Rickey Henderson	2.50
575	Tony Armas	.05
576	Dave Revering	.05
577	Jeff Newman	.05
578	Bob Lacey	.05
579	Brian Kingman (Photo actually Alan Wirth.)	.05
580	Mitchell Page	.05
581	Billy Martin	.25
582	Rob Picciolo	.05
583	Mike Heath	.05
584	Mickey Klutts	.05
585	Orlando Gonzalez	.05
586	Mike Davis RC	.05
587	Wayne Gross	.05
588	Matt Keough	.05
589	Steve McCatty	.05
590	Dwayne Murphy	.05
591	Mario Guerrero	.05
592	Dave McKay	.05
593	Jim Essian	.05
594	Dave Heaverlo	.05
595	Maury Wills	.10
596	Juan Beniquez	.05
597	Rodney Craig	.05
598	Jim Anderson	.05
599	Floyd Bannister	.05
600	Bruce Bochte	.05
601	Julio Cruz	.05
602	Ted Cox	.05
603	Dan Meyer	.05
604	Larry Cox	.05
605	Bill Stein	.05
606	Dave Garcia	.05
607	Dave Roberts	.05
608	Leon Roberts	.05
609	Reggie Walton	.05
610	Dave Edler	.05
611	Larry Milbourne	.05
612	Kim Allen	.05
613	Mario Mendoza	.05
614	Tom Paciorek	.05
615	Glenn Abbott	.05
616	Joe Simpson	.05
617	Mickey Rivers	.05
618	Jim Kern	.05
619	Jim Sundberg	.05
620	Richie Zisk	.05
621	Jon Matlack	.05
622	Fergie Jenkins	.75
623	Pat Corrales	.05
624	Ed Figueroa	.05
625	Buddy Bell	.05
626	Al Oliver	.05
627	Doc Medich	.05
628	Bump Wills	.05
629	Rusty Staub	.05
630	Pat Putnam	.05
631	John Grubb	.05
632	Danny Darwin	.05
633	Ken Clay	.05
634	Jim Norris	.05
635	John Butcher	.05
636	Dave Roberts	.05
637	Billy Sample	.05
638	Carl Yastrzemski	1.00
639	Cecil Cooper	.05
640	Mike Schmidt	2.00
641a	Checklist 1-50 (41 Hal McRae)	.10
641b	Checklist 1-50 (41 Hal McRae Double Threat)	.10
642	Checklist 51-109	.05
643	Checklist 110-168	.05
644a	Checklist 169-220 (202 George Foster)	.10
644b	Checklist 169-220 (202 George Foster "Slugger")	.10
(645a)	Triple Threat (Larry Bowa, Pete Rose, Mike Schmidt (No number on back.))	2.00
645b	Triple Threat (Pete Rose, Larry Bowa, Mike Schmidt (Number on back.))	2.00
646	Checklist 221-267	.05
647	Checklist 268-315	.05
648	Checklist 316-359	.05
649	Checklist 360-408	.05
650	Reggie Jackson	2.00
651	Checklist 409-458	.05
652a	Checklist 459-509 (483 Aurelio Lopez)	.10
652b	Checklist 459-506 (No 483.)	.10
653	Willie Wilson	.05
654a	Checklist 507-550 (514 Jerry Augustine)	.10
654b	Checklist 507-550 (514 Billy Travers)	.10
655	George Brett	3.00
656	Checklist 551-593	.05
657	Tug McGraw	.05
658	Checklist 594-637	.05
659a	Checklist 640-660 (Last number on front is 551.)	.10
659b	Checklist 640-660 (Last number on front is 483.)	.15
660a	Steve Carlton (Date 1066 on back.)	1.00
660b	Steve Carlton (Date 1966 on back.)	2.00

All-Star Game/Team Logo Stickers

Highlights of previous All-Star Games are presented in Robert Laughlin cartoons on the cardboard backings of these stickers which feature team logos, caps or patches. Though none of the players are named on the cards, many are identifiable by the pictures, uniform numbers and/or game-action descriptions on the cards. Where a specific player is clearly depicted, his name is listed.

		NM/M
Complete Set (47):		15.00
Common Card:		.50
1933	AL wins newsman's first "Dream Game" (Babe Ruth)	1.00
1934	out (Carl Hubbell, Babe Ruth, Lou Gehrig, Jimmie Foxx, Al Simmons, Joe Cronin)	.50
1935	in row (Mel Harder, Lefty Gomez)	.60
1936	first time (Dizzy Dean)	.75
1937	lineup (Lou Gehrig)	.75
1938	gets strong pitching (Johnny VanderMeer)	.60
1939	in World's Fair city (Joe DiMaggio)	.75
1940	shutout (Paul Derringer)	.50
1941	Two-out homer in 9th wins for AL (Ted Williams)	.65
1942	victory (Lou Boudreau, Rudy York)	.50
1943	anyway	.50
1944	easiest win	.50
1946	most lopsided win	.50
1947	AL pinch hits break up pitchers' battle	.50
1948	AL wins despite stars on injury list	.50
1949	gains 12-4 series lead (George Kell, Johnny Mize)	.50
1950	park	.50
1951	NL bombs rivals with four homers (Ralph Kiner)	.50
1952	Two NL homers win rain-shortened game (Jackie Robinson, Hank Sauer)	.65
1953	first eight innings (Red Schoendienst, Minnie Minoso)	.50
1954	slugfest (Al Rosen)	.50
1955	in 12th (Stan Musial)	.65
1956	NL scores in five straight innings (Ted Williams)	.75
1957	in ninth (Mickey Mantle)	1.00
1958	of no extra-base hits (Nellie Fox)	.65
1959	two games (Frank Robinson, Al Kaline)	.50
1960	NL wins both games in AL parks	.50
1961	for only tie (Stu Miller)	.50
1962	year of two games is split	.50
1963	NL is outhit 11-6 but wins anyway	.50
1964	All-Star series	.50
1965	All-Star series (Willie Mays)	.75
1966	NL takes pitchers' battle in 10th (Juan Marichal, Denny McLain)	.60
1967	30 batters fan in 15-inning marathon	.50
1968	AL scoreless streak reaches 18 innings	.50
1969	runaway (Willie McCovey)	.60
1970	12th (Bud Harrelson)	.50
1971	triumph from 1963 to 1980 (Reggie Jackson, Harmon Killebrew, Frank Robinson)	.65
1972	games (Hank Aaron)	.75
1973	they win again	.50
1974	Dodgers are heroes in easy NL victory	.50
1975	9th	.50
1976	NL breezes	.50
1977	win again	.50
1978	with four in 8th	.50
1979	row to win seesaw 50th game	.50
1980	series lead of 32-18 (1 tie)	.50

Star Stickers

The 128-card 1981 Fleer Star Sticker set was designed to allow the card fronts to be peeled away from the cardboard backs. Fronts feature color photos with blue and yellow trim. Backs are identical in design to the regular 1981 Fleer set except for color and numbering. The set contains three unnumbered checklist cards whose fronts depict Reggie Jackson, George Brett and Mike Schmidt. The sticker-cards, which are the standard 2-1/2" x 3-1/2", were issued in gum wax packs.

		NM/M
Complete Set (128):		15.00
Common Player:		.15
Wax Pack (5):		1.25
Wax Box (36):		15.00
1	Steve Garvey	.40
2	Ron LeFlore	.15
3	Ron Cey	.15
4	Dave Revering	.15
5	Tony Armas	.15
6	Mike Norris	.15
7	Steve Kemp	.15
8	Bruce Bochte	.15
9	Mike Schmidt	2.00
10	Scott McGregor	.15
11	Buddy Bell	.15
12	Carney Lansford	.15
13	Carl Yastrzemski	1.00
14	Ben Oglivie	.15
15	Willie Stargell	1.00
16	Cecil Cooper	.15
17	Gene Richards	.15
18	Jim Kern	.15
19	Jerry Koosman	.15
20	Larry Bowa	.15
21	Kent Tekulve	.15
22	Dan Driessen	.15
23	Phil Niekro	.75
24	Dan Quisenberry	.15
25	Dave Winfield	1.00
26	Dave Parker	.15
27	Rick Langford	.15
28	Amos Otis	.15
29	Bill Buckner	.15
30	Al Bumbry	.15
31	Bake McBride	.15
32	Mickey Rivers	.15
33	Rick Burleson	.15
34	Dennis Eckersley	.75
35	Cesar Cedeno	.15
36	Enos Cabell	.15
37	Johnny Bench	1.00
38	Robin Yount	1.00
39	Mark Belanger	.15
40	Rod Carew	1.00
41	George Foster	.15
42	Lee Mazzilli	.15
43	Triple Threat (Larry Bowa, Pete Rose, Mike Schmidt)	2.00
44	J.R. Richard	.15
45	Lou Piniella	.15
46	Ken Landreaux	.15
47	Rollie Fingers	.75
48	Joaquin Andujar	.15
49	Tom Seaver	1.00
50	Bobby Grich	.15
51	Jon Matlack	.15
52	Jack Clark	.15
53	Jim Rice	.15
54	Rickey Henderson	3.00
55	Roy Smalley	.15
56	Mike Flanagan	.15
57	Steve Rogers	.15
58	Carlton Fisk	1.00
59	Don Sutton	.75
60	Ken Griffey	.15
61	Burt Hooton	.15
62	Dusty Baker	.15
63	Vida Blue	.15
64	Al Oliver	.15
65	Jim Bibby	.15
66	Tony Perez	.75
67	Davy Lopes (Davey)	.15
68	Bill Russell	.15
69	Larry Parrish	.15
70	Garry Maddox	.15
71	Phil Garner	.15
72	Graig Nettles	.20
73	Gary Carter	.15

74	Pete Rose	3.00
75	Greg Luzinski	.15
76	Ron Guidry	.15
77	Gorman Thomas	.15
78	Jose Cruz	.15
79	Bob Boone	.15
80	Bruce Sutter	.75
81	Chris Chambliss	.15
82	Paul Molitor	1.00
83	Tug McGraw	.15
84	Ferguson Jenkins	.75
85	Steve Carlton	1.00
86	Miguel Dilone	.15
87	Reggie Smith	.15
88	Rick Cerone	.15
89	Alan Trammell	.15
90	Doug DeCinces	.15
91	Sparky Lyle	.15
92	Warren Cromartie	.15
93	Rick Reuschel	.15
94	Larry Hisle	.15
95	Paul Splittorff	.15
96	Manny Trillo	.15
97	Frank White	.15
98	Fred Lynn	.15
99	Bob Horner	.15
100	Omar Moreno	.15
101	Dave Concepcion	.15
102	Larry Gura	.15
103	Ken Singleton	.15
104	Steve Stone	.15
105	Richie Zisk	.15
106	Willie Wilson	.15
107	Willie Randolph	.15
108	Nolan Ryan	3.00
109	Joe Morgan	1.00
110	Bucky Dent	.20
111	Dave Kingman	.15
112	John Castino	.15
113	Joe Rudi	.15
114	Ed Farmer	.15
115	Reggie Jackson	2.50
116	George Brett	2.00
117	Eddie Murray	1.00
118	Rich Gossage	.20
119	Dale Murphy	.40
120	Ted Simmons	.15
121	Tommy John	.20
122	Don Baylor	.15
123	Andre Dawson	.60
124	Jim Palmer	1.00
125	Garry Templeton	.15
----	Checklist 1-42 (Reggie Jackson)	.50
----	Checklist 43-83 (George Brett)	.50
----	Checklist 84-125 (Mike Schmidt)	.50

Superstar Stickers

While these small (about 1-1/2" x 2") stickers carry the Fleer name and were, indeed, produced by Fleer, they are more akin to collectors' issues than a legitimate product. Wrappers of 1981 Fleer Star Stickers offered the opportunity to put one's own photo, or the photo of someone else, on 24 stickers for a couple of dollars and proofs of purchase. Some enterprising hobbyists sent in several different pictures of Mickey Mantle and pictures of then-current stars and had them made into stickers. Because they are un-authorized by Mantle, or the other players seen (Boggs, Mattingly, Yaz, etc.), there is no collector value.

1982 Fleer

Fleer's 1982 set did not match the quality of the previous year's effort. Many of the card photos are blurred and have muddied back-grounds. The 2-1/2" x 3-1/2" cards feature color photos bordered by a frame which is color-coded by team. Backs are blue, white, and yellow and contain the player's team logo plus the logos of Major League Baseball and the Major League Baseball Players Association. Due to a lawsuit by Topps, Fleer was forced to issue the set with team logo stick-

ers rather than gum. The complete set price does not include the higher priced variations.

		NM/M
Complete Set (660):		45.00
Common Player:		.05
Wax Pack (15):		3.00
Wax Box (36):		85.00
Cello Pack (28):		4.00
Cello Box (24):		85.00
Vending Box (500):		40.00

1	Dusty Baker	.05
2	Robert Castillo	.05
3	Ron Cey	.05
4	Terry Forster	.05
5	Steve Garvey	.30
6	Dave Goltz	.05
7	Pedro Guerrero	.05
8	Burt Hooton	.05
9	Steve Howe	.05
10	Jay Johnstone	.05
11	Ken Landreaux	.05
12	Davey Lopes	.05
13	Mike Marshall RC	.15
14	Bobby Mitchell	.05
15	Rick Monday	.05
16	Tom Niedenfuer RC	.05
17	Ted Power RC	.05
18	Jerry Reuss	.05
19	Ron Roenicke	.05
20	Bill Russell	.05
21	Steve Sax RC	.45
22	Mike Scioscia	.05
23	Reggie Smith	.05
24	Dave Stewart RC	1.50
25	Rick Sutcliffe	.05
26	Derrel Thomas	.05
27	Fernando Valenzuela	.10
28	Bob Welch	.05
29	Steve Yeager	.05
30	Bobby Brown	.05
31	Rick Cerone	.05
32	Ron Davis	.05
33	Bucky Dent	.10
34	Barry Foote	.05
35	George Frazier	.05
36	Oscar Gamble	.05
37	Rich Gossage	.10
38	Ron Guidry	.10
39	Reggie Jackson	1.50
40	Tommy John	.10
41	Rudy May	.05
42	Larry Milbourne	.05
43	Jerry Mumphrey	.05
44	Bobby Murcer	.10
45	Gene Nelson RC	.05
46	Graig Nettles	.10
47	Johnny Oates	.05
48	Lou Piniella	.10
49	Willie Randolph	.05
50	Rick Reuschel	.05
51	Dave Revering	.05
52	Dave Righetti RC	.45
53	Aurelio Rodriguez	.05
54	Bob Watson	.05
55	Dennis Werth	.05
56	Dave Winfield	1.00
57	Johnny Bench	1.00
58	Bruce Berenyi	.05
59	Larry Biittner	.05
60	Scott Brown	.05
61	Dave Collins	.05
62	Geoff Combe	.05
63	Dave Concepcion	.05
64	Dan Driessen	.05
65	Joe Edelen	.05
66	George Foster	.05
67	Ken Griffey	.05
68	Paul Householder	.05
69	Tom Hume	.05
70	Junior Kennedy	.05
71	Ray Knight	.05
72	Mike LaCoss	.05
73	Rafael Landestoy	.05
74	Charlie Leibrandt	.05
75	Sam Mejias	.05
76	Paul Moskau	.05
77	Joe Nolan	.05
78	Mike O'Berry	.05
79	Ron Oester	.05
80	Frank Pastore	.05
81	Joe Price	.05
82	Tom Seaver	1.00
83	Mario Soto	.05
84	Mike Vail	.05
85	Tony Armas	.05
86	Shooty Babitt	.05

87	Dave Beard	.05
88	Rick Bosetti	.05
89	Keith Drumright	.05
90	Wayne Gross	.05
91	Mike Heath	.05
92	Rickey Henderson	1.00
93	Cliff Johnson	.05
94	Jeff Jones	.05
95	Matt Keough	.05
96	Brian Kingman	.05
97	Mickey Klutts	.05
98	Rick Langford	.05
99	Steve McCatty	.05
100	Dave McKay	.05
101	Dwayne Murphy	.05
102	Jeff Newman	.05
103	Mike Norris	.05
104	Bob Owchinko	.05
105	Mitchell Page	.05
106	Rob Picciolo	.05
107	Jim Spencer	.05
108	Fred Stanley	.05
109	Tom Underwood	.05
110	Joaquin Andujar	.05
111	Steve Braun	.05
112	Bob Forsch	.05
113	George Hendrick	.05
114	Keith Hernandez	.05
115	Tom Herr	.05
116	Dane Iorg	.05
117	Jim Kaat	.10
118	Tito Landrum	.05
119	Sixto Lezcano	.05
120	Mark Littell	.05
121	John Martin	.05
122	Silvio Martinez	.05
123	Ken Oberkfell	.05
124	Darrell Porter	.05
125	Mike Ramsey	.05
126	Orlando Sanchez	.05
127	Bob Shirley	.05
128	Lary Sorensen	.05
129	Bruce Sutter	.75
130	Bob Sykes	.05
131	Garry Templeton	.05
132	Gene Tenace	.05
133	Jerry Augustine	.05
134	Sal Bando	.05
135	Mark Brouhard	.05
136	Mike Caldwell	.05
137	Reggie Cleveland	.05
138	Cecil Cooper	.05
139	Jamie Easterly	.05
140	Marshall Edwards	.05
141	Rollie Fingers	.75
142	Jim Gantner	.05
143	Moose Haas	.05
144	Larry Hisle	.05
145	Roy Howell	.05
146	Rickey Keeton	.05
147	Randy Lerch	.05
148	Paul Molitor	1.00
149	Don Money	.05
150	Charlie Moore	.05
151	Ben Oglivie	.05
152	Ted Simmons	.05
153	Jim Slaton	.05
154	Gorman Thomas	.05
155	Robin Yount	1.00
156	Pete Vukovich	.05
157	Benny Ayala	.05
158	Mark Belanger	.05
159	Al Bumbry	.05
160	Terry Crowley	.05
161	Rich Dauer	.05
162	Doug DeCinces	.05
163	Rick Dempsey	.05
164	Jim Dwyer	.05
165	Mike Flanagan	.05
166	Dave Ford	.05
167	Dan Graham	.05
168	Wayne Krenchicki	.05
169	John Lowenstein	.05
170	Dennis Martinez	.05
171	Tippy Martinez	.05
172	Scott McGregor	.05
173	Jose Morales	.05
174	Eddie Murray	1.00
175	Jim Palmer	1.00
176	Cal Ripken, Jr. RC	40.00
177	Gary Roenicke	.05
178	Lenn Sakata	.05
179	Ken Singleton	.05
180	Sammy Stewart	.05
181	Tim Stoddard	.05
182	Steve Stone	.05
183	Stan Bahnsen	.05
184	Ray Burris	.05
185	Gary Carter	1.00
186	Warren Cromartie	.05
187	Andre Dawson	.50
188	Terry Francona RC	.05
189	Woodie Fryman	.05
190	Bill Gullickson	.05
191	Grant Jackson	.05
192	Wallace Johnson	.05
193	Charlie Lea	.05
194	Bill Lee	.05
195	Jerry Manuel	.05
196	Brad Mills	.05
197	John Milner	.05
198	Rowland Office	.05
199	David Palmer	.05
200	Larry Parrish	.05
201	Mike Phillips	.05
202	Tim Raines	.25
203	Bobby Ramos	.05
204	Jeff Reardon	.05

205	Steve Rogers	.05
206	Scott Sanderson	.05
207	Rodney Scott (Photo actually Tim Raines.)	.10
208	Elias Sosa	.05
209	Chris Speier	.05
210	Tim Wallach RC	1.00
211	Jerry White	.05
212	Alan Ashby	.05
213	Cesar Cedeno	.05
214	Jose Cruz	.05
215	Kiko Garcia	.05
216	Phil Garner	.05
217	Danny Heep	.05
218	Art Howe	.05
219	Bob Knepper	.05
220	Frank LaCorte	.05
221	Joe Niekro	.05
222	Joe Pittman	.05
223	Terry Puhl	.05
224	Luis Pujols	.05
225	Craig Reynolds	.05
226	J.R. Richard	.05
227	Dave Roberts	.05
228	Vern Ruhle	.05
229	Nolan Ryan	3.00
230	Joe Sambito	.05
231	Tony Scott	.05
232	Dave Smith	.05
233	Harry Spilman	.05
234	Don Sutton	.75
235	Dickie Thon	.05
236	Denny Walling	.05
237	Gary Woods	.05
238	Luis Aguayo RC	.05
239	Ramon Aviles	.05
240	Bob Boone	.05
241	Larry Bowa	.05
242	Warren Brusstar	.05
243	Steve Carlton	1.00
244	Larry Christenson	.05
245	Dick Davis	.05
246	Greg Gross	.05
247	Sparky Lyle	.05
248	Gary Maddox	.05
249	Gary Matthews	.05
250	Bake McBride	.05
251	Tug McGraw	.05
252	Keith Moreland	.05
253	Dickie Noles	.05
254	Mike Proly	.05
255	Ron Reed	.05
256	Pete Rose	2.50
257	Dick Ruthven	.05
258	Mike Schmidt	2.00
259	Lonnie Smith	.05
260	Manny Trillo	.05
261	Del Unser	.05
262	George Vukovich	.05
263	Tom Brookens	.05
264	George Cappuzzello	.05
265	Marty Castillo	.05
266	Al Cowens	.05
267	Kirk Gibson	.05
268	Richie Hebner	.05
269	Ron Jackson	.05
270	Lynn Jones	.05
271	Steve Kemp	.05
272	Rick Leach RC	.25
273	Aurelio Lopez	.05
274	Jack Morris	.05
275	Kevin Saucier	.05
276	Lance Parrish	.05
277	Rick Peters	.05
278	Dan Petry	.05
279	David Rozema	.05
280	Stan Papi	.05
281	Dan Schatzeder	.05
282	Champ Summers	.05
283	Alan Trammell	.05
284	Lou Whitaker	.05
285	Milt Wilcox	.05
286	John Wockenfuss	.05
287	Gary Allenson	.05
288	Tom Burgmeier	.05
289	Bill Campbell	.05
290	Mark Clear	.05
291	Steve Crawford	.05
292	Dennis Eckersley	.75
293	Dwight Evans	.05
294	Rich Gedman RC	.10
295	Garry Hancock	.05
296	Glenn Hoffman	.05
297	Bruce Hurst	.05
298	Carney Lansford	.05
299	Rick Miller	.05
300	Reid Nichols	.05
301	Bob Ojeda RC	.25
302	Tony Perez	.75
303	Chuck Rainey	.05
304	Jerry Remy	.05
305	Jim Rice	.50
306	Joe Rudi	.05
307	Bob Stanley	.05
308	Dave Stapleton	.05
309	Frank Tanana	.05
310	Mike Torrez	.05
311	John Tudor	.05
312	Carl Yastrzemski	1.00
313	Buddy Bell	.05
314	Steve Comer	.05
315	Danny Darwin	.05
316	John Ellis	.05
317	John Grubb	.05
318	Rick Honeycutt	.05
319	Charlie Hough	.05
320	Fergie Jenkins	.75
321	John Henry Johnson	.05

322	Jim Kern	.05
323	Jon Matlack	.05
324	Doc Medich	.05
325	Mario Mendoza	.05
326	Al Oliver	.05
327	Pat Putnam	.05
328	Mickey Rivers	.05
329	Leon Roberts	.05
330	Billy Sample	.05
331	Bill Stein	.05
332	Jim Sundberg	.05
333	Mark Wagner	.05
334	Bump Wills	.05
335	Bill Almon	.05
336	Harold Baines	.05
337	Ross Baumgarten	.05
338	Tony Bernazard	.05
339	Britt Burns	.05
340	Richard Dotson	.05
341	Jim Essian	.05
342	Ed Farmer	.05
343	Carlton Fisk	1.00
344	Kevin Hickey	.05
345	Lamarr Hoyt (LaMarr)	.05
346	Lamar Johnson	.05
347	Jerry Koosman	.05
348	Rusty Kuntz	.05
349	Dennis Lamp	.05
350	Ron LeFlore	.05
351	Chet Lemon	.05
352	Greg Luzinski	.05
353	Bob Molinaro	.05
354	Jim Morrison	.05
355	Wayne Nordhagen	.05
356	Greg Pryor	.05
357	Mike Squires	.05
358	Steve Trout	.05
359	Alan Bannister	.05
360	Len Barker	.05
361	Bert Blyleven	.10
362	Joe Charboneau	.10
363	John Denny	.05
364	Bo Diaz	.05
365	Miguel Dilone	.05
366	Jerry Dybzinski	.05
367	Wayne Garland	.05
368	Mike Hargrove	.05
369	Toby Harrah	.05
370	Ron Hassey	.05
371	Von Hayes RC	.25
372	Pat Kelly	.05
373	Duane Kuiper	.05
374	Rick Manning	.05
375	Sid Monge	.05
376	Jorge Orta	.05
377	Dave Rosello	.05
378	Dan Spillner	.05
379	Mike Stanton	.05
380	Andre Thornton	.05
381	Tom Veryzer	.05
382	Rick Waits	.05
383	Doyle Alexander	.05
384	Vida Blue	.05
385	Fred Breining	.05
386	Enos Cabell	.05
387	Jack Clark	.05
388	Darrell Evans	.05
389	Tom Griffin	.05
390	Larry Herndon	.05
391	Al Holland	.05
392	Gary Lavelle	.05
393	Johnnie LeMaster	.05
394	Jerry Martin	.05
395	Milt May	.05
396	Greg Minton	.05
397	Joe Morgan	1.00
398	Joe Pettini	.05
399	Alan Ripley	.05
400	Billy Smith	.05
401	Rennie Stennett	.05
402	Ed Whitson	.05
403	Jim Wohlford	.05
404	Willie Aikens	.05
405	George Brett	2.00
406	Ken Brett	.05
407	Dave Chalk	.05
408	Rich Gale	.05
409	Cesar Geronimo	.05
410	Larry Gura	.05
411	Clint Hurdle	.05
412	Mike Jones	.05
413	Dennis Leonard	.05
414	Renie Martin	.05
415	Lee May	.05
416	Hal McRae	.05
417	Darryl Motley	.05
418	Rance Mulliniks	.05
419	Amos Otis	.05
420	Ken Phelps RC	.05
421	Jamie Quirk	.05
422	Dan Quisenberry	.05
423	Paul Splittorff	.05
424	U.L. Washington	.05
425	John Wathan	.05
426	Frank White	.05
427	Willie Wilson	.05
428	Brian Asselstine	.05
429	Bruce Benedict	.05
430	Tom Boggs	.05
431	Larry Bradford	.05
432	Rick Camp	.05
433	Chris Chambliss	.05
434	Gene Garber	.05
435	Preston Hanna	.05
436	Bob Horner	.05
437	Glenn Hubbard	.05
438a	Al Hrabosky (All Hrabosky, 5'1" on back.)	4.50

438b	Al Hrabosky (Al Hrabosky, 5'1" on back.)	1.00
438c	Al Hrabosky (Al Hrabosky, 5'10" on back.)	.25
439	Rufino Linares	.05
440	Rick Mahler RC	.05
441	Ed Miller	.05
442	John Montefusco	.05
443	Dale Murphy	.50
444	Phil Niekro	.75
445	Gaylord Perry	.75
446	Biff Pocoroba	.05
447	Rafael Ramirez	.05
448	Jerry Royster	.05
449	Claudell Washington	.05
450	Don Aase	.05
451	Don Baylor	.05
452	Juan Beniquez	.05
453	Rick Burleson	.05
454	Bert Campaneris	.05
455	Rod Carew	1.00
456	Bob Clark	.05
457	Brian Downing	.05
458	Dan Ford	.05
459	Ken Forsch	.05
460	Dave Frost	.05
461	Bobby Grich	.05
462	Larry Harlow	.05
463	John Harris	.05
464	Andy Hassler	.05
465	Butch Hobson	.05
466	Jesse Jefferson	.05
467	Bruce Kison	.05
468	Fred Lynn	.05
469	Angel Moreno	.05
470	Ed Ott	.05
471	Fred Patek	.05
472	Steve Renko	.05
473	Mike Witt RC	.10
474	Geoff Zahn	.05
475	Gary Alexander	.05
476	Dale Berra	.05
477	Kurt Bevacqua	.05
478	Jim Bibby	.05
479	John Candelaria	.05
480	Victor Cruz	.05
481	Mike Easler	.05
482	Tim Foli	.05
483	Lee Lacy	.05
484	Vance Law	.05
485	Bill Madlock	.05
486	Willie Montanez	.05
487	Omar Moreno	.05
488	Steve Nicosia	.05
489	Dave Parker	.05
490	Tony Pena	.05
491	Pascual Perez	.05
492	Johnny Ray RC	.05
493	Rick Rhoden	.05
494	Bill Robinson	.05
495	Don Robinson	.05
496	Enrique Romo	.05
497	Rod Scurry	.05
498	Eddie Solomon	.05
499	Willie Stargell	1.00
500	Kent Tekulve	.05
501	Jason Thompson	.05
502	Glenn Abbott	.05
503	Jim Anderson	.05
504	Floyd Bannister	.05
505	Bruce Bochte	.05
506	Jeff Burroughs	.05
507	Bryan Clark	.05
508	Ken Clay	.05
509	Julio Cruz	.05
510	Dick Drago	.05
511	Gary Gray	.05
512	Dan Meyer	.05
513	Jerry Narron	.05
514	Tom Paciorek	.05
515	Casey Parsons	.05
516	Lenny Randle	.05
517	Shane Rawley	.05
518	Joe Simpson	.05
519	Richie Zisk	.05
520	Neil Allen	.05
521	Bob Bailor	.05
522	Hubie Brooks	.05
523	Mike Cubbage	.05
524	Pete Falcone	.05
525	Doug Flynn	.05
526	Tom Hausman	.05
527	Ron Hodges	.05
528	Randy Jones	.05
529	Mike Jorgensen	.05
530	Dave Kingman	.05
531	Ed Lynch	.05
532	Mike Marshall	.05
533	Lee Mazzilli	.05
534	Dyar Miller	.05
535	Mike Scott	.05
536	Rusty Staub	.05
537	John Stearns	.05
538	Craig Swan	.05
539	Frank Taveras	.05
540	Alex Trevino	.05
541	Ellis Valentine	.05
542	Mookie Wilson	.05
543	Joel Youngblood	.05
544	Pat Zachry	.05
545	Glenn Adams	.05
546	Fernando Arroyo	.05
547	John Verhoeven	.05
548	Sal Butera	.05
549	John Castino	.05
550	Don Cooper	.05
551	Doug Corbett	.05
552	Dave Engle	.05

553	Roger Erickson	.05
554	Danny Goodwin	.05
555a	Darrell Jackson (Black cap.)	.65
555b	Darrell Jackson (Red cap w/speck of white.)	3.00
555c	Darrell Jackson (Red cap w/white T.)	.10
556	Pete Mackanin	.05
557	Jack O'Connor	.05
558	Hosken Powell	.05
559	Pete Redfern	.05
560	Roy Smalley	.05
561	Chuck Baker	.05
562	Gary Ward	.05
563	Rob Wilfong	.05
564	Al Williams	.05
565	Butch Wynegar	.05
566	Randy Bass	.05
567	Juan Bonilla	.05
568	Danny Boone	.05
569	John Curtis	.05
570	Juan Eichelberger	.05
571	Barry Evans	.05
572	Tim Flannery	.05
573	Ruppert Jones	.05
574	Terry Kennedy	.05
575	Joe Lefebvre	.05
576a	John Littlefield (Pitching lefty.)	80.00
576b	John Littlefield (Pitching righty.)	.05
577	Gary Lucas	.05
578	Steve Mura	.05
579	Broderick Perkins	.05
580	Gene Richards	.05
581	Luis Salazar	.05
582	Ozzie Smith	1.50
583	John Urrea	.05
584	Chris Welsh	.05
585	Rick Wise	.05
586	Doug Bird	.05
587	Tim Blackwell	.05
588	Bobby Bonds	.10
589	Bill Buckner	.05
590	Bill Caudill	.05
591	Hector Cruz	.05
592	Jody Davis RC	.10
593	Ivan DeJesus	.05
594	Steve Dillard	.05
595	Leon Durham	.05
596	Rawly Eastwick	.05
597	Steve Henderson	.05
598	Mike Krukow	.05
599	Mike Lum	.05
600	Randy Martz	.05
601	Jerry Morales	.05
602	Ken Reitz	.05
603a	Lee Smith RC (Cubs logo reversed on back.)	2.50
603b	Lee Smith RC (corrected)	2.50
604	Dick Tidrow	.05
605	Jim Tracy	.05
606	Mike Tyson	.05
607	Ty Waller	.05
608	Danny Ainge	.50
609	Jorge Bell RC	1.00
610	Mark Bomback	.05
611	Barry Bonnell	.05
612	Jim Clancy	.05
613	Damaso Garcia	.05
614	Jerry Garvin	.05
615	Alfredo Griffin	.05
616	Garth Iorg	.05
617	Luis Leal	.05
618	Ken Macha	.05
619	John Mayberry	.05
620	Joey McLaughlin	.05
621	Lloyd Moseby	.05
622	Dave Stieb	.05
623	Jackson Todd	.05
624	Willie Upshaw RC	.05
625	Otto Velez	.05
626	Ernie Whitt	.05
627	Al Woods	.05
628	1981 All-Star Game	.05
629	All-Star Infielders (Bucky Dent, Frank White)	.05
630	Big Red Machine (Dave Concepcion, Dan Driessen, George Foster)	.10
631	Top N.L. Relief Pitcher (Bruce Sutter)	.30
632	Steve & Carlton (Steve Carlton, Carlton Fisk)	.25
633	3000th Game, May 25, 1981 (Carl Yastrzemski)	.35
634	Dynamic Duo (Johnny Bench, Tom Seaver)	.30
635	West Meets East (Gary Carter, Fernando Valenzuela)	.20
636a	N.L. Strikeout King (Fernando Valenzuela ("…led the National League…"))	.50
636b	N.L. Strikeout King (Fernando Valenzuela ("… led the National League…"))	.25
637	Home Run King (Mike Schmidt)	.50
638	N.L. All-Stars (Gary Carter, Dave Parker)	.25
639	Perfect Game! (Len Barker, Bo Diaz)	.05
640	Pete Rose, Pete Rose, Jr. (Re-Pete)	2.00

641	Phillies' Finest (Steve Carlton, Mike Schmidt, Lonnie Smith)	.50
642	Red Sox Reunion (Dwight Evans, Fred Lynn)	.10
643	Most Hits and Runs (Rickey Henderson)	1.00
644	Most Saves 1981 A.L. (Rollie Fingers)	.15
645	Most 1981 Wins (Tom Seaver)	.25
646a	Yankee Powerhouse (Reggie Jackson, Dave Winfield (Comma after "outfielder" on back.))	1.50
646b	Yankee Powerhouse (Reggie Jackson, Dave Winfield (No comma.))	2.00
647	Checklist 1-56	.05
648	Checklist 57-109	.05
649	Checklist 110-156	.05
650	Checklist 157-211	.05
651	Checklist 212-262	.05
652	Checklist 263-312	.05
653	Checklist 313-358	.05
654	Checklist 359-403	.05
655	Checklist 404-449	.05
656	Checklist 450-501	.05
657	Checklist 502-544	.05
658	Checklist 545-585	.05
659	Checklist 586-627	.05
660	Checklist 628-646	.05

Proofs

Ken Griffey
REDS • OUTFIELD

More than two dozen proof cards which differ significantly from the issued versions in 1982 Fleer are known, though the quantities in which they have made their way into the hobby market are not known. Blank-backed and hand-cut from press sheets, the proofs include a number of Hall of Famers and high-demand stars. The manner in which the proof card differs from the issued version is listed parenthetically.

		NM/M
----	Dave Patterson (No issued version.)	75.00
4	Terry Forster (Green photo border.)	50.00
31	Rick Cerone/Catching (Game-action.)	75.00
37	Rich Gossage (Pose to knees.)	75.00
48	Lou Piniella/Trotting (Game-action.)	75.00
49	Willie Randolph/Btg (Game-action.)	75.00
61	Dave Collins/Btg (Game-action.)	50.00
67	Ken Griffey (Home uniform.)	60.00
82	Tom Seaver/Pitching (Game-action.)	60.00
312	Carl Yastrzemski (Misspelled "Yastremski.")	350.00
395	Milt May (Ed Whitson photo.)	60.00
402	Ed Whitson (Milt May photo.)	60.00
416	Hal McRae (Position: OF.)	25.00
427	Willie Wilson (Pose, no microphone.)	50.00
449	Claudell Washington (Game-action, batting.)	50.00
503	Jim Anderson (Incorrect name: Mike.)	25.00
555	Darrell Jackson (Pictures unidentified pitcher.)	45.00
629	All-Star Infielders (Captioned: "Dent & White.")	25.00
632	Steve & Carlton (Captioned: "Carlton & Steve / FISK & CARLTON.")	40.00
635	West Meets East (Captioned: "East Meets West.")	25.00
638	N.L. All-Stars (Captioned: "Parker & Carter.")	25.00
644	Most Saves 1981 (Captioned: "A.L. Most Saves in 1981.")	25.00

Test Cards

To test a proposed cardboard stock from International Paper Co., a run of 100 sheets of test cards was printed and delivered to Fleer officials. The cards on the sheet include various combinations of correct picture/name combinations, incorrect picture/name combinations and cards with no player identification. All cards have the words "TEST CARD" overprinted in black in the player identification area at bottom center, along with the letters "o," "n" or both vertically at the left end of the oblong. Backs are blank. At least half of the 132-card test sheets have made their way into the hobby where they are offered both as complete sheets and as hand-cut single cards or panels. A number of the photos seen on the test card did not appear in Fleer's 1982 card set. The checklist here is arranged by row and card number on the sheets. Player names are as printed, if the photo is not that player it is identified in parentheses. Each of the 66 cards is double-printed on the sheet.

		NM/M
	Complete Sheet (132):	1,500
	Complete Set (66):	900.00
	Common Card:	10.00
1-1	Jon Matlack (Steve Christmas)	10.00
1-2	Wayne Gross (Jose Brito)	10.00
1-3	Mario Mendoza (John Lickert)	10.00
1-4	Mike Heath (Daryl Sconiers)	10.00
1-5	Bump Wills (Lee Mazzilli)	10.00
1-6	Steve McCatty (Jose Rodriguez)	10.00
1-7	Steve Stone	25.00
1-8	No identification (Brian Harper)	10.00
1-9	Dennis Martinez (Cubs player)	15.00
1-10	No identification (Julio Valdez)	10.00
1-11	Jim Palmer (Del Unser)	25.00
2-1	Billy Sample (Bill Doran)	10.00
2-2	Tony Armas (Tony Armas)	10.00
2-3	Rick Honeycutt (Rick Honeycutt)	10.00
2-4	Cliff Jackson (Tim Ireland)	10.00
2-5	John Ellis (Floyd Rayford)	10.00
2-6	Dave McKay (Jim Wright)	10.00
2-7	Ken Singleton (Larry Milbourne)	10.00
2-8	No identification (Steve Balboni)	10.00
2-9	John Lowenstein (Mickey Mahler)	10.00
2-10	No identification (Ty Waller)	10.00
2-11	Doug DeCinces (Mike Patterson)	10.00
3-1	Mickey Rivers (Pat Putnam)	10.00
3-2	Rickey Henderson (Mike Norris)	25.00

646	Yankee Powerhouse (Captioned: "Winfield & Jackson.")	45.00
652	Checklist (Lists #275 as Stan Papi.)	15.00
655	Checklist (McRae's position: OF.)	15.00
660	Checklist (White border, incorrect captions as above.)	15.00

3-3	Jim Sundberg (Jim Kern)	10.00
3-4	Bob Owchinko (Fred Stanley)	10.00
3-5	Buddy Bell (Danny Darwin)	10.00
3-6	Shooty Babbitt (Rick Langford)	10.00
3-7	Sammy Stewart (Tippy Martinez)	10.00
3-8	No identification (Juan Eichelberger)	10.00
3-9	Lenn Sakata (Eddie Murray)	25.00
3-10	No identification (Juan Bonilla)	10.00
3-11	Benny Ayala (Terry Crowley)	10.00
4-1	Al Oliver (Bill Stein)	10.00
4-2	Dwayne Murphy (Matt Keough)	10.00
4-3	Leon Roberts (John Grubb)	10.00
4-4	Rob Picciolo (Brian Kingman)	10.00
4-5	Mark Wagner (Steve Comer)	10.00
4-6	Jeff Jones (Jeff Neumann)	10.00
4-7	Tim Stoddard (Mike Flanagan)	10.00
4-8	No identification (John Urrea)	10.00
4-9	Rick Dempsey (Mark Belanger)	10.00
4-10	No identification (Luis Salazar)	10.00
4-11	Dave Ford (Cal Ripken Jr.)	250.00
5-1	Pat Putnam	15.00
5-2	Mike Norris	15.00
5-3	Jim Kern	15.00
5-4	Fred Stanley	15.00
5-5	Danny Darwin	15.00
5-6	Rick Langford	15.00
5-7	Tippy Martinez	15.00
5-8	No identification (Juan Eichelberger)	10.00
5-9	Eddie Murray	30.00
5-10	No identification (Juan Bonilla)	10.00
5-11	Terry Crowley	15.00
6-1	Bill Stein	15.00
6-2	Matt Keough	15.00
6-3	John Grubb	15.00
6-4	Brian Kingman	15.00
6-5	Steve Comer	15.00
6-6	Jeff Neumann	15.00
6-7	Mike Flanagan	15.00
6-8	No identification (John Urrea)	15.00
6-9	Mark Belanger	15.00
6-10	No identification (Luis Salazar)	10.00
6-11	Cal Ripken, Jr.	400.00

1982 Fleer Stamps

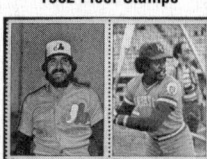

Issued by Fleer in 1982, this set consists of 242 player stamps, each measuring 1-13/16" x 2-1/2". Originally issued in perforated strips of 10, the full-color stamps are numbered in the lower-left corner and were designed to be placed in an album. Six stamps feature two players each.

		NM/M
	Complete Set (242):	10.00
	Common Player:	.05
	Stamp Album:	1.50
	Wax Pack (10):	.35
	Wax Box (60):	12.50
1	Fernando Valenzuela	.05
2	Rick Monday	.05
3	Ron Cey	.05
4	Dusty Baker	.05
5	Burt Hooton	.05
6	Pedro Guerrero	.05
7	Jerry Reuss	.05
8	Bill Russell	.05
9	Steve Garvey	.15
10	Davey Lopes	.05
11	Tom Seaver	.25
12	George Foster	.05
13	Frank Pastore	.05
14	Dave Collins	.05
15	Dave Concepcion	.05
16	Ken Griffey	.05
17	Johnny Bench	.25
18	Ray Knight	.05
19	Mario Soto	.05
20	Ron Oester	.05
21	Ken Oberkfell	.05
22	Bob Forsch	.05
23	Keith Hernandez	.05
24	Dane Iorg	.05
25	George Hendrick	.05

26	Gene Tenace	.05
27	Garry Templeton	.05
28	Bruce Sutter	.20
29	Darrell Porter	.05
30	Tom Herr	.05
31	Tim Raines	.25
32	Chris Speier	.05
33	Warren Cromartie	.05
34	Larry Parrish	.05
35	Andre Dawson	.25
36	Steve Rogers	.05
37	Jeff Reardon	.05
38	Rodney Scott	.05
39	Gary Carter	.25
40	Scott Sanderson	.05
41	Cesar Cedeno	.05
42	Nolan Ryan	1.00
43	Don Sutton	.20
44	Terry Puhl	.05
45	Joe Niekro	.05
46	Tony Scott	.05
47	Joe Sambito	.05
48	Art Howe	.05
49	Bob Knepper	.05
50	Jose Cruz	.05
51	Pete Rose	.50
52	Dick Ruthven	.05
53	Mike Schmidt	.35
54	Steve Carlton	.25
55	Tug McGraw	.05
56	Larry Bowa	.05
57	Garry Maddox	.05
58	Gary Matthews	.05
59	Manny Trillo	.05
60	Lonnie Smith	.05
61	Vida Blue	.05
62	Milt May	.05
63	Joe Morgan	.25
64	Enos Cabell	.05
65	Jack Clark	.05
66	Claudell Washington	.05
67	Gaylord Perry	.20
68	Phil Niekro	.20
69	Bob Horner	.05
70	Chris Chambliss	.05
71	Dave Parker	.25
72	Tony Pena	.05
73	Kent Tekulve	.05
74	Mike Easler	.05
75	Tim Foli	.05
76	Willie Stargell	.25
77	Bill Madlock	.05
78	Jim Bibby	.05
79	Omar Moreno	.05
80	Lee Lacy	.05
81	Hubie Brooks	.05
82	Rusty Staub	.05
83	Ellis Valentine	.05
84	Neil Allen	.05
85	Dave Kingman	.05
86	Mookie Wilson	.05
87	Doug Flynn	.05
88	Pat Zachry	.05
89	John Stearns	.05
90	Lee Mazzilli	.05
91	Ken Reitz	.05
92	Mike Krukow	.05
93	Jerry Morales	.05
94	Leon Durham	.05
95	Ivan DeJesus	.05
96	Bill Buckner	.05
97	Jim Tracy	.05
98	Steve Henderson	.05
99	Dick Tidrow	.05
100	Mike Tyson	.05
101	Ozzie Smith	.35
102	Ruppert Jones	.05
103	Broderick Perkins	.05
104	Gene Richrds	.05
105	Terry Kennedy	.05
106	Jim Bibby, Willie Stargell	.10
107	Larry Bowa, Pete Rose	.25
108	Warren Spahn, Fernando Valenzuela	.10
109	Dave Concepcion, Pete Rose	.25
110	Reggie Jackson, Dave Winfield	
111	Tom Lasorda, Fernando Valenzuela	
112	Reggie Jackson	.35
113	Dave Winfield	.25
114	Lou Piniella	.10
115	Tommy John	.10
116	Rich Gossage	.10
117	Ron Davis	.05
118	Rick Cerone	.05
119	Graig Nettles	.05
120	Ron Guidry	.05
121	Willie Randolph	.05
122	Dwayne Murphy	.05
123	Rickey Henderson	.25
124	Wayne Gross	.05
125	Mike Norris	.05
126	Rick Langford	.05
127	Jim Spencer	.05
128	Tony Armas	.05
129	Matt Keough	.05
130	Jeff Jones	.05
131	Steve McCatty	.05
132	Rollie Fingers	.20
133	Jim Gantner	.05
134	Gorman Thomas	.05
135	Robin Yount	.25
136	Paul Molitor	.25
137	Ted Simmons	.05
138	Ben Oglivie	.05
139	Moose Haas	.05

140	Cecil Cooper	.05
141	Pete Vuckovich	.05
142	Doug DeCinces	.05
143	Jim Palmer	.25
144	Steve Stone	.05
145	Mike Flanagan	.05
146	Rick Dempsey	.05
147	Al Bumbry	.05
148	Mark Belanger	.05
149	Scott McGregor	.05
150	Ken Singleton	.05
151	Eddie Murray	.25
152	Lance Parrish	.05
153	David Rozema	.05
154	Champ Summers	.05
155	Alan Trammell	.05
156	Lou Whitaker	.05
157	Milt Wilcox	.05
158	Kevin Saucier	.05
159	Jack Morris	.25
160	Steve Kemp	.05
161	Kirk Gibson	.05
162	Carl Yastrzemski	.25
163	Jim Rice	.20
164	Carney Lansford	.05
165	Dennis Eckersley	.20
166	Mike Torrez	.05
167	Dwight Evans	.05
168	Glenn Hoffman	.05
169	Bob Stanley	.05
170	Tony Perez	.05
171	Jerry Remy	.05
172	Buddy Bell	.05
173	Ferguson Jenkins	.20
174	Mickey Rivers	.05
175	Bump Wills	.05
176	Jon Matlack	.05
177	Steve Comer	.05
178	Al Oliver	.05
179	Bill Stein	.05
180	Pat Putnam	.05
181	Jim Sundberg	.05
182	Ron LeFlore	.05
183	Carlton Fisk	.25
184	Harold Baines	.05
185	Bill Almon	.05
186	Richard Dotson	.05
187	Greg Luzinski	.05
188	Mike Squires	.05
189	Britt Burns	.05
190	Lamarr Hoyt	.05
191	Chet Lemon	.05
192	Joe Charboneau	.10
193	Toby Harrah	.05
194	John Denny	.05
195	Rick Manning	.05
196	Miguel Dilone	.05
197	Bo Diaz	.05
198	Mike Hargrove	.05
199	Bert Blyleven	.05
200	Len Barker	.05
201	Andre Thornton	.05
202	George Brett	.35
203	U.L. Washington	.05
204	Dan Quisenberry	.05
205	Larry Gura	.05
206	Willie Aikens	.05
207	Willie Wilson	.05
208	Dennis Leonard	.05
209	Frank White	.05
210	Hal McRae	.05
211	Amos Otis	.05
212	Don Aase	.05
213	Butch Hobson	.05
214	Fred Lynn	.05
215	Brian Downing	.05
216	Dan Ford	.05
217	Rod Carew	.25
218	Bobby Grich	.05
219	Rick Burleson	.05
220	Don Baylor	.05
221	Ken Forsch	.05
222	Bruce Bochte	.05
223	Richie Zisk	.05
224	Tom Paciorek	.05
225	Julio Cruz	.05
226	Jeff Burroughs	.05
227	Doug Corbett	.05
228	Roy Smalley	.05
229	Gary Ward	.05
230	John Castino	.05
231	Rob Wilfong	.05
232	Dave Stieb	.05
233	Otto Velez	.05
234	Damaso Garcia	.05
235	John Mayberry	.05
236	Alfredo Griffin	.05
237	Ted Williams, Carl Yastrzemski	.50
238	Rick Cerone, Graig Nettles	.05
239	Buddy Bell, George Brett	.15
240	Steve Carlton, Jim Kaat	.10
241	Steve Carlton, Dave Parker	.10
242	Ron Davis, Nolan Ryan	.40

1983 Fleer Promo Sheet

The consumer, rather than dealer, was the target audience for this sheet premiering '83 Fleer. Six player cards, identical to the issued versions, appear on the 9-5/8" x 7-1/2" sheet, along with advertising messages on front and back. Versions of the sheet can be found with the name of hobby publications which inserted the sample into their issues.

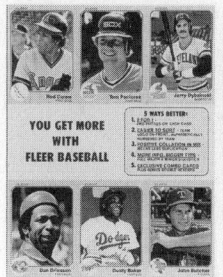

NM/M
Uncut Sheet: 5.00

1983 Fleer

The 1983 Fleer set features color photos set inside a light brown border. The cards are standard 2-1/2" x 3-1/2". A team logo is located at the card bottom and the word "Fleer" is found at the top. The card backs are designed on a vertical format and include a small black and white photo of the player along with biographical and statistical information. The reverses are done in two shades of brown on white stock. The set was issued with team logo stickers.

	NM/M
Complete Set (660):	40.00
Common Player:	.05
Wax Pack (15):	3.00
Wax Box (38):	100.00
Cello Pack (28):	4.00
Cello Box (24):	80.00
Vending Box (500):	35.00

No.	Player	Price
1	Joaquin Andujar	.05
2	Doug Bair	.05
3	Steve Braun	.05
4	Glenn Brummer	.05
5	Bob Forsch	.05
6	David Green	.05
7	George Hendrick	.05
8	Keith Hernandez	.05
9	Tom Herr	.05
10	Dane Iorg	.05
11	Jim Kaat	.10
12	Jeff Lahti	.05
13	Tito Landrum	.05
14	Dave LaPoint RC	.05
15	Willie McGee RC	1.50
16	Steve Mura	.05
17	Ken Oberkfell	.05
18	Darrell Porter	.05
19	Mike Ramsey	.05
20	Gene Roof	.05
21	Lonnie Smith	.05
22	Ozzie Smith	1.50
23	John Stuper	.05
24	Bruce Sutter	.65
25	Gene Tenace	.05
26	Jerry Augustine	.05
27	Dwight Bernard	.05
28	Mark Brouhard	.05
29	Mike Caldwell	.05
30	Cecil Cooper	.05
31	Jamie Easterly	.05
32	Marshall Edwards	.05
33	Rollie Fingers	.65
34	Jim Gantner	.05
35	Moose Haas	.05
36	Roy Howell	.05
37	Peter Ladd	.05
38	Bob McClure	.05
39	Doc Medich	.05
40	Paul Molitor	.75
41	Don Money	.05
42	Charlie Moore	.05
43	Ben Oglivie	.05
44	Ed Romero	.05
45	Ted Simmons	.65
46	Jim Slaton	.05
47	Don Sutton	.65
48	Gorman Thomas	.05
49	Pete Vuckovich	.05
50	Ned Yost	.05
51	Robin Yount	.75
52	Benny Ayala	.05
53	Bob Bonner	.05
54	Al Bumbry	.05
55	Terry Crowley	.05
56	Storm Davis RC	.10
57	Rich Dauer	.05
58	Rick Dempsey	.05
59	Jim Dwyer	.05
60	Mike Flanagan	.05
61	Dan Ford	.05
62	Glenn Gulliver	.05
63	John Lowenstein	.05
64	Dennis Martinez	.05
65	Tippy Martinez	.05
66	Scott McGregor	.05
67	Eddie Murray	.75
68	Joe Nolan	.05
69	Jim Palmer	.75
70	Cal Ripken, Jr.	6.00
71	Gary Roenicke	.05
72	Lenn Sakata	.05
73	Ken Singleton	.05
74	Sammy Stewart	.05
75	Tim Stoddard	.05
76	Don Aase	.05
77	Don Baylor	.05
78	Juan Beniquez	.05
79	Bob Boone	.05
80	Rick Burleson	.05
81	Rod Carew	.75
82	Bobby Clark	.05
83	Doug Corbett	.05
84	John Curtis	.05
85	Doug DeCinces	.05
86	Brian Downing	.05
87	Joe Ferguson	.05
88	Tim Foli	.05
89	Ken Forsch	.05
90	Dave Goltz	.05
91	Bobby Grich	.05
92	Andy Hassler	.05
93	Reggie Jackson	1.50
94	Ron Jackson	.05
95	Tommy John	.10
96	Bruce Kison	.05
97	Fred Lynn	.05
98	Ed Ott	.05
99	Steve Renko	.05
100	Luis Sanchez	.05
101	Rob Wilfong	.05
102	Mike Witt	.05
103	Geoff Zahn	.05
104	Willie Aikens	.05
105	Mike Armstrong	.05
106	Vida Blue	.05
107	Bud Black RC	.50
108	George Brett	2.00
109	Bill Castro	.05
110	Onix Concepcion	.05
111	Dave Frost	.05
112	Cesar Geronimo	.05
113	Larry Gura	.05
114	Steve Hammond	.05
115	Don Hood	.05
116	Dennis Leonard	.05
117	Jerry Martin	.05
118	Lee May	.05
119	Hal McRae	.05
120	Amos Otis	.05
121	Greg Pryor	.05
122	Dan Quisenberry	.05
123	Don Slaught RC	.20
124	Paul Splittorff	.05
125	U.L. Washington	.05
126	John Wathan	.05
127	Frank White	.05
128	Willie Wilson	.05
129	Steve Bedrosian	.05
130	Bruce Benedict	.05
131	Tommy Boggs	.05
132	Brett Butler	.05
133	Rick Camp	.05
134	Chris Chambliss	.05
135	Ken Dayley	.05
136	Gene Garber	.05
137	Terry Harper	.05
138	Bob Horner	.05
139	Glenn Hubbard	.05
140	Rufino Linares	.05
141	Rick Mahler	.05
142	Dale Murphy	.50
143	Phil Niekro	.65
144	Pascual Perez	.05
145	Biff Pocoroba	.05
146	Rafael Ramirez	.05
147	Jerry Royster	.05
148	Ken Smith	.05
149	Bob Walk	.05
150	Claudell Washington	.05
151	Bob Watson	.05
152	Larry Whisenton	.05
153	Porfirio Altamirano	.05
154	Marty Bystrom	.05
155	Steve Carlton	.75
156	Larry Christenson	.05
157	Ivan DeJesus	.05
158	John Denny	.05
159	Bob Dernier	.05
160	Bo Diaz	.05
161	Ed Farmer	.05
162	Greg Gross	.05
163	Mike Krukow	.05
164	Garry Maddox	.05
165	Gary Matthews	.05
166	Tug McGraw	.05
167	Bob Molinaro	.05
168	Sid Monge	.05
169	Ron Reed	.05
170	Bill Robinson	.05
171	Pete Rose	3.00
172	Dick Ruthven	.05
173	Mike Schmidt	2.00
174	Manny Trillo	.05
175	Ozzie Virgil	.05
176	George Vukovich	.05
177	Gary Allenson	.05
178	Luis Aponte	.05
179	Wade Boggs RC	10.00
180	Tom Burgmeier	.05
181	Mark Clear	.05
182	Dennis Eckersley	.65
183	Dwight Evans	.05
184	Rich Gedman	.05
185	Glenn Hoffman	.05
186	Bruce Hurst	.05
187	Carney Lansford	.05
188	Rick Miller	.05
189	Reid Nichols	.05
190	Bob Ojeda	.05
191	Tony Perez	.65
192	Chuck Rainey	.05
193	Jerry Remy	.05
194	Jim Rice	.35
195	Bob Stanley	.05
196	Dave Stapleton	.05
197	Mike Torrez	.05
198	John Tudor	.05
199	Julio Valdez	.05
200	Carl Yastrzemski	.75
201	Dusty Baker	.05
202	Joe Beckwith	.05
203	Greg Brock RC	.05
204	Ron Cey	.05
205	Terry Forster	.05
206	Steve Garvey	.30
207	Pedro Guerrero	.05
208	Burt Hooton	.05
209	Steve Howe	.05
210	Ken Landreaux	.05
211	Mike Marshall	.05
212	Candy Maldonado RC	.05
213	Rick Monday	.05
214	Tom Niedenfuer	.05
215	Jorge Orta	.05
216	Jerry Reuss	.05
217	Ron Roenicke	.05
218	Vicente Romo	.05
219	Bill Russell	.05
220	Steve Sax	.05
221	Mike Scioscia	.05
222	Dave Stewart	.05
223	Derrel Thomas	.05
224	Fernando Valenzuela	.05
225	Bob Welch	.05
226	Ricky Wright	.05
227	Steve Yeager	.05
228	Bill Almon	.05
229	Harold Baines	.05
230	Salome Barojas	.05
231	Tony Bernazard	.05
232	Britt Burns	.05
233	Richard Dotson	.05
234	Ernesto Escarrega	.05
235	Carlton Fisk	.75
236	Jerry Hairston Sr.	.05
237	Kevin Hickey	.05
238	LaMarr Hoyt	.05
239	Steve Kemp	.05
240	Jim Kern	.05
241	Ron Kittle RC	.25
242	Jerry Koosman	.05
243	Dennis Lamp	.05
244	Rudy Law	.05
245	Vance Law	.05
246	Ron LeFlore	.05
247	Greg Luzinski	.05
248	Tom Paciorek	.05
249	Aurelio Rodriguez	.05
250	Mike Squires	.05
251	Steve Trout	.05
252	Jim Barr	.05
253	Dave Bergman	.05
254	Fred Breining	.05
255	Bob Brenly	.05
256	Jack Clark	.05
257	Chili Davis	.05
258	Darrell Evans	.05
259	Alan Fowlkes	.05
260	Rich Gale	.05
261	Atlee Hammaker	.05
262	Al Holland	.05
263	Duane Kuiper	.05
264	Bill Laskey	.05
265	Gary Lavelle	.05
266	Johnnie LeMaster	.05
267	Renie Martin	.05
268	Milt May	.05
269	Greg Minton	.05
270	Joe Morgan	.75
271	Tom O'Malley	.05
272	Reggie Smith	.05
273	Guy Sularz	.05
274	Champ Summers	.05
275	Max Venable	.05
276	Jim Wohlford	.05
277	Ray Burris	.05
278	Gary Carter	.75
279	Warren Cromartie	.05
280	Andre Dawson	.40
281	Terry Francona	.05
282	Doug Flynn	.05
283	Woody Fryman	.05
284	Bill Gullickson	.05
285	Wallace Johnson	.05
286	Charlie Lea	.05
287	Randy Lerch	.05
288	Brad Mills	.05
289	Dan Norman	.05
290	Al Oliver	.05
291	David Palmer	.05
292	Tim Raines	.05
293	Jeff Reardon	.05
294	Steve Rogers	.05
295	Scott Sanderson	.05
296	Dan Schatzeder	.05
297	Bryn Smith	.05
298	Chris Speier	.05
299	Tim Wallach	.05
300	Jerry White	.05
301	Joel Youngblood	.05
302	Ross Baumgarten	.05
303	Dale Berra	.05
304	Jim Candelaria	.05
305	Dick Davis	.05
306	Mike Easler	.05
307	Richie Hebner	.05
308	Lee Lacy	.05
309	Bill Madlock	.05
310	Larry McWilliams	.05
311	John Milner	.05
312	Omar Moreno	.05
313	Jim Morrison	.05
314	Steve Nicosia	.05
315	Dave Parker	.05
316	Tony Pena	.05
317	Johnny Ray	.05
318	Rick Rhoden	.05
319	Don Robinson	.05
320	Enrique Romo	.05
321	Manny Sarmiento	.05
322	Rod Scurry	.05
323	Jim Smith	.05
324	Willie Stargell	.75
325	Jason Thompson	.05
326	Kent Tekulve	.05
327a	Tom Brookens (Narrow (1/4") brown box at bottom on back.)	.45
327b	Tom Brookens (Wide (1-1/4") brown box at bottom on back.)	
328	Enos Cabell	.05
329	Kirk Gibson	.05
330	Larry Herndon	.05
331	Mike Ivie	.05
332	Howard Johnson RC	1.00
333	Lynn Jones	.05
334	Rick Leach	.05
335	Chet Lemon	.05
336	Jack Morris	.05
337	Lance Parrish	.05
338	Larry Pashnick	.05
339	Dan Petry	.05
340	Dave Rozema	.05
341	Dave Rucker	.05
342	Elias Sosa	.05
343	Dave Tobik	.05
344	Alan Trammell	.05
345	Jerry Turner	.05
346	Jerry Ujdur	.05
347	Pat Underwood	.05
348	Lou Whitaker	.05
349	Milt Wilcox	.05
350	Glenn Wilson RC	.05
351	John Wockenfuss	.05
352	Kurt Bevacqua	.05
353	Juan Bonilla	.05
354	Floyd Chiffer	.05
355	Luis DeLeon	.05
356	Dave Dravecky RC	.30
357	Dave Edwards	.05
358	Juan Eichelberger	.05
359	Tim Flannery	.05
360	Tony Gwynn RC	15.00
361	Ruppert Jones	.05
362	Terry Kennedy	.05
363	Joe Lefebvre	.05
364	Sixto Lezcano	.05
365	Tim Lollar	.05
366	Gary Lucas	.05
367	John Montefusco	.05
368	Broderick Perkins	.05
369	Joe Pittman	.05
370	Gene Richards	.05
371	Luis Salazar	.05
372	Eric Show RC	.05
373	Garry Templeton	.05
374	Chris Welsh	.05
375	Alan Wiggins	.05
376	Rick Cerone	.05
377	Dave Collins	.05
378	Roger Erickson	.05
379	George Frazier	.05
380	Oscar Gamble	.05
381	Goose Gossage	.10
382	Ken Griffey	.05
383	Ron Guidry	.10
384	Dave LaRoche	.05
385	Rudy May	.05
386	John Mayberry	.05
387	Lee Mazzilli	.05
388	Mike Morgan	.05
389	Jerry Mumphrey	.05
390	Bobby Murcer	.10
391	Graig Nettles	.10
392	Lou Piniella	.05
393	Willie Randolph	.05
394	Shane Rawley	.05
395	Dave Righetti	.05
396	Andre Robertson	.05
397	Roy Smalley	.05
398	Dave Winfield	.75
399	Butch Wynegar	.05
400	Chris Bando	.05
401	Alan Bannister	.05
402	Len Barker	.05
403	Tom Brennan	.05
404	Carmelo Castillo RC	.05
405	Miguel Dilone	.05
406	Jerry Dybzinski	.05
407	Mike Fischlin	.05
408	Ed Glynn (Photo actually Bud Anderson.)	.05
409	Mike Hargrove	.05
410	Toby Harrah	.05
411	Ron Hassey	.05
412	Von Hayes	.05
413	Rick Manning	.05
414	Bake McBride	.05
415	Larry Milbourne	.05
416	Bill Nahorodny	.05
417	Jack Perconte	.05
418	Larry Sorensen	.05
419	Dan Spillner	.05
420	Rick Sutcliffe	.05
421	Andre Thornton	.05
422	Rick Waits	.05
423	Eddie Whitson	.05
424	Jesse Barfield	.05
425	Barry Bonnell	.05
426	Jim Clancy	.05
427	Damaso Garcia	.05
428	Jerry Garvin	.05
429	Alfredo Griffin	.05
430	Garth Iorg	.05
431	Roy Lee Jackson	.05
432	Luis Leal	.05
433	Buck Martinez	.05
434	Joey McLaughlin	.05
435	Lloyd Moseby	.05
436	Rance Mulliniks	.05
437	Dale Murray	.05
438	Wayne Nordhagen	.05
439	Gene Petralli RC	.05
440	Hosken Powell	.05
441	Dave Stieb	.05
442	Willie Upshaw	.05
443	Ernie Whitt	.05
444	Al Woods	.05
445	Alan Ashby	.05
446	Jose Cruz	.05
447	Kiko Garcia	.05
448	Phil Garner	.05
449	Danny Heep	.05
450	Art Howe	.05
451	Bob Knepper	.05
452	Alan Knicely	.05
453	Ray Knight	.05
454	Frank LaCorte	.05
455	Mike LaCoss	.05
456	Randy Moffitt	.05
457	Joe Niekro	.05
458	Terry Puhl	.05
459	Luis Pujols	.05
460	Craig Reynolds	.05
461	Bert Roberge	.05
462	Vern Ruhle	.05
463	Nolan Ryan	4.00
464	Joe Sambito	.05
465	Tony Scott	.05
466	Dave Smith	.05
467	Harry Spilman	.05
468	Dickie Thon	.05
469	Denny Walling	.05
470	Larry Andersen	.05
471	Floyd Bannister	.05
472	Jim Beattie	.05
473	Bruce Bochte	.05
474	Manny Castillo	.05
475	Bill Caudill	.05
476	Bryan Clark	.05
477	Al Cowens	.05
478	Julio Cruz	.05
479	Todd Cruz	.05
480	Gary Gray	.05
481	Dave Henderson	.05
482	Mike Moore RC	.05
483	Gaylord Perry	.65
484	Dave Revering	.05
485	Joe Simpson	.05
486	Mike Stanton	.05
487	Rick Sweet	.05
488	Ed Vande Berg RC	.05
489	Richie Zisk	.05
490	Doug Bird	.05
491	Larry Bowa	.05
492	Bill Buckner	.05
493	Bill Campbell	.05
494	Jody Davis	.05
495	Leon Durham	.05
496	Steve Henderson	.05
497	Willie Hernandez	.05
498	Fergie Jenkins	.65
499	Jay Johnstone	.05
500	Junior Kennedy	.05
501	Randy Martz	.05
502	Jerry Morales	.05
503	Keith Moreland	.05
504	Dickie Noles	.05
505	Mike Proly	.05
506	Allen Ripley	.05
507	Ryne Sandberg RC	10.00
508	Lee Smith	1.00
509	Pat Tabler	.05
510	Dick Tidrow	.05
511	Bump Wills	.05
512	Gary Woods	.05
513	Tony Armas	.05
514	Dave Beard	.05
515	Jeff Burroughs	.05
516	John D'Acquisto	.05
517	Wayne Gross	.05
518	Mike Heath	.05
519	Rickey Henderson	.75
520	Cliff Johnson	.05
521	Matt Keough	.05
522	Brian Kingman	.05
523	Rick Langford	.05
524	Davey Lopes	.05
525	Steve McCatty	.05
526	Dave McKay	.05
527	Dan Meyer	.05
528	Dwayne Murphy	.05
529	Jeff Newman	.05
530	Mike Norris	.05
531	Bob Owchinko	.05
532	Joe Rudi	.05
533	Jimmy Sexton	.05
534	Fred Stanley	.05
535	Tom Underwood	.05
536	Neil Allen	.05
537	Wally Backman	.05
538	Bob Bailor	.05
539	Hubie Brooks	.05
540	Carlos Diaz	.05
541	Pete Falcone	.05
542	George Foster	.05
543	Ron Gardenhire	.05
544	Brian Giles	.05
545	Ron Hodges	.05
546	Randy Jones	.05
547	Mike Jorgensen	.05
548	Dave Kingman	.05
549	Ed Lynch	.05
550	Jesse Orosco	.05
551	Rick Ownbey	.05
552	Charlie Puleo RC	.05
553	Gary Rajsich	.05
554	Mike Scott	.05
555	Rusty Staub	.05
556	John Stearns	.05
557	Craig Swan	.05
558	Ellis Valentine	.05
559	Tom Veryzer	.05
560	Mookie Wilson	.05
561	Pat Zachry	.05
562	Buddy Bell	.05
563	John Butcher	.05
564	Steve Comer	.05
565	Danny Darwin	.05
566	Bucky Dent	.05
567	John Grubb	.05
568	Rick Honeycutt	.05
569	Dave Hostetler	.05
570	Charlie Hough	.05
571	Lamar Johnson	.05
572	Jon Matlack	.05
573	Paul Mirabella	.05
574	Larry Parrish	.05
575	Mike Richardt	.05
576	Mickey Rivers	.05
577	Billy Sample	.05
578	Dave Schmidt RC	.05
579	Bill Stein	.05
580	Jim Sundberg	.05
581	Frank Tanana	.05
582	Mark Wagner	.05
583	George Wright	.05
584	Johnny Bench	.75
585	Bruce Berenyi	.05
586	Larry Biittner	.05
587	Cesar Cedeno	.05
588	Dave Concepcion	.05
589	Dan Driessen	.05
590	Greg Harris	.05
591	Ben Hayes	.05
592	Paul Householder	.05
593	Tom Hume	.05
594	Wayne Krenchicki	.05
595	Rafael Landestoy	.05
596	Charlie Leibrandt	.05
597	Eddie Milner RC	.05
598	Ron Oester	.05
599	Frank Pastore	.05
600	Joe Price	.05
601	Tom Seaver	.75
602	Bob Shirley	.05
603	Mario Soto	.05
604	Alex Trevino	.05
605	Mike Vail	.05
606	Duane Walker	.05
607	Tom Brunansky	.05
608	Bobby Castillo	.05
609	John Castino	.05
610	Ron Davis	.05
611	Lenny Faedo	.05
612	Terry Felton	.05
613	Gary Gaetti RC	.35
614	Mickey Hatcher	.05
615	Brad Havens	.05
616	Kent Hrbek	.05
617	Randy S. Johnson	.05
618	Tim Laudner	.05
619	Jeff Little	.05
620	Bob Mitchell	.05
621	Jack O'Connor	.05
622	John Pacella	.05
623	Pete Redfern	.05
624	Jesus Vega	.05
625	Frank Viola RC	1.00
626	Ron Washington	.05
627	Gary Ward	.05
628	Al Williams	.05
629	Red Sox All-Stars (Mark Clear, Dennis Eckersley, Carl Yastrzemski)	.25
630	300 Career Wins (Terry Bulling, Gaylord Perry)	.10

631 Pride of Venezuela (Dave Concepcion, Manny Trillo) .10
632 All-Star Infielders (Buddy Bell, Robin Yount) .20
633 Mr. Vet & Mr. Rookie (Kent Hrbek, Dave Winfield) .25
634 Fountain of Youth (Pete Rose, Willie Stargell) .40
635 Big Chiefs (Toby Harrah, Andre Thornton) .05
636 "Smith Bros." (Lonnie Smith, Ozzie Smith) .15
637 Base Stealers' Threat (Gary Carter, Bo Diaz) .10
638 All-Star Catchers (Gary Carter, Carlton Fisk) .15
639 Rickey Henderson/IA .50
640 Home Run Threats (Reggie Jackson, Ben Oglivie) .25
641 Two Teams - Same Day (Joel Youngblood) .05
642 Last Perfect Game (Len Barker, Ron Hassey) .05
643 Blue (Vida Blue) .05
644 Black & (Bud Black) .05
645 Power (Reggie Jackson) .30
646 Speed & (Rickey Henderson) .30
647 Checklist 1-51 .05
648 Checklist 52-103 .05
649 Checklist 104-152 .05
650 Checklist 153-200 .05
651 Checklist 201-251 .05
652 Checklist 252-301 .05
653 Checklist 302-351 .05
654 Checklist 352-399 .05
655 Checklist 400-444 .05
656 Checklist 445-489 .05
657 Checklist 490-535 .05
658 Checklist 536-583 .05
659 Checklist 584-628 .05
660 Checklist 629-646 .05

Star Stamps

The 1983 Fleer Stamp set consists of 288 stamps, including 224 player stamps and 64 team logo stamps. They were originally issued on four different sheets of 72 stamps each (checklisted below) and in "Vend-A-Stamp" dispensers of 18 stamps each. Sixteen different dispenser strips were needed to complete the set (strips 1-4 comprise Sheet 1; strips 5-8 comprise Sheet 2; strips 9-12 comprise Sheet 3; and strips 13-16 comprise Sheet 4.) Stamps measure 1-1/4" x 1-13/16".

NM/M
Complete Sheet Set (4): 5.00
Complete Vend-A-Stamp Set (288): 5.00
Common Sheet: 2.50
Common Stamp Dispenser: .35
Common Single Stamp: .01
1 Sheet 1 (A's Logo, Angels Logo, Astros Logo, Cardinals Logo, Cubs Logo, Dodgers Logo, Expos Logo, Giants Logo, Indians Logo, Mets Logo, Orioles Logo, Phillies Logo, Pirates Logo, Red Sox Logo, Twins Logo, White Sox Logo, Neil Allen, Harold Baines, Buddy Bell, Dale Berra, Wade Boggs, George Brett, Bill Buckner, Jack Clark, Dave Concepcion, Warren Cromartie, Doug DeCinces, Luis DeLeon, Brian Driessen, Dan Driessen, Mike Flanagan, Bob Forsch, Ken Forsch, Toby) 2.50
2 Sheet 2 (Angels Logo, Astros Logo, Braves Logo, Cardinals logo, Dodgers Logo, Expos Logo, Indians Logo, Mariners Logo, Mets Logo, Phillies Logo, Pirates Logo, Rangers Logo, Reds Logo, Royals Logo, Tigers Logo, Yankees Logo,

Willie Aikens, Bob Bailor, Dusty Baker, Floyd Bannister, Len Barker, Hubie Brooks, Tom Brunansky, Chris Chambliss, Mark Clear, Andre Dawson, Bo Diaz, Dennis Eckersley, Rollie Fingers, George Foster, Goose Gossage, Ken Griffey, Ron Guid) 2.50
3 Sheet 3 (A's Logo, Angels Logo, Blue Jays Logo, Braves Logo, Brewers Logo, Dodgers Logo, Giants Logo, Indians Logo, Mariners Logo, Orioles Logo, Padres Logo, Reds Logo, Royals Logo, Tigers Logo, Twins Logo, White Sox Logo, Alan Ashby, Dave Beard, Jim Beattie, Johnny Bench, Bob Boone, Rod Carew, Gary Carter, Bobby Castillo, Bill Caudill, Cecil Cooper, Mike Easler, Dwight Evans, Carlton Fisk, Gene Garber, Damaso Garcia, Larry Herndon, Al Hol) 2.50
4 Sheet 4 (Blue Jays Logo, Braves Logo, Brewers Logo, Cubs Logo, Expos Logo, Giants Logo, Padres Logo, Phillies Logo, Pirates Logo, Rangers Logo, Red Sox Logo, Reds Logo, Royals Logo, Twins Logo, White Sox Logo, Yankees Logo, Joaquin Andujar, Don Baylor, Vida Blue, Bruce Bochte, Larry Bowa, Al Bumbry, Jeff Burroughs, Enos Cabell, Steve Carlton, Cesar Cedeno, Rick Cerone, Ron Cey, Larry Christenson, Jim Clancy, Jose Cruz, Danny Darwin, Rich Dauer, Ron Davis,) 2.50

Star Stamps Poster

Available via a wrapper redemption offer, this huge (31-3/4" x 21-3/4") poster is printed in red and blue on glossy white paper stock. Besides blue-tone photos of each stamp, the poster has trivia questions and the logos of each team, league, MLB and the players' association. Sheets were folded to 9-1/2" x 12-1/2" for mailing.

NM/M
Star Stamp Poster 10.00

1983 Fleer Stickers

This 270-sticker set consists of both player stickers and team logo stickers, all measuring 1-13/16" x 2-1/2". The player stickers are numbered on the back. The front features a full-color photo surrounded by a blue border with two stars at the top. The stickers were issued in strips of 10 player stickers plus two team logo stickers. The 26 logo stickers have been assigned numbers 271 through 296.

NM/M
Complete Set (296): 10.00
Common Player: .05
Wax Pack (12): .30
Wax Box (48): 10.00
1 Bruce Sutter .20
2 Willie McGee .05
3 Darrell Porter .05
4 Lonnie Smith .05
5 Dane Iorg .05
6 Keith Hernandez .05
7 Joaquin Andujar .05
8 Ken Oberkfell .05
9 John Stuper .05
10 Ozzie Smith .40
11 Bob Forsch .05
12 Jim Gantner .05
13 Rollie Fingers .20
14 Pete Vuckovich .05
15 Ben Oglivie .05
16 Don Sutton .20
17 Bob McClure .05
18 Robin Yount .25
19 Paul Molitor .25
20 Gorman Thomas .05
21 Mike Caldwell .05
22 Ted Simmons .05
23 Cecil Cooper .05
24 Steve Renko .05
25 Tommy John .10
26 Rod Carew .25
27 Bruce Kison .05
28 Ken Forsch .05
29 Geoff Zahn .05
30 Doug DiCinces .05
31 Fred Lynn .05
32 Reggie Jackson .40
33 Don Baylor .05
34 Bob Boone .05
35 Brian Downing .05
36 Goose Gossage .05
37 Roy Smalley .05
38 Graig Nettles .25
39 Dave Winfield .25
40 Lee Mazzilli .05
41 Jerry Mumphrey .05
42 Dave Collins .05
43 Rick Cerone .05
44 Willie Randolph .05
45 Lou Piniella .10
46 Ken Griffey .05
47 Ron Guidry .05
48 Jack Clark .05
49 Reggie Smith .05
50 Atlee Hammaker .05
51 Fred Breining .05
52 Gary Lavelle .05
53 Chili Davis .05
54 Greg Minton .05
55 Joe Morgan .25
56 Al Holland .05
57 Bill Laskey .05
58 Duane Kuiper .05
59 Tom Burgmeier .05
60 Carl Yastrzemski .25
61 Mark Clear .05
62 Mike Torrez .05
63 Dennis Eckersley .20
64 Wade Boggs .50
65 Bob Stanley .05
66 Jim Rice .15
67 Carney Lansford .05
68 Jerry Remy .05
69 Dwight Evans .05
70 John Candelaria .05
71 Bill Madlock .05
72 Dave Parker .05
73 Kent Tekulve .05
74 Tony Pena .05
75 Manny Sarmiento .05
76 Johnny Ray .05
77 Dale Berra .05
78 Lee Lacy .05
79 Jason Thompson .05
80 Mike Easler .05
81 Willie Stargell .25
82 Rick Camp .05
83 Bob Watson .05
84 Bob Horner .05
85 Rafael Ramirez .05
86 Chris Chambliss .05
87 Gene Garber .05
88 Claudell Washington .05
89 Steve Bedrosian .05
90 Dale Murphy .15
91 Phil Niekro .05
92 Jerry Royster .05
93 Bob Walk .05
94 Frank White .05
95 Dennis Leonard .05
96 Vida Blue .05
97 U.L. Washington .05
98 George Brett .45
99 Amos Otis .05
100 Dan Quisenberry .05
101 Willie Aikens .05
102 Hal McRae .05
103 Larry Gura .05
104 Willie Wilson .05
105 Damaso Garcia .05
106 Hosken Powell .05
107 Joey McLaughlin .05
108 Jim Clancy .05
109 Barry Bonnell .05
110 Garth Iorg .05
111 Dave Stieb .05
112 Fernando Valenzuela .05
113 Steve Garvey .10
114 Rick Monday .05
115 Burt Hooton .05
116 Bill Russell .05
117 Pedro Guerrero .05
118 Steve Sax .05
119 Steve Howe .05
120 Ken Landreaux .05
121 Dusty Baker .05
122 Ron Cey .05
123 Jerry Reuss .05
124 Bump Wills .05
125 Keith Moreland .05
126 Dick Tidrow .05
127 Bill Campbell .05
128 Larry Bowa .05
129 Randy Martz .05
130 Ferguson Jenkins .20
131 Leon Durham .05
132 Bill Buckner .05
133 Ron Davis .05
134 Jack O'Connor .05
135 Kent Hrbek .05
136 Gary Ward .05
137 Al Williams .05
138 Tom Brunansky .05
139 Bobby Castillo .05
140 Dusty Baker, Dale Murphy .10
141 Nolan Ryan .65
142 Lee Lacey (Lacy), Omar Moreno .05
143 Al Oliver, Pete Rose .25
144 Rickey Henderson .25
145 Ray Knight, Pete Rose, Mike Schmidt .30
146 Hal McRae, Ben Oglivie .05
147 Tom Hume, Ray Knight .05
148 Buddy Bell, Carlton Fisk .05
149 Steve Kemp .05
150 Rudy Law .05
151 Ron LeFlore .05
152 Jerry Koosman .05
153 Carlton Fisk .25
154 Salome Barojas .05
155 Harold Baines .05
156 Britt Burns .05
157 Tom Paciorek .05
158 Greg Luzinski .05
159 LaMarr Hoyt .05
160 George Wright .05
161 Danny Darwin .05
162 Lamar Johnson .05
163 Charlie Hough .05
164 Buddy Bell .05
165 John Matlack (Jon) .05
166 Billy Sample .05
167 John Grubb .05
168 Larry Parrish .05
169 Ivan DeJesus .05
170 Mike Schmidt .45
171 Tug McGraw .05
172 Ron Reed .05
173 Garry Maddox .05
174 Pete Rose .50
175 Manny Trillo .05
176 Steve Carlton .25
177 Bo Diaz .05
178 Gary Matthews .05
179 Bill Caudill .05
180 Ed Vande Berg .05
181 Gaylord Perry .20
182 Floyd Bannister .05
183 Richie Zisk .05
184 Al Cowens .05
185 Bruce Bochte .05
186 Jeff Burroughs .05
187 Dave Beard .05
188 Davey Lopes .05
189 Dwayne Murphy .05
190 Rick Langford .05
191 Tom Underwood .05
192 Rickey Henderson .25
193 Mike Flanagan .05
194 Scott McGregor .05
195 Ken Singleton .05
196 Rich Dauer .05
197 John Lowenstein .05
198 Cal Ripken, Jr. 1.00
199 Dennis Martinez .05
200 Jim Palmer .25
201 Tippy Martinez .05
202 Eddie Murray .25
203 Al Bumbry .05
204 Dickie Thon .05
205 Phil Garner .05
206 Jose Cruz .05
207 Nolan Ryan .65
208 Ray Knight .05
209 Terry Puhl .05
210 Joe Niekro .05
211 Art Howe .05
212 Alan Ashby .05
213 Tom Hume .05
214 Johnny Bench .25
215 Larry Biittner .05
216 Mario Soto .05
217 Dan Driessen .05
218 Tom Seaver .25
219 Dave Concepcion .05
220 Wayne Krenchicki .05
221 Cesar Cedeno .05
222 Ruppert Jones .05
223 Terry Kennedy .05
224 Luis DeLeon .05
225 Eric Show .05
226 Tim Flannery .05
227 Garry Templeton .05
228 Tim Lollar .05
229 Sixto Lezcano .05
230 Bob Bailor .05
231 Craig Swan .05
232 Dave Kingman .05
233 Mookie Wilson .05
234 John Stearns .05
235 Ellis Valentine .05
236 Neil Allen .05
237 Pat Zachry .05
238 Rusty Staub .05
239 George Foster .05
240 Rick Sutcliffe .05
241 Andre Thornton .05
242 Mike Hargrove .05
243 Dan Spillner .05
244 Lary Sorensen .05
245 Len Barker .05
246 Rick Manning .05
247 Toby Harrah .05
248 Milt Wilcox .05
249 Lou Whitaker .05
250 Tom Brookens .05
251 Chet Lemon .05
252 Jack Morris .05
253 Alan Trammell .05
254 John Wockenfuss .05
255 Lance Parrish .05
256 Larry Herndon .05
257 Chris Speier .05
258 Woody Fryman .05
259 Scott Sanderson .05
260 Steve Rogers .05
261 Warren Cromartie .05
262 Gary Carter .25
263 Bill Gullickson .05
264 Andre Dawson .15
265 Tim Raines .05
266 Charlie Lea .05
267 Jeff Reardon .05
268 Al Oliver .05
269 George Hendrick .05
270 John Montefusco .05
(271) A's Logo .05
(272) Angels Logo .05
(273) Astros Logo .05
(274) Blue Jays Logo .05
(275) Braves Logo .05
(276) Brewers Logo .05
(277) Cardinals Logo .05
(278) Cubs Logo .05
(279) Dodgers Logo .05
(280) Expos Logo .05
(281) Giants Logo .05
(282) Indians Logo .05
(283) Mariners Logo .05
(284) Mets Logo .05
(285) Orioles Logo .05
(286) Padres Logo .05
(287) Phillies Logo .05
(288) Pirates Logo .05
(289) Rangers Logo .05
(290) Red Sox Logo .05
(291) Reds Logo .05
(292) Royals Logo .05
(293) Tigers Logo .05
(294) Twins Logo .05
(295) Yankees Logo .05
(296) White Sox Logo .05

1984 Fleer Sample Sheet

Reportedly available only as an insert in a trade magazine for the grocery industry, this full-color 7-7/8" x 10-7/8" sheet is printed on glossy paper rather than cardboard. The full-color front reproduces nine cards from the forthcoming '84 Fleer issue. The black and red back has details of the cards and ordering informarrtion.

NM/M
Sample Sheet:
George Foster, Keith Hernandez, Ron Oester, Charlie Puleo, Steve Rogers, Dan Schatzeder, Bill Scherrer, Bryn Smith, Darryl Strawberry 10.00

1984 Fleer

The 1984 Fleer set contained 660 cards for the fourth consecutive year. The 2-1/2" x 3-1/2" cards feature a color photo surrounded

Kent Hrbek
FIRST BASE

by white borders and horizontal dark blue stripes. The top stripe contains the word "Fleer" with the lower carrying the player's name. Backs have a small black-and-white player photo and are done in blue ink on white stock. The set was issued with team logo stickers.

NM/M
Complete Set (660): 40.00
Common Player: .05
Wax Pack (15): 2.50
Wax Box (36): 75.00
Cello Pack (28): 4.50
Cello Box (24): 85.00
Vending Box (500): 40.00
1 Mike Boddicker RC .05
2 Al Bumbry .05
3 Todd Cruz .05
4 Rich Dauer .05
5 Storm Davis .05
6 Rick Dempsey .05
7 Jim Dwyer .05
8 Mike Flanagan .05
9 Dan Ford .05
10 John Lowenstein .05
11 Dennis Martinez .05
12 Tippy Martinez .05
13 Scott McGregor .05
14 Eddie Murray 1.00
15 Joe Nolan .05
16 Jim Palmer 1.00
17 Cal Ripken, Jr. 4.00
18 Gary Roenicke .05
19 Lenn Sakata .05
20 John Shelby RC .05
21 Ken Singleton .05
22 Sammy Stewart .05
23 Tim Stoddard .05
24 Marty Bystrom .05
25 Steve Carlton 1.00
26 Ivan DeJesus .05
27 John Denny .05
28 Bob Dernier .05
29 Bo Diaz .05
30 Kiko Garcia .05
31 Greg Gross .05
32 Kevin Gross RC .05
33 Von Hayes .05
34 Willie Hernandez .05
35 Al Holland .05
36 Charles Hudson RC .05
37 Joe Lefebvre .05
38 Sixto Lezcano .05
39 Garry Maddox .05
40 Gary Matthews .05
41 Len Matuszek .05
42 Tug McGraw .05
43 Joe Morgan 1.00
44 Tony Perez .75
45 Ron Reed .05
46 Pete Rose 3.00
47 Juan Samuel RC .25
48 Mike Schmidt 2.50
49 Ozzie Virgil .05
50 Juan Agosto RC .05
51 Harold Baines .05
52 Floyd Bannister .05
53 Salome Barojas .05
54 Britt Burns .05
55 Julio Cruz .05
56 Richard Dotson .05
57 Jerry Dybzinski .05
58 Carlton Fisk 1.00
59 Scott Fletcher RC .05
60 Jerry Hairston Sr. .05
61 Kevin Hickey .05
62 Marc Hill .05
63 LaMarr Hoyt .05
64 Ron Kittle .05
65 Jerry Koosman .05
66 Dennis Lamp .05
67 Rudy Law .05
68 Vance Law .05
69 Greg Luzinski .05
70 Tom Paciorek .05
71 Mike Squires .05
72 Dick Tidrow .05
73 Greg Walker RC .05
74 Glenn Abbott .05
75 Howard Bailey .05
76 Doug Bair .05
77 Juan Berenguer .05
78 Tom Brookens .05
79 Enos Cabell .05
80 Kirk Gibson .05

#	Player	Price
81	John Grubb	.05
82	Larry Herndon	.05
83	Wayne Krenchicki	.05
84	Rick Leach	.05
85	Chet Lemon	.05
86	Aurelio Lopez	.05
87	Jack Morris	.05
88	Lance Parrish	.05
89	Dan Petry	.05
90	Dave Rozema	.05
91	Alan Trammell	.05
92	Lou Whitaker	.05
93	Milt Wilcox	.05
94	Glenn Wilson	.05
95	John Wockenfuss	.05
96	Dusty Baker	.05
97	Joe Beckwith	.05
98	Greg Brock	.05
99	Jack Fimple	.05
100	Pedro Guerrero	.05
101	Rick Honeycutt	.05
102	Burt Hooton	.05
103	Steve Howe	.05
104	Ken Landreaux	.05
105	Mike Marshall	.05
106	Rick Monday	.05
107	Jose Morales	.05
108	Tom Niedenfuer	.05
109	Alejandro Pena RC	.05
110	Jerry Reuss	.05
111	Bill Russell	.05
112	Steve Sax	.05
113	Mike Scioscia	.05
114	Derrel Thomas	.05
115	Fernando Valenzuela	.05
116	Bob Welch	.05
117	Steve Yeager	.05
118	Pat Zachry	.05
119	Don Baylor	.05
120	Bert Campaneris	.05
121	Rick Cerone	.05
122	Ray Fontenot RC	.05
123	George Frazier	.05
124	Oscar Gamble	.05
125	Goose Gossage	.10
126	Ken Griffey	.05
127	Ron Guidry	.10
128	Jay Howell RC	.05
129	Steve Kemp	.05
130	Matt Keough	.05
131	Don Mattingly RC	20.00
132	John Montefusco	.05
133	Omar Moreno	.05
134	Dale Murray	.05
135	Graig Nettles	.05
136	Lou Piniella	.10
137	Willie Randolph	.05
138	Shane Rawley	.05
139	Dave Righetti	.05
140	Andre Robertson	.05
141	Bob Shirley	.05
142	Roy Smalley	.05
143	Dave Winfield	1.00
144	Butch Wynegar	.05
145	Jim Acker RC	.05
146	Doyle Alexander	.05
147	Jesse Barfield	.05
148	George Bell	.05
149	Barry Bonnell	.05
150	Jim Clancy	.05
151	Dave Collins	.05
152	Tony Fernandez RC	.50
153	Damaso Garcia	.05
154	Dave Geisel	.05
155	Jim Gott RC	.05
156	Alfredo Griffin	.05
157	Garth Iorg	.05
158	Roy Lee Jackson	.05
159	Cliff Johnson	.05
160	Luis Leal	.05
161	Buck Martinez	.05
162	Joey McLaughlin	.05
163	Randy Moffitt	.05
164	Lloyd Moseby	.05
165	Rance Mulliniks	.05
166	Jorge Orta	.05
167	Dave Stieb	.05
168	Willie Upshaw	.05
169	Ernie Whitt	.05
170	Len Barker	.05
171	Steve Bedrosian	.05
172	Bruce Benedict	.05
173	Brett Butler	.05
174	Rick Camp	.05
175	Chris Chambliss	.05
176	Ken Dayley	.05
177	Pete Falcone	.05
178	Terry Forster	.05
179	Gene Garber	.05
180	Terry Harper	.05
181	Bob Horner	.05
182	Glenn Hubbard	.05
183	Randy Johnson	.05
184	Craig McMurtry RC	.05
185	Donnie Moore RC	.05
186	Dale Murphy	.60
187	Phil Niekro	.75
188	Pascual Perez	.05
189	Biff Pocoroba	.05
190	Rafael Ramirez	.05
191	Jerry Royster	.05
192	Claudell Washington	.05
193	Bob Watson	.05
194	Jerry Augustine	.05
195	Mark Brouhard	.05
196	Mike Caldwell	.05
197	Tom Candiotti RC	.25
198	Cecil Cooper	.05
199	Rollie Fingers	.75
200	Jim Gantner	.05
201	Bob L. Gibson	.05
202	Moose Haas	.05
203	Roy Howell	.05
204	Pete Ladd	.05
205	Rick Manning	.05
206	Bob McClure	.05
207	Paul Molitor	1.00
208	Don Money	.05
209	Charlie Moore	.05
210	Ben Oglivie	.05
211	Chuck Porter	.05
212	Ed Romero	.05
213	Ted Simmons	.05
214	Jim Slaton	.05
215	Don Sutton	.75
216	Tom Tellmann	.05
217	Pete Vuckovich	.05
218	Ned Yost	.05
219	Robin Yount	1.00
220	Alan Ashby	.05
221	Kevin Bass RC	.05
222	Jose Cruz	.05
223	Bill Dawley RC	.05
224	Frank DiPino	.05
225	Bill Doran RC	.05
226	Phil Garner	.05
227	Art Howe	.05
228	Bob Knepper	.05
229	Ray Knight	.05
230	Frank LaCorte	.05
231	Mike LaCoss	.05
232	Mike Madden	.05
233	Jerry Mumphrey	.05
234	Joe Niekro	.05
235	Terry Puhl	.05
236	Luis Pujols	.05
237	Craig Reynolds	.05
238	Vern Ruhle	.05
239	Nolan Ryan	4.00
240	Mike Scott	.05
241	Tony Scott	.05
242	Dave Smith	.05
243	Dickie Thon	.05
244	Denny Walling	.05
245	Dale Berra	.05
246	Jim Bibby	.05
247	John Candelaria	.05
248	Jose DeLeon RC	.05
249	Mike Easler	.05
250	Cecilio Guante RC	.05
251	Richie Hebner	.05
252	Lee Lacy	.05
253	Bill Madlock	.05
254	Milt May	.05
255	Lee Mazzilli	.05
256	Larry McWilliams	.05
257	Jim Morrison	.05
258	Dave Parker	.05
259	Tony Pena	.05
260	Johnny Ray	.05
261	Rick Rhoden	.05
262	Don Robinson	.05
263	Manny Sarmiento	.05
264	Rod Scurry	.05
265	Kent Tekulve	.05
266	Gene Tenace	.05
267	Jason Thompson	.05
268	Lee Tunnell RC	.05
269	Marvell Wynne RC	.05
270	Ray Burris	.05
271	Gary Carter	1.00
272	Warren Cromartie	.05
273	Andre Dawson	.30
274	Doug Flynn	.05
275	Terry Francona	.05
276	Bill Gullickson	.05
277	Bob James	.05
278	Charlie Lea	.05
279	Bryan Little	.05
280	Al Oliver	.05
281	Tim Raines	.05
282	Bobby Ramos	.05
283	Jeff Reardon	.05
284	Steve Rogers	.05
285	Scott Sanderson	.05
286	Dan Schatzeder	.05
287	Bryn Smith	.05
288	Chris Speier	.05
289	Manny Trillo	.05
290	Mike Vail	.05
291	Tim Wallach	.05
292	Chris Welsh	.05
293	Jim Wohlford	.05
294	Kurt Bevacqua	.05
295	Juan Bonilla	.05
296	Bobby Brown	.05
297	Luis DeLeon	.05
298	Dave Dravecky	.05
299	Tim Flannery	.05
300	Steve Garvey	.25
301	Tony Gwynn	2.00
302	Andy Hawkins RC	.10
303	Ruppert Jones	.05
304	Terry Kennedy	.05
305	Tim Lollar	.05
306	Gary Lucas	.05
307	Kevin McReynolds RC	.25
308	Sid Monge	.05
309	Mario Ramirez	.05
310	Gene Richards	.05
311	Luis Salazar	.05
312	Eric Show	.05
313	Elias Sosa	.05
314	Garry Templeton	.05
315	Mark Thurmond RC	.05
316	Ed Whitson	.05
317	Alan Wiggins	.05
318	Neil Allen	.05
319	Joaquin Andujar	.05
320	Steve Braun	.05
321	Glenn Brummer	.05
322	Bob Forsch	.05
323	David Green	.05
324	George Hendrick	.05
325	Tom Herr	.05
326	Dane Iorg	.05
327	Jeff Lahti	.05
328	Dave LaPoint	.05
329	Willie McGee	.05
330	Ken Oberkfell	.05
331	Darrell Porter	.05
332	Jamie Quirk	.05
333	Mike Ramsey	.05
334	Floyd Rayford	.05
335	Lonnie Smith	.05
336	Ozzie Smith	2.00
337	John Stuper	.05
338	Bruce Sutter	.75
339	Andy Van Slyke RC	1.00
340	Dave Von Ohlen	.05
341	Willie Aikens	.05
342	Mike Armstrong	.05
343	Bud Black	.05
344	George Brett	2.50
345	Onix Concepcion	.05
346	Keith Creel	.05
347	Larry Gura	.05
348	Don Hood	.05
349	Dennis Leonard	.05
350	Hal McRae	.05
351	Amos Otis	.05
352	Gaylord Perry	.75
353	Greg Pryor	.05
354	Dan Quisenberry	.05
355	Steve Renko	.05
356	Leon Roberts	.05
357	Pat Sheridan RC	.05
358	Joe Simpson	.05
359	Don Slaught	.05
360	Paul Splittorff	.05
361	U.L. Washington	.05
362	John Wathan	.05
363	Frank White	.05
364	Willie Wilson	.05
365	Jim Barr	.05
366	Dave Bergman	.05
367	Fred Breining	.05
368	Bob Brenly	.05
369	Jack Clark	.05
370	Chili Davis	.05
371	Mark Davis RC	.05
372	Darrell Evans	.05
373	Atlee Hammaker	.05
374	Mike Krukow	.05
375	Duane Kuiper	.05
376	Bill Laskey	.05
377	Gary Lavelle	.05
378	Johnnie LeMaster	.05
379	Jeff Leonard	.05
380	Randy Lerch	.05
381	Renie Martin	.05
382	Andy McGaffigan	.05
383	Greg Minton	.05
384	Tom O'Malley	.05
385	Max Venable	.05
386	Brad Wellman	.05
387	Joel Youngblood	.05
388	Gary Allenson	.05
389	Luis Aponte	.05
390	Tony Armas	.05
391	Doug Bird	.05
392	Wade Boggs	2.00
393	Dennis Boyd RC	.05
394	Mike Brown	.05
395	Mark Clear	.05
396	Dennis Eckersley	.75
397	Dwight Evans	.05
398	Rich Gedman	.05
399	Glenn Hoffman	.05
400	Bruce Hurst	.05
401	John Henry Johnson	.05
402	Ed Jurak	.05
403	Rick Miller	.05
404	Jeff Newman	.05
405	Reid Nichols	.05
406	Bob Ojeda	.05
407	Jerry Remy	.05
408	Jim Rice	.05
409	Bob Stanley	.05
410	Dave Stapleton	.05
411	John Tudor	.05
412	Carl Yastrzemski	1.50
413	Buddy Bell	.05
414	Larry Biittner	.05
415	John Butcher	.05
416	Danny Darwin	.05
417	Bucky Dent	.05
418	Dave Hostetler	.05
419	Charlie Hough	.05
420	Bobby Johnson	.05
421	Odell Jones	.05
422	Jon Matlack	.05
423	Pete O'Brien RC	.05
424	Larry Parrish	.05
425	Mickey Rivers	.05
426	Billy Sample	.05
427	Dave Schmidt	.05
428	Mike Smithson RC	.05
429	Bill Stein	.05
430	Dave Stewart	.05
431	Jim Sundberg	.05
432	Frank Tanana	.05
433	Dave Tobik	.05
434	Wayne Tolleson RC	.05
435	George Wright	.05
436	Bill Almon	.05
437	Keith Atherton RC	.05
438	Dave Beard	.05
439	Tom Burgmeier	.05
440	Jeff Burroughs	.05
441	Chris Codiroli RC	.05
442	Tim Conroy RC	.05
443	Mike Davis	.05
444	Wayne Gross	.05
445	Garry Hancock	.05
446	Mike Heath	.05
447	Rickey Henderson	1.00
448	Don Hill	.05
449	Bob Kearney	.05
450	Bill Krueger	.05
451	Rick Langford	.05
452	Carney Lansford	.05
453	Davey Lopes	.05
454	Steve McCatty	.05
455	Dan Meyer	.05
456	Dwayne Murphy	.05
457	Mike Norris	.05
458	Ricky Peters	.05
459	Tony Phillips	.05
460	Tom Underwood	.05
461	Mike Warren	.05
462	Johnny Bench	1.50
463	Bruce Berenyi	.05
464	Dann Bilardello	.05
465	Cesar Cedeno	.05
466	Dave Concepcion	.05
467	Dan Driessen	.05
468	Nick Esasky RC	.05
469	Rich Gale	.05
470	Ben Hayes	.05
471	Paul Householder	.05
472	Tom Hume	.05
473	Alan Knicely	.05
474	Eddie Milner	.05
475	Ron Oester	.05
476	Kelly Paris	.05
477	Frank Pastore	.05
478	Ted Power	.05
479	Joe Price	.05
480	Charlie Puleo	.05
481	Gary Redus RC	.05
482	Bill Scherrer	.05
483	Mario Soto	.05
484	Alex Trevino	.05
485	Duane Walker	.05
486	Larry Bowa	.05
487	Warren Brusstar	.05
488	Bill Buckner	.05
489	Bill Campbell	.05
490	Ron Cey	.05
491	Jody Davis	.05
492	Leon Durham	.05
493	Mel Hall RC	.05
494	Fergie Jenkins	.75
495	Jay Johnstone	.05
496	Craig Lefferts RC	.10
497	Carmelo Martinez RC	.05
498	Jerry Morales	.05
499	Keith Moreland	.05
500	Dickie Noles	.05
501	Mike Proly	.05
502	Chuck Rainey	.05
503	Dick Ruthven	.05
504	Ryne Sandberg	2.00
505	Lee Smith	.05
506	Steve Trout	.05
507	Gary Woods	.05
508	Juan Beniquez	.05
509	Bob Boone	.05
510	Rick Burleson	.05
511	Rod Carew	1.00
512	Bobby Clark	.05
513	John Curtis	.05
514	Doug DeCinces	.05
515	Brian Downing	.05
516	Tim Foli	.05
517	Ken Forsch	.05
518	Bobby Grich	.05
519	Andy Hassler	.05
520	Reggie Jackson	1.50
521	Ron Jackson	.05
522	Tommy John	.10
523	Bruce Kison	.05
524	Steve Lubratich	.05
525	Fred Lynn	.05
526	Gary Pettis RC	.05
527	Luis Sanchez	.05
528	Daryl Sconiers	.05
529	Ellis Valentine	.05
530	Rob Wilfong	.05
531	Mike Witt	.05
532	Geoff Zahn	.05
533	Bud Anderson	.05
534	Chris Bando	.05
535	Alan Bannister	.05
536	Bert Blyleven	.10
537	Tom Brennan	.05
538	Jamie Easterly	.05
539	Juan Eichelberger	.05
540	Jim Essian	.05
541	Mike Fischlin	.05
542	Julio Franco	.05
543	Mike Hargrove	.10
544	Toby Harrah	.05
545	Ron Hassey	.05
546	Neal Heaton RC	.05
547	Bake McBride	.05
548	Broderick Perkins	.05
549	Lary Sorensen	.05
550	Dan Spillner	.05
551	Rick Sutcliffe	.05
552	Pat Tabler	.05
553	Gorman Thomas	.05
554	Andre Thornton	.05
555	George Vukovich	.05
556	Darrell Brown	.05
557	Tom Brunansky	.05
558	Randy Bush RC	.05
559	Bobby Castillo	.05
560	John Castino	.05
561	Ron Davis	.05
562	Dave Engle	.05
563	Lenny Faedo	.05
564	Pete Filson	.05
565	Gary Gaetti	.05
566	Mickey Hatcher	.05
567	Kent Hrbek	.05
568	Rusty Kuntz	.05
569	Tim Laudner	.05
570	Rick Lysander	.05
571	Bobby Mitchell	.05
572	Ken Schrom	.05
573	Ray Smith	.05
574	Tim Teufel RC	.05
575	Frank Viola	.05
576	Gary Ward	.05
577	Ron Washington	.05
578	Len Whitehouse	.05
579	Al Williams	.05
580	Bob Bailor	.05
581	Mark Bradley	.05
582	Hubie Brooks	.05
583	Carlos Diaz	.05
584	George Foster	.05
585	Brian Giles	.05
586	Danny Heep	.05
587	Keith Hernandez	.05
588	Ron Hodges	.05
589	Scott Holman	.05
590	Dave Kingman	.05
591	Ed Lynch	.05
592	Jose Oquendo RC	.05
593	Jesse Orosco	.05
594	Junior Ortiz RC	.05
595	Tom Seaver	1.00
596	Doug Sisk RC	.05
597	Rusty Staub	.05
598	John Stearns	.05
599	Darryl Strawberry	.25
600	Craig Swan	.05
601	Walt Terrell RC	.05
602	Mike Torrez	.05
603	Mookie Wilson	.05
604	Jamie Allen	.05
605	Jim Beattie	.05
606	Tony Bernazard	.05
607	Manny Castillo	.05
608	Bill Caudill	.05
609	Bryan Clark	.05
610	Al Cowens	.05
611	Dave Henderson	.05
612	Steve Henderson	.05
613	Orlando Mercado	.05
614	Mike Moore	.05
615	Ricky Nelson	.05
616	Spike Owen RC	.10
617	Pat Putnam	.05
618	Ron Roenicke	.05
619	Mike Stanton	.05
620	Bob Stoddard	.05
621	Rick Sweet	.05
622	Roy Thomas	.05
623	Ed Vande Berg	.05
624	Matt Young RC	.05
625	Richie Zisk	.05
626	'83 All-Star Game Record Breaker (Fred Lynn)	.05
627	'83 All-Star Game Record Breaker (Manny Trillo)	.05
628	N.L. Iron Man (Steve Garvey)	.10
629	A.L. Batting Runner-Up (Rod Carew)	.15
630	A.L. Batting Champion (Wade Boggs)	.50
631	Letting Go Of The Raines (Tim Raines)	.05
632	Double Trouble (Al Oliver)	.05
633	All-Star Second Base (Steve Sax)	.05
634	All-Star Shortstop (Dickie Thon)	.05
635	Ace Firemen (Tippy Martinez, Dan Quisenberry)	.05
636	Reds Reunited (Joe Morgan, Tony Perez, Pete Rose)	.75
637	Backstop Stars (Bob Boone, Lance Parrish)	.05
638	The Pine Tar Incident, 7/24/83 (George Brett, Gaylord Perry)	.25
639	1983 No-Hitters (Bob Forsch, Dave Righetti, Mike Warren)	.05
640	Retiring Superstars (Johnny Bench, Carl Yastrzemski)	.50
641	Going Out In Style (Gaylord Perry)	.05
642	300 Club & Strikeout Record (Steve Carlton)	.10
643	The Managers (Joe Altobelli, Paul Owens)	.05
644	The MVP (Rick Dempsey)	.05
645	The Rookie Winner (Mike Boddicker)	.05
646	The Clincher (Scott McGregor)	.05
647	Checklist: Orioles/Royals (Joe Altobelli)	.05
648	Checklist: Phillies/Giants (Paul Owens)	.05
649	Checklist: White Sox/Red Sox (Tony LaRussa)	.05
650	Checklist: Tigers/Rangers (Sparky Anderson)	.10
651	Checklist: Dodgers/A's (Tommy Lasorda)	.10
652	Checklist: Yankees/Reds (Billy Martin)	.05
653	Checklist: Blue Jays/Cubs (Bobby Cox)	.10
654	Checklist: Braves/Angels (Joe Torre)	.10
655	Checklist: Brewers/Indians (Rene Lacheman)	.05
656	Checklist: Astros/Twins (Bob Lillis)	.05
657	Checklist: Pirates/Mets (Chuck Tanner)	.05
658	Checklist: Expos/Mariners (Bill Virdon)	.05
659	Checklist: Padres/Specials (Dick Williams)	.05
660	Checklist: Cardinals/Specials (Whitey Herzog)	.05

Fleer Update

Brett Butler
OUTFIELD

Following the lead of Topps, Fleer issued near the end of the baseball season a 132-card set to update player trades and include rookies not depicted in the regular issue. The cards are identical in design to the regular issue but are numbered U-1 through U-132. Available only as a boxed set through hobby dealers, the set was printed in limited quantities. Sets were not factory sealed.

#	Player	NM/M
	Complete Set (132):	220.00
	Common Player:	.25
1	Willie Aikens	.25
2	Luis Aponte	.25
3	Mark Bailey	.25
4	Bob Bailor	.25
5	Dusty Baker	.25
6	Steve Balboni	.25
7	Alan Bannister	.25
8	Marty Barrett	.25
9	Dave Beard	.25
10	Joe Beckwith	.25
11	Dave Bergman	.25
12	Tony Bernazard	.25
13	Bruce Bochte	.25
14	Barry Bonnell	.25
15	Phil Bradley	.25
16	Fred Breining	.25
17	Mike Brown	.25
18	Bill Buckner	.25
19	Ray Burris	.25
20	John Butcher	.25
21	Brett Butler	.25
22	Enos Cabell	.25
23	Bill Campbell	.25
24	Bill Caudill	.25
25	Bobby Clark	.25
26	Bryan Clark	.25
27	Roger Clemens RC	140.00
28	Jaime Cocanower	.25
29	Ron Darling RC	1.00
30	Alvin Davis RC	.25
31	Bob Dernier	.25
32	Carlos Diaz	.25
33	Mike Easler	.25
34	Dennis Eckersley	4.00
35	Jim Essian	.25
36	Darrell Evans	.25
37	Mike Fitzgerald	.25
38	Tim Foli	.25
39	John Franco RC	3.00
40	George Frazier	.25
41	Rich Gale	.25
42	Barbaro Garbey	.25
43	Dwight Gooden RC	7.50
44	Goose Gossage	.40
45	Wayne Gross	.25
46	Mark Gubicza RC	1.00
47	Jackie Gutierrez	.25
48	Toby Harrah	.25
49	Ron Hassey	.25
50	Richie Hebner	.25
51	Willie Hernandez	.25
52	Ed Hodge	.25

53	Ricky Horton	.25
54	Art Howe	.25
55	Dane Iorg	.25
56	Brook Jacoby	.25
57	Dion James RC	.25
58	Mike Jeffcoat RC	.25
59	Ruppert Jones	.25
60	Bob Kearney	.25
61	Jimmy Key RC	1.00
62	Dave Kingman	.25
63	Brad Komminsk RC	.25
64	Jerry Koosman	.25
65	Wayne Krenchicki	.25
66	Rusty Kuntz	.25
67	Frank LaCorte	.25
68	Dennis Lamp	.25
69	Tito Landrum	.25
70	Mark Langston RC	4.00
71	Rick Leach	.25
72	Craig Lefferts	.25
73	Gary Lucas	.25
74	Jerry Martin	.25
75	Carmelo Martinez	.25
76	Mike Mason RC	.25
77	Gary Matthews	.25
78	Andy McGaffigan	.25
79	Joey McLaughlin	.25
80	Joe Morgan	5.00
81	Darryl Motley	.25
82	Graig Nettles	.40
83	Phil Niekro	3.00
84	Ken Oberkfell	.25
85	Al Oliver	.25
86	Jorge Orta	.25
87	Amos Otis	.25
88	Bob Owchinko	.25
89	Dave Parker	.25
90	Jack Perconte	.25
91	Tony Perez	3.00
92	Gerald Perry	.25
93	Kirby Puckett RC	75.00
94	Shane Rawley	.25
95	Floyd Rayford	.25
96	Ron Reed	.25
97	R.J. Reynolds	.25
98	Gene Richards	.25
99	Jose Rijo RC	1.00
100	Jeff Robinson	.25
101	Ron Romanick	.25
102	Pete Rose	10.00
103	Bret Saberhagen RC	5.00
104	Scott Sanderson	.25
105	Dick Schofield RC	.25
106	Tom Seaver	7.50
107	Jim Slaton	.25
108	Mike Smithson	.25
109	Lary Sorensen	.25
110	Tim Stoddard	.25
111	Jeff Stone	.25
112	Champ Summers	.25
113	Jim Sundberg	.25
114	Rick Sutcliffe	.35
115	Craig Swan	.25
116	Derrel Thomas	.25
117	Gorman Thomas	.25
118	Alex Trevino	.25
119	Manny Trillo	.25
120	John Tudor	.25
121	Tom Underwood	.25
122	Mike Vail	.25
123	Tom Waddell	.25
124	Gary Ward	.25
125	Terry Whitfield	.25
126	Curtis Wilkerson	.25
127	Frank Williams	.25
128	Glenn Wilson	.25
129	John Wockenfuss	.25
130	Ned Yost	.25
131	Mike Young RC	.25
132	Checklist 1-132	.10

1984 Fleer Stickers

This set was designed to be housed in a special collector's album that was organized according to various league leader categories, resulting in some players being pictured on more than one sticker. Each full-color sticker measures 1-15/16" x 2-1/2" and is framed with a beige border. The stickers, which were sold in packs of six, are numbered on the back.

		NM/M
Complete Set (126):		9.00
Common Player:		.05
Sticker Album:		1.00

Wax Box (100):		12.00
1	Dickie Thon	.05
2	Ken Landreaux	.05
3	Darrell Evans	.05
4	Harold Baines	.05
5	Dave Winfield	.25
6	Bill Madlock	.05
7	Lonnie Smith	.05
8	Jose Cruz	.05
9	George Hendrick	.05
10	Ray Knight	.05
11	Wade Boggs	.30
12	Rod Carew	.25
13	Lou Whitaker	.05
14	Alan Trammell	.05
15	Cal Ripken, Jr.	.50
16	Mike Schmidt	.40
17	Dale Murphy	.20
18	Andre Dawson	.15
19	Pedro Guerrero	.15
20	Jim Rice	.15
21	Tony Armas	.05
22	Ron Kittle	.05
23	Eddie Murray	.25
24	Jose Cruz	.05
25	Andre Dawson	.15
26	Rafael Ramirez	.05
27	Al Oliver	.05
28	Wade Boggs	.30
29	Cal Ripken, Jr.	.50
30	Lou Whitaker	.05
31	Cecil Cooper	.05
32	Dale Murphy	.20
33	Andre Dawson	.15
34	Pedro Guerrero	.05
35	Mike Schmidt	.40
36	George Brett	.40
37	Jim Rice	.15
38	Eddie Murray	.25
39	Carlton Fisk	.25
40	Rusty Staub	.05
41	Duane Walker	.05
42	Steve Braun	.05
43	Kurt Bevacqua	.05
44	Hal McRae	.05
45	Don Baylor	.05
46	Ken Singleton	.05
47	Greg Luzinski	.05
48	Mike Schmidt	.40
49	Keith Hernandez	.05
50	Dale Murphy	.20
51	Tim Raines	.05
52	Wade Boggs	.30
53	Rickey Henderson	.25
54	Rod Carew	.25
55	Ken Singleton	.05
56	John Denny	.05
57	John Candelaria	.05
58	Larry McWilliams	.05
59	Pascual Perez	.05
60	Jesse Orosco	.05
61	Moose Haas	.05
62	Richard Dotson	.05
63	Mike Flanagan	.05
64	Scott McGregor	.05
65	Atlee Hammaker	.05
66	Rick Honeycutt	.05
67	Lee Smith	.05
68	Al Holland	.05
69	Greg Minton	.05
70	Bruce Sutter	.20
71	Jeff Reardon	.05
72	Frank DiPino	.05
73	Dan Quisenberry	.05
74	Bob Stanley	.05
75	Ron Davis	.05
76	Bill Caudill	.05
77	Peter Ladd	.05
78	Steve Carlton	.25
79	Mario Soto	.05
80	Larry McWilliams	.05
81	Fernando Valenzuela	.05
82	Nolan Ryan	.75
83	Jack Morris	.05
84	Floyd Bannister	.05
85	Dave Stieb	.05
86	Dave Righetti	.05
87	Rick Sutcliffe	.05
88	Tim Raines	.05
89	Alan Wiggins	.05
90	Steve Sax	.05
91	Mookie Wilson	.05
92	Rickey Henderson	.25
93	Rudy Law	.05
94	Willie Wilson	.05
95	Julio Cruz	.05
96	Johnny Bench	.30
97	Carl Yastrzemski	.25
98	Gaylord Perry	.15
99	Pete Rose	.45
100	Joe Morgan	.25
101	Steve Carlton	.25
102	Jim Palmer	.25
103	Rod Carew	.25
104	Darryl Strawberry	.20
105	Craig McMurtry	.05
106	Mel Hall	.05
107	Lee Tunnell	.05
108	Bill Dawley	.05
109	Ron Kittle	.05
110	Mike Boddicker	.05
111	Julio Franco	.05
112	Daryl Sconiers	.05
113	Neal Heaton	.05
114	John Shelby	.05
115	Rick Dempsey	.05
116	John Lowenstein	.05
117	Jim Dwyer	.05

118	Bo Diaz	.05
119	Pete Rose	.45
120	Joe Morgan	.25
121	Gary Matthews	.05
122	Garry Maddox	.05
123	Paul Owens	.05
124	Tom Lasorda	.05
125	Joe Altobelli	.05
126	Tony LaRussa	.05

1985 Fleer

The 1985 Fleer set consists of 660 cards, each measuring 2-1/2" x 3-1/2". Card fronts feature a color photo plus the player's team logo and the word "Fleer." The photos have a color-coded frame which corresponds to the player's team. A gray border surrounds the frame. Backs are similar in design to previous years, but have two shades of red and black ink on white stock. For the fourth consecutive year, Fleer included special cards and team checklists in the set. Also incorporated in a set for the first time were 10 "Major League Prospect" cards, each featuring two rookie hopefuls. The set was issued with team logo stickers.

		NM/M
Unopened Factory Set (660):		50.00
Complete Set (660):		40.00
Common Player:		.05
Wax Pack (15):		4.50
Wax Box (36):		150.00
Cello Pack (28):		6.00
Cello Box (24):		150.00
Rack Pack (45):		8.00
Vending Box (500):		35.00
1	Doug Bair	.05
2	Juan Berenguer	.05
3	Dave Bergman	.05
4	Tom Brookens	.05
5	Marty Castillo	.05
6	Darrell Evans	.05
7	Barbaro Garbey	.05
8	Kirk Gibson	.05
9	John Grubb	.05
10	Willie Hernandez	.05
11	Larry Herndon	.05
12	Howard Johnson	.05
13	Ruppert Jones	.05
14	Rusty Kuntz	.05
15	Chet Lemon	.05
16	Aurelio Lopez	.05
17	Sid Monge	.05
18	Jack Morris	.05
19	Lance Parrish	.05
20	Dan Petry	.05
21	Dave Rozema	.05
22	Bill Scherrer	.05
23	Alan Trammell	.05
24	Lou Whitaker	.05
25	Milt Wilcox	.05
26	Kurt Bevacqua	.05
27	Greg Booker RC	.05
28	Bobby Brown	.05
29	Luis DeLeon	.05
30	Dave Dravecky	.05
31	Tim Flannery	.05
32	Steve Garvey	.40
33	Goose Gossage	.10
34	Tony Gwynn	2.00
35	Greg Harris	.05
36	Andy Hawkins	.05
37	Terry Kennedy	.05
38	Craig Lefferts	.05
39	Tim Lollar	.05
40	Carmelo Martinez	.05
41	Kevin McReynolds	.05
42	Graig Nettles	.05
43	Luis Salazar	.05
44	Eric Show	.05
45	Garry Templeton	.05
46	Mark Thurmond	.05
47	Ed Whitson	.05
48	Alan Wiggins	.05
49	Rich Bordi	.05
50	Larry Bowa	.05
51	Warren Brusstar	.05
52	Ron Cey	.05
53	Henry Cotto RC	.05
54	Jody Davis	.05
55	Bob Dernier	.05

56	Leon Durham	.05
57	Dennis Eckersley	.75
58	George Frazier	.05
59	Richie Hebner	.05
60	Dave Lopes	.05
61	Gary Matthews	.05
62	Keith Moreland	.05
63	Rick Reuschel	.05
64	Dick Ruthven	.05
65	Ryne Sandberg	2.00
66	Scott Sanderson	.05
67	Lee Smith	.05
68	Tim Stoddard	.05
69	Rick Sutcliffe	.05
70	Steve Trout	.05
71	Gary Woods	.05
72	Wally Backman	.05
73	Bruce Berenyi	.05
74	Hubie Brooks	.05
75	Kelvin Chapman	.05
76	Ron Darling	.05
77	Sid Fernandez RC	.05
78	Mike Fitzgerald	.05
79	George Foster	.05
80	Brent Gaff	.05
81	Ron Gardenhire	.05
82	Dwight Gooden	.25
83	Tom Gorman	.05
84	Danny Heep	.05
85	Keith Hernandez	.05
86	Ray Knight	.05
87	Ed Lynch	.05
88	Jose Oquendo	.05
89	Jesse Orosco	.05
90	Rafael Santana RC	.05
91	Doug Sisk	.05
92	Rusty Staub	.05
93	Darryl Strawberry	.10
94	Walt Terrell	.05
95	Mookie Wilson	.05
96	Jim Acker	.05
97	Willie Aikens	.05
98	Doyle Alexander	.05
99	Jesse Barfield	.05
100	George Bell	.05
101	Jim Clancy	.05
102	Dave Collins	.05
103	Tony Fernandez	.05
104	Damaso Garcia	.05
105	Jim Gott	.05
106	Alfredo Griffin	.05
107	Garth Iorg	.05
108	Roy Lee Jackson	.05
109	Cliff Johnson	.05
110	Jimmy Key	.05
111	Dennis Lamp	.05
112	Rick Leach	.05
113	Luis Leal	.05
114	Buck Martinez	.05
115	Lloyd Moseby	.05
116	Rance Mulliniks	.05
117	Dave Stieb	.05
118	Willie Upshaw	.05
119	Ernie Whitt	.05
120	Mike Armstrong	.05
121	Don Baylor	.05
122	Marty Bystrom	.05
123	Rick Cerone	.05
124	Joe Cowley RC	.05
125	Brian Dayett RC	.05
126	Tim Foli	.05
127	Ray Fontenot	.05
128	Ken Griffey	.05
129	Ron Guidry	.10
130	Toby Harrah	.05
131	Jay Howell	.05
132	Steve Kemp	.05
133	Don Mattingly	2.50
134	Bobby Meacham	.05
135	John Montefusco	.05
136	Omar Moreno	.05
137	Dale Murray	.05
138	Phil Niekro	.05
139	Mike Pagliarulo RC	.20
140	Willie Randolph	.05
141	Dennis Rasmussen RC	.05
142	Dave Righetti	.05
143	Jose Rijo	.05
144	Andre Robertson	.05
145	Bob Shirley	.05
146	Dave Winfield	1.00
147	Butch Wynegar	.05
148	Gary Allenson	.05
149	Tony Armas	.05
150	Marty Barrett	.05
151	Wade Boggs	2.00
152	Dennis Boyd	.05
153	Bill Buckner	.05
154	Mark Clear	.05
155	Roger Clemens	25.00
156	Steve Crawford	.05
157	Mike Easler	.05
158	Dwight Evans	.05
159	Rich Gedman	.05
160	Jackie Gutierrez	.05
161	Bruce Hurst	.05
162	John Henry Johnson	.05
163	Rick Miller	.05
164	Reid Nichols	.05
165	Al Nipper RC	.05
166	Bob Ojeda	.05
167	Jerry Remy	.05
168	Jim Rice	.25
169	Bob Stanley	.05
170	Mike Boddicker	.05
171	Al Bumbry	.05
172	Todd Cruz	.05
173	Rich Dauer	.05

174	Storm Davis	.05
175	Rick Dempsey	.05
176	Jim Dwyer	.05
177	Mike Flanagan	.05
178	Dan Ford	.05
179	Wayne Gross	.05
180	John Lowenstein	.05
181	Dennis Martinez	.05
182	Tippy Martinez	.05
183	Scott McGregor	.05
184	Eddie Murray	1.00
185	Joe Nolan	.05
186	Floyd Rayford	.05
187	Cal Ripken, Jr.	4.00
188	Gary Roenicke	.05
189	Lenn Sakata	.05
190	John Shelby	.05
191	Ken Singleton	.05
192	Sammy Stewart	.05
193	Bill Swaggerty	.05
194	Tom Underwood	.05
195	Mike Young	.05
196	Steve Balboni	.05
197	Joe Beckwith	.05
198	Bud Black	.05
199	George Brett	2.50
200	Onix Concepcion	.05
201	Mark Gubicza RC	.50
202	Larry Gura	.05
203	Mark Huismann RC	.05
204	Dane Iorg	.05
205	Danny Jackson RC	.05
206	Charlie Leibrandt	.05
207	Hal McRae	.05
208	Darryl Motley	.05
209	Jorge Orta	.05
210	Greg Pryor	.05
211	Dan Quisenberry	.05
212	Bret Saberhagen	.25
213	Pat Sheridan	.05
214	Don Slaught	.05
215	U.L. Washington	.05
216	John Wathan	.05
217	Frank White	.05
218	Willie Wilson	.05
219	Neil Allen	.05
220	Joaquin Andujar	.05
221	Steve Braun	.05
222	Danny Cox RC	.05
223	Bob Forsch	.05
224	David Green	.05
225	George Hendrick	.05
226	Tom Herr	.05
227	Ricky Horton RC	.05
228	Art Howe	.05
229	Mike Jorgensen	.05
230	Kurt Kepshire	.05
231	Jeff Lahti	.05
232	Tito Landrum	.05
233	Dave LaPoint	.05
234	Willie McGee	.05
235	Tom Nieto RC	.05
236	Terry Pendleton RC	1.00
237	Darrell Porter	.05
238	Dave Rucker	.05
239	Lonnie Smith	.05
240	Ozzie Smith	2.00
241	Bruce Sutter	.75
242	Andy Van Slyke	.05
243	Dave Von Ohlen	.05
244	Larry Andersen	.05
245	Bill Campbell	.05
246	Steve Carlton	1.00
247	Tim Corcoran	.05
248	Ivan DeJesus	.05
249	John Denny	.05
250	Bo Diaz	.05
251	Greg Gross	.05
252	Kevin Gross	.05
253	Von Hayes	.05
254	Al Holland	.05
255	Charles Hudson	.05
256	Jerry Koosman	.05
257	Joe Lefebvre	.05
258	Sixto Lezcano	.05
259	Garry Maddox	.05
260	Len Matuszek	.05
261	Tug McGraw	.05
262	Al Oliver	.05
263	Shane Rawley	.05
264	Juan Samuel	.05
265	Mike Schmidt	2.50
266	Jeff Stone RC	.05
267	Ozzie Virgil	.05
268	Glenn Wilson	.05
269	John Wockenfuss	.05
270	Darrell Brown	.05
271	Tom Brunansky	.05
272	Randy Bush	.05
273	John Butcher	.05
274	Bobby Castillo	.05
275	Ron Davis	.05
276	Dave Engle	.05
277	Pete Filson	.05
278	Gary Gaetti	.05
279	Mickey Hatcher	.05
280	Ed Hodge	.05
281	Kent Hrbek	.05
282	Houston Jimenez	.05
283	Tim Laudner	.05
284	Rick Lysander	.05
285	Dave Meier	.05
286	Kirby Puckett	8.00
287	Pat Putnam	.05
288	Ken Schrom	.05
289	Mike Smithson	.05
290	Tim Teufel	.05
291	Frank Viola	.05

292	Ron Washington	.05
293	Don Aase	.05
294	Juan Beniquez	.05
295	Bob Boone	.05
296	Mike Brown	.05
297	Rod Carew	1.00
298	Doug Corbett	.05
299	Doug DeCinces	.05
300	Brian Downing	.05
301	Ken Forsch	.05
302	Bobby Grich	.05
303	Reggie Jackson	2.00
304	Tommy John	.10
305	Curt Kaufman	.05
306	Bruce Kison	.05
307	Fred Lynn	.05
308	Gary Pettis	.05
309	Ron Romanick RC	.05
310	Luis Sanchez	.05
311	Dick Schofield	.05
312	Daryl Sconiers	.05
313	Jim Slaton	.05
314	Derrel Thomas	.05
315	Rob Wilfong	.05
316	Mike Witt	.05
317	Geoff Zahn	.05
318	Len Barker	.05
319	Steve Bedrosian	.05
320	Bruce Benedict	.05
321	Rick Camp	.05
322	Chris Chambliss	.05
323	Jeff Dedmon RC	.05
324	Terry Forster	.05
325	Gene Garber	.05
326	Albert Hall RC	.05
327	Terry Harper	.05
328	Bob Horner	.05
329	Glenn Hubbard	.05
330	Randy Johnson	.05
331	Brad Komminsk	.05
332	Rick Mahler	.05
333	Craig McMurtry	.05
334	Donnie Moore	.05
335	Dale Murphy	.40
336	Ken Oberkfell	.05
337	Pascual Perez	.05
338	Gerald Perry	.05
339	Rafael Ramirez	.05
340	Jerry Royster	.05
341	Alex Trevino	.05
342	Claudell Washington	.05
343	Alan Ashby	.05
344	Mark Bailey RC	.05
345	Kevin Bass	.05
346	Enos Cabell	.05
347	Jose Cruz	.05
348	Bill Dawley	.05
349	Frank DiPino	.05
350	Bill Doran	.05
351	Phil Garner	.05
352	Bob Knepper	.05
353	Mike LaCoss	.05
354	Jerry Mumphrey	.05
355	Joe Niekro	.05
356	Terry Puhl	.05
357	Craig Reynolds	.05
358	Vern Ruhle	.05
359	Nolan Ryan	4.00
360	Joe Sambito	.05
361	Mike Scott	.05
362	Dave Smith	.05
363	Julio Solano RC	.05
364	Dickie Thon	.05
365	Denny Walling	.05
366	Dave Anderson	.05
367	Bob Bailor	.05
368	Greg Brock	.05
369	Carlos Diaz	.05
370	Pedro Guerrero	.05
371	Orel Hershiser RC	3.00
372	Rick Honeycutt	.05
373	Burt Hooton	.05
374	Ken Howell RC	.05
375	Ken Landreaux	.05
376	Candy Maldonado	.05
377	Mike Marshall	.05
378	Tom Niedenfuer	.05
379	Alejandro Pena	.05
380	Jerry Reuss	.05
381	R.J. Reynolds RC	.05
382	German Rivera	.05
383	Bill Russell	.05
384	Steve Sax	.05
385	Mike Scioscia	.05
386	Franklin Stubbs RC	.05
387	Fernando Valenzuela	.05
388	Bob Welch	.05
389	Terry Whitfield	.05
390	Steve Yeager	.05
391	Pat Zachry	.05
392	Fred Breining	.05
393	Gary Carter	1.00
394	Andre Dawson	.25
395	Miguel Dilone	.05
396	Dan Driessen	.05
397	Doug Flynn	.05
398	Terry Francona	.05
399	Bill Gullickson	.05
400	Bob James	.05
401	Charlie Lea	.05
402	Bryan Little	.05
403	Gary Lucas	.05
404	David Palmer	.05
405	Tim Raines	.25
406	Mike Ramsey	.05
407	Jeff Reardon	.05
408	Steve Rogers	.05
409	Dan Schatzeder	.05

No.	Player	Price
410	Bryn Smith	.05
411	Mike Stenhouse	.05
412	Tim Wallach	.05
413	Jim Wohlford	.05
414	Bill Almon	.05
415	Keith Atherton	.05
416	Bruce Bochte	.05
417	Tom Burgmeier	.05
418	Ray Burris	.05
419	Bill Caudill	.05
420	Chris Codiroli	.05
421	Tim Conroy	.05
422	Mike Davis	.05
423	Jim Essian	.05
424	Mike Heath	.05
425	Rickey Henderson	1.00
426	Donnie Hill	.05
427	Dave Kingman	.05
428	Bill Krueger	.05
429	Carney Lansford	.05
430	Steve McCatty	.05
431	Joe Morgan	1.00
432	Dwayne Murphy	.05
433	Tony Phillips	.05
434	Lary Sorensen	.05
435	Mike Warren	.05
436	Curt Young RC	.05
437	Luis Aponte	.05
438	Chris Bando	.05
439	Tony Bernazard	.05
440	Bert Blyleven	.10
441	Brett Butler	.05
442	Ernie Camacho	.05
443	Joe Carter	.25
444	Carmelo Castillo	.05
445	Jamie Easterly	.05
446	Steve Farr RC	.05
447	Mike Fischlin	.05
448	Julio Franco	.05
449	Mel Hall	.05
450	Mike Hargrove	.05
451	Neal Heaton	.05
452	Brook Jacoby	.05
453	Mike Jeffcoat RC	.05
454	Don Schulze RC	.05
455	Roy Smith	.05
456	Pat Tabler	.05
457	Andre Thornton	.05
458	George Vukovich	.05
459	Tom Waddell	.05
460	Jerry Willard	.05
461	Dale Berra	.05
462	John Candelaria	.05
463	Jose DeLeon	.05
464	Doug Frobel	.05
465	Cecilio Guante	.05
466	Brian Harper	.05
467	Lee Lacy	.05
468	Bill Madlock	.05
469	Lee Mazzilli	.05
470	Larry McWilliams	.05
471	Jim Morrison	.05
472	Tony Pena	.05
473	Johnny Ray	.05
474	Rick Rhoden	.05
475	Don Robinson	.05
476	Rod Scurry	.05
477	Kent Tekulve	.05
478	Jason Thompson	.05
479	John Tudor	.05
480	Lee Tunnell	.05
481	Marvell Wynne	.05
482	Salome Barojas	.05
483	Dave Beard	.05
484	Jim Beattie	.05
485	Barry Bonnell	.05
486	Phil Bradley RC	.05
487	Al Cowens	.05
488	Alvin Davis	.05
489	Dave Henderson	.05
490	Steve Henderson	.05
491	Bob Kearney	.05
492	Mark Langston	.15
493	Larry Milbourne	.05
494	Paul Mirabella	.05
495	Mike Moore	.05
496	Edwin Nunez RC	.05
497	Spike Owen	.05
498	Jack Perconte	.05
499	Ken Phelps	.05
500	Jim Presley RC	.05
501	Mike Stanton	.05
502	Bob Stoddard	.05
503	Gorman Thomas	.05
504	Ed Vande Berg	.05
505	Matt Young	.05
506	Juan Agosto	.05
507	Harold Baines	.05
508	Floyd Bannister	.05
509	Britt Burns	.05
510	Julio Cruz	.05
511	Richard Dotson	.05
512	Jerry Dybzinski	.05
513	Carlton Fisk	1.00
514	Scott Fletcher	.05
515	Jerry Hairston Sr.	.05
516	Marc Hill	.05
517	LaMarr Hoyt	.05
518	Ron Kittle	.05
519	Rudy Law	.05
520	Vance Law	.05
521	Greg Luzinski	.05
522	Gene Nelson	.05
523	Tom Paciorek	.05
524	Ron Reed	.05
525	Bert Roberge	.05
526	Tom Seaver	1.00
527	Roy Smalley	.05
528	Dan Spillner	.05
529	Mike Squires	.05
530	Greg Walker	.05
531	Cesar Cedeno	.05
532	Dave Concepcion	.05
533	Eric Davis RC	2.00
534	Nick Esasky	.05
535	Tom Foley	.05
536	John Franco	.05
537	Brad Gulden	.05
538	Tom Hume	.05
539	Wayne Krenchicki	.05
540	Andy McGaffigan	.05
541	Eddie Milner	.05
542	Ron Oester	.05
543	Bob Owchinko	.05
544	Dave Parker	.05
545	Frank Pastore	.05
546	Tony Perez	.75
547	Ted Power	.05
548	Joe Price	.05
549	Gary Redus	.05
550	Pete Rose	3.00
551	Jeff Russell RC	.05
552	Mario Soto	.05
553	Jay Tibbs RC	.05
554	Duane Walker	.05
555	Alan Bannister	.05
556	Buddy Bell	.05
557	Danny Darwin	.05
558	Charlie Hough	.05
559	Bobby Jones	.05
560	Odell Jones	.05
561	Jeff Kunkel RC	.05
562	Mike Mason RC	.05
563	Pete O'Brien	.05
564	Larry Parrish	.05
565	Mickey Rivers	.05
566	Billy Sample	.05
567	Dave Schmidt	.05
568	Donnie Scott	.05
569	Dave Stewart	.05
570	Frank Tanana	.05
571	Wayne Tolleson	.05
572	Gary Ward	.05
573	Curtis Wilkerson	.05
574	George Wright	.05
575	Ned Yost	.05
576	Mark Brouhard	.05
577	Mike Caldwell	.05
578	Bobby Clark	.05
579	Jaime Cocanower	.05
580	Cecil Cooper	.05
581	Rollie Fingers	.75
582	Jim Gantner	.05
583	Moose Haas	.05
584	Dion James	.05
585	Pete Ladd	.05
586	Rick Manning	.05
587	Bob McClure	.05
588	Paul Molitor	1.00
589	Charlie Moore	.05
590	Ben Oglivie	.05
591	Chuck Porter	.05
592	Randy Ready RC	.05
593	Ed Romero	.05
594	Bill Schroeder RC	.05
595	Ray Searage	.05
596	Ted Simmons	.05
597	Jim Sundberg	.05
598	Don Sutton	.75
599	Tom Tellmann	.05
600	Rick Waits	.05
601	Robin Yount	1.00
602	Dusty Baker	.05
603	Bob Brenly	.05
604	Jack Clark	.05
605	Chili Davis	.05
606	Mark Davis	.05
607	Dan Gladden RC	.25
608	Atlee Hammaker	.05
609	Mike Krukow	.05
610	Duane Kuiper	.05
611	Bob Lacey	.05
612	Bill Laskey	.05
613	Gary Lavelle	.05
614	Johnnie LeMaster	.05
615	Jeff Leonard	.05
616	Randy Lerch	.05
617	Greg Minton	.05
618	Steve Nicosia	.05
619	Gene Richards	.05
620	Jeff Robinson RC	.05
621	Scot Thompson	.05
622	Manny Trillo	.05
623	Brad Wellman	.05
624	Frank Williams RC	.05
625	Joel Youngblood	.05
626	Cal Ripken, Jr./IA	1.00
627	Mike Schmidt/IA	.50
628	Giving the Signs (Sparky Anderson)	.05
629	A.L. Pitcher's Nightmare (Rickey Henderson, Dave Winfield)	.50
630	N.L. Pitcher's Nightmare (Ryne Sandberg, Mike Schmidt)	1.00
631	N.L. All-Stars (Gary Carter, Steve Garvey, Ozzie Smith, Darryl Strawberry)	.25
632	All-Star Game Winning Battery (Gary Carter, Charlie Lea)	.10
633	N.L. Pennant Clinchers (Steve Garvey, Goose Gossage)	.10
634	N.L. Rookie Phenoms (Dwight Gooden, Juan Samuel)	.05
635	Toronto's Big Guns (Willie Upshaw)	.05
636	Toronto's Big Guns (Lloyd Moseby)	.05
637	Holland (Al Holland)	.05
638	Tunnell (Lee Tunnell)	.05
639	Reggie Jackson/IA	.50
640	Pete Rose/IA	.75
641	Father & Son (Cal Ripken, Jr., Cal Ripken, Sr.)	1.00
642	Cubs team	.10
643	1984's Two Perfect Games & One No-Hitter (Jack Morris, David Palmer, Mike Witt)	.05
644	Major League Prospect (Willie Lozado, Vic Mata)	.05
645	Major League Prospect (Kelly Gruber RC, Randy O'Neal RC)	.15
646	Major League Prospect (Jose Roman RC, Joel Skinner RC)	.05
647	Major League Prospect (Steve Kiefer RC, Danny Tartabull RC)	.50
648	Major League Prospect (Rob Deer RC, Alejandro Sanchez RC)	.25
649	Major League Prospect (Shawon Dunston RC, Bill Hatcher RC)	1.00
650	Major League Prospect (Mike Bielecki RC, Ron Robinson RC)	.10
651	Major League Prospect (Zane Smith RC, Paul Zuvella RC)	.10
652	Major League Prospect (Glenn Davis RC, Joe Hesketh RC)	.20
653	Major League Prospect (Steve Jeltz RC, John Russell RC)	.10
654	Checklist 1-95	.05
655	Checklist 96-195	.05
656	Checklist 196-292	.05
657	Checklist 293-391	.05
658	Checklist 392-481	.05
659	Checklist 482-575	.05
660	Checklist 576-660	.05

Fleer Update

For the second straight year, Fleer issued a 132-card update set. Cards portray traded players on their new teams and also include rookies not depicted in the regular issue. The cards are identical in design to the 1985 Fleer set but are numbered U-1 through U-132. The set was issued with team logo stickers in a specially designed box and was available only through hobby dealers.

		NM/M
Complete Set (132):		5.00
Common Player:		.10
1	Don Aase	.10
2	Bill Almon	.10
3	Dusty Baker	.10
4	Dale Berra	.10
5	Karl Best RC	.10
6	Tim Birtsas RC	.10
7	Vida Blue	.10
8	Rich Bordi	.10
9	Daryl Boston RC	.10
10	Hubie Brooks	.10
11	Chris Brown RC	.10
12	Tom Browning RC	.10
13	Al Bumbry	.10
14	Tim Burke RC	.10
15	Ray Burris	.10
16	Jeff Burroughs	.10
17	Ivan Calderon RC	.10
18	Jeff Calhoun	.10
19	Bill Campbell	.10
20	Don Carman RC	.10
21	Gary Carter	.50
22	Bobby Castillo	.10
23	Bill Caudill	.10
24	Rick Cerone	.10
25	Jack Clark	.10
26	Pat Clements RC	.10
27	Stewart Cliburn RC	.10
28	Vince Coleman RC	.10
29	Dave Collins	.10
30	Fritz Connally	.10
31	Henry Cotto RC	.10
32	Danny Darwin	.10
33	Darren Daulton RC	1.00
34	Jerry Davis	.10
35	Brian Dayett	.10
36	Ken Dixon RC	.10
37	Tommy Dunbar	.10
38	Mariano Duncan RC	.10
39	Bob Fallon	.10
40	Brian Fisher RC	.10
41	Mike Fitzgerald	.10
42	Ray Fontenot	.10
43	Greg Gagne RC	.10
44	Oscar Gamble	.10
45	Jim Gott	.10
46	David Green	.10
47	Alfredo Griffin	.10
48	Ozzie Guillen RC	2.00
49	Toby Harrah	.10
50	Ron Hassey	.10
51	Rickey Henderson	3.00
52	Steve Henderson	.10
53	George Hendrick	.10
54	Teddy Higuera RC	.10
55	Al Holland	.10
56	Burt Hooton	.10
57	Jay Howell	.10
58	LaMarr Hoyt	.10
59	Tim Hulett RC	.10
60	Bob James	.10
61	Cliff Johnson	.10
62	Howard Johnson	.10
63	Ruppert Jones	.10
64	Steve Kemp	.10
65	Bruce Kison	.10
66	Mike LaCoss	.10
67	Lee Lacy	.10
68	Dave LaPoint	.10
69	Gary Lavelle	.10
70	Vance Law	.10
71	Manny Lee RC	.10
72	Sixto Lezcano	.10
73	Tim Lollar	.10
74	Urbano Lugo RC	.10
75	Fred Lynn	.10
76	Steve Lyons RC	.10
77	Mickey Mahler	.10
78	Ron Mathis RC	.10
79	Len Matuszek	.10
80	Oddibe McDowell RC	.10
81	Roger McDowell RC	.10
82	Donnie Moore	.10
83	Ron Musselman	.10
84	Al Oliver	.10
85	Joe Orsulak RC	.10
86	Dan Pasqua RC	.10
87	Chris Pittaro RC	.10
88	Rick Reuschel	.10
89	Earnie Riles RC	.10
90	Jerry Royster	.10
91	Dave Rozema	.10
92	Dave Rucker	.10
93	Vern Ruhle	.10
94	Mark Salas RC	.10
95	Luis Salazar	.10
96	Joe Sambito	.10
97	Billy Sample	.10
98	Alex Sanchez	.10
99	Calvin Schiraldi RC	.10
100	Rick Schu RC	.10
101	Larry Sheets RC	.10
102	Ron Shepherd	.10
103	Nelson Simmons RC	.10
104	Don Slaught	.10
105	Roy Smalley	.10
106	Lonnie Smith	.10
107	Nate Snell RC	.10
108	Lary Sorensen	.10
109	Chris Speier	.10
110	Mike Stenhouse	.10
111	Tim Stoddard	.10
112	John Stuper	.10
113	Jim Sundberg	.10
114	Bruce Sutter	.10
115	Don Sutton	.50
116	Bruce Tanner RC	.10
117	Kent Tekulve	.10
118	Walt Terrell	.10
119	Mickey Tettleton RC	1.00
120	Rich Thompson	.10
121	Louis Thornton RC	.10
122	Alex Trevino	.10
123	John Tudor	.10
124	Jose Uribe RC	.10
125	Dave Valle RC	.10
126	Dave Von Ohlen	.10
127	Curt Wardle	.10
128	U.L. Washington	.10
129	Ed Whitson	.10
130	Herm Winningham RC	.10
131	Rich Yett RC	.10
132	Checklist	.10

1985 Fleer Limited Edition

The 1985 Fleer Limited Edition boxed set was distributed through several chains of retail stores. The cards, which are the standard 2-1/2" x 3-1/2", have full-color photos inside a red and yellow frame. The backs are set in black type against two different shades of yellow and contain the

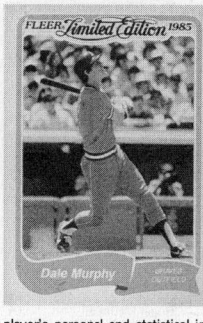

player's personal and statistical information. The set was issued in a specially designed box which carried the complete checklist for the set on the back. Six team logo stickers were also included with the set.

		NM/M
Complete Set (44):		4.00
Common Player:		.10
1	Buddy Bell	.10
2	Bert Blyleven	.15
3	Wade Boggs	.60
4	George Brett	.75
5	Rod Carew	.50
6	Steve Carlton	.50
7	Alvin Davis	.10
8	Andre Dawson	.25
9	Steve Garvey	.15
10	Goose Gossage	.15
11	Tony Gwynn	.60
12	Keith Hernandez	.10
13	Kent Hrbek	.10
14	Reggie Jackson	.60
15	Dave Kingman	.10
16	Ron Kittle	.10
17	Mark Langston	.10
18	Jeff Leonard	.10
19	Bill Madlock	.10
20	Don Mattingly	.75
21	Jack Morris	.10
22	Dale Murphy	.15
23	Eddie Murray	.50
24	Tony Pena	.10
25	Dan Quisenberry	.10
26	Tim Raines	.10
27	Jim Rice	.25
28	Cal Ripken, Jr.	1.00
29	Pete Rose	.85
30	Nolan Ryan	1.00
31	Ryne Sandberg	.60
32	Steve Sax	.10
33	Mike Schmidt	.75
34	Tom Seaver	.50
35	Ozzie Smith	.60
36	Mario Soto	.10
37	Dave Stieb	.10
38	Darryl Strawberry	.50
39	Rick Sutcliffe	.10
40	Alan Trammell	.10
41	Willie Upshaw	.10
42	Fernando Valenzuela	.10
43	Dave Winfield	.50
44	Robin Yount	.50

1985 Fleer Star Stickers

The 1985 Fleer sticker set consists of 126 player stickers, each measuring 1-15/16" x 2-1/2". Numbered on the back, the stickers were designed to be put in a special album. Distributed in packs of six, the 1985 stickers are the scarcest of all Fleer baseball sticker issues.

		NM/M
Complete Set (126):		12.50
Common Player:		.05
Sticker Album:		1.25
Wax Pack (6):		.25
Wax Box (100):		16.00
1	Pete Rose	1.00
2	Pete Rose	1.00
3	Pete Rose	1.00
4	Don Mattingly	1.50
5	Dave Winfield	.40
6	Wade Boggs	.50
7	Buddy Bell	.05
8	Tony Gwynn	.40
9	Lee Lacy	.05
10	Chili Davis	.05
11	Ryne Sandberg	.50
12	Tony Armas	.05
13	Jim Rice	.15
14	Dave Kingman	.05
15	Alvin Davis	.05
16	Gary Carter	.25
17	Mike Schmidt	1.00
18	Dale Murphy	.20
19	Ron Cey	.05
20	Eddie Murray	.40
21	Harold Baines	.05
22	Kirk Gibson	.05
23	Jim Rice	.15
24	Gary Matthews	.05
25	Keith Hernandez	.05
26	Gary Carter	.25
27	George Hendrick	.05
28	Tony Armas	.05
29	Dave Kingman	.05
30	Dwayne Murphy	.05
31	Lance Parrish	.05
32	Andre Thornton	.05
33	Dale Murphy	.20
34	Mike Schmidt	1.00
35	Gary Carter	.25
36	Darryl Strawberry	.05
37	Don Mattingly	1.50
38	Larry Parrish	.05
39	George Bell	.05
40	Dwight Evans	.05
41	Cal Ripken, Jr.	2.00
42	Tim Raines	.05
43	Johnny Ray	.05
44	Juan Samuel	.05
45	Ryne Sandberg	.50
46	Mike Easler	.05
47	Andre Thornton	.05
48	Dave Kingman	.05
49	Don Baylor	.05
50	Rusty Staub	.05
51	Steve Braun	.05
52	Kevin Bass	.05
53	Greg Gross	.05
54	Rickey Henderson	.40
55	Dave Collins	.05
56	Brett Butler	.05
57	Gary Pettis	.05
58	Tim Raines	.05
59	Juan Samuel	.05
60	Alan Wiggins	.05
61	Lonnie Smith	.05
62	Eddie Murray	.05
63	Eddie Murray	.05
64	Eddie Murray	.05
65	Eddie Murray	.05
66	Eddie Murray	.05
67	Eddie Murray	.05
68	Tom Seaver	.05
69	Tom Seaver	.05
70	Tom Seaver	.05
71	Tom Seaver	.05
72	Tom Seaver	.05
73	Tom Seaver	.05
74	Mike Schmidt	.25
75	Mike Schmidt	.25
76	Mike Schmidt	.25
77	Mike Schmidt	.25
78	Mike Schmidt	.25
79	Mike Schmidt	.25
80	Mike Boddicker	.05
81	Bert Blyleven	.05
82	Jack Morris	.05
83	Dan Petry	.05
84	Frank Viola	.05
85	Joaquin Andujar	.05
86	Mario Soto	.05
87	Dwight Gooden	.05
88	Joe Niekro	.05
89	Rick Sutcliffe	.05
90	Mike Boddicker	.05
91	Dave Stieb	.05
92	Bert Blyleven	.05
93	Phil Niekro	.25
94	Alejandro Pena	.05
95	Dwight Gooden	.05
96	Orel Hershiser	.15
97	Rick Rhoden	.05
98	John Candelaria	.05
99	Dan Quisenberry	.05
100	Bill Caudill	.05
101	Willie Hernandez	.05
102	Dave Righetti	.05
103	Ron Davis	.05
104	Bruce Sutter	.20
105	Lee Smith	.05
106	Jesse Orosco	.05
107	Al Holland	.05
108	Goose Gossage	.05
109	Mark Langston	.05
110	Dave Stieb	.05
111	Mike Witt	.05
112	Bert Blyleven	.05
113	Dwight Gooden	.05
114	Fernando Valenzuela	.05
115	Nolan Ryan	2.00
116	Mario Soto	.05
117	Ron Darling	.05
118	Dan Gladden	.05
119	Jeff Stone	.05
120	John Franco	.05
121	Barbaro Garbey	.05
122	Kirby Puckett	1.50
123	Roger Clemens	7.50
124	Bret Saberhagen	.05
125	Sparky Anderson	.05
126	Dick Williams	.05

1986 Fleer

The 1986 Fleer set contains 660 color cards measuring 2-1/2" x 3-1/2". The card fronts feature a player photo enclosed by a dark blue border. The card backs are minus the black-and-white photo that was included in past Fleer efforts. Player biographical and statistical information appear in black and yellow on white stock. As in 1985, Fleer devoted 10 cards, entitled "Major League Prospects," to 20 promising rookie players. The 1986 set, as in the previous four years was issued with team logo stickers.

	NM/M
Unopened Fact. Set (660):	30.00
Complete Set (660):	25.00
Common Player:	.05
Wax Pack (15):	1.50
Wax Box (36):	45.00
Cello Pack (28):	2.00
Cello Box (24):	40.00
Rack Pack (45):	4.00
Rack Box (24):	65.00

No.	Player	Price
1	Steve Balboni	.05
2	Joe Beckwith	.05
3	Buddy Biancalana	.05
4	Bud Black	.05
5	George Brett	2.00
6	Onix Concepcion	.05
7	Steve Farr	.05
8	Mark Gubicza	.05
9	Dane Iorg	.05
10	Danny Jackson	.05
11	Lynn Jones	.05
12	Mike Jones	.05
13	Charlie Leibrandt	.05
14	Hal McRae	.05
15	Omar Moreno	.05
16	Darryl Motley	.05
17	Jorge Orta	.05
18	Dan Quisenberry	.05
19	Bret Saberhagen	.05
20	Pat Sheridan	.05
21	Lonnie Smith	.05
22	Jim Sundberg	.05
23	John Wathan	.05
24	Frank White	.05
25	Willie Wilson	.05
26	Joaquin Andujar	.05
27	Steve Braun	.05
28	Bill Campbell	.05
29	Cesar Cedeno	.05
30	Jack Clark	.05
31	Vince Coleman	.05
32	Danny Cox	.05
33	Ken Dayley	.05
34	Ivan DeJesus	.05
35	Bob Forsch	.05
36	Brian Harper	.05
37	Tom Herr	.05
38	Ricky Horton	.05
39	Kurt Kepshire	.05
40	Jeff Lahti	.05
41	Tito Landrum	.05
42	Willie McGee	.05
43	Tom Nieto	.05
44	Terry Pendleton	.05
45	Darrell Porter	.05
46	Ozzie Smith	1.50
47	John Tudor	.05
48	Andy Van Slyke	.05
49	Todd Worrell RC	.25
50	Jim Acker	.05
51	Doyle Alexander	.05
52	Jesse Barfield	.05
53	George Bell	.05
54	Jeff Burroughs	.05
55	Bill Caudill	.05
56	Jim Clancy	.05
57	Tony Fernandez	.05
58	Tom Filer	.05
59	Damaso Garcia	.05
60	Tom Henke RC	.05
61	Garth Iorg	.05
62	Cliff Johnson	.05
63	Jimmy Key	.05
64	Dennis Lamp	.05
65	Gary Lavelle	.05
66	Buck Martinez	.05
67	Lloyd Moseby	.05
68	Rance Mulliniks	.05
69	Al Oliver	.05
70	Dave Stieb	.05
71	Louis Thornton	.05
72	Willie Upshaw	.05
73	Ernie Whitt	.05
74	Rick Aguilera RC	.75
75	Wally Backman	.05
76	Gary Carter	1.00
77	Ron Darling	.05
78	Len Dykstra RC	2.00
79	Sid Fernandez	.05
80	George Foster	.05
81	Dwight Gooden	.05
82	Tom Gorman	.05
83	Danny Heep	.05
84	Keith Hernandez	.05
85	Howard Johnson	.05
86	Ray Knight	.05
87	Terry Leach	.05
88	Ed Lynch	.05
89	Roger McDowell	.05
90	Jesse Orosco	.05
91	Tom Paciorek	.05
92	Ronn Reynolds	.05
93	Rafael Santana	.05
94	Doug Sisk	.05
95	Rusty Staub	.05
96	Darryl Strawberry	.05
97	Mookie Wilson	.05
98	Neil Allen	.05
99	Don Baylor	.05
100	Dale Berra	.05
101	Rich Bordi	.05
102	Marty Bystrom	.05
103	Joe Cowley	.05
104	Brian Fisher RC	.05
105	Ken Griffey	.05
106	Ron Guidry	.10
107	Ron Hassey	.05
108	Rickey Henderson	1.00
109	Don Mattingly	2.00
110	Bobby Meacham	.05
111	John Montefusco	.05
112	Phil Niekro	.75
113	Mike Pagliarulo	.05
114	Dan Pasqua	.05
115	Willie Randolph	.05
116	Dave Righetti	.05
117	Andre Robertson	.05
118	Billy Sample	.05
119	Bob Shirley	.05
120	Ed Whitson	.05
121	Dave Winfield	1.00
122	Butch Wynegar	.05
123	Dave Anderson	.05
124	Bob Bailor	.05
125	Greg Brock	.05
126	Enos Cabell	.05
127	Bobby Castillo	.05
128	Carlos Diaz	.05
129	Mariano Duncan	.05
130	Pedro Guerrero	.05
131	Orel Hershiser	.05
132	Rick Honeycutt	.05
133	Ken Howell	.05
134	Ken Landreaux	.05
135	Bill Madlock	.05
136	Candy Maldonado	.05
137	Mike Marshall	.05
138	Len Matuszek	.05
139	Tom Niedenfuer	.05
140	Alejandro Pena	.05
141	Jerry Reuss	.05
142	Bill Russell	.05
143	Steve Sax	.05
144	Mike Scioscia	.05
145	Fernando Valenzuela	.05
146	Bob Welch	.05
147	Terry Whitfield	.05
148	Juan Beniquez	.05
149	Bob Boone	.05
150	John Candelaria	.05
151	Rod Carew	1.00
152	Stewart Cliburn RC	.05
153	Doug DeCinces	.05
154	Brian Downing	.05
155	Ken Forsch	.05
156	Craig Gerber	.05
157	Bobby Grich	.05
158	George Hendrick	.05
159	Al Holland	.05
160	Reggie Jackson	1.50
161	Ruppert Jones	.05
162	Urbano Lugo RC	.05
163	Kirk McCaskill RC	.25
164	Donnie Moore	.05
165	Gary Pettis	.05
166	Ron Romanick	.05
167	Dick Schofield	.05
168	Daryl Sconiers	.05
169	Jim Slaton	.05
170	Don Sutton	.75
171	Mike Witt	.05
172	Buddy Bell	.05
173	Tom Browning	.05
174	Dave Concepcion	.05
175	Eric Davis	.05
176	Bo Diaz	.05
177	Nick Esasky	.05
178	John Franco	.05
179	Tom Hume	.05
180	Wayne Krenchicki	.05
181	Andy McGaffigan	.05
182	Eddie Milner	.05
183	Ron Oester	.05
184	Dave Parker	.05
185	Frank Pastore	.05
186	Tony Perez	.75
187	Ted Power	.05
188	Joe Price	.05
189	Gary Redus	.05
190	Ron Robinson	.05
191	Pete Rose	2.50
192	Mario Soto	.05
193	John Stuper	.05
194	Jay Tibbs	.05
195	Dave Van Gorder	.05
196	Max Venable	.05
197	Juan Agosto	.05
198	Harold Baines	.05
199	Floyd Bannister	.05
200	Britt Burns	.05
201	Julio Cruz	.05
202	Joel Davis RC	.05
203	Richard Dotson	.05
204	Carlton Fisk	1.00
205	Scott Fletcher	.05
206	Ozzie Guillen	.05
207	Jerry Hairston Sr.	.05
208	Tim Hulett	.05
209	Bob James	.05
210	Ron Kittle	.05
211	Rudy Law	.05
212	Bryan Little	.05
213	Gene Nelson	.05
214	Reid Nichols	.05
215	Luis Salazar	.05
216	Tom Seaver	1.00
217	Dan Spillner	.05
218	Bruce Tanner	.05
219	Greg Walker	.05
220	Dave Wehrmeister	.05
221	Juan Berenguer	.05
222	Dave Bergman	.05
223	Tom Brookens	.05
224	Darrell Evans	.05
225	Barbaro Garbey	.05
226	Kirk Gibson	.05
227	John Grubb	.05
228	Willie Hernandez	.05
229	Larry Herndon	.05
230	Chet Lemon	.05
231	Aurelio Lopez	.05
232	Jack Morris	.05
233	Randy O'Neal	.05
234	Lance Parrish	.05
235	Dan Petry	.05
236	Alex Sanchez	.05
237	Bill Scherrer	.05
238	Nelson Simmons	.05
239	Frank Tanana	.05
240	Walt Terrell	.05
241	Alan Trammell	.05
242	Lou Whitaker	.05
243	Milt Wilcox	.05
244	Hubie Brooks	.05
245	Tim Burke RC	.05
246	Andre Dawson	.35
247	Mike Fitzgerald	.05
248	Terry Francona	.05
249	Bill Gullickson	.05
250	Joe Hesketh	.05
251	Bill Laskey	.05
252	Vance Law	.05
253	Charlie Lea	.05
254	Gary Lucas	.05
255	David Palmer	.05
256	Tim Raines	.05
257	Jeff Reardon	.05
258	Bert Roberge	.05
259	Dan Schatzeder	.05
260	Bryn Smith	.05
261	Randy St. Claire RC	.05
262	Scot Thompson	.05
263	Tim Wallach	.05
264	U.L. Washington	.05
265	Mitch Webster RC	.05
266	Herm Winningham RC	.05
267	Floyd Youmans RC	.05
268	Don Aase	.05
269	Mike Boddicker	.05
270	Rich Dauer	.05
271	Storm Davis	.05
272	Rick Dempsey	.05
273	Ken Dixon	.05
274	Jim Dwyer	.05
275	Mike Flanagan	.05
276	Wayne Gross	.05
277	Lee Lacy	.05
278	Fred Lynn	.05
279	Tippy Martinez	.05
280	Dennis Martinez	.05
281	Scott McGregor	.05
282	Eddie Murray	1.00
283	Floyd Rayford	.05
284	Cal Ripken, Jr.	3.00
285	Gary Roenicke	.05
286	Larry Sheets	.05
287	John Shelby	.05
288	Nate Snell	.05
289	Sammy Stewart	.05
290	Alan Wiggins	.05
291	Mike Young	.05
292	Alan Ashby	.05
293	Mark Bailey	.05
294	Kevin Bass	.05
295	Jeff Calhoun	.05
296	Jose Cruz	.05
297	Glenn Davis	.05
298	Bill Dawley	.05
299	Frank DiPino	.05
300	Bill Doran	.05
301	Phil Garner	.05
302	Jeff Heathcock RC	.05
303	Charlie Kerfeld RC	.05
304	Bob Knepper	.05
305	Ron Mathis	.05
306	Jerry Mumphrey	.05
307	Jim Pankovits	.05
308	Terry Puhl	.05
309	Craig Reynolds	.05
310	Nolan Ryan	3.00
311	Mike Scott	.05
312	Dave Smith	.05
313	Dickie Thon	.05
314	Denny Walling	.05
315	Kurt Bevacqua	.05
316	Al Bumbry	.05
317	Jerry Davis	.05
318	Luis DeLeon	.05
319	Dave Dravecky	.05
320	Tim Flannery	.05
321	Steve Garvey	.30
322	Goose Gossage	.05
323	Tony Gwynn	1.50
324	Andy Hawkins	.05
325	LaMarr Hoyt	.05
326	Roy Lee Jackson	.05
327	Terry Kennedy	.05
328	Craig Lefferts	.05
329	Carmelo Martinez	.05
330	Lance McCullers RC	.05
331	Kevin McReynolds	.05
332	Graig Nettles	.05
333	Jerry Royster	.05
334	Eric Show	.05
335	Tim Stoddard	.05
336	Garry Templeton	.05
337	Mark Thurmond	.05
338	Ed Wojna	.05
339	Tony Armas	.05
340	Marty Barrett	.05
341	Wade Boggs	1.50
342	Dennis Boyd	.05
343	Bill Buckner	.05
344	Mark Clear	.05
345	Roger Clemens	2.00
346	Steve Crawford	.05
347	Mike Easler	.05
348	Dwight Evans	.05
349	Rich Gedman	.05
350	Jackie Gutierrez	.05
351	Glenn Hoffman	.05
352	Bruce Hurst	.05
353	Bruce Kison	.05
354	Tim Lollar	.05
355	Steve Lyons	.05
356	Al Nipper	.05
357	Bob Ojeda	.05
358	Jim Rice	.30
359	Bob Stanley	.05
360	Mike Trujillo	.05
361	Thad Bosley	.05
362	Warren Brusstar	.05
363	Ron Cey	.05
364	Jody Davis	.05
365	Bob Dernier	.05
366	Shawon Dunston	.05
367	Leon Durham	.05
368	Dennis Eckersley	.75
369	Ray Fontenot	.05
370	George Frazier	.05
371	Bill Hatcher	.05
372	Dave Lopes	.05
373	Gary Matthews	.05
374	Ron Meredith	.05
375	Keith Moreland	.05
376	Reggie Patterson	.05
377	Dick Ruthven	.05
378	Ryne Sandberg	1.50
379	Scott Sanderson	.05
380	Lee Smith	.05
381	Lary Sorensen	.05
382	Chris Speier	.05
383	Rick Sutcliffe	.05
384	Steve Trout	.05
385	Gary Woods	.05
386	Bert Blyleven	.10
387	Tom Brunansky	.05
388	Randy Bush	.05
389	John Butcher	.05
390	Ron Davis	.05
391	Dave Engle	.05
392	Frank Eufemia	.05
393	Pete Filson	.05
394	Gary Gaetti	.05
395	Greg Gagne	.05
396	Mickey Hatcher	.05
397	Kent Hrbek	.05
398	Tim Laudner	.05
399	Rick Lysander	.05
400	Dave Meier	.05
401	Kirby Puckett	1.50
402	Mark Salas	.05
403	Ken Schrom	.05
404	Roy Smalley	.05
405	Mike Smithson	.05
406	Mike Stenhouse	.05
407	Tim Teufel	.05
408	Frank Viola	.05
409	Ron Washington	.05
410	Keith Atherton	.05
411	Dusty Baker	.05
412	Tim Birtsas RC	.05
413	Bruce Bochte	.05
414	Chris Codiroli	.05
415	Dave Collins	.05
416	Mike Davis	.05
417	Alfredo Griffin	.05
418	Mike Heath	.05
419	Steve Henderson	.05
420	Donnie Hill	.05
421	Jay Howell	.05
422	Tommy John	.10
423	Dave Kingman	.05
424	Bill Krueger	.05
425	Rick Langford	.05
426	Carney Lansford	.05
427	Steve McCatty	.05
428	Dwayne Murphy	.05
429	Steve Ontiveros RC	.05
430	Tony Phillips	.05
431	Jose Rijo	.05
432	Mickey Tettleton	.05
433	Luis Aguayo	.05
434	Larry Andersen	.05
435	Steve Carlton	1.00
436	Don Carman RC	.05
437	Tim Corcoran	.05
438	Darren Daulton	.05
439	John Denny	.05
440	Tom Foley	.05
441	Greg Gross	.05
442	Kevin Gross	.05
443	Von Hayes	.05
444	Charles Hudson	.05
445	Garry Maddox	.05
446	Shane Rawley	.05
447	Dave Rucker	.05
448	John Russell	.05
449	Juan Samuel	.05
450	Mike Schmidt	2.00
451	Rick Schu	.05
452	Dave Shipanoff	.05
453	Dave Stewart	.05
454	Jeff Stone	.05
455	Kent Tekulve	.05
456	Ozzie Virgil	.05
457	Glenn Wilson	.05
458	Jim Beattie	.05
459	Karl Best	.05
460	Barry Bonnell	.05
461	Phil Bradley	.05
462	Ivan Calderon RC	.05
463	Al Cowens	.05
464	Alvin Davis	.05
465	Dave Henderson	.05
466	Bob Kearney	.05
467	Mark Langston	.05
468	Bob Long	.05
469	Mike Moore	.05
470	Edwin Nunez	.05
471	Spike Owen	.05
472	Jack Perconte	.05
473	Jim Presley	.05
474	Donnie Scott	.05
475	Bill Swift RC	.05
476	Danny Tartabull	.05
477	Gorman Thomas	.05
478	Roy Thomas	.05
479	Ed Vande Berg	.05
480	Frank Wills	.05
481	Matt Young	.05
482	Ray Burris	.05
483	Jaime Cocanower	.05
484	Cecil Cooper	.05
485	Danny Darwin	.05
486	Rollie Fingers	.75
487	Jim Gantner	.05
488	Bob Gibson	.05
489	Moose Haas	.05
490	Teddy Higuera RC	.05
491	Paul Householder	.05
492	Pete Ladd	.05
493	Rick Manning	.05
494	Bob McClure	.05
495	Paul Molitor	1.00
496	Charlie Moore	.05
497	Ben Oglivie	.05
498	Randy Ready	.05
499	Earnie Riles RC	.05
500	Ed Romero	.05
501	Bill Schroeder	.05
502	Ray Searage	.05
503	Ted Simmons	.05
504	Pete Vuckovich	.05
505	Rick Waits	.05
506	Robin Yount	1.00
507	Len Barker	.05
508	Steve Bedrosian	.05
509	Bruce Benedict	.05
510	Rick Camp	.05
511	Rick Cerone	.05
512	Chris Chambliss	.05
513	Jeff Dedmon	.05
514	Terry Forster	.05
515	Gene Garber	.05
516	Terry Harper	.05
517	Bob Horner	.05
518	Glenn Hubbard	.05
519	Joe Johnson RC	.05
520	Brad Komminsk	.05
521	Rick Mahler	.05
522	Dale Murphy	.30
523	Ken Oberkfell	.05
524	Pascual Perez	.05
525	Gerald Perry	.05
526	Rafael Ramirez	.05
527	Steve Shields RC	.05
528	Zane Smith	.05
529	Bruce Sutter	.75
530	Milt Thompson RC	.05
531	Claudell Washington	.05
532	Paul Zuvella	.05
533	Vida Blue	.05
534	Bob Brenly	.05
535	Chris Brown RC	.05
536	Chili Davis	.05
537	Mark Davis	.05
538	Rob Deer	.05
539	Dan Driessen	.05
540	Scott Garrelts	.05
541	Dan Gladden	.05
542	Jim Gott	.05
543	David Green	.05
544	Atlee Hammaker	.05
545	Mike Jeffcoat	.05
546	Mike Krukow	.05
547	Dave LaPoint	.05
548	Jeff Leonard	.05
549	Greg Minton	.05
550	Alex Trevino	.05
551	Manny Trillo	.05
552	Jose Uribe RC	.05
553	Brad Wellman	.05
554	Frank Williams	.05
555	Joel Youngblood	.05
556	Alan Bannister	.05
557	Glenn Brummer	.05
558	Steve Buechele RC	.05
559	Jose Guzman RC	.05
560	Toby Harrah	.05
561	Greg Harris	.05
562	Dwayne Henry RC	.05
563	Burt Hooton	.05
564	Charlie Hough	.05
565	Mike Mason	.05
566	Oddibe McDowell RC	.05
567	Dickie Noles	.05
568	Pete O'Brien	.05
569	Larry Parrish	.05
570	Dave Rozema	.05
571	Dave Schmidt	.05
572	Don Slaught	.05
573	Wayne Tolleson	.05
574	Duane Walker	.05
575	Gary Ward	.05
576	Chris Welsh	.05
577	Curtis Wilkerson	.05
578	George Wright	.05
579	Chris Bando	.05
580	Tony Bernazard	.05
581	Brett Butler	.05
582	Ernie Camacho	.05
583	Joe Carter	.05
584	Carmelo Castillo (Carmelo)	.05
585	Jamie Easterly	.05
586	Julio Franco	.05
587	Mel Hall	.05
588	Mike Hargrove	.05
589	Neal Heaton	.05
590	Brook Jacoby	.05
591	Otis Nixon RC	.25
592	Jerry Reed	.05
593	Vern Ruhle	.05
594	Pat Tabler	.05
595	Rich Thompson	.05
596	Andre Thornton	.05
597	Dave Von Ohlen	.05
598	George Vukovich	.05
599	Tom Waddell	.05
600	Curt Wardle	.05
601	Jerry Willard	.05
602	Bill Almon	.05
603	Mike Bielecki	.05
604	Sid Bream	.05
605	Mike Brown	.05
606	Pat Clements RC	.05
607	Jose DeLeon	.05
608	Denny Gonzalez	.05
609	Cecilio Guante	.05
610	Steve Kemp	.05
611	Sam Khalifa	.05
612	Lee Mazzilli	.05
613	Larry McWilliams	.05
614	Jim Morrison	.05
615	Joe Orsulak RC	.25
616	Tony Pena	.05
617	Johnny Ray	.05
618	Rick Reuschel	.05
619	R.J. Reynolds	.05
620	Rick Rhoden	.05
621	Don Robinson	.05
622	Jason Thompson	.05
623	Lee Tunnell	.05
624	Jim Winn	.05
625	Marvell Wynne	.05
626	Dwight Gooden/IA	.05
627	Don Mattingly/IA	.50
628	Pete Rose (4,192 Hits)	1.00
629	Rod Carew (3,000 Hits)	.25
630	Phil Niekro, Tom Seaver (300 Wins)	.25
631	Ouch! (Don Baylor)	.05
632	Instant Offense (Tim Raines, Darryl Strawberry)	.05
633	Shortstops Supreme (Cal Ripken, Jr., Alan Trammell)	1.00
634	Boggs & "Hero" (Wade Boggs, George Brett)	1.00
635	Braves Dynamic Duo (Bob Horner, Dale Murphy)	.25
636	Cardinal Ignitors (Vince Coleman, Willie McGee)	.25
637	Terror on the Basepaths (Vince Coleman)	.05
638	Charlie Hustle & Dr. K (Dwight Gooden, Pete Rose)	.50
639	1984 and 1985 A.L. Batting Champs (Wade Boggs, Don Mattingly)	1.00
640	N.L. West Sluggers (Steve Garvey, Dale Murphy, Dave Parker)	.25

641 Staff Aces (Dwight Gooden, Fernando Valenzuela) .10
642 Blue Jay Stoppers (Jimmy Key, Dave Stieb) .05
643 A.L. All-Star Backstops (Carlton Fisk, Rich Gedman)
644 Major League Prospect (Benito Santiago RC, Gene Walter RC) 1.00
645 Major League Prospect (Colin Ward RC, Mike Woodard RC) .10
646 Major League Prospect (Kal Daniels RC, Paul O'Neill RC) 2.00
647 Major League Prospect (Andres Galarraga RC, Fred Toliver RC) 3.00
648 Major League Prospect (Curt Ford RC, Bob Kipper RC)
649 Major League Prospect (Jose Canseco RC, Eric Plunk RC) 5.00
650 Major League Prospect (Mark McLemore RC, Gus Polidor RC) .75
651 Major League Prospect (Mickey Brantley RC, Rob Woodward RC) .10
652 Major League Prospect (Mark Funderburk RC, Billy Joe Robidoux RC) .10
653 Major League Prospect (Cecil Fielder RC, Cory Snyder RC) 1.50
654 Checklist 1-97 .05
655 Checklist 98-196 .05
656 Checklist 197-291 .05
657 Checklist 292-385 .05
658 Checklist 386-482 .05
659 Checklist 483-578 .05
660 Checklist 579-660 .05

All-Stars

Fleer's choices for a major league All-Star team make up this 12-card set. The cards were randomly inserted in 35¢ wax packs and 59¢ cello packs. The card fronts have a color photo set against a bright red background for A.L. players or a bright blue background for N.L. players. Backs feature the player's career highlights on a red and blue background.

NM/M
Complete Set (12): 7.50
Common Player: .10
1 Don Mattingly 2.00
2 Tom Herr .10
3 George Brett 2.00
4 Gary Carter .75
5 Cal Ripken, Jr. 4.00
6 Dave Parker .10
7 Rickey Henderson .75
8 Pedro Guerrero .10
9 Dan Quisenberry .10
10 Dwight Gooden .10
11 Gorman Thomas .10
12 John Tudor .10

Future Hall Of Famers

The 1986 Future Hall of Famers set is comprised of six players Fleer felt would gain eventual entrance into the Baseball Hall of Fame. The cards are the standard 2-1/2" x 3-1/2" and were randomly inserted in three-pack rack packs. Card fronts feature a player photo set against a blue background with horizontal light blue stripes. Backs are printed in black on blue and feature career highlights in narrative form.

NM/M
Complete Set (6): 5.00
Common Player: .75
1 Pete Rose 2.00
2 Steve Carlton .75
3 Tom Seaver .75
4 Rod Carew .75
5 Nolan Ryan 3.00
6 Reggie Jackson 1.00

Box Panels

Picking up on a Donruss idea, Fleer issued eight cards in panels of four on the bottoms of the wax and cello pack boxes. The cards are numbered C-1 through C-8 and are 2-1/2" x 3-1/2", with a complete panel measuring 5" x 7-1/8". Included in the eight cards are six players and two team logo/checklist cards.

NM/M
Complete Panel Set (2): 4.00
Complete Singles Set (8): 4.00
Common Single Player: .20
Panel 2.50
1 Royals Logo/Checklist .05
2 George Brett 2.00
3 Ozzie Guillen .20
4 Dale Murphy .40
Panel 1.50
5 Cardinals Logo/Checklist .05
6 Tom Browning .20
7 Gary Carter 1.00
8 Carlton Fisk 1.00

Fleer Update

Issued near the end of the baseball season, the 1986 Fleer Update set consists of cards numbered U-1 through U-132. The 2-1/2" x 3-1/2" cards are identical in design to the regular 1986 Fleer set. The purpose of the set is to update player trades and include rookies not depicted in the regular issue. The set was issued with team logo stickers in a specially designed box and was available only through hobby dealers.

NM/M
Unopened Fact. Set (132): 40.00
Complete Set (132): 30.00
Common Player: .05
1 Mike Aldrete RC .05
2 Andy Allanson RC .05
3 Neil Allen .05
4 Joaquin Andujar .05
5 Paul Assenmacher RC .05
6 Scott Bailes RC .05
7 Jay Baller RC .05
8 Scott Bankhead RC .05
9 Bill Bathe RC .05
10 Don Baylor .05
11 Billy Beane RC .05
12 Steve Bedrosian .05
13 Juan Beniquez .05
14 Barry Bonds RC 25.00
15 Bobby Bonilla RC 1.00
16 Rich Bordi .05
17 Bill Campbell .05
18 Tom Candiotti .05
19 John Cangelosi RC .05
20 Jose Canseco 4.00
21 Chuck Cary RC .05
22 Juan Castillo RC .05
23 Rick Cerone .05
24 John Cerutti RC .05
25 Will Clark RC 1.00
26 Mark Clear .05
27 Darnell Coles RC .05
28 Dave Collins .05
29 Tim Conroy .05
30 Ed Correa RC .05
31 Joe Cowley .05
32 Bill Dawley .05
33 Rob Deer .05
34 John Denny .05
35 Jim DeShaies .05
36 Doug Drabek RC 1.00
37 Mike Easler .05
38 Mark Eichhorn RC .05
39 Dave Engle .05
40 Mike Fischlin .05
41 Scott Fletcher .05
42 Terry Forster .05
43 Terry Francona .05
44 Andres Galarraga .50
45 Lee Guetterman RC .05
46 Bill Gullickson .05
47 Jackie Gutierrez .05
48 Moose Haas .05
49 Billy Hatcher .05
50 Mike Heath .05
51 Guy Hoffman RC .05
52 Tom Hume .05
53 Pete Incaviglia RC .50
54 Dane Iorg .05
55 Chris James RC .05
56 Stan Javier RC .05
57 Tommy John .15
58 Tracy Jones RC .05
59 Wally Joyner RC 1.00
60 Wayne Krenchicki .05
61 John Kruk RC 1.00
62 Mike LaCoss .05
63 Pete Ladd .05
64 Dave LaPoint .05
65 Mike LaValliere RC .05
66 Rudy Law .05
67 Dennis Leonard .05
68 Steve Lombardozzi RC .05
69 Aurelio Lopez .05
70 Mickey Mahler .05
71 Candy Maldonado .05
72 Roger Mason RC .05
73 Greg Mathews RC .05
74 Andy McGaffigan .05
75 Joel McKeon RC .05
76 Kevin Mitchell RC .50
77 Bill Mooneyham RC .05
78 Omar Moreno .05
79 Jerry Mumphrey .05
80 Al Newman RC .05
81 Phil Niekro .50
82 Randy Niemann .05
83 Juan Nieves RC .05
84 Bob Ojeda .05
85 Rick Ownbey .05
86 Tom Paciorek .05
87 David Palmer .05
88 Jeff Parrett RC .05
89 Pat Perry RC .05
90 Dan Plesac RC .05
91 Darrell Porter .05
92 Luis Quinones RC .05
93 Rey Quinonez RC .05
94 Gary Redus .05
95 Jeff Reed RC .05
96 Bip Roberts RC .05
97 Billy Joe Robidoux .05
98 Gary Roenicke .05
99 Ron Roenicke .05
100 Angel Salazar .05
101 Joe Sambito .05
102 Billy Sample .05
103 Dave Schmidt .05
104 Ken Schrom .05
105 Ruben Sierra RC .75
106 Ted Simmons .05
107 Sammy Stewart .05
108 Kurt Stillwell RC .05
109 Dale Sveum RC .05
110 Tim Teufel .05
111 Bob Tewksbury RC .05
112 Andres Thomas RC .05
113 Jason Thompson .05
114 Milt Thompson .05
115 Rob Thompson RC .05
116 Jay Tibbs .05
117 Fred Toliver RC .05
118 Wayne Tolleson .05
119 Alex Trevino .05
120 Manny Trillo .05
121 Ed Vande Berg .05
122 Ozzie Virgil .05
123 Tony Walker RC .05
124 Gene Walter RC .05
125 Duane Ward RC .05
126 Jerry Willard .05
127 Mitch Williams RC .05
128 Reggie Williams RC .05
129 Bobby Witt RC .05
130 Marvell Wynne .05
131 Steve Yeager .05
132 Checklist .05

Baseball's Best

The 1986 Fleer Baseball's Best set was produced for the McCrory's retail chain and its affiliated stores. Subtitled "Sluggers vs. Pitchers," the set contains 22 each of the game's best hitters and pitchers. The 2-1/2" x 3-1/2" cards have color action photos on front. Backs are done in blue and red and carry players' personal and statistical data. The sets were issued in a specially designed box with six team logo stickers.

NM/M
Complete Set (44): 4.00
Common Player: .10
1 Bert Blyleven .25
2 Wade Boggs .75
3 George Brett 1.00
4 Tom Browning .10
5 Jose Canseco .60
6 Will Clark .15
7 Roger Clemens 1.00
8 Alvin Davis .10
9 Julio Franco .10
10 Kirk Gibson .10
11 Dwight Gooden .10
12 Goose Gossage .10
13 Pedro Guerrero .10
14 Ron Guidry .10
15 Tony Gwynn .75
16 Orel Hershiser .10
17 Kent Hrbek .10
18 Reggie Jackson .75
19 Wally Joyner .15
20 Charlie Leibrandt .10
21 Don Mattingly 1.00
22 Willie McGee .10
23 Jack Morris .10
24 Dale Murphy .25
25 Eddie Murray .50
26 Jeff Reardon .10
27 Rick Reuschel .10
28 Cal Ripken, Jr. 2.00
29 Pete Rose 1.50
30 Nolan Ryan 2.00
31 Bret Saberhagen .10
32 Ryne Sandberg .40
33 Mike Schmidt 1.00
34 Tom Seaver .50
35 Bryn Smith .10
36 Mario Soto .10
37 Dave Stieb .10
38 Darryl Strawberry .10
39 Rick Sutcliffe .10
40 John Tudor .10
41 Fernando Valenzuela .10
42 Bobby Witt .10
43 Mike Witt .10
44 Robin Yount .50

League Leaders

Fleer's 1986 "League Leaders" set features 44 of the game's top players and was issued through the Walgreen's drug store chain. Fronts contain a color photo and feature player name, team and postition in a blue band near the bottom of the card. The words "League Leaders" appear in a red band at the top of the card. The background for the card fronts is alternating blue and white stripes. The card backs are printed in blue, red and white and carry statistical information and team logo. Cards are the standard 2-1/2" x 3-1/2". The set was issued in a special cardboard box, along with six team logo stickers.

NM/M
Complete Set (44): 4.00
Common Player: .10
1 Wade Boggs .60
2 George Brett .75
3 Jose Canseco .60
4 Rod Carew .40
5 Gary Carter .40
6 Jack Clark .10
7 Vince Coleman .10
8 Jose Cruz .10
9 Alvin Davis .10
10 Mariano Duncan .10
11 Leon Durham .10
12 Carlton Fisk .40
13 Julio Franco .10
14 Scott Garrelts .10
15 Steve Garvey .25
16 Dwight Gooden .10
17 Ozzie Guillen .10
18 Willie Hernandez .10
19 Bob Horner .10
20 Kent Hrbek .10
21 Charlie Leibrandt .10
22 Don Mattingly .75
23 Oddibe McDowell .10
24 Willie McGee .10
25 Keith Moreland .10
26 Lloyd Moseby .10
27 Dale Murphy .25
28 Phil Niekro .35
29 Joe Orsulak .10
30 Dave Parker .10
31 Lance Parrish .10
32 Kirby Puckett .60
33 Tim Raines .10
34 Earnie Riles .10
35 Cal Ripken, Jr. 1.50
36 Pete Rose 1.00
37 Bret Saberhagen .10
38 Juan Samuel .10
39 Ryne Sandberg .40
40 Tom Seaver .40
41 Lee Smith .10
42 Ozzie Smith .60
43 Dave Stieb .10
44 Robin Yount .40

Limited Edition

Produced for the McCrory's store chain and its affiliates for the second year in a row, the Limited Edition set contains 44 cards. In standard 2-1/2" x 3-1/2" size, cards have color photos enclosed by green, red and yellow trim. Backs carry black print on two shades of red. The set was issued in a special cardboard box, along with six team logo stickers.

NM/M
Complete Set (44): 4.00
Common Player: .10
1 Doyle Alexander .10
2 Joaquin Andujar .10
3 Harold Baines .10
4 Wade Boggs .60
5 Phil Bradley .10
6 George Brett .75
7 Hubie Brooks .10
8 Chris Brown .10
9 Tom Brunansky .10
10 Gary Carter .50
11 Vince Coleman .10
12 Cecil Cooper .10
13 Jose Cruz .10
14 Mike Davis .10
15 Carlton Fisk .50
16 Julio Franco .10
17 Damaso Garcia .10
18 Rich Gedman .10
19 Kirk Gibson .10
20 Dwight Gooden .10
21 Pedro Guerrero .10
22 Tony Gwynn .60
23 Rickey Henderson .50
24 Orel Hershiser .10
25 LaMarr Hoyt .10
26 Reggie Jackson .60
27 Don Mattingly .75
28 Oddibe McDowell .10
29 Willie McGee .10
30 Paul Molitor .50
31 Dale Murphy .20
32 Eddie Murray .50
33 Dave Parker .10
34 Tony Pena .10
35 Jeff Reardon .10
36 Cal Ripken, Jr. 1.50
37 Pete Rose 1.00
38 Bret Saberhagen .10
39 Juan Samuel .10
40 Ryne Sandberg .60
41 Mike Schmidt .75
42 Lee Smith .10
43 Don Sutton .40
44 Lou Whitaker .10

Mini

Fleer's 1986 "Classic Miniatures" set contains 120 cards that measure 1-13/16" x 2-9/16". The design of the high-gloss cards is identical to the regular 1986 Fleer set but the player photos are entirely different. The set, which was issued in a specially designed box along with 18 team logo stickers, was available only through hobby dealers.

NM/M
Complete Set (120): 3.50
Common Player: .05
1 George Brett .65
2 Dan Quisenberry .05
3 Bret Saberhagen .05
4 Lonnie Smith .05
5 Willie Wilson .05
6 Jack Clark .05
7 Vince Coleman .05
8 Tom Herr .05
9 Willie McGee .05
10 Ozzie Smith .50
11 John Tudor .05
12 Jesse Barfield .05
13 George Bell .05
14 Tony Fernandez .05
15 Damaso Garcia .05
16 Dave Stieb .05
17 Gary Carter .40
18 Ron Darling .05
19 Dwight Gooden .05
20 Keith Hernandez .05
21 Darryl Strawberry .05
22 Ron Guidry .05
23 Rickey Henderson .40
24 Don Mattingly .65
25 Dave Righetti .05
26 Dave Winfield .40
27 Mariano Duncan .05
28 Pedro Guerrero .05
29 Bill Madlock .05
30 Mike Marshall .05
31 Fernando Valenzuela .05
32 Reggie Jackson .50
33 Gary Pettis .05
34 Ron Romanick .05
35 Don Sutton .30
36 Mike Witt .05
37 Buddy Bell .05
38 Tom Browning .05
39 Dave Parker .05
40 Pete Rose .75
41 Mario Soto .05
42 Harold Baines .05
43 Carlton Fisk .40
44 Ozzie Guillen .05
45 Ron Kittle .05
46 Tom Seaver .40
47 Kirk Gibson .05
48 Jack Morris .05
49 Lance Parrish .05
50 Alan Trammell .05
51 Lou Whitaker .05
52 Hubie Brooks .05
53 Andre Dawson .25
54 Tim Raines .05

No	Player	Price
55	Bryn Smith	.05
56	Tim Wallach	.05
57	Mike Boddicker	.05
58	Eddie Murray	.40
59	Cal Ripken, Jr.	1.25
60	John Shelby	.05
61	Mike Young	.05
62	Jose Cruz	.05
63	Glenn Davis	.05
64	Phil Garner	.05
65	Nolan Ryan	1.25
66	Mike Scott	.05
67	Steve Garvey	.15
68	Goose Gossage	.05
69	Tony Gwynn	.50
70	Andy Hawkins	.05
71	Garry Templeton	.05
72	Wade Boggs	.50
73	Roger Clemens	.65
74	Dwight Evans	.05
75	Rich Gedman	.05
76	Jim Rice	.25
77	Shawon Dunston	.05
78	Leon Durham	.05
79	Keith Moreland	.05
80	Ryne Sandberg	.50
81	Rick Sutcliffe	.05
82	Bert Blyleven	.05
83	Tom Brunansky	.05
84	Kent Hrbek	.05
85	Kirby Puckett	.50
86	Bruce Bochte	.05
87	Jose Canseco	.40
88	Mike Davis	.05
89	Jay Howell	.05
90	Dwayne Murphy	.05
91	Steve Carlton	.40
92	Von Hayes	.05
93	Juan Samuel	.05
94	Mike Schmidt	.65
95	Glenn Wilson	.05
96	Phil Bradley	.05
97	Alvin Davis	.05
98	Jim Presley	.05
99	Danny Tartabull	.05
100	Cecil Cooper	.05
101	Paul Molitor	.40
102	Earnie Riles	.05
103	Robin Yount	.65
104	Bob Horner	.05
105	Dale Murphy	.20
106	Bruce Sutter	.30
107	Claudell Washington	.05
108	Chris Brown	.05
109	Chili Davis	.05
110	Scott Garrelts	.05
111	Oddibe McDowell	.05
112	Pete O'Brien	.05
113	Gary Ward	.05
114	Brett Butler	.05
115	Julio Franco	.05
116	Brook Jacoby	.05
117	Mike Brown	.05
118	Joe Orsulak	.05
119	Tony Pena	.05
120	R.J. Reynolds	.05

Star Stickers

STAR STICKER — STEVE GARVEY, PADRES, FIRST BASE

Fleer's 1986 sticker-card set again measures 2-1/2" x 3-1/2" and features color photos inside dark maroon borders. Backs are identical to the 1986 baseball card issue except for the 1-132 numbering system and blue ink instead of yellow. Card #132 is a multi-player card featuring Dwight Gooden and Dale Murphy on the front and a complete checklist for the set on the reverse. The cards were sold in wax packs with team logo stickers.

	NM/M
Complete Set (132):	7.00
Common Player:	.05
Wax Pack (5):	1.00
Wax Box (36):	12.00

No	Player	Price
1	Harold Baines	.05
2	Jesse Barfield	.05
3	Don Baylor	.05
4	Juan Beniquez	.05
5	Tim Birtsas	.05
6	Bert Blyleven	.10
7	Bruce Bochte	.05
8	Wade Boggs	.50
9	Dennis Boyd	.05
10	Phil Bradley	.05
11	George Brett	.65
12	Hubie Brooks	.05
13	Chris Brown	.05
14	Tom Browning	.05
15	Tom Brunansky	.05
16	Bill Buckner	.05
17	Britt Burns	.05
18	Brett Butler	.05
19	Jose Canseco	.40
20	Rod Carew	.40
21	Steve Carlton	.40
22	Don Carman	.05
23	Gary Carter	.40
24	Jack Clark	.05
25	Vince Coleman	.40
26	Cecil Cooper	.05
27	Jose Cruz	.05
28	Ron Darling	.05
29	Alvin Davis	.05
30	Jody Davis	.05
31	Mike Davis	.05
32	Andre Dawson	.25
33	Mariano Duncan	.05
34	Shawon Dunston	.05
35	Leon Durham	.05
36	Darrell Evans	.05
37	Tony Fernandez	.05
38	Carlton Fisk	.40
39	John Franco	.05
40	Julio Franco	.05
41	Damaso Garcia	.05
42	Scott Garrelts	.05
43	Steve Garvey	.15
44	Rich Gedman	.05
45	Kirk Gibson	.05
46	Dwight Gooden	.50
47	Pedro Guerrero	.05
48	Ron Guidry	.05
49	Ozzie Guillen	.05
50	Tony Gwynn	.50
51	Andy Hawkins	.05
52	Von Hayes	.05
53	Rickey Henderson	.40
54	Tom Henke	.05
55	Keith Hernandez	.05
56	Willie Hernandez	.05
57	Tom Herr	.05
58	Orel Hershiser	.05
59	Teddy Higuera	.05
60	Bob Horner	.05
61	Charlie Hough	.05
62	Jay Howell	.05
63	LaMarr Hoyt	.05
64	Kent Hrbek	.05
65	Reggie Jackson	.50
66	Bob James	.05
67	Dave Kingman	.05
68	Ron Kittle	.05
69	Charlie Leibrandt	.05
70	Fred Lynn	.05
71	Mike Marshall	.05
72	Don Mattingly	.65
73	Oddibe McDowell	.05
74	Willie McGee	.05
75	Scott McGregor	.05
76	Paul Molitor	.40
77	Donnie Moore	.05
78	Keith Moreland	.05
79	Jack Morris	.05
80	Dale Murphy	.15
81	Eddie Murray	.40
82	Phil Niekro	.35
83	Joe Orsulak	.05
84	Dave Parker	.05
85	Lance Parrish	.05
86	Larry Parrish	.05
87	Tony Pena	.05
88	Gary Pettis	.05
89	Jim Presley	.05
90	Kirby Puckett	.50
91	Dan Quisenberry	.05
92	Tim Raines	.05
93	Johnny Ray	.05
94	Jeff Reardon	.05
95	Rick Reuschel	.05
96	Jim Rice	.25
97	Dave Righetti	.05
98	Earnie Riles	.05
99	Cal Ripken, Jr.	1.25
100	Ron Romanick	.05
101	Pete Rose	.85
102	Nolan Ryan	1.25
103	Bret Saberhagen	.05
104	Mark Salas	.05
105	Juan Samuel	.05
106	Ryne Sandberg	.50
107	Mike Schmidt	.65
108	Mike Scott	.05
109	Tom Seaver	.40
110	Bryn Smith	.05
111	Dave Smith	.05
112	Lee Smith	.05
113	Ozzie Smith	.50
114	Mario Soto	.05
115	Dave Stieb	.05
116	Darryl Strawberry	.05
117	Bruce Sutter	.35
118	Garry Templeton	.05
119	Gorman Thomas	.05
120	Andre Thornton	.05
121	Alan Trammell	.05
122	John Tudor	.05
123	Fernando Valenzuela	.05
124	Frank Viola	.05
125	Gary Ward	.05
126	Lou Whitaker	.05
127	Frank White	.05
128	Glenn Wilson	.05
129	Willie Wilson	.05
130	Dave Winfield	.40
131	Robin Yount	.40
132	Dwight Gooden, Dale Murphy	.10

Star Stickers Box Panels

Four cards, numbered S-1 through S-4, were placed on the bottoms of 1986 Fleer Star Stickers wax pack boxes. The cards are nearly identical in format to the regular issue sticker cards. Individual cards measure 2-1/2" x 3-1/2" in size, while a complete panel of four measures 5" x 7-1/8".

	NM/M
Complete Panel Set:	2.00
Complete Singles Set (4):	2.00
Common Single Player:	.30

No	Player	Price
1	Dodgers Logo	.05
2	Wade Boggs	1.25
3	Steve Garvey	.30
4	Dave Winfield	1.00

1987 Fleer

TIM RAINES, OUTFIELD, EXPOS, FLEER

The 1987 Fleer set consists of 660 cards. Fronts feature a graduated blue-to-white border design. The player's name and position appear in the upper-left corner of the card; his team logo is located in the lower-right. Backs are done in blue, red and white and contain an innovative "Pro Scouts Report" feature which rates the player's batting or pitching skills. For the third year in a row, Fleer included its "Major League Prospects" subset. Fleer produced a glossy-finish Collectors Edition set which came housed in a specially-designed tin box. After experiencing a dramatic hike in price during 1987, the glossy set now sells for only a few dollars more than the regular issue.

	NM/M
Unopened Fact. Set (672):	65.00
Complete Set (660):	50.00
Common Player:	.05
Wax Pack (15/17):	3.00
Wax Box (36):	100.00
Cello Pack (28):	5.00
Cello Box (24):	100.00
Rack Pack (51):	8.00
Rack Box (24):	160.00

No	Player	Price
1	Rick Aguilera	.05
2	Richard Anderson	.05
3	Wally Backman	.05
4	Gary Carter	.75
5	Ron Darling	.05
6	Len Dykstra	.05
7	Kevin Elster RC	.05
8	Sid Fernandez	.05
9	Dwight Gooden	.50
10	Ed Hearn RC	.05
11	Danny Heep	.05
12	Keith Hernandez	.05
13	Howard Johnson	.05
14	Ray Knight	.05
15	Lee Mazzilli	.05
16	Roger McDowell	.05
17	Kevin Mitchell	.05
18	Randy Niemann	.05
19	Bob Ojeda	.05
20	Jesse Orosco	.05
21	Rafael Santana	.05
22	Doug Sisk	.05
23	Darryl Strawberry	.05
24	Tim Teufel	.05
25	Mookie Wilson	.05
26	Tony Armas	.05
27	Marty Barrett	.05
28	Don Baylor	.05
29	Wade Boggs	1.00
30	Oil Can Boyd	.05
31	Bill Buckner	.05
32	Roger Clemens	2.00
33	Steve Crawford	.05
34	Dwight Evans	.05
35	Rich Gedman	.05
36	Dave Henderson	.05
37	Bruce Hurst	.05
38	Tim Lollar	.05
39	Al Nipper	.05
40	Spike Owen	.05
41	Jim Rice	.30
42	Ed Romero	.05
43	Joe Sambito	.05
44	Calvin Schiraldi	.05
45	Tom Seaver	.75
46	Jeff Sellers RC	.05
47	Bob Stanley	.05
48	Sammy Stewart	.05
49	Larry Andersen	.05
50	Alan Ashby	.05
51	Kevin Bass	.05
52	Jeff Calhoun	.05
53	Jose Cruz	.05
54	Danny Darwin	.05
55	Glenn Davis	.05
56	Jim Deshaies RC	.10
57	Bill Doran	.05
58	Phil Garner	.05
59	Billy Hatcher	.05
60	Charlie Kerfeld	.05
61	Bob Knepper	.05
62	Dave Lopes	.05
63	Aurelio Lopez	.05
64	Jim Pankovits	.05
65	Terry Puhl	.05
66	Craig Reynolds	.05
67	Nolan Ryan	3.00
68	Mike Scott	.05
69	Dave Smith	.05
70	Dickie Thon	.05
71	Tony Walker	.05
72	Denny Walling	.05
73	Bob Boone	.05
74	Rick Burleson	.05
75	John Candelaria	.05
76	Doug Corbett	.05
77	Doug DeCinces	.05
78	Brian Downing	.05
79	Chuck Finley RC	1.00
80	Terry Forster	.05
81	Bobby Grich	.05
82	George Hendrick	.05
83	Jack Howell RC	.05
84	Reggie Jackson	1.00
85	Ruppert Jones	.05
86	Wally Joyner	.05
87	Gary Lucas	.05
88	Kirk McCaskill	.05
89	Donnie Moore	.05
90	Gary Pettis	.05
91	Vern Ruhle	.05
92	Dick Schofield	.05
93	Don Sutton	.65
94	Rob Wilfong	.05
95	Mike Witt	.05
96	Doug Drabek	.05
97	Mike Easler	.05
98	Mike Fischlin	.05
99	Brian Fisher	.05
100	Ron Guidry	.10
101	Rickey Henderson	.75
102	Tommy John	.10
103	Ron Kittle	.05
104	Don Mattingly	2.00
105	Bobby Meacham	.05
106	Joe Niekro	.05
107	Mike Pagliarulo	.05
108	Dan Pasqua	.05
109	Willie Randolph	.05
110	Dennis Rasmussen	.05
111	Dave Righetti	.05
112	Gary Roenicke	.05
113	Rod Scurry	.05
114	Bob Shirley	.05
115	Joel Skinner	.05
116	Tim Stoddard	.05
117	Bob Tewksbury RC	.35
118	Wayne Tolleson	.05
119	Claudell Washington	.05
120	Dave Winfield	.75
121	Steve Buechele	.05
122	Ed Correa RC	.05
123	Scott Fletcher	.05
124	Jose Guzman	.05
125	Toby Harrah	.05
126	Greg Harris	.05
127	Charlie Hough	.05
128	Pete Incaviglia	.05
129	Mike Mason	.05
130	Oddibe McDowell	.05
131	Dale Mohorcic RC	.05
132	Pete O'Brien	.05
133	Tom Paciorek	.05
134	Larry Parrish	.05
135	Geno Petralli	.05
136	Darrell Porter	.05
137	Jeff Russell	.05
138	Ruben Sierra RC	.05
139	Don Slaught	.05
140	Gary Ward	.05
141	Curtis Wilkerson	.05
142	Mitch Williams RC	.10
143	Bobby Witt RC	.10
144	Dave Bergman	.05
145	Tom Brookens	.05
146	Bill Campbell	.05
147	Chuck Cary RC	.05
148	Darnell Coles	.05
149	Dave Collins	.05
150	Darrell Evans	.05
151	Kirk Gibson	.05
152	John Grubb	.05
153	Willie Hernandez	.05
154	Larry Herndon	.05
155	Eric King RC	.05
156	Chet Lemon	.05
157	Dwight Lowry	.05
158	Jack Morris	.05
159	Randy O'Neal	.05
160	Lance Parrish	.05
161	Dan Petry	.05
162	Pat Sheridan	.05
163	Jim Slaton	.05
164	Frank Tanana	.05
165	Walt Terrell	.05
166	Mark Thurmond	.05
167	Alan Trammell	.05
168	Lou Whitaker	.05
169	Luis Aguayo	.05
170	Steve Bedrosian	.05
171	Don Carman	.05
172	Darren Daulton	.05
173	Greg Gross	.05
174	Kevin Gross	.05
175	Von Hayes	.05
176	Charles Hudson	.05
177	Tom Hume	.05
178	Steve Jeltz	.05
179	Mike Maddux RC	.05
180	Shane Rawley	.05
181	Gary Redus	.05
182	Ron Roenicke	.05
183	Bruce Ruffin RC	.10
184	John Russell	.05
185	Juan Samuel	.05
186	Dan Schatzeder	.05
187	Mike Schmidt	2.00
188	Rick Schu	.05
189	Jeff Stone	.05
190	Kent Tekulve	.05
191	Milt Thompson	.05
192	Glenn Wilson	.05
193	Buddy Bell	.05
194	Tom Browning	.05
195	Sal Butera	.05
196	Dave Concepcion	.05
197	Kal Daniels	.05
198	Eric Davis	.05
199	John Denny	.05
200	Bo Diaz	.05
201	Nick Esasky	.05
202	John Franco	.05
203	Bill Gullickson	.05
204	Barry Larkin RC	2.00
205	Eddie Milner	.05
206	Rob Murphy RC	.05
207	Ron Oester	.05
208	Dave Parker	.05
209	Tony Perez	.65
210	Ted Power	.05
211	Joe Price	.05
212	Ron Robinson	.05
213	Pete Rose	2.50
214	Mario Soto	.05
215	Kurt Stillwell RC	.05
216	Max Venable	.05
217	Chris Welsh	.05
218	Carl Willis RC	.05
219	Jesse Barfield	.05
220	George Bell	.05
221	Bill Caudill	.05
222	John Cerutti RC	.05
223	Jim Clancy	.05
224	Mark Eichhorn RC	.10
225	Tony Fernandez	.05
226	Damaso Garcia	.05
227	Kelly Gruber	.05
228	Tom Henke	.05
229	Garth Iorg	.05
230	Cliff Johnson	.05
231	Joe Johnson	.05
232	Jimmy Key	.05
233	Dennis Lamp	.05
234	Rick Leach	.05
235	Buck Martinez	.05
236	Lloyd Moseby	.05
237	Rance Mulliniks	.05
238	Dave Stieb	.05
239	Willie Upshaw	.05
240	Ernie Whitt	.05
241	Andy Allanson RC	.05
242	Scott Bailes RC	.05
243	Chris Bando	.05
244	Tony Bernazard	.05
245	John Butcher	.05
246	Brett Butler	.05
247	Ernie Camacho	.05
248	Tom Candiotti	.05
249	Joe Carter	.05
250	Carmen Castillo	.05
251	Julio Franco	.05
252	Mel Hall	.05
253	Brook Jacoby	.05
254	Phil Niekro	.65
255	Otis Nixon	.05
256	Dickie Noles	.05
257	Bryan Oelkers	.05
258	Ken Schrom	.05
259	Don Schulze	.05
260	Cory Snyder	.05
261	Pat Tabler	.05
262	Andre Thornton	.05
263	Rich Yett RC	.05
264	Mike Aldrete RC	.05
265	Juan Berenguer	.05
266	Vida Blue	.05
267	Bob Brenly	.05
268	Chris Brown	.05
269	Will Clark	.05
270	Chili Davis	.05
271	Mark Davis	.05
272	Kelly Downs RC	.05
273	Scott Garrelts	.05
274	Dan Gladden	.05
275	Mike Krukow	.05
276	Randy Kutcher RC	.05
277	Mike LaCoss	.05
278	Jeff Leonard	.05
279	Candy Maldonado	.05
280	Roger Mason	.05
281	Bob Melvin RC	.05
282	Greg Minton	.05
283	Jeff Robinson	.05
284	Harry Spilman	.05
285	Rob Thompson RC	.05
286	Jose Uribe	.05
287	Frank Williams	.05
288	Joel Youngblood	.05
289	Jack Clark	.05
290	Vince Coleman	.05
291	Tim Conroy	.05
292	Danny Cox	.05
293	Ken Dayley	.05
294	Curt Ford	.05
295	Bob Forsch	.05
296	Tom Herr	.05
297	Ricky Horton	.05
298	Clint Hurdle	.05
299	Jeff Lahti	.05
300	Steve Lake	.05
301	Tito Landrum	.05
302	Mike LaValliere RC	.05
303	Greg Mathews RC	.05
304	Willie McGee	.05
305	Jose Oquendo	.05
306	Terry Pendleton	.05
307	Pat Perry	.05
308	Ozzie Smith	1.50
309	Ray Soff	.05
310	John Tudor	.05
311	Andy Van Slyke	.05
312	Todd Worrell	.05
313	Dann Bilardello	.05
314	Hubie Brooks	.05
315	Tim Burke	.05
316	Andre Dawson	.35
317	Mike Fitzgerald	.05
318	Tom Foley	.05
319	Andres Galarraga	.05
320	Joe Hesketh	.05
321	Wallace Johnson	.05
322	Wayne Krenchicki	.05
323	Vance Law	.05
324	Dennis Martinez	.05
325	Bob McClure	.05
326	Andy McGaffigan	.05
327	Al Newman RC	.05
328	Tim Raines	.05
329	Jeff Reardon	.05
330	Luis Rivera RC	.05
331	Bob Sebra RC	.05
332	Bryn Smith	.05
333	Jay Tibbs	.05
334	Tim Wallach	.05
335	Mitch Webster	.05
336	Jim Wohlford	.05
337	Floyd Youmans	.05
338	Chris Bosio RC	.25
339	Glenn Braggs RC	.05
340	Rick Cerone	.05
341	Mark Clear	.05
342	Bryan Clutterbuck RC	.05
343	Cecil Cooper	.05
344	Rob Deer	.05
345	Jim Gantner	.05
346	Ted Higuera	.05
347	John Henry Johnson	.05
348	Tim Leary RC	.05
349	Rick Manning	.05
350	Paul Molitor	.75
351	Charlie Moore	.05
352	Juan Nieves	.05
353	Ben Oglivie	.05
354	Dan Plesac RC	.10
355	Ernest Riles	.05
356	Billy Joe Robidoux	.05
357	Bill Schroeder	.05
358	Dale Sveum RC	.05
359	Gorman Thomas	.05
360	Bill Wegman RC	.05
361	Robin Yount	.75
362	Steve Balboni	.05
363	Scott Bankhead RC	.05
364	Buddy Biancalana	.05
365	Bud Black	.05
366	George Brett	2.00
367	Steve Farr	.05
368	Mark Gubicza	.05
369	Bo Jackson	.75
370	Danny Jackson	.05

No.	Player	Price
371	Mike Kingery RC	.05
372	Rudy Law	.05
373	Charlie Leibrandt	.05
374	Dennis Leonard	.05
375	Hal McRae	.05
376	Jorge Orta	.05
377	Jamie Quirk	.05
378	Dan Quisenberry	.05
379	Bret Saberhagen	.05
380	Angel Salazar	.05
381	Lonnie Smith	.05
382	Jim Sundberg	.05
383	Frank White	.05
384	Willie Wilson	.05
385	Joaquin Andujar	.05
386	Doug Bair	.05
387	Dusty Baker	.05
388	Bruce Bochte	.05
389	Jose Canseco	.65
390	Chris Codiroli	.05
391	Mike Davis	.05
392	Alfredo Griffin	.05
393	Moose Haas	.05
394	Donnie Hill	.05
395	Jay Howell	.05
396	Dave Kingman	.05
397	Carney Lansford	.05
398	David Leiper RC	.05
399	Bill Mooneyham RC	.05
400	Dwayne Murphy	.05
401	Steve Ontiveros	.05
402	Tony Phillips	.05
403	Eric Plunk	.05
404	Jose Rijo	.05
405	Terry Steinbach RC	.50
406	Dave Stewart	.05
407	Mickey Tettleton	.05
408	Dave Von Ohlen	.05
409	Jerry Willard	.05
410	Curt Young	.05
411	Bruce Bochy	.05
412	Dave Dravecky	.05
413	Tim Flannery	.05
414	Steve Garvey	.25
415	Goose Gossage	.10
416	Tony Gwynn	1.50
417	Andy Hawkins	.05
418	LaMarr Hoyt	.05
419	Terry Kennedy	.05
420	John Kruk	.05
421	Dave LaPoint	.05
422	Craig Lefferts	.05
423	Carmelo Martinez	.05
424	Lance McCullers	.05
425	Kevin McReynolds	.05
426	Graig Nettles	.05
427	Bip Roberts	.05
428	Jerry Royster	.05
429	Benito Santiago	.05
430	Eric Show	.05
431	Bob Stoddard	.05
432	Garry Templeton	.05
433	Gene Walter	.05
434	Ed Whitson	.05
435	Marvell Wynne	.05
436	Dave Anderson	.05
437	Greg Brock	.05
438	Enos Cabell	.05
439	Mariano Duncan	.05
440	Pedro Guerrero	.05
441	Orel Hershiser	.05
442	Rick Honeycutt	.05
443	Ken Howell	.05
444	Ken Landreaux	.05
445	Bill Madlock	.65
446	Mike Marshall	.05
447	Len Matuszek	.05
448	Tom Niedenfuer	.05
449	Alejandro Pena	.05
450	Dennis Powell RC	.05
451	Jerry Reuss	.05
452	Bill Russell	.05
453	Steve Sax	.05
454	Mike Scioscia	.05
455	Franklin Stubbs	.05
456	Alex Trevino	.05
457	Fernando Valenzuela	.05
458	Ed Vande Berg	.05
459	Bob Welch	.05
460	Reggie Williams RC	.05
461	Don Aase	.05
462	Juan Beniquez	.05
463	Mike Boddicker	.05
464	Juan Bonilla	.05
465	Rich Bordi	.05
466	Storm Davis	.05
467	Rick Dempsey	.05
468	Ken Dixon	.05
469	Jim Dwyer	.05
470	Mike Flanagan	.05
471	Jackie Gutierrez	.05
472	Brad Havens	.05
473	Lee Lacy	.05
474	Fred Lynn	.05
475	Scott McGregor	.05
476	Eddie Murray	.75
477	Tom O'Malley	.05
478	Cal Ripken, Jr.	3.00
479	Larry Sheets	.05
480	John Shelby	.05
481	Nate Snell	.05
482	Jim Traber RC	.05
483	Mike Young	.05
484	Neil Allen	.05
485	Harold Baines	.05
486	Floyd Bannister	.05
487	Daryl Boston	.05
488	Ivan Calderon	.05

No.	Player	Price
489	John Cangelosi RC	.05
490	Steve Carlton	.75
491	Joe Cowley	.05
492	Julio Cruz	.05
493	Bill Dawley	.05
494	Jose DeLeon	.05
495	Richard Dotson	.05
496	Carlton Fisk	.75
497	Ozzie Guillen	.05
498	Jerry Hairston Sr.	.05
499	Ron Hassey	.05
500	Tim Hulett	.05
501	Bob James	.05
502	Steve Lyons	.05
503	Joel McKeon RC	.05
504	Gene Nelson	.05
505	Dave Schmidt	.05
506	Ray Searage	.05
507	Bobby Thigpen RC	.15
508	Greg Walker	.05
509	Jim Acker	.05
510	Doyle Alexander	.05
511	Paul Assenmacher RC	.05
512	Bruce Benedict	.05
513	Chris Chambliss	.05
514	Jeff Dedmon	.05
515	Gene Garber	.05
516	Ken Griffey	.05
517	Terry Harper	.05
518	Bob Horner	.05
519	Glenn Hubbard	.05
520	Rick Mahler	.05
521	Omar Moreno	.05
522	Dale Murphy	.35
523	Ken Oberkfell	.05
524	Ed Olwine	.05
525	David Palmer	.05
526	Rafael Ramirez	.05
527	Billy Sample	.05
528	Ted Simmons	.05
529	Zane Smith	.05
530	Bruce Sutter	.65
531	Andres Thomas RC	.05
532	Ozzie Virgil	.05
533	Allan Anderson RC	.05
534	Keith Atherton	.05
535	Billy Beane	.05
536	Bert Blyleven	.10
537	Tom Brunansky	.05
538	Randy Bush	.05
539	George Frazier	.05
540	Gary Gaetti	.05
541	Greg Gagne	.05
542	Mickey Hatcher	.05
543	Neal Heaton	.05
544	Kent Hrbek	.05
545	Roy Lee Jackson	.05
546	Tim Laudner	.05
547	Steve Lombardozzi	.05
548	Mark Portugal RC	.10
549	Kirby Puckett	1.50
550	Jeff Reed	.05
551	Mark Salas	.05
552	Roy Smalley	.05
553	Mike Smithson	.05
554	Frank Viola	.05
555	Thad Bosley	.05
556	Ron Cey	.05
557	Jody Davis	.05
558	Ron Davis	.05
559	Bob Dernier	.05
560	Frank DiPino	.05
561	Shawon Dunston	.05
562	Leon Durham	.05
563	Dennis Eckersley	.65
564	Terry Francona	.05
565	Dave Gumpert	.05
566	Guy Hoffman	.05
567	Ed Lynch	.05
568	Gary Matthews	.05
569	Keith Moreland	.05
570	Jamie Moyer RC	.05
571	Jerry Mumphrey	.05
572	Ryne Sandberg	1.00
573	Scott Sanderson	.05
574	Lee Smith	.05
575	Chris Speier	.05
576	Rick Sutcliffe	.05
577	Manny Trillo	.05
578	Steve Trout	.05
579	Karl Best	.05
580	Scott Bradley RC	.05
581	Phil Bradley	.05
582	Mickey Brantley	.05
583	Mike Brown	.05
584	Alvin Davis	.05
585	Lee Guetterman RC	.05
586	Mark Huismann	.05
587	Bob Kearney	.05
588	Pete Ladd	.05
589	Mark Langston	.05
590	Mike Moore	.05
591	Mike Morgan	.05
592	John Moses	.05
593	Ken Phelps	.05
594	Jim Presley	.05
595	Rey Quinonez (Quinones) RC	.05
596	Harold Reynolds	.05
597	Billy Swift	.05
598	Danny Tartabull	.05
599	Steve Yeager	.05
600	Matt Young	.05
601	Bill Almon	.05
602	Rafael Belliard RC	.05
603	Mike Bielecki	.05
604	Barry Bonds	40.00
605	Bobby Bonilla	.05

No.	Player	Price
606	Sid Bream	.05
607	Mike Brown	.05
608	Pat Clements	.05
609	Mike Diaz RC	.05
610	Cecilio Guante	.05
611	Barry Jones RC	.05
612	Bob Kipper	.05
613	Larry McWilliams	.05
614	Jim Morrison	.05
615	Joe Orsulak	.05
616	Junior Ortiz	.05
617	Tony Pena	.05
618	Johnny Ray	.05
619	Rick Reuschel	.05
620	R.J. Reynolds	.05
621	Rick Rhoden	.05
622	Don Robinson	.05
623	Bob Walk	.05
624	Jim Winn	.05
625	Youthful Power (Jose Canseco, Pete Incaviglia)	.15
626	300 Game Winners (Phil Niekro, Don Sutton)	.25
627	A.L. Firemen (Don Aase, Dave Righetti)	.05
628	Rookie All-Stars (Jose Canseco, Wally Joyner)	.15
629	Magic Mets (Gary Carter, Dwight Gooden, Keith Hernandez, Darryl Strawberry)	.15
630	N.L. Best Righties (Mike Krukow, Mike Scott)	.05
631	Sensational Southpaws (John Franco, Fernando Valenzuela)	.05
632	Count 'Em (Bob Horner)	.05
633	A.L. Pitcher's Nightmare (Jose Canseco, Kirby Puckett, Jim Rice)	.05
634	All-Star Battery (Gary Carter, Roger Clemens)	.50
635	4,000 Strikeouts (Steve Carlton)	.15
636	Big Bats At First Sack (Glenn Davis, Eddie Murray)	.15
637	On Base (Wade Boggs, Keith Hernandez)	.25
638	Sluggers From Left Side (Don Mattingly, Darryl Strawberry)	.50
639	Former MVP's (Dave Parker, Ryne Sandberg)	.25
640	Dr. K. & Super K (Roger Clemens, Dwight Gooden)	.50
641	A.L. West Stoppers (Charlie Hough, Mike Witt)	.05
642	Doubles & Triples (Tim Raines, Juan Samuel)	.05
643	Outfielders With Punch (Harold Baines, Jesse Barfield)	.05
644	Major League Prospects (Dave Clark RC, Greg Swindell RC)	.35
645	Major League Prospects (Ron Karkovice RC, Russ Morman RC)	.25
646	Major League Prospects (Willie Fraser RC, Devon White RC)	1.00
647	Major League Prospects (Jerry Browne RC, Mike Stanley RC)	.25
648	Major League Prospects (Phil Lombardi RC, Dave Magadan RC)	.20
649	Major League Prospects (Ralph Bryant RC, Jose Gonzalez RC)	.10
650	Major League Prospects (Randy Asadoor RC, Jimmy Jones RC)	.10
651	Major League Prospects (Marvin Freeman RC, Tracy Jones RC)	.10
652	Major League Prospects (Kevin Seitzer RC, John Stefero RC)	.25
653	Major League Prospects (Steve Fireovid RC, Rob Nelson RC)	.10
654	Checklist 1-95	.05
655	Checklist 96-192	.05
656	Checklist 193-288	.05
657	Checklist 289-384	.05
658	Checklist 385-483	.05
659	Checklist 484-578	.05
660	Checklist 579-660	.05

All-Stars

As in 1986, Fleer All-Star Team cards were randomly inserted in wax and cello packs. Twelve cards, measuring the standard 2-1/2" x 3-1/2", comprise the set. Fronts feature a full-color player photo set against a gray background for American League players and a black background for National Leaguers. Backs are printed in black, red and white

and feature a lengthy player biography. Fleer's choices for a major league All-Star team is once again the theme for the set.

		NM/M
Complete Set (12):		8.00
Common Player:		.25
1	Don Mattingly	2.00
2	Gary Carter	1.00
3	Tony Fernandez	.25
4	Steve Sax	.25
5	Kirby Puckett	1.50
6	Mike Schmidt	2.00
7	Mike Easler	.25
8	Todd Worrell	.25
9	George Bell	.25
10	Fernando Valenzuela	.25
11	Roger Clemens	2.00
12	Tim Raines	.25

Headliners

A continuation of the 1986 Future Hall of Famers idea, Fleer encountered legal problems with using the Hall of Fame name and abated them by entitling the set "Headliners." The cards were randomly inserted in three-pack rack packs. Fronts feature a player photo set against a beige background with bright red stripes. Backs are printed in black, red and gray and offer a brief biography with an emphasis on the player's performance during the 1986 season.

		NM/M
Complete Set (6):		4.00
Common Player:		.50
1	Wade Boggs	1.50
2	Jose Canseco	1.00
3	Dwight Gooden	.50
4	Rickey Henderson	1.00
5	Keith Hernandez	.50
6	Jim Rice	.75

'86 World Series

Fleer issued a set of 12 cards highlighting the 1986 World Series between the Boston Red Sox and New York Mets. The sets were available only with Fleer factory sets, both regular and glossy. The cards, 2-1/2" x 3-1/2", have either horizontal or vertical formats. The fronts are

bordered in red, white and blue stars and stripes with a thin gold frame around the photo. Backs are printed in red and blue on white stock and include information regarding the photo on the card fronts.

		NM/M
Complete Set, Regular (12):		6.00
Complete Set, Glossy (12):		6.00
Common Card:		.25
1	Left-Hand Finesse Beats Mets (Bruce Hurst)	.25
2	Wade Boggs, Keith Hernandez	1.25
3	Roger Clemens	4.00
4	Gary Carter	1.00
5	Ron Darling	.25
6	.433 Series Batting Average (Marty Barrett)	.25
7	Dwight Gooden	.50
8	Strategy At Work	.25
9	Dewey! (Dwight Evans)	.25
10	One Strike From Boston Victory (Dave Henderson, Spike Owen)	.25
11	Ray Knight, Darryl Strawberry	.25
12	Series M.V.P. (Ray Knight)	.25

Box Panels

For the second straight year, Fleer produced a special set of cards designed to stimulate sales of their wax and cello pack boxes. In 1987, Fleer issued 16 cards in panels of four on the bottoms of retail boxes. The cards are numbered C-1 through C-16 and are 2-1/2" x 3-1/2" in size. The cards have the same design as the regular issue set with the player photos and card numbers being different.

		NM/M
Complete Panel Set (4):		6.00
Complete Singles Set (16):		6.00
Common Panel:		1.50
Common Single Player:		.15
Panel		1.50
1	Mets Logo	.05
2	Keith Hernandez	.25
8	Dale Murphy	.45
14	Ryne Sandberg	1.00
Panel		2.50
3	Jesse Barfield	.15
5	George Brett	1.50
6	Red Sox Logo	.05
11	Kirby Puckett	1.00
Panel		1.50
4	Dwight Gooden	.15
9	Astros Logo	.05
10	Dave Parker	.15
15	Mike Schmidt	1.50
Panel		1.00
7	Wally Joyner	.25
12	Dave Righetti	.15
13	Angels Logo	.05
16	Robin Yount	.75

Glossy Tin

The three-year run of limited edition, glossy collectors' issues by Fleer from 1987-89 has become known to the hobby as "tins" for the colorful lithographed metal boxes in which complete sets were sold. In their debut year a reported 100,000 sets were made, each serial numbered on a sticker attached to the shrink-wrapped tin box. While the glossy version of the 1987 Fleer set once enjoyed a significant premium over regular cards, today that pre-

mium has evaporated and, indeed, it can be harder to find a buyer for the glossy version.

	NM/M
Unopened Set (672):	75.00
Complete Set (672):	50.00
Common Player:	.10

Fleer Update

The 1987 update edition brings the regular Fleer set up to date by including traded players and hot rookies. The cards measure 2-1/2" x 3-1/2" and are housed in a specially designed box with 25 team logo stickers. A glossy-coated Fleer Collectors Edition set was also produced.

		NM/M
Complete Set (132):		9.00
Common Player:		.05
1	Scott Bankhead	.05
2	Eric Bell RC	.05
3	Juan Beniquez	.05
4	Juan Berenguer	.05
5	Mike Birkbeck RC	.05
6	Randy Bockus RC	.05
7	Rod Booker RC	.05
8	Thad Bosley	.05
9	Greg Brock	.05
10	Bob Brower RC	.05
11	Chris Brown	.05
12	Jerry Browne	.05
13	Ralph Bryant	.05
14	DeWayne Buice RC	.05
15	Ellis Burks RC	.05
16	Casey Candaele RC	.05
17	Steve Carlton	.50
18	Juan Castillo RC	.05
19	Chuck Crim RC	.05
20	Mark Davidson RC	.05
21	Mark Davis	.05
22	Storm Davis	.05
23	Bill Dawley	.05
24	Andre Dawson	.30
25	Brian Dayett	.05
26	Rick Dempsey	.05
27	Ken Dowell RC	.05
28	Dave Dravecky	.05
29	Mike Dunne RC	.05
30	Dennis Eckersley	.40
31	Cecil Fielder	.05
32	Brian Fisher	.05
33	Willie Fraser	.05
34	Ken Gerhart RC	.05
35	Jim Gott	.05
36	Dan Gladden	.05
37	Mike Greenwell RC	.05
38	Cecilio Guante	.05
39	Albert Hall	.05
40	Atlee Hammaker	.05
41	Mickey Hatcher	.05
42	Mike Heath	.05
43	Neal Heaton	.05
44	Mike Henneman RC	.05
45	Guy Hoffman	.05
46	Charles Hudson	.05
47	Chuck Jackson RC	.05
48	Mike Jackson RC	.05
49	Reggie Jackson	.75
50	Chris James	.05
51	Dion James	.05
52	Stan Javier	.05
53	Stan Jefferson RC	.05
54	Jimmy Jones	.05
55	Tracy Jones	.05
56	Terry Kennedy	.05
57	Mike Kingery	.05
58	Ray Knight	.05
59	Gene Larkin RC	.05
60	Mike LaValliere	.05
61	Jack Lazorko RC	.05
62	Terry Leach	.05
63	Rick Leach	.05
64	Craig Lefferts	.05
65	Jim Lindeman RC	.05
66	Bill Long RC	.05
67	Mike Loynd RC	.05
68	Greg Maddux RC	8.00
69	Bill Madlock	.05
70	Dave Magadan	.05
71	Joe Magrane RC	.05
72	Fred Manrique RC	.05
73	Mike Mason	.05
74	Lloyd McClendon RC	.05

75	Fred McGriff RC	.05
76	Mark McGwire	3.00
77	Mark McLemore	.05
78	Kevin McReynolds	.05
79	Dave Meads RC	.05
80	Greg Minton	.05
81	John Mitchell RC	.05
82	Kevin Mitchell	.05
83	John Morris	.05
84	Jeff Musselman RC	.05
85	Randy Myers RC	.05
86	Gene Nelson	.05
87	Joe Niekro	.05
88	Tom Nieto	.05
89	Reid Nichols	.05
90	Matt Nokes RC	.05
91	Dickie Noles	.05
92	Edwin Nunez	.05
93	Jose Nunez RC	.05
94	Paul O'Neill	.05
95	Jim Paciorek RC	.05
96	Lance Parrish	.05
97	Bill Pecota RC	.05
98	Tony Pena	.05
99	Luis Polonia RC	.05
100	Randy Ready	.05
101	Jeff Reardon	.05
102	Gary Redus	.05
103	Rick Rhoden	.05
104	Wally Ritchie RC	.05
105	Jeff Robinson RC	.05
106	Mark Salas	.05
107	Dave Schmidt	.05
108	Kevin Seitzer	.05
109	John Shelby	.05
110	John Smiley RC	.05
111	Lary Sorenson	.05
112	Chris Speier	.05
113	Randy St. Claire	.05
114	Jim Sundberg	.05
115	B.J. Surhoff RC	.05
116	Greg Swindell	.05
117	Danny Tartabull	.05
118	Dorn Taylor RC	.05
119	Lee Tunnell	.05
120	Ed Vande Berg	.05
121	Andy Van Slyke	.05
122	Gary Ward	.05
123	Devon White	.05
124	Alan Wiggins	.05
125	Bill Wilkinson RC	.05
126	Jim Winn	.05
127	Frank Williams	.05
128	Ken Williams RC	.05
129	Matt Williams RC	1.00
130	Herm Winningham	.05
131	Matt Young	.05
132	Checklist 1-132	.05

Update Glossy Tin

The 1987 Fleer glossy tin update set is identical to the regular-issue updates, except for the high-gloss coating on the cards' fronts and the lithographed metal box in which the sets were sold. Production was estimated at 100,000. Because of perceived overproduction, the glossy tin update set and singles currently carry little, if any, premium over the regular-issue updates.

	NM/M
Unopened Set (132):	12.00
Complete Set (132):	7.50
Common Player:	.10

Award Winners

The 1987 Fleer Award Winners boxed set was prepared for distribution through 7-Eleven stores. The 2-1/2" x 3-1/2" cards feature players who have won various major league awards during their careers. Fronts contain full-color photos surrounded by a yellow border. The name of the award the player won is printed at the bottom of the card in an oval-shaped band designed to resemble a metal nameplate on a trophy. Backs are printed in black, yellow and white, and include lifetime major and minor league sta-

tistics along with typical personal information. Each boxed set contained six team logo stickers.

		NM/M
Complete Set (44):		5.00
Common Player:		.10
1	Marty Barrett	.10
2	George Bell	.10
3	Bert Blyleven	.20
4	Bob Boone	.10
5	John Candelaria	.10
6	Jose Canseco	.45
7	Gary Carter	.50
8	Joe Carter	.10
9	Roger Clemens	1.00
10	Cecil Cooper	.10
11	Eric Davis	.10
12	Tony Fernandez	.10
13	Scott Fletcher	.10
14	Bob Forsch	.10
15	Dwight Gooden	.10
16	Ron Guidry	.10
17	Ozzie Guillen	.10
18	Bill Gullickson	.10
19	Tony Gwynn	.75
20	Bob Knepper	.10
21	Ray Knight	.10
22	Mark Langston	.10
23	Candy Maldonado	.10
24	Don Mattingly	1.00
25	Roger McDowell	.10
26	Dale Murphy	.20
27	Dave Parker	.10
28	Lance Parrish	.10
29	Gary Pettis	.10
30	Kirby Puckett	.75
31	Johnny Ray	.10
32	Dave Righetti	.10
33	Cal Ripken, Jr.	1.50
34	Bret Saberhagen	.10
35	Ryne Sandberg	.75
36	Mike Schmidt	1.00
37	Mike Scott	.10
38	Ozzie Smith	.75
39	Robbie Thompson	.10
40	Fernando Valenzuela	.10
41	Mitch Webster	.10
42	Frank White	.10
43	Mike Witt	.10
44	Todd Worrell	.10

Baseball All-Stars

Produced by Fleer for exclusive distribution through Ben Franklin stores, the "Baseball All-Stars" set is comprised of 44 cards in the standard 2-1/2" x 3-1/2" format. Cards have full-color photos surrounded by a bright red border with white pinstripes at the top and bottom. Backs are printed in blue, white and dark red and include complete major and minor league statistics. The set was issued in a special cardboard box with a handful of team logo stickers.

		NM/M
Complete Set (44):		5.00
Common Player:		.10
1	Harold Baines	.10
2	Jesse Barfield	.10
3	Wade Boggs	.65
4	Dennis "Oil Can" Boyd	.10
5	Scott Bradley	.10
6	Jose Canseco	.40
7	Gary Carter	.50
8	Joe Carter	.10
9	Mark Clear	.10
10	Roger Clemens	.85
11	Jose Cruz	.10
12	Chili Davis	.10
13	Jody Davis	.10
14	Rob Deer	.10
15	Brian Downing	.10
16	Sid Fernandez	.10
17	John Franco	.10
18	Andres Galarraga	.10
19	Dwight Gooden	.10
20	Tony Gwynn	.65
21	Charlie Hough	.10
22	Bruce Hurst	.10
23	Wally Joyner	.10
24	Carney Lansford	.10
25	Fred Lynn	.10

26	Don Mattingly	.85
27	Willie McGee	.10
28	Jack Morris	.10
29	Dale Murphy	.20
30	Bob Ojeda	.10
31	Tony Pena	.10
32	Kirby Puckett	.65
33	Dan Quisenberry	.10
34	Tim Raines	.10
35	Willie Randolph	.10
36	Cal Ripken, Jr.	1.50
37	Pete Rose	1.00
38	Nolan Ryan	1.50
39	Juan Samuel	.10
40	Mike Schmidt	.85
41	Ozzie Smith	.65
42	Andres Thomas	.10
43	Fernando Valenzuela	.10
44	Mike Witt	.10

Baseball's Best

For a second straight baseball card season, Fleer produced for McCrory's stores and their affiliates a 44-card "Baseball's Best" set. Subtitled "Sluggers vs. Pitchers," 28 everyday players and 16 pitchers are featured. The card design is nearly identical to the previous year's effort. The cards were sold in a specially designed box along with six team logo stickers.

		NM/M
Complete Set (44):		4.00
Common Player:		.10
1	Kevin Bass	.10
2	Jesse Barfield	.10
3	George Bell	.10
4	Wade Boggs	.65
5	Sid Bream	.10
6	George Brett	.85
7	Ivan Calderon	.10
8	Jose Canseco	.10
9	Jack Clark	.10
10	Roger Clemens	.85
11	Eric Davis	.10
12	Andre Dawson	.25
13	Sid Fernandez	.10
14	John Franco	.10
15	Dwight Gooden	.10
16	Pedro Guerrero	.10
17	Tony Gwynn	.65
18	Rickey Henderson	.60
19	Tom Henke	.10
20	Ted Higuera	.10
21	Pete Incaviglia	.10
22	Wally Joyner	.10
23	Jeff Leonard	.10
24	Joe Magrane	.10
25	Don Mattingly	.85
26	Mark McGwire	1.00
27	Jack Morris	.10
28	Dale Murphy	.20
29	Dave Parker	.10
30	Ken Phelps	.10
31	Kirby Puckett	.65
32	Tim Raines	.10
33	Jeff Reardon	.10
34	Dave Righetti	.10
35	Cal Ripken, Jr.	1.50
36	Bret Saberhagen	.10
37	Mike Schmidt	.85
38	Mike Scott	.10
39	Kevin Seitzer	.10
40	Darryl Strawberry	.10
41	Rick Sutcliffe	.10
42	Pat Tabler	.10
43	Fernando Valenzuela	.10
44	Mike Witt	.10

Baseball's Best Box Bottom

These special cards were printed on the bottom of retail boxes of Fleer's "Baseball's Best" boxed sets. The box-bottom cards are in the same format as the boxed cards, with red, white and blue borders and a yellow title strip at top. Backs are also similar in design to the regular-issue cards, carrying player data and stats. Cards are numbered with a "M" prefix.

		NM/M
Complete Panel:		3.00
Complete Set (6):		3.00
Common Player:		.50
1	Steve Bedrosian	.50
2	Will Clark	1.00
3	Vince Coleman	.50
4	Bo Jackson	2.00
5	Cory Snyder	.50
---	K.C. Royals Logo	.10

Exciting Stars

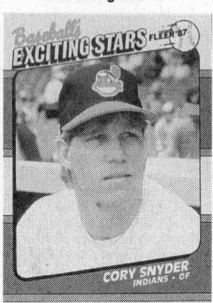

Another entry into the Fleer line-up of individual boxed sets, the "Baseball's Exciting Stars" set was produced for Cumberland Farms stores. The card fronts feature a red, white and blue border with the words "Exciting Stars" printed in yellow at the top. The backs are printed in red and blue and carry complete major and minor league statistics. Included with the boxed set of 44 cards were six team logo stickers.

		NM/M
Complete Set (44):		4.00
Common Player:		.10
1	Don Aase	.10
2	Rick Aguilera	.10
3	Jesse Barfield	.10
4	Wade Boggs	.65
5	Dennis "Oil Can" Boyd	.10
6	Sid Bream	.10
7	Jose Canseco	.45
8	Steve Carlton	.50
9	Gary Carter	.50
10	Will Clark	.85
11	Roger Clemens	.85
12	Danny Cox	.10
13	Alvin Davis	.10
14	Eric Davis	.10
15	Rob Deer	.10
16	Brian Downing	.10
17	Gene Garber	.10
18	Steve Garvey	.20
19	Dwight Gooden	.10
20	Mark Gubicza	.10
21	Mel Hall	.10
22	Terry Harper	.10
23	Von Hayes	.10
24	Rickey Henderson	.50
25	Tom Henke	.10
26	Willie Hernandez	.10
27	Ted Higuera	.10
28	Rick Honeycutt	.10
29	Kent Hrbek	.08
30	Wally Joyner	.10
31	Charlie Kerfeld	.10
32	Fred Lynn	.10
33	Don Mattingly	.85
34	Tim Raines	.10
35	Dennis Rasmussen	.10
36	Johnny Ray	.10
37	Jim Rice	.25
38	Pete Rose	1.00
39	Lee Smith	.10
40	Cory Snyder	.10
41	Darryl Strawberry	.10
42	Kent Tekulve	.10
43	Willie Wilson	.10
44	Bobby Witt	.10

Game Winners

The 1987 Fleer "Baseball's Game Winners" boxed set was produced for distribution through Bi-Mart Discount Drug, Pay'n-Save, Mott's 5 & 10, M.E. Moses, and Winn's stores. Cards have a light blue border with the player's name and game winning RBI or games-won

statistics in a yellow oval band at the top. Backs are similar to the regular-issue 1987 Fleer, with full professional stats. Included with the boxed set were six team logo stickers.

		NM/M
Complete Set (44):		4.00
Common Player:		.10
1	Harold Baines	.10
2	Don Baylor	.10
3	George Bell	.10
4	Tony Bernazard	.10
5	Wade Boggs	.75
6	George Brett	.85
7	Hubie Brooks	.10
8	Jose Canseco	.50
9	Gary Carter	.60
10	Roger Clemens	.85
11	Eric Davis	.10
12	Glenn Davis	.10
13	Shawon Dunston	.10
14	Mark Eichhorn	.10
15	Gary Gaetti	.10
16	Steve Garvey	.15
17	Kirk Gibson	.10
18	Dwight Gooden	.10
19	Von Hayes	.10
20	Willie Hernandez	.10
21	Ted Higuera	.10
22	Wally Joyner	.10
23	Bob Knepper	.10
24	Mike Krukow	.10
25	Jeff Leonard	.10
26	Don Mattingly	.85
27	Kirk McCaskill	.10
28	Kevin McReynolds	.10
29	Jim Morrison	.10
30	Dale Murphy	.15
31	Pete O'Brien	.10
32	Bob Ojeda	.10
33	Larry Parrish	.10
34	Ken Phelps	.10
35	Dennis Rasmussen	.10
36	Ernest Riles	.10
37	Cal Ripken, Jr.	1.00
38	Ron Robinson	.10
39	Steve Sax	.10
40	Mike Schmidt	.85
41	John Tudor	.10
42	Fernando Valenzuela	.10
43	Mike Witt	.10
44	Curt Young	.10

Hottest Stars

The "Baseball's Hottest Stars" set was produced by Fleer for the Revco Drug Store chain. Measuring the standard 2-1/2" x 3-1/2", the cards feature full-color photos surrounded by a red, white and blue border. Card backs are printed in red, white and black and contain the player's lifetime professional statistics. The set was sold in a special cardboard box with six team logo stickers.

		NM/M
Unopened Set (44):		45.00
Complete Set (44):		25.00
Common Player:		.10
1	Joaquin Andujar	.10
2	Harold Baines	.10
3	Kevin Bass	.10
4	Don Baylor	.10
5	Barry Bonds	20.00
6	George Brett	1.00

7	Tom Brunansky	.10
8	Brett Butler	.10
9	Jose Canseco	.60
10	Roger Clemens	1.00
11	Ron Darling	.10
12	Eric Davis	.10
13	Andre Dawson	.25
14	Doug DeCinces	.10
15	Leon Durham	.10
16	Mark Eichhorn	.10
17	Scott Garrelts	.10
18	Dwight Gooden	.10
19	Dave Henderson	.10
20	Rickey Henderson	.60
21	Keith Hernandez	.10
22	Ted Higuera	.10
23	Bob Horner	.10
24	Pete Incaviglia	.10
25	Wally Joyner	.10
26	Mark Langston	.10
27	Don Mattingly	1.00
28	Dale Murphy	.20
29	Kirk McCaskill	.10
30	Willie McGee	.10
31	Dave Righetti	.10
32	Pete Rose	1.50
33	Bruce Ruffin	.10
34	Steve Sax	.10
35	Mike Schmidt	1.00
36	Larry Sheets	.10
37	Eric Show	.10
38	Dave Smith	.10
39	Cory Snyder	.10
40	Frank Tanana	.10
41	Alan Trammell	.10
42	Reggie Williams	.10
43	Mookie Wilson	.10
44	Todd Worrell	.10

League Leaders

For a second year, Fleer produced a 44-card "League Leaders" set for Walgreens. The card fronts feature a border style which is identical to that used in 1986. However, a trapezoidal shaped full-color player photo is placed diagonally on the front. "1987 Fleer League Leaders" appears in the upper left corner of the front although nowhere on the card does it state in which pitching, hitting or fielding department was the player a league leader. Backs are printed in red and blue on white stock. The cards in the boxed set are the standard 2-1/2" x 3-1/2" size.

		NM/M
Complete Set (44):		4.00
Common Player:		.10
1	Jesse Barfield	.10
2	Mike Boddicker	.10
3	Wade Boggs	.65
4	Phil Bradley	.10
5	George Brett	.85
6	Hubie Brooks	.10
7	Chris Brown	.10
8	Jose Canseco	.50
9	Joe Carter	.10
10	Roger Clemens	.85
11	Vince Coleman	.10
12	Joe Cowley	.10
13	Kal Daniels	.10
14	Glenn Davis	.10
15	Jody Davis	.10
16	Darrell Evans	.10
17	Dwight Evans	.10
18	John Franco	.10
19	Julio Franco	.10
20	Dwight Gooden	.10
21	Goose Gossage	.10
22	Tom Herr	.10
23	Ted Higuera	.10
24	Bob Horner	.10
25	Pete Incaviglia	.10
26	Wally Joyner	.10
27	Dave Kingman	.10
28	Don Mattingly	.85
29	Willie McGee	.10
30	Donnie Moore	.10
31	Keith Moreland	.10
32	Eddie Murray	.60
33	Mike Pagliarulo	.10
34	Larry Parrish	.10
35	Tony Pena	.10
36	Kirby Puckett	.65

37	Pete Rose	1.00
38	Juan Samuel	.10
39	Ryne Sandberg	.65
40	Mike Schmidt	.85
41	Darryl Strawberry	.10
42	Greg Walker	.10
43	Bob Welch	.10
44	Todd Worrell	.10

Limited Edition

For the third straight year, Fleer produced a Limited Edition set for the McCrory's store chain and its affiliates. The cards are the standard 2-1/2" x 3-1/2" and feature light blue borders at the top and bottom and a diagonal red and white border running along both sides. The set was issued in a specially prepared cardboard box, along with six team logo stickers.

		NM/M
Complete Set (44):		4.00
Common Player:		.10
1	Floyd Bannister	.10
2	Marty Barrett	.10
3	Steve Bedrosian	.10
4	George Bell	.10
5	George Brett	.85
6	Jose Canseco	.40
7	Joe Carter	.10
8	Will Clark	.10
9	Roger Clemens	.85
10	Vince Coleman	.10
11	Glenn Davis	.10
12	Mike Davis	.10
13	Len Dykstra	.10
14	John Franco	.10
15	Julio Franco	.10
16	Steve Garvey	.25
17	Kirk Gibson	.10
18	Dwight Gooden	.10
19	Tony Gwynn	.65
20	Keith Hernandez	.10
21	Teddy Higuera	.10
22	Kent Hrbek	.10
23	Wally Joyner	.10
24	Mike Krukow	.10
25	Mike Marshall	.10
26	Don Mattingly	.85
27	Oddibe McDowell	.10
28	Jack Morris	.10
29	Lloyd Moseby	.10
30	Dale Murphy	.20
31	Eddie Murray	.50
32	Tony Pena	.10
33	Jim Presley	.10
34	Jeff Reardon	.10
35	Jim Rice	.25
36	Pete Rose	1.00
37	Mike Schmidt	.85
38	Mike Scott	.10
39	Lee Smith	.10
40	Lonnie Smith	.10
41	Gary Ward	.10
42	Dave Winfield	.50
43	Todd Worrell	.10
44	Robin Yount	.50

Limited Edition Box Bottom

These special cards were printed on the bottom of retail boxes of Fleer's "Limited Edition" boxed sets. The box-bottom cards are in the same format as the boxed cards, with red, white and blue borders. Backs are also similar in design to the regular-issue cards, carrying player data and stats.

		NM/M
Complete Panel:		2.00
Complete Set (6):		2.00
Common Player:		.50
C1	Ron Darling	.50
C2	Bill Buckner	.50
C3	John Candelaria	.50
C4	Jack Clark	.50
C5	Bret Saberhagen	.50
C6	Houston Astros Logo	.25

Mini

Continuing with an idea originated the previous year, the Fleer "Classic Miniatures" set consists of

Cecil Cooper

120 cards that measure 1-13/16" x 2-9/16". The cards are identical in design to the regular-issue set, but use completely different photos. The set was issued in a specially prepared collectors box along with 18 team logo stickers. The mini set was available only through hobby dealers.

		NM/M
Complete Set (120):		4.00
Common Player:		.05
1	Don Aase	.05
2	Joaquin Andujar	.05
3	Harold Baines	.05
4	Jesse Barfield	.05
5	Kevin Bass	.05
6	Don Baylor	.05
7	George Bell	.05
8	Tony Bernazard	.05
9	Bert Blyleven	.05
10	Wade Boggs	.65
11	Phil Bradley	.05
12	Sid Bream	.05
13	George Brett	.85
14	Hubie Brooks	.05
15	Chris Brown	.05
16	Tom Candiotti	.05
17	Jose Canseco	.40
18	Gary Carter	.50
19	Joe Carter	.05
20	Roger Clemens	.85
21	Vince Coleman	.05
22	Cecil Cooper	.05
23	Ron Darling	.05
24	Alvin Davis	.05
25	Chili Davis	.05
26	Eric Davis	.05
27	Glenn Davis	.05
28	Mike Davis	.05
29	Doug DeCinces	.05
30	Rob Deer	.05
31	Jim Deshaies	.05
32	Bo Diaz	.05
33	Richard Dotson	.05
34	Brian Downing	.05
35	Shawon Dunston	.05
36	Mark Eichhorn	.05
37	Dwight Evans	.05
38	Tony Fernandez	.05
39	Julio Franco	.05
40	Gary Gaetti	.05
41	Andres Galarraga	.05
42	Scott Garrelts	.05
43	Steve Garvey	.15
44	Kirk Gibson	.05
45	Dwight Gooden	.05
46	Ken Griffey	.05
47	Mark Gubicza	.05
48	Ozzie Guillen	.05
49	Bill Gullickson	.05
50	Tony Gwynn	.65
51	Von Hayes	.05
52	Rickey Henderson	.50
53	Keith Hernandez	.05
54	Willie Hernandez	.05
55	Ted Higuera	.05
56	Charlie Hough	.05
57	Kent Hrbek	.05
58	Pete Incaviglia	.05
59	Wally Joyner	.05
60	Bob Knepper	.05
61	Mike Krukow	.05
62	Mark Langston	.05
63	Carney Lansford	.05
64	Jim Lindeman	.05
65	Bill Madlock	.05
66	Don Mattingly	.85
67	Kirk McCaskill	.05
68	Lance McCullers	.05
69	Keith Moreland	.05
70	Jack Morris	.05
71	Jim Morrison	.05
72	Lloyd Moseby	.05
73	Jerry Mumphrey	.05
74	Dale Murphy	.15
75	Eddie Murray	.50
76	Pete O'Brien	.05
77	Bob Ojeda	.05
78	Jesse Orosco	.05
79	Dan Pasqua	.05
80	Dave Parker	.05
81	Larry Parrish	.05
82	Jim Presley	.05
83	Kirby Puckett	.65
84	Dan Quisenberry	.05
85	Tim Raines	.05
86	Dennis Rasmussen	.05
87	Johnny Ray	.05
88	Jeff Reardon	.05
89	Jim Rice	.25
90	Dave Righetti	.05
91	Earnest Riles	.05
92	Cal Ripken, Jr.	1.50
93	Ron Robinson	.05
94	Juan Samuel	.05
95	Ryne Sandberg	.65
96	Steve Sax	.05
97	Mike Schmidt	.85
98	Ken Schrom	.05
99	Mike Scott	.05
100	Ruben Sierra	.05
101	Lee Smith	.05
102	Ozzie Smith	.65
103	Cory Snyder	.05
104	Kent Tekulve	.05
105	Andres Thomas	.05
106	Rob Thompson	.05
107	Alan Trammell	.05
108	John Tudor	.05
109	Fernando Valenzuela	.05
110	Greg Walker	.05
111	Mitch Webster	.05
112	Lou Whitaker	.05
113	Frank White	.05
114	Reggie Williams	.05
115	Glenn Wilson	.05
116	Willie Wilson	.05
117	Dave Winfield	.50
118	Mike Witt	.05
119	Todd Worrell	.05
120	Floyd Youmans	.05

Record Setters

CHRIS BROWN
GIANTS • THIRD BASE
FLEER RECORD SETTERS

Produced by Fleer for the Eckerd Drug chain, the Record Setters set contains 44 cards in standard 2-1/2" x 3-1/2" size. Although the set is titled "Record Setters," the actual records the players have set is not specified anywhere on the cards. Given that several players included in the set were young prospects, a better title for those cards might have been "Possible Record Setters." The set came housed in a special cardboard box with six team logo stickers.

		NM/M
Complete Set (44):		4.00
Common Player:		.10
1	George Brett	.85
2	Chris Brown	.10
3	Jose Canseco	.40
4	Roger Clemens	.85
5	Alvin Davis	.10
6	Shawon Dunston	.10
7	Tony Fernandez	.10
8	Carlton Fisk	.45
9	Gary Gaetti	.10
10	Gene Garber	.10
11	Rich Gedman	.10
12	Dwight Gooden	.10
13	Ozzie Guillen	.10
14	Bill Gullickson	.10
15	Billy Hatcher	.10
16	Orel Hershiser	.10
17	Wally Joyner	.10
18	Ray Knight	.10
19	Craig Lefferts	.10
20	Don Mattingly	.85
21	Kevin Mitchell	.10
22	Lloyd Moseby	.10
23	Dale Murphy	.15
24	Eddie Murray	.45
25	Phil Niekro	.10
26	Ben Oglivie	.10
27	Jesse Orosco	.10
28	Joe Orsulak	.10
29	Larry Parrish	.10
30	Tim Raines	.10
31	Shane Rawley	.10
32	Dave Righetti	.10
33	Pete Rose	1.00
34	Steve Sax	.10
35	Mike Schmidt	.85
36	Mike Scott	.10
37	Don Sutton	.30
38	Alan Trammell	.10
39	John Tudor	.10
40	Gary Ward	.10
41	Lou Whitaker	.10
42	Willie Wilson	.10
43	Todd Worrell	.10
44	Floyd Youmans	.10

Star Stickers

ROGER CLEMENS

The 1987 Fleer Star Stickers set contains 132 cards which become stickers if the back is bent and peeled off. As in the previous year, the card backs are identical, save the numbering system, to the regular-issue cards. The cards measure 2-1/2" x 3-1/2" and were sold in wax packs with team logo stickers. The fronts have a green border with a red and white banner wrapped across the upper left corner and the sides. The backs are printed in green and yellow.

		NM/M
Complete Set (132):		6.00
Common Player:		.05
Wax Pack (5):		.50
Wax Box (36):		12.00
1	Don Aase	.05
2	Harold Baines	.05
3	Floyd Bannister	.05
4	Jesse Barfield	.05
5	Marty Barrett	.05
6	Kevin Bass	.05
7	Don Baylor	.05
8	Steve Bedrosian	.05
9	George Bell	.05
10	Bert Blyleven	.05
11	Mike Boddicker	.05
12	Wade Boggs	.65
13	Phil Bradley	.05
14	George Brett	.85
15	Hubie Brooks	.05
16	Tom Brunansky	.05
17	Tom Candiotti	.05
18	Jose Canseco	.40
19	Gary Carter	.05
20	Joe Carter	.05
21	Will Clark	.05
22	Mark Clear	.05
23	Roger Clemens	.85
24	Vince Coleman	.05
25	Jose Cruz	.05
26	Ron Darling	.05
27	Alvin Davis	.05
28	Chili Davis	.05
29	Eric Davis	.05
30	Glenn Davis	.05
31	Mike Davis	.05
32	Andre Dawson	.25
33	Doug DeCinces	.05
34	Brian Downing	.05
35	Shawon Dunston	.05
36	Mark Eichhorn	.05
37	Dwight Evans	.05
38	Tony Fernandez	.05
39	Bob Forsch	.05
40	John Franco	.05
41	Julio Franco	.05
42	Gary Gaetti	.05
43	Gene Garber	.05
44	Scott Garrelts	.05
45	Steve Garvey	.20
46	Kirk Gibson	.05
47	Dwight Gooden	.05
48	Ken Griffey	.05
49	Ozzie Guillen	.05
50	Bill Gullickson	.05
51	Tony Gwynn	.65
52	Mel Hall	.05
53	Greg Harris	.05
54	Von Hayes	.05
55	Rickey Henderson	.50
56	Tom Henke	.05
57	Keith Hernandez	.05
58	Willie Hernandez	.05
59	Ted Higuera	.05
60	Bob Horner	.05
61	Charlie Hough	.05
62	Jay Howell	.05
63	Kent Hrbek	.05
64	Bruce Hurst	.05
65	Pete Incaviglia	.05
66	Bob James	.05
67	Wally Joyner	.05
68	Mike Krukow	.05
70	Mark Langston	.05
71	Carney Lansford	.05
72	Fred Lynn	.05
73	Bill Madlock	.05
74	Don Mattingly	.85
75	Kirk McCaskill	.05
76	Lance McCullers	.05
77	Oddibe McDowell	.05
78	Paul Molitor	.50
79	Keith Moreland	.05
80	Jack Morris	.05
81	Jim Morrison	.05
82	Jerry Mumphrey	.05
83	Dale Murphy	.20
84	Eddie Murray	.50
85	Ben Oglivie	.05
86	Bob Ojeda	.05
87	Jesse Orosco	.05
88	Dave Parker	.05
89	Larry Parrish	.05
90	Tony Pena	.05
91	Jim Presley	.05
92	Kirby Puckett	.65
93	Dan Quisenberry	.05
94	Tim Raines	.05
95	Dennis Rasmussen	.05
96	Shane Rawley	.05
97	Johnny Ray	.05
98	Jeff Reardon	.05
99	Jim Rice	.25
100	Dave Righetti	.05
101	Cal Ripken, Jr.	2.00
102	Pete Rose	1.00
103	Nolan Ryan	2.00
104	Juan Samuel	.05
105	Ryne Sandberg	.65
106	Steve Sax	.05
107	Mike Schmidt	.85
108	Mike Scott	.05
109	Dave Smith	.05
110	Lee Smith	.05
111	Lonnie Smith	.05
112	Ozzie Smith	.65
113	Cory Snyder	.05
114	Darryl Strawberry	.05
115	Don Sutton	.45
116	Kent Tekulve	.05
117	Gorman Thomas	.05
118	Alan Trammell	.05
119	John Tudor	.05
120	Fernando Valenzuela	.05
121	Bob Welch	.05
122	Lou Whitaker	.05
123	Frank White	.05
124	Reggie Williams	.05
125	Willie Wilson	.05
126	Dave Winfield	.50
127	Mike Witt	.05
128	Todd Worrell	.05
129	Curt Young	.05
130	Robin Yount	.50
131	Checklist (Jose Canseco, Don Mattingly)	
132	Checklist (Bo Jackson, Eric Davis)	

Star Stickers Box Panels

WADE BOGGS

Fleer issued on the bottoms of its Fleer Star Stickers wax pack boxes six player cards plus two team logo/checklist cards. The cards, which measure 2-1/2" x 3-1/2", are numbered S-1 through S-8, and are identical in design to the Star Stickers.

		NM/M
Complete Panel Set (2):		2.50
Complete Singles Set (8):		2.50
Common Single Player:		.10
Panel		2.00
2	Wade Boggs	.75
3	Bert Blyleven	.10
6	Phillies Logo	.05
8	Don Mattingly	1.50
Panel		1.00
1	Tigers Logo	.05
4	Jose Cruz	.10
5	Glenn Davis	.10
8	Bob Horner	.05

1988 Fleer

A clean, uncluttered look was featured in the 1988 Fleer set. Cards in the standard 2-1/2" x 3-1/2" format feature blue and red diagonal lines on a white background. Player identification and team logo ap-

Alan Trammell
SHORTSTOP

pears at top. Backs include personal information and career statistics, plus a new feature called "At Their Best." This feature graphically shows a player's pitching or hitting statistics for home and road games and how he fared during day games as opposed to night contests. The set includes 19 special cards (#622-640) and 12 "Major League Prospects" cards.

		NM/M
Retail Factory Set (672):		12.00
Hobby Factory Set (672):		10.00
Complete Set (660):		8.00
Common Player:		.05
Wax Pack (15):		.75
Wax Box (36):		12.00
Cello Pack (28):		1.25
Cello Box (24):		16.00
1	Keith Atherton	.05
2	Don Baylor	.05
3	Juan Berenguer	.05
4	Bert Blyleven	.10
5	Tom Brunansky	.05
6	Randy Bush	.05
7	Steve Carlton	.50
8	Mark Davidson RC	.05
9	George Frazier	.05
10	Gary Gaetti	.05
11	Greg Gagne	.05
12	Dan Gladden	.05
13	Kent Hrbek	.05
14	Gene Larkin RC	.05
15	Tim Laudner	.05
16	Steve Lombardozzi	.05
17	Al Newman	.05
18	Joe Niekro	.05
19	Kirby Puckett	.65
20	Jeff Reardon	.05
21a	Dan Schatzader (Incorrect spelling.)	.10
21b	Dan Schatzeder (Correct spelling.)	.05
22	Roy Smalley	.05
23	Mike Smithson	.05
24	Les Straker RC	.05
25	Frank Viola	.05
26	Jack Clark	.05
27	Vince Coleman	.05
28	Danny Cox	.05
29	Bill Dawley	.05
30	Ken Dayley	.05
31	Doug DeCinces	.05
32	Curt Ford	.05
33	Bob Forsch	.05
34	David Green	.05
35	Tom Herr	.05
36	Ricky Horton	.05
37	Lance Johnson RC	.25
38	Steve Lake	.05
39	Jim Lindeman	.05
40	Joe Magrane RC	.10
41	Greg Mathews	.05
42	Willie McGee	.05
43	John Morris	.05
44	Jose Oquendo	.05
45	Tony Pena	.05
46	Terry Pendleton	.05
47	Ozzie Smith	.65
48	John Tudor	.05
49	Lee Tunnell	.05
50	Todd Worrell	.05
51	Doyle Alexander	.05
52	Dave Bergman	.05
53	Tom Brookens	.05
54	Darrell Evans	.05
55	Kirk Gibson	.05
56	Mike Heath	.05
57	Mike Henneman	.05
58	Willie Hernandez	.05
59	Larry Herndon	.05
60	Eric King	.05
61	Chet Lemon	.05
62	Scott Lusader RC	.05
63	Bill Madlock	.05
64	Jack Morris	.05
65	Jim Morrison	.05
66	Matt Nokes	.05
67	Dan Petry	.05
68a	Jeff Robinson RC (Born 12-13-60 on back.)	.25
68b	Jeff Robinson RC (Born 12/14/61 on back.)	.10
69	Pat Sheridan	.05
70	Nate Snell	.05

#	Player	Price
71	Frank Tanana	.05
72	Walt Terrell	.05
73	Mark Thurmond	.05
74	Alan Trammell	.05
75	Lou Whitaker	.05
76	Mike Aldrete	.05
77	Bob Brenly	.05
78	Will Clark	.05
79	Chili Davis	.05
80	Kelly Downs	.05
81	Dave Dravecky	.05
82	Scott Garrelts	.05
83	Atlee Hammaker	.05
84	Dave Henderson	.05
85	Mike Krukow	.05
86	Mike LaCoss	.05
87	Craig Lefferts	.05
88	Jeff Leonard	.05
89	Candy Maldonado	.05
90	Ed Milner	.05
91	Bob Melvin	.05
92	Kevin Mitchell	.05
93	Jon Perlman RC	.05
94	Rick Reuschel	.05
95	Don Robinson	.05
96	Chris Speier	.05
97	Harry Spilman	.05
98	Robbie Thompson	.05
99	Jose Uribe	.05
100	Mark Wasinger RC	.05
101	Matt Williams	.05
102	Jesse Barfield	.05
103	George Bell	.05
104	Juan Beniquez	.05
105	John Cerutti	.05
106	Jim Clancy	.05
107	Rob Ducey RC	.05
108	Mark Eichhorn	.05
109	Tony Fernandez	.05
110	Cecil Fielder	.05
111	Kelly Gruber	.05
112	Tom Henke	.05
113	Garth Iorg (Iorg)	.05
114	Jimmy Key	.05
115	Rick Leach	.05
116	Manny Lee	.05
117	Nelson Liriano RC	.05
118	Fred McGriff	.05
119	Lloyd Moseby	.05
120	Rance Mulliniks	.05
121	Jeff Musselman	.05
122	Jose Nunez RC	.05
123	Dave Stieb	.05
124	Willie Upshaw	.05
125	Duane Ward RC	.05
126	Ernie Whitt	.05
127	Rick Aguilera	.05
128	Wally Backman	.05
129	Mark Carreon RC	.10
130	Gary Carter	.50
131	David Cone RC	.05
132	Ron Darling	.05
133	Len Dykstra	.05
134	Sid Fernandez	.05
135	Dwight Gooden	.05
136	Keith Hernandez	.05
137	Gregg Jefferies RC	.50
138	Howard Johnson	.05
139	Terry Leach	.05
140	Barry Lyons RC	.05
141	Dave Magadan	.05
142	Roger McDowell	.05
143	Kevin McReynolds	.05
144	Keith Miller RC	.05
145	John Mitchell RC	.05
146	Randy Myers	.05
147	Bob Ojeda	.05
148	Jesse Orosco	.05
149	Rafael Santana	.05
150	Doug Sisk	.05
151	Darryl Strawberry	.05
152	Tim Teufel	.05
153	Gene Walter	.05
154	Mookie Wilson	.05
155	Jay Aldrich RC	.05
156	Chris Bosio	.05
157	Glenn Braggs	.05
158	Greg Brock	.05
159	Juan Castillo	.05
160	Mark Clear	.05
161	Cecil Cooper	.05
162	Chuck Crim RC	.05
163	Rob Deer	.05
164	Mike Felder	.05
165	Jim Gantner	.05
166	Ted Higuera	.05
167	Steve Kiefer	.05
168	Rick Manning	.05
169	Paul Molitor	.50
170	Juan Nieves	.05
171	Dan Plesac	.05
172	Earnest Riles	.05
173	Bill Schroeder	.05
174	Steve Stanicek RC	.05
175	B.J. Surhoff	.05
176	Dale Sveum	.05
177	Bill Wegman	.05
178	Robin Yount	.50
179	Hubie Brooks	.05
180	Tim Burke	.05
181	Casey Candaele	.05
182	Mike Fitzgerald	.05
183	Tom Foley	.05
184	Andres Galarraga	.05
185	Neal Heaton	.05
186	Wallace Johnson	.05
187	Vance Law	.05
188	Dennis Martinez	.05

#	Player	Price
189	Bob McClure	.05
190	Andy McGaffigan	.05
191	Reid Nichols	.05
192	Pascual Perez	.05
193	Tim Raines	.05
194	Jeff Reed	.05
195	Bob Sebra	.05
196	Bryn Smith	.05
197	Randy St. Claire	.05
198	Tim Wallach	.05
199	Mitch Webster	.05
200	Herm Winningham	.05
201	Floyd Youmans	.05
202	Brad Arnsberg RC	.05
203	Rick Cerone	.05
204	Pat Clements	.05
205	Henry Cotto	.05
206	Mike Easler	.05
207	Ron Guidry	.10
208	Bill Gullickson	.05
209	Rickey Henderson	.50
210	Charles Hudson	.05
211	Tommy John	.10
212	Roberto Kelly RC	.25
213	Ron Kittle	.05
214	Don Mattingly	.75
215	Bobby Meacham	.05
216	Mike Pagliarulo	.05
217	Dan Pasqua	.05
218	Willie Randolph	.05
219	Rick Rhoden	.05
220	Dave Righetti	.05
221	Jerry Royster	.05
222	Tim Stoddard	.05
223	Wayne Tolleson	.05
224	Gary Ward	.05
225	Claudell Washington	.05
226	Dave Winfield	.50
227	Buddy Bell	.05
228	Tom Browning	.05
229	Dave Concepcion	.05
230	Kal Daniels	.05
231	Eric Davis	.05
232	Bo Diaz	.05
233	Nick Esasky	.05
234	John Franco	.05
235	Guy Hoffman	.05
236	Tom Hume	.05
237	Tracy Jones	.05
238	Bill Landrum RC	.05
239	Barry Larkin	.05
240	Terry McGriff RC	.05
241	Rob Murphy	.05
242	Ron Oester	.05
243	Dave Parker	.05
244	Pat Perry	.05
245	Ted Power	.05
246	Dennis Rasmussen	.05
247	Ron Robinson	.05
248	Kurt Stillwell	.05
249	Jeff Treadway RC	.05
250	Frank Williams	.05
251	Steve Balboni	.05
252	Bud Black	.05
253	Thad Bosley	.05
254	George Brett	.75
255	John Davis RC	.05
256	Steve Farr	.05
257	Gene Garber	.05
258	Jerry Gleaton	.05
259	Mark Gubicza	.05
260	Bo Jackson	.10
261	Danny Jackson	.05
262	Ross Jones	.05
263	Charlie Leibrandt	.05
264	Bill Pecota RC	.05
265	Melido Perez RC	.05
266	Jamie Quirk	.05
267	Dan Quisenberry	.05
268	Bret Saberhagen	.05
269	Angel Salazar	.05
270	Kevin Seitzer	.05
271	Danny Tartabull	.05
272	Gary Thurman RC	.05
273	Frank White	.05
274	Willie Wilson	.05
275	Tony Bernazard	.05
276	Jose Canseco	.30
277	Mike Davis	.05
278	Storm Davis	.05
279	Dennis Eckersley	.40
280	Alfredo Griffin	.05
281	Rick Honeycutt	.05
282	Jay Howell	.05
283	Reggie Jackson	.65
284	Dennis Lamp	.05
285	Carney Lansford	.05
286	Mark McGwire	.85
287	Dwayne Murphy	.05
288	Gene Nelson	.05
289	Steve Ontiveros	.05
290	Tony Phillips	.05
291	Eric Plunk	.05
292	Luis Polonia	.15
293	Rick Rodriguez RC	.05
294	Terry Steinbach	.05
295	Dave Stewart	.05
296	Curt Young	.05
297	Luis Aguayo	.05
298	Steve Bedrosian	.05
299	Jeff Calhoun	.05
300	Don Carman	.05
301	Todd Frohwirth RC	.05
302	Greg Gross	.05
303	Kevin Gross	.05
304	Von Hayes	.05
305	Keith Hughes RC	.05
306	Mike Jackson RC	.05

#	Player	Price
307	Chris James	.05
308	Steve Jeltz	.05
309	Mike Maddux	.05
310	Lance Parrish	.05
311	Shane Rawley	.05
312	Wally Ritchie RC	.05
313	Bruce Ruffin	.05
314	Juan Samuel	.05
315	Mike Schmidt	.75
316	Rick Schu	.05
317	Jeff Stone	.05
318	Kent Tekulve	.05
319	Milt Thompson	.05
320	Glenn Wilson	.05
321	Rafael Belliard	.05
322	Barry Bonds	1.00
323	Bobby Bonilla	.05
324	Sid Bream	.05
325	John Cangelosi	.05
326	Mike Diaz	.05
327	Doug Drabek	.05
328	Mike Dunne RC	.05
329	Brian Fisher	.05
330	Brett Gideon RC	.05
331	Terry Harper	.05
332	Bob Kipper	.05
333	Mike LaValliere	.05
334	Jose Lind RC	.15
335	Junior Ortiz	.05
336	Vicente Palacios RC	.05
337	Bob Patterson RC	.05
338	Al Pedrique RC	.05
339	R.J. Reynolds	.05
340	John Smiley	.05
341	Andy Van Slyke	.05
342	Bob Walk	.05
343	Marty Barrett	.05
344	Todd Benzinger RC	.05
345	Wade Boggs	.65
346	Tom Bolton RC	.05
347	Oil Can Boyd	.05
348	Ellis Burks	.05
349	Roger Clemens	.75
350	Steve Crawford	.05
351	Dwight Evans	.05
352	Wes Gardner RC	.05
353	Rich Gedman	.05
354	Mike Greenwell	.05
355	Sam Horn RC	.05
356	Bruce Hurst	.05
357	John Marzano RC	.05
358	Al Nipper	.05
359	Spike Owen	.05
360	Jody Reed RC	.15
361	Jim Rice	.20
362	Ed Romero	.05
363	Kevin Romine RC	.05
364	Joe Sambito	.05
365	Calvin Schiraldi	.05
366	Jeff Sellers	.05
367	Bob Stanley	.05
368	Scott Bankhead	.05
369	Phil Bradley	.05
370	Scott Bradley	.05
371	Mickey Brantley	.05
372	Mike Campbell RC	.05
373	Alvin Davis	.05
374	Lee Guetterman	.05
375	Dave Hengel RC	.05
376	Mike Kingery	.05
377	Mark Langston	.05
378	Edgar Martinez RC	1.00
379	Mike Moore	.05
380	Mike Morgan	.05
381	John Moses	.05
382	Donnell Nixon RC	.05
383	Edwin Nunez	.05
384	Ken Phelps	.05
385	Jim Presley	.05
386	Rey Quinones	.05
387	Jerry Reed	.05
388	Harold Reynolds	.05
389	Dave Valle	.05
390	Bill Wilkinson RC	.05
391	Harold Baines	.05
392	Floyd Bannister	.05
393	Daryl Boston	.05
394	Ivan Calderon	.05
395	Jose DeLeon	.05
396	Richard Dotson	.05
397	Carlton Fisk	.50
398	Ozzie Guillen	.05
399	Ron Hassey	.05
400	Donnie Hill	.05
401	Bob James	.05
402	Dave LaPoint	.05
403	Bill Lindsey RC	.05
404	Bill Long RC	.05
405	Steve Lyons	.05
406	Fred Manrique RC	.05
407	Jack McDowell RC	.25
408	Gary Redus	.05
409	Ray Searage	.05
410	Bobby Thigpen	.05
411	Greg Walker	.05
412	Kenny Williams RC	.05
413	Jim Winn	.05
414	Jody Davis	.05
415	Andre Dawson	.25
416	Brian Dayett	.05
417	Bob Dernier	.05
418	Frank DiPino	.05
419	Shawon Dunston	.05
420	Leon Durham	.05
421	Les Lancaster RC	.05
422	Ed Lynch	.05
423	Greg Maddux	.75
424	Dave Martinez RC	.05

#	Player	Price
425a	Keith Moreland (Bunting, photo actually Jody Davis.)	2.00
425b	Keith Moreland (Standing upright, correct photo.)	.05
426	Jamie Moyer	.05
427	Jerry Mumphrey	.05
428	Paul Noce RC	.05
429	Rafael Palmeiro	.40
430	Wade Rowdon RC	.05
431	Ryne Sandberg	.65
432	Scott Sanderson	.05
433	Lee Smith	.05
434	Jim Sundberg	.05
435	Rick Sutcliffe	.05
436	Manny Trillo	.05
437	Juan Agosto	.05
438	Larry Andersen	.05
439	Alan Ashby	.05
440	Kevin Bass	.05
441	Ken Caminiti RC	.25
442	Rocky Childress RC	.05
443	Jose Cruz	.05
444	Danny Darwin	.05
445	Glenn Davis	.05
446	Jim Deshaies	.05
447	Bill Doran	.05
448	Ty Gainey	.05
449	Billy Hatcher	.05
450	Jeff Heathcock	.05
451	Bob Knepper	.05
452	Rob Mallicoat RC	.05
453	Dave Meads RC	.05
454	Craig Reynolds	.05
455	Nolan Ryan	1.00
456	Mike Scott	.05
457	Dave Smith	.05
458	Denny Walling	.05
459	Robbie Wine RC	.05
460	Gerald Young RC	.05
461	Bob Brower	.05
462a	Jerry Browne (White player, photo actually Bob Brower.)	2.00
462b	Jerry Browne (Black player, correct photo.)	.05
463	Steve Buechele	.05
464	Edwin Correa	.05
465	Cecil Espy RC	.05
466	Scott Fletcher	.05
467	Jose Guzman	.05
468	Greg Harris	.05
469	Charlie Hough	.05
470	Pete Incaviglia	.05
471	Paul Kilgus RC	.05
472	Mike Loynd	.05
473	Oddibe McDowell	.05
474	Dale Mohorcic	.05
475	Pete O'Brien	.05
476	Larry Parrish	.05
477	Geno Petralli	.05
478	Jeff Russell	.05
479	Ruben Sierra	.05
480	Mike Stanley	.05
481	Curtis Wilkerson	.05
482	Mitch Williams	.05
483	Bobby Witt	.05
484	Tony Armas	.05
485	Bob Boone	.05
486	Bill Buckner	.05
487	DeWayne Buice RC	.05
488	Brian Downing	.05
489	Chuck Finley	.05
490	Willie Fraser	.05
491	Jack Howell	.05
492	Ruppert Jones	.05
493	Wally Joyner	.05
494	Jack Lazorko	.05
495	Gary Lucas	.05
496	Kirk McCaskill	.05
497	Mark McLemore	.05
498	Darrell Miller	.05
499	Greg Minton	.05
500	Donnie Moore	.05
501	Gus Polidor	.05
502	Johnny Ray	.05
503	Mark Ryal RC	.05
504	Dick Schofield	.05
505	Don Sutton	.40
506	Devon White	.05
507	Mike Witt	.05
508	Dave Anderson	.05
509	Tim Belcher RC	.05
510	Ralph Bryant	.05
511	Tim Crews RC	.15
512	Mike Devereaux RC	.10
513	Mariano Duncan	.05
514	Pedro Guerrero	.05
515	Jeff Hamilton RC	.05
516	Mickey Hatcher	.05
517	Brad Havens	.05
518	Orel Hershiser	.05
519	Shawn Hillegas RC	.05
520	Ken Howell	.05
521	Tim Leary	.05
522	Mike Marshall	.05
523	Steve Sax	.05
524	Mike Scioscia	.05
525	Mike Sharperson RC	.05
526	John Shelby	.05
527	Franklin Stubbs	.05
528	Fernando Valenzuela	.05
529	Bob Welch	.05
530	Matt Young	.05
531	Jim Acker	.05
532	Paul Assenmacher	.05
533	Jeff Blauser RC	.10
534	Joe Boever RC	.05

#	Player	Price
535	Martin Clary RC	.05
536	Kevin Coffman RC	.05
537	Jeff Dedmon	.05
538	Ron Gant RC	.50
539	Tom Glavine RC	2.00
540	Ken Griffey	.05
541	Al Hall	.05
542	Glenn Hubbard	.05
543	Dion James	.05
544	Dale Murphy	.20
545	Ken Oberkfell	.05
546	David Palmer	.05
547	Gerald Perry	.05
548	Charlie Puleo	.05
549	Ted Simmons	.05
550	Zane Smith	.05
551	Andres Thomas	.05
552	Ozzie Virgil	.05
553	Don Aase	.05
554	Jeff Ballard RC	.05
555	Eric Bell	.05
556	Mike Boddicker	.05
557	Ken Dixon	.05
558	Jim Dwyer	.05
559	Ken Gerhart	.05
560	Rene Gonzales RC	.05
561	Mike Griffin	.05
562	John Hayban (Habyan)	.05
563	Terry Kennedy	.05
564	Ray Knight	.05
565	Lee Lacy	.05
566	Fred Lynn	.05
567	Eddie Murray	.50
568	Tom Niedenfuer	.05
569	Bill Ripken RC	.05
570	Cal Ripken, Jr.	1.00
571	Dave Schmidt	.05
572	Larry Sheets	.05
573	Pete Stanicek RC	.05
574	Mark Williamson RC	.05
575	Mike Young	.05
576	Shawn Abner RC	.05
577	Greg Booker	.05
578	Chris Brown	.05
579	Keith Comstock RC	.05
580	Joey Cora RC	.05
581	Mark Davis	.05
582	Tim Flannery	.05
583	Goose Gossage	.05
584	Mark Grant	.05
585	Tony Gwynn	.65
586	Andy Hawkins	.05
587	Stan Jefferson	.05
588	Jimmy Jones	.05
589	John Kruk	.05
590	Shane Mack RC	.10
591	Carmelo Martinez	.05
592	Lance McCullers	.05
593	Eric Nolte RC	.05
594	Randy Ready	.05
595	Luis Salazar	.05
596	Benito Santiago	.05
597	Eric Show	.05
598	Garry Templeton	.05
599	Ed Whitson	.05
600	Scott Bailes	.05
601	Chris Bando	.05
602	Jay Bell RC	.50
603	Brett Butler	.05
604	Tom Candiotti	.05
605	Joe Carter	.05
606	Carmen Castillo	.05
607	Brian Dorsett RC	.05
608	John Farrell RC	.05
609	Julio Franco	.05
610	Mel Hall	.05
611	Tommy Hinzo RC	.05
612	Brook Jacoby	.05
613	Doug Jones RC	.05
614	Ken Schrom	.05
615	Cory Snyder	.05
616	Sammy Stewart	.05
617	Greg Swindell	.05
618	Pat Tabler	.05
619	Ed Vande Berg	.05
620	Eddie Williams RC	.05
621	Rich Yett	.05
622	Slugging Sophomores (Wally Joyner, Cory Snyder)	.10
623	Dominican Dynamite (George Bell, Pedro Guerrero)	.05
624	Oakland's Power Team (Jose Canseco, Mark McGwire)	.50
625	Classic Relief (Dan Plesac, Dave Righetti)	.05
626	All-Star Righties (Jack Morris, Bret Saberhagen, Mike Witt)	.05
627	Game Closers (Steve Bedrosian, John Franco)	.05
628	Masters of the Double Play (Ryne Sandberg, Ozzie Smith)	.50
629	Rookie Record Setter (Mark McGwire)	.50
630	Changing the Guard in Boston (Todd Benzinger, Ellis Burks, Mike Greenwell)	.10
631	N.L. Batting Champs (Tony Gwynn, Tim Raines)	.20
632	Pitching Magic (Orel Hershiser, Mike Scott)	.05

#	Player	Price
633	Big Bats At First (Mark McGwire, Pat Tabler)	.50
634	Hitting King and the Thief (Tony Gwynn, Vince Coleman)	.15
635	A.L. Slugging Shortstops (Tony Fernandez, Cal Ripken, Jr., Alan Trammell)	.40
636	Tried and True Sluggers (Gary Carter, Mike Schmidt)	.40
637	Crunch Time (Eric Davis)	.05
638	A.L. All-Stars (Matt Nokes, Kirby Puckett)	.25
639	N.L. All-Stars (Keith Hernandez, Dale Murphy)	.10
640	The "O's" Brothers (Bill Ripken, Cal Ripken, Jr.)	.50
641	Major League Prospects (Mark Grace RC, Darrin Jackson RC)	1.00
642	Major League Prospects (Damon Berryhill RC, Jeff Montgomery RC)	.20
643	Major League Prospects (Felix Fermin RC, Jessie Reid RC)	.05
644	Major League Prospects (Greg Myers RC, Greg Tabor RC)	.05
645	Major League Prospects (Jim Eppard RC, Joey Meyer RC)	.05
646	Major League Prospects (Adam Peterson RC, Randy Velarde RC)	.10
647	Major League Prospects (Chris Gwynn RC, Peter Smith RC)	.15
648	Major League Prospects (Greg Jelks RC, Tom Newell RC)	.05
649	Major League Prospects (Mario Diaz RC, Clay Parker RC)	.05
650	Major League Prospects (Jack Savage RC, Todd Simmons RC)	.05
651	Major League Prospects (John Burkett RC, Kirt Manwaring RC)	.30
652	Major League Prospects (Dave Otto RC, Walt Weiss RC)	.25
653	Major League Prospects (Randell Byers (Randall) RC, Jeff King RC)	.25
654a	Checklist 1-101 (21 is Schatzader)	.10
654b	Checklist 1-101 (21 is Schatzeder)	.05
655	Checklist 102-201	.05
656	Checklist 202-296	.05
657	Checklist 297-390	.05
658	Checklist 391-483	.05
659	Checklist 484-575	.05
660	Checklist 576-660	.05

All-Stars

ALAN TRAMMELL

For the third consecutive year, Fleer randomly inserted All-Star Team cards in its wax and cello packs. Twelve cards make up the set, with players chosen for the set being Fleer's idea of a major league All-Star team.

	NM/M
Complete Set (12):	3.00
Common Player:	.10
1 Matt Nokes	.10
2 Tom Henke	.10
3 Ted Higuera	.10
4 Roger Clemens	1.50
5 George Bell	.10
6 Andre Dawson	.25
7 Eric Davis	.10
8 Wade Boggs	.85
9 Alan Trammell	.10
10 Juan Samuel	.10
11 Jack Clark	.10
12 Paul Molitor	.75

Headliners

This six-card set was inserted in Fleer three-packs, sold by retail outlets and hobby dealers nationwide. The card fronts feature crisp full-color player cut-outs printed on a gray and white facsimile sports page. "Fleer Headliners 1988" is printed in black and red on a white banner across the top of the card, both front and back. A similar white banner across the card bottom bears the black and white National or American League logo and a red player/team name. Card backs are black on gray with red accents and include the card number and a narrative career summary.

		NM/M
Complete Set (6):		3.00
Common Player:		.25
1	Don Mattingly	1.50
2	Mark McGwire	2.00
3	Jack Morris	.15
4	Darryl Strawberry	.15
5	Dwight Gooden	.15
6	Tim Raines	.15

'87 World Series

Highlights of the 1987 Series are captured in this full-color insert set found only in Fleer's regular 660-card factory sets. This second World Series edition by Fleer features cards framed in red, with a blue and white starred bunting draped over the upper edges of the photo and a brief photo caption printed on a yellow band across the lower border. Numbered card backs are red, white and blue and include a description of the action pictured on the front, with stats for the Series.

		NM/M
Complete Set (12):		2.50
Common Player:		.25
1	"Grand" Hero In Game 1 (Dan Gladden)	.25
2	The Cardinals "Bush" Whacked (Randy Bush, Tony Pena)	.25
3	Masterful Performance Turns Momentum (John Tudor)	.25
4	Ozzie Smith	1.00
5	Throw Smoke! (Tony Pena, Todd Worrell)	.25
6	Cardinal Attack - Disruptive Speed (Vince Coleman)	.25
7	Herr's Wallop (Dan Driessen, Tom Herr)	.25
8	Kirby Puckett	1.00
9	Kent Hrbek	.25
10	Rich Hacker/Coach, Tom Herr, Lee Weyer/Umpire	.25
11	Game 7's Play At The Plate (Don Baylor, Dave Phillips/Umpire)	.25
12	Frank Viola	.25

Box Panels

Fleer's third annual box-bottom issue once again included 16 full-color trading cards printed on the bottoms of four different wax and cello pack retail display boxes. Each box contains three player cards and one team logo card. Player cards follow the same design as the basic 1988 Fleer issue. Standard size, the cards are numbered C-1 through C-16.

		NM/M
Complete Panel Set (4):		4.00
Complete Singles Set (16):		4.00
Common Panel:		1.00
Common Single Player:		.10
Panel		1.50
1	Cardinals Logo	.05
11	Mike Schmidt	1.00
14	Dave Stewart	.10
15	Tim Wallach	.10
Panel		1.00
2	Dwight Evans	.10
5	Shane Rawley	.10
10	Ryne Sandberg	.75
13	Tigers Logo	.05
Panel		1.25
3	Andres Galarraga	.10
6	Dale Murphy	.45
9	Giants Logo	.05
12	Kevin Seitzer	.10
Panel		1.00
4	Wally Joyner	.10
5	Twins Logo	.05
7	Kirby Puckett	1.00
16	Todd Worrell	.10

Glossy Tin

In its second year of production, Fleer radically reduced production numbers on its glossy version of the 1988 baseball card set. With production estimates in the 60,000 set range, values of the '88 tin glossies are about double those of the regular issue cards. Once again the issue was sold only as complete sets in colorful lithographed metal boxes.

	NM/M
Complete Set (672):	20.00
Common Player:	.15

Update

This update set (numbered U-1 through U-132 are 2-1/2" x 3-1/2") features traded veterans and rookies in a mixture of full-color action shots and close-ups, framed by white borders with red and blue stripes. The backs are red, white and blue-gray and include personal info, along with yearly and "At Their Best" (day, night, home, road) stats charts. The set was packaged in white cardboard boxes with red and blue stripes. A glossy-coated edition of the update set was issued in its own box and is valued at two times the regular issue.

		NM/M
Complete Set (132):		5.00
Common Player:		.05
1	Jose Bautista RC	.05
2	Joe Orsulak	.05
3	Doug Sisk	.05
4	Craig Worthington RC	.05
5	Mike Boddicker	.05
6	Rick Cerone	.05
7	Larry Parrish	.05
8	Lee Smith	.10
9	Mike Smithson	.05
10	John Trautwein RC	.05
11	Sherman Corbett RC	.05
12	Chili Davis	.05
13	Jim Eppard	.05
14	Bryan Harvey RC	.05
15	John Davis	.05
16	Dave Gallagher RC	.05
17	Ricky Horton	.05
18	Dan Pasqua	.05
19	Melido Perez	.05
20	Jose Segura RC	.05
21	Andy Allanson	.05
22	Jon Perlman	.05
23	Domingo Ramos	.05
24	Rick Rodriguez	.05
25	Willie Upshaw	.05
26	Paul Gibson RC	.05
27	Don Heinkel RC	.05
28	Ray Knight	.05
29	Gary Pettis	.05
30	Luis Salazar	.05
31	Mike MacFarlane RC	.05
32	Jeff Montgomery	.05
33	Ted Power	.05
34	Israel Sanchez RC	.05
35	Kurt Stillwell	.05
36	Pat Tabler	.05
37	Don August RC	.05
38	Darryl Hamilton RC	.05
39	Jeff Leonard	.05
40	Joey Meyer	.05
41	Allan Anderson	.05
42	Brian Harper	.05
43	Tom Herr	.05
44	Charlie Lea	.05
45	John Moses	.05
46	John Candelaria	.05
47	Jack Clark	.05
48	Richard Dotson	.05
49	Al Leiter RC	.05
50	Rafael Santana	.05
51	Don Slaught	.05
52	Todd Burns RC	.05
53	Dave Henderson	.05
54	Doug Jennings RC	.05
55	Dave Parker	.05
56	Walt Weiss	.05
57	Bob Welch	.05
58	Henry Cotto	.05
59	Marion Diaz (Mario)	.05
60	Mike Jackson	.05
61	Bill Swift	.05
62	Jose Cecena RC	.05
63	Ray Hayward RC	.05
64	Jim Steels RC	.05
65	Pat Borders RC	.05
66	Sil Campusano RC	.05
67	Mike Flanagan	.05
68	Todd Stottlemyre RC	.05
69	David Wells RC	.05
70	Jose Alvarez RC	.05
71	Paul Runge	.05
72	Cesar Jimenez RC (German)	.05
73	Pete Smith	.05
74	John Smoltz RC	1.50
75	Damon Berryhill	.05
76	Goose Gossage	.05
77	Mark Grace	.10
78	Darrin Jackson	.05
79	Vance Law	.05
80	Jeff Pico RC	.05
81	Gary Varsho RC	.05
82	Tim Birtsas	.05
83	Rob Dibble RC	.05
84	Danny Jackson	.05
85	Paul O'Neill	.05
86	Jose Rijo	.05
87	Chris Sabo RC	.25
88	John Fishel RC	.05
89	Craig Biggio RC	4.00
90	Terry Puhl	.05
91	Rafael Ramirez	.05
92	Louie Meadows RC	.05
93	Kirk Gibson	.05
94	Alfredo Griffin	.05
95	Jay Howell	.05
96	Jesse Orosco	.05
97	Alejandro Pena	.05
98	Tracy Woodson RC	.05
99	John Dopson RC	.05
100	Brian Holman RC	.05
101	Rex Hudler RC	.05
102	Jeff Parrett RC	.05
103	Nelson Santovenia RC	.05
104	Kevin Elster	.05
105	Jeff Innis RC	.05
106	Mackey Sasser RC	.05
107	Phil Bradley	.05
108	Danny Clay RC	.05
109	Greg Harris	.05
110	Ricky Jordan RC	.05
111	David Palmer	.05
112	Jim Gott	.05
113	Tommy Gregg RC (Photo actually Randy Milligan.)	.05
114	Barry Jones	.05
115	Randy Milligan RC	.05
116	Luis Alicea RC	.05
117	Tom Brunansky	.05
118	John Costello RC	.05
119	Jose DeLeon	.05
120	Bob Horner	.05
121	Scott Terry RC	.05
122	Roberto Alomar RC	1.50
123	Dave Leiper	.05
124	Keith Moreland	.05
125	Mark Parent RC	.05
126	Dennis Rasmussen	.05
127	Randy Bockus	.05
128	Brett Butler	.05
129	Donell Nixon	.05
130	Earnest Riles	.05
131	Roger Samuels RC	.05
132	Checklist	.05

Update Glossy Tin

The glossy version of the 1988 Fleer Update set differs from the regular-issue Update set only in the high-gloss finish applied to the cards' fronts and the lithographed metal box in which sets were sold.

	NM/M
Complete Set (132):	9.00
Common Player:	.15

Award Winners

This limited edition boxed set of 1987 award-winning player cards also includes six team logo sticker cards. Red, white, blue and yellow bands border the sharp, full-color player photos printed below a "Fleer Award Winners 1988" banner. The player's name and award are printed beneath the photo. Flip sides are red, white and blue and list personal information, career data, team logo and card number. This set was sold exclusively at 7-11 stores nationwide.

		NM/M
Complete Set (44):		3.50
Common Player:		.05
1	Steve Bedrosian	.05
2	George Bell	.05
3	Wade Boggs	.65
4	Jose Canseco	.30
5	Will Clark	.05
6	Roger Clemens	.75
7	Kal Daniels	.05
8	Eric Davis	.05
9	Andre Dawson	.25
10	Mike Dunne	.05
11	Dwight Evans	.05
12	Carlton Fisk	.50
13	Julio Franco	.05
14	Dwight Gooden	.05
15	Pedro Guerrero	.05
16	Tony Gwynn	.65
17	Orel Hershiser	.05
18	Tom Henke	.05
19	Ted Higuera	.05
20	Charlie Hough	.05
21	Wally Joyner	.05
22	Jimmy Key	.05
23	Don Mattingly	.75
24	Mark McGwire	1.50
25	Paul Molitor	.50
26	Jack Morris	.05
27	Dale Murphy	.05
28	Terry Pendleton	.05
29	Kirby Puckett	.65
30	Tim Raines	.05
31	Jeff Reardon	.05
32	Harold Reynolds	.05
33	Dave Righetti	.05
34	Benito Santiago	.05
35	Mike Schmidt	.75
36	Mike Scott	.05
37	Kevin Seitzer	.05
38	Larry Sheets	.05
39	Ozzie Smith	.65
40	Darryl Strawberry	.05
41	Rick Sutcliffe	.05
42	Danny Tartabull	.05
43	Alan Trammell	.05
44	Tim Wallach	.05

Baseball All-Stars

This limited edition boxed set features major league All-Stars. The standard-size cards feature a sporty bright blue and yellow striped background. Card backs feature a blue and white striped design with a yellow highlighted section at the top that contains the player name, card number, team, position and personal data, followed by lifetime career stats. Fleer All-Stars are cello-wrapped in blue and yellow striped boxes with checklist backs. The set includes six team logo sticker cards that feature black-and-white aerial shots of major league ballparks. The set was marketed exclusively by Ben Franklin stores.

		NM/M
Complete Set (44):		4.00
Common Player:		.05
1	George Bell	.05
2	Wade Boggs	.65
3	Bobby Bonilla	.05
4	George Brett	.85
5	Jose Canseco	.05
6	Jack Clark	.05
7	Will Clark	.05
8	Roger Clemens	.85
9	Eric Davis	.05
10	Andre Dawson	.25
11	Julio Franco	.05
12	Dwight Gooden	.05
13	Tony Gwynn	.65
14	Orel Hershiser	.05
15	Teddy Higuera	.05
16	Charlie Hough	.05
17	Kent Hrbek	.05
18	Bruce Hurst	.05
19	Wally Joyner	.05
20	Mark Langston	.05
21	Dave LaPoint	.05
22	Candy Maldonado	.05
23	Don Mattingly	.85
24	Roger McDowell	.05
25	Mark McGwire	1.00
26	Jack Morris	.05
27	Dale Murphy	.20
28	Eddie Murray	.50
29	Matt Nokes	.05
30	Kirby Puckett	.65
31	Tim Raines	.05
32	Willie Randolph	.05
33	Jeff Reardon	.05
34	Nolan Ryan	1.00
35	Juan Samuel	.05
36	Mike Schmidt	.85
37	Mike Scott	.05
38	Kevin Seitzer	.05
39	Ozzie Smith	.65
40	Darryl Strawberry	.05
41	Rick Sutcliffe	.05
42	Alan Trammell	.05
43	Tim Wallach	.05
44	Dave Winfield	.05

Baseball's Best

This boxed set of 44 standard-size cards (2-1/2" x 3-1/2") and six team logo stickers is the third annual issue from Fleer highlighting the best major league sluggers and pitchers. Five additional player

cards were printed on retail display box bottoms, along with a checklist logo card (numbered C-1 through C-6). Full-color player photos are framed by a green border that fades to yellow. A red (slugger) or blue (pitcher) player name is printed beneath the photo. Backs are printed in green on a white background with yellow highlights. Card number, player name and personal info appear in a green vertical box on the left-hand side of the card back with a yellow cartoon-style team logo overprinted across a stats chart on the right. This set was produced by Fleer for exclusive distribution by McCrory's stores (McCrory, McClellan, J.J. Newberry, H.L. Green, TG&Y).

		NM/M
Complete Set (44):		4.00
Common Player:		.05
1	George Bell	.05
2	Wade Boggs	.65
3	Bobby Bonilla	.05
4	Tom Brunansky	.05
5	Ellis Burks	.05
6	Jose Canseco	.40
7	Joe Carter	.05
8	Will Clark	.05
9	Roger Clemens	.85
10	Eric Davis	.05
11	Glenn Davis	.05
12	Andre Dawson	.25
13	Dennis Eckersley	.45
14	Andres Galarraga	.05
15	Dwight Gooden	.05
16	Pedro Guerrero	.05
17	Tony Gwynn	.65
18	Orel Hershiser	.05
19	Ted Higuera	.05
20	Pete Incaviglia	.05
21	Danny Jackson	.05
22	Doug Jennings	.05
23	Mark Langston	.05
24	Dave LaPoint	.05
25	Mike LaValliere	.05
26	Don Mattingly	.85
27	Mark McGwire	1.00
28	Dale Murphy	.20
29	Ken Phelps	.05
30	Kirby Puckett	.65
31	Johnny Ray	.05
32	Jeff Reardon	.05
33	Dave Righetti	.05
34	Cal Ripken, Jr. (Ripken)	1.50
35	Chris Sabo	.05
36	Mike Schmidt	.85
37	Mike Scott	.05
38	Kevin Seitzer	.05
39	Dave Stewart	.05
40	Darryl Strawberry	.05
41	Greg Swindell	.05
42	Frank Tanana	.05
43	Dave Winfield	.50
44	Todd Worrell	.05

Baseball's Best Box Panel

Six cards were placed on the bottoms of retail boxes of the Fleer Baseball's Best boxed sets in 1988. The cards, 2-1/2" x 3-1/2", are identical in design to cards found in the 44-card set. The cards are numbered C-1 through C-6 and were produced for distribution by McCrory stores and its affiliates.

		NM/M
Complete Panel Set:		1.50
Complete Singles Set (6):		1.50
Common Single Player:		.10
1	Ron Darling	.10
2	Rickey Henderson	.75
3	Carney Lansford	.10
4	Rafael Palmeiro	.60
5	Frank Viola	.10
6	Minnesota Twins Logo	.05

Exciting Stars

This boxed set showcases star major leaguers. Player photos are slanted upwards to the right, framed by a blue border with a red and white stripe across the middle. Card backs are numbered and printed in red, white and blue. The set was packaged in a checklist box, with six team logo sticker cards featuring black-and-white stadium photos on the flip sides. Exciting Stars was distributed via Cumberland Farm stores throughout the northeastern U.S. and Florida.

		NM/M
Complete Set (44):		3.00
Common Player:		.05
1	Harold Baines	.05
2	Kevin Bass	.05
3	George Bell	.05
4	Wade Boggs	.65
5	Mickey Brantley	.05
6	Sid Bream	.05
7	Jose Canseco	.30
8	Jack Clark	.05
9	Will Clark	.05
10	Roger Clemens	.85
11	Vince Coleman	.05
12	Eric Davis	.05
13	Andre Dawson	.25
14	Julio Franco	.05
15	Dwight Gooden	.05
16	Mike Greenwell	.05
17	Tony Gwynn	.65
18	Von Hayes	.02
19	Tom Henke	.05
20	Orel Hershiser	.05
21	Teddy Higuera	.05
22	Brook Jacoby	.05
23	Wally Joyner	.05
24	Jimmy Key	.05
25	Don Mattingly	.85
26	Mark McGwire	1.00
27	Jack Morris	.05
28	Dale Murphy	.20
29	Matt Nokes	.05
30	Kirby Puckett	.65
31	Tim Raines	.05
32	Ryne Sandberg	.65
33	Benito Santiago	.05
34	Mike Schmidt	.85
35	Mike Scott	.05
36	Kevin Seitzer	.05
37	Larry Sheets	.05
38	Ruben Sierra	.05
39	Darryl Strawberry	.05
40	Rick Sutcliffe	.05
41	Danny Tartabull	.05
42	Alan Trammell	.05
43	Fernando Valenzuela	.05
44	Devon White	.05

Hottest Stars

MIKE GREENWELL RED SOX OUTFIELD

This boxed set of standard-size player cards and six team logo stickers was produced by Fleer for exclusive distribution at Revco drug stores nationwide. Card fronts feature full-color photos of players representing every major league team. Photos are framed in red, orange and yellow, with a blue-and-white player name printed at bottom. A flaming baseball logo bearing the words "Hottest Stars" appears in the lower-left corner of the photo. Card backs are red, white and blue. The player's name, position, card number and team logo are printed at top, followed by a

stats box and personal data. The set also includes six team logo sticker cards with flipside stadium photos in black-and-white.

		NM/M
Complete Set (44):		3.50
Common Player:		.05
1	George Bell	.05
2	Wade Boggs	.65
3	Bobby Bonilla	.05
4	George Brett	.85
5	Jose Canseco	.30
6	Will Clark	.05
7	Roger Clemens	.85
8	Eric Davis	.05
9	Andre Dawson	.25
10	Tony Fernandez	.05
11	Julio Franco	.05
12	Gary Gaetti	.05
13	Dwight Gooden	.05
14	Mike Greenwell	.05
15	Tony Gwynn	.65
16	Rickey Henderson	.50
17	Keith Hernandez	.05
18	Tom Herr	.05
19	Orel Hershiser	.05
20	Ted Higuera	.05
21	Wally Joyner	.05
22	Jimmy Key	.05
23	Mark Langston	.05
24	Don Mattingly	.85
25	Jack McDowell	.05
26	Mark McGwire	1.00
27	Kevin Mitchell	.05
28	Jack Morris	.05
29	Dale Murphy	.20
30	Kirby Puckett	.65
31	Tim Raines	.05
32	Shane Rawley	.05
33	Benito Santiago	.05
34	Mike Schmidt	.85
35	Mike Scott	.05
36	Kevin Seitzer	.05
37	Larry Sheets	.05
38	Ruben Sierra	.05
39	Dave Smith	.05
40	Ozzie Smith	.65
41	Darryl Strawberry	.05
42	Rick Sutcliffe	.05
43	Pat Tabler	.05
44	Alan Trammell	.05

League Leaders

JOSE CANSECO OAKLAND A's OUTFIELD

This boxed set is the third annual limited edition set from Fleer highlighting leading players. The 1988 edition contains the same type of information, front and back, as the previous sets, with a new color scheme and design. Card fronts have bright blue borders, solid on the lower portion, striped on the upper, with a gold bar separating the two sections. The full-color player photo is centered above a yellow name banner. The numbered card backs are blue, pink and white, and contain player stats and personal notes. Six team logo sticker cards, with flipside black-and-white photos of ballparks, accompany this set which was marketed exclusively by Walgreen drug stores.

		NM/M
Complete Set (44):		3.50
Common Player:		.05
1	George Bell	.05
2	Wade Boggs	.65
3	Ivan Calderon	.05
4	Jose Canseco	.30
5	Will Clark	.05
6	Roger Clemens	.85
7	Vince Coleman	.05
8	Eric Davis	.05
9	Andre Dawson	.25
10	Bill Doran	.05
11	Dwight Evans	.05
12	Julio Franco	.05
13	Gary Gaetti	.05
14	Andres Galarraga	.05
15	Dwight Gooden	.05
16	Tony Gwynn	.65
17	Tom Henke	.05
18	Keith Hernandez	.05
19	Orel Hershiser	.05
20	Ted Higuera	.05
21	Kent Hrbek	.05
22	Wally Joyner	.05
23	Jimmy Key	.05
24	Mark Langston	.05
25	Don Mattingly	.85
26	Mark McGwire	1.00
27	Paul Molitor	.50
28	Jack Morris	.05
29	Dale Murphy	.20
30	Kirby Puckett	.65
31	Tim Raines	.05
32	Rick Rueschel	.05
33	Bret Saberhagen	.05
34	Benito Santiago	.05
35	Mike Schmidt	.85
36	Mike Scott	.05
37	Kevin Seitzer	.05
38	Larry Sheets	.05
39	Ruben Sierra	.05
40	Darryl Strawberry	.05
41	Rick Sutcliffe	.05
42	Alan Trammell	.05
43	Andy Van Slyke	.05
44	Todd Worrell	.05

Mini

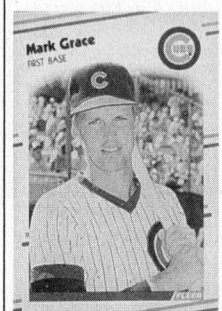

Mark Grace FIRST BASE

This third annual issue of miniatures (1-7/8" x 2-5/8") includes 120 high-gloss cards featuring new photos, not copies from the regular issue, although the card designs are identical. Card backs are red, white and blue and include personal data, yearly career stats and a stats breakdown of batting average, slugging percentage and on-base average, listed for day, night, home and road games. Card backs are numbered in alphabetical order by teams which are also listed alphabetically. The set includes 18 team logo stickers with black-and-white aerial stadium photos on the flip sides.

		NM/M
Complete Set (120):		3.50
Common Player:		.05
1	Eddie Murray	.50
2	Dave Schmidt	.05
3	Larry Sheets	.05
4	Wade Boggs	.65
5	Roger Clemens	.85
6	Dwight Evans	.05
7	Mike Greenwell	.05
8	Sam Horn	.05
9	Lee Smith	.05
10	Brian Downing	.05
11	Wally Joyner	.05
12	Devon White	.05
13	Mike Witt	.05
14	Ivan Calderon	.05
15	Ozzie Guillen	.05
16	Jack McDowell	.05
17	Kenny Williams	.05
18	Joe Carter	.05
19	Julio Franco	.05
20	Pat Tabler	.05
21	Doyle Alexander	.05
22	Jack Morris	.05
23	Matt Nokes	.05
24	Walt Terrell	.05
25	Alan Trammell	.05
26	Bret Saberhagen	.05
27	Kevin Seitzer	.05
28	Danny Tartabull	.05
29	Gary Thurman	.05
30	Ted Higuera	.05
31	Paul Molitor	.50
32	Dan Plesac	.05
33	Robin Yount	.50
34	Gary Gaetti	.05
35	Kent Hrbek	.05
36	Kirby Puckett	.65
37	Jeff Reardon	.05
38	Frank Viola	.05
39	Jack Clark	.05
40	Rickey Henderson	.50
41	Don Mattingly	.85
42	Willie Randolph	.05
43	Dave Righetti	.05
44	Dave Winfield	.50
45	Jose Canseco	.30
46	Mark McGwire	1.00
47	Dave Parker	.05
48	Dave Stewart	.05
49	Walt Weiss	.05
50	Bob Welch	.05
51	Mickey Brantley	.05
52	Mark Langston	.05
53	Harold Reynolds	.05
54	Scott Fletcher	.05
55	Charlie Hough	.05
56	Pete Incaviglia	.05
57	Larry Parrish	.05
58	Ruben Sierra	.05
59	George Bell	.05
60	Mark Eichhorn	.05
61	Tony Fernandez	.05
62	Tom Henke	.05
63	Jimmy Key	.05
64	Dion James	.05
65	Dale Murphy	.20
66	Zane Smith	.05
67	Andre Dawson	.25
68	Mark Grace	.25
69	Jerry Mumphrey	.05
70	Ryne Sandberg	.65
71	Rick Sutcliffe	.05
72	Kal Daniels	.05
73	Eric Davis	.05
74	John Franco	.05
75	Ron Robinson	.05
76	Jeff Treadway	.05
77	Kevin Bass	.05
78	Glenn Davis	.05
79	Nolan Ryan	1.00
80	Mike Scott	.05
81	Dave Smith	.05
82	Kirk Gibson	.05
83	Pedro Guerrero	.05
84	Orel Hershiser	.05
85	Steve Sax	.05
86	Fernando Valenzuela	.05
87	Tim Burke	.05
88	Andres Galarraga	.05
89	Neal Heaton	.05
90	Tim Raines	.05
91	Tim Wallach	.05
92	Dwight Gooden	.05
93	Keith Hernandez	.05
94	Gregg Jefferies	.10
95	Howard Johnson	.05
96	Roger McDowell	.05
97	Darryl Strawberry	.05
98	Steve Bedrosian	.05
99	Von Hayes	.05
100	Shane Rawley	.05
101	Juan Samuel	.05
102	Mike Schmidt	.85
103	Bobby Bonilla	.05
104	Mike Dunne	.05
105	Andy Van Slyke	.05
106	Vince Coleman	.05
107	Bob Horner	.05
108	Willie McGee	.05
109	Ozzie Smith	.65
110	John Tudor	.05
111	Todd Worrell	.05
112	Tony Gwynn	.65
113	John Kruk	.05
114	Lance McCullers	.05
115	Benito Santiago	.05
116	Will Clark	.05
117	Jeff Leonard	.05
118	Candy Maldonado	.05
119	Kirt Manwaring	.05
120	Don Robinson	.05

MVP

DAVE WINFIELD YANKEES OUTFIELD

This boxed set of 44 standard-size cards and six team logo stickers was produced by Fleer for exclusive distribution at Toys "R" Us stores. This premiere edition features full-color player photos framed by a yellow and blue border. Card backs are yellow and blue on a white background. The player's team, position and personal data are followed by stats, logo and a blue banner bearing the player's name, team logo and card number. The six sticker cards feature black-and-white stadium photos on the backs.

		NM/M
Complete Set (44):		3.50
Common Player:		.05
1	George Bell	.05
2	Wade Boggs	.65
3	Jose Canseco	.30
4	Ivan Calderon	.05
5	Will Clark	.05
6	Roger Clemens	.85
7	Vince Coleman	.05
8	Eric Davis	.05
9	Andre Dawson	.25
10	Dave Dravecky	.05
11	Mike Dunne	.05
12	Dwight Evans	.05
13	Sid Fernandez	.05
14	Tony Fernandez	.05
15	Julio Franco	.05
16	Dwight Gooden	.05
17	Tony Gwynn	.65
18	Ted Higuera	.05
19	Charlie Hough	.05
20	Wally Joyner	.05
21	Mark Langston	.05
22	Don Mattingly	.85
23	Mark McGwire	1.00
24	Jack Morris	.05
25	Dale Murphy	.20
26	Kirby Puckett	.65
27	Tim Raines	.05
28	Willie Randolph	.05
29	Ryne Sandberg	.65
30	Benito Santiago	.05
31	Mike Schmidt	.85
32	Mike Scott	.05
33	Kevin Seitzer	.05
34	Larry Sheets	.05
35	Ozzie Smith	.65
36	Dave Stewart	.05
37	Darryl Strawberry	.05
38	Rick Sutcliffe	.05
39	Alan Trammell	.05
40	Fernando Valenzuela	.05
41	Frank Viola	.05
42	Tim Wallach	.05
43	Dave Winfield	.50
44	Robin Yount	.50

Record Setters

1988 FLEER RECORD SETTERS — DALE MURPHY BRAVES OUTFIELD

For the second consecutive year, Fleer issued this set for exclusive distribution by Eckerd Drug stores. Cards are standard size with red and blue borders framing the full-color player photos. Card backs list personal information and career stats in red and blue on a white background. Each 44-card set comes cello-wrapped in a checklist box that contains six additional cards with peel-off team logo stickers. The sticker cards feature black-and-white aerial photos of major league ballparks, along with stadium statistics such as field size, seating capacity and date of the first game played.

		NM/M
Complete Set (44):		3.50
Common Player:		.05
1	Jesse Barfield	.05
2	George Bell	.05
3	Wade Boggs	.65
4	Jose Canseco	.35
5	Jack Clark	.05
6	Will Clark	.05
7	Roger Clemens	.85
8	Alvin Davis	.05
9	Eric Davis	.05
10	Andre Dawson	.25
11	Mike Dunne	.05
12	John Franco	.05
13	Julio Franco	.05
14	Dwight Gooden	.05
15	Mark Gubicza	.05
16	Ozzie Guillen	.05
17	Tony Gwynn	.65
18	Orel Hershiser	.05
19	Teddy Higuera	.05
20	Howard Johnson	.05
21	Wally Joyner	.05
22	Jimmy Key	.05
23	Jeff Leonard	.05
24	Don Mattingly	.85
25	Mark McGwire	1.00
26	Jack Morris	.05
27	Dale Murphy	.20
28	Larry Parrish	.05
29	Kirby Puckett	.65
30	Tim Raines	.05
31	Harold Reynolds	.05
32	Dave Righetti	.05
33	Cal Ripken, Jr.	1.00
34	Benito Santiago	.05
35	Mike Schmidt	.85
36	Mike Scott	.05
37	Kevin Seitzer	.05
38	Ozzie Smith	.65
39	Darryl Strawberry	.05
40	Rick Sutcliffe	.05
41	Alan Trammell	.05
42	Frank Viola	.05
43	Mitch Williams	.05
44	Todd Worrell	.05

Star Stickers

FLEER Star Stickers — ALAN TRAMMELL TIGERS SHORTSTOP

This set of 132 standard-size sticker cards (including a checklist card) features exclusive player photos, different from those in the Fleer regular issue. Card fronts have light gray borders sprinkled with multi-colored stars. Card backs are printed in red, gray and black on white and include personal data and a breakdown of pitching and batting stats into day, night, home and road categories. Cards were marketed in two different display boxes that feature six players and two team logos on the bottoms.

		NM/M
Complete Set (132):		7.50
Common Player:		.05
Wax Pack (5):		.50
Wax Box (36):		10.00
1	Mike Boddicker	.05
2	Eddie Murray	.50
3	Cal Ripken, Jr.	1.50
4	Larry Sheets	.05
5	Wade Boggs	.65
6	Ellis Burks	.05
7	Roger Clemens	.85
8	Dwight Evans	.05
9	Mike Greenwell	.05
10	Bruce Hurst	.05
11	Brian Downing	.05
12	Wally Joyner	.05
13	Mike Witt	.05
14	Ivan Calderon	.05
15	Jose DeLeon	.05
16	Ozzie Guillen	.05
17	Bobby Thigpen	.05
18	Joe Carter	.05
19	Julio Franco	.05
20	Brook Jacoby	.05
21	Cory Snyder	.05
22	Pat Tabler	.05
23	Doyle Alexander	.05
24	Kirk Gibson	.05
25	Mike Henneman	.05
26	Jack Morris	.05
27	Matt Nokes	.05
28	Walt Terrell	.05
29	Alan Trammell	.05
30	George Brett	.85
31	Charlie Leibrandt	.05
32	Bret Saberhagen	.05
33	Kevin Seitzer	.05
34	Danny Tartabull	.05
35	Frank White	.05
36	Rob Deer	.05
37	Ted Higuera	.05
38	Paul Molitor	.50
39	Dan Plesac	.05
40	Robin Yount	.50
41	Bert Blyleven	.05
42	Tom Brunansky	.05
43	Gary Gaetti	.05
44	Kent Hrbek	.05
45	Kirby Puckett	.65
46	Jeff Reardon	.05
47	Frank Viola	.05
48	Don Mattingly	.85
49	Mike Pagliarulo	.05
50	Willie Randolph	.05
51	Rick Rhoden	.05
52	Dave Righetti	.05
53	Dave Winfield	.50
54	Jose Canseco	.30
55	Carney Lansford	.05
56	Mark McGwire	1.00
57	Dave Stewart	.05

58	Curt Young	.05
59	Alvin Davis	.05
60	Mark Langston	.05
61	Ken Phelps	.05
62	Harold Reynolds	.05
63	Scott Fletcher	.05
64	Charlie Hough	.05
65	Pete Incaviglia	.05
66	Oddibe McDowell	.05
67	Pete O'Brien	.05
68	Larry Parrish	.05
69	Ruben Sierra	.05
70	Jesse Barfield	.05
71	George Bell	.05
72	Tony Fernandez	.05
73	Tom Henke	.05
74	Jimmy Key	.05
75	Lloyd Moseby	.05
76	Dion James	.05
77	Dale Murphy	.20
78	Zane Smith	.05
79	Andre Dawson	.25
80	Ryne Sandberg	.65
81	Rick Sutcliffe	.05
82	Kal Daniels	.05
83	Eric Davis	.05
84	John Franco	.05
85	Kevin Bass	.05
86	Glenn Davis	.05
87	Bill Doran	.05
88	Nolan Ryan	1.50
89	Mike Scott	.05
90	Dave Smith	.05
91	Pedro Guerrero	.05
92	Orel Hershiser	.05
93	Steve Sax	.05
94	Fernando Valenzuela	.05
95	Tim Burke	.05
96	Andres Galarraga	.05
97	Tim Raines	.05
98	Tim Wallach	.05
99	Mitch Webster	.05
100	Ron Darling	.05
101	Sid Fernandez	.05
102	Dwight Gooden	.05
103	Keith Hernandez	.05
104	Howard Johnson	.05
105	Roger McDowell	.05
106	Darryl Strawberry	.05
107	Steve Bedrosian	.05
108	Von Hayes	.05
109	Shane Rawley	.05
110	Juan Samuel	.05
111	Mike Schmidt	.85
112	Milt Thompson	.05
113	Sid Bream	.05
114	Bobby Bonilla	.05
115	Mike Dunne	.05
116	Andy Van Slyke	.05
117	Vince Coleman	.05
118	Willie McGee	.05
119	Terry Pendleton	.05
120	Ozzie Smith	.65
121	John Tudor	.05
122	Todd Worrell	.05
123	Tony Gwynn	.65
124	John Kruk	.05
125	Benito Santiago	.05
126	Will Clark	.05
127	Dave Dravecky	.05
128	Jeff Leonard	.05
129	Candy Maldonado	.05
130	Rick Rueschel	.05
131	Don Robinson	.05
132	Checklist	

Star Stickers Box Panels

RON GUIDRY

This set of eight box-bottom cards was printed on two different retail display boxes. Six players photos and two team logo sticker cards are included in the set, three player photos and one team photo per box. The full-color player photos are exclusive to the Fleer Star Sticker set. The cards, which measure 2-1/2" x 3-1/2", have a light gray border sprinkled with multi-color stars. The backs are printed in navy blue and red.

		NM/M
Complete Panel Set (2):		1.50
Complete Singles Set (8):		1.50
Common Singles Player:		.15
Panel		1.00
1	Eric Davis	.10
3	Kevin Mitchell	.10
5	Rickey Henderson	.75
7	Tigers Logo	.05
Panel		1.00
2	Gary Carter	.75
4	Ron Guidry	.05
6	Don Baylor	.10
8	Giants Logo	.05

Superstars

OREL HERSHISER
Dodgers • Pitcher

This is the fourth edition of Fleer boxed sets produced for distribution by McCrory's (1985-87 issues were titled "Fleer Limited Edition"). The Superstars standard-size card set features full-color player photos framed by red, white and blue striped top and bottom borders. Card fronts have a semi-glossy slightly textured finish. Card backs are red and blue on white and include card numbers, personal data and statistics. Six team logo sticker cards are also included in this set which was marketed in red, white and blue boxes with checklist backs. Boxed sets were sold exclusively at McCrory's stores and its affiliates.

		NM/M
Complete Set (44):		5.00
Common Player:		.10
1	Steve Bedrosian	.10
2	George Bell	.10
3	Wade Boggs	.65
4	Barry Bonds	1.50
5	Jose Canseco	.45
6	Joe Carter	.10
7	Jack Clark	.10
8	Will Clark	.10
9	Roger Clemens	.85
10	Alvin Davis	.10
11	Eric Davis	.10
12	Glenn Davis	.10
13	Andre Dawson	.25
14	Dwight Gooden	.10
15	Orel Hershiser	.10
16	Teddy Higuera	.10
17	Kent Hrbek	.10
18	Wally Joyner	.10
19	Jimmy Key	.10
20	John Kruk	.10
21	Jeff Leonard	.10
22	Don Mattingly	.85
23	Mark McGwire	1.00
24	Kevin McReynolds	.10
25	Dale Murphy	.15
26	Matt Nokes	.10
27	Terry Pendleton	.10
28	Kirby Puckett	.65
29	Tim Raines	.10
30	Rick Rhoden	.10
31	Cal Ripken, Jr.	1.50
32	Benito Santiago	.10
33	Mike Schmidt	.85
34	Mike Scott	.10
35	Kevin Seitzer	.10
36	Ruben Sierra	.10
37	Cory Snyder	.10
38	Darryl Strawberry	.10
39	Rick Sutcliffe	.10
40	Danny Tartabull	.10
41	Alan Trammell	.10
42	Ken Williams	.10
43	Mike Witt	.10
44	Robin Yount	.50

Superstars Box Panel

SHANE RAWLEY
Phillies • Pitcher

Six cards were placed on the bottoms of retail boxes of the Fleer Superstars boxed sets. in 1988. The cards, 2-1/2" x 3-1/2", are identical in design to cards found in the 44-card set. The cards are numbered C-1 through C-6 and were produced for distribution by McCrory stores and its affiliates.

		NM/M
Complete Panel:		2.50
Complete Set (6):		2.50
Common Player:		.25
C1	Pete Incaviglia	.15
C2	Rickey Henderson	1.00
C3	Tony Fernandez	.15
C4	Shane Rawley	.15
C5	Ryne Sandberg	1.50
C6	St. Louis Cardinals Logo/Checklist	.10

1989 Fleer

KEVIN ROMINE
OUTFIELD

This set includes 660 standard-size cards and was issued with 45 team logo stickers. Individual card fronts feature a gray and white striped background with full-color player photos framed by a bright line of color that slants upward to the right. The set also includes two subsets: 15 Major League Prospects and 12 SuperStar Specials. A special bonus set of 12 All-Star Team cards was randomly inserted in individual wax packs of 15 cards. The last seven cards in the set are checklists, with players listed alphabetically by teams.

		NM/M
Retail Factory Set (660):		17.50
Hobby Factory Set (672):		20.00
Complete Set (660):		15.00
Common Player:		.05
Wax Pack (15):		1.00
Wax Box (36):		25.00
Cello Pack (36):		1.50
Cello Box (24):		20.00
Rack Pack (42+1):		1.50
Rack Box (24):		25.00
1	Don Baylor	.05
2	Lance Blankenship RC	.05
3	Todd Burns RC	.05
4	Greg Cadaret RC	.05
5	Jose Canseco	.35
6	Storm Davis	.05
7	Dennis Eckersley	.35
8	Mike Gallego RC	.05
9	Ron Hassey	.05
10	Dave Henderson	.05
11	Rick Honeycutt	.05
12	Glenn Hubbard	.05
13	Stan Javier	.05
14	Doug Jennings RC	.05
15	Felix Jose RC	.05
16	Carney Lansford	.05
17	Mark McGwire	.65
18	Gene Nelson	.05
19	Dave Parker	.05
20	Eric Plunk	.05
21	Luis Polonia	.05
22	Terry Steinbach	.05
23	Dave Stewart	.05
24	Walt Weiss	.05
25	Bob Welch	.05
26	Curt Young	.05
27	Rick Aguilera	.05
28	Wally Backman	.05
29	Mark Carreon	.05
30	Gary Carter	.40
31	David Cone	.05
32	Ron Darling	.05
33	Len Dykstra	.05
34	Kevin Elster	.05
35	Sid Fernandez	.05
36	Dwight Gooden	.05
37	Keith Hernandez	.05
38	Gregg Jefferies	.05
39	Howard Johnson	.05
40	Terry Leach	.05
41	Dave Magadan	.05
42	Bob McClure	.05
43	Roger McDowell	.05
44	Kevin McReynolds	.05
45	Keith Miller	.05
46	Randy Myers	.05
47	Bob Ojeda	.05
48	Mackey Sasser	.05
49	Darryl Strawberry	.05
50	Tim Teufel	.05
51	Dave West RC	.05
52	Mookie Wilson	.05
53	Dave Anderson	.05
54	Tim Belcher	.05
55	Mike Davis	.05
56	Mike Devereaux	.05
57	Kirk Gibson	.05
58	Alfredo Griffin	.05
59	Chris Gwynn	.05
60	Jeff Hamilton	.05
61a	Danny Heep (Home: San Antonio, TX):	.25
61b	Danny Heep (Home: Lake Hills, TX):	.25
62	Orel Hershiser	.05
63	Brian Holton RC	.05
64	Jay Howell	.05
65	Tim Leary	.05
66	Mike Marshall	.05
67	Ramon Martinez RC	.25
68	Jesse Orosco	.05
69	Alejandro Pena	.05
70	Steve Sax	.05
71	Mike Scioscia	.05
72	Mike Sharperson	.05
73	John Shelby	.05
74	Franklin Stubbs	.05
75	John Tudor	.05
76	Fernando Valenzuela	.05
77	Tracy Woodson	.05
78	Marty Barrett	.05
79	Todd Benzinger	.05
80	Mike Boddicker	.05
81	Wade Boggs	.50
82	"Oil Can" Boyd	.05
83	Ellis Burks	.05
84	Rick Cerone	.05
85	Roger Clemens	.75
86	Steve Curry RC	.05
87	Dwight Evans	.05
88	Wes Gardner	.05
89	Rich Gedman	.05
90	Mike Greenwell	.05
91	Bruce Hurst	.05
92	Dennis Lamp	.05
93	Spike Owen	.05
94	Larry Parrish	.05
95	Carlos Quintana RC	.05
96	Jody Reed	.05
97	Jim Rice	.25
98a	Kevin Romine (Batting follow-thru, photo actually Randy Kutcher.)	.05
98b	Kevin Romine (Arms crossed on chest, correct photo.)	.25
99	Lee Smith	.05
100	Mike Smithson	.05
101	Bob Stanley	.05
102	Allan Anderson	.05
103	Keith Atherton	.05
104	Juan Berenguer	.05
105	Bert Blyleven	.10
106	Eric Bullock RC	.05
107	Randy Bush	.05
108	John Christensen RC	.05
109	Mark Davidson	.05
110	Gary Gaetti	.05
111	Greg Gagne	.05
112	Dan Gladden	.05
113	German Gonzalez RC	.05
114	Brian Harper	.05
115	Tom Herr	.05
116	Kent Hrbek	.05
117	Gene Larkin	.05
118	Tim Laudner	.05
119	Charlie Lea	.05
120	Steve Lombardozzi	.05
121a	John Moses (Home: Phoenix, AZ):	.25
121b	John Moses (Home: Tempe, AZ):	.25
122	Al Newman	.05
123	Mark Portugal	.05
124	Kirby Puckett	.50
125	Jeff Reardon	.05
126	Fred Toliver	.05
127	Frank Viola	.05
128	Doyle Alexander	.05
129	Dave Bergman	.05
130a	Tom Brookens (Mike Heath stats on back.)	.50
130b	Tom Brookens (Correct stats on back.)	.05
131	Paul Gibson RC	.05
132a	Mike Heath (Tom Brookens stats on back.)	.50
132b	Mike Heath (Correct stats on back.)	.05
133	Don Heinkel RC	.05
134	Mike Henneman	.05
135	Guillermo Hernandez	.05
136	Eric King	.05
137	Chet Lemon	.05
138	Fred Lynn	.05
139	Jack Morris	.05
140	Matt Nokes	.05
141	Gary Pettis	.05
142	Ted Power	.05
143	Jeff Robinson	.05
144	Luis Salazar	.05
145	Steve Searcy RC	.05
146	Pat Sheridan	.05
147	Frank Tanana	.05
148	Alan Trammell	.05
149	Walt Terrell	.05
150	Jim Walewander RC	.05
151	Lou Whitaker	.05
152	Tim Birtsas	.05
153	Tom Browning	.05
154	Keith Brown RC	.05
155	Norm Charlton RC	.15
156	Dave Concepcion	.05
157	Kal Daniels	.05
158	Eric Davis	.05
159	Bo Diaz	.05
160	Rob Dibble RC	.05
161	Nick Esasky	.05
162	John Franco	.05
163	Danny Jackson	.05
164	Barry Larkin	.05
165	Rob Murphy	.05
166	Paul O'Neill	.05
167	Jeff Reed	.05
168	Jose Rijo	.05
169	Ron Robinson	.05
170	Chris Sabo	.05
171	Candy Sierra RC	.05
172	Van Snider RC	.05
173a	Jeff Treadway (Blue "target" above head.)	75.00
173b	Jeff Treadway (No "target.")	.05
174	Frank Williams	.05
175	Herm Winningham	.05
176	Jim Adduci RC	.05
177	Don August	.05
178	Mike Birkbeck	.05
179	Chris Bosio	.05
180	Glenn Braggs	.05
181	Greg Brock	.05
182	Mark Clear	.05
183	Chuck Crim	.05
184	Rob Deer	.05
185	Tom Filer	.05
186	Jim Gantner	.05
187	Darryl Hamilton	.05
188	Ted Higuera	.05
189	Odell Jones	.05
190	Jeffrey Leonard	.05
191	Joey Meyer	.05
192	Paul Mirabella	.05
193	Paul Molitor	.40
194	Charlie O'Brien RC	.05
195	Dan Plesac	.05
196	Gary Sheffield RC	1.00
197	B.J. Surhoff	.05
198	Dale Sveum	.05
199	Bill Wegman	.05
200	Robin Yount	.40
201	Rafael Belliard	.05
202	Barry Bonds	.75
203	Bobby Bonilla	.05
204	Sid Bream	.05
205	Benny Distefano RC	.05
206	Doug Drabek	.05
207	Mike Dunne	.05
208	Felix Fermin	.05
209	Brian Fisher	.05
210	Jim Gott	.05
211	Bob Kipper	.05
212	Dave LaPoint	.05
213	Mike LaValliere	.05
214	Jose Lind	.05
215	Junior Ortiz	.05
216	Vicente Palacios	.05
217	Tom Prince RC	.05
218	Gary Redus	.05
219	R.J. Reynolds	.05
220	Jeff Robinson	.05
221	John Smiley	.05
222	Andy Van Slyke	.05
223	Bob Walk	.05
224	Glenn Wilson	.05
225	Jesse Barfield	.05
226	George Bell	.05
227	Pat Borders	.05
228	John Cerutti	.05
229	Jim Clancy	.05
230	Mark Eichhorn	.05
231	Tony Fernandez	.05
232	Cecil Fielder	.05
233	Mike Flanagan	.05
234	Kelly Gruber	.05
235	Tom Henke	.05
236	Jimmy Key	.05
237	Rick Leach	.05
238	Manny Lee	.05
239	Nelson Liriano	.05
240	Fred McGriff	.05
241	Lloyd Moseby	.05
242	Rance Mulliniks	.05
243	Jeff Musselman	.05
244	Dave Stieb	.05
245	Todd Stottlemyre RC	.05
246	Duane Ward	.05
247	David Wells	.05
248	Ernie Whitt	.05
249	Luis Aguayo	.05
250a	Neil Allen (Home: Sarasota, FL)	.25
250b	Neil Allen (Home: Syosset, NY)	.05
251	John Candelaria	.05
252	Jack Clark	.05
253	Richard Dotson	.05
254	Rickey Henderson	.40
255	Tommy John	.05
256	Roberto Kelly	.05
257	Al Leiter	.05
258	Don Mattingly	.60
259	Dale Mohorcic	.05
260	Hal Morris RC	.25
261	Scott Nielsen RC	.05
262	Mike Pagliarulo	.05
263	Hipolito Pena RC	.05
264	Ken Phelps	.05
265	Willie Randolph	.05
266	Rick Rhoden	.05
267	Dave Righetti	.05
268	Rafael Santana	.05
269	Steve Shields RC	.05
270	Joel Skinner	.05
271	Don Slaught	.05
272	Claudell Washington	.05
273	Gary Ward	.05
274	Dave Winfield	.40
275	Luis Aquino RC	.05
276	Floyd Bannister	.05
277	George Brett	.60
278	Bill Buckner	.05
279	Nick Capra RC	.05
280	Jose DeJesus RC	.05
281	Steve Farr	.05
282	Jerry Gleaton	.05
283	Mark Gubicza	.05
284	Tom Gordon RC	.25
285	Bo Jackson	.10
286	Charlie Leibrandt	.05
287	Mike Macfarlane RC	.10
288	Jeff Montgomery	.05
289	Bill Pecota	.05
290	Jamie Quirk	.05
291	Bret Saberhagen	.05
292	Kevin Seitzer	.05
293	Kurt Stillwell	.05
294	Pat Tabler	.05
295	Danny Tartabull	.05
296	Gary Thurman	.05
297	Frank White	.05
298	Willie Wilson	.05
299	Roberto Alomar	.20
300	Sandy Alomar, Jr. RC	.25
301	Chris Brown	.05
302	Mike Brumley RC	.05
303	Mark Davis	.05
304	Mark Grant	.05
305	Tony Gwynn	.50
306	Greg Harris RC	.05
307	Andy Hawkins	.05
308	Jimmy Jones	.05
309	John Kruk	.05
310	Dave Leiper	.05
311	Carmelo Martinez	.05
312	Lance McCullers	.05
313	Keith Moreland	.05
314	Dennis Rasmussen	.05
315	Randy Ready	.05
316	Benito Santiago	.05
317	Eric Show	.05
318	Todd Simmons	.05
319	Garry Templeton	.05
320	Dickie Thon	.05
321	Ed Whitson	.05
322	Marvell Wynne	.05
323	Mike Aldrete	.05
324	Brett Butler	.05
325	Will Clark	.05
326	Kelly Downs	.05
327	Dave Dravecky	.05
328	Scott Garrelts	.05
329	Atlee Hammaker	.05
330	Charlie Hayes RC	.10
331	Mike Krukow	.05
332	Craig Lefferts	.05
333	Candy Maldonado	.05
334	Kirt Manwaring	.05
335	Bob Melvin	.05
336	Kevin Mitchell	.05
337	Donell Nixon	.05
338	Tony Perezchica RC	.05
339	Joe Price	.05
340	Rick Reuschel	.05
341	Earnest Riles	.05
342	Don Robinson	.05
343	Chris Speier	.05
344	Robby Thompson	.05
345	Jose Uribe	.05
346	Matt Williams	.05
347	Trevor Wilson RC	.15
348	Juan Agosto	.05
349	Larry Andersen	.05
350a	Alan Ashby ("Throws Right")	.25
350b	Alan Ashby ("Throws Right")	.05
351	Kevin Bass	.05
352	Buddy Bell	.05
353	Craig Biggio	.05
354	Danny Darwin	.05
355	Glenn Davis	.05
356	Jim Deshaies	.05
357	Bill Doran	.05
358	John Fishel RC	.05
359	Billy Hatcher	.05
360	Bob Knepper	.05
361	Louie Meadows RC	.05
362	Dave Meads	.05
363	Jim Pankovits	.05
364	Terry Puhl	.05
365	Rafael Ramirez	.05
366	Craig Reynolds	.05
367	Mike Scott	.05
368	Nolan Ryan	.75
369	Dave Smith	.05
370	Gerald Young	.05
371	Hubie Brooks	.05
372	Tim Burke	.05
373	John Dopson RC	.05
374	Mike Fitzgerald	.05

375	Tom Foley	.05
376	Andres Galarraga	.05
377	Neal Heaton	.05
378	Joe Hesketh	.05
379	Brian Holman RC	.05
380	Rex Hudler	.05
381a	Randy Johnson RC (Marlboro ad on scoreboard.)	40.00
381b	Randy Johnson RC (Ad partially obscured.)	10.00
381c	Randy Johnson RC (Ad completely blacked out.)	3.00
382	Wallace Johnson	.05
383	Tracy Jones	.05
384	Dave Martinez	.05
385	Dennis Martinez	.05
386	Andy McGaffigan	.05
387	Otis Nixon	.05
388	Johnny Paredes RC	.05
389	Jeff Parrett	.05
390	Pascual Perez	.05
391	Tim Raines	.05
392	Luis Rivera	.05
393	Nelson Santovenia RC	.05
394	Bryn Smith	.05
395	Tim Wallach	.05
396	Andy Allanson	.05
397	Rod Allen RC	.05
398	Scott Bailes	.05
399	Tom Candiotti	.05
400	Joe Carter	.05
401	Carmen Castillo	.05
402	Dave Clark	.05
403	John Farrell	.05
404	Julio Franco	.05
405	Don Gordon	.05
406	Mel Hall	.05
407	Brad Havens	.05
408	Brook Jacoby	.05
409	Doug Jones	.05
410	Jeff Kaiser RC	.05
411	Luis Medina RC	.05
412	Cory Snyder	.05
413	Greg Swindell	.05
414	Ron Tingley RC	.05
415	Willie Upshaw	.05
416	Ron Washington	.05
417	Rich Yett	.05
418	Damon Berryhill	.05
419	Mike Bielecki	.05
420	Doug Dascenzo RC	.05
421	Jody Davis	.05
422	Andre Dawson	.25
423	Frank DiPino	.05
424	Shawon Dunston	.05
425	"Goose" Gossage	.10
426	Mark Grace	.05
427	Mike Harkey RC	.05
428	Darrin Jackson	.05
429	Les Lancaster	.05
430	Vance Law	.05
431	Greg Maddux	.50
432	Jamie Moyer	.05
433	Al Nipper	.05
434	Rafael Palmeiro	.35
435	Pat Perry	.05
436	Jeff Pico RC	.05
437	Ryne Sandberg	.50
438	Calvin Schiraldi	.05
439	Rick Sutcliffe	.05
440a	Manny Trillo ("Throws Rig")	.35
440b	Manny Trillo ("Throws Right")	.05
441	Gary Varsho RC	.05
442	Mitch Webster	.05
443	Luis Alicea	.05
444	Tom Brunansky	.05
445	Vince Coleman	.05
446	John Costello RC	.05
447	Danny Cox	.05
448	Ken Dayley	.05
449	Jose DeLeon	.05
450	Curt Ford	.05
451	Pedro Guerrero	.05
452	Bob Horner	.05
453	Tim Jones RC	.05
454	Steve Lake	.05
455	Joe Magrane	.05
456	Greg Mathews	.05
457	Willie McGee	.05
458	Larry McWilliams	.05
459	Jose Oquendo	.05
460	Tony Pena	.05
461	Terry Pendleton	.05
462	Steve Peters RC	.05
463	Ozzie Smith	.50
464	Scott Terry	.05
465	Denny Walling	.05
466	Todd Worrell	.05
467	Tony Armas	.05
468	Dante Bichette RC	.25
469	Bob Boone	.05
470	Terry Clark RC	.05
471	Stew Cliburn RC	.05
472	Mike Cook RC	.05
473	Sherman Corbett RC	.05
474	Chili Davis	.05
475	Brian Downing	.05
476	Jim Eppard	.05
477	Chuck Finley	.05
478	Willie Fraser	.05
479	Bryan Harvey	.05
480	Jack Howell	.05
481	Wally Joyner	.05
482	Jack Lazorko	.05
483	Kirk McCaskill	.05
484	Mark McLemore	.05

485	Greg Minton	.05
486	Dan Petry	.05
487	Johnny Ray	.05
488	Dick Schofield	.05
489	Devon White	.05
490	Mike Witt	.05
491	Harold Baines	.05
492	Daryl Boston	.05
493	Ivan Calderon	.05
494	Mike Diaz	.05
495	Carlton Fisk	.40
496	Dave Gallagher RC	.05
497	Ozzie Guillen	.05
498	Shawn Hillegas	.05
499	Lance Johnson	.05
500	Barry Jones	.05
501	Bill Long	.05
502	Steve Lyons	.05
503	Fred Manrique	.05
504	Jack McDowell	.05
505	Donn Pall RC	.05
506	Kelly Paris	.05
507	Dan Pasqua	.05
508	Ken Patterson RC	.05
509	Melido Perez	.05
510	Jerry Reuss	.05
511	Mark Salas	.05
512	Bobby Thigpen	.05
513	Mike Woodard	.05
514	Bob Brower	.05
515	Steve Buechele	.05
516	Jose Cecena RC	.05
517	Cecil Espy	.05
518	Scott Fletcher	.05
519	Cecilio Guante	.05
520	Jose Guzman	.05
521	Ray Hayward	.05
522	Charlie Hough	.05
523	Pete Incaviglia	.05
524	Mike Jeffcoat	.05
525	Paul Kilgus	.05
526	Chad Kreuter RC	.15
527	Jeff Kunkel	.05
528	Oddibe McDowell	.05
529	Pete O'Brien	.05
530	Geno Petralli	.05
531	Jeff Russell	.05
532	Ruben Sierra	.05
533	Mike Stanley	.05
534	Ed Vande Berg	.05
535	Curtis Wilkerson	.05
536	Mitch Williams	.05
537	Bobby Witt	.05
538	Steve Balboni	.05
539	Scott Bankhead	.05
540	Scott Bradley	.05
541	Mickey Brantley	.05
542	Jay Buhner	.05
543	Mike Campbell	.05
544	Darnell Coles	.05
545	Henry Cotto	.05
546	Alvin Davis	.05
547	Mario Diaz	.05
548	Ken Griffey Jr. RC	6.00
549	Erik Hanson RC	.05
550	Mike Jackson	.05
551	Mark Langston	.05
552	Edgar Martinez	.05
553	Bill McGuire RC	.05
554	Mike Moore	.05
555	Jim Presley	.05
556	Rey Quinones	.05
557	Jerry Reed	.05
558	Harold Reynolds	.05
559	Mike Schooler RC	.05
560	Bill Swift	.05
561	Dave Valle	.05
562	Steve Bedrosian	.05
563	Phil Bradley	.05
564	Don Carman	.05
565	Bob Dernier	.05
566	Marvin Freeman	.05
567	Todd Frohwirth	.05
568	Greg Gross	.05
569	Kevin Gross	.05
570	Greg Harris	.05
571	Von Hayes	.05
572	Chris James	.05
573	Steve Jeltz	.05
574	Ron Jones RC	.05
575	Ricky Jordan RC	.05
576	Mike Maddux	.05
577	David Palmer	.05
578	Lance Parrish	.05
579	Shane Rawley	.05
580	Bruce Ruffin	.05
581	Juan Samuel	.05
582	Mike Schmidt	.60
583	Kent Tekulve	.05
584	Milt Thompson	.05
585	Jose Alvarez RC	.05
586	Paul Assenmacher	.05
587	Bruce Benedict	.05
588	Jeff Blauser	.05
589	Terry Blocker RC	.05
590	Ron Gant	.05
591	Tom Glavine	.30
592	Tommy Gregg	.05
593	Albert Hall	.05
594	Dion James	.05
595	Rick Mahler	.05
596	Dale Murphy	.25
597	Gerald Perry	.05
598	Charlie Puleo	.05
599	Ted Simmons	.05
600	Pete Smith	.05
601	Zane Smith	.05
602	John Smoltz	.50

603	Bruce Sutter	.35
604	Andres Thomas	.05
605	Ozzie Virgil	.05
606	Brady Anderson	.05
607	Jeff Ballard	.05
608	Jose Bautista RC	.05
609	Ken Gerhart	.05
610	Terry Kennedy	.05
611	Eddie Murray	.40
612	Carl Nichols RC	.05
613	Tom Niedenfuer	.05
614	Joe Orsulak	.05
615	Oswaldo Peraza RC (Oswald)	.05
616a	Bill Ripken (Vulgarity on bat knob.)	8.00
616b	Bill Ripken (Scribble over vulgarity.)	6.00
616c	Bill Ripken (Black box over vulgarity.)	.10
616d	Bill Ripken (Vulgarity whited out.(Many fake "white out" cards exist, created by erasures.)	250.00
616e	Billy Ripken (Strip cut out of bottom of card.)	
617	Cal Ripken, Jr.	.75
618	Dave Schmidt	.05
619	Rick Schu	.05
620	Larry Sheets	.05
621	Doug Sisk	.05
622	Pete Stanicek	.05
623	Mickey Tettleton	.05
624	Jay Tibbs	.05
625	Jim Traber	.05
626	Mark Williamson	.05
627	Craig Worthington RC	.05
628	Speed and Power (Jose Canseco)	.20
629	Pitcher Perfect (Tom Browning)	.05
630	Like Father Like Sons (Roberto Alomar, Sandy Alomar, Jr.)	.20
631	N.L. All-Stars (Will Clark, Rafael Palmeiro)	.10
632	Homeruns Coast to Coast (Will Clark, Darryl Strawberry)	.05
633	Hot Corner's Hot Hitters (Wade Boggs, Carney Lansford)	.25
634	Triple A's (Jose Canseco, Mark McGwire, Terry Steinbach)	.40
635	Dual Heat (Mark Davis, Dwight Gooden)	.05
636	N.L. Pitching Power (David Cone, Danny Jackson)	.05
637	Cannon Arms (Bobby Bonilla, Chris Sabo)	.05
638	Double Trouble (Andres Galarraga, Gerald Perry)	.05
639	Power Center (Eric Davis)	.05
640	Major League Prospects (Cameron Drew RC, Steve Wilson RC)	.05
641	Major League Prospects (Kevin Brown, Kevin Reimer RC)	.30
642	Major League Prospects (Jerald Clark RC, Brad Pounders RC)	.05
643	Major League Prospects (Mike Capel RC, Drew Hall RC)	.05
644	Major League Prospects (Joe Girardi RC, Rolando Roomes RC)	.20
645	Major League Prospects (Marty Brown RC, Lenny Harris RC)	.15
646	Major League Prospects (Luis de los Santos RC, Jim Campbell RC)	.05
647	Major League Prospects (Miguel Garcia RC, Randy Kramer RC)	.05
648	Major League Prospects (Torey Lovullo RC, Robert Palacios RC)	.05
649	Major League Prospects (Jim Corsi RC, Bob Milacki RC)	.05
650	Major League Prospects (Grady Hall RC, Mike Rochford RC)	.05
651	Major League Prospects (Vance Lovelace RC, Terry Taylor RC)	.05
652	Major League Prospects (Dennis Cook RC, Ken Hill RC)	.20
653	Major League Prospects (Scott Service RC, Shane Turner RC)	.05
654	Checklist 1-101	.05
655	Checklist 102-200	.05
656	Checklist 201-298	.05
657	Checklist 299-395	.05
658	Checklist 396-490	.05
659	Checklist 491-584	.05
660	Checklist 585-660	.05

All-Star Team

This special 12-card set represents Fleer's choices for its 1989 Major League All-Star Team. For the fourth consecutive year, Fleer inserted the special cards randomly in wax and cello packs. The cards feature two player photos set against a green background with the "'89 Fleer All-Star Team" logo bannered across the top, and the player's name, position and team in the lower left corner. The backs contain a narrative player profile.

		NM/M
Complete Set (12):		2.50
Common Player:		.25
1	Bobby Bonilla	.25
2	Jose Canseco	.75
3	Will Clark	.40
4	Dennis Eckersley	.50
5	Julio Franco	.25
6	Mike Greenwell	.25
7	Orel Hershiser	.25
8	Paul Molitor	1.00
9	Mike Scioscia	.25
10	Darryl Strawberry	.25
11	Alan Trammell	.25
12	Frank Viola	.25

For The Record

Fleer's "For the Record" set features six players and their achievements from 1988. Fronts of the standard 2-1/2" x 3-1/2" cards feature a photo of the player set against a red scoreboard background. Card backs are grey and describe individual accomplishments. The cards were distributed randomly in rack packs.

		NM/M
Complete Set (6):		2.50
Common Player:		.25
1	Wade Boggs	.75
2	Roger Clemens	1.00
3	Andres Galarraga	.25
4	Kirk Gibson	.25
5	Greg Maddux	.75
6	Don Mattingly	1.00

World Series

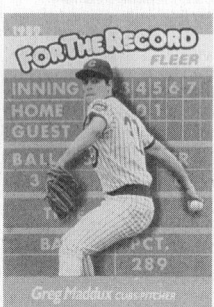

This 12-card set, which depicts highlights of the 1988 World Series, was included as a special sub-set with the regular and glossy factory-collated Fleer set. It was not available as individual cards in wax packs, cello packs or any other form.

		NM/M
Complete Set, Regular (12):		2.00
Common Card:		.10
1	Dodgers Secret Weapon (Mickey Hatcher)	.10
2	Rookie Starts Series (Tim Belcher)	.10
3	Jose Canseco	.25
4	Dramatic Comeback (Mike Scioscia)	.10
5	Kirk Gibson	.15
6	Orel Hershiser	.10
7	One Swings, Three RBIs (Mike Marshall)	.10
8	Mark McGwire	1.00
9	Sax's Speed Wins Game 4 (Steve Sax)	.10
10	Series Caps Award Winning Year (Walt Weiss)	.10
11	Orel Hershiser	.15
12	Dodger Blue, World Champs	.25

Box Panels

For the fourth consecutive year, Fleer issued a series of cards on the bottom panels of its regular 1989 wax pack boxes. The 28-card set includes 20 players and eight team logo cards, all designed in the identical style of the regular 1989 Fleer set. The box-bottom cards were randomly printed, four cards (three player cards and one team logo) on each bottom panel. Cards are numbered C-1 to C-28.

		NM/M
Complete Panel Set (7):		6.00
Complete Singles Set (28):		3.00
Common Single Player:		.15
.1	Mets Logo	.05
2	Wade Boggs	.75
3	George Brett	1.25
4	Jose Canseco	.50
5	A's Logo	.05
6	Will Clark	.10
7	David Cone	.10
8	Andres Galarraga	.10
9	Dodgers Logo	.05
10	Kirk Gibson	.10
11	Mike Greenwell	.10
12	Tony Gwynn	.75
13	Tigers Logo	.05
14	Orel Hershiser	.10
15	Danny Jackson	.05
16	Wally Joyner	.10
17	Red Sox Logo	.05
18	Yankees Logo	.05
19	Fred McGriff	.20
20	Kirby Puckett	.75
21	Chris Sabo	.10
22	Kevin Seitzer	.05
23	Pirates logo	.05
24	Astros Logo	.05
25	Darryl Strawberry	.10
26	Alan Trammell	.10
27	Andy Van Slyke	.10
28	Frank Viola	.10

Glossy Tin

The last of the limited-edition, collector-version glossy tin sets is estimated to have been produced in an edition of 30,000-60,000, creating a significant premium over their counterparts in the regular Fleer set. The issue was sold only in complete-set form in a lithographed metal box. The 1989 glossies differ from the regular cards on back in the use of blue, rather than yellow ink, and the appearance at center of a large baseball logo with 1989 / Collector's Edition / Fleer at center. No glossy

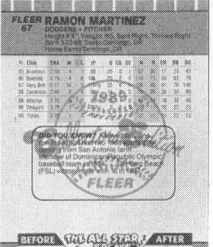

version of the '89 Update set was made. Fleer glossy sets were originally wholesaled at $40 each.

	NM/M
Unopened Set (672):	75.00
Complete Set (672):	50.00
Common Player:	.25

Update

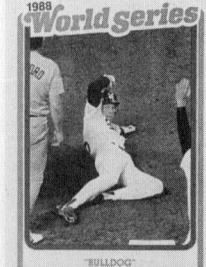

Fleer produced its sixth consecutive "Update" set in 1989 to supplement the company's regular set. As in the past, the set consisted of 132 cards (numbered U-1 through U-132) that were sold by hobby dealers in special collector's boxes.

		NM/M
Complete Set (132):		6.00
Common Player:		.05
1	Phil Bradley	.05
2	Mike Devereaux	.05
3	Steve Finley RC	.05
4	Kevin Hickey	.05
5	Bob Milacki	.05
6	Randy Milligan	.05
7	John Dopson	.05
8	Nick Esasky	.05
9	Rob Murphy	.05
10	Jim Abbott RC	.25
11	Bert Blyleven	.10
12	Jeff Manto RC	.05
13	Bob McClure	.05
14	Lance Parrish	.05
15	Lee Stevens RC	.05
16	Claudell Washington	.05
17	Mark Davis	.05
18	Eric King	.05
19	Ron Kittle	.05
20	Matt Merullo RC	.05
21	Steve Rosenberg RC	.05
22	Robin Ventura	.25
23	Keith Atherton	.05
24	Joey (Albert) Belle RC	1.00
25	Jerry Browne	.05
26	Felix Fermin	.05
27	Brad Komminsk	.05
28	Pete O'Brien	.05
29	Mike Brumley	.05
30	Tracy Jones	.05
31	Mike Schwabe RC	.05
32	Gary Ward	.05
33	Frank Williams	.05
34	Kevin Appier RC	.25
35	Bob Boone	.05
36	Luis de los Santos	.05
37	Jim Eisenreich RC	.05
38	Jaime Navarro RC	.05
39	Bill Spiers RC	.05
40	Greg Vaughn RC	.25
41	Randy Veres RC	.05
42	Wally Backman	.05
43	Shane Rawley	.05
44	Steve Balboni	.05
45	Jesse Barfield	.05
46	Alvaro Espinoza RC	.05
47	Bob Geren RC	.05
48	Mel Hall	.05
49	Andy Hawkins	.05
50	Hensley Meulens RC	.05
51	Steve Sax	.05
52	Deion Sanders RC	.75
53	Rickey Henderson	.40
54	Mike Moore	.05
55	Tony Phillips	.05
56	Greg Briley	.05

58	Gene Harris	.05
59	Randy Johnson	2.00
60	Jeffrey Leonard	.05
61	Dennis Powell	.05
62	Omar Vizquel	.05
63	Kevin Brown	.05
64	Julio Franco	.05
65	Jamie Moyer	.05
66	Rafael Palmeiro	.35
67	Nolan Ryan	1.00
68	Francisco Cabrera RC	.05
69	Junior Felix RC	.05
70	Al Leiter	.05
71	Alex Sanchez RC	.05
72	Geronimo Berroa RC	.05
73	Derek Lilliquist RC	.05
74	Lonnie Smith	.05
75	Jeff Treadway	.05
76	Paul Kilgus	.05
77	Lloyd McClendon	.05
78	Scott Sanderson	.05
79	Dwight Smith RC	.05
80	Jerome Walton RC	.05
81	Mitch Williams	.05
82	Steve Wilson	.05
83	Todd Benzinger	.05
84	Ken Griffey	.05
85	Rick Mahler	.05
86	Rolando Roomes	.05
87	Scott Scudder RC	.05
88	Jim Clancy	.05
89	Rick Rhoden	.05
90	Dan Schatzeder	.05
91	Mike Morgan	.05
92	Eddie Murray	.40
93	Willie Randolph	.05
94	Ray Searage	.05
95	Mike Aldrete	.05
96	Kevin Gross	.05
97	Mark Langston	.05
98	Spike Owen	.05
99	Zane Smith	.05
100	Don Aase	.05
101	Barry Lyons	.05
102	Juan Samuel	.05
103	Wally Whitehurst RC	.05
104	Dennis Cook	.05
105	Len Dykstra	.05
106	Charlie Hayes RC	.05
107	Tommy Herr	.05
108	Ken Howell	.05
109	John Kruk	.05
110	Roger McDowell	.05
111	Terry Mulholland RC	.05
112	Jeff Parrett	.05
113	Neal Heaton	.05
114	Jeff King	.05
115	Randy Kramer	.05
116	Bill Landrum	.05
117	Cris Carpenter RC	.05
118	Frank DiPino	.05
119	Ken Hill	.05
120	Dan Quisenberry	.05
121	Milt Thompson	.05
122	Todd Zeile RC	.25
123	Jack Clark	.05
124	Bruce Hurst	.05
125	Mark Parent	.05
126	Bip Roberts	.05
127	Jeff Brantley RC	.05
128	Terry Kennedy	.05
129	Mike LaCoss	.05
130	Greg Litton	.05
131	Mike Schmidt	.65
132	Checklist	.05

Bill Ripken FF 'Test'

At the height of the furor over the vulgarity shown on the initial print run of Bill Ripken's card, when genuine examples were selling for as high as $125, this fantasy card surfaced to prey on collectors. In standard size, the card is printed in black-and-white on front and back, reproducing a genuine card. On the back, typography was also added to make the piece look like a test card. This fraudulent product has no collectible value.

Baseball All-Stars

This specially-boxed set was produced by Fleer for the Ben Franklin store chain. The full-color play-

er photos are surrounded by a border of pink and yellow vertical bands. "Fleer Baseball All-Stars" appears along the top in red, white and blue. The set was sold in a box with a checklist on the back.

		NM/M
Complete Set (44):		4.00
Common Player:		.10
1	Doyle Alexander	.10
2	George Bell	.10
3	Wade Boggs	.65
4	Bobby Bonilla	.10
5	Jose Canseco	.40
6	Will Clark	.40
7	Roger Clemens	.75
8	Vince Coleman	.10
9	David Cone	.10
10	Mark Davis	.10
11	Andre Dawson	.25
12	Dennis Eckersley	.45
13	Andres Galarraga	.10
14	Kirk Gibson	.10
15	Dwight Gooden	.10
16	Mike Greenwell	.10
17	Mark Gubicza	.10
18	Ozzie Guillen	.10
19	Tony Gwynn	.65
20	Rickey Henderson	.50
21	Orel Hershiser	.10
22	Danny Jackson	.10
23	Doug Jones	.10
24	Ricky Jordan	.10
25	Bob Knepper	.10
26	Barry Larkin	.10
27	Vance Law	.10
28	Don Mattingly	.75
29	Mark McGwire	1.00
30	Paul Molitor	.50
31	Gerald Perry	.10
32	Kirby Puckett	.65
33	Johnny Ray	.10
34	Harold Reynolds	.10
35	Cal Ripken, Jr.	1.50
36	Don Robinson	.10
37	Ruben Sierra	.10
38	Dave Smith	.10
39	Darryl Strawberry	.10
40	Dave Steib	.10
41	Alan Trammell	.10
42	Andy Van Slyke	.10
43	Frank Viola	.10
44	Dave Winfield	.50

Exciting Stars

Sold exclusively in Cumberland Farm stores, this boxed set pictures the game's top stars. The card fronts feature a color player photo surrounded by a blue border with "Baseball's Exciting Stars" along the top. The cards were numbered alphabetically and packed in a special box with a complete checklist on the back.

		NM/M
Complete Set (44):		4.00
Common Player:		.10
1	Harold Baines	.10
2	Wade Boggs	.65
3	Jose Canseco	.50
4	Joe Carter	.10
5	Will Clark	.10
6	Roger Clemens	.75
7	Vince Coleman	.10

8	David Cone	.10
9	Eric Davis	.10
10	Glenn Davis	.10
11	Andre Dawson	.25
12	Dwight Evans	.10
13	Andres Galarraga	.10
14	Kirk Gibson	.10
15	Dwight Gooden	.10
16	Jim Gott	.10
17	Mark Grace	.10
18	Mike Greenwell	.10
19	Mark Gubicza	.10
20	Tony Gwynn	.65
21	Rickey Henderson	.60
22	Tom Henke	.10
23	Mike Henneman	.10
24	Orel Hershiser	.10
25	Danny Jackson	.10
26	Gregg Jefferies	.10
27	Ricky Jordan	.10
28	Wally Joyner	.10
29	Mark Langston	.10
30	Tim Leary	.10
31	Don Mattingly	.75
32	Mark McGwire	1.50
33	Dale Murphy	.15
34	Kirby Puckett	.65
35	Chris Sabo	.10
36	Kevin Seitzer	.10
37	Ruben Sierra	.10
38	Ozzie Smith	.65
39	Dave Stewart	.10
40	Darryl Strawberry	.10
41	Alan Trammell	.10
42	Frank Viola	.10
43	Dave Winfield	.60
44	Robin Yount	.60

Heroes of Baseball

This boxed set was produced by Fleer for the Woolworth store chain. The fronts of the cards are designed in a red and blue color scheme and feature full-color photos that fade into a soft focus on all edges. The set is numbered alphabetically and was packaged in a special box with a checklist on the back.

		NM/M
Complete Set (44):		4.00
Common Player:		.10
1	George Bell	.10
2	Wade Boggs	.75
3	Barry Bonds	1.50
4	Tom Brunansky	.10
5	Jose Canseco	.40
6	Joe Carter	.10
7	Will Clark	.10
8	Roger Clemens	.85
9	David Cone	.10
10	Eric Davis	.10
11	Glenn Davis	.10
12	Andre Dawson	.25
13	Dennis Eckersley	.50
14	John Franco	.10
15	Gary Gaetti	.10
16	Andres Galarraga	.10
17	Kirk Gibson	.10
18	Dwight Gooden	.10
19	Mike Greenwell	.10
20	Tony Gwynn	.75
21	Bryan Harvey	.10
22	Orel Hershiser	.10
23	Ted Higuera	.10
24	Danny Jackson	.10
25	Ricky Jordan	.10
26	Don Mattingly	.85
27	Fred McGriff	.10
28	Mark McGwire	1.00
29	Kevin McReynolds	.10
30	Gerald Perry	.10
31	Kirby Puckett	.75
32	Johnny Ray	.10
33	Harold Reynolds	.10
34	Cal Ripken, Jr.	1.50
35	Ryne Sandberg	.75
36	Kevin Seitzer	.10
37	Ruben Sierra	.10
38	Darryl Strawberry	.10
39	Bobby Thigpen	.10
40	Alan Trammell	.10
41	Andy Van Slyke	.10
42	Frank Viola	.10
43	Dave Winfield	.65
44	Robin Yount	.65

League Leaders

Robin Yount

Another of the various small, boxed sets issued by Fleer, "League Leaders" was produced for Walgreen stores. The standard-size cards feature color photos on the front surrounded by a red border with "Fleer League Leaders" across the top. The backs include player stats and data and the team logo. The cards are numbered and packaged in a special box that includes the full checklist on the back.

		NM/M
Complete Set (44):		5.00
Common Player:		.10
1	Steve Bedrosian	.10
2	George Bell	.10
3	Wade Boggs	.75
4	George Brett	.85
5	Hubie Brooks	.10
6	Jose Canseco	.50
7	Will Clark	.10
8	Roger Clemens	.85
9	Eric Davis	.10
10	Glenn Davis	.10
11	Andre Dawson	.25
12	Andres Galarraga	.10
13	Kirk Gibson	.10
14	Dwight Gooden	.10
15	Mark Grace	.10
16	Mike Greenwell	.10
17	Tony Gwynn	.75
18	Bryan Harvey	.10
19	Orel Hershiser	.10
20	Ted Higuera	.10
21	Danny Jackson	.10
22	Mike Jackson	.10
23	Doug Jones	.10
24	Greg Maddux	.75
25	Mike Marshall	.10
26	Don Mattingly	.85
27	Fred McGriff	.10
28	Mark McGwire	1.50
29	Kevin McReynolds	.10
30	Jack Morris	.10
31	Gerald Perry	.10
32	Kirby Puckett	.75
33	Chris Sabo	.10
34	Mike Scott	.10
35	Ruben Sierra	.10
36	Darryl Strawberry	.10
37	Danny Tartabull	.10
38	Bobby Thigpen	.10
39	Alan Trammell	.10
40	Andy Van Slyke	.10
41	Frank Viola	.10
42	Walt Weiss	.10
43	Dave Winfield	.65
44	Todd Worrell	.10

Superstars

WADE BOGGS
THIRD BASE

This boxed set was produced by Fleer for the McCrory store chain. The cards are standard 2-1/2" x 3-1/2" and the full-color player photos are outlined in red with a tan-and-white striped border. The backs carry yellow and white stripes and include the Fleer "SuperStars" logo, player stats and biographical information. The cards are numbered alphabetically and packaged in a special box that includes a checklist on the back.

		NM/M
Complete Set (44):		3.00
Common Player:		.10
1	Allan Anderson	.10
2	Wade Boggs	.75
3	Jose Canseco	.50
4	Will Clark	.10
5	Roger Clemens	.85
6	Vince Coleman	.10
7	David Cone	.10
8	Kal Daniels	.10
9	Chili Davis	.10
10	Eric Davis	.10
11	Glenn Davis	.10
12	Andre Dawson	.25
13	John Franco	.10
14	Andres Galarraga	.10
15	Kirk Gibson	.10
16	Dwight Gooden	.10
17	Mark Grace	.10
18	Mike Greenwell	.10
19	Tony Gwynn	.75
20	Orel Hershiser	.10
21	Pete Incaviglia	.10
22	Danny Jackson	.10
23	Gregg Jefferies	.10
24	Joe Magrane	.10
25	Don Mattingly	.85
26	Fred McGriff	.10
27	Mark McGwire	1.00
28	Dale Murphy	.15
29	Dan Plesac	.10
30	Kirby Puckett	.75
31	Harold Reynolds	.10
32	Cal Ripken, Jr.	1.50
33	Jeff Robinson	.10
34	Mike Scott	.10
35	Ozzie Smith	.75
36	Dave Stewart	.10
37	Darryl Strawberry	.10
38	Greg Swindell	.10
39	Bobby Thigpen	.10
40	Alan Trammell	.10
41	Andy Van Slyke	.10
42	Frank Viola	.10
43	Dave Winfield	.65
44	Robin Yount	.65

MVP

MIKE GREENWELL

Filled with superstars, this boxed set was produced by Fleer in 1989 for the Toys "R" Us chain. The fronts of the cards are designed in a yellow and green color scheme and include a "Fleer Baseball MVP" logo above the color player photo. The backs are printed in shades of green and yellow and include biographical notes and stats. The set was issued in a special box with a checklist on the back.

		NM/M
Complete Set (44):		4.00
Common Player:		.10
1	Roberto Alomar	.35
2	Harold Baines	.10
3	Tim Belcher	.10
4	Wade Boggs	.65
5	George Brett	.85
6	Jose Canseco	.50
7	Gary Carter	.60
8	Will Clark	.10
9	Roger Clemens	.85
10	Kal Daniels	.10
11	Eric Davis	.10
12	Andre Dawson	.25
13	Tony Fernandez	.10
14	Scott Fletcher	.10
15	Andres Galarraga	.10
16	Kirk Gibson	.10
17	Dwight Gooden	.10
18	Jim Gott	.10
19	Mark Grace	.10
20	Mike Greenwell	.10
21	Tony Gwynn	.75
22	Rickey Henderson	.60
23	Orel Hershiser	.10
24	Ted Higuera	.10
25	Gregg Jefferies	.10
26	Wally Joyner	.10
27	Mark Langston	.10
28	Greg Maddux	.75
29	Don Mattingly	.85
30	Fred McGriff	.10
31	Mark McGwire	1.50

32	Dan Plesac	.10
33	Kirby Puckett	.75
34	Jeff Reardon	.10
35	Chris Sabo	.10
36	Mike Schmidt	.85
37	Mike Scott	.10
38	Cory Snyder	.10
39	Darryl Strawberry	.10
40	Alan Trammell	.10
41	Frank Viola	.10
42	Walt Weiss	.10
43	Dave Winfield	.60
44	Todd Worrell	.10

1990 Fleer

George Brett
FIRST BASE

Fleer's 1990 set, its 10th annual baseball card offering, again consisted of 660 cards numbered by team. The front of the cards feature mostly action photos surrounded by one of several different color bands and a white border. The set includes various special cards, including a series of "Major League Prospects," Players of the Decade, team checklist cards and a series of multi-player cards. The backs include complete career stats, player data, and a special "Vital Signs" section showing on-base percentage, slugging percentage, etc. for batters; and strikeout and walk ratios, opposing batting averages, etc. for pitchers.

	NM/M
Factory Hobby Set (672):	12.50
Retail Hobby Set (660):	12.00
Complete Set (660):	10.00
Common Player:	.05
Wax Pack (15):	.50
Wax Box (36):	10.00
Cello Pack (33):	1.00
Cello Box (24):	12.00

1	Lance Blankenship	.05
2	Todd Burns	.05
3	Jose Canseco	.30
4	Jim Corsi	.05
5	Storm Davis	.05
6	Dennis Eckersley	.35
7	Mike Gallego	.05
8	Ron Hassey	.05
9	Dave Henderson	.05
10	Rickey Henderson	.40
11	Rick Honeycutt	.05
12	Stan Javier	.05
13	Felix Jose	.05
14	Carney Lansford	.05
15	Mark McGwire	.65
16	Mike Moore	.05
17	Gene Nelson	.05
18	Dave Parker	.05
19	Tony Phillips	.05
20	Terry Steinbach	.05
21	Dave Stewart	.05
22	Walt Weiss	.05
23	Bob Welch	.05
24	Curt Young	.05
25	Paul Assenmacher	.05
26	Damon Berryhill	.05
27	Mike Bielecki	.05
28	Kevin Blankenship	.05
29	Andre Dawson	.25
30	Shawon Dunston	.05
31	Joe Girardi	.05
32	Mark Grace	.05
33	Mike Harkey	.05
34	Paul Kilgus	.05
35	Les Lancaster	.05
36	Vance Law	.05
37	Greg Maddux	.50
38	Lloyd McClendon	.05
39	Jeff Pico	.05
40	Ryne Sandberg	.50
41	Scott Sanderson	.05
42	Dwight Smith	.05
43	Rick Sutcliffe	.05
44	Jerome Walton RC	.05
45	Mitch Webster	.05
46	Curt Wilkerson	.05
47	Dean Wilkins RC	.05
48	Mitch Williams	.05
49	Steve Wilson	.05
50	Steve Bedrosian	.05
51	Mike Benjamin RC	.05

#	Player	Price
52	Jeff Brantley RC	.10
53	Brett Butler	.05
54	Will Clark	.05
55	Kelly Downs	.05
56	Scott Garrelts	.05
57	Atlee Hammaker	.05
58	Terry Kennedy	.05
59	Mike LaCoss	.05
60	Craig Lefferts	.05
61	Greg Litton RC	.05
62	Candy Maldonado	.05
63	Kirt Manwaring	.05
64	Randy McCament RC	.05
65	Kevin Mitchell	.05
66	Donell Nixon	.05
67	Ken Oberkfell	.05
68	Rick Reuschel	.05
69	Ernest Riles	.05
70	Don Robinson	.05
71	Pat Sheridan	.05
72	Chris Speier	.05
73	Robby Thompson	.05
74	Jose Uribe	.05
75	Matt Williams	.05
76	George Bell	.05
77	Pat Borders	.05
78	John Cerutti	.05
79	Junior Felix RC	.05
80	Tony Fernandez	.05
81	Mike Flanagan	.05
82	Mauro Gozzo RC	.05
83	Kelly Gruber	.05
84	Tom Henke	.05
85	Jimmy Key	.05
86	Manny Lee	.05
87	Nelson Liriano	.05
88	Lee Mazzilli	.05
89	Fred McGriff	.05
90	Lloyd Moseby	.05
91	Rance Mulliniks	.05
92	Alex Sanchez	.05
93	Dave Steib	.05
94	Todd Stottlemyre	.05
95	Duane Ward	.05
96	David Wells	.05
97	Ernie Whitt	.05
98	Frank Wills	.05
99	Mookie Wilson	.05
100	Kevin Appier	.05
101	Luis Aquino	.05
102	Bob Boone	.05
103	George Brett	.60
104	Jose DeJesus	.05
105	Luis de los Santos	.05
106	Jim Eisenreich	.05
107	Steve Farr	.05
108	Tom Gordon	.05
109	Mark Gubicza	.05
110	Bo Jackson	.10
111	Terry Leach	.05
112	Charlie Leibrandt	.05
113	Rick Luecken RC	.05
114	Mike Macfarlane	.05
115	Jeff Montgomery	.05
116	Bret Saberhagen	.05
117	Kevin Seitzer	.05
118	Kurt Stillwell	.05
119	Pat Tabler	.05
120	Danny Tartabull	.05
121	Gary Thurman	.05
122	Frank White	.05
123	Willie Wilson	.05
124	Matt Winters RC	.05
125	Jim Abbott	.05
126	Tony Armas	.05
127	Dante Bichette	.05
128	Bert Blyleven	.10
129	Chili Davis	.05
130	Brian Downing	.05
131	Mike Fetters RC	.05
132	Chuck Finley	.05
133	Willie Fraser	.05
134	Bryan Harvey	.05
135	Jack Howell	.05
136	Wally Joyner	.05
137	Jeff Manto RC	.05
138	Kirk McCaskill	.05
139	Bob McClure	.05
140	Greg Minton	.05
141	Lance Parrish	.05
142	Dan Petry	.05
143	Johnny Ray	.05
144	Dick Schofield	.05
145	Lee Stevens RC	.05
146	Claudell Washington	.05
147	Devon White	.05
148	Mike Witt	.05
149	Roberto Alomar	.20
150	Sandy Alomar, Jr.	.05
151	Andy Benes	.05
152	Jack Clark	.05
153	Pat Clements	.05
154	Joey Cora	.05
155	Mark Davis	.05
156	Mark Grant	.05
157	Tony Gwynn	.50
158	Greg Harris	.05
159	Bruce Hurst	.05
160	Darrin Jackson	.05
161	Chris James	.05
162	Carmelo Martinez	.05
163	Mike Pagliarulo	.05
164	Mark Parent	.05
165	Dennis Rasmussen	.05
166	Bip Roberts	.05
167	Benito Santiago	.05
168	Calvin Schiraldi	.05
169	Eric Show	.05
170	Garry Templeton	.05
171	Ed Whitson	.05
172	Brady Anderson	.05
173	Jeff Ballard	.05
174	Phil Bradley	.05
175	Mike Devereaux	.05
176	Steve Finley	.05
177	Pete Harnisch RC	.05
178	Kevin Hickey	.05
179	Brian Holton	.05
180	Ben McDonald RC	.15
181	Bob Melvin	.05
182	Bob Milacki	.05
183	Randy Milligan	.05
184	Gregg Olson RC	.05
185	Joe Orsulak	.05
186	Bill Ripken	.05
187	Cal Ripken, Jr.	.75
188	Dave Schmidt	.05
189	Larry Sheets	.05
190	Mickey Tettleton	.05
191	Mark Thurmond	.05
192	Jay Tibbs	.05
193	Jim Traber	.05
194	Mark Williamson	.05
195	Craig Worthington	.05
196	Don Aase	.05
197	Blaine Beatty RC	.05
198	Mark Carreon	.05
199	Gary Carter	.40
200	David Cone	.05
201	Ron Darling	.05
202	Kevin Elster	.05
203	Sid Fernandez	.05
204	Dwight Gooden	.05
205	Keith Hernandez	.05
206	Jeff Innis RC	.05
207	Gregg Jefferies	.05
208	Howard Johnson	.05
209	Barry Lyons	.05
210	Dave Magadan	.05
211	Kevin McReynolds	.05
212	Jeff Musselman	.05
213	Randy Myers	.05
214	Bob Ojeda	.05
215	Juan Samuel	.05
216	Mackey Sasser	.05
217	Darryl Strawberry	.05
218	Tim Teufel	.05
219	Frank Viola	.05
220	Juan Agosto	.05
221	Larry Anderson	.05
222	Eric Anthony RC	.10
223	Kevin Bass	.05
224	Craig Biggio	.05
225	Ken Caminiti	.05
226	Jim Clancy	.05
227	Danny Darwin	.05
228	Glenn Davis	.05
229	Jim Deshaies	.05
230	Bill Doran	.05
231	Bob Forsch	.05
232	Brian Meyer	.05
233	Terry Puhl	.05
234	Rafael Ramirez	.05
235	Rick Rhoden	.05
236	Dan Schatzeder	.05
237	Mike Scott	.05
238	Dave Smith	.05
239	Alex Trevino	.05
240	Glenn Wilson	.05
241	Gerald Young	.05
242	Tom Brunansky	.05
243	Cris Carpenter	.05
244	Alex Cole RC	.05
245	Vince Coleman	.05
246	John Costello	.05
247	Ken Dayley	.05
248	Jose DeLeon	.05
249	Frank DiPino	.05
250	Pedro Guerrero	.05
251	Ken Hill	.05
252	Joe Magrane	.05
253	Willie McGee	.05
254	John Morris	.05
255	Jose Oquendo	.05
256	Tony Pena	.05
257	Terry Pendleton	.05
258	Ted Power	.05
259	Dan Quisenberry	.05
260	Ozzie Smith	.50
261	Scott Terry	.05
262	Milt Thompson	.05
263	Denny Walling	.05
264	Todd Worrell	.05
265	Todd Zeile	.05
266	Marty Barrett	.05
267	Mike Boddicker	.05
268	Wade Boggs	.50
269	Ellis Burks	.05
270	Rick Cerone	.05
271	Roger Clemens	.60
272	John Dopson	.05
273	Nick Esasky	.05
274	Dwight Evans	.05
275	Wes Gardner	.05
276	Rich Gedman	.05
277	Mike Greenwell	.05
278	Danny Heep	.05
279	Eric Hetzel	.05
280	Dennis Lamp	.05
281	Rob Murphy	.05
282	Joe Price	.05
283	Carlos Quintana	.05
284	Jody Reed	.05
285	Luis Rivera	.05
286	Kevin Romine	.05
287	Lee Smith	.05
288	Mike Smithson	.05
289	Bob Stanley	.05
290	Harold Baines	.05
291	Kevin Brown	.05
292	Steve Buechele	.05
293	Scott Coolbaugh RC	.05
294	Jack Daugherty RC	.05
295	Cecil Espy	.05
296	Julio Franco	.05
297	Juan Gonzalez RC	2.00
298	Cecilio Guante	.05
299	Drew Hall	.05
300	Charlie Hough	.05
301	Pete Incaviglia	.05
302	Mike Jeffcoat	.05
303	Chad Kreuter	.05
304	Jeff Kunkel	.05
305	Rick Leach	.05
306	Fred Manrique	.05
307	Jamie Moyer	.05
308	Rafael Palmeiro	.35
309	Geno Petralli	.05
310	Kevin Reimer	.05
311	Kenny Rogers RC	.10
312	Jeff Russell	.05
313	Nolan Ryan	.75
314	Ruben Sierra	.05
315	Bobby Witt	.05
316	Chris Bosio	.05
317	Glenn Braggs	.05
318	Greg Brock	.05
319	Chuck Crim	.05
320	Rob Deer	.05
321	Mike Felder	.05
322	Tom Filer	.05
323	Tony Fossas RC	.05
324	Jim Gantner	.05
325	Darryl Hamilton	.05
326	Ted Higuera	.05
327	Mark Knudson RC	.05
328	Bill Krueger	.05
329	Tim McIntosh RC	.05
330	Paul Molitor	.40
331	Jaime Navarro	.05
332	Charlie O'Brien	.05
333	Jeff Peterek RC	.05
334	Dan Plesac	.05
335	Jerry Reuss	.05
336	Gary Sheffield	.35
337	Bill Spiers RC	.05
338	B.J. Surhoff	.05
339	Greg Vaughn	.05
340	Robin Yount	.40
341	Hubie Brooks	.05
342	Tim Burke	.05
343	Mike Fitzgerald	.05
344	Tom Foley	.05
345	Andres Galarraga	.05
346	Damaso Garcia	.05
347	Marquis Grissom RC	.50
348	Kevin Gross	.05
349	Joe Hesketh	.05
350	Jeff Huson RC	.05
351	Wallace Johnson	.05
352	Mark Langston	.05
353a	Dave Martinez (Yellow 90.)	6.00
353b	Dave Martinez (Red 90.)	.05
354	Dennis Martinez	.05
355	Andy McGaffigan	.05
356	Otis Nixon	.05
357	Spike Owen	.05
358	Pascual Perez	.05
359	Tim Raines	.05
360	Nelson Santovenia	.05
361	Bryn Smith	.05
362	Zane Smith	.05
363	Larry Walker RC	.75
364	Tim Wallach	.05
365	Rick Aguilera	.05
366	Allan Anderson	.05
367	Wally Backman	.05
368	Doug Baker RC	.05
369	Juan Berenguer	.05
370	Randy Bush	.05
371	Carmen Castillo	.05
372	Mike Dyer RC	.05
373	Gary Gaetti	.05
374	Greg Gagne	.05
375	Dan Gladden	.05
376	German Gonzalez	.05
377	Brian Harper	.05
378	Kent Hrbek	.05
379	Gene Larkin	.05
380	Tim Laudner	.05
381	John Moses	.05
382	Al Newman	.05
383	Kirby Puckett	.50
384	Shane Rawley	.05
385	Jeff Reardon	.05
386	Roy Smith	.05
387	Gary Wayne RC	.05
388	Dave West	.05
389	Tim Belcher	.05
390	Tim Crews	.05
391	Mike Davis	.05
392	Rick Dempsey	.05
393	Kirk Gibson	.05
394	Jose Gonzalez	.05
395	Alfredo Griffin	.05
396	Jeff Hamilton	.05
397	Lenny Harris	.05
398	Mickey Hatcher	.05
399	Orel Hershiser	.05
400	Jay Howell	.05
401	Mike Marshall	.05
402	Ramon Martinez	.05
403	Mike Morgan	.05
404	Eddie Murray	.40
405	Alejandro Pena	.05
406	Willie Randolph	.05
407	Mike Scioscia	.05
408	Ray Searage	.05
409	Fernando Valenzuela	.05
410	Jose Vizcaino RC	.10
411	John Wetteland RC	.20
412	Jack Armstrong	.05
413	Todd Benzinger	.05
414	Tim Birtsas	.05
415	Tom Browning	.05
416	Norm Charlton	.05
417	Eric Davis	.05
418	Rob Dibble	.05
419	John Franco	.05
420	Ken Griffey Sr.	.05
421	Chris Hammond RC	.15
422	Danny Jackson	.05
423	Barry Larkin	.05
424	Tim Leary	.05
425	Rick Mahler	.05
426	Joe Oliver RC	.05
427	Paul O'Neill	.05
428	Luis Quinones	.05
429	Jeff Reed	.05
430	Jose Rijo	.05
431	Ron Robinson	.05
432	Rolando Roomes	.05
433	Chris Sabo	.05
434	Scott Scudder RC	.05
435	Herm Winningham	.05
436	Steve Balboni	.05
437	Jesse Barfield	.05
438	Mike Blowers RC	.05
439	Tom Brookens	.05
440	Greg Cadaret	.05
441	Alvaro Espinoza	.05
442	Bob Geren RC	.05
443	Lee Guetterman	.05
444	Mel Hall	.05
445	Andy Hawkins	.05
446	Roberto Kelly	.05
447	Don Mattingly	.60
448	Lance McCullers	.05
449	Hensley Meulens	.05
450	Dale Mohorcic	.05
451	Clay Parker	.05
452	Eric Plunk	.05
453	Dave Righetti	.05
454	Deion Sanders	.10
455	Steve Sax	.05
456	Don Slaught	.05
457	Walt Terrell	.05
458	Dave Winfield	.40
459	Jay Bell	.05
460	Rafael Belliard	.05
461	Barry Bonds	.75
462	Bobby Bonilla	.05
463	Sid Bream	.05
464	Benny Distefano	.05
465	Doug Drabek	.05
466	Jim Gott	.05
467	Billy Hatcher	.05
468	Neal Heaton	.05
469	Jeff King	.05
470	Bob Kipper	.05
471	Randy Kramer	.05
472	Bill Landrum	.05
473	Mike LaValliere	.05
474	Jose Lind	.05
475	Junior Ortiz	.05
476	Gary Redus	.05
477	Rick Reed RC	.05
478	R.J. Reynolds	.05
479	Jeff Robinson	.05
480	John Smiley	.05
481	Andy Van Slyke	.05
482	Bob Walk	.05
483	Andy Allanson	.05
484	Scott Bailes	.05
485	Albert Belle	.05
486	Bud Black	.05
487	Jerry Browne	.05
488	Tom Candiotti	.05
489	Joe Carter	.05
490	David Clark	.05
491	John Farrell	.05
492	Felix Fermin	.05
493	Brook Jacoby	.05
494	Dion James	.05
495	Doug Jones	.05
496	Brad Komminsk	.05
497	Rod Nichols	.05
498	Pete O'Brien	.05
499	Steve Olin RC	.05
500	Jesse Orosco	.05
501	Joel Skinner	.05
502	Cory Snyder	.05
503	Greg Swindell	.05
504	Rich Yett	.05
505	Scott Bankhead	.05
506	Scott Bradley	.05
507	Greg Briley	.05
508	Jay Buhner	.05
509	Darnell Coles	.05
510	Keith Comstock	.05
511	Henry Cotto	.05
512	Alvin Davis	.05
513	Ken Griffey Jr.	.65
514	Erik Hanson	.05
515	Gene Harris	.05
516	Brian Holman	.05
517	Mike Jackson	.05
518	Randy Johnson	.40
519	Jeffrey Leonard	.05
520	Edgar Martinez	.05
521	Dennis Powell	.05
522	Jim Presley	.05
523	Jerry Reed	.05
524	Harold Reynolds	.05
525	Mike Schooler	.05
526	Bill Swift	.05
527	David Valle	.05
528	Omar Vizquel	.05
529	Ivan Calderon	.05
530	Carlton Fisk	.40
531	Scott Fletcher	.05
532	Dave Gallagher	.05
533	Ozzie Guillen	.05
534	Greg Hibbard RC	.05
535	Shawn Hillegas	.05
536	Lance Johnson	.05
537	Eric King	.05
538	Ron Kittle	.05
539	Steve Lyons	.05
540	Carlos Martinez	.05
541	Tom McCarthy RC	.05
542	Matt Merullo RC	.05
543	Donn Pall	.05
544	Dan Pasqua	.05
545	Ken Patterson	.05
546	Melido Perez	.05
547	Steve Rosenberg	.05
548	Sammy Sosa RC	5.00
549	Bobby Thigpen	.05
550	Robin Ventura	.05
551	Greg Walker	.05
552	Don Carman	.05
553	Pat Combs RC	.05
554	Dennis Cook	.05
555	Darren Daulton	.05
556	Len Dykstra	.05
557	Curt Ford	.05
558	Charlie Hayes	.05
559	Von Hayes	.05
560	Tom Herr	.05
561	Ken Howell	.05
562	Steve Jeltz	.05
563	Ron Jones	.05
564	Ricky Jordan	.05
565	John Kruk	.05
566	Steve Lake	.05
567	Roger McDowell	.05
568	Terry Mulholland	.05
569	Dwayne Murphy	.05
570	Jeff Parrett	.05
571	Randy Ready	.05
572	Bruce Ruffin	.05
573	Dickie Thon	.05
574	Jose Alvarez	.05
575	Geronimo Berroa	.05
576	Jeff Blauser	.05
577	Joe Boever	.05
578	Marty Clary	.05
579	Jody Davis	.05
580	Mark Eichhorn	.05
581	Darrell Evans	.05
582	Ron Gant	.05
583	Tom Glavine	.25
584	Tommy Greene RC	.05
585	Tommy Gregg	.05
586	Dave Justice RC	.40
587	Mark Lemke RC	.05
588	Derek Lilliquist	.05
589	Oddibe McDowell	.05
590	Kent Mercker RC	.05
591	Dale Murphy	.20
592	Gerald Perry	.05
593	Lonnie Smith	.05
594	Pete Smith	.05
595	John Smoltz	.05
596	Mike Stanton RC	.05
597	Andres Thomas	.05
598	Jeff Treadway	.05
599	Doyle Alexander	.05
600	Dave Bergman	.05
601	Brian Dubois RC	.05
602	Paul Gibson	.05
603	Mike Heath	.05
604	Mike Henneman	.05
605	Guillermo Hernandez	.05
606	Shawn Holman	.05
607	Tracy Jones	.05
608	Chet Lemon	.05
609	Fred Lynn	.05
610	Jack Morris	.05
611	Matt Nokes	.05
612	Gary Pettis	.05
613	Kevin Ritz RC	.05
614	Jeff Robinson	.05
615	Steve Searcy	.05
616	Frank Tanana	.05
617	Alan Trammell	.05
618	Gary Ward	.05
619	Lou Whitaker	.05
620	Frank Williams	.05
621a	Players of the Decade/1980 (George Brett (... 10 .390 hitting ...))	1.00
621b	Players of the Decade/1980 (George Brett)	.25
622	Players of the Decade/1981 (Fernando Valenzuela)	.05
623	Players of the Decade/1982 (Dale Murphy)	.05
624a	Players of the Decade/1983 (Cal Ripkin, Jr. (Ripken))	1.50
624b	Players of the Decade/1983 (Cal Ripkin, Jr.)	.05
625	Players of the Decade/1984 (Ryne Sandberg)	.25
626	Players of the Decade/1985 (Don Mattingly)	.15
627	Players of the Decade/1986 (Roger Clemens)	.30
628	Players of the Decade/1987 (George Bell)	.05
629	Players of the Decade/1988 (Jose Canseco)	.10
630a	Players of the Decade/1989 (Will Clark (Total bases 32.))	.35
630b	Players of the Decade/1989 (Will Clark (Total bases 321.))	.05
631	Game Savers (Mark Davis, Mitch Williams)	.05
632	Boston Igniters (Wade Boggs, Mike Greenwell)	.15
633	Starter & Stopper (Mark Davis, Jeff Russell)	.05
634	League's Best Shortstops (Tony Fernandez, Cal Ripken Jr.)	.30
635	Human Dynamos (Kirby Puckett, Bo Jackson)	.20
636	300 Strikeout Club (Mike Scott, Nolan Ryan)	.30
637	The Dynamic Duo (Will Clark, Kevin Mitchell)	.15
638	A.L. All-Stars (Don Mattingly, Mark McGwire)	.65
639	N.L. East Rivals (Howard Johnson, Ryne Sandberg)	.20
640	Major League Prospects (Rudy Seanez RC, Colin Charland RC)	.05
641	Major League Prospects (George Canale RC, Kevin Maas RC)	.10
642	Major League Prospects (Kelly Mann RC, Dave Hansen RC)	.05
643	Major League Prospects (Greg Smith RC, Stu Tate RC)	
644	Major League Prospects (Tom Drees RC, Dan Howitt RC)	.05
645	Major League Prospects (Mike Roesler RC, Derrick May RC)	.05
646	Major League Prospects (Scott Hemond RC, Mark Gardner RC)	.10
647	Major League Prospects (John Orton RC, Scott Leius RC)	.10
648	Major League Prospects (Rich Monteleone RC, Dana Williams RC)	.05
649	Major League Prospects (Mike Huff RC, Steve Frey RC)	.05
650	Major League Prospects (Chuck McElroy RC, Moises Alou RC)	.50
651	Major League Prospects (Bobby Rose RC, Mike Hartley RC)	.10
652	Major League Prospects (Matt Kinzer RC, Wayne Edwards RC)	.05
653	Major League Prospects (Delino DeShields RC, Jason Grimsley RC)	.15
654	Athletics, Cubs, Giants & Blue Jays (Checklist)	.05
655	Royals, Angels, Padres & Orioles (Checklist)	.05
656	Mets, Astros, Cardinals & Red Sox (Checklist)	.05
657	Rangers, Brewers, Expos & Twins (Checklist)	.05
658	Dodgers, Reds, Yankees & Pirates (Checklist)	.05
659	Indians, Mariners, White Sox & Phillies (Checklist)	.05
660	Braves, Tigers & Special Cards (Checklist)	.05

All-Stars

MARK DAVIS PITCHER

The top players at each position, as selected by Fleer, are featured in this 12-card set inserted in cello packs and some wax packs. The cards measure 2-1/2" x 3-1/2" and feature a unique two-photo format on the card fronts.

	NM/M
Complete Set (12):	4.00
Common Player:	.20
1 Harold Baines	.20
2 Will Clark	.20
3 Mark Davis	.20
4 Howard Johnson	.20
5 Joe Magrane	.20
6 Kevin Mitchell	.20
7 Kirby Puckett	1.00
8 Cal Ripken	2.00
9 Ryne Sandberg	1.00
10 Mike Scott	.20
11 Ruben Sierra	.20
12 Mickey Tettleton	.20

League Standouts

DON MATTINGLY • 1B • YANKEES

Fleer's "League Standouts" are six of baseball's top players distributed randomly in Fleer rack packs. Fronts feature full color photos with a six-dimensional effect. A black and gold frame borders the photo. Backs are yellow and describe the player's accomplishments. The cards measure 2-1/2" x 3-1/2".

	NM/M
Complete Set (6):	3.00
Common Player:	.50
1 Barry Larkin	.50
2 Don Mattingly	1.50
3 Darryl Strawberry	.50
4 Jose Canseco	.75
5 Wade Boggs	1.00
6 Mark Grace	.50

Soaring Stars

Larry Walker OF • Montreal Expos

Cards from this 12-card set could be found in 1990 Fleer jumbo cello packs. The cards are styled with a cartoon flavor, featuring astronomical graphics surrounding the player. Backs feature information about the promising young player.

	NM/M
Complete Set (12):	5.00
Common Player:	.10
1 Todd Zeile	.25
2 Mike Stanton	.25
3 Larry Walker	.50
4 Robin Ventura	1.00
5 Scott Coolbaugh	.25
6 Ken Griffey Jr.	4.00
7 Tom Gordon	.25
8 Jerome Walton	.25
9 Junior Felix	.25
10 Jim Abbott	.25
11 Ricky Jordan	.25
12 Dwight Smith	.25

World Series

This 12-card set depicts highlights of the 1989 World Series and was included in the factory-collated Fleer set. Single World Series cards were discovered in cello and rack packs, but this was not intended to happen. Fronts of the 2-1/2" x 3-1/2" cards feature action photos set against a white background with a red and blue '"89 World Series" banner. Backs are pink and white and describe the events of the 1989 Fall Classic.

'89 WORLD SERIES — PARKER'S BAT PRODUCES POWER

	NM/M
Complete Set (12):	1.50
Common Player:	.10
1 The Final Piece To The Puzzle (Mike Moore)	.10
2 Kevin Mitchell	.15
3 Game Two's Crushing Blow	.20
4 Will Clark	.15
5 Jose Canseco	.75
6 Great Leather in the Field	.10
7 Game One And A's Break Out On Top	.10
8 Dave Stewart	.10
9 Parker's Bat Produces Power (Dave Parker)	.25
10 World Series Record Book Game 3	.10
11 Rickey Henderson	.75
12 Oakland A's - Baseball's Best In '89	.25

Box Panels

Don Mattingly FIRST BASE

For the fifth consecutive year, Fleer issued a series of cards on the bottom panels of its wax pack boxes. This 28-card set features both players and team logo cards. The cards were numbered C-1 to C-28.

	NM/M
Complete Set, Panels (7):	7.00
Complete Set, Singles (28):	7.00
Common Player:	.05
1 Giants Logo	.05
2 Tim Belcher	.05
3 Roger Clemens	1.00
4 Eric Davis	.05
5 Glenn Davis	.05
6 Cubs Logo	.05
7 John Franco	.05
8 Mike Greenwell	.05
9 Athletics Logo	.05
10 Ken Griffey Jr.	2.00
11 Pedro Guerrero	.05
12 Tony Gwynn	.75
13 Blue Jays Logo	.05
14 Orel Hershiser	.05
15 Bo Jackson	.10
16 Howard Johnson	.05
17 Mets Logo	.05
18 Cardinals Logo	.05
19 Don Mattingly	1.00
20 Mark McGwire	2.00
21 Kevin Mitchell	.05
22 Kirby Puckett	.75
23 Royals Logo	.05
24 Orioles Logo	.05
25 Ruben Sierra	.05
26 Dave Stewart	.05
27 Jerome Walton	.05
28 Robin Yount	.60

Printed in Canada

Drafted from Pirates organization in 1980.

ON BASE % .391
SLUGGING % .422
STRIKEOUT RATIO 8.6
© 1990 FLEER LTD./LTEE PTD. IN CANADA

Whether these cards were printed for distribution in Canada or simply the work of a Canadian printer engaged by Fleer to meet U.S. demand is unknown. Each of the 660 cards in the 1990 Fleer issue can be found with a "1990 FLEER LTD./LTEE PTD. IN CANADA" copyright notice on back in the bottom border. Except for various superstar cards, little demand attaches to this variation.

	NM/M
Complete Set (660):	25.00
Common Player:	.25
Wax Pack (10):	1.50
Wax Box (48):	50.00

Update

Fleer produced its seventh consecutive "Update" set in 1990. As in the past, the set consists of 132 cards (numbered U-1 through U-132) that were sold by hobby dealers in special collectors boxes. The cards are designed in the same style as the regular issue. A special Nolan Ryan commemorative card is included in the set.

	NM/M
Complete Set (132):	5.00
Common Player:	.05
1 Steve Avery RC	.05
2 Francisco Cabrera	.05
3 Nick Esasky	.05
4 Jim Kremers RC	.05
5 Greg Olson RC	.05
6 Jim Presley	.05
7 Shawn Boskie RC	.05
8 Joe Kraemer RC	.05
9 Luis Salazar	.05
10 Hector Villanueva RC	.05
11 Glenn Braggs	.05
12 Mariano Duncan	.05
13 Billy Hatcher	.05
14 Tim Layana RC	.05
15 Hal Morris	.05
16 Javier Ortiz RC	.05
17 Dave Rohde RC	.05
18 Eric Yelding RC	.05
19 Hubie Brooks	.05
20 Kal Daniels	.05
21 Dave Hansen	.05
22 Mike Hartley	.05
23 Stan Javier	.05
24 Jose Offerman RC	.05
25 Juan Samuel	.05
26 Dennis Boyd	.05
27 Delino DeShields	.05
28 Steve Frey	.05
29 Mark Gardner	.05
30 Chris Nabholz RC	.05
31 Bill Sampen RC	.05
32 Dave Schmidt	.05
33 Daryl Boston	.05
34 Chuck Carr RC	.05
35 John Franco	.05
36 Todd Hundley RC	.25
37 Julio Machado RC	.05
38 Alejandro Pena	.05
39 Darren Reed RC	.05
40 Kelvin Torve RC	.05
41 Darrel Akerfelds RC	.05
42 Jose DeJesus	.05
43 Dave Hollins RC	.05
44 Carmelo Martinez	.05
45 Brad Moore RC	.05
46 Dale Murphy	.15
47 Wally Backman	.05
48 Stan Belinda RC	.05
49 Bob Patterson	.05
50 Ted Power	.05
51 Don Slaught	.05
52 Geronimo Pena RC	.05
53 Lee Smith	.05
54 John Tudor	.05
55 Joe Carter	.05
56 Tom Howard RC	.05
57 Craig Lefferts	.05
58 Rafael Valdez RC	.05
59 Dave Anderson	.05
60 Kevin Bass	.05
61 John Burkett	.05
62 Gary Carter	.40
63 Rick Parker RC	.05
64 Trevor Wilson	.05
65 Chris Hoiles RC	.05
66 Tim Hulett	.05
67 Dave Johnson RC	.05
68 Curt Schilling RC	.35
69 David Segui RC	.05
70 Tom Brunansky	.05
71 Greg Harris	.05
72 Dana Kiecker RC	.05
73 Tim Naehring RC	.05
74 Tony Pena	.05
75 Jeff Reardon	.05
76 Jerry Reed	.05
77 Mark Eichhorn	.05
78 Mark Langston	.05
79 John Orton	.05
80 Luis Polonia	.05
81 Dave Winfield	.40
82 Cliff Young RC	.05
83 Wayne Edwards	.05
84 Alex Fernandez RC	.05
85 Craig Grebeck RC	.05
86 Scott Radinsky RC	.05
87 Frank Thomas RC	3.00
88 Beau Allred RC	.05
89 Sandy Alomar, Jr.	.05
90 Carlos Baerga RC	.10
91 Kevin Bearse RC	.05
92 Chris James	.05
93 Candy Maldonado	.05
94 Jeff Manto	.05
95 Cecil Fielder	.05
96 Travis Fryman RC	.25
97 Lloyd Moseby	.05
98 Edwin Nunez	.05
99 Tony Phillips	.05
100 Larry Sheets	.05
101 Mark Davis	.05
102 Storm Davis	.05
103 Gerald Perry	.05
104 Terry Shumpert RC	.05
105 Edgar Diaz RC	.05
106 Dave Parker	.05
107 Tim Drummond RC	.05
108 Junior Ortiz	.05
109 Park Pittman RC	.05
110 Kevin Tapani RC	.05
111 Oscar Azocar RC	.05
112 Jim Leyritz RC	.05
113 Kevin Maas RC	.05
114 Alan Mills RC	.05
115 Matt Nokes	.05
116 Pascual Perez	.05
117 Ozzie Canseco RC	.05
118 Scott Sanderson	.05
119 Tino Martinez RC	.05
120 Jeff Schaefer RC	.05
121 Matt Young	.05
122 Brian Bohanon RC	.05
123 Jeff Huson	.05
124 Ramon Manon RC	.05
125 Gary Mielke RC	.05
126 Willie Blair RC	.05
127 Glenallen Hill RC	.05
128 John Olerud RC	.35
129 Luis Sojo RC	.05
130 Mark Whiten RC	.05
131 Three Decades of No Hitters (Nolan Ryan)	1.00
132 Checklist	.05

Award Winners

BO JACKSON ROYALS OUTFIELD

Hill's department stores and 7-Eleven outlets exclusively sold the 1990 Fleer "Award Winners." This 44-card boxed set includes baseball's statistical leaders of 1989. Card fronts feature a full-color player photo framed by a winner's cup design and blue border. Backs showcase player statistics in blue on a yellow and white background. The cards measure 2-1/2" x 3-1/2". The checklist provided on the back of each box is not correct. It incorrectly lists Bob Boone's team as the Angels and card #10 as Ron Darling. Darryl Strawberry (#38) is not checklisted and all cards #10-38 are off by a number. This is one of the scarcer Fleer box sets of the era.

	NM/M
Complete Set (44):	6.00
Common Player:	.05
1 Jeff Ballard	.05
2 Tim Belcher	.05
3 Bert Blyleven	.05
4 Wade Boggs	.75
5 Bob Boone	.05
6 Jose Canseco	.50
7 Will Clark	.05
8 Jack Clark	.05
9 Vince Coleman	.05
10 Eric Davis	.05
11 Jose DeLeon	.05
12 Tony Fernandez	.05
13 Carlton Fisk	.60
14 Scott Garrelts	.05
15 Tom Gordon	.05
16 Ken Griffey Jr.	1.50
17 Von Hayes	.05
18 Rickey Henderson	.60
19 Bo Jackson	.10
20 Howard Johnson	.05
21 Don Mattingly	1.00
22 Fred McGriff	.05
23 Kevin Mitchell	.05
24 Gregg Olson	.05
25 Gary Pettis	.05
26 Kirby Puckett	.75
27 Harold Reynolds	.05
28 Jeff Russell	.05
29 Nolan Ryan	2.00
30 Bret Saberhagen	.05
31 Ryne Sandberg	.75
32 Benito Santiago	.05
33 Mike Scott	.05
34 Ruben Sierra	.05
35 Lonnie Smith	.05
36 Ozzie Smith	.75
37 Dave Stewart	.05
38 Darryl Strawberry	.05
39 Greg Swindell	.05
40 Andy Van Slyke	.05
41 Tim Wallach	.05
42 Jerome Walton	.05
43 Mitch Williams	.05
44 Robin Yount	.60

Baseball All-Stars

ERIC DAVIS REDS OUTFIELD

Sold exclusively in Ben Franklin stores, this boxed set showcases the game's top players. Fronts feature a player photo surrounded by a pin-striped tan border. Backs have statistics and data printed in shades of red and dark blue. The cards measure 2-1/2" x 3-1/2" and are packed in a special box with a complete checklist on the back. Like other Fleer boxed sets, the cards are numbered alphabetically. All cards carry a "Printed in Canada" note on back.

	NM/M
Complete Set (44):	6.00
Common Player:	.05
1 Wade Boggs	.75
2 Bobby Bonilla	.05
3 Tim Burke	.05
4 Jose Canseco	.50
5 Will Clark	.05
6 Eric Davis	.05
7 Glenn Davis	.05
8 Julio Franco	.05
9 Tony Fernandez	.05
10 Gary Gaetti	.05
11 Scott Garrelts	.05
12 Mark Grace	.05
13 Mike Greenwell	.05
14 Ken Griffey Jr.	1.00
15 Mark Gubicza	.05
16 Pedro Guerrero	.05
17 Von Hayes	.05
18 Orel Hershiser	.05
19 Bruce Hurst	.05
20 Bo Jackson	.10
21 Howard Johnson	.05
22 Doug Jones	.05
23 Barry Larkin	.05
24 Don Mattingly	.85
25 Mark McGwire	1.00
26 Kevin McReynolds	.05
27 Kevin Mitchell	.05
28 Dan Plesac	.05
29 Kirby Puckett	.75
30 Cal Ripken	1.50
31 Bret Saberhagen	.05
32 Ryne Sandberg	.75
33 Steve Sax	.05
34 Ruben Sierra	.05
35 Ozzie Smith	.75

League Leaders

TIM BELCHER DODGERS PITCHER

For the fifth consecutive year Fleer released a "League Leaders" boxed set of 44 top Major League players. Card number 42 (Jerome Walton) pictures a player other than Walton. The 2-1/2" x 3-1/2" cards display a full-color photo bordered by a blue frame. Backs feature complete statistics. The cards are numbered alphabetically and a complete checklist is displayed on the back of the box. The set was available at Walgreen drug stores. Cards carry a "Printed in Canada" notice on back.

	NM/M
Complete Set (44):	6.00
Common Player:	.10
1 Roberto Alomar	.25
2 Tim Belcher	.10
3 George Bell	.10
4 Wade Boggs	.75
5 Jose Canseco	.50
6 Will Clark	.10
7 David Cone	.10
8 Eric Davis	.10
9 Glenn Davis	.10
10 Nick Esasky	.10
11 Dennis Eckersley	.55
12 Mark Grace	.10
13 Mike Greenwell	.10
14 Ken Griffey Jr.	1.25
15 Mark Gubicza	.10
16 Pedro Guerrero	.10
17 Tony Gwynn	.75
18 Rickey Henderson	.60
19 Bo Jackson	.15
20 Doug Jones	.10
21 Ricky Jordan	.10
22 Barry Larkin	.10
23 Don Mattingly	.85
24 Fred McGriff	.10
25 Mark McGwire	1.25
26 Kevin Mitchell	.10
27 Jack Morris	.10
28 Gregg Olson	.10
29 Dan Plesac	.10
30 Kirby Puckett	.75
31 Nolan Ryan	1.50
32 Bret Saberhagen	.75
33 Ryne Sandberg	.75
34 Steve Sax	.10
35 Mike Scott	.10
36 Ruben Sierra	.10
37 Lonnie Smith	.10
38 Darryl Strawberry	.10
39 Bobby Thigpen	.10
40 Andy Van Slyke	.10
41 Tim Wallach	.10
42 Jerome Walton	.10
43 Devon White	.10
44 Robin Yount	.60

MVP

GEORGE BELL BLUE JAYS OUTFIELD

This 44-card boxed set was produced by Fleer for the Toys R Us chain. Fronts are designed with graduating black-to-white borders, surrounding a color player photo. Backs contain individual data and career statistics. The back of each box carries a checklist of all the players in the set. Six peel-off team logo stickers featuring a baseball trivia quiz on the back are also included with each set. The cards are 2-1/2" x 3-1/2" and numbered alphabetically. All cards carry a "Printed in Canada" notation on the back at bottom.

	NM/M
Complete Set (44):	6.00
Common Player:	.10

1	George Bell	.10
2	Bert Blyleven	.10
3	Wade Boggs	.65
4	Bobby Bonilla	.10
5	George Brett	.85
6	Jose Canseco	.45
7	Will Clark	.10
8	Roger Clemens	.85
9	Eric Davis	.10
10	Glenn Davis	.10
11	Tony Fernandez	.10
12	Dwight Gooden	.10
13	Mike Greenwell	.10
14	Ken Griffey Jr.	1.25
15	Pedro Guerrero	.10
16	Tony Gwynn	.65
17	Rickey Henderson	.50
18	Tom Herr	.10
19	Orel Hershiser	.10
20	Kent Hrbek	.10
21	Bo Jackson	.15
22	Howard Johnson	.10
23	Don Mattingly	.85
24	Fred McGriff	
25	Mark McGwire	1.25
26	Kevin Mitchell	.10
27	Paul Molitor	.50
28	Dale Murphy	.25
29	Kirby Puckett	.65
30	Tim Raines	.10
31	Cal Ripken, Jr.	1.50
32	Bret Saberhagen	.10
33	Ryne Sandberg	.65
34	Ruben Sierra	.10
35	Dwight Smith	
36	Ozzie Smith	.65
37	Darryl Strawberry	.10
38	Dave Stewart	.10
39	Greg Swindell	.10
40	Bobby Thigpen	.10
41	Alan Trammell	.10
42	Jerome Walton	.10
43	Mitch Williams	.10
44	Robin Yount	.50

1991 Fleer Promo Strip

This three-card strip was issued to introduce Fleer's 1991 baseball card set. The cards on the 7-1/2" x 3-1/2" strip are identical to the players' regular issue cards.

	NM/M
Three-Card Strip:	4.00

1991 Fleer

Fleer expanded its 1991 set to include 720 cards. The cards feature yellow borders surrounding full-color action photos. Backs feature a circular portrait photo, biographical information, complete statistics, and career information. Once again the cards are numbered alphabetically within team. Because Fleer used more than one printer, many minor variations in photo cropping and typography can be found. The most notable are included in the checklist here.

	NM/M
Unopened Factory Set (732):	12.00
Complete Set (720):	10.00
Common Player:	.05
Wax Pack (15):	.50
Wax Box (36):	12.50
Jumbo Wax Pack (53):	1.25
Jumbo Wax Box (24):	20.00
Cello Pack (30):	1.00
Cello Box (24):	16.00

1	Troy Afenir RC	.05
2	Harold Baines	.05
3	Lance Blankenship	.05
4	Todd Burns	.05
5	Jose Canseco	.30
6	Dennis Eckersley	.35
7	Mike Gallego	.05
8	Ron Hassey	.05
9	Dave Henderson	.05
10	Rickey Henderson	.40
11	Rick Honeycutt	.05
12	Doug Jennings	.05
13	Joe Klink RC	.05
14	Carney Lansford	.05
15	Darren Lewis RC	.05
16	Willie McGee	.05
17a	Mark McGwire (Six-line career summary.)	.65
17b	Mark McGwire (Seven-line career summary.)	.65
18	Mike Moore	.05
19	Gene Nelson	.05
20	Dave Otto	.05
21	Jamie Quirk	.05
22	Willie Randolph	.05
23	Scott Sanderson	.05
24	Terry Steinbach	.05
25	Dave Stewart	.05
26	Walt Weiss	.05
27	Bob Welch	.05
28	Curt Young	.05
29	Wally Backman	.05
30	Stan Belinda RC	.05
31	Jay Bell	.05
32	Rafael Belliard	.05
33	Barry Bonds	.75
34	Bobby Bonilla	.05
35	Sid Bream	.05
36	Doug Drabek	.05
37	Carlos Garcia RC	.10
38	Neal Heaton	.05
39	Jeff King	.05
40	Bob Kipper	.05
41	Bill Landrum	.05
42	Mike LaValliere	.05
43	Jose Lind	.05
44	Carmelo Martinez	.05
45	Bob Patterson	.05
46	Ted Power	.05
47	Gary Redus	.05
48	R.J. Reynolds	.05
49	Don Slaught	.05
50	John Smiley	.05
51	Zane Smith	.05
52	Randy Tomlin RC	.10
53	Andy Van Slyke	.05
54	Bob Walk	.05
55	Jack Armstrong	.05
56	Todd Benzinger	.05
57	Glenn Braggs	.05
58	Keith Brown	.05
59	Tom Browning	.05
60	Norm Charlton	.05
61	Eric Davis	.05
62	Rob Dibble	.05
63	Bill Doran	.05
64	Mariano Duncan	.05
65	Chris Hammond	.05
66	Billy Hatcher	.05
67	Danny Jackson	.05
68	Barry Larkin	.05
69	Tim Layana RC	.05
70	Terry Lee RC	.05
71	Rick Mahler	.05
72	Hal Morris	.05
73	Randy Myers	.05
74	Ron Oester	.05
75	Joe Oliver	.05
76	Paul O'Neill	.05
77	Luis Quinones	.05
78	Jeff Reed	.05
79	Jose Rijo	.05
80	Chris Sabo	.05
81	Scott Scudder	.05
82	Herm Winningham	.05
83	Larry Andersen	.05
84	Marty Barrett	.05
85	Mike Boddicker	.05
86	Wade Boggs	.50
87	Tom Bolton	.05
88	Tom Brunansky	.05
89	Ellis Burks	.05
90	Roger Clemens	.55
91	Scott Cooper RC	.05
92	John Dopson	.05
93	Dwight Evans	.05
94	Wes Gardner	.05
95	Jeff Gray RC	.05
96	Mike Greenwell	.05
97	Greg Harris	.05
98	Daryl Irvine RC	.05
99	Dana Kiecker RC	.05
100	Randy Kutcher	.05
101	Dennis Lamp	.05

102	Mike Marshall	.05
103	John Marzano	.05
104	Rob Murphy	.05
105a	Tim Naehring RC (Seven-line career summary.)	.05
105b	Tim Naehring RC (Nine-line career summary.)	.05
106	Tony Pena	.05
107	Phil Plantier RC	.05
108	Carlos Quintana	.05
109	Jeff Reardon	.05
110	Jerry Reed	.05
111	Jody Reed	.05
112	Luis Rivera	.05
113a	Kevin Romine (One-line career summary.)	.05
113b	Kevin Romine (Two-line career summary.)	.05
114	Phil Bradley	.05
115	Ivan Calderon	.05
116	Wayne Edwards	.05
117	Alex Fernandez	.05
118	Carlton Fisk	.40
119	Scott Fletcher	.05
120	Craig Grebeck RC	.05
121	Ozzie Guillen	.05
122	Greg Hibbard	.05
123	Lance Johnson	.05
124	Barry Jones	.05
125a	Ron Karkovice (Two-line career summary.)	.05
125b	Ron Karkovice (One-line career summary.)	.05
126	Eric King	.05
127	Steve Lyons	.05
128	Carlos Martinez	.05
129	Jack McDowell	.05
130	Donn Pall	.05
131	Dan Pasqua	.05
132	Ken Patterson	.05
133	Melido Perez	.05
134	Adam Peterson	.05
135	Scott Radinsky RC	.05
136	Sammy Sosa	.50
137	Bobby Thigpen	.05
138	Frank Thomas	.40
139	Robin Ventura	.05
140	Daryl Boston	.05
141	Chuck Carr RC	.05
142	Mark Carreon	.05
143	David Cone	.05
144	Ron Darling	.05
145	Kevin Elster	.05
146	Sid Fernandez	.05
147	John Franco	.05
148	Dwight Gooden	.05
149	Tom Herr	.05
150	Todd Hundley	.05
151	Gregg Jefferies	.05
152	Howard Johnson	.05
153	Dave Magadan	.05
154	Kevin McReynolds	.05
155	Keith Miller	.05
156	Bob Ojeda	.05
157	Tom O'Malley	.05
158	Alejandro Pena	.05
159	Darren Reed RC	.05
160	Mackey Sasser	.05
161	Darryl Strawberry	.05
162	Tim Teufel	.05
163	Kelvin Torve	.05
164	Julio Valera	.05
165	Frank Viola	.05
166	Wally Whitehurst	.05
167	Jim Acker	.05
168	Derek Bell RC	.10
169	George Bell	.05
170	Willie Blair RC	.05
171	Pat Borders	.05
172	John Cerutti	.05
173	Junior Felix	.05
174	Tony Fernandez	.05
175	Kelly Gruber	.05
176	Tom Henke	.05
177	Glenallen Hill	.05
178	Jimmy Key	.05
179	Manny Lee	.05
180	Fred McGriff	.05
181	Rance Mulliniks	.05
182	Greg Myers	.05
183	John Olerud	.05
184	Luis Sojo	.05
185	Dave Steib	.05
186	Todd Stottlemyre	.05
187	Duane Ward	.05
188	David Wells	.05
189	Mark Whiten RC	.05
190	Ken Williams	.05
191	Frank Wills	.05
192	Mookie Wilson	.05
193	Don Aase	.05
194	Tim Belcher	.05
195	Hubie Brooks	.05
196	Dennis Cook	.05
197	Tim Crews	.05
198	Kal Daniels	.05
199	Kirk Gibson	.05
200	Jim Gott	.05
201	Alfredo Griffin	.05
202	Chris Gwynn	.05
203	Dave Hansen	.05
204	Lenny Harris	.05
205	Mike Hartley	.05
206	Mickey Hatcher	.05
207	Carlos Hernandez RC	.05
208	Orel Hershiser	.05
209	Jay Howell	.05
210	Mike Huff	.05

211	Stan Javier	.05
212	Ramon Martinez	.05
213	Mike Morgan	.05
214	Eddie Murray	.40
215	Jim Neidlinger RC	.05
216	Jose Offerman	.05
217	Jim Poole RC	.05
218	Juan Samuel	.05
219	Mike Scioscia	.05
220	Ray Searage	.05
221	Mike Sharperson	.05
222	Fernando Valenzuela	.05
223	Jose Vizcaino	.05
224	Mike Aldrete	.05
225	Scott Anderson RC	.05
226	Dennis Boyd	.05
227	Tim Burke	.05
228	Delino DeShields	.05
229	Mike Fitzgerald	.05
230	Tom Foley	.05
231	Steve Frey	.05
232	Andres Galarraga	.05
233	Mark Gardner	.05
234	Marquis Grissom	.05
235	Kevin Gross	.05
236	Drew Hall	.05
237	Dave Martinez	.05
238	Dennis Martinez	.05
239	Dale Mohorcic	.05
240	Chris Nabholz RC	.05
241	Otis Nixon	.05
242	Junior Noboa RC	.05
243	Spike Owen	.05
244	Tim Raines	.05
245	Mel Rojas RC	.10
246	Scott Ruskin RC	.05
247	Bill Sampen RC	.05
248	Nelson Santovenia	.05
249	Dave Schmidt	.05
250	Larry Walker	.05
251	Tim Wallach	.05
252	Dave Anderson	.05
253	Kevin Bass	.05
254	Steve Bedrosian	.05
255	Jeff Brantley	.05
256	John Burkett	.05
257	Brett Butler	.05
258	Gary Carter	.40
259	Will Clark	.05
260	Steve Decker RC	.05
261	Kelly Downs	.05
262	Scott Garrelts	.05
263	Terry Kennedy	.05
264	Mike LaCoss (Photo on back actually Ken Oberkfell.)	.05
265	Mark Leonard RC	.05
266	Greg Litton	.05
267	Kevin Mitchell	.05
268	Randy O'Neal RC	.05
269	Rick Parker RC	.05
270	Rick Reuschel	.05
271	Ernest Riles	.05
272	Don Robinson	.05
273	Robby Thompson	.05
274	Mark Thurmond	.05
275	Jose Uribe	.05
276	Matt Williams	.05
277	Trevor Wilson	.05
278	Gerald Alexander RC	.05
279	Brad Arnsberg	.05
280	Kevin Belcher RC	.05
281	Joe Bitker RC	.05
282	Kevin Brown	.05
283	Steve Buechele	.05
284	Jack Daugherty	.05
285	Julio Franco	.05
286	Juan Gonzalez	.20
287	Bill Haselman RC	.05
288	Charlie Hough	.05
289	Jeff Huson	.05
290	Pete Incaviglia	.05
291	Mike Jeffcoat	.05
292	Jeff Kunkel	.05
293	Gary Mielke	.05
294	Jamie Moyer	.05
295	Rafael Palmeiro	.35
296	Geno Petralli	.05
297	Gary Pettis	.05
298	Kevin Reimer	.05
299	Kenny Rogers	.05
300	Jeff Russell	.05
301	John Russell	.05
302a	Nolan Ryan (First horizontal line between 1979/1980.)	.75
302b	Nolan Ryan (First horizontal line between 1980/1981.)	.75
303	Ruben Sierra	.05
304	Bobby Witt	.05
305	Jim Abbott	.05
306	Kent Anderson RC	.05
307	Dante Bichette	.05
308	Bert Blyleven	.05
309	Chili Davis	.05
310	Brian Downing	.05
311	Mark Eichhorn	.05
312	Mike Fetters	.05
313	Chuck Finley	.05
314	Willie Fraser	.05
315	Bryan Harvey	.05
316	Donnie Hill	.05
317	Wally Joyner	.05
318	Mark Langston	.05
319	Kirk McCaskill	.05
320	John Orton	.05
321	Lance Parrish	.05
322	Luis Polonia	.05
323	Johnny Ray	.05
324	Bobby Rose	.05

325	Dick Schofield	.05
326	Rick Schu	.05
327a	Lee Stevens (Six-line career summary.)	.05
327b	Lee Stevens (Seven-line career summary.)	.05
328	Devon White	.05
329	Dave Winfield	.40
330	Cliff Young RC	.05
331	Dave Bergman	.05
332	Phil Clark RC	.05
333	Darnell Coles	.05
334	Milt Cuyler RC	.05
335	Cecil Fielder	.05
336	Travis Fryman	.05
337	Paul Gibson	.05
338	Jerry Don Gleaton	.05
339	Mike Heath	.05
340	Mike Henneman	.05
341	Chet Lemon	.05
342	Lance McCullers	.05
343	Jack Morris	.05
344	Lloyd Moseby	.05
345	Edwin Nunez	.05
346	Clay Parker	.05
347	Dan Petry	.05
348	Tony Phillips	.05
349	Jeff Robinson	.05
350	Mark Salas	.05
351	Mike Schwabe RC	.05
352	Larry Sheets	.05
353	John Shelby	.05
354	Frank Tanana	.05
355	Alan Trammell	.05
356	Gary Ward	.05
357	Lou Whitaker	.05
358	Beau Allred	.05
359	Sandy Alomar, Jr.	.05
360	Carlos Baerga	.05
361	Kevin Bearse RC	.05
362	Tom Brookens	.05
363	Jerry Browne	.05
364	Tom Candiotti	.05
365	Alex Cole	.05
366	John Farrell	.05
367	Felix Fermin	.05
368	Keith Hernandez	.05
369	Brook Jacoby	.05
370	Chris James	.05
371	Dion James	.05
372	Doug Jones	.05
373	Candy Maldonado	.05
374	Steve Olin	.05
375	Jesse Orosco	.05
376	Rudy Seanez	.05
377	Joel Skinner	.05
378	Cory Snyder	.05
379	Greg Swindell	.05
380	Sergio Valdez RC	.05
381	Mike Walker RC	.05
382	Colby Ward RC	.05
383	Turner Ward RC	.05
384	Mitch Webster	.05
385	Kevin Wickander RC	.05
386	Darrel Akerfelds	.05
387	Joe Boever	.05
388a	Rod Booker (No 1981 stats.)	.05
388b	Rod Booker (1981 stats included)	.05
389	Sil Campusano	.05
390	Don Carman	.05
391	Wes Chamberlain RC	.05
392	Pat Combs	.05
393	Darren Daulton	.05
394	Jose DeJesus	.05
395	Len Dykstra	.05
396	Jason Grimsley	.05
397	Charlie Hayes	.05
398	Von Hayes	.05
399	Dave Hollins RC	.05
400	Ken Howell	.05
401	Ricky Jordan	.05
402	John Kruk	.05
403	Steve Lake	.05
404	Chuck Malone RC	.05
405	Roger McDowell	.05
406	Chuck McElroy	.05
407	Mickey Morandini RC	.05
408	Terry Mulholland	.05
409	Dale Murphy	.15
410	Randy Ready	.05
411	Bruce Ruffin	.05
412	Dickie Thon	.05
413	Paul Assenmacher	.05
414	Damon Berryhill	.05
415	Mike Bielecki	.05
416	Shawn Boskie RC	.05
417	Dave Clark	.05
418	Doug Dascenzo	.05
419a	Andre Dawson (No 1976 stats.)	.25
419b	Andre Dawson (1976 stats included)	.25
420	Shawon Dunston	.05
421	Joe Girardi	.05
422	Mark Grace	.05
423	Mike Harkey	.05
424	Les Lancaster	.05
425	Bill Long	.05
426	Greg Maddux	.50
427	Derrick May	.05
428	Jeff Pico	.05
429	Domingo Ramos	.05
430	Luis Salazar	.05
431	Ryne Sandberg	.50
432	Dwight Smith	.05
433	Greg Smith	.05

434	Rick Sutcliffe	.05
435	Gary Varsho	.05
436	Hector Villanueva RC	.05
437	Jerome Walton	.05
438	Curtis Wilkerson	.05
439	Mitch Williams	.05
440	Steve Wilson	.05
441	Marvell Wynne	.05
442	Scott Bankhead	.05
443	Scott Bradley	.05
444	Greg Briley	.05
445	Mike Brumley	.05
446	Jay Buhner	.05
447	Dave Burba RC	.05
448	Henry Cotto	.05
449	Alvin Davis	.05
450	Ken Griffey Jr.	.60
451	Erik Hanson	.05
452	Gene Harris	.05
453	Brian Holman	.05
454	Mike Jackson	.05
455	Randy Johnson	.40
456	Jeffrey Leonard	.05
457	Edgar Martinez	.05
458	Tino Martinez	.05
459	Pete O'Brien	.05
460	Harold Reynolds	.05
461	Mike Schooler	.05
462	Bill Swift	.05
463	David Valle	.05
464	Omar Vizquel	.05
465	Matt Young	.05
466	Brady Anderson	.05
467	Jeff Ballard	.05
468	Juan Bell RC	.05
469a	Mike Devereaux ("Six" last word in career summary top line.)	.05
469b	Mike Devereaux ("Runs" last word in career summary top line.)	.05
470	Steve Finley	.05
471	Dave Gallagher	.05
472	Leo Gomez RC	.05
473	Rene Gonzales	.05
474	Pete Harnisch	.05
475	Kevin Hickey	.05
476	Chris Hoiles RC	.10
477	Sam Horn	.05
478	Tim Hulett	.05
479	Dave Johnson	.05
480	Ron Kittle	.05
481	Ben McDonald	.05
482	Bob Melvin	.05
483	Bob Milacki	.05
484	Randy Milligan	.05
485	John Mitchell RC	.05
486	Gregg Olson	.05
487	Joe Orsulak	.05
488	Joe Price	.05
489	Bill Ripken	.05
490	Cal Ripken, Jr.	.75
491	Curt Schilling	.25
492	David Segui RC	.10
493	Anthony Telford RC	.05
494	Mickey Tettleton	.05
495	Mark Williamson	.05
496	Craig Worthington	.05
497	Juan Agosto	.05
498	Eric Anthony	.05
499	Craig Biggio	.05
500	Ken Caminiti	.05
501	Casey Candaele	.05
502	Andujar Cedeno RC	.05
503	Danny Darwin	.05
504	Mark Davidson	.05
505	Glenn Davis	.05
506	Jim Deshaies	.05
507	Luis Gonzalez RC	1.00
508	Bill Gullickson	.05
509	Xavier Hernandez RC	.05
510	Brian Meyer	.05
511	Ken Oberkfell	.05
512	Mark Portugal	.05
513	Rafael Ramirez	.05
514	Karl Rhodes RC	.10
515	Mike Scott	.05
516	Mike Simms RC	.05
517	Dave Smith	.05
518	Franklin Stubbs	.05
519	Glenn Wilson	.05
520	Eric Yelding	.05
521	Gerald Young	.05
522	Shawn Abner	.05
523	Roberto Alomar	.20
524	Andy Benes	.05
525	Joe Carter	.05
526	Jack Clark	.05
527	Joey Cora	.05
528	Paul Faries RC	.05
529	Tony Gwynn	.50
530	Atlee Hammaker	.05
531	Greg Harris	.05
532	Thomas Howard RC	.05
533	Bruce Hurst	.05
534	Craig Lefferts	.05
535	Derek Lilliquist	.05
536	Fred Lynn	.05
537	Mike Pagliarulo	.05
538	Mark Parent	.05
539	Dennis Rasmussen	.05
540	Bip Roberts	.05
541	Richard Rodriguez RC	.05
542	Benito Santiago	.05
543	Calvin Schiraldi	.05
544	Eric Show	.05
545	Phil Stephenson	.05
546	Garry Templeton	.05

547	Ed Whitson	.05
548	Eddie Williams	.05
549	Kevin Appier	.05
550	Luis Aquino	.05
551	Bob Boone	.05
552	George Brett	.55
553	Jeff Conine RC	.30
554	Steve Crawford	.05
555	Mark Davis	.05
556	Storm Davis	.05
557	Jim Eisenreich	.05
558	Steve Farr	.05
559	Tom Gordon	.05
560	Mark Gubicza	.05
561	Bo Jackson	.10
562	Mike Macfarlane	.05
563	Brian McRae RC	.10
564	Jeff Montgomery	.05
565	Bill Pecota	.05
566	Gerald Perry	.05
567	Bret Saberhagen	.05
568	Jeff Schulz RC	.05
569	Kevin Seitzer	.05
570	Terry Shumpert RC	.05
571	Kurt Stillwell	.05
572	Danny Tartabull	.05
573	Gary Thurman	.05
574	Frank White	.05
575	Willie Wilson	.05
576	Chris Bosio	.05
577	Greg Brock	.05
578	George Canale	.05
579	Chuck Crim	.05
580	Rob Deer	.05
581	Edgar Diaz RC	.05
582	Tom Edens RC	.05
583	Mike Felder	.05
584	Jim Gantner	.05
585	Darryl Hamilton	.05
586	Ted Higuera	.05
587	Mark Knudson	.05
588	Bill Krueger	.05
589	Tim McIntosh	.05
590	Paul Mirabella	.05
591	Paul Molitor	.40
592	Jaime Navarro	.05
593	Dave Parker	.05
594	Dan Plesac	.05
595	Ron Robinson	.05
596	Gary Sheffield	.30
597	Bill Spiers	.05
598	B.J. Surhoff	.05
599	Greg Vaughn	.05
600	Randy Veres	.05
601	Robin Yount	.40
602a	Rick Aguilera (Five-line career summary.)	.05
602b	Rick Aguilera (Four-line career summary.)	.05
603	Allan Anderson	.05
604	Juan Berenguer	.05
605	Randy Bush	.05
606	Carmen Castillo	.05
607	Tim Drummond	.05
608	Scott Erickson RC	.10
609	Gary Gaetti	.05
610a	Greg Gagne (Horizontal lines under 82 Ft. Lauderdale, 84 Toledo and 87 Twins.)	.05
610b	Greg Gagne (Horizontal lines under 82 Orlando, 84 Twins and 88 Twins.)	.05
611	Dan Gladden	.05
612	Mark Guthrie RC	.05
613	Brian Harper	.05
614	Kent Hrbek	.05
615	Gene Larkin	.05
616	Terry Leach	.05
617	Nelson Liriano	.05
618	Shane Mack	.05
619	John Moses	.05
620	Pedro Munoz RC	.05
621	Al Newman	.05
622	Junior Ortiz	.05
623	Kirby Puckett	.50
624	Roy Smith	.05
625	Kevin Tapani	.05
626	Gary Wayne	.05
627	David West	.05
628	Cris Carpenter	.05
629	Vince Coleman	.05
630	Ken Dayley	.05
631	Jose DeLeon	.05
632	Frank DiPino	.05
633	Bernard Gilkey RC	.25
634	Pedro Guerrero	.05
635	Ken Hill	.05
636	Felix Jose	.05
637	Ray Lankford RC	.25
638	Joe Magrane	.05
639	Tom Niedenfuer	.05
640	Jose Oquendo	.05
641	Tom Pagnozzi	.05
642	Terry Pendleton	.05
643	Mike Perez RC	.05
644	Bryn Smith	.05
645	Lee Smith	.05
646	Ozzie Smith	.50
647	Scott Terry	.05
648	Bob Tewksbury	.05
649	Milt Thompson	.05
650	John Tudor	.05
651	Denny Walling	.05
652	Craig Wilson RC	.05
653	Todd Worrell	.05
654	Todd Zeile	.05
655	Oscar Azocar RC	.05
656	Steve Balboni	.05

657	Jesse Barfield	.05
658	Greg Cadaret	.05
659	Chuck Cary	.05
660	Rick Cerone	.05
661	Dave Eiland RC	.05
662a	Alvaro Espinoza (No 1979-80 stats.)	.05
662b	Alvaro Espinoza (1979-80 stats included)	.05
663	Bob Geren	.05
664	Lee Guetterman	.05
665	Mel Hall	.05
666a	Andy Hawkins (No 1978 stats.)	.05
666b	Andy Hawkins (1978 stats included)	.05
667	Jimmy Jones	.05
668	Roberto Kelly	.05
669	Dave LaPoint	.05
670	Tim Leary	.05
671	Jim Leyritz RC	.10
672	Kevin Maas	.05
673	Don Mattingly	.60
674	Matt Nokes	.05
675	Pascual Perez	.05
676	Eric Plunk	.05
677	Dave Righetti	.05
678	Jeff Robinson	.05
679	Steve Sax	.05
680	Mike Witt	.05
681	Steve Avery	.05
682	Mike Bell	.05
683	Jeff Blauser	.05
684	Francisco Cabrera	.05
685	Tony Castillo RC	.05
686	Marty Clary	.05
687	Nick Esasky	.05
688	Ron Gant	.05
689	Tom Glavine	.25
690	Mark Grant	.05
691	Tommy Gregg	.05
692	Dwayne Henry	.05
693	Dave Justice	.05
694	Jimmy Kremers RC	.05
695	Charlie Leibrandt	.05
696	Mark Lemke	.05
697	Oddibe McDowell	.05
698	Greg Olson	.05
699	Jeff Parrett	.05
700	Jim Presley	.05
701	Victor Rosario RC	.05
702	Lonnie Smith	.05
703	Pete Smith	.05
704	John Smoltz	.05
705	Mike Stanton	.05
706	Andres Thomas	.05
707	Jeff Treadway	.05
708	Jim Vatcher RC	.05
709	Home Run Kings (Ryne Sandberg, Cecil Fielder)	.10
710	Second Generation Superstars (Barry Bonds, Ken Griffey Jr.)	.65
711	NLCS Team Leaders (Bobby Bonilla, Barry Larkin)	.05
712	Top Game Savers (Bobby Thigpen, John Franco)	.05
713	Chicago's 100 Club (Andre Dawson, Ryne Sandberg)	.10
714	Checklists (Athletics, Pirates, Reds, Red Sox)	.05
715	Dodgers	.05
716	Checklists (Expos, Giants, Rangers, Angels)	.05
717	Checklists (Tigers, Indians, Phillies, Cubs)	.05
718	Checklists (Mariners, Orioles, Astros, Padres)	.05
719	Checklists (Royals, Brewers, Twins, Cardinals)	.05
720	Checklists (Yankees, Braves, Super Stars)	.05

All-Stars

Three player photos are featured on each card in this special insert set. An action shot and portrait close-up are featured on the front, while a full-figure pose is showcased on the back. The cards were inserted into 1991 Fleer cello packs.

		NM/M
Complete Set (10):		5.00
Common Player:		.25
1	Ryne Sandberg	.75
2	Barry Larkin	.25
3	Matt Williams	.25
4	Cecil Fielder	.25
5	Barry Bonds	2.00
6	Rickey Henderson	.50
7	Ken Griffey Jr.	1.50
8	Jose Canseco	.25
9	Benito Santiago	.25
10	Roger Clemens	1.00

World Series

Once again Fleer released a set in honor of the World Series from the previous season. The 1991 issue features only eight cards compared to 12 in 1990. The cards feature white borders surrounding full-color action shots from the 1990 Fall Classic. The card backs feature an overview of the World Series action.

		NM/M
Complete Set (8):		1.50
Common Player:		.25
1	Eric Davis	.25
2	Billy Hatcher	.25
3	Jose Canseco	.35
4	Rickey Henderson	.45
5	Chris Sabo, Carney Lansford	.25
6	Dave Stewart	.25
7	Jose Rijo	.25
8	Reds Celebrate	.25

Box Panels

Unlike past box panel sets, the 1991 Fleer box panels feature a theme; 1990 no-hitters are celebrated on the three different boxes. The cards feature blank backs and are numbered in order of no-hitter on the front. A team logo was included on each box. The card fronts are styled after the 1991 Fleer cards. A special no-hitter logo appears in the lower left corner.

		NM/M
Complete Set, Singles (10):		3.00
Complete Set, Panels (3):		3.00
Common Player:		.10
1	Mark Langston, Mike Witt	.10
2	Randy Johnson	1.00
3	Nolan Ryan	2.00
4	Dave Stewart	.10
5	Fernando Valenzuela	.10
6	Andy Hawkins	.10
7	Melido Perez	.10
8	Terry Mulholland	.10
9	Dave Steib	.10
----	Team Logos	.05

Update

Fleer produced its eighth consecutive "Update" set in 1991 to supplement the company's regular set. As in the past, the set consists of 132 cards that were sold by hobby dealers in special collectors boxes. The cards are designed in the same style as the regular Fleer issue.

		NM/M
Complete Set (132):		3.00
Common Player:		.05
1	Glenn Davis	.05
2	Dwight Evans	.05
3	Jose Mesa RC	.05
4	Jack Clark	.05
5	Danny Darwin	.05
6	Steve Lyons	.05
7	Mo Vaughn RC	.05
8	Floyd Bannister	.05
9	Gary Gaetti	.05
10	Dave Parker	.05
11	Joey Cora	.05
12	Charlie Hough	.05
13	Matt Merullo	.05
14	Warren Newson RC	.05
15	Tim Raines	.05
16	Albert Belle	.05
17	Glenallen Hill	.05
18	Shawn Hillegas	.05
19	Mark Lewis RC	.05
20	Charles Nagy RC	.05
21	Mark Whiten	.05
22	John Cerutti	.05
23	Rob Deer	.05
24	Mickey Tettleton	.05
25	Warren Cromartie	.05
26	Kirk Gibson	.05
27	David Howard RC	.05
28	Brent Mayne RC	.05
29	Dante Bichette	.05
30	Mark Lee RC	.05
31	Julio Machado	.05
32	Edwin Nunez	.05
33	Willie Randolph	.05
34	Franklin Stubbs	.05
35	Bill Wegman	.05
36	Chili Davis	.05
37	Chuck Knoblauch RC	.05
38	Scott Leius	.05
39	Jack Morris	.05
40	Mike Pagliarulo	.05
41	Lenny Webster RC	.05
42	John Habyan RC	.05
43	Steve Howe	.05
44	Jeff Johnson RC	.05
45	Scott Kamieniecki RC	.05
46	Pat Kelly RC	.05
47	Hensley Meulens	.05
48	Wade Taylor RC	.05
49	Bernie Williams	.20
50	Kirk Dressendorfer RC	.05
51	Ernest Riles	.05
52	Rich DeLucia RC	.05
53	Tracy Jones	.05
54	Bill Krueger	.05
55	Alonzo Powell RC	.05
56	Jeff Schaefer	.05
57	Russ Swan RC	.05
58	John Barfield RC	.05
59	Rich Gossage	.10
60	Jose Guzman	.05
61	Dean Palmer RC	.05
62	Ivan Rodriguez RC	1.50
63	Roberto Alomar	.20
64	Tom Candiotti	.05
65	Joe Carter	.05
66	Ed Sprague RC	.05
67	Pat Tabler	.05
68	Mike Timlin RC	.05
69	Devon White	.05
70	Rafael Belliard	.05
71	Juan Berenguer	.05
72	Sid Bream	.05
73	Marvin Freeman	.05
74	Kent Mercker	.05
75	Otis Nixon	.05
76	Terry Pendleton	.05
77	George Bell	.05
78	Danny Jackson	.05
79	Chuck McElroy	.05
80	Gary Scott RC	.05
81	Heathcliff Slocumb RC	.05
82	Dave Smith	.05
83	Rick Wilkins RC	.05
84	Freddie Benavides RC	.05
85	Ted Power	.05
86	Mo Sanford RC	.05
87	Jeff Bagwell RC	2.00
88	Steve Finley	.05
89	Pete Harnisch	.05
90	Darryl Kile RC	.05
91	Brett Butler	.05
92	John Candelaria	.05
93	Gary Carter	.40
94	Kevin Gross	.05
95	Bob Ojeda	.05
96	Darryl Strawberry	.05
97	Ivan Calderon	.05
98	Ron Hassey	.05
99	Gilberto Reyes	.05
100	Hubie Brooks	.05
101	Rick Cerone	.05
102	Vince Coleman	.05
103	Jeff Innis	.05
104	Pete Schourek RC	.05
105	Andy Ashby RC	.05
106	Wally Backman	.05
107	Darrin Fletcher RC	.05
108	Tommy Greene	.05
109	John Morris	.05
110	Mitch Williams	.05
111	Lloyd McClendon	.05
112	Orlando Merced RC	.05
113	Vicente Palacios	.05
114	Gary Varsho	.05
115	John Wehner RC	.05
116	Rex Hudler	.05
117	Tim Jones	.05
118	Geronimo Pena RC	.05
119	Gerald Perry	.05
120	Larry Andersen	.05
121	Jerald Clark	.05
122	Scott Coolbaugh	.05
123	Tony Fernandez	.05
124	Darrin Jackson	.05
125	Fred McGriff	.05
126	Jose Mota RC	.05
127	Tim Teufel	.05
128	Bud Black	.05
129	Mike Felder	.05
130	Willie McGee	.05
131	Dave Righetti	.05
132	Checklist	.05

ProVisions

The illustrations of artist Terry Smith are showcased in this special set. Twelve fantasy portraits were produced for cards inserted into rack packs. Four other ProVision cards were inserted into factory sets. The rack pack cards feature black borders, while the factory set cards have white borders. Information on the card backs explains the manner in which Smith painted each player. Factory insert ProVisions are indicated by an "F" suffix in the checklist here.

		NM/M
Complete Set (12):		5.00
Common Player:		.15
Complete Factory Set (4):		5.00
Common Player:		.25
1	Kirby Puckett	.75
2	Will Clark	.15
3	Ruben Sierra	.15
4	Mark McGwire	1.50
5	Bo Jackson	.25
6	Jose Canseco	.50
7	Dwight Gooden	.15
8	Mike Greenwell	.15
9	Roger Clemens	1.00
10	Eric Davis	.15
11	Don Mattingly	1.00
12	Darryl Strawberry	.15
1F	Barry Bonds	3.50
2F	Rickey Henderson	.50
3F	Ryne Sandberg	1.00
4F	Dave Stewart	.25

1992 Fleer Promo

It has been reported that only 100 of this sample card were made for distribution at the 1991 FanFest event. The card differs from the issued Kirby Puckett card in the '92 Fleer set in the card number, absence of 1991 stats and the overprinting of a sample card notice, all on the back.

		NM/M
123	Kirby Puckett	400.00

1992 Fleer

For the second consecutive year, Fleer produced a 720-card set. The standard card fronts feature full-color action photos bordered in green with the player's name, position and team logo on the right border. The backs feature another full-color action photo,

biographical information and statistics. A special 12-card Roger Clemens subset is also included in the 1992 Fleer set. Three more Clemens cards were available through a mail-in offer, and 2,000 Roger Clemens autographed cards were inserted in 1992 packs. Once again the cards are numbered according to team. Subsets in the issue included Major League Propects (#652-680), Record Setters (#681-687), League Leaders (#688-697), Superstar Specials (#698-707) and ProVisions (#708-713), which for the first time were part of the regular numbered set rather than limited edition insert cards.

		NM/M
Unopened Factory Set (732):		17.50
Complete Set (720):		8.00
Common Player:		.05
Wax Pack (15):		.45
Wax Box (36):		10.00
Cello Pack (35):		1.00
Cello Box (24):		16.00
1	Brady Anderson	.05
2	Jose Bautista	.05
3	Juan Bell	.05
4	Glenn Davis	.05
5	Mike Devereaux	.05
6	Dwight Evans	.05
7	Mike Flanagan	.05
8	Leo Gomez	.05
9	Chris Hoiles	.05
10	Sam Horn	.05
11	Tim Hulett	.05
12	Dave Johnson	.05
13	Chito Martinez RC	.05
14	Ben McDonald	.05
15	Bob Melvin	.05
16	Luis Mercedes RC	.10
17	Jose Mesa	.05
18	Bob Milacki	.05
19	Randy Milligan	.05
20	Mike Mussina	.30
21	Gregg Olson	.05
22	Joe Orsulak	.05
23	Jim Poole	.05
24	Arthur Rhodes RC	.10
25	Billy Ripken	.05
26	Cal Ripken, Jr.	1.00
27	David Segui	.05
28	Roy Smith	.05
29	Anthony Telford	.05
30	Mark Williamson	.05
31	Craig Worthington	.05
32	Wade Boggs	.55
33	Tom Bolton	.05
34	Tom Brunansky	.05
35	Ellis Burks	.05
36	Jack Clark	.05
37	Roger Clemens	.60
38	Danny Darwin	.05
39	Mike Greenwell	.05
40	Joe Hesketh	.05
41	Daryl Irvine	.05
42	Dennis Lamp	.05
43	Tony Pena	.05
44	Phil Plantier	.05
45	Carlos Quintana	.05
46	Jeff Reardon	.05
47	Jody Reed	.05
48	Luis Rivera	.05
49	Mo Vaughn	.05
50	Jim Abbott	.05
51	Kyle Abbott	.05
52	Ruben Amaro Jr. RC	.05
53	Scott Bailes	.05
54	Chris Beasley RC	.05
55	Mark Eichhorn	.05
56	Mike Fetters	.05
57	Chuck Finley	.05
58	Gary Gaetti	.05
59	Dave Gallagher	.05
60	Donnie Hill	.05
61	Bryan Harvey	.05
62	Wally Joyner	.05
63	Mark Langston	.05
64	Kirk McCaskill	.05
65	John Orton	.05
66	Lance Parrish	.05
67	Luis Polonia	.05
68	Bobby Rose	.05
69	Dick Schofield	.05

#	Player	Price
70	Luis Sojo	.05
71	Lee Stevens	.05
72	Dave Winfield	.50
73	Cliff Young	.05
74	Wilson Alvarez	.05
75	Esteban Beltre RC	.05
76	Joey Cora	.05
77	Brian Drahman RC	.05
78	Alex Fernandez	.05
79	Carlton Fisk	.50
80	Scott Fletcher	.05
81	Craig Grebeck	.05
82	Ozzie Guillen	.05
83	Greg Hibbard	.05
84	Charlie Hough	.05
85	Mike Huff	.05
86	Bo Jackson	.10
87	Lance Johnson	.05
88	Ron Karkovice	.05
89	Jack McDowell	.05
90	Matt Merullo	.05
91	Warren Newson RC	.05
92	Donn Pall	.05
93	Dan Pasqua	.05
94	Ken Patterson	.05
95	Melido Perez	.05
96	Scott Radinsky	.05
97	Tim Raines	.05
98	Sammy Sosa	.55
99	Bobby Thigpen	.05
100	Frank Thomas	.50
101	Robin Ventura	.05
102	Mike Aldrete	.05
103	Sandy Alomar, Jr.	.05
104	Carlos Baerga	.05
105	Albert Belle	.05
106	Willie Blair	.05
107	Jerry Browne	.05
108	Alex Cole	.05
109	Felix Fermin	.05
110	Glenallen Hill	.05
111	Shawn Hillegas	.05
112	Chris James	.05
113	Reggie Jefferson RC	.05
114	Doug Jones	.05
115	Eric King	.05
116	Mark Lewis	.05
117	Carlos Martinez	.05
118	Charles Nagy	.05
119	Rod Nichols	.05
120	Steve Olin	.05
121	Jesse Orosco	.05
122	Rudy Seanez	.05
123	Joel Skinner	.05
124	Greg Swindell	.05
125	Jim Thome RC	.50
126	Mark Whiten	.05
127	Scott Aldred	.05
128	Andy Allanson	.05
129	John Cerutti	.05
130	Milt Cuyler	.05
131	Mike Dalton RC	.05
132	Rob Deer	.05
133	Cecil Fielder	.05
134	Travis Fryman	.05
135	Dan Gakeler RC	.05
136	Paul Gibson	.05
137	Bill Gullickson	.05
138	Mike Henneman	.05
139	Pete Incaviglia	.05
140	Mark Leiter RC	.05
141	Scott Livingstone RC	.10
142	Lloyd Moseby	.05
143	Tony Phillips	.05
144	Mark Salas	.05
145	Frank Tanana	.05
146	Walt Terrell	.05
147	Mickey Tettleton	.05
148	Alan Trammell	.05
149	Lou Whitaker	.05
150	Kevin Appier	.05
151	Luis Aquino	.05
152	Todd Benzinger	.05
153	Mike Boddicker	.05
154	George Brett	.60
155	Storm Davis	.05
156	Jim Eisenreich	.05
157	Kirk Gibson	.05
158	Tom Gordon	.05
159	Mark Gubicza	.05
160	David Howard RC	.05
161	Mike Macfarlane	.05
162	Brent Mayne	.05
163	Brian McRae	.05
164	Jeff Montgomery	.05
165	Bill Pecota	.05
166	Harvey Pulliam RC	.05
167	Bret Saberhagen	.05
168	Kevin Seitzer	.05
169	Terry Shumpert	.05
170	Kurt Stillwell	.05
171	Danny Tartabull	.05
172	Gary Thurman	.05
173	Dante Bichette	.05
174	Kevin Brown	.05
175	Chuck Crim	.05
176	Jim Gantner	.05
177	Darryl Hamilton	.05
178	Ted Higuera	.05
179	Darren Holmes	.05
180	Mark Lee	.05
181	Julio Machado	.05
182	Paul Molitor	.50
183	Jaime Navarro	.05
184	Edwin Nunez	.05
185	Dan Plesac	.05
186	Willie Randolph	.05
187	Ron Robinson	.05
188	Gary Sheffield	.30
189	Bill Spiers	.05
190	B.J. Surhoff	.05
191	Dale Sveum	.05
192	Greg Vaughn	.05
193	Bill Wegman	.05
194	Robin Yount	.50
195	Rick Aguilera	.05
196	Allan Anderson	.05
197	Steve Bedrosian	.05
198	Randy Bush	.05
199	Larry Casian RC	.05
200	Chili Davis	.05
201	Scott Erickson	.05
202	Greg Gagne	.05
203	Dan Gladden	.05
204	Brian Harper	.05
205	Kent Hrbek	.05
206	Chuck Knoblauch	.05
207	Gene Larkin	.05
208	Terry Leach	.05
209	Scott Leius	.05
210	Shane Mack	.05
211	Jack Morris	.05
212	Pedro Munoz RC	.05
213	Denny Neagle RC	.10
214	Al Newman	.05
215	Junior Ortiz	.05
216	Mike Pagliarulo	.05
217	Kirby Puckett	.55
218	Paul Sorrento	.05
219	Kevin Tapani	.05
220	Lenny Webster	.05
221	Jesse Barfield	.05
222	Greg Cadaret	.05
223	Dave Eiland	.05
224	Alvaro Espinoza	.05
225	Steve Farr	.05
226	Bob Geren	.05
227	Lee Guetterman	.05
228	John Habyan	.05
229	Mel Hall	.05
230	Steve Howe	.05
231	Mike Humphreys RC	.05
232	Scott Kamieniecki RC	.10
233	Pat Kelly	.05
234	Roberto Kelly	.05
235	Tim Leary	.05
236	Kevin Maas	.05
237	Don Mattingly	.60
238	Hensley Meulens	.05
239	Matt Nokes	.05
240	Pascual Perez	.05
241	Eric Plunk	.05
242	John Ramos RC	.05
243	Scott Sanderson	.05
244	Steve Sax	.05
245	Wade Taylor RC	.05
246	Randy Velarde	.05
247	Bernie Williams	.05
248	Troy Afenir	.05
249	Harold Baines	.05
250	Lance Blankenship	.05
251	Mike Bordick RC	.10
252	Jose Canseco	.30
253	Steve Chitren	.05
254	Ron Darling	.05
255	Dennis Eckersley	.45
256	Mike Gallego	.05
257	Dave Henderson	.05
258	Rickey Henderson	.50
259	Rick Honeycutt	.05
260	Brook Jacoby	.05
261	Carney Lansford	.05
262	Mark McGwire	.75
263	Mike Moore	.05
264	Gene Nelson	.05
265	Jamie Quirk	.05
266	Joe Slusarski RC	.10
267	Terry Steinbach	.05
268	Dave Stewart	.05
269	Todd Van Poppel RC	.05
270	Walt Weiss	.05
271	Bob Welch	.05
272	Curt Young	.05
273	Scott Bradley	.05
274	Greg Briley	.05
275	Jay Buhner	.05
276	Henry Cotto	.05
277	Alvin Davis	.05
278	Rich DeLucia	.05
279	Ken Griffey Jr.	.65
280	Erik Hanson	.05
281	Brian Holman	.05
282	Mike Jackson	.05
283	Randy Johnson	.50
284	Tracy Jones	.05
285	Bill Krueger	.05
286	Edgar Martinez	.05
287	Tino Martinez	.05
288	Rob Murphy	.05
289	Pete O'Brien	.05
290	Alonzo Powell	.05
291	Harold Reynolds	.05
292	Mike Schooler	.05
293	Russ Swan	.05
294	Bill Swift	.05
295	Dave Valle	.05
296	Omar Vizquel	.05
297	Gerald Alexander	.05
298	Brad Arnsberg	.05
299	Kevin Brown	.05
300	Jack Daugherty	.05
301	Mario Diaz	.05
302	Brian Downing	.05
303	Julio Franco	.05
304	Juan Gonzalez	.25
305	Rich Gossage	.10
306	Jose Guzman	.05
307	Jose Hernandez RC	.05
308	Jeff Huson	.05
309	Mike Jeffcoat	.05
310	Terry Mathews RC	.05
311	Rafael Palmeiro	.45
312	Dean Palmer	.05
313	Geno Petralli	.05
314	Gary Pettis	.05
315	Kevin Reimer	.05
316	Ivan Rodriguez	.45
317	Kenny Rogers	.05
318	Wayne Rosenthal RC	.05
319	Jeff Russell	.05
320	Nolan Ryan	1.00
321	Ruben Sierra	.05
322	Jim Acker	.05
323	Roberto Alomar	.20
324	Derek Bell	.05
325	Pat Borders	.05
326	Tom Candiotti	.05
327	Joe Carter	.05
328	Rob Ducey	.05
329	Kelly Gruber	.05
330	Juan Guzman RC	.25
331	Tom Henke	.05
332	Jimmy Key	.05
333	Manny Lee	.05
334	Al Leiter	.05
335	Bob MacDonald RC	.05
336	Candy Maldonado	.05
337	Rance Mulliniks	.05
338	Greg Myers	.05
339	John Olerud	.05
340	Ed Sprague RC	.10
341	Dave Stieb	.05
342	Todd Stottlemyre	.05
343	Mike Timlin RC	.10
344	Duane Ward	.05
345	David Wells	.05
346	Devon White	.05
347	Mookie Wilson	.05
348	Eddie Zosky	.05
349	Steve Avery	.05
350	Mike Bell RC	.05
351	Rafael Belliard	.05
352	Juan Berenguer	.05
353	Jeff Blauser	.05
354	Sid Bream	.05
355	Francisco Cabrera	.05
356	Marvin Freeman	.05
357	Ron Gant	.05
358	Tom Glavine	.30
359	Brian Hunter RC	.05
360	Dave Justice	.05
361	Charlie Leibrandt	.05
362	Mark Lemke	.05
363	Kent Mercker	.05
364	Keith Mitchell RC	.05
365	Greg Olson	.05
366	Terry Pendleton	.05
367	Armando Reynoso RC	.05
368	Deion Sanders	.10
369	Lonnie Smith	.05
370	Pete Smith	.05
371	John Smoltz	.05
372	Mike Stanton	.05
373	Jeff Treadway	.05
374	Mark Wohlers RC	.05
375	Paul Assenmacher	.05
376	George Bell	.05
377	Shawn Boskie	.05
378	Frank Castillo RC	.05
379	Andre Dawson	.25
380	Shawon Dunston	.05
381	Mark Grace	.05
382	Mike Harkey	.05
383	Danny Jackson	.05
384	Les Lancaster	.05
385	Cedric Landrum RC	.05
386	Greg Maddux	.55
387	Derrick May	.05
388	Chuck McElroy	.05
389	Ryne Sandberg	.55
390	Heathcliff Slocumb RC	.10
391	Dave Smith	.05
392	Dwight Smith	.05
393	Rick Sutcliffe	.05
394	Hector Villanueva	.05
395	Chico Walker	.05
396	Jerome Walton	.05
397	Rick Wilkins RC	.15
398	Jack Armstrong	.05
399	Freddie Benavides RC	.05
400	Glenn Braggs	.05
401	Tom Browning	.05
402	Norm Charlton	.05
403	Eric Davis	.05
404	Rob Dibble	.05
405	Bill Doran	.05
406	Mariano Duncan	.05
407	Kip Gross RC	.05
408	Chris Hammond	.05
409	Billy Hatcher	.05
410	Chris Jones RC	.05
411	Barry Larkin	.05
412	Hal Morris	.05
413	Randy Myers	.05
414	Joe Oliver	.05
415	Paul O'Neill	.05
416	Ted Power	.05
417	Luis Quinones	.05
418	Jeff Reed	.05
419	Jose Rijo	.05
420	Chris Sabo	.05
421	Reggie Sanders RC	.05
422	Scott Scudder	.05
423	Glenn Sutko	.05
424	Eric Anthony	.05
425	Jeff Bagwell	.50
426	Craig Biggio	.05
427	Ken Caminiti	.05
428	Casey Candaele	.05
429	Mike Capel	.05
430	Andujar Cedeno	.05
431	Jim Corsi	.05
432	Mark Davidson	.05
433	Steve Finley	.05
434	Luis Gonzalez	.05
435	Pete Harnisch	.05
436	Dwayne Henry	.05
437	Xavier Hernandez	.05
438	Jimmy Jones	.05
439	Darryl Kile RC	.05
440	Rob Mallicoat RC	.05
441	Andy Mota RC	.05
442	Al Osuna	.05
443	Mark Portugal	.05
444	Scott Servais RC	.10
445	Mike Simms	.05
446	Gerald Young	.05
447	Tim Belcher	.05
448	Brett Butler	.05
449	John Candelaria	.05
450	Gary Carter	.50
451	Dennis Cook	.05
452	Tim Crews	.05
453	Kal Daniels	.05
454	Jim Gott	.05
455	Alfredo Griffin	.05
456	Kevin Gross	.05
457	Chris Gwynn	.05
458	Lenny Harris	.05
459	Orel Hershiser	.05
460	Jay Howell	.05
461	Stan Javier	.05
462	Eric Karros	.05
463	Ramon Martinez	.05
464	Roger McDowell	.05
465	Mike Morgan	.05
466	Eddie Murray	.50
467	Jose Offerman	.05
468	Bob Ojeda	.05
469	Juan Samuel	.05
470	Mike Scioscia	.05
471	Darryl Strawberry	.05
472	Bret Barberie RC	.10
473	Brian Barnes	.05
474	Eric Bullock	.05
475	Ivan Calderon	.05
476	Delino DeShields	.05
477	Jeff Fassero RC	.10
478	Mike Fitzgerald	.05
479	Steve Frey	.05
480	Andres Galarraga	.05
481	Mark Gardner	.05
482	Marquis Grissom	.05
483	Chris Haney	.05
484	Barry Jones	.05
485	Dave Martinez	.05
486	Dennis Martinez	.05
487	Chris Nabholz	.05
488	Spike Owen	.05
489	Gilberto Reyes	.05
490	Mel Rojas	.05
491	Scott Ruskin	.05
492	Bill Sampen	.05
493	Larry Walker	.05
494	Tim Wallach	.05
495	Daryl Boston	.05
496	Hubie Brooks	.05
497	Tim Burke	.05
498	Mark Carreon	.05
499	Tony Castillo	.05
500	Vince Coleman	.05
501	David Cone	.05
502	Kevin Elster	.05
503	Sid Fernandez	.05
504	John Franco	.05
505	Dwight Gooden	.05
506	Todd Hundley	.05
507	Jeff Innis	.05
508	Gregg Jefferies	.05
509	Howard Johnson	.05
510	Dave Magadan	.05
511	Terry McDaniel RC	.05
512	Kevin McReynolds	.05
513	Keith Miller	.05
514	Charlie O'Brien	.05
515	Mackey Sasser	.05
516	Pete Schourek RC	.05
517	Julio Valera	.05
518	Frank Viola	.05
519	Wally Whitehurst	.05
520	Anthony Young RC	.05
521	Andy Ashby RC	.10
522	Kim Batiste RC	.05
523	Joe Boever	.05
524	Wes Chamberlain	.05
525	Pat Combs	.05
526	Danny Cox	.05
527	Darren Daulton	.05
528	Jose DeJesus	.05
529	Len Dykstra	.05
530	Darrin Fletcher	.05
531	Tommy Greene	.05
532	Jason Grimsley	.05
533	Charlie Hayes	.05
534	Von Hayes	.05
535	Dave Hollins	.05
536	Ricky Jordan	.05
537	John Kruk	.05
538	Jim Lindeman	.05
539	Mickey Morandini	.05
540	Terry Mulholland	.05
541	Dale Murphy	.20
542	Randy Ready	.05
543	Wally Ritchie	.05
544	Bruce Ruffin	.05
545	Steve Searcy	.05
546	Dickie Thon	.05
547	Mitch Williams	.05
548	Stan Belinda	.05
549	Jay Bell	.05
550	Barry Bonds	1.00
551	Bobby Bonilla	.05
552	Steve Buechele	.05
553	Doug Drabek	.05
554	Neal Heaton	.05
555	Jeff King	.05
556	Bob Kipper	.05
557	Bill Landrum	.05
558	Mike LaValliere	.05
559	Jose Lind	.05
560	Lloyd McClendon	.05
561	Orlando Merced	.05
562	Bob Patterson	.05
563	Joe Redfield RC	.05
564	Gary Redus	.05
565	Rosario Rodriguez	.05
566	Don Slaught	.05
567	John Smiley	.05
568	Zane Smith	.05
569	Randy Tomlin	.05
570	Andy Van Slyke	.05
571	Gary Varsho	.05
572	Bob Walk	.05
573	John Wehner RC	.05
574	Juan Agosto	.05
575	Cris Carpenter	.05
576	Jose DeLeon	.05
577	Rich Gedman	.05
578	Bernard Gilkey	.05
579	Pedro Guerrero	.05
580	Ken Hill	.05
581	Rex Hudler	.05
582	Felix Jose	.05
583	Ray Lankford	.05
584	Omar Olivares	.05
585	Jose Oquendo	.05
586	Tom Pagnozzi	.05
587	Geronimo Pena	.05
588	Mike Perez	.05
589	Gerald Perry	.05
590	Bryn Smith	.05
591	Lee Smith	.05
592	Ozzie Smith	.55
593	Scott Terry	.05
594	Bob Tewksbury	.05
595	Milt Thompson	.05
596	Todd Zeile	.05
597	Larry Andersen	.05
598	Oscar Azocar	.05
599	Andy Benes	.05
600	Ricky Bones RC	.05
601	Jerald Clark	.05
602	Pat Clements	.05
603	Paul Faries	.05
604	Tony Fernandez	.05
605	Tony Gwynn	.55
606	Greg Harris	.05
607	Thomas Howard	.05
608	Bruce Hurst	.05
609	Darrin Jackson	.05
610	Tom Lampkin	.05
611	Craig Lefferts	.05
612	Jim Lewis RC	.05
613	Mike Maddux	.05
614	Fred McGriff	.05
615	Jose Melendez RC	.05
616	Jose Mota RC	.05
617	Dennis Rasmussen	.05
618	Bip Roberts	.05
619	Rich Rodriguez	.05
620	Benito Santiago	.05
621	Craig Shipley RC	.05
622	Tim Teufel	.05
623	Kevin Ward RC	.05
624	Ed Whitson	.05
625	Dave Anderson	.05
626	Kevin Bass	.05
627	Rod Beck RC	.10
628	Bud Black	.05
629	Jeff Brantley	.05
630	John Burkett	.05
631	Will Clark	.05
632	Royce Clayton RC	.05
633	Steve Decker	.05
634	Kelly Downs	.05
635	Mike Felder	.05
636	Scott Garrelts	.05
637	Eric Gunderson	.05
638	Bryan Hickerson RC	.05
639	Darren Lewis	.05
640	Greg Litton	.05
641	Kirt Manwaring	.05
642	Paul McClellan RC	.05
643	Willie McGee	.05
644	Kevin Mitchell	.05
645	Francisco Olivares	.05
646	Mike Remlinger RC	.10
647	Dave Righetti	.05
648	Robby Thompson	.05
649	Jose Uribe	.05
650	Matt Williams	.05
651	Trevor Wilson	.05
652	Tom Goodwin RC (Prospects)	.05
653	Terry Bross RC (Prospects)	.05
654	Mike Christopher RC (Prospects)	.05
655	Kenny Lofton (Prospects)	.05
656	Chris Cron RC (Prospects)	.05
657	Willie Banks RC (Prospects)	.05
658	Pat Rice RC (Prospects) (Last name misspelled.)	.75
659a	Rob Mauer RC (Prospects) (Name misspelled)	
659b	Rob Maurer RC (Prospects)(Corrected)	.05
660	Don Harris RC (Prospects)	.05
661	Henry Rodriguez (Prospects)	.05
662	Cliff Brantley RC (Prospects)	.05
663	Mike Linskey RC (Prospects)	.05
664	Gary Disarcina RC (Prospects)	.05
665	Gil Heredia RC (Prospects)	.10
666	Vinny Castilla RC (Prospects)	.50
667	Paul Abbott RC (Prospects)	.05
668	Monty Fariss RC (Prospects)	.05
669	Jarvis Brown RC (Prospects)	.05
670	Wayne Kirby RC (Prospects)	.05
671	Scott Brosius RC (Prospects)	.05
672	Bob Hamelin (Prospects)	.05
673	Joel Johnston RC (Prospects)	.05
674	Tim Spehr RC (Prospects)	.05
675	Jeff Gardner RC (Prospects)	.05
676	Rico Rossy RC (Prospects)	.05
677	Roberto Hernandez RC (Prospects)	.20
678	Ted Wood RC (Prospects)	.05
679	Cal Eldred (Prospects)	.05
680	Sean Berry (Prospects)	.05
681	Rickey Henderson (Stolen Base Record)	.20
682	Nolan Ryan (Record 7th No-hitter)	.25
683	Dennis Martinez (Perfect Game)	.05
684	Wilson Alvarez (Rookie No-hitter)	.05
685	Joe Carter (3 100 RBI Seasons)	.05
686	Dave Winfield (400 Home Runs)	.20
687	David Cone (Ties NL Record Strikeouts)	.05
688	Jose Canseco (League Leaders)	.15
689	Howard Johnson (League Leaders)	.05
690	Julio Franco (League Leaders)	.05
691	Terry Pendleton (League Leaders)	.05
692	Cecil Fielder (League Leaders)	.05
693	Scott Erickson (League Leaders)	.05
694	Tom Glavine (League Leaders)	.05
695	Dennis Martinez (League Leaders)	.05
696	Bryan Harvey (League Leaders)	.05
697	Lee Smith (League Leaders)	.05
698	Super Siblings (Roberto & Sandy Alomar, Roberto & Sandy Alomar)	.10
699	The Indispensables (Bobby Bonilla, Will Clark)	.05
700	Teamwork (Mark Wohlers, Kent Mercker, Alejandro Pena)	.05
701	Tiger Tandems (Chris Jones, Bo Jackson, Gregg Olson, Frank Thomas)	.05
702	The Ignitors (Brett Butler, Paul Molitor)	.10
703	The Indispensables II (Cal Ripken Jr., Joe Carter)	.05
704	Power Packs (Barry Larkin, Kirby Puckett)	.15
705	Today and Tomorrow (Mo Vaughn, Cecil Fielder)	.05
706	Teenage Sensations (Ramon Martinez, Ozzie Guillen)	.05
707	Designated Hitters (Harold Baines, Wade Boggs)	.20
708	Robin Yount (ProVision)	.35
709	Ken Griffey Jr. (ProVision)	.60
710	Nolan Ryan (ProVision)	.75
711	Cal Ripken, Jr. (ProVision)	.75
712	Frank Thomas (ProVision)	.50
713	Dave Justice (ProVision)	.05
714	Checklist 1-101	.05
715	Checklist 102-194	.05
716	Checklist 195-296	.05
717	Checklist 297-397	.05
718	Checklist 398-494	.05
719	Checklist 495-596	.05
720a	Checklist 597-720 (659 Rob Mauer)	.05
720b	Checklist 597-720 (659 Rob Maurer)	.05

All-Stars

Black borders with gold highlights are featured on these special wax pack insert cards. The fronts feature glossy action photos with a portrait photo inset. Backs feature career highlights.

		NM/M
Complete Set (24):		8.00
Common Player:		.10
1	Felix Jose	.10
2	Tony Gwynn	1.25
3	Barry Bonds	3.00
4	Bobby Bonilla	.10
5	Mike LaValliere	.10
6	Tom Glavine	.40
7	Ramon Martinez	.10
8	Lee Smith	.10
9	Mickey Tettleton	.10
10	Scott Erickson	.10
11	Frank Thomas	.75
12	Danny Tartabull	.10
13	Will Clark	.10
14	Ryne Sandberg	1.25
15	Terry Pendleton	.10
16	Barry Larkin	.10
17	Rafael Palmeiro	.65
18	Julio Franco	.10
19	Robin Ventura	.10
20	Cal Ripken, Jr.	3.00
21	Joe Carter	.10
22	Kirby Puckett	1.25
23	Ken Griffey Jr.	2.25
24	Jose Canseco	.50

Roger Clemens

This set chronicles the career highlights of Roger Clemens. The initial 12 cards from the set were inserted in 1992 Fleer wax packs. A limited number of autographed cards were inserted as well. The additional three cards from the set were available through a mail-in offer. The card fronts feature black borders with metallic gold type. The flip side is yellow with black borders.

		NM/M
Complete Set (15):		6.00
Common Card:		.50
Autographed Card:		40.00
1	Quiet Storm	.50
2	Courted by the Mets and Twins	.50
3	The Show	.50
4	A Rocket Launched	.50
5	Time of Trial	.50
6	Break Through	.50
7	Play it Again Roger	.50
8	Business as Usual	.50
9	Heee's Back	.50
10	Blood, Sweat and Tears	.50
11	Prime of Life	.50
12	Man for Every Season	.50
13	Cooperstown Bound	1.50
14	The Heat of the Moment	1.50
15	Final Words	1.50

Lumber Co.

Baseball's top power hitters at each position are featured in this nine-card set. Fronts feature full-color action photos bordered in black. Backs feature posed player

photos and career highlights. The set was included only in factory sets released to the hobby trade.

		NM/M
Complete Set (9):		5.00
Common Player:		.25
1	Cecil Fielder	.25
2	Mickey Tettleton	.25
3	Darryl Strawberry	.25
4	Ryne Sandberg	1.00
5	Jose Canseco	.40
6	Matt Williams	.25
7	Cal Ripken, Jr.	2.00
8	Barry Bonds	2.00
9	Ron Gant	.25

Rookie Sensations

This 20-card set features the top rookies of 1991 and rookie prospects from 1992. The card fronts feature blue borders with "Rookie Sensations" in gold along the top border. The flip sides feature background information on the player. The cards were randomly inserted in 1992 Fleer cello packs. This issue saw very high prices when initially released then suffered long-term declines as the hobby became inundated with more and more insert sets.

		NM/M
Complete Set (20):		13.50
Common Player:		.35
1	Frank Thomas	6.00
2	Todd Van Poppel	.35
3	Orlando Merced	.35
4	Jeff Bagwell	6.00
5	Jeff Fassero	.35
6	Darren Lewis	.35
7	Milt Cuyler	.35
8	Mike Timlin	.35
9	Brian McRae	.35
10	Chuck Knoblauch	.35
11	Rich DeLucia	.35
12	Ivan Rodriguez	4.50
13	Juan Guzman	.35
14	Steve Chitren	.35
15	Mark Wohlers	.35
16	Wes Chamberlain	.35
17	Ray Lankford	.35
18	Chito Martinez	.35
19	Phil Plantier	.35
20	Scott Leius	.35

Smoke 'N Heat

This 12-card set of top pitchers was included in factory sets designated for sale within the general retail trade. Card numbers have an "S" prefix.

		NM/M
Complete Set (12):		7.50
Common Player:		.25
1	Lee Smith	.25
2	Jack McDowell	.25
3	David Cone	.25
4	Roger Clemens	2.00
5	Nolan Ryan	3.00
6	Scott Erickson	.25
7	Tom Glavine	.50
8	Dwight Gooden	.25
9	Andy Benes	.25

10	Steve Avery	.25
11	Randy Johnson	1.00
12	Jim Abbott	.25

Team Leaders

White and green borders highlight this insert set from Fleer. The card fronts also feature a special gold-foil "team leaders" logo beneath the full-color player photo. The card backs feature player information. The cards were randomly inserted in 1992 Fleer rack packs.

		NM/M
Complete Set (20):		10.00
Common Player:		.50
1	Don Mattingly	2.00
2	Howard Johnson	.50
3	Chris Sabo	.50
4	Carlton Fisk	1.25
5	Kirby Puckett	1.50
6	Cecil Fielder	.50
7	Tony Gwynn	1.50
8	Will Clark	.50
9	Bobby Bonilla	.50
10	Len Dykstra	.50
11	Tom Glavine	.75
12	Rafael Palmeiro	1.00
13	Wade Boggs	1.50
14	Joe Carter	.50
15	Ken Griffey Jr.	2.50
16	Darryl Strawberry	.50
17	Cal Ripken, Jr.	3.00
18	Danny Tartabull	.50
19	Jose Canseco	.75
20	Andre Dawson	.50

Update

This 132-card set was released in boxed set form and features traded players, free agents and top rookies from 1992. The cards are styled after the regular 1992 Fleer and are numbered alphabetically according to team. This set marks the ninth year that Fleer has released an update set. The set includes four black-bordered "Headliner" cards.

		NM/M
Complete Set (136):		60.00
Common Player:		.05
H1	1992 All-Star Game MVP (Ken Griffey Jr.)	1.50

H2	3000 Career Hits (Robin Yount)	.50
H3	Major League Career Saves Record (Jeff Reardon)	.10
H4	Record RBI Performance (Cecil Fielder)	.05
1	Todd Frohwirth	.05
2	Alan Mills	.05
3	Rick Sutcliffe	.05
4	John Valentin RC	.25
5	Frank Viola	.05
6	Bob Zupcic RC	.05
7	Mike Butcher RC	.05
8	Chad Curtis RC	.50
9	Damion Easley RC	.25
10	Tim Salmon RC	.50
11	Julio Valera	.05
12	George Bell	.05
13	Roberto Hernandez RC	.05
14	Shawn Jeter RC	.05
15	Thomas Howard	.05
16	Jesse Levis RC	.05
17	Kenny Lofton	.05
18	Paul Sorrento	.05
19	Rico Brogna RC	.05
20	John Doherty RC	.05
21	Dan Gladden	.05
22	Buddy Groom RC	.05
23	Shawn Hare RC	.05
24	John Kiely RC	.05
25	Kurt Knudsen RC	.05
26	Gregg Jefferies	.05
27	Wally Joyner	.05
28	Kevin Koslofski RC	.05
29	Kevin McReynolds	.05
30	Rusty Meacham	.05
31	Keith Miller	.05
32	Hipolito Pichardo RC	.05
33	James Austin RC	.05
34	Scott Fletcher	.05
35	John Jaha RC	.05
36	Pat Listach RC	.05
37	Dave Nilsson RC	.05
38	Kevin Seitzer	.05
39	Tom Edens	.05
40	Pat Mahomes RC	.05
41	John Smiley	.05
42	Charlie Hayes	.05
43	Sam Militello RC	.05
44	Andy Stankiewicz RC	.05
45	Danny Tartabull	.05
46	Bob Wickman RC	.05
47	Jerry Browne	.05
48	Kevin Campbell RC	.05
49	Vince Horsman RC	.05
50	Troy Neel RC	.05
51	Ruben Sierra	.05
52	Bruce Walton RC	.05
53	Willie Wilson	.05
54	Bret Boone RC	.50
55	Dave Fleming RC	.05
56	Kevin Mitchell	.05
57	Jeff Nelson RC	.05
58	Shane Turner RC	.05
59	Jose Canseco	.65
60	Jeff Frye RC	.05
61	Danilo Leon RC	.05
62	Roger Pavlik RC	.05
63	David Cone	.05
64	Pat Hentgen RC	.05
65	Randy Knorr RC	.05
66	Jack Morris	.05
67	Dave Winfield	1.00
68	David Nied RC	.05
69	Otis Nixon	.05
70	Alejandro Pena	.05
71	Jeff Reardon	.05
72	Alex Arias RC	.05
73	Jim Bullinger RC	.05
74	Mike Morgan	.05
75	Rey Sanchez RC	.05
76	Bob Scanlan	.05
77	Sammy Sosa	3.00
78	Scott Bankhead	.05
79	Tim Belcher	.05
80	Steve Foster RC	.05
81	Willie Greene RC	.05
82	Bip Roberts	.05
83	Scott Ruskin	.05
84	Greg Swindell	.05
85	Juan Guerrero RC	.05
86	Butch Henry RC	.05
87	Doug Jones	.05
88	Brian Williams RC	.05
89	Tom Candiotti	.05
90	Eric Davis	.05
91	Carlos Hernandez RC	.05
92	Mike Piazza RC	45.00
93	Mike Sharperson	.05
94	Eric Young RC	.05
95	Moises Alou	.05
96	Greg Colbrunn	.05
97	Wil Cordero RC	.05
98	Ken Hill	.05
99	John Vander Wal RC	.05
100	John Wetteland	.05
101	Bobby Bonilla	.05
102	Eric Hilman RC	.05
103	Pat Howell RC	.05
104	Jeff Kent RC	15.00
105	Dick Schofield	.05
106	Ryan Thompson RC	.05
107	Chico Walker	.05
108	Juan Bell	.05
109	Mariano Duncan	.05
110	Jeff Grotewold RC	.05
111	Ben Rivera RC	.05
112	Curt Schilling	.65

113	Victor Cole RC	.05
114	Al Martin RC	.05
115	Roger Mason	.05
116	Blas Minor RC	.05
117	Tim Wakefield RC	4.00
118	Mark Clark RC	.05
119	Rheal Cormier RC	.05
120	Donovan Osborne RC	.05
121	Todd Worrell	.05
122	Jeremy Hernandez RC	.05
123	Randy Myers	.05
124	Frank Seminara RC	.05
125	Gary Sheffield	.75
126	Dan Walters RC	.05
127	Steve Hosey RC	.05
128	Mike Jackson	.05
129	Jim Pena RC	.05
130	Cory Snyder	.05
131	Bill Swift	.05
132	Checklist	.05

7-Eleven

The 1992 Performer Collection was a combined effort from Fleer and 7-11. Customers at 7-11 stores received a packet of five cards with gasoline purchases to build the 24-card set of major stars. The cards are standard size, with virtually the identical design to the regular issue Fleer set of 1992, with only the addition of "The Performer" logo on the front of the card and a pair of sponsors' logos on back.

		NM/M
Complete Set (24):		9.00
Common Player:		.20
1	Nolan Ryan	1.50
2	Frank Thomas	.65
3	Ryne Sandberg	.75
4	Ken Griffey Jr.	1.00
5	Cal Ripken, Jr.	1.50
6	Roger Clemens	.85
7	Cecil Fielder	.20
8	Dave Justice	.20
9	Wade Boggs	.75
10	Tony Gwynn	.75
11	Kirby Puckett	.75
12	Darryl Strawberry	.20
13	Jose Canseco	.50
14	Barry Larkin	.20
15	Terry Pendleton	.20
16	Don Mattingly	.85
17	Rickey Henderson	.65
18	Ruben Sierra	.20
19	Jeff Bagwell	.65
20	Tom Glavine	.45
21	Ramon Martinez	.20
22	Will Clark	.20
23	Barry Bonds	1.50
24	Roberto Alomar	.40

1993 Fleer

The card fronts feature silver borders with the player's name, team and position in a banner along the left side of the card. The backs feature an action photo of the player with his name in bold behind him. A box featuring biographical information, statistics and player information is located to the right of the action photo. The cards are numbered alphabetically by team. The

basic Fleer issue for 1993 was issued in two series of 360 cards each. The 720-card set included a number of subsets and could be found in many different types of packaging with an unprecedented number of inserts sets to spice up each offering.

		NM/M
Complete Set (720):		10.00
Common Player:		.05
Series 1 or 2 Pack (15):		.50
Series 1 or 2 Box (36):		12.50
1	Steve Avery	.05
2	Sid Bream	.05
3	Ron Gant	.05
4	Tom Glavine	.25
5	Brian Hunter	.05
6	Ryan Klesko	.05
7	Charlie Leibrandt	.05
8	Kent Mercker	.05
9	David Nied	.05
10	Otis Nixon	.05
11	Greg Olson	.05
12	Terry Pendleton	.05
13	Deion Sanders	.10
14	John Smoltz	.05
15	Mike Stanton	.05
16	Mark Wohlers	.05
17	Paul Assenmacher	.05
18	Steve Buechele	.05
19	Shawon Dunston	.05
20	Mark Grace	.05
21	Derrick May	.05
22	Chuck McElroy	.05
23	Mike Morgan	.05
24	Rey Sanchez	.05
25	Ryne Sandberg	.60
26	Bob Scanlan	.05
27	Sammy Sosa	.60
28	Rick Wilkins	.05
29	Bobby Ayala RC	.05
30	Tim Belcher	.05
31	Jeff Branson RC	.05
32	Norm Charlton	.05
33	Steve Foster	.05
34	Willie Greene RC	.05
35	Chris Hammond	.05
36	Milt Hill RC	.05
37	Hal Morris	.05
38	Joe Oliver	.05
39	Paul O'Neill	.05
40	Tim Pugh RC	.05
41	Jose Rijo	.05
42	Bip Roberts	.05
43	Chris Sabo	.05
44	Reggie Sanders	.05
45	Eric Anthony	.05
46	Jeff Bagwell	.50
47	Craig Biggio	.05
48	Joe Boever	.05
49	Casey Candaele	.05
50	Steve Finley	.05
51	Luis Gonzalez	.05
52	Pete Harnisch	.05
53	Xavier Hernandez	.05
54	Doug Jones	.05
55	Eddie Taubensee	.05
56	Brian Williams	.05
57	Pedro Astacio RC	.10
58	Todd Benzinger	.05
59	Brett Butler	.05
60	Tom Candiotti	.05
61	Lenny Harris	.05
62	Carlos Hernandez	.05
63	Orel Hershiser	.05
64	Eric Karros	.05
65	Ramon Martinez	.05
66	Jose Offerman	.05
67	Mike Scioscia	.05
68	Mike Sharperson	.05
69	Eric Young RC	.10
70	Moises Alou	.05
71	Ivan Calderon	.05
72	Archi Cianfrocco RC	.05
73	Wil Cordero	.05
74	Delino DeShields	.05
75	Mark Gardner	.05
76	Ken Hill	.05
77	Tim Laker RC	.05
78	Chris Nabholz	.05
79	Mel Rojas	.05
80	John Vander Wal RC	.10
81	Larry Walker	.05
82	Tim Wallach	.05
83	John Wetteland	.05
84	Bobby Bonilla	.05
85	Daryl Boston	.05
86	Sid Fernandez	.05
87	Eric Hillman RC	.05
88	Todd Hundley	.05
89	Howard Johnson	.05
90	Jeff Kent	.05
91	Eddie Murray	.50
92	Bill Pecota	.05
93	Bret Saberhagen	.05
94	Dick Schofield	.05
95	Pete Schourek	.05
96	Anthony Young	.05
97	Ruben Amaro Jr.	.05
98	Juan Bell	.05
99	Wes Chamberlain	.05
100	Darren Daulton	.05
101	Mariano Duncan	.05
102	Mike Hartley	.05
103	Ricky Jordan	.05

No.	Player	Price
104	John Kruk	.05
105	Mickey Morandini	.05
106	Terry Mulholland	.05
107	Ben Rivera RC	.05
108	Curt Schilling	.25
109	Keith Shepherd RC	.05
110	Stan Belinda	.05
111	Jay Bell	.05
112	Barry Bonds	1.00
113	Jeff King	.05
114	Mike LaValliere	.05
115	Jose Lind	.05
116	Roger Mason	.05
117	Orlando Merced	.05
118	Bob Patterson	.05
119	Don Slaught	.05
120	Zane Smith	.05
121	Randy Tomlin	.05
122	Andy Van Slyke	.05
123	Tim Wakefield RC	.10
124	Rheal Cormier	.05
125	Bernard Gilkey	.05
126	Felix Jose	.05
127	Ray Lankford	.05
128	Bob McClure	.05
129	Donovan Osborne	.05
130	Tom Pagnozzi	.05
131	Geronimo Pena	.05
132	Mike Perez	.05
133	Lee Smith	.05
134	Bob Tewksbury	.05
135	Todd Worrell	.05
136	Todd Zeile	.05
137	Jerald Clark	.05
138	Tony Gwynn	.60
139	Greg Harris	.05
140	Jeremy Hernandez	.05
141	Darrin Jackson	.05
142	Mike Maddux	.05
143	Fred McGriff	.05
144	Jose Melendez	.05
145	Rich Rodriguez	.05
146	Frank Seminara	.05
147	Gary Sheffield	.35
148	Kurt Stillwell	.05
149	Dan Walters RC	.05
150	Rod Beck	.05
151	Bud Black	.05
152	Jeff Brantley	.05
153	John Burkett	.05
154	Will Clark	.05
155	Royce Clayton	.05
156	Mike Jackson	.05
157	Darren Lewis	.05
158	Kirt Manwaring	.05
159	Willie McGee	.05
160	Cory Snyder	.05
161	Bill Swift	.05
162	Trevor Wilson	.05
163	Brady Anderson	.05
164	Glenn Davis	.05
165	Mike Devereaux	.05
166	Todd Frohwirth	.05
167	Leo Gomez	.05
168	Chris Hoiles	.05
169	Ben McDonald	.05
170	Randy Milligan	.05
171	Alan Mills	.05
172	Mike Mussina	.30
173	Gregg Olson	.05
174	Arthur Rhodes	.05
175	David Segui	.05
176	Ellis Burks	.05
177	Roger Clemens	.65
178	Scott Cooper	.05
179	Danny Darwin	.05
180	Tony Fossas	.05
181	Paul Quantrill RC	.10
182	Jody Reed	.05
183	John Valentin RC	.10
184	Mo Vaughn	.05
185	Frank Viola	.05
186	Bob Zupcic	.05
187	Jim Abbott	.05
188	Gary DiSarcina	.05
189	Damion Easley RC	.10
190	Junior Felix	.05
191	Chuck Finley	.05
192	Joe Grahe	.05
193	Bryan Harvey	.05
194	Mark Langston	.05
195	John Orton	.05
196	Luis Polonia	.05
197	Tim Salmon	.05
198	Luis Sojo	.05
199	Wilson Alvarez	.05
200	George Bell	.05
201	Alex Fernandez	.05
202	Craig Grebeck	.05
203	Ozzie Guillen	.05
204	Lance Johnson	.05
205	Ron Karkovice	.05
206	Kirk McCaskill	.05
207	Jack McDowell	.05
208	Scott Radinsky	.05
209	Tim Raines	.05
210	Frank Thomas	.50
211	Robin Ventura	.05
212	Sandy Alomar Jr.	.05
213	Carlos Baerga	.05
214	Dennis Cook	.05
215	Thomas Howard	.05
216	Mark Lewis	.05
217	Derek Lilliquist	.05
218	Kenny Lofton	.05
219	Charles Nagy	.05
220	Steve Olin	.05
221	Paul Sorrento	.05
222	Jim Thome	.40
223	Mark Whiten	.05
224	Milt Cuyler	.05
225	Rob Deer	.05
226	John Doherty RC	.05
227	Cecil Fielder	.05
228	Travis Fryman	.05
229	Mike Henneman	.05
230	John Kiely RC	.05
231	Kurt Knudsen RC	.05
232	Scott Livingstone	.05
233	Tony Phillips	.05
234	Mickey Tettleton	.05
235	Kevin Appier	.05
236	George Brett	.65
237	Tom Gordon	.05
238	Gregg Jefferies	.05
239	Wally Joyner	.05
240	Kevin Koslofski RC	.05
241	Mike Macfarlane	.05
242	Brian McRae	.05
243	Rusty Meacham	.05
244	Keith Miller	.05
245	Jeff Montgomery	.05
246	Hipolito Pichardo RC	.05
247	Ricky Bones	.05
248	Cal Eldred	.05
249	Mike Fetters	.05
250	Darryl Hamilton	.05
251	Doug Henry	.05
252	John Jaha RC	.05
253	Pat Listach	.05
254	Paul Molitor	.50
255	Jaime Navarro	.05
256	Kevin Seitzer	.05
257	B.J. Surhoff	.05
258	Greg Vaughn	.05
259	Bill Wegman	.05
260	Robin Yount	.50
261	Rick Aguilera	.05
262	Chili Davis	.05
263	Scott Erickson	.05
264	Greg Gagne	.05
265	Mark Guthrie	.05
266	Brian Harper	.05
267	Kent Hrbek	.05
268	Terry Jorgensen	.05
269	Gene Larkin	.05
270	Scott Leius	.05
271	Pat Mahomes	.05
272	Pedro Munoz	.05
273	Kirby Puckett	.60
274	Kevin Tapani	.05
275	Carl Willis	.05
276	Steve Farr	.05
277	John Habyan	.05
278	Mel Hall	.05
279	Charlie Hayes	.05
280	Pat Kelly	.05
281	Don Mattingly	.65
282	Sam Militello	.05
283	Matt Nokes	.05
284	Melido Perez	.05
285	Andy Stankiewicz	.05
286	Danny Tartabull	.05
287	Randy Velarde	.05
288	Bob Wickman	.05
289	Bernie Williams	.05
290	Lance Blankenship	.05
291	Mike Bordick	.05
292	Jerry Browne	.05
293	Dennis Eckersley	.40
294	Rickey Henderson	.50
295	Vince Horsman RC	.05
296	Mark McGwire	.85
297	Jeff Parrett	.05
298	Ruben Sierra	.05
299	Terry Steinbach	.05
300	Walt Weiss	.05
301	Bob Welch	.05
302	Willie Wilson	.05
303	Bobby Witt	.05
304	Bret Boone	.05
305	Jay Buhner	.05
306	Dave Fleming	.05
307	Ken Griffey Jr.	.75
308	Erik Hanson	.05
309	Edgar Martinez	.05
310	Tino Martinez	.05
311	Jeff Nelson	.05
312	Dennis Powell	.05
313	Mike Schooler	.05
314	Russ Swan	.05
315	Dave Valle	.05
316	Omar Vizquel	.05
317	Kevin Brown	.05
318	Todd Burns	.05
319	Jose Canseco	.35
320	Julio Franco	.05
321	Jeff Frye	.05
322	Juan Gonzalez	.30
323	Jose Guzman	.05
324	Jeff Huson	.05
325	Dean Palmer	.05
326	Kevin Reimer	.05
327	Ivan Rodriguez	.40
328	Kenny Rogers	.05
329	Dan Smith RC	.05
330	Roberto Alomar	.20
331	Derek Bell	.05
332	Pat Borders	.05
333	Joe Carter	.05
334	Kelly Gruber	.05
335	Tom Henke	.05
336	Jimmy Key	.05
337	Manuel Lee	.05
338	Candy Maldonado	.05
339	John Olerud	.05
340	Todd Stottlemyre	.05
341	Duane Ward	.05
342	Devon White	.05
343	Dave Winfield	.50
344	Edgar Martinez (League Leaders)	.05
345	Cecil Fielder (League Leaders)	.05
346	Kenny Lofton (League Leaders)	.05
347	Jack Morris (League Leaders)	.05
348	Roger Clemens (League Leaders)	.35
349	Fred McGriff (Round Trippers)	.05
350	Barry Bonds (Round Trippers)	.60
351	Gary Sheffield (Round Trippers)	.05
352	Darren Daulton (Round Trippers)	.05
353	Dave Hollins (Round Trippers)	.05
354	Brothers In Blue (Pedro Martinez, Ramon Martinez)	.25
355	Power Packs (Ivan Rodriguez, Kirby Puckett)	.25
356	Triple Threats (Ryne Sandberg, Gary Sheffield)	.20
357	Infield Trifecta (Roberto Alomar, Chuck Knoblauch, Carlos Baerga)	.05
358	Checklist	.05
359	Checklist	.05
360	Checklist	.05
361	Rafael Belliard	.05
362	Damon Berryhill	.05
363	Mike Bielecki	.05
364	Jeff Blauser	.05
365	Francisco Cabrera	.05
366	Marvin Freeman	.05
367	Dave Justice	.05
368	Mark Lemke	.05
369	Alejandro Pena	.05
370	Jeff Reardon	.05
371	Lonnie Smith	.05
372	Pete Smith	.05
373	Shawn Boskie	.05
374	Jim Bullinger	.05
375	Frank Castillo	.05
376	Doug Dascenzo	.05
377	Andre Dawson	.25
378	Mike Harkey	.05
379	Greg Hibbard	.05
380	Greg Maddux	.60
381	Ken Patterson	.05
382	Jeff Robinson	.05
383	Luis Salazar	.05
384	Dwight Smith	.05
385	Jose Vizcaino	.05
386	Scott Bankhead	.05
387	Tom Browning	.05
388	Darnell Coles	.05
389	Rob Dibble	.05
390	Bill Doran	.05
391	Dwayne Henry	.05
392	Cesar Hernandez	.05
393	Roberto Kelly	.05
394	Barry Larkin	.05
395	Dave Martinez	.05
396	Kevin Mitchell	.05
397	Jeff Reed	.05
398	Scott Ruskin	.05
399	Greg Swindell	.05
400	Dan Wilson	.05
401	Andy Ashby	.05
402	Freddie Benavides	.05
403	Dante Bichette	.05
404	Willie Blair	.05
405	Denis Boucher	.05
406	Vinny Castilla	.05
407	Braulio Castillo	.05
408	Alex Cole	.05
409	Andres Galarraga	.05
410	Joe Girardi	.05
411	Butch Henry	.05
412	Darren Holmes	.05
413	Calvin Jones	.05
414	Steve Reed RC	.05
415	Kevin Ritz	.05
416	Jim Tatum RC	.05
417	Jack Armstrong	.05
418	Bret Barberie	.05
419	Ryan Bowen	.05
420	Cris Carpenter	.05
421	Chuck Carr	.05
422	Scott Chiamparino	.05
423	Jeff Conine	.05
424	Jim Corsi	.05
425	Steve Decker	.05
426	Chris Donnels	.05
427	Monty Fariss	.05
428	Bob Natal	.05
429	Pat Rapp RC	.05
430	Dave Weathers	.05
431	Nigel Wilson RC	.05
432	Ken Caminiti	.05
433	Andujar Cedeno	.05
434	Tom Edens	.05
435	Juan Guerrero	.05
436	Pete Incaviglia	.05
437	Jimmy Jones	.05
438	Darryl Kile	.05
439	Rob Murphy	.05
440	Al Osuna	.05
441	Mark Portugal	.05
442	Scott Servais	.05
443	John Candelaria	.05
444	Tim Crews	.05
445	Eric Davis	.05
446	Tom Goodwin	.05
447	Jim Gott	.05
448	Kevin Gross	.05
449	Dave Hansen	.05
450	Jay Howell	.05
451	Roger McDowell	.05
452	Bob Ojeda	.05
453	Henry Rodriguez	.05
454	Darryl Strawberry	.05
455	Mitch Webster	.05
456	Steve Wilson	.05
457	Brian Barnes	.05
458	Sean Berry	.05
459	Jeff Fassero	.05
460	Darrin Fletcher	.05
461	Marquis Grissom	.05
462	Dennis Martinez	.05
463	Spike Owen	.05
464	Matt Stairs	.05
465	Sergio Valdez	.05
466	Kevin Bass	.05
467	Vince Coleman	.05
468	Mark Dewey	.05
469	Kevin Elster	.05
470	Tony Fernandez	.05
471	John Franco	.05
472	Dave Gallagher	.05
473	Paul Gibson	.05
474	Dwight Gooden	.05
475	Lee Guetterman	.05
476	Jeff Innis	.05
477	Dave Magadan	.05
478	Charlie O'Brien	.05
479	Willie Randolph	.05
480	Mackey Sasser	.05
481	Ryan Thompson	.05
482	Chico Walker	.05
483	Kyle Abbott	.05
484	Bob Ayrault	.05
485	Kim Batiste	.05
486	Cliff Brantley	.05
487	Jose DeLeon	.05
488	Len Dykstra	.05
489	Tommy Greene	.05
490	Jeff Grotewold	.05
491	Dave Hollins	.05
492	Danny Jackson	.05
493	Stan Javier	.05
494	Tom Marsh	.05
495	Greg Matthews	.05
496	Dale Murphy	.15
497	Todd Pratt RC	.05
498	Mitch Williams	.05
499	Danny Cox	.05
500	Doug Drabek	.05
501	Carlos Garcia	.05
502	Lloyd McClendon	.05
503	Denny Neagle	.05
504	Gary Redus	.05
505	Bob Walk	.05
506	John Wehner	.05
507	Luis Alicea	.05
508	Mark Clark	.05
509	Pedro Guerrero	.05
510	Rex Hudler	.05
511	Brian Jordan	.05
512	Omar Olivares	.05
513	Jose Oquendo	.05
514	Gerald Perry	.05
515	Bryn Smith	.05
516	Craig Wilson	.05
517	Tracy Woodson	.05
518	Larry Anderson	.05
519	Andy Benes	.05
520	Jim Deshaies	.05
521	Bruce Hurst	.05
522	Randy Myers	.05
523	Benito Santiago	.05
524	Tim Scott	.05
525	Tim Teufel	.05
526	Mike Benjamin	.05
527	Dave Burba	.05
528	Craig Colbert	.05
529	Mike Felder	.05
530	Bryan Hickerson	.05
531	Chris James	.05
532	Mark Leonard	.05
533	Greg Litton	.05
534	Francisco Oliveras	.05
535	John Patterson	.05
536	Jim Pena	.05
537	Dave Righetti	.05
538	Robby Thompson	.05
539	Jose Uribe	.05
540	Matt Williams	.05
541	Storm Davis	.05
542	Sam Horn	.05
543	Tim Hulett	.05
544	Craig Lefferts	.05
545	Chito Martinez	.05
546	Mark McLemore	.05
547	Luis Mercedes	.05
548	Bob Milacki	.05
549	Joe Orsulak	.05
550	Billy Ripken	.05
551	Cal Ripken, Jr.	1.00
552	Rick Sutcliffe	.05
553	Jeff Tackett	.05
554	Wade Boggs	.60
555	Tom Brunansky	.05
556	Jack Clark	.05
557	John Dopson	.05
558	Mike Gardiner	.05
559	Mike Greenwell	.05
560	Greg Harris	.05
561	Billy Hatcher	.05
562	Joe Hesketh	.05
563	Tony Pena	.05
564	Phil Plantier	.05
565	Luis Rivera	.05
566	Herm Winningham	.05
567	Matt Young	.05
568	Bert Blyleven	.05
569	Mike Butcher	.05
570	Chuck Crim	.05
571	Chad Curtis RC	.15
572	Tim Fortugno	.05
573	Steve Frey	.05
574	Gary Gaetti	.05
575	Scott Lewis	.05
576	Lee Stevens	.05
577	Ron Tingley	.05
578	Julio Valera	.05
579	Shawn Abner	.05
580	Joey Cora	.05
581	Chris Cron	.05
582	Carlton Fisk	.50
583	Roberto Hernandez	.05
584	Charlie Hough	.05
585	Terry Leach	.05
586	Donn Pall	.05
587	Dan Pasqua	.05
588	Steve Sax	.05
589	Bobby Thigpen	.05
590	Albert Belle	.05
591	Felix Fermin	.05
592	Glenallen Hill	.05
593	Brook Jacoby	.05
594	Reggie Jefferson	.05
595	Carlos Martinez	.05
596	Jose Mesa	.05
597	Rod Nichols	.05
598	Junior Ortiz	.05
599	Eric Plunk	.05
600	Ted Power	.05
601	Scott Scudder	.05
602	Kevin Wickander	.05
603	Skeeter Barnes	.05
604	Mark Carreon	.05
605	Dan Gladden	.05
606	Bill Gullickson	.05
607	Chad Kreuter	.05
608	Mark Leiter	.05
609	Mike Munoz	.05
610	Rich Rowland	.05
611	Frank Tanana	.05
612	Walt Terrell	.05
613	Alan Trammell	.05
614	Lou Whitaker	.05
615	Luis Aquino	.05
616	Mike Boddicker	.05
617	Jim Eisenreich	.05
618	Mark Gubicza	.05
619	David Howard	.05
620	Mike Magnante	.05
621	Brent Mayne	.05
622	Kevin McReynolds	.05
623	Eddie Pierce RC	.05
624	Bill Sampen	.05
625	Steve Shifflett	.05
626	Gary Thurman	.05
627	Curtis Wikerson	.05
628	Chris Bosio	.05
629	Scott Fletcher	.05
630	Jim Gantner	.05
631	Dave Nilsson	.05
632	Jesse Orosco	.05
633	Dan Plesac	.05
634	Ron Robinson	.05
635	Bill Spiers	.05
636	Franklin Stubbs	.05
637	Willie Banks	.05
638	Randy Bush	.05
639	Chuck Knoblauch	.05
640	Shane Mack	.05
641	Mike Pagliarulo	.05
642	Jeff Reboulet	.05
643	John Smiley	.05
644	Mike Trombley RC	.05
645	Gary Wayne	.05
646	Lenny Webster	.05
647	Tim Burke	.05
648	Mike Gallego	.05
649	Dion James	.05
650	Jeff Johnson	.05
651	Scott Kamieniecki	.05
652	Kevin Maas	.05
653	Rich Monteleone	.05
654	Jerry Nielsen	.05
655	Scott Sanderson	.05
656	Mike Stanley	.05
657	Gerald Williams	.05
658	Curt Young	.05
659	Harold Baines	.05
660	Kevin Campbell	.05
661	Ron Darling	.05
662	Kelly Downs	.05
663	Eric Fox	.05
664	Dave Henderson	.05
665	Rick Honeycutt	.05
666	Mike Moore	.05
667	Jamie Quirk	.05
668	Jeff Russell	.05
669	Dave Stewart	.05
670	Greg Briley	.05
671	Dave Cochrane	.05
672	Henry Cotto	.05
673	Rich DeLucia	.05
674	Brian Fisher	.05
675	Mark Grant	.05
676	Randy Johnson	.50
677	Tim Leary	.05
678	Pete O'Brien	.05
679	Lance Parrish	.05
680	Harold Reynolds	.05
681	Shane Turner	.05
682	Jack Daugherty	.05
683	David Hulse RC	.05
684	Terry Mathews	.05
685	Al Newman	.05
686	Edwin Nunez	.05
687	Rafael Palmeiro	.40
688	Roger Pavlik	.05
689	Geno Petralli	.05
690	Nolan Ryan	1.00
691	David Cone	.05
692	Alfredo Griffin	.05
693	Juan Guzman	.05
694	Pat Hentgen	.05
695	Randy Knorr	.05
696	Bob MacDonald	.05
697	Jack Morris	.05
698	Ed Sprague	.05
699	Dave Stieb	.05
700	Pat Tabler	.05
701	Mike Timlin	.05
702	David Wells	.05
703	Eddie Zosky	.05
704	Gary Sheffield (League Leaders)	.05
705	Darren Daulton (League Leaders)	.05
706	Marquis Grissom (League Leaders)	.05
707	Greg Maddux (League Leaders)	.10
708	Bill Swift (League Leaders)	.05
709	Juan Gonzalez (Round Trippers)	.15
710	Mark McGwire (Round Trippers)	.50
711	Cecil Fielder (Round Trippers)	.05
712	Albert Belle (Round Trippers)	.05
713	Joe Carter (Round Trippers)	.05
714	Power Brokers (Frank Thomas, Cecil Fielder)	.10
715	Unsung Heroes (Larry Walker, Darren Daulton)	.05
716	Hot Corner Hammers (Edgar Martinez, Robin Ventura)	.05
717	Start to Finish (Roger Clemens, Dennis Eckersley)	.25
718	Checklist	.05
719	Checklist	.05
720	Checklist	.05

All-Stars

Horizontal-format All-Star cards comprised one of the many 1993 Fleer insert issues. Twelve cards of National League All-Stars were included in Series I wax packs, while a dozen American League All-Stars were found in Series II packs. They are among the more popular and valuable of the '93 Fleer inserts.

	NM/M
Complete Set A.L. (12):	6.00
Complete Set N.L. (12):	3.75
Common Player:	.15

AMERICAN LEAGUE

No.	Player	Price
1	Frank Thomas	.85
2	Roberto Alomar	.40
3	Edgar Martinez	.15
4	Pat Listach	.15
5	Cecil Fielder	.15
6	Juan Gonzalez	.40
7	Ken Griffey Jr.	2.00
8	Joe Carter	.15
9	Kirby Puckett	1.00
10	Brian Harper	.15
11	Dave Fleming	.15
12	Jack McDowell	.15

NATIONAL LEAGUE

No.	Player	Price
1	Fred McGriff	.15
2	Delino DeShields	.15
3	Gary Sheffield	.40
4	Barry Larkin	.15
5	Felix Jose	.15
6	Larry Walker	.15
7	Barry Bonds	2.50
8	Andy Van Slyke	.15
9	Darren Daulton	.15
10	Greg Maddux	.75
11	Tom Glavine	.25
12	Lee Smith	.15

Tom Glavine Career Highlights

This 15-card insert set spotlighted career highlights of Fleer's 1993 spokesman, Tom Glavine. Twelve cards were available in Series 1 and Series 2 packs; cards #13-15 could be obtained only via a special mail offer. A limited number of certified autograph cards were also inserted into packs. Cards #1-4 and 7-10 can each be found with two variations of the writeups on the back. The versions found in Series 2 packaging are the "correct" backs. Neither version carries a premium value.

	NM/M
Complete Set (15):	5.00
Common Card:	.50
Autographed Card:	30.00
1-15 Tom Glavine	.50

Golden Moments

Three cards of this insert set were available in both series of wax packs. Fronts feature black borders with gold-foil baseballs in the corners. The player's name appears in a "Golden Moments" banner at the bottom of the photo. Backs have a portrait photo of the player at top-center and a information on the highlight. The cards are unnumbered and are checklisted here alphabetically within series.

	NM/M
Complete Set (6):	4.00
Common Player:	.25
SERIES 1	2.00
(1) George Brett	1.50
(2) Mickey Morandini	.25
(3) Dave Winfield	.50
SERIES 2	2.00
(1) Dennis Eckersley	.40
(2) Bip Roberts	.25
(3) Frank Thomas, Juan Gonzalez	1.50

Major League Prospects

Rookie Sensations

Yet another way to package currently hot rookies and future prospects to increase sales of the base product, there were 18 insert cards found in each series' wax packs. Fronts are bordered in black and have gold-foil highlights. Most of the depicted players were a few seasons away from everyday play in the major leagues.

	NM/M
Complete Set (36):	7.50
Common Player:	.15
SERIES 1	5.00
1 Melvin Nieves	.15
2 Sterling Hitchcock	.15
3 Tim Costo	.15
4 Manny Alexander	.15
5 Alan Embree	.15
6 Kevin Young	.15
7 J.T. Snow	.15
8 Russ Springer	.15
9 Billy Ashley	.15
10 Kevin Rogers	.15
11 Steve Hosey	.15
12 Eric Wedge	.15
13 Mike Piazza	3.50
14 Jesse Levis	.15
15 Rico Brogna	.15
16 Alex Arias	.15
17 Rod Brewer	.15
18 Troy Neel	.15
SERIES 2	2.50
1 Scooter Tucker	.15
2 Kerry Woodson	.15
3 Greg Colbrunn	.15
4 Pedro Martinez	1.50
5 Dave Silvestri	.15
6 Kent Bottenfield	.15
7 Rafael Bournigal	.15
8 J.T. Bruett	.15
9 Dave Mlicki	.15
10 Paul Wagner	.15
11 Mike Williams	.15
12 Henry Mercedes	.15
13 Scott Taylor	.15
14 Dennis Moeller	.15
15 Javier Lopez	.15
16 Steve Cooke	.15
17 Pete Young	.15
18 Ken Ryan	.15

ProVisions

This three-card insert set in Series I wax packs features the baseball art of Wayne Still. Black-bordered fronts feature a player-fantasy painting at center, with the player's name gold-foil stamped beneath. Backs are also bordered in black and have a white box with a career summary.

	NM/M
Complete Set (6):	3.00
Common Player:	.40
SERIES 1	2.00
1 Roberto Alomar	.65
2 Dennis Eckersley	1.00
3 Gary Sheffield	.75
SERIES 2	1.00
1 Andy Van Slyke	.40
2 Tom Glavine	.75
3 Cecil Fielder	.40

Ten rookie sensations - some of whom had not been true rookies for several seasons - were featured in this insert issue packaged exclusively in Series 1 and Series 2 cello packs. Card fronts have a player photo set against a silver background and surrounded by a blue border. The player's name and other front printing are in gold foil. Backs are also printed in silver with a blue border. There is a player portrait photo and career summary.

	NM/M
Complete Set (20):	6.25
Common Player:	.25
SERIES 1	3.00
1 Kenny Lofton	.50
2 Cal Eldred	.25
3 Pat Listach	.25
4 Roberto Hernandez	.25
5 Dave Fleming	.25
6 Eric Karros	.25
7 Reggie Sanders	.25
8 Derrick May	.25
9 Mike Perez	.25
10 Donovan Osborne	.25
SERIES 2	2.00
1 Moises Alou	.50
2 Pedro Astacio	.25
3 Jim Austin	.25
4 Chad Curtis	.25
5 Gary DiSarcina	.25
6 Scott Livingstone	.25
7 Sam Militello	.25
8 Arthur Rhodes	.25
9 Tim Wakefield	.35
10 Bob Zupcic	.25

Team Leaders

This 20-card insert issue was exclusive to Series 1 and 2 rack packs. Fronts have a portrait photo, with a small action photo superimposed. At the side is a colored bar with the player's name and "Team Leaders" printed vertically. On back is a career summary. Card borders are a light metallic green and both sides of the card are UV coated.

	NM/M
Complete Set (20):	12.50
Common Player:	.40
SERIES 1	10.00
1 Kirby Puckett	1.25
2 Mark McGwire	3.00
3 Pat Listach	.40
4 Roger Clemens	1.50
5 Frank Thomas	1.00
6 Carlos Baerga	.40
7 Brady Anderson	.40
8 Juan Gonzalez	.50
9 Roberto Alomar	.60
10 Ken Griffey Jr.	2.00
SERIES 2	4.00
1 Will Clark	.40
2 Terry Pendleton	.40
3 Ray Lankford	.40
4 Eric Karros	.40
5 Gary Sheffield	.75
6 Ryne Sandberg	1.25
7 Marquis Grissom	.40
8 John Kruk	.40
9 Jeff Bagwell	1.00
10 Andy Van Slyke	.40

Final Edition

This 310-card set was sold as a complete set in its own box. Card numbers have the prefix "F." The set also includes 10 Diamond Tribute cards, which are numbered DT1-DT10.

	NM/M
Complete Set (310):	7.50
Common Player:	.05
1 Steve Bedrosian	.05
2 Jay Howell	.05
3 Greg Maddux	.05
4 Greg McMichael RC	.05
5 Tony Tarasco RC	.05
6 Jose Bautista	.05

7	Jose Guzman	.05
8	Greg Hibbard	.05
9	Candy Maldonado	.05
10	Randy Myers	.05
11	Matt Walbeck RC	.05
12	Turk Wendell	.05
13	Willie Nelson	.05
14	Greg Cadaret	.05
15	Roberto Kelly	.05
16	Randy Milligan	.05
17	Kevin Mitchell	.05
18	Jeff Reardon	.05
19	John Roper	.05
20	John Smiley	.05
21	Andy Ashby	.05
22	Dante Bichette	.05
23	Willie Blair	.05
24	Pedro Castellano	.05
25	Vinny Castilla	.05
26	Jerald Clark	.05
27	Alex Cole	.05
28	Scott Fredrickson RC	.05
29	Jay Gainer RC	.05
30	Andres Galarraga	.05
31	Joe Girardi	.05
32	Ryan Hawblitzel	.05
33	Charlie Hayes	.05
34	Darren Holmes	.05
35	Chris Jones	.05
36	David Nied	.05
37	J. Owens RC	.05
38	Lance Painter RC	.05
39	Jeff Parrett	.05
40	Steve Reed RC	.05
41	Armando Reynoso	.05
42	Bruce Ruffin	.05
43	Danny Sheaffer RC	.05
44	Keith Shepherd	.05
45	Jim Tatum	.05
46	Gary Wayne	.05
47	Eric Young	.05
48	Luis Aquino	.05
49	Alex Arias	.05
50	Jack Armstrong	.05
51	Bret Barberie	.05
52	Geronimo Berroa	.05
53	Ryan Bowen	.05
54	Greg Briley	.05
55	Chris Carpenter	.05
56	Chuck Carr	.05
57	Jeff Conine	.05
58	Jim Corsi	.05
59	Orestes Destrade	.05
60	Junior Felix	.05
61	Chris Hammond	.05
62	Bryan Harvey	.05
63	Charlie Hough	.05
64	Joe Klink	.05
65	Richie Lewis RC	.05
66	Mitch Lyden RC	.05
67	Bob Natal	.05
68	Scott Pose RC	.05
69	Rich Renteria	.05
70	Benito Santiago	.05
71	Gary Sheffield	.15
72	Matt Turner RC	.05
73	Walt Weiss	.05
74	Darrell Whitmore RC	.05
75	Nigel Wilson	.05
76	Kevin Bass	.05
77	Doug Drabek	.05
78	Tom Edens	.05
79	Chris James	.05
80	Greg Swindell	.05
81	Omar Daal RC	.05
82	Raul Mondesi	.05
83	Jody Reed	.05
84	Cory Snyder	.05
85	Rick Trlicek	.05
86	Tim Wallach	.05
87	Todd Worrell	.05
88	Tavo Alvarez	.05
89	Frank Bolick	.05
90	Kent Bottenfield	.05
91	Greg Colbrunn	.05
92	Cliff Floyd	.05
93	Lou Frazier RC	.05
94	Mike Gardiner	.05
95	Mike Lansing RC	.25
96	Bill Risley	.05
97	Jeff Shaw	.05
98	Kevin Baez	.05
99	Tim Bogar RC	.05
100	Jeromy Burnitz	.05
101	Mike Draper	.05
102	Darrin Jackson	.05
103	Mike Maddux	.05
104	Joe Orsulak	.05

105	Doug Saunders	.05
106	Frank Tanana	.05
107	Dave Telgheder	.05
108	Larry Anderson	.05
109	Jim Eisenreich	.05
110	Pete Incaviglia	.05
111	Danny Jackson	.05
112	David West	.05
113	Al Martin	.05
114	Blas Minor	.05
115	Dennis Moeller	.05
116	Will Pennyfeather	.05
117	Rich Robertson	.05
118	Ben Shelton	.05
119	Lonnie Smith	.05
120	Freddie Toliver	.05
121	Paul Wagner	.05
122	Kevin Young	.05
123	Rene Arocha RC	.05
124	Gregg Jefferies	.05
125	Paul Kilgus	.05
126	Les Lancaster	.05
127	Joe Magrane	.05
128	Rob Murphy	.05
129	Erik Pappas	.05
130	Stan Royer	.05
131	Ozzie Smith	.65
132	Tom Urbani	.05
133	Mark Whiten	.05
134	Derek Bell	.05
135	Doug Brocail	.05
136	Phil Clark	.05
137	Mark Ettles RC	.05
138	Jeff Gardner	.05
139	Pat Gomez RC	.05
140	Ricky Gutierrez	.05
141	Gene Harris	.05
142	Kevin Higgins RC	.05
143	Trevor Hoffman	.05
144	Phil Plantier	.05
145	Kerry Taylor RC	.05
146	Guillermo Velasquez	.05
147	Wally Whitehurst	.05
148	Tim Worrell RC	.05
149	Todd Benzinger	.05
150	Barry Bonds	2.00
151	Greg Brummett	.05
152	Mark Carreon	.05
153	Dave Martinez	.05
154	Jeff Reed	.05
155	Kevin Rogers	.05
156	Harold Baines	.05
157	Damon Buford	.05
158	Paul Carey RC	.05
159	Jeffrey Hammonds	.05
160	Jamie Moyer	.05
161	Sherman Obando RC	.05
162	John O'Donoghue RC	.05
163	Brad Pennington	.05
164	Jim Poole	.05
165	Harold Reynolds	.05
166	Fernando Valenzuela	.05
167	Jack Voight RC	.05
168	Mark Williamson	.05
169	Scott Bankhead	.05
170	Greg Blosser	.05
171	Jim Byrd	.05
172	Ivan Calderon	.05
173	Andre Dawson	.25
174	Scott Fletcher	.05
175	Jose Melendez	.05
176	Carlos Quintana	.05
177	Jeff Russell	.05
178	Aaron Sele	.05
179	Rod Correia RC	.05
180	Chili Davis	.05
181	Jim Edmonds RC	3.00
182	Rene Gonzales	.05
183	Hilly Hathaway RC	.05
184	Torey Lovullo	.05
185	Greg Myers	.05
186	Gene Nelson	.05
187	Troy Percival	.05
188	Scott Sanderson	.05
189	Darryl Scott RC	.05
190	J.T. Snow RC	.50
191	Russ Springer	.05
192	Jason Bere	.05
193	Rodney Bolton	.05
194	Ellis Burks	.05
195	Bo Jackson	.15
196	Mike LaValliere	.05
197	Scott Ruffcorn	.05
198	Jeff Schwartz RC	.05
199	Jerry DiPoto	.05
200	Alvaro Espinoza	.05
201	Wayne Kirby	.05
202	Tom Kramer RC	.05
203	Jesse Levis	.05
204	Manny Ramirez	.50
205	Jeff Treadway	.05
206	Bill Wertz RC	.05
207	Cliff Young	.05
208	Matt Young	.05
209	Kirk Gibson	.05
210	Greg Gohr	.05
211	Bill Krueger	.05
212	Bob MacDonald	.05
213	Mike Moore	.05
214	David Wells	.05
215	Billy Brewer RC	.05
216	David Cone	.05
217	Greg Gagne	.05
218	Mark Gardner	.05
219	Chris Haney	.05
220	Phil Hiatt	.05
221	Jose Lind	.05
222	Juan Bell	.05

223	Tom Brunansky	.05
224	Mike Ignasiak	.05
225	Joe Kmak	.05
226	Tom Lampkin	.05
227	Graeme Lloyd RC	.05
228	Carlos Maldonado	.05
229	Matt Mieske	.05
230	Angel Miranda	.05
231	Troy O'Leary RC	.10
232	Kevin Reimer	.05
233	Larry Casian	.05
234	Jim Deshaies	.05
235	Eddie Guardado RC	.10
236	Chip Hale	.05
237	Mike Maksudian RC	.05
238	David McCarty	.05
239	Pat Meares RC	.05
240	George Tsamis RC	.05
241	Dave Winfield	.50
242	Jim Abbott	.05
243	Wade Boggs	.65
244	Andy Cook RC	.05
245	Russ Davis RC	.10
246	Mike Humphreys	.05
247	Jimmy Key	.05
248	Jim Leyritz	.05
249	Bobby Munoz	.05
250	Paul O'Neil	.05
251	Spike Owen	.05
252	Dave Silvestri	.05
253	Marcos Armas RC	.05
254	Brent Gates	.05
255	Goose Gossage	.25
256	Scott Lydy RC	.05
257	Henry Mercedes	.05
258	Mike Mohler RC	.05
259	Troy Neel	.05
260	Edwin Nunez	.05
261	Craig Paquette	.05
262	Kevin Seitzer	.05
263	Rich Amaral	.05
264	Mike Blowers	.05
265	Chris Bosio	.05
266	Norm Charlton	.05
267	Jim Converse RC	.05
268	John Cummings RC	.05
269	Mike Felder	.05
270	Mike Hampton	.05
271	Bill Haselman	.05
272	Dwayne Henry	.05
273	Greg Litton	.05
274	Mackey Sasser	.05
275	Lee Tinsley	.05
276	David Wainhouse	.05
277	Jeff Bronkey RC	.05
278	Benji Gil	.05
279	Tom Henke	.05
280	Charlie Leibrandt	.05
281	Robb Nen	.05
282	Bill Ripken	.05
283	Jon Shave RC	.05
284	Doug Strange	.05
285	Matt Whiteside RC	.05
286	Scott Brow RC	.05
287	Willie Canate RC	.05
288	Tony Castillo	.05
289	Domingo Cedeno RC	.05
290	Darnell Coles	.05
291	Danny Cox	.05
292	Mark Eichhorn	.05
293	Tony Fernandez	.05
294	Al Leiter	.05
295	Paul Molitor	.50
296	Dave Stewart	.05
297	Woody Williams RC	.05
298	Checklist	.05
299	Checklist	.05
300	Checklist	.05
1DT	Wade Boggs	.65
2DT	George Brett	.75
3DT	Andre Dawson	.25
4DT	Carlton Fisk	.50
5DT	Paul Molitor	.50
6DT	Nolan Ryan	2.00
7DT	Lee Smith	.05
8DT	Ozzie Smith	.65
9DT	Dave Winfield	.50
10DT	Robin Yount	.50

Atlantic

The Atlantic Collectors Edition set of 1993 features 24 of the top players in the game (plus one checklist) portrayed in a style matching the regular-issue Fleer set, with the addition of the Atlantic logo and a gold border. The cards were given away five at a time with gasoline purchases at gas stations in New York and Pennsylvania during the summer.

		NM/M
Complete Set (25):		3.50
Common Player:		.12
1	Roberto Alomar	.20
2	Barry Bonds	1.00
3	Bobby Bonilla	.10
4	Will Clark	.10
5	Roger Clemens	.60
6	Darren Daulton	.10
7	Dennis Eckersley	.30
8	Cecil Fielder	.10
9	Tom Glavine	.25
10	Juan Gonzalez	.25
11	Ken Griffey Jr.	.75
12	John Kruk	.10
13	Greg Maddux	.50
14	Don Mattingly	.60
15	Fred McGriff	.10
16	Mark McGwire	.85
17	Terry Pendleton	.10
18	Kirby Puckett	.25
19	Cal Ripken Jr.	1.00
20	Nolan Ryan	1.00
21	Ryne Sandberg	.50
22	Gary Sheffield	.25
23	Frank Thomas	.40
24	Andy Van Slyke	.10
25	Checklist	.05

Fruit of the Loom

Fruit of the Loom and Fleer combined to create a 66-card baseball set in 1993 that featured many of the top players in the game. The cards, with the same design as the regular-issue Fleer cards, also display the Fruit of the Loom logo in the upper-left corner. Three cards were inserted in specially marked packages of the company's products.

		NM/M
Complete Set (66):		30.00
Common Player:		.25
1	Roberto Alomar	.45
2	Brady Anderson	.25
3	Jeff Bagwell	1.00
4	Albert Belle	.25
5	Craig Biggio	.25
6	Barry Bonds	3.00
7	George Brett	1.75
8	Brett Butler	.25
9	Jose Canseco	.65
10	Joe Carter	.25
11	Will Clark	.25
12	Roger Clemens	1.75
13	Darren Daulton	.25
14	Andre Dawson	.40
15	Delino DeShields	.25
16	Rob Dibble	.25
17	Doug Drabek	.25
18	Dennis Eckersley	.85
19	Cecil Fielder	.25
20	Travis Fryman	.25
21	Tom Glavine	.45
22	Juan Gonzalez	.50
23	Dwight Gooden	.25
24	Mark Grace	.25
25	Ken Griffey Jr.	2.00
26	Marquis Grissom	.25
27	Juan Guzman	.25
28	Tony Gwynn	1.50
29	Rickey Henderson	1.00
30	David Justice	.25
31	Eric Karros	.25
32	Chuck Knoblauch	.25
33	John Kruk	.25
34	Ray Lankford	.25
35	Barry Larkin	.25
36	Pat Listach	.25
37	Kenny Lofton	.25
38	Shane Mack	.25
39	Greg Maddux	1.50
40	Dennis Martinez	.25
41	Edgar Martinez	.25
42	Ramon Martinez	.25
43	Don Mattingly	1.75
44	Jack McDowell	.25
45	Fred McGriff	.25
46	Mark McGwire	2.50
47	Jeff Montgomery	.25
48	Eddie Murray	1.00
49	Charles Nagy	.25
50	Tom Pagnozzi	.25
51	Terry Pendleton	.25
52	Kirby Puckett	1.50
53	Jose Rijo	.25
54	Cal Ripken, Jr.	3.00
55	Nolan Ryan	3.00
56	Ryne Sandberg	1.50
57	Gary Sheffield	.65
58	Bill Swift	.25
59	Danny Tartabull	.25
60	Mickey Tettleton	.25
61	Frank Thomas	1.00
62	Andy Van Slyke	.25
63	Robin Ventura	.25
64	Larry Walker	.25
65	Robin Yount	1.00
66	Checklist	.05

1994 Fleer "Highlights" Promo Sheet

To introduce its special insert card series honoring 1993 A.L. Rookie of the Year Tim Salmon and Phillies stars John Kruk and Darren Daulton, Fleer issued this 5" x 7" promo sheet. The three player cards on the sheet are similar to the issued versions except they have black overprinting on front and back which reads, "PROMOTIONAL SAMPLE." The non-player segment of the sheet has details about the inserts and special mail-in offers for additional cards.

	NM/M
Sheet:	6.00

1994 Fleer

Fleer's 720-card 1994 set, released in one series, includes another 204 insert cards to be pursued by collectors. Every pack includes one of the cards, randomly inserted from among the 12 insert sets. Regular cards have action photos on front, with a team logo in one of the lower corners. The player's name and position is stamped in gold foil around the card. On back, another color player photo is overprinted with color boxes, data and stats, leaving a clear image of the player's face, 1-1/2" x 1-3/4" in size. Cards are UV coated on both sides.

		NM/M
Complete Set (720):		12.50
Common Player:		.05
Pack (15):		.50
Wax Box (36):		12.50
1	Brady Anderson	.05
2	Harold Baines	.05
3	Mike Devereaux	.05
4	Todd Frohwirth	.05
5	Jeffrey Hammonds	.05
6	Chris Hoiles	.05
7	Tim Hulett	.05
8	Ben McDonald	.05
9	Mark McLemore	.05
10	Alan Mills	.05
11	Jamie Moyer	.05
12	Mike Mussina	.40
13	Gregg Olson	.05
14	Mike Pagliarulo	.05
15	Brad Pennington	.05
16	Jim Poole	.05
17	Harold Reynolds	.05
18	Arthur Rhodes	.05
19	Cal Ripken, Jr.	2.00
20	David Segui	.05
21	Rick Sutcliffe	.05
22	Fernando Valenzuela	.05
23	Jack Voigt	.05
24	Mark Williamson	.05
25	Scott Bankhead	.05
26	Roger Clemens	1.00
27	Scott Cooper	.05
28	Danny Darwin	.05
29	Andre Dawson	.25
30	Rob Deer	.05
31	John Dopson	.05
32	Scott Fletcher	.05
33	Mike Greenwell	.05
34	Greg Harris	.05
35	Billy Hatcher	.05
36	Bob Melvin	.05
37	Tony Pena	.05
38	Paul Quantrill	.05
39	Carlos Quintana	.05
40	Ernest Riles	.05
41	Jeff Russell	.05
42	Ken Ryan	.05
43	Aaron Sele	.05
44	John Valentin	.05
45	Mo Vaughn	.05
46	Frank Viola	.05
47	Bob Zupcic	.05
48	Mike Butcher	.05
49	Rod Correia	.05
50	Chad Curtis	.05
51	Chili Davis	.05
52	Gary DiSarcina	.05
53	Damion Easley	.05
54	Jim Edmonds	.05
55	Chuck Finley	.05
56	Steve Frey	.05
57	Rene Gonzales	.05
58	Joe Grahe	.05
59	Hilly Hathaway	.05
60	Stan Javier	.05
61	Mark Langston	.05
62	Phil Leftwich	.05
63	Torey Lovullo	.05
64	Joe Magrane	.05
65	Greg Myers	.05
66	Ken Patterson	.05
67	Eduardo Perez	.05
68	Luis Polonia	.05
69	Tim Salmon	.05
69a	Tim Salmon/OPS	2.00
70	J.T. Snow	.05
71	Ron Tingley	.05
72	Julio Valera	.05
73	Wilson Alvarez	.05
74	Tim Belcher	.05
75	George Bell	.05
76	Jason Bere	.05
77	Rod Bolton	.05
78	Ellis Burks	.05
79	Joey Cora	.05
80	Alex Fernandez	.05
81	Craig Grebeck	.05
82	Ozzie Guillen	.05
83	Roberto Hernandez	.05
84	Bo Jackson	.10
85	Lance Johnson	.05
86	Ron Karkovice	.05
87	Mike LaValliere	.05
88	Kirk McCaskill	.05
89	Jack McDowell	.05
90	Warren Newson	.05
91	Dan Pasqua	.05
92	Scott Radinsky	.05
93	Tim Raines	.05
94	Steve Sax	.05
95	Jeff Schwarz	.05
96	Frank Thomas	.75
97	Robin Ventura	.05
98	Sandy Alomar, Jr.	.05
99	Carlos Baerga	.05
100	Albert Belle	.05
101	Mark Clark	.05
102	Jerry DiPoto	.05
103	Alvaro Espinoza	.05
104	Felix Fermin	.05
105	Jeremy Hernandez	.05
106	Reggie Jefferson	.05
107	Wayne Kirby	.05
108	Tom Kramer	.05
109	Mark Lewis	.05
110	Derek Lilliquist	.05
111	Kenny Lofton	.05
112	Candy Maldonado	.05
113	Jose Mesa	.05
114	Jeff Mutis	.05
115	Charles Nagy	.05
116	Bob Ojeda	.05
117	Junior Ortiz	.05
118	Eric Plunk	.05
119	Manny Ramirez	.75
120	Paul Sorrento	.05
121	Jim Thome	.60
122	Jeff Treadway	.05
123	Bill Wertz	.05
124	Skeeter Barnes	.05
125	Milt Cuyler	.05
126	Eric Davis	.05
127	John Doherty	.05
128	Cecil Fielder	.05
129	Travis Fryman	.05
130	Kirk Gibson	.05
131	Dan Gladden	.05
132	Greg Gohr	.05
133	Chris Gomez	.05
134	Bill Gullickson	.05
135	Mike Henneman	.05
136	Kurt Knudsen	.05
137	Chad Kreuter	.05
138	Bill Krueger	.05
139	Scott Livingstone	.05
140	Bob MacDonald	.05
141	Mike Moore	.05
142	Tony Phillips	.05
143	Mickey Tettleton	.05
144	Alan Trammell	.05
145	David Wells	.05
146	Lou Whitaker	.05
147	Kevin Appier	.05
148	Stan Belinda	.05
149	George Brett	1.00
150	Billy Brewer	.05
151	Hubie Brooks	.05
152	David Cone	.05
153	Gary Gaetti	.05
154	Greg Gagne	.05
155	Tom Gordon	.05
156	Mark Gubicza	.05
157	Chris Gwynn	.05
158	John Habyan	.05
159	Chris Haney	.05
160	Phil Hiatt	.05
161	Felix Jose	.05
162	Wally Joyner	.05
163	Jose Lind	.05
164	Mike Macfarlane	.05
165	Mike Magnante	.05
166	Brent Mayne	.05
167	Brian McRae	.05
168	Kevin McReynolds	.05
169	Keith Miller	.05
170	Jeff Montgomery	.05
171	Hipolito Pichardo	.05
172	Rico Rossy	.05
173	Juan Bell	.05
174	Ricky Bones	.05
175	Cal Eldred	.05
176	Mike Fetters	.05
177	Darryl Hamilton	.05
178	Doug Henry	.05
179	Mike Ignasiak	.05
180	John Jaha	.05
181	Pat Listach	.05
182	Graeme Lloyd	.05
183	Matt Mieske	.05
184	Angel Miranda	.05
185	Jaime Navarro	.05
186	Dave Nilsson	.05
187	Troy O'Leary	.05
188	Jesse Orosco	.05
189	Kevin Reimer	.05
190	Kevin Seitzer	.05
191	Bill Spiers	.05
192	B.J. Surhoff	.05
193	Dickie Thon	.05
194	Jose Valentin	.05
195	Greg Vaughn	.05
196	Bill Wegman	.05
197	Robin Yount	.75
198	Rick Aguilera	.05
199	Willie Banks	.05
200	Bernardo Brito	.05
201	Larry Casian	.05
202	Scott Erickson	.05
203	Eddie Guardado	.05
204	Mark Guthrie	.05
205	Chip Hale	.05
206	Brian Harper	.05
207	Mike Hartley	.05
208	Kent Hrbek	.05
209	Terry Jorgensen	.05
210	Chuck Knoblauch	.05
211	Gene Larkin	.05
212	Shane Mack	.05
213	David McCarty	.05
214	Pat Meares	.05
215	Pedro Munoz	.05
216	Derek Parks	.05
217	Kirby Puckett	.85
218	Jeff Reboulet	.05
219	Kevin Tapani	.05
220	Mike Trombley	.05
221	George Tsamis	.05
222	Carl Willis	.05
223	Dave Winfield	.75
224	Jim Abbott	.05
225	Paul Assenmacher	.05
226	Wade Boggs	.85
227	Russ Davis	.05
228	Steve Farr	.05
229	Mike Gallego	.05
230	Paul Gibson	.05
231	Steve Howe	.05
232	Dion James	.05
233	Domingo Jean	.05
234	Scott Kamieniecki	.05
235	Pat Kelly	.05
236	Jimmy Key	.05
237	Jim Leyritz	.05
238	Kevin Maas	.05
239	Don Mattingly	1.00
240	Rich Monteleone	.05
241	Bobby Munoz	.05
242	Matt Nokes	.05
243	Paul O'Neill	.05
244	Spike Owen	.05
245	Melido Perez	.05
246	Lee Smith	.05
247	Mike Stanley	.05
248	Danny Tartabull	.05
249	Randy Velarde	.05
250	Bob Wickman	.05
251	Bernie Williams	.20
252	Mike Aldrete	.05
253	Marcos Armas	.05
254	Lance Blankenship	.05
255	Mike Bordick	.05
256	Scott Brosius	.05
257	Jerry Browne	.05
258	Ron Darling	.05
259	Kelly Downs	.05
260	Dennis Eckersley	.60
261	Brent Gates	.05
262	Goose Gossage	.05
263	Scott Hemond	.05
264	Dave Henderson	.05
265	Rick Honeycutt	.05
266	Vince Horsman	.05
267	Scott Lydy	.05
268	Mark McGwire	1.50
269	Mike Mohler	.05
270	Troy Neel	.05
271	Edwin Nunez	.05
272	Craig Paquette	.05
273	Ruben Sierra	.05
274	Terry Steinbach	.05
275	Todd Van Poppel	.05
276	Bob Welch	.05
277	Bobby Witt	.05
278	Rich Amaral	.05
279	Mike Blowers	.05
280	Bret Boone	.05
281	Chris Bosio	.05
282	Jay Buhner	.05
283	Norm Charlton	.05
284	Mike Felder	.05
285	Dave Fleming	.05
286	Ken Griffey Jr.	1.25
287	Erik Hanson	.05
288	Bill Haselman	.05
289	Brad Holman RC	.05
290	Randy Johnson	.75
291	Tim Leary	.05
292	Greg Litton	.05
293	Dave Magadan	.05
294	Edgar Martinez	.05
295	Tino Martinez	.05
296	Jeff Nelson	.05
297	Erik Plantenberg RC	.05
298	Mackey Sasser	.05
299	Brian Turang RC	.05
300	Dave Valle	.05
301	Omar Vizquel	.05
302	Brian Bohanon	.05
303	Kevin Brown	.05
304	Jose Canseco	.40
305	Mario Diaz	.05
306	Julio Franco	.05
307	Juan Gonzalez	.75
308	Tom Henke	.05
309	David Hulse	.05
310	Manuel Lee	.05
311	Craig Lefferts	.05
312	Charlie Leibrandt	.05
313	Rafael Palmeiro	.75
314	Dean Palmer	.05
315	Roger Pavlik	.05
316	Dan Peltier	.05
317	Geno Petralli	.05
318	Gary Redus	.05
319	Ivan Rodriguez	.65
320	Kenny Rogers	.05
321	Nolan Ryan	2.00
322	Doug Strange	.05
323	Matt Whiteside	.05
324	Roberto Alomar	.30
325	Pat Borders	.05
326	Joe Carter	.05
327	Tony Castillo	.05
328	Darnell Coles	.05
329	Danny Cox	.05
330	Mark Eichhorn	.05
331	Tony Fernandez	.05
332	Alfredo Griffin	.05
333	Juan Guzman	.05
334	Rickey Henderson	.75
335	Pat Hentgen	.05
336	Randy Knorr	.05
337	Al Leiter	.05
338	Paul Molitor	.75
339	Jack Morris	.05
340	John Olerud	.05
341	Dick Schofield	.05
342	Ed Sprague	.05
343	Dave Stewart	.05
344	Todd Stottlemyre	.05
345	Mike Timlin	.05
346	Duane Ward	.05
347	Turner Ward	.05
348	Devon White	.05
349	Woody Williams	.05
350	Steve Avery	.05
351	Steve Bedrosian	.05
352	Rafael Belliard	.05
353	Damon Berryhill	.05
354	Jeff Blauser	.05
355	Sid Bream	.05
356	Francisco Cabrera	.05
357	Marvin Freeman	.05
358	Ron Gant	.05
359	Tom Glavine	.25
360	Jay Howell	.05
361	Dave Justice	.05
362	Ryan Klesko	.05
363	Mark Lemke	.05
364	Javier Lopez	.05
365	Greg Maddux	.85
366	Fred McGriff	.05
367	Greg McMichael	.05
368	Kent Mercker	.05
369	Otis Nixon	.05
370	Greg Olson	.05
371	Bill Pecota	.05
372	Terry Pendleton	.05
373	Deion Sanders	.05
374	Pete Smith	.05
375	John Smoltz	.05
376	Mike Stanton	.05
377	Tony Tarasco	.05
378	Mark Wohlers	.05
379	Jose Bautista	.05
380	Shawn Boskie	.05
381	Steve Buechele	.05
382	Frank Castillo	.05
383	Mark Grace	.10
384	Jose Guzman	.05
385	Mike Harkey	.05
386	Greg Hibbard	.05
387	Glenallen Hill	.05
388	Steve Lake	.05
389	Derrick May	.05
390	Chuck McElroy	.05
391	Mike Morgan	.05
392	Randy Myers	.05
393	Dan Plesac	.05
394	Kevin Roberson	.05
395	Rey Sanchez	.05
396	Ryne Sandberg	.85
397	Bob Scanlan	.05
398	Dwight Smith	.05
399	Sammy Sosa	1.25
400	Jose Vizcaino	.05
401	Rick Wilkins	.05
402	Willie Wilson	.05
403	Eric Yelding	.05
404	Bobby Ayala	.05
405	Jeff Branson	.05
406	Tom Browning	.05
407	Jacob Brumfield	.05
408	Tim Costo	.05
409	Rob Dibble	.05
410	Willie Greene	.05
411	Thomas Howard	.05
412	Roberto Kelly	.05
413	Bill Landrum	.05
414	Barry Larkin	.05
415	Larry Luebbers RC	.05
416	Kevin Mitchell	.05
417	Hal Morris	.05
418	Joe Oliver	.05
419	Tim Pugh	.05
420	Jeff Reardon	.05
421	Jose Rijo	.05
422	Bip Roberts	.05
423	John Roper	.05
424	Johnny Ruffin	.05
425	Chris Sabo	.05
426	Juan Samuel	.05
427	Reggie Sanders	.05
428	Scott Service	.05
429	John Smiley	.05
430	Jerry Spradlin RC	.05
431	Kevin Wickander	.05
432	Freddie Benavides	.05
433	Dante Bichette	.05
434	Willie Blair	.05
435	Daryl Boston	.05
436	Kent Bottenfield	.05
437	Vinny Castilla	.05
438	Jerald Clark	.05
439	Alex Cole	.05
440	Andres Galarraga	.05
441	Joe Girardi	.05
442	Greg Harris	.05
443	Charlie Hayes	.05
444	Darren Holmes	.05
445	Chris Jones	.05
446	Roberto Mejia	.05
447	David Nied	.05
448	J. Owens	.05
449	Jeff Parrett	.05
450	Steve Reed	.05
451	Armando Reynoso	.05
452	Bruce Ruffin	.05
453	Mo Sanford	.05
454	Danny Sheaffer	.05
455	Jim Tatum	.05
456	Gary Wayne	.05
457	Eric Young	.05
458	Luis Aquino	.05
459	Alex Arias	.05
460	Jack Armstrong	.05
461	Bret Barberie	.05
462	Ryan Bowen	.05
463	Chuck Carr	.05
464	Jeff Conine	.05
465	Henry Cotto	.05
466	Orestes Destrade	.05
467	Chris Hammond	.05
468	Bryan Harvey	.05
469	Charlie Hough	.05
470	Joe Klink	.05
471	Richie Lewis	.05
472	Bob Natal RC	.05
473	Pat Rapp RC	.05
474	Rich Renteria RC	.10
475	Rich Rodriguez	.05
476	Benito Santiago	.05
477	Gary Sheffield	.35
478	Matt Turner	.05
479	David Weathers	.05
480	Walt Weiss	.05
481	Darrell Whitmore	.05
482	Eric Anthony	.05
483	Jeff Bagwell	.75

484	Kevin Bass	.05
485	Craig Biggio	.05
486	Ken Caminiti	.05
487	Andujar Cedeno	.05
488	Chris Donnels	.05
489	Doug Drabek	.05
490	Steve Finley	.05
491	Luis Gonzalez	.25
492	Pete Harnisch	.05
493	Xavier Hernandez	.05
494	Doug Jones	.05
495	Todd Jones	.05
496	Darryl Kile	.05
497	Al Osuna	.05
498	Mark Portugal	.05
499	Scott Servais	.05
500	Greg Swindell	.05
501	Eddie Taubensee	.05
502	Jose Uribe	.05
503	Brian Williams	.05
504	Billy Ashley	.05
505	Pedro Astacio	.05
506	Brett Butler	.05
507	Tom Candiotti	.05
508	Omar Daal	.05
509	Jim Gott	.05
510	Kevin Gross	.05
511	Dave Hansen	.05
512	Carlos Hernandez	.05
513	Orel Hershiser	.05
514	Eric Karros	.05
515	Pedro Martinez	.75
516	Ramon Martinez	.05
517	Roger McDowell	.05
518	Raul Mondesi	.05
519	Jose Offerman	.05
520	Mike Piazza	1.25
521	Jody Reed	.05
522	Henry Rodriguez	.05
523	Mike Sharperson	.05
524	Cory Snyder	.05
525	Darryl Strawberry	.05
526	Rick Trlicek	.05
527	Tim Wallach	.05
528	Mitch Webster	.05
529	Steve Wilson	.05
530	Todd Worrell	.05
531	Moises Alou	.05
532	Brian Barnes	.05
533	Sean Berry	.05
534	Greg Colbrunn	.05
535	Delino DeShields	.05
536	Jeff Fassero	.05
537	Darrin Fletcher	.05
538	Cliff Floyd	.05
539	Lou Frazier	.05
540	Marquis Grissom	.05
541	Butch Henry	.05
542	Ken Hill	.05
543	Mike Lansing	.05
544	Brian Looney RC	.05
545	Dennis Martinez	.05
546	Chris Nabholz	.05
547	Randy Ready	.05
548	Mel Rojas	.05
549	Kirk Rueter	.05
550	Tim Scott	.05
551	Jeff Shaw	.05
552	Tim Spehr	.05
553	John VanderWal	.05
554	Larry Walker	.05
555	John Wetteland	.05
556	Rondell White	.05
557	Tim Bogar	.05
558	Bobby Bonilla	.05
559	Jeromy Burnitz	.05
560	Sid Fernandez	.05
561	John Franco	.05
562	Dave Gallagher	.05
563	Dwight Gooden	.05
564	Eric Hillman	.05
565	Todd Hundley	.05
566	Jeff Innis	.05
567	Darrin Jackson	.05
568	Howard Johnson	.05
569	Bobby Jones	.05
570	Jeff Kent	.05
571	Mike Maddux	.05
572	Jeff McKnight	.05
573	Eddie Murray	.75
574	Charlie O'Brien	.05
575	Joe Orsulak	.05
576	Bret Saberhagen	.05
577	Pete Schourek	.05
578	Dave Telgheder	.05
579	Ryan Thompson	.05
580	Anthony Young	.05
581	Ruben Amaro	.05
582	Larry Andersen	.05
583	Kim Batiste	.05
584	Wes Chamberlain	.05
585	Darren Daulton	.05
586	Mariano Duncan	.05
587	Len Dykstra	.05
588	Jim Eisenreich	.05
589	Tommy Greene	.05
590	Dave Hollins	.05
591	Pete Incaviglia	.05
592	Danny Jackson	.05
593	Ricky Jordan	.05
594	John Kruk	.05
595	Roger Mason	.05
596	Mickey Morandini	.05
597	Terry Mulholland	.05
598	Todd Pratt	.05
599	Ben Rivera	.05
600	Curt Schilling	.25
601	Kevin Stocker	.05

602	Milt Thompson	.05
603	David West	.05
604	Mitch Williams	.05
605	Jay Bell	.05
606	Dave Clark	.05
607	Steve Cooke	.05
608	Tom Foley	.05
609	Carlos Garcia	.05
610	Joel Johnston	.05
611	Jeff King	.05
612	Al Martin	.05
613	Lloyd McClendon	.05
614	Orlando Merced	.05
615	Blas Minor	.05
616	Denny Neagle	.05
617	Mark Petkovsek RC	.05
618	Tom Prince	.05
619	Don Slaught	.05
620	Zane Smith	.05
621	Randy Tomlin	.05
622	Andy Van Slyke	.05
623	Paul Wagner	.05
624	Tim Wakefield	.05
625	Bob Walk	.05
626	Kevin Young	.05
627	Luis Alicea	.05
628	Rene Arocha	.05
629	Rod Brewer	.05
630	Rheal Cormier	.05
631	Bernard Gilkey	.05
632	Lee Guetterman	.05
633	Gregg Jefferies	.05
634	Brian Jordan	.05
635	Les Lancaster	.05
636	Ray Lankford	.05
637	Rob Murphy	.05
638	Omar Olivares	.05
639	Jose Oquendo	.05
640	Donovan Osborne	.05
641	Tom Pagnozzi	.05
642	Erik Pappas	.05
643	Geronimo Pena	.05
644	Mike Perez	.05
645	Gerald Perry	.05
646	Ozzie Smith	.85
647	Bob Tewksbury	.05
648	Allen Watson	.05
649	Mark Whiten	.05
650	Tracy Woodson	.05
651	Todd Zeile	.05
652	Andy Ashby	.05
653	Brad Ausmus	.05
654	Billy Bean	.05
655	Derek Bell	.05
656	Andy Benes	.05
657	Doug Brocail	.05
658	Jarvis Brown	.05
659	Archi Cianfrocco	.05
660	Phil Clark	.05
661	Mark Davis	.05
662	Jeff Gardner	.05
663	Pat Gomez	.05
664	Ricky Gutierrez	.05
665	Tony Gwynn	.85
666	Gene Harris	.05
667	Kevin Higgins	.05
668	Trevor Hoffman	.05
669	Pedro A. Martinez RC	.05
670	Tim Mauser	.05
671	Melvin Nieves	.05
672	Phil Plantier	.05
673	Frank Seminara	.05
674	Craig Shipley	.05
675	Kerry Taylor	.05
676	Tim Teufel	.05
677	Guillermo Velasquez	.05
678	Wally Whitehurst	.05
679	Tim Worrell	.05
680	Rod Beck	.05
681	Mike Benjamin	.05
682	Todd Benzinger	.05
683	Bud Black	.05
684	Barry Bonds	2.00
685	Jeff Brantley	.05
686	Dave Burba	.05
687	John Burkett	.05
688	Mark Carreon	.05
689	Will Clark	.10
690	Royce Clayton	.05
691	Bryan Hickerson	.05
692	Mike Jackson	.05
693	Darren Lewis	.05
694	Kirt Manwaring	.05
695	Dave Martinez	.05
696	Willie McGee	.05
697	John Patterson	.05
698	Jeff Reed	.05
699	Kevin Rogers	.05
700	Scott Sanderson	.05
701	Steve Scarsone	.05
702	Billy Swift	.05
703	Robby Thompson	.05
704	Matt Williams	.05
705	Trevor Wilson	.05
706	"Brave New World" (Fred McGriff, Ron Gant, Dave Justice)	.10
707	"1-2 Punch" (Paul Molitor, John Olerud)	.10
708	"American Heat" (Mike Mussina, Jack McDowell)	.10
709	"Together Again" (Lou Whitaker, Alan Trammell)	.10
710	"Lone Star Lumber" (Rafael Palmeiro, Juan Gonzalez)	.20

711	"Batmen" (Brett Butler, Tony Gwynn)	.05
712	"Twin Peaks" (Kirby Puckett, Chuck Knoblauch)	.20
713	"Back to Back" (Mike Piazza, Eric Karros)	.25
714	Checklist	.05
715	Checklist	.05
716	Checklist	.05
717	Checklist	.05
718	Checklist	.05
719	Checklist	.05
720	Checklist	.05

All-Stars

Each league's 25 representatives for the 1993 All-Star Game are featured in this insert set. Fronts have a player action photo with a rippling American flag in the top half of the background. The '93 All-Star logo is featured at the bottom, along with a gold-foil impression of the player's name. The flag motif is repeated at top of the card back, along with a player portrait photo set against a red (American League) or blue (National League) background. Odds of finding one of the 50 All-Star inserts are one in every two 15-card foil packs.

		NM/M
	Complete Set (50):	10.00
	Common Player:	.10
1	Roberto Alomar	.20
2	Carlos Baerga	.10
3	Albert Belle	.10
4	Wade Boggs	.75
5	Joe Carter	.10
6	Scott Cooper	.10
7	Cecil Fielder	.10
8	Travis Fryman	.10
9	Juan Gonzalez	.60
10	Ken Griffey Jr.	1.50
11	Pat Hentgen	.10
12	Randy Johnson	.60
13	Jimmy Key	.10
14	Mark Langston	.10
15	Jack McDowell	.10
16	Paul Molitor	.60
17	Jeff Montgomery	.10
18	Mike Mussina	.10
19	John Olerud	.10
20	Kirby Puckett	.75
21	Cal Ripken, Jr.	2.00
22	Ivan Rodriguez	.50
23	Frank Thomas	.65
24	Greg Vaughn	.10
25	Duane Ward	.10
26	Steve Avery	.10
27	Rod Beck	.10
28	Jay Bell	.10
29	Andy Benes	.10
30	Jeff Blauser	.10
31	Barry Bonds	2.00
32	Bobby Bonilla	.10
33	John Burkett	.10
34	Darren Daulton	.10
35	Andres Galarraga	.10
36	Tom Glavine	.30
37	Mark Grace	.25
38	Marquis Grissom	.10
39	Tony Gwynn	.75
40	Bryan Harvey	.10
41	Dave Hollins	.10
42	Dave Justice	.10
43	Darryl Kile	.10
44	John Kruk	.10
45	Barry Larkin	.10
46	Terry Mulholland	.10
47	Mike Piazza	1.50
48	Ryne Sandberg	.75
49	Gary Sheffield	.30
50	John Smoltz	.10

Award Winners

The 1993 MVP, Cy Young and Rookie of the Year award winners from each league are featured in this insert set. Cards are UV coated on both sides. Three different croppings of the same player action photo are featured on the front, with the player's name and other print-

ing in gold foil. Backs have a player portrait and short summary of his previous season's performance. According to the company, odds of finding one of these horizontal-format inserts were one in 37 packs.

		NM/M
	Complete Set (6):	4.50
	Common Player:	.25
1	Frank Thomas	.75
2	Barry Bonds	2.00
3	Jack McDowell	.25
4	Greg Maddux	1.00
5	Tim Salmon	.50
6	Mike Piazza	1.50

Golden Moments

Ten highlights from the 1993 Major League baseball season are commemorated in this insert set. Each of the cards has a title which summarizes the historical moment. These inserts were available exclusively in Fleer cards packaged for large retail outlets.

		NM/M
	Complete Set (10):	5.00
	Common Player:	.10
1	"Four in One" (Mark Whiten)	.10
2	"Left and Right" (Carlos Baerga)	.10
3	"3,000 Hit Club" (Dave Winfield)	.50
4	"Eight Straight" (Ken Griffey Jr.)	1.50
5	"Triumphant Return" (Bo Jackson)	.25
6	"Farewell to Baseball" (George Brett)	1.00
7	"Farewell to Baseball" (Nolan Ryan)	2.00
8	"Thirty Times Six" (Fred McGriff)	.10
9	"Enters 5th Dimension" (Frank Thomas)	.75
10	"The No-Hit Parade" (Chris Bosio, Jim Abbott, Darryl Kile)	.10

Golden Moments Super

Super-size (3-1/2" x 5") versions of the Golden Moments insert set were included in hobby cases at the rate of one set, in a specially-printed folder, per 20-box case. Each card carries a serial number designating its position in an edition of 10,000.

	NM/M
Complete Set (10):	7.50
Common Player:	.50

1	"Four in One" (Mark Whiten)	.50
2	"Left and Right" (Carlos Baerga)	.50
3	"3,000 Hit Club" (Dave Winfield)	.75
4	"Eight Straight" (Ken Griffey Jr.)	2.00
5	"Triumphant Return" (Bo Jackson)	.75
6	"Farewell to Baseball" (George Brett)	1.50
7	"Farewell to Baseball" (Nolan Ryan)	2.50
8	"Thirty Times Six" (Fred McGriff)	.50
9	"Enters 5th Dimension" (Frank Thomas)	1.00
10	"The No-Hit Parade" (Chris Bosio, Jim Abbott, Darryl Kile)	.50

League Leaders

Twelve players who led the major leagues in various statistical categories in 1993 are featured in this insert set. Cards are UV coated and have gold-foil stamping on both sides. Within a light metallic green border, card fronts feature a color action photo superimposed over a similar photo in black-and-white. The category in which the player led his league is printed down the right border. Other printing is gold-foil. On back is a color photo and details of the league-leading performance. Stated odds of finding a League Leaders card were one per 17 packs.

		NM/M
	Complete Set (12):	3.00
	Common Player:	.10
1	John Olerud	.10
2	Albert Belle	.10
3	Rafael Palmeiro	.75
4	Kenny Lofton	.10
5	Jack McDowell	.10
6	Kevin Appier	.10
7	Andres Galarraga	.10
8	Barry Bonds	2.00
9	Len Dykstra	.10
10	Chuck Carr	.10
11	Tom Glavine	.30
12	Greg Maddux	1.00

Lumber Co.

This insert set features the major leagues' top home run hitters. Inserted only in 21-card jumbo packs, odds of finding one were given as one per five packs. Card fronts feature player action photos against a background resembling the label area of a baseball bat. On back is a background photo of a row of bats on the dirt. A player write-up and close-up photo complete the design.

		NM/M
	Complete Set (10):	7.50
	Common Player:	.40
1	Albert Belle	.40
2	Barry Bonds	2.50
3	Ron Gant	.40
4	Juan Gonzalez	1.00
5	Ken Griffey Jr.	2.00
6	Dave Justice	.40
7	Fred McGriff	.40
8	Rafael Palmeiro	.75
9	Frank Thomas	1.25
10	Matt Williams	.40

Major League Prospects

Thirty-five of the game's promising young stars are featured in this insert set. A light green metallic border frames a player photo, with his team logo lightly printed over the background. Most of the printing is gold-foil stamped. Backs have a player photo against a pinstriped background. A light blue box contains career details. Given odds of finding a "Major League Prospects" card are one in six packs.

		NM/M
	Complete Set (35):	4.00
	Common Player:	.10
1	Kurt Abbott	.10
2	Brian Anderson	.10
3	Rich Aude	.10
4	Cory Bailey	.10
5	Danny Bautista	.10
6	Marty Cordova	.10
7	Tripp Cromer	.10
8	Midre Cummings	.10
9	Carlos Delgado	1.50
10	Steve Dreyer	.10
11	Steve Dunn	.10
12	Jeff Granger	.10
13	Tyrone Hill	.10
14	Denny Hocking	.10
15	John Hope	.10
16	Butch Huskey	.10
17	Miguel Jimenez	.10
18	Chipper Jones	2.50
19	Steve Karsay	.10
20	Mike Kelly	.10
21	Mike Lieberthal	.20
22	Albie Lopez	.10
23	Jeff McNeely	.10
24	Dan Miceli	.10
25	Nate Minchey	.10
26	Marc Newfield	.10
27	Darren Oliver	.10
28	Luis Ortiz	.10
29	Curtis Pride	.10
30	Roger Salkeld	.10
31	Scott Sanders	.10
32	Dave Staton	.10
33	Salomon Torres	.10
34	Steve Trachsel	.10
35	Chris Turner	.10

ProVisions

Nine players are featured in this insert set. Cards feature the fantasy artwork of Wayne Still in a format that produces one large image when all nine cards are properly arranged. Besides the art, card fronts feature the player's name in gold-foil. Backs have a background in several shades of red, with the player's name and team at the top in white. A short career summary is printed in black. Odds of finding this particular insert in a pack are one in 12.

		NM/M
Complete Set (9):		4.00
Common Player:		.25
1	Darren Daulton	.25
2	John Olerud	.25
3	Matt Williams	.25
4	Carlos Baerga	.25
5	Ozzie Smith	1.00
6	Juan Gonzalez	.75
7	Jack McDowell	.25
8	Mike Piazza	2.00
9	Tony Gwynn	1.00

Rookie Sensations

This insert set features the top rookies from 1993. These inserts were available only in 21-card jumbo packs, with stated odds of one in four packs. Full-bleed fronts have a pair of player photos - one highlighted by a neon outline - superimposed on a graduated background approximating the team colors. Team uniform logo details appear vertically at the right or left side. The player's name is gold-foil stamped in a banner at bottom. The Rookie Sensations and Fleer logos are also gold-imprinted. On back, the team uniform logo is repeated on a white background, along with another player photo and a short write-up.

		NM/M
Complete Set (20):		6.00
Common Player:		.25
1	Rene Arocha	.25
2	Jason Bere	.25
3	Jeromy Burnitz	.25
4	Chuck Carr	.25
5	Jeff Conine	.25
6	Steve Cooke	.25
7	Cliff Floyd	.25
8	Jeffrey Hammonds	.25
9	Wayne Kirby	.25
10	Mike Lansing	.25
11	Al Martin	.25
12	Greg McMichael	.25
13	Troy Neel	.25
14	Mike Piazza	4.00
15	Armando Reynoso	.25
16	Kirk Rueter	.25
17	Tim Salmon	1.00
18	Aaron Sele	.25
19	J.T. Snow	.25
20	Kevin Stocker	.25

Tim Salmon A.L. Rookie of the Year

The popular Angels Rookie of the Year is featured in a 15-card set produced in what Fleer terms "metallized" format. The first 12 cards in the set were inserted into foil packs at the rate of about one card per box. Three additional cards could be obtained by sending $1.50 and 10 '94 Fleer wrappers to a mail-in offer. On

both front and back, the cards have a color player photo set against a metallic-image background.

		NM/M
Complete Set (15):		12.50
Common Card:		1.00
Autograph/2,000:		15.00
1-12	Tim Salmon	1.00
13-15	Tim Salmon	1.50

Smoke N' Heat

Among the scarcest of the '94 Fleer inserts, available at a stated rate of one per 30 packs, these feature 10 of the top strikeout pitchers in the major leagues. "Metallized" card fronts have a player photo set against an infernal background with large letters, "Smoke 'N Heat." The player's name is in gold foil at bottom. Backs have a similar chaotic hot-red background, a player photo and career summary.

		NM/M
Complete Set (12):		10.00
Common Player:		.20
1	Roger Clemens	4.00
2	David Cone	.25
3	Juan Guzman	.25
4	Pete Harnisch	.25
5	Randy Johnson	2.00
6	Mark Langston	.25
7	Greg Maddux	3.00
8	Mike Mussina	1.00
9	Jose Rijo	.25
10	Nolan Ryan	5.00
11	Curt Schilling	1.00
12	John Smoltz	.75

Team Leaders

A player from each major league team has been chosen for this 28-card insert set. Fronts feature a team logo against a backgound of graduated team colors. Player portrait and action photos are superimposed. At bottom is the player name, team and position, all in gold foil. Backs have a team logo and player photo set against a white background, with a short write-up justifying the player's selection as a "Team Leader". Odds of finding one of these inserts were given as one in eight packs.

		NM/M
Complete Set (28):		7.50
Common Player:		.10
1	Cal Ripken, Jr.	2.00
2	Mo Vaughn	.10
3	Tim Salmon	.15
4	Frank Thomas	.50
5	Carlos Baerga	.10
6	Cecil Fielder	.10
7	Brian McRae	.10
8	Greg Vaughn	.10
9	Kirby Puckett	.65
10	Don Mattingly	.75
11	Mark McGwire	1.50
12	Ken Griffey Jr.	1.00
13	Juan Gonzalez	.50
14	Paul Molitor	.50

15	Dave Justice	.10
16	Ryne Sandberg	.65
17	Barry Larkin	.10
18	Andres Galarraga	.10
19	Gary Sheffield	.25
20	Jeff Bagwell	.50
21	Mike Piazza	1.00
22	Marquis Grissom	.10
23	Bobby Bonilla	.10
24	Len Dykstra	.10
25	Jay Bell	.10
26	Gregg Jefferies	.10
27	Tony Gwynn	.65
28	Will Clark	.15

All-Rookie Team

Sharing the format of the basic 1994 Fleer issue, this nine-card set of rookies was available only by redemption of a trade card randomly inserted into foil packs. The exchange card expired Sept. 30, 1994. The cards are numbered with an "M" prefix.

		NM/M
Complete Set (9):		3.00
Common Player:		.25
Exchange Card:		.25
1	Kurt Abbott	.25
2	Rich Becker	.25
3	Carlos Delgado	2.00
4	Jorge Fabregas	.25
5	Bob Hamelin	.25
6	John Hudek	.25
7	Tim Hyers	.25
8	Luis Lopez	.25
9	James Mouton	.25

Update

Rookies, traded players and free agents who changed teams were included in the annual update issue. In the same format as the regular-issue '94 Fleer set, cards are numbered alphabetically within team. Ten special Diamond Tribute cards included in the Update set feature baseball's proven superstars.

		NM/M
Complete Set (210):		50.00
Common Player:		.05
1	Mark Eichhorn	.05
2	Sid Fernandez	.05
3	Leo Gomez	.05
4	Mike Oquist	.05
5	Rafael Palmeiro	.60
6	Chris Sabo	.05
7	Dwight Smith	.05
8	Lee Smith	.05
9	Damon Berryhill	.05
10	Wes Chamberlain	.05
11	Gar Finnvold	.05
12	Chris Howard	.05
13	Tim Naehring	.05
14	Otis Nixon	.05
15	Brian Anderson	.05
16	Jorge Fabregas	.05
17	Rex Hudler	.05
18	Bo Jackson	.15
19	Mark Leiter	.05
20	Spike Owen	.05
21	Harold Reynolds	.05
22	Chris Turner	.05
23	Dennis Cook	.05
24	Jose DeLeon	.05

25	Julio Franco	.05
26	Joe Hall	.05
27	Darrin Jackson	.05
28	Dane Johnson	.05
29	Norberto Martin	.05
30	Scott Sanderson	.05
31	Jason Grimsley	.05
32	Dennis Martinez	.05
33	Jack Morris	.05
34	Eddie Murray	.75
35	Chad Ogea	.05
36	Tony Pena	.05
37	Paul Shuey	.05
38	Omar Vizquel	.05
39	Danny Bautista	.05
40	Tim Belcher	.05
41	Joe Boever	.05
42	Storm Davis	.05
43	Junior Felix	.05
44	Mike Gardiner	.05
45	Buddy Groom	.05
46	Juan Samuel	.05
47	Vince Coleman	.05
48	Bob Hamelin	.05
49	Dave Henderson	.05
50	Rusty Meacham	.05
51	Terry Shumpert	.05
52	Jeff Bronkey	.05
53	Alex Diaz	.05
54	Brian Harper	.05
55	Jose Mercedes	.05
56	Jody Reed	.05
57	Bob Scanlan	.05
58	Turner Ward	.05
59	Rich Becker	.05
60	Alex Cole	.05
61	Denny Hocking	.05
62	Scott Leius	.05
63	Pat Mahomes	.05
64	Carlos Pulido	.05
65	Dave Stevens	.05
66	Matt Walbeck	.05
67	Xavier Hernandez	.05
68	Sterling Hitchcock	.05
69	Terry Mulholland	.05
70	Luis Polonia	.05
71	Gerald Williams	.05
72	Mark Acre	.05
73	Geronimo Berroa	.05
74	Rickey Henderson	.75
75	Stan Javier	.05
76	Steve Karsay	.05
77	Carlos Reyes	.05
78	Bill Taylor	.05
79	Eric Anthony	.05
80	Bobby Ayala	.05
81	Tim Davis	.05
82	Felix Fermin	.05
83	Reggie Jefferson	.05
84	Keith Mitchell	.05
85	Bill Risley	.05
86	Alex Rodriguez RC	40.00
87	Roger Salkeld	.05
88	Dan Wilson	.05
89	Cris Carpenter	.05
90	Will Clark	.10
91	Jeff Frye	.05
92	Rick Helling	.05
93	Chris James	.05
94	Oddibe McDowell	.05
95	Billy Ripken	.05
96	Carlos Delgado	.60
97	Alex Gonzalez	.50
98	Shawn Green	.50
99	Darren Hall	.05
100	Mike Huff	.05
101	Mike Kelly	.05
102	Roberto Kelly	.05
103	Charlie O'Brien	.05
104	Jose Oliva	.05
105	Gregg Olson	.05
106	Willie Banks	.05
107	Jim Bullinger	.05
108	Chuck Crim	.05
109	Shawon Dunston	.05
110	Karl Rhodes	.05
111	Steve Trachsel	.05
112	Anthony Young	.05
113	Eddie Zambrano	.05
114	Bret Boone	.05
115	Jeff Brantley	.05
116	Hector Carrasco	.05
117	Tony Fernandez	.05
118	Tim Fortugno	.05
119	Erik Hanson	.05
120	Chuck McElroy	.05
121	Deion Sanders	.05
122	Ellis Burks	.05
123	Marvin Freeman	.05
124	Mike Harkey	.05
125	Howard Johnson	.05
126	Mike Kingery	.05
127	Nelson Liriano	.05
128	Marcus Moore	.05
129	Mike Munoz	.05
130	Kevin Ritz	.05
131	Walt Weiss	.05
132	Kurt Abbott	.05
133	Jerry Browne	.05
134	Greg Colbrunn	.05
135	Jeremy Hernandez	.05
136	Dave Magadan	.05
137	Kurt Miller	.05
138	Robb Nen	.05
139	Jesus Tavarez	.05
140	Sid Bream	.05
141	Tom Edens	.05
142	Tony Eusebio	.05

143	John Hudek	.05
144	Brian Hunter	.05
145	Orlando Miller	.05
146	James Mouton	.05
147	Shane Reynolds	.05
148	Rafael Bournigal	.05
149	Delino DeShields	.05
150	Garey Ingram	.05
151	Chan Ho Park	.05
152	Wil Cordero	.05
153	Pedro Martinez	.75
154	Randy Milligan	.05
155	Lenny Webster	.05
156	Rico Brogna	.05
157	Josias Manzanillo	.05
158	Kevin McReynolds	.05
159	Mike Remlinger	.05
160	David Segui	.05
161	Pete Smith	.05
162	Kelly Stinnett	.05
163	Jose Vizcaino	.05
164	Billy Hatcher	.05
165	Doug Jones	.05
166	Mike Lieberthal	.05
167	Tony Longmire	.05
168	Bobby Munoz	.05
169	Paul Quantrill	.05
170	Heathcliff Slocumb	.05
171	Fernando Valenzuela	.05
172	Mark Dewey	.05
173	Brian Hunter	.05
174	Jon Lieber	.05
175	Ravelo Manzanillo	.05
176	Dan Miceli	.05
177	Rick White	.05
178	Bryan Eversgerd	.05
179	John Habyan	.05
180	Terry McGriff	.05
181	Vicente Palacios	.05
182	Rich Rodriguez	.05
183	Rick Sutcliffe	.05
184	Donnie Elliott	.05
185	Joey Hamilton	.05
186	Tim Hyers	.05
187	Luis Lopez	.05
188	Ray McDavid	.05
189	Bip Roberts	.05
190	Scott Sanders	.05
191	Eddie Williams	.05
192	Steve Frey	.05
193	Pat Gomez	.05
194	Rich Monteleone	.05
195	Mark Portugal	.05
196	Darryl Strawberry	.05
197	Salomon Torres	.05
198	W. Van Landingham	.05
199	Checklist	.05
200	Checklist	.05

DIAMOND TRIBUTE

DT1	Barry Bonds	2.00
DT2	Joe Carter	.05
DT3	Will Clark	.10
DT4	Roger Clemens	1.50
DT5	Tony Gwynn	1.00
DT6	Don Mattingly	1.50
DT7	Fred McGriff	.05
DT8	Eddie Murray	.75
DT9	Kirby Puckett	1.00
DT10	Cal Ripken Jr.	2.00

Atlantic

Five-card packs of this special Fleer set were given away with an eight-gallon premium gasoline purchase at Atlantic/Sunoco stations in the Eastern U.S. between June 1 and July 31. Many of the cards suffered damaged borders from the packaging process. Cards are in the basic 1994 Fleer format, though the name and position around the team logo at top are in white on these cards, rather than gold-foil. Different front and back photos are used in this set. Backs include the gas station logos at bottom.

		NM/M
Complete Set (25):		3.00
Common Player:		.10
1	Roberto Alomar	.20
2	Carlos Baerga	.10
3	Jeff Bagwell	.40
4	Jay Bell	.10
5	Barry Bonds	1.00
6	Joe Carter	.10

7	Roger Clemens	.60
8	Darren Daulton	.10
9	Lenny Dykstra	.10
10	Cecil Fielder	.10
11	Tom Glavine	.35
12	Juan Gonzalez	.40
13	Ken Griffey Jr.	.75
14	Dave Justice	.10
15	John Kruk	.10
16	Greg Maddux	.50
17	Don Mattingly	.60
18	Jack McDowell	.10
19	John Olerud	.10
20	Mike Piazza	.75
21	Kirby Puckett	.50
22	Tim Salmon	.25
23	Frank Thomas	.40
24	Andy Van Slyke	.10
25	Checklist	.05

Extra Bases

Extra Bases was a 400-card, oversized set, plus 80 insert cards in four different subsets. The cards, 4-11/16" by 2-1/2", have a full-bleed photo on the front and back, as well as UV coating and color coding by team. As was the case in other Fleer products, Extra Bases contained an insert card in every pack. All 80 insert cards feature gold or silver foil stamping.

		NM/M
Complete Set (400):		15.00
Common Player:		.10
Wax Pack:		.45
Wax Box (36):		10.00
1	Brady Anderson	.10
2	Harold Baines	.10
3	Mike Devereaux	.10
4	Sid Fernandez	.10
5	Jeffrey Hammonds	.10
6	Chris Hoiles	.10
7	Ben McDonald	.10
8	Mark McLemore	.10
9	Mike Mussina	.40
10	Mike Oquist	.10
11	Rafael Palmeiro	.75
12	Cal Ripken, Jr.	2.50
13	Chris Sabo	.10
14	Lee Smith	.10
15	Wes Chamberlain	.10
16	Roger Clemens	1.25
17	Scott Cooper	.10
18	Danny Darwin	.10
19	Andre Dawson	.25
20	Mike Greenwell	.10
21	Tim Naehring	.10
22	Otis Nixon	.10
23	Jeff Russell	.10
24	Ken Ryan	.10
25	Aaron Sele	.10
26	John Valentin	.10
27	Mo Vaughn	.10
28	Frank Viola	.10
29	Brian Anderson RC	.15
30	Chad Curtis	.10
31	Chili Davis	.10
32	Gary DiSarcina	.10
33	Damion Easley	.10
34	Jim Edmonds	.10
35	Chuck Finley	.10
36	Bo Jackson	.15
37	Mark Langston	.10
38	Harold Reynolds	.10
39	Tim Salmon	.20
40	Wilson Alvarez	.10
41	James Baldwin	.10
42	Jason Bere	.10
43	Joey Cora	.10
44	Ray Durham RC	.50
45	Alex Fernandez	.10
46	Julio Franco	.10
47	Ozzie Guillen	.10
48	Darrin Jackson	.10
49	Lance Johnson	.10
50	Ron Karkovice	.10
51	Jack McDowell	.10
52	Tim Raines	.10

#	Player	
53	Frank Thomas	.75
54	Robin Ventura	.10
55	Sandy Alomar Jr.	.10
56	Carlos Baerga	.10
57	Albert Belle	.10
58	Mark Clark	.10
59	Wayne Kirby	.10
60	Kenny Lofton	.10
61	Dennis Martinez	.10
62	Jose Mesa	.10
63	Jack Morris	.10
64	Eddie Murray	.75
65	Charles Nagy	.10
66	Manny Ramirez	.75
67	Paul Shuey	.10
68	Paul Sorrento	.10
69	Jim Thome	.50
70	Omar Vizquel	.10
71	Eric Davis	.10
72	John Doherty	.10
73	Cecil Fielder	.10
74	Travis Fryman	.10
75	Kirk Gibson	.10
76	Gene Harris	.10
77	Mike Henneman	.10
78	Mike Moore	.10
79	Tony Phillips	.10
80	Mickey Tettleton	.10
81	Alan Trammell	.10
82	Lou Whitaker	.10
83	Kevin Appier	.10
84	Vince Coleman	.10
85	David Cone	.10
86	Gary Gaetti	.10
87	Greg Gagne	.10
88	Tom Gordon	.10
89	Jeff Granger	.10
90	Bob Hamelin	.10
91	Dave Henderson	.10
92	Felix Jose	.10
93	Wally Joyner	.10
94	Jose Lind	.10
95	Mike Macfarlane	.10
96	Brian McRae	.10
97	Jeff Montgomery	.10
98	Ricky Bones	.10
99	Jeff Bronkey	.10
100	Alex Diaz	.10
101	Cal Eldred	.10
102	Darryl Hamilton	.10
103	Brian Harper	.10
104	John Jaha	.10
105	Pat Listach	.10
106	Dave Nilsson	.10
107	Jody Reed	.10
108	Kevin Seitzer	.10
109	Greg Vaughn	.10
110	Turner Ward	.10
111	Wes Weger	.10
112	Bill Wegman	.10
113	Rick Aguilera	.10
114	Rich Becker	.10
115	Alex Cole	.10
116	Scott Erickson	.10
117	Kent Hrbek	.10
118	Chuck Knoblauch	.10
119	Scott Leius	.10
120	Shane Mack	.10
121	Pat Mahomes	.10
122	Pat Meares	.10
123	Kirby Puckett	1.00
124	Kevin Tapani	.10
125	Matt Walbeck	.10
126	Dave Winfield	.75
127	Jim Abbott	.10
128	Wade Boggs	1.00
129	Mike Gallego	.10
130	Xavier Hernandez	.10
131	Pat Kelly	.10
132	Jimmy Key	.10
133	Don Mattingly	1.25
134	Terry Mulholland	.10
135	Matt Nokes	.10
136	Paul O'Neill	.10
137	Melido Perez	.10
138	Luis Polonia	.10
139	Mike Stanley	.10
140	Danny Tartabull	.10
141	Randy Velarde	.10
142	Bernie Williams	.20
143	Mark Acre	.10
144	Geronimo Berroa	.10
145	Mike Bordick	.10
146	Scott Brosius	.10
147	Ron Darling	.10
148	Dennis Eckersley	.65
149	Brent Gates	.10
150	Rickey Henderson	.75
151	Stan Javier	.10
152	Steve Karsay	.10
153	Mark McGwire	2.00
154	Troy Neel	.10
155	Ruben Sierra	.10
156	Terry Steinbach	.10
157	Bill Taylor	.10
158	Rich Amaral	.10
159	Eric Anthony	.10
160	Bobby Ayala	.10
161	Chris Bosio	.10
162	Jay Buhner	.10
163	Tim Davis	.10
164	Felix Fermin	.10
165	Dave Fleming	.10
166	Ken Griffey Jr.	1.50
167	Reggie Jefferson	.10
168	Randy Johnson	.75
169	Edgar Martinez	.10
170	Tino Martinez	.10
171	Bill Risley	.10
172	Roger Salkeld	.10
173	Mac Suzuki RC	.20
174	Dan Wilson	.10
175	Kevin Brown	.10
176	Jose Canseco	.40
177	Will Clark	.15
178	Juan Gonzalez	.75
179	Rick Helling	.10
180	Tom Henke	.10
181	Chris James	.10
182	Manuel Lee	.10
183	Dean Palmer	.10
184	Ivan Rodriguez	.65
185	Kenny Rogers	.10
186	Roberto Alomar	.20
187	Pat Borders	.10
188	Joe Carter	.10
189	Carlos Delgado	.50
190	Juan Guzman	.10
191	Pat Hentgen	.10
192	Paul Molitor	.75
192a	Paul Molitor (Promotional sample.)	2.00
193	John Olerud	.10
194	Ed Sprague	.10
195	Dave Stewart	.10
196	Todd Stottlemyre	.10
197	Duane Ward	.10
198	Devon White	.10
199	Steve Avery	.10
200	Jeff Blauser	.10
201	Tom Glavine	.30
202	Dave Justice	.10
203	Mike Kelly	.10
204	Roberto Kelly	.10
205	Ryan Klesko	.10
206	Mark Lemke	.10
207	Javier Lopez	.10
208	Greg Maddux	1.00
209	Fred McGriff	.10
210	Greg McMichael	.10
211	Kent Mercker	.10
212	Terry Pendleton	.10
213	John Smoltz	.10
214	Tony Tarasco	.10
215	Willie Banks	.10
216	Steve Buechele	.10
217	Shawon Dunston	.10
218	Mark Grace	.15
219	Brooks Kieschnick RC	.10
220	Derrick May	.10
221	Randy Myers	.10
222	Karl Rhodes	.10
223	Rey Sanchez	.10
224	Sammy Sosa	1.50
225	Steve Traschel	.10
226	Rick Wilkins	.10
227	Bret Boone	.15
228	Jeff Brantley	.10
229	Tom Browning	.10
230	Hector Carrasco	.10
231	Rob Dibble	.10
232	Erik Hanson	.10
233	Barry Larkin	.10
234	Kevin Mitchell	.10
235	Hal Morris	.10
236	Joe Oliver	.10
237	Jose Rijo	.10
238	Johnny Ruffin	.10
239	Deion Sanders	.15
240	Reggie Sanders	.10
241	John Smiley	.10
242	Dante Bichette	.10
243	Ellis Burks	.10
244	Andres Galarraga	.10
245	Joe Girardi	.10
246	Greg Harris	.10
247	Charlie Hayes	.10
248	Howard Johnson	.10
249	Roberto Mejia	.10
250	Marcus Moore	.10
251	David Nied	.10
252	Armando Reynoso	.10
253	Bruce Ruffin	.10
254	Mark Thompson	.10
255	Walt Weiss	.10
256	Kurt Abbott RC	.20
257	Bret Barberie	.10
258	Chuck Carr	.10
259	Jeff Conine	.10
260	Chris Hammond	.10
261	Bryan Harvey	.10
262	Jeremy Hernandez	.10
263	Charlie Hough	.10
264	Dave Magadan	.10
265	Benito Santiago	.10
266	Gary Sheffield	.25
267	David Weathers	.10
268	Jeff Bagwell	.75
269	Craig Biggio	.10
270	Ken Caminiti	.10
271	Andujar Cedeno	.10
272	Doug Drabek	.10
273	Steve Finley	.10
274	Luis Gonzalez	.20
275	Pete Harnisch	.10
276	John Hudek	.10
277	Darryl Kile	.10
278	Orlando Miller	.10
279	James Mouton	.10
280	Shane Reynolds	.10
281	Scott Servais	.10
282	Greg Swindell	.10
283	Pedro Astacio	.10
284	Brett Butler	.10
285	Tom Candiotti	.10
286	Delino DeShields	.10
287	Kevin Gross	.10
288	Orel Hershiser	.10
289	Eric Karros	.10
290	Ramon Martinez	.10
291	Raul Mondesi	.10
292	Jose Offerman	.10
293	Chan Ho Park RC	.75
294	Mike Piazza	1.50
295	Henry Rodriguez	.10
296	Cory Snyder	.10
297	Tim Wallach	.10
298	Todd Worrell	.10
299	Moises Alou	.10
300	Sean Berry	.10
301	Wil Cordero	.10
302	Joey Eischen	.10
303	Jeff Fassero	.10
304	Darrin Fletcher	.10
305	Cliff Floyd	.10
306	Marquis Grissom	.10
307	Ken Hill	.10
308	Mike Lansing	.10
309	Pedro Martinez	.75
310	Mel Rojas	.10
311	Kirk Rueter	.10
312	Larry Walker	.10
313	John Wetteland	.10
314	Rondell White	.10
315	Bobby Bonilla	.10
316	John Franco	.10
317	Dwight Gooden	.10
318	Todd Hundley	.10
319	Bobby Jones	.10
320	Jeff Kent	.10
321	Kevin McReynolds	.10
322	Bill Pulsipher	.10
323	Bret Saberhagen	.10
324	David Segui	.10
325	Pete Smith	.10
326	Kelly Stinnett	.10
327	Ryan Thompson	.10
328	Jose Vizcaino	.10
329	Ricky Bottalico	.10
330	Darren Daulton	.10
331	Mariano Duncan	.10
332	Len Dykstra	.10
333	Tommy Greene	.10
334	Billy Hatcher	.10
335	Dave Hollins	.10
336	Pete Incaviglia	.10
337	Danny Jackson	.10
338	Doug Jones	.10
339	Ricky Jordan	.10
340	John Kruk	.10
341	Curt Schilling	.30
342	Kevin Stocker	.10
343	Jay Bell	.10
344	Steve Cooke	.10
345	Carlos Garcia	.10
346	Brian Hunter	.10
347	Jeff King	.10
348	Al Martin	.10
349	Orlando Merced	.10
350	Denny Neagle	.10
351	Don Slaught	.10
352	Andy Van Slyke	.10
353	Paul Wagner	.10
354	Rick White	.10
355	Luis Alicea	.10
356	Rene Arocha	.10
357	Rheal Cormier	.10
358	Bernard Gilkey	.10
359	Gregg Jefferies	.10
360	Ray Lankford	.10
361	Tom Pagnozzi	.10
362	Mike Perez	.10
363	Ozzie Smith	1.00
364	Bob Tewksbury	.10
365	Mark Whiten	.10
366	Todd Zeile	.10
367	Andy Ashby	.10
368	Brad Ausmus	.10
369	Derek Bell	.10
370	Andy Benes	.10
371	Archi Cianfrocco	.10
372	Tony Gwynn	1.00
373	Trevor Hoffman	.10
374	Tim Hyers	.10
375	Pedro Martinez	.10
376	Phil Plantier	.10
377	Bip Roberts	.10
378	Scott Sanders	.10
379	Dave Staton	.10
380	Wally Whitehurst	.10
381	Rod Beck	.10
382	Todd Benzinger	.10
383	Barry Bonds	2.50
384	John Burkett	.10
385	Royce Clayton	.10
386	Bryan Hickerson	.10
387	Mike Jackson	.10
388	Darren Lewis	.10
389	Kirt Manwaring	.10
390	Willie McGee	.10
391	Mark Portugal	.10
392	Bill Swift	.10
393	Robby Thompson	.10
394	Salomon Torres	.10
395	Matt Williams	.10
396	Checklist	
397	Checklist	
398	Checklist	
399	Checklist	
400	Checklist	

Game Breakers

Game Breakers featured 30 big-name stars from both leagues who have exhibited offensive fire-power. This insert set was done in a horizontal format picturing the player in two different shots, one close-up and one slightly further away. The words "Game Breakers" is written across the bottom, with the player name and team in much smaller letters, printed under it.

		NM/M
Complete Set (30):		15.00
Common Player:		.25
1	Jeff Bagwell	.75
2	Rod Beck	.25
3	Albert Belle	.25
4	Barry Bonds	3.00
5	Jose Canseco	.65
6	Joe Carter	.25
7	Roger Clemens	1.50
8	Darren Daulton	.25
9	Len Dykstra	.25
10	Cecil Fielder	.25
11	Tom Glavine	.50
12	Juan Gonzalez	.75
13	Mark Grace	.35
14	Ken Griffey Jr.	2.00
15	Dave Justice	.25
16	Greg Maddux	1.25
17	Don Mattingly	1.50
18	Ben McDonald	.25
19	Fred McGriff	.25
20	Paul Molitor	.75
21	John Olerud	.25
22	Mike Piazza	2.00
23	Kirby Puckett	1.25
24	Cal Ripken, Jr.	3.00
25	Tim Salmon	.35
26	Gary Sheffield	.50
27	Frank Thomas	1.00
28	Mo Vaughn	.25
29	Matt Williams	.25
30	Dave Winfield	.75

Major League Hopefuls

Minor league standouts with impressive credentials were showcased in Major League Hopefuls. Each card in this insert set shows the player over a computer enhanced background, with three smaller photos running down the top half, on the left side of the card. The insert set title runs across the bottom and the player's name is just under it on a black strip.

		NM/M
Complete Set (10):		2.00
Common Player:		.25
1	James Baldwin	.25
2	Ricky Bottalico	.25
3	Ray Durham	.25
4	Joey Eischen	.25
5	Brooks Kieschnick	.25
6	Orlando Miller	.25
7	Bill Pulsipher	.25
8	Mac Suzuki	.25
9	Mark Thompson	.25
10	Wes Weger	.25

Rookie Standouts

Rookie Standouts highlights 20 of the best and brightest first-year players of the 1994 season. Cards picture the player on a baseball background, with a black,

jagged-edged "aura" around the player. Names and teams were placed in the bottom-left corner, running up the side. The Rookie Standouts logo, which is a gold glove with a baseball in it and "Rookie Standouts" printed under it, was placed in the bottom-right corner and the Extra Bases logo appears in the upper-left.

		NM/M
Complete Set (20):		7.50
Common Player:		.25
1	Kurt Abbott	.25
2	Brian Anderson	.25
3	Hector Carrasco	.25
4	Tim Davis	.25
5	Carlos Delgado	2.50
6	Cliff Floyd	.25
7	Bob Hamelin	.25
8	Jeffrey Hammonds	.25
9	Rick Helling	.25
10	Steve Karsay	.25
11	Ryan Klesko	.25
12	Javier Lopez	.25
13	Raul Mondesi	.25
14	James Mouton	.25
15	Chan Ho Park	.25
16	Manny Ramirez	3.00
17	Tony Tarasco	.25
18	Steve Trachsel	.25
19	Rick White	.25
20	Rondell White	.25

Second Year Stars

Second-Year Stars contains 1993 rookies who were expected to have an even bigger impact in the 1994 season. Each card features five photos of the player. Four are in a filmstrip down the left side; the remaining two-thirds of the card contain a larger photo. "Second-Year Stars" is printed across the bottom, along with the player name and team. Backs repeat the film-strip motif.

		NM/M
Complete Set (20):		5.00
Common Player:		.25
1	Bobby Ayala	.25
2	Jason Bere	.25
3	Chuck Carr	.25
4	Jeff Conine	.25
5	Steve Cooke	.25
6	Wil Cordero	.25
7	Carlos Garcia	.25
8	Brent Gates	.25
9	Trevor Hoffman	.25
10	Wayne Kirby	.25
11	Al Martin	.25

12	Pedro Martinez	1.50
13	Greg McMichael	.25
14	Troy Neel	.25
15	David Nied	.25
16	Mike Piazza	3.00
17	Kirk Rueter	.25
18	Tim Salmon	.50
19	Aaron Sele	.25
20	Kevin Stocker	.25

Pitcher's Duel

Pitcher's Duel was available to collectors who mailed in 10 Extra Bases wrappers. The set features 20 of the top pitchers in baseball. Contained in the set were five American League and five National League cards, with two pitchers from the same league on each card. The front background pictures a wide-angle photo of a major league stadium, viewed from above the diamond, behind home plate. Backs have two more action photos set against a sepia-toned background photo of an Old West street to enhance the shootout theme of the set. Cards are numbered with an "M" prefix.

		NM/M
Complete Set (10):		7.50
Common Player:		.50
1	Roger Clemens, Jack McDowell	2.50
2	Ben McDonald, Randy Johnson	1.50
3	Jimmy Key, David Cone	.50
4	Mike Mussina, Aaron Sele	1.00
5	Chuck Finley, Wilson Alvarez	.25
6	Steve Avery, Curt Schilling	.75
7	Greg Maddux, Jose Rijo	2.00
8	Bret Saberhagen, Bob Tewksbury	.50
9	Tom Glavine, Bill Swift	.75
10	Doug Drabek, Orel Hershiser	.50

1995 Fleer Promos

This eight-player (plus a header card), cello-wrapped promo set was included in a special "Fleer" national newsstand magazine in early 1995. At first glance the cards seem identical to the regularly issued cards of the same players, but there are subtle differences on the back of each card.

		NM/M
Complete Set (9):		4.00
Common Player:		.50
26	Roger Clemens (1988 291 SO and 1992 2.41 ERA boxed)	2.00
78	Paul O'Neill (1991 boxed)	.50
155	David Cone (1990 233 SO boxed, white shadow on team names)	.50
235	Tim Salmon (No box on 1992 101 R.)	.50
285	Juan Gonzalez (Black stats, 1993 boxed.)	1.00
351	Marquis Grissom (No box on 1988 291 AB.)	.50
509	Ozzie Smith (Black stats, no box on 1986 Cardinals.)	1.50
514	Dante Bichette (Black stats.)	.50
--	Header Card "Different by Design"	.05

1995 Fleer

Fleer baseball in 1995 offered six different designs, one for each division. The basic set contains 600 cards and was sold in 12- and 18-card packs. National League West cards feature many smaller pictures in the background that are identical to the picture in the forefront, while AL West cards contain an action photo over top of a close-up on the right side and a water colored look on the left side. AL Central cards exhibit numbers pertinent to each player throughout the front design, with the player in the middle. NL East players appear in action on the left half of the card with a colorful, encripted look on the rest. National League Central and American League East feature more standard designs with the player in the forefront, with vital numbers and a color background.

	NM/M
Complete Set (600):	15.00
Common Player:	.05
Pack (12):	.75
Wax Box (36):	17.50
1	Brady Anderson	.05
2	Harold Baines	.05
3	Damon Buford	.05
4	Mike Devereaux	.05
5	Mark Eichhorn	.05
6	Sid Fernandez	.05
7	Leo Gomez	.05
8	Jeffrey Hammonds	.05
9	Chris Hoiles	.05
10	Rick Krivda	.05
11	Ben McDonald	.05
12	Mark McLemore	.05
13	Alan Mills	.05
14	Jamie Moyer	.05
15	Mike Mussina	.40
16	Mike Oquist	.05
17	Rafael Palmeiro	.65
18	Arthur Rhodes	.05
19	Cal Ripken, Jr.	2.50
20	Chris Sabo	.05
21	Lee Smith	.05
22	Jack Voight	.05
23	Damon Berryhill	.05
24	Tom Brunansky	.05
25	Wes Chamberlain	.05
26	Roger Clemens	1.25
27	Scott Cooper	.05
28	Andre Dawson	.25
29	Gar Finnvold	.05
30	Tony Fossas	.05
31	Mike Greenwell	.05
32	Joe Hesketh	.05
33	Chris Howard	.05
34	Chris Nabholz	.05
35	Tim Naehring	.05
36	Otis Nixon	.05
37	Carlos Rodriguez	.05
38	Rich Rowland	.05
39	Ken Ryan	.05
40	Aaron Sele	.05
41	John Valentin	.05
42	Mo Vaughn	.05
43	Frank Viola	.05
44	Danny Bautista	.05
45	Joe Boeven	.05
46	Milt Cuyler	.05
47	Storm Davis	.05
48	John Doherty	.05
49	Junior Felix	.05
50	Cecil Fielder	.05
51	Travis Fryman	.05
52	Mike Gardiner	.05
53	Kirk Gibson	.05
54	Chris Gomez	.05
55	Buddy Groom	.05
56	Mike Henneman	.05
57	Chad Kreuter	.05
58	Mike Moore	.05
59	Tony Phillips	.05
60	Juan Samuel	.05
61	Mickey Tettleton	.05
62	Alan Trammell	.05
63	David Wells	.05
64	Lou Whitaker	.05

65	Jim Abbott	.05
66	Joe Ausanio	.05
67	Wade Boggs	1.00
68	Mike Gallego	.05
69	Xavier Hernandez	.05
70	Sterling Hitchcock	.05
71	Steve Howe	.05
72	Scott Kamieniecki	.05
73	Pat Kelly	.05
74	Jimmy Key	.05
75	Jim Leyritz	.05
76	Don Mattingly	1.25
77	Terry Mulholland	.05
78	Paul O'Neill	.05
79	Melido Perez	.05
80	Luis Polonia	.05
81	Mike Stanley	.05
82	Danny Tartabull	.05
83	Randy Velarde	.05
84	Bob Wickman	.05
85	Bernie Williams	.10
86	Gerald Williams	.05
87	Roberto Alomar	.10
88	Pat Borders	.05
89	Joe Carter	.05
90	Tony Castillo	.05
91	Brad Cornett	.05
92	Carlos Delgado	.50
93	Alex Gonzalez	.05
94	Shawn Green	.40
95	Juan Guzman	.05
96	Darren Hall	.05
97	Pat Hentgen	.05
98	Mike Huff	.05
99	Randy Knorr	.05
100	Al Leiter	.05
101	Paul Molitor	.75
102	John Olerud	.05
103	Dick Schofield	.05
104	Ed Sprague	.05
105	Dave Stewart	.05
106	Todd Stottlemyre	.05
107	Devon White	.05
108	Woody Williams	.05
109	Wilson Alvarez	.05
110	Paul Assenmacher	.05
111	Jason Bere	.05
112	Dennis Cook	.05
113	Joey Cora	.05
114	Jose DeLeon	.05
115	Alex Fernandez	.05
116	Julio Franco	.05
117	Craig Graboeck	.05
118	Ozzie Guillen	.05
119	Roberto Hernandez	.05
120	Darrin Jackson	.05
121	Lance Johnson	.05
122	Ron Karkovice	.05
123	Mike LaValliere	.05
124	Norberto Martin	.05
125	Kirk McCaskill	.05
126	Jack McDowell	.05
127	Tim Raines	.05
128	Frank Thomas	.75
129	Robin Ventura	.05
130	Sandy Alomar Jr.	.05
131	Carlos Baerga	.05
132	Albert Belle	.05
133	Mark Clark	.05
134	Alvaro Espinoza	.05
135	Jason Grimsley	.05
136	Wayne Kirby	.05
137	Kenny Lofton	.05
138	Albie Lopez	.05
139	Dennis Martinez	.05
140	Jose Mesa	.05
141	Eddie Murray	.75
142	Charles Nagy	.05
143	Tony Pena	.05
144	Eric Plunk	.05
145	Manny Ramirez	.75
146	Jeff Russell	.05
147	Paul Shuey	.05
148	Paul Sorrento	.05
149	Jim Thome	.65
150	Omar Vizquel	.05
151	Dave Winfield	.75
152	Kevin Appier	.05
153	Billy Brewer	.05
154	Vince Coleman	.05
155	David Cone	.05
156	Gary Gaetti	.05
157	Greg Gagne	.05
158	Tom Gordon	.05
159	Mark Gubicza	.05
160	Bob Hamelin	.05
161	Dave Henderson	.05
162	Felix Jose	.05
163	Wally Joyner	.05
164	Jose Lind	.05
165	Mike Macfarlane	.05
166	Mike Magnante	.05
167	Brent Mayne	.05
168	Brian McRae	.05
169	Rusty Meacham	.05
170	Jeff Montgomery	.05
171	Hipolito Pichardo	.05
172	Terry Shumpert	.05
173	Michael Tucker	.05
174	Ricky Bones	.05
175	Jeff Cirillo RC	.30
176	Alex Diaz	.05
177	Cal Eldred	.05
178	Mike Fetters	.05
179	Darryl Hamilton	.05
180	Brian Harper	.05
181	John Jaha	.05
182	Pat Listach	.05

183	Graeme Lloyd	.05
184	Jose Mercedes	.05
185	Matt Mieske	.05
186	Dave Nilsson	.05
187	Jody Reed	.05
188	Bob Scanlan	.05
189	Kevin Seitzer	.05
190	Bill Spiers	.05
191	B.J. Surhoff	.05
192	Jose Valentin	.05
193	Greg Vaughn	.05
194	Turner Ward	.05
195	Bill Wegman	.05
196	Rick Aguilera	.05
197	Rich Becker	.05
198	Alex Cole	.05
199	Marty Cordova	.05
200	Steve Dunn	.05
201	Scott Erickson	.05
202	Mark Guthrie	.05
203	Chip Hale	.05
204	LaTroy Hawkins	.05
205	Denny Hocking	.05
206	Chuck Knoblauch	.05
207	Scott Leius	.05
208	Shane Mack	.05
209	Pat Mahomes	.05
210	Pat Meares	.05
211	Pedro Munoz	.05
212	Kirby Puckett	1.00
213	Jeff Reboulet	.05
214	Dave Stevens	.05
215	Kevin Tapani	.05
216	Matt Walbeck	.05
217	Carl Willis	.05
218	Brian Anderson	.05
219	Chad Curtis	.05
220	Chili Davis	.05
221	Gary DiSarcina	.05
222	Damion Easley	.05
223	Jim Edmonds	.05
224	Chuck Finley	.05
225	Joe Grahe	.05
226	Rex Hudler	.05
227	Bo Jackson	.10
228	Mark Langston	.05
229	Phil Leftwich	.05
230	Mark Leiter	.05
231	Spike Owen	.05
232	Bob Patterson	.05
233	Troy Percival	.05
234	Eduardo Perez	.05
235	Tim Salmon	.10
236	J.T. Snow	.05
237	Chris Turner	.05
238	Mark Acre	.05
239	Geronimo Berroa	.05
240	Mike Bordick	.05
241	John Briscoe	.05
242	Scott Brosius	.05
243	Ron Darling	.05
244	Dennis Eckersley	.65
245	Brent Gates	.05
246	Rickey Henderson	.75
247	Stan Javier	.05
248	Steve Karsay	.05
249	Mark McGwire	2.00
250	Troy Neel	.05
251	Steve Ontiveros	.05
252	Carlos Reyes	.05
253	Ruben Sierra	.05
254	Terry Steinbach	.05
255	Bill Taylor	.05
256	Todd Van Poppel	.05
257	Bobby Witt	.05
258	Rich Amaral	.05
259	Eric Anthony	.05
260	Bobby Ayala	.05
261	Mike Blowers	.05
262	Chris Bosio	.05
263	Jay Buhner	.05
264	John Cummings	.05
265	Tim Davis	.05
266	Felix Fermin	.05
267	Dave Fleming	.05
268	Goose Gossage	.05
269	Ken Griffey Jr.	1.50
270	Reggie Jefferson	.05
271	Randy Johnson	.75
272	Edgar Martinez	.05
273	Tino Martinez	.05
274	Greg Pirkl	.05
275	Bill Risley	.05
276	Roger Salkeld	.05
277	Luis Sojo	.05
278	Mac Suzuki	.05
279	Dan Wilson	.05
280	Kevin Brown	.05
281	Jose Canseco	.40
282	Cris Carpenter	.05
283	Will Clark	.10
284	Jeff Frye	.05
285	Juan Gonzalez	.65
286	Rick Helling	.05
287	Tom Henke	.05
288	David Hulse	.05
289	Chris James	.05
290	Manuel Lee	.05
291	Oddibe McDowell	.05
292	Dean Palmer	.05
293	Roger Pavlik	.05
294	Bill Ripken	.05
295	Ivan Rodriguez	.05
296	Kenny Rogers	.05
297	Doug Strange	.05
298	Matt Whiteside	.05
299	Steve Avery	.05
300	Steve Bedrosian	.05

301	Rafael Belliard	.05
302	Jeff Blauser	.05
303	Dave Gallagher	.05
304	Tom Glavine	.30
305	Dave Justice	.05
306	Mike Kelly	.05
307	Roberto Kelly	.05
308	Ryan Klesko	.05
309	Mark Lemke	.05
310	Javier Lopez	.05
311	Greg Maddux	1.00
312	Fred McGriff	.05
313	Greg McMichael	.05
314	Kent Mercker	.05
315	Charlie O'Brien	.05
316	Jose Oliva	.05
317	Terry Pendleton	.05
318	John Smoltz	.05
319	Mike Stanton	.05
320	Tony Tarasco	.05
321	Terrell Wade	.05
322	Mark Wohlers	.05
323	Kurt Abbott	.05
324	Luis Aquino	.05
325	Bret Barberie	.05
326	Ryan Bowen	.05
327	Jerry Browne	.05
328	Chuck Carr	.05
329	Matias Carrillo	.05
330	Greg Colbrunn	.05
331	Jeff Conine	.05
332	Mark Gardner	.05
333	Chris Hammond	.05
334	Bryan Harvey	.05
335	Richie Lewis	.05
336	Dave Magadan	.05
337	Terry Mathews	.05
338	Robb Nen	.05
339	Yorkis Perez	.05
340	Pat Rapp	.05
341	Benito Santiago	.05
342	Gary Sheffield	.40
343	Dave Weathers	.05
344	Moises Alou	.05
345	Sean Berry	.05
346	Wil Cordero	.05
347	Joe Eischen	.05
348	Jeff Fassero	.05
349	Darrin Fletcher	.05
350	Cliff Floyd	.05
351	Marquis Grissom	.05
352	Butch Henry	.05
353	Gil Heredia	.05
354	Ken Hill	.05
355	Mike Lansing	.05
356	Pedro Martinez	.75
357	Mel Rojas	.05
358	Kirk Rueter	.05
359	Tim Scott	.05
360	Jeff Shaw	.05
361	Larry Walker	.05
362	Lenny Webster	.05
363	John Wetteland	.05
364	Rondell White	.05
365	Bobby Bonilla	.05
366	Rico Brogna	.05
367	Jeromy Burnitz	.05
368	John Franco	.05
369	Dwight Gooden	.05
370	Todd Hundley	.05
371	Jason Jacome	.05
372	Bobby Jones	.05
373	Jeff Kent	.05
374	Jim Lindeman	.05
375	Josias Manzanillo	.05
376	Roger Mason	.05
377	Kevin McReynolds	.05
378	Joe Orsulak	.05
379	Bill Pulsipher	.05
380	Bret Saberhagen	.05
381	David Segui	.05
382	Pete Smith	.05
383	Kelly Stinnett	.05
384	Ryan Thompson	.05
385	Jose Vizcaino	.05
386	Toby Borland	.05
387	Ricky Bettalico	.05
388	Darren Daulton	.05
389	Mariano Duncan	.05
390	Len Dykstra	.05
391	Jim Eisenreich	.05
392	Tommy Greene	.05
393	Dave Hollins	.05
394	Pete Incaviglia	.05
395	Danny Jackson	.05
396	Doug Jones	.05
397	Ricky Jordan	.05
398	John Kruk	.05
399	Mike Lieberthal	.05
400	Tony Longmire	.05
401	Mickey Morandini	.05
402	Bobby Munoz	.05
403	Curt Schilling	.25
404	Heathcliff Slocumb	.05
405	Kevin Stocker	.05
406	Fernando Valenzuela	.05
407	David West	.05
408	Willie Banks	.05
409	Jose Bautista	.05
410	Steve Buechele	.05
411	Jim Bullinger	.05
412	Chuck Crim	.05
413	Shawon Dunston	.05
414	Kevin Foster	.05
415	Mark Grace	.10
416	Jose Hernandez	.05
417	Glenallen Hill	.05
418	Brooks Kieschnick	.05

419	Derrick May	.05
420	Randy Myers	.05
421	Dan Plesac	.05
422	Karl Rhodes	.05
423	Rey Sanchez	.05
424	Sammy Sosa	1.50
425	Steve Trachsel	.05
426	Rick Wilkins	.05
427	Anthony Young	.05
428	Eddie Zambrano	.05
429	Bret Boone	.05
430	Jeff Branson	.05
431	Jeff Brantley	.05
432	Hector Carrasco	.05
433	Brian Dorsett	.05
434	Tony Fernandez	.05
435	Tim Fortugno	.05
436	Erik Hanson	.05
437	Thomas Howard	.05
438	Kevin Jarvis	.05
439	Barry Larkin	.05
440	Chuck McElroy	.05
441	Kevin Mitchell	.05
442	Hal Morris	.05
443	Jose Rijo	.05
444	John Roper	.05
445	Johnny Ruffin	.05
446	Deion Sanders	.05
447	Reggie Sanders	.05
448	Pete Schourek	.05
449	John Smiley	.05
450	Eddie Taubensee	.05
451	Jeff Bagwell	.75
452	Kevin Bass	.05
453	Craig Biggio	.05
454	Ken Caminiti	.05
455	Andujar Cedeno	.05
456	Doug Drabek	.05
457	Tony Eusebio	.05
458	Mike Felder	.05
459	Steve Finley	.05
460	Luis Gonzalez	.10
461	Mike Hampton	.05
462	Pete Harnisch	.05
463	John Hudek	.05
464	Todd Jones	.05
465	Darryl Kile	.05
466	James Mouton	.05
467	Shane Reynolds	.05
468	Scott Servais	.05
469	Greg Swindell	.05
470	Dave Veres	.05
471	Brian Williams	.05
472	Jay Bell	.05
473	Jacob Brumfield	.05
474	Dave Clark	.05
475	Steve Cooke	.05
476	Midre Cummings	.05
477	Mark Dewey	.05
478	Tom Foley	.05
479	Carlos Garcia	.05
480	Jeff King	.05
481	Jon Lieber	.05
482	Ravelo Manzanillo	.05
483	Al Martin	.05
484	Orlando Merced	.05
485	Danny Miceli	.05
486	Denny Neagle	.05
487	Lance Parrish	.05
488	Don Slaught	.05
489	Zane Smith	.05
490	Andy Van Slyke	.05
491	Paul Wagner	.05
492	Rick White	.05
493	Luis Alicea	.05
494	Rene Arocha	.05
495	Rheal Cormier	.05
496	Bryan Eversgerd	.05
497	Bernard Gilkey	.05
498	John Habyan	.05
499	Gregg Jefferies	.05
500	Brian Jordan	.05
501	Ray Lankford	.05
502	John Mabry	.05
503	Terry McGriff	.05
504	Tom Pagnozzi	.05
505	Vicente Palacios	.05
506	Geronimo Pena	.05
507	Gerald Perry	.05
508	Rich Rodriguez	.05
509	Ozzie Smith	1.00
510	Bob Tewksbury	.05
511	Allen Watson	.05
512	Mark Whiten	.05
513	Todd Zeile	.05
514	Dante Bichette	.05
515	Willie Blair	.05
516	Ellis Burks	.05
517	Marvin Freeman	.05
518	Andres Galarraga	.05
519	Joe Girardi	.05
520	Greg Harris	.05
521	Charlie Hayes	.05
522	Mike Kingery	.05
523	Nelson Liriano	.05
524	Mike Munoz	.05
525	David Nied	.05
526	Steve Reed	.05
527	Kevin Ritz	.05
528	Bruce Ruffin	.05
529	John Vander Wal	.05
530	Walt Weiss	.05
531	Eric Young	.05
532	Billy Ashley	.05
533	Pedro Astacio	.05
534	Rafael Bournigal	.05
535	Brett Butler	.05
536	Tom Candiotti	.05

537	Omar Daal	.05
538	Delino DeShields	.05
539	Darren Dreifort	.05
540	Kevin Gross	.05
541	Orel Hershiser	.05
542	Garey Ingram	.05
543	Eric Karros	.05
544	Ramon Martinez	.05
545	Raul Mondesi	.05
546	Chan Ho Park	.05
547	Mike Piazza	1.50
548	Henry Rodriguez	.05
549	Rudy Seanez	.05
550	Ismael Valdes	.05
551	Tim Wallach	.05
552	Todd Worrell	.05
553	Andy Ashby	.05
554	Brad Ausmus	.05
555	Derek Bell	.05
556	Andy Benes	.05
557	Phil Clark	.05
558	Donnie Elliott	.05
559	Ricky Gutierrez	.05
560	Tony Gwynn	1.00
561	Joey Hamilton	.05
562	Trevor Hoffman	.05
563	Luis Lopez	.05
564	Pedro Martinez	.05
565	Tim Mauser	.05
566	Phil Plantier	.05
567	Bip Roberts	.05
568	Scott Sanders	.05
569	Craig Shipley	.05
570	Jeff Tabaka	.05
571	Eddie Williams	.05
572	Rod Beck	.05
573	Mike Benjamin	.05
574	Barry Bonds	2.50
575	Dave Burba	.05
576	John Burkett	.05
577	Mark Carreon	.05
578	Royce Clayton	.05
579	Steve Frey	.05
580	Bryan Hickerson	.05
581	Mike Jackson	.05
582	Darren Lewis	.05
583	Kirt Manwaring	.05
584	Rich Monteleone	.05
585	John Patterson	.05
586	J.R. Phillips	.05
587	Mark Portugal	.05
588	Joe Rosselli	.05
589	Darryl Strawberry	.05
590	Bill Swift	.05
591	Robby Thompson	.05
592	William Van Landingham	.05
593	Matt Williams	.05
594	Checklist	.05
595	Checklist	.05
596	Checklist	.05
597	Checklist	.05
598	Checklist	.05
599	Checklist	.05
600	Checklist	.05

All-Stars

All-Stars are a horizontal, two-sided insert set consisting of 25 cards. A National League All-Star is on one side, while an American League All-Star is on the other, by position. All-Stars are the most common insert in Fleer 1995 baseball, with an insertion ratio of one per three packs.

	NM/M
Complete Set (25):	8.00
Common Card:	.20
1	Ivan Rodriguez,	
	Mike Piazza	.75
2	Frank Thomas,	
	Gregg Jefferies	.50
3	Roberto Alomar,	
	Mariano Duncan	.40
4	Wade Boggs,	
	Matt Williams	.65
5	Cal Ripken, Jr.,	
	Ozzie Smith	1.50
6	Joe Carter, Barry Bonds	1.50
7	Ken Griffey Jr.,	
	Tony Gwynn	.75
8	Kirby Puckett,	
	Dave Justice	.65
9	Jimmy Key, Greg Maddux	.65
10	Chuck Knoblauch,	
	Wil Cordero	.20
11	Scott Cooper,	
	Ken Caminiti	
12	Will Clark, Carlos Garcia	.50
13	Paul Molitor, Jeff Bagwell	.50
14	Travis Fryman,	
	Craig Biggio	.20
15	Mickey Tettleton,	
	Fred McGriff	.20
16	Kenny Lofton,	
	Moises Alou	.20

17 Albert Belle, Marquis Grissom .20
18 Paul O'Neill, Dante Bichette .20
19 David Cone, Ken Hill .20
20 Mike Mussina, Doug Drabek .50
21 Randy Johnson, John Hudek .50
22 Pat Hentgen, Danny Jackson .20
23 Wilson Alvarez, Rod Beck .20
24 Lee Smith, Randy Myers .20
25 Jason Bere, Doug Jones .20

Award Winners

Fleer Award Winners contain Fleer's choices of baseball's most outstanding players. This six-card set was only inserted at a rate of one per 24 packs. Each card has an embossed gold foil design, with the gold strip running up the left side and containing the words "Fleer Award Winner" and the player name.

	NM/M
Complete Set (6):	4.00
Common Player:	.25
1 Frank Thomas	1.50
2 Jeff Bagwell	1.50
3 David Cone	.25
4 Greg Maddux	2.00
5 Bob Hamelin	.25
6 Raul Mondesi	.25

League Leaders

League Leaders feature players on a horizontal format from 10 statistical categories from both leagues. "League Leader" is placed in a blue strip down the left-side of the card, with their respective league and their name in it. These were inserted at a rate of one per 12 packs.

	NM/M
Complete Set (10):	4.00
Common Player:	.25
1 Paul O'Neill	.25
2 Ken Griffey Jr.	1.50
3 Kirby Puckett	.75
4 Jimmy Key	.25
5 Randy Johnson	.65
6 Tony Gwynn	.75
7 Matt Williams	.25
8 Jeff Bagwell	.50
9 Greg Maddux, Ken Hill	.75
10 Andy Benes	.25

Lumber Company

Ten of the top longball hitters were featured in Lumber Co., which were inserted into every 24 12-card retailer packs. They show the power hitter in action, with a wood-grain Lumber Co. logo across the bottom, contain the player's name and team.

	NM/M
Complete Set (10):	12.00
Common Player:	.40
1 Jeff Bagwell	1.50
2 Albert Belle	.40
3 Barry Bonds	3.50
4 Jose Canseco	.75
5 Joe Carter	.40
6 Ken Griffey Jr.	2.50
7 Fred McGriff	.40
8 Kevin Mitchell	.40
9 Frank Thomas	1.75
10 Matt Williams	.40

Major League Prospects

Major League Prospects showcases 10 of 1995's most promising young players. The set title is repeatedly printed across the background, with the player's name and team in a gray strip across the bottom. These cards were inserted into one every six packs.

	NM/M
Complete Set (10):	6.00
Common Player:	.25
1 Garret Anderson	.50
2 James Baldwin	.25
3 Alan Benes	.25
4 Armando Benitez	.25
5 Ray Durham	.25
6 Brian Hunter	.25
7a Derek Jeter (No licensor logos on back.)	4.00
7b Derek Jeter (Licensor logos on back.)	4.00
8 Charles Johnson	.25
9 Orlando Miller	.25
10 Alex Rodriguez	3.00

Pro-Visions

Pro-Visions contain six interlocking cards that form one giant picture. These original art cards exhibit the fantasy art background and are inserted into every nine packs.

	NM/M
Complete Set (6):	2.00
Common Player:	.25
1 Mike Mussina	.40
2 Raul Mondesi	.25
3 Jeff Bagwell	.75
4 Greg Maddux	1.00
5 Tim Salmon	.25
6 Manny Ramirez	.75

Rookie Sensations

A perennial favorite within Fleer products, Rookie Sensations cards were inserted in 18-card packs only, at a rate of one per 16 packs. This 20-card set featured the top rookies from the 1994 season. The player's name and team run up the right side of the card, while the words "Rookie Sensations" appear in the bottom-left corner, separated by a colorful, zig-zagged image of a player.

	NM/M
Complete Set (20):	5.00

Common Player:	.25
1 Kurt Abbott	.25
2 Rico Brogna	.25
3 Hector Carrasco	.25
4 Kevin Foster	.25
5 Chris Gomez	.25
6 Darren Hall	.25
7 Bob Hamelin	.25
8 Joey Hamilton	.25
9 John Hudek	.25
10 Ryan Klesko	.25
11 Javier Lopez	.25
12 Matt Mieske	.25
13 Raul Mondesi	.25
14 Manny Ramirez	4.00
15 Shane Reynolds	.25
16 Bill Risley	.25
17 Johnny Ruffin	.25
18 Steve Trachsel	.25
19 William Van Landingham	.25
20 Rondell White	.25

Team Leaders

Team Leaders are two-player cards featuring the leading hitter and pitcher from each major league team, one on each side. Inserted at a rate of one per 24 packs, these are only found in 12-card hobby packs. Team Leaders consisted of 28 cards and included a Team Leader logo in the bottom-left corner.

	NM/M
Complete Set (28):	50.00
Common Card:	.50
1 Cal Ripken, Jr., Mike Mussina	7.50
2 Mo Vaughn, Roger Clemens	4.50
3 Tim Salmon, Chuck Finley	.75
4 Frank Thomas, Jack McDowell	2.50
5 Albert Belle, Dennis Martinez	.50
6 Cecil Fielder, Mike Moore	.50
7 Bob Hamelin, David Cone	.50
8 Greg Vaughn, Ricky Bones	.50
9 Kirby Puckett, Rick Aguilera	3.00
10 Don Mattingly, Jimmy Key	4.50
11 Ruben Sierra, Dennis Eckersley	1.50
12 Ken Griffey Jr., Randy Johnson	6.00
13 Jose Canseco, Kenny Rogers	1.00
14 Joe Carter, Pat Hentgen	.50
15 Dave Justice, Greg Maddux	3.00
16 Sammy Sosa, Steve Trachsel	5.00
17 Kevin Mitchell, Jose Rijo	.50
18 Dante Bichette, Bruce Ruffin	.50
19 Jeff Conine, Robb Nen	.50
20 Jeff Bagwell, Doug Drabek	2.50
21 Mike Piazza, Ramon Martinez	5.00
22 Moises Alou, Ken Hill	.50
23 Bobby Bonilla, Bret Saberhagen	.50
24 Darren Daulton, Danny Jackson	.50
25 Jay Bell, Zane Smith	.50
26 Gregg Jefferies, Bob Tewksbury	.50
27 Tony Gwynn, Andy Benes	3.00
28 Matt Williams, Rod Beck	.50

All-Fleer 9

Available only by mailing in 10 Fleer wrappers and $3, this set presents an all-star lineup in a unique design. Colored scribbles down one side of the card front offer a background for gold-foil printing of the card title, player name, position and team. Backs repeat the colored scribbles across virtually the entire surface, making it extremely difficult to read the career summary printed in white over it.

	NM/M
Complete Set (9):	4.00
Common Player:	.25
1 Mike Piazza	1.00
2 Frank Thomas	.50
3 Roberto Alomar	.40
4 Cal Ripken Jr.	2.50
5 Matt Williams	.25
6 Barry Bonds	2.50
7 Ken Griffey Jr.	1.00
8 Tony Gwynn	.65
9 Greg Maddux	.65

All-Rookies

This mail-in set was available by redeeming a randomly inserted trade card found in packs. The cards feature action player photos on a muted background, with the player ID in gold-foil beneath a huge rookie banner. Horizontal backs have a player photo at left and professional highlights at right. Cards have an "M" prefix to the card number.

	NM/M
Complete Set (9):	1.50
Common Player:	.25
Trade card: 2X	.12
1 Edgardo Alfonzo	.25
2 Jason Bates	.25
3 Brian Boehringer	.25
4 Darren Bragg	.25
5 Brad Clontz	.25
6 Jim Dougherty	.25
7 Todd Hollandsworth	.25
8 Rudy Pemberton	.25
9 Frank Rodriguez	.25

Update

Fleer carried its "different by design" concept of six formats (one for each division in each league) from the regular set into its 1995 Update issue. The issue consists of 200 cards of 1995's traded, rookie and free agent players, plus five different insert sets. One insert card was found in each regular (12-card, $1.49) and jumbo (18-card, $2.29) pack. Cards are numbered with a "U" prefix.

	NM/M
Complete Set (200):	7.00
Common Player:	.05

Pack (12):	.50
Wax Box (36):	7.50
1 Manny Alexander	.05
2 Bret Barberie	.05
3 Armando Benitez	.05
4 Kevin Brown	.05
5 Doug Jones	.05
6 Sherman Obando	.05
7 Andy Van Slyke	.05
8 Stan Belinda	.05
9 Jose Canseco	.30
10 Vaughn Eshelman	.05
11 Mike Macfarlane	.05
12 Troy O'Leary	.05
13 Steve Rodriguez	.05
14 Lee Tinsley	.05
15 Tim Vanegmond	.05
16 Mark Whiten	.05
17 Sean Bergman	.05
18 Chad Curtis	.05
19 John Flaherty	.05
20 Bob Higginson RC	.15
21 Felipe Lira	.05
22 Shannon Penn	.05
23 Todd Stevenson	.05
24 Sean Whiteside	.05
25 Tony Fernandez	.05
26 Jack McDowell	.05
27 Andy Petitte	.15
28 John Wetteland	.05
29 David Cone	.05
30 Mike Timlin	.05
31 Duane Ward	.05
32 Jim Abbott	.05
33 James Baldwin	.05
34 Mike Devereaux	.05
35 Ray Durham	.05
36 Tim Fortugno	.05
37 Scott Ruffcorn	.05
38 Chris Sabo	.05
39 Paul Assenmacher	.05
40 Bud Black	.05
41 Orel Hershiser	.05
42 Julian Tavarez	.05
43 Dave Winfield	.60
44 Pat Borders	.05
45 Melvin Bunch RC	.05
46 Tom Goodwin	.05
47 Jon Nunnally	.05
48 Joe Randa	.05
49 Dilson Torres RC	.05
50 Joe Vitiello	.05
51 David Hulse	.05
52 Scott Karl	.05
53 Mark Kiefer	.05
54 Derrick May	.05
55 Joe Oliver	.05
56 Al Reyes	.05
57 Steve Sparks RC	.05
58 Jerald Clark	.05
59 Eddie Guardado	.05
60 Kevin Maas	.05
61 David McCarty	.05
62 Brad Radke RC	.50
63 Scott Stahoviak	.05
64 Garret Anderson	.05
65 Shawn Boskie	.05
66 Mike James	.05
67 Tony Phillips	.05
68 Lee Smith	.05
69 Mitch Williams	.05
70 Jim Corsi	.05
71 Mark Harkey	.05
72 Dave Stewart	.05
73 Todd Stottlemyre	.05
74 Joey Cora	.05
75 Chad Kreuter	.05
76 Jeff Nelson	.05
77 Alex Rodriguez	2.00
78 Ron Villone	.05
79 Bob Wells RC	.05
80 Jose Alberro RC	.05
81 Terry Burrows	.05
82 Kevin Gross	.05
83 Wilson Heredia	.05
84 Mark McLemore	.05
85 Otis Nixon	.05
86 Jeff Russell	.05
87 Mickey Tettleton	.05
88 Bob Tewksbury	.05
89 Pedro Borbon	.05
90 Marquis Grissom	.05
91 Chipper Jones	.75
92 Mike Mordecai	.05
93 Jason Schmidt	.05
94 John Burkett	.05
95 Andre Dawson	.25
96 Matt Dunbar RC	.05
97 Charles Johnson	.05
98 Terry Pendleton	.05
99 Rich Scheid	.05
100 Quilvio Veras	.05
101 Bobby Witt	.05
102 Eddie Zosky	.05
103 Shane Andrews	.05
104 Reid Cornelius	.05
105 Chad Fonville RC	.05
106 Mark Grudzielanek RC	.25
107 Roberto Kelly	.05
108 Carlos Perez RC	.05
109 Tony Tarasco	.05
110 Brett Butler	.05
111 Carl Everett	.05
112 Pete Harnisch	.05
113 Doug Henry	.05
114 Kevin Lomon	.05
115 Blas Minor	.05
116 Dave Mlicki	.05
117 Ricky Otero RC	.05
118 Norm Charlton	.05
119 Tyler Green	.05
120 Gene Harris	.05
121 Charlie Hayes	.05
122 Gregg Jefferies	.05
123 Michael Mimbs RC	.05
124 Paul Quantrill	.05
125 Frank Castillo	.05
126 Brian McRae	.05
127 Jaime Navarro	.05
128 Mike Perez	.05
129 Tanyon Sturtze	.05
130 Ozzie Timmons	.05
131 John Courtright	.05
132 Ron Gant	.05
133 Xavier Hernandez	.05
134 Brian Hunter	.05
135 Benito Santiago	.05
136 Pete Smith	.05
137 Scott Sullivan	.05
138 Derek Bell	.05
139 Doug Brocail	.05
140 Ricky Gutierrez	.05
141 Pedro Martinez	.05
142 Orlando Miller	.05
143 Phil Plantier	.05
144 Craig Shipley	.05
145 Rich Aude	.05
146 Jason Christiansen RC	.05
147 Freddy Garcia RC	.25
148 Jim Gott	.05
149 Mark Johnson RC	.05
150 Esteban Loaiza	.05
151 Dan Plesac	.05
152 Gary Wilson RC	.05
153 Allen Battle	.05
154 Terry Bradshaw	.05
155 Scott Cooper	.05
156 Tripp Cromer	.05
157 John Frascatore	.05
158 John Habyan	.05
159 Tom Henke	.05
160 Ken Hill	.05
161 Danny Jackson	.05
162 Donovan Osborne	.05
163 Tom Urbani	.05
164 Roger Bailey	.05
165 Jorge Brito RC	.05
166 Vinny Castilla	.05
167 Darren Holmes	.05
168 Roberto Mejia	.05
169 Bill Swift	.05
170 Mark Thompson	.05
171 Larry Walker	.05
172 Greg Hansell	.05
173 Dave Hansen	.05
174 Carlos Hernandez	.05
175 Hideo Nomo RC	2.00
176 Jose Offerman	.05
177 Antonio Osuna	.05
178 Reggie Williams	.05
179 Todd Williams	.05
180 Andres Berumen	.05
181 Ken Caminiti	.05
182 Andujar Cedeno	.05
183 Steve Finley	.05
184 Bryce Florie	.05
185 Dustin Hermanson	.05
186 Ray Holbert	.05
187 Melvin Nieves	.05
188 Roberto Petagine	.05
189 Jody Reed	.05
190 Fernando Valenzuela	.05
191 Brian Williams	.05
192 Mark Dewey	.05
193 Glenallen Hill	.05
194 Chris Hook RC	.05
195 Terry Mulholland	.05
196 Steve Scarsone	.05
197 Trevor Wilson	.05
198 Checklist	.05
199 Checklist	.05
200 Checklist	.05

Update Diamond Tribute

Borderless action photos and gold-foil graphics are front features of this chase set honoring perhaps the 10 top names among baseball's veteran players. Backs have another photo and a few sentences describing what makes the player worthy of inclusion in such a set. The Diamond Tribute cards are found on the average of one per five packs.

		NM/M
Complete Set (10):		6.00
Common Player:		.25
1	Jeff Bagwell	.75
2	Albert Belle	.25
3	Barry Bonds	3.00
4	David Cone	.25
5	Dennis Eckersley	.50
6	Ken Griffey Jr.	1.50
7	Rickey Henderson	.60
8	Greg Maddux	1.00
9	Frank Thomas	.75
10	Matt Williams	.25

Update Headliners

The most common of the Fleer Update inserts are the Headliners cards found on average of one per three packs. Fronts have an action photo set against a collage of newspaper clippings. The graphics are gold-foil. Backs have another color photo and a "Fleer Times" newspaper background with career summary and/or quotes about the featured player.

		NM/M
Complete Set (20):		8.00
Common Player:		.10
1	Jeff Bagwell	.50
2	Albert Belle	.15
3	Barry Bonds	3.00
4	Jose Canseco	.40
5	Joe Carter	.15
6	Will Clark	.25
7	Roger Clemens	2.00
8	Lenny Dykstra	.15
9	Cecil Fielder	.15
10	Juan Gonzalez	.40
11	Ken Griffey Jr.	2.00
12	Kenny Lofton	.25
13	Greg Maddux	.75
14	Fred McGriff	.15
15	Mike Piazza	1.50
16	Kirby Puckett	.75
17	Tim Salmon	.15
18	Frank Thomas	.50
19	Mo Vaughn	.15
20	Matt Williams	.15

Update Rookie Update

Ten of 1995's top rookies are featured in this horizontally formatted insert set. Fronts have an action photo with a large gold-foil "ROOKIE UPDATE" headline at top. Backs have another photo and career summary. Rookie Update chase cards are found on the average of one per four packs.

		NM/M
Complete Set (10):		4.00
Common Player:		.10
1	Shane Andrews	.10
2	Ray Durham	.10
3	Shawn Green	.40
4	Charles Johnson	.10
5	Chipper Jones	1.50
6	Esteban Loaiza	.10
7	Hideo Nomo	1.00
8	Jon Nunnally	.10
9	Alex Rodriguez	2.00
10	Julian Tavarez	.10

Update Smooth Leather

These inserts featuring top fielders were found only in pre-priced (magazine) foil packs, at an average rate of one card per 12 packs. Fronts are highlighted with gold-foil graphics. Backs have a glove in the background and explain the player's defensive abilities.

		NM/M
Complete Set (10):		7.50
Common Player:		.25
1	Roberto Alomar	.50
2	Barry Bonds	2.50
3	Ken Griffey Jr.	1.50
4	Marquis Grissom	.25
5	Darren Lewis	.25
6	Kenny Lofton	.25
7	Don Mattingly	1.00
8	Cal Ripken Jr.	2.50
9	Ivan Rodriguez	.75
10	Matt Williams	.25

Update Soaring Stars

A metallic foil-etched background behind the color player action photo identifies this chase set as the toughest among those in the 1995 Fleer Update issue. The Soaring Star cards are found at the average rate of one per box. Backs are conventionally printed and featured a colorful posterized version of the front background, along with another color photo and a career summary.

		NM/M
Complete Set (9):		3.50
Common Player:		.15
1	Moises Alou	.35
2	Jason Bere	.25
3	Jeff Conine	.25
4	Cliff Floyd	.25
5	Pat Hentgen	.25
6	Kenny Lofton	.25
7	Raul Mondesi	.25
8	Mike Piazza	3.00
9	Tim Salmon	.35

Panini Stickers

Following Fleer's purchase of the well-known Italian sticker company, Panini, it was no surprise to see the companies produce a 1995 baseball issue. Titled "Major League Baseball All-Stars," the set consists of 156 player and team logo stickers. A 36-page color album to house the stickers was sold for $1.19. Sold in six-sticker packs for about .50, the indi-vidual stickers measure 1-15/16"x3". Borders are team color-coded and have the player name and team logo at bottom, with the position abbreviation in a diamond at top-right. Backs are printed in black-and-white and include a sticker number, copyright notice and large logos of the licensors and Fleer/Panini. Each sticker can be found with backs that do, or do not, include a promotional message beginning, "Collect all 156 . . ."

		NM/M
Complete Set (156):		3.00
Common Player:		.05
Album:		1.00
Wax Pack (6):		.25
Wax Box (100):		15.00
1	Tom Glavine	.15
2	Doug Drabek	.05
3	Rod Beck	.05
4	Pedro J. Martinez	.25
5	Danny Jackson	.05
6	Greg Maddux	.30
7	Bret Saberhagen	.05
8	Ken Hill	.05
9	Marvin Freeman	.05
10	Andy Benes	.05
11	Wilson Alvarez	.05
12	Jimmy Key	.05
13	Mike Mussina	.15
14	Roger Clemens	.35
15	Pat Hentgen	.05
16	Randy Johnson	.25
17	Lee Smith	.05
18	David Cone	.05
19	Jason Bere	.05
20	Dennis Martinez	.05
21	Darren Daulton	.05
22	Darrin Fletcher	.05
23	Tom Pagnozzi	.05
24	Mike Piazza	.40
25	Benito Santiago	.05
26	Sandy Alomar Jr.	.05
27	Chris Hoiles	.05
28	Ivan Rodriguez	.20
29	Mike Stanley	.05
30	Dave Nilsson	.05
31	Jeff Bagwell	.25
32	Mark Grace	.10
33	Gregg Jefferies	.05
34	Andres Galarraga	.05
35	Fred McGriff	.10
36	Will Clark	.10
37	Mo Vaughn	.05
38	Don Mattingly	.35
39	Frank Thomas	.25
40	Cecil Fielder	.05
41	Robby Thompson	.05
42	Delino DeShields	.05
43	Carlos Garcia	.05
44	Bret Boone	.05
45	Craig Biggio	.05
46	Roberto Alomar	.10
47	Chuck Knoblauch	.05
48	Jose Lind	.05
49	Carlos Baerga	.05
50	Lou Whitaker	.05
51	Bobby Bonilla	.05
52	Tim Wallach	.05
53	Todd Zeile	.05
54	Matt Williams	.05
55	Ken Caminiti	.05
56	Robin Ventura	.05
57	Wade Boggs	.30
58	Scott Cooper	.05
59	Travis Fryman	.05
60	Dean Palmer	.05
61	Jay Bell	.05
62	Barry Larkin	.05
63	Ozzie Smith	.30
64	Wil Cordero	.05
65	Royce Clayton	.05
66	Chris Gomez	.05
67	Ozzie Guillen	.05
68	Cal Ripken Jr.	.05
69	Omar Vizquel	.05
70	Gary DiSarcina	.05
71	Dante Bichette	.05
72	Lenny Dykstra	.05
73	Barry Bonds	.50
74	Gary Sheffield	.20
75	Larry Walker	.05
76	Raul Mondesi	.05
77	Dave Justice	.05
78	Moises Alou	.05
79	Tony Gwynn	.30
80	Deion Sanders	.05
81	Kenny Lofton	.05
82	Kirby Puckett	.30
83	Juan Gonzalez	.20
84	Jay Buhner	.05
85	Joe Carter	.05
86	Ken Griffey Jr.	.40
87	Ruben Sierra	.05
88	Tim Salmon	.05
89	Paul O'Neill	.05
90	Albert Belle	.05
91	Danny Tartabull	.05
92	Jose Canseco	.20
93	Harold Baines	.05
94	Kirk Gibson	.05
95	Chili Davis	.05
96	Eddie Murray	.25
97	Bob Hamelin	.05
98	Paul Molitor	.25
99	Raul Mondesi	.05
100	Ryan Klesko	.05
101	Cliff Floyd	.05
102	William Van Landingham	.05
103	Joey Hamilton	.05
104	John Hudek	.05
105	Manny Ramirez	.25
106	Bob Hamelin	.05
107	Rusty Greer	.05
108	Chris Gomez	.05
109	Greg Maddux	.20
110	Jeff Bagwell	.15
111	Raul Mondesi	.05
112	David Cone	.05
113	Frank Thomas	.25
114	Bob Hamelin	.05
115	Tony Gwynn	.20
116	Matt Williams	.05
117	Jeff Bagwell	.15
118	Craig Biggio	.05
119	Andy Benes	.05
120	Greg Maddux	.20
121	John Franco	.05
122	Paul O'Neill	.05
123	Ken Griffey Jr.	.35
124	Kirby Puckett	.20
125	Kenny Lofton	.05
126	Randy Johnson	.05
127	Jimmy Key	.05
128	Lee Smith	.05
129	San Francisco Giants Logo	.05
130	Montreal Expos Logo	.05
131	Cincinnati Reds Logo	.05
132	Los Angeles Dodgers Logo	.05
133	New York Mets Logo	.05
134	San Diego Padres Logo	.05
135	Colorado Rockies Logo	.05
136	Pittsburgh Pirates Logo	.05
137	Florida Marlins Logo	.05
138	Philadelphia Phillies Logo	.05
139	Atlanta Braves Logo	.05
140	Houston Astros Logo	.05
141	St. Louis Cardinals Logo	.05
142	Chicago Cubs Logo	.05
143	Cleveland Indians Logo	.05
144	New York Yankees Logo	.05
145	Kansas City Royals Logo	.05
146	Chicago White Sox Logo	.05
147	Baltimore Orioles Logo	.05
148	Seattle Mariners Logo	.05
149	Boston Red Sox Logo	.05
150	California Angels Logo	.05
151	Toronto Blue Jays Logo	.05
152	Detroit Tigers Logo	.05
153	Texas Rangers Logo	.05
154	Oakland A's Logo	.05
155	Milwaukee Brewers Logo	.05
156	Minnesota Twins Logo	.05

Revco Cleveland Indians

In the midst of their pennant winning season in 1995, the Cleveland Indians were the subject of a special "Update" set produced by Fleer and sold exclusively by Revco stores and the team itself. Seventeen of the 20 cards in the set are virtually identical to the regular-issue 1995 Fleer cards, except for a change in card number on the back, designating each card as "X of 20," and the use of silver foil on front, as opposed to the gold foil found on regular cards. The Dave Winfield card in the Update issue pictures him in an Indians uniform, instead of the Twins uniform in which he appears in the regular set. Logo and checklist cards were added to the team set. Cards were sold in 10-card foil packs.

		NM/M
Complete Set (20):		6.00
Common Player:		.10
1	Sandy Alomar Jr.	.10
2	Carlos Baerga	.10
3	Albert Belle	.10
4	Mark Clark	.10
5	Alvaro Espinoza	.10
6	Wayne Kirby	.10
7	Kenny Lofton	.10
8	Dennis Martinez	.10
9	Jose Mesa	.10
10	Eddie Murray	2.00
11	Charles Nagy	.10
12	Tony Pena	.10
13	Eric Plunk	.10
14	Manny Ramirez	2.00
15	Paul Sorrento	.10
16	Jim Thome	1.00
17	Omar Vizquel	.10
18	Dave Winfield	2.00
19	Indians/Fleer Logo Card	.05
20	Checklist/Indians Logo	.05

1996 Fleer

In a radical departure from the UV-coated standard for even base-brand baseball cards, Fleer's 1996 issue is printed on a matte surface. Fronts feature borderless game-action photos with minimal (player ID, Fleer logo) graphic enhancement in gold foil. Backs have a white background, a portrait photo, full pro stats and a few career highlights. The single-series set was sold in basic 11-card packs with one of nearly a dozen insert-set cards in each $1.49 pack. The set is arranged alphabetically by player within team and league. A glossy-surface Tiffany Collection parallel was included in each pack.

		NM/M
Complete Set (600):		20.00
Common Player:		.05
Complete Tiffany Set (600):		100.00
Tiffanies:		2X
Pack (11):		.75
Wax Box (36):		16.00
1	Manny Alexander	.05
2	Brady Anderson	.05
3	Harold Baines	.05
4	Armando Benitez	.05
5	Bobby Bonilla	.05
6	Kevin Brown	.05
7	Scott Erickson	.05
8	Curtis Goodwin	.05
9	Jeffrey Hammonds	.05
10	Jimmy Haynes	.05
11	Chris Hoiles	.05
12	Doug Jones	.05
13	Rick Krivda	.05
14	Jeff Manto	.05
15	Ben McDonald	.05
16	Jamie Moyer	.05
17	Mike Mussina	.50
18	Jesse Orosco	.05
19	Rafael Palmeiro	.65
20	Cal Ripken Jr.	2.50
20(p)	Cal Ripken Jr./OPS	2.50
21	Rick Aguilera	.05
22	Luis Alicea	.05
23	Stan Belinda	.05
24	Jose Canseco	.50
25	Roger Clemens	1.25
26	Vaughn Eshelman	.05
27	Mike Greenwell	.05
28	Erik Hanson	.05
29	Dwayne Hosey	.05
30	Mike Macfarlane	.05
31	Tim Naehring	.05
32	Troy O'Leary	.05
33	Aaron Sele	.05
34	Zane Smith	.05
35	Jeff Suppan	.05
36	Lee Tinsley	.05
37	John Valentin	.05
38	Mo Vaughn	.05
39	Tim Wakefield	.05
40	Jim Abbott	.05
41	Brian Anderson	.05
42	Garret Anderson	.05
43	Chili Davis	.05
44	Gary DiSarcina	.05
45	Damion Easley	.05
46	Jim Edmonds	.05
47	Chuck Finley	.05
48	Todd Greene	.05
49	Mike Harkey	.05
50	Mike James	.05
51	Mark Langston	.05
52	Greg Myers	.05
53	Orlando Palmeiro	.05
54	Bob Patterson	.05
55	Troy Percival	.05
56	Tony Phillips	.05
57	Tim Salmon	.10
58	Lee Smith	.05
59	J.T. Snow	.05
60	Randy Velarde	.05
61	Wilson Alvarez	.05
62	Luis Andujar RC	.05
63	Jason Bere	.05
64	Ray Durham	.05
65	Alex Fernandez	.05
66	Ozzie Guillen	.05
67	Roberto Hernandez	.05
68	Lance Johnson	.05
69	Matt Karchner	.05
70	Ron Karkovice	.05
71	Norberto Martin	.05
72	Dave Martinez	.05
73	Kirk McCaskill	.05
74	Lyle Mouton	.05
75	Tim Raines	.05
76	Mike Sirotka RC	.05
77	Frank Thomas	.75
78	Larry Thomas	.05
79	Robin Ventura	.05
80	Sandy Alomar Jr.	.05
81	Paul Assenmacher	.05
82	Carlos Baerga	.05
83	Albert Belle	.05
84	Mark Clark	.05
85	Alan Embree	.05
86	Alvaro Espinoza	.05
87	Orel Hershiser	.05
88	Ken Hill	.05
89	Kenny Lofton	.05
90	Dennis Martinez	.05
91	Jose Mesa	.05
92	Eddie Murray	.75
93	Charles Nagy	.05
94	Chad Ogea	.05
95	Tony Pena	.05
96	Herb Perry	.05
97	Eric Plunk	.05
98	Jim Poole	.05
99	Manny Ramirez	.75
100	Paul Sorrento	.05
101	Julian Travarez	.05
102	Jim Thome	.60
103	Omar Vizquel	.05
104	Dave Winfield	.75
105	Danny Bautista	.05
106	Joe Boever	.05
107	Chad Curtis	.05
108	John Doherty	.05
109	Cecil Fielder	.05
110	John Flaherty	.05
111	Travis Fryman	.05
112	Chris Gomez	.05
113	Bob Higginson	.05
114	Mark Lewis	.05
115	Jose Lima	.05
116	Felipe Lira	.05
117	Brian Maxcy	.05
118	C.J. Nitkowski	.05
119	Phil Plantier	.05
120	Clint Sodowsky	.05
121	Alan Trammell	.05
122	Lou Whitaker	.05
123	Kevin Appier	.05
124	Johnny Damon	.35
125	Gary Gaetti	.05
126	Tom Goodwin	.05
127	Tom Gordon	.05
128	Mark Gubicza	.05
129	Bob Hamelin	.05
130	David Howard	.05
131	Jason Jacome	.05
132	Wally Joyner	.05
133	Keith Lockhart	.05
134	Brent Mayne	.05
135	Jeff Montgomery	.05
136	Jon Nunnally	.05
137	Juan Samuel	.05
138	Mike Sweeney RC	.50
139	Michael Tucker	.05
140	Joe Vitiello	.05
141	Ricky Bones	.05
142	Chuck Carr	.05
143	Jeff Cirillo	.05
144	Mike Fetters	.05
145	Darryl Hamilton	.05
146	David Hulse	.05
147	John Jaha	.05
148	Scott Karl	.05
149	Mark Kiefer	.05
150	Pat Listach	.05

151	Mark Loretta	.05	269	Tony Castillo	.05	387	Chris Hammond	.05

No.	Player	Price	No.	Player	Price	No.	Player	Price	No.	Player	Price
151	Mark Loretta	.05	269	Tony Castillo	.05	387	Chris Hammond	.05	505	Mickey Morandini	.05
152	Mike Matheny	.05	270	Domingo Cedeno	.05	388	Charles Johnson	.05	506	Gene Schall	.05
153	Matt Mieske	.05	271	Timothy Crabtree	.05	389	Terry Mathews	.05	507	Curt Schilling	.25
154	Dave Nilsson	.05	272	Carlos Delgado	.60	390	Robb Nen	.05	508	Heathcliff Slocumb	.05
155	Joe Oliver	.05	273	Alex Gonzalez	.05	391	Joe Orsulak	.05	509	Kevin Stocker	.05
156	Al Reyes	.05	274	Shawn Green	.20	392	Terry Pendleton	.05	510	Andy Van Slyke	.05
157	Kevin Seitzer	.05	275	Juan Guzman	.05	393	Pat Rapp	.05	511	Lenny Webster	.05
158	Steve Sparks	.05	276	Pat Hentgen	.05	394	Gary Sheffield	.45	512	Mark Whiten	.05
159	B.J. Surhoff	.05	277	Al Leiter	.05	395	Jesus Tavarez	.05	513	Melvin Williams	.05
160	Jose Valentin	.05	278	Sandy Martinez RC	.05	396	Marc Valdes	.05	514	Jay Bell	.05
161	Greg Vaughn	.05	279	Paul Menhart	.05	397	Quilvio Veras	.05	515	Jacob Brumfield	.05
162	Fernando Vina	.05	280	John Olerud	.05	398	Randy Veres	.05	516	Jason Christiansen	.05
163	Rich Becker	.05	281	Paul Quantrill	.05	399	Devon White	.05	517	Dave Clark	.05
164	Ron Coomer	.05	282	Ken Robinson	.05	400	Jeff Bagwell	.75	518	Midre Cummings	.05
165	Marty Cordova	.05	283	Ed Sprague	.05	401	Derek Bell	.05	519	Angelo Encarnacion	.05
166	Chuck Knoblauch	.05	284	Mike Timlin	.05	402	Craig Biggio	.05	520	John Ericks	.05
167	Matt Lawton RC	.30	285	Steve Avery	.05	403	John Cangelosi	.05	521	Carlos Garcia	.05
168	Pat Meares	.05	286	Rafael Belliard	.05	404	Jim Dougherty	.05	522	Mark Johnson	.05
169	Paul Molitor	.75	287	Jeff Blauser	.05	405	Doug Drabek	.05	523	Jeff King	.05
170	Pedro Munoz	.05	288	Pedro Borbon	.05	406	Tony Eusebio	.05	524	Nelson Liriano	.05
171	Jose Parra	.05	289	Brad Clontz	.05	407	Ricky Gutierrez	.05	525	Esteban Loaiza	.05
172	Kirby Puckett	1.00	290	Mike Devereaux	.05	408	Mike Hampton	.05	526	Al Martin	.05
173	Brad Radke	.05	291	Tom Glavine	.25	409	Dean Hartgraves	.05	527	Orlando Merced	.05
174	Jeff Reboulet	.05	292	Marquis Grissom	.05	410	John Hudek	.05	528	Dan Miceli	.05
175	Rich Robertson	.05	293	Chipper Jones	1.00	411	Brian Hunter	.05	529	Ramon Morel	.05
176	Frank Rodriguez	.05	294	David Justice	.05	412	Todd Jones	.05	530	Denny Neagle	.05
177	Scott Stahoviak	.05	295	Mike Kelly	.05	413	Darryl Kile	.05	531	Steve Parris	.05
178	Dave Stevens	.05	296	Ryan Klesko	.05	414	Dave Magadan	.05	532	Dan Plesac	.05
179	Matt Walbeck	.05	297	Mark Lemke	.05	415	Derrick May	.05	533	Don Slaught	.05
180	Wade Boggs	1.00	298	Javier Lopez	.05	416	Orlando Miller	.05	534	Paul Wagner	.05
181	David Cone	.05	299	Greg Maddux	1.00	417	James Mouton	.05	535	John Wehner	.05
182	Tony Fernandez	.05	300	Fred McGriff	.05	418	Shane Reynolds	.05	536	Kevin Young	.05
183	Joe Girardi	.05	301	Greg McMichael	.05	419	Greg Swindell	.05	537	Allen Battle	.05
184	Derek Jeter	2.50	302	Kent Mercker	.05	420	Jeff Tabaka	.05	538	David Bell	.05
185	Scott Kamieniecki	.05	303	Mike Mordecai	.05	421	Dave Veres	.05	539	Alan Benes	.05
186	Pat Kelly	.05	304	Charlie O'Brien	.05	422	Billy Wagner	.05	540	Scott Cooper	.05
187	Jim Leyritz	.05	305	Eduardo Perez	.05	423	Donne Wall RC	.05	541	Tripp Cromer	.05
188	Tino Martinez	.05	306	Luis Polonia	.05	424	Rick Wilkins	.05	542	Tony Fossas	.05
189	Don Mattingly	1.25	307	Jason Schmidt	.05	425	Billy Ashley	.05	543	Bernard Gilkey	.05
190	Jack McDowell	.05	308	John Smoltz	.05	426	Mike Blowers	.05	544	Tom Henke	.05
191	Jeff Nelson	.05	309	Terrell Wade	.05	427	Brett Butler	.05	545	Brian Jordan	.05
192	Paul O'Neill	.05	310	Mark Wohlers	.05	428	Tom Candiotti	.05	546	Ray Lankford	.05
193	Melido Perez	.05	311	Scott Bullett	.05	429	Juan Castro	.05	547	John Mabry	.05
194	Andy Pettitte	.30	312	Jim Bullinger	.05	430	Jim Cummings	.05	548	T.J. Mathews	.05
195	Mariano Rivera	.15	313	Larry Casian	.05	431	Delino DeShields	.05	549	Mike Morgan	.05
196	Ruben Sierra	.05	314	Frank Castillo	.05	432	Joey Eischen	.05	550	Jose Oliva	.05
197	Mike Stanley	.05	315	Shawon Dunston	.05	433	Chad Fonville	.05	551	Jose Oquendo	.05
198	Darryl Strawberry	.05	316	Kevin Foster	.05	434	Greg Gagne	.05	552	Donovan Osborne	.05
199	John Wetteland	.05	317	Matt Franco	.05	435	Dave Hansen	.05	553	Tom Pagnozzi	.05
200	Bob Wickman	.05	318	Luis Gonzalez	.10	436	Carlos Hernandez	.05	554	Mark Petkovsek	.05
201	Bernie Williams	.10	319	Mark Grace	.05	437	Todd Hollandsworth	.05	555	Danny Sheaffer	.05
202	Mark Acre	.05	320	Jose Hernandez	.05	438	Eric Karros	.05	556	Ozzie Smith	1.00
203	Geronimo Berroa	.05	321	Mike Hubbard	.05	439	Roberto Kelly	.05	557	Mark Sweeney	.05
204	Mike Bordick	.05	322	Brian McRae	.05	440	Ramon Martinez	.05	558	Allen Watson	.05
205	Scott Brosius	.05	323	Randy Myers	.05	441	Raul Mondesi	.05	559	Andy Ashby	.05
206	Dennis Eckersley	.65	324	Jaime Navarro	.05	442	Hideo Nomo	.65	560	Brad Ausmus	.05
207	Brent Gates	.05	325	Mark Parent	.05	443	Antonio Osuna	.05	561	Willie Blair	.05
208	Jason Giambi	.60	326	Mike Perez	.05	444	Chan Ho Park	.05	562	Ken Caminiti	.05
209	Rickey Henderson	.75	327	Rey Sanchez	.05	445	Mike Piazza	1.75	563	Andujar Cedeno	.05
210	Jose Herrera	.05	328	Ryne Sandberg	1.00	446	Felix Rodriguez	.05	564	Glenn Dishman	.05
211	Stan Javier	.05	329	Scott Servais	.05	447	Kevin Tapani	.05	565	Steve Finley	.05
212	Doug Johns	.05	330	Sammy Sosa	1.50	448	Ismael Valdes	.05	566	Bryce Florie	.05
213	Mark McGwire	2.00	331	Ozzie Timmons	.05	449	Todd Worrell	.05	567	Tony Gwynn	1.00
214	Steve Ontiveros	.05	332	Steve Trachsel	.05	450	Moises Alou	.05	568	Joey Hamilton	.05
215	Craig Paquette	.05	333	Todd Zeile	.05	451	Shane Andrews	.05	569	Dustin Hermanson	.05
216	Ariel Prieto	.05	334	Bret Boone	.10	452	Yamil Benitez	.05	570	Trevor Hoffman	.05
217	Carlos Reyes	.05	335	Jeff Branson	.05	453	Sean Berry	.05	571	Brian Johnson	.05
218	Terry Steinbach	.05	336	Jeff Brantley	.05	454	Wil Cordero	.05	572	Marc Kroon	.05
219	Todd Stottlemyre	.05	337	Dave Burba	.05	455	Jeff Fassero	.05	573	Scott Livingstone	.05
220	Danny Tartabull	.05	338	Hector Carrasco	.05	456	Darrin Fletcher	.05	574	Marc Newfield	.05
221	Todd Van Poppel	.05	339	Mariano Duncan	.05	457	Cliff Floyd	.05	575	Melvin Nieves	.05
222	John Wasdin	.05	340	Ron Gant	.05	458	Mark Grudzielanek	.05	576	Jody Reed	.05
223	George Williams	.05	341	Lenny Harris	.05	459	Gil Heredia	.05	577	Bip Roberts	.05
224	Steve Wojciechowski	.05	342	Xavier Hernandez	.05	460	Tim Laker	.05	578	Scott Sanders	.05
225	Rich Amaral	.05	343	Thomas Howard	.05	461	Mike Lansing	.05	579	Fernando Valenzuela	.05
226	Bobby Ayala	.05	344	Mike Jackson	.05	462	Pedro Martinez	.75	580	Eddie Williams	.05
227	Tim Belcher	.05	345	Barry Larkin	.05	463	Carlos Perez	.05	581	Rod Beck	.05
228	Andy Benes	.05	346	Darren Lewis	.05	464	Curtis Pride	.05	582	Marvin Benard RC	.10
229	Chris Bosio	.05	347	Hal Morris	.05	465	Mel Rojas	.05	583	Barry Bonds	2.50
230	Darren Bragg	.05	348	Eric Owens	.05	466	Kirk Rueter	.05	584	Jamie Brewington	.05
231	Jay Buhner	.05	349	Mark Portugal	.05	467	F.P. Santangelo RC	.05	585	Mark Carreon	.05
232	Norm Charlton	.05	350	Jose Rijo	.05	468	Tim Scott	.05	586	Royce Clayton	.05
233	Vince Coleman	.05	351	Reggie Sanders	.05	469	David Segui	.05	587	Shawn Estes	.05
234	Joey Cora	.05	352	Benito Santiago	.05	470	Tony Tarasco	.05	588	Glenallen Hill	.05
235	Russ Davis	.05	353	Pete Schourek	.05	471	Rondell White	.05	589	Mark Leiter	.05
236	Alex Diaz	.05	354	John Smiley	.05	472	Edgardo Alfonzo	.05	590	Kirt Manwaring	.05
237	Felix Fermin	.05	355	Eddie Taubensee	.05	473	Tim Bogar	.05	591	David McCarty	.05
238	Ken Griffey Jr.	1.75	356	Jerome Walton	.05	474	Rico Brogna	.05	592	Terry Mulholland	.05
239	Sterling Hitchcock	.05	357	David Wells	.05	475	Damon Buford	.05	593	John Patterson	.05
240	Randy Johnson	.75	358	Roger Bailey	.05	476	Paul Byrd	.05	594	J.R. Phillips	.05
241	Edgar Martinez	.05	359	Jason Bates	.05	477	Carl Everett	.10	595	Deion Sanders	.05
242	Bill Risley	.05	360	Dante Bichette	.05	478	John Franco	.05	596	Steve Scarsone	.05
243	Alex Rodriguez	2.00	361	Ellis Burks	.05	479	Todd Hundley	.05	597	Robby Thompson	.05
244	Luis Sojo	.05	362	Vinny Castilla	.05	480	Butch Huskey	.05	598	Sergio Valdez	.05
245	Dan Wilson	.05	363	Andres Galarraga	.05	481	Jason Isringhausen	.05	599	William Van Landingham	.05
246	Bob Wolcott	.05	364	Darren Holmes	.05	482	Bobby Jones	.05	600	Matt Williams	.05
247	Will Clark	.10	365	Mike Kingery	.05	483	Chris Jones	.05			
248	Jeff Frye	.05	366	Curt Leskanic	.05	484	Jeff Kent	.10			
249	Benji Gil	.05	367	Quinton McCracken	.05	485	Dave Mlicki	.05			
250	Juan Gonzalez	.65	368	Mike Munoz	.05	486	Robert Person	.05			
251	Rusty Greer	.05	369	David Nied	.05	487	Bill Pulsipher	.05			
252	Kevin Gross	.05	370	Steve Reed	.05	488	Kelly Stinnett	.05			
253	Roger McDowell	.05	371	Bruce Rekar	.05	489	Ryan Thompson	.05			
254	Mark McLemore	.05	372	Kevin Ritz	.05	490	Jose Vizcaino	.05			
255	Otis Nixon	.05	373	Bruce Ruffin	.05	491	Howard Battle	.05			
256	Luis Ortiz	.05	374	Bret Saberhagen	.05	492	Toby Borland	.05			
257	Mike Pagliarulo	.05	375	Bill Swift	.05	493	Ricky Bottalico	.05			
258	Dean Palmer	.05	376	John Vander Wal	.05	494	Darren Daulton	.05			
259	Roger Pavlik	.05	377	Larry Walker	.05	495	Lenny Dykstra	.05			
260	Ivan Rodriguez	.65	378	Walt Weiss	.05	496	Jim Eisenreich	.05			
261	Kenny Rogers	.05	379	Eric Young	.05	497	Sid Fernandez	.05			
262	Jeff Russell	.05	380	Kurt Abbott	.05	498	Tyler Green	.05			
263	Mickey Tettleton	.05	381	Alex Arias	.05	499	Charlie Hayes	.05			
264	Bob Tewksbury	.05	382	Jerry Browne	.05	500	Gregg Jefferies	.05			
265	Dave Valle	.05	383	John Burkett	.05	501	Kevin Jordan	.05			
266	Matt Whiteside	.05	384	Greg Colbrunn	.05	502	Tony Longmire	.05			
267	Roberto Alomar	.30	385	Jeff Conine	.05	503	Tom Marsh	.05			
268	Joe Carter	.05	386	Andre Dawson	.35	504	Michael Mimbs	.05			

While Fleer's basic card set for 1996 feature matte-surface cards, a glossy version of each regular card was also issued as a parallel insert set. Other than the UV coating on front and back and the use of silver- rather than gold-foil typography on front, the cards are identical to the regular '96 Fleer player cards. One glossy version card is found in each pack.

	NM/M
Complete Set (600):	100.00
Common Player:	.15
Stars:	2X

Checklists

Checklist cards are treated as an insert set in 1996 Fleer, appearing on average once every six packs. Like all other Fleer hobby inserts in the baseball set, the checklists are UV-coated front and back, in contrast to the matte-finish regular issue cards. Checklists have borderless game-action photos on front, with gold-foil typography. Backs have a large Fleer logo and checklist data on a white background.

		NM/M
Complete Set (10):		5.00
Common Player:		.25
1	Barry Bonds	2.00
2	Ken Griffey Jr.	1.00
3	Chipper Jones	.75
4	Greg Maddux	.75
5	Mike Piazza	1.00
6	Manny Ramirez	.60
7	Cal Ripken Jr.	2.00
8	Frank Thomas	.60
9	Mo Vaughn	.25
10	Matt Williams	.25

Golden Memories

Some of the 1995 season's greatest moments are captured in this insert set, a one per 10 pack pick. Fronts have two photos of the player, one in full color in the foreground and one in monochrome as a backdrop. Typography is in prismatic foil vertically down one side. Backs have another color player photo, along with details of the milestone. Two of the cards feature multiple players.

		NM/M
Complete Set (10):		6.00
Common Player:		.10
1	Albert Belle	.10
2	Barry Bonds, Sammy Sosa	1.50
3	Greg Maddux	1.00
4	Edgar Martinez	.10
5	Ramon Martinez	.10
6	Mark McGwire	1.50
7	Eddie Murray	.50
8	Cal Ripken Jr.	2.00
9	Frank Thomas	.75
10	Alan Trammell, Lou Whitaker	.15

Tiffany

Lumber Company

Once again for 1996, a Fleer "Lumber Company" chase set honors the game's top sluggers. The '96 version has a horizontal format with a rather small player action photo on a background resembling the trademark area of a bat. The "trademark" is actually the player and team name along with the "Lumber Company" ID, printed in textured glossy black ink. Backs repeat the trademark motif and also include a close-up player photo and a few words about his power-hitting numbers. Lumber Company cards are a one per nine pack pick, on average, found only in retail packs.

		NM/M
Complete Set (12):		12.50
Common Player:		.50
1	Albert Belle	.50
2	Dante Bichette	.50
3	Barry Bonds	3.00
4	Ken Griffey Jr.	1.50
5	Mark McGwire	2.00
6	Mike Piazza	1.50
7	Manny Ramirez	1.00
8	Tim Salmon	.60
9	Sammy Sosa	1.25
10	Frank Thomas	1.00
11	Mo Vaughn	.50
12	Matt Williams	.50

Post-Season Glory

Highlights of the 1995 post-season are featured in this small chase card set. Against a stadium background are multiple photos of the featured player, arranged horizontally. The vertical backs have another player photo down one side, and a description of his playoff performance on the other. Stated odds of picking one of these cards are one per five packs.

		NM/M
Complete Set (5):		1.50
Common Player:		.15
1	Tom Glavine	.25
2	Ken Griffey Jr.	1.00
3	Orel Hershiser	.15
4	Randy Johnson	.50
5	Jim Thome	.50

Prospects

Minor leaguers who are expected to make it big in the big time are featured in this insert issue. Fronts feature large portrait photos against pastel backgrounds with player and set ID in prismatic foil. Backs have an action photo and repeat the front background color in a box which details the player's potential and career to date. Average odds of finding a Prospects card are one per six packs.

	NM/M
Complete Set (10):	1.00
Common Player:	.15
1 Yamil Benitez	.15
2 Roger Cedeno	.15
3 Tony Clark	.15
4 Micah Franklin	.15
5 Karim Garcia	.30
6 Todd Greene	.15
7 Alex Ochoa	.15
8 Ruben Rivera	.15
9 Chris Snopek	.15
10 Shannon Stewart	.15

Road Warriors

A black-and-white country highway photo is the background for the color player action photo on this insert set. Front typography is in silver foil. The players featured are those whose performance on the road is considered outstanding. Backs have a white background, portrait photo and stats bearing out the away-game superiority. These inserts are found at an average pace of one per 13 packs.

	NM/M
Complete Set (10):	9.00
Common Player:	.40
1 Derek Bell	.40
2 Tony Gwynn	1.25
3 Greg Maddux	1.25
4 Mark McGwire	2.50
5 Mike Piazza	2.00
6 Manny Ramirez	1.00
7 Tim Salmon	.50
8 Frank Thomas	1.00
9 Mo Vaughn	1.00
10 Matt Williams	.40

Rookie Sensations

Top rookies of the 1995 season are featured on this chase card set. Horizontally formatted, the cards have an action photo on one side and a large prismatic-foil end strip which displays the player name, team logo and card company identifiers. Backs have a portrait photo on a white background with a few sentences about the player's rookie season. Stated odds of finding one of these inserts is one per 11 packs, on average.

	NM/M
Complete Set (15):	5.00
Common Player:	.25
1 Garret Anderson	.40
2 Marty Cordova	.25
3 Johnny Damon	1.00
4 Ray Durham	.25
5 Carl Everett	.25
6 Shawn Green	.50
7 Brian Hunter	.25
8 Jason Isringhausen	.25
9 Charles Johnson	.25
10 Chipper Jones	2.00
11 John Mabry	.25
12 Hideo Nomo	1.00
13 Troy Percival	.25
14 Andy Pettitte	.50
15 Quilvio Veras	.25

Smoke 'N Heat

Once more using the "Smoke 'N Heat" identifier for a chase set of the game's hardest throwers, Fleer presents these select pitchers in action photos against a black-and-flame background. Front typography is in gold foil. Backs have a large portrait photo, repeat the flame motif as background and have a description of the pitcher's prowess in a black box. The cards are found, on average, once per nine packs.

	NM/M
Complete Set (10):	4.00
Common Player:	.15
1 Kevin Appier	.15
2 Roger Clemens	1.50
3 David Cone	.15
4 Chuck Finley	.15
5 Randy Johnson	.75
6 Greg Maddux	1.00
7 Pedro Martinez	.75
8 Hideo Nomo	.50
9 John Smoltz	.30
10 Todd Stottlemyre	.15

Team Leaders

One player from each club has been selected for inclusion in the "Team Leaders" chase set. Fronts have action player photos on a background of metallic foil littered with multiple representations of the team logo. Gold-foil lettering identifies the player, team and chase set. Backs have a white background, portrait photo and description of the player's leadership role. Stated rate of insertion for this set is one card per nine packs, on average, found only in hobby packs.

	NM/M
Complete Set (28):	30.00
Common Player:	.40
1 Cal Ripken Jr.	6.00
2 Mo Vaughn	.50
3 Jim Edmonds	1.00
4 Frank Thomas	2.00
5 Kenny Lofton	.50
6 Travis Fryman	.50
7 Gary Gaetti	.50
8 B.J. Surhoff	.50
9 Kirby Puckett	2.50
10 Don Mattingly	3.00
11 Mark McGwire	4.00
12 Ken Griffey Jr.	3.00
13 Juan Gonzalez	1.00
14 Joe Carter	.50
15 Greg Maddux	2.50
16 Sammy Sosa	3.00
17 Barry Larkin	.50
18 Dante Bichette	.50
19 Jeff Conine	.50
20 Jeff Bagwell	2.00
21 Mike Piazza	3.00
22 Rondell White	.50
23 Rico Brogna	.50
24 Darren Daulton	.50
25 Jeff King	.50
26 Ray Lankford	.50
27 Tony Gwynn	2.50
28 Barry Bonds	6.00

Tomorrow's Legends

In this insert set the projected stars of tomorrow are featured in action poses on a busy multi-colored, quartered background of baseball symbols and the globe. Typography is in silver foil. Backs have a portrait photo and large team logo along with an early-career summary. Odds of finding a "Tomorrow's Legends" card are posted at one per 13 packs, on average.

	NM/M
Complete Set (10):	3.50
Common Player:	.25
1 Garret Anderson	.25
2 Jim Edmonds	.50
3 Brian Hunter	.25
4 Jason Isringhausen	.25
5 Charles Johnson	.25
6 Chipper Jones	2.00
7 Ryan Klesko	.25
8 Hideo Nomo	1.00
9 Manny Ramirez	1.50
10 Rondell White	.25

Zone

The toughest pull (one in 90 packs, average) among the '96 Fleer chase cards is this set evoking the "zone" that the game's great players seek in which their performance is at its peak. The cards have action photos with a background of prismatic foil. Backs are conventionally printed but simulate the foil background and include a player portrait photo plus quotes about the player.

	NM/M
Complete Set (12):	20.00
Common Player:	.75
1 Albert Belle	.75
2 Barry Bonds	6.00
3 Ken Griffey Jr.	4.00
4 Tony Gwynn	3.00
5 Randy Johnson	2.00
6 Kenny Lofton	.50
7 Greg Maddux	3.00
8 Edgar Martinez	.75
9 Mike Piazza	4.00
10 Frank Thomas	2.00
11 Mo Vaughn	.75
12 Matt Williams	.75

Update

Fleer Update Baseball has 250 cards, including more than 55 rookies, plus traded players and free agents in their new uniforms, 35 Encore subset cards and five checklists. Each card in the regular-issue set also has a parallel "Tiffany Collection" version, which has UV coating and holographic foil stamping in contrast to the matte finish and gold foil of the regular cards. Insert cards include Diamond Tribute, New Horizons, Smooth Leather and Soaring Stars. Each pack also contains a Fleer "Thanks a Million" scratch-off game card, redeemable for prizes. Cards are numbered with a "U" prefix.

	NM/M
Complete Set (250):	12.00
Common Player:	.05
Complete Tiffany Set (250):	40.00
Tiffany Stars:	2X
Pack (11):	1.00
Wax Box (24):	15.00
1 Roberto Alomar	.10
2 Mike Devereaux	.05
3 Scott McClain RC	.05
4 Roger McDowell	.05
5 Kent Mercker	.05
6 Jimmy Myers	.05
7 Randy Myers	.05
8 B.J. Surhoff	.05
9 Tony Tarasco	.05
10 David Wells	.05
11 Wil Cordero	.05
12 Tom Gordon	.05
13 Reggie Jefferson	.05
14 Jose Malave	.05
15 Kevin Mitchell	.05
16 Jamie Moyer	.05
17 Heathcliff Slocumb	.05
18 Mike Stanley	.05
19 George Arias	.05
20 Jorge Fabregas	.05
21 Don Slaught	.05
22 Randy Velarde	.05
23 Harold Baines	.05
24 Mike Cameron RC	.75
25 Darren Lewis	.05
26 Tony Phillips	.05
27 Bill Simas	.05
28 Chris Snopek	.05
29 Kevin Tapani	.05
30 Danny Tartabull	.05
31 Julio Franco	.05
32 Jack McDowell	.05
33 Kimera Bartee	.05
34 Mark Lewis	.05
35 Melvin Nieves	.05
36 Mark Parent	.05
37 Eddie Williams	.05
38 Tim Belcher	.05
39 Sal Fasano	.05
40 Chris Haney	.05
41 Mike Macfarlane	.05
42 Jose Offerman	.05
43 Joe Randa	.05
44 Bip Roberts	.05
45 Chuck Carr	.05
46 Bobby Hughes	.05
47 Graeme Lloyd	.05
48 Ben McDonald	.05
49 Kevin Wickander	.05
50 Rick Aguilera	.05
51 Mike Durant	.05
52 Chip Hale	.05
53 LaTroy Hawkins	.05
54 Dave Hollins	.05
55 Roberto Kelly	.05
56 Paul Molitor	.75
57 Dan Naulty RC	.05
58 Mariano Duncan	.05
59 Andy Fox RC	.05
60 Jim Girardi	.05
61 Dwight Gooden	.05
62 Jimmy Key	.05
63 Matt Luke RC	.05
64 Tino Martinez	.05
65 Jeff Nelson	.05
66 Tim Raines	.05
67 Ruben Rivera	.05
68 Kenny Rogers	.05
69 Gerald Williams	.05
70 Tony Batista RC	.05
71 Allen Battle	.05
72 Jim Corsi	.05
73 Steve Cox	.05
74 Pedro Munoz	.05
75 Phil Plantier	.05
76 Scott Spiezio	.05
77 Ernie Young	.05
78 Russ Davis	.05
79 Sterling Hitchcock	.05
80 Edwin Hurtado	.05
81 Raul Ibanez RC	.05
82 Mike Jackson	.05
83 Ricky Jordan	.05
84 Paul Sorrento	.05
85 Doug Strange	.05
86 Mark Brandenburg	.05
87 Damon Buford	.05
88 Kevin Elster	.05
89 Darryl Hamilton	.05
90 Ken Hill	.05
91 Ed Vosberg	.05
92 Craig Worthington	.05
93 Tilson Brito	.05
94 Giovanni Carrara	.05
95 Felipe Crespo	.05
96 Erik Hanson	.05
97 Marty Janzen RC	.05
98 Otis Nixon	.05
99 Charlie O'Brien	.05
100 Robert Perez	.05
101 Paul Quantrill	.05
102 Bill Risley	.05
103 Juan Samuel	.05
104 Jermaine Dye	.05
105 Wonderful Monds	.05
106 Dwight Smith	.05
107 Jerome Walton	.05
108 Terry Adams	.05
109 Leo Gomez	.05
110 Robin Jennings RC	.05
111 Doug Jones	.05
112 Brooks Kieschnick	.05
113 Dave Magadan	.05
114 Jason Maxwell RC	.05
115 Rodney Myers	.05
116 Eric Anthony	.05
117 Vince Coleman	.05
118 Eric Davis	.05
119 Steve Gibralter	.05
120 Curtis Goodwin	.05
121 Willie Greene	.05
122 Mike Kelly	.05
123 Marcus Moore	.05
124 Chad Mottola	.05
125 Chris Sabo	.05
126 Roger Salkeld	.05
127 Pedro Castellano	.05
128 Trenidad Hubbard	.05
129 Jayhawk Owens	.05
130 Jeff Reed	.05
131 Kevin Brown	.05
132 Al Leiter	.05
133 Matt Mantei RC	.05
134 Dave Weathers	.05
135 Devon White	.05
136 Bob Abreu	.05
137 Sean Berry	.05
138 Doug Brocail	.05
139 Richard Hidalgo	.05
140 Alvin Morman	.05
141 Mike Blowers	.05
142 Roger Cedeno	.05
143 Greg Gagne	.05
144 Karim Garcia	.10
145 Wilton Guerrero RC	.05
146 Israel Alcantara RC	.05
147 Omar Daal	.05
148 Ryan McGuire	.05
149 Sherman Obando	.05
150 Jose Paniagua	.05
151 Henry Rodriguez	.05
152 Andy Stankiewicz	.05
153 Dave Veres	.05
154 Juan Acevedo	.05
155 Mark Clark	.05
156 Bernard Gilkey	.05
157 Pete Harnisch	.05
158 Lance Johnson	.05
159 Brent Mayne	.05
160 Rey Ordonez	.05
161 Kevin Roberson	.05
162 Paul Wilson	.05
163 David Doster RC	.05
164 Mike Grace RC	.05
165 Rich Hunter RC	.05
166 Pete Incaviglia	.05
167 Mike Lieberthal	.05
168 Terry Mulholland	.05
169 Ken Ryan	.05
170 Benito Santiago	.05
171 Kevin Sefcik RC	.05
172 Lee Tinsley	.05
173 Todd Zeile	.05
174 Francisco Cordova RC	.05
175 Danny Darwin	.05
176 Charlie Hayes	.05
177 Jason Kendall	.05
178 Mike Kingery	.05
179 Jon Lieber	.05
180 Zane Smith	.05
181 Luis Alicea	.05
182 Cory Bailey	.05
183 Andy Benes	.05
184 Pat Borders	.05
185 Mike Busby RC	.05
186 Royce Clayton	.05
187 Dennis Eckersley	.65
188 Gary Gaetti	.05
189 Ron Gant	.05
190 Aaron Holbert	.05
191 Willie McGee	.05
192 Miguel Mejia RC	.05
193 Jeff Parrett	.05
194 Todd Stottlemyre	.05
195 Sean Bergman	.05
196 Archi Cianfrocco	.05
197 Rickey Henderson	.75
198 Wally Joyner	.05
199 Craig Shipley	.05
200 Bob Tewksbury	.05
201 Tim Worrell	.05
202 Rich Aurilia RC	.05
203 Doug Creek	.05
204 Shawon Dunston	.05
205 Osvaldo Fernandez RC	.05
206 Mark Gardner	.05
207 Stan Javier	.05
208 Marcus Jensen	.05
209 Chris Singleton RC	.05
210 Allen Watson	.05
211 Jeff Bagwell (Encore)	.75
212 Derek Bell (Encore)	.05
213 Albert Belle (Encore)	.05
214 Wade Boggs (Encore)	1.00
215 Barry Bonds (Encore)	2.00
216 Jose Canseco (Encore)	.50
217 Marty Cordova (Encore)	.05
218 Jim Edmonds (Encore)	.05
219 Cecil Fielder (Encore)	.05
220 Andres Galarraga (Encore)	.05
221 Juan Gonzalez (Encore)	.65
222 Mark Grace (Encore)	.10
223 Ken Griffey Jr. (Encore)	1.50
224 Tony Gwynn (Encore)	1.00
225 Jason Isringhausen (Encore)	.05
226 Derek Jeter (Encore)	.75
227 Randy Johnson (Encore)	.75
228 Chipper Jones (Encore)	1.00
229 Ryan Klesko (Encore)	.05
230 Barry Larkin (Encore)	.05
231 Kenny Lofton (Encore)	.05
232 Greg Maddux (Encore)	1.00
233 Raul Mondesi (Encore)	.05
234 Hideo Nomo (Encore)	.65
235 Mike Piazza (Encore)	1.50
236 Manny Ramirez (Encore)	.75
237 Cal Ripken Jr. (Encore)	2.00
238 Tim Salmon (Encore)	.10
239 Ryne Sandberg (Encore)	1.00
240 Reggie Sanders (Encore)	.05
241 Gary Sheffield (Encore)	.30
242 Sammy Sosa (Encore)	.75
243 Frank Thomas (Encore)	.75
244 Mo Vaughn (Encore)	.05
245 Matt Williams (Encore)	.05
246 Checklist	.05
247 Checklist	.05
248 Checklist	.05
249 Checklist	.05
250 Checklist	.05

Update Tiffany

	NM/M
Complete Set (250):	45.00
Common Player:	.15
Glossy Stars:	2X

Update Diamond Tribute

These insert cards are the most difficult to pull from 1996 Fleer Update packs; they are seeded one per every 100 packs. The 10-card set features cards of future Hall of Famers on stock utilizing two different holographic foils and a diamond design, similar to the "Zone" insert cards in Fleer Baseball.

	NM/M
Complete Set (10):	50.00
Common Player:	4.00
1 Wade Boggs	6.00
2 Barry Bonds	10.00
3 Ken Griffey Jr.	7.50
4 Tony Gwynn	6.00
5 Rickey Henderson	4.00
6 Greg Maddux	6.00
7 Eddie Murray	4.00
8 Cal Ripken Jr.	10.00
9 Ozzie Smith	6.00
10 Frank Thomas	5.00

Update Headliners

These 20 cards feature newsmakers from 1996. The cards were random inserts in 1996 Fleer Update packs, one per every five retail packs.

	NM/M
Complete Set (20):	20.00

Common Player: .25

#	Player	Price
1	Roberto Alomar	.50
2	Jeff Bagwell	1.00
3	Albert Belle	.25
4	Barry Bonds	3.50
5	Cecil Fielder	.25
6	Juan Gonzalez	.75
7	Ken Griffey Jr.	2.25
8	Tony Gwynn	1.50
9	Randy Johnson	1.00
10	Chipper Jones	1.50
11	Ryan Klesko	.25
12	Kenny Lofton	.25
13	Greg Maddux	1.50
14	Hideo Nomo	.75
15	Mike Piazza	2.25
16	Manny Ramirez	1.00
17	Cal Ripken Jr.	3.50
18	Tim Salmon	.40
19	Frank Thomas	1.00
20	Matt Williams	.25

Update New Horizons

These 1996 Fleer Update inserts feature 20 promising youngsters with bright futures in the majors. The cards were seeded one per every five hobby packs.

NM/M
Complete Set (20): 2.00
Common Player: .25

#	Player	Price
1	Bob Abreu	.45
2	George Arias	.25
3	Tony Batista	.25
4	Steve Cox	.25
5	David Doster	.25
6	Jermaine Dye	.25
7	Andy Fox	.25
8	Mike Grace	.25
9	Todd Greene	.25
10	Wilton Guerrero	.25
11	Richard Hidalgo	.25
12	Raul Ibanez	.25
13	Robin Jennings	.25
14	Marcus Jensen	.25
15	Jason Kendall	.35
16	Brooks Kieschnick	.25
17	Ryan McGuire	.25
18	Miguel Mejia	.25
19	Rey Ordonez	.25
20	Paul Wilson	.25

Update Smooth Leather

Ten of the game's top fielders are showcased on these 1996 Fleer Update insert cards. The cards were seeded one per every five packs.

NM/M
Complete Set (10): 7.00
Common Player: .40

#	Player	Price
1	Roberto Alomar	.50
1p	Roberto Alomar (Promo)	2.00
2	Barry Bonds	2.50
3	Will Clark	.45
4	Ken Griffey Jr.	1.75
5	Kenny Lofton	.40
6	Greg Maddux	1.00
7	Raul Mondesi	.40
8	Rey Ordonez	.40
9	Cal Ripken Jr.	2.50
9p	Cal Ripken Jr. (Promo)	6.00
10	Matt Williams	.40

Update Soaring Stars

Ten of the game's top players are spotlighted on these 1996 Fleer Update inserts. The cards were seeded one per every 11 packs.

NM/M
Complete Set (10): 6.00
Common Player: .25

#	Player	Price
1	Jeff Bagwell	.75
2	Barry Bonds	2.00
3	Juan Gonzalez	.75

#	Player	Price
4	Ken Griffey Jr.	1.50
5	Chipper Jones	1.00
6	Greg Maddux	1.00
7	Mike Piazza	1.50
8	Manny Ramirez	.75
9	Frank Thomas	.75
10	Matt Williams	.25

Baseball '96

For a second consecutive year Fleer issued a special version of its Cleveland Indians cards for sale at Revco stores and Jacobs Field. Sold in 10-card packs with a suggested retail price of $1.49, the Revco version Indians team set differs from the regular Fleer cards in the application of UV coating on front and back, the use of silver- rather than gold-foil highlights and the numbering "X of 20." Following up on the Indians team-set issue, Fleer also issued 20-card sets for several other teams, distributed regionally. They were also sold in 10-card packs ($1.99 SRP) and feature UV coating, silver-foil graphics and special numbering. Some cards were updated and feature new photos reflecting trades, free agent signings, etc.

NM/M
Complete Set (180): 27.00
Common Player: .09

Atlanta Braves Team Set: 4.00

#	Player	Price
1	Steve Avery	.10
2	Jeff Blauser	.10
3	Brad Clontz	.10
4	Tom Glavine	.35
5	Marquis Grissom	.10
6	Chipper Jones	1.25
7	David Justice	.10
8	Ryan Klesko	.10
9	Mark Lemke	.10
10	Javier Lopez	.10
11	Greg Maddux	1.25
12	Fred McGriff	.10
13	Greg McMichael	.10
14	Eddie Perez	.10
15	Jason Schmidt	.10
16	John Smoltz	.10
17	Terrell Wade	.10
18	Mark Wohlers	.10
19	Logo Card	.10
20	Checklist	.10

Baltimore Orioles Team Set: 5.00

#	Player	Price
1	Roberto Alomar	.20
2	Brady Anderson	.10
3	Armando Benitez	.10
4	Bobby Bonilla	.10
5	Scott Erickson	.10
6	Jeffrey Hammonds	.10
7	Jimmy Haynes	.10
8	Chris Hoiles	.10
9	Rick Krivda	.10
10	Kent Mercker	.10
11	Mike Mussina	.45
12	Randy Myers	.10
13	Jesse Orosco	.10
14	Rafael Palmeiro	.75
15	Cal Ripken Jr.	2.50
16	B.J. Surhoff	.10
17	Tony Tarasco	.10
18	David Wells	.10
19	Logo Card	.10
20	Checklist	.10

Boston Red Sox Team Set: 3.00

#	Player	Price
1	Stan Belinda	.10
2	Jose Canseco	.50
3	Roger Clemens	2.00
4	Wil Cordero	.10
5	Vaughn Eshelman	.10
6	Tom Gordon	.10
7	Mike Greenwell	.10
8	Dwayne Hosey	.10
9	Kevin Mitchell	.10
10	Tim Naehring	.10
11	Troy O'Leary	.10
12	Aaron Sele	.10
13	Heathcliff Slocumb	.10
14	Mike Stanley	.10
15	Jeff Suppan	.10
16	John Valentin	.10
17	Mo Vaughn	.10
18	Tim Wakefield	.10
19	Logo Card	.10
20	Checklist	.10

Chicago Cubs Team Set: 4.00

#	Player	Price
1	Terry Adams	.10
2	Jim Bullinger	.10
3	Frank Castillo	.10
4	Kevin Foster	.10
5	Leo Gomez	.10
6	Luis Gonzalez	.20
7	Mark Grace	.15
8	Jose Hernandez	.10
9	Robin Jennings RC	.10
10	Doug Jones	.10
11	Brooks Kieschnick	.10
12	Brian McRae	.10
13	Jaime Navarro	.10
14	Rey Sanchez	.10
15	Ryne Sandberg	1.25
16	Scott Servais	.10
17	Sammy Sosa	1.50
18	Steve Trachsel	.10
19	Logo Card	.10
20	Checklist	.10

Chicago White Sox Team Set: 4.00

#	Player	Price
1	Wilson Alvarez	.10
2	Harold Baines	.10
3	Jason Bere	.10
4	Ray Durham	.10
5	Alex Fernandez	.10
6	Ozzie Guillen	.10
7	Roberto Hernandez	.10
8	Matt Karchner	.10
9	Ron Karkovice	.10
10	Darren Lewis	.10
11	Dave Martinez	.10
12	Lyle Mouton	.10
13	Tony Phillips	.10
14	Chris Snopek	.10
15	Kevin Tapani	.10
16	Danny Tartabull	.10
17	Frank Thomas	1.00
18	Robin Ventura	.10
19	Logo Card	.10
20	Checklist	.10

Cleveland Indians Team Set: 4.00

#	Player	Price
1	Sandy Alomar Jr.	.10
2	Paul Assenmacher	.10
3	Carlos Baerga	.10
4	Albert Belle	.09
5	Orel Hershiser	.10
6	Kenny Lofton	.10
7	Dennis Martinez	.10
8	Jose Mesa	.10
9	Eddie Murray	1.00
10	Charles Nagy	.10
11	Tony Pena	.10
12	Herb Perry	.10
13	Eric Plunk	.10
14	Jim Poole	.10
15	Manny Ramirez	1.00
16	Julian Tavarez	.10
17	Jim Thome	.75
18	Omar Vizquel	.10
19	Logo Card	.10
20	Checklist	.10

Colorado Rockies Team Set: 2.75

#	Player	Price
1	Jason Bates	.10
2	Dante Bichette	.10
3	Ellis Burks	.10
4	Vinny Castilla	.10
5	Andres Galarraga	.10
6	Darren Holmes	.10
7	Curt Leskanic	.10
8	Quinton McCracken	.10
9	Mike Munoz	.10
10	Jayhawk Owens	.10
11	Steve Reed	.10
12	Kevin Ritz	.10
13	Bret Saberhagen	.10
14	Bill Swift	.10
15	John Vander Wal	.10
16	Larry Walker	.10
17	Walt Weiss	.10
18	Eric Young	.10
19	Logo Card	.10
20	Checklist	.10

L.A. Dodgers Team Set: 4.00

#	Player	Price
1	Mike Blowers	.10
2	Brett Butler	.10
3	Tom Candiotti	.10
4	Roger Cedeno	.10
5	Delino DeShields	.10
6	Chad Fonville	.10
7	Greg Gagne	.10
8	Karim Garcia	.15
9	Todd Hollandsworth	.10
10	Eric Karros	.10
11	Ramon Martinez	.10
12	Raul Mondesi	.10
13	Hideo Nomo	.75
14	Antonio Osuna	.10
15	Chan Ho Park	.10
16	Mike Piazza	2.00
17	Ismael Valdes	.10
18	Todd Worrell	.10
19	Logo Card	.10
20	Checklist	.10

Texas Rangers Team Set: 2.75

#	Player	Price
1	Mark Brandenburg	.10
2	Damon Buford	.10
3	Will Clark	.15
4	Kevin Elster	.10
5	Benji Gil	.10
6	Juan Gonzalez	.75
7	Rusty Greer	.10
8	Kevin Gross	.10
9	Darryl Hamilton	.10
10	Ken Hill	.10
11	Mark McLemore	.10
12	Dean Palmer	.10
13	Roger Pavlik	.10
14	Ivan Rodriguez	.75
15	Mickey Tettleton	.10
16	Dave Valle	.10
17	Ed Vosberg	.10
18	Matt Whiteside	.10
19	Logo Card	.10
20	Checklist	.10

Panini Stickers

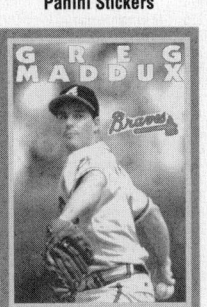

For the second year of distribution by Fleer/SkyBox, the annual baseball sticker set once again used Panini as the dominant brand identification. Printed in Italy, the stickers were sold in packs of six for 49 cents in the U.S., 69 cents in Canada. At 2-1/8" x 3", the basic player stickers have a green border around the color action photo; a second, ghosted, version of the photo appear in the background. Team logo and player ID are in a bat at bottom. Backs are printed in blue with the sticker number, Panini and licensor logos, along with copyright information. Team logo and special rookie stickers were printed on silver foil. A 60-page album was issued to house the set.

NM/M
Complete Set (246): 4.00
Common Player: .05
Album: .75

#	Player	Price
1	David Justice	.05
2	Tom Glavine	.20
3	Javier Lopez	.05
4	Greg Maddux	.45
5	Marquis Grissom	.05
6	Braves Logo	.05
7	Ryan Klesko	.05
8	Chipper Jones	.45
9	Quilvio Veras	.05
10	Chris Hammond	.05
11	Charles Johnson	.05
12	John Burkett	.05
13	Marlins Logo	.05
14	Jeff Conine	.05
15	Gary Sheffield	.25
16	Greg Colbrunn	.05
17	Moises Alou	.05
18	Pedro J. Martinez	.35
19	Rondell White	.05
20	Tony Tarasco	.05
21	Expos Logo	.05
22	Carlos Perez	.05
23	David Segui	.05
24	Wil Cordero	.05
25	Jason Isringhausen	.05
26	Rico Brogna	.05
27	Edgardo Alfonzo	.05
28	Todd Hundley	.05
29	Mets Logo	.05
30	Bill Pulsipher	.05
31	Carl Everett	.05
32	Jose Vizcaino	.05
33	Lenny Dykstra	.05
34	Charlie Hayes	.05
35	Heathcliff Slocumb	.05
36	Darren Daulton	.05
37	Phillies Logo	.05
38	Mickey Morandini	.05
39	Gregg Jefferies	.05
40	Jim Eisenreich	.05
41	Brian McRae	.05
42	Luis Gonzalez	.05
43	Randy Myers	.05
44	Shawon Dunston	.05
45	Cubs Logo	.05
46	Jaime Navarro	.05
47	Mark Grace	.05
48	Sammy Sosa	.50
49	Barry Larkin	.05
50	Pete Schourek	.05
51	John Smiley	.05
52	Reggie Sanders	.05
53	Reds Logo	.05
54	Hal Morris	.05
55	Ron Gant	.05
56	Bret Boone	.05
57	Craig Biggio	.05
58	Brian L. Hunter	.05
59	Jeff Bagwell	.35
60	Shane Reynolds	.05
61	Astros Logo	.05
62	Derek Bell	.05
63	Doug Drabek	.05
64	Orlando Miller	.05
65	Jay Bell	.05
66	Dan Miceli	.05
67	Orlando Merced	.05
68	Jeff King	.05
69	Carlos Garcia	.05
70	Pirates Logo	.05
71	Al Martin	.05
72	Denny Neagle	.05
73	Ray Lankford	.05
74	Ozzie Smith	.45
75	Bernard Gilkey	.05
76	John Mabry	.05
77	Cardinals Logo	.05
78	Brian Jordan	.05
79	Scott Cooper	.05
80	Allen Watson	.05
81	Dante Bichette	.05
82	Bret Saberhagen	.05
83	Walt Weiss	.05
84	Andres Galarraga	.05
85	Rockies Logo	.05
86	Larry Walker	.05
87	Bill Swift	.05
88	Vinny Castilla	.05
89	Raul Mondesi	.05
90	Roger Cedeno	.05
91	Chad Fonville	.05
92	Hideo Nomo	.30
93	Dodgers Logo	.05
94	Ramon Martinez	.05
95	Mike Piazza	.60
96	Eric Karros	.05
97	Tony Gwynn	.45
98	Brad Ausmus	.05
99	Trevor Hoffman	.05
100	Ken Caminiti	.05
101	Padres Logo	.05
102	Andy Ashby	.05
103	Steve Finley	.05
104	Joey Hamilton	.05
105	Matt Williams	.05
106	Rod Beck	.05
107	Barry Bonds	.75
108	William Van Landingham	.05
109	Giants Logo	.05
110	Deion Sanders	.05
111	Royce Clayton	.05
112	Glenallen Hill	.05
113	Tony Gwynn (League Leader - BA)	.20
114	Dante Bichette (League Leader - HR)	.05
115	Dante Bichette (League Leader - RBI)	.05
116	Quilvio Veras (League Leader - SB)	.05
117	Hideo Nomo (League Leader - K)	.15
118	Greg Maddux (League Leader - W)	.15
119	Randy Myers (League Leader - Saves)	.05
120	Edgar Martinez (League Leader - BA)	.05
121	Albert Belle (League Leader - HR)	.05
122	Mo Vaughn (League Leader - RBI)	.05
123	Kenny Lofton (League Leader - SB)	.05
124	Randy Johnson (League Leader - K)	.15
125	Mike Mussina (League Leader - W)	.10
126	Jose Mesa (League Leader - Saves)	.05
127	Mike Mussina	.20
128	Cal Ripken Jr.	.75
129	Rafael Palmeiro	.30
130	Ben McDonald	.05
131	Orioles Logo	.05
132	Chris Hoiles	.05
133	Bobby Bonilla	.05
134	Brady Anderson	.05
135	Jose Canseco	.20
136	Roger Clemens	.50
137	Mo Vaughn	.30
138	Mike Greenwell	.05
139	Red Sox Logo	.05
140	Tim Wakefield	.05
141	John Valentin	.05
142	Tim Naehring	.05
143	Travis Fryman	.05
144	Chad Curtis	.05
145	Felipe Lira	.05
146	Cecil Fielder	.05
147	Tigers Logo	.05
148	John Flaherty	.05
149	Chris Gomez	.05
150	Sean Bergman	.05
151	Don Mattingly	.50
152	Andy Pettitte	.15
153	Wade Boggs	.45
154	Paul O'Neill	.05
155	Yankees Logo	.05
156	Bernie Williams	.10
157	Jack McDowell	.05
158	David Cone	.05
159	Roberto Alomar	.10
160	Paul Molitor	.35
161	Shawn Green	.15
162	Joe Carter	.05
163	Blue Jays Logo	.05
164	Alex Gonzalez	.05
165	Al Leiter	.05
166	John Olerud	.05
167	Alex Fernandez	.05
168	Ray Durham	.05
169	Lance Johnson	.05
170	Ozzie Guillen	.05
171	White Sox Logo	.05
172	Robin Ventura	.05
173	Frank Thomas	.35
174	Tim Raines	.05
175	Albert Belle	.35
176	Manny Ramirez	.35
177	Eddie Murray	.35
178	Orel Hershiser	.05
179	Indians Logo	.05
180	Kenny Lofton	.05
181	Carlos Baerga	.05
182	Jose Mesa	.05
183	Gary Gaetti	.05
184	Tom Goodwin	.05
185	Kevin Appier	.05
186	Jon Nunnally	.05
187	Royals Logo	.05
188	Wally Joyner	.05
189	Jeff Montgomery	.05
190	Johnny Damon	.25
191	B.J. Surhoff	.05
192	Ricky Bones	.05
193	John Jaha	.05
194	Dave Nilsson	.05
195	Brewers Logo	.05
196	Greg Vaughn	.05
197	Kevin Seitzer	.05
198	Joe Oliver	.05
199	Chuck Knoblauch	.05
200	Kirby Puckett	.45
201	Marty Cordova	.05
202	Pat Meares	.05
203	Twins Logo	.05
204	Scott Stahoviak	.05
205	Matt Walbeck	.05
206	Pedro Munoz	.05
207	Garret Anderson	.05
208	Chili Davis	.05
209	Tim Salmon	.10
210	J.T. Snow	.05
211	Angels Logo	.05
212	Jim Edmonds	.05
213	Chuck Finley	.05
214	Mark Langston	.05
215	Dennis Eckersley	.30
216	Todd Stottlemyre	.05
217	Geronimo Berroa	.05
218	Mark McGwire	.65
219	A's Logo	.05
220	Brent Gates	.05
221	Terry Steinbach	.05
222	Rickey Henderson	.35
223	Ken Griffey Jr.	.60
224	Alex Rodriguez	.65
225	Tino Martinez	.05
226	Randy Johnson	.35
227	Mariners Logo	.05
228	Jay Buhner	.05
229	Vince Coleman	.05
230	Edgar Martinez	.05
231	Will Clark	.10
232	Juan Gonzalez	.35
233	Kenny Rogers	.05
234	Ivan Rodriguez	.30
235	Rangers Logo	.05
236	Mickey Tettleton	.05
237	Dean Palmer	.05
238	Otis Nixon	.05
239	Hideo Nomo (Rookie)	.20
240	Quilvio Veras (Rookie)	.05
241	Jason Isringhausen (Rookie)	.05
242	Andy Pettitte (Rookie)	.05
243	Chipper Jones (Rookie)	.25
244	Garret Anderson (Rookie)	.05
245	Charles Johnson (Rookie)	.05
246	Marty Cordova (Rookie)	.05

1997 Fleer

Fleer maintained its matte-finish coating for 1997 after it debuted in the 1996 product. The regular-issue Series 1 has 500 cards equipped with icons designating All-Stars, League Leaders and World Series cards. There were also 10 checklist cards in the regular-issue set, featuring stars on the front. Fleer arrived in 10-card packs and had a Tiffany Collection parallel set and six different insert sets, including Rookie Sensations, Golden Memories, Team Leaders, Night and Day, Zone and Lumber Company. Series 2 comprises 261 cards plus inserts Decade of Excellence, Bleacher Bashers, Diamond Tributes, Goudey Greats, Headliners, New Horizons and Soaring Stars.

	NM/M
Complete Set (761):	100.00
Complete Series 1 Set (500):	30.00
Complete Series 2 Set (261):	70.00
Common Player:	.05
Complete Tiffany Set (1-761):	500.00
Tiffany Stars/RC's:	8X
A. Jones Circa AU/200:	35.00
Series 2 Pack (10):	3.00
Series 2 Wax Box (36):	90.00

#	Player	Price
1	Roberto Alomar	.10
2	Brady Anderson	.05
3	Bobby Bonilla	.05
4	Rocky Coppinger	.05
5	Cesar Devarez	.05
6	Scott Erickson	.05
7	Jeffrey Hammonds	.05
8	Chris Hoiles	.05
9	Eddie Murray	1.00
10	Mike Mussina	.40
11	Randy Myers	.05
12	Rafael Palmeiro	.75
13	Cal Ripken Jr.	2.50
14	B.J. Surhoff	.05
15	David Wells	.05
16	Todd Zeile	.05
17	Darren Bragg	.05
18	Jose Canseco	.40
19	Roger Clemens	1.75
20	Wil Cordero	.05
21	Jeff Frye	.05
22	Nomar Garciaparra	1.75
23	Tom Gordon	.05
24	Mike Greenwell	.05
25	Reggie Jefferson	.05
26	Jose Malave	.05
27	Tim Naehring	.05
28	Troy O'Leary	.05
29	Heathcliff Slocumb	.05
30	Mike Stanley	.05
31	John Valentin	.05
32	Mo Vaughn	.05
33	Tim Wakefield	.05
34	Garret Anderson	.05
35	George Arias	.05
36	Shawn Boskie	.05
37	Chili Davis	.05
38	Jason Dickson	.05
39	Gary DiSarcina	.05
40	Jim Edmonds	.05
41	Darin Erstad	.10
42	Jorge Fabregas	.05
43	Chuck Finley	.05
44	Todd Greene	.05
45	Mike Holtz RC	.05
46	Rex Hudler	.05
47	Mike James	.05
48	Mark Langston	.05
49	Troy Percival	.05
50	Tim Salmon	.15
51	Jeff Schmidt	.05
52	J.T. Snow	.05
53	Randy Velarde	.05
54	Wilson Alvarez	.05
55	Harold Baines	.05
56	James Baldwin	.05
57	Jason Bere	.05
58	Mike Cameron	.05
59	Ray Durham	.05
60	Alex Fernandez	.05
61	Ozzie Guillen	.05
62	Roberto Hernandez	.05
63	Ron Karkovice	.05
64	Darren Lewis	.05
65	Dave Martinez	.05
66	Lyle Mouton	.05
67	Greg Norton	.05
68	Tony Phillips	.05
69	Chris Snopek	.05
70	Kevin Tapani	.05
71	Danny Tartabull	.05
72	Frank Thomas	1.00
73	Robin Ventura	.05
74	Sandy Alomar Jr.	.05
75	Albert Belle	.05
76	Mark Carreon	.05
77	Julio Franco	.05
78	Brian Giles RC	1.00
79	Orel Hershiser	.05
80	Kenny Lofton	.05
81	Dennis Martinez	.05
82	Jack McDowell	.05
83	Jose Mesa	.05
84	Charles Nagy	.05
85	Chad Ogea	.05
86	Eric Plunk	.05
87	Manny Ramirez	1.00
88	Kevin Seitzer	.05
89	Julian Tavarez	.05
90	Jim Thome	.65
91	Jose Vizcaino	.05
92	Omar Vizquel	.05
93	Brad Ausmus	.05
94	Kimera Bartee	.05
95	Raul Casanova	.05
96	Tony Clark	.05
97	John Cummings	.05
98	Travis Fryman	.05
99	Bob Higginson	.05
100	Mark Lewis	.05
101	Felipe Lira	.05
102	Phil Nevin	.05
103	Melvin Nieves	.05
104	Curtis Pride	.05
105	A.J. Sager	.05
106	Ruben Sierra	.05
107	Justin Thompson	.05
108	Alan Trammell	.05
109	Kevin Appier	.05
110	Tim Belcher	.05
111	Jaime Bluma	.05
112	Johnny Damon	.35
113	Tom Goodwin	.05
114	Chris Haney	.05
115	Keith Lockhart	.05
116	Mike Macfarlane	.05
117	Jeff Montgomery	.05
118	Jose Offerman	.05
119	Craig Paquette	.05
120	Joe Randa	.05
121	Bip Roberts	.05
122	Jose Rosado	.05
123	Mike Sweeney	.05
124	Michael Tucker	.05
125	Jeromy Burnitz	.05
126	Jeff Cirillo	.05
127	Jeff D'Amico	.05
128	Mike Fetters	.05
129	John Jaha	.05
130	Scott Karl	.05
131	Jesse Levis	.05
132	Mark Loretta	.05
133	Mike Matheny	.05
134	Ben McDonald	.05
135	Matt Mieske	.05
136	Marc Newfield	.05
137	Dave Nilsson	.05
138	Jose Valentin	.05
139	Fernando Vina	.05
140	Bob Wickman	.05
141	Gerald Williams	.05
142	Rick Aguilera	.05
143	Rich Becker	.05
144	Ron Coomer	.05
145	Marty Cordova	.05
146	Roberto Kelly	.05
147	Chuck Knoblauch	.05
148	Matt Lawton	.05
149	Pat Meares	.05
150	Travis Miller	.05
151	Paul Molitor	1.00
152	Greg Myers	.05
153	Dan Naulty	.05
154	Kirby Puckett	1.50
155	Brad Radke	.05
156	Frank Rodriguez	.05
157	Scott Stahoviak	.05
158	Dave Stevens	.05
159	Matt Walbeck	.05
160	Todd Walker	.05
161	Wade Boggs	1.50
162	David Cone	.05
163	Mariano Duncan	.05
164	Cecil Fielder	.05
165	Joe Girardi	.05
166	Dwight Gooden	.05
167	Charlie Hayes	.05
168	Derek Jeter	2.50
169	Jimmy Key	.05
170	Jim Leyritz	.05
171	Tino Martinez	.05
172	Ramiro Mendoza RC	.10
173	Jeff Nelson	.05
174	Paul O'Neill	.05
175	Andy Pettitte	.35
176	Mariano Rivera	.15
177	Ruben Rivera	.05
178	Kenny Rogers	.05
179	Darryl Strawberry	.05
180	John Wetteland	.05
181	Bernie Williams	.10
182	Willie Adams	.05
183	Tony Batista	.05
184	Geronimo Berroa	.05
185	Mike Bordick	.05
186	Scott Brosius	.05
187	Bobby Chouinard	.05
188	Jim Corsi	.05
189	Brent Gates	.05
190	Jason Giambi	.50
191	Jose Herrera	.05
192	Damon Mashore RC	.05
193	Mark McGwire	2.25
194	Mike Mohler	.05
195	Scott Spiezio	.05
196	Terry Steinbach	.05
197	Bill Taylor	.05
198	John Wasdin	.05
199	Steve Wojciechowski	.05
200	Ernie Young	.05
201	Rich Amaral	.05
202	Jay Buhner	.05
203	Norm Charlton	.05
204	Joey Cora	.05
205	Russ Davis	.05
206	Ken Griffey Jr.	2.00
207	Sterling Hitchcock	.05
208	Brian Hunter	.05
209	Raul Ibanez	.05
210	Randy Johnson	1.00
211	Edgar Martinez	.05
212	Jamie Moyer	.05
213	Alex Rodriguez	2.25
214	Paul Sorrento	.05
215	Matt Wagner	.05
216	Bob Wells	.05
217	Dan Wilson	.05
218	Damon Buford	.05
219	Will Clark	.10
220	Kevin Elster	.05
221	Juan Gonzalez	.75
222	Rusty Greer	.05
223	Kevin Gross	.05
224	Darryl Hamilton	.05
225	Mike Henneman	.05
226	Ken Hill	.05
227	Mark McLemore	.05
228	Darren Oliver	.05
229	Dean Palmer	.05
230	Roger Pavlik	.05
231	Ivan Rodriguez	.75
232	Mickey Tettleton	.05
233	Bobby Witt	.05
234	Jacob Brumfield	.05
235	Joe Carter	.05
236	Tim Crabtree	.05
237	Carlos Delgado	.50
238	Huck Flener	.05
239	Alex Gonzalez	.05
240	Shawn Green	.20
241	Juan Guzman	.05
242	Pat Hentgen	.05
243	Marty Janzen	.05
244	Sandy Martinez	.05
245	Otis Nixon	.05
246	Charlie O'Brien	.05
247	John Olerud	.05
248	Robert Perez	.05
249	Ed Sprague	.05
250	Mike Timlin	.05
251	Steve Avery	.05
252	Jeff Blauser	.05
253	Brad Clontz	.05
254	Jermaine Dye	.05
255	Tom Glavine	.30
256	Marquis Grissom	.05
257	Andruw Jones	1.00
258	Chipper Jones	1.50
259	David Justice	.05
260	Ryan Klesko	.05
261	Mark Lemke	.05
262	Javier Lopez	.05
263	Greg Maddux	1.50
264	Fred McGriff	.05
265	Greg McMichael	.05
266	Denny Neagle	.05
267	Terry Pendleton	.05
268	Eddie Perez	.05
269	John Smoltz	.05
270	Terrell Wade	.05
271	Mark Wohlers	.05
272	Terry Adams	.05
273	Brant Brown	.05
274	Leo Gomez	.05
275	Luis Gonzalez	.05
276	Mark Grace	.10
277	Tyler Houston	.05
278	Robin Jennings	.05
279	Brooks Kieschnick	.05
280	Brian McRae	.05
281	Jaime Navarro	.05
282	Ryne Sandberg	1.50
283	Scott Servais	.05
284	Sammy Sosa	1.75
285	Dave Swartzbaugh RC	.05
286	Amaury Telemaco	.05
287	Steve Trachsel	.05
288	Pedro Valdes RC	.05
289	Turk Wendell	.05
290	Bret Boone	.05
291	Jeff Branson	.05
292	Jeff Brantley	.05
293	Eric Davis	.05
294	Willie Greene	.05
295	Thomas Howard	.05
296	Barry Larkin	.05
297	Kevin Mitchell	.05
298	Hal Morris	.05
299	Chad Mottola	.05
300	Joe Oliver	.05
301	Mark Portugal	.05
302	Roger Salkeld	.05
303	Reggie Sanders	.05
304	Pete Schourek	.05
305	John Smiley	.05
306	Eddie Taubensee	.05
307	Dante Bichette	.05
308	Ellis Burks	.05
309	Vinny Castilla	.05
310	Andres Galarraga	.05
311	Curt Leskanic	.05
312	Quinton McCracken	.05
313	Neifi Perez	.05
314	Jeff Reed	.05
315	Steve Reed	.05
316	Armando Reynoso	.05
317	Kevin Ritz	.05
318	Bruce Ruffin	.05
319	Larry Walker	.05
320	Walt Weiss	.05
321	Jamey Wright	.05
322	Eric Young	.05
323	Kurt Abbott	.05
324	Alex Arias	.05
325	Kevin Brown	.05
326	Luis Castillo	.05
327	Greg Colbrunn	.05
328	Jeff Conine	.05
329	Andre Dawson	.25
330	Charles Johnson	.05
331	Al Leiter	.05
332	Ralph Milliard	.05
333	Robb Nen	.05
334	Pat Rapp	.05
335	Edgar Renteria	.05
336	Gary Sheffield	.35
337	Devon White	.05
338	Bob Abreu	.05
339	Jeff Bagwell	1.00
340	Derek Bell	.05
341	Sean Berry	.05
342	Craig Biggio	.05
343	Doug Drabek	.05
344	Tony Eusebio	.05
345	Ricky Gutierrez	.05
346	Mike Hampton	.05
347	Brian Hunter	.05
348	Todd Jones	.05
349	Darryl Kile	.05
350	Derrick May	.05
351	Orlando Miller	.05
352	James Mouton	.05
353	Shane Reynolds	.05
354	Billy Wagner	.05
355	Donne Wall	.05
356	Mike Blowers	.05
357	Brett Butler	.05
358	Roger Cedeno	.05
359	Chad Curtis	.05
360	Delino DeShields	.05
361	Greg Gagne	.05
362	Karim Garcia	.10
363	Wilton Guerrero	.05
364	Todd Hollandsworth	.05
365	Eric Karros	.05
366	Ramon Martinez	.05
367	Raul Mondesi	.05
368	Hideo Nomo	.75
369	Antonio Osuna	.05
370	Chan Ho Park	.05
371	Mike Piazza	2.00
372	Ismael Valdes	.05
373	Todd Worrell	.05
374	Moises Alou	.05
375	Shane Andrews	.05
376	Yamil Benitez	.05
377	Jeff Fassero	.05
378	Darrin Fletcher	.05
379	Cliff Floyd	.05
380	Mark Grudzielanek	.05
381	Mike Lansing	.05
382	Barry Manuel	.05
383	Pedro Martinez	1.00
384	Henry Rodriguez	.05
385	Mel Rojas	.05
386	F.P. Santangelo	.05
387	David Segui	.05
388	Ugueth Urbina	.05
389	Rondell White	.05
390	Edgardo Alfonzo	.05
391	Carlos Baerga	.05
392	Mark Clark	.05
393	Alvaro Espinoza	.05
394	John Franco	.05
395	Bernard Gilkey	.05
396	Pete Harnisch	.05
397	Todd Hundley	.05
398	Butch Huskey	.05
399	Jason Isringhausen	.05
400	Lance Johnson	.05
401	Bobby Jones	.05
402	Alex Ochoa	.05
403	Rey Ordonez	.05
404	Robert Person	.05
405	Paul Wilson	.05
406	Matt Beech	.05
407	Ron Blazier	.05
408	Ricky Bottalico	.05
409	Lenny Dykstra	.05
410	Jim Eisenreich	.05
411	Bobby Estalella	.05
412	Mike Grace	.05
413	Gregg Jefferies	.05
414	Mike Lieberthal	.05
415	Wendell Magee Jr.	.05
416	Mickey Morandini	.05
417	Ricky Otero	.05
418	Scott Rolen	.75
419	Ken Ryan	.05
420	Benito Santiago	.05
421	Curt Schilling	.25
422	Kevin Sefcik	.05
423	Jermaine Allensworth	.05
424	Trey Beamon	.05
425	Jay Bell	.05
426	Francisco Cordova	.05
427	Carlos Garcia	.05
428	Mark Johnson	.05
429	Jason Kendall	.05
430	Jeff King	.05
431	Jon Lieber	.05
432	Al Martin	.05
433	Orlando Merced	.05
434	Ramon Morel	.05
435	Matt Ruebel	.05
436	Jason Schmidt	.05
437	Marc Wilkins RC	.05
438	Alan Benes	.05
439	Andy Benes	.05
440	Royce Clayton	.05
441	Dennis Eckersley	.65
442	Gary Gaetti	.05
443	Ron Gant	.05
444	Aaron Holbert	.05
445	Brian Jordan	.05
447	Ray Lankford	.05
448	John Mabry	.05
448	T.J. Mathews	.05
449	Willie McGee	.05
450	Donovan Osborne	.05
451	Tom Pagnozzi	.05
452	Ozzie Smith	1.50
453	Todd Stottlemyre	.05
454	Mark Sweeney	.05
455	Dmitri Young	.05
456	Andy Ashby	.05
457	Ken Caminiti	.05
458	Archi Cianfrocco	.05
459	Steve Finley	.05
460	John Flaherty	.05
461	Chris Gomez	.05
462	Tony Gwynn	1.50
463	Joey Hamilton	.05
464	Rickey Henderson	1.00
465	Trevor Hoffman	.05
466	Brian Johnson	.05
467	Wally Joyner	.05
468	Jody Reed	.05
469	Scott Sanders	.05
470	Bob Tewksbury	.05
471	Fernando Valenzuela	.05
472	Greg Vaughn	.05
473	Tim Worrell	.05
474	Rich Aurilia	.05
475	Rod Beck	.05
476	Marvin Benard	.05
477	Barry Bonds	2.50
478	Jay Canizaro	.05
479	Shawon Dunston	.05
480	Shawn Estes	.05
481	Mark Gardner	.05
482	Glenallen Hill	.05
483	Stan Javier	.05
484	Marcus Jensen	.05
485	Bill Mueller RC	1.50
486	William Van Landingham	.05
487	Allen Watson	.05
488	Rick Wilkins	.05
489	Matt Williams	.05
489p	Matt Williams ("PROMOTIONAL SAMPLE")	1.50
490	Desi Wilson	.05
491	Checklist (Albert Belle)	.05
492	Checklist (Ken Griffey Jr.)	.85
493	Checklist (Andruw Jones)	.40
494	Checklist (Chipper Jones)	.60
495	Checklist (Mark McGwire)	1.00
496	Checklist (Paul Molitor)	.45
497	Checklist (Mike Piazza)	.85
498	Checklist (Cal Ripken Jr.)	1.25
499	Checklist (Alex Rodriguez)	1.00
500	Checklist (Frank Thomas)	.45
501	Kenny Lofton	.05
502	Carlos Perez	.05
503	Tim Raines	.05
504	Danny Patterson RC	.05
505	Derrick May	.05
506	Dave Hollins	.05
507	Felipe Crespo	.05
508	Brian Banks	.05
509	Jeff Kent	.05
510	Bubba Trammell RC	.25
511	Robert Person	.05
512	David Arias RC (Ortiz)	40.00
513	Ryan Jones	.05
514	David Justice	.05
515	Will Cunnane	.05
516	Russ Johnson	.05
517	John Burkett	.05
518	Robinson Checo RC	.05
519	Ricardo Rincon RC	.05
520	Woody Williams	.05
521	Rick Helling	.05
522	Jorge Posada	.05
523	Kevin Orie	.05
524	Fernando Tatis RC	.15
525	Jermaine Dye	.05
526	Brian Hunter	.05
527	Greg McMichael	.05
528	Matt Wagner	.05
529	Richie Sexson	.05
530	Scott Ruffcorn	.05
531	Luis Gonzalez	.10
532	Mike Johnson	.05
533	Mark Petkovsek	.05
534	Doug Drabek	.05
535	Jose Canseco	.40
536	Bobby Bonilla	.05
537	J.T. Snow	.05
538	Shawon Dunston	.05
539	John Ericks	.05
540	Terry Steinbach	.05
541	Jay Bell	.05
542	Joe Borowski	.05
543	David Wells	.05
544	Justin Towle RC	.10
545	Mike Blowers	.05
546	Shannon Stewart	.05
547	Rudy Pemberton	.05
548	Bill Swift	.05
549	Osvaldo Fernandez	.05
550	Eddie Murray	1.00
551	Don Wengert	.05
552	Brad Ausmus	.05
553	Carlos Garcia	.05
554	Jose Guillen	.05
555	Rheal Cormier	.05
556	Doug Brocail	.05
557	Rex Hudler	.05
558	Armando Benitez	.05
559	Elieser Marrero	.05
560	Ricky Ledee RC	.25
561	Bartolo Colon	.05
562	Quilvio Veras	.05
563	Alex Fernandez	.05
564	Darren Dreifort	.05
565	Benji Gil	.05
566	Kent Mercker	.05
567	Glendon Rusch	.05
568	Ramon Tatis RC	.05
569	Roger Clemens	1.75
570	Mark Lewis	.05
571	Emil Brown RC	.05
572	Jaime Navarro	.05
573	Sherman Obando	.05
574	John Wasdin	.05
575	Calvin Maduro	.05
576	Todd Jones	.05
577	Orlando Merced	.05
578	Cal Eldred	.05
579	Mark Gubicza	.05
580	Michael Tucker	.05
581	Tony Saunders RC	.05
582	Garvin Alston	.05
583	Joe Roa	.05
584	Brady Raggio RC	.05
585	Jimmy Key	.05
586	Marc Sagmoen RC	.05
587	Jim Bullinger	.05
588	Yorkis Perez	.05
589	Jose Cruz Jr. RC	.75
590	Mike Stanton	.05
591	Deivi Cruz RC	.25
592	Steve Karsay	.05
593	Mike Trombley	.05
594	Doug Glanville	.05
595	Scott Sanders	.05
596	Thomas Howard	.05
597	T.J. Staton	.05
598	Garrett Stephenson	.05
599	Rico Brogna	.05
600	Albert Belle	.05
601	Jose Vizcaino	.05
602	Chili Davis	.05
603	Shane Mack	.05
604	Jim Eisenreich	.05
605	Todd Zeile	.05
606	Brian Boehringer	.05
607	Paul Shuey	.05
608	Kevin Tapani	.05
609	John Wetteland	.05
610	Jim Leyritz	.05
611	Ray Montgomery	.05
612	Doug Bochtler	.05
613	Wady Almonte	.05
614	Danny Tartabull	.05
615	Orlando Miller	.05
616	Bobby Ayala	.05
617	Tony Graffanino	.05
618	Marc Valdes	.05
619	Ron Villone	.05
620	Derrek Lee	.05
621	Greg Colbrunn	.05
622	Felix Heredia RC	.10
623	Carl Everett	.05
624	Mark Thompson	.05
625	Jeff Granger	.05
626	Damian Jackson	.05
627	Mark Leiter	.05
628	Chris Holt	.05
629	Dario Veras RC	.05
630	Dave Burba	.05
631	Darryl Hamilton	.05
632	Mark Acre	.05
633	Fernando Hernandez	.05
634	Terry Mulholland	.05
635	Dustin Hermanson	.05
636	Delino DeShields	.05
637	Steve Avery	.05
638	Tony Womack RC	.10
639	Mark Whiten	.05
640	Marquis Grissom	.05
641	Xavier Hernandez	.05
642	Eric Davis	.05
643	Bob Tewksbury	.05
644	Dante Powell	.05
645	Carlos Castillo	.05
646	Chris Widger	.05
647	Moises Alou	.05
648	Pat Listach	.05
649	Edgar Ramos	.05
650	Deion Sanders	.05
651	John Olerud	.05
652	Todd Dunwoody	.05
653	Randall Simon RC	.10
654	Dan Carlson	.05
655	Matt Williams	.05
656	Jeff King	.05
657	Luis Alicea	.05
658	Brian Moehler	.05

659	Ariel Prieto	.05
660	Kevin Elster	.05
661	Mark Hutton	.05
662	Aaron Sele	.05
663	Graeme Lloyd	.05
664	John Burke	.05
665	Mel Rojas	.05
666	Sid Fernandez	.05
667	Pedro Astacio	.05
668	Jeff Abbott	.05
669	Darren Daulton	.05
670	Mike Bordick	.05
671	Sterling Hitchcock	.05
672	Damion Easley	.05
673	Armando Reynoso	.05
674	Pat Cline	.05
675	Orlando Cabrera RC	.50
676	Alan Embree	.05
677	Brian Bevil	.05
678	David Weathers	.05
679	Cliff Floyd	.05
680	Joe Randa	.05
681	Bill Haselman	.05
682	Jeff Fassero	.05
683	Matt Morris	.05
684	Mark Portugal	.05
685	Lee Smith	.05
686	Pokey Reese	.05
687	Benito Santiago	.05
688	Brian Johnson	.05
689	Brent Brede RC	.05
690	Shigetosi Hasegawa	.05
691	Julio Santana	.05
692	Steve Kline	.05
693	Julian Tavarez	.05
694	John Hudek	.05
695	Manny Alexander	.05
696	Roberto Alomar (Encore)	.10
697	Jeff Bagwell (Encore)	.45
698	Barry Bonds (Encore)	1.25
699	Ken Caminiti (Encore)	.05
700	Juan Gonzalez (Encore)	.35
701	Ken Griffey Jr. (Encore)	.85
702	Tony Gwynn (Encore)	.60
703	Derek Jeter (Encore)	1.25
704	Andruw Jones (Encore)	.45
705	Chipper Jones (Encore)	.60
706	Barry Larkin (Encore)	.05
707	Greg Maddux (Encore)	.60
708	Mark McGwire (Encore)	1.00
709	Paul Molitor (Encore)	.45
710	Hideo Nomo (Encore)	.35
711	Andy Pettitte (Encore)	.30
712	Mike Piazza (Encore)	.85
713	Manny Ramirez (Encore)	.45
714	Cal Ripken Jr. (Encore)	1.25
715	Alex Rodriguez (Encore)	1.00
716	Ryne Sandberg (Encore)	.60
717	John Smoltz (Encore)	.05
718	Frank Thomas (Encore)	.50
719	Mo Vaughn (Encore)	.05
720	Bernie Williams (Encore)	.10
721	Checklist (Tim Salmon)	.60
722	Checklist (Greg Maddux)	.60
723	Checklist (Cal Ripken Jr.)	1.25
724	Checklist (Mo Vaughn)	.50
725	Checklist (Ryne Sandberg)	.45
726	Checklist (Frank Thomas)	.50
727	Checklist (Barry Larkin)	.05
728	Checklist (Manny Ramirez)	.45
729	Checklist (Andres Galarraga)	.05
730	Checklist (Tony Clark)	.05
731	Checklist (Gary Sheffield)	.20
732	Checklist (Jeff Bagwell)	.40
733	Checklist (Kevin Appier)	.05
734	Checklist (Mike Piazza)	.85
735	Checklist (Jeff Cirillo)	.05
736	Checklist (Paul Molitor)	.40
737	Checklist (Henry Rodriguez)	.05
738	Checklist (Todd Hundley)	.05
739	Checklist (Derek Jeter)	1.25
740	Checklist (Mark McGwire)	1.00
741	Checklist (Curt Schilling)	.15
742	Checklist (Jason Kendall)	.05
743	Checklist (Tony Gwynn)	.60
744	Checklist (Barry Bonds)	1.25
745	Checklist (Ken Griffey Jr.)	.85
746	Checklist (Brian Jordan)	.05
747	Checklist (Juan Gonzalez)	.40
748	Checklist (Joe Carter)	.05
749	Arizona Diamondbacks	.05
750	Tampa Bay Devil Rays	.05
751	Hideki Irabu RC	.15
752	Jeremi Gonzalez RC	.15
753	Mario Valdez RC	.05
754	Aaron Boone	.05
755	Brett Tomko	.05
756	Jaret Wright RC	1.00
757	Ryan McGuire	.05
758	Jason McDonald	.05
759	Adrian Brown RC	.05
760	Keith Foulke RC	.25
761	Checklist	.05

Tiffany

Insertion odds were considerably lengthened for the UV-coated Tiffany Collection parallels in 1997 Fleer - to one card per 20 packs.

		NM/M
Complete Set (761):		500.00
Common Player:		1.00
Stars/Rcs:		8X
512	David Arias (Ortiz)	140.00

Bleacher Blasters

This 10-card insert features some of the game's top power hitters and was found in retail packs only. Cards featured a die-cut "burst" pattern on an etched foil background. Backs have a portrait photo and career highlights. Cards were inserted 1:36 packs.

		NM/M
Complete Set (10):		40.00
Common Player:		1.50
1	Albert Belle	1.50
2	Barry Bonds	10.00
3	Juan Gonzalez	2.00
4	Ken Griffey Jr.	6.00
5	Mark McGwire	8.00
6	Mike Piazza	6.00
7	Alex Rodriguez	8.00
8	Frank Thomas	4.00
9	Mo Vaughn	1.50
10	Matt Williams	1.50

Decade of Excellence

A 12-card insert found 1:36 in hobby shop packs, cards are in a format similar to the 1987 Fleer set and feature vintage photos of players who started their careers no later than the '87 season. Ten percent of the press run (1:360 packs) received a special foil treatment and designation as "Rare Traditions."

		NM/M
Complete Set (12):		35.00
Common Player:		1.50
Rare Tradition:		12X
1	Wade Boggs	4.50
2	Barry Bonds	9.00
3	Roger Clemens	6.00
4	Tony Gwynn	4.50
5	Rickey Henderson	3.00
6	Greg Maddux	4.50
7	Mark McGwire	6.00
8	Paul Molitor	3.00
9	Eddie Murray	3.00
10	Cal Ripken Jr.	9.00
11	Ryne Sandberg	4.50
12	Matt Williams	1.50

Diamond Tribute

Twelve of the game's top stars are highlighted in this set. Fronts feature an embossed rainbow pris-

matic foil background and gold lettering. Backs have an action photo and a few sentences about the player. They were inserted 1:288 packs.

		NM/M
Complete Set (12):		120.00
Common Player:		3.00
1	Albert Belle	3.00
2	Barry Bonds	20.00
3	Juan Gonzalez	5.00
4	Ken Griffey Jr.	12.50
5	Tony Gwynn	10.00
6	Greg Maddux	10.00
7	Mark McGwire	15.00
8	Eddie Murray	8.00
9	Mike Piazza	12.50
10	Cal Ripken Jr.	20.00
11	Alex Rodriguez	15.00
12	Frank Thomas	15.00

Golden Memories

Golden Memories captures 10 different highlights from the 1996 season, and is inserted one per 16 packs. Moments like Dwight Gooden's no hitter, Paul Molitor's 3000th hit and Eddie Murray's 500th home run are highlighted on a horizontal format.

		NM/M
Complete Set (10):		6.00
Common Player:		.25
1	Barry Bonds	2.00
2	Dwight Gooden	.25
3	Todd Hundley	.25
4	Mark McGwire	1.50
5	Paul Molitor	.75
6	Eddie Murray	.75
7	Hideo Nomo	.50
8	Mike Piazza	1.25
9	Cal Ripken Jr.	2.00
10	Ozzie Smith	1.00

Goudey Greats

Using a 2-3/8" x 2-7/8" format reminiscent of 1933 Goudey cards, this 15-card insert offers today's top players in classic old-time design. Cards were inserted 1:8 packs. A limited number (1 percent of press run) of cards received a special gold-foil treatment and were found only in hobby packs.

		NM/M
Complete Set (15):		20.00
Common Player:		.50
Foils:		15X
1	Barry Bonds	4.00
2	Ken Griffey Jr.	3.00
3	Tony Gwynn	4.00
4	Derek Jeter	4.00
5	Chipper Jones	2.00
6	Kenny Lofton	.50
7	Greg Maddux	3.50
8	Mark McGwire	3.50
9	Eddie Murray	1.50
10	Mike Piazza	3.00
11	Cal Ripken Jr.	4.00
12	Alex Rodriguez	3.50
13	Ryne Sandberg	2.00
14	Frank Thomas	1.50
15	Mo Vaughn	.50

Headliners

This 20-card insert highlights the personal achievements of each of the players depicted. Cards were inserted 1:2 packs and feature multi-color foil stamping on the fronts and a newspaper-style account of the player's achievement on the back.

		NM/M
Complete Set (20):		5.00
Common Player:		.10
1	Jeff Bagwell	.25
2	Albert Belle	.10
3	Barry Bonds	1.00
4	Ken Caminiti	.10
5	Juan Gonzalez	.20
6	Ken Griffey Jr.	.60
7	Tony Gwynn	.40
8	Derek Jeter	1.00
9	Andruw Jones	.25
10	Chipper Jones	.40
11	Greg Maddux	.40
12	Mark McGwire	.75
13	Paul Molitor	.25
14	Eddie Murray	.25
15	Mike Piazza	.60
16	Cal Ripken Jr.	1.00
17	Alex Rodriguez	.75
18	Ryne Sandberg	.40
19	John Smoltz	.05
20	Frank Thomas	.25

Lumber Company

Lumber Company inserts were found every 48 retail packs. The cards were printed on a die-cut, spherical wood-like pattern, with the player imposed on the left side. Eighteen of the top power hitters in baseball are highlighted.

		NM/M
Complete Set (18):		45.00
Common Player:		1.00
1	Brady Anderson	1.00
2	Jeff Bagwell	3.00
3	Albert Belle	1.00
4	Barry Bonds	8.00
5	Jay Buhner	1.00
6	Ellis Burks	1.00
7	Andres Galarraga	1.00
8	Juan Gonzalez	2.00
9	Ken Griffey Jr.	5.00
10	Todd Hundley	1.00
11	Ryan Klesko	1.00
12	Mark McGwire	5.00
13	Mike Piazza	5.00
14	Alex Rodriguez	6.00
15	Gary Sheffield	2.00
16	Sammy Sosa	4.00
17	Frank Thomas	3.00
18	Mo Vaughn	1.00

Million Dollar Moments

By assembling a complete set of 50 baseball "Million Dollar Moments" cards prior to July 31, 1998, a collector could win $50,000 a year through 2018. The catch, of course, is that cards #46-50 were printed in very limited quantities, with only one card #50. (Stated odds of winning the million were one in nearly 46,000,000.) The Moments cards have player ac-

tion photos on front vignetted into a black border. The Fleer Million Dollar Moments logo is at top, with the player name and the date and details of his highlight at bottom in orange and white. Backs have the contest rules in fine print. Instant Win versions of some cards were also issued.

		NM/M
Complete Set (45):		2.00
Common Player:		.05
1	Checklist	.05
2	Derek Jeter	.45
3	Babe Ruth	.25
4	Barry Bonds	.45
5	Brooks Robinson	.05
6	Todd Hundley	.05
7	Johnny Vander Meer	.05
8	Cal Ripken Jr.	.45
9	Bill Mazeroski	.05
10	Chipper Jones	.25
11	Frank Robinson	.05
12	Roger Clemens	.35
13	Bob Feller	.05
14	Mike Piazza	.30
15	Joe Nuxhall	.05
16	Hideo Nomo	.15
17	Jackie Robinson	.25
18	Orel Hershiser	.05
19	Bobby Thomson	.05
20	Joe Carter	.05
21	Al Kaline	.05
22	Bernie Williams	.05
23	Don Larsen	.05
24	Rickey Henderson	.15
25	Maury Wills	.05
26	Andruw Jones	.15
27	Bobby Richardson	.05
28	Alex Rodriguez	.35
29	Jim Bunning	.05
30	Ken Caminiti	.05
31	Bob Gibson	.05
32	Frank Thomas	.20
33	Mickey Lolich	.05
34	John Smoltz	.05
35	Ron Swoboda	.05
36	Albert Belle	.05
37	Chris Chambliss	.05
38	Juan Gonzalez	.10
39	Ron Blomberg	.05
40	John Wetteland	.05
41	Carlton Fisk	.05
42	Mo Vaughn	.05
43	Bucky Dent	.05
44	Greg Maddux	.25
45	Willie Stargell	.05

New Horizons

Rookies and prospects expected to make an impact during the 1996 season were featured in this 15-card insert set. Card fronts feature a rainbow foil background with the words "New Horizon" featured prominently on the bottom under the player's name. Cards were inserted 1:4 packs.

		NM/M
Complete Set (15):		2.00
Common Player:		.05
1	Bob Abreu	.05
2	Jose Cruz Jr.	.10
3	Darin Erstad	.10
4	Nomar Garciaparra	.75
5	Vladimir Guerrero	.60
6	Wilton Guerrero	.05
7	Jose Guillen	.05
8	Hideki Irabu	.05
9	Andruw Jones	.60
10	Kevin Orie	.05
11	Scott Rolen	.50
12	Scott Spiezio	.05
13	Bubba Trammell	.05
14	Todd Walker	.05
15	Dmitri Young	.05

Night & Day

Night and Day spotlighted 10 stars with unusual prowess during night or day games. These lenticular cards carried the toughest insert ratios in Fleer Baseball at one per 288 packs.

Complete Set (10): 45.00
Common Player: 1.00

		NM/M
Complete Set (10):		45.00
Common Player:		1.00
1	Barry Bonds	12.00
2	Ellis Burks	1.00
3	Juan Gonzalez	2.00
4	Ken Griffey Jr.	6.00
5	Mark McGwire	7.50
6	Mike Piazza	6.00
7	Manny Ramirez	4.00
8	Alex Rodriguez	8.00
9	John Smoltz	2.00
10	Frank Thomas	4.00

Rookie Sensations

Rookies Sensations showcased 20 of the top up-and-coming stars in baseball. Appearing every six packs, these inserts have the feaured player in the foreground, with the background look of painted brush strokes.

		NM/M
Complete Set (20):		6.00
Common Player:		.25
1	Jermaine Allensworth	.25
2	James Baldwin	.25
3	Alan Benes	.25
4	Jermaine Dye	.25
5	Darin Erstad	.50
6	Todd Hollandsworth	.25
7	Derek Jeter	2.50
8	Jason Kendall	.25
9	Alex Ochoa	.25
10	Rey Ordonez	.25
11	Edgar Renteria	.25
12	Bob Abreu	.50
13	Nomar Garciaparra	1.50
14	Wilton Guerrero	.25
15	Andruw Jones	1.00
16	Wendell Magee	.25
17	Neifi Perez	.25
18	Scott Rolen	.75
19	Scott Spiezio	.25
20	Todd Walker	.25

Soaring Stars

A 12-card insert found 1:12 packs designed to profile players with outstanding statistical performances early in their careers. Fronts have player action photos set against a background of rainbow holographic stars which appear, disappear and twinkle as the viewing angle is changed. Conventionally printed backs have another player photo and a few sentences about his career. A parallel version on which the background stars glow was issued at a greatly reduced rate.

	NM/M
Complete Set (12):	10.00
Common Player:	.25
Glowing:	6X
1 Albert Belle	.25
2 Barry Bonds	2.00
3 Juan Gonzalez	.50
4 Ken Griffey Jr.	1.25
5 Derek Jeter	2.00
6 Andruw Jones	.60
7 Chipper Jones	1.00
8 Greg Maddux	1.00
9 Mark McGwire	1.50
10 Mike Piazza	1.25
11 Alex Rodriguez	1.50
12 Frank Thomas	.75

Team Leaders

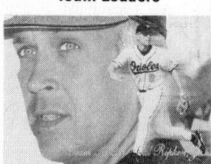

Team Leaders captured the statistical and/or inspirational leaders from all 28 teams. Inserted every 20 packs, these inserts were printed on a horizontal format, with the player's face die-cut in the perimeter of the card.

	NM/M
Complete Set (28):	25.00
Common Player:	.25
1 Cal Ripken Jr.	5.00
2 Mo Vaughn	.25
3 Jim Edmonds	.40
4 Frank Thomas	1.50
5 Albert Belle	.25
6 Bob Higginson	.25
7 Kevin Appier	.25
8 John Jaha	.25
9 Paul Molitor	1.50
10 Andy Pettitte	.65
11 Mark McGwire	4.00
12 Ken Griffey Jr.	3.00
13 Juan Gonzalez	.75
14 Pat Hentgen	.25
15 Chipper Jones	2.00
16 Mark Grace	.35
17 Barry Larkin	.25
18 Ellis Burks	.25
19 Gary Sheffield	.60
20 Jeff Bagwell	1.50
21 Mike Piazza	3.00
22 Henry Rodriguez	.25
23 Todd Hundley	.25
24 Curt Schilling	.60
25 Jeff King	.25
26 Brian Jordan	.25
27 Tony Gwynn	1.50
28 Barry Bonds	5.00

Zone

Twenty of the top hitters in baseball are featured on these holographic cards with the words Zone printed across the front. Zone inserts were found only in hobby packs at a rate of one per 80.

	NM/M
Complete Set (20):	80.00
Common Player:	1.50
1 Jeff Bagwell	5.00
2 Albert Belle	1.50
3 Barry Bonds	15.00
4 Ken Caminiti	1.50
5 Andres Galarraga	1.50
6 Juan Gonzalez	2.50
7 Ken Griffey Jr.	8.00
8 Tony Gwynn	6.00
9 Chipper Jones	6.00
10 Greg Maddux	6.00
11 Mark McGwire	10.00
12 Dean Palmer	1.50
13 Andy Petitte	3.00
14 Mike Piazza	8.00
15 Alex Rodriguez	12.00
16 Gary Sheffield	2.50
17 John Smoltz	2.50
18 Frank Thomas	5.00
19 Jim Thome	4.00
20 Matt Williams	1.50

1998 Fleer

Fleer was issued in two series in 1998, with 350 cards in Series 1 and 250 in Series 2. Each card features a borderless color action shot, with backs containing player information. Subsets in Series 1 included Smoke 'N Heat (301-310), Golden Memories (311-320) and Tale of the Tape (321-340). Golden Memories (1:6 packs) and Tale of the Tape (1:4) were shortprinted. Series 2 subsets included 25 short-printed (1:4) Unforgettable Moments (571-595). Inserts in Series 1 were Vintage '63, Vintage '63 Classic, Decade of Excellence, Decade of Excellence Rare Traditions, Diamond Ink, Diamond Standouts, Lumber Company, Power Game, Rookie Sensations and Zone. Series 2 inserts include: Vintage '63, Vintage '63 Classic, Promising Forecast, In the Clutch, Mickey Mantle: Monumental Moments, Mickey Mantle: Monumental Moments Gold Edition, Diamond Tribute and Diamond Ink.

	NM/M
Complete Set (600):	65.00
Complete Series 1 (350):	40.00
Complete Series 2 (250):	25.00
Common Player:	.05
Series 1 or 2 Pack (10):	1.00
Series 1 or 2 Wax Box (36):	20.00
1 Ken Griffey Jr.	1.50
2 Derek Jeter	2.50
3 Gerald Williams	.05
4 Carlos Delgado	.50
5 Nomar Garciaparra	1.50
6 Gary Sheffield	.30
7 Jeff King	.05
8 Cal Ripken Jr.	2.50
9 Matt Williams	.25
10 Chipper Jones	1.00
11 Chuck Knoblauch	.05
12 Mark Grudzielanek	.05
13 Edgardo Alfonzo	.05
14 Andres Galarraga	.05
15 Tim Salmon	.15
16 Reggie Sanders	.05
17 Tony Clark	.05
18 Jason Kendall	.05
19 Juan Gonzalez	.65
20 Ben Grieve	.10
21 Roger Clemens	1.25
22 Raul Mondesi	.05
23 Robin Ventura	.05
24 Derrek Lee	.05
25 Mark McGwire	2.00
26 Luis Gonzalez	.10
27 Kevin Brown	.05
28 Kirk Rueter	.05
29 Bobby Estalella	.05
30 Shawn Green	.35
31 Greg Maddux	1.00
32 Jorge Velandia	.05
33 Larry Walker	.05
34 Joey Cora	.05
35 Frank Thomas	.85
36 Curtis King RC	.05
37 Aaron Boone	.05
38 Curt Schilling	.25
39 Bruce Aven	.05
40 Ben McDonald	.05
41 Andy Ashby	.05
42 Jason McDonald	.05
43 Eric Davis	.05
44 Mark Grace	.10
45 Pedro Martinez	.75
46 Lou Collier	.05
47 Chan Ho Park	.05
48 Shane Halter	.05
49 Brian Hunter	.05
50 Jeff Bagwell	.75
51 Bernie Williams	.10
52 J.T. Snow	.05
53 Todd Greene	.05
54 Shannon Stewart	.05
55 Darren Bragg	.05
56 Fernando Tatis	.05
57 Darryl Kile	.05
59 Javier Valentin	.05
60 Brian McRae	.05
61 Tom Evans	.05
62 Randall Simon	.05
63 Darrin Fletcher	.05
64 Jaret Wright	.05
65 Luis Ordaz	.05
66 Jose Canseco	.40
67 Edgar Renteria	.05
68 Jay Buhner	.05
69 Paul Konerko	.10
70 Adrian Brown	.05
71 Chris Carpenter	.05
72 Mike Lieberthal	.05
73 Dean Palmer	.05
74 Jorge Fabregas	.05
75 Stan Javier	.05
76 Damion Easley	.05
77 David Cone	.05
78 Aaron Sele	.05
79 Antonio Alfonseca	.05
80 Bobby Jones	.05
81 David Justice	.05
82 Jeffrey Hammonds	.05
83 Doug Glanville	.05
84 Jason Dickson	.05
85 Brad Radke	.05
86 David Segui	.05
87 Greg Vaughn	.05
88 Mike Cather RC	.05
89 Alex Fernandez	.05
90 Billy Taylor	.05
91 Jason Schmidt	.05
92 Mike DeJean RC	.05
93 Domingo Cedeno	.05
94 Jeff Cirillo	.05
95 Manny Aybar RC	.10
96 Jaime Navarro	.05
97 Dennis Reyes	.05
98 Barry Larkin	.05
99 Troy O'Leary	.05
100 Alex Rodriguez	2.00
100p Alex Rodriguez/OPS	2.00
101 Pat Hentgen	.05
102 Bubba Trammell	.05
103 Glendon Rusch	.05
104 Kenny Lofton	.05
105 Craig Biggio	.05
106 Kelvim Escobar	.05
107 Mark Kotsay	.05
108 Rondell White	.05
109 Darren Oliver	.05
110 Jim Thome	.65
111 Rich Becker	.05
112 Chad Curtis	.05
113 Dave Hollins	.05
114 Bill Mueller	.05
115 Antone Williamson	.05
116 Tony Womack	.05
117 Randy Myers	.05
118 Rico Brogna	.05
119 Pat Watkins	.05
120 Eli Marrero	.05
121 Jay Bell	.05
122 Kevin Tapani	.05
123 Todd Erdos RC	.10
124 Neifi Perez	.05
125 Todd Hundley	.05
126 Jeff Abbott	.05
127 Todd Zeile	.05
128 Travis Fryman	.05
129 Sandy Alomar	.05
130 Fred McGriff	.05
131 Richard Hidalgo	.05
132 Scott Spiezio	.05
133 John Valentin	.05
134 Quilvio Veras	.05
135 Mike Lansing	.05
136 Paul Molitor	.75
137 Randy Johnson	.75
138 Harold Baines	.05
139 Doug Jones	.05
140 Abraham Nunez	.05
141 Alan Benes	.05
142 Matt Perisho	.05
143 Chris Clemons	.05
144 Andy Pettitte	.30
145 Jason Giambi	.40
146 Moises Alou	.05
147 Chad Fox RC	.05
148 Felix Martinez	.05
149 Carlos Mendoza RC	.05
150 Scott Rolen	.65
151 Jose Cabrera RC	.05
152 Justin Thompson	.05
153 Ellis Burks	.05
154 Pokey Reese	.05
155 Bartolo Colon	.05
156 Ray Durham	.05
157 Ugueth Urbina	.05
158 Tom Goodwin	.05
159 David Dellucci RC	.25
160 Rod Beck	.05
161 Ramon Martinez	.05
162 Joe Carter	.05
163 Kevin Orie	.05
164 Trevor Hoffman	.05
165 Emil Brown	.05
166 Robb Nen	.05
167 Paul O'Neill	.05
168 Ryan Long	.05
169 Ray Lankford	.05
170 Ivan Rodriguez	.65
171 Rick Aguilera	.05
172 Deivi Cruz	.05
173 Ricky Bottalico	.05
174 Garret Anderson	.05
175 Jose Vizcaino	.05
176 Omar Vizquel	.05
177 Jeff Blauser	.05
178 Orlando Cabrera	.05
179 Russ Johnson	.05
180 Matt Stairs	.05
181 Will Cunnane	.05
182 Adam Riggs	.05
183 Matt Morris	.05
184 Mario Valdez	.05
185 Larry Sutton	.05
186 Marc Pisciotta RC	.05
187 Dan Wilson	.05
188 John Franco	.05
189 Darren Daulton	.05
190 Todd Helton	.75
191 Brady Anderson	.05
192 Ricardo Rincon	.05
193 Kevin Stocker	.05
194 Jose Valentin	.05
195 Ed Sprague	.05
196 Ryan McGuire	.05
197 Scott Eyre RC	.05
198 Steve Finley	.05
199 T.J. Mathews	.05
200 Mike Piazza	1.50
201 Mark Wohlers	.05
202 Brian Giles	.05
203 Eduardo Perez	.05
204 Shigetosi Hasegawa	.05
205 Mariano Rivera	.15
206 Jose Rosado	.05
207 Michael Coleman	.05
208 James Baldwin	.05
209 Russ Davis	.05
210 Billy Wagner	.05
211 Sammy Sosa	1.50
212 Frank Catalanotto RC	.15
213 Delino DeShields	.05
214 John Olerud	.05
215 Heath Murray	.05
216 Jose Vidro	.05
217 Jim Edmonds	.05
218 Shawon Dunston	.05
219 Homer Bush	.05
220 Midre Cummings	.05
221 Tony Saunders	.05
222 Jeromy Burnitz	.05
223 Enrique Wilson	.05
224 Chili Davis	.05
225 Jerry DiPoto	.05
226 Dante Powell	.05
227 Javier Lopez	.05
228 Kevin Polcovich RC	.10
229 Deion Sanders	.05
230 Jimmy Key	.05
231 Rusty Greer	.05
232 Reggie Jefferson	.05
233 Ron Coomer	.05
234 Bobby Higginson	.05
235 Magglio Ordonez RC	2.00
236 Miguel Tejada	.25
237 Rick Gorecki	.05
238 Charles Johnson	.05
239 Lance Johnson	.05
240 Derek Bell	.05
241 Will Clark	.10
242 Brady Raggio	.05
243 Orel Hershiser	.05
244 Vladimir Guerrero	.75
245 John LeRoy	.05
246 Shawn Estes	.05
247 Brett Tomko	.05
248 Dave Nilsson	.05
249 Edgar Martinez	.05
250 Tony Gwynn	1.00
251 Mark Bellhorn	.05
252 Jed Hansen	.05
253 Butch Huskey	.05
254 Eric Young	.05
255 Vinny Castilla	.05
256 Hideki Irabu	.05
257 Mike Cameron	.05
258 Juan Encarnacion	.05
259 Brian Rose	.05
260 Brad Ausmus	.05
261 Dan Serafini	.05
262 Willie Greene	.05
263 Troy Percival	.05
264 Jeff Wallace RC	.05
265 Richie Sexson	.05
266 Rafael Palmeiro	.65
267 Brad Fullmer	.05
268 Jeremi Gonzalez	.05
269 Rob Stanifer RC	.05
270 Mickey Morandini	.05
271 Andruw Jones	.75
272 Royce Clayton	.05
273 Takashi Kashiwada	.05
274 Steve Woodard RC	.10
275 Jose Cruz Jr.	.05
276 Keith Foulke	.05
277 Brad Rigby	.05
278 Tino Martinez	.05
279 Todd Jones	.05
280 John Wetteland	.05
281 Alex Gonzalez	.05
282 Ken Cloude	.05
283 Jose Guillen	.05
284 Danny Clyburn	.05
285 David Ortiz	.05
286 John Thomson	.05
287 Kevin Appier	.05
288 Ismael Valdes	.05
289 Gary DiSarcina	.05
290 Todd Dunwoody	.05
291 Wally Joyner	.05
292 Charles Nagy	.05
293 Jeff Shaw	.05
294 Kevin Millwood RC	1.00
295 Rigo Beltran RC	.05
296 Jeff Frye	.05
297 Oscar Henriquez	.05
298 Mike Thurman	.05
299 Garrett Stephenson	.05
300 Barry Bonds	2.50
301 Roger Clemens (Smoke 'N Heat)	.75
302 David Cone (Smoke 'N Heat)	.05
303 Hideki Irabu (Smoke 'N Heat)	.05
304 Randy Johnson (Smoke 'N Heat)	.40
305 Greg Maddux (Smoke 'N Heat)	.50
306 Pedro Martinez (Smoke 'N Heat)	.35
307 Mike Mussina (Smoke 'N Heat)	.25
308 Andy Pettitte (Smoke 'N Heat)	.15
309 Curt Schilling (Smoke 'N Heat)	.10
310 John Smoltz (Smoke 'N Heat)	.05
311 Roger Clemens (Golden Memories)	1.00
312 Jose Cruz Jr. (Golden Memories)	.25
313 Nomar Garciaparra (Golden Memories)	1.00
314 Ken Griffey Jr. (Golden Memories)	1.00
315 Tony Gwynn (Golden Memories)	.75
316 Hideki Irabu (Golden Memories)	.25
317 Randy Johnson (Golden Memories)	.60
318 Mark McGwire (Golden Memories)	1.50
319 Curt Schilling (Golden Memories)	.35
320 Larry Walker (Golden Memories)	.15
321 Jeff Bagwell (Tale of the Tape)	.60
322 Albert Belle (Tale of the Tape)	.15
323 Barry Bonds (Tale of the Tape)	1.50
324 Jay Buhner (Tale of the Tape)	.15
325 Tony Clark (Tale of the Tape)	.15
326 Jose Cruz Jr. (Tale of the Tape)	.15
327 Andres Galarraga (Tale of the Tape)	.15
328 Juan Gonzalez (Tale of the Tape)	.30
329 Ken Griffey Jr. (Tale of the Tape)	.85
330 Andruw Jones (Tale of the Tape)	.60
331 Tino Martinez (Tale of the Tape)	.15
332 Mark McGwire (Tale of the Tape)	1.00
333 Rafael Palmeiro (Tale of the Tape)	.50
334 Mike Piazza (Tale of the Tape)	.85
335 Manny Ramirez (Tale of the Tape)	.65
336 Alex Rodriguez (Tale of the Tape)	1.00
337 Frank Thomas (Tale of the Tape)	.65
338 Jim Thome (Tale of the Tape)	.65
339 Mo Vaughn (Tale of the Tape)	.15
340 Larry Walker (Tale of the Tape)	.15
341 Checklist (Jose Cruz Jr.)	.15
342 Checklist (Ken Griffey Jr.)	.60
343 Checklist (Derek Jeter)	1.00
344 Checklist (Andruw Jones)	.40
345 Checklist (Chipper Jones)	.50
346 Checklist (Greg Maddux)	.50
347 Checklist (Mike Piazza)	.65
348 Checklist (Cal Ripken Jr.)	1.00
349 Checklist (Alex Rodriguez)	.75
350 Checklist (Frank Thomas)	.45
351 Mo Vaughn	.05
352 Andres Galarraga	.05
353 Roberto Alomar	.10
354 Darin Erstad	.10
355 Albert Belle	.05
356 Matt Williams	.05
357 Darryl Kile	.05
358 Kenny Lofton	.05
359 Orel Hershiser	.05
360 Bob Abreu	.05
361 Chris Widger	.05
362 Glenallen Hill	.05
363 Chili Davis	.05
364 Kevin Brown	.05
365 Marquis Grissom	.05
366 Livan Hernandez	.05
367 Moises Alou	.05
368 Matt Lawton	.05
369 Rey Ordonez	.05
370 Kenny Rogers	.05
371 Lee Stevens	.05
372 Wade Boggs	1.00
373 Luis Gonzalez	.05
374 Jeff Conine	.05
375 Esteban Loaiza	.05
376 Jose Canseco	.40
377 Henry Rodriguez	.05
378 Dave Burba	.05
379 Todd Hollandsworth	.05
380 Ron Gant	.05
381 Pedro Martinez	.75
382 Ryan Klesko	.05
383 Derrek Lee	.05
384 Doug Glanville	.05
385 David Wells	.05
386 Ken Caminiti	.05
387 Damon Hollins	.05
388 Manny Ramirez	.75
389 Mike Mussina	.45
390 Jay Bell	.05
391 Mike Piazza	1.50
392 Mike Lansing	.05
393 Mike Hampton	.05
394 Geoff Jenkins	.05
395 Jimmy Haynes	.05
396 Scott Servais	.05
397 Kent Mercker	.05
398 Jeff Kent	.05
399 Kevin Elster	.05
400 Masato Yoshii RC	.50
401 Jose Vizcaino	.05
402 Javier Martinez	.05
403 David Segui	.05
404 Tony Saunders	.05
405 Karim Garcia	.05
406 Armando Benitez	.05
407 Joe Randa	.05
408 Vic Darensbourg	.05
409 Sean Casey	.20
410 Eric Milton	.05
411 Trey Moore	.05
412 Mike Stanley	.05
413 Tom Gordon	.05
414 Hal Morris	.05
415 Braden Looper	.05
416 Mike Kelly	.05
417 John Smoltz	.05
418 Roger Cedeno	.05
419 Al Leiter	.05
420 Chuck Knoblauch	.05
421 Felix Rodriguez	.05
422 Bip Roberts	.05
423 Ken Hill	.05
424 Jermaine Allensworth	.05
425 Esteban Yan	.05
426 Scott Karl	.05
427 Sean Berry	.05
428 Rafael Medina	.05
429 Javier Vazquez	.05
430 Rickey Henderson	.75
431 Adam Butler RC	.05
432 Todd Stottlemyre	.05
433 Yamil Benitez	.05
434 Sterling Hitchcock	.05
435 Paul Sorrento	.05
436 Bobby Ayala	.05
437 Tim Raines	.05
438 Chris Hoiles	.05
439 Rod Beck	.05
440 Donnie Sadler	.05
441 Charles Johnson	.05
442 Russ Ortiz	.05
443 Pedro Astacio	.05
444 Wilson Alvarez	.05
445 Mike Blowers	.05
446 Todd Zeile	.05
447 Mel Rojas	.05
448 F.P. Santangelo	.05
449 Dmitri Young	.05
450 Brian Anderson	.05
451 Cecil Fielder	.05
452 Roberto Hernandez	.05
453 Todd Walker	.05
454 Tyler Green	.05
455 Jorge Posada	.05
456 Geronimo Berroa	.05
457 Jose Silva	.05
458 Bobby Bonilla	.05
459 Walt Weiss	.05
460 Darren Dreifort	.05
461 B.J. Surhoff	.05
462 Quinton McCracken	.05
463 Derek Lowe	.05
464 Jorge Fabregas	.05
465 Joey Hamilton	.05
466 Brian Jordan	.05
467 Allen Watson	.05
468 John Jaha	.05
469 Heathcliff Slocumb	.05
470 Gregg Jefferies	.05
471 Scott Brosius	.05
472 Chad Ogea	.05
473 A.J. Hinch	.05
474 Bobby Smith	.05
475 Brian Moehler	.05
476 DaRond Stovall	.05
477 Kevin Young	.05
478 Jeff Suppan	.05
479 Marty Cordova	.05

480	John Halama RC	.25
481	Bubba Trammell	.05
482	Mike Caruso	.05
483	Eric Karros	.05
484	Jamey Wright	.05
485	Mike Sweeney	.05
486	Aaron Sele	.05
487	Cliff Floyd	.05
488	Jeff Brantley	.05
489	Jim Leyritz	.05
490	Denny Neagle	.05
491	Travis Fryman	.05
492	Carlos Baerga	.05
493	Eddie Taubensee	.05
494	Darryl Strawberry	.05
495	Brian Johnson	.05
496	Randy Myers	.05
497	Jeff Blauser	.05
498	Jason Wood	.05
499	Rolando Arrojo RC	.25
500	Johnny Damon	.05
501	Jose Mercedes	.05
502	Tony Batista	.05
503	Mike Piazza	1.50
504	Hideo Nomo	.65
505	Chris Gomez	.05
506	Jesus Sanchez RC	.05
507	Al Martin	.05
508	Brian Edmondson	.05
509	Joe Girardi	.05
510	Shayne Bennett	.05
511	Joe Carter	.05
512	Dave Mlicki	.05
513	Rich Butler RC	.10
514	Dennis Eckersley	.65
515	Travis Lee	.10
516	John Mabry	.05
517	Jose Mesa	.05
518	Phil Nevin	.05
519	Raul Casanova	.05
520	Mike Fetters	.05
521	Gary Sheffield	.30
522	Terry Steinbach	.05
523	Steve Trachsel	.05
524	Josh Booty	.05
525	Darryl Hamilton	.05
526	Mark McLemore	.05
527	Kevin Stocker	.05
528	Bret Boone	.05
529	Shane Andrews	.05
530	Robb Nen	.05
531	Carl Everett	.05
532	LaTroy Hawkins	.05
533	Fernando Vina	.05
534	Michael Tucker	.05
535	Mark Langston	.05
536	Mickey Mantle	2.00
537	Bernard Gilkey	.05
538	Francisco Cordova	.05
539	Mike Bordick	.05
540	Fred McGriff	.05
541	Cliff Politte	.05
542	Jason Varitek	.05
543	Shawon Dunston	.05
544	Brian Meadows	.05
545	Pat Meares	.05
546	Carlos Perez	.05
547	Desi Relaford	.05
548	Antonio Osuna	.05
549	Devon White	.05
550	Sean Runyan	.05
551	Mickey Morandini	.05
552	Dave Martinez	.05
553	Jeff Fassero	.05
554	Ryan Jackson RC	.05
555	Stan Javier	.05
556	Jaime Navarro	.05
557	Jose Offerman	.05
558	Mike Lowell RC	1.00
559	Darrin Fletcher	.05
560	Mark Lewis	.05
561	Dante Bichette	.05
562	Chuck Finley	.05
563	Kerry Wood	.35
564	Andy Benes	.05
565	Freddy Garcia	.05
566	Tom Glavine	.25
567	Jon Nunnally	.05
568	Miguel Cairo	.05
569	Shane Reynolds	.05
570	Roberto Kelly	.05
571	Checklist (Jose Cruz Jr.)	.25
572	Checklist (Ken Griffey Jr.)	.65
573	Checklist (Mark McGwire)	.75
574	Checklist (Cal Ripken Jr.)	1.00
575	Checklist (Frank Thomas)	.45
576	Jeff Bagwell (Unforgettable Moments)	1.00
577	Barry Bonds (Unforgettable Moments)	3.00
578	Tony Clark (Unforgettable Moments)	.25
579	Roger Clemens (Unforgettable Moments)	2.00
580	Jose Cruz Jr. (Unforgettable Moments)	.25
581	Nomar Garciaparra (Unforgettable Moments)	1.50
582	Juan Gonzalez (Unforgettable Moments)	1.00
583	Ben Grieve (Unforgettable Moments)	.25
584	Ken Griffey Jr. (Unforgettable Moments)	2.00
585	Tony Gwynn (Unforgettable Moments)	1.50
586	Derek Jeter (Unforgettable Moments)	3.00

587	Randy Johnson (Unforgettable Moments)	1.00
588	Chipper Jones (Unforgettable Moments)	1.50
589	Greg Maddux (Unforgettable Moments)	1.50
590	Mark McGwire (Unforgettable Moments)	2.50
591	Andy Pettitte (Unforgettable Moments)	.45
592	Paul Molitor (Unforgettable Moments)	1.00
593	Cal Ripken Jr. (Unforgettable Moments)	3.00
594	Alex Rodriguez (Unforgettable Moments)	2.50
595	Scott Rolen (Unforgettable Moments)	.50
596	Curt Schilling (Unforgettable Moments)	.50
597	Frank Thomas (Unforgettable Moments)	1.25
598	Jim Thome (Unforgettable Moments)	.75
599	Larry Walker (Unforgettable Moments)	.25
600	Bernie Williams (Unforgettable Moments)	.30

Decade of Excellence

Decade of Excellence inserts were found in one per 72 Series 1 hobby packs of Fleer Tradition. The 12-card set features 1988 season photos in Fleer's 1988 card design. The set includes only those current players who have been in baseball for 10 years or more. The use of blue and red metallic foil stripes in the background differentiates a scarcer (1:720 hobby packs) "Rare Traditions" parallel to the insert.

		NM/M
Complete Set (12):		35.00
Common Player:		1.00
Inserted 1:72		
Rare Traditions:		3X
Inserted 1:720		
1	Roberto Alomar	1.50
2	Barry Bonds	8.00
3	Roger Clemens	5.00
4	David Cone	1.00
5	Andres Galarraga	1.00
6	Mark Grace	1.00
7	Tony Gwynn	4.00
8	Randy Johnson	3.00
9	Greg Maddux	4.00
10	Mark McGwire	6.00
11	Paul O'Neill	1.00
12	Cal Ripken Jr.	8.00

Diamond Ink

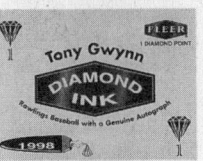

These one-per-pack inserts offer collectors a chance to acquire genuine autographed baseballs. Issued in denominations of 1, 5 and 10 points, the cards had to be accumulated to a total of 500 points of the same player to be redeemed for an autographed ball of that player. Cards are the standard 3-1/2" x 2-1/2" and are printed in black and purple on front and black and yellow on back. The point value of each card is embossed at center to prevent counterfeiting. The rules of the exchange program are printed on back. The deadline for redemption was Dec. 31, 1998. Values shown are for 1-pt. cards. The unnumbered players in the series are listed alphabetically.

Diamond Standouts

Diamond Standouts were inserted into Series I packs at a rate of one per 12. The 20-card insert set features players over a diamond design silver foil background.

		NM/M
Complete Set (20):		25.00
Common Player:		.50
1	Jeff Bagwell	1.00
2	Barry Bonds	4.00
3	Roger Clemens	2.00
4	Jose Cruz Jr.	.50
5	Andres Galarraga	.50
6	Nomar Garciaparra	2.00
7	Juan Gonzalez	.75
8	Ken Griffey Jr.	2.00
9	Derek Jeter	4.00
10	Randy Johnson	1.00
11	Chipper Jones	1.50
12	Kenny Lofton	.50
13	Greg Maddux	1.50
14	Pedro Martinez	1.00
15	Mark McGwire	3.00
16	Mike Piazza	2.00
17	Alex Rodriguez	3.00
18	Curt Schilling	.75
19	Frank Thomas	1.50
20	Larry Walker	.50

Diamond Tribute

This 10-card insert was exclusive to Series 2 packs and seeded one per 300 packs. Cards were printed on a leather-like laminated stock and had silver holofoil stamping.

		NM/M
Complete Set (10):		90.00
Common Player:		5.00
DT1	Jeff Bagwell	7.50
DT2	Roger Clemens	10.00
DT3	Nomar Garciaparra	10.00
DT4	Juan Gonzalez	5.00
DT5	Ken Griffey Jr.	12.00
DT6	Mark McGwire	15.00
DT7	Mike Piazza	12.00
DT8	Cal Ripken Jr.	20.00
DT9	Alex Rodriguez	15.00
DT10	Frank Thomas	7.50

Heroes For Kids Commemorative Card

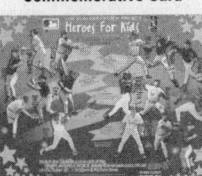

More than two dozen nominees for Players Choice Awards are featured in action photos on both sides of this 11" x 8-1/2" card.

	NM/M
Complete Set, 1 pt. (11):	1.00
Common Player, 1 pt.:	.05
5-pt. Cards:	5X
10-pt. Cards:	10X
(1) Jay Buhner	.20
(2) Roger Clemens	.20
(3) Jose Cruz Jr.	.05
(4) Nomar Garciaparra	.20
(5) Tony Gwynn	.15
(6) Roberto Hernandez	.05
(7) Greg Maddux	.15
(8) Cal Ripken Jr.	.30
(9) Alex Rodriguez	.25
(10) Scott Rolen	.10
(11) Tony Womack	.05

In the Clutch

	NM/M
Commemorative Card:	3.00

This Series 2 insert features stars who can stand up to pressure of big league ball. Fronts have embossed action photos on a prismatic metallic foil background. Backs have a portrait photo and a few words about the player. Stated insertion rate for the inserts was one per 20 packs on average.

		NM/M
Complete Set (15):		25.00
Common Player:		.40
IC1	Jeff Bagwell	1.00
IC2	Barry Bonds	5.00
IC3	Roger Clemens	2.00
IC4	Jose Cruz Jr.	.40
IC5	Nomar Garciaparra	2.00
IC6	Juan Gonzalez	.75
IC7	Ken Griffey Jr.	2.50
IC8	Tony Gwynn	1.50
IC9	Derek Jeter	5.00
IC10	Chipper Jones	1.50
IC11	Greg Maddux	1.50
IC12	Mark McGwire	4.00
IC13	Mike Piazza	2.50
IC14	Frank Thomas	1.00
IC15	Larry Walker	.40

Lumber Company

This 15-card set was exclusive to Series I retail packs and inserted one per 36 packs. It included power hitters and featured the insert name in large letters across the top.

		NM/M
Complete Set (15):		50.00
Common Player:		.75
Inserted 1:36 R		
1	Jeff Bagwell	2.50
2	Barry Bonds	8.00
3	Jose Cruz Jr.	.75
4	Nomar Garciaparra	4.00
5	Juan Gonzalez	1.50
6	Ken Griffey Jr.	5.00
7	Tony Gwynn	3.00
8	Chipper Jones	.75
9	Tino Martinez	.75
10	Mark McGwire	6.00
11	Mike Piazza	5.00
12	Cal Ripken Jr.	8.00
13	Alex Rodriguez	6.00
14	Frank Thomas	2.50
15	Larry Walker	.75

Mickey Mantle Monumental Moments

This 10-card insert honors Hall of Famer Mickey Mantle's legendary career and was seeded one per 68 packs of Series 2. Fleer/SkyBox worked closely with Mantle's family with each photo in the set personally selected by them. A gold-enhanced version was issued with each card serially numbered to 51.

	NM/M
Complete Set (10):	40.00
Common Card:	5.00
Inserted 1:68	

Gold (51 Sets):		3X
1	Armed and Dangerous	5.00
2	Getting Ready in Spring Training	5.00
3	Mantle and Rizzuto Celebrate	5.00
4	Posed for Action	5.00
5	Signed, Sealed and Ready to Deliver	5.00
6	Triple Crown 1956 Season	5.00
7	Number 7 . . . Mantle's Powerful Swing . . .	5.00
8	Old-Timers Day Introduction	5.00
9	Portrait of Determination	5.00

Promising Forecast

Potential future stars are showcased in this Series 2 insert. Both front and back have a background of a colorful weather map. Fronts have a glossy player action photo on a matte-finish background. Backs are all-glossy and have a second photo and a few words about the player's potential. Average odds of pulling a Promising Forecast card were stated as one per 12 packs.

		NM/M
Complete Set (20):		7.00
Common Player:		.25
Inserted 1:12		
PF1	Rolando Arrojo	.25
PF2	Sean Casey	.40
PF3	Brad Fullmer	.25
PF4	Karim Garcia	.35
PF5	Ben Grieve	.25
PF6	Todd Helton	3.00
PF7	Richard Hidalgo	.25
PF8	A.J. Hinch	.25
PF9	Paul Konerko	.35
PF10	Mark Kotsay	.25
PF11	Derrek Lee	1.00
PF12	Travis Lee	.35
PF13	Eric Milton	.25
PF14	Magglio Ordonez	.50
PF15	David Ortiz	.50
PF16	Brian Rose	.25
PF17	Miguel Tejada	.40
PF18	Jason Varitek	.35
PF19	Enrique Wilson	.25
PF20	Kerry Wood	1.00

Rookie Sensations

Rookie Sensations included 20 gray-bordered cards of the 1997 most promising players who were eligible for the Rookie of the Year award. Each card contained a multicolored background and was inserted one per 18 packs.

		NM/M
Complete Set (20):		12.00
Common Player:		.50
Inserted 1:18		
1	Mike Cameron	.50
2	Jose Cruz Jr.	.50
3	Jason Dickson	.50
4	Kelvim Escobar	.50
5	Nomar Garciaparra	3.00
6	Ben Grieve	.50
7	Vladimir Guerrero	3.00
8	Wilton Guerrero	.50
9	Jose Guillen	.50
10	Todd Helton	2.00
11	Livan Hernandez	.50
12	Hideki Irabu	.50
13	Andruw Jones	3.00
14	Matt Morris	.50
15	Magglio Ordonez	1.00
16	Neifi Perez	.50
17	Scott Rolen	2.00
18	Fernando Tatis	.50
19	Brett Tomko	.50
20	Jaret Wright	.50

The Power Game

Pitchers and hitters are pictured over a purple metallic background with UV coating in this 20-card insert. Power Game inserts were exclusive to Series I and seeded one per 36 packs.

		NM/M
Complete Set (20):		30.00
Common Player:		.50
Inserted 1:36		
1	Jeff Bagwell	2.00
2	Albert Belle	.50
3	Barry Bonds	6.00
4	Tony Clark	.50
5	Roger Clemens	3.50
6	Jose Cruz Jr.	.50
7	Andres Galarraga	.50
8	Nomar Garciaparra	3.50
9	Juan Gonzalez	1.00
10	Ken Griffey Jr.	4.00
11	Randy Johnson	2.00
12	Greg Maddux	3.00
13	Pedro Martinez	2.00
14	Tino Martinez	.50
15	Mark McGwire	5.00
16	Mike Piazza	4.00
17	Curt Schilling	.75
18	Frank Thomas	2.00
19	Jim Thome	2.00
20	Larry Walker	.50

Vintage '63

MARK McGWIRE
St. Louis Cardinals ⸱ 1B

Vintage featured 126 different players, with 63 in Series I and 63 in Series II, on the design of 1963 Fleer cards. The insert commemorated the 35th anniversary of Fleer and was seeded one per hobby pack. In addition, Series II featured Mickey Mantle on card No. 67, which completed the original 1963

Fleer set that ended at card No. 66 and wasn't able to include Mantle for licensing reasons. The Mantle card was printed in vintage looking stock and was purposely made to look and feel like the originals. Fleer also printed a Classic parallel version to this insert that contained gold foil on the front and was sequentially numbered to 63 with a "C" prefix on the back.

		NM/M
Complete Set (126):		20.00
Complete Series 1 (63):		10.00
Complete Series 2 (63):		10.00
Common Player:		.10
Classics (63 sets):		20X
1	Jason Dickson	.10
2	Tim Salmon	.25
3	Andruw Jones	.75
4	Chipper Jones	1.00
5	Kenny Lofton	.10
6	Greg Maddux	1.00
7	Rafael Palmeiro	.65
8	Cal Ripken Jr.	2.50
9	Nomar Garciaparra	1.25
10	Mark Grace	.10
11	Sammy Sosa	1.25
12	Frank Thomas	.75
13	Deion Sanders	.10
14	Sandy Alomar	.10
15	David Justice	.10
16	Jim Thome	.75
17	Matt Williams	.10
18	Jaret Wright	.10
19	Vinny Castilla	.10
20	Andres Galarraga	.10
21	Todd Helton	.75
22	Larry Walker	.10
23	Tony Clark	.10
24	Moises Alou	.10
25	Kevin Brown	.10
26	Charles Johnson	.10
27	Edgar Renteria	.10
28	Gary Sheffield	.50
29	Jeff Bagwell	.75
30	Craig Biggio	.10
31	Raul Mondesi	.10
32	Mike Piazza	1.50
33	Chuck Knoblauch	.10
34	Paul Molitor	.75
35	Vladimir Guerrero	.75
36	Pedro Martinez	.75
37	Todd Hundley	.10
38	Derek Jeter	2.50
39	Tino Martinez	.10
40	Paul O'Neill	.10
41	Andy Pettitte	.35
42	Mariano Rivera	.20
43	Bernie Williams	.20
44	Ben Grieve	.10
45	Scott Rolen	.65
46	Curt Schilling	.45
47	Jason Kendall	.10
48	Tony Womack	.10
49	Ray Lankford	.10
50	Mark McGwire	2.00
51	Matt Morris	.10
52	Tony Gwynn	1.00
53	Barry Bonds	2.50
54	Jay Buhner	.10
55	Ken Griffey Jr.	1.50
56	Randy Johnson	.75
57	Edgar Martinez	.10
58	Alex Rodriguez	2.00
59	Juan Gonzalez	.65
60	Rusty Greer	.10
61	Ivan Rodriguez	.65
62	Roger Clemens	1.25
63	Jose Cruz Jr.	.10
	Checklist #1-63	.10
64	Darin Erstad	.20
65	Jay Bell	.10
66	Andy Benes	.10
67	Mickey Mantle	2.00
68	Karim Garcia	.10
69	Travis Lee	.10
70	Matt Williams	.10
71	Andres Galarraga	.10
72	Tom Glavine	.35
73	Ryan Klesko	.10
74	Denny Neagle	.10
75	John Smoltz	.10
76	Roberto Alomar	.20
77	Joe Carter	.10
78	Mike Mussina	.50
79	B.J. Surhoff	.10
80	Dennis Eckersley	.65
81	Pedro Martinez	.10
82	Mo Vaughn	.10
83	Jeff Blauser	.10
84	Henry Rodriguez	.10
85	Albert Belle	.10
86	Sean Casey	.25
87	Travis Fryman	.10
88	Kenny Lofton	.10
89	Darryl Kile	.10
90	Mike Lansing	.10
91	Bobby Bonilla	.10
92	Cliff Floyd	.10
93	Livan Hernandez	.10
94	Derrek Lee	.10
95	Moises Alou	.10
96	Shane Reynolds	.10
97	Jeff Conine	.10

98	Johnny Damon	.35
99	Eric Karros	.10
100	Hideo Nomo	.65
101	Marquis Grissom	.10
102	Matt Lawton	.10
103	Todd Walker	.10
104	Gary Sheffield	.50
105	Bernard Gilkey	.10
106	Rey Ordonez	.10
107	Chili Davis	.10
108	Chuck Knoblauch	.10
109	Charles Johnson	.10
110	Rickey Henderson	.75
111	Bob Abreu	.10
112	Doug Glanville	.10
113	Gregg Jefferies	.10
114	Al Martin	.10
115	Kevin Young	.10
116	Ron Gant	.10
117	Kevin Brown	.10
118	Ken Caminiti	.10
119	Joey Hamilton	.10
120	Jeff Kent	.10
121	Wade Boggs	1.00
122	Quinton McCracken	.10
123	Fred McGriff	.50
124	Paul Sorrento	.10
125	Jose Canseco	.50
126	Randy Myers	.10
	Checklist #64-126	.10

Vintage '63 Classic

Vintage '63 Classic paralleled all 126 Vintage '63 inserts throughout Series 1 and 2, plus the checklists. These cards feature gold-foil stamping on front, specifically around the diamond in the lower-left corner, and are sequentially numbered to 63 sets. Cards have a "C" suffix to the card number.

		NM/M
Complete Set (128):		650.00
Common Player:		4.00
Stars/RC's:		20X

Zone

Inserted in one per 288 packs of Series I Fleer Tradition, Zone featured 15 top players printed on rainbow foil and etching.

		NM/M
Complete Set (15):		130.00
Common Player:		4.00
Inserted 1:288		
1	Jeff Bagwell	7.50
2	Barry Bonds	25.00
3	Roger Clemens	10.00
4	Jose Cruz Jr.	4.00
5	Nomar Garciaparra	10.00
6	Juan Gonzalez	6.00
7	Ken Griffey Jr.	12.00
8	Tony Gwynn	9.00
9	Chipper Jones	9.00
10	Greg Maddux	9.00
11	Mark McGwire	15.00
12	Mike Piazza	12.00
13	Alex Rodriguez	20.00
14	Frank Thomas	7.50
15	Larry Walker	4.00

Update

Fleer's first Update set since 1994 is this 100-card boxed set. It arrived soon after the conclusion of the 1998 World Series and focused on rookies who made their major league debut in September and had not yet had a rookie card. The set had 70 rookies, including 15 making their major league debut, 20 traded players and free agents. There was one subset called Season's Highlights that focused on feats like Mark McGwire's 70th home run, Sammy Sosa's single-month home run record and Kerry Wood's 20 strikeout performance.

		NM/M
Complete Set (100):		12.50
Common Player:		.05
U1	Mark McGwire (Season Highlights)	.75
U2	Sammy Sosa (Season Highlights)	.45
U3	Roger Clemens (Season Highlights)	.45
U4	Barry Bonds (Season Highlights)	1.00
U5	Kerry Wood (Season Highlights)	
U6	Paul Molitor (Season Highlights)	.25
U7	Ken Griffey Jr. (Season Highlights)	.50
U8	Cal Ripken Jr. (Season Highlights)	1.00
U9	David Wells (Season Highlights)	.05
U10	Alex Rodriguez (Season Highlights)	.75
U11	Angel Pena RC	.05
U12	Bruce Chen	.05
U13	Craig Wilson	.05
U14	Orlando Hernandez RC	1.50
U15	Aramis Ramirez	.10
U16	Aaron Boone	.05
U17	Bob Henley	.05
U18	Juan Guzman	.05
U19	Darryl Hamilton	.05
U20	Jay Payton	.05
U21	Jeremy Powell RC	.05
U22	Ben Davis	.05
U23	Preston Wilson	.10
U24	Jim Parque RC	.15
U25	Odalis Perez RC	.25
U26	Ron Belliard	.05
U27	Royce Clayton	.05
U28	George Lombard	.05
U29	Tony Phillips	.05
U30	Fernando Seguignol RC	.15
U31	Armando Rios RC	.10
U32	Jerry Hairston Jr. RC	.25
U33	Justin Baughman RC	.05
U34	Seth Greisinger	.05
U35	Alex Gonzalez	.05
U36	Michael Barrett	.05
U37	Carlos Beltran	.35
U38	Ellis Burks	.05
U39	Jose Jimenez	.05
U40	Carlos Guillen	.05
U41	Marlon Anderson	.05
U42	Scott Elarton	.05
U43	Glenallen Hill	.05
U44	Shane Monahan	.05
U45	Dennis Martinez	.05
U46	Carlos Febles RC	.05
U47	Carlos Perez	.05
U48	Wilton Guerrero	.05
U49	Randy Johnson	.45
U50	Brian Simmons RC	.05
U51	Carlton Loewer	.05
U52	Mark DeRosa RC	.50
U53	Tim Young RC	.05
U54	Gary Gaetti	.05
U55	Eric Chavez	.25
U56	Carl Pavano	.05
U57	Mike Stanley	.05
U58	Todd Stottlemyre	.05
U59	Gabe Kapler RC	.50
U60	Mike Jerzembeck RC	.15
U61	Mitch Meluskey RC	.15
U62	Bill Pulsipher	.05
U63	Derrick Gibson	.05
U64	John Rocker RC	.75

U65	Calvin Pickering	.05
U66	Blake Stein	.05
U67	Fernando Tatis	.05
U68	Gabe Alvarez	.05
U69	Jeffrey Hammonds	.05
U70	Adrian Beltre	.25
U71	Ryan Bradley RC	.10
U72	Edgar Clemente RC	.05
U73	Rick Croushore RC	.05
U74	Matt Clement	.15
U75	Dermal Brown	.05
U76	Paul Bako	.05
U77	Placido Polanco RC	1.00
U78	Jay Tessmer	.05
U79	Jarrod Washburn	.05
U80	Kevin Witt	.05
U81	Mike Metcalfe	.05
U82	Daryle Ward	.05
U83	Benj Sampson RC	.05
U84	Mike Kinkade RC	.20
U85	Randy Winn	.05
U86	Jeff Shaw	.05
U87	Troy Glaus RC	4.00
U88	Hideo Nomo	.35
U89	Mark Grudzielanek	.05
U90	Mike Frank RC	.05
U91	Bobby Howry RC	.05
U92	Ryan Minor RC	.15
U93	Corey Koskie RC	1.00
U94	Matt Anderson RC	.20
U95	Joe Carter	.05
U96	Paul Konerko	.15
U97	Sidney Ponson	.05
U98	Jeremy Giambi RC	.25
U99	Jeff Kubenka RC	.05
U100	J.D. Drew RC	5.00

Diamond Skills Commemorative Sheet

In conjunction with its sponsorship of the Diamond Skills program, Fleer and its 2,500 direct dealers distributed this eight-player sheet to 7-14 year olds participating in the event. Participants could get a sheet by redeeming Fleer wrappers at a local card store. The 10" x 9" sheet features full size Fleer Tradition card reproductions. At top is a list of 1997 Diamond Skills winners.

	NM/M
Complete Sheet:	2.00

Mantle & Sons

As part of its participation in SportsFest in May, 1998, Fleer issued a promotional card featuring a vintage color photo of Mickey Mantle and his sons, David and Danny. The back of the card announced Fleer's first-ever inclusion of Mickey Mantle cards in some of its forthcoming releases.

	NM/M
Mickey Mantle, Danny Mantle, David Mantle	3.00

Mickey Mantle Promo Postcard

This 4-1/4" x 5-1/2" color postcard was sent to Fleer dealers to announce a Mickey Mantle commemorative series in its Series 2 product. The address side has the Fleer Tradition logo in black, blue and red. The picture side has a color photo of one of the Mantle cards to be issued in

the format of the 1963 Fleer issue. Cards are individually serial numbered within an edition of 3,500.

	NM/M
Mickey Mantle	4.00

Mark McGwire 62nd HR 23K Gold Commemorative

Marketed as a retail-exclusive "Official 62nd HR 23 Kt. Gold Commemorative Card," this 2-1/2" x 3-1/2" card was sold in a colorful blister pack. Embossed in 23-karat gold foil is an image of McGwire in action. Also on front are a 62-HR logo and a facsimile autograph, along with the legend "Smashing the Record." On back is a small picture of McGwire with the large 9-8-98 date and the details of the record blast. There are appropriate licensing logos and a serial number from within an edition of 200,000.

	NM/M
Mark McGwire	5.00

National Convention Commemorative Set

In conjunction with its participation at the 19th National Sports Collectors Convention in Chicago in August 1998, Fleer distributed this commemorative set to persons purchasing VIP admission packages. The set includes a specially numbered (NC1) Fleer Tradition Mickey Mantle card, a card picturing Mick with his sons, one of seven large-format (3-1/2" x 5") cards reproducing Mantle Monumental Moments inserts, and an unnumbered header card. The Monumental Moments reproductions are printed on a pin-striped-sky background.

		NM/M
Complete Set (8):		15.00
Common Card:		2.25
NC1	Mickey Mantle (Fleer Tradition)	2.25
NC2	Mickey Mantle (With sons.)	2.25
NC3	Mickey Mantle (Monumental Moments - accepting trophy.)	2.25
NC4	Mickey Mantle (Monumental Moments - making a throw.)	2.25
NC5	Mickey Mantle (Monumental Moments - in sliding pit.)	2.25
NC6	Mickey Mantle (Monumental Moments - batting.)	2.25
NC7	Mickey Mantle (Monumental Moments - number retired.)	2.25
	Header Card	.25

1999 Fleer

Released as a single series in 10-card packs with a suggested retail price of $1.59, the base set consists of 600 cards, including 10 checklists and a 15-card Franchise Futures subset. Cards are UV coated, with borderless photos and gold-foil graphics. Backs have personal bio-information along with year-by-year career stats and a small photo. There are two parallels, Starting Nine, which are hobby-exclusive, numbered to nine sets with blue foil stamping and Warning Track. Found exclusively in retail packs, Warning Tracks can be identified by red foil stamping and a Warning Track logo.

		NM/M
Complete Set (600):		25.00
Common Player:		.05
Warning Track:		2X
Inserted 1:1 R		
Pack (10):		1.00
Wax Box (36):		25.00
1	Mark McGwire	2.00
2	Sammy Sosa	1.25
3	Ken Griffey Jr.	1.50
4	Kerry Wood	.30
5	Derek Jeter	2.50
6	Stan Musial	2.00
7	J.D. Drew	.65
7p	J.D. Drew/OPS	1.50
8	Cal Ripken Jr.	2.50
9	Alex Rodriguez	2.00
10	Travis Lee	.15
11	Andres Galarraga	.05
12	Nomar Garciaparra	1.25
13	Albert Belle	.05
14	Barry Larkin	.05
15	Dante Bichette	.05
16	Tony Clark	.05
17	Moises Alou	.05
18	Rafael Palmeiro	.65
19	Raul Mondesi	.05
20	Vladimir Guerrero	.75
21	John Olerud	.05
22	Bernie Williams	.05
23	Ben Grieve	.05
24	Scott Rolen	.05
25	Jeromy Burnitz	.05
26	Ken Caminiti	.05
27	Barry Bonds	2.50
28	Todd Helton	.75
29	Juan Gonzalez	.65
30	Roger Clemens	1.25
31	Andruw Jones	.75
32	Mo Vaughn	.05
33	Larry Walker	.75
34	Frank Thomas	.75
35	Manny Ramirez	.75
36	Randy Johnson	.75
37	Vinny Castilla	.05
38	Juan Encarnacion	.05
39	Jeff Bagwell	.75
40	Gary Sheffield	.50
41	Mike Piazza	1.50
42	Richie Sexson	.05
43	Tony Gwynn	1.00
44	Chipper Jones	1.00
45	Jim Thome	.65

No	Player	Price
46	Craig Biggio	.05
47	Carlos Delgado	.40
48	Greg Vaughn	.05
49	Greg Maddux	1.00
50	Troy Glaus	.65
51	Roberto Alomar	.10
52	Dennis Eckersley	.60
53	Mike Caruso	.05
54	Bruce Chen	.05
55	Aaron Boone	.05
56	Bartolo Colon	.05
57	Derrick Gibson	.05
58	Brian Anderson	.05
59	Gabe Alvarez	.05
60	Todd Dunwoody	.05
61	Rod Beck	.05
62	Derek Bell	.05
63	Francisco Cordova	.05
64	Johnny Damon	.25
65	Adrian Beltre	.15
66	Garret Anderson	.05
67	Armando Benitez	.05
68	Edgardo Alfonzo	.05
69	Ryan Bradley	.05
70	Eric Chavez	.30
71	Bobby Abreu	.05
72	Andy Ashby	.05
73	Ellis Burks	.05
74	Jeff Cirillo	.05
75	Jay Buhner	.05
76	Ron Gant	.05
77	Rolando Arrojo	.10
78	Will Clark	.10
79	Chris Carpenter	.05
80	Jim Edmonds	.05
81	Tony Batista	.05
82	Shane Andrews	.05
83	Mark DeRosa	.05
84	Brady Anderson	.05
85	Tony Gordon	.05
86	Brant Brown	.05
87	Ray Durham	.05
88	Ron Coomer	.05
89	Bret Boone	.05
90	Travis Fryman	.05
91	Darryl Kile	.05
92	Paul Bako	.05
93	Cliff Floyd	.05
94	Scott Elarton	.05
95	Jeremy Giambi	.05
96	Darren Dreifort	.05
97	Marquis Grissom	.05
98	Marty Cordova	.05
99	Fernando Seguignol	.05
100	Orlando Hernandez	.05
101	Jose Cruz Jr.	.05
102	Jason Giambi	.60
103	Damion Easley	.05
104	Freddy Garcia	.05
105	Marlon Anderson	.05
106	Kevin Brown	.05
107	Joe Carter	.05
108	Russ Davis	.05
109	Brian Jordan	.05
110	Wade Boggs	1.00
111	Tom Goodwin	.05
112	Scott Brosius	.05
113	Darin Erstad	.10
114	Jay Bell	.05
115	Tom Glavine	.25
116	Pedro Martinez	.75
117	Mark Grace	.10
118	Russ Ortiz	.05
119	Magglio Ordonez	.10
120	Sean Casey	.15
121	Rafael Roque RC	.05
122	Brian Giles	.05
123	Mike Lansing	.05
124	David Cone	.05
125	Alex Gonzalez	.05
126	Carl Everett	.05
127	Jeff King	.05
128	Charles Johnson	.05
129	Geoff Jenkins	.05
130	Corey Koskie	.05
131	Brad Fullmer	.05
132	Al Leiter	.05
133	Rickey Henderson	.75
134	Rico Brogna	.05
135	Jose Guillen	.05
136	Matt Clement	.05
137	Carlos Guillen	.05
138	Orel Hershiser	.05
139	Ray Lankford	.05
140	Miguel Cairo	.05
141	Chuck Finley	.05
142	Rusty Greer	.05
143	Kelvim Escobar	.05
144	Ryan Klesko	.05
145	Andy Benes	.05
146	Eric Davis	.05
147	David Wells	.05
148	Trot Nixon	.05
149	Jose Hernandez	.05
150	Mark Johnson	.05
151	Mike Frank	.05
152	Joey Hamilton	.05
153	David Justice	.15
154	Mike Mussina	.40
155	Neifi Perez	.05
156	Luis Gonzalez	.10
157	Livan Hernandez	.05
158	Dermal Brown	.05
159	Jose Lima	.05
160	Eric Karros	.05
161	Ronnie Belliard	.05
162	Matt Lawton	.05
163	Dustin Hermanson	.05
164	Brian McRae	.05
165	Mike Kinkade	.05
166	A.J. Hinch	.05
167	Doug Glanville	.05
168	Hideo Nomo	.65
169	Jason Kendall	.05
170	Steve Finley	.05
171	Jeff Kent	.05
172	Ben Davis	.05
173	Edgar Martinez	.05
174	Eli Marrero	.05
175	Quinton McCracken	.05
176	Rick Helling	.05
177	Tom Evans	.05
178	Carl Pavano	.10
179	Todd Greene	.05
180	Omar Daal	.05
181	George Lombard	.05
182	Ryan Minor	.05
183	Troy O'Leary	.05
184	Robb Nen	.05
185	Mickey Morandini	.05
186	Robin Ventura	.05
187	Pete Harnisch	.05
188	Kenny Lofton	.05
189	Eric Milton	.05
190	Bobby Higginson	.05
191	Jamie Moyer	.05
192	Mark Kotsay	.05
193	Shane Reynolds	.05
194	Carlos Febles	.05
195	Jeff Kubenka	.05
196	Chuck Knoblauch	.05
197	Kenny Rogers	.05
198	Bill Mueller	.05
199	Shane Monahan	.05
200	Matt Morris	.05
201	Fred McGriff	.05
202	Ivan Rodriguez	.65
203	Kevin Witt	.05
204	Troy Percival	.05
205	David Dellucci	.05
206	Kevin Millwood	.05
207	Jerry Hairston Jr.	.05
208	Mike Stanley	.05
209	Henry Rodriguez	.05
210	Trevor Hoffman	.05
211	Craig Wilson	.05
212	Reggie Sanders	.05
213	Carlton Loewer	.05
214	Omar Vizquel	.05
215	Gabe Kapler	.05
216	Derrek Lee	.05
217	Billy Wagner	.05
218	Dean Palmer	.05
219	Chan Ho Park	.05
220	Fernando Vina	.05
221	Roy Halladay	.05
222	Paul Molitor	.75
223	Ugueth Urbina	.05
224	Rey Ordonez	.05
225	Ricky Ledee	.05
226	Scott Spiezio	.05
227	Wendell Magee Jr.	.05
228	Aramis Ramirez	.05
229	Brian Simmons	.05
230	Fernando Tatis	.05
231	Bobby Smith	.05
232	Aaron Sele	.05
233	Shawn Green	.20
234	Mariano Rivera	.15
235	Tim Salmon	.10
236	Andy Fox	.05
237	Denny Neagle	.05
238	John Valentin	.05
239	Kevin Tapani	.05
240	Paul Konerko	.10
241	Robert Fick	.05
242	Edgar Renteria	.05
243	Brett Tomko	.05
244	Daryle Ward	.05
245	Carlos Beltran	.30
246	Angel Pena	.05
247	Steve Woodard	.05
248	David Ortiz	.05
249	Justin Thompson	.05
250	Rondell White	.05
251	Jaret Wright	.05
252	Ed Sprague	.05
253	Jay Payton	.05
254	Mike Lowell	.05
255	Orlando Cabrera	.05
256	Jason Schmidt	.05
257	David Segui	.05
258	Paul Sorrento	.05
259	John Wetteland	.05
260	Devon White	.05
261	Odalis Perez	.05
262	Calvin Pickering	.05
263	Alex Ramirez	.05
264	Preston Wilson	.05
265	Brad Radke	.05
266	Walt Weiss	.05
267	Tim Young	.05
268	Tino Martinez	.05
269	Matt Stairs	.05
270	Curt Schilling	.25
271	Tony Womack	.05
272	Ismael Valdes	.05
273	Wally Joyner	.05
274	Armando Rios	.05
275	Andy Pettitte	.25
276	Bubba Trammell	.05
277	Todd Zeile	.05
278	Shannon Stewart	.05
279	Matt Williams	.05
280	John Rocker	.05
281	B.J. Surhoff	.05
282	Eric Young	.05
283	Dmitri Young	.05
284	John Smoltz	.05
285	Todd Walker	.05
286	Paul O'Neill	.05
287	Blake Stein	.05
288	Kevin Young	.05
289	Quilvio Veras	.05
290	Kirk Rueter	.05
291	Randy Winn	.05
292	Miguel Tejada	.05
293	J.T. Snow	.05
294	Michael Tucker	.05
295	Jay Tessmer	.05
296	Scott Erickson	.05
297	Tim Wakefield	.05
298	Jeff Abbott	.05
299	Eddie Taubensee	.05
300	Darryl Hamilton	.05
301	Kevin Orie	.05
302	Jose Offerman	.05
303	Scott Karl	.05
304	Chris Widger	.05
305	Todd Hundley	.05
306	Desi Relaford	.05
307	Sterling Hitchcock	.05
308	Delino DeShields	.05
309	Alex Gonzalez	.05
310	Justin Baughman	.05
311	Jamey Wright	.05
312	Wes Helms	.05
313	Dante Powell	.05
314	Jim Abbott	.05
315	Manny Alexander	.05
316	Harold Baines	.05
317	Danny Graves	.05
318	Sandy Alomar	.05
319	Pedro Astacio	.05
320	Jermaine Allensworth	.05
321	Matt Anderson	.05
322	Chad Curtis	.05
323	Antonio Osuna	.05
324	Brad Ausmus	.05
325	Steve Trachsel	.05
326	Mike Blowers	.05
327	Brian Bohanon	.05
328	Chris Gomez	.05
329	Valerio de los Santos	.05
330	Rich Aurilia	.05
331	Michael Barrett	.05
332	Rick Aguilera	.05
333	Adrian Brown	.05
334	Bill Spiers	.05
335	Matt Beech	.05
336	David Bell	.05
337	Juan Acevedo	.05
338	Jose Canseco	.50
339	Wilson Alvarez	.05
340	Luis Alicea	.05
341	Jason Dickson	.05
342	Mike Bordick	.05
343	Ben Ford	.05
344	Keith Lockhart	.05
345	Jason Christiansen	.05
346	Darren Bragg	.05
347	Doug Brocail	.05
348	Jeff Blauser	.05
349	James Baldwin	.05
350	Jeffrey Hammonds	.05
351	Ricky Bottalico	.05
352	Russ Branyan	.05
353	Mark Brownson	.05
354	Dave Berg	.05
355	Sean Bergman	.05
356	Jeff Conine	.05
357	Shayne Bennett	.05
358	Bobby Bonilla	.05
359	Bob Wickman	.05
360	Carlos Baerga	.05
361	Chris Fussell	.05
362	Chili Davis	.05
363	Jerry Spradlin	.05
364	Carlos Hernandez	.05
365	Roberto Hernandez	.05
366	Marvin Benard	.05
367	Ken Cloude	.05
368	Tony Fernandez	.05
369	John Burkett	.05
370	Gary DiSarcina	.05
371	Alan Benes	.05
372	Karim Garcia	.05
373	Carlos Perez	.05
374	Damon Buford	.05
375	Mark Clark	.05
376	Edgard Clemente RC	.05
377	Chad Bradford	.05
378	Frank Catalanotto	.05
379	Vic Darensbourg	.05
380	Sean Berry	.05
381	Dave Burba	.05
382	Sal Fasano	.05
383	Steve Parris	.05
384	Roger Cedeno	.05
385	Chad Fox	.05
386	Wilton Guerrero	.05
387	Dennis Cook	.05
388	Joe Girardi	.05
389	LaTroy Hawkins	.05
390	Ryan Christenson	.05
391	Paul Byrd	.05
392	Lou Collier	.05
393	Jeff Fassero	.05
394	Jim Leyritz	.05
395	Shawn Estes	.05
396	Mike Kelly	.05
397	Rich Croushore	.05
398	Royce Clayton	.05
399	Rudy Seanez	.05
400	Darrin Fletcher	.05
401	Shigetosi Hasegawa	.05
402	Bernard Gilkey	.05
403	Juan Guzman	.05
404	Jeff Frye	.05
405	Marino Santana	.05
406	Alex Fernandez	.05
407	Gary Gaetti	.05
408	Dan Miceli	.05
409	Mike Cameron	.05
410	Mike Remlinger	.05
411	Joey Cora	.05
412	Mark Gardner	.05
413	Aaron Ledesma	.05
414	Jerry Dipoto	.05
415	Ricky Gutierrez	.05
416	John Franco	.05
417	Mendy Lopez	.05
418	Hideki Irabu	.05
419	Mark Grudzielanek	.05
420	Bobby Hughes	.05
421	Pat Meares	.05
422	Jimmy Haynes	.05
423	Bob Henley	.05
424	Bobby Estalella	.05
425	Jon Lieber	.05
426	Giomar Guevara RC	.05
427	Jose Jimenez	.05
428	Deivi Cruz	.05
429	Jonathan Johnson	.05
430	Ken Hill	.05
431	Craig Grebeck	.05
432	Jose Rosado	.05
433	Danny Klassen	.05
434	Bobby Howry	.05
435	Gerald Williams	.05
436	Omar Olivares	.05
437	Chris Hoiles	.05
438	Seth Greisinger	.05
439	Scott Hatteberg	.05
440	Jeremi Gonzalez	.05
441	Wil Cordero	.05
442	Jeff Montgomery	.05
443	Chris Stynes	.05
444	Tony Saunders	.05
445	Einar Diaz	.05
446	Laril Gonzalez	.05
447	Ryan Jackson	.05
448	Mike Hampton	.05
449	Todd Hollandsworth	.05
450	Gabe White	.05
451	John Jaha	.05
452	Bret Saberhagen	.05
453	Otis Nixon	.05
454	Steve Kline	.05
455	Butch Huskey	.05
456	Mike Jerzembeck	.05
457	Wayne Gomes	.05
458	Mike Macfarlane	.05
459	Jesus Sanchez	.05
460	Al Martin	.05
461	Dwight Gooden	.05
462	Ruben Rivera	.05
463	Pat Hentgen	.05
464	Jose Valentin	.05
465	Vladimir Nunez	.05
466	Charlie Hayes	.05
467	Jay Powell	.05
468	Raul Ibanez	.05
469	Kent Mercker	.05
470	John Mabry	.05
471	Woody Williams	.05
472	Roberto Kelly	.05
473	Jim Mecir	.05
474	Dave Hollins	.05
475	Rafael Medina	.05
476	Darren Lewis	.05
477	Felix Heredia	.05
478	Brian Hunter	.05
479	Matt Mantei	.05
480	Richard Hidalgo	.05
481	Bobby Jones	.05
482	Hal Morris	.05
483	Ramiro Mendoza	.05
484	Matt Luke	.05
485	Esteban Loaiza	.05
486	Mark Loretta	.05
487	A.J. Pierzynski	.05
488	Charles Nagy	.05
489	Kevin Sefcik	.05
490	Jason McDonald	.05
491	Jeremy Powell	.05
492	Scott Servais	.05
493	Abraham Nunez	.05
494	Stan Spencer	.05
495	Stan Javier	.05
496	Jose Paniagua	.05
497	Gregg Jefferies	.05
498	Gregg Olson	.05
499	Derek Lowe	.05
500	Willis Otanez	.05
501	Brian Moehler	.05
502	Glenallen Hill	.05
503	Bobby Jones	.05
504	Greg Norton	.05
505	Mike Jackson	.05
506	Kirt Manwaring	.05
507	Eric Weaver	.05
508	Mitch Meluskey	.05
509	Todd Jones	.05
510	Mike Matheny	.05
511	Benj Sampson	.05
512	Tony Phillips	.05
513	Mike Thurman	.05
514	Jorge Posada	.05
515	Bill Taylor	.05
516	Mike Sweeney	.05
517	Jose Silva	.05
518	Mark Lewis	.05
519	Chris Peters	.05
520	Brian Johnson	.05
521	Mike Timlin	.05
522	Mark McLemore	.05
523	Dan Plesac	.05
524	Kelly Stinnett	.05
525	Sidney Ponson	.05
526	Jim Parque	.05
527	Tyler Houston	.05
528	John Thomson	.05
529	Mike Metcalfe	.05
530	Robert Person	.05
531	Marc Newfield	.05
532	Javier Vazquez	.05
533	Terry Steinbach	.05
534	Turk Wendell	.05
535	Tim Raines	.05
536	Brian Meadows	.05
537	Mike Lieberthal	.05
538	Ricardo Rincon	.05
539	Dan Wilson	.05
540	John Johnstone	.05
541	Todd Stottlemyre	.05
542	Kevin Stocker	.05
543	Ramon Martinez	.05
544	Mike Simms	.05
545	Paul Quantrill	.05
546	Matt Walbeck	.05
547	Turner Ward	.05
548	Bill Pulsipher	.05
549	Donnie Sadler	.05
550	Lance Johnson	.05
551	Bill Simas	.05
552	Jeff Reed	.05
553	Jeff Shaw	.05
554	Joe Randa	.05
555	Paul Shuey	.05
556	Mike Redmond	.05
557	Sean Runyan	.05
558	Enrique Wilson	.05
559	Scott Radinsky	.05
560	Larry Sutton	.05
561	Masato Yoshii	.05
562	David Nilsson	.05
563	Mike Trombley	.05
564	Darryl Strawberry	.05
565	Dave Mlicki	.05
566	Placido Polanco	.05
567	Yorkis Perez	.05
568	Esteban Yan	.05
569	Lee Stevens	.05
570	Steve Sinclair	.05
571	Jarrod Washburn	.05
572	Lenny Webster	.05
573	Mike Sirotka	.05
574	Jason Varitek	.05
575	Terry Mulholland	.05
576	Adrian Beltre (Franchise Futures)	.10
577	Eric Chavez (Franchise Futures)	.20
578	J.D. Drew (Franchise Futures)	.35
579	Juan Encarnacion (Franchise Futures)	.05
580	Nomar Garciaparra (Franchise Futures)	.65
581	Troy Glaus (Franchise Futures)	.35
582	Ben Grieve (Franchise Futures)	.05
583	Vladimir Guerrero (Franchise Futures)	.40
584	Todd Helton (Franchise Futures)	.35
585	Derek Jeter (Franchise Futures)	1.25
586	Travis Lee (Franchise Futures)	.10
587	Alex Rodriguez (Franchise Futures)	1.00
588	Scott Rolen (Franchise Futures)	.30
589	Richie Sexson (Franchise Futures)	.05
590	Kerry Wood (Franchise Futures)	.20
591	Ken Griffey Jr. (Checklist)	.75
592	Chipper Jones (Checklist)	.50
593	Alex Rodriguez (Checklist)	1.00
594	Sammy Sosa (Checklist)	.65
595	Mark McGwire (Checklist)	1.00
596	Cal Ripken Jr. (Checklist)	1.25
597	Nomar Garciaparra (Checklist)	.65
598	Derek Jeter (Checklist)	1.25
599	Kerry Wood (Checklist)	.20
600	J.D. Drew (Checklist)	.40

NM/M
Common Player: 20.00

Warning Track Collection

Each of the cards in '99 Fleer Tradition was paralleled in this retail-only issue found one per pack. Warning Track cards are distinguished by the use of red metallic foil on front for the player's name, team, position that are in gold-foil on the regular version. There is also a special "Warning Track Collection" logo in red foil at bottom-right. On back, WTC cards have a "W" suffix to the card number.

NM/M
Complete Set (600): 160.00
Common Player: .50
Stars: 2X

Fleer Date With Destiny

This 10-card set takes a look at what Hall of Fame plaques might look like for some of today's great players. These are serially numbered to 100 sets.

NM/M
Complete Set (10): 300.00
Common Player: 20.00
Production 100 Sets

1	Barry Bonds	60.00
2	Roger Clemens	35.00
3	Ken Griffey Jr.	40.00
4	Tony Gwynn	30.00
5	Greg Maddux	30.00
6	Mark McGwire	50.00
7	Mike Piazza	40.00
8	Cal Ripken Jr.	60.00
9	Alex Rodriguez	50.00
10	Frank Thomas	20.00

Diamond Magic

A multi-layer card, where collectors turn a "wheel" for a kaleidoscope effect behind the player image. These are seeded 1:96 packs.

NM/M
Complete Set (15): 50.00
Common Player: 1.00
Inserted 1:96

1	Barry Bonds	9.00
2	Roger Clemens	4.50

Starting Nine

This ultra-scarce, hobby-only parallel insert, found at the rate of about two cards per case, includes just nine cards of each player. Sharing the basic design of the Fleer Traditional set, the cards have blue metallic foil printing on front, including a "STARTING 9 NINE" logo at lower-right. At bottom right, the card's individual serial number from within the edition of nine is printed. Backs have an "S" suffix to the card number.

Diamond Magic

Chipper Jones

3	Nomar Garciaparra	4.50
4	Ken Griffey Jr.	5.00
5	Tony Gwynn	3.75
6	Orlando Hernandez	1.00
7	Derek Jeter	9.00
8	Randy Johnson	3.00
9	Chipper Jones	3.75
10	Greg Maddux	3.75
11	Mark McGwire	6.00
12	Alex Rodriguez	7.50
13	Sammy Sosa	4.50
14	Bernie Williams	1.50
15	Kerry Wood	2.00

Going Yard

This 15-card set features the top home run hitters from the '98 season. These 1:18 pack inserts unfold to be twice as wide as regular cards and takes an unorthodox look at how far the longest home runs went.

		NM/M
Complete Set (15):		4.00
Common Player:		.10
Inserted 1:18		
1	Moises Alou	.10
2	Albert Belle	.10
3	Jose Canseco	.30
4	Vinny Castilla	.10
5	Andres Galarraga	.10
6	Juan Gonzalez	.20
7	Ken Griffey Jr.	.75
8	Chipper Jones	.50
9	Mark McGwire	1.00
10	Rafael Palmeiro	.35
11	Mike Piazza	.75
12	Alex Rodriguez	1.00
13	Sammy Sosa	.65
14	Greg Vaughn	.10
15	Mo Vaughn	.10

Golden Memories

This 15-card set pays tribute to the great moments from the 1998 season including David Wells' perfect game and McGwire's record breaking season. These are seeded 1:54 packs on an embossed frame design.

		NM/M
Complete Set (15):		45.00
Common Player:		.75
Inserted 1:54		
1	Albert Belle	.75
2	Barry Bonds	7.50
3	Roger Clemens	4.50
4	Nomar Garciaparra	4.50

5	Juan Gonzalez	1.50
6	Ken Griffey Jr.	3.75
7	Randy Johnson	2.75
8	Greg Maddux	3.25
9	Mark McGwire	5.00
10	Mike Piazza	3.75
11	Cal Ripken Jr.	7.50
12	Alex Rodriguez	6.00
13	Sammy Sosa	4.50
14	David Wells	.75
15	Kerry Wood	2.00

Home Run Heroes

These cards were part of an unannounced multi-manufacturer (Fleer, Upper Deck, Topps, Pacific) insert program which was exclusive to Wal-Mart. Each company produced cards of Mark McGwire and Sammy Sosa, along with two other premier sluggers. Each company's cards share a "Power Elite" logo at top and "Home Run Heroes" logo vertically at right.

		NM/M
Complete Set (4):		7.50
Common Player:		1.50
1	Mark McGwire (Tradition)	3.00
2	Sammy Sosa (Sports Illustrated)	2.00
3	Mike Piazza (SkyBox Thunder)	2.00
4	Nomar Garciaparra (SkyBox Thunder)	2.00

Stan Musial Monumental Moments

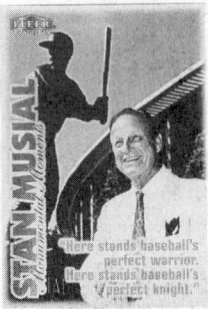

Great moments and insight from and about the St. Louis Cardinals great. This 10-card tribute set chronicles Musial's legendary career. These are seeded 1:36 packs with 500 autographed cards randomly seeded.

		NM/M
Complete Set (10):		15.00
Common Musial:		2.00
Autographed Card:		60.00
1	Life in Donora	2.00
2	Values	2.00
3	In the Beginning	2.00
4	In the Navy	2.00
5	The 1948 Season (W/Red Schoendienst.)	2.00
6	Success Stories (W/Pres. Kennedy.)	2.00
7	Mr. Cardinal	2.00
8	Most Valuable Player	2.00
9	... baseball's perfect knight	2.00
10	Hall of Fame	2.00

Rookie Flashback

This 15-card set features the impact rookies from the 1998 season. These are seeded 1:6 packs and feature sculpture embossing.

		NM/M
Complete Set (15):		5.00
Common Player:		.25
Inserted 1:6		
1	Matt Anderson	.25

2	Rolando Arrojo	.25
3	Adrian Beltre	.50
4	Mike Caruso	.25
5	Eric Chavez	.40
6	J.D. Drew	.75
7	Juan Encarnacion	.25
8	Brad Fullmer	.25
9	Troy Glaus	1.50
10	Ben Grieve	.25
11	Todd Helton	1.50
12	Orlando Hernandez	.25
13	Travis Lee	.40
14	Richie Sexson	.25
15	Kerry Wood	.65

Vintage '61

Todd Helton

This 50-card set takes the first 50 cards from the base set and showcases them in the 1961 Fleer "Baseball Greats" card design. These are seeded one per hobby pack.

		NM/M
Complete Set (50):		7.50
Common Player:		.05
Inserted 1:1		
1	Mark McGwire	.75
2	Sammy Sosa	.50
3	Ken Griffey Jr.	.60
4	Kerry Wood	.25
5	Derek Jeter	1.00
6	Stan Musial	.75
7	J.D. Drew	.30
8	Cal Ripken Jr.	1.00
9	Alex Rodriguez	.75
10	Travis Lee	.10
11	Andres Galarraga	.05
12	Nomar Garciaparra	.50
13	Albert Belle	.05
14	Barry Larkin	.05
15	Dante Bichette	.05
16	Tony Clark	.05
17	Moises Alou	.05
18	Rafael Palmeiro	.30
19	Raul Mondesi	.05
20	Vladimir Guerrero	.35
21	John Olerud	.05
22	Bernie Williams	.10
23	Ben Grieve	.05
24	Scott Rolen	.30
25	Jeromy Burnitz	.05
26	Ken Caminiti	.05
27	Barry Bonds	1.00
28	Todd Helton	.35
29	Juan Gonzalez	.25
30	Roger Clemens	.50
31	Andruw Jones	.35
32	Mo Vaughn	.05
33	Larry Walker	.05
34	Frank Thomas	.35
35	Manny Ramirez	.35
36	Randy Johnson	.35
37	Vinny Castilla	.05
38	Juan Encarnacion	.05
39	Jeff Bagwell	.35
40	Gary Sheffield	.25
41	Mike Piazza	.60
42	Richie Sexson	.05
43	Tony Gwynn	.45
44	Chipper Jones	.45
45	Jim Thome	.15
46	Craig Biggio	.05
47	Carlos Delgado	.25
48	Greg Vaughn	.05
49	Greg Maddux	.45
50	Troy Glaus	.35

Update

Alfonso Soriano

Distributed as a 150-card boxed set, the main focus for this release is the inclusion of rookie cards of players called up late in the '99 season, including Rick Ankiel. Besides rookies, the set also features 10 traded players/ free agents and a 10-card Season Highlights subset.

		NM/M
Complete Set (150):		25.00
Common Player:		.10
1	Rick Ankiel **RC**	5.00
2	Peter Bergeron **RC**	.25
3	Pat Burrell **RC**	1.50
4	Eric Munson **RC**	.35
5	Alfonso Soriano **RC**	3.00
6	Tim Hudson **RC**	2.00
7	Erubiel Durazo **RC**	.25
8	Chad Hermansen **RC**	.10
9	Jeff Zimmerman **RC**	.10
10	Jesus Pena **RC**	.10
11	Ramon Hernandez **RC**	.10
12	Trent Durrington **RC**	.25
13	Tony Armas Jr. **RC**	.10
14	Mike Fyhrie **RC**	.10
15	Danny Kolb **RC**	.25
16	Mike Porzio **RC**	.10
17	Will Brunson **RC**	.10
18	Mike Duvall **RC**	.10
19	Doug Mientkiewicz **RC**	.75
20	Gabe Molina **RC**	.15
21	Luis Vizcaino **RC**	.20
22	Robinson Cancel **RC**	.10
23	Brett Laxton **RC**	.10
24	Joe McEwing **RC**	.25
25	Justin Speier **RC**	.20
26	Kip Wells **RC**	.12
27	Armando Almanza **RC**	.10
28	Joe Davenport **RC**	.10
29	Yamid Haad **RC**	.10
30	John Halama	.10
31	Adam Kennedy	.10
32	Vicente Padilla **RC**	.25
33	Travis Dawkins **RC**	.25
34	Ryan Rupe **RC**	.25
35	B.J. Ryan **RC**	.10
36	Chance Sanford **RC**	.10
37	Anthony Shumaker **RC**	.10
38	Ryan Glynn **RC**	.10
39	Matt Herges **RC**	.20
40	Ben Molina	.10
41	Scott Williamson	.10
42	Eric Gagne **RC**	1.50
43	John McDonald **RC**	.10
44	Scott Sauerbeck **RC**	.10
45	Mike Venafro **RC**	.10
46	Edwards Guzman **RC**	.10
47	Richard Barker **RC**	.10
48	Braden Looper	.10
49	Chad Meyers **RC**	.10
50	Scott Strickland **RC**	.10
51	Billy Koch	.10
52	Dave Newhan **RC**	.10
53	David Riske **RC**	.10
54	Jose Santiago	.10
55	Miguel Del Toro **RC**	.10
56	Orber Moreno **RC**	.10
57	Dave Roberts **RC**	.10
58	Tim Byrdak **RC**	.10
59	David Lee **RC**	.10
60	Guillermo Mota **RC**	.15
61	Wilton Veras **RC**	.15
62	Joe Mays **RC**	.15
63	Jose Fernandez **RC**	.15
64	Ray King **RC**	.10
65	Chris Petersen **RC**	.10
66	Vernon Wells	.10
67	Ruben Mateo	.10
68	Ben Petrick	.10
69	Chris Tremie **RC**	.10
70	Lance Berkman	.10
71	Dan Smith	.10
72	Carlos Hernandez **RC**	.10
73	Chad Harville **RC**	.25
74	Damaso Marte	.10
75	Aaron Myette **RC**	.15
76	Willis Roberts **RC**	.10
77	Erik Sabel **RC**	.10
78	Hector Almonte **RC**	.10
79	Kris Benson	.10
80	Pat Daneker **RC**	.10
81	Freddy Garcia **RC**	.50
82	Byung-Hyun Kim **RC**	.25
83	Wily Pena **RC**	1.00

84	Dan Wheeler **RC**	.15
85	Tim Harikkala **RC**	.10
86	Derrin Ebert **RC**	.10
87	Horacio Estrada **RC**	.10
88	Liu Rodriguez **RC**	.10
89	Jordan Zimmerman **RC**	.10
90	A.J. Burnett **RC**	.40
91	Doug Davis **RC**	.10
92	Robert Ramsey **RC**	.10
93	Ryan Franklin **RC**	.10
94	Charlie Greene **RC**	.10
95	Bo Porter **RC**	.10
96	Jorge Toca **RC**	.10
97	Casey Blake **RC**	.20
98	Amaury Garcia **RC**	.10
99	Jose Molina **RC**	.10
100	Melvin Mora **RC**	1.00
101	Joe Nathan **RC**	.10
102	Juan Pena **RC**	.25
103	Dave Borkowski **RC**	.10
104	Eddie Gaillard **RC**	.10
105	Rob Radlosky **RC**	.10
106	Brett Hinchliffe **RC**	.10
107	Carlos Lee	.10
108	Rob Ryan **RC**	.10
109	Jeff Weaver **RC**	.50
110	Ed Yarnall	.10
111	Nelson Cruz **RC**	.10
112	Cleatus Davidson **RC**	.10
113	Tim Kubinski **RC**	.10
114	Sean Spencer **RC**	.10
115	Joe Winkelsas **RC**	.10
116	Chris Clapinski **RC**	.10
117	Tom Davey **RC**	.10
118	Warren Morris	.10
119	Dan Murray **RC**	.10
120	Jose Nieves **RC**	.10
121	Mark Quinn **RC**	.50
122	Josh Beckett **RC**	10.00
123	Chad Allen **RC**	.10
124	Mike Figga	.10
125	Beiker Graterol **RC**	.10
126	Aaron Scheffer **RC**	.10
127	Wiki Gonzalez **RC**	.10
128	Ramon E. Martinez	.10
129	Matt Riley **RC**	.25
130	Chris Woodward **RC**	.10
131	Albert Belle	.10
132	Roger Cedeno	.10
133	Roger Clemens	.75
134	Brian Giles	.10
135	Rickey Henderson	.60
136	Randy Johnson	.60
137	Brian Jordan	.10
138	Paul Konerko	.15
139	Hideo Nomo	.50
140	Kenny Rogers	.10
141	Wade Boggs	.65
142	Jose Canseco	.45
143	Roger Clemens	.75
144	David Cone	.10
145	Tony Gwynn	.65
146	Mark McGwire	1.00
147	Cal Ripken Jr.	1.50
148	Alex Rodriguez	.10
149	Fernando Tatis	.10
150	Robin Ventura	.10

Millennium

Kerry Wood Checklist

This special edition of '99 Fleer Tradition was issued only in factory sets, for sale on Shop at Home. Besides the 600 cards in the regular Tradition issue, these sets include 20 renumbered rookie and highlight cards from the Fleer Update set. Each set is sealed with gold-foil on which is a serial number from with an edition of 5,000 sets. Each card in the edition has a special gold-foil "2000" logo on front.

		NM/M
Complete Factory Set (620):		30.00
Common Player:		.50
Stars:		5X
601	Rick Ankiel	.75
602	Peter Bergeron	.50
603	Pat Burrell	2.00
604	Eric Munson	.50
605	Alfonso Soriano	2.00
606	Tim Hudson	1.25
607	Erubiel Durazo	.50
608	Chad Hermansen	.50
609	Jeff Zimmerman	.50
610	Jesus Pena	.50

611	Wade Boggs (Highlights)	.75
612	Jose Canseco (Highlights)	.50
613	Roger Clemens (Highlights)	1.00
614	David Cone (Highlights)	.50
615	Tony Gwynn (Highlights)	.75
616	Mark McGwire (Highlights)	1.50
617	Cal Ripken Jr. (Highlights)	2.00
618	Alex Rodriguez (Highlights)	1.50
619	Fernando Tatis (Highlights)	.50
620	Robin Ventura (Highlights)	.50

Brilliants Sample

To preview the introduction of its Brilliants brand of premium quality cards into baseball, Fleer issued a promo card of J.D. Drew. Like the issued cards, the sample is printed on plastic with a mirrored silver background on front. Both front and back are overprinted, "PROMOTIONAL SAMPLE."

	NM/M
J.D. Drew	3.00

1999 Fleer Brilliants

This 175-card set features an action photo on a complete silver-foiled background swirl pattern. The featured player's name, team and postion are stamped in gold foil. Card backs have a small photo, vital information, 1998 statistics and a brief overview of the player's '98 season. Cards numbered 126-175 are part of a short-printed Rookies subset and are seeded 1:2 packs.

		NM/M
Complete Set (175):		60.00
Common Player:		.25
Common SP (126-175):		.50
Blues (1:3):		1.5X
SP Blues (1:6):		1X
Golds:		8X
SP Golds:		3X
Production 99 Sets		
24 Karat Golds:		40X
SP's:		15X
Production 24 Sets		
Pack (5):		2.00
Wax Box (24):		32.50
1	Mark McGwire	2.50
2	Derek Jeter	3.00
3	Nomar Garciaparra	1.75
4	Travis Lee	.25
5	Jeff Bagwell	.75
6	Andres Galarraga	.25
7	Pedro Martinez	.75
8	Cal Ripken Jr.	3.00
9	Vladimir Guerrero	.75
10	Chipper Jones	1.50
11	Rusty Greer	.25
12	Omar Vizquel	.25
13	Quinton McCracken	.25
14	Jaret Wright	.25
15	Mike Mussina	.50
16	Jason Giambi	.60
17	Tony Clark	.25
18	Troy O'Leary	.25
19	Troy Percival	.25

20	Kerry Wood	.50
21	Vinny Castilla	.25
22	Chris Carpenter	.25
23	Richie Sexson	.25
24	Ken Griffey Jr.	2.00
25	Barry Bonds	3.00
26	Carlos Delgado	.60
27	Frank Thomas	.75
28	Manny Ramirez	.75
29	Shawn Green	.50
30	Mike Piazza	2.00
31	Tino Martinez	.25
32	Dante Bichette	.25
33	Scott Rolen	.65
34	Gabe Alvarez	.25
35	Raul Mondesi	.25
36	Damion Easley	.25
37	Jeff Kent	.25
38	Al Leiter	.25
39	Alex Rodriguez	2.50
40	Jeff King	.25
41	Mark Grace	.25
42	Larry Walker	.25
43	Moises Alou	.25
44	Juan Gonzalez	.65
45	Rolando Arrojo	.25
46	Tom Glavine	.45
47	Johnny Damon	.45
48	Livan Hernandez	.25
49	Craig Biggio	.25
50	Dmitri Young	.25
51	Chan Ho Park	.25
52	Todd Walker	.25
53	Derrek Lee	.25
54	Todd Helton	.75
55	Ray Lankford	.25
56	Jim Thome	.65
57	Matt Lawton	.25
58	Matt Anderson	.25
59	Jose Offerman	.25
60	Eric Karros	.25
61	Orlando Hernandez	.25
62	Ben Grieve	.25
63	Bobby Abreu	.25
64	Kevin Young	.25
65	John Olerud	.25
66	Sammy Sosa	1.75
67	Andy Ashby	.25
68	Juan Encarnacion	.25
69	Shane Reynolds	.25
70	Bernie Williams	.35
71	Mike Cameron	.25
72	Troy Glaus	.75
73	Gary Sheffield	.60
74	Jeromy Burnitz	.25
75	Mike Caruso	.25
76	Chuck Knoblauch	.25
77	Kenny Rogers	.25
78	David Cone	.25
79	Tony Gwynn	1.50
80	Aramis Ramirez	.25
81	Paul O'Neill	.25
82	Charles Nagy	.25
83	Javy Lopez	.25
84	Scott Erickson	.25
85	Trevor Hoffman	.25
86	Andruw Jones	.75
87	Ray Durham	.25
88	Jorge Posada	.25
89	Edgar Martinez	.25
90	Tim Salmon	.35
91	Bobby Higginson	.25
92	Adrian Beltre	.45
93	Jason Kendall	.25
94	Henry Rodriguez	.25
95	Greg Maddux	1.50
96	David Justice	.25
97	Ivan Rodriguez	.65
98	Curt Schilling	.45
99	Matt Williams	.25
100	Darin Erstad	.25
101	Rafael Palmeiro	.65
102	David Wells	.25
103	Barry Larkin	.25
104	Robin Ventura	.25
105	Edgar Renteria	.25
106	Andy Pettitte	.50
107	Albert Belle	.50
108	Steve Finley	.25
109	Fernando Vina	.25
110	Rondell White	.25
111	Kevin Brown	.25
112	Jose Canseco	.50
113	Roger Clemens	1.75
114	Todd Hundley	.25
115	Will Clark	.35
116	Jim Edmonds	.25
117	Randy Johnson	.75
118	Denny Neagle	.25
119	Brian Jordan	.25
120	Dean Palmer	.25
121	Roberto Alomar	.45
122	Ken Caminiti	.25
123	Brian Giles	.25
124	Todd Stottlemyre	.25
125	Mo Vaughn	.25
126	J.D. Drew	1.00
127	Ryan Minor	.50
128	Gabe Kapler	.50
129	Jeremy Giambi	.50
130	Eric Chavez	.50
131	Ben Davis	.50
132	Rob Fick	.50
133	George Lombard	.50
134	Calvin Pickering	.50
135	Preston Wilson	.50
136	Corey Koskie	.75
137	Russell Branyan	.50

138	Bruce Chen	.50
139	Matt Clement	.75
140	Pat Burrell **RC**	2.50
141	Freddy Garcia **RC**	1.00
142	Brian Simmons	.50
143	Carlos Febles	.50
144	Carlos Guillen	.50
145	Fernando Seguignol	.50
146	Carlos Beltran	1.00
147	Edgard Clemente	.50
148	Mitch Meluskey	.50
149	Ryan Bradley	.50
150	Marlon Anderson	.50
151	A.J. Burnett **RC**	1.00
152	Scott Hunter **RC**	.50
153	Mark Johnson	.50
154	Angel Pena	.50
155	Roy Halladay	.75
156	Chad Allen **RC**	.50
157	Trot Nixon	.75
158	Ricky Ledee	.50
159	Gary Bennett **RC**	.50
160	Micah Bowie **RC**	.50
161	Doug Mientkiewicz	.60
162	Danny Klassen	.50
163	Willis Otanez	.50
164	Jin Ho Cho	.50
165	Mike Lowell	.60
166	Armando Rios	.50
167	Tom Evans	.50
168	Michael Barrett	.50
169	Alex Gonzalez	.50
170	Masao Kida **RC**	.60
171	Peter Tucci **RC**	.50
172	Luis Saturria	.50
173	Kris Benson	.50
174	Mario Encarnacion **RC**	.50
175	Roosevelt Brown **RC**	.50

Blue/Golds

The 175 Fleer Brilliants base cards are paralleled in three insert sets of differing degrees of scarcity. Brilliant Blue parallels have a mirrored blue foil background on front and a "B" suffix to the card number on back. They are seeded one per three packs (125 veterans) and one per six packs (50 rookies). Gold parallels are printed with gold foil background and a "G" suffix. Each card is serially numbered on back within an edition of 99. The 24-karat Gold parallels have gold rainbow holographic foil backgrounds, a 24-karat gold logo and are serially numbered to just 24 of each card; numbers have a TG suffix.

	NM/M
Brilliants Blue Common:	.50
Brilliants Blue Stars:	1.5X
Brilliants Blue Rookies:	1X
Brilliants Gold Common:	3.00
Brilliants Gold Stars:	8X
Brilliants Gold Rookies:	3X
Brilliants 24K Gold Common:	10.00
Brilliants 24K Gold Stars:	40X
Brilliants 24K Gold Rookies:	15X

Illuminators

This 15-card set highlights baseball's top young prospects on a team color-coded fully foiled

front. Card backs are numbered with an "I" suffix and are inserted 1:10 packs.

	NM/M
Complete Set (15):	10.00
Common Player:	.75
Inserted 1:10	
1	Kerry Wood	2.00
2	Ben Grieve	.75
3	J.D. Drew	1.50
4	Juan Encarnacion	.75
5	Travis Lee	.75
6	Todd Helton	3.00
7	Troy Glaus	2.00
8	Ricky Ledee	.75
9	Eric Chavez	1.50
10	Ben Davis	.75
11	George Lombard	.75
12	Jeremy Giambi	.75
13	Richie Sexson	.75
14	Corey Koskie	.75
15	Russell Branyan	.75

Shining Stars

Shining Stars is a 15-card set printed on styrene with two-sided mirrored foil. Card backs are numbered with a "S" suffix and are seeded 1:20 packs. Pulsars are a parallel set that are printed on two-sided rainbow holographic foil and styrene with an embossed star pattern in the background. Pulsars are seeded 1:400 packs.

	NM/M
Complete Set (15):	30.00
Common Player:	1.50
Inserted 1:20	
Pulsars:	4X
Inserted 1:400	
1	Ken Griffey Jr.	2.50
2	Mark McGwire	3.00
3	Sammy Sosa	2.25
4	Derek Jeter	4.00
5	Nomar Garciaparra	2.25
6	Alex Rodriguez	3.00
7	Mike Piazza	2.50
8	Juan Gonzalez	1.50
9	Chipper Jones	2.00
10	Cal Ripken Jr.	4.00
11	Frank Thomas	1.50
12	Greg Maddux	2.00
13	Roger Clemens	2.25
14	Vladimir Guerrero	1.50
15	Manny Ramirez	1.50

1999 Fleer Mystique

The "Mystique" of this issue lay partly in the fact that each four-card $4.99 pack included a card which was covered with a peel-off coating, either a short-printed star card from the #1-100 base set, one of the short-printed Rookie (#101-150) or Stars (#151-160) cards or one of the inserts. The Rookie cards are serial numbered to 2,999 apiece, while the red-foil highlighted Stars cards are in an edition of 2,500 each. Fronts have metallic foil backgrounds, backs have a player portrait photo, biographical and career notes and stats.

	NM/M
Complete Set (160):	125.00
Common Player:	.20
Common SP (1-100):	.75
Common (101-150):	1.00
Production 2,999 Sets	
Common (151-160):	2.00
Production 2,500 Sets	
Pack (4):	3.00
Wax Box (24):	60.00
1	Ken Griffey Jr./SP	2.50
2	Livan Hernandez	.20
3	Jeff Kent	.20
4	Brian Jordan	.20
5	Kevin Young	.20
6	Vinny Castilla	.20
7	Orlando Hernandez/SP	.75
8	Bobby Abreu	.20
9	Vladimir Guerrero/SP	1.50
10	Chuck Knoblauch	.20
11	Nomar Garciaparra/SP	2.25
12	Jeff Bagwell	1.00
13	Todd Walker	.20
14	Johnny Damon	.45
15	Mike Caruso	.20
16	Cliff Floyd	.20
17	Andy Pettitte	.35
18	Cal Ripken Jr./SP	4.00
19	Brian Giles	.20
20	Robin Ventura	.20
21	Alex Gonzalez	.20
22	Randy Johnson	.75
23	Raul Mondesi	.20
24	Ken Caminiti	.20
25	Tom Glavine	.40
26	Derek Jeter/SP	4.00
27	Carlos Delgado	.50
28	Adrian Beltre	.35
29	Tino Martinez	.20
30	Todd Helton	1.00
31	Juan Gonzalez/SP	1.25
32	Henry Rodriguez	.20
33	Jim Thome	.65
34	Paul O'Neill	.20
35	Scott Rolen/SP	1.25
36	Rafael Palmeiro	.65
37	Will Clark	.20
38	Todd Hundley	.20
39	Andruw Jones/SP	1.50
40	Luis Rolando Arrojo	.20
41	Barry Larkin	.20
42	Tim Salmon	.25
43	Rondell White	.20
44	Curt Schilling	.40
45	Chipper Jones/SP	2.00
46	Jeromy Burnitz	.20
47	Mo Vaughn	.20
48	Tony Clark	.20
49	Fernando Tatis	.20
50	Dmitri Young	.20
51	Wade Boggs	1.50
52	Rickey Henderson	.75
53	Manny Ramirez/SP	1.50
54	Edgar Martinez	.20
55	Jason Giambi	.65
56	Jason Kendall	.20
57	Eric Karros	.20
58	Jose Canseco/SP	1.00
59	Shawn Green	.40
60	Ellis Burks	.20
61	Derek Bell	.20
62	Shannon Stewart	.20
63	Roger Clemens/SP	2.25
64	Sean Casey/SP	.75
65	Jose Offerman	.20
66	Sammy Sosa/SP	2.25
67	Frank Thomas/SP	1.50
68	Tony Gwynn/SP	2.00
69	Roberto Alomar	.35
70	Mark McGwire/SP	3.00
71	Troy Glaus	1.00
72	Ray Durham	.20
73	Jeff Cirillo	.20
74	Alex Rodriguez/SP	3.00
75	Jose Cruz Jr.	.20
76	Juan Encarnacion	.20
77	Mark Grace	.20
78	Barry Bonds/SP	4.00
79	Ivan Rodriguez/SP	1.25
80	Greg Vaughn	.20
81	Greg Maddux/SP	2.00
82	Albert Belle	.20
83	John Olerud	.20
84	Kenny Lofton	.20
85	Bernie Williams	.30
86	Matt Williams	.20
87	Ray Lankford	.20
88	Darin Erstad	.40
89	Ben Grieve	.20
90	Craig Biggio	.20
91	Dean Palmer	.20
92	Reggie Sanders	.20
93	Dante Bichette	.20
94	Pedro Martinez/SP	1.50
95	Larry Walker	.20
96	David Wells	.20
97	Travis Leev	.75
98	Mike Piazza/SP	2.50
99	Mike Mussina	.45
100	Kevin Brown	.20
101	Ruben Mateo (Rookie)	1.00
102	Roberto Ramirez (Rookie)	1.00
103	Glen Barker **RC** (Rookie)	1.00
104	Clay Bellinger **RC** (Rookie)	1.00
105	Carlos Guillen (Rookie)	1.00

106	Scott Schoeneweis (Rookie)	1.00
107	Creighton Gubanich (Rookie)	1.00
108	Scott Williamson (Rookie)	1.00
109	Edwards Guzman **RC** (Rookie)	1.00
110	A.J. Burnett **RC** (Rookie)	4.00
111	Jeremy Giambi (Rookie)	1.50
112	Trot Nixon (Rookie)	1.50
113	J.D. Drew (Rookie)	3.00
114	Roy Halladay (Rookie)	1.50
115	Jose Macias **RC** (Rookie)	2.00
116	Corey Koskie (Rookie)	1.50
117	Ryan Rupe **RC** (Rookie)	1.50
118	Scott Hunter (Rookie)	1.00
119	Rob Fick (Rookie)	1.00
120	McKay Christensen (Rookie)	1.50
121	Carlos Febles (Rookie)	2.00
122	Gabe Kapler (Rookie)	1.50
123	Jeff Liefer (Rookie)	1.00
124	Warren Morris (Rookie)	1.00
125	Chris Pritchett (Rookie)	1.00
126	Torii Hunter (Rookie)	3.00
127	Armando Rios (Rookie)	1.00
128	Ricky Ledee (Rookie)	1.00
129	Kelly Dransfeldt **RC** (Rookie)	1.00
130	Jeff Zimmerman (Rookie)	1.50
131	Eric Chavez (Rookie)	1.50
132	Freddy Garcia (Rookie)	3.00
133	Jose Jimenez (Rookie)	1.00
134	Pat Burrell **RC** (Rookie)	20.00
135	Joe McEwing **RC** (Rookie)	1.50
136	Kris Benson (Rookie)	1.50
137	Joe Mays **RC** (Rookie)	2.00
138	Rafael Roque (Rookie)	1.00
139	Cristian Guzman (Rookie)	1.50
140	Michael Barrett (Rookie)	1.50
141	Doug Mientkiewicz (Rookie)	1.50
142	Jeff Weaver **RC** (Rookie)	4.00
143	Mike Lowell (Rookie)	1.50
144	Jason Phillips **RC** (Rookie)	2.00
145	Marlon Anderson (Rookie)	1.50
146	Brett Hinchliffe **RC** (Rookie)	1.00
147	Matt Clement (Rookie)	1.50
148	Terrence Long (Rookie)	1.50
149	Carlos Beltran (Rookie)	2.50
150	Preston Wilson (Rookie)	1.50
151	Ken Griffey Jr. (Stars)	3.00
152	Mark McGwire (Stars)	3.00
153	Sammy Sosa (Stars)	1.50
154	Mike Piazza (Stars)	3.00
155	Alex Rodriguez (Stars)	3.00
156	Nomar Garciaparra (Stars)	1.50
157	Cal Ripken Jr. (Stars)	4.00
158	Greg Maddux (Stars)	1.50
159	Derek Jeter (Stars)	4.00
160	Juan Gonzalez (Stars)	1.00
	Checklist Card	.10

Mystique Gold

The first 100 cards of the base set are paralleled in this insert which features gold-foil highlights on front. Gold versions are found in one of eight packs, on average.

	NM/M
Common Player:	1.00
Stars (1-100):	1.5X
Inserted 1:8	

Masterpiece

Each of the cards in Fleer Mystique was also produced in a unique Masterpiece version. The super-rarities are labeled on front "The Only 1 of 1 / Masterpiece."

	NM/M
Common Player:	50.00

Mystique Destiny

A silver holofoil background on front and a serial number within an edition of 999 each marks this insert set. Backs have another photo along with career highlights.

	NM/M
Complete Set (10):	35.00
Common Player:	2.00
Production 999 Sets	
1	Tony Gwynn	5.00
2	Juan Gonzalez	3.00
3	Scott Rolen	4.00
4	Nomar Garciaparra	6.00
5	Orlando Hernandez	2.00
6	Andruw Jones	4.00
7	Vladimir Guerrero	4.00
8	Darin Erstad	4.00
9	Manny Ramirez	4.00
10	Roger Clemens	6.00

Established

A plastic stock, red holofoil background and silver foil highlights complement the action photo of a top star in this insert set. Backs have another photo, some career highlights and a serial number from within an edition of 100 each.

	NM/M
Complete Set (10):	300.00
Common Player:	15.00
Production 100 Sets	
1	Ken Griffey Jr.	30.00
2	Derek Jeter	60.00
3	Chipper Jones	20.00
4	Greg Maddux	20.00
5	Mark McGwire	45.00
6	Mike Piazza	30.00
7	Cal Ripken Jr.	60.00
8	Alex Rodriguez	45.00
9	Sammy Sosa	25.00
10	Frank Thomas	15.00

Feel the Game

Swatches of various game-used equipment are featured in this insert series. Each card is hand-numbered from editions which range between 345 and 450.

	NM/M
Common Player:	10.00
Adrian Beltre/Shoe/430	15.00
J.D. Drew/Jsy/450	15.00
Juan Gonzalez/Bat Glv/415	15.00
Tony Gwynn/Jsy/435	15.00
Kevin Millwood/Jsy/435	10.00
Alex Rodriguez/Bat Glv/345	30.00
Frank Thomas/Jsy/450	15.00

Fresh Ink

These inserts, found about one per 48 packs, have a white oval at bottom front containing an autograph of the player pictured. At bottom is a white panel with a hand-printed serial number from within each card's edition, which ranged from 140 to 1,000. Backs have a Fleer seal and statement of authenticity pertinent to the autograph. The unnumbered cards are listed here in alphabetical order.

	NM/M
Complete Set (26):	300.00
Common Player:	4.00
Inserted 1:48	
Roberto Alomar/500	10.00
Michael Barrett/1,000	6.00
Kris Benson/500	8.00
Micah Bowie/1,000	4.00
A.J. Burnett/500	10.00
Pat Burrell/500	15.00
Ken Caminiti/250	10.00
Jose Canseco/250	25.00
Sean Casey/1,000	8.00
Edgard Clemente/1,000	4.00
Bartolo Colon/500	8.00
J.D. Drew/400	15.00
Juan Encarnacion/1,000	4.00
Troy Glaus/400	15.00
Juan Gonzalez/250	15.00
Shawn Green/250	15.00
Tony Gwynn/250	30.00
Chipper Jones/500	35.00
Gabe Kapler/750	6.00
Barry Larkin/250	25.00
Doug Mientkiewicz/500	6.00
Alex Rodriguez/200	80.00
Scott Rolen/140	30.00
Fernando Tatis/750	4.00
Robin Ventura/500	5.00
Todd Walker/1,000	6.00

Prophetic

Blue holofoil with silver highlights is the graphic treatment found on this insert set of young stars. Each card is numbered on front from within an edition of 1,999. Backs have a portrait photo and a few words about the player.

	NM/M
Complete Set (10):	15.00
Common Player:	1.00
Production 1,999 Sets	
1 Eric Chavez	1.50
2 J.D. Drew	2.00
3 A.J. Burnett	1.00
4 Ben Grieve	1.00
5 Gabe Kapler	1.00
6 Todd Helton	2.50
7 Troy Glaus	4.00
8 Travis Lee	1.00
9 Pat Burrell	5.00
10 Kerry Wood	1.50

Diamond Skills Commemorative Sheet

In conjunction with its sponsorship of the Diamond Skills program, Fleer distributed this eight-player sheet to 7-14 year olds par-

ticipating in the event. Participants could get a sheet by redeeming Fleer wrappers at a local card store. The 10" x 9" sheet features full size Fleer Tradition cards. At top is a list of 1997 Diamond Skills winners.

	NM/M
Complete Sheet:	3.00

National Convention Commemorative Set

In conjunction with its participation at the 20th National Sports Collectors Convention in Atlanta in July 1999 Fleer distributed this cello-wrapped commemorative set to persons purchasing VIP admission packages. The set includes a specially-numbered (NC1) version of the Stan Musial card from '99 Fleer Tradition, three large-format (3-1/2"x5") cards reproducing Musial Monumental Moments inserts, and an un-numbered header card. The Monumental Moments reproductions are printed on a red background with the famed St. Louis arch.

	NM/M
Complete Set (5):	10.00
Common Card:	2.00
NC1 Stan Musial (Fleer Tradition)	2.00
NC2 Stan Musial (Life in Donora - Monumental Moment)	2.00
NC3 Stan Musial (The 1948 Season - Monumental Moment)	2.00
NC4 Stan Musial (Hall of Fame - Monumental Season)	2.00
Header Card	.25

2000 Fleer Focus

The 250-card base set has two versions for the Prospects subset card numbers 226-250. The portrait versions are serial numbered from 1-999, while the remaining serial numbered from 1,000 to 3,999 capture an action shot. The base set design has a white border with gold foil stamping. Card backs have complete year-by-year statistics along with a career note and small photo.

	NM/M
Complete Set (250):	100.00
Common Player:	.15
Common Prospect (226-250):	4.00
Production 2,999 Sets	
Common Portrait (226-250):	8.00
Portraits:	2X
Production 999 Sets	
Pack:	2.00
Wax Box (24):	35.00
1 Nomar Garciaparra	1.25
2 Adrian Beltre	.35
3 Miguel Tejada	.35
4 Joe Randa	.15
5 Larry Walker	.15
6 Jeff Weaver	.15
7 Jay Bell	.15
8 Ivan Rodriguez	.50
9 Edgar Martinez	.15
10 Desi Relaford	.15
11 Derek Jeter	2.50
12 Delino DeShields	.15
13 Craig Biggio	.15
14 Chuck Knoblauch	.15
15 Chuck Finley	.15
16 Brett Tomko	.15
17 Bobby Higginson	.15
18 Pedro Martinez	.75
19 Troy O'Leary	.15
20 Rickey Henderson	.75
21 Robb Nen	.15
22 Rolando Arrojo	.15
23 Rondell White	.15
24 Royce Clayton	.15
25 Rusty Greer	.15
26 Stan Spencer	.15
27 Steve Finley	.15
28 Tom Goodwin	.15
29 Troy Percival	.15
30 Wilton Guerrero	.15
31 Roberto Alomar	.30
32 Mike Hampton	.15
33 Michael Barrett	.15
34 Curt Schilling	.40
35 Bill Mueller	.15
36 Bernie Williams	.30
37 John Smoltz	.15
38 B.J. Surhoff	.15
39 Pete Harnisch	.15
40 Juan Encarnacion	.15
41 Derrek Lee	.15
42 Jeff Shaw	.15
43 David Cone	.15
44 Jason Christiansen	.15
45 Jeff Kent	.15
46 Randy Johnson	.75
47 Todd Walker	.15
48 Jose Lima	.15
49 Jason Giambi	.50
50 Ken Griffey Jr.	1.50
51 Bartolo Colon	.15
52 Mike Lieberthal	.15
53 Shane Reynolds	.15
54 Travis Lee	.15
55 Travis Fryman	.15
56 John Valentin	.15
57 Joey Hamilton	.15
58 Jay Buhner	.15
59 Brad Radke	.15
60 A.J. Burnett	.15
61 Roy Halladay	.25
62 Raul Mondesi	.15
63 Matt Mantei	.15
64 Mark Grace	.15
65 David Justice	.15
66 Billy Wagner	.15
67 Eric Milton	.15
68 Eric Chavez	.25
69 Doug Glanville	.15
70 Ray Durham	.15
71 Mike Sirotka	.15
72 Greg Vaughn	.15
73 Brian Jordan	.15
74 Alex Gonzalez	.15
75 Alex Rodriguez	2.00
76 David Nilsson	.15
77 Robin Ventura	.15
78 Kevin Young	.15
79 Wilson Alvarez	.15
80 Matt Williams	.15
81 Ismael Valdes	.15
82 Kenny Lofton	.15
83 Carlos Beltran	.45
84 Doug Mientkiewicz	.15
85 Wally Joyner	.15
86 J.D. Drew	.35
87 Carlos Delgado	.50
88 Tony Womack	.15
89 Eric Young	.15
90 Manny Ramirez	.75
91 Johnny Damon	.15
92 Torii Hunter	.25
93 Kenny Rogers	.15
94 Trevor Hoffman	.15
95 John Wetteland	.15
96 Ray Lankford	.15
97 Tom Glavine	.30
98 Carlos Lee	.15
99 Richie Sexson	.15
100 Carlos Febles	.15
101 Chad Allen	.15
102 Sterling Hitchcock	.15
103 Joe McEwing	.15
104 Justin Thompson	.15
105 Jim Edmonds	.15
106 Kerry Wood	.40
107 Jim Thome	.65
108 Jeremy Giambi	.15
109 Mike Piazza	1.50
110 Darryl Kile	.15
111 Darin Erstad	.30
112 Kyle Farnsworth	.15
113 Omar Vizquel	.15
114 Orber Moreno	.15
115 Al Leiter	.15
116 John Olerud	.15
117 Aaron Sele	.15
118 Chipper Jones	1.00
119 Paul Konerko	.25
120 Chris Singleton	.15
121 Fernando Vina	.15
122 Andy Ashby	.15
123 Eli Marrero	.15
124 Edgar Renteria	.15
125 Roberto Hernandez	.15
126 Andruw Jones	.75
127 Magglio Ordonez	.25
128 Bob Wickman	.15
129 Tony Gwynn	1.00
130 Mark McGwire	2.00
131 Albert Belle	.15
132 Pokey Reese	.15
133 Tony Clark	.15
134 Jeff Bagwell	.75
135 Mark Grudzielanek	.15
136 Dustin Hermanson	.15
137 Reggie Sanders	.15
138 Ryan Rupe	.15
139 Kevin Millwood	.15
140 Bret Saberhagen	.15
141 Juan Guzman	.15
142 Alex Gonzalez	.15
143 Gary Sheffield	.30
144 Roger Clemens	1.25
145 Ben Grieve	.15
146 Bobby Abreu	.15
147 Brian Giles	.15
148 Quinton McCracken	.15
149 Freddy Garcia	.15
150 Erubiel Durazo	.15
151 Sidney Ponson	.15
152 Scott Williamson	.15
153 Ken Caminiti	.15
154 Vladimir Guerrero	.75
155 Andy Pettitte	.25
156 Edwards Guzman	.15
157 Shannon Stewart	.15
158 Greg Maddux	1.00
159 Mike Stanley	.15
160 Sean Casey	.25
161 Cliff Floyd	.15
162 Devon White	.15
163 Scott Brosius	.15
164 Marlon Anderson	.15
165 Jason Kendall	.15
166 Ryan Klesko	.15
167 Sammy Sosa	1.25
168 Frank Thomas	.75
169 Geoff Jenkins	.15
170 Jason Schmidt	.15
171 Dan Wilson	.15
172 Jose Canseco	.40
173 Troy Glaus	.75
174 Mariano Rivera	.20
175 Scott Rolen	.65
176 J.T. Snow	.15
177 Rafael Palmeiro	.65
178 A.J. Hinch	.15
179 Jose Offerman	.15
180 Jeff Cirillo	.15
181 Dean Palmer	.15
182 Jose Rosado	.15
183 Armando Benitez	.15
184 Brady Anderson	.15
185 Cal Ripken Jr.	2.50
186 Barry Larkin	.15
187 Damion Easley	.15
188 Moises Alou	.15
189 Todd Hundley	.15
190 Tim Hudson	.25
191 Livan Hernandez	.15
192 Fred McGriff	.15
193 Orlando Hernandez	.25
194 Tim Salmon	.20
195 Mike Mussina	.40
196 Todd Helton	.75
197 Juan Gonzalez	.50
198 Kevin Brown	.15
199 Ugueth Urbina	.15
200 Matt Stairs	.15
201 Shawn Estes	.15
202 Gabe Kapler	.15
203 Javy Lopez	.15
204 Henry Rodriguez	.15
205 Dante Bichette	.15
206 Jeromy Burnitz	.15
207 Todd Zeile	.15
208 Rico Brogna	.15
209 Warren Morris	.15
210 David Segui	.15
211 Vinny Castilla	.15
212 Mo Vaughn	.15
213 Charles Johnson	.15
214 Neifi Perez	.15
215 Shawn Green	.40
216 Carl Pavano	.15
217 Tino Martinez	.15
218 Barry Bonds	2.50
219 David Wells	.15
220 Paul O'Neill	.15
221 Masato Yoshii	.15
222 Kris Benson	.15
223 Fernando Tatis	.15
224 Lee Stevens	.15
225 Jose Cruz Jr.	.15
226 Rick Ankiel (Prospect)	4.00
227 Matt Riley (Prospect)	4.00
228 Norm Hutchins (Prospect)	4.00
229 Ruben Mateo (Prospect)	4.00
230 Ben Petrick (Prospect)	4.00
231 Mario Encarnacion (Prospect)	4.00
232 Nick Johnson (Prospect)	6.00
233 Adam Piatt (Prospect)	6.00
234 Mike Darr (Prospect)	4.00
235 Chad Hermansen (Prospect)	4.00
236 Wily Pena (Prospect)	6.00
237 Octavio Dotel (Prospect)	4.00
238 Vernon Wells (Prospect)	6.00
239 Daryle Ward (Prospect)	4.00
240 Adam Kennedy (Prospect)	4.00
241 Angel Pena (Prospect)	4.00
242 Lance Berkman (Prospect)	6.00
243 Gabe Molina (Prospect)	4.00
244 Steve Lomasney (Prospect)	4.00
245 Jacob Cruz (Prospect)	4.00
246 Mark Quinn (Prospect)	4.00
247 Eric Munson (Prospect)	4.00
248 Alfonso Soriano (Prospect)	6.00
249 Kip Wells (Prospect)	4.00
250 Josh Beckett (Prospect)	6.00
Checklist #171	.05
Checklist #172-25, Inserts	.05
Checklist Inserts	.05

Green

Green, rather than gold, ink is used on front for the player name, team and position to distinguish this parallel insert set. On back, each card is numbered from within an edition of 300 each.

	NM/M
Common Player:	3.00
Stars:	5-10X
Yng Stars & RC's (226-250):	1-2X
Production 300 Sets	

Masterpiece

Each of the cards in Fleer Focus was issued in a parallel edition of just one piece each. Fronts of Masterpiece 1/1s have purple metallic ink, instead of gold, for the player identification. On back, there is a notation "The Only 1 of 1 Masterpiece" along with an "M" suffix to the card number. An error version has all the attributes of the true Masterpiece, but lacks the "Only 1 . . ." notation on back (see 2000 Fleer Focus Masterpiece Errors).

	NM/M
Common Player:	100.00

Masterpiece Errors

Thousands of collectors' hopes were crushed when it was determined that an unknown number of uncompleted Masterpiece 1-of-1 cards were erroneously inserted in Focus foil packs. Like the true Masterpiece cards, the fronts of the error cards have the player name, team and position at bottom front in purple, rather than gold foil. On back, the cards even have the "M"

suffix to the card number at lower-right. Unfortunately, these do not have the foil-stamped "The Only 1 of 1 Masterpiece" notation on back; greatly reducing the value.

	NM/M
Complete Set (25):	250.00
Common Player:	4.00
50M Ken Griffey Jr.	100.00
202M Gabe Kapler	8.00
203M Javy Lopez	6.00
204M Henry Rodriguez	4.00
205M Dante Bichette	5.00
206M Jeromy Burnitz	5.00
207M Todd Zeile	4.00
208M Rico Brogna	4.00
209M Warren Morris	4.00
210M David Segui	5.00
211M Vinny Castilla	5.00
212M Mo Vaughn	6.00
213M Charles Johnson	5.00
214M Neifi Perez	5.00
215M Shawn Green	20.00
216M Carl Pavano	4.00
217M Tino Martinez	5.00
218M Barry Bonds	30.00
219M David Wells	8.00
220M Paul O'Neill	8.00
221M Masato Yoshii	5.00
222M Kris Benson	8.00
223M Fernando Tatis	6.00
224M Lee Stevens	4.00
225M Jose Cruz Jr.	6.00

Club 3000

These inserts are die-cut around the numbers 3,000 and features three players who either have 3,000 hits or strikeouts, this set spotlights Stan Musial, Steve Carlton and Paul Molitor. These were seeded 1:36 packs.

	NM/M
Complete Set (3):	4.00
Common Player:	1.50
(1) Steve Carlton	1.50
(2) Paul Molitor	1.50
(3) Stan Musial	1.50

Club 3000 Memorabilia

Five tiers featuring memorabilia from game-used bats, caps etc... make up this hand numbered set. Besides a bat and cap insert others include jersey, bat and jersey combo and a bat, jersey and cap combo.

	NM/M
Steve Carlton/Bat/325	25.00
Steve Carlton/Hat/65	75.00
Steve Carlton/Jsy/750	20.00
Steve Carlton/Bat/ Hat/Jsy/25	200.00
Paul Molitor/Bat/355	30.00
Paul Molitor/Hat/65	85.00
Paul Molitor/Jsy/975	20.00
Paul Molitor/Bat/ Jsy/100	60.00
Stan Musial/Bat/325	50.00
Stan Musial/Hat/65	125.00
Stan Musial/Jsy/975	35.00
Stan Musial/Bat/ Jsy/100	80.00

Feel the Game

This 10-card set offers pieces of player-worn jersey from some of baseball's biggest stars embedded into the card front. These were seeded 1:288 packs.

	NM/M
Common Player:	5.00
Inserted 1:288	
Adrian Beltre	7.50
Tom Glavine	10.00
Vladimir Guerrero	15.00
Randy Johnson	15.00
Javy Lopez	5.00
Alex Rodriguez	30.00

Scott Rolen 10.00
Cal Ripken Jr. 40.00
Tim Salmon 6.00
Miguel Tejada 10.00

Focal Points

This 15-card set has silver foil etching around the border and silver foil stamping. These were seeded 1:6 packs and are numbered with an "F" suffix on the card back.

		NM/M
Complete Set (15):		15.00
Common Player:		.75
Inserted 1:6		
1	Mark McGwire	2.50
2	Tony Gwynn	1.00
3	Nomar Garciaparra	2.00
4	Juan Gonzalez	.75
5	Jeff Bagwell	.75
6	Chipper Jones	1.00
7	Cal Ripken Jr.	3.00
8	Alex Rodriguez	2.50
9	Scott Rolen	.75
10	Vladimir Guerrero	.75
11	Mike Piazza	1.50
12	Frank Thomas	.75
13	Ken Griffey Jr.	1.50
14	Sammy Sosa	1.50
15	Derek Jeter	3.00

Focus Pocus

This 10-card set has a silver prismatic, holofoil background with silver foil stamping. These were seeded 1:14 packs and are numbered with an "FP" suffix.

		NM/M
Complete Set (10):		12.00
Common Player:		1.00
Inserted 1:14		
1	Cal Ripken Jr.	3.00
2	Tony Gwynn	1.50
3	Nomar Garciaparra	2.00
4	Juan Gonzalez	1.00
5	Mike Piazza	2.00
6	Mark McGwire	2.50
7	Chipper Jones	1.50
8	Ken Griffey Jr.	2.00
9	Derek Jeter	3.00
10	Alex Rodriguez	2.50

Fresh Ink

These autographed inserts are seeded 1:96 packs.

	NM/M
Common Player:	5.00
Inserted 1:96	
Chad Allen	5.00
Michael Barrett	5.00
Josh Beckett	30.00
Rob Bell	5.00
Adrian Beltre	15.00
Milton Bradley	8.00
Rico Brogna	5.00
Mike Cameron	8.00
Eric Chavez	15.00
Bruce Chen	5.00
Johnny Damon	20.00
Ben Davis	5.00
J.D. Drew	15.00
Erubiel Durazo	10.00
Jeremy Giambi	6.00
Jason Giambi	25.00
Doug Glanville	6.00
Troy Glaus	25.00
Shawn Green	20.00
Mike Hampton	10.00
Tim Hudson	15.00
John Jaha	5.00
Derek Jeter	150.00
D'Angelo Jimenez	5.00
Nick Johnson	8.00
Andruw Jones	20.00
Jason Kendall	10.00
Adam Kennedy	6.00
Mike Lieberthal	8.00
Edgar Martinez	15.00
Aaron McNeal	5.00
Kevin Millwood	10.00
Mike Mussina	30.00
Magglio Ordonez	15.00
Eric Owens	5.00
Rafael Palmeiro	20.00
Wily Pena	15.00
Adam Piatt	8.00
Cal Ripken Jr.	100.00
Alex Rodriguez	65.00
Scott Rolen	20.00
Tim Salmon	15.00
Chris Singleton	5.00
Mike Sweeney	10.00
Jose Vidro	8.00
Rondell White	8.00
Jaret Wright	5.00

Future Vision

This 15-card set highlights the top prospects over a holo-foiled background with red foil etching and stamping. These were seeded 1:9 packs and are numbered with an "FV" suffix.

		NM/M
Complete Set (15):		8.00
Common Player:		.40
Inserted 1:9		
1	Rick Ankiel	.50
2	Matt Riley	.40
3	Ruben Mateo	.40
4	Ben Petrick	.40
5	Mario Encarnacion	.40
6	Octavio Dotel	.40
7	Vernon Wells	.65
8	Adam Kennedy	.40
9	Lance Berkman	.40
10	Chad Hermansen	.40
11	Mark Quinn	.40
12	Eric Munson	.40
13	Alfonso Soriano	2.00
14	Kip Wells	.40
15	Josh Beckett	.75

2000 Fleer Gamers

The 120-card base set has silver foil etching down the left portion of the card with vertical stripes running down the right portion of the card front. The card back has career statistical totals as well as a small photo. Two short-printed subsets also make up the 120-card set. Next Gamers (91-110) are seeded 1:3 packs and Fame Game (111-120) are seeded 1:8 packs.

		NM/M
Complete Set (120):		50.00
Common Player (1-90):		.15
Common (91-110):		1.00
Inserted 1:3		
Common (111-120):		1.50
Inserted 1:8		
Pack:		2.00
Wax Box:		35.00
1	Cal Ripken Jr.	2.00
2	Derek Jeter	2.00
3	Alex Rodriguez	1.50
4	Alex Gonzalez	.15
5	Nomar Garciaparra	1.25
6	Brian Giles	.15
7	Chris Singleton	.15
8	Kevin Brown	.15
9	J.D. Drew	.25
10	Raul Mondesi	.15
11	Sammy Sosa	1.25
12	Carlos Beltran	.50
13	Eric Chavez	.25
14	Gabe Kapler	.15
15	Tim Salmon	.25
16	Manny Ramirez	.75
17	Orlando Hernandez	.15
18	Jeff Kent	.15
19	Juan Gonzalez	.75
20	Moises Alou	.15
21	Jason Giambi	.50
22	Ivan Rodriguez	.60
23	Geoff Jenkins	.15
24	Ken Griffey Jr.	1.25
25	Mark McGwire	1.50
26	Jose Canseco	.40
27	Roberto Alomar	.40
28	Craig Biggio	.15
29	Scott Rolen	.65
30	Vinny Castilla	.15
31	Greg Maddux	1.00
32	Pedro J. Martinez	.75
33	Mike Piazza	1.25
34	Albert Belle	.25
35	Frank Thomas	.75
36	Bobby Abreu	.15
37	Edgar Martinez	.15
38	Pokey Reese	.15
39	Preston Wilson	.15
40	Mike Lieberthal	.15
41	Andruw Jones	.75
42	Damion Easley	.15
43	Mike Cameron	.15
44	Todd Walker	.15
45	Jason Kendall	.15
46	Sean Casey	.25
47	Corey Koskie	.15
48	Warren Morris	.15
49	Andres Galarraga	.15
50	Dean Palmer	.15
51	Jose Vidro	.15
52	Brian Jordan	.15
53	Tony Clark	.15
54	Vladimir Guerrero	.75
55	Mo Vaughn	.15
56	Richie Sexson	.15
57	Tino Martinez	.15
58	Eric Owens	.15
59	Matt Williams	.15
60	Omar Vizquel	.15
61	Rickey Henderson	.75
62	J.T. Snow	.15
63	Mark Grace	.25
64	Carlos Febles	.15
65	Paul O'Neill	.15
66	Randy Johnson	.75
67	Kenny Lofton	.15
68	Roger Cedeno	.15
69	Shawn Green	.35
70	Chipper Jones	1.00
71	Jeff Cirillo	.15
72	Robin Ventura	.15
73	Paul Konerko	.15
74	Jeromy Burnitz	.15
75	Ben Grieve	.15
76	Troy Glaus	.75
77	Jim Thome	.15
78	Bernie Williams	.25
79	Barry Bonds	2.00
80	Ray Durham	.15
81	Adrian Beltre	.15
82	Ray Lankford	.15
83	Carlos Delgado	.50
84	Erubiel Durazo	.15
85	Larry Walker	.15
86	Edgardo Alfonzo	.15
87	Rafael Palmeiro	.65
88	Magglio Ordonez	.25
89	Jeff Bagwell	.75
90	Tony Gwynn	1.00
91	Norm Hutchins (Next Gamers)	1.00
92	Derrick Turnbow RC (Next Gamers)	1.00
93	Matt Riley (Next Gamers)	1.00
94	David Eckstein (Next Gamers)	1.00
95	Dernell Stenson (Next Gamers)	1.00
96	Joe Crede (Next Gamers)	1.00
97	Ben Petrick (Next Gamers)	1.00
98	Eric Munson (Next Gamers)	1.00
99	Pablo Ozuna (Next Gamers)	1.00
100	Josh Beckett (Next Gamers)	3.00
101	Aaron McNeal RC (Next Gamers)	1.50
102	Milton Bradley (Next Gamers)	1.50
103	Alex Escobar (Next Gamers)	1.50
104	Alfonso Soriano (Next Gamers)	4.00
105	Wily Pena (Next Gamers)	1.50
106	Nick Johnson (Next Gamers)	1.50
107	Adam Piatt (Next Gamers)	1.00
108	Pat Burrell (Next Gamers)	2.00
109	Rick Ankiel (Next Gamers)	1.00
110	Vernon Wells (Next Gamers)	2.00
111	Alex Rodriguez (Fame Game)	3.00
112	Cal Ripken Jr. (Fame Game)	4.00
113	Mark McGwire (Fame Game)	3.00
114	Ken Griffey Jr. (Fame Game)	2.00
115	Mike Piazza (Fame Game)	2.00
116	Nomar Garciaparra (Fame Game)	3.00
117	Derek Jeter (Fame Game)	4.00
118	Chipper Jones (Fame Game)	1.50
119	Sammy Sosa (Fame Game)	2.00
120	Tony Gwynn (Fame Game)	1.50

Extra

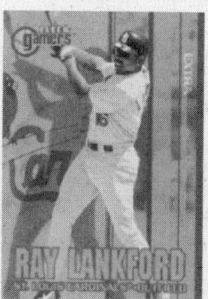

A parallel to the 120-card base set, the gold foiled card front and "Extra" written down the right portion of the card can be used to differentiate these from regular cards. "Extra" is also written underneath the card number on the back as well. Extras 1-90 are seeded 1:24 packs and numbers 91-120 are seeded 1:36 packs.

Stars (1-90):	5-10X
Inserted 1:24	
Next Gamers (91-110):	1-2X
Inserted 1:36	
Fame Game (110-120):	1-2X
Inserted 1:36	

Cal to Greatness

This 15-card tribute insert set to baseball's "Iron Man" is broken into three tiers. Cards 1-5 are seeded 1:9 packs, cards 6-10 are found

1:25 packs and cards 11-15 are inserted 1:144 packs. Card backs are numbered with a "C" suffix.

		NM/M
Complete Set (15):		100.00
Common Ripken (1-5):		3.00
Inserted 1:9		
Common Ripken (6-10):		6.00
Inserted 1:25		
Common Ripken (11-15):		20.00
Inserted 1:144		
1-5	Cal Ripken Jr.	3.00
6-10	Cal Ripken Jr.	6.00
11-15	Cal Ripken Jr.	20.00

Change the Game

This 15-card set has a holofoiled front with Change the Game printed behind the player image. Seeded 1:24 packs, card backs are numbered with a "CG" suffix.

		NM/M
Complete Set (15):		50.00
Common Player:		1.50
Inserted 1:24		
1	Alex Rodriguez	6.00
2	Cal Ripken Jr.	7.50
3	Chipper Jones	3.00
4	Derek Jeter	7.50
5	Ken Griffey Jr.	6.00
6	Mark McGwire	6.00
7	Mike Piazza	4.00
8	Nomar Garciaparra	4.00
9	Sammy Sosa	4.00
10	Tony Gwynn	3.00
11	Ivan Rodriguez	1.50
12	Pedro Martinez	2.00
13	Juan Gonzalez	2.00
14	Vladimir Guerrero	2.00
15	Manny Ramirez	2.00

Determined

This 15-card set has a holofoiled front with two player images on the card front. The second player photo is smaller than the primary image and is a close-up shot. Card backs are numbered with a "D" suffix and are seeded 1:12 packs.

		NM/M
Complete Set (15):		25.00
Common Player:		.50
Inserted 1:12		
1	Nomar Garciaparra	2.50
2	Chipper Jones	2.00
3	Derek Jeter	4.00
4	Mike Piazza	2.50
5	Jeff Bagwell	1.00
6	Mark McGwire	3.00
7	Greg Maddux	2.00
8	Sammy Sosa	2.50
9	Ken Griffey Jr.	2.50
10	Alex Rodriguez	3.00
11	Tony Gwynn	2.00
12	Cal Ripken Jr.	4.00
13	Barry Bonds	4.00
14	Juan Gonzalez	1.00
15	Sean Casey	.50

Lumber

Seeded 1:36 packs, these inserts have a piece of game-used bat embedded into the card front and are numbered with an "GL" suffix.

		NM/M
Common Player:		5.00
Inserted 1:36		
1	Alex Rodriguez	30.00
2	Carlos Delgado	10.00
3	Jose Vidro	5.00
4	Carlos Febles	5.00
5	J.D. Drew	7.50
6	Mike Cameron	5.00
7	Derek Jeter	40.00
8	Eric Chavez	6.00
9	Cal Ripken Jr.	40.00
10	Gabe Kapler	5.00
11	Damion Easley	5.00
12	Frank Thomas	15.00
13	Chris Singleton	5.00
14	Norm Hutchins	5.00
15	Pokey Reese	5.00
16	Rafael Palmeiro	12.00
17	Ray Durham	5.00
18	Ray Lankford	5.00
19	Roger Cedeno	5.00
20	Shawn Green	5.00
21	Wade Boggs	20.00
22	Roberto Alomar	7.50
23	Moises Alou	5.00
24	Adrian Beltre	6.00
25	Barry Bonds	40.00
26	Jason Giambi	10.00
27	Jason Kendall	5.00
28	Paul Konerko	5.00
29	Mike Lieberthal	5.00
30	Edgar Martinez	5.00
31	Raul Mondesi	5.00
32	Scott Rolen	12.00
33	Alfonso Soriano	10.00
34	Ivan Rodriguez	10.00
35	Magglio Ordonez	7.50
36	Chipper Jones	20.00
37	Sean Casey	6.00
38	Edgardo Alfonzo	5.00
39	Robin Ventura	5.00
40	Bernie Williams	6.00
41	Vladimir Guerrero	15.00
42	Tony Clark	5.00
43	Carlos Beltran	10.00
44	Warren Morris	5.00
45	Jim Thome	5.00
46	Jeromy Burnitz	5.00
47	Matt Williams	5.00
48	Erubiel Durazo	5.00

Lumber Autograph

Twelve players also signed a limited number of their Lumber inserts. The number signed by each player is listed after the player name. These were seeded 1:287 packs.

		NM/M
Common Player:		15.00
Inserted 1:287		
1	Derek Jeter	150.00
2	Eric Chavez	20.00
3	Rafael Palmeiro	40.00
4	Shawn Green	35.00
5	Roberto Alomar	45.00
6	Paul Konerko	15.00
7	Sean Casey	15.00
8	Alex Rodriguez	80.00
9	Robin Ventura	20.00
10	Erubiel Durazo	15.00
11	Tony Clark	15.00
12	Alfonso Soriano	60.00

2000 Fleer Greats of the Game

Satchel Paige
of the
St. Louis Browns

The base set consists of 107-cards of retired stars. Card fronts have a brown border with "Fleer Greats of the Game" stamped in silver foil. Backs have a small photo along with complete career statistics and a brief career highlight.

		NM/M
Complete Set (108):		50.00
Common Player:		.50
Pack (6):		10.00
Wax Box (24):		200.00
1	Mickey Mantle	8.00
2	Gil Hodges	1.00
3	Monte Irvin	1.00
4	Satchel Paige	2.50
5	Roy Campanella	2.00
6	Richie Ashburn	1.00
7	Roger Maris	3.00
8	Ozzie Smith	2.00
9	Reggie Jackson	2.50
10	Eddie Mathews	2.50
11	Dave Righetti	.50
12	Dave Winfield	1.00
13	Lou Whitaker	.50
14	Phil Garner	.50
15	Ron Cey	.50
16	Brooks Robinson	2.50
17	Bruce Sutter	.50
18	Dave Parker	.50
19	Johnny Bench	2.50
20	Fernando Valenzuela	.50
21	George Brett	4.00
22	Paul Molitor	2.00
23	Hoyt Wilhelm	.50
24	Luis Aparicio	.50
25	Frank White	.50
26	Herb Score	.50
27	Kirk Gibson	.50
28	Mike Schmidt	3.00
29	Don Baylor	.50
30	Joe Pepitone	.50
31	Hal McRae	.50
32	Lee Smith	.50
33	Nolan Ryan	7.00
33	Nolan Ryan/OPS	5.00
34	Bill Mazeroski	.75
35	Bobby Doerr	.50
36	Duke Snider	1.00
37	Dick Groat	.50
38	Larry Doby	.50
39	Kirby Puckett	2.00
40	Steve Carlton	1.00
41	Dennis Eckersley	.50
42	Jim Bunning	.50
43	Ron Guidry	.50
44	Alan Trammell	1.00
45	Bob Feller	1.50
46	Dave Concepcion	.50
47	Dwight Evans	.50
48	Enos Slaughter	.50
49	Tom Seaver	2.50
50	Tony Oliva	1.00
51	Mel Stottlemyre	.50
52	Tommy John	.50
53	Willie McCovey	1.00
54	Red Schoendienst	.50
55	Gorman Thomas	.50
56	Ralph Kiner	1.00
57	Robin Yount	2.00
58	Andre Dawson	1.00
59	Al Kaline	2.50
60	Dom DiMaggio	.50
61	Juan Marichal	1.00
62	Jack Morris	.50
63	Warren Spahn	1.50
64	Preacher Roe	.50
65	Darrell Evans	.50
66	Jim Bouton	.50
67	Rocky Colavito	.75
68	Bob Gibson	1.50
69	Whitey Ford	1.50
70	Moose Skowron	.50
71	Boog Powell	1.00
72	Al Lopez	.50
73	Lou Brock	1.00
74	Mickey Lolich	.50
75	Rod Carew	2.00
76	Bob Lemon	.50
77	Frank Howard	.50
78	Phil Rizzuto	1.50
79	Carl Yastrzemski	2.00
80	Rico Carty	.50
81	Jim Kaat	.50

82	Bert Blyleven	.50
83	George Kell	.50
84	Jim Palmer	1.00
85	Maury Wills	1.00
86	Jim Rice	.50
87	Joe Carter	.50
88	Clete Boyer	.50
89	Yogi Berra	2.00
90	Cecil Cooper	.50
91	Davey Johnson	.50
92	Lou Boudreau	.50
93	Orlando Cepeda	1.00
94	Tommy Henrich	.50
95	Hank Bauer	.50
96	Don Larsen	1.50
97	Vida Blue	1.00
98	Ben Oglivie	.50
99	Don Mattingly	5.00
100	Dale Murphy	1.00
101	Ferguson Jenkins	1.00
102	Bobby Bonds	.75
103	Dick Allen	.50
104	Stan Musial	3.00
105	Gaylord Perry	.50
106	Willie Randolph	.50
107	Willie Stargell	1.50
108	Checklist	.50

Autographs

George Brett

Seeded in every six packs, Autographs feature the signature on the bottom half of the card front in black Sharpie. The autographed set features 89 retired players. Some cards were issued in considerably lower quantities than others, as noted in the checklist.

		NM/M
Common Player:		10.00
Inserted 1:6		
	Luis Aparicio	25.00
	Hank Bauer	10.00
	Don Baylor	20.00
	Johnny Bench	200.00
	Yogi Berra	180.00
	Vida Blue	20.00
	Bert Blyleven	10.00
	Bobby Bonds	40.00
	Lou Boudreau	120.00
	Jim Bouton	20.00
	Clete Boyer	15.00
	George Brett	
	(275 or less)	300.00
	Lou Brock	40.00
	Jim Bunning	40.00
	Rod Carew	50.00
	Steve Carlton	20.00
	Joe Carter/SP	75.00
	Orlando Cepeda	25.00
	Ron Cey	15.00
	Rocky Colavito	30.00
	Dave Concepcion	
	(Black autograph.)	15.00
	Dave Concepcion	
	(Red autograph.)	15.00
	Cecil Cooper	10.00
	Andre Dawson	25.00
	Dom DiMaggio	75.00
	Bobby Doerr	15.00
	Darrell Evans	15.00
	Bob Feller	30.00
	Whitey Ford	
	(300 or less)	150.00
	Phil Garner	10.00
	Bob Gibson	40.00
	Kirk Gibson	20.00
	Dick Groat	25.00
	Ron Guidry	20.00
	Tommy Henrich	
	(300 or less)	180.00
	Frank Howard	20.00
	Reggie Jackson	
	(250 or less)	180.00
	Ferguson Jenkins	20.00
	Tommy John	10.00
	Davey Johnson	10.00
	Jim Kaat	20.00
	Al Kaline	50.00
	George Kell	20.00
	Ralph Kiner	30.00
	Don Larsen	25.00
	Mickey Lolich	10.00
	Juan Marichal	40.00
	Eddie Mathews	150.00
	Don Mattingly	
	(300 or less)	350.00

	Bill Mazeroski	50.00
	Willie McCovey	150.00
	Hal McRae	10.00
	Paul Molitor	50.00
	Jack Morris	10.00
	Dale Murphy	40.00
	Stan Musial	150.00
	Ben Oglivie	10.00
	Tony Oliva	15.00
	Jim Palmer/SP	150.00
	Dave Parker	20.00
	Joe Pepitone	10.00
	Gaylord Perry	15.00
	Boog Powell	15.00
	Kirby Puckett	
	(200 or less)	350.00
	Willie Randolph	20.00
	Jim Rice	30.00
	Dave Righetti	15.00
	Phil Rizzuto	
	(200 or less)	200.00
	Brooks Robinson	40.00
	Preacher Roe	15.00
	Nolan Ryan	180.00
	Mike Schmidt	
	(175 or less)	500.00
	Red Schoendienst	20.00
	Herb Score	25.00
	Tom Seaver	100.00
	Moose Skowron	20.00
	Enos Slaughter	30.00
	Lee Smith	10.00
	Ozzie Smith/SP	200.00
	Duke Snider/SP	200.00
	Warren Spahn/SP	275.00
	Bruce Sutter	15.00
	Gorman Thomas	10.00
	Alan Trammell	20.00
	Frank White	10.00
	Hoyt Wilhelm	15.00
	Maury Wills	15.00
	Dave Winfield	300.00
	Carl Yastrzemski	75.00
	Robin Yount/SP	250.00

Memorable Moments Auto.

		NM/M
Common Player:		60.00
1	Ron Guidry/78	75.00
2	Nolan Ryan/99	300.00
3	Herb Score/55	40.00
4	Tom Seaver/69	180.00

Retrospection

REGGIE JACKSON

The 15-card Retrospection insert set highlights some of the all-time greats with a design borrowed from 1960 Fleer. Former greats including Stan Musial and Al Kaline are featured. They were seeded 1:6 packs.

		NM/M
Complete Set (15):		75.00
Common Player:		4.00
Inserted 1:6		
1	Rod Carew	4.00
2	Stan Musial	8.00
3	Nolan Ryan	15.00
4	Tom Seaver	6.00
5	Brooks Robinson	5.00
6	Al Kaline	6.00
7	Mike Schmidt	10.00
8	Thurman Munson	8.00
9	Steve Carlton	4.00
10	Roger Maris	8.00
11	Duke Snider	5.00
12	Yogi Berra	6.00
13	Carl Yastrzemski	5.00
14	Reggie Jackson	6.00
15	Johnny Bench	8.00

Yankees Clippings

Yankees Clippings

This 15-card memorabilia insert features an actual piece of New York Yankee uniform worn by former stars. The jersey swatch is

formed in the shape of the interlocking "NY" logo and are seeded 1:48 packs.

		NM/M
Common Player:		20.00
Inserted 1:48		
1	Mickey Mantle	200.00
2	Ron Guidry	40.00
3	Don Larsen	40.00
4	Elston Howard	40.00
5	Mel Stottlemyre	25.00
6	Don Mattingly	100.00
7	Reggie Jackson	50.00
8	Tommy John	20.00
9	Dave Winfield	25.00
10	Willie Randolph	20.00
11	Tommy Henrich	20.00
12	Billy Martin	50.00
13	Dave Righetti	20.00
14	Joe Pepitone	20.00
15	Thurman Munson	80.00

2000 Fleer Impact

Roger Clemens P

The base set consists of 200 cards with 25 of those being Prospect subset cards. The featured player's team logo appears beside the player name on the bottom portion with the Impact logo on the top left portion. Card backs have a maximum of 10 years of statistics along with a small photo and vital information. Impact was sold in 10-card packs with an SRP of $.99 per pack.

		NM/M
Complete Set (200):		15.00
Common Player:		.10
Pack (10):		1.00
Box (36):		20.00
1	Cal Ripken Jr.	1.50
2	Jose Canseco	.25
3	Manny Ramirez	.60
4	Bernie Williams	.30
5	Troy Glaus	.60
6	Jeff Bagwell	.60
7	Corey Koskie	.10
8	Barry Larkin	.10
9	Mark Quinn	.10
10	Russ Ortiz	.10
11	Tim Salmon	.15
12	Preston Wilson	.10
13	Mo Vaughn	.15
14	Ray Lankford	.10
15	Sterling Hitchcock	.10
16	Al Leiter	.10
17	Jim Morris	.10
18	Freddy Garcia	.10
19	Adrian Beltre	.20
20	Eric Chavez	.20
21	Robinson Cancel	.10
22	Edgar Renteria	.10
23	John Jaha	.10
24	Chuck Finley	.10
25	Andres Galarraga	.10
26	Paul Byrd	.10
27	John Halama	.10
28	Eric Karros	.10
29	Mike Piazza	1.00
30	Ryan Rupe	.10
31	Frank Thomas	.60
32	Randy Velarde	.10
33	Bobby Abreu	.10
34	Randy Johnson	.50
35	Matt Williams	.10
36	Tony Gwynn	.75
37	Dean Palmer	.10
38	Aaron Sele	.10
39	Rondell White	.10
40	Erubiel Durazo	.10
41	Curt Schilling	.25
42	Kip Wells	.10
43	Craig Biggio	.10
44	Tom Glavine	.25
45	Trevor Hoffman	.10
46	Greg Vaughn	.10
47	Edgar Martinez	.20
48	Magglio Ordonez	.20
49	Mark Mulder	.10
50	John Rocker	.10
51	Kenny Rogers	.10
52	Gary Sheffield	.25
53	Brian Simmons	.10
54	Tony Womack	.10
55	Ken Caminiti	.10
56	Jeff Cirillo	.10

57	Ray Durham	.10
58	Mike Lieberthal	.10
59	Ruben Mateo	.10
60	Mike Cameron	.10
61	Rusty Greer	.10
62	Alex Rodriguez	1.25
63	Robin Ventura	.10
64	Pokey Reese	.10
65	Jose Lima	.10
66	Neifi Perez	.10
67	Rafael Palmeiro	.50
68	Scott Rolen	.50
69	Mike Hampton	.10
70	Sammy Sosa	1.00
71	Mike Stanley	.10
72	Dan Wilson	.10
73	Kerry Wood	.50
74	Mike Mussina	.30
75	Masato Yoshii	.10
76	Peter Bergeron	.10
77	Carlos Delgado	.50
78	Juan Encarnacion	.10
79	Nomar Garciaparra	1.00
80	Jason Kendall	.10
81	Pedro Martinez	.60
82	Darin Erstad	.40
83	Larry Walker	.10
84	Rick Ankiel	.10
85	Scott Erickson	.10
86	Roger Clemens	.85
87	Matt Lawton	.10
88	Jon Lieber	.10
89	Shane Reynolds	.10
90	Ivan Rodriguez	.50
91	Pat Burrell	.50
92	Kent Bottenfield	.10
93	David Cone	.10
94	Mark Grace	.15
95	Paul Konerko	.10
96	Eric Milton	.10
97	Lee Stevens	.10
98	B.J. Surhoff	.10
99	Billy Wagner	.10
100	Ken Griffey Jr.	1.00
101	Randy Wolf	.10
102	Henry Rodriguez	.10
103	Carlos Beltran	.40
104	Rich Aurilia	.10
105	Chipper Jones	.75
106	Homer Bush	.10
107	Johnny Damon	.10
108	J.D. Drew	.40
109	Orlando Hernandez	.10
110	Brad Radke	.10
111	Wilton Veras	.10
112	Dmitri Young	.10
113	Jermaine Dye	.10
114	Kris Benson	.10
115	Derek Jeter	1.50
116	Cole Liniak	.10
117	Jim Thome	.10
118	Pedro Astacio	.10
119	Carlos Febles	.10
120	Darryl Kile	.10
121	Alfonso Soriano	.50
122	Michael Barrett	.10
123	Ellis Burks	.10
124	Chad Hermansen	.10
125	Trot Nixon	.10
126	Bobby Higginson	.10
127	Rick Helling	.10
128	Chris Carpenter	.10
129	Vinny Castilla	.10
130	Brian Giles	.10
131	Todd Helton	.60
132	Jason Varitek	.10
133	Rob Ducey	.10
134	Octavio Dotel	.10
135	Adam Kennedy	.10
136	Jeff Kent	.10
137	Aaron Boone	.10
138	Todd Walker	.10
139	Jeromy Burnitz	.10
140	Roberto Hernandez	.10
141	Matt LeCroy	.10
142	Ugueth Urbina	.10
143	David Wells	.10
144	Luis Gonzalez	.25
145	Andruw Jones	.50
146	Juan Gonzalez	.60
147	Moises Alou	.10
148	Michael Tejera	.10
149	Brian Jordan	.10
150	Mark McGwire	1.25
151	Shawn Green	.25
152	Jay Bell	.10
153	Fred McGriff	.10
154	Rey Ordonez	.10
155	Matt Stairs	.10
156	A.J. Burnett	.10
157	Omar Vizquel	.10
158	Damion Easley	.10
159	Dante Bichette	.10
160	Javy Lopez	.10
161	Fernando Seguignol	.10
162	Richie Sexson	.10
163	Vladimir Guerrero	.60
164	Kevin Young	.10
165	Josh Beckett	.10
166	Albert Belle	.10
167	Cliff Floyd	.10
168	Gabe Kapler	.10
169	Nick Johnson	.15
170	Raul Mondesi	.10
171	Warren Morris	.10
172	Kenny Lofton	.10
173	Reggie Sanders	.10
174	Mike Sweeney	.10

175	Robert Fick	.10
176	Barry Bonds	1.50
177	Luis Castillo	.10
178	Roger Cedeno	.10
179	Jim Edmonds	.10
180	Geoff Jenkins	.10
181	Adam Piatt	.10
182	Phil Nevin	.10
183	Roberto Alomar	.30
184	Kevin Brown	.10
185	D.T. Cromer	.10
186	Jason Giambi	.50
187	Fernando Tatis	.10
188	Brady Anderson	.10
189	Tony Clark	.10
190	Alex Fernandez	.10
191	Matt Blank	.10
192	Greg Maddux	.75
193	Kevin Millwood	.10
194	Jason Schmidt	.10
195	Shannon Stewart	.10
196	Rolando Arrojo	.10
197	Darren Dreifort	.10
198	Ben Grieve	.10
199	Bartolo Colon	.10
200	Sean Casey	.10

Autographics

This autographed set has the player signature on the bottom portion of the card. These were seeded 1:216 packs.

		NM/M
Common Player:		5.00
Inserted 1:216		
Silvers:		1-2X
Production 250 Sets		
Golds:		1-2X
Production 50 Sets		
1	Bobby Abreu	15.00
2	Marlon Anderson	5.00
3	Rick Ankiel	15.00
4	Rob Bell	5.00
5	Carlos Beltran	25.00
6	Wade Boggs	30.00
7	Barry Bonds	200.00
8	Milton Bradley	8.00
9	Pat Burrell	25.00
10	Orlando Cabrera	10.00
11	Chris Carpenter	5.00
12	Sean Casey	8.00
13	Carlos Delgado	20.00
14	J.D. Drew	15.00
15	Ray Durham	8.00
16	Kelvim Escobar	5.00
17	Vladimir Guerrero	30.00
18	Tony Gwynn	35.00
19	Jerry Hairston Jr.	5.00
20	Todd Helton	25.00
21	Nick Johnson	8.00
22	Jason Kendall	8.00
23	Mark Kotsay	8.00
24	Cole Liniak	5.00
25	Jose Macias	5.00
26	Greg Maddux	60.00
27	Ruben Mateo	8.00
28	Ober Moreno	5.00
29	Eric Munson	8.00
30	Joe Nathan	5.00
31	Angel Pena	5.00
32	Adam Piatt	6.00
33	Matt Riley	5.00
34	Cal Ripken Jr.	100.00
35	Alex Rodriguez	75.00
36	Scott Rolen	25.00
37	Jimmy Rollins	15.00
38	B.J. Ryan	5.00
39	Alfonso Soriano	40.00
40	Frank Thomas	25.00
41	Wilton Veras	5.00
42	Billy Wagner	10.00
43	Jeff Weaver	5.00
44	Scott Williamson	6.00

Genuine Coverage

This memorabilia insert set has pieces of game-used batting gloves embedded into the card front. They were seeded 1:720 packs.

		NM/M
Common Player:		5.00
Inserted 1:720		
1	Alex Rodriguez	65.00
2	Cole Liniak	5.00
3	Barry Bonds	75.00

#	Player	Price
4	Ben Davis	5.00
5	Bobby Abreu	7.50
6	Mike Sweeney	7.50
7	Rafael Palmeiro	35.00
8	Carlos Lee	5.00
9	Glen Barker	5.00
10	Jason Giambi	30.00
11	Jacque Jones	7.50
12	Joe Nathan	5.00
13	Jason LaRue	5.00
14	Magglio Ordonez	7.50
15	Shannon Stewart	5.00
16	Matt Lawton	5.00
17	Trevor Hoffman	5.00

Mighty Fine in '99

This 40-card set honors the 1999 World Series Champion New York Yankees as well as other various award winners from the '99 season. These were seeded one per pack.

		NM/M
Complete Set (40):		8.00
Common Player:		.15
Inserted 1:1		
1	Clay Bellinger	.15
2	Scott Brosius	.15
3	Roger Clemens	.75
4	David Cone	.15
5	Chad Curtis	.15
6	Chili Davis	.15
7	Joe Girardi	.15
8	Jason Grimsley	.15
9	Orlando Hernandez	.15
10	Hideki Irabu	.15
11	Derek Jeter	2.00
12	Chuck Knoblauch	.15
13	Ricky Ledee	.15
14	Jim Leyritz	.15
15	Tino Martinez	.15
16	Ramiro Mendoza	.15
17	Jeff Nelson	.15
18	Paul O'Neill	.15
19	Andy Pettitte	.25
20	Jorge Posada	.25
21	Mariano Rivera	.25
22	Luis Sojo	.15
23	Mike Stanton	.15
24	Allen Watson	.15
25	Bernie Williams	.30
26	Chipper Jones	.60
27	Ivan Rodriguez	.45
28	Randy Johnson	.50
29	Pedro Martinez	.50
30	Scott Williamson	.15
31	Carlos Beltran	.40
32	Mark McGwire	1.50
33	Ken Griffey Jr.	1.00
34	Robin Ventura	.15
35	Tony Gwynn	.60
36	Wade Boggs	.60
37	Cal Ripken Jr.	2.00
38	Jose Canseco	.40
39	Alex Rodriguez	1.50
40	Fernando Tatis	.15

Point of Impact

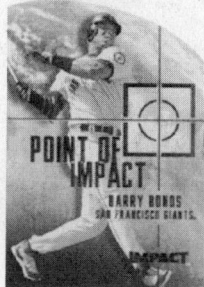

Point of Impact honors some of the game's top sluggers on a die-cut design. Card fronts have silver foil stamping and cross hairs where the featured player finds his sweet spot. These were seeded 1:30 packs and are numbered with an "PI" suffix on the card back.

		NM/M
Complete Set (10):		20.00
Common Player:		1.00
Inserted 1:30		
1	Ken Griffey Jr.	2.00
2	Mark McGwire	3.00
3	Sammy Sosa	2.00
4	Jeff Bagwell	1.00
5	Derek Jeter	4.00
6	Chipper Jones	1.50
7	Nomar Garciaparra	2.00
8	Cal Ripken Jr.	4.00
9	Barry Bonds	4.00
10	Alex Rodriguez	3.00

2000 Fleer Mystique

The base set consists of 175-cards including a 50-card Prospects subset that each card is serially numbered to 2,000 and covered. The card fronts have a full bleed design with gold foil stamping. Card backs have complete year-by-year statistics and a small photo.

		NM/M
Complete Set (175):		350.00
Common Player:		.20
Common 126-175:		6.00
Production 2,000 sets		
Pack (5):		3.00
Box (20):		50.00
1	Derek Jeter	3.00
2	David Justice	.20
3	Kevin Brown	.20
4	Jason Giambi	.75
5	Jose Canseco	.50
6	Mark Grace	.30
7	Hideo Nomo	.65
8	Edgardo Alfonzo	.20
9	Barry Bonds	3.00
10	Pedro Martinez	1.00
11	Juan Gonzalez	1.00
12	Vladimir Guerrero	1.00
13	Chuck Finley	.20
14	Brian Jordan	.20
15	Richie Sexson	.20
16	Chan Ho Park	.20
17	Tim Hudson	.40
18	Fred McGriff	.60
19	Darin Erstad	.60
20	Chris Singleton	.20
21	Jeff Bagwell	1.00
22	David Cone	.20
23	Edgar Martinez	.20
24	Greg Maddux	1.50
25	Jim Thome	.20
26	Eric Karros	.20
27	Bobby Abreu	.20
28	Greg Vaughn	.20
29	Kevin Millwood	.20
30	Omar Vizquel	.20
31	Marquis Grissom	.20
32	Mike Lieberthal	.20
33	Gabe Kapler	.20
34	Brady Anderson	.20
35	Jeff Cirillo	.20
36	Geoff Jenkins	.20
37	Scott Rolen	.75
38	Rafael Palmeiro	.65
39	Randy Johnson	1.00
40	Barry Larkin	.20
41	Johnny Damon	.40
42	Andy Pettitte	.40
43	Mark McGwire	2.50
44	Albert Belle	.20
45	Derrick Gibson	.20
46	Corey Koskie	.20
47	Curt Schilling	.50
48	Ivan Rodriguez	.65
49	Mike Mussina	.50
50	Todd Helton	1.00
51	Matt Lawton	.20
52	Jason Kendall	.20
53	Kenny Rogers	.20
54	Cal Ripken Jr.	3.00
55	Larry Walker	.20
56	Eric Milton	.20
57	Warren Morris	.20
58	Carlos Delgado	.50
59	Kerry Wood	.65
60	Cliff Floyd	.20
61	Mike Piazza	2.00
62	Jeff Kent	.20
63	Sammy Sosa	2.00
64	Alex Fernandez	.20
65	Mike Hampton	.20
66	Livan Hernandez	.20
67	Matt Williams	.20
68	Roberto Alomar	.45
69	Jermaine Dye	.20
70	Bernie Williams	.35
71	Edgar Renteria	.20
72	Tom Glavine	.40
73	Bartolo Colon	.20
74	Jason Varitek	.20
75	Eric Chavez	.40
76	Fernando Tatis	.20
77	Adrian Beltre	.40
78	Paul Konerko	.20
79	Mike Lowell	.20
80	Robin Ventura	.20
81	Russ Ortiz	.20
82	Troy Glaus	1.00
83	Frank Thomas	1.00
84	Craig Biggio	.20
85	Orlando Hernandez	.20
86	John Olerud	.20
87	Chipper Jones	1.50
88	Manny Ramirez	1.00
89	Shawn Green	.40
90	Ben Grieve	.20
91	Vinny Castilla	.20
92	Tim Salmon	.35
93	Dante Bichette	.20
94	Ken Caminiti	.20
95	Andruw Jones	.75
96	Alex Rodriguez	2.50
97	Erubiel Durazo	.30
98	Sean Casey	.30
99	Carlos Beltran	.50
100	Paul O'Neill	.20
101	Ray Lankford	.20
102	Troy O'Leary	.20
103	Bobby Higginson	.20
104	Rondell White	.20
105	Tony Gwynn	1.50
106	Jim Edmonds	.20
107	Magglio Ordonez	.40
108	Preston Wilson	.20
109	Roger Clemens	1.75
110	Ken Griffey Jr.	2.00
111	Nomar Garciaparra	2.00
112	Juan Encarnacion	.20
113	Michael Barrett	.20
114	Matt Clement	.20
115	David Wells	.20
116	Mo Vaughn	.20
117	Mike Cameron	.20
118	Jose Lima	.20
119	Tino Martinez	.20
120	J.D. Drew	.40
121	Carl Everett	.20
122	Tony Clark	.20
123	Brad Radke	.20
124	Kevin Young	.20
125	Raul Mondesi	.20
126	Cole Liniak (Prospects)	6.00
127	Alfonso Soriano (Prospects)	8.00
128	Lance Berkman (Prospects)	8.00
129	Danny Young (Prospects)	6.00
130	Francisco Cordero (Prospects)	6.00
131	Rob Fick (Prospects)	6.00
132	Matt LeCroy (Prospects)	6.00
133	Adam Piatt (Prospects)	6.00
134	Derrick Turnbow RC (Prospects)	6.00
135	Mark Quinn (Prospects)	6.00
136	Kip Wells (Prospects)	6.00
137	Rob Bell (Prospects)	6.00
138	Brad Penny (Prospects)	6.00
139	Pat Burrell (Prospects)	10.00
140	Danys Baez RC (Prospects)	6.00
141	Chad Hermansen (Prospects)	6.00
142	Steve Lomasney (Prospects)	6.00
143	Peter Bergeron (Prospects)	6.00
144	Jimmy Anderson (Prospects)	6.00
145	Mike Darr (Prospects)	6.00
146	Jacob Cruz (Prospects)	6.00
147	Kazuhiro Sasaki RC (Prospects)	10.00
148	Ben Petrick (Prospects)	6.00
149	Rick Ankiel (Prospects)	8.00
150	Aaron McNeal RC (Prospects)	6.00
151	Octavio Dotel (Prospects)	6.00
152	Juan Pena (Prospects)	6.00
153	Nick Johnson (Prospects)	8.00
154	Wilton Veras (Prospects)	6.00
155	Wily Pena (Prospects)	6.00
156	Mark Mulder (Prospects)	6.00
157	Daryle Ward (Prospects)	6.00
158	Chad Durbin RC (Prospects)	6.00
159	Angel Pena (Prospects)	6.00
160	Dewayne Wise (Prospects)	6.00
161	Tarrik Brock (Prospects)	6.00
162	Marcus Jensen (Prospects)	6.00
163	Kevin Barker (Prospects)	6.00
164	B.J. Ryan (Prospects)	6.00
165	Cesar King (Prospects)	6.00
166	Geoff Blum (Prospects)	6.00
167	Ruben Mateo (Prospects)	6.00
168	Ramon Ortiz (Prospects)	6.00
169	Eric Munson (Prospects)	6.00
170	Josh Beckett (Prospects)	8.00
171	Rafael Furcal (Prospects)	6.00
172	Matt Riley (Prospects)	6.00
173	Johan Santana RC (Prospects)	60.00
174	Mark Johnson (Prospects)	6.00
175	Adam Kennedy (Prospects)	6.00

Gold

These parallel inserts to the 175-card base set are identical to the base cards besides gold highlights throughout the background of the player photo. The word "Gold" also appears underneath the card number on the back. These were seeded 1:20 packs.

Stars (1-125):	4-8X
SP's (126-175):	1X
Inserted 1:20	

Club 3000

This three-card set is die-cut around the 3,000 numerals with a date on the left side when the featured player reached the 3,000 milestone. The player name is stamped in silver holo-foil. Card backs are not numbered and have a brief career note. These were seeded 1:20 packs.

		NM/M
Complete Set (3):		6.00
Common Player:		1.50
Inserted 1:20		
1	Cal Ripken Jr.	5.00
2	Bob Gibson	1.50
3	Dave Winfield	1.50

Club 3000 Memorabilia

Five different memorabilia versions of each player exist, using pieces of game-used bat, jersey and cap which are embedded into each card. The amount of each card produced is listed after the player name.

	NM/M
Cal Ripken Jr./Jsy/825	40.00
Cal Ripken Jr./Bat/265	75.00
Cal Ripken Jr./Hat/55	120.00
Cal Ripken Jr./Bat/Jsy/100	100.00
Bob Gibson/Jsy/825	20.00
Bob Gibson/Bat/265	30.00
Bob Gibson/Bat/Jsy/100	50.00
Bob Gibson/Hat/Jsy/100	50.00
Bob Gibson/Hat/55	75.00
Dave Winfield/Jsy/825	15.00
Dave Winfield/Bat/270	25.00
Dave Winfield/Bat/Jsy/100	50.00
Dave Winfield/Hat/55	60.00

Diamond Dominators

This 10-card set spotlights baseball's most dominating performers. Card fronts have a holofoil appearance. These were seeded 1:5 packs and are numbered with an "DD" suffix.

		NM/M
Complete Set (10):		15.00
Common Player:		.75
Inserted 1:5		
1	Manny Ramirez	1.00
2	Pedro Martinez	1.00
3	Sean Casey	.75
4	Vladimir Guerrero	1.00
5	Sammy Sosa	1.50
6	Nomar Garciaparra	1.50
7	Mark McGwire	2.50
8	Ken Griffey Jr.	1.50
9	Derek Jeter	3.00
10	Alex Rodriguez	2.50

Feel the Game

This game-used memorabilia set features either game-used jerseys or bats from today's top stars. These were seeded 1:120 packs.

		NM/M
Common Player:		5.00
Inserted 1:120		
1	Tony Gwynn/Jsy	20.00
2	Alex Rodriguez/Jsy	25.00
3	Chipper Jones/Jsy	20.00
4	Cal Ripken Jr./Jsy	40.00
5	Derek Jeter/Pants	40.00
6	Alex Rodriguez/Bat	30.00
7	Frank Thomas/Bat	15.00
8	Barry Bonds/Bat	40.00
9	Carlos Beltran/Bat	5.00
10	Shawn Green/Bat	8.00
11	Michael Barrett/Bat	5.00
12	Rafael Palmeiro/Bat	10.00
13	Vladimir Guerrero/Bat	15.00
14	Pat Burrell/Bat	12.00

Fresh Ink

This autographed set features signatures from many of the game's top players and are seeded 1:40 packs.

		NM/M
Common Player:		5.00
Inserted 1:40		
1	Chad Allen	5.00
2	Glen Barker	5.00
3	Michael Barrett	5.00
4	Josh Beckett	30.00
5	Rob Bell	5.00
6	Lance Berkman	25.00
7	Kent Bottenfield	5.00
8	Milton Bradley	8.00
9	Orlando Cabrera	5.00
10	Sean Casey	10.00
11	Roger Cedeno	6.00
12	Will Clark	25.00
13	Russ Davis	5.00
14	Carlos Delgado	15.00
15	Einar Diaz	5.00
16	J.D. Drew	10.00
17	Erubiel Durazo	10.00
18	Damion Easley	5.00
19	Carlos Febles	5.00
20	Doug Glanville	6.00
21	Alex Gonzalez	5.00
22	Tony Gwynn	40.00
23	Mike Hampton	5.00
24	Bobby Howry	5.00
25	John Jaha	5.00
26	Nick Johnson	10.00
27	Andruw Jones	20.00
28	Adam Kennedy	8.00
29	Mike Lieberthal	8.00
30	Jose Macias	5.00
31	Ruben Mateo	5.00
32	Raul Mondesi	8.00
33	Heath Murray	5.00
34	Mike Mussina	30.00
35	Hideo Nomo	250.00
36	Magglio Ordonez	15.00
37	Eric Owens	5.00
38	Adam Piatt	5.00
39	Cal Ripken Jr.	100.00
40	Tim Salmon	15.00
41	Chris Singleton	5.00
42	J.T. Snow	8.00
43	Mike Sweeney	10.00
44	Wilton Veras	5.00
45	Jose Vidro	8.00
46	Rondell White	10.00
47	Jaret Wright	5.00

High Praise

This 10-card set has a holo-foiled card front with a "sky" background. These were inserted 1:20 packs and are numbered on the card back with an "HP" suffix.

		NM/M
Complete Set (10):		18.00
Common Player:		.75
Inserted 1:20		
1	Mark McGwire	3.00
2	Ken Griffey Jr.	2.00
3	Alex Rodriguez	3.00
4	Derek Jeter	4.00
5	Sammy Sosa	2.00
6	Mike Piazza	2.00
7	Nomar Garciaparra	2.00
8	Cal Ripken Jr.	4.00
9	Tony Gwynn	1.50
10	Shawn Green	.75

Rookie I.P.O.

This 10-card set highlights the top young rookies on a holofoil design. Card backs are numbered with an "RI" suffix and are seeded 1:10 packs.

		NM/M
Complete Set (10):		8.00
Common Player:		.50
Inserted 1:10		
1	Josh Beckett	1.00
2	Eric Munson	.50
3	Pat Burrell	2.00
4	Alfonso Soriano	1.50
5	Rick Ankiel	.50
6	Ruben Mateo	.50
7	Mark Quinn	.50
8	Kip Wells	.50
9	Ben Petrick	.50
10	Nick Johnson	.75

Seismic Activity

This 10-card set spotlights the top power hitters in the game. The player image is in the foreground of a warp like setting with golden highlights. Card backs are numbered with an "SA" suffix and are seeded 1:40 packs. A serial numbered parallel called Richter 100 is randomly seeded and is limited to 100 serial numbered sets.

	NM/M
Complete Set (10):	45.00
Common Player:	3.00
Inserted 1:40	
Richter Parallel:	3-5X

Production 100 Sets
		NM/M
1	Ken Griffey Jr.	5.00
2	Sammy Sosa	5.00
3	Derek Jeter	10.00
4	Mark McGwire	8.00
5	Manny Ramirez	3.00
6	Mike Piazza	5.00
7	Vladimir Guerrero	3.00
8	Chipper Jones	5.00
9	Alex Rodriguez	8.00
10	Jeff Bagwell	3.00

Supernaturals

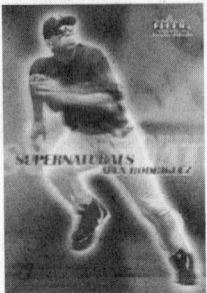

This 10-card set has a warp like image of the player on the front with silver holo-foil highlights around the player image and gold foil stamping. Card backs are numbered with an "S" suffix. These were seeded 1:10 packs.

		NM/M
Complete Set (10):		15.00
Common Player:		1.00
Inserted 1:10		
1	Alex Rodriguez	3.00
2	Chipper Jones	1.75
3	Derek Jeter	4.00
4	Ivan Rodriguez	1.00
5	Ken Griffey Jr.	2.00
6	Mark McGwire	3.00
7	Mike Piazza	2.00
8	Nomar Garciaparra	2.00
9	Sammy Sosa	2.00
10	Vladimir Guerrero	1.50

Dave Winfield Auto. Memorabilia

This two-card set consists of 40 game-used helmet Winfield cards and 20 game-used ball cards.

		NM/M
Complete Set (2):		
1	Dave Winfield/Bat/20	140.00
2	Dave Winfield/Helmet/40	125.00

2000 Fleer Showcase

The base set consists of 140 cards, including 40 Prospect Showcase subset cards. Cards 101-115 are serially numbered to 1,000 and cards 116-140 are serially numbered to 2,000. The card fronts are holo-foiled, with the player name and team stamped in gold foil. Card backs have year-by-year statistics and a small close-up photo. Five-card packs carried an SRP of $4.99.

		NM/M
Complete Set (140):		200.00
Common Player (1-100):		.25
Common (101-115):		6.00
Production 1,000 Sets		
Common (116-140):		4.00
Production 2,000 Sets		
Pack (5):		2.50
Box (24):		50.00
1	Alex Rodriguez	2.50
2	Derek Jeter	3.00
3	Jeromy Burnitz	.25
4	John Olerud	.25
5	Paul Konerko	.25
6	Johnny Damon	.40
7	Curt Schilling	.50
8	Barry Larkin	.25
9	Adrian Beltre	.40
10	Scott Rolen	.75
11	Carlos Delgado	.50
12	Pedro J. Martinez	1.00
13	Todd Helton	1.00
14	Jacque Jones	.25
15	Jeff Kent	.25
16	Darin Erstad	.65
17	Juan Encarnacion	.25
18	Roger Clemens	1.75
19	Tony Gwynn	1.50
20	Nomar Garciaparra	2.00
21	Roberto Alomar	.40
22	Matt Lawton	.25
23	Rich Aurilia	.25
24	Charles Johnson	.25
25	Jim Thome	.25
26	Eric Milton	.25
27	Barry Bonds	3.00
28	Albert Belle	.25
29	Travis Fryman	.25
30	Ken Griffey Jr.	2.00
31	Phil Nevin	.25
32	Chipper Jones	1.50
33	Craig Biggio	.25
34	Mike Hampton	.25
35	Fred McGriff	.25
36	Cal Ripken Jr.	3.00
37	Manny Ramirez	1.00
38	Jose Vidro	.25
39	Trevor Hoffman	.25
40	Tom Glavine	.50
41	Frank Thomas	1.00
42	Chris Widger	.25
43	J.D. Drew	.50
44	Andres Galarraga	.25
45	Pokey Reese	.25
46	Mike Piazza	2.00
47	Kevin Young	.25
48	Sean Casey	.25
49	Carlos Beltran	.60
50	Jason Kendall	.25
51	Vladimir Guerrero	1.00
52	Jermaine Dye	.25
53	Brian Giles	.25
54	Andruw Jones	1.00
55	Richard Hidalgo	.25
56	Robin Ventura	.25
57	Ivan Rodriguez	.65
58	Greg Maddux	1.50
59	Billy Wagner	.25
60	Ruben Mateo	.25
61	Troy Glaus	1.00
62	Dean Palmer	.25
63	Eric Chavez	.40
64	Edgar Martinez	.25
65	Randy Johnson	1.00
66	Preston Wilson	.25
67	Orlando Hernandez	.25
68	Jim Edmonds	.25
69	Carl Everett	.25
70	Larry Walker	.25
71	Ron Belliard	.25
72	Sammy Sosa	2.00
73	Matt Williams	.25
74	Cliff Floyd	.25
75	Bernie Williams	.40
76	Fernando Tatis	.25
77	Steve Finley	.25
78	Jeff Bagwell	1.00
79	Edgardo Alfonzo	.40
80	Jose Canseco	.40
81	Magglio Ordonez	.40
82	Shawn Green	.40
83	Bobby Abreu	.25
84	Tony Batista	.25
85	Mo Vaughn	.25
86	Juan Gonzalez	1.00
87	Paul O'Neill	.25
88	Mark McGwire	2.50
89	Mark Grace	.35
90	Kevin Brown	.25
91	Ben Grieve	.25
92	Shannon Stewart	.25
93	Erubiel Durazo	.25
94	Antonio Alfonseca	.25
95	Jeff Cirillo	.25
96	Greg Vaughn	.25
97	Kerry Wood	.60
98	Geoff Jenkins	.25
99	Jason Giambi	.75
100	Rafael Palmeiro	.65
101	Rafael Furcal	6.00
102	Pablo Ozuna	6.00
103	Brad Penny	6.00
104	Mark Mulder	8.00
105	Adam Piatt	6.00
106	Mike Lamb RC	6.00
107	Kazuhiro Sasaki RC	15.00
108	Aaron McNeal RC	6.00
109	Pat Burrell	8.00
110	Rick Ankiel	6.00
111	Eric Munson	6.00
112	Josh Beckett	6.00
113	Adam Kennedy	6.00
114	Alex Escobar	8.00
115	Chad Hermansen	6.00
116	Kip Wells	4.00
117	Matt LeCroy	4.00
118	Julio Ramirez	4.00
119	Ben Petrick	4.00
120	Nick Johnson	6.00
121	Gookie Dawkins	4.00
122	Julio Zuleta RC	4.00
123	Alfonso Soriano	8.00
124	Keith McDonald RC	4.00
125	Kory DeHaan	4.00
126	Vernon Wells	6.00
127	Dernell Stenson	4.00
128	David Eckstein	4.00
129	Robert Fick	4.00
130	Cole Liniak	4.00
131	Mark Quinn	4.00
132	Eric Gagne	5.00
133	Wily Pena	4.00
134	Andy Thompson RC	4.00
135	Steve Sisco RC	4.00
136	Paul Rigdon RC	4.00
137	Rob Bell	4.00
138	Carlos Guillen	5.00
139	Jimmy Rollins	5.00
140	Jason Conti	4.00

Legacy

A parallel to the 140-card base set these feature a matte and holo-foil design and are serially numbered to 20.

Stars (1-100):	30-50X
Prospects (101-140):	3-6X
Production 20 Sets	

Masterpiece

Each card in 2000 Showcase was issued in a unique Masterpiece edition. The front is enhanced with gold ink and on back is printed the notice "The Only 1 Of 1 / Masterpiece."

Prospect Showcase First

A parallel of the 40-card Prospects subset. These differ from the base cards in that they have a horizontal format and are serially numbered to 500.

Prospects (101-140):	1-2X
Production 500 Sets	

Club 3000

This two-card set pays tribute to Lou Brock and Nolan Ryan. Each card is die-cut around the numerals 3,000 with a date displaying the day Brock or Ryan reached their 3,000 milestone. The player name is stamped in silver holo-foil. These were inserted 1:24 packs.

	NM/M
Common Player:	3.00

Club 3000 Memorabilia

These inserts feature actual game-used pieces of memorabilia from Nolan Ryan and Lou Brock and are serial numbered. The number produced is listed after the player name.

	NM/M
Lou Brock/Jsy/680	15.00
Lou Brock/Bat/270	25.00
Lou Brock/Hat/Bat/Jsy/25	100.00
Nolan Ryan/Jsy/780	40.00
Nolan Ryan/Hat/65	120.00
Nolan Ryan - Bat/265	60.00
Nolan Ryan/Bat/Jsy/100	120.00

Consummate Prose

This 15-card set has an image of a worn scroll of paper with consummate prose written on it in the background of the player image. The Showcase logo, player name and Consummate Prose are stamped in gold foil. Card backs are numbered with an "CP" suffix and are inserted 1:6 packs.

		NM/M
Complete Set (15):		20.00
Common Player:		.50
Inserted 1:6		
1	Jeff Bagwell	1.50
2	Alex Rodriguez	3.00
3	Chipper Jones	2.00
4	Derek Jeter	4.00
5	Manny Ramirez	1.50
6	Tony Gwynn	2.00
7	Sammy Sosa	2.50
8	Ivan Rodriguez	1.00
9	Greg Maddux	2.00
10	Ken Griffey Jr.	2.50
11	Rick Ankiel	.50
12	Cal Ripken Jr.	4.00
13	Pedro Martinez	1.50
14	Mike Piazza	2.50
15	Mark McGwire	3.00

Feel the Game

This set has swatches of game worn jersey embedded into the card front.

		NM/M
Common Player:		5.00
Inserted 1:72		
1	Barry Bonds	30.00
2	Gookie Dawkins	5.00
3	Darin Erstad	8.00
4	Troy Glaus	10.00
5	Scott Rolen	8.00
6	Alex Rodriguez	25.00
7	Andruw Jones	8.00
8	Robin Ventura	5.00
9	Sean Casey	5.00
10	Cal Ripken Jr.	40.00

Final Answer

These foiled inserts have a green border with the player inside a frame with question marks in the background. The card backs have trivia questions about the featured player. Card backs are numbered with a "FA" suffix. These were seeded 1:10 packs.

		NM/M
Complete Set (10):		20.00
Common Player:		1.00
Inserted 1:10		
1	Alex Rodriguez	3.00
2	Vladimir Guerrero	1.00
3	Cal Ripken Jr.	4.00
4	Sammy Sosa	2.00
5	Barry Bonds	2.00
6	Derek Jeter	4.00
7	Ken Griffey Jr.	2.00
8	Mike Piazza	2.00
9	Nomar Garciaparra	2.00
10	Mark McGwire	3.00

Fresh Ink

These autographed inserts are inserted 1:24 packs.

		NM/M
Common Player:		5.00
Inserted 1:24		
1	Rick Ankiel	20.00
2	Josh Beckett	30.00
3	Barry Bonds	200.00
4	A.J. Burnett	10.00
5	Pat Burrell	15.00
6	Ken Caminiti	8.00
7	Sean Casey	10.00
8	Jose Cruz Jr.	10.00
9	Gookie Dawkins	10.00
10	Erubiel Durazo	10.00
11	Juan Encarnacion	8.00
12	Darin Erstad	15.00
13	Rafael Furcal	15.00
14	Nomar Garciaparra	100.00
15	Jason Giambi	20.00
16	Jeremy Giambi	6.00
17	Brian Giles	15.00
18	Troy Glaus	20.00
20	Vladimir Guerrero	30.00
21	Chad Hermansen	5.00
23	Trevor Hoffman	5.00
24	Randy Johnson	60.00
25	Andruw Jones	15.00
26	Jason Kendall	8.00
27	Paul Konerko	10.00
28	Mike Lowell	10.00
29	Aaron McNeal	5.00
30	Warren Morris	5.00
31	Paul O'Neill	20.00
32	Magglio Ordonez	10.00
33	Pablo Ozuna	5.00
34	Brad Penny	8.00
35	Ben Petrick	5.00
36	Pokey Reese	5.00
37	Cal Ripken Jr.	125.00
38	Alex Rodriguez	75.00
39	Scott Rolen	30.00
40	Jose Vidro	5.00
41	Kip Wells	5.00

License to Skill

License to Skill have a rounded, die-cut top with a concentric-circles background. Silver and gold

foil etching and foil stamping are used as well. Card backs are numbered with an "LS" suffix.

		NM/M
Complete Set (10):		25.00
Common Player:		1.50
Inserted 1:20		
1	Vladimir Guerrero	2.00
2	Pedro J. Martinez	2.00
3	Nomar Garciaparra	4.00
4	Ivan Rodriguez	1.50
5	Mark McGwire	5.00
6	Derek Jeter	6.00
7	Ken Griffey Jr.	4.00
8	Randy Johnson	2.00
9	Sammy Sosa	4.00
10	Alex Rodriguez	5.00

Long Gone

These inserts are die-cut around the card top to mimic the outfield dimensions of the featured players' stadium. Gold foil stamping is also used. Card backs are numbered with an "LG" suffix and have an insertion ratio of 1:20 packs.

		NM/M
Complete Set (10):		25.00
Common Player:		2.00
Inserted 1:20		
1	Sammy Sosa	4.00
2	Derek Jeter	6.00
3	Nomar Garciaparra	4.00
4	Juan Gonzalez	2.00
5	Vladimir Guerrero	2.00
6	Barry Bonds	6.00
7	Jeff Bagwell	2.00
8	Alex Rodriguez	5.00
9	Ken Griffey Jr.	4.00
10	Mark McGwire	5.00

Noise of Summer

This 10-card set has a kaleidoscope background with the insert name stamped in red foil and the logo, player name and team name stamped in gold foil. Card backs are numbered with an "NS" suffix. These were seeded 1:10 packs.

		NM/M
Complete Set (10):		15.00
Common Player:		1.00
Inserted 1:10		
1	Chipper Jones	1.50
2	Jeff Bagwell	

3 Manny Ramirez 1.00
4 Mark McGwire 3.00
5 Ken Griffey Jr. 2.00
6 Mike Piazza 2.00
7 Pedro J. Martinez 1.00
8 Alex Rodriguez 3.00
9 Derek Jeter 4.00
10 Randy Johnson 1.00

Sweet Sigs

These autographed inserts have the featured players' autograph on an actual "sweet spot" from an authentic Major League baseball. These have an insertion ratio of 1:250 packs.

	NM/M
Common Player:	10.00
Inserted 1:250	
1 Nomar Garciaparra/53	150.00
2 Alex Rodriguez/67	200.00
3 Tony Gwynn	40.00
4 Roger Clemens/79	140.00
5 Scott Rolen	50.00
6 Greg Maddux	80.00
7 Jose Cruz Jr.	15.00
8 Tony Womack	10.00
9 Jay Buhner	10.00
10 Nolan Ryan	125.00

2000 Fleer Tradition

The Fleer Tradition base set consists of 450 cards including a 30-card rookies/prospects subset, 30 team cards, 10 league leaders, 6 award winners, 10 postseason recaps and 86 checklists. The card fronts have a close-up photo of the featured player as well as a small action photo surrounded by a white border. Like the fronts the card backs have a "throwback" look, which includes complete year-by-year statistics, a brief career note and vital information. 10-card packs had a SRP of $1.49.

	NM/M
Complete Set (450):	50.00
Common Player:	.10
Complete Glossy Factory Set (500):	450.00
Complete Glossy Factory Set (455):	75.00
Glossy (1-450):	1-2X
Common Glossy (451-500):	.50
Five Glossy (451-500) per factory set. 1,000 produced (451-500)	
Pack (10):	1.50
Wax Box:	35.00

1 AL HRs .50
2 NL HRs .50
3 AL RBIs .50
4 NL RBIs .50
5 AL Avg. .50
6 NL Avg. .15
7 AL Wins .20
8 NL Wins .40
9 AL ERA .20
10 NL ERA .25
11 Matt Mantei .10
12 John Rocker .10
13 Kyle Farnsworth .10
14 Juan Guzman .10
15 Manny Ramirez .75
16 Matt Riley-P, Calvin Pickering-1B .10
17 Tony Clark .10
18 Brian Meadows .10
19 Orber Moreno .10
20 Eric Karros .10
21 Steve Woodard .10
22 Scott Brosius .10
23 Gary Bennett .10
24 Jason Wood-3B, Dave Borkowski-P .10
25 Joe McEwing .10
26 Juan Gonzalez .75
27 Roy Halladay .25
28 Trevor Hoffman .10
29 Arizona Diamondbacks .10
30 Domingo Guzman-P RC, Wiki Gonzalez-C .25
31 Bret Boone .10
32 Nomar Garciaparra 2.00
33 Bo Porter .10
34 Eddie Taubensee .10
35 Pedro Astacio .10
36 Derek Bell .10
37 Jacque Jones .10
38 Ricky Ledee .10
39 Jeff Kent .10
40 Matt Williams .10
41 Alfonso Soriano-SS, D'Angelo Jimenez-3B .75
42 B.J. Surhoff .10
43 Denny Neagle .10
44 Omar Vizquel .10
45 Jeff Bagwell .75
46 Mark Grudzielanek .10
47 LaTroy Hawkins .10
48 Orlando Hernandez .10
49 Ken Griffey Jr. 2.00
50 Fernando Tatis .10
51 Quilvio Veras .10
52 Wayne Gomes .10
53 Rick Helling .10
54 Shannon Stewart .10
55 Dermal Brown-OF, Mark Quinn-OF .20
56 Randy Johnson 1.00
57 Greg Maddux 1.50
58 Mike Cameron .10
59 Matt Anderson .10
60 Milwaukee Brewers .10
61 Derrek Lee .10
62 Mike Sweeney .10
63 Fernando Vina .10
64 Orlando Cabrera .20
65 Doug Glanville .10
66 Stan Spencer .10
67 Ray Lankford .10
68 Kelly Dransfeldt .10
69 Alex Gonzalez .10
70 Russell Branyan-3B, Danny Peoples-OF .10
71 Jim Edmonds .10
72 Brady Anderson .10
73 Mike Stanley .10
74 Travis Fryman .10
75 Carlos Febles .10
76 Bobby Higginson .10
77 Carlos Perez .10
78 Steve Cox-1B, Alex Sanchez-OF .10
79 Dustin Hermanson .10
80 Kenny Rogers .10
81 Miguel Tejada .25
82 Ben Davis .10
83 Reggie Sanders .10
84 Eric Davis .10
85 J.D. Drew .45
86 Ryan Rupe .10
87 Bobby Smith .10
88 Jose Cruz Jr. .10
89 Carlos Delgado .50
90 Toronto Blue Jays .10
91 Denny Stark-P RC, Gil Meche-P .25
92 Randy Velarde .10
93 Aaron Boone .10
94 Javy Lopez .10
95 Johnny Damon .25
96 Jon Lieber .10
97 Montreal Expos .10
98 Mark Kotsay .10
99 Luis Gonzalez .25
100 Larry Walker .10
101 Adrian Beltre .25
102 Alex Ochoa .10
103 Michael Barrett .10
104 Tampa Bay Devil Rays .10
105 Rey Ordonez .10
106 Derek Jeter 3.00
107 Mike Lieberthal .10
108 Ellis Burks .10
109 Steve Finley .10
110 Ryan Klesko .10
111 Steve Avery .10
112 Dave Veres .10
113 Cliff Floyd .10
114 Shane Reynolds .10
115 Kevin Brown .10
116 David Nilsson .10
117 Mike Trombley .10
118 Todd Walker .10
119 John Olerud .10
120 Chuck Knoblauch .10
121 Nomar Garciaparra 2.00
122 Trot Nixon .10
123 Erubiel Durazo .10
124 Edwards Guzman .10
125 Curt Schilling .50
126 Brian Jordan .10
127 Cleveland Indians .10
128 Benito Santiago .10
129 Frank Thomas .75
130 Neifi Perez .10
131 Alex Fernandez .10
132 Jose Lima .10
133 Jorge Toca-1B, Melvin Mora-OF .10
134 Scott Karl .10
135 Brad Radke .10
136 Paul O'Neill .10
137 Kris Benson .10
138 Colorado Rockies .10
139 Jason Phillips .10
140 Robb Nen .10
141 Ken Hill .10
142 Charles Johnson .10
143 Paul Konerko .10
144 Dmitri Young .10
145 Justin Thompson .10
146 Mark Loretta .10
147 Edgardo Alfonzo .10
148 Armando Benitez .10
149 Octavio Dotel .10
150 Wade Boggs 1.50
151 Ramon Hernandez .10
152 Freddy Garcia .10
153 Edgar Martinez .10
154 Ivan Rodriguez .65
155 Kansas City Royals .10
156 Cleatus Davidson-2B, Cristian Guzman-SS .10
157 Andy Benes .10
158 Todd Dunwoody .10
159 Pedro Martinez 1.00
160 Mike Caruso .10
161 Mike Sirotka .10
162 Darryl Kile .10
163 Chipper Jones 1.50
164 Carl Everett .15
165 Geoff Jenkins .10
166 Dan Perkins .10
167 Andy Pettitte .25
168 Francisco Cordova .10
169 Jay Buhner .10
170 Jay Bell .10
171 Andruw Jones .75
172 Bobby Howry .10
173 Chris Singleton .10
174 Todd Helton .75
175 A.J. Burnett .10
176 Marquis Grissom .10
177 Eric Milton .10
178 Los Angeles Dodgers .10
179 Kevin Appier .10
180 Brian Giles .10
181 Tom Davey .10
182 Mo Vaughn .10
183 Jose Hernandez .10
184 Jim Parque .10
185 Derrick Gibson .10
186 Bruce Aven .10
187 Jeff Cirillo .10
188 Doug Mientkiewicz .10
189 Eric Chavez .25
190 Al Martin .10
191 Tom Glavine .25
192 Butch Huskey .10
193 Ray Durham .10
194 Greg Vaughn .10
195 Vinny Castilla .10
196 Ken Caminiti .10
197 Joe Mays .10
198 Chicago White Sox .10
199 Mariano Rivera .20
200 Mark McGwire 2.50
201 Pat Meares .10
202 Andres Galarraga .10
203 Tom Gordon .10
204 Henry Rodriguez .10
205 Brett Tomko .10
206 Dante Bichette .10
207 Craig Biggio .10
208 Matt Lawton .10
209 Tino Martinez .10
210 Aaron Myette-P, Josh Paul-C .10
211 Warren Morris .10
212 San Diego Padres .10
213 Ramon E. Martinez .10
214 Troy Percival .10
215 Jason Johnson .10
216 Carlos Lee .10
217 Scott Williamson .10
218 Jeff Weaver .10
219 Ronnie Belliard .10
220 Jason Giambi .65
221 Ken Griffey Jr. 2.00
222 John Halama .10
223 Brett Hinchliffe .10
224 Wilson Alvarez .10
225 Rolando Arrojo .10
226 Ruben Mateo .10
227 Rafael Palmeiro .65
228 David Wells .10
229 Eric Gagne-P, Jeff Williams-P .10
231 Tim Salmon .30
232 Mike Mussina .50
233 Magglio Ordonez .25
234 Ron Villone .10
235 Antonio Alfonseca .10
236 Jeromy Burnitz .10
237 Ben Grieve .10
238 Giomar Guevara .10
239 Garret Anderson .10
240 John Smoltz .10
241 Mark Grace .15
242 Cole Liniak-3B, Jose Molina-C .10
243 Damion Easley .10
244 Jeff Montgomery .10
245 Kenny Lofton .10
246 Masato Yoshii .10
247 Philadelphia Phillies .10
248 Raul Mondesi .10
249 Marlon Anderson .10
250 Shawn Green .40
251 Sterling Hitchcock .10
252 Randy Wolf-P, Anthony Shumaker-P .10
253 Jeff Fassero .10
254 Eli Marrero .10
255 Cincinnati Reds .10
256 Rick Ankiel-P, Adam Kennedy-2B .50
257 Darin Erstad .60
258 Albert Belle .20
259 Bartolo Colon .10
260 Bret Saberhagen .10
261 Carlos Beltran .50
262 Glenallen Hill .10
263 Gregg Jefferies .10
264 Matt Clement .10
265 Miguel Del Toro .10
266 Robinson Cancel-C, Kevin Barker-1B .10
267 San Francisco Giants .10
268 Kent Bottenfield .10
269 Fred McGriff .10
270 Chris Carpenter .10
271 Atlanta Braves .10
272 Wilton Veras-3B, Tomokazu Ohka-P RC .50
273 Will Clark .20
274 Troy O'Leary .10
275 Sammy Sosa 2.00
276 Travis Lee .15
277 Sean Casey .25
278 Ron Gant .10
279 Roger Clemens 1.75
280 Phil Nevin .10
281 Mike Piazza 2.00
282 Mike Lowell .10
283 Kevin Millwood .10
284 Joe Randa .10
285 Jeff Shaw .10
286 Jason Varitek .10
287 Harold Baines .10
288 Gabe Kapler .10
289 Chuck Finley .10
290 Carl Pavano .10
291 Brad Ausmus .10
292 Brad Fullmer .10
293 Boston Red Sox .10
294 Bob Wickman .10
295 Billy Wagner .10
296 Shawn Estes .10
297 Gary Sheffield .40
298 Fernando Seguignol .10
299 Omar Olivares .10
300 Baltimore Orioles .10
301 Matt Stairs .10
302 Andy Ashby .10
303 Todd Greene .10
304 Jesse Garcia .10
305 Kerry Wood .50
306 Roberto Alomar .40
307 New York Mets .10
308 Dean Palmer .10
309 Mike Hampton .10
310 Devon White .10
311 Chad Hermansen-OF, Mike Garcia-P .10
312 Tim Hudson .40
313 John Franco .10
314 Jason Schmidt .10
315 J.T. Snow .10
316 Ed Sprague .10
317 Chris Widger .10
318 Ben Petrick-C, Luther Hackman-P RC .25
319 Jose Mesa .10
320 Jose Canseco .50
321 John Wetteland .10
322 Minnesota Twins .10
323 Jeff DaVanon-OF RC, Brian Cooper-P .25
324 Tony Womack .10
325 Rod Beck .10
326 Mickey Morandini .10
327 Pokey Reese .10
328 Jaret Wright .10
329 Glen Barker .10
330 Darren Dreifort .10
331 Torii Hunter .15
332 Tony Armas Jr.-P, Peter Bergeron-OF .10
333 Hideki Irabu .10
334 Desi Relaford .10
335 Barry Bonds 3.00
336 Gary DiSarcina .10
337 Gerald Williams .10
338 John Valentin .10
339 David Justice .10
340 Juan Encarnacion .10
341 Jeremy Giambi .10
342 Chan Ho Park .10
343 Vladimir Guerrero 1.00
344 Robin Ventura .10
345 Bobby Abreu .10
346 Tony Gwynn 1.50
347 Jose Jimenez .10
348 Royce Clayton .10
349 Kelvim Escobar .10
350 Chicago Cubs .10
351 Travis Dawkins-SS, Jason LaRue-C .10
352 Barry Larkin .25
353 Cal Ripken Jr. 3.00
353a Cal Ripken Jr./OPS 4.00
354 Alex Rodriguez 2.50
355 Todd Stottlemyre .10
356 Terry Adams .10
357 Pittsburgh Pirates .10
358 Jim Thome .10
359 Corey Lee-P, Doug Davis-P .10
360 Moises Alou .10
361 Todd Hollandsworth .10
362 Marty Cordova .10
363 David Cone .10
364 Joe Nathan-P, Wilson Delgado-SS .10
365 Paul Byrd .10
366 Edgar Renteria .10
367 Rusty Greer .10
368 David Segui .10
369 New York Yankees .50
370 Daryle Ward-OF/1B, Carlos Hernandez-2B .10
371 Troy Glaus .75
372 Delino DeShields .10
373 Jose Offerman .10
374 Sammy Sosa 2.00
375 Sandy Alomar Jr. .10
376 Masao Kida .10
377 Richard Hidalgo .10
378 Ismael Valdes .10
379 Ugueth Urbina .10
380 Darryl Hamilton .10
381 John Jaha .10
382 St. Louis Cardinals .10
383 Scott Sauerbeck .10
384 Russ Ortiz .10
385 Jamie Moyer .10
386 Dave Martinez .10
387 Todd Zeile .10
388 Anaheim Angels .10
389 Rob Ryan-OF, Nick Bierbrodt-P .10
390 Rickey Henderson .75
391 Alex Rodriguez 2.50
392 Texas Rangers .10
393 Roberto Hernandez .10
394 Tony Batista .10
395 Oakland Athletics .10
396 Randall Simon-1B, David Cortes-P RC .20
397 Gregg Olson .10
398 Sidney Ponson .10
399 Micah Bowie .10
400 Mark McGwire 2.50
401 Florida Marlins .10
402 Chad Allen .10
403 Casey Blake-3B, Vernon Wells-OF .10
404 Pete Harnisch .10
405 Preston Wilson .10
406 Richie Sexson .10
407 Rico Brogna .10
408 Todd Hundley .10
409 Wally Joyner .10
410 Tom Goodwin .10
411 Joey Hamilton .10
412 Detroit Tigers .10
413 Michael Tejera-P RC, Ramon Castro-C .25
414 Alex Gonzalez .10
415 Jermaine Dye .10
416 Jose Rosado .10
417 Wilton Guerrero .10
418 Rondell White .10
419 Al Leiter .10
420 Bernie Williams .25
421 A.J. Hinch .10
422 Pat Burrell .10
423 Scott Rolen .65
424 Jason Kendall .10
425 Kevin Young .10
426 Eric Owens .10
427 Derek Jeter 1.00
428 Livan Hernandez .10
429 Russ Davis .10
430 Dan Wilson .10
431 Quinton McCracken .10
432 Homer Bush .10
433 Seattle Mariners .10
434 Chad Harville-P, Luis Vizcaino-P .10
435 Carlos Beltran .45
436 Scott Williamson .10
437 Pedro Martinez .75
438 Randy Johnson .75
439 Ivan Rodriguez .60
440 Chipper Jones .75
441 AL Division (Bernie Williams) .15
442 AL Division (Pedro Martinez) .50
443 AL Champ (Derek Jeter) 1.00
444 NL Division (Brian Jordan) .10
445 NL Division (Todd Pratt) .10
446 NL Champ (Kevin Millwood) .10
447 World Series (Orlando Hernandez) .10
448 World Series (Derek Jeter) 1.00
449 World Series (Chad Curtis) .10
450 World Series (Roger Clemens) .75
451 Carlos Casimiro RC 8.00
452 Adam Melhuse RC 8.00
453 Adam Bernero RC 8.00
454 Dusty Allen RC 8.00
455 Chan Perry RC 8.00
456 Damian Rolls RC 8.00
457 Josh Phelps RC 10.00
458 Barry Zito RC 25.00
459 Hector Ortiz RC 8.00
460 Juan Pierre RC 15.00
461 Jose Ortiz RC 15.00
462 Chad Zerbe RC 8.00
463 Julio Zuleta RC 8.00
464 Eric Byrnes RC 25.00
465 Wilfredo Rodriguez RC 10.00
466 Wascar Serrano RC 8.00
467 Aaron McNeal RC 8.00
468 Paul Rigdon RC 8.00
469 John Snyder RC 8.00
470 J.C. Romero RC 8.00
471 Talmadge Nunnari RC 8.00
472 Mike Lamb RC 8.00
473 Ryan Kohlmeier RC 8.00
474 Rodney Lindsey RC 8.00
475 Elvis Pena RC 8.00
476 Alex Cabrera RC 10.00
477 Chris Richard RC 8.00
478 Pedro Feliz RC 10.00
479 Ross Gload RC 8.00
480 Timoniel Perez RC 8.00
481 Jason Woolf RC 8.00
482 Kenny Kelly RC 8.00
483 Sang-Hoon Lee RC 8.00
484 John Riedling RC 8.00
485 Chris Wakeland RC 8.00
486 Britt Reames RC 8.00
487 Greg LaRocca RC 8.00
488 Randy Keisler RC 8.00
489 Xavier Nady RC 20.00
490 Keith Ginter RC 10.00
491 Joey Nation RC 8.00
492 Kazuhiro Sasaki RC 8.00
493 Lesli Brea RC 8.00
494 Jace Brewer RC 8.00
495 Yohanny Valera RC 8.00
496 Adam Piatt RC 10.00
497 Nate Rolison RC 8.00
498 Aubrey Huff RC 8.00
499 Jason Tyner RC 8.00
500 Corey Patterson RC 10.00

Club 3000

The Club 3000 inserts are die-cut around the number 3,000, commemmorating their reaching the 3,000 hit achievement. These are seeded 1:36 packs and features George Brett, Rod Carew and Robin Yount.

	NM/M
Complete Set (3):	5.00
Common Player:	3.00
Inserted 1:36	
(1) George Brett	4.00
(2) Rod Carew	2.00
(3) Robin Yount	2.00

Club 3000 Memorabilia

These are a parallel to the base version and has five different memorabilia based tiers. Level 2 (cap), Level 3 (bat), Level 4 (jersey), Level 5 (bat and jersey) and Level 6 (bat, jersey and cap). Each card is hand-numbered.

	NM/M
George Brett/Bat/250	60.00
George Brett/Hat/100	75.00
George Brett/Jsy/445	30.00
George Brett/Bat/Jsy/100	90.00
Rod Carew/Bat/225	50.00
Rod Carew/Hat/100	50.00
Rod Carew/Jsy/440	30.00
Rod Carew/Bat/Jsy/100	65.00
Robin Yount/Bat/250	40.00
Robin Yount/Hat/100	30.00
Robin Yount/Jsy/440	30.00
Robin Yount/Bat/Jsy/100	75.00

Dividends

This insert set consists of 15 cards and spotlights the top players on a horizontal format. Card fronts have silver foil stamping, a red border and are seeded 1:6 packs. They are numbered on the back with a "D" suffix.

		NM/M
Complete Set (15):		15.00
Common Player:		.50
Inserted 1:6		
1	Alex Rodriguez	2.50
2	Ben Grieve	.50
3	Cal Ripken Jr.	3.00
4	Chipper Jones	1.50
5	Derek Jeter	3.00
6	Frank Thomas	1.00
7	Jeff Bagwell	1.00
8	Sammy Sosa	2.00
9	Tony Gwynn	1.50
10	Scott Rolen	.75
11	Nomar Garciaparra	2.00
12	Mike Piazza	2.00
13	Mark McGwire	2.50
14	Ken Griffey Jr.	2.00
15	Juan Gonzalez	1.00

Fresh Ink

This autographed insert set consists of 38 cards on a vertical format with the autograph on the bottom third of the card below the player image. These were inserted 1:144 packs.

	NM/M
Common Player:	5.00
Inserted 1:144	
Rick Ankiel	15.00
Carlos Beltran	25.00
Pat Burrell	15.00
Miguel Cairo	5.00
Sean Casey	8.00
Will Clark	30.00
Mike Darr	5.00
J.D. Drew	10.00
Erubiel Durazo	10.00
Carlos Febles	5.00
Freddy Garcia	8.00
Greg Maddux	80.00
Jason Grilli	5.00
Vladimir Guerrero	35.00
Tony Gwynn	40.00
Jerry Hairston Jr.	8.00
Tim Hudson	15.00
John Jaha	5.00
D'Angelo Jimenez	5.00
Andruw Jones	20.00
Gabe Kapler	6.00
Cesar King	5.00
Jason LaRue	5.00
Mike Lieberthal	8.00
Pedro Martinez	50.00
Gary Matthews Jr.	5.00
Orber Moreno	5.00
Eric Munson	5.00
Rafael Palmeiro	35.00
Jim Parque	6.00
Willi Mo Pena	15.00
Cal Ripken Jr.	100.00
Alex Rodriguez	80.00
Tim Salmon	15.00
Chris Singleton	5.00
Alfonso Soriano	50.00
Ed Yarnall	5.00

Grasskickers

This 15-card set has a close-up photo of the featured player with holographic silver foil stamping. These are seeded 1:30 packs and are numbered on the back with a "GK" suffix.

		NM/M
Complete Set (15):		50.00
Common Player:		2.00
Inserted 1:30		
1	Tony Gwynn	3.00
2	Scott Rolen	2.00
3	Nomar Garciaparra	4.00
4	Mike Piazza	4.00
5	Mark McGwire	6.00
6	Frank Thomas	2.00
7	Cal Ripken Jr.	8.00

Hall's Well

This 15-card set spotlights superstars destined for Cooperstown, featured on a transparent plastic stock with overlays of silver foil stamping. These were seeded 1:30 packs and are numbered with a "HW" suffix.

		NM/M
Complete Set (15):		50.00
Common Player:		1.50
Inserted 1:30		
1	Mark McGwire	6.00
2	Alex Rodriguez	6.00
3	Cal Ripken Jr.	8.00
4	Chipper Jones	3.00
5	Derek Jeter	8.00
6	Frank Thomas	2.00
7	Greg Maddux	3.00
8	Juan Gonzalez	2.00
9	Ken Griffey Jr.	4.00
10	Mike Piazza	4.00
11	Nomar Garciaparra	4.00
12	Sammy Sosa	4.00
13	Roger Clemens	3.50
14	Ivan Rodriguez	1.50
15	Tony Gwynn	3.00

Opening Day 2K

As part of a multi-manufacturer promotion, Fleer issued eight cards of an "Opening Day 2K" set. Packages containing some of the 32 cards in the issue were distributed by MLB teams early in the season. The cards were also available exclusively as inserts in packs sold at KMart stores early in the season. The Fleer Tradition OD2K cards have gold-foil graphic highlights on front. Backs are in the basic format of the rest of the Tradition issue, and are numbered "XX of 32/OD."

		NM/M
Complete Set (8):		6.00
Common Player:		.50
9	Cal Ripken Jr.	2.00
10	Alex Rodriguez	2.00
11	Mike Piazza	1.00
12	Jeff Bagwell	.75
13	Randy Johnson	.75
14	Jason Kendall	.50
15	Magglio Ordonez	.50
16	Carlos Delgado	.50

Ripken Collection

This 10-card set is devoted to Cal Ripken Jr. and features 10 different Fleer retro designs. These were seeded 1:30 packs.

		NM/M
Complete Set (10):		50.00
Common Card:		6.00
Inserted 1:30		
8	Chipper Jones	3.00
9	Greg Maddux	3.00
10	Ken Griffey Jr.	4.00
11	Juan Gonzalez	2.00
12	Derek Jeter	8.00
13	Sammy Sosa	4.00
14	Roger Clemens	3.50
15	Alex Rodriguez	6.00

Ten-4

This 10-card insert set focuses on baseball's home run kings on a die-cut design enhanced with silver foil stamping. These were seeded 1:18 packs and are numbered on the card back with a "TF" suffix.

		NM/M
Complete Set (10):		20.00
Common Player:		2.00
Inserted 1:18		
1	Sammy Sosa	2.00
2	Nomar Garciaparra	2.00
3	Mike Piazza	2.00
4	Mark McGwire	3.00
5	Ken Griffey Jr.	2.00
6	Juan Gonzalez	1.00
7	Derek Jeter	4.00
8	Chipper Jones	1.50
9	Cal Ripken Jr.	4.00
10	Alex Rodriguez	3.00

Who To Watch

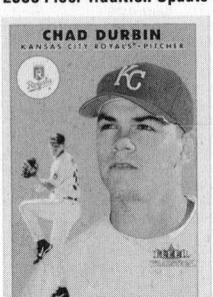

Top prospects for the 2000 season are highlighted in this 15-card set, including Rick Ankiel. They have a die-cut design with gold foil stamping. These were inserted 1:3 packs and numbered on the back with a "WW" suffix.

		NM/M
Complete Set (15):		5.00
Common Player:		.25
Inserted 1:3		
1	Rick Ankiel	.40
2	Matt Riley	.25
3	Wilton Veras	.25
4	Ben Petrick	.25
5	Chad Hermansen	.25
6	Peter Bergeron	.25
7	Mark Quinn	.25
8	Russell Branyan	.25
9	Alfonso Soriano	1.50
10	Randy Wolf	.50
11	Ben Davis	.25
12	Jeff DaVanon	.25
13	D'Angelo Jimenez	.25
14	Vernon Wells	1.00
15	Adam Kennedy	.40

Glossy Lumberjacks

	NM/M
Common Player:	8.00

One per factory set.
Production Listed

1	Edgardo Alfonzo/145	10.00
2	Roberto Alomar/627	10.00
3	Moises Alou/529	8.00
4	Carlos Beltran/489	8.00
5	Adrian Beltre/127	10.00
6	Barry Bonds/305	40.00
7	Pat Burrell/45	25.00
9	Sean Casey/50	10.00
11	Eric Chavez/259	10.00
12	Tony Clark/70	8.00
13	Carlos Delgado/70	20.00
14	J.D. Drew/135	10.00
15	Erubiel Durazo/70	10.00
17	Carlos Febles/120	10.00
18	Jason Giambi/220	15.00
19	Shawn Green/429	10.00
20	Vladimir Guerrero/809	15.00
21	Derek Jeter/180	50.00
22	Chipper Jones/725	15.00
23	Gabe Kapler/160	8.00
25	Paul Konerko/70	10.00
27	Mike Lieberthal/45	10.00
28	Edgar Martinez/211	10.00
29	Raul Mondesi/458	8.00
30	Warren Morris/35	10.00
31	Magglio Ordonez/190	10.00
32	Rafael Palmeiro/49	15.00
33	Pokey Reese/110	8.00
34	Cal Ripken/235	50.00
35	Alex Rodriguez/292	25.00
36	Ivan Rodriguez/602	10.00
37	Scott Rolen/502	10.00
38	Chris Singleton/68	8.00
39	Alfonso Soriano/285	15.00
40	Frank Thomas/489	10.00
41	Jim Thome/479	10.00
42	Robin Ventura/114	10.00
43	Jose Vidro/60	10.00
44	Bernie Williams/215	10.00
45	Matt Williams/152	8.00

2000 Fleer Tradition Update

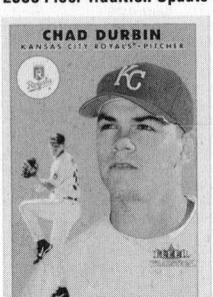

Card #50 was supposed to be Indians prospect C.C. Sabathia but it was never issued because he was not called up during the 2000 season.

		NM/M
Complete Set (150):		20.00
Common Player:		.15
1	Ken Griffey Jr.	
	(Season Highlights)	.50
2	Cal Ripken Jr.	
	(Season Highlights)	1.00
3	Randy Velarde	
	(Season Highlights)	.15
4	Fred McGriff	
	(Season Highlights)	.15
5	Derek Jeter	
	(Season Highlights)	1.00
6	Tom Glavine	
	(Season Highlights)	.25
7	Brent Mayne	
	(Season Highlights)	.15
8	Alex Ochoa	
	(Season Highlights)	.15
9	Scott Sheldon	
	(Season Highlights)	.15
10	Randy Johnson	
	(Season Highlights)	.35
11	Daniel Garibay RC	.15
12	Brad Fullmer	.15
13	Kazuhiro Sasaki RC	.50
14	Andy Tracy	.15
15	Bret Boone	.15
16	Chad Durbin RC	.25
17	Mark Buehrle RC	1.50
18	Julio Zuleta RC	.15
19	Jeremy Giambi	.15
20	Gene Stechschulte RC	.15
21	Lou Pote, Bengie Molina	.15
22	Darrell Einertson	.15
23	Ken Griffey Jr.	.75
24	Jeff Sparks RC,	
	Dan Wheeler	.25
25	Aaron Fultz RC	.15

26	Derek Bell	.15
27	Rob Bell, D.T. Cromer	.15
28	Rob Fick	.15
29	Darryl Kile	.15
30	Clayton Andrews,	
	John Bate	.15
31	Dave Veres	.15
32	Hector Mercado RC	.15
33	Willie Morales	.15
34	Kelly Wunsch, Kip Wells	.15
35	Hideki Irabu	.15
36	Sean DePaula	.15
37	Dewayne Wise,	
	Chris Woodward	.15
38	Curt Schilling	.25
39	Mark Johnson	.15
40	Mike Cameron	.15
41	Scott Sheldon, Tom Evans	.15
42	Brett Tomko	.15
43	Johan Santana RC	15.00
44	Andy Benes	.15
45	Matt LeCroy,	
	Mark Redman	.15
46	Ryan Klesko	.15
47	Andy Ashby	.15
48	Octavio Dotel	.15
49	Eric Byrnes RC	1.00
51	Kenny Rogers	.15
52	Ben Weber	.15
53	Matt Blank,	
	Scott Strickland	.15
54	Tom Goodwin	.15
55	Jim Edmonds	.15
56	Derrick Turnbow RC	.25
57	Mark Mulder	.15
58	Tarrik Brock,	
	Ruben Quevedo	.15
59	Danny Young	.15
60	Fernando Vina	.15
61	Justin Brunette RC	.15
62	Jimmy Anderson	.15
63	Reggie Sanders	.15
64	Adam Kennedy	.15
65	Jesse Garcia, B.J. Ryan	.15
66	Al Martin	.15
67	Kevin Walker	.15
68	Brad Penny	.15
69	B.J. Surhoff	.15
70	Geoff Blum,	
	Trace Coquillette	.15
71	Jose Jimenez	.15
72	Chuck Finley	.15
73	Valerio De Los Santos,	
	Everett Stull	.15
74	Terry Adams	.15
75	Rafael Furcal	.15
76	Mike Darr, John Roskos	.15
77	Quilvio Veras	.15
78	Armando Almanza	.15
79	Greg Vaughn	.15
80	Keith McDonald RC	.15
81	Eric Cammack	.15
82	Horacio Estrada, Ray King	.15
83	Kory DeHaan	.15
84	Kevin Hodges	.15
85	Mike Lamb RC	.25
86	Shawn Green	.40
87	Dan Reichert,	
	Jason Rakers	.15
88	Adam Piatt	.15
89	Mike Garcia	.15
90	Rodrigo Lopez RC	1.00
91	John Olerud	.15
92	Barry Zito, Terrence Long	.25
93	Jimmy Rollins	1.00
94	Denny Neagle	.15
95	Rickey Henderson	.50
96	Adam Eaton,	
	Buddy Carlyle	.15
97	Brian O'Connor	.15
98	Andy Thompson	.15
99	Jason Boyd	.15
100	Carlos Guillen,	
	Joel Piniero	.15
101	Raul Gonzalez	.15
102	Brandon Kolb RC	.25
103	Jason Maxwell,	
	Mike Lincoln	.15
104	Luis Matos RC	.50
105	Morgan Burkhart RC	.25
106	Ismael Villegas,	
	Steve Sisco	.15
107	David Justice	.15
108	Pablo Ozuna	.15
109	Jose Canseco	.40
110	Alex Cora, Shawn Gilbert	.15
111	Will Clark	.25
112	Keith Luuloa, Eric Weaver	.15
113	Bruce Chen	.15
114	Adam Hyzdu	.15
115	Yovanny Lara,	
	Scott Forster	.15
116	Allen McDill, Jose Macias	.15
117	Kevin Nicholson	.15
118	Israel Alcantara,	
	Tim Young	.15
119	Juan Alvarez	.15
120	Julio Lugo,	
	Mitch Meluskey	.15
121	B.J. Waszgis	.15
122	Jeff D'Amico, Brett Laxton	.15
123	Ricky Ledee	.15
124	Mark DeRosa,	
	Jason Marquis	.15
125	Alex Cabrera RC	.50
126	Gary Matthews,	
	Augie Ojeda	.15
127	Richie Sexson	.15

128	Santiago Perez,	
	Hector Ramirez	.15
129	Rondell White	.15
130	Craig House RC	.15
131	Kevin Beirne, Jon Garland	.15
132	Wayne Franklin	.15
133	Henry Rodriguez	.15
134	Jay Payton, Jim Mann	.15
135	Ron Gant	.15
136	Paxton Crawford RC,	
	Sang-Hoon Lee	.25
137	Kent Bottenfield	.15
138	Rocky Biddle RC	.15
139	Travis Lee	.15
140	Ryan Vogelsong	.15
141	Jason Conti,	
	Geraldo Guzman	.15
142	Tim Drew, Mark Watson	.15
143	John Parrish RC,	
	Chris Richard	.15
144	Javier Cardona RC,	
	Brandon Villafuetre	.15
145	Tike Redman RC,	
	Steve Sparks	.15
146	Brian Schneider,	
	Matt Skrmetta	.15
147	Pasqual Coco RC,	
	Leo Estrella	.15
148	Lorenzo Barcelo RC,	
	Joe Crede	.15
149	Jace Brewer RC	.25
150	Milton Bradley,	
	Tomas de la Rosa	.15

Update Mantle Pieces

		NM/M
Inserted 1:80 Sets		
1	Mickey Mantle	150.00

Diamond Skills Commemorative Sheet

Utilizing the same format and card reproductions as the souvenir sheet issued in conjunction with the season-opener Cubs-Mets series in Japan, Fleer issued this commemorative sheet for distribution to participants in the 2000 Diamond Skills competition. The 10" x 9" sheets depict star cards from Fleer's 2000 Tradition set.

	NM/M
Derek Jeter, Chipper Jones,	
Pedro Martinez, Mike Piazza,	
Cal Ripken Jr.,	
Ivan Rodriguez, Sammy Sosa,	
Mo Vaughn	10.00

Japan Commemorative Sheet

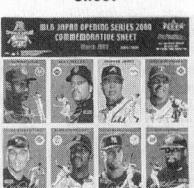

To commemorate the opening of the 2000 Major League Baseball season with a Cubs-Mets series in Japan, Fleer created this commemorative sheet for distribution at the opening game on March 29 (20,000) and at the Xebio Sporting Goods stores and Pro Pacific Hobby stores in Japan (5,000 each). The 10"x 9" sheets depict on front cards from Fleer's 2000 Tradition set.

	NM/M
Ivan Rodriguez, Sammy Sosa,	
Mo Vaughn, Derek Jeter,	
Chipper Jones,	
Pedro Martinez, Mike Piazza,	
Cal Ripken Jr.	20.00

Oreo

In a nationwide promotional contest in which children stacked Oreo cookies at grocery stores, a pair of hot star cards were given away as consolation prizes. Each 2-1/2" x 3-1/2" card has blue borders with a color photo at center. Jeter's card shows him stacking cookies, while Junior's card (in his new Reds uniform) shows him holding a bag of cookies. Backs have personal information, stats, an action photo and logos of MLB, Fleer and Oreo.

		NM/M
Complete Set (2):		6.00
(1)	Ken Griffey Jr.	3.00
(2)	Derek Jeter	3.00

SportsCards Greats of the Game

The first-ever fully-licensed baseball card set to be issued in the form of a magazine insert, this set comprises the game's top players in the design of Fleer's very popular Greats of the Game issue (which depicted only former stars). The cards were issued six per month in uncut sheet form (8-1/4" x 11-1/8") in SportsCards magazine dated February through July 2001. The cards were only inserted in newsstand and card-shop copies. Persons who subscribed to the magazine in a special offer received the complete set in unbound format. If cut from the sheet, individual cards measure the standard 2-1/2" x 3-1/2". On front are action photos on a white background with maroon borders. Backs have player identification, licensor logos and 2000 season stats.

		NM/M
Complete Set, Sheets (6):		35.00
Complete Set, Singles (36):		25.00
Common Player:		.50
	Sheet 1, February	6.00
1	Rick Ankiel	.75
2	Jeff Bagwell	1.00
3	Barry Bonds	3.00
4	Pat Burrell	.65
5	Roger Clemens	1.50
6	Carlos Delgado	.65
	Sheet 2, March	4.00
7	J.D. Drew	.65
8	Jim Edmonds	.50
9	Darin Erstad	.65
10	Andres Galarraga	.50
11	Nomar Garciaparra	2.00
12	Jason Giambi	.75
	Sheet 3, April	6.00
13	Troy Glaus	1.00
14	Roberto Alomar	.50
15	Ken Griffey Jr.	2.00
16	Vladimir Guerrero	1.00
17	Tony Gwynn	1.25
18	Todd Helton	1.00
	Sheet 4, May	7.50
19	Derek Jeter	3.00
20	Randy Johnson	1.00
21	Chipper Jones	1.25
22	Andruw Jones	1.00
23	Greg Maddux	1.25
24	Pedro Martinez	1.00
	Sheet 5, June	10.00
25	Mark McGwire	2.50
26	Magglio Ordonez	.50
27	Mike Piazza	2.00
28	Manny Ramirez	1.00
29	Cal Ripken Jr.	3.00
30	Alex Rodriguez	2.50
	Sheet 6, July	4.00
31	Ivan Rodriguez	.65

32	Jeff Kent	.50
33	Gary Sheffield	.50
34	Sammy Sosa	2.00
35	Frank Thomas	1.00
36	Bernie Williams	.50

2000 Fleer/Twizzlers

A dozen of baseball's biggest stars are reproduced in a format only slightly different from 2000 Fleer Tradition for inclusion in packages of Twizzlers candy. The candy version features UV coating on both front and back, has a small Twizzlers logo at lower-right on back and is numbered "X of 12." Cards were included in large (26.5 oz.) packages of candy or a complete set could be obtained for $1.50 and 15 proofs of purchase from smaller packages.

		NM/M
Complete Set (12):		7.50
Common Player:		.25
1	Mark McGwire	1.50
2	Cal Ripken Jr.	2.00
3	Chipper Jones	.75
4	Bernie Williams	.35
5	Alex Rodriguez	1.50
6	Curt Schilling	.35
7	Ken Griffey Jr.	1.00
8	Sammy Sosa	1.00
9	Mike Piazza	1.00
10	Pedro Martinez	.50
11	Kenny Lofton	.25
12	Larry Walker	.25

1992 Flopps Promos

Prior to the 1992 season, Pro Set announced plans to produce a set of 66 cards parodying contemporary baseball All-Stars and teams. The name "Flopps" was used instead of Pro Set, which does not appear anywhere on the cards. While the announced checklist included players such as Craig Piggio, George Brat and Cal Ripped-One, only five promo cards were produced before the Players Union complained and the idea was dropped. Pro Set didn't want to offend the union at the time because they were attempting to get a baseball card license. Cards pictured caricatures of the players on front and funny biographies on back, all in color in the standard 2-1/2" x 3-1/2" format.

		NM/M
Complete Set (5):		6.00
Common Player:		.50
(1)	Barry Bones	4.00
(2)	Wade Bugs	2.50
(3)	Ken Groovy, Jr.	3.00
(4)	Stickey Henderson	1.50
(5)	Lance Perishable	.50

1993 Florida Agriculture Dept. Braves/Marlins

A pair of eight-card team panels of the Atlanta Braves and Florida Marlins was issued by the Florida

Department of Agriculture and Consumer Services to promote the state's fruit and vegetable products. Individual cards show the player posing - sometimes comically - with one of the state's agricultural products. The photos are bordered in team colors and have a "Fresh 2 U" logo in the upper-left consisting of a fruit or vegetable superimposed on a ball diamond and crossed bats. Backs have the player's name, uniform number, and a short career summary at top. In center is a baseball with the result of an at-bat. In the bottom panel is a statistic about one of the state's crops. A card number is at top. Individual cards measure the standard 2-1/2" x 3-1/2", with the eight-card perforated sheets measuring 10" x 7". The card sheets were distributed during the Sunshine State Games in Tallahassee.

		NM/M
Complete Set (16):		18.00
Common Player:		1.00
Atlanta Braves Team Set:		10.00
1	Team Logo Card	1.00
2	Steve Avery	1.00
3	Jeff Blauser	1.00
4	Sid Bream	1.00
5	Tom Glavine	4.00
6	Mark Lemke	1.00
7	Greg Olson	1.00
8	Terry Pendleton	1.00
Florida Marlins Team Set:		9.00
1	Team Logo Card	1.00
2	Billy the Marlin (Mascot)	1.00
3	Ryan Bowen	1.00
4	Benito Santiago	1.00
5	Richie Lewis	1.00
6	Bret Barbarie	1.00
7	Rich Renteria	1.00
8	Jeff Conine	1.00

1987 Red Foley Stickers

Individual player stickers were inserted in sheets within the pages of "Red Foley's Best Baseball Book Ever." The 8-1/2" x 11", 96-page softbound book offered games, quizzes and trivia, with a space to put each sticker. Individual stickers measure about 1-3/8" x 1-3/4". Stickers have color photos on front with a number in the white border at bottom. Player identification does not appear on the sticker. Cover price of the book in 1987 was about $7.

		NM/M
Complete Book:		9.00
Complete Sticker Set (130):		7.50
Common Player:		.05
1	Julio Franco	.05
2	Willie Randolph	.05
3	Jesse Barfield	.05
4	Mike Witt	.05
5	Orel Hershiser	.05
6	Dwight Gooden	.50
7	Dan Quisenberry	.05
8	Vince Coleman	.05

9	Rich Gossage	.05
10	Kirk Gibson	.05
11	Joaquin Andujar	.05
12	Dave Concepcion	.05
13	Andre Dawson	.25
14	Tippy Martinez	.05
15	Bob James	.05
16	Ryne Sandberg	1.00
17	Bob Knepper	.05
18	Bob Stanley	.05
19	Jim Presley	.05
20	Greg Gross	.05
21	Bob Horner	.05
22	Paul Molitor	.75
23	Kirby Puckett	1.00
24	Scott Garrelts	.05
25	Tony Pena	.05
26	Charlie Hough	.05
27	Joe Carter	.05
28	Dave Winfield	.75
29	Tony Fernandez	.05
30	Bobby Grich	.05
31	Mike Marshall	.05
32	Keith Hernandez	.05
33	Dennis Leonard	.05
34	John Tudor	.05
35	Kevin McReynolds	.05
36	Lance Parrish	.05
37	Carney Lansford	.05
38	Buddy Bell	.05
39	Tim Raines	.05
40	Mike Boddicker	.05
41	Carlton Fisk	.75
42	Lee Smith	.05
43	Glenn Davis	.05
44	Jim Rice	.25
45	Mark Langston	.05
46	Mike Schmidt	1.50
47	Dale Murphy	.45
48	Cecil Cooper	.05
49	Kent Hrbek	.05
50	Will Clark	.10
51	Johnny Ray	.05
52	Darrell Porter	.05
53	Brook Jacoby	.05
54	Ron Guidry	.05
55	Lloyd Moseby	.05
56	Donnie Moore	.05
57	Fernando Valenzuela	.05
58	Darryl Strawberry	.05
59	Hal McRae	.05
60	Tommy Herr	.05
61	Steve Garvey	.35
62	Alan Trammell	.05
63	Jose Canseco	.50
64	Pete Rose	1.75
65	Jeff Reardon	.05
66	Eddie Murray	.75
67	Ozzie Guillen	.05
68	Jody Davis	.05
69	Bill Doran	.05
70	Roger Clemens	1.25
71	Alvin Davis	.05
72	Von Hayes	.05
73	Zane Smith	.05
74	Ted Higuera	.05
75	Tom Brunansky	.05
76	Chili Davis	.05
77	R.J. Reynolds	.05
78	Oddibe McDowell	.05
79	Brett Butler	.05
80	Rickey Henderson	.75
81	Dave Steib	.05
82	Wally Joyner	.05
83	Pedro Guerrero	.05
84	Jesse Orosco	.05
85	Steve Balboni	.05
86	Willie McGee	.05
87	Graig Nettles	.05
88	Lou Whitaker	.05
89	Jay Howell	.05
90	Dave Parker	.05
91	Hubie Brooks	.05
92	Rick Dempsey	.05
93	Neil Allen	.05
94	Shawon Dunston	.05
95	Jose Cruz	.05
96	Wade Boggs	1.00
97	Danny Tartabull	.05
98	Steve Bedrosian	.05
99	Ken Oberkfell	.05
100	Ben Oglivie	.05
101	Bert Blyleven	.05
102	Jeff Leonard	.05
103	Rick Rhoden	.05
104	Larry Parrish	.05
105	Tony Bernazard	.05
106	Don Mattingly	1.50
107	Willie Upshaw	.05
108	Reggie Jackson	1.00
109	Bill Madlock	.05
110	Gary Carter	.75
111	George Brett	1.50
112	Ozzie Smith	1.00
113	Tony Gwynn	.75
114	Jack Morris	.05
115	Dave Kingman	.05
116	John Franco	.05
117	Tim Wallach	.05
118	Cal Ripken Jr.	2.00
119	Harold Baines	.05
120	Leon Durham	.05
121	Nolan Ryan	2.00
122	Dennis (Oil Can) Boyd	.05
123	Matt Young	.05
124	Shane Rawley	.05
125	Bruce Sutter	.65
126	Robin Yount	.75

127	Frank Viola	.05
128	Vida Blue	.05
129	Rick Reuschel	.05
130	Pete Incaviglia	.05

1988 Red Foley Stickers

Identical in format to the previous year's issues, the 104 player and 26 team logo stickers in this set were bound into a 96-page, 8-1/2" x 11" softbound book titled "Red Foley's Best Baseball Book Ever." Each 1-3/8" x 1-3/4" sticker could be placed in the book as an answer to trivia questions, quizzes, games, etc. Stickers have color player photos with a number in the white border at bottom. There is no player identification on the stickers. Original issue price was about $8.

		NM/M
Complete Book:		9.00
Complete Sticker Set (130):		6.00
Common Player:		.05
1	Mike Aldrete	.05
2	Andy Ashby	.05
3	Harold Baines	.05
4	Floyd Bannister	.05
5	Buddy Bell	.05
6	George Bell	.05
7	Barry Bonds	2.00
8	Scott Bradley	.05
9	Bob Brower	.05
10	Ellis Burks	.05
11	Casey Candaele	.05
12	Jack Clark	.05
13	Roger Clemens	1.25
14	Kal Daniels	.05
15	Eric Davis	.05
16	Mike Davis	.05
17	Andre Dawson	.25
18	Rob Deer	.05
19	Brian Downing	.05
20	Doug Drabek	.05
21	Dwight Evans	.05
22	Sid Fernandez	.05
23	Carlton Fisk	.75
24	Scott Fletcher	.05
25	Julio Franco	.05
26	Gary Gaetti	.05
27	Ken Gerhardt	.05
28	Ken Griffey	.05
29	Pedro Guerrero	.05
30	Billy Hatcher	.05
31	Mike Heath	.05
32	Neal Heaton	.05
33	Tom Henke	.05
34	Larry Herndon	.05
35	Brian Holton	.05
36	Glenn Hubbard	.05
37	Bruce Hurst	.05
38	Bo Jackson	.10
39	Michael Jackson	.05
40	Howard Johnson	.05
41	Wally Joyner	.05
42	Jimmy Key	.05
43	Ray Knight	.05
44	John Kruk	.05
45	Mike Krukow	.05
46	Mark Langston	.05
47	Gene Larkin	.05
48	Jeff Leonard	.05
49	Bill Long	.05
50	Fred Lynn	.05
51	Dave Magadan	.05
52	Joe Magrane	.05
53	Don Mattingly	1.50
54	Fred McGriff	.05
55	Mark McGwire	1.75
56	Kevin McReynolds	.05
57	Dave Meads	.05
58	Keith Moreland	.05
59	Dale Murphy	.30
60	Juan Nieves	.05
61	Paul Noce	.05
62	Matt Nokes	.05
63	Pete O'Brien	.05
64	Paul O'Neill	.05
65	Lance Parrish	.05
66	Larry Parrish	.05
67	Tony Pena	.05
68	Terry Pendleton	.05
69	Ken Phelps	.05
70	Dan Plesac	.05
71	Luis Polonia	.05
72	Kirby Puckett	1.00

73	Jeff Reardon	.05
74	Rick Rhoden	.05
75	Dave Righetti	.05
76	Cal Ripken Jr.	2.00
77	Bret Saberhagen	.05
78	Benito Santiago	.05
79	Mike Schmidt	1.50
80	Dick Schofield	.05
81	Mike Scott	.05
82	John Smiley	.05
83	Cory Snyder	.05
84	Franklin Stubbs	.05
85	B.J. Surhoff	.05
86	Rick Sutcliffe	.05
87	Pat Tabler	.05
88	Jose Tartabull (Danny)	.05
89	Garry Templeton	.05
90	Walt Terrell	.05
91	Andre Thornton	.05
92	Andy Van Slyke	.05
93	Ozzie Virgil	.05
94	Tim Wallach	.05
95	Gary Ward	.05
96	Mark Wasinger	.05
97	Mitch Webster	.05
98	Bob Welch	.05
99	Devon White	.05
100	Frank White	.05
101	Ed Whitson	.05
102	Bill Wilkinson	.05
103	Glenn Wilson	.05
104	Curt Young	.05
105	Braves Logo	.05
106	Phillies Logo	.05
107	Padres Logo	.05
108	Giants Logo	.05
109	Orioles Logo	.05
110	Tigers Logo	.05
111	Pirates Logo	.05
112	Royals Logo	.05
113	Astros Logo	.05
114	Indians Logo	.05
115	Brewers Logo	.05
116	Cardinals Logo	.05
117	White Sox Logo	.05
118	Blue Jays Logo	.05
119	Red Sox Logo	.05
120	Athletics Logo	.05
121	Cubs Logo	.05
122	Mariners Logo	.05
123	Rangers Logo	.05
124	Dodgers Logo	.05
125	Yankees Logo	.05
126	Mets Logo	.05
127	Twins Logo	.05
128	Expos Logo	.05
129	Angels Logo	.05
130	Reds Logo	.05

1989 Red Foley Stickers

In its third consecutive year of publication, "Red Foley's Best Baseball Book Ever" retained its 96-page softbound 8-1/2" x 11" format of trivia, quizzes and games to be illustrated by placing one or more of 130 player stickers in the book. Individual stickers are 1-3/8" x 1-3/4" and feature color photos with a white border. Sticker number appears in the bottom-right. There is no player identification on the sticker. Original price of the book is about $8.

		NM/M
Complete Book:		9.00
Complete Sticker Set (130):		7.50
Common Player:		.05
1	Doyle Alexander	.05
2	Luis Alicea	.05
3	Roberto Alomar	.15
4	Andy Ashby	.05
5	Floyd Bannister	.05
6	Jesse Barfield	.05
7	George Bell	.05
8	Wade Boggs	1.00
9	Barry Bonds	2.00
10	Bobby Bonilla	.05
11	Chris Bosio	.05
12	George Brett	1.50
13	Hubie Brooks	.05
14	Tom Brunansky	.05
15	Tim Burke	.05
16	Ivan Calderon	.05
17	Tom Candiotti	.05
18	Jose Canseco	.50
19	Gary Carter	.75

20	Joe Carter	.05
21	Jack Clark	.05
22	Will Clark	.10
23	Roger Clemens	1.25
24	David Cone	.05
25	Ed Correa	.05
26	Kal Daniels	.05
27	Al Davis	.05
28	Chili Davis	.05
29	Eric Davis	.05
30	Glen Davis	.05
31	Jody Davis	.05
32	Mark Davis	.05
33	Andre Dawson	.25
34	Rob Deer	.05
35	Jose DeLeon	.05
36	Bo Diaz	.05
37	Bill Doran	.05
38	Shawon Dunston	.05
39	Dennis Eckersley	.60
40	Dwight Evans	.05
41	Tony Fernandez	.05
42	Brian Fisher	.05
43	Carlton Fisk	.75
44	Mike Flanagan	.05
45	John Franco	.05
46	Gary Gaetti	.05
47	Andres Galarraga	.05
48	Scott Garrelts	.05
49	Kirk Gibson	.05
50	Dan Gladden	.05
51	Dwight Gooden	.05
52	Pedro Guerrero	.05
53	Ozzie Guillen	.05
54	Tony Gwynn	1.00
55	Mel Hall	.05
56	Von Hayes	.05
57	Keith Hernandez	.05
58	Orel Hershiser	.05
59	Ted Higuera	.05
60	Charlie Hough	.05
61	Jack Howell	.05
62	Kent Hrbek	.05
63	Pete Incaviglia	.05
64	Bo Jackson	.10
65	Brook Jacoby	.05
66	Chris James	.05
67	Lance Johnson	.05
68	Wally Joyner	.05
69	John Kruk	.05
70	Mike LaCoss	.05
71	Mark Langston	.05
72	Carney Lansford	.05
73	Barry Larkin	.05
74	Mike LaValliere	.05
75	Jose Lind	.05
76	Fred Lynn	.05
77	Greg Maddux	1.00
78	Candy Maldonado	.05
79	Don Mattingly	1.50
80	Mark McGwire	1.75
81	Paul Molitor	.75
82	Jack Morris	.05
83	Lloyd Moseby	.05
84	Dale Murphy	.30
85	Eddie Murray	.75
86	Matt Nokes	.05
87	Pete O'Brien	.05
88	Rafael Palmeiro	.65
89	Melido Perez	.05
90	Gerald Perry	.05
91	Tim Raines	.05
92	Willie Randolph	.05
93	Johnny Ray	.05
94	Jeff Reardon	.05
95	Jody Reed	.05
96	Harold Reynolds	.05
97	Dave Righetti	.05
98	Billy Ripken	.05
99	Cal Ripken Jr.	2.00
100	Nolan Ryan	2.00
101	Juan Samuel	.05
102	Benito Santiago	.05
103	Steve Sax	.05
104	Mike Schmidt	1.50
105	Rick Schu	.05
106	Mike Scott	.05
107	Kevin Seitzer	.05
108	Ruben Sierra	.05
109	Lee Smith	.05
110	Ozzie Smith	1.00
111	Zane Smith	.05
112	Dave Stewart	.05
113	Darryl Strawberry	.05
114	Bruce Sutter	.65
115	Bill Swift	.05
116	Greg Swindell	.05
117	Frank Tanana	.05
118	Danny Tartabull	.05
119	Milt Thompson	.05
120	Rob Thompson	.05
121	Alan Trammell	.05
122	John Tudor	.05
123	Fernando Valenzuela	.05
124	Dave Valle	.05
125	Frank Viola	.05
126	Ozzie Virgil	.05
127	Tim Wallach	.05
128	Dave Winfield	.75
129	Mike Witt	.05
130	Robin Yount	.75

1990 Red Foley Stickers

In its fourth consecutive year of publication, "Red Foley's Best Baseball Book Ever" retained its 96-page softbound 8-1/2" x 11" format of triv-

ia, quizzes and games to be illustrated by placing one of 104 player or 26 team logo stickers in the book. Individual stickers are 1-3/8" x 1-3/4" and feature color photos with a white border. Sticker number appears in the bottom-right. There is no player identification on the sticker.

		NM/M
Complete Book:		9.00
Complete Sticker Set (130):		7.00
Common Player:		.05
1	Allan Anderson	.05
2	Scott Bailes	.05
3	Jeff Ballard	.05
4	Jesse Barfield	.05
5	Bert Blyleven	.05
6	Wade Boggs	1.00
7	Barry Bonds	2.00
8	Chris Bosio	.05
9	George Brett	1.50
10	Tim Burke	.05
11	Ellis Burks	.05
12	Brett Butler	.05
13	Ivan Calderon	.05
14	Jose Canseco	.50
15	Joe Carter	.05
16	Jack Clark	.05
17	Will Clark	.10
18	Roger Clemens	1.25
19	Vince Coleman	.05
20	Eric Davis	.05
21	Glenn Davis	.05
22	Mark Davis	.05
23	Andre Dawson	.25
24	Rob Deer	.05
25	Jose DeLeon	.05
26	Jim Deshaies	.05
27	Doug Drabek	.05
28	Lenny Dykstra	.05
29	Dennis Eckersley	.65
30	Steve Farr	.05
31	Tony Fernandez	.05
32	Carlton Fisk	.75
33	John Franco	.05
34	Julio Franco	.05
35	Andres Galarraga	.05
36	Tom Glavine	.25
37	Dwight Gooden	.05
38	Mark Grace	.10
39	Mike Greenwell	.05
40	Ken Griffey Jr.	1.25
41	Kelly Gruber	.05
42	Pedro Guerrero	.05
43	Tony Gwynn	1.00
44	Bryan Harvey	.05
45	Von Hayes	.05
46	Willie Hernandez	.05
47	Tommy Herr	.05
48	Orel Hershiser	.05
49	Jay Howell	.05
50	Kent Hrbek	.05
51	Bo Jackson	.10
52	Steve Jeltz	.05
53	Jimmy Key	.05
54	Ron Kittle	.05
55	Mark Langston	.05
56	Carney Lansford	.05
57	Barry Larkin	.05
58	Jeffrey Leonard	.05
59	Don Mattingly	1.50
60	Fred McGriff	.05
61	Mark McGwire	1.75
62	Kevin McReynolds	.05
63	Randy Myers	.05
64	Kevin Mitchell	.05
65	Paul Molitor	.05
66	Mike Morgan	.05
67	Dale Murphy	.30
68	Eddie Murray	.75
69	Matt Nokes	.05
70	Greg Olson	.05
71	Paul O'Neill	.05
72	Rafael Palmeiro	.65
73	Lance Parrish	.05
74	Dan Plesac	.05
75	Kirby Puckett	1.00
76	Jeff Reardon	.05
77	Rick Reuschel	.05
78	Cal Ripken Jr.	2.00
79	Dave Righetti	.05
80	Jeff Russell	.05
81	Nolan Ryan	2.00
82	Benito Santiago	.05
83	Steve Sax	.05
84	Mike Schooler	.05
85	Mike Scott	.05
86	Kevin Seitzer	.05
87	Dave Smith	.05
88	Lonnie Smith	.05
89	Ozzie Smith	1.00
90	John Smoltz	.05
91	Cory Snyder	.05
92	Darryl Strawberry	.05
93	Greg Swindell	.05
94	Mickey Tettleton	.05
95	Bobby Thigpen	.05
96	Alan Trammell	.05
97	Dave Valle	.05
98	Andy Van Slyke	.05
99	Tim Wallach	.05
100	Jerome Walton	.05
101	Lou Whitaker	.05
102	Devon White	.05
103	Mitch Williams	.05
104	Glen Wilson	.05
105	Indians Logo	.05
106	Rangers Logo	.05
107	Reds Logo	.05
108	Orioles Logo	.05
109	Red Sox Logo	.05
110	White Sox Logo	.05
111	Dodgers Logo	.05
112	Tigers Logo	.05
113	Mariners Logo	.05
114	Blue Jays Logo	.05
115	Expos Logo	.05
116	Pirates Logo	.05
117	Astros Logo	.05
118	Cardinals Logo	.05
119	Padres Logo	.05
120	Angels Logo	.05
121	Yankees Logo	.05
122	Cubs Logo	.05
123	Brewers Logo	.05
124	Twins Logo	.05
125	Giants Logo	.05
126	Royals Logo	.05
127	A's Logo	.05
128	Mets Logo	.05
129	Phillies Logo	.05
130	Braves Logo	.05

1991 Red Foley Stickers

76

In its fifth consecutive year of publication, "Red Foley's Best Baseball Book Ever" retained its 96-page softbound 8-1/2" x 11" format of trivia, quizzes and games to be illustrated by placing one of 112 regular or 18 All-Star (#113-130) stickers in the book. Individual stickers are 1-3/8" x 1-3/4" and feature color photos with a white border. Sticker number appears in the bottom-right. There is no player identification on the sticker.

		NM/M
Complete Book:		10.00
Comlete Sticker Set (130):		8.00
Common Player:		.05
1	Jim Abbott	.05
2	Rick Aguilera	.05
3	Roberto Alomar	.30
4	Rob Dibble	.05
5	Wally Backman	.05
6	Harold Baines	.05
7	Steve Bedrosian	.05
8	Craig Biggio	.05
9	Wade Boggs	1.00
10	Bobby Bonilla	.05
11	George Brett	1.25
12	Greg Brock	.05
13	Hubie Brooks	.05
14	Tom Brunansky	.05
15	Tim Burke	.05
16	Tom Candiotti	.05
17	Jose Canseco	.50
18	Jack Clark	.05
19	Will Clark	.10
20	Roger Clemens	1.25
21	Vince Coleman	.05
22	Kal Daniels	.05
23	Glenn Davis	.05
24	Mark Davis	.05
25	Andre Dawson	.05
26	Rob Deer	.05
27	Delino DeShields	.05
28	Doug Drabek	.05
29	Shawon Dunston	.05
30	Lenny Dykstra	.05
31	Dennis Eckersley	.35
32	Kevin Elster	.05
33	Tony Fernandez	.05
34	Cecil Fielder	.05
35	Chuck Finley	.05
36	Carlton Fisk	.75
37	Greg Gagne	.05
38	Ron Gant	.05
39	Dan Gladden	.05
40	Dwight Gooden	.05
41	Ken Griffey Jr.	1.50
42	Kelly Gruber	.05
43	Pedro Guerrero	.05
44	Ozzie Guillen	.05
45	Pete Harnisch	.05
46	Billy Hatcher	.05
47	Von Hayes	.05
48	Rickey Henderson	.75
49	Mike Henneman	.05
50	Kent Hrbek	.05
51	Pete Incaviglia	.05
52	Howard Johnson	.05
53	Randy Johnson	.75
54	Doug Jones	.05
55	Ricky Jordan	.05
56	Wally Joyner	.05
57	Roberto Kelly	.05
58	Barry Larkin	.05
59	Craig Lefferts	.05
60	Candy Maldonado	.05
61	Don Mattingly	1.25
62	Oddibe McDowell	.05
63	Roger McDowell	.05
64	Willie McGee	.05
65	Fred McGriff	.05
66	Kevin Mitchell	.05
67	Mike Morgan	.05
68	Eddie Murray	.75
69	Gregg Olson	.05
70	Joe Orsulak	.05
71	Dan Petry	.05
72	Dan Plesac	.05
73	Jim Presley	.05
74	Kirby Puckett	1.00
75	Tim Raines	.05
76	Jeff Reardon	.05
77	Dave Righetti	.05
78	Cal Ripken Jr.	2.00
79	Nolan Ryan	2.00
80	Bret Saberhagen	.05
81	Chris Sabo	.05
82	Ryne Sandberg	1.00
83	Benito Santiago	.05
84	Steve Sax	.05
85	Mike Schooler	.05
86	Mike Scott	.05
87	Ruben Sierra	.05
88	Cory Snyder	.05
89	Dave Steib	.05
90	Dave Stewart	.05
91	Kurt Stillwell	.05
92	Bobby Thigpen	.05
93	Alan Trammell	.05
94	John Tudor	.05
95	Dave Valle	.05
96	Andy Van Slyke	.05
97	Robin Ventura	.05
98	Frank Viola	.05
99	Tim Wallach	.05
100	Matt Williams	.05
101	Mitch Williams	.05
102	Dave Winfield	.05
103	Eric Yelding	.05
104	Robin Yount	.75
105	Steve Avery	.05
106	Travis Fryman	.05
107	Juan Gonzalez	.40
108	Todd Hundley	.05
109	Ben McDonald	.05
110	Jose Offerman	.05
111	Frank Thomas	.75
112	Bernie Williams	.10
113	Sandy Alomar Jr.	.05
114	Jack Armstrong	.05
115	Wade Boggs	.40
116	Jose Canseco	.25
117	Will Clark	.10
118	Andre Dawson	.05
119	Lenny Dykstra	.05
120	Ken Griffey Jr.	.65
121	Rickey Henderson	.40
122	Mark McGwire	1.75
123	Kevin Mitchell	.05
124	Cal Ripken Jr.	1.00
125	Chris Sabo	.05
126	Ryne Sandberg	.50
127	Steve Sax	.05
128	Mike Scoscia	.05
129	Ozzie Smith	.50
130	Bob Welch	.05

1992 Red Foley Stickers

The format was unchanged when "Red Foley's Best Baseball Book Ever" was published in 1992. The 96-page, 8-1/2" x 11" softcover book features 96 pages of quizzes, trivia and games, along with 130 player stickers (#105-130 are All-Star stickers) to be placed on the proper pages. Single stickers measure 1-3/8" x 1-3/4" and have color photos with a white border. A sticker number is in the bottom-right. No player identification appears on the stickers. Issue price of the book was about $9.

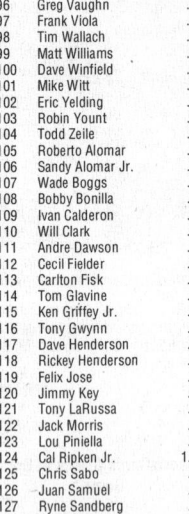

		NM/M
Complete Book:		12.00
Complete Sticker Set (130):		10.00
Common Player:		.05
1	Jim Abbott	.05
2	Roberto Alomar	.15
3	Sandy Alomar Jr.	.05
4	Eric Anthony	.05
5	Kevin Appier	.05
6	Jack Armstrong	.05
7	Steve Avery	.05
8	Carlos Baerga	.05
9	Scott Bankhead	.05
10	George Bell	.05
11	Albert Belle	.05
12	Andy Benes	.05
13	Craig Biggio	.05
14	Wade Boggs	1.00
15	Barry Bonds	2.00
16	Bobby Bonilla	.05
17	Sid Bream	.05
18	George Brett	1.25
19	Hubie Brooks	.05
20	Ellis Burks	.05
21	Brett Butler	.05
22	Jose Canseco	.40
23	Joe Carter	.05
24	Jack Clark	.05
25	Will Clark	.10
26	Roger Clemens	1.25
27	Vince Coleman	.05
28	Eric Davis	.05
29	Glenn Davis	.05
30	Andre Dawson	.25
31	Rob Deer	.05
32	Delino DeShields	.05
33	Lenny Dykstra	.05
34	Scott Erickson	.05
35	Cecil Fielder	.05
36	Carlton Fisk	.75
37	Travis Fryman	.05
38	Greg Gagne	.05
39	Juan Gonzalez	.40
40	Tommy Greene	.05
41	Ken Griffey Jr.	1.50
42	Kent Hrbek	.05
43	Kelly Gruber	.05
44	Tony Gwynn	1.00
45	Dave Henderson	.05
46	Rickey Henderson	.75
47	Orel Hershiser	.05
48	Marquis Grissom	.05
49	Howard Johnson	.05
50	Felix Jose	.05
51	Wally Joyner	.05
52	David Justice	.05
53	Roberto Kelly	.05
54	Ray Lankford	.05
55	Barry Larkin	.05
56	Mark Lewis	.05
57	Kevin Maas	.05
58	Greg Maddux	1.00
59	Dennis Martinez	.05
60	Edgar Martinez	.05
61	Don Mattingly	1.50
62	Ben McDonald	.05
63	Jack McDowell	.05
64	Willie McGee	.05
65	Fred McGriff	.05
66	Brian McRae	.05
67	Mark McGwire	1.75
68	Kevin Mitchell	.05
69	Terry Mulholland	.05
70	Dale Murphy	.25
71	Eddie Murray	.75
72	John Olerud	.05
73	Rafael Palmeiro	.65
74	Terry Pendleton	.05
75	Luis Polonia	.05
76	Mark Portugal	.05
77	Kirby Puckett	1.00
78	Tim Raines	.05
79	Harold Reynolds	.05
80	Billy Ripken	.05
81	Cal Ripken Jr.	2.00
82	Nolan Ryan	2.00
83	Chris Sabo	.05
84	Ryne Sandberg	1.00
85	Benito Santiago	.05
86	Kevin Seitzer	.05
87	Gary Sheffield	.30
88	Ruben Sierra	.05
89	John Smiley	.05
90	Ozzie Smith	1.00
91	Darryl Strawberry	.05
92	B.J. Surhoff	.05
93	Frank Thomas	.75
94	Alan Trammell	.05
95	Andy Van Slyke	.05
96	Greg Vaughn	.05
97	Frank Viola	.05
98	Tim Wallach	.05
99	Matt Williams	.05
100	Dave Winfield	.75
101	Mike Witt	.05
102	Eric Yelding	.05
103	Robin Yount	.75
104	Todd Zeile	.05
105	Roberto Alomar	.10
106	Sandy Alomar Jr.	.05
107	Wade Boggs	.50
108	Bobby Bonilla	.05
109	Ivan Calderon	.05
110	Will Clark	.05
111	Andre Dawson	.05
112	Cecil Fielder	.05
113	Carlton Fisk	.30
114	Tom Glavine	.25
115	Ken Griffey Jr.	.65
116	Tony Gwynn	.50
117	Dave Henderson	.05
118	Rickey Henderson	.30
119	Felix Jose	.05
120	Jimmy Key	.05
121	Tony LaRussa	.05
122	Jack Morris	.05
123	Lou Piniella	.05
124	Cal Ripken Jr.	1.00
125	Chris Sabo	.05
126	Juan Samuel	.05
127	Ryne Sandberg	.50
128	Benito Santiago	.05
129	Ozzie Smith	.50
130	Danny Tartabull	.05

1993 Red Foley Stickers

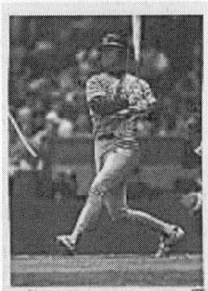

67

The format was unchanged when "Red Foley's Best Baseball Book Ever" was published in 1993. The 96-page, 8-1/2" x 11" softcover book features 96 pages of quizzes, trivia and games, along with 130 player stickers (#105-130 are All-Star stickers) to be placed on the proper pages. Single stickers measure 1-3/8" x 1-3/4" and have color photos with a white border. A sticker number is in the bottom-right. No player identification appears on the stickers.

		NM/M
Complete Book:		10.00
Complete Sticker Set (130):		9.00
Common Player:		.05
1	Jim Abbott	.05
2	Roberto Alomar	.15
3	Sandy Alomar Jr.	.05
4	Steve Avery	.05
5	Jeff Bagwell	.75
6	Harold Baines	.05
7	Bret Barberie	.05
8	Derek Bell	.05
9	Jay Bell	.05
10	Albert Belle	.05
11	Andy Benes	.05
12	Craig Biggio	.05
13	Wade Boggs	1.00
14	Barry Bonds	2.00
15	Bobby Bonilla	.05
16	Jose Canseco	.40
17	Joe Carter	.05
18	Wes Chamberlain	.05
19	Will Clark	.10
20	Roger Clemens	1.25
21	Milt Cuyler	.05
22	Eric Davis	.05
23	Delino DeShields	.05
24	Rob Dibble	.05
25	Doug Drabek	.05
26	Shawon Dunston	.05
27	Lenny Dykstra	.05
28	Scott Erickson	.05
29	Cecil Fielder	.05
30	Steve Finley	.05
31	Tom Glavine	.25
32	Dwight Gooden	.05
33	Mark Grace	.05
34	Ken Griffey Jr.	1.50
35	Marquis Grissom	.05
36	Kelly Gruber	.05
37	Mark Gubicza	.05
38	Tony Gwynn	1.00
39	Mel Hall	.05
40	Pete Harnisch	.05

41 Brian Harper .05
42 Bryan Harvey .05
43 Rickey Henderson .75
44 Orel Hershiser .05
45 Gregg Jefferies .05
46 Howard Johnson .05
47 Felix Jose .05
48 Wally Joyner .05
49 David Justice .05
50 Roberto Kelly .05
51 Chuck Knoblauch .05
52 John Kruk .05
53 Barry Larkin .05
54 Kenny Lofton .05
55 Greg Maddux 1.00
56 Dennis Martinez .05
57 Edgar Martinez .05
58 Tino Martinez .05
59 Don Mattingly 1.25
60 Jack McDowell .05
61 Willie McGee .05
62 Fred McGriff .05
63 Mark McGwire 1.75
64 Brian McRae .05
65 Randy Milligan .05
66 Kevin Mitchell .05
67 Paul Molitor .75
68 Dale Murphy .25
69 Mike Mussina .40
70 Charles Nagy .05
71 Gregg Olson .05
72 Rafael Palmeiro .65
73 Dean Palmer .05
74 Phil Plantier .05
75 Luis Polonia .05
76 Kirby Puckett 1.00
77 Tim Raines .05
78 Cal Ripken Jr. 2.00
79 Bip Roberts .05
80 Ivan Rodriguez .65
81 Nolan Ryan 2.00
82 Bret Saberhagen .05
83 Ryne Sandberg 1.00
84 Deion Sanders .10
85 Reggie Sanders .05
86 Benito Santiago .05
87 Mike Scoscia .05
88 Lee Smith .05
89 Ozzie Smith 1.00
90 Lee Stevens .05
91 Darryl Strawberry .05
92 B.J. Surhoff .05
93 Danny Tartabull .05
94 Mickey Tettleton .05
95 Frank Thomas .75
96 Robby Thompson .05
97 Alan Trammell .05
98 Greg Vaughn .05
99 Mo Vaughn .05
100 Andy Van Slyke .05
101 Robin Ventura .05
102 Matt Williams .05
103 Robin Yount .75
104 Todd Zeile .05
105 Roberto Alomar .15
106 Sandy Alomar Jr. .05
107 Wade Boggs .50
108 Kevin Brown .05
109 Joe Carter .05
110 Will Clark .05
111 Bobby Cox .05
112 Dennis Eckersley .40
113 Tony Fernandez .05
114 Tom Glavine .05
115 Ken Griffey Jr. .65
116 Tony Gwynn .50
117 Tom Kelly .05
118 John Kruk .05
119 Fred McGriff .05
120 Mark McGwire .75
121 Kirby Puckett .50
122 Cal Ripken Jr. 1.00
123 Bip Roberts .05
124 Ivan Rodriguez .20
125 Gary Sheffield .25
126 Ruben Sierra .05
127 Ozzie Smith .50
128 Andy Van Slyke .05
129 Robin Ventura .05
130 Larry Walker .05

1994 Red Foley

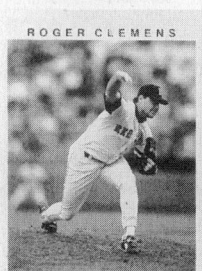

Beginning in 1994, major changes were seen in "Red Foley's Best Baseball Book Ever." The book remained in 8-1/2" x 11" format, but was downsized to 64 pages. The previous years' stickers were replaced with four nine-card sheets of perforated baseball cards. When separated from the sheets, cards measure the standard 2-1/2" x 3-1/2". The unnumbered cards appear in two types. "Superstar" cards feature a single player in a color action photo on front. "Team Leaders" cards have two teammates on front. Red and black printing on backs give personal data and career highlights. Original retail cost of the book was $8.95.

NM/M
Complete Book: 15.00
Complete Set (36): 12.00
Common Card: .25
(1) Barry Bonds 2.00
(2) Joe Carter .25
(3) Roger Clemens 1.25
(4) Juan Gonzalez .60
(5) Ken Griffey Jr. 1.50
(6) Fred McGriff .25
(7) Jose Rijo .25
(8) Ryne Sandberg 1.00
(9) Angels (Tim Salmon, Mark Langston) .25
(10) Astros (Jeff Bagwell, Doug Drabek) .50
(11) Athletics (Mark McGwire, Dennis Eckersley) .75
(12) Blue Jays (Roberto Alomar, John Olerud) .30
(13) Braves (Greg Maddux, Tom Glavine) .60
(14) Brewers (Robin Yount, Cal Eldred) .50
(15) Cardinals (Ray Lankford, Ozzie Smith) .60
(16) Cubs (Mark Grace, Randy Myers) .30
(17) Dodgers (Mike Piazza, Orel Hershiser) .65
(18) Expos (Larry Walker, Marquis Grissom) .25
(19) Giants (Will Clark, Matt Williams) .25
(20) Indians (Albert Belle, Carlos Baerga) .25
(21) Mariners (Jay Buhner, Randy Johnson) .40
(22) Marlins (Gary Sheffield, Bryan Harvey) .25
(23) Mets (Bobby Bonilla, Dwight Gooden) .25
(24) Orioles (Cal Ripken Jr., Mike Mussina) 1.00
(25) Padres (Andy Benes, Tony Gwynn) .60
(26) Phillies (John Kruk, Tommy Greene) .25
(27) Pirates (Jay Bell, Andy Van Slyke) .25
(28) Rangers (Jose Canseco, Kevin Brown) .35
(29) Reds (Barry Larkin, Reggie Sanders) .25
(30) Red Sox (Mo Vaughn, Frank Viola) .25
(31) Rockies (Charlie Hayes, Andres Galarraga) .25
(32) Royals (Brian McRae, David Cone) .25
(33) Tigers (Cecil Fielder, Mike Henneman) .25
(34) Twins (Kirby Puckett, Rick Aguilera) .60
(35) White Sox (Frank Thomas, Jack McDowell) .50
(36) Yankees (Don Mattingly, Jim Abbott) .75

1995 Red Foley

The Red Foley book of children's games, quizzes, trivia and other baseball related entertainment reprised its 1994 format for 1995. The 36 perforated insert cards, 2-1/2" x 3-1/2", were again divided into single-player "Superstar" and two-player "Team Leaders" types. Designs were identical to the previous year, with color action photos on front and career highlights on back. The unnumbered cards are checklisted here in alphabetical order by type.

NM/M
Complete Book: 15.00
Complete Set (36): 12.00
Common Card: .25
(1) Barry Bonds 2.00
(2) Joe Carter .25
(3) Roger Clemens 1.00
(4) Juan Gonzalez .60
(5) Ken Griffey Jr. 1.50
(6) Fred McGriff .25
(7) Cal Ripken Jr. 2.00
(8) Frank Thomas .75
(9) Angels (Tim Salmon, Steve Finley) .35
(10) Astros (Jeff Bagwell, Craig Biggio) .50
(11) Athletics (Mark McGwire, Dennis Eckersley) .75
(12) Blue Jays (Roberto Alomar, John Olerud) .35
(13) Braves (Greg Maddux, David Justice) .60
(14) Brewers (Cal Eldred, Dave Nillson) .25
(15) Cardinals (Ozzie Smith, Gregg Jefferies) .60
(16) Cubs (Mark Grace, Randy Myers) .35
(17) Dodgers (Mike Piazza, Orel Hershiser) .65
(18) Expos (Larry Walker, Ken Hill) .25
(19) Giants (Matt Williams, Rod Beck) .25
(20) Indians (Albert Belle, Carlos Baerga) .25
(21) Mariners (Jay Buhner, Randy Johnson) .25
(22) Marlins (Gary Sheffield, Benito Santiago) .25
(23) Mets (Bret Saberhagen, Bobby Bonilla) .25
(24) Orioles (Rafael Palmeiro, Mike Mussina) .40
(25) Padres (Tony Gwynn, Andy Benes) .60
(26) Phillies (John Kruk, Lenny Dykstra) .25
(27) Pirates (Andy Van Slyke, Al Martin) .25
(28) Rangers (Jose Canseco, Will Clark) .35
(29) Reds (Barry Larkin, Jose Rijo) .25
(30) Red Sox (Mo Vaughn, Aaron Sele) .25
(31) Rockies (Andres Galarraga, Dante Bichette) .25
(32) Royals (Brian McRae, David Cone) .25
(33) Tigers (Cecil Fielder, Travis Fryman) .25
(34) Twins (Kirby Puckett, Rick Aguilera) .60
(35) White Sox (Robin Ventura, Wilson Alvarez) .25
(36) Yankees (Don Mattingly, Jimmy Key) .65

1996 Red Foley

The Red Foley book of children's games, quizzes, trivia and other baseball related entertainment changed little for its 1996 edition. The number of cards was decreased to 32 and the size to a 2" x 2-3/4" perforated format. Only single-player cards were produced. Designs were nearly identical to the previous year, with color action photos on front and career highlights on back. The unnumbered cards are checklisted here in alphabetical order.

NM/M
Complete Book: 12.00
Complete Set (32): 9.00
Common Player: .25
(1) Roberto Alomar .30
(2) Moises Alou .25
(3) Carlos Baerga .25
(4) Jay Bell .25
(5) Craig Biggio .25
(6) Barry Bonds 1.50
(7) Jeff Conine .25
(8) Lenny Dykstra .25
(9) Cecil Fielder .25
(10) Ken Griffey Jr. 1.00
(11a) Tony Gwynn (Red) .75
(11b) Tony Gwynn (Purple) .75
(12) Rickey Henderson .65
(13) Wally Joyner .25
(14) Barry Larkin .25
(15) Mark McGwire 1.25
(16) Eddie Murray .65
(17) Rafael Palmeiro .25
(18) Mike Piazza 1.00
(19) Greg Maddux .75
(20) Paul O'Neill .25
(21) Kirby Puckett .25
(22) Bill Pulsipher .25
(23) Cal Ripken Jr. 1.50
(24) Ivan Rodriguez .50
(25) Kenny Rogers .25
(26) Tim Salmon .30
(27) Kevin Seitzer .25
(28) Ozzie Smith .25
(29) Sammy Sosa .90
(30) Frank Thomas .65
(31) Mo Vaughn .25
(32) Larry Walker .25

1988 Foot Locker Slam Fest

Two baseball players are among the athletes pictured in this Foot Locker set issued in conjunction with the shoe store chain's Slam Fest competition. Cards were given away at local stores. The 2-1/2" x 3-1/2" cards have color player portrait photos on a semi-gloss front. All athletes are pictured in Slam Dunk basketball jerseys. A sponsor's banner is at top; the chain's referee logo at lower-left. Backs are printed in blue with information about the televised competition and the player's career.

NM/M
Complete Set (9): 6.00
Common Player: .50
(1) Carl Banks (Football) .50
(2) Mike Conley/SP (Track) .50
(3) Thomas Hearns (Boxing) 2.00
(4) Bo Jackson 2.00
(5) Keith Jackson (Football) .50
(6) Karch Kiraly (Volleyball) .50
(7) Ricky Sanders (Football) .50
(8) Dwight Stones (Track) .50
(9) Devon White 1.00

1989 Foot Locker Slam Fest

One baseball player is among the athletes pictured in this Foot Locker set issued in conjunction with the shoe store chain's Slam Fest competition. Cards were given away at local stores. The 2-1/2" x 3-1/2" cards have color player portrait photos on a semi-gloss front. All athletes are pictured in Slam Dunk basketball jerseys. A sponsor's banner is at top. Backs have information about the televised competition and the player's career.

NM/M
Complete Set (10): 3.00
Common Player: .35
1 Mike Conley (Track) .40
2 Keith Jackson (Football) .75
3 Vince Coleman 1.00
4 Eric Dickerson (Football) 2.00
5 Steve Timmons (Volleyball) .40
6 Matt Biondi (Swimming) .50
7 Carl Lewis (Track) .75
8 Mike Quick (Football) .50
9 Mike Powell (Track) .50
10 Checklist .05

1991 Foot Locker Slam Fest

A number of baseball players were included among the various current and former athletes in this set of three 10-card series produced in conjunction with the sporting gear retailer's Slam Fest charity event. Players are pictured in color on the 2-1/2" x 3-1/2" cards wearing Nike basketball uniforms.

NM/M
Complete Set (30): 5.00
Common Player: .03
1-1 Ken Griffey Jr. 1.50
1-2 Delino DeShields .10
1-3 Barry Bonds 4.00
1-4 Jack Armstrong .10
1-5 Dave Justice .10
1-6 Deion Sanders .50
1-7 Michael Dean Perry (Football) .10
1-8 Tim Brown (Football) .10
1-9 Mike Conley (Track) .10
1-10 Mike Powell (Track) .10
10-1 Wilt Chamberlain (Basketball) 1.00
10-2 Carl Ramsey (Basketball) .10
10-3 Bobby Jones (Basketball) .10
10-4 John Havlicek (Basketball) .10
10-5 Calvin Murphy (Basketball) .10
10-6 Nate Thurmond (Basketball) .10
10-7 John Havlicek (Basketball) .10
10-8 Checklist Series 1 .05
10-9 Checklist Series 2 .05
10-10 Checklist Series 3 .05
20-1 Jerry Lucas (Basketball) .10
20-2 Bo Jackson .10
20-3 Elvin Hayes (Basketball) .10
20-4 Thomas Hearns (Boxing) .25
20-5 Matt Biondi (Swimming) .10
20-6 Earl Monroe (Basketball) .10
20-7 Eric Dickerson (Football) .50
20-8 Carl Lewis (Track) .25
20-9 Wilt and Company (Basketball) .10
20-10 TV Schedule .05

1989 Foxes Holsum Super Stars Discs

(See 1989 Holsum for checklist and price guide. Distributed in Carolinas.)

1981 Franchise 1966 Baltimore Orioles

One of the lesser-known producers of collectors' issues in the early 1980s was "The Franchise." Most of their card sets featured subjects of special interest to their home (Maryland) area. This set, for example, features the 1966 Baltimore Orioles World Champions. In 2-1/2" x 3-1/2" size, cards have black-and-white player photos on front surrounded by orange borders. Black-and-white backs are somewhat in the style of 1953 Bowman, with personal data, career highlights and 1966/Lifetime stats.

NM/M
Complete Set (32): 13.50
Common Player: .50
1 World Champs 1966 .50
2 Team Photo .50
3 Luis Aparicio 2.50
4 Steve Barber .50
5 Hank Bauer .50
6 Paul Blair .50
7 Curt Blefary .50
8 Sam Bowens .50
9 Gene Brabender .50
10 Harry Brecheen .50
11 Wally Bunker .50
12 Moe Drabowsky .50
13 Andy Etchebarren .50
14 Eddie Fisher .50
15 Dick Hall .50
16 Larry Haney .50
17 Woody Held .50
18 Billy Hunter .50
19 Bob Johnson .50
20 Dave Johnson .50
21 Sherman Lollar .50
22 Dave McNally .50
23 John Miller .50
24 Stu Miller .50
25 Jim Palmer 2.50
26 Boog Powell 1.50
27 Brooks Robinson 3.00
28 Frank Robinson 3.00
29 Vic Roznovsky .50
30 Russ Snyder .50
31 Eddie Watt .50
32 Gene Woodling .50

1983 Franchise Brooks Robinson

This collectors' issue was produced by a Maryland company which specialized in sets of local interest. Cards detail the career of the Orioles Hall of Famer. Fronts of the 2-1/2" x 3-1/2" cards have a black-and-white photo with orange graphics. Backs are printed in black, white and orange and provide a title and details about the front photo.

NM/M
Complete Set (40): 35.00
Common Card: 1.00
1 Professional record 1.00
2 Youngest on team 1.00
3 All-state performer 1.00
4 Teen-ager in Texas 1.00
5 First spring training 1.00
6 Another uniform 1.00
7 First solid infield 1.00
8 Celebration time 1.00
9 Instinctive baserunner 1.00
10 Wedding day 1.00
11 First business partner 1.00
12 Second solid infield 1.00
13 Two Baltimore heroes 1.00
14 Enjoying the kids 1.00
15 Playing every game 1.00
16 Upsetting the Yankees 1.00
17 Tag out at third 1.00
18 Getting net results 1.00
19 The future MVPs 1.50
20 The original Rocky 1.00
21 Bauer's gloveman 1.00
22 World Series infield 1.00
23 Orioles' power parade 1.00
24 All-star trio 1.50
25 Lethal lumber 1.00
26 Belanger joins infield 1.00
27 Respect for Oliva 1.00
28 Out of Harm's way 1.00
29 Master trader 1.00
30 Eastern Shore visit 1.00
31 Gloves of gold 1.00
32 Ripping the Reds 1.00
33 Rappin' with Willie 2.00
34 Using the body 1.00
35 Getting the umps' attention 1.00
36 Respect from teammate 1.00
37 Touch of class 1.00
38 Bubble never burst 1.00
39 Honored by Yankees 1.00
40 Two greats at third 1.00

2002 Franz Bread Seattle Mariners

This team set was produced by Upper Deck and issued regionally with individually cello-wrapped cards inserted into loaves of bread. The cards have game-action photos which are borderless at top and sides. In a wide white strip at bottom are the team name, player name, position and uniform number and a Franz logo. In the upper corners are UD and Mariners 25th Anniversary logos. Backs have a portrait photo, a few words about the player, previous season's stats and various logos and copyright information.

		NM/M
Complete Set (16):		10.00
Common Player:		.50
1	Ichiro	5.00
2	Edgar Martinez	1.00
3	John Olerud	.75
4	Bret Boone	.75
5	Jeff Cirillo	.50
6	Carlos Guillen	.50
7	Mike Cameron	.50
8	Ruben Sierra	.50
9	Ben Davis	.50
10	Freddy Garcia	.50
11	Kazuhiro Sasaki	1.00
12	Jamie Moyer	.50
13	James Baldwin	.50
14	Jeff Nelson	.50
15	Dan Wilson	.50
16	Mark McLemore	.50

1987 French/Bray Orioles

8 CAL RIPKEN, IF
Compliments of
FRENCH/BRAY, INC.

The Baltimore Orioles and French Bray, Inc. issued a baseball card set to be handed out to fans in attendance at Memorial Stadium on July 26th. Thirty perforated, detachable cards were printed within a three-panel fold-out piece measuring 9-1/2" x 11-1/4". The card fronts feature full-color player photos surrounded by an orange border. The French/Bray logo appears on the card front. The backs are of simple design, containing only the player's name, uniform number, position and professional record.

		NM/M
Complete Set, Panel:		45.00
Complete Set, Singles (30):		40.00
Common Player:		1.00
2	Alan Wiggins	1.00
3	Bill Ripken	1.00
6	Floyd Rayford	1.00
7	Cal Ripken, Sr.	1.00
8	Cal Ripken, Jr.	25.00
9	Jim Dwyer	1.00
10	Terry Crowley	1.00
15	Terry Kennedy	1.00
16	Scott McGregor	1.00
18	Larry Sheets	1.00
19	Fred Lynn	1.00
20	Frank Robinson	4.00
24	Dave Schmidt	1.00
25	Ray Knight	1.00
27	Lee Lacy	1.00
31	Mark Wiley	1.00
32	Mark Williamson	1.00
33	Eddie Murray	12.50
38	Ken Gerhart	1.00
39	Ken Dixon	1.00
40	Jimmy Williams	1.00
42	Mike Griffin	1.00
43	Mike Young	1.00
44	Elrod Hendricks	1.00
45	Eric Bell	1.00

		(col 2)
46	Mike Flanagan	1.00
49	Tom Niedenfuer	1.00
52	Mike Boddicker	1.00
54	John Habyan	1.00
57	Tony Arnold	1.00

1988 French/Bray Orioles

52 MIKE BODDICKER, RHS
Compliments of
FRENCH/BRAY, INC.

French-Bray sponsored a full-color brochure that was distributed to fans during an in-stadium promotion. A blue and orange front cover features inset photos of the Orioles in action on the upper left in a filmstrip motif. To the right is the Orioles logo and their 1988 slogan, "You Gotta Be There" above a baseball glove and ball. The 3-panel foldout measures approximately 9-1/2" x 11-1/4" and includes a team photo on the inside cover, with two perforated pages of individual cards featuring players, coaches and the team manager. Individual cards measure 2-1/4" x 3-1/8", with close-ups framed in white with an orange accent line. The player name and sponsor logo are printed beneath the photo. The black-and-white backs are numbered by player uniform and provide career stats. Additional copies of the brochure were made available from the Orioles Baseball Store following the free giveaway.

		NM/M
Complete Set, Panel:		70.00
Complete Set, Singles (31):		60.00
Common Player:		1.00
2	Don Buford	1.00
6	Joe Orsulak	1.00
7	Bill Ripken	1.00
8	Cal Ripken, Jr.	40.00
9	Jim Dwyer	1.00
10	Terry Crowley	1.00
12	Mike Morgan	1.00
14	Mickey Tettleton	1.00
15	Terry Kennedy	1.00
17	Pete Stanicek	1.00
18	Larry Sheets	1.00
19	Fred Lynn	1.00
20	Frank Robinson	5.00
23	Ozzie Peraza	1.00
24	Dave Schmidt	1.00
25	Rich Schu	1.00
28	Jim Traber	1.00
31	Herm Starrette	1.00
33	Eddie Murray	15.00
34	Jeff Ballard	1.00
41	Ken Gerhart	1.00
40	Minnie Mendoza	1.00
44	Don Aase	1.00
44	Elrod Hendricks	1.00
47	John Hart	1.00
41	Jose Bautista	1.00
49	Tom Niedenfuer	1.00
52	Mike Boddicker	1.00
53	Jay Tibbs	1.00
88	Rene Gonzales	1.00
---	Team Photo	5.00

1989 French/Bray Orioles

16 PHIL BRADLEY, OF
Compliments of
French-Bray, Incorporated
Wilcox Walter Furlong Paper Co.

This 32-card team set was co-sponsored by French-Bray and the Wilcox Walter Furlong Paper Co., and was distributed as an in-stadium promotion to fans attending the

May 12 game. Smaller than standard size, the cards measure 2-1/4" x 3" and feature a full-color player photo with number, name and position below. The backs, done in black-and-white, include brief player data and complete major and minor league stats.

		NM/M
Complete Set (32):		20.00
Common Player:		.50
3	Bill Ripken	.50
6	Joe Orsulak	.50
7	Cal Ripken, Sr.	.50
8	Cal Ripken, Jr.	15.00
9	Brady Anderson	1.50
10	Steve Finley	.50
11	Craig Worthington	.50
12	Mike Devereaux	.50
14	Mickey Tettleton	.50
15	Randy Milligan	.50
16	Phil Bradley	.50
18	Bob Milacki	.50
19	Larry Sheets	.50
20	Frank Robinson	4.50
21	Mark Thurmond	.50
23	Kevin Hickey	.50
24	Dave Schmidt	.50
28	Jim Traber	.50
29	Jeff Ballard	.50
30	Gregg Olson	.50
31	Al Jackson	.50
32	Mark Williamson	.50
36	Bob Melvin	.50
37	Brian Holton	.50
40	Tom McCraw	.50
42	Pete Harnisch	.50
43	Fransisco Melendez	.50
44	Elrod Hendricks	.50
46	Johnny Oates	.50
48	Jose Bautista	.50
88	Rene Gonzales	.50
---	Sponsor's Card	.50

1992 French's Mustard

In 1992 French's gave away a promotional card with the purchase of its mustard products. Each of the cards displays photographs of two players. The cards, which have team insignias airbrushed out, feature a green border, color photos and the players' statistics on the back.

		NM/M
Complete Set (18):		4.00
Common Card:		.10
1	Jeff Bagwell, Chuck Knoblauch	.50
2	Roger Clemens, Tom Glavine	.65
3	Julio Franco, Terry Pendleton	.10
4	Howard Johnson, Jose Canseco	.35
5	John Smiley, Scott Erickson	.10
6	Bryan Harvey, Lee Smith	.10
7	Kirby Puckett, Barry Bonds	1.00
8	Robin Ventura, Matt Williams	.10
9	Tony Pena, Tom Pagnozzi	.10
10	Benito Santiago, Sandy Alomar, Jr.	.10
11	Don Mattingly, Will Clark	.75
12	Ryne Sandberg, Roberto Alomar	.60
13	Cal Ripken, Jr., Ozzie Smith	1.00
14	Wade Boggs, Chris Sabo	.60
15	Ken Griffey Jr., David Justice	.75
16	Joe Carter, Tony Gwynn	.60
17	Rickey Henderson, Darryl Strawberry	.50
18	Jack Morris, Steve Avery	.10

2003 French's Mustard N.Y. Yankees

This six-card set sponsored by Yankee Stadium's long-time condiments concessionaire was distirubted to fans 14 and under. Produced by Donruss, the standard-sized cards have game-action photos on front with the sponsor's ad message at bottom. Backs have player personal data, career highlights and career stats.

		NM/M
Complete Set (6):		5.00
Common Player:		.25
1	Derek Jeter	4.00
2	Alfonso Soriano	1.00
3	Jorge Posada	.25
4	Jose Contreras	.50
5	Jeff Weaver	.25
6	Steve Karsay	.25
--	Header Card	.05

1983 Fritsch One-Year Winners

Benny Valenzuela

Larry Fritsch Cards continued its series of collector's issues under the banner of "One-Year Winners" with a 64-card color issue in 1983. Most of the player photos featured are unused Topps pictures. As in previous issues, the set features players with short major league careers, few of whom appear on any contemporary baseball card. In the style of 1966 Topps cards, the set has large player photos bordered in white with a diagonal blue strip in an upper corner containing the initials OYW. A blue strip beneath the photo has the player name in black. Backs are in red, black and white with personal data, stats and career highlights.

		NM/M
Complete Set (64):		35.00
Common Player:		2.00
55	Don Prince	2.00
56	Tom Gramly	2.00
57	Roy Heiser	2.00
58	Hank Izquierdo	2.00
59	Rex Johnston	2.00
60	Jack Damaska	2.00
61	John Flavin	2.00
62	John Glenn	2.00
63	Stan Johnson	2.00
64	Don Choate	2.00
65	Bill Kern	2.00
66	Dick Luebke	2.00
67	Glen Clark	2.00
68	Lamar Jacobs	2.00
69	Rick Herrscher	2.00
70	Jim McManus	2.00
71	Len Church	2.00
72	Larry Stubing	2.00
73	Cal Emery	2.00
74	Lee Gregory	2.00
75	Mike Page	2.00
76	Benny Valenzuela	2.00
77	John Papa	2.00
78	Jim Stump	2.00
79	Brian McCall	2.00
80	Al Kenders	2.00
81	Corky Withrow	2.00
82	Verle Tiefenthaler	2.00
83	Dave Wissman	2.00
84	Tom Fletcher	2.00
85	Dale Willis	2.00
86	Larry Foster	2.00
87	Johnnie Seale	2.00
88	Jim Lehew	2.00
89	Charlie Shoemaker	2.00
90	Don Arlick	2.00
91	George Gerberman	2.00
92	John Prenzenger	2.00
93	Merlin Nippert	2.00
94	Steve Demeter	2.00
95	John Paciorek	2.00

		(col 4)
96	Larry Loughlin	2.00
97	Alan Brice	2.00
98	Chet Boak	2.00
99	Alan Koch	2.00
100	Dan Thomas	2.00
101	Elder White	2.00
102	Jim Snyder	2.00
103	Ted Schreiber	2.00
104	Evans Killeen	2.00
105	Ray Daviault	2.00
106	Larry Foss	2.00
107	Wayne Graham	2.00
108	Santiago Rosario	2.00
109	Bob Sprout	2.00
110	Tom Hughes	2.00
111	Em Lindbeck	2.00
112	Ray Blemker	2.00
113	Shaun Fitzmaurice	2.00
114	Ron Stillwell	2.00
115	Carl Thomas	2.00
116	Mike DeGerick	2.00
117	Jay Dahl	2.00
118	Al Lary	2.00

1983 Fritsch 1953 Boston/Milwaukee Braves

This collectors' issue commemorates the 30th anniversary of the move of the Boston Braves to Milwaukee. The black-and-white photos on the front of the cards (bordered in blue) were taken in spring training, with players still wearing Boston caps. Card backs have personal data and detailed career highlights. Cards measure about 2-5/8" x 3-3/4", which was the standard prior to 1957.

		NM/M
Complete Set (33):		8.00
Common Player:		.25
1	Joe Adcock	.35
2	John Antonelli	.25
3	Billy Bruton	.25
4	Bob Buhl	.25
5	Lew Burdette	.35
6	Paul Burris	.25
7	Dave Cole	.25
8	Johnny Cooney	.25
9	Walker Cooper	.25
10	Del Crandall	.35
11	George Crowe	.25
12	Jack Dittmer	.25
13	Dick Donovan	.25
14	Sid Gordon	.25
15	Virgil Jester	.25
16	Ernie Johnson	.25
17	Dave Jolly	.25
18	Billy Klaus	.25
19	Don Liddle	.25
20	Johnny Logan	.25
21	Luis Marquez	.25
21s	Luis Marquez (Sample overprint.)	.25
22	Eddie Mathews	1.00
22s	Eddie Mathews (Sample overprint.)	.25
23	Andy Pafko	.35
24	Jim Pendleton	.25
25	Ebba St. Claire	.25
26	Sibby Sisti	.25
27	Warren Spahn	1.00
28	Max Surkont	.25
29	Bob Thorpe	.25
30	Murray Wall	.25
31	Bucky Walters	.25
32	Jim Wilson	.25
33	1953 Braves Team	.25

1986 Fritsch Negro League BasebAll-Stars

One of the most comprehensive collectors' issues to feature the stars of the Negro Leagues, the Fritsch set features black-and-white photos of varying quality; most of the photos are contemporary with the players' careers from the 1920s into the 1950s, with a few of the segregated leagues' earlier pioneers also included. Fronts are highlighted with red graphics. Backs are printed in blue and present a brief summary

Satchel Paige

of the player's career and a list of the teams on which he played. Cards are in standard 2-1/2" x 3-1/2" format.

		NM/M
Complete Set (119):		15.00
Common Player:		.10
1	Buck Leonard	.15
2	Ted Page	.15
3	Cool Papa Bell	.15
4	Oscar Charleston, Josh Gibson, Ted Page, Judy Johnson	.15
5	Judy Johnson	.15
6	Monte Irvin	.15
7	Ray Dandridge	.15
8	Oscar Charleston	.15
9	Josh Gibson	.15
10	Satchel Paige	.25
10s	Satchel Paige (SAMPLE on back.)	2.50
11	Jackie Robinson	.50
12	Piper Davis	.10
13	Josh Johnson	.10
14	Lou Dials	.10
15	Andy Porter	.10
16	Pop Lloyd	.15
17	Andy Watts	.10
18	Rube Foster	.10
19	Martin Dihigo	.15
20	Lou Dials	.15
21	Satchel Paige	.25
22	Crush Holloway	.10
23	Josh Gibson	.15
24	Oscar Charleston	.15
25	Jackie Robinson	.50
26	Larry Brown	.10
27	Hilton Smith	.15
28	Moses Fleetwood Walker	.25
29	Jimmie Crutchfield	.10
30	Josh Gibson	.15
30s	Josh Gibson (SAMPLE on back.)	2.00
31	Josh Gibson	.15
32	Bullet Rogan	.15
33	Clint Thomas	.10
34	Rats Henderson	.10
35	Pat Scantlebury	.10
36	Sidney Morton	.10
37	Larry Kimbrough	.10
38	Sam Jethroe	.10
39	Normal "Tweed" Webb	.10
40	Mahlon Duckett	.10
41	Andy Anderson	.10
42	Buster Haywood	.10
43	Bob Trice	.10
44	Bus Clarkson	.10
45	Buck O'Neil	.10
46	Jim Zapp	.10
47	Piper Davis	.10
48	Ed Steel	.10
49	Bob Boyd	.10
50	Marlin Carter	.10
51	George Giles	.10
52	Bill Byrd	.10
53	Art Pennington	.10
54	Max Manning	.10
55	Ron Teasley	.10
56	Ziggy Marcell	.10
57	Bill Cash	.10
58	Joe Scott	.10
59	Joe Fillmore	.10
60	Bob Thurman	.10
61	Larry Kimbrough	.10
62	Verdell Mathis	.10
63	Josh Johnson	.10
64	Double Duty Radcliffe	.15
65	William Bobby Robinson	.10
66	Bingo DeMoss	.10
67	John Beckwith	.10
68	Bill Jackman	.10
69	Bill Drake	.10
70	Charles Grant	.15
71	Willie Wells	.25
72	Jose Fernandez	.10
73	Isidro Fabri	.10
74	Frank Austin	.10
75	Richard Lundy	.10
76	Junior Gilliam	.15
77	John Donaldson	.10
78	Herb Dixon	.10
79	Slim Jones	.10
80	Sam Jones	.10
81	Dave Hoskins	.10
82	Jerry Benjamin	.10
83	Luke Easter	.10
84	Ramon Herrera	.10
85	Matthew Carlisle	.10

Negro League Baseball Stars

Satchel Paige

86	Smoky Joe Williams	.25
87	Marv Williams	.10
88	William Yancey	.10
89	Monte Irvin	.15
89s	Monte Irvin (SAMPLE on back.)	1.00
90	Cool Papa Bell	.15
91	Biz Mackey	.25
92	Harry Simpson	.10
93	Lazario Salazar	.10
94	Bill Perkins	.10
95	Johnny Davis	.10
96	Jelly Jackson	.10
97	Sam Bankhead	.10
98	Hank Thompson	.10
99	William Bell	.10
100	Cliff Bell	.10
101	Dave Barnhill	.10
102	Dan Bankhead	.10
103	Lloyd Bassett	.10
104	Newt Allen	.10
105	George Jefferson	.10
106	Pat Paterson	.10
107	Goose Tatum	.15
108	Dave Malarcher	.10
109	Home Run Johnson	.10
110	Bill Monroe	.10
111	Sammy Hughes	.10
112	Dick Redding	.10
113	Fats Jenkins	.10
114	Jimmie Lyons	.10
115	Mule Suttles	.10
116	Ted Trent	.10
117	George Sweatt	.10
118	Frank Duncan	.10
119	Checklist	.05

1991 Front Row Ken Griffey Jr.

Production of this collectors' set and related promo cards was reported at 25,000 sets each. Cards trace the three-year career of Junior in photos, stats, highlights and biographic details. Fronts have various posed and color action photos, complete with team logos, and a white border. Horizontal backs are printed in black on a light blue background. Promo cards have a large "PROMO" printed on a baseball at center. Size is 2-1/2" x 3-1/2".

		NM/M
Complete Set (10):		2.00
Complete Promo Set (5):		1.00
Common Card:		.25
Common Promo:		.25
1	Ken Griffey Jr./AS	.25
1	Ken Griffey Jr./AS (Promo)	.25
2	Ken Griffey Jr. (The Breakdown)	.25
2	Ken Griffey Jr. (The Breakdown)(Promo)	.25
3	Ken Griffey Jr. (Homers)	.25
3	Ken Griffey Jr. (Homers)(Promo)	.25
4	Ken Griffey Jr. (Gold Glv)	.25
4	Ken Griffey Jr. (Gold Glv)(Promo)	.25
5	Ken Griffey Jr. (Drafted)	.25
5	Ken Griffey Jr. (Drafted)(Promo)	.25
6	Ken Griffey Jr. (Up Close and Personal)	.25
7	Ken Griffey Jr. (Background)	.25
8	Ken Griffey Jr. (The Majors)	.25
9	Ken Griffey Jr. (Career Highlights)	.25
10	Ken Griffey Jr. (The American League)	.25

1992-95 Front Row All-Time Great Series

Some of baseball's greatest living former stars were featured in this run of five-card sets. Originally intended to encompass 100 players, the issue was cut considerably short. Each single-player set contains five cards featuring black-and-white and/or color photos on front. Backs have a photo in the

BUCK LEONARD

background, overprinted with statistical, biographical or career information. Major league uniform logos have been removed from photos for lack of licensing by MLB. Each set was issued in an edition of 25,000, with an illustrated, numbered certificate of authenticity included. Each set was also produced with the top card authentically autographed. The Perry and Spahn sets were issued some time after the first 37 players. Sets are checklisted here alphabetically; single cards are not listed because the cards are usually sold only as sets.

		NM/M
Common Player Set:		.25
(1)	Hank Aaron (5-card set)	1.00
(1a)	Hank Aaron/Auto.	40.00
(2)	Ernie Banks (5-card set)	.75
(2a)	Ernie Banks/Auto.	15.00
(3)	Al Barlick (5-card set)	.25
(3a)	Al Barlick/Auto.	25.00
(4)	Johnny Bench (5-card set)	.75
(4a)	Johnny Bench/Auto.)	20.00
(5)	Yogi Berra (5-card set)	.75
(5a)	Yogi Berra/Auto.	20.00
(6)	Lou Boudreau (5-card set)	.25
(6a)	Lou Boudreau/Auto.	16.00
(7)	Lou Brock (5-card set)	.25
(7a)	Lou Brock/Auto.	12.50
(8)	Roy Campanella (5-card set)	.75
(8a)	Roy Campanella/Auto.	150.00
(9)	Rod Carew (5-card set)	.35
(9a)	Rod Carew/Auto.	20.00
(10)	Ray Dandridge (5-card set)	.25
(10a)	Ray Dandridge/Auto.	17.50
(11)	Bobby Doerr (5-card set)	.25
(11a)	Bobby Doerr/Auto.	12.50
(12)	Rick Ferrell (5-card set)	.25
(12a)	Rick Ferrell/Auto.	30.00
(13)	Rollie Fingers (5-card set)	.25
(13a)	Rollie Fingers/Auto.	12.50
(14)	Whitey Ford (5-card set)	.50
(14a)	Whitey Ford/Auto.	22.50
(15)	George Foster (5-card set)	.25
(15a)	George Foster/Auto.	10.00
(16)	Catfish Hunter (5-card set)	.25
(16a)	Catfish Hunter/Auto.	15.00
(17)	Monte Irvin (5-card set)	.25
(17a)	Monte Irvin/Auto.	5.00
(18)	Al Kaline (5-card set)	.50
(18a)	Al Kaline/Auto.15.00 (19)	
(19a)	George Kell (5-card set)	.25
	George Kell/Auto.	12.50
(20)	Ralph Kiner (5-card set)	.25
(20a)	Ralph Kiner/Auto.	30.00
(21)	Don Larsen (5-card set)	.25
(21a)	Don Larsen/Auto.	15.00
(22)	Bob Lemon (5-card set)	.25
(22a)	Bob Lemon/Auto.	25.00
(23)	Buck Leonard (5-card set)	.25
(23a)	Buck Leonard/Auto.	22.50
(23p)	Buck Leonard ("PROMO" on back.)	1.00
(24)	Juan Marichal (5-card set)	.35
(24a)	Juan Marichal/Auto.	15.00
(25)	Joe Morgan (5-card set)	.25
(25a)	Joe Morgan/Auto.	25.00
(26)	Stan Musial (5-card set)	.50
(26a)	Stan Musial/Auto.	40.00
(27)	Hal Newhouser (5-card set)	.25
(27a)	Hal Newhouser/Auto.	15.00
(28)	Jim Palmer (5-card set)	.25
(28a)	Jim Palmer/Auto.	12.50
(29)	Tony Perez (5-card set)	.25
(29a)	Tony Perez/Auto.	12.50
(30)	Gaylord Perry (5-card set)	.25
(30a)	Gaylord Perry/Auto.	12.50
(31)	Pee Wee Reese (5-card set)	.35
(32a)	Pee Wee Reese/Auto.	40.00
(32)	Phil Rizzuto (5-card set)	.50
(32a)	Phil Rizzuto/Auto.	20.00
(33)	Brooks Robinson (5-card set)	.35
(33a)	Brooks Robinson/Auto.	12.50
(34)	Frank Robinson (5-card set)	.35
(34a)	Frank Robinson/Auto.	15.00

(35)	Red Schoendienst (5-card set)	.25
(35a)	Red Schoendienst/Auto.	40.00
(36)	Tom Seaver (5-card set)	.35
(36a)	Tom Seaver/Auto.	17.50
(37)	Warren Spahn (5-card set)	.50
(37a)	Warren Spahn/Auto.	30.00
(38)	Willie Stargell (5-card set)	.25
(38a)	Willie Stargell/Auto.	15.00
(39)	Carl Yastrzemski (5-card set)	.35
(39a)	Carl Yastrzemski/Auto.	30.00

1992 Front Row Club House Series Ken Griffey, Jr.

Ten cards tracing the life and career of Ken Griffey Jr. comprise this collectors' issue. Cards are standard 2-1/2" x 3-1/2" with borderless color action and posed photos. Uniform logos have been removed from the photos since the set is not licensed by MLB. A Club House Series logo is on front at bottom-right. Horizontal backs have a color photo of Griffey ghosted in the background. Printed over that are personal data, career highlights and stats.

		NM/M
Complete Set (10):		1.00
Common Player:		.15
1	Ken Griffey Jr. (Background)	.15
2	Ken Griffey Jr. (Drafted)	.15
3	Ken Griffey Jr. (The Majors)	.15
4	Ken Griffey Jr. (The Breakdown)	.15
5	Ken Griffey Jr. (The American League)	.15
6	Ken Griffey Jr./AS	.15
7	Ken Griffey Jr. (Gold Glv)	.15
8	Ken Griffey Jr. (Homers)	.15
9	Ken Griffey Jr. (Career Highlights)	.15
10	Ken Griffey Jr. (A Closer Look)	.15

1992 Front Row Ken Griffey Jr. Holograms

This set of collectors' edition cards was produced in an issue of 50,000, with each set including a numbered certificate of authenticity. In standard 2-1/2" x 3-1/2" size, the cards have a borderless hologram picture on front. Conventionally printed backs have a color photo of the player and a few sentences about his career. Team logos have been removed from the pictures because the cards were not licensed by MLB.

		NM/M
Complete Set (3):		3.00
Common Card:		1.00
1	Ken Griffey Jr. (Making History)	1.00
2	Ken Griffey Jr. (Rewriting the Record Book)	1.00
3	Ken Griffey Jr. (Turning Up Gold)	1.00

1992 Front Row Ken Griffey Jr. Pure Gold

KEN GRIFFEY, JR.

This set of collectors' edition cards was produced in an issue of 20,000, with each set including a numbered certificate of authenticity. In standard 2-1/2" x 3-1/2" size, the cards have wide gold-foil borders on front. Backs have stats or a few sentences about his career. Team logos have been removed from the pictures because the cards were not licensed by MLB.

		NM/M
Complete Set (3):		3.00
Common Card:		1.00
1	Ken Griffey Jr. (Gold Glv)	1.00
2	Ken Griffey Jr. (Background)	1.00
3	Ken Griffey Jr. (Drafted)	1.00

1992 Front Row Holograms

The "career" seasons of three Hall of Famers are remembered in this series of cards. In standard 2-1/2" x 3-1/2" format, fronts have a borderless hologram featuring a vintage action photo. Conventionally printed backs have a color photo, a recap and stats from the named season, and a foil holographic serial number tag designating the card's place in an edition of 100,000 each.

		NM/M
Complete Set (3):		1.50
Common Player:		.50
(1)	Hank Aaron	.70
(2)	Roy Campanella	.50
(3)	Tom Seaver	.50

1992 Front Row Pure Gold

Each of these 2-1/2" x 3-1/2" cards features 23-K gold borders on front, surrounding a color action photo on which uniform details have been airbrushed away. Backs have player information.

		NM/M
Complete Set (6):		15.00
Common Player:		3.00
(1)	Hank Aaron	3.00
(2)	Roy Campanella	3.00
(3)	Tom Seaver	3.00
	Frank Thomas Strip (3):	10.00
(4)	Frank Thomas/Btg	3.00
(5)	Frank Thomas/Standing	3.00
(6)	Frank Thomas/Fldg	3.00

1992 Front Row Frank Thomas

Budding super slugger Frank Thomas is featured in this collectors' issue. The 2-1/2" x 3-1/2" cards have color photos on front, from which team logos have been airbrushed because the set is licensed only by the player, and not by MLB. Horizontally formatted backs have a second color photo along with a headline and a few sen-

FRANK THOMAS

tences about his career to that point. The set was released in an edition of 30,000 and each was sold with a serial-numbered certificate of authenticity.

		NM/M
Complete Set (7):		3.00
Common Card:		.50
Autographed (# to 4,000):		15.00
1	Frank Thomas (A Good Start)	.50
nno	Frank Thomas (A Good Start-promo overprint on back.)	.50
2	Frank Thomas (Multi-Talented)	.50
3	Frank Thomas (Auburn Career)	.50
4	Frank Thomas (Accomplishments)	.50
5	Frank Thomas (Individual Honors)	.50
6	Frank Thomas (Minor League Stats)	.50
7	Frank Thomas (Major League Stats)	.50

1993 Front Row Gold Collection

Rollie Fingers

Five borderless color photos (uniform logos removed) of Rollie Fingers are featured on the cards in this set. At bottom in a dark green stripe is the player name and, at left, the Front Row logo and the word "PREMIUM." Vertically at left is "The Gold Collection." All front printing is in gold foil. Backs have dark green borders with a ghost-image action photo and a few sentences about the player. A baseball at top carries the legend, "All Time Great / Series." Production was reported as 5,000 sets.

		NM/M
Complete Set (5):		2.00
Common Card:		.50
1-5	Rollie Fingers	.50

1999 FroZsnack's High-Screamers Lids

KERRY WOOD

These 3-1/4" plastic lids were found on ice cream snacks sold at ballparks and possibly other outlets. A player photo with uniform logos covered is featured at center with personal data and 1998 stats on the side. The player name is in

a banner at top, his team, position and career highlights are in a banner at bottom.

		NM/M
Complete Set (40):		30.00
Common Player:		.75
(1)	Roberto Alomar	.75
(2)	Jeff Bagwell	1.25
(3)	Albert Belle	.75
(4)	Dante Bichette	.75
(5)	Craig Biggio	.75
(6)	Barry Bonds	2.50
(7)	Kevin Brown	.75
(8)	Jose Canseco	1.00
(9)	Vinny Castilla	.75
(10)	Tony Clark	.75
(11)	Francisco Cordova	.75
(12)	Eric Davis	.75
(13)	Nomar Garciaparra	1.75
(14)	Tom Glavine	1.00
(15)	Ben Grieve	.75
(16)	Ken Griffey Jr.	2.00
(17)	Tony Gwynn	1.50
(18)	Rickey Henderson	1.25
(19)	Livan Hernandez	.75
(20)	Derek Jeter	2.50
(21)	Jason Kendall	.75
(22)	Randy Johnson	1.25
(23)	Barry Larkin	.75
(24)	Greg Maddux	1.50
(25)	Tino Martinez	.75
(26)	Mark McGwire	2.25
(27)	Robb Nen	.75
(28)	Mike Piazza	2.00
(29)	Manny Ramirez	1.25
(30)	Cal Ripken Jr.	2.50
(31)	Alex Rodriguez	2.25
(32)	Scott Rolen	1.00
(33)	Sammy Sosa	1.75
(34)	Frank Thomas	1.25
(35)	Greg Vaughn	.75
(36)	Fernando Vina	.75
(37)	Omar Vizquel	.75
(38)	Larry Walker	.75
(39)	Matt Williams	.75
(40)	Kerry Wood	1.00

1998 Fruit Roll-Ups All-Stars

Perforated panels of eight small (1-1/2" x 2") cards bearing the Topps logo were found on 38-count boxes of Fruit Roll-Ups snacks early in the 1998 season. The blank-back cards are printed on a 6" x 4" panel which can be removed from the box back. The front of the box pictures Rodriguez, Thomas and McGwire.

		NM/M
Complete Box:		5.00
Complete Panel:		4.00
Complete Set, Singles (8):		3.50
Common Player:		.50
(1)	Tony Gwynn	1.00
(2)	Derek Jeter	1.50
(3)	Kenny Lofton	.50
(4)	Mark McGwire	1.25
(5)	Mike Piazza	1.25
(6)	Cal Ripken Jr.	1.50
(7)	Ivan Rodriguez	.65
(8)	Frank Thomas	.75

1985 Fun Food Buttons

DWIGHT GOODEN
NEW YORK METS

Fun Foods of Little Silver, N.J., issued a set of 133 full-color metal pins in 1985. The buttons, which are 1-1/4" in diameter and have a "safety pin" back, have bright borders which correspond to the player's team colors. The button backs are numbered and contain the player's 1984 batting or earned run average. The buttons were available as complete sets through hobby dealers and were also distributed in packs of three through retail stores.

Cardboard 1-1/2" x 1-1/2" square proofs of the buttons' fronts are also seen in the hobby; their value is 2-3X that of the corresponding button, with production reported to be only 2,000 cardboard proofs.

		NM/M
Complete Set (133):		20.00
Common Player:		.10
Wax Pack (3):		.50
Wax Box (36):		9.00
1	Dave Winfield	1.00
2	Lance Parrish	.10
3	Gary Carter	1.00
4	Pete Rose	2.00
5	Jim Rice	.35
6	George Brett	1.75
7	Fernando Valenzuela	.10
8	Darryl Strawberry	.10
9	Steve Garvey	.45
10	Rollie Fingers	.75
11	Mike Schmidt	1.75
12	Kent Tekulve	.10
13	Ryne Sandberg	1.50
14	Bruce Sutter	.75
15	Tom Seaver	1.00
16	Reggie Jackson	1.50
17	Rickey Henderson	1.00
18	Mark Langston	.10
19	Jack Clark	.10
20	Willie Randolph	.10
21	Kirk Gibson	.10
22	Andre Dawson	.35
23	Dave Concepcion	.10
24	Tony Armas	.10
25	Dan Quisenberry	.10
26	Pedro Guerrero	.10
27	Dwight Gooden	.10
28	Tony Gwynn	1.50
29	Robin Yount	1.00
30	Steve Carlton	1.00
31	Bill Madlock	.10
32	Rick Sutcliffe	.10
33	Willie McGee	.10
34	Greg Luzinski	.10
35	Rod Carew	1.00
36	Dave Kingman	.10
37	Alvin Davis	.10
38	Chili Davis	.10
39	Don Baylor	.10
40	Alan Trammell	.10
41	Tim Raines	.10
42	Cesar Cedeno	.10
43	Wade Boggs	1.50
44	Frank White	.10
45	Steve Sax	.10
46	George Foster	.10
47	Terry Kennedy	.10
48	Cecil Cooper	.10
49	John Denny	.10
50	John Candelaria	.10
51	Jody Davis	.10
52	George Hendrick	.10
53	Ron Kittle	.10
54	Fred Lynn	.10
55	Carney Lansford	.10
56	Gorman Thomas	.10
57	Manny Trillo	.10
58	Steve Kemp	.10
59	Jack Morris	.10
60	Dan Petry	.10
61	Mario Soto	.10
62	Dwight Evans	.10
63	Hal McRae	.10
64	Mike Marshall	.10
65	Mookie Wilson	.10
66	Graig Nettles	.10
67	Ben Oglivie	.10
68	Juan Samuel	.10
69	Johnny Ray	.10
70	Gary Matthews	.10
71	Ozzie Smith	1.50
72	Carlton Fisk	1.00
73	Doug DeCinces	.10
74	Joe Morgan	1.00
75	Dave Stieb	.10
76	Buddy Bell	.10
77	Don Mattingly	1.75
78	Lou Whitaker	.10
79	Willie Hernandez	.10
80	Dave Parker	.10
81	Bob Stanley	.10
82	Willie Wilson	.10
83	Orel Hershiser	.10
84	Rusty Staub	.10
85	Goose Gossage	.10
86	Don Sutton	.75
87	Al Holland	.10
88	Tony Pena	.10
89	Ron Cey	.10
90	Joaquin Andujar	.10
91	LaMarr Hoyt	.10
92	Tommy John	.10
93	Dwayne Murphy	.10
94	Willie Upshaw	.10
95	Gary Ward	.10
96	Ron Guidry	.10
97	Chet Lemon	.10
98	Aurelio Lopez	.10
99	Tony Perez	.75
100	Bill Buckner	.10
101	Mike Hargrove	.10
102	Scott McGregor	.10
103	Dale Murphy	.50
104	Keith Hernandez	.10
105	Paul Molitor	1.00
106	Bert Blyleven	.10
107	Leon Durham	.10
108	Lee Smith	.10
109	Nolan Ryan	3.00
110	Harold Baines	.10
111	Kent Hrbek	.10
112	Ron Davis	.10
113	George Bell	.10
114	Charlie Hough	.10
115	Phil Niekro	.75
116	Dave Righetti	.10
117	Darrell Evans	.10
118	Cal Ripken, Jr.	3.00
119	Eddie Murray	1.00
120	Storm Davis	.10
121	Mike Boddicker	.10
122	Bob Horner	.10
123	Chris Chambliss	.10
124	Ted Simmons	.10
125	Andre Thornton	.10
126	Larry Bowa	.10
127	Bob Dernier	.10
128	Joe Niekro	.10
129	Jose Cruz	.10
130	Tom Brunansky	.10
131a	Garry Gaetti	50.00
131b	Gary Gaetti	.10
132	Lloyd Moseby	.10
133	Frank Tanana	.10

G

1982 Renata Galasso 20 Years of Met Baseball

RICHIE ASHBURN
OUTFIELDER

The original New York Mets team of 1962 is featured on this 20-year anniversary set. The 2-1/2" x 3-1/2" cards have black-and-white photos with blue borders. The player name and position is in orange at bottom. Backs repeat the team colors with blue and orange printing on white cardboard. Card and uniform numbers appear in the top corners, there is a career summary, 1962 and career stats and a trivia question. Production was reported as 2,500 sets.

		NM/M
Complete Set (30):		10.00
Common Player:		.50
1	Marv Throneberry	.75
2	Richie Ashburn	2.00
3	Charlie Neal	.50
4	Cliff Cook	.50
5	Elio Chacon	.50
6	Chris Cannizzaro	.50
7	Jim Hickman	.50
8	Rod Kanehl	.50
9	Gene Woodling	.50
10	Gil Hodges	2.00
11	Al Jackson	.50
12	Sammy Taylor	.50
13	Felix Mantilla	.50
14	Ken MacKenzie	.50
15	Craig Anderson	.50
16	Bob Moorhead	.50
17	Joe Christopher	.50
18	Bob Miller	.50
19	Frank Thomas	.75
20	Vinegar Bend Mizell	.50
21	Bill Hunter	.50
22	Roger Craig	.50
23	Jay Hook	.50
24	Meet The Mets (Team card.)	.75
25	Choo Choo Coleman	.50
26	Casey Stengel	2.00
27	Solly Hemus	.50
28	Rogers Hornsby	2.00
29	Red Ruffing	.50
30	George Weiss	.50

1983 Renata Galasso 1933 All-Stars

The premiere All-Star Game in 1933 is commemorated in this 50th anniversary collectors' issue. In standard 2-1/2" x 3-1/2" format (though not uniformly cut to exact

CHUCK KLEIN
OUTFIELDER — NATIONAL LEAGUE

size), the cards feature black-and-white portrait photos on front. Many of the National League All-Stars are pictured in their special NL uniforms. In the wide white border at bottom is the player's name, position and league. Backs are printed in red, white and blue with a large Galasso ad and a short career summary; there is little mention of the 1933 All-Star Game. Two unnumbered cards issued with the set have N.L. and A.L. team photos on front and blue-tone backs showing A-S managers Connie Mack and John McGraw "choosing up sides."

		NM/M
Complete Set (45):		15.00
Common Player:		1.00
1	Tony Cuccinello	1.00
2	Lon Warenke (Warneke)	1.00
3	Hal Schumacher	1.00
4	Wally Berger	1.00
5	Lefty O'Doul	1.00
6	Chuck Klein	1.00
7	Chick Hafey	1.00
8	Jimmie Wilson	1.00
9	John McGraw	1.00
10	Max Carey	1.00
11	Bill McKechnie	1.00
12	Dick Bartell	1.00
13	Bill Hallahan	1.00
14	Woody English	1.00
15	Paul Waner	1.00
16	Carl Hubbell	1.50
17	Frank Frisch	1.00
18	Gabby Hartnett	1.00
19	Pie Traynor	1.00
20	Bill Terry	1.00
21	Pepper Martin	1.00
22	Earl Averill	1.00
23	Jimmy Dykes	1.00
24	Charlie Gehringer	1.50
25	Rich Ferrell (Rick)	1.00
26	Joe Cronin	1.00
27	Ben Chapman	1.00
28	Eddie Rommel	1.00
29	Lefty Grove	1.50
30	Connie Mack	1.00
31	Babe Ruth	5.00
32	Sam West	1.00
33	Tony Lazzeri	1.00
34	Al Simmons	1.00
35	Wes Ferrell	1.00
36	Bill Dickey	1.00
37	General Crowder	1.00
38	Oral Hildebrand	1.00
39	Lefty Gomez	1.00
40	Jimmie Foxx	1.50
41	Art Fletcher	1.00
42	Eddie Collins	1.00
43	Lou Gehrig	3.00
(44)	1933 N.L. All-Star Team	2.00
(45)	1933 A.L. All-Star Team	2.00

1983 Renata Galasso 1969 Seattle Pilots

JIM BOUTON
PITCHER

The one-year American League franchise in Seattle is recalled with this collectors' issue. Full-color photos of the peripatetic Pilots are framed in team-color blue and gold on a beige background in standard 2-1/2" x 3-1/2" size. Backs

are printed in red and blue on white and feature a career summary and 1969 stats. For some players, this represents their only baseball card appearance and for many more, it is their only card in a Pilots' uniform. Many of the sets were originally sold with the #1 Jim Bouton card personally autographed.

		NM/M
Complete Set (43):		15.00
Common Player:		.50
1	Jim Bouton	2.00
1(a)	Jim Bouton/Auto.	15.00
2	Joe Schultz	.50
3	Bill Edgerton	.70
4	Gary Timberlake	.70
5	Dick Baney	.50
6	Mike G. Marshall	1.00
7	Jim Gosger	.50
8	Mike Hegan	.50
9	Steve Hovley	.50
10	Don Mincher	.50
11	Miguel Fuentes	.50
12	Charlie Bates	.50
13	John O'Donoghue	.50
14	Tommy Davis	.75
15	Jerry McNertney	.50
16	Rich Rollins	.50
17	Fred Talbot	.50
18	John Gelnar	.50
19	Bob Locker	.50
20	Frank Crosetti	.75
21	Sal Maglie	.75
22	Sibby Sisti	.50
23	Ron Plaza	.50
24	Federico Velazquez	.50
25	Diego Segui	.50
26	Steve Barber	.50
27	Jack Aker	.50
28	Marty Pattin	.50
29	Ray Oyler	.50
30	Danny Walton	.75
31	Merritt Ranew	.50
32	John Donaldson	.50
33	Greg Goossen	.50
34	Gary Bell	.50
35	Jim Pagliaroni	.50
36	Mike Ferraro	.50
37	Tommy Harper	.75
38	John Morris	.50
39	Larry Haney	.50
40	Ron Clark	.50
41	Steve Whitaker	.50
42	Wayne Comer	.50
43	Gene Brabender	.50

1984 Renata Galasso Baseball Collector Series

Some of baseball's best are presented in this glossy-front black-and-white, 2-3/8" x 3-1/2", collectors' set, patterned after the 1953 Bowmans. Backs are in red and black with a career summary and lifetime stats.

		NM/M
Complete Set (20):		15.00
Common Player:		.50
1	Roberto Clemente	1.50
2	Duke Snider	.75
3	Sandy Koufax	1.50
4	Carl Hubbell	.50
5	Ty Cobb	1.00
6	Willie Mays	1.50
7	Jackie Robinson	1.50
8	Joe DiMaggio	3.00
9	Stan Musial	1.00
10	Pie Traynor	.50
11	Yogi Berra	.75
12	Babe Ruth	3.00
13	Brooks Robinson	.50
14	Walter Johnson	.50
15	Ted Williams	1.50
16	Bill Dickey	.50
17	Lou Gehrig	2.00
18	Hank Aaron	1.50
19	Eddie Mathews	.50
20	Mickey Mantle	5.00

Hall of Fame Art Card Series

Painting on these 2-7/8" x 5" deckle-edge cards are by Ron Lewis and depict Hall of Famers induction between 1936-46. There are no graphics or player identification on the front. Backs are printed in red and black and have player personal data, career highlights and lifetime stats within a decorative shield.

		NM/M
Complete Set (45):		15.00
Common Player:		.50
1	Ty Cobb	3.00
2	Babe Ruth	5.00
3	Walter Johnson	1.50
4	Christy Mathewson	1.50
5	Honus Wagner	1.50
6	Napoleon Lajoie	.75
7	Tris Speaker	.75
8	Cy Young	1.50
9	Morgan Bulkeley	.50
10	Ban Johnson	.50
11	John McGraw	.50
12	Connie Mack	.50
13	George Wright	.50
14	Grover Alexander	1.00
15	Alexander Cartwright	.50
16	Henry Chadwick	.50
17	Eddie Collins	.50
18	Lou Gehrig	4.00
19	Willie Keeler	.50
20	George Sisler	.50
21	Cap Anson	.50
22	Charles Comiskey	.50
23	Candy Cummings	.50
24	Buck Ewing	.50
25	Charlie Radbourne	.50
26	A.G. Spalding	.50
27	Roger (Rogers) Hornsby	.75
28	Kenesaw M. Landis	.50
29	Roger Bresnahan	.50
30	Dan Brouthers	.50
31	Fred Clarke	.50
32	Jimmy Collins	.50
33	Ed Delahanty	.50
34	Hugh Duffy	.50
35	Mike "King" Kelly	.50
36	Hughie Jennings	.50
37	Jim O'Rourke	.50
38	Wilbert Robinson	.50
39	Jesse Burkett	.50
40	Frank Chance	.50
41	Jack Chesbro	.50
42	Johnny Evers	.50
43	Joe Tinker	.50
44	Eddie Plank	.50
45	Checklist	.50

Reggie Jackson

This collectors' issue chronicling the career of "Mr. October" was produced in two sizes - the standard 2-1/2" x 3-1/2" and the Topps' "mini" format of 2-1/4" x 3-1/8". Both sizes share the same design of a color or black-and-white photo on a blue border with "Reggie 44" at bottom, along with a photo of his classic swing. Backs have statistical

data, career summary or part of a puzzle showing all of Jackson's Topps cards to that point. The full-size set was limited to 10,000, with 500 featuring a genuine autograph on card #1; the mini set was issued in an edition of 5,000.

	NM/M
Complete Standard-Size Set (30):	7.50
Complete Set w/Auto. #1:	45.00
Complete Mini Set (30):	10.00
Common Card:	.40

Willie Mays Story

Color and black-and-white photos from the Hall of Famer's career and off-field life are featured in this collectors' set. Each photo is surrounded by a red frame and white border. Many of the photos will be familiar to collectors as having earlier appeared on Topps cards. Backs of the first 45 cards are in red, black and white, with biographical information or a description of the front photo. Backs of cards #46-90 can be assembled into a full-color puzzle of Mays' baseball cards from Topps, Bowman and others. Card #1 in each set is authentically autographed by Mays. Retail price at issue was $20.

	NM/M
Complete Set (90):	35.00
Common Card:	.50

1927 N.Y. Yankees

Paintings by Ron Lewis adorn this collectors' issue honoring what may have been baseball's best team ever. The 2-1/2" x 3-1/2" cards have blue borders with the player's name in a banner at bottom. Backs have typical player data plus 1927 and career stats. The set was originally issued at about $5.

		NM/M
Complete Set (30):		18.00
Common Player:		.50
1	Lou Gehrig	5.00
2	Babe Ruth	7.50
3	Earle Combs	1.00
4	Ed Barrow	.50
5	Bob Shawkey	.50
6	Bob Meusel	.50
7	Urban Shocker	.50
8	Ben Paschal	.50
9	John Grabowski	.50
10	Jacob Ruppert	.50
11	Herb Pennock	1.00
12	Miller Huggins	1.00
13	Wilcy Moore	.50
14	Walter Beall	.50
15	Cedric Durst	.50
16	Tony Lazzeri	1.00
17	Mark Koenig	.50
18	Waite Hoyt	1.00
19	Myles Thomas	.50
20	Joe Dugan	.50
21	Art Fletcher	.50
22	Charlie O'Leary	.50
23	Ray Morehart	.50
24	Benny Bengough	.50
25	Pat Collins	.50
26	Dutch Reuther (Ruether)	.50
27	George Pipgras	.50
28	Mike Gazella	.50
29	Julian Wera	.50
30	Joe Giard	.50

1985 Renata Galasso Dwight Gooden

This collectors' issue was produced by Brooklyn dealer Renata Galasso as one of several to capitalize on Gooden's early fame. Card #1 features a Ron Lewis painting of Gooden, the others feature color photos from his boyhood and early career.

(Card #16 pictures him shaking hands with Henry Aaron.) Photos are surrounded on front with a border of blue squares. A pink "DR. K" logo is at bottom-right. Backs are in blue and white and feature a question and answer session with the pitcher, stats, or part of a nine-piece puzzle. Five thousand sets were produced, with 500 of them featuring Gooden's autograph on Card #1. Issue price was about $11.

	NM/M
Complete Set (30):	4.00
Complete Autographed Set:	15.00
Single Card:	.15

1986 Renata Galasso Dwight Gooden

Dr. K's Cy Young Season in 1985 is recalled in this collectors' set. Numbered from 31-60, picking up where the 1985 set had left off, the series share a similar format. Fronts have black-and-white or color photos surrounded by a frame of blue dots and larger orange squares. A blue "Dr. K" appears in the lower-right corner. Backs are in blue and orange on white and narrate the 1985 season. The final nine cards in the set have pieces forming a puzzle picture of Gooden.

	NM/M
Complete Set (30):	4.00
Single Card:	.15

Don Mattingly

The life and career of the Yankees superstar is traced in this collectors' issue. The 2-1/2" x 3-1/2" cards have a mix of black-and-white and color photos on a white background with blue pinstripes. A yellow circle in a bottom corner of each card front has "THE HIT MAN" in red. Backs are printed in blue, with 21 of them featuring a question-and-answer format and nine forming a puzzle picture of Mattingly.

	NM/M
Complete Set (30):	6.00
Single Card:	.50

1986 Renata Galasso 1961 Yankees Black-and-White

Illustrating one of the problems with collectors' issues, a person holding one of these cards might assume it is of 1961 or 1962 vintage because there is no date of actual issue, which occurred around 1986, anywhere on the cards. In a format similar to Topps' 1961 cards, this set features large black-and-white player photos on a 2-1/2" x 3-1/2" glossy stock. The player name and position are in a pair of color bars at bottom. Backs are in red and black and have personal data, season and career stats, a 1961 season summary and a trivia question. Reported production was 2,500.

	NM/M
Complete Set (30):	20.00
Common Player:	.50
1 Roger Maris	3.00
2 Bobby Richardson	.75
3 Tony Kubek	.75
4 Elston Howard	.75
5 Bill Skowron	.75
6 Clete Boyer	.50
7 Mickey Mantle	7.50
8 Yogi Berra	2.00
9 Johnny Blanchard	.50
10 Hector Lopez	.50
11 Whitey Ford	2.00
12 Ralph Terry	.50
13 Bill Stafford	.50
14 Bud Daley	.50
15 Billy Gardner	.50
16 Jim Coates	.50
17 Luis Arroyo	.50
18 Tex Clevenger	.50
19 Bob Cerv	.50
20 Art Ditmar	.50
21 Bob Turley	.50
22 Joe DeMaestri	.50
23 Rollie Sheldon	.50
24 Earl Torgeson	.50
25 Hal Reniff	.50
26 Ralph Houk	.50
27 Jim Hegan	.50
28 Johnny Sain	.60
29 Frank Crosetti	.50
30 Wally Moses	.50

1961 Yankees Color

The World Champion N.Y. Yankees of 1961 are remembered in this collectors' set. The 2-1/2" x 3-1/2" cards borrow the design of Topps' 1961 issue, with a large color photo at top and red and yellow boxes below with player name and position in contrasting color. Backs are printed in blue and red with a few biographical details, 1961 and career stats and a career summary.

	NM/M
Complete Set (37):	15.00
Common Player:	.25

1	Roger Maris	3.00
2	Yogi Berra	1.50
3	Whitey Ford	1.50
4	Hector Lopez	.25
5	Bob Turley	.25
6	Frank Crosetti	.25
7	Bob Cerv	.25
8	Jack Reed	.25
9	Luis Arroyo	.25
10	Danny McDevitt	.25
11	Duke Maas	.25
12	Jesse Gonder	.25
13	Ralph Terry	.25
14	Deron Johnson	.25
15	Johnny Blanchard	.25
16	Bill Stafford	.25
17	Earl Torgeson	.25
18	Tony Kubek	.40
19	Rollie Sheldon	.25
20	Tex Clevenger	.25
21	Art Ditmar	.25
22	Bud Daley	.25
23	Jim Coates	.25
24	Al Downing	.25
25	Johnny Sain	.25
26	Jim Hegan	.25
27	Wally Moses	.25
28	Ralph Houk	.25
29	Bill Skowron	.40
30	Bobby Richardson	.40
31	Johnny James	.25
32	Hal Reniff	.25
33	Mickey Mantle	6.00
34	Clete Boyer	.25
35	Elston Howard	.35
36	Joe DeMaestri	.25
37	Billy Gardner	.25

1983 Gardner's Brewers

Topps produced in 1983 for Gardner's Bakery of Madison Wis., a 22-card set featuring the American League champion Milwaukee Brewers. The cards, which measure 2-1/2" x 3-1/2", have colorful fronts which contain the player's name, team and position plus the Brewers and Gardner's logos. The card backs are identical to the regular Topps issue but are numbered 1-22. The cards were inserted in specially marked packages of Gardner's bread products and were susceptible to grease stains.

	NM/M
Complete Set (22):	8.00
Common Player:	.25
1 Harvey Kuenn	.25
2 Dwight Bernard	.25
3 Mark Brouhard	.25
4 Mike Caldwell	.25
5 Cecil Cooper	.25
6 Marshall Edwards	.25
7 Rollie Fingers	1.00
8 Jim Gantner	.25
9 Moose Haas	.25
10 Bob McClure	.25
11 Paul Molitor	4.00
12 Don Money	.25
13 Charlie Moore	.25
14 Ben Oglivie	.25
15 Ed Romero	.25
16 Ted Simmons	.25
17 Jim Slaton	.25
18 Don Sutton	1.00
19 Gorman Thomas	.25
20 Pete Vuckovich	.25
21 Ned Yost	.25
22 Robin Yount	3.00

1984 Gardner's Brewers

For the second straight year, Gardner's Bakery inserted baseball cards featuring the Milwaukee Brewers with its bread products. The 22-card set, entitled "1984 Series II," have multi-colored fronts that include the Brewers and Gardner's logos. The card backs are identical to the regular 1984 Topps issue except for the 1-22 numbering system. The Topps-produced cards are the standard 2-1/2" x 3-1/2" size. The

cards are sometimes found with grease stains, resulting from contact with the bread.

	NM/M
Complete Set (22):	5.00
Common Player:	.25
1 Rene Lachemann	.25
2 Mark Brouhard	.25
3 Mike Caldwell	.25
4 Bobby Clark	.25
5 Cecil Cooper	.25
6 Rollie Fingers	.50
7 Jim Gantner	.25
8 Moose Haas	.25
9 Roy Howell	.25
10 Pete Ladd	.25
11 Rick Manning	.25
12 Bob McClure	.25
13 Paul Molitor	3.00
14 Charlie Moore	.25
15 Ben Oglivie	.25
16 Ed Romero	.25
17 Ted Simmons	.25
18 Jim Sundberg	.25
19 Don Sutton	.50
20 Tom Tellmann	.25
21 Pete Vuckovich	.25
22 Robin Yount	3.00

1985 Gardner's Brewers

Gardner's Bakery issued a 22-card set featuring the Milwaukee Brewers for the third consecutive year in 1985. The set was produced by Topps and is designed in a horizontal format. The card fronts feature color photos inside blue, red and yellow frames. The player's name and position are placed in orange boxes to the right of the photo and are accompanied by the Brewers and Gardner's logos. The card backs are identical to the regular 1985 Topps set but are blue rather than green and are numbered 1-22. The cards, which were inserted in specially marked bread products, are often found with grease stains.

	NM/M
Complete Set (22):	5.00
Common Player:	.25
1 George Bamberger	.25
2 Mark Brouhard	.25
3 Bob Clark	.25
4 Jaime Cocanower	.25
5 Cecil Cooper	.25
6 Rollie Fingers	.50
7 Jim Gantner	.25
8 Moose Haas	.25
9 Dion James	.25
10 Pete Ladd	.25
11 Rick Manning	.25
12 Bob McClure	.25
13 Paul Molitor	3.00
14 Charlie Moore	.25
15 Ben Oglivie	.25
16 Chuck Porter	.25
17 Ed Romero	.25
18 Bill Schroeder	.25
19 Ted Simmons	.25
20 Tom Tellmann	.25
21 Pete Vuckovich	.25
22 Robin Yount	3.00

1989 Gardner's Brewers

Returning after a three-year hiatus, Gardner's Bread of Madison, Wis., issued a 15-card Milwaukee Brewers set in 1989. The blue and white-bordered cards are the standard size and feature posed portrait photos with all Brewer logos air-

brushed from the players' caps. The Gardner's logo appears at the top of the card, while the player's name is below the photo. The set, which was produced in conjunction with Mike Schechter Associates, was issued with loaves of bread or packages of buns, one card per package.

	NM/M
Complete Set (15):	5.00
Common Player:	.25
1 Paul Molitor	2.50
2 Robin Yount	2.50
3 Jim Gantner	.25
4 Rob Deer	.25
5 B.J. Surhoff	.25
6 Dale Sveum	.25
7 Ted Higuera	.25
8 Dan Plesac	.25
9 Bill Wegman	.25
10 Juan Nieves	.25
11 Greg Brock	.25
12 Glenn Braggs	.25
13 Joey Meyer	.25
14 Ernest Riles	.25
15 Don August	.25

1986 Gatorade Cubs

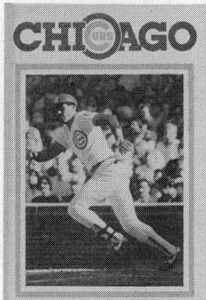

(19) MANNY TRILLO, IF

Gatorade sponsored this set which was given away at the July 17, 1986, Cubs game. Cards measure 2-7/8" x 4-1/4" and feature color photos inside red and white frames. The Cubs logo appears at the top of the card. Backs include statistical information and the Gatorade logo. This set marked the fifth consecutive year the Cubs had held a baseball card giveaway promotion.

	NM/M
Complete Set (28):	12.00
Common Player:	.25
1 Gene Michael	.25
6 Keith Moreland	.25
9 Jody Davis	.25
10 Leon Durham	.25
11 Ron Cey	.25
12 Shawon Dunston	.25
15 Davey Lopes	.25
16 Terry Francona	.25
18 Steve Christmas	.25
19 Manny Trillo	.25
20 Bob Dernier	.25
21 Scott Sanderson	.25
22 Jerry Mumphrey	.25
23 Ryne Sandberg	9.00
27 Thad Bosley	.25
28 Chris Speier	.25
29 Steve Lake	.25
31 Ray Fontenot	.25
34 Steve Trout	.25
36 Gary Matthews	.25
39 George Frazier	.25
40 Rick Sutcliffe	.25
43 Dennis Eckersley	1.50
46 Lee Smith	.35
48 Jay Baller	.25
49 Jamie Moyer	.25
52 Guy Hoffman	.25

The Coaching Staff (Ruben Amaro, Billy Connors, Johnny Oates, John Vukovich, Billy Williams) .25

1987 Gatorade Indians

(28) CORY SNYDER, IF   COMPLIMENTS OF Gatorade

For the second year in a row, the Indians gave out a perforated set of baseball cards to fans attending the Team Photo/Baseball Card Day promotion. Sponsored by Gatorade, the individual cards measure 2-1/2" x 3-1/8". Fronts contain a color photo surrounded by a red frame inside a white border. The player's name, uniform number and the Gatorade logo are also on front. Backs are printed in black, blue and red and carry a facsimile autograph and the player's stats.

	NM/M
Complete Set, Foldout:	6.00
Complete Set, Singles (31):	6.00
Common Player:	.25
2 Brett Butler	.25
4 Tony Bernazard	.25
6 Andy Allanson	.25
7 Pat Corrales	.25
8 Carmen Castillo	.25
10 Pat Tabler	.25
11 Jamie Easterly	.25
12 Dave Clark	.25
13 Ernie Camacho	.25
14 Julio Franco	.35
17 Junior Noboa	.25
18 Ken Schrom	.25
20 Otis Nixon	.25
21 Greg Swindell	.25
22 Frank Wills	.25
23 Chris Bando	.25
24 Rick Dempsey	.25
26 Brook Jacoby	.25
27 Mel Hall	.25
28 Cory Snyder	.25
29 Andre Thornton	.35
30 Joe Carter	.75
35 Phil Niekro	.75
36 Ed Vande Berg	.25
42 Rich Yett	.25
43 Scott Bailes	.25
46 Doug Jones	.25
49 Tom Candiotti	.25
54 Tom Waddell	.25
Manager and Coaching Staff (Jack Aker, Bobby Bonds, Pat Corrales, Doc Edwards, Johnny Goryl)	.25
--- Team Photo	

1988 Gatorade Indians

(52) JOHN FARRELL, P   COMPLIMENTS OF Gatorade

This three-panel foldout was sponsored by Gatorade for distribution during an in-stadium giveaway. The cover includes four game-action photos. One panel of the 9-1/2" x 11-1/4" glossy color foldout features a team photo (with checklist), two panels consist of 30 perforated baseball cards (2-1/4" x 3") featuring team members. Posed portrait photos are framed in red on a white background. The player's name and uniform number are printed below the photo. Backs are printed in red, blue and black. A facsimile autograph appears at the top-right of the card back, opposite the player uniform number, name and position. Both major and minor league stats are listed.

		NM/M
Complete Set, Foldout:		5.00
Complete Set, Singles (31):		5.00
Common Player:		.25
2	Tom Spencer	.25
6	Andy Allanson	.25
7	Luis Issac	.25
8	Carmen Castillo	.25
9	Charlie Manuel	.25
10	Pat Tabler	.25
11	Doug Jones	.25
14	Julio Franco	.50
15	Ron Washington	.25
16	Jay Bell	.75
17	Bill Laskey	.25
20	Willie Upshaw	.25
21	Greg Swindell	.25
23	Chris Bando	.25
25	Dave Clark	.25
26	Brook Jacoby	.25
27	Mel Hall	.25
28	Cory Snyder	.25
30	Joe Carter	.75
31	Dan Schatzeder	.25
32	Doc Edwards	.25
33	Ron Kittle	.25
35	Mark Wiley	.25
42	Rich Yett	.25
43	Scott Bailes	.25
45	Johnny Goryl	.25
47	Jeff Kaiser	.25
49	Tom Candiotti	.25
50	Jeff Dedmon	.25
52	John Farrell	.25
---	Team Photo	2.00

1993 Gatorade Detroit Tigers

Color action photos are featured on these oversized (2-7/8" x 4-1/4") cards. The pictures are framed in team-color navy and orange pinstripes with a white border. Player name is in white in a navy border below the photo, with the position printed in orange at bottom. A large team logo appears in the upper-right corner. Backs are printed in orange and black and include a Gatorade logo, player identification and stats. Cards are listed here by uniform number.

		NM/M
Complete Set (28):		4.00
Common Player:		.25
1	Lou Whitaker	.75
3	Alan Trammell	1.00
4	Tony Phillips	.25
7	Scott Livingstone	.25
9	Skeeter Barnes	.25
11	Sparky Anderson	.75
15	Gary Thurman	.25
16	David Wells	.25
18	David Haas	.25
19	Chad Kreuter	.25
20	Mickey Tettleton	.25
21	Mike Moore	.25
22	Milt Cuyler	.25
23a	Kirk Gibson	.50
23b	Mark Leiter	.50
24	Travis Fryman	.50
27	Kurt Knudsen	.25
28	Rob Deer	.25
30	Bill Krueger	.25
32	Dan Gladden	.25
36	Bill Gullickson	.25
38	Bob MacDonald	.25
39	Mike Henneman	.25
42	Buddy Groom	.25
44	John Doherty	.25
45	Cecil Fielder	.50
49	Tom Bolton	.25
---	Coaches (Dick Tracewksi, Billy Muffett, Larry Herndon, Gene Roof, Dan Whitmer)	.25

1995 Gatorade Cubs

SHAWON DUNSTON-12
INFIELDER

Fans attending the August 24 game at Wrigley Field received a set of oversized (2-7/8" x 4-1/4") cards of the Chicago Cubs, sponsored by Gatorade. Cards feature a color action photo at top, with the player's name, position and uniform number in a blue box at bottom. Backs have a small black-and-white portrait photo, complete minor and major league stats and the team and sponsor logos. Cards are checklisted here by player uniform number.

		NM/M
Complete Set (27):		5.00
Common Player:		.25
5	Jim Riggleman	.25
9	Scott Servais	.25
10	Scott Bullett	.25
11	Rey Sanchez	.25
12	Shawon Dunston	.25
13	Turk Wendell	.25
16	Anthony Young	.25
17	Mark Grace	.50
18	Jose Hernandez	.25
20	Howard Johnson	.25
21	Sammy Sosa	4.00
25	Luis Gonzalez	.50
27	Todd Zeile	.25
28	Randy Myers	.25
29	Jose Guzman	.25
30	Ozzie Timmons	.25
32	Kevin Foster	.25
38	Jaime Navarro	.25
46	Steve Trachsel	.25
47	Mike Perez	.25
49	Frank Castillo	.25
52	Jim Bullinger	.25
53	Chris Nabholz	.25
55	Larry Casian	.25
56	Brian McRae	.25
57	Rich Garces	.25
---	Cubs Coaches (Dave Bialas, Fergie Jenkins, Tony Muser, Max Oliveras, Dan Radison, Billy Williams)	.25

1997 Gatorade Cubs

This postcard-size set was a stadium give-away. Fronts have game-action photos on a green ivy background. Backs have player data and stats. The set is arranged here alphabetically.

		NM/M
Complete Set (26):		8.00
Common Player:		.25
(1)	Terry Adams	.25
(2)	Kent Bottenfield	.25
(3)	Brant Brown	.25
(4)	Dave Clark	.25
(5)	Shawon Dunston	.25
(6)	Kevin Foster	.25
(7)	Doug Glanville	.25
(8)	Jeremi Gonzalez	.25
(9)	Mark Grace	.50
(10)	Dave Hansen	.25
(11)	Jose Hernandez	.25
(12)	Tyler Houston	.25
(13)	Brian McRae	.25
(14)	Kevin Orie	.25
(15)	Bob Patterson	.25
(16)	Jim Riggleman	.25
(17)	Mel Rojas	.25
(18)	Rey Sanchez	.25
(19)	Ryne Sandberg	4.00
(20)	Scott Servais	.25
(21)	Sammy Sosa	4.00
(22)	Kevin Tapani	.25
(23)	Ramon Tatis	.25
(24)	Steve Traschel	.25
(25)	Turk Wendell	.25
(26)	Cubs Coaches (Rick Kranitz, Jeff Pentland, Mako Oliveras, Dan Radison, Phil Regan, Billy Williams)	.25

1985 General Mills Stickers

General Mills of Canada inserted a panel of two cellophane-wrapped baseball stickers in each box of Cheerios in 1985. The full-color sticker panels, measuring 2-3/8" x 3-3/4", are blank-backed and unnumbered and contain the player's name, team and position in both English and French. The General Mills logo appears at the top of each sticker. All team insignia on the players' uniforms and caps have been airbrushed off.

		NM/M
Complete Panel Set (15):		10.00
Complete Singles Set (26):		7.00
Common Panel:		.50
Common Player:		.25
Panel (1)		1.25
(1)	Gary Carter	.50
(2)	Tom Brunansky	.25
Panel (2)		1.25
(1)	Gary Carter	.50
(3)	Dave Steib	.25
Panel (3)		1.00
(4)	Andre Dawson	.35
(5)	Alvin Davis	.25
Panel (4)		1.00
(4)	Andre Dawson	.35
(3)	Dave Steib	.25
Panel (5)		1.00
(6)	Steve Garvey	.35
(7)	Buddy Bell	.25
Panel (6)		1.25
(6)	Steve Garvey	.35
(8)	Jim Rice	.30
Panel (7)		1.00
(9)	Jeff Leonard	.25
(10)	Eddie Murray	.50
Panel (8)		1.50
(11)	Dale Murphy	.35
(12)	Robin Yount	.50
Panel (9)		1.50
(13)	Terry Puhl	.25
(14)	Reggie Jackson	.60
Panel (10)		.50
(15)	Johnny Ray	.25
(16)	Lou Whitaker	.25
Panel (11)		1.00
(17)	Ryne Sandberg	.75
(18)	Mike Hargrove	.25
Panel (12)		2.00
(19)	Mike Schmidt	.75
(20)	George Brett	.75
Panel (13)		2.00
(21)	Ozzie Smith	.60
(22)	Dave Winfield	.75
Panel (14)		1.25
(23)	Mario Soto	.25
(24)	Carlton Fisk	.50
Panel (15)		1.00
(25)	Fernando Valenzuela	.50
(26)	Dwayne Murphy	.25

1986 General Mills Booklets

BASEBALL PLAYERS BOOKLET
LIVRET DES JOUEURS DE BASEBALL 5

National League Players
WEST/OUEST
Joueurs de la Ligue nationale

In 1986, General Mills of Canada inserted six different "Baseball Players Booklets" in specially marked boxes of Cheerios. Ten different players are featured in each booklet, with statistics for the 1985 season in both English and French. The booklet, when opened fully, measures 3-3/4" x 15". Also included in the booklet is a contest sponsored by Petro-Canada service stations to win a day with a major league player at his 1987 spring training site in Florida. Team insignias have been airbrushed off the players' uniforms and caps.

		NM/M
Complete Set (6):		12.50
Common Booklet:		1.25

1987 General Mills Booklets

BASEBALL PLAYERS
JOUEURS DE BASEBALL 3

For a second straight year, General Mills of Canada inserted one of six different "Baseball Super-Stars Booklets" in specially marked boxes of Cheerios and Honey Nut Cheerios cereal. Each booklet contains ten full-color photos for a total of 60 players. The booklets, when completely unfolded, measure 15" x 3-3/4". Written in both English and French, the set was produced by Mike Schechter and Associates. All team insignias have been airbrushed off the photos.

		NM/M
Complete Set (6):		9.00
Common Booklet:		2.00
1	Toronto Blue Jays (Jesse Barfield, George Bell, Tony Fernandez, Kelly Gruber, Tom Henke, Jimmy Key, Lloyd Moseby, Dave Stieb, Willie Upshaw, Ernie Whitt)	2.00
2	A.L. East (Wade Boggs, Roger Clemens, Kirk Gibson, Rickey Henderson, Don Mattingly, Jack Morris, Eddie Murray, Pat Tabler, Dave Winfield, Robin Yount)	4.00
3	A.L. West (Phil Bradley, George Brett, Jose Canseco, Carlton Fisk, Reggie Jackson, Wally Joyner, Kirk McCaskill, Larry Parrish, Kirby Puckett, Dan Quisenberry)	2.50
4	Montreal Expos (Hubie Brooks, Mike Fitzgerald, Andres Galarraga, Vance Law, Andy McGaffigan, Bryn Smith, Jason Thompson, Tim Wallach, Mitch Webster, Floyd Youmans)	2.00
1	A.L. East (Wade Boggs, Kirk Gibson, Rickey Henderson, Don Mattingly, Jack Morris, Lance Parrish, Jim Rice, Dave Righetti, Cal Ripken, Lou Whitaker)	4.00
2	A.L. West (Harold Baines, Phil Bradley, George Brett, Carlton Fisk, Ozzie Guillen, Kent Hrbek, Reggie Jackson, Dan Quisenberry, Bret Saberhagen, Frank White)	2.50
3	Toronto Blue Jays (Jesse Barfield, George Bell, Bill Caudill, Tony Fernandez, Damaso Garcia, Lloyd Moseby, Rance Mulliniks, Dave Stieb, Willie Upshaw, Ernie Whitt)	2.00
4	N.L. East (Gary Carter, Jack Clark, George Foster, Dwight Gooden, Gary Matthews, Willie McGee, Ryne Sandberg, Mike Schmidt, Lee Smith, Ozzie Smith)	2.50
5	N.L. West (Dave Concepcion, Pedro Guerrero, Terry Kennedy, Dale Murphy, Graig Nettles, Dave Parker, Tony Perez, Steve Sax, Bruce Sutter, Fernando Valenzuela)	1.25
6	Montreal Expos (Hubie Brooks, Andre Dawson, Mike Fitzgerald, Vance Law, Tim Raines, Jeff Reardon, Bryn Smith, Jason Thompson, Tim Wallach, Mitch Webster)	2.00
5	N.L. East (Gary Carter, Dwight Gooden, Keith Hernandez, Willie McGee, Tim Raines, R.J. Reynolds, Ryne Sandberg, Mike Schmidt, Ozzie Smith, Darryl Strawberry)	2.50
6	N.L. West (Kevin Bass, Chili Davis, Bill Doran, Pedro Guerrero, Tony Gwynn, Dale Murphy, Dave Parker, Steve Sax, Mike Scott, Fernando Valenzuela)	2.00

1990 Giant Eagle Roberto Clemente Stickers

The Giant Eagle food stores around Pittsburgh issued a collectors' poster and set of 18 stickers circa 1990. Each of the 2-1/2" x 3-1/2" stickers features one of Roberto Clemente's regular-issue Topps cards 1955-72. The stickers were originally issued in strips of three. Backs are blank. The issue was almost certainly not authorized by Topps or the Clemente estate.

		NM/M
Complete Set, Strips (6):		20.00
Common Sticker:		2.00
Poster:		16.00

1981 Granny Goose Potato Chips A's

MIKE NORRIS
17 PITCHER

The 1981 Granny Goose set features the Oakland A's. The 2-1/2" x 3-1/2" cards were issued in bags of potato chips and are sometimes found with grease stains. The cards have full color fronts with the graphics done in the team's green and yellow colors. The backs contain the A's logo and a short player biography. The Revering card was withdrawn from the set shortly after he was traded and is in shorter supply than the rest of the cards in the set. The cards are numbered in the checklist that follows by the player's uniform number.

1982 Granny Goose Potato Chips A's

RICKEY HENDERSON
35 OUTFIELD

Granny Goose repeated its promotion from the previous year and issued another set featuring the Oakland A's. The 2-1/2" x 3-1/2" cards were distributed in two fashions - in bags of potato chips and at Fan Appreciation Day at Oakland-Alameda Coliseum. The cards are identical in design to the 1981 set and can be distinguished from it by the date on the copyright on the bottom of the card reverse. The cards are numbered in the checklist that follows by the player's uniform number.

		NM/M
Complete Set (15):		100.00
Common Player:		2.00
1	Billy Martin	8.00
2	Mike Heath	2.00
5	Jeff Newman	2.00
8	Mitchell Page	2.00
8	Rob Picciolo	2.00
10	Wayne Gross	2.00
12	Dave Revering	40.00
17	Mike Norris	2.00
20	Tony Armas	2.00
21	Dwayne Murphy	2.00
22	Rick Langford	2.00
27	Matt Keough	2.00
35	Rickey Henderson	35.00
39	Dave McKay	2.00
54	Steve McCatty	2.00

1982 Granny Goose Potato Chips A's

		NM/M
Complete Set (15):		7.50
Common Player:		.50
1	Billy Martin	1.00
2	Mike Heath	.50
5	Jeff Newman	.50
8	Rob Picciolo	.50
10	Wayne Gross	.50
11	Fred Stanley	.50
15	Davey Lopes	.50
17	Mike Norris	.50
20	Tony Armas	.50
21	Dwayne Murphy	.50
22	Rick Langford	.50
27	Matt Keough	.50
35	Rickey Henderson	6.00
44	Cliff Johnson, Jr.	.50
54	Steve McCatty	.50

1982 Granny Goose Signature Set

The cards from this very scarce 15-card set are identical to the regular Granny Goose cards, but contain a facsimile autograph on the front. The cards were initially intended as special prize-redemption inserts from Granny Goose potato chips, but were never released in any quantity.

		NM/M
Complete Set (15):		125.00
Common Player:		5.00
1	Billy Martin	30.00
2	Mike Heath	5.00
5	Jeff Newman	5.00
8	Rob Picciolo	5.00
10	Wayne Gross	5.00
11	Fred Stanley	7.50
15	Davey Lopes	5.00
17	Mike Norris	5.00
20	Tony Armas	5.00
21	Dwayne Murphy	5.00
22	Rick Langford	5.00
27	Matt Keough	5.00
35	Rickey Henderson	45.00
44	Cliff Johnson, Jr.	5.00
54	Steve McCatty	5.00

1983 Granny Goose Potato Chips A's

For the third consecutive year, Granny Goose issued a set of baseball cards featuring the Oakland A's. The cards were issued with or without a detachable coupon found

at the bottom of each card. Issued in bags of potato chips were the coupon cards, which contain a scratch-off section offering prizes. The cards without the coupon section were given away to fans at Oakland-Alameda Coliseum on July 3, 1983. Cards with the detachable coupon command a 50 per cent premium over the coupon-less variety. The cards in the following checklist are numbered by the player's uniform number.

		NM/M
Complete Set (15):		8.00
Common Player:		.50
2	Mike Heath	.50
4	Carney Lansford	.50
10	Wayne Gross	.50
14	Steve Boros	.50
15	Davey Lopes	.50
16	Mike Davis	.50
17	Mike Norris	.50
21	Dwayne Murphy	.50
22	Rick Langford	.50
27	Matt Keough	.50
31	Tom Underwood	.50
33	Dave Beard	.50
35	Rickey Henderson	6.00
39	Tom Burgmeier	.50
54	Steve McCatty	.50

1999 GTE Tampa Bay Devil Rays

This team set was a stadium giveaway. Fronts have game-action color photos. On back are complete minor and major league stats along with team and sponsor logos.

		NM/M
Complete Set (30):		10.00
Common Player:		.25
1	Scott Aldred	.25
2	Wilson Alvarez	.25
3	Rolando Arrojo	.25
4	Wade Boggs	3.00
5	Miguel Cairo	.25
6	Jose Canseco	2.00
7	Coaches (Orlando Gomez, Billy Hatcher, Frank Howard, Greg Riddoch, Leon Roberts, Rick Williams)	.25
8	Mike DiFelice	.25
9	John Flaherty	.25
10	Roberto Hernandez	.25
11	David Lamb	.25
12	Aaron Ledesma	.25
13	Albie Lopez	.25
14	Dave Martinez	.25
15	Quinton McCracken	.35
16	Fred McGriff	.35
17	Herbert Perry	.25
18	Bryan Rekar	.25
19	Larry Rothschild	.25
20	Ryan Rupe	.25
21	Julio Santana	.25
22	Tony Saunders	.25
23	Paul Sorrento	.25
24	Kevin Stocker	.25
25	Rick White	.25
26	Randy Winn	.25
27	Bobby Witt	.25
28	Esteban Yan	.25
---	Literacy Champion (Quinton McCracken)	.25
---	Sponsor's Card	.25

H

1981-89 Hall of Fame Metallic Plaque-cards

Between 1981-89, the National Baseball Hall of Fame & Museum issued a set of metallic baseball cards reproducing the plaques of the baseball greats inducted. The plaques are pictured on 2-1/2" x 3-1/2" blank-backed gold anodized aluminum. Every detail of the plaque is fully and faithfully reproduced. The set was sold in series through the Hall of Fame's gift shop. The series was discontinued for economic reasons in 1989. Only 1,000 plaques of each player were produced. Values are, to some extent, based not only on player popularity, but on year of issue; later plaques tend to be more expensive because fewer were sold.

		NM/M
Complete Set (204):		650.00
Common Player:		3.00
(1)	Hank Aaron/1983	20.00
(2)	Grover Alexander/1982	5.00
(3)	Walter Alston/1984	4.00
(4)	Cap Anson/1981	4.00
(5)	Luis Aparicio/1984	6.50
(6)	Luke Appling/1982	3.50
(7)	Earl Averill/1983	3.00
(8)	"Home Run" Baker/1983	3.00
(9)	David Bancroft/1982	3.00
(10)	Ernie Banks/1982	8.00
(11)	Al Barlick/1989	4.50
(12)	Ed Barrow/1982	3.00
(13)	Jacob Beckley/1982	3.00
(14)	Cool Papa Bell/1981	6.00
(15)	Johnny Bench/1989	15.00
(16)	"Chief" Bender/1982	3.50
(17)	Yogi Berra/1982	12.00
(18)	Jim Bottomley/1981	4.00
(19)	Lou Boudreau/1982	3.00
(20)	Roger Bresnahan/1982	3.00
(21)	Lou Brock/1986	12.00
(22)	Dan Brouthers/1982	3.00
(23)	Mordecai Brown/1981	4.00
(24)	Morgan Burkeley/1981	3.00
(25)	Jesse Burkett/1982	3.00
(26)	Roy Campanella/1981	12.50
(27)	Max Carey/1982	4.00
(28)	Alexander Cartwright/1981	3.00
(29)	Henry Chadwick/1982	3.00
(30)	Frank Chance/1981	4.50
(31)	Happy Chandler/1983	3.00
(32)	Oscar Charleston/1982	4.00
(33)	Jack Chesbro/1982	3.50
(34)	Fred Clarke/1983	3.00
(35)	John Clarkson/1982	3.00
(36)	Roberto Clemente/1982	30.00
(37)	Ty Cobb/1981	30.00
(38)	Mickey Cochrane/1983	5.00
(39)	Eddie Collins/1981	3.00
(40)	James Collins/1982	3.00
(41)	Earle Combs/1983	3.00
(42)	Charles Comiskey/1982	3.00
(43)	Jocko Conlan/1981	3.00
(44)	Thomas Connolly/1982	3.00
(45)	Roger Connor/1982	3.00
(46)	Stan Coveleski/1982	3.00
(47)	Sam Crawford/1983	3.50
(48)	Joe Cronin/1981	5.00
(49)	Candy Cummings/1982	3.00
(50)	Kiki Cuyler/1983	4.00
(51)	Ray Dandridge (1989)	6.00
(52)	Dizzy Dean/1983	10.00
(53)	Ed Delahanty/1981	3.00
(54)	Bill Dickey/1981	5.00
(55)	Martin Dihigo/1982	6.50
(56)	Joe DiMaggio/1983	35.00
(57)	Bobby Doerr/1986	4.00
(58)	Don Drysdale/1984	10.00
(59)	Hugh Duffy/1982	3.00
(60)	Bill Evans/1983	3.00
(61)	John Evers/1982	4.50
(62)	Buck Ewing/1981	3.00
(63)	Urban Faber/1983	3.00
(64)	Bob Feller/1981	6.50
(65)	Rick Ferrell/1984	4.00
(66)	Elmer Flick/1982	3.00
(67)	Whitey Ford/1983	10.00
(68)	Rube Foster/1983	3.00
(69)	Jimmie Foxx/1982	7.50
(70)	Ford Frick/1981	3.00
(71)	Frank Frisch/1981	3.00
(72)	Pud Galvin/1982	3.00
(73)	Lou Gehrig/1982	35.00
(74)	Charles Gehringer/1983	6.50
(75)	Bob Gibson/1982	6.50
(76)	Josh Gibson/1981	6.50
(77)	Warren Giles/1983	3.00
(78)	Lefty Gomez/1981	4.00
(79)	Goose Goslin/1982	4.00
(80)	Hank Greenberg/1981	8.00
(81)	Clark Griffith/1982	3.00
(82)	Burleigh Grimes/1982	3.00
(83)	Lefty Grove/1981	4.50
(84)	Chick Hafey/1982	3.00
(85)	Pop Haines/1982	3.00
(86)	William Hamilton/1982	3.00
(87)	William Harridge/1982	3.00
(88)	Bucky Harris/1982	4.00
(89)	Gabby Hartnett/1982	3.50
(90)	Harry Heilmann/1983	3.00
(91)	Bill Herman/1982	3.00
(92)	Harry Hooper/1982	3.00
(93)	Rogers Hornsby/1981	8.00
(94)	Schoolboy Hoyt/1983	3.00
(95)	Cal Hubbard/1982	3.00
(96)	Carl Hubbell/1981	3.50
(97)	Miller Huggins/1982	3.50
(98)	Catfish Hunter/1989	6.00
(99)	Monte Irvin/1981	3.50
(100)	Travis Jackson/1983	3.00
(101)	Hugh Jennings/1983	3.00
(102)	Ban Johnson/1981	3.00
(103)	Judy Johnson/1981	3.00
(104)	Walter Johnson/1982	10.00
(105)	Addie Joss/1981	3.00
(106)	Al Kaline/1981	8.00
(107)	Timothy Keefe/1983	3.00
(108)	Willie Keeler/1982	4.00
(109)	George Kell/1984	4.00
(110)	Joe Kelley/1983	3.00
(111)	Highpockets Kelly (?)	3.00
(112)	King Kelly/1981	4.00
(113)	Harmon Killebrew/1984	6.50
(114)	Ralph Kiner/1982	3.00
(115)	Chuck Klein/1983	4.00
(116)	Bill Klem/1981	3.00
(117)	Sandy Koufax/1982	25.00
(118)	Nap Lajoie/1982	5.00
(119)	Kenesaw Landis/1981	3.00
(120)	Buck Leonard/1982	3.50
(121)	Bob Lemon/1981	3.00
(122)	Fred Linstrom/1982	3.00
(123)	Pop Lloyd/1981	3.00
(124)	Ernie Lombardi/1986	3.00
(125)	Al Lopez/1981	3.00
(126)	Ted Lyons/1983	3.00
(127)	Connie Mack/1981	3.00
(128)	Larry MacPhail/1983	3.00
(129)	Mickey Mantle/1983	40.00
(130)	Heinie Manush/1981	3.00
(131)	Rabbit Maranville/1981	4.00
(132)	Juan Marichal/1984	5.00
(133)	Rube Marquard/1983	3.50
(134)	Eddie Mathews/1983	3.50
(135)	Christy Mathewson/1981	10.00
(136)	Willie Mays/1981	20.00
(137)	Joe McCarthy/1983	3.00
(138)	Thomas McCarthy/1983	3.00
(139)	Willie McCovey/1986	3.50
(140)	Iron Man McGinnity/1982	3.00
(141)	John McGraw/1982	3.00
(142)	Bill McKechnie/1982	3.00
(143)	Joe Medwick/1983	3.00
(144)	Johnny Mize/1982	3.00
(145)	Stan Musial/1981	15.00
(146)	Kid Nichols/1983	4.00
(147)	James O'Rourke/1982	3.00
(148)	Mel Ott/1981	4.00
(149)	Satchel Paige/1981	12.50
(150)	Herb Pennock/1983	3.00
(151)	Eddie Plank/1982	3.00
(152)	Hoss Radbourne/1983	3.00
(153)	Pee Wee Reese/1984	3.50
(154)	Sam Rice/1983	3.00
(155)	Branch Rickey/1981	3.00
(156)	Eppa Rixey/1983	3.00
(157)	Robin Roberts/1982	5.00
(158)	Brooks Robinson/1984	6.00
(159)	Frank Robinson/1983	6.50
(160)	Jackie Robinson/1981	20.00
(161)	Wilbert Robinson/1982	3.50
(162)	Edd Roush/1982	3.00
(163)	Red Ruffing/1982	4.00
(164)	Amos Rusie/1983	3.00
(165)	Babe Ruth/1981	40.00
(166)	Ray Schalk/1982	3.00
(167)	Red Schoendienst/1989	8.00
(168)	Joe Sewell/1982	3.00
(169)	Al Simmons/1982	5.00
(170)	George Sisler/1981	3.00
(171)	Enos Slaughter/1986	8.00
(172)	Duke Snider/1981	8.00
(173)	Warren Spahn/1982	8.00
(174)	Al Spalding/1982	4.00
(175)	Tris Speaker/1982	6.50
(176)	Willie Stargell/1989	3.00
(177)	Casey Stengel/1981	6.50
(178)	Bill Terry/1981	3.00
(179)	Sam Thompson/1983	3.00
(180)	Joe Tinker/1982	6.00
(181)	Pie Traynor/1982	6.00
(182)	Dazzy Vance/1983	4.00
(183)	Arky Vaughan/1986	3.00
(184)	Rube Waddell/1983	4.00
(185)	Honus Wagner/1982	15.00
(186)	Roderick Wallace/1982	3.00
(187)	Ed Walsh/1982	3.00
(188)	Lloyd Waner/1981	4.00
(189)	Paul Waner/1981	5.00
(190)	John Ward/1982	3.00
(191)	George Weiss/1983	3.00
(192)	Mickey Welch/1983	3.00
(193)	Zack Wheat/1982	4.00
(194)	Hoyt Wilhelm/1986	6.50
(195)	Billy Williams/1989	8.00
(196)	Ted Williams/1981	27.50
(197)	Hack Wilson/1982	4.00
(198)	George Wright/1982	3.00
(199)	Harry Wright/1983	3.00
(200)	Early Wynn/1982	4.00
(201)	Carl Yastrzemski/1989	12.00
(202)	Tom Yawkey/1982	3.00
(203)	Cy Young/1981	10.00
(204)	Ross Youngs/1982	3.00

1995 Baseball's Hall of Famers Creating History

This boxed set of large-format (2-7/8" x 4-1/2") round-cornered cards was designated "Flash-Pack / Knowledge in a Nutshell." It was described as the the first in a series. Card fronts feature borderless black-and-white or color photos with no player identification or other graphics. Black-and-white backs identify the player, provide a career summary and date of selection to the Hall of Fame. The unnumbered cards are listed here alphabetically. The boxed set originally retailed for $9.95.

		NM/M
Complete Set (36):		20.00
Common Player:		.50
(1)	Cap Anson	.50
(2)	Ernie Banks	2.00
(3)	Edward G. Barrow	.50
(4)	Roger Bresnahan	.50
(5)	Lou Brock	1.00
(6)	Roy Campanella	2.00
(7)	Alexander Cartwright	.50
(8)	Henry Chadwick	.50
(9)	Oscar Charleston	.50
(10)	Jack Chesbro	.50
(11)	Roberto Clemente	4.00
(12)	Charles Comiskey	.50
(13)	Candy Cummings	.50
(14)	Andrew "Rube" Foster	.50
(15)	Ford Frick	.50
(16)	Josh Gibson	1.00
(17)	Burleigh Grimes	.50
(18)	Cal Hubbard	.50
(19)	Carl Hubbell	.50
(20)	Willie Keeler	.50
(21)	Bill Klem	.50
(22)	Kenesaw M. Landis	.50
(23)	Larry MacPhail	.50
(24)	Juan Marichal	1.00
(25)	Willie Mays	3.00
(26)	John McGraw	.50
(27)	Stan Musial	2.00
(28)	Charles Radbourne	.50
(29)	Branch Rickey	.50
(30)	Robin Roberts	1.00
(31)	Brooks Robinson	1.00
(32)	Warren Spahn	1.00
(33)	Albert Spalding	.50
(34)	Willie Stargell	1.00
(35)	Rube Waddell	.50
(36)	Harry Wright	.50

1998 Hamburger Helper Home Run Heroes

Eight top sluggers are featured in this box-back set from Hamburger Helper. The 2-1/2" x 3-1/2" cards are printed on the backs of various flavors of the skillet meal boxes. Unlike many similar issues these are fully licensed by Major League Baseball, as well as the Players Association, and the player photos have uniform logos. Also unusual is that the cards have a printed back in black-and-white offering personal data, career highlights and stats.

		NM/M
Complete Set, Boxes (8):		15.00
Complete Set, Singles (8):		15.00
Common Player:		.50
1	Mark McGwire	3.00
2	Rafael Palmeiro	1.25
3	Tino Martinez	.50
4	Barry Bonds	4.00
5	Larry Walker	.50
6	Juan Gonzalez	1.25
7	Mike Piazza	2.00
8	Frank Thomas	1.50

1988 Hardee's/Coke Conlon

Regionally issued in a promotion sponsored by Hardee's restaurants and Coca-Cola, this six-card set features the photos of Charles Martin Conlon and is closely related to the Sporting News-Wide World Conlon issues of the time. The cards feature sepia photos on front and career stats and summary on back. The unnumbered cards are checklisted here alphabetically.

		NM/M
Complete Set (6):		3.00
Common Player:		.40
(1)	Cool Papa Bell	.40
(2)	Ty Cobb	1.25
(3)	Lou Gehrig	1.50
(4)	Connie Mack	.40
(5)	Casey Stengel	.40
(6)	Rube Waddell	.40

1996 Hebrew National Detroit Tigers

One of the team's hot dog concessionaires sponsored a set of Tiger cards given away at the September 1 game. Originally intended to be 28 cards, only 26 were issued due to late-season trades. Cards are in a larger than normal 2-7/8" x 4-1/4" format with game-action photo on front. Down one side in team colors are the player name and position, with the stalking tiger logo at bottom. Backs have a large light blue gothic "D" in the background with player personal data and major/minor league stats and team/sponsor logos.

		NM/M
Complete Set (26):		12.00
Common Player:		.50
1	Kimera Bartee	.50
2	Jose Lima	.50
3	Tony Clark	.50
5	Travis Fryman	.50
7	Bobby Higginson	.50
8	Greg Keagle	.50
9	Mark Lewis	.50
10	Richie Lewis	.50
11	Felipe Lira	.50
12	Mike Myers	.50
13	Melvin Nieves	.50
14	Alan Trammell	1.00
15	Tom Urbani	.50
16	Brian Williams	.50
17	Eddie Williams	.50
18	Curtis Pride	.50
19	Mark Parent	.50
20	Raul Casanova	.50
21	Omar Olivares	.50
22	Gregg Olson	.50
23	Justin Thompson	.50
24	Brad Ausmus	.50
25	Andujar Cedeno	.50
26	Buddy Bell	.50
27	Paws (Mascot)	.50
28	Detroit Tigers Coaches (Glenn Ezell, Terry Francona, Larry Herndon, Fred Kendall, John (Jon) Matlack, Ron Oester)	.50

1997 Hebrew National Detroit Tigers

The hot dog concessionaire at Tiger Stadium produced a second annual team set in 1997, giving the cards away at the June 22 game. Cards feature borderless color action photos on front, with a tiny black-and-white portrait photo at bottom-right. Backs are printed in blue and yellow and have player data, complete major and minor league stats and the team and sponsor logos.

		NM/M
Complete Set (28):		12.00
Common Player:		.50
1	Jose Bautista	.50
2	Willie Blair	.50
3	Doug Brocail	.50
4	Raul Casanova	.50
5	Tony Clark	.50
6	Deivi Cruz	.50
7	John Cummings	.50
8	Damion Easley	.50
9	Travis Fryman	.50
10	Bobby Higginson	.50
11	Brian Hunter	.50
12	Todd Johnson	.50
13	Todd Jones	.50
14	Felipe Lira	.50
15	Dan Miceli	.50
16	Brian Moehler	.50
17	Mike Myers	.50
18	Phil Nevin	.50
19	Melvin Nieves	.50
20	Omar Oliveras	.50
21	Curtis Pride	.50
22	A.J. Sager	.50
23	Justin Thompson	.50
24	Matt Walbeck	.50
25	Jody Reed	.50

26 Bob Hamelin .50
27 Buddy Bell .50
28 Tigers Coaches (Rick Adair, Larry Herndon, Perry Hill, Fred Kendall, Larry Parrish, Jerry White) .50

1998 Hershey's Baltimore Orioles

This team set was a stadium giveaway at a late-season game. The 2-1/2" x 3-1/2" cards have portrait or game-action photos bordered in black. An orange stripe vertically at left has the player name. Backs have a red border around complete major and minor league stats. Team and Hershey's logos are at bottom.

	NM/M
Complete Set (25):	15.00
Common Player:	.50
(1) Roberto Alomar	.75
(2) Brady Anderson	.75
(3) Harold Baines	.75
(4) Rich Becker	.50
(5) Armando Benitez	.50
(6) Mike Bordick	.50
(7) Eric Davis	.60
(8) Doug Drabek	.50
(9) Scott Erickson	.50
(10) Chris Hoiles	.50
(11) Doug Johns	.50
(12) Scott Kamienicki	.50
(13) Jimmy Key	.50
(14) Alan Mills	.50
(15) Mike Mussina	2.00
(16) Jesse Orosco	.50
(17) Rafael Palmeiro	2.00
(18) Sidney Ponson	.50
(19) Jeff Reboulet	.50
(20) Arthur Rhodes	.50
(21) Cal Ripken	4.00
(22) Pete Smith	.50
(23) B.J. Surhoff	.50
(24) Lenny Webster	.50
(25) Orioles Coaches (Carlos Bernhardt, Rick Down, Mike Flanagan, Elrod Hendricks, Eddie Murray, Sam Perlozzo)	.50

1993 Highland Mint Mint-Cards

The Highland Mint produced replicas of several Topps rookie cards and other prominent cards in bronze and silver. Limited to 1,000 in silver and 5,000 in bronze, the company produced cards of many current stars along with a replica of Brooks Robinson's 1957 rookie card. The cards carried a suggested retail price of $235 for the silver and $50 for the bronze. Cards measure 2-1/2" x 3-1/2" and are 1/10" thick. Each Mint-Card has a serial number engraved on the edge and is sold in a heavy lucite holder, packaged with a certificate of authenticity in a plastic book-style folder.

	NM/M
Common Player, Silver:	70.00
Common Player, Bronze:	12.50
(1s) Brooks Robinson (1957 Topps, silver edition of 796)	110.00
(1b) Brooks Robinson (1957 Topps, bronze edition of 2,043)	20.00
(2s) Dave Winfield (1974 Topps, silver edition of 266)	200.00
(2b) Dave Winfield (1974 Topps, bronze edition of 1,216)	20.00
(3s) George Brett (1975 Topps, silver edition of 999)	100.00
(3b) George Brett (1975 Topps, bronze edition of 3,560)	20.00
(4s) Robin Yount (1975 Topps silver edition of 349)	110.00
(4b) Robin Yount (1975 Topps, bronze edition of 1,564)	40.00
(5s) Ozzie Smith (1979 Topps, silver edition of 211)	245.00
(5b) Ozzie Smith (1979 Topps, bronze edition of 1,088)	35.00
(6s) Don Mattingly (1984 Topps, silver edition of 414)	75.00
(6b) Don Mattingly (1984 Topps, bronze edition of 1,550)	40.00
(7s) Roger Clemens (1985 Topps, silver edition of 432)	140.00
(7b) Roger Clemens (1985 Topps, bronze edition of 1,789)	25.00
(8s) Kirby Puckett (1985 Topps, silver edition of 359)	85.00
(8b) Kirby Puckett (1985 Topps, bronze edition of 1,723)	20.00
(9s) Barry Bonds (1986 Topps Traded, silver edition of 596)	125.00
(9b) Barry Bonds (1986 Topps Traded, bronze edition of 2,677)	50.00
(10s) Will Clark (1986 Topps Traded, silver edition of 150)	225.00
(10b) Will Clark (1986 Topps Traded, bronze edition of 1,0444)	20.00
(11s) Roberto Alomar (1988 Topps Traded, silver edition of 214)	90.00
(11b) Roberto Alomar (1988 Topps Traded, bronze edition of 928)	20.00
(12s) Juan Gonzalez (1990 Topps, silver edition of 365)	65.00
(12b) Juan Gonzalez (1990 Topps, bronze edition of 1,899)	15.00
(13s) Ken Griffey Jr. (1992 Topps, silver edition of 1,000)	100.00
(13b) Ken Griffey Jr. (1992 Topps, bronze edition of 5,000)	15.00
(13g) Ken Griffey Jr. (1992 Topps, gold edition of 500)	200.00
(14s) Cal Ripken, Jr. (1992 Topps, silver edition of 1,000)	100.00
(14b) Cal Ripken, Jr. (1992 Topps, bronze edition of 4,065)	15.00
(15s) Nolan Ryan (1992 Topps, silver edition of 999)	150.00
(15b) Nolan Ryan (1992 Topps, bronze edition of 5,000)	25.00
(16s) Ryne Sandberg (1992 Topps, silver edition of 430)	145.00
(16b) Ryne Sandberg (1992 Topps, bronze edition of 1,932)	15.00
(17s) Frank Thomas (1992 Topps, silver edition of 1,000)	85.00
(17b) Frank Thomas (1992 Topps, bronze edition of 5,000)	12.50
(17g) Frank Thomas (1992 Topps, gold edition of 500)	150.00

1994 Highland Mint Mint-Cards

In 1994 the Highland Mint continued its production of Mint-Cards, licensed metal replicas of Topps baseball, football and hockey cards. Maximum production of baseball players in the series was reduced to 750 in silver and halved to 2,500 in bronze. Suggested retail prices remained at $235 and $50, respectively. Once again cards were produced in the same 2-1/2" x 3-1/2" format as original Topps cards and were minted to a thickness of 1/10", with a serial number engraved on the edge. Mintcards were sold in a heavy lucite holder, packaged with a certificate of authenticity in a plastic book-style holder. In mid-year, the company announced it was ceasing production of Topps-replica baseball cards and that henceforth all baseball Mint-Cards would reproduce the designs of Pinnacle brand cards.

	NM/M
Common Player, Silver:	50.00
Common Player, Bronze:	12.00
Common Player, Gold:	200.00
(1a) Ernie Banks (1954 Topps, silver edition of 437)	65.00
(1b) Ernie Banks (1954 Topps, bronze edition of 920)	25.00
(2a) Carl Yastrzemski (1960 Topps, silver edition of 500)	75.00
(2b) Carl Yastrzemski (1960 Topps, bronze edition of 1,072)	30.00
(3a) Johnny Bench (1969 Topps, silver edition of 500)	75.00
(3b) Johnny Bench (1969 Topps, bronze edition of 1,384)	22.50
(4a) Mike Schmidt (1974 Topps, silver edition of 500)	75.00
(4b) Mike Schmidt (1974 Topps, bronze edition of 1,641)	20.00
(5a) Paul Molitor (1979 Topps, silver edition of 260)	175.00
(5b) Paul Molitor (1979 Topps, bronze edition of 639)	17.50
(6a) Deion Sanders (1989 Topps, silver edition of 187)	60.00
(6b) Deion Sanders (1989 Topps, bronze edition of 668)	12.50
(7a) Dave Justice (1990 Topps, silver edition of 265)	75.00
(7b) Dave Justice (1990 Topps, bronze edition of 1,396)	12.50
(8a) Jeff Bagwell (1992 Pinnacle, silver edition of 750)	50.00
(8b) Jeff Bagwell (1992 Pinnacle, bronze edition of 2,500)	15.00
(9a) Greg Maddux (1992 Pinnacle, silver edition of 750)	175.00
(9b) Greg Maddux (1992 Pinnacle, bronze edition of 2,500)	25.00
(10a) Mike Piazza (1992 Topps, silver edition of 750)	75.00
(10b) Mike Piazza (1992 Topps, bronze edition of 2,500)	20.00
(10c) Mike Piazza (1992 Topps, gold edition of 374)	300.00
(12a) Nolan Ryan (1992 Pinnacle Then and Now, silver edition of 1,000)	75.00
(12b) Nolan Ryan (1992 Pinnacle Then and Now, bronze edition of 5,000)	15.00
(12c) Nolan Ryan (1992 Pinnacle Then & Now, gold edition 500)	200.00
(13a) Tim Salmon (1993 Topps, silver edition of 264)	110.00
(13b) Tim Salmon (1993 Topps, bronze edition of 768)	10.00

1995 Highland Mint Mint-Cards

For 1995, the Highland Mint continued its series of precious-metal editions of cards in all major team sports. The 2-1/2" x 3-1/2" cards contain 4-1/4 oz. of bronze or silver or 24-K gold plating on silver. Each Mint-card is sold in a heavy plastic holder within a numbered album and with a certificate of authenticity. Only the firm's baseball cards are listed here.

	NM/M
38b Michael Jordan (Upper Deck Rare Air, bronze, edition of 5,000)	15.00
38s Michael Jordan (Upper Deck Rare Air, silver, edition of 1,000.)	100.00
38g Michael Jordan (Upper Deck Rare Air, gold, edition of 500.)	300.00
Mickey Mantle (1992 Pinnacle, bronze edition of 1,000)	20.00
Mickey Mantle (1992 Pinnacle, silver edition of 1,000)	75.00
Mickey Mantle (1992 Pinnacle, gold edition of 500)	300.00

1992 High 5 Decals

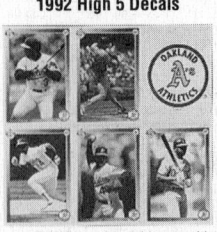

This issue of peelable, reusable "decals" was sold in both team sets and superstar panels. Each $2.99 panel contains five player decals and a team logo decal. The backing paper has a color 5" x 7" photo of a superstar that can be cut out and framed. Overall dimensions of the decal sheet are 7-1/2" x 7". The unnumbered decals are checklisted here in alphabetical order within team.

	NM/M
Complete Set (156):	30.00
Common Player:	.25
(1) Baltimore Orioles Logo	.25
(2) Mike Devereaux	.25
(3) Ben McDonald	.25
(4) Gregg Olson	.25
(5) Joe Orsulak	.25
(6) Cal Ripken Jr.	3.00
(7) Boston Red Sox Logo	.25
(8) Wade Boggs	2.00
(9) Roger Clemens	2.25
(10) Phil Plantier	.25
(11) Jeff Reardon	.25
(12) Mo Vaughn	.25
(13) California Angels Logo	.25
(14) Jim Abbott	.25
(15) Chuck Finley	.25
(16) Bryan Harvey	.25
(17) Mark Langston	.25
(18) Dave Winfield	1.50
(19) Chicago White Sox Logo	.25
(20) Carlton Fisk	1.50
(21) Jack McDowell	.25
(22) Bobby Thigpen	.25
(23) Frank Thomas	1.50
(24) Robin Ventura	.25
(25) Cleveland Indians Logo	.25
(26) Sandy Alomar Jr.	.25
(27) Carlos Baerga	.25
(28) Albert Belle	.25
(29) Alex Cole	.25
(30) Charles Nagy	.25
(31) Detroit Tigers Logo	.25
(32) Cecil Fielder	.25
(33) Travis Fryman	.25
(34) Tony Phillips	.25
(35) Alan Trammell	.25
(36) Lou Whitaker	.25
(37) Kansas City Royals Logo	.25
(38) George Brett	2.50
(39) Jim Eisenreich	.25
(40) Brian McRae	.25
(41) Jeff Montgomery	.25
(42) Bret Saberhagen	.25
(43) Milwaukee Brewers Logo	.25
(44) Chris Bosio	.25
(45) Paul Molitor	1.50
(46) B.J. Surhoff	.25
(47) Greg Vaughn	.25
(48) Robin Yount	1.50
(49) Minnesota Twins Logo	.25
(50) Rick Aguilera	.25
(51) Scott Erickson	.25
(52) Kent Hrbek	.25
(53) Kirby Puckett	2.00
(54) Kevin Tapani	.25
(55) New York Yankees Logo	.25
(56) Mel Hall	.25
(57) Roberto Kelly	.25
(58) Kevin Maas	.25
(59) Don Mattingly	2.50
(60) Steve Sax	.25
(61) Oakland A's Logo	.25
(62) Harold Baines	.25
(63) Jose Canseco	.75
(64) Dennis Eckersley	1.25
(65) Dave Henderson	.25
(66) Rickey Henderson	1.50
(67) Seattle Mariners Logo	.25
(68) Jay Buhner	.25
(69) Ken Griffey Jr.	2.75
(70) Randy Johnson	1.50
(71) Edgar Martinez	.25
(72) Harold Reynolds	.25
(73) Texas Rangers Logo	.25
(74) Julio Franco	.25
(75) Juan Gonzalez	1.25
(76) Rafael Palmeiro	1.25
(77) Nolan Ryan	3.00
(77p) Nolan Ryan (Prototype)	6.50
(78) Ruben Sierra	.25
(79) Toronto Blue Jays Logo	.25
(80) Roberto Alomar	.50
(81) Joe Carter	.25
(82) Kelly Gruber	.25
(83) John Olerud	.25
(84) Devon White	.25
(85) Atlanta Braves Logo	.25
(86) Steve Avery	.25
(87) Ron Gant	.25
(88) Tom Glavine	.40
(89) David Justice	.25
(90) Terry Pendleton	.25
(91) Chicago Cubs Logo	.25
(92) George Bell	.25
(93) Andre Dawson	.30
(94) Mark Grace	.25
(95) Greg Maddux	2.00
(96) Ryne Sandberg	2.00
(97) Cincinnati Reds Logo	.25
(98) Eric Davis	.25
(99) Barry Larkin	.25
(100) Hal Morris	.25
(101) Jose Rijo	.25
(102) Chris Sabo	.25
(103) Houston Astros Logo	.25
(104) Jeff Bagwell	1.50
(105) Craig Biggio	.25
(106) Ken Caminiti	.25
(107) Luis Gonzalez	.50
(108) Pete Harnisch	.25
(109) Los Angeles Dodgers Logo	.25
(110) Brett Butler	.25
(111) Lenny Harris	.25
(112) Ramon Martinez	.25
(113) Eddie Murray	1.50
(114) Darryl Strawberry	.25
(115) Montreal Expos Logo	.25
(116) Ivan Calderon	.25
(117) Delino DeShields	.25
(118) Marquis Grissom	.25
(119) Dennis Martinez	.25
(120) Larry Walker	.25
(121) New York Mets Logo	.25
(122) David Cone	.25
(123) Dwight Gooden	.25
(124) Gregg Jefferies	.25
(125) Howard Johnson	.25
(126) Kevin McReynolds	.25
(127) Philadelphia Phillies Logo	.25
(128) Wes Chamberlain	.25
(129) Lenny Dykstra	.25
(130) John Kruk	.25
(131) Terry Mulholland	.25
(132) Mitch Williams	.25
(133) Pittsburgh Pirates Logo	.25
(134) Barry Bonds	3.00
(135) Doug Drabek	.25
(136) John Smiley	.25
(137) Zane Smith	.25
(138) Andy Van Slyke	.25
(139) St. Louis Cardinals Logo	.25
(140) Felix Jose	.25
(141) Ray Lankford	.25
(142) Lee Smith	.25
(143) Ozzie Smith	2.00
(144) Todd Zeile	.25
(145) San Diego Padres Logo	.25
(146) Tony Fernandez	.25
(147) Tony Gwynn	2.00
(148) Bruce Hurst	.25
(149) Fred McGriff	.25
(150) Gary Sheffield	.50
(151) San Francisco Giants Logo	.25
(152) Will Clark	.30
(152p) Will Clark (Prototype)	1.50
(153) Willie McGee	.25
(154) Kevin Mitchell	.25
(155) Robby Thompson	.25
(156) Matt Williams	.25

1989 Hills Team MVP's

This high-gloss, boxed set of superstars was produced by Topps for the Hills department store chain. The words "Hills Team MVP's" appear above the player photos, while the player's name and team are printed below. The front of the card carries a red, white and blue color scheme with yellow and gold accents. The horizontal backs include player data set against a green playing field background.

	NM/M
Complete Set (33):	4.00
Common Player:	.10
1 Harold Baines	.10
2 Wade Boggs	.75
3 George Brett	1.00
4 Tom Brunansky	.10
5 Jose Canseco	.35
6 Joe Carter	.10
7 Will Clark	.15
8 Roger Clemens	.85
9 Dave Cone	.10
10 Glenn Davis	.10
11 Andre Dawson	.25
12 Dennis Eckersley	.40
13 Andres Galarraga	.10
14 Kirk Gibson	.10
15 Mike Greenwell	.10
16 Tony Gwynn	.75
17 Orel Hershiser	.10
18 Danny Jackson	.10
19 Mark Langston	.10
20 Fred McGriff	.10
21 Dale Murphy	.50
22 Eddie Murray	.50
23 Kirby Puckett	.75
24 Johnny Ray	.10
25 Juan Samuel	.10
26 Ruben Sierra	.10
27 Dave Stewart	.10
28 Darryl Strawberry	.10
29 Alan Trammell	.10
30 Andy Van Slyke	.10
31 Frank Viola	.10
32 Dave Winfield	.50
33 Robin Yount	.50

1990 Hills Hit Men

The 33 slugging percentage leaders are featured in this high-gloss boxed set. The cards were produced by Topps for the Hills department store chain. Fronts feature "Hit Men" in a bat design above the photo. The player's name appears on a band below the photo. Horizontal backs feature a breakdown of the player's slugging percentage and also display career statistics.

	NM/M
Complete Set (33):	5.00
Common Player:	.10
1 Eric Davis	.10
2 Will Clark	.15
3 Don Mattingly	.75
4 Darryl Strawberry	.10
5 Kevin Mitchell	.10
6 Pedro Guerrero	.10
7 Jose Canseco	.35
8 Jim Rice	.15
9 Danny Tartabull	.10
10 George Brett	.75
11 Kent Hrbek	.10
12 George Bell	.10
13 Eddie Murray	.50
14 Fred Lynn	.10
15 Andre Dawson	.25
16 Dale Murphy	.15
17 Dave Winfield	.50
18 Jack Clark	.10
19 Wade Boggs	.65
20 Ruben Sierra	.10
21 Dave Parker	.10
22 Glenn Davis	.10
23 Dwight Evans	.10
24 Jesse Barfield	.10
25 Kirk Gibson	.10
26 Alvin Davis	.10
27 Kirby Puckett	.65
28 Joe Carter	.10
29 Carlton Fisk	.50
30 Harold Baines	.10
31 Andres Galarraga	.10
32 Cal Ripken, Jr.	1.50
33 Howard Johnson	.10

1993 Hills Pirates Kids Club

DENNY NEAGLE

Stars of the Eastern Division N.L. champions are picutred on this 12-card issue. The set was issued in the form of a perforated 10" x 10-1/2" panel. Fronts have player action photos with orange frames, white borders and a team logo. Black-and-white backs have a player portrait, personal data and stats, and the Hills Pirates Kids Club logo. Cards are numbered by uniform number.

		NM/M
Complete Set, Sheet:		7.00
Complete Set, Singles (12):		6.00
Common Player:		.50
6	Orlando Merced	.50
7	Jeff King	.50
10	Jim Leyland	.50
14	Tom Prince	.50
23	Lloyd McClendon	.50
26	Steve Cooke	.50
28	Al Martin	.50
32	Denny Neagle	.50
36	Kevin Young	.50
45	John Candelaria	.50
50	Stan Belinda	.50
55	Blas Minor	.50

Hillshire Farm Home Run Heroes

ERNIE BANKS

Via a special offer on packages of Hillshire Farm meats, collectors could order an autographed card of several star sluggers of the 1960s. Cards were available by sending in a package coupon and $4 for handling. The 2-1/2" x 3-1/2" cards have color player photos on which uniform logos have been removed. Borders are black and enhanced with gold foil. Black and gold backs offer lifetime stats and career highlights.

		NM/M
Complete Set (4):		30.00
Common Player:		7.50
(1)	Ernie Banks	10.00
(2)	Harmon Killebrew	7.50
(3)	Frank Robinson	7.50
(4)	Willie Stargell	12.00

1988 Historic Limited Editions Brooklyn Dodgers

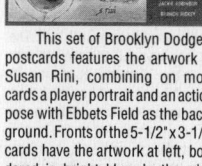

This set of Brooklyn Dodgers postcards features the artwork of Susan Rini, combining on most cards a player portrait and an action pose with Ebbets Field as the background. Fronts of the 5-1/2" x 3-1/2" cards have the artwork at left, bordered in bright blue. In the wide right border, the team name and

logo, and the player name, are printed in white. Postcard-style backs are printed in blue. The cards were issued in three series of 12 each, but are checklisted here in alphabetical order. Two different cards each exist for Erskine and Lavagetto. Production of the series was limited to 5,000 sets; 2,000 sets were produced with a low-gloss finish to facilitate autographing, while the remaining 3,000 sets were high-gloss. Either sold for $20 at time of issue. Two hundred uncut sheets of each series were sold for $30 apiece. A special album was also made available.

		NM/M
Complete Set (36):		10.00
Common Player:		.50
(1)	Cal Abrams	.50
(2)	Sandy Amoros	.50
(3)	Red Barber (Announcer)	.50
(4)	Ralph Branca	.50
(5)	Chuck Connors	.75
(6)	Roger Craig	.50
(7)	Roy Campanella	1.50
(8)	Don Drysdale	1.00
(9)	Leo Durocher	.50
(10)	Carl Erskine	.50
(11)	Carl Erskine	.50
(12)	Carl Furillo	.50
(13)	Gene Hermanski	.50
(14)	Gil Hodges	1.00
(15)	Clyde King	.50
(16)	Clem Labine	.50
(17)	Tommy Lasorda	.75
(18)	Cookie Lavagetto	.50
(19)	Cookie Lavagetto	.50
(20)	Larry MacPhail (GM)	.50
(21)	Sal Maglie	.50
(22)	Eddie Miksis	.50
(23)	Don Newcombe	.60
(24)	Walter O'Malley (Owner)	.50
(25)	Mickey Owen	.50
(26)	Andy Pafko	.50
(27)	Johnny Podres	.50
(28)	Pee Wee Reese	1.00
(29)	Preacher Roe	.50
(30)	Jackie Robinson	2.50
(31)	George Shuba	.50
(32)	Duke Snider	1.50
(33)	Red Barber, Leo Durocher	.50
(34)	Jackie Robinson, Branch Rickey	1.00
(35)	Ebbets Field	.50
(36)	Dodgers Sym-Phony Band	.50

Historic Limited Editions Lou Gehrig Postcards

LOU GEHRIG

This set of postcards combines portrait and action art with a Yankee Stadium backdrop in paintings by Susan Rini. The art is set towards the top of the 3-1/2" x 5-1/2" cards which have a pinstripe background, player name beneath the art and team name and logo at bottom. Horizontal backs are postcard-style and printed in blue with appropriate credit lines, copyright notice and logos. Original issue price was $10 per set, with uncut sheets available for $15.

		NM/M
Complete Set (8):		6.00
Common Card:		1.00

Don Mattingly Series 1

One of the most popular Yankees of the past 25 years is honored on this set of postcards. The 3-1/2" x 5-1/2" cards feature the artwork of Susan Rini on each card. Mattingly is shown in portrait and action art on most of the cards, though sometimes the picture of another Yankee great takes the place of the action picture. Background on the front is white with

DON MATTINGLY

blue pinstripes. Postcard-style backs are printed in blue and announce an edition of 5,000 sets. Price at issue was about $10, with uncut sheets of the cards available for $24.

	NM/M
Complete Set (12):	6.00
Common Card:	.50

Negro Leagues Postcards

WILLIE WELLS

NEGRO LEAGUE

Both well-known and obscure players of the segregated Negro Leagues are included in this series of color postcards. Fronts of the 3-1/2" x 5-1/2" cards have portrait and action paintings of the players on a peach-colored background. Postcard-style backs are printed in blue and indicate a limit of 5,000 sets were produced. An edition of 200 uncut sheets was also produced.

		NM/M
Complete Set (12):		7.00
Common Player:		.50
Uncut Sheet:		10.00
1	Monte Irvin	1.00
2	Martin Dihigo	.85
3	Clint Thomas	.50
4	Buster Haywood	.50
5	George Giles	.50
6	Isidro Fabri	.50
7	James (Cool Papa) Bell	.65
8	Josh Gibson	1.50
9	Lou Dials	.50
10	Willie Wells	.75
11	Walter (Buck) Leonard	.75
12	Jose Fernandez	.50

1990 Historic Limited Editions Roberto Clemente

ROBERTO CLEMENTE

PITTSBURGH PIRATES

This set of 3-1/2" x 5-1/2" postcards details the career of the Pirates outfielder. Background of each card is beige. At top is an approximately 3" x 3-1/2" color painting of Clemente in both portrait and

action poses, created by sports artist Susan Rini. Player and team name, and team logo are at bottom. Postcard-style backs are printed in blue with appropriate credit lines and copyright data. Production was reported at 5,000 sets.

	NM/M
Complete Set (12):	12.50
Common Card:	1.50

Thurman Munson Postcards

THURMAN MUNSON

New York Yankees

The late, great Yankees catcher is memorialized in this set of color postcards from sports artist Susan Rini. Fronts of the 3-1/2" x 5-1/2" cards have a combination portrait/action painting toward the top, on a background of pinstripes. Player and team names and the Yankees logo are at bottom. Horizontal backs are in postcard style, printed in blue with appropriate licensing, copyright and credit data, and logos. Production was limited to 5,000 sets and 200 complete-set uncut sheets.

		NM/M
Complete Set (12):		10.00
Common Card:		1.25
Uncut Sheet:		55.00
1-12	Thurman Munson	1.25

Nolan Ryan Series 1

NOLAN RYAN

The Mets and Rangers years are graphically depicted on this set of postcards in combined portrait and action paintings by sports artist Susan Rini. The 3-1/2" x 5-1/2" cards have a light blue background on front, with the player and team name, and the team logo at bottom. Postcard-style backs are printed in blue with copyright and licensing information, along with a notice that the set is limited to an edition of 10,000.

	NM/M
Complete Set (12):	10.00
Common Card:	1.00

Nolan Ryan Series 2

The Astros and Angels years are graphically depicted on this set of postcards in combined portrait and action paintings by Susan Rini. The 3-1/2" x 5-1/2" cards have a beige background on front, with the player and team name, and the team logo at bottom. Postcard-style backs are printed in blue and offer copyright and licensing information, along with a notice that the set is limited to an edition of 10,000.

		NM/M
Complete Set (36):		11.00
Common Player:		.50
1	Championship Trophy	.50
2	Shea Stadium	.50
3	Tommie Agee	.50
4	Ken Boswell	.50

NOLAN RYAN

Astros

NOLAN RYAN

	NM/M
Complete Set (12):	10.00
Common Card:	1.00

Yankees Monuments

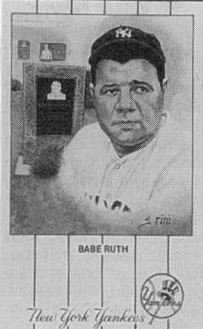

BABE RUTH

New York Yankees

Those honored with plaques in Monument Park behind the center field wall at Yankee Stadium are presented in this series of postcards. On a pinstriped background, the fronts of the 3-1/2" x 5-1/2" cards have a portrait of the person with his plaque in the background, the work of Susan Rini. The team name and logo are at bottom. Postcard-style backs are printed in blue with various copyright and creator notices, MLB logo and an indication that the cards were produced in an edition of 5,000. At time of issue, complete sets sold for about $10; uncut sheets were available for $20.

		NM/M
Complete Set (12):		12.00
Common Player:		.70
1	Lou Gehrig	2.25
2	Babe Ruth	3.00
3	Thurman Munson	1.50
4	Elston Howard	.70
5	Phil Rizzuto	.70
6	Mickey Mantle	4.50
7	Bill Dickey	.70
8	Lefty Gomez	.70
9	Pope Paul VI	2.25
10	Jacob Ruppert	.70
11	Roger Maris	2.25
12	Joe DiMaggio	3.00

1969 Mets Postcards

This set commemorates the Amazin' Mets World Championship team of 1969. The 5-1/2" x 3-1/2" cards have bright blue front borders. At left is a portrait/action painting of the players by sports artist Susan Rini. Postcard-style backs are printed in blue with copyright and credit data, card number, logos, etc. The issue was limited to 5,000 sets and originally sold for about $20. Uncut sheets were available for $25.

5	Ed Charles	.50
6	Don Cardwell	.50
7	Donn Clendenon	.65
8	Jack DiLauro	.50
9	Duffy Dyer	.50
10	Wayne Garrett	.50
11	Jerry Grote	.50
12	Rod Gaspar	.50
13	Gary Gentry	.50
14	Bud Harrelson	.65
15	Gil Hodges	1.00
16	Cleon Jones	.65
17	Ed Kranepool	.65
18	Cal Koonce	.50
19	Jerry Koosman	.65
20	Jim McAndrew	.50
21	Tug McGraw	.75
22	J.C. Martin	.50
23	Bob Pfeil	.50
24	Nolan Ryan	4.00
25	Ron Swoboda	.50
26	Tom Seaver	1.50
27	Art Shamsky	.50
28	Ron Taylor	.50
29	Al Weis	.50
30	Joe Pignatano	.50
31	Eddie Yost	.50
32	Ralph Kiner (Announcer)	.50
33	Bob Murphy (Writer)	.50
34	Lindsey Nelson (Announcer)	.50
35	Yogi Berra	1.00
36	Rube Walker	.50

1991 Historic Limited Editions Brooklyn Dodgers

Three additional series of 12-card player postcard sets in 1991 were issued as a follow-up to the company's debut issue of 1988. Identical in format, the 5-1/2" x 3-1/2" cards have a Dodger blue background on front. At the left end is artwork by Susan Rini combining portrait and action pictures of the player against a background of Ebbets Field. Player and team identification are in white at right. Postcard backs are printed in blue with credits, copyright data, logos and series and card numbers.

		NM/M
Complete Set (36):		20.00
Common Player:		.50
SERIES 2		5.00
1	Charley Dressen	.50
2	John Roseboro	.50
3	Eddie Stanky	.50
4	Goody Rosen	.50
5	Ed Head	.50
6	Dick Williams	.50
7	Clarence (Bud) Podbielan	.50
8	Erv Palica	.50
9	Augie Galan	.50
10	Billy Loes	.50
11	Billy Cox	.50
12	Phil Phifer	.50
SERIES 3		5.00
1	Joe Black	.75
2	Jack Banta	.50
3	Whitlow Wyatt	.50
4	Gino Cimoli	.50
5	Dolph Camilli (Dolf)	.50
6	Dan Bankhead	.50
7	Henry Behrman	.50
8	Pete Reiser	.50
9	Chris Van Cuyk	.50
10	James (Junior) Gilliam	.75
11	Don Zimmer	.75
12	Ed Roebuck	.50
SERIES 4		5.00
1	Billy Herman	.50
2	Rube Walker	.50
3	Tommy Brown	.50
4	Charlie Neal	.50
5	Kirby Higbe	.50
6	Bruce Edwards	.50
7	Joe Hatten	.50
8	Rex Barney	.50
9	Al Gionfriddo	.50
10	Luis Olmo	.50
11	Dixie Walker	.50
12	Walter Alston	1.00

Don Mattingly Series 2

Two years after the release of the first series, another 12 Mattingly postcards were issued. The 3-1/2" x 5-1/2" cards feature the artwork of Susan Rini on each card. Mattingly is shown in portrait and action art on each of the cards. Background on the front is white with blue pinstripes. Postcard-style backs are printed in blue and announce an edi-

DON MATTINGLY

New York Yankees

tion of 5,000 sets. Price at issue was about $10, with uncut sheets of the cards available for $24.

	NM/M
Complete Set (12):	6.00
Common Card:	.50
1-12 Don Mattingly	.50

1961 Yankees Postcards

New York Yankees

Three series of 12 postcards each were issued to commemorate the '61 Yanks. All cards are 5-1/2" x 3-1/2", with a pinstriped border design. At left front are combination portrait/action paintings by Susan Rini. Team name and logo are at right, along with player identification. Backs are printed in blue, in postcard style, with copyright, credits, logos, etc.

	NM/M
Complete Set (36):	16.00
Common Player:	.25
SERIES 1	3.00
1 Yogi Berra	1.00
2 Tom Tresh	.45
3 Bill Skowron	.45
4 Al Downing	.25
5 Jim Coates	.25
6 Luis Arroyo	.25
7 Johnny Blanchard	.25
8 Hector Lopez	.25
9 Tony Kubek	.50
10 Ralph Houk	.25
11 Bobby Richardson	.50
12 Clete Boyer	.35
SERIES 2	8.00
1 Roger Maris	6.00
2 Jesse Gonder	.25
3 Danny McDevitt	.25
4 Leroy Thomas	.25
5 Billy Gardner	.25
6 Ralph Terry	.25
7 Hal Reniff	.25
8 Earl Torgeson	.25
9 Art Ditmar	.25
10 Jack Reed	.25
11 Johnny James	.25
12 Elston Howard	.25
SERIES 3	6.00
1 Mickey Mantle	5.00
2 Deron Johnson	.25
3 Bob Hale	.25
4 Bill Stafford	.25
5 Duke Maas	.25
6 Bob Cerv	.25
7 Roland Sheldon	.35
8 Ryne Duren	.35
9 Bob Turley	.35
10 Whitey Ford	1.00
11 Bud Daley	.25
12 Joe DeMaestri	.25

1989 Holsum/Schafer's Super Stars Discs

SUPER STARS

Holsum Schafer's

WALLY JOYNER

This version of the 1989 MSA bakeries disc set was issued in Canada by Ben's bakeries. The discs are

nearly identical to the other regional variations except for the appearance of a red "Schafer's" logo at top.

	NM/M
Complete Set (20):	9.00
Common Player:	.25
1 Wally Joyner	.25
2 Wade Boggs	1.00
3 Ozzie Smith	1.00
4 Don Mattingly	1.25
5 Jose Canseco	.50
6 Tony Gwynn	1.00
7 Eric Davis	.25
8 Kirby Puckett	1.00
9 Kevin Seitzer	.25
10 Darryl Strawberry	.25
11 Gregg Jefferies	.25
12 Mark Grace	.25
13 Matt Nokes	.25
14 Mark McGwire	2.00
15 Don Mattingly	1.25
16 Roger Clemens	1.25
17 Frank Viola	.25
18 Orel Hershiser	.25
19 Dave Cone	.25
20 Kirk Gibson	.25

1989 Holsum Bakeries Super Stars Discs

This set of 2-3/4" diameter discs was manufactured by Mike Schechter Associates for Holsum bakeries' inclusion in various bread brands. Because the cards are licensed only by the Players Association and not MLB, the player photos have been airbrushed to remove cap and uniform logos. Cards feature white borders with red, yellow and blue decorations. Backs are printed in dark blue and include a few 1988 and career stats and some player vitals. The set was distributed in Michigan.

	NM/M
Complete Set (20):	12.00
Common Player:	.50
1 Wally Joyner	.50
2 Wade Boggs	2.00
3 Ozzie Smith	2.00
4 Don Mattingly	2.50
5 Jose Canseco	1.00
6 Tony Gwynn	2.00
7 Eric Davis	.50
8 Kirby Puckett	2.00
9 Kevin Seitzer	.50
10 Darryl Strawberry	.50
11 Gregg Jefferies	.50
12 Mark Grace	.50
13 Matt Nokes	.50
14 Mark McGwire	3.00
15 Bobby Bonilla	.50
16 Roger Clemens	2.50
17 Frank Viola	.50
18 Orel Hershiser	.50
19 Dave Cone	.50
20 Kirk Gibson	.50

1990 Holsum Bakeries Super Stars Discs

Holsum

SUPERSTARS

MARK DAVIS

Players in this disc set are featured in round portrait photos on which uniform logos have been painted over for lack of a license from Major League Baseball (the set is licensed by the Players Union and bears their logo on back). Most of the front border on these 2-3/4" diameter discs is in red, with yellow stars and white baseballs around the portrait and the bakery's logo at top. A yellow banner beneath the photo has the "Superstars" logo. At bottom, in the white portion of the border, the player's name is presented in red, with his team and position in blue. Backs are printed in blue and include 1989 and career stats, a few biographical details, the card number and appropriate copyrights.

	NM/M
Complete Set (20):	4.00
Common Player:	.25
1 George Bell	.25
2 Tim Raines	.25

3 Tom Henke	.25
4 Andres Galarraga	.25
5 Bret Saberhagen	.25
6 Mark Davis	.25
7 Robin Yount	.75
8 Rickey Henderson	.75
9 Kevin Mitchell	.25
10 Howard Johnson	.25
11 Will Clark	.30
12 Orel Hershiser	.25
13 Fred McGriff	.25
14 Dave Stewart	.25
15 Vince Coleman	.25
16 Steve Sax	.25
17 Kirby Puckett	1.00
18 Tony Gwynn	1.00
19 Jerome Walton	.25
20 Gregg Olson	.25

1991 Holsum Bakeries Super Stars Discs

SUPER STARS

TIM WALLACH

MONTREAL EXPOS THIRD BASE

Similar to the previous year's issue, the 20 discs in the 1991 bakery set feature a color player photo (uniform logos airbrushed off) at center, with a wide white border to the edge of the 2-3/4" diameter cardboard. The player's name appears in a yellow stripe at bottom, along with his team and position. Backs are printed in dark blue and include a few stats from the previous season. The issue was distributed in Canada for Ben's Bakeries.

	NM/M
Complete Set (20):	45.00
Common Player:	.75
1 Darryl Strawberry	.75
2 Eric Davis	.75
3 Tim Wallach	.75
4 Kevin Mitchell	.75
5 Tony Gwynn	4.50
6 Ryne Sandberg	4.50
7 Doug Drabek	.75
8 Randy Myers	.75
9 Ken Griffey Jr.	6.50
10 Alan Trammell	.75
11 Ken Griffey Sr.	.75
12 Rickey Henderson	3.00
13 Roger Clemens	5.50
14 Bob Welch	.75
15 Kelly Gruber	.75
16 Mark McGwire	7.50
17 Cecil Fielder	.75
18 Dave Steib	.75
19 Nolan Ryan	9.00
20 Cal Ripken, Jr.	9.00

1983 Homeplate Sports Cards Al Kaline Story

Commemorating Al Kaline's 30th anniversary with the Detroit Tigers, this set chronicles his life and career. The 2-1/2" x 3-1/2" cards have either black-and-white front photos with orange borders or color photos with black borders. Backs reverse the color scheme and provide details about the photo on front. The first card in each set has been personally autographed by Kaline.

	NM/M
Complete Set (73):	15.00
Common Card:	.25
1a 30 Years a Tiger/Auto.	12.00
1b I'd play baseball for nothing	.25
2 Sandlot days in Baltimore	.25

3 MVP trophy winner	.25
4 Learning the ropes	.25
5 Working for a living	.25
6 Pleasing a young fan	.25
7 Al and Louise - the newlyweds	.25
8 Al and Pat Mullin	.25
9 How Al does it #1	.25
10 How Al does it #2	.25
11 Silver Bat for the Champ	.25
12 Al and George Stark	.25
13 Al watches Gordie Howe swing a bat	2.00
14 Kaline and Mantle - Batting Champs	1.00
15 Kaline	.25
16 Martin, Kaline, Kuenn, Mantle, Ford	.50
17 Crossing the plate	.25
18 1959 All-Star Game (W/Bill Skowron.)	.25
19 Cash, Colavito, Kaline	.50
20 Kaline slides under Nellie Fox	.25
21 One of many awards	.25
22 Kaline, Jim Campbell, Norm Cash - 1962	.25
23 Costly catch - 1962	.25
24 Jim Bunning, Al, Norm Cash in Japan	.25
25 Perfect form	.25
26 Ernie Harwell, Al, George Kell	.25
27 Life isn't always easy	.25
28 Al, Michael and Mark Kaline	.25
29 Al and Charlie Dressen - 1965	.25
30 George Kell and Al - Fielding masters	.25
31 Al and Hal Newhouser	.25
32 Michael, Louise, Al and Mark Kaline	.25
33 Al, Charlie Gehringer, Bill Freehan	.25
34 Rapping a hit in 1967	.25
35 Veteran rivals Mantle and Kaline	1.00
36 Al homers against Boston - 1968	.25
37 1968 World Series homer	.25
38 Premier fielder	.25
39 All-Time All-Stars (W/Hank Greenberg, etc.)	.50
40 Part of the game	.25
41 Family portrait	.25
42 Spring training tribute	.25
43 Billy Martin and Al	.25
44 First $100,000 Tiger	.25
45 On deck - 1972	.25
46 A close call	.25
47 On deck in Baltimore - 1974	.25
48 Hit number 3,000 - 1974	.25
49 April 17, 1955 - 3 Homers	.25
50 All-Star Game record	.25
51 1968 Series action - Cepeda	.25
52 Celebrating 1968	.25
53 Al Kaline Day	.25
54 3,000 Hit Day	.25
55 Thank you - Sept. 29, 1974	.25
56 Silver salute - Sept. 29, 1974	.25
57 Al and Kell - a new career	.25
58 Voices of the Tigers	.25
59 Tiger record setter	.25
60 1970 AL All-Star team	.25
61 Pat Mullin and Al	.25
62 Al and Lolich - Aug., 1980	.25
63 Hall of Fame plaque	.25
64 Al and Bowie Kuhn - Aug. 4, 1980	.25
65 Al and parents - Aug., 1980	.25
66 Fame	.25
67 "The Man" and the Boy (W/Stan Musial.)	.50
68 Two Kids - Ted Williams and Kaline	.50
69 Master glovemen (W/Brooks Robinson.)	.45
70 Coach and Pupil - Al and Pat Underwood	.25
71 Kaline career records	.25
72 A Tiger Forever	.25

1990 Homers Cookies Pittsburgh Pirates

This set of 4" x 6" color cards was a stadium giveaway. Fronts have borderless game-action front photos. Backs are in black, white and green and have player biographical data, major and minor league stats, career highlights and a sponsor's logo.

	NM/M
Complete Set (31):	20.00
Common Player:	.50
(1) Wally Backman	.50
(2) Doug Bair	.50
(3) Jay Bell	.50
(4) Rafael Belliard	.50
(5) Barry Bonds	8.00
(6) Bobby Bonilla	.50

BARRY BONDS

(7) Sid Bream	.50
(8) John Cangelosi	.50
(9) Rich Donnelly	.50
(10) Doug Drabek	.50
(11) Billy Hatcher	.50
(12) Neal Heaton	.50
(13) Jeff King	.50
(14) Bob Kipper	.50
(15) Randy Kramer	.50
(16) Gene Lamont	.50
(17) Bill Landrum	.50
(18) Mike LaValliere	.50
(19) Jim Leyland	.50
(20) Jose Lind	.50
(21) Milt May	.50
(22) Ray Miller	.50
(23) Ted Power	.50
(24) Gary Redus	.50
(25) R.J. Reynolds	.50
(26) Tommy Sandt	.50
(27) Don Slaught	.50
(28) John Smiley	.50
(29) Walt Terrell	.50
(30) Andy Van Slyke	.50
(31) Bob Walk	.50

1991 Homers Cookies

SATCHEL PAIGE

One Hall of Famer's card was inserted in each box of Homers Cookies. The cards measure 2-1/2" x 3-1/2" and feature sepia-toned photos. The card backs feature lifetime statistics and career highlights. The cards are also numbered on the back and a checklist is featured on the back of each card.

	NM/M
Complete Set (9):	5.00
Common Player:	.50
1 Babe Ruth	2.00
2 Satchel Paige	.75
3 Lefty Gomez	.50
4 Ty Cobb	1.00
5 Cy Young	.50
6 Bob Feller	.50
7 Roberto Clemente	2.00
8 Dizzy Dean	.50
9 Lou Gehrig	1.50

1999 Homers Cookies

WILLIE STARGELL   1st BASE

HOMERS

Former stars are featured in this set of cards inserted into specially marked boxes of cookies (suggested retail about $1). The 2-1/2" x 3-1/2"

cards have color player photos (without uniform logos) with a white border. At top is player identification, at bottom is a red stripe with "HOMERS." Horizontal backs have a cartoon, career data, biographical information and a checklist.

	NM/M
Complete Set (9):	7.50
Common Player:	1.00
1 Vida Blue	1.00
2 Orlando Cepeda	1.00
3 Darrell Evans	1.00
4 Harmon Killebrew	1.00
5 Dave Kingman	1.00
6 Eddie Murray	1.50
7 Frank Robinson	1.50
8 Willie Stargell	1.50
9 Carl Yastrzemski	1.50

1985 Hostess Braves

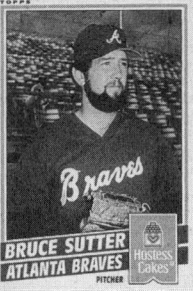

BRUCE SUTTER   ATLANTA BRAVES   PITCHER

Hostess Cakes

After a five-year hiatus, Hostess returned to the production of baseball cards in 1985 with an Atlanta Braves team set. The 22 cards in the set were printed by Topps and inserted into packages of snack cake products, three cello-wrapped player cards and a header card per box. The 2-1/2" x 3-1/2" cards share a common back design with the regular-issue Topps cards of 1985.

	NM/M
Complete Set (22):	4.00
Common Player:	.35
1 Eddie Haas	.35
2 Len Barker	.35
3 Steve Bedrosian	.35
4 Bruce Benedict	.35
5 Rick Camp	.35
6 Rick Cerone	.35
7 Chris Chambliss	.35
8 Terry Forster	.35
9 Gene Garber	.35
10 Albert Hall	.35
11 Bob Horner	.50
12 Glenn Hubbard	.35
13 Brad Komminsk	.35
14 Rick Mahler	.35
15 Craig McMurtry	.35
16 Dale Murphy	3.00
17 Ken Oberkfell	.35
18 Pascual Perez	.35
19 Gerald Perry	.35
20 Rafael Ramirez	.35
21 Bruce Sutter	2.50
22 Claudell Washington	.35
--- Header Card	.05

1987 Hostess Stickers

RYNE SANDBERG

Hostess of Canada issued a 30-card set of stickers in specially marked bags of potato chips. One sticker, measuring 1-3/4" x 1-3/8" in size, was found in each bag. The stickers have full-color fronts with the player's name appearing in black type in a white band. The Hostess logo and the sticker number are also included on the fronts. The backs are written in both English and French and contain the player's name, position and team.

		NM/M
Complete Set (30):		12.00
Common Player:		.25
1	Jesse Barfield	.25
2	Ernie Whitt	.25
3	George Bell	.25
4	Hubie Brooks	.25
5	Tim Wallach	.25
6	Floyd Youmans	.25
7	Dale Murphy	.50
8	Ryne Sandberg	2.25
9	Eric Davis	.25
10	Mike Scott	.25
11	Fernando Valenzuela	.25
12	Gary Carter	1.50
13	Mike Schmidt	2.50
14	Tony Pena	.25
15	Ozzie Smith	2.00
16	Tony Gwynn	2.00
17	Mike Krukow	.25
18	Eddie Murray	1.50
19	Wade Boggs	2.00
20	Wally Joyner	.25
21	Harold Baines	.25
22	Brook Jacoby	.25
23	Lou Whitaker	.25
24	George Brett	2.50
25	Robin Yount	1.50
26	Kirby Puckett	2.00
27	Don Mattingly	2.50
28	Jose Canseco	.75
29	Phil Bradley	.25
30	Pete O'Brien	.25

1988 Hostess Potato Chips Expos/Blue Jays

The Expos and Blue Jays are showcased in this set of 24 discs (1-1/2" diameter). Full-color portraits are framed in white, surrounded by red stars. A yellow-banner "1988 Collectors Edition" label is printed (English and French) beneath the photo, followed by the player's name in black. Numbered disc backs are bilingual, blue and white, and include player name and stats. The set was distributed inside Hostess potato chip packages sold in Canada.

		NM/M
Complete Panel Set (12):		6.50
Complete Singles Set (24):		4.50
Common Panel:		.50
Common Player:		.35
Panel 1		.50
1	Mitch Webster	.35
20	Lloyd Moseby	.35
Panel 2		.50
2	Tim Burke	.35
23	Tom Henke	.35
Panel 3		.50
3	Tom Foley	.35
13	Jim Clancy	.35
Panel 4		.50
4	Herm Winningham	.35
14	Rance Mulliniks	.35
Panel 5		.75
5	Hubie Brooks	.35
24	Jimmy Key	.35
Panel 6		.75
6	Mike Fitzgerald	.35
17	Dave Steib	.35
Panel 7		1.50
7	Tim Wallach	.35
15	Fred McGriff	.50
Panel 8		1.50
8	Andres Galarraga	.45
21	Tony Fernandez	.35
Panel 9		.50
9	Floyd Youmans	.35
18	Mark Eichhorn	.35
Panel 10		.50
10	Neal Heaton	.35
19	Jesse Barfield	.35
Panel 11		1.00
11	Tim Raines	.45
16	Ernie Whitt	.35
Panel 12		.75
12	Casey Candaele	.35
22	George Bell	.35

1990 Hostess Blue Jays Highlight Stickers

Team history highlights through the 1980 season are featured in this set of stickers. The set was produced and distributed in 1989 in strips of three 2-1/4" x 3-1/4" stickers, some oriented horizontally, some vertically. Fronts have color photos with a light blue box beneath containing the highlight printed in both English and French. Black-and-white Hostess and team logos are at the left and right, respectively. Backs

are blank. The set is checklisted here alphabetically based on the title of the sticker at top or left of the strip.

		NM/M
Complete Set (18):		15.00
Common Sticker:		.50
Panel 1		2.00
(1)	First AL East Pennant (Dave Steib)	.50
(2)	Killer Bees Born (George Bell, Lloyd Moseby, Jesse Barfield)	1.00
(3)	AL Home Run Champ (Jesse Barfield)	1.00
Panel 2		2.00
(4)	First Home Run in Skydome (Fred McGriff)	1.50
(5)	Club Save Leader (Tom Henke)	.50
(6)	Three Winning Openers in a Row (Jimmy Key)	1.00
Panel 3		2.00
(7)	First 100 Wins (Jim Clancy)	.50
(8)	ML Home Run Record (Ernie Whitt)	.50
(9)	AL East Champs Again (Tom Henke)	.50
Panel 4		2.00
(10)	Home Run on First Pitch (Junior Felix)	.50
(11)	Almost Perfect (Dave Steib)	.50
(12)	First Game at Skydome (Dave Steib)	.50
Panel 5		2.00
(13)	Most Double Plays (Damaso Garcia)	.50
(14)	M.V.P. (George Bell)	.50
(15)	Hits the Cycle (Kelly Gruber)	.50
Panel 6		2.00
(16)	Stolen Bases (Dave Collins)	.50
(17)	Gold Glove Winners (Jesse Barfield, Tony Fernandez)	.50
(18)	Goodbye to Exhibition Stadium	.50

1993 Hostess Twinkies

The Continental Baking Co., makers of Hostess Twinkies and cupcakes, returned to the baseball card market in 1993 with a 32-card set issued in two series. The promotion began around opening day with the first series; the second series was made available after the All-Star break. The cards were packaged in multi-packs with cupcakes that look like baseballs, with three cards in a box of eight cupcakes.

	NM/M
Complete Set (32):	4.00
Common Player:	.10
Uncut Sheet:	9.00

1	Andy Van Slyke	.10
2	Ryne Sandberg	.65
3	Bobby Bonilla	.10
4	John Kruk	.10
5	Ray Lankford	.10
6	Gary Sheffield	.25
7	Darryl Strawberry	.10
8	Barry Larkin	.10
9	Terry Pendleton	.10
10	Jose Canseco	.40
11	Dennis Eckersley	.50
12	Brian McRae	.10
13	Frank Thomas	.60
14	Roberto Alomar	.25
15	Cecil Fielder	.10
16	Carlos Baerga	.10
17	Will Clark	.15
18	Andres Galarraga	.10
19	Jeff Bagwell	.60
20	Brett Butler	.10
21	Benito Santiago	.10
22	Tom Glavine	.25
23	Rickey Henderson	.60
24	Wally Joyner	.10
25	Ken Griffey Jr.	.85
26	Cal Ripken Jr.	1.00
27	Roger Clemens	.75
28	Don Mattingly	.75
29	Kirby Puckett	.65
30	Larry Walker	.10
31	Jack McDowell	.10
32	Pat Listach	.10

1986 Houston Astros Police

This full-color police safety set was issued by the Houston Police Department and sponsored by Kool-Aid. The set was distributed at the Astrodome on June 14, when 15,000 sets of the first 12 cards were given away. The balance of the set was distributed throughout the summer by police. The cards feature player photos on the fronts and a safety tip on the back. The cards measure 4-1/8" x 2-5/8".

	NM/M
Complete Set (26):	4.00
Common Player:	.25
1	Jim Pankovits	.25
2	Nolan Ryan	3.00
3	Mike Scott	.25
4	Kevin Bass	.25
5	Bill Doran	.25
6	Hal Lanier	.25
7	Denny Walling	.25
8	Alan Ashby	.25
9	Phil Garner	.25
10	Charlie Kerfeld	.25
11	Dave Smith	.25
12	Jose Cruz	.25
13	Craig Reynolds	.25
14	Mark Bailey	.25
15	Bob Knepper	.25
16	Julio Solano	.25
17	Dickie Thon	.25
18	Mike Madden	.25
19	Jeff Calhoun	.25
20	Tony Walker	.25
21	Terry Puhl	.25
22	Glenn Davis	.25
23	Billy Hatcher	.25
24	Jim Deshaies	.25
25	Frank DiPino	.25
26	Coaching Staff (Yogi Berra, Matt Galante, Denis Menke, Les Moss, Gene Tenace)	.25

1987 Houston Astros Police

The 1987 Astros safety set was produced through the combined efforts of the team, Deer Park Hospital and Sportsmedia Presentations. Cards #1-12 were handed out to youngsters 14 and under at the Astrodome on July 14. The balance of the distribution was handled by Deer Park Hospital. The cards, which measure 2-5/8" x 4-1/8", contain full-color

photos. The backs offer a brief team/player history and a "Tips From The Dugout" anti-drug message.

	NM/M
Complete Set (26):	5.00
Common Player:	.25
1	Larry Andersen	.25
2	Mark Bailey	.25
3	Jose Cruz	.25
4	Danny Darwin	.25
5	Bill Doran	.25
6	Billy Hatcher	.25
7	Hal Lanier	.25
8	Davey Lopes	.25
9	Dave Meads	.25
10	Craig Reynolds	.25
11	Mike Scott	.25
12	Denny Walling	.25
13	Aurelio Lopez	.25
14	Dickie Thon	.25
15	Terry Puhl	.25
16	Nolan Ryan	4.00
17	Dave Smith	.25
18	Julio Solano	.25
19	Jim Deshaies	.25
20	Bob Knepper	.25
21	Alan Ashby	.25
22	Kevin Bass	.25
23	Glenn Davis	.25
24	Phil Garner	.25
25	Jim Pankovits	.25
26	Coaching Staff (Yogi Berra, Matt Galante, Denis Menke, Les Moss, Gene Tenace)	.25

1988 Houston Astros Police

This set of full-color cards highlighting the Houston Astros was produced by the team, in conjunction with Deer Park Hospital and Sportsmedia Promotions for distribution to fans 14 years and younger at a ball-park giveaway. The 2-5/8" x 4-1/8" cards feature full-color player photos framed by a narrow blue border with an orange player/team name block below the photo. Blue-and-white backs have orange borders with player information, career highlights and anti-drug tips.

	NM/M
Complete Set (26):	5.00
Common Player:	.25
1	Juan Agosto	.25
2	Larry Andersen	.25
3	Joaquin Andujar	.25
4	Alan Ashby	.25
5	Mark Bailey	.25
6	Kevin Bass	.25
7	Danny Darwin	.25
8	Glenn Davis	.25
9	Jim Deshaies	.25
10	Bill Doran	.25
11	Billy Hatcher	.25
12	Jeff Heathcock	.25
13	Steve Henderson	.25
14	Chuck Jackson	.25
15	Bob Knepper	.25
16	Jim Pankovits	.25
17	Terry Puhl	.25

18	Rafael Ramirez	.25
19	Craig Reynolds	.25
20	Nolan Ryan	4.00
21	Mike Scott	.25
22	Dave Smith	.25
23	Denny Walling	.25
24	Gerald Young	.25
25	Hal Lanier	.25
26	Coaching Staff (Yogi Berra, Gene Clines, Matt Galante, Marc Hill, Denis Menke, Les Moss)	.25

2005 Houston Astros Card Deck

This stadium giveaway was sponsored by Academy Sports+ Outdoors. Cards are 2-1/2" x 3-1/2" with rounded corners. Backs have a baseball in the background with team and sponsor's logos. Fronts have game-action photos. Many players have two cards in the deck, most with the same photo.

		NM/M
Complete Set (56):		12.00
Common Player:		.25
AS	Roger Clemens	3.00
2S	Russ Springer	.25
3S	Chad Harville	.25
4S	Brad Lidge	.35
5S	Jeff Bagwell	1.00
6S	Jason Lane	.25
7S	Luke Scott	.25
8S	Brad Lidge	.35
9S	Roger Clemens	3.00
10S	Jason Lane	.25
JS	Luke Scott	.25
QS	Minute Maid Park	.25
KS	Jeff Bagwell	1.00
AD	Roy Oswalt	.50
2D	Brad Ausmus	.25
3D	Russ Springer	.25
4D	Raul Chavez	.25
5D	Morgan Ensberg	.25
6D	Brandon Duckworth	.25
7D	Orlando Palmeiro	.25
8D	Brandon Duckworth	.25
9D	Roy Oswalt	.50
10D	Orlando Palmeiro	.25
JD	Morgan Ensberg	.25
QD	Minute Maid Park	.25
KD	Brad Ausmus	.25
AC	Brandon Backe	.25
2C	Chris Burke	.25
3C	Dan Wheeler	.25
4C	Eric Bruntlett	.25
5C	Jose Vizcaino	.25
6C	Dan Wheeler	.25
7C	Craig Biggio	.50
8C	Willy Taveras	.25
9C	Brandon Backe	.25
10C	Jose Vizcaino	.25
JC	Willy Taveras	.25
QC	Minute Maid Park	.25
KC	Craig Biggio	.50
AH	Andy Pettitte	.35
2H	Raul Chavez	.25
3H	Chad Qualls	.25
4H	John Franco	.25
5H	Mike Lamb	.25
6H	Adam Everett	.25
7H	John Franco	.25
8H	Lance Berkman	.50
9H	Andy Pettitte	.35
10H	Mike Lamb	.25
JH	Adam Everett	.25
QH	Minute Maid Park	.25
KH	Lance Berkman	.50
---	Phil Garner	.25
---	Phil Garner	.25
---	NL Wild Cardb 04	.05
---	NL Wild Card 04	.05

1989 Houston Colt .45s Fire Safety

The expansion Houston Colt .45s of 1962 are featured in this 1989 fire safety issue. The 2-1/2" x 3-1/2" cards have sepia player photos on front, with blue pistol frames and team logo, an orange name banner and brown Smokey logo. Backs are in black-and-white with

a fire prevention cartoon, Forest Service logos and the player name, position and uniform number. Cards numbers are at upper-right.

		NM/M
Complete Set (29):		12.50
Common Player:		.50
1	Bob Bruce	.50
2	Al Cicotte	.50
3	Dave Giusti	.50
4	Jim Golden	.50
5	Ken Johnson	.50
6	Tom Borland	.50
7	Bobby Shantz	.50
8	Dick Farrell	.50
9	Jim Umbricht	.50
10	Hal Woodeshick	.50
11	Merritt Ranew	.50
12	Hal Smith	.50
13	Jim Campbell	.50
14	Norm Larker	.75
15	Joe Amalfitano	.50
16	Bob Aspromonte	.75
17	Bob Lillis	.50
18	Dick Gernert	.50
19	Don Buddin	.50
20	Pidge Browne	.50
21	Von McDaniel	.50
22	Don Taussig	.50
23	Al Spangler	.50
24	Al Heist	.50
25	Jim Pendleton	.50
26	Johnny Weekly	.50
27	Harry Craft	.50
28	.45s Coaches (Lum Harris, Bobby Bragan, Jim Busby, Cot Deal, Jim Adair)	.50
29	Team Photo	.50

1993 Hoyle Legends of Baseball

Specially marked decks of Hoyle playing cards contained one of nine Hall of Famer's cards. In the 2-1/2" x 3-1/2" round-cornered poker-size format, the cards have oft-seen black-and-white photos on a glossy front. Backs have a facsimile autograph, biographical data, some stats and career highlights.

		NM/M
Complete Set (9):		12.00
Common Player:		1.00
(1)	Ty Cobb	2.00
(2)	Dizzy Dean	1.00
(3)	Lou Gehrig	2.00
(4)	Walter Johnson	1.00
(5)	Satchel Paige	1.00
(6)	Babe Ruth	3.00
(7)	Casey Stengel	1.00
(8)	Honus Wagner	1.50
(9)	Cy Young	1.00

1993 Humpty Dumpty

The Canadian potato chip company Humpty Dumpty issued a 50-card set of miniature cards in 1993. The UV coated cards measure 1-7/16" x 1-15/16", with a full-bleed color photo on the front along with the team logo. The backs have three-year statistics and biographical information about the player, are printed on heavy paper, with round corners. Backs are printed in French, and contain an offer for an album to house the set.

		NM/M
Complete Set (24):		15.00
Common Player:		1.00
Album:		5.00
0	Al Oliver	2.00
4	Chris Speier	1.00
5	John Milner	1.00
6	Jim Fanning	1.00
8	Gary Carter	7.50
10	Andre Dawson	5.00
11	Frank Tavaras (Taveras)	1.00
16	Terry Francona	1.00
17	Tim Blackwell	1.00
18	Jerry White	1.00
20	Bob James	1.00
21	Scott Sanderson	1.00
24	Brad Mills	1.00
29	Tim Wallach	1.00
30	Tim Raines	3.00
34	Bill Gullickson	1.00
35	Woodie Fryman	1.00
38	Bryn Smith	1.00
41	Jeff Reardon	1.00
44	Dan Norman	1.00
45	Steve Rogers	1.00
48	Ray Burris	1.00
49	Warren Cromartie	1.00
53	Charlie Lea	1.00

1987 Hygrade Baseball's All-Time Greats

(See "Baseball's All-Time Greats" for checklist and values.)

I

1994 Innovative Confections Sucker Savers

These 2-3/8" diameter discs were included in a plastic snap-top lollipop holder. A yellow strip which intersects the red border at the top contains the player name and team, while a yellow diamond graphic surrounds the player photo. Produced by Michael Schechter Assoc., the discs are licensed by the Players Union but not MLB, so team uniform logos are airbrushed off the photos. Backs are printed in blue and have 1993 and career stats. Square "proof" versions are common in the hobby and carry little or no premium.

		NM/M
Complete Set (20):		25.00
Common Player:		1.00
1	Rickey Henderson	2.00
2	Ken Caminiti	1.00
3	Terry Pendleton	1.00
4	Tim Raines	1.00
5	Joe Carter	1.00
6	Benito Santiago	1.00
7	Jim Abbott	1.00
8	Ozzie Smith	2.50
9	Don Slaught	1.00
10	Tony Gwynn	2.50
11	Mark Langston	1.00
12	Darryl Strawberry	1.00
13	David Justice	1.00
14	Cecil Fielder	1.00
15	Cal Ripken Jr.	4.00
16	Jeff Bagwell	2.00
17	Mike Piazza	3.00
18	Bobby Bonilla	1.00
19	Barry Bonds	4.00
20	Roger Clemens	2.75

1991 International Playing Card Co. All-Stars

(See 1991 U.S. Playing Card All-Stars for checklist and price guide.)

along with appropriate product and baseball logos and a card number. Besides being packed one per bag in chips, the complete set was also available via a mail-in offer with a plastic album.

		NM/M
Complete Set (50):		10.00
Complete Set, W/Album:		15.00
Common Player:		.25
1	Cal Ripken, Jr.	3.00
2	Mike Mussina	.50
3	Roger Clemens	2.25
4	Chuck Finley	.25
5	Sandy Alomar	.25
6	Frank Thomas	1.00
7	Robin Ventura	.25
8	Cecil Fielder	.25
9	George Brett	2.00
10	Cal Eldred	.25
11	Kirby Puckett	1.50
12	Dave Winfield	1.00
13	Jim Abbott	.25
14	Rickey Henderson	1.00
15	Ken Griffey Jr.	2.50
16	Nolan Ryan	3.00
17	Ivan Rodriguez	.75
18	Paul Molitor	1.00
19	John Olerud	.25
20	Joe Carter	.25
21	Jack Morris	.25
22	Roberto Alomar	.40
23	Pat Borders	.25
24	Devon White	.25
25	Juan Guzman	.25
26	Steve Avery	.25
27	John Smoltz	.25
28	Mark Grace	.25
29	Jose Rijo	.25
30	Dave Nied	.25
31	Benito Santiago	.25
32	Jeff Bagwell	1.00
33	Tim Wallach	.25
34	Eric Karros	.25
35	Delino DeShields	.25
36	Wilfredo Cordero	.25
37	Marquis Grissom	.25
38a	Ken Hill (Weight: 1915)	.50
38b	Ken Hill (Weight: 195)	.25
39	Moises Alou	.25
40	Chris Nabholz	.25
41	Dennis Martinez	.25
42	Larry Walker	.25
43	Bobby Bonilla	.25
44	Lenny Dykstra	.25
45	Tim Wakefield	.25
46	Andy Van Slyke	.25
47	Tony Gwynn	1.50
48	Fred McGriff	.25
49	Barry Bonds	3.00
50	Ozzie Smith	1.50
---	Checklist	.10

1982 Hygrade Expos

Gary Carter 8

This Montreal Expos team set was the object of intense collector speculation when it was first issued. Single cello-wrapped cards were included in packages of Hygrade luncheon meat in the province of Quebec only. A mail-in offer for the complete set appeared later in the season. It remains a relatively scarce issue today. The 2" x 3" cards

1994 International Playing Cards Toronto Blue Jays

ROBERTO ALOMAR ♣ 2B

Virtually identical to the team and mixed stars playing card sets issued by U.S. Playing Card Co., this Toronto team set was issued for the Canadian market. In playing card format at 2-1/2" x 3-1/2" with rounded corners, the set features Blue Jays players on front with their name and position in white in a blue stripe beneath the photo. Backs are bright blue with the team logo at top-center and sponsors' logos along the bottom. The set was sold in a colorful cardboard box.

		NM/M
Complete Set (55):		4.00
Common Player:		.05
AC	John Olerud	.15
2C	Al Leiter	.05
3C	Dave Stewart	.10
4C	Pat Borders	.05
5C	Devon White	.10
6C	Joe Carter	.10
7C	Roberto Alomar	.35
8C	Woody Williams	.05
9C	Eddie Zosky	.05
10C	Willie Canate	.05
JC	Danny Cox	.05
QC	Todd Stottlemyre	.10
KC	Ed Sprague	.05
AS	Paul Molitor	1.00
2S	Michael Timlin	.05
3S	Randy Knorr	.05
4S	Pat Hentgen	.05
5S	Darnell Coles	.05
6S	Juan Guzman	.05
7S	Roberto Alomar	.35
8S	Joe Carter	.10
9S	Scott Brow	.05
10S	Dick Schofield	.05
JS	Rob Butler	.05
QS	Tony Castillo	.05
KS	Duane Ward	.05
AH	Joe Carter	.10
2H	Woody Williams	.05
3H	Danny Cox	.05
4H	Todd Stottlemyre	.10
5H	Ed Sprague	.05
6H	John Olerud	.15
7H	Paul Molitor	1.00
8H	Scott Brow	.05
9H	Pat Hentgen	.05
10H	Al Leiter	.05
JH	Dave Stewart	.10
QH	Pat Borders	.05
KH	Devon White	.10
AD	Roberto Alomar	.35
2D	Eddie Zosky	.05
3D	Rob Butler	.05
4D	Tony Castillo	.05
5D	Duane Ward	.05
6D	Paul Molitor	1.00
7D	John Olerud	.15
8D	Carlos Delgado	.75
9D	Michael Timlin	.05
10D	Randy Knorr	.05
JD	Pat Hentgen	.05
QD	Darnell Coles	.05
KD	Juan Guzman	.05
Joker	Team Name	.05
Joker	A.L. Logo	.05
---	Checklist	.05

1995 International Playing Cards Toronto Blue Jays

For a second year the Canadian affiliate of the U.S. Playing Card Co. issued a team set of Blue Jays. Fronts have color portrait and action photos - up to three for popular players - with player identification and traditional playing card suit and value indicators in opposite corners. Cards are in 2-1/2" x 3-1/2" round-cornered format and were sold in a colorful flip-top box.

	NM/M
Complete Set (56):	4.00
Common Player:	.05

AC	John Olerud	.15
2C	Pat Hentgen	.05
3C	Juan Guzman	.05
4C	Cecil Fielder	.10
5C	Roberto Alomar	.35
6C	Joe Carter	.10
7C	Mark Eichhorn	.05
8C	Carlos Delgado	.75
9C	Tom Candiotti	.05
10C	Dave Stewart	.10
JC	Tony Fernandez	.05
QC	Pat Borders	.05
KC	Dave Winfield	1.00
AS	Paul Molitor	1.00
2S	Todd Stottlemyre	.10
3S	Rickey Henderson	1.00
4S	Tom Henke	.05
5S	Fred McGriff	.10
6S	Devon White	.10
7S	Duane Ward	.05
8S	David Wells	.05
9S	David Cone	.10
10S	Mike Timlin	.05
JS	Ed Sprague	.05
QS	Jack Morris	.05
KS	Jimmy Key	.10
AH	Roberto Alomar	.35
2H	Candy Maldonado	.05
3H	Mike Timlin	.05
4H	Ed Sprague	.05
5H	Pat Borders	.05
6H	Jimmy Key	.10
7H	Paul Molitor	1.00
8H	Candy Maldonado	.05
9H	Danny Cox	.05
10H	Todd Stottlemyre	.05
JH	Rickey Henderson	1.00
QH	Tom Henke	.05
KH	Cecil Fielder	.10
AD	Joe Carter	.10
2D	Duane Ward	.05
3D	Dave Stewart	.10
4D	Tony Fernandez	.05
5D	Jack Morris	.05
6D	Dave Winfield	1.00
7D	John Olerud	.15
8D	Manny Lee	.05
9D	Pat Hentgen	.05
JD	Randy Knorr	.05
JD	Juan Guzman	.05
QD	Fred McGriff	.10
KD	Devon White	.10
---	Toronto Blue Jays	.05
---	Team Logo Card	.05
---	A.L. Logo Card	.05
---	Checklist	.05

J

1984 Jarvis Press Rangers

BILLY SAMPLE OF Rangers

For its second annual "Baseball Card Day" game promotional set, the Rangers picked up a new sponsor, Jarvis Press of Dallas. The 30 cards in the set include 27 players, the manager, trainer and a group card of the coaches. Cards measure 2-3/8" x 3-1/2". Color game-action photos make up the card fronts. Backs, printed in black and white, include a portrait photo of the player. A source close to the promotion indicated 10,000 sets were produced.

	NM/M
Complete Set (30):	4.00
Common Player:	.35

1	Bill Stein	.35
2	Alan Bannister	.35
3	Wayne Tolleson	.35
5	Billy Sample	.35
6	Bobby Jones	.35
7	Ned Yost	.35
9	Pete O'Brien	.35
11	Doug Rader	.35
13	Tommy Dunbar	.35
14	Jim Anderson	.35
15	Larry Parrish	.35
16	Mike Mason	.35

17	Mickey Rivers	.35
19	Curtis Wilkerson	.35
20	Jeff Kunkel	.35
21	Odell Jones	.35
24	Dave Schmidt	.35
25	Buddy Bell	.35
26	George Wright	.35
28	Frank Tanana	.35
30	Marv Foley	.35
31	Dave Stewart	.50
32	Gary Ward	.35
38	Dickie Noles	.35
43	Donnie Scott	.35
44	Danny Darwin	.35
49	Charlie Hough	.35
53	Joey McLaughlin	.35
---	Coaching Staff (Rich Donnelly, Glenn Ezell, Merv Rettenmund, Dick Such, Wayne Terwilliger)	.35
---	Trainer (Bill Zeigler)	.35

1986 Jays Potato Chips

TEDDY HIGUERA MILWAUKEE BREWERS PITCHER

One of a handful of round baseball cards produced for inclusion in boxes of potato chips on a regional basis in 1986, the Jays set of 2-7/8" discs is believed to be the scarcest of the type. The 20 cards in the issue include the most popular Milwaukee Brewers and Chicago Cubs and White Sox players; the set having been distributed in the southern Wisconsin- northern Illinois area. Like many contemporary sets produced by Mike Schechter Associates, the '86 Jays cards feature player photos on which the team logos have been airbrushed off the caps.

		NM/M
Complete Set (20):		17.50
Common Player:		.50
(1)	Harold Baines	.50
(2)	Cecil Cooper	.50
(3)	Jody Davis	.50
(4)	Bob Dernier	.50
(5)	Richard Dotson	.50
(6)	Shawon Dunston	.50
(7)	Carlton Fisk	3.00
(8)	Jim Gantner	.50
(9)	Ozzie Guillen	.50
(10)	Teddy Higuera	.50
(11)	Ron Kittle	.50
(12)	Paul Molitor	3.00
(13)	Keith Moreland	.50
(14)	Ernie Riles	.50
(15)	Ryne Sandberg	6.00
(16)	Tom Seaver	3.00
(17)	Lee Smith	.50
(18)	Rick Sutcliffe	.50
(19)	Greg Walker	.50
(20)	Robin Yount	3.00

1984 Jewel Food Chicago Cubs/White Sox

Similar in format to previous issues by the Midwestern food company, these 16-piece sets of Chicago's National and American League teams are printed on 6" x 9" paper. Fronts feature a chest-to-cap color player photo with a dark facsimile autograph. A logo and copyright notice by the Players Association is at upper-left. Backs are

blank. Cards were distributed four per week with the purchase of specific sale products.

		NM/M
Complete Cubs Set (16):		12.00
Complete White Sox Set (16):		12.50
Common Player:		.50
(1)	Larry Bowa	.50
(2)	Ron Cey	.50
(3)	Jody Davis	.50
(4)	Bob Dernier	.50
(5)	Leon Durham	.50
(6)	Dennis Eckersley	2.50
(7)	Richie Hebner	.50
(8)	Gary Matthews	.50
(9)	Keith Moreland	.50
(10)	Ryne Sandberg	6.00
(11)	Scott Sanderson	.50
(12)	Lee Smith	.75
(13)	Tom Stoddard	.50
(14)	Rick Sutcliffe	.75
(15)	Steve Trout	.50
(16)	Gary Woods	.50
(1)	Harold Baines	.50
(2)	Alan Bannister	.50
(3)	Julio Cruz	.50
(4)	Richard Dotson	.50
(5)	Jerry Dybzinski	.50
(6)	Carlton Fisk	4.00
(7)	Scott Fletcher	.50
(8)	LaMarr Hoyt	.50
(9)	Ron Kittle	.50
(10)	Rudy Law	.50
(11)	Vance Law	.50
(12)	Greg Luzinski	.50
(13)	Tom Paciorek	.50
(14)	Tom Seaver	4.00
(15)	Mike Squires	.50
(16)	Greg Walker	.50

1986 Jiffy Pop/MSA Promos

NOLAN RYAN PITCHER HOUSTON ASTROS

This 20-card set was produced by Mike Schecter Associates in 1986 to provide attendees at a restaurant and food trade show with examples of his card promotions. The promos have the same fronts as the 1986 Jiffy Pop discs on a 2-7/8" diameter format. The backs have an advertisement for MSA's services. Like the regular issues, the uniform logos have been airbrushed from the discs due to lack of a license from Major League Baseball (the issue is licensed by the Players Union). The unnumbered promo discs are checklisted here alphabetically.

		NM/M
Complete Set (20):		175.00
Common Player:		4.00
(1)	Wade Boggs	10.00
(2)	George Brett	15.00
(3)	Gary Carter	10.00
(4)	Steve Garvey	6.00
(5)	Dwight Gooden	4.00
(6)	Reggie Jackson	12.50
(7)	Don Mattingly	15.00
(8)	Willie McGee	4.00
(9)	Dale Murphy	6.00
(10)	Eddie Murray	10.00
(11)	Lance Parrish	4.00
(12)	Jim Rice	6.00
(13)	Cal Ripken, Jr.	25.00
(14)	Pete Rose	20.00
(15)	Nolan Ryan	25.00
(16)	Ryne Sandberg	12.50
(17)	Mike Schmidt	15.00
(18)	Fernando Valenzuela	4.00
(19)	Dave Winfield	10.00
(20)	Robin Yount	10.00

1986 Jiffy Pop

DAVE WINFIELD OUTFIELDER NEW YORK YANKEES

One of the scarcer of the 1986 regionals, the Jiffy Pop discs were inserted in packages of heat-and-eat popcorn. A production of Mike Schechter Associates, the 2-7/8" diameter discs feature 20 popular stars, many in the same pictures found in other '86 regionals. Like other MSA issues, caps have had the team logos erased, allowing Jiffy Pop to avoid paying a licensing fee to the teams. Backs have a few biographical details and stats.

		NM/M
Complete Set (20):		15.00
Common Player:		.50
1	Jim Rice	.65
2	Wade Boggs	1.00
3	Lance Parrish	.50
4	George Brett	2.00
5	Robin Yount	1.00
6	Don Mattingly	2.00
7	Dave Winfield	1.00
8	Reggie Jackson	1.50
9	Cal Ripken	3.50
10	Eddie Murray	1.00
11	Pete Rose	2.50
12	Ryne Sandberg	1.50
13	Nolan Ryan	3.50
14	Fernando Valenzuela	.50
15	Willie McGee	.50
16	Dale Murphy	.75
17	Mike Schmidt	2.00
18	Steve Garvey	.50
19	Gary Carter	1.00
20	Dwight Gooden	.50

1987 Jiffy Pop

For a second year, Jiffy Pop inserted player discs in its packages of popcorn. The full-color discs measure 2-7/8" in diameter and were produced by Mike Schechter Associates. Titled "2nd Annual Collectors' Edition," the card fronts feature player photos with all team insignias airbrushed away. Information on the backs of the discs is printed in bright red on white stock. Die-cut 16-1/4" x 14" press sheets containing all 20 discs were available via a mail-in offer.

		NM/M
Complete Set (20):		20.00
Uncut Sheet:		25.00
Common Player:		.75
1	Ryne Sandberg	2.00
2	Dale Murphy	1.25
3	Jack Morris	.75
4	Keith Hernandez	.75
5	George Brett	2.50
6	Don Mattingly	2.50
7	Ozzie Smith	2.00
8	Cal Ripken, Jr.	3.50
9	Dwight Gooden	.75
10	Pedro Guerrero	.75
11	Lou Whitaker	.75
12	Roger Clemens	2.50
13	Lance Parrish	.75
14	Rickey Henderson	2.00
15	Fernando Valenzuela	.75
16	Mike Schmidt	2.50
17	Darryl Strawberry	.75
18	Mike Scott	.75
19	Jim Rice	1.00
20	Wade Boggs	2.00

1988 Jiffy Pop

This 20-disc set is the third Jiffy Pop issue spotlighting leading players. Discs are 2-1/2" in diameter with a semi-gloss finish and feature full-color closeups on white stock. Team logos have been airbrushed off the player's caps. Fronts have a curved label "3rd Annual Collector's Edition." Disc backs are white, with dark blue lettering, and contain player information, stats and disc number. An uncut sheet (16" x 14-1/2") with all 20 discs was available in a mail-in redemption offer.

		NM/M
Complete Set (20):		9.00
Uncut Sheet:		10.00
Common Player:		.35
1	Buddy Bell	.35
2	Wade Boggs	1.25
3	Gary Carter	1.25
4	Jack Clark	.35
5	Will Clark	.45
6	Roger Clemens	2.00
7	Vince Coleman	.35
8	Andre Dawson	.50
9	Keith Hernandez	.35
10	Kent Hrbek	.35
11	Wally Joyner	.35
12	Paul Molitor	1.25
13	Eddie Murray	1.25
14	Tim Raines	.35
15	Bret Saberhagen	.35
16	Alan Trammell	.35
17	Ozzie Virgil	.35
18	Tim Wallach	.35
19	Dave Winfield	1.25
20	Robin Yount	1.25

Ronnie Joyner St. Louis Browns Heads-Up

Though there is nothing on the cards themselves to identify their origins, this set is the work of sports artist Ronnie Joyner, produced in co-operation with the St. Louis Browns Historical Society. They approximate the 1938 Goudey Heads-Up format in 2-1/2" x 2-7/8" size with sepia portraits and orange backgrounds. Backs have a vintage look with player personal data, a career summary and trivia question. Cards were sold as complete sets.

		NM/M
Complete Set (20):		10.00
Common Player:		.50
1	Hank Arft	.50
2	Ellis Clary	.50
3	Jim Delsing	.50
4	Ned Garver	.65
5	Don Gutteridge	.50
6	Red Hayworth	.50
7	Bill Jennings	.50
8	Dick Kryhoski	.50
9	Don Lenhardt	.50
10	Bob Mahoney	.50
11	Frank Mancuso	.50
12	Babe Martin	.50
13	Ed Mickelson	.50
14	J.W. Porter	.50
15	Roy Sievers	.75
16	Virgil Trucks	.65
17	Al Widmar	.50
18	Jerry Witte	.50
19	Arthur Richman (Number One Fan)	.50
20	Stan Musial (Cross Town Rival)	5.00

2003 Ronnie Joyner 1953 St. Louis Browns

Though there is nothing on the cards themselves to identify their origins, or even that they do not actually date from 1953, this set is the work of sports artist Ronnie Joyner, who produced two other Brownies sets in previous years in co-operation with the St. Louis Browns Historical Society. The cards are in the modern 2-1/2" x 3-1/2" format with colorful fronts featuring Joyner portraits of the players and cartoon-style names. Backs have a vintage look with player personal data, a car-

toon about the player, a career summary and 1953 and lifetime stats. Cards were sold as complete sets.

		NM/M
Complete Set (40):		15.00
Common Player:		.50
1	Satchel Paige	5.00
2	Les Moss	.50
3	Roy Sievers	.65
4	Bobby Young	.50
5	Marlin Stuart	.50
6	Billy Hunter	.50
7	Don Lenhardt	.50
8	Johnny Groth	.50
9	Vic Wertz	.50
10	Don Larsen	1.00
11	Clint Courtney	.50
12	Dick Kryhoski	.50
13	Neil Berry	.50
14	Bob Cain	.50
15	Willie Miranda	.50
16	Hank Edwards	.50
17	Dick Kokos	.50
18	Jim Pisoni	.50
19	Harry Brecheen	.50
20	Browns 1953 Season Summary	.50
21	Checklist	.50
22	Lou Kretlow	.50
23	Babe Martin	.50
24	Ed Mickelson	.50
25	Frank Kellert	.50
26	Virgil Trucks	.65
27	Dick Littlefield	.50
28	Jim Dyck	.50
29	Mike Blyzka	.50
30	Bob Habenicht	.75
31	Max Lanier	.50
32	Bob Elliott	.50
33	Duane Pillette	.50
34	Johnny Lipon	.50
35	Bob Turley	.50
36	Vern Stephens	.50
37	Hal White	.50
38	Dixie Upright	.75
39	Bobo Holloman	.50
40	Marty Marion	.65

1990 Jumbo Sunflower Seeds

The 1990 "Autograph Series" of 24 cards came in packages of sunflower seeds and were produced by Mike Schecter Associates for Stagi & Scriven Farms Inc. The cards were found in specially-marked packages of Jumbo California Sunflower Seeds, three cards per package. Standard size with MLB logos airbrushed out, the cards are blue with a white frame. The numbered backs contain yearly statistics and biographical information along with a facsimile autograph.

		NM/M
Complete Set (24):		10.00
Common Player:		.25
(1)	Kevin Mitchell	.25
(2)	Ken Griffey Jr.	1.75
(3)	Howard Johnson	.25
(4)	Bo Jackson	.35
(5)	Kirby Puckett	1.25
(6)	Robin Yount	1.00
(7)	Dave Stieb	.25
(8)	Don Mattingly	1.50
(9)	Barry Bonds	2.00
(10)	Pedro Guerrero	.25
(11)	Tony Gwynn	1.25
(12)	Von Hayes	.25
(13)	Rickey Henderson	1.00
(14)	Tim Raines	.25
(15)	Alan Trammell	.25
(16)	Dave Stewart	.25
(17)	Will Clark	.35
(18)	Roger Clemens	1.50
(19)	Wally Joyner	.25
(20)	Ryne Sandberg	1.25
(21)	Eric Davis	.25
(22)	Mike Scott	.25
(23)	Cal Ripken, Jr.	2.00
(24)	Eddie Murray	1.00

1991 Jumbo Sunflower Seeds

In its second year of baseball card production, Jumbo California Sunflower Seeds maintained the same basic format for its cards. Player photos, with uniform logos airbrushed away, in a white frame are surrounded by a red border with yellow pinstripe. At top left is the issuer's logo; above the photo in white is "Autograph Series II." A facsimile autograph is printed over the photo. Beneath the picture are the player's name, team and position. Backs are printed in red and include major league stats and a career summary.

		NM/M
Complete Set (24):		7.50
Common Player:		.25
1	Ozzie Smith	1.00
2	Wade Boggs	1.00
3	Bobby Bonilla	.25
4	George Brett	1.25
5	Kal Daniels	.25
6	Glenn Davis	.25
7	Chuck Finley	.25
8	Cecil Fielder	.25
9	Len Dykstra	.25
10	Dwight Gooden	.25
11	Ken Griffey Jr.	1.50
12	Kelly Gruber	.25
13	Kent Hrbek	.25
14	Andre Dawson	.35
15	Dave Justice	.50
16	Barry Larkin	.25
17	Ben McDonald	.25
18	Mark McGwire	1.75
19	Roberto Alomar	.50
20	Nolan Ryan	2.00
21	Sandy Alomar, Jr.	.25
22	Bobby Thigpen	.25
23	Tim Wallach	.25
24	Mitch Williams	.25

1992 Jumbo Sunflower Seeds

The basic format used in 1990-91 was returned for 1992 when Michael Schecter Associates produced another 24-card set for inclusion in packages of Jumbo Sunflower Seeds (the "California" identifier was dropped in 1992). Cards feature a player photo on which the uniform logos have been eliminated. Across the photo in black is a facsimile autograph. Around the photo are borders of, successively, white, blue, yellow and white. In the upper-left corner is the issuer's logo. "Autograph Series III" appears in red at upper-right. Beneath the picture, the player's name is printed in red, with his team and position in white. Backs are printed in blue, with major league stats and a career summary, along with a few personal data and the appropriate logos.

		NM/M
Complete Set (24):		6.00
Common Player:		.25
1	Jeff Reardon	.25
2	Bill Gullickson	.25
3	Todd Zeile	.25
4	Terry Mulholland	.25
5	Kirby Puckett	1.00
6	Howard Johnson	.25
7	Terry Pendleton	.25
8	Will Clark	.35
9	Cal Ripken, Jr.	2.00
10	Chris Sabo	.25
11	Jim Abbott	.25
12	Joe Carter	.25
13	Paul Molitor	.75
14	Ken Griffey Jr.	1.50
15	Randy Johnson	.75
16	Bobby Bonilla	.25
17	John Smiley	.25
18	Jose Canseco	.50
19	Tom Glavine	.50
20	Darryl Strawberry	.25
21	Brett Butler	.25
22	Devon White	.25
23	Scott Erickson	.25
24	Willie McGee	.25

K

1987 Kahn's Reds

(44) ERIC DAVIS, OF

After a nearly 20-year layoff, Kahn's Wieners sponsored a baseball card set in 1987. The hot dog concessionaire sponsored a Reds team set that was distributed to fans attending the August 2 game at Riverfront Stadium. Cards are the standard 2-1/2" x 3-1/2" size. The fronts offer a full-color player photo bordered in red and white. Backs carry the Kahn's logo, a portrait photo of the player and career stats.

		NM/M
Complete Set (26):		9.00
Common Player:		.25
6	Bo Diaz	.25
10	Terry Francona	.25
11	Kurt Stillwell	.25
12	Nick Esasky	.25
13	Dave Concepcion	.25
15	Barry Larkin	3.00
16	Ron Oester	.25
21	Paul O'Neill	1.00
23	Lloyd McClendon	.25
25	Buddy Bell	.25
28	Kal Daniels	.25
29	Tracy Jones	.25
30	Guy Hoffman	.25
31	John Franco	.25
32	Tom Browning	.25
33	Ron Robinson	.25
34	Bill Gullickson	.25
35	Pat Pacillo	.25
39	Dave Parker	.25
43	Bill Landrum	.25
44	Eric Davis	.50
46	Rob Murphy	.25
47	Frank Williams	.25
48	Ted Power	.25
---	Pete Rose (Manager)	3.00
---	Reds Coaches (Scott Breeden, Billy DeMars, Tommy Helms, Bruce Kimm, Jim Lett, Tony Perez)	.25

1988 Kahn's Mets

Approximately 50,000 Mets fans received this complimentary card set during a ballpark promotion sponsored by Kahn's Wieners. Twenty-five players are featured in the set, along with manager Davey Johnson, four coaches and a team photo. Card fronts have a dark blue border with an orange rectangle framing the color player photo; players' uniform numbers are printed in white in the upper-right corner, beside the team logo. Backs are black-and-white with red accents. In addition to player acquisition date, birthday and residence, a paragraph-style career summary is included. Cards measure 2-1/2" x 3-1/2".

		NM/M
Complete Set (31):		4.00
Common Player:		.25
1	Mookie Wilson	.25
2	Mackey Sasser	.25
3	Bud Harrelson	.25
4	Lenny Dykstra	.35
5	Davey Johnson	.25
6	Wally Backman	.25
8	Gary Carter	3.00
11	Tim Teufel	.25
12	Ron Darling	.25
13	Lee Mazzilli	.25
15	Rick Aguilera	.25
16	Dwight Gooden	.50
17	Keith Hernandez	.35
18	Darryl Strawberry	.50
19	Bob Ojeda	.25
20	Howard Johnson	.30
21	Kevin Elster	.25
22	Kevin McReynolds	.25
26	Terry Leach	.25
28	Bill Robinson	.25
29	Dave Magadan	.25
30	Mel Stottlemyre	.25
31	Gene Walter	.25
33	Barry Lyons	.25
34	Sam Perlozzo	.25
42	Roger McDowell	.25
44	David Cone	.50
48	Randy Myers	.25
50	Sid Fernandez	.25
52	Greg Pavlick	.25
---	Team Photo	.25

Reds

(17) CHRIS SABO, IF

This 26-card team set was a giveaway during the Aug. 14, 1988 Cincinnati Reds game. The glossy cards (2-1/2" x 3-1/2") feature color action photos inside red and white borders. The Reds logo, player uniform number, name and position are printed below the photo. The backs are black and white, with small player close-ups and career stats. A promotional 25-cent coupon for Kahn's Wieners was included with each set.

		NM/M
Complete Set (26):		6.00
Common Player:		.25
6	Bo Diaz	.25

8	Terry McGriff	.25
9	Eddie Milner	.25
10	Leon Durham	.25
11	Barry Larkin	.50
12	Nick Esasky	.25
13	Dave Concepcion	.25
14	Pete Rose	3.00
15	Jeff Treadway	.25
17	Chris Sabo	.30
20	Danny Jackson	.25
21	Paul O'Neill	.30
22	Dave Collins	.25
27	Jose Rijo	.25
28	Kal Daniels	.25
29	Tracy Jones	.25
30	Lloyd McClendon	.25
31	John Franco	.25
32	Tom Browning	.25
33	Ron Robinson	.25
40	Jack Armstrong	.25
44	Eric Davis	.30
46	Rob Murphy	.25
47	Frank Williams	.25
48	Tim Birtsas	.25
---	Coaches (Danny Breeden, Tommy Helms, Bruce Kimm, Jim Lett, Lee May, Tony Perez)	.25

1989 Kahn's Cooperstown Collection

This 11-player card set was available through a mail-in offer. One dollar and three proofs of purchase from Hillshire Farms were needed to obtain the set. The card fronts feature paintings of recent Hall of Fame inductees. A coupon card was also included with each set.

		NM/M
Complete Set (11):		3.00
Common Player:		.50
(1)	Cool Papa Bell	.50
(2)	Johnny Bench	.75
(3)	Lou Brock	.60
(4)	Whitey Ford	.75
(5)	Bob Gibson	.65
(6)	Billy Herman	.50
(7)	Harmon Killebrew	.75
(8)	Eddie Mathews	.65
(9)	Brooks Robinson	.65
(10)	Willie Stargell	.65
(11)	Carl Yastrzemski	.75

1989 Kahn's Mets

This team set was sponsored by Kahn's Wieners and given to fans attending the July 6 game at Shea Stadium. Standard-size cards feature a color photo surrounded by a blue and orange border with the player's name and uniform number across the top. Backs include the Kahn's logo, along with player information and complete Major League stats. Four update cards were later added to the set.

		NM/M
Complete Set (35):		4.00
Common Player:		.20
1	Mookie Wilson	.25
2	Mackey Sasser	.20
3	Bud Harrelson	.20
5	Davey Johnson	.20

7	Juan Samuel	.20
8	Gary Carter	1.00
9	Gregg Jefferies	.50
11	Tim Teufel	.20
12	Ron Darling	.20
13	Lee Mazzilli	.20
16	Dwight Gooden	.30
17	Keith Hernandez	.20
18	Darryl Strawberry	.30
19	Bob Ojeda	.20
20	Howard Johnson	.20
21	Kevin Elster	.20
22	Kevin McReynolds	.20
28	Bill Robinson	.20
29	Dave Magadan	.20
30	Mel Stottlemyre	.20
32	Mark Carreon	.20
33	Barry Lyons	.20
34	Sam Perlozzo	.20
38	Rick Aguilera	.20
44	David Cone	.50
46	Dave West	.20
48	Randy Myers	.20
49	Don Aase	.20
50	Sid Fernandez	.20
52	Greg Pavlick	.20
---	Team Card	.20
13	Jeff Musselman	.20
25	Keith Miller	.50
28	Frank Viola	.50
40	Jeff Innis	.50

Reds

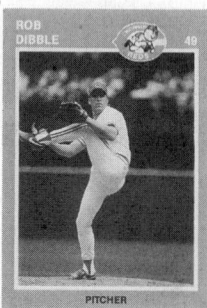

ROB DIBBLE 49

PITCHER

This team set, sponsored by Kahn's Wieners, was distributed to fans attending the August 6 Reds game at Riverfront Stadium. The standard-size, red-bordered cards feature action photos with the player's name in the upper-left corner, his uniform number in the upper-right and the Reds logo in the middle. Backs include a black-and-white portrait, player data and complete major and minor league stats. The Kahn's logo appears in the upper-right corner of the back.

		NM/M
Complete Set (26):		6.00
Common Player:		.20
6	Bo Diaz	.20
7	Lenny Harris	.25
11	Barry Larkin	.50
12	Joel Youngblood	.20
14	Pete Rose	3.00
16	Ron Oester	.20
17	Chris Sabo	.20
20	Danny Jackson	.20
21	Paul O'Neill	.40
25	Todd Benzinger	.20
27	Jose Rijo	.20
28	Kal Daniels	.20
29	Herm Winningham	.20
30	Ken Griffey	.25
31	John Franco	.20
32	Tom Browning	.20
33	Ron Robinson	.20
34	Jeff Reed	.20
36	Rolando Roomes	.20
37	Norm Charlton	.20
42	Rick Mahler	.20
43	Kent Tekulve	.20
44	Eric Davis	.30
48	Tim Birtsas	.20
49	Rob Dibble	.25
---	Coaches (Danny Breeden, Dave Bristol, Tommy Helms, Jim Lett, Lee May, Tony Perez)	.25

1990 Kahn's Mets

For the third consecutive year, Kahn's issued a team set of Mets baseball cards. The sets were distrubted at Shea Stadium on May 3, prior to the Mets/Reds game. Cards feature blue and orange (team colors) graphics and are numbered according to uniform number. Two coupon cards were also included with each set.

	NM/M
Complete Set (34):	3.00

Mets

DAVID CONE 44

Common Player:		.20
1	Lou Thornton	.20
2	Mackey Sasser	.20
3	Bud Harrelson	.20
4	Mike Cubbage	.20
5	Davey Johnson	.20
6	Mike Marshall	.20
9	Gregg Jefferies	.50
10	Dave Magadan	.20
11	Tim Teufel	.20
12	Jeff Musselman	.20
15	Ron Darling	.20
16	Dwight Gooden	.30
18	Darryl Strawberry	.30
19	Bob Ojeda	.20
20	Howard Johnson	.20
21	Kevin Elster	.20
22	Kevin McReynolds	.20
25	Keith Miller	.20
26	Alejandro Pena	.20
27	Tom O'Malley	.20
29	Frank Viola	.20
30	Mel Stottlemyre	.20
31	John Franco	.20
32	Doc Edwards	.20
33	Barry Lyons	.20
45	Orlando Mercado	.20
40	Jeff Innis	.20
44	David Cone	.35
45	Mark Carreon	.20
48	Wally Whitehurst	.20
48	Julio Machado	.20
50	Sid Fernandez	.20
52	Greg Pavlick	.20
---	Team Card	.20

Reds

CINCINNATI REDS

(44) Eric Davis, OF

This team set marks the fourth consecutive year in which Kahn's released a modern Reds issue. The cards feature color photos, red and white borders and the player's name, number, and postion on the card front. The flip sides feature biographical information, statistics, a posed photo and the Kahn's logo. The set is numbered by uniform.

		NM/M
Complete Set (27):		4.00
Common Player:		.25
7	Mariano Duncan	.25
9	Joe Oliver	.25
10	Luis Quinones	.25
11	Barry Larkin	.50
15	Glenn Braggs	.25
16	Ron Oester	.25
17	Chris Sabo	.25
20	Danny Jackson	.25
21	Paul O'Neill	.40
22	Billy Hatcher	.25
23	Hal Morris	.25
25	Todd Benzinger	.25
27	Jose Rijo	.25
28	Randy Myers	.25
29	Herm Winningham	.25
30	Ken Griffey	.25
32	Tom Browning	.25
34	Jeff Reed	.25
37	Norm Charlton	.25
40	Jack Armstrong	.25
41	Lou Pinella	.30
42	Rick Mahler	.25
43	Tim Layana	.25
44	Eric Davis	.35
48	Tim Birtsas	.25
49	Rob Dibble	.25

---	Coaches (Jackie Moore, Tony Perez, Sam Perlozzo, Larry Rothschild, Stan Williams)	.25

1991 Kahn's Mets

Mets

Howard Johnson IF

20

Kahn's kept its tradition in 1991 with the release of this set featuring members of the New York Mets. Cards measure 2 1/2" x 3 1/2" and the fronts feature a pinstripe design. The backs are printed horizontally and feature complete statistics. The cards are numbered according to uniform number. The complete set was distributed at a 1991 home game.

		NM/M
Complete Set (33):		4.00
Common Player:		.20
1	Vince Coleman	.20
2	Mackey Sasser	.20
3	Bud Harrelson	.20
4	Mike Cubbage	.20
5	Charlie O'Brien	.20
7	Hubie Brooks	.20
8	Daryl Boston	.20
9	Gregg Jefferies	.30
10	Dave Magadan	.20
11	Tim Teufel	.20
13	Rick Cerone	.20
15	Ron Darling	.20
16	Dwight Gooden	.30
17	David Cone	.50
20	Howard Johnson	.20
21	Kevin Elster	.20
22	Kevin McReynolds	.20
25	Keith Miller	.20
26	Alejandro Pena	.20
28	Tom Herr	.20
37	Frank Viola	.20
30	Mel Stottlemyre	.20
31	John Franco	.20
32	Doc Edwards	.20
40	Jeff Innis	.20
43	Doug Simons	.20
45	Mark Carreon	.20
47	Wally Whitehurst	.20
48	Pete Schourek	.20
50	Sid Fernandez	.20
51	Tom Spencer	.20
52	Greg Pavlick	.20
---	Team Card	.20

Reds

BARRY LARKIN Shortstop (11)

WORLD CHAMPION CINCINNATI REDS

The World Champion Cincinnati Reds are showcased in this 28-card set. The card fronts feature small color action photos on white stock. Backs feature statistics, biographical information and the Kahn's logo. A special card of team mascot Schottzie is included in this set.

		NM/M
Complete Set (28):		4.00
Common Player:		.25
7	Mariano Duncan	.25
9	Joe Oliver	.25
10	Luis Quinones	.25
11	Barry Larkin	.50
15	Glenn Braggs	.25
17	Chris Sabo	.25
19	Bill Doran	.25
21	Paul O'Neill	.30
22	Billy Hatcher	.25

23	Hal Morris	.25
25	Todd Benzinger	.25
27	Jose Rijo	.25
28	Randy Myers	.25
29	Herm Winningham	.25
32	Tom Browning	.25
34	Jeff Reed	.25
36	Don Carman	.25
37	Norm Charlton	.25
40	Jack Armstrong	.25
41	Lou Piniella	.30
44	Eric Davis	.30
45	Chris Hammond	.25
47	Scott Scudder	.25
48	Ted Power	.25
49	Rob Dibble	.25
57	Freddie Benavides	.25
---	Schottzie (Mascot)	.25
---	Coaches (Jackie Moore, Tony Perez, Sam Perlozzo, Larry Rothschild, Stan Williams)	.25

1992 Kahn's Mets

Mets

TODD HUNDLEY 9

A Mets' blue border surrounds the game-action photos in this team set. Backs are horizontally formatted and present full major league stats and the '92 Mets team slogan, "Hardball is Back." A baseball on front carries the uniform number by which the set is checklisted here. Cents-offs coupons for Kahn's hot dogs and corn dogs were packaged with the set when it was distributed at a home game, but are not considered part of the set.

		NM/M
Complete Set (33):		4.00
Common Player:		.20
1	Vince Coleman	.20
2	Mackey Sasser	.20
3	Junior Noboa	.20
4	Mike Cubbage	.20
6	Daryl Boston	.20
8	Dave Gallagher	.20
9	Todd Hundley	.35
10	Jeff Torborg	.20
11	Dick Schofield	.20
12	Willie Randolph	.20
15	Kevin Elster	.20
16	Dwight Gooden	.20
17	David Cone	.50
18	Bret Saberhagen	.35
19	Anthony Young	.20
20	Howard Johnson	.20
22	Charlie O'Brien	.20
25	Bobby Bonilla	.20
26	Barry Foote	.20
27	Tom McCraw	.20
28	Dave LaRoche	.20
29	Dave Magadan	.20
30	Mel Stottlemyre	.20
31	John Franco	.20
32	Bill Pecota	.20
33	Eddie Murray	1.00
40	Jeff Innis	.20
44	Tim Burke	.20
45	Paul Gibson	.20
47	Wally Whitehurst	.20
50	Sid Fernandez	.20
51	John Stephenson	.20
---	Mets Team	.20

Reds

CINCINNATI REDS

(37) NORM CHARLTON P

	Coaches (Jackie Moore, John McLaren, Sam Perlozzo, Tony Perez, Larry Rothschild)	.25

1993 Kahn's Mets

IF EDDIE MURRAY 33

Mets

The Mets distributed the 1993 Kahn's team set to fans on May 23 at Shea Stadium. Cards feature color photos and a white border. The Mets logo is at the bottom center and the player's name, position and uniform number at the top. Backs include career statistics and biography inside a red border. Also included in the set is a team photo card and a title card which features the New York skyline and the stadium. Apparently not all cards, such as those of coaches, were issued in all sets.

		NM/M
Complete Set (36):		7.50
Common Player:		.25
1	Tony Fernandez	.25
4	Mike Cubbage	.50
6	Joe Orsulak	.25
7	Jeff McKnight	.25
8	Dave Gallagher	.25
9	Todd Hundley	.50
10	Jeff Torborg	.50
11	Vince Coleman	.50
12	Jeff Kent	1.00
16	Dwight Gooden	.25
18	Bret Saberhagen	.35
19	Anthony Young	.25
20	Howard Johnson	.25
21	Darren Reed	.25
22	Charlie O'Brien	.25
23	Tim Bogar	.25
25	Bobby Bonilla	.50
26	Barry Foote	.50
27	Tom McCraw	.50
28	Dave LaRoche	.50
29	Frank Tanana	.50
30	Mel Stottlemyre	.50
31	John Franco	.25

This 27-card set (two coupon cards distributed with the team set are not considered part of the set) was given to fans at a promotional home date. The 2-1/2" x 3-1/2" cards have a red border with the team name at top and player name at bottom in white. The player's uniform number and position in black flank his name. A team logo appears in the lower-left corner of the photo. Backs are printed in red and black and have complete pro stats, a few biographical details and the logo of the Riverfront Stadium hot dog concessionaire. The checklist presented here is in order of uniform number.

		NM/M
Complete Set (27):		4.00
Common Player:		.25
2	Schottzie (Mascot)	.25
9	Joe Oliver	.25
10	Bip Roberts	.25
11	Barry Larkin	.45
12	Freddie Benavides	.25
15	Glenn Braggs	.25
16	Reggie Sanders	.25
17	Chris Sabo	.25
19	Bill Doran	.25
21	Paul O'Neill	.35
23	Hal Morris	.25
25	Scott Bankhead	.25
26	Darnell Coles	.25
27	Jose Rijo	.25
28	Scott Ruskin	.25
29	Greg Swindell	.25
30	Dave Martinez	.25
31	Tim Belcher	.25
32	Tom Browning	.25
34	Jeff Reed	.25
37	Norm Charlton	.25
38	Troy Afenir	.25
41	Lou Piniella	.30
45	Chris Hammond	.25
48	Dwayne Henry	.25
49	Rob Dibble	.25

33	Eddie Murray	1.50
34	Chico Walker	.25
40	Jeff Innis	.25
44	Ryan Thompson	.25
47	Mike Draper	.25
48	Pete Schourek	.25
50	Sid Fernandez	.25
51	Mike Maddux	.25
---	John Stephenson	.50
---	Team Photo	.25
---	Header Card	.10
---	Corn Dog Coupon	.05
---	Hot Dog Coupon	.05

Reds

Kahn's produced a Reds team set which was given away to fans at Riverfront Stadium on August 1. The cards, organized by player's uniform number, show a photo of the player on the front with the player's name at the top and the Reds logo in the lower left corner, surrounded by a pinstripe border. Card backs have the player's lifetime statistics and biography. Card #2 in the set portrays team owner Marge Schott and her dog Schottzie II. Coupon cards good for discounts on packages of Kahn's hot dogs and corn dogs were packaged with the set but are not considered part of the set.

		NM/M
Complete Set (28):		6.00
Common Player:		.25
2	Schottzie (Mascot) (Marge Schott)	.25
7	Kevin Mitchell	.25
8	Juan Samuel	.25
9	Joe Oliver	.25
10	Bip Roberts	.25
11	Barry Larkin	.40
15	Davey Johnson	.25
16	Reggie Sanders	.25
17	Chris Sabo	.25
19	Randy Milligan	.25
20	Jeff Branson	.25
23	Hal Morris	.25
25	Greg Cadaret	.25
27	Jose Rijo	.25
30	Bobby Kelly	.25
31	Tim Belcher	.25
32	Tom Browning	.25
40	Tim Pugh	.25
41	Jeff Reardon	.25
42	Gary Varsho	.25
43	Bill Landrum	.25
46	Jacob Brumfield	.25
49	Rob Dibble	.25
53	Kevin Wickander	.25
57	John Smiley	.25
59	Bobby Ayala	.25
---	Coaches (Jose Cardenal, Don Gullett, Ray Knight, Bobby Valentine, Dave Miley)	.25
---	Broadcasters (Marty Brennaman, Joe Nuxhall)	.25

Reds

Distributed at a promotional game and sponsored by the hot dog concessionaire at Riverfront Stadi-

---

um this was the eighth consecutive Reds team set produced by Kahn's. Cards feature a player action photo with a red stripe superimposed near the left border. The stripe contains the player name and position at top and the team logo at bottom. Backs are printed in red and black and include full minor and major league stats. Cards are numbered by uniform number printed on back.

		NM/M
Complete Set (31):		4.00
Common Player:		.20
2	Schottzie (Mascot)	.20
4	Jacob Brumfield	.20
7	Kevin Mitchell	.20
9	Joe Oliver	.20
10	Eddie Taubensee	.20
11	Barry Larkin	.35
12	Deion Sanders	.50
15	Davey Johnson	.20
16	Reggie Sanders	.20
19	Jerome Walton	.20
20	Jeff Branson	.20
21	Tony Fernandez	.20
22	Thomas Howard	.20
23	Hal Morris	.20
27	Jose Rijo	.20
28	Lenny Harris	.20
29	Brett Boone	.50
31	Chuck McElroy	.20
32	Tom Browning	.20
33	Brian Dorsett	.20
39	Erik Hanson	.20
40	Tim Pugh	.20
44	John Roper	.20
45	Jeff Brantley	.20
46	Pete Schourek	.20
47	Johnny Ruffin	.20
49	Rob Dibble	.20
55	Tim Fortugno	.20
57	John Smiley	.20
58	Hector Carrasco	.20
---	Reds Coaching Staff (Bob Boone, Don Gullett, Grant Jackson, Ray Knight, Joel Youngblood)	.20

1995 Kahn's Mets

Game-action photos are featured in this edition of the annual tradition of cards sponsored by the Mets hot dog concessionaire. In standard 2-1/2" x 3-1/2" format the cards have a gray background with navy pinstripes. The player's name, uniform number and position are in team colors of blue and orange at bottom. Backs are in red, black and white with personal data, previous-year or career stats and team and sponsor logos. The cards are checklisted here by uniform number.

		NM/M
Complete Set (36):		4.00
Common Player:		.25
1	Ricky Otero	.25
4	Mike Cubbage	.25
5	Chris Jones	.25
6	Joe Orsulak	.25
7	Bobby Wine	.25
8	Steve Swisher	.25
9	Todd Hundley	.30
10	Tom McCraw	.25
11	Aaron Ledesma	.25
12	Jeff Kent	.75
13	Edgardo Alfonzo	.60
15	Jose Vizcaino	.25
17	Bret Saberhagen	.35
18	Jeff Barry	.25
19	Bill Spiers	.25
20	Ryan Thompson	.25
21	Bill Pulsipher	.25
22	Brett Butler	.25
23	Tim Bogar	.25
25	Bobby Bonilla	.25
26	Rico Brogna	.25
27	Pete Harnisch	.25
28	Bobby Jones	.25
31	John Franco	.25
33	Kelly Stinnett	.25
34	Blas Minor	.25

35	Doug Henry	.25
38	Dave Mlicki	.25
40	Eric Gunderson	.25
44	Jason Isringhausen	.25
45	Jerry DiPoto	.25
52	Dallas Green	.25
55	Greg Pavlick	.25
---	Frank Howard	.25
---	50-Cent Hot Dog Coupon	.05
---	50-Cent Corn Dog Coupon	.05

Reds

This team set continues the tradition of baseball card sponsorship by Kahn's Meats. The set was given away at the August 6 game. Team name and the year are printed in the white border above the photo; the player's name and position are in white in a red strip at bottom. A Reds logo appears in the upper-right corner of the photo, with the player's uniform number below in white. Backs have complete minor and major league stats, along with a few biographical details and the Reds and Kahn's logos. The checklist is presented here by uniform number. Two Kahn's coupons were included in each cello-wrapped set.

		NM/M
Complete Set (34):		4.50
Common Player:		.15
02	Schottzie (02)	.15
6	Ron Gant	.30
8	Damon Berryhill	.15
9	Eric Anthony	.15
10	Eddie Taubensee	.15
11	Barry Larkin	.40
12	Willie Greene	.15
15	Davey Johnson	.15
16	Reggie Sanders	.15
17	Mark Lewis	.15
18	Benito Santiago	.15
19	Jerome Walton	.15
20	Jeff Branson	.15
21	Deion Sanders	.30
22	Thomas Howard	.15
23	Hal Morris	.15
26	Johnny Ruffin	.15
27	Jose Rijo	.15
28	Lenny Harris	.15
29	Brett Boone	.40
30	Brian Hunter	.15
31	Chuck McElroy	.15
36	Kevin Jarvis	.15
37	Xavier Hernandez	.15
40	Tim Pugh	.15
41	Brad Pennington	.15
42	Mike Jackson	.15
44	John Roper	.15
45	Jeff Brantley	.15
46	Pete Schourek	.15
49	C.J. Nitkowski	.15
57	John Smiley	.15
58	Hector Carrasco	.15
---	Reds Coaches (Ray Knight, Don Gullett, Grant Jackson, Hal McRae, Joel Youngblood)	.15

1996 Kahn's Mets

This team set was handed out to attendees at the August 3 game at Shea Stadium. Sponsored by the

---

Mets' hot dog concessionaire, the set features the players, coaches and manager in color action photos. Borders are in dark shades and include a Mets logo at lower-right. The player name and uniform number are in white. Backs are in black, red and white with personal data, 1995 stats and sponsors logos. The uniform number is repeated at lower-left. Cards are checklisted here in alphabetical order. The set was distributed cello-wrapped with two 50-cent hot dogs coupons.

		NM/M
Complete Set (32):		5.00
Common Player:		.25
(1)	Edgardo Alfonzo	.25
(2)	Tim Bogar	.25
(3)	Rico Brogna	.25
(4)	Paul Byrd	.25
(5)	Mark Clark	.25
(6)	Mike Cubbage	.25
(7)	Jerry Dipoto	.25
(8)	Carl Everett	.25
(9)	John Franco	.25
(10)	Bernard Gilkey	.25
(11)	Dallas Green	.25
(12)	Pete Harnisch	.25
(13)	Doug Henry	.25
(14)	Frank Howard	.25
(15)	Todd Hundley	.25
(16)	Butch Huskey	.25
(17)	Jason Isringhausen	.25
(18)	Lance Johnson	.25
(19)	Bobby Jones	.25
(20)	Chris Jones	.25
(21)	Brent Mayne	.25
(22)	Tom McCraw	.25
(23)	Dave Mlicki	.25
(24)	Alex Ochoa	.25
(25)	Rey Ordonez	.25
(26)	Greg Pavlick	.25
(27)	Robert Person	.25
(28)	Bill Pulsipher	.25
(29)	Steve Swisher	.25
(30)	Andy Tomberlin	.25
(31)	Paul Wilson	.25
(32)	Bobby Wine	.25

Reds

The players, manager, coaches and mascot are once again featured in a Cincinnati Reds team set sponsored by the team's hot dog concessionaire and given away to fans at the August 4 game. The 2-1/2" x 3-1/2" cards have color game-action photos on front. A red stripe at top has the team logo, player name, position and uniform number. A stripe beneath the photo has team name and year. Backs are printed in black and red on white and include personal data and complete major and minor league stats. Cards are checklisted here by uniform number.

		NM/M
Complete Set (34):		5.00
Common Player:		.25
02	Schottzie (Mascot)	.25
7	Curtis Goodwin	.25
9a	Eric Anthony	.25
9b	Joe Oliver	.25
10	Eddie Taubensee	.25
11	Barry Larkin	.45
12	Willie Greene	.25
16	Reggie Sanders	.25
17	Chris Sabo	.25
18	Eric Owens	.25
20	Jeff Branson	.25
22	Mark Portugal	.25
22	Thomas Howard	.25
23	Hal Morris	.25
25	Ray Knight	.25
26	Johnny Ruffin	.25
27	Jose Rijo	.25
28	Lenny Harris	.25
29	Brett Boone	.50
30	Eduardo Perez	.25
32	Kevin Jarvis	.25

34	Dave Burba	.25
36	Scott Service	.25
41	Jeff Shaw	.25
42	Roger Salkeld	.25
44	Eric Davis	.30
45	Jeff Brantley	.25
46	Pete Schourek	.25
57	John Smiley	.25
58	Hector Carrasco	.25
69	Tim Belk	.25
---	Coaches (Marc Bombard, Don Gullett, Tom Hume, Jim Lett, Hal McRae)	.25
---	Bernie Stowe (Equipment Manager)	.25

Reds

This team set was given away to fans at the August 3 game, sponsored by the Reds' hot dog concessionaire. The 2-1/2" x 3-1/2" cards have game action player photos at right and the player's name, position and uniform number in a two-toned red stripe vertically at left. Backs are printed in red and black and include complete major and minor league stats. Cards are listed here according to uniform number.

		NM/M
Complete Set (34):		5.00
Common Player:		.25
00	Curtis Goodwin	.25
02	Schottzie (Mascot)	.25
3	Pokey Reese	.25
4	Brook Fordyce	.25
7	Joe Oliver	.25
9	Terry Pendleton	.25
10	Eddie Taubensee	.25
11	Barry Larkin	.35
12	Willie Greene	.25
15	Mike Kelly	.25
16	Reggie Sanders	.25
17	Aaron Boone	.50
20	Jeff Branson	.25
21	Deion Sanders	.35
23	Hal Morris	.25
25	Ray Knight	.25
27	Jose Rijo	.25
28	Lenny Harris	.25
29	Brett Boone	.50
33	Steve Gibralter	.25
34	Dave Burba	.25
36	Mike Morgan	.25
37	Stan Belinda	.25
38	Kent Mercker	.25
39	Eduardo Perez	.25
42	Brett Tomko	.25
41	Jeff Shaw	.25
45	Mike Remlinger	.25
45	Jeff Brantley	.25
46	Pete Schourek	.25
56	Scott Sullivan	.25
57	John Smiley	.25
58	Felix Rodriguez	.25
---	Ken Griffey Sr., Don Gullett, Tom Hume, Denis Menke, Joel Youngblood	.25

Reds

For the 12th consecutive year, the Reds hot dog concessionaire issued a team set, given away at an August 9 promotional game. The 2-1/2" x3-1/2" cards have game-action pho-

---

tos at right, borderless at top, bottom and right. At left is a vertical red stripe with player name and uniform number. Horizontal backs have player data and complete major and minor league stats overprinted on a Kahn's logo. Backs are printed in red, black and white.

		NM/M
Complete Set (34):		5.00
Common Player:		.25
3	Pokey Reese	.25
4	Damian Jackson	.25
6	Brook Fordyce	.25
9	Pat Watkins	.25
10	Ed Taubensee	.25
11	Barry Larkin	.35
13	Willie Greene	.25
15	Jack McKeon	.25
16	Reggie Sanders	.25
17	Aaron Boone	.25
21	Sean Casey	.75
22	Jon Nunnally	.25
23	Chris Stynes	.25
25	Dmitri Young	.25
26	Steve Cooke	.25
29	Paul Konerko	.75
29	Bret Boone	.50
31	Scott Sullivan	.25
32	Danny Graves	.25
33	John Hudek	.25
34	Mike Frank	.25
36	Gabe White	.25
37	Stan Belinda	.25
38	Pete Harnisch	.25
39	Eduardo Perez	.25
40	Brett Tomko	.25
43	Mike Remlinger	.25
44	Scott Winchester	.25
46	Melvin Nieves	.25
48	Rick Krivda	.25
53	Todd Williams	.25
58	Steve Parris	.25
---	Reds Coaches (Harry Dunlop, Ken Griffey, Don Gullett, Tom Hume, Ron Oester)	.25
02	Schottzie (Mascot)	.25

Reds

Distribution of a Kahn's team set for the Reds attained its 13th annual celebration July 31 when the cards were handed out to fans at Cinergy Field. Cards have player action photos which are borderless at top and right. At left is a ragged-edged red strip with player identification. Team identification is in a red strip at bottom. Backs are in red and black on white with a large Kahn's logo ghosted at center. Player data and complete professional stats are provided. Cards are checklisted here by uniform number.

		NM/M
Complete Set (34):		5.00
Common Player:		.25
02	Schottzie (Mascot)	.25
3	Pokey Reese	.25
4	Jeffrey Hammonds	.25
9	Hal Morris	.25
10	Eddie Taubensee	.25
11	Barry Larkin	.35
12	Chris Stynes	.25
15	Denny Neagle	.25
17	Aaron Boone	.25
21	Sean Casey	.50
23	Greg Vaughn	.25
25	Dmitri Young	.25
26	Jason LaRue	.25
28	Mark Lewis	.25
29	Brian Johnson	.25
31	Jack McKeon	.25
32	Danny Graves	.25
33	Steve Avery	.25
34	Michael Tucker	.25
36	Gabe White	.25
37	Stan Belinda	.25
38	Pete Harnisch	.25
40	Brett Tomko	.25
41	Ron Villone	.25
43	Mark Wohlers	.25
44	Mike Cameron	.25

46	Jason Bere	.25
48	Scott Williamson	.25
49	Dennis Reyes	.25
56	Scott Sullivan	.25
58	Steve Parris	.25
---	Marty Brennaman, Joe Nuxhall (Broadcasters)	.25
---	Ken Griffey Sr., Ron Oester, Denis Menke, Dave Collins (Reds Coaches)	

Reds

Some 42,500 sets of Reds cards were distributed to fans at the July 22 game at Cinergy Field. Sponsored for the 14th consecutive year by Kahn's meats, the cards do not have a Kahn's logo. Fronts have game action photos with the team logo at top-left, the player name at top-right, his position and uniform number at lower-right and "2000 Cincinnati Reds" vertically in a red stripe at left. Backs have a ghosted team logo, player data and stats. The checklist here is presented by uniform number.

		NM/M
Complete Set (34):		5.00
Common Player:		.25
3	Pokey Reese	.25
4	Chris Stynes	.25
6	Benito Santiago	.25
8	Alex Ochoa	.25
9	Dante Bichette	.25
10	Eddie Taubensee	.25
11	Barry Larkin	.45
12	Juan Castro	.25
15	Denny Neagle	.25
17	Aaron Boone	.25
21	Sean Casey	.65
23	Hal Morris	.25
25	Dmitri Young	.25
29	Rob Bell	.25
30	Ken Griffey Jr.	3.00
31	Jack McKeon	.25
32	Danny Graves	.25
34	Michael Tucker	.25
36	Manny Aybar	.25
38	Pete Harnisch	.25
41	Ron Villone	.25
43	Osvaldo Fernandez	.25
45	Elmer Dessens	.25
48	Scott Williamson	.25
49	Dennis Reyes	.25
56	Scott Sullivan	.25
58	Steve Parris	.25
---	Coaching Staff (Ken Griffey Sr., Denis Menke, Ron Oester, Dave Collins)	.25
---	Coaching Staff (Don Gullett, Harry Dunlop, Tom Hume, Mark Berry)	.25
---	Marty Brennaman, Joe Nuxhall (Broadcasters)	.25
---	Red (Mascot)	.25
---	Kahnlee (Mascot)	.25
---	Coupon	.05
---	Coupon	.05

1981 Kansas City Royals Police

Ten of the most popular Royals players are featured in this 2-1/2" x 4-1/8" set. Card fronts feature full-color photos with player name, position, facsimile autograph and team logo. Backs include player statistics, a tip from the Royals and list the four sponsoring organizations. The set was issued by the Ft. Myers, Fla., Police Department near the Royals' spring training headquarters.

		NM/M
Complete Set (10):		20.00
Common Player:		1.00
(1)	Willie Mays Aikens	1.00
(2)	George Brett	15.00
(3)	Rich Gale	1.00
(4)	Clint Hurdle	1.00

CLINT HURDLE
Outfielder
6'-3"
195 lbs.

(5)	Dennis Leonard	1.00
(6)	Hal McRae	1.00
(7)	Amos Otis	1.00
(8)	U.L. Washington	1.00
(9)	Frank White	1.00
(10)	Willie Wilson	1.50

1983 Kansas City Royals Police

JOHN WATHAN
Catcher
6' 2"
205 lbs.

After skipping the 1982 season, the Ft. Myers, Fla., Police Department issued a Royals safety set in 1983 that is almost identical to their 1981 set. Cards are again 2-1/2" x 4-1/8" and include just 10 players. Cards are unnumbered, with vertical fronts and horizontal backs. Fronts have team logos, player name and position and facsimile autographs. Backs list the four sponsoring organizations, a "Tip from the Royals" and a "Kids and Cops Fact" about each player.

		NM/M
Complete Set (10):		15.00
Common Player:		.50
(1)	Willie Mays Aikens	.50
(2)	George Brett	13.50
(3)	Dennis Leonard	.50
(4)	Hal McRae	.50
(5)	Amos Otis	.50
(6)	Dan Quisenberry	.50
(7)	U.L. Washington	.50
(8)	John Wathan	.50
(9)	Frank White	.50
(10)	Willie Wilson	.75

1983 Kansas City Royals Fire Safety

BO JACKSON

This set featuring full-color player caricatures by K.K. Goodale was produced for an in-stadium promotion August 14. The 3" x 5" cards depict players, manager and coaches in action poses against a white background with a Royals

logo at upper-left, opposite the Smokey Bear logo. Backs are black-and-white and contain brief player data and a Smokey cartoon.

		NM/M
Complete Set (28):		7.50
Common Player:		.25
1	John Wathan	.25
2	Coaches (Frank Funk, Adrian Garrett, Mike Lum, Ed Napolean, Bob Schaefer, Jim Schaefer)	.25
3	Willie Wilson	.35
4	Danny Tartabull	.25
5	Bo Jackson	1.50
6	Gary Thurman	.25
7	Jerry Don Gleaton	.25
8	Floyd Bannister	.25
9	Buddy Black	.25
10	Steve Farr	.25
11	Gene Garber	.25
12	Mark Gubicza	.25
13	Charlie Liebrandt	.25
14	Ted Power	.25
15	Dan Quisenberry	.25
16	Bret Saberhagen	.35
17	Mike Macfarlane	.25
18	Scotti Madison	.25
19	Jamie Quirk	.25
20	George Brett	5.00
21	Kevin Seitzer	.25
22	Bill Pecota	.25
23	Kurt Stillwell	.25
24	Brad Wellman	.25
25	Frank White	.25
26	Jim Eisenreich	.25
27	Smokey Bear	.10
---	Checklist	.10

1991 Kansas City Royals Police

#16 Bo Jackson

Bo Jackson's release by the Royals in spring training caused his card to be withdrawn from distribution with the other 26 cards in this set. The 2-5/8" x 4-1/8" cards feature a color action photo on front, with the team name in royal blue and the player name and uniform number in black in the bottom border. Backs are printed in blue on white and feature a large cartoon safety message at center, career stats and bio at top, and the logos of the set's sponsors, Kansas City Life Insurance Co., and the Metro Chiefs and Sheriffs Assn., at bottom. Complete sets were distributed in a white paper envelope with team and sponsor logos.

		NM/M
Complete Set (27) (W/Bo Jackson):		5.00
Complete Set (26) (No Bo Jackson):		3.00
Common Player:		.10
1	Kurt Stillwell	.10
3	Terry Shumpert	.10
4	Danny Tartabull	.10
5	George Brett	3.00
8	Jim Eisenreich	.10
12	John Wathan	.10
14	Storm Davis	.10
15	Mike MacFarlane	.10
16	Bo Jackson	3.00
18	Bret Saberhagen	.25
21	Jeff Montgomery	.10
23	Mark Gubicza	.10
25	Gary Thurman	.10
27	Luis Aquino	.10
28	Steve Crawford	.10
30	Kirk Gibson	.15
31	Bill Pecota	.10
33	Kevin Seitzer	.10
36	Tom Gordon	.10
38	Andy McGaffigan	.10
44	Mark Davis	.10
52	Mike Boddicker	.10
55	Kevin Appier	.15
56	Brian McRae	.10

---	Royals Coaches (Pat Dobson, Adrian Garrett)	.10
---	Royals Coaches (Glenn Ezell, Lynn Jones, Bob Schaefer)	.10
---	Header Card - Royals Stadium	.10

1992 Kansas City Royals Police

Royals #5 George Brett

Sponsored by K.C. Life Insurance and distributed by the Metropolitan Chiefs and Sheriffs Association, this 27-card set was distributed at a promotional game. Though they are checklisted, it is rumored that the cards of Kevin Seitzer (traded) and Kirk Gibson (released) were withdrawn early in the promotion, though both names appear on the checklist. The cards are numbered to match the player's uniform numbers. Cards are in the popular police-set format of 2-5/8" x 4-1/8" with white borders around color action photos. Backs have player data, stats, a fire safety message and sponsor's information.

		NM/M
Complete Set (27):		5.00
Common Player:		.25
2	Bob Melvin	.25
3	Terry Shumpert	.25
5	George Brett	3.00
8	Jim Eisenreich	.25
9	Gregg Jefferies	.35
11	Hal McRae	.25
12	Wally Joyner	.35
13	David Howard	.25
16	Mike McFarlane	.25
16	Keith Miller	.25
21	Jeff Montgomery	.25
22	Kevin McReynolds	.25
23	Mark Gubicza	.25
24	Brent Mayne	.25
25	Gary Thomas	.25
27	Luis Aquino	.25
29	Chris Gwynn	.25
30	Kirk Gibson	.35
33	Kevin Seitzer	.25
36	Tom Gordon	.25
37	Joel Johnson	.25
48	Mark Davis	.25
52	Mike Boddicker	.25
55	Kevin Appier	.25
56	Brian McRae	.25
57	Mike Magnante	.25
---	Coaches (Glenn Ezell, Adrian Garrett, Guy Hansen, Lynn Jones, Bruce Kison, Lee May)	.25

1993 Kansas City Royals Police

ROYALS

GEORGE BRETT
INF/DH • 5

One of the longest-running police/fire safety issues continued in 1993 with a set marking the team's 25th anniversary season. The 2-5/8" x 4" cards have a light blue border, a color photo at center, an anniver-

sary logo at lower-left and the player's name, position and uniform number at lower-right. All typography is in royal blue. Backs are printed in blue on white and feature career stats and highlights, a few biographical notes and a large safety message. Logos of the set's sponsors, Kansas City Life Insurance and the Metro Police Chiefs and Sheriffs Assn. are featured at bottom.

		NM/M
Complete Set (27):		4.00
Common Player:		.15
5	George Brett	3.00
7	Greg Gagne	.15
9	Craig Wilson	.15
11	Hal McRae	.15
12	Wally Joyner	.25
13	Jose Lind	.15
14	Chris Gwynn	.15
15	Mike MacFarlane	.15
16	Keith Miller	.15
17	David Cone	.25
19	Curtis Wilkerson	.15
21	Jeff Montgomery	.15
22	Kevin McReynolds	.15
23	Mark Gubicza	.15
24	Brent Mayne	.15
27	Luis Aquino	.15
28	Rusty Meacham	.15
33	Chris Haney	.15
35	Felix Jose	.15
35	Hipolito Pichardo	.15
36	Tom Gordon	.15
37	Mark Gardner	.15
42	Kevin Koslofski	.15
52	Mike Boddicker	.15
55	Kevin Appier	.15
56	Brian McRae	.15
---	Royals Coaches (Steve Boros, Glenn Ezell, Guy Hansen, Bruce Kison, Lee May)	.15

1994 Kansas City Royals Police

Royals KC

Gary Gaetti
3rd Base

The team's long run of police/fire safety issues continued in 1994. The 2-5/8" x 4" cards have a pale yellow background with vertical light blue stripe, a color photo at center, team logo at top and the player's name, position and uniform number at bottom. Backs are printed in blue on white and feature career stats and highlights, a few biographical notes and a large safety message. Logos of the set's sponsors, Kansas City Life Insurance and the Metro Police Chiefs and Sheriffs Assn. are featured at bottom.

		NM/M
Complete Set (27):		8.00
Common Player:		.25
3	Bob Hamelin	.25
6	David Howard	.25
7	Greg Gagne	.25
8	Gary Gaetti	.25
11	Hal McRae	.25
12	Wally Joyner	.25
13	Jose Lind	.25
15	Mike McFarlane	.25
16	Keith Miller	.25
21	Jeff Montgomery	.25
22	David Cone	.25
23	Mark Gubicza	.25
24	Brent Mayne	.25
29	Vince Coleman	.25
33	Chris Haney	.25
34	Felix Jose	.25
35	Hipolito Pichardo	.25
36	Tom Gordon	.25
40	Kevin Koslofski	.25
41	Billy Brewer	.25
42	Dave Henderson	.25
44	Stan Belinda	.25
55	Kevin Appier	.25
56	Brian McRae	.25
'94	Royals Coaches (Steve Boros, Glenn Ezell, Bruce Kison, Lee May, Jamie Quirk)	.25

---	George Brett (Royals Hall of Fame)	3.00
---	Frank White (Royals Hall of Fame)	.50

1995 Kansas City Royals Police

In 1995, the Royals safety set was sponsored by Kansas City Life Insurance Co., and distributed by law enforcement agencies in the greater Kansas City area. The cards measure about 2-5/8" x 4" and feature action photos on front. The team name is scripted at bottom with logo and the player's last name and "1995" are vertically at right. Backs have a few vital data, a career stats line, a safety message and sponsor's logo. Cards are listed here in alphabetical order.

		NM/M
Complete Set (12):		4.00
Common Player:		.50
(1)	Kevin Appier	.50
(2)	Bob Boone	.65
(3)	Vince Coleman	.50
(4)	Gary Gaetti	.50
(5)	Greg Gagne	.50
(6)	Tom Gordon	.50
(7)	Mark Gubicza	.50
(8)	Chris Haney	.50
(9)	Wally Joyner	.65
(10)	Brent Mayne	.50
(11)	Jeff Montgomery	.50
(12)	Hipolito Pichardo	.50

1996 Kansas City Royals Police

Royals Nunnally • 22

The 1997 Royals safety set issue is a 23-card presentation given to young fans at a promotional game. The 2-5/8" x 4" cards have game-action color photo bordered in white. Backs are in blue on white with a few personal data, career highlights and record, a cartoon safety message and the logo of sponsoring Kansas City Life Insurance, which provided the cards for distribution by the Metropolitan Chiefs and Sheriffs Assn. Cards are checklisted here alphabetically.

		NM/M
Complete Set (27):		4.00
Common Player:		.25
1	Bip Roberts	.25
3	Bob Hamelin	.25
4	Keith Lockhart	.25
6	David Howard	.25
8	Bob Boone	.45
15	Mike Macfarlane	.25
16	Joe Randa	.25
17	Kevin Appier	.25
18	Johnny Damon	1.50
21	Jeff Montgomery	.25
22	Jon Nunnally	.25
23	Mark Gubicza	.25
25	Terry Clark	.25
25	Les Norman	.25
28	Rusty Meacham	.25
30	Jose Offerman	.25
33	Michael Tucker	.25
33	Chris Haney	.25
35	Hipolito Pichardo	.25
37	Rick Huisman	.25
38	Jim Converse	.25
41	Tim Belcher	.25
42	Tom Goodwin	.25
43	Joe Vitiello	.25
44	Jason Jacome	.25
45	Melvin Bunch	.25
57	Mike Magnante	.25

1997 Kansas City Royals Police

In 1996 the Royals returned to safety set issue with this 27-card presentation given to fans 14 and under at the April 20 game. The 2-5/8" x 4" cards have game-action color photo bordered in white. Backs are in blue on white with a few personal data, career highlights and record, a cartoon safety message and the logo of sponsoring Kansas City Life Insurance, which provided the cards for distribution by the Metropolitan Chiefs and Sheriffs Assn. Cards are checklisted here by uniform number.

		NM/M
Complete Set (23):		4.00
Common Player:		.25
(1)	Kevin Appier	.25
(2)	Tim Belcher	.25
(3)	Jay Bell	.25
(4)	Jaime Bluma	.25
(5)	Bob Boone	.50
(6)	Johnny Damon	1.50
(7)	Chili Davis	.25
(8)	Tom Goodwin	.25
(9)	Chris Haney	.25
(10)	David Howard	.25
(11)	Rick Huisman	.25
(12)	Jason Jacome	.25
(13)	Jeff King	.25
(14)	Mike Macfarlane	.25
(15)	Jeff Montgomery	.25
(16)	Jose Offerman	.25
(17)	Craig Paquette	.25
(18)	Hipolito Pichardo	.25
(19)	Bip Roberts	.25
(20)	Jose Rosado	.25
(21)	Sluggerrr (Mascot)	.25
(22)	Mike Sweeney	.25
(23)	Joe Vitiello	.25

1998 Kansas City Royals Police

In 1998 the Royals issued this safety set to fans 14 and under at a promotional game. The 2-5/8" x 4" cards have game-action color photo bordered in white. Backs are in blue on white with a few bits of personal data, a cartoon safety message and the logo of sponsoring Kansas City Life Insurance, which provided the cards for distribution by the Metropolitan Chiefs and Sheriffs Assn. Cards are checklisted here by uniform number.

		NM/M
Complete Set (26):		4.00
Common Player:		.25
2	Jed Hansen	.25
4	Shane Halter	.25
7	Jeff King	.35
14	Felix Martinez	.25
15	Mike Macfarlane	.25
16	Dean Palmer	.25
17	Kevin Appier	.25
18	Johnny Damon	1.50
19	Jeff Conine	.50
21	Jeff Montgomery	.25
22	Larry Sutton	.25
23	Hal Morris	.25
24	Jermaine Dye	.25
27	Joe Vitiello	.25
29	Mike Sweeney	.25
30	Jose Offerman	.25
33	Chris Haney	.25
35	Hipolito Pichardo	.25
40	Tony Muser	.25
41	Tim Belcher	.25
43	Roderick Myers	.25
47	Brian Bevil	.25
50	Jose Rosado	.25
53	Glendon Rusch	.25
56	Matt Whisenant	.25
	Sluggerrr (Mascot)	.25

2000 Kansas City Royals Police

The Royals issued this safety set to the first 10,000 fans 14 and under at an April 30 promotional game. The 2-5/8" x 4" cards have game-action color photo bordered in white. Backs are in blue on white

with a few bits of personal data, a cartoon safety message and the logo of sponsoring Kansas City Life Insurance, which provided the cards for distribution by the Metropolitan Chiefs and Sheriffs Assn. Cards are checklisted here by uniform number.

		NM/M
Complete Set (25):		4.00
Common Player:		.25
1	Rey Sanchez	.25
3	Carlos Febles	.50
4	Ray Holbert	.25
6	Todd Dunwoody	.25
12	Jeff Reboulet	.25
14	Mark Quinn	.25
15	Carlos Beltran	3.00
16	Joe Randa	.25
18	Johnny Damon	1.00
19	Brian Johnson	.25
24	Jermaine Dye	.25
28	Jay Witasick	.25
29	Mike Sweeney	.25
33	Chad Durbin	.25
34	Blake Stein	.25
37	Jeff Suppan	.25
38	Scott Pose	.25
40	Tony Muser	.25
41	Dan Reichert	.25
46	Jose Santiago	.25
48	Jerry Spradlin	.25
49	Chris Fussell	.25
50	Jose Rosado	.25
52	Ricky Bottalico	.25
	Sluggerrr (Mascot)	.25

1993 Kansas City Star Royals All-Time Team

On the occasion of the team's 25th anniversary the Kansas City Star newspaper issued a sheet honoring the All-Time Team. The 10-3/8" x 14-3/8" sheet is perforated to allow separation of the individual 2-1/2" x 3-1/2" cards. Fronts have color photos at center with royal blue borders at the sides and gold at top and bottom. A Royals 25th anniversary logo is at lower-right. Backs are printed in black and blue on white with a career summary and the player's K.C. stats. The unnumbered cards are checklisted here alphabetically.

		NM/M
Uncut Sheet:		12.00
Complete Set (16):		10.00
Common Player:		.50
(1)	George Brett	6.00
(2)	Steve Busby	.50
(3)	Al Cowens	.50
(4)	Dick Howser	.50
(5)	Dennis Leonard	.50
(6)	John Mayberry	.50
(7)	Hal McRae	.75
(8)	Amos Otis	.50
(9)	Fred Patek	.50
(10)	Darrell Porter	.50
(11)	Dan Quisenberry	.75
(12)	Bret Saberhagen	1.00
(13)	Paul Splittorff	.50

(14)	Frank White	.75
(15)	Willie Wilson	1.00
(16)	25th Anniversary Logo	.50

1985 Kas Potato Chips Discs

One of a pair of nearly identical (see Kitty Clover) sets issued by midwestern potato chip companies, this issue features top stars of the day on 2-3/4" cardboard discs. The discs have a player portrait at center, with uniform logos airbrushed away because the producer was licensed only by the MLB Players Association and not Major League Baseball. The player's name, team and position are printed in a white diamond around the photo. The sponsor's logo is in the orange border. Backs are in black-and-white and have a few biographical data, a 1984 stats line and a Snack Time logo. The unnumbered discs are checklisted here in alphabetical order. Square versions of the discs, which have been cut from press sheets are known within the hobby and carry a small premium. KAS was based in St. Louis.

		NM/M
Complete Set (25):		4.00
Common Player:		.25
1	Rey Sanchez	.25
3	Carlos Febles	.50
4	Ray Holbert	.25
6	Todd Dunwoody	.25
12	Jeff Reboulet	.25
14	Mark Quinn	.25
15	Carlos Beltran	3.00
16	Joe Randa	.25
18	Johnny Damon	1.00
19	Brian Johnson	.25
24	Jermaine Dye	.25
28	Jay Witasick	.25
29	Mike Sweeney	.25
33	Chad Durbin	.25
34	Blake Stein	.25
37	Jeff Suppan	.25
38	Scott Pose	.25
40	Tony Muser	.25
41	Dan Reichert	.25
46	Jose Santiago	.25
48	Jerry Spradlin	.25
49	Chris Fussell	.25
50	Jose Rosado	.25
52	Ricky Bottalico	.25
	Sluggerrr (Mascot)	.25

1986 Kas Potato Chips Cardinals

One of several of 2-7/8" round baseball card discs created by Mike Schecter Associates for inclusion in packages of potato chips, the 20-card Kas set features players of the defending National League Champion St. Louis Cardinals. Fronts feature color photos on which the team logos have been removed from the caps by airbrushing the photos' uniform logos. Card backs have minimal personal data and 1985 stats.

		NM/M
Complete Set (20):		16.00
Common Player:		.50
1	Vince Coleman	1.00
2	Ken Dayley	.50
3	Tito Landrum	.50
4	Steve Braun	.50
5	Danny Cox	.50
6	Bob Forsch	.50
7	Ozzie Smith	9.00
8	Brian Harper	.50
9	Jack Clark	.50
10	Todd Worrell	.50
11	Joaquin Andujar	.50
12	Tom Nieto	.50

13	Kurt Kepshire	.50
14	Terry Pendleton	.50
15	Tom Herr	.50
16	Darrell Porter	.50
17	John Tudor	.50
18	Jeff Lahti	.50
19	Andy Van Slyke	1.00
20	Willie McGee	1.00

1986 Kay Bee Young Superstars

One of the most-widely distributed of the specialty boxed sets of 1986, the Kay Bee toy store chain set of "Young Superstars of Baseball" was produced by Topps. The 2-1/2" x 3-1/2" cards are printed on white stock with a glossy surface finish. Backs, printed in red and black, are strongly reminiscent of the 1971 Topps cards. While the set concentrated on "young" stars of the game, few of the year's top rookies were included.

		NM/M
Complete Set (33):		2.00
Common Player:		.05
1	Rick Aguilera	.05
2	Chris Brown	.05
3	Tom Browning	.05
4	Tom Brunansky	.05
5	Vince Coleman	.05
6	Ron Darling	.05
7	Alvin Davis	.05
8	Mariano Duncan	.05
9	Shawon Dunston	.05
10	Sid Fernandez	.05
11	Tony Fernandez	.05
12	Brian Fisher	.05
13	John Franco	.05
14	Julio Franco	.05
15	Dwight Gooden	.05
16	Ozzie Guillen	.05
17	Tony Gwynn	.75
18	Jimmy Key	.05
19	Don Mattingly	1.50
20	Oddibe McDowell	.05
21	Roger McDowell	.05
22	Dan Pasqua	.05
23	Terry Pendleton	.05
24	Jim Presley	.05
25	Kirby Puckett	.75
26	Earnie Riles	.05
27	Bret Saberhagen	.05
28	Mark Salas	.05
29	Juan Samuel	.05
30	Jeff Stone	.05
31	Darryl Strawberry	.05
32	Andy Van Slyke	.05
33	Frank Viola	.05

1987 Kay Bee Superstars of Baseball

For a second year, Topps produced a boxed set for the Kay Bee toy store chain. Called "Superstars of Baseball," cards in the set measure 2-1/2" x 3-1/2". The glossy-coated fronts carry a color player photo plus the Kay Bee logo. Backs, reminiscent of those found in the 1971 Topps set, offer a black-and-white portrait of the player along

with his name, postion, personal information, playing record and a brief biography.

		NM/M
Complete Set (33):		3.00
Common Player:		.05
1	Harold Baines	.05
2	Jesse Barfield	.05
3	Don Baylor	.05
4	Wade Boggs	.65
5	George Brett	.75
6	Hubie Brooks	.05
7	Jose Canseco	.30
8	Gary Carter	.50
9	Joe Carter	.50
10	Roger Clemens	.75
11	Vince Coleman	.05
12	Glenn Davis	.05
13	Dwight Gooden	.05
14	Pedro Guerrero	.05
15	Tony Gwynn	.65
16	Rickey Henderson	.50
17	Keith Hernandez	.05
18	Wally Joyner	.05
19	Don Mattingly	.75
20	Jack Morris	.05
21	Dale Murphy	.15
22	Eddie Murray	.50
23	Dave Parker	.05
24	Kirby Puckett	.65
25	Tim Raines	.05
26	Jim Rice	.05
27	Dave Righetti	.05
28	Ryne Sandberg	.65
29	Mike Schmidt	.75
30	Mike Scott	.05
31	Darryl Strawberry	.05
32	Fernando Valenzuela	.05
33	Dave Winfield	.50

1988 Kay Bee Superstars of Baseball

This boxed set was produced by Topps for exclusive distribution via Kay Bee toy stores nationwide. Card fronts are super glossy and feature color player action photos below a bright red and yellow player name banner. Photos are framed in green above a large, cartoon-style Kay Bee logo. Backs feature player closeups in a horizontal layout in blue ink on a green and white background. Backs are numbered and carry biographical information, career data and major league batting stats.

		NM/M
Complete Set (33):		3.00
Common Player:		.05
1	George Bell	.05
2	Wade Boggs	.65
3	Jose Canseco	.30
4	Joe Carter	.50
5	Jack Clark	.05
6	Eric Davis	.05
7	Andre Dawson	.25
8	Darrell Evans	.05
9	Dwight Evans	.05
10	Gary Gaetti	.05
11	Tony Gwynn	.65
12	Howard Johnson	.05
13	Wally Joyner	.05
14	Don Mattingly	.75
15	Willie McGee	.05
16	Mark McGwire	.85
17	Paul Molitor	.50
18	Dale Murphy	.25
19	Dave Parker	.05
20	Lance Parrish	.05
21	Kirby Puckett	.65
22	Tim Raines	.05
23	Cal Ripken, Jr.	1.00
24	Juan Samuel	.05
25	Mike Schmidt	.75
26	Mike Scott	.05
27	Ruben Sierra	.05
28	Darryl Strawberry	.05
29	Danny Tartabull	.05
30	Alan Trammell	.05
31	Tim Wallach	.05
32	Dave Winfield	.50

1988 Kay Bee Team Leaders

This boxed edition of 44 player and six team logo cards was produced by Fleer for distribution by Kay Bee toy stores nationwide. Color player photos are framed in black against a bright red border. "Fleer Team Leaders 1988" and Kay Bee logos appear on the front. Backs, (red, white and pink) repeat the Team Leaders logo, followed by stats, personal data, team and MLB logos. The player's name, card number and position are listed on the lower border. The set includes six team logo sticker cards that feature black-and-white stadium photos on the backs.

		NM/M
Complete Set (44):		3.00
Common Player:		.05
1	George Bell	.05
2	Wade Boggs	.65
3	Jose Canseco	.40
4	Will Clark	.10
5	Roger Clemens	.75
6	Eric Davis	.05
7	Andre Dawson	.25
8	Julio Franco	.05
9	Andres Galarraga	.05
10	Dwight Gooden	.05
11	Tony Gwynn	.65
12	Tom Henke	.05
13	Orel Hershiser	.05
14	Kent Hrbek	.05
15	Ted Higuera	.05
16	Wally Joyner	.05
17	Jimmy Key	.05
18	Mark Langston	.05
19	Don Mattingly	.75
20	Willie McGee	.05
21	Mark McGwire	.85
22	Paul Molitor	.50
23	Jack Morris	.05
24	Dale Murphy	.25
25	Larry Parrish	.05
26	Kirby Puckett	.65
27	Tim Raines	.05
28	Jeff Reardon	.05
29	Dave Righetti	.05
30	Cal Ripken, Jr.	1.00
31	Don Robinson	.05
32	Bret Saberhagen	.05
33	Juan Samuel	.05
34	Mike Schmidt	.75
35	Mike Scott	.05
36	Kevin Seitzer	.05
37	Dave Smith	.05
38	Ozzie Smith	.65
39	Zane Smith	.05
40	Darryl Strawberry	.05
41	Rick Sutcliffe	.05
42	Bobby Thigpen	.05
43	Alan Trammell	.05
44	Andy Van Slyke	.05

1989 Kay Bee Superstars of Baseball

The top stars of baseball are featured in this boxed set produced by Topps for the Kay Bee Toy store chain. The glossy, standard-size cards display the Kay Bee logo below the player photo on the front. The top of the card is headlined "Superstars of Baseball," with the player's name underneath. Backs include a small black-and-white player photo and personal data.

DAVE HOSTETLER

		NM/M
Complete Set (33):		3.00
Common Player:		.05
1	Wade Boggs	.65
2	George Brett	.75
3	Jose Canseco	.30
4	Gary Carter	.50
5	Jack Clark	.05
6	Will Clark	.10
7	Roger Clemens	.75
8	Eric Davis	.05
9	Andre Dawson	.25
10	Dwight Evans	.05
11	Carlton Fisk	.05
12	Andres Galarraga	.05
13	Kirk Gibson	.05
14	Dwight Gooden	.05
15	Mike Greenwell	.05
16	Pedro Guerrero	.05
17	Tony Gwynn	.65
18	Rickey Henderson	.50
19	Orel Hershiser	.05
20	Don Mattingly	.50
21	Mark McGwire	.85
22	Dale Murphy	.25
23	Eddie Murray	.50
24	Kirby Puckett	.65
25	Tim Raines	.05
26	Ryne Sandberg	.65
27	Mike Schmidt	.75
28	Ozzie Smith	.65
29	Darryl Strawberry	.05
30	Alan Trammell	.05
31	Frank Viola	.05
32	Dave Winfield	.50
33	Robin Yount	.50

1990 Kay Bee Kings

DWIGHT EVANS

This boxed set was the fifth annual issue produced by Topps for the Kay Bee toy store chain. The 2-1/2" x 3-1/2" cards feature color action photos on the front and complete statistics on the flip sides. The cards are numbered alphabetically.

		NM/M
Complete Set (33):		4.00
Common Player:		.05
1	Doyle Alexander	.05
2	Bert Blyleven	.05
3	Wade Boggs	.65
4	George Brett	.75
5	John Candelaria	.05
6	Gary Carter	.50
7	Vince Coleman	.05
8	Andre Dawson	.25
9	Dennis Eckersley	.40
10	Darrell Evans	.05
11	Dwight Evans	.05
12	Carlton Fisk	.50
13	Ken Griffey	.05
14	Tony Gwynn	.65
15	Rickey Henderson	.50
16	Keith Hernandez	.05
17	Charlie Hough	.05
18	Don Mattingly	.75
19	Jack Morris	.05
20	Dale Murphy	.25
21	Eddie Murray	.50
22	Dave Parker	.05
23	Kirby Puckett	.65
24	Tim Raines	.05
25	Rick Reuschel	.05
26	Jerry Reuss	.05
27	Jim Rice	.15
28	Nolan Ryan	1.00
29	Ozzie Smith	.65
30	Frank Tanana	.05
31	Willie Wilson	.05
32	Dave Winfield	.50
33	Robin Yount	.50

1993 Keebler Texas Rangers

Over a series of eight home dates in Arlington Stadium's final season, the Keebler baking company along with a group of rotating co-sponsors produced and distributed a team set featuring "all players, manager and coaches who have ever appeared in a Rangers game." Besides the player cards there were checklists, team photo cards, team-leader cards, logo cards and other specials. The cards were made up into 8-1/2" x 11" booklets, with the cards perforated for removal. Series 2 and 3 booklets had 72 cards; the other series had 54 cards each. Single cards measure 2-1/2" x 3-1/2". Sepia-toned player portraits are featured with red frames. A blue banner at top has the team name. The player name is printed in black in the white bottom border. The Keebler logo is at the photo's lower-left, while the player's position is in a baseball diamond diagram at lower-right. Backs are printed in black, include a few biographical details and the player's Rangers' and major league career stats. The Keebler logo is repreated on the back, along with the logo of the co-sponsor of that particular series. A total of 42,000 of the first series booklets were distributed; 35,000 each of the other seven series were produced.

		NM/M
Complete Set (468):		35.00
Common Player:		.10
1	Ted Williams	5.00
2	Larry Biitner	.10
3	Rich Billings	.10
4	Dick Bosman	.10
5	Pete Broberg	.10
6	Jeff Burroughs	.10
7	Casey Cox	.10
8	Jim Driscoll	.10
9	Jan Dukes	.10
10	Bill Fahey	.10
11	Ted Ford	.10
12	Bill Gogolewski	.10
13	Tom Grieve	.10
14	Rich Hand	.10
15	Toby Harrah	.25
16	Vic Harris	.10
17	Rich Hinton	.10
18	Frank Howard	.25
19	Gerry Janeski	.10
20	Dalton Jones	.10
21	Hal King	.10
22	Ted Kubiak	.10
23	Steve Lawson	.10
24	Paul Lindblad	.10
25	Joe Lovitto	.10
26	Elliott Maddox	.10
27	Marty Martinez	.10
28	Jim Mason	.10
29	Don Mincher	.10
30	Dave Nelson	.10
31	Jim Panther	.10
32	Mike Paul	.10
33	Horacio Pina	.10
34	Tom Ragland	.10
35	Lenny Randle	.10
36	Jim Roland	.10
37	Jim Shellenback	.10
38	Don Stanhouse	.10
39	Ken Suarez	.10
40	Joe Camacho	.10
41	Nellie Fox	2.00
42	Sid Hudson	.10
43	George Susce	.10
44	Wayne Terwilliger	.10
45	Darrel Akerfelds	.10
46	Doyle Alexander	.10
47	Gerald Alexander	.10
48	Brian Allard	.10
49	Lloyd Allen	.10
50	Sandy Alomar	.10
51	Wilson Alvarez	.10
52	Jim Anderson	.10
53	Scott Anderson	.10
54	Brad Arnsberg	.10
55	Tucker Ashford	.10
56	Doug Ault	.10
57	Bob Babcock	.10
58	Mike Bacsik	.10
59	Harold Baines	.10
60	Alan Bannister	.10
61	Floyd Bannister	.10
62	John Barfield	.10
63	Len Barker	.10
64	Steve Barr	.10
65	Randy Bass	.10
66	Lew Beasley	.10
67	Kevin Belcher	.10
68	Buddy Bell	.10
69	Juan Beniquez	.10
70	Kurt Bevacqua	.10
71	Jim Bibby	.10
72	Joe Bitker	.10
73	Larvell Blanks	.10
74	Bert Blyleven	.25
75	Terry Bogener	.10
76	Tommy Boggs	.10
77	Dan Boitano	.10
78	Bobby Bonds	.25
79	Thad Bosley	.10
80	Dennis Boyd	.10
81	Nelson Briles	.10
82	Ed Brinkman	.10
83	Bob Brower	.10
84	Jackie Brown	.10
85	Larry Brown	.10
86	Jerry Browne	.10
87	Glenn Brummer	.10
88	Kevin Buckley	.10
89	Steve Buechele	.10
90	Ray Burris	.10
91	John Butcher	.10
92	Bert Campaneris	.10
93	Mike Campbell	.10
94	John Cangelosi	.10
95	Nick Capra	.10
96	Leo Cardenas	.10
97	Don Carman	.10
98	Rico Carty	.10
99	Don Castle	.10
100	Jose Cecena	.10
101	Dave Chalk	.10
102	Scott Chiamparino	.10
103	Ken Clay	.10
104	Reggie Cleveland	.10
105	Gene Clines	.10
106	David Clyde	.10
107	Cris Colon	.10
108	Merrill Combs	.10
109	Steve Comer	.10
110	Glen Cook	.10
111	Scott Coolbaugh	.10
112	Pat Corrales	.10
113	Edwin Correa	.10
114	Larry Cox	.10
115	Keith Creel	.10
116	Victor Cruz	.10
117	Mike Cubbage	.10
118	Bobby Cuellar	.10
119	Danny Darwin	.10
120	Jack Daugherty	.10
121	Doug Davis	.10
122	Odie Davis	.10
123	Willie Davis	.10
124	Bucky Dent	.10
125	Adrian Devine	.10
126	Mario Diaz	.10
127	Rich Donnelly	.10
128	Brian Downing	.10
129	Tommy Dunbar	.10
130	Steve Dunning	.10
131	Dan Duran	.10
132	Don Durham	.10
133	Dick Egan	.10
134	Dock Ellis	.10
135	John Ellis	.10
136	Mike Epstein	.10
137	Cecil Espy	.10
138	Chuck Estrada	.10
139	Glenn Ezell	.10
140	Hector Fajardo	.10
141	Monty Fariss	.10
142	Ed Farmer	.10
143	Jim Farr	.10
144	Joe Ferguson	.10
145	Ed Figueroa	.10
146	Steve Fireovid	.10
147	Scott Fletcher	.10
148	Doug Flynn	.10
149	Marv Foley	.10
150	Tim Foli	.10
151	Tony Fossas	.10
152	Steve Foucault	.10
153	Art Fowler	.10
154	Jim Fregosi	.10
155	Pepe Frias	.10
156	Oscar Gamble	.10
157	Barbaro Garbey	.10
158	Dick Gernert	.10
159	Jim Gideon	.10
160	Jerry Don Gleaton	.10
161	Orlando Gomez	.10
162	Rich Gossage	.25
163	Gary Gray	.10
164	Gary Green	.10
165	John Grubb	.10
166	Cecilio Guante	.10
167	Jose Guzman	.10
168	Drew Hall	.10
169	Bill Hands	.10
170	Steve Hargan	.10
171	Mike Hargrove	.10
172	Toby Harrah	.25
173	Bud Harrelson	.10
174	Donald Harris	.10
175	Greg Harris	.10
176	Mike Hart	.10
177	Bill Haselman	.10
178	Ray Hayward	.10
179	Tommy Helms	.10
180	Ken Henderson	.10
181	Rick Henninger	.10
182	Dwayne Henry	.10
183	Jose Hernandez	.10
184	Whitey Herzog	.10
185	Chuck Hiller	.10
186	Joe Hoerner	.10
187	Guy Hoffman	.10
188	Gary Holle	.10
189	Rick Honeycutt	.10
190	Burt Hooton	.10
191	John Hoover	.10
192	Willie Horton	.10
193	Dave Hostetler	.10
194	Charlie Hough	.10
195	Tom House	.10
196	Art Howe	.10
197	Steve Howe	.10
198	Roy Howell	.10
199	Charles Hudson	.10
200	Billy Hunter	.10
201	Pete Incaviglia	.25
202	Mike Jeffcoat	.10
203	Ferguson Jenkins	2.00
204	Alex Johnson	.10
205	Bobby Johnson	.10
206	Cliff Johnson	.10
207	Darrell Johnson	.10
208	John Henry Johnson	.10
209	Lamar Johnson	.10
210	Bobby Jones	.10
211	Odell Jones	.10
212	Mike Jorgensen	.10
213	Don Kainer	.10
214	Mike Kekich	.10
215	Steve Kemp	.10
216	Jim Kern	.10
217	Paul Kilgus	.10
218	Ed Kirkpatrick	.10
219	Darold Knowles	.10
220	Fred Koenig	.10
221	Jim Kremmel	.10
222	Chad Kreuter	.10
223	Jeff Kunkel	.10
224	Bob Lacey	.10
225	Al Lachowicz	.10
226	Joe Lahoud	.10
227	Rick Leach	.10
228	Danny Leon	.10
229	Dennis Lewallyn	.10
230	Rick Lisi	.10
231	Davey Lopes	.10
232	John Lowenstein	.10
233	Mike Loynd	.10
234	Frank Lucchesi	.10
235	Sparky Lyle	.10
236	Pete Mackanin	.10
237	Bill Madlock	.25
238	Greg Mahlberg	.10
239	Mickey Mahler	.10
240	Bob Malloy	.10
241	Ramon Manon	.10
242	Fred Manrique	.10
243	Barry Manuel	.10
244	Mike Marshall	.10
245	Billy Martin	.50
246	Mike Mason	.10
247	Terry Mathews	.10
248	Jon Matlack	.10
249	Rob Maurer	.10
250	Dave May	.10
251	Scott May	.10
252	Lee Mazzilli	.10
253	Larry McCall	.10
254	Lance McCullers	.10
255	Oddibe McDowell	.10
256	Russ McGinnis	.10
257	Joey McLaughlin	.10
258	Craig McMurtry	.10
259	Doc Medich	.10
260	Dave Meier	.10
261	Mario Mendoza	.10
262	Orlando Mercado	.10
263	Mark Mercer	.10
264	Ron Meridith	.10
265	Jim Merritt	.10
266	Gary Mielke	.10
267	Eddie Miller	.10
268	Paul Mirabella	.10
269	Dave Moates	.10
270	Dale Mohorcic	.10
271	Willie Montanez	.10
272	Tommy Moore	.10
273	Roger Moret	.10
274	Jamie Moyer	.10
275	Dale Murray	.10
276	Al Newman	.10
277	Dickie Noles	.10
278	Eric Nolte	.10
279	Nelson Norman	.10
280	Jim Norris	.10
281	Edwin Nunez	.10
282	Pete O'Brien	.10
283	Al Oliver	.25
284	Tom O'Malley	.10
285	Tom Paciorek	.10
286	Ken Pape	.10
287	Mark Parent	.10
288	Larry Parrish	.10
289	Gaylord Perry	2.00
290	Stan Perzanowski	.10
291	Fritz Peterson	.10
292	Mark Petkovsek	.10
293	Gary Pettis	.10
294	Jim Piersall	.25
295	John Poloni	.10
296	Jim Poole	.10
297	Tom Poquette	.10
298	Darrell Porter	.10
299	Ron Pruitt	.10
300	Greg Pryor	.10
301	Luis Pujols	.10
302	Pat Putnam	.10
303	Doug Rader	.10
304	Dave Rajsich	.10
305	Kevin Reimer	.10
306	Merv Rettenmund	.10
307	Mike Richardt	.10
308	Mickey Rivers	.10
309	Dave Roberts	.10
310	Leon Roberts	.10
311	Jeff Robinson	.10
312	Tom Robson	.10
313	Wayne Rosenthal	.10
314	Dave Rozema	.10
315	Jeff Russell	.10
316	Connie Ryan	.10
317	Billy Sample	.10
318	Jim Schaffer	.10
319	Calvin Schiraldi	.10
320	Dave Schmidt	.10
321	Donnie Scott	.10
322	Tony Scruggs	.10
323	Bob Sebra	.10
324	Larry See	.10
325	Sonny Siebert	.10
326	Ruben Sierra	.10
327	Charlie Silvera	.10
328	Duke Sims	.10
329	Bill Singer	.10
330	Craig Skok	.10
331	Don Slaught	.10
332	Roy Smalley	.10
333	Dan Smith	.10
334	Keith Smith	.10
335	Mike Smithson	.10
336	Eric Soderholm	.10
337	Sammy Sosa	4.00
338	Jim Spencer	.10
339	Dick Such	.10
340	Eddie Stanky	.10
341	Mike Stanley	.10
342	Rusty Staub	.35
343	James Steels	.10
344	Bill Stein	.10
345	Rick Stelmaszek	.10
346	Ray Stephens	.10
347	Dave Stewart	.10
348	Jeff Stone	.10
349	Bill Sudakis	.10
350	Jim Sundberg	.10
351	Rich Surhoff	.10
352	Greg Tabor	.10
353	Frank Tanana	.10
354	Jeff Terpko	.10
355	Stan Thomas	.10
356	Bobby Thompson	.10
357	Danny Thompson	.10
358	Dickie Thon	.10
359	Dave Tobik	.10
360	Wayne Tolleson	.10
361	Cesar Tovar	.10
362	Jim Umbarger	.10
363	Bobby Valentine	.10
364	Ellis Valentine	.10
365	Ed Vande Berg	.10
366	Dewayne Vaughn	.10
367	Mark Wagner	.10
368	Rick Waits	.10
369	Duane Walker	.10
370	Mike Wallace	.10
371	Denny Walling	.10
372	Danny Walton	.10
373	Gary Ward	.10
374	Claudell Washington	.10
375	Larue Wasington	.10
376	Chris Welsh	.10
377	Don Werner	.10
378	Len Whitehouse	.10
379	Del Wilber	.10
380	Curtis Wilkerson	.10
381	Matt Williams	.10
382	Mitch Williams	.10
383	Bump Wills	.10
384	Paul Wilmet	.10
385	Steve Wilson	.10
386	Bobby Witt	.10
387	Clyde Wright	.10
388	George Wright	.10
389	Ricky Wright	.10
390	Ned Yost	.10
391	Don Zimmer	.10
392	Richie Zisk	.10
393	Kevin Kennedy	.10
394	Steve Balboni	.10
395	Brian Bohanon	.10
396	Jeff Bronkey	.10
397	Kevin Brown	.10
398	Todd Burns	.10
399	Jose Canseco	.75
400	Cris Carpenter	.10
401	Doug Dascenzo	.10
402	Butch Davis	.10
403	Steve Dreyer	.10
404	Rob Ducey	.10
405	Julio Franco	.10
406	Jeff Frye	.10
407	Benji Gil	.10
408	Juan Gonzalez	3.00
409	Tom Henke	.10
410	David Hulse	.10
411	Jeff Huson	.10
412	Chris James	.10
413	Manuel Lee	.10
414	Craig Lefferts	.10
415	Charlie Leibrandt	.10
416	Gene Nelson	.10
417	Robb Nen	.10
418	Darren Oliver	.10
419	Rafael Palmeiro	2.00
420	Dean Palmer	.10
421	Bob Patterson	.10
422	Roger Pavlik	.10
423	Dan Peltier	.10
424	Geno Petralli	.10
425	Gary Redus	.10
426	Rick Reed	.10
427	Bill Ripken	.10
428	Ivan Rodriguez	3.00
429	Kenny Rogers	.10
430	John Russell	.10
431	Nolan Ryan	6.00
432	Mike Schooler	.10
433	Jon Shave	.10
434	Doug Strange	.10
435	Matt Whiteside	.10
436	Mickey Hatcher	.10
437	Perry Hill	.10
438	Jackie Moore	.10
439	Dave Oliver	.10
440	Claude Osteen	.10
441	Willie Upshaw	.10
442	Checklist 1-112	.10
443	Checklist 113-224	.10
444	Checklist 225-336	.10
445	Checklist 337-446	.10
446	Arlington Stadium	.10

Los Angeles Dodgers

RAUL MONDESI

In a promotion similar to those of Mother's Cookies in the past, Keebler sponsored a kids' trading card day August 15 distributing 28-card packs to fans 14 and under. Each pack contained 21 different cards and seven duplicates to trade in an effort to complete the set. The 2-1/2" x 3-1/2" cards have borderless player photos on front with a Dodgers logo ad team-color red and blue stripes at bottom in which the player's name appears. Color backs have a team logo, a Keebler's elf logo and a few bits of player biographical data.

		NM/M
Complete Set (28):		10.00
Common Player:		.50
1	Davey Johnson	.50
2	Eric Karros	.50
3	Gary Sheffield	.75
4	Raul Mondesi	.50
5	Kevin Brown	.60
6	Mark Grudzielanek	.50
7	Todd Hollandsworth	.50
8	Todd Hundley	.50
9	Jeff Shaw	.50
10	Pedro Borbon	.50
11	Chan Ho Park	.75
12	Jose Vizcaino	.50
13	Devon White	.50
14	Darren Dreifort	.50
15	Onan Masaoka	.50
16	Dave Hansen	.50
17	Adrian Beltre	1.50
18	Ismael Valdes	.50
19	Alan Mills	.50
20	Eric Young	.50
21	Mike Maddux	.50
22	Carlos Perez	.50
23	Tripp Cromer	.50
24	Jamie Arnold	.50
25	Angel Pena	.50
26	Trenidad Hubbard	.50
27	Doug Bochtler	.50
28	Coaches/Checklist (Rick Dempsey, Rich Down, Glenn Hoffman, Manny Mota, Claude Osteen, John Shelby, Jim Tracy)	.50

San Diego Padres

In a promotion similar to those of Mother's Cookies in the past, Keebler sponsored a kids' trading card day August 1 distributing 28-card packs to fans 14 and under. Each

TONY GWYNN

MOLITOR
INFIELD

RELIEF PITCHER

pack contained 21 different cards and seven duplicates to trade in an effort to complete the set. The 2-1/2" x 3-1/2" cards have borderless player photos on front with a Padres logo and team-color orange and blue stripes at bottom in which the player's name appears. Color backs have a Padres 1969-1999 logo, a Keebler's elf logo and a few bits of player biographical data.

		NM/M
Complete Set (28):		10.00
Common Player:		.50
1	Bruce Bochy	.50
2	Tony Gwynn	4.00
3	Wally Joyner	.50
4	Sterling Hitchcock	.50
5	Jim Leyritz	.50
6	Trevor Hoffman	.75
7	Quilvio Veras	.50
8	Dave Magadan	.50
9	Andy Ashby	.50
10	Damian Jackson	.50
11	Dan Miceli	.50
12	Reggie Sanders	.50
13	Chris Gomez	.50
14	Ruben Rivera	.50
15	Greg Myers	.50
16	Ed Vosberg	.50
17	John Vander Wal	.50
18	Donne Wall	.50
19	Eric Owens	.50
20	Brian Boehringer	.50
21	Woody Williams	.50
22	Matt Clement	.50
23	Carlos Reyes	.50
24	Stan Spencer	.50
25	George Arias	.50
26	Carlos Almanzar	.50
27	Phil Nevin	.50
28	Greg Booker, Tim Flannery, Davey Lopes, Rob Picciolo, Merv Rettenmund, Dave Smith (Padres Coaches)	.50

S.F. Giants

ROBB NEN

In a promotion similar to those of Mother's Cookies in the past, Keebler sponsored a kids' trading card day distributing 28-card packs to fans 14 and under. Each pack contained 21 different cards and seven duplicates to trade in an effort to complete the set. The 2-1/2" x 3-1/2" cards have borderless player photos on front with a farewell to Candlestick Park logo and team-color orange and black stripes at bottom in which the player's name appears. Color backs have a Keebler's elf logo and a few bits of player biographical data.

		NM/M
Complete Set (28):		12.50
Common Player:		.50
1	Dusty Baker	.50
2	Barry Bonds	7.50
3	Jeff Kent	.75
4	Robb Nen	.50
5	Bill Mueller	.50
6	Russ Ortiz	.50

7	Ellis Burks	.50
8	Marvin Benard	.50
9	Kirk Rueter	.50
10	J.T. Snow	.50
11	Stan Javier	.50
12	Chris Brock	.50
13	Charlie Hayes	.50
14	Joe Nathan	.50
15	Rich Rodriguez	.50
16	Brent Mayne	.50
17	Shawn Estes	.50
18	Rich Aurilia	.50
19	Mark Gardner	.50
20	Scott Servais	.50
21	John Johnstone	.50
22	Felix Rodriguez	.50
23	Armando Rios	.50
24	Alan Embree	.50
25	F.P. Santangelo	.50
26	Jerry Spradlin	.50
27	Lon Simmons (Broadcaster)	.50
28	Giants Coaches (Carlos Alfonso, Gene Clines, Sonny Jackson, Juan Lopez, Ron Perranoski, Ron Wotus)	.50

2000 Keebler Arizona Diamondbacks

Keebler cookies sponsored a kids' trading card day, distributing 28-card packs to fans 14 and under. Each pack contained 21 different cards and seven duplicates to trade in an effort to complete the set. Round-cornered cards have borderless portrait photos with a stripe at bottom featuring player identification and team logo. Backs have player data, uniform number, biographical information and Keebler's logo.

		NM/M
Complete Set (28):		10.00
Common Player:		.50
1	Buck Showalter	.50
2	Randy Johnson	3.00
3	Luis Gonzalez	.65
4	Todd Stottlemyre	.50
5	Matt Williams	.75
6	Curt Schilling	1.50
7	Jay Bell	.50
8	Steve Finley	.50
9	Brian Anderson	.50
10	Tony Womack	.50
11	Mike Morgan	.50
12	Damian Miller	.50
13	Greg Swindell	.50
14	Greg Colbrunn	.50
15	Dan Plesac	.50
16	Craig Counsell	.50
17	Russ Springer	.50
18	Kelly Stinnett	.50
19	Alex Cabrera	.50
20	Matt Mantei	.50
21	Danny Klassen	.50
22	Hanley Frias	.50
23	Byung-Hyun Kim	.50
24	Jason Conti	.50
25	Danny Bautista	.50
26	Erubiel Durazo	.50
27	Armando Reynoso	.50
28	Coaches/Checklist	.50

L.A. Dodgers

GARY SHEFFIELD

Keebler cookies sponsored a kids' trading card day August 20, distributing 28-card packs to fans 14 and under. Each pack contained 21 different cards and seven duplicates to trade in an effort to complete the set. Round-cornered cards have borderless portrait photos with a red stripe at bottom featuring player identification and team logo. Backs have player data, uniform number, biographical information and Keebler's logo.

		NM/M
Complete Set (28):		10.00
Common Player:		.50
1	Davey Johnson	.50
2	Eric Karros	.50

3	Gary Sheffield	.75
4	Kevin Brown	.60
5	Shawn Green	2.50
6	Mark Grudzielanek	.50
7	Todd Hollandsworth	.50
8	Todd Hundley	.50
9	Jeff Shaw	.50
10	Adrian Beltre	1.00
11	Chan Ho Park	.60
12	Jose Vizcaino	.50
13	Devon White	.50
14	Darren Dreifort	.50
15	Onan Masaoka	.50
16	Dave Hansen	.50
17	Kevin Elster	.50
18	Antonio Osuna	.50
19	Geronimo Berroa	.50
20	Orel Hershiser	.65
21	Chad Kreuter	.50
22	Carlos Perez	.50
23	F.P. Santangelo	.50
24	Terry Adams	.50
25	Alex Cora	.50
26	Matt Herges	.50
27	Mike Fetters	.50
28	Coaches/Checklist (Rick Dempsey, Claude Osteen, Rick Down, Manny Mota, Jim Tracy, Glenn Hoffman, John Shelby)	.50

San Diego Padres

RYAN KLESKO

Keebler cookies sponsored a kids' trading card day July 16 distributing 28-card packs to fans 14 and under. Each pack contained 21 different cards and seven duplicates to trade in an effort to complete the set. Fronts of the round-cornered 2-1/2" x 3-1/2" cards have posed photos with team-color orange and blue bars at bottom with player name and team logo. Backs have player ID, jersey number and team logo.

		NM/M
Complete Set (28):		10.00
Common Player:		.50
1	Bruce Bochy	.50
2	Tony Gwynn	4.00
3	Ryan Klesko	.50
4	Sterling Hitchcock	.50
5	Al Martin	.50
6	Trevor Hoffman	.75
7	Bret Boone	.65
8	Dave Magadan	.50
9	Steve Montgomery	.50
10	Damian Jackson	.50
11	Woody Williams	.50
12	Wiki Gonzalez	.50
13	Chris Gomez	.50
14	Ruben Rivera	.50
15	Ed Sprague	.50
16	Carlton Loewer	.50
17	Kory DeHaan	.50
18	Donne Wall	.50
19	Eric Owens	.50
20	Brian Boehringer	.50
21	Phil Nevin	.50
22	Matt Clement	.50
23	Brian Meadows	.50
24	Vincente Palacios	.50
25	Carlos Hernandez	.50
26	Carlos Almanzar	.50
27	Kevin Walker	.50
28	Coaches/Checklist (Greg Booker, Tim Flannery, Ben Oglivie, Rob Picciolo, Dave Smith, Alan Trammell)	.50

S.F. Giants

Keebler cookies sponsored a trading card day August 6, distributing 25,000 28-card packs to fans. Each pack contained 21 different cards and seven duplicates to trade in an effort to complete the set.

		NM/M
Complete Set (28):		10.00
Common Player:		.50
1	Dusty Baker	.50
2	Barry Bonds	5.00
3	Jeff Kent	.75

4	Robb Nen	.50
5	J.T. Snow	.50
6	Russ Ortiz	.50
7	Ellis Burks	.50
8	Bill Mueller	.50
9	Shawn Estes	.50
10	Marvin Benard	.50
11	Kirk Rueter	.50
12	Bobby Estalella	.50
13	Livan Hernandez	.50
14	Rich Aurilia	.50
15	Alan Embree	.50
16	Armando Rios	.50
17	Felix Rodriguez	.50
18	Doug Mirabelli	.50
19	John Johnstone	.50
20	Russ Davis	.50
21	Joe Nathan	.50
22	Aaron Fultz	.50
23	Felipe Crespo	.50
24	Mark Gardner	.50
25	Ramon Martinez	.50
26	Calvin Murray	.50
27	Carlos Alfonso	.50
28	Giants Coaches (Gene Clines, Sonny Jackson, Juan Lopez, Dave Righetti, Robby Thompson, Ron Wotus)	.50

Seattle Mariners

Keebler cookies sponsored a trading card day at a home game August 13, distributing 20,000 28-card packs to fans. Each pack contained 21 different cards and seven duplicates to trade in an effort to complete the set. Cards are 2-1/2" x 3-1/2" with rounded corners. Fronts have borderless posed photos with a team logo at lower-left and the player name in white in a dark blue strip. Backs have a color Keebler logo and basic player information.

		NM/M
Complete Set (28):		15.00
Common Player:		.50
1	Lou Piniella	.50
2	Alex Rodriguez	6.00
3	Jamie Moyer	.50
4	Edgar Martinez	.50
5	Kazuhiro Sasaki	.75
6	Jay Buhner	.50
7	Rickey Henderson	2.50
8	John Olerud	.50
9	Aaron Sele	.50
10	Charles Gipson	.50
11	Arthur Rhodes	.50
12	Dan Wilson	.50
13	Jose Mesa	.50
14	Mike Cameron	.50
15	John Halama	.50
16	Mark McLemore	.50
17	Brett Tomko	.50
18	Tom Lampkin	.50
19	Freddy Garcia	.50
20	John Mabry	.50
21	Paul Abbott	.50
22	Stan Javier	.50
23	Gil Meche	.50
24	David Bell	.50
25	Frankie Rodriguez	.50
26	Raul Ibanez	.50
27	Jose Paniagua	.50
28	Coaches/Checklist	.50

1986 Keller's Butter Phillies

Kellers SUPER STARS SERIES Beatrice 1985		
MIKE SCHMIDT PHILADELPHIA PHILLIES 3rd BASE		

It's a good thing the Keller's Butter set of six Philadelphia Phillies players is downright unattractive or their value would be sky high. One card was printed on each one pound package of butter. The 2-1/2" x 2-3/4" cards feature crude drawings of the players, the backs are blank.

		NM/M
Complete Set (6):		15.00
Common Player:		1.00
(1)	Steve Carlton	4.00
(2)	Von Hayes	1.00
(3)	Gary Redus	1.00
(4)	Juan Samuel	1.00
(5)	Mike Schmidt	8.00
(6)	Glenn Wilson	1.00

1981 Kellogg's

"Bigger" is the word to best describe Kellogg's 1981 card set. Not only were the cards themselves larger than ever before at 2-1/2" x 3-1/2", but the size of the set was increased to 66, the largest since the 75-card issues of 1970-71. The '81 Kellogg's set was available only as complete sets by mail. It is thought that the wider format of the 1981s may help prevent the problems of curling and cracking from which other years of Kellogg's issues suffer.

		NM/M
Complete Set (66):		15.00
Common Player:		.50
1	George Foster	.50
2	Jim Palmer	1.50
3	Reggie Jackson	2.50
4	Al Oliver	.50
5	Mike Schmidt	3.00
6	Nolan Ryan	7.50
7	Bucky Dent	.50
8	George Brett	3.00
9	Jim Rice	.75
10	Steve Garvey	.75
11	Willie Stargell	1.50
12	Phil Niekro	1.00
13	Dave Parker	.50
14	Cesar Cedeno	.50
15	Don Baylor	.50
16	J.R. Richard	.50
17	Tony Perez	1.00
18	Eddie Murray	1.50
19	Chet Lemon	.50
20	Ben Oglivie	.50
21	Dave Winfield	1.50
22	Joe Morgan	1.50
23	Vida Blue	.50
24	Willie Wilson	.50
25	Steve Henderson	.50
26	Rod Carew	1.50
27	Garry Templeton	.50
28	Dave Concepcion	.50
29	Davey Lopes	.50
30	Ken Landreaux	.50
31	Keith Hernandez	.50
32	Cecil Cooper	.50
33	Rickey Henderson	3.00
34	Frank White	.50
35	George Hendrick	.50
36	Reggie Smith	.50
37	Tug McGraw	.50
38	Tom Seaver	1.50
39	Ken Singleton	.50
40	Terry Puhl	.50
41	Rich "Goose" Gossage	.50
42	Larry Bowa	.50
43	Phil Garner	.50
44	Ron Guidry	.50
45	Lee Mazzilli	.50
46	Dave Kingman	.50
47	Carl Yastrzemski	2.00
48	Rick Burleson	.50
49	Steve Carlton	1.50
50	Alan Trammell	.75
51	Tommy John	.50
52	Paul Molitor	1.50
53	Joe Charboneau	1.00
54	Rick Langford	.50
55	Bruce Sutter	.50
56	Robin Yount	1.50
57	Steve Stone	.50
58	Larry Gura	.50
59	Mike Flanagan	.50
60	Bob Horner	.50
61	Bruce Bochte	.50
62	Pete Rose	6.00
63	Buddy Bell	.50
64	Johnny Bench	2.00
65	Mike Hargrove	.50

1982 Kellogg's

For the second straight year in 1982, Kellogg's cards were not inserted into cereal boxes, but had to be obtained by sending cash and box tops to the company for complete sets. The '82 cards were downsized both in number of cards in the set - 64 - and in physical dimensions, 2-1/8" x 3-1/4".

3-D SUPER STARS

	NM/M
Complete Set (64):	15.00
Common Player:	.25
1 Richie Zisk	.25
2 Bill Buckner	.25
3 George Brett	3.00
4 Rickey Henderson	1.50
5 Jack Morris	.25
6 Ozzie Smith	2.00
7 Rollie Fingers	1.00
8 Tom Seaver	2.00
9 Fernando Valenzuela	.25
10 Hubie Brooks	.25
11 Nolan Ryan	7.50
12 Dave Winfield	1.50
13 Bob Horner	.25
14 Reggie Jackson	2.50
15 Burt Hooton	.25
16 Mike Schmidt	3.00
17 Bruce Sutter	1.00
18 Pete Rose	6.00
19 Dave Kingman	.25
20 Neil Allen	.25
21 Don Sutton	1.00
22 Dave Concepcion	.25
23 Keith Hernandez	.25
24 Gary Carter	1.50
25 Carlton Fisk	1.50
26 Ron Guidry	.25
27 Steve Carlton	1.50
28 Robin Yount	1.50
29 John Castino	.25
30 Johnny Bench	2.00
31 Bob Knepper	.25
32 Rich "Goose" Gossage	.25
33 Buddy Bell	.25
34 Art Howe	.25
35 Tony Armas	.25
36 Phil Niekro	1.00
37 Len Barker	.25
38 Bobby Grich	.25
39 Steve Kemp	.25
40 Kirk Gibson	.25
41 Carney Lansford	.25
42 Jim Palmer	1.50
43 Carl Yastrzemski	2.00
44 Rick Burleson	.25
45 Dwight Evans	.25
46 Ron Cey	.25
47 Steve Garvey	.50
48 Dave Parker	.25
49 Mike Easler	.25
50 Dusty Baker	.25
51 Rod Carew	1.50
52 Chris Chambliss	.25
53 Tim Raines	.25
54 Chet Lemon	.25
55 Bill Madlock	.25
56 George Foster	.25
57 Dwayne Murphy	.25
58 Ken Singleton	.25
59 Mike Norris	.25
60 Cecil Cooper	.25
61 Al Oliver	.25
62 Willie Wilson	.25
63 Vida Blue	.25
64 Eddie Murray	1.50

1983 Kellogg's

MORRIS
PITCHER

In its 14th consecutive year of baseball card issue, Kellogg's returned to the policy of inserting single cards into cereal boxes, as well as offering complete sets by a mail-in box top redemption offer. The 3-D cards themselves returned to a narrow 1-7/8" x 3-1/4" format, while the set size was reduced to 60 cards.

		NM/M
Complete Set (60):		15.00
Common Player:		.40
1	Rod Carew	1.50
2	Rollie Fingers	1.00
3	Reggie Jackson	2.50
4	George Brett	3.00
5	Hal McRae	.40
6	Pete Rose	6.00
7	Fernando Valenzuela	.40
8	Rickey Henderson	1.50
9	Carl Yastrzemski	2.00
10	Rich "Goose" Gossage	.40
11	Eddie Murray	1.50
12	Buddy Bell	.40
13	Jim Rice	.60
14	Robin Yount	1.50
15	Dave Winfield	1.50
16	Harold Baines	.40
17	Garry Templeton	.40
18	Bill Madlock	.40
19	Pete Vuckovich	.40
20	Pedro Guerrero	.40
21	Ozzie Smith	2.00
22	George Foster	.40
23	Willie Wilson	.40
24	Johnny Ray	.40
25	George Hendrick	.40
26	Andre Thornton	.40
27	Leon Durham	.40
28	Cecil Cooper	.40
29	Don Baylor	.40
30	Lonnie Smith	.40
31	Nolan Ryan	7.50
32	Dan Quiesenberry (Quisenberry)	.40
33	Len Barker	.40
34	Neil Allen	.40
35	Jack Morris	.40
36	Dave Stieb	.40
37	Bruce Sutter	1.00
38	Jim Sundberg	.40
39	Jim Palmer	1.50
40	Lance Parrish	.40
41	Floyd Bannister	.40
42	Larry Gura	.40
43	Britt Burns	.40
44	Toby Harrah	.40
45	Steve Carlton	1.50
46	Greg Minton	.40
47	Gorman Thomas	.40
48	Jack Clark	.40
49	Keith Hernandez	.40
50	Greg Luzinski	.40
51	Fred Lynn	.40
52	Dale Murphy	.75
53	Kent Hrbek	.40
54	Bob Horner	.40
55	Gary Carter	1.50
56	Carlton Fisk	1.50
57	Dave Concepcion	.40
58	Mike Schmidt	3.00
59	Bill Buckner	.40
60	Bobby Grich	.40

1991 Kellogg's Baseball Greats

Six Hall of Famers are featured on the backs of 7- and 12-ounce Corn Flakes boxes. The photos are designed to be cut out and assembled as a stand-up figure. A career summary also appears on the box back.

		NM/M
Complete Set (6):		12.00
Common Player:		2.00
(1)	Hank Aaron	4.00
(2)	Ernie Banks	2.50
(3)	Yogi Berra	2.50
(4)	Lou Brock	2.00
(5)	Steve Carlton	2.00
(6)	Bob Gibson	2.00

1991 Kellogg's Leyendas

These bilingual (English/Spanish) cards honoring past Hispanic stars were inserted in several brands of Kellogg's cereal in selected geographic areas. Fronts have an action player photo, while

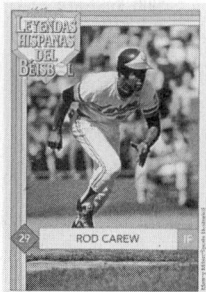

backs have a black-and-white portrait photo, biographical details, career stats and highlights.

		NM/M
Complete Set (11):		9.00
Common Player:		.50
(1)	Bert Campaneris	.50
(2)	Rod Carew	1.00
(3)	Rico Carty	.50
(4)	Cesar Cedeno	.50
(5)	Orlando Cepeda	1.00
(6)	Roberto Clemente	6.00
(7)	Mike Cuellar	.50
(8)	Ed Figueroa	.40
(9)	Minnie Minoso	.75
(10)	Manny Sanguillen	.50
(11)	Header card	.25

1991 Kellogg's 3-D

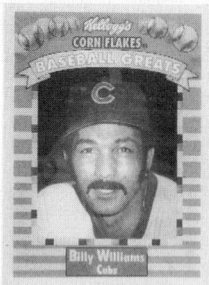

In 1991, specially-marked packages of Kellogg's Corn Flakes included 3-D baseball cards, resuming a tradition that began in 1970 and continued without interruption until 1983. In the 1991 edition, there are 15 cards to collect, featuring many of the greatest living retired stars in the game. Most of the players are in the Hall of Fame. The card fronts show two pictures of the player, while the backs include career highlights and a portrait. The cards are 2-1/2" x 3-5/16", numbered and were made by Sportflics. A complete set was available via a mail-in offer for $4.95 plus proofs of purchase.

		NM/M
Complete Set (15):		4.50
Common Player:		.25
1	Gaylord Perry	.25
2	Hank Aaron	1.00
3	Willie Mays	1.00
4	Ernie Banks	.75
5	Bob Gibson	.50
6	Harmon Killebrew	.50
7	Rollie Fingers	.50
8	Steve Carlton	.50
9	Billy Williams	.25
10	Lou Brock	.25
11	Yogi Berra	.75
12	Warren Spahn	.50
13	Boog Powell	.25
14	Don Baylor	.25
15	Ralph Kiner	.25

1992 Kellogg's 3-D

Kellogg's cereal company created a 10-card 1992 All-Star set of retired stars, with one card inserted in specially-marked boxes of corn flakes, and complete sets available by mail. The cards, produced by Sportflics, feature two sequential action images on each front. Red, white and blue designs comprise the border, with yellow bands above and beneath the photo. On back is a black-and-white portrait photo, plus a career summary, a few stats, and the logos of the cereal company, the Major League Baseball Players Alumni and Sportflics. As in the previous year, cards are slightly longer,

at 2-1/2" x 2-5/16", than standard size. Also available by mail was a large, colorful cardboard display in which the cards could be placed.

		NM/M
Complete Set (10):		2.00
Common Player:		.25
1	Willie Stargell	.50
2	Tony Perez	.50
3	Jim Palmer	.50
4	Rod Carew	.50
5	Tom Seaver	.65
6	Phil Niekro	.50
7	Bill Madlock	.25
8	Jim Rice	.35
9	Dan Quisenberry	.25
10	Mike Schmidt	1.00

3-D Canadian

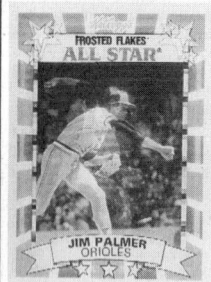

Very similar in format to the American version, 3-D cards of 10 basebAll-Stars of the past were found in packages of Kellogg's Frosted Flakes. Backs of the Canadian cards are printed in both English and French, which left no room for a card number, so the checklist provided here is alphabetical.

		NM/M
Complete Set (10):		8.00
Common Player:		.75
(1)	Rod Carew	1.00
(2)	Bill Madlock	.75
(3)	Phil Niekro	1.00
(4)	Jim Palmer	1.00
(5)	Tony Perez	1.00
(6)	Dan Quisenberry	.75
(7)	Jim Rice	.75
(8)	Mike Schmidt	1.50
(9)	Tom Seaver	1.50
(10)	Willie Stargell	1.00

1994 Kellogg's Clemente Collection

To commemorate the life and career of its greatest sports hero, special boxes of Kellogg's Corn Flakes sold in Puerto Rico for a time in 1994 contained one of three special cards in a cello pack. The 2-1/2" x 3-1/2" cards have color photos on front bordered in bright colors. A home plate design at top-left reads: "Kellogg's Clemente Coleccion Classico." Black-

and-white backs are printed in Spanish, have personal data, career stats, highlights and a portrait photo.

		NM/M
Complete Set (3):		35.00
Common Card:		12.50
1	Roberto Clemente (Bat on shoulder.)	12.50
2	Roberto Clemente/Running (Black helmet.)	12.50
3	Roberto Clemente/Running (Yyellow version.)	12.50

1987 Key Food Discs

(See 1987 Super Stars Discs for checklist and price guide.)

1988 Key Food Discs

(See 1988 Super Stars Discs for checklist and price guide.)

1988 King-B

Created by Mike Schechter Associates, this set consists of 24 numbered discs, 2-3/4" in diameter. The cards were inserted in specially marked 7/16 ounce tubs of Jerky Stuff (shredded beef jerky). Fronts feature full-color photos surrounded by a blue border. The King-B logo appears in the upper left portion of the disc. Backs are printed in blue on white stock and carry player personal and playing information. Team insignias have been airbrushed from the players' caps and jerseys.

		NM/M
Complete Set (24):		15.00
Common Player:		.50
Uncut Sheet:		20.00
1	Mike Schmidt	1.50
2	Dale Murphy	.65
3	Kirby Puckett	1.00
4	Ozzie Smith	1.00
5	Tony Gwynn	1.00
6	Mark McGwire	2.50
7	George Brett	1.50
8	Darryl Strawberry	.50
9	Wally Joyner	.50
10	Cory Snyder	.50
11	Barry Bonds	3.00
12	Darrell Evans	.50
13	Mike Scott	.50
14	Andre Dawson	.65
15	Don Mattingly	1.50
16	Candy Maldonado	.50
17	Alvin Davis	.50
18	Carlton Fisk	.75
19	Fernando Valenzuela	.50
20	Roger Clemens	1.50
21	Larry Parrish	.50
22	Eric Davis	.50
23	Paul Molitor	.50
24	Cal Ripken, Jr.	3.00

1989 King-B

The second King-B set created by Mike Schechter Associates again consists of 24 circular baseball player discs in cans of shredded

cards measuring 2-3/4" in diameter. The cards were inserted into specially-marked tubs of "Jerky Stuff." Fronts feature full-color photos bordered in red. The King-B logo appears in the upper left portion of the disc. Like the 1988 set, the team insignias have airbrushed from uniforms and caps. The backs are printed in red and display personal information and stats.

		NM/M
Complete Set (24):		15.00
Common Player:		.50
1	Kirk Gibson	.50
2	Eddie Murray	1.50
3	Wade Boggs	2.00
4	Mark McGwire	3.00
5	Ryne Sandberg	2.00
6	Ozzie Guillen	.50
7	Chris Sabo	.50
8	Joe Carter	.50
9	Alan Trammell	.50
10	Nolan Ryan	4.00
11	Bo Jackson	.75
12	Orel Hershiser	.50
13	Robin Yount	1.50
14	Frank Viola	.50
15	Darryl Strawberry	.50
16	Dave Winfield	1.50
17	Jose Canseco	.75
18	Von Hayes	.50
19	Andy Van Slyke	.50
20	Pedro Guerrero	.50
21	Tony Gwynn	2.00
22	Will Clark	.50
23	Danny Jackson	.50
24	Pete Incaviglia	.50

1990 King-B

King-B meat products offered baseball player discs inside specially-marked packages in 1990, the third year in a row the company inserted the discs with shredded beef jerky. Each disc measures 2-3/4" across and uses full-color pictures on the front. The backs have biographical information and statistics. Team insignias have been airbrushed from caps and uniforms. As in the first two years of the promotion, there are 24 cards in the set.

		NM/M
Complete Set (24):		8.00
Common Player:		.50
1	Mike Scott	.50
2	Kevin Mitchell	.50
3	Tony Gwynn	.75
4	Ozzie Smith	.75
5	Kirk Gibson	.50
6	Tim Raines	.50
7	Von Hayes	.50
8	Bobby Bonilla	.50
9	Wade Boggs	.75
10	Chris Sabo	.50
11	Dale Murphy	.65
12	Cory Snyder	.50
13	Fred McGriff	1.00
14	Don Mattingly	1.00
15	Jerome Walton	.50
16	Ken Griffey Jr.	2.50
17	Bo Jackson	.65
18	Robin Yount	.65
19	Rickey Henderson	.50
20	Jim Abbott	.50
21	Kirby Puckett	.75
22	Nolan Ryan	3.00
23	Gregg Olson	.50
24	Lou Whitaker	.50

1991 King-B

The 1991 release of baseball player discs in cans of shredded

beef snack was labeled "Fourth Annual Collectors' Edition." Once again the discs are 2-3/8" in diameter and feature player photos on which uniform logos have been removed for lack of an MLB license. Front border is in green; backs are printed in blue and include 1990 and major league cumulative stats. One player from each major league team is included in the set.

		NM/M
Complete Set (24):		15.00
Common Player:		.50
1	Willie McGee	.50
2	Kevin Seitzer	.50
3	Kevin Maas	.50
4	Ben McDonald	.50
5	Rickey Henderson	1.00
6	Ken Griffey Jr.	2.00
7	John Olerud	.50
8	Dwight Gooden	.50
9	Ruben Sierra	.50
10	Luis Polonia	.50
11	Wade Boggs	1.50
12	Ramon Martinez	.50
13	Craig Biggio	.50
14	Cecil Fielder	.50
15	Will Clark	.50
16	Matt Williams	.50
17	Sandy Alomar Jr.	.50
18	David Justice	.50
19	Ryne Sandberg	1.50
20	Benito Santiago	.50
21	Barry Bonds	3.00
22	Carlton Fisk	1.00
23	Kirby Puckett	1.50
24	Jose Rijo	.50

1992 King-B

Labeled the "Fifth Annual Collectors' Edition," the 1992 King-B discs were again packaged in plastic containers of shredded beef snack. The 2-3/8" diameter discs have a color player portrait at center. Uniform logos have been removed from the photos for lack of an MLB licensing agreement. The player's name and team are in white in a blue banner above his photo. Backs are printed in blue and include previous year and career stats along with a few biographical details and appropriate logos.

		NM/M
Complete Set (24):		15.00
Common Player:		.50
1	Terry Pendleton	.50
2	Chris Sabo	.50
3	Frank Thomas	1.00
4	Todd Zeile	.50
5	Bobby Bonilla	.50
6	Howard Johnson	.50
7	Nolan Ryan	3.00
8	Ken Griffey Jr.	2.00
9	Roger Clemens	1.75
10	Tony Gwynn	1.50
11	Steve Avery	.50
12	Cal Ripken Jr.	3.00
13	Danny Tartabull	.50
14	Paul Molitor	1.00
15	Willie McGee	.50
16	Wade Boggs	1.50
17	Cecil Fielder	.50
18	Jack Morris	.50
19	Ryne Sandberg	1.50
20	Kirby Puckett	1.50
21	Craig Biggio	.50
22	Harold Baines	.50
23	Scott Erickson	.50
24	Joe Carter	.50

1993 King-B

The sixth annual edition of baseball player discs inserted into packages of King-B meat snacks followed the format of previous issues. Measuring 2-3/8" in diameter, the cards have a photo (with uniform logos airbrushed away) in a yellow baseball diamond design at center. The disc is bordered in black. Backs are printed in red and contain 1992 and career stats.

		NM/M
Complete Set (24):		9.00
Common Player:		1.00
1	Barry Bonds	2.00
2	Ken Griffey Jr.	1.50
3	Cal Ripken, Jr.	2.00
4	Frank Thomas	.75
5	Steve Avery	.50
6	Benito Santiago	.50
7	Luis Polonia	.50
8	Jose Rijo	.50
9	George Brett	1.25
10	Darren Daulton	.50
11	Cecil Fielder	.50
12	Ozzie Smith	1.00
13	Joe Carter	.50
14	Dwight Gooden	.50
15	Tom Henke	.50
16	Brett Butler	.50
17	Nolan Ryan	2.00
18	Sandy Alomar, Jr.	.50
19	Tom Glavine	.60
20	Rafael Palmeiro	.75
21	Roger Clemens	1.25
22	Ryne Sandberg	1.00
23	Doug Drabek	.50
24	Chuck Knoblauch	.50

1994 King-B

King-B once again created and inserted discs of 24 major league stars with its products in 1994. The entire set was also available in uncut sheet form which was found in each case. Discs measure 2-3/8" diameter and have a broad purple border with yellow and white typography surrounding the player photo at center. A black glove holds a King-B logo at bottom. Uniform logos have been airbrushed from the photos. Backs are printed in purple and include 1993 and career stats.

		NM/M
Complete Set (24):		6.00
Common Player:		.50
1	Fred McGriff	.50
2	Paul Molitor	.75
3	Jack McDowell	.50
4	Darren Daulton	.50
5	Wade Boggs	1.00
6	Ken Griffey Jr.	2.00
7	Tim Salmon	.50
8	Dennis Eckersley	.65
9	Albert Belle	.50
10	Travis Fryman	.50
11	Chris Hoiles	.50
12	Kirby Puckett	1.00
13	John Olerud	.50
14	Frank Thomas	.75
15	Lenny Dykstra	.50
16	Andres Galarraga	.50
17	Barry Larkin	.50
18	Greg Maddux	1.00
19	Mike Piazza	1.50
20	Roberto Alomar	.50
21	Robin Ventura	.50
22	Ryne Sandberg	1.00
23	Andy Van Slyke	.50
24	Barry Bonds	3.00

1995 King-B

A wood-grain background distinguishes the eighth annual baseball disc issue packaged inside shredded beef snack tins. Because they are licensed only by the Players Association, and not MLB, cards in the set have had team logos removed from the color player photos at the center of the 2-3/8" diameter discs. Backs are printed in red and have a few personal bits

---

of data, previous season and career stats and the logos of King-B and the MLBPA.

		NM/M
Complete Set (24):		15.00
Common Player:		.35
1	Roberto Alomar	.35
2	Jeff Bagwell	.75
3	Wade Boggs	1.50
4	Barry Bonds	3.00
5	Joe Carter	.35
6	Mariano Duncan	.35
7	Lenny Dykstra	.35
8	Andres Galarraga	.35
9	Matt Williams	.35
10	Raul Mondesi	.35
11	Ken Griffey Jr.	2.00
12	Gregg Jefferies	.35
13	Fred McGriff	.35
14	Paul Molitor	.75
15	Dave Justice	.35
16	Mike Piazza	1.75
17	Kirby Puckett	1.50
18	Cal Ripken Jr.	3.00
19	Ivan Rodriguez	.65
20	Ozzie Smith	1.50
21	Gary Sheffield	.50
22	Frank Thomas	.75
23	Greg Maddux	1.50
24	Jimmy Key ("JIIMY" on back.)	.35

1996 King-B

The "9th Annual Collectors Edition" of King-B discs once again features player photos on which uniform insignia have been airbrushed away. The cards are licensed by Michael Schechter Associates only with the Players Union, not MLB, and so cannot display team logos. The 2-5/8" cardboard discs are packaged in plastic cannisters of shredded dried meat. Fronts have the 1996 date at left in a black and gold pinstriped area. The backs are in black and white with 1995 and career stats, along with a few vital data and appropriate logos and copyright information.

		NM/M
Complete Set (24):		15.00
Common Player:		.50
1	Roger Clemens	1.75
2	Mo Vaughn	.50
3	Dante Bichette	.50
4	Jeff Bagwell	1.00
5	Randy Johnson	1.00
6	Ken Griffey Jr.	2.00
7	Kirby Puckett	1.50
8	Orel Hershiser	.50
9	Albert Belle	.50
10	Tony Gwynn	1.50
11	Tom Glavine	.65
12	Jim Abbott	.50
13	Andres Galarraga	.50
14	Frank Thomas	1.00
15	Barry Larkin	.50
16	Mike Piazza	1.75
17	Matt Williams	.50
18	Greg Maddux	1.50
19	Hideo Nomo	.75
20	Roberto Alomar	.50
21	Ivan Rodriguez	.50
22	Cal Ripken Jr.	3.00
23	Barry Bonds	3.00
24	Mark McGwire	2.50

1997 King-B

The shredded beef product issued its 10th Anniversary set of player discs in 1997. The discs are packed inside the plastic canisters of the snack food and measure 2-3/8" in di-

---

ameter. The '97 discs have a player action photo on front against a gold and black marbled background. Backs are in black-and-white and repeat the photo in the background, along with a few stats and personal data, logos and a disc number. One player from each team is represented in the checklist.

		NM/M
Complete Set (28):		15.00
Common Player:		.50
1	Brady Anderson	.50
2	Barry Bonds	3.00
3	Travis Fryman	.50
4	Rey Ordonez	.50
5	Kenny Lofton	.50
6	Mark McGwire	2.50
7	Jeff Bagwell	1.00
8	Roger Clemens	1.75
9	Juan Gonzalez	.75
10	Mike Piazza	1.75
11	Tim Salmon	.50
12	Jeff Montgomery	.50
13	Joe Carter	.50
14	David Cone	.50
15	Frank Thomas	1.00
16	Mickey Morandini	.50
17	Ray Lankford	.50
18	Pedro Martinez	1.00
19	Tom Glavine	.65
20	Chuck Knoblauch	.50
21	Dan Wilson	.50
22	Gary Sheffield	.65
23	Dante Bichette	.50
24	Al Martin	.50
25	Barry Larkin	.50
26	Ryne Sandberg	1.50
27	Steve Finley	.50
28	Matt Mieske	.50

1998 King-B

Except for the expansion teams, each Major League team has one player in this issue of player discs which were packed inside plastic canisters of the snack food. The cards measure 2-3/8" in diameter with a color player action photo on front (uniform logos have been removed). Backs have a few stats and personal data, logos plus a disc number.

		NM/M
Complete Set (28):		12.50
Common Player:		.50
1	Brady Anderson	.50
2	Barry Bonds	3.00
3	Tony Clark	.50
4	Rey Ordonez	.50
5	Travis Fryman	.50
6	Jason Giambi	.75
7	Jeff Bagwell	1.00
8	Tim Naehring	.50
9	Juan Gonzalez	.75
10	Mike Piazza	1.50
11	Tim Salmon	.50
12	Jeff Montgomery	.50
13	Tom Glavine	.65
14	Chuck Knoblauch	.50
15	Dan Wilson	.50
16	Gary Sheffield	.65
17	Dante Bichette	.50
18	Al Martin	.50
19	Roger Clemens	1.50
20	David Cone	.50
21	Frank Thomas	1.00
22	Mike Lieberthal	.50
23	Ray Lankford	.50
24	Rondell White	.50
25	Barry Larkin	.50
26	Matt Mieske	.50
27	Steve Finley	.50
28	Fernando Vina	.50

1999 King-B

The shredded beef product issued its 12th set of cardboard player discs in 1999. The discs are packed inside plastic canisters of the snack food and measure 2-3/8" in diameter. The cards have a color player action photo on front. Uniform logos are removed and team names are nowhere to be seen on the cards. Backs repeat the front photo in black-and-white in the background, along with a few stats and personal data, logos and a disc number. One player from each team is represented in the checklist.

		NM/M
Complete Set (30):		15.00
Common Player:		.50
1	Brady Anderson	.50
2	Barry Bonds	3.00
3	Scott Rolen	.75
4	Tony Clark	.50
5	Jeff Bagwell	1.00
6	Roberto Alomar	.50
7	Mark Kotsay	.50
8	Juan Gonzalez	.75
9	Tim Salmon	.50
10	Tom Glavine	.65
11	Frank Thomas	1.00
12	Dan Wilson	.50
13	Dante Bichette	.50
14	Mickey Morandini	.50
15	Fred McGriff	.50
16	Andy Benes	.50
17	Jeff Montgomery	.50
18	Pedro Martinez	1.00
19	Barry Larkin	.50
20	Carlos Delgado	.75
21	Mike Myers	.50
22	Ray Lankford	.50
23	Brad Radke	.50
24	Al Martin	.50
25	Raul Mondesi	.50
26	Ugueth Urbina	.50
27	Derek Jeter	3.00
28	Ben Grieve	.50
29	Mike Piazza	1.75
30	Wally Joyner	.50

2000 King-B

The shredded beef product issued its 13th annual set of cardboard player discs in 2000. The discs are packed inside plastic canisters of the snack food and measure 2-3/8" in diameter. The cards have a color player action photo on front. Uniform logos are removed and team names are nowhere to be seen on the cards. Backs have a black-and-white portrait photo, along with a few stats and personal data, logos and a disc number. One player from each team is represented in the checklist.

		NM/M
Complete Set (30):		15.00
Common Player:		.50
1	Nomar Garciaparra	1.50
2	Larry Walker	.50
3	Manny Ramirez	.75
4	Carlos Beltran	.65
5	Mark McGwire	2.00
6	Jeromy Burnitz	.50
7	Carlos Delgado	.50
8	Tom Glavine	.65
9	Shawn Green	.60
10	Mark Kotsay	.50
11	Warren Morris	.50
12	Fred McGriff	.50
13	Brady Anderson	.50
14	Jeff Bagwell	.75
15	Tony Clark	.50

16	Ben Grieve	.50
17	Vladimir Guerrero	.75
18	Tony Gwynn	1.00
19	Derek Jeter	3.00
20	Barry Larkin	.50
21	Rafael Palmeiro	.65
22	Mike Piazza	1.50
23	Brad Radke	.50
24	Scott Rolen	.65
25	Tim Salmon	.50
26	Frank Thomas	.75
27	Mark Grace	.50
28	Jeff Kent	.50
29	Dan Wilson	.50
30	Jay Bell	.50

1985 Kitty Clover Potato Chips Discs

One of a pair of nearly identical (see KAS) sets issued by midwestern potato chip companies, this issue features top stars of the day on 2-3/4" cardboard discs. The discs have a player portrait at center, with uniform logos airbrushed away because the producer was licensed only by the Players Association and not Major League Baseball. The player's name, team and position are printed in a white diamond around the photo. The sponsor's logo is in the yellow border. Backs are in black-and-white and have a few biographical data, a 1984 stats line and a Snack Time logo. The unnumbered discs are checklisted here in alphabetical order. Square versions of the discs, which have been cut from press sheets are known within the hobby and carry a small premium. Kitty Clover was based in Omaha.

		NM/M
Complete Set (30):		15.00
Common Player:		.50
1	Brady Anderson	.50
2	Barry Bonds	3.00
3	Scott Rolen	.75
4	Tony Clark	.50
5	Jeff Bagwell	1.00
6	Roberto Alomar	.50
7	Mark Kotsay	.50
8	Juan Gonzalez	.75
9	Tim Salmon	.50
10	Tom Glavine	.65
11	Frank Thomas	1.00
12	Dan Wilson	.50
13	Dante Bichette	.50
14	Mickey Morandini	.50
15	Fred McGriff	.50
16	Andy Benes	.50
17	Jeff Montgomery	.50
18	Pedro Martinez	1.00
19	Barry Larkin	.50
20	Carlos Delgado	.75
21	Mike Myers	.50
22	Ray Lankford	.50
23	Brad Radke	.50
24	Al Martin	.50
25	Raul Mondesi	.50
26	Ugueth Urbina	.50
27	Derek Jeter	3.00
28	Ben Grieve	.50
29	Mike Piazza	1.75
30	Wally Joyner	.50

1986 Kitty Clover Potato Chips Royals

Twenty players of the 1985 World's Champion Kansas City Royals are featured in a round card set inserted into packages of potato chips in the K.C. area. The 2-7/8" discs were similar to other contemporary snack issues produced by Mike Schechter Associates in that team logos have been airbrushed off the players' caps. The photos of some of the players can be found on other regional issues of 1986.

		NM/M
Complete Set (20):		15.00

Common Player:		.75
1	Lonnie Smith	.75
2	Buddy Biancalana	.75
3	Bret Saberhagen	1.00
4	Hal McRae	.75
5	Onix Concepcion	.75
6	Jorge Orta	.75
7	Bud Black	.75
8	Dan Quisenberry	.75
9	Dane Iorg	.75
10	Charlie Leibrandt	.75
11	Pat Sheridan	.75
12	John Wathan	.75
13	Frank White	.75
14	Darryl Motley	.75
15	Willie Wilson	1.00
16	Danny Jackson	.75
17	Steve Balboni	.75
18	Jim Sundberg	.75
19	Mark Gubicza	.75
20	George Brett	6.00

1996 Klosterman Baking Big Red Machine

Twenty years after The Big Red Machine captured the World's Championship, the 1976 Cincinnati Reds were honored on a card set issued by this Queen City bakery. One card was included with each 20-oz. loaf of bread during the run of the promotion. Cards are 2-3/8" x 3-1/2". Fronts feature color game-action photos with a large headline above and the player's name and position in white on a red strip at bottom. The Reds logo is in an upper corner of the photo, with the player's uniform number beneath. Backs have career summary and stats for the 1976 season and M.L. career, along with sponsors' logos and copyright information.

		NM/M
Complete Set (10):		10.00
Common Player:		.50
5	Johnny Bench	4.00
8	Joe Morgan	1.50
10	Sparky Anderson	1.00
13	Dave Concepcion	.50
15	George Foster	.50
20	Cesar Geronimo	.50
24	Tony Perez	1.00
30	Ken Griffey	.50
35	Don Gullett	.50
----	The Big Four (Tony Perez, Johnny Bench, Joe Morgan, Pete Rose)	3.00

2000 Klosterman Bakery Big Red Machine

The 25th anniversary of Cincinnati's 1975 World Series championship is marked with this issue by a regional bakery. The cards are printed on thin stock in a size 2-3/8" x 3-1/2" format. Fronts have vintage game-action photos with red borders and a Big Red Machine 25th anniversary logo. Backs recap the player's 1975 season in words and stats. The cards were distributed singly in loaves of bread. The unnumbered cards are listed here in alphabetical order.

		NM/M
Complete Set (10):		5.00
Common Player:		.50
(1)	Sparky Anderson	.65
(2)	Johnny Bench	1.00
(3)	Jack Billingham	.50
(4)	Dave Concepcion	.50
(5)	George Foster	.50
(6)	Cesar Geronimo	.50
(7)	Ken Griffey	.50
(8)	Joe Morgan	.75
(9)	Tony Perez	.65
(10)	Pete Rose, Joe Morgan, Johnny Bench	1.00

1982 K-Mart

The first of what became dozens of boxed sets specially produced for retail chain stores by the major card producers, the 1982 K-Mart set has enjoyed little collector popularity. The theme of the set is Most Valuable Players and selected record-breaking performances of the 1962-1981 seasons. The design used miniature reproductions of Topps cards of the era, except in a few cases where designs had to be created because original cards were never issued (1962 Maury Wills, 1975 Fred Lynn). Originally sold for about $2 per boxed set of 44, large quantities were bought up by speculators who got burned when over-production and lack of demand caused the set to drop as low as 10¢. The 2-1/2" x 3-1/2" cards were printed by Topps.

		NM/M
Complete Set (44):		3.00
Common Player:		.10
1	Mickey Mantle	2.00
2	Maury Wills	.10
3	Elston Howard	.10
4	Sandy Koufax	.50
5	Brooks Robinson	.10
6	Ken Boyer	.10
7	Zoilo Versalles	.10
8	Willie Mays	.50
9	Frank Robinson	.10
10	Bob Clemente	.50
11	Carl Yastrzemski	.25
12	Orlando Cepeda	.10
13	Denny McLain	.10
14	Bob Gibson	.10
15	Harmon Killebrew	.10
16	Willie McCovey	.10
17	Boog Powell	.10
18	Johnny Bench	.10
19	Vida Blue	.10
20	Joe Torre	.10
21	Rich Allen	.10
22	Johnny Bench	.10
23	Reggie Jackson	.25
24	Pete Rose	.45
25	Jeff Burroughs	.10
26	Steve Garvey	.10
27	Fred Lynn	.10
28	Joe Morgan	.10
29	Thurman Munson	.10
30	Joe Morgan	.10
31	Rod Carew	.10
32	George Foster	.10
33	Jim Rice	.10
34	Dave Parker	.10
35	Don Baylor	.10
36	Keith Hernandez	.10
37	Willie Stargell	.10
38	George Brett	.50
39	Mike Schmidt	.50
40	Rollie Fingers	.10
41	Mike Schmidt	.50
42	Don Drysdale	.10
43	Hank Aaron	.50
44	Pete Rose	.45

1987 K-Mart

ROGER MARIS

Produced by Topps for K-Mart, the 1987 K-Mart set was distributed by the department stores to celebrate their 25th anniversary. Entitled "Baseball's Stars of the Decades," the 33-card set was issued in a special cardboard box with one stick of bubblegum. Fronts feature a full-color photo set diagonally against a red background. The backs contain career highlights plus pitching or batting statistics for the decade in which the player enjoyed his greatest success. Cards are the standard 2-1/2" x 3-1/2".

		NM/M
Complete Set (33):		3.00
Common Player:		.10
1	Hank Aaron	.60
2	Roberto Clemente	.75
3	Bob Gibson	.10
4	Harmon Killebrew	.10
5	Mickey Mantle	2.00
6	Juan Marichal	.10
7	Roger Maris	.25
8	Willie Mays	.60
9	Brooks Robinson	.10
10	Frank Robinson	.10
11	Carl Yastrzemski	.25
12	Johnny Bench	.10
13	Lou Brock	.10
14	Rod Carew	.10
15	Steve Carlton	.10
16	Reggie Jackson	.25
17	Jim Palmer	.10
18	Jim Rice	.10
19	Pete Rose	.60
20	Nolan Ryan	.75
21	Tom Seaver	.10
22	Willie Stargell	.10
23	Wade Boggs	.25
24	George Brett	.50
25	Gary Carter	.10
26	Dwight Gooden	.10
27	Rickey Henderson	.10
28	Don Mattingly	.50
29	Dale Murphy	.10
30	Eddie Murray	.10
31	Mike Schmidt	.50
32	Darryl Strawberry	.10
33	Fernando Valenzuela	.10

1988 K-Mart

memorable moments

ROBIN YOUNT

This 33-card boxed set, titled "Memorable Moments," was produced by Topps for distribution via K-Mart. The 1988 cards are standard-size with red, white and blue borders and a super glossy coating. Numbered card backs are printed in red and blue on white and highlight special events in the featured players' careers. The set was marketed in a bright yellow and green checklist box (gum included).

		NM/M
Complete Set (33):		2.00
Common Player:		.10
1	George Bell	.10
2	Wade Boggs	.45
3	George Brett	.50

4	Jose Canseco	.25
5	Jack Clark	.10
6	Will Clark	.50
7	Roger Clemens	.50
8	Vince Coleman	.10
9	Andre Dawson	.15
10	Dwight Gooden	.10
11	Pedro Guerrero	.10
12	Tony Gwynn	.45
13	Rickey Henderson	.35
14	Keith Hernandez	.10
15	Don Mattingly	.50
16	Mark McGwire	.75
17	Paul Molitor	.35
18	Dale Murphy	.15
19	Tim Raines	.10
20	Dave Righetti	.10
21	Cal Ripken, Jr.	1.00
22	Pete Rose	.60
23	Nolan Ryan	1.00
24	Benny Santiago	.10
25	Mike Schmidt	.50
26	Mike Scott	.10
27	Kevin Seitzer	.10
28	Ozzie Smith	.45
29	Darryl Strawberry	.10
30	Rick Sutcliffe	.10
31	Fernando Valenzuela	.10
32	Todd Worrell	.10
33	Robin Yount	.35

1989 K-Mart

DreamTeam
KIRBY PUCKETT

This 33-card, glossy set was produced by Topps for K-Mart, where it was sold in stores nationwide. The standard-size cards feature mostly action shots on the front, and include the Topps "Dream Team" logo at the top, with the K-Mart logo in the lower right corner. The first 11 cards in the set picture the top rookies of 1988, while the next 11 picture the top A.L. rookies of the '80s, and the final 11 cards highlight the top N.L. rookies of the decade.

		NM/M
Complete Set (33):		2.00
Common Player:		.10
1	Mark Grace	.10
2	Ron Gant	.10
3	Chris Sabo	.10
4	Walt Weiss	.10
5	Jay Buhner	.10
6	Cecil Espy	.10
7	Dave Gallagher	.10
8	Damon Berryhill	.10
9	Tim Belcher	.10
10	Paul Gibson	.10
11	Gregg Jefferies	.10
12	Don Mattingly	.75
13	Harold Reynolds	.10
14	Wade Boggs	.60
15	Cal Ripken, Jr.	1.00
16	Kirby Puckett	.60
17	George Bell	.10
18	Jose Canseco	.25
19	Terry Steinbach	.10
20	Roger Clemens	.65
21	Mark Langston	.10
22	Harold Baines	.10
23	Will Clark	.60
24	Ryne Sandberg	.60
25	Tim Wallach	.10
26	Shawon Dunston	.10
27	Tim Raines	.10
28	Darryl Strawberry	.10
29	Tony Gwynn	.60
30	Tony Pena	.10
31	Doc Gooden	.10
32	Fernando Valenzuela	.10
33	Pedro Guerrero	.10

1990 K-Mart

This 33-card glossy set was produced by Topps for K-Mart, where it was available nationwide. The set is subtitled "Superstars" and features 16 A.L. players, 16 N.L. stars and a managers' card featuring both Tony LaRussa and Roger Craig. A special Superstars logo is featured on the card fronts. The 1990 issue

Kmart 1990 A.L.
SUPER STARS
RICKEY HENDERSON • OF

marks the fourth consecutive year that Topps has produced a set in co-operation with K-Mart.

		NM/M
Complete Set (33):		3.00
Common Player:		.10
1	Will Clark	.10
2	Ryne Sandberg	.50
3	Howard Johnson	.10
4	Ozzie Smith	.50
5	Tony Gwynn	.50
6	Kevin Mitchell	.10
7	Jerome Walton	.10
8	Craig Biggio	.10
9	Mike Scott	.10
10	Dwight Gooden	.10
11	Sid Fernandez	.10
12	Joe Magrane	.10
13	Jay Howell	.10
14	Mark Davis	.10
15	Pedro Guerrero	.10
16	Glenn Davis	.10
17	Don Mattingly	.65
18	Julio Franco	.10
19	Wade Boggs	.50
20	Cal Ripken, Jr.	1.00
21	Jose Canseco	.25
22	Kirby Puckett	.50
23	Rickey Henderson	.35
24	Mickey Tettleton	.10
25	Nolan Ryan	1.00
26	Bret Saberhagen	.10
27	Jeff Ballard	.10
28	Chuck Finley	.10
29	Dennis Eckersley	.30
30	Dan Plesac	.10
31	Fred McGriff	.10
32	Mark McGwire	.75
33	Managers (Tony LaRussa, Roger Craig)	.10

1988 Kodak White Sox

These blank-back large format (8" x 12") cards feature borderless color action photos of team stars, overprinted with team and sponsor logos and a facsimile autograph. At top is a line of type with the card number and a "1988 Kodak Collectible Series" title.

		NM/M
Complete Set (5):		10.00
Common Player:		2.00
1	Ozzie Guillen	2.00
2	Carlton Fisk	4.00
3	Rick Horton	2.00
4	Ivan Calderon	2.00
5	Harold Baines	2.00

1989 Kodak White Sox

1989 Kodak Collectible Series #1

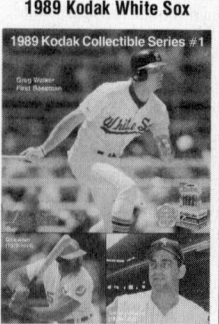

A series of six collectible pictures was given to fans over the course of the 1989 season. Sponsored by Kodak and Osco drug stores, the 8" x 12" sheets combine pictures of a current White Sox star with those of two former stars who played the same position. Ads for the sponsors appear on the photos' fronts, while there is a modicum of information about the former stars accompanying their portraits, including the years they played for the Sox.

		NM/M
Complete Set (6):		10.00
Common Card:		2.00
1	Greg Walker, Dick Allen, Ted Kluszewski	2.50
2	Steve Lyons, Eddie Collins, Nellie Fox	2.50
3	Carlton Fisk, Sherm Lollar, Ray Schalk	2.50
4	Harold Baines, Minnie Minoso, Jim Landis	2.00
5	Bobby Thigpen, Gerry Staley, Hoyt Wilhelm	2.00
6	Ozzie Guillen, Luke Appling, Luis Aparicio	2.00

1990 Kodak White Sox

1990 Kodak Collectible Series #5

Scott Fletcher
Second Baseman

Again utilizing a large format (7" x 11") with borderless color action photos, the "1990 Kodak Collectible Series" features top stars of the South Siders. Player name and position, along with team and sponsor's logos, are superimposed over the photo, along with the title line and card number. The blank-back cards were distributed over the course of the season at various home games.

		NM/M
Complete Set (6):		10.00
Common Player:		2.00
1	Carlton Fisk	4.00
2	Melido Perez	2.00
3	Ozzie Guillen	2.00
4	Ron Kittle	2.00
5	Scott Fletcher	2.00
6	Comiskey Park	2.00

1991 Kodak White Sox

35 FRANK THOMAS

For a fourth year in a row, Kodak sponsored a White Sox team set in 1991. Fronts feature a full-bleed color action photo with the player's name and uniform number at the bottom and a commemorative logo for new Comiskey Park's inaugural season at top. Black-and-white backs have a few stats, personal details and career highlights along with the Kodak logo.

		NM/M
Complete Set (30):		24.00
Common Player:		.50
1	Lance Johnson	.50
5	Matt Merullo	.50
7	Scott Fletcher	.50
8	Bo Jackson	1.50
10	Jeff Torborg	.50
12	Ozzie Guillen	.50
20	Craig Grebeck	.50
20	Ron Karkovice	.50
21	Joey Cora	.50
22	Donn Pall	.50
23	Robin Ventura	1.00
25	Sammy Sosa	10.00
27	Greg Hibbard	.50
28	Cory Snyder	.50
29	Jack McDowell	.50
30	Tim Raines	.50
31	Scott Radinsky	.50

32	Alex Fernandez	.50
33	Melido Perez	.50
34	Ken Patterson	.50
35	Frank Thomas	5.00
37	Bobby Thigpen	.50
44	Dan Pasqua	.50
45	Wayne Edwards	.50
49	Charlie Hough	.50
50	Brian Drahman	.50
72	Carlton Fisk	3.00
---	White Sox Coaches (Terry Bevington, Sammy Ellis, Barry Foote, Walt Hriniak, Dave Laroche, Joe Nossek, John Stephenson)	.50
---	Co-captains (Ozzie Guillen, Carlton Fisk)	.50
---	No. 1 Draft Choices (Alex Fernandez, Jack McDowell, Frank Thomas, Robin Ventura)	1.00

1992 Kodak White Sox

GOOD GUYS WEAR BLACK

FISK 72

With the theme of "Good Guys Wear Black," this set depicts the Chicago southsiders in photos featuring the team's Sunday-best black uniform jerseys. Photos on the cards are full-bleed with the GGWB logo in the upper-left corner of each card. At bottom is a black strip with the player's last name and uniform number. On back are the player's 1991 and career stats, a few biographical details, a trivia question and Kodak logo. At 2-5/8" x 3-1/2", the cards are slightly wider than current standard.

		NM/M
Complete Set (30):		10.00
Common Player:		.25
1	Lance Johnson	.25
5	Matt Merullo	.25
7	Steve Sax	.25
8	Mike Huff	.25
13	Ozzie Guillen	.25
20	Craig Grebeck	.25
20	Ron Karkovice	.25
21	George Bell	.25
22	Donn Pall	.25
23	Robin Ventura	.50
24	Warren Newson	.25
25	Kirk McCaskill	.25
27	Greg Hibbard	.25
28	Joey Cora	.25
29	Jack McDowell	.25
30	Tim Raines	.25
31	Scott Radinsky	.25
32	Alex Fernandez	.25
33	Gene Lamont	.25
34	Terry Leach	.25
35	Frank Thomas	4.00
37	Bobby Thigpen	.25
39	Roberto Hernandez	.25
40	Wilson Alvarez	.25
44	Dan Pasqua	.25
45	Shawn Abner	.25
49	Charlie Hough	.25
72	Carlton Fisk	2.50
00	Waldo (Cartoon mascot.)	.25
---	Mike Squires, Terry Bevington, Gene Lamont, Joe Nossek, Jackie Brown, Walt Hriniak, Doug Mansolino, Dave Huppert	.25

1993 Kodak White Sox

Kodak produced a White Sox set of 30 cards in 1993 that was given away prior to the July 23 game between Chicago and Milwaukee. The full color cards are slightly oversized at 2-5/8" x 3-1/2" and are printed on a very heavy card stock. The photo on the front is full bleed, with the White Sox logo appearing in the upper corner and a metallic blue stripe at the card bottom displaying the player's uniform number, name and position. The backs are white with gray borders and a Kodak logo, with year and career statistics and biographical information. The cards are unnumbered.

		NM/M
Complete Set (30):		10.00
Common Player:		.25
1	Lance Johnson	.25
7	Steve Sax	.25
8	Bo Jackson	.75
10	Mike LaValliere	.25
12	Mike Huff	.25
13	Ozzie Guillen	.25
14	Craig Grebeck	.25
20	Ron Karkovice	.25
21	George Bell	.25
22	Donn Pall	.25
23	Robin Ventura	.50
25	Kirk McCaskill	.25
26	Ellis Burks	.25
28	Joey Cora	.25
29	Jack McDowell	.25
30	Tim Raines	.25
31	Scott Radinsky	.25
32	Alex Fernandez	.25
33	Gene Lamont	.25
34	Terry Leach	.25
35	Frank Thomas	4.00
37	Bobby Thigpen	.25
39	Roberto Hernandez	.25
40	Wilson Alvarez	.25
42	Rod Bolton	.25
44	Dan Pasqua	.25
45	Chuck Cary	.25
49	Jeff Schwartz	.25
51	Jason Bere	.25
---	1993 Coaching Staff (Gene Lamont, Jackie Brown, Terry Bevington, Joe Nossek, Walt Hriniak, Doug Mansolino, Dewey Robinson, Jose Antigua)	.25

1994 Kodak White Sox

Slightly wider than standard cards, at 2-5/8" x 3-1/2" cards, this team set features borderless game-action photos on front with a silver facsimile autograph. Backs are bordered in silver and have a few stats, player personal data, career highlights and logos of the team and sponsor.

		NM/M
Complete Set (30):		12.00
Common Player:		.50
(1)	Wilson Alvarez	.50
(2)	Paul Assenmacher	.50
(3)	Jason Bere	.50
(4)	Dennis Cook	.50
(5)	Joey Cora	.50
(6)	Jose DeLeon	.50
(7)	Alex Fernandez	.50
(8)	Julio Franco	.50
(9)	Craig Grebeck	.50
(10)	Ozzie Guillen	.50
(11)	Joe Hall	.50
(12)	Roberto Hernandez	.50
(13)	Dann Howitt	.50
(14)	Darrin Jackson	.50
(15)	Dane Johnson	.50
(16)	Lance Johnson	.50
(17)	Ron Karkovice	.50
(18)	Gene Lamont	.50
(19)	Mike LaValliere	.50
(20)	Norberto Martin	.50
(21)	Kirk McCaskill	.50
(22)	Jack McDowell	.50
(23)	Warren Newson	.50
(24)	Dan Pasqua	.50
(25)	Tim Raines	.50
(26)	Scott Sanderson	.50
(27)	Frank Thomas	4.00
(28)	Robin Ventura	.75
(29)	Bob Zupcic	.50
(30)	Coaches (Terry Bevington, Jackie Brown, Roly de Armas, Walt Hriniak, Gene Lamont, Doug Mansolino, Joe Nossek, Rick Peterson)	.50

1995 Kodak Pittsburgh Pirates

This 13-1/2" x 20-1/4" perforated sheet containing 30 player and staff cards and sponsor advertising was issued to persons attending a July 23 promotional game. Individual cards measure 2-1/4" x 3-1/4". Player photos at center are flanked by the team name in gold with the player name in yellow in a red banner above. Backs are in black-and-white with just a few biographical notes and team and sponsor logos. The unnumbered cards are checklisted here alphabetically.

		NM/M
Complete Set, Sheet:		6.00
Complete Set, Singles (30):		6.00
Common Player:		.25
(1)	Rich Aude	.25
(2)	Jay Bell	.50
(3)	Jacob Brumfield	.25
(4)	Jason Christiansen	.25
(5)	Dave Clark	.25
(6)	Steve Cooke	.25
(7)	Midre Cummings	.25
(8)	Mike Dyer	.25
(9)	Angelo Encarnacion	.25
(10)	Carlos Garcia	.25
(11)	Freddy Garcia	.25
(12)	Jim Gott	.25
(13)	Mark Johnson	.25
(14)	Jeff King	.25
(15)	Jim Leyland	.25
(16)	Jon Lieber	.25
(17)	Nelson Liriano	.25
(18)	Esteban Loaiza	.25
(19)	Al Martin	.25
(20)	Jeff McCurry	.25
(21)	Orlando Merced	.25
(22)	Dan Miceli	.25
(23)	Denny Neagle	.25
(24)	Mark Parent	.25
(25)	Steve Pegues	.25
(26)	Dan Plesac	.25
(27)	Don Slaught	.25
(28)	Paul Wagner	.25
(29)	Rick White	.25
(30)	Gary Wilson	.25

1995 Kodak White Sox

Fans attending the July 21 game at Comiskey Park received a cello-wrapped 30-card team set. Fronts of the 2-5/8" x 3-1/2" cards have color player photos that are borderless at top and sides. At bottom the player's name appears in black-and-white. Backs are in black-and-white and feature the sponsor's logo and the team's 95-year anniversary logo. There are also a few biographical details, 1994 and career stats and a player trivia question. Cards are numbered by player uniform number.

		NM/M
Complete Set (30):		9.00
Common Player:		.15
1	Lance Johnson	.15
5	Ray Durham	.30
7	Norberto Martin	.15

8	Mike Devereaux	.15
10	Mike Lavalliere	.15
12	Craig Grebeck	.15
13	Ozzie Guillen	.15
14	Dave Martinez	.15
15	Kirk McCaskill	.15
18	Terry Bevington	.15
19	Ron Karkovice	.15
23	Robin Ventura	.25
24	Warren Newson	.15
25	Jim Abbott	.15
26	Brian Keyser	.15
28	John Kruk	.15
30	Tim Raines	.15
31	Scott Radinsky	.15
32	Alex Fernandez	.15
35	Frank Thomas	4.00
39	Roberto Hernandez	.15
40	Wilson Alvarez	.15
46	Jason Bere	.15
48	Jose DeLeon	.15
49	Rob Dibble	.15
51	Tim Fortugno	.15
---	Frank Thomas (1995 All-Star)	2.00
---	White Sox Coaching Staff (Terry Bevington, Don Cooper, Roly DeArmas, Walt Hriniak, Ron Jackson, Doug Mansolino, Joe Nossek, Mark Salas)	.15
---	Trainers (Herm Schneider, Mark Anderson)	.15
---	Director of Conditioning (Steve Odgers)	.15

1985 Kondritz Vince Coleman

The debut season of 1985 N.L. Rookie of the Year Vince Coleman is traced in this 20-card set issued by Illinois dealer Kondritz Trading Cards. Fronts of the 2-1/2" x 3-1/2" cards have player posed or action photos surrounded by a wide red border. Backs are in black-and-white with a few sentences about Coleman, a card number, large "Invincible" and copyright data. Sets were originally sold for about $10.

	NM/M
Complete Set (20):	5.00
Common Card:	.25

1986 Kondritz Ozzie Smith

The career of future Hall of Fame Cardinals shortstop Ozzie Smith is traced in this 20-card set issued by Illinois dealer Kondritz Trading Cards. Fronts of the 2-1/2" x 3-1/2" cards have player posed or action photos surrounded by a wide red border. Backs are in black-and-white with a few sentences about Smith, a card number, a large "THE WIZARD" and copyright data. Sets were originally sold for about $10.

	NM/M
Complete Set (20):	20.00
Common Card:	1.50
1-20 Ozzie Smith	1.50

1987 Kraft Home Plate Heroes

Kraft Foods issued a 48-card set on specially marked packages of macaroni & cheese dinners. Titled "Home Plate Heroes," 24 two-card panels measuring 3-1/2" x 7-1/8" make up the set. Individual cards measure 2-1/4" x 3-1/2". The blank-backed cards feature fronts with full-color photos, although all team insignias have been erased. In conjunction with the card set, Kraft offered a contest to "Win A Day With A Major Leaguer." Mike Schechter Associates produced the set for Kraft. A total of 120 different panel combinations (five with each player) can be found.

		NM/M
Complete Set, Panels:		20.00
Complete Set, Singles (48):		16.00
Common Player:		.25
1	Eddie Murray	.50
2	Dale Murphy	.40
3	Cal Ripken, Jr.	1.00
4	Mike Scott	.25
5	Jim Rice	.35
6	Jody Davis	.25
7	Wade Boggs	.60
8	Ryne Sandberg	.60
9	Wally Joyner	.25
10	Eric Davis	.25
11	Ozzie Guillen	.25
12	Tony Pena	.25
13	Harold Baines	.25
14	Johnny Ray	.25
15	Joe Carter	.25
16	Ozzie Smith	.60
17	Cory Snyder	.25
18	Vince Coleman	.25
19	Kirk Gibson	.25
20	Steve Garvey	.35
21	George Brett	.75
22	John Tudor	.25
23	Robin Yount	.50
24	Von Hayes	.25
25	Kent Hrbek	.25
26	Darryl Strawberry	.60
27	Kirby Puckett	.60
28	Ron Darling	.25
29	Don Mattingly	.75
30	Mike Schmidt	.75
31	Rickey Henderson	.50
32	Fernando Valenzuela	.25
33	Dave Winfield	.50
34	Pete Rose	.85
35	Jose Canseco	.40
36	Glenn Davis	.25
37	Alvin Davis	.25
38	Steve Sax	.25
39	Pete Incaviglia	.25
40	Jeff Reardon	.25
41	Jesse Barfield	.25
42	Hubie Brooks	.25
43	George Bell	.25
44	Tony Gwynn	.60
45	Roger Clemens	.65
46	Chili Davis	.25
47	Mike Witt	.25
48	Nolan Ryan	1.00

1993 Kraft Pop-Up Action

Kraft released a set of Pop-Up Action baseball cards in 1993 that was available in specially-marked packages of Kraft Singles. The cards are similar to the 1992 Canadian Post Cereal cards with a pop-up tab. The set is made up of 15 players each from the American and National Leagues.

		NM/M
Complete Set (30):		12.00
Common Player:		.35
American League		
(1)	Jim Abbott	.35
(2)	Roberto Alomar	.35
(3)	Sandy Alomar Jr.	.35
(4)	George Brett	.75
(5)	Roger Clemens	.75
(6)	Dennis Eckersley	.50
(7)	Cecil Fielder	.35
(8)	Ken Griffey Jr.	1.00
(9)	Don Mattingly	.75
(10)	Mark McGwire	1.50
(11)	Kirby Puckett	.65
(12)	Cal Ripken, Jr.	2.00
(13)	Nolan Ryan	2.00
(14)	Robin Ventura	.35
(15)	Robin Yount	.60
National League		
(1)	Bobby Bonilla	.35
(2)	Ken Caminiti	.35
(3)	Will Clark	.35
(4)	Darren Daulton	.35
(5)	Doug Drabek	.35
(6)	Delino DeShields	.35
(7)	Tom Glavine	.45
(8)	Tony Gwynn	.65
(9)	Orel Hershiser	.35
(10)	Barry Larkin	.35
(11)	Terry Pendleton	.35
(12)	Ryne Sandberg	.65
(13)	Gary Sheffield	.50
(14)	Lee Smith	.35
(15)	Andy Van Slyke	.35

1994 Kraft Pop-Ups

Kraft offered a 30-card set in 1994 featuring major stars in a pop-up format. The cards show the players in action shots front and back, with the front picture "popping up." Kraft Singles consumers could find one 2-1/2" x 3-3/8" card in each package of cheese, with 15 players from each league. The cards were licensed by the Major League Baseball Players Association, but not by Major League Baseball, so the team logos were airbrushed from player's caps and uniforms. Through an on-pack and in-store mail-in offer, collectors could order complete sets of the cards for $1.95 per league (15 cards), plus the appropriate proofs of purchase. In a somewhat unusual move, officials of Kraft USA announced that the print run would be eight million cards, which works out to about 266,000 sets.

		NM/M
Complete Set (30):		7.50
Common Player:		.25
1	Carlos Baerga	.25
2	Dennis Eckersley	.50
3	Cecil Fielder	.25
4	Juan Gonzalez	.50
5	Ken Griffey Jr.	1.00
6	Mark Langston	.25
7	Brian McRae	.25
8	Paul Molitor	.60
9	Kirby Puckett	.75
10	Cal Ripken Jr.	1.50
11	Danny Tartabull	.25
12	Frank Thomas	.60
13	Greg Vaughn	.25
14	Mo Vaughn	.25
15	Dave Winfield	.60
16	Jeff Bagwell	.60
17	Barry Bonds	1.50
18	Bobby Bonilla	.25
19	Delino DeShields	.25
20	Lenny Dykstra	.25

21	Andres Galarraga	.25
22	Tom Glavine	.25
23	Mark Grace	.25
24	Tony Gwynn	.75
25	David Justice	.25
26	Barry Larkin	.25
27	Mike Piazza	.90
28	Gary Sheffield	.40
29	Ozzie Smith	.75
30	Andy Van Slyke	.25

1995 Kraft Singles Superstars

Once again incorporating a pop-up center action figure, these cards were available both in packages of cheese slices and via a mail-in offer. The 2-1/2" x 3-1/2" cards have a second player photo in the center which is revealed by pushing down the hinged front and back of the card, creating a stand. All photos have had uniform logos removed. A baseball design is at the bottom of each player photo. Back of the card has abbreviated stats and career highlights. The back of the pop-up figure has a paragraph about the player titled, "What Singles Him Out." Besides being packaged with cheese, the cards were available by sending in proofs of purchase and $1.95 for each 15-player A.L. or N.L. set.

		NM/M
Complete Set (30):		7.50
Common Player:		.25
1	Roberto Alomar	.25
2	Joe Carter	.25
3	Cecil Fielder	.25
4	Juan Gonzalez	.50
5	Ken Griffey Jr.	1.25
6	Jimmy Key	.25
7	Chuck Knoblauch	.25
8	Kenny Lofton	.25
9	Mike Mussina	.40
10	Paul O'Neill	.25
11	Kirby Puckett	.75
12	Cal Ripken Jr.	1.50
13	Ivan Rodriguez	.50
14	Frank Thomas	.60
15	Mo Vaughn	.25
16	Moises Alou	.25
17	Jeff Bagwell	.60
18	Barry Bonds	1.50
19	Jeff Conine	.25
20	Lenny Dykstra	.25
21	Andres Galarraga	.25
22	Tony Gwynn	.75
23	Gregg Jefferies	.25
24	Barry Larkin	.25
25	Greg Maddux	.75
26	Mike Piazza	1.00
27	Bret Saberhagen	.25
28	Ozzie Smith	.75
29	Sammy Sosa	1.00
30	Matt Williams	.25

1994 KVTU-TV San Francisco Giants

This short set was sponsored by the Giants' television broadcasting partner. Eight of the team's top names are featured on the 2-1/2" x

3-1/2" cards. Fronts have action photos framed in orange and brown with white borders. Black-and-white backs have a few career highlights and the TV station's logo.

		NM/M
Complete Set (9):		12.00
Common Player:		1.00
(1)	Dusty Baker	1.00
(2)	Rod Beck	1.00
(3)	Barry Bonds	7.50
(4)	Bobby Bonds	1.00
(5)	John Burkett	1.00
(6)	Billy Swift	1.00
(7)	Robby Thompson	1.00
(8)	Matt Williams	1.00
(9)	Header Card	.50

L

1981 L.A. Dodgers Police

TOM LASORDA
No. 2 — Manager
LAPD SALUTES THE 1981
Dodgers

Similar in format to the previous year's set, the Dodgers 1981 police set grew to 32 cards due to the acquisitions of Ken Landreaux and Dave Stewart shortly before printing of the sets. These two cards may even have been added after the initial printing run, making them slightly more difficult to obtain. The full-color cards are again 2-13/16" x 4-1/8", with a safety tip on the card back. Each card front has the line "LAPD Salutes the 1981 Dodgers."

		NM/M
Complete Set (32):		6.00
Common Player:		.25
2	Tom Lasorda	.50
3	Rudy Law	.25
5	Steve Garvey	3.00
7	Steve Yeager	.25
9	Reggie Smith	.25
10	Ron Cey	.25
12	Dusty Baker	.35
14	Joe Ferguson	.25
14	Mike Scioscia	.25
15	Davey Lopes	.25
16	Rick Monday	.25
18	Bill Russell	.25
21	Jay Johnstone	.25
26	Don Stanhouse	.25
28	Joe Beckwith	.25
28	Pete Guerrero	.25
30	Derrel Thomas	.25
34	Fernando Valenzuela	1.50
36	Bob Welch	.25
36	Pepe Frias	.25
37	Robert Castillo	.25
38	Dave Goltz	.25
41	Jerry Reuss	.25
43	Rick Sutcliffe	.25
44a	Mickey Hatcher	.25
44b	Ken Landreaux	1.25
46	Burt Hooton	.25
48	Dave Stewart	1.50
51	Terry Forster	.25
57	Steve Howe	.25
---	Coaching Staff	
	(Monty Basgall, Mark Cresse,	
	Tom Lasorda, Manny Mota,	
	Danny Ozark,	
	Ron Perranoski)	.25
---	Team Photo/Checklist	.25

1982 L.A. Dodgers Police

Again issued in the same 2-13/16" x 4-1/8" size of the '80 and '81 sets, the 1982 Los Angeles set commemorates the team's 1981 World Championship. In addition to the 26 cards numbered by uniform for players and manager Tom Lasorda, there are four unnumbered cards which feature the team winning the division, league and World Series titles, plus one of the

World Series trophy. The full-color card photos are once again vivid portraits on a clean white card stock. Card backs offer brief biographies and stadium information in addition to a safety tip.

		NM/M
Complete Set (30):		5.00
Common Player:		.25
2	Tom Lasorda	.50
6	Steve Garvey	2.00
7	Steve Yeager	.25
8	Mark Belanger	.25
10	Ron Cey	.25
12	Dusty Baker	.35
14	Mike Scioscia	.25
16	Rick Monday	.25
18	Bill Russell	.25
21	Jay Johnstone	.25
26	Alejandro Pena	.25
28	Pedro Guerrero	.25
30	Derrel Thomas	.25
31	Jorge Orta	.25
34	Fernando Valenzuela	.75
35	Bob Welch	.25
38	Dave Goltz	.25
40	Ron Roenicke	.25
41	Jerry Reuss	.25
44	Ken Landreaux	.25
46	Burt Hooton	.25
48	Dave Stewart	.35
49	Tom Niedenfuer	.25
51	Terry Forster	.25
52	Steve Sax	.35
57	Steve Howe	.25
---	Division Championship	.25
---	League Championship	.25
---	World Series	
	Championship	.25
---	Trophy Card/Checklist	.25

1983 L.A. Dodgers Police

FERNANDO VALENZUELA 34
1983 Dodgers

While these full-color cards remained 2-13/16" x 4-1/8" and card fronts were similar to those of previous years, the card backs are quite different. Card backs are in a horizontal design for the first time, and include a small head portrait photo of the player in the upper left corner. Fairly complete player statistics are included but there is no safety tip. The 30 cards are numbered by uniform number, with an unnumbered coaches card also included. Fronts include the year, team logo, player name and number.

		NM/M
Complete Set (30):		6.00
Common Player:		.25
2	Tom Lasorda	.50
3	Steve Sax	.25
5	Mike Marshall	.25
7	Steve Yeager	.25
12	Dusty Baker	.35
14	Mike Scioscia	.25
16	Rick Monday	.25
17	Greg Brock	.25
18	Bill Russell	.25
20	Candy Maldonado	.25
21	Ricky Wright	.25
22	Mark Bradley	.25

23	Dave Sax	.25
26	Alejandro Pena	.25
27	Joe Beckwith	.25
28	Pedro Guerrero	.25
30	Derrel Thomas	.25
34	Fernando Valenzuela	.75
35	Bob Welch	.25
38	Pat Zachry	.25
40	Ron Roenicke	.25
41	Jerry Reuss	.25
43	Jose Morales	.25
44	Ken Landreaux	.25
46	Burt Hooton	.25
47	Larry White	.25
48	Dave Stewart	.35
49	Tom Niedenfuer	.25
57	Steve Howe	.25
---	Coaches Card	
	(Joe Amalfitano,	
	Monty Basgall, Mark Cresse,	
	Manny Mota,	
	Ron Perranoski)	.25

1984 L.A. Dodgers Fire Safety

S A X

Unlike the California Angels and San Diego Padres sets issued in conjunction with the Forestry Service in 1984, the Los Angeles Dodgers set contains only three players, pictured on much larger 5" x 7" cards. Each player is pictured with Smokey in a forest scene on the full-color card fronts. Backs of the unnumbered cards have brief biographical information and lifetime statistics. The cards were distributed at a Dodgers home game.

		NM/M
Complete Set (4):		7.00
Common Player:		2.50
(1)	Ken Landreaux	2.50
(2)	Tom Niedenfuer	2.50
(3)	Steve Sax	2.50
(4)	Smokey Bear	.50

1984 L.A. Dodgers Police

MIKE MARSHALL
Dodgers
1984 5

This was the fifth yearly effort of the Dodgers and the Los Angeles Police Department. There are 30 cards in the set, which remains 2-13/16" x 4-1/8". Card fronts are designed somewhat differently than previous years, with more posed photos, bolder player names and numbers and a different team logo. Card backs again feature a small portrait photo in the upper left corner, along with brief biographical information and an anti-drug tip. Card backs are in Dodger blue. Cards are numbered by uniform number, with an unnumbered coaches card also included.

		NM/M
Complete Set (30):		4.00
Common Player:		.25
2	Tom Lasorda	.50
3	Steve Sax	.25
5	Mike Marshall	.25
7	Steve Yeager	.25
9	Greg Brock	.25
10	Dave Anderson	.25
14	Mike Scioscia	.25

16	Rick Monday	.25
17	Rafael Landestoy	.25
18	Bill Russell	.25
20	Candy Maldonado	.25
25	Bob Bailor	.25
25	German Rivera	.25
26	Alejandro Pena	.25
27	Carlos Diaz	.25
28	Pedro Guerrero	.25
31	Jack Fimple	.25
34	Fernando Valenzuela	.75
35	Bob Welch	.25
38	Pat Zachry	.25
40	Rick Honeycutt	.25
41	Jerry Reuss	.25
43	Jose Morales	.25
44	Ken Landreaux	.25
45	Terry Whitfield	.25
46	Burt Hooton	.25
49	Tom Niedenfuer	.25
55	Orel Hershiser	3.00
56	Richard Rodas	.25
---	Coaches Card	
	(Joe Amalfitano,	
	Monty Basgall, Mark Cresse,	
	Manny Mota,	
	Ron Perranoski)	.25

1986 L.A. Dodgers Police

Dodgers
1986

MIKE MARSHALL 5

After skipping the 1985 season, the Los Angeles Dodgers once again issued baseball cards related to police safety. The 1986 set features 30 full-color glossy cards measuring 2-1/4" x 4-1/8", numbered according to player uniforms. The backs feature brief player data and a safety tip from the Los Angeles Police Department. The sets were given away May 18 during Baseball Card Day at Dodger Stadium.

		NM/M
Complete Set (30):		4.00
Common Player:		.20
2	Tom Lasorda	.40
3	Steve Sax	.20
5	Mike Marshall	.20
9	Greg Brock	.20
10	Dave Anderson	.20
12	Bill Madlock	.20
14	Mike Scioscia	.20
17	Len Matuszek	.20
18	Bill Russell	.20
22	Franklin Stubbs	.20
23	Enos Cabell	.20
25	Mariano Duncan	.20
26	Alejandro Pena	.20
27	Carlos Diaz	.20
28	Pedro Guerrero	.20
29	Alex Trevino	.20
31	Ed Vande Berg	.20
34	Fernando Valenzuela	.50
35	Bob Welch	.20
40	Rick Honeycutt	.20
41	Jerry Reuss	.20
44	Ken Howell	.20
44	Ken Landreaux	.20
45	Terry Whitfield	.20
48	Dennis Powell	.20
49	Tom Niedenfuer	.20
51	Reggie Williams	.20
55	Orel Hershiser	.50
---	Team Photo/Checklist	.20
---	Coaching Staff	
	(Joe Amalfitano,	
	Monty Basgall, Mark Cresse,	
	Ben Hines, Don McMahon,	
	Manny Mota,	
	Ron Perranoski)	.20

1987 L.A. Dodgers All-Stars Fire Safety

This fire safety set features "25 Years of Dodger All-Stars." The cards, which measure 2-1/2" x 3-3/4", were given out to fans 14 and younger at the September 18 game at Dodgers stadium. Fronts have full-color photos set in the shape of Dodger Stadium and have attractive silver borders. Backs carry the player's All-Star Game record plus a fire prevention message. Many of the

SANDY KOUFAX
25 Years of Dodger All-Stars

photos used in the set were from team-issued picture packs sold by the Dodgers in the past.

		NM/M
Complete Set (40):		7.50
Common Player:		.25
(1)	Walt Alston	.45
(2)	Dusty Baker	.30
(3)	Jim Brewer	.25
(4)	Ron Cey	.25
(5)	Tommy Davis	.25
(6)	Willie Davis	.25
(7)	Don Drysdale	2.00
(8)	Steve Garvey	1.50
(9)	Bill Grabarkewitz	.25
(10)	Pedro Guerrero	.25
(11)	Tom Haller	.25
(12)	Orel Hershiser	.45
(13)	Burt Hooton	.25
(14)	Steve Howe	.25
(15)	Tommy John	.30
(16)	Sandy Koufax	5.00
(17)	Tom Lasorda	.45
(18)	Jim Lefebvre	.25
(19)	Davey Lopes	.25
(20)	Mike Marshall/Outfielder	.25
(21)	Mike Marshall/Pitcher	.25
(22)	Andy Messersmith	.25
(23)	Rick Monday	.25
(24)	Manny Mota	.25
(25)	Claude Osteen	.25
(26)	Johnny Podres	.30
(27)	Phil Regan	.25
(28)	Jerry Reuss	.25
(29)	Rick Rhoden	.25
(30)	John Roseboro	.25
(31)	Bill Russell	.25
(32)	Steve Sax	.25
(33)	Bill Singer	.25
(34)	Reggie Smith	.25
(35)	Don Sutton	1.00
(36)	Fernando Valenzuela	.50
(37)	Bob Welch	.25
(38)	Maury Wills	.45
(39)	Jim Wynn	.25
(40)	Logo Card/Checklist	.10

Police

JOSE GONZALEZ 47

Producing a police set for the seventh time in eight years, the 1987 edition contains 30 cards which measure 2-13/16" x 4-1/8". The set includes a special Dodger Stadium 25th Anniversary card. The card fronts contain a full-color photo plus the Dodger Stadium 25th Anniversary logo. The photos are a mix of action and posed shots. The backs contain personal player data plus a police safety tip. The cards were given out April 24th at Dodger Stadium and were distributed by the Los Angeles police department at a rate of two cards per week.

		NM/M
Complete Set (30):		4.00
Common Player:		.20
2	Tom Lasorda	.50
3	Steve Sax	.25
5	Mike Marshall	.25

10	Dave Anderson	.25
12	Bill Madlock	.25
14	Mike Scioscia	.25
15	Gilberto Reyes	.25
17	Len Matuszek	.25
21	Reggie Williams	.25
22	Franklin Stubbs	.25
23	Tim Leary	.25
25	Mariano Duncan	.25
26	Alejandro Pena	.25
28	Pedro Guerrero	.25
29	Alex Trevino	.25
33	Jeff Hamilton	.25
34	Fernando Valenzuela	.50
35	Bob Welch	.25
36	Matt Young	.25
40	Rick Honeycutt	.25
41	Jerry Reuss	.25
43	Ken Howell	.25
44	Ken Landreaux	.25
46	Ralph Bryant	.25
47	Jose Gonzalez	.25
49	Tom Niedenfuer	.25
51	Brian Holton	.25
55	Orel Hershiser	.60
---	Coaching Staff	
	(Joe Amalfitano, Mark Cresse,	
	Tom Lasorda, Don McMahon,	
	Manny Mota, Ron Perranoski,	
	Bill Russell)	.25
---	Dodger Stadium/Checklist	.25

1988 L.A. Dodgers Fire Safety

STEVE SAX
L.A. Dodgers Record-Breaker

Record-breaking Dodgers from the past three decades are featured on this perforated sheet. Individual cards measure 2-1/2" x 4" and are printed on a light blue background in a design similar to the previous year's All-Star set. Black-and-white card backs contain the player name, a summary of the player's record-breaking performance and a reproduction of one of a number of Smokey Bear fire prevention posters printed during the 1950s-1980s. The sheets were distributed to fans in Dodger Stadium.

		NM/M
Complete Set, Foldout:		9.00
Complete Set, Singles (32):		7.50
Common Player:		.25
1	Walter Alston	.30
2	John Roseboro	.25
3	Frank Howard	.30
4	Sandy Koufax	5.00
5	Manny Mota	.25
6	Record Pitchers	
	(Sandy Koufax, Jerry Reuss,	
	Bill Singer)	.35
7	Maury Wills	.30
8	Tommy Davis	.25
9	Phil Regan	.25
10	Wes Parker	.25
11	Don Drysdale	1.50
12	Willie Davis	.25
13	Bill Russell	.25
14	Jim Brewer	.25
15	Record Fielders (Ron Cey,	
	Steve Garvey, Davey Lopes,	
	Bill Russell)	.25
16	Mike Marshall/Pitcher	.25
17	Steve Garvey	.75
18	Davey Lopes	.25
19	Burt Hooton	.25
20	Jim Wynn	.25
21	Record Hitters (Dusty Baker,	
	Ron Cey, Steve Garvey,	
	Reggie Smith)	.25
22	Dusty Baker	.30
23	Tom Lasorda	.40
24	Fernando Valenzuela	.50
25	Steve Sax	.25
26	Dodger Stadium	.25
27	Ron Cey	.25
28	Pedro Guerrero	.25
29	Mike Marshall/Outfielder	.25
30	Don Sutton	.75
---	Logo Card/Checklist	.10
---	Smokey Bear	.10

Police

DON SUTTON 20

The Los Angeles Police Department sponsored this 30-card set (2-3/4" x 4-1/8") for use in a local crime prevention promotion. The sets include an unnumbered manager/coaches photo and three double-photo cards. The double cards feature posed closeups; the rest are action photos. The card fronts have white borders, with the team logo lower right and a bold black player name lower left. Card backs are black and white with a small close-up photo of the player, followed by personal and career info, a crime prevention tip and a LAPD badge logo. Card numbers refer to players' uniform numbers (the double-photo cards carry two numbers on both front and back).

		NM/M
Complete Set (30):		6.00
Common Player:		.15
2	Tom Lasorda	.30
3	Steve Sax	.15
5	Mike Marshall	.15
7	Alfredo Griffin	.15
9	Mickey Hatcher	.15
10	Dave Anderson	.15
12	Danny Heep	.15
14	Mike Scioscia	.15
17/21	Tito Landrum, Len Matuszek	.15
20	Don Sutton	.60
22	Franklin Stubbs	.15
23	Kirk Gibson	.40
25	Mariano Duncan	.15
26	Alejandro Pena	.15
27/52	Tim Crews, Mike Sharperson	.25
28	Pedro Guerrero	.15
29	Alex Trevino	.15
31	John Shelby	.15
33	Jeff Hamilton	.15
34	Fernando Valenzuela	.50
37	Mike Davis	.15
41	Brad Havens	.15
43	Ken Howell	.15
47	Jesse Orosco	.15
49/57	Tim Belcher, Shawn Hillegas	.15
50	Jay Howell	.15
51	Brian Holton	.15
54	Tim Leary	.15
55	Orel Hershiser	.40
---	Manager/Coaches (Joe Amalfitano, Steve Boros, Mark Cresse, Joe Ferguson, Tom Lasorda, Manny Mota, Ron Perranoski, Bill Russell)	.15

1989 L.A. Dodgers Greats Fire Safety

The largest baseball card set ever issued in conjunction with the U.S. Forest Service's Smokey the Bear fire prevention campaign was this 104-card issue featuring great players of the Brooklyn and L.A. Dodgers. Issued on perforated sheets, individual cards measure 2-1/2" x 3-1/2". White-bordered fronts have a sepia-toned photo of the player, with Dodger blue rules on the top and sides. Beneath the photo is a baseball-and-banner logo, "A Century of Dodger Greats." The player's name is beneath the ball with Smokey at left and the team logo at right. Backs are printed in blue, feature career stats and highlights and include a Smokey fire safety cartoon.

		NM/M
Complete Set (104):		20.00
Common Player:		.10
1	Tommy Lasorda, Walter Alston, Burt Shotton	.50
2	David Bancroft	.10
3	Dan Brouthers	.10
4	Roy Campanella	2.00
5	Max Carey	.10
6	Hazen "Kiki" Cuyler	.10
7	Don Drysdale	1.00
8	Burleigh Grimes	.10
9	Billy Herman	.10
10	Waite Hoyt	.10
11	Hughie Jennings	.10
12	Willie Keeler	.10
13	Joseph Kelley	.10
14	George Kelly	.10
15	Sandy Koufax	3.00
16	Heinie Manush	.10
17	Juan Marichal	.75
18	Walter Maranville	.10
19	Rube Marquard	.10
20	Thomas McCarthy	.10
21	Joseph McGinnity	.10
22	Joe Medwick	.10
23	Pee Wee Reese	2.00
24	Frank Robinson	1.00
25	Jackie Robinson	3.50
26	Babe Ruth	4.00
27	Duke Snider	2.00
28	Casey Stengel	.25
29	Dazzy Vance	.10
30	Arky Vaughan	.10
31	Mike Scioscia	.10
32	Lloyd Waner, Paul Waner	.10
33	John Monte Ward	.10
34	Zack Wheat	.10
35	Hoyt Wilhelm	.10
36	Hack Wilson	.10
37	Tony Cuccinello	.10
38	Al Lopez	.10
39	Leo Durocher	.25
40	Cookie Lavagetto	.10
41	Babe Phelps	.10
42	Dolf Camilli	.10
43	Whit Wyatt	.10
44	Mickey Owen	.10
45	Van Mungo	.10
46	Pete Coscarart	.10
47	Pete Reiser	.10
48	Augie Galan	.10
49	Dixie Walker	.10
50	Kirby Higbe	.10
51	Ralph Branca	.10
52	Bruce Edwards	.10
53	Eddie Stanky	.10
54	Gil Hodges	1.50
55	Don Newcombe	.50
56	Preacher Roe	.25
57	Willie Randolph	.10
58	Carl Furillo	.50
59	Charles Dressen	.10
60	Carl Erskine	.25
61	Clem Labine	.15
62	Gino Cimoli	.10
63	Johnny Podres	.25
64	Johnny Roseboro	.15
65	Wally Moon	.10
66	Charlie Neal	.10
67	Norm Larker	.10
68	Stan Williams	.10
69	Maury Wills	.20
70	Tommy Davis	.15
71	Jim Lefebvre	.10
72	Phil Regan	.10
73	Claude Osteen	.10
74	Tom Haller	.10
75	Bill Singer	.10
76	Bill Grabarkewitz	.10
77	Willie Davis	.15
78	Don Sutton	.50
79	Jim Brewer	.10
80	Manny Mota	.15
81	Bill Russell	.10
82	Ron Cey	.15
83	Steve Garvey	.50
84	Mike G. Marshall	.10
85	Andy Messersmith	.10
86	Jimmy Wynn	.10
87	Rick Rhoden	.10
88	Reggie Smith	.15
89	Jay Howell	.10
90	Rick Monday	.10
91	Tommy John	.15
92	Bob Welch	.15
93	Dusty Baker	.20
94	Pedro Guerrero	.15
95	Burt Hooton	.10
96	Davey Lopes	.10
97	Fernando Valenzuela	.20
98	Steve Howe	.10
99	Steve Sax	.10
100	Orel Hershiser	.40
101	Mike A. Marshall	.10
102	Wilbert Robinson	.10
103	Fred Lindstrom	.10
104	Ernie Lombardi	.10

Police

MIKE SCIOSCIA 14

The Los Angeles Dodgers and the L.A. Police Department teamed up in 1989 to produce a 30-card police set. The cards, which measure 4-1/4" x 2-5/8", feature color action photos with the player's name and uniform number below. The Dodgers logo and "1989" appear in the upper left. The backs include player information plus a safety message.

		NM/M
Complete Set (30):		3.00
Common Player:		.15
2	Tom Lasorda	.30
3	Jeff Hamilton	.15
5	Mike Marshall	.15
7	Alfredo Griffin	.15
9	Mickey Hatcher	.15
10	Dave Anderson	.15
12	Willie Randolph	.15
14	Mike Scioscia	.15
17	Rick Dempsey	.15
20	Mike Davis	.15
21	Tracy Woodson	.15
22	Franklin Stubbs	.15
23	Kirk Gibson	.30
25	Mariano Duncan	.15
26	Alejandro Pena	.15
27	Mike Sharperson	.15
29	Ricky Horton	.15
30	John Tudor	.15
31	John Shelby	.15
33	Eddie Murray	2.00
34	Fernando Valenzuela	.35
36	Mike Morgan	.15
48	Ramon Martinez	.35
49	Tim Belcher	.15
50	Jay Howell	.15
52	Tim Crews	.15
54	Tim Leary	.15
55	Orel Hershiser	.35
57	Ray Searage	.15
---	Dodger Coaches (Joe Amalfitano, Mark Cresse, Joe Ferguson, Ben Hines, Tommy Lasorda, Manny Mota, Ron Perranoski, Bill Russell)	.15

1990 L.A. Dodgers Police

CENTENNIAL CELEBRATION

HUBIE BROOKS 21

This set honors the centennial celebration of the Los Angeles Dodgers. A special 100 Anniversary logo appears on the card fronts. The cards measure 2-3/4" x 4-1/4" and feature full-color photos. The card backs are printed horizontally and contain a special safety tip or anti-drug message along with player information. The L.A.P.D. logo is featured on the bottom of the card back.

		NM/M
Complete Set (30):		3.00

Common Player:		.15
2	Tommy Lasorda	.30
3	Jeff Hamilton	.15
5	Alfredo Griffin	.15
9	Mickey Hatcher	.15
11	Juan Samuel	.15
12	Willie Randolph	.15
14	Mike Scioscia	.15
16	Chris Gwynn	.15
17	Rick Dempsey	.15
19	Hubie Brooks	.15
22	Franklin Stubbs	.15
23	Kirk Gibson	.25
27	Mike Sharperson	.15
28	Kal Daniels	.15
29	Lenny Harris	.15
31	John Shelby	.15
33	Eddie Murray	2.00
34	Fernando Valenzuela	.40
35	Jim Gott	.15
36	Mike Morgan	.15
40	Jose Gonzalez	.15
46	Mike Hartley	.15
48	Ramon Martinez	.15
49	Tim Belcher	.15
50	Jay Howell	.15
52	Tim Crews	.15
55	Orel Hershiser	.25
57	John Wetteland	.35
59	Ray Searage	.15
---	Dodgers Coaches (Joe Amalfitano, Mark Cresse, Joe Ferguson, Ben Hines, Tommy Lasorda, Manny Mota, Ron Perranoski, Bill Russell)	.15

1991 L.A. Dodgers Police

EDDIE MURRAY 33

One of the longest-running police/fire safety sets continued in 1991 with this 30-card set. Players are featured in color action photos set in a tombstone shape against a white background. The date is in a banner at top with the player name, team logo and uniform number at bottom. All typography is printed in Dodger blue. Backs are printed in black-and-white and include biographical data, an anti-drug message and an LAPD badge. Cards measure 2-13/16" x 4-1/8".

		NM/M
Complete Set (30):		4.00
Common Player:		.15
3	Jeff Hamilton	.15
5	Stan Javier	.15
7	Alfredo Griffin	.15
10	Juan Samuel	.15
12	Gary Carter	1.50
14	Mike Scioscia	.15
15	Chris Gwynn	.15
17	Bob Ojeda	.15
22	Brett Butler	.15
23	Dennis Cook	.15
27	Mike Sharperson	.15
28	Kal Daniels	.15
29	Lenny Harris	.15
30	Jose Offerman	.15
31	Jim Neidlinger	.15
33	Eddie Murray	1.50
35	Jim Gott	.15
36	Mike Morgan	.15
38	Jose Gonzalez	.15
40	Barry Lyons	.15
44	Darryl Strawberry	.45
45	Kevin Gross	.15
46	Mike Hartley	.15
48	Ramon Martinez	.15
49	Tim Belcher	.15
50	Jay Howell	.15
52	Tim Crews	.15
54	John Candelaria	.15
55	Orel Hershiser	.35
---	Dodgers Coaches (Ben Hines, Ron Perranoski, Mark Cresse, Manny Mota, Mike Sharperson, Tommy Lasorda, Joe Amalfitano, Joe Ferguson, Bill Russell)	.15

1992 L.A. Dodgers Police

ERIC KARROS

The 1992 Dodgers Police set consists of 30 cards numbered to correspond to the player's uniform number. The set includes a card of manager Tommy Lasorda and Dodgers coaches. They were given out at promotional dates at Dodger Stadium.

		NM/M
Complete Set (30):		4.00
Common Player:		.25
2	Tommy Lasorda	.35
3	Jeff Hamilton	.25
5	Stan Javier	.25
7	Juan Samuel	.25
14	Mike Scioscia	.25
15	Dave Hansen	.25
17	Bob Ojeda	.25
20	Mitch Webster	.25
22	Brett Butler	.25
23	Eric Karros	.50
27	Mike Sharperson	.25
28	Kal Daniels	.25
29	Lenny Harris	.25
30	Jose Offerman	.25
31	Roger McDowell	.25
33	Eric Davis	.25
35	Jim Gott	.25
36	Todd Benzinger	.25
38	Steve Wilson	.25
41	Carlos Hernandez	.25
44	Darryl Strawberry	.35
45	Kevin Gross	.25
48	Ramon Martinez	.25
49	Tom Candiotti	.25
50	Jay Howell	.25
52	Tim Crews	.25
54	John Candelaria	.25
55	Orel Hershiser	.40
57	Kip Gross	.25
---	Coaches (Joe Amalfitano, Mark Cresse, Joe Ferguson, Ben Hines, Tommy Lasorda, Manny Mota, Ron Perranoski, Ron Roenicke)	.25

1993 L.A. Dodgers Police

LANCE PARRISH 12

The 1993 Los Angeles Dodgers Police Set consisted of 29 cards, including cards of manager Tommy Lasorda and his coaches. The fronts of the cards have a photo surrounded by a blue border, with the Dodgers logo and the player's name on the bottom. The set is not numbered, but the player's uniform number does appear on the front of the cards.

		NM/M
Complete Set (29):		6.00
Common Player:		.25
2	Tommy Lasorda	.35
3	Jody Reed	.25
5	Dave Hansen	.25
12	Lance Parrish	.25
17	Roger McDowell	.25
20	Mitch Webster	.25
22	Brett Butler	.25
23	Eric Karros	.25
25	Tim Wallach	.25
26	Henry Rodriguez	.25
27	Mike Sharperson	.25
28	Cory Snyder	.25
29	Lenny Harris	.25
30	Jose Offerman	.25

1994 L.A. Dodgers Police

This 30-card set was distributed to all fans attending the Dodgers May 27 home game. Cards were produced in the form of a perforated sheet. Fronts have mostly game-action photos surrounded by a Dodger-blue border. The player's uniform number is in red in a baseball in the upper-left corner. At bottom is the team logo and the player's name in black on a yellow strip. Backs are in black on white, have a few career and biographical notes and an anti-drug message from the L.A.P.D. and the D.A.R.E. program. When removed from the sheet, cards measure the standard 2-1/2" x 3-1/2". They are checklisted here by uniform number.

		NM/M
Uncut Sheet:		6.00
Complete Set (30):		5.00
Common Player:		.25
2	Tommy Lasorda	.35
5	Dave Hansen	.25
7	Billy Ashley	.25
10	Chris Gwynn	.25
12	Jeff Treadway	.25
14	Delino DeShields	.25
15	Tom Prince	.25
17	Roger McDowell	.25
20	Mitch Webster	.25
21	Rafael Bournigal	.25
22	Brett Butler	.25
23	Eric Karros	.25
26	Carlos Hernandez	.25
28	Cory Snyder	.25
29	Tim Wallach	.25
30	Jose Offerman	.25
31	Mike Piazza	2.50
35	Jim Gott	.25
37	Darren Dreifort	.25
38	Todd Worrell	.25
40	Henry Rodriguez	.25
43	Raul Mondesi	.50
46	Kevin Gross	.25
47	Garey Wayne	.25
48	Ramon Martinez	.25
49	Tom Candiotti	.25
55	Orel Hershiser	.35
56	Pedro Astacio	.25
61	Chan Ho Park	.75
---	Coaches (Mark Cresse, Manny Mota, Bill Russell, Reggie Smith, Joe Ferguson, Ron Perranoski, Tommy Lasorda, Joe Amalfitano)	.25

1995 L.A. Dodgers Limited Edition

This special high-tech set of Brooklyn/Los Angeles Dodgers rookie of the year winners between 1947-94 was given to Dodger season ticket purchasers prior to the strike-shortened 1995 baseball season. Produced in a technique similar to Topps Finest, the cards have on front metallic backgrounds in red, green, blue or purple. A color player action photo is

Also listed for the far-right top column (1994 section continues in text), and column values:

31	Mike Piazza	3.00
33	Eric Davis	.25
35	Jim Gott	.25
38	Todd Worrell	.25
41	Carlos Hernandez	.25
45	Pedro Martinez	2.00
46	Kevin Gross	.25
47	Tom Goodwin	.25
48	Ramon Martinez	.25
49	Tom Candiotti	.25
55	Steve Wilson	.25
55	Orel Hershiser	.45
56	Pedro Astacio	.25
57	Kip Gross	.25
---	Coaches (Joe Amalfitano, Mark Cresse, Joe Ferguson, Ben Hines, Tommy Lasorda, Manny Mota, Ron Perranoski, Ron Roenicke)	.25

featured. Faux granite strips at bottom have the player's name and year of his ROY award in gold. Backs have a color portrait photo in a gold frame with career stats and highlights and a few personal details. The primary front background color is repeated on the back. A header card printed in blue on white linen-texture paper accompanies the set.

		NM/M
Complete Set (14):		50.00
Common Player:		2.00
1	Jackie Robinson	15.00
2	Don Newcombe	4.00
3	Joe Black	4.00
4	Jim Gilliam	4.00
5	Frank Howard	4.00
6	Jim Lefebvre	2.00
7	Ted Sizemore	2.00
8	Rick Sutcliffe	3.00
9	Steve Howe	2.00
10	Fernando Valenzuela	5.00
11	Steve Sax	3.00
12	Eric Karros	3.00
13	Mike Piazza	15.00
14	Raul Mondesi	3.00
---	Header Card	.10

1995 L.A. Dodgers Police

Action photos of the L.A. Dodgers are featured on this 30-card safety set which was given away to some 40,000 fans attending an early-season game. The set was produced as a perforated sheet measuring 14-13/16" x 17-1/2", with individual cards measuring 2-1/2" x 3-1/2". Fronts feature a Dodger-blue border with the player name in black in a yellow stripe at bottom. The player's uniform number is in red in a baseball in the upper-right. Backs are in black-and-white and have a few player biographical details along with an anti-drug safety message and the logos of the LAPD and D.A.R.E.

		NM/M
Uncut Sheet:		6.00
Complete Set (30):		6.00
Common Player:		.25
2	Tommy Lasorda	.35
4	Eddie Pye	.25
5	Dave Hansen	.25
7	Billy Ashley	.25
12	Jeff Treadway	.25
14	Delino DeShields	.25
16	Hideo Nomo	2.00
21	Rafael Bournigal	.25
23	Eric Karros	.25
25	Ron Coomer	.25
28	Carlos Hernandez	.25
28	Todd Hollandsworth	.25
29	Tim Wallach	.25
30	Jose Offerman	.25
31	Mike Piazza	2.00
37	Todd Worrell	.25
40	Henry Rodriguez	.25
43	Raul Mondesi	.35
45	Al Osuna	.25
48	Ramon Martinez	.25
49	Tom Candiotti	.25

50	Antonio Osuna	.25
52	Greg Hansell	.25
54	Omar Daal	.25
56	Pedro Astacio	.25
57	Rudy Seanez	.25
59	Ismael Valdes	.25
61	Chan Ho Park	.50
66	Todd Williams	.25
---	Coaches (Mark Cresse, Manny Mota, Bill Russell, Reggie Smith, Tommy Lasorda, Joe Amalfitano, Dave Wallace, Ralph Avila)	.25

1996 L.A. Dodgers Police

For the 16th time in 17 years (they skipped 1985), the Dodgers issued a safety set to fans attending the April 11 game. As in recent years, the set was issued in the form of a perforated 30-card sheet. Each card measures just under 2-1/2" wide and is 3-1/2" tall; sheet dimensions are 14-7/8" x 17-1/2". Game-action photos are bordered in Dodger blue with the uniform number in red at upper-left. Backs are in black-and-white with a few vital stats and an anti-drug abuse, anti-gang message from D.A.R.E.

		NM/M
Uncut Sheet:		6.50
Complete Set (30):		6.00
Common Player:		.10
2	Tommy Lasorda	.25
3	Chad Fonville	.10
5	Dave Hansen	.10
9	Greg Gagne	.10
12	Karim Garcia	.25
13	Antonio Osuna	.10
14	Delino DeShields	.10
16	Hideo Nomo	2.00
20	Mike Blowers	.10
21	Billy Ashley	.10
22	Brett Butler	.10
23	Eric Karros	.10
25	Mike Busch	.10
26	Carlos Hernandez	.10
27	Roger Cedeno	.10
28	Todd Hollandsworth	.10
29	Milt Thompson	.10
31	Mike Piazza	2.00
33	Garey Ingram	.10
38	Todd Worrell	.10
41	John Cummings	.10
43	Raul Mondesi	.10
44	Mark Guthrie	.10
48	Ramon Martinez	.10
49	Tom Candiotti	.10
51	Joey Eischen	.10
52	Darren Hall	.10
56	Pedro Astacio	.10
59	Ismael Valdes	.10
---	Dodgers Coaches (Joe Amalfitano, Mark Cresse, Tommy Lasorda, Manny Mota, Bill Russell, Reggie Smith, Dave Wallace)	.10

Rookies of the Year

This card was inserted into a die-cut space in the 1996 holiday greetings card sent out by the L.A.

Dodgers. In 2-1/2" x 3-1/2 format it features portrait photos of the 1992-96 National League Rookies of the Year - all Dodgers. Overall background of the front is green. Back has information on previous Dodgers ROYs and the rookie season stats of the 1992-96 winners.

	NM/M
Dodger Rookies of the Year: (Eric Karros/1992, Mike Piazza/1993, Raul Mondesi/1994, Hideo Nomo/1995, Todd Hollandsworth/1996)	15.00

1997 L.A. Dodgers Fan Appreciation Days

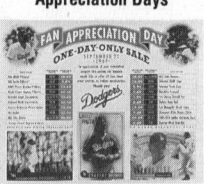

Fans attending the September 21 game were given this 11" x 8-1/2" sheet announcing a one-day sale of Dodgers souvenirs. At bottom are three differently styled cards of some of the team's most popular players. All are in color and standard 2-1/2" x 3-1/2" size, perforated for easy separation from the sheet. Card backs are in black-and-white with drawings of the players in the upper-left, biographical data and trivia. Cards are numbered by uniform number.

		NM/M
Complete Sheet:		6.00
Complete Set, Singles (3):		6.00
16	Hideo Nomo	3.00
31	Mike Piazza	4.00
61	Chan Ho Park	1.50

Police

Action photos of the 1997 Dodgers are featured on this set distributed at the April 23 game to nearly 30,500 fans. The 14-3/4" x 17-1/2" sheet has 30 cards, perforated on two, three or four sides, depending on position on the sheet. Individual cards measure 2-1/2" x 3-1/2". A central photo is surrounded with a white border. A ball with the player's uniform number in red is at top-left. At bottom is the team logo and player name. Backs are in black-and-white with biographical notes, an anti-drug message from each player and the logos of LAPD and DARE. Cards are checklisted here by uniform number.

		NM/M
Uncut Sheet:		7.00
Complete Set (30):		6.00
Common Player:		.20
3	Chad Fonville	.20
5	Chip Hale	.20
9	Greg Gagne	.20
12	Karim Garcia	.20
13	Anthony Osuna	.20
15	Tom Prince	.20
16	Hideo Nomo	1.50
18	Bill Russell	.20
21	Billy Ashley	.20
22	Brett Butler	.20
23	Eric Karros	.20
25	Juan Castro	.20
27	Todd Zeile	.20
28	Todd Hollandsworth	.20
30	Wilton Guerrero	.20
31	Mike Piazza	2.50
35	Wayne Kirby	.20

36	Scott Radinsky	.20
37	Darren Dreifort	.20
40	Todd Worrell	.20
43	Raul Mondesi	.20
44	Mark Guthrie	.20
46	Nelson Liriano	.20
48	Ramon Martinez	.20
52	Tom Candiotti	.20
52	Darren Hall	.20
56	Pedro Astacio	.20
59	Ismael Valdes	.20
61	Chan Ho Park	.20
---	Coaches (Joe Amalfitano, Mark Cresse, Manny Mota, Mike Scioscia, Reggie Smith, Dave Wallace)	.20

1998 L.A. Dodgers Fan Appreciation Days

Fans attending the Dodgers' final homestand were given this 11" x 8-1/2" sheet announcing a sale of Dodgers souvenirs. At bottom are three cards of some of the team's most popular players. All are in color and standard 2-1/2" x 3-1/2" size, perforated for easy separation from the sheet. Card backs are in black-and-white with personal data, a facsimile autograph and trivia. Cards are numbered by uniform number.

		NM/M
Complete Sheet:		6.00
Complete Set, (3):		4.00
Common Player:		2.00
10	Gary Sheffield	2.50
23	Eric Karros	2.00
43	Raul Mondesi	2.00

Police

Repeating the format used in recent years, a 30-card perforated sheet, the Dodgers issued their annual D.A.R.E. drug-awareness set in April. Individual cards are the standard 2-1/2" x 3-1/2" on the 15" x 17-1/2" sheet. Fronts have action photos with blue borders. A baseball at top-left has the player's uniform number in red, by which the set is checklisted here.

		NM/M
Uncut Sheet:		7.00
Complete Set (30):		6.00
Common Player:		.25
7	Paul Konerko	.50
10	Jose Vizcaino	.25
12	Mike Devereaux	.25
13	Antonio Osuna	.25
15	Tom Prince	.25
16	Hideo Nomo	2.00
18	Bill Russell	.25
22	Thomas Howard	.25
23	Eric Karros	.25
25	Juan Castro	.25
26	Eric Young	.25
27	Todd Zeile	.25
28	Todd Hollandsworth	.25
30	Wilton Guerrero	.25
31	Mike Piazza	3.00
36	Scott Radinsky	.25
37	Darren Dreifort	.25
40	Matt Luke	.25
41	Tripp Cromer	.25
43	Raul Mondesi	.25
44	Mark Guthrie	.25
46	Roger Cedeno	.25
47	Jim Bruske	.25
47	Trenidad Hubbard	.25
48	Ramon Martinez	.25
49	Frank Lankford	.25

52	Darren Hall	.25
59	Ismael Valdes	.25
61	Chan Ho Park	.25
---	Joe Amalfitano, Mark Cresse, Glenn Gregson, Manny Mota, Mike Scioscia, Reggie Smith	.25

Record Breakers

This set of motion cards was distributed one per month to members of the Dodgers Kids Clubhouse when they attended a game. The 3-1/2" x 2-1/2" cards have a borderless front with an action scene viewed by changing the angle of the card. The team logo appears in an upper corner. Backs repeat the logo and have personal data and details of the record performance. The cards are unnumbered. Distribution of the Nomo and Piazza cards was cut short when those players were traded in mid-season.

		NM/M
Complete Set (5):		17.50
Common Player:		2.00
(1)	Ramon Martinez	2.00
(2)	Raul Mondesi/Action	2.00
(3)	Raul Mondesi/Portrait (Membership card.)	2.00
(4)	Hideo Nomo	6.00
(5)	Mike Piazza	7.50

1999 L.A. Dodgers Concession Stand Cards

During the first five home games of the 1999 season, fans visiting the concession stands at Dodgers Stadium could receive a free player card. Fronts have color action photos on a white background with blue borders. The player's first name is printed at bottom, and a catchword at top. Backs are horizontal in black-and-white with a portrait photo career highlights and personal data, plus team and Dodger Stadium logos.

		NM/M
Complete Set (5):		4.00
Common Player:		1.00
1	Kevin Brown	1.50
2	Chan Ho Park	1.00
3	Ismael Valdes	1.00
4	Carlos Perez	1.00
5	Darren Dreifort	1.00

Fan Appreciation Days

Fans attending the Dodgers' final homestand were given this 11" x 8-1/2" sheet announcing special sales of Dodgers souvenirs. At bottom are three cards of some of the team's most popular players. All are in color and standard 2-1/2" x 3-1/2" size, perforated for easy separation from the sheet. The card

---

fronts are in the style of 1953 Topps while backs are in black-and-white 1951-Bowman format with personal data, and a career summary.

		NM/M
Complete Sheet:		5.00
Complete Set (3):		4.00
1	Adrian Beltre	2.00
2	Kevin Brown	1.00
3	Eric Karros	1.00

Library Card

As part of a promotion to draw youngsters to the library to receive a free baseball bat, these sheets were given away at a promotional game at Dodger Stadium. The 8-1/2" x 4-3/4" sheet has a standard-size card perforated for easy removal. Front has an action photo. On back is another photo overprinted with stats.

		NM/M
(1)	Eric Karros	3.00

Police

Repeating the format used in recent years, a 30-card perforated sheet, the Dodgers issued their annual D.A.R.E. drug-awareness set in April. Individual cards are the standard 2-1/2" x 3-1/2" on the 15" x 17-1/2" sheet. Fronts have action photos with blue borders. A baseball at top-left has the player's uniform number, by which the set is checklisted here. Backs are in black-and-white with LAPD and D.A.R.E. logos, player data and a safety message.

		NM/M
Uncut Sheet:		7.00
Complete Set (30):		6.00
Common Player:		.25
5	Jose Vizcaino	.25
7	Tripp Cromer	.25
8	Mark Grudzielanek	.25
10	Todd Hundley	.25
10	Gary Sheffield	.75
13	Antonio Osuna	.25
14	Adam Riggs	.25
15	Davey Johnson	.25
16	Paul LoDuca	.75
17	Juan Castro	.25
21	Eric Young	.25
22	Devon White	.25
23	Eric Karros	.25
25	Dave Hansen	.25
27	Kevin Brown	.45
28	Todd Hollandsworth	.25
29	Adrian Beltre	2.00
33	Carlos Perez	.25
37	Darren Dreifort	.25
41	Jeff Shaw	.25
43	Raul Mondesi	.25
46	Rick Wilkins	.25
48	Jacob Brumfield	.25
50	Pedro Borbon	.25
51	Onan Masaoka	.25
59	Ismael Valdes	.25
61	Chan Ho Park	.20
63	Angel Pena	.25
75	Alan Mills	.25
---	Coaches (Rick Dempsey, Rick Down, Glenn Hoffman, Charlie Hough, Manny Mota, John Shelby, Jim Tracy)	

2000 L.A. Dodgers Fan Appreciation Days

Shawn Green

Fans attending late-season Dodgers' games were given this 11" x 8-1/2" sheet announcing special sales of Dodgers souvenirs. At bottom are three cards of some of the team's most popular players. All are in color and standard 2-1/2" x 3-1/2" size, perforated for easy separation from the sheet. Card fronts have portrait and action photos while backs have 1/3 of a color team photo.

	NM/M
Complete Sheet:	5.00
Complete Set (3):	4.00
10 Gary Sheffield	1.00
15 Shawn Green	2.00
23 Eric Karros	1.00

Library Cards

As part of a promotion to draw youngsters to the library to receive a free baseball, this sheet was given away at a promotional game at Dodger Stadium. The 8-1/2" x 4-3/4" sheet has a standard-size card perforated for easy removal. Front has both portrait and action photos. On back is another photo overprinted with stats.

	NM/M
Complete Set (2):	4.00
Common Player:	2.00
(1) Kevin Brown	2.00
(2) Gary Sheffield	2.00

Police

SHAWN GREEN

Repeating the format used in recent years, a 30-card 14-7/8" x 17-1/2" perforated sheet, the Dodgers issued their annual D.A.R.E. drug-awareness set in April. Individual cards are the standard 2-1/2" x 3-1/2". Fronts have game-action photos with blue borders. A baseball at top-left has the player's uniform number, by which the set is checklisted here. Backs are in black-and-white with LAPD and D.A.R.E. logos, player data and a safety message.

	NM/M
Uncut Sheet:	7.00
Complete Set (30):	6.00
Common Player:	
3 Alex Cora	.25
7 Jose Vizcaino	.25
8 Mark Grudzielanek	.25
9 Todd Hundley	.25
10 Gary Sheffield	.75
13 Antonio Osuna	.25
14 F.P. Santangelo	.25

15	Shawn Green	1.00
16	Paul LoDuca	.75
21	Chad Kreuter	.25
22	Devon White	.25
23	Eric Karros	.25
25	Dave Hansen	.25
27	Kevin Brown	.60
28	Todd Hollandsworth	.25
29	Adrian Beltre	1.00
30	Gregg Olson	.25
33	Carlos Perez	.25
36	Angel Pena	.25
37	Darren Dreifort	.25
40	Onan Masaoka	.25
41	Jeff Shaw	.25
43	Kevin Elster	.25
48	Eric Gagne	.75
51	Terry Adams	.25
55	Orel Hershiser	.50
56	Mike Fetters	.25
61	Chan Ho Park	.25
75	Alan Mills	.25
	Coaches (Rick Down, Glenn Hoffman, Davey Johnson, Manny Mota, Claude Osteen, John Shelby, Jim Tracy)	.25

1997 LaSalle Bank Ryne Sandberg

RYNE SANDBERG

#23

FOR 15 YEARS, A CLASSIC CUB

This card was part of a souvenir tribute distributed to more than 30,000 persons attending Ryne Sandberg's final game at Wrigley Field on September 20. A commemorative program and this card marked Ryno's 15 years as a Chicago Cub. The 2-1/2" x 3-1/2" card is printed on heavy, UV-coated cardboard. The front features a borderless color action photo. On the full-color back are portrait and action photos, career highlights and stats through September 14.

	NM/M
Ryne Sandberg	7.50

1985 Leaf-Donruss

KENT HRBEK 1B

In an attempt to share in the Canadian baseball card market, Donruss issued a 264-card version of its regular set to be sold in Canada. Fronts of the 2-1/2" x 3-1/2" cards are virtually identical to the regular '85 Donruss cards of the same players, except that a green stylized leaf has been added to the logo in the upper-left. On back, player biographies have been rewritten to accomodate both English and French versions, and new card numbers have been assigned. The 264 cards in this shortened set concentrate on star-caliber players, as well as those of Canada's two major league teams. A special two-card subset, "Canadian Greats," featured paintings of Dave Stieb and Tim Raines. The Leaf-Donruss cards were widely distributed in the U.S. through hobby dealers.

		NM/M
Complete Set (264):		35.00
Common Player:		.05
Wax Pack (12):		2.50
Wax Box (36):		75.00
1	Ryne Sandberg/DK	1.25
2	Doug DeCinces/DK	.05
3	Rich Dotson/DK	.05
4	Bert Blyleven/DK	.05
5	Lou Whitaker/DK	.05
6	Dan Quisenberry/DK	.05
7	Don Mattingly/DK	2.00
8	Carney Lansford/DK	.05
9	Frank Tanana/DK	.05
10	Willie Upshaw/DK	.05
11	Claudell Washington/DK	.05
12	Mike Marshall/DK	.05
13	Joaquin Andujar/DK	.05
14	Cal Ripken, Jr./DK	5.00
15	Jim Rice/DK	.25
16	Don Sutton/DK	.60
17	Frank Viola/DK	.05
18	Alvin Davis/DK	.05
19	Mario Soto/DK	.05
20	Jose Cruz/DK	.05
21	Charlie Lea/DK	.05
22	Jesse Orosco/DK	.05
23	Juan Samuel/DK	.05
24	Tony Pena/DK	.05
25	Tony Gwynn/DK	1.25
26	Bob Brenly/DK	.05
27	Steve Kiefer/RR	.05
28	Joe Morgan	.60
29	Luis Leal	.05
30	Dan Gladden	.05
31	Shane Rawley	.05
32	Mark Clear	.05
33	Terry Kennedy	.05
34	Hal McRae	.05
35	Mickey Rivers	.05
36	Tom Brunansky	.05
37	LaMarr Hoyt	.05
38	Orel Hershiser	1.00
39	Chris Bando	.05
40	Lee Lacy	.05
41	Lance Parrish	.05
42	George Foster	.05
43	Kevin McReynolds	.05
44	Robin Yount	.60
45	Craig McMurtry	.05
46	Mike Witt	.05
47	Gary Redus	.05
48	Dennis Rasmussen	.05
49	Gary Woods	.05
50	Phil Bradley	.05
51	Steve Bedrosian	.05
52	Duane Walker	.05
53	Geoff Zahn	.05
54	Dave Stieb	.05
55	Pascual Perez	.05
56	Mark Langston	.25
57	Bob Dernier	.05
58	Joe Cowley	.05
59	Dan Schatzeder	.05
60	Ozzie Smith	1.25
61	Bob Knepper	.05
62	Keith Hernandez	.05
63	Rick Rhoden	.05
64	Alejandro Pena	.05
65	Damaso Garcia	.05
66	Chili Davis	.05
67	Al Oliver	.05
68	Alan Wiggins	.05
69	Darryl Motley	.05
70	Gary Ward	.05
71	John Butcher	.05
72	Scott McGregor	.05
73	Bruce Hurst	.05
74	Dwayne Murphy	.05
75	Greg Luzinski	.05
76	Pat Tabler	.05
77	Chet Lemon	.05
78	Jim Sundberg	.05
79	Wally Backman	.05
80	Terry Puhl	.05
81	Storm Davis	.05
82	Jim Wohlford	.05
83	Willie Randolph	.05
84	Ron Cey	.05
85	Jim Beattie	.05
86	Rafael Ramirez	.05
87	Cesar Cedeno	.05
88	Bobby Grich	.05
89	Jason Thompson	.05
90	Steve Sax	.05
91	Tony Fernandez	.15
92	Jeff Leonard	.05
93	Von Hayes	.05
94	Steve Garvey	.30
95	Steve Balboni	.05
96	Larry Parrish	.05
97	Tim Teufel	.05
98	Sammy Stewart	.05
99	Roger Clemens	30.00
100	Steve Kemp	.05
101	Tom Seaver	1.00
102	Andre Thornton	.05
103	Kirk Gibson	.05
104	Ted Simmons	.05
105	David Palmer	.05
106	Roy Lee Jackson	.05
107	Kirby Puckett	4.00
108	Charlie Hough	.05
109	Mike Boddicker	.05
110	Willie Wilson	.05
111	Tim Lollar	.05
112	Tony Armas	.05

113	Steve Carlton	.60
114	Gary Lavelle	.05
115	Cliff Johnson	.05
116	Ray Burris	.05
117	Rudy Law	.05
118	Mike Scioscia	.05
119	Kent Tekulve	.05
120	George Vukovich	.05
121	Barbaro Garbey	.05
122	Mookie Wilson	.05
123	Ben Oglivie	.05
124	Jerry Mumphrey	.05
125	Willie McGee	.05
126	Jeff Reardon	.05
127	Dave Winfield	1.00
128	Lee Smith	.10
129	Ken Phelps	.05
130	Rick Camp	.05
131	Dave Concepcion	.05
132	Rod Carew	.60
133	Andre Dawson	.25
134	Doyle Alexander	.05
135	Miguel Dilone	.05
136	Jim Gott	.05
137	Eric Show	.05
138	Phil Niekro	.45
139	Rick Sutcliffe	.05
140	Two For The Title (Don Mattingly, Dave Winfield)	3.00
141	Ken Oberkfell	.05
142	Jack Morris	.05
143	Lloyd Moseby	.05
144	Pete Rose	2.00
145	Gary Gaetti	.05
146	Don Baylor	.05
147	Bobby Meacham	.05
148	Frank White	.05
149	Mark Thurmond	.05
150	Dwight Evans	.05
151	Al Holland	.05
152	Joel Youngblood	.05
153	Rance Mulliniks	.05
154	Bill Caudill	.05
155	Carlton Fisk	.60
156	Rick Honeycutt	.05
157	John Candelaria	.05
158	Alan Trammell	.05
159	Darryl Strawberry	.05
160	Aurelio Lopez	.05
161	Enos Cabell	.05
162	Dion James	.05
163	Bruce Sutter	.75
164	Razor Shines	.05
165	Butch Wynegar	.05
166	Rich Bordi	.05
167	Spike Owen	.05
168	Chris Chambliss	.05
169	Dave Parker	.05
170	Reggie Jackson	1.00
171	Bryn Smith	.05
172	Dave Collins	.05
173	Dave Engle	.05
174	Buddy Bell	.05
175	Mike Flanagan	.05
176	George Brett	1.50
177	Graig Nettles	.05
178	Jerry Koosman	.05
179	Wade Boggs	1.25
180	Jody Davis	.05
181	Ernie Whitt	.05
182	Dave Kingman	.05
183	Vance Law	.05
184	Fernando Valenzuela	.05
185	Bill Madlock	.05
186	Brett Butler	.05
187	Doug Sisk	.05
188	Dan Petry	.05
189	Joe Niekro	.05
190	Rollie Fingers	.45
191	David Green	.05
192	Steve Rogers	.05
193	Ken Griffey	.05
194	Scott Sanderson	.05
195	Barry Bonnell	.05
196	Bruce Benedict	.05
197	Keith Moreland	.05
198	Fred Lynn	.05
199	Tim Wallach	.20
200	Kent Hrbek	.05
201	Pete O'Brien	.05
202	Bud Black	.05
203	Eddie Murray	.60
204	Goose Gossage	.05
205	Mike Schmidt	1.50
206	Mike Easler	.05
207	Jack Clark	.05
208	Rickey Henderson	1.00
209	Jesse Barfield	.15
210	Ron Kittle	.05
211	Pedro Guerrero	.05
212	Johnny Ray	.05
213	Julio Franco	.05
214	Hubie Brooks	.05
215	Darrell Evans	.05
216	Nolan Ryan	5.00
217	Jim Gantner	.05
218	Tim Raines	.20
219	Dave Righetti	.05
220	Gary Matthews	.05
221	Jack Perconte	.05
222	Dale Murphy	.30
223	Brian Downing	.05
224	Mickey Hatcher	.05
225	Lonnie Smith	.05
226	Jorge Orta	.05
227	Milt Wilcox	.05
228	John Denny	.05

229	Marty Barrett	.05
230	Alfredo Griffin	.05
231	Harold Baines	.05
232	Bill Russell	.05
233	Marvell Wynne	.05
234	Dwight Gooden	.50
235	Willie Hernandez	.05
236	Bill Gullickson	.05
237	Ron Guidry	.05
238	Leon Durham	.05
239	Al Cowens	.05
240	Bob Horner	.05
241	Gary Carter	1.00
242	Glenn Hubbard	.05
243	Steve Trout	.05
244	Jay Howell	.05
245	Terry Francona	.05
246	Cecil Cooper	.05
247	Larry McWilliams	.05
248	George Bell	.15
249	Larry Herndon	.05
250	Ozzie Virgil	.05
251	Dave Stieb (Canadian Great)	.50
252	Tim Raines (Canadian Great)	2.00
253	Ricky Horton	.05
254	Bill Buckner	.05
255	Dan Driessen	.05
256	Ron Darling	.05
257	Doug Flynn	.05
258	Darrell Porter	.05
259	George Hendrick	.05
653	Lou Gehrig Puzzle Card	.05
----	Checklist 1-26 DK	.05
----	Checklist 27-102	.05
----	Checklist 103-178	.05
----	Checklist 179-259	.05

1986 Leaf

STARATED ROOKIE

ANDRES GALARRAGA RR

For its second Canadian card set the Donruss name was removed from the front of the company's 264-card issue, identifying the cards as "Leaf '86." Again concentrating on big-name stars and players from the Expos and Blue Jays, the 2-1/2" x 3-1/2" cards feature a design identical to the 1986 Donruss cards. Backs were altered to allow the publication of career highlights in both English and French, and card numbers were changed. The "Canadian Greats" cards in the 1986 Leaf set, painted portraits rather than photos, were Jesse Barfield and Jeff Reardon. Besides being sold in its intended market in Canada, the set was widely distributed in the U.S. through hobby vendors.

		NM/M
Complete Set (264):		12.00
Common Player:		.05
Wax Pack:		1.00
Wax Box (36):		20.00
1	Kirk Gibson/DK	.05
2	Goose Gossage/DK	.05
3	Willie McGee/DK	.05
4	George Bell/DK	.10
5	Tony Armas/DK	.05
6	Chili Davis/DK	.05
7	Cecil Cooper/DK	.05
8	Mike Boddicker/DK	.05
9	Davey Lopes/DK	.05
10	Bill Doran/DK	.05
11	Bret Saberhagen/DK	.05
12	Brett Butler/DK	.05
13	Harold Baines/DK	.05
14	Mike Davis/DK	.05
15	Tony Perez/DK	.35
16	Willie Randolph/DK	.05
17	Bob Boone/DK	.05
18	Orel Hershiser/DK	.05
19	Johnny Ray/DK	.05
20	Gary Ward/DK	.05
21	Rick Mahler/DK	.05
22	Phil Bradley/DK	.05
23	Jerry Koosman/DK	.05
24	Tom Brunansky/DK	.05
25	Andre Dawson/DK	.35
26	Dwight Gooden/DK	.05
27	Andres Galarraga/RR	2.00
28	Fred McGriff/RR	4.00

29	Dave Shipanoff/RR	.05
30	Danny Jackson	.05
31	Robin Yount	.50
32	Mike Fitzgerald	.05
33	Lou Whitaker	.05
34	Alfredo Griffin	.05
35	"Oil Can" Boyd	.05
36	Ron Guidry	.05
37	Rickey Henderson	.75
38	Jack Morris	.05
39	Brian Downing	.05
40	Mike Marshall	.05
41	Tony Gwynn	1.00
42	George Brett	1.25
43	Jim Gantner	.05
44	Hubie Brooks	.05
45	Tony Fernandez	.10
46	Oddibe McDowell	.05
47	Ozzie Smith	1.00
48	Ken Griffey	.05
49	Jose Cruz	.05
50	Mariano Duncan	.05
51	Mike Schmidt	1.25
52	Pat Tabler	.05
53	Pete Rose	1.50
54	Frank White	.05
55	Carney Lansford	.05
56	Steve Garvey	.15
57	Vance Law	.05
58	Tony Pena	.05
59	Wayne Tolleson	.05
60	Dale Murphy	.20
61	LaMarr Hoyt	.05
62	Ryne Sandberg	1.00
63	Gary Carter	1.00
64	Lee Smith	.05
65	Alvin Davis	.05
66	Edwin Nunez	.05
67	Kent Hrbek	.05
68	Dave Stieb	.05
69	Kirby Puckett	1.00
70	Paul Molitor	.75
71	Glenn Hubbard	.05
72	Lloyd Moseby	.05
73	Mike Smithson	.05
74	Jeff Leonard	.05
75	Danny Darwin	.05
76	Kevin McReynolds	.05
77	Bill Buckner	.05
78	Ron Oester	.05
79	Tommy Herr	.05
80	Mike Pagliarulo	.05
81	Ron Romanick	.05
82	Brook Jacoby	.05
83	Eddie Murray	.50
84	Gary Pettis	.05
85	Chet Lemon	.05
86	Toby Harrah	.05
87	Mike Scioscia	.05
88	Bert Blyleven	.05
89	Dave Righetti	.05
90	Bob Knepper	.05
91	Fernando Valenzuela	.05
92	Dave Dravecky	.05
93	Julio Franco	.05
94	Keith Moreland	.05
95	Darryl Motley	.05
96	Jack Clark	.05
97	Tim Wallach	.05
98	Steve Balboni	.05
99	Storm Davis	.05
100	Jay Howell	.05
101	Alan Trammell	.05
102	Willie Hernandez	.05
103	Don Mattingly	1.25
104	Lee Lacy	.05
105	Pedro Guerrero	.05
106	Willie Wilson	.05
107	Craig Reynolds	.05
108	Tim Raines	.15
109	Shane Rawley	.05
110	Larry Parrish	.05
111	Eric Show	.05
112	Mike Witt	.05
113	Dennis Eckersley	.35
114	Mike Moore	.05
115	Vince Coleman	.05
116	Damaso Garcia	.05
117	Steve Carlton	.50
118	Floyd Bannister	.05
119	Mario Soto	.05
120	Fred Lynn	.05
121	Bob Horner	.05
122	Rick Sutcliffe	.05
123	Walt Terrell	.05
124	Keith Hernandez	.05
125	Dave Winfield	.75
126	Frank Viola	.05
127	Dwight Evans	.05
128	Willie Upshaw	.05
129	Andre Thornton	.05
130	Donnie Moore	.05
131	Darryl Strawberry	.05
132	Nolan Ryan	2.00
133	Garry Templeton	.05
134	John Tudor	.05
135	Dave Parker	.05
136	Larry McWilliams	.05
137	Terry Pendleton	.05
138	Terry Puhl	.05
139	Bob Dernier	.05
140	Ozzie Guillen	.05
141	Jim Clancy	.05
142	Cal Ripken, Jr.	2.00
143	Mickey Hatcher	.05
144	Dan Petry	.05
145	Rich Gedman	.05
146	Jim Rice	.10

#	Player	Price
147	Butch Wynegar	.05
148	Donnie Hill	.05
149	Jim Sundberg	.05
150	Joe Hesketh	.05
151	Chris Codiroli	.05
152	Charlie Hough	.05
153	Herman Winningham	.05
154	Dave Rozema	.05
155	Don Slaught	.05
156	Juan Beniquez	.05
157	Ted Higuera	.05
158	Andy Hawkins	.05
159	Don Robinson	.05
160	Glenn Wilson	.05
161	Earnest Riles	.05
162	Nick Esasky	.05
163	Carlton Fisk	.50
164	Claudell Washington	.05
165	Scott McGregor	.05
166	Nate Snell	.05
167	Ted Simmons	.05
168	Wade Boggs	1.00
169	Marty Barrett	.05
170	Bud Black	.05
171	Charlie Leibrandt	.05
172	Charlie Lea	.05
173	Reggie Jackson	.50
174	Bryn Smith	.05
175	Glenn Davis	.05
176	Von Hayes	.05
177	Danny Cox	.05
178	Sam Khalifa	.05
179	Tom Browning	.05
180	Scott Garrelts	.05
181	Shawon Dunston	.05
182	Doyle Alexander	.05
183	Jim Presley	.05
184	Al Cowens	.05
185	Mark Salas	.05
186	Tom Niedenfuer	.05
187	Dave Henderson	.05
188	Lonnie Smith	.05
189	Bruce Bochte	.05
190	Leon Durham	.05
191	Terry Francona	.05
192	Bruce Sutter	.75
193	Steve Crawford	.05
194	Bob Brenly	.05
195	Dan Pasqua	.05
196	Juan Samuel	.05
197	Floyd Rayford	.05
198	Tim Burke	.05
199	Ben Oglivie	.05
200	Don Carman	.05
201	Lance Parrish	.05
202	Terry Forster	.05
203	Neal Heaton	.05
204	Ivan Calderon	.05
205	Jorge Orta	.05
206	Tom Henke	.05
207	Rick Reuschel	.05
208	Dan Quisenberry	.05
209	Ty-Breaking Hit (Pete Rose)	.25
210	Floyd Youmans	.05
211	Tom Filer	.05
212	R.J. Reynolds	.05
213	Gorman Thomas	.05
214	Canadian Great (Jeff Reardon (Canadian Great))	.45
215	Chris Brown	.05
216	Rick Aguilera	.05
217	Ernie Whitt	.05
218	Joe Orsulak	.05
219	Jimmy Key	.05
220	Atlee Hammaker	.05
221	Ron Darling	.05
222	Zane Smith	.05
223	Bob Welch	.05
224	Reid Nichols	.05
225	Fleet Feet (Vince Coleman, Willie McGee)	.10
226	Mark Gubicza	.05
227	Tim Birtsas	.05
228	Mike Hargrove	.05
229	Randy St. Claire	.05
230	Larry Herndon	.05
231	Dusty Baker	.05
232	Mookie Wilson	.05
233	Jeff Lahti	.05
234	Tom Seaver	.50
235	Mike Scott	.05
236	Don Sutton	.35
237	Roy Smalley	.05
238	Bill Madlock	.05
239	Charles Hudson	.05
240	John Franco	.05
241	Frank Tanana	.05
242	Sid Fernandez	.05
243	Knuckle Brothers (Joe Niekro, Phil Niekro)	.10
244	Dennis Lamp	.05
245	Gene Nelson	.05
246	Terry Harper	.05
247	Vida Blue	.05
248	Roger McDowell	.05
249	Tony Bernazard	.05
250	Cliff Johnson	.05
251	Hal McRae	.05
252	Garth Iorg	.05
253	Mitch Webster	.05
254	Jesse Barfield (Canadian Great)	.35
255	Dan Driessen	.05
256	Mike Brown	.05
257	Ron Kittle	.05
258	Bo Diaz	.05
259	Hank Aaron Puzzle Card	.05
260	Pete Rose (King of Kings)	1.50
----	Checklist 1-26 DK	.05
----	Checklist 27-106	.05
----	Checklist 107-186	.05
----	Checklist 187-260	.05

1987 Leaf

For the third consecutive season, Leaf-Donruss issued a Canadian baseball card set. These cards are nearly identical to the American set except for the name "Leaf" which appears on the front in place of "Donruss." The set contains 264 cards, each measuring 2-1/2" x 3-1/2", with a special emphasis being placed on players from the Montreal and Toronto teams. Backs feature career highlights in both English and French. As in the previous years, two "Canadian Greats" cards appear in the set. These painted portraits feature Mark Eichhorn and Floyd Youmans.

		NM/M
Unopened Factory Set (264)		25.00
Complete Set (264)		17.50
Common Player:		.05
Wax Pack:		1.50
Wax Box (36):		30.00
1	Wally Joyner/DK	.05
2	Roger Clemens/DK	1.00
3	Dale Murphy/DK	.15
4	Darryl Strawberry/DK	.05
5	Ozzie Smith/DK	.65
6	Jose Canseco/DK	.40
7	Charlie Hough/DK	.05
8	Brook Jacoby/DK	.05
9	Fred Lynn/DK	.05
10	Rick Rhoden/DK	.05
11	Chris Brown/DK	.05
12	Von Hayes/DK	.05
13	Jack Morris/DK	.10
14	Kevin McReynolds/DK	.05
15	George Brett/DK	.75
16	Ted Higuera/DK	.05
17	Hubie Brooks/DK	.05
18	Mike Scott/DK	.05
19	Kirby Puckett/DK	.65
20	Dave Winfield/DK	.75
21	Lloyd Moseby/DK	.10
22	Eric Davis/DK	.05
23	Jim Presley/DK	.05
24	Keith Moreland/DK	.05
25	Greg Walker/DK	.05
26	Steve Sax/DK	.05
27	Checklist 1-27	.05
28	B.J. Surhoff/RR	.05
29	Randy Myers/RR	.05
30	Ken Gerhart/RR	.05
31	Benito Santiago/RR	.05
32	Greg Swindell/RR	.05
33	Mike Birkbeck/RR	.05
34	Terry Steinbach/RR	.05
35	Bo Jackson/RR	.25
36	Greg Maddux/RR	2.00
37	Jim Lindeman/RR	.05
38	Devon White/RR	.75
39	Eric Bell/RR	.05
40	Will Fraser/RR	.05
41	Jerry Browne/RR	.05
42	Chris James/RR	.05
43	Rafael Palmeiro/RR	1.00
44	Pat Dodson/RR	.05
45	Duane Ward/RR	.25
46	Mark McGwire/RR	4.00
47	Bruce Fields/RR (Photo actually Darnell Coles.)	.05
48	Jody Davis	.05
49	Roger McDowell	.05
50	Jose Guzman	.05
51	Oddibe McDowell	.05
52	Harold Baines	.05
53	Dave Righetti	.05
54	Moose Haas	.05
55	Mark Langston	.05
56	Kirby Puckett	.65
57	Dwight Evans	.05
58	Willie Randolph	.05
59	Wally Backman	.05
60	Bryn Smith	.05
61	Tim Wallach	.05
62	Joe Hesketh	.05
63	Garry Templeton	.05
64	Rob Thompson	.05
65	Canadian Greats (Floyd Youmans)	.10
66	Ernest Riles	.05
67	Robin Yount	.50
68	Darryl Strawberry	.05
69	Ernie Whitt	.05
70	Dave Winfield	.65
71	Paul Molitor	.75
72	Dave Stieb	.05
73	Tom Henke	.05
74	Frank Viola	.05
75	Scott Garrelts	.05
76	Mike Boddicker	.05
77	Keith Moreland	.05
78	Lou Whitaker	.05
79	Dave Parker	.05
80	Lee Smith	.05
81	Tom Candiotti	.05
82	Greg Harris	.05
83	Fred Lynn	.05
84	Dwight Gooden	.05
85	Ron Darling	.05
86	Mike Krukow	.05
87	Spike Owen	.05
88	Len Dykstra	.05
89	Rick Aguilera	.05
90	Jim Clancy	.05
91	Joe Johnson	.05
92	Damaso Garcia	.05
93	Sid Fernandez	.05
94	Bob Ojeda	.05
95	Ted Higuera	.05
96	George Brett	.75
97	Willie Wilson	.05
98	Cal Ripken	1.50
99	Kent Hrbek	.05
100	Bert Blyleven	.05
101	Ron Guidry	.05
102	Andy Allanson	.05
103	Dave Henderson	.05
104	Kirk Gibson	.05
105	Lloyd Moseby	.05
106	Tony Fernandez	.05
107	Lance Parrish	.05
108	Ozzie Smith	.75
109	Gary Carter	.05
110	Eddie Murray	.50
111	Mike Witt	.05
112	Bobby Witt	.05
113	Willie McGee	.05
114	Steve Garvey	.10
115	Glenn Davis	.05
116	Jose Cruz	.05
117	Ozzie Guillen	.05
118	Alvin Davis	.05
119	Jose Rijo	.05
120	Bill Madlock	.05
121	Tommy Herr	.05
122	Mike Schmidt	.75
123	Mike Scioscia	.05
124	Terry Pendleton	.05
125	Leon Durham	.05
126	Alan Trammell	.05
127	Jesse Barfield	.05
128	Shawon Dunston	.05
129	Pete Rose	1.25
130	Von Hayes	.05
131	Julio Franco	.05
132	Juan Samuel	.05
133	Joe Carter	.10
134	Brook Jacoby	.05
135	Jack Morris	.05
136	Bob Horner	.05
137	Calvin Schiraldi	.05
138	Tom Browning	.05
139	Shane Rawley	.05
140	Mario Soto	.05
141	Dale Murphy	.15
142	Hubie Brooks	.05
143	Jeff Reardon	.05
144	Will Clark	.15
145	Ed Correa	.05
146	Glenn Wilson	.05
147	Johnny Ray	.05
148	Fernando Valenzuela	.05
149	Tim Raines	.10
150	Don Mattingly	.75
151	Jose Canseco	.40
152	Gary Pettis	.05
153	Don Sutton	.30
154	Jim Presley	.05
155	Checklist 28-105	.05
156	Dale Sveum	.05
157	Cory Snyder	.05
158	Jeff Sellers	.05
159	Denny Walling	.05
160	Danny Cox	.05
161	Bob Forsch	.05
162	Joaquin Andujar	.05
163	Roberto Clemente Puzzle Card	.10
164	Paul Assenmacher	.05
165	Marty Barrett	.05
166	Ray Knight	.05
167	Rafael Santana	.05
168	Bruce Ruffin	.05
169	Buddy Bell	.05
170	Kevin Mitchell	.05
171	Ken Oberkfell	.05
172	Gene Garber	.05
173	Canadian Greats (Mark Eichhorn)	.15
174	Don Carman	.05
175	Jesse Orosco	.05
176	Mookie Wilson	.05
177	Gary Ward	.05
178	John Franco	.05
179	Eric Davis	.05
180	Walt Terrell	.05
181	Phil Niekro	.30
182	Pat Tabler	.05
183	Brett Butler	.05
184	George Bell	.10
185	Pete Incaviglia	.05
186	Pete O'Brien	.05
187	Jimmy Key	.05
188	Frank White	.05
189	Mike Pagliarulo	.05
190	Roger Clemens	1.00
191	Rickey Henderson	.75
192	Mike Easler	.05
193	Wade Boggs	.75
194	Vince Coleman	.05
195	Charlie Kerfeld	.05
196	Dickie Thon	.05
197	Bill Doran	.05
198	Alfredo Griffin	.05
199	Carlton Fisk	.50
200	Phil Bradley	.05
201	Reggie Jackson	.65
202	Bob Boone	.05
203	Steve Sax	.05
204	Tom Niedenfuer	.05
205	Tim Burke	.05
206	Floyd Youmans	.05
207	Jay Tibbs	.05
208	Chili Davis	.05
209	Larry Parrish	.05
210	John Cerutti	.05
211	Kevin Bass	.05
212	Andre Dawson	.25
213	Bob Sebra	.05
214	Kevin McReynolds	.05
215	Jim Morrison	.05
216	Candy Maldonado	.05
217	John Kruk	.05
218	Todd Worrell	.05
219	Barry Bonds	10.00
220	Andy McGaffigan	.05
221	Andres Galarraga	.10
222	Mike Fitzgerald	.05
223	Kirk McCaskill	.05
224	Dave Smith	.05
225	Ruben Sierra	.05
226	Scott Fletcher	.05
227	Chet Lemon	.05
228	Dan Petry	.05
229	Mark Eichhorn	.05
230	Cecil Cooper	.05
231	Willie Upshaw	.05
232	Don Baylor	.05
233	Keith Hernandez	.05
234	Ryne Sandberg	.75
235	Tony Gwynn	.65
236	Chris Brown	.05
237	Pedro Guerrero	.05
238	Mark Gubicza	.05
239	Sid Bream	.05
240	Joe Cowley	.05
241	Bill Buckner	.05
242	John Candelaria	.05
243	Scott McGregor	.05
244	Tom Brunansky	.05
245	Gary Gaetti	.05
246	Orel Hershiser	.05
247	Jim Rice	.10
248	Oil Can Boyd	.05
249	Bob Knepper	.05
250	Danny Tartabull	.05
251	John Cangelosi	.05
252	Wally Joyner	.05
253	Bruce Hurst	.05
254	Rich Gedman	.05
255	Jim Deshaies	.05
256	Tony Pena	.05
257	Nolan Ryan	1.50
258	Mike Scott	.05
259	Checklist 106-183	.05
260	Dennis Rasmussen	.05
261	Bret Saberhagen	.05
262	Steve Balboni	.05
263	Tom Seaver	.50
264	Checklist 184-264	.05

1987 Leaf Candy City Team

Leaf produced this set as part of its endorsement for the Special Olympics. Twelve cards feature Baseball Hall of Famers. The cards measure 2-1/2" x 3-1/2" and are numbered H1-H12. The remaining six cards in the set are numbered S1-S6 and feature unnamed Special Olympics champions. All cards feature the artwork of Dick Perez. The cards were available through a mail-in offer advertised at special store displays. Only the baseball-related subjects are listed in the checklist.

		NM/M
Complete Set (12):		3.00
Common Player:		.15
H1	Mickey Mantle	1.00
H2	Yogi Berra	.35
H3	Roy Campanella	.35
H4	Stan Musial	.50
H5	Ted Williams	.60
H6	Duke Snider	.35
H7	Hank Aaron	.60
H8	Pee Wee Reese	.35
H9	Brooks Robinson	.25
H10	Al Kaline	.25
H11	Willie McCovey	.25
H12	Cool Papa Bell	.15

1988 Leaf

This 264-card set features color player photos from among the 1988 Donruss 660-card standard issue, with emphasis on players from Montreal and Toronto. A border of red, blue and black stripes duplicates the design of the Donruss set, with the exception of a "Leaf '88" logo in the upper-left corner that replaces the Donruss logo. Two special Canadian Greats cards are included in this set: Perez-Steele portraits of Tim Wallach and George Bell. The set also includes the portrait-style Diamond Kings cards (the set's first 26 cards, one for each team). The DK's carry the Donruss logo above the gold DK banner. All card backs are bilingual (French/English), numbered, and printed in black on white stock with a light blue border. This set was sold in 10-card wax packs with one triple-piece puzzle card per pack and was distributed via larger hobby and retail shops in the U.S. and Canada.

		NM/M
Complete Set (264):		6.00
Common Player:		.05
Wax Pack (15):		.50
Wax Box (36):		9.00
1	Mark McGwire/DK	1.25
2	Tim Raines/DK	.20
3	Benito Santiago/DK	.05
4	Alan Trammell/DK	.05
5	Danny Tartabull/DK	.05
6	Ron Darling/DK	.05
7	Paul Molitor/DK	.75
8	Devon White/DK	.20
9	Andre Dawson/DK	.25
10	Julio Franco/DK	.05
11	Scott Fletcher/DK	.05
12	Tony Fernandez/DK	.10
13	Shane Rawley /DK	.05
14	Kal Daniels/DK	.05
15	Jack Clark/DK	.05
16	Dwight Evans/DK	.05
17	Tommy John/DK	.05
18	Andy Van Slyke/DK	.05
19	Gary Gaetti/DK	.05
20	Mark Langston/DK	.05
21	Will Clark/DK	.15
22	Glenn Hubbard/DK	.05
23	Billy Hatcher/DK	.05
24	Bob Welch/DK	.05
25	Ivan Calderon/DK	.05
26	Cal Ripken, Jr./DK	1.50
27	Checklist 1-27	.05
28	Mackey Sasser/RR	.05
29	Jeff Treadway/RR	.05
30	Mike Campbell/RR	.05
31	Lance Johnson/RR	.05
32	Nelson Liriano/RR	.05
33	Shawn Abner/RR	.05
34	Roberto Alomar/RR	2.50
35	Shawn Hillegas/RR	.05
36	Joey Meyer/RR	.05
37	Kevin Elster/RR	.05
38	Jose Lind/RR	.05
39	Kirt Manwaring/RR	.05
40	Mark Grace/RR	.75
41	Jody Reed/RR	.05
42	John Farrell/RR	.05
43	Al Leiter/RR	.25
44	Gary Thurman/RR	.05
45	Vincente Palacios/RR	.05
46	Eddie Williams/RR	.05
47	Jack McDowell/RR	.20
48	Dwight Gooden	.05
49	Mike Witt	.05
50	Wally Joyner	.05
51	Brook Jacoby	.05
52	Bert Blyleven	.05
53	Ted Higuera	.05
54	Mike Scott	.05
55	Jose Guzman	.05
56	Roger Clemens	1.25
57	Dave Righetti	.05
58	Benito Santiago	.05
59	Ozzie Guillen	.05
60	Matt Nokes	.05
61	Fernando Valenzuela	.05
62	Orel Hershiser	.05
63	Sid Fernandez	.05
64	Ozzie Virgil	.05
65	Wade Boggs	.50
66	Floyd Youmans	.05
67	Jimmy Key	.05
68	Bret Saberhagen	.05
69	Jody Davis	.05
70	Shawon Dunston	.05
71	Julio Franco	.05
72	Danny Cox	.05
73	Jim Clancy	.05
74	Mark Eichhorn	.05
75	Scott Bradley	.05
76	Charlie Leibrandt	.05
77	Nolan Ryan	1.50
78	Ron Darling	.05
79	John Franco	.05
80	Dave Stieb	.05
81	Mike Fitzgerald	.05
82	Steve Bedrosian	.05
83	Dale Murphy	.20
84	Tim Burke	.05
85	Jack Morris	.05
86	Greg Walker	.05
87	Kevin Mitchell	.05
88	Doug Drabek	.05
89	Charlie Hough	.05
90	Tony Gwynn	.75
91	Rick Sutcliffe	.05
92	Shane Rawley	.05
93	George Brett	1.00
94	Frank Viola	.05
95	Tony Pena	.05
96	Jim Deshaies	.05
97	Mike Scioscia	.05
98	Rick Rhoden	.05
99	Terry Kennedy	.05
100	Cal Ripken	1.50
101	Pedro Guerrero	.05
102	Andy Van Slyke	.05
103	Willie McGee	.05
104	Mike Kingery	.05
105	Kevin Seitzer	.05
106	Robin Yount	.50
107	Tracy Jones	.05
108	Dave Magadan	.05
109	Mel Hall	.05
110	Billy Hatcher	.05
111	Todd Benzinger	.05
112	Mike LaValliere	.05
113	Barry Bonds	1.50
114	Tim Raines	.20
115	Ozzie Smith	.25
116	Dave Winfield	.75
117	Keith Hernandez	.05
118	Jeffrey Leonard	.05
119	Larry Parrish	.05
120	Rob Thompson	.05
121	Andres Galarraga	.15
122	Mickey Hatcher	.05
123	Mark Langston	.05
124	Mike Schmidt	1.00
125	Cory Snyder	.05
126	Andre Dawson	.15
127	Devon White	.15
128	Vince Coleman	.05
129	Bryn Smith	.05
130	Lance Parrish	.05
131	Willie Upshaw	.05
132	Pete O'Brien	.05
133	Tony Fernandez	.10
134	Billy Ripken	.05
135	Len Dykstra	.05
136	Kirk Gibson	.05
137	Kevin Bass	.05
138	Jose Canseco	.50
139	Kent Hrbek	.05
140	Lloyd Moseby	.05
141	Marty Barrett	.05
142	Carmelo Martinez	.05
143	Tom Foley	.05
144	Kirby Puckett	.75
145	Rickey Henderson	.75
146	Juan Samuel	.05
147	Pete Incaviglia	.05
148	Greg Brock	.05
149	Eric Davis	.05
150	Kal Daniels	.05
151	Bob Boone	.05
152	John Cerutti	.05
153	Mike Greenwell	.05
154	Oddibe McDowell	.05
155	Scott Fletcher	.05
156	Gary Carter	.75
157	Harold Baines	.05
158	Greg Swindell	.05

Mark McGwire 1B / OAKLAND ATHLETICS / BLUE CHIP CARDS / Leaf.

"The Blue Chip cards are printed on heavier stock and have a blue background on the back. Why they were produced and apparently not distributed is not known. It is presumed, though not confirmed, that all 12 Grand Slammers cards can also be found in the Blue Chip version.

		NM/M
Complete Set (12):		1,200
Common Player:		60.00
1	Jose Canseco	125.00
2	Mike Marshall	60.00
3	Walt Weiss	60.00
4	Kevin McReynolds	60.00
5	Mike Greenwell	60.00
6	Dave Winfield	150.00
7	Mark McGwire	400.00
8	Keith Hernandez	75.00
9	Franklin Stubbs	60.00
10	Danny Tartabull	60.00
11	Jesse Barfield	60.00
12	Ellis Burks	60.00

1990 Leaf Previews

JOE CARTER OF

This 12-card set was produced for dealer distribution to introduce Leaf as Donruss' premium-quality brand in mid-1990. Cards have the same format as the regular-issue versions with metallic silver ink highlights on front and back. The preview cards have a white undertype on back over the stats and career highlights. It reads "Special Preview Card."

		NM/M
Complete Set (12):		275.00
Common Player:		12.50
1	Steve Sax	12.50
2	Joe Carter	12.50
3	Dennis Eckersley	20.00
4	Ken Griffey Jr.	200.00
5	Barry Larkin	12.50
6	Mark Langston	12.50
7	Eric Anthony	12.50
8	Robin Ventura	12.50
9	Greg Vaughn	12.50
10	Bobby Bonilla	12.50
11	Gary Gaetti	12.50
12	Ozzie Smith	75.00

1990 Leaf

BOB TEWKSBURY P

1989 Leaf Blue Chip Cards

Unknown until 2001, these cards are a variation of the 1989 Donruss Grand Slammers insert set and share the back design with that issue. Instead of the GS logo in the lower-left corner of the photo, these cards have a black, white and blue logo reading "Blue Chip /

This 528-card set was issued in two 264-card series. The cards were printed on heavy quality stock and both the card fronts and backs have full color player photos. Cards also have an ultra-glossy finish on both the fronts and the backs. A high-tech foil Hall of Fame puzzle features former Yankee great Yogi Berra.

		NM/M
Complete Set (528):		75.00
Series 1 (264):		50.00
Series 2 (264):		25.00
Common Player:		.10
Series 1 Foil Pack (15):		4.00
Series 1 Foil Box (36):		80.00
Series 2 Foil Pack (15):		2.50
Series 2 Foil Box (36):		60.00

#	Name	Price
159	Mark McLemore	.05
160	Keith Moreland	.05
161	Jim Gantner	.05
162	Willie Randolph	.05
163	Fred Lynn	.05
164	B.J. Surhoff	.05
165	Ken Griffey	.05
166	Chet Lemon	.05
167	Alan Trammell	.05
168	Paul Molitor	.75
169	Lou Whitaker	.05
170	Will Clark	.10
171	Dwight Evans	.05
172	Eddie Murray	.50
173	Darrell Evans	.05
174	Ellis Burks	.05
175	Ivan Calderon	.05
176	John Kruk	.05
177	Don Mattingly	1.00
178	Dick Schofield	.05
179	Bruce Hurst	.05
180	Ron Guidry	.05
181	Jack Clark	.05
182	Franklin Stubbs	.05
183	Bill Doran	.05
184	Joe Carter	.05
185	Steve Sax	.05
186	Glenn Davis	.05
187	Bo Jackson	.10
188	Bobby Bonilla	.05
189	Willie Wilson	.05
190	Danny Tartabull	.05
191	Bo Diaz	.05
192	Buddy Bell	.05
193	Tim Wallach	.05
194	Mark McGwire	1.25
195	Carney Lansford	.05
196	Alvin Davis	.05
197	Von Hayes	.05
198	Mitch Webster	.05
199	Casey Candaele	.05
200	Gary Gaetti	.05
201	Tommy Herr	.05
202	Wally Backman	.05
203	Brian Downing	.05
204	Rance Mulliniks	.05
205	Craig Reynolds	.05
206	Ruben Sierra	.05
207	Ryne Sandberg	.75
208	Carlton Fisk	.50
209	Checklist 28-107	.05
210	Gerald Young	.05
211	MVP (Tim Raines)	.25
212	John Tudor	.05
213	Canadian Greats (George Bell)	.60
214	MVP (George Bell)	.25
215	Jim Rice	.10
216	Gerald Perry	.05
217	Dave Stewart	.05
218	Jose Uribe	.05
219	Rick Rueschel	.05
220	Darryl Strawberry	.05
221	Chris Brown	.05
223	Lee Mazzilli	.05
224	Denny Walling	.05
225	Jesse Barfield	.05
226	Barry Larkin	.05
227	Harold Reynolds	.05
228	Kevin McReynolds	.05
229	Todd Worrell	.05
230	Tommy John	.05
231	Rick Aguilera	.05
232	Bill Madlock	.05
233	Roy Smalley	.05
234	Jeff Musselman	.05
235	Mike Dunne	.05
236	Jerry Browne	.05
237	Sam Horn	.05
238	Howard Johnson	.05
239	Candy Maldonado	.05
240	Nick Esasky	.05
241	Geno Petralli	.05
242	Herm Winningham	.05
243	Roger McDowell	.05
244	Brian Fisher	.05
245	John Marzano	.05
246	Terry Pendleton	.05
247	Rick Leach	.05
248	Pascual Perez	.05
249	Mookie Wilson	.05
250	Ernie Whitt	.05
251	Ron Kittle	.05
252	Oil Can Boyd	.05
253	Jim Gott	.05
254	George Bell	.10
255	Canadian Greats (Tim Wallach)	.60
256	Luis Polonia	.05
257	Hubie Brooks	.05
258	Mickey Brantley	.05
259	Gregg Jefferies	.25
260	Johnny Ray	.05
261	Checklist 108-187	.05
262	Dennis Martinez	.05
263	Stan Musial Puzzle Card	.05
264	Checklist 188-264	.05

#	Name	Price
1	Introductory Card	.10
2	Mike Henneman	.10
3	Steve Bedrosian	.10
4	Mike Scott	.10
5	Allan Anderson	.10
6	Rick Sutcliffe	.10
7	Gregg Olson	.10
8	Kevin Elster	.10
9	Pete O'Brien	.10
10	Carlton Fisk	1.00
11	Joe Magrane	.10
12	Roger Clemens	2.50
13	Tom Glavine	.35
14	Tom Gordon	.10
15	Todd Benzinger	.10
16	Hubie Brooks	.10
17	Roberto Kelly	.10
18	Barry Larkin	.10
19	Mike Boddicker	.10
20	Roger McDowell	.10
21	Nolan Ryan	5.00
22	John Farrell	.10
23	Bruce Hurst	.10
24	Wally Joyner	.10
25	Greg Maddux	2.00
26	Chris Bosio	.10
27	John Cerutti	.10
28	Tim Burke	.10
29	Dennis Eckersley	.75
30	Glenn Davis	.10
31	Jim Abbott	.10
32	Mike LaValliere	.10
33	Andres Thomas	.10
34	Lou Whitaker	.10
35	Alvin Davis	.10
36	Melido Perez	.10
37	Craig Biggio	.10
38	Rick Aguilera	.10
39	Pete Harnisch	.10
40	David Cone	.10
41	Scott Garrelts	.10
42	Jay Howell	.10
43	Eric King	.10
44	Pedro Guerrero	.10
45	Mike Bielecki	.10
46	Bob Boone	.10
47	Kevin Brown	.10
48	Jerry Browne	.10
49	Mike Scioscia	.10
50	Chuck Cary	.10
51	Wade Boggs	2.00
52	Von Hayes	.10
53	Tony Fernandez	.10
54	Dennis Martinez	.10
55	Tom Candiotti	.10
56	Andy Benes	.10
57	Rob Dibble	.10
58	Chuck Crim	.10
59	John Smoltz	.60
60	Mike Heath	.10
61	Kevin Gross	.10
62	Mark McGwire	3.50
63	Bert Blyleven	.10
64	Bob Walk	.10
65	Mickey Tettleton	.10
66	Sid Fernandez	.10
67	Terry Kennedy	.10
68	Fernando Valenzuela	.10
69	Don Mattingly	2.50
70	Paul O'Neill	.10
71	Robin Yount	1.00
72	Bret Saberhagen	.10
73	Geno Petralli	.10
74	Brook Jacoby	.10
75	Roberto Alomar	.25
76	Devon White	.10
77	Jose Lind	.10
78	Pat Combs	.10
79	Dave Steib	.10
80	Tim Wallach	.10
81	Dave Stewart	.10
82	Eric Anthony RC	.10
83	Randy Bush	.10
84	Checklist	.10
85	Jaime Navarro	.10
86	Tommy Gregg	.10
87	Frank Tanana	.10
88	Omar Vizquel	.10
89	Ivan Calderon	.10
90	Vince Coleman	.10
91	Barry Bonds	5.00
92	Randy Milligan	.10
93	Frank Viola	.10
94	Matt Williams	.10
95	Alfredo Griffin	.10
96	Steve Sax	.10
97	Gary Gaetti	.10
98	Ryne Sandberg	2.00
99	Danny Tartabull	.10
100	Rafael Palmeiro	1.00
101	Jesse Orosco	.10
102	Garry Templeton	.10
103	Frank DiPino	.10
104	Tony Pena	.10
105	Dickie Thon	.10
106	Kelly Gruber	.10
107	Marquis Grissom RC	.10
108	Jose Canseco	.60
109	Mike Blowers	.10
110	Tom Browning	.10
111	Greg Vaughn	.10
112	Oddibe McDowell	.10
113	Gary Ward	.10
114	Jay Buhner	.10
115	Eric Show	.10
116	Bryan Harvey	.10
117	Andy Van Slyke	.10
118	Jeff Ballard	.10
119	Barry Lyons	.10
120	Kevin Mitchell	.10
121	Mike Gallego	.10
122	Dave Smith	.10
123	Kirby Puckett	2.00
124	Jerome Walton	.10
125	Bo Jackson	.20
126	Harold Baines	.10
127	Scott Bankhead	.10
128	Ozzie Guillen	.10
129	Jose Oquendo	.10
130	John Dopson	.10
131	Charlie Hayes	.10
132	Fred McGriff	.10
133	Chet Lemon	.10
134	Gary Carter	1.00
135	Rafael Ramirez	.10
136	Shane Mack	.10
137	Mark Grace	.10
138	Phil Bradley	.10
139	Dwight Gooden	.10
140	Harold Reynolds	.10
141	Scott Fletcher	.10
142	Ozzie Smith	2.00
143	Mike Greenwell	.10
144	Pete Smith	.10
145	Mark Gubicza	.10
146	Chris Sabo	.10
147	Ramon Martinez	.10
148	Tim Leary	.10
149	Randy Myers	.10
150	Jody Reed	.10
151	Bruce Ruffin	.10
152	Jeff Russell	.10
153	Doug Jones	.10
154	Tony Gwynn	2.00
155	Mark Langston	.10
156	Mitch Williams	.10
157	Gary Sheffield	.60
158	Tom Henke	.10
159	Oil Can Boyd	.10
160	Rickey Henderson	1.00
161	Bill Doran	.10
162	Chuck Finley	.10
163	Jeff King	.10
164	Nick Esasky	.10
165	Cecil Fielder	.10
166	Dave Valle	.10
167	Robin Ventura	.10
168	Jim Deshaies	.10
169	Juan Berenguer	.10
170	Craig Worthington	.10
171	Gregg Jefferies	.10
172	Will Clark	.10
173	Kirk Gibson	.10
174	Checklist	.10
175	Bobby Thigpen	.10
176	John Tudor	.10
177	Andre Dawson	.35
178	George Brett	2.50
179	Steve Buechele	.10
180	Albert Belle	.10
181	Eddie Murray	1.00
182	Bob Geren	.10
183	Rob Murphy	.10
184	Tom Herr	.10
185	George Bell	.10
186	Spike Owen	.10
187	Cory Snyder	.10
188	Fred Lynn	.10
189	Eric Davis	.10
190	Dave Parker	.10
191	Jeff Blauser	.10
192	Matt Nokes	.10
193	Delino DeShields RC	.50
194	Scott Sanderson	.10
195	Lance Parrish	.10
196	Bobby Bonilla	.10
197	Cal Ripken, Jr.	5.00
198	Kevin McReynolds	.10
199	Robby Thompson	.10
200	Tim Belcher	.10
201	Jesse Barfield	.10
202	Mariano Duncan	.10
203	Bill Spiers	.10
204	Frank White	.10
205	Julio Franco	.10
206	Greg Swindell	.10
207	Benito Santiago	.10
208	Johnny Ray	.10
209	Gary Redus	.10
210	Jeff Parrett	.10
211	Jimmy Key	.10
212	Tim Raines	.10
213	Carney Lansford	.10
214	Gerald Young	.10
215	Gene Larkin	.10
216	Dan Plesac	.10
217	Lonnie Smith	.10
218	Alan Trammell	.10
219	Jeffrey Leonard	.10
220	Sammy Sosa RC	20.00
221	Todd Zeile	.10
222	Bill Landrum	.10
223	Mike Devereaux	.10
224	Mike Marshall	.10
225	Jose Uribe	.10
226	Juan Samuel	.10
227	Mel Hall	.10
228	Kent Hrbek	.10
229	Shawon Dunston	.10
230	Kevin Seitzer	.10
231	Pete Incaviglia	.10
232	Sandy Alomar	.10
233	Bip Roberts	.10
234	Scott Terry	.10
235	Dwight Evans	.10
236	Ricky Jordan	.10
237	John Olerud RC	5.00
238	Zane Smith	.10
239	Walt Weiss	.10
240	Alvaro Espinoza	.10
241	Billy Hatcher	.10
242	Paul Molitor	1.00
243	Dale Murphy	.30
244	Dave Bergman	.10
245	Ken Griffey Jr.	3.00
246	Ed Whitson	.10
247	Kirk McCaskill	.10
248	Jay Bell	.10
249	Ben McDonald RC	.50
250	Darryl Strawberry	.10
251	Brett Butler	.10
252	Terry Steinbach	.10
253	Ken Caminiti	.10
254	Dan Gladden	.10
255	Dwight Smith	.10
256	Kurt Stillwell	.10
257	Ruben Sierra	.10
258	Mike Schooler	.10
259	Lance Johnson	.10
260	Terry Pendleton	.10
261	Ellis Burks	.10
262	Len Dykstra	.10
263	Mookie Wilson	.10
264	Checklist (Nolan Ryan)	.10
265	Nolan Ryan (No-Hit King)	2.00
266	Brian DuBois	.10
267	Don Robinson	.10
268	Glenn Wilson	.10
269	Kevin Tapani RC	.25
270	Marvell Wynne	.10
271	Billy Ripken	.10
272	Howard Johnson	.10
273	Brian Holman	.10
274	Dan Pasqua	.10
275	Ken Dayley	.10
276	Jeff Reardon	.10
277	Jim Presley	.10
278	Jim Eisenreich	.10
279	Danny Jackson	.10
280	Orel Hershiser	.10
281	Andy Hawkins	.10
282	Jose Rijo	.10
283	Luis Rivera	.10
284	John Kruk	.10
285	Jeff Huson	.10
286	Joel Skinner	.10
287	Jack Clark	.10
288	Chili Davis	.10
289	Joe Girardi	.10
290	B.J. Surhoff	.10
291	Luis Sojo	.10
292	Tom Foley	.10
293	Mike Moore	.10
294	Ken Oberkfell	.10
295	Luis Polonia	.10
296	Doug Drabek	.10
297	Dave Justice RC	2.00
298	Paul Gibson	.10
299	Edgar Martinez	.10
300	Frank Thomas RC	20.00
301	Eric Yelding	.10
302	Greg Gagne	.10
303	Brad Komminsk	.10
304	Ron Darling	.10
305	Kevin Bass	.10
306	Jeff Hamilton	.10
307	Ron Karkovice	.10
308	Milt Thompson	.10
309	Mike Harkey	.10
310	Mel Stottlemyre	.10
311	Kenny Rogers	.10
312	Mitch Webster	.10
313	Kal Daniels	.10
314	Matt Nokes	.10
315	Dennis Lamp	.10
316	Ken Howell	.10
317	Glenallen Hill	.10
318	Dave Martinez	.10
319	Chris James	.10
320	Mike Pagliarulo	.10
321	Hal Morris	.10
322	Rob Deer	.10
323	Greg Olson	.10
324	Tony Phillips	.10
325	Larry Walker RC	8.00
326	Ron Hassey	.10
327	Jack Howell	.10
328	John Smiley	.10
329	Steve Finley	.10
330	Dave Magadan	.10
331	Greg Litton	.10
332	Mickey Hatcher	.10
333	Lee Guetterman	.10
334	Norm Charlton	.10
335	Edgar Diaz	.10
336	Willie Wilson	.10
337	Bobby Witt	.10
338	Candy Maldonado	.10
339	Craig Lefferts	.10
340	Dante Bichette	.10
341	Wally Backman	.10
342	Dennis Cook	.10
343	Pat Borders	.10
344	Wallace Johnson	.10
345	Willie Randolph	.10
346	Danny Darwin	.10
347	Al Newman	.10
348	Mark Knudson	.10
349	Joe Boever	.10
350	Larry Sheets	.10
351	Mike Jackson	.10
352	Wayne Edwards	.10
353	Bernard Gilkey RC	.50
354	Don Slaught	.10
355	Joe Orsulak	.10
356	John Franco	.10
357	Jeff Brantley	.10
358	Mike Morgan	.10
359	Deion Sanders	.10
360	Terry Leach	.10
361	Les Lancaster	.10
362	Storm Davis	.10
363	Scott Coolbaugh	.10
364	Checklist	.10
365	Cecilio Guante	.10
366	Joey Cora	.10
367	Willie McGee	.10
368	Jerry Reed	.10
369	Darren Daulton	.10
370	Manny Lee	.10
371	Mark Gardner	.10
372	Rick Honeycutt	.10
373	Steve Balboni	.10
374	Jack Armstrong	.10
375	Charlie O'Brien	.10
376	Ron Gant	.10
377	Lloyd Moseby	.10
378	Gene Harris	.10
379	Joe Carter	.10
380	Scott Bailes	.10
381	R.J. Reynolds	.10
382	Bob Melvin	.10
383	Tim Teufel	.10
384	John Burkett	.10
385	Felix Jose	.10
386	Larry Andersen	.10
387	David West	.10
388	Luis Salazar	.10
389	Mike Macfarlane	.10
390	Charlie Hough	.10
391	Greg Briley	.10
392	Donn Pall	.10
393	Bryn Smith	.10
394	Carlos Quintana	.10
395	Steve Lake	.10
396	Mark Whiten RC	.15
397	Edwin Nunez	.10
398	Rick Parker	.10
399	Mark Portugal	.10
400	Roy Smith	.10
401	Hector Villanueva	.10
402	Bob Milacki	.10
403	Alejandro Pena	.10
404	Scott Bradley	.10
405	Ron Kittle	.10
406	Bob Tewksbury	.10
407	Wes Gardner	.10
408	Ernie Whitt	.10
409	Terry Shumpert	.10
410	Tim Layana	.10
411	Chris Gwynn	.10
412	Jeff Robinson	.10
413	Scott Scudder	.10
414	Kevin Romine	.10
415	Jose DeJesus	.10
416	Mike Jeffcoat	.10
417	Rudy Seanez	.10
418	Mike Dunne	.10
419	Dick Schofield	.10
420	Steve Wilson	.10
421	Bill Krueger	.10
422	Junior Felix	.10
423	Drew Hall	.10
424	Curt Young	.10
425	Franklin Stubbs	.10
426	Dave Winfield	1.00
427	Rick Reed	.10
428	Charlie Leibrandt	.10
429	Jeff Robinson	.10
430	Erik Hanson	.10
431	Barry Jones	.10
432	Alex Trevino	.10
433	John Moses	.10
434	Dave Johnson	.10
435	Mackey Sasser	.10
436	Rick Leach	.10
437	Lenny Harris	.10
438	Carlos Martinez	.10
439	Rex Hudler	.10
440	Domingo Ramos	.10
441	Gerald Perry	.10
442	John Russell	.10
443	Carlos Baerga RC	.50
444	Checklist	.10
445	Stan Javier	.10
446	Kevin Maas RC	.10
447	Tom Brunansky	.10
448	Carmelo Martinez	.10
449	Willie Blair RC	.10
450	Andres Galarraga	.10
451	Bud Black	.10
452	Greg Harris	.10

453	Joe Oliver	.10
454	Greg Brock	.10
455	Jeff Treadway	.10
456	Lance McCullers	.10
457	Dave Schmidt	.10
458	Todd Burns	.10
459	Max Venable	.10
460	Neal Heaton	.10
461	Mark Williamson	.10
462	Keith Miller	.10
463	Mike LaCoss	.10
464	Jose Offerman RC	.25
465	Jim Leyritz RC	.50
466	Glenn Braggs	.10
467	Ron Robinson	.10
468	Mark Davis	.10
469	Gary Pettis	.10
470	Keith Hernandez	.10
471	Dennis Rasmussen	.10
472	Mark Eichhorn	.10
473	Ted Power	.10
474	Terry Mulholland	.10
475	Todd Stottlemyre	.10
476	Jerry Goff	.10
477	Gene Nelson	.10
478	Rich Gedman	.10
479	Brian Harper	.10
480	Mike Felder	.10
481	Steve Avery	.10
482	Jack Morris	.10
483	Randy Johnson	1.00
484	Scott Radinsky	.10
485	Jose DeLeon	.10
486	Stan Belinda RC	.10
487	Brian Holton	.10
488	Mark Carreon	.10
489	Trevor Wilson	.10
490	Mike Sharperson	.10
491	Alan Mills RC	.10
492	John Candelaria	.10
493	Paul Assenmacher	.10
494	Steve Crawford	.10
495	Brad Arnsberg	.10
496	Sergio Valdez	.10
497	Mark Parent	.10
498	Tom Pagnozzi	.10
499	Greg Harris	.10
500	Randy Ready	.10
501	Duane Ward	.10
502	Nelson Santovenia	.10
503	Joe Klink	.10
504	Eric Plunk	.10
505	Jeff Reed	.10
506	Ted Higuera	.10
507	Joe Hesketh	.10
508	Dan Petry	.10
509	Matt Young	.10
510	Jerald Clark RC	.10
511	John Orton RC	.10
512	Scott Ruskin	.10
513	Chris Hoiles RC	.50
514	Daryl Boston	.10
515	Francisco Oliveras	.10
516	Ozzie Canseco	.10
517	Xavier Hernandez RC	.10
518	Fred Manrique	.10
519	Shawn Boskie	.10
520	Jeff Montgomery	.10
521	Jack Daugherty	.10
522	Keith Comstock	.10
523	Greg Hibbard RC	.10
524	Lee Smith	.10
525	Dana Kiecker	.10
526	Darrel Akerfelds	.10
527	Greg Myers	.10
528	Checklist	.10

1991 Leaf Previews

RYNE SANDBERG 2B

Cello packs of four cards previewing the 1991 Leaf set were included in each 1991 Donruss hobby factory set. The cards are identical in format to the regular 1991 Leafs, except there is a notation, "1991 PREVIEW CARD" in white print beneath the statistics and career information on the back.

		NM/M
Complete Set (26):		20.00
Common Player:		.50
1	Dave Justice	.50
2	Ryne Sandberg	1.50
3	Barry Larkin	.50
4	Craig Biggio	.50
5	Ramon Martinez	.50
6	Tim Wallach	.50

7	Dwight Gooden	.50
8	Len Dykstra	.50
9	Barry Bonds	4.00
10	Ray Lankford	.50
11	Tony Gwynn	1.50
12	Will Clark	.60
13	Leo Gomez	.50
14	Wade Boggs	1.50
15	Chuck Finley	.50
16	Carlton Fisk	1.00
17	Sandy Alomar, Jr.	.50
18	Cecil Fielder	.50
19	Bo Jackson	.75
20	Paul Molitor	1.00
21	Kirby Puckett	1.50
22	Don Mattingly	2.00
23	Rickey Henderson	1.00
24	Tino Martinez	.50
25	Nolan Ryan	4.00
26	Dave Steib	.50

1991 Leaf

JOHN OLERUD 1B

Silver borders and black insets surround the color action photos on the 1991 Leaf cards. The set was once again released in two series. Series I consists of cards 1-264. Card backs feature an additional player photo, biographical information, statistics and career highlights. The 1991 issue is not considered as scarce as the 1990 release.

		NM/M
Complete Set (528):		8.00
Common Player:		.05
Series 1 or 2 Pack (15):		.05
Series 1 or 2 Box (36):		12.50
1	The Leaf Card	.05
2	Kurt Stillwell	.05
3	Bobby Witt	.05
4	Tony Phillips	.05
5	Scott Garrelts	.05
6	Greg Swindell	.05
7	Billy Ripken	.05
8	Dave Martinez	.05
9	Kelly Gruber	.05
10	Juan Samuel	.05
11	Brian Holman	.05
12	Craig Biggio	.05
13	Lonnie Smith	.05
14	Ron Robinson	.05
15	Mike LaValliere	.05
16	Mark Davis	.05
17	Jack Daugherty	.05
18	Mike Henneman	.05
19	Mike Greenwell	.05
20	Dave Magadan	.05
21	Mark Williamson	.05
22	Marquis Grissom	.05
23	Pat Borders	.05
24	Mike Scioscia	.05
25	Shawon Dunston	.05
26	Randy Bush	.05
27	John Smoltz	.05
28	Chuck Crim	.05
29	Don Slaught	.05
30	Mike Macfarlane	.05
31	Wally Joyner	.05
32	Pat Combs	.05
33	Tony Pena	.05
34	Howard Johnson	.05
35	Leo Gomez	.05
36	Spike Owen	.05
37	Eric Davis	.05
38	Roberto Kelly	.05
39	Jerome Walton	.05
40	Shane Mack	.05
41	Kent Mercker	.05
42	B.J. Surhoff	.05
43	Jerry Browne	.05
44	Lee Smith	.05
45	Chuck Finley	.05
46	Terry Mulholland	.05
47	Tom Bolton	.05
48	Tom Herr	.05
49	Jim Deshaies	.05
50	Walt Weiss	.05
51	Hal Morris	.05
52	Lee Guetterman	.05
53	Paul Assenmacher	.05
54	Brian Harper	.05
55	Paul Gibson	.05
56	John Burkett	.05
57	Doug Jones	.05
58	Jose Oquendo	.05
59	Dick Schofield	.05

60	Dickie Thon	.05
61	Ramon Martinez	.05
62	Jay Buhner	.05
63	Mark Portugal	.05
64	Bob Welch	.05
65	Chris Sabo	.05
66	Chuck Cary	.05
67	Mark Langston	.05
68	Joe Boever	.05
69	Jody Reed	.05
70	Alejandro Pena	.05
71	Jeff King	.05
72	Tom Pagnozzi	.05
73	Joe Oliver	.05
74	Mike Witt	.05
75	Hector Villanueva	.05
76	Dan Gladden	.05
77	Dave Justice	.05
78	Mike Gallego	.05
79	Tom Candiotti	.05
80	Ozzie Smith	.60
81	Luis Polonia	.05
82	Randy Ready	.05
83	Greg Harris	.05
84	Checklist (Dave Justice)	.05
85	Kevin Mitchell	.05
86	Mark McLemore	.05
87	Terry Steinbach	.05
88	Tom Browning	.05
89	Matt Nokes	.05
90	Mike Harkey	.05
91	Omar Vizquel	.05
92	Dave Bergman	.05
93	Matt Williams	.05
94	Steve Olin	.05
95	Craig Wilson	.05
96	Dave Stieb	.05
97	Ruben Sierra	.05
98	Jay Howell	.05
99	Scott Bradley	.05
100	Eric Yelding	.05
101	Rickey Henderson	.45
102	Jeff Reed	.05
103	Jimmy Key	.05
104	Terry Shumpert	.05
105	Kenny Rogers	.05
106	Cecil Fielder	.05
107	Robby Thompson	.05
108	Alex Cole	.05
109	Randy Milligan	.05
110	Andres Galarraga	.05
111	Bill Spiers	.05
112	Kal Daniels	.05
113	Henry Cotto	.05
114	Casy Candaele	.05
115	Jeff Blauser	.05
116	Robin Yount	.45
117	Ben McDonald	.05
118	Bret Saberhagen	.05
119	Juan Gonzalez	.35
120	Lou Whitaker	.05
121	Ellis Burks	.05
122	Charlie O'Brien	.05
123	John Smiley	.05
124	Tim Burke	.05
125	John Olerud	.05
126	Eddie Murray	.45
127	Greg Maddux	.60
128	Kevin Tapani	.05
129	Ron Gant	.05
130	Jay Bell	.05
131	Chris Hoiles	.05
132	Tom Gordon	.05
133	Kevin Seitzer	.05
134	Jeff Huson	.05
135	Jerry Don Gleaton	.05
136	Jeff Brantley	.05
137	Felix Fermin	.05
138	Mike Devereaux	.05
139	Delino DeShields	.05
140	David Wells	.05
141	Tim Crews	.05
142	Erik Hanson	.05
143	Mark Davidson	.05
144	Tommy Gregg	.05
145	Jim Gantner	.05
146	Jose Lind	.05
147	Danny Tartabull	.05
148	Geno Petralli	.05
149	Travis Fryman	.05
150	Tim Naehring	.05
151	Kevin McReynolds	.05
152	Joe Orsulak	.05
153	Steve Frey	.05
154	Duane Ward	.05
155	Stan Javier	.05
156	Damon Berryhill	.05
157	Gene Larkin	.05
158	Greg Olson	.05
159	Mark Knudson	.05
160	Carmelo Martinez	.05
161	Storm Davis	.05
162	Jim Abbott	.05
163	Len Dykstra	.05
164	Tom Brunansky	.05
165	Dwight Gooden	.05
166	Jose Mesa	.05
167	Oil Can Boyd	.05
168	Barry Larkin	.05
169	Scott Sanderson	.05
170	Mark Grace	.05
171	Mark Guthrie	.05
172	Tom Glavine	.15
173	Gary Sheffield	.30
174	Checklist (Roger Clemens)	.25
175	Chris James	.05
176	Milt Thompson	.05
177	Donnie Hill	.05

178	Wes Chamberlain	.05
179	John Marzano	.05
180	Frank Viola	.05
181	Eric Anthony	.05
182	Jose Canseco	.30
183	Scott Scudder	.05
184	Dave Eiland	.05
185	Luis Salazar	.05
186	Pedro Munoz	.05
187	Steve Searcy	.05
188	Don Robinson	.05
189	Sandy Alomar	.05
190	Jose DeLeon	.05
191	John Orton	.05
192	Darren Daulton	.05
193	Mike Morgan	.05
194	Greg Briley	.05
195	Karl Rhodes	.05
196	Harold Baines	.05
197	Bill Doran	.05
198	Alvaro Espinoza	.05
199	Kirk McCaskill	.05
200	Jose DeJesus	.05
201	Jack Clark	.05
202	Daryl Boston	.05
203	Randy Tomlin	.05
204	Pedro Guerrero	.05
205	Billy Hatcher	.05
206	Tim Leary	.05
207	Ryne Sandberg	.60
208	Kirby Puckett	.60
209	Charlie Leibrandt	.05
210	Rick Honeycutt	.05
211	Joel Skinner	.05
212	Rex Hudler	.05
213	Bryan Harvey	.05
214	Charlie Hayes	.05
215	Matt Young	.05
216	Terry Kennedy	.05
217	Carl Nichols	.05
218	Mike Moore	.05
219	Paul O'Neill	.05
220	Steve Sax	.05
221	Shawn Boskie	.05
222	Rich DeLucia	.05
223	Lloyd Moseby	.05
224	Mike Kingery	.05
225	Carlos Baerga	.05
226	Bryn Smith	.05
227	Todd Stottlemyre	.05
228	Julio Franco	.05
229	Jim Gott	.05
230	Mike Schooler	.05
231	Steve Finley	.05
232	Dave Henderson	.05
233	Luis Quinones	.05
234	Mark Whiten	.05
235	Brian McRae	.05
236	Rich Gossage	.05
237	Rob Deer	.05
238	Will Clark	.10
239	Albert Belle	.05
240	Bob Melvin	.05
241	Larry Walker	.05
242	Dante Bichette	.05
243	Orel Hershiser	.05
244	Pete O'Brien	.05
245	Pete Harnisch	.05
246	Jeff Treadway	.05
247	Julio Machado	.05
248	Dave Johnson	.05
249	Kirk Gibson	.05
250	Kevin Brown	.05
251	Milt Cuyler	.05
252	Jeff Reardon	.05
253	David Cone	.05
254	Gary Redus	.05
255	Junior Noboa	.05
256	Greg Myers	.05
257	Dennis Cook	.05
258	Joe Girardi	.05
259	Allan Anderson	.05
260	Paul Marak	.05
261	Barry Bonds	2.00
262	Juan Bell	.05
263	Russ Morman	.05
264	Checklist (George Brett)	.25
265	Jerald Clark	.05
266	Dwight Evans	.05
267	Roberto Alomar	.15
268	Danny Jackson	.05
269	Brian Downing	.05
270	John Cerutti	.05
271	Robin Ventura	.05
272	Gerald Perry	.05
273	Wade Boggs	.60
274	Dennis Martinez	.05
275	Andy Benes	.05
276	Tony Fossas	.05
277	Franklin Stubbs	.05
278	John Kruk	.05
279	Kevin Gross	.05
280	Von Hayes	.05
281	Frank Thomas	.45
282	Rob Dibble	.05
283	Mel Hall	.05
284	Rick Mahler	.05
285	Dennis Eckersley	.35
286	Bernard Gilkey	.05
287	Dan Plesac	.05
288	Jason Grimsley	.05
289	Mark Lewis	.05
290	Tony Gwynn	.60
291	Jeff Russell	.05
292	Curt Schilling	.25
293	Pascual Perez	.05
294	Jack Morris	.05
295	Hubie Brooks	.05

296	Alex Fernandez	.05
297	Harold Reynolds	.05
298	Craig Worthington	.05
299	Willie Wilson	.05
300	Mike Maddux	.05
301	Dave Righetti	.05
302	Paul Molitor	.45
303	Gary Gaetti	.05
304	Terry Pendleton	.05
305	Kevin Elster	.05
306	Scott Fletcher	.05
307	Jeff Robinson	.05
308	Jesse Barfield	.05
309	Mike LaCoss	.05
310	Andy Van Slyke	.05
311	Glenallen Hill	.05
312	Bud Black	.05
313	Kent Hrbek	.05
314	Tim Teufel	.05
315	Tony Fernandez	.05
316	Beau Allred	.05
317	Curtis Wilkerson	.05
318	Bill Sampen	.05
319	Randy Johnson	.45
320	Mike Heath	.05
321	Sammy Sosa	1.00
322	Mickey Tettleton	.05
323	Jose Vizcaino	.05
324	John Candelaria	.05
325	David Howard	.05
326	Jose Rijo	.05
327	Todd Zeile	.05
328	Gene Nelson	.05
329	Dwayne Henry	.05
330	Mike Boddicker	.05
331	Ozzie Guillen	.05
332	Sam Horn	.05
333	Wally Whitehurst	.05
334	Dave Parker	.05
335	George Brett	.75
336	Bobby Thigpen	.05
337	Ed Whitson	.05
338	Ivan Calderon	.05
339	Mike Pagliarulo	.05
340	Jack McDowell	.05
341	Dana Kiecker	.05
342	Fred McGriff	.05
343	Mark Lee	.05
344	Alfredo Griffin	.05
345	Scott Bankhead	.05
346	Darrin Jackson	.05
347	Rafael Palmeiro	.35
348	Steve Farr	.05
349	Hensley Meulens	.05
350	Danny Cox	.05
351	Alan Trammell	.05
352	Edwin Nunez	.05
353	Joe Carter	.05
354	Eric Show	.05
355	Vance Law	.05
356	Jeff Gray	.05
357	Bobby Bonilla	.05
358	Ernest Riles	.05
359	Ron Hassey	.05
360	Willie McGee	.05
361	Mackey Sasser	.05
362	Glenn Braggs	.05
363	Mario Diaz	.05
364	Checklist (Barry Bonds)	.35
365	Kevin Bass	.05
366	Pete Incaviglia	.05
367	Luis Sojo	.05
368	Lance Parrish	.05
369	Mark Leonard	.05
370	Heathcliff Slocumb	.05
371	Jimmy Jones	.05
372	Ken Griffey Jr.	1.00
373	Chris Hammond	.05
374	Chili Davis	.05
375	Joey Cora	.05
376	Ken Hill	.05
377	Darryl Strawberry	.05
378	Ron Darling	.05
379	Sid Bream	.05
380	Bill Swift	.05
381	Shawn Abner	.05
382	Eric King	.05
383	Mickey Morandini	.05
384	Carlton Fisk	.45
385	Steve Lake	.05
386	Mike Jeffcoat	.05
387	Darren Holmes	.05
388	Tim Wallach	.05
389	George Bell	.05
390	Craig Lefferts	.05
391	Ernie Whitt	.05
392	Felix Jose	.05
393	Kevin Maas	.05
394	Devon White	.05
395	Otis Nixon	.05
396	Chuck Knoblauch	.05
397	Scott Coolbaugh	.05
398	Glenn Davis	.05
399	Manny Lee	.05
400	Andre Dawson	.20
401	Scott Chiamparino	.05
402	Bill Gullickson	.05
403	Lance Johnson	.05
404	Juan Agosto	.05
405	Danny Darwin	.05
406	Barry Jones	.05
407	Larry Andersen	.05
408	Luis Rivera	.05
409	Jaime Navarro	.05
410	Roger McDowell	.05
411	Brett Butler	.05
412	Dale Murphy	.15
413	Tim Raines	.05

414	Norm Charlton	.05
415	Greg Cadaret	.05
416	Chris Nabholz	.05
417	Dave Stewart	.05
418	Rich Gedman	.05
419	Willie Randolph	.05
420	Mitch Williams	.05
421	Brook Jacoby	.05
422	Greg Harris	.05
423	Nolan Ryan	2.00
424	Dave Rohde	.05
425	Don Mattingly	.75
426	Greg Gagne	.05
427	Vince Coleman	.05
428	Dan Pasqua	.05
429	Alvin Davis	.05
430	Cal Ripken, Jr.	2.00
431	Jamie Quirk	.05
432	Benito Santiago	.05
433	Jose Uribe	.05
434	Candy Maldonado	.05
435	Junior Felix	.05
436	Deion Sanders	.05
437	John Franco	.05
438	Greg Hibbard	.05
439	Floyd Bannister	.05
440	Steve Howe	.05
441	Steve Decker	.05
442	Vicente Palacios	.05
443	Pat Tabler	.05
444	Checklist (Darryl Strawberry)	.05
445	Mike Felder	.05
446	Al Newman	.05
447	Chris Donnels	.05
448	Rich Rodriguez	.05
449	Turner Ward	.05
450	Bob Walk	.05
451	Gilberto Reyes	.05
452	Mike Jackson	.05
453	Rafael Belliard	.05
454	Wayne Edwards	.05
455	Andy Allanson	.05
456	Dave Smith	.05
457	Gary Carter	.45
458	Warren Cromartie	.05
459	Jack Armstrong	.05
460	Bob Tewksbury	.05
461	Joe Klink	.05
462	Xavier Hernandez	.05
463	Scott Radinsky	.05
464	Jeff Robinson	.05
465	Gregg Jefferies	.05
466	Denny Neagle	.05
467	Carmelo Martinez	.05
468	Donn Pall	.05
469	Bruce Hurst	.05
470	Eric Bullock	.05
471	Rick Aguilera	.05
472	Charlie Hough	.05
473	Carlos Quintana	.05
474	Marty Barrett	.05
475	Kevin Brown	.05
476	Bobby Ojeda	.05
477	Edgar Martinez	.05
478	Bip Roberts	.05
479	Mike Flanagan	.05
480	John Habyan	.05
481	Larry Casian	.05
482	Wally Backman	.05
483	Doug Dascenzo	.05
484	Rick Dempsey	.05
485	Ed Sprague	.05
486	Steve Chitren	.05
487	Mark McGwire	1.50
488	Roger Clemens	.75
489	Orlando Merced	.05
490	Rene Gonzales	.05
491	Mike Stanton	.05
492	Al Osuna	.05
493	Rick Cerone	.05
494	Mariano Duncan	.05
495	Zane Smith	.05
496	John Morris	.05
497	Frank Tanana	.05
498	Junior Ortiz	.05
499	Dave Winfield	.45
500	Gary Varsho	.05
501	Chico Walker	.05
502	Ken Caminiti	.05
503	Ken Griffey Sr.	.05
504	Randy Myers	.05
505	Steve Bedrosian	.05
506	Cory Snyder	.05
507	Cris Carpenter	.05
508	Tim Belcher	.05
509	Jeff Hamilton	.05
510	Steve Avery	.05
511	Dave Valle	.05
512	Tom Lampkin	.05
513	Shawn Hillegas	.05
514	Reggie Jefferson	.05
515	Ron Karkovice	.05
516	Doug Drabek	.05
517	Tom Henke	.05
518	Chris Bosio	.05
519	Gregg Olson	.05
520	Bob Scanlan	.05
521	Alonzo Powell	.05
522	Jeff Ballard	.05
523	Ray Lankford	.05
524	Tommy Greene	.05
525	Mike Timlin	.05
526	Juan Berenguer	.05
527	Scott Erickson	.05
528	Checklist (Sandy Alomar Jr.)	.05

Gold Rookies

MO VAUGHN 1B

Special gold rookie and gold bonus cards were randomly inserted in 1991 Leaf packs. Backs have a design similar to the regular-issue cards, but have gold, rather than silver background. Fronts have gold-foil highlights. Card numbers of the issued version have a "BC" prefix, but there is a much rarer second version of the Series 1 cards, which carry card numbers between 265-276.

		NM/M
Complete Set (26):		10.00
Common Player:		.10
1	Scott Leius	.10
2	Luis Gonzalez	.40
3	Wil Cordero	.10
4	Gary Scott	.10
5	Willie Banks	.10
6	Arthur Rhodes	.10
7	Mo Vaughn	.25
8	Henry Rodriguez	.10
9	Todd Van Poppel	.10
10	Reggie Sanders	.10
11	Rico Brogna	.10
12	Mike Mussina	2.00
13	Kirk Dressendorfer	.10
14	Jeff Bagwell	6.00
15	Pete Schourek	.10
16	Wade Taylor	.10
17	Pat Kelly	.10
18	Tim Costo	.10
19	Roger Salkeld	.10
20	Andujar Cedeno	.10
21	Ryan Klesko	.10
22	Mike Huff	.10
23	Anthony Young	.10
24	Eddie Zosky	.10
25	Nolan Ryan (7th no-hitter)	.50
26	Rickey Henderson (Record Steal)	.25
	Plooey (Babe Ruth)	.01
265	Scott Leius	4.00
266	Luis Gonzalez	6.00
267	Wil Cordero	4.00
268	Gary Scott	4.00
269	Willie Banks	4.00
270	Arthur Rhodes	4.00
271	Mo Vaughn	10.00
272	Henry Rodriguez	4.00
273	Todd Van Poppel	4.00
274	Reggie Sanders	4.00
275	Rico Brogna	4.00
276	Mike Mussina	30.00

1992 Leaf Previews

FRED McGRIFF 1B PADRES

In a format identical to the regular-issue 1992 Leaf cards, this 26-card preview set was issued as a bonus in packs of four cards in each 1992 Donruss hobby factory set.

		NM/M
Complete Set (26):		15.00
Common Player:		.25
1	Steve Avery	.25
2	Ryne Sandberg	1.00
3	Chris Sabo	.25
4	Jeff Bagwell	.75
5	Darryl Strawberry	.25
6	Bret Barberie	.25
7	Howard Johnson	.25
8	John Kruk	.25
9	Andy Van Slyke	.25
10	Felix Jose	.25
11	Fred McGriff	.25
12	Will Clark	.35
13	Cal Ripken, Jr.	3.00
14	Phil Plantier	.25
15	Lee Stevens	.25
16	Frank Thomas	.75
17	Mark Whiten	.25
18	Cecil Fielder	.25
19	George Brett	1.50
20	Robin Yount	.75
21	Scott Erickson	.25
22	Don Mattingly	1.50
23	Jose Canseco	.50
24	Ken Griffey Jr.	2.00
25	Nolan Ryan	3.00
26	Joe Carter	.25

1992 Leaf

TRAVIS FRYMAN 3B

Two 264-card series comprise this 528-card set. The cards feature action photos on both the front and the back. Silver borders surround the photo on the card front. Each leaf card was also produced in a gold foil version. One gold card was issued per pack and a complete Leaf Gold Edition set can be assembled. Traded players and free agents are shown in uniform with their new teams.

		NM/M
Complete Set (528):		7.50
Common Player:		.05
Series 1 or 2 Pack:		.40
Series 1 or 2 Wax Box:		7.50
1	Jim Abbott	.05
2	Cal Eldred	.05
3	Bud Black	.05
4	Dave Howard	.05
5	Luis Sojo	.05
6	Gary Scott	.05
7	Joe Oliver	.05
8	Chris Gardner	.05
9	Sandy Alomar	.05
10	Greg Harris	.05
11	Doug Drabek	.05
12	Darryl Hamilton	.05
13	Mike Mussina	.30
14	Kevin Tapani	.05
15	Ron Gant	.05
16	Mark McGwire	1.00
17	Robin Ventura	.05
18	Pedro Guerrero	.05
19	Roger Clemens	.65
20	Steve Farr	.05
21	Frank Tanana	.05
22	Joe Hesketh	.05
23	Erik Hanson	.05
24	Greg Cadaret	.05
25	Rex Hudler	.05
26	Mark Grace	.05
27	Kelly Gruber	.05
28	Jeff Bagwell	.45
29	Darryl Strawberry	.05
30	Dave Smith	.05
31	Kevin Appier	.05
32	Steve Chitren	.05
33	Kevin Gross	.05
34	Rick Aguilera	.05
35	Juan Guzman	.05
36	Joe Orsulak	.05
37	Tim Raines	.05
38	Harold Reynolds	.05
39	Charlie Hough	.05
40	Tony Phillips	.05
41	Nolan Ryan	1.50
42	Vince Coleman	.05
43	Andy Van Slyke	.05
44	Tim Burke	.05
45	Luis Polonia	.05
46	Tom Browning	.05
47	Willie McGee	.05
48	Gary DiSarcina	.05
49	Mark Lewis	.05
50	Phil Plantier	.05
51	Doug Dascenzo	.05
52	Cal Ripken, Jr.	1.50
53	Pedro Munoz	.05
54	Carlos Hernandez	.05
55	Jerald Clark	.05
56	Jeff Brantley	.05
57	Don Mattingly	.65
58	Roger McDowell	.05
59	Steve Avery	.05
60	John Olerud	.05
61	Bill Gullickson	.05
62	Juan Gonzalez	.30
63	Felix Jose	.05
64	Robin Yount	.45
65	Greg Briley	.05
66	Steve Finley	.05
67	Checklist	.05
68	Tom Gordon	.05
69	Rob Dibble	.05
70	Glenallen Hill	.05
71	Calvin Jones	.05
72	Joe Girardi	.05
73	Barry Larkin	.05
74	Andy Benes	.05
75	Milt Cuyler	.05
76	Kevin Bass	.05
77	Pete Harnisch	.05
78	Wilson Alvarez	.05
79	Mike Devereaux	.05
80	Doug Henry	.05
81	Orel Hershiser	.05
82	Shane Mack	.05
83	Mike Macfarlane	.05
84	Thomas Howard	.05
85	Alex Fernandez	.05
86	Reggie Jefferson	.05
87	Leo Gomez	.05
88	Mel Hall	.05
89	Mike Greenwell	.05
90	Jeff Russell	.05
91	Steve Buechele	.05
92	David Cone	.05
93	Kevin Reimer	.05
94	Mark Lemke	.05
95	Bob Tewksbury	.05
96	Zane Smith	.05
97	Mark Eichhorn	.05
98	Kirby Puckett	.60
99	Paul O'Neill	.05
100	Dennis Eckersley	.35
101	Duane Ward	.05
102	Matt Nokes	.05
103	Mo Vaughn	.05
104	Pat Kelly	.05
105	Ron Karkovice	.05
106	Bill Spiers	.05
107	Gary Gaetti	.05
108	Mackey Sasser	.05
109	Robby Thompson	.05
110	Marvin Freeman	.05
111	Jimmy Key	.05
112	Dwight Gooden	.05
113	Charlie Leibrandt	.05
114	Devon White	.05
115	Charles Nagy	.05
116	Rickey Henderson	.45
117	Paul Assenmacher	.05
118	Junior Felix	.05
119	Julio Franco	.05
120	Norm Charlton	.05
121	Scott Servais	.05
122	Gerald Perry	.05
123	Brian McRae	.05
124	Don Slaught	.05
125	Juan Samuel	.05
126	Harold Baines	.05
127	Scott Livingstone	.05
128	Jay Buhner	.05
129	Darrin Jackson	.05
130	Luis Mercedes	.05
131	Brian Harper	.05
132	Howard Johnson	.05
133	Checklist	.05
134	Dante Bichette	.05
135	Dave Righetti	.05
136	Jeff Montgomery	.05
137	Joe Grahe	.05
138	Delino DeShields	.05
139	Jose Rijo	.05
140	Ken Caminiti	.05
141	Steve Olin	.05
142	Kurt Stillwell	.05
143	Jay Bell	.05
144	Jaime Navarro	.05
145	Ben McDonald	.05
146	Greg Gagne	.05
147	Jeff Blauser	.05
148	Carney Lansford	.05
149	Ozzie Guillen	.05
150	Milt Thompson	.05
151	Jeff Reardon	.05
152	Scott Sanderson	.05
153	Cecil Fielder	.05
154	Greg Harris	.05
155	Rich DeLucia	.05
156	Roberto Kelly	.05
157	Bryn Smith	.05
158	Chuck McElroy	.05
159	Tom Henke	.05
160	Luis Gonzalez	.25
161	Steve Wilson	.05
162	Shawn Boskie	.05
163	Mark Davis	.05
164	Mike Moore	.05
165	Mike Scioscia	.05
166	Scott Erickson	.05
167	Todd Stottlemyre	.05
168	Alvin Davis	.05
169	Greg Hibbard	.05
170	David Valle	.05
171	Dave Winfield	.45
172	Alan Trammell	.05
173	Kenny Rogers	.05
174	John Franco	.05
175	Jose Lind	.05
176	Pete Schourek	.05
177	Von Hayes	.05
178	Chris Hammond	.05
179	John Burkett	.05
180	Dickie Thon	.05
181	Joel Skinner	.05
182	Scott Cooper	.05
183	Andre Dawson	.25
184	Billy Ripken	.05
185	Kevin Mitchell	.05
186	Brett Butler	.05
187	Tony Fernandez	.05
188	Cory Snyder	.05
189	John Habyan	.05
190	Dennis Martinez	.05
191	John Smoltz	.05
192	Greg Myers	.05
193	Rob Deer	.05
194	Ivan Rodriguez	.45
195	Ray Lankford	.05
196	Bill Wegman	.05
197	Edgar Martinez	.05
198	Darryl Kile	.05
199	Checklist	.05
200	Brent Mayne	.05
201	Larry Walker	.05
202	Carlos Baerga	.05
203	Russ Swan	.05
204	Mike Morgan	.05
205	Hal Morris	.05
206	Tony Gwynn	.60
207	Mark Leiter	.05
208	Kirt Manwaring	.05
209	Al Osuna	.05
210	Bobby Thigpen	.05
211	Chris Hoiles	.05
212	B.J. Surhoff	.05
213	Lenny Harris	.05
214	Scott Leius	.05
215	Gregg Jefferies	.05
216	Bruce Hurst	.05
217	Steve Sax	.05
218	Dave Otto	.05
219	Sam Horn	.05
220	Charlie Hayes	.05
221	Frank Viola	.05
222	Jose Guzman	.05
223	Gary Redus	.05
224	Dave Gallagher	.05
225	Dean Palmer	.05
226	Greg Olson	.05
227	Jose DeLeon	.05
228	Mike LaValliere	.05
229	Mark Langston	.05
230	Chuck Knoblauch	.05
231	Bill Doran	.05
232	Dave Henderson	.05
233	Roberto Alomar	.20
234	Scott Fletcher	.05
235	Tim Naehring	.05
236	Mike Gallego	.05
237	Lance Johnson	.05
238	Paul Molitor	.45
239	Dan Gladden	.05
240	Willie Randolph	.05
241	Will Clark	.10
242	Sid Bream	.05
243	Derek Bell	.05
244	Bill Pecota	.05
245	Terry Pendleton	.05
246	Randy Ready	.05
247	Jack Armstrong	.05
248	Todd Van Poppel	.05
249	Shawon Dunston	.05
250	Bobby Rose	.05
251	Jeff Huson	.05
252	Bip Roberts	.05
253	Doug Jones	.05
254	Lee Smith	.05
255	George Brett	.65
256	Randy Tomlin	.05
257	Todd Benzinger	.05
258	Dave Stewart	.05
259	Mark Carreon	.05
260	Pete O'Brien	.05
261	Tim Teufel	.05
262	Bob Milacki	.05
263	Mark Guthrie	.05
264	Darrin Fletcher	.05
265	Omar Vizquel	.05
266	Chris Bosio	.05
267	Jose Canseco	.30
268	Mike Boddicker	.05
269	Lance Parrish	.05
270	Jose Vizcaino	.05
271	Chris Sabo	.05
272	Royce Clayton	.05
273	Marquis Grissom	.05
274	Fred McGriff	.05
275	Barry Bonds	1.50
276	Greg Vaughn	.05
277	Gregg Olson	.05
278	Dave Hollins	.05
279	Tom Glavine	.25
280	Bryan Hickerson	.05
281	Scott Radinsky	.05
282	Omar Olivares	.05
283	Ivan Calderon	.05
284	Kevin Maas	.05
285	Mickey Tettleton	.05
286	Wade Boggs	.60
287	Stan Belinda	.05
288	Jose Oquendo	.05
289	Frank Castillo	.05
290	Dave Stieb	.05
291	Dave Smith	.05
292	Tommy Greene	.05
293	Eric Karros	.05
294	Greg Maddux	.60
295	Jim Eisenreich	.05
296	Rafael Palmeiro	.35
297	Ramon Martinez	.05
298	Tim Wallach	.05
299	Jim Thome	.45
300	Chito Martinez	.05
301	Mitch Williams	.05
302	Randy Johnson	.45
303	Carlton Fisk	.45
304	Travis Fryman	.05
305	Bobby Witt	.05
306	Dave Magadan	.05
307	Alex Cole	.05
308	Bobby Bonilla	.05
309	Bryan Harvey	.05
310	Rafael Belliard	.05
311	Mariano Duncan	.05
312	Chuck Crim	.05
313	John Kruk	.05
314	Ellis Burks	.05
315	Craig Biggio	.05
316	Glenn Davis	.05
317	Ryne Sandberg	.60
318	Mike Sharperson	.05
319	Rich Rodriguez	.05
320	Lee Guetterman	.05
321	Benito Santiago	.05
322	Jose Offerman	.05
323	Tony Pena	.05
324	Pat Borders	.05
325	Mike Henneman	.05
326	Kevin Brown	.05
327	Chris Nabholz	.05
328	Franklin Stubbs	.05
329	Tino Martinez	.05
330	Mickey Morandini	.05
331	Checklist	.05
332	Mark Gubicza	.05
333	Bill Landrum	.05
334	Mark Whiten	.05
335	Darren Daulton	.05
336	Rick Wilkins	.05
337	Brian Jordan RC	.25
338	Kevin Ward	.05
339	Ruben Amaro	.05
340	Trevor Wilson	.05
341	Andujar Cedeno	.05
342	Michael Huff	.05
343	Brady Anderson	.05
344	Craig Grebeck	.05
345	Bobby Ojeda	.05
346	Mike Pagliarulo	.05
347	Terry Shumpert	.05
348	Dann Bilardello	.05
349	Frank Thomas	.45
350	Albert Belle	.05
351	Jose Mesa	.05
352	Rich Monteleone	.05
353	Bob Walk	.05
354	Monty Fariss	.05
355	Luis Rivera	.05
356	Anthony Young	.05
357	Geno Petralli	.05
358	Otis Nixon	.05
359	Tom Pagnozzi	.05
360	Reggie Sanders	.05
361	Lee Stevens	.05
362	Kent Hrbek	.05
363	Orlando Merced	.05
364	Mike Bordick	.05
365	Dion James	.05
366	Jack Clark	.05
367	Mike Stanley	.05
368	Randy Velarde	.05
369	Dan Pasqua	.05
370	Pat Listach	.05
371	Mike Fitzgerald	.05
372	Tom Foley	.05
373	Matt Williams	.05
374	Brian Hunter	.05
375	Joe Carter	.05
376	Bret Saberhagen	.05
377	Mike Stanton	.05
378	Hubie Brooks	.05
379	Eric Bell	.05
380	Walt Weiss	.05
381	Danny Jackson	.05
382	Manuel Lee	.05
383	Ruben Sierra	.05
384	Greg Swindell	.05
385	Ryan Bowen	.05
386	Kevin Ritz	.05
387	Curtis Wilkerson	.05
388	Gary Varsho	.05
389	Dave Hansen	.05
390	Bob Welch	.05
391	Lou Whitaker	.05
392	Ken Griffey Jr.	.75
393	Mike Maddux	.05
394	Arthur Rhodes	.05
395	Chili Davis	.05
396	Eddie Murray	.45
397	Checklist	.05
398	Dave Cochrane	.05
399	Kevin Seitzer	.05
400	Ozzie Smith	.60
401	Paul Sorrento	.05
402	Les Lancaster	.05
403	Junior Noboa	.05
404	Dave Justice	.05
405	Andy Ashby	.05
406	Danny Tartabull	.05
407	Bill Swift	.05
408	Craig Lefferts	.05
409	Tom Candiotti	.05
410	Lance Blankenship	.05
411	Jeff Tackett	.05
412	Sammy Sosa	.65
413	Jody Reed	.05
414	Bruce Ruffin	.05
415	Gene Larkin	.05
416	John Vanderwal	.05
417	Tim Belcher	.05
418	Steve Frey	.05
419	Dick Schofield	.05
420	Jeff King	.05
421	Kim Batiste	.05
422	Jack McDowell	.05
423	Damon Berryhill	.05
424	Gary Wayne	.05
425	Jack Morris	.05
426	Moises Alou	.05
427	Mark McLemore	.05
428	Juan Guerrero	.05
429	Scott Scudder	.05
430	Eric Davis	.05
431	Joe Slusarski	.05
432	Todd Zeile	.05
433	Dwayne Henry	.05
434	Cliff Brantley	.05
435	Butch Henry	.05
436	Todd Worrell	.05
437	Bob Scanlan	.05
438	Wally Joyner	.05
439	John Flaherty	.05
440	Brian Downing	.05
441	Darren Lewis	.05
442	Gary Carter	.45
443	Wally Ritchie	.05
444	Chris Jones	.05
445	Jeff Kent	.05
446	Gary Sheffield	.30
447	Ron Darling	.05
448	Deion Sanders	.05
449	Andres Galarraga	.05
450	Chuck Finley	.05
451	Derek Lilliquist	.05
452	Carl Willis	.05
453	Wes Chamberlain	.05
454	Roger Mason	.05
455	Spike Owen	.05
456	Thomas Howard	.05
457	Dave Martinez	.05
458	Pete Incaviglia	.05
459	Keith Miller	.05
460	Mike Fetters	.05
461	Paul Gibson	.05
462	George Bell	.05
463	Checklist	.05
464	Terry Mulholland	.05
465	Storm Davis	.05
466	Gary Pettis	.05
467	Randy Bush	.05
468	Ken Hill	.05
469	Rheal Cormier	.05
470	Andy Stankiewicz	.05
471	Dave Burba	.05
472	Henry Cotto	.05
473	Dale Sveum	.05
474	Rich Gossage	.05
475	William Suero	.05
476	Doug Strange	.05
477	Bill Krueger	.05
478	John Wetteland	.05
479	Melido Perez	.05
480	Lonnie Smith	.05
481	Mike Jackson	.05
482	Mike Gardiner	.05
483	David Wells	.05
484	Barry Jones	.05
485	Scott Bankhead	.05
486	Terry Leach	.05
487	Vince Horsman	.05
488	Dave Eiland	.05
489	Alejandro Pena	.05
490	Julio Valera	.05
491	Joe Boever	.05
492	Paul Miller	.05
493	Arci Cianfrocco RC	.05
494	Dave Fleming	.05
495	Kyle Abbott	.05
496	Chad Kreuter	.05
497	Chris James	.05
498	Donnie Hill	.05
499	Jacob Brumfield	.05
500	Ricky Bones	.05
501	Terry Steinbach	.05
502	Bernard Gilkey	.05
503	Dennis Cook	.05
504	Len Dykstra	.05
505	Mike Bielecki	.05
506	Bob Kipper	.05
507	Jose Melendez	.05
508	Rick Sutcliffe	.05
509	Ken Patterson	.05
510	Andy Allanson	.05
511	Al Newman	.05
512	Mark Gardner	.05
513	Jeff Schaefer	.05
514	Jim McNamara	.05
515	Peter Hoy	.05
516	Curt Schilling	.30
517	Kirk McCaskill	.05
518	Chris Gwynn	.05
519	Sid Fernandez	.05
520	Jeff Parrett	.05
521	Scott Ruskin	.05
522	Kevin McReynolds	.05
523	Rick Cerone	.05
524	Jesse Orosco	.05
525	Troy Afenir	.05
526	John Smiley	.05
527	Dale Murphy	.25
528	Leaf Set Card	.05

Gold Previews

In the same format as the chase cards which would be included in the regular 1992 Leaf packs, this preview set was produced for distribution to the Donruss dealer network. Cards feature the same black borders and gold highlights as the regular-issue Leaf Gold cards, but are numbered "X of 33" on the back.

		NM/M
Complete Set (33):		30.00
Common Player:		.50
1	Steve Avery	.50
2	Ryne Sandberg	2.00
3	Chris Sabo	.50
4	Jeff Bagwell	1.50
5	Darryl Strawberry	.50
6	Bret Barbarie	.50
7	Howard Johnson	.50
8	John Kruk	.50
9	Andy Van Slyke	.50
10	Felix Jose	.50
11	Fred McGriff	.50
12	Will Clark	.60
13	Cal Ripken, Jr.	4.00
14	Phil Plantier	.50
15	Lee Stevens	.50
16	Frank Thomas	1.50
17	Mark Whiten	.50
18	Cecil Fielder	.50
19	George Brett	2.50
20	Robin Yount	1.50
21	Scott Erickson	.50
22	Don Mattingly	2.50
23	Jose Canseco	1.00
24	Ken Griffey Jr.	3.00
25	Nolan Ryan	4.00
26	Joe Carter	.50
27	Deion Sanders	.50
28	Dean Palmer	.50
29	Andy Benes	.50
30	Gary DiSarcina	.50
31	Chris Hoiles	.50
32	Mark McGwire	3.00
33	Reggie Sanders	.50

Gold Edition

This set is a parallel version of Leaf's regular 1992 set. Card fronts do not have silver borders like the regular cards do; black borders and gold foil highlights are seen instead. A Gold Edition card was inserted in each 15-card 1992 Leaf foil pack.

	NM/M
Complete Set (528):	35.00
Common Player:	.10
Stars/Rookies:	3X

Gold Rookies

Two dozen of the major leagues' most promising players are featured in this insert set. Cards 1-12 were randomly included in Series 1 foil packs, while cards 13-24 were in Series 2 packs. Cards, numbered with a BC prefix, are standard size and enhanced with gold foil.

	NM/M
Complete Set (24):	4.00
Common Player:	.25

PAT MAHOMES RHP

Jumbo:		1.5X
1	Chad Curtis	.25
2	Brent Gates	.25
3	Pedro Martinez	3.00
4	Kenny Lofton	.35
5	Turk Wendell	.25
6	Mark Hutton	.25
7	Todd Hundley	.25
8	Matt Stairs	.25
9	Ed Taubensee	.25
10	David Nied	.25
11	Salomon Torres	.25
12	Bret Boone	.50
13	John Ruffin	.25
14	Ed Martel	.25
15	Rick Trlicek	.25
16	Raul Mondesi	.25
17	Pat Mahomes	.25
18	Dan Wilson	.25
19	Donovan Osborne	.25
20	Dave Silvestri	.25
21	Gary DiSarcina	.25
22	Denny Neagle	.25
23	Steve Hosey	.25
24	John Doherty	.25

1993 Leaf Promo

This unmarked promo of company spokesman Frank Thomas can be distinguished from the issued version of his card #195 by the presence of the Franklin logo on the batting glove he wears. The logo was airbrushed away from the issued card.

		NM/M
195	Frank Thomas	10.00

1993 Leaf

JUAN GONZALEZ RANGERS

Leaf issued this set in three series: two 220-card series and a 110-card update set. Card fronts have full-bleed action photos and players' names stamped in gold foil. Color-coded slate corners are used to differentiate teams. Backs have player photos against city-scapes or landmarks from the team's home city, a holographic embossed team logo and 1992 and career statistics. Players from the National League's expansion teams, the Colorado Rockies and Florida Marlins, along with the Cincinnati Reds, California Angels and Seattle Mariners were featured in Series II packs so they could be pictured in their new uniforms. The Update series included a specially numbered "DW" insert card honoring Dave Winfield's 3,000-hit landmark, plus 3,500 special Frank Thomas autographed cards.

	NM/M
Complete Set (550):	12.50
Common Player:	.05
Series 1 or 2 Pack (14):	.65
Series 1 or 2 Box (36):	12.50
Update Pack (14):	1.50
Update Box (36):	25.00
1	Ben McDonald	.05
2	Sid Fernandez	.05
3	Juan Guzman	.05

4	Curt Schilling	.40
5	Ivan Rodriguez	.65
6	Don Slaught	.05
7	Terry Steinbach	.05
8	Todd Zeile	.05
9	Andy Stankiewicz	.05
10	Tim Teufel	.05
11	Marvin Freeman	.05
12	Jim Austin	.05
13	Bob Scanlan	.05
14	Rusty Meacham	.05
15	Casey Candaele	.05
16	Travis Fryman	.05
17	Jose Offerman	.05
18	Albert Belle	.05
19	John Vander Wahl (Vander Wal)	.05
20	Dan Pasqua	.05
21	Frank Viola	.05
22	Terry Mulholland	.05
23	Gregg Olson	.05
24	Randy Tomlin	.05
25	Todd Stottlemyre	.05
26	Jose Oquendo	.05
27	Julio Franco	.05
28	Tony Gwynn	1.00
29	Ruben Sierra	.05
30	Robby Thompson	.05
31	Jim Bullinger	.05
32	Rick Aguilera	.05
33	Scott Servais	.05
34	Cal Eldred	.05
35	Mike Piazza	1.50
36	Brent Mayne	.05
37	Wil Cordero	.05
38	Milt Cuyler	.05
39	Howard Johnson	.05
40	Kenny Lofton	.05
41	Alex Fernandez	.05
42	Denny Neagle	.05
43	Tony Pena	.05
44	Bob Tewksbury	.05
45	Glenn Davis	.05
46	Fred McGriff	.05
47	John Olerud	.05
48	Steve Hosey	.05
49	Rafael Palmeiro	.65
50	Dave Justice	.05
51	Pete Harnisch	.05
52	Sam Militello	.05
53	Orel Hershiser	.05
54	Pat Mahomes	.05
55	Greg Colbrunn	.05
56	Greg Vaughn	.05
57	Vince Coleman	.05
58	Brian McRae	.05
59	Len Dykstra	.05
60	Dan Gladden	.05
61	Ted Power	.05
62	Donovan Osborne	.05
63	Ron Karkovice	.05
64	Frank Seminara	.05
65	Bob Zupcic	.05
66	Kirt Manwaring	.05
67	Mike Devereaux	.05
68	Mark Lemke	.05
69	Devon White	.05
70	Sammy Sosa	1.25
71	Pedro Astacio	.05
72	Dennis Eckersley	.60
73	Chris Nabholz	.05
74	Melido Perez	.05
75	Todd Hundley	.05
76	Kent Hrbek	.05
77	Mickey Morandini	.05
78	Tim McIntosh	.05
79	Andy Van Slyke	.05
80	Kevin McReynolds	.05
81	Mike Henneman	.05
82	Greg Harris	.05
83	Sandy Alomar Jr.	.05
84	Mike Jackson	.05
85	Ozzie Guillen	.05
86	Jeff Blauser	.05
87	John Valentin	.05
88	Rey Sanchez	.05
89	Rick Sutcliffe	.05
90	Luis Gonzalez	.25
91	Jeff Fassero	.05
92	Kenny Rogers	.05
93	Bret Saberhagen	.05
94	Bob Welch	.05
95	Darren Daulton	.05
96	Mike Gallego	.05
97	Orlando Merced	.05
98	Chuck Knoblauch	.05
99	Bernard Gilkey	.05
100	Billy Ashley	.05
101	Kevin Appier	.05
102	Jeff Brantley	.05
103	Bill Gullickson	.05
104	John Smoltz	.05
105	Paul Sorrento	.05
106	Steve Buechele	.05
107	Steve Sax	.05
108	Andujar Cedeno	.05
109	Billy Hatcher	.05
110	Checklist	.05
111	Alan Mills	.05
112	John Franco	.05
113	Jack Morris	.05
114	Mitch Williams	.05
115	Nolan Ryan	2.50
116	Jay Bell	.05
117	Mike Bordick	.05
118	Geronimo Pena	.05
119	Danny Tartabull	.05
120	Checklist	.05

121	Steve Avery	.05
122	Ricky Bones	.05
123	Mike Morgan	.05
124	Jeff Montgomery	.05
125	Jeff Bagwell	.75
126	Tony Phillips	.05
127	Lenny Harris	.05
128	Glenallen Hill	.05
129	Marquis Grissom	.05
130	Gerald Williams (Photo, stats actually Bernie Williams.)	.20
131	Greg Harris	.05
132	Tommy Greene	.05
133	Chris Hoiles	.05
134	Bob Walk	.05
135	Duane Ward	.05
136	Tom Pagnozzi	.05
137	Jeff Huson	.05
138	Kurt Stillwell	.05
139	Dave Henderson	.05
140	Darrin Jackson	.05
141	Frank Castillo	.05
142	Scott Erickson	.05
143	Darryl Kile	.05
144	Bill Wegman	.05
145	Steve Wilson	.05
146	George Brett	1.25
147	Moises Alou	.05
148	Lou Whitaker	.05
149	Chico Walker	.05
150	Jerry Browne	.05
151	Kirk McCaskill	.05
152	Zane Smith	.05
153	Matt Young	.05
154	Lee Smith	.05
155	Leo Gomez	.05
156	Dan Walters	.05
157	Pat Borders	.05
158	Matt Williams	.05
159	Dean Palmer	.05
160	John Patterson	.05
161	Doug Jones	.05
162	John Habyan	.05
163	Pedro Martinez	.75
164	Carl Willis	.05
165	Darrin Fletcher	.05
166	B.J. Surhoff	.05
167	Eddie Murray	.75
168	Keith Miller	.05
169	Ricky Jordan	.05
170	Juan Gonzalez	.65
171	Charles Nagy	.05
172	Mark Clark	.05
173	Bobby Thigpen	.05
174	Tim Scott	.05
175	Scott Cooper	.05
176	Royce Clayton	.05
177	Brady Anderson	.05
178	Sid Bream	.05
179	Derek Bell	.05
180	Otis Nixon	.05
181	Kevin Gross	.05
182	Ron Darling	.05
183	John Wetteland	.05
184	Mike Stanley	.05
185	Jeff Kent	.05
186	Brian Harper	.05
187	Mariano Duncan	.05
188	Robin Yount	.75
189	Al Martin	.05
190	Eddie Zosky	.05
191	Mike Munoz	.05
192	Andy Benes	.05
193	Dennis Cook	.05
194	Bill Swift	.05
195	Frank Thomas	.75
196	Damon Berryhill	.05
197	Mike Greenwell	.05
198	Mark Grace	.05
199	Darryl Hamilton	.05
200	Derrick May	.05
201	Ken Hill	.05
202	Kevin Brown	.05
203	Dwight Gooden	.05
204	Bobby Witt	.05
205	Juan Bell	.05
206	Kevin Maas	.05
207	Jeff King	.05
208	Scott Leius	.05
209	Rheal Cormier	.05
210	Darryl Strawberry	.05
211	Tom Gordon	.05
212	Bud Black	.05
213	Mickey Tettleton	.05
214	Pete Smith	.05
215	Felix Fermin	.05
216	Rick Wilkins	.05
217	George Bell	.05
218	Eric Anthony	.05
219	Pedro Munoz	.05
220	Checklist	.05
221	Lance Blankenship	.05
222	Deion Sanders	.10
223	Craig Biggio	.05
224	Ryne Sandberg	1.00
225	Ron Gant	.05
226	Tom Brunansky	.05
227	Chad Curtis	.05
228	Joe Carter	.05
229	Brian Jordan	.05
230	Brett Butler	.05
231	Frank Bolick	.05
232	Rod Beck	.05
233	Carlos Baerga	.05
234	Eric Karros	.05
235	Jack Armstrong	.05
236	Bobby Bonilla	.05
237	Don Mattingly	1.25

238	Jeff Gardner	.05
239	Dave Hollins	.05
240	Steve Cooke	.05
241	Jose Canseco	.35
242	Ivan Calderon	.05
243	Tim Belcher	.05
244	Freddie Benavides	.05
245	Roberto Alomar	.25
246	Rob Deer	.05
247	Will Clark	.10
248	Mike Felder	.05
249	Harold Baines	.05
250	David Cone	.05
251	Mark Guthrie	.05
252	Ellis Burks	.05
253	Jim Abbott	.05
254	Chili Davis	.05
255	Chris Bosio	.05
256	Bret Barberie	.05
257	Hal Morris	.05
258	Dante Bichette	.05
259	Storm Davis	.05
260	Gary DiSarcina	.05
261	Ken Caminiti	.05
262	Paul Molitor	.75
263	Joe Oliver	.05
264	Pat Listach	.05
265	Gregg Jefferies	.05
266	Jose Guzman	.05
267	Eric Davis	.05
268	Delino DeShields	.05
269	Barry Bonds	2.50
270	Mike Bielecki	.05
271	Jay Buhner	.05
272	Scott Pose RC	.05
273	Tony Fernandez	.05
274	Chito Martinez	.05
275	Phil Plantier	.05
276	Pete Incaviglia	.05
277	Carlos Garcia	.05
278	Tom Henke	.05
279	Roger Clemens	1.25
280	Rob Dibble	.05
281	Daryl Boston	.05
282	Greg Gagne	.05
283	Cecil Fielder	.05
284	Carlton Fisk	.75
285	Wade Boggs	1.00
286	Damion Easley	.05
287	Norm Charlton	.05
288	Jeff Conine	.05
289	Roberto Kelly	.05
290	Jerald Clark	.05
291	Rickey Henderson	.75
292	Chuck Finley	.05
293	Doug Drabek	.05
294	Dave Stewart	.05
295	Tom Glavine	.35
296	Jaime Navarro	.05
297	Ray Lankford	.05
298	Greg Hibbard	.05
299	Jody Reed	.05
300	Dennis Martinez	.05
301	Dave Martinez	.05
302	Reggie Jefferson	.05
303	John Cummings RC	.05
304	Orestes Destrade	.05
305	Mike Maddux	.05
306	David Segui	.05
307	Gary Sheffield	.35
308	Danny Jackson	.05
309	Craig Lefferts	.05
310	Andre Dawson	.20
311	Barry Larkin	.05
312	Alex Cole	.05
313	Mark Gardner	.05
314	Kirk Gibson	.05
315	Shane Mack	.05
316	Bo Jackson	.10
317	Jimmy Key	.05
318	Greg Myers	.05
319	Ken Griffey Jr.	1.50
320	Monty Fariss	.05
321	Kevin Mitchell	.05
322	Andres Galarraga	.05
323	Mark McGwire	2.00
324	Mark Langston	.05
325	Steve Finley	.05
326	Greg Maddux	1.00
327	Dave Nilsson	.05
328	Ozzie Smith	1.00
329	Candy Maldonado	.05
330	Checklist	.05
331	Tim Pugh RC	.05
332	Joe Girardi	.05
333	Junior Feliz	.05
334	Greg Swindell	.05
335	Ramon Martinez	.05
336	Sean Berry	.05
337	Joe Orsulak	.05
338	Wes Chamberlain	.05
339	Stan Belinda	.05
340	Checklist	.05
341	Bruce Hurst	.05
342	John Burkett	.05
343	Mike Mussina	.40
344	Scott Fletcher	.05
345	Rene Gonzales	.05
346	Roberto Hernandez	.05
347	Carlos Martinez	.05
348	Bill Krueger	.05
349	Felix Jose	.05
350	John Jaha	.05
351	Willie Banks	.05
352	Matt Nokes	.05
353	Kevin Seitzer	.05
354	Erik Hanson	.05
355	David Hulse RC	.05

356	Domingo Martinez RC	.05
357	Greg Olson	.05
358	Randy Myers	.05
359	Tom Browning	.05
360	Charlie Hayes	.05
361	Bryan Harvey	.05
362	Eddie Taubensee	.05
363	Tim Wallach	.05
364	Mel Rojas	.05
365	Frank Tanana	.05
366	John Kruk	.05
367	Tim Laker RC	.05
368	Rich Rodriguez	.05
369	Darren Lewis	.05
370	Harold Reynolds	.05
371	Jose Melendez	.05
372	Joe Grahe	.05
373	Lance Johnson	.05
374	Jose Mesa	.05
375	Scott Livingstone	.05
376	Wally Joyner	.05
377	Kevin Reimer	.05
378	Kirby Puckett	1.00
379	Paul O'Neill	.05
380	Randy Johnson	.75
381	Manuel Lee	.05
382	Dick Schofield	.05
383	Darren Holmes	.05
384	Charlie Hough	.05
385	John Orton	.05
386	Edgar Martinez	.05
387	Terry Pendleton	.05
388	Dan Plesac	.05
389	Jeff Reardon	.05
390	David Nied	.05
391	Dave Magadan	.05
392	Larry Walker	.05
393	Ben Rivera	.05
394	Lonnie Smith	.05
395	Craig Shipley	.05
396	Willie McGee	.05
397	Arthur Rhodes	.05
398	Mike Stanton	.05
399	Luis Polonia	.05
400	Jack McDowell	.05
401	Mike Moore	.05
402	Jose Lind	.05
403	Bill Spiers	.05
404	Kevin Tapani	.05
405	Spike Owen	.05
406	Tino Martinez	.05
407	Charlie Leibrandt	.05
408	Ed Sprague	.05
409	Bryn Smith	.05
410	Benito Santiago	.05
411	Jose Rijo	.05
412	Pete O'Brien	.05
413	Willie Wilson	.05
414	Bip Roberts	.05
415	Eric Young	.05
416	Walt Weiss	.05
417	Milt Thompson	.05
418	Chris Sabo	.05
419	Scott Sanderson	.05
420	Tim Raines	.05
421	Alan Trammell	.05
422	Mike Macfarlane	.05
423	Dave Winfield	.75
424	Bob Wickman	.05
425	David Valle	.05
426	Gary Redus	.05
427	Turner Ward	.05
428	Reggie Sanders	.05
429	Todd Worrell	.05
430	Julio Valera	.05
431	Cal Ripken, Jr.	2.50
432	Mo Vaughn	.05
433	John Smiley	.05
434	Omar Vizquel	.05
435	Billy Ripken	.05
436	Cory Snyder	.05
437	Carlos Quintana	.05
438	Omar Olivares	.05
439	Robin Ventura	.05
440	Checklist	.05
441	Kevin Higgins	.05
442	Carlos Hernandez	.05
443	Dan Peltier	.05
444	Derek Lilliquist	.05
445	Tim Salmon	.05
446	Sherman Obando RC	.05
447	Pat Kelly	.05
448	Todd Van Poppel	.05
449	Mark Whiten	.05
450	Checklist	.05
451	Pat Meares	.05
452	Tony Tarasco RC	.05
453	Chris Gwynn	.05
454	Armando Reynoso	.05
455	Danny Darwin	.05
456	Willie Greene	.05
457	Mike Blowers	.05
458	Kevin Roberson RC	.05
459	Graeme Lloyd RC	.05
460	David West	.05
461	Joey Cora	.05
462	Alex Arias	.05
463	Chad Kreuter	.05
464	Mike Lansing	.05
465	Mike Timlin	.05
466	Paul Wagner	.05
467	Mark Portugal	.05
468	Jim Leyritz	.05
469	Ryan Klesko	.05
470	Mario Diaz	.05
471	Guillermo Velasquez	.05
472	Fernando Valenzuela	.05
473	Raul Mondesi	.05

474	Mike Pagliarulo	.05
475	Chris Hammond	.05
476	Torey Lovullo	.05
477	Trevor Wilson	.05
478	Marcos Armas **RC**	.05
479	Dave Gallagher	.05
480	Jeff Treadway	.05
481	Jeff Branson	.05
482	Dickie Thon	.05
483	Eduardo Perez	.05
484	David Wells	.05
485	Brian Williams	.05
486	Domingo Cedeno	.05
487	Tom Candiotti	.05
488	Steve Frey	.05
489	Greg McMichael	.05
490	Marc Newfield	.05
491	Larry Andersen	.05
492	Damon Buford	.05
493	Ricky Gutierrez	.05
494	Jeff Russell	.05
495	Vinny Castilla	.05
496	Wilson Alvarez	.05
497	Scott Bullett	.05
498	Larry Casian	.05
499	Jose Vizcaino	.05
500	J.T. Snow **RC**	.75
501	Bryan Hickerson	.05
502	Jeremy Hernandez	.05
503	Jeromy Burnitz	.05
504	Steve Farr	.05
505	J. Owens	.05
506	Craig Paquette	.05
507	Jim Eisenreich	.05
508	Matt Whiteside	.05
509	Luis Aquino	.05
510	Mike LaValliere	.05
511	Jim Gott	.05
512	Mark McLemore	.05
513	Randy Milligan	.05
514	Gary Gaetti	.05
515	Lou Frazier	.05
516	Rich Amaral	.05
517	Gene Harris	.05
518	Aaron Sele	.05
519	Mark Wohlers	.05
520	Scott Kamieniecki	.05
521	Kent Mercker	.05
522	Jim Deshaies	.05
523	Kevin Stocker	.05
524	Jason Bere	.05
525	Tim Bogar	.05
526	Brad Pennington	.05
527	Curt Leskanic **RC**	.05
528	Wayne Kirby	.05
529	Tim Costo	.05
530	Doug Henry	.05
531	Trevor Hoffman	.05
532	Kelly Gruber	.05
533	Mike Harkey	.05
534	John Doherty	.05
535	Erik Pappas	.05
536	Brent Gates	.05
537	Roger McDowell	.05
538	Chris Haney	.05
539	Blas Minor	.05
540	Pat Hentgen	.05
541	Chuck Carr	.05
542	Doug Strange	.05
543	Xavier Hernandez	.05
544	Paul Quantrill	.05
545	Anthony Young	.05
546	Bret Boone	.05
547	Dwight Smith	.05
548	Bobby Munoz	.05
549	Russ Springer	.05
550	Roger Pavlik	.05
----	Dave Winfield (3,000 Hits)	2.00

Fasttrack

This 20-card insert set was released in two series; cards 1-10 were randomly included in Leaf Series I retail packs, while 11-20 were in Series II packs. Card fronts and backs are similar with a player photo and a diagonal white strip with "on the Fasttrack" printed in black and red. Fronts have the gold embossed Leaf logo, backs have the silver holographic team logo.

		NM/M
Complete Set (20):		15.00
Common Player:		.60
1	Frank Thomas	3.00

2	Tim Wakefield	.60
3	Kenny Lofton	.60
4	Mike Mussina	1.00
5	Juan Gonzalez	2.50
6	Chuck Knoblauch	.60
7	Eric Karros	.60
8	Ray Lankford	.60
9	Juan Guzman	.60
10	Pat Listach	.60
11	Carlos Baerga	.60
12	Felix Jose	.60
13	Steve Avery	.60
14	Robin Ventura	.60
15	Ivan Rodriguez	2.50
16	Cal Eldred	.60
17	Jeff Bagwell	3.00
18	Dave Justice	.60
19	Travis Fryman	.60
20	Marquis Grissom	.60

Gold All-Stars

Cards 1-10 in this insert set were randomly inserted one per Leaf Series I jumbo packs, while cards 11-20 were in Series II jumbo packs. Cards feature two players per card, one on each side. Only one side is numbered, but both sides have gold foil.

		NM/M
Complete Set (20):		15.00
Common Player:		.25
1	Ivan Rodriguez, Darren Daulton	.75
2	Don Mattingly, Fred McGriff	1.50
3	Cecil Fielder, Jeff Bagwell	.75
4	Carlos Baerga, Ryne Sandberg	1.00
5	Chuck Knoblauch, Delino DeShields	.25
6	Robin Ventura, Terry Pendleton	.25
7	Ken Griffey Jr., Andy Van Slyke	2.00
8	Joe Carter, Dave Justice	.25
9	Jose Canseco, Tony Gwynn	1.00
10	Dennis Eckersley, Rob Dibble	.60
11	Mark McGwire, Will Clark	2.50
12	Frank Thomas, Mark Grace	.75
13	Roberto Alomar, Craig Biggio	.50
14	Barry Larkin, Cal Ripken, Jr.	3.00
15	Gary Sheffield, Edgar Martinez	.50
16	Juan Gonzalez, Barry Bonds	3.00
17	Kirby Puckett, Marquis Grissom	1.00
18	Jim Abbott, Tom Glavine	.40
19	Nolan Ryan, Greg Maddux	3.00
20	Roger Clemens, Doug Drabek	1.50

Gold Rookies

These cards, numbered 1 of 20 etc., feature 1993 rookies and were randomly inserted into hobby foil packs, 10 players per series. Card fronts feature action photos, while the backs show a player photo

Heading for the Hall

Ten players on the way to the Baseball Hall of Fame are featured in this insert set. Series I Leaf packs had cards 1-5 randomly included; Series II packs had cards 6-10.

		NM/M
Complete Set (10):		10.00
Common Player:		1.00
1	Nolan Ryan	2.50
2	Tony Gwynn	1.00
3	Robin Yount	1.00
4	Eddie Murray	1.00
5	Cal Ripken, Jr.	2.50
6	Roger Clemens	2.00
7	George Brett	2.00
8	Ryne Sandberg	1.00
9	Kirby Puckett	1.00
10	Ozzie Smith	1.00

Frank Thomas

Leaf signed Frank Thomas as its spokesman for 1993, and honored him with a 10-card insert set. Cards 1-5 were randomly included in Series I packs; cards 6-10 were in Series II packs. A large "Frank" logo in a holographic foil stamp is featured on each card front along with a one-word character trait. On back is a color portrait photo of Thomas superimposed on a Chicago skyline. A paragraph on back describes how the character trait on front applies to Thomas.

		NM/M
Complete Set (10):		4.50
Common Card:		.75
Autographed Card:		30.00
1	Aggressive (Frank Thomas)	.75
2	Serious (Frank Thomas)	.75
3	Intense (Frank Thomas)	.75
4	Confident (Frank Thomas)	.75

against a landmark from his team's city. Jumbo versions in 3-1/2" x 5" format were produced as special retail box toppers, in a numbered edition of 5,000 each.

		NM/M
Complete Set (20):		5.00
Common Player:		.25
1	Kevin Young	.25
2	Wil Cordero	.25
3	Mark Kiefer	.25
4	Gerald Williams	.25
5	Brandon Wilson	.25
6	Greg Gohr	.25
7	Ryan Thompson	.25
8	Tim Wakefield	.25
9	Troy Neel	.25
10	Tim Salmon	.50
11	Kevin Rogers	.25
12	Rod Bolton	.25
13	Ken Ryan	.25
14	Phil Hiatt	.25
15	Rene Arocha	.25
16	Nigel Wilson	.25
17	J.T. Snow	.50
18	Benji Gil	.25
19	Chipper Jones	3.00
20	Darrell Sherman	.25

Update Gold All-Stars

These 10 cards, featuring 20 all-stars, were randomly inserted in Leaf Update packs. Each card features two players, one on each side. Cards are distinguished from the regular Gold All-Stars by indicating on the front the card is number X of 10, with a tiny white "Update" in the red stripe above the card number.

		NM/M
Complete Set (10):		7.50
Common Player:		.25
1	Mark Langston, Terry Mulholland	.25
2	Ivan Rodriguez, Darren Daulton	.50
3	John Olerud, John Kruk	.25
4	Roberto Alomar, Ryne Sandberg	1.00
5	Wade Boggs, Gary Sheffield	.75
6	Cal Ripken, Jr., Barry Larkin	3.00
7	Kirby Puckett, Barry Bonds	2.50
8	Marquis Grissom, Ken Griffey Jr.	2.00
9	Joe Carter, Dave Justice	.25
10	Mark Grace, Paul Molitor	.75

Update Gold Rookies

These five cards were randomly inserted in Leaf Update packs. Cards are similiar in design to the regular Gold Rookies cards, except the logo on the card back indicates they are from the Update series. Jumbo 3-1/2" x 5" versions were produced as special retail box toppers in a numbered edition of 5,000 each.

		NM/M
Complete Set (5):		3.50
Common Player:		.25
Jumbos:		1.5X
1	Allen Watson	.25
2	Jeffrey Hammonds	.25
3	David McCarty	.25
4	Mike Piazza	3.00
5	Roberto Meija	.25

Update Frank Thomas Autograph

This card was a random insert in '93 Leaf Update packs and features a genuine Frank Thomas autograph on front. Unlike the other cards in the set, this has a silver-gray border on front and back. Front has a gold-foil seal in upper-left. Back has a photo of Thomas in his batting follow-through. At bot-

tom on back is a white strip bearing the card's individual serial number from an edition of 3,500.

		NM/M
FT	Frank Thomas	35.00

Update Frank Thomas Super

This 10-card insert set features Leaf's 1993 spokesman, Frank Thomas. Cards, which measure 5" x 7", were included one per every Leaf Update foil box and are identical to the inserts found in Series I and II except in size. Cards are individually numbered. Thomas autographed 3,500 cards.

		NM/M
Complete Set (10):		17.50
Common Card:		2.00
1	Aggressive (Frank Thomas)	2.00
2	Serious (Frank Thomas)	2.00
3	Intense (Frank Thomas)	2.00
4	Confident (Frank Thomas)	2.00
5	Assertive (Frank Thomas)	2.00
6	Power (Frank Thomas)	2.00
7	Control (Frank Thomas)	2.00
8	Strength (Frank Thomas)	2.00
9	Concentration (Frank Thomas)	2.00
10	Preparation (Frank Thomas)	2.00

1994 Leaf Promos

Identical in format to the regular issue, this nine-card set was produced as a preview for the 1994 Leaf cards. The only differences on the promo cards are a large, black "Promotional Sample" notice overprinted diagonally on both the front and back of the cards. Instead of the regular card numbers, the promos are numbered "X of 9" at top to the left of the team logo hologram.

		NM/M
Complete Set (9):		7.50
Common Player:		.25
1	Roberto Alomar	.75
2	Darren Daulton	.25
3	Ken Griffey Jr.	2.00

4	David Justice	.25
5	Don Mattingly	1.50
6	Mike Piazza	2.00
7	Cal Ripken, Jr.	3.00
8	Ryne Sandberg	1.25
9	Frank Thomas	1.00

1994 Leaf

Donruss returned its premium-brand Leaf set in 1994 with an announced 25 percent production cut from the previous season - fewer than 20,000 20-box cases of each 220-card series. Game-action photos dominate the fronts of the cards, borderless at the top and sides. At bottom are team color-coded faux-marble borders with the player's name (last name in gold foil) and team. Backs have a background of the player's home stadium with another action photo superimposed. In a ticket-stub device at upper-left is a portrait photo and a few personal numbers. Previous season and career stats are in white stripes at bottom. The team logo is presented in holographic foil at upper-right. To feature 1994's new stadiums and uniforms, cards of the Indians, Rangers, Brewers and Astros were included only in the second series. Seven different types of insert cards were produced and distributed among the various types of Leaf packaging.

		NM/M
Complete Set (440):		10.00
Common Player:		.05
Series 1 or 2 Pack (12):		.75
Series 1 or 2 Box (36):		12.50
1	Cal Ripken, Jr.	2.50
2	Tony Tarasco	.05
3	Joe Girardi	.05
4	Bernie Williams	.20
5	Chad Kreuter	.05
6	Troy Neel	.05
7	Tom Pagnozzi	.05
8	Kirk Rueter	.05
9	Chris Bosio	.05
10	Dwight Gooden	.05
11	Mariano Duncan	.05
12	Jay Bell	.05
13	Lance Johnson	.05
14	Richie Lewis	.05
15	Dave Martinez	.05
16	Orel Hershiser	.05
17	Rob Butler	.05
18	Glenallen Hill	.05
19	Chad Curtis	.05
20	Mike Stanton	.05
21	Tim Wallach	.05
22	Milt Thompson	.05
23	Kevin Young	.05
24	John Smiley	.05
25	Jeff Montgomery	.05
26	Robin Ventura	.05
27	Scott Lydy	.05
28	Todd Stottlemyre	.05
29	Mark Whiten	.05
30	Robby Thompson	.05
31	Bobby Bonilla	.05
32	Andy Ashby	.05
33	Greg Myers	.05
34	Billy Hatcher	.05
35	Brad Holman	.05
36	Mark McLemore	.05
37	Scott Sanders	.05
38	Jim Abbott	.05
39	David Wells	.05
40	Roberto Kelly	.05
41	Jeff Conine	.05
42	Sean Berry	.05
43	Mark Grace	.25
44	Eric Young	.05
45	Rick Aguilera	.05
46	Chipper Jones	1.00
47	Mel Rojas	.05
48	Ryan Thompson	.05
49	Al Martin	.05
50	Cecil Fielder	.05
51	Pat Kelly	.05
52	Kevin Tapani	.05
53	Tim Costo	.05

#	Player		#	Player		#	Player		#	Player	
54	Dave Hollins	.05	172	Geronimo Pena	.05	290	Brian Harper	.05	408	Chuck Carr	.05
55	Kirt Manwaring	.05	173	Gary DiSarcina	.05	291	Chris Turner	.05	409	Ozzie Smith	1.00
56	Gregg Jefferies	.05	174	Marquis Grissom	.05	292	Luis Gonzalez	.25	410	Kent Mercker	.05
57	Ron Darling	.05	175	Joey Cora	.05	293	Kenny Rogers	.05	411	Andy Van Slyke	.05
58	Bill Haselman	.05	176	Jim Eisenreich	.05	294	Kirby Puckett	1.00	412	Jimmy Key	.05
59	Phil Plantier	.05	177	Brad Pennington	.05	295	Mike Stanley	.05	413	Pat Mahomes	.05
60	Frank Viola	.05	178	Terry Steinbach	.05	296	Carlos Reyes	.05	414	John Wetteland	.05
61	Todd Zeile	.05	179	Pat Borders	.05	297	Charles Nagy	.05	415	Todd Jones	.05
62	Bret Barberie	.05	180	Steve Buechele	.05	298	Reggie Jefferson	.05	416	Greg Harris	.05
63	Roberto Mejia	.05	181	Jeff Fassero	.05	299	Bip Roberts	.05	417	Kevin Stocker	.05
64	Chuck Knoblauch	.05	182	Mike Greenwell	.05	300	Darrin Jackson	.05	418	Juan Gonzalez	.65
65	Jose Lind	.05	183	Mike Henneman	.05	301	Mike Jackson	.05	419	Pete Smith	.05
66	Brady Anderson	.05	184	Ron Karkovice	.05	302	Dave Nilsson	.05	420	Pat Listach	.05
67	Ruben Sierra	.05	185	Pat Hentgen	.05	303	Ramon Martinez	.05	421	Trevor Hoffman	.05
68	Jose Vizcaino	.05	186	Jose Guzman	.05	304	Bobby Jones	.05	422	Scott Fletcher	.05
69	Joe Grahe	.05	187	Brett Butler	.05	305	Johnny Ruffin	.05	423	Mark Lewis	.05
70	Kevin Appier	.05	188	Charlie Hough	.05	306	Brian McRae	.05	424	Mickey Morandini	.05
71	Wilson Alvarez	.05	189	Terry Pendleton	.05	307	Bo Jackson	.10	425	Ryne Sandberg	1.00
72	Tom Candiotti	.05	190	Melido Perez	.05	308	Dave Stewart	.05	426	Erik Hanson	.05
73	John Burkett	.05	191	Orestes Destrade	.05	309	John Smoltz	.05	427	Gary Gaetti	.05
74	Anthony Young	.05	192	Mike Morgan	.05	310	Dennis Martinez	.05	428	Harold Reynolds	.05
75	Scott Cooper	.05	193	Joe Carter	.05	311	Dean Palmer	.05	429	Mark Portugal	.05
76	Nigel Wilson	.05	194	Jeff Blauser	.05	312	David Nied	.05	430	David Valle	.05
77	John Valentin	.05	195	Chris Hoiles	.05	313	Eddie Murray	.75	431	Mitch Williams	.05
78	Dave McCarty	.05	196	Ricky Gutierrez	.05	314	Darryl Kile	.05	432	Howard Johnson	.05
79	Archi Cianfrocco	.05	197	Mike Moore	.05	315	Rick Sutcliffe	.05	433	Hal Morris	.05
80	Lou Whitaker	.05	198	Carl Willis	.05	316	Shawon Dunston	.05	434	Tom Henke	.05
81	Dante Bichette	.05	199	Aaron Sele	.05	317	John Jaha	.05	435	Shane Mack	.05
82	Mark Dewey	.05	200	Checklist	.05	318	Salomon Torres	.05	436	Mike Piazza	1.50
83	Danny Jackson	.05	201	Tim Naehring	.05	319	Gary Sheffield	.45	437	Bret Saberhagen	.05
84	Harold Baines	.05	202	Scott Livingstone	.05	320	Curt Schilling	.30	438	Jose Mesa	.05
85	Todd Benzinger	.05	203	Luis Alicea	.05	321	Greg Vaughn	.05	439	Jaime Navarro	.05
86	Damion Easley	.05	204	Torey Lovullo RC	.05	322	Jay Howell	.05	440	Checklist	.05
87	Danny Cox	.05	205	Jim Gott	.05	323	Todd Hundley	.05			
88	Jose Bautista	.05	206	Bob Wickman	.05	324	Chris Sabo	.05			
89	Mike Lansing	.05	207	Greg McMichael	.05	325	Stan Javier	.05			
90	Phil Hiatt	.05	208	Scott Brosius	.05	326	Willie Greene	.05			
91	Tim Pugh	.05	209	Chris Gwynn	.05	327	Hipolito Pichardo	.05			
92	Tino Martinez	.05	210	Steve Sax	.05	328	Doug Strange	.05			
93	Raul Mondesi	.05	211	Dick Schofield	.05	329	Dan Wilson	.05			
94	Greg Maddux	1.00	212	Robb Nen	.05	330	Checklist	.05			
95	Al Leiter	.05	213	Ben Rivera	.05	331	Omar Vizquel	.05			
96	Benito Santiago	.05	214	Vinny Castilla	.05	332	Scott Servais	.05			
97	Len Dykstra	.05	215	Jamie Moyer	.05	333	Bob Tewksbury	.05			
98	Sammy Sosa	1.25	216	Wally Whitehurst	.05	334	Matt Williams	.05			
99	Tim Bogar	.05	217	Frank Castillo	.05	335	Tom Foley	.05			
100	Checklist	.05	218	Mike Blowers	.05	336	Jeff Russell	.05			
101	Deion Sanders	.10	219	Tim Scott	.05	337	Scott Leius	.05			
102	Bobby Witt	.05	220	Paul Wagner	.05	338	Ivan Rodriguez	.65			
103	Wil Cordero	.05	221	Jeff Bagwell	.75	339	Kevin Seitzer	.05			
104	Rich Amaral	.05	222	Ricky Bones	.05	340	Jose Rijo	.05			
105	Mike Mussina	.50	223	Sandy Alomar Jr.	.05	341	Eduardo Perez	.05			
106	Reggie Sanders	.05	224	Rod Beck	.05	342	Kirk Gibson	.05			
107	Ozzie Guillen	.05	225	Roberto Alomar	.20	343	Randy Milligan	.05			
108	Paul O'Neill	.05	226	Jack Armstrong	.05	344	Edgar Martinez	.05			
109	Tim Salmon	.05	227	Scott Erickson	.05	345	Fred McGriff	.05			
110	Rheal Cormier	.05	228	Rene Arocha	.05	346	Kurt Abbott	.05			
111	Billy Ashley	.05	229	Eric Anthony	.05	347	John Kruk	.05			
112	Jeff Kent	.05	230	Jeromy Burnitz	.05	348	Mike Felder	.05			
113	Derek Bell	.05	231	Kevin Brown	.05	349	Dave Staton	.05			
114	Danny Darwin	.05	232	Tim Belcher	.05	350	Kenny Lofton	.05			
115	Chip Hale	.05	233	Bret Boone	.05	351	Graeme Lloyd	.05			
116	Tim Raines	.05	234	Dennis Eckersley	.60	352	David Segui	.05			
117	Ed Sprague	.05	235	Tom Glavine	.30	353	Danny Tartabull	.05			
118	Darrin Fletcher	.05	236	Craig Biggio	.05	354	Bob Welch	.05			
119	Darren Holmes	.05	237	Pedro Astacio	.05	355	Duane Ward	.05			
120	Alan Trammell	.05	238	Ryan Bowen	.05	356	Tuffy Rhodes	.05			
121	Don Mattingly	1.25	239	Brad Ausmus	.05	357	Lee Smith	.05			
122	Greg Gagne	.05	240	Vince Coleman	.05	358	Chris James	.05			
123	Jose Offerman	.05	241	Jason Bere	.05	359	Walt Weiss	.05			
124	Joe Orsulak	.05	242	Ellis Burks	.05	360	Pedro Munoz	.05			
125	Jack McDowell	.05	243	Wes Chamberlain	.05	361	Paul Sorrento	.05			
126	Barry Larkin	.05	244	Ken Caminiti	.05	362	Todd Worrell	.05			
127	Ben McDonald	.05	245	Willie Banks	.05	363	Bob Hamelin	.05			
128	Mike Bordick	.05	246	Sid Fernandez	.05	364	Julio Franco	.05			
129	Devon White	.05	247	Carlos Baerga	.05	365	Roberto Petagine	.05			
130	Mike Perez	.05	248	Carlos Garcia	.05	366	Willie McGee	.05			
131	Jay Buhner	.05	249	Jose Canseco	.50	367	Pedro Martinez	.75			
132	Phil Leftwich	.05	250	Alex Diaz	.05	368	Ken Griffey Jr.	1.50			
133	Tommy Greene	.05	251	Albert Belle	.05	369	B.J. Surhoff	.05			
134	Charlie Hayes	.05	252	Moises Alou	.05	370	Kevin Mitchell	.05			
135	Don Slaught	.05	253	Bobby Ayala	.05	371	John Doherty	.05			
136	Mike Gallego	.05	254	Tony Gwynn	1.00	372	Manuel Lee	.05			
137	Dave Winfield	.75	255	Roger Clemens	1.25	373	Terry Mulholland	.05			
138	Steve Avery	.05	256	Eric Davis	.05	374	Zane Smith	.05			
139	Derrick May	.05	257	Wade Boggs	1.00	375	Otis Nixon	.05			
140	Bryan Harvey	.05	258	Chili Davis	.05	376	Jody Reed	.05			
141	Wally Joyner	.05	259	Rickey Henderson	.75	377	Doug Jones	.05			
142	Andre Dawson	.20	260	Andujar Cedeno	.05	378	John Olerud	.05			
143	Andy Benes	.05	261	Cris Carpenter	.05	379	Greg Swindell	.05			
144	John Franco	.05	262	Juan Guzman	.05	380	Checklist	.05			
145	Jeff King	.05	263	Dave Justice	.05	381	Royce Clayton	.05			
146	Joe Oliver	.05	264	Barry Bonds	2.50	382	Jim Thome	.65			
147	Bill Gullickson	.05	265	Pete Incaviglia	.05	383	Steve Finley	.05			
148	Armando Reynoso	.05	266	Tony Fernandez	.05	384	Ray Lankford	.05			
149	Dave Fleming	.05	267	Cal Eldred	.05	385	Henry Rodriguez	.05			
150	Checklist	.05	268	Alex Fernandez	.05	386	Dave Magadan	.05			
151	Todd Van Poppel	.05	269	Kent Hrbek	.05	387	Gary Redus	.05			
152	Bernard Gilkey	.05	270	Steve Farr	.05	388	Orlando Merced	.05			
153	Kevin Gross	.05	271	Doug Drabek	.05	389	Tom Gordon	.05			
154	Mike Devereaux	.05	272	Brian Jordan	.05	390	Luis Polonia	.05			
155	Tim Wakefield	.05	273	Xavier Hernandez	.05	391	Mark McGwire	2.00			
156	Andres Galarraga	.05	274	David Cone	.05	392	Mark Lemke	.05			
157	Pat Meares	.05	275	Brian Hunter	.05	393	Doug Henry	.05			
158	Jim Leyritz	.05	276	Mike Harkey	.05	394	Chuck Finley	.05			
159	Mike Macfarlane	.05	277	Delino DeShields	.05	395	Paul Molitor	.75			
160	Tony Phillips	.05	278	David Hulse	.05	396	Randy Myers	.05			
161	Brent Gates	.05	279	Mickey Tettleton	.05	397	Larry Walker	.05			
162	Mark Langston	.05	280	Kevin McReynolds	.05	398	Pete Harnisch	.05			
163	Allen Watson	.05	281	Darryl Hamilton	.05	399	Darren Lewis	.05			
164	Randy Johnson	.75	282	Ken Hill	.05	400	Frank Thomas	.75			
165	Doug Brocail	.05	283	Wayne Kirby	.05	401	Jack Morris	.05			
166	Rob Dibble	.05	284	Chris Hammond	.05	402	Greg Hibbard	.05			
167	Roberto Hernandez	.05	285	Mo Vaughn	.05	403	Jeffrey Hammonds	.05			
168	Felix Jose	.05	286	Ryan Klesko	.05	404	Will Clark	.10			
169	Steve Cooke	.05	287	Rick Wilkins	.05	405	Travis Fryman	.05			
170	Darren Daulton	.05	288	Bill Swift	.05	406	Scott Sanderson	.05			
171	Eric Karros	.05	289	Rafael Palmeiro	.65	407	Gene Harris	.05			

Clean-Up Crew

The number four spot in the line-up is featured on this 12-card insert set (six per series) found only in magazine distributor packaging. Fronts are gold-foil enhanced; backs feature an action photo set against a background of a lineup card on which the player is penciled into the #4 spot. His 1993 stats when batting clean-up are presented.

		NM/M
	Complete Set (12):	8.00
	Common Player:	1.00
1	Larry Walker	1.00
2	Andres Galarraga	1.00
3	Dave Hollins	1.00
4	Bobby Bonilla	1.00
5	Cecil Fielder	1.00
6	Danny Tartabull	1.00
7	Juan Gonzalez	2.00
8	Joe Carter	1.00
9	Fred McGriff	1.00
10	Matt Williams	1.00
11	Albert Belle	1.00
12	Harold Baines	1.00

Gamers

Leaf jumbo packs are the exclusive venue for the six cards of this insert set which were issued in each series.

		NM/M
	Complete Set (12):	30.00
	Common Player:	1.00
1	Ken Griffey Jr.	6.00
2	Len Dykstra	1.00
3	Juan Gonzalez	3.00
4	Don Mattingly	6.00
5	Dave Justice	1.00
6	Mark Grace	1.00
7	Frank Thomas	4.00
8	Barry Bonds	7.50
9	Kirby Puckett	4.50
10	Will Clark	1.00
11	John Kruk	1.00
12	Mike Piazza	6.00

Gold Rookies

A gold-foil rendered stadium background and huge black "94 Gold Leaf Rookie" serve as a backdrop for a player photo on these insert cards found at the rate of about one per 18 foil packs. The player's name and team are in silver at bottom. Horizontal backs have a ghosted action photo of the player in the background. A portrait photo is in the upper-right corner, above some personal data and stats. Cards are numbered "X of 20."

		NM/M
	Complete Set (20):	6.00
	Common Player:	.25
1	Javier Lopez	.25
2	Rondell White	.25
3	Butch Huskey	.25
4	Midre Cummings	.25
5	Scott Ruffcorn	.25
6	Manny Ramirez	3.50
7	Danny Bautista	.25
8	Russ Davis	.25
9	Steve Karsay	.25
10	Carlos Delgado	2.50
11	Bob Hamelin	.25
12	Marcus Moore	.25
13	Miguel Jimenez	.25
14	Matt Walbeck	.25
15	James Mouton	.25
16	Rich Becker	.25
17	Brian Anderson	.25
18	Cliff Floyd	.25
19	Steve Trachsel	.25
20	Hector Carrasco	.25

Gold Stars

The "Cadillac" of 1994 Leaf inserts, this 15-card series (#1-8 in Series 1; 9-15 in Series 2) is found on average of one card per 90 packs. The edition of 10,000 of each player's card is serially numbered. Fronts feature a rather small photo in a diamond-shaped frame against a green marble-look background. The border, facsimile autograph and several other graphic elements are presented in prismatic foil. The back repeats the basic front design with a few sentences about the player and a serial number strip at bottom.

		NM/M
	Complete Set (15):	60.00
	Common Player:	3.00
1	Roberto Alomar	4.00
2	Barry Bonds	12.00
3	Dave Justice	3.00
4	Ken Griffey Jr.	9.00
5	Len Dykstra	3.00
6	Don Mattingly	7.50
7	Andres Galarraga	3.00
8	Greg Maddux	6.00
9	Carlos Baerga	3.00
10	Paul Molitor	5.00
11	Frank Thomas	5.00
12	John Olerud	3.00
13	Juan Gonzalez	4.00
14	Fred McGriff	3.00
15	Jack McDowell	3.00

MVP Contenders

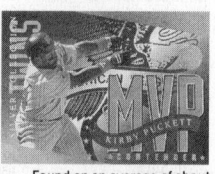

Found on an average of about once per 36-pack foil box, these inserts were produced in an edition of 10,000 each. Cards found in packs were marked "Silver Collection" on the horizontal fronts, and featured a silver-foil Leaf seal and other enhancements. Persons holding cards of the players selected as N.L. and A.L. MVPs could trade in their Contender card for an individually numbered 5" x 7" card of Leaf spokesman Frank Thomas and be entered in a drawing for one of 5,000 Gold Collection MVP Contender 28-card sets. Winning cards were punch-cancelled and returned to the winner along with his prize.

		NM/M
	Complete Set, Silver (30):	20.00
	Complete Set, Gold (30):	40.00
	Common Player, Silver:	.25
	Common Player, Gold:	.50
	AMERICAN LEAGUE	2.00
1a	Albert Belle/Silver	.25
1b	Albert Belle/Gold	.50
2a	Jose Canseco/Silver	1.25
2b	Jose Canseco/Gold	2.00
3a	Joe Carter/Silver	.25
3b	Joe Carter/Gold	.50
4a	Will Clark/Silver	.35
4b	Will Clark/Gold	.60
5a	Cecil Fielder/Silver	.25
5b	Cecil Fielder/Gold	.50
6a	Juan Gonzalez/Silver	1.50
6b	Juan Gonzalez/Gold	2.50
7a	Ken Griffey Jr./Silver	4.00
7b	Ken Griffey Jr./Gold	7.50
8a	Paul Molitor/Silver	4.00
8b	Paul Molitor/Gold	4.00
9a	Rafael Palmeiro/Silver	1.50
9b	Rafael Palmeiro/Gold	2.50
10a	Kirby Puckett/Silver	2.50
10b	Kirby Puckett/Gold	5.00
11a	Cal Ripken, Jr./Silver	6.00
11b	Cal Ripken, Jr./Gold	12.50
12a	Frank Thomas/Silver	4.00
12b	Frank Thomas/Gold	4.00
13a	Mo Vaughn/Silver	.25
13b	Mo Vaughn/Gold	.50
14a	Carlos Baerga/Silver	.25
14b	Carlos Baerga/Gold	.50
15	AL Bonus Card/Silver	.60
	NATIONAL LEAGUE	.60
1a	Gary Sheffield/Silver	.35
1b	Gary Sheffield/Gold	.65
2a	Jeff Bagwell/Silver	2.00
2b	Jeff Bagwell/Gold	4.00
3a	Dante Bichette/Silver	.25
3b	Dante Bichette/Gold	.50
4a	Barry Bonds/Silver	6.00
4b	Barry Bonds/Gold	12.50
5a	Darren Daulton/Silver	.25
5b	Darren Daulton/Gold	.25
6a	Andres Galarraga/Silver	.25
6b	Andres Galarraga/Gold	.50
7a	Gregg Jefferies/Silver	.25
7b	Gregg Jefferies/Gold	.50
8a	Dave Justice (Silver)	.25
8b	Dave Justice/Gold	.50
9a	Ray Lankford/Silver	.25
9b	Ray Lankford/Gold	.50
10a	Fred McGriff/Silver	.25
10b	Fred McGriff/Gold	.50
11a	Barry Larkin/Silver	.25
11b	Barry Larkin/Gold	.50
12a	Mike Piazza/Silver	4.00
12b	Mike Piazza/Gold	7.50
13a	Deion Sanders/Silver	.25
13b	Deion Sanders/Gold	.50
14a	Matt Williams/Silver	.50
14b	Matt Williams/Gold	.50
15	NL Bonus Card/Silver	.25

Power Brokers

This insert set was unique to Leaf Series 2 and features top sluggers. Horizontal fronts have a player photo at left, depicting his power stroke. A fireworks display is featured in the large letters of "POWER" at top. Other gold and silver foil highlights are featured on the black

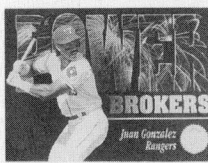

background. Backs have pie charts showing home run facts along with another player photo and a few stats. Stated odds of finding a Power Brokers insert card were one per dozen packs, on average.

		NM/M
Complete Set (10):		8.00
Common Player:		.40
1	Frank Thomas	.75
2	Dave Justice	.40
3	Barry Bonds	3.00
4	Juan Gonzalez	.65
5	Ken Griffey Jr.	2.00
6	Mike Piazza	2.00
7	Cecil Fielder	.40
8	Fred McGriff	.40
9	Joe Carter	.40
10	Albert Belle	.40

Slide Show

A new level of high-tech insert card production values was reached with the creation of Leaf's "Slide Show" cards, featuring a printed acetate center sandwiched between cardboard front and back. The see-through portion of the card is bordered in white to give it the appearance of a slide. The player's name, location and date of the photo are printed on the front of the "slide," with the card number on back. The pseudo-slide is bordered in black (Series 1) or white (Series 2), with a blue "Slide Show" logo at bottom and a silver-foil Leaf logo. Backs of the Slide Show inserts have a few sentences about the featured player from Frank Thomas, Leaf's official spokesman again in 1994. The first five cards were released in Series 1; cards 6-10 in Series 2. Stated odds of finding a Slide Show insert are one per 54 packs.

		NM/M
Complete Set (10):		9.00
Common Player:		.25
1	Frank Thomas	1.00
2	Mike Piazza	2.00
3	Darren Daulton	.25
4	Ryne Sandberg	1.50
5	Roberto Alomar	.50
6	Barry Bonds	3.00
7	Juan Gonzalez	.75
8	Tim Salmon	.25
9	Ken Griffey Jr.	2.00
10	Dave Justice	.25

Statistical Standouts

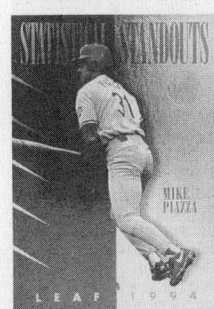

Significant statistical achievements of the 1993 season are marked in this insert set found in both retail and hobby packs at a rate of about once every 12 packs. Fronts feature player action photos set against a foil background of silver at right and a team color at left. A gold embossed Leaf seal is at upper-left. Backs are bordered in the complementary team color at right, silver at left and have a vertical player photo along with the statistical achievement. Cards are numbered "X-10."

		NM/M
Complete Set (10):		10.00
Common Player:		.40
1	Frank Thomas	.75
2	Barry Bonds	2.50
3	Juan Gonzalez	.65
4	Mike Piazza	2.00
5	Greg Maddux	1.00
6	Ken Griffey Jr.	2.00
7	Joe Carter	.40
8	Dave Winfield	.75
9	Tony Gwynn	1.00
10	Cal Ripken, Jr.	2.50

Frank Thomas Super

An edition of 20,000 super-size versions of Frank Thomas' 1994 Leaf card was produced for inclusion in Series II hobby boxes as a bonus. Except for its 5" x 7" format and a white strip on back bearing a serial number, the card is identical to the normal-size issue.

		NM/M
400	Frank Thomas	5.00

5th Anniversary

The card which insured the success of the Leaf brand name when it was re-introduced in 1990, the Frank Thomas rookie card, was re-issued in a 5th anniversary commemorative form as an insert in the 1994 set. On the chase card, silver foil rays emanate from the White Sox logo at lower-left, while a silver-foil 5th anniversary logo at upper-right replaces the Leaf script on the 1990 version. The card back carries a 1994 copyright. The Thomas anniversary card is found on average of once every 36 Series I hobby packs.

		NM/M
300	Frank Thomas	2.50

1994 Leaf/Limited Promo

A single, unlabeled promo card was issued by Leaf to preview its Limited brand. The front is printed on a matte finish background as opposed to the shiny silver of the issued versions, but is otherwise identical. On back there are subtle differences in the cropping of the background photo, and a Total

Bases stat is provided instead of Slugging Percentage as on the issued card. The principal difference is the use of card number 1 on the promo; the issued card is #24.

		NM/M
1	Frank Thomas	100.00

1994 Leaf/Limited

Leaf Limited is a 160-card super-premium set printed on the highest quality board stock ever used by Donruss. Production was limited to 3,000 20-box case equivalents, making this the most limited product up to that point from Donruss. Fronts feature silver holographic Spectra Tech foiling and a silhouetted player action photo over full silver foil. The team name and logo in silver and player name in black at the bottom of the card. Leaf Limited appears in silver at the top. Backs are dull gray with a quote from a baseball personality and a player picture in the top-right corner.

		NM/M
Complete Set (160):		35.00
Common Player:		.25
Pack (5):		2.50
Wax Box (20):		40.00
1	Jeffrey Hammonds	.25
2	Ben McDonald	.25
3	Mike Mussina	.75
4	Rafael Palmeiro	1.50
5	Cal Ripken, Jr.	6.00
6	Lee Smith	.25
7	Roger Clemens	3.00
8	Scott Cooper	.25
9	Andre Dawson	.40
10	Mike Greenwell	.25
11	Aaron Sele	.25
12	Mo Vaughn	.25
13	Brian Anderson RC	.25
14	Chad Curtis	.25
15	Chili Davis	.25
16	Gary DiSarcina	.25
17	Mark Langston	.25
18	Tim Salmon	.25
19	Wilson Alvarez	.25
20	Jason Bere	.25
21	Julio Franco	.25
22	Jack McDowell	.25
23	Tim Raines	.25
24	Frank Thomas	2.00
25	Robin Ventura	.25
26	Carlos Baerga	.25
27	Albert Belle	.25
28	Kenny Lofton	.25
29	Eddie Murray	2.00
30	Manny Ramirez	2.00
31	Cecil Fielder	.25
32	Travis Fryman	.25
33	Mickey Tettleton	.25
34	Alan Trammell	.25
35	Lou Whitaker	.25
36	David Cone	.25
37	Gary Gaetti	.25
38	Greg Gagne	.25
39	Bob Hamelin	.25
40	Wally Joyner	.25
41	Brian McRae	.25
42	Ricky Bones	.25
43	Brian Harper	.25

44	John Jaha	.25
45	Pat Listach	.25
46	Dave Nilsson	.25
47	Greg Vaughn	.25
48	Kent Hrbek	.25
49	Chuck Knoblauch	.25
50	Shane Mack	.25
51	Kirby Puckett	2.50
52	Dave Winfield	2.00
53	Jim Abbott	.25
54	Wade Boggs	2.50
55	Jimmy Key	.25
56	Don Mattingly	3.00
57	Paul O'Neill	.25
58	Danny Tartabull	.25
59	Dennis Eckersley	1.50
60	Rickey Henderson	2.00
61	Mark McGwire	5.00
62	Troy Neel	.25
63	Ruben Sierra	.25
64	Eric Anthony	.25
65	Jay Buhner	.25
66	Ken Griffey Jr.	4.00
67	Randy Johnson	2.00
68	Edgar Martinez	.25
69	Tino Martinez	.25
70	Jose Canseco	.75
71	Will Clark	.35
72	Juan Gonzalez	1.50
73	Dean Palmer	.25
74	Ivan Rodriguez	1.50
75	Roberto Alomar	.40
76	Joe Carter	.25
77	Carlos Delgado	1.00
78	Paul Molitor	2.00
79	John Olerud	.25
80	Devon White	.25
81	Steve Avery	.25
82	Tom Glavine	.50
83	Dave Justice	.25
84	Roberto Kelly	.25
85	Ryan Klesko	.25
86	Javier Lopez	.25
87	Greg Maddux	2.50
88	Fred McGriff	.25
89	Shawon Dunston	.25
90	Mark Grace	.25
91	Derrick May	.25
92	Sammy Sosa	3.00
93	Rick Wilkins	.25
94	Bret Boone	.25
95	Barry Larkin	.25
96	Kevin Mitchell	.25
97	Hal Morris	.25
98	Deion Sanders	.25
99	Reggie Sanders	.25
100	Dante Bichette	.25
101	Ellis Burks	.25
102	Andres Galarraga	.25
103	Joe Girardi	.25
104	Charlie Hayes	.25
105	Chuck Carr	.25
106	Jeff Conine	.25
107	Bryan Harvey	.25
108	Benito Santiago	.25
109	Gary Sheffield	.60
110	Jeff Bagwell	2.00
111	Craig Biggio	.25
112	Ken Caminiti	.25
113	Andujar Cedeno	.25
114	Doug Drabek	.25
115	Luis Gonzalez	.40
116	Brett Butler	.25
117	Delino DeShields	.25
118	Eric Karros	.25
119	Raul Mondesi	.25
120	Mike Piazza	4.00
121	Henry Rodriguez	.25
122	Tim Wallach	.25
123	Moises Alou	.25
124	Cliff Floyd	.25
125	Marquis Grissom	.25
126	Ken Hill	.25
127	Larry Walker	.25
128	John Wetteland	.25
129	Bobby Bonilla	.25
130	John Franco	.25
131	Jeff Kent	.25
132	Bret Saberhagen	.25
133	Ryan Thompson	.25
134	Darren Daulton	.25
135	Mariano Duncan	.25
136	Len Dykstra	.25
137	Danny Jackson	.25
138	John Kruk	.25
139	Jay Bell	.25
140	Jeff King	.25
141	Al Martin	.25
142	Orlando Merced	.25
143	Andy Van Slyke	.25
144	Bernard Gilkey	.25
145	Gregg Jefferies	.25
146	Ray Lankford	.25
147	Ozzie Smith	2.50
148	Mark Whiten	.25
149	Todd Zeile	.25
150	Derek Bell	.25
151	Andy Benes	.25
152	Tony Gwynn	2.50
153	Phil Plantier	.25
154	Bip Roberts	.25
155	Rod Beck	.25
156	Barry Bonds	6.00
157	John Burkett	.25
158	Royce Clayton	.25
159	Bill Swift	.25
160	Matt Williams	.25

Gold

Leaf Limited Gold was an 18-card insert set randomly packed into Leaf Limited. All cards are individually numbered and feature the starting lineups at each position in the National League and American League for the 1994 All-Star Game. There were only 10,000 cards of each player produced in this insert set.

		NM/M
Complete Set (18):		20.00
Common Player:		.25
1	Frank Thomas	1.50
2	Gregg Jefferies	.25
3	Roberto Alomar	.50
4	Mariano Duncan	.25
5	Wade Boggs	2.00
6	Matt Williams	.25
7	Cal Ripken, Jr.	4.00
8	Ozzie Smith	2.00
9	Kirby Puckett	2.00
10	Barry Bonds	4.00
11	Ken Griffey Jr.	3.00
12	Tony Gwynn	2.00
13	Joe Carter	.25
14	Dave Justice	.25
15	Ivan Rodriguez	1.25
16	Mike Piazza	3.00
17	Jimmy Key	.25
18	Greg Maddux	2.00

Rookies

Similar in format to the super-premium Leaf Limited issue, this separate issue features 80 of baseball's brightest young talents. Total production was reported as 30,000 serial numbered 20-pack foil boxes.

		NM/M
Complete Set (80):		17.50
Common Player:		.25
Pack (5):		3.00
Box (20):		60.00
1	Charles Johnson	.25
2	Rico Brogna	.25
3	Melvin Nieves	.25
4	Rich Becker	.25
5	Russ Davis	.25
6	Matt Mieske	.25
7	Paul Shuey	.25
8	Hector Carrasco	.25
9	J.R. Phillips	.25
10	Scott Ruffcorn	.25
11	Kurt Abbott	.25
12	Danny Bautista	.25
13	Rick White	.25
14	Steve Dunn	.25
15	Joe Ausanio	.25
16	Salomon Torres	.25
17	Rick Bottalico	.25
18	Johnny Ruffin	.25
19	Kevin Foster	.25
20	W. Van Landingham RC	.25
21	Troy O'Leary	.25
22	Mark Acre	.25
23	Norberto Martin	.25
24	Jason Jacome RC	.25
25	Steve Trachsel	.25
26	Denny Hocking	.25
27	Mike Lieberthal	.25
28	Gerald Williams	.25
29	John Mabry	.25
30	Greg Blosser	.25

31	Carl Everett	.25
32	Steve Karsay	.25
33	Jose Valentin	.25
34	Jon Lieber	.25
35	Chris Gomez	.25
36	Jesus Tavarez	.25
37	Tony Longmire	.25
38	Luis Lopez	.25
39	Matt Walbeck	.25
40	Rikkert Faneyte	.25
41	Shane Reynolds	.25
42	Joey Hamilton	.25
43	Ismael Valdes	.25
44	Danny Miceli	.25
45	Darren Bragg	.25
46	Alex Gonzalez	.25
47	Rick Helling	.25
48	Jose Oliva	.25
49	Jim Edmonds	4.00
50	Miguel Jimenez	.25
51	Tony Eusebio	.25
52	Shawn Green	4.00
53	Billy Ashley	.25
54	Rondell White	.25
55	Cory Bailey	.25
56	Tim Davis	.25
57	John Hudek	.25
58	Darren Hall	.25
59	Darren Dreifort	.25
60	Mike Kelly	.25
61	Marcus Moore	.25
62	Garret Anderson	.25
63	Brian Hunter	.25
64	Mark Smith	.25
65	Garey Ingram	.25
66	Rusty Greer RC	.25
67	Marc Newfield	.25
68	Gar Finnvold	.25
69	Paul Spoljaric	.25
70	Ray McDavid	.25
71	Orlando Miller	.25
72	Jorge Fabregas	.25
73	Ray Holbert	.25
74	Armando Benitez	.25
75	Ernie Young	.25
76	James Mouton	.25
77	Robert Perez RC	.25
78	Chan Ho Park RC	1.00
79	Roger Salkeld	.25
80	Tony Tarasco	.25

Rookies Rookie Phenoms

Similar in format to the other Leaf Limited cards for 1994, these Phenom inserts feature gold-foil background and graphics, rather than silver. Each card is numbered from within an edition of 5,000 of each player.

		NM/M
Complete Set (10):		260.00
Common Player:		1.00
Production 5,000 Sets		
1	Raul Mondesi	1.00
2	Bob Hamelin	1.00
3	Midre Cummings	1.00
4	Carlos Delgado	8.00
5	Cliff Floyd	1.00
6	Jeffrey Hammonds	1.00
7	Ryan Klesko	1.00
8	Javier Lopez	1.00
9	Manny Ramirez	10.00
10	Alex Rodriguez	250.00

1995 Leaf Promos

The lack of a "Sample" or "Promotional Card" notice makes these promos difficult to spot. They can be detected by the placement of the Registered symbol farther down and to the right compared to regular-issue cards. Also the thin line inside the gold-foil stamping enclosing the Leaf logo and inner "95" diamond is missing on the promos.

		NM/M
Complete Set (9):		35.00
Common Player:		2.00
1	Frank Thomas	4.00
10	Joe Carter	2.00
28	Matt Williams	2.00
40	Wade Boggs	6.00
60	Raul Mondesi	2.00
115	Greg Maddux	6.00

119	Jeff Bagwell	4.00
134	Cal Ripken Jr.	12.00
183	Kirby Puckett	6.00

1995 Leaf

Two series of 200 basic cards each, plus numerous insert sets, are featured in 1995 Leaf. The basic card design has a borderless action photo on front, with a small portrait photo printed at upper-left on holographic silver foil. The team name is printed in the same foil in large letters down the left side. A script rendition of the player's name is at bottom-right, with the Leaf logo under the portrait photo; both elements are in gold foil. Backs have a couple more player photos. The card number is in white in a silver-foil seal at upper-right. Previous season and career stats are at lower-left. Several of the insert sets are unique to various package configurations, while others are found in all types of packs.

	NM/M
Complete Set (400):	12.50
Common Player:	.05
Series 1 or 2 Pack (12):	.75
Series 1 or 2 Wax Box (36):	15.00

1	Frank Thomas	.75
2	Carlos Garcia	.05
3	Todd Hundley	.05
4	Damion Easley	.05
5	Roberto Mejia	.05
6	John Mabry	.05
7	Aaron Sele	.05
8	Kenny Lofton	.05
9	John Doherty	.05
10	Joe Carter	.05
11	Mike Lansing	.05
12	John Valentin	.05
13	Ismael Valdes	.05
14	Dave McCarty	.05
15	Melvin Nieves	.05
16	Bobby Jones	.05
17	Trevor Hoffman	.05
18	John Smoltz	.05
19	Leo Gomez	.05
20	Roger Pavlik	.05
21	Dean Palmer	.05
22	Rickey Henderson	.75
23	Eddie Taubensee	.05
24	Damon Buford	.05
25	Mark Wohlers	.05
26	Jim Edmonds	.05
27	Wilson Alvarez	.05
28	Matt Williams	.05
29	Jeff Montgomery	.05
30	Shawon Dunston	.05
31	Tom Pagnozzi	.05
32	Jose Lind	.05
33	Royce Clayton	.05
34	Cal Eldred	.05
35	Chris Gomez	.05
36	Henry Rodriguez	.05
37	Dave Fleming	.05
38	Jon Lieber	.05
39	Scott Servais	.05
40	Wade Boggs	1.00
41	John Olerud	.05
42	Eddie Williams	.05
43	Paul Sorrento	.05
44	Ron Karkovice	.05
45	Kevin Foster	.05
46	Miguel Jimenez	.05
47	Reggie Sanders	.05
48	Rondell White	.05
49	Scott Leius	.05
50	Jose Valentin	.05
51	William Van Landingham	.05
52	Denny Hocking	.05
53	Jeff Fassero	.05
54	Chris Hoiles	.05
55	Walt Weiss	.05
56	Geronimo Berroa	.05
57	Rich Rowland	.05
58	Dave Weathers	.05
59	Sterling Hitchcock	.05
60	Raul Mondesi	.05
61	Rusty Greer	.05
62	Dave Justice	.05
63	Cecil Fielder	.05

64	Brian Jordan	.05
65	Mike Lieberthal	.05
66	Rick Aguilera	.05
67	Chuck Finley	.05
68	Andy Ashby	.05
69	Alex Fernandez	.05
70	Ed Sprague	.05
71	Steve Buechele	.05
72	Willie Greene	.05
73	Dave Nilsson	.05
74	Bret Saberhagen	.05
75	Jimmy Key	.05
76	Darren Lewis	.05
77	Steve Cooke	.05
78	Kirk Gibson	.05
79	Ray Lankford	.05
80	Paul O'Neill	.05
81	Mike Bordick	.05
82	Wes Chamberlain	.05
83	Rico Brogna	.05
84	Kevin Appier	.05
85	Juan Guzman	.05
86	Kevin Seitzer	.05
87	Mickey Morandini	.05
88	Pedro Martinez	.75
89	Matt Mieske	.05
90	Tino Martinez	.05
91	Paul Shuey	.05
92	Bip Roberts	.05
93	Chili Davis	.05
94	Deion Sanders	.05
95	Darrell Whitmore	.05
96	Joe Orsulak	.05
97	Bret Boone	.05
98	Kent Mercker	.05
99	Scott Livingstone	.05
100	Brady Anderson	.05
101	James Mouton	.05
102	Jose Rijo	.05
103	Bobby Munoz	.05
104	Ramon Martinez	.05
105	Bernie Williams	.10
106	Troy Neel	.05
107	Ivan Rodriguez	.65
108	Salomon Torres	.05
109	Johnny Ruffin	.05
110	Darryl Kile	.05
111	Bobby Ayala	.05
112	Ron Darling	.05
113	Jose Lima	.05
114	Joey Hamilton	.05
115	Greg Maddux	1.00
116	Greg Colbrunn	.05
117	Ozzie Guillen	.05
118	Brian Anderson	.05
119	Jeff Bagwell	.75
120	Pat Listach	.05
121	Sandy Alomar	.05
122	Jose Vizcaino	.05
123	Rick Helling	.05
124	Allen Watson	.05
125	Pedro Munoz	.05
126	Craig Biggio	.05
127	Kevin Stocker	.05
128	Wil Cordero	.05
129	Rafael Palmeiro	.65
130	Gar Finnvold	.05
131	Darren Hall	.05
132	Heath Slocumb	.05
133	Darrin Fletcher	.05
134	Cal Ripken Jr.	2.50
135	Dante Bichette	.05
136	Don Slaught	.05
137	Pedro Astacio	.05
138	Ryan Thompson	.05
139	Greg Gohr	.05
140	Javier Lopez	.05
141	Lenny Dykstra	.05
142	Pat Rapp	.05
143	Mark Kiefer	.05
144	Greg Gagne	.05
145	Eduardo Perez	.05
146	Felix Fermin	.05
147	Jeff Frye	.05
148	Terry Steinbach	.05
149	Jim Eisenreich	.05
150	Brad Ausmus	.05
151	Randy Myers	.05
152	Rick White	.05
153	Mark Portugal	.05
154	Delino DeShields	.05
155	Scott Cooper	.05
156	Pat Hentgen	.05
157	Mark Gubicza	.05
158	Carlos Baerga	.05
159	Joe Girardi	.05
160	Rey Sanchez	.05
161	Todd Jones	.05
162	Luis Polonia	.05
163	Steve Trachsel	.05
164	Roberto Hernandez	.05
165	John Patterson	.05
166	Rene Arocha	.05
167	Will Clark	.10
168	Jim Leyritz	.05
169	Todd Van Poppel	.05
170	Robb Nen	.05
171	Midre Cummings	.05
172	Jay Buhner	.05
173	Kevin Tapani	.05
174	Mark Lemke	.05
175	Marcus Moore	.05
176	Wayne Kirby	.05
177	Rich Amaral	.05
178	Lou Whitaker	.05
179	Jay Bell	.05
180	Rick Wilkins	.05
181	Paul Molitor	.75

182	Gary Sheffield	.35
183	Kirby Puckett	1.00
184	Cliff Floyd	.05
185	Darren Oliver	.05
186	Tim Naehring	.05
187	John Hudek	.05
188	Eric Young	.05
189	Roger Salkeld	.05
190	Kirt Manwaring	.05
191	Kurt Abbott	.05
192	David Nied	.05
193	Todd Zeile	.05
194	Wally Joyner	.05
195	Dennis Martinez	.05
196	Billy Ashley	.05
197	Ben McDonald	.05
198	Bob Hamelin	.05
199	Chris Turner	.05
200	Lance Johnson	.05
201	Willie Banks	.05
202	Juan Gonzalez	.50
203	Scott Sanders	.05
204	Scott Brosius	.05
205	Curt Schilling	.25
206	Alex Gonzalez	.05
207	Travis Fryman	.05
208	Tim Raines	.05
209	Steve Avery	.05
210	Hal Morris	.05
211	Ken Griffey Jr.	1.50
212	Ozzie Smith	1.00
213	Chuck Carr	.05
214	Ryan Klesko	.05
215	Robin Ventura	.05
216	Luis Gonzalez	.20
217	Ken Ryan	.05
218	Mike Piazza	1.50
219	Matt Walbeck	.05
220	Jeff Kent	.05
221	Orlando Miller	.05
222	Kenny Rogers	.05
223	J.T. Snow	.05
224	Alan Trammell	.05
225	John Franco	.05
226	Gerald Williams	.05
227	Andy Benes	.05
228	Dan Wilson	.05
229	Dave Hollins	.05
230	Vinny Castilla	.05
231	Devon White	.05
232	Fred McGriff	.05
233	Quilvio Veras	.05
234	Tom Candiotti	.05
235	Jason Bere	.05
236	Mark Langston	.05
237	Mel Rojas	.05
238	Chuck Knoblauch	.05
239	Bernard Gilkey	.05
240	Mark McGwire	2.00
241	Kirk Rueter	.05
242	Pat Kelly	.05
243	Ruben Sierra	.05
244	Randy Johnson	.75
245	Shane Reynolds	.05
246	Danny Tartabull	.05
247	Darryl Hamilton	.05
248	Danny Bautista	.05
249	Tom Gordon	.05
250	Tom Glavine	.25
251	Orlando Merced	.05
252	Eric Karros	.05
253	Benji Gil	.05
254	Sean Bergman	.05
255	Roger Clemens	1.25
256	Roberto Alomar	.20
257	Benito Santiago	.05
258	Robby Thompson	.05
259	Marvin Freeman	.05
260	Jose Offerman	.05
261	Greg Vaughn	.05
262	David Segui	.05
263	Geronimo Pena	.05
264	Tim Salmon	.05
265	Eddie Murray	.75
266	Mariano Duncan	.05
267	Hideo Nomo RC	2.50
268	Derek Bell	.05
269	Mo Vaughn	.05
270	Jeff King	.05
271	Edgar Martinez	.05
272	Sammy Sosa	1.25
273	Scott Ruffcorn	.05
274	Darren Daulton	.05
275	John Jaha	.05
276	Andres Galarraga	.05
277	Mark Grace	.05
278	Mike Moore	.05
279	Barry Bonds	2.50
280	Manny Ramirez	.75
281	Ellis Burks	.05
282	Greg Swindell	.05
283	Barry Larkin	.05
284	Albert Belle	.35
285	Shawn Green	.05
286	John Roper	.05
287	Scott Erickson	.05
288	Moises Alou	.05
289	Mike Blowers	.05
290	Brent Gates	.05
291	Sean Berry	.05
292	Mike Stanley	.05
293	Jeff Conine	.05
294	Tim Wallach	.05
295	Bobby Bonilla	.05
296	Bruce Ruffin	.05
297	Chad Curtis	.05
298	Mike Greenwell	.05
299	Tony Gwynn	1.00

300	Russ Davis	.05
301	Danny Jackson	.05
302	Pete Harnisch	.05
303	Don Mattingly	1.25
304	Rheal Cormier	.05
305	Larry Walker	.05
306	Hector Carrasco	.05
307	Jason Jacome	.05
308	Phil Plantier	.05
309	Harold Baines	.05
310	Mitch Williams	.05
311	Charles Nagy	.05
312	Ken Caminiti	.05
313	Alex Rodriguez	2.00
314	Chris Sabo	.05
315	Gary Gaetti	.05
316	Andre Dawson	.25
317	Mark Clark	.05
318	Vince Coleman	.05
319	Brad Clontz	.05
320	Steve Finley	.05
321	Doug Drabek	.05
322	Mark McLemore	.05
323	Stan Javier	.05
324	Ron Gant	.05
325	Charlie Hayes	.05
326	Carlos Delgado	.50
327	Ricky Bottalico	.05
328	Rod Beck	.05
329	Mark Acre	.05
330	Chris Bosio	.05
331	Tony Phillips	.05
332	Garret Anderson	.05
333	Pat Meares	.05
334	Todd Worrell	.05
335	Marquis Grissom	.05
336	Brent Mayne	.05
337	Lee Tinsley	.05
338	Terry Pendleton	.05
339	David Cone	.05
340	Tony Fernandez	.05
341	Jim Bullinger	.05
342	Armando Benitez	.05
343	John Smiley	.05
344	Dan Miceli	.05
345	Charles Johnson	.05
346	Lee Smith	.05
347	Brian McRae	.05
348	Jim Thome	.65
349	Jose Oliva	.05
350	Terry Mulholland	.05
351	Tom Henke	.05
352	Dennis Eckersley	.65
353	Sid Fernandez	.05
354	Paul Wagner	.05
355	John Dettmer	.05
356	John Wetteland	.05
357	John Burkett	.05
358	Marty Cordova	.05
359	Norm Charlton	.05
360	Mike Devereaux	.05
361	Alex Cole	.05
362	Brett Butler	.05
363	Mickey Tettleton	.05
364	Al Martin	.05
365	Tony Tarasco	.05
366	Pat Mahomes	.05
367	Gary DiSarcina	.05
368	Bill Swift	.05
369	Chipper Jones	1.00
370	Orel Hershiser	.05
371	Kevin Gross	.05
372	Dave Winfield	.75
373	Andujar Cedeno	.05
374	Jim Abbott	.05
375	Glenallen Hill	.05
376	Otis Nixon	.05
377	Roberto Kelly	.05
378	Chris Hammond	.05
379	Mike Macfarlane	.05
380	J.R. Phillips	.05
381	Luis Alicea	.05
382	Bret Barberie	.05
383	Tom Goodwin	.05
384	Mark Whiten	.05
385	Jeffrey Hammonds	.05
386	Omar Vizquel	.05
387	Mike Mussina	.35
388	Rickey Bones	.05
389	Steve Ontiveros	.05
390	Jeff Blauser	.05
391	Jose Canseco	.35
392	Bob Tewksbury	.05
393	Jacob Brumfield	.05
394	Doug Jones	.05
395	Ken Hill	.05
396	Pat Borders	.05
397	Carl Everett	.05
398	Gregg Jefferies	.05
399	Jack McDowell	.05
400	Denny Neagle	.05

Checklists

Honoring the major 1994 award winners in the American (Series I) and National (Series II) Leagues, checklists for the 1995 Leaf set are not numbered among the regular issue. Horizontal cards have a player action photo at left with his name and team in gold foil at bottom. The award is printed vertically at left with the checklist beginning on the right. Backs continue the checklist on a graduated purple background with the checklist number in a silver-foil seal at top-right.

	NM/M
Complete Set (8):	1.50
Common Player:	.25

1	Checklist 1-67 (Bob Hamelin) (Rookie of the Year)	.25
2	Checklist 68-134 (David Cone (Cy Young))	.25
3	Checklist 135-200 (Frank Thomas (MVP))	.45
4	Series II inserts checklist (Paul O'Neill) (Batting title.)	.25
5	Checklist 201-267 (Raul Mondesi) (Rookie of the Year)	.25
6	Checklist 268-334 (Greg Maddux) (Cy Young)	.50
7	Checklist 335-400 (Jeff Bagwell (MVP))	.45
8	Series 2 inserts checklist (Tony Gwynn) (Batting title.)	.50

Cornerstones

Cornerstones, six of the best first baseman-third baseman combos in baseball, is a six-card insert series found, on average, once every 18 packs in Series I Leaf. Card fronts are horizontally oriented and have a silver prismatic border and player names. Player defensive action photos are set against a background resembling their team logo chiseled into a stone block. Backs have player batting photos at each end with offensive and defensive stats from 1994, and a few words about the duo.

	NM/M
Complete Set (6):	3.50
Common Player:	.40

1	Frank Thomas, Robin Ventura	.75
2	Cecil Fielder, Travis Fryman	.40
3	Don Mattingly, Wade Boggs	2.00
4	Jeff Bagwell, Ken Caminiti	.75
5	Will Clark, Dean Palmer	.40
6	J.R. Phillips, Matt Williams	.40

Gold Stars

Once again the toughest pull among the Leaf inserts are the Gold Leaf Stars found in both series. Found on average of one card per 90-270 packs, depending on pack card count, each of these chase cards is numbered on back within an edition of 10,000. Cards have fronts printed on metallic foil with the player name at top, the series title at bottom and a vertical stars and stripe device at right all printed in gold foil. A die-cut star appears at bottom-left. Backs are conventionally printed with another player

photo and a few sentences about the star. The serial number is in gold foil in a white strip at top.

	NM/M
Complete Set (14):	35.00
Common Player:	1.00

1	Jeff Bagwell	2.50
2	Albert Belle	1.00
3	Tony Gwynn	3.50
4	Ken Griffey Jr.	4.50
5	Barry Bonds	6.00
6	Don Mattingly	4.00
7	Raul Mondesi	1.00
8	Joe Carter	1.00
9	Greg Maddux	3.50
10	Frank Thomas	2.50
11	Mike Piazza	4.50
12	Jose Canseco	1.50
13	Kirby Puckett	3.50
14	Matt Williams	1.00

Gold Rookies

Every other pack of Series I Leaf Series I is seeded with a Gold Leaf Rookie card. Fronts have a largely white background with a large player photo at left-center and a smaller picture in a rectangle at upper-right. A team-color stripe is at left, while a smaller gray stripe is at top-right. The team name is printed in large gray letters across the center of the card, with the player name in a team color beneath that and above the gold-foil Leaf logo at lower-left. "Gold Leaf Rookies" is printed in gold foil down the right side. Backs repeat the team-color motif with a large action photo of the player in a single color and a smaller color portrait. Full career stats are at bottom.

	NM/M
Complete Set (16):	3.00
Common Player:	.10

1	Alex Rodriguez	2.50
2	Garret Anderson	.25
3	Shawn Green	.50
4	Armando Benitez	.10
5	Darren Dreifort	.10
6	Orlando Miller	.10
7	Jose Oliva	.10
8	Ricky Bottalico	.10
9	Charles Johnson	.10
10	Brian Hunter	.10
11	Ray McDavid	.10
12	Chan Ho Park	.10
13	Mike Kelly	.10
14	Cory Bailey	.10
15	Alex Gonzalez	.10
16	Andrew Lorraine	.10

Great Gloves

While the stated emphasis is on fielding prowess in this Series II chase set, players who don't also swing a big stick are ignored. Found as frequently as one per two packs, cards have a detail photo of a glove at left, with an action photo at right. The player name in the Great Gloves logo at bottom-right is in gold foil,

game's top sluggers. Backs have another photo against a background of tree trunks. A white stripe at bottom carries each card's unique serial number within an edition of 5,000.

		NM/M
Complete Set (16):		55.00
Common Player:		2.00
1	Albert Belle	2.00
2	Barry Bonds	12.00
3	Juan Gonzalez	3.50
4	Ken Griffey Jr.	7.50
5	Fred McGriff	2.00
6	Mike Piazza	7.50
7	Kirby Puckett	6.00
8	Mo Vaughn	
9	Frank Thomas	4.50
10	Jeff Bagwell	4.50
11	Matt Williams	2.00
12	Jose Canseco	3.00
13	Raul Mondesi	2.00
14	Manny Ramirez	4.50
15	Cecil Fielder	2.00
16	Cal Ripken Jr.	12.00

Opening Day

Issued in celebration of the 1995's season's delayed debut, this set was only available via a mail-in offer for $2 and eight wrappers. Cards were advertised as featuring front and back photos shot on opening day. Fronts feature a player photo bordered on the left with a vertical "1995 Opening Day" stripe featuring exploding fireworks at the bottom. The player's name and position appear in a silver-foil strip at bottom; a silver-foil Leaf logo is at upper-right. Backs have a player action photo set against a background of exploding fireworks and a re-cap of the player's 1995 Opening Day performance.

		NM/M
Complete Set (8):		6.00
Common Player:		.25
1	Frank Thomas	.50
2	Jeff Bagwell	.50
3	Barry Bonds	2.00
5	Ken Griffey Jr.	1.00
5	Mike Piazza	1.00
6	Cal Ripken Jr.	2.00
7	Jose Canseco	.35
8	Larry Walker	.25

1996 Leaf

Reverting to a single-series issue of 220 basic cards, plus numerous insert set bells and whistles, this was the final Leaf set under Donruss' ownership. Regular cards offer large action photos on front and back with a side and bottom border subdued through darkening (front) or lightening (back). Fronts feature silver prismatic-foil graphic highlights while the back includes a circular portrait photo with vital data around. Leaf was sold in both hobby and retail versions, each with some

unique inserts. Basic unit was the 12-card foil pack, with suggested retail of $2.49.

		NM/M
Complete Set (220):		10.00
Common Player:		.05
Complete Gold Set (220):		100.00
Common Golds:		1.00
Gold Press Proofs:		15X
Complete Silver Set (220):		50.00
Common Silvers:		.50
Silver Press Proofs:		6X
Complete Bronze Set (220):		40.00
Common Bronze:		.25
Bronze Press Proofs:		4X
Pack (12):		.25
Wax Box (30):		25.00
1	John Smoltz	.10
2	Dennis Eckersley	.60
3	Delino DeShields	.05
4	Cliff Floyd	.05
5	Chuck Finley	.05
6	Cecil Fielder	.05
7	Tim Naehring	.05
8	Carlos Perez	.05
9	Brad Ausmus	.05
10	Matt Lawton **RC**	.15
11	Alan Trammell	.05
12	Steve Finley	.05
13	Paul O'Neill	.05
14	Gary Sheffield	.40
15	Mark McGwire	1.50
16	Bernie Williams	.05
17	Jeff Montgomery	.05
18	Chan Ho Park	.05
19	Greg Vaughn	.05
20	Jeff Kent	.05
21	Cal Ripken Jr.	2.00
22	Charles Johnson	.05
23	Eric Karros	.05
24	Alex Rodriguez	1.50
25	Chris Snopek	.05
26	Jason Isringhausen	.05
27	Chili Davis	.05
28	Chipper Jones	.75
29	Bret Saberhagen	.05
30	Tony Clark	.05
31	Marty Cordova	.05
32	Dwayne Hosey	.05
33	Fred McGriff	.05
34	Deion Sanders	.05
35	Orlando Merced	.05
36	Brady Anderson	.05
37	Ray Lankford	.05
38	Manny Ramirez	.65
39	Alex Fernandez	.05
40	Greg Colbrunn	.05
41	Ken Griffey Jr.	1.00
42	Mickey Morandini	.05
43	Chuck Knoblauch	.05
44	Quinton McCracken	.05
45	Tim Salmon	.05
46	Jose Mesa	.05
47	Marquis Grissom	.05
48	Checklist	.05
49	Raul Mondesi	.05
50	Mark Grudzielanek	.05
51	Ray Durham	.05
52	Matt Williams	.05
53	Bob Hamelin	.05
54	Lenny Dykstra	.05
55	Jeff King	.05
56	LaTroy Hawkins	.05
57	Terry Pendleton	.05
58	Kevin Stocker	.05
59	Ozzie Timmons	.05
60	David Justice	.05
61	Ricky Bottalico	.05
62	Andy Ashby	.05
63	Larry Walker	.05
64	Jose Canseco	.40
65	Bret Boone	.05
66	Shawn Green	.35
67	Chad Curtis	.05
68	Travis Fryman	.05
69	Roger Clemens	1.00
70	David Bell	.05
71	Rusty Greer	.05
72	Bob Higginson	.05
73	Joey Hamilton	.05
74	Kevin Seitzer	.05
75	Julian Tavarez	.05
76	Troy Percival	.05
77	Kirby Puckett	.75
78	Barry Bonds	2.00
79	Michael Tucker	.05

80	Paul Molitor	.65
81	Carlos Garcia	.05
82	Johnny Damon	.35
83	Mike Hampton	.05
84	Ariel Prieto	.05
85	Tony Tarasco	.05
86	Pete Schourek	.05
87	Tom Glavine	.30
88	Rondell White	.05
89	Jim Edmonds	.05
90	Robby Thompson	.05
91	Wade Boggs	.75
92	Pedro Martinez	.65
93	Gregg Jefferies	.05
94	Albert Belle	.05
95	Benji Gil	.05
96	Denny Neagle	.05
97	Mark Langston	.05
98	Sandy Alomar	.05
99	Tony Gwynn	.75
100	Todd Hundley	.05
101	Dante Bichette	.05
102	Eddie Murray	.05
103	Lyle Mouton	.05
104	John Jaha	.05
105	Checklist	.05
106	Jon Nunnally	.05
107	Juan Gonzalez	.50
108	Kevin Appier	.05
109	Brian McRae	.05
110	Lee Smith	.05
111	Tim Wakefield	.05
112	Sammy Sosa	1.00
113	Jay Buhner	.05
114	Garret Anderson	.05
115	Edgar Martinez	.05
116	Edgardo Alfonzo	.05
117	Billy Ashley	.05
118	Joe Carter	.05
119	Javy Lopez	.05
120	Bobby Bonilla	.05
121	Ken Caminiti	.05
122	Barry Larkin	.05
123	Shannon Stewart	.05
124	Orel Hershiser	.05
125	Jeff Conine	.05
126	Mark Grace	.05
127	Kenny Lofton	.05
128	Luis Gonzalez	.25
129	Rico Brogna	.05
130	Mo Vaughn	.05
131	Brad Radke	.05
132	Jose Herrera	.05
133	Rick Aguilera	.05
134	Gary DiSarcina	.05
135	Andres Galarraga	.05
136	Carl Everett	.05
137	Steve Avery	.05
138	Vinny Castilla	.05
139	Dennis Martinez	.05
140	John Wetteland	.05
141	Alex Gonzalez	.05
142	Brian Jordan	.05
143	Todd Hollandsworth	.05
144	Terrell Wade	.05
145	Wilson Alvarez	.05
146	Reggie Sanders	.05
147	Will Clark	.10
148	Hideo Nomo	.50
149	J.T. Snow	.05
150	Frank Thomas	.65
151	Ivan Rodriguez	.60
152	Jay Bell	.05
153	Checklist	.05
154	David Cone	.05
155	Roberto Alomar	.20
156	Carlos Delgado	.40
157	Carlos Baerga	.05
158	Geronimo Berroa	.05
159	Joe Vitiello	.05
160	Terry Steinbach	.05
161	Doug Drabek	.05
162	David Segui	.05
163	Ozzie Smith	.05
164	Kurt Abbott	.05
165	Randy Johnson	.65
166	John Valentin	.05
167	Mickey Tettleton	.05
168	Ruben Sierra	.05
169	Jim Thome	.60
170	Mike Greenwell	.05
171	Quilvio Veras	.05
172	Robin Ventura	.05
173	Bill Pulsipher	.05
174	Rafael Palmeiro	.60
175	Hal Morris	.05
176	Ryan Klesko	.05
177	Eric Young	.05
178	Shane Andrews	.05
179	Brian Hunter	.05
180	Brett Butler	.05
181	John Olerud	.05
182	Moises Alou	.05
183	Glenallen Hill	.05
184	Ismael Valdes	.05
185	Andy Pettitte	.25
186	Yamil Benitez	.05
187	Jason Bere	.05
188	Dean Palmer	.05
189	Jimmy Haynes	.05
190	Trevor Hoffman	.05
191	Mike Mussina	.40
192	Greg Maddux	.75
193	Ozzie Guillen	.05
194	Pat Listach	.05
195	Derek Bell	.05
196	Darren Daulton	.05
197	John Mabry	.05

198	Ramon Martinez	.05
199	Jeff Bagwell	.65
200	Mike Piazza	1.00
201	Al Martin	.05
202	Aaron Sele	.05
203	Ed Sprague	.05
204	Rod Beck	.05
205	Checklist	.05
206	Mike Lansing	.05
207	Craig Biggio	.05
208	Jeffrey Hammonds	.05
209	Dave Nilsson	.05
210	Checklist, Inserts (Dante Bichette, Albert Belle)	.05
211	Derek Jeter	2.00
212	Alan Benes	.05
213	Jason Schmidt	.05
214	Alex Ochoa	.05
215	Ruben Rivera	.05
216	Roger Cedeno	.05
217	Jeff Suppan	.05
218	Billy Wagner	.05
219	Mark Loretta	.05
220	Karim Garcia	.10

Press Proofs

Carrying the parallel edition concept to its inevitable next level, '96 Leaf offered the Press Proof insert cards in three degrees of scarcity, each highlighted with appropriate holographic foil. At the top of the line are Gold Press Proofs in an edition of only 500 of each card. Silver and Bronze versions were produced in editions of 1,000 and 2,000, respectively. Press Proofs are inserted into both hobby and retail packs at an average rate of one card per 10 packs.

	NM/M
Complete Set, Gold (220):	200.00
Complete Set, Silver (220):	100.00
Complete Set, Bronze (220):	75.00
Common Player, Gold:	1.00
Common Player, Silver:	.50
Common Player, Bronze:	.25

All-Star MVP Contenders

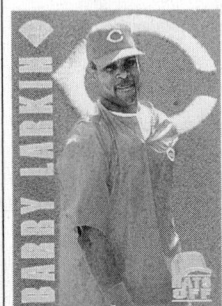

A surprise insert in Leaf boxes was this interactive redemption issue. Twenty leading candidates for MVP honors at the 1996 All-Star Game in Philadelphia were presented in a silver-foil highlighted horizontal format. The player's league logo serves as a background to the color action photo on front. Backs have details of the redemption offer which expired Aug. 15, 1996. The first 5,000 persons who sent in the Mike Piazza card for redemption received a gold version of the set and had their Piazza card punch-cancelled and returned.

		NM/M
Complete Set (20):		12.50
Common Card:		.25
Golds:		1.5X
1	Frank Thomas	.75
2	Mike Piazza	1.50
2c	Mike Piazza (Redeemed and punch-cancelled.)	1.00
3	Sammy Sosa	1.50
4	Cal Ripken Jr.	2.00
5	Jeff Bagwell	.75
6	Reggie Sanders	.25
7	Mo Vaughn	.25
8	Tony Gwynn	1.00
9	Dante Bichette	.25
10	Tim Salmon	.25

11	Chipper Jones	1.00
12	Kenny Lofton	.25
13	Manny Ramirez	.75
14	Barry Bonds	2.00
15	Raul Mondesi	.25
16	Kirby Puckett	1.00
17	Albert Belle	.25
18	Ken Griffey Jr.	1.50
19	Greg Maddux	1.00
20	Bonus Card	.10

Gold Leaf Stars

A vignetted background of embossed gold metallic cardboard and a Gold Leaf Stars logo in 22-K gold foil are featured on this limited (2,500 of each) edition insert. Backs include a second color photo of the player and a serial number from within the edition. Gold Leaf Stars were included in both hobby and retail packaging, with an average insertion rate of one per 210 packs.

		NM/M
Complete Set (15):		125.00
Common Player:		3.00
1	Frank Thomas	9.00
2	Dante Bichette	3.00
3	Sammy Sosa	15.00
4	Ken Griffey Jr.	15.00
5	Mike Piazza	15.00
6	Tim Salmon	3.00
7	Hideo Nomo	6.00
8	Cal Ripken Jr.	20.00
9	Chipper Jones	12.00
10	Albert Belle	3.00
11	Tony Gwynn	12.00
12	Mo Vaughn	3.00
13	Barry Larkin	3.00
14	Manny Ramirez	9.00
15	Greg Maddux	12.00

Hats Off

The most technically innovative inserts of 1996 have to be the Hats Off series exclusive to Leaf retail packs. Front player photos are on a background that is both flocked to simulate the cloth of a baseball cap, plus enhanced with a stiched team logo. The graphics are all in raised textured gold foil. Backs are conventionally printed and include a gold-foil serial number placing each card within an edition of 5,000 per player.

		NM/M
Complete Set (8):		30.00
Common Player:		3.00
1	Cal Ripken Jr.	12.00
2	Barry Larkin	3.00
3	Frank Thomas	4.50
4	Mo Vaughn	3.00
5	Ken Griffey Jr.	7.50
6	Hideo Nomo	4.00
7	Albert Belle	3.00
8	Greg Maddux	6.00

Picture Perfect

Leaf calls the glossy central area of these inserts "pearlized foil," which allows the player action photo to stand out in contrast to the

actual wood veneer background. Gold-foil highlights complete the design. Backs are conventionally printed and include a gold-foil serial number from within the edition of 5,000 of each player's card. Cards #1-6 are hobby-only inserts, while #7-12 are found in retail packs. Average insertion rate is one per 140 packs. A promo version of each card was also issued.

		NM/M
Complete Set (12):		22.50
Common Player:		1.00
Promos:		2X
1	Frank Thomas	2.00
2	Cal Ripken Jr.	5.00
3	Greg Maddux	2.50
4	Manny Ramirez	2.00
5	Chipper Jones	2.50
6	Tony Gwynn	2.50
7	Ken Griffey Jr.	3.00
8	Albert Belle	1.00
9	Jeff Bagwell	2.00
10	Mike Piazza	2.00
11	Mo Vaughn	1.00
12	Barry Bonds	5.00

Statistical Standouts

The feel of leather complements the game-used baseball background on these hobby-only inserts featuring the game's top names. Backs offer statistical data and a gold-foil serial number placing the card within an edition of 2,500 for each player. Average insertion rate is one per 210 packs.

		NM/M
Complete Set (8):		60.00
Common Player:		3.00
1	Cal Ripken Jr.	20.00
2	Tony Gwynn	10.00
3	Frank Thomas	7.50
4	Ken Griffey Jr.	13.50
5	Hideo Nomo	6.00
6	Greg Maddux	10.00
7	Albert Belle	3.00
8	Chipper Jones	10.00

Frank Thomas' Greatest Hits

Die-cut plastic with a background of prismatic foil to simulate a segment of a compact disc is the format for this insert issue chronicling the career-to-date of Frank Thomas. Backs include a few stats and a portrait photo, plus a gold-foil serial number from within an edition of 5,000. Cards #1-4 are found only in hobby packs; cards #5-7 are exclusive to retail packs (average insertion rate one per 210 packs) and card #8 could be had only through a wrapper redemption.

		NM/M
Complete Set (8):		12.50
Common Card:		2.00
1	1990	2.00
2	1991	2.00
3	1992	2.00
4	1993	2.00
5	1994	2.00
6	1995	2.00
7	Career	2.00
8	MVP	2.00

Total Bases

Total-base leaders from 1991-95 are featured in this hobby-only insert set. Card fronts are printed on textured canvas to simulate a base image. Fronts are highlighted with gold foil. Backs have stats ranking the player in this category plus a gold-foil serial number from an edition of 5,000 of each player. Total Bases inserts are seeded at an average rate of one per 72 packs. Each player can also be found in a promo card version, marked as such on each side.

		NM/M
Complete Set (12):		25.00
Common Player:		1.00
Promos:		2X
1	Frank Thomas	2.50
2	Albert Belle	1.00
3	Rafael Palmeiro	2.00
4	Barry Bonds	6.00
5	Kirby Puckett	3.00
6	Joe Carter	1.00
7	Paul Molitor	2.50
8	Fred McGriff	1.00
9	Ken Griffey Jr.	4.00
10	Carlos Baerga	1.00
11	Juan Gonzalez	2.00
12	Cal Ripken Jr.	6.00

1996 Leaf/Limited

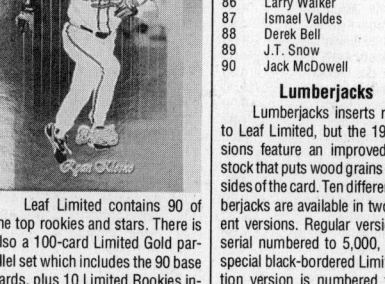

Leaf Limited contains 90 of the top rookies and stars. There is also a 100-card Limited Gold parallel set which includes the 90 base cards, plus 10 Limited Rookies inserts. The gold parallel cards are seeded one per 11 packs. Regular Limited Rookies inserts were seeded one per seven packs. Other insert sets were two versions of Lumberjacks and Pennant Craze.

		NM/M
Complete Set (90):		15.00
Common Player:		.10
Gold Set (90):		50.00
Gold Stars/Rookies:		3X
Pack (5):		1.50
Wax Box (14):		20.00
1	Ivan Rodriguez	.60
2	Roger Clemens	1.50
3	Gary Sheffield	.40
4	Tino Martinez	.10
5	Sammy Sosa	1.50
6	Reggie Sanders	.10
7	Ray Lankford	.10
8	Manny Ramirez	.75
9	Jeff Bagwell	1.00
10	Greg Maddux	1.00
11	Ken Griffey Jr.	1.50
12	Rondell White	.10
13	Mike Piazza	1.50
14	Marc Newfield	.10
15	Cal Ripken Jr.	3.00
16	Carlos Delgado	.40
17	Tim Salmon	.10
18	Andres Galarraga	.10
19	Chuck Knoblauch	.10
20	Matt Williams	.10
21	Mark McGwire	2.00
22	Ben McDonald	.10
23	Frank Thomas	.75
24	Johnny Damon	.35
25	Gregg Jefferies	.10
26	Travis Fryman	.10
27	Chipper Jones	1.00
28	David Cone	.10
29	Kenny Lofton	.10
30	Mike Mussina	.30
31	Alex Rodriguez	2.00
32	Carlos Baerga	.10
33	Brian Hunter	.10
34	Juan Gonzalez	.60
35	Bernie Williams	.10
36	Wally Joyner	.10
37	Fred McGriff	.10
38	Randy Johnson	.75
39	Marty Cordova	.10
40	Garret Anderson	.10
41	Albert Belle	.10
42	Edgar Martinez	.10
43	Barry Larkin	.10
44	Paul O'Neill	.10
45	Cecil Fielder	.10
46	Rusty Greer	.10
47	Mo Vaughn	.10
48	Dante Bichette	.10
49	Ryan Klesko	.10
50	Roberto Alomar	.25
51	Raul Mondesi	.10
52	Robin Ventura	.10
53	Tony Gwynn	1.00
54	Mark Grace	.10
55	Jim Thome	.60
56	Jason Giambi	.50
57	Tom Glavine	.25
58	Jim Edmonds	.10
59	Pedro Martinez	.75
60	Charles Johnson	.10
61	Wade Boggs	1.00
62	Orlando Merced	.10
63	Craig Biggio	.10
64	Brady Anderson	.10
65	Hideo Nomo	.60
66	Ozzie Smith	1.00
67	Eddie Murray	.75
68	Will Clark	.15
69	Jay Buhner	.10
70	Kirby Puckett	1.00
71	Barry Bonds	3.00
72	Ray Durham	.10
73	Sterling Hitchcock	.10
74	John Smoltz	.10
75	Andre Dawson	.35
76	Joe Carter	.10
77	Ryne Sandberg	1.00
78	Rickey Henderson	.75
79	Brian Jordan	.10
80	Greg Vaughn	.10
81	Andy Pettitte	.25
82	Dean Palmer	.10
83	Paul Molitor	.75
84	Rafael Palmeiro	.60
85	Henry Rodriguez	.10
86	Tony Walker	.10
87	Ismael Valdes	.10
88	Derek Bell	.10
89	J.T. Snow	.10
90	Jack McDowell	.10

Lumberjacks

Lumberjacks inserts returned to Leaf Limited, but the 1996 versions feature an improved maple stock that puts wood grains on both sides of the card. Ten different Lumberjacks are available in two different versions. Regular versions are serial numbered to 5,000, while a special black-bordered Limited Edition version is numbered to 500. Each Lumberjacks card was also produced in a promo card version, appropriately marked on each side.

		NM/M
Complete Set (10):		40.00
Common Player:		1.50

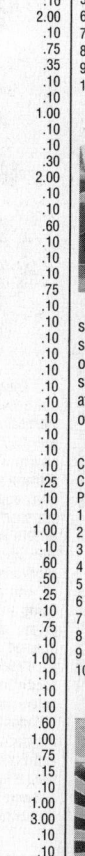

Lumberjack Blacks (500):		2X
Promos:		2X
1	Ken Griffey Jr.	5.00
2	Sammy Sosa	5.00
3	Cal Ripken Jr.	7.50
4	Frank Thomas	3.00
5	Alex Rodriguez	6.00
6	Mo Vaughn	1.50
7	Chipper Jones	4.00
8	Mike Piazza	5.00
9	Jeff Bagwell	3.00
10	Mark McGwire	6.00

Pennant Craze

Each card in this insert set is sequentially numbered to 2,500 in silver foil on the back. The top-front of the cards have a die-cut pennant shape and is felt-textured. Appropriately marked promotional versions of each card can also be found.

		NM/M
Complete Set (10):		20.00
Common Player:		1.00
Promos:		2X
1	Juan Gonzalez	1.25
2	Cal Ripken Jr.	4.00
3	Frank Thomas	1.50
4	Ken Griffey Jr.	2.50
5	Albert Belle	1.00
6	Greg Maddux	2.00
7	Paul Molitor	1.50
8	Alex Rodriguez	3.00
9	Barry Bonds	4.00
10	Chipper Jones	2.00

Rookies

There are two versions of this 1996 Limited insert set. The cards are reprinted as part of a Limited Gold parallel set, which also includes the regular issue's 90 cards. The gold cards are seeded one per every 11 packs. The top young players are also featured on regular Limited Rookies inserts; these versions are seeded one per every seven packs.

		NM/M
Complete Set (10):		7.50
Common Player:		.50
Limited Gold:		3X
1	Alex Ochoa	.50
2	Darin Erstad	1.00
3	Ruben Rivera	.50
4	Derek Jeter	5.00
5	Jermaine Dye	.50
6	Jason Kendall	.50
7	Mike Grace	.50
8	Andruw Jones	2.50
9	Rey Ordonez	.50
10	George Arias	.50

1996 Leaf/Preferred

Leaf Preferred consists of 150 cards, a Press Proof parallel set and three insert sets, one of which has its own parallel set, too. While no individual odds are given for insert sets, the overall odds of getting an insert card are one per 10 packs. The Press Proof inserts replace the silver foil name and strip down the left side of the card with gold foil. Press Proof parallels were limited to 250 sets. Another insert set, Silver Leaf Steel, has a card seeded one per pack. This insert set is paralleled by a Gold Leaf Steel set, which appears in much more limited numbers. The two other insert sets are Steel Power and Staremaster.

		NM/M
Complete Set (150):		15.00
Common Player:		.05
Press Proofs:		12X
Pack (6):		1.00
Wax Box (24):		20.00
1	Ken Griffey Jr.	1.25
2	Rico Brogna	.05
3	Gregg Jefferies	.05
4	Reggie Sanders	.05
5	Manny Ramirez	.75
6	Shawn Green	.40
7	Tino Martinez	.05
8	Jeff Bagwell	.75
9	Marc Newfield	.05
10	Ray Lankford	.05
11	Jay Bell	.05
12	Greg Maddux	.50
13	Frank Thomas	.75
14	Travis Fryman	.05
15	Mark McGwire	1.50
16	Chuck Knoblauch	.05
17	Sammy Sosa	1.25
18	Matt Williams	.05
19	Roger Clemens	1.25
20	Rondell White	.05
21	Ivan Rodriguez	.65
22	Cal Ripken Jr.	2.00
23	Ben McDonald	.05
24	Kenny Lofton	.05
25	Mike Piazza	1.25
26	David Cone	.05
27	Gary Sheffield	.40
28	Tim Salmon	.05
29	Andres Galarraga	.05
30	Johnny Damon	.35
31	Ozzie Smith	1.00
32	Carlos Baerga	.05
33	Raul Mondesi	.05
34	Moises Alou	.05
35	Alex Rodriguez	1.50
36	Mike Mussina	.40
37	Jason Isringhausen	.05
38	Barry Larkin	.05
39	Bernie Williams	.05
40	Chipper Jones	1.00
41	Joey Hamilton	.05
42	Charles Johnson	.05
43	Juan Gonzalez	.50
44	Greg Vaughn	.05
45	Robin Ventura	.05
46	Albert Belle	.05
47	Rafael Palmeiro	.65
48	Brian Hunter	.05
49	Mo Vaughn	.05
50	Paul O'Neill	.05
51	Mark Grace	.05
52	Randy Johnson	.75
53	Pedro Martinez	.75
54	Marty Cordova	.05
55	Garret Anderson	.05
56	Joe Carter	.05
57	Jim Thome	.05
58	Edgardo Alfonzo	.05
59	Dante Bichette	.05
60	Darryl Hamilton	.05
61	Roberto Alomar	.20
62	Fred McGriff	.05
63	Kirby Puckett	1.00
64	Hideo Nomo	.60
65	Alex Fernandez	.05
66	Ryan Klesko	.05
67	Wade Boggs	1.00
68	Eddie Murray	.75
69	Eric Karros	.05
70	Jim Edmonds	.05
71	Edgar Martinez	.05
72	Andy Pettitte	.30
73	Mark Grudzielanek	.05
74	Tom Glavine	.25
75	Ken Caminiti	.05
76	Will Clark	.10
77	Craig Biggio	.05
78	Brady Anderson	.05
79	Tony Gwynn	1.00
80	Larry Walker	.05
81	Brian Jordan	.05
82	Lenny Dykstra	.05
83	Butch Huskey	.05
84	Jack McDowell	.05
85	Cecil Fielder	.05
86	Jose Canseco	.40
87	Jason Giambi	.50
88	Rickey Henderson	.75
89	Kevin Seitzer	.05
90	Carlos Delgado	.40
91	Ryne Sandberg	1.00
92	Dwight Gooden	.05
93	Michael Tucker	.05
94	Barry Bonds	2.00
95	Eric Young	.05
96	Dean Palmer	.05
97	Henry Rodriguez	.05
98	John Mabry	.05
99	J.T. Snow	.05
100	Andre Dawson	.25
101	Ismael Valdes	.05
102	Charles Nagy	.05
103	Jay Buhner	.05
104	Derek Bell	.05
105	Paul Molitor	.75
106	Hal Morris	.05
107	Ray Durham	.05
108	Bernard Gilkey	.05
109	John Valentin	.05
110	Melvin Nieves	.05
111	John Smoltz	.05
112	Terrell Wade	.05
113	Chad Mottola	.05
114	Tony Clark	.05
115	John Wasdin	.05
116	Derek Jeter	2.00
117	Rey Ordonez	.05
118	Jason Thompson	.05
119	Robin Jennings **RC**	.05
120	Rocky Coppinger **RC**	.05
121	Billy Wagner	.05
122	Steve Gibralter	.05
123	Jermaine Dye	.05
124	Jason Kendall	.05
125	Mike Grace **RC**	.05
126	Jason Schmidt	.05
127	Paul Wilson	.05
128	Alan Benes	.05
129	Justin Thompson	.05
130	Brooks Kieschnick	.05
131	George Arias	.05
132	Osvaldo Fernandez **RC**	.20
133	Todd Hollandsworth	.05
134	Chan Ho Park	.05
135	Mark Loretta	.05
136	Ruben Rivera	.05
137	Jeff Suppan	.05
138	Ugueth Urbina	.05
139	LaTroy Hawkins	.05
140	Chris Snopek	.05
141	Edgar Renteria	.05
142	Raul Casanova	.05
143	Jose Herrera	.05
144	Matt Lawton **RC**	.05
145	Ralph Milliard **RC**	.05
146	Checklist (Frank Thomas)	.05
147	Checklist (Jeff Bagwell)	.05
148	Checklist (Ken Griffey Jr.)	.05
149	Checklist (Mike Piazza)	.05
150	—	

Press Proofs

Inserted at a rate of about one per 48 packs, Press Proof parallels of the 150 cards in Leaf Preferred are identifiable only by the use of gold foil, rather than silver, on the card fronts, and gold ink on back. The cards are not otherwise marked or numbered. It is believed the issue was limited to 250-500 of each card.

		NM/M
Complete Set (150):		100.00
Common Player:		.50
Stars/Rookies:		12X

Leaf Steel Promos

Each of the 77 gold cards in the Preferred Steel set can also be found in gold, silver and bronze promo card versions. The samples differ from the issued versions only in an overprint diagonally on the back which reads "PROMOTIONAL CARD." This parallel promo edition represents one of the largest promo card issues of the mid-1990s. Cards were reportedly distributed to dealers on the basis of one gold promo per three-case order. The silver and bronze versions were reportedly never officially released, though examples have found their way into the market in some quantity.

		NM/M
Complete Gold Set (77):		625.00
Common Gold Player:		4.00
Silver: Values Undetermined		
Bronze: Values Undetermined		
1	Frank Thomas	15.00
2	Paul Molitor	15.00
3	Kenny Lofton	4.00
4	Travis Fryman	4.00
5	Jeff Conine	4.00
6	Barry Bonds	50.00
7	Gregg Jefferies	4.00
8	Alex Rodriguez	40.00
9	Wade Boggs	20.00
10	David Justice	4.00
11	Hideo Nomo	12.50
12	Roberto Alomar	6.00
13	Todd Hollandsworth	4.00
14	Mark McGwire	40.00
15	Rafael Palmeiro	12.50
16	Will Clark	4.00
17	Cal Ripken Jr.	50.00
18	Derek Bell	4.00
19	Gary Sheffield	7.50
20	Juan Gonzalez	12.50
21	Garret Anderson	4.00
22	Mo Vaughn	4.00
23	Robin Ventura	4.00
24	Carlos Baerga	4.00
25	Tim Salmon	4.00
26	Matt Williams	4.00
27	Fred McGriff	4.00
28	Rondell White	4.00
29	Ray Lankford	4.00
30	Lenny Dykstra	4.00
31	J.T. Snow	4.00
32	Sammy Sosa	25.00
33	Chipper Jones	20.00
34	Bobby Bonilla	4.00
35	Paul Wilson	4.00
36	Darren Daulton	4.00
37	Larry Walker	4.00
38	Raul Mondesi	4.00
39	Jeff Bagwell	15.00
40	Derek Jeter	50.00
41	Kirby Puckett	20.00
42	Jason Isringhausen	4.00
43	Vinny Castilla	4.00
44	Jim Edmonds	4.00
45	Ron Gant	4.00
46	Carlos Delgado	7.50
47	Jose Canseco	7.50
48	Tony Gwynn	20.00
49	Mike Mussina	7.50
50	Charles Johnson	4.00
51	Mike Piazza	25.00
52	Ken Griffey Jr.	25.00
53	Greg Maddux	20.00
54	Mark Grace	4.00
55	Ryan Klesko	4.00
56	Dennis Eckersley	12.50
57	Rickey Henderson	15.00
58	Michael Tucker	4.00
59	Joe Carter	4.00
60	Randy Johnson	15.00
61	Brian Jordan	4.00
62	Shawn Green	7.50
63	Roger Clemens	22.50
64	Andres Galarraga	4.00
65	Johnny Damon	7.50
66	Ryne Sandberg	20.00
67	Alan Benes	4.00
68	Albert Belle	4.00
69	Barry Larkin	4.00
70	Marty Cordova	4.00
71	Dante Bichette	4.00
72	Craig Biggio	4.00

73	Reggie Sanders	4.00
74	Moises Alou	4.00
75	Chuck Knoblauch	4.00
76	Cecil Fielder	4.00
77	Manny Ramirez	15.00

Leaf Steel

This 77-card insert set has two versions - a silver one and a much more limited gold one. A Silver Leaf Steel card is included in every pack; the parallel versions appear about one per 24 packs.

		NM/M
Complete Set (77):		25.00
Common Player:		.15
Gold:		2X
1	Frank Thomas	1.00
2	Paul Molitor	1.00
3	Kenny Lofton	.15
4	Travis Fryman	.15
5	Jeff Conine	.15
6	Barry Bonds	3.00
7	Gregg Jefferies	.15
8	Alex Rodriguez	2.50
9	Wade Boggs	1.50
10	David Justice	.15
11	Hideo Nomo	.75
12	Roberto Alomar	.30
13	Todd Hollandsworth	.15
14	Mark McGwire	2.50
15	Rafael Palmeiro	.75
16	Will Clark	.25
17	Cal Ripken Jr.	3.00
18	Derek Bell	.15
19	Gary Sheffield	.50
20	Juan Gonzalez	.65
21	Garret Anderson	.15
22	Mo Vaughn	.15
23	Robin Ventura	.15
24	Carlos Baerga	.15
25	Tim Salmon	.15
26	Matt Williams	.15
27	Fred McGriff	.15
28	Rondell White	.15
29	Ray Lankford	.15
30	Lenny Dykstra	.15
31	J.T. Snow	.15
32	Sammy Sosa	2.00
33	Chipper Jones	1.50
34	Bobby Bonilla	.15
35	Paul Wilson	.15
36	Darren Daulton	.15
37	Larry Walker	.15
38	Raul Mondesi	.15
39	Jeff Bagwell	1.00
40	Derek Jeter	3.00
41	Kirby Puckett	1.50
42	Jason Isringhausen	.15
43	Vinny Castilla	.15
44	Jim Edmonds	.15
45	Ron Gant	.15
46	Carlos Delgado	.50
47	Jose Canseco	.40
48	Tony Gwynn	1.50
49	Mike Mussina	.50
50	Charles Johnson	.15
51	Mike Piazza	2.00
52	Ken Griffey Jr.	2.00
53	Greg Maddux	1.50
54	Mark Grace	.15
55	Ryan Klesko	.15
56	Dennis Eckersley	.75
57	Rickey Henderson	1.00
58	Michael Tucker	.15
59	Joe Carter	.15
60	Randy Johnson	1.00
61	Brian Jordan	.15
62	Shawn Green	.50
63	Roger Clemens	2.00
64	Andres Galarraga	.15
65	Johnny Damon	.40
66	Ryne Sandberg	1.50
67	Alan Benes	.15
68	Albert Belle	.15
69	Barry Larkin	.15
70	Marty Cordova	.15
71	Dante Bichette	.15
72	Craig Biggio	.15
73	Reggie Sanders	.15
74	Moises Alou	.15
75	Chuck Knoblauch	.15
76	Cecil Fielder	.15
77	Manny Ramirez	1.00

Staremaster

These 1996 Leaf Preferred inserts provide a photographic tribute to the stares of 12 top players. Each card is printed on silver holographic card stock and is numbered up to 2,500.

		NM/M
Complete Set (12):		50.00
Common Player:		3.00
1	Chipper Jones	5.00
2	Alex Rodriguez	7.50
3	Derek Jeter	10.00
4	Tony Gwynn	5.00
5	Frank Thomas	4.00
6	Ken Griffey Jr.	6.00
7	Cal Ripken Jr.	10.00
8	Greg Maddux	5.00
9	Albert Belle	3.00
10	Barry Bonds	10.00
11	Jeff Bagwell	4.00
12	Mike Piazza	6.00

Steel Power

This eight-card Leaf Steel insert set combines micro-etched foil with interior die-cutting to honor the game's top power hitters. Each insert card carries a serial number up to 5,000.

		NM/M
Complete Set (8):		17.50
Common Player:		1.00
1	Albert Belle	1.00
2	Mo Vaughn	1.00
3	Ken Griffey Jr.	3.50
4	Cal Ripken Jr.	5.00
5	Mike Piazza	3.50
6	Barry Bonds	5.00
7	Jeff Bagwell	2.50
8	Frank Thomas	2.50

1996 Leaf/Signature Series

The base set which rode along with the autographed cards of more than 250 Major League players in Leaf's Signature Series (at least one authentic signature is guaranteed in every pack) features action photos with silver-foil highlights. Horizontal backs have a large photo along with a few stats and bits of personal data. One out of every 48 packs is a super pack containing nothing but autographed cards. The 150-card base set is paralleled in Gold and Platinum Press Proof insert sets. The gold version is seeded one per 12 packs in Series 1 and one per eight in the Extended Series. Platinums were issued in an edition of 150 of each of the 150 cards and are found only in the Extended Series at the rate of one per 24 packs. Four-card packs of Leaf Signature Series carried a suggested retail price at issue of $9.99.

		NM/M
Complete Set (150):		30.00
Complete 1st Series (100):		20.00
Complete Extended Series (50):		10.00
Common Player:		.05
Gold PP Stars/Rookies:		8X
Platinum PP Stars/Rookies:		20X
Pack (4):		5.00
Wax Box (12):		50.00
1	Mike Piazza	1.25
2	Juan Gonzalez	.65
3	Greg Maddux	1.00
4	Marc Newfield	.05
5	Wade Boggs	1.00
6	Ray Lankford	.05
7	Frank Thomas	.75
8	Rico Brogna	.05
9	Tim Salmon	.05
10	Ken Griffey Jr.	1.25
11	Manny Ramirez	.75
12	Cecil Fielder	.05
13	Gregg Jefferies	.05
14	Rondell White	.05
15	Cal Ripken Jr.	2.00
16	Alex Rodriguez	1.50
17	Bernie Williams	.05
18	Andres Galarraga	.05
19	Mike Mussina	.50
20	Chuck Knoblauch	.05
21	Joe Carter	.05
22	Jeff Bagwell	.75
23	Mark McGwire	1.50
24	Sammy Sosa	1.00
25	Reggie Sanders	.05
26	Chipper Jones	1.00
27	Jeff Cirillo	.05
28	Roger Clemens	1.25
29	Craig Biggio	.05
30	Gary Sheffield	.45
31	Paul O'Neill	.05
32	Johnny Damon	.35
33	Jason Isringhausen	.05
34	Jay Bell	.05
35	Henry Rodriguez	.05
36	Matt Williams	.05
37	Randy Johnson	.75
38	Fred McGriff	.05
39	Jason Giambi	.60
40	Ivan Rodriguez	.65
41	Raul Mondesi	.05
42	Barry Larkin	.05
43	Ryan Klesko	.05
44	Joey Hamilton	.05
45	Todd Hundley	.05
46	Jim Edmonds	.05
47	Dante Bichette	.05
48	Roberto Alomar	.20
49	Mark Grace	.05
50	Brady Anderson	.05
51	Hideo Nomo	.65
52	Ozzie Smith	1.00
53	Robin Ventura	.05
54	Andy Pettitte	.35
55	Kenny Lofton	.05
56	John Mabry	.05
57	Paul Molitor	.75
58	Rey Ordonez	.05
59	Albert Belle	.05
60	Charles Johnson	.05
61	Edgar Martinez	.05
62	Derek Bell	.05
63	Carlos Delgado	.50
64	Raul Casanova	.05
65	Ismael Valdes	.05
66	J.T. Snow	.05
67	Derek Jeter	2.00
68	Jason Kendall	.05
69	John Smoltz	.05
70	Chad Mottola	.05
71	Jim Thome	.60
72	Will Clark	.10
73	Mo Vaughn	.05
74	John Wasdin	.05
75	Rafael Palmeiro	.65
76	Mark Grudzielanek	.05
77	Larry Walker	.05
78	Alan Benes	.05
79	Michael Tucker	.05
80	Billy Wagner	.05
81	Paul Wilson	.05
82	Greg Vaughn	.05
83	Dean Palmer	.05
84	Ryne Sandberg	1.00
85	Eric Young	.05
86	Jay Buhner	.05
87	Tony Clark	.05
88	Jermaine Dye	.05
89	Barry Bonds	2.00
90	Ugueth Urbina	.05
91	Charles Nagy	.05
92	Ruben Rivera	.05
93	Todd Hollandsworth	.05
94	Darin Erstad RC	1.50
95	Brooks Kieschnick	.05
96	Edgar Renteria	.05
97	Lenny Dykstra	.05
98	Tony Gwynn	1.00
99	Kirby Puckett	1.00
100	Checklist	.05
101	Andruw Jones	.75
102	Alex Ochoa	.05
103	David Cone	.05
104	Rusty Greer	.05
105	Jose Canseco	.45
106	Ken Caminiti	.05
107	Mariano Rivera	.15
108	Ron Gant	.05
109	Darryl Strawberry	.05
110	Vladimir Guerrero	.75
111	George Arias	.05
112	Jeff Conine	.05
113	Bobby Higginson	.05
114	Eric Karros	.05
115	Brian Hunter	.05
116	Eddie Murray	.75
117	Todd Walker	.05
118	Chan Ho Park	.05
119	John Jaha	.05
120	David Justice	.05
121	Makoto Suzuki	.05
122	Scott Rolen	.65
123	Tino Martinez	.25
124	Kimera Bartee	.05
125	Garret Anderson	.05
126	Brian Jordan	.05
127	Andre Dawson	.30
128	Javier Lopez	.05
129	Bill Pulsipher	.05
130	Dwight Gooden	.05
131	Al Martin	.05
132	Terrell Wade	.05
133	Steve Gibralter	.05
134	Tom Glavine	.35
135	Kevin Appier	.05
136	Tim Raines	.05
137	Curtis Pride	.05
138	Todd Greene	.05
139	Bobby Bonilla	.05
140	Trey Beamon	.05
141	Marty Cordova	.05
142	Rickey Henderson	.75
143	Ellis Burks	.05
144	Dennis Eckersley	.65
145	Kevin Brown	.05
146	Carlos Baerga	.05
147	Brett Butler	.05
148	Marquis Grissom	.05
149	Karim Garcia	.05
150	Checklist	.05

Press Proofs

The 150-card base set of Leaf/Signature was paralleled in a pair of Press Proof versions. Identical in format to the regular issue, the Press Proofs have an embossed gold- or platinum-foil oval seal at left and "PRESS PROOF" vertically at right in the same color foil. Backs are identical to the regular version. Gold Press Proofs were inserted one per 12 packs of Series 1 and one per eight packs of Extended. Platinum Proofs are found only in Extended Series packs, at an average rate of one per 24. Total production of Platinum Press proofs was 150 of each card.

	NM/M
Common Gold:	2.00
Gold Stars:	8X
Common Platinum:	4.00
Platinum Stars:	20X

Autographs Promos

To introduce its Autograph Series, Leaf sent dealers one of two promo card versions of the Frank Thomas card. Most received a card with a pre-printed facsimile autograph, duly noted in small type beneath the signature. Others (500) received a genuine Frank Thomas autograph on

their promo. All of the cards are marked "PROMOTIONAL CARD" diagonally on both front and back.

	NM/M
Frank Thomas (Facsimile signature.)	4.00
Frank Thomas (Genuine autograph.)	50.00

Autographs

Every pack of 1996 Leaf Signature Series includes at least one authentically signed card from one of over 250 players. There were 240 players who signed three versions in these quantities: 500 Gold, 1,000 Silver and 3,500 Bronze. There are also short-printed autographs for 10 players in quantities of 100 Gold, 200 Silver and 700 Bronze. The short-printed players are designated with an "SP" in the checklist. Cards are numbered alphabetically in the checklist since the autographed cards are unnumbered. Each major leaguer signed a notarized affidavit to guarantee each signature was authentic. Series 1 cards of Carlos Delgado, Brian Hunter, Phil Plantier, Jim Thome, Terrell Wade and Ernie Young were signed too late for inclusion in Series 1 packs, and were inserted with Extended. No Bronze cards of Thome were signed.

		NM/M
Common Bronze Player:		4.00
Silver:		1.5X
Gold:		2X
SPs: 100 Gold, 200 Silver, 700 Bronze		
(1)	Kurt Abbott	4.00
(2)	Juan Acevedo	4.00
(3)	Terry Adams	4.00
(4)	Manny Alexander	4.00
(5)	Roberto Alomar/SP	35.00
(6)	Moises Alou	12.00
(7)	Wilson Alvarez	4.00
(8)	Garret Anderson	10.00
(9)	Shane Andrews	4.00
(10)	Andy Ashby	4.00
(11)	Pedro Astacio	4.00
(12)	Brad Ausmus	4.00
(13)	Bobby Ayala	4.00
(14)	Carlos Baerga	4.00
(15)	Harold Baines	10.00
(16)	Jason Bates	4.00
(17)	Allen Battle	4.00
(18)	Rich Becker	4.00
(19)	David Bell	4.00
(20)	Rafael Belliard	4.00
(21)	Andy Benes	4.00
(22)	Armando Benitez	4.00
(23)	Jason Bere	4.00
(24)	Geronimo Berroa	4.00
(25)	Willie Blair	4.00
(26)	Mike Blowers	4.00
(27)	Wade Boggs/SP	50.00
(28)	Ricky Bones	4.00
(29)	Mike Bordick	4.00
(30)	Toby Borland	4.00
(31)	Ricky Bottalico	4.00
(32)	Darren Bragg	4.00
(33)	Jeff Branson	4.00
(34)	Tilson Brito	4.00
(35)	Rico Brogna	4.00
(36)	Scott Brosius	7.50
(37)	Damon Buford	4.00
(38)	Mike Busby	4.00
(39)	Tom Candiotti	4.00
(41)	Andujar Cedeno	4.00
(42)	Domingo Cedeno	4.00
(43)	Roger Cedeno	4.00
(44)	Norm Charlton	4.00
(45)	Jeff Cirillo	4.00
(46)	Will Clark	10.00
(47)	Jeff Conine	4.00
(48)	Steve Cooke	4.00
(49)	Joey Cora	4.00
(50)	Marty Cordova	4.00
(51)	Rheal Cormier	4.00
(52)	Felipe Crespo	4.00
(53)	Chad Curtis	4.00
(54)	Johnny Damon	15.00
(55)	Russ Davis	4.00
(56)	Andre Dawson	10.00
(57a)	Carlos Delgado (Black autograph.)	
(57b)	Carlos Delgado (Blue autograph.)	15.00
(58)	Doug Drabek	4.00
(59)	Darren Dreifort	4.00
(60)	Shawon Dunston	4.00
(61)	Ray Durham	4.00
(62)	Jim Edmonds	12.00
(63)	Joey Eischen	4.00
(64)	Jim Eisenreich	4.00
(65)	Sal Fasano	4.00
(66)	Jeff Fassero	4.00
(67)	Alex Fernandez	4.00
(68)	Darrin Fletcher	4.00
(69)	Chad Fonville	4.00
(70)	Kevin Foster	4.00
(71)	John Franco	4.00
(72)	Julio Franco	10.00
(74)	Marvin Freeman	4.00
(75)	Travis Fryman	4.00
(76)	Gary Gaetti	4.00
(77)	Carlos Garcia	4.00
(78)	Jason Giambi	10.00
(79)	Benji Gil	4.00
(80)	Greg Gohr	4.00
(81)	Chris Gomez	4.00
(82)	Leo Gomez	4.00
(83)	Tom Goodwin	4.00
(84)	Mike Grace	4.00
(85)	Mike Greenwell	6.00
(86)	Rusty Greer	4.00
(87)	Mark Grudzielanek	4.00
(88)	Mark Gubicza	4.00
(89)	Juan Guzman	4.00
(90)	Darryl Hamilton	4.00
(91)	Joey Hamilton	4.00
(92)	Chris Hammond	4.00
(93)	Mike Hampton	7.50
(94)	Chris Haney	4.00
(95)	Todd Haney	4.00
(96)	Erik Hanson	4.00
(97)	Pete Harnisch	4.00
(98)	LaTroy Hawkins	4.00
(99)	Charlie Hayes	4.00
(100)	Jimmy Haynes	4.00
(101)	Roberto Hernandez	4.00
(102)	Bobby Higginson	4.00
(103)	Glenallen Hill	4.00
(104)	Ken Hill	4.00
(105)	Sterling Hitchcock	4.00
(106)	Trevor Hoffman	10.00
(107)	Dave Hollins	4.00
(108)	Dwayne Hosey	4.00
(109)	Thomas Howard	4.00
(110)	Steve Howe	6.00
(111)	John Hudek	4.00
(112)	Rex Hudler	4.00
(113)	Brian Hunter	4.00
(114)	Butch Huskey	4.00
(115)	Mark Hutton	4.00
(116)	Jason Jacome	4.00
(117)	John Jaha	4.00
(118)	Reggie Jefferson	4.00
(119)	Derek Jeter/SP	150.00
(120)	Bobby Jones	4.00
(121)	Todd Jones	4.00
(122)	Brian Jordan	5.00
(123)	Kevin Jordan	4.00
(124)	Jeff Juden	4.00
(125)	Ron Karkovice	4.00
(126)	Roberto Kelly	4.00
(127)	Mark Kiefer	4.00
(128)	Brooks Kieschnick	4.00
(129)	Jeff King	4.00
(130)	Mike Lansing	4.00
(131)	Matt Lawton	7.50
(132)	Al Leiter	6.00
(133)	Mark Leiter	4.00
(134)	Curtis Leskanic	4.00
(135)	Darren Lewis	4.00
(136)	Mark Lewis	4.00
(137)	Felipe Lira	4.00
(138)	Pat Listach	4.00
(139)	Keith Lockhart	4.00
(140)	Kenny Lofton/SP	25.00
(141)	John Mabry	4.00
(142)	Mike Macfarlane	4.00
(143)	Kirt Manwaring	4.00
(144)	Al Martin	4.00
(145)	Norberto Martin	4.00
(146)	Dennis Martinez	5.00
(147)	Pedro Martinez	40.00
(148)	Sandy Martinez	4.00
(149)	Mike Matheny	4.00
(150)	T.J. Mathews	4.00

(150)	David McCarty	4.00
(151)	Ben McDonald	4.00
(152)	Pat Meares	4.00
(153)	Orlando Merced	4.00
(154)	Jose Mesa	4.00
(155)	Matt Mieske	4.00
(156)	Orlando Miller	4.00
(157)	Mike Mimbs	4.00
(158)	Paul Molitor/SP	40.00
(159)	Raul Mondesi/SP	20.00
(160)	Jeff Montgomery	4.00
(161)	Mickey Morandini	4.00
(162)	Lyle Mouton	4.00
(163)	James Mouton	4.00
(164)	Jamie Moyer	4.00
(165)	Rodney Myers	4.00
(166)	Denny Neagle	4.00
(167)	Robb Nen	4.00
(168)	Marc Newfield	4.00
(169)	Dave Nilsson	4.00
(170)	Jon Nunnally	4.00
(171)	Chad Ogea	4.00
(172)	Troy O'Leary	4.00
(173)	Rey Ordonez	4.00
(174)	Jayhawk Owens	4.00
(175)	Tom Pagnozzi	4.00
(176)	Dean Palmer	4.00
(177)	Roger Pavlik	4.00
(178)	Troy Percival	4.00
(179)	Carlos Perez	4.00
(180)	Robert Perez	4.00
(181)	Andy Pettitte	30.00
(182)	Phil Plantier	4.00
(183)	Mike Potts	4.00
(184)	Curtis Pride	4.00
(185)	Ariel Prieto	4.00
(186)	Bill Pulsipher	4.00
(187)	Brad Radke	4.00
(188)	Manny Ramirez/SP	35.00
(189)	Joe Randa	4.00
(190)	Pat Rapp	4.00
(191)	Bryan Rekar	4.00
(192)	Shane Reynolds	4.00
(193)	Arthur Rhodes	4.00
(194)	Mariano Rivera	45.00
(195a)	Alex Rodriguez/SP (Black autograph.)	120.00
(195b)	Alex Rodriguez/SP (Blue autograph.)	120.00
(196)	Frank Rodriguez	4.00
(197)	Mel Rojas	4.00
(198)	Ken Ryan	4.00
(199)	Bret Saberhagen	4.00
(200)	Tim Salmon	5.00
(201)	Rey Sanchez	4.00
(202)	Scott Sanders	4.00
(203)	Steve Scarsone	4.00
(204)	Curt Schilling	25.00
(205)	Jason Schmidt	20.00
(206)	David Segui	4.00
(207)	Kevin Seitzer	4.00
(208)	Scott Servais	4.00
(209)	Don Slaught	4.00
(210)	Zane Smith	4.00
(211)	Paul Sorrento	4.00
(212)	Scott Stahoviak	4.00
(213)	Mike Stanley	4.00
(214)	Terry Steinbach	4.00
(215)	Kevin Stocker	4.00
(216)	Jeff Suppan	4.00
(217)	Bill Swift	4.00
(218)	Greg Swindell	4.00
(219)	Kevin Tapani	4.00
(220)	Danny Tartabull	4.00
(221)	Julian Tavarez	4.00
(222a)	Frank Thomas/SP (Blue autograph.)	40.00
(222b)	Frank Thomas/SP (Black autograph.)	40.00
(223)	Jim Thome/SP/Silver	40.00
(224)	Ozzie Timmons	4.00
(225a)	Michael Tucker (Black autograph.)	4.00
(225b)	Michael Tucker (Blue autograph.)	.
(226)	Ismael Valdez	4.00
(227)	Jose Valentin	4.00
(228)	Todd Van Poppel	4.00
(229)	Mo Vaughn/SP	15.00
(230)	Quilvio Veras	4.00
(231)	Fernando Vina	4.00
(232)	Joe Vitiello	4.00
(233)	Jose Vizcaino	4.00
(234)	Omar Vizquel	12.00
(235)	Terrell Wade	4.00
(236)	Paul Wagner	4.00
(237)	Matt Walbeck	4.00
(238)	Jerome Walton	4.00
(239)	Turner Ward	4.00
(240)	Allen Watson	4.00
(241)	David Weathers	4.00
(242)	Walt Weiss	4.00
(244)	Turk Wendell	4.00
(244)	Rondell White	5.00
(245)	Brian Williams	4.00
(246)	George Williams	4.00
(247)	Paul Wilson	4.00
(248)	Bobby Witt	4.00
(249)	Bob Wolcott	4.00
(250)	Eric Young	4.00
(251)	Ernie Young	4.00
(252)	Gregg Zaun	4.00
---	Frank Thomas (Auto. jumbo edition of 1,500.)	25.00

1996 Leaf/Signature Series Extended Autographs

Signature Series Extended Autograph cards comprise 30 short-printed stars and top prospects, and 187 other major leaguers. Most players signed 5,000 cards each, while other signees' totals are listed in parentheses. Signature cards for Alex Rodriguez, Juan Gonzalez and Andruw Jones were only available through mail-in redemption. Autographed cards were a different design from Series 1 and were seeded two per pack in Extended. The un-numbered cards are checklisted here in alphabetical order.

		NM/M
Common Player:		4.00
Extended Pack:		20.00
Extended Box:		150.00
(1)	Scott Aldred	4.00
(2)	Mike Aldrete	4.00
(3)	Rich Amaral	4.00
(4)	Alex Arias	4.00
(5)	Paul Assenmacher	4.00
(6)	Roger Bailey	4.00
(7)	Erik Bennett	4.00
(8)	Sean Bergman	4.00
(9)	Doug Bochtler	4.00
(10)	Tim Bogar	4.00
(11)	Pat Borders	4.00
(12)	Pedro Borbon	4.00
(13)	Shawn Boskie	4.00
(14)	Rafael Bournigal	4.00
(15)	Mark Brandenburg	4.00
(16)	John Briscoe	4.00
(17)	Jorge Brito	4.00
(18)	Doug Brocail	4.00
(19)	Jay Buhner/SP/1,000	17.50
(20)	Scott Bullett	4.00
(21)	Dave Burba	4.00
(22)	Ken Caminiti/SP/1,000	25.00
(23)	John Cangelosi	4.00
(24)	Cris Carpenter	4.00
(25)	Chuck Carr	4.00
(26)	Larry Casian	4.00
(27)	Tony Castillo	4.00
(28)	Jason Christiansen	4.00
(29)	Archi Cianfrocco	4.00
(30)	Mark Clark	4.00
(31)	Terry Clark	4.00
(32)	Roger Clemens/SP/1,000	150.00
(33)	Jim Converse	4.00
(34)	Dennis Cook	4.00
(35)	Francisco Cordova	4.00
(36)	Jim Corsi	4.00
(37)	Tim Crabtree	4.00
(38)	Doug Creek/SP/1,950	8.00
(39)	John Cummings	4.00
(40)	Omar Daal	4.00
(41)	Rich DeLucia	4.00
(42)	Mark Dewey	4.00
(43)	Alex Diaz	4.00
(44)	Jermaine Dye/SP/2,500	12.00
(45)	Ken Edenfield	4.00
(46)	Mark Eichhorn	4.00
(47)	John Ericks	4.00
(48)	Darin Erstad	10.00
(49)	Alvaro Espinoza	4.00
(50)	Jorge Fabregas	4.00
(51)	Mike Fetters	4.00
(52)	John Flaherty	4.00
(53)	Bryce Florie	4.00
(54)	Tony Fossas	4.00
(55)	Lou Frazier	4.00
(56)	Mike Gallego	4.00
(57)	Karim Garcia/SP/2,500	6.00
(58)	Jason Giambi	12.00
(59)	Ed Giovanola	4.00
(60)	Tom Glavine/SP/1,250	40.00
(61)	Juan Gonzalez/SP/1,000	30.00
(61)	Juan Gonzalez (Redemption card.)	5.00
(62)	Craig Grebeck	4.00
(63)	Buddy Groom	4.00
(64)	Kevin Gross	4.00
(65)	Eddie Guardado	4.00
(66)	Mark Guthrie	4.00
(67)	Tony Gwynn/SP/1,000	60.00
(68)	Chip Hale	4.00
(69)	Darren Hall	4.00
(70)	Lee Hancock	4.00
(71)	Dave Hansen	4.00
(72)	Bryan Harvey	4.00
(73)	Bill Haselman	4.00
(74)	Mike Henneman	4.00
(75)	Doug Henry	4.00
(76)	Gil Heredia	4.00
(77)	Carlos Hernandez	4.00
(78)	Jose Hernandez	4.00
(79)	Darren Holmes	4.00
(80)	Mark Holzemer	4.00
(81)	Rick Honeycutt	4.00
(82)	Chris Hook	4.00
(83)	Chris Howard	4.00
(84)	Jack Howell	4.00
(85)	David Hulse	4.00
(86)	Edwin Hurtado	4.00
(87)	Jeff Huson	4.00
(88)	Mike James	4.00
(89)	Derek Jeter/SP/1,000	160.00
(90)	Brian Johnson	4.00
(91)	Randy Johnson/SP/1,000	125.00
(92)	Mark Johnson	4.00
(93)	Andruw Jones/SP/2,000	30.00
(93)	Andruw Jones (Redemption card.)	5.00
(94)	Chris Jones	4.00
(95)	Ricky Jordan	4.00
(96)	Matt Karchner	4.00
(97)	Scott Karl	4.00
(98)	Jason Kendall/SP/2,500	10.00
(99)	Brian Keyser	4.00
(100)	Mike Kingery	4.00
(101)	Wayne Kirby	4.00
(102)	Ryan Klesko/SP/1,000	17.50
(103)	Chuck Knoblauch/SP/1,000	15.00
(104)	Chad Kreuter	4.00
(105)	Tom Lampkin	4.00
(106)	Scott Leius	4.00
(107)	Jon Lieber	4.00
(108)	Nelson Liriano	4.00
(109)	Scott Livingstone	4.00
(110)	Graeme Lloyd	4.00
(111)	Kenny Lofton/SP/1,000	10.00
(112)	Luis Lopez	4.00
(113)	Torey Lovullo	4.00
(114)	Greg Maddux/SP/500	250.00
(115)	Mike Maddux	4.00
(116)	Dave Magadan	4.00
(117)	Mike Magnante	4.00
(118)	Joe Magrane	4.00
(119)	Pat Mahomes	4.00
(120)	Matt Mantei	4.00
(121)	John Marzano	4.00
(122)	Terry Matthews	4.00
(123)	Chuck McElroy	4.00
(124)	Fred McGriff/SP/1,000	35.00
(125)	Mark McLemore	4.00
(126)	Greg McMichael	4.00
(127)	Blas Minor	4.00
(128)	Dave Mlicki	4.00
(129)	Mike Mohler	4.00
(130)	Paul Molitor /SP/1,000	25.00
(131)	Steve Montgomery	4.00
(132)	Mike Mordecai	4.00
(133)	Mike Morgan	4.00
(134)	Mike Munoz	4.00
(135)	Greg Myers	4.00
(136)	Jimmy Myers	4.00
(137)	Mike Myers	4.00
(138)	Bob Natal	4.00
(139)	Dan Naulty	4.00
(140)	Jeff Nelson	4.00
(141)	Warren Newson	4.00
(142)	Chris Nichting	4.00
(143)	Melvin Nieves	4.00
(144)	Charlie O'Brien	4.00
(145)	Alex Ochoa	4.00
(146)	Omar Olivares	4.00
(147)	Joe Oliver	4.00
(148)	Lance Painter	4.00
(149)	Rafael Palmeiro/SP/2,000	35.00
(150)	Mark Parent	4.00
(151)	Steve Parris/SP/1,800	7.50
(152)	Bob Patterson	4.00
(153)	Tony Pena	7.50
(154)	Eddie Perez	4.00
(155)	Yorkis Perez	4.00
(156)	Robert Person	4.00
(157)	Mark Petkovsek	4.00
(158)	Andy Pettitte/SP/1,000	60.00
(159)	J.R. Phillips	4.00
(160)	Hipolito Pichardo	4.00
(161)	Eric Plunk	4.00
(162)	Jimmy Poole	4.00
(163)	Kirby Puckett/SP/1,000	80.00
(164)	Paul Quantrill	4.00
(165)	Tom Quinlan	4.00
(166)	Jeff Reboulet	4.00
(167)	Jeff Reed	4.00
(168)	Steve Reed	4.00
(169)	Carlos Reyes	4.00
(170)	Bill Risley	4.00
(171)	Kevin Ritz	4.00
(172)	Kevin Roberson	4.00
(173)	Rich Robertson	4.00
(174)	Alex Rodriguez/SP/500	180.00
(174)	Alex Rodriguez (Redemption card.)	15.00
(175)	Ivan Rodriguez/SP/1,250	40.00
(176)	Bruce Ruffin	4.00
(177)	Juan Samuel	4.00
(178)	Tim Scott	4.00
(179)	Kevin Sefcik	4.00
(180)	Jeff Shaw	4.00
(181)	Danny Sheaffer	4.00
(182)	Craig Shipley	4.00
(183)	Dave Silvestri	4.00
(184)	Aaron Small	4.00
(185)	Jim Smoltz/SP/1,000	90.00
(186)	Luis Sojo	4.00
(187)	Sammy Sosa/SP/1,000	160.00
(188)	Steve Sparks	4.00
(189)	Tim Spehr	4.00
(190)	Russ Springer	4.00
(191)	Matt Stairs	4.00
(192)	Andy Stankiewicz	4.00
(193)	Mike Stanton	4.00
(194)	Kelly Stinnett	4.00
(195)	Doug Strange	4.00
(196)	Mark Sweeney	4.00
(197)	Jeff Tabaka	4.00
(198)	Jesus Tavarez	4.00
(199)	Frank Thomas/SP/1,000	45.00
(200)	Larry Thomas	4.00
(201)	Mark Thompson	4.00
(202)	Mike Timlin	4.00
(203)	Steve Trachsel	4.00
(204)	Tom Urbani	4.00
(205)	Julio Valera	4.00
(206)	Dave Valle	4.00
(207)	William Van Landingham	4.00
(208)	Mo Vaughn/SP/1,000	10.00
(209)	Dave Veres	4.00
(210)	Ed Vosberg	4.00
(211)	Don Wengert	4.00
(212)	Matt Whiteside	4.00
(213)	Bob Wickman	4.00
(214)	Matt Williams/SP/1,250	12.00
(215)	Mike Williams	4.00
(216)	Woody Williams	4.00
(217)	Craig Worthington	4.00
---	Frank Thomas (Auto. jumbo edition of 1,500.)	30.00

Extended Autographs - Century Marks

Century Marks represent the first 100 autographs by the 30 short-printed stars and prospects, plus Alex Ochoa. These are designated with a blue holographic foil "Century Marks" logo. Cards of Gonzalez, Jeter, Andruw Jones, Palmeiro and Alex Rodriguez were available only via mail-in redemption cards.

		NM/M
Common Player:		15.00
(1)	Jay Buhner	30.00
(2)	Ken Caminiti	30.00
(3)	Roger Clemens	250.00
(4)	Jermaine Dye	30.00
(5)	Darin Erstad	45.00
(6)	Karim Garcia	30.00
(7)	Jason Giambi	75.00
(8)	Tom Glavine	90.00
(9)	Juan Gonzalez	90.00
(9)	Juan Gonzalez (Redemption card.)	7.50
(10)	Tony Gwynn	150.00
(11)	Derek Jeter	350.00
(11)	Derek Jeter (Redemption card.)	15.00
(12)	Randy Johnson	185.00
(13)	Andruw Jones	150.00
(13)	Andruw Jones (Redemption card.)	7.50
(14)	Jason Kendall	30.00
(15)	Ryan Klesko	30.00
(16)	Chuck Knoblauch	30.00
(17)	Kenny Lofton	30.00
(18)	Greg Maddux	200.00
(19)	Fred McGriff	30.00
(20)	Paul Molitor	110.00
(21)	Alex Ochoa	15.00
(22)	Rafael Palmeiro	110.00
(22)	Rafael Palmeiro (Redemption card.)	7.50
(23)	Andy Pettitte	75.00
(24)	Kirby Puckett	185.00
(25)	Alex Rodriguez	350.00
(25)	Alex Rodriguez (Redemption card.)	15.00
(26)	Ivan Rodriguez	100.00
(27)	John Smoltz	100.00
(28)	Sammy Sosa	350.00
(29)	Frank Thomas	135.00
(30)	Mo Vaughn	30.00
(31)	Matt Williams	30.00

Frank Thomas The Big Heart

In one of several specialty card charitable endeavors, Frank Thomas and Leaf teamed up to issue this set as a fund raiser for "The Big Hurt's" charitable foundation. Each of the cards was available in an edition limited to 3,500 each for a $20 donation. Cards are standard 2-1/2" x 3-1/2" with posed photos on front and "THE BIG HEART," a play on his nickname. Backs have information on the foundation.

		NM/M
Complete Set (4):		35.00
Common Card:		10.00
(1)	Frank Thomas (Bat on shoulder.)	10.00
(2)	Frank Thomas (Holding glove.)	10.00
(3)	Frank Thomas (Horizontal)	10.00
(4)	Frank Thomas (Seated)	10.00

1997 Leaf

Leaf produced a 400-card set in two series in 1997. The cards feature a gray border with the player photo vignetted at center. The player's name, team and a Leaf logo are displayed at bottom in silver foil. A team logo is in the upper-right corner. Besides the base cards, 10-card packs retailing for $2.99 could contain one of the following inserts: Banner Season, Dress for Success, Get-A-Grip, Knot-hole Gang, Statistical Standouts, Fractal Matrix or Fractal Matrix Die-cut.

	NM/M
Complete Set (400):	25.00
Common Player:	.05
Jackie Robinson 1948 Leaf Reprint:	10.00
Series 1 Pack (12):	2.00
Series 1 Wax Box (18):	30.00
Series 2 Pack (12):	1.50
Series 2 Wax Box (24):	30.00
1 Wade Boggs	1.50
2 Brian McRae	.05
3 Jeff D'Amico	.05
4 George Arias	.05
5 Billy Wagner	.05
6 Ray Lankford	.05
7 Will Clark	.10
8 Edgar Renteria	.05
9 Alex Ochoa	.05
10 Roberto Hernandez	.05
11 Joe Carter	.05
12 Gregg Jefferies	.05
13 Mark Grace	.05
14 Roberto Alomar	.10
15 Joe Randa	.05
16 Alex Rodriguez	2.50
17 Tony Gwynn	1.50
18 Steve Gibralter	.05
19 Scott Stahoviak	.05
20 Matt Williams	.05
21 Quinton McCracken	.05
22 Ugueth Urbina	.05
23 Jermaine Allensworth	.05
24 Paul Molitor	.75
25 Carlos Delgado	.50
26 Bob Abreu	.05
27 John Jaha	.05
28 Rusty Greer	.05
29 Kimera Bartee	.05
30 Ruben Rivera	.05
31 Jason Kendall	.05
32 Lance Johnson	.05
33 Robin Ventura	.05
34 Kevin Appier	.05
35 John Mabry	.05
36 Ricky Otero	.05
37 Mike Lansing	.05
38 Mark McGwire	2.50
39 Tim Naehring	.05
40 Tom Glavine	.30
41 Rey Ordonez	.05
42 Tony Clark	.25
43 Rafael Palmeiro	.65
44 Pedro Martinez	.75
45 Keith Lockhart	.05
46 Dan Wilson	.05
47 John Wetteland	.05
48 Chan Ho Park	.05
49 Gary Sheffield	.40
50 Shawn Estes	.05
51 Royce Clayton	.05
52 Jaime Navarro	.05
53 Raul Casanova	.05
54 Jeff Bagwell	1.00
55 Barry Larkin	.05
56 Charles Nagy	.05
57 Ken Caminiti	.05
58 Todd Hollandsworth	.05
59 Pat Hentgen	.05
60 Jose Valentin	.05
61 Frank Rodriguez	.05
62 Mickey Tettleton	.05
63 Marty Cordova	.05
64 Cecil Fielder	.05
65 Barry Bonds	3.00
66 Scott Servais	.05
67 Ernie Young	.05
68 Wilson Alvarez	.05
69 Mike Grace	.05
70 Shane Reynolds	.05
71 Henry Rodriguez	.05
72 Eric Karros	.05
73 Mark Langston	.05
74 Scott Karl	.05
75 Trevor Hoffman	.05
76 Orel Hershiser	.05
77 John Smoltz	.05
78 Raul Mondesi	.05
79 Jeff Brantley	.05
80 Donne Wall	.05
81 Joey Cora	.05
82 Mel Rojas	.05
83 Chad Mottola	.05
84 Omar Vizquel	.05
85 Greg Maddux	1.50
86 Jamey Wright	.05
87 Chuck Finley	.05
88 Brady Anderson	.05
89 Alex Gonzalez	.05
90 Andy Benes	.05
91 Reggie Jefferson	.05
92 Paul O'Neill	.05
93 Javier Lopez	.05
94 Mark Grudzielanek	.05
95 Marc Newfield	.05
96 Kevin Ritz	.05
97 Fred McGriff	.05
98 Dwight Gooden	.05
99 Hideo Nomo	.65
100 Steve Finley	.05
101 Juan Gonzalez	.65
102 Jay Buhner	.05
103 Paul Wilson	.05
104 Alan Benes	.05
105 Manny Ramirez	1.00
106 Kevin Elster	.05
107 Frank Thomas	1.00
108 Orlando Miller	.05
109 Ramon Martinez	.05
110 Kenny Lofton	.05
111 Bernie Williams	.05
112 Robby Thompson	.05
113 Bernard Gilkey	.05
114 Ray Durham	.05
115 Jeff Cirillo	.05
116 Brian Jordan	.05
117 Rich Becker	.05
118 Al Leiter	.05
119 Mark Johnson	.05
120 Ellis Burks	.05
121 Sammy Sosa	2.00
122 Willie Greene	.05
123 Michael Tucker	.05
124 Eddie Murray	.75
125 Joey Hamilton	.05
126 Antonio Osuna	.05
127 Bobby Higginson	.05
128 Tomas Perez	.05
129 Tim Salmon	.05
130 Mark Wohlers	.05
131 Charles Johnson	.05
132 Randy Johnson	.75
133 Brooks Kieschnick	.05
134 Al Martin	.05
135 Dante Bichette	.05
136 Andy Pettitte	.30
137 Jason Giambi	.60
138 James Baldwin	.05
139 Ben McDonald	.05
140 Shawn Green	.35
141 Geronimo Berroa	.05
142 Jose Offerman	.05
143 Curtis Pride	.05
144 Terrell Wade	.05
145 Ismael Valdes	.05
146 Mike Mussina	.40
147 Mariano Rivera	.15
148 Ken Hill	.05
149 Darin Erstad	.25
150 Jay Bell	.05
151 Mo Vaughn	.05
152 Ozzie Smith	1.50
153 Jose Mesa	.05
154 Osvaldo Fernandez	.05
155 Vinny Castilla	.05
156 Jason Isringhausen	.05
157 B.J. Surhoff	.05
158 Robert Perez	.05
159 Ron Coomer	.05
160 Darren Oliver	.05
161 Mike Mohler	.05
162 Russ Davis	.05
163 Bret Boone	.05

164	Ricky Bottalico	.05
165	Derek Jeter	3.00
166	Orlando Merced	.05
167	John Valentin	.05
168	Andruw Jones	1.00
169	Angel Echevarria	.05
170	Todd Walker	.05
171	Desi Relaford	.05
172	Trey Beamon	.05
173	Brian Giles RC	.75
174	Scott Rolen	.60
175	Shannon Stewart	.05
176	Dmitri Young	.05
177	Justin Thompson	.05
178	Trot Nixon	.05
179	Josh Booty	.05
180	Robin Jennings	.05
181	Marvin Benard	.05
182	Luis Castillo	.05
183	Wendell Magee	.05
184	Vladimir Guerrero	1.00
185	Nomar Garciaparra	2.00
186	Ryan Hancock	.05
187	Mike Cameron	.05
188	Cal Ripken Jr. (Legacy)	1.50
189	Chipper Jones (Legacy)	.75
190	Albert Belle (Legacy)	.05
191	Mike Piazza (Legacy)	1.00
192	Chuck Knoblauch (Legacy)	1.00
193	Ken Griffey Jr. (Legacy)	1.00
194	Ivan Rodriguez (Legacy)	.30
195	Jose Canseco (Legacy)	.25
196	Ryne Sandberg (Legacy)	.75
197	Jim Thome (Legacy)	.05
198	Andy Pettitte (Checklist)	.05
199	Andruw Jones (Checklist)	.05
200	Derek Jeter (Checklist)	1.50
201	Chipper Jones	1.50
202	Albert Belle	.05
203	Mike Piazza	2.00
204	Ken Griffey Jr.	2.00
205	Ryne Sandberg	1.50
206	Jose Canseco	.40
207	Chili Davis	.05
208	Roger Clemens	2.00
209	Deion Sanders	.05
210	Darryl Hamilton	.05
211	Jermaine Dye	.05
212	Matt Williams	.05
213	Kevin Elster	.05
214	John Wetteland	.05
215	Garret Anderson	.05
216	Kevin Brown	.05
217	Matt Lawton	.05
218	Cal Ripken Jr.	3.00
219	Moises Alou	.05
220	Chuck Knoblauch	.05
221	Ivan Rodriguez	.65
222	Travis Fryman	.05
223	Jim Thome	.65
224	Eddie Murray	.75
225	Eric Young	.05
226	Ron Gant	.05
227	Tony Phillips	.05
228	Reggie Sanders	.05
229	Johnny Damon	.35
230	Bill Pulsipher	.05
231	Jim Edmonds	.05
232	Melvin Nieves	.05
233	Ryan Klesko	.05
234	David Cone	.05
235	Derek Bell	.05
236	Julio Franco	.05
237	Juan Guzman	.05
238	Larry Walker	.05
239	Delino DeShields	.05
240	Troy Percival	.05
241	Andres Galarraga	.05
242	Rondell White	.05
243	John Burkett	.05
244	J.T. Snow	.05
245	Alex Fernandez	.05
246	Edgar Martinez	.05
247	Craig Biggio	.05
248	Todd Hundley	.05
249	Jimmy Key	.05
250	Cliff Floyd	.05
251	Jeff Conine	.05
252	Curt Schilling	.35
253	Jeff King	.05
254	Tino Martinez	.05
255	Carlos Baerga	.05
256	Jeff Fassero	.05
257	Dean Palmer	.05
258	Robb Nen	.05
259	Sandy Alomar Jr.	.05
260	Carlos Perez	.05
261	Rickey Henderson	.75
262	Bobby Bonilla	.05
263	Darren Daulton	.05
264	Jim Leyritz	.05
265	Dennis Martinez	.05
266	Butch Huskey	.05
267	Joe Vitiello	.05
268	Steve Trachsel	.05
269	Glenallen Hill	.05
270	Terry Steinbach	.05
271	Mark McLemore	.05
272	Devon White	.05
273	Jeff Kent	.05
274	Tim Raines	.05
275	Carlos Garcia	.05
276	Hal Morris	.05
277	Gary Gaetti	.05
278	John Olerud	.05
279	Wally Joyner	.05
280	Brian Hunter	.05
281	Steve Karsay	.05

282	Denny Neagle	.05
283	Jose Herrera	.05
284	Todd Stottlemyre	.05
285	Bip Roberts	.05
286	Kevin Seitzer	.05
287	Benji Gil	.05
288	Dennis Eckersley	.65
289	Brad Ausmus	.05
290	Otis Nixon	.05
291	Darryl Strawberry	.05
292	Marquis Grissom	.05
293	Darryl Kile	.05
294	Quilvio Veras	.05
295	Tom Goodwin	.05
296	Benito Santiago	.05
297	Mike Bordick	.05
298	Roberto Kelly	.05
299	David Justice	.05
300	Carl Everett	.05
301	Mark Whiten	.05
302	Aaron Sele	.05
303	Darren Dreifort	.05
304	Bobby Jones	.05
305	Fernando Vina	.05
306	Ed Sprague	.05
307	Andy Ashby	.05
308	Tony Fernandez	.05
309	Roger Pavlik	.05
310	Mark Clark	.05
311	Mariano Duncan	.05
312	Tyler Houston	.05
313	Eric Davis	.05
314	Greg Vaughn	.05
315	David Segui	.05
316	Dave Nilsson	.05
317	F.P. Santangelo	.05
318	Wilton Guerrero	.05
319	Jose Guillen	.05
320	Kevin Orie	.05
321	Derrek Lee	.05
322	Bubba Trammell RC	.50
323	Pokey Reese	.05
324	Hideki Irabu RC	.25
325	Scott Spiezio	.05
326	Bartolo Colon	.05
327	Damon Mashore	.05
328	Ryan McGuire	.05
329	Chris Carpenter	.05
330	Jose Cruz Jr. RC	.50
331	Todd Greene	.05
332	Brian Moehler	.05
333	Mike Sweeney	.05
334	Neifi Perez	.05
335	Matt Morris	.05
336	Marvin Benard	.05
337	Karim Garcia	.05
338	Jason Dickson	.05
339	Brant Brown	.05
340	Jeff Suppan	.05
341	Deivi Cruz RC	.25
342	Antone Williamson	.05
343	Curtis Goodwin	.05
344	Brooks Kieschnick	.05
345	Tony Womack RC	.25
346	Rudy Pemberton	.05
347	Todd Dunwoody	.05
348	Frank Thomas (Legacy)	.50
349	Andruw Jones (Legacy)	.50
350	Alex Rodriguez (Legacy)	1.25
351	Greg Maddux (Legacy)	.75
352	Jeff Bagwell (Legacy)	.50
353	Juan Gonzalez (Legacy)	.35
354	Barry Bonds (Legacy)	1.50
355	Mark McGwire (Legacy)	1.25
356	Tony Gwynn (Legacy)	.75
357	Gary Sheffield (Legacy)	.25
358	Derek Jeter (Legacy)	1.50
359	Manny Ramirez (Legacy)	.50
360	Hideo Nomo (Legacy)	.30
361	Sammy Sosa (Legacy)	1.00
362	Paul Molitor (Legacy)	.40
363	Kenny Lofton (Legacy)	.40
364	Eddie Murray (Legacy)	.40
365	Barry Larkin (Legacy)	.40
366	Roger Clemens (Legacy)	1.00
367	John Smoltz (Legacy)	.05
368	Alex Rodriguez (Gamers)	1.50
369	Frank Thomas (Gamers)	.40
370	Cal Ripken Jr. (Gamers)	1.50
371	Ken Griffey Jr. (Gamers)	1.50
372	Greg Maddux (Gamers)	.75
373	Mike Piazza (Gamers)	1.25
374	Chipper Jones (Gamers)	.50
375	Albert Belle (Gamers)	.05
376	Chuck Knoblauch (Gamers)	.05
377	Brady Anderson (Gamers)	.05
378	David Justice (Gamers)	.05
379	Randy Johnson (Gamers)	.40
380	Wade Boggs (Gamers)	.75
381	Kevin Brown (Gamers)	.05
382	Tom Glavine (Gamers)	.05
383	Raul Mondesi (Gamers)	.05
384	Ivan Rodriguez (Gamers)	.30
385	Larry Walker (Gamers)	.05
386	Bernie Williams (Gamers)	.05
387	Rusty Greer (Gamers)	.05
388	Rafael Palmeiro (Gamers)	.05
389	Matt Williams (Gamers)	.05
390	Eric Young (Gamers)	.05
391	Fred McGriff (Gamers)	.05
392	Ken Caminiti (Gamers)	.05
393	Roberto Alomar (Gamers)	.05
394	Brian Jordan (Gamers)	.05
395	Mark Grace (Gamers)	.05
396	Jim Edmonds (Gamers)	.05
397	Deion Sanders (Gamers)	.05

398	Checklist (Vladimir Guerrero)	.50
399	Checklist (Darin Erstad)	.10
400	Checklist (Nomar Garciaparra)	1.00

Fractal Matrix

Leaf introduced Fractal Matrix inserts, a 400-card parallel set broken down into three colors and three unique die-cuts. One "fracture" breaks the insert set down by foil background color (80 Gold, 120 Silver and 200 Bronze). A second fracture breaks those cards down into X, Y and Z "axis" variations. There are no markings on the cards to segregate the X, Y and Z groups, though that information was printed on the box bottoms. No production numbers or insert ratios were released for either fracture. Each player is available in only one color/axis combination. The incredibly convoluted nature of the issue insured that virtually nobody understood the concept, putting a damper on collector interest.

		NM/M
	Common Bronze:	.35
	Common Silver:	.50
	Common Gold:	1.25
1	Wade Boggs G/Y	8.00
2	Brian McRae B/Y	.35
3	Jeff D'Amico B/Y	.35
4	George Arias S/Y	.50
5	Billy Wagner S/Y	.50
6	Ray Lankford B/Z	.35
7	Will Clark S/Y	.60
8	Edgar Renteria S/Y	.50
9	Alex Ochoa S/Y	.50
10	Roberto Hernandez B/X	.35
11	Joe Carter S/Y	.50
12	Gregg Jefferies B/X	.35
13	Mark Grace S/Y	.75
14	Roberto Alomar G/Y	2.00
15	Joe Randa B/X	.35
16	Alex Rodriguez G/Z	10.00
17	Tony Gwynn G/Z	6.00
18	Steve Gibralter B/Y	.35
19	Scott Stahoviak B/X	.35
20	Matt Williams S/Y	.50
21	Quinton McCracken B/Y	.35
22	Ugueth Urbina B/X	.35
23	Jermaine Allensworth S/X	.50
24	Paul Molitor G/X	5.00
25	Carlos Delgado S/Y	1.00
26	Bob Abreu S/Y	.50
27	John Jaha B/Y	.35
28	Rusty Greer S/Z	.50
29	Kimera Bartee B/X	.35
30	Ruben Rivera S/Y	.50
31	Jason Kendall S/Y	.50
32	Lance Johnson B/X	.35
33	Robin Ventura B/X	.35
34	Kevin Appier S/X	.50
35	John Mabry S/Y	.50
36	Ricky Otero B/X	.35
37	Mike Lansing B/X	.35
38	Mark McGwire G/Z	10.00
39	Tim Naehring B/X	.35
40	Tom Glavine S/Z	1.00
41	Rey Ordonez S/Y	.50
42	Tony Clark S/Y	.50
43	Rafael Palmeiro B/Z	2.00
44	Pedro Martinez B/X	2.00
45	Keith Lockhart B/X	.35
46	Dan Wilson B/X	.35
47	John Wetteland B/X	.35
48	Chan Ho Park B/X	.35
49	Gary Sheffield G/Z	3.00
50	Shawn Estes B/Y	.35
51	Royce Clayton B/Y	.35
52	Jaime Navarro B/Y	.35
53	Raul Casanova B/Y	.35
54	Jeff Bagwell G/Z	5.00
55	Barry Larkin G/Z	1.25
56	Charles Nagy B/X	.35
57	Ken Caminiti S/Y	1.25
58	Todd Hollandsworth S/Z	.50
59	Pat Hentgen S/X	.35
60	Jose Valentin B/X	.35
61	Frank Rodriguez B/X	.35
62	Mickey Tettleton B/X	.35

63	Marty Cordova G/X	1.25
64	Cecil Fielder S/Y	.50
65	Barry Bonds G/X	13.50
66	Scott Servais B/X	.35
67	Ernie Young B/X	.35
68	Wilson Alvarez B/X	.35
69	Mike Grace B/X	.35
70	Shane Reynolds S/X	.50
71	Henry Rodriguez S/Y	.50
72	Eric Karros B/X	.35
73	Mark Langston B/X	.35
74	Scott Karl B/X	.35
75	Trevor Hoffman B/X	.50
76	Orel Hershiser S/Y	.50
77	John Smoltz G/Y	1.50
78	Raul Mondesi G/Z	1.25
79	Jeff Brantley B/X	.35
80	Donne Wall B/X	.35
81	Joey Cora B/X	.35
82	Mel Rojas B/X	.35
83	Chad Mottola B/X	.35
84	Omar Vizquel B/X	.35
85	Greg Maddux G/Z	6.00
86	Jamey Wright S/Y	.35
87	Chuck Finley B/X	.35
88	Brady Anderson G/Y	1.25
89	Alex Gonzalez S/X	.50
90	Andy Benes B/X	.35
91	Reggie Jefferson B/X	.35
92	Paul O'Neill S/X	.35
93	Javier Lopez S/X	.50
94	Mark Grudzielanek S/X	.50
95	Marc Newfield B/X	.35
96	Kevin Ritz B/X	.35
97	Fred McGriff G/Y	1.25
98	Dwight Gooden S/X	.50
99	Hideo Nomo S/Y	1.50
100	Steve Finley B/X	.35
101	Juan Gonzalez G/Z	4.00
102	Jay Buhner S/Z	.50
103	Paul Wilson S/Y	.50
104	Alan Benes B/Y	.35
105	Manny Ramirez G/X	5.00
106	Kevin Elster S/X	.35
107	Frank Thomas G/X	5.00
108	Orlando Miller B/X	.35
109	Ramon Martinez B/X	.35
110	Kenny Lofton G/Z	1.25
111	Bernie Williams G/Y	1.25
112	Robby Thompson B/X	.35
113	Bernard Gilkey B/Z	.35
114	Ray Durham B/X	.35
115	Jeff Cirillo S/Z	.50
116	Brian Jordan G/Z	1.25
117	Rich Becker S/Y	.50
118	Al Leiter B/X	.35
119	Mark Johnson B/X	.35
120	Ellis Burks B/Y	.35
121	Sammy Sosa G/X	7.50
122	Willie Greene B/X	.35
123	Michael Tucker B/X	.35
124	Eddie Murray G/Y	6.00
125	Joey Hamilton S/Y	.50
126	Antonio Osuna B/X	.35
127	Bobby Higginson S/Y	.50
128	Tomas Perez B/X	.35
129	Tim Salmon G/Z	1.25
130	Mark Wohlers B/X	.35
131	Charles Johnson S/X	.50
132	Randy Johnson S/Y	2.00
133	Brooks Kieschnick S/X	.50
134	Al Martin S/Y	.35
135	Dante Bichette B/X	.50
136	Andy Pettitte G/Z	2.00
137	Jason Giambi G/Y	4.00
138	James Baldwin S/X	.50
139	Ben McDonald B/X	.35
140	Shawn Green S/X	1.00
141	Geronimo Berroa B/Y	.35
142	Jose Offerman B/X	.35
143	Curtis Pride B/X	.35
144	Terrell Wade B/X	.35
145	Ismael Valdes S/X	.50
146	Mike Mussina S/Y	1.25
147	Mariano Rivera S/X	.75
148	Ken Hill B/Y	.35
149	Darin Erstad G/Z	4.00
150	Jay Bell B/X	.35
151	Mo Vaughn S/Y	1.25
152	Ozzie Smith G/Y	8.00
153	Jose Mesa B/X	.35
154	Osvaldo Fernandez B/X	.35
155	Vinny Castilla B/Y	.35
156	Jason Isringhausen S/Y	.50
157	B.J. Surhoff B/X	.35
158	Robert Perez B/X	.35
159	Ron Coomer B/X	.35
160	Darren Oliver B/X	.35
161	Mike Mohler B/X	.35
162	Russ Davis B/X	.35
163	Bret Boone B/X	.35
164	Ricky Bottalico B/X	.35
165	Derek Jeter G/Z	13.50
166	Orlando Merced B/X	.35
167	John Valentin B/X	.35
168	Andruw Jones G/X	5.00
169	Angel Echevarria B/X	.35
170	Todd Walker S/Z	1.25
171	Desi Relaford B/X	.35
172	Trey Beamon S/X	.50
173	Brian Giles B/X	.35
174	Scott Rolen G/Z	3.50
175	Shannon Stewart S/Z	.50
176	Dmitri Young S/Y	1.25
177	Justin Thompson B/X	.35
178	Trot Nixon S/Y	.50
179	Josh Booty S/Y	.50
180	Robin Jennings B/X	.35

181	Marvin Benard B/X	.35
182	Luis Castillo B/Y	.35
183	Wendell Magee B/X	.35
184	Vladimir Guerrero G/X	5.00
185	Nomar Garciaparra G/X	12.50
186	Ryan Hancock B/X	.35
187	Mike Cameron S/X	.50
188	Cal Ripken Jr. B/Z	5.00
189	Chipper Jones G/X (Legacy)	4.00
190	Albert Belle S/Z (Legacy)	1.00
191	Mike Piazza B/Z (Legacy)	4.00
192	Chuck Knoblauch S/Y (Legacy)	.50
193	Ken Griffey Jr. B/Z (Legacy)	3.50
194	Ivan Rodriguez G/Z (Legacy)	4.00
195	Jose Canseco S/X (Legacy)	1.25
196	Ryne Sandberg S/X (Legacy)	3.00
197	Jim Thome G/Y (Legacy)	1.50
198	Checklist (Andy Pettitte B/Y)	.75
199	Checklist (Andruw Jones B/Y)	2.00
200	Checklist (Derek Jeter S/Y)	2.00
201	Chipper Jones G/X	10.00
202	Albert Belle G/Y	1.25
203	Mike Piazza G/X	3.00
204	Ken Griffey Jr. G/X	15.00
205	Ryne Sandberg G/Z	6.00
206	Jose Canseco S/Y	.75
207	Chili Davis S/X	.50
208	Roger Clemens G/Z	6.50
209	Deion Sanders G/Z	1.50
210	Darryl Hamilton B/X	.35
211	Jermaine Dye B/X	.35
212	Matt Williams G/Y	1.25
213	Kevin Elster B/X	.35
214	John Wetteland S/X	.35
215	Garret Anderson G/Z	1.25
216	Kevin Brown G/Y	1.25
217	Matt Lawton S/Y	.35
218	Cal Ripken Jr. G/X	16.50
219	Moises Alou B/X	.35
220	Chuck Knoblauch G/Z	1.25
221	Ivan Rodriguez S/Y	5.50
222	Travis Fryman B/Y	.35
223	Jim Thome G/Z	2.00
224	Eddie Murray S/Z	3.00
225	Eric Young G/Z	1.25
226	Ron Gant S/X	.50
227	Tony Phillips B/X	.35
228	Reggie Sanders B/Y	.35
229	Johnny Damon S/Z	1.00
230	Bill Pulsipher B/X	.35
231	Jim Edmonds G/Z	1.25
232	Melvin Nieves B/X	.35
233	Ryan Klesko G/Z	1.25
234	David Cone S/X	.50
235	Derek Bell B/Y	.35
236	Julio Franco S/X	.35
237	Juan Guzman B/X	.35
238	Larry Walker G/Z	1.25
239	Delino DeShields B/X	.35
240	Troy Percival S/X	.35
241	Andres Galarraga G/Z	1.25
242	Rondell White G/Z	1.25
243	John Burkett B/X	.35
244	J.T. Snow S/Y	.50
245	Alex Fernandez S/X	.50
246	Edgar Martinez S/X	.50
247	Craig Biggio G/Z	1.25
248	Todd Hundley S/X	1.25
249	Jimmy Key S/X	.50
250	Cliff Floyd B/Y	.35
251	Jeff Conine B/Y	.35
252	Curt Schilling B/X	.65
253	Jeff King B/X	.35
254	Tino Martinez G/Z	1.25
255	Carlos Baerga S/X	.50
256	Jeff Fassero B/X	.35
257	Dean Palmer S/Y	.50
258	Robb Nen B/X	.35
259	Sandy Alomar Jr. S/Y	.50
260	Carlos Perez B/X	.35
261	Rickey Henderson S/Y	2.00
262	Bobby Bonilla S/X	.50
263	Darren Daulton B/X	.35
264	Jim Leyritz B/X	.35
265	Dennis Martinez B/X	.35
266	Butch Huskey B/X	.35
267	Joe Vitiello S/X	.50
268	Steve Trachsel B/X	.35
269	Glenallen Hill B/X	.35
270	Terry Steinbach B/X	.35
271	Mark McLemore B/X	.35
272	Devon White B/X	.35
273	Jeff Kent B/X	.35
274	Tim Raines B/X	.35
275	Carlos Garcia B/X	.35
276	Hal Morris B/X	.35
277	Gary Gaetti B/X	.35
278	John Olerud S/Y	.50
279	Wally Joyner B/X	.35
280	Brian Hunter S/X	.50
281	Steve Karsay B/X	.35
282	Denny Neagle S/X	.50
283	Jose Herrera B/X	.35
284	Todd Stottlemyre B/X	.35
285	Bip Roberts B/X	.35
286	Kevin Seitzer B/X	.35
287	Benji Gil B/X	.35
288	Dennis Eckersley B/X	.50

289	Brad Ausmus B/X	.35
290	Otis Nixon B/X	.35
291	Darryl Strawberry B/X	.50
292	Marquis Grissom S/Y	.50
293	Darryl Kile B/X	.35
294	Quilvio Veras B/X	.35
295	Tom Goodwin B/X	.35
296	Benito Santiago B/X	.35
297	Mike Bordick B/X	.35
298	Roberto Kelly B/X	.35
299	David Justice G/Z	1.25
300	Carl Everett B/X	.35
301	Mark Whiten B/X	.35
302	Aaron Sele B/X	.35
303	Darren Dreifort B/X	.35
304	Bobby Jones B/X	.35
305	Fernando Vina B/X	.35
306	Ed Sprague B/X	.35
307	Andy Ashby S/X	.50
308	Tony Fernandez B/X	.35
309	Roger Pavlik B/X	.35
310	Mark Clark B/X	.35
311	Mariano Duncan B/X	.35
312	Tyler Houston B/X	.35
313	Eric Davis S/Y	.50
314	Greg Vaughn B/Y	.35
315	David Segui S/Y	.50
316	Dave Nilsson B/X	.35
317	F.P. Santangelo S/X	.50
318	Wilton Guerrero G/Z	1.25
319	Jose Guillen G/Z	1.25
320	Kevin Orie S/Y	.50
321	Derrek Lee G/Z	2.50
322	Bubba Trammell S/Y	.50
323	Pokey Reese S/Y	1.25
324	Hideki Irabu G/X	1.25
325	Scott Spiezio S/Y	.50
326	Bartolo Colon G/Z	1.25
327	Damon Mashore S/Y	.50
328	Ryan McGuire S/Y	.50
329	Chris Carpenter B/X	.35
330	Jose Cruz, Jr. G/X	2.50
331	Todd Greene S/Z	.50
332	Brian Moehler B/X	.35
333	Mike Sweeney B/Y	.35
334	Neifi Perez G/Z	1.25
335	Matt Morris S/Y	.50
336	Marvin Benard B/X	.35
337	Karim Garcia S/Y	.75
338	Jason Dickson S/Y	.50
339	Brant Brown S/Y	.50
340	Jeff Suppan S/Z	.50
341	Deivi Cruz B/X	.35
342	Antone Williamson G/Z	1.25
343	Curtis Goodwin B/X	.35
344	Brooks Kieschnick S/Y	.50
345	Tony Womack B/X	.35
346	Rudy Pemberton B/X	.35
347	Todd Dunwoody B/X	.35
348	Frank Thomas S/Y (Legacy)	2.25
349	Andruw Jones S/X (Legacy)	2.00
350	Alex Rodriguez S/Y (Legacy)	4.00
351	Greg Maddux S/Y (Legacy)	3.00
352	Jeff Bagwell B/Y (Legacy)	2.25
353	Juan Gonzalez S/Y (Legacy)	1.50
354	Barry Bonds B/Y (Legacy)	5.00
355	Mark McGwire B/Y (Legacy)	4.00
356	Tony Gwynn B/Y (Legacy)	3.00
357	Gary Sheffield B/X (Legacy)	.75
358	Derek Jeter S/X (Legacy)	4.00
359	Manny Ramirez S/Y (Legacy)	2.00
360	Hideo Nomo G/Z (Legacy)	4.00
361	Sammy Sosa B/X (Legacy)	3.50
362	Paul Molitor S/Z (Legacy)	3.00
363	Kenny Lofton B/Y (Legacy)	.35
364	Eddie Murray B/X (Legacy)	2.00
365	Barry Larkin S/Z (Legacy)	.50
366	Roger Clemens B/X (Legacy)	3.50
367	John Smoltz B/Z (Legacy)	.35
368	Alex Rodriguez S/X (Gamers)	3.25
369	Frank Thomas B/X (Gamers)	2.25
370	Cal Ripken Jr. S/Y (Gamers)	4.00
371	Ken Griffey Jr. S/Y (Gamers)	3.25
372	Greg Maddux B/X (Gamers)	3.00
373	Mike Piazza B/Y (Gamers)	3.25
374	Chipper Jones B/Y (Gamers)	3.00
375	Albert Belle B/X (Gamers)	.50
376	Chuck Knoblauch B/X (Gamers)	.35
377	Brady Anderson B/Z (Gamers)	.35
378	David Justice S/X (Gamers)	.50

379 Randy Johnson B/Z (Gamers) 2.00
380 Wade Boggs B/X (Gamers) 3.00
381 Kevin Brown B/X (Gamers) .35
382 Tom Glavine G/Y (Gamers) 3.00
383 Raul Mondesi S/X (Gamers) .50
384 Ivan Rodriguez S/X (Gamers) 1.25
385 Larry Walker B/Y (Gamers) .35
386 Bernie Williams B/Z (Gamers) .45
387 Rusty Greer G/Y (Gamers) 1.25
388 Rafael Palmeiro G/Y (Gamers) 4.50
389 Matt Williams B/X (Gamers) .35
390 Eric Young B/X (Gamers) .35
391 Fred McGriff B/X (Gamers) .35
392 Ken Caminiti B/X (Gamers) .35
393 Roberto Alomar B/Z (Gamers) .75
394 Brian Jordan B/X (Gamers) .35
395 Mark Grace G/Z (Gamers) 1.25
396 Jim Edmonds B/Y (Gamers) .35
397 Deion Sanders S/Y (Gamers) .50
398 Checklist (Vladimir Guerrero S/Z) 1.25
399 Checklist (Darin Erstad S/Y) 1.00
400 Checklist (Nomar Garciaparra S/Z) 2.00

Fractal Matrix Die-Cut

A second parallel set to the Leaf product, the Fractal Matrix Die-Cuts offer three different die-cut designs with three colors for each. The Axis-X die-cuts comprise 200 players (150 Bronze, 40 Silver and 10 Gold), the Axis-Y die-cuts has 120 players (60 Silver, 40 Bronze, 20 Gold), and the Axis-Z die-cuts consist of 80 players (50 Gold, 20 Silver, 10 Bronze). Odds of finding any of these inserts are 1:6 packs. Each player was issued in only one color/cut combination.

NM/M
Common X- or Y-Axis: .75
Common Z-Axis: 1.25
1 Wade Boggs B/X 6.00
2 Brian McRae B/Y .75
3 Jeff D'Amico B/Y .75
4 George Arias S/Y .75
5 Billy Wagner S/Y .75
6 Ray Lankford B/Z 1.25
7 Will Clark S/Y .75
8 Edgar Renteria S/Y .75
9 Alex Ochoa B/Y .75
10 Joe Carter B/X .75
11 Gregg Jefferies B/Y .75
12 Mark Grace S/Y .75
13 Roberto Alomar G/Y 1.50
14 Joe Randa B/Y .75
15 Alex Rodriguez G/Z 12.50
16 Tony Gwynn G/Z 7.50
17 Steve Gibralter B/Y .75
18 Scott Stahoviak B/X .75
19 Matt Williams B/Z 1.25
20 Quinton McCracken B/Y .75
21 Ugueth Urbina B/Y .75
22 Jermaine Allensworth S/X .75
23 Paul Molitor S/X 5.00
24 Carlos Delgado S/Y 2.00
25 Bob Abreu S/Y .75
26 John Jaha S/Y .75
27 Rusty Greer S/Z 1.25
28 Kimera Bartee B/X .75
29 Ruben Rivera B/X .75
30 Jason Kendall S/Y .75
31 Lance Johnson B/X .75
32 Robin Ventura B/Y .75
33 Kevin Appier S/X .75
34 John Mabry S/Y .75
35 Ricky Otero B/X .75

37 Mike Lansing B/X .75
38 Mark McGwire G/Z 12.50
39 Tim Naehring B/X .75
40 Tom Glavine S/Z 3.00
41 Rey Ordonez S/Y .75
42 Tony Clark S/Y .75
43 Rafael Palmeiro S/Z 4.00
44 Pedro Martinez B/X 5.00
45 Keith Lockhart B/X .75
46 Dan Wilson B/Y .75
47 John Wetteland B/Y .75
48 Chan Ho Park B/X .75
49 Gary Sheffield G/Z 2.50
50 Shawn Estes B/X .75
51 Royce Clayton B/X .75
52 Jaime Navarro B/X .75
53 Raul Casanova B/X .75
54 Jeff Bagwell G/Z 6.00
55 Barry Larkin S/X .75
56 Charles Nagy B/Y .75
57 Ken Caminiti B/X .75
58 Todd Hollandsworth S/Z 1.25
59 Pat Hentgen S/X .75
60 Jose Valentin B/X .75
61 Frank Rodriguez B/X .75
62 Mickey Tettleton B/X .75
63 Marty Cordova G/X .75
64 Cecil Fielder S/X .75
65 Barry Bonds B/X 15.00
66 Scott Servais B/X .75
67 Ernie Young B/X .75
68 Wilson Alvarez B/X .75
69 Mike Grace B/X .75
70 Shane Reynolds S/X .75
71 Henry Rodriguez S/Y .75
72 Eric Karros B/X .75
73 Mark Langston B/X .75
74 Scott Karl B/X .75
75 Trevor Hoffman B/X .75
76 Orel Hershiser S/X .75
77 John Smoltz G/Y .75
78 Raul Mondesi G/Z 1.25
79 Jeff Brantley B/X .75
80 Donne Wall B/X .75
81 Joey Cora B/X .75
82 Mel Rojas B/X .75
83 Chad Mottola B/X .75
84 Omar Vizquel B/X .75
85 Greg Maddux G/Z 7.50
86 Jamey Wright B/X .75
87 Chuck Finley B/X .75
88 Alex Gonzalez S/X .75
89 Andy Benes B/X .75
90 Reggie Jefferson B/X .75
91 Paul O'Neill B/Y .75
92 Javier Lopez S/X .75
93 Mark Grudzielanek S/X .75
94 Marc Newfield B/X .75
95 Kevin Ritz B/X .75
96 Fred McGriff G/Y .75
97 Dwight Gooden S/X .75
98 Hideo Nomo S/Y 4.00
99 Steve Finley B/X .75
100 Juan Gonzalez G/Z 4.00
101 Jay Buhner S/Z 1.25
102 Paul Wilson B/Y .75
103 Alan Benes B/Y .75
104 Manny Ramirez G/Z 6.00
105 Kevin Elster B/X .75
106 Frank Thomas G/Z 6.00
107 Orlando Miller B/X .75
108 Ramon Martinez B/X .75
109 Kenny Lofton G/Z 1.25
110 Bernie Williams B/X .75
111 Robby Thompson B/X .75
112 Bernard Gilkey B/Z 1.25
113 Ray Durham B/X .75
114 Jeff Cirillo S/Z .75
115 Brian Jordan B/Z 1.25
116 Rich Becker S/Y .75
117 Al Leiter B/X .75
118 Mark Johnson B/X .75
119 Ellis Burks B/Y .75
120 Sammy Sosa G/X 9.00
121 Willie Greene B/X .75
122 Michael Tucker B/X .75
123 Eddie Murray S/X 5.00
124 Joey Hamilton S/Y .75
125 Antonio Osuna B/X .75
126 Bobby Higginson S/Y .75
127 Tomas Perez B/X .75
128 Tim Salmon G/Z 1.25
129 Mark Wohlers B/X .75
130 Charles Johnson B/X .75
131 Randy Johnson S/Y 5.00
132 Brooks Kieschnick B/X .75
133 Al Martin S/Y .75
134 Dante Bichette B/X .75
135 Andy Pettitte G/Z 3.00
136 Jason Giambi S/Y 2.00
137 James Baldwin S/X .75
138 Ben McDonald B/X .75
139 Shawn Green B/X .75
140 Geronimo Berroa B/Y .75
141 Jose Offerman B/X .75
142 Curtis Pride B/Y .75
143 Terrell Wade B/X .75
144 Ismael Valdes B/X .75
145 Mike Mussina B/X 2.00
146 Mariano Rivera S/X 1.00
147 Ken Hill B/Y .75
148 Darin Erstad S/Z 2.50
149 Jay Bell B/X .75
150 Mo Vaughn G/X 2.50
151 Ozzie Smith G/Y 6.00
152 Jose Mesa B/X .75
153 Osvaldo Fernandez B/X .75
154 [.75]

155 Vinny Castilla B/Y .75
156 Jason Isringhausen S/Y .75
157 B.J. Surhoff B/X .75
158 Robert Perez B/X .75
159 Ron Coomer B/X .75
160 Darren Oliver B/X .75
161 Mike Mohler B/X .75
162 Russ Davis B/X .75
163 Bret Boone B/X .75
164 Ricky Bottalico B/X .75
165 Derek Jeter G/Z 15.00
166 Orlando Merced B/X .75
167 John Valentin B/X .75
168 Andruw Jones G/Z 6.00
169 Angel Echevarria B/X .75
170 Todd Walker G/Z 1.25
171 Desi Relaford B/Y .75
172 Trey Beamon S/X .75
173 Brian Giles S/Y .75
174 Scott Rolen G/Z 4.00
175 Shannon Stewart S/Z 1.25
176 Dmitri Young G/Z 1.25
177 Justin Thompson B/X .75
178 Trot Nixon S/Y 1.00
179 Josh Booty B/X .75
180 Robin Jennings B/X .75
181 Marvin Benard B/X .75
182 Luis Castillo B/Y .75
183 Wendell Magee B/X .75
184 Vladimir Guerrero G/X 5.00
185 Nomar Garciaparra G/X 7.50
186 Ryan Hancock B/X .75
187 Mike Cameron S/X .75
188 Cal Ripken Jr. B/Z (Legacy) 15.00
189 Chipper Jones B/X (Legacy) 7.50
190 Albert Belle S/Z (Legacy) 1.25
191 Mike Piazza B/Z (Legacy) 12.50
192 Chuck Knoblauch S/Y (Legacy) .75
193 Ken Griffey Jr. B/Z (Legacy) 10.00
194 Ivan Rodriguez G/Z (Legacy) 5.00
195 Jose Canseco S/X (Legacy) 1.50
196 Ryne Sandberg S/X (Legacy) 5.00
197 Jim Thome G/Y (Legacy) .75
198 Checklist (Andy Pettitte B/Y) 1.00
199 Checklist (Andruw Jones B/Y) 5.00
200 Checklist (Derek Jeter S/Y) 7.50
201 Chipper Jones G/X 6.00
202 Albert Belle G/Y .75
203 Mike Piazza G/Y 10.00
204 Ken Griffey Jr. G/X 7.50
205 Ryne Sandberg G/X 6.00
206 Jose Canseco S/Y 1.50
207 Chili Davis B/X .75
208 Roger Clemens B/Y 9.00
209 Deion Sanders G/Z 1.50
210 Darryl Hamilton B/X .75
211 Jermaine Dye S/X .75
212 Matt Williams G/Y .75
213 Kevin Elster B/X .75
214 John Wetteland S/X .75
215 Garret Anderson G/Z 1.25
216 Kevin Brown G/Y .75
217 Matt Lawton S/Y .75
218 Cal Ripken Jr. G/X 12.50
219 Moises Alou G/Y .75
220 Chuck Knoblauch G/Z 1.25
221 Ivan Rodriguez G/Z 4.00
222 Travis Fryman B/Y .75
223 Jim Thome G/Z 2.50
224 Eddie Murray S/Z 6.00
225 Eric Young G/Z 1.25
226 Ron Gant S/X .75
227 Tony Phillips B/X .75
228 Reggie Sanders B/Y .75
229 Johnny Damon S/Z 1.25
230 Bill Pulsipher B/X .75
231 Jim Edmonds G/Z 1.25
232 Melvin Nieves B/X .75
233 Ryan Klesko B/X .75
234 David Cone S/X .75
235 Derek Bell B/X .75
236 Julio Franco S/X .75
237 Juan Guzman B/X .75
238 Larry Walker G/Z 1.25
239 Delino DeShields B/X .75
240 Troy Percival B/X .75
241 Andres Galarraga G/Z 1.25
242 Rondell White G/Z 1.25
243 John Burkett B/X .75
244 J.T. Snow B/Y .75
245 Alex Fernandez S/Y .75
246 Edgar Martinez G/Z 1.25
247 Craig Biggio G/X 1.25
248 Todd Hundley G/Y .75
249 Jimmy Key S/X .75
250 Cliff Floyd B/Y .75
251 Jeff Conine B/Y .75
252 Curt Schilling B/X 1.50
253 Jeff King B/X .75
254 Tino Martinez B/Y 1.25
255 Carlos Baerga S/Y .75
256 Jeff Fassero B/X .75
257 Dean Palmer S/Y .75
258 Robb Nen B/X .75
259 Sandy Alomar Jr. S/Y .75
260 Carlos Perez B/X .75
261 Rickey Henderson S/Y 5.00

262 Bobby Bonilla S/Y .75
263 Darren Daulton B/X .75
264 Jim Leyritz B/X .75
265 Dennis Martinez B/X .75
266 Butch Huskey B/X .75
267 Joe Vitiello S/Y .75
268 Steve Trachsel B/X .75
269 Glenallen Hill B/X .75
270 Terry Steinbach B/X .75
271 Mark McLemore B/X .75
272 Devon White B/X .75
273 Jeff Kent B/X .75
274 Tim Raines S/Y .75
275 Carlos Garcia B/X .75
276 Hal Morris B/X .75
277 Gary Gaetti B/X .75
278 John Olerud B/X .75
279 Wally Joyner B/X .75
280 Brian Hunter S/X .75
281 Steve Karsay B/X .75
282 Denny Neagle S/Y .75
283 Jose Herrera B/X .75
284 Todd Stottlemyre B/X .75
285 Bip Roberts S/X .75
286 Kevin Seitzer B/X .75
287 Benji Gil B/Y .75
288 Dennis Eckersley S/X .75
289 Brad Ausmus B/X .75
290 Otis Nixon B/X .75
291 Darryl Strawberry B/X .75
292 Marquis Grissom S/Y .75
293 Darryl Kile B/X .75
294 Quilvio Veras B/X .75
295 Tom Goodwin B/X .75
296 Benito Santiago B/X .75
297 Mike Bordick B/X .75
298 Roberto Kelly B/X .75
299 David Justice G/Z 1.25
300 Carl Everett B/X .75
301 Mark Whiten B/X .75
302 Aaron Sele B/X .75
303 Darren Dreifort B/X .75
304 Bobby Jones B/X .75
305 Fernando Vina B/X .75
306 Ed Sprague B/X .75
307 Andy Ashby S/X .75
308 Tony Fernandez B/X .75
309 Roger Pavlik B/X .75
310 Mark Clark B/X .75
311 Mariano Duncan B/X .75
312 Tyler Houston B/X .75
313 Eric Davis S/Y .75
314 Greg Vaughn B/Y .75
315 David Segui B/X .75
316 Dave Nilsson S/X .75
317 F.P. Santangelo S/X .75
318 Wilton Guerrero G/Z 1.25
319 Jose Guillen G/Z 1.25
320 Kevin Orie S/Y .75
321 Derrek Lee G/Z 2.50
322 Bubba Trammell S/Y .75
323 Pokey Reese G/Z 1.25
324 Hideki Irabu G/X .75
325 Scott Spiezio G/Z 1.25
326 Bartolo Colon G/Z 1.25
327 Damon Mashore S/Y .75
328 Ryan McGuire S/Y .75
329 Chris Carpenter B/X .75
330 Jose Cruz, Jr. G/X .75
331 Todd Greene B/X 1.25
332 Brian Moehler B/X .75
333 Mike Sweeney B/X .75
334 Neifi Perez G/Z 1.25
335 Matt Morris S/Y .75
336 Marvin Benard B/Y .75
337 Karim Garcia S/Y .75
338 Jason Dickson S/Y .75
339 Brant Brown S/Y .75
340 Jeff Suppan S/Z 1.25
341 Deivi Cruz B/X .75
342 Antone Williamson G/Z 1.25
343 Curtis Goodwin B/X .75
344 Brooks Kieschnick S/Y .75
345 Tony Womack S/X .75
346 Rudy Pemberton B/X .75
347 Todd Dunwoody B/X .75
348 Frank Thomas S/Y (Legacy) 5.00
349 Andruw Jones S/X (Legacy) 5.00
350 Alex Rodriguez B/Y (Legacy) 10.00
351 Greg Maddux S/Y (Legacy) 6.00
352 Jeff Bagwell B/Y (Legacy) 5.00
353 Juan Gonzalez S/Y (Legacy) 4.00
354 Barry Bonds B/Y (Legacy) 12.50
355 Mark McGwire B/Y (Legacy) 10.00
356 Tony Gwynn B/Y (Legacy) 6.00
357 Gary Sheffield B/X (Legacy) 1.50
358 Derek Jeter S/X (Legacy) 12.50
359 Manny Ramirez B/Y (Legacy) 5.00
360 Hideo Nomo G/Z (Legacy) 4.00
361 Sammy Sosa B/X (Legacy) 6.50
362 Paul Molitor S/Z (Legacy) 6.00
363 Kenny Lofton B/X (Legacy) .75

364 Eddie Murray B/X (Legacy) 5.00
365 Barry Larkin S/Z (Legacy) 1.25
366 Roger Clemens S/Y (Legacy) 6.50
367 John Smoltz B/Z (Legacy) 1.25
368 Alex Rodriguez S/X (Gamers) 10.00
369 Frank Thomas B/X (Gamers) 5.00
370 Cal Ripken Jr. S/Y (Gamers) 12.50
371 Ken Griffey Jr. S/Y (Gamers) 7.50
372 Greg Maddux B/X (Gamers) 6.00
373 Mike Piazza S/X (Gamers) 10.00
374 Chipper Jones B/Y (Gamers) 6.00
375 Albert Belle B/X (Gamers) .75
376 Chuck Knoblauch B/X (Gamers) .75
377 Brady Anderson B/Z (Gamers) 1.25
378 David Justice S/X (Gamers) .75
379 Randy Johnson B/Z (Gamers) 6.00
380 Wade Boggs B/X (Gamers) 6.00
381 Kevin Brown B/X (Gamers) .75
382 Tom Glavine B/X (Gamers) 2.00
383 Raul Mondesi S/X (Gamers)
384 Ivan Rodriguez S/X (Gamers) 4.00
385 Larry Walker B/Y (Gamers)
386 Bernie Williams B/Z (Gamers) 1.25
387 Rusty Greer G/Y (Gamers) .75
388 Rafael Palmeiro G/Y (Gamers) 4.00
389 Matt Williams B/X (Gamers) .75
390 Eric Young B/X (Gamers) .75
391 Fred McGriff B/X (Gamers) .75
392 Ken Caminiti B/X (Gamers) .75
393 Roberto Alomar B/Z (Gamers) 2.00
394 Brian Jordan B/X (Gamers) 1.25
395 Mark Grace G/Z (Gamers) 1.25
396 Jim Edmonds B/Y (Gamers) .75
397 Deion Sanders S/Y (Gamers) .75
398 Checklist (Vladimir Guerrero S/Z) 3.00
399 Checklist (Darin Erstad S/Y) 1.00
400 Checklist (Nomar Garciaparra S/Z) 4.00

Banner Season

Banner Season was a 15-card insert set that was die-cut and printed on a canvas card stock. Only 2,500 individually numbered sets were produced, with cards only found in pre-priced packs.

NM/M
Complete Set (15): 30.00
Common Player: .50
1 Jeff Bagwell 2.50
2 Ken Griffey Jr. 5.00
3 Juan Gonzalez 1.50
4 Frank Thomas 2.50
5 Alex Rodriguez 6.00
6 Kenny Lofton .50
7 Chuck Knoblauch .50
8 Mo Vaughn .50
9 Chipper Jones 4.00
10 Ken Caminiti .50
11 Craig Biggio .50
12 John Smoltz .50
13 Pat Hentgen .50
14 Derek Jeter 7.50
15 Todd Hollandsworth .50

Dress for Success

Exclusive to retail packs was an insert called Dress for Success. It included 18 players printed on nylon and flocking card stock. Dress for Success was limited to 3,500 individually numbered sets.

NM/M
Complete Set (18): 17.50
Common Player: .25
1 Greg Maddux 1.50
2 Cal Ripken Jr. 3.00
3 Albert Belle .25
4 Frank Thomas 1.00
5 Dante Bichette .25
6 Gary Sheffield .50
7 Jeff Bagwell 1.00
8 Mike Piazza 2.00
9 Mark McGwire 2.25
10 Ken Caminiti .25
11 Alex Rodriguez 2.50
12 Ken Griffey Jr. 2.00
13 Juan Gonzalez .75
14 Brian Jordan .25
15 Mo Vaughn .75
16 Ivan Rodriguez .75
17 Andruw Jones 1.00
18 Chipper Jones 1.50

Get-A-Grip

Get a Grip included 16 double-sided cards, with a star hitter on one side and a star pitcher on the other. The card slated the two stars against each other and explained how the hitter would hit against the pitcher, while featuring the pitcher's top pitch. This insert was printed on silver foilboard with the right side die-cut, and limited to 3,500 numbered sets found only in hobby packs.

NM/M
Complete Set (16): 30.00
Common Card: 1.00
1 Ken Griffey Jr., Greg Maddux 3.00
2 John Smoltz, Frank Thomas 1.50
3 Mike Piazza, Andy Pettitte 3.00
4 Randy Johnson, Chipper Jones 2.50
5 Tom Glavine, Alex Rodriguez 4.00
6 Pat Hentgen, Jeff Bagwell 1.50
7 Kevin Brown, Juan Gonzalez 1.25
8 Barry Bonds, Mike Mussina 5.00
9 Hideo Nomo, Albert Belle 1.25
10 Troy Percival, Andruw Jones 1.50
11 Roger Clemens, Brian Jordan 3.00
12 Paul Wilson, Ivan Rodriguez 1.25
13 Andy Benes, Mo Vaughn 1.25
14 Al Leiter, Derek Jeter 5.00
15 Bill Pulsipher, Cal Ripken Jr. 5.00
16 Mariano Rivera, Ken Caminiti 1.00

Knot-Hole Gang

Knot-Hole Gang pictures 12 hitters viewed through a wood picket fence. Cards are die-cut along the top of the fence and printed on a wood stock. Production was limited to 5,000 numbered sets. A "SAMPLE" marked promo card exists for each.

		NM/M
Complete Set (12):		18.00
Common Player:		.50
Promos:		2X
1	Chuck Knoblauch	.50
2	Ken Griffey Jr.	3.50
3	Frank Thomas	1.50
4	Tony Gwynn	2.50
5	Mike Piazza	3.50
6	Jeff Bagwell	1.50
7	Rusty Greer	.50
8	Cal Ripken Jr.	5.00
9	Chipper Jones	2.50
10	Ryan Klesko	.50
11	Barry Larkin	.50
12	Paul Molitor	1.50

Leagues of the Nation

A 15-card insert set featuring a double-sided die-cut design. The players on each card represent matchups from the initial rounds of interleague play. Cards were numbered to 2,500 and feature a flocked texture.

		NM/M
Complete Set (15):		60.00
Common Card:		1.50
1	Juan Gonzalez, Barry Bonds	10.00
2	Cal Ripken Jr., Chipper Jones	10.00
3	Mark McGwire, Ken Caminiti	7.00
4	Derek Jeter, Kenny Lofton	10.00
5	Ivan Rodriguez, Mike Piazza	6.00
6	Ken Griffey Jr., Larry Walker	6.00
7	Frank Thomas, Sammy Sosa	5.00
8	Paul Molitor, Barry Larkin	3.00
9	Albert Belle, Deion Sanders	1.50
10	Matt Williams, Jeff Bagwell	3.00
11	Mo Vaughn, Gary Sheffield	1.50
12	Alex Rodriguez, Tony Gwynn	7.50
13	Tino Martinez, Scott Rolen	2.00
14	Darin Erstad, Wilton Guerrero	2.00
15	Tony Clark, Vladimir Guerrero	3.00

Statistical Standouts

Statistical Standouts were limited to only 1,000 individually numbered sets. Inserts were printed on leather and die-cut. The set included 15 top stars who excelled beyond their competition in many statistical categories.

		NM/M
Complete Set (15):		175.00
Common Player:		4.00
1	Albert Belle	4.00
2	Juan Gonzalez	9.00
3	Ken Griffey Jr.	20.00

4	Alex Rodriguez	25.00
5	Frank Thomas	12.00
6	Chipper Jones	15.00
7	Greg Maddux	15.00
8	Mike Piazza	20.00
9	Cal Ripken Jr.	30.00
10	Mark McGwire	25.00
11	Barry Bonds	30.00
12	Derek Jeter	30.00
13	Ken Caminiti	4.00
14	John Smoltz	4.00
15	Paul Molitor	12.00

Thomas Collection

This six-card insert from Series 2 features pieces of various game-used Frank Thomas items built into the texture of each card. Jerseys, bats, hats, batting gloves and sweatbands are all featured on the various cards, which are numbered to 100 each.

		NM/M
Complete Set (6):		360.00
Common Card:		60.00
1	Frank Thomas/Hat	60.00
2	Frank Thomas/ Home Jsy	80.00
3	Frank Thomas/Btg Glv	60.00
4	Frank Thomas/Bat	60.00
5	Frank Thomas/ Sweatband	60.00
6	Frank Thomas/Away Jsy	80.00

Warning Track

A 12-card insert printed on embossed canvas depicting players who are known for making tough catches. Cards were numbered to 3,500.

		NM/M
Complete Set (18):		40.00
Common Player:		1.00
1	Ken Griffey Jr.	6.00
2	Albert Belle	1.00
3	Barry Bonds	7.50
4	Andruw Jones	4.00
5	Kenny Lofton	1.00
6	Tony Gwynn	5.00
7	Manny Ramirez	4.00
8	Rusty Greer	1.00
9	Bernie Williams	1.00
10	Gary Sheffield	2.00
11	Juan Gonzalez	2.50
12	Raul Mondesi	1.00
13	Brady Anderson	1.00
14	Rondell White	1.00
15	Sammy Sosa	6.00
16	Deion Sanders	1.00
17	David Justice	1.00
18	Jim Edmonds	1.00

22kt Gold Stars

A 36-card insert from Series II Leaf, each card features a special 22-K. gold foil embossed stamp on front which is printed on gold foil cardboard. Horizontal backs have a portrait photo on a dark background and are serially numbered to a limit of 2,500 each.

		NM/M
Complete Set (36):		115.00
Common Player:		1.00
1	Frank Thomas	4.00
2	Alex Rodriguez	8.00
3	Ken Griffey Jr.	6.50
4	Andruw Jones	4.00
5	Chipper Jones	6.00
6	Jeff Bagwell	3.00
7	Derek Jeter	10.00
8	Deion Sanders	1.00
9	Ivan Rodriguez	3.50
10	Juan Gonzalez	3.00
11	Greg Maddux	5.50
12	Andy Pettitte	2.50
13	Roger Clemens	6.00
14	Hideo Nomo	1.00
15	Tony Gwynn	5.50
16	Barry Bonds	10.00
17	Kenny Lofton	1.00
18	Paul Molitor	4.00
19	Jim Thome	3.00
20	Albert Belle	1.00
21	Cal Ripken Jr.	10.00
22	Mark McGwire	8.00
23	Barry Larkin	1.00
24	Mike Piazza	6.50
25	Darin Erstad	2.00
26	Chuck Knoblauch	1.00
27	Vladimir Guerrero	4.00
28	Tony Clark	1.00
29	Scott Rolen	3.00
30	Nomar Garciaparra	6.50
31	Eric Young	1.00
32	Ryne Sandberg	5.50
33	Roberto Alomar	2.00
34	Eddie Murray	4.00
35	Rafael Palmeiro	3.50
36	Jose Guillen	1.00

1998 Leaf

The 50th Anniversary edition of Leaf Baseball consists of a 200-card base set with three subsets, three parallels and four inserts. The base set has 148 regular cards, a 10-card Curtain Calls subset, Gold Leaf Stars subset (20 cards), Gold Leaf Rookies subset (20 cards) and three checklists. The subsets cards #148-197 are short-printed in relation to the rest of the set. Card #42 does not exist because Leaf retired the number in honor of Jackie Robinson. The base set was paralleled in Fractal Matrix, Fractal Matrix Die-Cuts and Fractal Diamond Axis. Inserts include Crusade, Heading for the Hall, State Representatives and Statistical Standouts.

		NM/M
Complete Set (200):		40.00
Common Player:		.05

Common SP (#148-197):		.40
Pack (10):		2.00
Wax Box (24):		40.00
1	Rusty Greer	.05
2	Tino Martinez	.05
3	Bobby Bonilla	.05
4	Jason Giambi	.50
5	Matt Morris	.05
6	Craig Counsell	.05
7	Reggie Jefferson	.05
8	Brian Rose	.05
9	Ruben Rivera	.05
10	Shawn Estes	.05
11	Tony Gwynn	1.00
12	Jeff Abbott	.05
13	Jose Cruz Jr.	.05
14	Francisco Cordova	.05
15	Ryan Klesko	.05
16	Tim Salmon	.05
17	Brett Tomko	.05
18	Matt Williams	.05
19	Joe Carter	.05
20	Harold Baines	.05
21	Gary Sheffield	.50
22	Charles Johnson	.05
23	Aaron Boone	.05
24	Eddie Murray	.75
25	Matt Stairs	.05
26	David Cone	.05
27	Jon Nunnally	.05
28	Chris Stynes	.05
29	Enrique Wilson	.05
30	Randy Johnson	.75
31	Garret Anderson	.05
32	Manny Ramirez	.75
33	Jeff Suppan	.05
34	Rickey Henderson	.75
35	Scott Spiezio	.05
36	Rondell White	.05
37	Todd Greene	.05
38	Delino DeShields	.05
39	Kevin Brown	.05
40	Chili Davis	.05
41	Jimmy Key	.05
43	Mike Mussina	.40
44	Joe Randa	.05
45	Chan Ho Park	.40
46	Brad Radke	.05
47	Geronimo Berroa	.05
48	Wade Boggs	1.00
49	Kevin Appier	.05
50	Moises Alou	.05
51	David Justice	.05
52	Ivan Rodriguez	.65
53	J.T. Snow	.05
54	Brian Giles	.05
55	Will Clark	.10
56	Justin Thompson	.05
57	Javier Lopez	.05
58	Hideki Irabu	.05
59	Mark Grudzielanek	.05
60	Abraham Nunez	.05
61	Todd Hollandsworth	.05
62	Jay Bell	.05
63	Nomar Garciaparra	1.25
64	Vinny Castilla	.05
65	Lou Collier	.05
66	Kevin Orie	.05
67	John Valentin	.05
68	Robin Ventura	.05
69	Denny Neagle	.05
70	Tony Womack	.05
71	Dennis Reyes	.05
72	Wally Joyner	.05
73	Kevin Brown	.05
74	Ray Durham	.05
75	Mike Cameron	.05
76	Dante Bichette	.05
77	Jose Guillen	.05
78	Carlos Delgado	.50
79	Paul Molitor	.75
80	Jason Kendall	.05
81	Mark Belhorn	.05
82	Damian Jackson	.05
83	Bill Mueller	.05
84	Kevin Young	.05
85	Curt Schilling	.25
86	Jeffrey Hammonds	.05
87	Sandy Alomar Jr.	.05
88	Bartolo Colon	.05
89	Wilton Guerrero	.05
90	Bernie Williams	.05
91	Deion Sanders	.05
92	Mike Piazza	1.25
93	Butch Huskey	.05
94	Edgardo Alfonzo	.05
95	Alan Benes	.05
96	Craig Biggio	.25
97	Mark Grace	.25
98	Shawn Green	.25
99	Derrek Lee	.60
100	Ken Griffey Jr.	1.25
101	Tim Raines	.05
102	Pokey Reese	.05
103	Lee Stevens	.05
104	Shannon Stewart	.05
105	John Smoltz	.05
106	Frank Thomas	.75
107	Jeff Fassero	.05
108	Jay Buhner	.05
109	Jose Canseco	.50
110	Omar Vizquel	.05
111	Travis Fryman	.05
112	Dave Nilsson	.05
113	John Olerud	.05
114	Larry Walker	.05
115	Jim Edmonds	.05
116	Bobby Higginson	.05

117	Todd Hundley	.05
118	Paul O'Neill	.05
119	Bip Roberts	.05
120	Ismael Valdes	.05
121	Pedro Martinez	.75
122	Jeff Cirillo	.05
123	Andy Benes	.05
124	Bobby Jones	.05
125	Brian Hunter	.05
126	Darryl Kile	.05
127	Pat Hentgen	.05
128	Marquis Grissom	.05
129	Eric Davis	.05
130	Chipper Jones	1.00
131	Edgar Martinez	.05
132	Andy Pettitte	.20
133	Cal Ripken Jr.	2.00
134	Scott Rolen	.65
135	Ron Coomer	.05
136	Luis Castillo	.05
137	Fred McGriff	.05
138	Neifi Perez	.05
139	Eric Karros	.05
140	Alex Fernandez	.05
141	Jason Dickson	.05
142	Lance Johnson	.05
143	Ray Lankford	.05
144	Sammy Sosa	1.25
145	Eric Young	.05
146	Bubba Trammell	.05
147	Todd Walker	.05
148	Mo Vaughn/CC	.40
149	Jeff Bagwell/CC	1.00
150	Kenny Lofton/CC	.40
151	Raul Mondesi/CC	.40
152	Mike Piazza/CC	2.00
153	Chipper Jones/CC	1.50
154	Larry Walker/CC	.40
155	Greg Maddux/CC	1.50
156	Ken Griffey Jr./CC	2.00
157	Frank Thomas/CC	1.00
158	Darin Erstad/GLS	.75
159	Roberto Alomar/GLS	.60
160	Albert Belle/GLS	.40
161	Jim Thome/GLS	.75
162	Tony Clark/GLS	.40
163	Chuck Knoblauch/GLS	.40
164	Derek Jeter/GLS	3.00
165	Alex Rodriguez/GLS	2.50
166	Tony Gwynn/GLS	1.50
167	Roger Clemens/GLS	2.00
168	Barry Larkin/GLS	.40
169	Andres Galarraga/GLS	.40
170	Vladimir Guerrero/GLS	1.00
171	Mark McGwire/GLS	2.50
172	Barry Bonds/GLS	3.00
173	Juan Gonzalez/GLS	.75
174	Andruw Jones/GLS	1.00
175	Paul Molitor/GLS	1.00
176	Hideo Nomo/GLS	.75
177	Cal Ripken Jr./GLS	3.00
178	Brad Fullmer/GLR	.40
179	Jaret Wright/GLR	.40
180	Bobby Estalella/GLR	.40
181	Ben Grieve/GLR	.40
182	Paul Konerko/GLR	.60
183	David Ortiz/GLR	.75
184	Todd Helton/GLR	1.00
185	Juan Encarnacion/GLR	.40
186	Miguel Tejada/GLR	.60
187	Jacob Cruz/GLR	.40
188	Mark Kotsay/GLR	.40
189	Fernando Tatis/GLR	.40
190	Ricky Ledee/GLR	.40
191	Richard Hidalgo/GLR	.40
192	Richie Sexson/GLR	.40
193	Luis Ordaz/GLR	.40
194	Eli Marrero/GLR	.40
195	Livan Hernandez/GLR	.40
196	Homer Bush/GLR	.40
197	Raul Ibanez/GLR	.40
198	Checklist (Nomar Garciaparra)	.60
199	Checklist (Scott Rolen)	.30
200	Checklist (Jose Cruz Jr.)	.05
201	Al Martin	.05

Crusade

Thirty cards from the cross-brand Crusade insert appear in 1998 Leaf. The cards had Green (250 sets), Purple (100 sets) and Red (25 sets) versions. Forty Crusade cards were in 1998 Donruss and 30 each in 1998 Donruss Update and Leaf Rookies & Stars.

		NM/M
Complete Set (30):		400.00
Common Player:		6.00
Purples:		3X
Reds:		12X
3	Jim Edmonds	7.50
4	Darin Erstad	7.50
12	Mike Mussina	15.00
15	Albert Belle	6.00
17	Manny Ramirez	25.00
19	Jim Thome	20.00
24	Bubba Trammell	6.00
27	Bobby Higginson	6.00
28	Paul Molitor	25.00
30	Todd Walker	6.00
34	Andy Pettitte	10.00
35	Wade Boggs	30.00
38	Alex Rodriguez	60.00
41	Randy Johnson	25.00
44	Ivan Rodriguez	20.00
48	Roger Clemens	40.00
54	John Smoltz	6.00
56	Andruw Jones	25.00
58	Javier Lopez	6.00
59	Fred McGriff	6.00
66	Pokey Reese	6.00
68	Andres Galarraga	6.00
70	Eric Young	6.00
73	Moises Alou	6.00
78	Ben Grieve	6.00
79	Mike Piazza	50.00
82	Jason Kendall	6.00
95	Alan Benes	6.00
97	Tony Gwynn	30.00
98	Ken Caminiti	6.00

Heading for the Hall

This 20-card insert features players destined for the Hall of Fame. The set is sequentially numbered to 3,500. Each card is also found in a "SAMPLE" marked edition with no serial number.

		NM/M
Complete Set (20):		35.00
Common Player:		.75
Samples:		1X
1	Roberto Alomar	1.00
2	Jeff Bagwell	1.50
3	Albert Belle	.75
4	Wade Boggs	2.00
5	Barry Bonds	5.00
6	Roger Clemens	2.50
7	Juan Gonzalez	1.50
9	Ken Griffey Jr.	3.00
9	Tony Gwynn	2.00
10	Barry Larkin	.75
11	Kenny Lofton	.75
12	Greg Maddux	2.00
13	Mark McGwire	4.00
14	Paul Molitor	1.50
15	Eddie Murray	1.50
16	Mike Piazza	3.00
17	Cal Ripken Jr.	5.00
18	Ivan Rodriguez	1.25
19	Ryne Sandberg	2.00
20	Frank Thomas	1.50

State Representatives/ Provincial Powers

This 30-card insert features top players. The background has a picture of the state or, in the case of Canadian teams, the province in which he plays. "State Representatives" or "Provincial Powers" is printed at the top with the player's name at the bottom. This set is sequentially numbered to 5,000.

		NM/M
Complete Set (30)		40.00
Common Player:		.50
1	Ken Griffey Jr.	3.00
2	Frank Thomas	2.00
3	Alex Rodriguez	4.00
4	Cal Ripken Jr.	5.00
5	Chipper Jones	2.50
6	Andruw Jones	2.00
7	Scott Rolen	1.50
8	Nomar Garciaparra	3.00
9	Tim Salmon	.50
10	Manny Ramirez	2.00
11	Jose Cruz Jr.	.50
12	Vladimir Guerrero	2.00
13	Tino Martinez	.50
14	Larry Walker	.50
15	Mo Vaughn	.50
16	Jim Thome	1.50
17	Tony Clark	.50
18	Derek Jeter	5.00
19	Juan Gonzalez	1.00
20	Jeff Bagwell	2.00
21	Ivan Rodriguez	1.50
22	Mark McGwire	4.00
23	David Justice	.50
24	Chuck Knoblauch	.50
25	Andy Pettitte	.75
26	Raul Mondesi	.50
27	Randy Johnson	2.00
28	Greg Maddux	2.50
29	Bernie Williams	.50
30	Rusty Greer	.50

Statistical Standouts

This 24-card insert features players with impressive statistics. The cards have a horizontal layout and the feel of leather. The background has a ball and glove with the player's facsimile signature on the ball. Statistical Standouts is numbered to 2,500. A parallel die-cut version of each card comprises the first 250 numbered cards.

		NM/M
Complete Set (24)		55.00
Common Player:		1.00
Die-Cuts:		2X
1	Frank Thomas	2.50
2	Ken Griffey Jr.	4.00
3	Alex Rodriguez	5.00
4	Mike Piazza	4.00
5	Greg Maddux	3.00
6	Cal Ripken Jr.	6.00
7	Chipper Jones	3.00
8	Juan Gonzalez	2.00
9	Jeff Bagwell	2.50
10	Mark McGwire	5.00
11	Tony Gwynn	3.00
12	Mo Vaughn	1.00
13	Nomar Garciaparra	4.00
14	Jose Cruz Jr.	1.00
15	Vladimir Guerrero	2.50
16	Scott Rolen	2.00
17	Andy Pettitte	1.50
18	Randy Johnson	2.50
19	Larry Walker	1.00
20	Kenny Lofton	1.00
21	Tony Clark	1.00
22	David Justice	1.00
23	Derek Jeter	6.00
24	Barry Bonds	6.00

Fractal Foundation

Fractal Foundation is a stand-alone product but it parallels the 1998 Leaf set. It contains the Curtain Calls, Gold Leaf Stars and Gold Leaf Rookies subsets and is missing card #42 which Leaf retired in honor of Jackie Robinson. The set was printed on foil board and each card is numbered to 3,999. The set is paralleled in Fractal Materials, Fractal Materials Die-Cuts and Fractal Materials Z2 Axis.

		NM/M
Complete Set (200)		60.00
Common Player:		.20
Semistars:		.60
Unlisted Stars:		1.00
Pack (3):		2.00
Wax Box (18):		35.00
1	Rusty Greer	.20
2	Tino Martinez	.20
3	Bobby Bonilla	.20
4	Jason Giambi	.60
5	Matt Morris	.20
6	Craig Counsell	.20
7	Reggie Jefferson	.20
8	Brian Rose	.20
9	Ruben Rivera	.20
10	Shawn Estes	.20
11	Tony Gwynn	1.50
12	Jeff Abbott	.20
13	Jose Cruz Jr.	.20
14	Francisco Cordova	.20
15	Ryan Klesko	.20
16	Tim Salmon	.20
17	Brett Tomko	.20
18	Matt Williams	.20
19	Joe Carter	.20
20	Harold Baines	.20
21	Gary Sheffield	.50
22	Charles Johnson	.20
23	Aaron Boone	.20
24	Eddie Murray	1.00
25	Matt Stairs	.20
26	David Cone	.20
27	Jon Nunnally	.20
28	Chris Stynes	.20
29	Enrique Wilson	.20
30	Randy Johnson	1.00
31	Garret Anderson	.20
32	Manny Ramirez	1.00
33	Jeff Suppan	.20
34	Rickey Henderson	1.00
35	Scott Spiezio	.20
36	Rondell White	.20
37	Todd Greene	.20
38	Delino DeShields	.20
39	Kevin Brown	.20
40	Chili Davis	.20
41	Jimmy Key	.20
43	Mike Mussina	.40
44	Joe Randa	.20
45	Chan Ho Park	.20
46	Brad Radke	.20
47	Geronimo Berroa	.20
48	Wade Boggs	1.50
49	Kevin Appier	.20
50	Moises Alou	.20
51	David Justice	.20
52	Ivan Rodriguez	.75
53	J.T. Snow	.20
54	Brian Giles	.20
55	Will Clark	.20
56	Justin Thompson	.20
57	Javier Lopez	.20
58	Hideki Irabu	.20
59	Mark Grudzielanek	.20
60	Abraham Nunez	.20
61	Todd Hollandsworth	.20
62	Jay Bell	.20
63	Nomar Garciaparra	1.75
64	Vinny Castilla	.20
65	Lou Collier	.20
66	Kevin Orie	.20
67	John Valentin	.20
68	Robin Ventura	.20
69	Denny Neagle	.20
70	Tony Womack	.20
71	Dennis Reyes	.20
72	Wally Joyner	.20
73	Kevin Brown	.20
74	Ray Durham	.20
75	Mike Cameron	.20
76	Dante Bichette	.20
77	Jose Guillen	.20
78	Carlos Delgado	.50
79	Paul Molitor	1.00
80	Jason Kendall	.20
81	Mark Belhorn	.20
82	Damian Jackson	.20
83	Bill Mueller	.20
84	Kevin Young	.20
85	Curt Schilling	.40
86	Jeffrey Hammonds	.20
87	Sandy Alomar Jr.	.20
88	Bartolo Colon	.20
89	Wilton Guerrero	.20
90	Bernie Williams	.20
91	Deion Sanders	.20
92	Mike Piazza	2.00
93	Butch Huskey	.20
94	Edgardo Alfonzo	.20
95	Alan Benes	.20
96	Craig Biggio	.20
97	Mark Grace	.20
98	Shawn Green	.40
99	Derrek Lee	.50
100	Ken Griffey Jr.	2.00
101	Tim Raines	.20
102	Pokey Reese	.20
103	Lee Stevens	.20
104	Shannon Stewart	.20
105	John Smoltz	.20
106	Frank Thomas	1.00
107	Jeff Fassero	.20
108	Jay Buhner	.20
109	Jose Canseco	.40
110	Omar Vizquel	.20
111	Travis Fryman	.20
112	Dave Nilsson	.20
113	John Olerud	.20
114	Larry Walker	.20
115	Jim Edmonds	.20
116	Bobby Higginson	.20
117	Todd Hundley	.20
118	Paul O'Neill	.20
119	Bip Roberts	.20
120	Ismael Valdes	.20
121	Pedro Martinez	1.00
122	Jeff Cirillo	.20
123	Andy Benes	.20
124	Bobby Jones	.20
125	Brian Hunter	.20
126	Darryl Kile	.20
127	Pat Hentgen	.20
128	Marquis Grissom	.20
129	Eric Davis	.20
130	Chipper Jones	1.50
131	Edgar Martinez	.20
132	Andy Pettitte	.35
133	Cal Ripken Jr.	3.00
134	Scott Rolen	.75
135	Ron Coomer	.20
136	Luis Castillo	.20
137	Fred McGriff	.20
138	Neifi Perez	.20
139	Eric Karros	.20
140	Alex Fernandez	.20
141	Jason Dickson	.20
142	Lance Johnson	.20
143	Ray Lankford	.20
144	Sammy Sosa	1.75
145	Eric Young	.20
146	Bubba Trammell	.20
147	Todd Walker	.20
148	Mo Vaughn/CC	.20
149	Jeff Bagwell/CC	1.00
150	Kenny Lofton/CC	.20
151	Raul Mondesi/CC	.20
152	Mike Piazza/CC	2.00
153	Chipper Jones/CC	1.50
154	Larry Walker/CC	.20
155	Greg Maddux/CC	1.50
156	Ken Griffey Jr./CC	2.00
157	Frank Thomasv	.50
158	Darin Erstad/GLS	.50
159	Roberto Alomar/GLS	.40
160	Albert Belle/GLS	.20
161	Jim Thome/GLS	.75
162	Tony Clark/GLS	.20
163	Chuck Knoblauch/GLS	.20
164	Derek Jeterv	3.00
165	Alex Rodriguez/GLS	2.50
166	Tony Gwynn/GLS	1.50
167	Roger Clemens/GLS	1.75
168	Barry Larkinv	.20
169	Andres Galarraga/GLS	.20
170	Vladimir Guerrero/GLS	1.00
171	Mark McGwire/GLS	2.50
172	Barry Bonds/GLS	3.00
173	Juan Gonzalez/GLS	.75
174	Andruw Jones/GLS	1.00
175	Paul Molitor/GLS	1.00
176	Hideo Nomo/GLS	.75
177	Cal Ripken Jr./GLS	.75
178	Brad Fullmer/GLR	.20
179	Jaret Wright/GLR	.20
180	Bobby Estalella/GLR	.20
181	Ben Grieve/GLR	.20
182	Paul Konerko/GLR	.40
183	David Ortiz/GLR	.75
184	Todd Helton/GLR	1.00
185	Juan Encarnacion/GLR	.20
186	Miguel Tejada/GLR	.40
187	Jacob Cruz/GLR	.20
188	Mark Kotsay/GLR	.20
189	Fernando Tatis/GLR	.20
190	Ricky Ledee/GLR	.20
191	Richard Hidalgo/GLR	.20
192	Richie Sexson/GLR	.20
193	Luis Ordaz/GLR	.20
194	Eli Marrero/GLR	.20
195	Livan Hernandez/GLR	.20
196	Homer Bush/GLR	.20
197	Raul Ibanez/GLR	.20
198	Checklist (Nomar Garciaparra)	1.00
199	Checklist (Scott Rolen)	.30
200	Checklist (Jose Cruz Jr.)	.20

1998 Leaf Fractal Materials Samples

Each of the 50 Leather cards in Fractal Materials can be found in a sample version, prominently marked as such on back.

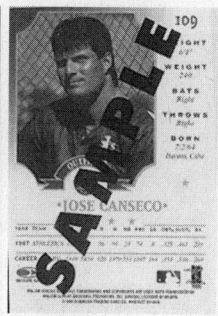

		NM/M
Complete Set (50):		100.00
Common Player:		2.00
5	Matt Morris	2.00
9	Ruben Rivera	2.00
10	Shawn Estes	2.00
15	Ryan Klesko	2.00
17	Brett Tomko	2.00
22	Charles Johnson	2.00
33	Jeff Suppan	2.00
36	Rondell White	2.00
39	Kevin Brown	2.00
53	J.T. Snow	2.00
55	Will Clark	2.00
58	Hideki Irabu	2.00
66	Kevin Orie	2.00
70	Tony Womack	2.00
76	Dante Bichette	2.00
78	Carlos Delgado	3.50
87	Sandy Alomar Jr.	2.00
93	Butch Huskey	2.00
94	Edgardo Alfonzo	2.00
95	Alan Benes	2.00
97	Mark Grace	2.00
99	Derrek Lee	4.00
105	John Smoltz	2.00
108	Jay Buhner	2.00
109	Jose Canseco	3.50
116	Bobby Higginson	2.00
117	Todd Hundley	2.00
136	Luis Castillo	2.00
137	Fred McGriff	2.00
138	Neifi Perez	2.00
146	Bubba Trammell	2.00
147	Todd Walker	2.00
158	Darin Erstad/GLS	3.50
160	Albert Belle/GLS	2.00
161	Jim Thome/GLS	4.00
162	Tony Clark/GLS	2.00
163	Chuck Knoblauch/GLS	2.00
167	Roger Clemens/GLS	6.50
170	Vladimir Guerrero/GLS	4.00
171	Mark McGwire/GLS	7.50
172	Barry Bonds/GLS	10.00
176	Hideo Nomo/GLS	4.00
189	Fernando Tatis/GLR	2.00
194	Eli Marrero/GLR	2.00
195	Livan Hernandez/GLR	2.00
201	Al Martin	2.00

1998 Leaf Fractal Materials

The Fractal Materials set fully parallels Fractal Foundations. Each of the inserts is sequentially numbered. The 200 card chase set was printed on four different materials: 100 plastic cards (numbered to 3,250), 50 leather (1,000), 30 nylon (500) and 20 wood (250). These parallels were inserted one per pack of Fractal Foundations. Each of the Leather cards can be found in a sample version marked as such on back.

		NM/M
Complete Set (200):		375.00
Complete Plastic Set (100):		65.00
Common Plastic (3,250):		.35
Complete Leather Set (50):		55.00
Common Leather (1,000):		.75
Complete Nylon Set (30):		60.00
Common Nylon (500):		1.25
Complete Wood Set (20):		200.00
Common Wood (250):		5.00
Wax Box:		120.00
1	Rusty Greer/N	1.25
2	Tino Martinez/N	5.00
3	Bobby Bonilla/N	1.25
4	Jason Giambi/N	4.00
5	Matt Morris/L	.75
6	Craig Counsell/P	.35
7	Reggie Jefferson/P	.35
8	Brian Rose/P	.35
9	Ruben Rivera/L	.75
10	Shawn Estes/L	.75
11	Tony Gwynn/P	20.00
12	Jeff Abbott/P	.35
13	Jose Cruz Jr./W	5.00
14	Francisco Cordova/P	.35
15	Ryan Klesko/L	.75
16	Tim Salmon/W	5.00
17	Brett Tomko/L	.35
18	Matt Williams/L	1.25
19	Joe Carter/P	.35
20	Harold Baines/P	.35
21	Gary Sheffield/N	2.50
22	Charles Johnson/L	.75
23	Aaron Boone/P	.35
24	Eddie Murray/N	5.00
25	Matt Stairs/P	.35
26	David Cone/P	.35
27	Jon Nunnally/P	.35
28	Chris Stynes/P	.35
29	Enrique Wilson/P	.35
30	Randy Johnson/W	15.00
31	Garret Anderson/N	1.25
32	Manny Ramirez/W	15.00
33	Jeff Suppan/L	.75
34	Rickey Henderson/N	5.00
35	Scott Spiezio/P	.35
36	Rondell White/L	.75
37	Todd Greene/N	1.25
38	Delino DeShields/P	.35
39	Kevin Brown/L	.75
40	Chili Davis/P	.35
41	Jimmy Key/P	.35
43	Mike Mussina/P	4.00
44	Joe Randa/P	.35
45	Chan Ho Park/N	1.25
46	Brad Radke/P	.35
47	Geronimo Berroa/P	.35
48	Wade Boggs/N	6.00
49	Kevin Appier/P	.35
50	Moises Alou/P	1.25
51	David Justice/P	.35
52	Ivan Rodriguez/W	12.50
53	J.T. Snow/L	.75
54	Brian Giles/P	.35
55	Will Clark/L	.75
56	Justin Thompson/P	1.25
57	Javier Lopez/P	.35
58	Hideki Irabu/L	.75
59	Mark Grudzielanek/P	.35
60	Abraham Nunez/P	.35
61	Todd Hollandsworth/P	.35
62	Jay Bell/P	.35
63	Nomar Garciaparra/W	20.00
64	Vinny Castilla/P	.35
65	Lou Collier/P	.35
66	Kevin Orie/L	.75
67	John Valentin/P	.35
68	Robin Ventura/P	.35
69	Denny Neagle/P	.35
70	Tony Womack/L	.75
71	Dennis Reyes/P	.35
72	Wally Joyner/P	.35
73	Kevin Brown/P	.35
74	Ray Durham/P	.35
75	Mike Cameron/N	1.25
76	Dante Bichette/L	.75
77	Jose Guillen/N	1.25
78	Carlos Delgado/L	1.50
79	Paul Molitor/W	15.00
80	Jason Kendall/P	.35
81	Mark Belhorn/L	.75
82	Damian Jackson/P	.35
83	Bill Mueller/P	.35
84	Kevin Young/P	.35
85	Curt Schilling/P	.60
86	Jeffrey Hammonds/P	.35
87	Sandy Alomar Jr./L	.75
88	Bartolo Colon/P	.35
89	Wilton Guerrero/P	.35
90	Bernie Williams/N	1.25
91	Deion Sanders/N	1.25
92	Mike Piazza/W	25.00
93	Butch Huskey/L	.75
94	Edgardo Alfonzo/L	.75
95	Alan Benes/L	.75
96	Craig Biggio/N	1.25
97	Mark Grace/L	.75
98	Shawn Green/L	1.25
99	Derrek Lee/L	2.00
100	Ken Griffey Jr./W	25.00
101	Tim Raines/P	.35
102	Pokey Reese/P	.35
103	Lee Stevens/P	.35
104	Shannon Stewart/N	1.25
105	John Smoltz/L	.75
106	Frank Thomas/W	15.00
107	Jeff Fassero/P	.35
108	Jay Buhner/L	.75
109	Jose Canseco/L	1.50
110	Omar Vizquel/P	.35
111	Travis Fryman/P	.35
112	Dave Nilsson/P	.35
113	John Olerud/P	.35
114	Larry Walker/W	5.00
115	Jim Edmonds/N	1.25
116	Bobby Higginson/L	.75
117	Todd Hundley/L	.75
118	Paul O'Neill/P	.35
119	Bip Roberts/P	.35
120	Ismael Valdes/P	.35
121	Pedro Martinez/N	5.00
122	Jeff Cirillo/P	.35
123	Andy Benes/P	.35
124	Bobby Jones/P	.35
125	Brian Hunter/P	.35
126	Darryl Kile/P	.35
127	Pat Hentgen/P	.35
128	Marquis Grissom/P	.35
129	Eric Davis/P	.35
130	Chipper Jones/W	20.00
131	Edgar Martinez/N	1.25
132	Andy Pettitte/W	10.00
133	Cal Ripken Jr./W	35.00
134	Scott Rolen/W	12.50
135	Ron Coomer/P	.35
136	Luis Castillo/L	.75
137	Fred McGriff/L	.75
138	Neifi Perez/L	.75
139	Eric Karros/P	.35
140	Alex Fernandez/P	.35
141	Jason Dickson/P	.35
142	Lance Johnson/P	.35
143	Ray Lankford/P	.35
144	Sammy Sosa/N	7.00
145	Eric Young/P	.35
146	Bubba Trammell/L	.75
147	Todd Walker/L	.75
148	Mo Vaughn/P/CC	.35
149	Jeff Bagwell/P/CC	3.00
150	Kenny Lofton/P/CC	.35
151	Raul Mondesi/P/CC	.35
152	Mike Piazza/P/CC	5.00
153	Chipper Jones/P/CC	4.00
154	Larry Walker/P/CC	.35
155	Greg Maddux/P/CC	4.00
156	Ken Griffey Jr./P/CC	5.00
157	Frank Thomas/P/CC	3.00
158	Darin Erstad/P/CC	2.00
159	Roberto Alomar/P/GLS	.65
160	Albert Belle/L/GLS	.75
161	Jim Thome/L/GLS	.75
162	Tony Clark/L/GLS	.75
163	Chuck Knoblauch/L/GLS	.75
164	Derek Jeter/P/GLS	7.50
165	Alex Rodriguez/P/GLS	6.00
166	Tony Gwynn/P/GLS	4.00
167	Roger Clemens/L/GLS	5.00
168	Barry Larkin/P/GLS	.35
169	Andres Galarraga/P/GLS	.35
170	Vladimir Guerrero/L/GLS	4.00
171	Mark McGwire/L/GLS	6.00
172	Barry Bonds/L/GLS	7.50
173	Juan Gonzalez/P/GLS	2.00
174	Andruw Jones/P/GLS	3.00
175	Paul Molitor/P/GLS	3.00
176	Hideo Nomo/L/GLS	2.00
177	Cal Ripken Jr./P/GLS	7.50
178	Brad Fullmer/P/GLR	.35
179	Jaret Wright/P/GLR	1.25
180	Bobby Estalella/P/GLR	.35
181	Ben Grieve/W/GLR	5.00
182	Paul Konerko/W/GLR	6.00
183	David Ortiz/N/GLR	2.50
184	Todd Helton/N/GLR	10.00
185	Juan Encarnacion/N/GLR	1.25
186	Miguel Tejada/N/GLR	1.50
187	Jacob Cruz/P/GLR	.35
188	Mark Kotsay/N/GLR	1.25
189	Fernando Tatis/P/GLR	.75
190	Ricky Ledee/P/GLR	.75
191	Richard Hidalgo/P/GLR	.35
192	Richie Sexson/P/GLR	.35
193	Luis Ordaz/P/GLR	.35
194	Eli Marrero/L/GLR	.75
195	Livan Hernandez/L/GLR	.75
196	Homer Bush/P/GLR	.35
197	Raul Ibanez/P/GLR	.35
198	Checklist (Nomar Garciaparra/P)	3.00
199	Checklist (Scott Rolen/P)	.40
200	Checklist (Jose Cruz Jr./P)	.35
201	Al Martin/L	.75

Fractal Materials Die-Cut

This parallel set adds a die-cut to the Fractal Materials set. The first 200 of 75 plastic, 15 leather, 5 nylon and 5 wood cards have an x-axis die-cut. The first 100 of 20 plastic, 25 leather, 10 nylon and 5 wood cards have a y-axis die-cut. The first 50 of 5 plastic, 10 leather, 15 nylon and 10 wood cards have a z-axis die-cut. The serial numbers on the backs of the die-cut cards are meaningless because they were printed prior to the die-cut fracture. This compounds the confusion engendered among collectors which has had a significant dampening effect on demand and, thus, market values.

	NM/M
Common X (200 of each):	1.50

Common Y (100): 3.00
Common Z (50): 6.00
1 Rusty Greer/Z 6.00
2 Tino Martinez/Y 3.00
3 Bobby Bonilla/Y 3.00
4 Jason Giambi/X 20.00
5 Matt Morris/Y 3.00
6 Craig Counsell/X 1.50
7 Reggie Jefferson/X 1.50
8 Brian Rose/X 1.50
9 Ruben Rivera/Y 3.00
10 Shawn Estes/Y 3.00
11 Tony Gwynn/X 12.50
12 Jeff Abbott/Y 3.00
13 Jose Cruz Jr./Z 6.00
14 Francisco Cordova/Y 1.50
15 Ryan Klesko/X 1.50
16 Tim Salmon/Y 3.00
17 Brett Tomko/Y 3.00
18 Matt Williams/Y 3.00
19 Joe Carter/X 1.50
20 Harold Baines/X 1.50
21 Gary Sheffield/Z 12.00
22 Charles Johnson/Y 3.00
23 Aaron Boone/Y 3.00
24 Eddie Murray/Y 10.00
25 Matt Stairs/Y 1.50
26 David Cone/X 1.50
27 Jon Nunnally/X 1.50
28 Chris Stynes/X 1.50
29 Enrique Wilson/Y 3.00
30 Randy Johnson/Y 10.00
31 Garret Anderson/X 3.00
32 Manny Ramirez/Y 10.00
33 Jeff Suppan/Y 3.00
34 Rickey Henderson/X 10.00
35 Scott Spiezio/Y 3.00
36 Rondell White/Y 3.00
37 Todd Greene/Z 3.00
38 Delino DeShields/Y 3.00
39 Kevin Brown/Y 1.50
40 Chili Davis/X 1.50
41 Jimmy Key/X 1.50
42 Mike Mussina/Y 20.00
43 Joe Randa/X 1.50
44 Chan Ho Park/Y 3.00
45 Brad Radke/X 1.50
46 Geronimo Berroa/X 1.50
47 Wade Boggs/Y 12.50
48 Kevin Appier/X 1.50
49 Moises Alou/X 1.50
50 David Justice/Z 6.00
51 Ivan Rodriguez/X 7.50
52 J.T. Snow/Y 1.50
53 Brian Giles/Y 1.50
54 Will Clark/X 1.50
55 Justin Thompson/Y 3.00
56 Javier Lopez/Y 1.50
57 Hideki Irabu/Y 1.50
58 Mark Grudzielanek/X 1.50
59 Abraham Nunez/Z 6.00
60 Todd Hollandsworth/Y 1.50
61 Jay Bell/Y 1.50
62 Nomar Garciaparra/Z 45.00
63 Nomar Garciaparra/Z 45.00
64 Vinny Castilla/Y 3.00
65 Lou Collier/Y 3.00
66 Kevin Orie/Y 1.50
67 John Valentin/X 1.50
68 Robin Ventura/X 1.50
69 Denny Neagle/X 1.50
70 Tony Womack/X 1.50
71 Dennis Reyes/Y 1.50
72 Wally Joyner/X 1.50
73 Kevin Brown/Y 1.50
74 Ray Durham/X 3.00
75 Mike Cameron/Y 3.00
76 Dante Bichette/Y 1.50
77 Jose Guillen/Z 6.00
78 Carlos Delgado/Y 10.00
79 Paul Molitor/X 10.00
80 Jason Kendall/Y 1.50
81 Mark Belhorn/Y 1.50
82 Damian Jackson/Y 3.00
83 Bill Mueller/Y 1.50
84 Kevin Young/Y 1.50
85 Curt Schilling/X 1.50
86 Jeffrey Hammonds/X 1.50
87 Sandy Alomar Jr./Y 3.00
88 Bartolo Colon/Y 3.00
89 Wilton Guerrero/Y 3.00
90 Bernie Williams/Z 6.00
91 Deion Sanders/Y 3.00
92 Mike Piazza/Y 55.00
93 Butch Huskey/Y 1.50
94 Edgardo Alfonzo/Y 3.00
95 Alan Benes/Y 1.50
96 Craig Biggio/Y 1.50
97 Mark Grace/Y 3.00
98 Shawn Green/Y 5.00
99 Derrek Lee/Y 6.00
100 Ken Griffey Jr./Z 55.00
101 Tim Raines/Y 1.50
102 Pokey Reese/Y 1.50
103 Lee Stevens/Y 1.50
104 Shannon Stewart/X 1.50
105 John Smoltz/Y 1.50
106 Frank Thomas/Y 30.00
107 Jeff Fassero/Y 1.50
108 Jay Buhner/Y 1.50
109 Jose Canseco/Y 3.00
110 Omar Vizquel/X 1.50
111 Travis Fryman/X 1.50
112 Dave Nilsson/X 1.50
113 John Olerud/X 1.50
114 Larry Walker/X 1.50
115 Jim Edmonds/X 3.00
116 Bobby Higginson/Y 3.00
117 Todd Hundley/Z 6.00

118 Paul O'Neill/X 1.50
119 Bip Roberts/X 1.50
120 Ismael Valdes/X 1.50
121 Pedro Martinez/X 10.00
122 Jeff Cirillo/X 1.50
123 Andy Benes/X 1.50
124 Bobby Jones/X 1.50
125 Brian Hunter/X 1.50
126 Darryl Kile/X 1.50
127 Pat Hentgen/X 1.50
128 Marquis Grissom/X 1.50
129 Eric Davis/X 1.50
130 Chipper Jones/X 45.00
131 Edgar Martinez/Z 6.00
132 Andy Pettitte/Y 6.00
133 Cal Ripken Jr./Z 75.00
134 Scott Rolen/Y 7.50
135 Ron Coomer/Y 1.50
136 Luis Castillo/X 1.50
137 Fred McGriff/X 1.50
138 Neifi Perez/Y 3.00
139 Eric Karros/X 1.50
140 Alex Fernandez/X 1.50
141 Jason Dickson/X 1.50
142 Lance Johnson/X 1.50
143 Ray Lankford/X 3.00
144 Sammy Sosa/Y 17.50
145 Eric Young/Y 3.00
146 Bubba Trammell/Z 6.00
147 Todd Walker/Z 6.00
148 Mo Vaughn/X /CC
149 Jeff Bagwell/X/CC 10.00
150 Kenny Lofton/X/CC 1.50
151 Raul Mondesi/X/CC 1.50
152 Mike Piazza/X/CC
153 Chipper Jones/X/CC 12.50
154 Larry Walker/X/CC 1.50
155 Greg Maddux/X/CC 12.50
156 Ken Griffey Jr./X/CC 15.00
157 Frank Thomas/X/CC 10.00
158 Darin Erstad/Y/GLS 4.00
159 Roberto Alomar/X/GLS 2.00
160 Albert Belle/X/GLS 1.50
161 Jim Thome/X/GLS 6.00
162 Tony Clark/Z/GLS 6.00
163 Chuck Knoblauch/Z/GLS 8.00
164 Derek Jeter/X/GLS 25.00
165 Alex Rodriguez/Y/GLS 30.00
166 Tony Gwynn/X/GLS 12.50
167 Roger Clemens/Y/GLS 17.50
168 Barry Larkin/Y/GLS 3.00
169 Andres Galarraga/Y/GLS 3.00
170 Vladimir Guerrero/Y/GLS 10.00
171 Mark McGwire/Z/GLS 65.00
172 Barry Bonds/X/GLS 35.00
173 Juan Gonzalez/Y/GLS 7.50
174 Andruw Jones/X/GLS 10.00
175 Paul Molitor/X/GLS 10.00
176 Hideo Nomo/B/GLS 25.00
177 Cal Ripken Jr./X/GLS 25.00
178 Brad Fullmer/Z/GLR 6.00
179 Jaret Wright/Z/GLR 6.00
180 Bobby Estalella/Y/GLR 3.00
181 Ben Grieve/Z/GLR 6.00
182 Paul Konerko/Z/GLR 7.50
183 David Ortiz/X/GLR 10.00
184 Todd Helton/Z/GLR 20.00
185 Juan Encarnacion/Z/GLR 6.00
186 Miguel Tejada/Z/GLR 12.00
187 Jacob Cruz/X/GLR 1.50
188 Mark Kotsay/Z/GLR 3.00
189 Fernando Tatis/Y/GLR 3.00
190 Ricky Ledee/X/GLR 1.50
191 Richard Hidalgo/Z/GLR 6.00
192 Richie Sexson/Z/GLR 6.00
193 Luis Ordaz/Y/GLR 3.00
194 Eli Marrero/Y/GLR 6.00
195 Livan Hernandez/Z/GLR 6.00
196 Homer Bush/X/GLR 1.50
197 Raul Ibanez/Y/GLR 1.50
198 Checklist (Nomar Garciaparra/X) 7.50
199 Checklist (Scott Rolen/Z) 7.50
200 Checklist (Jose Cruz Jr./X) 1.50
201 Al Martin/Y 3.00

Fractal Materials Z2 Axis

This 200-card set parallels Leaf Fractal Materials and was numbered to 20 sets.

	NM/M
Common Player:	10.00
Z2 Stars:	10X
Production 20 Sets	

Fractal Matrix

Fractal Matrix is a parallel insert set to 1998 Leaf. Cards have a metallic finish, with 100 done in bronze, 60 in silver and 40 in gold, and each color having some cards in X, Y and Z axis. Stated print runs are: Bronze: X - 1,600; Y - 1,800; Z - 1,900. Silver: X - 600; Y - 800; Z - 900. Gold: X - 100; Y - 300; Z - 400. Each player is found only in a single color/axis combination.

	NM/M
Complete Set (200):	250.00
Common Bronze:	.25
Common Silver:	.75
Common Gold:	2.00

1 Rusty Greer G/Z 2.00
2 Tino Martinez G/Z 2.00
3 Bobby Bonilla S/Y .75
4 Jason Giambi S/Y 1.25
5 Matt Morris S/Y .75
6 Craig Counsell B/X .25
7 Reggie Jefferson B/X .25
8 Brian Rose B/X .75
9 Ruben Rivera B/X .25
10 Shawn Estes S/Y .75
11 Tony Gwynn G/Z 10.00
12 Jeff Abbott B/Y .25
13 Jose Cruz Jr. G/Z 2.00
14 Francisco Cordova B/X .25
15 Ryan Klesko B/X .25
16 Tim Salmon G/Y 2.00
17 Brett Tomko B/X .25
18 Matt Williams S/Y .75
19 Joe Carter B/X .25
20 Harold Baines B/X .25
21 Gary Sheffield S/X 1.25
22 Charles Johnson S/Y .75
23 Aaron Boone B/X .25
24 Eddie Murray G/Y 7.50
25 Matt Stairs B/Y .25
26 David Cone B/X .25
27 Jon Nunnally B/X .25
28 Chris Stynes B/Y .25
29 Enrique Wilson B/Y .25
30 Randy Johnson S/Z 2.00
31 Garret Anderson S/Y .75
32 Manny Ramirez G/Z 7.50
33 Jeff Suppan B/X .25
34 Rickey Henderson B/X 1.00
35 Scott Spiezio B/X .25
36 Rondell White S/Y .75
37 Todd Greene S/Z .75
38 Delino DeShields B/X .25
39 Kevin Brown S/Y .75
40 Chili Davis B/X .25
41 Jimmy Key B/X .25
42 Mike Mussina G/Y 5.00
43 Joe Randa B/X .25
44 Chan Ho Park S/Y .75
45 Brad Radke B/X .25
46 Geronimo Berroa B/X .25
47 Wade Boggs S/Y 2.50
48 Kevin Appier B/X .25
49 Moises Alou S/Y .75
50 David Justice G/Y 2.00
51 Ivan Rodriguez G/Z 6.00
52 J.T. Snow B/X .25
53 Brian Giles B/X .25
54 Will Clark B/X .25
55 Justin Thompson S/Y .75
56 Javier Lopez S/X .75
57 Hideki Irabu B/Y .25
58 Mark Grudzielanek B/X .25
59 Abraham Nunez B/X .25
60 Todd Hollandsworth B/X .25
61 Jay Bell B/X .25
62 Nomar Garciaparra G/Z 10.00
63 Vinny Castilla B/Y .25
64 Lou Collier B/Y .25
65 Kevin Orie S/X .75
66 John Valentin B/X .25
67 Robin Ventura B/X .25
68 Denny Neagle B/Y .25
69 Tony Womack S/Y .75
70 Dennis Reyes S/Y .75
71 Wally Joyner B/Y .25
72 Kevin Brown S/Y .75
73 Ray Durham B/X .25
74 Mike Cameron S/Z .75
75 Dante Bichette B/X .25
76 Jose Guillen G/Y 2.00
77 Carlos Delgado B/Y .50
79 Paul Molitor G/Z 7.50

80 Jason Kendall B/X .25
81 Mark Belhorn B/X .25
82 Damian Jackson B/X .25
83 Bill Mueller B/X .25
84 Kevin Young B/X .25
85 Curt Schilling B/X .40
86 Jeffrey Hammonds B/X .25
87 Sandy Alomar Jr. S/Y .75
88 Bartolo Colon B/Y .50
89 Wilton Guerrero B/Y .25
90 Bernie Williams G/Y 2.00
91 Deion Sanders S/Y .75
92 Mike Piazza G/X 12.50
93 Butch Huskey B/X .25
94 Edgardo Alfonzo S/X .75
95 Alan Benes B/X .25
96 Craig Biggio S/Y .75
97 Mark Grace S/Y .75
98 Shawn Green S/Y 1.50
99 Derrek Lee S/Y .75
100 Ken Griffey Jr. G/Z 12.50
101 Tim Raines B/X .25
102 Pokey Reese S/X .75
103 Lee Stevens S/X .75
104 Shannon Stewart S/Y .75
105 John Smoltz S/Y .75
106 Frank Thomas G/X 7.50
107 Jeff Fassero B/X .25
108 Jay Buhner B/X .25
109 Jose Canseco B/X .50
110 Omar Vizquel B/X .25
111 Travis Fryman B/X .25
112 Dave Nilsson B/X .25
113 John Olerud B/X .25
114 Larry Walker G/Z 2.00
115 Jim Edmonds S/Y .75
116 Bobby Higginson S/X .75
117 Todd Hundley S/X .75
118 Paul O'Neill B/X .25
119 Bip Roberts B/X .25
120 Ismael Valdes B/X .25
121 Pedro Martinez S/Y 2.00
122 Jeff Cirillo B/X .25
123 Andy Benes B/X .25
124 Bobby Jones B/X .25
125 Brian Hunter B/X .25
126 Darryl Kile B/X .25
127 Pat Hentgen B/X .25
128 Marquis Grissom B/X .25
129 Eric Davis B/X .25
130 Chipper Jones G/Z 10.00
131 Edgar Martinez S/Z .75
132 Andy Pettitte B/X 3.00
133 Cal Ripken Jr. G/X 20.00
134 Scott Rolen G/Z 6.00
135 Ron Coomer B/X .25
136 Luis Castillo B/X .25
137 Fred McGriff B/Y .25
138 Neifi Perez B/Y .25
139 Eric Karros B/X .25
140 Alex Fernandez B/X .25
141 Jason Dickson B/X .25
142 Lance Johnson B/X .25
143 Ray Lankford B/X .25
144 Sammy Sosa G/Y 10.00
145 Eric Young B/Y .25
146 Bubba Trammell S/Y .75
147 Todd Walker S/Y .75
148 Mo Vaughn S/X .75
149 Jeff Bagwell S/X/CC 2.00
150 Kenny Lofton S/X/CC .75
151 Raul Mondesi S/X/CC .75
152 Mike Piazza S/X/CC 4.00
153 Chipper Jones S/X/CC 3.00
154 Larry Walker S/X/CC .75
155 Greg Maddux S/X/CC 3.00
156 Ken Griffey Jr. S/X/CC 4.00
157 Frank Thomas S/X/CC 2.00
158 Darin Erstad B/Z/GLS .50
159 Roberto Alomar B/Y/GLS .35
160 Albert Belle B/Y/GLS .75
161 Jim Thome G/Y/GLS 4.00
162 Tony Clark G/Y/GLS 4.00
163 Chuck Knoblauch B/Y/GLS .25
164 Derek Jeter G/Z/GLS 20.00
165 Alex Rodriguez G/Z/GLS 15.00
166 Tony Gwynn B/X/GLS 1.25
167 Roger Clemens G/Z/GLS 12.00
168 Barry Larkin B/Y/GLS .25
169 Andres Galarraga B/Y/GLS .25
170 Vladimir Guerrero G/Z/GLS 7.50
171 Mark McGwire B/Z/GLS 2.00
172 Barry Bonds B/Z/GLS 3.00
173 Juan Gonzalez G/Z/GLS 4.00
174 Andruw Jones B/Z/GLS 7.50
175 Paul Molitor B/X/GLS 1.00
176 Hideo Nomo B/Z/GLS .75
177 Cal Ripken Jr. B/X/GLS 2.25
178 Brad Fullmer S/Z/GLR .75
179 Jaret Wright G/Z/GLR 2.00
180 Bobby Estalella B/Y/GLR .25
181 Ben Grieve B/X/GLR 2.00
182 Paul Konerko G/Z/GLR 3.00
183 David Ortiz G/X/GLR 6.00
184 Todd Helton G/Z/GLR 5.00
185 Juan Encarnacion G/Z/GLR 2.00
186 Miguel Tejada G/Z/GLR 4.00
187 Jacob Cruz B/X/GLR .25
188 Mark Kotsay B/Z/GLR 2.00
189 Fernando Tatis S/Y/GLR .75
190 Ricky Ledee S/Y/GLR .75
191 Richard Hidalgo S/Y/GLR .75
192 Richie Sexson S/Y/GLR .75
193 Luis Ordaz B/X/GLR .25
194 Eli Marrero S/Z/GLR .75

195 Livan Hernandez S/Z/GLR .75
196 Homer Bush B/X/GLR .25
197 Raul Ibanez B/X/GLR .25
198 Checklist (Nomar Garciaparra/X) .75
199 Checklist (Scott Rolen/B/X) .35
200 Checklist (Jose Cruz Jr. B/X) .25
201 Al Martin B/X .25

Fractal Matrix Die-Cut

This parallel set adds a die-cut to the Fractal Matrix set. Three different die-cut versions were created: X-axis, Y-axis and Z-axis. An X-axis die-cut was added to 75 bronze, 20 silver and 5 gold cards. A Y-axis die-cut was added to 20 bronze, 30 silver and 10 gold cards. Of the 40 Z-axis cards, 5 are bronze, 10 silver and 25 gold. Stated print runs were 400 of each X-axis card; 200 Y and 100 Z.

	NM/M
Complete Set (200):	950.00
Common X-Axis:	2.00
Common Y-Axis:	3.00
Common Z-Axis:	5.00

1 Rusty Greer G/Z 5.00
2 Tino Martinez G/Z 5.00
3 Bobby Bonilla S/Y 3.00
4 Jason Giambi S/Y 7.50
5 Matt Morris S/Y 3.00
6 Craig Counsell B/X 2.00
7 Reggie Jefferson B/X 2.00
8 Brian Rose B/X 2.00
9 Ruben Rivera B/X 2.00
10 Shawn Estes S/Y 3.00
11 Tony Gwynn G/Z 35.00
12 Jeff Abbott B/Y 3.00
13 Jose Cruz Jr. G/Z 5.00
14 Francisco Cordova B/X 2.00
15 Ryan Klesko B/X 2.00
16 Tim Salmon G/Y 4.00
17 Brett Tomko B/X 2.00
18 Matt Williams S/Y 3.00
19 Joe Carter B/X 2.00
20 Harold Baines B/X 2.00
21 Gary Sheffield S/Z 15.00
22 Charles Johnson S/X 2.00
23 Aaron Boone B/X 2.00
24 Eddie Murray G/Y 10.00
25 Matt Stairs B/Y 2.00
26 David Cone B/X 2.00
27 Jon Nunnally B/X 2.00
28 Chris Stynes B/X 2.00
29 Enrique Wilson B/Y 2.00
30 Randy Johnson S/Z 30.00
31 Garret Anderson S/Y 3.00
32 Manny Ramirez G/Z 30.00
33 Jeff Suppan B/X 2.00
34 Rickey Henderson B/X 6.00
35 Scott Spiezio B/X 2.00
36 Rondell White S/Y 3.00
37 Todd Greene S/Z 5.00
38 Delino DeShields B/X 2.00
39 Kevin Brown S/Y 3.00
40 Chili Davis B/X 2.00
41 Jimmy Key B/X 2.00
42 Mike Mussina G/Y 7.50
43 Joe Randa B/X 2.00
44 Chan Ho Park S/Z 5.00
45 Brad Radke B/X 2.00
46 Geronimo Berroa B/X 2.00
47 Wade Boggs S/Y 12.00
48 Kevin Appier B/X 2.00
49 Moises Alou S/Y 3.00
50 David Justice G/Y 3.00
51 Ivan Rodriguez G/Z 25.00
52 J.T. Snow B/X 2.00
53 Brian Giles B/X 2.00
54 Will Clark B/Y 4.00
55 Justin Thompson S/Y 2.00
56 Javier Lopez S/X 2.00
57 Hideki Irabu B/Y 2.00
58 Mark Grudzielanek B/X 2.00
59 Abraham Nunez S/X 2.00
60 Todd Hollandsworth B/X 2.00
61 Jay Bell B/X 2.00
62 Nomar Garciaparra G/Z 40.00
63 Vinny Castilla B/Y 2.00
64 Lou Collier B/Y 2.00
65 Kevin Orie S/X 2.00
66 John Valentin B/X 2.00
67 Robin Ventura B/X 2.00

69 Denny Neagle B/X 2.00
70 Tony Womack S/Y 3.00
71 Dennis Reyes S/Y 3.00
72 Wally Joyner B/X 2.00
73 Kevin Brown B/Y 3.00
74 Ray Durham B/X 2.00
75 Mike Cameron S/Z 3.00
76 Dante Bichette B/X 2.00
77 Jose Guillen G/Y 3.00
78 Carlos Delgado B/X 2.00
79 Paul Molitor G/Z 30.00
80 Jason Kendall B/X 2.00
81 Mark Belhorn B/X 2.00
82 Damian Jackson B/X 2.00
83 Bill Mueller B/X 2.00
84 Kevin Young B/X 2.00
85 Curt Schilling B/X 2.00
86 Jeffrey Hammonds B/X 2.00
87 Sandy Alomar Jr. S/Y 3.00
88 Bartolo Colon B/Y 3.00
89 Wilton Guerrero B/Y 3.00
90 Bernie Williams G/Y 4.00
91 Deion Sanders S/Y 3.00
92 Mike Piazza G/X 20.00
93 Butch Huskey B/X 2.00
94 Edgardo Alfonzo S/X 2.00
95 Alan Benes S/Y 3.00
96 Craig Biggio S/Y 3.00
97 Mark Grace S/Y 4.00
98 Shawn Green S/Y 5.00
99 Derrek Lee S/Y 3.00
100 Ken Griffey Jr. G/Z 40.00
101 Tim Raines B/X 2.00
102 Pokey Reese S/X 2.00
103 Lee Stevens S/X 2.00
104 Shannon Stewart S/Y 3.00
105 John Smoltz S/Y 3.00
106 Frank Thomas G/X 6.00
107 Jeff Fassero B/Y 2.00
108 Jay Buhner B/Y 3.00
109 Jose Canseco B/X 4.50
110 Omar Vizquel B/X 2.00
111 Travis Fryman B/X 2.00
112 Dave Nilsson B/X 2.00
113 John Olerud B/X 2.00
114 Larry Walker G/Z 5.00
115 Jim Edmonds S/Y 3.00
116 Bobby Higginson S/X 2.00
117 Todd Hundley S/Y 2.00
118 Paul O'Neill B/X 2.00
119 Bip Roberts B/X 2.00
120 Ismael Valdes B/X 2.00
121 Pedro Martinez S/Y 10.00
122 Jeff Cirillo B/X 2.00
123 Andy Benes B/X 2.00
124 Bobby Jones B/X 2.00
125 Brian Hunter B/X 2.00
126 Darryl Kile B/X 2.00
127 Pat Hentgen B/X 2.00
128 Marquis Grissom B/X 2.00
129 Eric Davis B/X 2.00
130 Chipper Jones G/Z 35.00
131 Edgar Martinez S/Z 3.00
132 Andy Pettitte B/X 10.00
133 Cal Ripken Jr. G/X 25.00
134 Scott Rolen G/Z 25.00
135 Ron Coomer B/X 2.00
136 Luis Castillo B/Y 3.00
137 Fred McGriff B/Y 3.00
138 Neifi Perez B/Y 3.00
139 Eric Karros B/X 2.00
140 Alex Fernandez B/X 2.00
141 Jason Dickson B/X 2.00
142 Lance Johnson B/X 2.00
143 Ray Lankford B/Y 3.00
144 Sammy Sosa G/Y 20.00
145 Eric Young G/Y 3.00
146 Bubba Trammell S/Y 3.00
147 Todd Walker S/Y 3.00
148 Mo Vaughn S/X 3.00
149 Jeff Bagwell S/X/CC 6.00
150 Kenny Lofton S/X/CC 2.00
151 Raul Mondesi S/X/CC 2.00
152 Mike Piazza S/X/CC 20.00
153 Chipper Jones S/X/CC 10.00
154 Larry Walker S/X/CC 2.00
155 Greg Maddux S/X/CC 5.00
156 Ken Griffey Jr. S/X/CC 15.00
157 Frank Thomas S/X/CC 6.00
158 Darin Erstad B/Z/GLS 4.00
159 Roberto Alomar B/Y/GLS 2.00
160 Albert Belle G/Y/GLS 3.50
161 Jim Thome G/Y/GLS 5.00
162 Tony Clark G/Z/GLS 3.00
163 Chuck Knoblauch B/Y/GLS 3.00
164 Derek Jeter G/Z/GLS 50.00
165 Alex Rodriguez G/Z/GLS 45.00
166 Tony Gwynn B/X/GLS 10.00
167 Roger Clemens G/Z/GLS 37.50
168 Barry Larkin B/Y/GLS 3.00
169 Andres Galarraga B/Y/GLS 3.00
170 Vladimir Guerrero G/Z/GLS 30.00
171 Mark McGwire B/Z/GLS 45.00
172 Barry Bonds B/Z/GLS 30.00
173 Juan Gonzalez G/Z/GLS 30.00
174 Andruw Jones G/Z/GLS 30.00
175 Paul Molitor B/Z/GLS 30.00
176 Hideo Nomo B/Z/GLS 30.00
177 Cal Ripken Jr. B/X/GLS 50.00
178 Brad Fullmer S/Z/GLR 3.00
179 Jaret Wright G/Z/GLR 3.00
180 Bobby Estalella B/Y/GLS 3.00
181 Ben Grieve G/X/GLS 2.00
182 Paul Konerko G/Z/GLR

183	David Ortiz G/Z/GLR	7.50
184	Todd Helton G/X/GLR	6.00
185	Juan Encarnacion G/Z/GLR	5.00
186	Miguel Tejada G/Z/GLR	10.00
187	Jacob Cruz B/Y/GLR	3.00
188	Mark Kotsay G/Z/GLR	5.00
189	Fernando Tatis S/Z/GLR	5.00
190	Ricky Ledee S/Y/GLR	3.00
191	Richard Hidalgo S/Y/GLR	3.00
192	Richie Sexson S/Y/GLR	3.00
193	Luis Ordaz B/X/GLR	5.00
194	Eli Marrero S/Z/GLR	5.00
195	Livan Hernandez S/Z/GLR	5.00
196	Homer Bush B/X/GLR	2.00
197	Raul Ibanez B/X/GLR	2.00
198	Checklist (Nomar Garciaparra B/X)	5.00
199	Checklist (Scott Rolen B/X)	2.00
200	Checklist (Jose Cruz Jr. B/X)	2.00
201	Al Martin B/X	2.00

Fractal Matrix Diamond Axis

Production of this blue-foil finished top-shelf parallel within the 1998 Leaf set was limited to 50 serially numbered examples of each card.

	NM/M
Common Player:	7.50
Stars/Rookies:	20X
SP (148-177):	12X

1998 Leaf Limited Star Factor Sample

This sample card was intended to preview the 1998 Leaf Limited issue which was never released due to Pinnacle's bankruptcy. The card is printed with a refractive foil background and hundreds of embossed stars front and back. The back has a large "SAMPLE" overprint and is numbered "000."

	NM/M
000 Frank Thomas	4.00

1998 Leaf Rookies & Stars

This 339-card set consists of three subsets: Power Tools, Lineup Card and Rookies. Fronts feature full-bleed photos and silver-foil graphics. Backs have complete year-by-year statistics and a small photo. The base set has short-printed base cards, numbers 131-230, 301-339, which are seeded 1:2 packs. Rookies and Stars has two parallels to the base set: True Blue and Longevity. True Blue's feature blue foil stamping and are each numbered "1 of 500" on the card back. Longevity's are printed on a full-foiled card front with gold foil stamping and limited to 50 serially numbered sets.

	NM/M
Complete Set (339):	200.00
Common Player:	.10
Common SP (131-230):	.20
Common SP (301-339):	.50
Inserted 1:2	
True Blues:	12X
SP True Blues:	2X
Production 500 Sets	
Longevitys:	50X
SP Longevitys:	15X
Production 50 Sets	
Pack (9):	7.50
Wax Box (24):	150.00
1 Andy Pettitte	.30
2 Roberto Alomar	.20
3 Randy Johnson	.75
4 Manny Ramirez	.75
5 Paul Molitor	.75
6 Mike Mussina	.50
7 Jim Thome	.65
8 Tino Martinez	.10
9 Gary Sheffield	.50
10 Chuck Knoblauch	.10
11 Bernie Williams	.10
12 Tim Salmon	.10
13 Sammy Sosa	1.25
14 Wade Boggs	1.00
15 Andres Galarraga	.10
16 Pedro Martinez	.75
17 David Justice	.10
18 Chan Ho Park	.10
19 Jay Buhner	.10
20 Ryan Klesko	.10
21 Barry Larkin	.10
22 Will Clark	.15
23 Raul Mondesi	.10
24 Rickey Henderson	.75
25 Jim Edmonds	.10
26 Ken Griffey Jr.	1.25
27 Frank Thomas	.75
28 Cal Ripken Jr.	2.00
29 Alex Rodriguez	1.50
30 Mike Piazza	1.25
31 Greg Maddux	1.00
32 Chipper Jones	1.00
33 Tony Gwynn	1.00
34 Derek Jeter	2.00
35 Jeff Bagwell	.75
36 Juan Gonzalez	.50
37 Nomar Garciaparra	1.00
38 Andruw Jones	.75
39 Hideo Nomo	.60
40 Roger Clemens	1.25
41 Mark McGwire	1.50
42 Scott Rolen	.60
43 Vladimir Guerrero	.75
44 Barry Bonds	2.00
45 Darin Erstad	.25
46 Albert Belle	.10
47 Kenny Lofton	.10
48 Mo Vaughn	.10
49 Ivan Rodriguez	.60
50 Jose Cruz Jr.	.10
51 Tony Clark	.10
52 Larry Walker	.10
53 Mark Grace	.10
54 Edgar Martinez	.10
55 Fred McGriff	.10
56 Rafael Palmeiro	.60
57 Matt Williams	.10
58 Craig Biggio	.10
59 Ken Caminiti	.10
60 Jose Canseco	.40
61 Brady Anderson	.10
62 Moises Alou	.10
63 Justin Thompson	.10
64 John Smoltz	.10
65 Carlos Delgado	.50
66 J.T. Snow	.10
67 Jason Giambi	.50
68 Garret Anderson	.10
69 Rondell White	.10
70 Eric Karros	.10
71 Javier Lopez	.10
72 Pat Hentgen	.10
73 Dante Bichette	.10
74 Charles Johnson	.10
75 Tom Glavine	.30
76 Rusty Greer	.10
77 Travis Fryman	.10
78 Todd Hundley	.10
79 Ray Lankford	.10
80 Denny Neagle	.10
81 Henry Rodriguez	.10
82 Sandy Alomar Jr.	.10
83 Robin Ventura	.10
84 John Olerud	.10
85 Omar Vizquel	.10
86 Darren Dreifort	.10
87 Kevin Brown	.10
88 Curt Schilling	.35
89 Francisco Cordova	.10
90 Brad Radke	.10
91 David Cone	.10
92 Paul O'Neill	.10
93 Vinny Castilla	.10
94 Marquis Grissom	.10
95 Brian Hunter	.10
96 Kevin Appier	.10
97 Bobby Bonilla	.10
98 Eric Young	.10
99 Jason Kendall	.10
100 Shawn Green	.40
101 Edgardo Alfonzo	.10
102 Alan Benes	.10
103 Bobby Higginson	.10
104 Todd Greene	.10
105 Jose Guillen	.15
106 Neifi Perez	.10
107 Edgar Renteria	.10
108 Chris Stynes	.10
109 Todd Walker	.10
110 Brian Jordan	.10
111 Joe Carter	.10
112 Ellis Burks	.10
113 Brett Tomko	.10
114 Mike Cameron	.10
115 Shannon Stewart	.10
116 Kevin Orie	.10
117 Brian Giles	.10
118 Hideki Irabu	.10
119 Delino DeShields	.10
120 David Segui	.10
121 Dustin Hermanson	.10
122 Kevin Young	.10
123 Jay Bell	.10
124 Doug Glanville	.10
125 John Roskos RC	.10
126 Damon Hollins RC	.10
127 Matt Stairs	.10
128 Cliff Floyd	.10
129 Derek Bell	.10
130 Darryl Strawberry	.10
131 Ken Griffey Jr. (Power Tools)	1.25
132 Tim Salmon (Power Tools)	.20
133 Manny Ramirez (Power Tools)	.75
134 Paul Konerko (Power Tools)	.30
135 Frank Thomas (Power Tools)	.75
136 Todd Helton (Power Tools)	.75
137 Larry Walker (Power Tools)	.20
138 Mo Vaughn (Power Tools)	.20
139 Travis Lee (Power Tools)	.20
140 Ivan Rodriguez (Power Tools)	.60
141 Ben Grieve (Power Tools)	.20
142 Brad Fullmer (Power Tools)	.20
143 Alex Rodriguez (Power Tools)	1.50
144 Mike Piazza (Power Tools)	1.25
145 Greg Maddux (Power Tools)	1.00
146 Chipper Jones (Power Tools)	1.00
147 Kenny Lofton (Power Tools)	.20
148 Albert Belle (Power Tools)	.20
149 Barry Bonds (Power Tools)	2.00
150 Vladimir Guerrero (Power Tools)	.75
151 Tony Gwynn (Power Tools)	1.00
152 Derek Jeter (Power Tools)	2.00
153 Jeff Bagwell (Power Tools)	.75
154 Juan Gonzalez (Power Tools)	.60
155 Nomar Garciaparra (Power Tools)	1.00
156 Andruw Jones (Power Tools)	.75
157 Hideo Nomo (Power Tools)	.60
158 Roger Clemens (Power Tools)	1.25
159 Mark McGwire (Power Tools)	1.50
160 Scott Rolen (Power Tools)	.60
161 Travis Lee (Team Line-Up)	.20
162 Ben Grieve (Team Line-Up)	.20
163 Jose Guillen (Team Line-Up)	.20
164 John Olerud (Team Line-Up)	.20
165 Kevin Appier (Team Line-Up)	.20
166 Marquis Grissom (Team Line-Up)	.20
167 Rusty Greer (Team Line-Up)	.20
168 Ken Caminiti (Team Line-Up)	.20
169 Craig Biggio (Team Line-Up)	.20
170 Ken Griffey Jr. (Team Line-Up)	1.25
171 Larry Walker (Team Line-Up)	.20
172 Barry Larkin (Team Line-Up)	.20
173 Andres Galarraga (Team Line-Up)	.20
174 Wade Boggs (Team Line-Up)	1.00
175 Sammy Sosa (Team Line-Up)	1.25
176 Mike Piazza (Team Line-Up)	1.50
177 Jim Thome (Team Line-Up)	.60
178 Paul Molitor (Team Line-Up)	.75
179 Tony Clark (Team Line-Up)	.20
180 Jose Cruz Jr. (Team Line-Up)	.20
181 Darin Erstad (Team Line-Up)	.25
182 Barry Bonds (Team Line-Up)	2.00
183 Vladimir Guerrero (Team Line-Up)	.75
184 Scott Rolen (Team Line-Up)	.60
185 Mark McGwire (Team Line-Up)	1.50
186 Nomar Garciaparra (Team Line-Up)	1.00
187 Gary Sheffield (Team Line-Up)	.50
188 Cal Ripken Jr. (Team Line-Up)	2.00
189 Frank Thomas (Team Line-Up)	.75
190 Andy Petitte (Team Line-Up)	.30
191 Paul Konerko	.35
192 Todd Helton	1.50
193 Mark Kotsay	.20
194 Brad Fullmer	.20
195 Kevin Millwood RC	8.00
196 David Ortiz	3.00
197 Kerry Wood	1.50
198 Miguel Tejada	.40
199 Fernando Tatis	.20
200 Jaret Wright	.20
201 Ben Grieve	.20
202 Travis Lee	.20
203 Wes Helms	.20
204 Geoff Jenkins	.20
205 Russell Branyan	.20
206 Esteban Yan RC	.20
207 Ben Ford RC	.20
208 Rich Butler RC	.75
209 Ryan Jackson RC	.50
210 A.J. Hinch	.20
211 Magglio Ordonez RC	25.00
212 David Dellucci RC	.50
213 Billy McMillon	.20
214 Mike Lowell RC	10.00
215 Todd Erdos RC	.20
216 Carlos Mendoza RC	.25
217 Frank Catalanotto RC	.75
218 Julio Ramirez RC	.20
219 John Halama RC	.50
220 Wilson Delgado	.20
221 Mike Judd RC	.20
222 Rolando Arrojo RC	1.00
223 Jason LaRue RC	.50
224 Manny Aybar RC	.50
225 Jorge Velandia	.20
226 Mike Kinkade RC	.50
227 Carlos Lee RC	15.00
228 Bobby Hughes	.20
229 Ryan Christenson RC	.50
230 Masato Yoshii RC	1.00
231 Richard Hidalgo	.10
232 Rafael Medina	.10
233 Damian Jackson	.10
234 Derek Lowe	.15
235 Mario Valdez	.10
236 Eli Marrero	.10
237 Juan Encarnacion	.10
238 Livan Hernandez	.10
239 Bruce Chen	.10
240 Eric Milton	.10
241 Jason Varitek	.10
242 Scott Elarton	.10
243 Manuel Barrios RC	.10
244 Mike Caruso	.10
245 Tom Evans	.10
246 Pat Cline	.10
247 Matt Clement	.15
248 Karim Garcia	.15
249 Richie Sexson	.10
250 Sidney Ponson	.10
251 Randall Simon	.10
252 Tony Saunders	.10
253 Javier Valentin	.10
254 Danny Clyburn	.10
255 Michael Coleman	.10
256 Hanley Frias RC	.10
257 Miguel Cairo	.10
258 Rob Stanifer RC	.10
259 Lou Collier	.10
260 Abraham Nunez	.10
261 Ricky Ledee	.10
262 Carl Pavano	.10
263 Derrek Lee	.10
264 Jeff Abbott	.10
265 Bob Abreu	.10
266 Bartolo Colon	.10
267 Mike Drumright	.10
268 Daryle Ward	.10
269 Gabe Alvarez	.10
270 Josh Booty	.10
271 Damian Moss	.10
272 Brian Rose	.10
273 Jarrod Washburn	.10
274 Bobby Estalella	.10
275 Enrique Wilson	.10
276 Derrick Gibson	.10
277 Ken Cloude	.10
278 Kevin Witt	.10
279 Donnie Sadler	.10
280 Sean Casey	.20
281 Jacob Cruz	.10
282 Ron Wright	.10
283 Jeremi Gonzalez	.10
284 Desi Relaford	.10
285 Bobby Smith	.10
286 Javier Vazquez	.10
287 Steve Woodard RC	.20
288 Greg Norton	.10
289 Cliff Politte	.10
290 Felix Heredia	.10
291 Braden Looper	.10
292 Felix Martinez	.10
293 Brian Meadows	.10
294 Edwin Diaz	.10
295 Pat Watkins	.10
296 Marc Pisciotta RC	.10
297 Rick Gorecki	.10
298 DaRond Stovall	.10
299 Andy Larkin	.10
300 Felix Rodriguez	.10
301 Blake Stein	.50
302 John Rocker RC	1.00
303 Justin Baughman RC	.50
304 Jesus Sanchez RC	.50
305 Randy Winn	.50
306 Lou Merloni	.50
307 Jim Parque RC	1.00
308 Dennis Reyes	.50
309 Orlando Hernandez RC	10.00
310 Jason Johnson	.50
311 Torii Hunter	1.00
312 Mike Piazza	2.50
313 Mike Frank RC	.50
314 Troy Glaus RC	60.00
315 Jin Cho RC	.75
316 Ruben Mateo RC	1.00
317 Ryan Minor RC	1.00
318 Aramis Ramirez	.75
319 Adrian Beltre	1.00
320 Matt Anderson RC	1.00
321 Gabe Kapler RC	2.00
322 Jeremy Giambi RC	1.00
323 Carlos Beltran	1.00
324 Dermal Brown	.50
325 Ben Davis	.50
326 Eric Chavez	1.50
327 Bob Howry RC	.50
328 Roy Halladay	1.00
329 George Lombard	.50
330 Michael Barrett	.50
331 Fernando Seguignol RC	1.00
332 J.D. Drew RC	20.00
333 Odalis Perez RC	4.00
334 Alex Cora RC	1.00
335 Placido Polanco RC	8.00
336 Armando Rios RC	.50
337 Sammy Sosa (HR Commemorative)	3.00
338 Mark McGwire (HR Commemorative)	4.00
339 Sammy Sosa, Mark McGwire (Checklist)	4.00

Longevity

Only 50 sets of this parallel edition were issued. Each card is serially numbered on back. Fronts are printed with gold foil background and have LONGEVITY printed at top. Special Longevity holographic 1 of 1 cards exist, but cannot be priced due to rarity.

	NM/M
Common Player:	3.00
Stars:	50X
SP Stars (131-230):	15X
SP Stars (301-339):	5X

True Blue

This parallel edition of the Rookies & Stars base set is labeled at top-back "1 of 500." The parallels feature blue foil graphic highlights on front with TRUE BLUE at top.

	NM/M
Common Player:	1.00
Stars:	12X
SP Stars (131-230; 301-339):	2X

Cross Training

This 10-card insert set highlights players who excel at multiple aspects of the game. Card fronts are full-foiled and sequentially numbered on the card back to 1,000.

	NM/M
Complete Set (10):	30.00
Common Player:	1.50
Production 1,000 Sets	
1 Kenny Lofton	1.50
2 Ken Griffey Jr.	5.00
3 Alex Rodriguez	6.00
4 Greg Maddux	4.00
5 Barry Bonds	7.50
6 Ivan Rodriguez	2.50
7 Chipper Jones	4.00
8 Jeff Bagwell	3.00
9 Nomar Garciaparra	4.00
10 Derek Jeter	7.50

Crusade

This 30-card set is a continuation of this cross-brand insert. Cards are printed on a holographic green foil front and limited to 250 serial numbered sets. Two parallels are also randomly seeded: Purple and Red. Purples have purple holographic foil fronts and limited to 100 serial numbered sets. Reds are printed on red holographic foil fronts and limited to 25 serial numbered sets.

	NM/M
Complete Green Set (30):	225.00
Common Player:	7.50
Production 250 Sets	
Purples (100 Sets):	3X
Reds (25 Sets):	10X
101 Richard Hidalgo	7.50
102 Paul Konerko	15.00
103 Miguel Tejada	15.00
104 Fernando Tatis	7.50
105 Travis Lee	7.50
106 Wes Helms	7.50
107 Rich Butler	7.50
108 Mark Kotsay	7.50
109 Eli Marrero	7.50
110 David Ortiz	15.00
111 Juan Encarnacion	7.50

112	Jaret Wright	7.50
113	Livan Hernandez	7.50
114	Ron Wright	7.50
115	Ryan Christenson	7.50
116	Eric Milton	7.50
117	Brad Fullmer	7.50
118	Karim Garcia	10.00
119	Abraham Nunez	7.50
120	Ricky Ledee	7.50
121	Carl Pavano	7.50
122	Derrek Lee	15.00
123	A.J. Hinch	7.50
124	Brian Rose	7.50
125	Bobby Estalella	7.50
126	Kevin Millwood	10.00
127	Kerry Wood	30.00
128	Sean Casey	12.50
129	Russell Branyan	7.50
130	Magglio Ordonez	20.00

Leaf Rookies & Stars Extreme Measures

These inserts are printed on a full-foiled card front. Each card highlights an outstanding statistic for the featured player and is sequentially numbered to 1,000, minus the number of die-cut versions produced for each.

		NM/M
Complete Set (10):		50.00
Common Player:		3.00
1	Ken Griffey Jr./944	7.50
2	Frank Thomas/653	5.00
3	Tony Gwynn/628	6.00
4	Mark McGwire/942	9.00
5	Larry Walker/280	3.00
6	Mike Piazza/960	7.50
7	Roger Clemens/708	6.50
8	Greg Maddux/980	5.00
9	Jeff Bagwell/873	4.50
10	Nomar Garciaparra/989	6.50

Leaf Rookies & Stars Extreme Measures Die-Cuts

Each card highlights an outstanding statistic for each featured player, is die-cut and serially numbered to the limit of the particular statistic as shown.

		NM/M
Complete Set (10):		375.00
Common Player:		2.50
1	Ken Griffey Jr./56	65.00
2	Frank Thomas/347	11.00
3	Tony Gwynn/372	13.50
4	Mark McGwire/58	80.00
5	Larry Walker/720	2.50
6	Mike Piazza/40	75.00
7	Roger Clemens/292	16.00
8	Greg Maddux/20	100.00
9	Jeff Bagwell/127	20.00
10	Nomar Garciaparra/11	125.00

Freshman Orientation

Card fronts are printed on holographic foil with silver foil stamping and feature top prospects. Card backs highlight the date of the featured player's Major League debut, have a small photo and are serially numbered to 5,000 sets. Each card was also issued in an appropriately labeled sample version.

		NM/M
Complete Set (20):		20.00
Common Player:		.75
Production 5,000 Sets		
Samples:		1X
1	Todd Helton	4.00
2	Ben Grieve	.75
3	Travis Lee	.75
4	Paul Konerko	1.50
5	Jaret Wright	.75
6	Livan Hernandez	.75
7	Brad Fullmer	.75
8	Carl Pavano	.75
9	Richard Hidalgo	.75
10	Miguel Tejada	1.50
11	Mark Kotsay	.75
12	David Ortiz	1.50
13	Juan Encarnacion	.75
14	Fernando Tatis	.75
15	Kevin Millwood	1.50
16	Kerry Wood	2.50
17	Magglio Ordonez	1.50
18	Derrek Lee	1.50
19	Jose Cruz Jr.	.75
20	A.J. Hinch	.75

Great American Heroes

Card fronts are stamped with a holographic silver foil and done on a horizontal format. Card backs have a photo and are serially numbered to 2,500. Each card was also produced in an appropriately marked sample version.

		NM/M
Complete Set (20):		35.00
Common Player:		.75
Production 2,500 Sets		
Samples:		1X
1	Frank Thomas	1.75
2	Cal Ripken Jr.	5.00
3	Ken Griffey Jr.	3.00
4	Alex Rodriguez	4.00
5	Greg Maddux	2.25
6	Mike Piazza	3.00
7	Chipper Jones	3.00
8	Tony Gwynn	2.25
9	Jeff Bagwell	1.75
10	Juan Gonzalez	1.25
11	Hideo Nomo	1.25
12	Roger Clemens	2.50
13	Mark McGwire	4.00
14	Barry Bonds	5.00
15	Kenny Lofton	.75
16	Larry Walker	.75
17	Paul Molitor	1.75
18	Wade Boggs	2.25
19	Barry Larkin	.75
20	Andres Galarraga	.75

Greatest Hits

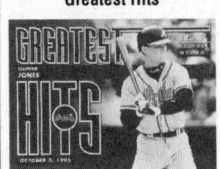

These inserts feature holographic silver foil stamping on the card front done on a horizontal format. Card backs have a photo and are serially numbered to 2,500.

		NM/M
Complete Set (20):		30.00
Common Player:		.50
Production 2,500 Sets		
1	Ken Griffey Jr.	2.50
2	Frank Thomas	1.50
3	Cal Ripken Jr.	4.00
4	Alex Rodriguez	3.00
5	Ben Grieve	.50
6	Mike Piazza	2.50
7	Chipper Jones	2.00
8	Tony Gwynn	2.00
9	Derek Jeter	4.00
10	Jeff Bagwell	1.50
11	Tino Martinez	.50
12	Juan Gonzalez	.75
13	Nomar Garciaparra	2.00
14	Mark McGwire	3.00
15	Scott Rolen	.75
16	David Justice	.50
17	Darin Erstad	.75
18	Mo Vaughn	.50
19	Ivan Rodriguez	.75
20	Travis Lee	.50

Home Run Derby

This 20-card set spotlights the top home run hitters on a bronze full-foiled card front. Card backs have a portrait photo and are serially numbered to 2,500.

		NM/M
Complete Set (20):		30.00
Common Player:		.75

1	Tino Martinez	.75
2	Jim Thome	1.25
3	Larry Walker	.75
4	Tony Clark	.75
5	Jose Cruz Jr.	.75
6	Barry Bonds	5.00
7	Scott Rolen	1.00
8	Paul Konerko	1.25
9	Travis Lee	.75
10	Todd Helton	1.25
11	Mark McGwire	4.00
12	Andruw Jones	1.50
13	Nomar Garciaparra	2.50
14	Juan Gonzalez	1.00
15	Jeff Bagwell	1.50
16	Chipper Jones	2.50
17	Mike Piazza	3.00
18	Frank Thomas	1.50
19	Ken Griffey Jr.	3.00
20	Albert Belle	.75

ML Hard Drives

Card fronts are stamped with silver holographic foil. Card backs detail to which field (left, center and right) the featured player hit each of his singles, doubles, triples and home runs. Each card is serially numbered to 2,500. Each card was also produced in an appropriately marked sample version.

		NM/M
Complete Set (20):		30.00
Common Player:		.75
Production 2,500 Sets		
Samples:		1X
1	Jeff Bagwell	1.50
2	Juan Gonzalez	1.00
3	Nomar Garciaparra	2.00
4	Ken Griffey Jr.	3.00
5	Frank Thomas	1.50
6	Cal Ripken Jr.	4.50
7	Alex Rodriguez	3.50
8	Mike Piazza	3.00
9	Chipper Jones	2.00
10	Tony Gwynn	2.00
11	Derek Jeter	4.50
12	Mo Vaughn	.75
13	Ben Grieve	.75
14	Manny Ramirez	1.50
15	Vladimir Guerrero	1.50
16	Scott Rolen	1.00
17	Darin Erstad	.75
18	Kenny Lofton	.75
19	Brad Fullmer	.75
20	David Justice	.75

MVPs

This 20-card set is printed on a full silver-foil card stock and sequentially numbered to 5,000. The first 500 of each card is treated with a "Pennant Edition" logo and unique color coating.

		NM/M
Complete Set (20):		35.00
Common Player:		.50
Production 4,500 Sets		
Pennant Editions:		2X
Production 500 Sets		
1	Frank Thomas	2.00
2	Chuck Knoblauch	.50
3	Cal Ripken Jr.	5.00
4	Alex Rodriguez	4.00

5	Ivan Rodriguez	1.50
6	Albert Belle	.50
7	Ken Griffey Jr.	3.00
8	Juan Gonzalez	1.50
9	Roger Clemens	2.75
10	Mo Vaughn	.50
11	Jeff Bagwell	2.00
12	Craig Biggio	.50
13	Chipper Jones	2.50
14	Barry Larkin	.50
15	Mike Piazza	3.00
16	Barry Bonds	5.00
17	Andruw Jones	2.00
18	Tony Gwynn	2.50
19	Greg Maddux	2.50
20	Mark McGwire	4.00

Standing Ovation

Card fronts are stamped with silver holographic foil and card backs have a small photo of the featured player and are serially numbered to 5,000. Each card was also produced in an appropriately labeled sample version.

		NM/M
Complete Set (10):		12.50
Common Player:		.75
Production 5,000 Sets		
Samples:		1X
1	Barry Bonds	3.00
2	Mark McGwire	2.50
3	Ken Griffey Jr.	2.00
4	Frank Thomas	1.00
5	Tony Gwynn	1.50
6	Cal Ripken Jr.	1.50
7	Greg Maddux	1.50
8	Roger Clemens	1.75
9	Paul Molitor	1.00
10	Ivan Rodriguez	.75

Ticket Masters

Card fronts are printed on a full-foiled card stock with silver foil stamping and have a photo of one of the two players featured from the same team. Card backs have a photo of the other featured player and are serially numbered to 2,500. The first 250 of each card are die-cut.

		NM/M
Complete Set (20):		32.50
Common Card:		.50
Production 2,250 Sets		
Die-Cuts:		1.5X
Production 250 Sets		
1	Ken Griffey Jr., Alex Rodriguez	4.00
2	Frank Thomas, Albert Belle	1.50
3	Cal Ripken Jr., Roberto Alomar	5.00
4	Greg Maddux, Chipper Jones	2.00
5	Tony Gwynn, Ken Caminiti	2.00
6	Derek Jeter, Andy Pettitte	5.00
7	Jeff Bagwell, Craig Biggio	1.50
8	Juan Go nzalez, Ivan Rodriguez	1.25
9	Nomar Garciaparra, Mo Vaughn	2.00
10	Vladimir Guerrero, Brad Fullmer	1.50
11	Andruw Jones, Andres Galarraga	1.50
12	Tino Martinez, Chuck Knoblauch	.50
13	Raul Mondesi, Paul Konerko	.75
14	Roger Clemens, Jose Cruz Jr.	2.25
15	Mark McGwire, Brian Jordan	4.00
16	Kenny Lofton, Manny Ramirez	1.50
17	Larry Walker, Todd Helton	1.25
18	Darin Erstad, Tim Salmon	.75
19	Travis Lee, Matt Williams	.50
20	Ben Grieve, Jason Giambi	1.00

1996 Legends of the Negro Leagues Playing Cards

This set of playing cards depicting ballplayers of the pre-integration Negro Leagues was issued as a fundraiser by the International Society of Athletes in conjunction with a reunion of the players. In standard playing card finish and round-corner format, the cards have black-and-white photos at center. Backs are in black with gold printing. Size is 2-1/2" x 3-1/2". The deck's queens feature notable females of the Negro Leagues and the sponsor.

		NM/M
Complete Set (56):		10.00
Common Player:		.15
AS	Satchel Paige	1.00
2S	James "Joe" Greene	.15
3S	James "Red" Moore	.15
4S	Othello "Chico" Renfroe	.15
5S	William "Judy" Johnson	.25
6S	Willie "The Devil" Wells	.25
7S	Gene Benson	.15
8S	Willard "Sunnie" Brown	.15
9S	Martin Dihigo	.25
10S	Don Newcombe	.25
JS	Ray "Hooks" Dandridge	.25
QS	Billie Harden	.15
KS	Roy "Campy" Campanella	.75
AD	Jack "Jackie" Robinson	2.00
2D	Sam Haynes	.15
3D	Bob "The Rope" Boyd	.15
4D	William "Bonnie" Serrell	.15
5D	Orestes "Minnie" Minoso	.20
6D	Pop Lloyd	.15
7D	Art "Superman" Pennington	.15
8D	Francisco "Pancho" Coimbre	.15
9D	Sam "Jet" Jethroe	.20
10D	Joe Black	.25
JD	Monte Irvin	.25
QD	Effa "Effie" Manley	.25
KD	Henry "Hank" Aaron	1.50
AC	Joshua "Josh" Gibson	.25
2C	William "Bill" Cash	.15
3C	Francis "Fran" Matthews	.15
4C	Fred "Leap" Bankhead	.15
5C	Alex Radcliffe	.15
6C	Authur "Artie" Wilson (Arthur)	.20
7C	James "Jim" Zapp	.15
8C	Henry "Kimmie" Kimbro	.15
9C	Chester "Chet" Brewer	.15
10C	Verdell "Lefty" Mathis	.15
JC	James "Junior" Gilliam	.25
QC	Marcenia "Toni" Stone	.15
KC	Willie Mays	1.50
AH	James "Cool Papa" Bell	.25
2H	Samuel "Harriston" Hairston	.20
3H	John "Buck" O'Neil	.25
4H	Lorenzo "Piper" Davis	.15
5H	Parnell Woods	.15
6H	Thomas "Pee Wee" Butts	.15
7H	Oscar Charleston	.25
8H	Lawrence "Larry" Doby	1.00
9H	Hilton Smith	.25
10H	Leon Day	.25
JH	Walter "Buck" Leonard	.25
QH	Pamela Pryor-Fuller	.15
KH	Ernest "Ernie" Banks	.75
---	Joker (Ted "Double Duty" Radcliffe)	.25
---	Super Joker (Andrew "Rube" Foster)	.25
---	Wilmer "Red" Fields	.25
---	Clifford "Connie" Johnson	.15

2001 Legends European Tour

This two-play, four-card set was issued in conjunction with the 8th annual Baseball Legends European Tour which made a goodwill swing through 11 military bases in Germany in June. Cards feature borderless vintage color photos on front. Team logos have been airbrushed away. A Legends tour logo appears in one corner. Backs have career stats and highlights and some of the tour sponsor's logos. The cards were given away at autograph sessions, baseball clinics, softball games and other events.

		NM/M
Complete Set (4):		10.00
Common Player:		2.00
(1)	Vida Blue (Green jersey)	3.00
(2)	Vida Blue (Yellow jersey)	3.00
(3)	Manny Sanguillen/Btg	2.00
(4)	Manny Sanguillen/ Catching	2.00

1998 Lemon Chill Chicago White Sox

In standard 2-1/2" x 3-1/2" format, this team set was a stadium giveaway. Fronts feature game-action photos with a stylized flame-like effect at left and bottom. The team logo is at lower-left, with the player name at bottom right. Backs have player personal data, stats, career highlights and a large sponsor's logo. The cards were checklisted here in alphabetical order.

		NM/M
Complete Set (30):		12.00
Common Player:		.50
(1)	Jeff Abbott	.50
(2)	Mark Anderson (Trainer), Steve Odgers (Strength Coach), Mark Salas, Herm Schneider (Trainer)	.50
(3)	James Baldwin	.50
(4)	Albert Belle	.50
(5)	Mike Cameron	.50

(6)	Mike Caruso	.50
(7)	Carlos Castillo	.50
(8)	Nardi Contreras, Von Joshua	.50
(9)	Wil Cordero	.50
(10)	Ray Durham	.50
(11)	Scott Eyre	.50
(12)	Keith Foulke	.50
(13)	Bob Howry	.50
(14)	Wallace Johnson, Bryan Little	.50
(15)	Matt Karchner	.50
(16)	Chad Kreuter	.50
(17)	Art Kusnyer, Joe Nossek	.50
(18)	Jerry Manuel	.50
(19)	Jaime Navarro	.50
(20)	Greg Norton	.50
(21)	Charlie O'Brien	.50
(22)	Magglio Ordonez	2.00
(23)	Jim Parque	.50
(24)	Bill Simas	.50
(25)	Mike Sirotka	.50
(26)	Chris Snopek	.50
(27)	John Snyder	.50
(28)	Frank Thomas	4.00
(29)	Robin Ventura	.50
(30)	Bryan Ward	.50

1999 Lemon Chill Chicago White Sox

In standard 2-1/2" x 3-1/2" format, this team set was a stadium giveaway. Fronts feature game-action photos on a borderless ghost-photo background with the team motto, "The Kids Can Play" and logo at lower-left, with the player name at top-left in red. Backs have a red duotone photo, '98 stats, uniform and card numbers and a large sponsor's logo. A five-card 1959 World Series commemorative subset was also included.

		NM/M
Complete Set (33):		10.00
Common Player:		.25
1	Brook Fordyce	.25
2	Carlos Lee	.50
3	Greg Norton	.25
4	John Snyder	.25
5	Craig Wilson	.25
6	Chris Singleton	.25
7	Liu Rodriguez	.25
8	Magglio Ordonez	1.00
9	Mike Sirotka	.25
10	Jaime Navarro	.25
11	Mark Johnson	.25
12	Jim Parque	.25
13	Jeff Liefer	.25
14	Mike Caruso	.25
15	Ray Durham	.25
17	Bob Howry	.25
18	James Baldwin	.25
19	Jerry Manuel	.25
20	Bill Simas	.25
21	Frank Thomas	2.00
22	Bryan Ward	.25
23	Scott Eyre	.25
24	Paul Konerko	1.00
25	Sean Lowe	.25
26	Keith Foulke	.25
---	Von Joshua, Nardi Contreras	.25
---	Joe Nossek, Art Kusnyer	.25
---	Herm Schneider (Trainer), Steve Odgers (Conditioning), Mark Salas (Bullpen), Mark Anderson (Trainer)	.25
1 of 5	1959 World Series Recap	.25
2 of 5	Billy Pierce	.25
3 of 5	Jim Landis	.25
4 of 5	Al Smith	.25
5 of 5	Al Lopez	.25

2000 Lemon Chill Chicago White Sox

The first 20,000 fans through the gates of Comiskey Park on July 16 received this team set. On front a color action photo stands out from the black-and-white background and is vignetted with black borders. The player name is in purple at bottom. A black-and-white

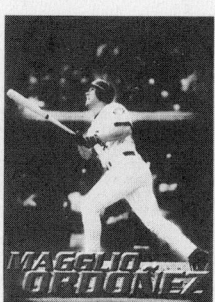

portrait photo is featured on back along with player data, 1999 stats and the sponsor's logo.

		NM/M
Complete Set (31):		10.00
Common Player:		.35
1	James Baldwin	.35
2	Herbert Perry	.35
3	Keith Foulke	.35
4	Tony Graffanino	.35
5	Kip Wells	.35
6	Mark Johnson	.35
7	Chris Singleton	.35
8	Ray Durham	.35
9	Jose Valentin	.35
10	Kevin Beirne	.35
11	Paul Konerko	1.00
12	Greg Norton	.35
13	Bill Simas	.35
14	Jeff Abbott	.35
15	Frank Thomas	3.00
16	Mike Sirotka	.35
17	Brook Fordyce	.35
18	Cal Eldred	.35
19	Bob Howry	.35
20	Jerry Manuel	.35
21	Kelly Wunsch	.35
22	Bryan Little, Wallace Johnson	.35
23	Joe Nossek, Art Kusnyer	.35
24	Jim Parque	.35
25	Carlos Lee	.50
26	Von Joshua, Nardi Contreras	.35
27	Sean Lowe	.35
28	Magglio Ordonez	1.00
29	Jesus Pena	.35
30	Craig Wilson	.35
31	Mark Anderson, Herm Schneider, Man Soo Lee, Steve Odgers	.35

1989 Lennox/HSE Astros

Formatted similar to a police/fire safety set, this Astros team issue is sponsored instead by a furnace company and the team's cable TV outlet. Cards measure 2-5/8" x 4-1/8" and feature portrait photos on front with orange and black team color pinstripes. Backs have biographical data, career summary and sponsors' logos.

		NM/M
Complete Set (26):		10.00
Common Player:		.25
1	Billy Hatcher	.25
2	Greg Gross	.25
3	Rick Rhoden	.25
4	Mike Scott	.25
5	Kevin Bass	.25
6	Alex Trevino	.25
7	Jim Clancy	.25
8	Bill Doran	.25
9	Dan Schatzeder	.25
10	Bob Knepper	.25
11	Jim Deshaies	.25
12	Eric Yelding	.25
13	Danny Darwin	.25
14	Coaches	.25
15	Craig Reynolds	.25
16	Rafael Ramirez	.25

17	Juan Agosto	.25
18	Larry Andersen	.25
19	Dave Smith	.25
20	Gerald Young	.25
21	Ken Caminiti	.50
22	Terry Puhl	.25
23	Bob Forsch	.25
24	Craig Biggio	6.00
25	Art Howe	.25
26	Glenn Davis	.25

1990 Lennox/HSE Astros

Ken Oberkfell   #10 - Infielder

For a second straight year Lennox, the furnace people, and HSE, the Astros cable TV outlet, sponsored a team set in an oversize (3-1/2" x 5") format on thin, semi-gloss stock. Fronts feature color player portrait photos, backs have a few biographical notes and logos for all parties. Cards are checklisted here by uniform numbers which appear on front and back.

		NM/M
Complete Set (29):		15.00
Common Player:		.50
1	Casey Candaele	.50
6	David Rohde	.50
7	Craig Biggio	5.00
9	Alex Trevino	.50
10	Ken Oberkfell	.50
11	Ken Caminiti	.50
12	Glenn Wilson	.50
13	Gerald Young	.50
15	Eric Yelding	.50
16	Rafael Ramirez	.50
17	Art Howe	.50
19	Bill Doran	.50
20	Dan Schatzeder	.50
21	Terry Puhl	.50
22	Mark Davidson	.50
26	Eric Anthony	.50
24	Franklin Stubbs	.50
27	Glenn Davis	.50
31	Xavier Hernandez	.50
33	Mike Scott	.50
36	Bill Gullickson	.50
38	Jim Clancy	.50
42	Jose Cano	.50
43	Jim Deshaies	.50
44	Danny Darwin	.50
45	Dave Smith	.50
47	Larry Andersen	.50
49	Juan Agosto	.50
51	Mark Portugal	.50

1990 Ron Lewis 1961 N.Y. Yankees

The World's Champion 1961 N.Y. Yankees are featured in this set of cards by sports artist Ron Lewis. The 42-card set contains cards of individual players, coaches and the manager, plus a team picture. The 3-1/2" x 5-1/2" cards were sold only in a complete boxed set edition of 10,000. Cards have oil painted portraits of the players set against a blue background. The card borders are pinstriped in dark blue. At bottom is a blank panel for autograph-

ing. Backs are printed in red and blue and have personal data, career summary, 1961 and career stats.

		NM/M
Complete Boxed Set (42):		10.00
Common Player:		.50
1	1961 N.Y. Yankees Team	3.00
2	Bobby Richardson	.50
3	Roger Maris	2.00
4	Elston Howard	.75
5	Bill Skowron	.60
6	Clete Boyer	.50
7	Mickey Mantle	4.00
8	Yogi Berra	1.00
9	Johnny Blanchard	.50
10	Hector Lopez	.50
11	Whitey Ford	1.00
12	Ralph Terry	.50
13	Bill Stafford	.50
14	Bud Daley	.50
15	Billy Gardner	.50
16	Jim Coates	.50
17	Luis Arroyo	.50
18	Tex Clevenger	.50
19	Bob Cerv	.50
20	Art Ditmar	.50
21	Bob Turley	.50
22	Joe DeMaestri	.50
23	Rollie Sheldon	.50
24	Earl Torgeson	.50
25	Hal Reniff	.50
26	Ralph Houk	.50
27	Johnny James	.50
28	Bob Hale	.50
29	Danny McDevitt	.50
30	Duke Maas	.50
31	Jim Hegan	.50
32	Wally Moses	.50
33	Frank Crosetti	.50
34	Lee Thomas	.50
35	Al Downing	.50
36	Jack Reed	.50
37	Ryne Duren	.50
38	Tom Tresh	.50
39	Johnny Sain	.50
40	Jesse Gonder	.50
41	Deron Johnson	.50
42	Tony Kubek	.60

1991 Ron Lewis Negro Leagues Postcards

Willie Mays

The 1991 Negro League Living Legends Postcard Set features paintings by artist Ron Lewis. Cards measure 3-1/2" x 5-1/2" and are stamped with a number within the 10,000 sets produced. Between each player's image and the player's name at the bottom of the card, is ample space for an autograph. The set, originally sold for $27, was created as a fund raiser for the Negro League Baseball Players Association. Two hundred uncut sheets were offered at $100 each.

		NM/M
Complete Set (30):		30.00
Common Player:		.75
1	George Giles	.75
2	Bill Cash	.75
3	Bob Harvey	.75
4	Lyman Bostock Sr.	.90
5	Ray Dandridge	2.50
6	Leon Day	2.00
7	Verdell "Lefty" Mathis	.75
8	Jimmie Crutchfield	.75
9	Clyde McNeal	.75
10	Bill Wright	.75
11	Mahlon Duckett	.75
12	William "Bobby" Robinson	.75
13	Max Manning	.75
14	Armando Vazquez	.75
15	Jehosie Heard	.75
16	Quincy Trouppe	.90
17	Wilmer Fields	.75
18	Lonnie Blair	.75
19	Garnett Blair	.75
20	Monte Irvin	2.50
21	Willie Mays	7.50
22	Buck Leonard	4.00
23	Frank Evans	.75
24	Josh Gibson Jr.	5.00

25	Ted "Double Duty" Radcliffe	1.50
26	Josh Johnson	.75
27	Gene Benson	.75
28	Lester Lockett	.75
29	Cowan "Bubba" Hyde	.75
30	Rufus Lewis	.75

1994 Ron Lewis Negro Leagues Postcards

BUCK O'NEILL

A second series of postcards honoring players of the Negro Leagues was produced by artist Ron Lewis in September 1994. In this set, more emphasis was placed on multi-player cards. Many of the cards also feature detailed backgrounds of street scenes with vintage vehicles, old-time stadiums, etc. Cards measure 3-1/2" x 5-1/2" and have a wide front border with the player(s) name printed at bottom and space above for autographing. Postcard backs are printed in black and include a few career stats, a card number and the card's position among the limited edition of 10,000.

		NM/M
Complete Set (32):		25.00
Common Card:		1.00
1	Willie Mays, Ernie Banks, Hank Aaron	4.00
1p	2-1/2"	1.00
2	Bill Wright, Lester Lockett, Lyman Bostock, Sr.	1.00
3	Josh Gibson, Josh Gibson Jr., Buck Leonard	2.50
4	Max Manning, Monte Irvin, Leon Day	1.50
5	Armando Vazquez, Minnie Minoso, Martin Dihigo	1.50
6	Ted "Double Duty" Radcliffe	1.50
7	Bill Owens, Turkey Stearnes, Bobby Robinson	1.00
8	Wilmer Fields, Edsall Walker, Josh Johnson	1.00
9	Artie Wilson, Lionel Hampton	1.50
10	Earl Taborn	1.00
11	Barney "Bonnie" Serrell	1.00
12	Rodolfo "Rudy" Fernandez	1.00
13	Willie Pope	1.00
14	Ray Noble	1.00
15	Jim "Fireball" Cohen	1.00
16	Henry Kimbro	1.00
17	Charlie Biot	1.00
18	Al Wilmore	1.00
19	Sam Jethroe	1.50
20	Tommy Sampson	1.00
21	Charlie Rivera	1.00
22	Claro Duany	1.00
23	Russell Awkard	1.00
24	Art "Superman" Pennington	1.00
25	Wilmer Harris	1.00
26	Napoleon "Nap" Gulley	1.00
27	Emilio Navarro	1.00
28	Andy Porter	1.00
29	Willie Grace	1.00
30	Red Moore	1.00
31	Buck O'Neill	2.00
32	Stanley Glenn	1.00

1996 Liberty Satellite Sports

This business-to-business promotion for a cable sports network content provider features on card fronts the logo of different cable networks. Space on back is shared by player data and stats and information about a local cable network.

		NM/M
Complete Set (21):		125.00
Common Player:		2.00
1	Cal Ripken Jr.	40.00
2	Paul O'Neill	2.00
3	Mo Vaughn	2.00
4	Travis Fryman	2.00

5	Brian Jordan	2.00
6	Ken Griffey Jr.	20.00
7	Craig Biggio	2.00
8	Chili Davis	2.00
9	Greg Maddux	15.00
10	Gary Sheffield	4.00
11	Frank Thomas	10.00
12	Barry Larkin	2.00
13	John Franco	2.00
14	Albert Belle	2.00
15	Mark McGwire	20.00
16	Barry Bonds	40.00
17	Lenny Dykstra	2.00
(18)	Mickey Lopez	2.00
(19)	Tim Salmon	2.00
(20)	Matt Williams	2.00
(21)	Header Card	.35

1992 Lime Rock Griffey Baseball Holograms

This set of three hologram cards features the Griffey family of pro players. Each card carries a "GRIFFEY BASEBALL" headline at top, with a large central action photo of one of the family and his facsimile autograph. The backs have a color photo, career highlights and stats. The cards were issued in several different versions as noted below.

		NM/M
Complete Set, Holograms (3):		3.00
Complete Set, Gold Holograms (3):		10.00
Complete Set, Autographed (3):		35.00
Complete Set, Blank-backed Promos (3):		6.00
Three-card strip, edition of 5,000:		6.50
1	Ken Griffey Sr. (Silver hologram, edition of 250,000.)	.50
1	Ken Griffey Sr. (Gold hologram, edition of 1,000.)	1.50
1	Ken Griffey Sr. (Auto. edition of 2,500.)	5.00
1	Ken Griffey Sr. (Blank-back promo, edition of 750.)	1.50
2	Ken Griffey Jr./Silver	2.50
2	Ken Griffey Jr./Gold	9.00
2	Ken Griffey Jr./Auto.	30.00
2	Ken Griffey Jr. (Promo)	9.00
3	Craig Griffey/Silver	.50
3	Craig Griffey/Gold	1.50
3	Craig Griffey/Auto.	2.00
3	Craig Griffey (Promo)	1.50

1991 Line Drive

This set of "old-timers" includes many Hall of Famers, as well as stars who had played into the late 1980s. In standard 2-1/2" x 3-1/2", the cards have color or sepia photos framed in blue and bordered in white. Horizontal backs have biographical and career notes and stats.

		NM/M
Complete Set (50):		6.00
Common Player:		.10
1	Don Drysdale	.25
2	Joe Torre	.15
3	Bob Gibson	.25

		NM/M
4	Bobby Richardson	.25
5	Ron Santo	.25
6	Eric Soderholm	.10
7	Yogi Berra	.35
8	Steve Garvey	.15
9	Steve Carlton	.25
10	Toby Harrah	.10
11	Luis Tiant	.10
12	Earl Weaver	.10
13	Bill Mazeroski	.10
14	Don Baylor	.10
15	Lew Burdette	.10
16	Jim Lonborg	.10
17	Jerry Grote	.10
18	Ernie Banks	.35
19	Doug DeCinces	.10
20	Jimmy Piersall	.10
21	Ken Holtzman	.10
22	Manny Mota	.10
23	Alvin Dark	.10
24	Lou Brock	.25
25	Ralph Houk	.15
26	Graig Nettles	.15
27	Bill White	.10
28	Billy Williams	.25
29	Willie Horton	.10
30	Tommie Agee	.10
31	Rico Petrocelli	.10
32	Julio Cruz	.10
33	Robin Roberts	.25
34	Dave Johnson	.10
35	Wilbur Wood	.10
36	Cesar Cedeno	.10
37	George Foster	.10
38	Thurman Munson	.25
39	Roberto Clemente	2.00
40	Eddie Mathews	.25
41	Harmon Killebrew	.25
42	Monte Irvin	.25
43	Bob Feller	2.00
44	Jimmie Foxx	1.00
45	Walter Johnson	1.00
46	Casey Stengel	.25
47	Satchel Paige	1.00
48	Ty Cobb	2.00
49	Mickey Cochrane	.25
50	Dizzy Dean	.35

1991 Line Drive Mickey Mantle

This 20-card set was part of a collector's kit featuring the Yankees superstar. Fronts of the 2-1/2" x 3-1/2" cards have sepia or color poses or action photos. The player's name appears in white in a blue panel at bottom. Red striping seperates the graphics from the white border. The Line Drive logo appears in an upper corner. Backs are printed in red and blue and feature a facsimile autograph, a few sentences about Mantle's career, manufacturer's and licensor's logos, and a card number. The same basic cards were included in a Collectors Marketing Corp. (see CMC) in 1989, lacking the Line Drive logo on front and the Impel logo and 1991 dates on back.

	NM/M
Complete Set (20):	15.00
Common Card:	2.00
1-20 Mickey Mantle	2.00

1991 Line Drive Don Mattingly

This 20-card set was part of a collectors kit featuring the Yankees' star. Fronts of the 2-1/2" x 3-1/2" cards have color poses or action photos. The player's name appears in white in a blue panel at bottom along with the Line Drive logo in red and white. Backs are printed in red and blue and feature a facsimile autograph, a few sentences about Mattingly's career, manufacturer's and licensor's logos, and a card number.

	NM/M
Complete Set (20):	3.00
Common Card:	.15
1-20 Don Mattingly	.25

1991 Line Drive Ryne Sandberg

This 20-card set was part of a collectors kit featuring the Cubs Hall of Fame second baseman. Fronts of the 2-1/2" x 3-1/2" cards have color poses or action photos. The player's name appears in blue and red in the white border above the photo. Backs are printed in red and blue and feature a few sentences about Sandberg's career, along with manufacturer's and licensor's logos, and a card number.

	NM/M
Complete Set (20):	10.00
Common Card:	.50
1-20 Ryne Sandberg	.50

1986 Lite Beer Astros

This regional set of the Houston Astros was sponsored by Lite Beer and given away in a special stadium promotion. The 4-1/2" x 6-3/4" cards feature full-color photos surrounded by a wide, white border. Diagonal color bands of yellow, orange, red and purple extend throught the upper-right and lower-left corners of the card, which also displays the Astros' 25th Anniversa-

ry logo and the Lite Beer logo in opposite corners. The backs include player information and statistics.

		NM/M
Complete Set (22):		25.00
Common Player:		1.00
3	Phil Garner	1.00
6	Mark Bailey	1.00
10	Dickie Thon	1.00
11	Frank DiPino	1.00
12	Craig Reynolds	1.00
14	Alan Ashby	1.00
17	Kevin Bass	1.00
19	Bill Doran	1.00
20	Jim Pankovits	1.00
21	Terry Puhl	1.00
22	Hal Lanier	1.00
25	Jose Cruz	1.00
27	Glenn Davis	1.00
28	Billy Hatcher	1.00
30	Denny Walling	1.00
33	Mike Scott	1.00
34	Nolan Ryan	15.00
37	Charlie Kerfeld	1.00
42	Bob Knepper	1.00
43	Jim Deshaies	1.00
45	Dave Smith	1.00
53	Mike Madden	1.00

Rangers

This postcard-size (approximately 4" x 6") set of Texas Rangers cards was sponsored by Lite Beer and was available by mail directly from the team. Fronts feature full-color photos surrounded by a wide, white border with the player's name, uniform number and postion appearing below. The Rangers logo is displayed in the lower-left corner, while the Lite Beer logo is in the lower-right. Backs offer personal information and stats.

		NM/M
Complete Set (28):		20.00
Common Player:		1.00
0	Oddibe McDowell	1.00
1	Scott Fletcher	1.00
2	Bobby Valentine	1.00
4	Don Slaught	1.00
5	Pete Incaviglia	2.00
6	Pete O'Brien	1.00
10	Art Howe	1.00
11	Toby Harrah	1.00
12	Geno Petralli	1.00
13	Joe Ferguson	1.00
14	Tim Foli	1.00
15	Larry Parrish	1.00
16	Mike Mason	1.00
17	Darrell Porter	1.00
19	Ed Correa	1.00
19	Curtis Wilkerson	1.00
22	Steve Buechele	1.00
24	Jose Guzman	1.00
24	Ricky Wright	1.00
27	Greg Harris	1.00
31	Tom Robson	1.00
32	Gary Ward	1.00
35	Tom House	1.00
44	Tom Paciorek	1.00
45	Dwayne Henry	1.00
48	Bobby Witt	1.00
49	Charlie Hough	1.00
---	Arlington Stadium	1.00

1994 Lite Beer Milwaukee Brewers

The 1994 baseball strike interrupted the issue of this four-series commemorative set advertised as including "Every Player in the Brewers Twenty-Five Year History." The set was produced in four booklets of 94 cards each. Individual 2-1/2" x 3-1/2" cards were perforated for easy detachment from the 13" x 7" booklets. Cards feature black-and-white player photos against a gold border. A blue, green and gold Brewers 25th anniversary logo is in the upper-left corner on

front. Half of the cards (Series I, II) have a Lite beer logo at top, while half (Series III, IV) have a Miller Genuine Draft logo. Backs are in black-and-white and include a few biographical bits, a line of career stats, the years played with the Brewers and team and brewery logos. Books I and II were issued as planned to adults attending the April 24 and June 26, 1994 games. The Series IV book, containing 10 special cards honoring the Brewers 25th Anniversary Team, was given away at a June 1995 game and Book III was distributed in August of 1995. Individual cards are unnumbered and are presented here in alphabetical order within series. Cards of Bobby Clark, Tom Edens, Ken McMullen and Danny Walton, which appear in Series I or III are repeated in Series IV.

		NM/M
Complete Set, Booklets (4):		30.00
Complete Set, Singles (376):		24.00
Common Player:		.10
Series I		.10
	Complete Book:	10.00
(1)	Hank Aaron	5.00
(2)	Jim Adduci	.10
(3)	Jay Aldrich	.10
(4)	Andy Allanson	.10
(5)	Dave Baldwin	.10
(6)	Sal Bando	.10
(7)	Len Barker	.10
(8)	Kevin Bass	.10
(9)	Ken Berry	.10
(10)	George Canale	.10
(11)	Tom Candiotti	.10
(12)	Mike Capel	.10
(13)	Bobby Darwin	.10
(14)	Danny Darwin	.10
(15)	Brock Davis	.10
(16)	Dick Davis	.10
(17)	Jamie Easterley	.10
(18)	Tom Edens	.10
(19)	Marshall Edwards	.10
(20)	Cal Eldred	.10
(21)	Bob Ellis	.10
(22)	Ed Farmer	.10
(23)	Mike Felder	.10
(24)	John Felske	.10
(25)	Mike Ferraro	.10
(26)	Mike Fetters	.10
(27)	Danny Frisella	.10
(28)	Bob Galasso	.10
(29)	Jim Gantner	.10
(30)	Pedro Garcia	.10
(31)	Bob Gardner	.10
(32)	John Gelnar	.10
(33)	Moose Haas	.10
(34)	Darryl Hamilton	.10
(35)	Larry Haney	.10
(36)	Jim Hannan	.10
(37)	Bob Hansen	.10
(38)	Mike Ignasiak	.10
(39)	John Jaha	.10
(40)	Dion James	.10
(41)	Deron Johnson	.10
(42)	John Henry Johnson	.10
(43)	Tim Johnson	.10
(44)	Rickey Keeton	.10
(45)	John Kennedy	.10
(46)	Jim Kern	.10
(47)	Pete Ladd	.10
(48)	Joe Lahoud	.10
(49)	Tom Lampkin	.10
(50)	Dave LaPoint	.10
(51)	George Lauzerique	.10
(52)	Julio Machado	.10
(53)	Alex Madrid	.10
(54)	Candy Maldonado	.10
(55)	Carlos Maldonado	.10
(56)	Rick Manning	.10
(57)	Jaime Navarro	.10
(58)	Ray Newman	.10
(59)	Juan Nieves	.10
(60)	Dave Nilsson	.10
(61)	Charlie O'Brien	.10
(62)	Syd O'Brien	.10
(63)	John O'Donoghue	.10
(64)	Jim Paciorek	.10

(65)	Dave Parker	.10
(66)	Bill Parsons	.10
(67)	Marty Pattin	.10
(68)	Jamie Quirk	.10
(69)	Willie Randolph	.10
(70)	Paul Ratliff	.10
(71)	Lance Rautzhan	.10
(72)	Randy Ready	.10
(73)	Ray Sadecki	.10
(74)	Lenn Sakata	.10
(75)	Ken Sanders	.10
(76)	Ted Savage	.10
(77)	Dick Schofield	.10
(78)	Jim Tatum	.10
(79)	Chuck Taylor	.10
(80)	Tom Tellmann	.10
(81)	Frank Tepedino	.10
(82)	Sandy Valdespino	.10
(83)	Jose Valentin	.10
(84)	Greg Vaughn	.10
(85)	Carlos Velazquez	.10
(86)	Rick Waits	.10
(87)	Danny Walton	.10
(88)	Floyd Weaver	.10
(89)	Bill Wegman	.10
(90)	Floyd Wicker	.10
(91)	Al Yates	.10
(92)	Ned Yost	.10
(93)	Mike Young	.10
(94)	Robin Yount	3.00
Series II		.10
	Complete Book:	8.00
(95)	Hank Allen	.10
(96)	Felipe Alou	.25
(97)	Max Alvis	.10
(98)	Larry Anderson	.10
(99)	Rick Auerbach	.10
(100)	Don August	.10
(101)	Billy Bates	.10
(102)	Gary Beare	.10
(103)	Larry Bearnarth	.10
(104)	Andy Beene	.10
(105)	Jerry Bell	.10
(106)	Juan Bell	.10
(107)	Dwight Bernard	.10
(108)	Bernie Carbo	.10
(109)	Jose Cardenal	.10
(110)	Matias Carrillo	.10
(111)	Juan Castillo	.10
(112)	Bill Castro	.10
(113)	Rick Cerone	.10
(114)	Rob Deer	.10
(115)	Rick Dempsey	.10
(116)	Alex Diaz	.10
(117)	Dick Ellsworth	.10
(118)	Narciso Elvira	.10
(119)	Tom Filer	.10
(120)	Rollie Fingers	.75
(121)	Scott Fletcher	.10
(122)	John Flinn	.10
(123)	Rich Folkers	.10
(124)	Tony Fossas	.10
(125)	Chris George	.10
(126)	Bob L. Gibson	.10
(127)	Gus Gil	.10
(128)	Tommy Harper	.10
(129)	Vic Harris	.10
(130)	Paul Hartzell	.10
(131)	Tom Hausman	.10
(132)	Neal Heaton	.10
(133)	Mike Hegan	.10
(134)	Jack Heidemann	.10
(135)	Doug Jones	.10
(136)	Mark Kiefer	.10
(137)	Steve Kiefer	.10
(138)	Ed Kirkpatrick	.10
(139)	Joe Kmak	.10
(140)	Mark Knudson	.10
(141)	Kevin Kobel	.10
(142)	Pete Koegel	.10
(143)	Jack Lazorko	.10
(144)	Tim Leary	.10
(145)	Mark Lee	.10
(146)	Jeffrey Leonard	.10
(147)	Randy Lerch	.10
(148)	Brad Lesley	.10
(149)	Sixto Lezcano	.10
(150)	Josias Manzanillo	.10
(151)	Buck Martinez	.10
(152)	Tom Matchick	.10
(153)	Davey May	.10
(154)	Matt Maysey	.10
(155)	Bob McClure	.10
(156)	Tim McIntosh	.10
(157)	Tim Nordbrook	.10
(158)	Ben Oglivie	.10
(159)	Jim Olander	.10
(160)	Troy O'Leary	.10
(161)	Roberto Pena	.10
(162)	Jeff Peterek	.10
(163)	Ray Peters	.10
(164)	Rob Picciolo	.10
(165)	John Poff	.10
(166)	Gus Polidor	.10
(167)	Dan Plesac	.10
(168)	Kevin Reimer	.10
(169)	Andy Replogle	.10
(170)	Jerry Reuss	.10
(171)	Archie Reynolds	.10
(172)	Bob Reynolds	.10
(173)	Ken Reynolds	.10
(174)	Tommie Reynolds	.10
(175)	Ernest Riles	.10
(176)	Bill Schroeder	.10
(177)	George Scott	.15
(178)	Ray Searage	.10
(179)	Bob Sebra	.10
(180)	Kevin Seitzer	.10

(181)	Dick Selma	.10
(182)	Bill Sharp	.10
(183)	Ron Theobald	.10
(184)	Dan Thomas	.10
(185)	Gorman Thomas	.15
(186)	Randy Veres	.10
(187)	Bill Voss	.10
(188)	Jim Wohlford	.10
Series III		.10
	Complete Book:	8.00
(189)	Jerry Augustine	.10
(190)	James Austin	.10
(191)	Rick Austin	.10
(192)	Kurt Bevacqua	.10
(193)	Tom Bianco	.10
(194)	Dante Bichette	.10
(195)	Mike Birkbeck	.10
(196)	Dan Boitano	.10
(197)	Bobby Bolin	.10
(198)	Mark Bomback	.10
(199)	Ricky Bones	.10
(200)	Chris Bosio	.10
(201)	Thad Bosley	.10
(202)	Steve Bowling	.10
(203)	Gene Brabender	.10
(204)	Glenn Braggs	.10
(205)	Mike Caldwell	.10
(206)	Billy Champion	.10
(207)	Mark Ciardi	.10
(208)	Bobby Clark	.10
(209)	Ron Clark	.10
(210)	Mark Clear	.10
(211)	Reggie Cleveland	.10
(212)	Bryan Clutterbuck	.10
(213)	Jaime Cocanower	.10
(214)	Jim Colborn	.10
(215)	Cecil Cooper	.15
(216)	Edgar Diaz	.10
(217)	Frank DiPino	.10
(218)	Dave Engle	.10
(219)	Ray Fosse	.10
(220)	Terry Francona	.10
(221)	Tito Francona	.10
(222)	LaVel Freeman	.10
(223)	Brian Giles	.10
(224)	Bob Heise	.10
(225)	Doug Henry	.10
(226)	Mike Hershberger	.10
(227)	Teddy Higuera	.10
(228)	Sam Hinds	.10
(229)	Fred Holdsworth	.10
(230)	Darren Holmes	.10
(231)	Paul Householder	.10
(232)	Odell Jones	.10
(233)	Brad Komminsk	.10
(234)	Andy Kosco	.10
(235)	Lew Krausse	.10
(236)	Ray Krawczyk	.10
(237)	Bill Krueger	.10
(238)	Ted Kubiak	.10
(239)	Jack Lind	.10
(240)	Frank Linzy	.10
(241)	Pat Listach	.10
(242)	Graeme Lloyd	.10
(243)	Bob Locker	.10
(244)	Skip Lockwood	.10
(245)	Ken McMullen	.10
(246)	Jerry McNertney	.10
(247)	Doc Medich	.10
(248)	Bob Meyer	.10
(249)	Joey Meyer	.10
(250)	Matt Mieske	.10
(251)	Roger Miller	.10
(252)	Paul Mirabella	.10
(253)	Angel Miranda	.10
(254)	Bobby Mitchell	.10
(255)	Paul Mitchell	.10
(256)	Paul Molitor	3.00
(257)	Rafael Novoa	.10
(258)	Jesse Orosco	.10
(259)	Carlos Ponce	.10
(260)	Chuck Porter	.10
(261)	Darrell Porter	.10
(262)	Billy Jo Robidoux	.10
(263)	Ron Robinson	.10
(264)	Eduardo Rodriguez	.10
(265)	Ellie Rodriguez	.10
(266)	Rich Rollins	.10
(267)	Ed Romero	.10
(268)	Gary Sheffield	1.00
(269)	Bob Sheldon	.10
(270)	Chris Short	.10
(271)	Bob Skube	.10
(272)	Jim Slaton	.10
(273)	Bernie Smith	.10
(274)	Russ Snyder	.10
(275)	Lary Sorensen	.10
(276)	Billy Spiers	.10
(277)	Ed Sprague	.10
(278)	Dickie Thon	.10
(279)	Bill Travers	.10
(280)	Pete Vuckovich	.10
(281)	Clyde Wright	.10
(282)	Jeff Yurak	.10
Series IV		
	Complete Book:	8.00
(283)	Joe Azcue	.10
(284)	Mike Boddicker	.10
(285)	Ken Brett	.10
(286)	John Briggs	.10
(287)	Pete Broberg	.10
(288)	Greg Brock	.10
(289)	Jeff Bronkey	.10
(290)	Mark Brouhard	.10
(291)	Kevin Brown	.10
(292)	Ollie Brown	.10
(293)	Bruce Brubaker	.10
(294)	Tom Brunansky	.10

(295)	Steve Brye	.10
(296)	Bob Burda	.10
(297)	Ray Burris	.10
(298)	Jeff Cirillo	.10
(299)	Bobby Clark	.10
(300)	Bob Coluccio	.10
(301)	Wayne Comer	.10
(302)	Billy Conigliaro	.10
(303)	Cecil Cooper	
	(25th Anniversary Team)	.10
(304)	Barry Cort	.10
(305)	Chuck Crim	.10
(306)	Lafayette Currence	.10
(307)	Kiki Diaz	.10
(308)	Bill Doran	.10
(309)	Al Downing	.10
(310)	Tom Edens	.10
(311)	Andy Etchebarren	.10
(312)	Rollie Fingers (25th)	.50
(313)	Jim Gantner (25th)	.10
(314)	Greg Goossen	.10
(315)	Brian Harper	.10
(316)	Larry Hisle	.10
(317)	Steve Hovley	.10
(318)	Wilbur Howard	.10
(319)	Roy Howell	.10
(320)	Bob Humphreys	.10
(321)	Jim Hunter	.10
(322)	Dave Huppert	.10
(323)	Von Joshua	.10
(324)	Art Kusnyer	.10
(325)	Doug Loman	.10
(326)	Jim Lonborg	.10
(327)	Marcelino Lopez	.10
(328)	Willie Lozado	.10
(329)	Mike Matheny	.10
(330)	Ken McMullen	.10
(331)	Jose Mercedes	.10
(332)	Paul Molitor (25th)	1.50
(333)	Don Money	.10
(334)	Don Money (25th)	.10
(335)	Charlie Moore	.10
(336)	Donnie Moore	.10
(337)	John Morris	.10
(338)	Curt Motton	.10
(339)	Willie Mueller	.10
(340)	Tom Murphy	.10
(341)	Tony Muser	.10
(342)	Edwin Nunez	.10
(343)	Ben Oglivie (25th)	.10
(344)	Pat Osborn (Osburn)	.10
(345)	Dennis Powell	.10
(346)	Jody Reed	.10
(347)	Phil Roof	.10
(348)	Jimmy Rosario	.10
(349)	Bruce Ruffin	.10
(350)	Gary Ryerson	.10
(351)	Bob Scanlan	.10
(352)	Ted Simmons	.10
(353)	Ted Simmons (25th)	.10
(354)	Duane Singleton	.10
(355)	Steve Stanicek	.10
(356)	Fred Stanley	.10
(357)	Dave Stapleton	.10
(358)	Randy Stein	.10
(359)	Earl Stephenson	.10
(360)	Franklin Stubbs	.10
(361)	William Suero	.10
(362)	Jim Sundberg	.10
(363)	B.J. Surhoff	.10
(364)	Gary Sutherland	.10
(365)	Don Sutton	.50
(366)	Dale Sveum	.10
(367)	Gorman Thomas (25th)	.10
(368)	Wayne Twitchell	.10
(369)	Dave Valle	.10
(370)	Greg Vaughn (25th)	.10
(371)	John Vukovich	.10
(372)	Danny Walton	.10
(373)	Turner Ward	.10
(374)	Rick Wrona	.10
(375)	Jim Wynn	.10
(376)	Robin Yount (25th)	1.50

1990 Little Big Leaguers

This set was issued on a series of five nine-card perforated panels at the back of a book titled, "little BIG LEAGUERS / Amazing Boyhood Stories of Today's BasebAll-Stars." The 96 text pages of the book offer inspiring boyhood baseball tales as well as childhood and major league photos of the players. The tear-out cards measure 2-1/2" x 3-1/2" and are perforated on all

four sides. Fronts have a black-and-white childhood photo of the player, nearly all in baseball uniform. The player's name is in white in a red strip at top, with the set name at bottom. Backs have the same red strips. At center in black-and-white are biographical data and career highlights. The unnumbered cards are checklisted here alphabetically.

		NM/M
Complete Set, Book:		6.00
Complete Set (45):		6.00
Common Player:		.25
(1)	Todd Benzinger	.25
(2)	Bud Black	.25
(3)	Wade Boggs	.75
(4)	Chris Bosio	.25
(5)	George Brett	2.00
(6)	Brett Butler	.25
(7)	Jose Canseco	.65
(8)	Gary Carter	.75
(9)	Joe Carter	.25
(10)	Eric Davis	.25
(11)	Glenn Davis	.25
(12)	Storm Davis	.25
(13)	Kevin Elster	.25
(14)	Tony Fernandez	.25
(15)	John Franco	.25
(16)	Gary Gaetti	.25
(17)	Mark Gubicza	.25
(18)	Tony Gwynn	1.00
(19)	Bruce Hurst	.25
(20)	Bo Jackson	.60
(21)	Bob Kipper	.25
(22)	Ron Kittle	.25
(23)	Carney Lansford	.25
(24)	Jeffrey Leonard	.25
(25)	Mike A. Marshall	.25
(26)	Lloyd McClendon	.25
(27)	Andy McGaffigan	.25
(28)	Keith Moreland	.25
(29)	Lloyd Moseby	.25
(30)	Dale Murphy	.50
(31)	Pete O'Brien	.25
(32)	Mike Pagliarulo	.25
(33)	Tim Raines	.25
(34)	Dennis Rasmussen	.25
(35)	Harold Reynolds	.25
(36)	Billy Ripken	.25
(37)	Nolan Ryan	3.00
(38)	Steve Sax	.25
(39)	Ozzie Smith	1.00
(40)	Jim Sundberg	.25
(41)	Rick Sutcliffe	.25
(42)	Dave Valle	.25
(43)	Andy Van Slyke	.25
(44)	Glenn Wilson	.25
(45)	Todd Worrell	.25

1991 Little Big Leaguers

This set was issued on a series of five nine-card perforated panels at the back of a book titled, "little BIG LEAGUERS / Amazing Boyhood Stories of Today's BasebAll-Stars." The 96 text pages of the book offer inspiring boyhood baseball tales as well as childhood and major league photos of the players. The tear-out cards measure 2-1/2" x 3-1/2" and are perforated on all

		NM/M
(7)	Tom Brunansky	.25
(8)	Ken Caminiti	.25
(9)	Will Clark	.35
(10)	Vince Coleman	.25
(11)	David Cone	.25
(12)	Alvin Davis	.25
(13)	Andre Dawson	.50
(14)	Bill Doran	.25
(15)	Nick Esasky	.25
(16)	Dwight Gooden	.25
(17)	Tom Gordon	.25
(18)	Ken Griffey Jr.	2.50
(19)	Kevin Gross	.25
(20)	Kelly Gruber	.25
(21)	Lee Guetterman	.25
(22)	Terry Kennedy	.25
(23)	John Kruk	.25
(24)	Bill Landrum	.25
(25)	Mark Langston	.25
(26)	Barry Larkin	.25
(27)	Dave Magadan	.25
(28)	Don Mattingly	2.00
(29)	Mark McGwire	3.00
(30)	Kevin Mitchell	.25
(31)	Bob Ojeda	.25
(32)	Gregg Olson	.25
(33)	Terry Pendleton	.25
(34)	Ted Power	.25
(35)	Kirby Puckett	1.50
(36)	Terry Puhl	.25
(37)	Bret Saberhagen	.25
(38)	Chris Sabo	.25
(39)	Kevin Seitzer	.25
(40)	Don Slaught	.25
(41)	Lonnie Smith	.25
(42)	Darryl Strawberry	.25
(43)	Mickey Tettleton	.25
(44)	Bobby Thigpen	.25
(45)	Frank White	.25

2005 Los Angeles Angels Card Deck

This stadium giveaway was sponsored by ValleyCrest Companies, a golf course design firm. Cards are 2-1/4" x 3-7/16" with rounded corners. Red backs have team and sponsor's logos. Each player appears four times in the deck, with an identical portrait photo on the same value card in each suit. Two wild cards complete the boxed set.

		NM/M
Complete Set (54):		10.00
Common Player:		.25
2	Adam Kennedy	.25
3	Darin Erstad	.25
4	Kelvim Escobar	.25
5	Bengie Molina	.25
6	Orlando Cabrera	.25
7	Garret Anderson	.25
8	Steve Finley	.25
9	Bartolo Colon	.25
10	Francisco Rodriguez	.25
J	Chone Figgins	.25
Q	Rally Money (Mascot)	.25
K	Mike Scioscia	.25
A	Vladimir Guerrero	.50
WC	Mascot	
	(Brendan Donnelly)	.25
WC	Mascot	
	(Brendan Donnelly)	.25

1981-93 Louisville Slugger

		NM/M
Complete Book:		6.00
Complete Set (45):		6.00
Common Player:		.25
(1)	Jim Abbott	.25
(2)	Jesse Barfield	.25
(3)	Kevin Bass	.25
(4)	Craig Biggio	.25
(5)	Phil Bradley	.25
(6)	Jeff Brantley	.25

Hillerich & Bradsby, makers of Louisville Slugger bats and gloves, produced these cards to be attached to the company's baseball gloves. A small round hole is punched in the upper-left corner of each standard-size card to enable them to be attached to the gloves. Undamaged cards are hard to find. All cards follow the same basic design - bright blue and green borders, player name and position above the full-color photo (with autograph overprint), yellow Louisville Slugger logo across the bottom border. Beneath the logo are the words "Member Louisville Slugger Bat & Glove Advisory Staff." The card backs are blue and green and include the player name, short biography and a list of personal records and information. Cards were printed with a glossy finish through 1987, when a flat finish was adopted as production moved from Taiwan to the Philippines.

		NM/M
Common Player:		2.00
(1)	Steve Garvey/Dodgers	5.00
(2)	Graig Nettles/Yankees	4.00
(1)	Pedro Guerrero/Dodgers	2.00
(2)	Fred Lynn/Angels	2.00
(1)	Ray Knight/Astros	5.00
(1)	Ray Knight/Mets	2.25
(3)	Graig Nettles/Padres	3.25
(1)	Steve Garvey/Padres	3.25
(2)	Gary Matthews/Cubs	2.00
(2)	Orel Hershiser/Dodgers	2.00
(2)	Rick Rhoden/Pirates	2.00
(1)	Eric Davis/Reds	2.00
(1)	Eric Davis/Reds	2.00
(2)	Steve Garvey/Padres	4.00
(4)	Orel Hershiser/Dodgers	2.00
(1)	Mike Pagliarulo/Yankees	2.00
(1)	Orel Hershiser/Dodgers	2.00
(1)	Orel Hershiser/Dodgers	2.00
(3)	Andy Van Slyke/Pirates	2.00
(3)	Lou Whitaker/Tigers	3.00
(1)	Wade Boggs/Red Sox	5.00
(1)	Eric Davis/Dodgers	2.00
(2)	Jack McDowell/	
	White Sox	2.00

1990s Louisville Slugger TPX Advisory Staff

This series of cards issued sometime, or over a period of time, in the 1990s depicts members of Hillerich & Bradsby's Pro Advisory Staff for its TPX line-up of baseball equipment. Cards are in standard 2-1/2" x 3-1/2" format with game-action or posed color photos and a facsimile autograph on front. Backs picture a bat, glove and bat bag.

		NM/M
Common Player:		3.00
(1)	Brett Butler/Dodgers	3.00
(2)	Bobby Jones/Mets	3.00
(3)	Reggie Sanders/Reds	3.00
(4)	Todd Stottlemyre/	
	Cardinals	3.00
(5)	Robin Ventura/White Sox	3.00

1992 Lykes Braves Team Photo Set

When Lykes Meats was awarded the Braves hot dog contract for 1992 they continued the previous years' baseball card promotions, including this early-May team photo/player card panel. Three 9-1/2" x 10-1/2" panels feature a team photo and 30 player cards. The cards have player portraits against a blue background in a tombstone shape. A blue ball at lower-left has the player's uniform number, while his name is in white in a red strip beneath the photo.

		NM/M
Complete Set (37):		12.00
Common Player:		.25
(1)	Steve Avery	.25
(2)	Jim Beauchamp	.25
(3)	Rafael Belliard	.25
(4)	Juan Berenguer	.25
(5)	Damon Berryhill	.25
(6)	Mike Bielecki	.25
(7)	Jeff Blauser	.25
(8)	Sid Bream	.25
(9)	Francisco Cabrera	.25
(10)	Pat Corrales	.25
(11)	Bobby Cox	.25
(12)	Marvin Freeman	.25
(13)	Ron Gant	.40
(14)	Tom Glavine	1.50
(15)	Tommy Gregg	.25
(16)	Brian Hunter	.25
(17)	Clarence Jones	.25
(18)	David Justice	.75
(19)	Charlie Leibrandt	.25
(20)	Mark Lemke	.25
(21)	Leo Mazzone	.25
(22)	Kent Mercker	.25
(23)	Otis Nixon	.25
(24)	Greg Olson	.25
(25)	Alejandro Pena	.25
(26)	Terry Pendleton	.25
(27)	Deion Sanders	.50

Red logos of the team and hot dog vendor are at bottom. Backs are printed in red and dark blue and feature stats, player data and a facsimile autograph. These cards are much more common than the Lykes singles distributed later in the season. The checklist here is alphabetized.

		NM/M
Complete Foldout Set:		6.00
Common Player:		.15
(1)	Steve Avery	.15
(2)	Rafael Belliard	.15
(3)	Juan Berenguer	.15
(4)	Damon Berryhill	.15
(5)	Mike Bielecki	.15
(6)	Jeff Blauser	.15
(7)	Sid Bream	.15
(8)	Francisco Cabrera	.15
(9)	Bobby Cox	.15
(10)	Nick Esasky	.15
(11)	Marvin Freeman	.15
(12)	Ron Gant	.15
(13)	Tom Glavine	1.00
(14)	Tommy Gregg	.15
(15)	Brian Hunter	.15
(16)	David Justice	.25
(17)	Charlie Leibrandt	.15
(18)	Mark Lemke	.15
(19)	Kent Mercker	.15
(20)	Otis Nixon	.15
(21)	Greg Olson	.15
(22)	Alejandro Pena	.15
(23)	Terry Pendleton	.15
(24)	Deion Sanders	.25
(25)	Lonnie Smith	.15
(26)	John Smoltz	1.00
(27)	Mike Stanton	.15
(28)	Jeff Treadway	.15
(29)	Jerry Willard	.15
(30)	Mark Wohlers	.15
(31)	Team Photo	.50

1992 Lykes Braves

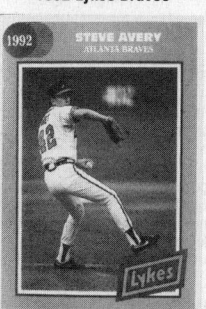

Though Braves players no longer appeared at an autograph booth or card giveaway days in 1992, the team's hot dog vendor continued to offer small groups of cards to kids attending Tuesday home games. This distribution makes assembling complete sets very challenging. In standard 2-1/2" x 3-1/2" size, the cards have a player photo border in, successively, white, dark blue, red and white. A red-and-blue Lykes logo is at lower-right. Above is a blue ball with the year of issue, and the team and player name printed in white. Backs are in black with the player's uniform number, full minor and major league stats, and biographical vitae.

(28)	Lonnie Smith	.25
(29)	John Smoltz	1.50
(30)	Mike Stanton	.25
(31)	Jeff Treadway	.25
(32)	Jerry Willard	.25
(33)	Jimy Williams	.25
(34)	Mark Wohlers	.25
(35)	Ned Yost	.25
(36)	Homer the Brave (Mascot)	.25
(37)	Rally (Mascot)	.25

1993 Lykes Braves

Each Tuesday home game during the 1993 season, three player cards were distributed to youngsters, sponsored by the team's hot dog vendor. This style of distribution makes collecting a complete 38-card set very challenging. Standard 2-1/2" x 3-1/2" size cards have a player portrait photo against a blue background. The card's front border is a darker blue separated from the photo by a yellow stripe. Red-white-and-blue team and vendor logos appear at the corners and the player's name and position are in white at lower-left. Backs are printed in black with complete career stats, biographical data and sponsors' logos. The unnumbered cards are checklisted here alphabetically. The final Tuesday's handouts, Lopez, McGriff and Tarasco have slightly different back printing and are somewhat scarcer than other cards.

		NM/M
Complete Set (38):		20.00
Common Player:		.50
(1)	Steve Avery	.50
(2)	Jim Beauchamp	.50
(3)	Steve Bedrosian	.50
(4)	Rafael Belliard	.50
(5)	Damon Berryhill	.50
(6)	Jeff Blauser	.50
(7)	Sid Bream	.50
(8)	Francisco Cabrera	.50
(9)	Pat Corrales	.50
(10)	Bobby Cox	.50
(11)	Marvin Freeman	.50
(12)	Ron Gant	.50
(13)	Tom Glavine	1.50
(14)	Jay Howell	.50
(15)	Brian Hunter	.50
(16)	Clarence Jones	.50
(17)	David Justice	.60
(18)	Mark Lemke	.50
(19)	Javier Lopez	1.00
(20)	Greg Maddux	2.50
(21)	Leo Mazzone	.50
(22)	Fred McGriff	1.00
(23)	Greg McMichael	.50
(24)	Kent Mercker	.50
(25)	Otis Nixon	.50
(26)	Greg Olson	.50
(27)	Bill Pecota	.50
(28)	Terry Pendleton	.50
(29)	Deion Sanders	1.00
(30)	Pete Smith	.50
(31)	John Smoltz	1.50
(32)	Mike Stanton	.50
(33)	Tony Tarasco	1.00
(34)	Jimy Williams	.50
(35)	Mark Wohlers	.50
(36)	Ned Yost	.50
(37)	Homer the Brave (Mascot)	.50
(38)	Rally (Mascot)	.50

Team Photo Set

The Atlanta Braves offered a perforated, uncut sheet team set in 1992 that was handed out in an early season game. The set, sponsored by Lykes, includes 30 cards and a team photo and carries the player's name and uniform number on the front of the card along with the Braves and Lykes logos. The backs contain the player's biography, career statistics and a facsimile autograph. The first card of Fred

McGriff as a Brave appears in this promotional set issued later in the season than in previous years. The 30 individual player cards also include Ryan Klesko, who was not in the single-card season-long giveaways. Three 9-1/2" x 10-1/2" panels comprise this issue, with each of the player cards perforated at the edges. Also for the first time in 1992, the same photos were used for the team sheet and single card promotions. Single cards measure 2-1/4" x 3-1/2" and are checklisted alphabetically here.

		NM/M
Complete Foldout Set:		5.00
Common Player:		.15
(1)	Steve Avery	.15
(2)	Steve Bedrosian	.15
(3)	Rafael Belliard	.15
(4)	Damon Berryhill	.15
(5)	Jeff Blauser	.15
(6)	Sid Bream	.15
(7)	Francisco Cabrera	.15
(8)	Bobby Cox	.15
(9)	Marvin Freeman	.15
(10)	Ron Gant	.15
(11)	Tom Glavine	1.00
(12)	Jay Howell	.15
(13)	Brian Hunter	.15
(14)	David Justice	.25
(15)	Ryan Klesko	.15
(16)	Mark Lemke	.15
(17)	Greg Maddux	2.00
(18)	Fred McGriff	.25
(19)	Greg McMichael	.15
(20)	Kent Mercker	.15
(21)	Otis Nixon	.15
(22)	Greg Olson	.15
(23)	Bill Pecota	.15
(24)	Terry Pendleton	.25
(25)	Deion Sanders	.25
(26)	Pete Smith	.15
(27)	John Smoltz	1.00
(28)	Mike Stanton	.15
(29)	Tony Tarasco	.15
(30)	Mark Wohlers	.15
(31)	Team Photo	.50

1994 Lykes Braves

While 34 cards were printed, only 27 were publicly released prior to the beginning of the 1994 baseball strike. Sponsored by the Braves' stadium hot dog concessionaire, the cards were given away at the rate of three per Tuesday home game. Because of the strike, the cards of Cox, Hill, Chipper Jones, Mike Kelly, Klesko, McGriff and Sanders were not officially released and are scarcer than the other 27. Card fronts feature a chest-to-cap player portrait photo set agaonst a blue background with an orange border and vertical blue stripe at right bearing the player's name. Backs are printed in black-and-white and have full major and minor league stats along with a few biographical details. There is no card or uniform number on the cards. They are presented here alphabetically.

		NM/M
Complete Set (34):		40.00
Common Player:		.25
(1)	Steve Avery	.25
(2)	Jim Beauchamp	.25
(3)	Steve Bedrosian	.25
(4)	Rafael Belliard	.25
(5)	Mike Bielecki	.25
(6)	Jeff Blauser	.25
(7)	Pat Corrales	.25
(8)	Bobby Cox	2.00
(9)	Dave Gallagher	.25
(10)	Tom Glavine	1.50
(11)	Milt Hill	2.00
(12)	Chipper Jones	10.00
(13)	Clarence Jones	.25
(14)	David Justice	.50
(15)	Mike Kelly	2.00

(16)	Ryan Klesko	6.00
(17)	Mark Lemke	.25
(18)	Javy Lopez	.25
(19)	Greg Maddux	3.00
(20)	Leo Mazzone	.25
(21)	Greg McMichael	.25
(22)	Fred McGriff	6.00
(23)	Kent Mercker	.25
(24)	Charlie O'Brien	.25
(25)	Gregg Olson	.25
(26)	Bill Pecota	.25
(27)	Terry Pendleton	.25
(28)	Deion Sanders	6.00
(29)	John Smoltz	1.50
(30)	Mike Stanton	.25
(31)	Tony Tarasco	.25
(32)	Jimy Williams	.25
(33)	Mark Wohlers	.25
(34)	Ned Yost	.25

1994 Lykes Braves Team Photo Set

Few of these team photo/player card sets have found their way into the hobby because they were intended for distribution at the August 14 Sunday home game which fell after the beginning of the 1994 baseball strike. As in past years, the set was produced as a fold-out containing a team photo and 35 player cards. Unlike previous editions, however, the player cards are identical in format to the single cards given away during the season, except that they are printed in red and blue on the back and are slightly smaller, at 2-1/8" x 3-1/8". The cards are checklisted here alphabeitcally.

		NM/M
Complete Foldout Set:		17.50
Common Player:		.25
(1)	Steve Avery	.25
(2)	Jim Beauchamp	.25
(3)	Steve Bedrosian	.25
(4)	Rafael Belliard	.25
(5)	Mike Bielecki	.25
(6)	Jeff Blauser	.25
(7)	Pat Corrales	.25
(8)	Bobby Cox	.25
(9)	Dave Gallagher	.25
(10)	Tom Glavine	1.50
(11)	Chipper Jones	3.50
(12)	Clarence Jones	.25
(13)	David Justice	.50
(14)	Mike Kelly	.25
(15)	Roberto Kelly	.25
(16)	Ryan Klesko	.25
(17)	Mark Lemke	.25
(18)	Javy Lopez	.25
(19)	Greg Maddux	3.50
(20)	Leo Mazzone	.25
(21)	Greg McMichael	.25
(22)	Fred McGriff	.25
(23)	Kent Mercker	.25
(24)	Mike Mordecai	.25
(25)	Charlie O'Brien	.25
(26)	Jose Oliva	.25
(27)	Gregg Olson	.25
(28)	Bill Pecota	.25
(29)	Terry Pendleton	.25
(30)	John Smoltz	1.50
(31)	Mike Stanton	.25
(32)	Tony Tarasco	.25
(33)	Jimy Williams	.25
(34)	Mark Wohlers	.25
(35)	Ned Yost	.25
(36)	Team Photo	.50

1995 Lykes Braves

For the only time since Atlanta's hot dog concessionaires began issuing cards in 1989, the team honored past, as well as current players, as part of its 30th anniversary celebration. The cards were distributed at Tuesday home games, usually three at a time, making assembly of a complete set difficult. Thus, this checklist may or may not be complete. Fronts have game-action photos with a black

strip at bottom bearing the player name. A 30th anniversary logo is at top, the sponsor's logo appears over a baseball in a lower corner. Black-and-white backs have player personal data and career record.

		NM/M
Complete Set (30):		10.00
Common Player:		.25
(1)	Hank Aaron	2.50
(2)	Steve Avery	.25
(3)	Steve Bedrosian	.25
(4)	Jeff Blauser	.25
(5)	Sid Bream	.25
(6)	Francisco Cabrera	.25
(7)	Chris Chambliss	.25
(8)	Bobby Cox	.25
(9)	Ron Gant	.25
(10)	Tom Glavine	1.50
(11)	Marquis Grissom	.25
(12)	Bob Horner	.25
(13)	Glenn Hubbard	.25
(14)	Chipper Jones	2.00
(15)	David Justice	.25
(16)	Ryan Klesko	.25
(17)	Mark Lemke	.25
(18)	Javy Lopez	.25
(19)	Greg Maddux	2.00
(20)	Fred McGriff	.25
(21)	Kent Mercker	.25
(22)	Dale Murphy	1.50
(23)	Phil Niekro	.40
(24)	Otis Nixon	.25
(25)	Charlie O'Brien	.25
(26)	Greg Olson	.25
(27)	Pascual Perez	.25
(28)	Lonnie Smith	.25
(29)	John Smoltz	1.50
(30)	Mark Wohlers	.25

Team Photo Set

Once again this promotional giveaway by the team's hot dog concessionaire took the form of a three-panel cardboard poster. Overall 10-3/4" x 28", the foldout features a color team photo at top and 30 individual player portrait cards below. Each card is 2-1/8" x 3-1/8" and perforated for separation. Backs are printed in red, white and blue with a few stats and vital data, along with team and sponsor logos. The unnumbered cards are checklisted here alphabetically.

		NM/M
Complete Foldout Set:		8.00
Common Player:		.10
(1)	Steve Avery	.10
(2)	Jim Beauchamp	.10
(3)	Rafael Belliard	.10
(4)	Jeff Blauser	.10
(5)	Pedro Borbon	.10
(6)	Brad Clontz	.10
(7)	Pat Corrales	.10
(8)	Bobby Cox	.10
(9)	Tom Glavine	.75
(10)	Marquis Grissom	.10
(11)	Chipper Jones	2.00
(12)	Clarence Jones	.25
(13)	David Justice	.25
(14)	Mike Kelly	.10
(15)	Ryan Klesko	.25
(16)	Mark Lemke	.10

(17)	Javier Lopez	.10
(18)	Greg Maddux	1.50
(19)	Leo Mazzone	.10
(20)	Fred McGriff	.10
(21)	Greg McMichael	.10
(22)	Kent Mercker	.10
(23)	Mike Mordecai	.10
(24)	Charlie O'Brien	.10
(25)	Jason Schmidt	.10
(26)	Dwight Smith	.10
(27)	John Smoltz	.75
(28)	Jimy Williams	.10
(29)	Mark Wohlers	.10
(30)	Ned Yost	.10
(31)	Team Photo	.25

1996 Lykes Braves Team Photo Set

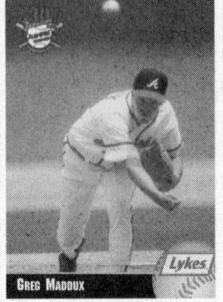

The Braves offered a perforated, four-panel 10-3/4" x 31-1/4" uncut sheet team set in 1996 that was handed out to children 12 and under at an early season game. The set was sponsored by Lykes, the team's hot dog concessionaire. There are 35 individual player and staff portrait cards in 2-1/8" x 3-1/8" format, and a 10-3/4" x 9-1/2" team photo panel. Each card carries the player's name, position and uniform number on the front, along with the Lykes logo. Black, white and blue backs contain biographical data, 1995 and career major and minor league statistics and team and sponsor logos. The cards are checklisted alphabetically here.

		NM/M
Complete Foldout Set:		8.00
Common Player:		.10
(1)	Steve Avery	.10
(2)	Danny Bautista	.10
(3)	Jim Beauchamp	.10
(4)	Rafael Belliard	.10
(5)	Mike Bielecki	.10
(6)	Jeff Blauser	.10
(7)	Pedro Borbon	.10
(8)	Brad Clontz	.10
(9)	Pat Corrales	.10
(10)	Bobby Cox	.10
(11)	Jermaine Dye	.10
(12)	Frank Fultz	.10
(13)	Tom Glavine	1.25
(14)	Marquis Grissom	.10
(15)	Chipper Jones	3.00
(16)	Clarence Jones	.10
(17)	David Justice	.25
(18)	Ryan Klesko	.10
(19)	Mark Lemke	.10
(20)	Javy Lopez	.10
(21)	Greg Maddux	2.50
(22)	Leo Mazzone	.10
(23)	Fred McGriff	.10
(24)	Greg McMichael	.10
(25)	Mike Mordecai	.10
(26)	Eddie Perez	.10
(27)	Jason Schmidt	.10
(28)	Dwight Smith	.10
(29)	John Smoltz	1.25
(30)	Terrell Wade	.10
(31)	Jerome Walton	.10
(32)	Mark Whiten	.10
(33)	Jimy Williams	.10
(34)	Mark Wohlers	.10
(35)	Ned Yost	.10
(36)	Team Photo	.50

M

1987 M & M's

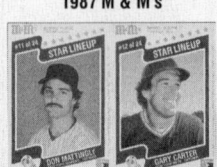

The M&M's "Star Lineup" set consists of 12 two-card panels inserted in specially marked packages of large M&M's candy. The two-card panels measure 5" x 3-1/2" with individual cards measuring 2-1/2" x 3-1/2" in size. The full-color photos are enclosed by a wavy blue frame and a white border. Card backs are printed in red ink on white stock and carry the player's career statistics and highlights. All team insignias have been airbrushed away. The set was designed and produced by Mike Schechter and Associates.

		NM/M
Complete Panel Set (12):		5.00
Complete Singles Set (24):		4.00
Common Panel:		1.00
Common Single Player:		.10
PANEL 1		
1	Wally Joyner	.25
2	Tony Pena	.10
PANEL 2		
3	Mike Schmidt	1.25
4	Ryne Sandberg	.50
PANEL 3		.40
5	Wade Boggs	.65
6	Jack Morris	.40
PANEL 4		.10
7	Roger Clemens	.65
8	Harold Baines	.45
PANEL 5		.10
9	Dale Murphy	.60
10	Jose Canseco	.25
PANEL 6		.20
11	Don Mattingly	.75
12	Gary Carter	.45
PANEL 7		.35
13	Cal Ripken Jr.	2.00
14	George Brett	1.00
PANEL 8		.50
15	Kirby Puckett	.65
16	Joe Carter	.40
PANEL 9		.10
17	Mike Witt	.25
18	Mike Scott	.10
PANEL 10		.10
19	Fernando Valenzuela	.45
20	Steve Garvey	.15
PANEL 11		.15
21	Steve Sax	1.50
22	Nolan Ryan	.10
PANEL 12		1.00
23	Tony Gwynn	1.25
24	Ozzie Smith	.40
		.40

2005 Major League Baseball Superstars Medallions

Coupons in USA Today between July 11 and August 19 allowed to collectors to purchase these medallions on a one-per-day basis for $2.99 at 7-Eleven, Super-America and Speedway convenience stores.

		NM/M
Complete Set (30):		100.00
Common Player:		3.00
(1)	Roger Clemens	6.00
(2)	Ichiro Suzuki	7.50
(3)	Derek Jeter	8.00
(4)	Curt Schilling	3.00
(5)	Albert Pujols	8.00
(6)	Randy Johnson	3.00
(7)	Ivan Rodriguez	3.00
(8)	Eric Gagne	3.00
(9)	Kerry Wood	3.00
(10)	Ben Sheets	3.00
(11)	John Smoltz	3.00
(12)	Vladimir Guerrero	3.00
(13)	Torii Hunter	3.00
(14)	David Ortiz	3.00
(15)	Carlos Delgado	3.00
(16)	Scott Rolen	3.00
(17)	Jason Schmidt	3.00
(18)	Sammy Sosa	3.00
(19)	Carlos Beltran	3.00
(20)	Luis Gonzalez	3.00
(21)	Ken Griffey Jr.	4.50
(22)	Todd Helton	3.00
(23)	Alfonso Soriano	3.00
(24)	Pedro Martinez	3.00
(25)	Jim Thome	3.00
(26)	Manny Ramirez	3.00
(27)	Johan Santana	3.00
(28)	Eric Chavez	3.00

(29)	Mark Prior	3.00
(30)	Alex Rodriguez	7.50

1997-2002 Major League Dad

To promote responsible fatherhood the California Department of Child Support Services issued a series of cards picturing big league players and their children. Issued in a variety of designs, all have the phrase "Major League Dad" on front.

		NM/M
Complete Set (10):		20.00
Common Player:		2.00
(1)	Garret Anderson/2000	2.00
(2)	Marvin Benard/2000	2.00
(3)	Mike Fetters/1998	2.00
(4)	Mark Gardner/1998	2.00
(5)	Wally Joyner	2.00
(6)	Chad Kreuter	2.00
(7)	Tim Salmon	2.00
(8)	Jeff Shaw/2000	2.00
(9)	Matt Stairs/2000	2.00
(10)	Greg Vaughn/1998	2.00

1988 Mickey Mantle's Restaurant

To promote the grand opening of Mickey Mantle's restaurant in New York City, this promotional card was issued by an Oklahoma public relations firm to members of the media. In round-cornered 2-1/2" x 3-1/2" format on thin, semi-gloss cardboard, the front has a posed color photo of Mantle. The back has details of the restaurant opening and a design reminiscent of the Yankee Stadium facade, printed in white on a dark blue background.

	NM/M
Mickey Mantle	7.50

1989 Marathon Cubs

This colorful 25-card Cubs team set was sponsored by Marathon and was distributed as a stadium promotion to fans attending the Aug. 10, 1989, game at Chicago's Wrigley Field. The oversize (2-3/4" x 4-1/4") feature an action photo inside a diagonal box on the card front, with the Chicago Cubs logo at the top and the player's uniform number, name and position along the bottom. The backs include a small black-and-white photo, player data and the Cubs and Marathon logos.

		NM/M
Complete Set (25):		12.00
Common Player:		.50
2	Vance Law	.50
4	Don Zimmer	.50
7	Joe Girardi	.50
8	Andre Dawson	2.50
9	Damon Berryhill	.50
10	Lloyd McClendon	.50
12	Shawon Dunston	.50
15	Domingo Ramos	.50
17	Mark Grace	.75
18	Dwight Smith	.50
19	Curt Wilkerson	.50
20	Jerome Walton	.50
21	Scott Sanderson	.50
23	Ryne Sandberg	6.50
28	Mitch Williams	.50
31	Greg Maddux	6.00
32	Calvin Schiraldi	.50
33	Mitch Webster	.50
36	Mike Bielecki	.50
39	Paul Kilgus	.50
40	Rick Sutcliffe	.50
41	Jeff Pico	.50
44	Steve Wilson	.50
50	Les Lancaster	.50
---	Coaches (Joe Altobelli, Chuck Cottier, Larry Cox, Jose Martinez, Dick Pole)	.50

1989 Marathon Tigers

(39) MIKE HENNEMAN—P

Marathon sponsored this giveaway set for a 1989 Tigers home game. The oversized cards feature thin white stock and full-color player photos. The cards are numbered according to uniform number.

		NM/M
Complete Set (28):		9.00
Common Player:		.50
1	Lou Whitaker	.75
3	Alan Trammell	1.00
8	Mike Heath	.50
9	Fred Lynn	.50
10	Keith Moreland	.50
11	Sparky Anderson	.75
12	Mike Brumley	.50
14	Dave Bergman	.50
15	Pat Sheridan	.50
17	Al Pedrique	.50
18	Ramon Pena	.50
19	Doyle Alexander	.50
21	Guillermo Hernandez	.50
23	Torey Lovullo	.50
24	Gary Pettis	.50
25	Ken Williams	.50
26	Frank Tanana	.50
27	Charles Hudson	.50
32	Gary Ward	.50
33	Matt Nokes	.50
34	Chet Lemon	.50
35	Rick Schu	.50
36	Frank Williams	.50
39	Mike Henneman	.50
44	Jeff Robinson	.50
47	Jack Morris	.50
48	Paul Gibson	.50
---	Coaches (Billy Consolo, Alex Grammas, Billy Muffett, Vada Pinson, Dick Tracewksi)	.50

1990 Marathon Cubs

Marathon sponsored its second consecutive Chicago Cubs team set. The oversized cards feature thin white stock and full-color photos. The cards are numbered according to uniform number, and were distributed at a Cubs home game.

		NM/M
Complete Set (28):		6.00
Common Player:		.25
4	Don Zimmer	.35
7	Joe Girardi	.25
8	Andre Dawson	1.50

10	Lloyd McClendon	.25
11	Luis Salazar	.25
12	Shawon Dunston	.25
15	Domingo Ramos	.25
17	Mark Grace	.35
18	Dwight Smith	.25
19	Curtis Wilkerson	.25
20	Jerome Walton	.25
22	Mike Harkey	.25
23	Ryne Sandberg	4.50
25	Marvell Wynne	.25
28	Mitch Williams	.25
30	Doug Dascenzo	.25
30	Dave Clark	.25
31	Greg Maddux	4.00
32	Hector Villanueva	.25
36	Mike Bielecki	.25
37	Bill Long	.25
40	Rick Sutcliffe	.25
41	Jeff Pico	.25
44	Steve Wilson	.25
45	Paul Assenmacher	.25
47	Shawn Boskie	.25
50	Les Lancaster	.25
---	Coaches (Joe Altobelli, Chuck Cottier, Jose Martinez, Dick Pole, Phil Roof)	.25

1991 Marathon Cubs

GREG MADDUX
PITCHER

Marathon Oil once again sponsored a set featuring the Chicago Cubs. This 28-card release features oversized cards measuring 2-7/8" x 4-1/4". The card fronts feature full-color action photos. The flip sides feature complete statistics. The cards are numbered according to uniform number. This number appears on both the front and back of the card.

		NM/M
Complete Set (28):		12.50
Common Player:		.50
7	Joe Girardi	.50
8	Andre Dawson	2.50
9	Damon Berryhill	.50
10	Luis Salazar	.50
11	George Bell	.50
12	Shawon Dunston	.50
16	Jose Vizcaino	.50
17	Mark Grace	.65
18	Dwight Smith	.50
19	Hector Villanueva	.50
20	Jerome Walton	.50
22	Mike Harkey	.50
23	Ryne Sandberg	6.50
24	Chico Walker	.50
29	Doug Dascenzo	.50
30	Bob Scanlan	.50
31	Greg Maddux	6.00
32	Danny Jackson	.50
35	Chuck McElroy	.50
36	Mike Bielecki	.50
40	Rick Sutcliffe	.50
41	Jim Essian	.50
42	Dave Smith	.50
45	Paul Assenmacher	.50
47	Shawn Boskie	.50
50	Les Lancaster	.50
51	Heathcliff Slocumb	.50
---	Coaches (Joe Altobelli, Billy Connors, Chuck Cottier, Jose Martinez, Phil Roof, Richie Zisk)	.50

1992 Marathon Cubs

SAMMY SOSA

The fourth consecutive year of a Cubs team set sponsored by Marathon Oil consists of 28 cards, including manager Jim Lefebvre and his coaching staff. The set was originally given away at the July 10, 1993 game at Wrigley Field. Cards are checklisted here by uniform number.

		NM/M
Complete Set (28):		9.00
Common Player:		.25
1	Doug Strange	.30
2	Frank Castillo	.30
5	Jim Lefebvre	.30
6	Rey Sanchez	.30
7	Joe Girardi	.30
8	Andre Dawson	.75
10	Luis Salazar	.30
12	Shawon Dunston	.30
16	Jose Vazcaino	.30
17	Mark Grace	.45
18	Dwight Smith	.30
19	Hector Villanueva	.30
20	Jerome Walton	.30
21	Sammy Sosa	3.50
23	Ryne Sandberg	3.50
27	Derrick May	.30
29	Doug Dascenzo	.30
30	Bob Scanlan	.30
31	Greg Maddux	3.00
32	Danny Jackson	.30
34	Ken Patterson	.30
35	Chuck McElroy	.30
36	Mike Morgan	.30
38	Jeff Robinson	.30
42	Dave Smith	.30
45	Paul Assenmacher	.30
47	Shawn Boskie	.30
---	Coaches (Tom Treblehorn, Jose Martinez, Billy Williams, Sammy Ellis, Chuck Cottier, Billy Connors)	.30

1993 Marathon Cubs

ASSENMACHER

The Cubs distributed the 1993 Marathon Oil set on July 28 in a game against the Padres. The cards, measuring an oversized 4-1/4" x 2-7/8", are unnumbered, with uniform numbers appearing on the back. The cards have a vertical blue stripe down the right side with the player's last name in large, white letters. Backs carry complete major and minor league statistics. There are 27 cards in the set. The checklist is presented here by uniform number.

		NM/M
Complete Set (27):		7.50
Common Player:		.25
2	Rick Wilkins	.25
5	Jim Lefebvre	.25
6	Willie Wilson	.25
10	Steve Lake	.25
11	Rey Sanchez	.25
16	Jose Vizcaino	.25
17	Mark Grace	.35
18	Dwight Smith	.25
19	Eric Yelding	.25
21	Sammy Sosa	3.50

22	Mike Harkey	.25
23	Ryne Sandberg	3.50
24	Steve Buechele	.25
25	Candy Maldonado	.25
27	Derrick May	.25
28	Randy Myers	.25
29	Jose Guzman	.25
30	Bob Scanlan	.25
32	Dan Plesac	.25
36	Mike Morgan	.25
37	Greg Hibbard	.25
38	Jose Bautista	.25
45	Paul Assenmacher	.25
49	Frank Castillo	.25
53	Doug Jennings	.25
---	Coaches (Billy Williams, Jose Martinez, Billy Connors, Tony Muser)	.25
---	Coaches (Dan Simonds, Tom Treblehorn, Chuck Cottier)	.25

2004 Maryland Lottery Golden Ticket Baltimore Orioles

DON BAYLOR

In conjunction with the 50th anniversary of the Baltimore Orioles, the Maryland Lottery issued a set of baseball cards depicting great moments and players from the past. They were issued in a four-card foil pack with the purchase of a $10 Golden Ticket scratch-off card. Cards #1-45 were reported issued in quantities of 50,000 to 100,000 each. The team highlight cards, #45-48 were issued in an edition of 25,000 each. Fifteen thousand of the Ripken Ironman card #49 were produced. Card #50, Babe Ruth (shown on a 1914 Orioles minor league baseball card), was produced in an edition of 10,000. The first 100 persons turning in a complete set won $1,000 and an Orioles prize package. Cards are in the standard 2-1/2" x 3-1/2" format, printed on thin cardboard UV-coated on both sides.

		NM/M
Complete Set (50):		40.00
Common Player:		.50
1	Luis Aparicio	.75
2	Steve Barber	.50
3	Don Baylor	.50
4	Mark Belanger	.50
5	Mike Boddicker	.50
6	Don Buford	.50
7	Al Bumbry	.50
8	Mike Cuellar	.50
9	Rich Dauer	.50
10	Storm Davis	.50
11	Doug DeCinces	.50
12	Pat Dobson	.50
13	Moe Drabowsky	.50
14	Andy Etchebarren	.50
15	Bobby Grich	.50
16	George Kell	.50
17	Tito Landrum	.50
18	Lee MacPhail	.50
19	Tippy Martinez	.50
20	Scott McGregor	.50
21	Dave McNally	.50
22	Milt Pappas	.50
23	Paul Richards	.50
24	Gary Roenicke	.50
25	Dave Schmidt	.50
26	Steve Stone	.50
27	Gus Triandos	.50
28	Gene Woodling	.50
29	Terry Crowley	.50
31	Elrod Hendricks	.50
33	Memorial Stadium	.50
32	Orioles Park	.50
33	Rex Barney	.50
34	Rick Dempsey	.50
35	Mike Flanagan	.50
36	Jim Gentile	.50
37	Reggie Jackson	2.00
38	Frank Robinson	2.00
39	Chuck Thompson	.50
40	Earl Weaver	.50
41	Opening Day 1954	.50

22	Mike Harkey	.25
23	Ryne Sandberg	3.50
24	Steve Buechele	.25
25	Candy Maldonado	.25
27	Derrick May	.25
28	Randy Myers	.25
29	Jose Guzman	.25
30	Bob Scanlan	.25
32	Dan Plesac	.25
36	Mike Morgan	.25
37	Greg Hibbard	.25
38	Jose Bautista	.25
45	Paul Assenmacher	.25
49	Frank Castillo	.25
53	Doug Jennings	.25

42	Brady Anderson	.50
43	Boog Powell	.65
44	Brooks Robinson	2.00
45	Jim Palmer	1.50
46	1966 World Series	7.50
47	1970 World Series	7.50
48	1983 World Series	7.50
49	2131 Ironman Breaks Record	7.50
50	Babe Ruth	15.00
---	Checklist/Rules	.10

1988 Master Bread Twins

KENT HRBEK
MINNESOTA TWINS

This set of 12 cardboard discs (2-3/4" diameter) features full-color photos of Minnesota Twins team members. Fronts have a bright blue background with red, yellow and black printing. The player photo (with team logos airbrushed off) is centered beneath a "Master Is Good Bread" headliner and a vivid yellow player/team name banner. Backs are black-and-white with five stars printed above the player's name, team, personal data, disc number, stats and "1988 Collector's Edition" banner. The discs were printed in Canada and marketed exclusively in Minnesota in packages of Master Bread, one disc per loaf. Squares cut from sheets are known in the hobby, valued about 50 percent of the issued version.

		NM/M
Complete Set (12):		12.00
Common Player:		1.00
1	Bert Blyleven	1.00
3	Frank Viola	1.00
3	Juan Berenguer	1.00
4	Jeff Reardon	1.00
5	Tim Laudner	1.00
6	Steve Lombardozzi	1.00
7	Randy Bush	1.00
8	Kirby Puckett	5.00
9	Gary Gaetti	1.00
10	Kent Hrbek	1.00
11	Greg Gagne	1.00
12	Tom Brunansky	1.00

1989 Master Bread

JULIO FRANCO
CLEVELAND INDIANS

For a second year Master Bread packages in the Twin Cities area contained a baseball player disc in 1989. The 2-3/4" discs are in the familiar Mike Schechter Associates format and, unlike the '88 set, featured American League players other than Twins. The issue is among the scarcer of the MSA disc issues. Fronts are trimmed in yellow banners and blue stars. Backs are in blue and have a few stats and player data, along with a disc number.

		NM/M
Complete Set (12):		20.00
Common Player:		1.00
1	Frank Viola	1.00
2	Kirby Puckett	4.00
3	Gary Gaetti	1.00
4	Alan Trammell	1.00
5	Wade Boggs	4.00
6	Don Mattingly	5.00
7	Wally Joyner	1.00
8	Paul Molitor	3.50
9	George Brett	5.00
10	Jose Canseco	2.00
11	Julio Franco	1.00
12	Cal Ripken Jr.	7.50

1989 MasterCard Masters of the Game

CHARLES DILLON (CASEY) STENGEL
OUTFIELD
NEW YORK GIANTS

The reason for issue and method of distribution for this set is not known. The issue was in the form of a 7-1/2" x 10-1/2" sheet on thin cardboard, picturing eight Hall of Famers around a title card. If cut from the unperforated sheet, single cards measure the standard 2-1/2" x 3-1/2". Fronts have familiar black-and-white photos with a gold border. Backs are in black, white and red with a repeat of the Masters of the Game logo, a few biographical details, lifetime stats and an MLB licensee logo. The unnumbered cards are checklisted here in alphabetical order.

		NM/M
Uncut Sheet:		6.00
Complete Set (9):		6.00
Common Player:		1.00
(1)	Ty Cobb	1.50
(2)	Lou Gehrig	1.50
(3)	Rogers Hornsby	1.00
(4)	Christy Mathewson	1.00
(5)	Satchel Paige	1.00
(6)	Babe Ruth	2.00
(7)	Casey Stengel	1.00
(8)	Cy Young	1.00
(9)	Title Card	.05

1985 Thom McAn Discs

ALAN TRAMMELL
INFIELDER

One of the more obscure 1985 issues, this 47-card set of "Pro Player Discs" was issued by Thom McAn as a promotion for its "Jox" tennis shoes, which are advertised on the back of the cards. The discs, which measure 2-3/4" in diameter, feature black-and-white player photos against a background of either gold, yellow, red, pink, green or blue. Although not included in the "official" checklist released by the company, cards of George Brett have also been reported. Many of the Latin players' discs are quite scarce and are believed to have been issued in more limited quantities in Hispanic communities. The discs are unnumbered and checklisted here alphabetically.

		NM/M
Complete Set (47):		50.00
Common Player:		1.00
(1)	Benny Ayala	1.25
(2)	Buddy Bell	1.00
(3)	Juan Beniquez	1.25
(4)	Tony Bernazard	1.25
(5)	Mike Boddicker	1.00
(6)	George Brett	9.00
(7)	Bill Buckner	1.00
(8)	Rod Carew	6.00
(9)	Steve Carlton	6.00
(10)	Caesar Cedeno (Cesar)	1.00
(11)	Onix Concepcion	1.00
(12)	Cecil Cooper	1.00
(13)	Al Cowens	1.00
(14)	Jose Cruz	1.25
(15)	Ivan DeJesus	1.25
(16)	Luis DeLeon	1.25
(17)	Rich Gossage	1.25
(18)	Pedro Guerrero	1.25
(19)	Ron Guidry	1.00
(20)	Tony Gwynn	7.50

(21)	Mike Hargrove	1.00
(22)	Keith Hernandez	1.25
(23)	Bob Horner	1.00
(24)	Kent Hrbek	1.00
(25)	Rick Langford	1.00
(26)	Jeff Leonard	1.00
(27)	Willie McGee	1.00
(28)	Jack Morris	1.00
(29)	Jesse Orosco	1.25
(30)	Junior Ortiz	1.00
(31)	Terry Puhl	1.00
(32)	Dan Quisenberry	1.00
(33)	Johnny Ray	1.00
(34)	Cal Ripken	12.00
(35)	Ed Romero	1.25
(36)	Ryne Sandberg	7.50
(37)	Mike Schmidt	9.00
(38)	Tom Seaver	6.00
(39)	Rick Sutcliffe	1.00
(40)	Bruce Sutter	4.50
(41)	Alan Trammell	1.00
(42)	Fernando Valenzuela	2.00
(43)	Ozzie Virgil	1.25
(44)	Greg Walker	1.00
(45)	Willie Wilson	1.00
(46)	Dave Winfield	6.00
(47)	Geoff Zahn	1.00

1990 McDonald's

RAMON MARTINEZ

This 25-card set was released exclusively at 11 McDonald's restaurants in Idaho and eastern Oregon. Four cards were given with a large fries-soda purchase. Production was reported as 4,000 each. The cards have front borders of graduated purple shades around a game-action photo. Backs are similar in format to regular 1990 Score cards and include a portrait photo. The McDonald's logo appears on front and back. Fifteen World Series trivia cards were part of the promotion.

		NM/M
Complete Set (25):		50.00
Common Player:		1.25
Trivia Card:		.60
1	Will Clark	1.25
2	Sandy Alomar, Jr.	1.25
3	Julio Franco	1.25
4	Carlton Fisk	5.00
5	Rickey Henderson	5.00
6	Matt Williams	1.25
7	John Franco	1.25
8	Ryne Sandberg	6.00
9	Kelly Gruber	1.25
10	Andre Dawson	3.00
11	Barry Bonds	12.00
12	Gary Sheffield	3.00
13	Ramon Martinez	1.25
14	Len Dykstra	1.25
15	Benito Santiago	1.25
16	Cecil Fielder	1.25
17	John Olerud	1.25
18	Roger Clemens	7.50
19	George Brett	10.00
20	George Bell	1.25
21	Ozzie Guillen	1.25
22	Steve Sax	1.25
23	Dave Stewart	1.25
24	Ozzie Smith	6.00
25	Robin Yount	5.00

1991 McDonald's Cleveland Indians

(9) Carlos Baerga Infielder

Distributed only at northern Ohio area McDonalds, this set features the players, coaches and manager of the Indians on an oversize (2-7/8" x 4-1/4") format. Color photos on front are framed in white and red with a white border all around. In the upper-left corner is a "Tribe Kids Fan Club" logo, while the McDonald's logo appears at lower-right. The player's uniform number, name and position are in black at lower-left. Backs are printed in black and have complete major and minor league statistics.

		NM/M
Complete Set (30):		5.00
Common Player:		.25
1	John McNamara	.25
4	Alex Cole	.25
5	Joel Skinner	.25
6	Jose Escobar	.25
7	Chris James	.25
8	Albert Belle	.50
9	Carlos Baerga	.25
11	Doug Jones	.25
14	Jerry Browne	.25
15	Sandy Alomar	.25
16	Felix Fermin	.25
20	Turner Ward	.25
21	Greg Swindell	.25
23	Mitch Webster	.25
26	Brook Jacoby	.25
27	Dave Otto	.25
31	Steve Olin	.25
37	Beau Allred	.25
38	Shawn Hillegas	.25
40	Eric King	.25
41	Charles Nagy	.25
44	Mike Huff	.25
45	Jeff Manto	.25
46	Bruce Egloff	.25
47	Jesse Orosco	.25
48	Mike Walker	.25
49	Tom Candiotti	.25
52	John Farrell	.25
54	Rod Nichols	.25
---	Coaches (Billy Williams, Jose Morales, Rich Dauer, Mike Hargrove, Luis Isaac, Mark Wiley)	.25

1992 McDonald's Baseball's Best

Sold in five-card cello packs with a food purchase at McDonald's stores in New York, New Jersey and Connecticut, this 44-card set was produced by Topps and carries the Topps logo, along with the Golden Arches, on front and back. Player photos on front are framed in yellow, surrounded by a black border. A red and blue "Baseball's Best" logo appears at top-right of the photo. Above that is a gold-foil stripe announcing "Limited Edition." At lower-right is another gold-foil stripe with the McDonald's logo and the player's name embossed thereon. On cards #34-44, which were distributed one per pack, there is an additional gold embossed "Rookie" shield at upper-left. Backs have a red border with a yellow stat box at center framed in white.

		NM/M
Complete Set (44):		6.00
Common Player:		.10
1	Cecil Fielder	.10
2	Benito Santiago	.10
3	Rickey Henderson	.60
4	Roberto Alomar	.20
5	Ryne Sandberg	.75
6	George Brett	1.25
7	Terry Pendleton	.10
8	Ken Griffey Jr.	1.25
9	Bobby Bonilla	.10
10	Roger Clemens	1.00
11	Ozzie Smith	.75
12	Barry Bonds	1.50
13	Cal Ripken, Jr.	1.50
14	Ron Gant	.10
15	Carlton Fisk	.60
16	Steve Avery	.10
17	Robin Yount	.60
18	Will Clark	.10
19	Kirby Puckett	.75
20	Jim Abbott	.10
21	Barry Larkin	.10
22	Jose Canseco	.45
23	Howard Johnson	.10
24	Nolan Ryan	1.50
25	Frank Thomas	.60
27	Danny Tartabull	.10
27	Julio Franco	.10
28	David Justice	.10
29	Joe Carter	.10
30	Dale Murphy	.35
31	Andre Dawson	.25
32	Dwight Gooden	.10
33	Bo Jackson	.20
34	Jeff Bagwell	.60
35	Chuck Knoblauch	.10
36	Derek Bell	.10
37	Jim Thome	.10
38	Royce Clayton	.10
39	Ryan Klesko	.10
40	Chito Martinez	.10
41	Ivan Rodriguez	.50
42	Todd Hundley	.10
43	Eric Karros	.10
44	Todd Van Poppel	.10

Cardinals

TIM McCARVER CATCHER

Pacific Trading Cards and McDonald's combined in 1992 to produce this 55-card (plus checklist) team set for the benefit of Ronald McDonald Children's Charities on the occasion of the St. Louis Cardinals' 100th anniversary. Sets were sold initially for $1.49. Cards are standard 2-1/2" x 3-1/2" size and UV coated on each side. There is a sepia-toned or color photo on both front and back; generally an action photo on front and a portrait on back. Player selection is largely weighted to the last half of the 20th Century, with only a few cards of players pre-dating the Gashouse Gang era. The front design is completed with a Cardinals anniversary logo in the upper-left corner, a McDonald's logo at lower-right and gold stripes top and bottom. The player's name and position appear in red at the bottom of the photo. Besides the portrait photo, backs have a career summary stats for the player's Cardinals year and major league career and all appropriate logos.

		NM/M
Complete Set (55):		6.00
Common Player:		.10
1	Jim Bottomley	.15
2	Rip Collins	.10
3	Johnny Mize	.25
4	Rogers Hornsby	.25
5	Miller Huggins	.10
6	Marty Marion	.10
7	Frank Frisch	.25
8	Whitey Kurowski	.10
9	Joe Medwick	.10
10	Terry Moore	.10
11	Chick Hafey	.25
12	Pepper Martin	.10
13	Bob O'Farrell	.10
14	Walker Cooper	.10
15	Dizzy Dean	.50
16	Grover Cleveland Alexander	.25
17	Jesse Haines	.25
18	Bill Hallahan	.10
19	Mort Cooper	.10
20	Burleigh Grimes	.25
21	Red Schoendienst	.25
22	Stan Musial	3.00
23	Enos Slaughter	.25
24	Keith Hernandez	.25
25	Bill White	.25
26	Orlando Cepeda	.25
27	Julian Javier	.10
28	Dick Groat	.25
29	Ken Boyer	.20
30	Lou Brock	.50
31	Mike Shannon	.25
32	Curt Flood	.25
33	Joe Cunningham	.10
34	Reggie Smith	.10
35	Ted Simmons	.10
36	Tim McCarver	.25
37	Tom Herr	.10
38	Ozzie Smith	2.00
39	Joe Torre	.45
41	Terry Pendleton	.20
41	Ken Reitz	.10
42	Vince Coleman	.10
43	Willie McGee	.25
45	Bake McBride	.10
45	George Hendrick	.10
46	Bob Gibson	1.00
47	Whitey Herzog	.10
48	Harry Brecheen	.10
49	Howard Pollet	.10
50	John Tudor	.10
51	Bob Forsch	.10
52	Bruce Sutter	.50
53	Lee Smith	.15
54	Todd Worrell	.10
55	Al Hrabosky	.10
---	Checklist	.02

Ken Griffey, Jr. Pin/Cards

1992 Limited Edition Collector Pin #1

This set of three card-pin combinations saw limited distribution in the Northwestern U.S., with sales benefitting the Ronald McDonald Children's Charities. Cards measure 2-1/2" x 3-1/2" and have the same color photo of Ken Griffey, Jr. on the front. Fronts also have a McDonald's logo and facsimile autograph. Uniform logos have been removed from the player's photo. Backs have a description of the charity and the logo "Griffey's Golden Moments," along with a 1992 Alrak Enterprises copyright. The pins were fastened through the cardboard of the card, leaving each with a hole. Prices quoted are for card/pin combinations.

		NM/M
Complete Set (3):		7.50
Common Card/Pin:		2.50
1-3	Ken Griffey Jr.	2.50

MVP

DEVON WHITE

McDonald's restaurants in Ontario released a 26-card All-Star baseball card set in 1992 featuring many of the top players in the game. The cards were sold at Canadian McDonald's in packs of four with the purchase of a meal. Additionally, the company offered a six-card Toronto Blue Jays subset. The cards were produced by Donruss.

		NM/M
Complete Set (33):		8.00
Common Player:		.25
1	Cal Ripken, Jr.	1.50
2	Frank Thomas	.65
3	George Brett	1.00
4	Roberto Kelly	.25
5	Nolan Ryan	1.50
6	Ryne Sandberg	.75
7	Darryl Strawberry	.25
8	Len Dykstra	.25
9	Fred McGriff	.25
10	Roger Clemens	.85
11	Sandy Alomar Jr.	.25
12	Robin Yount	.65
13	Jose Canseco	.45
14	Jimmy Key	.25
16	Barry Larkin	.25
16	Dennis Martinez	.25
17	Andy Van Slyke	.25
18	Will Clark	.25
19	Mark Langston	.25
20	Cecil Fielder	.25
21	Kirby Puckett	.75
22	Ken Griffey Jr.	1.00
23	David Justice	.25
24	Jeff Bagwell	.65
25	Howard Johnson	.25
26	Ozzie Smith	.75
1	Roberto Alomar	.25
2	Joe Carter	.25
3	Kelly Gruber	.25
4	Jack Morris	.25
5	Tom Henke	.25
6	Devon White	.25

WUAB Cleveland Indians

Jack ARMSTRONG 77

These larger-than-standard (2-7/8" x 4-1/4") cards were given to members of the Tribe Kids Fan Club, sponsored by McDonald's and television station WUAB, whose logos appear on front and back, respectively. Cards have poses or game photos with red frames, white borders and a row of vertical blue diamonds on front. Horizontally formatted backs are in black-and-white with complete career stats. Cards are listed here in order of the uniform numbers which appear on front.

		NM/M
Complete Set (30):		6.00
Common Player:		.25
0	Junior Ortiz	.25
1	Glenallen Hill	.25
2	Alex Cole	.25
4	Bob Skinner	.25
6	Kenny Lofton	.40
8	Albert Belle	.35
9	Carlos Baerga	.25
10	Mark Lewis	.25
11	Paul Sorrento	.25
15	Sandy Alomar Jr.	.25
16	Felix Fermin	.25
20	Tony Perezchica	.25
21	Mike Hargrove	.25
22	Mark Whiten	.25
25	Jim Thome	2.50
26	Brook Jacoby	.25
27	Dave Otto	.25
31	Derek Lilliquist	.25
33	Steve Olin	.25
33	Thomas Howard	.25
39	Brad Arnsberg	.25
39	Dennis Cook	.25
44	Charles Nagy	.25
44	Reggie Jefferson	.25
47	Scott Scudder	.25
48	Ted Power	.25
54	Rod Nichols	.25
63	Eric Bell	.25
77	Jack Armstrong	.25
---	The Coaches (Rick Adair, Ken Bolek, Dom Chiti, Ron Clark, Jose Morales, Dave Nelson, Jeff Newman)	.25

Cy Young

This pair of cards honoring a local hero was issued by McDonald's of Tuscarawas and Coshocton Counties in Ohio. A blue border card shows Young at bat and measures about 3-1/2" x 6". A red-bordered card has a commonly seen pitching pose and is about 3-3/4" x 5-15/16". A banner in front of crossed bats on front has his birth and death dates with a pair of McDonald's logos near the bottom. Backs are identical with biographical and statistical information.

		NM/M
Complete Set (2):		5.00
(1)	Cy Young/Btg	3.00
(2)	Cy Young/Pitching	3.00

1993 McDonald's Blue Jays

JACK MORRIS

This 36-card set was produced by Donruss and distributed by McDonald's of Canada. The set features two distinct styles of cards. The first 26 are "Great Moments" cards which feature team highlights of the 1985-1992 seasons. These cards have gold-foil embossed on front with a team logo/Great Moments seal. Backs have a description of the highlight. Cards #27-35 are individual player cards. They feature full-bleed color action photos on front. Backs have a second photo and recent stats. All cards have the McDonald's and Donruss logos on front. The 36th card in the set is a header card with a checklist on back.

		NM/M
Complete Set (36):		5.00
Common Card:		.15
1	First Title/1985 (Doyle Alexander)	.15
2	Home Run King/1986 (Jesse Barfield)	.15
3	Major League Home Run Record/1987 (Fred McGriff)	.15
4	Opening Bell/1988 (George Bell)	.35
5	First Cycle/1989 (Kelly Gruber)	.15
6	Unbelievable Comeback - 1989 (Ernie Whitt)	.15
7	Winners Again/1989 (Tom Henke)	.15
8	First No-Hitter/1990 (Dave Stieb)	.15
9	First 20-Gamer (Jack Morris)	.15
10	FANtastic/1992	.15
11	Sudden Impact/1992 (Pat Borders, Mark McGwire)	.50
12	The Turning Point/1992 (Roberto Alomar)	.35
13	On to Atlanta/1992 (Candy Maldonado)	.15
14	Instant Hero/1992 (Ed Sprague)	.15
15	Old Friends/1992 (Cito Gaston, Bobby Cox)	.15
16	The Catch/1992 (Devon White)	.15
17	Near Triple Play/1992 (Kelly Gruber, Deion Sanders)	.15
18	Winning Welcome/1992 (Roberto Alomar)	.35
19	Winning Slide/1992 (Kelly Gruber)	.15
20	Final Farewell/1992 (Jimmy Key)	.15
21	Winning RBI/1992 (Devon White, Candy Maldonado)	.15
22	Clincher/1992 (Joe Carter)	.35
23	World Chamions/1992	.15
24	Trophy Presentation/1992 (Cito Gaston, Bobby Brown)	.15
25	MVP - 1992 (Pat Borders)	.15
26	Heroes' Welcome/1992 (Roberto Alomar)	.35
	PLAYER CARDS	.15
27	John Olerud	.35
28	Roberto Alomar	.40
29	Ed Sprague	.15
30	Dick Schofield	.15
31	Devon White	.15
32	Joe Carter	.15
33	Darrin Jackson	.15
34	Pat Borders	.15

35	Paul Molitor	1.00
36	Checklist	.05

Expos

Top players and manager's from the team's 25 years were featured in a 33-card set produced by Donruss and distributed by Canadian McDonald's outlets. Card fronts feature a full-color borderless photo with the McDonald's and Donruss logos at top. A blue strip at bottom contains the player name and uniform number. At lower-left is an embossed silver-foil 25th anniversary logo. Fronts of the 2-1/2" x 3-1/2" cards are UV coated. Backs are printed in English and French and include a career summary and the player's stats while with the Expos. Appropriate sponsor, team and licensor logos also appear. Autographed cards of Expos manager Felipe Alou were randomly packaged.

		NM/M
Complete Set (33):		12.00
Common Player:		.25
1	Moises Alou	.75
2	Andre Dawson	1.50
3	Delino DeShields	.25
4	Andres Galarraga	.50
5	Marquis Grissom	.50
6	Tim Raines	.50
7	Larry Walker	1.00
8	Tim Wallach	.25
9	Ken Hill	.25
10	Dennis Martinez	.35
11	Jeff Reardon	.25
12	Gary Carter	4.00
13	Dave Cash	.25
14	Warren Cromartie	.25
15	Mack Jones	.25
16	Al Oliver	.35
17	Larry Parrish	.25
18	Rodney Scott	.25
19	Ken Singleton	.25
20	Rusty Staub	.35
21	Ellis Valentine	.25
22	Woody Fryman	.25
23	Charlie Lea	.25
24	Bill Lee	.25
25	Mike G. Marshall	.25
26	Claude Raymond	.25
27	Steve Renko	.25
28	Steve Rogers	.25
29	Bill Stoneman	.25
30	Gene Mauch	.25
31	Felipe Alou	.45
31a	Felipe Alou/Auto.	20.00
32	Buck Rodgers	.25
33	Checklist	.05

1997 McDonald's N.Y. Yankees

Three popular Yankees stars of the 1996 World Championship team are featured in this issue which raised funds for Ronald McDonald House Charities. The 2-1/2" x 3-1/2" cards have color action photos on front with dark blue borders, a facsimile autograph and McDonald's logo. Uniform and cap

logos have been removed from the photos. Backs are printed in blue with a cartoon of Ronald McDonald in baseball gear, a few biographical details about the player and some information about the charity.

		NM/M
Complete Set (3):		10.00
Common Player:		4.00
(1)	Dwight Gooden	4.00
(2)	Tino Martinez	4.00
(3)	Andy Pettitte	4.00

1998 McDonald's Arizona Diamondbacks

Marking the team's first year in the National League, this card set was given away to children 14 and under at an August 14 promotional game. In standard 2-1/2" x 3-1/2" format, the cards feature color portrait photos. Team and sponsor logos are in the left corners, with player identification in a green stripe at bottom. Backs have a desert scene background over which is printed personal data and professional stats. At bottom is a "Diamondbacks' Fact." Cards are listed here according to uniform number appearing on front.

		NM/M
Complete Set (24):		7.50
Common Player:		.50
5	Andy Stankiewicz	.50
6	Andy Fox	.50
9	Matt Williams	.75
10	Tony Batista	.50
11	Buck Showalter	.50
12	Jorge Fabregas	.50
15	Brent Brede	.50
16	Travis Lee	1.00
19	Willie Blair	.50
20	Jeff Suppan	.50
22	Devon White	.50
24	Karim Garcia	.75
25	David Dellucci	.50
26	Damian Miller	.50
30	Gregg Olson	.50
33	Jay Bell	.50
34	Brian Anderson	.50
35	Kelly Stinnett	.50
36	Clint Sodowsky	.50
37	Omar Daal	.50
38	Joel Adamson	.50
45	Andy Benes	.50
43	Yamil Benitez	.50
47	Felix Rodriguez	.50

1999 McDonald's St. Louis Cardinals

A late-season promotion at McDonald's restaurants in the St. Louis area offered six-card packs of Upper Deck Cardinal cards at $2.49, or $1.99 with a purchase. Cards are in the basic style of UD's 1999 MVP issue, but lack the silver-foil highlights on front. Backs are also nearly identical, but include a McDonald's logo at bottom-right.

Both front and back photos on the McDonald's cards differ from those used on UD MVP. Each foil pack contains four of the 15 player cards, plus two of the special Mark McGwire Milestone inserts. Checklist cards are a one-in-nine pack insert.

		NM/M
Complete Set (16):		4.00
Common Player:		.15
1	J.D. Drew	1.00
2	Jose Jiminez	.15
3	Mark McGwire	1.50
4	Fernando Tatis	.15
5	Edgar Renteria	.15
6	Ray Lankford	.15
7	Willie McGee	.15
8	Ricky Bottalico	.15
9	Eli Marrero	.15
10	Kent Bottenfield	.15
11	Eric Davis	.15
12	Darren Bragg	.15
13	Joe McEwing	.15
14	Shawon Dunston	.15
15	Darren Oliver	.15
---	Checklist	.05

1999 McDonald's Mark McGwire Milestones

A late-season promotion at McDonald's restaurants in the St. Louis area offered six-card packs of Upper Deck Cardinal cards at $2.49, or $1.99 with a purchase. Each foil pack contains four of the 15 player cards, plus two special Mark McGwire Milestone inserts. Horizontally formatted, the Milestones inserts have an action photo of McGwire on a silver metallic-foil background with red, blue and black high-tech graphic designs. The cards mark one of McGwire important home runs of 1998. Backs have a portrait photo and recount some of his career highlights. A McDonald's logo appears in the lower-right corner.

		NM/M
Complete Set (9):		7.00
Common Card:		1.00
M1	Mark McGwire/#50	1.00
M2	Mark McGwire/#60	1.00
M3	Mark McGwire/#61	1.00
M4	Mark McGwire/#62	1.50
M5	Mark McGwire/#63	1.00
M6	Mark McGwire/#67	1.00
M7	Mark McGwire/#68	1.00
M8	Mark McGwire/#69	1.00
M9	Mark McGwire/#70	1.50

2000 McDonald's Negro League Baseball

A set of 10 cards of former Negro Leagues ballplayers was issued by McDonald's in Milwaukee. The 2-1/2" x 3-1/2" cards have black-and-white oval photos at center, bordered in blue. A color logo reading "Yesterday's / Negro League Baseball / Players Wall of Fame" appears at top. A red starburst has the year the player was active in the Negro League. Below the photo are the McDonald's logo, the player's name and the years he was active in the Negro League. The red-on-white backs have biographical and career information and

stats. Cards originally sold in one-card packs for 99 cents, or the set of 10 for about $9.

		NM/M
Complete Set (10):		20.00
Common Player:		2.00
1	William "Bobby" Robinson	2.00
2	Mamie "Peanut" Johnson	2.00
3	Carl Long	2.00
4	John "Mule" Miles	2.00
5	Sherwood Brewer	2.00
6	Ira McKnight	2.00
7	Gordon Hopkins	2.00
8	Johnny Washington	2.00
9	Jim Robinson	2.00
10	Dennis "Bose" Biddle	2.00

St. Louis Cardinals Coin/Cards

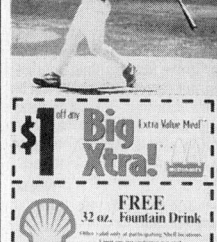

At a series of promotional games during the season, the Cardinals distributed these coin/cards. Wrapped in cellophane was a 2-1/2" x 4" card and a 39mm (about 1-1/2") bronze medallion. The card was horizontally perforated so it could be seperated into a 2-1/2" x 2" player card and two 2-1/2" x 1" coupons. The player card has a game action photo on front. On back is the player name and career highlights. The coupons are for $1 off a McDonald's meal and for a free soft drink at Shell gas stations. Coins have the team logo on front, a player image roughly the same as pictured on the card, and the player uniform number. Back of the coin has the team and sponsor logos and the date the coin was distributed.

		NM/M
Complete Set (4):		20.00
Common Player:		4.00
1	Willie McGee (May 13)	4.00
2	Fernando Vina (June 24)	4.00
3	Jim Edmonds (July 9)	6.00
4	Mark McGwire (September 3)	8.00

2003 McDonald's N.Y. Yankees

Beginning July 28, and extending until 8.75 million cards were given away, these Upper Deck-produced cards were available at 600+ McDonald's in the metro New York area with the purchase of a special Yankees-themed Happy Meal. Cards were issued in either singly in a cello pack, or in a pack with a scratch-off game card. Fronts have an action photo with a large ghost-image team logo behind. Also on front are the Yankee's 100th anniversary logo and logos

of UD and McDonald's. Backs have another player photo, stats, personal data and the logos.

		NM/M
Complete Set (24):		8.00
Common Player:		.25
1	Juan Acevedo	.25
2	Roger Clemens	1.50
3	John Flaherty	.25
4	Jason Giambi	.50
5	Chris Hammond	.25
6	Sterling Hitchcock	.25
7	Derek Jeter	2.50
8	Nick Johnson	.25
9	Steve Karsay	.25
10	Hideki Matsui	1.50
11	Raul Mondesi	.25
12	Mike Mussina	.35
13	Antonio Osuna	.25
14	Andy Petitte	.35
15	Jorge Posada	.35
16	Mariano Rivera	.35
17	Alfonso Soriano	.50
18	Bubba Trammell	.25
19	Robin Ventura	.25
20	Jeff Weaver	.25
21	David Wells	.25
22	Bernie Williams	.35
23	Enrique Wilson	.25
24	Todd Zeile	.25

2004 McDonald's Philadelphia Phillies

A two-card pack was given away with each Extra Value Meal purchase at Philly area McDonald's in July. Production of 170,000 of each card was reported. Upper Deck created the cards for the promotion.

		NM/M
Complete Set (27):		6.00
Common Player:		.50
1	Jim Thome	1.00
2	Placido Polanco	.50
3	Jimmy Rollins	1.00
4	David Bell	.50
5	Bobby Abreu	.50
6	Pat Burrell	1.00
7	Marlon Byrd	.50
8	Mike Lieberthal	.75
9	Kevin Millwood	.50
10	Randy Wolf	.50
11	Vicente Padilla	.50
12	Eric Milton	.50
13	Brett Myers	.50
15	Billy Wagner	.50
16	Tim Worrell	.50
17	Rheal Cormier	.50
18	Roberto Hernandez	.50
19	Ryan Madson	.50
20	Amaury Telemaco	.50
21	Tomas Perez	.50
22	Shawn Wooten	.50
23	Doug Glanville	.50
24	Ricky Ledee	.50
25	Jason Michaels	.50
26	Todd Pratt	.50
27	Larry Bowa	.50
---	Citizens Bank Park/ Checklist	.50

1992 MCI Ambassadors

Issued in conjunction with the MCI-sponsored Ambassadors of Baseball World Tour of overseas

military bases, this set features retired players who participated in the tour. Cards feature color photos with a white border, a color tour logo in the lower-left and a banner across the upper-left reading, "Support MWR With MCI." The player's name and position appear in the bottom border. Horizontally oriented backs have career stats and highlights and the logos of MCI and the Major League Baseball Players Alumni in black-and-white.

		NM/M
Complete Set (16):		35.00
Common Player:		2.00
1	Earl Weaver	3.00
2	Steve Garvey	6.00
3	Doug Flynn	2.00
4	Bert Campaneris	2.00
5	Bill Madlock	2.00
6	Graig Nettles	2.00
7	Dave Kingman	3.00
8	Paul Blair	2.00
9	Jeff Burroughs	2.00
10	Rick Waits	2.00
11	Elias Sosa	2.00
12	Tug McGraw	2.00
13	Ferguson Jenkins (Photo)	4.00
14	Bob Feller	6.00
	Ferguson Jenkins (Art)	4.00
---	Header Card	.50

1993 MCI Ambassadors

The Major League Baseball Players Alumni Association produced a set of 13 former players who were featured in 1993's MCI Ambassadors of Baseball World Tour. The card set was available free to military personnel who completed an MCI application. The tour of military bases worldwide included appearances by the players at base exchanges, clinics for dependent children and a softball game against base all-stars. The cards feature a photo of the player on the front with logos from the Ambassador tour and MCI in opposite corners.

		NM/M
Complete Set (14):		20.00
Common Player:		1.25
1	Vida Blue	1.25
2	Paul Blair	1.25
3	Mudcat Grant	1.25
4	Phil Niekro	2.00
5	Bob Feller	3.00
6	Joe Charboneau	2.00
7	Joe Rudi	1.25
8	Catfish Hunter	2.00
9	Manny Sanguillen	1.25
10	Harmon Killebrew	3.00
11	Al Oliver	1.25
12	Bob Dernier	1.25
13	Graig Nettles, Sparky Lyle	1.75
----	Header Card	.10

1994 MCI Ambassadors

Once again in 1994, the old-timers' tour of overseas military bases sponsored by MCI spawned a card set. The '94 set is similar to previous years' issues except that color player photos have had the uniform logos airbrushed away. MCI and tour logos appear in color on the front; backs are in black-and-white and contain career data and highlights along with MCI and Major League Baseball Players Alumni logos. Besides 11 numbered cards, there are four unnumbered cards in the 1994 set which include a pair honoring major leaguers who served in the military during World War II.

		NM/M
Complete Set (15):		30.00
Common Player:		2.00
1	Sparky Lyle	2.00
2	John Stearns	2.00
3	Bobby Thomson	3.00
4	Jimmy Wynn	2.00
5	Ferguson Jenkins	4.00
6	Tug McGraw	2.00
7	Paul Blair	2.00
8	Ron LeFlore	2.00
9	Manny Sanguillen	2.00
10	Doug Flynn	2.00
11	Bill North	2.00
----	Manny Sanguillen (Signing autographs.)	2.00
----	Doug Flynn (Instructing children.)	2.00
----	American Leaguers in WWII	2.00
----	National Leaguers in WWII	2.00

1995 MCI Ambassadors

For a fourth year, Major League Baseball, the Players' Union and the long distance phone provider issued a card set in conjunction with its series of softball games at military bases. Approximately 2,000 sets were issued. The 2-1/2" x 3-1/2" cards have player photos on front with MCI and the baseball tour logos in opposite corners. Backs have biographical and career information about the retired stars.

		NM/M
Complete Set (16):		30.00
Common Player:		2.00
1	Vida Blue	2.00
2	Bert Campaneris	2.00
3	Tug McGraw	2.00
4	Doug Flynn	2.00
5	Paul Blair	2.00
6	Harmon Killebrew	5.00
7	Sparky Lyle	2.00
8	Steve Garvey	4.00
9	Bert Blyleven	2.00
10	Omar Moreno	2.00
11	Bill Lee	2.00
12	Maury Wills	2.00
13	Dave Parker	2.00
14	Luis Aparicio	5.00
15	Brooks Robinson	5.00
16	George Foster	2.00

1996 MCI Ambassadors

This set of former players cards was issued in conjunction with a tour of overseas U.S. military bases by members of the Major League Baseball Players Alumni Association. Players taking part in the tour are featured on the card fronts in photos contemporary with their major league days. Backs have career summaries and stats along with sponsors logos. The cards were virtually all distributed overseas.

		NM/M
Complete Set (8):		30.00
Common Player:		5.00
(1)	Tommy Davis	6.00

(2)	Darrell Evans	6.00
(3)	Jay Howell	5.00
(4)	John Montefusco	5.00
(5)	Graig Nettles	6.00
(6)	Jim Sundberg	5.00
(7)	Header Card	.50
(8)	American Airlines Sponsor Card	.50

1991 MDA All-Stars

Though the Muscular Dystrophy Association isn't mentioned on the player cards, it was the beneficiary of this set produced by Smith-Kline Beecham. Card fronts feature color photos of the players during their active careers. Because the set was not licensed by MLB, team uniform logos have been airbrushed off the photos. Black-and-white backs have a recent portrait photo of the player, along with biographical and career data. The set was available by mail for $3.99 plus proofs of purchase from Tums antacid.

		NM/M
Complete Set (20):		15.00
Common Player:		.50
1	Steve Carlton	1.00
2	Ted Simmons	.50
3	Willie Stargell	1.00
4	Bill Mazeroski	1.00
5	Ron Santo	.75
6	Dave Concepcion	.50
7	Bobby Bonds	.50
8	George Foster	.50
9	Billy Williams	1.00
10	Whitey Ford	2.00
11	Yogi Berra	2.00
12	Boog Powell	.60
13	Davey Johnson	.50
14	Brooks Robinson	1.00
15	Jim Fregosi	.50
16	Harmon Killebrew	1.00
17	Ted Williams	3.00
18	Al Kaline	1.00
---	MDA Fact Card (Brooks Robinson)	.50
---	Header Card	.25

1992 MVP for MDA

The Muscular Dystrophy Association was the beneficiary of this set sponsored by SmithKline Beecham. Card fronts feature color photos of the players during their active careers. Because the set was not licensed by MLB, team uniform logos have been airbrushed off the photos. Black-and-white backs have a portrait photo of the player, along with biographical and career data. A vinyl album to house the set was included in the mail-in offer.

		NM/M
Complete Set (20):		9.00
Common Player:		1.00
Album:		4.50
1	Yogi Berra	2.00
2	Dick Groat	1.00
3	Maury Wills	1.00
4	Brooks Robinson	1.50
5	Orlando Cepeda	1.00
6	Harmon Killebrew	1.50
7	Boog Powell	1.00
8	Vida Blue	1.00
9	Jeff Burroughs	1.00
10	George Foster	1.00
11	Rod Carew	1.50
12	Jim Rice	1.00
13	Don Baylor	1.00
14	Willie Stargell	1.50
15	Rollie Fingers	1.00
16	Ray Knight	1.00
17	History of the MVP	.25
18	MVP Trivia	.25
19	Harmon Killebrew (W/1992 MDA Poster Child.)	1.00
20	MLB Players Assn. Alumni Info	.25

1986 Meadow Gold Blank Backs

This was the second set to be distributed by Meadow Gold Dairy (Beatrice Foods) in 1986. It was issued on Double Play ice cream cartons, one card per package. Full-color player photos have team logos and insignias airbrushed away. This 16-card set is very similar to the Meadow Gold popsicle set, but the photos are different in some instances. The cards measure 2-3/8" x 3-1/2". The Willie McGee card is reportedly tougher to find than other cards in the set.

		NM/M
Complete Singles Set (16):		20.00
Complete Carton Set (16):		22.50
Common Player:		.75
(1)	George Brett	2.50
(2)	Wade Boggs	2.00
(3)	Carlton Fisk	1.50
(4)	Steve Garvey	1.00
(5)	Dwight Gooden	.75
(6)	Pedro Guerrero	.75
(7)	Reggie Jackson	2.50
(8)	Don Mattingly	2.50
(9)	Willie McGee	.75
(10)	Dale Murphy	1.00
(11)	Cal Ripken, Jr.	3.00
(12)	Pete Rose	3.00
(13)	Ryne Sandberg	2.00
(14)	Mike Schmidt	2.50
(15)	Fernando Valenzuela	.75
(16)	Dave Winfield	1.50

Statistic Backs

Beatrice Foods produced this set of 20 cards on specially marked boxes of Meadow Gold Double Play popsicles, fudgesicles and bubble gum coolers. They came in two-card panels and have full-color player pictures with player name, team and position printed below the photo. Card backs are printed in red ink and feature player career highlights. The cards measure 2-3/8" x 3-1/2" and were distributed in the West and Midwest. It is considered one of the toughest 1986 regional sets to complete.

		NM/M
Complete Panel Set (10):		10.00
Complete Singles Set (20):		10.00
Common Panel:		1.00
Common Single:		.30
PANEL 1		2.00
1	George Brett	1.50
2	Fernando Valenzuela	.30
PANEL 2		1.00
3	Dwight Gooden	.30
4	Dale Murphy	.75
PANEL 3		3.50
5	Don Mattingly	1.50
6	Reggie Jackson	1.50
PANEL 4		3.00
7	Dave Winfield	1.00
8	Pete Rose	1.50
PANEL 5		1.50

9	Wade Boggs	1.25
10	Willie McGee	.30
PANEL 6		5.00
11	Cal Ripkin (Ripken)	3.00
12	Ryne Sandberg	1.25
PANEL 7		1.50
13	Carlton Fisk	1.00
14	Jim Rice	.50
PANEL 8		2.50
15	Steve Garvey	.50
16	Mike Schmidt	1.50
PANEL 9		1.00
17	Bruce Sutter	.75
18	Pedro Guerrero	.30
PANEL 10		1.00
19	Rick Sutcliff (Sutcliffe)	.75
20	Rich Gossage	.30

Milk

The third set from Meadow Gold from 1986 came on milk cartons; on pint, quart and half-gallon size containers. The cards measure 2-1/2" x 3-1/2" and feature drawings instead of photographs. Different dairies distributed the cards in various colors of ink. The cards can be found printed in red, brown or black ink. The crude drawings have prevented this rare set from being higher in price.

		NM/M
Complete Set (11):		75.00
Common Player:		3.50
(1)	Wade Boggs	9.00
(2)	George Brett	12.00
(3)	Steve Carlton	7.50
(4)	Dwight Gooden	3.50
(5)	Willie McGee	3.50
(6)	Dale Murphy	6.00
(7)	Cal Ripken, Jr.	17.50
(8)	Pete Rose	15.00
(9)	Ryne Sandberg	9.00
(10)	Mike Schmidt	12.00
(11)	Fernando Valenzuela	3.50

1992 Megacards Babe Ruth Prototypes

Basically identical to the regularly issued versions, these sample cards were distributed to hobby dealers to introduce Megacards Babe Ruth Collection. Most of the prototypes have different card numbers than those in the regular set, and all carry a large gray diagonal "PROTOTYPE" on back.

		NM/M
Complete Set (9):		7.50
Common Card:		1.00
14	Year in Review/1921 (Babe Ruth)	1.00
31	World Series/1916 (Babe Ruth)	1.00
75	Place in History/1928 (Babe Ruth)	1.00
106	Career Highlights/1927 (Babe Ruth)	1.00
124	Trivia/1926 (Babe Ruth)	1.00
129	Sultan of Swat/1925 (Babe Ruth)	1.00
134	Being Remembered/1948 - George Bush (Babe Ruth)	1.00

138	Being Remembered/1923 - Grantland Rice (Babe Ruth)	1.00
154	The Bambino - The Man (Babe Ruth, Lou Gehrig)	1.25

1992 Megacards Babe Ruth

This 165-card set chronicles the life and times of Babe Ruth. The set was produced by Megacards and is officially entitled "The Babe Ruth Collection." The cards feature classic black and white photos with black borders and captions below the photo. The card backs feature coordinating statistics and information.

		NM/M
Complete Set (165):		15.00
Complete Set, Tin:		20.00
Common Card:		.10
Wax Box (48):		20.00
1	Lifetime Pitching Statistics	.10
2	Lifetime Batting Statistics	.10
3	Lifetime - World Series Pitching	.10
4	Lifetime World Series Batting	.10
5	22-9 Record in the Minors	.10
6	2-1 Record First Year in the Majors	.10
7	Won 17 of his Last 21 Decisions	.10
8	Led League with 1.75 ERA and 9 Shutouts	.10
9	Defeats Walter Johnson for 6th Time	.10
10	Doubles as Pitcher and a Regular	.10
11	First Season in the Outfield	.10
12	Sold to Yankees for $100,000	.10
13	The Best Year Any Batter Ever Had	.10
14	Suspended for First 38 Games	.10
15	Wins American League MVP	.10
16	Wins Only Batting Title - .378	.10
17	The "Million Dollar Stomachache"	.10
18	Bats .372 with a .737 Slugging Average	.10
19	The Best Baseball Team in History	.20
20	Tops 50 Home Runs - 4th Time	.10
21	Clubs 500th Home Run	.10
22	Bam Bams Nine in a Week	.10
23	.700 Slugging Average for 9th Time	.10
24	Blasts Over 40 Homers for 11th Time	.10
25	Over 100 RBIs for 13th Time	.10
26	Tops 2,000 Career Walks	.10
27	Babe Retires	.10
28	Babe Coaches the Dodgers	.10
29	The Babe in Retirement	.10
30	1915 World Series - Warms Bench	.10
31	1916 World Series - Hurls 14-Inning Win	.10
32	1918 World Series - Scoreless Innings	.10
33	1921 World Series - Yankees' First	.10
34	1922 World Series - Back to the Farm	.10
35	1923 World Series - First Championship	.10
36	1926 World Series - 4 HR in Losing Cause	.10
37	1927 World Series - Destroy Bucs in Four	.15
38	1928 World Series - .625 BA and 1.375 SA	.10
39	1932 World Series - Yanks Sweep Cubs	.15
40	Lifetime - 2,056 Walks	.10
41	First to Fan 1,000 Times	.10
42	Lifetime - 2,174 Runs Scored	.15

43	Lifetime - 5,793 Total Bases	.15
44	Lifetime - 1,356 Extra-Base Hits	.10
45	Lifetime - 714 Home Runs	.10
46	Lifetime - 16 Grand Slams	.10
47	Lifetime - 8.5 Home Run Percentage	.15
48	Lifetime - Most Games, 2 or More HR	.10
49	Lifetime - 11 Seasons with 40+ HRs	.15
50	Lifetime - 2,211 RBIs	.15
51	Lifetime - .342 Batting Average	.15
52	Lifetime - .690 Slugging Average	.15
53	Season - Nine Shutouts	.10
54	Season - 170 Walks	.10
55	Season - 177 Runs Scored	.20
56	Season - .545 On-Base Percentage	.10
57	Season - 457 Total Bases	.15
58	Season - 119 Extra-Base Hits	.15
59	Season - 171 Runs Batted In	.15
60	Season - 60 Home Runs	.10
61	Season - 11.8 Home Run Percentage	.10
62	Season - .847 Slugging Average	.15
63	World Series 3-0 Record	.10
64	World Series - 0.87 ERA	.10
65	World Series - 33 Walks	.10
66	World Series - 37 Runs	.10
67	World Series - 96 Total Bases	.10
68	World Series - 15 Home Runs	.10
69	World Series - 33 RBIs	.10
70	World Series - .744 Slugging Average	.20
71	1914 - First Major League Victory	.10
72	1915 - First Major League Home Run	.10
73	1916 - Babe Derails "Big Train"	.10
74	1919 - Leads League in Fielding	.10
75	1919 First Home Run Record	.10
76	1920 - Babe Becomes a Yankee	.10
77	1923 - First Home Run in Yankee Stadium	.10
78	1923 - American League MVP	.10
79	1924 - Wins Only Batting Title	.15
80	1926 - Hits 3 Home Runs in Series Game	.10
81	1927 - Babe and Lou Smack 107 Home Runs (Lou Gehrig)	.20
82	1927 - The Babe's 60th Home Run	.20
83	1928 - Three HR in World Series Game	.10
84	1932 - Early "Called Shots" by the Bam	.10
85	1932 - The "Called Shot" - The Legend	.10
86	1932 - The "Called Shot" - The Believers	.10
87	1932 - The "Called Shot" - The Doubters	.10
88	1932 - The "Called Shot" - Babe's View	.10
89	1933 - First HR in an All-Star Game	.15
90	1933 - Last Time on the Mound	.10
91	1934 - Babe Hits 700th Home Run	.10
92	1934 - The Babe in Japan	.10
93	1935 - Last Major League Homers	.10
94	1939 - Inaugurated into Hall of Fame	.10
95	1942 - Faces Johnson Again in Exhibition	.10
96	1947 - Babe Ruth Day	.10
97	1948 - Babe's Farewell	.25
98	A Perfect Punch	.10
99	Yankees Best Base Thief	.10
100	Hub Pruett: Babe Buster	.10
101	Babe Caught Stealing, Ends 1926 Series	.10
102	Never Won a Triple Crown	.10
103	Babe Used a 54-Ounce Bat	.10
104	Babe Bats Righty	.10
105	Babe's Greatness	.10
106	The Babe's Best	.10
107	Outslugged Entire Teams	.10
108	First to Hit 30, 40, 50 and 60 Home Runs	.10
109	The Pitkin Study	.10
110	First to Put the Ball Into Orbit	.10
111	Afraid to Kill Somebody	.10
112	The Wonder Years: 1926-31	.10
113	Hit .422 With 7 Homers on Opening Days	.10
114	Babe at Bat	.10

115	"Greatest Ballplayer the Game Has Known"	.10
116	The Babe's Early Childhood	.10
117	St. Mary's Industrial School	.10
118	Babe and Brother Matthias	.10
119	The Babe's Nicknames	.10
120	Babe's First Wife, Helen	.10
121	Babe's Second Wife, Claire	.10
122	Lou Gehrig Appreciation Day	.20
123	Babe's Friendship With Herb Pennock	.10
124	The Babe and Miller Huggins	.10
125	The Babe and Ty Cobb	.15
126	Babe and Walter Johnson	.15
127	Baseball's Biggest Drawing Card	.10
128	Babe's Barnstorming	.10
129	Costly Confrontation	.10
130	He Often Played Hurt	.10
131	Babe's Big Bucks	.10
132	Want to be a Manager	.10
133	The Babe on the Links	.10
134	Babe in the Movies	.10
135	Babe Contributes to War Effort	.10
136	The Babe - Peace Negotiator	.10
137	Everyone Loved the Babe	.10
138	He Brought Children Joy	.10
139	He Always Had Time for Kids	.10
140	The Johnny Sylvester Story	.10
141	Moving with the Great	.10
142	Babe Ruth and the American Dream	.10
143	Being Remembered - Bill James	.10
144	Being Remembered - Bill James	.10
145	Being Remembered - Bill James	.10
146	Being Remembered - Mel Allen	.10
147	Being Remembered - Mel Allen	.10
148	Being Remembered - Wes Ferrell	.10
149	Being Remembered - George Bush	.50
150	Being Remembered - Ethan Allen	.20
151	Being Remembered - Daughter Dorothy	.10
152	Being Remembered - Daughter Julia	.10
153	Being Remembered - Daughter Julia	.10
154	Being Remembered - Mark Koenig	.10
155	Being Remembered - Donald Honig	.10
156	Being Remembered - L. Waner, Waite Hoyt	.10
157	Being Remembered - Waite Hoyt	.10
158	Being Remembered - Bill Dickey	.10
159	Being Remembered - Bob Meusel	.10
160	Being Remembered - Jim Chapman	.10
161	Being Remembered - Christy Walsh	.10
162	Being Remembered - The Babe Passes Away	.10
163	Being Remembered - Grantland Rice	.10
164	Checklist 1-83	.10
165	Checklist 84-165	.10

1995 Megacards Ken Griffey, Jr. MegaCaps

Three different "MegaCaps" picturing Ken Griffey, Jr., were prepared for insertion into blister packs containing full sets of the Ken Griffey Jr. Wish List Collection. Each of the 1-5/8" diameter cardboard discs has a color photo of Junior on front. Backs have trademark information. Reported print run for each of the three versions was 34,000.

		NM/M
Complete Set:		1.50
Common Cap:		.50
1	Ken Griffey Jr.	.50
2	Ken Griffey Jr.	.50
3	Ken Griffey Jr.	.50

1995 Megacards Ken Griffey, Jr. Wish List

Sold only as a complete set in a clam-shell plastic blister pack, this set has two areas of focus. The first 14 cards details Griffey's hopes for his baseball career and his life; the second 11 cards feature projections on Junior's possible career stats based on numbers generated by baseball statistician Bill James. Each card has a different action photo of Griffey on the front. Backs have a smaller version of the front photo in the upper-right corner, and a muted background photo of Griffey at bat. Card fronts are gold-foil enhanced. Packed with each set was one of three "MegaCaps" with Griffey's picture. With a reported print run of 100,000 sets, the issue sold for about $10 retail, with part of the purchase price going to the Make a Wish Foundation for seriously ill children.

		NM/M
Complete Set (27):		7.50
Common Card:		.50
1	Introduction (Ken Griffey Jr.)	.50
2	Make-A-Wish Foundation (Ken Griffey Jr.)	.50
3	To Make Dreams Come True (Ken Griffey Jr.)	.50
4	To Play With Dad (Ken Griffey Jr. (W/Ken Griffey, Sr.))	.50
5	"The Best I Can Be" (Ken Griffey Jr.)	.50
6	To Make the Majors (Ken Griffey Jr.)	.50
7	To Play for a Winner (Ken Griffey Jr.)	.50
8	To Assist B.A.T. (Ken Griffey Jr.)	.50
9	To Enrich Inner-City Baseball (Ken Griffey Jr.)	.50
10	A Lot to Live For (Ken Griffey Jr.)	.50
11	To Be an All-Around Player (Ken Griffey Jr.)	.50
12	To Be #1 in the Draft (Ken Griffey Jr.)	.50
13	To Win the Gold (Ken Griffey Jr.)	.50
14	Most Home Runs by Father/Son (Ken Griffey Jr. (W/Ken Griffey, Sr.))	.50
15	The Field of Possibilities (Ken Griffey Jr.)	.50
16	The Griffey Forecast (Ken Griffey Jr.)	.50
17	3,598 Career Games (Ken Griffey Jr.)	.50
18	2,361 Career Runs (Ken Griffey Jr.)	.50
19	3,947 Career Hits (Ken Griffey Jr.)	.50
20	777 Career Doubles (Ken Griffey Jr.)	.50
21	699 Career Home Runs (Ken Griffey Jr.)	.50
22	2,234 Career RBIs (Ken Griffey Jr.)	.50
24	1,541 Career Extra Base Hits (Ken Griffey Jr.)	.50
24	40 or More Home Runs 5 Times (Ken Griffey Jr.)	.50
25	28 Career Grand Slams (Ken Griffey Jr.)	.50
---	Contest Card	.05
---	Merchandise Order Card	.05

1995 Megacards Babe Ruth 100th Anniversary

Marking the centennial of Babe Ruth's birth, Megacards issued this 25-card set chronicling the life and career of baseball's all-time greatest player. Most of the cards feature on

front black-and-white photos of Ruth, although there are several colorized pictures scattered through the set. Fronts have gold-foil frames, captions and Ruth Centennial logo. Reverses have a background photo of Ruth's classic swing and a detailed vignette pertinent to the card's theme. The Babe Ruth 100th Anniversary Collection set was sold in a plastic clam-shell package containing one of three Babe Ruth "Megacaps." The edition was limited to 100,000 sets.

		NM/M
Complete Set (27):		5.00
Common Card:		.25
1	Baseball's Greatest Ever? (Babe Ruth)	.25
2	60 Home Run Club (Babe Ruth)	.25
3	No Slugger Comes Close (Babe Ruth (With Jimmie Foxx, Lou Gehrig, Al Simmons.))	.25
4	History's Most Frequent Home Run Threat (Babe Ruth)	.25
5	He Knew the Way Home (Babe Ruth)	.25
6	He Didn't Leave Them Stranded (Babe Ruth (With Lou Gehrig.))	.25
7	50 Home Run King (Babe Ruth)	.25
8	Long Ball Legend (Babe Ruth)	.25
9	.342 Plus Power (Babe Ruth (With Lloyd Waner, Paul Waner, Lou Gehrig.))	.25
10	No One Hit 'Em More Often (Babe Ruth)	.25
11	Greatest Pitching Prospect (Babe Ruth (Colorized, Red Sox pitcher.))	.25
12	Career Year (Babe Ruth (Colorized, fishing with Lou Gehrig.))	.25
13	Mr. Yankee (Babe Ruth (With Lou Gehrig; Don Mattingly superimposed.))	.50
14	Babe and "The Kid" (Babe Ruth (Ken Griffey, Jr., superimposed))	.50
15	Everyone Loved the Babe (Babe Ruth)	.50
16	The Babe Played Hurt (Babe Ruth)	.25
17	He Did It His Way (Babe Ruth)	.25
18	The Rewards of Greatness (Babe Ruth)	.25
19	Babe and Today's Rules (Babe Ruth)	.25
20	Babe in Today's Ballparks (Babe Ruth)	.25
21	Babe and Today's Best (Babe Ruth (Colorized, Ken Griffey Jr. superimposed.))	.75
22	Babe vs. Today's Pitching (Babe Ruth)	.25
23	The Babe and Father Time (Babe Ruth)	.25
24	How He Changed the Game (Babe Ruth (Colorized, with Dizzy Dean, Frank Frisch, Mickey Cochrane, Schoolboy Rowe.))	.25
25	Will There Be Another Babe? (Babe Ruth)	.25
---	Sweepstakes Card	.05
---	Babe Ruth Merchandise Order Card	.05

Babe Ruth MegaCaps

One of three different 1-5/8" "MegaCaps" picturing Babe Ruth was packaged in each set of Babe Ruth 100th Anniversary Collection cards. The discs feature a photo of Ruth on front and trademark information on the back. Each cap was produced in an edition of 34,000.

		NM/M
Complete Set (3):		1.50
Common Cap:		.50
1	Babe Ruth	.50
2	Babe Ruth	.50
3	Babe Ruth	.50

1994 Mellon Bank Phillies

This set sponsored by "The Official Bank of the Phillies" was issued in the form of a perforated fold-out, with individual cards in the standard 2-1/2" x 3-1/2" size. One panel is a 12-1/2" x 7" team photo. Fronts have game-action photos with a border of red pinstripes on white. The team name is in a box at top, the player name is in a banner at bottom. On back are personal data, stats and career highlights, along with the logos of the team, the sponsor and MLB's 125th Anniversary.

		NM/M
Foldout:		12.00
Complete Set, Singles (26):		8.00
Common Player:		.50
(1)	Larry Anderson	.50
(2)	Kim Batiste	.50
(3)	Shawn Boskie	.50
(4)	Darren Daulton	.75
(5)	Mariano Duncan	.50
(6)	Lenny Dykstra	.75
(7)	Jim Eisenreich	.50
(8)	Tommy Greene	.50
(9)	Dave Hollins	.50
(10)	Pete Incaviglia	.50
(11)	Danny Jackson	.50
(12)	Doug Jones	.50
(13)	Ricky Jordan	.50
(14)	John Kruk	.75
(15)	Tony Longmire	.50
(16)	Mickey Morandini	.50
(17)	Bobby Munoz	.50
(18)	Todd Pratt	.50
(19)	Paul Quantrill, Billy Hatcher	.50
(20)	Curt Schilling	1.50
(21)	Heathcliff Slocumb	.50
(22)	Kevin Stocker	.50
(23)	Milt Thompson	.50
(24)	David West	.50
(25)	Mike Williams	.50
(26)	Team photo	2.00

1995 Mellon Bank Phillies

This set was issued in the form of a perforated fold-out, with individual cards in the standard 2-1/2" x 3-1/2" size. Fronts have game-action

photos with a border of red pinstripes on white. The team name is in a box at top, the player name is in a banner at bottom. On back are personal data and stats, along with the logos of the team, the sponsor and the Phillies "Silver Season." The unnumbered cards are checklisted here alphabetically.

		NM/M
Foldout:		10.00
Complete Set, Singles (25):		8.00
Common Player:		.50
(1)	Kyle Abbott	.50
(2)	Toby Borland	.50
(3)	Ricky Bottalico	.50
(4)	Norm Charlton	.50
(5)	Darren Daulton	.75
(6)	Mariano Duncan	.50
(7)	Lenny Dykstra	.75
(8)	Jim Eisenreich	.50
(9)	Dave Gallagher	.50
(10)	Tyler Green	.50
(11)	Gene Harris	.50
(12)	Charlie Hayes	.50
(13)	Dave Hollins	.50
(14)	Gregg Jefferies	.50
(15)	Tony Longmire	.50
(16)	Michael Mimbs	.50
(17)	Mickey Morandini	.50
(18)	Paul Quantrill	.50
(19)	Randy Ready	.50
(20)	Curt Schilling	1.50
(21)	Heathcliff Slocumb	.50
(22)	Kevin Stocker	.50
(23)	Gary Varsho	.50
(24)	Lenny Webster	.50
(25)	David West	.50

2003 Merrick Mint Laser Line Gold Cards

These 2-1/2" x 3-1/2" cards are produced from 23-K gold foil in an intaglio printing process which gives them an engraved look and feel. Because the set is licensed only by the Player's Association, and not MLB, team logos and nicknames are not shown. Fronts have a portrait photo and facsimile autograph. Backs have information on the production process. The unnumbered cards are checklisted here alphabetically. Cards were issued in an acrylic case at an original price of about $15.

		NM/M
Complete Set (17):		75.00
Common Player:		3.00
(1)	Roger Clemens	5.00
(2)	Nomar Garciaparra	5.00
(3)	Ken Griffey Jr.	6.00
(4)	Vladimir Guerrero	4.00
(5)	Derek Jeter	10.00
(6)	Randy Johnson	4.00
(7)	Pedro Martinez	4.00
(8)	Hideki Matsui	4.00
(9)	Mike Piazza	6.00
(10)	Mark Prior	3.00
(11)	Albert Pujols	8.00
(12)	Alex Rodriguez	8.00
(13)	Alfonso Soriano	3.00
(14)	Sammy Sosa	5.00
(15)	Ichiro Suzuki	4.00
(16)	Jim Thome	3.00
(17)	Dontrelle Willis	3.00

2003 Merrick Mint N.Y. Yankees Stickers/Cards

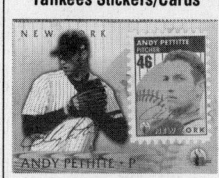

To commemorate the 100th anniversary of the N.Y. Yankees, this set of stickers and cards was

produced. Each player is represented on a self-adhesive 1-3/8" x 1-7/8" sticker and a 3-1/2" x 2-1/2" blank-backed card on which the sticker could be placed. Stickers were issued in sheets of nine or 16, and cards on perforated sheets of four or nine. The stickers have portrait photos, a facsimile autograph and uniform number. Cards have an action photo and facsimile autograph. Because the issued was licensed only by the Players Union and not MLB, uniform logos have been excised and the team nickname "Yankees" is nowhere to be seen. The issue was sold in sheets in either 5" x 7" or 8" x 10" format.

		NM/M
Set 8x10 Sheets (2):		7.00
Set 5x7 Sheets (4):		6.00
Complete Set Stickers (17):		2.00
Common Sticker:		.25
Complete Set Cards (17):		5.00
Common Card:		.50
2	Derek Jeter	1.00
6	Joe Torre	.25
12	Alfonso Soriano	.50
18	Jeff Weaver	.25
19	Robin Ventura	.25
20	Jorge Posada	.25
22	Jason Giambi	.50
25	Roger Clemens	.75
33	David Wells	.25
35	Mike Mussina	.35
36	Nick Johnson	.25
42	Mariano Rivera	.35
43	Raul Mondesi	.25
46	Andy Pettitte	.35
51	Bernie Williams	.25
55	Hideki Matsui	.50
---	100th Anniversary Logo	2.00
2	Derek Jeter	2.00
6	Joe Torre	.50
12	Alfonso Soriano	.75
18	Jeff Weaver	.50
19	Robin Ventura	.50
20	Jorge Posada	.50
22	Jason Giambi	.75
25	Roger Clemens	1.00
33	David Wells	.50
35	Mike Mussina	.60
36	Nick Johnson	.60
42	Mariano Rivera	.60
43	Raul Mondesi	.60
46	Andy Pettitte	.60
51	Bernie Williams	.60
55	Hideki Matsui	.75
---	100th Anniversary Logo	.50

Stickers/Cards

This issue comprises several types of collectibles in one cellobagged package. Each pack consists of nine self-adhesive 1-1/2" x 2" stickers, nine 3-1/2" x 2-1/2" blank-backed cards on which the sticker could be placed, one 2-1/2" x 5" "Colossal" sticker and one of seven 2-1/2" x 1-7/8" "Rookie Star" sticker of Hideki Matsui. The stickers have color portrait and black-and-white game action photos and a facsimile autograph. Cards have a color version of the action photo. Because the issued was licensed only by the Players Union and not MLB, uniform logos have been excised and team nicknames are nowhere to be seen.

		NM/M
Complete Set, Sheets (7):		20.00
Common Player Sticker + Card:		.50
Package 1		5.00
(C1)	Derek Jeter (Colossal)	1.00
RS1	Hideki Matsui/Btg (Rookie Star) (One hand visible.))	.50
(1)	Barry Bonds (Facing his right.)	1.50
(2)	Roger Clemens/DP	.75
(3)	Ken Griffey Jr./TP	.75
(4)	Randy Johnson	.65

(5) Pedro Martinez/DP .60
(6) Mike Piazza/DP 1.00
(7) Mark Prior .50
(8) Sammy Sosa/DP .75
(9) Ichiro/DP 1.00
Package 2 3.50
(C2) Alex Rodriguez (Colossal) .75
(RS2) Hideki Matsui/Btg
(Rookie Star)
(No hands visible.) .50
(10) Barry Bonds/DP
(Arms up.) 1.00
(11) Pat Burrell .50
(12) Jose Contreras .50
(13) Jim Edmonds .50
(14) Todd Helton .65
(15) Austin Kearns .50
(16) Greg Maddux .75
(17) Sammy Sosa/DP .75
(18) Mike Sweeney .50
Package 3 3.75
(C3) Nomar Garciaparra
(Colossal) .50
(RS3) Hideki Matsui/Throwing
(Rookie Star) .50
(19) Jeff Bagwell .65
(20) Barry Bonds/DP
(Arms up.) 1.00
(21) Ken Griffey Jr./TP .75
(22) Rafael Palmeiro .60
(23) Albert Pujols 1.25
(24) Alfonso Soriano .50
(25) Miguel Tedaja (Tejada) .50
(26) Larry Walker .50
(27) Dontrelle Willis .50
Package 4 3.25
(C4) Sammy Sosa (Colossal) .50
(RS4) Hideki Matsui
(Rookie Star)(Thumb up.)) .50
(28) Roger Clemen/DP .75
(29) Adam Dunn .50
(30) Vladimir Guerrero .65
(31) Torii Hunter .50
(32) Pedro Martinez/DP .60
(33) Magglio Ordonez .50
(34) Mike Piazza/DP 1.00
(35) Ivan Rodriguez .60
(36) John Smoltz .50
Package 5 3.50
(C5) Barry Bonds (Colossal) 1.00
(RS5) Hideki Matsui/Fldg
(Rookie Star)(Running.) .50
(37) Lance Berkman .50
(38) Eric Chavez .50
(39) Troy Glaus .50
(40) Shawn Green .50
(41) Andruw Jones .65
(42) Manny Ramirez .65
(43) Curt Schilling .50
(44) Ichiro/DP 1.00
(45) Bernie Williams .50
Package 6 3.75
(C6) Mike Piazza (Colossal) .50
(RS6) Hideki Matsui/Fldg
(Rookie Star)(Standing.) .50
(46) Garret Anderson .50
(47) Rocco Baldelli .50
(48) Nomar Garciaparra 1.00
(49) Juan Gonzalez .50
(50) Ken Griffey Jr./TP .75
(51) Derek Jeter 1.50
(52) Gary Sheffield .50
(53) Frank Thomas .50
(54) Jim Thome .65
Package 7 3.25
(C7) Ichiro (Colossal) .50
(RS7) Hideki Matsui/Btg (Rookie
Star)(Both hands visible.) .50
(55) Carlos Delgado .50
(56) Jason Giambi .60
(57) Tom Glavine .50
(58) Luis Gonzalez .50
(59) Chipper Jones .75
(60) Mike Mussina .50
(61) Alex Rodriguez 1.25
(62) Scott Rolen .60
(63) Barry Zito .50

1993 Metallic Images Cooperstown Collection

This set of retired players is produced of durable, embossed metal with rolled edges. Limited to 49,900, it came packaged in a collectors' tin with a numbered certificate of authenticity. The cards feature full-color photos on the front

and back and statistics on the reverse. Half of the players in the set are members of the Hall of Fame.

		NM/M
Complete Set (20):		5.00
Common Player:		.10
1	Hank Aaron	1.50
2	Vida Blue	.10
3	Yogi Berra	.50
4	Bobby Bonds	.10
5	Lou Brock	.20
6	Lew Burdette	.10
7	Rod Carew	.20
8	Rocky Colavito	.20
9	George Foster	.10
10	Bob Gibson	.20
11	Mickey Lolich	.10
12	Willie Mays	1.50
13	Johnny Mize	.20
14	Don Newcombe	.15
15	Gaylord Perry	.20
16	Boog Powell	.20
17	Bill Skowron	.15
18	Warren Spahn	.35
19	Willie Stargell	.20
20	Luis Tiant	.10
P1	Willie Mays	1.25

1995 Metallic Images Babe Ruth

This five-card set of metal cards honors Babe Ruth in the 100th anniversary of his birth. The cards are 2-5/8" x 3-9/16" and featured gold-toned rolled edges. Fronts have familiar sepia-toned photos of the Babe with colorized backgrounds. "Cooperstown Collection" logos appear on front and back. Backs have an overall background of a ghost-image picture of Ruth at bat, along with a small sepia portrait photo, career summary and, on some cards, a few stats. The set was issued in a black embossed tin box, with cards in a cello wrapper.

		NM/M
Complete Boxed Set (5):		5.00
Common Card:		1.00
1	Babe Ruth (Batting follow-through.)	1.00
2	Babe Ruth (Seated with bat on shoulders.)	1.00
3	Babe Ruth (Batting follow-through.)	1.00
4	Babe Ruth (Standing behind 10 bats.)	1.00
5	Babe Ruth (Batting follow-through.)	1.00

Impressions Willie Mays

As part of its Cooperstown Collection series of embossed metal cards, this set traces Willie Mays' career. The set was originally marketed by Avon cosmetics and sold in a lithographed steel box with pictures of Mays on the top and sides. Each of the cards inside was sealed in a cellophane wrapper. Cards measure about 2-5/8" x 3-5/8" and feature monochrome or color photos lithographed on steel. Borders and other design details are embossed. A second photo of Mays is on back, along with a few sentences about his life and career.

		NM/M
Complete Boxed Set (5):		4.00
Common Card:		1.00
1	Willie Mays (Negro Leagues)	1.00
2	Willie Mays (Minor Leagues)	1.00
3	Willie Mays (Rookie Year)	1.00
4	Willie Mays (New York Mets)	1.00
5	Willie Mays (Willie, Mickey, and the Duke)	1.00

1996 Metallic Impressions Ken Griffey, Jr.

This set of metal cards was sold in a lithographed steel box with pictures of Griffey on the top and sides. Each of the cards inside was sealed in a cellophane wrapper. Cards measure about 2-5/8" x 3-5/8" and feature color photos lithographed on steel. Borders and other design details are embossed. Two more photos of Griffey are on back, along with a few sentences about his life and career.

		NM/M
Complete Boxed Set (5):		3.00
Common Card:		1.00
1	Ken Griffey Jr. (At bat.)	1.00
2	Ken Griffey Jr./Throwing	1.00
3	Ken Griffey Jr./Running	1.00
4	Ken Griffey Jr./Fldg	1.00
5	Ken Griffey Jr./Swinging	1.00

Iron Men of Baseball

Originally sold by Avon, this set of embossed metal cards was sold in a lithographed steel box with player pictures on the top and sides. Each of the cards inside was sealed in in a cellophane wrapper. Cards measure about 2-5/8" x 3-5/8" and feature black-and-white or color photos lithographed on steel. Borders and other design details are embossed. A pair of photos is on back, along with details of each player's consecutive games streak.

		NM/M
Complete Boxed Set (5):		6.00
Common Card:		1.50
1	Lou Gehrig	1.50
2	Lou Gehrig	1.50
3	Cal Ripken Jr.	1.50
4	Cal Ripken Jr.	1.50
5	Lou Gehrig, Cal Ripken Jr.	1.50

Cal Ripken, Jr.

Two versions of this set were produced, a five-card set (#1-5) and a 10-card set (#1-10). Highlights of Cal Ripken's career are presented on these metallic baseball cards. Each 2-5/8" x 3-5/8" card has a color photo at center, surrounded by team-colored borders. Embossed at the bottom is a script version of Ripken's name with an oriole atop. In the lower-right corner is a metallic-looking home plate with "Iron Oriole." Backs repeat some of the front graphics and have identical portrait and action photos of Ripken and the magic number "2131" in lights at top. A paragraph at bottom describes a career milestone or highlight. The sets were sold in embossed lithographed metal boxes. The 10-card set is accompanied by a serial numbered certificate from an edition of 29,950.

		NM/M
Complete Boxed Set (10):		7.50
Complete Boxed Set (5):		4.00
Common Card:		1.00
1	Cal Ripken Jr. (Major League debut.)	1.00

2	Cal Ripken Jr. (1982 - Opening Day 3B)	1.00
3	Cal Ripken Jr. (Streak begins.)	1.00
4	Cal Ripken Jr. (Rookie of the Year)	1.00
5	Cal Ripken Jr. (1983)	1.00
6	Cal Ripken Jr. (Consecutive innings streak.)	1.00
7	Cal Ripken Jr. (1991 MVP)	1.00
8	Cal Ripken Jr. (Gold Glover)	1.00
9	Cal Ripken Jr. (Game 2,130.)	1.00
10	Cal Ripken Jr. (Game 2,131.)	1.00

1996 Metallic Impressions 1936 Hall of Fame Electees

As part of its Cooperstown Collection series of embossed metal cards, this set was released in the 60th anniversary year of the first Hall of Fame selections. The set was sold in a lithographed steel box with player pictures on the top and sides. Each of the cards inside was sealed in a cellophane wrapper. Cards measure about 2-5/8" x 3-5/8" and feature black-and-white photos lithographed on steel. Borders and other design details are embossed. A black-and-white photo is on back, along with "Peak Performance" stats and a career summary. Sets were originally sold through Avon.

		NM/M
Complete Boxed Set (5):		4.50
Common Player:		1.00
1	Babe Ruth	2.00
2	Ty Cobb	1.50
3	Christy Mathewson	1.00
4	Walter Johnson	1.00
5	Honus Wagner	1.00

1997 Metallic Impressions Jackie Robinson

As part of its Cooperstown Collection series of embossed metal cards, this set was released in the 50th anniversary year of Jackie Robinson's entry into the major leagues. The set was sold in a lithographed steel box with pictures of Robinson on the top and sides. Each of the cards inside was sealed in a cellophane wrapper. Cards measure about 2-5/8" x 3-5/8" and feature monochrome or color photos lithographed on steel. Borders and other design details are embossed. A black-and-white photo of Robinson is on back, along with a few sentences about his life and career.

		NM/M
Complete Boxed Set (5):		5.00
Common Card:		1.25
1	Jackie Robinson (Thigh-to-cap portrait.)	1.25
2	Jackie Robinson (Chest-to-cap portrait.)	1.25
3	Jackie Robinson/Btg (Color)	1.25
4	Jackie Robinson/Fldg	1.25
5	Jackie Robinson/Btg (B/w)	1.2

1996 Metal Universe Sample Sheet

To introduce its premiere edition of Metal Universe baseball cards, Fleer sent a nine-card sample sheet to dealers. The 8" x 11" sheet has a black border on each side of each card. The cards are identical in format to the issued version, printed on etched foil and overprinted "PROMOTIONAL SAMPLE" in gold diagonally on front and back.

	NM/M
Complete Sheet:	10.00

1996 Metal Universe

One of the most unusual baseball card issues of its era, Fleer's Metal Universe set is distinguished by its colored, textured metallic-foil backgrounds created by comic book illustrators. The effects range from gaudy to grotesque. Glossy player action photos are featured on front, with a steel-colored metallic strip at bottom carrying set and player ID. Conventionally printed backs have a heavy-metal theme with a color player portrait photo and a few stats and personal data around. The issue was sold in hobby and retail packaging with the basic eight-card pack at a suggested retail price of $2.49. Several insert sets were included, along with a platinum parallel edition of the player cards.

		NM/M
Complete Set (250):		17.50
Common Player:		.10
Platinum Set (250):		75.00
Common Platinum:		.25
Platinums:		5X
Pack (8):		1.50
Wax Box (24):		17.50
1	Roberto Alomar	.20
2	Brady Anderson	.10
3	Bobby Bonilla	.10
4	Chris Holles	.10
5	Ben McDonald	.10
6	Mike Mussina	.40
7	Randy Myers	.10
8	Rafael Palmeiro	.60
9	Cal Ripken Jr.	2.50
10	B.J. Surhoff	.10
11	Luis Alicea	.10
12	Jose Canseco	.50
13	Roger Clemens	1.25
14	Wil Cordero	.10
15	Tom Gordon	.10
16	Mike Greenwell	.10
17	Tim Naehring	.10
18	Troy O'Leary	.10
19	Mike Stanley	.10
20	John Valentin	.10
21	Mo Vaughn	.10
22	Tim Wakefield	.10
23	Garret Anderson	.10
24	Chili Davis	.10
25	Gary DiSarcina	.10
26	Jim Edmonds	.10
27	Chuck Finley	.10
28	Todd Greene	.10
29	Mark Langston	.10
30	Troy Percival	.10
31	Tony Phillips	.10
32	Tim Salmon	.10
33	Lee Smith	.10
34	J.T. Snow	.10
35	Ray Durham	.10
36	Alex Fernandez	.10
37	Ozzie Guillen	.10
38	Roberto Hernandez	.10
39	Lyle Mouton	.10
40	Frank Thomas	.75
41	Robin Ventura	.10
42	Sandy Alomar	.10
43	Carlos Baerga	.10

44	Albert Belle	.10
45	Orel Hershiser	.10
46	Kenny Lofton	.10
47	Dennis Martinez	.10
48	Jack McDowell	.10
49	Jose Mesa	.10
50	Eddie Murray	.75
51	Charles Nagy	.10
52	Manny Ramirez	.75
53	Julian Tavarez	.10
54	Jim Thome	.60
55	Omar Vizquel	.10
56	Chad Curtis	.10
57	Cecil Fielder	.10
58	John Flaherty	.10
59	Travis Fryman	.10
60	Chris Gomez	.10
61	Felipe Lira	.10
62	Kevin Appier	.10
63	Johnny Damon	.35
64	Tom Goodwin	.10
65	Mark Gubicza	.10
66	Jeff Montgomery	.10
67	Jon Nunnally	.10
68	Ricky Bones	.10
69	Jeff Cirillo	.10
70	John Jaha	.10
71	Dave Nilsson	.10
72	Joe Oliver	.10
73	Kevin Seitzer	.10
74	Greg Vaughn	.10
75	Marty Cordova	.10
76	Chuck Knoblauch	.10
77	Pat Meares	.10
78	Paul Molitor	.75
79	Pedro Munoz	.10
80	Kirby Puckett	1.00
81	Brad Radke	.10
82	Scott Stahoviak	.10
83	Matt Walbeck	.10
84	Wade Boggs	1.00
85	David Cone	.10
86	Joe Girardi	.10
87	Derek Jeter	2.50
88	Jim Leyritz	.10
89	Tino Martinez	.10
90	Don Mattingly	1.50
91	Paul O'Neill	.10
92	Andy Pettitte	.25
93	Tim Raines	.10
94	Kenny Rogers	.10
95	Ruben Sierra	.10
96	John Wetteland	.10
97	Bernie Williams	.10
98	Geronimo Berroa	.10
99	Dennis Eckersley	.65
100	Brent Gates	.10
101	Mark McGwire	2.00
102	Steve Ontiveros	.10
103	Terry Steinbach	.10
104	Jay Buhner	.10
105	Vince Coleman	.10
106	Joey Cora	.10
107	Ken Griffey Jr.	1.50
108	Randy Johnson	.75
109	Edgar Martinez	.10
110	Alex Rodriguez	2.00
111	Paul Sorrento	.10
112	Will Clark	.10
113	Juan Gonzalez	.50
114	Rusty Greer	.10
115	Dean Palmer	.10
116	Ivan Rodriguez	.65
117	Mickey Tettleton	.10
118	Joe Carter	.10
119	Alex Gonzalez	.10
120	Shawn Green	.30
121	Erik Hanson	.10
122	Pat Hentgen	.10
123	Sandy Martinez RC	.10
124	Otis Nixon	.10
125	John Olerud	.40
126	Steve Avery	.10
127	Tom Glavine	.40
128	Marquis Grissom	.10
129	Chipper Jones	1.00
130	David Justice	.10
131	Ryan Klesko	.10
132	Mark Lemke	.10
133	Javier Lopez	.10
134	Greg Maddux	1.00
135	Fred McGriff	.10
136	John Smoltz	.10
137	Mark Wohlers	.10
138	Frank Castillo	.10
139	Shawon Dunston	.10
140	Luis Gonzalez	.20
141	Mark Grace	.10
142	Brian McRae	.10
143	Jaime Navarro	.10
144	Rey Sanchez	.10
145	Ryne Sandberg	1.00
146	Sammy Sosa	1.25
147	Bret Boone	.10
148	Curtis Goodwin	.10
149	Barry Larkin	.10
150	Hal Morris	.10
151	Reggie Sanders	.10
152	Pete Schourek	.10
153	John Smiley	.10
154	Dante Bichette	.10
155	Vinny Castilla	.10
156	Andres Galarraga	.10
157	Bret Saberhagen	.10
158	Bill Swift	.10
159	Larry Walker	.10
160	Walt Weiss	.10
161	Kurt Abbott	.10

162	John Burkett	.10
163	Greg Colbrunn	.10
164	Jeff Conine	.10
165	Chris Hammond	.10
166	Charles Johnson	.10
167	Al Leiter	.10
168	Pat Rapp	.10
169	Gary Sheffield	.40
170	Quilvio Veras	.10
171	Devon White	.10
172	Jeff Bagwell	.75
173	Derek Bell	.10
174	Sean Berry	.10
175	Craig Biggio	.75
176	Doug Drabek	.10
177	Tony Eusebio	.10
178	Brian Hunter	.10
179	Orlando Miller	.10
180	Shane Reynolds	.10
181	Mike Blowers	.10
182	Roger Cedeno	.10
183	Eric Karros	.10
184	Ramon Martinez	.10
185	Raul Mondesi	.10
186	Hideo Nomo	.60
187	Mike Piazza	1.50
188	Moises Alou	.10
189	Yamil Benitez	.10
190	Darrin Fletcher	.10
191	Cliff Floyd	.10
192	Pedro Martinez	.75
193	Carlos Perez	.10
194	David Segui	.10
195	Tony Tarasco	.10
196	Rondell White	.10
197	Edgardo Alfonzo	.10
198	Rico Brogna	.10
199	Carl Everett	.10
200	Todd Hundley	.10
201	Jason Isringhausen	.10
202	Lance Johnson	.10
203	Bobby Jones	.10
204	Jeff Kent	.10
205	Bill Pulsipher	.10
206	Jose Vizcaino	.10
207	Ricky Bottalico	.10
208	Darren Daulton	.10
209	Lenny Dykstra	.10
210	Jim Eisenreich	.10
211	Gregg Jefferies	.10
212	Mickey Morandini	.10
213	Heathcliff Slocumb	.10
214	Jay Bell	.10
215	Carlos Garcia	.10
216	Jeff King	.10
217	Al Martin	.10
218	Orlando Merced	.10
219	Dan Miceli	.10
220	Denny Neagle	.10
221	Andy Benes	.10
222	Royce Clayton	.10
223	Gary Gaetti	.10
224	Ron Gant	.10
225	Bernard Gilkey	.10
226	Brian Jordan	.10
227	Ray Lankford	.10
228	John Mabry	.10
229	Ozzie Smith	1.00
230	Todd Stottlemyre	.10
231	Andy Ashby	.10
232	Brad Ausmus	.10
233	Ken Caminiti	.10
234	Steve Finley	.10
235	Tony Gwynn	1.00
236	Joey Hamilton	.10
237	Rickey Henderson	.75
238	Trevor Hoffman	.10
239	Wally Joyner	.10
240	Rod Beck	.10
241	Barry Bonds	2.50
242	Glenallen Hill	.10
243	Stan Javier	.10
244	Mark Leiter	.10
245	Deion Sanders	.15
246	William VanLandingham	.10
247	Matt Williams	.10
248	Checklist	.10
249	Checklist	.10
250	Checklist	.10

Platinum Edition

One of the eight cards in each pack of Fleer Metal baseball is a Platinum Edition parallel insert. Each of the 247 player cards (no checklists) in this special version has the textured foil background

rendered only in silver. The second line of the logo/ID strip at bottom also identifies the card as part of the Platinum Edition.

	NM/M
Complete Set (247):	75.00
Common Player:	.25
Stars:	5X

Heavy Metal

Some of the game's biggest hitters are included in this insert set. Action photos of players at bat are set on a silver-foil background on front. Backs have a close-up photo down one side, with praise for the player's power potential down the other. The Heavy Metal inserts can be expected to turn up at an average rate of one per eight packs.

		NM/M
Complete Set (10):		5.00
Common Player:		.35
1	Albert Belle	.35
2	Barry Bonds	1.50
3	Juan Gonzalez	.50
4	Ken Griffey Jr.	1.00
5	Mark McGwire	1.25
6	Mike Piazza	1.00
7	Sammy Sosa	.90
8	Frank Thomas	.60
9	Mo Vaughn	.35
10	Matt Williams	.35

Mining for Gold

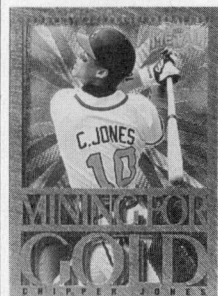

Available only in retail packs, at an average rate of one per dozen packs, the Mining for Gold insert series focuses on 1995's top rookies. Fronts have player action photos frame and backgrounded with several different gold tones in etched metal foil. Backs are conventionally printed, carrying on the same format with a portrait photo and a few words about the player.

		NM/M
Complete Set (12):		12.50
Common Player:		.75
1	Yamil Benitez	.75
2	Marty Cordova	.75
3	Shawn Green	2.00
4	Todd Greene	.75
5	Brian Hunter	.75
6	Derek Jeter	7.50
7	Charles Johnson	.75
8	Chipper Jones	3.50
9	Hideo Nomo	2.50
10	Alex Ochoa	.75
11	Andy Pettitte	1.00
12	Quilvio Veras	.75

Mother Lode

Medieval designs rendered in textured silver-foil on a plain white background are the setting for the color player photos in this hobby-only insert set. Backs also have a silver and white background along with another player photo and some

kind words about his skills. The cards are found at an average rate of one per 12 packs.

		NM/M
Complete Set (12):		15.00
Common Player:		.75
1	Barry Bonds	4.50
2	Jim Edmonds	.75
3	Ken Griffey Jr.	3.50
4	Kenny Lofton	.75
5	Raul Mondesi	.75
6	Rafael Palmeiro	1.50
7	Manny Ramirez	2.00
8	Cal Ripken Jr.	4.50
9	Tim Salmon	.75
10	Ryne Sandberg	3.00
11	Frank Thomas	2.00
12	Matt Williams	.75

Platinum Portraits

Close-up color photos on a plain metallic-foil background are featured in this insert set. The checklist is heavy in rookie and sophomore players, who are featured in an action photo on back, with a few career details. Platinum Portraits inserts are found in every fourth pack, on average.

		NM/M
Complete Set (10):		4.00
Common Player:		.40
1	Garret Anderson	.40
2	Marty Cordova	.40
3	Jim Edmonds	.40
4	Jason Isringhausen	.40
5	Chipper Jones	2.25
6	Ryan Klesko	.40
7	Hideo Nomo	1.00
8	Carlos Perez	.40
9	Manny Ramirez	1.50
10	Rondell White	.40

1996 Metal Universe Titanium

A huge purple-highlighted silver baseball in a star-studded night sky is the background for the action photos of the game's biggest names in this insert series. Backs have a second, more up-close, photo and a few words about the player. Titanium inserts are found in Metal Universe packs at an average rate of one per 24 packs.

		NM/M
Complete Set (10):		15.00
Common Player:		.50
1	Albert Belle	.50
2	Barry Bonds	4.00
3	Ken Griffey Jr.	2.50
4	Tony Gwynn	1.50

5	Greg Maddux	1.50
6	Mike Piazza	2.50
7	Cal Ripken Jr.	4.00
8	Frank Thomas	1.00
9	Mo Vaughn	.50
10	Matt Williams	.50

1997 Metal Universe

Metal Universe Baseball arrived in a 250-card set, including three checklists. Each card is printed on 100-percent etched foil with "comic book" art full-bleed backgrounds, with the player's name, team, position and the Metal Universe logo near the bottom of the card. Backs contain another player photo and key statistics. Metal Universe sold in eight-card packs and contained six different insert sets. They included: Blast Furnace, Magnetic Field, Mining for Gold, Mother Lode, Platinum Portraits and Titanium.

		NM/M
Complete Set (250):		17.50
Common Player:		.10
Pack (8):		1.50
Wax Box (24):		18.00
1	Roberto Alomar	.20
2	Brady Anderson	.10
3	Rocky Coppinger	.10
4	Chris Hoiles	.10
5	Eddie Murray	.60
6	Mike Mussina	.40
7	Rafael Palmeiro	.50
8	Cal Ripken Jr.	2.00
9	B.J. Surhoff	.10
10	Brant Brown	.10
11	Mark Grace	.10
12	Brian McRae	.10
13	Jaime Navarro	.10
14	Ryne Sandberg	.75
15	Sammy Sosa	1.00
16	Amaury Telemaco	.10
17	Steve Trachsel	.10
18	Darren Bragg	.10
19	Jose Canseco	.40
20	Roger Clemens	1.00
21	Nomar Garciaparra	1.00
22	Tom Gordon	.10
23	Tim Naehring	.10
24	Mike Stanley	.10
25	John Valentin	.10
26	Mo Vaughn	.40
27	Jermaine Dye	.10
28	Tom Glavine	.30
29	Marquis Grissom	.10
30	Andruw Jones	.60
31	Chipper Jones	.75
32	Ryan Klesko	.10
33	Greg Maddux	.75
34	Fred McGriff	.10
35	John Smoltz	.10
36	Garret Anderson	.10
37	George Arias	.10
38	Gary DiSarcina	.10
39	Jim Edmonds	.10
40	Darin Erstad	.25
41	Chuck Finley	.10
42	Troy Percival	.10
43	Tim Salmon	.10
44	Bret Boone	.10
45	Jeff Brantley	.10
46	Eric Davis	.10
47	Barry Larkin	.10
48	Hal Morris	.10
49	Mark Portugal	.10
50	Reggie Sanders	.10
51	John Smiley	.10
52	Wilson Alvarez	.10
53	Harold Baines	.10
54	James Baldwin	.10
55	Albert Belle	.10
56	Mike Cameron	.10
57	Ray Durham	.10
58	Alex Fernandez	.10
59	Roberto Hernandez	.10
60	Tony Phillips	.10
61	Frank Thomas	.60
62	Robin Ventura	.10
63	Jeff Cirillo	.10
64	Jeff D'Amico	.10
65	John Jaha	.10
66	Scott Karl	.10
67	Ben McDonald	.10

68	Marc Newfield	.10
69	Dave Nilsson	.10
70	Jose Valentin	.10
71	Dante Bichette	.10
72	Ellis Burks	.10
73	Vinny Castilla	.10
74	Andres Galarraga	.10
75	Kevin Ritz	.10
76	Larry Walker	.10
77	Walt Weiss	.10
78	Jamey Wright	.10
79	Eric Young	.10
80	Julio Franco	.10
81	Orel Hershiser	.10
82	Kenny Lofton	.10
83	Jack McDowell	.10
84	Jose Mesa	.10
85	Charles Nagy	.10
86	Manny Ramirez	.60
87	Jim Thome	.50
88	Omar Vizquel	.10
89	Matt Williams	.10
90	Kevin Appier	.10
91	Johnny Damon	.35
92	Chili Davis	.10
93	Tom Goodwin	.10
94	Keith Lockhart	.10
95	Jeff Montgomery	.10
96	Craig Paquette	.10
97	Jose Rosado	.10
98	Michael Tucker	.10
99	Wilton Guerrero	.10
100	Todd Hollandsworth	.10
101	Eric Karros	.10
102	Ramon Martinez	.10
103	Raul Mondesi	.10
104	Hideo Nomo	.60
105	Mike Piazza	1.25
106	Ismael Valdes	.10
107	Todd Worrell	.10
108	Tony Clark	.10
109	Travis Fryman	.10
110	Bob Higginson	.10
111	Mark Lewis	.10
112	Melvin Nieves	.10
113	Justin Thompson	.10
114	Wade Boggs	.75
115	David Cone	.10
116	Cecil Fielder	.10
117	Dwight Gooden	.10
118	Derek Jeter	2.00
119	Tino Martinez	.10
120	Paul O'Neill	.10
121	Andy Pettitte	.20
122	Mariano Rivera	.20
123	Darryl Strawberry	.10
124	John Wetteland	.10
125	Bernie Williams	.10
126	Tony Batista	.10
127	Geronimo Berroa	.10
128	Scott Brosius	.10
129	Jason Giambi	.50
130	Jose Herrera	.10
131	Mark McGwire	1.50
132	John Wasdin	.10
133	Bob Abreu	.10
134	Jeff Bagwell	.60
135	Derek Bell	.10
136	Craig Biggio	.10
137	Brian Hunter	.10
138	Darryl Kile	.10
139	Orlando Miller	.10
140	Shane Reynolds	.10
141	Billy Wagner	.10
142	Donne Wall	.10
143	Jay Buhner	.10
144	Jeff Fassero	.10
145	Ken Griffey Jr.	1.25
146	Sterling Hitchcock	.10
147	Randy Johnson	.60
148	Edgar Martinez	.10
149	Alex Rodriguez	1.50
149p	Alex Rodriguez/OPS	1.50
150	Paul Sorrento	.10
151	Dan Wilson	.10
152	Moises Alou	.10
153	Darrin Fletcher	.10
154	Cliff Floyd	.10
155	Mark Grudzielanek	.10
156	Vladimir Guerrero	.60
157	Mike Lansing	.10
158	Pedro Martinez	.60
159	Henry Rodriguez	.10
160	Rondell White	.10
161	Will Clark	.10
162	Juan Gonzalez	.50
163	Rusty Greer	.10
164	Ken Hill	.10
165	Mark McLemore	.10
166	Dean Palmer	.10
167	Roger Pavlik	.10
168	Ivan Rodriguez	.50
169	Mickey Tettleton	.10
170	Bobby Bonilla	.10
171	Kevin Brown	.10
172	Greg Colbrunn	.10
173	Jeff Conine	.10
174	Jim Eisenreich	.10
175	Charles Johnson	.10
176	Al Leiter	.10
177	Robb Nen	.10
178	Edgar Renteria	.10
179	Gary Sheffield	.40
180	Devon White	.10
181	Joe Carter	.10
182	Carlos Delgado	.40
183	Alex Gonzalez	.10
184	Shawn Green	.35

185	Juan Guzman	.10
186	Pat Hentgen	.10
187	Orlando Merced	.10
188	John Olerud	.10
189	Robert Perez	.10
190	Ed Sprague	.10
191	Mark Clark	.10
192	John Franco	.10
193	Bernard Gilkey	.10
194	Todd Hundley	.10
195	Lance Johnson	.10
196	Bobby Jones	.10
197	Alex Ochoa	.10
198	Rey Ordonez	.10
199	Paul Wilson	.10
200	Ricky Bottalico	.10
201	Gregg Jefferies	.10
202	Wendell Magee Jr.	.10
203	Mickey Morandini	.10
204	Ricky Otero	.10
205	Scott Rolen	.50
206	Benito Santiago	.10
207	Curt Schilling	.25
208	Rich Becker	.10
209	Marty Cordova	.10
210	Chuck Knoblauch	.10
211	Pat Meares	.10
212	Paul Molitor	.60
213	Frank Rodriguez	.10
214	Terry Steinbach	.10
215	Todd Walker	.10
216	Andy Ashby	.10
217	Ken Caminiti	.10
218	Steve Finley	.10
219	Tony Gwynn	.75
220	Joey Hamilton	.10
221	Rickey Henderson	.60
222	Trevor Hoffman	.10
223	Wally Joyner	.10
224	Scott Sanders	.10
225	Fernando Valenzuela	.10
226	Greg Vaughn	.10
227	Alan Benes	.10
228	Andy Benes	.10
229	Dennis Eckersley	.50
230	Ron Gant	.10
231	Brian Jordan	.10
232	Ray Lankford	.10
233	John Mabry	.10
234	Tom Pagnozzi	.10
235	Todd Stottlemyre	.10
236	Jermaine Allensworth	.10
237	Francisco Cordova	.10
238	Jason Kendall	.10
239	Jeff King	.10
240	Al Martin	.10
241	Rod Beck	.10
242	Barry Bonds	2.00
243	Shawn Estes	.10
244	Mark Gardner	.10
245	Glenallen Hill	.10
246	Bill Mueller	.10
247	J.T. Snow	.10
248	Checklist	.10
249	Checklist	.10
250	Checklist	.10

Blast Furnace

Blast Furnace inserts were found only in hobby packs, at a rate of one per 48 packs. The 12-card set was printed on a red-tinted plastic, with the words "Blast Furnace" near the bottom in gold foil with a fire-like border.

		NM/M
Complete Set (12):		40.00
Common Player:		1.50
1	Jeff Bagwell	4.00
2	Albert Belle	1.50
3	Barry Bonds	7.50
4	Andres Galarraga	1.50
5	Juan Gonzalez	2.50
6	Ken Griffey Jr.	5.00
7	Todd Hundley	1.50
8	Mark McGwire	6.00
9	Mike Piazza	5.00
10	Alex Rodriguez	6.00
11	Frank Thomas	4.00
12	Mo Vaughn	1.50

Emerald Autograph Redemption

Six different young stars were featured in this insert, which was found every 480 hobby packs of Metal Universe. The cards are similar to regular-issue cards, but have green foil highlights. Redemption cards are numbered AU1-AU6. The redemption period expired Jan. 15, 1998.

		NM/M
Complete Set (6):		10.00
Common Player:		1.00
1	Darin Erstad	1.50
2	Todd Hollandsworth	1.00
3	Alex Ochoa	.75
4	Alex Rodriguez	7.50
5	Scott Rolen	1.50
6	Todd Walker	1.00

Emerald Autographs

Six different young stars were featured in this insert, which was found every 480 hobby packs of Metal Universe. The cards are similar to regular-issue cards, but have a green foil finish and autograph on the front. Redemption cards are numbered AU1-AU6, the autographed cards have a notation on back, "Certified Emerald Autograph Card."

		NM/M
Complete Set (6):		75.00
Common Autograph:		4.00
1	Darin Erstad	6.00
2	Todd Hollandsworth	4.00
3	Alex Ochoa	4.00
4	Alex Rodriguez	60.00
5	Scott Rolen	10.00
6	Todd Walker	4.00

Magnetic Field

Magnetic Field inserts are printed in a horizontal format with prismatic foil backgrounds. This 10-card insert was found every 12 packs of Metal Universe.

		NM/M
Complete Set (10):		15.00
Common Player:		.75
1	Roberto Alomar	.75
2	Jeff Bagwell	1.25
3	Barry Bonds	.75
4	Ken Griffey Jr.	2.00
5	Derek Jeter	3.00
6	Kenny Lofton	.75
7	Edgar Renteria	.75
8	Cal Ripken Jr.	3.00
9	Alex Rodriguez	2.50
10	Matt Williams	.75

Mining for Gold

Mining for Gold was a 10-card insert that featured some of baseball's brightest stars on a die-cut "ingot" design with pearlized gold coating. This insert was found every nine packs.

		NM/M
Complete Set (10):		12.00
Common Player:		.75
1	Bob Abreu	.75
2	Kevin Brown	.75
3	Nomar Garciaparra	3.50
4	Vladimir Guerrero	3.00
5	Wilton Guerrero	.75
6	Andruw Jones	3.00
7	Curt Lyons	.75
8	Neifi Perez	.75
9	Scott Rolen	2.00
10	Todd Walker	.75

Mother Lode

Mother lode was the most difficult insert out of Metal Universe with a one per 288 pack insertion ratio. Each card in this 10-card inert was printed on etched foil with a plant-type monument in back of the player.

		NM/M
Complete Set (12):		80.00
Common Player:		2.00
1	Roberto Alomar	2.50
2	Jeff Bagwell	6.00
3	Barry Bonds	15.00
4	Ken Griffey Jr.	10.00
5	Andruw Jones	6.00
6	Chipper Jones	8.00
7	Kenny Lofton	2.00
8	Mike Piazza	10.00
9	Cal Ripken Jr.	15.00
10	Alex Rodriguez	12.50
11	Frank Thomas	6.00
12	Matt Williams	2.00

Platinum Portraits

Each card in the Platinum Portraits insert is printed on a background of platinum-colored etched foil. The 10-card set includes some of the top prospects and rising stars in baseball, and is included every 36 packs.

		NM/M
Complete Set (10):		10.00

Common Player:	.60
1 James Baldwin	.60
2 Jermaine Dye	.60
3 Todd Hollandsworth	.60
4 Derek Jeter	5.00
5 Chipper Jones	2.00
6 Jason Kendall	.60
7 Rey Ordonez	.60
8 Andy Pettitte	1.00
9 Edgar Renteria	.60
10 Alex Rodriguez	3.25

Titanium

These retail exclusive inserts include 10 cards and were found every 24 packs. Each card is die-cut on the top-left and bottom-right corner with a silver foil background. Titanium includes some of the most popular players in baseball on cards that are also embossed.

		NM/M
Complete Set (10):		24.00
Common Player:		1.50
1	Jeff Bagwell	2.00
2	Albert Belle	1.50
3	Ken Griffey Jr.	3.00
4	Chipper Jones	2.50
5	Greg Maddux	2.50
6	Mark McGwire	4.00
7	Mike Piazza	3.00
8	Cal Ripken Jr.	5.00
9	Alex Rodriguez	4.00
10	Frank Thomas	2.00

1998 Metal Universe

This 220-card single series release captured players over a foil etched, art background that related in some way to them or the city they played in. Metal Universe included a 15-card Hardball Galaxy subset and dealers and media were given an Alex Rodriguez promo card that was identical the base card except for the words "Promotional Sample" written across the back. The set arrived with a parallel called Precious Metal Gems, and included the following insert sets: All-Galactic Team, Diamond Heroes, Platinum Portraits, Titanium and Universal Language.

		NM/M
Complete Set (220):		15.00
Common Player:		.10
Pack (8):		1.50
Wax Box (24):		20.00
1	Jose Cruz Jr.	.10
2	Jeff Abbott	.10
3	Rafael Palmeiro	.65
4	Ivan Rodriguez	.65
5	Jaret Wright	.10
6	Derek Bell	.10
7	Chuck Finley	.10
8	Travis Fryman	.10
9	Randy Johnson	.75
10	Derrek Lee	.50
11	Bernie Williams	.10
12	Carlos Baerga	.10
13	Ricky Bottalico	.10
14	Ellis Burks	.10
15	Russ Davis	.10
16	Nomar Garciaparra	1.00
17	Joey Hamilton	.10
18	Jason Kendall	.10
19	Darryl Kile	.10
20	Edgardo Alfonzo	.10
21	Moises Alou	.10
22	Bobby Bonilla	.10
23	Jim Edmonds	.10
24	Jose Guillen	.10
25	Chuck Knoblauch	.10
26	Javy Lopez	.10
27	Billy Wagner	.10
28	Kevin Appier	.10
29	Joe Carter	.10
30	Todd Dunwoody	.10
31	Gary Gaetti	.10
32	Juan Gonzalez	.60
33	Jeffrey Hammonds	.10
34	Roberto Hernandez	.10
35	Dave Nilsson	.10
36	Manny Ramirez	.75
37	Robin Ventura	.10
38	Rondell White	.10
39	Vinny Castilla	.10
40	Will Clark	.10
41	Scott Hatteberg	.10
42	Russ Johnson	.10
43	Ricky Ledee	.10
44	Kenny Lofton	.10
45	Paul Molitor	.75
46	Justin Thompson	.10
47	Craig Biggio	.10
48	Damion Easley	.10
49	Brad Radke	.10
50	Ben Grieve	.10
51	Mark Bellhorn	.10
52	Henry Blanco RC	.10
53	Mariano Rivera	.20
54	Reggie Sanders	.10
55	Paul Sorrento	.10
56	Terry Steinbach	.10
57	Mo Vaughn	.10
58	Brady Anderson	.10
59	Tom Glavine	.40
60	Sammy Sosa	1.25
61	Larry Walker	.10
62	Rod Beck	.10
63	Jose Canseco	.45
64	Steve Finley	.10
65	Pedro Martinez	.75
66	John Olerud	.10
67	Scott Rolen	.60
68	Ismael Valdes	.10
69	Andrew Vessel	.10
70	Mark Grudzielanek	.10
71	Eric Karros	.10
72	Jeff Shaw	.10
73	Lou Collier	.10
74	Edgar Martinez	.10
75	Vladimir Guerrero	.75
76	Paul Konerko	.25
77	Kevin Orie	.10
78	Kevin Polcovich	.10
79	Brett Tomko	.10
80	Jeff Bagwell	.75
81	Barry Bonds	2.50
82	David Justice	.10
83	Hideo Nomo	.60
84	Ryne Sandberg	1.00
85	Shannon Stewart	.10
86	Derek Wallace	.10
87	Tony Womack	.10
88	Jason Giambi	.50
89	Mark Grace	.10
90	Pat Hentgen	.10
91	Raul Mondesi	.10
92	Matt Morris	.10
93	Matt Perisho	.10
94	Tim Salmon	.10
95	Jeremi Gonzalez	.10
96	Shawn Green	.25
97	Todd Greene	.10
98	Ruben Rivera	.10
99	Deion Sanders	.10
100	Alex Rodriguez	2.00
101	Will Cunnane	.10
102	Ray Lankford	.10
103	Ryan McGuire	.10
104	Charles Nagy	.10
105	Rey Ordonez	.10
106	Mike Piazza	1.50
107	Tony Saunders	.10
108	Curt Schilling	.25
109	Fernando Tatis	.10
110	Mark McGwire	2.00
111	David Dellucci RC	.10
112	Garret Anderson	.10
113	Shane Bowers	.10
114	David Cone	.10
115	Jeff King	.10
116	Matt Williams	.10
117	Aaron Boone	.10
118	Dennis Eckersley	.65
119	Livan Hernandez	.10
120	Richard Hidalgo	.10
121	Bobby Higginson	.10
122	Tino Martinez	.10
123	Tim Naehring	.10
124	Jose Vidro	.10
125	John Wetteland	.10
126	Jay Bell	.10
127	Albert Belle	.10
128	Marty Cordova	.10
129	Chili Davis	.10
130	Jason Dickson	.10
131	Rusty Greer	.10
132	Hideki Irabu	.10
133	Greg Maddux	1.00
134	Billy Taylor	.10
135	Jim Thome	.60
136	Gerald Williams	.10
137	Jeff Cirillo	.10
138	Delino DeShields	.10
139	Andres Galarraga	.10
140	Willie Greene	.10
141	John Jaha	.10
142	Charles Johnson	.10
143	Ryan Klesko	.10
144	Paul O'Neill	.10
145	Robinson Checo	.10
146	Roberto Alomar	.20
147	Wilson Alvarez	.10
148	Bobby Jones	.10
149	Raul Casanova	.10
150	Andruw Jones	.75
151	Mike Lansing	.10
152	Mickey Morandini	.10
153	Neifi Perez	.10
154	Pokey Reese	.10
155	Edgar Renteria	.10
156	Eric Young	.10
157	Darin Erstad	.20
158	Kelvim Escobar	.10
159	Carl Everett	.10
160	Tom Gordon	.10
161	Ken Griffey Jr.	1.50
162	Al Martin	.10
163	Bubba Trammell	.10
164	Carlos Delgado	.30
165	Kevin Brown	.10
166	Ken Caminiti	.10
167	Roger Clemens	1.25
168	Ron Gant	.10
169	Jeff Kent	.10
170	Mike Mussina	.40
171	Dean Palmer	.10
172	Henry Rodriguez	.10
173	Matt Stairs	.10
174	Jay Buhner	.10
175	Frank Thomas	.75
176	Mike Cameron	.10
177	Johnny Damon	.35
178	Tony Gwynn	1.00
179	John Smoltz	.10
180	B.J. Surhoff	.10
181	Antone Williamson	.10
182	Alan Benes	.10
183	Jeromy Burnitz	.10
184	Tony Clark	.10
185	Shawn Estes	.10
186	Todd Helton	.65
187	Todd Hundley	.10
188	Chipper Jones	1.00
189	Mark Kotsay	.10
190	Barry Larkin	.10
191	Mike Lieberthal	.10
192	Andy Pettitte	.25
193	Gary Sheffield	.35
194	Jeff Suppan	.10
195	Mark Wohlers	.10
196	Dante Bichette	.10
197	Trevor Hoffman	.10
198	J.T. Snow	.10
199	Derek Jeter	2.50
200	Cal Ripken Jr.	2.50
201	Steve Woodard RC	.25
202	Ray Durham	.10
203	Barry Bonds (Hardball Galaxy)	1.50
204	Tony Clark (Hardball Galaxy)	.10
205	Roger Clemens (Hardball Galaxy)	.65
206	Ken Griffey Jr. (Hardball Galaxy)	.75
207	Tony Gwynn (Hardball Galaxy)	.50
208	Derek Jeter (Hardball Galaxy)	1.50
209	Randy Johnson (Hardball Galaxy)	.40
210	Mark McGwire (Hardball Galaxy)	1.00
211	Hideo Nomo (Hardball Galaxy)	.30
212	Mike Piazza (Hardball Galaxy)	.75
213	Cal Ripken Jr. (Hardball Galaxy)	1.50
214	Alex Rodriguez (Hardball Galaxy)	1.00
215	Frank Thomas (Hardball Galaxy)	.40
216	Mo Vaughn (Hardball Galaxy)	.10
217	Larry Walker (Hardball Galaxy)	.10
218	Checklist (Ken Griffey Jr.)	.50
219	Checklist (Alex Rodriguez)	.60
220	Checklist (Frank Thomas)	.30

Precious Metal Gems

Precious Metal Gems includes 217 (no checklists) player cards from Metal Universe and are serial numbered to 50 sets. Because there were five Ultimate Metal Gems redemption cards (good for a complete set of Metal Gems) available, only serial numbers 1-45 were found in packs (46-50 were held back for the exchange program).

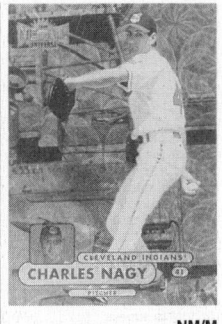

CHARLES NAGY

Common Player:	3.00
Stars:	25X
Production 50 Sets	

All-Galactic Team

This 18-card insert captures players over a planet holofoil background. Cards were inserted one per 192 packs.

		NM/M
Complete Set (18):		140.00
Common Player:		3.00
Inserted 1:192		
1	Ken Griffey Jr.	12.50
2	Frank Thomas	7.50
3	Chipper Jones	10.00
4	Albert Belle	3.00
5	Juan Gonzalez	5.00
6	Jeff Bagwell	7.50
7	Andruw Jones	7.50
8	Cal Ripken Jr.	20.00
9	Derek Jeter	20.00
10	Nomar Garciaparra	10.00
11	Darin Erstad	4.00
12	Greg Maddux	10.00
13	Alex Rodriguez	15.00
14	Mike Piazza	12.50
15	Vladimir Guerrero	7.50
16	Jose Cruz Jr.	3.00
17	Mark McGwire	15.00
18	Scott Rolen	5.00

Diamond Heroes

Diamond Heroes displayed six players in a comic book setting. This insert was seeded one per 18 packs and contained a foil etched image of a Marvel comic in the background.

		NM/M
Complete Set (6):		8.00
Common Player:		.50
Inserted 1:18		
1	Ken Griffey Jr.	2.00
2	Frank Thomas	1.50
3	Andruw Jones	1.50
4	Alex Rodriguez	2.50
5	Jose Cruz Jr.	.50
6	Cal Ripken Jr.	3.00

Platinum Portraits

This 12-card insert set featured color portraits of top players highlighted with a platinum-colored etched foil frame over it. Platinum Portraits are seeded one per 360 packs of Metal Universe.

	NM/M
Complete Set (12):	90.00
Common Player:	4.00
Inserted 1:360	
1 Ken Griffey Jr.	12.00
2 Frank Thomas	7.50
3 Chipper Jones	10.00
4 Jose Cruz Jr.	4.00
5 Andruw Jones	7.50
6 Cal Ripken Jr.	17.50
7 Derek Jeter	17.50
8 Darin Erstad	4.00
9 Greg Maddux	9.00
10 Alex Rodriguez	15.00
11 Mike Piazza	12.00
12 Vladimir Guerrero	7.50

Titanium

This die-cut 15-card insert contained color photos printed on embossed, sculpted cards on etched foil. Titanium inserts were seeded one per 96 packs.

	NM/M
Complete Set (15):	50.00
Common Player:	2.00
Inserted 1:96	
1 Ken Griffey Jr.	5.00
2 Frank Thomas	3.00
3 Chipper Jones	4.00
4 Jose Cruz Jr.	2.00
5 Juan Gonzalez	2.50
6 Scott Rolen	2.50
7 Andruw Jones	3.00
8 Cal Ripken Jr.	7.50
9 Derek Jeter	7.50
10 Nomar Garciaparra	4.00
11 Darin Erstad	2.50
12 Greg Maddux	4.00
13 Alex Rodriguez	6.00
14 Mike Piazza	5.00
15 Vladimir Guerrero	3.00

Universal Language

This 20-card insert features illustration and copy done in the player's native language. Cards were die-cut and inserted one per six packs.

	NM/M
Complete Set (20):	16.00
Common Player:	.40
Inserted 1:6	

1	Ken Griffey Jr.	1.25
2	Frank Thomas	.75
3	Chipper Jones	1.00
4	Albert Belle	.40
5	Juan Gonzalez	.60
6	Jeff Bagwell	.75
7	Andruw Jones	.75
8	Cal Ripken Jr.	2.00
9	Derek Jeter	2.00
10	Nomar Garciaparra	1.00
11	Darin Erstad	.50
12	Greg Maddux	1.00
13	Alex Rodriguez	1.50
14	Mike Piazza	1.25
15	Vladimir Guerrero	.75
16	Jose Cruz Jr.	.40
17	Hideo Nomo	.60
18	Kenny Lofton	.40
19	Tony Gwynn	1.00
20	Scott Rolen	.60

1999 Metal Universe Sample Sheet

To introduce its annual issue of embossed cards this six-card sheet of Metal Universe samples was issued. The 5" x 10-1/2" sheet has five regular cards and an example of the Building Blocks insert set. Cards on the sheet are virtually identical to the issued versions except they have the word "SAMPLE" on back in place of card numbers. At the February Hawaii trade show, 325 sheets with a special gold seal, serial numbered and autographed by J.D. Drew were distributed to attendees.

	NM/M
Complete Sheet:	7.50
Complete Autographed Sheet:	60.00

1999 Metal Universe

The 300-card base set offers 232 player cards and three subsets: Building Blocks, M.L.P.D. and Caught on the Fly. Base cards feature an action photo framed in an etched-foil and metallic, embossed name plate. Packs consist of eight cards with an S.R.P. of $2.69. There are two parallels, Precious Metal Gems and Gem Masters. Metal Gems are numbered to 50 with gold-foil etching. Gem Masters are limited to only one set, with silver foil etching and serial numbered "one of one."

	NM/M
Complete Set (300):	15.00
Common Player:	.10
Pack (8):	1.00
Wax Box (24):	20.00
1 Mark McGwire	1.50
2 Jim Edmonds	.10

3	Travis Fryman	.10
4	Tom Gordon	.10
5	Jeff Bagwell	.65
6	Rico Brogna	.10
7	Tom Evans	.10
8	John Franco	.10
9	Juan Gonzalez	.50
10	Paul Molitor	.65
11	Roberto Alomar	.20
12	Mike Hampton	.10
13	Orel Hershiser	.10
14	Todd Stottlemyre	.10
15	Robin Ventura	.10
16	Todd Walker	.10
17	Bernie Williams	.10
18	Shawn Estes	.10
19	Richie Sexson	.10
20	Kevin Millwood	.10
21	David Ortiz	.50
22	Mariano Rivera	.15
23	Ivan Rodriguez	.60
24	Mike Sirotka	.10
25	David Justice	.10
26	Carl Pavano	.10
27	Albert Belle	.10
28	Will Clark	.10
29	Jose Cruz Jr.	.40
30	Trevor Hoffman	.10
31	Dean Palmer	.10
32	Edgar Renteria	.10
33	David Segui	.10
34	B.J. Surhoff	.10
35	Miguel Tejada	.15
36	Bob Wickman	.10
37	Charles Johnson	.10
38	Andruw Jones	.65
39	Mike Lieberthal	.10
40	Eli Marrero	.10
41	Neifi Perez	.10
42	Jim Thome	.50
43	Barry Bonds	2.00
44	Carlos Delgado	.30
45	Chuck Finley	.10
46	Brian Meadows	.10
47	Tony Gwynn	.75
48	Jose Offerman	.10
49	Cal Ripken Jr.	2.00
50	Alex Rodriguez	1.50
51	Esteban Yan	.10
52	Matt Stairs	.10
53	Fernando Vina	.10
54	Rondell White	.10
55	Kerry Wood	.30
56	Dmitri Young	.10
57	Ken Caminiti	.10
58	Alex Gonzalez	.10
59	Matt Mantei	.10
60	Tino Martinez	.10
61	Hal Morris	.10
62	Rafael Palmeiro	.60
63	Troy Percival	.10
64	Bobby Smith	.10
65	Ed Sprague	.10
66	Brett Tomko	.10
67	Steve Trachsel	.10
68	Ugueth Urbina	.10
69	Jose Valentin	.10
70	Kevin Brown	.10
71	Shawn Green	.30
72	Dustin Hermanson	.10
73	Livan Hernandez	.10
74	Geoff Jenkins	.10
75	Jeff King	.10
76	Chuck Knoblauch	.10
77	Edgar Martinez	.10
78	Fred McGriff	.10
79	Mike Mussina	.40
80	Dave Nilsson	.10
81	Kenny Rogers	.10
82	Tim Salmon	.10
83	Reggie Sanders	.10
84	Wilson Alvarez	.10
85	Rod Beck	.10
86	Jose Guillen	.10
87	Bob Higginson	.10
88	Gregg Olson	.10
89	Jeff Shaw	.10
90	Masato Yoshii	.10
91	Todd Helton	.50
92	David Dellucci	.10
93	Johnny Damon	.35
94	Cliff Floyd	.10
95	Ken Griffey Jr.	1.00
96	Juan Guzman	.10
97	Derek Jeter	2.00
98	Barry Larkin	.10
99	Quinton McCracken	.10
100	Sammy Sosa	.85
101	Kevin Young	.10
102	Jay Bell	.10
103	Jay Buhner	.10
104	Jeff Conine	.10
105	Ryan Jackson	.10
106	Sidney Ponson	.10
107	Jeromy Burnitz	.10
108	Roberto Hernandez	.10
109	A.J. Hinch	.10
110	Hideki Irabu	.10
111	Paul Konerko	.20
112	Henry Rodriguez	.10
113	Shannon Stewart	.10
114	Tony Womack	.10
115	Wilton Guerrero	.10
116	Andy Benes	.10
117	Jeff Cirillo	.10
118	Chili Davis	.10
119	Eric Davis	.10
120	Vladimir Guerrero	.65

121	Dennis Reyes	.10
122	Rickey Henderson	.65
123	Mickey Morandini	.10
124	Jason Schmidt	.10
125	J.T. Snow	.10
126	Justin Thompson	.10
127	Billy Wagner	.10
128	Armando Benitez	.10
129	Sean Casey	.15
130	Brad Fullmer	.10
131	Ben Grieve	.10
132	Robb Nen	.10
133	Shane Reynolds	.10
134	Todd Zeile	.10
135	Brady Anderson	.10
136	Aaron Boone	.10
137	Orlando Cabrera	.10
138	Jason Giambi	.50
139	Randy Johnson	.65
140	Jeff Kent	.10
141	John Wetteland	.10
142	Rolando Arrojo	.10
143	Scott Brosius	.10
144	Mark Grace	.10
145	Jason Kendall	.10
146	Travis Lee	.10
147	Gary Sheffield	.40
148	David Cone	.10
149	Jose Hernandez	.10
150	Todd Jones	.10
151	Al Martin	.10
152	Ismael Valdes	.10
153	Wade Boggs	.75
154	Garret Anderson	.10
155	Bobby Bonilla	.10
156	Darryl Kile	.10
157	Ryan Klesko	.10
158	Tim Wakefield	.10
159	Kenny Lofton	.10
160	Jose Canseco	.40
161	Doug Glanville	.10
162	Todd Hundley	.10
163	Brian Jordan	.10
164	Steve Finley	.10
165	Tom Glavine	.25
166	Al Leiter	.10
167	Raul Mondesi	.10
168	Desi Relaford	.10
169	Bret Saberhagen	.10
170	Omar Vizquel	.10
171	Larry Walker	.10
172	Bobby Abreu	.10
173	Moises Alou	.10
174	Mike Caruso	.10
175	Royce Clayton	.10
176	Bartolo Colon	.10
177	Marty Cordova	.10
178	Darin Erstad	.30
179	Nomar Garciaparra	.75
180	Andy Ashby	.10
181	Dan Wilson	.10
182	Larry Sutton	.10
183	Tony Clark	.10
184	Andres Galarraga	.10
185	Ray Durham	.10
186	Hideo Nomo	.60
187	Steve Woodard	.10
188	Scott Rolen	.35
189	Mike Stanley	.10
190	Jaret Wright	.10
191	Vinny Castilla	.10
192	Jason Christiansen	.10
193	Paul Bako	.10
194	Carlos Perez	.10
195	Mike Piazza	1.00
196	Fernando Tatis	.10
197	Mo Vaughn	.10
198	Devon White	.10
199	Ricky Gutierrez	.10
200	Charlie Hayes	.10
201	Brad Radke	.10
202	Rick Helling	.10
203	John Smoltz	.10
204	Frank Thomas	.65
205	David Wells	.10
206	Roger Clemens	.85
207	Mark Grudzielanek	.10
208	Chipper Jones	.75
209	Ray Lankford	.10
210	Pedro Martinez	.65
211	Manny Ramirez	.65
212	Greg Vaughn	.10
213	Craig Biggio	.10
214	Rusty Greer	.10
215	Greg Maddux	.75
216	Rick Aguilera	.10
217	Andy Pettitte	.20
218	Dante Bichette	.10
219	Damion Easley	.10
220	Matt Morris	.10
221	John Olerud	.10
222	Chan Ho Park	.10
223	Curt Schilling	.25
224	John Valentin	.10
225	Matt Williams	.10
226	Ellis Burks	.10
227	Tom Goodwin	.10
228	Javy Lopez	.10
229	Eric Milton	.10
230	Paul O'Neill	.10
231	Magglio Ordonez	.15
232	Derek Lee	.45
233	Ken Griffey Jr. (Caught on the Fly)	.60
234	Randy Johnson (Caught on the Fly)	.30
235	Alex Rodriguez (Caught on the Fly)	.75

236	Darin Erstad (Caught on the Fly)	.15
237	Juan Gonzalez (Caught on the Fly)	.20
238	Derek Jeter (Caught on the Fly)	.40
239	Tony Gwynn (Caught on the Fly)	.20
240	Kerry Wood (Caught on the Fly)	.20
241	Cal Ripken Jr. (Caught on the Fly)	1.00
242	Sammy Sosa (Caught on the Fly)	.50
243	Greg Maddux (Caught on the Fly)	.40
244	Mark McGwire (Caught on the Fly)	.75
245	Chipper Jones (Caught on the Fly)	.40
246	Barry Bonds (Caught on the Fly)	1.00
247	Ben Grieve (Caught on the Fly)	.10
248	Ben Davis (Building Blocks)	.10
249	Robert Fick (Building Blocks)	.10
250	Carlos Guillen (Building Blocks)	.10
251	Mike Frank (Building Blocks)	.10
252	Ryan Minor (Building Blocks)	.10
253	Troy Glaus (Building Blocks)	.65
254	Matt Anderson (Building Blocks)	.10
255	Josh Booty (Building Blocks)	.10
256	Gabe Alvarez (Building Blocks)	.10
257	Gabe Kapler (Building Blocks)	.10
258	Enrique Wilson (Building Blocks)	.10
259	Alex Gonzalez (Building Blocks)	.10
260	Preston Wilson (Building Blocks)	.10
261	Eric Chavez (Building Blocks)	.20
262	Adrian Beltre (Building Blocks)	.30
263	Corey Koskie (Building Blocks)	.10
264	Robert Machado RC (Building Blocks)	.10
265	Orlando Hernandez (Building Blocks)	.10
266	Matt Clement (Building Blocks)	.10
267	Luis Ordaz (Building Blocks)	.10
268	Jeremy Giambi (Building Blocks)	.10
269	J.D. Drew (Building Blocks)	.50
269a	J.D. Drew (Building Blocks "Sample" autographed edition of 35.)	30.00
270	Cliff Politte (Building Blocks)	.10
271	Carlton Loewer (Building Blocks)	.10
272	Aramis Ramirez (Building Blocks)	.10
273	Ken Griffey Jr. (M.L.P.D.)	.60
274	Randy Johnson (M.L.P.D.)	.30
275	Alex Rodriguez (M.L.P.D.)	.75
276	Darin Erstad (M.L.P.D.)	.20
277	Scott Rolen (M.L.P.D.)	.25
278	Juan Gonzalez (M.L.P.D.)	.20
279	Jeff Bagwell (M.L.P.D.)	.30
280	Mike Piazza (M.L.P.D.)	.65
281	Derek Jeter (M.L.P.D.)	1.00
282	Travis Lee (M.L.P.D.)	.10
283	Tony Gwynn (M.L.P.D.)	.40
284	Kerry Wood (M.L.P.D.)	.20
285	Albert Belle (M.L.P.D.)	.10
286	Sammy Sosa (M.L.P.D.)	.50
287	Mo Vaughn (M.L.P.D.)	.20
288	Nomar Garciaparra (M.L.P.D.)	.45
289	Frank Thomas (M.L.P.D.)	.50
290	Cal Ripken Jr. (M.L.P.D.)	1.00
291	Greg Maddux (M.L.P.D.)	.40
292	Chipper Jones (M.L.P.D.)	.40
293	Ben Grieve (M.L.P.D.)	.10
294	Andruw Jones (M.L.P.D.)	.30
295	Mark McGwire (M.L.P.D.)	.75
296	Roger Clemens (M.L.P.D.)	.50
297	Barry Bonds (M.L.P.D.)	1.00
298	Ken Griffey Jr.-Checklist (M.L.P.D.)	.60
299	Kerry Wood-Checklist (M.L.P.D.)	.20
300	Alex Rodriguez-Checklist (M.L.P.D.)	.75

Precious Metal Gems

A 300-card parallel of the base set, these cards feature gold-foil etching and are inserted exclusively in hobby packs. Each card is serially numbered to 50. A Gem Master 1 of 1 parallel was also issued, but is too rare to value.

	NM/M
Common Player:	3.00
Stars:	25X
Gem Master 1 of 1:	
(Value Undetermined)	

Boyz With The Wood

The top hitters in the game are featured on these folded cards with four sides. These are inserted 1:18.

	NM/M
Complete Set (15):	17.50
Common Player:	.60
Inserted 1:18	
1 Ken Griffey Jr.	2.00
2 Frank Thomas	1.00
3 Jeff Bagwell	1.00
4 Juan Gonzalez	.75
5 Mark McGwire	2.50
6 Scott Rolen	.60
7 Travis Lee	.60
8 Tony Gwynn	2.00
9 Mike Piazza	2.00
10 Chipper Jones	2.00
11 Nomar Garciaparra	2.00
12 Derek Jeter	3.00
13 Cal Ripken Jr.	3.00
14 Andruw Jones	1.00
15 Alex Rodriguez	2.50

Diamond Soul

Utilizing lenticular technology these inserts showcase a soulful "galactic" design. The set consists of 15 cards which are seeded at 1:72 packs.

	NM/M
Complete Set (15):	60.00
Common Player:	1.50
Inserted 1:72	
1 Cal Ripken Jr.	12.00
2 Alex Rodriguez	9.00
3 Chipper Jones	6.00
4 Derek Jeter	12.00
5 Frank Thomas	4.00
6 Greg Maddux	6.00
7 Juan Gonzalez	3.00
8 Ken Griffey Jr.	7.50
9 Kerry Wood	3.00
10 Mark McGwire	9.00
11 Mike Piazza	7.50
12 Nomar Garciaparra	6.00
13 Scott Rolen	2.50

| 14 | Tony Gwynn | 6.00 |
| 15 | Travis Lee | 1.50 |

Linchpins

This 10-card set features a laser die-cut background and highlights key players who hold their teams together on the field and in the clubhouse. These are seeded 1:360 packs.

		NM/M
Complete Set (10):		75.00
Common Player:		5.00
Inserted 1:360		
1	Mike Piazza	10.00
2	Mark McGwire	12.50
3	Kerry Wood	5.00
4	Ken Griffey Jr.	10.00
5	Greg Maddux	7.50
6	Frank Thomas	6.00
7	Derek Jeter	15.00
8	Chipper Jones	7.50
9	Cal Ripken Jr.	15.00
10	Alex Rodriguez	12.50

Neophytes

This 15-card insert set showcases young stars like J.D. Drew and Troy Glaus. The cards feature silver foil stamping on a horizontal format, found on an average of 1:6 packs.

		NM/M
Complete Set (15):		7.50
Common Player:		.35
Inserted 1:6		
1	Troy Glaus	3.00
2	Travis Lee	.75
3	Scott Elarton	.35
4	Ricky Ledee	.35
5	Richard Hidalgo	.35
6	J.D. Drew	1.50
7	Paul Konerko	.75
8	Orlando Hernandez	.75
9	Mike Caruso	.35
10	Mike Frank	.35
11	Miguel Tejada	.50
12	Matt Anderson	.35
13	Kerry Wood	1.00
14	Gabe Alvarez	.35
15	Adrian Beltre	.50

Planet Metal

These die-cut cards feature a metallic view of the planet behind pop-out action photography. The 15-card set features the top players in the game and are seeded 1:36 packs.

		NM/M
Complete Set (15):		45.00
Common Player:		1.50
Inserted 1:36		
1	Alex Rodriguez	9.00
2	Andruw Jones	3.50
3	Cal Ripken Jr.	12.00
4	Chipper Jones	5.00

5	Darin Erstad	2.00
6	Derek Jeter	12.00
7	Frank Thomas	3.50
8	Travis Lee	1.50
9	Scott Rolen	2.50
10	Nomar Garciaparra	5.00
11	Mike Piazza	6.50
12	Mark McGwire	9.00
13	Ken Griffey Jr.	6.50
14	Juan Gonzalez	2.50
15	Jeff Bagwell	3.50

2000 Metal

		NM/M
Complete Set (250):		20.00
Common Player:		.10
Common Prospect (201-250):		.50
Inserted 1:2		
Pack (10):		1.50
Wax Box (28):		25.00
1	Tony Gwynn	1.00
2	Derek Jeter	2.50
3	Johnny Damon	.35
4	Javy Lopez	.10
5	Preston Wilson	.10
6	Derek Bell	.10
7	Richie Sexson	.10
8	Vinny Castilla	.10
9	Billy Wagner	.10
10	Carlos Beltran	.50
11	Chris Singleton	.10
12	Nomar Garciaparra	1.00
13	Carlos Febles	.10
14	Jason Varitek	.10
15	Luis Gonzalez	.20
16	Jon Lieber	.10
17	Mo Vaughn	.10
18	Dave Burba	.10
19	Brady Anderson	.10
20	Carlos Lee	.20
21	Chuck Finley	.10
22	Alex Gonzalez	.10
23	Matt Williams	.10
24	Chipper Jones	1.00
25	Pokey Reese	.10
26	Todd Helton	.65
27	Mike Mussina	.40
28	Butch Huskey	.10
29	Jeff Bagwell	.75
30	Juan Encarnacion	.10
31	A.J. Burnett	.10
32	Micah Bowie	.10
33	Brian Jordan	.10
34	Scott Erickson	.10
35	Sean Casey	.25
36	John Smoltz	.10
37	Edgard Clemente	.10
38	Mike Hampton	.10
39	Tom Glavine	.35
40	Albert Belle	.10
41	Jim Thome	.60
42	Jermaine Dye	.10
43	Sammy Sosa	1.25
44	Pedro Martinez	.75
45	Paul Konerko	.20
46	Damion Easley	.10
47	Cal Ripken Jr.	2.50
48	Jose Lima	.10
49	Mike Lowell	.10
50	Randy Johnson	.75
51	Dean Palmer	.10
52	Tim Salmon	.10
53	Kevin Millwood	.10
54	Mark Grace	.10
55	Aaron Boone	.10
56	Omar Vizquel	.10
57	Moises Alou	.10
58	Travis Fryman	.10
59	Erubiel Durazo	.10
60	Carl Everett	.10
61	Charles Johnson	.10
62	Trot Nixon	.10
63	Andres Galarraga	.10
64	Magglio Ordonez	.10
65	Pedro Astacio	.10
66	Roberto Alomar	.20
67	Pete Harnisch	.10
68	Scott Williamson	.10
69	Alex Fernandez	.10
70	Robin Ventura	.10
71	Chad Allen	.10
72	Darin Erstad	.20
73	Ron Coomer	.10
74	Ellis Burks	.10
75	Kent Bottenfield	.10
76	Ken Griffey Jr.	1.50
77	Mike Piazza	1.50
78	Jorge Posada	.20

79	Dante Bichette	.10
80	Adrian Beltre	.25
81	Andruw Jones	.75
82	Wilson Alvarez	.10
83	Edgardo Alfonzo	.10
84	Brian Giles	.10
85	Gary Sheffield	.25
86	Matt Stairs	.10
87	Bret Boone	.10
88	Kenny Rogers	.10
89	Barry Bonds	2.50
90	Scott Rolen	.60
91	Edgar Renteria	.10
92	Larry Walker	.10
93	Roger Cedeno	.10
94	Kevin Brown	.10
95	Lee Stevens	.10
96	Brad Radke	.10
97	Andy Pettitte	.25
98	Bobby Higginson	.10
99	Eric Chavez	.25
100	Alex Rodriguez	2.00
100s	Alex Rodriguez/OPS	2.00
101	Shannon Stewart	.10
102	Ryan Rupe	.10
103	Freddy Garcia	.10
104	John Jaha	.10
105	Greg Maddux	1.00
106	Hideki Irabu	.10
107	Rey Ordonez	.10
108	Troy O'Leary	.10
109	Frank Thomas	.75
110	Corey Koskie	.10
111	Bernie Williams	.10
112	Barry Larkin	.10
113	Kevin Appier	.10
114	Curt Schilling	.35
115	Bartolo Colon	.10
116	Edgar Martinez	.10
117	Ray Lankford	.10
118	Todd Walker	.10
119	John Wetteland	.10
120	David Nilsson	.10
121	Tino Martinez	.10
122	Phil Nevin	.10
123	Ben Grieve	.10
124	Ron Gant	.10
125	Jeff Kent	.10
126	Rick Helling	.10
127	Russ Ortiz	.10
128	Troy Glaus	.65
129	Chan Ho Park	.10
130	Jeromy Burnitz	.10
131	Aaron Sele	.10
132	Mike Sirotka	.10
133	Brad Ausmus	.10
134	Jose Rosado	.10
135	Mariano Rivera	.25
136	Jason Giambi	.50
137	Mike Lieberthal	.10
138	Chris Carpenter	.10
139	Henry Rodriguez	.10
140	Mike Sweeney	.10
141	Vladimir Guerrero	.75
142	Charles Nagy	.10
143	Jason Kendall	.10
144	Matt Lawton	.10
145	Michael Barrett	.10
146	David Cone	.10
147	Bobby Abreu	.10
148	Fernando Tatis	.10
149	Jose Canseco	.40
150	Craig Biggio	.10
151	Matt Mantei	.10
152	Jacque Jones	.10
153	John Halama	.10
154	Trevor Hoffman	.10
155	Rondell White	.10
156	Reggie Sanders	.10
157	Steve Finley	.10
158	Roberto Hernandez	.10
159	Geoff Jenkins	.10
160	Chris Widger	.10
161	Orel Hershiser	.10
162	Tim Hudson	.20
163	Kris Benson	.10
164	Kevin Young	.10
165	Rafael Palmeiro	.60
166	David Wells	.10
167	Ben Davis	.10
168	Jamie Moyer	.10
169	Randy Wolf	.10
170	Jeff Cirillo	.10
171	Warren Morris	.10
172	Billy Koch	.10
173	Marquis Grissom	.10
174	Geoff Blum	.10
175	Octavio Dotel	.10
176	Orlando Hernandez	.25
177	J.D. Drew	.25
178	Carlos Delgado	.40
179	Sterling Hitchcock	.10
180	Shawn Green	.25
181	Tony Clark	.10
182	Joe McEwing	.10
183	Fred McGriff	.10
184	Tony Batista	.10
185	Al Leiter	.10
186	Roger Clemens	1.25
187	Al Martin	.10
188	Eric Milton	.10
189	Bobby Smith	.10
190	Rusty Greer	.10
191	Shawn Estes	.10
192	Ken Caminiti	.10
193	Eric Karros	.10
194	Manny Ramirez	.75
195	Jim Edmonds	.10

196	Paul O'Neill	.10
197	Rico Brogna	.10
198	Ivan Rodriguez	.60
199	Doug Glanville	.10
200	Mark McGwire	2.00
201	Mark Quinn (Prospect)	.50
202	Norm Hutchins (Prospect)	.50
203	Ramon Ortiz (Prospect)	.50
204	Brett Laxton (Prospect)	.50
205	Jimmy Anderson (Prospect)	.50
206	Calvin Murray (Prospect)	.50
207	Wilton Veras (Prospect)	.50
208	Chad Hermansen (Prospect)	.50
209	Nick Johnson (Prospect)	.50
210	Kevin Barker (Prospect)	.50
211	Casey Blake (Prospect)	.50
212	Chad Meyers (Prospect)	.50
213	Kip Wells (Prospect)	.50
214	Eric Munson (Prospect)	.50
215	Lance Berkman (Prospect)	.50
216	Wily Pena (Prospect)	.50
217	Gary Matthews Jr. (Prospect)	.50
218	Travis Dawkins (Prospect)	.50
219	Josh Beckett (Prospect)	.75
220	Tony Armas Jr. (Prospect)	.50
221	Alfonso Soriano (Prospect)	1.00
222	Pat Burrell (Prospect)	1.00
223	Danys Baez **RC** (Prospect)	.50
224	Adam Kennedy (Prospect)	.50
225	Ruben Mateo (Prospect)	.50
226	Vernon Wells (Prospect)	.75
227	Brian Cooper (Prospect)	.50
228	Jeff DaVanon **RC** (Prospect)	.50
229	Glen Barker (Prospect)	.50
230	Robinson Cancel (Prospect)	.50
231	D'Angelo Jimenez (Prospect)	.50
232	Adam Piatt (Prospect)	.50
233	Buddy Carlyle (Prospect)	.50
234	Chad Hutchinson (Prospect)	.50
235	Matt Riley (Prospect)	.50
236	Cole Liniak (Prospect)	.50
237	Ben Petrick (Prospect)	.50
238	Peter Bergeron (Prospect)	.50
239	Cesar King (Prospect)	.50
240	Aaron Myette (Prospect)	.50
241	Eric Gagne (Prospect)	.60
242	Joe Nathan (Prospect)	.50
243	Bruce Chen (Prospect)	.50
244	Rob Bell (Prospect)	.50
245	Juan Sosa **RC** (Prospect)	.60
246	Julio Ramirez (Prospect)	.50
247	Wade Miller (Prospect)	.50
248	Trace Coquillette **RC** (Prospect)	.50
249	Robert Ramsay (Prospect)	.50
250	Rick Ankiel (Prospect)	.60

Emerald

A green tone at the top 1/4 of the card fronts, and a small circled "E" at top-right on back differentiate these parallels from the regular-issue cards. The first 200 cards in the set are found in this version about one every four packs. The odds double for the Prospects cards (#201-250) that were short-printed in the regular version as well.

	NM/M
Complete Set (250):	100.00
Common Player:	.25
Stars:	2.5X
Inserted 1:4	
Prospects (201-250):	2.5X
Inserted 1:8	

Fusion

		NM/M
Complete Set (15):		12.50
Common Player:		.50
Inserted 1:4		
1	Ken Griffey Jr., Alex Rodriguez	2.00
2	Mark McGwire, Rick Ankiel	2.00
3	Scott Rolen, Curt Schilling	.50
4	Pedro Martinez, Nomar Garciaparra	1.25
5	Carlos Beltran, Carlos Febles	.60
6	Sammy Sosa, Mark Grace	1.50
7	Vladimir Guerrero, Ugueth Urbina	1.00
8	Roger Clemens, Derek Jeter	3.00
9	Jeff Bagwell, Craig Biggio	1.00
10	Chipper Jones, Andruw Jones	1.50
11	Cal Ripken Jr., Mike Mussina	2.50
12	Manny Ramirez, Roberto Alomar	1.00
13	Sean Casey, Barry Larkin	.50
14	Ivan Rodriguez, Rafael Palmeiro	.75
15	Mike Piazza, Robin Ventura	1.50

Autographics

		NM/M
Common Player:		4.00
	Bobby Abreu	8.00
	Chad Allen	4.00
	Marlon Anderson	4.00
	Rick Ankiel	10.00
	Glen Barker	4.00
	Rob Bell	4.00
	Mark Bellhorn	5.00
	Peter Bergeron	4.00
	Lance Berkman	8.00
	Wade Boggs	25.00
	Barry Bonds	150.00
	Kent Bottenfield	4.00
	Pat Burrell	10.00
	Miguel Cairo	4.00
	Mike Cameron	6.00
	Chris Carpenter	6.00
	Roger Cedeno	4.00
	Mike Darr	6.00
	Einar Diaz	4.00
	J.D. Drew	15.00
	Erubiel Durazo	6.00
	Ray Durham	4.00
	Damion Easley	4.00
	Scott Elarton	4.00
	Jeremy Giambi	4.00
	Doug Glanville	4.00
	Shawn Green	10.00
	Jerry Hairston Jr.	4.00
	Bob Howry	4.00
	Norm Hutchins	4.00
	Randy Johnson	40.00
	Jacque Jones	4.00
	Gabe Kapler	6.00
	Cesar King	4.00
	Mark Kotsay	4.00
	Cole Liniak	4.00
	Greg Maddux	50.00
	Pedro Martinez	30.00
	Ruben Mateo	4.00
	Warren Morris	4.00
	Heath Murray	4.00
	Joe Nathan	4.00
	Jim Parque	4.00
	Angel Pena	4.00
	Cal Ripken Jr.	100.00
	Alex Rodriguez	60.00
	Ryan Rupe	4.00
	Randall Simon	4.00
	Chris Singleton	4.00
	Mike Sweeney	6.00
	Wilton Veras	4.00
	Scott Williamson	4.00
	Randy Wolf	6.00
	Tony Womack	6.00

Base Shredders

		NM/M
Complete Set (18):		160.00
Common Player:		5.00
Inserted 1:288		
(1)	Roberto Alomar	7.50
(2)	Michael Barrett	5.00
(3)	Tony Clark	5.00
(4)	Ben Davis	5.00
(5)	Erubiel Durazo	5.00
(6)	Troy Glaus	12.50
(7)	Ben Grieve	5.00
(8)	Vladimir Guerrero	15.00
(9)	Tony Gwynn	25.00
(10)	Todd Helton	12.50
(11)	Eric Munson	5.00
(12)	Rafael Palmeiro	10.00
(13)	Manny Ramirez	20.00
(14)	Ivan Rodriguez	10.00
(15)	Miguel Tejada	7.50
(16)	Mo Vaughn	5.00
(17)	Larry Walker	5.00
(18)	Matt Williams	5.00

Heavy Metal

		NM/M
Complete Set (10):		15.00
Common Player:		1.50
Inserted 1:20		
1	Sammy Sosa	2.25
2	Mark McGwire	3.00
3	Ken Griffey Jr.	2.50
4	Mike Piazza	2.50
5	Nomar Garciaparra	2.00
6	Alex Rodriguez	3.00
7	Manny Ramirez	1.50
8	Jeff Bagwell	1.50
9	Chipper Jones	2.00
10	Vladimir Guerrero	1.50

Hit Machines

		NM/M
Complete Set (10):		20.00
Common Player:		1.00
Inserted 1:20		
1	Ken Griffey Jr.	3.00
2	Mark McGwire	4.00
3	Frank Thomas	1.50
4	Tony Gwynn	2.00
5	Rafael Palmeiro	1.25
6	Bernie Williams	1.00
7	Derek Jeter	6.00
8	Sammy Sosa	2.50
9	Mike Piazza	3.00
10	Chipper Jones	2.00

Platinum Portraits

		NM/M
Complete Set (10):		6.00
Common Player:		.25
Inserted 1:8		
1	Carlos Beltran	.50
2	Vladimir Guerrero	.75
3	Manny Ramirez	.75
4	Ivan Rodriguez	.65
5	Sean Casey	.40
6	Alex Rodriguez	1.50
7	Derek Jeter	2.00
8	Nomar Garciaparra	1.00
9	Vernon Wells	.25
10	Shawn Green	.50

Talent Show

		NM/M
Complete Set (15):		6.00
Common Player:		.30
Inserted 1:4		
1	Rick Ankiel	.50
2	Matt Riley	.30
3	Chad Hermansen	.30
4	Ruben Mateo	.30
5	Eric Munson	.30
6	Alfonso Soriano	1.50
7	Wilton Veras	.30
8	Vernon Wells	.75
9	Erubiel Durazo	.30
10	Pat Burrell	1.50
11	Ben Davis	.30
12	A.J. Burnett	.30
13	Peter Bergeron	.30
14	Mark Quinn	.30
15	Ben Petrick	.30

1993 Metz Bakeries

Metz Baking Co. of Sioux City, Iowa, produced this set utilizing drawings of players rather than photos. The company also made available uncut sheets of the sets via a mail-in offer. Cards have either a yellow background with blue pinstripes or a blue background with yellow pinstripes. Players are shown in a red, white and black porthole at center. Backs are printed in black-and-white with complete major and minor league stats. Because the cards are licensed only by the Players Union and not Major League Baseball, the player paintings omit uniform logos. The un-

numbered cards are checklisted here in alphabetical order. A special collectors tin to house the set was also available.

		NM/M
Complete Set (40):		35.00
Common Player:		.75
(1)	Dante Bichette	.75
(2)	Wade Boggs	2.00
(3)	Barry Bonds	4.00
(4)	Bobby Bonilla	.75
(5)	Jose Canseco	1.00
(6)	Joe Carter	.75
(7)	Will Clark	.75
(8)	Roger Clemens	2.25
(9)	Doug Drabek	.75
(10)	Shawon Dunston	.75
(11)	Dennis Eckersley	1.25
(12)	Cecil Fielder	.75
(13)	Carlton Fisk	1.50
(14)	Andres Galarraga	.75
(15)	Kirk Gibson	.75
(16)	Dwight Gooden	.75
(17)	Mark Grace	.75
(18)	Ken Griffey Jr.	2.50
(19)	Tony Gwynn	2.00
(20)	Rickey Henderson	1.50
(21)	Kent Hrbek	.75
(22)	Howard Johnson	.75
(23)	Wally Joyner	.75
(24)	Dave Justice	.75
(25)	Barry Larkin	.75
(26)	Don Mattingly	2.50
(27)	Jack McDowell	.75
(28)	Paul Molitor	1.50
(29)	Terry Pendleton	.75
(30)	Kirby Puckett	2.00
(31)	Cal Ripken, Jr.	4.00
(32)	Nolan Ryan	4.00
(33)	Ryne Sandberg	2.00
(34)	Ozzie Smith	2.00
(35)	Darryl Strawberry	.75
(36)	Danny Tartabull	.75
(37)	Mickey Tettleton	.75
(38)	Alan Trammell	.75
(39)	Andy Van Slyke	.75
(40)	Dave Winfield	1.50

1993 Milk Bone Super Stars

Milk Bone Flavor Snacks and Dog Treats issued a 20-card Super Stars set in 1993 in a format comparable to the NFL Pro Line cards. The cards show the player at home with his dog, with the player shown in an action photo in the lower left corner of the card. The card backs have the player's stats and biography, along with information about the pet and a quote from the player about his dog. The cards were available, two at a time, in specially-marked packages of the company's products. The set also could be obtained through the mail by following instructions on the boxes.

		NM/M
Complete Set (20):		12.50
Common Player:		.50
(1)	Paul Molitor	1.00
(2)	Tom Glavine	.65
(3)	Barry Larkin	.50
(4)	Mark McGwire	2.50
(5)	Bill Swift	.50
(6)	Ken Caminiti	.50
(7)	Will Clark	.50
(8)	Rafael Palmeiro	.75
(9)	Matt Young	.50
(10)	Todd Zeile	.50
(11)	Wally Joyner	.50
(12)	Cal Ripken Jr.	3.50
(13)	Tom Foley	.50
(14)	Ben McDonald	.50
(15)	Larry Walker	.50
(16)	Rob Dibble	.50
(17)	Brett Butler	.50
(18)	Joe Girardi	.50
(19)	Brady Anderson	.50
(20)	Craig Biggio	.50

1989 Milk Duds Pittsburgh Pirates

John SMILEY

This set of Pirates photocards carries on its backs advertising for various brands of Leaf candies, principally Milk Duds. The 3-3/8" x 5-1/2" cards have color portrait photo on front with the player's name near the bottom and a team logo at bottom center. Backs have a few vital statistics, candy advertising and/or free ticket or contest offers. The cards are numbered by uniform number, but are listed here in alphabetical order.

		NM/M
Complete Set (38):		20.00
Common Player:		.75
(1)	Pirate Parrot (Mascot)	.75
(2)	Rafael Belliard	.75
(3)	Dann Bilardello	.75
(4)	Barry Bonds	9.00
(5)	Sid Bream	.75
(6)	Bobby Bonilla	1.00
(7)	John Cangelosi	.75
(8)	Benny Distefano	.75
(9)	Rich Donnelly	.75
(10)	Doug Drabek	.75
(11)	Brian Fisher	.75
(12)	Miguel Garcia	.75
(13)	Jim Gott	.75
(14)	Neal Heaton	.75
(15)	Bruce Kimm	.75
(16)	Jeff King	1.00
(17)	Bob Kipper	.75
(18)	Randy Kramer	.75
(19)	Gene Lamont	.75
(20)	Bill Landrum	.75
(21)	Mike LaValliere	.75
(22)	Jim Leyland	.75
(23)	Jose Lind	.75
(24)	Morris Madden	.75
(25)	Milt May	.75
(26)	Ray Miller	.75
(27)	Junior Ortiz	.75
(28)	Tom Prince	.75
(29)	Rey Quinones	.75
(30)	Gary Redus	.75
(31)	R.J. Reynolds	.75
(32)	Jeff Robinson	.75
(33)	Tommy Sandt	.75
(34)	John Smiley	.75
(35)	Dorn Taylor	.75
(36)	Andy Van Slyke	1.00
(37)	Bob Walk	.75
(38)	Glenn Wilson	.75

1997 Milk Mustache Trading Cards

MILK

ALEX RODRIGUEZ

shortstop SEATTLE MARINERS

Sponsored by the National Fluid Milk Processor Promotion Board (really), this nine-card panel was an advertising insert in the October 1997 issue of Sports Illustrated for Kids. The perforated panel measures about 7-1/2" x 10-1/2", with each card measuring the standard 2-1/2" x 3-1/2" and perforated on two, three or four sides, depending on its placement on the sheet. Player portrait photos are set on a

silver-look background. Cap and uniform logos have been eliminated and a milk moustache added. "MILK" appears in white in a purple stripe at the top of each player's card. Backs have a baseball tip and a milk tip ascribed to each player.

		NM/M
Complete Sheet:		5.00
Complete Set (9):		5.00
Common Player:		.25
1	Alex Rodriguez	2.50
2	Nomar Garciaparra	1.00
3	Andy Pettitte	.35
4	Darin Erstad	.45
5	Jason Kendall	.25
6	Vladimir Guerrero	1.00
7	Scott Rolen	.60
8	Tony Clark	.25
--	Header Card	.05

1990 Miller Beer Milwaukee Brewers

GARY SHEFFIELD
INFIELD

This 32-card set was given away with an album to adults attending an August Brewers game. Cards are standard 2-1/2" x 3-1/2" and feature borderless color photos above gold and black bottom stripes. The beer company's logo is featured in the upper-right corner, with the team logo at lower-left. Black-and-white backs feature player stats. The set has been checklisted below in alphabetical order. Cards are not numbered.

		NM/M
Complete Set w/Album (32):		10.00
Common Player:		.25
(1)	Chris Bosio	.25
(2)	Greg Brock	.25
(3)	Chuck Crim	.25
(4)	Rob Deer	.25
(5)	Edgar Diaz	.25
(6)	Tom Edens	.25
(7)	Mike Felder	.25
(8)	Tom Filer	.25
(9)	Jim Gantner	.25
(10)	Darryl Hamilton	.25
(11)	Teddy Higuera	.25
(12)	Mark Knudson	.25
(13)	Bill Krueger	.25
(14)	Paul Mirabella	.25
(15)	Paul Molitor	4.00
(16)	Jaime Navarro	.25
(17)	Charlie O'Brien	.25
(18)	Dave Parker	.25
(19)	Dan Plesac	.25
(20)	Dennis Powell	.25
(21)	Ron Robinson	.25
(22)	Bob Sebra	.25
(23)	Gary Sheffield	2.00
(24)	Bill Spiers	.25
(25)	B.J. Surhoff	.25
(26)	Dale Sveum	.25
(27)	Tom Trebelhorn	.25
(28)	Greg Vaughn	.25
(29)	Randy Veres	.25
(30)	Bill Wegman	.25
(31)	Robin Yount	4.00
(32)	Coaches (Don Baylor, Ray Burris, Duffy Dyer, Andy Etchebarren, Larry Haney)	.25

1991 Miller Beer Milwaukee Brewers

The Miller High Life Brewing Co., in conjunction with the Milwaukee Brewers, sponsored a 32-card limited edition baseball card set in 1991. The set, which features 30 cards of Brewer players plus additional cards of manager Tom Trebelhorn and his coaching staff, employs a home plate window for the front photo, with the player's name and words "Miller High Life" along the bottom of the card. Complete major

'91 BREWERS

PAUL
MOLITOR ■ IF

Miller HIGH LIFE

and minor league stats are printed on the black-and-white backs, which also include sponsors' logos.

		NM/M
Complete Set w/Album (32):		10.00
Common Player:		.25
(1)	Don August	.25
(2)	James Austin	.25
(3)	Dante Bichette	.35
(4)	Chris Bosio	.25
(5)	Kevin Brown	.25
(6)	Chuck Crim	.25
(7)	Rick Dempsey	.25
(8)	Jim Gantner	.25
(9)	Darryl Hamilton	.25
(10)	Teddy Higuera	.25
(11)	Darren Holmes	.25
(12)	Jim Hunter	.25
(13)	Mark Knudson	.25
(14)	Mark Lee	.25
(15)	Julio Machado	.25
(16)	Candy Maldonado	.25
(17)	Paul Molitor	4.00
(18)	Jaime Navarro	.25
(19)	Edwin Nunez	.25
(20)	Dan Plesac	.25
(21)	Willie Randolph	.25
(22)	Ron Robinson	.25
(23)	Gary Sheffield	1.00
(24)	Bill Spiers	.25
(25)	Franklin Stubbs	.25
(26)	B.J. Surhoff	.25
(27)	Dale Sveum	.25
(28)	Tom Treblehorn	.25
(29)	Greg Vaughn	.25
(30)	Bill Wegman	.25
(31)	Robin Yount	4.00

1994 Miller Genuine Draft Milwaukee Brewers

(See 1994 Lite Beer Milwaukee Brewers.)

1984 Milton Bradley

Championship Baseball BY MILTON BRADLEY

AL SUPER STAR

SHORTSTOP
ROBIN YOUNT

In 1984 Milton Bradley printed their baseball game cards in full-color and adopted the standard baseball card size of 2-1/2" x 3-1/2". A total of 30 cards were in the set. The card fronts show the player photos with the team insignias and logos airbrushed away. The game is called Championship Baseball. Card backs varied in style; some had player statistics plus game information, and others only game information.

	NM/M
Complete Boxed Set:	12.00
Complete Card Set (30):	7.50
Common Player:	.25
(1)	Wade Boggs	.75
(2)	George Brett	1.50
(3)	Rod Carew	.50
(4)	Steve Carlton	.50
(5)	Gary Carter	.50
(6)	Dave Concepcion	.25
(7)	Cecil Cooper	.25
(8)	Andre Dawson	.40
(9)	Carlton Fisk	.50
(10)	Steve Garvey	.40
(11)	Pedro Guerrero	.25
(12)	Ron Guidry	.25
(13)	Rickey Henderson	.50
(14)	Reggie Jackson	1.50
(15)	Ron Kittle	.25
(16)	Bill Madlock	.25
(17)	Dale Murphy	.40
(18)	Al Oliver	.25
(19)	Darrell Porter	.25
(20)	Cal Ripken, Jr.	2.50
(21)	Pete Rose	1.50
(22)	Steve Sax	.25
(23)	Mike Schmidt	1.50
(24)	Ted Simmons	.25
(25)	Ozzie Smith	.75
(26)	Dave Stieb	.25
(27)	Fernando Valenzuela	.25
(28)	Lou Whitaker	.25
(29)	Dave Winfield	.50
(30)	Robin Yount	.50

1982 Milwaukee Brewers Police

ROBIN YOUNT
No. 19 — Shortstop
New Berlin Police Department
Salutes The 1982
Milwaukee Brewers

The inaugural Milwaukee Brewers police set contains 30 cards in a 2-13/16" x 4-1/8" format. There are 26 players included in the set, which are numbered by player uniform number. Unnumbered cards were also issued for general manager Harry Dalton, manager Buck Rodgers, the coaches and a team card with checklist. The full-color photos are especially attractive, printed on the cards' crisp white stock. A number of Wisconsin law enforcement agencies distributed the cards and credit lines on the card fronts were changed accordingly.

		NM/M
Complete Set (30):		12.00
Common Player:		.25
4	Paul Molitor	4.00
5	Ned Yost	.25
7	Don Money	.25
9	Larry Hisle	.25
10	Bob McClure	.25
11	Ed Romero	.25
13	Roy Howell	.25
15	Cecil Cooper	.25
17	Jim Gantner	.25
19	Robin Yount	4.00
20	Gorman Thomas	.25
22	Charlie Moore	.25
23	Ted Simmons	.25
24	Ben Oglivie	.25
26	Kevin Bass	.25
28	Jamie Easterly	.25
29	Mark Brouhard	.25
30	Moose Haas	.25
34	Rollie Fingers	2.00
37	Randy Lerch	.25
37	Buck Rodgers	.25
41	Jim Slaton	.25
45	Doug Jones	.25
46	Jerry Augustine	.25
47	Dwight Bernard	.25
48	Mike Caldwell	.25
50	Pete Vuckovich	.25
---	Team Photo/Checklist	.25
---	Harry Dalton (General Mgr.)	.25
---	Coaches Card (Pat Dobson, Larry Haney, Ron Hansen, Cal McLish, Buck Rogers, Harry Warner)	.25

1983 Milwaukee Brewers Police

16 MARSHALL EDWARDS — OF
The Milwaukee Police Department
Presents The 1983
Milwaukee Brewers

Similar to 1982, a number of issuer variations exist for the 1983 Brewers police set, as law enforcement agencies throughout the state distributed the set with their own credit lines on the cards. At least 28 variations are known to exist, with those issued by smaller agencies being scarcest. Prices quoted below are for the most common variations, generally the Milwaukee Police Department and a few small-town departments whose entire supply of police cards seem to have fallen into dealers' hands. Some specialists are willing to pay a premium for the scarcer departments' issues. The 30, 2-13/16" x 4-1/8" cards include 29 players and coaches, along with a team card (with a checklist back). The team card and group coaches' card are unnumbered, while the others are numbered by uniform number.

		NM/M
Complete Set (30):		6.00
Common Player:		.25
4	Paul Molitor	3.00
5	Ned Yost	.25
7	Don Money	.25
8	Rob Picciolo	.25
10	Bob McClure	.25
11	Ed Romero	.25
13	Roy Howell	.25
15	Cecil Cooper	.25
16	Marshall Edwards	.25
17	Jim Gantner	.25
19	Robin Yount	3.00
20	Gorman Thomas	.25
21	Don Sutton	1.00
22	Charlie Moore	.25
23	Ted Simmons	.25
24	Ben Oglivie	.25
26	Bob Skube	.25
27	Pete Ladd	.25
28	Jamie Easterly	.25
30	Moose Haas	.25
32	Harvey Kuenn	.25
34	Rollie Fingers	1.00
40	Bob L. Gibson	.25
41	Jim Slaton	.25
42	Tom Tellmann	.25
46	Jerry Augustine	.25
48	Mike Caldwell	.25
50	Pete Vuckovich	.25
---	Team Photo/Checklist	.25
---	Coaches Card (Pat Dobson, Dave Garcia, Larry Haney, Ron Hansen)	.25

1984 Milwaukee Brewers Police

20 DON SUTTON — P
The Winneconne Police Department
Presents The 1984
MILWAUKEE BREWERS

The king of the variations again in 1984, the Milwaukee Brewers set has been found with 57 different police agencies' credit lines on the front of the cards. Once again, law enforcement agencies statewide participated in distributing the sets. Some departments also include a badge of the participating agency on the card backs. The full-color cards measure 2-13/16" x 4-1/8". There are 28 numbered player and manager cards, along with an unnumbered coaches card and a team card. Player names, uniform numbers and positions are listed on each card front. Prices listed are for the most common variety (Milwaukee Police Department); sets issued by smaller departments may be worth a premium to specialists. Reported print runs varied from 120,000 sets for the Milwaukee P.D. to just 500 sets for the community of Verona.

		NM/M
Complete Set (30):		6.00

Common Player:		.15
2	Randy Ready	.15
4	Paul Molitor	2.50
9	Jim Sundberg	.15
9	Rene Lachemann	.15
10	Bob McClure	.15
11	Ed Romero	.15
13	Roy Howell	.15
14	Dion James	.15
15	Cecil Cooper	.15
17	Jim Gantner	.15
19	Robin Yount	2.50
20	Don Sutton	1.00
21	Bill Schroeder	.15
22	Charlie Moore	.15
23	Ted Simmons	.15
24	Ben Oglivie	.15
25	Bobby Clark	.15
27	Pete Ladd	.15
28	Rick Manning	.15
29	Mark Brouhard	.15
30	Moose Haas	.15
34	Rollie Fingers	1.00
42	Tom Tellmann	.15
43	Chuck Porter	.15
46	Jerry Augustine	.15
47	Jaime Cocanower	.15
48	Mike Caldwell	.15
50	Pete Vuckovich	.15
---	Team Photo/Checklist	.15
---	Coaches Card (Pat Dobson, Dave Garcia, Larry Haney, Tom Trebelhorn)	.15

1985 Milwaukee Brewers Police

49 Ted Higuera P
The Milwaukee Police Department and The Milwaukee Journal
present the 1985
Milwaukee Brewers

The Brewers changed the size of their annual police set in 1985, but almost imperceptibly. The full-color cards are 2-3/4" x 4-1/8", a slight 1/16" narrower than the four previous efforts. Player and team name on the card fronts are much bolder than in previous years. Once again, numerous area police groups distributed the sets, leading to nearly 60 variations, as each agency put their own credit line on the cards. Card backs include the Brewers logo, a safety tip and, in some cases, a badge of the participating law enforcement group. There are 27 numbered player cards (by uniform number) and three unnumbered cards - team roster, coaches and a newspaper carrier card. Prices are for the most common departments.

		NM/M
Complete Set (30):		6.00
Common Player:		.15
2	Randy Ready	.15
4	Paul Molitor	2.50
5	Doug Loman	.15
7	Paul Householder	.15
10	Bob McClure	.15
11	Ed Romero	.15
14	Dion James	.15
15	Cecil Cooper	.15
17	Jim Gantner	.15
18	Danny Darwin	.15
19	Robin Yount	2.50
21	Bill Schroeder	.15
22	Charlie Moore	.15
23	Ted Simmons	.15
24	Ben Oglivie	.15
25	Brian Giles	.15
27	Pete Ladd	.15
28	Rick Manning	.15
29	Mark Brouhard	.15
30	Moose Haas	.15
31	George Bamberger	.15
34	Rollie Fingers	1.00
40	Bob L. Gibson	.15
41	Ray Searage	.15
47	Jaime Cocanower	.15
48	Ray Burris	.15
49	Ted Higuera	.15
50	Pete Vuckovich	.15

---	Coaches Card (Andy Etchebarren, Larry Haney, Frank Howard, Tony Muser, Herm Starrette)	.15
---	Team Photo	.15

1986 Milwaukee Brewers Police

45 Rob Deer OF
The Fond du Lac Police Dept., KFIZ Radio,
and National Exchange Bank & Trust
present the 1986
Milwaukee Brewers

The Milwaukee Brewers, in conjunction with the Milwaukee Police Department, WTMJ Radio and Kinney Shoes, produced this attractive police safety set of 30 cards. The cards measure 2-13/16" x 4-1/2". A thin black border encloses a full-color player photo on the front. The card backs give a safety tip and promos for the sponsor. The cards were distributed throughout the state of Wisconsin by numerous police departments; those of the smaller departments generally being scarcer than those issued in the big cities. Prices quoted below are for the most common departments' issues.

		NM/M
Complete Set (30):		4.00
Common Player:		.15
1	Ernest Riles	.15
2	Randy Ready	.15
3	Juan Castillo	.15
4	Paul Molitor	2.00
7	Paul Householder	.15
10	Bob McClure	.15
13	Rick Cerone	.15
15	Billy Jo Robidoux	.15
15	Cecil Cooper	.15
16	Mike Felder	.15
17	Jim Gantner	.15
18	Danny Darwin	.15
19	Robin Yount	2.00
21	Juan Nieves	.15
21	Bill Schroeder	.15
22	Charlie Moore	.15
24	Ben Oglivie	.15
25	Mark Clear	.15
28	Rick Manning	.15
31	George Bamberger	.15
32	Dan Plesac	.15
39	Tim Leary	.15
41	Ray Searage	.15
43	Chuck Porter	.15
45	Rob Deer	.15
47	Bill Wegman	.15
47	Jamie Cocanower	.15
49	Ted Higuera	.15
---	Coaches Card (Andy Etcheberren, Larry Haney, Frank Howard, Tony Muser, Herm Starrette)	.15
---	Team Photo/Roster	.15

1987 Milwaukee Brewers Police

5 B.J. Surhoff C
The Milwaukee Police Department
Kinney Shoes and WTMJ Radio
present the 1987
Milwaukee Brewers

The Milwaukee Brewers issued a safety set in 1987 for the sixth consecutive year. As in the past, many local police departments throughout Wisconsin participated in the giveaway program.

The Milwaukee version was sponsored by Kinney Shoe Stores and WTMJ Radio and was handed out to youngsters attending the Baseball Card Day at County Stadium on May 9th. The cards, which measure 2-1/4" x 4-1/8", feature full-color photos plus a safety tip on the backs. Chris Bosio can be found with a uniform number of 26 or 29. The card was corrected to #29 in later printings.

		NM/M
Complete Set (30):		5.00
Common Player:		.15
1	Ernest Riles	.15
2	Edgar Diaz	.15
3	Juan Castillo	.15
4	Paul Molitor	2.00
5	B.J. Surhoff	.15
7	Dale Sveum	.15
9	Greg Brock	.15
13	Billy Jo Robidoux	.15
15	Jim Paciorek	.15
15	Cecil Cooper	.15
16	Mike Felder	.15
17	Jim Gantner	.15
19	Robin Yount	2.00
20	Juan Nieves	.15
21	Bill Schroeder	.15
25	Mark Clear	.15
26a	Glenn Braggs	.15
26b	Chris Bosio	.30
28	Rick Manning	.15
29	Chris Bosio	.30
32	Chuck Crim	.15
34	Mark Ciardi	.15
37	Dan Plesac	.15
38	John Henry Johnson	.15
42	Mike Birbeck	.15
42	Tom Trebelhorn	.15
45	Rob Deer	.15
46	Bill Wegman	.15
49	Ted Higuera	.15
---	Coaches Card (Andy Etcheberren, Larry Haney, Chuck Hartenstein, Dave Hilton, Tony Muser)	.15
---	Team Photo/Roster	.15

1988 Milwaukee Brewers Police

3 Juan Castillo IF
The Marathon County Sheriff's Dept. and
Brickner Chrysler Center Inc.
2525 Avenue, Wausau, WI 54401
present the 1988
Milwaukee Brewers

This 30-card set is the 7th annual issue sponsored by the Milwaukee Police Department for local distribution during a crime prevention promotion. The full-color card fronts (2-3/4" x 4-1/8") feature the same design as the 1987 set with white borders and a black frame outlining the player photo and name. Sponsor credits and the team name are listed below the photo. The vertical card backs are blue on white with messages from the player and sponsors. Two group photos - one of the team's five coaches and one of the team (with a checklist back) - are unnumbered and printed horizontally. Card numbers refer to the players' uniform numbers.

		NM/M
Complete Set (30):		4.00
Common Player:		.15
1	Ernest Riles	.15
3	Juan Castillo	.15
4	Paul Molitor	2.00
5	B.J. Surhoff	.15
7	Dale Sveum	.15
9	Greg Brock	.15
11	Charlie O'Brien	.15
14	Jim Adduci	.15
16	Mike Felder	.15
17	Jim Gantner	.15
19	Robin Yount	2.00
20	Juan Nieves	.15
21	Bill Schroeder	.15
23	Joey Meyer	.15

25	Mark Clear	.15
26	Glenn Braggs	.15
28	Odell Jones	.15
29	Chris Bosio	.15
30	Steve Kiefer	.15
32	Chuck Crim	.15
33	Jay Aldrich	.15
37	Dan Plesac	.15
40	Mike Birkbeck	.15
42	Tom Trebelhorn	.15
43	Dave Stapleton	.15
45	Rob Deer	.15
46	Bill Wegman	.15
49	Ted Higuera	.15
---	Coaches Card (Andy Etcheberren, Larry Haney, Chuck Hartenstein, Dave Hilton, Tony Muser)	.15
---	Team Photo	.15

1989 Milwaukee Brewers Police

30 Terry Francona OF
Iola, Manawa & Marion Police Depts.
and Wisconsin Power and Light
present the 1989
Milwaukee Brewers

The Milwaukee Brewers, in conjunction with various corporate and civic sponsors, issued a 30-card police set in 1989, the eighth consecutive police set issued by the club. Some 95 law enforcement agencies in Wisconsin participated in the program, each releasing their own version of the same set. The cards measure 2-13/16" x 4-1/8" and feature full-color action photos with the player's name, uniform number and position below, along with the sponsoring agencies. The backs include the traditional safety messages. The cards were distributed in complete sets at a stadium promotion and also handed out individually over the course of the summer by uniformed police officers in various Wisconsin cities and counties.

		NM/M
Complete Set (30):		5.00
Common Player:		.15
1	Gary Sheffield	2.00
4	Paul Molitor	1.50
5	B.J. Surhoff	.15
6	Bill Spiers	.15
7	Dale Sveum	.15
9	Greg Brock	.15
14	Gus Polidor	.15
16	Mike Felder	.15
17	Jim Gantner	.15
19	Robin Yount	1.50
20	Juan Nieves	.15
22	Charlie O'Brien	.15
23	Joey Meyer	.15
25	Dave Engle	.15
26	Glenn Braggs	.15
27	Paul Mirabella	.15
29	Chris Bosio	.15
30	Terry Francona	.15
32	Chuck Crim	.15
37	Dan Plesac	.15
40	Mike Birkbeck	.15
41	Mark Knudson	.15
42	Tom Trebelhorn	.15
45	Rob Deer	.15
46	Bill Wegman	.15
48	Bryan Clutterbuck	.15
49	Teddy Higuera	.15
---	Team Photo	.15
---	Coaching Staff	.15

Yearbook Cards

Included in the team's special 20th anniversary edition yearbook was a set of 18 player cards stapled into the center of the book. Printed on a 16-1/2" x 11" cardboard sheet, there are nine cards per page, perforated on two, three or four sides, depending on sheet position. Cards have a pale yellow background. A blue and bright yellow 20th Anniversary team logo appears in the lower-right corner with the player's uniform number, name and position

---

4
Paul Molitor
Infielder

stacked at left in black. All but one of the photos are game-action shots. Backs are printed in black and include complete major and minor league stats. Cards are checklisted here by uniform number.

		NM/M
Complete Set, Singles (18):		8.00
Complete Yearbook:		10.00
Common Player:		.25
1	Gary Sheffield	2.00
4	Paul Molitor	4.00
5	B.J. Surhoff	.25
7	Dale Sveum	.25
9	Greg Brock	.25
17	Jim Gantner	.25
19	Robin Yount	4.00
20	Juan Nieves	.25
26	Glenn Braggs	.25
29	Chris Bosio	.25
32	Chuck Crim	.25
37	Dan Plesac	.25
38	Don August	.25
40	Mike Birkbeck	.25
42	Tom Trebelhorn	.25
45	Rob Deer	.25
46	Bill Wegman	.25
49	Teddy Higuera	.25

1990 Milwaukee Brewers Police

4 Paul Molitor IF
The Chilton Police Department
Chilton Food Mart & Valley Bank - Chilton
present the 1990
Milwaukee Brewers

Blue borders are featured on the front of the 1990 Brewer Police/Fire Safety set. The cards are numbered according to uniform number and public service messages appear on the card backs. The 2-13/16" x 4-1/8" cards were distributed by various Wisconsin police departments.

		NM/M
Complete Set (30):		4.00
Common Player:		.15
2	Eddie Diaz	.15
4	Paul Molitor	1.50
6	B. J. Surhoff	.15
6	Bill Spiers	.15
7	Dale Sveum	.15
9	Greg Brock	.15
11	Gary Sheffield	.75
14	Gus Polidor	.15
16	Mike Felder	.15
17	Jim Gantner	.15
19	Robin Yount	1.50
22	Charlie O'Brien	.15
23	Greg Vaughn	.15
26	Glenn Braggs	.15
27	Paul Mirabella	.15
28	Tom Filer	.15
29	Chris Bosio	.15
31	Jaime Navarro	.15
32	Chuck Crim	.15
34	Billy Bates	.15
37	Tony Fossas	.15
38	Dan Plesac	.15
38	Don August	.15
40	Dave Parker	.15
41	Mark Knudson	.15
42	Tom Trebelhorn	.15
45	Rob Deer	.15
49	Ted Higuera	.15

---	Coaches (Don Baylor, Ray Burris, Duffy Dyer, Larry Haney, Andy Etchebarren)	.15
---	Team photo/roster card	.15

Yearbook Cards

Printed on cardboard stock and stapled into the center of the team's 1990 yearbook was a set of 18 cards. The sheet is 16-1/2" x 11" overall. Each page has nine 2-5/8" x 3-1/2" cards perforated on two, three or four sides, depending on sheet position. Above-left and below-right of the color player poses are yellow triangles with blue pinstripes. The team's scrip logo is in the same team colors in the lower-left of the photo. The player's name, position abbreviation and uniform number are in yellow in the upper-right corner. Backs are printed in blue and include complete major and minor league stats. The checklist is presented here by uniform number.

		NM/M
Complete Set, Singles (18):		8.00
Complete Yearbook:		10.00
Common Player:		.25
4	Paul Molitor	4.00
5	B.J. Surhoff	.25
6	Bill Spiers	.25
7	Dale Sveum	.25
9	Greg Brock	.25
17	Jim Gantner	.25
19	Robin Yount	4.00
26	Glenn Braggs	.25
28	Tom Filer	.25
29	Chris Bosio	.25
31	Jaime Navarro	.25
32	Chuck Crim	.25
37	Dan Plesac	.25
38	Don August	.25
39	Dave Parker	.25
42	Tom Trebelhorn	.25
45	Rob Deer	.25
49	Ted Higuera	.25

1991 Milwaukee Brewers Police

The Milwaukee Brewers are featured on a 1991 team set sponsored by several Milwaukee area police departments and Delicious Brand Cookies and Crackers. The 30-card set is in full color with light gray border on the front and the backs are unnumbered and contain safety tips from the players.

		NM/M
Complete Set (30):		4.00
Common Player:		.25
(1)	Robin Yount	1.50
(2)	Rick Dempsey	.25
(3)	Jamie Navarro	.25
(4)	Darryl Hamilton	.25
(5)	Bill Spiers	.25
(6)	Dante Bichette	.25
(7)	Dan Plesac	.25
(8)	Don August	.25
(9)	Willie Randolph	.25
(10)	Franklin Stubbs	.25
(11)	Julio Machado	.25
(12)	Greg Vaughn	.25
(13)	Chris Bosio	.25
(14)	Mark Knudson	.25
(15)	Paul Molitor	1.50
(16)	Kevin Brown	.25
(17)	Ron Robinson	.25
(18)	Bill Wegman	.25
(19)	Teddy Higuera	.25
(20)	Mark Lee	.25
(21)	B.J. Surhoff	.25
(22)	Candy Maldonado	.25
(23)	Chuck Crim	.25
(24)	Dale Sveum	.25
(25)	Jim Gantner	.25
(26)	Greg Brock	.25
(27)	Gary Sheffield	.75
(28)	Edwin Nunez	.25
(29)	Tom Trebelhorn	.25
(30)	Coaches (Don Baylor, Ray Burris, Duffy Dyer, Andy Etchebarren, Larry Haney, Fred Stanley)	.25

1992 Milwaukee Brewers Police

The 1992 Milwaukee Brewers Police set consists of 30-cards in the standard, 2-1/2" x 3-1/2" format. The yellow-bordered cards were produced by Delicious Brand Cookies and Crackers and distributed by local Wisconsin police departments in co-operation with the Brewers.

		NM/M
Complete Set (30):		4.00
Common Player:		.15
(1)	Andy Allanson	.15
(2)	James Austin	.15
(3)	Dante Bichette	.15
(4)	Ricky Bones	.15
(5)	Chris Bosio	.15
(6)	Mike Fetters	.15
(7)	Scott Fletcher	.15
(8)	Jim Gantner	.15
(9)	Phil Garner	.15
(10)	Darryl Hamilton	.15
(11)	Doug Henry	.15
(12)	Teddy Higuera	.15
(13)	Pat Listach	.15
(14)	Jamie Navarro	.15
(15)	Edwin Nunez	.15
(16)	Tim McIntosh	.15
(17)	Paul Molitor	1.50
(18)	Jesse Orosco	.15
(19)	Dan Plesac	.15
(20)	Ron Robinson	.15
(21)	Bruce Ruffin	.15
(22)	Kevin Seitzer	.15
(23)	Bill Spiers	.15
(24)	Franklin Stubbs	.15
(25)	William Suero	.15
(26)	B.J. Surhoff	.15
(27)	Greg Vaughn	.15
(28)	Bill Wegman	.15
(29)	Robin Yount	1.50
(30)	Coaches (Bill Castro, Duffy Dyer, Mike Easler, Tim Foli, Don Rowe)	.15

1993 Milwaukee Brewers Police

The 1993 Milwaukee Brewers Police set included 30 cards with a graduated blue border. The left side has a '93 Brewers flag along the border in yellow, with the player's name in the upper right corner in white. The backs, which are white with black print, feature quotes from the player pictured. The cards are not numbered and the set also includes a card commemorating Robin Yount's 3,000th hit.

		NM/M
Complete Set (30):		3.00
Common Player:		.15
(1)	Bernie Brewer (Mascot)	.15
(2)	Phil Garner	.15
(3)	Yount's 3,000th Hit (Robin Yount)	1.00
(4)	Mark Kiefer	.15
(5)	Bill Spiers	.15
(6)	John Jaha	.15
(7)	Bill Wegman	.15
(8)	Ted Higuera	.15
(9)	Greg Vaughn	.15
(10)	Kevin Reimer	.15
(11)	Doug Henry	.15
(12)	William Suero	.15
(13)	Dave Nilsson	.15
(14)	James Austin	.15
(15)	Mike Fetters	.15
(16)	Ricky Bones	.15
(17)	Jaime Navarro	.15
(18)	Jesse Orosco	.15
(19)	Darryl Hamilton	.15
(20)	Cal Eldred	.15
(21)	Tim McIntosh	.15
(22)	Dickie Thon	.15
(23)	Graeme Lloyd	.15
(24)	Pat Listach	.15
(25)	Joe Kmak	.15
(26)	Alex Diaz	.15
(27)	Robin Yount	1.50
(28)	Tom Brunansky	.15
(29)	B.J. Surhoff	.15
(30)	Bill Doran	.15

1994 Milwaukee Brewers Police

All youngsters attending the April 23 Brewers game received this 30-card set sponsored by Pick'n Save supermarkets and Snickers candy bar, whose logos appear on both front and back. Cards featured posed player photos in their new 25th anniversary uniforms, against a lime green fabric backdrop or game action photos. Two green borders surround the photos. Navy blue bars above and below the photo have the player's name, team and uniform number. A 25th anniversary logo is at lower-right. The name of one of the many Wisconsin police agencies which distributed the cards is printed in black at bottom. Backs are printed in black-on-white and feature full major and minor league stats. The traditional safety message or anti-drug warning is not included on this issue. Cards are checklisted here by uniform number. Cards are in the 2-1/2" x 3-1/2" format.

		NM/M
Complete Set (30):		3.00
Common Player:		.25
2	Jose Valentin	.25
3	Phil Garner	.25
5	B.J. Surhoff	.25
8	Jody Reed	.25
9	Bill Spiers	.25
11	Dave Nilsson	.25
12	Brian Harper	.25
16	Pat Listach	.25
18	Tom Brunansky	.25
20	Kevin Seitzer	.25
21	Cal Eldred	.25
23	Greg Vaughn	.25
24	Darryl Hamilton	.25
25	Ricky Bones	.25
27	Turner Ward	.25
28	Doug Henry	.25
29	Jeff Bronkey	.25
30	Matt Mieske	.25
31	Jaime Navarro	.25
32	John Jaha	.25
36	Mike Fetters	.25
37	Graeme Lloyd	.25
39	Bob Scanlan	.25
40	Mike Ignasiak	.25
43	Mark Kiefer	.25
46	Bill Wegman	.25
47	Jesse Orosco	.25
49	Teddy Higuera	.25
63	Jeff D'Amico, Kelly Wunsch	.25
---	Bernie Brewer (Mascot)	.25

1995 Milwaukee Brewers Police

Some of the finest portrait photos seen on modern baseball cards are combined with game-action shots in the annual Brewers police set, sponsored by Old Fashioned Foods (makers of Squeeze Cheese). The 2-1/2" x 3-1/2" cards feature forest green borders with the player and team name, and uniform number in white on a deep blue band beneath. A tan panel at bottom has the name of the Milwaukee P.D. Many of the cards are presented in horizontal format. Backs are in black-and-white and include career stats and a safety tip. Cards are checklisted here according to uniform number.

		NM/M
Complete Set (33):		3.00
Common Player:		.25
1	Fernando Vina	.25
2	Jose Valentin	.25
3	Phil Garner	.25
5	B.J. Surhoff	.25
9	Joe Oliver	.25
10	Brewers Coaches (Bill Castro, Duffy Dyer, Tim Foli, Lamar Johnson, Don Rowe)	.25
11	Dave Nilsson	.25
12	Derrick May	.25
15	Dave Hulse	.25
16	Pat Listach	.25
20	Kevin Seitzer	.25
21	Cal Eldred	.25
22	Mike Matheny, Jeff Cirillo	.25
23	Greg Vaughn	.25
24	Darryl Hamilton	.25
25	Ricky Bones	.25
27	Turner Ward	.25
29	Jeff Bronkey	.25
30	Matt Mieske	.25
32	John Jaha	.25
36	Mike Fetters	.25
37	Graeme Lloyd	.25
38	Angel Miranda	.25
39	Bob Scanlan	.25
40	Michael Ignasiak	.25
41	Jose Mercedes, Mark Kiefer	.25
42	Scott Karl, Al Reyes, Steve Sparks	.25
46	Bill Wegman	.25
---	Bob Uecker (Announcer)	1.50
---	Charlie the Mouse (Sponsor)	.05
---	Iris the Cow (Sponsor)	.05
---	Squeezasaurus (Sponsor)	.05
---	Squeeze Cheese (Coupon)	.05

1996 Milwaukee Brewers Police

Metallic gold borders are featured on the Brewers' 14th annual safety set issued June 16 as a stadium giveaway. Cards are a mix of horizontal and vertical design with a large color photo at left. In a gold strip at right is the team logotype, player name, position and uniform number. Backs are in black-and-white with a safety message from the pictured player and the team logo. No sponsoring company or police agency is mentioned on the card. A special card in the set illustrates the proposed new Brewers stadium. Cards are listed here by uniform number.

		NM/M
Complete Set (30):		3.00
Common Player:		.15
1	Fernando Vina	.15
2	Jose Valentin	.15
3	Phil Garner	.15
4	Pat Listach	.15
8	Mark Loretta	.15
14	Dave Nilsson	.15
15	David Hulse	.15
16	Jesse Levis	.15
20	Kevin Seitzer	.15
21	Cal Eldred	.15
22	Mike Matheny	.15
23	Greg Vaughn	.15
24	Chuckie Carr	.15
25	Ricky Bones	.15
26	Jeff Cirillo	.15
27	Turner Ward	.15
30	Matt Mieske	.15
32	John Jaha	.15
36	Mike Fetters	.15
37	Graeme Lloyd	.15
38	Angel Miranda	.15
40	Ben McDonald	.15
42	Scott Karl	.15
48	Marshall Boze	.15
49	Mike Potts	.15
50	Steve Sparks	.15
51	Ramon Garcia	.15
52	Kevin Wickander	.15
---	Brewers Coaches	.15
---	Miller Park	.15

1997 Milwaukee Brewers Police

One of the more attractive safety sets of recent years, the 1997 Brewers team issue features action photos of each player in the standard 2-1/2" x 3-1/2" format. Down one side of the photo is the player's name in outline type. A team logo is at bottom-right. Backs are in black-and-white with a few bits of personal data and a cartoon figure presenting a safety tip for youngsters. The set was distributed to children attending the May 30 game at County Stadium. The checklist here is arranged by uniform number.

		NM/M
Complete Set (30):		3.00
Common Player:		.25
1	Fernando Vina	.25
2	Jose Valentin	.25
3	Phil Garner	.25
8	Mark Loretta	.25
9	Tim Unroe	.25
10	Marc Newfield	.25
13	Jeff D'Amico	.25
14	Dave Nillson	.25
15	Jeff Huson	.25
16	Jesse Levis	.25
20	Jeromy Burnitz	.50
21	Cal Eldred	.25
22	Mike Matheny	.25
24	Chuckie Carr	.25
25	Angel Miranda	.25
26	Jeff Cirillo	.25
27	Bob Wickman	.25
29	Gerald Williams	.25
30	Matt Mieske	.25
32	John Jaha	.25
36	Mike Fetters	.25
39	Bryce Florie	.25
40	Ben McDonald	.25
41	Jose Mercedes	.25
42a	Scott Karl	.25
42b	Jackie Robinson (Tribute)	2.00
43	Doug Jones	.25
49	Ron Villone	.25
51	Eddy Diaz	.25
---	Coaches (Chris Bando, Bill Castro, Jim Gantner, Lamar Johnson, Don Rowe)	.25

1998 Milwaukee Brewers Diamond Celebration

Persons attending a January 30 banquet in Milwaukee received a set of these cards highlighting the team's award winners for 1997. The set was sponsored by the Milwaukee Metropolitan Association of Commerce; their logo appears on the back. Fronts have color photos centered on a white background. The players are pictured in action, the staff in portraits. "Diamond Celebration" and the name are in script. The banquet date and specific honor also appear on front. Backs are in black-and-white with season highlights. The unnumbered cards are checklisted here alphabetically.

		NM/M
Complete Set (10):		15.00
Common Card:		.50
(1)	Hank Aaron	6.00
(2)	Jeromy Burnitz	2.00
(3)	Jeff Cirillo	2.00
(4)	Dick Hackett (Staff)	.50
(5)	Bill Haig (Staff)	.50
(6)	John Jaha	1.00
(7)	Doug Jones (MV Pitcher)	1.00
(8)	Doug Jones (MVP)	1.00
(9)	Bob Uecker (MC)	3.00
(10)	Bob Wickman	1.00

Police

For 1998, the Brewers cable television outlet sponsored the team's annual safety set, given away to kids at the June 21 game. Card fronts have player action photos vignetted on a close-up baseball background. Team and sponsor logos appear in opposite corners. Backs have a few bits of player data, a safety tip, sponsor's logo and uniform number.

		NM/M
Complete Set (30):		3.00
Common Player:		.25
1	Fernando Vina	.25
2	Jose Valentin	.25
3	Phil Garner	.25
5	Geoff Jenkins	.60
7	Dave Nilsson	.25
8	Mark Loretta	.25
9	Marquis Grissom	.25
10	Marc Newfield	.25
13	Jeff D'Amico	.25
14	Jeff Juden	.25

16	Jesse Levis	.25
20	Jeromy Burnitz	.50
21	Cal Eldred	.25
22	Mike Matheny	.25
24	Darrin Jackson	.25
26	Jeff Cirillo	.25
27	Bob Wickman	.25
28	Mike Myers	.25
30	Bob Hamelin	.25
32	John Jaha	.25
33/39	Bobby Hughes, Eric Owens	.25
37	Steve Woodard	.25
40	Chad Fox	.25
41	Jose Mercedes	.25
42	Scott Karl	.25
43	Doug Jones	.25
46	Paul Wagner	.25
47	Al Reyes	.25
48/30	Brad Woodall, Bronswell Patrick	.25
---	Coaches (Chris Bando, Bill Castro, Lamar Johnson, Doug Mansolino, Don Rowe, Joel Youngblood)	.25

1999 Milwaukee Brewers Diamond Celebration

Robin Yount
Hall of Famer

Persons attending a January 22 banquet in Milwaukee received a set of these cards highlighting the team's award winners for 1997. The set was sponsored by the Milwaukee Metropolitan Association of Commerce, whose logo appears on the back. Fronts have color photos. The players are pictured in action, the staff in portraits. "Diamond Celebration" and team logo are at left. The specific honor also appears on front. Backs are in black-and-white with season highlights. The unnumbered cards are checklisted here alphabetically.

		NM/M
Complete Set (11):		15.00
Common Player:		.50
(1)	Bob Betts (P.A. Announcer)	.50
(2)	Jeromy Burnitz (HR Champ)	2.00
(3)	Jeromy Burnitz (MVP)	2.00
(4)	Jeff Cirillo	1.00
(5)	Peter Gammons (Writer)	.50
(6)	Mark Loretta (Manager's award.)	1.00
(7)	Mark Loretta (Community service.)	1.00
(8)	Bud Selig (Owner)	.50
(9)	Bob Wickman	1.00
(10)	Steve Woodard	1.00
(11)	Robin Yount	6.00

Police

Sean Berry 7 '99

Presented by:
Midwest Sports Channel
and The Milwaukee Brewers

The regional cable station which carries Brewers games was the principal sponsor of the team's safety set given to fans on May 29. Cards feature color player poses against a sepia background showing Milwaukee County Stadium throughout the course of its 46-year history. Sponsor and team logos are in various corners on

---

front along with the player's name and uniform number. Backs have a few bits of personal data, a safety message and an ad from the sponsor. Cards are checklisted here in order of uniform number.

		NM/M
Complete Set (30):		3.00
Common Player:		.25
1	Fernando Vina	.25
2	Jose Valentin	.25
3	Phil Garner	.25
5	Geoff Jenkins	.60
7	Sean Berry	.25
8	Mark Loretta	.25
9	Marquis Grissom	.25
14	David Nilsson	.25
16	Lou Collier	.25
18	Jeromy Burnitz	.50
21	Cal Eldred	.25
22/48	Rich Becker, Steve Falteisek	.25
23	Brian Banks	.25
24	Alex Ochoa	.25
25	Jim Abbott	.35
26	Jeff Cirillo	.25
27	Bob Wickman	.25
28	Mike Myers	.25
31	Bobby Hughes	.25
37	Steve Woodard	.25
38	Eric Plunk	.25
40	Chad Fox	.25
42	Scott Karl	.25
46	Bill Pulsipher	.25
47	Al Reyes	.25
49	David Weathers	.25
52	Rafael Roque	.25
58	Valerio de los Santos	.25
---	Coaches (Bill Campbell, Bill Castro, Ron Jackson, Jim Lefebvre, Doug Mansolino, Bob Melvin)	.25
---	Milwaukee County Stadium	.25

2000 Milwaukee Brewers Diamond Celebration

26
Jeff Cirillo

Brewers
January 21 - 2000

Winners of various annual awards by the Milwaukee Brewers are featured in this standard-size card set which was issued at the team's Diamond Celebration dinner on January 21. A large portrait photo is featured along the left or right edge on front. Down the other side is player identification and the name of the award won. Backs have season highlights. The unnumbered cards are checklisted here alphabetically.

		NM/M
Complete Set (10):		15.00
Common Player:		.50
(1)	Kevin Barker	1.50
(2)	Ron Belliard	1.50
(3)	Jeromy Burnitz (HR Champ)	2.50
(4)	Jeromy Burnitz (MVP)	2.50
(5)	Jeff Cirillo	1.50
(6)	Marquis Grissom	1.50
(7)	Geoff Jenkins	3.00
(8)	Tim Kurkjian	.50
(9)	Dean Taylor, Davey Lopes	.50
(10)	Bob Wickman	1.00

Police

In its third season of sponsoring the team's safety set, the Brewers' cable franchisee offered the cards to the first 10,000 youngsters at a May promotional game. Other sets were distributed by police agencies. Card fronts have the players posed in their dark blue jerseys against a black background lit by a colorful Milwaukee Brewers neon sign. In a lower corner are the sponsor's logo, player name and uniform number. A Time-Warner Cable logo is in the white border at bottom. Backs have player

---

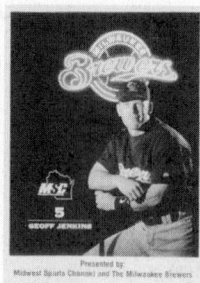

Presented by:
Midwest Sports Channel and the Milwaukee Brewers

identification and a safety message. Cards are checklisted here by uniform number.

		NM/M
Complete Set (30):		3.00
Common Player:		.25
00	Curtis Leskanic	.25
1	Luis Lopez	.25
2	Tyler Houston	.25
5	Geoff Jenkins	.50
7	Sean Berry	.25
8	Mark Loretta	.25
9	Marquis Grissom	.25
10	Ron Belliard	.25
12	Henry Blanco	.25
14	Charlie Hayes	.25
18	Jose Hernandez	.25
22	Jeromy Burnitz	.45
24	Kevin Barker	.25
26	James Mouton	.25
27	Bob Wickman	.25
28	Valerio de los Santos	.25
30	Davey Lopes	.25
31	Everett Stull	.25
33	Lyle Mouton	.25
37	Steve Woodard	.25
41	Jaime Navarro	.25
41	Matt Williams	.25
48	Jason Bere	.25
49	David Weathers	.25
51	Jimmy Haynes	.25
53	Juan Acevedo	.25
59	John Snyder	.25
88	Jim Bruske	.25
---	Coaches (Jerry Royster, Rod Carew, Bill Castro, Bob Apodaca, Chris Speier, Gary Allenson)	.25
---	Matt Vasgersian, Bill Schroeder (Broadcasters)	.25

2000 Milwaukee Journal Sentinel 1970s Brewers

ALL-DECADES TEAM
1970's

44

Henry Aaron
Designated Hitter

MILWAUKEE
JOURNAL SENTINEL

As selected by fan balloting, an All-Decade team of 1970s Milwaukee Brewers is honored on this set of cards given to fans at a promotional game in July. The standard 2-1/2" x 3-1/2" cards have borderless game-action photos on front with a gold-foil diamond naming the player, his position and uniform number. The newspaper sponsor's logo is at bottom. Backs have a team logo, player personal data, stats and career highlights. The unnumbered cards are checklisted here in alphabetical order.

		NM/M
Complete Set (13):		12.00
Common Player:		.50
(1)	Hank Aaron	6.00
(2)	George Bamberger	.50
(3)	Mike Caldwell	.50
(4)	Cecil Cooper	.75
(5)	Tommy Harper	.50
(6)	Larry Hisle	.50
(7)	Sixto Lezcano	.50
(8)	Don Money	.50
(9)	Charlie Moore	.50
(10)	Ken Sanders	.50
(11)	Jim Slaton	.50
(12)	Gorman Thomas	.50
(13)	Robin Yount	4.00

1980s Brewers

ALL-DECADES TEAM
1980's

Rollie Fingers
34

MILWAUKEE
JOURNAL SENTINEL

As selected by fan balloting, an All-Decade team of 1980s Milwaukee Brewers is honored on this set of cards given to fans at a promotional game August 11. The standard 2-1/2" x 3-1/2" cards have game-action photos on front with a gold-foil diamond naming the player, his position and uniform number. The newspaper sponsor's logo is at bottom. Backs have a team logo, player personal data, stats and career highlights. The unnumbered cards are checklisted here in alphabetical order.

		NM/M
Complete Set (13):		12.00
Common Player:		.50
(1)	Mike Caldwell	.50
(2)	Cecil Cooper	.50
(3)	Rollie Fingers	.75
(4)	Jim Gantner	.50
(5)	Harvey Kuenn	.50
(6)	Paul Molitor (DH)	3.00
(7)	Paul Molitor (3B)	3.00
(8)	Ben Oglivie	.50
(9)	Ted Simmons	.50
(10)	Gorman Thomas	.50
(11)	Pete Vuckovich	.50
(12)	Robin Yount (OF)	3.00
(13)	Robin Yount (SS)	3.00

1990s Brewers

As selected by fan balloting, an All-Decade team of 1990s Milwaukee Brewers is honored on this set of cards given to fans at a promotional game September 8. The standard 2-1/2" x 3-1/2" cards have game-action photos on front with a gold-foil diamond naming the player, his position and uniform number. The newspaper sponsor's logo is at bottom. Backs have a team logo, player personal data, stats and career highlights. The unnumbered cards are checklisted here in alphabetical order.

		NM/M
Complete Set (13):		9.00
Common Player:		.50
(1)	Chris Bosio	.50
(2)	Jeromy Burnitz	1.00
(3)	Jeff Cirillo	.50
(4)	Phil Garner	.50
(5)	John Jaha	.50
(6)	Geoff Jenkins	2.00
(7)	David Nilsson	.50
(8)	B.J. Surhoff	.50
(9)	Jose Valentin	.50
(10)	Fernando Vina	.50
(11)	Bill Wegman	.50
(12)	Bob Wickman	.50
(13)	Robin Yount	3.00

1983 Minnesota Twins Team Issue

2

The Minnesota Twins produced a 36-card set in 1983 to be sold at concession stands and

Complete Set (36):		7.50
Common Player:		.25
1	John Castino	.25
2	Jim Eisenreich	.35
3	Al Jimenez	.25
4	Dave Meier	.25
5	Gary Gaetti	.50
6	Mickey Hatcher	.25
7	Jeff Reed	.25
8	Tim Teufel	.25
9	Len Faedo	.25
10	Kent Hrbek	1.00
11	Tim Laudner	.25
12	Frank Viola	.50
13	Ken Schrom	.25
14	Larry Pashnick	.25
15	Dave Engle	.25
16	Keith Comstock	.25
17	Pete Filson	.25
18	Tom Brunansky	.25
19	Randy Bush	.25
20	Darrell Brown	.25
21	Al Williams	.25
22	Mike Walters	.25
23	John Butcher	.25
24	Bobby Castillo	.25

---

through the mail. The full-color borderless cards measure 2-1/2" x 3-1/2" and displayed the player's uniform number on a white Twins jersey at the bottom of the card. The backs contain full career statistics.

		NM/M
Complete Set (36):		7.00
Common Player:		.25
1	John Castino	.25
2	Jim Eisenreich	.50
3	Ray Smith	.25
4	Scott Ullger	.25
5	Gary Gaetti	.75
6	Mickey Hatcher	.25
7	Bobby Mitchell	.25
8	Len Faedo	.25
9	Kent Hrbek	2.00
10	Tim Laudner	.25
11	Frank Viola	1.00
12	Bryan Oelkers	.25
13	Rick Lysander	.25
14	Dave Engle	.25
15	Len Whitehouse	.25
16	Pete Filson	.25
17	Tom Brunansky	.25
18	Randy Bush	.25
19	Brad Havens	.25
20	Al Williams	.25
21	Gary Ward	.25
22	Jack O'Connor	.25
23	Bobby Castillo	.25
24	Ron Washington	.25
25	Ron Davis	.25
26	Tom Kelly	.25
27	Billy Gardner	.25
28	Rick Stelmaszek	.25
29	Jim Lemon	.25
30	Johnny Podres	.25
31	Minnesota's Native Sons (Jim Eisenreich, Kent Hrbek, Tim Laudner)	.50
32	Twins' Catchers (Dave Engle, Tim Laudner)	.25
33	The Lumber Company (Tom Brunansky, Gary Gaetti, Kent Hrbek, Gary Ward)	.75
34	Twins' Coaches (Billy Gardner, Tom Kelly, Jim Lemon, Johnny Podres, Rick Stelmaszek)	.25
35	Team Photo	.25
36	Metrodome/Checklist	.25

1984 Minnesota Twins Team Issue

Twins
16

This team-issued set from the Minnesota Twins consists of 36 full-color, borderless cards, each measuring 2-1/2" x 3-1/2". As in the previous year, the player's uniform number appears on a white Twins jersey at the bottom of the card. The backs are printed in red and blue on white stock and include career stats. The set features several special cards, including one of Harmon Killebrew.

		NM/M
Complete Set (36):		15.00
Common Player:		.20
1	Alvaro Espinoza	.25
2	Roy Smalley	.25
3	Pedro Oliva	.75
4	Dave Meier	.25
5	Gary Gaetti	.50
6	Mickey Hatcher	.25
7	Jeff Reed	.25
8	Tim Teufel	.25
9	Mark Salas	.25
10	Kent Hrbek	1.00
11	Tim Laudner	.25
12	Frank Viola	.50
13	Ken Schrom	.25
14	Rick Lysander	.25
15	Dave Engle	.25
16	Andre David	.25
17	Len Whitehouse	.25
18	Pete Filson	.25
19	Tom Brunansky	.25
20	Randy Bush	.25
21	Greg Gagne	.75
22	John Butcher	.25
23	Mike Stenhouse	.25
24	Kirby Puckett	10.00
25	Tom Klawitter	.25
26	Curt Wardle	.25
27	Rich Yett	.25
28	Ron Washington	.25
29	Ron Davis	.25
30	Tom Kelly	.25
31	Billy Gardner	.25
32	Rick Stelmaszek	.25
33	Johnny Podres	.40
34	Mike Smithson	.25
35	1985 All-Star Game Logo Card	.25
36	Twins Logo/Checklist	.25

25	Ron Washington	.25
26	Ron Davis	.25
27	Tom Kelly	.25
28	Billy Gardner	.25
29	Rick Stelmaszek	.25
30	Jim Lemon	.25
31	Johnny Podres	.25
32	Mike Smithson	.25
33	Harmon Killebrew	4.00
34	Team Photo	.50
35	Logo Card	.25
36	Metrodome/Checklist	.25

1985 Minnesota Twins Team Issue

Twins
9

Similar in format to the previous two years, this 36-card team-issued set features full-color, borderless cards. The player's uniform number is again displayed on a white Twins jersey in the lower right corner, and the 1985 All-Star Game logo is shown in the lower left. The All-Star Game logo also appears on a special card in the set that lists on the back all Twins who have been selected for previous All-Star Games. The set was sold at ballpark concession stands and through the mail.

		NM/M
Complete Set (36):		15.00
Common Player:		.20
1	Alvaro Espinoza	.25
2	Roy Smalley	.25
3	Pedro Oliva	.75
4	Dave Meier	.25
5	Gary Gaetti	.50
6	Mickey Hatcher	.25
7	Jeff Reed	.25
8	Tim Teufel	.25
9	Mark Salas	.25
10	Kent Hrbek	1.00
11	Tim Laudner	.25
12	Frank Viola	.50
13	Ken Schrom	.25
14	Rick Lysander	.25
15	Dave Engle	.25
16	Andre David	.25
17	Len Whitehouse	.25
18	Pete Filson	.25
19	Tom Brunansky	.25
20	Randy Bush	.25
21	Greg Gagne	.75
22	John Butcher	.25
23	Mike Stenhouse	.25
24	Kirby Puckett	10.00
25	Tom Klawitter	.25
26	Curt Wardle	.25
27	Rich Yett	.25
28	Ron Washington	.25
29	Ron Davis	.25
30	Tom Kelly	.25
31	Billy Gardner	.25
32	Rick Stelmaszek	.25
33	Johnny Podres	.40
34	Mike Smithson	.25
35	1985 All-Star Game Logo Card	.25
36	Twins Logo/Checklist	.25

1986 Minnesota Twins Team Issue

Twins
34

This team-issued set contains 36 2-9/16" x 3-1/2" full-color cards. Fronts feature the Twins 25th anniversary logo and a jersey at the bottom of each card with the player's uniform number. All cards, except an action shot of Bert Blyleven, are posed photos, with a facsimile autograph on each. The set also includes a checklist and a team photo.

		NM/M
Complete Set (36):		6.00
Common Player:		.15
1	Chris Pittaro	.15
2	Steve Lombardozzi	.15
3	Roy Smalley	.15
4	Pedro Oliva	.50
5	Gary Gaetti	.30
6	Mickey Hatcher	.15
7	Jeff Reed	.15
8	Mark Salas	.15
9	Kent Hrbek	.50
10	Tim Laudner	.15
11	Frank Viola	.30
12	Dennis Burtt	.15
13	Alex Sanchez	.15
14	Roy Smith	.15
15	Billy Beane	.15
16	Pete Filson	.15
17	Tom Brunansky	.15
18	Randy Bush	.15
19	Frank Eufemia	.15
20	Mark Davidson	.15
21	Bert Blyleven	.40
22	Greg Gagne	.15
23	John Butcher	.15
24	Kirby Puckett	5.00
25	Bill Latham	.15
26	Ron Washington	.15
27	Ron Davis	.15
28	Tom Kelly	.15
29	Dick Such	.15
30	Rick Stelmaszek	.15
31	Ray Miller	.15
32	Wayne Terwilliger	.15
33	Mike Smithson	.15
34	Alvis Woods	.15
35	Team Photo	.25
36	Twins Logo/Checklist	.15

1987 Minnesota Twins Team Issue

The Minnesota Twins produced a 32-card set of 2-1/2" x 3-1/2" full-color baseball cards to be sold at the ballpark and through their souvenir catalog. The card fronts are borderless, containing only the player photo. The backs are printed in blue and red on white card stock and carry the player's personal data and career record. The Twins also produced a post card set that was similar in design to the standard-size card set, but utilized different photos.

		NM/M
Complete Set (33):		12.50
Common Player:		.25
1	Steve Lombardozzi	.25
2	Roy Smalley	.25
3	Pedro Oliva	.50
4	Greg Gagne	.25
5	Gary Gaetti	.30
6	Tom Kelly	.25
7	Tom Nieto	.25
8	Mark Salas	.25
9	Kent Hrbek	.50
10	Tim Laudner	.25
11	Frank Viola	.35
12	Les Straker	.25
13	George Frazier	.25
14	Keith Atherton	.25
15	Tom Brunansky	.25
16	Randy Bush	.25
17	Al Newman	.25
18	Mark Davidson	.25
19	Bert Blyleven	.35
20	Dan Gladden	.25
21	Kirby Puckett	7.50
22	Mark Portugal	.25
23	Juan Berenguer	.25
24	Jeff Reardon	.25
25	Dick Such	.25
26	Rick Stelmaszek	.25
27	Rick Renick	.25
28	Wayne Terwilliger	.25

29	Joe Klink	.25
30	Mike Smithson	.25
31	Team Photo	.25
32	Twins Champions Logo	.25
33	Twins Logo/Checklist	.25

1988 Minnesota Twins Fire Safety

This 8-1/4" x 3-3/4" booklet contains a dozen postcards called Color-Grams featuring caricatures (suitable for coloring) of star players. Postcards are attached along a perforated edge to a baseball card-size stub with a black-and-white photo of the featured player. Backs include the player name and personal information. The card stubs include the same information, along with a fire prevention tip. Twins Color-Grams were produced as a public service by the U.S. Forest Service and Dept. of Agriculture and were distributed to fans at the Metrodome.

		NM/M
Complete Booklet:		10.00
Complete Set, Singles (12):		7.50
Common Player:		.50
(1)	Bert Blyleven	.75
(2)	Randy Bush	.50
(3)	Gary Gaetti	.60
(4)	Greg Gagne	.50
(5)	Dan Gladden	.50
(6)	Kent Hrbek	1.00
(7)	Gene Larkin	.50
(8)	Tim Laudner	.50
(9)	Al Newman	.50
(10)	Kirby Puckett	4.00
(11)	Jeff Reardon	.50
(12)	Frank Viola	.50

1988 Minnesota Twins Team Issue

The Twins issued this set to commemorate the team's 1987 World Series victory. The slightly oversized cards (2-5/8" x 3-7/16") feature color player photos printed on heavy stock with a gold-embossed "1987 World Champions" logo in the lower-left corner. Numbered card backs are red, white and blue and contain player name, personal info and stats. A limited edition of 5000 sets were printed but only a few hundred were sold before the cards were taken off the market due to Major League Baseball licensing restrictions on the use of the World Series logo.

		NM/M
Complete Set (33):		60.00
Common Player:		1.50
1	Steve Lombardozzi	1.50
2	Roy Smalley	1.50
3	Pedro Oliva	4.00
4	Greg Gagne	3.00
5	Gary Gaetti	2.00
6	Gene Larkin	2.00
7	Tom Kelly	2.00
8	Kent Hrbek	6.00
9	Tim Laudner	2.00
10	Frank Viola	4.00
11	Les Straker	1.50
12	Don Baylor	4.00
13	George Frazier	1.50
14	Keith Atherton	1.50
15	Tom Brunansky	1.50
16	Randy Bush	1.50
17	Al Newman	1.50
18	Mark Davidson	1.50
19	Bert Blyleven	4.00
20	Dan Schatzeder	1.50
21	Dan Gladden	2.00
22	Sal Butera	1.50
23	Kirby Puckett	25.00
24	Joe Niekro	2.00
25	Juan Berenguer	1.50
26	Jeff Reardon	3.00
27	Dick Such	1.50
28	Rick Stelmaszek	1.50
29	Rick Renick	1.50
30	Wayne Terwilliger	1.50
31	Team Photo	1.50
32	World Champions Team Logo Card	1.50
33	Team Logo Card/ Checklist	1.50

1997 Minnesota Twins 10th Anniversary

The 10th anniversary of the team's 1987 World Series victory is recalled with this set given to fans on August 8 during the reunion weekend at the Metrodome. The 2-1/2" x 3-1/2" cards have 10-year-old color action photos on front with the anniversary logo and player identification. On back are a black-and-white portrait photo, uniform number, biographical details, the player's 1987 season and post-season performance and the sponsor's logo. The cards are checklisted here in alphabetical order.

		NM/M
Complete Set (25):		10.00
Common Player:		.25
(1)	Keith Atherton	.25
(2)	Don Baylor	.40
(3)	Juan Berenguer	.25
(4)	Bert Blyleven	.35
(5)	Tom Brunansky	.25
(6)	Randy Bush	.25
(7)	Sal Butera	.25
(8)	Mark Davidson	.25
(9)	George Frazier	.25
(10)	Gary Gaetti	.50
(11)	Greg Gagne	.50
(12)	Dan Gladden	.25
(13)	Kent Hrbek	1.00
(14)	Tom Kelly	.25
(15)	Gene Larkin	.25
(16)	Tim Laudner	.25
(17)	Steve Lombardozzi	.25
(18)	Al Newman	.25
(19)	Joe Niekro	.40
(20)	Kirby Puckett	5.00
(21)	Jeff Reardon	.25
(22)	Dan Schatzeder	.25
(23)	Roy Smalley	.25
(24)	Les Straker	.25
(25)	Frank Viola	.40

2002 Minnesota Twins Police

More than 300 agencies comprising the Minnesota Crime Prevention Association distributed this multi-sport set. Eight players each from the Twins, Vikings and Wild were included, along with McGruff the Crime Dog. Distribution of the baseball players cards was between August 6-19. The baseball cards have game-action photos which are borderless at top and sides. Two team logos are in the top corners and a blue strip at bottom has player name, uniform number and position. Backs have a black-and-white portrait photo, a safety tip and sponsors logos. Only the baseball players from the issue are listed here.

		NM/M
Complete (Baseball) Set (8):		5.00
Common Player:		.50
1	Eddie Guardado	.50
2	Cristian Guzman	1.00
3	Jacque Jones	1.00
4	Corey Koskie	1.00

5	Doug Mientkiewicz	.50
6	A.J. Pierzynski	.50
7	Luis Rivas	.50
8	Torii Hunter	1.50

2003 Minnesota Twins Police

#47 • Corey Koskie • Third Base

Sponsored by the Minnesota Crime Prevention Association, this set features eight popular players and McGruff the Crime Dog. Standard 2-1/2" x 3-1/2" cards have game-action photos on front, borderless at top and sides. A blue stripe at bottom has uniform number, player name and position. The team's 2002 A.L. Central Division Champions logo and "Gotta See 'Em" 2003 season logo are in the top corners. A facsimile autograph appears on front. Backs are in black, white and blue with a portrait photo, player data and a safety tip, along with the sponsor's and printer's logos.

		NM/M
Complete Set (9):		5.00
Common Player:		.50
1	Torii Hunter	1.00
2	Doug Mientkiewicz	.75
3	Corey Koskie	.75
4	A.J. Pierzynski	.75
5	Brad Radke	.75
6	Jacque Jones	.75
7	Eddie Guardado	.50
8	Eric Milton	.50
9	McGruff the Crime Dog	.50

2004 Minnesota Twins Police

Sponsored by the Minnesota Crime Prevention Association, this set features eight popular players. Standard 2-1/2" x 3-1/2" cards have game-action photos on front, borderless at top and sides. A blue stripe at bottom has uniform number, player name and position. The team's 2003 A.L. Central Division Champions logo is in the top-right corner. A facsimile autograph appears on front. Backs are in black and white with a portrait photo, player data and a safety tip, along with the sponsor's and printer's logos.

		NM/M
Complete Set (8):		5.00
Common Player:		.50
1	Torii Hunter	.75
2	Doug Mientkiewicz	.50
3	Corey Koskie	.50
4	Shannon Stewart	.50
5	Brad Radke	.50
6	Cristian Guzman	.50
7	Johan Santana	2.00
8	Kyle Lohse	.50

2004 Minnesota Twins Team Issue

To build support in its drive to retain Major League Baseball in the Twin Cities and build a new outdoor stadium, the team issued this card set at its winter TwinsFest. Cards are

2-1/2" x 3-1/2" printed on thin semigloss stock. There are five player cards and seven depicting artists' views of the proposed ballpark.

		NM/M
Complete Set (12):		6.00
Common Player:		.50
21	Doug Mientkiewicz	.50
22	Brad Radke	.50
23	Shannon Stewart	.75
47	Corey Koskie	.75
48	Torii Hunter	1.00
---	A Ballpark for Minnesota ("As the new home . . .")	.50
---	A Ballpark for Minnesota ("Got off the bench . . .")	.50
---	A Ballpark for Minnesota ("Minnesota's new ballpark will honor . . .")	.50
---	A Ballpark for Minnesota ("Minnesota's new ballpark will mark . . .")	.50
---	A Ballpark for Minnesota ("Much like those . . .")	.50
---	A Ballpark for Minnesota ("The exterior . . .")	.50
---	A Ballpark for Minnesota ("With total seating . . .")	.50

2005 Star Tribune Minnesota Twins Medallion Collection

A set of 21 commemorative medallions was sponsored by the Star Tribune in this promotion. Coupons found in the newspaper between May 2-25 could be redeemed at newsstands (along with $2.99) for that day's medallion. Larger and thicker than a quarter, the 1-3/16" diameter medals are struck in nickel and have on their fronts an enameled portrait photo. A team logo dominates the back. A colorful, photofilled 7-3/4" x 13" album was available to house the pieces. The medals are listed here in alphabetical order.

		NM/M
Complete Set (21):		90.00
Common Player:		3.00
Album:		3.00
(1)	Grant Balfour	3.00
(2)	Juan Castro	3.00
(3)	Michael Cuddyer	3.00
(4)	Lew Ford	3.00
(5)	Ron Gardenhire	3.00
(6)	Torii Hunter	4.50
(7)	Jacque Jones	4.50
(8)	Matthew LeCroy	3.00
(9)	Kyle Lohse	3.00
(10)	Joe Mauer	10.00
(11)	Joe Mays	3.00
(12)	Justin Morneau	10.00
(13)	Joe Nathan	3.00
(14)	Brad Radke	4.50
(15)	Juan Rincon	3.00
(16)	Luis Rivas	3.00
(17)	J.C. Romero	3.00
(18)	Johan Santana	12.50
(19)	Carlos Silva	3.00
(20)	Shannon Stewart	3.00
(21)	Twins Back To Back To Back Championships	3.00

2005 Minnesota Twins Police

48 Torii Hunter •Centerfielder

Sponsored by the Minnesota Crime Prevention Association, this set features seven popular players and McGruff the Crime Dog. Standard 2-1/2" x 3-1/2" cards have game-action photos on front, bordered in dark blue. A strip at bottom has uniform number, player name and position. Team logos are in each upper corner. Backs are in black-and-white with a small portrait photo, player information, safety tip, along with the sponsor's and printer's logos. The set was distributed by area police agencies and at a Twins game in May.

		NM/M
Complete Set (8):		8.00
Common Player:		1.00
7	Joe Mauer	2.00
22	Brad Radke	1.00
23	Shannon Stewart	1.00
36	Joe Nathan	1.50
48	Torii Hunter	1.50
49	Kyle Lohse	1.00
57	Johan Santana	1.50
---	McGruff The Crime Dog	1.00

1992 MJB Holoprisms

The Holoprism set consists of two four-card hologram sets of Rookies of the Year Jeff Bagwell and Chuck Knoblauch. Each player set was packaged in a special plastic case. The production was limited to 250,000 of each set, numbered and with a letter of authenticity. Each player autographed 500 cards, which were randomly inserted.

		NM/M
Complete Bagwell Set (4):		6.00
Common Bagwell Card:		1.50
Complete Knoblauch Set (4):		6.00
Common Knoblauch Card:		1.00
Autographed Bagwell Card:		75.00
Autographed Knoblauch Card:		40.00
R1	Jeff Bagwell/Btg	2.00
R1a	Jeff Bagwell (Overprinted "PROTOTYPE" on back.)	2.00
R2	Jeff Bagwell/Fldg	2.00
R3	Jeff Bagwell/Btg	2.00
R4	Jeff Bagwell/Btg	2.00
R1	Chuck Knoblauch/Btg	1.00
R1a	Chuck Knoblauch (Overprinted "PROTOTYPE" on back.)	1.00
R2	Chuck Knoblauch/Fldg	1.00
R3	Chuck Knoblauch/Btg	1.00
R4	Chuck Knoblauch/Btg	1.00

2000 MLB Showdown Promos

To introduce its baseball card game, Wizards of the Coast produced a series of promo cards that were locally distributed to hobby stores to encourage people to join gaming leagues. The promos differ from the issued cards in the use of silver-foil highlights and the presence of large "FUTURE STAR" or "DIAMOND STAR" in the background, instead of a team logo, or "HOME RUN HITTER" at top. Because of the manner of distribution, some promos are more difficult to find in the hobby market.

	NM/M
Complete Set (43):	10.00
Common Player:	.40
(1) Sandy Alomar Jr.	.40
(2) Craig Biggio	.40
(3) Carlos Delgado	.60
(4) Damion Easley	.40
(5) Mark Grace	.40
(6) Rusty Greer	.40
(7) Tony Gwynn	.60
(8a) Andruw Jones (8 OB)	.60
(8b) Andruw Jones (10 OB)	1.00
(9) Chipper Jones	1.00
(10) Jeff Kent	.40
(11) Edgar Martinez	.40
(12) Gary Sheffield	.60
(13) B.J. Surhoff	.40
(14) Jason Varitek	.40
(15) Robin Ventura	.40
(16) Bernie Williams	.40
(1) Bob Abreu	.40
(2) Ron Belliard	.40
(3) Sean Casey	.40
(4) Luis Castillo	.40
(5) J.D. Drew	.60
(6) Erubiel Durazo	.40
(7) Carlos Febles	.40
(8) Troy Glaus	.65
(9) Ben Grieve	.40
(10) Todd Helton	.65
(11) Corey Koskie	.40
(12) Warren Morris	.40
1 Barry Bonds	2.00
2 Jose Canseco	.60
3 Nomar Garciaparra	1.00
4 Jason Giambi	.60
5 Shawn Green	.50
6 Ken Griffey Jr.	1.25
7 Andruw Jones	.75
8 Chipper Jones	1.00
9 Mark McGwire	1.50
10 Rafael Palmeiro	.65
11 Mike Piazza	1.25
12 Manny Ramirez	1.00
13 Alex Rodriguez	1.50
14 Sammy Sosa	1.00

2000 MLB Showdown 1st Edition

Yet another attempt to bridge the gap between baseball cards as player-related collectibles and as interactive game, MLB Showdown from veteran gamers Wizards of the Coast enjoyed significant initial interest. Issued as a starter deck and in nine-card booster packs, the debut set has 462 player cards, including 63 premium holofoil star cards and 75 strategy cards. The holo premium foils were inserted in booster packs at a rate of 1:3. Promo cards were locally distributed. While collectors compete with gamers for these cards in the market, relative values placed on the cards by each group of buyers will differ. Cards without the silver-foil

"1st Edition" logo were released in booster packs and are worth about half the values shown here.

	NM/M
Complete Set (517):	200.00
Common Player:	.15
Starter Box:	6.00
Starter Deck:	2.00
Booster Box (36):	25.00
Booster Pack (9):	1.00
1 Garret Anderson	.15
2 Tim Belcher	.15
3 Gary DiSarcina (Photo is Tim Salmon.)	.15
4 Darin Erstad	.30
5 Chuck Finley (Foil)	2.00
6 Troy Glaus	.65
7 Todd Greene	.15
8 Jeff Huson	.15
9 Orlando Palmeiro	.15
10 Troy Percival	.15
11 Mark Petkovsek	.15
12 Tim Salmon	.15
13 Steve Sparks	.15
14 Mo Vaughn	.15
15 Matt Walbeck	.15
16 Jay Bell (Foil)	2.00
17 Andy Benes	.15
18 Omar Daal	.15
19 Steve Finley	.15
20 Andy Fox	.15
21 Hanley Frias	.15
22 Bernard Gilkey	.15
23 Luis Gonzalez (Foil)	2.00
24 Randy Johnson (Foil)	3.00
25 Travis Lee	.15
26 Matt Mantei	.15
27 Dan Plesac	.15
28 Kelly Stinnett	.15
29 Greg Swindell	.15
30 Matt Williams (Foil)	2.00
31 Tony Womack	.15
32 Bret Boone	.15
33 Tom Glavine	.40
34 Jose Hernandez	.15
35 Brian Hunter	.15
36 Andruw Jones	.75
37 Chipper Jones (Foil)	4.00
38 Brian Jordan	.15
39 Ryan Klesko	.15
40 Keith Lockhart	.15
41 Greg Maddux (Foil)	4.00
42 Kevin Millwood (Foil)	2.00
43 Eddie Perez	.15
44 Mike Remlinger	.15
45 John Rocker	.15
46 John Smoltz	.15
47 Walt Weiss	.15
48 Gerald Williams	.15
49 Rich Amaral	.15
50 Brady Anderson	.15
51 Albert Belle	.15
52 Mike Bordick	.15
53 Jeff Conine	.15
54 Delino DeShields	.15
55 Scott Erickson	.15
56 Charles Johnson	.15
57 Mike Mussina	.35
58 Jesse Orosco	.15
59 Sidney Ponson	.15
60 Jeff Reboulet	.15
61 Cal Ripken Jr. (Foil)	7.00
62 B.J. Surhoff	.15
63 Mike Timlin	.15
64 Rod Beck	.15
65 Damon Buford	.15
66 Rheal Cormier	.15
67 Nomar Garciaparra (Foil)	4.00
68 Butch Huskey	.15
69 Darren Lewis	.15
70 Derek Lowe	.15
71 Pedro Martinez (Foil)	3.00
72 Trot Nixon	.15
73 Jose Offerman	.15
74 Troy O'Leary	.15
75 Mark Portugal	.15
76 Pat Rapp	.15
77 Mike Stanley	.15
78 John Valentin	.15
79 Jason Varitek	.25
80 Tim Wakefield	.15
81 Rick Aguilera	.15
82 Jeff Blauser	.15
83 Kyle Farnsworth	.15
84 Gary Gaetti	.15
85 Mark Grace	.15
86 Lance Johnson	.15
87 Jon Lieber	.15
88 Mickey Morandini	.15
89 Jose Nieves	.15
90 Jeff Reed	.15
91 Henry Rodriguez	.15
92 Scott Sanders	.15
93 Benito Santiago	.15
94 Sammy Sosa	4.50
95 Steve Trachsel	.15
96 James Baldwin	.15
97 Mike Caruso	.15
98 Ray Durham	.15
99 Brook Fordyce	.15
100 Bob Howry	.15
101 Paul Konerko	.50
102 Carlos Lee	.35
103 Greg Norton	.15
104 Magglio Ordonez	.15
105 Jim Parque	.15
106 Bill Simas	.15

107 Chris Singleton	.15
108 Mike Sirotka	.15
109 Frank Thomas (Foil)	3.00
110 Craig Wilson	.15
111 Aaron Boone	.15
112 Mike Cameron	.15
113 Sean Casey (Foil)	2.00
114 Danny Graves	.15
115 Pete Harnisch	.15
116 Barry Larkin (Foil)	2.00
117 Pokey Reese	.15
118 Scott Sullivan	.15
119 Eddie Taubensee	.15
120 Brett Tomko	.15
121 Michael Tucker	.15
122 Greg Vaughn	.15
123 Ron Villone	.15
124 Scott Williamson (Foil)	2.00
125 Dmitri Young	.15
126 Roberto Alomar (Foil)	2.00
127 Harold Baines	.15
128 Dave Burba	.15
129 Bartolo Colon	.15
130 Einar Diaz	.15
131 Travis Fryman	.15
132 Mike Jackson	.15
133 David Justice	.15
134 Kenny Lofton (Foil)	2.00
135 Charles Nagy	.15
136 Manny Ramirez (Foil)	3.00
137 Richie Sexson	.15
138 Paul Shuey	.15
139 Jim Thome (Foil)	2.50
140 Omar Vizquel	.15
141 Enrique Wilson	.15
142 Kurt Abbott	.15
143 Pedro Astacio	.15
144 Jeff Barry	.15
145 Dante Bichette	.15
146 Henry Blanco	.15
147 Brian Bohanon	.15
148 Vinny Castilla	.15
149 Jerry Dipoto	.15
150 Todd Helton	.65
151 Darryl Kile	.15
152 Curtis Leskanic	.15
153 Neifi Perez	.15
154 Terry Shumpert	.15
155 Dave Veres	.15
156 Larry Walker (Foil)	2.00
157 Brad Ausmus	.15
158 Frank Catalanotto	.15
159 Tony Clark	.15
160 Deivi Cruz	.15
161 Damion Easley	.15
162 Juan Encarnacion	.15
163 Karim Garcia	.15
164 Bobby Higginson	.15
165 Todd Jones	.15
166 Gabe Kapler	.15
167 Dave Mlicki	.15
168 Brian Moehler	.15
169 C.J. Nitkowski	.15
170 Dean Palmer (Foil)	2.00
171 Jeff Weaver	.15
172 Antonio Alfonseca	.15
173 Bruce Aven	.15
174 Dave Berg	.15
175 Luis Castillo (Foil)	2.00
176 Ryan Dempster	.15
177 Brian Edmondson	.15
178 Alex Gonzalez	.15
179 Mark Kotsay	.15
180 Derrek Lee	.50
181 Braden Looper	.15
182 Mike Lowell	.15
183 Brian Meadows	.15
184 Mike Redmond	.15
185 Dennis Springer	.15
186 Preston Wilson	.15
187 Jeff Bagwell (Foil)	3.00
188 Derek Bell	.15
189 Craig Biggio	.15
190 Tim Bogar	.15
191 Ken Caminiti	.15
192 Scott Elarton	.15
193 Tony Eusebio	.15
194 Carl Everett (Foil)	2.00
195 Mike Hampton (Foil)	2.00
196 Richard Hidalgo	.15
197 Stan Javier	.15
198 Jose Lima	.15
199 Jay Powell	.15
200 Shane Reynolds	.15
201 Bill Spiers	.15
202 Billy Wagner (Foil)	2.00
203 Carlos Beltran (Foil)	2.50
204 Johnny Damon	.35
205 Jermaine Dye	.15
206 Carlos Febles	.15
207 Jeremy Giambi	.15
208 Chad Kreuter	.15
209 Jeff Montgomery	.15
210 Joe Randa	.15
211 Jose Rosado	.15
212 Rey Sanchez	.15
213 Scott Service	.15
214 Tim Spehr	.15
215 Jeff Suppan	.15
216 Mike Sweeney	.15
217 Jay Witasick	.15
218 Adrian Beltre	.50
219 Pedro Borbon	.15
220 Kevin Brown (Foil)	2.00
221 Mark Grudzielanek	.15
222 Dave Hansen	.15
223 Todd Hundley	.15
224 Eric Karros	.15

225 Raul Mondesi	.15
226 Chan Ho Park	.15
227 Jeff Shaw	.15
228 Gary Sheffield (Foil)	2.50
229 Ismael Valdes	.15
230 Jose Vizcaino	.15
231 Devon White	.15
232 Eric Young	.15
233 Ron Belliard	.15
234 Sean Berry	.15
235 Jeromy Burnitz (Foil)	2.00
236 Jeff Cirillo	.15
237 Marquis Grissom	.15
238 Geoff Jenkins	.15
239 Scott Karl	.15
240 Mark Loretta	.15
241 Mike Myers	.15
242 David Nilsson (Foil)	2.00
243 Hideo Nomo	.50
244 Alex Ochoa	.15
245 Jose Valentin	.15
246 Bob Wickman	.15
247 Steve Woodard	.15
248 Chad Allen	.15
249 Ron Coomer	.15
250 Cristian Guzman	.15
251 Denny Hocking	.15
252 Torii Hunter	.15
253 Corey Koskie	.15
254 Matt Lawton	.15
255 Joe Mays	.15
256 Doug Mientkiewicz	.15
257 Eric Milton	.15
258 Brad Radke (Foil)	2.00
259 Terry Steinbach	.15
260 Mike Trombley	.15
261 Todd Walker	.15
262 Bob Wells	.15
263 Shane Andrews	.15
264 Michael Barrett	.15
265 Orlando Cabrera	.15
266 Brad Fullmer	.15
267 Vladimir Guerrero (Foil)	3.00
268 Wilton Guerrero	.15
269 Dustin Hermanson	.15
270 Steve Kline	.15
271 Manny Martinez	.15
272 Mike Thurman	.15
273 Ugueth Urbina	.15
274 Javier Vazquez	.15
275 Jose Vidro	.15
276 Rondell White	.15
277 Chris Widger	.15
278 Edgardo Alfonzo (Foil)	2.00
279 Armando Benitez	.15
280 Roger Cedeno	.15
281 Dennis Cook	.15
282 Shawon Dunston	.15
283 Matt Franco	.15
284 Darryl Hamilton	.15
285 Rickey Henderson (Foil)	3.00
286 Orel Hershiser	.15
287 Al Leiter	.15
288 John Olerud	.15
289 Rey Ordonez	.15
290 Mike Piazza (Foil)	5.00
291 Kenny Rogers	.15
292 Robin Ventura	.15
293 Turk Wendell	.15
294 Masato Yoshii	.15
295 Scott Brosius	.15
296 Roger Clemens (Foil)	4.50
297 David Cone (Foil)	2.00
298 Chad Curtis	.15
299 Chili Davis	.15
300 Orlando Hernandez	.15
301 Derek Jeter (Foil)	7.00
302 Chuck Knoblauch	.15
303 Ricky Ledee	.15
304 Tino Martinez	.15
305 Ramiro Mendoza	.15
306 Paul O'Neill	.15
307 Andy Pettitte	.35
308 Jorge Posada	.15
309 Mariano Rivera (Foil)	2.00
310 Mike Stanton	.15
311 Bernie Williams (Foil)	2.00
312 Kevin Appier	.15
313 Eric Chavez	.25
314 Ryan Christenson	.15
315 Jason Giambi	2.50
316 Ben Grieve	.15
317 Buddy Groom	.15
318 Gil Heredia	.15
319 A.J. Hinch	.15
320 John Jaha	.15
321 Doug Jones	.15
322 Omar Olivares	.15
323 Tony Phillips	.15
324 Matt Stairs	.15
325 Miguel Tejada	.15
326 Randy Velarde (Foil)	2.00
327 Bobby Abreu (Foil)	2.00
328 Marlon Anderson	.15
329 Alex Arias	.15
330 Rico Brogna	.15
331 Paul Byrd	.15
332 Ron Gant	.15
333 Doug Glanville	.15
334 Wayne Gomes	.15
335 Kevin Jordan	.15
336 Mike Lieberthal	.15
337 Steve Montgomery	.15
338 Chad Ogea	.15
339 Scott Rolen	.15
340 Curt Schilling (Foil)	2.50
341 Kevin Sefcik	.15
342 Mike Benjamin	.15

343 Kris Benson	.15
344 Adrian Brown	.15
345 Brant Brown	.15
346 Brad Clontz	.15
347 Brian Giles (Foil)	2.00
348 Jason Kendall (Foil)	2.00
349 Al Martin	.15
350 Warren Morris	.15
351 Todd Ritchie	.15
352 Scott Sauerbeck	.15
353 Jason Schmidt	.15
354 Ed Sprague	.15
355 Mike Williams	.15
356 Kevin Young	.15
357 Andy Ashby	.15
358 Ben Davis	.15
359 Tony Gwynn (Foil)	4.00
360 Sterling Hitchcock	.15
361 Trevor Hoffman (Foil)	2.00
362 Damian Jackson	.15
363 Wally Joyner	.15
364 Phil Nevin	.15
365 Eric Owens	.15
366 Ruben Rivera	.15
367 Reggie Sanders	.15
368 John Vander Wal	.15
369 Quilvio Veras	.15
370 Matt Whisenant	.15
371 Woody Williams	.15
372 Rich Aurilia	.15
373 Marvin Benard	.15
374 Barry Bonds (Foil)	7.00
375 Ellis Burks	.15
376 Alan Embree	.15
377 Shawn Estes	.15
378 John Johnstone	.15
379 Jeff Kent	.15
380 Brent Mayne	.15
381 Bill Mueller	.15
382 Robb Nen	.15
383 Russ Ortiz	.15
384 Kirk Rueter	.15
385 F.P. Santangelo	.15
386 J.T. Snow	.15
387 David Bell	.15
388 Jay Buhner	.15
389 Russ Davis	.15
390 Freddy Garcia	.15
391 Ken Griffey Jr. (Foil)	5.00
392 John Halama	.15
393 Brian L. Hunter	.15
394 Raul Ibanez	.15
395 Tom Lampkin	.15
396 Edgar Martinez (Foil)	2.00
397 Jose Mesa	.15
398 Jamie Moyer	.15
399 Jose Paniagua	.15
400 Alex Rodriguez (Foil)	6.00
401 Dan Wilson	.15
402 Manny Aybar	.15
403 Ricky Bottalico	.15
404 Kent Bottenfield	.15
405 Darren Bragg	.15
406 Alberto Castillo	.15
407 J.D. Drew	.60
408 Jose Jiminez	.15
409 Ray Lankford	.15
410 Joe McEwing	.15
411 Willie McGee	.15
412 Mark McGwire (Foil)	6.00
413 Darren Oliver	.15
414 Lance Painter	.15
415 Edgar Renteria	.15
416 Fernando Tatis (Foil)	2.00
417 Wilson Alvarez	.15
418 Rolando Arrojo	.15
419 Wade Boggs	1.00
420 Miguel Cairo	.15
421 Jose Canseco (Foil)	2.50
422 John Flaherty	.15
423 Roberto Hernandez	.15
424 Dave Martinez	.15
425 Fred McGriff	.15
426 Paul Sorrento	.15
427 Kevin Stocker	.15
428 Bubba Trammell	.15
429 Rick White	.15
430 Randy Winn	.15
431 Bobby Witt	.15
432 Royce Clayton	.15
433 Tim Crabtree	.15
434 Juan Gonzalez	.45
435 Tom Goodwin	.15
436 Rusty Greer	.15
437 Rick Helling	.15
438 Mark McLemore	.15
439 Mike Morgan	.15
440 Rafael Palmeiro (Foil)	3.00
441 Ivan Rodriguez (Foil)	3.00
442 Aaron Sele	.15
443 Lee Stevens	.15
444 Mike Venafro	.15
445 John Wetteland	.15
446 Todd Zeile	.15
447 Jeff Zimmerman (Foil)	2.00
448 Tony Batista	.15
449 Homer Bush	.15
450 Jose Cruz Jr.	.15
451 Carlos Delgado	.40
452 Kelvim Escobar	.15
453 Tony Fernandez (Foil)	2.00
454 Darrin Fletcher	.15
455 Shawn Green (Foil)	2.00
456 Pat Hentgen	.15
457 Billy Koch	.15
458 Graeme Lloyd	.15
459 Brian McRae	.15
460 David Segui	.15

461 Shannon Stewart	.15
462 David Wells	.15
S1 Bad Call (Umpire)	.10
S2 Big Inning (Mike Stanley)	.10
S3 Bobbled in the Outfield (Tony Phillips)	.10
S4 Clutch Hitting (Manny Ramirez)	.10
S5 Do or Die (Chuck Knoblauch)	.10
S6 Down the Middle (?)	.10
S7 Ducks on the Pond (Carl Everett)	.10
S8 Favorable Matchup (Barry Bonds)	.30
S9 Free Steal (Juan Encarnacion)	.10
S10 Get Under It (Jose Offerman)	.10
S11 Great Lead (Rickey Henderson)	.20
S12 Hard Slide (Damian Jackson)	.10
S13 High Fives (Derek Jeter)	.10
S14 Last Chance (Paul O'Neill)	.15
S15 Long Single (Derek Jeter)	.30
S16 Out of Gas (Jeff Zimmerman)	.10
S17 Out of Position (Rickey Henderson, Ryan Klesko)	.15
S18 Play the Percentages (Chipper Jones)	.10
S19 Rally Cap (Omar Vizquel)	.10
S20 Rattled (Mike Henneman)	.10
S21 Runner Not Held (Miguel Tejada)	.10
S22 Slow Roller (Brian Bohanon)	.10
S23 Stick a Fork in Him (Kevin Millwood)	.10
S24 Swing for the Fences (Sammy Sosa)	.15
S25 To the Warning Track (Ricky Ledee)	.10
S26 Whiplash (Mark McGwire)	.25
S27 Wide Throw (Roberto Alomar)	.10
S28 Wild Pitch (Eddie Taubensee)	.10
S29 By the Book (Walt Weiss)	.10
S30 Dominating (Billy Wagner)	.10
S31 Full Windup (Orlando Hernandez)	.10
S32 Good Fielding (Rey Ordonez, Ryan Klesko)	.10
S33 Gun 'Em Down! (Jason Kendall)	.10
S34 He's Got a Gun (Sammy Sosa)	.10
S35 In the Groove (David Cone)	.10
S36 In the Zone (Pedro Martinez)	.10
S37 Infield In (S.F. Giants)	.10
S38 Intimidation (Randy Johnson)	.15
S39 Just Over the Wall (Ken Griffey, Jr.)	.25
S40 Knock the Ball Down (?)	.10
S41 Lefty Specialist (Jesse Orosco)	.10
S42 Nerves of Steel (Mariano Rivera)	.10
S43 Nothing but Heat (Randy Johnson)	.10
S44 Pitch Out (Bobby Hughes)	.10
S45 Pumped Up (John Rocker)	.10
S46 Quick Pitch (Greg Maddux)	.10
S47 Rally Killer (Carlos Baerga)	.10
S48 Short Fly (Chuck Knoblauch, Bernie Williams)	.10
S49 Three Up, Three Down (Pedro Martinez)	.10
S50 Trick Pitch (Derek Jeter)	.10
S51 Belt-High (Sammy Sosa)	.15
S52 Change In Strategy (Joe Torre)	.10
S53 Grounder to Second (Pokey Reese)	.10
S54 Stealing Signals (Mark Grace)	.10
S55 Swing at Anything (Cal Ripken, Jr.)	.30

2000 MLB Showdown Pennant Run Promos

To promote its forthcoming Pennant Run edition, Wizards of the Coast issued eight specially marked sample cards. The promos have silver-foil player names and a large "W." The promos were issued one per copy of TopDeck magazine (a gamer's publication) which carried a $5.99 cover price.

	NM/M
Complete Set (8):	3.00
Common Player:	.50
1 Peter Bergeron	.50
2 Matt Clement	.50
3 Ramon Hernandez	.50
4 Gabe Kapler	.50
5 Adam Kennedy	.50

6	Sean Lowe	.50
7	Joe Nathan	.50
8	Daryle Ward	.50

2000 MLB Showdown Pennant Run

Issued just after the 2000 season opened, this is essentially an update to the interactive game MLB Showdown from veteran gamers Wizards of the Coast. Players in the set are generally those who changed teams during the off-season, or promising rookies. The Pennant Run edition was issued in a Booster box of 36 nine-card (seven player, two strategy) packs. The set has 130 "regular" player cards, 20 premium holofoil star cards and 25 strategy cards. The holo premium cards were inserted in packs at a rate of 1:3. While collectors compete with gamers for these cards in the market, relative values placed on the cards by each group of buyers may differ.

		NM/M
Complete Set (175):		30.00
Common Player:		.15
Booster Pack (9):		1.00
Booster Box (36):		20.00
1	Kent Bottenfield	.15
2	Ken Hill	.15
3	Adam Kennedy	.15
4	Ben Molina	.15
5	Scott Spiezio	.15
6	Brian Anderson	.15
7	Erubiel Durazo (Foil)	1.00
8	Armando Reynoso	.15
9	Russ Springer	.15
10	Todd Stottlemyre	.15
11	Tony Womack	.15
12	Andres Galarraga (Foil)	1.00
13	Javy Lopez (Foil)	1.00
14	Kevin McGlinchy	.15
15	Terry Mulholland	.15
16	Reggie Sanders	.15
17	Harold Baines	.15
18	Will Clark	.15
19	Mike Trombley	.15
20	Manny Alexander	.15
21	Carl Everett (Foil)	1.00
22	Ramon Martinez (Foil)	1.00
23	Bret Saberhagen	.15
24	John Wasdin	.15
25	Joe Girardi	.15
26	Ricky Gutierrez	.15
27	Glenallen Hill	.15
28	Kevin Tapani	.15
29	Kerry Wood (Foil)	2.00
30	Eric Young	.15
31	Keith Foulke (Foil)	1.00
32	Mark Johnson	.15
33	Sean Lowe	.15
34	Jose Valentin	.15
35	Dante Bichette	.15
36	Ken Griffey Jr. (Foil)	6.00
37	Denny Neagle	.15
38	Steve Parris	.15
39	Dennis Reyes	.15
40	Sandy Alomar Jr.	.15
41	Chuck Finley (Foil)	1.00
42	Steve Karsay	.15
43	Steve Reed	.15
44	Jaret Wright	.15
45	Jeff Cirillo	.15
46	Tom Goodwin	.15
47	Jeffrey Hammonds	.15
48	Mike Lansing	.15
49	Aaron Ledesma	.15
50	Brent Mayne	.15
51	Doug Brocail	.15
52	Robert Fick	.15
53	Juan Gonzalez	.60
54	Hideo Nomo	.60
55	Luis Polonia	.15
56	Brant Brown	.15
57	Alex Fernandez	.15
58	Cliff Floyd	.15
59	Dan Miceli	.15
60	Vladimir Nunez	.15
61	Moises Alou (Foil)	1.00
62	Roger Cedeno (Foil)	1.00
63	Octavio Dotel	.15
64	Mitch Meluskey	.15

65	Daryle Ward	.15
66	Mark Quinn (Foil)	1.00
67	Brad Rigby	.15
68	Blake Stein	.15
69	Mac Suzuki	.15
70	Terry Adams	.15
71	Darren Dreifort	.15
72	Kevin Elster	.15
73	Shawn Green (Foil)	1.50
74	Todd Hollandsworth	.15
75	Gregg Olson	.15
76	Kevin Barker	.15
77	Jose Hernandez	.15
78	Dave Weathers	.15
79	Hector Carrasco	.15
80	Eddie Guardado	.15
81	Jacque Jones	.25
82	David Ortiz	.15
83	Peter Bergeron	.15
84	Hideki Irabu	.15
85	Lee Stevens	.15
86	Anthony Telford	.15
87	Derek Bell	.15
88	John Franco	.15
89	Mike Hampton (Foil)	1.00
90	Bobby J. Jones	.15
91	Todd Pratt	.15
92	Todd Zeile	.15
93	Jason Grimsley	.15
94	Roberto Kelly	.15
95	Jim Leyritz	.15
96	Ramiro Mendoza	.15
97	Rich Becker	.15
98	Ramon Hernandez	.15
99	Tim Hudson (Foil)	2.00
100	Jason Isringhausen	.15
101	Mike Magnante	.15
102	Olmedo Saenz	.15
103	Mickey Morandini	.15
104	Robert Person	.15
105	Desi Relaford	.15
106	Jason Christiansen	.15
107	Wil Cordero	.15
108	Francisco Cordova	.15
109	Chad Hermansen	.15
110	Pat Meares	.15
111	Aramis Ramirez	.15
112	Bret Boone	.15
113	Matt Clement	.15
114	Carlos Hernandez	.15
115	Ryan Klesko	.15
116	Dave Magadan	.15
117	Al Martin	.15
118	Bobby Estalella	.15
119	Livan Hernandez	.15
120	Doug Mirabelli	.15
121	Joe Nathan	.15
122	Mike Cameron	.15
123	Mark McLemore	.15
124	Gil Meche	.15
125	John Olerud	.15
126	Arthur Rhodes	.15
127	Aaron Sele (Foil)	1.00
128	Jim Edmonds (Foil)	1.00
129	Pat Hentgen	.15
130	Darryl Kile	.15
131	Eli Marrero	.15
132	Dave Veres	.15
133	Fernando Vina	.15
134	Vinny Castilla	.15
135	Juan Guzman	.15
136	Ryan Rupe	.15
137	Greg Vaughn (Foil)	1.00
138	Gerald Williams	.15
139	Esteban Yan	.15
140	Tom Evans	.15
141	Gabe Kapler	.15
142	Ruben Mateo (Foil)	1.00
143	Kenny Rogers	.15
144	David Segui	.15
145	Tony Batista	.15
146	Chris Carpenter	.15
147	Brad Fullmer	.15
148	Alex Gonzalez	.15
149	Roy Halladay	.15
150	Raul Mondesi (Foil)	1.00
S1	Afterburners (Aaron Boone)	.10
S2	Change Sides (Chipper Jones)	.45
S3	Patience is a Virtue (Bob Abreu)	.10
S4	Payoff Pitch (Fernando Tatis)	.10
S5	Pointers (Rod Carew)	.35
S6	Professional Baserunner (J.D. Drew)	.10
S7	Professional Hitter (John VanderWal)	.10
S8	Protect the Runner (Pokey Reese)	.10
S9	Rough Outing (Greg Maddux)	.45
S10	Shelled (Cincinnati Reds)	.10
S11	Take What is Given (Larry Walker)	.25
S12	Tricky Hop (Alex Rodriguez)	.40
S13	Aggressive Coaching (Alex Rodriguez)	.40
S14	Cut Off in the Gap (N.Y. Mets)	.10
S15	Great Start (Kevin Brown)	.10
S16	Insult to Injury (Paul O'Neill)	.10
S17	Job Well Done (Scott Williamson)	.15

S18	Low and Away (Jamie Moyer)	.10
S19	Outfield In (Bernie Williams)	.10
S20	Put Out the Fire (John Franco)	.10
S21	Rotation Play (Pittsburgh Pirates)	.10
S22	Swiss Army Closer (John Rocker)	.10
S23	Whoops (Mike Lansing)	.10
S24	Pep Talk (Roger Clemens, Joe Torre)	.15
S25	Revenue Sharing (Derek Jeter)	.50

1992 Modell's Team Mets

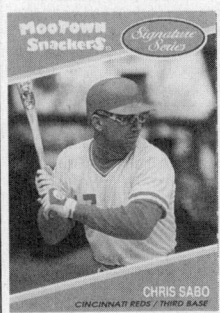

Team Mets, the junior fan club, included in its 1992 membership benefits a nine-card perforated sheet sponsored by Modell's Sporting Goods. Cards feature color action photos highlighted by team-color stripes of blue and orange, with a white outer border. The 7-1/2" x 10-1/2" sheet can be separated into standard-size 2-1/2" x 3-1/2" cards. Team Mets and Modell's logos are featured on back, along with 1991 stats and highlights, career numbers and personal data. Cards are checklisted here according to the uniform numbers found on the front.

		NM/M
Complete Set (9):		5.00
Common Player:		.50
1	Vince Coleman	.50
9	Todd Hundley	.50
12	Willie Randolph	.50
16	Dwight Gooden	.50
17	David Cone	.50
18	Bret Saberhagen	.50
20	Howard Johnson	.50
25	Bobby Bonilla	.50
33	Eddie Murray	2.00

1991 MooTown Snackers

Produced by the Sargento Cheese Co., cards were available in Mootown Snacker packages or by sending in a special set redemption coupon from a package to obtain the entire set for $5.95 and three UPCs. Fronts feature action photos with uniform logos airbrushed off. Photos are bordered at top and bottom in red. Backs are in red, black and white and feature statistics and a facsimile autograph. Each player card is attached to a perforated panel on its right which has the checklist and a coupon to order the complete set. Cards without the offer coupon still attached are worth 50% of the values quoted here.

		NM/M
Complete Set (24):		10.00
Common Player:		.25
1	Jose Canseco	.50
2	Kirby Puckett	1.00
3	Barry Bonds	2.00

4	Ken Griffey Jr.	1.50
5	Ryne Sandberg	1.00
6	Tony Gwynn	1.00
7	Kal Daniels	.25
8	Ozzie Smith	1.00
9	Dave Justice	.25
10	Sandy Alomar, Jr.	.25
11	Wade Boggs	1.00
12	Ozzie Guillen	.25
13	Dave Magadan	.25
14	Cal Ripken, Jr.	2.00
15	Don Mattingly	1.25
16	Ruben Sierra	.25
17	Robin Yount	.25
18	Len Dykstra	.25
19	George Brett	1.25
20	Lance Parrish	.25
21	Chris Sabo	.25
22	Craig Biggio	.25
23	Kevin Mitchell	.25
24	Cecil Fielder	.25

1992 MooTown Snackers

The unusual venue of cheese snack packs was the source for these cards. Produced as two-piece panels, there is a player card attached by perforations to a card offering a complete set for $7 and proofs of purchase. The player cards have cheese-yellow borders at top and bottom with an action photo at center. Produced by Michael Schecter Assoc., the cards have had uniform and cap logos removed because they are licensed only by the Players Association and not by MLB. Backs are printed in black and yellow on white and include a facsimile autograph. Cards with the complete set offer no longer attached are worth 50 percent of the values shown here.

		NM/M
Complete Set (24):		7.50
Common Player:		.25
1	Albert Belle	.25
2	Jeff Bagwell	.75
3	Jose Rijo	.25
4	Roger Clemens	1.25
5	Kevin Maas	.25
6	Kirby Puckett	1.00
7	Ken Griffey Jr.	1.50
8	Will Clark	.25
9	Felix Jose	.25
10	Cecil Fielder	.25
11	Darryl Strawberry	.25
12	John Smiley	.25
13	Roberto Alomar	.35
14	Paul Molitor	.75
15	Andre Dawson	.25
16	Terry Mulholland	.25
17	Fred McGriff	.25
18	Dwight Gooden	.25
19	Rickey Henderson	.75
20	Nolan Ryan	2.00
21	George Brett	1.25
22	Tom Glavine	.40
23	Cal Ripken Jr.	2.00
24	Frank Thomas	.75

1983 Mother's Cookies Giants

JACK CLARK

After putting out Pacific Coast League sets in 1952-53, Mother's Cookies distributed this full-color set of 20 San Francisco Giants cards three decades later. The 2-1/2" x 3-1/2" cards were produced by hobbyist Barry Colla and include the Giants logo and player's name on the card fronts. Backs are numbered and contain biographical information, sponsor's logo and a space for the player's autograph. Fifteen cards were given to every fan at the Aug. 7, 1983, Giants game, with each fan also receiving a coupon good for five additional cards.

		NM/M
Complete Set (20):		6.00
Common Player:		.35
1	Frank Robinson	2.00
2	Jack Clark	.50
3	Chili Davis	.45
4	Johnnie LeMaster	.35
5	Greg Minton	.35
6	Bob Brenly	.35
7	Fred Breining	.35
8	Jeff Leonard	.35
9	Darrell Evans	.50
10	Tom O'Malley	.35
11	Duane Kuiper	.35
12	Mike Krukow	.35
13	Atlee Hammaker	.35
14	Gary Lavelle	.35
15	Bill Laskey	.35
16	Max Venable	.35
17	Joel Youngblood	.35
18	Dave Bergman	.35
19	Mike Vail	.35
20	Andy McGaffigan	.35

1984 Mother's Cookies A's

DAVE KINGMAN

Following the success of their one set in 1983, Mother's Cookies issued five more team sets of cards in 1984. Cards measure 2-1/2" x 3-1/2" with rounded corners. Fronts feature unbordered color photos. Horizontal backs have biographical data, card number, Mother's Cookies logo and space for player autograph. There are 28 cards in the A's set, with 20 of the cards distributed during a stadium promotion. Fans also received a coupon redeemable for eight additional cards. Since those cards did not necessarily complete collectors' sets, Mother's Cookies cards become very popular among card traders. The A's set includes cards for the manager, coaches and a checklist.

		NM/M
Complete Set (28):		9.00
Common Player:		.25
1	Steve Boros	.25
2	Rickey Henderson	5.00
3	Joe Morgan	2.00
4	Dwayne Murphy	.25
5	Mike Davis	.25
6	Bruce Bochte	.25
7	Carney Lansford	.25
8	Steve McCatty	.25
9	Mike Heath	.25
10	Chris Codiroli	.25
11	Bill Almon	.25
12	Bill Caudill	.25
13	Donnie Hill	.25
14	Lary Sorensen	.25
15	Dave Kingman	.50
16	Garry Hancock	.25
17	Jeff Burroughs	.25
18	Tom Burgmeier	.25
19	Jim Essian	.25
20	Mike Warren	.25
21	Davey Lopes	.25
22	Ray Burris	.25
23	Tony Phillips	.25
24	Tim Conroy	.25
25	Jeff Bettendorf	.25
26	Keith Atherton	.25

27	A's Coaches (Clete Boyer, Bob Didier, Jackie Moore, Ron Schueler, Billy Williams)	.25
28	Oakland Coliseum/Checklist	.25

Astros

JOE NIEKRO Astros

Mother's Cookies issued a full-color team set for the Astros in 1984. Cards measure 2-1/2" x 3-1/2" with rounded corners. Card fronts feature unbordered color photos. Horizontal backs have biographical data, card number, Mother's Cookies logo and space for player autograph. There are 28 cards in the Astros set, with 20 of the cards distributed during a stadium promotion. Fans also received a coupon redeemable for eight additional cards. Since those cards did not necessarily complete collectors' sets, Mother's Cookies cards became very popular among traders. The Astros set includes one card for the coaches and a checklist.

		NM/M
Complete Set (28):		7.00
Common Player:		.25
1	Nolan Ryan	6.00
2	Joe Niekro	.25
3	Alan Ashby	.25
4	Bill Doran	.25
5	Phil Garner	.25
6	Ray Knight	.25
7	Dickie Thon	.25
8	Jose Cruz	.25
9	Jerry Mumphrey	.25
10	Terry Puhl	.25
11	Enos Cabell	.25
12	Harry Spilman	.25
13	Dave Smith	.25
14	Mike Scott	.25
15	Bob Lillis	.25
16	Bob Knepper	.25
17	Frank DiPino	.25
18	Tom Wieghaus	.25
19	Denny Walling	.25
20	Tony Scott	.25
21	Alan Bannister	.25
22	Bill Dawley	.25
23	Vern Ruhle	.25
24	Mike LaCoss	.25
25	Mike Madden	.25
26	Craig Reynolds	.25
27	Astros Coaches (Cot Deal, Don Leppert, Denis Menke, Les Moss, Jerry Walker)	.25
28	Astros Logo/Checklist	.25

Giants

JUAN MARICHAL Giants All-Star

Mother's Cookies issued a second annual full-color card set for the S.F. Giants in 1984. Cards measure 2-1/2" x 3-1/2" with rounded corners. Fronts feature drawings of former Giant All-Star team selections. Horizontal backs have brief biographical information, card number and Mother's Cookies logo and autograph space. There are 28 cards in the Giants set, with 20 of the cards distributed during a stadium promotion. Fans also received a coupon redeemable for eight additional cards. Since those cards did not necessarily complete collectors' sets, Mother's Cookies cards became very popular among card traders.

		NM/M
Complete Set (28):		7.50
Common Player:		.15
1	Willie Mays	4.50
2	Willie McCovey	1.00
3	Juan Marichal	.50
4	Gaylord Perry	.50
5	Tom Haller	.15
6	Jim Davenport	.15
7	Jack Clark	.25
8	Greg Minton	.15
9	Atlee Hammaker	.15
10	Gary Lavelle	.15
11	Orlando Cepeda	.50
12	Bobby Bonds	.25
13	John Antonelli	.15
14	Bob Schmidt (Photo actually Wes Westrum.)	.15
15	Sam Jones	.15
16	Mike McCormick	.15
17	Ed Bailey	.15
18	Stu Miller	.15
19	Felipe Alou	.25
20	Jim Hart	.15
21	Dick Dietz	.15
22	Chris Speier	.15
23	Bobby Murcer	.25
24	John Montefusco	.15
25	Vida Blue	.15
26	Ed Whitson	.15
27	Darrell Evans	.25
28	All-Star Game Logo/ Checklist	.15

Mariners

Mother's Cookies issued a full-color set for the Mariners in 1984. Cards measure 2-1/2" x 3-1/2" with rounded corners. Fronts feature unbordered color photos. Horizontal backs have brief biographical data, card number, Mother's Cookies logo and space for player autograph. There are 28 cards in the set with 20 of the cards distributed during a stadium promotion. Fans also received a coupon redeemable for eight additional cards. Since those cards did not necessarily complete collectors' sets, Mother's Cookies became very popular among traders. The set includes one card each for the manager, coaches and a checklist.

		NM/M
Complete Set (28):		6.00
Common Player:		.25
1	Del Crandall	.25
2	Barry Bonnell	.25
3	Dave Henderson	.25
4	Bob Kearney	.25
5	Mike Moore	.25
6	Spike Owen	.25
7	Gorman Thomas	.25
8	Ed Vande Berg	.25
9	Matt Young	.25
10	Larry Milbourne	.25
11	Dave Beard	.25
12	Jim Beattie	.25
13	Mark Langston	.25
14	Orlando Mercado	.25
15	Jack Perconte	.25
16	Pat Putnam	.25
17	Paul Mirabella	.25
18	Domingo Ramos	.25
19	Al Cowens	.25
20	Mike Stanton	.25
21	Steve Henderson	.25
22	Bob Stoddard	.25
23	Alvin Davis	.25
24	Phil Bradley	.25
25	Roy Thomas	.25
26	Darnell Coles	.25
27	Mariners Coaches (Chuck Cottier, Frank Funk, Ben Hines, Phil Roof, Rick Sweet)	.25
28	Seattle Kingdome/ Checklist	.25

Padres

Mother's Cookies issued a full-color set for the Padres in 1984. Cards measure 2-1/2" x 3-1/2", with rounded corners. Fronts feature unbordered color photos. Horizontal backs have brief biographical data, card number, sponsor's logo and space for player autograph. There are 28 cards in the set, with 20 of the cards distributed during a stadium promotion. Fans also received a coupon redeemable for eight additional cards. Since those cards did not necessarily complete collectors' sets, Mother's Cookies cards became very popular among traders. The Padres set includes one card each for the manager, coaches and a checklist.

		NM/M
Complete Set (28):		9.00
Common Player:		.25
1	Dick Williams	.25
2	Rich Gossage	.50
3	Tim Lollar	.25
4	Eric Show	.25
5	Terry Kennedy	.25
6	Kurt Bevacqua	.25
7	Steve Garvey	1.50
8	Garry Templeton	.25
9	Tony Gwynn	5.00
10	Alan Wiggins	.25
11	Dave Dravecky	.25
12	Tim Flannery	.25
13	Kevin McReynolds	.25
14	Bobby Brown	.25
15	Ed Whitson	.25
16	Doug Gwosdz	.25
17	Luis DeLeon	.25
18	Andy Hawkins	.25
19	Craig Lefferts	.25
20	Carmelo Martinez	.25
21	Sid Monge	.25
22	Graig Nettles	.25
23	Mario Ramirez	.25
24	Luis Salazar	.25
25	Champ Summers	.25
26	Mark Thurmond	.25
27	Padres Coaches (Harry Dunlop, Deacon Jones, Jack Krol, Norm Sherry, Ozzie Virgil)	.25
28	Jack Murphy Stadium/Checklist	.25

1985 Mother's Cookies A's

Mother's Cookies again issued five full-color sets for Major League teams in 1985. Cards measure 2-1/2" x 3-1/2" with rounded corners. Fronts feature unbordered color photos. Horizontal backs have brief biographical data, card number, Mother's Cookies logo and space for player autograph. The set was distributed in its entirety during a stadium promotion.

		NM/M
Complete Set (28):		7.00
Common Player:		.25
1	Jackie Moore	.25
2	Dave Kingman	.40

3	Don Sutton	1.25
4	Mike Heath	.25
5	Alfredo Griffin	.25
6	Dwayne Murphy	.25
7	Mike Davis	.25
8	Carney Lansford	.25
9	Chris Codiroli	.25
10	Bruce Bochte	.25
11	Mickey Tettleton	.25
12	Donnie Hill	.25
13	Rob Picciolo	.25
14	Dave Collins	.25
15	Dusty Baker	.50
16	Tim Conroy	.25
17	Keith Atherton	.25
18	Jay Howell	.25
19	Mike Warren	.25
20	Steve McCatty	.25
21	Bill Krueger	.25
22	Curt Young	.25
23	Dan Meyer	.25
24	Mike Gallego	.25
25	Jeff Kaiser	.25
26	Steve Henderson	.25
27	A's Coaches (Clete Boyer, Bob Didier, Dave McKay, Wes Stock, Billy Williams)	.25
28	Oakland Coliseum/ Checklist	.25

Astros

Mother's Cookies issued a second annual full-color set for the Astros in 1985. Cards measure 2-1/2" x 3-1/2" with rounded corners. Fronts feature unbordered color photos. Horizontal backs have biographical information, card number, Mother's Cookies logo and space for player autograph. The set was distributed in its entirety during a stadium promotion.

		NM/M
Complete Set (28):		8.00
Common Player:		.25
1	Bob Lillis	.25
2	Nolan Ryan	7.50
3	Phil Garner	.25
4	Jose Cruz	.25
5	Denny Walling	.25
6	Joe Niekro	.30
7	Terry Puhl	.25
8	Bill Doran	.25
9	Dickie Thon	.25
10	Enos Cabell	.25
11	Frank Dipino (DiPino)	.25
12	Julio Solano	.25
13	Alan Ashby	.25
14	Craig Reynolds	.25
15	Jerry Mumphrey	.25
16	Bill Dawley	.25
17	Mark Bailey	.25
18	Mike Scott	.25
19	Harry Spilman	.25
20	Bob Knepper	.25
21	Dave Smith	.25
22	Kevin Bass	.25
23	Tim Tolman	.25
24	Jeff Calhoun	.25
25	Jim Pankovits	.25
26	Ron Mathis	.25
27	Astros Coaches (Cot Deal, Matt Galante, Don Leppert, Denis Menke, Jerry Walker)	.25
28	Astros Logo/Checklist	.25

Giants

Mother's Cookies issued a third annual full-color set for the Giants in 1985. Cards measure 2-1/2" x 3-1/2" with rounded corners. Fronts feature unbordered color photos. Horizontal backs have brief biographical information, card number, Mother's Cookies logo and space for player autograph. The set was distributed in its entirety during a stadium promotion.

		NM/M
Complete Set (28):		6.00
Common Player:		.25
1	Jim Davenport	.25
2	Chili Davis	.25

3	Dan Gladden	.25
4	Jeff Leonard	.25
5	Manny Trillo	.25
6	Atlee Hammaker	.25
7	Bob Brenly	.25
8	Greg Minton	.25
9	Bill Laskey	.25
10	Vida Blue	.30
11	Mike Krukow	.25
12	Frank Williams	.25
13	Jose Uribe	.25
14	Johnnie LeMaster	.25
15	Scot Thompson	.25
16	Dave LaPoint	.25
17	David Green	.25
18	Chris Brown	.25
19	Joel Youngblood	.25
20	Mark Davis	.25
21	Jim Gott	.25
22	Doug Gwosdz	.25
23	Scott Garrelts	.25
24	Gary Rajsich	.25
25	Rob Deer	.25
26	Brad Wellman	.25
27	Coaches (Rocky Bridges, Chuck Hiller, Tom McCraw, Bob Miller, Jack Mull)	.25
28	Candlestick Park/Checklist	.25

Mariners

Mother's Cookies issued a second annual full-color set for the Mariners in 1985. Cards measure 2-1/2" x 3-1/2" with rounded corners. Fronts feature unbordered color photos. Horizontal backs have biographical information, card number, Mother's Cookies logo and space for player autograph. The set was distributed in its entirety during a stadium promotion.

		NM/M
Complete Set (28):		6.00
Common Player:		.25
1	Chuck Cottier	.25
2	Alvin Davis	.25
3	Mark Langston	.25
4	Dave Henderson	.25
5	Ed Vande Berg	.25
6	Al Cowens	.25
7	Spike Owen	.25
8	Mike Moore	.25
9	Gorman Thomas	.25
10	Barry Bonnell	.25
11	Jack Perconte	.25
12	Domingo Ramos	.25
13	Bob Kearney	.25
14	Matt Young	.25
15	Jim Beattie	.25
16	Mike Stanton	.25
17	David Valle	.25
18	Ken Phelps	.25
19	Salome Barojas	.25
20	Jim Presley	.25
21	Phil Bradley	.25
22	Dave Geisel	.25
23	Harold Reynolds	.50
24	Edwin Nunez	.25
25	Mike Morgan	.25
26	Ivan Calderon	.25
27	Mariners Coaches (Deron Johnson, Jim Mahoney, Marty Martinez, Phil Regan, Phil Roof)	.25
28	Seattle Kingdome/ Checklist	.25

Padres

Mother's Cookies issued a second annual full-color Padres team set in 1985. Cards have rounded corners and measure 2-1/2" x 3-1/2". Glossy fronts feature unbordered color photos. Horizontal backs have biographical data, card number, Mother's Cookies logo and space for player autograph. The set was distributed in its entirety during a stadium promotion.

		NM/M
Complete Set (28):		6.00
Common Player:		.25
1	Dick Williams	.25
2	Tony Gwynn	4.50
3	Kevin McReynolds	.25
4	Graig Nettles	.25
5	Rich Gossage	.40
6	Steve Garvey	1.50
7	Garry Templeton	.25
8	Dave Dravecky	.25
9	Eric Show	.25
10	Terry Kennedy	.25
11	Luis DeLeon	.25
12	Bruce Bochy	.25
13	Andy Hawkins	.25
14	Kurt Bevacqua	.25
15	Craig Lefferts	.25
16	Mario Ramirez	.25
17	LaMarr Hoyt	.25
18	Jerry Royster	.25
19	Tim Stoddard	.25
20	Tim Flannery	.25
21	Mark Thurmond	.25
22	Greg Booker	.25
23	Bobby Brown	.25
24	Carmelo Martinez	.25
25	Al Bumbry	.25
26	Jerry Davis	.25
27	Padres Coaches (Galen Cisco, Harry Dunlop, Deacon Jones, Jack Krol, Ozzie Virgil)	.25
28	Jack Murphy Stadium/Checklist	.25

1986 Mother's Cookies A's

Mother's Cookies produced four full-color team sets in 1986, with only the San Diego Padres not repeating from the 1985 group. The third annual set for the Oakland A's measures 2-1/2" x 3-1/2" with rounded corners. Glossy fronts feature unbordered color photos. Horizontal backs have brief biographical information, card number and Mother's Cookies logo. There are 28 cards in the A's set, with 20 of the cards distributed during a stadium promotion. Each fan also received a coupon redeemable for eight additional cards which could be traded to complete a set.

		NM/M
Complete Set (28):		10.00
Common Player:		.25
1	Jackie Moore	.25
2	Dave Kingman	.40
3	Dusty Baker	.40
4	Joaquin Andujar	.25
5	Alfredo Griffin	.25
6	Dwayne Murphy	.25

7	Mike Davis	.25
8	Carney Lansford	.25
9	Jose Canseco	6.00
10	Bruce Bochte	.25
11	Mickey Tettleton	.25
12	Donnie Hill	.25
13	Jose Rijo	.25
14	Rick Langford	.25
15	Chris Codiroli	.25
16	Moose Haas	.25
17	Keith Atherton	.25
18	Jay Howell	.25
19	Tony Phillips	.25
20	Steve Henderson	.25
21	Bill Krueger	.25
22	Steve Ontiveros	.25
23	Bill Bathe	.25
24	Rickey Peters	.25
25	Tim Birtsas	.25
26	Trainers (Frank Ciensczyk, Larry Davis, Steve Vucinich, Barry Weinberg)	.25
27	Coaches (Bob Didier, Dave McKay, Jeff Newman, Ron Plaza, Wes Stock, Bob Watson)	.25
28	Oakland Coliseum/ Checklist	.25

Astros

Mother's Cookies produced a third annual Astros team set in 1985. The round-cornered, glossy front 2-1/2" x 3-1/2" cards feature unbordered color paintings of Houston's past All-Star Game performers. Backs have biographical information, card number and Mother's Cookies logo. There are 28 cards in the set, with 20 of the cards distributed during a stadium promotion. Each fan also received a coupon redeemable for eight additional cards that could be traded to complete a set.

		NM/M
Complete Set (28):		9.00
Common Player:		.25
1	Dick Farrell	.25
2	Hal Woodeschick (Woodeshick)	.25
3	Joe Morgan	1.00
4	Claude Raymond	.25
5	Mike Cuellar	.25
6	Rusty Staub	.25
7	Jimmy Wynn	.25
8	Larry Dierker	.25
9	Denis Menke	.25
10	Don Wilson	.25
11	Cesar Cedeno	.25
12	Lee May	.25
13	Bob Watson	.25
14	Ken Forsch	.25
15	Joaquin Andujar	.25
16	Terry Puhl	.25
17	Joe Niekro	.30
18	Craig Reynolds	.25
19	Joe Sambito	.25
20	Jose Cruz	.25
21	J.R. Richard	.30
22	Bob Knepper	.25
23	Nolan Ryan	7.50
24	Ray Knight	.25
25	Bill Dawley	.25
26	Dickie Thon	.25
27	Jerry Mumphrey	.25
28	Astros Logo/Checklist	.25

Giants

Mother's Cookies produced a fourth annual set for the Giants in 1985. Round-cornered, glossy front cards measure 2-1/2" x 3-1/2" and feature unbordered color photos. Horizontal backs have biographical data, card number, and Mother's Cookies logo. There are 28 cards in the set, with 20 of the cards distributed during a stadium promotion. Each fan also received a coupon redeemable for eight additional cards which could be traded to complete the set.

NM/M
Complete Set (28): 6.00
Common Player: .25
1 Roger Craig .25
2 Chili Davis .25
3 Dan Gladden .25
4 Jeff Leonard .25
5 Bob Brenly .25
6 Atlee Hammaker .25
7 Will Clark 5.00
8 Greg Minton .25
9 Candy Maldonado .25
10 Vida Blue .25
11 Mike Krukow .25
12 Bob Melvin .25
13 Jose Uribe .25
14 Dan Driessen .25
15 Jeff Robinson .25
16 Rob Thompson .25
17 Mike LaCoss .25
18 Chris Brown .25
19 Scott Garrelts .25
20 Mark Davis .25
21 Jim Gott .25
22 Brad Wellman .25
23 Roger Mason .25
24 Bill Laskey .25
25 Brad Gulden .25
26 Joel Youngblood .25
27 Juan Berenguer .25
28 Coaches/Checklist (Bill Fahey, Bob Lillis, Gordy MacKenzie, Jose Morales, Norm Sherry) .25

Mariners

Mother's Cookies produced a third annual set for the M's in 1985. Round-cornered, glossy front cards measure 2-1/2" x 3-1/2" and feature unbordered color photos. Horizontal backs have brief biographical information, card number and sponsor's logo. There are 28 cards in the set, with 20 distributed during a stadium promotion. Each fan also received a coupon redeemable for eight additional cards which could be traded to complete the set.

NM/M
Complete Set (28): 6.00
Common Player: .25
1 Dick Williams .25
2 Alvin Davis .25
3 Mark Langston .25
4 Dave Henderson .25
5 Steve Yeager .25
6 Al Cowens .25
7 Jim Presley .25
8 Phil Bradley .25
9 Gorman Thomas .25
10 Barry Bonnell .25
11 Milt Wilcox .25
12 Domingo Ramos .25
13 Paul Mirabella .25
14 Matt Young .25
15 Ivan Calderon .25
16 Bill Swift .25
17 Pete Ladd .25
18 Ken Phelps .25
19 Karl Best .25
20 Spike Owen .25
21 Mike Moore .25
22 Danny Tartabull .25
23 Bob Kearney .25
24 Edwin Nunez .25

25 Mike Morgan .25
26 Roy Thomas .25
27 Jim Beattie .25
28 Coaches/Checklist (Deron Johnson, Marty Martinez, Phil Regan, Phil Roof, Ozzie Virgil) .25

1987 Mother's Cookies A's

Continuing with a tradition of producing beautiful baseball cards, Mother's Cookies of Oakland, Calif. issued a 28-card set featuring every Oakland A's player to have been elected to the All-Star Game since 1968. The full-color photos came from the private collection of nationally known photographer Doug McWilliams. Twenty of the 28 cards were given out to fans attending the A's game on July 5. An additional eight cards were available by redeeming a mail-in certificate. The cards measure 2-1/2" x 3-1/2" and feature rounded corners. Backs carry the player's All-Star Game statistics.

NM/M
Complete Set (28): 12.00
Common Player: .25
1 Bert Campaneris .25
2 Rick Monday .25
3 John Odom .25
4 Sal Bando .25
5 Reggie Jackson 2.50
6 Catfish Hunter 1.00
7 Vida Blue .25
8 Dave Duncan .25
9 Joe Rudi .25
10 Rollie Fingers .75
11 Ken Holtzman .25
12 Dick Williams .25
13 Alvin Dark .25
14 Gene Tenace .25
15 Claudell Washington .25
16 Phil Garner .25
17 Wayne Gross .25
18 Matt Keough .25
19 Jeff Newman .25
20 Rickey Henderson 1.50
21 Tony Armas .25
22 Mike Norris .25
23 Billy Martin .40
24 Bill Caudill .25
25 Jay Howell .25
26 Jose Canseco 2.00
27 Jose and Reggie (Jose Canseco, Reggie Jackson) 2.50
28 A's Logo/Checklist .25

Astros

Twenty of 28 cards featuring Astros players were given out to the first 25,000 fans attending the July 17 game at the Astrodome. An additional eight cards (though not necessarily the exact eight needed to complete a set) were available from the sponsor by redeeming a mail-in certificate. The cards have rounded corners, glossy fronts and measure 2-1/2" x 3-1/2". Backs are printed in purple and orange and contain personal data, the Mother's Cookies logo, card number and a spot for the player's autograph.

NM/M
Complete Set (28): 10.00
Common Player: .25
1 Hal Lanier .25
2 Mike Scott .25
3 Jose Cruz .25
4 Bill Doran .25
5 Bob Knepper .25
6 Phil Garner .25
7 Terry Puhl .25
8 Nolan Ryan 7.50
9 Kevin Bass .25
10 Glenn Davis .25
11 Alan Ashby .25
12 Charlie Kerfeld .25
13 Denny Walling .25
14 Danny Darwin .25
15 Mark Bailey .25
16 Davey Lopes .25
17 Dave Meads .25
18 Aurelio Lopez .25
19 Craig Reynolds .25
20 Dave Smith .25
21 Larry Anderson (Andersen) .25
22 Jim Pankovits .25
23 Jim Deshaies .25
24 Bert Pena .25
25 Dickie Thon .25
26 Billy Hatcher .25
27 Coaches (Yogi Berra, Matt Galante, Denis Menke, Les Moss, Gene Tenace) .25
28 Houston Astrodome/Checklist .25

Dodgers

Mother's Cookies produced for the first time in 1987 a team set featuring the L.A. Dodgers. Twenty of the 28 cards were given to youngsters 14 and under at Dodger Stadium on August 9. An additional eight cards were available from Mother's Cookies via a mail-in coupon. The borderless, full-color cards measure 2-1/2" x 3-1/2" and have rounded corners. A special album designed to house the set was available for $3.95 through a mail-in offer.

NM/M
Complete Set (28): 10.00
Common Player: .25
1 Tom Lasorda .40
2 Pedro Guerrero .25
3 Steve Sax .25
4 Fernando Valenzuela .25
5 Mike Marshall .25
6 Orel Hershiser .75
7 Mariano Duncan .25
8 Bill Madlock .25
9 Bob Welch .25
10 Mike Scioscia .25
11 Mike Ramsey .25
12 Matt Young .25
13 Franklin Stubbs .25
14 Tom Niedenfuer .25
15 Reggie Williams .25
16 Rick Honeycutt .25
17 Dave Anderson .25
18 Alejandro Pena .25
19 Ken Howell .25
20 Len Matuszek .25
21 Tim Leary .25
22 Tracy Woodson .25
23 Alex Trevino .25
24 Ken Landreaux .25
25 Mickey Hatcher .25
26 Brian Holton .25
27 Coaches (Joey Amalfitano, Mark Cresse, Don McMahon, Manny Mota, Ron Perranoski, Bill Russell) .25
28 Dodger Stadium/Checklist .25

Giants

Distribution of the 1987 Mother's Cookies Giants cards took place at Candlestick Park on June 27. Twenty of the 28 cards in the set were given to the first 25,000 fans entering

the park. The starter packet of 20 cards contained a mail-in coupon card which was good for an additional eight cards. The glossy-front cards measure 2-1/2" x 3-1/2" with rounded corners. Backs are printed in red and purple and contain personal and statistical information along with the Mother's Cookies logo.

NM/M
Complete Set (28): 9.00
Common Player: .25
1 Roger Craig .25
2 Will Clark 1.00
3 Chili Davis .25
4 Bob Brenly .25
5 Chris Brown .25
6 Mike Krukow .25
7 Candy Maldonado .25
8 Jeffrey Leonard .25
9 Greg Minton .25
10 Robby Thompson .25
11 Scott Garrelts .25
12 Bob Melvin .25
13 Jose Uribe .25
14 Mark Davis .25
15 Eddie Milner .25
16 Harry Spilman .25
17 Kelly Downs .25
18 Chris Speier .25
19 Jim Gott .25
20 Joel Youngblood .25
21 Mike LaCoss .25
22 Matt Williams 3.00
23 Roger Mason .25
24 Mike Aldrete .25
25 Jeff Robinson .25
26 Mark Grant .25
27 Coaches (Bill Fahey, Bob Lillis, Gordon MacKenzie, Jose Morales, Norm Sherry, Don Zimmer) .25
28 Candlestick Park/Checklist .25

Mariners

For the fourth consecutive year, Mother's Cookies issued a team set featuring the Mariners. Twenty of the 28 cards were distributed to the first 20,000 fans entering the Kingdome on August 9. An additional eight cards (though not necessarily the eight cards needed to complete the set) were available by redeeming a mail-in certificate. Collectors were encouraged to trade to complete a set. The 2-1/2" x 3-1/2" full-color cards feature glossy fronts and rounded corners. A specially designed album to house the set was available.

NM/M
Complete Set (28): 6.00
Common Player: .25
1 Dick Williams .25
2 Alvin Davis .25
3 Mike Moore .25
4 Jim Presley .25
5 Mark Langston .25
6 Phil Bradley .25
7 Ken Phelps .25
8 Mike Morgan .25
9 David Valle .25
10 Harold Reynolds .40
11 Edwin Nunez .25
12 Bob Kearney .25
13 Scott Bankhead .25
14 Scott Bradley .25
15 Mickey Brantley .25
16 Mark Huismann .25
17 Mike Kingery .25
18 John Moses .25
19 Donell Nixon .25
20 Rey Quinones .25
21 Domingo Ramos .25
22 Jerry Reed .25
23 Rich Renteria .25
24 Rich Monteleone .25
25 Mike Trujillo .25
26 Bill Wilkinson .25
27 John Christensen .25
28 Coaches/Checklist (Billy Connors, Frank Howard, Phil Roof, Bobby Tolan, Ozzie Virgil) .25

Rangers

While Mother's Cookies of Oakland had produced high-quality baseball card sets of various teams since 1983, the Rangers participated in the promotion for the first time in 1987. Twenty cards from the 28-card set were handed out to the first 25,000 fans entering Arlington Stadium on July 17. An additional eight cards (though not necessarily those needed to complete a set) were available by redeeming a mail-in certificate. The cards measure 2-1/2" x 3-1/2" with rounded corners and glossy finish, like all Mother's Cookies issued in 1987.

NM/M
Complete Set (28): 9.00
Common Player: .25
1 Bobby Valentine .25
2 Pete Incaviglia .50
3 Charlie Hough .25
4 Oddibe McDowell .25
5 Larry Parrish .25
6 Scott Fletcher .25
7 Steve Buechele .25
8 Tom Paciorek .25
9 Pete O'Brien .25
10 Darrell Porter .25
11 Greg Harris .25
12 Don Slaught .25
13 Ruben Sierra .50
14 Curtis Wilkerson .25
15 Dale Mohorcic .25
16 Ron Meredith .25
17 Mitch Williams .25
18 Bob Brower .25
19 Edwin Correa .25
20 Geno Petralli .25
21 Mike Loynd .25
22 Jerry Browne .25
23 Jose Guzman .25
24 Jeff Kunkel .25
25 Bobby Witt .25
26 Jeff Russell .25
27 Trainers (Danny Wheat, Bill Zeigler) .25
28 Coaches/Checklist (Joe Ferguson, Tim Foli, Tom House, Art Howe, Dave Oliver, Tom Robson) .25

Mark McGwire

A four-card set featuring outstanding rookie Mark McGwire of the Oakland A's was produced by Mother's Cookies in 1987. Cards are 2-1/2" x 3-1/2" and have rounded corners and glossy finish like other Mother's issues. The set was obtainable by sending in eight proof-of-purchase seals or could be secured at the National Sports Collectors Convention held July 9-12 in San Francisco. Convention goers received one card as a bonus for each Mother's Cookies baseball card album purchased.

NM/M
Complete Set (4): 10.00

Uncut Strip: 10.00
Common Card: 3.00
1 Mark McGwire/Portrait 3.00
2 Mark McGwire (Leaning on bat rack.) 3.00
3 Mark McGwire (Beginning batting swing.) 3.00
4 Mark McGwire (Batting follow-through.) 3.00

1988 Mother's Cookies A's

Complete at 28 cards, the 1988 Mother's Cookies A's set features full-color, borderless cards with rounded corners in the standard 2-1/2" x 3-1/2" format. Backs are printed in red and purple and include biographical information, the Mother's Cookies logo and card number. Starter sets of 20 cards were distributed at the stadium along with a promotional card redeemable for another eights cards (not necessarily those needed to complete the set). An album to house the cards was also available.

NM/M
Complete Set (28): 16.00
Common Player: .35
1 Tony LaRussa .50
2 Mark McGwire 6.00
3 Dave Stewart .35
4 Mickey Tettleton .35
5 Dave Parker .35
6 Carney Lansford .35
7 Jose Canseco .75
8 Don Baylor .50
9 Bob Welch .35
10 Dennis Eckersley 1.25
11 Walt Weiss .50
12 Tony Phillips .35
13 Steve Ontiveros .35
14 Dave Henderson .35
15 Stan Javier .35
16 Ron Hassey .35
17 Curt Young .35
18 Glenn Hubbard .35
19 Storm Davis .35
20 Eric Plunk .35
21 Matt Young .35
22 Mike Gallego .35
23 Rick Honeycutt .35
24 Doug Jennings .35
25 Gene Nelson .35
26 Greg Cadaret .35
27 Coaches (Dave Duncan, Rene Lachemann, Jim Lefebvre, Dave McKay, Mike Paul, Bob Watson) .35
28 Jose Canseco, Mark McGwire 2.50

Astros

One of six team sets issued by Mother's Cookies in 1988, the 28-card Astros set is similar in design to other Mother's Cookies sets. Glossy-front cards are 2-1/2" x 3-1/2" size with rounded corners and feature full-color, borderless photos on the fronts. Backs feature red and purple printing and include brief biographical information, the Mother's logo and card number. Twenty of the cards were distributed in a stadium promotion, along with a redemption card that could be exchanged for an additional eight cards (but not necessarily the eight needed to complete the set). An album was also available to house the set.

		NM/M
Complete Set (28):		12.00
Common Player:		.35
1	Hal Lanier	.35
2	Mike Scott	.35
3	Gerald Young	.35
4	Bill Doran	.35
5	Bob Knepper	.35
6	Billy Hatcher	.35
7	Terry Puhl	.35
8	Nolan Ryan	10.00
9	Kevin Bass	.35
10	Glenn Davis	.35
11	Alan Ashby	.35
12	Steve Henderson	.35
13	Denny Walling	.35
14	Danny Darwin	.35
15	Mark Bailey	.35
16	Ernie Camacho	.35
17	Rafael Ramirez	.35
18	Jeff Heathcock	.35
19	Craig Reynolds	.35
20	Dave Smith	.35
21	Larry Andersen	.35
22	Jim Pankovits	.35
23	Jim Deshaies	.35
24	Juan Agosto	.35
26	Chuck Jackson	.35
26	Joaquin Andujar	.35
27	Coaches (Yogi Berra, Gene Clines, Matt Galante, Marc Hill, Denis Menke, Les Moss)	.35
28	Trainers/Checklist (Doc Ewell, Dave Labossiere, Dennis Liborio)	.35

Dodgers

Similar in design to other Mother's Cookies sets, the 1988 Dodgers issue features full-color, borderless photos with backs printed in red and purple. The 28 cards in the set measure 2-1/2" x 3-1/2" with rounded corners. Starter packs of 20 cards were distributed at a ballpark promotion along with a coupon card that could be exchanged for an additional eight cards at a local card show or through the mail. Backs include brief player information, the Mother's Cookies logo and card number. The promotion also included a special album to house the set.

		NM/M
Complete Set (28):		8.00
Common Player:		.35
1	Tom Lasorda	.45
2	Pedro Guerrero	.35
3	Steve Sax	.35
4	Fernando Valenzuela	.35
5	Mike Marshall	.35
6	Orel Hershiser	.50
7	Alfredo Griffin	.35
8	Kirk Gibson	.35

9	Don Sutton	1.25
10	Mike Scioscia	.35
11	Franklin Stubbs	.35
12	Mike Davis	.35
13	Jesse Orosco	.35
14	John Shelby	.35
15	Rick Dempsey	.35
16	Jay Howell	.35
17	Dave Anderson	.35
18	Alejandro Pena	.35
19	Jeff Hamilton	.35
20	Danny Heep	.35
21	Tim Leary	.35
22	Brad Havens	.35
23	Tim Belcher	.35
24	Ken Howell	.35
25	Mickey Hatcher	.35
26	Brian Holton	.35
27	Mike Devereaux	.35
28	Coaches/Checklist (Joe Amalfitano, Mark Cresse, Joe Ferguson, Ben Hines, Manny Mota, Ron Perranoski, Bill Russell)	.35

Giants

One of six team sets issued in 1988 by Mother's Cookies, this 28-card Giants set featured full-color borderless photos on a standard-size card with rounded corners. Backs, printed in red and purple, include brief player data, the Mother's Cookies logo and card number. Twenty different cards were distributed as a starter set at a stadium promotion along with a coupon card that could be redeemed for an additional eight cards (not necessarily those needed to complete the set). The redemption cards could be exchanged through the mail or redeemed at a local card show.

		NM/M
Complete Set (28):		10.00
Common Player:		.35
1	Roger Craig	.35
2	Will Clark	.75
3	Kevin Mitchell	.35
4	Bob Brenly	.35
5	Mike Aldrete	.35
6	Mike Krukow	.35
7	Candy Maldonado	.35
8	Jeffrey Leonard	.35
9	Dave Dravecky	.35
10	Robby Thompson	.35
11	Scott Garrelts	.35
12	Bob Melvin	.35
13	Jose Uribe	.35
14	Brett Butler	.35
15	Rick Reuschel	.35
16	Harry Spilman	.35
17	Kelly Downs	.35
18	Chris Speier	.35
19	Atlee Hammaker	.35
20	Joel Youngblood	.35
21	Mike LaCoss	.35
22	Don Robinson	.35
23	Mark Wasinger	.35
24	Craig Lefferts	.35
25	Phil Garner	.35
26	Joe Price	.35
27	Coaches (Dusty Baker, Bill Fahey, Bob Lillis, Gordie MacKenzie, Jose Morales, Norm Sherry)	.35
28	Logo Card/Checklist	.35

Mariners

Similar in design to other Mother's Cookies sets, the 28-card Mariners issue features full-color, borderless photos on a 2-1/2" x 3-1/2" card with rounded corners. Backs, printed in red and purple, include brief biographical information, the Mother's Cookies logo and card number. Twenty-card starter packs were distributed at a stadium promotion, where fans also received a coupon card that could be exchanged for an additional eight cards (not necessar-

ily those needed to complete the set). The coupon card could be redeemed through the mail or exchanged at a local baseball card show. As with the rest of the 1988 Mother's Cookies sets, an album was also available to house the cards.

		NM/M
Complete Set (28):		6.00
Common Player:		.35
1	Dick Williams	.35
2	Alvin Davis	.35
3	Mike Moore	.35
4	Jim Presley	.35
5	Mark Langston	.35
6	Henry Cotto	.35
7	Ken Phelps	.35
8	Steve Trout	.35
9	David Valle	.35
10	Harold Reynolds	.50
11	Edwin Nunez	.35
12	Glenn Wilson	.35
13	Scott Bankhead	.35
14	Scott Bradley	.35
15	Mickey Brantley	.35
16	Bruce Fields	.35
17	Mike Kingery	.35
18	Mike Campbell	.35
19	Mike Jackson	.35
20	Rey Quinones	.35
21	Mario Diaz	.35
22	Jerry Reed	.35
23	Rich Renteria	.35
24	Julio Solano	.35
25	Bill Swift	.35
26	Bill Wilkinson	.35
27	Coaches (Billy Connors, Frank Howard, Phil Roof, Jim Snyder, Ozzie Virgil)	.35
28	Trainers/Checklist (Henry Genzale, Rick Griffin)	.35

Rangers

This 28-card issue was one of six team sets issued in 1988 by Mother's Cookies. The Rangers issue features full-color, borderless cards printed in standard 2-1/2" x 3-1/2" format with rounded corners. Backs are printed in red and purple and include player information, Mother's Cookies logo and card number. Twenty-card starter packs were distributed as a stadium promotion that included a redemption card good for another eight cards (not necessarily those needed to complete the set) either through the mail or at a local card show.

		NM/M
Complete Set (28):		7.00
Common Player:		.35
1	Bobby Valentine	.35
2	Pete Incaviglia	.35
3	Charlie Hough	.35
4	Oddibe McDowell	.35
5	Larry Parrish	.35
6	Scott Fletcher	.35
7	Steve Buechele	.35
8	Steve Kemp	.35
9	Pete O'Brien	.35
10	Ruben Sierra	.35
11	Mike Stanley	.35
12	Jose Cecena	.35

13	Cecil Espy	.35
14	Curtis Wilkerson	.35
15	Dale Mohorcic	.35
16	Ray Hayward	.35
17	Mitch Williams	.35
18	Bob Brower	.35
19	Paul Kilgus	.35
20	Geno Petralli	.35
21	James Steels	.35
22	Jerry Browne	.35
23	Jose Guzman	.35
24	DeWayne Vaughn	.35
25	Bobby Witt	.35
26	Jeff Russell	.35
27	Coaches (Richard Egan, Tom House, Art Howe, Davey Lopes, David Oliver, Tom Robson)	.35
28	Trainers/Checklist (Danny Wheat, Bill Zeigler)	.35

Will Clark

In a baseball spring training-related promotion, Mother's Cookies of Oakland, Calif. produced a full-color four-card set featuring San Francisco Giants first baseman Will Clark. The cards, which have glossy finishes and rounded corners, came cellophane-wrapped in specially marked 18-ounce packages of Mother's Cookies products. The cards are identical in style to the other Mother's Cookies issues.

		NM/M
Complete Set (4):		4.00
4-Card Uncut Panel:		4.00
Common Card:		1.00
1	Will Clark (Bat on shoulder.)	1.00
2	Will Clark/Kneeling	1.00
3	Will Clark (Batting follow-through.)	1.00
4	Will Clark (Heading for first base.)	1.00

Mark McGwire

For the second consecutive year, Mother's Cookies devoted a four-card set to Oakland A's slugger Mark McGwire. The full-color cards have rounded corners and measure 2-1/2" x 3-1/2". The cards were issued in specially marked 18-ounce packages of Mother's Cookies products in the northern California area. The cards are identical in design to the team issues produced by Mother's.

		NM/M
Complete Set (4):		7.00
4-Card Uncut Panel:		9.00
Common Card:		2.00
1	Mark McGwire (Holding oversized bat.)	2.00
2	Mark McGwire/Fldg	2.00
3	Mark McGwire/Kneeling	2.00
4	Mark McGwire (Bat in air.)	2.00

1989 Mother's Cookies A's

The 1989 Mother's Cookies A's set consists of 28 cards designed in the traditional style: a glossy 2-1/2" x 3-1/2" card with a borderless photo and rounded corners. A starter set of the cards was used as a stadium promotion and distributed to fans attending the July 30 Oakland game.

		NM/M
Complete Set (28):		13.50
Common Player:		.35
1	Tony LaRussa	.35
2	Mark McGwire	5.00
3	Terry Steinbach	.35
4	Dave Parker	.35
5	Carney Lansford	.35
6	Dave Stewart	.35
7	Jose Canseco	1.00
8	Walt Weiss	.35
9	Bob Welch	.35
10	Dennis Eckersley	1.25
11	Tony Phillips	.35
12	Mike Moore	.35
13	Dave Henderson	.35
14	Curt Young	.35
15	Ron Hassey	.35
16	Eric Plunk	.35
17	Luis Polonia	.35
18	Storm Davis	.35
19	Glenn Hubbard	.35
20	Greg Cadaret	.35
21	Stan Javier	.35
22	Felix Jose	.35
23	Mike Gallego	.35
24	Todd Burns	.35
25	Rick Honeycutt	.35
26	Gene Nelson	.35
27	A's Coaches (Dave Duncan, Rene Lacheman, Art Kusnyer, Tommie Reynolds, Merv Rettenmund)	.35
28	Walt Weiss, Mark McGwire, Jose Canseco	2.50

Astros

The 1989 Astros team set issued by Mother's Cookies consists of 28 cards in 2-1/2" x 3-1/2" format in the traditional style of glossy borderless photos and rounded corners. Partial sets were distributed to fans attending the July 22 game at the Astrodome. The cards feature the photography of Barry Colla and display the Mother's Cookies logo on the back.

		NM/M
Complete Set (28):		11.00
Common Player:		.35
1	Art Howe	.35
2	Mike Scott	.35
3	Gerald Young	.35
4	Bill Doran	.35
5	Billy Hatcher	.35
6	Terry Puhl	.35
7	Bob Knepper	.35
8	Kevin Bass	.35
9	Glenn Davis	.35
10	Alan Ashby	.35
11	Bob Forsch	.35
12	Greg Gross	.35
13	Danny Darwin	.35
14	Craig Biggio	3.00
15	Jim Clancy	.35
16	Rafael Ramirez	.35
17	Alex Trevino	.35
18	Craig Reynolds	.35
19	Dave Smith	.35
20	Larry Andersen	.35
21	Eric Yelding	.35
22	Jim Deshaies	.35
23	Juan Agosto	.35
24	Rick Rhoden	.35
25	Ken Caminiti	1.00
26	Dave Meads	.35
27	Astros Coaches (Yogi Berra, Matt Galante, Phil Garner, Les Moss, Ed Napoleon, Ed Ott)	.35
28	Trainers/Checklist (Dave Labossiere, Doc Ewell, Dennis Liborio)	.35

Dodgers

This 28-card set features the players and coaches of the L.A. Dodgers. The cards follow the traditional Mother's Cookies style featuring rounded corners, borderless color photos, horizontal backs and 2-1/2" x 3-1/2" size. Initially 20 cards were given away as starter sets at Dodger Stadium.

		NM/M
Complete Set (28):		9.00
Common Player:		.35
1	Tom Lasorda	.40
2	Eddie Murray	2.00
3	Mike Scioscia	.35
4	Fernando Valenzuela	.35
5	Mike Marshall	.35
6	Orel Hershiser	.50
7	Alfredo Griffin	.35
8	Kirk Gibson	.35
9	John Tudor	.35
10	Willie Randolph	.35
11	Franklin Stubbs	.35
12	Mike Davis	.35
13	Mike Morgan	.35
14	John Shelby	.35
15	Rick Dempsey	.35
16	Jay Howell	.35
17	Dave Anderson	.35
18	Alejandro Pena	.35
19	Jeff Hamilton	.35
20	Ricky Horton	.35
21	Tim Leary	.35
22	Ray Searage	.35
23	Tim Belcher	.35
24	Tim Crews	.35
25	Mickey Hatcher	.35
26	Mariano Duncan	.35
27	Coaches (Joe Amalfitano, Mark Cresse, Joe Ferguson, Ben Hines, Manny Mota, Ron Perranoski, Bill Russell)	.35
28	Checklist	.35

Giants

The 1989 Mother's Cookies Giants set consists of 28 cards, all featuring borderless, color photos with rounded corners. Starter sets of the cards were distributed as a stadium promotion to fans attending the August 6 game at Candlestick Park.

		NM/M
Complete Set (28):		9.00
Common Player:		.35
1	Roger Craig	.35
2	Will Clark	1.00
3	Kevin Mitchell	.35
4	Kelly Downs	.35
5	Brett Butler	.35
6	Mike Krukow	.35
7	Candy Maldonado	.35
8	Terry Kennedy	.35
9	Dave Dravecky	.35
10	Robby Thompson	.35
11	Scott Garrelts	.35
12	Matt Williams	1.00
13	Jose Uribe	.35
14	Tracy Jones	.35
15	Rick Reuschel	.35
16	Ernest Riles	.35
17	Jeff Brantley	.35
18	Chris Speier	.35
19	Atlee Hammaker	.35
20	Ed Jurak	.35
21	Mike LaCoss	.35
22	Don Robinson	.35
23	Kirt Manwaring	.35
24	Craig Lefferts	.35
25	Donnell Nixon	.35
26	Joe Price	.35
27	Rich Gossage	.75
28	Coaches/Checklist (Bill Fahey, Dusty Baker, Bob Lillis, Wendell Kim, Norm Sherry)	.35

Mariners

For the sixth straight season, Mother's Cookies released a Mariners team set. The 1989 issue features 28 cards. Starter sets of 20 cards were distributed at a Mariners home game. The cards are 2-1/2" x 3-1/2" and feature borderless, glossy full color photos. Card backs are horizontal. Rookie sensation Ken Griffey Jr. was included in the 1989 issue.

		NM/M
Complete Set (28):		12.50
Common Player:		.35
1	Jim Lefebvre	.35
2	Alvin Davis	.35
3	Ken Griffey Jr.	9.00
4	Jim Presley	.35
5	Mark Langston	.35
6	Henry Cotto	.35
7	Mickey Brantley	.35
8	Jeffrey Leonard	.35
9	Dave Valle	.35
10	Harold Reynolds	.50
11	Edgar Martinez	3.00
12	Tom Niedenfuer	.35
13	Scott Bankhead	.35
14	Scott Bradley	.35
15	Omar Vizquel	.35
16	Erik Hanson	.35
17	Bill Swift	.35
18	Mike Campbell	.35
19	Mike Jackson	.35
20	Rich Renteria	.35
21	Mario Diaz	.35
22	Jerry Reed	.35
23	Darnell Coles	.35
24	Steve Trout	.35
25	Mike Schooler	.35
26	Julio Solano	.35
27	Coaches (Gene Clines, Bob Didier, Rusty Kuntz, Mike Paul, Bill Plummer)	.35
28	Checklist/Trainers (Henry Genzale, Rick Griffin)	.35

Rangers

The 1989 Mother's Cookies Rangers team set features the traditional glossy borderless photos and rounded corners. The 2-1/2" x 3-1/2" set of 28 cards features the photography of Barry Colla. Partial sets were distributed to fans attending the July 30 game at Arlington Stadium.

		NM/M
Complete Set (28):		8.00
Common Player:		.35
1	Bobby Valentine	.35
2	Nolan Ryan	6.00
3	Julio Franco	.35
4	Charlie Hough	.35
5	Rafael Palmeiro	4.00
6	Jeff Russell	.35
7	Ruben Sierra	.35
8	Steve Buechele	.35
9	Buddy Bell	.35
10	Pete Incaviglia	.35
11	Geno Petralli	.35
12	Cecil Espy	.35
13	Scott Fletcher	.35
14	Bobby Witt	.35
15	Brad Arnsberg	.35
16	Rick Leach	.35
17	Jamie Moyer	.35
18	Kevin Brown	.35
19	Jeff Kunkel	.35
20	Craig McMurtry	.35
21	Kenny Rogers	.35
22	Mike Stanley	.35
23	Cecilio Guante	.35
24	Jim Sundberg	.35
25	Jose Guzman	.35
26	Jeff Stone	.35
27	Coaches (Dick Egan, Tom Robson, Toby Harrah, Dave Oliver, Tom House, Davey Lopes)	.35
28	Trainers/Checklist (Bill Ziegler, Danny Wheat)	.35

Jose Canseco

This special insert glossy set features Canseco in two posed (one standing, one kneeling) and two action (one batting, one running) shots. Full-color card fronts have

---

rounded corners. Flip sides are numbered, printed in red and purple, and carry 1988 stats and career notes. Cards are individually cellowrapped and inserted in Mother's Fudge 'N Chips, Oatmeal Raisin and Cocadas cookie bags.

		NM/M
Complete Set (4):		5.00
Four-Card Panel:		6.00
Common Card:		1.50
1	Jose Canseco (Ball in hand.)	1.50
2	Jose Canseco (On one knee grasping bat.)	1.50
3	Jose Canseco (Swinging-in action.)	1.50
4	Jose Canseco (Baserunning)	1.50

Will Clark

Will Clark is featured on a special-edition glossy set inserted in Mother's big bag chocolate chip cookies. The standard-size (2-1/2" x 3-1/2") cards feature Clark in two posed (batting and catching) and two action (batting and running) shots. Purple and red backs list 1986-88 stats.

		NM/M
Complete Set (4):		4.00
Four-Card Uncut Panel:		4.00
Common Card:		1.00
1	Will Clark (Displaying ball in glove.)	1.00
2	Will Clark (Batting stance.)	1.00
3	Will Clark (In action-after swing.)	1.00
4	Will Clark (Heading towards first.)	1.00

Ken Griffey, Jr.

This set featuring Ken Griffey, Jr. was issued by Mother's Cookies and was available only in cookie packages in Washington and Oregon. The cards were also available at a Seattle Mariners Kingdome baseball card show on August 20, where the set was introduced. The cards were then packed inside specially marked bags of cookies, one card per bag.

		NM/M
Complete Set (4):		15.00
Four-Card Uncut Panel:		20.00
Common Card:		5.00
1	Ken Griffey Jr. (Arms folded.)	5.00
2	Ken Griffey Jr. (Ball in hand.)	5.00
3	Ken Griffey Jr. (Bat over left shoulder.)	5.00
4	Ken Griffey Jr. (Back of jersey showing.)	5.00

Mark McGwire

This special edition features full-color glossy player photos by Barry Colla on standard-size (2-1/2" x 3-1/2") cards with rounded corners. Photos feature four different batting poses. Numbered flip sides, printed in purple and red, carry 1987-88 statistics. Cards are individually cello-wrapped and were inserted in Mother's Cookie Parade variety cookie bags.

		NM/M
Complete Set (4):		6.00
Common Player:		1.50
1	Mark McGwire (Bat on shoulder.)	1.50
2	Mark McGwire (Batting stance.)	1.50
3	Mark McGwire (Bat in front.)	1.50
4	Mark McGwire (Batting follow through.)	1.50

Rookies of the Year

This four-card set features the American League Rookies of the Year for 1986, 1987 and 1988, all members of the Oakland A's. The 2-1/2" x 3-1/2" cards feature full color photos in the traditional Mother's Cookies format. One card was devoted to each player along with a special card showcasing all three players. The cards were distributed one per box in Mother's Cookies.

		NM/M
Complete Set (4):		15.00
Four-Card Uncut Panel:		15.00
Common Card:		.75
1	Jose Canseco	2.25
2	Mark McGwire	7.50
3	Walt Weiss	.75
4	Walt Weiss, Mark McGwire, Jose Canseco	5.50

1990 Mother's Cookies A's

This 28-card set features cards distributed at an A's home game. Cards measure 2-1/2" x 3-1/2" and feature rounded corners. Backs include biographical information and autograph space.

		NM/M
Complete Set (28):		15.00
Common Player:		.35
1	Tony LaRussa	.35
2	Mark McGwire	4.00
3	Terry Steinbach	.35
4	Rickey Henderson	2.00
5	Dave Stewart	.35
6	Jose Canseco	.75
7	Dennis Eckersley	1.00
8	Carney Lansford	.35
9	Mike Moore	.35
10	Walt Weiss	.35
11	Scott Sanderson	.35
12	Ron Hassey	.35
13	Rick Honeycutt	.35
14	Ken Phelps	.35
15	Jamie Quirk	.35
16	Bob Welch	.35
17	Felix Jose	.35
18	Dave Henderson	.35
19	Mike Norris	.35
20	Todd Burns	.35
21	Lance Blankenship	.35
22	Gene Nelson	.35
23	Stan Javier	.35
24	Curt Young	.35
25	Mike Gallego	.35
26	Joe Klink	.35
27	Coaches (Dave Duncan, Art Kuysner, Rene Lacheman, Dave McKay, Merv Rettenmund, Tommie Reynolds)	.35
28	Checklist/Trainers (Frank Ciensczyk, Larry Davis, Steve Vucinich, Barry Weinberg)	.35

Astros

This 28-card set features cards styled like past Mother's Cookies releases. The cards were distributed

---

in 20-card packs at an Astros home game. The cards were never distributed in complete set form.

		NM/M
Complete Set (28):		10.00
Common Player:		.35
1	Art Howe	.35
2	Glenn Davis	.35
3	Eric Anthony	.35
4	Mike Scott	.35
5	Craig Biggio	2.00
6	Ken Caminiti	.50
7	Bill Doran	.35
8	Gerald Young	.35
9	Terry Puhl	.35
10	Mark Portugal	.35
11	Mark Davidson	.35
12	Jim Deshaies	.35
13	Bill Gullickson	.35
14	Franklin Stubbs	.35
15	Danny Darwin	.35
16	Ken Oberkfell	.35
17	Dave Smith	.35
18	Dan Schatzeder	.35
19	Rafael Ramirez	.35
20	Larry Andersen	.35
21	Alex Trevino	.35
22	Glenn Wilson	.35
23	Jim Clancy	.35
24	Eric Yelding	.35
25	Casey Candaele	.35
26	Juan Agosto	.35
27	Coaches (Bill Bowman, Bob Cluck, Phil Garner, Matt Galante, Rudy Jaramillo, Ed Napoleon)	.35
28	Checklist/Trainers (Doc Ewell, Dave Labossiere, Dennis Liborio)	.35

Dodgers

Distributed as a promotional item, these cards are styled like past Mother's Cookies releases. Fans 14 and under received a 20-card pack at a Dodgers home game. Cards were also available at a Labor Day card show in Anaheim. The cards were not distributed in complete set form.

		NM/M
Complete Set (28):		10.00
Common Player:		.35
1	Tom Lasorda	.45
2	Fernando Valenzuela	.35
3	Kal Daniels	.35
4	Mike Scioscia	.35
5	Eddie Murray	3.00
6	Mickey Hatcher	.35
7	Juan Samuel	.35
8	Alfredo Griffin	.35
9	Tim Belcher	.35
10	Hubie Brooks	.35
11	Jose Gonzalez	.35
12	Orel Hershiser	.45
13	Kirk Gibson	.35
14	Chris Gwynn	.35
15	Jay Howell	.35
16	Rick Dempsey	.35
17	Ramon Martinez	.50
18	Lenny Harris	.35
19	John Wetteland	.35
20	Mike Sharperson	.35
21	Mike Morgan	.35
22	Ray Searage	.35
23	Jeff Hamilton	.35
24	Jim Gott	.35
25	John Shelby	.35
26	Tim Crews	.35
27	Don Aase	.35
28	Coaches (Joe Amalfitano, Mark Cresse, Joe Ferguson, Ben Hines, Manny Mota, Ron Perranoski, Bill Russell)	.35

Giants

Like the other Mother's Cookies issues of 1990, Giants cards were distributed as a promotional item. Fans 14 and under were given a 20-card starter set at a Giants game. Cards could also be obtained

---

at the Labor Day card show in San Francisco. The cards were not released in complete set form.

		NM/M
Complete Set (28):		10.00
Common Player:		.35
1	Roger Craig	.35
2	Will Clark	1.00
3	Gary Carter	3.00
4	Kelly Downs	.35
5	Kevin Mitchell	.35
6	Steve Bedrosian	.35
7	Brett Butler	.35
8	Rick Reuschel	.35
9	Matt Williams	1.00
10	Robby Thompson	.35
11	Mike LaCoss	.35
12	Terry Kennedy	.35
13	Atlee Hammaker	.35
14	Rick Leach	.35
15	Ernest Riles	.35
16	Scott Garrelts	.35
17	Jose Uribe	.35
18	Greg Litton	.35
19	Dave Anderson	.35
20	Don Robinson	.35
21	Coaches (Dusty Baker, Bill Fahey, Wendell Kim, Bob Lillis, Norm Sherry)	.35
22	Bill Bathe	.35
23	Randy O'Neal	.35
24	Kevin Bass	.35
25	Jeff Brantley	.35
26	John Burkett	.35
27	Ernie Camacho	.35
28	Checklist	.35

Mariners

This 28-card set features the traditional Mother's Cookies style with borderless full-color photos with rounded corners. Backs feature biographical information and autograph space. The cards were released as a promotion at a Mariners home game and at a Kingdome card show.

		NM/M
Complete Set (28):		17.50
Common Player:		.35
1	Jim Lefebvre	.35
2	Alvin Davis	.35
3	Ken Griffey Jr.	7.00
4	Jeffrey Leonard	.35
5	David Valle	.35
6	Harold Reynolds	.35
7	Jay Buhner	.75
8	Erik Hanson	.35
9	Henry Cotto	.35
10	Edgar Martinez	.35
11	Bill Swift	.35
12	Omar Vizquel	.75
13	Randy Johnson	5.00
14	Greg Briley	.35
15	Gene Harris	.35
16	Matt Young	.35
17	Pete O'Brien	.35
18	Brent Knackert	.35
19	Mike Jackson	.35
20	Brian Holman	.35
21	Mike Schooler	.35
22	Darnell Coles	.35
23	Keith Comstock	.35
24	Scott Bankhead	.35
25	Scott Bradley	.35
26	Mike Brumley	.35
27	Coaches (Gene Clines, Bob Didier, Rusty Kuntz, Mike Paul, Bill Plummer)	.35
28	Checklist/Trainers (Henry Genzale, Rick Griffin, Tom Newberg)	.35

Rangers

Putting together a complete set of these cards was not an easy task. The cards were distributed in 20-card packs at a Rangers home game and also could be obtained at a Dallas card convention. The cards were not released in complete set form. The cards feature the traditional Mother's Cookies style of glossy photos and rounded corners.

		NM/M
Complete Set (28):		12.50
Common Player:		.35
1	Bobby Valentine	.35
2	Nolan Ryan	6.00
3	Ruben Sierra	.35
4	Pete Incaviglia	.35
5	Charlie Hough	.35
6	Harold Baines	.35
7	Gino Petralli	.35
8	Jeff Russell	.35
9	Rafael Palmeiro	2.00
10	Julio Franco	.35
11	Jack Daugherty	.35
12	Gary Pettis	.35
13	Brian Bohanon	.35
14	Steve Buechele	.35
15	Bobby Witt	.35
16	Thad Bosley	.35
17	Gary Mielke	.35
18	Jeff Kunkel	.35
19	Mike Jeffcoat	.35
20	Mike Stanley	.35
21	Kevin Brown	.35
22	Kenny Rogers	.35
23	Jeff Huson	.35
24	Jamie Moyer	.35
25	Cecil Espy	.35
26	John Russell	.35
27	Coaches (Toby Harrah, Tom House, Davey Lopes, Dave Oliver, Tom Robson)	.35
28	Checklist/Trainers (Joe Macko, Marty Stajduhar, Danny Wheat, Bill Zeigler)	.35

Jose Canseco

This special insert glossy set features Canseco in four posed shots. Full-color card fronts have rounded corners. Flip sides are numbered, printed in red and purple and feature the Mother's Cookies logo. The cards are individually cello-wrapped and inserted one per Mother's Cookies bag.

		NM/M
Complete Set (4):		4.00
Four-Card Uncut Panel:		5.00
Common Card:		1.50
1	Jose Canseco/Sitting (Bat on shoulder.)	1.50
2	Jose Canseco (Bat behind neck.)	1.50
3	Jose Canseco (Batting stance.)	1.50
4	Jose Canseco (On dugout step.)	1.50

Will Clark

1990 marks the third consecutive year that Mother's Cookies devoted a set to Giants slugger Will Clark. The set features four posed full-color shots. The cards follow the same design as all recent Mother's Cookies cards.

		NM/M
Complete Set (4):		4.00
Four-Card Uncut Panel:		4.00
Common Card:		1.00
1	Will Clark (Bat on shoulder.)	1.00
2	Will Clark (Closeup in stance.)	1.00
3	Will Clark (Open in stance.)	1.00
4	Will Clark (Bat behind neck.)	1.00

Mark McGwire

1990 marks the fourth year that A's slugger Mark McGwire was featured on a special four-card Mother's Cookies set. The photos for the cards were once again by Barry Colla. Four different posed shots of McGwire are showcased.

		NM/M
Complete Set (4):		6.00
Four-Card Uncut Panel:		7.50
Common Card:		2.00

1	Mark McGwire (Bat on shoulder.)	2.00
2	Mark McGwire (Leaning against bat rack.)	2.00
3	Mark McGwire (Glove in hand.)	2.00
4	Mark McGwire (On dugout step.)	2.00

Nolan Ryan

Unlike other special Mother's Cookies player sets, the Nolan Ryan cards feature "5000 K's" along with his name and team on the card fronts. The set honors the strikeout king's monumental feat. The cards follow the classic Mother's Cookies style.

		NM/M
Complete Set (4):		4.00
Four-Card Uncut Panel:		5.00
Common Card:		2.00
1	Nolan Ryan (Facing with ball in hand.)	2.00
2	Nolan Ryan (Standing in dugout.)	2.00
3	Nolan Ryan (Gripping ball behind back.)	2.00
4	Nolan Ryan (Sitting on dugout step.)	2.00

Matt Williams

Matt Williams made his Mother's Cookies single-player card set debut in 1990. Four posed shots of the Giants third baseman are showcased. Williams is featured twice in batting poses and twice as a fielder on the glossy, round-cornered 2-1/2" x 3-1/2" cards.

		NM/M
Complete Set (4):		2.50
Four-Card Uncut Panel:		2.50
Common Card:		.75
1	Matt Williams (Bat on shoulder.)	.75
2	Matt Williams (In batting stance.)	.75
3	Matt Williams (Glove in hand.)	.75
4	Matt Williams/Fldg	.75

1991 Mother's Cookies A's

The incomparable photography of Barry Colla captures the Oakland A's in their home-field environs for the 28 cards in this set. Glossy fronts feature borderless posed photos. The player's name and team appear in white in an upper corner. Backs have minimal biographical data, player position, uniform and card numbers and appropriate logos.

		NM/M
Complete Set (28):		12.00
Common Player:		.25
1	Tony LaRussa	.25
2	Mark McGwire	3.50
3	Terry Steinbach	.25
4	Rickey Henderson	1.50
5	Dave Stewart	.25
6	Jose Canseco	.75
7	Dennis Eckersley	1.00

8	Carney Lansford	.25
9	Bob Welch	.25
10	Walt Weiss	.25
11	Mike Moore	.25
12	Vance Law	.25
13	Rick Honeycutt	.25
14	Harold Baines	.25
15	Jamie Quirk	.25
16	Ernest Riles	.25
17	Willie Wilson	.25
18	Dave Henderson	.25
19	Kirk Dressendorfer	.25
20	Todd Burns	.25
21	Lance Blankenship	.25
22	Gene Nelson	.25
23	Eric Show	.25
24	Curt Young	.25
25	Mike Gallego	.25
26	Joe Klink	.25
27	Steve Chitren	.25
28	Coaches/Checklist (Rene Lacheman, Dave Duncan, Dave McKay, Tommie Reynolds, Art Kuysner, Reggie Jackson, Rick Burleson)	.25

Astros

This 28-card set was produced in the now-familiar Mother's Cookies card format. Glossy fronts feature rounded corners and full-bleed posed color photos (apparently taken at San Francisco's Candlestick Park, home base of photographer Barry Colla) with the player's name and team in white in an upper corner. Backs are printed in red and purple and include a few biographical details, along with cookie company and MLB logos, uniform and card numbers and a line for autographing.

		NM/M
Complete Set (28):		10.00
Common Player:		.25
1	Art Howe	.25
2	Steve Finley	.25
3	Pete Harnisch	.25
4	Mike Scott	.25
5	Craig Biggio	.50
6	Ken Caminiti	.25
7	Eric Yelding	.25
8	Jeff Bagwell	6.00
9	Jim Deshaies	.25
10	Mark Portugal	.25
11	Mark Davidson	.25
12	Jimmy Jones	.25
13	Luis Gonzalez	2.00
14	Karl Rhodes	.25
15	Curt Schilling	.25
16	Ken Oberkfell	.25
17	Mark McLemore	.25
18	David Rohde	.25
19	Rafael Ramirez	.25
20	Al Osuna	.25
21	Jim Corsi	.25
22	Carl Nichols	.25
23	Jim Clancy	.25
24	Dwayne Henry	.25
25	Casey Candaele	.25
26	Xavier Hernandez	.25
27	Darryl Kile	.25
28	Coaches/Checklist (CluckGalante, Rudy Jaramillo, Phil Garner, Bob Cluck, Ed Ott)	.25

Dodgers

Dodger Stadium is the background for Barry Colla's portraits of the Los Angeles manager, coaches and players appearing in this 28-card set. Standard-size cards with rounded corners feature borderless UV-coated fronts on which the only printing is the player's name and team in white in an upper corner. Backs are in red and purple and include a few biographical details, position, uniform and card numbers, a space for an autograph and the logos of the cookie company and MLB.

		NM/M
Complete Set (28):		7.50
Common Player:		.25
1	Tom Lasorda	.40
2	Darryl Strawberry	.25
3	Kal Daniels	.25
4	Mike Scioscia	.25
5	Eddie Murray	2.00
6	Brett Butler	.25
7	Juan Samuel	.25
8	Alfredo Griffin	.25
9	Tim Belcher	.25
10	Ramon Martinez	.25
11	Jose Gonzalez	.25
12	Orel Hershiser	.40
13	Bob Ojeda	.25
14	Chris Gwynn	.25
15	Jay Howell	.25
16	Gary Carter	2.00
17	Kevin Gross	.25
18	Lenny Harris	.25
19	Mike Hartley	.25
20	Mike Sharperson	.25
21	Mike Morgan	.25
22	John Candelaria	.25
23	Jeff Hamilton	.25
24	Jim Gott	.25
25	Barry Lyons	.25
26	Tim Crews	.25
27	Stan Javier	.25
28	Coaches/Checklist (Ron Perranoski, Bill Russell, Manny Mota, Joe Ferguson, Ben Hines, Joe Amalfitano, Mark Cresse)	.25

Giants

For the ninth consecutive year Mother's Cookies sponsored a promotional card set for the Giants. As in the beginning, the cards highlight the work of photographer Barry Colla with posed portraits of the personnel in Candlestick Park. Fronts of the round-cornered borderless cards are UV-coated and have the player's name and team printed in white in an upper corner. Backs are in red and purple and include cookie company and Major League Baseball logos along with a few biographical details and both uniform and card numbers.

		NM/M
Complete Set (28):		7.00
Common Player:		.25
1	Roger Craig	.25
2	Will Clark	.50
3	Steve Decker	.25
4	Kelly Downs	.25
5	Kevin Mitchell	.25
6	Willie McGee	.25
7	Buddy Black	.25
8	Dave Righetti	.25
9	Matt Williams	.50
10	Robby Thompson	.25
11	Mike LaCoss	.25
12	Terry Kennedy	.25
13	Mark Leonard	.25
14	Rick Reuschel	.25
15	Mike Felder	.25
16	Scott Garrelts	.25
17	Jose Uribe	.25
18	Greg Litton	.25
19	Dave Anderson	.25

20	Don Robinson	.25
21	Mike Kingery	.25
22	Trevor Wilson	.25
23	Kirt Manwaring	.25
24	Kevin Bass	.25
25	Jeff Brantley	.25
26	John Burkett	.25
27	Coaches (Norm Sherry, Wendell Kim, Bob Lillis, Dusty Baker, Bill Fahey)	.25
28	Trainers/Checklist (Mark Letendre, Greg Lynn)	.25

Rangers

The unusual venue of the players' locker room provides the backdrop for photos for this 28-card set sponsored by Mother's Cookies. Besides a look at the player's wardrobe, the full-bleed glossy front photos feature the player's name and position vertically along the left side. Backs have uniform and card numbers, some biographical data and logos of the cookie company and Major League Baseball.

		NM/M
Complete Set (28):		12.50
Common Player:		.25
1	Bobby Valentine	.25
2	Nolan Ryan	6.00
3	Ruben Sierra	.25
4	Juan Gonzalez	3.00
5	Steve Buechele	.25
6	Bobby Witt	.25
7	Geno Petralli	.25
8	Jeff Russell	.25
9	Rafael Palmeiro	2.00
10	Julio Franco	.25
11	Jack Daugherty	.25
12	Gary Pettis	.25
13	John Barfield	.25
14	Scott Chiamparino	.25
15	Kevin Reimer	.25
16	Rich Gossage	.25
17	Brian Downing	.25
18	Denny Walling	.25
19	Mike Jeffcoat	.25
20	Mike Stanley	.25
21	Kevin Brown	.25
22	Kenny Rogers	.25
23	Jeff Huson	.25
24	Mario Diaz	.25
25	Brad Arnsberg	.25
26	John Russell	.25
27	Gerald Alexander	.25
28	Coaches/Checklist (Orlando Gomez, Toby Harrah, Tom House, Davey Lopes, Dave Oliver, Tom Robson)	.25

Griffeys

This four-card set was packaged with Mother's Cookies sold in the Pacific Northwest. Each card features a borderless glossy posed photo on front. The traditional rounded corners of Mother's cards are found on the issue. Backs have a few stats and career notes.

	NM/M
Complete Set, Singles (4):	5.00

Complete Set, Uncut Strip:		5.00
Common Card:		1.00
1	Ken Griffey Jr.	3.00
2	Ken Griffey, Sr.	1.00
3	Ken Griffey Jr., Ken Griffey Sr. (Holding gloves.)	1.00
4	Ken Griffey Jr., Ken Griffey Sr. (Holding bats.)	1.50

Nolan Ryan 300 Wins

Mother's Cookies in 1991 created a four-card Nolan Ryan set honoring baseball's most recent 300-game winner. One card was included in specially marked packages of cookies. Card fronts have the traditional Mother's Cookies look: Barry Colla photography on full-bleed cards with rounded corners. Backs have a few statistics and career notes.

		NM/M
Complete Set (4):		2.00
Four-Card Uncut Panel:		2.00
Common Card:		.75
1	Nolan Ryan/Standing (Front view.)	.75
2	Nolan Ryan/Kneeling	.75
3	Nolan Ryan/Standing (Side view.)	.75
4	Nolan Ryan (Gripping "300" ball.)	.75

1992 Mother's Cookies A's

The commemorative patch marking the Oakland A's 25th season on the West Coast is visible on several of Barry Colla's photos in this 28-card issue. The traditional Mother's Cookies card format of 2-1/2" x 3-1/2", round-cornered cards with UV-coated borderless front photos is followed in this set. The player's name and team are in white in an upper corner. Backs have cookie company and Major League Baseball logos, along with the player's position, uniform and card numbers, space for an autograph and minimal biographical data. Back printing is in red and purple on white.

		NM/M
Complete Set (28):		7.50
Common Player:		.25
1	Tony LaRussa	.25
2	Mark McGwire	3.50
3	Terry Steinbach	.25
4	Rickey Henderson	1.50
5	Dave Stewart	.25
6	Jose Canseco	.75
7	Dennis Eckersley	1.00
8	Carney Lansford	.25
9	Bob Welch	.25
10	Walt Weiss	.25
11	Mike Moore	.25
12	Goose Gossage	.25
13	Rick Honeycutt	.25
14	Harold Baines	.25
15	Jamie Quirk	.25
16	Jeff Parrett	.25
17	Willie Wilson	.25

18	Dave Henderson	.25
19	Joe Slusarski	.25
20	Mike Bordick	.25
21	Lance Blankenship	.25
22	Gene Nelson	.25
23	Vince Horsman	.25
24	Ron Darling	.25
25	Randy Ready	.25
26	Scott Hemond	.25
27	Scott Brosius	.25
28	Coaches/Checklist (Tommie Reynolds, Dave Duncan, Doug Rader, Rene Lacheman, Art Kusnyer, Dave McKay)	.25

Astros

The Astrodome provides the backdrop for Barry Colla's photos of Astros personnel seen on this 28-card set sponsored by Mother's Cookies. Cards are in standard 2-1/2" x 3-1/2" and feature rounded corners. Glossy fronts are borderless and have no graphics except the player's name and team in an upper corner. Backs are printed in red and purple and have a few biographical details along with uniform and card numbers, the player's position, an autograph line and the logos of the cookie company and MLB.

		NM/M
Complete Set (28):		7.50
Common Player:		.25
1	Art Howe	.25
2	Steve Finley	.25
3	Pete Harnisch	.25
4	Pete Incaviglia	.25
5	Craig Biggio	.50
6	Ken Caminiti	.25
7	Eric Anthony	.25
8	Jeff Bagwell	4.00
9	Andujar Cedeno	.25
10	Mark Portugal	.25
11	Eddie Taubensee	.25
12	Jimmy Jones	.25
13	Joe Boever	.25
14	Benny Distefano	.25
15	Juan Guerrero	.25
16	Doug Jones	.25
17	Scott Servais	.25
18	Butch Henry	.25
19	Rafael Ramirez	.25
20	Al Osuna	.25
21	Rob Murphy	.25
22	Chris Jones	.25
23	Rob Mallicoat	.25
24	Darryl Kile	.25
25	Casey Candaele	.25
26	Xavier Hernandez	.25
27	Coaches (Bob Cluck, Matt Galante, Rudy Jaramillo, Ed Ott, Tom Spencer)	.25
28	Trainers / Checklist (Doc Ewell, Dennis Liborio, Dave Labossiere)	.25

Dodgers

A commemorative patch marking Dodger Stadium's 30th anniversary is featured on some of the Barry Colla photos seen on this 28-card set. Cards have the now-traditional round-corner, glossy-front borderless format with player name and team in white in an upper corner. Printed in red and purple, the backs have a few biographical details along with uniform and card numbers and appropriate logos.

		NM/M
Complete Set (28):		6.00
Common Player:		.25
1	Tom Lasorda	.35
2	Brett Butler	.25
3	Tom Candiotti	.25
4	Eric Davis	.25
5	Lenny Harris	.25
6	Orel Hershiser	.35
7	Ramon Martinez	.25
8	Jose Offerman	.25
9	Mike Scioscia	.25
10	Darryl Strawberry	.25
11	Todd Benzinger	.25
12	John Candelaria	.25
13	Tim Crews	.25
14	Kal Daniels	.25
15	Jim Gott	.25
16	Kevin Gross	.25
17	Dave Hansen	.25
18	Carlos Hernandez	.25
19	Jay Howell	.25
20	Stan Javier	.25
21	Eric Karros	.50
22	Roger McDowell	.25
23	Bob Ojeda	.25
24	Juan Samuel	.25
25	Mike Sharperson	.25
26	Mitch Webster	.25
27	Steve Wilson	.25
28	Coaches/Checklist (Joe Amalfitano, Mark Cresse, Joe Ferguson, Ben Hines, Manny Mota, Ron Perranoski, Ron Roenicke)	.25

Giants

In 1983 Mother's Cookies re-entered the baseball card world with a set of S.F. Giants cards. In 1992, the company sponsored its 10th consecutive Giants team issue. As in the '83 set, the cards feature the photography of Barry Colla. In 2-1/2" x 3-1/2" size with rounded corners and UV-coating on the borderless fronts, the cards continue the format used since 1984. Backs are also in the familiar style, with a bit of biographical data and appropriate logos.

		NM/M
Complete Set (28):		7.50
Common Player:		.25
1	Roger Craig	.25
2	Will Clark	.50
3	Bill Swift	.25
4	Royce Clayton	.25
5	John Burkett	.25
6	Willie McGee	.25
7	Buddy Black	.25
8	Dave Righetti	.25
9	Matt Williams	.50
10	Robby Thompson	.25
11	Darren Lewis	.25
12	Mike Jackson	.25
13	Mark Leonard	.25
14	Rod Beck	.25
15	Mike Felder	.25
16	Bryan Hickerson	.25
17	Jose Uribe	.25
18	Greg Litton	.25
19	Cory Snyder	.25
20	Jim McNamara	.25
21	Kelly Downs	.25
22	Trevor Wilson	.25
23	Kirt Manwaring	.25
24	Kevin Bass	.25
25	Jeff Brantley	.25
26	Dave Burba	.25
27	Chris James	.25
28	Coaches/Checklist (Carlos Alfonso, Dusty Baker, Bob Brenly, Wendell Kim, Bob Lillis)	.25

Mariners

After a one-year absence from the Mother's Cookies lineup, the M's returned in 1992 with a set. Standard-size cards have rounded corners and UV-coated fronts. The only graphics appearing on the borderless fronts are the player and team name in white in an upper corner. Backs are printed in red and purple and have basic biographical data, uniform and card numbers, space for an autograph and appropriate sponsor and licensor logos.

		NM/M
Complete Set (28):		12.50
Common Player:		.25
1	Bill Plummer	.25
2	Ken Griffey Jr.	4.00
3	Harold Reynolds	.25
4	Kevin Mitchell	.25
5	David Valle	.25
6	Jay Buhner	.40
7	Erik Hanson	.25
8	Pete O'Brien	.25
9	Henry Cotto	.25
10	Mike Schooler	.25
11	Tino Martinez	1.00
12	Dennis Powell	.25
13	Randy Johnson	2.00
14	Dave Cochrane	.25
15	Greg Briley	.25
16	Omar Vizquel	.40
17	Dave Fleming	.25
18	Matt Sinatro	.25
19	Jeff Nelson	.25
20	Edgar Martinez	.25
21	Calvin Jones	.25
22	Russ Swan	.25
23	Jim Acker	.25
24	Jeff Schaffer	.25
25	Clay Parker	.25
26	Brian Holman	.25
27	Coaches (Marty Martinez, Gene Clines, Roger Hansen, Dan Warthen, Russ Nixon, Rusty Kuntz)	.25
28	Mascot/Checklist	.25

Padres

The Padres ended a six-year hiatus when they re-appeared in the Mother's Cookies lineup for 1992. The 28-card set follows the traditional Mother's format: 2-1/2" x 3-1/2" cards with rounded corners, glossy borderless front photos and the player and team name in white in an upper corner. Backs have appropriate logos, uniform and card numbers, player data and room for an autograph, all printed in red and purple.

		NM/M
Complete Set (28):		10.00
Common Player:		.25
1	Greg Riddoch	.25
2	Greg Harris	.25
3	Gary Sheffield	1.00
4	Fred McGriff	.40
5	Kurt Stillwell	.25
6	Benito Santiago	.25
7	Tony Gwynn	4.00
8	Tony Fernandez	.25

9	Jerald Clark	.25
10	Dave Eiland	.25
11	Randy Myers	.25
12	Oscar Azocar	.25
13	Dann Bilardello	.25
14	Jose Melendez	.25
15	Darrin Jackson	.25
16	Andy Benes	.25
17	Tim Teufel	.25
18	Jeremy Hernandez	.25
19	Kevin Ward	.25
20	Bruce Hurst	.25
21	Larry Andersen	.25
22	Rich Rodriguez	.25
23	Pat Clements	.25
24	Craig Lefferts	.25
25	Craig Shipley	.25
26	Mike Maddux	.25
27	Coaches (Bruce Kimm, Rob Picciolo, Merv Rettenmund, Mike Roarke, Jim Snyder)	.25
28	Team Logo/Checklist	.25

Rangers

The clubhouse wall provides the universal backdrop for the posed photos in this 28-card set. Standard-size cards have a high-gloss borderless front photo with rounded corners and the player and team name in white in an upper corner. Backs are in red and purple and have a few player biographical details along with uniform and card numbers, space for an autograph and the logos of the sponsor and licensor.

		NM/M
Complete Set (28):		15.00
Common Player:		.25
1	Bobby Valentine	.25
2	Nolan Ryan	5.00
3	Ruben Sierra	.25
4	Juan Gonzalez	2.00
5	Ivan Rodriguez	4.00
6	Bobby Witt	.25
7	Geno Petralli	.25
8	Jeff Russell	.25
9	Rafael Palmeiro	1.50
10	Julio Franco	.25
11	Jack Daugherty	.25
12	Dickie Thon	.25
13	Floyd Bannister	.25
14	Scott Chiamparino	.25
15	Kevin Reimer	.25
16	Jeff Robinson	.25
17	Brian Downing	.25
18	Brian Bohanon	.25
19	Jose Guzman	.25
20	Terry Mathews	.25
21	Kevin Brown	.25
22	Kenny Rogers	.25
23	Jeff Huson	.25
24	Monty Fariss	.25
25	Al Newman	.25
26	Dean Palmer	.25
27	John Cangelosi	.25
28	Coaches/Checklist (Ray Burris, Orlando Gomez, Toby Harrah, Tom House, Dave Oliver, Tom Robson)	.25

Jeff Bagwell

The set consists of four standard-size cards with a full-bleed color photo on the fronts of the cards and rounded corners. Bagwell's name appears horizontally in white on the front of the card and the backs are printed in purple and red. Along with the Major League merchandise logo on the bottom of the card there is an area for the player's autograph.

		NM/M
Complete Set (4):		9.00
Four-Card Uncut Panel:		10.00
Common Card:		2.50
1	Jeff Bagwell (Head and shoulders.)	2.50
2	Jeff Bagwell (Bat on shoulder.)	2.50
3	Jeff Bagwell (Waist-up.)	2.50
4	Jeff Bagwell (Ball in glove.)	2.50

Chuck Knoblauch

American League 1991 Rookie of the Year Chuck Knoblauch is featured in this four-card set. Similar in format to other Mother's cards, the glossy fronts have rounded corners and feature full-bleed color photos. The red and purple backs have statistical and biographical data along with appropriate logos.

		NM/M
Complete Set (4):		4.00
Common Card:		1.00
1	Chuck Knoblauch (Bat on shoulder.)	1.00
2	Chuck Knoblauch (Head and shoulders.)	1.00
3	Chuck Knoblauch (Waist-up.)	1.00
4	Chuck Knoblauch/Fldg	1.00

Nolan Ryan 7 No-Hitters

Mother's Cookie Co. produced an eight-card set in 1992 commemorating Nolan Ryan's seven no-hitters. Cards were found in specially marked packages of Mother's Cookies. The company also made available uncut sheets of the eight cards through the mail. Fronts feature photos contemporary with Ryan's no-hitters in a borderless, round-cornered format with glossy surface. "Nolan Ryan/7 No-Hitters" appears in white vertically in the upper-left corner. Backs are printed in red and purple and include a bit of biographical data along with details of each no-hitter. The eighth card in the set offers room to write in information about a future no-hitter which never materialized prior to Ryan's retirement following the 1993 season.

	NM/M
Complete Set (8):	6.00
Eight-Card Uncut Panel:	6.00

		NM/M
Common Card:		1.00
1	Nolan Ryan/Portrait/Angels	1.00
2	Nolan Ryan/Ptchg/Angels	1.00
3	Nolan Ryan/Waving/Angels	1.00
4	Nolan Ryan/Angels (Holding four "0" balls.)	1.00
5	Nolan Ryan/Astros	1.00
6	Nolan Ryan/Pitching/Rangers	1.00
7	Nolan Ryan/Pitching/Rangers	1.00
8	Nolan Ryan/Rangers (Palms up.)	1.00

1993 Mother's Cookies Angels

In its 11th year of renewed baseball card production, Mother's Cookies sponsored seven major league teams including, for the first time, the California Angels. At special promotional games, youngsters entering the ballpark were given packs of 28 cards. Each of the paper envelopes contained 20 different player cards and eight cards of another player. Instructions on the envelope encouraged trading to complete a set of 28. All of the team sets were identical in format. Cards measure the standard 2-1/2" x 3-1/2" with rounded corners. Fronts feature borderless posed photos, the work of photographer Barry Colla. The only graphic elements on the front are the player's name and team in white, generally in an upper corner. In 1993 the Mother's cards featured a somewhat less glossy front finish than in previous years. Backs are printed in red and purple. Data includes the player's position, uniform and card numbers, a few biographical bits, a "How Obtained" statement and a space for an autograph, along with the logos of the cookie company and Major League Baseball.

		NM/M
Complete Set (28):		9.00
Common Player:		.25
1	Buck Rodgers	.25
2	Gary DiSarcina	.25
3	Chuck Finley	.25
4	J.T. Snow	.50
5	Gary Gaetti	.25
6	Chili Davis	.25
7	Tim Salmon	2.50
8	Mark Langston	.25
9	Scott Sanderson	.25
10	John Orton	.25
11	Julio Valera	.25
12	Chad Curtis	.25
13	Kelly Gruber	.25
14	Rene Gonzalez	.25
15	Luis Polonia	.25
16	Greg Myers	.25
17	Gene Nelson	.25
18	Torey Lovullo	.25
19	Scott Lewis	.25
20	Chuck Crim	.25
21	John Farrell	.25
22	Steve Frey	.25
23	Stan Javier	.25
24	Ken Patterson	.25
25	Ron Tingley	.25
26	Damion Easley	.25
27	Joe Grahe	.25
28	Coaches/Checklist (Jimmie Reese, Rod Carew, Bobby Knoop, Chuck Hernandez, Ken Macha, John Wathan, Rick Turner)	.25

A's

	NM/M
Complete Set (28):	6.00
Common Player:	.25
1 Tony LaRussa	.25

2	Mark McGwire	2.00
3	Terry Steinbach	.25
4	Dennis Eckersley	.75
5	Ruben Sierra	.25
6	Rickey Henderson	1.00
7	Mike Bordick	.25
8	Rick Honeycutt	.25
9	Dave Henderson	.25
10	Bob Welch	.25
11	Dale Sveum	.25
12	Ron Darling	.25
13	Jerry Browne	.25
14	Bobby Witt	.25
15	Troy Neel	.25
16	Goose Gossage	.25
17	Brent Gates	.25
18	Storm Davis	.25
19	Scott Hemond	.25
20	Kelly Downs	.25
21	Kevin Seitzer	.25
22	Lance Blankenship	.25
23	Mike Mohler	.25
24	Edwin Nunez	.25
25	Joe Boever	.25
26	Shawn Hillegas	.25
27	Coaches (Dave Duncan, Art Kusnyer, Greg Luzinski, Dave McKay, Tommie Reynolds)	.25
28	Checklist (Frank Ciensczyk (equipment manager))	.25

Astros

		NM/M
Complete Set (28):		9.00
Common Player:		.25
1	Art Howe	.25
2	Steve Finley	.25
3	Pete Harnisch	.25
4	Craig Biggio	.50
5	Doug Drabek	.25
6	Scott Servais	.25
7	Jeff Bagwell	2.50
8	Eric Anthony	.25
9	Ken Caminiti	.25
10	Andujar Cedeno	.25
11	Mark Portugal	.25
12	Jose Uribe	.25
13	Rick Parker	.25
14	Doug Jones	.25
15	Luis Gonzalez	.50
16	Kevin Bass	.25
17	Greg Swindell	.25
18	Eddie Taubensee	.25
19	Darryl Kile	.25
20	Brian Williams	.25
21	Chris James	.25
22	Chris Donnels	.25
23	Xavier Hernandez	.25
24	Casey Candaele	.25
25	Eric Bell	.25
26	Mark Grant	.25
27	Tom Edens	.25
28	Coaches/Checklist (Bill Bowman, Bob Cluck, Matt Galante, Rudy Jaramillo, Ed Ott, Tom Spencer)	.25

Dodgers

	NM/M
Complete Set (28):	20.00
Common Player:	.25
1 Tommy Lasorda	.35
2 Eric Karros	.25
3 Brett Butler	.25
4 Mike Piazza	9.00
5 Jose Offerman	.25
6 Tim Wallach	.25

7	Eric Davis	.25
8	Darryl Strawberry	.25
9	Jody Reed	.25
10	Orel Hershiser	.35
11	Tom Candiotti	.25
12	Ramon Martinez	.25
13	Lenny Harris	.25
14	Mike Sharperson	.25
15	Omar Daal	.25
16	Pedro Martinez	6.00
17	Jim Gott	.25
18	Carlos Hernandez	.25
19	Kevin Gross	.25
20	Cory Snyder	.25
21	Todd Worrell	.25
22	Mitch Webster	.25
23	Steve Wilson	.25
24	Dave Hansen	.25
25	Roger McDowell	.25
26	Pedro Astacio	.25
27	Rick Trlicek	.25
28	Coaches/Checklist (Joe Amalfitano, Mark Cresse, Joe Ferguson, Ben Hines, Manny Mota, Ron Perranoski, Ron Roenicke)	.25

Giants

		NM/M
Complete Set (28):		8.00
Common Player:		.25
1	Dusty Baker	.40
2	Will Clark	.50
3	Matt Williams	.50
4	Barry Bonds	7.50
5	Bill Swift	.25
6	Royce Clayton	.25
7	John Burkett	.25
8	Willie McGee	.25
9	Kirt Manwaring	.25
10	Dave Righetti	.25
11	Todd Benzinger	.25
12	Rod Beck	.25
13	Darren Lewis	.25
14	Robby Thompson	.25
15	Mark Carreon	.25
16	Dave Martinez	.25
17	Jeff Brantley	.25
18	Dave Burba	.25
19	Mike Benjamin	.25
20	Mike Jackson	.25
21	Craig Colbert	.25
22	Bud Black	.25
23	Trevor Wilson	.25
24	Kevin Rogers	.25
25	Jeff Reed	.25
26	Bryan Hickerson	.25
27	Gino Minutelli	.25
28	Coaches / Checklist (Bobby Bonds, Bob Brenly, Wendell Kim, Bob Lillis, Dick Pole, Denny Sommers)	.25

Mariners

		NM/M
Complete Set (28):		10.00
Common Player:		.25
1	Lou Piniella	.25
2	Dave Fleming	.25
3	Pete O'Brien	.25
4	Ken Griffey Jr.	6.00
5	Henry Cotto	.25
6	Jay Buhner	.25
7	David Valle	.25
8	Dwayne Henry	.25
9	Mike Felder	.25
10	Norm Charlton	.25
11	Edgar Martinez	.25
12	Erik Hanson	.25
13	Mike Blowers	.25
14	Omar Vizquel	.25
15	Randy Johnson	2.00
16	Russ Swan	.25
17	Tino Martinez	.25
18	Rich DeLucia	.25
19	Jeff Nelson	.25
20	Chris Bosio	.25
21	Tim Leary	.25
22	Mackey Sasser	.25
23	Dennis Powell	.25
24	Mike Hampton	.25
25	Fernando Vina	.25
26	John Cummings	.25
27	Rich Amaral	.25
28	Coaches/Checklist (Sammy Ellis, John McLaren, Ken Griffey Sr., Sam Perlozzo, Sam Mejias, Lee Elia)	.25

Padres

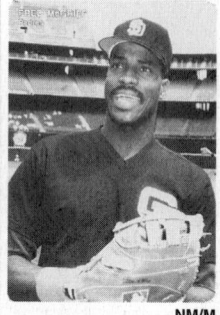

		NM/M
Complete Set (28):		10.00
Common Player:		.25
1	Jim Riggleman	.25
2	Gary Sheffield	1.00
3	Tony Gwynn	6.00
4	Fred McGriff	.25
5	Greg Harris	.25
6	Tim Teufel	.25
7	Dave Eiland	.25
8	Phil Plantier	.25
9	Bruce Hurst	.25
10	Ricky Gutierrez	.25
11	Rich Rodriguez	.25
12	Derek Bell	.25
13	Bob Geren	.25
14	Andy Benes	.25
15	Darrell Sherman	.25
16	Frank Seminara	.25
17	Guillermo Velasquez	.25
18	Gene Harris	.25
19	Dan Walters	.25
20	Craig Shipley	.25
21	Phil Clark	.25
22	Jeff Gardner	.25
23	Mike Scioscia	.25
24	Wally Whitehurst	.25
25	Roger Mason	.25
26	Kerry Taylor	.25
27	Tim Scott	.25
28	Coaches/Checklist (Dave Bialas, Bruce Bochy, Rob Picciolo, Dan Radison, Merv Rettenmund, Mike Roarke)	.25

Nolan Ryan Farewell

Nolan Ryan's final 10 major league seasons with the Astros and Rangers are captured in this set. Cards are in standard Mother's Cookies format: 2-1/2" x 3-1/2" with rounded corners, borderless front photos and UV-coated. Each card has a "Nolan Ryan Farewell Set" diamond logo in an upper corner. Backs are printed in red and purple and have a few biographical details along with the year the picture on front was created. Each card has stats for one year from 1984-1992 or cumulative All-Star stats along with Major League totals. Cards were available either cello-wrapped singly in cookie packages or as a complete set via a mail-in offer.

		NM/M
Complete Set (10):		6.00
Uncut Sheet (10):		6.00
Common Card:		.75
1	Nolan Ryan (1984 Astros)	.75
2	Nolan Ryan (1985 Astros)	.75
3	Nolan Ryan (1986 Astros)	.75
4	Nolan Ryan (1987 Astros)	.75
5	Nolan Ryan (1988 Astros)	.75
6	Nolan Ryan (1989 Rangers)	.75
7	Nolan Ryan (1990 Rangers)	.75
8	Nolan Ryan (1991 Rangers)	.75
9	Nolan Ryan (1992 Rangers)	.75
10	Nolan Ryan (All-Star Stats)	.75

1994 Mother's Cookies Angels

Originally scheduled to be given away at a promotional date during the 1994 season, these cards were caught in the strike and not distributed until the March 30-April 1 home-and-home series between the replacement players of the Angels and those of the Oakland A's. The cards were distributed in a paper envelope containing 20 different cards and eight cards of a 21st player. The idea was to trade to complete a set. The 2-1/2" x 3-1/2" cards have rounded corners and feature borderless color photos on front with the player's name and team in one of the corners. Backs are printed in red and purple and include some biographical data, uniform and card numbers, logos of Mother's Cookies and Major League Baseball and a line for an autograph.

		NM/M
Complete Set (28):		12.50
Common Player:		.25
1	Marcel Lachemann	.25
2	Mark Langston	.25
3	J.T. Snow	.25
4	Chad Curtis	.25
5	Tim Salmon	1.00
6	Gary DiSarcina	.25
7	Bo Jackson	2.50
8	Dwight Smith	.25
9	Chuck Finley	.25
10	Rod Correia	.25
11	Spike Owen	.25
12	Harold Reynolds	.25
13	Chris Turner	.25
14	Chili Davis	.25
15	Bob Patterson	.25
16	Jim Edmonds	4.00
17	Joe Magrane	.25
18	Craig Lefferts	.25
19	Scott Lewis	.25
20	Rex Hudler	.25
21	Mike Butcher	.25
22	Brian Anderson	.25
23	Greg Myers	.25
24	Mark Leiter	.25
25	Joe Grahe	.25
26	Jorge Fabregas	.25
27	John Dopson	.25
28	Angels Coaches/Checklist (Chuck Hernandez, Ken Macha, Bobby Knoop, Joe Maddon, Rod Carew, Max Oliveras)	.25

A's

Departing little from previous years, this 28-card set of the players, manager and coaches of the Oakland A's features the inimitable photography of Barry Colla. Cards are 2-1/2" x 3-1/2" with rounded corners and borderless photos. The player's name and team are in white in one of the corners. Backs

MARK McGWIRE Athletics

are printed in red and purple and feature a few biographical bits, a uniform number and card number, a line for an autograph and the logos of Mother's Cookies and Major League Baseball. Originally intended to be given away at a game during the strike-shortened 1994 season, the cards were instead given out at the March 30-April 1 home-and-home exhibition series between the A's and the California Angels. To promote old-fashioned card trading, each package of cards contained 20 different cards, plus eight cards of a 21st player. Considerable trading was thus required to complete a set.

		NM/M
Complete Set (28):		12.00
Common Player:		.25
1	Tony LaRussa	.25
2	Mark McGwire	5.00
3	Terry Steinbach	.25
4	Dennis Eckersley	1.50
5	Mike Bordick	.25
6	Rickey Henderson	2.00
7	Ruben Sierra	.25
8	Stan Javier	.25
9	Todd Van Poppel	.25
10	Bob Welch	.25
11	Miguel Jiminez	.25
12	Steve Karsay	.25
13	Geronimo Berroa	.25
14	Bobby Witt	.25
15	Troy Neel	.25
16	Ron Darling	.25
17	Scott Hemond	.25
18	Steve Ontiveros	.25
19	Mike Aldrete	.25
20	Carlos Reyes	.25
21	Brent Gates	.25
22	Mark Acre	.25
23	Eric Helfand	.25
24	Vince Horsman	.25
25	Bill Taylor	.25
26	Scott Brosius	.25
27	John Briscoe	.25
28	Athletics' Coaches/Checklist (Dave Duncan, Jim Lefebvre, Carney Lansford, Tommie Reynolds, Art Kusnyer, Dave McKay)	.25

Astros

JEFF BAGWELL Astros

Distributed at an early 1995 game because the 1994 strike wiped out the planned promotional date, these cards were handed out in packages that contained 20 different cards and eight cards of a 21st player. The idea was to trade the duplicates to form a team set. The round-cornered 2-1/2" x 3-1/2" cards have a borderless color photo on front. Backs are printed in red and purple and include a few biographical notes, uniform and card numbers, a line for an autograph and logos of Mother's Cookies and Major League Baseball.

		NM/M
Complete Set (28):		10.00
Common Player:		.25
1	Terry Collins	.25
2	Mitch Williams	.25
3	Jeff Bagwell	2.50
4	Luis Gonzalez	.50
5	Craig Biggio	.50
6	Darryl Kile	.25
7	Ken Caminiti	.25
8	Steve Finley	.25
9	Pete Harnisch	.25
10	Sid Bream	.25
11	Mike Felder	.25
12	Tom Edens	.25
13	James Mouton	.25
14	Doug Drabek	.25
15	Greg Swindell	.25
16	Chris Donnels	.25
17	John Hudek	.25
18	Andujar Cedeno	.25
19	Scott Servais	.25
20	Todd Jones	.25
21	Kevin Bass	.25
22	Shane Reynolds	.25
23	Brian Williams	.25
24	Tony Eusebio	.25
25	Mike Hampton	.25
26	Andy Stankiewicz	.25
27	Astros Coaches (Ben Hines, Julio Linares, Matt Galante, Steve Henderson, Mel Stottlemyre, Sr.)	.25
28	Astros Trainers/Checklist (Dave Labossiere, Dennis Liborio, Rex Jones)	.25

Dodgers

MIKE PIAZZA NL 1993 R.O.Y.

Plans to distribute this set were postponed when the players' strike wiped out the latter part of the 1994 season. Instead, the cards were distributed at an early 1995 promotional contest. Each package of 28 cards contained 20 different cards and eight cards of a 21st player. This required extensive trading to complete a team set. Cards feature borderless color photos on a 2-1/2" x 3-1/2" round-cornered format. Backs are printed in red and purple and include uniform and card numbers, biographical data, an autograph line and the logos of Mother's Cookies and Major League Baseball.

		NM/M
Complete Set (28):		9.00
Common Player:		.25
1	Tommy Lasorda	.25
2	Mike Piazza	5.00
3	Delino DeShields	.25
4	Eric Karros	.25
5	Jose Offerman	.25
6	Brett Butler	.25
7	Orel Hershiser	.35
8	Henry Rodriguez	.25
9	Raul Mondesi	.25
10	Tim Wallach	.25
11	Ramon Martinez	.25
12	Mitch Webster	.25
13	Todd Worrell	.25
14	Jeff Treadway	.25
15	Tom Candiotti	.25
16	Pedro Astacio	.25
17	Chris Gwynn	.25
18	Jim Gott	.25
19	Omar Daal	.25
20	Cory Snyder	.25
21	Kevin Gross	.25
22	Dave Hansen	.25
23	Al Osuna	.25
24	Darren Dreifort	.25
25	Roger McDowell	.25
26	Carlos Hernandez	.25
27	Gary Wayne	.25
28	Dodgers Coaches/Checklist (Ron Perranoski, Joe Amalfitano, Reggie Smith, Joe Ferguson, Bill Russell, Mark Cresse)	.25

Giants

BARRY BONDS Giants

Unable to distribute these cards in 1994 because the strike wiped out a promotional date, the Giants gave away the cards at an early 1995 game. Cards were distributed in packages containing 20 different players and eight cards of a 21st player; requiring extensive trading to complete a team set. The 2-1/2" x 3-1/2" round-cornered cards feature borderless color photos on front. Backs have red and purple printing and include a few biographical notes, card and uniform numbers, Mother's Cookies and Major League Baseball logos and a line for an autograph.

		NM/M
Complete Set (28):		15.00
Common Player:		.25
1	Dusty Baker	.40
2	Robby Thompson	.25
3	Barry Bonds	7.50
4	Royce Clayton	.25
5	John Burkett	.25
6	Bill Swift	.25
7	Matt Williams	.50
8	Rod Beck	.25
9	Steve Scarsone	.25
10	Mark Portugal	.25
11	John Patterson	.25
12	Darren Lewis	.25
13	Kirt Manwaring	.25
14	Salomon Torres	.25
15	Willie McGee	.25
16	Dave Martinez	.25
17	Darryl Strawberry	.25
18	Steve Frey	.25
19	Rich Monteleone	.25
20	Todd Benzinger	.25
21	Jeff Reed	.25
22	Mike Benjamin	.25
23	Mike Jackson	.25
24	Pat Gomez	.25
25	Dave Burba	.25
26	Bryan Hickerson	.25
27	Mark Carreon	.25
28	Giants Coaches/Checklist (Bobby Bonds, Bob Lillis, Wendell Kim, Bob Brenly, Dick Pole, Denny Sommers)	.25

Mariners

LOU PINIELLA Mariners

When the players struck on Aug. 12, 1994, it killed the Mariners' plans to distribute these cards at a promotional game. Instead, packages of the cards were given away during the winter as players and management toured the Northwest drumming up fan interest. Cards were issued in a group containing 20 different players and eight cards of a 21st player. It was necessary to trade the duplicates to finish a team set. Cards are 2-1/2" x 3-1/2" with round corners and feature borderless color photos on front. Backs are in red and purple and include biographical bits, uniform and card numbers and the logos of Mother's Cookies and Major League Baseball.

		NM/M
Complete Set (28):		10.00
Common Player:		.25
1	Lou Piniella	.25
2	Randy Johnson	2.00
3	Eric Anthony	.25
4	Ken Griffey Jr.	5.00
5	Felix Fermin	.25
6	Jay Buhner	.25
7	Chris Bosio	.25
8	Reggie Jefferson	.25
9	Greg Hibbard	.25
10	Dave Fleming	.25
11	Rich Amaral	.25
12	Rich Gossage	.25
13	Edgar Martinez	.25
14	Bobby Ayala	.25
15	Darren Bragg	.25
16	Tino Martinez	.25
17	Mike Blowers	.25
18	John Cummings	.25
19	Keith Mitchell	.25
20	Bill Haselman	.25
21	Greg Pirkl	.25
22	Mackey Sasser	.25
23	Tim Davis	.25
24	Dan Wilson	.25
25	Jeff Nelson	.25
26	Kevin King	.25
28	Torey Lovullo	.25
	Mariners Coaches/Checklist (Sam Perlozzo, Lee Elia, Sammy Ellis, John McLaren, Sam Mejias)	.25

Padres

The cancellation of the latter part of the 1994 season by the players' strike wiped out a planned promotional date on which these cards were to have been given out. Instead, the cards were distributed at an early 1995 game. Packages were given out consisting of 20 different cards plus eight cards of a 21st player, which could be traded to complete a team set. Cards are 2-1/2" x 3-1/2" with rounded corners and a borderless color photo on front. Backs are printed in red and purple and have a few biographical notes, card and uniform numbers, an autograph line and logos of Mother's Cookies and Major League Baseball.

		NM/M
Complete Set (28):		9.00
Common Player:		.25
1	Jim Riggleman	.25
2	Tony Gwynn	5.00
3	Andy Benes	.25
4	Bip Roberts	.25
5	Phil Clark	.25
6	Wally Whitehurst	.25
7	Archi Cianfrocco	.25
8	Derek Bell	.25
9	Ricky Gutierrez	.25
10	Mark Davis	.25
11	Phil Plantier	.25
12	Brian Johnson	.25
13	Billy Bean	.25
14	Craig Shipley	.25
15	Tim Hyers	.25
16	Gene Harris	.25
17	Scott Sanders	.25
18	A.J. Sager	.25
19	Keith Lockhart	.25
20	Tim Mauser	.25
21	Andy Ashby	.25
22	Brad Ausmus	.25
23	Trevor Hoffman	.25
24	Luis Lopez	.25
25	Doug Brocail	.25
26	Dave Staton	.25
27	Pedro A. Martinez	.25
28	Padres Coaches/Checklist (Sonny Siebert, Rob Picciolo, Dave Bialas, Dan Radison, Merv Rettenmund, Bruce Bochy)	.25

Rookies of the Year

In 1994 Mother's Cookies issued three different four-card sets of the 1993 Rookies of the Year. Cards of Mike Piazza of the Dodgers and Tim Salmon of California were available, one per package, in each of six varieties of Mother's Big Cookies. There was also a four-card set featuring both players on each of the four cards. These cards were packaged one per bag of Mother's Major League Double Headers. The specially marked packages with the trading cards inside also carried details about Mother's Commemorative Uncut Strips of each of the three different sets in a mail-in offer. In addition, the company created two chase cards designed to put the real cookie fans to the test. The "One in a Thousand - Rookies of the Year" foil trading cards were inserted one in every 1,000 packages, with either blue or red foil, and fewer than 10,000 of the foil cards produced.

		NM/M
Complete Set (12):		8.00
Four-Card Uncut Piazza Panel:		6.00
Four-Card Uncut Salmon Panel:		2.00
Four-Card Uncut Piazza-Salmon Panel:		4.00
Common Player:		.50
1	Tim Salmon (Bat on shoulder.)	.50
2	Tim Salmon (Batting stance.)	.50
3	Tim Salmon (Dugout pose.)	.50
4	Tim Salmon/Fldg	.50
5	Mike Piazza (Bat on shoulder.)	1.50
6	Mike Piazza (Batting stance.)	1.50
7	Mike Piazza (Dugout pose.)	1.50
8	Mike Piazza/Catching	1.50
9	Tim Salmon, Mike Piazza (Bats on shoulders.)	.50
10	Tim Salmon, Mike Piazza (Arm around shoulder.)	.50
11	Tim Salmon, Mike Piazza (Shaking hands.)	.50
12	Tim Salmon, Mike Piazza (Back to back.)	.50
BF	Tim Salmon, Mike Piazza (Shaking hands; 1 in 1,000 blue foil.)	9.00
RF	Tim Salmon, Mike Piazza/Kneeling (1 in 1,000 red foil.)	9.00

Nolan Ryan Final Farewell

A virtual reprint of the 1993 Farewell Set, the 1994 version uses the same photos and, except for card #10, presents the same information on the card backs. Card #10 in the 1994 set offers 1993 season and final Major League stats instead of the All-Star stats on the 1993 version. Some minor differ-

ences in photo cropping between the two sets will be noticed, as well as the fact that many of the back elements which had been printed in red on the 1993 cards are in purple on the 1994 cards, and vice versa. Cards can be distinguished by the presence of a 1993 or 1994 copyright line on the back.

		NM/M
Complete Set (10):		6.00
10-Card Uncut Panel:		10.00
Common Card:		1.00
1	Nolan Ryan (1984 Astros)	1.00
2	Nolan Ryan (1985 Astros)	1.00
3	Nolan Ryan (1986 Astros)	1.00
4	Nolan Ryan (1987 Astros)	1.00
5	Nolan Ryan (1988 Astros)	1.00
6	Nolan Ryan (1989 Rangers)	1.00
7	Nolan Ryan (1990 Rangers)	1.00
8	Nolan Ryan (1991 Rangers)	1.00
9	Nolan Ryan (1992 Rangers)	1.00
10	Nolan Ryan (1993 Rangers)	1.00

1995 Mother's Cookies Angels

Seven teams in the Western U.S. participated in Mother's Cookies 13th season of sponsoring team sets. Virtually identical in format to previous years, the 2-1/2" x 3-1/2" round-cornered cards were given away at promotional dates. To promote old-fashioned card trading, the cards were distributed in a paper envelope containing 20 different cards, plus eight cards of a 21st player. Considerable trading was thus required to complete a team set. As in previous years, Barry Colla's superb photos capture the players, manager and coaches of each team in a 28-card set. Backs are again printed in red and purple with a few bits of biographical data, uniform and card numbers and space for an autograph, along with the sponsor's logo.

		NM/M
Complete Set (28):		9.00
Common Player:		.25
1	Marcel Lachemann	.25
2	Mark Langston	.25
3	J.T. Snow	.25
4	Tim Salmon	1.50
5	Chili Davis	.25
6	Gary DiSarcina	.25
7	Tony Phillips	.25
8	Jim Edmonds	2.50
9	Chuck Finley	.25
10	Mark Dalesandro	.25
11	Greg Myers	.25
12	Spike Owen	.25
13	Lee Smith	.25
14	Eduardo Perez	.25
15	Bob Patterson	.25
16	Mitch Williams	.25
17	Garret Anderson	.50
18	Mike Bielecki	.25
19	Shawn Boskie	.25
20	Damion Easley	.25
21	Mike Butcher	.25
22	Brian Anderson	.25
23	Andy Allanson	.25
24	Scott Sanderson	.25
25	Troy Percival	.25
26	Rex Hudler	.25
27	Mike James	.25
28	Coaches/checklist (Mick Billmeyer, Rick Burleson, Rod Carew,

Chuck Hernandez, Bobby Knoop, Bill Lachemann, Joe Maddon) .25

A's

		NM/M
Complete Set (29):		7.50
Common Player:		.25
1	Tony LaRussa	.25
2	Mark McGwire	2.50
3	Terry Steinbach	.25
4	Dennis Eckersley	.75
5	Rickey Henderson	1.00
6	Ron Darling	.25
7	Ruben Sierra	.25
8	Mike Aldrete	.25
9	Stan Javier	.25
10	Mike Bordick	.25
11	Dave Stewart	.25
12	Geronimo Berroa	.25
13	Todd Van Poppel	.25
14	Todd Stottlemyre	.25
15	Eric Helfand	.25
16	Dave Leiper	.25
17	Rick Honeycutt	.25
18	Steve Ontiveros	.25
19	Mike Gallego	.25
20	Carlos Reyes	.25
21	Brent Gates	.25
22	Craig Paquette	.25
23	Mike Harkey	.25
24	Andy Tomberlin	.25
25	Jim Corsi	.25
26	Mark Acre	.25
27	Scott Brosius	.25
28	Coaches/Checklist (Dave Duncan, Art Kusnyer, Carney Lansford, Jim Lefebvre, Dave McKay, Tommie Reynolds)	.25
29	Ariel Prieto (Late-season update.)	2.50
---	Mother's Coupon (Spanish)	.05

Astros

		NM/M
Complete Set (28):		9.00
Common Player:		.25
1	Terry Collins	.25
2	Jeff Bagwell	2.50
3	Luis Gonzalez	.50
4	Darryl Kile	.25
5	Derek Bell	.25
6	Scott Servais	.25
7	Craig Biggio	.50
8	Dave Magadan	.25
9	Milt Thompson	.25
10	Derrick May	.25
11	Doug Drabek	.25
12	Tony Eusebio	.25
13	Phil Nevin	.25
14	James Mouton	.25
15	Phil Plantier	.25
16	Pedro Martinez	.25
17	Orlando Miller	.25
18	John Hudek	.25
19	Doug Brocail	.25
20	Craig Shipley	.25
21	Shane Reynolds	.25
22	Mike Hampton	.25
23	Todd Jones	.25
24	Greg Swindell	.25
25	Jim Dougherty	.25
26	Brian Hunter	.25
27	Dave Veres	.25

Dodgers

		NM/M
Complete Set (28):		12.00
Common Player:		.25
1	Tommy Lasorda	.25
2	Mike Piazza	4.00
3	Raul Mondesi	.25
4	Ramon Martinez	.25
5	Eric Karros	.25
6	Roberto Kelly	.25
7	Tim Wallach	.25
8	Jose Offerman	.25
9	Delino DeShields	.25
10	Dave Hansen	.25
11	Pedro Astacio	.25
12	Mitch Webster	.25
13	Hideo Nomo	6.00
14	Billy Ashley	.25
15	Chris Gwynn	.25
16	Todd Hollandsworth	.25
17	Omar Daal	.25
18	Todd Worrell	.25
19	Todd Williams	.25
20	Carlos Hernandez	.25
21	Tom Candiotti	.25
22	Antonio Osuna	.25
23	Ismael Valdes	.25
24	Rudy Seanez	.25
25	Joey Eischen	.25
26	Greg Hansell	.25
27	Rick Parker	.25
28	Coaches/Checklist (Joe Amalfitano, Mark Cresse, Manny Mota, Bill Russell, Reggie Smith, Dave Wallace)	.25

Giants

		NM/M
Complete Set (28):		12.00
Common Player:		.25
1	Dusty Baker	.40
2	Robby Thompson	.25
3	Barry Bonds	6.00
4	Royce Clayton	.25
5	Glenallen Hill	.25
6	Terry Mulholland	.25
7	Matt Williams	.50
8	Mark Portugal	.25
9	John Patterson	.25
10	Rod Beck	.25
11	Mark Leiter	.25
12	Kirt Manwaring	.25
13	Steve Scarsone	.25
14	Darren Lewis	.25
15	Tom Lampkin	.25
16	William Van Landingham	.25
17	Joe Rosselli	.25
18	Chris Hook	.25
19	Mark Dewey	.25
20	J.R. Phillips	.25
21	Jeff Reed	.25
22	Pat Gomez	.25
23	Mike Benjamin	.25
24	Trevor Wilson	.25
25	Dave Burba	.25
26	Jose Bautista	.25
27	Mark Carreon	.25
28	Coaches/Checklist (Bobby Bonds, Bob Brenly, Wendell Kim, Bob Lillis, Dick Pole)	.25

28 Coaches/Checklist (Jesse Barfield, Matt Galante, Steve Henderson, Julio Linares, Mel Stottlemyre) .25

Mariners

		NM/M
Complete Set (28):		12.00
Common Player:		.25
1	Lou Piniella	.25
2	Randy Johnson	2.00
3	Dave Fleming	.25
4	Ken Griffey Jr.	4.00
5	Edgar Martinez	.25
6	Jay Buhner	.25
7	Alex Rodriguez	7.50
8	Joey Cora	.25
9	Tim Davis	.25
10	Mike Blowers	.25
11	Chris Bosio	.25
12	Dan Wilson	.25
13	Rich Amaral	.25
14	Bobby Ayala	.25
15	Darren Bragg	.25
16	Bob Wells	.25
17	Doug Strange	.25
18	Chad Kreuter	.25
19	Rafael Carmona	.25
20	Luis Sojo	.25
21	Tim Belcher	.25
22	Steve Frey	.25
23	Tino Martinez	.25
24	Felix Fermin	.25
25	Jeff Nelson	.25
26	Alex Diaz	.25
27	Bill Risley	.25
28	Coaches/Checklist (Bobby Cuellar, Lee Elia, John McLaren, Sam Mejias, Sam Perlozzo, Matt Sinatro)	.25

Padres

		NM/M
Complete Set (28):		9.00
Common Player:		.25
1	Bruce Bochy	.25
2	Tony Gwynn	4.00
3	Ken Caminiti	.25
4	Bip Roberts	.25
5	Andujar Cedeno	.25
6	Andy Benes	.25
7	Phil Clark	.25
8	Fernando Valenzuela	.25
9	Roberto Petagine	.25
10	Brian Johnson	.25
11	Scott Livingstone	.25
12	Brian Williams	.25
13	Jody Reed	.25
14	Steve Finley	.25
15	Jeff Tabaka	.25
16	Ray Holbert	.25
17	Tim Worrell	.25
18	Eddie Williams	.25
19	Brad Ausmus	.25
20	Willie Blair	.25
21	Trevor Hoffman	.25
22	Scott Sanders	.25
23	Andy Ashby	.25
24	Joey Hamilton	.25
25	Andres Berumen	.25
26	Melvin Nieves	.25
27	Bryce Florie	.25
28	Coaches/Checklist (Davey Lopes, Graig Nettles, Rob Picciolo, Merv Rettenmund, Sonny Siebert)	.25

1996 Mother's Cookies Angels

After a four-year absence, the California Angels returned to participate in Mother's Cookies 14th season of sponsoring team sets. Virtually identical in format to previous years, the 2-1/2" x 3-1/2" round-cornered cards were given away at promotional dates. To promote old-fashioned card trading, the cards were distributed in a paper envelope containing 20 different cards, plus eight cards of a 21st player. Considerable trading was thus required to complete a team set. As in previous years, superb photos capture the players, manager and coaches of each team in a 28-card set. Backs are again printed in red and purple with a few bits of biographical data, uniform and card numbers and space for an autograph, along with the sponsor's logo.

		NM/M
Complete Set (28):		7.50
Common Player:		.25
1	Marcel Lachemann	.25
2	Chili Davis	.25
3	Mark Langston	.25
4	Tim Salmon	.75
5	Jim Abbott	.25
6	Jim Edmonds	1.00
7	Gary DiSarcina	.25
8	J.T. Snow	.25
9	Chuck Finley	.25
10	Tim Wallach	.25
11	Lee Smith	.25
12	George Arias	.25
13	Troy Percival	.25
14	Randy Velarde	.25
15	Garret Anderson	.35
16	Jorge Fabregas	.25
17	Shawn Boskie	.25
18	Mark Eichhorn	.25
19	Jack Howell	.25
20	Jason Grimsley	.25
21	Rex Hudler	.25
22	Mike Aldrete	.25
23	Mike James	.25
24	Scott Sanderson	.25
25	Don Slaught	.25
26	Mark Holzemer	.25
27	Dick Schofield	.25
28	Coaches/Checklist (Mick Billmeyer, Rick Burleson, Rod Carew, Chuck Hernandez, Bobby Knoop, Bill Lachemann, Joe Maddon)	.25

A's

		NM/M
Complete Set (28):		7.50
Common Player:		.25
1	Art Howe	.25
2	Mark McGwire	2.00
3	Jason Giambi	2.50
4	Terry Steinbach	.25
5	Mike Bordick	.25
6	Brent Gates	.25
7	Scott Brosius	.25

8	Doug Johns	.25
9	Jose Herrera	.25
10	John Wasdin	.25
11	Ernie Young	.25
12	Pedro Munoz	.25
13	Steve Wojciechowski	.25
14	Geronimo Berroa	.25
15	Phil Plantier	.25
16	Bobby Chouinard	.25
17	George Williams	.25
18	Jim Corsi	.25
19	Mike Mohler	.25
20	Torey Lovullo	.25
21	Carlos Reyes	.25
22	Buddy Groom	.25
23	Don Wengert	.25
24	Bill Taylor	.25
25	Todd Van Poppel	.25
26	Rafael Bournigal	.25
27	Damon Mashore	.25
28	Coaches/Checklist (Bob Alejo, Bob Cluck, Duffy Dyer, Brad Fischer, Denny Walling, Ron Washington)	.25

Astros

		NM/M
Complete Set (28):		7.50
Common Player:		.25
1	Terry Collins	.25
2	Jeff Bagwell	2.50
3	Craig Biggio	.50
4	Derek Bell	.25
5	Darryl Kile	.25
6	Sean Berry	.25
7	Doug Drabek	.25
8	Derrick May	.25
9	Orlando Miller	.25
10	Mike Hampton	.25
11	Rick Wilkins	.25
12	Brian Hunter	.25
13	Shane Reynolds	.25
14	James Mouton	.25
15	Greg Swindell	.25
16	Bill Spiers	.25
17	Alvin Morman	.25
18	Tony Eusebio	.25
19	John Hudek	.25
20	Doug Brocail	.25
21	Anthony Young	.25
22	John Cangelosi	.25
23	Jeff Tabaka	.25
24	Mike Simms	.25
25	Todd Jones	.25
26	Ricky Gutierrez	.25
27	Mark Small	.25
28	Coaches/Checklist (Matt Galante, Steve Henderson, Julio Linares, Brent Strom, Rick Sweet)	.25

Dodgers

		NM/M
Complete Set (28):		10.00
Common Player:		.25
1	Tommy Lasorda	.25
2	Mike Piazza	4.00
3	Hideo Nomo	2.50
4	Raul Mondesi	.25
5	Eric Karros	.25
6	Delino DeShields	.25
7	Greg Gagne	.25
8	Brett Butler	.25
9	Todd Hollandsworth	.25
10	Mike Blowers	.25
11	Ismael Valdes	.25
12	Pedro Astacio	.25

13	Billy Ashley	.25
14	Tom Candiotti	.25
15	Dave Hansen	.25
16	Joey Eischen	.25
17	Milt Thompson	.25
18	Chan Ho Park	1.50
19	Antonio Osuna	.25
20	Carlos Hernandez	.25
21	Ramon Martinez	.25
22	Scott Radinsky	.25
23	Chad Fonville	.25
24	Darren Hall	.25
25	Todd Worrell	.25
26	Mark Guthrie	.25
27	Roger Cedeno	.25
28	Coaches/Checklist (Joe Amalfitano, Mark Cresse, Manny Mota, Bill Russell, Reggie Smith, Dave Wallace)	.25

Giants

		NM/M
Complete Set (28):		9.00
Common Player:		.25
1	Dusty Baker	.40
2	Barry Bonds	5.00
3	Rod Beck	.50
4	Matt Williams	.50
5	Robby Thompson	.25
6	Glenallen Hill	.25
7	Mark Carreon	.25
8	Osvaldo Fernandez	.25
9	J.R. Phillips	.25
10	Shawon Dunston	.25
11	Mark Leiter	.25
12	William Van Landingham	.25
13	Stan Javier	.25
14	Allen Watson	.25
15	Mel Hall	.25
16	Doug Creek	.25
17	Steve Scarsone	.25
18	Mark Dewey	.25
19	Mark Gardner	.25
20	David McCarty	.25
21	Tom Lampkin	.25
22	Jeff Juden	.25
23	Steve Decker	.25
24	Rich DeLucia	.25
25	Kim Batiste	.25
26	Steve Bourgeois	.25
27		
28	Checklist/Coaches (Carlos Alfonso, Bobby Bonds, Jim Davenport, Wendell Kim, Bob Lillis, Juan Lopez, Dick Pole, Mike Sadek)	.25

Mariners

		NM/M
Complete Set (28):		15.00
Common Player:		.25
1	Lou Piniella	.25
2	Randy Johnson	1.00
3	Jay Buhner	.25
4	Ken Griffey Jr.	3.00
5	Ricky Jordan	.25
6	Rich Amaral	.25
7	Edgar Martinez	.25
8	Joey Cora	.25
9	Alex Rodriguez	6.00
10	Sterling Hitchcock	.25
11	Chris Bosio	.25
12	John Marzano	.25
13	Bob Wells	.25
14	Rafael Carmona	.25
15	Dan Wilson	.25

16	Norm Charlton	.25
17	Paul Sorrento	.25
18	Mike Jackson	.25
19	Luis Sojo	.25
20	Bobby Ayala	.25
21	Alex Diaz	.25
22	Doug Strange	.25
23	Bob Wolcott	.25
24	Darren Bragg	.25
25	Paul Menhart	.25
26	Edwin Hurtado	.25
27	Russ Davis	.25
28	Coaches/Checklist (Bobby Cuellar, Lee Elia, John McLaren, Sam Mejias, Matt Sinatro, Steve Smith)	.25

Padres

		NM/M
Complete Set (28):		9.00
Common Player:		.25
1	Bruce Bochy	.25
2	Tony Gwynn	3.50
3	Wally Joyner	.25
4	Rickey Henderson	1.50
5	Ken Caminiti	.25
6	Scott Sanders	.25
7	Steve Finley	.25
8	Fernando Valenzuela	.25
9	Brian Johnson	.25
10	Jody Reed	.25
11	Bob Tewksbury	.25
12	Andujar Cedeno	.25
13	Sean Bergman	.25
14	Marc Newfield	.25
15	Craig Shipley	.25
16	Scott Livingstone	.25
17	Trevor Hoffman	.25
18	Doug Bochtler	.25
19	Archi Cianfrocco	.25
20	Joey Hamilton	.25
21	Andy Ashby	.25
22	Chris Gwynn	.25
23	Luis Lopez	.25
24	Tim Worrell	.25
25	Brad Ausmus	.25
26	Willie Blair	.25
27	Bryce Florie	.25
28	Coaches/Checklist (Tim Flannery, Grady Little, Davey Lopes, Rob Picciolo, Merv Rettenmund, Dan Warthen)	.25

Rangers

		NM/M
Complete Set (28):		9.00
Common Player:		.25
1	Johnny Oates	.25
2	Will Clark	.50
3	Juan Gonzalez	2.50
4	Ivan Rodriguez	3.50
5	Darryl Hamilton	.25
6	Dean Palmer	.25
7	Mickey Tettleton	.25
8	Craig Worthington	.25
9	Rusty Greer	.25
10	Kevin Gross	.25
11	Rick Helling	.25
12	Kevin Elster	.25
13	Bobby Witt	.25
14	Mark McLemore	.25
15	Warren Newson	.25
16	Mike Henneman	.25
17	Ken Hill	.25
18	Gil Heredia	.25
19	Roger Pavlik	.25
20	Dave Valle	.25

21	Mark Brandenburg	.25
22	Kurt Stillwell	.25
23	Ed Vosberg	.25
24	Dennis Cook	.25
25	Damon Buford	.25
26	Benji Gil	.25
27	Darren Oliver	.25
28	Coaches/Checklist (Dick Bosman, Bucky Dent, Larry Hardy, Rudy Jaramillo, Ed Napoleon, Jerry Narron)	.25

1997 Mother's Cookies Angels

Fans attending the August 3 game at Anaheim Stadium received a starter set of 21 of the 28 cards in this team set, plus seven duplicates. They were encouraged to trade to fill their sets. The 2-1/2" x 3-1/2" round-corner cards have player portrait photos on front. To the left and bottom are red and blue stripes. The player name is at bottom in white, and the team logo is at bottom-right. Backs have minimal player data, a sponsor's logo and space for an autograph.

		NM/M
Complete Set (28):		7.50
Common Player:		.25
1	Terry Collins	.25
2	Tim Salmon	.50
3	Eddie Murray	2.50
4	Mark Langston	.25
5	Jim Edmonds	.75
6	Tony Phillips	.25
7	Gary DiSarcina	.25
8	Garret Anderson	.25
9	Chuck Finley	.25
10	Darin Erstad	2.00
11	Jim Leyritz	.25
12	Shigetosi Hasegawa	.25
13	Luis Alicea	.25
14	Troy Percival	.25
15	Allen Watson	.25
16	Craig Grebeck	.25
17	Mike Holtz	.25
18	Chad Kreuter	.25
19	Dennis Springer	.25
20	Jason Dickson	.25
21	Mike James	.25
22	Orlando Palmeiro	.25
23	Dave Hollins	.25
24	Mark Gubicza	.25
25	Pep Harris	.25
26	Jack Howell	.25
27	Rich DeLucia	.25
28	Angels Coaches/Checklist (Larry Bowa, Rod Carew, Joe Coleman, Marcel Lachemann, Joe Maddon, Dave Parker)	.25

A's

Fans attending the August 10 game at the Coliseum received a starter set of 21 of the 28 cards in this team set, plus seven duplicates. They were encouraged to trade to fill their sets. The 2-1/2" x 3-1/2" round-corner cards have player portrait photos on front. To the left and bottom are green and

gold stripes. The player name is at bottom in white, and the team logo is at bottom-right. Backs have minimal player data, a sponsor's logo and space for an autograph.

		NM/M
Complete Set (28):		9.00
Common Player:		.25
1	Art Howe	.25
2	Mark McGwire	2.50
3	Jose Canseco	1.00
4	Jason Giambi	1.50
5	Geronimo Berroa	.25
6	Ernie Young	.25
7	Scott Brosius	.25
8	Dave Magadan	.25
9	Mike Mohler	.25
10	George Williams	.25
11	Tony Batista	.25
12	Steve Karsay	.25
13	Rafael Bournigal	.25
14	Ariel Prieto	.25
15	Buddy Groom	.25
16	Matt Stairs	.25
17	Brent Mayne	.25
18	Bill Taylor	.25
19	Scott Spiezio	.25
20	Richie Lewis	.25
21	Mark Acre	.25
22	Dave Telgheder	.25
23	Willie Adams	.25
24	Izzy Molina	.25
25	Don Wengert	.25
26	Damon Mashore	.25
27	Aaron Small	.25
28	A's Coaches/Checklist (Bob Alejo, Bob Cluck, Duffy Dyer, Brad Fischer, Denny Walling, Ron Washington)	.25

Astros

Children attending a promotional game at the Astrodome received a starter set of 21 of the 28 cards in this team set, plus seven duplicates. They were encouraged to trade to fill their sets. The 2-1/2" x 3-1/2" round-corner cards have portrait photos on front. To the left and bottom are navy and gold stripes. The player name is at bottom in white, and the team logo is at bottom-right. Backs have minimal player data, a sponsor's logo and space for an autograph.

		NM/M
Complete Set (28):		9.00
Common Player:		.25
1	Larry Dierker	.25
2	Jeff Bagwell	2.50
3	Craig Biggio	.50
4	Darryl Kile	.25
5	Luis Gonzalez	.50
6	Shane Reynolds	.25
7	James Mouton	.25
8	Sean Berry	.25
9	Billy Wagner	.75
10	Ricky Gutierrez	.25
11	Mike Hampton	.25
12	Tony Eusebio	.25
13	Derek Bell	.25
14	Ray Montgomery	.25
15	Bill Spiers	.25
16	Sid Fernandez	.25
17	Brad Ausmus	.25
18	John Hudek	.25
19	Bob Abreu	.25
20	Russ Springer	.25
21	Chris Holt	.25
22	Tom Martin	.25
23	Donne Wall	.25
24	Thomas Howard	.25
25	Jose Lima	.25
26	Pat Listach	.25
27	Ramon Garcia	.25
28	Astros Coaches/Checklist (Alan Ashby, Jose Cruz, Mike Cubbage, Tom McCraw, Vern Ruhle, Bill Virdon)	.25

Dodgers

HIDEO NOMO

Children attending the July 13 game at Dodger Stadium received a starter set of 21 of the 28 cards in this team set, plus seven duplicates. They were encouraged to trade to fill their sets. The 2-1/2" x 3-1/2" round-corner cards have player portrait photos on front. To the left and bottom are red and blue stripes. The player name is at bottom in white, and the team logo is at bottom-right. Backs have minimal player data, a sponsor's logo and space for an autograph.

		NM/M
Complete Set (28):		12.00
Common Player:		.25
1	Bill Russell	.25
2	Eric Karros	.25
3	Mike Piazza	4.00
4	Raul Mondesi	.25
5	Hideo Nomo	2.00
6	Todd Hollandsworth	.25
7	Greg Gagne	.25
8	Brett Butler	.25
9	Ramon Martinez	.25
10	Todd Zeile	.25
11	Ismael Valdes	.25
12	Chip Hale	.25
13	Tom Candiotti	.25
14	Billy Ashley	.25
15	Chan Ho Park	.50
16	Wayne Kirby	.25
17	Mark Guthrie	.25
18	Juan Castro	.25
19	Todd Worrell	.25
20	Tom Prince	.25
21	Scott Radinsky	.25
22	Pedro Astacio	.25
23	Wilton Guerrero	.25
24	Darren Hall	.25
25	Darren Dreifort	.25
26	Nelson Liriano	.25
27	Dodgers Coaches (Joe Amalfitano, Mark Cresse, Manny Mota, Mike Scioscia, Reggie Smith, Dave Wallace)	.25
28	Robinson 50th Anniversary Logo/Checklist	.25

Giants

MARVIN BENARD   GIANTS

Twenty thousand fans attending the July 27 game at 3Com Park received a starter set of 21 of the 28 cards in this team set, plus seven duplicates. They were encouraged to trade to fill their sets. The 2-1/2" x 3-1/2" round-corner cards have player portrait photos on front. To the left and bottom are black and orange stripes. The player name is at bottom in white, and the team logo is at bottom-right. Backs have minimal player data, a sponsor's logo and space for an autograph.

		NM/M
Complete Set (28)		10.00
Common Player:		.25
1	Dusty Baker	.25
2	Barry Bonds	5.00

3	J.T. Snow	.25
4	Rod Beck	.25
5	Glenallen Hill	.25
6	Rick Wilkins	.25
7	Jeff Kent	.50
8	Shawn Estes	.25
9	Darryl Hamilton	.25
10	Jose Vizcaino	.25
11	Julian Tavares	.25
12	Mark Gardner	.25
13	Stan Javier	.25
14	Osvaldo Fernandez	.25
15	Jim Poole	.25
16	Marvin Benard	.25
17	William Van Landingham	.25
18	Bill Mueller	.25
19	Mark Lewis	.25
20	Damon Berryhill	.25
21	Doug Henry	.25
22	Rich Rodriguez	.25
23	Kirk Rueter	.25
24	Rich Aurilia	.25
25	Joe Roa	.25
26	Marcus Jensen	.25
27	Miguel Murphy (Equipment Manager)	.25
28	Giants Coaches/Checklist (Carlos Alfonso, Gene Clines, Sonny Jackson, Juan Lopez, Ron Perranoski, Dick Pole)	.25

Padres

TONY GWYNN   PADRES

Partial sets of Mother's Cookies Padres were given to children 14 and under attending the June 22 game at Jack Murphy Stadium. Team colors of royal blue and orange form border strips to the left and bottom of the posed photo. A team logo appears at lower-right.

		NM/M
Complete Set (28):		9.00
Common Player:		.25
1	Bruce Bochy	.25
2	Tony Gwynn	3.00
3	Ken Caminiti	.25
4	Wally Joyner	.25
5	Rickey Henderson	1.50
6	Greg Vaughn	.25
7	Steve Finley	.25
8	Fernando Valenzuela	.25
9	John Flaherty	.25
10	Sterling Hitchcock	.25
11	Quilvio Veras	.25
12	Don Slaught	.25
13	Sean Bergman	.25
14	Chris Gomez	.25
15	Craig Shipley	.25
16	Joey Hamilton	.25
17	Scott Livingstone	.25
18	Trevor Hoffman	.25
19	Doug Bochtler	.25
20	Chris Jones	.25
21	Andy Ashby	.25
22	Archi Cianfrocco	.25
23	Tim Worrell	.25
24	Will Cunnane	.25
25	Carlos Hernandez	.25
26	Tim Scott	.25
27	Dario Veras	.25
28	Coaches/Checklist (Greg Booker, Tim Flannery, Davey Lopes, Rob Picciolo, Merv Rettenmund, Dan Warthen)	.25

Rangers

Fans attending a promotional game at the Ballpark in Arlington received a starter set of 21 of the 28 cards in this team set, plus seven duplicates. They were encouraged to trade to fill their sets. The 2-1/2" x 3-1/2" round-corner cards have player portrait photos on front. To the left and bottom are red and blue stripes. The player name is at bottom in white, and the team logo is at bottom-right. Backs have minimal player data, a sponsor's logo and space for an autograph.

IVAN RODRIGUEZ

		NM/M
Complete Set (28):		8.00
Common Player:		.25
1	Johnny Oates	.25
2	Will Clark	.50
3	Juan Gonzalez	2.50
4	Ivan Rodriguez	3.50
5	John Wetteland	.25
6	Mickey Tettleton	.25
7	Dean Palmer	.25
8	Rusty Greer	.25
9	Ed Vosberg	.25
10	Lee Stevens	.25
11	Benji Gil	.25
12	Mike Devereaux	.25
13	Bobby Witt	.25
14	Mark McLemore	.25
15	Warren Newson	.25
16	Eric Gunderson	.25
17	Ken Hill	.25
18	Damon Buford	.25
19	Roger Pavlik	.25
20	Billy Ripken	.25
21	John Burkett	.25
22	Darren Oliver	.25
23	Mike Simms	.25
24	Julio Santana	.25
25	Henry Mercedes	.25
26	Xavier Hernandez	.25
27	Danny Patterson	.25
28	Rangers Coaches/Checklist (Dick Bosman, Bucky Dent, Larry Hardy, Rudy Jaramillo, Ed Napoleon, Jerry Narron)	.25

1998 Mother's Cookies A's

TOM CANDIOTTI

The first 25,000 fans at the August 2 game in Oakland received a starter set of 21 of the 28 cards in this team set, plus seven duplicates. They were encouraged to trade to fill their sets. The 2-1/2" x 3-1/2" round-corner cards have player portrait photos on front. To the left and bottom are green and gold stripes. The player name is at the bottom in white, and the team logo is at bottom-left. Backs have minimal player data, a sponsor's logo and space for an autograph, all printed in red and purple on a purple background.

		NM/M
Complete Set (28):		8.00
Common Player:		.25
1	Art Howe	.25
2	Rickey Henderson	1.00
3	Jason Giambi	2.00
4	Tom Candiotti	.25
5	Matt Stairs	.25
6	Kenny Rogers	.25
7	Scott Spiezio	.50
8	Ben Grieve	.25
9	Kevin Mitchell	.25
10	A.J. Hinch	.25
11	Bill Taylor	.25
12	Rafael Bournigal	.25
13	Miguel Tejada	3.00
14	Kurt Abbott	.25
15	Buddy Groom	.25
16	Dave Magadan	.25
17	Mike Oquist	.25
18	Mike Macfarlane	.25
19	Mike Fetters	.25

20	Ryan Christenson	.25
21	T.J. Mathews	.25
22	Mike Mohler	.25
23	Jason McDonald	.25
24	Blake Stein	.25
25	Mike Blowers	.25
26	Jimmy Haynes	.25
27	Aaron Small	.25
28	Coaches/Checklist (Duffy Dyer, Brad Fischer, Gary Jones, Rick Peterson, Denny Walling, Ron Washington)	.25

Astros

JEFF BAGWELL

The first 25,000 fans at the September 13 game at the Astrodome received a starter set of 21 of the 28 cards in this team set, plus seven duplicates. They were encouraged to trade to fill their sets. The 2-1/2" x 3-1/2" round-corner cards have player portrait photos on front. To the left and bottom are team-color blue and gold stripes. The player name is at the bottom in white, and the team logo is at bottom-left. Backs have minimal player data, a sponsor's logo and space for an autograph, all printed in red and purple on a purple background.

		NM/M
Complete Set (28):		9.00
Common Player:		.25
1	Larry Dierker	.25
2	Jeff Bagwell	3.00
3	Craig Biggio	.50
4	Derek Bell	.25
5	Shane Reynolds	.25
6	Sean Berry	.25
7	Moises Alou	.25
8	Carl Everett	.25
9	Billy Wagner	.25
10	Tony Eusebio	.25
11	Mike Hampton	.25
12	Ricky Gutierrez	.25
13	Jose Lima	.25
14	Brad Ausmus	.25
15	Bill Spiers	.25
16	C.J. Nitkowski	.25
17	Randy Johnson	4.00
18	Mike Magnante	.25
19	Dave Clark	.25
20	Sean Bergman	.25
21	Richard Hidalgo	.25
22	Pete Shourek	.25
23	Jay Powell	.25
24	Trever Miller	.25
25	Tim Bogar	.25
26	Doug Henry	.25
27	Scott Elarton	.25
28	Coaches (Jose Cruz, Mike Cubbage, Dave Engle, Matt Galante, Tom McCraw, Vern Ruhle)	.25

Dodgers

CHARLES JOHNSON

The first 25,000 kids at the August 16 game in Los Angeles received a starter set of 21 of the 28 cards in this team set, plus seven duplicates. They were encouraged to trade to fill their sets. The 2-1/2" x 3-1/2" round-corner cards have player portrait photos on front. To the left and bottom

1	Dusty Baker	.25
2	Barry Bonds	5.00
3	Shawn Estes	.25
4	Jeff Kent	.50
5	Orel Hershiser	.25
6	Brian Johnson	.25
7	J.T. Snow	.25
8	Bill Mueller	.25
9	Kirk Rueter	.25
10	Darryl Hamilton	.25
11	Rich Aurilia	.25
12	Mark Gardner	.25
13	Stan Javier	.25
14	Robb Nen	.25
15	Rich Rodriguez	.25
16	Brent Mayne	.25
17	Julian Tavares	.25
18	Rey Sanchez	.25
19	Chris Jones	.25
20	Charlie Hayes	.25
21	Danny Darwin	.25
22	Jim Poole	.25
23	Marvin Benard	.25
24	Steve Reed	.25
25	Alex Diaz	.25
26	John Johnstone	.25

are red and blue stripes. The player name is at the bottom in white, and the team logo is at bottom-left. Backs have minimal player data, a sponsor's logo and space for an autograph, all printed in red and purple on a purple background.

		NM/M
Complete Set (28):		7.50
Common Player:		.25
1	Glenn Hoffman	.25
2	Eric Karros	.25
3	Bobby Bonilla	.25
4	Raul Mondesi	.25
5	Gary Sheffield	1.00
6	Ramon Martinez	.25
7	Charles Johnson	.25
8	Jose Vizcaino	.25
9	Scott Radinsky	.25
10	Jim Eisenreich	.25
11	Ismael Valdes	.25
12	Eric Young	.25
13	Chan Ho Park	.25
14	Roger Cedeno	.25
15	Antonio Osuna	.25
16	Dave Mlicki	.25
17	Mark Guthrie	.25
18	Juan Castro	.25
19	Darren Dreifort	.25
20	Tom Prince	.25
21	Jeff Shaw	.25
22	Alex Cora	.25
23	Matt Luke	.25
24	Darren Hall	.25
25	Trenidad Hubbard	.25
26	Jim Bruske	.25
27	Tripp Cromer	.25
28	Dodgers Coaches (Joe Amalfitano, Mickey Hatcher, Charlie Hough, Manny Mota, Mike Scioscia, John Shelby)	.25

Giants

SHAWN ESTES   GIANTS

The first 25,000 fans at the July 26 game at 3Com Park received a starter set of 21 of the 28 cards in this team set, plus seven duplicates. They were encouraged to trade to fill their sets. The 2-1/2" x 3-1/2" round-corner cards have player portrait photos on front. To the left and bottom are black and orange stripes. The player name is at the bottom in white, and the team logo is at bottom-left. Backs have minimal player data, a sponsor's logo and space for an autograph, all printed in red and purple on a purple background.

		NM/M
Complete Set (28):		9.00
Common Player:		.25
1	Dusty Baker	.25
2	Barry Bonds	5.00

27	Rene De La Rosa, Mike Krukow, Duane Kuiper, Jon Miller, Amaury Pi-Gonzalez, Ted Robinson (Broadcasters)	.25
28	Giants Coaches/Checklist (Carlos Alfonso, Gene Clines, Sonny Jackson, Juan Lopez, Ron Perranoski, Ron Wotus)	.25

Padres

Fans at a designated Pads' home game received a starter set of 21 of the 28 cards in this team set, plus seven duplicates. They were encouraged to trade to fill their sets. The 2-1/2" x 3-1/2" round-corner cards have player portrait photos on front. To the left and bottom are blue and orange stripes. The player name is at the bottom in white, and the team logo is at bottom-left. Backs have minimal player data, a sponsor's logo and space for an autograph, all printed in red and purple on a purple background.

		NM/M
Complete Set (28):		9.00
Common Player:		.25
1	Bruce Bochy	.25
2	Tony Gwynn	4.00
3	Ken Caminiti	.25
4	Kevin Brown	.40
5	Wally Joyner	.25
6	Sterling Hitchcock	.25
7	Greg Vaughn	.25
8	Steve Finley	.25
9	Joey Hamilton	.25
10	Carlos Hernandez	.25
11	Quilvio Veras	.25
12	Trevor Hoffman	.25
13	Chris Gomez	.25
14	Andy Ashby	.25
15	Greg Myers	.25
16	Mark Langston	.25
17	Andy Sheets	.25
18	Dan Miceli	.25
19	James Mouton	.25
20	Brian Boehringer	.25
21	Archi Cianfrocco	.25
22	Mark Sweeney	.25
23	Pete Smith	.25
24	Eddie Williams	.25
25	Ed Giovanola	.25
26	Carlos Reyes	.25
27	Donne Wall	.25
28	Padres Coaches (Greg Booker, Tim Flannery, Davey Lopes, Rob Picciolo, Merv Rettenmund, Dave Stewart)	.25

1998 Mr. Sub Roger Clemens

The date attributed is speculative, since the cards carry no copyright. This set appears to have been issued by a Canadian sub sandwich chain to honor Roger Clemens first four Cy Young Awards. Borderless fronts of the 2-1/2" x 3-1/2" cards have color portrait and action artwork of Clemens in a Blue Jays uniform, with a sepia multi-exposure image of Cy Young in the background, all four cards in the set share the front design, with the only difference being the card number at top-left. Backs are dominated by a large coin-like design with black-and-white artwork of Clemens. The first three cards have back pictures in a Red Sox uniform, the last card shows him with Toronto. The date of his CY Award is shown on each "coin." Beneath the central design on the graduated blue background are MLB and Mr. Sub logos and "www.RocketRoger.com."

		NM/M
Complete Set (4):		6.00
Common Card:		1.50
1	Roger Clemens/1986	1.50
2	Roger Clemens/1987	1.50
3	Roger Clemens/1991	1.50
4	Roger Clemens/1997	1.50

1992 Mr. Turkey

Mr. Turkey, a division of Sara Lee, offered a set of Major League Superstar cards during the 1992 season. A total of 26 cards, one player representing each team, were included in various Mr. Turkey meat packages. The cardboard packaging allows for the printing directly on the carton instead of inserting the cards inside the package. Collectors were able to collect the cards individually or as an uncut sheet, available by sending to the company.

		NM/M
Complete Set (26):		10.00
Uncut Sheet:		15.00
Common Player:		.35
1	Jim Abbott	.40
2	Roberto Alomar	.50
3	Sandy Alomar, Jr.	.40
4	Craig Biggio	.40
5	George Brett	2.00
6	Will Clark	.40
7	Roger Clemens	2.00
8	Cecil Fielder	.40
9	Carlton Fisk	1.00
10	Andres Galarraga	.40
11	Dwight Gooden	.40
12	Ken Griffey Jr.	3.00
13	Tony Gwynn	1.50
14	Rickey Henderson	1.00
15	Dave Justice	.40
16	Don Mattingly	2.00
17	Dale Murphy	.75
18	Kirby Puckett	1.50
19	Cal Ripken, Jr.	3.50
20	Nolan Ryan	3.50
21	Chris Sabo	.40
22	Ryne Sandberg	1.50
23	Ozzie Smith	1.50
24	Darryl Strawberry	.40
25	Andy Van Slyke	.40
26	Robin Yount	1.00

1995 Mr. Turkey

Five retired players are featured in this issue. The 2-1/2" x 3-1/2" cards have a sepia or color photo on front, along with a Baseball Greats logo. Uniform logos have been removed from the photos. Backs have personal and career data, and logos of the sponsor and the players' licensing agent. The cards are unnumbered.

		NM/M
Complete Set (5):		10.00
Common Player:		2.00
(1)	Bob Feller	2.00
(2)	Al Kaline	2.00
(3)	Tug McGraw	2.00
(4)	Boog Powell	2.00
(5)	Warren Spahn	4.00

1983 Mr. Z's Pizza Milwaukee Brewers

These 5" x 7" color cards were given away (bagged in cellophane) with the purchase of frozen pizzas.

		NM/M
Complete Set (3):		7.50
Common Player:		1.00
(1)	Cecil Cooper	1.00
(2)	Paul Molitor	4.00
(3)	Robin Yount	4.00

1984 Mr. Z's Pizza Milwaukee Brewers

These 5" x 7" color cards were given away with the purchase of frozen pizza and other Brewer-logo food products.

		NM/M
Complete Set (3):		4.00
Common Player:		1.00
(1)	George Bamberger	1.00
(2)	Rollie Fingers	2.00
(3)	Jim Gantner	1.00

1985 Mr. Z's Pizza Pete Rose

These 5" x 7" cards were issued in Mr. Z's pizzas, each one picturing Pete Rose. Fronts have borderless action photos with a headline in black or white and a facsimile autograph. Backs have a red border with photos of Reds team merchandise which could be obtained by saving pizza labels.

		NM/M
Complete Set (11):		35.00
Common Player:		4.00
(1)	Another Hit! (Pete Rose)	4.00
(2)	Classic Rose (Pete Rose)	4.00
(3)	Lay One Down (Pete Rose)	4.00
(4)	Line Up Time (Pete Rose)	4.00
(5)	On Deck (Pete Rose)	4.00
(6)	One Hit Closer! (Pete Rose No facsimile autograph.)	4.00
(7)	Pete's Back (Pete Rose)	4.00
(8)	Play Ball! (Pete Rose)	4.00
(9)	Player-Manager (Pete Rose)	4.00

(10)	Rounding Third Heading for Home (Pete Rose)	4.00
(11)	Send in the Lefty (Pete Rose)	4.00

1981 MSA Discs

Unlike the contemporary Peter Pan/Sunbeam blank-back discs, this set of 2-3/4" diameter discs carry on their backs the advertising of Michael Schechter Associates, their producer.

		NM/M
Complete Set (3):		7.50
Common Player:		1.00
(1)	Cecil Cooper	1.00
(2)	Paul Molitor	4.00
(3)	Robin Yount	4.00

		NM/M
Complete Set (32):		135.00
Common Player:		4.00
(1)	Buddy Bell	4.00
(2)	Johnny Bench	8.00
(3)	Bruce Bochte	4.00
(4)	George Brett	12.50
(5)	Bill Buckner	4.00
(6)	Rod Carew	8.00
(7)	Steve Carlton	8.00
(8)	Cesar Cedeno	4.00
(9)	Jack Clark	4.00
(10)	Cecil Cooper	4.00
(11)	Bucky Dent	4.00
(12)	Carlton Fisk	8.00
(13)	Steve Garvey	6.50
(14)	Goose Gossage	4.00
(15)	Mike Hargrove	4.00
(16)	Keith Hernandez	4.00
(17)	Bob Horner	4.00
(18)	Reggie Jackson	12.50
(19)	Steve Kemp	4.00
(20)	Ron LeFlore	4.00
(21)	Fred Lynn	4.00
(22)	Lee Mazzilli	4.00
(23)	Eddie Murray	8.00
(24)	Mike Norris	4.00
(25)	Dave Parker	4.00
(26)	J.R. Richard	4.00
(27)	Pete Rose	15.00
(28)	Mike Schmidt	12.50
(29)	Tom Seaver	9.00
(30)	Roy Smalley	4.00
(31)	Willie Stargell	8.00
(32)	Garry Templeton	4.00

1981 MSA/Peter Pan-Sunbeam Bakery Discs

Only the MSA copyright is found on these 2-3/4" diameter player discs, the names of Peter Pan or Sunbeam Bakery, the sponsors that packed the discs in loaves of bread, are nowhere to be seen. Like other MSA disc issues, the black-and-white player picture appears on a baseball design with side panels in various colors. Player information appears at each side and in the center panel, along with the Players Association logo. Because the discs are not licensed by the leagues, uniform logos have been removed from the photos. Backs are blank. The unnumbered discs are checklisted here in alphabetical order. A 16-3/4" x 22-5/8" red, white and blue display poster with slots for inserting the discs is known bearing the Peter Pan advertising.

		NM/M
Complete Set (32):		75.00
Common Player:		2.00
Pete Pan Poster:		25.00
(1)	Buddy Bell	2.00
(2)	Johnny Bench	4.50
(3)	Bruce Bochte	2.00
(4)	George Brett	7.50
(5)	Bill Buckner	2.00
(6)	Rod Carew	4.50
(7)	Steve Carlton	4.50

(8)	Cesar Cedeno	2.00
(9)	Jack Clark	2.00
(10)	Cecil Cooper	2.00
(11)	Bucky Dent	2.00
(12)	Carlton Fisk	4.50
(13)	Steve Garvey	3.50
(14)	Goose Gossage	2.00
(15)	Mike Hargrove	2.00
(16)	Keith Hernandez	2.00
(17)	Bob Horner	2.00
(18)	Reggie Jackson	7.50
(19)	Steve Kemp	2.00
(20)	Ron LeFlore	2.00
(21)	Fred Lynn	2.00
(22)	Lee Mazzilli	2.00
(23)	Eddie Murray	4.50
(24)	Mike Norris	2.00
(25)	Dave Parker	2.00
(26)	J.R. Richard	2.00
(27)	Pete Rose	9.00
(28)	Mike Schmidt	7.50
(29)	Tom Seaver	5.00
(30)	Roy Smalley	2.00
(31)	Willie Stargell	4.50
(32)	Garry Templeton	2.00

1985 MSA/Subway Sandwiches Discs

Identical in form and format to other Schechter discs of the era, the Subway giveaways are nowhere marked as such, only the MSA copyright appears. The 2-3/4" diameter discs have black-and-white player portraits in the white center panel of a baseball design. The variously colored end panels contain player information and a 1985 date. The Players Association logo appears beneath the photo. Because the discs are not licensed by Major League Baseball, team logos have been airbrushed off uniforms. The unnumbered, blank-backed discs are checklisted here in alphabetical order.

		NM/M
Complete Set (36):		95.00
Common Player:		3.00
(1)	Buddy Bell	3.00
(2)	Mike Boddicker	3.00
(3)	George Brett	10.00
(4)	Bill Buckner	3.00
(5)	Rod Carew	6.50
(6)	Steve Carlton	6.50
(7)	Cesar Cedeno	3.00
(8)	Dave Concepcion	3.00
(9)	Cecil Cooper	3.00
(10)	Al Cowens	3.00
(11)	Goose Gossage	3.00
(12)	Pedro Guerrero	3.00
(13)	Ron Guidry	3.00
(14)	Tony Gwynn	9.00
(15)	Mike Hargrove	3.00
(16)	Bob Horner	3.00
(17)	Kent Hrbek	3.00
(18)	Rick Langford	3.00
(19)	Dennis Leonard	3.00
(20)	Willie McGee	3.00
(21)	Jack Morris	3.00
(22)	Terry Puhl	3.00
(23)	Dan Quisenberry	3.00
(24)	Johnny Ray	3.00
(25)	Cal Ripken Jr.	15.00
(26)	Ryne Sandberg	9.00
(27)	Mike Schmidt	10.00
(28)	Tom Seaver	6.50
(29)	Rick Sutcliffe	3.00
(30)	Bruce Sutter	4.50
(31)	Alan Trammell	3.00
(32)	Fernando Valenzuela	3.00
(33)	Greg Walker	3.00
(34)	Willie Wilson	3.00
(35)	Dave Winfield	6.50
(36)	Geoff Zahn	3.00

1992 MTV Rock n' Jock

The third annual softball charity game featuring music and sports personalities was the occasion for issue of this three-card set. Fronts have a multi-colored player action photo (presumably taken at the previous year's game). Backs are in black-and-white with the MTV and event logos, the date and place of the game and the notation that the card is from a "Limited Edition of 20,000."

		NM/M
Complete Set (3):		6.00
Common Player:		.50
1	M.C. Hammer	.50
2	Frank Thomas	2.00
3	Ken Griffey Jr.	4.00

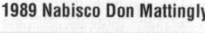

1989 Nabisco Don Mattingly

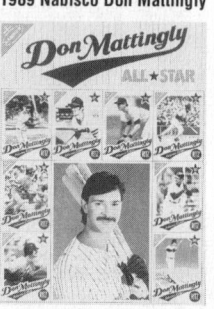

Issued as a mail-in premium for Ritz cracker proofs of purchase, this sheet measures 10-5/8" x 13-15/16" and includes eight 2-1/2" x 3-1/2" cards and a 5"x7" card. The individual cards are not perforated and are seldom seen cut from the sheet. For lack of licensing by Major League Baseball, the photos on front have generally had the team logos airbrushed away. Cards are numbered on front and back with a year identifying the photo. Backs are printed in red, white and blue and contain biographical data and career highlights on the small cards, while the large card offers complete major and minor league stats and major awards won. The sheet was produced for Nabisco by Topps.

		NM/M
Complete Sheet:		7.50
Common Card:		1.00
72	Don Mattingly (Boyhood photo.)	1.00
81	Don Mattingly (Minor league photo.)	1.00
84	Don Mattingly/Fldg	1.00
85-89	Don Mattingly/Btg	1.00
----	Don Mattingly (5"x7" pose)	1.00

1992 Nabisco Canadian Tradition

Nabisco released a 36-card set of former Toronto Blue Jays and Montreal Expos inside several of its products in 1992. A colorful 9" x 12"

album with plastic sheets was available via a mail-in offer. The cards are artist renderings of the players, similar in style to the famous sports drawings that appeared on the pages of the Sporting News over the years. Text on the drawings is in both English and French. Backs are printed in red, white and blue and include the team and Nabisco logos along with English and French descriptions of the Famous Moment.

		NM/M
Complete Set (36):		25.00
Common Player:		.75
Album:		7.50
1	Bill Lee	.75
2	Cliff Johnson	.75
3	Ken Singleton	.75
4	Al Woods	.75
5	Ron Hunt	.75
6	Barry Bonnell	.75
7	Tony Perez	4.00
8	Willie Upshaw	.75
9	Coco Laboy	.75
10	Famous Moments (Blue Jays Win A.L. East/1985)	.75
11	Bob Bailey	.75
12	Dave McKay	.75
13	Rodney Scott	.75
14	Jerry Garvin	.75
15	Famous Moments (Expos Win N.L. East/1981)	.75
16	Rick Bosetti	.75
17	Larry Parrish	.75
18	Bill Singer	.75
19	Ron Fairly	.75
20	Damaso Garcia	.75
21	Al Oliver	1.50
22	Famous Moments (Blue Jays Win Eastern Division/1989)	.75
23	Claude Raymond	.75
24	Buck Martinez	.75
25	Rusty Staub	1.50
26	Otto Velez	.75
27	Mack Jones	.75
28	Garth Iorg	.75
29	Bill Stoneman	.75
30	Doug Ault	.75
31	Famous Moments (Expos Host All-Star Game/1982)	.75
32	Jesse Jefferson	.75
33	Steve Rogers	.75
34	Ernie Whitt	.75
35	John Boccabella	.75
36	Bill Bailor	.75

1993 Nabisco All-Star Autographs

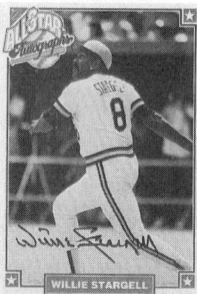

In a promotion with the Major League Baseball Players Alumni, Nabisco produced this six-card set of former stars. For $5 and proofs of purchase, collectors could receive an authentically autographed card. The 2-1/2" x 3-1/2" cards featured color photos on front on which the team logos have been airbrushed away, since Major League Baseball did not license the issue. Backs gave biographical and career information along with a black-and-white childhood photo of the player. The unnumbered cards are checklisted here in alphabetical order. Don Drysdale's death on July 3, in the midst of the promotion, curtailed availability of cards with his autograph. Each card came cased with a certificate of authenticity. Unautographed cards and 12-card uncut sheets are known.

		NM/M
Complete Set (6):		90.00
Common Player:		6.00
(1)	Ernie Banks	13.50
(2)	Don Drysdale	45.00
(3)	Catfish Hunter	20.00
(4)	Phil Niekro	6.00

(5)	Brooks Robinson	7.50
(6)	Willie Stargell	25.00

1994 Nabisco All-Star Legends Autographs

For a second year in 1994, Nabisco continued its program of offering autographed cards of former stars for $5 and proofs of purchase from its snack products. Cards retained the same basic format of using airbrushed color photos on front and black-and-white childhood photos on back. Fronts have a "Nabisco All-Star Legends" logo in the upper-left. Backs have career and biographical data and the logos of the sponsor and the Major League Baseball Players Alumni. The unnumbered cards are checklisted here alphabetically. Each card came with a certificate of authenticity. The Sparky Lyle card was not part of the mail-in promotion but was distributed in person during the Legends' tour. Unautographed cards and 12-card uncut sheets are also known.

		NM/M
Complete Set (5):		30.00
Common Player:		6.00
(1)	Bob Gibson	9.00
(2)	Sparky Lyle	12.00
(3)	Jim Palmer	6.00
(4)	Frank Robinson	8.00
(5)	Duke Snider	10.00

2000 Team Nabisco All-Stars

This series was issued in Nabisco snack and cookie packages. Fronts have color photos on which team logos have been removed. The player figure is set against a background that has a large purple-blue baseball at bottom and red and white rays at top. The sponsor logo is at top-right. Backs have a smaller version of the photo, career stats and highlights. The unnumbered cards are checklisted here alphabetically.

		NM/M
Complete Set (11):		9.00
Common Player:		.50
(1)	Lawrence "Yogi" Berra	1.50
(2)	Gary Carter	1.00
(3)	Orlando Cepeda	1.00
(4)	George Foster	.50
(5)	Steve Garvey	.75
(6)	John Kruk	.50
(7)	Joe Morgan	1.00
(8)	Dot Richardson	.50
(9)	Brooks Robinson	1.00
(10)	Mike Schmidt	2.00
(11)	Ozzie Smith	2.00

1983 Nalley Potato Chips Mariners

These large (8-11/16" x 10-11/16") photo cards were issued only in the area of Washington state by Nalley Potato Chips. The six Seattle Mariners are pictured in full color on the entire back panel of each box. On the side panels, detailed player stats and biographies are listed on one side, with a Mariners schedule and ticket discount offer on the other side.

		NM/M
Complete Set (6):		45.00
Common Player:		7.50
8	Rick Sweet	7.50
16	Al Cowens	7.50
21	Todd Cruz	7.50
22	Richie Zisk	7.50
36	Gaylord Perry	20.00
37	Bill Caudill	7.50

1995 National Packtime

An unusual joint venture by the six major baseball card licensees resulted in this 18-card set which was available only via a mail-in offer. The set was obtained by sending in $2 and 28 wrappers from any of the companies' 1995 baseball cards prior to June 30, 1995. Most of the card designs were similar to the respective company's regular issues of the same brand. Each card is gold-foil enhanced and each carries the crossed-bats National Packtime logo on front. Cards are numbered on back from 1-18. A reported 130,000 of the sets were exchanged for wrappers.

		NM/M
Complete Set (18):		3.00
Common Player:		.15
1	Frank Thomas (Donruss)	.40
2	Matt Williams (Fleer Ultra)	.15
3	Juan Gonzalez (Pacific Crown)	.35
4	Bob Hamelin (Pinnacle)	.15
5	Mike Piazza (Topps)	.50
6	Ken Griffey Jr. (Upper Deck)	.75
7	Barry Bonds (Donruss)	.25
8	Tim Salmon (Fleer Ultra)	.15
9	Jose Canseco (Pacific Crown)	.25
10	Cal Ripken Jr. (Pinnacle)	.75
11	Raul Mondesi (Topps)	.15
12	Alex Rodriguez (Upper Deck)	.60
13	Will Clark (Donruss)	.20
14	Fred McGriff (Fleer Ultra)	.15
15	Tony Gwynn (Pacific Crown)	.45
16	Kenny Lofton (Pinnacle)	.15
17	Deion Sanders (Topps)	.20
18	Jeff Bagwell (Upper Deck)	.40

Welcome to the Show

This special set was another joint venture by the major card manufacturers, Major League Baseball and the Players Association. Sets of six cards were given to attendees at the National Sports Collectors Convention. In designs similar to the companies' regular-issue cards of 1995, these handouts carry a National Packtime logo on front and a red, white and black "WELCOME TO THE SHOW" logo on back. Cards are various numbered "of" 5, 6 or 8, though only six were issued. A paper accompanying the six-card packs assured collectors they were receiving the entire set.

		NM/M
Complete Set (6):		3.00
Common Player:		.50
1 of 6	Greg Maddux (Leaf)	1.00
1/8	Albert Belle (Upper Deck)	.60
2 of 6	Darren Daulton (Ultra)	.50
2 of 6	Don Mattingly (Topps)	1.50
3 of 5	Hideo Nomo (Pinnacle)	.75
3 of 6	Randy Johnson (Pacific)	.75

1986 National Photo Royals

These 2-7/8" x 4-1/4" cards were a team issue produced in conjunction with National Photo. The 24-card set includes 21 players, manager Dick Howser, a Royals' 1985 World Championship commemorative card and a discount offer card from National Photo. Card fronts feature full-color action photos with a blue "Kansas City Royals" at the top of each card. Each player's name, number and position are also included. Card backs list complete professional career statistics, along with the National Photo logo.

		NM/M
Complete Set (24):		3.50
Common Player:		.15
1	Buddy Biancalana	.15
3	Jorge Orta	.15
4	Greg Pryor	.15
5	George Brett	3.00
6	Willie Wilson	.25
8	Jim Sundberg	.15
10	Dick Howser	.15
11	Hal McRae	.15
20	Frank White	.15
22	Lonnie Smith	.15
23	Dennis Leonard	.15
24	Mark Gubicza	.15
24	Darryl Motley	.15
26	Danny Jackson	.15
25	Steve Farr	.15
29	Dan Quisenberry	.25
31	Bret Saberhagen	.25
35	Lynn Jones	.15
37	Charlie Leibrandt	.15
38	Mark Huismann	.15
40	Buddy Black	.15
45	Steve Balboni	.15

----	Header Card	.15
----	Discount Card	.15

1988 Negro League Stars

Players associated with the segregated Negro Leagues around Pittsburgh are featured on this set sponsored by the Duquesne Light Co. and the Pittsburgh Pirates and handed out at the September 10 Pirates game. The 2-1/2" x 3-1/2" cards were issued on a perforated sheet. Fronts have sepia photos. A yellow banner at top reads "NEGRO LEAGUE STARS," a commemorative circle logo appears at lower-right. Backs are in black-and-white with a career summary, biographical data, and the Pirates logo.

		NM/M
Complete Set (20):		12.00
Uncut Sheet:		12.50
Common Player:		.40
1	Rube Foster	.60
2	1913 Homestead Grays	.40
3	Cum Posey	.75
4	1926 Pittsburgh Crawford	.40
5	Gus Greenlee	.40
6	Pop Lloyd	.60
7	Oscar Charleston	.60
8	Smoky Joe Williams	.60
9	Judy Johnson	.60
10	Martin Dihigo	.60
11	Satchel Paige	1.50
12	Josh Gibson	1.50
13	Sam Streeter	.40
14	Cool Papa Bell	.60
15	Ted Page	.40
16	Buck Leonard	1.00
17	Ray Dandridge	.60
18	Lefty Melix, Willis Moody	.40
19	Harold Tinker	.40
20	Monte Irvin	.80

1984 Nestle

The 792 cards in the 1984 Nestle set are identical to the Topps regular issue except that the candy company's logo replaces the Topps logo in the upper-right corner of the front. The set was offered as a premium in uncut 132-card sheet form (24" x 48"). A few enterprising individuals bought up the majority of the reported 4,000 set production and had the sheets cut into single cards. Due to the ease in handling individual cards, as opposed to large press sheets, sets of single cards sell for more than sheet sets.

	NM/M
Complete Set, Sheets (6)	100.00
Complete Set, Singles (792)	130.00
Common Player:	.15
Sheet A:	60.00
Sheet B:	10.00
Sheet C:	10.00
Sheet D:	10.00
Sheet E:	10.00
Sheet F:	10.00

Don Mattingly "Proof/Test"

This fantasy card has been frequently encountered in the market since the days of Mattingly's dominance in the baseball card world in the late 1980s. The card is seen in several variations, always in black-and-white with a blank-back. Some versions of this unauthorized collectors issues carry notations of proof- or test-card status on front and/or back.

Dream Team

This set was issued by the Nestle candy company in conjunction with Topps. Cards are in standard 2-1/2" x 3-1/2" size and feature the top 22 players of 1984, 11 from each league. This full-color "Dream Team" includes one player at each position, plus right- and left-handed starting pitchers and one reliever. Card fronts and backs each have a Nestle logo. An unnumbered checklist was included with the set.

		NM/M
Complete Set (23):		9.00
Common Player:		.35
Uncut Sheet:		10.00
1	Eddie Murray	.75
2	Lou Whitaker	.35
3	George Brett	2.00
4	Cal Ripken	3.50
5	Jim Rice	.50
6	Dave Winfield	.75
7	Lloyd Moseby	.35
8	Lance Parrish	.35
9	LaMarr Hoyt	.35
10	Ron Guidry	.35
11	Dan Quisenberry	.35
12	Steve Garvey	.50
13	Johnny Ray	.35
14	Mike Schmidt	2.00
15	Ozzie Smith	1.50
16	Andre Dawson	.50
17	Tim Raines	.35
18	Dale Murphy	.50
19	Tony Pena	.35
20	John Denny	.35
21	Steve Carlton	.75
22	Al Holland	.35
----	Checklist	.05

1987 Nestle

Nestle, in conjunction with Topps, issued a 33-card set in 1987. Cards #1-11 feature black-and-white photos of players from the "Golden Era." Cards #12-33 feature full-color photos of American (12-22) and National League (23-33) players from the "Modern Era" of baseball. The cards measure 2-1/2" x 3-1/2" and have all team emblems airbrushed away. Three cards were inserted in specially marked six-packs of various Nestle candy bars. Two complete sets were available through a mail-in offer for $1.50 and three proofs of purchase.

		NM/M
Complete Set (33):		10.00
Common Player:		.30
1	Lou Gehrig	.75
2	Rogers Hornsby	.30
3	Pie Traynor	.30
4	Honus Wagner	.50
5	Babe Ruth	2.00
6	Tris Speaker	.30
7	Ty Cobb	.65
8	Mickey Cochrane	.30
9	Walter Johnson	.30
10	Carl Hubbell	.30
11	Jimmie Foxx	.30
12	Rod Carew	.30
13	Nellie Fox	.30
14	Brooks Robinson	.30
15	Luis Aparicio	.30
16	Frank Robinson	.30
17	Mickey Mantle	3.00
18	Ted Williams	.75
19	Yogi Berra	.30
20	Bob Feller	.30
21	Whitey Ford	.30
22	Harmon Killebrew	.30
23	Stan Musial	.60
24	Jackie Robinson	.75
25	Eddie Mathews	.30
26	Ernie Banks	.30
27	Roberto Clemente	1.50
28	Willie Mays	.75
29	Hank Aaron	.75
30	Johnny Bench	.30
31	Bob Gibson	.30
32	Warren Spahn	.30
33	Duke Snider	.30

1988 Nestle

This 44-card set was produced by Mike Schechter Associates for Nestle. "Dream Team" packets of three player cards and one checklist card were inserted in six-packs of Nestle's candy bars. The issue features current players divided into four Dream Teams (East and West teams for each league). The "1988 Nestle" header appears at the top of the red and yellow-bordered cards. Below the player closeup (in an airbrushed cap) is a blue oval player name banner. Card backs are red, white and blue with personal stats, career highlights and major league totals. The bright red, blue and yellow checklist card outlines two special offers; one for an uncut sheet of all 44 player cards and one for a 1988 replica autographed baseball.

		NM/M
Complete Set, Singles (44):		10.00
Complete Set, Uncut Sheet:		10.00
Common Player:		.25
1	Roger Clemens	2.25
2	Dale Murphy	.50
3	Eric Davis	.25
4	Gary Gaetti	.25
5	Ozzie Smith	2.00
6	Mike Schmidt	2.25
7	Ozzie Guillen	.25
8	John Franco	.25
9	Andre Dawson	.25

10	Mark McGwire	2.50
11	Bret Saberhagen	.25
12	Benny Santiago	.25
13	Jose Uribe	.25
14	Will Clark	.25
15	Don Mattingly	2.25
16	Juan Samuel	.25
17	Jack Clark	.25
18	Darryl Strawberry	.25
19	Bill Doran	.25
20	Pete Incaviglia	.25
21	Dwight Gooden	.25
22	Willie Randolph	.25
23	Tim Wallach	.25
24	Pedro Guerrero	.25
25	Steve Bedrosian	.25
26	Gary Carter	1.00
27	Jeff Reardon	.25
28	Dave Righetti	.25
29	Frank White	.25
30	Buddy Bell	.25
31	Tim Raines	.25
32	Wade Boggs	2.00
33	Dave Winfield	1.00
34	George Bell	.25
35	Alan Trammell	.25
36	Joe Carter	.25
37	Jose Canseco	.75
38	Carlton Fisk	1.00
39	Kirby Puckett	2.00
40	Tony Gwynn	2.00
41	Matt Nokes	.25
42	Keith Hernandez	.25
43	Nolan Ryan	3.00
44	Wally Joyner	.25

2002 Nestle

Specially marked boxes of Nestle's ice cream novelties contained one of six Topps-produced cards sealed to the cardboard in a protective plastic pouch. The 2-1/2" x 3-1/2" cards have a color action photo and black-and-white portrait photo on front. Both pictures have had uniform logos removed because the cards are licensed only by the players, and not by MLB. Topps and Nestle's logos appear at top. Backs have another color photo, biographical data, recent stats, career highlights and sponsor/copyright information. Authentically autographed A-Rod and Chipper cards were random inserts.

		NM/M
Complete Set (6):		12.00
Common Player:		2.00
1	Barry Bonds	3.50
2	Chipper Jones	2.00
2	Chipper Jones/Auto.	35.00
3	Mike Piazza	2.50
4	Alex Rodriguez	2.50
4	Alex Rodriguez/Auto.	60.00
5	Sammy Sosa	2.00
6	Ichiro	3.00

1991-1992 NewSport

This set of glossy player cards was issued in France as four-card panels stapled into issues of a monthly magazine devoted to American sports; hence all of the text is

in French. The approximately 4" x 6" cards have a month of issue in tiny type on the back. Fronts have large color game-action photos or poses bordered in white. At top is the player's last name and initial, and his position. The NewSport and MLB logos are at bottom. Backs are in black-and-white with biographical details, major league stats and career summary. The unnumbered cards are checklisted here in alphabetical order. In 2001 a hoard of more than 14,000 of the cards, comprising 175 sets and thousands of four-card panels, was offered in a major hobby auction but did not meet a $5,000 minimum bid.

		NM/M
Complete Set (32):		55.00
Common Player:		1.00
(1)	Roberto Alomar	1.50
(2)	Wade Boggs	4.00
(3)	George Brett	4.50
(4)	Will Clark	1.00
(5)	Eric Davis	1.00
(6)	Rob Dibble	1.00
(7)	Doug Drabek	1.00
(8)	Cecil Fielder	1.00
(9)	Julio Franco	1.00
(10)	Ken Griffey Jr.	5.00
(11)	Rickey Henderson	3.00
(12)	Kent Hrbek	1.00
(13)	Bo Jackson	1.50
(14)	Howard Johnson	1.00
(15)	Barry Larkin	1.00
(16)	Don Mattingly	4.50
(17)	Fred McGriff	1.00
(18)	Mark McGwire	6.00
(19)	Jack Morris	1.00
(20)	Lloyd Moseby	1.00
(21)	Terry Pendleton	1.00
(22)	Kirby Puckett	4.00
(23)	Cal Ripken Jr.	7.50
(24)	Nolan Ryan	7.50
(25)	Bret Saberhagen	1.00
(26)	Ryne Sandberg	4.00
(27)	Benito Santiago	1.00
(28)	Mike Scioscia	1.00
(29)	Ozzie Smith	4.00
(30)	Darryl Strawberry	1.00
(31)	Andy Van Slyke	1.00
(32)	Frank Viola	1.00

1989 J.J. Nissen Super Stars

Distributed with bakery products, these standard-size cards feature central color photos on which uniform logos have been airbrushed away due to lack of a Major League Baseball license by Michael Schechter Associates, the cards' manufacturer. Front graphics are in shades of red, orange and yellow. Backs are printed in black-and-white. The complete set price does not include the Mark Grace card with Vance Law's photo.

		NM/M
Complete Set (20):		7.00
Common Player:		.25
1	Wally Joyner	.25
2	Wade Boggs	1.00
3	Ellis Burks	.25
4	Don Mattingly	1.25
5	Jose Canseco	.75
6	Mike Greenwell	.25
7	Eric Davis	.25
8	Kirby Puckett	1.00
9	Kevin Seitzer	.25
10	Darryl Strawberry	.25
11	Gregg Jefferies	.25
12a	Mark Grace (Photo actually Vance Law.)	3.00
12b	Mark Grace (Correct photo.)	.35
13	Matt Nokes	.25
14	Mark McGwire	1.50
15	Bobby Bonilla	.25
16	Roger Clemens	1.25
17	Frank Viola	.25
18	Orel Hershiser	.25

19	David Cone	.25
20	Ted Williams	2.00

2001 Norstan Milwaukee Brewers Walk of Fame

To commemorate the Walk of Fame in their newly opened ballpark, the Brewers gave this set of inaugural inductees' cards to the first 30,000 fans at the July 12 game. Sponsored by Norstan, whose logo appears in red on front, the 2-1/2" x 3-1/2" cards have sepia toned game-action photos on front with facsimile autograph; at left is a vertical bar with player name and uniform number. Black-and-white backs have another action photo.

		NM/M
Complete Set (4):		8.00
Common Player:		1.00
(1)	Hank Aaron	4.00
(2)	Rollie Fingers	1.00
(3)	Paul Molitor	2.00
(4)	Robin Yount	2.00

1984 N.Y. Mets M.V.P. Club

This nine-card, uncut panel was issued - along with other souvenir items - as a promotion by the New York Mets M.V.P. (Most Valuable Person) Club. Available from the club by mail, the perforated panel features eight full-color player cards, plus a special promotional card in the center. The full panel measures 7-1/2" x 10-1/2", with individual cards measuring the standard 2-1/2" x 3-1/2". Card backs are numbered in the upper right corner and include player stats and career highlights.

		NM/M
Complete Singles Set (9):		3.00
Common Player:		.25
Panel:		4.50
1	Dave Johnson	.25
2	Ron Darling	.25
3	George Foster	.25
4	Keith Hernandez	.50
5	Jesse Orosco	.25
6	Rusty Staub	.40
7	Darryl Strawberry	1.50
8	Mookie Wilson	.35
----	Membership Card	.05

1985 N.Y. Mets Super Fan Club

This nine-card panel was issued as part of a souvenir package by the New York Mets Super Fan Club. The full-color, perforated panel measures 7-1/2" x 10-1/2" and features eight standard-size player cards, plus a special promotional card in the center. The uncut sheet was available by mail directly from the club. The backs are numbered in the upper right corner and include player statistics and career highlights.

		NM/M
Complete Singles Set (9):		3.50
Common Player:		.25
Panel:		4.50
1	Wally Backman	.25
2	Bruce Berenyi	.25
3	Gary Carter	1.00
4	George Foster	.25
5	Dwight Gooden	1.00
6	Keith Hernandez	.50
7	Doug Sisk	.25
8	Darryl Strawberry	.35
----	Membership Card	.05

1985 N.Y. Mets Police

This collectors' issue came out of Florida, where the Mets conducted spring training. The cards were not authorized by the team, the Kiwanis Club or any police agency; they were manufactured strictly for sale to unsuspecting collectors. In format they resemble contemporary safety issues, measuring 2-5/8" x 4-1/4" with color player photos on front and an anti-drug message on back (ironic, considering the percentage of players in the set who had well-publicized substance abuse problems). Because of their unlicensed nature no collectible value is quoted.

Complete Set (6):

1986 N.Y. Mets Super Fan Club

This special nine-card panel was issued by the fan club of the 1986 World Champion New York Mets, along with other souvenir items gained with membership in the club. Included in the full-color set are eight top Mets players, with a promotional card in the center of the panel. Individual cards measure 2-1/2" x 3-1/2", and are perforated at the edges to facilitate separation. The full panel measures 70-1/2" x 10-1/2". Card fronts feature posed photos of each player, along with

name, position and team logo. Backs feature career and personal data, and are printed in the team's blue and orange colors.

		NM/M
Complete Singles Set (9):		2.00
Common Player:		.15
Panel:		2.00
1	Wally Backman	.25
2	Gary Carter	1.00
3	Ron Darling	.25
4	Dwight Gooden	.35
5	Keith Hernandez	.45
6	Howard Johnson	.25
7	Roger McDowell	.25
8	Darryl Strawberry	.35
----	Membership Card	.05

1992 N.Y. Mets Spring Training Superstars

A series of large-format (13-3/4" x 22-3/4") color pictures of Mets players was issued during spring training 1992 by the Port St. Lucie News and The Stuart News in Florida. The pictures are printed on heavy newspaper stock and feature color action photos with a light blue frame and white border. A box at bottom has the player's major league career stats. Various advertisements appear on back. The unnumbered pictures are listed here alphabetically and it is possible this list is not complete.

		NM/M
Complete Set (9):		35.00
Common Player:		4.00
(1)	Bobby Bonilla	4.00
(2)	Kevin Elster	4.00
(3)	John Franco	4.00
(4)	Todd Hundley	4.00
(5)	Howard Johnson	4.00
(6)	Dave Magadan	4.00
(7)	Eddie Murray	8.00
(8)	Willie Randolph	4.00
(9)	Bret Saberhagen	6.00

1997 N.Y. Mets Motion Cards

This issue was handed out to fans as a stadium promotion. The 3-1/2" x 2-1/2" cards have a borderless action scene on front, in which the players move when the card is tilted. Backs are conventionally printed with another player action photo, 1996 stats and biographical details.

		NM/M
Complete Set (4):		9.00
Common Player:		2.00
0	Rey Ordonez	3.00
1	Lance Johnson	2.00
9	Todd Hundley	2.50
31	John Franco	2.00

1982 N.Y. Yankees Yearbook

American League stars of the 1940s-1960s are featured in a two-page cardboard panel stapled into the Yankees yearbook in 1982. The cards were the work of TCMA and done in the style of early-1950s Bowman cards, although the size is the standard 2-1/2" x 3-1/2". Like the '51 Bowmans, the yearbook cards have a color painting of the

player on front with his name in a black strip near the bottom. Backs have a career summary and a bit of personal data along with the TCMA copyright notice. The yearbook originally sold for $3.

		NM/M
Complete Yearbook:		18.00
Complete Set, Singles (18):		16.00
Common Player:		1.00
1	Joe DiMaggio	6.00
2	Billy Pierce	1.00
3	Phil Rizzuto	2.00
4	Ted Williams	5.00
5	Billy Martin	1.50
6	Mel Parnell	1.00
7	Harmon Killebrew	1.50
8	Yogi Berra	2.00
9	Roy Sievers	1.00
10	Bill Dickey	1.50
11	Hank Greenberg	2.00
12	Allie Reynolds	1.00
13	Joe Sewell	1.00
14	Virgil Trucks	1.00
15	Mickey Mantle	8.00
16	Boog Powell	1.00
17	Whitey Ford	1.50
18	Lou Boudreau	1.00

1985 N.Y. Yankees Police

This collectors' issue came out of Florida, where the Yankees conducted spring training. The cards were not authorized by the team, the Kiwanis Club of any police agency; they were manufactured strictly for sale to unsuspecting collectors. In format they resemble contemporary safety issues, measuring 2-5/8" x 4-1/4" with color player photos on front and an anti-drug message on back. Because they are unlicensed, no collector value is attributed.

Complete Set (6):

1981 O-Pee-Chee

The Canadian version of the 1981 Topps set consists of 374 cards. This O-Pee-Chee set features many cards which note a player team change on front. These notations could be accomplished as the OPC cards were printed after the Topps. The cards measure 2-1/2" x 3-1/2" and have texts that are written in both English and French. The cards were printed on both white and gray stock. Cards with gray stock are valued 2-3X those with white stock.

		NM/M
Complete Set (374):		40.00
Common Player:		.10

Wax Pack (8): 2.50
Wax Box (36): 60.00

1 Frank Pastore .10
2 Phil Huffman .10
3 Len Barker .10
4 Robin Yount 2.00
5 Dave Stieb .45
6 Gary Carter 4.00
7 Butch Hobson .10
8 Lance Parrish .10
9 Bruce Sutter 1.50
10 Mike Flanagan .10
11 Paul Mirabella .10
12 Craig Reynolds .10
13 Joe Charboneau .50
14 Dan Driessen .10
15 Larry Parrish .10
16 Ron Davis .10
17 Cliff Johnson .10
18 Bruce Bochte .10
19 Jim Clancy .10
20 Bill Russell .10
21 Ron Oester .10
22 Danny Darwin .10
23 Willie Aikens .10
24 Don Stanhouse .10
25 Sixto Lezcano .10
26 U.L. Washington .10
27 Champ Summers .10
28 Enrique Romo .10
29 Gene Tenace .10
30 Jack Clark .10
31 Checklist 1-125 .10
32 Ken Oberkfell .10
33 Rick Honeycutt .10
34 Al Bumbry .10
35 John Tamargo .10
36 Ed Farmer .10
37 Gary Roenicke .10
38 Tim Foli .10
39 Eddie Murray 2.00
40 Roy Howell .10
41 Bill Gullickson .15
42 Jerry White .10
43 Tim Blackwell .10
44 Steve Henderson .10
45 Enos Cabell .10
46 Rick Bossetti .10
47 Bill North .10
48 Rich Gossage .15
49 Bob Shirley .10
50 Dave Lopes .10
51 Shane Rawley .10
52 Lloyd Moseby .75
53 Burt Hooton .10
54 Ivan DeJesus .10
55 Mike Norris .10
56 Del Unser .10
57 Dave Revering .10
58 Joel Youngblood .10
59 Steve McCatty .10
60 Willie Randolph .10
61 Butch Wynegar .10
62 Gary Lavelle .10
63 Willie Montanez .10
64 Terry Puhl .10
65 Scott McGregor .10
66 Buddy Bell .10
67 Toby Harrah .10
68 Jim Rice .45
69 Darrell Evans .10
70 Al Oliver .10
71 Hal Dues .10
72 Barry Evans .10
73 Doug Bair .10
74 Mike Hargrove .10
75 Reggie Smith .10
76 Mario Mendoza .10
77 Mike Barlow .10
78 Garth Iorg .10
79 Jeff Reardon 1.00
80 Roger Erickson .10
81 Dave Stapleton .10
82 Barry Bonnell .10
83 Dave Concepcion .10
84 Johnnie LeMaster .10
85 Mike Caldwell .10
86 Wayne Gross .10
87 Rick Camp .10
88 Joe Lefebvre .10
89 Darrell Jackson .10
90 Bake McBride .10
91 Tim Stoddard .10
92 Mike Easler .10
93 Jim Bibby .10
94 Kent Tekulve .10
95 Jim Sundberg .10
96 Tommy John .15

97 Chris Speier .10
98 Clint Hurdle .10
99 Phil Garner .10
100 Rod Carew 2.00
101 Steve Stone .10
102 Joe Niekro .10
103 Jerry Martin .10
104 Ron LeFlore .10
105 Jose Cruz .10
106 Don Money .10
107 Bobby Brown .10
108 Larry Herndon .10
109 Dennis Eckersley 1.50
110 Carl Yastrzemski 2.50
111 Greg Minton .10
112 Dan Schatzeder .10
113 George Brett 4.00
114 Tom Underwood .10
115 Roy Smalley .10
116 Carlton Fisk 2.00
117 Pete Falcone .10
118 Dale Murphy 1.00
119 Tippy Martinez .10
120 Larry Bowa .10
121 Julio Cruz .10
122 Jim Gantner .10
123 Al Cowens .10
124 Jerry Garvin .10
125 Andre Dawson 3.00
126 Charlie Leibrandt .10
127 Willie Stargell 2.00
128 Andre Thornton .10
129 Art Howe .10
130 Larry Gura .10
131 Jerry Remy .10
132 Rick Dempsey .10
133 Alan Trammell .15
134 Mike LaCoss .10
135 Gorman Thomas .10
136 Expos Future Stars
(Bobby Pate, Tim Raines,
Roberto Ramos) 3.00
137 Bill Madlock .10
138 Rich Dotson .10
139 Oscar Gamble .10
140 Bob Forsch .10
141 Miguel Dilone .10
142 Jackson Todd .10
143 Dan Meyer .10
144 Garry Templeton .10
145 Mickey Rivers .10
146 Alan Ashby .10
147 Dale Berra .10
148 Randy Jones .10
149 Joe Nolan .10
150 Mark Fidrych .25
151 Tony Armas .10
152 Steve Kemp .10
153 Jerry Reuss .10
154 Rick Langford .10
155 Chris Chambliss .10
156 Bob McClure .10
157 John Wathan .10
158 John Curtis .10
159 Steve Howe .10
160 Garry Maddox .10
161 Dan Graham .10
162 Doug Corbett .10
163 Rob Dressler .10
164 Bucky Dent .10
165 Alvis Woods .10
166 Floyd Bannister .10
167 Lee Mazzilli .10
168 Don Robinson .10
169 John Mayberry .10
170 Woodie Fryman .10
171 Gene Richards .10
172 Rick Burleson .10
173 Bump Wills .10
174 Glenn Abbott .10
175 Dave Collins .10
176 Mike Krukow .10
177 Rick Monday .10
178 Dave Parker .10
179 Rudy May .10
180 Pete Rose 6.00
181 Elias Sosa .10
182 Bob Grich .10
183 Fred Norman .10
184 Jim Dwyer .10
185 Dennis Leonard .10
186 Gary Matthews .10
187 Ron Hassey .10
188 Doug DeCinces .10
189 Craig Swan .10
190 Cesar Cedeno .10
191 Rick Sutcliffe .10
192 Kiko Garcia .10
193 Pete Vuckovich .10
194 Tony Bernazard .10
195 Keith Hernandez .10
196 Jerry Mumphrey .10
197 Jim Kern .10
198 Jerry Dybzinski .10
199 John Lowenstein .10
200 George Foster .10
201 Phil Niekro 1.50
202 Bill Buckner .10
203 Steve Carlton 2.00
204 John D'Acquisto .10
205 Rick Reuschel .10
206 Dan Quisenberry .10
207 Mike Schmidt 4.00
208 Bob Watson .10
209 Jim Spencer .10
210 Jim Palmer 1.50
211 Derrel Thomas .10
212 Steve Nicosia .10

213 Omar Moreno .10
214 Richie Zisk .10
215 Larry Hisle .10
216 Mike Torrez .10
217 Rich Hebner .10
218 Britt Burns .10
219 Ken Landreaux .10
220 Tom Seaver 2.00
221 Bob Davis .10
222 Jorge Orta .10
223 Bobby Bonds .10
224 Pat Zachry .10
225 Ruppert Jones .10
226 Duane Kuiper .10
227 Rodney Scott .10
228 Tom Paciorek .10
229 Rollie Fingers 1.50
230 George Hendrick .10
231 Tony Perez 2.50
232 Grant Jackson .10
233 Damaso Garcia .10
234 Lou Whitaker .10
235 Scott Sanderson .10
236 Mike Ivie .10
237 Charlie Moore .10
238 Blue Jays Future Stars
(Luis Leal, Brian Milner,
Ken Schrom) .45
239 Rick Miller .10
240 Nolan Ryan 9.00
241 Checklist 126-250 .10
242 Chet Lemon .10
243 Dave Palmer .10
244 Ellis Valentine .10
245 Carney Lansford .10
246 Ed Ott .10
247 Glenn Hubbard .10
248 Joey McLaughlin .10
249 Jerry Narron .10
250 Ron Guidry .10
251 Steve Garvey .75
252 Victor Cruz .10
253 Bobby Murcer .10
254 Ozzie Smith 3.00
255 John Stearns .10
256 Bill Campbell .10
257 Rennie Stennett .10
258 Rick Waits .10
259 Gary Lucas .10
260 Ron Cey .10
261 Rickey Henderson 8.00
262 Sammy Stewart .10
263 Brian Downing .10
264 Mark Bomback .10
265 John Candelaria .10
266 Renie Martin .10
267 Stan Bahnsen .10
268 Expos Team .50
269 Ken Forsch .10
270 Greg Luzinski .10
271 Ron Jackson .10
272 Wayne Garland .10
273 Milt May .10
274 Rick Wise .10
275 Dwight Evans .10
276 Sal Bando .10
277 Alfredo Griffin .10
278 Rick Sofield .10
279 Bob Knepper .10
280 Ken Griffey .10
281 Ken Singleton .10
282 Ernie Whitt .10
283 Billy Sample .10
284 Jack Morris .10
285 Dick Ruthven .10
286 Johnny Bench 2.00
287 Dave Smith .10
288 Amos Otis .10
289 Dave Goltz .10
290 Bob Boone .10
291 Aurelio Lopez .10
292 Tom Hume .10
293 Charlie Lea .10
294 Bert Blyleven .10
295 Hal McRae .10
296 Bob Stanley .10
297 Bob Bailor .10
298 Jerry Koosman .10
299 Eliott Maddox .10
300 Paul Molitor 2.50
301 Matt Keough .10
302 Pat Putnam .10
303 Dan Ford .10
304 John Castino .10
305 Barry Foote .10
306 Lou Piniella .15
307 Gene Garber .10
308 Rick Manning .10
309 Don Baylor .10
310 Vida Blue .10
311 Doug Flynn .10
312 Rick Rhoden .10
313 Fred Lynn .10
314 Rich Dauer .10
315 Kirk Gibson 2.50
316 Ken Reitz .10
317 Lonnie Smith .10
318 Steve Yeager .10
319 Rowland Office .10
320 Tom Burgmeier .10
321 Leon Durham .10
322 Neil Allen .10
323 Ray Burris .10
324 Mike Willis .10
325 Ray Knight .10
326 Rafael Landestoy .10
327 Moose Haas .10
328 Ross Baumgarten .10

329 Joaquin Andujar .10
330 Frank White .10
331 Blue Jays Team .50
332 Dick Drago .10
333 Sid Monge .10
334 Joe Sambito .10
335 Rick Cerone .10
336 Eddie Whitson .10
337 Sparky Lyle .10
338 Checklist 251-374 .10
339 Jon Matlack .10
340 Ben Oglivie .10
341 Dwayne Murphy .10
342 Terry Crowley .10
343 Frank Taveras .10
344 Steve Rogers .10
345 Warren Cromartie .10
346 Bill Caudill .10
347 Harold Baines 1.50
348 Frank LaCorte .10
349 Glenn Hoffman .10
350 J.R. Richard .10
351 Otto Velez .10
352 Ted Simmons .10
353 Terry Kennedy .10
354 Al Hrabosky .10
355 Bob Horner .10
356 Cecil Cooper .10
357 Bob Welch .10
358 Paul Moskau .10
359 Dave Rader .10
360 Willie Wilson .10
361 Dave Kingman .10
362 Joe Rudi .10
363 Rich Gale .10
364 Steve Trout .10
365 Graig Nettles .10
366 Lamar Johnson .10
367 Denny Martinez .10
368 Manny Trillo .10
369 Frank Tanana .10
370 Reggie Jackson 2.50
371 Bill Lee .10
372 Jay Johnstone .10
373 Jason Thompson .10
374 Tom Hutton .10

Posters

Inserted inside the regular 1981 O-Pee-Chee wax packs, these full-color posters measure approximately 4-7/8" x 6-7/8". The set is complete at 24 posters and includes 12 players each from the Blue Jays and Expos. The blank-backed posters are numbered in the border below the photo where the caption is written in both French and English. The photos are surrounded by a blue border for Blue Jays players or a red border for Expos. Because they were inserted in wax packs, the posters are usually found quarter-folded; such folds are not considered in grading.

NM/M
Complete Set (24): 10.00
Common Player: .50

1 Willie Montanez .50
2 Rodney Scott .50
3 Chris Speier .50
4 Larry Parrish .50
5 Warren Cromartie .50
6 Andre Dawson 2.00
7 Ellis Valentine .50
8 Gary Carter 5.00
9 Steve Rogers .50
10 Woodie Fryman .50
11 Jerry White .50
12 Scott Sanderson .50
13 John Mayberry .50
14 Damasa Garcia (Damaso) .50
15 Alfredo Griffin .50
16 Garth Iorg .50
17 Alvis Woods .50
18 Rick Bosetti .50
19 Barry Bonnell .50
20 Ernie Whitt .50
21 Jim Clancy .50
22 Dave Stieb 1.50
23 Otto Velez .50
24 Lloyd Moseby .50

1982 O-Pee-Chee

The 1982 O-Pee-Chee set, complete at 396 cards, is nearly identical in design to the 1982 Topps set, except the Canadian-issued cards display the O-Pee-Chee logo on the front of the card and list the player's position in both French and English. The backs of the cards, which measure the standard 2-1/2" x 3-1/2", are also bilingual. Some of the cards carry an extra line on the front indicating an off-season team change.

NM/M
Complete Set (396): 35.00
Common Player: .10
Wax Pack: 1.50
Wax Box (36): 40.00

1 Dan Spillner .10
2 Ken Singleton/AS .10
3 John Candelaria .10
4 Frank Tanana .10
5 Reggie Smith .10
6 Rick Monday .10
7 Scott Sanderson .10
8 Rich Gauer .10
9 Ron Guidry .15
10 Ron Guidry/IA .10
11 Tom Brookens .10
12 Moose Haas .10
13 Chet Lemon .10
14 Steve Howe .10
15 Ellis Valentine .10
16 Toby Harrah .10
17 Darrell Evans .10
18 Johnny Bench 2.00
19 Ernie Whitt .10
20 Garry Maddox .10
21 Graig Nettles/IA .10
22 Al Oliver/IA .10
23 Bob Boone .10
24 Pete Rose/IA 2.00
25 Jerry Remy .10
26 Jorge Orta .10
27 Bobby Bonds .10
28 Jim Clancy .10
29 Dwayne Murphy .10
30 Tom Seaver 2.00
31 Tom Seaver/IA 1.00
32 Claudell Washington .10
33 Bob Shirley .10
34 Bob Forsch .10
35 Willie Aikens .10
36 Rod Carew/AS .60
37 Willie Randolph .10
38 Charlie Lea .10
39 Lou Whitaker .10
40 Dave Parker .10
41 Dave Parker/IA .10
42 Mark Belanger .10
43 Rick Langford .10
44 Rollie Fingers/IA .10
45 Rick Cerone .10
46 Johnny Wockenfuss .10
47 Jack Morris/AS .10
48 Cesar Cedeno .10
49 Alvis Woods .10
50 Buddy Bell .10
51 Mickey Rivers/IA .10
52 Steve Rogers .10
53 Blue Jays Team .50
54 Ron Hassey .10
55 Rick Burleson .10
56 Harold Baines .10
57 Craig Reynolds .10
58 Carlton Fisk/AS .60
59 Jim Kern .10
60 Tony Armas .10
61 Warren Cromartie .10
62 Graig Nettles .10
63 Jerry Koosman .10
64 Pat Zachry .10
65 Terry Kennedy .10
66 Richie Zisk .10
67 Rich Gale .10
68 Steve Carlton 2.00
69 Greg Luzinski/IA .10
70 Tim Raines 2.00
71 Roy Lee Jackson .10
72 Carl Yastrzemski 2.00
73 John Castino .10
74 Joe Niekro .10
75 Tommy John .15
76 Miguel Dilone .10
77 Gary Gray .10

79 Tom Hume .10
80 Jim Palmer 1.50
81 Jim Palmer/IA .75
82 Vida Blue/IA .10
83 Garth Iorg .10
84 Rennie Stennett .10
85 Davey Lopes/IA .10
86 Dave Concepcion .10
87 Matt Keough .10
88 Jim Spencer .10
89 Steve Henderson .10
90 Nolan Ryan 7.50
91 Carney Lansford .10
92 Bake McBride .10
93 Dave Stapleton .10
94 Expos Team .50
95 Ozzie Smith 4.00
96 Rich Hebner .10
97 Tim Foli .10
98 Darrell Porter .10
99 Barry Bonnell .10
100 Mike Schmidt 3.00
101 Mike Schmidt/IA 1.50
102 Dan Briggs .10
103 Al Cowens .10
104 Grant Jackson .10
105 Kirk Gibson .10
106 Dan Schatzeder .10
107 Juan Berenguer .10
108 Jack Morris .15
109 Dave Revering .10
110 Carlton Fisk 2.00
111 Carlton Fisk/IA 1.00
112 Billy Sample .10
113 Steve McCatty .10
114 Ken Landreaux .10
115 Gaylord Perry 1.00
116 Elias Sosa .10
117 Rich Gossage/IA .10
118 Expos Future Stars
(Terry Francona, Brad Mills,
Bryn Smith) .25
119 Billy Almon .10
120 Gary Lucas .10
121 Ken Oberkfell .10
122 Steve Carlton/IA 1.00
123 Jeff Reardon .50
124 Bill Buckner .10
125 Danny Ainge 2.50
126 Paul Splittorff .10
127 Lonnie Smith .10
128 Rudy May .10
129 Checklist 1-132 .10
130 Julio Cruz .10
131 Stan Bahnsen .10
132 Pete Vuckovich .10
133 Luis Salazar .10
134 Dan Ford .10
135 Denny Martinez .10
136 Lary Sorensen .10
137 Fergie Jenkins 1.50
138 Rick Camp .10
139 Wayne Nordhagen .10
140 Ron LeFlore .10
141 Rick Sutcliffe .10
142 Rick Waits .10
143 Mookie Wilson .10
144 Greg Minton .10
145 Bob Horner .10
146 Joe Morgan/IA 1.00
147 Larry Gura .10
148 Alfredo Griffin .10
149 Pat Putnam .10
150 Ted Simmons .10
151 Gary Matthews .10
152 Greg Luzinski .10
153 Mike Flanagan .10
154 Jim Morrison .10
155 Otto Velez .10
156 Frank White .10
157 Doug Corbett .10
158 Brian Downing .10
159 Willie Randolph/IA .10
160 Luis Tiant .10
161 Andre Thornton .10
162 Amos Otis .10
163 Paul Mirabella .10
164 Bert Blyleven .10
165 Rowland Office .10
166 Gene Tenace .10
167 Cecil Cooper .10
168 Bruce Benedict .10
169 Mark Clear .10
170 Jim Bibby .10
171 Ken Griffey Sr./IA .10
172 Bill Gullickson .10
173 Mike Scioscia .10
174 Doug DeCinces .10
175 Jerry Mumphrey .10
176 Rollie Fingers 1.00
177 George Foster/IA .10
178 Mitchell Page .10
179 Steve Garvey .50
180 Steve Garvey/IA .25
181 Woodie Fryman .10
182 Larry Herndon .10
183 Frank White/IA .10
184 Alan Ashby .10
185 Phil Niekro 1.00
186 Leon Roberts .10
187 Rod Carew 2.00
188 Willie Stargell/IA 1.00
189 Joel Youngblood .10
190 J.R. Richard .10
191 Tim Wallach .50
192 Broderick Perkins .10
193 Johnny Grubb .10
194 Larry Bowa .10

195 Paul Molitor 3.00
196 Willie Upshaw .10
197 Roy Smalley .10
198 Chris Speier .10
199 Don Aase .10
200 George Brett 3.00
201 George Brett/IA 1.50
202 Rick Manning .10
203 Blue Jays Future Stars (Jesse Barfield, Brian Milner, Boomer Wells) 2.00
204 Rick Reuschel .10
205 Neil Allen .10
206 Leon Durham .10
207 Jim Gantner .10
208 Joe Morgan 2.00
209 Gary Lavelle .10
210 Keith Hernandez .10
211 Joe Charboneau .10
212 Mario Mendoza .10
213 Willie Randolph/AS .10
214 Lance Parrish .10
215 Mike Krukow .10
216 Ron Cey .10
217 Ruppert Jones .10
218 Dave Lopes .10
219 Steve Yeager .10
220 Manny Trillo .10
221 Dave Concepcion/IA .10
222 Butch Wynegar .10
223 Lloyd Moseby .20
224 Bruce Bochte .10
225 Ed Ott .10
226 Checklist 133-264 .10
227 Ray Burris .10
228 Reggie Smith/IA .10
229 Oscar Gamble .10
230 Willie Wilson .10
231 Brian Kingman .10
232 John Stearns .10
233 Duane Kuiper .10
234 Don Baylor .10
235 Mike Easler .10
236 Lou Piniella .10
237 Robin Yount 2.00
238 Kevin Saucier .10
239 Jon Matlack .10
240 Bucky Dent .10
241 Bucky Dent/IA .10
242 Milt May .10
243 Lee Mazzilli .10
244 Gary Carter 3.00
245 Ken Reitz .10
246 Scott McGregor/AS .10
247 Pedro Guerrero .10
248 Art Howe .10
249 Dick Tidrow .10
250 Tug McGraw .10
251 Fred Lynn .10
252 Fred Lynn/IA .10
253 Gene Richards .10
254 Jorge Bell 4.00
255 Tony Perez 2.50
256 Tony Perez/IA .10
257 Rich Dotson .10
258 Bo Diaz .10
259 Rodney Scott .10
260 Bruce Sutter 1.50
261 George Brett/AS 1.00
262 Rick Dempsey .10
263 Mike Phillips .10
264 Jerry Garvin .10
265 Al Bumbry .10
266 Hubie Brooks .10
267 Vida Blue .10
268 Rickey Henderson 3.00
269 Rick Peters .10
270 Rusty Staub .20
271 Sixto Lezcano .10
272 Bump Wills .10
273 Gary Allenson .10
274 Randy Jones .10
275 Bob Watson .10
276 Dave Kingman .10
277 Terry Puhl .10
278 Jerry Reuss .10
279 Sammy Stewart .10
280 Ben Oglivie .10
281 Kent Tekulve .10
282 Ken Macha .10
283 Ron Davis .10
284 Bob Grich .10
285 Sparky Lyle .10
286 Rich Gossage/AS .10
287 Dennis Eckersley 1.00
288 Garry Templeton .10
289 Bob Stanley .10
290 Ken Singleton .10
291 Mickey Hatcher .10
292 Dave Palmer .10
293 Damaso Garcia .10
294 Don Money .10
295 George Hendrick .10
296 Steve Kemp .10
297 Dave Smith .10
298 Bucky Dent/AS .10
299 Steve Trout .10
300 Reggie Jackson 2.50
301 Reggie Jackson/IA 1.00
302 Doug Flynn .10
303 Wayne Gross .10
304 Johnny Bench/IA 1.00
305 Don Sutton 1.00
306 Don Sutton/IA .40
307 Mark Bomback .10
308 Charlie Moore .10
309 Jeff Burroughs .10
310 Mike Hargrove .10

311 Enos Cabell .10
312 Lenny Randle .10
313 Ivan DeJesus .10
314 Buck Martinez .10
315 Burt Hooton .10
316 Scott McGregor .10
317 Dick Ruthven .10
318 Mike Heath .10
319 Ray Knight .10
320 Chris Chambliss .10
321 Chris Chambliss/IA .10
322 Ross Baumgarten .10
323 Bill Lee .10
324 Gorman Thomas .10
325 Jose Cruz .10
326 Al Oliver .10
327 Jackson Todd .10
328 Ed Farmer .10
329 U.L. Washington .10
330 Ken Griffey .10
331 John Milner .10
332 Don Robinson .10
333 Cliff Johnson .10
334 Fernando Valenzuela .15
335 Jim Sundberg .10
336 George Foster .10
337 Pete Rose/AS 1.50
338 Davey Lopes/AS .10
339 Mike Schmidt/AS 1.00
340 Dave Concepcion/AS .10
341 Andre Dawson/AS .25
342 George Foster /AS .10
343 Dave Parker/AS .10
344 Gary Carter/AS 1.00
345 Fernando Valenzuela/AS .10
346 Tom Seaver/AS .60
347 Bruce Sutter/AS .75
348 Darrell Porter/IA .10
349 Dave Collins .10
350 Amos Otis/IA .10
351 Frank Taveras .10
352 Dave Winfield 3.00
353 Larry Parrish .10
354 Roberto Ramos .10
355 Dwight Evans .10
356 Mickey Rivers .10
357 Butch Hobson .10
358 Carl Yastrzemski/IA 1.00
359 Ron Jackson .10
360 Len Barker .10
361 Pete Rose 4.00
362 Kevin Hickey .10
363 Rod Carew/IA 1.00
364 Hector Cruz .10
365 Bill Madlock .10
366 Jim Rice .40
367 Ron Cey (IA) .10
368 Luis Leal .10
369 Dennis Leonard .10
370 Mike Norris .10
371 Tom Paciorek .10
372 Willie Stargell 2.00
373 Dan Driessen .10
374 Larry Bowa/IA .10
375 Dusty Baker .10
376 Joey McLaughlin .10
377 Reggie Jackson/AS .60
378 Mike Caldwell .10
379 Andre Dawson 1.00
380 Dave Stieb .20
381 Alan Trammell .10
382 John Mayberry .10
383 John Wathan .10
384 Hal McRae .10
385 Ken Forsch .10
386 Jerry White .10
387 Tom Veryzer .10
388 Joe Rudi .10
389 Bob Knepper .10
390 Eddie Murray 2.00
391 Dale Murphy .50
392 Bob Boone/IA .10
393 Al Hrabosky .10
394 Checklist 265-396 .10
395 Omar Moreno .10
396 Rich Gossage .15

Posters

MONTREAL EXPOS ... GARY CARTER

The 24 posters in this Canadian set, which features 12 players from the Expos and 12 from the Blue Jays, were inserted in regular 1982 O-Pee-Chee wax packs. The posters measure approximately 4-7/8" x 6-7/8" and are usually found quarter-folded for pack insertion. Such fold lines are not considered in grading. The blank-backed posters are numbered in the bottom border where the captions appear in both French and English. Red borders surround the photos of Blue Jays players, while blue borders are used for the Expos.

NM/M
Complete Set (24): 12.00
Common Player: .50
1 John Mayberry .50
2 Damaso Garcia .50
3 Ernie Whitt .50
4 Lloyd Moseby .50
5 Alvis Woods .50
6 Dave Stieb .75
7 Roy Lee Jackson .50
8 Joey McLaughlin .50
9 Luis Leal .50
10 Aurelio Rodriguez .50
11 Otto Velez .50
12 Juan Berenger (Berenguer) .50
13 Warren Cromartie .50
14 Rodney Scott .50
15 Larry Parrish .50
16 Gary Carter 5.00
17 Tim Raines 2.00
18 Andre Dawson 2.00
19 Terry Francona .50
20 Steve Rogers .50
21 Bill Gullickson .50
22 Scott Sanderson .50
23 Jeff Reardon .50
24 Jerry White .50

Stickers

The Canadian OPC stickers are identical to the Topps version except for the bi-lingual printing on backs.

1983 O-Pee-Chee

Again complete at 396 cards, the 1983 O-Pee-Chee set borrows its design from the 1983 Topps set, except the Canadian-issued cards display the O-Pee-Chee logo on the front of the card and show the player's position in both French and English. The backs of the cards are also printed in both languages. The cards measure the standard 2-1/2" x 3-1/2". Some cards carry the extra line on the front indicating an off-season trade.

NM/M
Complete Set (396): 30.00
Common Player: .05
Wax Pack: 3.00
Wax Box (36): 60.00
1 Rusty Staub .15
2 Larry Parrish .05
3 George Brett 1.75
4 Carl Yastrzemski 1.50
5 Al Oliver (Super Veteran) .05
6 Bill Virdon .05
7 Gene Richards .05
8 Steve Balboni .05
9 Joey McLaughlin .05
10 Gorman Thomas .05
11 Chris Chambliss .05
12 Ray Burris .05
13 Larry Herndon .05
14 Ozzie Smith 1.50
15 Ron Cey .05
16 Willie Wilson .05
17 Kent Tekulve .05
18 Kent Tekulve (Super Veteran) .05
19 Oscar Gamble .05
20 Carlton Fisk 1.25
21 Dale Murphy/AS .05
22 Randy Lerch .05
23 Dale Murphy .45
24 Steve Mura .05
25 Hal McRae .05
26 Dennis Lamp .05
27 Ron Washington .05
28 Bruce Bochte .05
29 Randy Jones .05
30 Jim Rice .15
31 Bill Gullickson .05
32 Dave Concepcion/AS .05
33 Ted Simmons (Super Veteran) .05

34 Bobby Cox .05
35 Rollie Fingers .60
36 Rollie Fingers (Super Veteran) .10
37 Mike Hargrove .05
38 Roy Smalley .05
39 Terry Puhl .05
40 Fernando Valenzuela .05
41 Garry Maddox .05
42 Dale Murray .05
43 Bob Dernier .05
44 Don Robinson .05
45 John Mayberry .05
46 Richard Dotson .05
47 Wayne Nordhagen .05
48 Lary Sorenson .05
49 Willie McGee .15
50 Bob Horner .05
51 Rusty Staub (Super Veteran) .05
52 Tom Seaver 1.25
53 Chet Lemon .05
54 Scott Sanderson .05
55 Mookie Wilson .05
56 Reggie Jackson 1.50
57 Tim Blackwell .05
58 Keith Moreland .05
59 Alvis Woods .05
60 Johnny Bench 1.25
61 Johnny Bench (Super Veteran) .30
62 Jim Gott .05
63 Rick Monday .05
64 Gary Matthews .05
65 Jack Morris .15
66 Lou Whitaker .05
67 U.L. Washington .05
68 Eric Show .05
69 Lee Lacy .05
70 Steve Carlton 1.25
71 Steve Carlton (Super Veteran) .10
72 Tom Paciorek .05
73 Manny Trillo .05
74 Tony Perez (Super Veteran) .05
75 Amos Otis .05
76 Rick Mahler .05
77 Hosken Powell .05
78 Bill Caudill .05
79 Dan Petry .05
80 George Foster .05
81 Joe Morgan .05
82 Burt Hooton .05
83 Ryne Sandberg 8.00
84 Alan Ashby .05
85 Ken Singleton .05
86 Tom Hume .05
87 Dennis Leonard .05
88 Jim Gantner .05
89 Leon Roberts .05
90 Jerry Reuss .05
91 Ben Oglivie .05
92 Sparky Lyle (Super Veteran) .05
93 John Castino .05
94 Phil Niekro .60
95 Alan Trammell .10
96 Gaylord Perry .05
97 Tom Herr .05
98 Vance Law .05
99 Dickie Noles .05
100 Pete Rose 2.00
101 Pete Rose (Super Veteran) .50
102 Dave Concepcion .05
103 Darrell Porter .05
104 Ron Guidry .05
105 Don Baylor .05
106 Steve Rogers/AS .05
107 Greg Minton .05
108 Glenn Hoffman .05
109 Luis Leal .05
110 Ken Griffey .05
111 Expos Team .05
112 Luis Pujols .05
113 Julio Cruz .05
114 Jim Slaton .05
115 Chili Davis .05
116 Pedro Guerrero .05
117 Mike Ivie .05
118 Chris Welsh .05
119 Frank Pastore .05
120 Len Barker .05
121 Chris Speier .05
122 Bobby Murcer .05
123 Bill Russell .05
124 Lloyd Moseby .05
125 Leon Durham .05
126 Carl Yastrzemski (Super Veteran) .05
127 John Candelaria .05
128 Phil Garner .05
129 Checklist 1-132 .05
130 Dave Stieb .10
131 Geoff Zahn .05
132 Todd Cruz .05
133 Tony Pena .05
134 Hubie Brooks .05
135 Dwight Evans .05
136 Willie Aikens .05
137 Woodie Fryman .05
138 Rick Dempsey .05
139 Bruce Berenyi .05
140 Willie Randolph .05
141 Eddie Murray 1.25
142 Mike Caldwell .05
143 Tony Gwynn 8.00

144 Tommy John (Super Veteran) .05
145 Don Sutton .60
146 Don Sutton (Super Veteran) .10
147 Rick Manning .05
148 George Hendrick .05
149 Johnny Ray .05
150 Bruce Sutter 1.00
151 Bruce Sutter (Super Veteran) .25
152 Jay Johnstone .05
153 Jerry Koosman .05
154 Johnnie LeMaster .05
155 Dan Quisenberry .05
156 Luis Salazar .05
157 Steve Bedrosian .05
158 Jim Sundberg .05
159 Gaylord Perry (Super Veteran) .10
160 Dave Kingman .05
161 Dave Kingman (Super Veteran) .05
162 Mark Clear .05
163 Cal Ripken 8.00
164 Dave Palmer .05
165 Dan Driessen .05
166 Tug McGraw .05
167 Denny Martinez .10
168 Juan Eichelberger .05
169 Doug Flynn .05
170 Steve Howe .05
171 Frank White .05
172 Mike Flanagan .05
173 Andre Dawson/AS .15
174 Manny Trillo/AS .05
175 Bo Diaz .05
176 Dave Righetti .05
177 Harold Baines .05
178 Vida Blue .05
179 Luis Tiant (Super Veteran) .05
180 Rickey Henderson 1.50
181 Rick Rhoden .05
182 Fred Lynn .05
183 Ed Vande Berg .05
184 Dwayne Murphy .05
185 Tim Lollar .05
186 Dave Tobik .05
187 Tug McGraw (Super Veteran) .05
188 Rick Miller .05
189 Dan Schatzeder .05
190 Cecil Cooper .05
191 Jim Beattie .05
192 Rich Dauer .05
193 Al Cowens .05
194 Roy Lee Jackson .05
195 Mike Gates .05
196 Tommy John .10
197 Bob Forsch .05
198 Steve Garvey .15
199 Brad Mills .05
200 Rod Carew 1.25
201 Rod Carew (Super Veteran) .05
202 Blue Jays Team .05
203 Floyd Bannister .05
204 Bruce Benedict .05
205 Dave Parker .05
206 Ken Oberkfell .05
207 Graig Nettles (Super Veteran) .05
208 Sparky Lyle .05
209 Jason Thompson .05
210 Jack Clark .05
211 Jim Kaat .05
212 John Stearns .05
213 Tom Burgmeier .05
214 Jerry White .05
215 Mario Soto .05
216 Scott McGregor .05
217 Tim Stoddard .05
218 Bill Laskey .05
219 Reggie Jackson (Super Veteran) .05
220 Dusty Baker .05
221 Joe Niekro .05
222 Damaso Garcia .05
223 John Montefusco .05
224 Mickey Rivers .05
225 Enos Cabell .05
226 LaMarr Hoyt .05
227 Tim Raines .20
228 Joaquin Andujar .05
229 Tim Wallach .15
230 Fergie Jenkins .05
231 Fergie Jenkins (Super Veteran) .05
232 Tom Brunansky .05
233 Ivan DeJesus .05
234 Bryn Smith .05
235 Claudell Washington .05
236 Steve Renko .05
237 Dan Norman .05
238 Cesar Cedeno .05
239 Dave Stapleton .05
240 Rich Gossage .10
241 Rich Gossage (Super Veteran) .05
242 Bob Stanley .05
243 Rich Gale .05
244 Sixto Lezcano .05
245 Steve Sax .05
246 Jerry Mumphrey .05
247 Dave Smith .05
248 Bake McBride .05
249 Checklist 133-264 .05
250 Bill Buckner .05

251 Kent Hrbek .05
252 Gene Tenace .05
253 Charlie Lea .05
254 Rick Cerone .05
255 Gene Garber .05
256 Gene Garber (Super Veteran) .05
257 Jesse Barfield .30
258 Dave Winfield 1.50
259 Don Money .05
260 Steve Kemp .05
261 Steve Yeager .05
262 Keith Hernandez .05
263 Tippy Martinez .05
264 Joe Morgan (Super Veteran) .05
265 Joel Youngblood .05
266 Bruce Sutter/AS .25
267 Terry Francona .05
268 Neil Allen .05
269 Ron Oester .05
270 Dennis Eckersley .60
271 Dale Berra .05
272 Al Bumbry .05
273 Lonnie Smith .05
274 Terry Kennedy .05
275 Ray Knight .05
276 Mike Norris .05
277 Rance Mulliniks .05
278 Dan Spillner .05
279 Bucky Dent .05
280 Bert Blyleven .05
281 Barry Bonnell .05
282 Reggie Smith .05
283 Reggie Smith (Super Veteran) .05
284 Ted Simmons .05
285 Lance Parrish .05
286 Larry Christenson .05
287 Ruppert Jones .05
288 Bob Welch .05
289 John Wathan .05
290 Jeff Reardon .05
291 Dave Revering .05
292 Craig Swan .05
293 Graig Nettles .05
294 Alfredo Griffin .05
295 Jerry Remy .05
296 Joe Sambito .05
297 Ron LeFlore .05
298 Brian Downing .05
299 Jim Palmer 1.00
300 Mike Schmidt 1.75
301 Mike Schmidt (Super Veteran) .35
302 Ernie Whitt .05
303 Andre Dawson .75
304 Bobby Murcer (Super Veteran) .05
305 Larry Bowa .05
306 Lee Mazzilli .05
307 Lou Piniella .05
308 Buck Martinez .05
309 Jerry Martin .05
310 Greg Luzinski .05
311 Al Oliver .05
312 Mike Torrez .05
313 Dick Ruthven .05
314 Gary Carter/AS .05
315 Rick Burleson .05
316 Phil Niekro (Super Veteran) .10
317 Moose Haas .05
318 Carney Lansford .05
319 Tim Foli .05
320 Steve Rogers .05
321 Kirk Gibson .05
322 Glenn Hubbard .05
323 Luis DeLeon .05
324 Mike Marshall .05
325 Von Hayes .05
326 Garth Iorg .05
327 Jose Cruz .05
328 Jim Palmer (Super Veteran) .10
329 Darrell Evans .05
330 Buddy Bell .05
331 Mike Krukow .05
332 Omar Moreno .05
333 Dave LaRoche .05
334 Dave LaRoche (Super Veteran) .05
335 Bill Madlock .05
336 Garry Templeton .05
337 John Lowenstein .05
338 Willie Upshaw .05
339 Dave Hostetler .05
340 Larry Gura .05
341 Doug DeCinces .05
342 Mike Schmidt/AS .25
343 Charlie Hough .05
344 Andre Thornton .05
345 Jim Clancy .05
346 Ken Forsch .05
347 Sammy Stewart .05
348 Alan Bannister .05
349 Checklist 265-396 .05
350 Robin Yount 1.25
351 Warren Cromartie .05
352 Tim Raines/AS .05
353 Tony Armas .05
354 Tom Seaver (Super Veteran) .30
355 Tony Perez 1.00
356 Toby Harrah .05
357 Dan Ford .05
358 Charlie Puleo .05
359 Dave Collins .05

#	Player	Price
360	Nolan Ryan	6.00
361	Nolan Ryan (Super Veteran)	2.50
362	Bill Almon	.05
363	Eddie Milner	.05
364	Gary Lucas	.05
365	Dave Lopes	.05
366	Bob Boone	.05
367	Biff Pocoroba	.05
368	Richie Zisk	.05
369	Tony Bernazard	.05
370	Gary Carter	1.50
371	Paul Molitor	1.50
372	Art Howe	.05
373	Pete Rose/AS	.50
374	Glenn Adams	.05
375	Pete Vukovich	.05
376	Gary Lavelle	.05
377	Lee May	.05
378	Lee May (Super Veteran)	.05
379	Butch Wynegar	.05
380	Ron Davis	.05
381	Bob Grich	.05
382	Gary Roenicke	.05
383	Jim Kaat	.10
384	Steve Carlton/AS	.05
385	Mike Easler	.05
386	Rod Carew/AS	.05
387	Bobby Grich/AS	.05
388	George Brett/AS	.25
389	Robin Yount/AS	.05
390	Reggie Jackson/AS	.05
391	Rickey Henderson/AS	.25
392	Fred Lynn/AS	.05
393	Carlton Fisk/AS	.05
394	Pete Vuckovich/AS	.05
395	Larry Gura /AS	.05
396	Dan Quisenberry/AS	.05

1984 O-Pee-Chee

Almost identical in design to the 1984 Topps set, the 1984 O-Pee-Chee set contains 396 cards. The O-Pee-Chee cards display the Canadian company's logo in the upper right corner and the backs of the cards are printed in both English and French. The cards measure 2-1/2" x 3-1/2", and some include the extra line on the front of the card to indicate a trade.

		NM/M
Complete Set (396):		22.50
Common Player:		.05
Wax Pack:		1.00
Wax Box (36):		25.00
1	Pascual Perez	.10
2	Cal Ripken	6.00
3	Lloyd Moseby	.15
4	Mel Hall	.05
5	Willie Wilson	.05
6	Mike Morgan	.05
7	Gary Lucas	.05
8	Don Mattingly	8.00
9	Jim Gott	.05
10	Robin Yount	1.50
11	Joey McLaughlin	.05
12	Billy Sample	.05
13	Oscar Gamble	.05
14	Bill Russell	.05
15	Burt Hooton	.05
16	Omar Moreno	.05
17	Dave Lopes	.05
18	Dale Berra	.05
19	Rance Mulliniks	.05
20	Greg Luzinski	.05
21	Doug Sisk	.05
22	Don Robinson	.05
23	Keith Moreland	.05
24	Richard Dotson	.05
25	Glenn Hubbard	.05
26	Rod Carew	1.50
27	Alan Wiggins	.05
28	Frank Viola	.05
29	Phil Niekro	1.00
30	Wade Boggs	2.50
31	Dave Parker	.05
32	Bobby Ramos	.05
33	Tom Burgmeier	.05
34	Eddie Milner	.05
35	Don Sutton	1.00
36	Glenn Wilson	.05
37	Mike Krukow	.05
38	Dave Collins	.05
39	Garth Iorg	.05
40	Dusty Baker	.05
41	Tony Bernazard	.05
42	Claudell Washington	.05
43	Cecil Cooper	.05
44	Dan Driessen	.05
45	Jerry Mumphrey	.05
46	Rick Rhoden	.05
47	Rudy Law	.05
48	Julio Franco	.05
49	Mike Norris	.05
50	Chris Chambliss	.05
51	Pete Falcone	.05
52	Mike Marshall	.05
53	Amos Otis	.05
54	Jesse Orosco	.05
55	Dave Concepcion	.05
56	Gary Allenson	.05
57	Dan Schatzeder	.05
58	Jerry Remy	.05
59	Carney Lansford	.05
60	Paul Molitor	2.50
61	Chris Codiroli	.05
62	Dave Hostetler	.05
63	Ed Vande Berg	.05
64	Ryne Sandberg	2.50
65	Kirk Gibson	.05
66	Nolan Ryan	6.00
67	Gary Ward	.05
68	Luis Salazar	.05
69	Dan Quisenberry	.05
70	Gary Matthews	.05
71	Pete O'Brien	.05
72	John Wathan	.05
73	Jody Davis	.05
74	Kent Tekulve	.05
75	Bob Forsch	.05
76	Alfredo Griffin	.05
77	Bryn Smith	.05
78	Mike Torrez	.05
79	Mike Hargrove	.05
80	Steve Rogers	.05
81	Bake McBride	.05
82	Doug DeCinces	.05
83	Richie Zisk	.05
84	Randy Bush	.05
85	Atlee Hammaker	.05
86	Chet Lemon	.05
87	Frank Pastore	.05
88	Alan Trammell	.05
89	Terry Francona	.05
90	Pedro Guerrero	.05
91	Dan Spillner	.05
92	Lloyd Moseby	.05
93	Bob Knepper	.05
94	Ted Simmons	.05
95	Aurelio Lopez	.05
96	Bill Buckner	.05
97	LaMarr Hoyt	.05
98	Tom Brunansky	.05
99	Ron Oester	.05
100	Reggie Jackson	1.50
101	Ron Davis	.05
102	Ken Oberkfell	.05
103	Dwayne Murphy	.05
104	Jim Slaton	.05
105	Tony Armas	.05
106	Ernie Whitt	.05
107	Johnnie LeMaster	.05
108	Randy Moffitt	.05
109	Terry Forster	.05
110	Ron Guidry	.05
111	Bill Virdon	.05
112	Doyle Alexander	.05
113	Lonnie Smith	.05
114	Checklist	
115	Andre Thornton	.05
116	Jeff Reardon	.15
117	Tom Herr	.05
118	Charlie Hough	.05
119	Phil Garner	.05
120	Keith Hernandez	.05
121	Rich Gossage	.10
122	Ted Simmons	.05
123	Butch Wynegar	.05
124	Damaso Garcia	.05
125	Britt Burns	.05
126	Bert Blyleven	.05
127	Carlton Fisk	1.50
128	Rick Manning	.05
129	Bill Laskey	.05
130	Ozzie Smith	2.50
131	Bo Diaz	.05
132	Tom Paciorek	.05
133	Dave Rozema	.05
134	Dave Stieb	.15
135	Brian Downing	.05
136	Rick Camp	.05
137	Willie Aikens	.05
138	Charlie Moore	.05
139	George Frazier	.05
140	Storm Davis	.05
141	Glenn Hoffman	.05
142	Charlie Lea	.05
143	Mike Vail	.05
144	Steve Sax	.05
145	Gary Lavelle	.05
146	Gorman Thomas	.05
147	Dan Petry	.05
148	Mark Clear	.05
149	Dave Beard	.05
150	Dale Murphy	.75
151	Steve Trout	.05
152	Tony Pena	.05
153	Geoff Zahn	.05
154	Dave Henderson	.05
155	Frank White	.05
156	Dick Ruthven	.05
157	Gary Gaetti	.05
158	Lance Parrish	.05
159	Joe Price	.05
160	Mario Soto	.05
161	Tug McGraw	.05
162	Bob Ojeda	.05
163	George Hendrick	.05
164	Scott Sanderson	.05
165	Ken Singleton	.05
166	Terry Kennedy	.05
167	Gene Garber	.05
168	Juan Bonilla	.05
169	Larry Parrish	.05
170	Jerry Reuss	.05
171	John Tudor	.05
172	Dave Kingman	.05
173	Garry Templeton	.05
174	Bob Boone	.05
175	Graig Nettles	.05
176	Lee Smith	.05
177	LaMarr Hoyt	.05
178	Bill Krueger	.05
179	Buck Martinez	.05
180	Manny Trillo	.05
181	Lou Whitaker	.05
182	Darryl Strawberry	1.00
183	Neil Allen	.05
184	Jim Rice	.25
185	Sixto Lezcano	.05
186	Tom Hume	.05
187	Garry Maddox	.05
188	Bryan Little	.05
189	Jose Cruz	.05
190	Ben Oglivie	.05
191	Cesar Cedeno	.05
192	Nick Esasky	.05
193	Ken Forsch	.05
194	Jim Palmer	1.25
195	Jack Morris	.15
196	Steve Howe	.05
197	Harold Baines	.05
198	Bill Doran	.05
199	Willie Hernandez	.05
200	Andre Dawson	1.25
201	Bruce Kison	.05
202	Bobby Cox	.05
203	Matt Keough	.05
204	Ron Guidry	.05
205	Greg Minton	.05
206	Al Holland	.05
207	Luis Leal	.05
208	Jose Oquendo	.05
209	Leon Durham	.05
210	Joe Morgan	1.50
211	Lou Whitaker/AS	.05
212	George Brett/AS	.75
213	Bruce Hurst	.05
214	Steve Carlton	1.50
215	Tippy Martinez	.05
216	Ken Landreaux	.05
217	Alan Ashby	.05
218	Dennis Eckersley	1.00
219	Craig McMurtry	.05
220	Fernando Valenzuela	.05
221	Cliff Johnson	.05
222	Rick Honeycutt	.05
223	George Brett	3.00
224	Rusty Staub	.20
225	Lee Mazzilli	.05
226	Pat Putnam	.05
227	Bob Welch	.05
228	Rick Cerone	.05
229	Lee Lacy	.05
230	Rickey Henderson	2.50
231	Gary Redus	.05
232	Tim Wallach	.25
233	Checklist	
234	Rafael Ramirez	.05
235	Matt Young	.05
236	Ellis Valentine	.05
237	John Castino	.05
238	Eric Show	.05
239	Bob Horner	.05
240	Eddie Murray	1.50
241	Billy Almon	.05
242	Greg Brock	.05
243	Bruce Sutter	1.00
244	Dwight Evans	.05
245	Rick Sutcliffe	.05
246	Terry Crowley	.05
247	Fred Lynn	.05
248	Bill Dawley	.05
249	Dave Stapleton	.05
250	Bill Madlock	.05
251	Jim Sundberg	.05
252	Steve Yeager	.05
253	Jim Wohlford	.05
254	Shane Rawley	.05
255	Bruce Benedict	.05
256	Dave Geisel	.05
257	Julio Cruz	.05
258	Luis Sanchez	.05
259	Von Hayes	.05
260	Scott McGregor	.05
261	Tom Seaver	1.50
262	Doug Flynn	.05
263	Wayne Gross	.05
264	Larry Gura	.05
265	John Montefusco	.05
266	Dave Winfield/AS	1.00
267	Tim Lollar	.05
268	Ron Washington	.05
269	Mickey Rivers	.05
270	Mookie Wilson	.05
271	Moose Haas	.05
272	Rick Dempsey	.05
273	Dan Quisenberry	.05
274	Steve Henderson	.05
275	Len Matuszek	.05
276	Frank Tanana	.05
277	Dave Righetti	.05
278	Jorge Bell	.35
279	Ivan DeJesus	.05
280	Floyd Bannister	.05
281	Dale Murray	.05
282	Andre Robertson	.05
283	Rollie Fingers	1.00
284	Tommy John	.10
285	Darrell Porter	.05
286	Lary Sorensen	.05
287	Warren Cromartie	.05
288	Jim Beattie	.05
289	Blue Jays Team	.25
290	Dave Dravecky	.05
291	Eddie Murray/AS	.50
292	Greg Bargar	.05
293	Tom Underwood	.05
294	U.L. Washington	.05
295	Mike Flanagan	.05
296	Rich Gedman	.05
297	Bruce Berenyi	.05
298	Jim Gantner	.05
299	Bill Caudill	.05
300	Pete Rose	4.00
301	Steve Kemp	.05
302	Barry Bonnell	.05
303	Joel Youngblood	.05
304	Rick Langford	.05
305	Roy Smalley	.05
306	Ken Griffey	.05
307	Al Oliver	.05
308	Ron Hassey	.05
309	Len Barker	.05
310	Willie McGee	.05
311	Jerry Koosman	.05
312	Jorge Orta	.05
313	Pete Vuckovich	.05
314	George Wright	.05
315	Bob Grich	.05
316	Jesse Barfield	.25
317	Willie Upshaw	.05
318	Bill Gullickson	.10
319	Ray Burris	.05
320	Bob Stanley	.05
321	Ken Schrom	.05
322	Ken Schrom	.05
323	Johnny Ray	.05
324	Brian Giles	.05
325	Darrell Evans	.05
326	Mike Caldwell	.05
327	Ruppert Jones	.05
328	Chris Speier	.05
329	Bobby Castillo	.05
330	John Candelaria	.05
331	Bucky Dent	.05
332	Expos Team	.25
333	Larry Herndon	.05
334	Chuck Rainey	.05
335	Don Baylor	.05
336	Bob James	.05
337	Jim Clancy	.05
338	Duane Kuiper	.05
339	Roy Lee Jackson	.05
340	Bob McClure	.05
341	Larry McWilliams	.05
342	Tim Foli	.05
343	Fergie Jenkins	2.00
344	Dickie Thon	.05
345	Kent Hrbek	.05
346	Larry Bowa	.05
347	Buddy Bell	.05
348	Toby Harrah	.05
349	Dan Ford	.05
350	George Foster	.05
351	Lou Piniella	.05
352	Dave Stewart	.25
353	Mike Easler	.05
354	Jeff Burroughs	.05
355	Jason Thompson	.05
356	Glenn Abbott	.05
357	Ron Cey	.05
358	Bob Dernier	.05
359	Jim Acker	.05
360	Willie Randolph	.05
361	Mike Schmidt	3.00
362	David Green	.05
363	Cal Ripken Jr./AS	2.00
364	Jim Rice/AS	.05
365	Steve Bedrosian	.05
366	Gary Carter	2.50
367	Chili Davis	.05
368	Hubie Brooks	.05
369	Steve McCatty	.05
370	Tim Raines	.35
371	Joaquin Andujar	.05
372	Gary Roenicke	.05
373	Ron Kittle	.05
374	Rich Dauer	.05
375	Dennis Leonard	.05
376	Rick Burleson	.05
377	Eric Rasmussen	.05
378	Dave Winfield	2.50
379	Checklist	
380	Steve Garvey	.50
381	Jack Clark	.05
382	Odell Jones	.05
383	Terry Puhl	.05
384	Joe Niekro	.05
385	Tony Perez	2.00
386	George Hendrick/AS	.05
387	Johnny Ray/AS	.05
388	Mike Schmidt/AS	.75
389	Ozzie Smith/AS	.75
390	Tim Raines/AS	.25
391	Dale Murphy/AS	.25
392	Andre Dawson/AS	.35
393	Gary Carter/AS	1.00
394	Steve Rogers/AS	.15
395	Steve Carlton/AS	.50
396	Jesse Orosco/AS	.05

Stickers

Bi-lingual backs are the only difference between the OPC 1984 sticker set and the Topps issue. The sets share a checklist and, generally, values, although some Blue Jays and Expos stars may command a small premium in the Canadian version.

1985 O-Pee-Chee

This 396-card set is almost identical in design to the 1985 Topps set. Measuring 2-1/2" x 3-1/2", the fronts of the Canadian-issued cards display the O-Pee-Chee logo in the upper left corner, and the backs of the cards are printed in both French and English. A "traded" line appears on the front of some of the cards to indicate a change in teams.

		NM/M
Complete Set (396):		15.00
Common Player:		.05
Wax Pack (15):		1.50
Wax Box (36):		40.00
1	Tom Seaver	1.50
2	Gary Lavelle	.05
3	Tim Wallach	.15
4	Jim Wohlford	.05
5	Jeff Robinson	.05
6	Willie Wilson	.05
7	Cliff Johnson	.05
8	Willie Randolph	.05
9	Larry Herndon	.05
10	Kirby Puckett	4.00
11	Mookie Wilson	.05
12	Dave Lopes	.05
13	Tim Lollar	.05
14	Chris Bando	.05
15	Jerry Koosman	.05
16	Bobby Meacham	.05
17	Mike Scott	.05
18	Rich Gedman	.05
19	George Frazier	.05
20	Chet Lemon	.05
21	Dave Concepcion	.05
22	Jason Thompson	.05
23	Bret Saberhagen	.05
24	Jesse Barfield	.15
25	Steve Bedrosian	.05
26	Roy Smalley	.05
27	Bruce Berenyi	.05
28	Butch Wynegar	.05
29	Alan Ashby	.05
30	Cal Ripken	4.00
31	Luis Leal	.05
32	Dave Dravecky	.05
33	Tito Landrum	.05
34	Pedro Guerrero	.05
35	Graig Nettles	.05
36	Fred Breining	.05
37	Roy Lee Jackson	.05
38	Steve Henderson	.05
39	Gary Pettis	.05
40	Phil Niekro	.75
41	Dwight Gooden	.10
42	Luis Sanchez	.05
43	Lee Smith	.05
44	Dickie Thon	.05
45	Greg Minton	.05
46	Mike Flanagan	.05
47	Bud Black	.05
48	Tony Fernandez	.50
49	Carlton Fisk	1.50
50	John Candelaria	.05
51	Bob Watson	.05
52	Rick Leach	.05
53	Rick Rhoden	.05
54	Cesar Cedeno	.05
55	Frank Tanana	.05
56	Larry Bowa	.05
57	Willie McGee	.05
58	Rich Dauer	.05
59	Jorge Bell	.35
60	George Hendrick	.05
61	Donnie Moore	.05
62	Mike Ramsey	.05
63	Nolan Ryan	4.00
64	Mark Bailey	.05
65	Bill Buckner	.05
66	Jerry Reuss	.05
67	Mike Schmidt	2.50
68	Von Hayes	.05
69	Phil Bradley	.05
70	Don Baylor	.05
71	Julio Cruz	.05
72	Rick Sutcliffe	.05
73	Storm Davis	.05
74	Mike Krukow	.05
75	Willie Upshaw	.05
76	Craig Lefferts	.05
77	Lloyd Moseby	.05
78	Ron Davis	.05
79	Rick Mahler	.05
80	Keith Hernandez	.05
81	Vance Law	.05
82	Joe Price	.05
83	Dennis Lamp	.05
84	Gary Ward	.05
85	Mike Marshall	.05
86	Marvell Wynne	.05
87	David Green	.05
88	Bryn Smith	.05
89	Sixto Lezcano	.05
90	Rich Gossage	.10
91	Jeff Burroughs	.05
92	Bobby Brown	.05
93	Oscar Gamble	.05
94	Rick Dempsey	.05
95	Jose Cruz	.05
96	Johnny Ray	.05
97	Joel Youngblood	.05
98	Eddie Whitson	.05
99	Milt Wilcox	.05
100	George Brett	2.50
101	Jim Acker	.05
102	Jim Sundberg	.05
103	Ozzie Virgil	.05
104	Mike Fitzgerald	.05
105	Ron Kittle	.05
106	Pascual Perez	.05
107	Barry Bonnell	.05
108	Lou Whitaker	.05
109	Gary Roenicke	.05
110	Alejandro Pena	.05
111	Doug DeCinces	.05
112	Doug Flynn	.05
113	Tom Herr	.05
114	Bob James	.05
115	Rickey Henderson	2.00
116	Pete Rose	3.00
117	Greg Gross	.05
118	Eric Show	.05
119	Buck Martinez	.05
120	Steve Kemp	.05
121	Checklist 1-132	
122	Tom Brunansky	.05
123	Dave Kingman	.05
124	Garry Templeton	.05
125	Kent Tekulve	.05
126	Darryl Strawberry	.05
127	Mark Gubicza	.05
128	Ernie Whitt	.05
129	Don Robinson	.05
130	Al Oliver	.05
131	Mario Soto	.05
132	Jeff Leonard	.05
133	Andre Dawson	.35
134	Bruce Hurst	.05
135	Bobby Cox	.05
136	Matt Young	.05
137	Bob Forsch	.05
138	Ron Darling	.05
139	Steve Trout	.05
140	Geoff Zahn	.05
141	Ken Forsch	.05
142	Jerry Willard	.05
143	Bill Gullickson	.05
144	Mike Mason	.05
145	Alvin Davis	.05
146	Gary Redus	.05
147	Willie Aikens	.05
148	Steve Yeager	.05
149	Dickie Noles	.05
150	Jim Rice	.25
151	Moose Haas	.05
152	Steve Balboni	.05
153	Frank LaCorte	.05
154	Argenis Salazar	.05
155	Bob Grich	.05
156	Craig Reynolds	.05
157	Bill Madlock	.05
158	Pat Tabler	.05
159	Don Slaught	.05
160	Lance Parrish	.05
161	Ken Schrom	.05
162	Wally Backman	.05
163	Dennis Eckersley	.75
164	Dave Collins	.05
165	Dusty Baker	.05
166	Claudell Washington	.05
167	Rick Cerone	.05
168	Garth Iorg	.05
169	Shane Rawley	.05
170	George Foster	.05
171	Tony Bernazard	.05
172	Don Sutton	.75
173	Jerry Remy	.05
174	Rick Honeycutt	.05

175 Dave Parker .05
176 Buddy Bell .05
177 Steve Garvey .20
178 Miguel Dilone .05
179 Tommy John .10
180 Dave Winfield 2.00
181 Alan Trammell .05
182 Rollie Fingers .75
183 Larry McWilliams .05
184 Carmen Castillo .05
185 Al Holland .05
186 Jerry Mumphrey .05
187 Chris Chambliss .05
188 Jim Clancy .05
189 Glenn Wilson .05
190 Rusty Staub .05
191 Ozzie Smith 2.00
192 Howard Johnson .05
193 Jimmy Key 1.00
194 Terry Kennedy .05
195 Glenn Hubbard .05
196 Pete O'Brien .05
197 Keith Moreland .05
198 Eddie Milner .05
199 Dave Engle .05
200 Reggie Jackson 1.50
201 Burt Hooton .05
202 Gorman Thomas .05
203 Larry Parrish .05
204 Bob Stanley .05
205 Steve Rogers .05
206 Phil Garner .05
207 Ed Vande Berg .05
208 Jack Clark .05
209 Bill Campbell .05
210 Gary Matthews .05
211 Dave Palmer .05
212 Tony Perez 1.50
213 Sammy Stewart .05
214 John Tudor .05
215 Bob Brenly .05
216 Jim Gantner .05
217 Bryan Clark .05
218 Doyle Alexander .05
219 Bo Diaz .05
220 Fred Lynn .05
221 Eddie Murray 1.50
222 Hubie Brooks .05
223 Tom Hume .05
224 Al Cowens .05
225 Mike Boddicker .05
226 Len Matuszek .05
227 Danny Darwin .05
228 Scott McGregor .05
229 Dave LaPoint .05
230 Gary Carter 2.00
231 Joaquin Andujar .05
232 Rafael Ramirez .05
233 Wayne Gross .05
234 Neil Allen .05
235 Gary Maddox .05
236 Mark Thurmond .05
237 Julio Franco .05
238 Ray Burris .05
239 Tim Teufel .05
240 Dave Stieb .15
241 Brett Butler .05
242 Greg Brock .05
243 Barbaro Garbey .05
244 Greg Walker .05
245 Chili Davis .05
246 Darrell Porter .05
247 Tippy Martinez .05
248 Terry Forster .05
249 Harold Baines .05
250 Jesse Orosco .05
251 Brad Gulden .05
252 Mike Hargrove .05
253 Nick Esasky .05
254 Frank Williams .05
255 Lonnie Smith .05
256 Daryl Sconiers .05
257 Bryan Little .05
258 Terry Francona .05
259 Mark Langston .15
260 Dave Righetti .05
261 Checklist 133-264 .05
262 Bob Horner .05
263 Mel Hall .05
264 John Shelby .05
265 Juan Samuel .05
266 Frank Viola .05
267 Jim Fanning .05
268 Dick Ruthven .05
269 Bobby Ramos .05
270 Dan Quisenberry .05
271 Dwight Evans .05
272 Andre Thornton .05
273 Orel Hershiser .50
274 Ray Knight .05
275 Bill Caudill .05
276 Charlie Hough .05
277 Tim Raines .25
278 Mike Squires .05
279 Alex Trevino .05
280 Ron Romanick .05
281 Tom Niedenfuer .05
282 Mike Stenhouse .05
283 Terry Puhl .05
284 Hal McRae .05
285 Dan Driessen .05
286 Rudy Law .05
287 Walt Terrell .05
288 Jeff Kunkel .05
289 Bob Kennedy .05
290 Cecil Cooper .05
291 Bob Welch .05
292 Frank Pastore .05

293 Dan Schatzeder .05
294 Tom Nieto .05
295 Joe Niekro .05
296 Ryne Sandberg 2.00
297 Gary Lucas .05
298 John Castino .05
299 Bill Doran .05
300 Rod Carew 1.50
301 John Montefusco .05
302 Johnnie LeMaster .05
303 Jim Beattie .05
304 Gary Gaetti .05
305 Dale Berra .05
306 Rick Reuschel .05
307 Ken Oberkfell .05
308 Kent Hrbek .05
309 Mike Witt .05
310 Manny Trillo .05
311 Jim Gott .05
312 LaMarr Hoyt .05
313 Dave Schmidt .05
314 Ron Oester .05
315 Doug Sisk .05
316 John Lowenstein .05
317 Derrel Thomas .05
318 Ted Simmons .05
319 Darrell Evans .05
320 Dale Murphy .50
321 Ricky Horton .05
322 Ken Phelps .05
323 Lee Mazzilli .05
324 Don Mattingly 2.50
325 John Denny .05
326 Ken Singleton .05
327 Brook Jacoby .05
328 Greg Luzinski .05
329 Bob Ojeda .05
330 Leon Durham .05
331 Bill Laskey .05
332 Ben Oglivie .05
333 Willie Hernandez .05
334 Bob Dernier .05
.335 Bruce Benedict .05
336 Rance Mulliniks .05
337 Rick Cerone .05
338 Britt Burns .05
339 Danny Heep .05
340 Robin Yount 1.50
341 Andy Van Slyke .05
342 Curt Wilkerson .05
343 Bill Russell .05
344 Dave Henderson .05
345 Charlie Lea .05
346 Terry Pendleton .05
347 Carney Lansford .05
348 Bob Boone .05
349 Mike Easler .05
350 Wade Boggs 2.00
351 Atlee Hammaker .05
352 Joe Morgan 1.50
353 Damaso Garcia .05
354 Floyd Bannister .05
355 Bert Blyleven .05
356 John Butcher .05
357 Fernando Valenzuela .05
358 Tony Pena .05
359 Mike Smithson .05
360 Steve Carlton 1.50
361 Alfredo Griffin .05
362 Craig McMurtry .05
363 Bill Dawley .05
364 Richard Dotson .05
365 Carmelo Martinez .05
366 Ron Cey .05
367 Tony Scott .05
368 Dave Bergman .05
369 Steve Sax .05
370 Bruce Sutter 1.00
371 Mickey Rivers .05
372 Kirk Gibson .05
373 Scott Sanderson .05
374 Brian Downing .05
375 Jeff Reardon .15
376 Frank DiPino .05
377 Checklist 265-396 .05
378 Alan Wiggins .05
379 Charles Hudson .05
380 Ken Griffey .05
381 Tom Paciorek .05
382 Jack Morris .15
383 Tony Gwynn 2.00
384 Jody Davis .05
385 Jose DeLeon .05
386 Bob Kearney .05
387 George Wright .05
388 Ron Guidry .05
389 Rick Manning .05
390 Sid Fernandez .05
391 Bruce Bochte .05
392 Dan Petry .05
393 Tim Stoddard .05
394 Tony Armas .05
395 Paul Molitor 2.00
396 Mike Heath .05

TORONTO BLUE JAYS

player photos are surrounded by a red border for Expos and a blue border for Blue Jays.

NM/M

Complete Set (24): 9.00
Common Player: .50
1 Mike Fitzgerald .50
2 Dan Driessen .50
3 Dave Palmer .50
4 U.L. Washington .50
5 Hubie Brooks .50
6 Tim Wallach .75
7 Tim Raines 2.50
8 Herm Winningham .50
9 Andre Dawson 2.50
10 Charlie Lea .50
11 Steve Rogers .50
12 Jeff Reardon .60
13 Buck Martinez .50
14 Willie Upshaw .50
15 Damaso Garcia .50
16 Tony Fernandez 1.00
17 Rance Mulliniks .50
18 George Bell 1.00
19 Lloyd Moseby .50
20 Jesse Barfield .60
21 Doyle Alexander .50
22 Dave Stieb .85
23 Bill Caudill .50
24 Gary Lavelle .50

Stickers

Bi-lingual backs are the only difference between the OPC 1985 sticker set and the Topps issue. The sets share a checklist and, generally, values, although some Blue Jays and Expos stars may command a small premium in the Canadian version.

1986 O-Pee-Chee

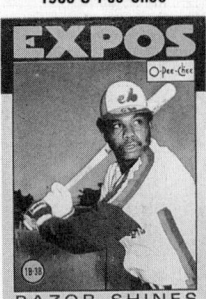

EXPOS
RAZOR SHINES

As usual, the 1986 O-Pee-Chee set was issued in close simulation of the Topps cards for the same year. The 396 cards in the set are 2-1/2" x 3-1/2" and use almost all of the same pictures as the Topps set. The O-Pee-Chee cards, being a Canadian issue, list player information in both English and French. There is an abundance of players from the two Canadian teams - Toronto and Montreal. As the O-Pee-Chee set was issued later in the year than the Topps regular issue, players who changed teams after the printing date are noted with a traded line at the bottom of the player photo. O-Pee-Chee's logo appears in the upper right of each card front.

NM/M

Complete Set (396): 12.00
Common Player: .05
Wax Box (36): 16.00
1 Pete Rose 1.50
2 Ken Landreaux .05
3 Rob Picciolo .05
4 Steve Garvey .10
5 Andy Hawkins .05
6 Rudy Law .05
7 Lonnie Smith .05
8 Dwayne Murphy .05
9 Moose Haas .05
10 Tony Gwynn 1.00

Posters

The 1985 O-Pee-Chee poster set consists of 12 players each from the Expos and Blue Jays. The blank-backed posters measure approximately 4-7/8" x 6-7/8" and generally have fold marks because they were inserted in the OPC wax packs. The card number, written in both French and English, appears in the bottom border. The full-color

11 Bob Ojeda .05
12 Jose Uribe .05
13 Bob Kearney .05
14 Julio Cruz .05
15 Eddie Whitson .05
16 Rick Schu .05
17 Mike Stenhouse .05
18 Lou Thornton .05
19 Ryne Sandberg 1.00
20 Lou Whitaker .05
21 Mark Brouhard .05
22 Gary Lavelle .05
23 Manny Lee .05
24 Don Slaught .05
25 Willie Wilson .05
26 Mike Marshall .05
27 Ray Knight .05
28 Mario Soto .05
29 Dave Anderson .05
30 Eddie Murray .75
31 Dusty Baker .05
32 Steve Yeager .05
33 Andy Van Slyke .05
34 Dave Righetti .05
35 Jeff Reardon .05
36 Burt Hooton .05
37 Johnny Ray .05
38 Glenn Hoffman .05
39 Rick Mahler .05
40 Ken Griffey .05
41 Brad Wellman .05
42 Joe Hesketh .05
43 Mark Salas .05
44 Jorge Orta .05
45 Damaso Garcia .05
46 Jim Acker .05
47 Bill Madlock .05
48 Bill Almon .05
49 Rick Manning .05
50 Dan Quisenberry .05
51 Jim Gantner .05
52 Kevin Bass .05
53 Len Dykstra .05
54 John Franco .05
55 Fred Lynn .05
56 Jim Morrison .05
57 Bill Doran .05
58 Leon Durham .05
59 Andre Thornton .05
60 Dwight Evans .05
61 Larry Herndon .05
62 Bob Boone .05
63 Kent Hrbek .05
64 Floyd Bannister .05
65 Harold Baines .05
66 Pat Tabler .05
67 Carmelo Martinez .05
68 Ed Lynch .05
69 George Foster .05
70 Dave Winfield 1.00
71 Ken Schrom .05
72 Toby Harrah .05
73 Jackie Gutierrez .05
74 Rance Mulliniks .05
75 Jose DeLeon .05
76 Ron Romanick .05
77 Charlie Leibrandt .05
78 Bruce Benedict .05
79 Dave Schmidt .05
80 Darryl Strawberry .05
81 Wayne Krenchicki .05
82 Tippy Martinez .05
83 Phil Garner .05
84 Darrell Porter .05
85 Tony Perez 1.00
86 Tom Waddell .05
87 Tim Hulett .05
88 Barbaro Garbey .05
89 Randy St. Claire .05
90 Garry Templeton .05
91 Tim Teufel .05
92 Al Cowens .05
93 Scot Thompson .05
94 Tom Herr .05
95 Ozzie Virgil .05
96 Jose Cruz .05
97 Gary Gaetti .05
98 Roger Clemens 2.00
99 Vance Law .05
100 Nolan Ryan 2.50
101 Mike Smithson .05
102 Rafael Santana .05
103 Darrell Evans .05
104 Rich Gossage .05
105 Gary Ward .05
106 Jim Gott .05
107 Rafael Ramirez .05
108 Ted Power .05
109 Ron Guidry .05
110 Scott McGregor .05
111 Mike Scioscia .05
112 Glenn Hubbard .05
113 U.L. Washington .05
114 Al Oliver .05
115 Jay Howell .05
116 Brook Jacoby .05
117 Willie McGee .05
118 Jerry Royster .05
119 Barry Bonnell .05
120 Steve Carlton .75
121 Alfredo Griffin .05
122 David Green .05
123 Greg Walker .05
124 Frank Tanana .05
125 Dave Lopes .05
126 Mike Krukow .05
127 Jack Howell .05
128 Greg Harris .50

129 Herm Winningham .05
130 Alan Trammell .05
131 Checklist 1-132 .05
132 Razor Shines .05
133 Bruce Sutter .65
134 Carney Lansford .05
135 Joe Niekro .05
136 Ernie Whitt .05
137 Charlie Moore .05
138 Mel Hall .05
139 Roger McDowell .05
140 John Candelaria .05
141 Bob Rodgers .05
142 Manny Trillo .05
143 Dave Palmer .05
144 Robin Yount .75
145 Pedro Guerrero .05
146 Von Hayes .05
147 Lance Parrish .05
148 Mike Heath .05
149 Brett Butler .05
150 Joaquin Andujar .05
151 Graig Nettles .05
152 Pete Vuckovich .05
153 Jason Thompson .05
154 Bert Roberge .05
155 Bob Grich .05
156 Roy Smalley .05
157 Ron Hassey .05
158 Bob Stanley .05
159 Orel Hershiser .05
160 Chet Lemon .05
161 Terry Puhl .05
162 Dave LaPoint .05
163 Onix Concepcion .05
164 Steve Balboni .05
165 Mike Davis .05
166 Dickie Thon .05
167 Zane Smith .05
168 Jeff Burroughs .05
169 Alex Trevino .05
170 Gary Carter 1.00
171 Tito Landrum .05
172 Sammy Stewart .05
173 Wayne Gross .05
174 Britt Burns .05
175 Steve Sax .05
176 Jody Davis .05
177 Joel Youngblood .05
178 Fernando Valenzuela .05
179 Storm Davis .05
180 Don Mattingly 1.25
181 Steve Bedrosian .05
182 Jesse Orosco .05
183 Gary Roenicke .05
184 Don Baylor .05
185 Rollie Fingers .50
186 Ruppert Jones .05
187 Scott Fletcher .05
188 Bob Dernier .05
189 Mike Mason .05
190 George Hendrick .05
191 Wally Backman .05
192 Oddibe McDowell .05
193 Bruce Hurst .05
194 Ron Cey .05
195 Dave Concepcion .05
196 Doyle Alexander .05
197 Dale Murray .05
198 Mark Langston .05
199 Dennis Eckersley .50
200 Mike Schmidt 1.50
201 Nick Esasky .05
202 Ken Dayley .05
203 Rick Cerone .05
204 Larry McWilliams .05
205 Brian Downing .05
206 Danny Darwin .05
207 Bill Caudill .05
208 Dave Rozema .05
209 Eric Show .05
210 Brad Komminsk .05
211 Chris Bando .05
212 Chris Speier .05
213 Jim Clancy .05
214 Randy Bush .05
215 Frank White .05
216 Dan Petry .05
217 Tim Wallach .05
218 Mitch Webster .05
219 Dennis Lamp .05
220 Bob Horner .05
221 Dave Henderson .05
222 Dave Smith .05
223 Willie Upshaw .05
224 Cesar Cedeno .05
225 Ron Darling .05
226 Lee Lacy .05
227 John Tudor .05
228 Jim Presley .05
229 Bill Gullickson .05
230 Terry Kennedy .05
231 Bob Knepper .05
232 Rick Rhoden .05
233 Richard Dotson .05
234 Jesse Barfield .10
235 Butch Wynegar .05
236 Jerry Reuss .05
237 Juan Samuel .05
238 Larry Parrish .05
239 Bill Buckner .05
240 Pat Sheridan .05
241 Tony Fernandez .05
242 Rich Thompson .05
243 Rickey Henderson 1.00
244 Craig Lefferts .05
245 Jim Sundberg .05
246 Phil Niekro .50

247 Terry Harper .05
248 Spike Owen .05
249 Bret Saberhagen .05
250 Dwight Gooden .05
251 Rich Dauer .05
252 Keith Hernandez .05
253 Bo Diaz .05
254 Ozzie Guillen .05
255 Tony Armas .05
256 Andre Dawson .25
257 Doug DeCinces .05
258 Tim Burke .05
259 Dennis Boyd .05
260 Tony Pena .05
261 Sal Butera .05
262 Wade Boggs 1.00
263 Checklist 133-254 .05
264 Ron Oester .05
265 Ron Davis .05
266 Keith Moreland .05
267 Paul Molitor 1.00
268 John Denny .05
269 Frank Viola .05
270 Jack Morris .10
271 Dave Collins .05
272 Bert Blyleven .05
273 Jerry Willard .05
274 Matt Young .05
275 Charlie Hough .05
276 Dave Dravecky .05
277 Garth Iorg .05
278 Hal McRae .05
279 Curt Wilkerson .05
280 Tim Raines .20
281 Bill Laskey .05
282 Jerry Mumphrey .05
283 Pat Clements .05
284 Bob James .05
285 Buddy Bell .05
286 Tom Brookens .05
287 Dave Parker .05
288 Ron Kittle .05
289 Johnnie LeMaster .05
290 Carlton Fisk .75
291 Jimmy Key .05
292 Gary Matthews .05
293 Marvell Wynne .05
294 Danny Cox .05
295 Kirk Gibson .05
296 Mariano Duncan .05
297 Ozzie Smith 1.00
298 Craig Reynolds .05
299 Bryn Smith .05
300 George Brett 1.50
301 Walt Terrell .05
302 Greg Gross .05
303 Claudell Washington .05
304 Howard Johnson .05
305 Phil Bradley .05
306 R.J. Reynolds .05
307 Bob Brenly .05
308 Hubie Brooks .05
309 Alvin Davis .05
310 Donnie Hill .05
311 Dick Schofield .05
312 Tom Filer .05
313 Mike Fitzgerald .05
314 Marty Barrett .05
315 Mookie Wilson .05
316 Alan Knicely .05
317 Ed Romero .05
318 Glenn Wilson .05
319 Bud Black .05
320 Jim Rice .20
321 Terry Pendleton .05
322 Dave Kingman .05
323 Gary Pettis .05
324 Dan Schatzeder .05
325 Juan Beniquez .05
326 Kent Tekulve .05
327 Mike Pagliarulo .05
328 Pete O'Brien .05
329 Kirby Puckett 1.00
330 Rick Sutcliffe .05
331 Alan Ashby .05
332 Willie Randolph .05
333 Tom Henke .05
334 Ken Oberkfell .05
335 Don Sutton .50
336 Dan Gladden .05
337 George Vukovich .05
338 Jorge Bell .10
339 Jim Dwyer .05
340 Cal Ripken 2.50
341 Willie Hernandez .05
342 Gary Redus .05
343 Jerry Koosman .05
344 Jim Wohlford .05
345 Donnie Moore .05
346 Floyd Youmans .05
347 Gorman Thomas .05
348 Cliff Johnson .05
349 Ken Howell .05
350 Jack Clark .05
351 Gary Lucas .05
352 Bob Clark .05
353 Dave Stieb .05
354 Tony Bernazard .05
355 Lee Smith .05
356 Mickey Hatcher .05
357 Ed Vande Berg .05
358 Rick Dempsey .05
359 Bobby Cox .05
360 Lloyd Moseby .05
361 Shane Rawley .05
362 Garry Maddox .05
363 Buck Martinez .05
364 Ed Nunez .05

365	Luis Leal	.05
366	Dale Berra	.05
367	Mike Boddicker	.05
368	Greg Brock	.05
369	Al Holland	.05
370	Vince Coleman	.05
371	Rod Carew	.75
372	Ben Oglivie	.05
373	Lee Mazzilli	.05
374	Terry Francona	.05
375	Rich Gedman	.05
376	Charlie Lea	.05
377	Joe Carter	.50
378	Bruce Bochte	.05
379	Bobby Meacham	.05
380	LaMarr Hoyt	.05
381	Jeff Leonard	.05
382	Ivan Calderon	.05
383	Chris Brown	.05
384	Steve Trout	.05
385	Cecil Cooper	.05
386	Cecil Fielder	1.50
387	Tim Flannery	.05
388	Chris Codiroli	.05
389	Glenn Davis	.05
390	Tom Seaver	.75
391	Julio Franco	.05
392	Tom Brunansky	.05
393	Rob Wilfong	.05
394	Reggie Jackson	.75
395	Scott Garrelts	.05
396	Checklist 255-396	.05

Box Panels

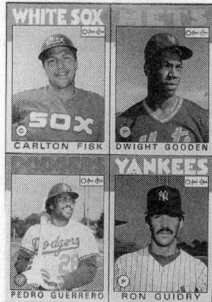

The Canadian card company licensed by Topps to distribute cards in Canada is O-Pee-Chee. In 1986, O-Pee-Chee issued wax pack boxes with baseball cards printed on the box bottoms. Four cards appear on four different boxes making a complete set of 16. The cards are identical to the 1986 Topps wax box issue with the exception of the OPC logo replacing Topps' and the addition of French on the card backs. These bilingual cards were issued in Canada but are readily available in the USA. The cards are the standard 2-1/2" x 3-1/2" size, printed in full-color with black and red backs. The panel cards are not numbered but instead are lettered from A through P.

		NM/M
Complete Panel Set (4):		12.00
Complete Singles Set (16):		11.00
Common Panel:		3.50
Common Single Player:		.15
Panel		4.50
A	Jorge Bell	.50
B	Wade Boggs	1.00
C	George Brett	1.50
D	Vince Coleman	.20
Panel		3.50
E	Carlton Fisk	1.00
F	Dwight Gooden	.20
G	Pedro Guerrero	.20
H	Ron Guidry	.20
Panel		4.00
I	Reggie Jackson	1.50
J	Don Mattingly	2.00
K	Oddibe McDowell	.15
L	Willie McGee	.15
Panel		3.00
M	Dale Murphy	.65
N	Pete Rose	2.50
O	Bret Saberhagen	.15
P	Fernando Valenzuela	.15

Stickers

Bi-lingual backs are the only difference between the OPC 1986 sticker set and the Topps issue. The sets share a checklist and, generally, values, although some Blue Jays and Expos stars may command a small premium in the Canadian version.

	NM/M
Complete Set:	15.00
Common Player:	.05
Album:	2.00

Tattoos

Topps and its Canadian shadow O-Pee-Chee returned to tattoos in 1986, marketing a set of 24 different tattoo sheets. Each sheet of tattoos measures 3-7/16" x 14" and includes both player portrait and smaller generic action tattoos. The player tattoos measure about 1-1/2" x 2-1/2". With 24 sheets, eight players per sheet, there are 192 players represented in the set. The sheets are numbered. The OPC version is distinguished from Topps by copyright notice.

1987 O-Pee-Chee

O-Pee-Chee of London, Ont., under license from the Topps Chewing Gum Co., continued a practice started in 1965 by issuing a baseball card set for 1987. The 396-card set is identical in design to the regular Topps set, save the name "O-Pee-Chee" replacing "Topps" in the lower right corner. Because the set is issued after its American counterpart, several cards appear with trade notations and corrected logos on the fronts. The cards, which are printed on white stock and are the standard 2-1/2" x 3-1/2", feature backs written in both English and French.

		NM/M
Complete Set (396):		15.00
Common Player:		.05
Wax Pack:		1.00
Wax Box (36):		17.50

1	Ken Oberkfell	.05
2	Jack Howell	.05
3	Hubie Brooks	.05
4	Bob Grich	.05
5	Rick Leach	.05
6	Phil Niekro	.50
7	Rickey Henderson	1.00
8	Terry Pendleton	.05
9	Jay Tibbs	.05
10	Cecil Cooper	.05
11	Mario Soto	.05
12	George Bell	.15
13	Nick Esasky	.05
14	Larry McWilliams	.05
15	Dan Quisenberry	.05
16	Ed Lynch	.05
17	Pete O'Brien	.05
18	Luis Aguayo	.05
19	Matt Young	.05
20	Gary Carter	1.00
21	Tom Paciorek	.05
22	Doug DeCinces	.05
23	Lee Smith	.05
24	Jesse Barfield	.05
25	Bert Blyleven	.05
26	Greg Brock	.05
27	Dan Petry	.05
28	Rick Dempsey	.05
29	Jimmy Key	.05
30	Tim Raines	.15
31	Bruce Hurst	.05
32	Manny Trillo	.05
33	Andy Van Slyke	.05
34	Ed Vande Berg	.05
35	Sid Bream	.05
36	Dave Winfield	1.00
37	Scott Garrelts	.05
38	Dennis Leonard	.05
39	Marty Barrett	.05
40	Dave Righetti	.05
41	Bo Diaz	.05
42	Gary Redus	.05
43	Tom Niedenfuer	.05
44	Greg Harris	.05
45	Jim Presley	.05
46	Danny Gladden	.05
47	Roy Smalley	.05
48	Wally Backman	.05
49	Tom Seaver	.75
50	Dave Smith	.05
51	Mel Hall	.05
52	Tim Flannery	.05
53	Julio Cruz	.05
54	Dick Schofield	.05
55	Tim Wallach	.05
56	Glenn Davis	.05
57	Darren Daulton	.05
58	Chico Walker	.05
59	Garth Iorg	.05
60	Tony Pena	.05
61	Ron Hassey	.05
62	Dave Dravecky	.05
63	Jorge Orta	.05
64	Al Nipper	.05
65	Tom Browning	.05
66	Marc Sullivan	.05
67	Todd Worrell	.05
68	Glenn Hubbard	.05
69	Carney Lansford	.05
70	Charlie Hough	.05
71	Lance McCullers	.05
72	Walt Terrell	.05
73	Bob Kearney	.05
74	Dan Pasqua	.05
75	Ron Darling	.05
76	Robin Yount	.75
77	Pat Tabler	.05
78	Tom Foley	.05
79	Juan Nieves	.05
80	Wally Joyner	.05
81	Wayne Krenchicki	.05
82	Kirby Puckett	1.00
83	Bob Ojeda	.05
84	Mookie Wilson	.05
85	Kevin Bass	.05
86	Kent Tekulve	.05
87	Mark Salas	.05
88	Brian Downing	.05
89	Ozzie Guillen	.05
90	Dave Stieb	.05
91	Rance Mulliniks	.05
92	Mike Witt	.05
93	Charlie Moore	.05
94	Jose Uribe	.05
95	Oddibe McDowell	.05
96	Ray Soff	.05
97	Glenn Wilson	.05
98	Brook Jacoby	.05
99	Darryl Motley	.05
100	Steve Garvey	.10
101	Frank White	.05
102	Mike Moore	.05
103	Rick Aguilera	.05
104	Buddy Bell	.05
105	Floyd Youmans	.05
106	Lou Whitaker	.05
107	Ozzie Smith	1.00
108	Jim Gantner	.05
109	R.J. Reynolds	.05
110	John Tudor	.05
111	Alfredo Griffin	.05
112	Mike Flanagan	.05
113	Neil Allen	.05
114	Ken Griffey	.05
115	Donnie Moore	.05
116	Bob Horner	.05
117	Ron Shepherd	.05
118	Cliff Johnson	.05
119	Vince Coleman	.05
120	Eddie Murray	.75
121	Dwayne Murphy	.05
122	Jim Clancy	.05
123	Ken Landreaux	.05
124	Tom Nieto	.05
125	Bob Brenly	.05
126	George Brett	1.25
127	Vance Law	.05
128	Checklist 1-132	.05
129	Bob Knepper	.05
130	Dwight Gooden	.05
131	Juan Bonilla	.05
132	Tim Burke	.05
133	Bob McClure	.05
134	Scott Bailes	.05
135	Mike Easler	.05
136	Ron Romanick	.05
137	Rich Gedman	.05
138	Bob Dernier	.05
139	John Denny	.05
140	Bret Saberhagen	.05
141	Herm Winningham	.05
142	Rick Sutcliffe	.05
143	Ryne Sandberg	1.00
144	Mike Scioscia	.05
145	Charlie Kerfeld	.05
146	Jim Rice	.15
147	Steve Trout	.05
148	Jesse Orosco	.05
149	Mike Boddicker	.05
150	Wade Boggs	1.00
151	Dane Iorg	.05
152	Rick Burleson	.05
153	Duane Ward	.05
154	Rick Reuschel	.05
155	Nolan Ryan	2.00
156	Bill Caudill	.05
157	Danny Darwin	.05
158	Ed Romero	.05
159	Bill Almon	.05
160	Julio Franco	.05
161	Kent Hrbek	.05
162	Chill Davis	.05
163	Kevin Gross	.05
164	Carlton Fisk	.75
165	Jeff Reardon	.05
166	Bob Boone	.05
167	Rick Honeycutt	.05
168	Dan Schatzeder	.05
169	Jim Wohlford	.05
170	Phil Bradley	.05
171	Ken Schrom	.05
172	Ron Oester	.05
173	Juan Beniquez	.05
174	Tony Armas	.05
175	Bob Stanley	.05
176	Steve Buechele	.05
177	Keith Moreland	.05
178	Cecil Fielder	.50
179	Gary Gaetti	.05
180	Chris Brown	.05
181	Tom Herr	.05
182	Lee Lacy	.05
183	Ozzie Virgil	.05
184	Paul Molitor	1.00
185	Roger McDowell	.05
186	Mike Marshall	.05
187	Ken Howell	.05
188	Rob Deer	.05
189	Joe Hesketh	.05
190	Jim Sundberg	.05
191	Kelly Gruber	.10
192	Cory Snyder	.05
193	Dave Concepcion	.05
194	Kirk McCaskill	.05
195	Mike Pagliarulo	.05
196	Rick Manning	.05
197	Brett Butler	.05
198	Tony Gwynn	1.00
199	Mariano Duncan	.05
200	Pete Rose	1.25
201	John Cangelosi	.05
202	Danny Cox	.05
203	Butch Wynegar	.05
204	Chris Chambliss	.05
205	Graig Nettles	.05
206	Chet Lemon	.05
207	Don Aase	.05
208	Mike Mason	.05
209	Alan Trammell	.05
210	Lloyd Moseby	.05
211	Richard Dotson	.05
212	Mike Fitzgerald	.05
213	Darrell Porter	.05
214	Checklist 133-264	.05
215	Mark Langston	.05
216	Steve Farr	.05
217	Dann Bilardello	.05
218	Gary Ward	.05
219	Cecilio Guante	.05
220	Joe Carter	.15
221	Ernie Whitt	.05
222	Denny Walling	.05
223	Charlie Leibrandt	.05
224	Wayne Tolleson	.05
225	Mike Smithson	.05
226	Zane Smith	.05
227	Terry Puhl	.05
228	Eric Davis	.05
229	Don Mattingly	1.25
230	Don Baylor	.05
231	Frank Tanana	.05
232	Tom Brookens	.05
233	Steve Bedrosian	.05
234	Wallace Johnson	.05
235	Alvin Davis	.05
236	Tommy John	.05
237	Jim Morrison	.05
238	Ricky Horton	.05
239	Shane Rawley	.05
240	Steve Balboni	.05
241	Mike Krukow	.05
242	Rick Mahler	.05
243	Bill Doran	.05
244	Mark Clear	.05
245	Willie Upshaw	.05
246	Hal McRae	.05
247	Jose Canseco	.45
248	George Hendrick	.05
249	Doyle Alexander	.05
250	Teddy Higuera	.05
251	Tom Hume	.05
252	Denny Martinez	.05
253	Eddie Milner	.05
254	Steve Sax	.05
255	Juan Samuel	.05
256	Dave Bergman	.05
257	Bob Forsch	.05
258	Steve Yeager	.05
259	Don Sutton	.50
260	Vida Blue	.05
261	Tom Brunansky	.05
262	Joe Sambito	.05
263	Mitch Webster	.05
264	Checklist 265-396	.05
265	Darrell Evans	.05
266	Dave Kingman	.05
267	Howard Johnson	.05
268	Greg Pryor	.05
269	Tippy Martinez	.05
270	Jody Davis	.05
271	Steve Carlton	.75
272	Andres Galarraga	.15
273	Fernando Valenzuela	.05
274	Jeff Hearron	.05
275	Ray Knight	.05
276	Bill Madlock	.05
277	Tom Henke	.05
278	Gary Pettis	.05
279	Jimy Williams	.05
280	Jeffrey Leonard	.05
281	Bryn Smith	.05
282	John Cerutti	.05
283	Gary Roenicke	.05
284	Joaquin Andujar	.05
285	Dennis Boyd	.05
286	Tim Hulett	.05
287	Craig Lefferts	.05
288	Tito Landrum	.05
289	Manny Lee	.05
290	Leon Durham	.05
291	Johnny Ray	.05
292	Franklin Stubbs	.05
293	Bob Rodgers	.05
294	Terry Francona	.05
295	Len Dykstra	.05
296	Tom Candiotti	.05
297	Frank DiPino	.05
298	Craig Reynolds	.05
299	Jerry Hairston Sr.	.05
300	Reggie Jackson	1.00
301	Luis Aquino	.05
302	Greg Walker	.05
303	Terry Kennedy	.05
304	Phil Garner	.05
305	John Franco	.05
306	Bill Buckner	.05
307	Kevin Mitchell	.05
308	Don Slaught	.05
309	Harold Baines	.05
310	Frank Viola	.05
311	Dave Lopes	.05
312	Cal Ripken	2.00
313	John Candelaria	.05
314	Bob Sebra	.05
315	Bud Black	.05
316	Brian Fisher	.05
317	Clint Hurdle	.05
318	Ernie Riles	.05
319	Dave LaPoint	.05
320	Barry Bonds	6.00
321	Tim Stoddard	.05
322	Ron Cey	.05
323	Al Newman	.05
324	Jerry Royster	.05
325	Garry Templeton	.05
326	Mark Gubicza	.05
327	Andre Thornton	.05
328	Bob Welch	.05
329	Tony Fernandez	.05
330	Mike Scott	.05
331	Jack Clark	.05
332	Danny Tartabull	.05
333	Greg Minton	.05
334	Ed Correa	.05
335	Candy Maldonado	.05
336	Dennis Lamp	.05
337	Sid Fernandez	.05
338	Greg Gross	.05
339	Willie Hernandez	.05
340	Roger Clemens	1.50
341	Mickey Hatcher	.05
342	Bob James	.05
343	Jose Cruz	.05
344	Bruce Sutter	.65
345	Andre Dawson	.25
346	Shawon Dunston	.05
347	Scott McGregor	.05
348	Carmelo Martinez	.05
349	Storm Davis	.05
350	Keith Hernandez	.05
351	Andy McGaffigan	.05
352	Dave Parker	.05
353	Ernie Camacho	.05
354	Eric Show	.05
355	Don Carman	.05
356	Floyd Bannister	.05
357	Willie McGee	.05
358	Atlee Hammaker	.05
359	Dale Murphy	.30
360	Pedro Guerrero	.05
361	Will Clark	.10
362	Bill Campbell	.05
363	Alejandro Pena	.05
364	Dennis Rasmussen	.05
365	Rick Rhoden	.05
366	Randy St. Claire	.05
367	Willie Wilson	.05
368	Dwight Evans	.05
369	Moose Haas	.05
370	Fred Lynn	.05
371	Mark Eichhorn	.05
372	Dave Schmidt	.05
373	Jerry Reuss	.05
374	Lance Parrish	.05
375	Ron Guidry	.05
376	Jack Morris	.05
377	Willie Randolph	.05
378	Joel Youngblood	.05
379	Darryl Strawberry	.05
380	Rich Gossage	.05
381	Dennis Eckersley	.50
382	Gary Lucas	.05
383	Ron Davis	.05
384	Pete Incaviglia	.05
385	Orel Hershiser	.10
386	Kirk Gibson	.05
387	Don Robinson	.05
388	Darnell Coles	.05
389	Von Hayes	.05
390	Gary Matthews	.05
391	Jay Howell	.05
392	Tim Laudner	.05
393	Rod Scurry	.05
394	Tony Bernazard	.05
395	Damaso Garcia	.05
396	Mike Schmidt	1.25

Box Panels

For the second consecutive year, O-Pee-Chee placed baseball cards on the bottoms of its wax pack boxes. The 2-1/8" x 3" cards were issued in panels of four and are slightly smaller in size than the regular issue OPC cards. The card fronts are identical in design to the regular issue, while the backs contain a newspaper-type commentary in both French and English. Collectors may note the 1987 Topps wax box cards were issued on side panels as opposed to box bottoms. Because the OPC wax boxes are smaller in size than their U.S. counterparts, printing cards on side panels was not possible.

		NM/M
Complete Panel Set (2):		5.00
Complete Singles Set (8):		5.00
Common Single Player:		.15
Panel		2.00
A	Don Baylor	.15
B	Steve Carlton	.50
C	Ron Cey	.15
D	Cecil Cooper	.15
Panel		4.00
E	Rickey Henderson	1.00
F	Jim Rice	.35
G	Don Sutton	.50
H	Dave Winfield	1.00

Stickers

Bi-lingual backs are the only difference between the OPC 1987 sticker set and the Topps issue. The sets share a checklist and, generally, values, although some Blue Jays and Expos stars may command a small premium in the Canadian version.

1988 O-Pee-Chee

Under license from Topps, O-Pee-Chee uses the same player photos as the Topps issue, but the Canadian edition includes only 396 cards (one-half the number in the Topps set). The OPC set was printed after the U.S. press run, so several cards carry overprints on the fronts, indicating changes in players' teams. New teams are named in the overprints; card headers bear the former team names. This set follows the same basic design as the 1988 Topps cards. The OPC logo appears in place of the Topps logo, both front and back. A four-card subset consists of #1 and #2 draft choices for the Expos (Nathan Minchey and Delino DeShields) and Blue Jays (Alex Sanchez and Derek

Bell). These cards are distinguished by a yellow or orange triangle in the lower-right corner bearing the player's name above the words "Choisi au repechage." Card backs are bilingual (English-French) and printed in black on orange. This series was marketed primarily in Canada in four separate display boxes, with four cards printed one each box bottom. Individual card packs contain seven cards and one stick of gum.

	NM/M
Unopened Fact. Set (396):	9.00
Complete Set (396):	7.50
Common Player:	.05
Wax Pack (7):	.25
Wax Box (48):	7.50

#	Player	Price
1	Chris James	.05
2	Steve Buechele	.05
3	Mike Henneman	.05
4	Eddie Murray	.60
5	Bret Saberhagen	.05
6	Nathan Minchey (Draft Pick)	.05
7	Harold Reynolds	.05
8	Bo Jackson	.10
9	Mike Easler	.05
10	Ryne Sandberg	.75
11	Mike Young	.05
12	Tony Phillips	.05
13	Andres Thomas	.05
14	Tim Burke	.05
15	Chili Davis	.05
16	Jim Lindeman	.05
17	Ron Oester	.05
18	Craig Reynolds	.05
19	Juan Samuel	.05
20	Kevin Gross	.05
21	Cecil Fielder	.25
22	Greg Swindell	.05
23	Jose DeLeon	.05
24	Jim Deshaies	.05
25	Andres Galarraga	.10
26	Mitch Williams	.05
27	R.J. Reynolds	.05
28	Jose Nuñez	.05
29	Angel Salazar	.05
30	Sid Fernandez	.05
31	Keith Moreland	.05
32	John Kruk	.05
33	Rob Deer	.05
34	Ricky Horton	.05
35	Harold Baines	.05
36	Jamie Moyer	.05
37	Kevin McReynolds	.05
38	Ozzie Smith	.75
39	Ron Darling	.05
40	Orel Hershiser	.05
41	Bob Melvin	.05
42	Alfredo Griffin	.05
43	Dick Schofield	.05
44	Terry Steinbach	.05
45	Kent Hrbek	.05
46	Darnell Coles	.05
47	Jimmy Key	.05
48	Alan Ashby	.05
49	Julio Franco	.05
50	Hubie Brooks	.05
51	Chris Bando	.05
52	Fernando Valenzuela	.05
53	Kal Daniels	.05
54	Jim Clancy	.05
55	Phil Bradley	.05
56	Andy McGaffigan	.05
57	Mike LaValliere	.05
58	Dave Magadan	.05
59	Danny Cox	.05
60	Rickey Henderson	.75
61	Jim Rice	.20
62	Calvin Schiraldi	.05
63	Jerry Mumphrey	.05
64	Ken Caminiti	.05
65	Leon Durham	.05
66	Shane Rawley	.05
67	Ken Oberkfell	.05
68	Keith Hernandez	.05
69	Bob Brenly	.05
70	Roger Clemens	.90
71	Gary Pettis	.05
72	Dennis Eckersley	.50
73	Dave Smith	.05
74	Cal Ripken	1.00
75	Joe Carter	.15
76	Denny Martinez	.05
77	Juan Beniquez	.05
78	Tim Laudner	.05
79	Ernie Whitt	.05
80	Mark Langston	.05
81	Dale Sveum	.05
82	Dion James	.05
83	Dave Valle	.05
84	Bill Wegman	.05
85	Howard Johnson	.05
86	Benito Santiago	.05
87	Casey Candaele	.05
88	Delino DeShields (Draft Pick)	3.00
89	Dave Winfield	.75
90	Dale Murphy	.50
91	Jay Howell	.05
92	Ken Williams	.05
93	Bob Sebra	.05
94	Tim Wallach	.10
95	Lance Parrish	.05
96	Todd Benzinger	.05
97	Scott Garrelts	.05
98	Jose Guzman	.05
99	Jeff Reardon	.05
100	Jack Clark	.05
101	Tracy Jones	.05
102	Barry Larkin	.05
103	Curt Young	.05
104	Juan Nieves	.05
105	Terry Pendleton	.05
106	Rob Ducey	.05
107	Scott Bailes	.05
108	Eric King	.05
109	Mike Pagliarulo	.05
110	Teddy Higuera	.05
111	Pedro Guerrero	.05
112	Chris Brown	.05
113	Kelly Gruber	.05
114	Jack Howell	.05
115	Johnny Ray	.05
116	Mark Eichhorn	.05
117	Tony Pena	.05
118	Bob Welch	.05
119	Mike Kingery	.05
120	Kirby Puckett	.75
121	Charlie Hough	.05
122	Tony Bernazard	.05
123	Tom Candiotti	.05
124	Ray Knight	.05
125	Bruce Hurst	.05
126	Steve Jeltz	.05
127	Ron Guidry	.05
128	Duane Ward	.05
129	Greg Minton	.05
130	Buddy Bell	.05
131	Denny Walling	.05
132	Donnie Hill	.05
133	Wayne Tolleson	.05
134	Bob Rodgers	.05
135	Todd Worrell	.05
136	Brian Dayett	.05
137	Chris Bosio	.05
138	Mitch Webster	.05
139	Jerry Browne	.05
140	Jesse Barfield	.05
141	Doug DeCinces	.05
142	Andy Van Slyke	.05
143	Doug Drabek	.05
144	Jeff Parrett	.05
145	Bill Madlock	.05
146	Larry Herndon	.05
147	Bill Buckner	.05
148	Carmelo Martinez	.05
149	Ken Howell	.05
150	Eric Davis	.05
151	Randy Ready	.05
152	Jeffrey Leonard	.05
153	Dave Steib	.05
154	Jeff Stone	.05
155	Dave Righetti	.05
156	Gary Matthews	.05
157	Gary Carter	.75
158	Bob Boone	.05
159	Glenn Davis	.05
160	Willie McGee	.05
161	Bryn Smith	.05
162	Mark McLemore	.05
163	Dale Mohorcic	.05
164	Mike Flanagan	.05
165	Robin Yount	.60
166	Bill Doran	.05
167	Rance Mulliniks	.05
168	Wally Joyner	.05
169	Cory Snyder	.05
170	Rich Gossage	.05
171	Rick Mahler	.05
172	Henry Cotto	.05
173	George Bell	.15
174	B.J. Surhoff	.05
175	Kevin Bass	.05
176	Jeff Reed	.05
177	Frank Tanana	.05
178	Darryl Strawberry	.05
179	Lou Whitaker	.05
180	Terry Kennedy	.05
181	Mariano Duncan	.05
182	Ken Phelps	.05
183	Bob Dernier	.05
184	Ivan Calderon	.05
185	Rick Rhoden	.05
186	Rafael Palmeiro	.50
187	Kelly Downs	.05
188	Spike Owen	.05
189	Bobby Bonilla	.05
190	Candy Maldonado	.05
191	John Cerutti	.05
192	Devon White	.25
193	Brian Fisher	.05
194	Alex Sanchez (Draft Pick)	.20
195	Dan Quisenberry	.05
196	Dave Engle	.05
197	Lance McCullers	.05
198	Franklin Stubbs	.05
199	Scott Bradley	.05
200	Wade Boggs	.75
201	Kirk Gibson	.05
202	Brett Butler	.05
203	Dave Anderson	.05
204	Donnie Moore	.05
205	Nelson Liriano	.05
206	Danny Gladden	.05
207	Dan Pasqua	.05
208	Robbie Thompson	.05
209	Richard Dotson	.05
210	Willie Randolph	.05
211	Danny Tartabull	.05
212	Greg Brock	.05
213	Albert Hall	.05
214	Dave Schmidt	.05
215	Von Hayes	.05
216	Herm Winningham	.05
217	Mike Davis	.05
218	Charlie Leibrandt	.05
219	Mike Stanley	.05
220	Tom Henke	.05
221	Dwight Evans	.05
222	Willie Wilson	.05
223	Stan Jefferson	.05
224	Mike Dunne	.05
225	Mike Scioscia	.05
226	Larry Parrish	.05
227	Mike Scott	.05
228	Wallace Johnson	.05
229	Jeff Musselman	.05
230	Pat Tabler	.05
231	Paul Molitor	.75
232	Bob James	.05
233	Joe Niekro	.05
234	Oddibe McDowell	.05
235	Gary Ward	.05
236	Ted Power	.05
237	Pascual Perez	.05
238	Luis Polonia	.05
239	Mike Diaz	.05
240	Lee Smith	.05
241	Willie Upshaw	.05
242	Tom Neidenfuer	.05
243	Tim Raines	.20
244	Jeff Robinson	.05
245	Rich Gedman	.05
246	Scott Bankhead	.05
247	Andre Dawson	.25
248	Brook Jacoby	.05
249	Mike Marshall	.05
250	Nolan Ryan	1.00
251	Tom Foley	.05
252	Bob Brower	.05
253	Checklist 1-132	.05
254	Scott McGregor	.05
255	Ken Griffey	.05
256	Ken Schrom	.05
257	Gary Gaetti	.05
258	Ed Nunez	.05
259	Frank Viola	.05
260	Vince Coleman	.05
261	Reid Nichols	.05
262	Tim Flannery	.05
263	Glenn Braggs	.05
264	Garry Templeton	.05
265	Bo Diaz	.05
266	Matt Nokes	.05
267	Barry Bonds	1.00
268	Bruce Ruffin	.05
269	Ellis Burks	.05
270	Mike Witt	.05
271	Ken Gerhart	.05
272	Lloyd Moseby	.05
273	Garth Iorg	.05
274	Mike Greenwell	.05
275	Kevin Seitzer	.05
276	Luis Salazar	.05
277	Shawon Dunston	.05
278	Rick Reuschel	.05
279	Randy St. Claire	.05
280	Pete Incaviglia	.05
281	Mike Boddicker	.05
282	Jay Tibbs	.05
283	Shane Mack	.05
284	Walt Terrell	.05
285	Jim Presley	.05
286	Greg Walker	.05
287	Dwight Gooden	.05
288	Jim Morrison	.05
289	Gene Garber	.05
290	Tony Fernandez	.05
291	Ozzie Virgil	.05
292	Carney Lansford	.05
293	Jim Acker	.05
294	Tommy Hinzo	.05
295	Bert Blyleven	.05
296	Ozzie Guillen	.05
297	Zane Smith	.05
298	Milt Thompson	.05
299	Len Dykstra	.05
300	Don Mattingly	.85
301	Bud Black	.05
302	Jose Uribe	.05
303	Manny Lee	.05
304	Sid Bream	.05
305	Steve Sax	.05
306	Billy Hatcher	.05
307	John Shelby	.05
308	Lee Mazzilli	.05
309	Bill Long	.05
310	Tom Herr	.05
311	Derek Bell (Draft Pick)	3.00
312	George Brett	.85
313	Bob McClure	.05
314	Jimy Williams	.05
315	Dave Parker	.05
316	Doyle Alexander	.05
317	Dan Plesac	.05
318	Mel Hall	.05
319	Ruben Sierra	.05
320	Alan Trammell	.05
321	Mike Schmidt	.85
322	Wally Ritchie	.05
323	Rick Leach	.05
324	Danny Jackson	.05
325	Glenn Hubbard	.05
326	Frank White	.05
327	Larry Sheets	.05
328	John Cangelosi	.05
329	Bill Gullickson	.05
330	Eddie Whitson	.05
331	Brian Downing	.05
332	Gary Redus	.05
333	Wally Backman	.05
334	Dwayne Murphy	.05
335	Claudell Washington	.05
336	Dave Concepcion	.05
337	Jim Gantner	.05
338	Marty Barrett	.05
339	Mickey Hatcher	.05
340	Jack Morris	.05
341	John Franco	.05
342	Ron Robinson	.05
343	Greg Gagne	.05
344	Steve Bedrosian	.05
345	Scott Fletcher	.05
346	Vance Law	.05
347	Joe Johnson	.05
348	Jim Eisenreich	.05
349	Alvin Davis	.05
350	Will Clark	.10
351	Mike Aldrete	.05
352	Billy Ripken	.05
353	Dave Stewart	.05
354	Neal Heaton	.05
355	Roger McDowell	.05
356	John Tudor	.05
357	Floyd Bannister	.05
358	Rey Quinones	.05
359	Glenn Wilson	.05
360	Tony Gwynn	.75
361	Greg Maddux	.75
362	Juan Castillo	.05
363	Willie Fraser	.05
364	Nick Esasky	.05
365	Floyd Youmans	.05
366	Chet Lemon	.05
367	Matt Young	.05
368	Gerald Young	.05
369	Bob Stanley	.05
370	Jose Canseco	.45
371	Joe Hesketh	.05
372	Rick Sutcliffe	.05
373	Checklist 133-264	.05
374	Checklist 265-396	.05
375	Tom Brunansky	.05
376	Jody Davis	.05
377	Sam Horn	.05
378	Mark Gubicza	.05
379	Rafael Ramirez	.05
380	Joe Magrane	.05
381	Pete O'Brien	.05
382	Lee Guetterman	.05
383	Eric Bell	.05
384	Gene Larkin	.05
385	Carlton Fisk	.60
386	Mike Fitzgerald	.05
387	Kevin Mitchell	.05
388	Jim Winn	.05
389	Mike Smithson	.05
390	Darrell Evans	.05
391	Terry Leach	.05
392	Charlie Kerfeld	.05
393	Mike Krukow	.05
394	Mark McGwire	.90
395	Fred McGriff	.10
396	DeWayne Buice	.05

Box Panels

A Topps licensee, O-Pee-Chee of Canada issued this 16-card set on wax display box bottoms. Cards feature popular current players and are identified by alphabet (A-P) rather than numbers. Player photos are the same ones used on the Topps U.S. issue and cards follow the same design as Topps' regular issue set. The OPC logo replaces the Topps logo on both front and back. Orange and black card backs are bilingual (French/English) and include complete major and minor league career stats.

	NM/M
Complete Panel Set (4):	8.00
Complete Singles Set (16):	8.00
Common Single Player:	.10
Panel	1.00
A Don Baylor	.10
B Steve Bedrosian	.05
C Juan Beniquez	.10
D Bob Boone	.15
Panel	2.00
E Darrell Evans	.10
F Tony Gwynn	1.00
G John Kruk	.10
H Marvell Wynne	.10
Panel	1.00
I Joe Carter	.25
J Eric Davis	.10
K Howard Johnson	.10
L Darryl Strawberry	.10
Panel	5.00
M Rickey Henderson	1.00
N Nolan Ryan	3.00
O Mike Schmidt	1.50
P Kent Tekulve	.10

Stickers/Stickercards

This is the Canadian version of Topps' sticker issue for 1988, virtually identical except for the substitution of the OPC logo and copyright notice on the front of the stickercard. The Canadian version shares the Topps' checklists and, essentially, the price structure, although Canadian star players command a small premium in the OPC version.

1989 O-Pee-Chee

At 396 cards, the 1989 O-Pee-Chee issue is half the size of the corresponding Topps set. As in previous years, the design of the OPC cards is virtually identical to the Topps version, though the Topps logo on front has been replaced with an O-Pee-Chee logo in one of the upper corners and the backs are printed in both English and French for the Canadian market. Cards of players who changed teams often contain an overprint indicating the player's new team and date of the transaction.

	NM/M
Complete Set (396):	10.00
Common Player:	.05
Wax Box (48):	12.00

#	Player	Price
1	Brook Jacoby	.05
2	Atlee Hammaker	.05
3	Jack Clark	.05
4	Dave Steib	.10
5	Bud Black	.05
6	Damon Berryhill	.05
7	Mike Scioscia	.05
8	Jose Uribe	.05
9	Mike Aldrete	.05
10	Andre Dawson	.25
11	Bruce Sutter	.45
12	Dale Sveum	.05
13	Dan Quisenberry	.05
14	Tom Niedenfuer	.05
15	Robby Thompson	.05
16	Ron Robinson	.05
17	Brian Downing	.05
18	Rick Rhoden	.05
19	Greg Gagne	.05
20	Allan Anderson	.05
21	Eddie Whitson	.05
22	Billy Ripken	.05
23	Mike Fitzgerald	.05
24	Shane Rawley	.05
25	Frank White	.05
26	Don Mattingly	.75
27	Fred Lynn	.05
28	Mike Moore	.05
29	Kelly Gruber	.05
30	Dwight Gooden	.05
31	Dan Pasqua	.05
32	Dennis Rasmussen	.05
33	B.J. Surhoff	.05
34	Sid Fernandez	.05
35	John Tudor	.05
36	Mitch Webster	.05
37	Doug Drabek	.05
38	Bobby Witt	.05
39	Mike Maddux	.05
40	Steve Sax	.05
41	Orel Hershiser	.05
42	Pete Incaviglia	.05
43	Guillermo Hernandez	.05
44	Kevin Coffman	.05
45	Kal Daniels	.05
46	Carlton Fisk	.50
47	Carney Lansford	.05
48	Tim Burke	.05
49	Alan Trammell	.05
50	George Bell	.15
51	Tony Gwynn	.60
52	Bob Brenly	.05
53	Ruben Sierra	.05
54	Otis Nixon	.05
55	Julio Franco	.05
56	Pat Tabler	.05
57	Alvin Davis	.05
58	Kevin Seitzer	.05
59	Mark Davis	.05
60	Tom Brunansky	.05
61	Jeff Treadway	.05
62	Alfredo Griffin	.05
63	Keith Hernandez	.05
64	Alex Trevino	.05
65	Rick Reuschel	.05
66	Bob Walk	.05
67	Dave Palmer	.05
68	Pedro Guerrero	.05
69	Jose Oquendo	.05
70	Mark McGwire	.85
71	Mike Boddicker	.05
72	Wally Backman	.05
73	Pascual Perez	.05
74	Joe Hesketh	.05
75	Tom Henke	.05
76	Nelson Liriano	.05
77	Doyle Alexander	.05
78	Tim Wallach	.10
79	Scott Bankhead	.05
80	Cory Snyder	.05
81	Dave Magadan	.05
82	Randy Ready	.05
83	Steve Buechele	.05
84	Bo Jackson	.10
85	Kevin McReynolds	.05
86	Jeff Reardon	.05
87	Tim Raines	.25
88	Melido Perez	.05
89	Dave LaPoint	.05
90	Vince Coleman	.05
91	Floyd Youmans	.05
92	Buddy Bell	.05
93	Andres Galarraga	.15
94	Tony Pena	.05
95	Gerald Young	.05
96	Rick Cerone	.05
97	Ken Oberkfell	.05
98	Larry Sheets	.05
99	Chuck Crim	.05
100	Mike Schmidt	.75
101	Ivan Calderon	.05
102	Kevin Bass	.05
103	Chili Davis	.05
104	Randy Myers	.05
105	Ron Darling	.05
106	Willie Upshaw	.05
107	Jose DeLeon	.05
108	Fred Manrique	.05
109	Johnny Ray	.05
110	Paul Molitor	.60
111	Rance Mulliniks	.05
112	Jim Presley	.05
113	Lloyd Moseby	.05
114	Lance Parrish	.05
115	Jody Davis	.05
116	Matt Nokes	.05
117	Dave Anderson	.05
118	Checklist	.05
119	Rafael Belliard	.05
120	Frank Viola	.05
121	Roger Clemens	.85
122	Luis Salazar	.05
123	Mike Stanley	.05
124	Jim Traber	.05
125	Mike Krukow	.05
126	Sid Bream	.05
127	Joel Skinner	.05
128	Milt Thompson	.05
129	Terry Clark	.05
130	Gerald Perry	.05
131	Bryn Smith	.05
132	Kirby Puckett	.60
133	Bill Long	.05
134	Jim Gantner	.05
135	Jose Rijo	.05
136	Joey Meyer	.05
137	Geno Petralli	.05
138	Wallace Johnson	.05
139	Mike Flanagan	.05
140	Shawon Dunston	.05
141	Eric Plunk	.05
142	Bobby Bonilla	.05
143	Jack McDowell	.05
144	Mookie Wilson	.05
145	Dave Stewart	.10
146	Gary Pettis	.05
147	Eric Show	.05
148	Eddie Murray	.50
149	Lee Smith	.05
150	Fernando Valenzuela	.05
151	Bob Walk	.05
152	Harold Baines	.05
153	Albert Hall	.05
154	Don Carman	.05
155	Marty Barrett	.05
156	Chris Sabo	.05
157	Bret Saberhagen	.05

158	Danny Cox	.05
159	Tom Foley	.05
160	Jeffrey Leonard	.05
161	Brady Anderson	.05
162	Rich Gossage	.05
163	Greg Brock	.05
164	Joe Carter	.10
165	Mike Dunne	.05
166	Jeff Russell	.05
167	Dan Plesac	.05
168	Willie Wilson	.05
169	Mike Jackson	.05
170	Tony Fernandez	.05
171	Jamie Moyer	.05
172	Jim Gott	.05
173	Mel Hall	.05
174	Mark McGwire	.85
175	John Shelby	.05
176	Jeff Parrett	.05
177	Tim Belcher	.05
178	Rich Gedman	.05
179	Ozzie Virgil	.05
180	Mike Scott	.05
181	Dickie Thon	.05
182	Rob Murphy	.05
183	Oddibe McDowell	.05
184	Wade Boggs	.60
185	Claudell Washington	.05
186	Randy Johnson	2.00
187	Paul O'Neill	.05
188	Todd Benzinger	.05
189	Kevin Mitchell	.05
190	Mike Witt	.05
191	Sil Campusano	.05
192	Ken Gerhart	.05
193	Bob Rodgers	.05
194	Floyd Bannister	.05
195	Ozzie Guillen	.05
196	Ron Gant	.05
197	Neal Heaton	.05
198	Bill Swift	.05
199	Dave Parker	.05
200	George Brett	.75
201	Bo Diaz	.05
202	Brad Moore	.05
203	Rob Ducey	.05
204	Bert Blyleven	.05
205	Dwight Evans	.05
206	Roberto Alomar	.60
207	Henry Cotto	.05
208	Harold Reynolds	.05
209	Jose Guzman	.05
210	Dale Murphy	.15
211	Mike Pagliarulo	.05
212	Jay Howell	.05
213	Rene Gonzalez	.05
214	Scott Garrelts	.05
215	Kevin Gross	.05
216	Jack Howell	.05
217	Kurt Stillwell	.05
218	Mike LaValliere	.05
219	Jim Clancy	.05
220	Gary Gaetti	.05
221	Hubie Brooks	.05
222	Bruce Ruffin	.05
223	Jay Buhner	.05
224	Cecil Fielder	.15
225	Willie McGee	.05
226	Bill Doran	.05
227	John Farrell	.05
228	Nelson Santovenia	.05
229	Jimmy Key	.05
230	Ozzie Smith	.60
231	Dave Schmidt	.05
232	Jody Reed	.05
233	Gregg Jefferies	.05
234	Tom Browning	.05
235	John Kruk	.05
236	Charles Hudson	.05
237	Todd Stottlemyre	.10
238	Don Slaught	.05
239	Tim Laudner	.05
240	Greg Maddux	.60
241	Brett Butler	.05
242	Checklist	.05
243	Bob Boone	.05
244	Willie Randolph	.05
245	Jim Rice	.15
246	Rey Quinones	.05
247	Checklist	.05
248	Stan Javier	.05
249	Tim Leary	.05
250	Cal Ripken, Jr.	1.00
251	John Dopson	.05
252	Billy Hatcher	.05
253	Robin Yount	.50
254	Mickey Hatcher	.05
255	Bob Horner	.05
256	Benito Santiago	.05
257	Luis Rivera	.05
258	Fred McGriff	.05
259	Dave Wells	.10
260	Dave Winfield	.60
261	Rafael Ramirez	.05
262	Nick Esasky	.05
263	Barry Bonds	1.00
264	Joe Magrane	.05
265	Kent Hrbek	.05
266	Jack Morris	.10
267	Jeff Robinson	.05
268	Ron Kittle	.05
269	Candy Maldonado	.05
270	Wally Joyner	.05
271	Glenn Braggs	.05
272	Ron Hassey	.05
273	Jose Lind	.05
274	Mark Eichhorn	.05
275	Danny Tartabull	.05

276	Paul Kilgus	.05
277	Mike Davis	.05
278	Andy McGaffigan	.05
279	Scott Bradley	.05
280	Bob Knepper	.05
281	Gary Redus	.05
282	Rickey Henderson	.60
283	Andy Allenson	.05
284	Rick Leach	.05
285	John Candelaria	.05
286	Dick Schofield	.05
287	Bryan Harvey	.05
288	Randy Bush	.05
289	Ernie Whitt	.05
290	John Franco	.05
291	Todd Worrell	.05
292	Teddy Higuera	.05
293	Keith Moreland	.05
294	Juan Berenguer	.05
295	Scott Fletcher	.05
296	Roger McDowell	.05
297	Mark Grace	.10
298	Chris James	.05
299	Frank Tanana	.05
300	Darryl Strawberry	.05
301	Charlie Leibrandt	.05
302	Gary Ward	.05
303	Brian Fisher	.05
304	Terry Steinbach	.05
305	Dave Smith	.05
306	Greg Minton	.05
307	Lance McCullers	.05
308	Phil Bradley	.05
309	Terry Kennedy	.05
310	Rafael Palmeiro	.45
311	Ellis Burks	.05
312	Doug Jones	.05
313	Dennis Martinez	.10
314	Pete O'Brien	.05
315	Greg Swindell	.05
316	Walt Weiss	.05
317	Pete Stanicek	.05
318	Gene Nelson	.05
319	Danny Jackson	.05
320	Lou Whitaker	.05
321	Will Clark	.05
322	John Smiley	.05
323	Mike Marshall	.05
324	Gary Carter	.60
325	Jesse Barfield	.05
326	Dennis Boyd	.05
327	Dave Henderson	.05
328	Chet Lemon	.05
329	Bob Melvin	.05
330	Eric Davis	.05
331	Ted Power	.05
332	Carmelo Martinez	.05
333	Bob Ojeda	.05
334	Steve Lyons	.05
335	Dave Righetti	.05
336	Steve Balboni	.05
337	Calvin Schiraldi	.05
338	Vance Law	.05
339	Zane Smith	.05
340	Kirk Gibson	.05
341	Jim Deshaies	.05
342	Tom Brookens	.05
343	Pat Borders	.05
344	Devon White	.10
345	Charlie Hough	.05
346	Rex Hudler	.05
347	John Cerutti	.05
348	Kirk McCaskill	.05
349	Len Dykstra	.05
350	Andy Van Slyke	.05
351	Jeff Robinson	.05
352	Rick Schu	.05
353	Bruce Benedict	.05
354	Bill Wegman	.05
355	Mark Langston	.05
356	Steve Farr	.05
357	Richard Dotson	.05
358	Andres Thomas	.05
359	Alan Ashby	.05
360	Ryne Sandberg	.60
361	Kelly Downs	.05
362	Jeff Musselman	.05
363	Barry Larkin	.05
364	Rob Deer	.05
365	Mike Henneman	.05
366	Nolan Ryan	1.00
367	Johnny Paredes	.05
368	Bobby Thigpen	.05
369	Mickey Brantley	.05
370	Dennis Eckersley	.45
371	Manny Lee	.05
372	Juan Samuel	.05
373	Tracy Jones	.05
374	Mike Greenwell	.05
375	Terry Pendleton	.05
376	Steve Lombardozzi	.05
377	Mitch Williams	.05
378	Glenn Davis	.05
379	Mark Gubicza	.05
380	Orel Hershiser	.05
381	Jimy Williams	.05
382	Kirk Gibson	.05
383	Howard Johnson	.05
384	Dave Cone	.05
385	Von Hayes	.05
386	Luis Polonia	.05
387	Dan Gladden	.05
388	Pete Smith	.05
389	Jose Canseco	.35
390	Mickey Hatcher	.05
391	Wil Tejada	.05
392	Duane Ward	.05
393	Rick Mahler	.05

394	Rick Sutcliffe	.05
395	Dave Martinez	.05
396	Ken Dayley	.05

Box Panels

Continuing its practice of printing baseball cards on the bottom panels of its wax pack boxes, OPC in 1989 issued a special 16-card set, printing four cards on each of four different box-bottom panels. The cards are identical in design to the regular 1989 OPC cards. They are designated by letter (from A through P) rather than by number.

	NM/M
Complete Panel Set (4):	10.00
Complete Singles Set (16):	10.00
Common Panel:	1.50
Common Single Player:	.10

Panel		2.50
A	George Brett	1.50
B	Bill Buckner	.10
C	Darrell Evans	.10
D	Rich Gossage	.10
Panel		1.50
E	Greg Gross	.10
F	Rickey Henderson	1.00
G	Keith Hernandez	.10
H	Tom Lasorda	.25
Panel		7.50
I	Jim Rice	.50
J	Cal Ripken, Jr.	3.00
K	Nolan Ryan	3.00
L	Mike Schmidt	1.50
Panel		1.50
M	Bruce Sutter	.75
N	Don Sutton	.50
O	Kent Tekulve	.10
P	Dave Winfield	1.00

Stickers/Stickercards

Once again sharing a checklist with the 1989 Topps sticker issue, the OPC version differs only in the substitution of the O-Pee-Chee logo and copyright notice on the front of the stickercard. Values are also essentially the same, although Expos and Blue Jay stars carry a small premium in the OPC version.

1990 O-Pee-Chee

Box Panels / descriptions

Virtually identical to the contemporary 1990 Topps set, the OPC issue features the same 792 cards. On most cards the fronts are indistinguishable, even to the use of a Topps logo on the Canadian product. A number of the OPC cards differ from their Topps counterparts in that there is a notice of team change printed in black on the front. Backs of the OPC cards feature a few lines of French in areas such as the stat headings, the career summary and monthly scoreboard. The OPC cards omit the Topps copyright line and feature an OPC copyright line on back.

	NM/M
Unopened Fact. Set (792):	15.00
Complete Set (792):	12.00
Common Player:	.05
Wax Pack:	.75
Wax Box (36):	20.00

Stickers

Once again sharing a checklist with the 1990 Topps sticker issue, the OPC version differs only in the substitution of the O-Pee-Chee logo and copyright notice on the stickercard. Values are also essentially the same, although Expos and Blue Jays stars carry a small premium in the OPC version.

Sample Sheet

This 7-1/2" x 10-1/2" sample sheet debuts the 1991 OPC set. Fronts reproduce the basic design while the back, printed in blue on white, contains an ad for OPC.

	NM/M
Complete Sheet:	5.00

1991 O-Pee-Chee

Once again for 1991, OPC utilized the contemporary Topps set of 792 cards as the basis for its own issue. The OPC cards are again printed on a lighter, whiter stock and differ from the Topps cards in the addition of French to the card backs, along with the OPC copyright. Many card fronts in OPC carry a small black typographical notice concerning team changes by the players.

	NM/M
Complete Set (792):	10.00
Common Player:	.05
Wax Box (36):	9.00

Premier

The O-Pee-Chee Co. of London, Ontario, Canada produced this 132-card set. The card fronts feature action photos, while the flip sides display a posed photo and career statistics. The cards were packaged seven cards per pack in a tamper-

proof foil wrap. Several Expo and Blue Jay players are featured. Two special cards are included in this set. Card #62 honors Rickey Henderson's stolen base record, while card #102 commemorates Nolan Ryan's seventh no-hitter. Traded players and free agents are featured with their new teams.

	NM/M
Unopened Fact. Set (132):	4.00
Complete Set (132):	3.00
Common Player:	.05
Wax Pack (7):	.75
Wax Box (36):	9.00

1	Roberto Alomar	.40
2	Sandy Alomar	.05
3	Moises Alou	.20
4	Brian Barnes	.05
5	Steve Bedrosian	.05
6	George Bell	.10
7	Juan Bell	.05
8	Albert Belle	.05
9	Bud Black	.05
10	Mike Boddicker	.05
11	Wade Boggs	.75
12	Barry Bonds	1.00
13	Denis Boucher	.10
14	George Brett	.85
15	Hubie Brooks	.05
16	Brett Butler	.05
17	Ivan Calderon	.05
18	Jose Canseco	.25
19	Gary Carter	.75
20	Joe Carter	.10
21	Jack Clark	.05
22	Will Clark	.05
23	Roger Clemens	.90
24	Alex Cole	.05
25	Vince Coleman	.05
26	Jeff Conine	.05
27	Milt Cuyler	.05
28	Danny Darwin	.05
29	Eric Davis	.05
30	Glenn Davis	.05
31	Andre Dawson	.25
32	Ken Dayley	.05
33	Steve Decker	.05
34	Delino DeShields	.10
35	Lance Dickson	.05
36	Kirk Dressendorfer	.05
37	Shawon Dunston	.05
38	Dennis Eckersley	.50
39	Dwight Evans	.05
40	Howard Farmer	.05
41	Junior Felix	.05
42	Alex Fernandez	.10
43	Tony Fernandez	.05
44	Cecil Fielder	.15
45	Carlton Fisk	.60
46	Willie Fraser	.05
47	Gary Gaetti	.05
48	Andres Galarraga	.10
49	Ron Gant	.05
50	Kirk Gibson	.05
51	Bernard Gilkey	.05
52	Leo Gomez	.05
53	Rene Gonzalez	.05
54	Juan Gonzalez	.45
55	Doc Gooden	.05
56	Ken Griffey Jr.	.90
57	Kelly Gruber	.05
58	Pedro Guerrero	.05
59	Tony Gwynn	.75
60	Chris Hammond	.05
61	Ron Hassey	.05
62	Rickey Henderson	.75
63	Tom Henke	.05
64	Orel Hershiser	.05
65	Chris Hoiles	.05
66	Todd Hundley	.05
67	Pete Incaviglia	.05
68	Danny Jackson	.05
69	Barry Jones	.05
70	David Justice	.05
71	Jimmy Key	.05
72	Ray Lankford	.05
73	Darren Lewis	.05
74	Kevin Maas	.05
75	Denny Martinez	.05
76	Tino Martinez	.05
77	Don Mattingly	.85
78	Willie McGee	.05
79	Fred McGriff	.15
80	Hensley Meulens	.05

81	Kevin Mitchell	.05
82	Paul Molitor	.75
83	Mickey Morandini	.05
84	Jack Morris	.05
85	Dale Murphy	.15
86	Eddie Murray	.60
87	Chris Nabholz	.05
88	Tim Naehring	.05
89	Otis Nixon	.05
90	Jose Offerman	.05
91	Bob Ojeda	.05
92	John Olerud	.15
93	Gregg Olson	.05
94	Dave Parker	.05
95	Terry Pendleton	.05
96	Kirby Puckett	.75
97	Rock Raines	.10
98	Jeff Reardon	.05
99	Dave Righetti	.05
100	Cal Ripken	1.00
101	Mel Rojas	.10
102	Nolan Ryan	1.00
103	Ryne Sandberg	.75
104	Scott Sanderson	.05
105	Benito Santiago	.05
106	Pete Schourek	.05
107	Gary Scott	.05
108	Terry Shumpert	.05
109	Ruben Sierra	.05
110	Doug Simons	.05
111	Dave Smith	.05
112	Ozzie Smith	.75
113	Cory Snyder	.05
114	Luis Sojo	.05
115	Dave Stewart	.10
116	Dave Stieb	.05
117	Darryl Strawberry	.05
118	Pat Tabler	.05
119	Wade Taylor	.05
120	Bobby Thigpen	.05
121	Frank Thomas	.60
122	Mike Timlin	.05
123	Alan Trammell	.05
124	Mo Vaughn	.05
125	Tim Wallach	.05
126	Devon White	.05
127	Mark Whiten	.05
128	Bernie Williams	.10
129	Willie Wilson	.05
130	Dave Winfield	.75
131	Robin Yount	.60
132	Checklist	.05

1992 O-Pee-Chee

Once again closely following the format of the 1992 Topps set, and for the most part corresponding to its 792-card checklist, the 1992 OPCs differ on the front only in the substitution of an O-Pee-Chee logo for the Topps logo, and in the inclusion of team-change information for many of the players who moved after the Topps cards were printed. On backs, the light blue "Topps" logo printed behind the stats has been removed, and the logo beneath the card number changed from "Topps" to "O-Pee-Chee." The addition of a few lines of French above the stats and in the career summary can be seen on the OPC cards, as well as the substitution of an OPC copyright line for that of Topps. Where the 1992 Topps set features All-Star cards in the number range 386-407, the OPC set has a group of player cards who are not represented in the Topps set, including four "Tribute" cards honoring Gary Carter. Card #45 in the OPC set is also a Carter Trbitue card, whereas in the Topps set it is a regular card.

	NM/M
Unopened Fact. Set (792):	15.00
Complete Set (792):	10.00
Common Player:	.05
Wax Box (36):	12.00
45	Gary Carter - Tribute	1.00
386	Lance Blankenship	.10
387	Gary Carter - Tribute	1.00
388	Ron Tingley	.10

#	Player	Price
389	Gary Carter - Tribute	1.00
390	Gene Harris	.10
391	Jeff Schaefer	.10
392	Mark Grant	.10
393	Carl Willis	.10
394	Al Leiter	.25
395	Ron Robinson	.10
396	Tim Hullett	.10
397	Craig Worthington	.10
398	John Orton	.10
399	Gary Carter - Tribute	1.00
400	John Dopson	.10
401	Moises Alou	.60
402	Gary Carter - Tribute	1.00
403	Matt Young	.10
404	Wayne Edwards	.10
405	Nick Esasky	.10
406	Dave Eiland	.10
407	Mike Brumley	.10

Premier

JOSE MELENDEZ

O-Pee-Chee increased the number of cards in its premier set to 198 for 1992. The cards feature white borders surrounding full-color player photos. The O-Pee-Chee banner appears at the top of the card and the player's name and position appear at the bottom. The backs feature an additional player photo, statistics and player information. Traded players and free agents are featured with their new teams.

		NM/M
Factory Set (198):		5.00
Complete Set (198):		4.00
Common Player:		.10
Wax Box (36):		9.00
1	Wade Boggs	.75
2	John Smiley	.10
3	Checklist	.10
4	Ron Gant	.10
5	Mike Bordick	.10
6	Charlie Hayes	.10
7	Kevin Morton	.10
8	Checklist	.10
9	Chris Gwynn	.10
10	Melido Perez	.10
11	Danny Gladden	.10
12	Brian McRae	.10
13	Denny Martinez	.15
14	Bob Scanlan	.10
15	Julio Franco	.10
16	Ruben Amaro	.10
17	Mo Sanford	.10
18	Scott Bankhead	.10
19	Dickie Thon	.10
20	Chris James	.10
21	Mike Huff	.10
22	Orlando Merced	.10
23	Chris Sabo	.10
24	Jose Canseco	.40
25	Reggie Sanders	.10
26	Chris Nabholz	.10
27	Kevin Seitzer	.10
28	Ryan Bowen	.10
29	Gary Carter	.75
30	Wayne Rosenthal	.10
31	Alan Trammell	.10
32	Doug Drabek	.10
33	Craig Shipley	.10
34	Ryne Sandberg	.75
35	Chuck Knoblauch	.10
36	Bret Barberie	.10
37	Tim Naehring	.10
38	Omar Olivares	.10
39	Royce Clayton	.10
40	Brent Mayne	.10
41	Darrin Fletcher	.10
42	Howard Johnson	.10
43	Steve Sax	.10
44	Greg Swindell	.10
45	Andre Dawson	.25
46	Kent Hrbek	.10
47	Doc Gooden	.10
48	Mark Leiter	.10
49	Tom Glavine	.25
50	Mo Vaughn	.10
51	Doug Jones	.10
52	Brian Barnes	.10
53	Rob Dibble	.10
54	Kevin McReynolds	.10
55	Ivan Rodriguez	.50
56	Scott Livingstone	.10
57	Mike Magnante	.10
58	Pete Schourek	.10
59	Frank Thomas	.60
60	Kirk McCaskill	.10
61	Wally Joyner	.10
62	Rick Aguilera	.10
63	Eric Karros	.10
64	Tino Martinez	.10
65	Bryan Hickerson	.10
66	Ruben Sierra	.10
67	Willie Randolph	.10
68	Bill Landrum	.10
69	Bip Roberts	.10
70	Cecil Fielder	.15
71	Pat Kelly	.10
72	Kenny Lofton	.10
73	John Franco	.10
74	Phil Plantier	.10
75	Dave Martinez	.10
76	Warren Newson	.10
77	Chito Martinez	.10
78	Brian Hunter	.10
79	Jack Morris	.10
80	Eric King	.10
81	Nolan Ryan	1.50
82	Bret Saberhagen	.10
83	Roberto Kelly	.10
84	Ozzie Smith	.75
85	Chuck McElroy	.10
86	Carlton Fisk	.60
87	Mike Mussina	.50
88	Mark Carreon	.10
89	Ken Hill	.10
90	Rick Cerone	.10
91	Deion Sanders	.15
92	Don Mattingly	.85
93	Danny Tartabull	.10
94	Keith Miller	.10
95	Gregg Jefferies	.10
96	Barry Larkin	.10
97	Kevin Mitchell	.10
98	Rick Sutcliffe	.10
99	Mark McGwire	1.25
100	Albert Belle	.10
101	Gregg Olson	.10
102	Kirby Puckett	.75
103	Luis Gonzalez	.10
104	Randy Myers	.10
105	Roger Clemens	.90
106	Tony Gwynn	.75
107	Jeff Bagwell	.60
108	John Wetteland	.10
109	Bernie Williams	.10
110	Scott Kamieniecki	.10
111	Robin Yount	.60
112	Dean Palmer	.10
113	Tim Belcher	.10
114	George Brett	.85
115	Frank Viola	.10
116	Kelly Gruber	.10
117	David Justice	.10
118	Scott Leius	.10
119	Jeff Fassero	.10
120	Sammy Sosa	.90
121	Al Osuna	.10
122	Wilson Alvarez	.10
123	Jose Offerman	.10
124	Mel Rojas	.10
125	Shawon Dunston	.10
126	Pete Incaviglia	.10
127	Von Hayes	.10
128	Dave Gallagher	.10
129	Eric Davis	.10
130	Roberto Alomar	.35
131	Mike Gallego	.10
132	Robin Ventura	.10
133	Bill Swift	.10
134	John Kruk	.10
135	Craig Biggio	.10
136	Eddie Taubensee	.10
137	Cal Ripken, Jr.	1.50
138	Charles Nagy	.10
139	Jose Melendez	.10
140	Jim Abbott	.10
141	Paul Molitor	.75
142	Tom Candiotti	.10
143	Bobby Bonilla	.10
144	Matt Williams	.10
145	Brett Butler	.10
146	Will Clark	.10
147	Rickey Henderson	.75
148	Ray Lankford	.10
149	Bill Pecota	.10
150	Dave Winfield	.75
151	Darren Lewis	.10
152	Bob MacDonald	.10
153	David Segui	.10
154	Benny Santiago	.10
155	Chuck Finley	.10
156	Andujar Cedeno	.10
157	Barry Bonds	1.50
158	Joe Grahe	.10
159	Frank Castillo	.10
160	Dave Burba	.10
161	Leo Gomez	.10
162	Orel Hershiser	.10
163	Delino DeShields	.15
164	Sandy Alomar	.10
165	Denny Neagle	.10
166	Fred McGriff	.15
167	Ken Griffey Jr.	1.00
168	Juan Guzman	.10
169	Bobby Rose	.10
170	Steve Avery	.10
171	Rich DeLucia	.10
172	Mike Timlin	.10
173	Randy Johnson	.65
174	Paul Gibson	.10
175	David Cone	.10
176	Marquis Grissom	.15
177	Kurt Stillwell	.10
178	Mark Whiten	.10
179	Darryl Strawberry	.10
180	Mike Morgan	.10
181	Scott Scudder	.10
182	George Bell	.15
183	Alvin Davis	.10
184	Len Dykstra	.10
185	Kyle Abbott	.10
186	Chris Haney	.10
187	Junior Noboa	.10
188	Dennis Eckersley	.50
189	Derek Bell	.20
190	Lee Smith	.10
191	Andres Galarraga	.15
192	Jack Armstrong	.10
193	Eddie Murray	.60
194	Joe Carter	.15
195	Terry Pendleton	.10
196	Darryl Kile	.10
197	Rod Beck	.10
198	Hubie Brooks	.10

1993 O-Pee-Chee

DEVON WHITE OUTFIELDER

For the first time in history, the 1993 O-Pee-Chee set differed significantly from the Topps set; photographs and designs are entirely different. Team names are scripted across the top, but a yellow triangle with a new team name appears on the front for players who have been traded. Two insert sets honoring the 1992 World Champion Toronto Blue Jays were also produced.

		NM/M
Complete Set (396):		15.00
Common Player:		.10
Wax Pack (8):		.75
Wax Box:		15.00
1	Jim Abbott	.10
2	Eric Anthony	.10
3	Harold Baines	.10
4	Roberto Alomar	.45
5	Steve Avery	.10
6	James Austin	.10
7	Mark Wohlers	.10
8	Steve Buechele	.10
9	Pedro Astacio	.10
10	Moises Alou	.20
11	Rod Beck	.10
12	Sandy Alomar	.10
13	Brett Boone	.10
14	Bryan Harvey	.10
15	Bobby Bonilla	.10
16	Brady Anderson	.10
17	Andy Benes	.10
18	Ruben Amaro	.10
19	Jay Bell	.10
20	Kevin Brown	.10
21	Scott Bankhead	.10
22	Dennis Boucher	.10
23	Kevin Appier	.10
24	Pat Kelly	.10
25	Rick Aguilera	.10
26	George Bell	.10
27	Steve Farr	.10
28	Chad Curtis	.10
29	Jeff Bagwell	.60
30	Lance Blankenship	.10
31	Derek Bell	.10
32	Damon Berryhill	.10
33	Ricky Bones	.10
34	Rheal Cormier	.10
35	Andre Dawson	.30
36	Brett Butler	.10
37	Sean Berry	.10
38	Bud Black	.10
39	Carlos Baerga	.10
40	Jay Buhner	.10
41	Charlie Hough	.10
42	Sid Fernandez	.10
43	Luis Mercedes	.10
44	Jerald Clark	.10
45	Wes Chamberlain	.10
46	Barry Bonds	1.50
47	Jose Canseco	.30
48	Tim Belcher	.10
49	David Nied	.10
50	George Brett	.85
51	Cecil Fielder	.30
52	Chili Davis	.10
53	Alex Fernandez	.10
54	Charlie Hayes	.10
55	Rob Ducey	.10
56	Craig Biggio	.10
57	Mike Bordick	.10
58	Pat Borders	.10
59	Jeff Blauser	.10
60	Chris Bosio	.10
61	Bernard Gilkey	.10
62	Shawon Dunston	.10
63	Tom Candiotti	.10
64	Darrin Fletcher	.10
65	Jeff Brantley	.10
66	Albert Belle	.10
67	Dave Fleming	.10
68	John Franco	.10
69	Glenn Davis	.10
70	Tony Fernandez	.10
71	Darren Daulton	.10
72	Doug Drabek	.10
73	Julio Franco	.10
74	Tom Browning	.10
75	Tom Gordon	.10
76	Travis Fryman	.10
77	Scott Erickson	.10
78	Carlton Fisk	.60
79	Roberto Kelly	.10
80	Gary DiSarcina	.10
81	Ken Caminiti	.10
82	Ron Darling	.10
83	Joe Carter	.15
84	Sid Bream	.10
85	Cal Eldred	.10
86	Mark Grace	.10
87	Eric Davis	.10
88	Ivan Calderon	.10
89	John Burkett	.10
90	Felix Fermin	.10
91	Ken Griffey Jr.	1.00
92	Doc Gooden	.10
93	Mike Devereaux	.10
94	Tony Gwynn	.75
95	Mariano Duncan	.10
96	Jeff King	.10
97	Juan Gonzalez	.50
98	Norm Charlton	.10
99	Mark Gubicza	.10
100	Danny Gladden	.10
101	Greg Gagne	.10
102	Ozzie Guillen	.10
103	Don Mattingly	.85
104	Damion Easley	.10
105	Casey Candaele	.10
106	Dennis Eckersley	.50
107	David Cone	.10
108	Ron Gant	.10
109	Mike Fetters	.10
110	Mike Harkey	.10
111	Kevin Gross	.10
112	Archi Cianfrocco	.10
113	Will Clark	.10
114	Glenallen Hill	.10
115	Erik Hanson	.10
116	Todd Hundley	.10
117	Leo Gomez	.10
118	Bruce Hurst	.10
119	Len Dykstra	.10
120	Jose Lind	.10
121	Jose Guzman	.10
122	Rob Dibble	.10
123	Gregg Jefferies	.10
124	Bill Gullickson	.10
125	Brian Harper	.10
126	Roberto Hernandez	.10
127	Sam Militello	.10
128	Junior Felix	.10
129	Andujar Cedeno	.10
130	Rickey Henderson	.75
131	Bob MacDonald	.10
132	Tom Glavine	.25
133	Scott Fletcher	.10
134	Brian Jordan	.10
135	Greg Maddux	.75
136	Orel Hershiser	.10
137	Greg Colbrunn	.10
138	Royce Clayton	.10
139	Thomas Howard	.10
140	Randy Johnson	.75
141	Jeff Innis	.10
142	Chris Hoiles	.10
143	Darrin Jackson	.10
144	Tommy Greene	.10
145	Mike LaValliere	.10
146	David Hulse	.10
147	Barry Larkin	.10
148	Wally Joyner	.10
149	Mike Henneman	.10
150	Kent Hrbek	.10
151	Bo Jackson	.15
152	Rich Monteleone	.10
153	Chuck Finley	.10
154	Steve Finley	.10
155	Dave Henderson	.10
156	Kelly Gruber	.10
157	Brian Hunter	.10
158	Darryl Hamilton	.10
159	Derrick May	.10
160	Jay Howell	.10
161	Wil Cordero	.10
162	Bryan Hickerson	.10
163	Reggie Jefferson	.10
164	Edgar Martinez	.10
165	Nigel Wilson	.10
166	Howard Johnson	.10
167	Tim Hulett	.10
168	Mike Maddux	.10
169	Dave Hollins	.10
170	Zane Smith	.10
171	Rafael Palmeiro	.45
172	Dave Martinez	.10
173	Rusty Meacham	.10
174	Mark Leiter	.10
175	Chuck Knoblauch	.10
176	Lance Johnson	.10
177	Matt Nokes	.10
178	Luis Gonzalez	.10
179	Jack Morris	.10
180	David Justice	.10
181	Doug Henry	.10
182	Felix Jose	.10
183	Roberto DeShields	.15
184	Rene Gonzales	.10
185	Pete Harnisch	.10
186	Mike Moore	.10
187	Juan Guzman	.10
188	John Olerud	.20
189	Ryan Klesko	.10
190	John Jaha	.10
191	Ray Lankford	.10
192	Jeff Fassero	.10
193	Darren Lewis	.10
194	Mark Lewis	.10
195	Alan Mills	.10
196	Wade Boggs	.75
197	Hal Morris	.10
198	Ron Karkovice	.10
199	John Grahe	.10
200	Butch Henry	.10
201	Mark McGwire	1.25
202	Tom Henke	.10
203	Ed Sprague	.10
204	Charlie Leibrandt	.10
205	Pat Listach	.10
206	Omar Olivares	.10
207	Mike Morgan	.10
208	Eric Karros	.10
209	Marquis Grissom	.15
210	Willie McGee	.10
211	Derek Lilliquist	.10
212	Tino Martinez	.10
213	Jeff Kent	.10
214	Mike Mussina	.35
215	Randy Myers	.10
216	John Kruk	.10
217	Tom Brunansky	.10
218	Paul O'Neill	.10
219	Scott Livingstone	.10
220	John Valentin	.10
221	Eddie Zosky	.10
222	Pete Smith	.10
223	Bill Wegman	.10
224	Todd Zeile	.10
225	Tim Wallach	.10
226	Mitch Williams	.10
227	Tim Wakefield	.10
228	Frank Viola	.10
229	Nolan Ryan	1.50
230	Kirk McCaskill	.10
231	Melido Perez	.10
232	Mark Langston	.10
233	Xavier Hernandez	.10
234	Jerry Browne	.10
235	Dave Stieb	.15
236	Mark Lemke	.10
237	Paul Molitor	.75
238	Geronimo Pena	.10
239	Ken Hill	.10
240	Jack Clark	.10
241	Greg Myers	.10
242	Pete Incaviglia	.10
243	Ruben Sierra	.10
244	Todd Stottlemyre	.10
245	Pat Hentgen	.10
246	Melvin Nieves	.10
247	Jaime Navarro	.10
248	Donovan Osborne	.10
249	Brian Barnes	.10
250	Cory Snyder	.10
251	Kenny Lofton	.10
252	Kevin Mitchell	.10
253	Dave Magadan	.10
254	Ben McDonald	.10
255	Fred McGriff	.20
256	Mickey Morandini	.10
257	Randy Tomlin	.10
258	Dean Palmer	.10
259	Roger Clemens	1.00
260	Joe Oliver	.10
261	Jeff Montgomery	.10
262	Tony Phillips	.10
263	Shane Mack	.10
264	Jack McDowell	.10
265	Mike Macfarlane	.10
266	Luis Polonia	.10
267	Doug Jones	.10
268	Terry Steinbach	.10
269	Jimmy Key	.10
270	Pat Tabler	.10
271	Otis Nixon	.10
272	Dave Nilsson	.10
273	Tom Pagnozzi	.10
274	Ryne Sandberg	.75
275	Ramon Martinez	.10
276	Tim Laker	.10
277	Bill Swift	.10
278	Charles Nagy	.10
279	Harold Reynolds	.10
280	Eddie Murray	.60
281	Gregg Olson	.10
282	Frank Seminara	.10
283	Terry Mulholland	.10
284	Kevin Palmer	.10
285	Mike Greenwell	.10
286	Jose Rijo	.10
287	Brian McRae	.10
288	Frank Tanana	.10
289	Pedro Munoz	.10
290	Tim Raines	.15
291	Andy Stankiewicz	.10
292	Tim Salmon	.10
293	Jimmy Jones	.10
294	Dave Stewart	.15
295	Mike Timlin	.10
296	Greg Olson	.10
297	Dan Plesac	.10
298	Mike Perez	.10
299	Jose Offerman	.10
300	Denny Martinez	.15
301	Robby Thompson	.10
302	Bret Saberhagen	.10
303	Joe Orsulak	.10
304	Tim Naehring	.10
305	Bip Roberts	.10
306	Kirby Puckett	.75
307	Steve Sax	.10
308	Danny Tartabull	.10
309	Jeff Juden	.10
310	Duane Ward	.10
311	Alejandro Pena	.10
312	Kevin Seitzer	.10
313	Ozzie Smith	.75
314	Mike Piazza	1.00
315	Chris Nabholz	.10
316	Tony Pena	.10
317	Gary Sheffield	.25
318	Mark Portugal	.10
319	Walt Weiss	.10
320	Manuel Lee	.10
321	David Wells	.15
322	Terry Pendleton	.10
323	Billy Spiers	.10
324	Lee Smith	.10
325	Bob Scanlan	.10
326	Mike Scioscia	.10
327	Spike Owen	.10
328	Mackey Sasser	.10
329	Arthur Rhodes	.10
330	Ben Rivera	.10
331	Ivan Rodriguez	.50
332	Phil Plantier	.10
333	Chris Sabo	.10
334	Mickey Tettleton	.10
335	John Smiley	.10
336	Bobby Thigpen	.10
337	Randy Velarde	.10
338	Luis Sojo	.10
339	Scott Servais	.10
340	Bob Welch	.10
341	Devon White	.15
342	Jeff Reardon	.10
343	B.J. Surhoff	.10
344	Bob Tewksbury	.10
345	Jose Vizcaino	.10
346	Mike Sharperson	.10
347	Mel Rojas	.10
348	Matt Williams	.10
349	Steve Olin	.10
350	Mike Schooler	.10
351	Ryan Thompson	.10
352	Cal Ripken	1.50
353	Benny Santiago	.10
354	Curt Schilling	.25
355	Andy Van Slyke	.10
356	Kenny Rogers	.10
357	Jody Reed	.10
358	Reggie Sanders	.10
359	Kevin McReynolds	.10
360	Alan Trammell	.10
361	Kevin Tapani	.10
362	Frank Thomas	.60
363	Bernie Williams	.10
364	John Smoltz	.10
365	Robin Yount	.60
366	John Wetteland	.10
367	Bob Zupcic	.10
368	Julio Valera	.10
369	Brian Williams	.10
370	Willie Wilson	.10
371	Dave Winfield	.75
372	Deion Sanders	.10
373	Greg Vaughn	.10
374	Todd Worrell	.10
375	Darryl Strawberry	.10
376	John Vander Wal	.10
377	Mike Benjamin	.10
378	Mark Whiten	.10
379	Omar Vizquel	.10
380	Anthony Young	.10
381	Rick Sutcliffe	.10
382	Candy Maldonado	.10
383	Francisco Cabrera	.10
384	Larry Walker	.20
385	Scott Cooper	.10
386	Gerald Williams	.10
387	Robin Ventura	.10
388	Carl Willis	.10
389	Lou Whitaker	.10
390	Hipolito Pichardo	.10
391	Rudy Seanez	.10
392	Greg Swindell	.10
393	Mo Vaughn	.10
394	Checklist 1 of 3	.10
395	Checklist 2 of 3	.10
396	Checklist 3 of 3	.10

World Champs

This 18-card insert set commemorates the Toronto Blue Jays' 1992 World Series victory; 17 players and Manager Cito Gaston are featured. Cards were randomly inserted, one World Champs or World Series Heroes card per every 69-cent, eight-card pack. Fronts and backs each feature the World's Championship logo. Backs include stats from the 1992 ALCS and World Series.

	NM/M
Complete Set (18):	4.00
Common Player:	.25
1 Roberto Alomar	1.00
2 Pat Borders	.25
3 Joe Carter	.65
4 David Cone	.35
5 Kelly Gruber	.25
6 Juan Guzman	.25
7 Tom Henke	.25
8 Jimmy Key	.35
9 Manuel Lee	.25
10 Candy Maldonado	.25
11 Jack Morris	.35
12 John Olerud	.50
13 Ed Sprague	.25
14 Todd Stottlemyre	.25
15 Duane Ward	.25
16 Devon White	.35
17 Dave Winfield	1.50
18 Cito Gaston	.25

World Series Heroes

This insert set honors four of the Toronto Blue Jays' World Series stars. Cards were randomly inserted in every 69-cent, eight-card pack, one World Champs or World Series Heroes card per pack.

	NM/M
Complete Set (4):	1.50
Common Player:	.25
1 Pat Borders	.25
2 Jimmy Key	.25
3 Ed Sprague	.25
4 Dave Winfield	1.50

Premier

For the third consecutive year, O-Pee-Chee produced a set under its Premier brand name. The regular set, issued in three series, has 132 cards and 48 insert cards. The insert sets are titled Star Performers (gold borders), Foil Star Performers (full-bleed photos and gold stamping), and Top Draft Picks (two each featuring the Toronto Blue Jays and Montreal Expos top picks). O-Pee-Chee announced it produced only 4,000 cases for this set.

	NM/M
Complete Set (132):	4.00
Common Player:	.05
Wax Box:	8.00
1 Barry Bonds	1.50
2 Chad Curtis	.05
3 Chris Bosio	.05
4 Cal Eldred	.05
5 Dan Walter	.05
6 Rene Arocha	.05
7 Delino DeShields	.05
8 Spike Owen	.05
9 Jeff Russell	.05
10 Phil Plantier	.05
11 Mike Christopher	.05
12 Darren Daulton	.05
13 Scott Cooper	.05
14 Paul O'Neill	.05
15 Jimmy Key	.05
16 Dickie Thon	.05
17 Greg Gohr	.05
18 Andre Dawson	.05
19 Steve Cooke	.05
20 Tony Fernandez	.05
21 Mark Gardner	.05
22 Dave Martinez	.05
23 Jose Guzman	.05
24 Chili Davis	.05
25 Randy Knorr	.05
26 Mike Piazza	1.00
27 Benji Gil	.05
28 Dave Winfield	.45
29 Wil Cordero	.05
30 Butch Henry	.05
31 Eric Young	.05
32 Orestes Destrade	.05
33 Randy Myers	.05
34 Tom Brunansky	.05
35 Dan Wilson	.05
36 Juan Guzman	.05
37 Tim Salmon	.05
38 Bill Krueger	.05
39 Larry Walker	.25
40 David Hulse	.05
41 Ken Ryan	.05
42 Jose Lind	.05
43 Benny Santiago	.05
44 Ray Lankford	.05
45 Dave Stewart	.05
46 Don Mattingly	.60
47 Fernando Valenzuela	.05
48 Scott Fletcher	.05
49 Wade Boggs	.50
50 Norm Charlton	.05
51 Carlos Baerga	.05
52 John Olerud	.15
53 Willie Wilson	.05
54 Dennis Moeller	.05
55 Joe Orsulak	.05
56 John Smiley	.05
57 Al Martin	.05
58 Andres Galarraga	.15
59 Billy Ripken	.05
60 Dave Stieb	.05
61 Dave Magadan	.05
62 Todd Worrell	.05
63 Sherman Obando	.05
64 Kent Bottenfield	.05
65 Vinny Castilla	.05
66 Charlie Hayes	.05
67 Mike Hartley	.05
68 Harold Baines	.05
69 John Cummings	.05
70 J.T. Snow	.05
71 Graeme Lloyd	.05
72 Frank Bolick	.05
73 Doug Drabek	.05
74 Milt Thompson	.05
75 Tim Pugh	.05
76 John Kruk	.05
77 Tom Henke	.05
78 Kevin Young	.05
79 Ryan Thompson	.05
80 Mike Hampton	.05
81 Jose Canseco	.30
82 Mike Lansing	.15
83 Candy Maldonado	.05
84 Alex Arias	.05
85 Troy Neel	.05
86 Greg Swindell	.05
87 Tim Wallach	.05
88 Andy Van Slyke	.05
89 Harold Baines	.05
90 Bryan Harvey	.05
91 Jerald Clark	.05
92 David Cone	.05
93 Ellis Burks	.05
94 Scott Bankhead	.05
95 Pete Incaviglia	.05
96 Cecil Fielder	.10
97 Sean Berry	.05
98 Gregg Jefferies	.05
99 Billy Brewer	.05
100 Scott Sanderson	.05
101 Walt Weiss	.05
102 Travis Fryman	.05
103 Barry Larkin	.05
104 Darren Holmes	.05
105 Ivan Calderon	.05
106 Terry Jorgensen	.05
107 David Nied	.05
108 Tim Bogar	.05
109 Roberto Kelly	.05
110 Mike Moore	.05
111 Carlos Garcia	.05
112 Mike Bielecki	.05
113 Trevor Hoffman	.05

	NM/M
114 Rich Amaral	.05
115 Jody Reed	.05
116 Charlie Leibrandt	.05
117 Greg Gagne	.05
118 Darrell Sherman	.05
119 Jeff Conine	.05
120 Tim Laker	.05
121 Kevin Seitzer	.05
122 Jeff Mutis	.05
123 Rico Rossy	.05
124 Paul Molitor	.45
125 Cal Ripken	1.50
126 Greg Maddux	.60
127 Greg McMichael	.05
128 Felix Jose	.05
129 Dick Schofield	.05
130 Jim Abbott	.05
131 Kevin Reimer	.05
132 Checklist	.05

Premier Star Performers

O-Pee-Chee released a 22-card insert set in two forms: Star Performers (featuring a gold border design) and Foil Star Performers (featuring full-bleed photos and gold stamping). The players are identical in both sets, but foil cards are generally worth more. There are 34 Star Performers per 36-card wax box and one Foil Star Performer card per box.

	NM/M
Complete Set (22):	4.50
Common Player:	.10
Foil:	6X
1 Frank Thomas	.50
2 Fred McGriff	.15
3 Roberto Alomar	.40
4 Ryne Sandberg	.65
5 Gary Sheffield	.25
6 Juan Gonzalez	.40
7 Eric Karros	.10
8 Ken Griffey Jr.	.75
9 Deion Sanders	.05
10 Kirby Puckett	.65
11 Will Clark	.10
12 Joe Carter	.15
13 Cal Ripken	1.50
14 Barry Bonds	1.50
15 Pat Listach	.10
16 Mark McGwire	1.00
17 Kenny Lofton	.10
18 Roger Clemens	.75
19 Greg Maddux	.65
20 Nolan Ryan	1.50
21 Tom Glavine	.20
22 Dennis Eckersley	.40

Premier Top Draft Picks

These randomly inserted cards feature four prospects; two each for Montreal and Toronto. Card fronts are foil-stamped and have a vertical banner with the player's name. The OPC Premier logo is in the corner. On back is another player photo, a team logo and a bi-lingual rationale for the player's draft status.

	NM/M
Complete Set (4):	2.50
Common Player:	.50
1 B.J. Wallace	.50
2 Shannon Stewart	2.00
3 Rod Henderson	.50
4 Todd Steverson	.50

1994 O-Pee-Chee Sample Sheet

The basic '94 OPC card set and all of its chase card sets were previewed on this sample sheet sent to dealers. Measuring 8"x11", the sheet's cards vary slightly from issued cards in terms of foil highlights. Card fronts on the sample sheet are highlighted in red foil while there is no foil on the backs. Each of the card backs (except the jumbo All-Star) includes the notation "Pre-Production Sample."

	NM/M
Complete Sheet:	6.00

1994 O-Pee-Chee

Limited to 2,500 cases (about 112,000 of each card in the regular 270-card set) the '94 OPC issue features color photos on front and back along with complete major league stats (and some minor league stats) on back. Team names are in a color-coded strip at left. Career summaries and some other data are printed in both English and French.

	NM/M
Complete Set (270):	15.00
Common Player:	.05
Wax Pack (15):	.75
Wax Box (36):	15.00
1 Paul Molitor	.75
2 Kirt Manwaring	.05
3 Brady Anderson	.05
4 Scott Cooper	.05
5 Kevin Stocker	.05
6 Alex Fernandez	.05
7 Jeff Montgomery	.05
8 Danny Tartabull	.05
9 Damion Easley	.05
10 Andujar Cedeno	.05
11 Steve Karsay	.05
12 Dave Stewart	.05
13 Fred McGriff	.05
14 Jaime Navarro	.05
15 Allen Watson	.05
16 Ryne Sandberg	.75
17 Arthur Rhodes	.05
18 Marquis Grissom	.05
19 John Burkett	.05
20 Robby Thompson	.05
21 Denny Martinez	.05
22 Ken Griffey Jr.	1.00
23 Orestes Destrade	.05
24 Dwight Gooden	.05
25 Rafael Palmeiro	.40
26 Pedro Martinez	.05
27 Wes Chamberlain	.05
28 Juan Gonzalez	.50
29 Kevin Mitchell	.05
30 Dante Bichette	.05
31 Howard Johnson	.05
32 Mickey Tettleton	.05
33 Robin Ventura	.05
34 Terry Mulholland	.05
35 Bernie Williams	.05
36 Eduardo Perez	.05
37 Rickey Henderson	.65
38 Terry Pendleton	.05
39 John Smoltz	.05
40 Derrick May	.05
41 Pedro Martinez	.60
42 Mark Portugal	.05
43 Albert Belle	.05
44 Edgar Martinez	.05
45 Gary Sheffield	.35
46 Bret Saberhagen	.05
47 Ricky Gutierrez	.05
48 Orlando Merced	.05
49 Mike Greenwell	.05
50 Jose Rijo	.05
51 Jeff Granger	.05
52 Mike Henneman	.05
53 Dave Winfield	.65
54 Don Mattingly	.85
55 J.T. Snow	.05
56 Todd Van Poppel	.05
57 Chipper Jones	.75
58 Darryl Hamilton	.05
59 Delino DeShields	.05
60 Rondell White	.05
61 Eric Anthony	.05
62 Charlie Hough	.05
63 Sid Fernandez	.05
64 Derek Bell	.05
65 Phil Plantier	.05
66 Curt Schilling	.20
67 Roger Clemens	1.00
68 Jose Lind	.05
69 Andres Galarraga	.05
70 Tim Belcher	.05
71 Ron Karkovice	.05
72 Alan Trammell	.05
73 Pete Harnisch	.05
74 Mark McGwire	1.50
75 Ryan Klesko	.05
76 Ramon Martinez	.05
77 Gregg Jefferies	.05
78 Steve Buechele	.05
79 Bill Swift	.05
80 Matt Williams	.05
81 Randy Johnson	.60
82 Mike Mussina	.50
83 Andy Benes	.05
84 Dave Staton	.05
85 Steve Cooke	.05
86 Andy Van Slyke	.05
87 Ivan Rodriguez	.50
88 Frank Viola	.05
89 Aaron Sele	.05
90 Ellis Burks	.05
91 Wally Joyner	.05
92 Rick Aguilera	.05
93 Kirby Puckett	.75
94 Roberto Hernandez	.05
95 Mike Stanley	.05
96 Roberto Alomar	.25
97 James Mouton	.05
98 Chad Curtis	.05
99 Mitch Williams	.05
100 Carlos Delgado	.40
101 Greg Maddux	.75
102 Brian Harper	.05
103 Tom Pagnozzi	.05
104 Jose Offerman	.05
105 John Wetteland	.05
106 Carlos Baerga	.05
107 Dave Magadan	.05
108 Bobby Jones	.05
109 Tony Gwynn	.75
110 Jeromy Burnitz	.05
111 Bip Roberts	.05
112 Carlos Garcia	.05
113 Jeff Russell	.05
114 Armando Reynoso	.05
115 Ozzie Guillen	.05
116 Bo Jackson	.10
117 Terry Steinbach	.05
118 Deion Sanders	.05
119 Randy Myers	.05
120 Mark Whiten	.05
121 Manny Ramirez	.60
122 Ben McDonald	.05
123 Darren Daulton	.05
124 Kevin Young	.05
125 Barry Larkin	.05
126 Cecil Fielder	.05
127 Frank Thomas	.60
128 Luis Polonia	.05
129 Steve Finley	.05
130 John Olerud	.05
131 John Jaha	.05
132 Darren Lewis	.05
133 Orel Hershiser	.05
134 Chris Bosio	.05
135 Ryan Thompson	.05
136 Chris Sabo	.05
137 Tommy Greene	.05
138 Andre Dawson	.25
139 Bobby Kelly	.05
140 Ken Hill	.05
141 Greg Gagne	.05
142 Julio Franco	.05
143 Chili Davis	.05
144 Dennis Eckersley	.50
145 Joe Carter	.05
146 Mark Grace	.05
147 Mike Piazza	.90
148 J.R. Phillips	.05
149 Rich Amaral	.05
150 Benny Santiago	.05
151 Jeff King	.05
152 Dean Palmer	.05
153 Hal Morris	.05
154 Mike MacFarlane	.05
155 Chuck Knoblauch	.05
156 Pat Kelly	.05
157 Greg Swindell	.05
158 Chuck Finley	.05
159 Devon White	.05
160 Duane Ward	.05
161 Sammy Sosa	.85
162 Javier Lopez	.05
163 Eric Karros	.05
164 Royce Clayton	.05
165 Salomon Torres	.05
166 Jeff Kent	.05
167 Chris Hoiles	.05
168 Len Dykstra	.05
169 Jose Canseco	.35
170 Bret Boone	.05
171 Charlie Hayes	.05
172 Lou Whitaker	.05
173 Jack McDowell	.05
174 Jimmy Key	.05
175 Mark Langston	.05
176 Darryl Kile	.05
177 Juan Guzman	.05
178 Pat Borders	.05
179 Cal Eldred	.05
180 Jose Guzman	.05
181 Ozzie Smith	.75
182 Rod Beck	.05
183 Dave Fleming	.05
184 Eddie Murray	.60
185 Cal Ripken	2.00
186 Dave Hollins	.05
187 Will Clark	.05
188 Otis Nixon	.05
189 Joe Oliver	.05
190 Roberto Mejia	.05
191 Felix Jose	.05
192 Tony Phillips	.05
193 Wade Boggs	.75
194 Tim Salmon	.05
195 Ruben Sierra	.05
196 Steve Avery	.05
197 B.J. Surhoff	.05
198 Todd Zeile	.05
(199) Raul Mondesi (No card number on back.)	.25
200 Barry Bonds	2.00
201 Sandy Alomar	.05
202 Bobby Bonilla	.05
203 Mike Devereaux	.05
204 Rickey Bottalico	.05
205 Kevin Brown	.05
206 Jason Bere	.05
207 Reggie Sanders	.05
208 David Nied	.05
209 Travis Fryman	.05
210 James Baldwin	.05
211 Jim Abbott	.05
212 Jeff Bagwell	.60
213 Bob Welch	.05
214 Jeff Blauser	.05
215 Brett Butler	.05
216 Pat Listach	.05
217 Bob Tewksbury	.05
218 Mike Lansing	.05
219 Wayne Kirby	.05
220 Chuck Carr	.05
221 Harold Baines	.05
222 Jay Bell	.05
223 Cliff Floyd	.05
224 Rob Dibble	.05
225 Kevin Appier	.05
226 Eric Davis	.05
227 Matt Walbeck	.05
228 Tim Raines	.05
229 Paul O'Neill	.05
230 Craig Biggio	.05
231 Brent Gates	.05
232 Rob Butler	.05
233 Dave Justice	.05
234 Rene Arocha	.05
235 Mike Morgan	.05
236 Denis Boucher	.05
237 Kenny Lofton	.05
238 Jeff Conine	.05
239 Bryan Harvey	.05
240 Danny Jackson	.05
241 Al Martin	.05
242 Tom Henke	.05
243 Erik Hanson	.05
244 Walt Weiss	.05
245 Brian McRae	.05
246 Kevin Tapani	.05
247 David McCarty	.05
248 Doug Drabek	.05
249 Troy Neel	.05
250 Tom Glavine	.20
251 Ray Lankford	.05
252 Wil Cordero	.05
253 Larry Walker	.05
254 Charles Nagy	.05
255 Kirk Rueter	.05
256 John Franco	.05
257 John Kruk	.05
258 Alex Gonzalez	.05
259 Mo Vaughn	.05
260 David Cone	.05
261 Kent Hrbek	.05
262 Lance Johnson	.05
263 Luis Gonzalez	.10
264 Mike Bordick	.05
265 Ed Sprague	.05
266 Moises Alou	.05
267 Omar Vizquel	.05
268 Jay Buhner	.05
269 Checklist	.05
270 Checklist	.05

All-Star Redemption Cards

A series of 25 All-Star redemption cards was one of the several inserts which were found at the rate of one per pack in '94 OPC foil. Fronts feature a color photo floating over a white background. The player's name is displayed in gold script at top and the card number is repeated along the top and left or right of the photo. Backs have information on how to redeem the cards for a super-size version of the set. Approximately 78,000 of each of the 25 cards in the insert set were produced.

		NM/M
Complete Set (25):		9.00
Common Player:		.50
1	Frank Thomas	.65
2	Paul Molitor	1.00
3	Barry Bonds	2.50
4	Juan Gonzalez	.60
5	Jeff Bagwell	.75
6	Carlos Baerga	.50
7	Ryne Sandberg	1.00
8	Ken Griffey Jr.	2.00
9	Mike Piazza	1.50
10	Tim Salmon	.50
11	Marquis Grissom	.50
12	Albert Belle	.50
13	Fred McGriff	.50
14	Jack McDowell	.50
14p	Jack McDowell ("Pre-Production Sample")	
15	Cal Ripken, Jr.	2.50
16	John Olerud	.50
17	Kirby Puckett	1.00
18	Roger Clemens	1.50
19	Larry Walker	.60
20	Cecil Fielder	.50
21	Roberto Alomar	.60
22	Greg Maddux	1.00
23	Joe Carter	.50
24	Dave Justice	.50
25	Kenny Lofton	.50

Jumbo All-Stars

Each of the 60,000 foil-pack boxes of '94 OPC contained one jumbo (5" x 7") All-Star card from a set of 25. Fronts are identical to the All-Star redemption card inserts found in foil packs, with a UV coating. Backs are blank. Each of the jumbo All-Stars was produced in a quantity of 2,400. A factory-set version of the jumbo All-Stars was also available by redeeming five of the AS inserts and $20. The factory-set AS jumbos differ from the box-toppers in that they have gold-foil enhancements and are numbered to 5,000 each.

		NM/M
Complete Set (25):		75.00
Common Player:		2.00
Complete Factory Set:		35.00
Factory Set Singles:		.75X
1	Frank Thomas	4.00
2	Paul Molitor	5.00
3	Barry Bonds	9.00
4	Juan Gonzalez	3.00

5	Jeff Bagwell	4.00
6	Carlos Baerga	2.00
7	Ryne Sandberg	5.00
8	Ken Griffey Jr.	7.50
9	Mike Piazza	6.00
10	Tim Salmon	2.00
11	Marquis Grissom	2.50
12	Albert Belle	2.00
13	Fred McGriff	2.50
14	Jack McDowell	2.00
15	Cal Ripken	9.00
16	John Olerud	2.50
17	Kirby Puckett	5.00
18	Roger Clemens	6.00
19	Larry Walker	2.50
20	Cecil Fielder	2.50
21	Roberto Alomar	3.00
22	Greg Maddux	5.00
23	Joe Carter	2.50
24	Dave Justice	2.50
25	Kenny Lofton	2.00

Diamond Dynamos

"Baseball's brightest new stars" was the stated criteria for inclusion in this chase card set. Fronts feature a full-bleed action photo with the player's name and "Diamond Dynamos" logo at bottom in red foil. Backs have a second player photo, personal data, a bi-lingual career summary and gold-foil presentation of the player's name and "Twenty-first Century Stars." An average of 1-2 of the cards was inserted per foil box, creating a production run of 5,000 of each card.

		NM/M
Complete Set (18):		5.00
Common Player:		.25
1	Mike Piazza	4.00
2	Roberto Mejia	.25
3	Wayne Kirby	.25
4	Kevin Stocker	.25
5	Chris Gomez	.25
6	Bobby Jones	.25
7	David McCarty	.25
8	Kirk Rueter	.25
9	J.T. Snow	.25
10	Wil Cordero	.25
11	Tim Salmon	.25
12	Jeff Conine	.25
13	Jason Bere	.25
14	Greg McMichael	.25
15	Brent Gates	.25
16	Allen Watson	.25
17	Aaron Sele	.25
18	Carlos Garcia	.25

Hot Prospects

Nine of 1994's hottest rookies are featured in this insert set. Fronts feature full-bleed photos with the player's name in gold foil at bottom. An "O-Pee-Chee Hot Prospects" logo appears in an upper corner. Backs are in shades of red, yellow and orange and include another player photo, biographical data, a career summary and complete minor league stats.

	NM/M
Complete Set (9):	7.50

Toronto Blue Jays

The Blue Jays' starting line-up for the final game of the 1993 World Series is honored on this insert set. Fronts have a blue typographic background of "World Series Champions '92 & '93." There is a color player photo with his name in red foil at bottom. Backs repeat the typographic background in black and include 1992 and 1993 World Series stats along with the player's Series highlights in both English and French. A gold-foil seal marking the back-to-back championships is at top center. Stated odds of finding a Blue Jays insert card are one per foil box, indicating a production of about 6,666 of each card.

		NM/M
Complete Set (9):		6.00
Common Player:		.50
1	Rickey Henderson	2.00
2	Devon White	.75
3	Paul Molitor	2.00
4	Joe Carter	.75
5	John Olerud	1.00
6	Roberto Alomar	1.50
7	Ed Sprague	.50
8	Pat Borders	.50
9	Tony Fernandez	.50

1987 Oakland Athletics Fire Safety

The 1987 Smokey Bear A's set is not comparable to earlier Forestry Service issues. The cards are bound together in a book titled "Smokey Bear's Fire Prevention Color-Grams." Each Color-Gram features two cards in one. A near-standard size (2-1/2" x 3-3/4") black-and-white card is attached to a large perforated (3-3/4"x 6") card, also black-and-white. The large card, which has a postcard back, features a caricature of the player and is intended to be colored and mailed. Backs contain personal and statistical information and carry a Smokey the Bear cartoon fire safety message. The books were distributed at an A's game during the 1987 season.

	NM/M
Complete Book:	4.50
Complete Singles Set (12):	3.00
Common Player:	.25

(1)	Joaquin Andujar	.25
(2)	Jose Canseco	1.50
(3)	Mike Davis	.25
(4)	Alfredo Griffin	.25
(5)	Moose Haas	.25
(6)	Jay Howell	.25
(7)	Reggie Jackson	1.50
(8)	Carney Lansford	.25
(9)	Dwayne Murphy	.25
(10)	Tony Phillips	.25
(11)	Dave Stewart	.25
(12)	Curt Young	.25

1992 Oakland A's Dream Team

Following fan balloting in 1991, the Oakland A's named an all-time Dream Team for their 25th anniversary season in 1992 and issued a card set of those players. Cards were distributed in two versions. Perforated sheets of eight cards each were included in the second and third editions of the team's magazine. Imperforate four-card strips were also handed out to the first 10,000 fans attending each of four selected home games in 1992. Cards measure 2-9/16" x 3-3/4". Fronts have gray borders. At upper-left is a green and yellow Dream Team pennant; a 25th anniversary logo at lower-right is also in team colors. A red box beneath the color player photo has the name and position in red and white. Black-and-white backs have uniform and card numbers, career stats and highlights and a few biographical bits.

		NM/M
Complete Set (16):		20.00
Common Player:		1.00
1	Mark McGwire	5.00
2	Mike Gallego	1.00
3	Bert Campaneris	1.00
4	Carney Lansford	1.00
5	Reggie Jackson	4.00
6	Rickey Henderson	3.00
7	Jose Canseco	3.00
8	Dave Parker	1.00
9	Terry Steinbach	1.00
10	Dave Stewart	1.00
11	Jim "Catfish" Hunter	2.00
12	Vida Blue	1.00
13	Bob Welch	1.00
14	Dennis Eckersley	2.00
15	Rollie Fingers	2.00
16	Tony LaRussa	1.00

1995 Oakland A's CHP

This safety set was sponsored by the California Highway Patrol. Fronts of the 2-1/2" x 3-1/2" cards have borderless game-action photos with a pair of team logos in the upper corner, a CHiPs badge at bottom-left and the player's name at lower-right. Black-and-white backs have player data and a driving safety tip.

	NM/M
Complete Set (8):	15.00

1999 Plumbers Local 342 Oakland A's

Borrowing from the concept used for many years by Mother's Cookies, this team set was designed to encourage trading when it was distributed to 15,000 fans on May 2. Cards were given away in shrink-wrapped packs of 28, containing 20 single cards and eight of one of the others. Sponsored by a trade union, the Plumbers Steamfitters Refrigeration Local 342, the set has color photos on front, surrounded by borders which morph from yellow to dark green. A "Generation '99 A's" logo is at lower-left. Backs have minimal player data.

		NM/M
Complete Set (28):		12.50
Common Player:		.25
1	Art Howe	.25
2	Ben Grieve	.50
3	Jason Giambi	3.00
4	Kenny Rogers	.25
5	Matt Stairs	.25
6	Tom Candiotti	.25
7	Tony Phillips	.25
8	Eric Chavez	1.50
9	Tim Raines	.50
10	A.J. Hinch	.25
11	Bill Taylor	.25
12	Miguel Tejada	1.50
13	Tim Worrell	.25
14	Scott Spezio	.25
15	Buddy Groom	.25
16	Olmedo Saenz	.25
17	T.J. Mathews	.25
18	Mike Macfarlane	.25
19	Brad Rigby	.25
20	Ryan Christenson	.25
21	Doug Jones	.25
22	Terry Clark	.25
23	Jorge Velandia	.25
24	Gil Heredia	.25
25	John Jaha	.25
26	Jimmy Haynes	.25
27	Jason McDonald	.25
28	A's Coaches/Checklist (Thad Bosley, Brad Fischer, Dave Hudgens, Ken Macha, Rick Peterson, Ron Washington)	.25

2000 Plumbers Local 342 Oakland A's

This team set was designed to encourage trading when it was distributed to fans at a promotional game. Cards were given away in packs of 28, containing 20 single cards and eight of one of the others. Sponsored by a trade union, the Plumbers Steamfitters Refrigeration Local 342, the set has color photos on front, surrounded by green borders. Backs have minimal player data.

		NM/M
Complete Set (28):		15.00
Common Player:		.50
1	Art Howe	.50
2	Jason Giambi	4.00
3	Tim Hudson	2.00
4	Matt Stairs	.50
5	Kevin Appier	.50
6	Ben Grieve	.50
7	Randy Velarde	.50
8	Eric Chavez	1.50
9	Mark Mulder	.75
10	Sal Fasano	.50
11	Doug Jones	.50
12	Miguel Tejada	1.50

13	Omar Oliveres	.50
14	Jeremy Giambi	.50
15	Gil Heredia	.50
16	Olmedo Saenz	.50
17	T.J. Mathews	.50
18	Ramon Hernandez	.50
19	Jeff Tam	.50
20	Ryan Christenson	.50
21	John Jaha	.50
22	Rich Sauveur	.50
23	Terrence Long	.50
24	Mike Magnante	.50
25	Scott Service	.50
26	Frank Menechino	.50
27	Jason Isringhausen	.50
28	Coaches/Checklist	.50

2001 Oakland A's Cal Ripken Farewell

To mark his final trip to Oakland as a player, the A's issued these cards to the first 20,000 fans at the September 3-5 games. The cards commemorate career highlights. Fronts have action photos from earlier seasons and a smaller second photo of more current vintage. Red-and-black backs have a ghost-image photo details of the highlight and specifics of the giveaway.

		NM/M
Complete Set (3):		9.00
Common Card:		3.00
1	Cal Ripken Jr. (Rookie Season 1982)	3.00
2	Cal Ripken Jr. (All-Star Game 1987)	3.00
3	Cal Ripken Jr. (2,131 - Record Breaker)	3.00

2002 Plumbers Local 342 Oakland A's

This team set was designed to encourage trading when it was distributed to 15,000 fans on August 18. Cards were given away in shrink-wrapped packs of 28, containing 20 single cards and eight of one of the others. Sponsored by a trade union, the Plumbers Steamfitters Refrigeration Local 342, the set has borderless color photos on front. A team-colors green and gold strip at bottom has the the player name and "BASEBALL A's STYLE." Backs are in black, green and gold with player data and a large union logo.

		NM/M
Complete Set (28):		15.00
Common Player:		.50
1	Art Howe	.50
2	Tim Hudson	2.00
3	David Justice	.50
4	Mark Mulder	.50
5	Jermaine Dye	.50
6	Barry Zito	.50
7	Miguel Tejada	1.50
8	Eric Chavez	1.50
9	Terrence Long	.50
10	John Mabry	.50
11	Billy Koch	.50
12	Adam Piatt	.50

13	Ramon Hernandez	.50
14	Randy Velarde	.50
15	Scott Hatteberg	.50
16	Mike Magnante	.50
17	Greg Myers	.50
18	Cory Lidle	.50
19	Olmedo Saenz	.50
20	Jim Mecir	.50
21	Eric Byrnes	.50
22	Mark Ellis	.50
23	Mike Venafro	.50
24	Carlos Pena	.50
25	Mike Fyhrie	.50
26	Aaron Harang	.50
27	Chad Bradford	.50
28	A's Coaches (Thad Bosley, Brad Fischer, Ken Macha, Rick Peterson, Mike Quade, Ron Washington)	.50

2003 Plumbers Local 342 Oakland A's

MARK MULDER LHP

This team set was designed to encourage trading when it was distributed to fans at a promotional game. Twenty-eight cards were given away in paper envelopes, containing 20 single cards and eight of one of the others. Sponsored by the Plumbers Steamfitters Refrigeration Local 342, the set has borderless color photos on front. A team-colors green and gold strip at bottom has the player name, position and team logo. Backs are in white, green and gold with player data and a large union logo.

		NM/M
Complete Set (28):		15.00
Common Player:		.50
1	Ken Macha	.50
2	Tim Hudson	2.00
3	Miguel Tejada	1.50
4	Mark Mulder	.75
5	Ramon Hernandez	.50
6	Barry Zito	2.00
7	Jose Guillen	.50
8	Eric Chavez	1.50
9	Terrence Long	.50
10	Ricardo Rincon	.50
11	Erubiel Durazo	.50
12	Mark Ellis	.50
13	Keith Foulke	.50
14	Eric Byrnes	.50
15	Ted Lilly	.50
16	Scott Hatteberg	.50
17	Rich Harden	1.00
18	Chris Singleton	.50
19	Chad Bradford	.50
20	Jermaine Dye	.50
21	Chad Harville	.50
22	Adam Melhuse	.50
23	Jim Mecir	.50
24	John Halama	.50
25	Mike Neu	.50
26	Billy McMillon	.50
27	Frank Menechino	.50
28	A's Coaches (Brad Fischer, Terry Francona, Bob Geren, Dave Hudgens, Rick Peterson, Ron Washington)	.50

1983 O'Connell & Son Ink Baseball Greats

AL KALINE

Detroit Tigers

This set of 4-1/2" x 6-1/2" blank-back cards features the artwork of T.S. O'Connell done in the style of 1959 Topps cards. Player portraits are in black-and-white, while backgrounds and team logos are in color. Production was limited to 2,000 sets.

		NM/M
Complete Set (20):		65.00
Common Player:		2.50
(1)	Hank Aaron	6.50
(2)	Johnny Bench	2.50
(3)	Yogi Berra	3.50
(4)	George Brett	4.50
(5)	Roy Campanella	3.50
(6)	Rod Carew	2.50
(7)	Roberto Clemente	10.00
(8)	Bob Gibson	2.50
(9)	Al Kaline	3.00
(10)	Mickey Mantle	12.50
(11)	Joe Morgan	2.50
(12)	Stan Musial	3.50
(13)	Jim Rice	2.50
(14)	Frank Robinson	2.50
(15)	Pete Rose	6.50
(16)	Tom Seaver	2.50
(17)	Duke Snider	3.50
(18)	Honus Wagner	4.50
(19)	Carl Yastrzemski	2.50
(20)	Robin Yount	2.50

1984-91 O'Connell & Son Ink Mini Prints

ryne sandberg

202

This series of 2-1/2" x 3-1/2" blank-backed cards was issued over the period of 1984-91. Cards #1-180 were sold in annual series of 36 each from 1984-88; the 21-card Sixth Series was issued in 1990. The final 43 cards, plus unnumbered checklists for the first six series were distributed in issues of the company's newsletter, "The Infield Dirt." All cards feature black-and-white pen-and-ink player portraits by T.S. O'Connell and have only the player name and card number on front. Several styles of background, some in color, are found among the various series. Production was limited to 2,000 of each card.

		NM/M
Complete Set (250):		450.00
Common Player:		1.50
	First Series	45.00
1	Ted Williams	7.50
2	Minnie Minoso	1.50
3	Sandy Koufax	9.00
4	Al Kaline	4.50
5	Whitey Ford	3.00
6	Wade Boggs	3.00
7	Nolan Ryan	12.00
8	Greg Luzinski	1.50
9	Cal Ripken	12.00
10	Carl Yastrzemski	4.50
11	Dale Murphy	2.00
12	Rocky Colavito	7.50
13	George Brett	7.50
14	Willie McCovey	3.00
15	Rod Carew	2.50
16	Bob Gibson	2.50
17	Robin Yount	3.00
18	Steve Carlton	2.50
19	Harmon Killebrew	2.50
20	Willie Mays	7.50
21	Reggie Jackson	5.00
22	Eddie Mathews	2.50
23	Eddie Murray	2.50
24	Johnny Bench	2.50
25	Mickey Mantle	18.00
26	Willie Stargell	2.50
27	Rickey Henderson	2.50
28	Roger Maris	6.00
29	Darryl Strawberry	1.50
30	Pete Rose	9.00
31	Jim Rice	1.50
32	Thurman Munson	3.00
33	Brooks Robinson	2.50
34	Fernando Valenzuela	1.50
35	Tony Oliva	1.50
36	Hank Aaron	7.50
	Second Series	45.00
37	Joe Morgan	2.50

38	Kent Hrbek	1.50
39	Yogi Berra	3.00
40	Stan Musial	7.50
41	Gary Matthews	1.50
42	Larry Doby	1.50
43	Steve Garvey	2.50
44	Bob Horner	1.50
45	Ron Guidry	1.50
46	Ernie Banks	3.00
47	Carlton Fisk	2.50
48	"Pee Wee" Reese	2.50
49	Bobby Shantz	1.50
50	Joe DiMaggio	12.00
51	Enos Slaughter	1.50
52	Gary Carter	2.50
53	Bob Feller	1.50
54	Phil Rizzuto	2.50
55	Dave Concepcion	1.50
56	Ron Kittle	1.50
57	Dwight Evans	1.50
58	Johnny Mize	1.50
59	Richie Ashburn	2.50
60	Roberto Clemente	12.00
61	Fred Lynn	1.50
62	Billy Williams	1.50
63	Dave Winfield	2.50
64	Robin Roberts	2.50
65	Billy Martin	1.50
66	Duke Snider	3.00
67	Luis Aparicio	2.50
68	Mickey Vernon	1.50
69	Mike Schmidt	6.00
70	Frank Robinson	2.50
71	Bill Madlock	1.50
72	Rollie Fingers	1.50
	Third Series	45.00
73	Rod Carew	2.50
74	Carl Erskine	1.50
75	Lou Brock	2.50
76	Brooks Robinson	2.50
77	Roberto Clemente	12.00
78	Nellie Fox	2.50
79	Bud Harrelson	1.50
80	Ted Williams	7.50
81	Walter Johnson	2.50
82	Cal Ripken	12.00
83	Lefty Grove	2.00
84	Lou Whitaker	1.50
85	Johnny Bench	2.50
86	Ty Cobb	6.00
87	Mike Schmidt	6.00
88	George Brett	7.50
89	Jim Bunning	2.50
90	Babe Ruth	12.00
91	Satchel Paige	5.00
92	Warren Spahn	1.50
93	Dale Murphy	2.50
94	Early Wynn	1.50
95	Reggie Jackson	2.50
96	Charlie Gehringer	1.50
97	Jackie Robinson	9.00
98	Lou Gehrig	10.00
99	Hank Aaron	7.50
100	Mickey Mantle	18.00
101	Sandy Koufax	9.00
102	Ryne Sandberg	4.00
103	Don Mattingly	6.00
104	Darryl Strawberry	1.50
105	Tom Seaver	2.50
106	Bill Klem	1.50
107	Dwight Gooden	1.50
108	Pete Rose	9.00
	Fourth Series	45.00
109	Elston Howard	2.50
110	Honus Wagner	3.00
111	Waite Hoyt	1.50
112	Bill Bruton	1.50
113	Gil Hodges	2.50
114	Vic Power	1.50
115	Al Kaline	4.50
116	Al Lopez	1.50
117	Rocky Bridges	1.50
118	Jim Gilliam	1.50
119	Christy Mathewson	2.50
120	Hank Greenberg	2.50
121	Eddie Mathews	2.50
122	Van Mungo	1.50
123	Harry Simpson	1.50
124	Carl Yastrzemski	2.50
125	Pete Rose	9.00
126	Dizzy Dean	3.00
127	Chi Chi Olivo	1.50
128	Johnny Vander Meer	1.50
129	Roberto Clemente	12.00
130	Carl Hubbell	1.50
131	Willie Mays	7.50
132	Willie Stargell	2.50
133	Sam Jethroe	1.50
134	Pete Rose	9.00
135	Jackie Robinson	9.00
136	Yogi Berra	3.00
137	Grover Alexander	2.00
138	Joe Morgan	2.50
139	Rube Foster	1.50
140	Mickey Mantle	18.00
141	Ted Williams	7.50
142	Jimmie Foxx	2.50
143	Pepper Martin	1.50
144	Hank Aaron	7.50
	Fifth Series	45.00
145	Vida Blue	1.50
146	Carl Furillo	2.00
147	Lloyd Waner	1.50
148	Eddie Dyer	1.50
149	Casey Stengel	2.50
150	Mickey Mantle	18.00
151	Gil Hodges	2.50
152	Don Mossi	1.50

153	Ron Swoboda	1.50
154	Hoyt Wilhelm	1.50
155	Ed Roush (Edd)	1.50
156	Mickey Lolich	2.00
157	Jim Palmer	2.50
158	Thurman Munson	3.00
159	Don Zimmer	1.50
160	Hank Aaron	7.50
161	Johnny Bench	2.50
162	Orlando Cepeda	1.50
163	Honus Wagner	3.00
164	Tom Seaver	2.50
165	Willie Mays	7.50
166	Elmer Riddle	1.50
167	Tony Oliva	1.50
168	Elmer Flick	1.50
169	Curt Flood	1.50
170	Carl Yastrzemski	2.50
171	Charlie Keller	1.50
172	Christy Mathewson	2.50
173	Eddie Plank	1.50
174	Lou Gehrig	10.00
175	John McGraw	1.50
176	Mule Haas	1.50
177	Paul Waner	1.50
178	Steve Blass	1.50
179	Honus Wagner	3.00
180	Jack Barry	1.50
	Sixth Series	45.00
181	Rocky Colavito	4.50
182	Danny Murtaugh	1.50
183	John Edwards	1.50
184	Pete Rose	9.00
185	Roy Campanella	3.00
186	Jerry Grote	1.50
187	Leo Durocher	1.50
188	Rollie Fingers	2.50
189	Wes Parker	1.50
190	Joe Rudi	1.50
191	Bill Veeck	2.50
192	Mark Fidrych	2.50
193	George Foster	1.50
194	Early Wynn	1.50
195	Frank Howard	1.50
196	Graig Nettles	2.50
197	Juan Pizzaro	1.50
198	Jose Cruz	1.50
199	Joe Jackson	12.00
200	Stan Musial	7.50
201	Chuck Klein	1.50
	Seventh Series	45.00
202	Ryne Sandberg	6.00
203	Richie Allen	2.50
204	Bo Jackson	2.50
205	Kevin Mitchell	1.50
206	Al Smith, Early Wynn, Larry Doby	1.50
207	Mickey Mantle	18.00
208	Will Clark	2.50
209	Cecil Fielder	1.50
210	Bobby Richardson	2.50
211	Nolan Ryan	12.00
212	Casey Stengel	2.50
213	Ted Kluszewski	3.00
214	Gaylord Perry	2.50
215	Johnny Vander Meer	1.50
216	Willie Mays	7.50
217	Goose Goslin	1.50
218	Bobby Shantz	1.50
219	Terry Pendleton	1.50
220	Richie Ashburn	2.50
221	Robin Yount	2.50
222	Cal Ripken	12.00
223	Danny Ainge	1.50
224	Bob Friend	1.50
225	Orel Hershiser	2.50
226	Wade Boggs	3.00
227	Bill Mazeroski (1960 World Series home run.)	3.00
228	Stan Musial	7.50
229	Chris Short	1.50
230	Johnny Bench	2.50
231	Nellie Fox	2.50
232	Ron Santo	2.50
233	Tony Gwynn	6.00
234	Phil Niekro	2.50
235	Frank Thomas	4.50
236	Greg Gross	1.50
237	Ken Griffey Jr.	9.00
238	Benito Santiago	1.50
239	Dwight Gooden	1.50
240	Darryl Strawberry	1.50
241	Roy Campanella	3.00
242	Roger Clemens	6.00
243	Kirby Puckett	7.50
244	Nolan Ryan	12.00
---	First Series Checklist	.25
---	Second Series Checklist	.25
---	Third Series Checklist	.25
---	Fourth Series Checklist	.25
---	Fifth Series Checklist	.25
---	Sixth Series Checklist	.25

1986 Oh Henry! Cleveland Indians

This 30-card set of Cleveland Indians players was distributed by the team at a special Photo/Baseball Card Day at Municipal Stadium. The cards were printed on an 11" x 29" three-panel, perforated foldout piece which featured four action shots of the Indians on the cover. Unfolded, there are two panels containing the baseball cards and a third which contains a team photo.

1986 CLEVELAND INDIANS

THE TRIBE

Cards measure 2-1/4" x 3-1/8". The players' studio portraits are framed in blue with a white border and list player name, number and position. Card fronts also include a picture of the sponsoring candy bar. Card backs include facsimile autograph and professional records. Each card is perforated for separation.

		NM/M
Complete Set, Foldout:		9.00
Common Player:		.40
2	Brett Butler	.40
4	Tony Bernazard	.40
6	Andy Allanson	.40
7	Pat Corrales	.40
8	Carmen Castillo	.40
10	Pat Tabler	.40
13	Ernie Camacho	.40
14	Julio Franco	.50
15	Dan Rohn	.40
18	Ken Schrom	.40
20	Otis Nixon	.40
22	Fran Mullins	.40
23	Chris Bando	.40
24	Ed Williams	.40
26	Brook Jacoby	.40
27	Mel Hall	.40
30	Andre Thornton	.50
32	Joe Carter	.75
35	Phil Niekro	2.00
36	Jamie Easterly	.40
37	Don Schulze	.40
42	Rich Yett	.40
43	Scott Bailes	.40
44	Neal Heaton	.40
48	Jim Kern	.40
48	Dickie Noles	.40
53	Tom Candiotti	.40
53	Reggie Ritter	.40
54	Tom Waddell	.40
---	Coaching Staff (Jack Aker, Bobby Bonds, Doc Edwards, John Goryl)	.40
---	Team Photo	2.00

1995 Oh Henry! Toronto Blue Jays

Michael Huff 25

The candy bar company, Oh Henry!, sponsored this card set giveaway. The 2-1/2" x 3-1/2" cards have an action photo on a green background with the team name repeated in white diagonally. A large colorful "LET'S PLAY BALL" team logo is at top-left. The player name and uniform number are overprinted at bottom. Backs are printed in black-and-

white with personal data, career highlights, stats, and sponsor's logo. Cards are listed here alphabetically.

		NM/M
Complete Set (36):		12.00
Common Player:		.25
(1)	Roberto Alomar	.75
(2)	Bob Bailor	.25
(3)	Howard Battle	.25
(4)	Joe Carter	.45
(5)	Tony Castillo	.25
(6)	Domingo Cedeno	.25
(7)	Galen Cisco	.25
(8)	David Cone	.35
(9)	Brad Cornett	.25
(10)	Danny Cox	.25
(11)	Tim Crabtree	.25
(12)	Carlos Delgado	1.00
(13)	Cito Gaston	.25
(14)	Alex Gonzalez	.50
(15)	Shawn Green	2.00
(16)	Juan Guzman	.25
(17)	Darren Hall	.25
(18)	Pat Hentgen	.25
(19)	Larry Hisle	.25
(20)	Dennis Holmberg	.25
(21)	Michael Huff	.25
(22)	Randy Knorr	.25
(23)	Al Leiter	.25
(24)	Nick Leyva	.25
(25)	Angel Martinez	.25
(26)	Paul Molitor	2.50
(27)	John Olerud	.50
(28)	Tomas Perez	.25
(29)	Aaron Small	.25
(30)	Paul Spoljaric	.25
(31)	Ed Sprague	.25
(32)	Gene Tenace	.25
(33)	Mike Timlin	.25
(34)	Duane Ward	.25
(35)	Devon White	.40
(36)	Woody Williams	.25

1996 Oh Henry! Toronto Blue Jays

Carlos Delgado 21

In celebration of the team's 20th anniversary, Oh Henry! sponsored a card set giveaway at SkyDome on June 11. The first 25,000 fans received a boxed set of current and former players. The 2-1/2" x 3-1/2" cards have a borderless photo on front. The central portion of the picture is in color, the edges are in black-and-white. The player name and uniform number are overprinted at bottom. The team's anniversary logo is in the upper-left corner. On former players' cards there is a gold "ALUMNI" banner under the logo ball. Backs are printed in blue and white with career summary and stats, a few bits of personal data and logos of the team and sponsor. Cards are listed here alphabetically.

		NM/M
Complete Set (36):		8.00
Common Player:		.25
(1)	George Bell	.35
(2)	Brian Bohanon	.25
(3)	Joe Carter	.40
(4)	Tony Castillo	.25
(5)	Domingo Cedeno	.25
(6)	Tim Crabtree	.25
(7)	Felipe Crespo	.25
(8)	Carlos Delgado	1.50
(9)	Cito Gaston	.25
(10)	Alex Gonzalez	.50
(11)	Shawn Green	1.00
(12)	Alfredo Griffin	.25
(13)	Kelly Gruber	.25
(14)	Juan Guzman	.25
(15)	Erik Hanson	.25
(16)	Pat Hentgen	.25
(17)	Marty Janzen	.25
(18)	Nick Leyva	.25
(19)	Sandy Martinez	.25
(20)	Lloyd Moseby	.35
(21)	Otis Nixon	.25
(22)	Charlie O'Brien	.25
(23)	John Olerud	.75
(24)	Robert Perez	.25

(25)	Paul Quantrill	.25
(26)	Mel Queen	.25
(27)	Bill Risley	.25
(28)	Juan Samuel	.25
(29)	Ed Sprague	.25
(30)	Dave Steib	.35
(31)	Gene Tenace	.25
(32)	Mike Timlin	.25
(33)	Willie Upshaw	.25
(34)	Jeffrey Ware	.25
(35)	Ernie Whitt	.25
(36)	Woody Williams	.25

1997 Oh Henry! Toronto Blue Jays

The first 25,000 fans entering SkyDome for the Blue Jays' May 6 game received a team card set sponsored by the candy bar company. In 2-1/2" x 3-1/2" size, fronts feature color action photos with a splash of "infield dirt" vertically at left. The player's name and uniform number appear at top-left. "Oh!" and the team logo are printed in bottom corners. Backs are printed in blue and white with a few personal data, stats and career highlights.

		NM/M
	Complete Set (36):	7.50
	Common Player:	.25
2	Otis Nixon	.25
3	Felipe Crespo	.25
4	Alfredo Griffin	.25
5	Jacob Brumfield	.25
6	Orlando Merced	.25
7	Shannon Stewart	.50
8	Alex Gonzalez	.40
9	Jim Lett	.25
11	Juan Samuel	.25
12	Tilson Brito	.25
13	Carlos Garcia	.25
15	Shawn Green	1.00
16	Nick Leyva	.25
17	Robert Perez	.25
18	Benito Santiago	.25
19	Dan Plesac	.25
21	Roger Clemens	2.50
23	Charlie O'Brien	.25
24	Paul Spoljaric	.25
25	Carlos Delgado	1.50
26	Willie Upshaw	.25
29	Joe Carter	.30
31	Robert Person	.25
33	Ed Sprague	.25
36	Mel Queen	.25
37	Tim Crabtree	.25
39	Erik Hanson	.25
40	Mike Timlin	.25
41	Pat Hentgen	.25
43	Cito Gaston	.25
44	Gene Tenace	.25
48	Paul Quantrill	.25
49	Luis Andujar	.25
54	Woody Williams	.25
55	Bill Risley	.25
57	Juan Guzman	.25

1998 Oh Henry! Toronto Blue Jays

This stadium giveaway card set was issued in a flip-top cardboard box decorated with the team logo and checklist. The 2-1/2" x 3-1/2" cards have (mostly) game action photos on their borderless fronts. Sponsor logo at player name and uniform number are at top, team logo and motto "BRING IT ON" are at bottom. Backs are blue-and-white with player data, stats and career highlights. The checklist is arranged by uniform number.

		NM/M
	Complete Set (36):	7.50
	Common Player:	.25
1	Tony Fernandez	.25
2	Felipe Crespo	.25
4	Craig Grebeck	.25
7	Mark Dalesandro	.25
8	Eddie Rodriguez	.25
9	Alex Gonzalez	.45
9	Darren Fletcher	.25
10	Jim Lett	.25
11	Juan Samuel	.25
14	Kevin Brown	.25
15	Shawn Green	1.00
16	Jack Hubbard	.25
17	Tim Johnson	.25
18	Benito Santiago	.25
19	Dan Plesac	.25
20	Mike Stanley	.25
21	Roger Clemens	3.00
22	Sal Butera	.25
23	Jose Cruz Jr.	.35
24	Shannon Stewart	.35
25	Carlos Delgado	1.50
27	Chris Carpenter	.25
28	Randy Myers	.25
30	Woody Williams	.25
31	Robert Person	.25
33	Ed Sprague	.25
34	Mel Queen	.25
38	Gary Matthews	.25
39	Erik Hanson	.25
40	Carlos Almanzar	.25
41	Pat Hentgen	.25
44	Jose Canseco	1.00
45	Kelvim Escobar	.25
48	Paul Quantrill	.25
55	Bill Risley	.25
57	Juan Guzman	.25

1999 Oh Henry! Toronto Blue Jays

This boxed set was a stadium give-away. Fronts of the 2-1/2" x 3-1/2" cards have game-action photos on a wood-look background. Backs have personal data, career highlights and stats printed in blue. The checklist is arranged by uniform number.

		NM/M
	Complete Set (36):	7.50
	Common Player:	.25
1	Tony Fernandez	.25
2	Norberto Martin	.25
4	Craig Grebeck	.25
5	Mark Dalesandro	.25
7	Pat Kelly	.25
8	Alex Gonzalez	.25
9	Darrin Fletcher	.25
10	Jim Lett	.25
11	Jim Fregosi	.25
12	Willie Greene	.25
13	Pete Munro	.25
15	Shawn Green	.75
16	Lloyd Moseby	.25
17	Dave Hollins	.25
18	Homer Bush	.25
19	Dan Plesac	.25
22	Mike Matheny	.25
23	Jose Cruz	.25
24a	Paul Spoljaric	.25
24b	Shannon Stewart	.35
25	Carlos Delgado	1.50
26	Chris Carpenter	.25
29	Geronimo Berroa	.25
30	Marty Pevey	.25
32	Roy Halladay	.75
34	Mel Queen	.25
35	Terry Bevington	.25
38	Gary Matthews	.25
37	Graeme Lloyd	.25
41	Pat Hentgen	.25
43	Tom Davey	.25
47	Kelvim Escobar	.25
48	Paul Quantrill	.25
50	Joey Hamilton	.25
77	Bill Risley	.25

2000 Oh Henry! Toronto Blue Jays

This boxed set was a stadium give-away. Fronts of the 2-1/2" x 3-1/2" cards have game-action photos on a dark blue background. Backs have personal data, career highlights and stats printed in blue.

		NM/M
	Complete Set (36):	10.00
	Common Player:	.25
3	Lee Elia	.25
4	Craig Grebeck	.25
7	Tony Batista	.25
8	Alex Gonzalez	.25
9	Darrin Fletcher	.25
10	Vernon Wells	.50
11	Jim Fregosi	.25
13	Peter Munro	.25
15	Marty Cordova	.25
18	Homer Bush	.25
20	Brad Fullmer	.25
22	Rick Langford	.25
23	Jose Cruz	.25
24	Shannon Stewart	.25
25	Carlos Delgado	1.50
26	Chris Carpenter	.25
28	Lance Painter	.25
29	Bobby Knoop	.25
30	Alberto Castillo	.25
32	Roy Halladay	.75
33	David Wells	.50
34	Clayton Andrews	.25
35	Terry Bevington	.25
37	Frank Castillo	.25
41	Cito Gaston	.25
43	Raul Mondesi	.25
44	Billy Koch	.25
47	Kelvim Escobar	.25
48	Paul Quantrill	.25
49	John Bale	.25
50	Joey Hamilton	.25
51	Pedro Borbon	.25
52	John Frascatore	.25
55	DeWayne Wise	.25
56	Roly de Armas	.25
77/00	Diamond / Ace (Mascots)	.25

2001 Oh Henry! Toronto Blue Jays

The team's 25th season is commemorated with this stadium give-away boxed set. Fronts have action photos on a blue background with team and sponsor logos. Backs have a large 25th anniversary logo, complete stats, personal data and career highlights.

		NM/M
	Complete Set (36):	8.00
	Common Player:	.25
1	Cookie Rojas	.25
2	Jeff Frye	.25
5	Chris Woodward	.25
7	Tony Batista	.25
8	Alex Gonzalez	.35
9	Darrin Fletcher	.25
13	Buck Martinez	.25
14	Ryan Freel	.25
16	Garth Iorg	.25
17	Chris Michalak	.25
18	Homer Bush	.25
19	Dan Plesac	.25
20	Brad Fullmer	.25
21	Esteban Loaiza	.25
22	Brian Simmons	.25
23	Jose Cruz Jr.	.25
24	Shannon Stewart	.50
25	Carlos Delgado	1.00
26	Chris Carpenter	.25
28	Lance Painter	.25
30	Alberto Castillo	.25
33	Mike Sirotka	.25
35	Terry Bevington	.25
39	Steve Parris	.25
41	Cito Gaston	.25
43	Raul Mondesi	.25
44	Billy Koch	.25
45	Kelvim Escobar	.25
47	Gil Patterson	.25
48	Paul Quantrill	.25
50	Joey Hamilton	.25
51	Pedro Borbon	.25
52	John Frascatore	.25
53	Mark Connor	.25
---	First Pitch (Bill Singer)	.25
---	Home Run Record (Raul Mondesi, Tony Batista, Jose Cruz Jr., Carlos Delgado)	.25

1982-1988 Ohio Baseball Hall of Fame

Ohio natives and players who made their mark playing in the Buckeye State are featured in this collectors' issue, along with executives and a few other figures. Fronts of the 3-3/8" x 5-5/8" cards have black-and-white player photos surrounded by red borders. The player's name and year of induction are at bottom. Black-and-white backs have lengthy career summaries. Original production was 2,500 sets which were sold into the hobby at $7 apiece. Later inductees were added to the set through at least 1988, but the checklist after #65 is incomplete and may represent skip-numbering.

		NM/M
	Complete Set (93):	100.00
	Common Player:	.25
1	Ohio Baseball Hall of Fame	2.00
2	Checklist	.50
3	Nick Cullop	2.00
4	Dean Chance	2.00
5	Bob Feller	3.00
6	Jesse Haines	2.00
7	Waite Hoyt	2.00
8	Ernie Lombardi	2.00
9	Mike Powers	2.00
10	Edd Roush	2.00
11	Red Ruffing	2.00
12	Luke Sewell	2.00
13	Tris Speaker	2.00
14	Cy Young	3.00
15	Walter Alston	2.00
16	Lou Boudreau	2.00
17	Warren Giles	2.00
18	Ted Kluszewski	3.00
19	William McKinley	2.00
20	Roger Peckinpaugh	2.00
21	Johnny Vander Meer	2.00
22	Early Wynn	2.00
23	Earl Averill	2.00
24	Stan Coveleski	2.00
25	Lefty Grove	2.00
26	Nap Lajoie	2.00
27	Al Lopez	2.00
28	Eddie Onslow	2.00
29	Branch Rickey	2.00
30	Frank Robinson	3.00
31	George Sisler	2.00
32	Bob Lemon	2.00
33	Satchel Paige	3.00
34	Bucky Walters	2.00
35	Gus Bell	2.00
36	Rocky Colavito	3.00
37	Mel Harder	2.00
38	Tommy Henrich	2.00
39	Miller Huggins	2.00
40	Fred Hutchinson	2.00
41	Eppa Rixey	2.00
42	Joe Sewell	2.00
43	George Uhle	2.00
44	Bill Veeck	2.00
45	Estel Crabtree	2.00
46	Harvey Haddix	2.00
47	Noodles Hahn	2.00
48	Joe Jackson	4.00
49	Kenesaw Landis	2.00
50	Thurman Munson	3.00
51	Gabe Paul	2.00
52	Vada Pinson	2.00
53	Wally Post	2.00
54	Vic Wertz	2.00
55	Paul Derringer	2.00
56	John Galbreath	2.00
57	Richard Marquard	2.00
58	Bill McKechnie	2.00
59	Rocky Nelson	2.00
60	Al Rosen	2.00
61	Lew Fonseca	2.00
62	Larry MacPhail	2.00
63	Joe Nuxhall	2.00
64	Birdie Tebbetts	2.00
65	Gene Woodling	2.00
66	Ethan Allen	2.00
67	Mike Garcia	2.00
68	Bob Howsam	2.00
69	Addie Joss	2.00
70	Ken Keltner	2.00
71	"Tot" Pressnell	2.00
72	Roger Bresnahan	2.00
73	Bill Mazeroski	3.00
75a	Frank McCormick	2.00
75b	George H. Sisler	2.00
76	Bill Wambsganss	2.00
79	Woody English	2.00
80	Roy McMillan	3.00
81	Frank Baumholtz	2.00
83	Sam McDowell	2.50
84	James Campbell	2.00
86	Ned Garver	2.00
87	Bob Purkey	2.00
90	Harold Cooper	2.00
91	Dennis Galehouse	2.00
92	Brooks Lawrence	2.50
93	Tony Lucadello	2.00

1992 Old Style Chicago Cubs

More than two dozens Cubs stars are featured in this set of 2-1/2" x 3-1/2" cards. Front have sepia player photos with their years at Chicago indicated on top. Backs are printed in black, red and blue on white with a few stats and career highlights, sponsor and team logos and a picture of the Cubs uniform in the player's debut year. The unnumbered cards are checklisted here in alphabetical order.

		NM/M
	Complete Set (28):	15.00
	Common Player:	.50
(1)	Grover Alexander	.50
(2)	Cap Anson	.50
(3)	Ernie Banks	3.00
(4)	Mordecai Brown	.50
(5)	Phil Cavarretta	.50
(6)	Frank Chance	.50
(7)	Kiki Cuyler	.50
(8)	Johnny Evers	.50
(9)	Charlie Grimm	.50
(10)	Stan Hack	.50
(11)	Gabby Hartnett	.50
(12)	Billy Herman	.50
(13)	Rogers Hornsby	.50
(14)	Ken Hubbs	1.00
(15)	Randy Hundley	.50
(16)	Fergie Jenkins	.75
(17)	Bill Lee	.50
(18)	Andy Pafko	.50
(19)	Rick Reuschel	.50
(20)	Charlie Root	.50
(21)	Ron Santo	.75
(22)	Hank Sauer	.50
(23)	Riggs Stephenson	.50
(24)	Bruce Sutter	.75
(25)	Joe Tinker	.50
(26)	Hippo Vaughn	.50
(27)	Billy Williams	1.00
(28)	Hack Wilson	.50

1993 Old Style Billy Williams

The career of long-time Cubs star, batting coach and Hall of Famer Billy Williams is traced in this four-card set given to fans attending the Aug. 17, 1993, game at Wrigley Field between the Cubs and Expos. Fronts of the first three cards have black-and-white photos, the last card is in color. Backs have biographical and career information along with the sponsor's logo.

		NM/M
	Complete Set (4):	8.00
	Common Card:	2.00
(1)	Billy Williams/ Btg/Personal	2.00
(2)	Billy Williams/ Fldg/Playing Career	2.00
(3)	Billy Williams/ Btg/Playing Career	2.00
(4)	Billy Williams/Portrait/ Coaching Career	2.00

1999 Old Style Chicago Cubs All-Century Team

Cubs greats of the 20th Century are featured in this stadium give-away card set. The set was distributed over the course of three games at Wrigley Field in seven-card cello-wrapped packs. With the exception of all-time manager Frank Chance, the cards were packaged alphabetically; Chance was included in the third "series" pack. Fronts of the 2-1/2" x 3-1/2" cards have black-and-white or color photos in a fancy white frame on a tan background. Color team and sponsor logos appear in the left-hand corners. Black-and-white backs have player data, career highlights and lifetime Cubs stats. The player's uniform number, if any, appears on both front and back. Cards have a glossy surface on both front and back.

		NM/M
	Complete Set (21):	20.00
	Common Player:	.50
(1)	Grover Alexander	.50
(2)	Ernie Banks	2.50
(3)	Mordecai Brown	.50
(4)	Phil Cavarretta	.50
(5)	Frank Chance	.50
(6)	Andre Dawson	1.00
(7)	Mark Grace	2.00
(8)	Charlie Grimm	.50
(9)	Stan Hack	.50
(10)	Gabby Hartnett	.50
(11)	Billy Herman	.50
(12)	Fergie Jenkins	.75
(13)	Andy Pafko	.50
(14)	Ryne Sandberg	2.50
(15)	Ron Santo	1.50
(16)	Lee Smith	.50
(17)	Sammy Sosa	3.00
(18)	Bruce Sutter	.75

(19) Joe Tinker .50
(20) Billy Williams .75
(21) Hack Wilson .50

1982 On Deck Cookies Discs

These 2-3/4" discs were packaged with a large cookie and sold for 25-29 cents in areas including Florida and New Jersey. The fronts have a 1981 copyright date, but the backs indicate "1982 Collectors Series." Fronts have black-and-white player portraits in the center panel of a baseball design. The end panels can be any one of several pastel colors. Backs are in red and black and repeat the baseball motif and include a copyright for "All sports baking Co., Inc." Each side carries the Players Union logo through which the discs were licensed by Michael Schechter Associates. Because they are not licensed through Major League Baseball, player pictures have no uniform logos.

		NM/M
Complete Set (32):		60.00
Common Player:		1.50
(1)	Buddy Bell	1.50
(2)	Johnny Bench	4.00
(3)	Bruce Bochte	1.50
(4)	George Brett	7.50
(5)	Bill Buckner	1.50
(6)	Rod Carew	4.00
(7)	Steve Carlton	4.00
(8)	Cesar Cedeno	1.50
(9)	Jack Clark	1.50
(10)	Cecil Cooper	1.50
(11)	Bucky Dent	1.50
(12)	Carlton Fisk	4.00
(13)	Steve Garvey	2.50
(14)	Goose Gossage	1.50
(15)	Mike Hargrove	1.50
(16)	Keith Hernandez	1.50
(17)	Bob Horner	1.50
(18)	Reggie Jackson	7.50
(19)	Steve Kemp	1.50
(20)	Ron LeFlore	1.50
(21)	Fred Lynn	1.50
(22)	Lee Mazilli	1.50
(23)	Eddie Murray	4.00
(24)	Mike Norris	1.50
(25)	Dave Parker	1.50
(26)	J.R. Richard	1.50
(27)	Pete Rose	9.00
(28)	Mike Schmidt	7.50
(29)	Tom Seaver	4.00
(30)	Willie Stargell	4.00
(31)	Roy Smalley	1.50
(32)	Garry Templeton	1.50

1994 Oscar Mayer Superstar Pop-Ups

Oscar Mayer Bologna packages in 1994 included one pop-up card in each, but unlike the similar Kraft cards, in this case it was 30 round cards (2-1/2 inches in diameter), with the Oscar Mayer logo on the front and trivia questions on the backs. The promotion ran from April through May, or as long as the supplies lasted. The cards were licensed by the Major League Baseball Players Association, but not by Major League Baseball, so the team logos were airbrushed from player's caps and uniforms. Through an on-pack and in-store mail-in offer, collectors could order complete sets of cards for $1.95 per league (15 cards), plus the appropriate proofs of purchase. Officials of Kraft USA, parent company of Oscar Mayer, announced that they printed 266,000 sets.

		NM/M
Complete Set (30):		10.00
Common Player:		.50
1	Jim Abbott	.50
2	Kevin Appier	.50
3	Roger Clemens	1.25
4	Cecil Fielder	.60
5	Juan Gonzalez	.60
6	Ken Griffey Jr.	1.50
7	Kenny Lofton	.50
8	Jack McDowell	.50
9	Paul Molitor	.75
10	Kirby Puckett	1.00
11	Cal Ripken Jr.	2.00
12	Tim Salmon	.50
13	Ruben Sierra	.50
14	Frank Thomas	.75
15	Greg Vaughn	.50
16	Jeff Bagwell	.75
17	Barry Bonds	2.00
18	Bobby Bonilla	.50
19	Jeff Conine	.50
20	Lenny Dykstra	.50
21	Andres Galarraga	.50
22	Marquis Grissom	.50
23	Tony Gwynn	1.00
24	Gregg Jefferies	.50
25	John Kruk	.50
26	Greg Maddux	1.00
27	Mike Piazza	1.25
28	Jose Rijo	.50
29	Ryne Sandberg	1.00
30	Andy Van Slyke	.50

1987-89 Our Own Tea Discs

Our Own Tea was one of the regional brands which appears on the series of player disc folders which were packaged with various iced tea mixes and other products between 1987-89.

1988 Pacific Baseball Legends

Pacific Trading Cards rounded up 110 photos of the greatest baseball players from the past 40 years for its 1988 "Baseball Legends" set. All players featured in the set are (or were) members of the Major League Baseball Alumni Association. Card fronts feature silver outer borders and large, clear full-color player photos outlined in black against colorful banner-style inner borders of red, blue, green, orange or gold. The player's name and position are printed in white letters on the lower portion of the banner. Card backs are numbered and carry the Baseball Legends logo, player biography, major league career stats, and personal information. The cards are sold in boxed sets via candy wholesalers, with emphasis on Midwest and New England states. Complete collector sets in clear plastic boxes were made available via dealers or directly from Pacific Trading Cards. Four cards were issued in both error and corrected versions.

		NM/M
Complete Set (110)		
(No checklist.):		15.00
Common Player:		.10
Wax Pack (10):		.75
Wax Box (36):		15.00
1	Hank Aaron	2.00
2	Red Shoendienst (Schoendienst)	.30
3	Brooks Robinson	.50
4	Luke Appling	.30
5	Gene Woodling	.30
6	Stan Musial	1.00
7	Mickey Mantle	6.00
8	Richie Ashburn	.50
9	Ralph Kiner	.40
10	Phil Rizzuto	.50
11	Harvey Haddix	.10
12	Ken Boyer	.20
13	Clete Boyer	.10
14	Ken Harrelson	.20
15	Robin Roberts	.40
16	Catfish Hunter	.40
17	Frank Howard	.20
18	Jim Perry	.10
19a	Elston Howard (Reversed photo.)	.20
19b	Elston Howard (Correct photo.)	.20
20	Jim Bouton	.20
21	Pee Wee Reese	.50
22a	Mel Stottlemyer	.20
22b	Mel Stottlemyre	.20
23	Hank Sauer	.10
24	Willie Mays	1.00
25	Tom Tresh	.20
26	Roy Sievers	.10
27	Leo Durocher	.30
28	Al Dark	.20
29	Tony Kubek	.30
30	Johnny Vander Meer	.20
31	Joe Adcock	.20
32	Bob Lemon	.40
33	Don Newcombe	.40
34	Thurman Munson	.50
35	Earl Battey	.10
36	Ernie Banks	.60
37	Matty Alou	.10
38	Dave McNally	.10
39	Mickey Lolich	.10
40	Jackie Robinson	1.00
41	Allie Reynolds	.30
42a	Don Larson	.20
42b	Don Larsen	.20
43	Fergie Jenkins	.30
44	Jim Gilliam	.20
45	Bobby Thomson	.20
46	Sparky Anderson	.20
47	Roy Campanella	.60
48	Marv Throneberry	.20
49	Bill Virdon	.10
50	Ted Williams	1.00
51	Minnie Minoso	.20
52	Bob Turley	.20
53	Yogi Berra	.60
54	Juan Marichal	.40
55	Duke Snider	.60
56	Harvey Kuenn	.20
57	Nellie Fox	.40
58	Felipe Alou	.20
59	Tony Oliva	.20
60	Bill Mazeroski	.40
61	Bobby Shantz	.20
62	Mark Fidrych	.20
63	Johnny Mize	.30
64	Ralph Terry	.10
65	Gus Bell	.20
66	Jerry Koosman	.20
67	Mike McCormick	.10
68	Lou Burdette	.20
69	George Kell	.30
70	Vic Raschi	.20
71	Chuck Connors	.40
72	Ted Kluszewski	.30
73	Bobby Doerr	.30
74	Bobby Richardson	.30
75	Carl Erskine	.30
76	Hoyt Wilhelm	.40
77	Bob Purkey	.10
78	Bob Friend	.10
79	Monte Irvin	.30
80a	Jim Longborg	.20
80b	Jim Lonborg	.20
81	Wally Moon	.10
82	Moose Skowron	.20
83	Tommy Davis	.20
84	Enos Slaughter	.40
85	Sal Maglie	.20
86	Harmon Killebrew	.50
87	Gil Hodges	.40
88	Jim Kaat	.30
89	Roger Maris	.50
90	Billy Williams	.40
91	Luis Aparicio	.40
92	Jim Bunning	.40
93	Bill Freehan	.20
94	Orlando Cepeda	.30
95	Early Wynn	.40
96	Tug McGraw	.20
97	Ron Santo	.30
98	Del Crandall	.10
99	Sal Bando	.10
100	Joe DiMaggio	2.00
101	Bob Feller	.50
102	Larry Doby	.40
103	Rollie Fingers	.30
104	Al Kaline	.60
105	Johnny Podres	.20
106	Lou Boudreau	.30
107	Zoilo Versalles	.10
108	Dick Groat	.10
109	Warren Spahn	.50
110	Johnny Bench	.60
----	Checklist	2.00

1989 Pacific Legends II

Pacific Trading Cards issued its Baseball Legends II set as a carry over of its initial set. The photos are printed on silver background and have colorful inner borders of red, blue, orange or gold. Players' names and positions are printed in white letters below the photos. The card backs once again present the "Baseball Legends" logo, player biography, major league career statistics, and personal information. The Baseball Legends II are numbered 110-220 and were available in wax packs at a limited number of retail chains. The complete set was also made available via dealers or could be ordered directly from Pacific Trading Cards.

		NM/M
Complete Set (110)		
(No checklist.):		12.50
Common Player:		.10
Wax Pack (10):		.75
Wax Box (36):		15.00
111	Reggie Jackson	.50
112	Rich Reese	.10
113	Frankie Frisch	.10
114	Ed Kranepool	.10
115	Al Hrabosky	.10
116	Eddie Mathews	.20
117	Ty Cobb	1.00
118	Jim Davenport	.10
119	Buddy Lewis	.10
120	Virgil Trucks	.10
121	Del Ennis	.10
122	Dick Radatz	.10
123	Andy Pafko	.10
124	Wilbur Wood	.10
125	Joe Sewell	.10
126	Herb Score	.10
127	Paul Waner	.10
128	Lloyd Waner	.10
129	Brooks Robinson	.20
130	Bo Belinsky	.10
131	Phil Cavaretta	.10
132	Claude Osteen	.10
133	Tito Francona	.10
134	Billy Pierce	.10
135	Roberto Clemente	3.00
136	Spud Chandler	.10
137	Enos Slaughter	.20
138	Ken Holtzman	.10
139	John Hopp	.10
140	Tony LaRussa	.20
141	Ryne Duren	.10
142	Glenn Beckert	.10
143	Ken Keltner	.10
144	Hank Bauer	.10
145	Roger Craig	.10
146	Frank Baker	.10
147	Jim O'Toole	.10
148	Rogers Hornsby	.20
149	Jose Cardenal	.10
150	Bobby Doerr	.10
151	Mickey Cochrane	.20
152	Gaylord Perry	.20
153	Frank Thomas	.10
154	Ted Williams	1.00
155	Sam McDowell	.10
156	Bob Feller	.20
157	Bert Campaneris	.10
158	Thornton Lee	.10
159	Gary Peters	.10
160	Joe Medwick	.10
161	Joe Nuxhall	.10
162	Joe Schultz	.10
163	Harmon Killebrew	.20
164	Bucky Walters	.10
165	Bobby Allison	.10
166	Lou Boudreau	.10
167	Joe Cronin	.10
168	Mike Torrez	.10
169	Rich Rollins	.10
170	Tony Cuccinello	.10
171	Hoyt Wilhelm	.10
172	Ernie Harwell	.10
173	George Foster	.10
174	Lou Gehrig	1.50
175	Dave Kingman	.10
176	Babe Ruth	2.00
177	Joe Black	.10
178	Roy Face	.10
179	Earl Weaver	.10
180	Johnny Mize	.10
181	Roger Cramer	.10
182	Jim Piersall	.10
183	Ned Garver	.10
184	Billy Williams	.10
185	Lefty Grove	.10
186	Jim Grant	.10
187	Elmer Valo	.10
188	Ewell Blackwell	.10
189	Mel Ott	.10
190	Harry Walker	.10
191	Bill Campbell	.10
192	Walter Johnson	.40
193	Jim "Catfish" Hunter	.10
194	Charlie Keller	.10
195	Hank Greenberg	.40
196	Bobby Murcer	.10
197	Al Lopez	.10
198	Vida Blue	.10
199	Shag Crawford	.10
200	Arky Vaughan	.10
201	Smoky Burgess	.10
202	Rip Sewell	.10
203	Earl Averill	.10
204	Milt Pappas	.10
205	Mel Harder	.10
206	Sam Jethroe	.10
207	Randy Hundley	.10
208	Jessie Haines	.10
209	Jack Brickhouse	.10
210	Whitey Ford	.20
211	Honus Wagner	1.25
212	Phil Niekro	.10
213	Gary Bell	.10
214	Jon Matlack	.10
215	Moe Drabowsky	.10
216	Edd Roush	.10
217	Joel Horlen	.10
218	Casey Stengel	.20
219	Burt Hooton	.10
220	Joe Jackson	3.00
----	Checklist	2.00

1990 Pacific Legends

The cards in this 110-card set feature the same style as the previous Pacific Legends releases. The cards were available in wax packs as well as in complete set form. Several players found in the first two legends releases are also found in this issue along with new players.

		NM/M
Complete Set (110):		10.00
Common Player:		.10
Wax Pack (10):		.50
Wax Box (36):		12.50
1	Hank Aaron	2.00
2	Tommie Agee	.10
3	Luke Appling	.20
4	Sal Bando	.10
5	Ernie Banks	1.00
6	Don Baylor	.20
7	Yogi Berra	.75
8	Vida Blue	.10
9	Lou Boudreau	.10
10	Clete Boyer	.10
11	George Bamberger	.10
12	Lou Brock	.30
13	Ralph Branca	.10
14	Carl Erskine	.10
15	Bert Campaneris	.10
16	Steve Carlton	.50
17	Rod Carew	.50
18	Rocky Colovito	.40
19	Frank Crosetti	.10
20	Larry Doby	.10
21	Bobby Doerr	.10
22	Walt Dropo	.10
23	Rick Ferrell	.10
24	Joe Garagiola	.50
25	Ralph Garr	.10
26	Dick Groat	.10
27	Steve Garvey	.40
28	Bob Gibson	.50
29	Don Drysdale	.40
30	Billy Herman	.10
31	Bobby Grich	.10
32	Monte Irvin	.20
33	Dave Johnson	.10
34	Don Kessinger	.10
35	Harmon Killebrew	.50
36	Ralph Kiner	.20
37	Vern Law	.10
38	Ed Lopat	.10
39	Bill Mazeroski	.40
40	Rick Monday	.10
41	Manny Mota	.10
42	Don Newcombe	.20
43	Gaylord Perry	.20
44	Jim Piersall	.10
45	Johnny Podres	.20
46	Boog Powell	.20
47	Robin Roberts	.20
48	Ron Santo	.30
49	Herb Score	.20
50	Enos Slaughter	.20
51	Warren Spahn	.50
52	Rusty Staub	.20
53	Frank Torre	.10
54	Bob Horner	.10
55	Lee May	.10
56	Bill White	.10
57	Hoyt Wilhelm	.20
58	Billy Williams	.20
59	Ted Williams	1.50
60	Tom Seaver	.50
61	Carl Yastrzemski	.75
62	Marv Throneberry	.10
63	Steve Stone	.10
64	Rico Petrocelli	.10
65	Orlando Cepeda	.30
66	Eddie Mathews	.50
67	Joe Sewell	.10
68	Jim "Catfish" Hunter	.20
69	Alvin Dark	.10
70	Richie Ashburn	.30
71	Dusty Baker	.10
72	George Foster	.10
73	Eddie Yost	.10
74	Buddy Bell	.10
75	Manny Sanguillen	.10
76	Jim Bunning	.20
77	Smoky Burgess	.20
78	Al Rosen	.20
79	Gene Conley	.10
80	Dave Dravecky	.10
81	Charlie Gehringer	.20
82	Billy Pierce	.10
83	Willie Horton	.10
84	Ron Hunt	.10
85	Bob Feller	.40
86	George Kell	.20
87	Dave Kingman	.20
88	Jerry Koosman	.10
89	Clem Labine	.10
90	Tony LaRussa	.20
91	Dennis Leonard	.10
92	Dale Long	.10
93	Sparky Lyle	.10
94	Gil McDougald	.10
95	Don Mossi	.10
96	Phil Niekro	.20
97	Tom Paciorek	.10
98	Mel Parnell	.10
99	Lou Pinella	.20
100	Bobby Richardson	.20
101	Phil Rizzuto	.60
102	Brooks Robinson	.40
103	Pete Runnels	.10
104	Diego Segui	.10
105	Bobby Shantz	.10
106	Bobby Thomson	.10
107	Joe Torre	.30
108	Earl Weaver	.30
109	Willie Wilson	.10
110	Jesse Barfield	.10

Senior League

An early supporter of the short-lived "old-timers" league, Pacific issued a card set depicting the players of the Senior Professional Baseball Association. Sold in wax packs as well as complete boxed sets, the cards have silver borders on front with yellow stars above and to the right of the player photo. Color team logos are at bottom-left. Red, white and blue backs have appropriate logos, card number, a few biographical details and a short career summary in a horizontal format. The cards were issued with a set of 15 team logo stickers with a puzzle back. Shades of the 1989 Fleer Billy Ripken card, the card of Jim Nettles contains a photo which shows a vulgarity written on the knob of his bat. A cleaned-up version was issued later, and is much scarcer. Many other errors from the regular-edition set were corrected in a glossy edition of 20,000 complete sets, while several new errors were created.

		NM/M
Complete Set (220):		4.00
Common Player:		.05
Glossy:		2X
1	Bobby Tolan	.05
2	Sergio Ferrer	.05
3	David Rajsich	.05
4	Ron LeFlore	.10
5	Steve Henderson	.05
6	Jerry Martin	.05
7	Gary Rajsich	.05
8	Elias Sosa	.05
9	Jon Matlack	.05
10	Steve Kemp	.05
11	Lenny Randle	.05
12	Roy Howell	.05
13	Milt Wilcox	.05
14	Alan Bannister	.05
15	Dock Ellis	.05
16	Mike Williams	.05
17	Luis Gomez	.05
18	Joe Sambito	.05
19	Bake McBride	.05
20a	Pat Zachry (Photo actually Dick Bosman.)	.05
20b	Dick Bosman	.10
21	Dwight Lowry	.05
22	Ozzie Virgil Sr.	.05
23	Randy Lerch	.05
24	Butch Benton	.05
25	Tom Zimmer	.05
26a	Al Holland (Photo actually Nardi Contreras.)	.05
26b	Nardi Contreras	.10
27	Sammy Stewart	.05
28	Bill Lee	.05
29	Ferguson Jenkins	.50
30	Leon Roberts	.05
31	Rick Wise	.05
32	Butch Hobson	.05
33	Pete LaCock	.05
34	Bill Campbell	.05
35	Doug Simunic	.05
36	Mario Guerrero	.05
37	Jim Willoughby	.05
38	Joe Pittman	.05
39	Mark Bomback	.05
40	Tommy McMillian	.05
41	Gary Allanson	.05
42	Cecil Cooper	.10
43	John LaRosa	.05
44	Darrell Brandon	.05
45	Bernie Carbo	.05
46	Mike Cuellar	.10
47	Al Bumbry	.05
48a	Gene Richards (Photo actually Tony Scott.)	.05
49b	Tony Scott	.10
49	Pedro Borbon	.05
50	Julio Solo	.05
51a	Ed Nottle (Back reads Sun Sox.)	.05
51b	Ed Nottle (Back reads Super Sox.)	.10
52	Jim Bibby	.05
53	Doug Griffin	.05
54	Ed Clements	.05
55	Dalton Jones	.05
56	Earl Weaver	.25
57	Jesus DeLaRosa	.05
58	Paul Casanova	.05
59	Frank Riccelli	.05
60	Rafael Landestoy	.05
61	George Hendrick	.05
62	Cesar Cedeno	.10
63	Bert Campaneris	.10
64	Derrel Thomas	.05
65	Bobby Ramos	.05
66	Grant Jackson	.05
67	Steve Whitaker	.05
68	Pedro Ramos	.05
69	Joe Hicks	.05
70	Taylor Duncan	.05
71	Tom Shopay	.05
72	Ken Clay	.05
73	Mike Kekich	.05
74	Ed Halicki	.05
75	Ed Figueroa	.05
76	Paul Blair	.05
77	Luis Tiant	.10
78	Stan Bahnsen	.05
79	Rennie Stennett	.05
80	Bobby Molinaro	.05
81	Jim Gideon	.05
82	Orlando Gonzalez	.05
83	Amos Otis	.05
84	Dennis Leonard	.05

85	Pat Putman	.05
86	Rick Manning	.05
87	Pat Dobson	.05
88	Marty Castillo	.05
89	Steve McCatty	.05
90	Doug Bird	.05
91	Rick Waits	.05
92	Ron Jackson	.05
93	Tim Hosley	.05
94	Steve Luebber	.05
95	Rich Gale	.05
96	Champ Summers	.05
97	Dave LaRoche	.05
98	Bobby Jones	.05
99	Kim Allen	.05
100	Wayne Garland	.05
101	Tom Spencer	.05
102	Dan Driessen	.05
103	Ron Pruitt	.05
104	Tim Ireland	.05
105	Dan Driessen	.05
106	Pepe Frias	.05
107	Eric Rasmussen	.05
108	Don Hood	.05
109a	Joe Coleman (Photo actually Tony Torchia.)	.05
109b	Tony Torchia	.10
110	Jim Slaton	.05
111	Clint Hurdle	.05
112	Larry Milbourne	.05
113	Al Holland	.05
114	George Foster	.05
115	Graig Nettles	.10
116	Oscar Gamble	.05
117	Ross Grimsley	.05
118	Bill Travers	.05
119	Jose Beniquez	.05
120a	Jerry Grote (In Action)	.05
120b	Jerry Grote (Catcher)	.10
121	John D'Acquisto	.05
122	Tom Murphy	.05
123	Walt Williams	.05
124	Roy Thomas	.05
125a	Jerry Grote (Photo actually Fred Stanley.)	.05
125b	Fred Stanley (Jerry Grote back.)	.10
126a	Jim Nettles (Vulgarity on bat knob.)	.50
126b	Jim Nettles (No vulgarity.)	3.00
127	Randy Niemann	.05
128a	Bobby Bonds	.05
128b	Bobby Bonds (No name/position on front.)	.50
129	Ed Glynn	.05
130	Ed Hicks	.05
131	Ivan Murrell	.05
132	Graig Nettles	.10
133	Hal McRae	.20
134	Pat Kelly	.05
135	Sammy Stewart	.05
136	Bruce Kison	.05
137	Jim Morrison	.05
138	Omar Moreno	.05
139	Tom Brown	.05
140	Steve Dillard	.05
141	Gary Alexander	.05
142	Al Oliver	.10
143	Rick Lysander	.05
144	Tippy Martinez	.05
145	Al Cowens	.05
146	Gene Clines	.05
147	Willie Aikens	.05
148	Tommy Moore	.05
149	Clete Boyer	.05
150	Stan Cliburn	.05
151	Ken Kravec	.05
152	Garth Iorg	.05
153	Rick Peterson	.05
154	Wayne Nordhagen	.05
155	Danny Meyer	.05
156	Wayne Garrett	.05
157	Wayne Krenchicki	.05
158	Graig Nettles	.10
159	Earl Stephenson	.05
160	Carl Taylor	.05
161	Rollie Fingers	.50
162	Toby Harrah	.10
163	Mickey Rivers	.05
164	Dave Kingman	.10
165	Paul Mirabella	.05
166	Dick Williams	.05
167	Luis Pujols	.05
168	Tito Landrum	.05
169	Tom Underwood	.05
170	Mark Wagner	.05
171	Odell Jones	.05
172	Doug Capilla	.05
173	Alfie Rondon	.05
174	Lowell Palmer	.05
175	Juan Eichelberger	.05
176	Wes Clements	.05
177	Rodney Scott	.05
178	Ron Washington	.05
179	Al Hrabosky	.05
180	Sid Monge	.05
181	Randy Johnson	.05
182	Tim Stoddard	.05
183	Dick Williams	.05
184	Lee Lacy	.05
185	Jerry White	.05
186	Dave Kingman	.10
187	Checklist 1-110	.05
188	Jose Cruz	.10
189	Jamie Easterly	.05
190	Ike Blessit	.05
191	Johnny Grubb	.05

192	Dave Cash	.05
193	Doug Corbett	.05
194	Bruce Bochy	.05
195	Mark Corey	.05
196	Gil Rondon	.05
197	Jerry Martin	.05
198	Gerry Pirtle	.05
199	Gates Brown	.05
200	Bob Galasso	.05
201	Bake McBride	.05
202	Wayne Granger	.05
203	Larry Milbourne	.05
204	Tom Paciorek	.05
205	U.L. Washington	.05
206	Larvell Blanks	.05
207	Bob Shirley	.05
208	Pete Falcone	.05
209	Sal Butera	.05
210	Roy Branch	.05
211	Dyar Miller	.05
212	Paul Siebert	.05
213	Ken Reitz	.05
214	Bill Madlock	.10
215	Vida Blue	.15
216	Dave Hilton	.05
217	Pedro Ramos, Charlie Bree	.05
218	Checklist 111-220	.05
219	Pat Dobson, Earl Weaver	.25
220	Curt Flood	.15

1991 Pacific Senior League

In 1991 Pacific Trading Cards produced its second set of cards of Senior Professional Baseball Association players. The cards feature color photos on the front, with the player's name and position along the bottom and team nickname and logo on a banner vertically on the left side. There are 160 cards in the glossy set, with some multi-player and in-action cards included. For reasons unknown, some of the cards (including those of Rice, Fingers, Blue, Dave Cash, Dan Norman, Ron LeFlore, Cesar Cedeno, Rafael Landestoy and Dan Driessen) were apparently printed in two versions.

		NM/M
Complete Set (160):		3.00
Common Player:		.05
1	Dan Driessen	.05
2	Marty Castillo	.05
3	Jerry White	.05
4	Bud Anderson	.05
5	Ron Jackson	.05
6	Fred Stanley	.05
7	Steve Luebber	.05
8	Jery Terrell	.05
9	Pat Dobson	.05
10	Ken Kravec	.05
11	Gil Rondon	.05
12	Dyar Miller	.05
13	Bobby Molinaro	.05
14	Jerry Martin	.05
15	Rick Waits	.05
16	Steve McCatty	.05
17	Roger Slagle	.05
18	Mike Ramsey	.05
19	Rich Gale	.05
20	Larry Harlow	.05
21	Dan Rohn	.05
22	Don Cooper	.05
23	Marv Foley	.05
24	Rafael Landestoy	.05
25	Eddie Milner	.05
26a	Amos Otis (Green jersey pose.)	.05
26b	Amos Otis (White jersey action.)	.05
27	Odell Jones	.05
28	Tippy Martinez	.05
29	Stu Cliburn	.05
30	Stan Cliburn	.05
31	Tony Cloninger	.05
32	Jeff Jones	.05
33	Ken Reitz	.05
34	Dave Sax	.05
35	Orlando Gonzalez	.05
36	Jose Cruz	.10
37	Mickey Mahler	.05
38	Derek Botelho	.05
39	Rick Lysander	.05
40	Cesar Cedeno	.10

41	Garth Iorg	.05
42	Wayne Krenchicki	.05
43	Clete Boyer	.05
44	Dan Boone	.05
45	George Vukovich	.05
46	Omar Moreno	.05
47	Ron Washington	.05
48	Ron Washington (MVP)	.05
49	Rick Peterson	.05
50	Tack Wilson	.05
51	Stan Cliburn, Stu Cliburn	.05
52	Rick Lysander (POY)	.05
53	Cesar Cedeno, Pete LaCock	.05
54	Jim Marshall, Clete Boyer	.05
55	Doug Simunic	.05
56	Pat Kelly	.05
57	Roy Branch	.05
58	Dave Cash	.05
59	Bobby Jones	.05
60	Hector Cruz	.05
61	Reggie Cleveland	.05
62	Gary Lance	.05
63	Ron LeFlore	.05
64	Dan Norman	.05
65	Renie Martin	.05
66	Pete Mackanin	.05
67	Frank Riccelli	.05
68	Alfie Rondon	.05
69	Rodney Scott	.05
70	Jim Tracy	.05
71	Ed Dennis	.05
72	Rick Lindell	.05
73	Stu Pepper	.05
74	Jeff Youngbauer	.05
75	Russ Foster	.05
76	Jeff Capriati	.05
77	Art DeFreites	.05
78	Alfie Rondon/Action	.05
79	Reggie Cleveland/Action	.05
80	Dave Cash/Action	.05
81	Vida Blue	.15
82	Ed Glynn	.05
83	Bob Owchinko	.05
84	Bill Fleming	.05
85	Ron Roenicke, Gary Roenicke	.05
86	Tom Thompson	.05
87	Derrell Thomas	.05
88	Jim Willoughby	.05
89	Jim Pankovits	.05
90	Jack Cooley	.05
91	Lenn Sakata	.05
92	Mike Brocki	.05
93	Chuck Fick	.05
94	Tom Benedict	.05
95	Anthony Davis	.05
96	Cardell Camper	.05
97	Leon Roberts	.05
98	Roger Erickson	.05
99	Kim Allen	.05
100	Dave Skaggs	.05
101	Joe Decker	.05
102	U.L. Washington	.05
103	Don Fletcher	.05
104	Gary Roenicke	.05
105	Rich Dauer	.05
106	Ron Roenicke	.05
107	Mike Norris	.05
108	Ferguson Jenkins	.50
109	Ronn Reynolds	.05
110	Pete Falcone	.05
111	Gary Allenson	.05
112	Mark Wagner	.05
113	Jack Lazorko	.05
114	Bob Galasso	.05
115	Ron Davis	.05
116	Lenny Randle	.05
117	Ricky Peters	.05
118	Jim Dwyer	.05
119	Juan Eichelberger	.05
120	Pete LaCock	.05
121	Tony Scott	.05
122	Rick Lancellotti	.05
123	Barry Bonnell	.05
124	Dave Hilton	.05
125	Bill Campbell	.05
126	Rollie Fingers	.50
127	Jim Marshall	.05
128	Razor Shines	.05
129	Guy Sularz	.05
130	Roy Thomas	.05
131	Joel Youngblood	.05
132	Ernie Camacho	.05
133	Dave Hilton, Jim Marshall, Fred Stanley	.05
134	Ken Landreaux	.05
135	Dave Rozema	.05
136	Tom Zimmer	.05
137	Elias Sosa	.05
138	Ozzie Virgil Sr.	.05
139	Al Holland	.05
140	Milt Wilcox	.05
141	Jerry Reed	.05
142	Chris Welch	.05
143	Luis Gomez	.05
144	Steve Henderson	.05
145	Butch Benton	.05
146	Bill Lee	.05
147	Todd Cruz	.05
148	Jim Rice	.45
149	Tito Landrum	.05
150	Ozzie Virgil Jr.	.05
151	Joe Pittman	.05
152	Bobby Tolan	.05
153	Len Barker	.05
154	Dave Rajsich	.05
155	Glenn Gulliver	.05

156	Gary Rajsich	.05
157	Joe Sambito	.05
158	Frank Vito	.05
159	Ozzie Virgil Sr., Ozzie Virgil Jr.	.05
160	Dave Rajsich, Gary Rajsich	.05

Nolan Ryan

The career and family life of Nolan Ryan (to 1991) were the subject matter of this 110-card set by Pacific Trading Card Co. Sold in both foil packs and factory sets, the cards have a UV-coated front featuring a photo flanked on the left by "Nolan Ryan" printed vertically in a color accent stripe. At lower left is a flaming baseball "Texas Express" logo. A photo caption appears beneath the photo. On back the blazing ball motif is repeated, with a photo or career highlights in its center.

		NM/M
Factory Set (110):		8.00
Complete Set (110):		5.00
Common Card:		.10
Wax Pack (12):		.50
Wax Box (36):		12.00
1	Future Hall of Famer	.10
2	From Little League to the Major Leagues	.10
3	A Dream Come True	.10
4	Signed by the Mets	.10
5	Fireball Pitcher	.10
6	Mets Rookie Pitcher	.10
7	First Major League Win	.10
8	Early in 1969	.10
9	Tensions of a Pennant Race	.10
10	Mets Clinch NL East	.10
11	Keep the Ball Down	.10
12	Playoff Victory	.10
13	World Series Victory	.10
14	The Amazin' Mets	.10
15	Met Strikeout Record	.10
16	One of the Worst Trades in Baseball	.10
17	Slow Start with Mets	.10
18	Pitcher New York Mets	.10
19	Traded to the Angels	.10
20	Meeting New Friends	.10
21	Throwing Fast Balls	.10
22	Move the Ball Around	.10
23	Nolan Heat	.10
24	No-Hitter Number 1	.10
25	Looking Back on Number 1	.10
26	No-Hitter Number 2	.10
27	Single Season Strikeout Record	.10
28	21 Wins in 1973	.10
29	Fastest Pitch Ever Thrown at 100.9 MPH	.10
30	No-Hitter Number 3	.10
31	No-Hitter Number 4	.10
32	Ryan and Tanana	.10
33	Learning Change-Up	.10
34	Pitcher California Angels	.10
35	Nolan Joins Astros	.10
36	Starting Pitcher Nolan Ryan	.10
37	Taking Batting Practice	.10
38	The Game's Greatest Power Pitcher	.10
39	3000 Career Strikeouts	.10
40	A Ryan Home Run	.10
41	The Fast Ball Grip	.10
42	Record 5th No-Hitter	.10
43	No-Hitter Number 5	.10
44	A Dream Fulfilled	.10
45	Nolan Passes Walter Johnson	.10
46	Strikeout 4000	.10
47	Astros Win Western Division Title	.10
48	Pitcher Houston Astros	.10
49	Milestone Strikeouts	.10
50	Post Season Participant	.10
51	Hurling for Houston	.10
52	135 N.L. Wins	.10
53	Through with Chew	.10
54	Signed by Rangers 1989	.10
55	Pleasant Change for Nolan	.10
56	Real Special Moment	.10
57	1989 All-Star Game	.10

58	Pitching in 1989 All-Star Game	.10
59	5000 Strikeouts; A Standing Ovation	.10
60	Great Moments in 1989	.10
61	Nolan with Dan Smith, Rangers First Pic	.10
62	Ranger Club Record 16 Strikeouts	.10
63	Last Pitch No-Hitter Number 6	.10
64	Sweet Number 6	.10
65	Oldest to Throw No-Hitter	.10
66	Another Ryan Win	.10
67	20th Pitcher to Win 300	.10
68	300 Win Battery	.10
69	300 Game Winner	.10
70	Perfect Mechanics	.10
71	22 Seasons with 100 or more Strikeouts	.10
72	11th Strikeout Title	.10
73	232 Strikeouts, 1990	.10
74	The 1990 Season	.10
75	Pitcher Texas Rangers	.10
76	1991, Nolan's 25th Season	.10
77	Throwing Spirals	.10
78	Running the Steps	.10
79	Hard Work and Conditioning	.10
80	The Rigid Workout	.10
81	Ryan's Routine	.10
82	Ryan's Routine Between Starts	.10
83	Running in Outfield	.10
84	B.P. in Texas	.10
85	18 Career Low-Hitters	.10
86	My Job is to Give My Team/Chance to Win	.10
87	The Spring Workout	.10
88	Power versus Power	.10
89	Awesome Power	.10
90	Blazing Speed	.10
91	The Pick Off	.10
92	Real Gamer	.10
93	Ranger Battery Mates	.10
94	The Glare	.10
95	The High Leg Kick	.10
96	Day Off	.10
97	A New Ball	.10
98	Going to Rosin Bag	.10
99	Time for Relief	.10
100	Lone Star Legend	.10
101	Fans' Favorite	.10
102	Watching Nolan Pitch	.10
103	Our Family of Five	.10
104	Texas Beefmaster	.10
105	Gentleman Rancher	.10
106	Texas Cowboy Life	.10
107	The Ryan Family	.10
108	Participating in Cutting Horse Contest	.10
109	Nolan Interviews	.10
110	Lynn Nolan Ryan	.10

Nolan Ryan Milestones

Issued as inserts in the 1991 Nolan Ryan foil packs was this set of eight career highlight cards. The format is basically the same as the regular-issue cards, except that the inserts are bordered in either silver (edition of 10,000) or gold (edition of 1,000). The unnumbered cards are checklisted here in chronolgical order. The inserts were found only in foil and wax packs.

		NM/M
Complete Set, Silver (8):		50.00
Complete Set, Gold (8):		65.00
Common Card, Silver:		7.50
Common Card, Gold:		12.00
(1a)	Rookie Pitcher/Silver	7.50
(1b)	Rookie Pitcher/Gold	12.00
(2a)	No-Hitter 1/Silver	7.50
(2b)	No-Hitter 1/Gold	12.00
(3a)	No-Hitter 2/Silver	7.50
(3b)	No-Hitter 2/Gold	12.00
(4a)	No-Hitter 3/Silver	7.50
(4b)	No-Hitter 3/Gold	12.00
(5a)	No-Hitter 4/Silver	7.50
(5b)	No-Hitter 4/Gold	12.00
(6a)	No-Hitter 5/Silver	7.50
(6b)	No-Hitter 5/Gold	12.00
(7a)	Sweet 6/Silver	7.50
(7b)	Sweet 6/Gold	12.00

(8a)	25th Season/Silver	7.50
(8b)	25th Season/Gold	12.00

Nolan Ryan 7th No-Hitter

Number Seven

On May 1, 1991, before the home crowd at Arlington, Nolan Ryan posted his seventh career no-hitter, blanking the Blue Jays. In commemoration of the event, Pacific produced a seven-card insert set for random inclusion in its Nolan Ryan "Texas Express" foil packs. Each card was produced in an edition of 10,000 silver-foil bordered cards and 1,000 with gold-foil borders. The design follows the basic format of the regular Ryan issue, with the flaming baseball series logo at lower-left on the front, the card's title in a colored stripe beneath the photo, and Ryan's name printed vertically in a colored stripe at left. Backs repeat the flaming ball design at center, containing information about the no-hitter.

		NM/M
Complete Set, Silver (7):		50.00
Complete Set, Gold (7):		125.00
Common Card, Silver:		12.00
Common Card, Gold:		25.00
1a	Last Pitch/Silver	12.00
1b	Last Pitch/Gold	25.00
2a	No-Hitter #7/Silver	12.00
2b	No-Hitter #7/Gold	25.00
3a	The Best/Silver	12.00
3b	The Best/Gold	25.00
4a	Time to Celebrate/Silver	12.00
4b	Time to Celebrate/Gold	25.00
5a	Congratulations from Rangers Fans/Silver	12.00
5b	Congratulations from Rangers Fans/Gold	25.00
6a	Catcher Mike Stanley/Silver	12.00
6b	Catcher Mike Stanley/Gold	25.00
7a	All in a Day's Work/Silver	12.00
7b	All in a Day's Work/Gold	25.00

Nolan Ryan 7th No-Hitter Hologram

No-Hitter #7

Even more elusive and exclusive than the gold- and silver-foil bordered "7th No-Hitter" inserts found in wax and foil packs was this edition produced with gold and silver holographic borders (1,000 each in gold and silver). The hologram 7th No-Hitter inserts were found only in 99-cent cello packs.

		NM/M
Complete Set, Silver (7):		300.00
Complete Set, Gold (7):		300.00
Common Card, Silver:		50.00
Common Card, Gold:		50.00
1a	Last Pitch/Silver	50.00
1b	Last Pitch/Gold	50.00
2a	No-Hitter #7/Silver	50.00
2b	No-Hitter #7/Gold	50.00
3a	The Best/Silver	50.00
3b	The Best/Gold	50.00

4a	Time to Celebrate/Silver	50.00
4b	Time to Celebrate/Gold	50.00
5a	Congratulations from Rangers Fans/Silver	50.00
5b	Congratulations from Rangers Fans/Gold	50.00
6a	Catcher Mike Stanley/Silver	50.00
6b	Catcher Mike Stanley/Gold	50.00
7a	All in a Day's Work/Silver	50.00
7b	All in a Day's Work/Gold	50.00

1992 Pacific Nolan Ryan

The 1992 Nolan Ryan "Texas Express" Series 2 is numbered 111 to 220, featuring the same design as the original 110-card issue of 1991. The set includes photos of Ryan from boyhood to his seventh no-hitter, and two bonus subsets were also randomly inserted in the foil packs.

		NM/M
Complete Set (110):		6.00
Common Player:		.10
111	The Golden Arm	.10
112	Little League All-Star	.10
113	All-State Pitcher	.10
114	Nolan Ryan Field	.10
115	Nolan at Age 20	.10
116	Nolan Ryan Jacksonville Suns	.10
117	Surrounded By Friends	.10
118	Nolan the Cowboy	.10
119	The Simple Life	.10
120	Nolan Loves Animals	.10
121	Growing Up in New York	.10
122	New York Strikeout Record	.10
123	Traded	.10
124	Hall of Fame Victims	.10
125	Number 500	.10
126	California Victory	.10
127	20 Win Season	.10
128	Throwing Heat	.10
129	Strikeout Record	.10
130	Number One	.10
131	1,000th Strikeout	.10
132	Number Two	.10
133	2,000th Strikeout	.10
134	Number Three	.10
135	Pure Speed	.10
136	Independence Day Fireworks	.10
137	Fast Ball Pitcher	.10
138	Number Four	.10
139	Free Agent	.10
140	Houston Bound	.10
141	Big Dollars	.10
142	Strong Houston Staff	.10
143	Number Five	.10
144	Astro MVp	.10
145	Western Division Game	.10
146	National League All-Star	.10
147	Major League Record	.10
148	Nolan Breaks Johnson's Record	.10
149	Reese and Nolan	.10
150	100th National League Win	.10
151	4,000th Strikeout	.10
152	League Leader	.10
153	250th Career Win	.10
154	The Seldom of Swat	.10
155	4,500th Strikeout	.10
156	Like Father Like Son	.10
157	Spoiled in the Ninth	.10
158	Leaving Houston	.10
159	Houston Star	.10
160	Ryan Test Free Agency	.10
161	Awesome Heat	.10
162	Brotherly Love	.10
163	Astros Return	.10
164	Texas Size Decision	.10
165	Texas Legend	.10
166	Drawing a Crowd	.10
167	Great Start	.10
168	5,000th Strikeout	.10
169	Texas All-Star	.10
170	Number Six	.10
171	300th Win	.10
172	1990 League Leader	.10
173	Man of the Year	.10
174	Spring Training 1991	.10
175	Fast Ball Grip	.10
176	Strong Arm	.10
177	Stanley's Delight	.10
178	After Nolan's 7th No-Hitter	.10
179	Stretching Before the Game	.10
180	The Rangers Sign Nolan for 1992 and 199	.10
181	Heading to the Bullpen	.10
182	Nolan Ryan - Banker	.10
183	Time with Fans	.10
184	Solid 1992 Season	.10
185	Ranger Team Leader	.10
186	More Records	.10
187	Number Seven	.10
188	Nolan Passes Niekro	.10
189	Ryan Trails Sutton	.10
190	Ranger Strikeout Mark	.10
191	Consecutive K's	.10
192	5,500th Strikeout	.10
193	Twenty-Five First Timers	.10

194	No-Hitters Ended in the Ninth	.10
195	Constant Work-Outs	.10
196	Nolan in Motion	.10
197	Pitching in Fenway Park	.10
198	Goose and Nolan	.10
199	Talking Over Strategy	.10
200	Don't Mess With Texas	.10
201	314-278 Thru 1991	.10
202	All-Time Leader	.10
203	High Praise	.10
204	Manager's Delight	.10
205	733 Major League Starts	.10
206	Ryan the Quarterback	.10
207	Hard Work Pays Off	.10
208	Passing Along Wisdom	.10
209	Still Dominant	.10
210	Nolan's Fast Ball	.10
211	Seven No-Hitters	.10
212	Training for Perfection	.10
213	Nolan's Edge - Speed	.10
214	This One was for Them	.10
215	Another Day's Work	.10
216	Pick Off at Third	.10
217	Ready to Pitch	.10
218	Spring Training 1992	.10
219	Nolan Receives The Victor Award	.10
220	Nolan's 26th Season	.10

Nolan Ryan Gold Inserts

Number Two

Pacific produced this insert set for the 1992 Nolan Ryan "Texas Express" sequel. There are eight different gold-foil bordered cards, one for each of Ryan's no-hitters, plus an additional card combining all seven. Design is similar to the 1991-92 Ryan cards from Pacific. Backs feature box scores of the no-hitters. The cards are unnumbered. According to the manufacturer, 10,000 of each insert were produced.

		NM/M
Complete Set (8):		65.00
Common Ryan:		10.00
(1)	Number One	10.00
(2)	Number Two	10.00
(3)	Number Three	10.00
(4)	Number Four	10.00
(5)	Number Five	10.00
(6)	Number Six	10.00
(7)	Number Seven	10.00
(8)	Seven No-Hitters	10.00

Nolan Ryan Limited

One of two insert sets included in both regular and jumbo foil packs of 1992 Pacific Nolan Ryan cards was this six-card presentation. Cards have the basic format of the regular issue except the "Texas Express" logo on front has been replaced by a Rangers team logo. Vertically formatted backs have a color photo at left and a few paragraphs of career summary at center. Each card was printed in an edition of 3,000, and Ryan personally autographed 1,000 of card #1. A second version of these cards, without the words "Limited Edition" on back beneath the Rangers and MLB logos,

was produced for inclusion in the July 1992 issue of "Trading Cards" magazine. The magazine versions of these cards are worth about 10 percent of the inserts.

		NM/M
Complete Set (6):		30.00
Common Card:		7.50
1	Nolan Ryan	7.50
1a	Nolan Ryan/Auto.	90.00
2	Nolan Ryan	7.50
3	The Texas Express	7.50
4	Seventh No-Hitter	7.50
5	Texas Legacy	7.50
6	Quarter Century	7.50

1992 Pacific Tom Seaver

16 WINS IN 1968

In a style similar to its popular Nolan Ryan sets, Pacific produced a Tom Seaver set of 110 cards in 1992. The company also produced two limited edition subsets as part of the "Tom Terrific" card series. Cards were sold in both foil packs and factory sets. UV-coated fronts have white borders with silver, violet or magenta highlight stripes. A baseball symbol at lower-left has "Tom" above and "Terrific" beneath. This image is duplicated on back, with the ball containing either a photo or career highlights.

		NM/M
Complete Set (110):		4.00
Common Player:		.05
1	Stand-out High School Basketball Player	.05
2	Pro Ball Player	.05
3	Destined to be a Met	.05
4	Brave or Met	.05
5	Mets Luck of the Draw.	.05
6	Sent to Jacksonville	.05
7	First Major League Win	.05
8	1967 Rookie of the Year	.05
9	Humble Beginnings	.05
10	Predicting the Future	.05
11	Rookie All-Star	.05
12	16 Wins in 1968	.05
13	1968 N.L. All-Star	.05
14	The Amazing Mets	.05
15	1969 Cy Young Winner	.05
16	Pitcher of the Year	.05
17	Strikeout Leader	.05
18	Ties Major League Record	.05
19	Mr. Consistency	.05
20	Finishing in Style	.05
21	Twenty-Game Winner	.05
22	Second Cy Young Award	.05
23	Batting Star	.05
24	At Bat in the World Series	.05
25	Championship Series Record	.05
26	Injury Plagued Season	.05
27	Comeback	.05
28	Super September	.05
29	Sporting News All-Star	.05
30	Strikeout Record	.05
31	USC Alumni Star	.05
32	Winning Smile	.05
33	One-Hitter	.05
34	Traded to the Reds	.05
35	New York Mets Pitcher	.05
36	Winning with the Reds	.05
37	No-Hitter	.05
38	N.L. Leader	.05
39	Smooth Swing	.05
40	No Decision in the Championship Series	.05
41	Injury Shortened Season	.05
42	Bouncing Back	.05
43	Eighth All-Star Appearance	.05
44	Spring Training 1982	.05
45	Back to New York	.05
46	Cincinnati Reds Pitcher	.05
47	Back in the Big Apple	.05
48	Opening Day Star	.05
49	Not Much Run Support	.05
50	Pair of Shutouts	.05
51	4,000 Inning Mark	.05
52	One Season in New York	.05
53	Chicago Bound	.05
54	Chicago White Sox Pitcher	.05
55	Win 300	.05
56	16 Wins in 1985	.05

57	Blast From the Past	.05
58	Moving Up in the Record Book	.05
59	Cy Young Winners	.05
60	Two Legends of the Game	.05
61	Singing Praise	.05
62	300th Win Tribute	.05
63	The Seaver Family	.05
64	20th Major League Season	.05
65	Traded to the Red Sox	.05
66	Chicago White Sox Career Record	.05
67	Red Sox Man	.05
68	Boston Red Sox Pitcher	.05
69	One Last Try	.05
70	Major League Records	.05
71	Lowest N.L. Career ERA	.05
72	Pitching in Comiskey Park	.05
73	273 N.L. Wins	.05
74	300 Win Honors	.05
75	311 Major League Wins	.05
76	41 Retired	.05
77	Championship Series 2.84 ERA	.05
78	June 1976 Age 32	.05
79	8-Time N.L. All-Star	.05
80	Broadcasting Career	.05
81	300th Win Celebration	.05
82	Tom and Nolan	.05
83	4th Best ERA All-Time	.05
84	15th All-Time in Victories	.05
85	300 Win Club	.05
86	Hall of Fame	.05
87	Pitching in Wrigley Field	.05
88	Power Pitching	.05
89	Spring Training 1980	.05
90	Pitching in Riverfront Stadium 1980	.05
91	Tom Terrific	.05
92	Super Seaver	.05
93	Top 10 All-Time	.05
94	16 Opening Day Starts	.05
95	3,272 Strikeouts	.05
96	Six Opening Day Wins	.05
97	239 Innings Pitched in 1985	.05
98	A Day Off	.05
99	Concentration (You Can't Let Up)	.05
100	Velocity, Movement, and Location	.05
101	Strikeout King	.05
102	The Most Important Pitch	.05
103	Cincinnati Reds Number 41	.05
104	George Thomas Seaver	.05
105	Dazzling Dean of the Reds' Staff	.05
106	Tom Receives the Judge Emil Fuchs Award	.05
107	Boston Mound Ace	.05
108	Fly Ball to Center	.05
109	August 4, 1985 Yankee Stadium	.05
110	Breaking Walter Johnson's Record	.05

Tom Seaver Milestones

Inserted into foil packs of its 1992 Seaver set, Pacific produced a gold-foil bordered set limited to 10,000 each of six different cards featuring career milestones. A white-bordered version of 3,000 cards each was also produced. One thousand of the "Rookie Phenomenon" cards were personally autographed by Seaver among the inserts. On each card, an action photo of Seaver is flanked at left with his name vertically printed in a fading color stripe. The "Tom Terrific" baseball logo carried is carried over from the regular set at lower-left. Backs have a second photo at left, and a summary of the career highlight.

		NM/M
Complete Set (6):		12.50
Complete Set, Gold (6):		15.00
Common Card:		2.50
Common Card, Gold:		3.50
1a	Rookie Phenomenon	2.50
1b	Rookie Phenomenon/Gold	3.50

1c	Rookie Phenomenon (Auto. edition of 1,000.)	25.00
2a	Miracle Mets	2.50
2b	Miracle Mets/Gold	3.50
3a	Strikeout Record	2.50
3b	Strikeout Record/Gold	3.50
4a	No-Hitter	2.50
4b	No-Hitter/Gold	3.50
5a	300th Win	2.50
5b	300th Win/Gold	3.50
6a	Hall of Fame	2.50
6b	Hall of Fame/Gold	3.50

1993 Pacific Nolan Ryan 27th Season

Rangers' Opening Night Pitcher

Pacific marked the record-breaking 27th season of Nolan Ryan's career by re-issuing all 220 cards in its popular Nolan Ryan set with a special logo. The first series of the set (110 cards) had been issued in 1991 and the second series was issued in 1992 and numbered 111-220. In 1993 the company released a 30-card update for the pitcher's final season, complete with the special logo. Later the company decided to reissue cards 1-220 with the same logo because of the demand for the cards. Refer to 1991 and 1992 sets for card 1-220 checklists.

		NM/M
Complete Set (250):		10.00
Common Player:		.10
221	Rangers' Opening Night	.10
222	Slow Start in 1992	.10
223	Still Productive	.10
224	Getting Hot	.10
225	Closing Strong	.10
226	No Decision	.10
227	No Run Support	.10
228	Two Complete Games	.10
229	8-2/3 Inning Shutout	.10
230	Multiple Stikeout Games	.10
231	Ejected	.10
232	319 and Counting	.10
233	Strikeout	.10
234	24 of 26 Seasons	.10
235	Smile, Nolan	.10
236	Texas Ranger Marks	.10
237	Ranger Ace	.10
238	Another Record	.10
239	6th Place All-Time Innings Pitched	.10
240	27 Games Started in 1992	.10
241	Seaver & Ryan	.10
242	Angels' Number 30 Retired	.10
243	Angels' Nolan Ryan Night	.10
244	Angels' Hall of Fame	.10
245	Great Friends	.10
246	Cowboys	.10
247	Spring Training	.10
248	Smokin' Fastball	.10
249	The Texas Express	.10
250	Pacific Pride	.10

Limited

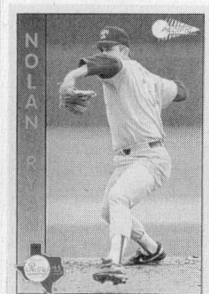

Continuing with its "Limited Edition" insert set from the 1992 Nolan Ryan issue, this insert set picks up with numbers 7-12, featuring 1992 highlights in Ryan's career.

	NM/M
Complete Set (6):	20.00
Common Player:	5.00
7-12 Nolan Ryan	5.00

Limited Gold

A gold-foil bordered version of the six 1993 Nolan Ryan "Limited Edition" insert cards was created as a card show give-away and random pack insert. Gold versions of cards #7-9 were given out at a Bellevue, Wash., show, while gold cards of #10-12 were found in foil packs. Just 3,000 of each foil-pack insert was produced.

	NM/M
Complete Set (6):	35.00
Common Player:	7.50
7-12 Nolan Ryan	7.50

Prism

An insert set unique to the 1993 Pacific Nolan Ryan 27th Season set was this issue of 20 prism cards. Fronts feature an action photo of Ryan against a prismatic background. Backs have another photo and a few brief biographical notes on a marbled background. Each prism card was produced in a silver edition of 10,000, a gold edition of 1,500 and a gold-edition uncut sheet of 20 cards serially numbered to 1,000. The prism cards were inserted into 25-cent foil packs of Pacific's 1993 Nolan Ryan issue.

	NM/M
Complete Set (Silver)(20):	55.00
Common Card (Silver):	3.50
1	Nolan Ryan/Silver	3.50
1a	Nolan Ryan/Gold	6.00
2	Nolan Ryan/Silver	3.50
2a	Nolan Ryan/Gold	6.00
3	Nolan Ryan/Silver	3.50
3a	Nolan Ryan/Gold	6.00
4	Nolan Ryan/Silver	3.50
4a	Nolan Ryan/Gold	6.00
5	Nolan Ryan/Silver	3.50
5a	Nolan Ryan/Gold	6.00
6	Nolan Ryan/Silver	3.50
6a	Nolan Ryan/Gold	6.00
7	Nolan Ryan/Silver	3.50
7a	Nolan Ryan/Gold	6.00
8	Nolan Ryan/Silver	3.50
8a	Nolan Ryan/Gold	6.00
9	Nolan Ryan/Silver	3.50
9a	Nolan Ryan/Gold	6.00
10	Nolan Ryan/Silver	3.50
10a	Nolan Ryan/Gold	6.00
11	Nolan Ryan/Silver	3.50
11a	Nolan Ryan/Gold	6.00
12	Nolan Ryan/Silver	3.50
12a	Nolan Ryan/Gold	6.00
13	Nolan Ryan/Silver	3.50
13a	Nolan Ryan/Gold	6.00
14	Nolan Ryan/Silver	3.50
14a	Nolan Ryan/Gold	6.00
15	Nolan Ryan/Silver	3.50
15a	Nolan Ryan/Gold	6.00
16	Nolan Ryan/Silver	3.50
16a	Nolan Ryan/Gold	6.00
17	Nolan Ryan/Silver	3.50
17a	Nolan Ryan/Gold	6.00
18	Nolan Ryan/Silver	3.50
18a	Nolan Ryan/Gold	6.00
19	Nolan Ryan/Silver	3.50
19a	Nolan Ryan/Gold	6.00
20	Nolan Ryan/Silver	3.50
20a	Nolan Ryan/Gold	6.00
Complete Set (Gold)(20):		85.00
Common Card (Gold):		6.00
Uncut Sheet (Gold):		110.00

1993 Pacific/McCormick Nolan Ryan Milestones

Great moments in Nolan Ryan's career are featured in this set produced by Pacific for McCormick & Co., a food products company. Fronts are similar to several of Pacific's other Ryan issues and include a "Farewell to a Legend" logo in the lower-left corner. The career highlight represented by the photo is named in a red strip at bottom. Backs share an action photo of Ryan over which are printed stats, information about the highlight or other data. Sponsors' logos are in the corners. Cards are UV coated on both sides.

	NM/M
Complete Set (21):	7.50
Common Player:	.50
1	No-Hitter #1 (Nolan Ryan)	.50
2	No-Hitter #2 (Nolan Ryan)	.50
3	No-Hitter #3 (Nolan Ryan)	.50
4	No-Hitter #4 (Nolan Ryan)	.50
5	No-Hitter #5 (Nolan Ryan)	.50
6	Last Pitch No-Hitter #6 (Nolan Ryan)	.50
7	No-Hitter #7 (Nolan Ryan)	.50
8	1st Strikeout (Nolan Ryan)	.50
9	1,000 Strikeout (Nolan Ryan)	.50
10	2,000 Strikeout (Nolan Ryan)	.50
11	3,000 Strikeout (Nolan Ryan)	.50
12	Nolan Breaks Johnson's Record (Nolan Ryan)	.50
13	4,000 Strikeout (Nolan Ryan)	.50
14	5,000 Strikeout (Nolan Ryan)	.50
15	5,500th Strikeout (Nolan Ryan)	.50
16	First Major League Win (Nolan Ryan)	.50
17	250th Career Win (Nolan Ryan)	.50
18	300th Win (Nolan Ryan)	.50
19	100.9 MPH Pitch (Nolan Ryan)	.50
20	Lone Star Legend (Nolan Ryan)	.50
---	Header Card	.10

1993 Pacific

This set marks the first time a major league set was designed entirely for the Spanish-speaking market. Distribution areas included retail markets in the United States, Mexico, South America and the Caribbean. The cards are glossy and feature Spanish text on both sides. Cards are numbered in alphabetical order by team, beginning with Atlanta. Insert sets are: Prism (20 cards featuring Spanish players and their accomplishments), Beisbol De Estrella (Stars of Baseball), Hot Players and Amigos (a 30-card set which features two or more players per card).

	NM/M
Complete Set (660):	20.00
Common Player:	.05
1	Rafael Belliard	.05
2	Sid Bream	.05
3	Francisco Cabrera	.05
4	Marvin Freeman	.05
5	Ron Gant	.05
6	Tom Glavine	.25
7	Brian Hunter	.05
8	Dave Justice	.05
9	Ryan Klesko	.05
10	Melvin Nieves	.05
11	Deion Sanders	.05
12	John Smoltz	.05
13	Mark Wohlers	.05
14	Brady Anderson	.05
15	Glenn Davis	.05
16	Mike Devereaux	.05
17	Leo Gomez	.05
18	Chris Hoiles	.05
19	Chito Martinez	.05
20	Ben McDonald	.05
21	Mike Mussina	.40
22	Gregg Olson	.05
23	Joe Orsulak	.05
24	Cal Ripken, Jr.	1.50
25	David Segui	.05
26	Rick Sutcliffe	.05
27	Wade Boggs	.65
28	Tom Brunansky	.05
29	Ellis Burks	.05
30	Roger Clemens	.75
31	John Dopson	.05
32	John Flaherty	.05
33	Mike Greenwell	.05
34	Tony Pena	.05
35	Carlos Quintana	.05
36	Luis Rivera	.05
37	Mo Vaughn	.05
38	Frank Viola	.05
39	Matt Young	.05
40	Scott Bailes	.05
41	Bert Blyleven	.05
42	Chad Curtis	.05
43	Gary DiSarcina	.05
44	Chuck Finley	.05
45	Mike Fitzgerald	.05
46	Gary Gaetti	.05
47	Rene Gonzales	.05
48	Mark Langston	.05
49	Scott Lewis	.05
50	Luis Polonia	.05
51	Tim Salmon	.05
52	Lee Stevens	.05
53	Steve Buechele	.05
54	Frank Castillo	.05
55	Doug Dascenzo	.05
56	Andre Dawson	.25
57	Shawon Dunston	.05
58	Mark Grace	.05
59	Mike Morgan	.05
60	Luis Salazar	.05
61	Rey Sanchez	.05
62	Ryne Sandberg	.65
63	Dwight Smith	.05
64	Jerome Walton	.05
65	Rick Wilkins	.05
66	Wilson Alvarez	.05
67	George Bell	.05
68	Joey Cora	.05
69	Alex Fernandez	.05
70	Carlton Fisk	.50
71	Craig Grebeck	.05
72	Ozzie Guillen	.05
73	Jack McDowell	.05
74	Scott Radinsky	.05
75	Tim Raines	.05
76	Bobby Thigpen	.05
77	Frank Thomas	.50
78	Robin Ventura	.05
79	Tom Browning	.05
80	Jacob Brumfield	.05
81	Rob Dibble	.05
82	Bill Doran	.05
83	Billy Hatcher	.05
84	Barry Larkin	.05
85	Hal Morris	.05
86	Joe Oliver	.05
87	Jeff Reed	.05
88	Jose Rijo	.05
89	Bip Roberts	.05
90	Chris Sabo	.05
91	Sandy Alomar, Jr.	.05
92	Brad Arnsberg	.05
93	Carlos Baerga	.05
94	Albert Belle	.05
95	Felix Fermin	.05
96	Mark Lewis	.05
97	Kenny Lofton	.05
98	Carlos Martinez	.05
99	Rod Nicholas	.05
100	Dave Rohde	.05
101	Scott Scudder	.05
102	Paul Sorrento	.05
103	Mark Whiten	.05
104	Mark Carreon	.05
105	Milt Cuyler	.05
106	Rob Deer	.05
107	Cecil Fielder	.05
108	Travis Fryman	.05
109	Dan Gladden	.05
110	Bill Gullickson	.05
111	Les Lancaster	.05
112	Mark Leiter	.05
113	Tony Phillips	.05
114	Mickey Tettleton	.05
115	Alan Trammell	.05
116	Lou Whitaker	.05
117	Jeff Bagwell	.50
118	Craig Biggio	.05
119	Joe Boever	.05
120	Casey Candaele	.05
121	Andujar Cedeno	.05
122	Steve Finley	.05
123	Luis Gonzalez	.05
124	Pete Harnisch	.05
125	Jimmy Jones	.05
126	Mark Portugal	.05
127	Rafael Ramirez	.05
128	Mike Simms	.05
129	Eric Yelding	.05
130	Luis Aquino	.05
131	Kevin Appier	.05
132	Mike Boddicker	.05
133	George Brett	.75
134	Tom Gordon	.05
135	Mark Gubicza	.05
136	David Howard	.05
137	Gregg Jefferies	.05
138	Wally Joyner	.05
139	Brian McRae	.05
140	Jeff Montgomery	.05
141	Terry Shumpert	.05
142	Curtis Wilkerson	.05
143	Brett Butler	.05
144	Eric Davis	.05
145	Kevin Gross	.05
146	Dave Hansen	.05
147	Lenny Harris	.05
148	Carlos Hernandez	.05
149	Orel Hershiser	.05
150	Jay Howell	.05
151	Eric Karros	.05
152	Ramon Martinez	.05
153	Jose Offerman	.05
154	Mike Sharperson	.05
155	Darryl Strawberry	.05
156	Jim Gantner	.05
157	Darryl Hamilton	.05
158	Doug Henry	.05
159	John Jaha	.05
160	Pat Listach	.05
161	Jaime Navarro	.05
162	Dave Nilsson	.05
163	Jesse Orosco	.05
164	Kevin Seitzer	.05
165	B.J. Surhoff	.05
166	Greg Vaughn	.05
167	Robin Yount	.50
168	Rick Aguilera	.05
169	Scott Erickson	.05
170	Mark Guthrie	.05
171	Kent Hrbek	.05
172	Chuck Knoblauch	.05
173	Gene Larkin	.05
174	Shane Mack	.05
175	Pedro Munoz	.05
176	Mike Pagliarulo	.05
177	Kirby Puckett	.65
178	Kevin Tapani	.05
179	Gary Wayne	.05
180	Moises Alou	.05
181	Brian Barnes	.05
182	Archie Cianfrocco	.05
183	Delino DeShields	.05
184	Darrin Fletcher	.05
185	Marquis Grissom	.05
186	Ken Hill	.05
187	Dennis Martinez	.05
188	Bill Sampen	.05
189	John VanderWal	.05
190	Larry Walker	.05
191	Tim Wallach	.05
192	Bobby Bonilla	.05
193	Daryl Boston	.05
194	Vince Coleman	.05
195	Kevin Elster	.05
196	Sid Fernandez	.05
197	John Franco	.05
198	Dwight Gooden	.05
199	Howard Johnson	.05
200	Willie Randolph	.05
201	Bret Saberhagen	.05
202	Dick Schofield	.05
203	Pete Schourek	.05
204	Greg Cadaret	.05
205	John Habyan	.05
206	Pat Kelly	.05
207	Kevin Maas	.05
208	Don Mattingly	.75
209	Matt Nokes	.05
210	Melido Perez	.05
211	Scott Sanderson	.05
212	Andy Stankiewicz	.05
213	Danny Tartabull	.05
214	Randy Velarde	.05
215	Bernie Williams	.05
216	Harold Baines	.05
217	Mike Bordick	.05
218	Scott Brosius	.05
219	Jerry Browne	.05
220	Ron Darling	.05
221	Dennis Eckersley	.40
222	Rickey Henderson	.50
223	Rick Honeycutt	.05
224	Mark McGwire	1.25
225	Ruben Sierra	.05
226	Terry Steinbach	.05
227	Bob Welch	.05
228	Willie Wilson	.05
229	Ruben Amaro	.05
230	Kim Batiste	.05
231	Juan Bell	.05
232	Wes Chamberlain	.05
233	Darren Daulton	.05
234	Mariano Duncan	.05
235	Len Dykstra	.05
236	Dave Hollins	.05
237	Stan Javier	.05
238	John Kruk	.05
239	Mickey Morandini	.05
240	Terry Mulholland	.05
241	Mitch Williams	.05
242	Stan Belinda	.05
243	Jay Bell	.05
244	Carlos Garcia	.05
245	Jeff King	.05
246	Mike LaValliere	.05
247	Lloyd McClendon	.05
248	Orlando Merced	.05
249	Paul Miller	.05
250	Gary Redus	.05
251	Don Slaught	.05
252	Zane Smith	.05
253	Andy Van Slyke	.05
254	Tim Wakefield	.05
255	Andy Benes	.05
256	Dann Bilardello	.05
257	Tony Gwynn	.65
258	Greg Harris	.05
259	Darrin Jackson	.05
260	Mike Maddux	.05
261	Fred McGriff	.05
262	Rich Rodriguez	.05
263	Benito Santiago	.05
264	Gary Sheffield	.35
265	Kurt Stillwell	.05
266	Tim Teufel	.05
267	Bud Black	.05
268	John Burkett	.05
269	Will Clark	.05
270	Royce Calyton	.05
271	Bryan Hickerson	.05
272	Chris James	.05
273	Darren Lewis	.05
274	Willie McGee	.05
275	Jim McNamara	.05
276	Francisco Oliveras	.05
277	Robby Thompson	.05
278	Matt Williams	.05
279	Trevor Wilson	.05
280	Bret Boone	.05
281	Greg Briley	.05
282	Jay Buhner	.05
283	Henry Cotto	.05
284	Rich DeLucia	.05
285	Dave Fleming	.05
286	Ken Griffey Jr.	1.00
287	Erik Hanson	.05
288	Randy Johnson	.50
289	Tino Martinez	.05
290	Edgar Martinez	.05
291	Dave Valle	.05
292	Omar Vizquel	.05
293	Luis Alicea	.05
294	Bernard Gilkey	.05
295	Felix Jose	.05
296	Ray Lankford	.05
297	Omar Olivares	.05
298	Jose Oquendo	.05
299	Tom Pagnozzi	.05
300	Geronimo Pena	.05
301	Gerald Perry	.05
302	Ozzie Smith	.65
303	Lee Smith	.05
304	Bob Tewksbury	.05
305	Todd Zeile	.05
306	Kevin Brown	.05
307	Todd Burns	.05
308	Jose Canseco	.35
309	Hector Fajardo	.05
310	Julio Franco	.05
311	Juan Gonzalez	.25
312	Jeff Huson	.05
313	Rob Maurer	.05
314	Rafael Palmeiro	.45
315	Dean Palmer	.05
316	Ivan Rodriguez	.45
317	Nolan Ryan	1.50
318	Dickie Thon	.05
319	Roberto Alomar	.20
320	Derek Bell	.05
321	Pat Borders	.05
322	Joe Carter	.05
323	Kelly Gruber	.05
324	Juan Guzman	.05
325	Manny Lee	.05
326	Jack Morris	.05
327	John Olerud	.05
328	Ed Sprague	.05
329	Todd Stottlemyre	.05
330	Duane Ward	.05
331	Steve Avery	.05
332	Damon Berryhill	.05
333	Jeff Blauser	.05
334	Mark Lemke	.05
335	Greg Maddux	.65
336	Kent Mercker	.05
337	Otis Nixon	.05
338	Greg Olson	.05
339	Bill Pecota	.05
340	Terry Pendleton	.05
341	Mike Stanton	.05
342	Todd Frohwirth	.05
343	Tim Hulett	.05
344	Mark McLemore	.05
345	Luis Mercedes	.05
346	Alan Mills	.05
347	Sherman Obando	.05
348	Jim Poole	.05
349	Harold Reynolds	.05
350	Arthur Rhodes	.05
351	Jeff Tackett	.05
352	Fernando Valenzuela	.05
353	Scott Bankhead	.05
354	Ivan Calderon	.05
355	Scott Cooper	.05
356	Danny Darwin	.05
357	Scott Fletcher	.05
358	Tony Fossas	.05
359	Greg Harris	.05
360	Joe Hesketh	.05
361	Jose Melendez	.05
362	Paul Quantrill	.05
363	John Valentin	.05
364	Mike Butcher	.05
365	Chuck Crim	.05
366	Chili Davis	.05
367	Damion Easley	.05
368	Steve Frey	.05
369	Joe Grahe	.05
370	Greg Myers	.05
371	John Orton	.05
372	J.T. Snow	.05
373	Ron Tingley	.05
374	Julio Valera	.05
375	Paul Assenmacher	.05
376	Jose Bautista	.05
377	Jose Guzman	.05
378	Greg Hibbard	.05
379	Candy Maldonado	.05
380	Derrick May	.05
381	Dan Plesac	.05
382	Tommy Shields	.05
383	Sammy Sosa	.75
384	Jose Vizcaino	.05
385	Greg Walbeck	.05
386	Ellis Burks	.05
387	Roberto Hernandez	.05
388	Mike Huff	.05
389	Bo Jackson	.10
390	Lance Johnson	.05
391	Ron Karkovice	.05
392	Kirk McCaskill	.05
393	Donn Pall	.05
394	Dan Pasqua	.05
395	Steve Sax	.05
396	Dave Stieb	.05
397	Bobby Ayala	.05
398	Tim Belcher	.05
399	Jeff Branson	.05
400	Cesar Hernandez	.05
401	Roberto Kelly	.05
402	Randy Milligan	.05
403	Kevin Mitchell	.05
404	Juan Samuel	.05
405	Reggie Sanders	.05
406	John Smiley	.05
407	Dan Wilson	.05
408	Mike Christopher	.05
409	Dennis Cook	.05
410	Alvaro Espinoza	.05
411	Glenallen Hill	.05
412	Reggie Jefferson	.05
413	Derek Lilliquist	.05
414	Jose Mesa	.05
415	Charles Nagy	.05
416	Junior Ortiz	.05
417	Eric Plunk	.05
418	Ted Power	.05
419	Scott Aldred	.05
420	Andy Ashby	.05
421	Freddie Benavides	.05
422	Dante Bichette	.05
423	Willie Blair	.05
424	Vinny Castilla	.05
425	Jerald Clark	.05
426	Alex Cole	.05
427	Andres Galarraga	.05
428	Joe Girardi	.05
429	Charlie Hayes	.05
430	Butch Henry	.05
431	Darren Holmes	.05
432	Dale Murphy	.20
433	David Nied	.05
434	Jeff Parrett	.05
435	Steve Reed RC	.05
436	Armando Reynoso	.05
437	Bruce Ruffin	.05
438	Bryn Smith	.05
439	Jim Tatum	.05
440	Eric Young	.05
441	Skeeter Barnes	.05
442	Tom Bolton	.05
443	Kirk Gibson	.05
444	Chad Krueter	.05
445	Bill Krueger	.05
446	Scott Livingstone	.05
447	Bob MacDonald	.05
448	Mike Moore	.05
449	Mike Munoz	.05
450	Gary Thurman	.05
451	David Wells	.05
452	Alex Arias	.05
453	Jack Armstrong	.05
454	Bret Barberie	.05
455	Ryan Bowen	.05
456	Cris Carpenter	.05
457	Chuck Carr	.05
458	Jeff Conine	.05

459	Steve Decker	.05
460	Orestes Destrade	.05
461	Monty Fariss	.05
462	Junior Felix	.05
463	Bryan Harvey	.05
464	Trevor Hoffman	.05
465	Charlie Hough	.05
466	Dave Magadan	.05
467	Bob McClure	.05
468	Rob Natal	.05
469	Scott Pose	.05
470	Rich Renteria	.05
471	Benito Santiago	.05
472	Matt Turner	.05
473	Walt Weiss	.05
474	Eric Anthony	.05
475	Chris Donnels	.05
476	Doug Drabek	.05
477	Xavier Hernandez	.05
478	Doug Jones	.05
479	Darryl Kile	.05
480	Scott Servais	.05
481	Greg Swindell	.05
482	Eddie Taubensee	.05
483	Jose Uribe	.05
484	Brian Williams	.05
485	Billy Brewer	.05
486	David Cone	.05
487	Greg Gagne	.05
488	Phil Hiatt	.05
489	Jose Lind	.05
490	Brent Mayne	.07
491	Kevin McReynolds	.05
492	Keith Miller	.05
493	Hipolito Pichardo	.05
494	Harvey Pulliam	.05
495	Rico Rossay	.05
496	Pedro Astacio	.05
497	Tom Candiotti	.05
498	Tom Goodwin	.05
499	Jim Gott	.05
500	Pedro Martinez	.50
501	Roger McDowell	.05
502	Mike Piazza	.75
503	Jody Reed	.05
504	Rick Trlicek	.05
505	Mitch Webster	.05
506	Steve Wilson	.05
507	James Austin	.05
508	Ricky Bones	.05
509	Alex Diaz	.05
510	Mike Fetters	.05
511	Teddy Higuera	.05
512	Graeme Lloyd	.05
513	Carlos Maldonado	.05
514	Josias Manzanillo	.05
515	Kevin Reimer	.05
516	Bill Spiers	.05
517	Bill Wegman	.05
518	Willie Banks	.05
519	J.T. Bruett	.05
520	Brian Harper	.05
521	Terry Jorgensen	.05
522	Scott Leius	.05
523	Pat Mahomes	.05
524	Dave McCarty	.05
525	Jeff Reboulet	.05
526	Mike Trombley	.05
527	Carl Willis	.05
528	Dave Winfield	.50
529	Sean Berry	.05
530	Frank Bolick	.05
531	Kent Bottenfield	.05
532	Wil Cordero	.05
533	Jeff Fassero	.05
534	Tim Laker	.05
535	Mike Lansing	.05
536	Chris Nabholz	.05
537	Mel Rojas	.05
538	John Wetteland	.05
539	Ted Wood (Front photo actually Frank Bollick.)	.05
540	Mike Draper	.05
541	Tony Fernandez	.05
542	Todd Hundley	.05
543	Jeff Innis	.05
544	Jeff McKnight	.05
545	Eddie Murray	.50
546	Charlie O'Brien	.05
547	Frank Tanana	.05
548	Ryan Thompson	.05
549	Chico Walker	.05
550	Anthony Young	.05
551	Jim Abbott	.05
552	Wade Boggs	.75
553	Steve Farr	.05
554	Neal Heaton	.05
555	Steve Howe	.05
556	Dion James	.05
557	Scott Kamieniecki	.05
558	Jimmy Key	.05
559	Jim Leyritz	.05
560	Paul O'Neill	.05
561	Spike Owen	.05
562	Lance Blankenship	.05
563	Joe Boever	.05
564	Storm Davis	.05
565	Kelly Downs	.05
566	Eric Fox	.05
567	Rich Gossage	.05
568	Dave Henderson	.05
569	Shawn Hillegas	.05
570	Mike Mohler **RC**	.05
571	Troy Neel	.05
572	Dale Sveum	.05
573	Larry Anderson	.05
574	Bob Ayrault	.05
575	Jose DeLeon	.05

576	Jim Eisenreich	.05
577	Pete Incaviglia	.05
578	Danny Jackson	.05
579	Ricky Jordan	.05
580	Ben Rivera	.05
581	Curt Schilling	.25
582	Milt Thompson	.05
583	David West	.05
584	John Candelaria	.05
585	Steve Cooke	.05
586	Tom Foley	.05
587	Al Martin	.05
588	Blas Minor	.05
589	Dennis Moeller	.05
590	Denny Neagle	.05
591	Tom Prince	.05
592	Randy Tomlin	.05
593	Bob Walk	.05
594	Kevin Young	.05
595	Pat Gomez	.05
596	Ricky Gutierrez	.05
597	Gene Harris	.05
598	Jeremy Hernandez	.05
599	Phil Plantier	.05
600	Tim Scott	.05
601	Frank Seminara	.05
602	Darrell Sherman	.05
603	Craig Shipley	.05
604	Guillermo Velasquez	.05
605	Dan Walters	.05
606	Mike Benjamin	.05
607	Barry Bonds	1.50
608	Jeff Brantley	.05
609	Dave Burba	.05
610	Craig Colbert	.05
611	Mike Jackson	.05
612	Kirt Manwaring	.05
613	Dave Martinez	.05
614	Dave Righetti	.05
615	Kevin Rogers	.05
616	Bill Swift	.05
617	Rich Amaral	.05
618	Mike Blowers	.05
619	Chris Bosio	.05
620	Norm Charlton	.05
621	John Cummings	.05
622	Mike Felder	.05
623	Bill Haselman	.05
624	Tim Leary	.05
625	Pete O'Brien	.05
626	Russ Swan	.05
627	Fernando Vina	.05
628	Rene Arocha	.05
629	Rod Brewer	.05
630	Ozzie Canseco	.05
631	Rheal Cormier	.05
632	Brian Jordan	.05
633	Joe Magrane	.05
634	Donovan Osborne	.05
635	Mike Perez	.05
636	Stan Royer	.05
637	Hector Villanueva	.05
638	Tracy Woodson	.05
639	Benji Gil	.05
640	Tom Henke	.05
641	David Hulse	.05
642	Charlie Leibrandt	.05
643	Robb Nen	.05
644	Dan Peltier	.05
645	Billy Ripken	.05
646	Kenny Rogers	.05
647	John Russell	.05
648	Dan Smith	.05
649	Matt Whiteside	.05
650	William Canate	.05
651	Darnell Coles	.05
652	Al Leiter	.05
653	Dominigo Martinez	.05
654	Paul Molitor	.50
655	Luis Sojo	.05
656	Dave Stewart	.05
657	Mike Timlin	.05
658	Turner Ward	.05
659	Devon White	.05
660	Eddie Zosky	.05

Beisbol Amigos

In groups of two, three or more, and generally from the same team, Latin players are paired in this second series insert set. The cards feature player photos (sometimes posed, sometimes superimposed) on a background of red, white and black baseballs. The players' last names and a card title are printed in Spanish on front and repeated on back. Also on back a few career highlights and stats are printed in red on a marbled background - again all in Spanish.

		NM/M
Complete Set (30):		7.50
Common Player:		.50

1	Edgar Martinez	.50
2	Luis Polonia, Stan Javier	.50
3	George Bell, Julio Franco	.50
4	Ozzie Guillen, Ivan Rodriguez	.60
5	Carlos Baerga, Sandy Alomar Jr.	.50
6	Sandy Alomar Jr., Alvaro Espinoza, Paul Sorrento, Carlos Baerga, Felix Fermin, Junior Ortiz, Jose Mesa, Carlos Martinez	.50
7	Sandy Alomar Jr., Roberto Alomar	1.00
8	Jose Lind, Felix Jose	.50
9	Ricky Bones, Jaime Navarro	.50
10	Jaime Navarro, Jesse Orosco	.50
11	Tino Martinez, Edgar Martinez	.50
12	Juan Gonzalez, Ivan Rodriguez	.75
13	Juan Gonzalez, Julio Franco	.60
14	Julio Franco, Jose Canseco, Rafael Palmeiro	.60
15	Juan Gonzalez, Jose Canseco	.65
16	Ivan Rodriguez, Benji Gil	.60
17	Jose Guzman, Frank Castillo	.50
18	Rey Sanchez, Jose Vizcaino	.50
19	Derrick May, Sammy Sosa	2.00
20	Sammy Sosa, Candy Maldonado	2.00
21	Jose Rijo, Juan Samuel	.50
22	Freddie Benavides, Andres Galarraga	.50
23	Guillermo Velasquez, Benito Santiago	.50
24	Luis Gonzalez, Andujar Cedeno	.50
25	Wil Cordero, Dennis Martinez	.50
26	Moises Alou, Wil Cordero	.50
27	Ozzie Canseco, Jose Canseco	.75
28	Jose Oquendo, Luis Alicea	.50
29	Luis Alicea, Rene Arocha	.50
30	Geronimo Pena, Luis Alicea	.50

Estrellas de Beisbol

Pacific produced a gold-foil "Stars of Baseball" set of 20 that was randomly inserted as part of the company's first series Spanish language set in 1993. Each card features a color action photo on the front surrounded by a gold-foil border. Production was limited to 10,000 of each card.

		NM/M
Complete Set (20):		6.00
Common Player:		.50

1	Moises Alou	.50
2	Bobby Bonilla	.50
3	Tony Fernandez	.50
4	Felix Jose	.50
5	Dennis Martinez	.50
6	Orlando Merced	.50
7	Jose Oquendo	.50
8	Geronimo Pena	.50
9	Jose Rijo	.50
10	Benito Santiago	.65
11	Sandy Alomar Jr.	.50
12	Carlos Baerga	.50
13	Jose Canseco	1.50
14	Juan "Igor" Gonzalez	2.00
15	Juan Guzman	.50
16	Edgar Martinez	.50
17	Rafael Palmeiro	2.00
18	Ruben Sierra	.50
19	Danny Tartabull	.50
20	Omar Vizquel	.50

Jugadores Calientes

Three dozen "hot players" with a decidedly Hispanic predominance are featured in this glittery Series 2 insert set. Player action

photos appear in front of a silver prismatic foil background. Names appear at bottom in boldly styled, but hard to read, letters in bright colors. Horizontal backs have a pair of player photos and a large team logo, along with a few stats, all printed in Spanish.

		NM/M
Complete Set (36):		20.00
Common Player:		.50

1	Rich Amaral	.50
2	George Brett	1.75
3	Jay Buhner	.50
4	Roger Clemens	2.00
5	Kirk Gibson	.50
6	Juan Gonzalez	1.00
7	Ken Griffey Jr.	2.00
8	Bo Jackson	.75
9	Kenny Lofton	.50
10	Mark McGwire	2.25
11	Sherman Obando	.50
12	John Olerud	.50
13	Carlos Quintana	.50
14	Ivan Rodriguez	1.00
15	Nolan Ryan	2.50
16	J.T. Snow	.50
17	Fernando Valenzuela	.50
18	Dave Winfield	1.25
19	Moises Alou	.50
20	Jeff Bagwell	1.25
21	Barry Bonds	2.50
22	Bobby Bonilla	.50
23	Vinny Castilla	.50
24	Andujar Cedeno	.50
25	Orestes Destrade	.50
26	Andres Galarraga	.50
27	Mark Grace	.50
28	Tony Gwynn	1.50
29	Roberto Kelly	.50
30	John Kruk	.50
31	Dave Magadan	.50
32	Derrick May	.50
33	Orlando Merced	.50
34	Mike Piazza	2.00
35	Armadno Reynoso	.50
36	Jose Vizcaino	.50

Prism Insert

Pacific produced a prism card that was randomly inserted in its Series 1 Spanish-language set in 1993. Each of the 20 cards has a color photo of a star Latino player on the front superimposed over a prismatic silver-foil background. Card backs contain an action photo and a brief player biography on a marbled background. Production was limited to 10,000 of each card.

		NM/M
Complete Set (20):		60.00
Common Player:		3.00

1	Francisco Cabrera	3.00
2	Jose Lind	3.00
3	Dennis Martinez	3.00
4	Ramon Martinez	3.00
5	Jose Rijo	3.00
6	Benito Santiago	3.00
7	Roberto Alomar	9.00
8	Sandy Alomar Jr.	3.00
9	Carlos Baerga	3.00
10	George Bell	3.00
11	Jose Canseco	6.00

1994 Pacific Crown Promos

Virtually identical in format to the regular 1994 Pacific Crown issue, the eight cards in the promo set have a "P-" prefix to the card number. Each side has a large "For Promotional Use Only" printed diagonally in black. The cards were sent to dealers as a preview to Pacific's 1994 bilingual issue.

		NM/M
Complete Set (8):		6.00
Common Player:		.75

1	Carlos Baerga	.75
2	Joe Carter	.75
3	Juan Gonzalez	.75
4	Ken Griffey Jr.	2.00
5	Greg Maddux	1.50
6	Mike Piazza	1.75
7	Tim Salmon	.75
8	Frank Thomas	1.25

1994 Pacific Crown

Following its 1993 Spanish-language set, Pacific's 1994 "Crown Collection" offering is bilingual, featuring both English and Spanish for most of the back printing. Fronts have an action photo which is borderless at the top and sides. A gold-foil line separates the bottom of the photo from a marbled strip that is color-coded by team. The player's name appears in two lines at the left of the strip, a gold-foil crown logo is at left. A Pacific logo appears in one of the upper corners of the photo. Backs have a photo, again borderless at top and sides, with a Pacific logo in one upper corner and the card number and MLB logos in the lower corners. At bottom is a gray marble strip with a few biographical details, 1993 and career stats and a ghost-image color team logo. The 660 cards in the set were issued in a single series.

		NM/M
Complete Set (660):		20.00
Common Player:		.05
Pack (12):		1.00
Wax Box (36):		20.00

1	Steve Avery	.05
2	Steve Bedrosian	.05
3	Damon Berryhill	.05
4	Jeff Blauser	.05
5	Sid Bream	.05
6	Francisco Cabrera	.05
7	Ramon Caraballo	.05
8	Ron Gant	.05
9	Tom Glavine	.25
10	Chipper Jones	.75
11	Dave Justice	.05
12	Ryan Klesko	.05
13	Mark Lemke	.05
14	Javier Lopez	.05
15	Greg Maddux	.75
16	Fred McGriff	.05
17	Greg McMichael	.05
18	Kent Mercker	.05
19	Otis Nixon	.05
20	Terry Pendleton	.05
21	Deion Sanders	.05
22	John Smoltz	.05
23	Tony Tarasco	.05
24	Manny Alexander	.05
25	Brady Anderson	.05
26	Harold Baines	.05
27	Damion Buford (Damon)	.05
28	Paul Carey	.05
29	Mike Devereaux	.05
30	Todd Frohwirth	.05
31	Leo Gomez	.05
32	Jeffrey Hammonds	.05
33	Chris Hoiles	.05
34	Tim Hullett	.05
35	Ben McDonald	.05
36	Mark McLemore	.05
37	Alan Mills	.05
38	Mike Mussina	.35
39	Sherman Obando	.05
40	Gregg Olson	.05
41	Mike Pagliarulo	.05
42	Jim Poole	.05
43	Harold Reynolds	.05
44	Cal Ripken, Jr.	2.00
45	David Segui	.05
46	Fernando Valenzuela	.05
47	Jack Voight	.05
48	Scott Bankhead	.05
49	Roger Clemens	1.00
50	Scott Cooper	.05
51	Danny Darwin	.05
52	Andre Dawson	.20
53	John Dopson	.05
54	Scott Fletcher	.05
55	Tony Fossas	.05
56	Mike Greenwell	.05
57	Billy Hatcher	.05
58	Jeff McNeely	.05
59	Jose Melendez	.05
60	Tim Naehring	.05
61	Tony Pena	.05
62	Carlos Quintana	.05
63	Paul Quantrill	.05
64	Luis Rivera	.05
65	Jeff Russell	.05
66	Aaron Sele	.05
67	John Valentin	.05
68	Mo Vaughn	.05
69	Frank Viola	.05
70	Bob Zupcic	.05
71	Mike Butcher	.05
72	Ron Correia	.05
73	Chad Curtis	.05
74	Chili Davis	.05
75	Gary DiSarcina	.05
76	Damion Easley	.05
77	John Farrell	.05
78	Chuck Finley	.05
79	Joe Grahe	.05
80	Stan Javier	.05
81	Mark Langston	.05
82	Phil Leftwich	.05
83	Torey Lovullo	.05
84	Joe Magrane	.05
85	Greg Myers	.05
86	Eduardo Perez	.05
87	Luis Polonia	.05
88	Tim Salmon	.05
89	J.T. Snow	.05
90	Kurt Stillwell	.05
91	Ron Tingley	.05
92	Chris Turner	.05
93	Julio Valera	.05
94	Jose Bautista	.05
95	Shawn Boskie	.05
96	Steve Buechele	.05
97	Frank Castillo	.05
98	Mark Grace	.05
99	Jose Guzman	.05
100	Mike Harkey	.05
101	Greg Hibbard	.05
102	Doug Jennings	.05
103	Derrick May	.05
104	Mike Morgan	.05
105	Randy Myers	.05
106	Karl Rhodes	.05
107	Kevin Roberson	.05
108	Rey Sanchez	.05
109	Ryne Sandberg	.75
110	Tommy Shields	.05
111	Dwight Smith	.05
112	Sammy Sosa	.75
113	Jose Vizcaino	.05
114	Turk Wendell	.05
115	Rick Wilkins	.05
116	Willie Wilson	.05
117	Eddie Zambrano	.05
118	Wilson Alvarez	.05
119	Tim Belcher	.05
120	Jason Bere	.05
121	Rodney Bolton	.05
122	Ellis Burks	.05
123	Joey Cora	.05
124	Alex Fernandez	.05
125	Ozzie Guillen	.05
126	Craig Grebeck	.05
127	Roberto Hernandez	.05
128	Bo Jackson	.10
129	Lance Johnson	.05

12	Alex Fernandez	3.00
13	Julio Franco	3.00
14	Igor (Juan) Gonzalez	12.00
15	Ozzie Guillen	3.00
16	Teddy Higuera	3.00
17	Edgar Martinez	3.00
18	Hipolito Pichardo	3.00
19	Luis Polonia	3.00
20	Ivan Rodriguez	7.50

#	Player	Price
130	Ron Karkovice	.05
131	Mike Lavalliere	.05
132	Norberto Martin	.05
133	Kirk McCaskill	.05
134	Jack McDowell	.05
135	Scott Radinsky	.05
136	Tim Raines	.05
137	Steve Sax	.05
138	Frank Thomas	.60
139	Dan Pasqua	.05
140	Robin Ventura	.05
141	Jeff Branson	.05
142	Tom Browning	.05
143	Jacob Brumfield	.05
144	Tim Costo	.05
145	Rob Dibble	.05
146	Brian Dorsett	.05
147	Steve Foster	.05
148	Cesar Hernandez	.05
149	Roberto Kelly	.05
150	Barry Larkin	.05
151	Larry Luebbers	.05
152	Kevin Mitchell	.05
153	Joe Oliver	.05
154	Tim Pugh	.05
155	Jeff Reardon	.05
156	Jose Rijo	.05
157	Bip Roberts	.05
158	Chris Sabo	.05
159	Juan Samuel	.05
160	Reggie Sanders	.05
161	John Smiley	.05
162	Jerry Spradlin	.05
163	Gary Varsho	.05
164	Sandy Alomar Jr.	.05
165	Carlos Baerga	.05
166	Albert Belle	.05
167	Mark Clark	.05
168	Alvaro Espinoza	.05
169	Felix Fermin	.05
170	Reggie Jefferson	.05
171	Wayne Kirby	.05
172	Tom Kramer	.05
173	Jesse Levis	.05
174	Kenny Lofton	.05
175	Candy Maldonado	.05
176	Carlos Martinez	.05
177	Jose Mesa	.05
178	Jeff Mutis	.05
179	Charles Nagy	.05
180	Bob Ojeda	.05
181	Junior Ortiz	.05
182	Eric Plunk	.05
183	Manny Ramirez	.60
184	Paul Sorrento	.05
185	Jeff Treadway	.05
186	Bill Wertz	.05
187	Freddie Benavides	.05
188	Dante Bichette	.05
189	Willie Blair	.05
190	Daryl Boston	.05
191	Pedro Castellano	.05
192	Vinny Castilla	.05
193	Jerald Clark	.05
194	Alex Cole	.05
195	Andres Galarraga	.05
196	Joe Girardi	.05
197	Charlie Hayes	.05
198	Darren Holmes	.05
199	Chris Jones	.05
200	Curt Leskanic	.05
201	Roberto Mejia	.05
202	David Nied	.05
203	J. Owens	.05
204	Steve Reed	.05
205	Armando Reynoso	.05
206	Bruce Ruffin	.05
207	Keith Shepherd	.05
208	Jim Tatum	.05
209	Eric Young	.05
210	Skeeter Barnes	.05
211	Danny Bautista	.05
212	Tom Bolton	.05
213	Eric Davis	.05
214	Storm Davis	.05
215	Cecil Fielder	.05
216	Travis Fryman	.05
217	Kirk Gibson	.05
218	Dan Gladden	.05
219	John Doherty	.05
220	Chris Gomez	.05
221	David Haas	.05
222	Bill Krueger	.05
223	Chad Kreuter	.05
224	Mark Leiter	.05
225	Bob MacDonald	.05
226	Mike Moore	.05
227	Tony Phillips	.05
228	Rich Rowland	.05
229	Mickey Tettleton	.05
230	Alan Trammell	.05
231	David Wells	.05
232	Lou Whitaker	.05
233	Luis Aquino	.05
234	Alex Arias	.05
235	Jack Armstrong	.05
236	Ryan Bowen	.05
237	Chuck Carr	.05
238	Matias Carrillo	.05
239	Jeff Conine	.05
240	Henry Cotto	.05
241	Orestes Destrade	.05
242	Chris Hammond	.05
243	Bryan Harvey	.05
244	Charlie Hough	.05
245	Richie Lewis	.05
246	Mitch Lyden	.05
247	Dave Magadan	.05

#	Player	Price
248	Bob Natal	.05
249	Benito Santiago	.05
250	Gary Sheffield	.30
251	Matt Turner	.05
252	David Weathers	.05
253	Walt Weiss	.05
254	Darrell Whitmore	.05
255	Nigel Wilson	.05
256	Eric Anthony	.05
257	Jeff Bagwell	.60
258	Kevin Bass	.05
259	Craig Biggio	.05
260	Ken Caminiti	.05
261	Andujar Cedeno	.05
262	Chris Donnels	.05
263	Doug Drabek	.05
264	Tom Edens	.05
265	Steve Finley	.05
266	Luis Gonzalez	.05
267	Pete Harnisch	.05
268	Xavier Hernandez	.05
269	Todd Jones	.05
270	Darryl Kile	.05
271	Al Osuna	.05
272	Rick Parker	.05
273	Mark Portugal	.05
274	Scott Servais	.05
275	Greg Swindell	.05
276	Eddie Taubensee	.05
277	Jose Uribe	.05
278	Brian Williams	.05
279	Kevin Appier	.05
280	Billy Brewer	.05
281	David Cone	.05
282	Greg Gagne	.05
283	Tom Gordon	.05
284	Chris Gwynn	.05
285	John Habyan	.05
286	Chris Haney	.05
287	Phil Hiatt	.05
288	David Howard	.05
289	Felix Jose	.05
290	Wally Joyner	.05
291	Kevin Koslofski	.05
292	Jose Lind	.05
293	Brent Mayne	.05
294	Mike Mcfarlane	.05
295	Brian McRae	.05
296	Kevin McReynolds	.05
297	Keith Miller	.05
298	Jeff Montgomery	.05
299	Hipolito Pichardo	.05
300	Rico Rossy	.05
301	Curtis Wilkerson	.05
302	Pedro Astacio	.05
303	Rafael Bournigal	.05
304	Brett Butler	.05
305	Tom Candiotti	.05
306	Omar Daal	.05
307	Jim Gott	.05
308	Kevin Gross	.05
309	Dave Hansen	.05
310	Carlos Hernandez	.05
311	Orel Hershiser	.05
312	Eric Karros	.05
313	Pedro Martinez	.60
314	Ramon Martinez	.05
315	Roger McDowell	.05
316	Raul Mondesi	.05
317	Jose Offerman	.05
318	Mike Piazza	1.00
319	Jody Reed	.05
320	Henry Rodriguez	.05
321	Cory Snyder	.05
322	Darryl Strawberry	.05
323	Tim Wallach	.05
324	Steve Wilson	.05
325	Juan Bell	.05
326	Ricky Bones	.05
327	Alex Diaz	.05
328	Cal Eldred	.05
329	Darryl Hamilton	.05
330	Doug Henry	.05
331	John Jaha	.05
332	Pat Listach	.05
333	Graeme Lloyd	.05
334	Carlos Maldonado	.05
335	Angel Miranda	.05
336	Jaime Navarro	.05
337	Dave Nilsson	.05
338	Rafael Novoa	.05
339	Troy O'Leary	.05
340	Jesse Orosco	.05
341	Kevin Seitzer	.05
342	Bill Spiers	.05
343	William Suero	.05
344	B.J. Surhoff	.05
345	Dickie Thon	.05
346	Jose Valentin	.05
347	Greg Vaughn	.05
348	Robin Yount	.60
349	Willie Banks	.05
350	Bernardo Brito	.05
351	Scott Erickson	.05
352	Mark Guthrie	.05
353	Chip Hale	.05
354	Brian Harper	.05
355	Kent Hrbek	.05
356	Terry Jorgenson	.05
357	Chuck Knoblauch	.05
358	Gene Larkin	.05
359	Scott Leius	.05
360	Shane Mack	.05
361	David McCarty	.05
362	Pat Meares	.05
363	Pedro Munoz	.05
364	Derek Parks	.05
365	Kirby Puckett	.75

#	Player	Price
366	Jeff Reboulet	.05
367	Kevin Tapani	.05
368	Mike Trombley	.05
369	George Tsamis	.05
370	Carl Willis	.05
371	Dave Winfield	.60
372	Moises Alou	.05
373	Brian Barnes	.05
374	Sean Berry	.05
375	Frank Bolick	.05
376	Wil Cordero	.05
377	Delino DeShields	.05
378	Jeff Fassero	.05
379	Darren Fletcher	.05
380	Cliff Floyd	.05
381	Lou Frazier	.05
382	Marquis Grissom	.05
383	Gil Heredia	.05
384	Mike Lansing	.05
385	Oreste Marrero	.05
386	Dennis Martinez	.05
387	Curtis Pride	.05
388	Mel Rojas	.05
389	Kirk Rueter	.05
390	Joe Siddall	.05
391	John Vander Wal	.05
392	Larry Walker	.05
393	John Wetteland	.05
394	Rondell White	.05
395	Tom Bogar	.05
396	Bobby Bonilla	.05
397	Jeromy Burnitz	.05
398	Mike Draper	.05
399	Sid Fernandez	.05
400	John Franco	.05
401	Dave Gallagher	.05
402	Dwight Gooden	.05
403	Eric Hillman	.05
404	Todd Hundley	.05
405	Butch Huskey	.05
406	Jeff Innis	.05
407	Howard Johnson	.05
408	Jeff Kent	.05
409	Ced Landrum	.05
410	Mike Maddux	.05
411	Josias Manzanillo	.05
412	Jeff McKnight	.05
413	Eddie Murray	.60
414	Tito Navarro	.05
415	Joe Orsulak	.05
416	Bret Saberhagen	.05
417	Dave Telgheder	.05
418	Ryan Thompson	.05
419	Chico Walker	.05
420	Jim Abbott	.05
421	Wade Boggs	.75
422	Mike Gallego	.05
423	Mark Hutton	.05
424	Dion James	.05
425	Domingo Jean	.05
426	Pat Kelly	.05
427	Jimmy Key	.05
428	Jim Leyritz	.05
429	Kevin Maas	.05
430	Don Mattingly	1.00
431	Bobby Munoz	.05
432	Matt Nokes	.05
433	Paul O'Neill	.05
434	Spike Owen	.05
435	Melido Perez	.05
436	Lee Smith	.05
437	Andy Stankiewicz	.05
438	Mike Stanley	.05
439	Danny Tartabull	.05
440	Randy Velarde	.05
441	Bernie Williams	.05
442	Gerald Williams	.05
443	Mike Witt	.05
444	Marcos Armas	.05
445	Lance Blankenship	.05
446	Mike Bordick	.05
447	Ron Darling	.05
448	Dennis Eckersley	.45
449	Brent Gates	.05
450	Goose Gossage	.05
451	Scott Hemond	.05
452	Dave Henderson	.05
453	Shawn Hillegas	.05
454	Rick Honeycutt	.05
455	Scott Lydy	.05
456	Mark McGwire	1.50
457	Henry Mercedes	.05
458	Mike Mohler	.05
459	Troy Neel	.05
460	Edwin Nunez	.05
461	Craig Paquette	.05
462	Ruben Sierra	.05
463	Terry Steinbach	.05
464	Todd Van Poppel	.05
465	Bob Welch	.05
466	Bobby Witt	.05
467	Ruben Amaro	.05
468	Larry Anderson	.05
469	Kim Batiste	.05
470	Wes Chamberlain	.05
471	Darren Daulton	.05
472	Mariano Duncan	.05
473	Len Dykstra	.05
474	Jim Eisenreich	.05
475	Tommy Greene	.05
476	Dave Hollins	.05
477	Pete Incaviglia	.05
478	Danny Jackson	.05
479	John Kruk	.05
480	Tony Longmire	.05
481	Jeff Manto	.05
482	Mike Morandini	.05
483	Terry Mulholland	.05

#	Player	Price
484	Todd Pratt	.05
485	Ben Rivera	.05
486	Curt Schilling	.25
487	Kevin Stocker	.05
488	Milt Thompson	.05
489	David West	.05
490	Mitch Williams	.05
491	Jeff Ballard	.05
492	Jay Bell	.05
493	Scott Bullett	.05
494	Dave Clark	.05
495	Steve Cooke	.05
496	Midre Cummings	.05
497	Mark Dewey	.05
498	Carlos Garcia	.05
499	Jeff King	.05
500	Al Martin	.05
501	Lloyd McClendon	.05
502	Orlando Merced	.05
503	Blas Minor	.05
504	Denny Neagle	.05
505	Tom Prince	.05
506	Don Slaught	.05
507	Zane Smith	.05
508	Randy Tomlin	.05
509	Andy Van Slyke	.05
510	Paul Wagner	.05
511	Tim Wakefield	.05
512	Bob Walk	.05
513	John Wehner	.05
514	Kevin Young	.05
515	Billy Bean	.05
516	Andy Benes	.05
517	Derek Bell	.05
518	Doug Brocail	.05
519	Jarvis Brown	.05
520	Phil Clark	.05
521	Mark Davis	.05
522	Jeff Gardner	.05
523	Pat Gomez	.05
524	Ricky Gutierrez	.05
525	Tony Gwynn	.75
526	Gene Harris	.05
527	Kevin Higgins	.05
528	Trevor Hoffman	.05
529	Luis Lopez	.05
530	Pedro A. Martinez	.05
531	Melvin Nieves	.05
532	Phil Plantier	.05
533	Frank Seminara	.05
534	Craig Shipley	.05
535	Tim Tuefel	.05
536	Guillermo Velasquez	.05
537	Wally Whitehurst	.05
538	Rod Beck	.05
539	Todd Benzinger	.05
540	Barry Bonds	2.00
541	Jeff Brantley	.05
542	Dave Burba	.05
543	John Burkett	.05
544	Will Clark	.05
545	Royce Clayton	.05
546	Brian Hickerson (Bryan)	.05
547	Mike Jackson	.05
548	Darren Lewis	.05
549	Kirt Manwaring	.05
550	Dave Martinez	.05
551	Willie McGee	.05
552	Jeff Reed	.05
553	Dave Righetti	.05
554	Kevin Rogers	.05
555	Steve Scarsone	.05
556	Bill Swift	.05
557	Robby Thompson	.05
558	Salomon Torres	.05
559	Matt Williams	.05
560	Trevor Wilson	.05
561	Rich Amaral	.05
562	Mike Blowers	.05
563	Chris Bosio	.05
564	Jay Buhner	.05
565	Norm Charlton	.05
566	Jim Converse	.05
567	Rich DeLucia	.05
568	Mike Felder	.05
569	Dave Fleming	.05
570	Ken Griffey Jr.	1.00
571	Bill Haselman	.05
572	Dwayne Henry	.05
573	Brad Holman	.05
574	Randy Johnson	.60
575	Greg Litton	.05
576	Edgar Martinez	.05
577	Tino Martinez	.05
578	Jeff Nelson	.05
579	Mark Newfield	.05
580	Roger Salkeld	.05
581	Mackey Sasser	.05
582	Brian Turang	.05
583	Omar Vizquel	.05
584	Dave Valle	.05
585	Luis Alicea	.05
586	Rene Arocha	.05
587	Rheal Cormier	.05
588	Tripp Cromer	.05
589	Bernard Gilkey	.05
590	Lee Guetterman	.05
591	Gregg Jefferies	.05
592	Tim Jones	.05
593	Paul Kilgus	.05
594	Les Lancaster	.05
595	Omar Olivares	.05
596	Jose Oquendo	.05
597	Donovan Osborne	.05
598	Tom Pagnozzi	.05
599	Erik Pappas	.05
600	Geronimo Pena	.05
601	Mike Perez	.05

#	Player	Price
602	Gerald Perry	.05
603	Stan Royer	.05
604	Ozzie Smith	.75
605	Bob Tewksbury	.05
606	Allen Watson	.05
607	Mark Whiten	.05
608	Todd Zeile	.05
609	Jeff Bronkey	.05
610	Kevin Brown	.05
611	Jose Canseco	.35
612	Doug Dascenzo	.05
613	Butch Davis	.05
614	Mario Diaz	.05
615	Julio Franco	.05
616	Benji Gil	.05
617	Juan Gonzalez	.30
618	Tom Henke	.05
619	Jeff Huson	.05
620	David Hulse	.05
621	Craig Lefferts	.05
622	Rafael Palmeiro	.50
623	Dean Palmer	.05
624	Bob Patterson	.05
625	Roger Pavlik	.05
626	Gary Redus	.05
627	Ivan Rodriguez	.50
628	Kenny Rogers	.05
629	Jon Shave	.05
630	Doug Strange	.05
631	Matt Whiteside	.05
632	Roberto Alomar	.15
633	Pat Borders	.05
634	Scott Brow	.05
635	Rob Butler	.05
636	Joe Carter	.05
637	Tony Castillo	.05
638	Mark Eichhorn	.05
639	Tony Fernandez	.05
640	Huck Flener **RC**	.05
641	Alfredo Griffin	.05
642	Juan Guzman	.05
643	Rickey Henderson	.60
644	Pat Hentgen	.05
645	Pat Knorr	.05
646	Al Leiter	.05
647	Domingo Martinez	.05
648	Paul Molitor	.60
649	Jack Morris	.05
650	John Olerud	.05
651	Ed Sprague	.05
652	Dave Stewart	.05
653	Devon White	.05
654	Woody Williams	.05
655	Barry Bonds (MVP)	1.00
656	Greg Maddux (CY)	.40
657	Jack McDowell (CY)	.05
658	Mike Piazza (ROY)	.65
659	Tim Salmon (ROY)	.05
660	Frank Thomas (MVP)	.25

All Latino All-Star Team

Latino All-Stars is the theme of the third insert set found randomly packed in Pacific Spanish for 1994. Cards feature a player action photo on front, with a gold foil pinstripe around the sides and top. The player's name appears in gold script at bottom and there is a baseball logo in the corner. On backs a portrait photo of the player is set against a background of his native flag. Season highlights of 1993 are presented in English and Spanish. Eight thousand sets were produced.

		NM/M
Complete Set (20):		4.00
Common Player:		.25
1	Benito Santiago	.25
2	Dave Magadan	.25
3	Andres Galarraga	.25
4	Luis Gonzalez	.25
5	Jose Offerman	.25
6	Bobby Bonilla	.25
7	Dennis Martinez	.25
8	Mariano Duncan	.25
9	Orlando Merced	.25
10	Jose Rijo	.25
11	Danny Tartabull	.25
12	Ruben Sierra	.25
13	Ivan Rodriguez	1.00
14	Juan Gonzalez	1.00
15	Jose Canseco	.50
16	Rafael Palmeiro	1.00
17	Roberto Alomar	.50

#	Player	Price
18	Eduardo Perez	.25
19	Alex Fernandez	.25
20	Omar Vizquel	.25

Homerun Leaders

A gold prismatic background behind a color action player photo is the featured design on this Pacific insert set. Backs have another player photo against a ballfield backdrop. A huge baseball is overprinted with the player's name and number of 1993 homers. A league designation is among the logos featured on back. A total of 8,000 of these inserts sets was the announced production.

		NM/M
Complete Set (20):		25.00
Common Player:		1.00
1	Juan Gonzalez	1.50
2	Ken Griffey Jr.	3.00
3	Frank Thomas	2.50
4	Albert Belle	1.00
5	Rafael Palmeiro	1.50
6	Joe Carter	1.00
7	Dean Palmer	1.00
8	Mickey Tettleton	1.00
9	Tim Salmon	1.00
10	Danny Tartabull	1.00
11	Barry Bonds	5.00
12	Dave Justice	1.00
13	Matt Williams	1.00
14	Fred McGriff	1.00
15	Ron Gant	1.00
16	Mike Piazza	3.00
17	Bobby Bonilla	1.00
18	Phil Plantier	1.00
19	Sammy Sosa	3.00
20	Rick Wilkins	1.00

Jewels of the Crown

One of three inserts into 1994 Pacific Spanish foil packs. The design features a player action photo set against a silver prismatic background. On back is another color player photo against a background of colored silk and a large jewel. Season highlight stats and awards won are presented in both English and Spanish. The announced production run of these inserts was 8,000 sets.

		NM/M
Complete Set (36):		40.00
Common Player:		1.00
1	Robin Yount	2.50
2	Juan Gonzalez	1.25
3	Rafael Palmeiro	2.00
4	Paul Molitor	2.50
5	Roberto Alomar	1.25
6	John Olerud	1.00
7	Randy Johnson	2.50
8	Ken Griffey Jr.	4.00
9	Wade Boggs	3.00
10	Don Mattingly	3.50
11	Kirby Puckett	3.00
12	Tim Salmon	2.50
13	Frank Thomas	2.50
14	Fernando Valenzuela (Comeback Player)	1.00
15	Cal Ripken, Jr.	6.00
16	Carlos Baerga	1.00
17	Kenny Lofton	1.00

18	Cecil Fielder	1.00
19	John Burkett	1.00
20	Andres Galarraga (Comeback Player)	1.00
21	Charlie Hayes	1.00
22	Orestes Destrade	1.00
23	Jeff Conine	1.00
24	Jeff Bagwell	2.50
25	Mark Grace	1.00
26	Ryne Sandberg	3.00
27	Gregg Jefferies	1.00
28	Barry Bonds	6.00
29	Mike Piazza	3.50
30	Greg Maddux	3.00
31	Darren Daulton	1.00
32	John Kruk	1.00
33	Len Dykstra	1.00
34	Orlando Merced	1.00
35	Tony Gwynn	3.00
36	Robby Thompson	1.00

Jewels of the Crown - Retail

Using the same design, photos, graphics and card numbers, the retail version of the Jewels of the Crown insert set varies only in the silver prismatic foil background on front. While the scarcer hobby version has a diamond-shaped pattern to the foil, the retail version has numerous circles as a background pattern. The retail cards were inserted one per pack of retail product and are thus much more common than the hobby version.

		NM/M
Complete Set (36):		40.00
Common Player:		.75
1	Robin Yount	2.50
2	Juan Gonzalez	1.25
3	Rafael Palmeiro	1.25
4	Paul Molitor	2.50
5	Roberto Alomar	1.00
6	John Olerud	.75
7	Randy Johnson	2.50
8	Ken Griffey Jr.	4.00
9	Wade Boggs	3.00
10	Don Mattingly	3.50
11	Kirby Puckett	3.00
12	Tim Salmon	.75
13	Frank Thomas	2.50
14	Fernando Valenzuela (Comeback Player)	.75
15	Cal Ripken, Jr.	5.00
16	Carlos Baerga	.75
17	Kenny Lofton	.75
18	Cecil Fielder	.75
19	John Burkett	.75
20	Andres Galarraga (Comeback Player)	.75
21	Charlie Hayes	.75
22	Orestes Destrade	.75
23	Jeff Conine	.75
24	Jeff Bagwell	2.50
25	Mark Grace	.75
26	Ryne Sandberg	3.00
27	Gregg Jefferies	.75
28	Barry Bonds	5.00
29	Mike Piazza	3.50
30	Greg Maddux	3.00
31	Darren Daulton	.75
32	John Kruk	.75
33	Len Dykstra	.75
34	Orlando Merced	.75
35	Tony Gwynn	3.00
36	Robby Thompson	.75

1995 Pacific

The base cards in Pacific's Crown Collection baseball issue for 1995 feature borderless color action photos on front, graphically highlighted by the player name at bottom in gold foil and a color team logo in a baseball at lower-left. Backs have a playing field design in the background with a portrait photo at left. At right are 1994 stats, career highlights and a ghosted image of the team logo. Most back printing is in both English and Spanish. The 450 cards in the series are arranged alphabetically within team, with the

teams arranged in city-alpha order. Several chase cards series are found in the 12-card foil packs.

		NM/M
Complete Set (450):		20.00
Common Player:		.05
Pack (12):		1.00
Wax Box (36):		20.00
1	Steve Avery	.05
2	Rafael Belliard	.05
3	Jeff Blauser	.05
4	Tom Glavine	.05
5	Dave Justice	.05
6	Mike Kelly	.05
7	Roberto Kelly	.05
8	Ryan Klesko	.05
9	Mark Lemke	.05
10	Javier Lopez	.05
11	Greg Maddux	.75
12	Fred McGriff	.05
13	Greg McMichael	.05
14	Jose Oliva	.05
15	John Smoltz	.05
16	Tony Tarasco	.05
17	Brady Anderson	.05
18	Harold Baines	.05
19	Armando Benitez	.05
20	Mike Devereaux	.05
21	Leo Gomez	.05
22	Jeffrey Hammonds	.05
23	Chris Hoiles	.05
24	Ben McDonald	.05
25	Mark McLemore	.05
26	Jamie Moyer	.05
27	Mike Mussina	.40
28	Rafael Palmeiro	.50
29	Jim Poole	.05
30	Cal Ripken Jr.	2.00
31	Lee Smith	.05
32	Mark Smith	.05
33	Jose Canseco	.35
34	Roger Clemens	1.00
35	Scott Cooper	.05
36	Andre Dawson	.25
37	Tony Fossas	.05
38	Mike Greenwell	.05
39	Chris Howard	.05
40	Jose Melendez	.05
41	Nate Minchey	.05
42	Tim Naehring	.05
43	Otis Nixon	.05
44	Carlos Rodriguez	.05
45	Aaron Sele	.05
46	Lee Tinsley	.05
47	Sergio Valdez	.05
48	John Valentin	.05
49	Mo Vaughn	.05
50	Brian Anderson	.05
51	Garret Anderson	.05
52	Rod Correia	.05
53	Chad Curtis	.05
54	Mark Dalesandro	.05
55	Chili Davis	.05
56	Gary DiSarcina	.05
57	Damion Easley	.05
58	Jim Edmonds	.05
59	Jorge Fabregas	.05
60	Chuck Finley	.05
61	Bo Jackson	.10
62	Mark Langston	.05
63	Eduardo Perez	.05
64	Tim Salmon	.05
65	J.T. Snow	.05
66	Willie Banks	.05
67	Jose Bautista	.05
68	Shawon Dunston	.05
69	Kevin Foster	.05
70	Mark Grace	.05
71	Jose Guzman	.05
72	Jose Hernandez	.05
73	Blaise Ilsley	.05
74	Derrick May	.05
75	Randy Myers	.05
76	Karl Rhodes	.05
77	Kevin Roberson	.05
78	Rey Sanchez	.05
79	Sammy Sosa	.75
80	Steve Trachsel	.05
81	Eddie Zambrano	.05
82	Wilson Alvarez	.05
83	Jason Bere	.05
84	Joey Cora	.05
85	Jose DeLeon	.05
86	Alex Fernandez	.05
87	Julio Franco	.05
88	Ozzie Guillen	.05
89	Joe Hall	.05

90	Roberto Hernandez	.05
91	Darrin Jackson	.05
92	Lance Johnson	.05
93	Norberto Martin	.05
94	Jack McDowell	.05
95	Tim Raines	.05
96	Olmedo Saenz	.05
97	Frank Thomas	.60
98	Robin Ventura	.05
99	Bret Boone	.05
100	Jeff Brantley	.05
101	Jacob Brumfield	.05
102	Hector Carrasco	.05
103	Brian Dorsett	.05
104	Tony Fernandez	.05
105	Willie Greene	.05
106	Erik Hanson	.05
107	Kevin Jarvis	.05
108	Barry Larkin	.05
109	Kevin Mitchell	.05
110	Hal Morris	.05
111	Jose Rijo	.05
112	Johnny Ruffin	.05
113	Deion Sanders	.05
114	Reggie Sanders	.05
115	Sandy Alomar Jr.	.05
116	Ruben Amaro	.05
117	Carlos Baerga	.05
118	Albert Belle	.05
119	Alvaro Espinoza	.05
120	Rene Gonzales	.05
121	Wayne Kirby	.05
122	Kenny Lofton	.05
123	Candy Maldonado	.05
124	Dennis Martinez	.05
125	Eddie Murray	.60
126	Charles Nagy	.05
127	Tony Pena	.05
128	Manny Ramirez	.60
129	Paul Sorrento	.05
130	Jim Thome	.40
131	Omar Vizquel	.05
132	Dante Bichette	.05
133	Ellis Burks	.05
134	Vinny Castilla	.05
135	Marvin Freeman	.05
136	Andres Galarraga	.05
137	Joe Girardi	.05
138	Charlie Hayes	.05
139	Mike Kingery	.05
140	Nelson Liriano	.05
141	Roberto Mejia	.05
142	David Nied	.05
143	Steve Reed	.05
144	Armando Reynoso	.05
145	Bruce Ruffin	.05
146	John Vander Wal	.05
147	Walt Weiss	.05
148	Skeeter Barnes	.05
149	Tim Belcher	.05
150	Junior Felix	.05
151	Cecil Fielder	.05
152	Travis Fryman	.05
153	Kirk Gibson	.05
154	Chris Gomez	.05
155	Buddy Groom	.05
156	Chad Kreuter	.05
157	Mike Moore	.05
158	Tony Phillips	.05
159	Juan Samuel	.05
160	Mickey Tettleton	.05
161	Alan Trammell	.05
162	David Wells	.05
163	Lou Whitaker	.05
164	Kurt Abbott	.05
165	Luis Aquino	.05
166	Alex Arias	.05
167	Bret Barberie	.05
168	Jerry Browne	.05
169	Chuck Carr	.05
170	Matias Carrillo	.05
171	Greg Colbrunn	.05
172	Jeff Conine	.05
173	Carl Everett	.05
174	Robb Nen	.05
175	Yorkis Perez	.05
176	Pat Rapp	.05
177	Benito Santiago	.05
178	Gary Sheffield	.35
179	Darrell Whitmore	.05
180	Jeff Bagwell	.60
181	Kevin Bass	.05
182	Craig Biggio	.05
183	Andujar Cedeno	.05
184	Doug Drabek	.05
185	Tony Eusebio	.05
186	Steve Finley	.05
187	Luis Gonzalez	.05
188	Pete Harnisch	.05
189	John Hudek	.05
190	Orlando Miller	.05
191	James Mouton	.05
192	Roberto Petagine	.05
193	Shane Reynolds	.05
194	Greg Swindell	.05
195	Dave Veres	.05
196	Kevin Appier	.05
197	Stan Belinda	.05
198	Vince Coleman	.05
199	David Cone	.05
200	Gary Gaetti	.05
201	Greg Gagne	.05
202	Mark Gubicza	.05
203	Bob Hamelin	.05
204	Dave Henderson	.05
205	Felix Jose	.05
206	Wally Joyner	.05
207	Jose Lind	.05

208	Mike Macfarlane	.05
209	Brian McRae	.05
210	Jeff Montgomery	.05
211	Hipolito Pichardo	.05
212	Pedro Astacio	.05
213	Brett Butler	.05
214	Omar Daal	.05
215	Delino DeShields	.05
216	Darren Dreifort	.05
217	Carlos Hernandez	.05
218	Orel Hershiser	.05
219	Garey Ingram	.05
220	Eric Karros	.05
221	Ramon Martinez	.05
222	Raul Mondesi	.05
223	Jose Offerman	.05
224	Mike Piazza	1.00
225	Henry Rodriguez	.05
226	Ismael Valdes	.05
227	Tim Wallach	.05
228	Jeff Cirillo	.05
229	Alex Diaz	.05
230	Cal Eldred	.05
231	Mike Fetters	.05
232	Brian Harper	.05
233	Ted Higuera	.05
234	John Jaha	.05
235	Graeme Lloyd	.05
236	Jose Mercedes	.05
237	Jaime Navarro	.05
238	Dave Nilsson	.05
239	Jesse Orosco	.05
240	Jody Reed	.05
241	Jose Valentin	.05
242	Greg Vaughn	.05
243	Turner Ward	.05
244	Rick Aguilera	.05
245	Rich Becker	.05
246	Jim Deshaies	.05
247	Steve Dunn	.05
248	Scott Erickson	.05
249	Kent Hrbek	.05
250	Chuck Knoblauch	.05
251	Scott Leius	.05
252	David McCarty	.05
253	Pat Meares	.05
254	Pedro Munoz	.05
255	Kirby Puckett	.75
256	Carlos Pulido	.05
257	Kevin Tapani	.05
258	Matt Walbeck	.05
259	Dave Winfield	.60
260	Moises Alou	.05
261	Juan Bell	.05
262	Freddie Benavides	.05
263	Sean Berry	.05
264	Wil Cordero	.05
265	Jeff Fassero	.05
266	Darrin Fletcher	.05
267	Cliff Floyd	.05
268	Marquis Grissom	.05
269	Gil Heredia	.05
270	Ken Hill	.05
271	Pedro Martinez	.05
272	Mel Rojas	.05
273	Larry Walker	.05
274	John Wetteland	.05
275	Rondell White	.05
276	Tim Bogar	.05
277	Bobby Bonilla	.05
278	Rico Brogna	.05
279	Jeromy Burnitz	.05
280	John Franco	.05
281	Eric Hillman	.05
282	Todd Hundley	.05
283	Jeff Kent	.05
284	Mike Maddux	.05
285	Joe Orsulak	.05
286	Luis Rivera	.05
287	Bret Saberhagen	.05
288	David Segui	.05
289	Ryan Thompson	.05
290	Fernando Vina	.05
291	Jose Vizcaino	.05
292	Jim Abbott	.05
293	Wade Boggs	.75
294	Russ Davis	.05
295	Mike Gallego	.05
296	Xavier Hernandez	.05
297	Steve Howe	.05
298	Jimmy Key	.05
299	Don Mattingly	1.00
300	Terry Mulholland	.05
301	Paul O'Neill	.05
302	Luis Polonia	.05
303	Mike Stanley	.05
304	Danny Tartabull	.05
305	Randy Velarde	.05
306	Bob Wickman	.05
307	Bernie Williams	.05
308	Mark Acre	.05
309	Geronimo Berroa	.05
310	Mike Bordick	.05
311	Dennis Eckersley	.50
312	Rickey Henderson	.60
313	Stan Javier	.05
314	Miguel Jimenez	.05
315	Francisco Matos	.05
316	Mark McGwire	1.50
317	Troy Neel	.05
318	Steve Ontiveros	.05
319	Carlos Reyes	.05
320	Ruben Sierra	.05
321	Terry Steinbach	.05
322	Bob Welch	.05
323	Bobby Witt	.05
324	Larry Andersen	.05
325	Kim Batiste	.05

326	Darren Daulton	.05
327	Mariano Duncan	.05
328	Lenny Dykstra	.05
329	Jim Eisenreich	.05
330	Danny Jackson	.05
331	John Kruk	.05
332	Tony Longmire	.05
333	Tom Marsh	.05
334	Mickey Morandini	.05
335	Bobby Munoz	.05
336	Todd Pratt	.05
337	Tom Quinlan	.05
338	Kevin Stocker	.05
339	Fernando Valenzuela	.05
340	Jay Bell	.05
341	Dave Clark	.05
342	Steve Cooke	.05
343	Carlos Garcia	.05
344	Jeff King	.05
345	Jon Lieber	.05
346	Ravelo Manzanillo	.05
347	Al Martin	.05
348	Orlando Merced	.05
349	Denny Neagle	.05
350	Alejandro Pena	.05
351	Don Slaught	.05
352	Zane Smith	.05
353	Andy Van Slyke	.05
354	Rick White	.05
355	Kevin Young	.05
356	Andy Ashby	.05
357	Derek Bell	.05
358	Andy Benes	.05
359	Phil Clark	.05
360	Donnie Elliott	.05
361	Ricky Gutierrez	.05
362	Tony Gwynn	.75
363	Trevor Hoffman	.05
364	Tim Hyers	.05
365	Luis Lopez	.05
366	Jose Martinez	.05
367	Pedro A. Martinez	.05
368	Phil Plantier	.05
369	Bip Roberts	.05
370	A.J. Sager	.05
371	Jeff Tabaka	.05
372	Todd Benzinger	.05
373	Barry Bonds	2.00
374	John Burkett	.05
375	Mark Carreon	.05
376	Royce Clayton	.05
377	Pat Gomez	.05
378	Erik Johnson	.05
379	Darren Lewis	.05
380	Kirt Manwaring	.05
381	Dave Martinez	.05
382	John Patterson	.05
383	Mark Portugal	.05
384	Darryl Strawberry	.05
385	Salomon Torres	.05
386	Bill Van Landingham	.05
387	Matt Williams	.05
388	Rich Amaral	.05
389	Bobby Ayala	.05
390	Mike Blowers	.05
391	Chris Bosio	.05
392	Jay Buhner	.05
393	Jim Converse	.05
394	Tim Davis	.05
395	Felix Fermin	.05
396	Dave Fleming	.05
397	Goose Gossage	.05
398	Ken Griffey Jr.	1.00
399	Randy Johnson	.60
400	Edgar Martinez	.05
401	Tino Martinez	.05
402	Alex Rodriguez	1.50
403	Dan Wilson	.05
404	Luis Alicea	.05
405	Rene Arocha	.05
406	Bernard Gilkey	.05
407	Gregg Jefferies	.05
408	Ray Lankford	.05
409	Terry McGriff	.05
410	Omar Olivares	.05
411	Jose Oquendo	.05
412	Vicente Palacios	.05
413	Geronimo Pena	.05
414	Mike Perez	.05
415	Gerald Perry	.05
416	Ozzie Smith	.75
417	Bob Tewksbury	.05
418	Mark Whiten	.05
419	Todd Zeile	.05
420	Esteban Beltre	.05
421	Kevin Brown	.05
422	Cris Carpenter	.05
423	Will Clark	.05
424	Hector Fajardo	.05
425	Jeff Frye	.05
426	Juan Gonzalez	.30
427	Rusty Greer	.05
428	Rick Honeycutt	.05
429	David Hulse	.05
430	Manny Lee	.05
431	Junior Ortiz	.05
432	Dean Palmer	.05
433	Ivan Rodriguez	.50
434	Dan Smith	.05
435	Roberto Alomar	.15
436	Pat Borders	.05
437	Scott Brow	.05
438	Rob Butler	.05
439	Joe Carter	.05
440	Tony Castillo	.05
441	Domingo Cedeno	.05
442	Brad Cornett	.05
443	Carlos Delgado	.35

444	Alex Gonzalez	.05
445	Juan Guzman	.05
446	Darren Hall	.05
447	Paul Molitor	.60
448	John Olerud	.05
449	Robert Perez	.05
450	Devon White	.05

Gold Crown Die-Cut

A die-cut gold holographic foil crown in the background is featured in this chase set. The player's name at bottom is rendered in the same foil. Backs have a dark blue background, a portrait photo and a 1994 season recap.

		NM/M
Complete Set (20):		30.00
Common Player:		.45
1	Greg Maddux	2.50
2	Fred McGriff	.45
3	Rafael Palmeiro	1.50
4	Cal Ripken Jr.	4.50
5	Jose Canseco	1.00
6	Frank Thomas	2.00
7	Albert Belle	.45
8	Manny Ramirez	2.00
9	Andres Galarraga	.45
10	Jeff Bagwell	2.00
11	Chan Ho Park	.45
12	Raul Mondesi	.45
13	Mike Piazza	3.00
14	Kirby Puckett	2.50
15	Barry Bonds	4.50
16	Ken Griffey Jr.	3.00
17	Alex Rodriguez	3.50
18	Juan Gonzalez	1.00
19	Roberto Alomar	1.00
20	Carlos Delgado	1.25

Hot Hispanics

Acknowledging its bilingual card license and market niche, this insert set of Latinos Destacados (Hot Hispanics) features top Latin players in the majors. The series logo and a gold-foil holographic player name rise from a row of flames at bottom-front. On the reverse is another player photo, on an inferno background, along with 1994 season highlights and a large team logo.

		NM/M
Complete Set (36):		20.00
Common Player:		.25
1	Roberto Alomar	1.25
2	Moises Alou	.25
3	Wilson Alvarez	.25
4	Carlos Baerga	.25
5	Geronimo Berroa	.25
6	Jose Canseco	1.00
7	Hector Carrasco	.25
8	Wil Cordero	.25
9	Carlos Delgado	1.50
10	Damion Easley	.25
11	Tony Eusebio	.25
12	Hector Fajardo	.25
13	Andres Galarraga	.25
14	Carlos Garcia	.25
15	Chris Gomez	.25
16	Alex Gonzalez	.25
17	Juan Gonzalez	1.25
18	Luis Gonzalez	.25
19	Felix Jose	.25
20	Javier Lopez	.25

21	Luis Lopez	.25
22	Dennis Martinez	.25
23	Orlando Miller	.25
24	Raul Mondesi	.25
25	Jose Oliva	.25
26	Rafael Palmeiro	2.00
27	Yorkis Perez	.25
28	Manny Ramirez	2.50
29	Jose Rijo	.25
30	Alex Rodriguez	4.00
31	Ivan Rodriguez	2.00
32	Carlos Rodriguez	.25
33	Sammy Sosa	3.00
34	Tony Tarasco	.25
35	Ismael Valdes	.25
36	Bernie Williams	.25

Marquee Prism

Etched gold holographic foil is the background to the action photos in this insert set. Player names at bottom-front are shadowed in team colors. Backs repeat the front photo in miniature version in a box at one side that offers career stats and a highlight. On the other end is a portrait photo on a background of baseballs.

		NM/M
Complete Set (36):		22.50
Common Player:		.35
1	Jose Canseco	.65
2	Gregg Jefferies	.35
3	Fred McGriff	.35
4	Joe Carter	.35
5	Tim Salmon	.35
6	Wade Boggs	1.25
7	Dave Winfield	1.00
8	Bob Hamelin	.35
9	Cal Ripken Jr.	3.00
10	Don Mattingly	1.50
11	Juan Gonzalez	.50
12	Carlos Delgado	.65
13	Barry Bonds	3.00
14	Albert Belle	.35
15	Raul Mondesi	.35
16	Jeff Bagwell	1.00
17	Mike Piazza	1.50
18	Rafael Palmeiro	.75
19	Frank Thomas	1.00
20	Matt Williams	.35
21	Ken Griffey Jr.	2.00
22	Will Clark	.35
23	Bobby Bonilla	.35
24	Kenny Lofton	.35
25	Paul Molitor	1.00
26	Kirby Puckett	1.25
27	Dave Justice	.35
28	Jeff Conine	.35
29	Bret Boone	.35
30	Larry Walker	.35
31	Cecil Fielder	.35
32	Manny Ramirez	1.00
33	Javier Lopez	.35
34	Jimmy Key	.35
35	Andres Galarraga	.35
36	Tony Gwynn	1.25

1995 Pacific Prism

The rainbow prismatic foil background on the card fronts provides the visual punch to Pacific's premium brand cards. In a throwback to the 1950s, the cards were sold in single-card packs for $1.75. Production was limited to 2,999 cases of 36-pack boxes. Backs have a large portrait photo on a conventionally printed rainbow background. In keeping with the company's license, the 1994 season summary printed at bottom on back is in both English and Spanish. One checklist, team or Pacific logo was inserted into each pack to protect the Prism card.

		NM/M
Complete Set (144):		65.00
Common Player:		.25
Pack (2):		.60
Wax Box (36):		12.50
1	Dave Justice	.25
2	Ryan Klesko	.25
3	Javier Lopez	.25
4	Greg Maddux	2.00
5	Fred McGriff	.25
6	Tony Tarasco	.25
7	Jeffrey Hammonds	.25
8	Mike Mussina	.75
9	Rafael Palmeiro	1.25
10	Cal Ripken Jr.	5.00
11	Lee Smith	.25
12	Roger Clemens	2.50
13	Scott Cooper	.25
14	Mike Greenwell	.25
15	Carlos Rodriguez	.25
16	Mo Vaughn	.25
17	Chili Davis	.25
18	Jim Edmonds	.25
19	Jorge Fabregas	.25
20	Bo Jackson	.35
21	Tim Salmon	.25
22	Mark Grace	.25
23	Jose Guzman	.25
24	Randy Myers	.25
25	Rey Sanchez	.25
26	Sammy Sosa	2.50
27	Wilson Alvarez	.25
28	Julio Franco	.25
29	Ozzie Guillen	.25
30	Jack McDowell	.25
31	Frank Thomas	1.50
32	Bret Boone	.25
33	Barry Larkin	.25
34	Hal Morris	.25
35	Jose Rijo	.25
36	Deion Sanders	.25
37	Carlos Baerga	.25
38	Albert Belle	.25
39	Kenny Lofton	.25
40	Dennis Martinez	.25
41	Manny Ramirez	1.50
42	Omar Vizquel	.25
43	Dante Bichette	.25
44	Marvin Freeman	.25
45	Andres Galarraga	.25
46	Mike Kingery	.25
47	Danny Bautista	.25
48	Cecil Fielder	.25
49	Travis Fryman	.25
50	Tony Phillips	.25
51	Alan Trammell	.25
52	Lou Whitaker	.25
53	Alex Arias	.25
54	Bret Barberie	.25
55	Jeff Conine	.25
56	Charles Johnson	.25
57	Gary Sheffield	.65
58	Jeff Bagwell	1.50
59	Craig Biggio	.25
60	Doug Drabek	.25
61	Tony Eusebio	.25
62	Luis Gonzalez	.25
63	David Cone	.25
64	Bob Hamelin	.25
65	Felix Jose	.25
66	Wally Joyner	.25
67	Brian McRae	.25
68	Brett Butler	.25
69	Garey Ingram	.25
70	Ramon Martinez	.25
71	Raul Mondesi	.25
72	Mike Piazza	2.50
73	Henry Rodriguez	.25
74	Ricky Bones	.25
75	Pat Listach	.25
76	Dave Nilsson	.25
77	Jose Valentin	.25
78	Rick Aguilera	.25
79	Denny Hocking	.25
80	Shane Mack	.25
81	Pedro Munoz	.25
82	Kirby Puckett	2.00
83	Dave Winfield	1.50
84	Moises Alou	.25
85	Wil Cordero	.25
86	Cliff Floyd	.25
87	Marquis Grissom	.25
88	Pedro Martinez	1.50
89	Larry Walker	.25
90	Bobby Bonilla	.25
91	Jeromy Burnitz	.25
92	John Franco	.25
93	Jeff Kent	.25
94	Jose Vizcaino	.25
95	Wade Boggs	2.00
96	Jimmy Key	.25
97	Don Mattingly	2.50
98	Paul O'Neill	.25
99	Luis Polonia	.25
100	Danny Tartabull	.25
101	Geronimo Berroa	.25
102	Rickey Henderson	1.50
103	Ruben Sierra	.25
104	Terry Steinbach	.25
105	Darren Daulton	.25
106	Mariano Duncan	.25
107	Lenny Dykstra	.25
108	Mike Lieberthal	.25
109	Tony Longmire	.25
110	Tom Marsh	.25
111	Jay Bell	.25
112	Carlos Garcia	.25
113	Orlando Merced	.25
114	Andy Van Slyke	.25
115	Derek Bell	.25
116	Tony Gwynn	2.00
117	Luis Lopez	.25
118	Bip Roberts	.25
119	Rod Beck	.25
120	Barry Bonds	5.00
121	Darryl Strawberry	.25
122	Bill Van Landingham	.25
123	Matt Williams	.25
124	Jay Buhner	.25
125	Felix Fermin	.25
126	Ken Griffey Jr.	3.00
127	Randy Johnson	1.50
128	Edgar Martinez	.25
129	Alex Rodriguez	4.00
130	Rene Arocha	.25
131	Gregg Jefferies	.25
132	Mike Perez	.25
133	Ozzie Smith	2.00
134	Jose Canseco	.65
135	Will Clark	.25
136	Juan Gonzalez	1.00
137	Ivan Rodriguez	1.25
138	Roberto Alomar	.50
139	Joe Carter	.25
140	Carlos Delgado	.75
141	Alex Gonzalez	.25
142	Juan Guzman	.25
143	Paul Molitor	1.50
144	John Olerud	.25

Team Logos

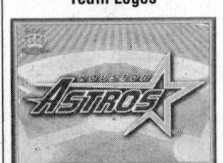

Inserted one card per pack to provide some protection to the Prism card, this was a checklist, team or Pacific logo card. The large color logos are on a background of a playing field. Backs have a short English/Spanish history of the team.

		NM/M
Complete Set (31):		2.00
Common Player:		.10
1	Baltimore Orioles	.10
2	Boston Red Sox	.10
3	California Angels	.10
4	Chicago White Sox	.10
5	Cleveland Indians	.10
6	Detroit Tigers	.10
7	Kansas City Royals	.10
8	Milwaukee Brewers	.10
9	Minnesota Twins	.10
10	New York Yankees	.10
11	Oakland Athletics	.10
12	Seattle Mariners	.10
13	Texas Rangers	.10
14	Toronto Blue Jays	.10
15	Atlanta Braves	.10
16	Chicago Cubs	.10
17	Cincinnati Reds	.10
18	Colorado Rockies	.10
19	Florida Marlins	.10
20	Houston Astros	.10
21	Los Angeles Dodgers	.10
22	Montreal Expos	.10
23	New York Mets	.10
24	Philadelphia Phillies	.10
25	Pittsburgh Pirates	.10
26	St. Louis Cardinals	.10
27	San Diego Padres	.10
28	San Francisco Giants	.10
1	Checklist 1-72	.05
2	Checklist 73-144	.05
---	Pacific Logo Card	.05

Mariners Memories

To commemorate the M's magical 1995 season leading up to the A.L. Western Division pennant and the American League championship series, Pacific issued this boxed set. The first 17 cards in the set depict post-season action, with backs done in newspaper style. The rest of the set features the individual players in borderless action photos on front and smaller color portraits on back. All cards feature silver-foil highlights on front. The set was sold in a team-colors cardboard box. The set was released in late December and includes full 1995 stats for the players.

		NM/M
Complete Set (50):		10.00
Common Player:		.25
1	Griffey slams M's to brink (Ken Griffey Jr.)	.50
2	Mariners clinch tie in Texas (Vince Coleman)	.10
3	Mariners win the West (Luis Sojo)	.10
4	At last, something to celebrate (Randy Johnson)	.25
5	Johnson stands tall (Randy Johnson)	.25
6	Griffey has big debut (Ken Griffey Jr.)	.50
7	Tino ignites Mariners (Edgar Martinez, Tino Martinez)	.10
8	Mariners tie Yankee series (Edgar Martinez)	.10
9	Griffey scores winning run (Ken Griffey Jr.)	.50
10	Thunder in the Kingdome	.10
11	Series win ends years of futility	.10
12	Bob who? beats Cleveland (Bob Wolcott)	.10
13	Buhner rocks Cleveland (Jay Buhner)	.10
14	Johnson salutes Kingdome crowd (Randy Johnson)	.25
15	Fans give their all (Lou Piniella)	.10
16	Cora eludes tag (Joey Cora)	.10
17	Voice of M's calls winner (Dave Niehaus)	.10
18	Rich Amaral	.10
19	Bobby Ayala	.10
20	Tim Belcher	.10
21	Andy Benes	.10
22	Mike Blowers	.10
23	Chris Bosio	.10
24	Darren Bragg	.10
25	Jay Buhner	.25
26	Rafael Carmona	.10
27	Norm Charlton	.10
28	Vince Coleman	.10
29	Joey Cora	.10
30	Alex Diaz	.10
31	Felix Fermin	.10
32	Ken Griffey Jr.	3.00
33	Lee Guetterman	.10
34	Randy Johnson	3.00
35	Edgar Martinez	.25
36	Tino Martinez	.25
37	Jeff Nelson	.10
38	Warren Newson	.10
39	Greg Pirkl	.10
40	Arquimedez Pozo	.10
41	Bill Risley	.10
42	Alex Rodriquez (Rodriguez)	5.00
43	Luis Sojo	.10
44	Doug Strange	.10
45	Salomon Torres	.10
46	Bob Wells	.10
47	Chris Widger	.10
48	Dan Wilson	.10
49	Bob Wolcott	.10
50	Lou Piniella	.25

1996 Pacific Crown Collection

Pacific's base set for 1996 features 450 gold-foil enhanced cards. Fronts have borderless game-action photos with the issuer's logo in an upper corner and the player's name at bottom center in gold. Horizontal backs have a portrait photo at right, career highlights in both English and Spanish at left, and 1995 stats at top. Cards were sold in 12-card foil packs which could include one of six types of insert cards.

		NM/M
Complete Set (450):		17.50
Common Player:		.05
Pack (12):		1.00
Wax Box (36):		25.00
1	Steve Avery	.05
2	Ryan Klesko	.05
3	Pedro Borbon	.05
4	Chipper Jones	1.00
5	Kent Mercker	.05
6	Greg Maddux	1.00
7	Greg McMichael	.05
8	Mark Wohlers	.05
9	Fred McGriff	.05
10	John Smoltz	.05
11	Rafael Belliard	.05
12	Mark Lemke	.05
13	Tom Glavine	.30
14	Javier Lopez	.05
15	Jeff Blauser	.05
16	Dave Justice	.05
17	Marquis Grissom	.05
18	Greg Maddux (NL Cy Young)	.50
19	Randy Myers	.05
20	Scott Servais	.05
21	Sammy Sosa	1.00
22	Kevin Foster	.05
23	Jose Hernandez	.05
24	Jim Bullinger	.05
25	Mike Perez	.05
26	Shawon Dunston	.05
27	Rey Sanchez	.05
28	Frank Castillo	.05
29	Jaime Navarro	.05
30	Brian McRae	.05
31	Mark Grace	.05
32	Roberto Rivera	.05
33	Luis Gonzalez	.05
34	Hector Carrasco	.05
35	Bret Boone	.05
36	Thomas Howard	.05
37	Hal Morris	.05
38	John Smiley	.05
39	Jeff Brantley	.05
40	Barry Larkin	.05
41	Mariano Duncan	.05
42	Xavier Hernandez	.05
43	Pete Schourek	.05
44	Reggie Sanders	.05
45	Dave Burba	.05
46	Jeff Branson	.05
47	Mark Portugal	.05
48	Ron Gant	.05
49	Benito Santiago	.05
50	Barry Larkin (NL MVP)	.05
51	Steve Reed	.05
52	Kevin Ritz	.05
53	Dante Bichette	.05
54	Darren Holmes	.05
55	Ellis Burks	.05
56	Walt Weiss	.05
57	Armando Reynoso	.05
58	Vinny Castilla	.05
59	Jason Bates	.05
60	Mike Kingery	.05
61	Bryan Rekar	.05
62	Curtis Leskanic	.05
63	Bret Saberhagen	.05
64	Andres Galarraga	.05
65	Larry Walker	.05
66	Joe Girardi	.05
67	Quilvio Veras	.05
68	Robb Nen	.05
69	Mario Diaz	.05
70	Chuck Carr	.05
71	Alex Arias	.05
72	Pat Rapp	.05
73	Rich Garces	.05
74	Kurt Abbott	.05
75	Andre Dawson	.25
76	Greg Colbrunn	.05
77	John Burkett	.05
78	Terry Pendleton	.05
79	Jesus Tavarez	.05
80	Charles Johnson	.05
81	Yorkis Perez	.05
82	Jeff Conine	.05
83	Gary Sheffield	.45
84	Brian Hunter	.05
85	Derrick May	.05
86	Greg Swindell	.05
87	Derek Bell	.05
88	Dave Veres	.05
89	Jeff Bagwell	.75
90	Todd Jones	.05
91	Orlando Miller	.05
92	Pedro A. Martinez	.05
93	Tony Eusebio	.05
94	Craig Biggio	.05
95	Shane Reynolds	.05
96	James Mouton	.05
97	Doug Drabek	.05
98	Dave Magadan	.05
99	Ricky Gutierrez	.05
100	Hideo Nomo	.50
101	Delino DeShields	.05
102	Tom Candiotti	.05
103	Mike Piazza	1.50
104	Ramon Martinez	.05
105	Pedro Astacio	.05
106	Chad Fonville	.05
107	Raul Mondesi	.05
108	Ismael Valdes	.05
109	Jose Offerman	.05
110	Todd Worrell	.05
111	Eric Karros	.05
112	Brett Butler	.05
113	Juan Castro	.05
114	Roberto Kelly	.05
115	Omar Daal	.05
116	Antonio Osuna	.05
117	Hideo Nomo (NL Rookie of Year)	.50
118	Mike Lansing	.05
119	Mel Rojas	.05
120	Sean Berry	.05
121	David Segui	.05
122	Tavo Alvarez	.05
123	Pedro Martinez	.75
124	F.P. Santangelo RC	.05
125	Rondell White	.05
126	Cliff Floyd	.05
127	Henry Rodriguez	.05
128	Tony Tarasco	.05
129	Yamil Benitez	.05
130	Carlos Perez	.05
131	Wil Cordero	.05
132	Jeff Fassero	.05
133	Moises Alou	.05
134	John Franco	.05
135	Rico Brogna	.05
136	Dave Mlicki	.05
137	Bill Pulsipher	.05
138	Jose Vizcaino	.05
139	Carl Everett	.05
140	Edgardo Alfonzo	.05
141	Bobby Jones	.05
142	Alberto Castillo	.05
143	Joe Orsulak	.05
144	Jeff Kent	.05
145	Ryan Thompson	.05
146	Jason Isringhausen	.05
147	Todd Hundley	.05
148	Alex Ochoa	.05
149	Charlie Hayes	.05
150	Michael Mimbs	.05
151	Darren Daulton	.05
152	Toby Borland	.05
153	Andy Van Slyke	.05
154	Mickey Morandini	.05
155	Sid Fernandez	.05
156	Tom Marsh	.05
157	Kevin Stocker	.05
158	Paul Quantrill	.05
159	Gregg Jefferies	.05
160	Ricky Bottalico	.05
161	Lenny Dykstra	.05
162	Mark Whiten	.05
163	Tyler Green	.05
164	Jim Eisenreich	.05
165	Heathcliff Slocumb	.05
166	Esteban Loaiza	.05
167	Rich Aude	.05
168	Jason Christiansen	.05
169	Ramon Morel	.05
170	Orlando Merced	.05
171	Paul Wagner	.05
172	Jeff King	.05
173	Jay Bell	.05
174	Jacob Brumfield	.05
175	Nelson Liriano	.05
176	Dan Miceli	.05
177	Carlos Garcia	.05
178	Denny Neagle	.05
179	Angelo Encarnacion	.05
180	Al Martin	.05
181	Midre Cummings	.05
182	Eddie Williams	.05
183	Roberto Petagine	.05
184	Tony Gwynn	1.00
185	Andy Ashby	.05
186	Melvin Nieves	.05
187	Phil Clark	.05
188	Brad Ausmus	.05
189	Bip Roberts	.05
190	Fernando Valenzuela	.05
191	Marc Newfield	.05
192	Steve Finley	.05
193	Trevor Hoffman	.05
194	Andujar Cedeno	.05
195	Jody Reed	.05
196	Ken Caminiti	.05
197	Joey Hamilton	.05
198	Tony Gwynn (NL Batting Champ)	.50
199	Shawn Barton	.05
200	Deion Sanders	.05
201	Rikkert Faneyte	.05
202	Barry Bonds	2.50
203	Matt Williams	.05
204	Jose Bautista	.05
205	Mark Leiter	.05
206	Mark Carreon	.05
207	Robby Thompson	.05
208	Terry Mulholland	.05
209	Rod Beck	.05
210	Royce Clayton	.05
211	J.R. Phillips	.05
212	Kirt Manwaring	.05
213	Glenallen Hill	.05
214	William Van Landingham	.05
215	Scott Cooper	.05
216	Bernard Gilkey	.05
217	Allen Watson	.05

218	Donovan Osborne	.05
219	Ray Lankford	.05
220	Tony Fossas	.05
221	Tom Pagnozzi	.05
222	John Mabry	.05
223	Tripp Cromer	.05
224	Mark Petkovsek	.05
225	Mike Morgan	.05
226	Ozzie Smith	1.00
227	Tom Henke	.05
228	Jose Oquendo	.05
229	Brian Jordan	.05
230	Cal Ripken Jr.	2.50
231	Scott Erickson	.05
232	Harold Baines	.05
233	Jeff Manto	.05
234	Jesse Orosco	.05
235	Jeffrey Hammonds	.05
236	Brady Anderson	.05
237	Manny Alexander	.05
238	Chris Hoiles	.05
239	Rafael Palmeiro	.60
240	Ben McDonald	.05
241	Curtis Goodwin	.05
242	Bobby Bonilla	.60
243	Mike Mussina	.60
244	Kevin Brown	.05
245	Armando Benitez	.05
246	Jose Canseco	.50
247	Erik Hanson	.05
248	Mo Vaughn	.05
249	Tim Naehring	.05
250	Vaughn Eshelman	.05
251	Mike Greenwell	.05
252	Troy O'Leary	.05
253	Tim Wakefield	.05
254	Dwayne Hosey	.05
255	John Valentin	.05
256	Rick Aguilera	.05
257	Mike MacFarlane	.05
258	Roger Clemens	1.50
259	Luis Alicea	.05
260	Mo Vaughn (AL MVP)	.05
261	Mark Langston	.05
262	Jim Edmonds	.05
263	Rod Correia	.05
264	Tim Salmon	.05
265	J.T. Snow	.05
266	Orlando Palmeiro	.05
267	Jorge Fabregas	.05
268	Jim Abbott	.05
269	Eduardo Perez	.05
270	Lee Smith	.05
271	Gary DiSarcina	.05
272	Damion Easley	.05
273	Tony Phillips	.05
274	Garret Anderson	.05
275	Chuck Finley	.05
276	Chili Davis	.05
277	Lance Johnson	.05
278	Alex Fernandez	.05
279	Robin Ventura	.05
280	Chris Snopek	.05
281	Brian Keyser	.05
282	Lyle Mouton	.05
283	Luis Andujar RC	.05
284	Tim Raines	.05
285	Larry Thomas	.05
286	Ozzie Guillen	.05
287	Frank Thomas	.75
288	Roberto Hernandez	.05
289	Dave Martinez	.05
290	Ray Durham	.05
291	Ron Karkovice	.05
292	Wilson Alvarez	.05
293	Omar Vizquel	.05
294	Eddie Murray	.75
295	Sandy Alomar	.05
296	Orel Hershiser	.05
297	Jose Mesa	.05
298	Julian Tavarez	.05
299	Dennis Martinez	.05
300	Carlos Baerga	.05
301	Manny Ramirez	.75
302	Jim Thome	.60
303	Kenny Lofton	.05
304	Tony Pena	.05
305	Alvaro Espinoza	.05
306	Paul Sorrento	.05
307	Albert Belle	.05
308	Danny Bautista	.05
309	Chris Gomez	.05
310	Jose Lima	.05
311	Phil Nevin	.05
312	Alan Trammell	.05
313	Chad Curtis	.05
314	John Flaherty	.05
315	Travis Fryman	.05
316	Todd Steverson	.05
317	Brian Bohanon	.05
318	Lou Whitaker	.05
319	Bobby Higginson	.05
320	Steve Rodriguez	.05
321	Cecil Fielder	.05
322	Felipe Lira	.05
323	Juan Samuel	.05
324	Bob Hamelin	.05
325	Tom Goodwin	.05
326	Johnny Damon	.25
327	Hipolito Pichardo	.05
328	Dilson Torres	.05
329	Kevin Appier	.05
330	Mark Gubicza	.05
331	Jon Nunnally	.05
332	Gary Gaetti	.05
333	Brent Mayne	.05
334	Brent Cookson	.05
335	Tom Gordon	.05

336	Wally Joyner	.05
337	Greg Gagne	.05
338	Fernando Vina	.05
339	Joe Oliver	.05
340	John Jaha	.05
341	Jeff Cirillo	.05
342	Pat Listach	.05
343	Dave Nilsson	.05
344	Steve Sparks	.05
345	Ricky Bones	.05
346	David Hulse	.05
347	Scott Karl	.05
348	Darryl Hamilton	.05
349	B.J. Surhoff	.05
350	Angel Miranda	.05
351	Sid Roberson	.05
352	Matt Mieske	.05
353	Jose Valentin RC	.05
354	Matt Lawton RC	.25
355	Eddie Guardado	.05
356	Brad Radke	.05
357	Pedro Munoz	.05
358	Scott Stahoviak	.05
359	Erik Schullstrom	.05
360	Pat Meares	.05
361	Marty Cordova	.05
362	Scott Leius	.05
363	Matt Walbeck	.05
364	Rich Becker	.05
365	Kirby Puckett	1.00
366	Oscar Munoz	.05
367	Chuck Knoblauch	.05
368	Marty Cordova (AL Rookie of Year)	.05
369	Bernie Williams	.05
370	Mike Stanley	.05
371	Andy Pettitte	.25
372	Jack McDowell	.05
373	Sterling Hitchcock	.05
374	David Cone	.05
375	Randy Velarde	.05
376	Don Mattingly	1.50
377	Melido Perez	.05
378	Wade Boggs	1.00
379	Ruben Sierra	.05
380	Tony Fernandez	.05
381	John Wetteland	.05
382	Mariano Rivera	.15
383	Derek Jeter	2.50
384	Paul O'Neill	.05
385	Mark McGwire	2.00
386	Scott Brosius	.05
387	Don Wengert	.05
388	Terry Steinbach	.05
389	Brent Gates	.05
390	Craig Paquette	.05
391	Mike Bordick	.05
392	Ariel Prieto	.05
393	Dennis Eckersley	.65
394	Carlos Reyes	.05
395	Todd Stottlemyre	.05
396	Rickey Henderson	.75
397	Geronimo Berroa	.05
398	Steve Ontiveros	.05
399	Mike Gallego	.05
400	Stan Javier	.05
401	Randy Johnson	.75
402	Norm Charlton	.05
403	Mike Blowers	.05
404	Tino Martinez	.05
405	Dan Wilson	.05
406	Andy Benes	.05
407	Alex Diaz	.05
408	Edgar Martinez	.05
409	Chris Bosio	.05
410	Ken Griffey Jr.	1.50
411	Luis Sojo	.05
412	Bob Wolcott	.05
413	Vince Coleman	.05
414	Rich Amaral	.05
415	Jay Buhner	.05
416	Alex Rodriguez	2.00
417	Joey Cora	.05
418	Randy Johnson (AL Cy Young)	.25
419	Edgar Martinez (AL Batting Champ)	.05
420	Ivan Rodriguez	.65
421	Mark McLemore	.05
422	Mickey Tettleton	.05
423	Juan Gonzalez	.40
424	Will Clark	.05
425	Kevin Gross	.05
426	Dean Palmer	.05
427	Kenny Rogers	.05
428	Bob Tewksbury	.05
429	Benji Gil	.05
430	Jeff Russell	.05
431	Rusty Greer	.05
432	Roger Pavlik	.05
433	Esteban Beltre	.05
434	Otis Nixon	.05
435	Paul Molitor	.75
436	Carlos Delgado	.50
437	Ed Sprague	.05
438	Juan Guzman	.05
439	Domingo Cedeno	.05
440	Pat Hentgen	.05
441	Tomas Perez	.05
442	John Olerud	.05
443	Shawn Green	.25
444	Al Leiter	.05
445	Joe Carter	.05
446	Robert Perez	.05
447	Devon White	.05
448	Tony Castillo	.05
449	Alex Gonzalez	.05
450	Roberto Alomar	.20
450p	Roberto Alomar (Unmarked promo card, "Games: 128" on back.)	1.50

Cramer's Choice

One of the most unusually shaped baseball cards of all time is the Cramer's Choice insert set from the 1996 Pacific Crown Collection. The set features the 10 best players as chosen by Pacific founder and president, Mike Cramer. Cards are in a die-cut pyramidal design 3-1/2" tall and 2-1/2" at the base. The player picture on front is set against a silver-foil background, while the player name and other information is in gold foil on a faux marble base; the effect is a simulation of a trophy. Backs repeat the marbled background and have a bilingual justification from Cramer concerning his choice of the player as one of the 10 best. Average insertion rate is one card per case (720 packs). Cards are numbered with a "CC" prefix.

		NM/M
Complete Set (10):		150.00
Common Player:		6.00
1	Roberto Alomar	7.50
2	Wade Boggs	15.00
3	Cal Ripken Jr.	30.00
4	Greg Maddux	15.00
5	Frank Thomas	12.50
6	Tony Gwynn	15.00
7	Mike Piazza	20.00
8	Ken Griffey Jr.	25.00
9	Manny Ramirez	12.50
10	Edgar Martinez	6.00

Estrellas Latinas

Three dozen of the best contemporary Latino ballplayers are honored in this chase set. Cards feature action photos silhouetted on a black background shot through with gold-foil streaks and stars. The player name, set and insert set logos are in gold at left. Backs have a portrait photo and English/Spanish career summary. The Latino Stars insert cards are inserted at an average rate of one per nine packs; about four per foil box. Cards are numbered with an "EL" prefix.

		NM/M
Complete Set (36):		16.00
Common Player:		.25
1	Roberto Alomar	.50
2	Moises Alou	.25
3	Carlos Baerga	.25
4	Geronimo Berroa	.25
5	Ricky Bones	.25
6	Bobby Bonilla	.25
7	Jose Canseco	.65
8	Vinny Castilla	.25
9	Pedro Martinez	1.50
10	John Valentin	.25
11	Andres Galarraga	.25
12	Juan Gonzalez	.75
13	Ozzie Guillen	.25
14	Esteban Loaiza	.25
15	Javier Lopez	.25
16	Dennis Martinez	.25

17	Edgar Martinez	.25
18	Tino Martinez	.25
19	Orlando Merced	.25
20	Jose Mesa	.25
21	Raul Mondesi	.25
22	Jaime Navarro	.25
23	Rafael Palmeiro	.75
24	Carlos Perez	.25
25	Manny Ramirez	1.50
26	Alex Rodriguez	3.50
27	Ivan Rodriguez	1.25
28	David Segui	.25
29	Ruben Sierra	.25
30	Sammy Sosa	2.00
31	Julian Tavarez	.25
32	Ismael Valdes	.25
33	Fernando Valenzuela	.25
34	Quilvio Veras	.25
35	Omar Vizquel	.25
36	Bernie Williams	.25

Gold Crown Die-Cuts

One of Pacific's most popular inserts of the previous year returns in 1996. The Gold Crown die-cuts have the top of the card cut away to form a gold-foil crown design with an action photo below. The player's name is also in gold foil. Backs repeat the gold crown design at top, have a portrait photo at lower-right and a few words about the player, in both English and Spanish. Insertion rate was advertised as one per 37 packs, on average. Cards are numbered with a "DC" prefix.

		NM/M
Complete Set (36):		45.00
Common Player:		.75
1	Roberto Alomar	1.00
2	Will Clark	.75
3	Johnny Damon	1.00
4	Don Mattingly	2.50
5	Edgar Martinez	.75
6	Manny Ramirez	1.50
7	Mike Piazza	2.50
8	Quilvio Veras	.75
9	Rickey Henderson	1.50
10	Jeff Bagwell	1.50
11	Andres Galarraga	.75
12	Tim Salmon	.75
13	Ken Griffey Jr.	2.50
14	Sammy Sosa	2.00
15	Cal Ripken Jr.	4.50
16	Raul Mondesi	.75
17	Jose Canseco	1.00
18	Frank Thomas	1.50
19	Hideo Nomo	1.00
20	Wade Boggs	2.00
21	Reggie Sanders	.75
22	Carlos Baerga	.75
23	Mo Vaughn	.75
24	Ivan Rodriguez	1.25
25	Kirby Puckett	2.00
26	Albert Belle	.75
27	Vinny Castilla	.75
28	Greg Maddux	2.00
29	Dante Bichette	.75
30	Deion Sanders	.75
31	Chipper Jones	2.00
32	Cecil Fielder	.75
33	Randy Johnson	1.50
34	Mark McGwire	3.50
35	Tony Gwynn	2.00
36	Barry Bonds	4.50

Hometown of the Players

The hometown roots of 20 top players are examined in this chase set. Fronts have action photos with large areas of the background replaced with textured gold foil, including solid and outline versions of the player's name. Backs have a portrait photo, a representation of the player's native flag and a few words about his hometown. Card numbers have an "HP" prefix and are inserted at an average rate of one per 18 packs; about two per box.

		NM/M
Complete Set (20):		15.00
Common Player:		.50
1	Mike Piazza	1.50
2	Greg Maddux	1.00
3	Tony Gwynn	1.00
4	Carlos Baerga	.50
5	Don Mattingly	1.50
6	Cal Ripken Jr.	2.50
7	Chipper Jones	1.00
8	Andres Galarraga	.50
9	Manny Ramirez	.75
10	Roberto Alomar	.60
11	Ken Griffey Jr.	1.50
12	Jose Canseco	.60
13	Frank Thomas	.75
14	Vinny Castilla	.50
15	Roberto Kelly	.50
16	Dennis Martinez	.50
17	Kirby Puckett	1.00
18	Raul Mondesi	.50
19	Hideo Nomo	.60
20	Edgar Martinez	.50

Milestones

A textured metallic blue-foil background is featured on this insert set. Behind the player action photo is a spider's web design with flying baseballs, team logo and a number representing the milestone. The player's name is in purple foil, outlined in white, vertically at right. Backs have a portrait photo and bi-lingual description of the milestone. Average insertion rate for this insert series is one per 37 packs. Cards are numbered with a "M" prefix.

		NM/M
Complete Set (10):		12.50
Common Player:		.50
1	Albert Belle	.50
2	Don Mattingly	2.25
3	Tony Gwynn	2.00
4	Jose Canseco	1.00
5	Marty Cordova	.50
6	Wade Boggs	2.00
7	Greg Maddux	2.00
8	Eddie Murray	1.50
9	Ken Griffey Jr.	2.50
10	Cal Ripken Jr.	3.00

October Moments

Post-season baseball has never been better represented on a card than in Pacific's "October Moments" chase set. Action photos are set against a background of a stadium decked in the traditional

Fall Classic bunting, all rendered in metallic copper foil. At bottom is a textured silver strip with the player name in copper and a swirl of fallen leaves. Backs have a repeat of the leaves and bunting themes with a player portrait at center and English/Spanish description of his October heroics. These cards are found at an average rate of once per 37 packs. Cards are numbered with an "OM" prefix.

		NM/M
Complete Set (20):		30.00
Common Player:		.60
1	Carlos Baerga	.60
2	Albert Belle	.75
3	Dante Bichette	.60
4	Jose Canseco	1.25
5	Tom Glavine	1.00
6	Ken Griffey Jr.	5.00
7	Randy Johnson	2.50
8	Chipper Jones	3.50
9	Dave Justice	.60
10	Ryan Klesko	.60
11	Kenny Lofton	.60
12	Javier Lopez	.60
13	Greg Maddux	3.50
14	Edgar Martinez	.60
15	Don Mattingly	4.00
16	Hideo Nomo	1.25
17	Mike Piazza	4.00
18	Manny Ramirez	2.50
19	Reggie Sanders	.60
20	Jim Thome	1.50

1996 Pacific Prism

Only the best in baseball make the cut for the Prism checklist. Sold in one-card foil packs the cards feature action photos set against an etched silver-foil background highlighted by slashes approximating team colors. Backs are conventionally printed in a horizontal format with a player portrait photo at left center on a purple background. A short 1995 season recap is feature in both English and Spanish. Card numbers are prefixed with a "P."

		NM/M
Complete Set (144):		50.00
Common Player:		.35
Golds:		1.5X
Pack (2):		.65
Wax Box (36):		20.00
1	Tom Glavine	.75
2	Chipper Jones	2.00
3	David Justice	.35
4	Ryan Klesko	.35
5	Javier Lopez	.35
6	Greg Maddux	2.00
7	Fred McGriff	.35
8	Frank Castillo	.35
9	Luis Gonzalez	.35
10	Mark Grace	.35
11	Brian McRae	.35
12	Jaime Navarro	.35
13	Sammy Sosa	2.00
14	Bret Boone	.35
15	Ron Gant	.35
16	Barry Larkin	.35
17	Reggie Sanders	.35
18	Benito Santiago	.35
19	Dante Bichette	.35
20	Vinny Castilla	.35
21	Andres Galarraga	.35
22	Bryan Rekar	.35
23	Roberto Alomar	.35
23p	Roberto Alomar ("Azulejos" rather than "Los Azulajos" on back, unmarked promo card.)	1.00
24	Jeff Conine	.35
25	Andre Dawson	.50
26	Charles Johnson	.35
27	Gary Sheffield	1.00
28	Quilvio Veras	.35
29	Jeff Bagwell	1.50
30	Derek Bell	.35
31	Craig Biggio	.35
32	Tony Eusebio	.35
33	Karim Garcia	.35

34 Eric Karros .35
35 Ramon Martinez .35
36 Raul Mondesi .35
37 Hideo Nomo 1.00
38 Mike Piazza 3.00
39 Ismael Valdes .35
40 Moises Alou .35
41 Wil Cordero .35
42 Pedro Martinez 1.50
43 Mel Rojas .35
44 David Segui .35
45 Edgardo Alfonzo .35
46 Rico Brogna .35
47 John Franco .35
48 Jason Isringhausen .35
49 Jose Vizcaino .35
50 Ricky Bottalico .35
51 Darren Daulton .35
52 Lenny Dykstra .35
53 Tyler Green .35
54 Gregg Jefferies .35
55 Jay Bell .35
56 Jason Christiansen .35
57 Carlos Garcia .35
58 Esteban Loaiza .35
59 Orlando Merced .35
60 Andujar Cedeno .35
61 Tony Gwynn 2.00
62 Melvin Nieves .35
63 Phil Plantier .35
64 Fernando Valenzuela .35
65 Barry Bonds 4.50
66 J.R. Phillips .35
67 Deion Sanders .35
68 Matt Williams .35
69 Bernard Gilkey .35
70 Tom Henke .35
71 Brian Jordan .35
72 Ozzie Smith 2.00
73 Manny Alexander .35
74 Bobby Bonilla .35
75 Mike Mussina 1.00
76 Rafael Palmeiro 1.00
77 Cal Ripken Jr. 4.50
78 Jose Canseco 1.00
79 Roger Clemens 2.50
80 John Valentin .35
81 Mo Vaughn .35
82 Tim Wakefield .35
83 Garret Anderson .35
84 Damion Easley .35
85 Jim Edmonds .35
86 Tim Salmon .35
87 Wilson Alvarez .35
88 Alex Fernandez .35
89 Ozzie Guillen .35
90 Roberto Hernandez .35
91 Frank Thomas 1.50
92 Robin Ventura .35
93 Carlos Baerga .35
94 Albert Belle .35
95 Kenny Lofton .35
96 Dennis Martinez .35
97 Eddie Murray 1.50
98 Manny Ramirez 1.50
99 Omar Vizquel .35
100 Chad Curtis .35
101 Cecil Fielder .35
102 Felipe Lira .35
103 Alan Trammell .35
104 Kevin Appier .35
105 Johnny Damon .35
106 Gary Gaetti .35
107 Wally Joyner .35
108 Ricky Bones .35
109 John Jaha .35
110 B.J. Surhoff .35
111 Jose Valentin .35
112 Fernando Vina .35
113 Marty Cordova .35
114 Chuck Knoblauch .35
115 Scott Leius .35
116 Pedro Munoz .35
117 Kirby Puckett 2.00
118 Wade Boggs 2.00
119 Don Mattingly 2.50
120 Jack McDowell .35
121 Paul O'Neill .35
122 Ruben Rivera .35
123 Bernie Williams .35
124 Geronimo Berroa .35
125 Rickey Henderson 1.50
126 Mark McGwire 3.50
127 Terry Steinbach .35
128 Danny Tartabull .35
129 Jay Buhner .35
130 Joey Cora .35
131 Ken Griffey Jr. 3.00
132 Randy Johnson 1.50
133 Edgar Martinez .35
134 Tino Martinez .35
135 Will Clark .35
136 Juan Gonzalez .75
137 Dean Palmer .35
138 Ivan Rodriguez 1.25
139 Mickey Tettleton .35
140 Larry Walker .35
141 Joe Carter .35
142 Carlos Delgado 1.00
143 Alex Gonzalez .35
144 Paul Molitor 1.50

Gold

Exactly paralleling the cards in the regular Prism set, this chase card insert replaces the silver foil on front with gold foil. All else re-

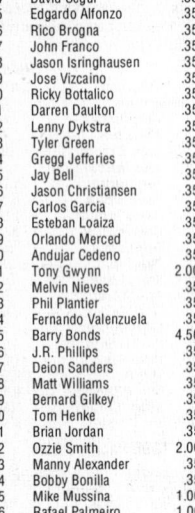

4 Randy Johnson 4.50
5 Greg Maddux 6.00
6 Ramon Martinez 1.50
7 Jose Mesa 1.50
8 Mike Mussina 2.50
9 Hideo Nomo 3.00
10 Jose Rijo 1.50

mains the same. Stated odds of picking a Gold Prism parallel card are about one per 18 packs, on average (two per box).

	NM/M
Complete Set (144):	100.00
Common Player:	.50
Stars:	1.5X

Fence Busters

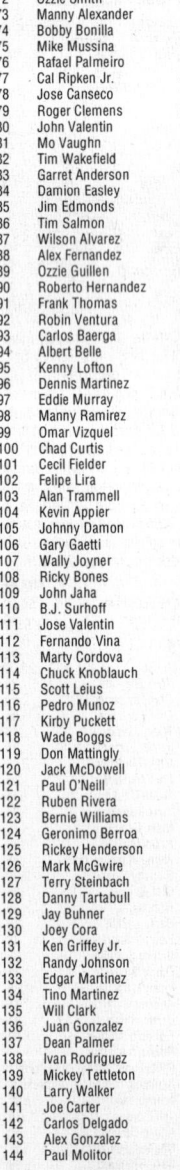

Home run heroes are featured in this insert set. The player's big swing is photographed in the foreground while a baseball flies out of the etched metallic foil stadium background. The player's name is in blue foil. Backs have another player photo and details of his 1995 season home run output, in both English and Spanish. Cards are numbered with an FB prefix. Stated odds of finding a Fence Busters insert are one per 37 packs, on average.

	NM/M
Complete Set (19):	50.00
Common Player:	1.50

1 Albert Belle 1.50
2 Dante Bichette 1.50
3 Barry Bonds 7.50
4 Jay Buhner 1.50
5 Jose Canseco 2.25
6 Ken Griffey Jr. 5.00
7 Chipper Jones 4.00
8 David Justice 1.50
9 Eric Karros 1.50
10 Edgar Martinez 1.50
11 Mark McGwire 6.00
12 Eddie Murray 3.00
13 Mike Piazza 5.00
14 Kirby Puckett 4.00
15 Cal Ripken Jr. 7.50
16 Tim Salmon 1.50
17 Sammy Sosa 4.00
18 Frank Thomas 3.00
19 Mo Vaughn 1.50

Flame Throwers

Burning baseballs are the background for the game's best pitchers in this die-cut insert set. The gold-foil highlighted flames have their tails die-cut at the card's left end. The featured pitcher is shown in action in the foreground. The name at bottom and company logo are in gold foil. Backs are conventionally printed with another action photo and 1995 highlight printed in both English and Spanish. Card numbers carry an FT prefix. Stated odds of finding a Flame Throwers card are one in 73 packs, about every two boxes.

	NM/M
Complete Set (10):	25.00
Common Player:	1.50

1 Roger Clemens 6.50
2 David Cone 1.50
3 Tom Glavine 2.50

Red Hot Stars

Bright red metallic foil provides the background for these inserts. Color action photos are in the foreground, while player name and multiple team logos are worked into the background. Backs are conventionally printed with another player photo and a few words - in both English and Spanish - about the player's 1995 season. Card numbers have an RH prefix. Stated odds of finding a Red Hot Stars insert are one per 37 packs.

	NM/M
Complete Set (20):	25.00
Common Player:	.50

1 Roberto Alomar .75
2 Jeff Bagwell 1.50
3 Albert Belle .50
4 Wade Boggs 2.00
5 Barry Bonds 4.00
6 Jose Canseco 1.00
7 Ken Griffey Jr. 2.50
8 Tony Gwynn 2.00
9 Randy Johnson 1.50
10 Chipper Jones 2.00
11 Greg Maddux 2.00
12 Edgar Martinez .50
13 Don Mattingly 2.50
14 Mike Piazza 2.50
15 Kirby Puckett 2.00
16 Manny Ramirez 1.50
17 Cal Ripken Jr. 4.00
18 Tim Salmon .50
19 Frank Thomas 1.50
20 Mo Vaughn .50

Carlos Baerga Celebrities Softball

This set was produced for distribution to fans attending the second annual Carlos Baerga Celebrities Softball Game in Puerto Rico. Packs were handed out containing two of the cards from this set, a regular Pacific Crown Collection card, a Pacific logo card and an information card about card shops on the island. The softball celebrities cards have a blue and red marbled border with player names at bottom in gold foil. Players are shown in action during the '95 game. Backs feature a portrait photo of the player and English/Spanish description of his participation in the event.

	NM/M
Complete Set (8):	12.00
Common Player:	1.00

1 Carlos Baerga 1.00
2 Mike Piazza 4.00
3 Bernie Williams 1.00
4 Frank Thomas 2.50

5 Roberto Alomar 1.25
6 Edgar Martinez 1.00
7 Kenny Lofton 1.00
8 Sammy Sosa 4.00

Nolan Ryan Career Highlights

Nolan Ryan KING OF K'S

Highlights of Ryan's career with the Texas Rangers are featured in this 11-card set given to fans attending the September 13 game at Arlington during Nolan Ryan Appreciation Week, when the team retired his jersey. Ten cards feature action photos on front with gold-foil graphics. Backs share a background photo of Ryan's classic windup and describe the action pictured on front. Sponsors' and licensors' logos are at top and bottom. An 11th unnumbered card is a checklist.

	NM/M
Complete Set (11):	9.00
Common Player:	1.00

--- Header Card/Checklist .25
1 King of K's (Nolan Ryan) 1.00
2 324 Career Wins (Nolan Ryan) 1.00
3 Miracle Man (Nolan Ryan) 1.00
4 Low-Hit Nolan (Nolan Ryan) 1.00
5 Milestone K's (Nolan Ryan) 1.00
6 Pure Heat (Nolan Ryan) 1.00
7 No-Hit Nolan (Nolan Ryan) 1.00
8 Ryan's Farewell (Nolan Ryan) 1.00
9 Legendary Career (Nolan Ryan) 1.00
10 Retiring #34 (Nolan Ryan) 1.00

Advil Nolan Ryan

Advil Ryan Home Run

Nolan Ryan, who starred in TV commercials for Advil pain reliever at the end of his career continued his association with the product via a baseball card set in 1996. A pair of cards marking the all-time strikeout leader's first and last Ks were available in-store with the purchase of a bottle of Advil. A 27-card set of career highlight cards was available by mail for $5.50 and proof of purchase. All of the Ryan cards have full-bleed front photos with gold-foil highlights and the Advil and Pacific logos. Backs have a background photo of Ryan pitching, with a description of the highlight. Cards are UV coated on each side. The mail-in set was issued in a collector's box.

	NM/M
Complete Set (29):	6.00
Common Player:	.25

IN-STORE CARDS
1a First Strikeout (Nolan Ryan) .50
2a Last strikeout (Nolan Ryan) .50

MAIL-IN SET
1 New York Mets Rookie Pitcher (Nolan Ryan) .25
2 California Angels (Nolan Ryan) .25
3 Houston Astros (Nolan Ryan) .25
4 Texas Rangers (Nolan Ryan) .25
5 No-Hitter #1 (Nolan Ryan) .25
6 No-Hitter #2 (Nolan Ryan) .25
7 No-Hitter #3 (Nolan Ryan) .25
8 No-Hitter #4 (Nolan Ryan) .25
9 No-Hitter #5 (Nolan Ryan) .25
10 No-Hitter #6 (Nolan Ryan) .25
11 No-Hitter #7 (Nolan Ryan) .25
12 First Major League Win (Nolan Ryan) .25
13 250th Win (Nolan Ryan) .25
14 300th Win (Nolan Ryan) .25
15 324th Win (Nolan Ryan) .25
16 1,000th Strikeout (Nolan Ryan) .25
17 2,000th Strikeout (Nolan Ryan) .25
18 3,000th Strikeout (Nolan Ryan) .25
19 Nolan Breaks Johnson Record (Nolan Ryan) .25
20 4,000th Strikeout (Nolan Ryan) .25
21 5,000th Strikeout (Nolan Ryan) .25
22 World Series Victory (Nolan Ryan) .25
23 Fastest Pitch Ever Thrown (Nolan Ryan) .25
24 Ryan Home Run (Nolan Ryan) .25
25 The Greatest Power Pitcher (Nolan Ryan) .25
26 1989 All-Star Game (Nolan Ryan) .25
27 Last Appearance (Nolan Ryan) .25

1997 Pacific Crown

The 450-card, regular-sized set was available in 12-card packs. The card fronts feature the player's name in gold foil along the left border with the team logo in the bottom right corner. The card backs feature a head shot of the player in the lower left quadrant with a short highlight in both Spanish and English. Inserted in packs were: Card-Supials, Cramer's Choice, Latinos Of The Major Leagues, Fireworks Die-Cuts, Gold Crown Die-Cuts and Triple Crown Die-Cuts. A parallel silver version (67 sets) was available.

	NM/M
Complete Set (450):	30.00
Common Player:	.05
Silver Stars/RC's:	15X
Light Blue:	1X
Pack (12):	1.25
Wax Box (36):	32.50

1 Garret Anderson .05
2 George Arias .05
3 Chili Davis .05
4 Gary DiSarcina .05
5 Jim Edmonds .05
6 Darin Erstad .15
7 Jorge Fabregas .05
8 Chuck Finley .05
9 Rex Hudler .05
10 Mark Langston .05
11 Orlando Palmeiro .05
12 Troy Percival .05
13 Tim Salmon .05
14 J.T. Snow .05
15 Randy Velarde .05
16 Manny Alexander .05
17 Roberto Alomar .25
18 Brady Anderson .05
19 Armando Benitez .05
20 Bobby Bonilla .05
21 Rocky Coppinger .05
22 Scott Erickson .05
23 Jeffrey Hammonds .05
24 Chris Hoiles .05
25 Eddie Murray .75
26 Mike Mussina .60
27 Randy Myers .05
28 Rafael Palmeiro .65
29 Cal Ripken Jr. 2.50
30 B.J. Surhoff .05
31 Tony Tarasco .05
32 Esteban Beltre .05
33 Darren Bragg .05
34 Jose Canseco .60
35 Roger Clemens 1.50
36 Wil Cordero .05
37 Alex Delgado .05
38 Jeff Frye .05
39 Nomar Garciaparra 1.00
40 Tom Gordon .05
41 Mike Greenwell .05
42 Reggie Jefferson .05
43 Tim Naehring .05
44 Troy O'Leary .05
45 Heathcliff Slocumb .05
46 Lee Tinsley .05
47 John Valentin .05
48 Mo Vaughn .05
49 Wilson Alvarez .05
50 Harold Baines .05
51 Ray Durham .05
52 Alex Fernandez .05
53 Ozzie Guillen .05
54 Roberto Hernandez .05
55 Ron Karkovice .05
56 Darren Lewis .05
57 Norberto Martin .05
58 Dave Martinez .05
59 Lyle Mouton .05
60 Jose Munoz .05
61 Tony Phillips .05
62 Rich Sauveur .05
63 Danny Tartabull .05
64 Frank Thomas .75
65 Robin Ventura .05
66 Sandy Alomar Jr. .05
67 Albert Belle .05
68 Julio Franco .05
69 Brian Giles RC .50
70 Danny Graves .05
71 Orel Hershiser .05
72 Jeff Kent .05
73 Kenny Lofton .05
74 Dennis Martinez .05
75 Jack McDowell .05
76 Jose Mesa .05
77 Charles Nagy .05
78 Manny Ramirez .75
79 Julian Tavarez .05
80 Jim Thome .60
81 Jose Vizcaino .05
82 Omar Vizquel .05
83 Brad Ausmus .05
84 Kimera Bartee .05
85 Raul Casanova .05
86 Tony Clark .05
87 Travis Fryman .05
88 Bobby Higginson .05
89 Mark Lewis .05
90 Jose Lima .05
91 Felipe Lira .05
92 Phil Nevin .05
93 Melvin Nieves .05
94 Curtis Pride .05
95 Ruben Sierra .05
96 Alan Trammell .05
97 Kevin Appier .05
98 Tim Belcher .05
99 Johnny Damon .35
100 Tom Goodwin .05
101 Bob Hamelin .05
102 David Howard .05
103 Jason Jacome .05
104 Keith Lockhart .05
105 Mike Macfarlane .05
106 Jeff Montgomery .05
107 Jose Offerman .05
108 Hipolito Pichardo .05
109 Joe Randa .05
110 Bip Roberts .05
111 Chris Stynes .05
112 Mike Sweeney .05
113 Joe Vitiello .05
114 Jeromy Burnitz .05
115 Chuck Carr .05
116 Jeff Cirillo .05
117 Mike Fetters .05
118 David Hulse .05
119 John Jaha .05
120 Scott Karl .05
121 Jesse Levis .05
122 Mark Loretta .05
123 Mike Matheny .05
124 Ben McDonald .05
125 Matt Mieske .05
126 Angel Miranda .05
127 Dave Nilsson .05
128 Jose Valentin .05
129 Fernando Vina .05
130 Ron Villone .05
131 Gerald Williams .05
132 Rick Aguilera .05
133 Rich Becker .05
134 Ron Coomer .05
135 Marty Cordova .05
136 Eddie Guardado .05
137 Denny Hocking .05
138 Roberto Kelly .05
139 Chuck Knoblauch .05
140 Matt Lawton .05
141 Pat Meares .05
142 Paul Molitor .75

#	Player	Price
143	Greg Myers	.05
144	Jeff Reboulet	.05
145	Scott Stahoviak	.05
146	Todd Walker	.05
147	Wade Boggs	1.00
148	David Cone	.05
149	Mariano Duncan	.05
150	Cecil Fielder	.05
151	Dwight Gooden	.05
152	Derek Jeter	2.50
153	Jim Leyritz	.05
154	Tino Martinez	.05
155	Paul O'Neill	.05
156	Andy Pettitte	.25
157	Tim Raines	.05
158	Mariano Rivera	.15
159	Ruben Rivera	.05
160	Kenny Rogers	.05
161	Darryl Strawberry	.05
162	John Wetteland	.05
163	Bernie Williams	.05
164	Tony Batista	.05
165	Geronimo Berroa	.05
166	Mike Bordick	.05
167	Scott Brosius	.05
168	Brent Gates	.05
169	Jason Giambi	.65
170	Jose Herrera	.05
171	Brian Lesher	.05
172	Damon Mashore RC	.05
173	Mark McGwire	2.00
174	Ariel Prieto	.05
175	Carlos Reyes	.05
176	Matt Stairs	.05
177	Terry Steinbach	.05
178	John Wasdin	.05
179	Ernie Young	.05
180	Rich Amaral	.05
181	Bobby Ayala	.05
182	Jay Buhner	.05
183	Rafael Carmona	.05
184	Norm Charlton	.05
185	Joey Cora	.05
186	Ken Griffey Jr.	1.50
187	Sterling Hitchcock	.05
188	Dave Hollins	.05
189	Randy Johnson	.75
190	Edgar Martinez	.05
191	Jamie Moyer	.05
192	Alex Rodriguez	2.00
193	Paul Sorrento	.05
194	Salomon Torres	.05
195	Bob Wells	.05
196	Dan Wilson	.05
197	Will Clark	.05
198	Kevin Elster	.05
199	Rene Gonzales	.05
200	Juan Gonzalez	.40
201	Rusty Greer	.05
202	Darryl Hamilton	.05
203	Mike Henneman	.05
204	Ken Hill	.05
205	Mark McLemore	.05
206	Darren Oliver	.05
207	Dean Palmer	.05
208	Roger Pavlik	.05
209	Ivan Rodriguez	.65
210	Kurt Stillwell	.05
211	Mickey Tettleton	.05
212	Bobby Witt	.05
213	Tilson Brito	.05
214	Jacob Brumfield	.05
215	Miguel Cairo	.05
216	Joe Carter	.05
217	Felipe Crespo	.05
218	Carlos Delgado	.60
219	Alex Gonzalez	.05
220	Shawn Green	.15
221	Juan Guzman	.05
222	Pat Hentgen	.05
223	Charlie O'Brien	.05
224	John Olerud	.05
225	Robert Perez	.05
226	Tomas Perez	.05
227	Juan Samuel	.05
228	Ed Sprague	.05
229	Mike Timlin	.05
230	Rafael Belliard	.05
231	Jermaine Dye	.05
232	Tom Glavine	.25
233	Marquis Grissom	.05
234	Andruw Jones	.75
235	Chipper Jones	1.00
236	David Justice	.05
237	Ryan Klesko	.05
238	Mark Lemke	.05
239	Javier Lopez	.05
240	Greg Maddux	1.00
241	Fred McGriff	.05
242	Denny Neagle	.05
243	Eddie Perez	.05
244	John Smoltz	.05
245	Mark Wohlers	.05
246	Brant Brown	.05
247	Scott Bullett	.05
248	Leo Gomez	.05
249	Luis Gonzalez	.05
250	Mark Grace	.05
251	Jose Hernandez	.05
252	Brooks Kieschnick	.05
253	Brian McRae	.05
254	Jaime Navarro	.05
255	Mike Perez	.05
256	Rey Sanchez	.05
257	Ryne Sandberg	1.00
258	Scott Servais	.05
259	Sammy Sosa	1.00
260	Pedro Valdes RC	.05

#	Player	Price
261	Turk Wendell	.05
262	Bret Boone	.05
263	Jeff Branson	.05
264	Jeff Brantley	.05
265	Dave Burba	.05
266	Hector Carrasco	.05
267	Eric Davis	.05
268	Willie Greene	.05
269	Lenny Harris	.05
270	Thomas Howard	.05
271	Barry Larkin	.05
272	Hal Morris	.05
273	Joe Oliver	.05
274	Eric Owens	.05
275	Jose Rijo	.05
276	Reggie Sanders	.05
277	Eddie Taubensee	.05
278	Jason Bates	.05
279	Dante Bichette	.05
280	Ellis Burks	.05
281	Vinny Castilla	.05
282	Andres Galarraga	.05
283	Quinton McCracken	.05
284	Jayhawk Owens	.05
285	Jeff Reed	.05
286	Bryan Rekar	.05
287	Armando Reynoso	.05
288	Kevin Ritz	.05
289	Bruce Ruffin	.05
290	John Vander Wal	.05
291	Larry Walker	.05
292	Walt Weiss	.05
293	Eric Young	.05
294	Kurt Abbott	.05
295	Alex Arias	.05
296	Miguel Batista	.05
297	Kevin Brown	.05
298	Luis Castillo	.05
299	Greg Colbrunn	.05
300	Jeff Conine	.05
301	Charles Johnson	.05
302	Al Leiter	.05
303	Robb Nen	.05
304	Joe Orsulak	.05
305	Yorkis Perez	.05
306	Edgar Renteria	.05
307	Gary Sheffield	.30
308	Jesus Tavarez	.05
309	Quilvio Veras	.05
310	Devon White	.05
311	Jeff Bagwell	.75
312	Derek Bell	.05
313	Sean Berry	.05
314	Craig Biggio	.05
315	Doug Drabek	.05
316	Tony Eusebio	.05
317	Ricky Gutierrez	.05
318	Xavier Hernandez	.05
319	Brian L. Hunter	.05
320	Darryl Kile	.05
321	Derrick May	.05
322	Orlando Miller	.05
323	James Mouton	.05
324	Bill Spiers	.05
325	Pedro Astacio	.05
326	Brett Butler	.05
327	Juan Castro	.05
328	Roger Cedeno	.05
329	Delino DeShields	.05
330	Karim Garcia	.10
331	Todd Hollandsworth	.05
332	Eric Karros	.05
333	Oreste Marrero	.05
334	Ramon Martinez	.05
335	Raul Mondesi	.05
336	Hideo Nomo	.50
337	Antonio Osuna	.05
338	Chan Ho Park	.05
339	Mike Piazza	1.50
340	Ismael Valdes	.05
341	Moises Alou	.05
342	Omar Daal	.05
343	Jeff Fassero	.05
344	Cliff Floyd	.05
345	Mark Grudzielanek	.05
346	Mike Lansing	.05
347	Pedro Martinez	.75
348	Sherman Obando	.05
349	Jose Paniagua	.05
350	Henry Rodriguez	.05
351	Mel Rojas	.05
352	F.P. Santangelo	.05
353	Dave Segui	.05
354	Dave Silvestri	.05
355	Ugueth Urbina	.05
356	Rondell White	.05
357	Edgardo Alfonzo	.05
358	Carlos Baerga	.05
359	Tim Bogar	.05
360	Rico Brogna	.05
361	Alvaro Espinoza	.05
362	Carl Everett	.05
363	John Franco	.05
364	Bernard Gilkey	.05
365	Todd Hundley	.05
366	Butch Huskey	.05
367	Jason Isringhausen	.05
368	Bobby Jones	.05
369	Lance Johnson	.05
370	Brent Mayne	.05
371	Alex Ochoa	.05
372	Rey Ordonez	.05
373	Ron Blazier	.05
374	Ricky Bottalico	.05
375	David Doster	.05
376	Lenny Dykstra	.05
377	Jim Eisenreich	.05
378	Bobby Estalella	.05

#	Player	Price
379	Gregg Jefferies	.05
380	Kevin Jordan	.05
381	Ricardo Jordan	.05
382	Mickey Morandini	.05
383	Ricky Otero	.05
384	Benito Santiago	.05
385	Gene Schall	.05
386	Curt Schilling	.25
387	Kevin Sefcik	.05
388	Kevin Stocker	.05
389	Jermaine Allensworth	.05
390	Jay Bell	.05
391	Jason Christiansen	.05
392	Francisco Cordova	.05
393	Mark Johnson	.05
394	Jason Kendall	.05
395	Jeff King	.05
396	Jon Lieber	.05
397	Nelson Liriano	.05
398	Esteban Loaiza	.05
399	Al Martin	.05
400	Orlando Merced	.05
401	Ramon Morel	.05
402	Luis Alicea	.05
403	Alan Benes	.05
404	Andy Benes	.05
405	Terry Bradshaw	.05
406	Royce Clayton	.05
407	Dennis Eckersley	.65
408	Gary Gaetti	.05
409	Mike Gallego	.05
410	Ron Gant	.05
411	Brian Jordan	.05
412	Ray Lankford	.05
413	John Mabry	.05
414	Willie McGee	.05
415	Tom Pagnozzi	.05
416	Ozzie Smith	1.00
417	Todd Stottlemyre	.05
418	Mark Sweeney	.05
419	Andy Ashby	.05
420	Ken Caminiti	.05
421	Archi Cianfrocco	.05
422	Steve Finley	.05
423	Chris Gomez	.05
424	Tony Gwynn	1.00
425	Joey Hamilton	.05
426	Rickey Henderson	.75
427	Trevor Hoffman	.05
428	Brian Johnson	.05
429	Wally Joyner	.05
430	Scott Livingstone	.05
431	Jody Reed	.05
432	Craig Shipley	.05
433	Fernando Valenzuela	.05
434	Greg Vaughn	.05
435	Rich Aurilia	.05
436	Kim Batiste	.05
437	Jose Bautista	.05
438	Rod Beck	.05
439	Marvin Benard	.05
440	Barry Bonds	2.50
441	Shawon Dunston	.05
442	Shawn Estes	.05
443	Osvaldo Fernandez	.05
444	Stan Javier	.05
445	David McCarty	.05
446	Bill Mueller RC	.15
447	Steve Scarsone	.05
448	Robby Thompson	.05
449	Rick Wilkins	.05
450	Matt Williams	.05

Light Blue

This parallel insert was produced exclusively for insertion in Wal-Mart/Sam's jumbo packs at the rate of one per pack. Following the format of the regular-issue, they use light blue foil, rather than the standard gold. Light blue inserts should not be confused with the much scarcer silver inserts which are visually similar.

	NM/M
Complete Set (450):	60.00
Common Player:	.25
Stars:	1X

Silver

This parallel insert was produced in an edition of only 67 cards per player. Following the format of the regular-issue, they use silver foil, rather than the standard gold. Silver

parallels were inserted at an advertised rate of one per 73 packs. Silver inserts should not be confused with the much more common light blue inserts which are visually similar.

	NM/M
Common Player:	1.00
Stars/Rookies:	12X

Card-Supials

The 36-card, regular-sized set was inserted every 37 packs of 1997 Pacific Crown baseball. The card fronts feature a gold-foil spiral with the player's name printed along a curve on the bottom edge. The team logo appears in the lower right corner. The card backs feature an action shot and are numbered "x of 36." The cards come with a mini (1-1/4" x 1-3/4") card that slides into a pocket on the back. The mini cards depict the same action shot as the larger card backs.

	NM/M
Complete Set (72):	80.00
Complete Large Set (36):	60.00
Complete Small Set (36):	45.00
Common Large:	.75
Small Cards: 75 Percent	
1 Roberto Alomar	1.00
2 Brady Anderson	.75
3 Eddie Murray	2.00
4 Cal Ripken Jr.	5.00
5 Jose Canseco	1.00
6 Mo Vaughn	.75
7 Frank Thomas	2.00
8 Albert Belle	.75
9 Omar Vizquel	.75
10 Chuck Knoblauch	.75
11 Paul Molitor	2.00
12 Wade Boggs	2.50
13 Derek Jeter	5.00
14 Andy Pettitte	1.00
15 Mark McGwire	3.50
16 Jay Buhner	.75
17 Ken Griffey Jr.	3.00
18 Alex Rodriguez	3.50
19 Juan Gonzalez	1.00
20 Ivan Rodriguez	1.50
21 Andruw Jones	2.00
22 Chipper Jones	2.50
23 Ryan Klesko	.75
24 Greg Maddux	2.50
25 Ryne Sandberg	2.50
26 Andres Galarraga	.75
27 Gary Sheffield	1.00
28 Jeff Bagwell	2.00
29 Todd Hollandsworth	.75
30 Hideo Nomo	1.00
31 Mike Piazza	3.00
32 Todd Hundley	.75
33 Dennis Eckersley	1.50
34 Ken Caminiti	.75
35 Tony Gwynn	2.50
36 Barry Bonds	5.00

Cramer's Choice Awards

The 10-card, regular-sized set was inserted every 721 packs and features a die-cut pyramid design. A color player photo is imaged over silver foil with the player's name and position in gold foil over a green marble background along the bottom. The card backs feature a headshot with a brief career highlight in both Spanish and English. The cards are numbered with a "CC" prefix.

	NM/M
Complete Set (10):	75.00

		NM/M
Common Player:		4.50
1	Roberto Alomar	5.00
2	Frank Thomas	9.00
3	Albert Belle	4.50
4	Andy Pettitte	4.50
5	Ken Griffey Jr.	17.50
6	Alex Rodriguez	25.00
7	Chipper Jones	12.00
8	John Smoltz	4.50
9	Mike Piazza	15.00
10	Tony Gwynn	12.00

Fireworks Die-Cuts

The 20-card, regular-sized, die-cut set was inserted every 73 packs of 1997 Crown. The card fronts feature a color action shot with generic fireworks over a stadium on the upper half. The horizontal card backs contain close-up shots with highlights in Spanish and English. The cards are numbered with the "FW" prefix.

		NM/M
Complete Set (20):		40.00
Common Player:		.75
1	Roberto Alomar	1.00
2	Brady Anderson	.75
3	Eddie Murray	2.50
4	Cal Ripken Jr.	7.50
5	Frank Thomas	2.50
6	Albert Belle	.75
7	Derek Jeter	7.50
8	Andy Pettitte	1.00
9	Bernie Williams	.75
10	Mark McGwire	6.50
11	Ken Griffey Jr.	5.00
12	Alex Rodriguez	6.50
13	Juan Gonzalez	1.25
14	Andruw Jones	2.50
15	Chipper Jones	3.50
16	Hideo Nomo	1.25
17	Mike Piazza	5.00
18	Henry Rodriguez	.75
19	Tony Gwynn	3.50
20	Barry Bonds	7.50

Gold Crown Die-Cuts

The 36-card, regular-sized, die-cut set was inserted every 37 packs. The card fronts feature a die-cut, gold-foil crown on the top border and the player's name appears in gold along the bottom edge. The

card backs contain a headshot and a Spanish/English highlight and are numbered with the "GC" prefix.

		NM/M
Complete Set (36):		65.00
Common Player:		1.00
1	Roberto Alomar	1.25
2	Brady Anderson	1.00
3	Mike Mussina	1.50
4	Eddie Murray	2.75
5	Cal Ripken Jr.	8.50
6	Jose Canseco	2.00
7	Frank Thomas	2.75
8	Albert Belle	1.00
9	Omar Vizquel	1.00
10	Wade Boggs	3.50
11	Derek Jeter	8.50
12	Andy Pettitte	1.25
13	Mariano Rivera	1.25
14	Bernie Williams	1.00
15	Mark McGwire	6.50
16	Ken Griffey Jr.	5.00
17	Edgar Martinez	1.00
18	Alex Rodriguez	6.50
19	Juan Gonzalez	1.50
20	Ivan Rodriguez	2.50
21	Andruw Jones	2.75
22	Chipper Jones	3.50
23	Ryan Klesko	1.00
24	John Smoltz	1.00
25	Ryne Sandberg	3.50
26	Andres Galarraga	1.00
27	Edgar Renteria	1.00
28	Jeff Bagwell	2.75
29	Todd Hollandsworth	1.00
30	Hideo Nomo	1.50
31	Mike Piazza	5.00
32	Todd Hundley	1.00
33	Brian Jordan	1.00
34	Ken Caminiti	1.00
35	Tony Gwynn	3.50
36	Barry Bonds	8.50

Latinos of the Major Leagues

The 36-card, regular-sized set was inserted twice every 37 packs. The card fronts feature a color action shot over the player's name in gold foil. The card backs have another action shot and a Spanish/English highlight.

		NM/M
Complete Set (36):		45.00
Common Player:		1.00
1	George Arias	1.00
2	Roberto Alomar	1.50
3	Rafael Palmeiro	2.50
4	Bobby Bonilla	1.00
5	Jose Canseco	2.00
6	Wilson Alvarez	1.00
7	Dave Martinez	1.00
8	Julio Franco	1.00
9	Manny Ramirez	3.00
10	Omar Vizquel	1.00
11	Marty Cordova	1.00
12	Roberto Kelly	1.00
13	Tino Martinez	1.00
14	Mariano Rivera	1.50
15	Ruben Rivera	1.00
16	Bernie Williams	1.00
17	Geronimo Berroa	1.00
18	Joey Cora	1.00
19	Edgar Martinez	1.00
20	Alex Rodriguez	6.00
21	Juan Gonzalez	2.00
22	Ivan Rodriguez	2.50
23	Andruw Jones	3.00
24	Javier Lopez	1.00
25	Sammy Sosa	4.50
26	Vinny Castilla	1.00
27	Andres Galarraga	1.00
28	Ramon Martinez	1.00
29	Raul Mondesi	1.00
30	Ismael Valdes	1.00
31	Pedro Martinez	3.00
32	Henry Rodriguez	1.00
33	Carlos Baerga	1.00
34	Rey Ordonez	1.00
35	Fernando Valenzuela	1.00
36	Osvaldo Fernandez	1.00

Triple Crown Die-Cuts

The 20-card, regular-sized, die-cut set was inserted every 145 packs of Crown baseball. The horizontal card fronts feature the same gold-foil, die-cut crown as on the Gold Crown Die-Cut inserts. The card backs feature a headshot, Spanish/English text and are numbered with the "TC" prefix.

		NM/M
Complete Set (20):		75.00
Common Player:		2.00
1	Brady Anderson	2.00
2	Rafael Palmeiro	4.00
3	Mo Vaughn	2.00
4	Frank Thomas	5.00
5	Albert Belle	2.00
6	Jim Thome	4.00
7	Cecil Fielder	2.00
8	Mark McGwire	10.00
9	Ken Griffey Jr.	7.50
10	Alex Rodriguez	10.00
11	Juan Gonzalez	3.00
12	Andruw Jones	5.00
13	Chipper Jones	6.00
14	Dante Bichette	2.00
15	Ellis Burks	2.00
16	Andres Galarraga	2.00
17	Jeff Bagwell	5.00
18	Mike Piazza	7.50
19	Ken Caminiti	2.00
20	Barry Bonds	12.50

1997 Pacific Invincible

The 1997 Pacific Invincible 150-card set was sold in three-card packs. The card fronts feature gold foil parallel lines with a color action shot. The bottom right quadrant contains a transparent cel headshot. The card backs have Spanish/English text and another color action shot. The reverse cel has the player's hat team logo air-brushed off to prevent reverse print. Insert sets are: Sluggers & Hurlers, Sizzling Lumber, Gate Attractions, Gems of the Diamond (2:1), and Light Blue (retail only) and Platinum (hobby) parallel sets of the 150 base cards.

		NM/M
Complete Set (150):		30.00
Common Player:		.25
Light Blues:		1X
Platinums:		2X
Pack (3):		1.00
Wax Box (36):		25.00
1	Chili Davis	.25
2	Jim Edmonds	.25
3	Darin Erstad	.50
4	Orlando Palmeiro	.25
5	Tim Salmon	.25
6	J.T. Snow	.25
7	Roberto Alomar	.50
8	Brady Anderson	.25
9	Eddie Murray	1.50
10	Mike Mussina	1.00
11	Rafael Palmeiro	1.25
12	Cal Ripken Jr.	4.00
13	Jose Canseco	1.00
14	Roger Clemens	2.50
15	Nomar Garciaparra	2.00
16	Reggie Jefferson	.25
17	Mo Vaughn	.25
18	Wilson Alvarez	.25
19	Harold Baines	.25
20	Alex Fernandez	.25
21	Danny Tartabull	.25
22	Frank Thomas	1.50
23	Robin Ventura	.25
24	Sandy Alomar Jr.	.25

25	Albert Belle	.25
26	Kenny Lofton	.25
27	Jim Thome	.75
28	Omar Vizquel	.25
29	Raul Casanova	.25
30	Tony Clark	.25
31	Travis Fryman	.25
32	Bobby Higginson	.25
33	Melvin Nieves	.25
34	Justin Thompson	.25
35	Johnny Damon	.50
36	Tom Goodwin	.25
37	Jeff Montgomery	.25
38	Jose Offerman	.25
39	John Jaha	.25
40	Jeff Cirillo	.25
41	Dave Nilsson	.25
42	Jose Valentin	.25
43	Fernando Vina	.25
44	Marty Cordova	.25
45	Roberto Kelly	.25
46	Chuck Knoblauch	.25
47	Paul Molitor	1.50
48	Todd Walker	.25
49	Wade Boggs	2.00
50	Cecil Fielder	.25
51	Derek Jeter	4.00
52	Tino Martinez	.25
53	Andy Pettitte	.40
54	Mariano Rivera	.40
55	Bernie Williams	.25
56	Tony Batista	.25
57	Geronimo Berroa	.25
58	Jason Giambi	.75
59	Mark McGwire	3.00
60	Terry Steinbach	.25
61	Jay Buhner	.25
62	Joey Cora	.25
63	Ken Griffey Jr.	2.50
64	Edgar Martinez	.25
65	Alex Rodriguez	3.00
66	Paul Sorrento	.25
67	Will Clark	.25
68	Juan Gonzalez	.75
69	Rusty Greer	.25
70	Dean Palmer	.25
71	Ivan Rodriguez	1.25
72	Joe Carter	.25
73	Carlos Delgado	.75
74	Juan Guzman	.25
75	Pat Hentgen	.25
76	Ed Sprague	.25
77	Jermaine Dye	.25
78	Andruw Jones	1.50
79	Chipper Jones	2.00
80	Ryan Klesko	.25
81	Javier Lopez	.25
82	Greg Maddux	2.00
83	John Smoltz	.25
84	Mark Grace	.25
85	Luis Gonzalez	.25
86	Brooks Kieschnick	.25
87	Jaime Navarro	.25
88	Ryne Sandberg	2.00
89	Sammy Sosa	2.00
90	Bret Boone	.25
91	Jeff Brantley	.25
92	Eric Davis	.25
93	Barry Larkin	.25
94	Reggie Sanders	.25
95	Ellis Burks	.25
96	Dante Bichette	.25
97	Vinny Castilla	.25
98	Andres Galarraga	.25
99	Eric Young	.25
100	Kevin Brown	.25
101	Jeff Conine	.25
102	Charles Johnson	.25
103	Edgar Renteria	.25
104	Gary Sheffield	.75
105	Jeff Bagwell	1.50
106	Derek Bell	.25
107	Sean Berry	.25
108	Craig Biggio	.25
109	Shane Reynolds	.25
110	Karim Garcia	.25
111	Todd Hollandsworth	.25
112	Ramon Martinez	.25
113	Raul Mondesi	.25
114	Hideo Nomo	.75
115	Mike Piazza	2.50
116	Ismael Valdes	.25
117	Moises Alou	.25
118	Mark Grudzielanek	.25
119	Pedro Martinez	1.50
120	Henry Rodriguez	.25
121	F.P. Santangelo	.25
122	Carlos Baerga	.25
123	Bernard Gilkey	.25
124	Todd Hundley	.25
125	Lance Johnson	.25
126	Alex Ochoa	.25
127	Rey Ordonez	.25
128	Lenny Dykstra	.25
129	Gregg Jefferies	.25
130	Ricky Otero	.25
131	Benito Santiago	.25
132	Jermaine Allensworth	.25
133	Francisco Cordova	.25
134	Carlos Garcia	.25
135	Jason Kendall	.25
136	Al Martin	.25
137	Dennis Eckersley	1.25
138	Ron Gant	.25
139	Brian Jordan	.25
140	John Mabry	.25
141	Ozzie Smith	2.00
142	Ken Caminiti	.25

143	Steve Finley	.25
144	Tony Gwynn	2.00
145	Wally Joyner	.25
146	Fernando Valenzuela	.25
147	Barry Bonds	4.00
148	Jacob Cruz	.25
149	Osvaldo Fernandez	.25
150	Matt Williams	.25

Gate Attractions

The 32-card, regular-sized set was inserted every 73 packs of Pacific Invincible baseball. The card fronts feature a generic baseball glove background with the player's name and position in a gold-foil circle. The center of the card is a cel action shot within a common baseball image. The player's team logo appears in the upper right corner. The card backs contain a headshot in the upper left corner with highlights in Spanish and English. The player's image in the cel is etched in gray in reverse. The cards are numbered with the "GA" prefix.

		NM/M
Complete Set (32):		80.00
Common Player:		1.00
1	Roberto Alomar	1.00
2	Brady Anderson	1.00
3	Cal Ripken Jr.	8.00
4	Frank Thomas	2.50
5	Kenny Lofton	1.00
6	Omar Vizquel	1.00
7	Paul Molitor	2.50
8	Wade Boggs	3.00
9	Derek Jeter	8.00
10	Andy Pettitte	1.50
11	Bernie Williams	1.00
12	Geronimo Berroa	1.00
13	Mark McGwire	6.00
14	Ken Griffey Jr.	4.50
15	Alex Rodriguez	4.50
16	Juan Gonzalez	1.50
17	Andruw Jones	2.50
18	Chipper Jones	3.00
19	Greg Maddux	3.00
20	Ryne Sandberg	3.00
21	Sammy Sosa	3.00
22	Andres Galarraga	1.00
23	Jeff Bagwell	2.50
24	Todd Hollandsworth	1.00
25	Hideo Nomo	3.00
26	Mike Piazza	4.50
27	Todd Hundley	1.00
28	Lance Johnson	1.00
29	Ozzie Smith	3.00
30	Ken Caminiti	1.00
31	Tony Gwynn	3.00
32	Barry Bonds	8.00

Gems of the Diamond

Essentially the base set for 1997 Pacific Prism Invincible, these cards are found two per three-card pack. Fronts of the 2-1/2" x 3-1/2" cards have action photos with earth-tone borders and a color team logo at bottom. Backs have a large player portrait photos in a diamond at right-center and are numbered with a "GD-" prefix.

		NM/M
Complete Set (220):		20.00

	Common Player:	.10
1	Jim Abbott	.10
2	Shawn Boskie	.10
3	Gary DiSarcina	.10
4	Jim Edmonds	.10
5	Todd Greene	.10
6	Jack Howell	.10
7	Jeff Schmidt	.10
8	Shad Williams	.10
9	Roberto Alomar	.35
10	Cesar Devarez	.10
11	Alan Mills	.10
12	Eddie Murray	.75
13	Jesse Orosco	.10
14	Arthur Rhodes	.10
15	Bill Ripken	.10
16	Cal Ripken Jr.	2.50
17	Mark Smith	.10
18	Roger Clemens	1.50
19	Vaughn Eshelman	.10
20	Rich Garces	.10
21	Bill Haselman	.10
22	Dwayne Hosey	.10
23	Mike Maddux	.10
24	Jose Malave	.10
25	Aaron Sele	.10
26	James Baldwin	.10
27	Pat Borders	.10
28	Mike Cameron	.10
29	Tony Castillo	.10
30	Domingo Cedeno	.10
31	Greg Norton	.10
32	Frank Thomas	.75
33	Albert Belle	.10
34	Einar Diaz	.10
35	Alan Embree	.10
36	Albie Lopez	.10
37	Chad Ogea	.10
38	Tony Pena	.10
39	Joe Roa	.10
40	Fausto Cruz	.10
41	Joey Eischen	.10
42	Travis Fryman	.10
43	Mike Myers	.10
44	A.J. Sager	.10
45	Duane Singleton	.10
46	Justin Thompson	.10
47	Jeff Granger	.10
48	Les Norman	.10
49	Jon Nunnally	.10
50	Craig Paquette	.10
51	Michael Tucker	.10
52	Julio Valera	.10
53	Kevin Young	.10
54	Cal Eldred	.10
55	Ramon Garcia	.10
56	Marc Newfield	.10
57	Al Reyes	.10
58	Tim Unroe	.10
59	Tim Vanegmond	.10
60	Turner Ward	.10
61	Bob Wickman	.10
62	Chuck Knoblauch	.10
63	Paul Molitor	.75
64	Kirby Puckett	1.00
65	Tom Quinlan	.10
66	Rich Robertson	.10
67	Dave Stevens	.10
68	Matt Walbeck	.10
69	Wade Boggs	1.00
70	Tony Fernandez	.10
71	Andy Fox	.10
72	Joe Girardi	.10
73	Charlie Hayes	.10
74	Pat Kelly	.10
75	Jeff Nelson	.10
76	Melido Perez	.10
77	Mark Acre	.10
78	Allen Battle	.10
79	Rafael Bournigal	.10
80	Mark McGwire	2.00
81	Pedro Munoz	.10
82	Scott Spiezio	.10
83	Don Wengert	.10
84	Steve Wojciechowski	.10
85	Alex Diaz	.10
86	Ken Griffey Jr.	1.50
87	Raul Ibanez	.10
88	Mike Jackson	.10
89	John Marzano	.10
90	Greg McCarthy	.10
91	Alex Rodriguez	2.00
92	Andy Sheets	.10
93	Makoto Suzuki	.10
94	Benji Gil	.10
95	Juan Gonzalez	.40
96	Kevin Gross	.10
97	Gil Heredia	.10
98	Luis Ortiz	.10
99	Jeff Russell	.10
100	Dave Valle	.10
101	Marty Janzen	.10
102	Sandy Martinez	.10
103	Julio Mosquera	.10
104	Otis Nixon	.10
105	Paul Spoljaric	.10
106	Shannon Stewart	.10
107	Woody Williams	.10
108	Steve Avery	.10
109	Mike Bielecki	.10
110	Pedro Borbon	.10
111	Ed Giovanola	.10
112	Chipper Jones	1.00
113	Greg Maddux	1.00
114	Mike Mordecai	.10
115	Terrell Wade	.10
116	Terry Adams	.10
117	Brian Dorsett	.10

118	Doug Glanville	.10
119	Tyler Houston	.10
120	Robin Jennings	.10
121	Ryne Sandberg	1.00
122	Terry Shumpert	.10
123	Amaury Telemaco	.10
124	Steve Trachsel	.10
125	Curtis Goodwin	.10
126	Mike Kelly	.10
127	Chad Mottola	.10
128	Mark Portugal	.10
129	Roger Salkeld	.10
130	John Smiley	.10
131	Lee Smith	.10
132	Roger Bailey	.10
133	Andres Galarraga	.10
134	Darren Holmes	.10
135	Curtis Leskanic	.10
136	Mike Munoz	.10
137	Jeff Reed	.10
138	Mark Thompson	.10
139	Jamey Wright	.10
140	Andre Dawson	.25
141	Craig Grebeck	.10
142	Matt Mantei	.10
143	Billy McMillon	.10
144	Kurt Miller	.10
145	Ralph Milliard	.10
146	Bob Natal	.10
147	Joe Siddall	.10
148	Bob Abreu	.25
149	Doug Brocail	.10
150	Danny Darwin	.10
151	Mike Hampton	.10
152	Todd Jones	.10
153	Kirt Manwaring	.10
154	Alvin Morman	.10
155	Billy Ashley	.10
156	Tom Candiotti	.10
157	Darren Dreifort	.10
158	Greg Gagne	.10
159	Wilton Guerrero	.10
160	Hideo Nomo	.40
161	Mike Piazza	1.50
162	Tom Prince	.10
163	Todd Worrell	.10
164	Moises Alou	.10
165	Shane Andrews	.10
166	Derek Aucoin	.10
167	Raul Chavez	.10
168	Darrin Fletcher	.10
169	Mark Leiter	.10
170	Henry Rodriguez	.10
171	Dave Veres	.10
172	Paul Byrd	.10
173	Alberto Castillo	.10
174	Mark Clark	.10
175	Rey Ordonez	.10
176	Roberto Petagine	.10
177	Andy Tomberlin	.10
178	Derek Wallace	.10
179	Paul Wilson	.10
180	Ruben Amaro Jr.	.10
181	Toby Borland	.10
182	Rich Hunter	.10
183	Tony Longmire	.10
184	Wendell Magee Jr.	.10
185	Bobby Munoz	.10
186	Scott Rolen	.60
187	Mike Williams	.10
188	Trey Beamon	.10
189	Jason Christiansen	.10
190	Elmer Dessens	.10
191	Angelo Encarnacion	.10
192	Carlos Garcia	.10
193	Mike Kingery	.10
194	Chris Peters	.10
195	Tony Womack	.10
196	Brian Barber	.10
197	David Bell	.10
198	Tony Fossas	.10
199	Rick Honeycutt	.10
200	T.J. Mathews	.10
201	Miguel Mejia	.10
202	Donovan Osborne	.10
203	Ozzie Smith	1.00
204	Andres Berumen	.10
205	Ken Caminiti	.10
206	Chris Gwynn	.10
207	Tony Gwynn	1.00
208	Rickey Henderson	.75
209	Scott Sanders	.10
210	Jason Thompson	.10
211	Fernando Valenzuela	.10
212	Tim Worrell	.10
213	Barry Bonds	2.50
214	Jay Canizaro	.10
215	Doug Creek	.10
216	Jacob Cruz	.10
217	Glenallen Hill	.10
218	Tom Lampkin	.10
219	Jim Poole	.10
220	Desi Wilson	.10

Sizzling Lumber

The 36-card, regular-sized, die-cut set was inserted every 37 packs of Invincible. The cards have die-cut flames along the right border with a bat running parallel. The player's name appears in gold foil along the top border with his position in English and Spanish in gold foil along the bottom. The card backs feature a headshot in the

upper half and contain Spanish and English text. The cards are numbered with the "SL" prefix.

		NM/M
Complete Set (36):		50.00
Common Player:		.50
1A	Cal Ripken Jr.	6.50
1B	Rafael Palmeiro	2.50
1C	Roberto Alomar	1.00
2A	Frank Thomas	3.00
2B	Robin Ventura	.50
2C	Harold Baines	.50
3A	Albert Belle	.50
3B	Manny Ramirez	3.00
3C	Kenny Lofton	.50
4A	Derek Jeter	6.50
4B	Bernie Williams	.50
4C	Wade Boggs	3.50
5A	Mark McGwire	5.00
5B	Jason Giambi	2.00
5C	Geronimo Berroa	.50
6A	Ken Griffey Jr.	4.00
6B	Alex Rodriguez	5.00
6C	Jay Buhner	.50
7A	Juan Gonzalez	1.50
7B	Dean Palmer	.50
7C	Ivan Rodriguez	2.50
8A	Ryan Klesko	.50
8B	Chipper Jones	3.50
9A	Andruw Jones	3.00
9B	Dante Bichette	.50
9C	Andres Galarraga	.50
9C	Vinny Castilla	.50
10A	Jeff Bagwell	3.00
10B	Craig Biggio	.50
10C	Derek Bell	.50
11A	Mike Piazza	4.00
11B	Raul Mondesi	.50
11C	Karim Garcia	.50
12A	Tony Gwynn	3.50
12B	Ken Caminiti	.50
12C	Greg Vaughn	.50

Sluggers & Hurlers

The 24-card, regular-sized set was inserted every 145 packs of Pacific Invincible baseball. The cards are numbered with an "SH-xA" or "SH-xaB." Each "A" card is the left half of a two-card set with the two players from the same team having their logo in the fit-together center. Each card has the player's name printed in gold foil along the bottom border with gold-foil swirls around the team logo. The card backs have a circular headshot with text in English and Spanish.

		NM/M
Complete Set (24):		80.00
Common Player:		2.00
SH-1a	Cal Ripken Jr.	10.00
SH-1b	Mike Mussina	2.50
SH-2a	Jose Canseco	2.50
SH-2b	Roger Clemens	6.00
SH-3a	Frank Thomas	3.50
SH-3b	Wilson Alvarez	2.00
SH-4a	Kenny Lofton	2.00
SH-4b	Orel Hershiser	2.00
SH-5a	Derek Jeter	10.00
SH-5b	Andy Pettitte	2.00
SH-6a	Ken Griffey Jr.	6.00
SH-6b	Randy Johnson	3.50
SH-7a	Alex Rodriguez	7.50

SH-7b	Jamie Moyer	2.00
SH-8a	Andruw Jones	3.50
SH-8b	Greg Maddux	4.50
SH-9a	Chipper Jones	4.50
SH-9b	John Smoltz	2.00
SH-10a	Jeff Bagwell	3.50
SH-10b	Shane Reynolds	2.00
SH-11a	Mike Piazza	6.00
SH-11b	Hideo Nomo	2.50
SH-12a	Tony Gwynn	4.50
SH-12b	Fernando Valenzuela	2.00

Carlos Baerga Celebrities Softball

This set was produced for distribution to fans attending the third annual Carlos Baerga Celebrities Softball Game in Puerto Rico on December 14. Packs were handed out containing two cards from this set, a 1997 Pacific Crown Collection card, a '97 Pacific Invincible card, a Pacific logo card and an information card about card shops on the island. The softball celebrities cards have gold-foil highlighted borderless action photos from the 1996 game. Pacific and the charity game's logos are in upper-right and lower left. Horizontal backs have a player portrait photo at left and English/Spanish description of his participation in the event.

		NM/M
	Complete Set (10):	16.00
	Common Player:	1.00
1	Carlos Baerga	1.00
2	Bernie Williams	1.00
3	Ivan Rodriguez	5.00
4	Sandy Alomar Jr.	1.00
5	Joey Cora	1.00
6	Roberto Alomar	1.50
7	Moises Alou	1.00
8	Rey Ordonez	1.00
9	Derek Jeter	10.00
10	David Justice	1.00

NationsBank Florida Marlins

Certainly one of the nicest team card sets ever given away at a promotional game was this Marlins set produced by Pacific and sponsored by NationsBank. The cello-wrapped set was given out to the first 16,000 children attending the June 27 Marlins game. The 2-1/2" x 3-1/2" cards are UV-coated on both sides with a gold-foil "wave" containing the player names on front. The producer, sponsor and team logos also appear on front. Backs have a swirling teal background with a player color portrait in the upper-right. Personal data, 1996 and career stats and a short career summary - are also found on back.

		NM/M
	Complete Set (33):	6.00
	Common Player:	.25
1	Kurt Abbott	.25

2	Moises Alou	.25
3	Alex Arias	.25
4	Bobby Bonilla	.25
5	Kevin Brown	.25
6	John Cangelosi	.25
7	Luis Castillo	.25
8	Jeff Conine	.25
9	Jim Eisenreich	.25
10	Alex Fernandez	.25
11	Cliff Floyd	.25
12	Rick Helling	.25
13	Felix Heredia	.25
14	Mark Hutton	.25
15	Charles Johnson	.25
16	Al Leiter	.25
17	Robb Nen	.25
18	Jay Powell	.25
19	Pat Rapp	.25
20	Edgar Renteria	.25
21	Tony Saunders	.25
22	Gary Sheffield	.75
23	Devon White	.25
24	Gregg Zaun	.25
25	Jim Leyland	.25
26	Rich Donnelly	.25
27	Bruce Kimm	.25
28	Jerry Manuel	.25
29	Milt May	.25
30	Larry Rothschild	.25
31	Tommy Sandt	.25
32	Billy the Marlin (Mascot)	.25
(33)	Header Card/Checklist	.10

1998 Pacific

Pacific Baseball for 1998 is a 450-card, bilingual set. The base set features full-bleed photos with the Pacific Crown Collection logo in the upper-left and the player's name, position and team at the bottom. Inserts include Cramer's Choice Awards, In The Cage Laser-Cuts, Home Run Hitters, Team Checklist Laser-Cuts, Gold Crown Die-Cuts and Latinos of the Major Leagues. Three foil-color parallels were issued: Reds were found one per Wal-Mart exclusive retail pack; Silvers were found one per Hobby pack. Platinum Blues, numbered to 67 each, were found one per 73 packs.

	NM/M
Complete Set (450):	40.00
Common Player:	.05
Silvers:	3X
Inserted 1:1 H	
Reds:	6X
Inserted 1:1 R	
Platinum Blues:	15X
Inserted 1:73	
Pack (12):	1.00
Wax Box (36):	20.00

1	Luis Alicea	.05
2	Garret Anderson	.05
3	Jason Dickson	.05
4	Gary DiSarcina	.05
5	Jim Edmonds	.05
6	Darin Erstad	.15
7	Chuck Finley	.05
8	Shigetosi Hasegawa	.05
9	Rickey Henderson	.75
10	Dave Hollins	.05
11	Mark Langston	.05
12	Orlando Palmeiro	.05
13	Troy Percival	.05
14	Tony Phillips	.05
15	Tim Salmon	.05
16	Allen Watson	.05
17	Roberto Alomar	.25
18	Brady Anderson	.05
19	Harold Baines	.05
20	Armando Benitez	.05
21	Geronimo Berroa	.05
22	Mike Bordick	.05
23	Eric Davis	.05
24	Scott Erickson	.05
25	Chris Hoiles	.05
26	Jimmy Key	.05
27	Aaron Ledesma	.05
28	Mike Mussina	.50
29	Randy Myers	.05
30	Jesse Orosco	.05
31	Rafael Palmeiro	.65
32	Jeff Reboulet	.05
33	Cal Ripken Jr.	2.00

34	B.J. Surhoff	.05
35	Steve Avery	.05
36	Darren Bragg	.05
37	Wil Cordero	.05
38	Jeff Frye	.05
39	Nomar Garciaparra	1.00
40	Tom Gordon	.05
41	Bill Haselman	.05
42	Scott Hatteberg	.05
43	Butch Henry	.05
44	Reggie Jefferson	.05
45	Tim Naehring	.05
46	Troy O'Leary	.05
47	Jeff Suppan	.05
48	John Valentin	.05
49	Mo Vaughn	.05
50	Tim Wakefield	.05
51	James Baldwin	.05
52	Albert Belle	.05
53	Tony Castillo	.05
54	Doug Drabek	.05
55	Ray Durham	.05
56	Jorge Fabregas	.05
57	Ozzie Guillen	.05
58	Matt Karchner	.05
59	Norberto Martin	.05
60	Dave Martinez	.05
61	Lyle Mouton	.05
62	Jaime Navarro	.05
63	Frank Thomas	.75
64	Mario Valdez	.05
65	Robin Ventura	.05
66	Sandy Alomar Jr.	.05
67	Paul Assenmacher	.05
68	Tony Fernandez	.05
69	Brian Giles	.05
70	Marquis Grissom	.05
71	Orel Hershiser	.05
72	Mike Jackson	.05
73	David Justice	.05
74	Albie Lopez	.05
75	Jose Mesa	.05
76	Charles Nagy	.05
77	Chad Ogea	.05
78	Manny Ramirez	.75
79	Jim Thome	.60
80	Omar Vizquel	.05
81	Matt Williams	.05
82	Jaret Wright	.05
83	Willie Blair	.05
84	Raul Casanova	.05
85	Tony Clark	.05
86	Deivi Cruz	.05
87	Damion Easley	.05
88	Travis Fryman	.05
89	Bobby Higginson	.05
90	Brian Hunter	.05
91	Todd Jones	.05
92	Dan Miceli	.05
93	Brian Moehler	.05
94	Melvin Nieves	.05
95	Jody Reed	.05
96	Justin Thompson	.05
97	Bubba Trammell	.05
98	Kevin Appier	.05
99	Jay Bell	.05
100	Yamil Benitez	.05
101	Johnny Damon	.35
102	Chili Davis	.05
103	Jermaine Dye	.05
104	Jed Hansen	.05
105	Jeff King	.05
106	Mike Macfarlane	.05
107	Felix Martinez	.05
108	Jeff Montgomery	.05
109	Jose Offerman	.05
110	Dean Palmer	.05
111	Hipolito Pichardo	.05
112	Jose Rosado	.05
113	Jeromy Burnitz	.05
114	Jeff Cirillo	.05
115	Cal Eldred	.05
116	John Jaha	.05
117	Doug Jones	.05
118	Scott Karl	.05
119	Jesse Levis	.05
120	Mark Loretta	.05
121	Ben McDonald	.05
122	Jose Mercedes	.05
123	Matt Mieske	.05
124	Dave Nilsson	.05
125	Jose Valentin	.05
126	Fernando Vina	.05
127	Gerald Williams	.05
128	Rick Aguilera	.05
129	Rich Becker	.05
130	Ron Coomer	.05
131	Marty Cordova	.05
132	Eddie Guardado	.05
133	LaTroy Hawkins	.05
134	Denny Hocking	.05
135	Chuck Knoblauch	.05
136	Matt Lawton	.05
137	Pat Meares	.05
138	Paul Molitor	.75
139	David Ortiz	.50
140	Brad Radke	.05
141	Terry Steinbach	.05
142	Bob Tewksbury	.05
143	Javier Valentin	.05
144	Wade Boggs	1.00
145	David Cone	.05
146	Chad Curtis	.05
147	Cecil Fielder	.05
148	Joe Girardi	.05
149	Dwight Gooden	.05
150	Hideki Irabu	.05
151	Derek Jeter	2.00

152	Tino Martinez	.05
153	Ramiro Mendoza	.05
154	Paul O'Neill	.05
155	Andy Pettitte	.20
156	Jorge Posada	.05
157	Mariano Rivera	.15
158	Rey Sanchez	.05
159	Luis Sojo	.05
160	David Wells	.05
161	Bernie Williams	.05
162	Rafael Bournigal	.05
163	Scott Brosius	.05
164	Jose Canseco	.50
165	Jason Giambi	.60
166	Ben Grieve	.05
167	Dave Magadan	.05
168	Brent Mayne	.05
169	Jason McDonald	.05
170	Izzy Molina	.05
171	Ariel Prieto	.05
172	Carlos Reyes	.05
173	Scott Spiezio	.05
174	Matt Stairs	.05
175	Bill Taylor	.05
176	Dave Telgheder	.05
177	Steve Wojciechowski	.05
178	Rich Amaral	.05
179	Bobby Ayala	.05
180	Jay Buhner	.05
181	Rafael Carmona	.05
182	Ken Cloude	.05
183	Joey Cora	.05
184	Russ Davis	.05
185	Jeff Fassero	.05
186	Ken Griffey Jr.	1.25
187	Raul Ibanez	.05
188	Randy Johnson	.75
189	Roberto Kelly	.05
190	Edgar Martinez	.05
191	Jamie Moyer	.05
192	Omar Olivares	.05
193	Alex Rodriguez	1.50
194	Heathcliff Slocumb	.05
195	Paul Sorrento	.05
196	Dan Wilson	.05
197	Scott Bailes	.05
198	John Burkett	.05
199	Domingo Cedeno	.05
200	Will Clark	.05
201	Hanley Frias RC	.05
202	Juan Gonzalez	.40
203	Tom Goodwin	.05
204	Rusty Greer	.05
205	Wilson Heredia	.05
206	Darren Oliver	.05
207	Billy Ripken	.05
208	Ivan Rodriguez	.65
209	Lee Stevens	.05
210	Fernando Tatis	.05
211	John Wetteland	.05
212	Bobby Witt	.05
213	Jacob Brumfield	.05
214	Joe Carter	.05
215	Roger Clemens	1.25
216	Felipe Crespo	.05
217	Jose Cruz Jr.	.05
218	Carlos Delgado	.50
219	Mariano Duncan	.05
220	Carlos Garcia	.05
221	Alex Gonzalez	.05
222	Juan Guzman	.05
223	Pat Hentgen	.05
224	Orlando Merced	.05
225	Tomas Perez	.05
226	Paul Quantrill	.05
227	Benito Santiago	.05
228	Woody Williams	.05
229	Rafael Belliard	.05
230	Jeff Blauser	.05
231	Pedro Borbon	.05
232	Tom Glavine	.25
233	Tony Graffanino	.05
234	Andruw Jones	.75
235	Chipper Jones	1.00
236	Ryan Klesko	.05
237	Mark Lemke	.05
238	Kenny Lofton	.05
239	Javier Lopez	.05
240	Fred McGriff	.05
241	Greg Maddux	1.00
242	Denny Neagle	.05
243	John Smoltz	.05
244	Michael Tucker	.05
245	Mark Wohlers	.05
246	Manny Alexander	.05
247	Miguel Batista	.05
248	Mark Clark	.05
249	Doug Glanville	.05
250	Jeremi Gonzalez	.05
251	Mark Grace	.05
252	Jose Hernandez	.05
253	Lance Johnson	.05
254	Brooks Kieschnick	.05
255	Kevin Orie	.05
256	Ryne Sandberg	1.00
257	Scott Servais	.05
258	Sammy Sosa	1.00
259	Kevin Tapani	.05
260	Ramon Tatis	.05
261	Bret Boone	.05
262	Dave Burba	.05
263	Brook Fordyce	.05
264	Willie Greene	.05
265	Barry Larkin	.05
266	Pedro A. Martinez	.05
267	Hal Morris	.05
268	Joe Oliver	.05
269	Eduardo Perez	.05

270	Pokey Reese	.05
271	Felix Rodriguez	.05
272	Deion Sanders	.05
273	Reggie Sanders	.05
274	Jeff Shaw	.05
275	Scott Sullivan	.05
276	Brett Tomko	.05
277	Roger Bailey	.05
278	Dante Bichette	.05
279	Ellis Burks	.05
280	Vinny Castilla	.05
281	Frank Castillo	.05
282	Mike DeJean RC	.05
283	Andres Galarraga	.05
284	Darren Holmes	.05
285	Kirt Manwaring	.05
286	Quinton McCracken	.05
287	Neifi Perez	.05
288	Steve Reed	.05
289	John Thomson	.05
290	Larry Walker	.05
291	Walt Weiss	.05
292	Kurt Abbott	.05
293	Antonio Alfonseca	.05
294	Moises Alou	.05
295	Alex Arias	.05
296	Bobby Bonilla	.05
297	Kevin Brown	.05
298	Craig Counsell	.05
299	Darren Daulton	.05
300	Jim Eisenreich	.05
301	Alex Fernandez	.05
302	Felix Heredia	.05
303	Livan Hernandez	.05
304	Charles Johnson	.05
305	Al Leiter	.05
306	Robb Nen	.05
307	Edgar Renteria	.05
308	Gary Sheffield	.45
309	Devon White	.05
310	Bob Abreu	.10
311	Brad Ausmus	.05
312	Jeff Bagwell	.75
313	Derek Bell	.05
314	Sean Berry	.05
315	Craig Biggio	.05
316	Ramon Garcia	.05
317	Luis Gonzalez	.05
318	Ricky Gutierrez	.05
319	Mike Hampton	.05
320	Richard Hidalgo	.05
321	Thomas Howard	.05
322	Darryl Kile	.05
323	Jose Lima	.05
324	Shane Reynolds	.05
325	Bill Spiers	.05
326	Tom Candiotti	.05
327	Roger Cedeno	.05
328	Greg Gagne	.05
329	Karim Garcia	.05
330	Wilton Guerrero	.05
331	Todd Hollandsworth	.05
332	Eric Karros	.05
333	Ramon Martinez	.05
334	Raul Mondesi	.05
335	Otis Nixon	.05
336	Hideo Nomo	.40
337	Antonio Osuna	.05
338	Chan Ho Park	.05
339	Mike Piazza	1.25
340	Dennis Reyes	.05
341	Ismael Valdes	.05
342	Todd Worrell	.05
343	Todd Zeile	.05
344	Darrin Fletcher	.05
345	Mark Grudzielanek	.05
346	Vladimir Guerrero	.75
347	Dustin Hermanson	.05
348	Mike Lansing	.05
349	Pedro Martinez	.75
350	Ryan McGuire	.05
351	Jose Paniagua	.05
352	Carlos Perez	.05
353	Henry Rodriguez	.05
354	F.P. Santangelo	.05
355	David Segui	.05
356	Ugueth Urbina	.05
357	Marc Valdes	.05
358	Jose Vidro	.05
359	Rondell White	.05
360	Juan Acevedo	.05
361	Edgardo Alfonzo	.05
362	Carlos Baerga	.05
363	Carl Everett	.05
364	John Franco	.05
365	Bernard Gilkey	.05
366	Todd Hundley	.05
367	Butch Huskey	.05
368	Bobby Jones	.05
369	Takashi Kashiwada	.05
370	Greg McMichael	.05
371	Brian McRae	.05
372	Alex Ochoa	.05
373	John Olerud	.05
374	Rey Ordonez	.05
375	Turk Wendell	.05
376	Ricky Bottalico	.05
377	Rico Brogna	.05
378	Lenny Dykstra	.05
379	Bobby Estalella	.05
380	Wayne Gomes	.05
381	Tyler Green	.05
382	Gregg Jefferies	.05
383	Mark Leiter	.05
384	Mike Lieberthal	.05
385	Mickey Morandini	.05
386	Scott Rolen	.60
387	Curt Schilling	.25

388	Kevin Stocker	.05
389	Danny Tartabull	.05
390	Jermaine Allensworth	.05
391	Adrian Brown	.05
392	Jason Christiansen	.05
393	Steve Cooke	.05
394	Francisco Cordova	.05
395	Jose Guillen	.05
396	Jason Kendall	.05
397	Jon Lieber	.05
398	Esteban Loaiza	.05
399	Al Martin	.05
400	Kevin Polcovich RC	.05
401	Joe Randa	.05
402	Ricardo Rincon	.05
403	Tony Womack	.05
404	Kevin Young	.05
405	Andy Benes	.05
406	Royce Clayton	.05
407	Delino DeShields	.05
408	Mike Difelice	.05
409	Dennis Eckersley	.60
410	John Frascatore	.05
411	Gary Gaetti	.05
412	Ron Gant	.05
413	Brian Jordan	.05
414	Ray Lankford	.05
415	Willie McGee	.05
416	Mark McGwire	1.50
417	Matt Morris	.05
418	Luis Ordaz	.05
419	Todd Stottlemyre	.05
420	Andy Ashby	.05
421	Jim Bruske	.05
422	Ken Caminiti	.05
423	Will Cunnane	.05
424	Steve Finley	.05
425	John Flaherty	.05
426	Chris Gomez	.05
427	Tony Gwynn	1.00
428	Joey Hamilton	.05
429	Carlos Hernandez	.05
430	Sterling Hitchcock	.05
431	Trevor Hoffman	.05
432	Wally Joyner	.05
433	Greg Vaughn	.05
434	Quilvio Veras	.05
435	Wilson Alvarez	.05
436	Rod Beck	.05
437	Barry Bonds	2.00
438	Jacob Cruz	.05
439	Shawn Estes	.05
440	Darryl Hamilton	.05
441	Roberto Hernandez	.05
442	Glenallen Hill	.05
443	Stan Javier	.05
444	Brian Johnson	.05
445	Jeff Kent	.05
446	Bill Mueller	.05
447	Kirk Rueter	.05
448	J.T. Snow	.05
449	Julian Tavarez	.05
450	Jose Vizcaino	.05

Red/Silver/Blue

Red, Silver and Platinum Blue parallels were printed for all 450 cards in Pacific, with the gold foil found on base cards being replaced by one of those foils. Red foil versions were inserted one per Wal-Mart pack (retail). Silver versions were inserted one per hobby pack. Platinum Blues, limited to 67 sets, were a one per 73 pack insert.

	NM/M
Common Red:	1.50
Red Stars:	6X
Common Silver:	.75
Silver Stars:	3X
Common Platinum Blue:	3.00
Platinum Blue Stars:	15X

Cramer's Choice

Cramer's Choice Awards is a 10-card die-cut insert. The cards feature the top player at each position as selected by Pacific CEO Mike Cramer. Each card is shaped like a trophy.

		NM/M
	Complete Set (10):	150.00
	Common Player:	7.50
	Inserted 1:721	
1	Greg Maddux	15.00
2	Roberto Alomar	7.50

3	Cal Ripken Jr.	30.00
4	Nomar Garciaparra	15.00
5	Larry Walker	7.50
6	Mike Piazza	17.50
7	Mark McGwire	25.00
8	Tony Gwynn	15.00
9	Ken Griffey Jr.	20.00
10	Roger Clemens	17.50

Gold Crown Die-Cuts

Gold Crown Die-Cuts is a 36-card insert seeded one per 37 packs. Each card has a holographic silver foil background and gold etching. The cards are die-cut around a crown design at the top.

		NM/M
Complete Set (36):		85.00
Common Player:		1.50
1	Chipper Jones	4.00
2	Greg Maddux	4.00
3	Denny Neagle	1.50
4	Roberto Alomar	2.00
5	Rafael Palmeiro	2.50
6	Cal Ripken Jr.	8.00
7	Nomar Garciaparra	4.00
8	Mo Vaughn	1.50
9	Frank Thomas	3.00
10	Sandy Alomar Jr.	1.50
11	David Justice	1.50
12	Manny Ramirez	3.00
13	Andres Galarraga	1.50
14	Larry Walker	1.50
15	Moises Alou	1.50
16	Livan Hernandez	1.50
17	Gary Sheffield	2.00
18	Jeff Bagwell	3.00
19	Raul Mondesi	1.50
20	Hideo Nomo	2.00
21	Mike Piazza	4.50
22	Derek Jeter	8.00
23	Tino Martinez	1.50
24	Bernie Williams	1.50
25	Ben Grieve	1.50
26	Mark McGwire	6.50
27	Tony Gwynn	4.00
28	Barry Bonds	8.00
29	Ken Griffey Jr.	5.00
30	Randy Johnson	3.00
31	Edgar Martinez	1.50
32	Alex Rodriguez	6.50
33	Juan Gonzalez	2.00
34	Ivan Rodriguez	2.50
35	Roger Clemens	4.50
36	Jose Cruz Jr.	1.50

Home Run Hitters

This 20-card set was inserted one per 73 packs. The full-foil cards feature a color player photo with their home run total from 1997 embossed in the background.

		NM/M
Complete Set (20):		50.00
Common Player:		1.00
1	Rafael Palmeiro	3.00
2	Mo Vaughn	1.00
3	Sammy Sosa	4.00
4	Albert Belle	1.00
5	Frank Thomas	3.50
6	David Justice	1.00
7	Jim Thome	3.00
8	Matt Williams	1.00
9	Vinny Castilla	1.00
10	Andres Galarraga	1.00
11	Larry Walker	1.00
12	Jeff Bagwell	3.50
13	Mike Piazza	4.50
14	Tino Martinez	1.00
15	Mark McGwire	6.00
16	Barry Bonds	7.50
17	Jay Buhner	1.00
18	Ken Griffey Jr.	5.00
19	Alex Rodriguez	6.00
20	Juan Gonzalez	2.00

In the Cage

This insert set features top players in a die-cut batting cage. The netting on the cage is laser-cut. In The Cage laser-cuts were inserted one per 145 packs.

		NM/M
Complete Set (20):		175.00
Common Player:		4.00
1	Chipper Jones	12.00
2	Roberto Alomar	4.00
3	Cal Ripken Jr.	25.00
4	Nomar Garciaparra	12.00
5	Frank Thomas	10.00
6	Sandy Alomar Jr.	4.00
7	David Justice	4.00
8	Larry Walker	4.00
9	Bobby Bonilla	4.00
10	Mike Piazza	16.00
11	Tino Martinez	4.00
12	Bernie Williams	4.00
13	Mark McGwire	20.00
14	Tony Gwynn	12.00
15	Barry Bonds	25.00
16	Ken Griffey Jr.	16.00
17	Edgar Martinez	4.00
18	Alex Rodriguez	20.00
19	Juan Gonzalez	6.00
20	Ivan Rodriguez	7.50

Latinos of the Major Leagues

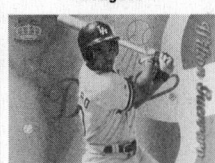

This 36-card set features Major League players of Hispanic descent. The background has a world map on the left, the player's team logo in the center and an American flag on the right.

		NM/M
Complete Set (36):		30.00
Common Player:		.50
Inserted 2:37		
1	Andruw Jones	2.50
2	Javier Lopez	.50
3	Roberto Alomar	1.25
4	Geronimo Berroa	.50
5	Rafael Palmeiro	2.00
6	Nomar Garciaparra	3.00
7	Sammy Sosa	3.00
8	Ozzie Guillen	.50
9	Sandy Alomar Jr.	.50
10	Manny Ramirez	2.50
11	Omar Vizquel	.50
12	Vinny Castilla	.50
13	Andres Galarraga	.50
14	Moises Alou	.50
15	Bobby Bonilla	.50
16	Livan Hernandez	.50
17	Edgar Renteria	.50
18	Wilton Guerrero	.50
19	Raul Mondesi	.50
20	Ismael Valdes	.50
21	Fernando Vina	.50
22	Pedro Martinez	2.50
23	Edgardo Alfonzo	.50
24	Carlos Baerga	.50
25	Rey Ordonez	.50
26	Tino Martinez	.50
27	Mariano Rivera	1.00
28	Bernie Williams	.50
29	Jose Canseco	1.50
30	Joey Cora	.50
31	Roberto Kelly	.50
32	Edgar Martinez	.50
33	Alex Rodriguez	3.50
34	Juan Gonzalez	1.50
35	Ivan Rodriguez	2.00
36	Jose Cruz Jr.	.50

Team Checklists

Team Checklists is a 30-card insert in the bilingual Pacific Baseball set. One card was created for each team. A player photo is featured on the right with the team logo laser-cut into a bat barrel design on the left.

		NM/M
Complete Set (30):		60.00
Common Player:		.50
1	Tim Salmon, Jim Edmonds	.50
2	Cal Ripken Jr., Roberto Alomar	6.00
3	Nomar Garciaparra, Mo Vaughn	3.50
4	Frank Thomas, Albert Belle	2.50
5	Sandy Alomar Jr., Manny Ramirez	2.50
6	Justin Thompson, Tony Clark	.50
7	Johnny Damon, Jermaine Dye	.75
8	Dave Nilsson, Jeff Cirillo	.50
9	Paul Molitor, Chuck Knoblauch	2.50
10	Tino Martinez, Derek Jeter	6.00
11	Ben Grieve, Jose Canseco	1.00
12	Ken Griffey Jr., Alex Rodriguez	5.00
13	Juan Gonzalez, Ivan Rodriguez	2.00
14	Jose Cruz Jr., Roger Clemens	4.00
15	Greg Maddux, Chipper Jones	3.50
16	Sammy Sosa, Mark Grace	3.50
17	Barry Larkin, Deion Sanders	.50
18	Larry Walker, Andres Galarraga	.50
19	Moises Alou, Bobby Bonilla	.50
20	Jeff Bagwell, Craig Biggio	2.50
21	Mike Piazza, Hideo Nomo	4.00
22	Pedro Martinez, Henry Rodriguez	2.50
23	Rey Ordonez, Carlos Baerga	.50
24	Curt Schilling, Scott Rolen	1.50
25	Al Martin, Tony Womack	.50
26	Mark McGwire, Dennis Eckersley	5.00
27	Tony Gwynn, Wally Joyner	3.50
28	Barry Bonds, J.T. Snow	6.00
29	Matt Williams, Jay Bell	.50
30	Fred McGriff, Roberto Hernandez	.50

1998 Pacific Aurora

The Aurora base set consists of 200 cards printed on 24-point board. The cards have a color photo bordered on two sides by a thick green (National League) or red (A.L.) border. A portrait photo appears in the upper-right corner. Back has another portrait photo, 1997 and career stats, career highlights and personal data. Aurora was sold in six-card foil packs. Inserts include Pennant Fever (with three parallels), Hardball Cel-Fusions, Kings of the Major Leagues, On Deck Laser-Cuts and Pacific Cubes.

		NM/M
Complete Set (200):		20.00
Common Player:		.05
Pack (6):		1.00
Wax Box (36):		20.00
1	Garret Anderson	.05
2	Jim Edmonds	.05
3	Darin Erstad	.15
4	Cecil Fielder	.05
5	Chuck Finley	.05
6	Todd Greene	.05
7	Ken Hill	.05
8	Tim Salmon	.05
9	Roberto Alomar	.20
10	Brady Anderson	.05
11	Joe Carter	.05
12	Mike Mussina	.35
13	Rafael Palmeiro	.65
14	Cal Ripken Jr.	2.50
15	B.J. Surhoff	.05
16	Steve Avery	.05
17	Nomar Garciaparra	1.00
18	Pedro Martinez	.75
19	John Valentin	.05
20	Jason Varitek	.05
21	Mo Vaughn	.05
22	Albert Belle	.05
23	Ray Durham	.05
24	Magglio Ordonez **RC**	1.50
25	Frank Thomas	.75
26	Robin Ventura	.05
27	Sandy Alomar Jr.	.05
28	Travis Fryman	.05
29	Dwight Gooden	.05
30	David Justice	.05
31	Kenny Lofton	.05
32	Manny Ramirez	.75
33	Jim Thome	.60
34	Omar Vizquel	.05
35	Enrique Wilson	.05
36	Jaret Wright	.05
37	Tony Clark	.05
38	Bobby Higginson	.05
39	Brian Hunter	.05
40	Bip Roberts	.05
41	Justin Thompson	.05
42	Jeff Conine	.05
43	Johnny Damon	.35
44	Jermaine Dye	.05
45	Jeff King	.05
46	Jeff Montgomery	.05
47	Hal Morris	.05
48	Dean Palmer	.05
49	Terry Pendleton	.05
50	Rick Aguilera	.05
51	Marty Cordova	.05
52	Paul Molitor	.75
53	Otis Nixon	.05
54	Brad Radke	.05
55	Terry Steinbach	.05
56	Todd Walker	.05
57	Chili Davis	.05
58	Derek Jeter	2.50
59	Chuck Knoblauch	.05
60	Tino Martinez	.05
61	Paul O'Neill	.05
62	Andy Pettitte	.20
63	Mariano Rivera	.15
64	Bernie Williams	.05
65	Jason Giambi	.50
66	Ben Grieve	.50
67	Rickey Henderson	.75
68	A.J. Hinch	.05
69	Kenny Rogers	.05
70	Jay Buhner	.05
71	Joey Cora	.05
72	Ken Griffey Jr.	1.50
73	Randy Johnson	.75
74	Edgar Martinez	.05
75	Jamie Moyer	.05
76	Alex Rodriguez	2.00
77	David Segui	.05
78	Rolando Arrojo **RC**	.35
79	Wade Boggs	1.00
80	Roberto Hernandez	.05
81	Dave Martinez	.05
82	Fred McGriff	.05
83	Paul Sorrento	.05
84	Kevin Stocker	.05
85	Will Clark	.05
86	Juan Gonzalez	.40
87	Tom Goodwin	.05
88	Rusty Greer	.05
89	Ivan Rodriguez	.65
90	John Wetteland	.05
91	Jose Canseco	.40
92	Roger Clemens	1.25
93	Jose Cruz Jr.	.50
94	Carlos Delgado	.50
95	Pat Hentgen	.05
96	Jay Bell	.05
97	Andy Benes	.05
98	Karim Garcia	.05
99	Travis Lee	.50
100	Devon White	.05
101	Matt Williams	.05
102	Andres Galarraga	.05
103	Tom Glavine	.30
104	Andruw Jones	.75
105	Chipper Jones	1.00
106	Ryan Klesko	.05
107	Javy Lopez	.05
108	Greg Maddux	1.50
109	Walt Weiss	.05
110	Rod Beck	.05
111	Jeff Blauser	.05
112	Mark Grace	.05
113	Lance Johnson	.05
114	Mickey Morandini	.05
115	Henry Rodriguez	.05
116	Sammy Sosa	1.00
117	Kerry Wood	.35
118	Lenny Harris	.05
119	Damian Jackson	.05
120	Barry Larkin	.05
121	Reggie Sanders	.05
122	Brett Tomko	.05
123	Dante Bichette	.05
124	Ellis Burks	.05
125	Vinny Castilla	.05
126	Todd Helton	.75
127	Darryl Kile	.05
128	Larry Walker	.05
129	Bobby Bonilla	.05
130	Livan Hernandez	.05
131	Charles Johnson	.05
132	Derek Lee	.50
133	Edgar Renteria	.05
134	Gary Sheffield	.35
135	Moises Alou	.05
136	Jeff Bagwell	.75
137	Derek Bell	.05
138	Craig Biggio	.05
139	John Halama **RC**	.15
140	Mike Hampton	.05
141	Richard Hidalgo	.05
142	Wilton Guerrero	.05
143	Todd Hollandsworth	.05
144	Eric Karros	.05
145	Paul Konerko	.05
146	Raul Mondesi	.05
147	Hideo Nomo	.40
148	Chan Ho Park	.05
149	Mike Piazza	1.25
150	Jeromy Burnitz	.05
151	Todd Dunn	.05
152	Marquis Grissom	.05
153	John Jaha	.05
154	Dave Nilsson	.05
155	Fernando Vina	.05
156	Mark Grudzielanek	.05
157	Vladimir Guerrero	.75
158	F.P. Santangelo	.05
159	Jose Vidro	.05
160	Rondell White	.05
161	Edgardo Alfonzo	.05
162	Carlos Baerga	.05
163	John Franco	.05
164	Todd Hundley	.05
165	Brian McRae	.05
166	John Olerud	.05
167	Rey Ordonez	.05
168	Masato Yoshii **RC**	.25
169	Ricky Bottalico	.05
170	Doug Glanville	.05
171	Gregg Jefferies	.05
172	Desi Relaford	.05
173	Scott Rolen	.60
174	Curt Schilling	.30
175	Jose Guillen	.05
176	Jason Kendall	.05
177	Al Martin	.05
178	Abraham Nunez	.05
179	Kevin Young	.05
180	Royce Clayton	.05
181	Delino DeShields	.05
182	Gary Gaetti	.05
183	Ron Gant	.05
184	Brian Jordan	.05
185	Ray Lankford	.05
186	Willie McGee	.05
187	Mark McGwire	2.00
188	Kevin Brown	.05
189	Ken Caminiti	.05
190	Steve Finley	.05
191	Tony Gwynn	1.00
192	Wally Joyner	.05
193	Ruben Rivera	.05
194	Quilvio Veras	.05
195	Barry Bonds	2.50
196	Shawn Estes	.05
197	Orel Hershiser	.05
198	Jeff Kent	.05
199	Robb Nen	.05
200	J.T. Snow	.05

Cubes

A cardboard cube presenting player photos on top and three sides, plus a side of stats was created as a hobby-only insert for Pacific Aurora. The assembled, shrink-wrapped cubes were packed one per box.

		NM/M
Complete Set (20):		75.00
Common Player:		1.50
Inserted 1:Box		
1	Travis Lee	1.50
2	Chipper Jones	4.00
3	Greg Maddux	4.00
4	Cal Ripken Jr.	6.00
5	Nomar Garciaparra	4.00
6	Frank Thomas	3.00
7	Manny Ramirez	3.00
8	Larry Walker	1.50
9	Hideo Nomo	2.00
10	Mike Piazza	5.00
11	Derek Jeter	10.00
12	Ben Grieve	1.50
13	Mark McGwire	7.50
14	Tony Gwynn	4.00
15	Barry Bonds	10.00
16	Ken Griffey Jr.	6.00
17	Alex Rodriguez	7.50
18	Wade Boggs	4.00
19	Juan Gonzalez	2.00
20	Jose Cruz Jr.	1.50

Hardball Cel-Fusion

Hardball Cel-Fusion features a die-cut celluloid baseball fused to a foiled and etched card.

		NM/M
Complete Set (20):		60.00
Common Player:		2.00
Inserted 1:73		
1	Travis Lee	2.00
2	Chipper Jones	6.00
3	Greg Maddux	6.00
4	Cal Ripken Jr.	15.00
5	Nomar Garciaparra	6.00
6	Frank Thomas	4.50
7	David Justice	2.00
8	Jeff Bagwell	4.50
9	Hideo Nomo	3.00
10	Mike Piazza	7.50
11	Derek Jeter	15.00
12	Ben Grieve	3.00
13	Scott Rolen	3.00
14	Mark McGwire	12.00
15	Tony Gwynn	6.00
16	Ken Griffey Jr.	9.00
17	Alex Rodriguez	12.00
18	Ivan Rodriguez	3.50
19	Roger Clemens	7.50
20	Jose Cruz Jr.	2.00

Kings of the Major Leagues

This 10-card insert features star players on fully-foiled cards. A marble-look semi-circular panel at bottom has the player identification. The action photo at center is set against a bronze orb and concentric circles of gold-foil repeat the "Kings of the Major Leagues" title. Backs have a color portrait on a red and black background along with a few sentences about the player.

		NM/M
Complete Set (10):		75.00
Common Player:		7.50
Inserted 1:361		
1	Chipper Jones	9.00
2	Greg Maddux	9.00
3	Cal Ripken Jr.	20.00
4	Nomar Garciaparra	9.00
5	Frank Thomas	7.50
6	Mike Piazza	10.00
7	Mark McGwire	15.00
8	Tony Gwynn	9.00
9	Ken Griffey Jr.	12.00
10	Alex Rodriguez	15.00

On Deck Laser-Cut

On Deck Laser-Cut is a 20-card insert in packs of 1998 Pacific Aurora. Fronts have an action photo at top, with an intricately die-cut pattern in gold foil below. Backs feature a portrait photo.

		NM/M
Complete Set (20):		30.00
Common Player:		.60
Inserted 1:9		
1	Travis Lee	.60
2	Chipper Jones	2.25
3	Greg Maddux	2.25
4	Cal Ripken Jr.	6.00
5	Nomar Garciaparra	2.25
6	Frank Thomas	1.50
7	Manny Ramirez	1.50
8	Larry Walker	.60
9	Hideo Nomo	1.00
10	Mike Piazza	2.50
11	Derek Jeter	6.00
12	Ben Grieve	.60
13	Mark McGwire	4.50
14	Tony Gwynn	2.25
15	Barry Bonds	6.00
16	Ken Griffey Jr.	3.00
17	Alex Rodriguez	4.50
18	Wade Boggs	2.25
19	Juan Gonzalez	1.00
20	Jose Cruz Jr.	.60

Pennant Fever

Pennant Fever is a 50-card insert seeded one per pack. Each card is fully foiled and etched. The color player image is duplicated in the upper-left corner with an image stamped in gold foil. Pennant Fever has four parallels. Red cards are a 1:4 retail insert. The Silver retail parallel is numbered to 250. Platinum Blue is numbered to 100 and the Copper hobby parallel is numbered to 20. Tony Gwynn signed his card serially numbered one in each insert.

		NM/M
Complete Set (50):		25.00
Common Player:		.20
Inserted 1:1		
Reds (1:4 Retail):		2X
Silvers (250 Sets):		4X
Platinum Blues (100 Sets):		12X
Coppers (20 Sets):		40X
1	Tony Gwynn	1.00
2	Derek Jeter	2.00
3	Alex Rodriguez	1.50
4	Paul Molitor	.75
5	Nomar Garciaparra	1.00
6	Jeff Bagwell	.75
7	Ivan Rodriguez	.65
8	Cal Ripken Jr.	2.00
9	Matt Williams	.20
10	Chipper Jones	1.00
11	Edgar Martinez	.20
12	Wade Boggs	1.00
13	Paul Konerko	.30
14	Ben Grieve	.20
15	Sandy Alomar Jr.	.20
16	Travis Lee	.20
17	Scott Rolen	.65
18	Ryan Klesko	.20
19	Juan Gonzalez	.40
20	Albert Belle	.20
21	Roger Clemens	1.25
22	Javy Lopez	.20
23	Jose Cruz Jr.	.20
24	Ken Griffey Jr.	1.25
25	Mark McGwire	1.50
26	Brady Anderson	.20
27	Jaret Wright	.20
28	Roberto Alomar	.30
29	Joe Carter	.20
30	Hideo Nomo	.40
31	Mike Piazza	1.25
32	Andres Galarraga	.20
33	Larry Walker	.20
34	Tim Salmon	.20
35	Frank Thomas	.75
36	Moises Alou	.20
37	David Justice	.20
38	Manny Ramirez	.75
39	Jim Edmonds	.20
40	Barry Bonds	2.00
41	Jim Thome	.65
42	Mo Vaughn	.20
43	Rafael Palmeiro	.65
44	Darin Erstad	.30
45	Pedro Martinez	.75
46	Greg Maddux	1.00
47	Jose Canseco	.45
48	Vladimir Guerrero	.75
49	Bernie Williams	.20
50	Randy Johnson	.75

1998 Pacific Crown Royale

The Crown Royale base set consists of 144 die-cut cards. The cards have a horizontal layout and are die-cut around a crown design at the top. The cards are double-foiled and etched. Inserts include Diamond Knights, Pillars of the Game, Race to the Record, All-Star Die-Cuts, Firestone on Baseball and Cramer's Choice Awards.

		NM/M
Complete Set (144):		60.00
Common Player:		.20
Pack (6):		1.00
Wax Box (24):		20.00
1	Garret Anderson	.20
2	Jim Edmonds	.20
3	Darin Erstad	.50
4	Tim Salmon	.20
5	Jarrod Washburn	.20
6	David Dellucci	.20
7	Travis Lee	.20
8	Devon White	.20
9	Matt Williams	.20
10	Andres Galarraga	.20
11	Tom Glavine	.35
12	Andruw Jones	2.00
13	Chipper Jones	3.00
14	Ryan Klesko	.20
15	Javy Lopez	.20
16	Greg Maddux	3.00
17	Walt Weiss	.20
18	Roberto Alomar	.75
19	Harold Baines	.20
20	Eric Davis	.20
21	Mike Mussina	1.00
22	Rafael Palmeiro	1.50
23	Cal Ripken Jr.	5.00
24	Nomar Garciaparra	3.00
25	Pedro Martinez	2.00
26	Troy O'Leary	.20
27	Mo Vaughn	.20
28	Tim Wakefield	.20
29	Mark Grace	.20
30	Mickey Morandini	.20
31	Sammy Sosa	3.00
32	Kerry Wood	.50
33	Albert Belle	.20
34	Mike Caruso	.20
35	Ray Durham	.20
36	Frank Thomas	2.00
37	Robin Ventura	.20
38	Bret Boone	.20
39	Sean Casey	.25
40	Barry Larkin	.20
41	Reggie Sanders	.20
42	Sandy Alomar Jr.	.20
43	David Justice	.20
44	Kenny Lofton	.20
45	Manny Ramirez	2.00
46	Jim Thome	1.00
47	Omar Vizquel	.20
48	Jaret Wright	.20
49	Dante Bichette	.20
50	Ellis Burks	.20
51	Vinny Castilla	.20
52	Todd Helton	2.00
53	Larry Walker	.20
54	Tony Clark	.20
55	Damion Easley	.20
56	Bobby Higginson	.20
57	Cliff Floyd	.20
58	Livan Hernandez	.20
59	Derek Lee	.75
60	Edgar Renteria	.20
61	Moises Alou	.20
62	Jeff Bagwell	2.00
63	Derek Bell	.20
64	Craig Biggio	.20
65	Johnny Damon	.35
66	Jeff King	.20
67	Hal Morris	.20
68	Dean Palmer	.20
69	Bobby Bonilla	.20
70	Eric Karros	.20
71	Raul Mondesi	.20
72	Gary Sheffield	.75
73	Jeromy Burnitz	.20
74	Jeff Cirillo	.20
75	Marquis Grissom	.20
76	Fernando Vina	.20
77	Marty Cordova	.20
78	Pat Meares	.20
79	Paul Molitor	2.00
80	Terry Steinbach	.20
81	Todd Walker	.20
82	Brad Fullmer	.20
83	Vladimir Guerrero	2.00
84	Carl Pavano	.20
85	Rondell White	.20
86	Carlos Baerga	.20
87	Hideo Nomo	1.00
88	John Olerud	.20
89	Rey Ordonez	.20
90	Mike Piazza	3.00
91	Masato Yoshii RC	.75
92	Orlando Hernandez RC	.75
93	Hideki Irabu	.20
94	Derek Jeter	5.00
95	Chuck Knoblauch	.20
96	Ricky Ledee	.20
97	Tino Martinez	.20
98	Paul O'Neill	.20
99	Bernie Williams	.20
100	Jason Giambi	1.25
101	Ben Grieve	.20
102	Rickey Henderson	2.00
103	Matt Stairs	.20
104	Bob Abreu	.25
105	Doug Glanville	.20
106	Scott Rolen	1.50
107	Curt Schilling	.35
108	Jose Guillen	.20
109	Jason Kendall	.20
110	Jason Schmidt	.20
111	Kevin Young	.20
112	Delino DeShields	.20
113	Brian Jordan	.20
114	Ray Lankford	.20
115	Mark McGwire	4.00
116	Tony Gwynn	3.00
117	Wally Joyner	.20
118	Ruben Rivera	.20
119	Greg Vaughn	.20
120	Rich Aurilia	.20
121	Barry Bonds	5.00
122	Bill Mueller	.20
123	Robb Nen	.20
124	Jay Buhner	.20
125	Ken Griffey Jr.	3.50
126	Edgar Martinez	.20
127	Shane Monahan	.20
128	Alex Rodriguez	4.00
129	David Segui	.20
130	Rolando Arrojo RC	.75
131	Wade Boggs	3.00
132	Quinton McCracken	.20
133	Fred McGriff	.20
134	Bobby Smith	.20
135	Will Clark	.20
136	Juan Gonzalez	1.00
137	Rusty Greer	.20
138	Ivan Rodriguez	1.50
139	Aaron Sele	.20
140	John Wetteland	.20
141	Jose Canseco	1.00
142	Roger Clemens	3.50
143	Carlos Delgado	1.25
144	Shawn Green	.50

All-Stars

This 20-card insert was seeded one per 25 packs. The featured players all participated in the 1998 All-Star Game. The background features the sun rising over a mountain with a die-cut at the top of the card.

		NM/M
Complete Set (20):		110.00
Common Player:		1.50
Inserted 1:25		
1	Roberto Alomar	2.00
2	Cal Ripken Jr.	15.00
3	Kenny Lofton	1.50
4	Jim Thome	5.00
5	Derek Jeter	15.00
6	David Wells	1.50
7	Ken Griffey Jr.	10.00
8	Alex Rodriguez	12.00
9	Juan Gonzalez	4.00
10	Ivan Rodriguez	5.00
11	Gary Sheffield	2.50
12	Chipper Jones	7.50
13	Greg Maddux	7.50
14	Walt Weiss	1.50
15	Larry Walker	1.50
16	Craig Biggio	1.50
17	Mike Piazza	10.00
18	Mark McGwire	12.00
19	Tony Gwynn	7.50
20	Barry Bonds	15.00

Cramer's Choice Awards

Premium-sized Cramer's Choice Awards were inserted one per box. The 10 players in the set are featured on a die-cut card designed to resemble a trophy. Pacific CEO Mike Cramer signed and hand-numbered ten sets of Cramer's Choice Awards.

		NM/M
Complete Set (10):		65.00
Common Player:		4.00
Inserted 1:box		
1	Cal Ripken Jr.	15.00
2	Ken Griffey Jr.	9.00
3	Alex Rodriguez	12.00
4	Juan Gonzalez	5.00
5	Travis Lee	4.00
6	Chipper Jones	7.50
7	Greg Maddux	7.50
8	Kerry Wood	5.00
9	Mark McGwire	12.00
10	Tony Gwynn	7.50

Diamond Knights

Diamond Knights is a 25-card, one per pack insert. Each card features a color action photo and the player's name, team and position listed on a Medieval-type border at the bottom.

		NM/M
Complete Set (25):		20.00
Common Player:		.35
Inserted 1:1		
1	Andres Galarraga	.35
2	Chipper Jones	1.00
3	Greg Maddux	1.00
4	Cal Ripken Jr.	2.50
5	Nomar Garciaparra	1.50
6	Mo Vaughn	.35
7	Kerry Wood	.45
8	Frank Thomas	.75
9	Vinny Castilla	.35
10	Jeff Bagwell	.35
11	Craig Biggio	.35
12	Paul Molitor	.75
13	Mike Piazza	1.50
14	Orlando Hernandez	.35
15	Derek Jeter	2.50
16	Ricky Ledee	.35
17	Mark McGwire	2.00
18	Tony Gwynn	1.00
19	Barry Bonds	2.50
20	Ken Griffey Jr.	1.75
21	Alex Rodriguez	2.00
22	Wade Boggs	1.00
23	Juan Gonzalez	.45
24	Ivan Rodriguez	.65
25	Jose Canseco	.50

Firestone on Baseball

This 26-card insert features star players with commentary by sports personality Roy Firestone. The fronts have a color photo of the player and a portrait of Firestone in the lower-right corner. The card backs have text by Firestone on what makes the featured player great. Firestone signed a total of 300 cards in this insert.

		NM/M
Complete Set (26):		50.00
Common Player:		.35
Firestone Auto. Card:		18.00
Inserted 1:12		
1	Travis Lee	.35
2	Chipper Jones	3.00
3	Greg Maddux	3.00
4	Cal Ripken Jr.	6.00
5	Nomar Garciaparra	3.00
6	Mo Vaughn	.35
7	Kerry Wood	1.00
8	Frank Thomas	2.25
9	Manny Ramirez	2.25
10	Larry Walker	.35
11	Gary Sheffield	1.00
12	Paul Molitor	2.25
13	Hideo Nomo	1.50
14	Mike Piazza	3.50
15	Ben Grieve	.35
16	Mark McGwire	5.00
17	Tony Gwynn	3.00
18	Barry Bonds	6.00
19	Ken Griffey Jr.	4.00
20	Randy Johnson	2.25
21	Alex Rodriguez	5.00
22	Wade Boggs	3.00
23	Juan Gonzalez	1.50
24	Ivan Rodriguez	1.75
25	Roger Clemens	3.50
26	Roy Firestone	.35

Home Run Fever

Home Run Fever features players who had a shot at breaking Roger Maris' home run record in 1998. Fronts have a player photo on the left and a blackboard with numbers from 1 to 60 on the right. Ten circles featuring disappearing ink contained numbers 61 through 70. Collectors could rub the circles to reveal the player's potential record home run total.

		NM/M
Complete Set (10):		30.00
Common Player:		1.50
Inserted 1:73		
1	Andres Galarraga	1.50
2	Sammy Sosa	4.50
3	Albert Belle	1.50
4	Jim Thome	3.00
5	Mark McGwire	7.50
6	Greg Vaughn	1.50
7	Ken Griffey Jr.	6.00
8	Alex Rodriguez	7.50
9	Juan Gonzalez	2.50
10	Jose Canseco	2.50

Pillars of the Game

1998 Pacific Invincible

Invincible consists of a 150-card base set with a horizontal format featuring a player photo on the left and a portrait in a cel window on the right. The regular cards were inserted one per five-card pack. Silver (2:37) and Platinum Blue (1:73) parallels were also created. Inserts include Moments in Time, Team Checklists, Photoengravings, Interleague Players, Gems of the Diamond and Cramer's Choice Awards.

		NM/M
Complete Set (150):		60.00
Common Player:		.20
Silvers:		4X
Inserted 2:37		
Platinum Blues:		6X
Inserted 1:73		
Pack (5):		1.25
Wax Box (36):		32.50
1	Garret Anderson	.20
2	Jim Edmonds	.20
3	Darin Erstad	.35
4	Chuck Finley	.20
5	Tim Salmon	.35
6	Roberto Alomar	.35
7	Brady Anderson	.20
8	Geronimo Berroa	.20
9	Eric Davis	.20
10	Mike Mussina	.50
11	Rafael Palmeiro	1.00
12	Cal Ripken Jr.	6.00
13	Steve Avery	.20
14	Nomar Garciaparra	2.50
15	John Valentin	.20
16	Mo Vaughn	.20
17	Albert Belle	.20
18	Ozzie Guillen	.20
19	Norberto Martin	.20
20	Frank Thomas	1.50
21	Robin Ventura	.20
22	Sandy Alomar Jr.	.20
23	David Justice	.20
24	Kenny Lofton	.20
25	Manny Ramirez	1.50
26	Jim Thome	1.00
27	Omar Vizquel	.20
28	Matt Williams	.20
29	Jaret Wright	.20
30	Raul Casanova	.20
31	Tony Clark	.20
32	Deivi Cruz	.20
33	Bobby Higginson	.20
34	Justin Thompson	.20
35	Yamil Benitez	.20
36	Johnny Damon	.35
37	Jermaine Dye	.20
38	Jed Hansen	.20
39	Larry Sutton	.20
40	Jeromy Burnitz	.20
41	Jeff Cirillo	.20
42	Dave Nilsson	.20
43	Jose Valentin	.20
44	Fernando Vina	.20
45	Marty Cordova	.20
46	Chuck Knoblauch	.20
47	Paul Molitor	1.50

48	Brad Radke	.20
49	Terry Steinbach	.20
50	Wade Boggs	2.50
51	Hideki Irabu	.20
52	Derek Jeter	6.00
53	Tino Martinez	.20
54	Andy Pettitte	.30
55	Mariano Rivera	.30
56	Bernie Williams	.20
57	Jose Canseco	.75
58	Jason Giambi	.75
59	Ben Grieve	.20
60	Aaron Small	.20
61	Jay Buhner	.20
62	Ken Cloude	.20
63	Joey Cora	.20
64	Ken Griffey Jr.	3.50
65	Randy Johnson	1.50
66	Edgar Martinez	.20
67	Alex Rodriguez	5.00
68	Will Clark	.20
69	Juan Gonzalez	.75
70	Rusty Greer	.20
71	Ivan Rodriguez	1.00
72	Joe Carter	.20
73	Roger Clemens	3.00
74	Jose Cruz Jr.	.20
75	Carlos Delgado	.75
76	Andruw Jones	1.50
77	Chipper Jones	2.50
78	Ryan Klesko	.20
79	Javier Lopez	.20
80	Greg Maddux	2.50
81	Miguel Batista	.20
82	Jeremi Gonzalez	.20
83	Mark Grace	.20
84	Kevin Orie	.20
85	Sammy Sosa	2.50
86	Barry Larkin	.20
87	Deion Sanders	.20
88	Reggie Sanders	.20
89	Chris Stynes	.20
90	Dante Bichette	.20
91	Vinny Castilla	.20
92	Andres Galarraga	.20
93	Neifi Perez	.20
94	Larry Walker	.20
95	Moises Alou	.20
96	Bobby Bonilla	.20
97	Kevin Brown	.20
98	Craig Counsell	.20
99	Livan Hernandez	.20
100	Edgar Renteria	.20
101	Gary Sheffield	.60
102	Jeff Bagwell	1.50
103	Craig Biggio	.20
104	Luis Gonzalez	.20
105	Darryl Kile	.20
106	Wilton Guerrero	.20
107	Eric Karros	.20
108	Ramon Martinez	.20
109	Raul Mondesi	.20
110	Hideo Nomo	.75
111	Chan Ho Park	.20
112	Mike Piazza	3.00
113	Mark Grudzielanek	.20
114	Vladimir Guerrero	1.50
115	Pedro Martinez	1.50
116	Henry Rodriguez	.20
117	David Segui	.20
118	Edgardo Alfonzo	.20
119	Carlos Baerga	.20
120	John Franco	.20
121	John Olerud	.20
122	Rey Ordonez	.20
123	Ricky Bottalico	.20
124	Gregg Jefferies	.20
125	Mickey Morandini	.20
126	Scott Rolen	1.00
127	Curt Schilling	.45
128	Jose Guillen	.20
129	Esteban Loaiza	.20
130	Al Martin	.20
131	Tony Womack	.20
132	Dennis Eckersley	1.00
133	Gary Gaetti	.20
134	Curtis King	.20
135	Ray Lankford	.20
136	Mark McGwire	5.00
137	Ken Caminiti	.20
138	Steve Finley	.20
139	Tony Gwynn	2.50
140	Carlos Hernandez	.20
141	Wally Joyner	.20
142	Barry Bonds	6.00
143	Jacob Cruz	.20
144	Shawn Estes	.20
145	Stan Javier	.20
146	J.T. Snow	.20
147	Nomar Garciaparra (ROY)	1.00
148	Scott Rolen (ROY)	.60
149	Ken Griffey Jr. (MVP)	1.75
150	Larry Walker (MVP)	.20

Cramer's Choice

The 10-card Cramer's Choice Awards insert features top players on cards with a die-cut trophy design. This set has six different foil variations, each with a different production number. Green (99 hand-numbered sets), Dark Blue (80), Light Blue (50), Red (25), Gold (15) and Purple (10) versions were included in Invincible.

		NM/M
Complete Green Set (10):		200.00
Common Green (99 Sets):		10.00
Dark Blues (80 Sets):		1X
Light Blues (50 Sets):		1.5X
Reds (25 Sets):		2X
Golds (15 Sets):		3X
Purples (10 Sets):		5X
1	Greg Maddux	20.00
2	Roberto Alomar	10.00
3	Cal Ripken Jr.	40.00
4	Nomar Garciaparra	20.00
5	Larry Walker	10.00
6	Mike Piazza	22.50
7	Mark McGwire	30.00
8	Tony Gwynn	20.00
9	Ken Griffey Jr.	25.00
10	Roger Clemens	22.50

Gems of the Diamond

Gems of the Diamond is a 220-card insert seeded four per pack. The cards feature a color photo inside a white border.

		NM/M
Complete Set (220):		20.00
Common Player:		.10
1	Jim Edmonds	.10
2	Todd Greene	.10
3	Ken Hill	.10
4	Mike Holtz	.10
5	Mike James	.10
6	Chad Kreuter	.10
7	Tim Salmon	.10
8	Roberto Alomar	.20
9	Brady Anderson	.10
10	David Dellucci	.10
11	Jeffrey Hammonds	.10
12	Mike Mussina	.40
13	Rafael Palmeiro	.65
14	Arthur Rhodes	.10
15	Cal Ripken Jr.	2.50
16	Nerio Rodriguez	.10
17	Tony Tarasco	.10
18	Lenny Webster	.10
19	Mike Benjamin	.10
20	Rich Garces	.10
21	Nomar Garciaparra	1.00
22	Shane Mack	.10
23	Jose Malave	.10
24	Jesus Tavarez	.10
25	Mo Vaughn	.75
26	John Wasdin	.10
27	Jeff Abbott	.10
28	Albert Belle	.75
29	Mike Cameron	.10
30	Al Levine	.10
31	Robert Machado	.10
32	Greg Norton	.10
33	Magglio Ordonez	.20
34	Mike Sirotka	.10
35	Frank Thomas	.75
36	Mario Valdez	.10
37	Sandy Alomar Jr.	.20
38	David Justice	.20
39	Jack McDowell	.10
40	Eric Plunk	.10
41	Manny Ramirez	.75
42	Kevin Seitzer	.10
43	Paul Shuey	.10
44	Omar Vizquel	.10
45	Kimera Bartee	.10
46	Glenn Dishman	.10
47	Orlando Miller	.10
48	Mike Myers	.10
49	Phil Nevin	.10
50	A.J. Sager	.10

51	Ricky Bones	.10
52	Scott Cooper	.10
53	Shane Halter	.10
54	David Howard	.10
55	Glendon Rusch	.10
56	Joe Vitiello	.10
57	Jeff D'Amico	.10
58	Mike Fetters	.10
59	Mike Matheny	.10
60	Jose Mercedes	.10
61	Ron Villone	.10
62	Jack Voigt	.10
63	Brent Brede	.10
64	Chuck Knoblauch	.40
65	Paul Molitor	.75
66	Todd Ritchie	.10
67	Frankie Rodriguez	.10
68	Scott Stahoviak	.10
69	Greg Swindell	.10
70	Todd Walker	.10
71	Wade Boggs	1.00
72	Hideki Irabu	.10
73	Derek Jeter	2.50
74	Pat Kelly	.10
75	Graeme Lloyd	.10
76	Tino Martinez	.10
77	Jeff Nelson	.10
78	Scott Pose	.10
79	Mike Stanton	.10
80	Darryl Strawberry	.10
81	Bernie Williams	.10
82	Tony Batista	.10
83	Mark Bellhorn	.10
84	Ben Grieve	.10
85	Pat Lennon	.10
86	Brian Lesher	.10
87	Miguel Tejada	.20
88	George Williams	.10
89	Joey Cora	.10
90	Rob Ducey	.10
91	Ken Griffey Jr.	1.50
92	Randy Johnson	.75
93	Edgar Martinez	.10
94	John Marzano	.10
95	Greg McCarthy	.10
96	Alex Rodriguez	2.00
97	Andy Sheets	.10
98	Mike Timlin	.10
99	Lee Tinsley	.10
100	Damon Buford	.10
101	Alex Diaz	.10
102	Benji Gil	.10
103	Juan Gonzalez	.40
104	Eric Gunderson	.10
105	Danny Patterson	.10
106	Ivan Rodriguez	.65
107	Mike Simms	.10
108	Luis Andujar	.10
109	Joe Carter	.10
110	Roger Clemens	1.25
111	Jose Cruz Jr.	.10
112	Shawn Green	.30
113	Robert Perez	.10
114	Juan Samuel	.10
115	Ed Sprague	.10
116	Shannon Stewart	.10
117	Danny Bautista	.10
118	Chipper Jones	1.00
119	Ryan Klesko	.10
120	Keith Lockhart	.10
121	Javier Lopez	.10
122	Greg Maddux	1.00
123	Kevin Millwood	.10
124	Mike Mordecai	.10
125	Eddie Perez	.10
126	Randall Simon	.10
127	Miguel Cairo	.10
128	Dave Clark	.10
129	Kevin Foster	.10
130	Mark Grace	.10
131	Tyler Houston	.10
132	Mike Hubbard	.10
133	Kevin Orie	.10
134	Ryne Sandberg	1.00
135	Sammy Sosa	1.00
136	Lenny Harris	.10
137	Kent Mercker	.10
138	Mike Morgan	.10
139	Deion Sanders	.10
140	Chris Stynes	.10
141	Gabe White	.10
142	Jason Bates	.10
143	Vinny Castilla	.10
144	Andres Galarraga	.10
145	Curtis Leskanic	.10
146	Jeff McCurry	.10
147	Mike Munoz	.10
148	Larry Walker	.10
149	Jamey Wright	.10
150	Moises Alou	.10
151	Bobby Bonilla	.10
152	Kevin Brown	.10
153	John Cangelosi	.10
154	Jeff Conine	.10
155	Cliff Floyd	.10
156	Jay Powell	.10
157	Edgar Renteria	.10
158	Tony Saunders	.10
159	Gary Sheffield	.40
160	Jeff Bagwell	.75
161	Tim Bogar	.10
162	Tony Eusebio	.10
163	Chris Holt	.10
164	Ray Montgomery	.10
165	Luis Rivera	.10
166	Eric Anthony	.10
167	Brett Butler	.10
168	Juan Castro	.10

169	Tripp Cromer	.10
170	Raul Mondesi	.10
171	Hideo Nomo	.40
172	Mike Piazza	1.25
173	Tom Prince	.10
174	Adam Riggs	.10
175	Shane Andrews	.10
176	Shayne Bennett	.10
177	Raul Chavez	.10
178	Pedro Martinez	.75
179	Sherman Obando	.10
180	Andy Stankiewicz	.10
181	Alberto Castillo	.10
182	Shawn Gilbert	.10
183	Luis Lopez	.10
184	Roberto Petagine	.10
185	Armando Reynoso	.10
186	Midre Cummings	.10
187	Kevin Jordan	.10
188	Desi Relaford	.10
189	Scott Rolen	.65
190	Ken Ryan	.10
191	Kevin Sefcik	.10
192	Emil Brown	.10
193	Lou Collier	.10
194	Francisco Cordova	.10
195	Kevin Elster	.10
196	Mark Smith	.10
197	Marc Wilkins	.10
198	Manny Aybar	.10
199	Jose Bautista	.10
200	David Bell	.10
201	Rigo Beltran	.10
202	Delino DeShields	.10
203	Dennis Eckersley	.65
204	John Mabry	.10
205	Eli Marrero	.10
206	Willie McGee	.10
207	Mark McGwire	2.00
208	Ken Caminiti	.10
209	Tony Gwynn	1.00
210	Chris Jones	.10
211	Craig Shipley	.10
212	Pete Smith	.10
213	Jorge Velandia	.10
214	Dario Veras	.10
215	Rich Aurilia	.10
216	Damon Berryhill	.10
217	Barry Bonds	2.50
218	Osvaldo Fernandez	.10
219	Dante Powell	.10
220	Rich Rodriguez	.10

Interleague Players

Interleague Players is a 30-card insert featuring 15 sets of players - one National League and one American League player. The dark blue backgrounds have red lightning bolts and the white borders are made of a leather-like material. When a set of players is placed next to each other, they form the MLB Interleague logo in the center. Interleague Players cards were inserted one per 73 packs.

		NM/M
Complete Set (30):		120.00
Common Player:		1.50
Inserted 1:73		
1A	Roberto Alomar	2.50
1N	Craig Biggio	1.50
2A	Cal Ripken Jr.	12.00
2N	Chipper Jones	6.00
3A	Nomar Garciaparra	6.00
3N	Scott Rolen	3.50
4A	Mo Vaughn	1.50
4N	Andres Galarraga	1.50
5A	Frank Thomas	4.50
5N	Tony Gwynn	6.00
6A	Albert Belle	1.50
6N	Barry Bonds	12.00
7A	Hideki Irabu	1.50
7N	Hideo Nomo	2.50
8A	Derek Jeter	12.00
8N	Rey Ordonez	1.50
9A	Tino Martinez	1.50
9N	Mark McGwire	10.00
10A	Alex Rodriguez	10.00
10N	Edgar Renteria	1.50
11A	Ken Griffey Jr.	7.50
11N	Larry Walker	1.50
12A	Randy Johnson	4.50
12N	Greg Maddux	6.00
13A	Ivan Rodriguez	3.50
13N	Mike Piazza	6.50
14A	Roger Clemens	6.50
14N	Pedro Martinez	4.50
15A	Jose Cruz Jr.	1.50
15N	Wilton Guerrero	1.50

Moments in Time

Moments in Time (20 cards, 1:145) is designed as a baseball scoreboard. The cards have a horizontal layout with the date of an important game in the player's career at the top. The player's stats from the game are featured and a picture is located on the scoreboard screen.

		NM/M
Complete Set (20):		100.00
Common Player:		3.00
Inserted 1:145		
1	Chipper Jones	10.00
2	Cal Ripken Jr.	17.50
3	Frank Thomas	7.50
4	David Justice	3.00
5	Andres Galarraga	3.00
6	Larry Walker	3.00
7	Livan Hernandez	3.00
8	Wilton Guerrero	3.00
9	Hideo Nomo	4.50
10	Mike Piazza	12.00
11	Pedro Martinez	7.50
12	Bernie Williams	3.00
13	Ben Grieve	3.00
14	Scott Rolen	6.00
15	Mark McGwire	15.00
16	Tony Gwynn	10.00
17	Ken Griffey Jr.	13.50
18	Alex Rodriguez	15.00
19	Juan Gonzalez	4.50
20	Jose Cruz Jr.	3.00

Photoengravings

Photoengravings is an 18-card insert seeded one per 37 packs. Each card has a unique "old-style" design with a player photo in a frame in the center.

		NM/M
Complete Set (18):		50.00
Common Player:		1.00
Inserted 1:37		
1	Greg Maddux	3.50
2	Cal Ripken Jr.	7.50
3	Nomar Garciaparra	3.50
4	Frank Thomas	2.50
5	Larry Walker	1.00
6	Mike Piazza	4.00
7	Hideo Nomo	2.00
8	Pedro Martinez	2.50
9	Derek Jeter	7.50
10	Tino Martinez	1.00
11	Mark McGwire	6.00
12	Tony Gwynn	3.50
13	Barry Bonds	7.50
14	Ken Griffey Jr.	5.00
15	Alex Rodriguez	6.00
16	Ivan Rodriguez	2.25
17	Roger Clemens	4.00
18	Jose Cruz Jr.	1.00

Team Checklists

Team Checklists is a 30-card insert seeded 2:37. The fronts feature a player collage with the team logo in

the background. The back has a complete checklist for that team in Invincible and more player photos.

		NM/M
Complete Set (30):		60.00
Common Player:		1.00
Inserted 2:37		
1	Anaheim Angels (Jim Edmonds, Tim Salmon, Darin Erstad, Garret Anderson, Rickey Henderson)	2.50
2	Atlanta Braves (Greg Maddux, Chipper Jones, Javy Lopez, Ryan Klesko, Andruw Jones)	3.00
3	Baltimore Orioles (Cal Ripken Jr., Roberto Alomar, Brady Anderson, Mike Mussina, Rafael Palmeiro)	6.00
4	Boston Red Sox (Nomar Garciaparra, Mo Vaughn, Steve Avery, John Valentin)	3.00
5	Chicago Cubs (Sammy Sosa, Mark Grace, Ryne Sandberg, Jeremi Gonzalez)	3.00
6	Chicago White Sox (Frank Thomas, Albert Belle, Robin Ventura, Ozzie Guillen)	2.50
7	Cincinnati Reds (Barry Larkin, Deion Sanders, Reggie Sanders, Brett Tomko)	1.00
8	Cleveland Indians (Sandy Alomar Jr., Manny Ramirez, David Justice, Jim Thome, Omar Vizquel)	2.50
9	Colorado Rockies (Andres Galarraga, Larry Walker, Vinny Castilla, Dante Bichette, Ellis Burks)	1.00
10	Detroit Tigers (Jason Thompson, Tony Clark, Deivi Cruz, Bobby Higginson)	1.00
11	Florida Marlins (Gary Sheffield, Edgar Renteria, Livan Hernandez, Charles Johnson, Bobby Bonilla)	1.00
12	Houston Astros (Jeff Bagwell, Craig Biggio, Richard Hidalgo, Darryl Kile)	2.50
13	Kansas City Royals (Johnny Damon, Jermaine Dye, Chili Davis, Jose Rosado)	1.00
14	Los Angeles Dodgers (Mike Piazza, Wilton Guerrero, Raul Mondesi, Hideo Nomo, Ramon Martinez)	4.00
15	Milwaukee Brewers (David Nilsson, Fernando Vina, Jeromy Burnitz, Julio Franco, Jeff Cirillo)	1.00
16	Minnesota Twins (Paul Molitor, Chuck Knoblauch, Brad Radke, Terry Steinbach, Marty Cordova)	2.50
17	Montreal Expos (Henry Rodriguez, Vladimir Guerrero, Pedro Martinez, David Segui, Mark Grudzielanek)	2.50
18	New York Mets (Carlos Baerga, Todd Hundley, Rey Ordonez, John Olerud, Edgardo Alfonzo)	1.00
19	New York Yankees (Derek Jeter, Tino Martinez, Bernie Williams, Andy Pettitte, Mariano Rivera)	6.00
20	Oakland Athletics (Jose Canseco, Ben Grieve, Jason Giambi, Matt Stairs)	1.75
21	Philadelphia Phillies (Curt Schilling, Scott Rolen, Gregg Jefferies, Lenny Dykstra, Ricky Bottalico)	1.75
22	Pittsburgh Pirates (Al Martin, Tony Womack, Jose Guillen, Esteban Loaiza)	1.00
23	St. Louis Cardinals (Mark McGwire, Dennis Eckersley, Delino DeShields, Willie McGee, Ray Lankford)	4.50
24	San Diego Padres (Tony Gwynn, Ken Caminiti, Wally Joyner, Steve Finley)	3.00

25 San Francisco Giants (Barry Bonds, J.T. Snow, Stan Javier, Rod Beck, Jose Vizcaino) 6.00
26 Seattle Mariners (Ken Griffey Jr., Alex Rodriguez, Edgar Martinez, Randy Johnson, Jay Buhner) 4.50
27 Texas Rangers (Juan Gonzalez, Ivan Rodriguez, Will Clark, John Wetteland, Rusty Greer) 2.00
28 Toronto Blue Jays (Jose Cruz Jr., Roger Clemens, Pat Hentgen, Joe Carter) 4.00
29 Arizona Diamondbacks (Yamil Benitez, Devon White, Matt Williams, Jay Bell) 1.00
30 Tampa Bay Devil Rays (Wade Boggs, Paul Sorrento, Fred McGriff, Roberto Hernandez) 3.00

1998 Pacific Omega

The Omega base set consists of 250 three-image cards. The horizontal cards feature a color player photo in the center with the image duplicated in foil on the right. Another color photo is on the left. The photos are divided by a baseball seam design. Red-foil parallels were a 1:4 pack insert in Wal-Mart exclusive packaging.

NM/M
Complete Set (250): 25.00
Common Player: .10
Reds: 4X
Pack (6): 1.00
Wax Box (36): 15.00
1 Garret Anderson .10
2 Gary DiSarcina .10
3 Jim Edmonds .10
4 Darin Erstad .20
5 Cecil Fielder .10
6 Chuck Finley .10
7 Shigetosi Hasegawa .10
8 Tim Salmon .10
9 Brian Anderson .10
10 Jay Bell .10
11 Andy Benes .10
12 Yamil Benitez .10
13 Jorge Fabregas .10
14 Travis Lee .10
15 Devon White .10
16 Matt Williams .10
17 Andres Galarraga .10
18 Tom Glavine .35
19 Andruw Jones .75
20 Chipper Jones 1.00
21 Ryan Klesko .10
22 Javy Lopez .10
23 Greg Maddux 1.00
24 Kevin Millwood RC .50
25 Denny Neagle .10
26 John Smoltz .10
27 Roberto Alomar .20
28 Brady Anderson .10
29 Joe Carter .10
30 Eric Davis .10
31 Jimmy Key .10
32 Mike Mussina .40
33 Rafael Palmeiro .65
34 Cal Ripken Jr. 2.50
35 B.J. Surhoff .10
36 Dennis Eckersley .65
37 Nomar Garciaparra 1.00
38 Reggie Jefferson .10
39 Derek Lowe .10
40 Pedro Martinez .75
41 Brian Rose .10
42 John Valentin .10
43 Jason Varitek .10
44 Mo Vaughn .10
45 Jeff Blauser .10
46 Jeremi Gonzalez .10
47 Mark Grace .10
48 Lance Johnson .10
49 Kevin Orie .10
50 Henry Rodriguez .10
51 Sammy Sosa 1.00
52 Kerry Wood .35
53 Albert Belle .10
54 Mike Cameron .10
55 Mike Caruso .10
56 Ray Durham .10
57 Jaime Navarro .10
58 Greg Norton .10
59 Magglio Ordonez RC 1.50
60 Frank Thomas .75
61 Robin Ventura .10

62 Bret Boone .10
63 Willie Greene .10
64 Barry Larkin .10
65 Jon Nunnally .10
66 Eduardo Perez .10
67 Reggie Sanders .10
68 Brett Tomko .10
69 Sandy Alomar Jr. .10
70 Travis Fryman .10
71 David Justice .10
72 Kenny Lofton .10
73 Charles Nagy .10
74 Manny Ramirez .75
75 Jim Thome .65
76 Omar Vizquel .10
77 Enrique Wilson .10
78 Jaret Wright .10
79 Dante Bichette .10
80 Ellis Burks .10
81 Vinny Castilla .10
82 Todd Helton .75
83 Darryl Kile .10
84 Mike Lansing .10
85 Neifi Perez .10
86 Larry Walker .10
87 Raul Casanova .10
88 Tony Clark .10
89 Luis Gonzalez .10
90 Bobby Higginson .10
91 Brian Hunter .10
92 Bip Roberts .10
93 Justin Thompson .10
94 Josh Booty .10
95 Craig Counsell .10
96 Livan Hernandez .10
97 Ryan Jackson RC .10
98 Mark Kotsay .10
99 Derrek Lee .50
100 Mike Piazza 1.25
101 Edgar Renteria .10
102 Cliff Floyd .10
103 Moises Alou .10
104 Jeff Bagwell .75
105 Derrick Bell .10
106 Sean Berry .10
107 Craig Biggio .10
108 John Halama RC .15
109 Richard Hidalgo .10
110 Shane Reynolds .10
111 Tim Belcher .10
112 Brian Bevil .10
113 Jeff Conine .10
114 Johnny Damon .25
115 Jeff King .10
116 Jeff Montgomery .10
117 Dean Palmer .10
118 Terry Pendleton .10
119 Bobby Bonilla .10
120 Wilton Guerrero .10
121 Todd Hollandsworth .10
122 Charles Johnson .10
123 Eric Karros .10
124 Paul Konerko .20
125 Ramon Martinez .10
126 Raul Mondesi .10
127 Hideo Nomo .40
128 Gary Sheffield .45
129 Ismael Valdes .10
130 Jeromy Burnitz .10
131 Jeff Cirillo .10
132 Todd Dunn .10
133 Marquis Grissom .10
134 John Jaha .10
135 Scott Karl .10
136 Dave Nilsson .10
137 Jose Valentin .10
138 Fernando Vina .10
139 Rick Aguilera .10
140 Marty Cordova .10
141 Pat Meares .10
142 Paul Molitor .75
143 David Ortiz .50
144 Brad Radke .10
145 Terry Steinbach .10
146 Todd Walker .10
147 Shane Andrews .10
148 Brad Fullmer .10
149 Mark Grudzielanek .10
150 Vladimir Guerrero .75
151 F.P. Santangelo .10
152 Jose Vidro .10
153 Rondell White .10
154 Carlos Baerga .10
155 Bernard Gilkey .10
156 Todd Hundley .10
157 Butch Huskey .10
158 Bobby Jones .10
159 Brian McRae .10
160 John Olerud .10
161 Rey Ordonez .10
162 Masato Yoshii RC .25
163 David Cone .10
164 Hideki Irabu .10
165 Derek Jeter 2.50
166 Chuck Knoblauch .10
167 Tino Martinez .10
168 Paul O'Neill .30
169 Andy Pettitte .30
170 Mariano Rivera .15
171 Darryl Strawberry .10
172 David Wells .10
173 Bernie Williams .10
174 Ryan Christenson RC .15
175 Jason Giambi .60
176 Ben Grieve .10
177 Rickey Henderson .75
178 A.J. Hinch .10
179 Kenny Rogers .10

180 Ricky Bottalico .10
181 Rico Brogna .10
182 Doug Glanville .10
183 Gregg Jefferies .10
184 Mike Lieberthal .10
185 Scott Rolen .65
186 Curt Schilling .35
187 Jermaine Allensworth .10
188 Lou Collier .10
189 Jose Guillen .10
190 Jason Kendall .10
191 Al Martin .10
192 Tony Womack .10
193 Kevin Young .10
194 Royce Clayton .10
195 Delino DeShields .10
196 Gary Gaetti .10
197 Ron Gant .10
198 Brian Jordan .10
199 Ray Lankford .10
200 Mark McGwire 2.00
201 Todd Stottlemyre .10
202 Kevin Brown .10
203 Ken Caminiti .10
204 Steve Finley .10
205 Tony Gwynn 1.00
206 Carlos Hernandez .10
207 Wally Joyner .10
208 Greg Vaughn .10
209 Barry Bonds 2.50
210 Shawn Estes .10
211 Orel Hershiser .10
212 Stan Javier .10
213 Jeff Kent .10
214 Bill Mueller .10
215 Robb Nen .10
216 J.T. Snow .10
217 Jay Buhner .10
218 Ken Cloude .10
219 Joey Cora .10
220 Ken Griffey Jr. 1.50
221 Glenallen Hill .10
222 Randy Johnson .75
223 Edgar Martinez .10
224 Jamie Moyer .10
225 Alex Rodriguez 2.00
226 David Segui .10
227 Dan Wilson .10
228 Rolando Arrojo RC .25
229 Wade Boggs 1.00
230 Miguel Cairo .10
231 Roberto Hernandez .10
232 Quinton McCracken .10
233 Fred McGriff .10
234 Paul Sorrento .10
235 Kevin Stocker .10
236 Will Clark .10
237 Juan Gonzalez .40
238 Rusty Greer .10
239 Rick Helling .10
240 Roberto Kelly .10
241 Ivan Rodriguez .65
242 Aaron Sele .10
243 John Wetteland .10
244 Jose Canseco .50
245 Roger Clemens 1.25
246 Jose Cruz Jr. .10
247 Carlos Delgado .50
248 Alex Gonzalez .10
249 Ed Sprague .10
250 Shannon Stewart .10

EO Portraits

EO Portraits is a 20-card insert seeded 1:73. Each card has a color action photo with a player portrait laser-cut into the card. A "1-of-1" parallel features a laser-cut number on the card as well. The "EO" stands for "Electro Optical" technology.

NM/M
Complete Set (20): 70.00
Common Player: 1.25
Inserted 1:73
1 Cal Ripken Jr. 10.00
2 Nomar Garciaparra 5.00
3 Mo Vaughn 1.25
4 Frank Thomas 4.00
5 Manny Ramirez 4.00
6 Ben Grieve 1.25
7 Ken Griffey Jr. 7.50
8 Alex Rodriguez 7.50
9 Juan Gonzalez 2.00
10 Ivan Rodriguez 3.50
11 Travis Lee 1.25
12 Greg Maddux 5.00

13 Chipper Jones 5.00
14 Kerry Wood 2.00
15 Larry Walker 1.25
16 Jeff Bagwell 4.00
17 Mike Piazza 6.00
18 Mark McGwire 7.50
19 Tony Gwynn 5.00
20 Barry Bonds 10.00

Face to Face

Face to Face features two star players on each card. It is a 10-card insert seeded one per 145 packs.

NM/M
Complete Set (10): 50.00
Common Player: 2.00
Inserted 1:145
1 Alex Rodriguez, Nomar Garciaparra 9.00
2 Mark McGwire, Ken Griffey Jr. 9.00
3 Mike Piazza, Sandy Alomar Jr. 6.00
4 Kerry Wood, Roger Clemens 6.00
5 Cal Ripken Jr., Paul Molitor 10.00
6 Tony Gwynn, Wade Boggs 5.00
7 Frank Thomas, Chipper Jones 5.00
8 Travis Lee, Ben Grieve 2.00
9 Hideo Nomo, Hideki Irabu 3.50
10 Juan Gonzalez, Manny Ramirez 3.50

Online

Online is a 36-card insert seeded about one per nine packs. The foiled and etched cards feature a color player photo in front of a hi-tech designed background. The card fronts also include the internet address for the player's web site on bigleaguers.com.

NM/M
Complete Set (36): 35.00
Common Player: .45
Inserted 1:9
1 Cal Ripken Jr. 5.00
2 Nomar Garciaparra 2.00
3 Pedro Martinez 1.50
4 Mo Vaughn .45
5 Frank Thomas 1.50
6 Sandy Alomar Jr. .45
7 Manny Ramirez 1.50
8 Jaret Wright .45
9 Paul Molitor 1.50
10 Derek Jeter 5.00
11 Bernie Williams .45
12 Ben Grieve .45
13 Ken Griffey Jr. 3.00
14 Edgar Martinez .45
15 Alex Rodriguez 4.00
16 Wade Boggs 2.00
17 Juan Gonzalez .75
18 Ivan Rodriguez 1.00
19 Roger Clemens 2.50
20 Travis Lee .45
21 Matt Williams .45
22 Andres Galarraga .45
23 Chipper Jones 2.00
24 Greg Maddux 2.00
25 Sammy Sosa 2.00
26 Kerry Wood .75
27 Barry Larkin .45
28 Larry Walker .45
29 Derek Lee 1.00
30 Jeff Bagwell 1.50
31 Hideo Nomo .75
32 Mike Piazza 2.50
33 Scott Rolen 1.00
34 Mark McGwire 4.00
35 Tony Gwynn 2.00
36 Barry Bonds 5.00

Prism

This 20-card insert was seeded one per 37 packs. Horizontal card fronts feature prismatic foil technology.

NM/M
Complete Set (20): 30.00
Common Player: .75
Inserted 1:37
1 Cal Ripken Jr. 4.50
2 Nomar Garciaparra 2.50
3 Pedro Martinez 1.50
4 Frank Thomas 1.50
5 Manny Ramirez 1.50
6 Brian Giles .75
7 Derek Jeter 4.50
8 Ben Grieve .75
9 Ken Griffey Jr. 3.00
10 Alex Rodriguez 3.50
11 Juan Gonzalez 1.00
12 Travis Lee .75
13 Chipper Jones 2.50
14 Greg Maddux 2.50
15 Kerry Wood 1.00
16 Larry Walker .75
17 Hideo Nomo 1.00
18 Mike Piazza 2.50
19 Mark McGwire 3.50
20 Tony Gwynn 2.50

Rising Stars

Rising Stars is a multi-tiered hobby-only insert. The 20 base cards are found about 1:9 packs. Each card has two or three prospects from the same team. Five tiers of partial parallels of the insert are sequentially numbered.

NM/M
Complete Set (30): 15.00
Common Player: .50
Inserted 1:9
Tier 1 (# to 100): 3X
Tier 2 (# to 75): 4X
Tier 3 (# to 50): 5X
Tier 4 (# to 25): 10X
Tier 5 (1 of 1): Value Undetermined
1 Nerio Rodriguez, Sidney Ponson .50
2 Frank Catalanotto, Roberto Duran, Sean Runyan .50
3 Kevin L. Brown, Carlos Almanzar .50
4 Aaron Boone, Pat Watkins, Scott Winchester .50
5 Brian Meadows, Andy Larkin, Antonio Alfonseca .50
7 DaRond Stovall, Trey Moore, Shayne Bennett .50
7 Felix Martinez, Larry Sutton, Brian Bevil .50
8 Homer Bush, Mike Buddie .50
9 Rich Butler, Esteban Yan .50
10 Damon Hollins, Brian Edmondson .50
11 Lou Collier, Jose Silva, Javier Martinez .50
12 Steve Sinclair, Mark Dalesandro .50
13 Jason Varitek, Brian Rose, Brian Shouse .50
14 Mike Caruso, Jeff Abbott, Tom Fordham .50
15 Jason Johnson, Bobby Smith .50
16 Dave Berg, Mark Kotsay, Jesus Sanchez .50
17 Richard Hidalgo, John Halama, Trever Miller .50
18 Geoff Jenkins, Bobby Hughes, Steve Woodard .50
19 Eli Marrero, Cliff Politte, Mike Busby .50
20 Desi Relaford, Darrin Winston .50
21 Todd Helton, Bobby Jones 1.50
22 Rolando Arrojo, Miguel Cairo, Dan Carlson .50
23 David Ortiz, Javier Valentin, Eric Milton 1.25

24 Magglio Ordonez, Greg Norton 1.00
25 Brad Fullmer, Javier Vazquez, Rick DeHart .50
26 Paul Konerko, Matt Luke 1.00
27 Derrek Lee, Ryan Jackson, John Roskos 1.25
28 Ben Grieve, A.J. Hinch, Ryan Christenson .50
29 Travis Lee, Karim Garcia, David Dellucci .65
30 Kerry Wood, Marc Pisciotta 1.00

1998 Pacific Online

Online consists of an 800-card base set featuring 750 players on cards that list the internet address of the player's home page on the bigleaguers.com web site. Twenty players have two cards, each with different front and back photos but sharing a card number. Each of the 30 teams has a checklist that lists the team's web site. The Web Cards set parallels the 750 player cards. It has a serial number that can be entered at the bigleaguers.com Web site to determine if a prize has been won. Red-foil versions of each card were produced for retail-only jumbo packs; they may carry a modest premium.

NM/M
Complete Set (800): 60.00
Common Player: .05
Web Stars/RC's: 2X
Inserted 1:1
Pack (9): .75
Wax Box (36): 20.00
1 Garret Anderson .05
2 Rich DeLucia RC .05
3 Jason Dickson .05
4 Gary DiSarcina .05
5 Jim Edmonds .05
6 Darin Erstad .15
7 Cecil Fielder .05
8 Chuck Finley .05
9 Carlos Garcia .05
10 Shigetosi Hasegawa .05
11 Ken Hill .05
12 Dave Hollins .05
13 Mike Holtz .05
14 Mike James .05
15 Norberto Martin .05
16 Damon Mashore .05
17 Jack McDowell .05
18 Phil Nevin .05
19 Omar Olivares .05
20 Troy Percival .05
21 Rich Robertson .05
22 Tim Salmon .05
23 Craig Shipley .05
24 Matt Walbeck .05
25 Allen Watson .05
26 Jim Edmonds (Angels Checklist) .05
27 Brian Anderson .05
28 Tony Batista .05
29 Jay Bell .05
30 Andy Benes .05
31 Yamil Benitez .05
32 Willie Blair .05
33 Brent Brede .05
34 Scott Brow .05
35 Omar Daal .05
36 David Dellucci .05
37 Edwin Diaz .05
38 Jorge Fabregas .05
39 Andy Fox .05
40 Karim Garcia .05
41a Travis Lee/Btg .05
41b Travis Lee/Fldg .05
42 Barry Manuel .05
43 Gregg Olson .05
44 Felix Rodriguez .05
45 Clint Sodowsky .05
46 Russ Springer .05
47 Andy Stankiewicz .05
48 Kelly Stinnett .05
49 Jeff Suppan .05
50 Devon White .05
51 Matt Williams .05
52 Travis Lee (Diamondbacks Checklist) .05

#	Player	Price	#	Player	Price	#	Player	Price	#	Player	Price	#	Player	Price	#	Player	Price
53	Danny Bautista	.05	160	James Baldwin	.05	270	Roberto Duran	.05	383	Tom Prince	.05	494	Mike Piazza		606	Mike Busby	.05
54	Rafael Belliard	.05	161	Albert Belle	.05	271	Damion Easley	.05	384	Scott Radinsky	.05		(Mets Checklist)	.45	607	Royce Clayton	.05
55	Adam Butler **RC**	.10	162	Jason Bere	.05	272	Bryce Florie	.05	385	Gary Sheffield	.40	495	Willie Banks	.05	608	Delino DeShields	.05
56	Mike Cather	.05	163	Mike Cameron	.05	273	Luis Gonzalez	.05	386	Ismael Valdes	.05	496	Scott Brosius	.05	609	John Frascatore	.05
57	Brian Edmondson	.05	164	Mike Caruso	.05	274	Bob Higginson	.05	387	Jose Vizcaino	.05	497	Mike Buddie	.05	610	Gary Gaetti	.05
58	Alan Embree	.05	165	Carlos Castillo	.05	275	Brian Hunter	.05	388	Eric Young	.05	498	Homer Bush	.05	611	Ron Gant	.05
59	Andres Galarraga	.05	166	Tony Castillo	.05	276	Todd Jones	.05	389	Gary Sheffield		499	David Cone	.05	612	David Howard	.05
60	Tom Glavine	.35	167	Ray Durham	.05	277	Greg Keagle	.05		(Dodgers Checklist)	.10	500	Chad Curtis	.05	613	Brian Hunter	.05
61	Tony Graffanino	.05	168	Scott Eyre	.05	278	Jeff Manto	.05	390	Jeromy Burnitz	.05	501	Chili Davis	.05	614	Brian Jordan	.05
62	Andruw Jones	.05	169	Tom Fordham	.05	279	Brian Moehler	.05	391	Jeff Cirillo	.05	502	Joe Girardi	.05	615	Tom Lampkin	.05
63a	Chipper Jones/Btg	.75	170	Keith Foulke	.05	280	Joe Oliver	.05	392	Cal Eldred	.05	503	Darren Holmes	.05	616	Ray Lankford	.05
63b	Chipper Jones/Fldg	.75	171	Lou Frazier	.05	281	Joe Randa	.05	393	Chad Fox	.05	504	Hideki Irabu	.05	617	Braden Looper	.05
64	Ryan Klesko	.05	172	Matt Karchner	.05	282	Billy Ripken	.05	394	Marquis Grissom	.05	505a	Derek Jeter/Btg	2.00	618	John Mabry	.05
65	Keith Lockhart	.05	173	Chad Kreuter	.05	283	Bip Roberts	.05	395	Bob Hamelin	.05	505b	Derek Jeter/Fldg	2.00	619	Eli Marrero	.05
66	Javy Lopez	.05	174	Jaime Navarro	.05	284	Sean Runyan	.05	396	Bobby Hughes	.05	506	Chuck Knoblauch	.05	620	Willie McGee	.05
67a	Greg Maddux/Btg	.75	175	Greg Norton	.05	285	A.J. Sager	.05	397	Darrin Jackson	.05	507	Graeme Lloyd	.05	621a	Mark McGwire/Btg	1.50
67b	Greg Maddux/Pitching	.75	176	Charlie O'Brien	.05	286	Justin Thompson	.05	398	John Jaha	.05	508	Tino Martinez	.05	621b	Mark McGwire/Fldg	1.50
68	Dennis Martinez	.05	177	Magglio Ordonez	.15	287	Tony Clark		399	Geoff Jenkins	.05	509	Ramiro Mendoza	.05	622	Kent Mercker	.05
69	Kevin Millwood **RC**	.50	178	Ruben Sierra	.05		(Tigers Checklist)	.05	400	Doug Jones	.05	510	Jeff Nelson	.05	623	Matt Morris	.05
70	Denny Neagle	.05	179	Bill Simas	.05	288	Antonio Alfonseca	.05	401	Jeff Juden	.05	511	Paul O'Neill	.05	624	Donovan Osborne	.05
71	Eddie Perez	.05	180	Mike Sirotka	.05	289	Dave Berg	.05	402	Scott Karl	.05	512	Andy Pettitte	.20	625	Tom Pagnozzi	.05
72	Curtis Pride	.05	181	Chris Snopek	.05	290	Josh Booty	.05	403	Jesse Levis	.05	513	Jorge Posada	.05	626	Lance Painter	.05
73	John Smoltz	.05	182a	Frank Thomas		291	John Cangelosi	.05	404	Mark Loretta	.05	514	Tim Raines	.05	627	Mark Petkovsek	.05
74	Michael Tucker	.05		(In batter's box.)	.65	292	Craig Counsell	.05	405	Mike Matheny	.05	515	Mariano Rivera	.15	628	Todd Stottlemyre	.05
75	Walt Weiss	.05	182b	Frank Thomas/Swinging	.65	293	Vic Darensbourg	.05	406	Jose Mercedes	.05	516	Luis Sojo	.05	629	Mark McGwire	
76	Gerald Williams	.05	183	Robin Ventura	.05	294	Cliff Floyd	.05	407	Mike Myers	.05	517	Mike Stanton	.05		(Cardinals Checklist)	.75
77	Mark Wohlers	.05	184	Frank Thomas		295	Oscar Henriquez	.05	408	Matt Newfield	.05	518	Darryl Strawberry	.05	630	Andy Ashby	.05
78	Chipper Jones			(White Sox Checklist)	.40	296	Felix Heredia	.05	409	Dave Nilsson	.05	519	Dale Sveum	.05	631	Brian Boehringer	.05
	(Braves Checklist)	.40	185	Stan Belinda	.05	297	Ryan Jackson **RC**	.05	410	Al Reyes	.05	520	David Wells	.05	632	Kevin Brown	.05
79	Roberto Alomar	.15	186	Aaron Boone	.05	298	Mark Kotsay	.05	411	Jose Valentin	.05	521	Bernie Williams	.05	633	Ken Caminiti	.05
80	Brady Anderson	.05	187	Bret Boone	.05	299	Andy Larkin	.05	412	Fernando Vina	.05	522	Bernie Williams		634	Steve Finley	.05
81	Harold Baines	.05	188	Brook Fordyce	.05	300	Derrek Lee	.60	413	Paul Wagner	.05		(Yankees Checklist)	.05	635	Ed Giovanola	.05
82	Armando Benitez	.05	189	Willie Greene	.05	301	Brian Meadows	.05	414	Bob Wickman	.05	523	Kurt Abbott	.05	636	Chris Gomez	.05
83	Mike Bordick	.05	190	Pete Harnisch	.05	302	Rafael Medina	.05	415	Steve Woodard	.05	524	Mike Blowers	.05	637a	Tony Gwynn (Blue jersey.)	.75
84	Joe Carter	.05	191	Lenny Harris	.05	303	Jay Powell	.05	416	Marquis Grissom		525	Rafael Bournigal	.05	637b	Tony Gwynn	
85	Norm Charlton	.05	192	Mark Hutton	.05	304	Edgar Renteria	.05		(Brewers Checklist)	.05	526	Tom Candiotti	.05		(White jersey.)	.75
86	Eric Davis	.05	193	Damian Jackson	.05	305	Jesus Sanchez **RC**	.05	417	Rick Aguilera	.05	527	Ryan Christenson	.05		SAMPLE Tony Gwynn (SAMPLE	
87	Doug Drabek	.05	194	Ricardo Jordan	.05	306	Rob Stanifer	.05	418	Ron Coomer	.05	528	Mike Fetters	.05		overprint on back.)	1.00
88	Scott Erickson	.05	195	Barry Larkin	.05	307	Gregg Zaun	.05	419	Marty Cordova	.05	529	Jason Giambi	.50	638	Joey Hamilton	.05
89	Jeffrey Hammonds	.05	196	Eduardo Perez	.05	308	Derrek Lee		420	Brent Gates	.05	530a	Ben Grieve/Btg	.05	639	Carlos Hernandez	.05
90	Chris Hoiles	.05	197	Pokey Reese	.05		(Marlins Checklist)	.30	421	Eddie Guardado	.05	530b	Ben Grieve/Running	.05	640	Sterling Hitchcock	.05
91	Scott Kamienicki	.05	198	Mike Remlinger	.05	309	Moises Alou	.05	422	Denny Hocking	.05	531	Buddy Groom	.05	641	Trevor Hoffman	.05
92	Jimmy Key	.05	199	Reggie Sanders	.05	310	Brad Ausmus	.05	423	Matt Lawton	.05	532	Jimmy Haynes	.05	642	Wally Joyner	.05
93	Terry Mathews	.05	200	Jeff Shaw	.05	311a	Jeff Bagwell/Btg	.65	424	Pat Meares	.05	533	Rickey Henderson	.65	643	Dan Miceli	.05
94	Alan Mills	.05	201	Chris Stynes	.05	311b	Jeff Bagwell/Fldg	.65	425	Orlando Merced	.05	534	A.J. Hinch	.05	644	James Mouton	.05
95	Mike Mussina	.25	202	Scott Sullivan	.05	312	Derek Bell	.05	426	Eric Milton	.05	535	Mike Macfarlane	.05	645	Greg Myers	.05
96	Jesse Orosco	.05	203	Eddie Taubensee	.05	313	Sean Bergman	.05	427	Paul Molitor	.65	536	Dave Magadan	.05	646	Carlos Reyes	.05
97	Rafael Palmeiro	.60	204	Brett Tomko	.05	314	Sean Berry	.05	428	Mike Morgan	.05	537	T.J. Mathews	.05	647	Andy Sheets	.05
98	Sidney Ponson	.05	205	Pat Watkins	.05	315	Craig Biggio	.05	429	Dan Naulty	.05	538	Jason McDonald	.05	648	Pete Smith	.05
99	Jeff Reboulet	.05	206	David Weathers	.05	316	Tim Bogar	.05	430	Otis Nixon	.05	539	Kevin Mitchell	.05	649	Mark Sweeney	.05
100	Arthur Rhodes	.05	207	Gabe White	.05	317	Jose Cabrera	.05	431	Alex Ochoa	.05	540	Mike Mohler	.05	650	Greg Vaughn	.05
101a	Cal Ripken Jr./Btg	2.00	208	Scott Winchester	.05	318	Dave Clark	.05	432	David Ortiz	.40	541	Mike Oquist	.05	651	Quilvio Veras	.05
101b	Cal Ripken Jr./Btg		209	Barry Larkin		319	Tony Eusebio	.05	433	Brad Radke	.05	542	Ariel Prieto	.05	652	Tony Gwynn	
	(Close-up.)	2.00		(Reds Checklist)	.05	320	Carl Everett	.05	434	Todd Ritchie	.05	543	Kenny Rogers	.05		(Padres Checklist)	.40
102	Nerio Rodriguez	.05	210	Sandy Alomar Jr.	.05	321	Ricky Gutierrez	.05	435	Frank Rodriguez	.05	544	Aaron Small	.05	653	Rich Aurilia	.05
103	B.J. Surhoff	.05	211	Paul Assenmacher	.05	322	John Halama	.05	436	Terry Steinbach	.05	545	Scott Spiezio	.05	654	Marvin Benard	.05
104	Lenny Webster	.05	212	Geronimo Berroa	.05	323	Mike Hampton	.05	437	Greg Swindell	.05	546	Matt Stairs	.05	655a	Barry Bonds/Btg	2.00
105	Cal Ripken Jr.		213	Pat Borders	.05	324	Doug Henry	.05	438	Bob Tewksbury	.05	547	Bill Taylor	.05	655b	Barry Bonds/Btg	
	(Orioles Checklist)	1.00	214	Jeff Branson	.05	325	Richard Hidalgo	.05	439	Mike Trombley	.05	548	Dave Telgheder	.05		(Close-up.)	2.00
106	Steve Avery	.05	215	Dave Burba	.05	326	Jack Howell	.05	440	Javier Valentin	.05	549	Jack Voigt	.05	656	Danny Darwin	.05
107	Mike Benjamin	.05	216	Bartolo Colon	.05	327	Jose Lima	.05	441	Todd Walker	.05	550	Ben Grieve (A's Checklist)	.05	657	Shawn Estes	.05
108	Darren Bragg	.05	217	Shawon Dunston	.05	328	Mike Magnante	.05	442	Paul Abreu	.10	551	Ruben Amaro	.05	658	Mark Gardner	.05
109	Damon Buford	.05	218	Travis Fryman	.05	329	Trever Miller	.05		(Twins Checklist)	.40	552	Ruben Amaro	.05	659	Darryl Hamilton	.05
110	Jim Corsi	.05	219	Brian Giles	.05	330	C.J. Nitkowski	.05	443	Shane Andrews	.05	553	Alex Arias	.05	660	Charlie Hayes	.05
111	Dennis Eckersley	.60	220	Dwight Gooden	.05	331	Shane Reynolds	.05	444	Miguel Batista	.05	554	Matt Beech	.05	661	Orel Hershiser	.05
112	Rich Garces	.05	221	Mike Jackson	.05	332	Bill Spiers	.05	445	Shayne Bennett	.05	555	Ricky Bottalico	.05	662	Stan Javier	.05
113a	Nomar Garciaparra/Btg	.75	222	David Justice	.05	333	Billy Wagner	.05	446	Rick DeHart	.05	556	Billy Brewer	.05	663	Brian Johnson	.05
113b	Nomar Garciaparra/Fldg	.75	223	Kenny Lofton	.05	334	Jeff Bagwell		447	Brad Fullmer	.05	557	Rico Brogna	.05	664	John Johnstone	.05
114	Tom Gordon	.05	224	Jose Mesa	.05		(Astros Checklist)	.40	448	Mark Grudzielanek	.05	558	Doug Glanville	.05	665	Jeff Kent	.05
115	Scott Hatteberg	.05	225	Alvin Morman	.05	335	Tim Belcher	.05	449	Vladimir Guerrero	.65	559	Wayne Gomes	.05	666	Brent Mayne	.05
116	Butch Henry	.05	226	Charles Nagy	.05	336	Brian Bevil	.05	450	Dustin Hermanson	.05	560	Mike Grace	.05	667	Bill Mueller	.05
117	Reggie Jefferson	.05	227	Chad Ogea	.05	337	Johnny Damon	.35	451	Steve Kline	.05	561	Tyler Green	.05	668	Robb Nen	.05
118	Mark Lemke	.05	228	Eric Plunk	.05	338	Jermaine Dye	.05	452	Scott Livingstone	.05	562	Rex Hudler	.05	669	Jim Poole	.05
119	Darren Lewis	.05	229	Manny Ramirez	.65	339	Sal Fasano	.05	453	Mike Maddux	.05	563	Gregg Jefferies	.05	670	Steve Reed	.05
120	Jim Leyritz	.05	230	Paul Shuey	.05	340	Shane Halter	.05	454	Derrick May	.05	564	Kevin Jordan	.05	671	Rich Rodriguez	.05
121	Derek Lowe	.05	231	Jim Thome	.65	341	Chris Haney	.05	455	Ryan McGuire	.05	565	Mark Leiter	.05	672	Kirk Rueter	.05
122	Pedro Martinez	.65	232	Ron Villone	.05	342	Jed Hansen	.05	456	Trey Moore	.05	566	Mark Lewis	.05	673	Rey Sanchez	.05
123	Troy O'Leary	.05	233	Omar Vizquel	.05	343	Jeff King	.05	457	Mike Mordecai	.05	567	Mike Lieberthal	.05	674	J.T. Snow	.05
124	Brian Rose	.05	234	Enrique Wilson	.05	344	Jeff Montgomery	.05	458	Carl Pavano	.05	568	Mark Parent	.05	675	Julian Tavarez	.05
125	Bret Saberhagen	.05	235	Jaret Wright	.05	345	Hal Morris	.05	459	Carlos Perez	.05	569	Yorkis Perez	.05	676	Barry Bonds	
126	Donnie Sadler	.05	236	Manny Ramirez		346	Jose Offerman	.05	460	F.P. Santangelo	.05	570	Desi Relaford	.05		(Giants Checklist)	1.00
127	Brian Shouse	.05		(Indians Checklist)	.40	347	Dean Palmer	.05	461	DaRond Stovall	.05	571	Scott Rolen	.50	677	Rich Amaral	.05
128	John Valentin	.05	237	Pedro Astacio	.05	348	Terry Pendleton	.05	462	Anthony Telford	.05	572	Curt Schilling	.35	678	Bobby Ayala	.05
129	Jason Varitek	.05	238	Jason Bates	.05	349	Hipolito Pichardo	.05	463	Ugueth Urbina	.05	573	Kevin Sefcik	.05	679	Jay Buhner	.05
130	Mo Vaughn	.05	239	Dante Bichette	.05	350	Jim Pittsley	.05	464	Marc Valdes	.05	574	Jerry Spradlin	.05	680	Ken Cloude	.05
131	Tim Wakefield	.05	240	Ellis Burks	.05	351	Pat Rapp	.05	465	Jose Vidro	.05	575	Garrett Stephenson	.05	681	Joey Cora	.05
132	John Wasdin	.05	241	Vinny Castilla	.05	352	Jose Rosado	.05	466	Rondell White	.05	576	Darrin Winston	.05	682	Russ Davis	.05
133	Nomar Garciaparra		242	Greg Colbrunn	.05	353	Glendon Rusch	.05	467	Chris Widger	.05	577	Scott Rolen		683	Rob Ducey	.05
	(Red Sox Checklist)	.45	243	Mike DeJean	.05	354	Scott Service	.05	468	Vladimir Guerrero			(Phillies Checklist)	.20	684	Jeff Fassero	.05
134	Terry Adams	.05	244	Jerry Dipoto	.05	355	Larry Sutton	.05		(Expos Checklist)	.40	578	Jermaine Allensworth	.05	685	Tony Fossas	.05
135	Manny Alexander	.05	245	Curtis Goodwin	.05	356	Mike Sweeney	.05	469	Edgardo Alfonzo	.05	579	Jason Christiansen	.05	686a	Ken Griffey Jr./Btg	1.25
136	Rod Beck	.05	246	Todd Helton	.65	357	Joe Vitiello	.05	470	Carlos Baerga	.05	580	Lou Collier	.05	686b	Ken Griffey Jr./Fldg	1.25
137	Jeff Blauser	.05	247	Bobby Jones	.05	358	Matt Whisenant	.05	471	Rich Becker	.05	581	Francisco Cordova	.05	687	Glenallen Hill	.05
138	Brant Brown	.05	248	Darryl Kile	.05	359	Ernie Young	.05	472	Brian Bohanon	.05	582	Elmer Dessens	.05	688	Jeff Huson	.05
139	Mark Clark	.05	249	Mike Lansing	.05	360	Jeff King		473	Alberto Castillo	.05	583	Freddy Garcia	.05	689	Randy Johnson	.65
140	Jeremi Gonzalez	.05	250	Curtis Leskanic	.05		(Royals Checklist)	.05	474	Dennis Cook	.05	584	Jose Guillen	.05	690	Edgar Martinez	.05
141	Mark Grace	.05	251	Nelson Liriano	.05	361	Bobby Bonilla	.05	475	John Franco	.05	585	Jason Kendall	.05	691	John Marzano	.05
142	Jose Hernandez	.05	252	Kirt Manwaring	.05	362	Jim Bruske	.05	476	Matt Franco	.05	586	Jon Lieber	.05	692	Jamie Moyer	.05
143	Tyler Houston	.05	253	Chuck McElroy	.05	363	Juan Castro	.05	477	Bernard Gilkey	.05	587	Esteban Loaiza	.05	693a	Alex Rodriguez/Btg	1.50
144	Lance Johnson	.05	254	Mike Munoz	.05	364	Roger Cedeno	.05	478	John Hudek	.05	588	Al Martin	.05	693b	Alex Rodriguez/Fldg	1.50
145	Sandy Martinez	.05	255	Neifi Perez	.05	365	Mike Devereaux	.05	479	Butch Huskey	.05	589	Javier Martinez	.05	694	David Segui	.05
146	Matt Mieske	.05	256	Jeff Reed	.05	366	Darren Dreifort	.05	480	Bobby Jones	.05	590	Chris Peters **RC**	.05	695	Heathcliff Slocumb	.05
147	Mickey Morandini	.05	257	Mark Thompson	.05	367	Jim Eisenreich	.05	481	Al Leiter	.05	591	Kevin Polcovich	.05	696	Paul Spoljaric	.05
148	Terry Mulholland	.05	258	John Vander Wal	.05	368	Wilton Guerrero	.05	482	Luis Lopez	.05	592	Ricardo Rincon	.05	697	Bill Swift	.05
149	Kevin Orie	.05	259	Dave Veres	.05	369	Mark Guthrie	.05	483	Brian McRae	.05	593	Jason Schmidt	.05	698	Mike Timlin	.05
150	Bob Patterson	.05	260a	Larry Walker/Btg	.05	370	Darren Hall	.05	484	Dave Mlicki	.05	594	Jose Silva	.05	699	Bob Wells	.05
151	Marc Pisciotta	.05	260b	Larry Walker/Btg		371	Todd Hollandsworth	.05	485	John Olerud	.05	595	Mark Smith	.05	700	Dan Wilson	.05
152	Henry Rodriguez	.05		(Close-up.)	.05	372	Thomas Howard	.05	486	Rey Ordonez	.05	596	Doug Strange	.05	701	Ken Griffey Jr.	
153	Scott Servais	.05	261	Jamey Wright	.05	373	Trenidad Hubbard	.05	487	Craig Paquette	.05	597	Turner Ward	.05		(Mariners Checklist)	.05
154	Sammy Sosa	.75	262	Larry Walker		374	Charles Johnson	.05	488a	Mike Piazza/Btg	1.00	598	Marc Wilkins	.05	702	Wilson Alvarez	.05
155	Kevin Tapani	.05		(Rockies Checklist)	.05	375	Eric Karros	.05	488b	Mike Piazza/Btg		599	Mike Williams	.05	703	Rolando Arrojo **RC**	.30
156	Steve Trachsel	.05	263	Kimera Bartee	.05	376	Paul Konerko	.20		(Close-up.)	1.00	600	Tony Womack	.05	704a	Wade Boggs/Btg	.75
157a	Kerry Wood/Pitching	.30	264	Doug Brocail	.05	377	Matt Luke	.05	489	Todd Pratt	.05	601	Kevin Young	.05	704b	Wade Boggs/Fldg	.75
157b	Kerry Wood/Pitching		265	Raul Casanova	.05	378	Ramon Martinez	.05	490	Mel Rojas	.05	602	Tony Womack		705	Rich Butler	.05
	(Close-up.)	.30	266	Frank Castillo	.05	379	Raul Mondesi	.05	491	Tim Spehr	.05		(Pirates Checklist)	.05	706	Miguel Cairo	.05
158	Kerry Wood		267	Frank Catalanotto	.05	380	Hideo Nomo	.35	492	Turk Wendell	.05	603	Manny Aybar	.05	707	Mike Difelice	.05
	(Cubs Checklist)	.20	268	Tony Clark	.05	381	Antonio Osuna	.05	493	Masato Yoshii **RC**	.25	604	Kent Bottenfield	.05	708	John Flaherty	.05
159	Jeff Abbott	.05	269	Deivi Cruz	.05	382	Chan Ho Park	.05				605	Jeff Brantley	.05	709	Roberto Hernandez	.05

710	Mike Kelly	.05
711	Aaron Ledesma	.05
712	Albie Lopez	.05
713	Dave Martinez	.05
714	Quinton McCracken	.05
715	Fred McGriff	.05
716	Jim Mecir	.05
717	Tony Saunders	.05
718	Bobby Smith	.05
719	Paul Sorrento	.05
720	Dennis Springer	.05
721	Kevin Stocker	.05
722	Ramon Tatis	.05
723	Bubba Trammell	.05
724	Esteban Yan	.05
725	Wade Boggs (Devil Rays Checklist)	.40
726	Luis Alicea	.05
727	Scott Bailes	.05
728	John Burkett	.05
729	Domingo Cedeno	.05
730	Will Clark	.05
731	Kevin Elster	.05
732a	Juan Gonzalez (Bat.)	.35
732b	Juan Gonzalez (No bat.)	.35
733	Tom Goodwin	.05
734	Rusty Greer	.05
735	Eric Gunderson	.05
736	Bill Haselman	.05
737	Rick Helling	.05
738	Roberto Kelly	.05
739	Mark McLemore	.05
740	Darren Oliver	.05
741	Danny Patterson	.05
742	Roger Pavlik	.05
743a	Ivan Rodriguez/Btg	.60
743b	Ivan Rodriguez/Fldg	.60
744	Aaron Sele	.05
745	Mike Simms	.05
746	Lee Stevens	.05
747	Fernando Tatis	.05
748	John Wetteland	.05
749	Bobby Witt	.05
750	Juan Gonzalez (Rangers Checklist)	.20
751	Carlos Almanzar	.05
752	Kevin Brown	.05
753	Jose Canseco	.40
754	Chris Carpenter	.05
755	Roger Clemens	1.00
756	Felipe Crespo	.05
757	Jose Cruz Jr.	.05
758	Mark Dalesandro	.05
759	Carlos Delgado	.50
760	Kelvim Escobar	.05
761	Tony Fernandez	.05
762	Darrin Fletcher	.05
763	Alex Gonzalez	.05
764	Craig Grebeck	.05
765	Shawn Green	.35
766	Juan Guzman	.05
767	Erik Hanson	.05
768	Pat Hentgen	.05
769	Randy Myers	.05
770	Robert Person	.05
771	Dan Plesac	.05
772	Paul Quantrill	.05
773	Bill Risley	.05
774	Juan Samuel	.05
775	Steve Sinclair	.05
776	Ed Sprague	.05
777	Mike Stanley	.05
778	Shannon Stewart	.05
779	Woody Williams	.05
780	Roger Clemens (Blue Jays Checklist)	.45

Web Cards

This 800-card parallel set allowed collectors to use Pacific's web site to find out the prize they had won. The cards used gold foil on the front instead of the silver foil used on base cards, and contained an eight-digit code on the back that was the claim number.

	NM/M
Web Stars/RC's:	2X
Inserted 1:1	

1998 Pacific Paramount

Paramount was Pacific's first fully-licensed baseball card product. The 250 base cards feature full-bleed photos with the player's name and team listed at the bottom. The base set is paralleled three times.

Gold retail (1:1), Copper hobby (1:1) and Platinum Blue (1:73) versions were included. Inserts in the product are Special Delivery Die-Cuts, Team Checklist Die-Cuts, Cooperstown Bound, Fielder's Choice Laser-Cuts and Inaugural Issue.

	NM/M
Complete Set (250):	20.00
Common Player:	.10
Gold (1:1R):	1X
Copper (1:1H):	1X
Red (1:1 ANCO):	2X
Platinum Blue (1:73):	4X
Holographic Silver:	20X
Production 99 Sets	
Pack (6):	1.00
Wax Box (36):	15.00

1	Garret Anderson	.10
2	Gary DiSarcina	.10
3	Jim Edmonds	.10
4	Darin Erstad	.20
5	Cecil Fielder	.10
6	Chuck Finley	.10
7	Todd Greene	.10
8	Shigetosi Hasegawa	.10
9	Tim Salmon	.10
10	Roberto Alomar	.10
11	Brady Anderson	.10
12	Joe Carter	.10
13	Eric Davis	.10
14	Ozzie Guillen	.10
15	Mike Mussina	.40
16	Rafael Palmeiro	.65
17	Cal Ripken Jr.	2.50
18	B.J. Surhoff	.10
19	Steve Avery	.10
20	Nomar Garciaparra	1.00
21	Reggie Jefferson	.10
22	Pedro Martinez	.75
23	Tim Naehring	.10
24	John Valentin	.10
25	Mo Vaughn	.10
26	James Baldwin	.10
27	Albert Belle	.10
28	Ray Durham	.10
29	Benji Gil	.10
30	Jaime Navarro	.10
31	Magglio Ordonez RC	1.50
32	Frank Thomas	.75
33	Robin Ventura	.10
34	Sandy Alomar Jr.	.10
35	Geronimo Berroa	.10
36	Travis Fryman	.10
37	David Justice	.10
38	Kenny Lofton	.10
39	Charles Nagy	.10
40	Manny Ramirez	.75
41	Jim Thome	.65
42	Omar Vizquel	.10
43	Jaret Wright	.10
44	Raul Casanova	.10
45	Frank Catalanotto RC	.20
46	Tony Clark	.10
47	Bobby Higginson	.10
48	Brian Hunter	.10
49	Todd Jones	.10
50	Bip Roberts	.10
51	Justin Thompson	.10
52	Kevin Appier	.10
53	Johnny Damon	.35
54	Jermaine Dye	.10
55	Jeff King	.10
56	Jeff Montgomery	.10
57	Dean Palmer	.10
58	Jose Rosado	.10
59	Larry Sutton	.10
60	Rick Aguilera	.10
61	Marty Cordova	.10
62	Pat Meares	.10
63	Paul Molitor	.75
64	Otis Nixon	.10
65	Brad Radke	.10
66	Terry Steinbach	.10
67	Todd Walker	.10
68	Hideki Irabu	.10
69	Derek Jeter	2.50
70	Chuck Knoblauch	.10
71	Tino Martinez	.10
72	Paul O'Neill	.10
73	Andy Pettitte	.20
74	Mariano Rivera	.15
75	Bernie Williams	.10
76	Mark Bellhorn	.10
77	Tom Candiotti	.10
78	Jason Giambi	.50

79	Ben Grieve	.10
80	Rickey Henderson	.75
81	Jason McDonald	.10
82	Aaron Small	.10
83	Miguel Tejada	.20
84	Jay Buhner	.10
85	Joey Cora	.10
86	Jeff Fassero	.10
87	Ken Griffey Jr.	1.50
88	Randy Johnson	.75
89	Edgar Martinez	.10
90	Alex Rodriguez	2.00
91	David Segui	.10
92	Dan Wilson	.10
93	Wilson Alvarez	.10
94	Wade Boggs	1.00
95	Miguel Cairo	.10
96	John Flaherty	.10
97	Dave Martinez	.10
98	Quinton McCracken	.10
99	Fred McGriff	.10
100	Paul Sorrento	.10
101	Kevin Stocker	.10
102	John Burkett	.10
103	Will Clark	.10
104	Juan Gonzalez	.40
105	Rusty Greer	.10
106	Roberto Kelly	.10
107	Ivan Rodriguez	.65
108	Fernando Tatis	.10
109	John Wetteland	.10
110	Jose Canseco	.40
111	Roger Clemens	1.25
112	Jose Cruz Jr.	.10
113	Carlos Delgado	.50
114	Alex Gonzalez	.10
115	Pat Hentgen	.10
116	Ed Sprague	.10
117	Shannon Stewart	.10
118	Brian Anderson	.10
119	Jay Bell	.10
120	Andy Benes	.10
121	Yamil Benitez	.10
122	Jorge Fabregas	.10
123	Travis Lee	.10
124	Devon White	.10
125	Matt Williams	.10
126	Bob Wolcott	.10
127	Andres Galarraga	.10
128	Tom Glavine	.35
129	Andruw Jones	.75
130	Chipper Jones	1.00
131	Ryan Klesko	.10
132	Javy Lopez	.10
133	Greg Maddux	1.00
134	Denny Neagle	.10
135	John Smoltz	.10
136	Rod Beck	.10
137	Jeff Blauser	.10
138	Mark Grace	.10
139	Lance Johnson	.10
140	Mickey Morandini	.10
141	Kevin Orie	.10
142	Sammy Sosa	1.00
143	Aaron Boone	.10
144	Bret Boone	.10
145	Dave Burba	.10
146	Lenny Harris	.10
147	Barry Larkin	.10
148	Reggie Sanders	.10
149	Brett Tomko	.10
150	Pedro Astacio	.10
151	Dante Bichette	.10
152	Ellis Burks	.10
153	Vinny Castilla	.10
154	Todd Helton	.75
155	Darryl Kile	.10
156	Jeff Reed	.10
157	Larry Walker	.10
158	Bobby Bonilla	.10
159	Todd Dunwoody	.10
160	Livan Hernandez	.10
161	Charles Johnson	.10
162	Mark Kotsay	.10
163	Derrek Lee	.60
164	Edgar Renteria	.10
165	Gary Sheffield	.50
166	Moises Alou	.10
167	Jeff Bagwell	.75
168	Derek Bell	.10
169	Craig Biggio	.10
170	Mike Hampton	.10
171	Richard Hidalgo	.10
172	Chris Holt	.10
173	Shane Reynolds	.10
174	Wilton Guerrero	.10
175	Eric Karros	.10
176	Paul Konerko	.20
177	Ramon Martinez	.10
178	Raul Mondesi	.10
179	Hideo Nomo	.40
180	Chan Ho Park	.10
181	Mike Piazza	1.25
182	Ismael Valdes	.10
183	Jeromy Burnitz	.10
184	Jeff Cirillo	.10
185	Todd Dunn	.10
186	Marquis Grissom	.10
187	John Jaha	.10
188	Doug Jones	.10
189	Dave Nilsson	.10
190	Jose Valentin	.10
191	Fernando Vina	.10
192	Orlando Cabrera	.10
193	Steve Falteisek	.10
194	Mark Grudzielanek	.10
195	Vladimir Guerrero	.75
196	Carlos Perez	.10

197	F.P. Santangelo	.10
198	Jose Vidro	.10
199	Rondell White	.10
200	Edgardo Alfonzo	.10
201	Carlos Baerga	.10
202	John Franco	.10
203	Bernard Gilkey	.10
204	Todd Hundley	.10
205	Butch Huskey	.10
206	Bobby Jones	.10
207	Brian McRae	.10
208	John Olerud	.10
209	Rey Ordonez	.10
210	Ricky Bottalico	.10
211	Bobby Estalella	.10
212	Doug Glanville	.10
213	Gregg Jefferies	.10
214	Mike Lieberthal	.10
215	Desi Relaford	.10
216	Scott Rolen	.65
217	Curt Schilling	.35
218	Adrian Brown	.10
219	Emil Brown	.10
220	Francisco Cordova	.10
221	Jose Guillen	.10
222	Al Martin	.10
223	Abraham Nunez	.10
224	Tony Womack	.10
225	Kevin Young	.10
226	Alan Benes	.10
227	Royce Clayton	.10
228	Gary Gaetti	.10
229	Ron Gant	.10
230	Brian Jordan	.10
231	Ray Lankford	.10
232	Mark McGwire	2.00
233	Todd Stottlemyre	.10
234	Kevin Brown	.10
235	Ken Caminiti	.10
236	Steve Finley	.10
237	Tony Gwynn	1.00
238	Wally Joyner	.10
239	Ruben Rivera	.10
240	Greg Vaughn	.10
241	Quilvio Veras	.10
242	Barry Bonds	2.50
243	Jacob Cruz	.10
244	Shawn Estes	.10
245	Orel Hershiser	.10
246	Stan Javier	.10
247	Brian Johnson	.10
248	Jeff Kent	.10
249	Robb Nen	.10
250	J.T. Snow	.10

Gold/Copper/Red

Gold, Copper and Red foil versions of all 250 cards in Paramount were inserted at a rate of one per pack. Gold versions were retail exclusive, Copper versions were hobby exclusive and Red versions were ANCO pack exclusive. The only difference is these parallels use a different color foil than the base cards.

	NM/M
Common Gold/Copper Player:	.25
Gold/Copper Stars:	1X
Inserted 1:1	
Common Red Player:	.30
Red Stars:	2X

Holographic Silver

Holographics Silver parallel cards were issued for all 250 cards in the Paramount set. These were inserted in hobby packs, with only 99 sets produced.

	NM/M
Common Player:	.10
Holographic Silver Stars:	20X
Production 99 Sets	

Platinum Blue

This parralled set reprinted all 250 cards in Paramount using blue foil stamping on the card front. These were inserted one per 73 packs.

	NM/M
Common Platinum Blue Player:	1.00
Platinum Blue Stars:	4X
Inserted 1:73	

Cooperstown Bound

Cooperstown Bound is a 10-card insert seeded one per 361 packs. Each card features a color player photo with a silver foil column on the left. The cards are fully foiled and etched.

	NM/M
Complete Set (10):	60.00
Common Player:	8.00
Inserted 1:361	
Pacific Proofs:	6X
Production 20 Sets	

1	Greg Maddux	10.00
2	Cal Ripken Jr.	15.00
3	Frank Thomas	8.00
4	Mike Piazza	8.00
5	Paul Molitor	8.00
6	Mark McGwire	12.00
7	Tony Gwynn	8.00
8	Barry Bonds	15.00
9	Ken Griffey Jr.	10.00
10	Wade Boggs	8.00

Fielder's Choice

Fielder's Choice Laser-Cuts is a 20-card insert seeded one per 73 packs. Each card is die-cut around a baseball glove that appears in the background. The webbing of the glove is laser-cut.

	NM/M
Complete Set (20):	45.00
Common Player:	.75
Inserted 1:73	
1	Chipper Jones	3.00
2	Greg Maddux	3.00
3	Cal Ripken Jr.	6.00
4	Nomar Garciaparra	3.00
5	Frank Thomas	2.50
6	David Justice	.75
7	Larry Walker	.75
8	Jeff Bagwell	2.50
9	Hideo Nomo	1.25
10	Mike Piazza	3.50
11	Derek Jeter	6.00
12	Ben Grieve	.75
13	Mark McGwire	4.50
14	Tony Gwynn	3.00
15	Barry Bonds	6.00
16	Ken Griffey Jr.	4.00
17	Alex Rodriguez	4.50

18	Wade Boggs	3.00
19	Ivan Rodriguez	2.00
20	Jose Cruz Jr.	.75

Special Delivery

Special Delivery cards are die-cut to resemble a postage stamp. Each card front is foiled and etched and features three photos of the player. Special Delivery is a 20-card insert seeded one per 37 packs.

	NM/M
Complete Set (20):	30.00
Common Player:	.50
Inserted 1:37	
1	Chipper Jones	2.50
2	Greg Maddux	2.50
3	Cal Ripken Jr.	5.00
4	Nomar Garciaparra	2.50
5	Pedro Martinez	2.00
6	Frank Thomas	2.00
7	David Justice	.50
8	Jeff Bagwell	2.00
9	Hideo Nomo	1.00
10	Mike Piazza	3.00
11	Vladimir Guerrero	2.00
12	Derek Jeter	5.00
13	Ben Grieve	.50
14	Mark McGwire	4.00
15	Tony Gwynn	2.50
16	Barry Bonds	2.50
17	Ken Griffey Jr.	3.50
18	Alex Rodriguez	4.00
19	Jose Cruz Jr.	.50

Team Checklists

Team Checklists (30 cards, 2:37) feature a player photo surrounded by two bats. The card is die-cut around the photo and the bats at the top. The bottom has the player's name, position and team.

	NM/M
Complete Set (30):	25.00
Common Player:	.25
Inserted 1:18	
1	Tim Salmon	.25
2	Cal Ripken Jr.	4.00
3	Nomar Garciaparra	1.50
4	Frank Thomas	1.00
5	Manny Ramirez	1.00
6	Tony Clark	.25
7	Dean Palmer	.25
8	Paul Molitor	1.00
9	Derek Jeter	4.00
10	Ben Grieve	.25
11	Ken Griffey Jr.	2.50
12	Wade Boggs	1.50
13	Ivan Rodriguez	.75
14	Roger Clemens	2.00
15	Matt Williams	.25
16	Chipper Jones	1.50
17	Sammy Sosa	1.50
18	Barry Larkin	.25
19	Larry Walker	.25
20	Livan Hernandez	.25
21	Jeff Bagwell	1.00
22	Mike Piazza	.25
23	John Jaha	.25
24	Vladimir Guerrero	1.00
25	Todd Hundley	.25
26	Scott Rolen	.75
27	Kevin Young	.25
28	Mark McGwire	3.00
29	Tony Gwynn	1.50
30	Barry Bonds	4.00

1998 Pacific Revolution

Pacific Revolution consists of a 150-card base set. The base cards are dual-foiled, etched and embossed. Inserts include Showstoppers, Prime Time Performers Laser-Cuts, Foul Pole Laser-Cuts, Major League Icons and Shadow Series.

		NM/M
Complete Set (150):		65.00
Common Player:		.25
Pack (3):		1.00
Wax Box (24):		20.00
1	Garret Anderson	.25
2	Jim Edmonds	.25
3	Darin Erstad	.40
4	Chuck Finley	.25
5	Tim Salmon	.25
6	Jay Bell	.25
7	Travis Lee	.25
8	Devon White	.25
9	Matt Williams	.25
10	Andres Galarraga	.45
11	Tom Glavine	.25
12	Andruw Jones	2.50
13	Chipper Jones	3.50
14	Ryan Klesko	.25
15	Javy Lopez	.25
16	Greg Maddux	3.50
17	Walt Weiss	.25
18	Roberto Alomar	.40
19	Joe Carter	.25
20	Mike Mussina	1.25
21	Rafael Palmeiro	2.00
22	Cal Ripken Jr.	6.00
23	B.J. Surhoff	.25
24	Nomar Garciaparra	3.00
25	Reggie Jefferson	.25
26	Pedro Martinez	2.50
27	Troy O'Leary	.25
28	Mo Vaughn	.25
29	Mark Grace	.25
30	Mickey Morandini	.25
31	Henry Rodriguez	.25
32	Sammy Sosa	3.00
33	Kerry Wood	1.25
34	Albert Belle	.25
35	Ray Durham	.25
36	Magglio Ordonez RC	2.00
37	Frank Thomas	2.50
38	Robin Ventura	.25
39	Bret Boone	.25
40	Barry Larkin	.25
41	Reggie Sanders	.25
42	Brett Tomko	.25
43	Sandy Alomar	.25
44	David Justice	.25
45	Kenny Lofton	.25
46	Manny Ramirez	2.50
47	Jim Thome	2.00
48	Omar Vizquel	.25
49	Jaret Wright	.25
50	Dante Bichette	.25
51	Ellis Burks	.25
52	Vinny Castilla	.25
53	Todd Helton	2.50
54	Larry Walker	.25
55	Tony Clark	.25
56	Deivi Cruz	.25
57	Damion Easley	.25
58	Bobby Higginson	.25
59	Brian Hunter	.25
60	Cliff Floyd	.25
61	Livan Hernandez	.25
62	Derrek Lee	1.50
63	Edgar Renteria	.25
64	Moises Alou	.25
65	Jeff Bagwell	2.50
66	Derek Bell	.25
67	Craig Biggio	.25
68	Richard Hidalgo	.25
69	Johnny Damon	.40
70	Jeff King	.25
71	Hal Morris	.25
72	Dean Palmer	.25
73	Bobby Bonilla	.25
74	Charles Johnson	.25
75	Paul Konerko	.35
76	Raul Mondesi	.25
77	Gary Sheffield	.75
78	Jeromy Burnitz	.25
79	Marquis Grissom	.25
80	Dave Nilsson	.25
81	Fernando Vina	.25
82	Marty Cordova	.25
83	Pat Meares	.25
84	Paul Molitor	2.50
85	Brad Radke	.25
86	Terry Steinbach	.25
87	Todd Walker	.25
88	Brad Fullmer	.25
89	Vladimir Guerrero	2.50

90	Carl Pavano	.25
91	Rondell White	.25
92	Bernard Gilkey	.25
93	Hideo Nomo	1.25
94	John Olerud	.25
95	Rey Ordonez	.25
96	Mike Piazza	4.00
97	Masato Yoshii RC	.65
98	Hideki Irabu	.25
99	Derek Jeter	6.00
100	Chuck Knoblauch	.25
101	Tino Martinez	.25
102	Paul O'Neill	.25
103	Darryl Strawberry	.25
104	Bernie Williams	.25
105	Jason Giambi	1.50
106	Ben Grieve	.25
107	Rickey Henderson	2.50
108	Matt Stairs	.25
109	Doug Glanville	.25
110	Desi Relaford	.25
111	Scott Rolen	1.50
112	Curt Schilling	.45
113	Jason Kendall	.25
114	Al Martin	.25
115	Jason Schmidt	.25
116	Kevin Young	.25
117	Delino DeShields	.25
118	Gary Gaetti	.25
119	Brian Jordan	.25
120	Ray Lankford	.25
121	Mark McGwire	5.00
122	Kevin Brown	.25
123	Steve Finley	.25
124	Tony Gwynn	3.50
125	Wally Joyner	.25
126	Greg Vaughn	.25
127	Barry Bonds	6.00
128	Orel Hershiser	.25
129	Jeff Kent	.25
130	Bill Mueller	.25
131	Jay Buhner	.25
132	Ken Griffey Jr.	4.50
133	Randy Johnson	2.50
134	Edgar Martinez	.25
135	Alex Rodriguez	5.00
136	David Segui	.25
137	Rolando Arrojo RC	.75
138	Wade Boggs	3.50
139	Quinton McCracken	.25
140	Fred McGriff	.25
141	Will Clark	.25
142	Juan Gonzalez	1.25
143	Tom Goodwin	.25
144	Ivan Rodriguez	2.00
145	Aaron Sele	.25
146	John Wetteland	.25
147	Jose Canseco	.50
148	Roger Clemens	4.00
149	Jose Cruz Jr.	.25
150	Carlos Delgado	.65

Shadows

Shadows is a full parallel of the Revolution base set. Limited to 99 sequentially numbered sets, each card is embossed with a special "Shadow Series" stamp.

	NM/M
Common Player:	2.00
Stars/Rookies:	6X

Foul Pole

Foul Pole Laser-Cuts is a 20-card insert seeded one per 49 packs. Each card features a color player

photo on the left and a foul pole on the right. The foul pole design includes netting that is laser cut.

		NM/M
Complete Set (20):		100.00
Common Player:		2.00
Inserted 1:49		
1	Cal Ripken Jr.	15.00
2	Nomar Garciaparra	7.50
3	Mo Vaughn	2.00
4	Frank Thomas	6.00
5	Manny Ramirez	6.00
6	Bernie Williams	2.00
7	Ben Grieve	2.00
8	Ken Griffey Jr.	10.00
9	Alex Rodriguez	12.00
10	Juan Gonzalez	3.00
11	Ivan Rodriguez	5.00
12	Travis Lee	2.00
13	Chipper Jones	7.50
14	Sammy Sosa	7.50
15	Vinny Castilla	2.00
16	Moises Alou	2.00
17	Gary Sheffield	3.00
18	Mike Piazza	9.00
19	Mark McGwire	12.00
20	Barry Bonds	15.00

Major League Icons

Major League Icons is a 10-card insert seeded one per 121 packs. Each card features a player photo on a die-cut shield, with the shield on a flaming stand.

		NM/M
Complete Set (10):		50.00
Common Player:		4.50
Inserted 1:121		
1	Cal Ripken Jr.	15.00
2	Nomar Garciaparra	7.50
3	Frank Thomas	6.00
4	Ken Griffey Jr.	10.00
5	Alex Rodriguez	12.50
6	Chipper Jones	7.50
7	Kerry Wood	4.50
8	Mike Piazza	9.00
9	Mark McGwire	12.50
10	Tony Gwynn	7.50

Prime Time Performers

Prime Time Performers is a 20-card insert seeded one per 25 packs. The cards are designed like a TV program guide with the team logo laser-cut on the TV screen. The color player photo is located on the left.

		NM/M
Complete Set (20):		25.00
Common Player:		.50
Inserted 1:25		
1	Cal Ripken Jr.	4.50
2	Nomar Garciaparra	2.00
3	Frank Thomas	1.50
4	Jim Thome	1.25
5	Hideki Irabu	.50
6	Derek Jeter	4.50
7	Ben Grieve	.50
8	Ken Griffey Jr.	3.00
9	Alex Rodriguez	3.50
10	Juan Gonzalez	.75
11	Ivan Rodriguez	1.25
12	Travis Lee	.50
13	Chipper Jones	2.00
14	Greg Maddux	2.00
15	Kerry Wood	.75
16	Larry Walker	.50
17	Jeff Bagwell	1.50
18	Mike Piazza	2.50
19	Mark McGwire	3.50
20	Tony Gwynn	2.00

Rookies and Hardball Heroes

This hobby-only insert combines 20 hot prospects with 10 veteran stars. Horizontal cards have action photos on a flashy metallic-foil background. A portrait photo is on back. The first 20 cards in the set, the youngsters, are paralleled in a gold edition which was limited to just 50 cards of each.

		NM/M
Complete Set (30):		20.00
Common Player:		.25
Inserted 1:6		
Gold (1-20):		10X
Production 50 Sets		
1	Justin Baughman	.25
2	Jarrod Washburn	.25
3	Travis Lee	.25
4	Kerry Wood	.50
5	Magglio Ordonez	.50
6	Todd Helton	1.00
7	Derrek Lee	.25
8	Richard Hidalgo	.25
9	Mike Caruso	.25
10	David Ortiz	.75
11	Brad Fullmer	.25
12	Masato Yoshii	.25
13	Orlando Hernandez	.25
14	Ricky Ledee	.25
15	Ben Grieve	.25
16	Carlton Loewer	.25
17	Desi Relaford	.25
18	Ruben Rivera	.25
19	Rolando Arrojo	.25
20	Matt Perisho	.25
21	Chipper Jones	2.00
22	Greg Maddux	2.00
23	Cal Ripken Jr.	5.00
24	Nomar Garciaparra	2.00
25	Frank Thomas	1.00
26	Mark McGwire	4.00
27	Tony Gwynn	2.00
28	Ken Griffey Jr.	3.00
29	Alex Rodriguez	4.00
30	Juan Gonzalez	.50

Showstoppers

This 36-card insert was seeded two per 25 packs. The cards feature holographic foil. The color photo is centered above the team logo and the Showstoppers logo.

		NM/M
Complete Set (36):		30.00
Common Player:		.45
Inserted 1:12		
1	Cal Ripken Jr.	5.00
2	Nomar Garciaparra	2.50
3	Pedro Martinez	2.00
4	Mo Vaughn	.45
5	Frank Thomas	2.00
6	Manny Ramirez	2.00
7	Jim Thome	1.75
8	Jaret Wright	.45
9	Paul Molitor	2.00
10	Orlando Hernandez	.60
11	Derek Jeter	5.00
12	Bernie Williams	.45
13	Ben Grieve	.45
14	Ken Griffey Jr.	3.50
15	Alex Rodriguez	4.00
16	Wade Boggs	2.50
17	Juan Gonzalez	1.00
18	Ivan Rodriguez	1.75
19	Jose Canseco	.75
20	Roger Clemens	3.00
21	Travis Lee	.45
22	Andres Galarraga	.45
23	Chipper Jones	2.50
24	Greg Maddux	2.50
25	Sammy Sosa	2.50
26	Kerry Wood	.75
27	Vinny Castilla	.45
28	Larry Walker	.45
29	Moises Alou	.45
30	Raul Mondesi	.45
31	Gary Sheffield	.75
32	Hideo Nomo	1.00
33	Mike Piazza	3.00
34	Mark McGwire	4.00
35	Tony Gwynn	2.50
36	Barry Bonds	5.00

Nestle's Latinos

Produced by Pacific this set of Latino ballplayers' cards was issued in three-card packs with the purchase of certain Nestle's food products in Los Angeles, Miami, Houston and San Antonio. Cards are found in two styles. Five of the cards have gold-foil graphic highlights on both top and bottom on front. On back the card number is in a white circle. The second style has foil on at bottom front and on back the card number is in a black circle. Both types have Pacific and Nestle logos on front and back.

		NM/M
Complete Set (20):		8.00
Common Player:		.25
1	Ismael Valdes	.25
2	Juan Gonzalez	.50
3	Ivan Rodriguez	.65
4	Joey Cora	.25
5	Livan Hernandez	.25
1	Tino Martinez	.25
4	Alex Rodriguez	1.50
5	Edgar Martinez	.25
4	Andres Galarraga	.25
6	Manny Ramirez	.75
7	Carlos Baerga	.25
8	Pedro Martinez	.75
9	Vinny Castilla	.25
10	Sammy Sosa	1.00
11	Nomar Garciaparra	1.00
12	Javy Lopez	.25
13	Sandy Alomar	.25
14	Roberto Alomar	.40
15	Jose Canseco	.50

Home Run Heroes

This retail exclusive product was sold as a complete set sealed in a tin lithographed can. The 2-1/2" x 3-1/2" cards have color action photos on front of the players in the followthrough of their home run swing. The figures are set on an artificial background which includes a sign giving the date and distance of their final home run of the 1998 season. Their team logo is in the "turf" at their feet. Fronts are highlighted with gold foil. On back are a portrait photo, a season summary and 1998 stats, along with appropriate licensor and manufacturer logos.

		NM/M
Complete Set (6):		2.50
Common Player:		.25
1	Mark McGwire	

2	Sammy Sosa	.65
3	Ken Griffey Jr.	.75
4	Greg Vaughn	.25
5	Albert Belle	.25
6	Jose Canseco	.50

Home Run History

This boxed set commemorating the great home run chase of 1998 was an exclusive to one of the television home-shopping shows. Each player is featured on 35 cards, with several depicting both players. Fronts have portraits or action shots which are borderless at the top and sides. At bottom is a gold-foil highlighted panel with the player's name, card title and date. Backs have another photo and details of the highlight. A pair of die-cut bonus cards were included in the boxed set.

		NM/M
Complete Set (70+2):		10.00
Common Card:		.50
1	Mark McGwire (Portrait of a Hero)	.50
2	Sammy Sosa (Portrait of a Hero)	.50
3	Mark McGwire (Fan Favorite)	.50
4	Sammy Sosa (Fan Favorite)	.50
5	Mark McGwire (Well-Rounded Superstar)	.50
6	Sammy Sosa (Well-Rounded Superstar)	.50
7	Mark McGwire (Cardinals Slugger)	.50
8	Sammy Sosa (Cubs Slugger)	.50
9	Mark McGwire (Home Run #48)	.50
10	Sammy Sosa (20 HRs in June)	.50
11	Mark McGwire (Home Run #50)	.50
12	Sammy Sosa (Home Run #50)	.50
13	Mark McGwire (Home Run #57)	.50
14	Sammy Sosa (Home Run #51)	.50
15	Mark McGwire (Home Run #58)	.50
16	Sammy Sosa (Home Run #56)	.50
17	Mark McGwire (Home Run #59)	.50
18	Sammy Sosa (Home Run #59)	.50
19	Mark McGwire (Home Run #60)	.50
20	Sammy Sosa (Home Run #60)	.50
21	Mark McGwire (Home Run #61)	.50
22	Sammy Sosa (Home Run #61)	.50
23	Mark McGwire (Home Run #62)	.50
24	Sammy Sosa (Home Run #62)	.50
25	Mark McGwire (The Record Falls)	.50
26	Sammy Sosa (Tied at 62!)	.50
27	Mark McGwire (The Home Run Ball)	.50
28	Sammy Sosa (Sammy Sosa Day)	.50
29	Mark McGwire (Achievement Award)	.50
30	Sammy Sosa (Achievement Award)	.50
31	Mark McGwire (What a Ride!)	.50
32	Sammy Sosa (A Season of Accolades)	.50
33	Mark McGwire (Home Run #63)	.50
34	Sammy Sosa (Sammy, You're the Man)	.50
35	Mark McGwire (Home Run #64)	.50
36	Sammy Sosa (Home Run #63)	.50

No.	Player	Price
37	Mark McGwire (Home Run #65)	.50
38	Sammy Sosa (Home Run #64)	.50
39	Mark McGwire (Home Run #67)	.50
40	Sammy Sosa (Home Run #65)	.50
41	Mark McGwire (Home Run #68)	.50
42	Sammy Sosa (Home Run #66)	.50
43	Mark McGwire (70!!!)	.50
44	Sammy Sosa (Cubs Win Wild Card)	.50
45	Mark McGwire (Last Swing of the Bat)	.50
46	Sammy Sosa (18 Stolen Bases)	.50
47	Mark McGwire (Power at the Plate)	.50
48	Sammy Sosa (Grand Sam)	.50
49	Mark McGwire (130 Runs Scored)	.50
50	Sammy Sosa (134 Runs Scored)	.50
51	Mark McGwire (32 HRs on the Road)	.50
52	Sammy Sosa (31 HRs on the Road)	.50
53	Mark McGwire (38 HRs at Home)	.50
54	Sammy Sosa (35 HRs at Home)	.50
55	Mark McGwire (11 First-Inning Home Runs)	.50
56	Sammy Sosa (12 First-Inning Home Runs)	.50
57	Mark McGwire (10 Multiple-HR Games)	.50
58	Sammy Sosa (11 Multiple-HR Games)	.50
59	Mark McGwire (545-Foot Blast)	.50
60	Sammy Sosa (500-Foot Blast)	.50
61	Mark McGwire (St. Louis' Favorite Son)	.50
62	Sammy Sosa (Chicago's Favorite Son)	.50
63	Mark McGwire (A Season of Celebration)	.50
64	Sammy Sosa (A Season of Celebration)	.50
65	Mark McGwire (Curtain Call)	.50
66	Sammy Sosa (Curtain Call)	.50
67	Mark McGwire, Sammy Sosa (Awesome Power)	.50
68	Mark McGwire, Sammy Sosa (Ambassadors of the Game)	.50
69	Mark McGwire, Sammy Sosa (Transcending Sports)	.50
70	Mark McGwire, Sammy Sosa (Friends to the End/Checklist)	.50

Home Run History Bonus Cards

Though they are not identified as such, this pair of Gold Crown-style die-cut cards are bonus inserts in the Home Run History boxed set. Fronts have gold-foil highlights with the pivotal number in blue-sky tones. Backs have portrait photos and a few words about the remarkable record.

		NM/M
1	Mark McGwire (Home Run Champ)	1.50
1	Cal Ripken Jr. (Consecutive Games)	2.00

National Convention Redemption

This card of Pacific spokesman Tony Gwynn was given away at the card company's booth in a redemption program during the 1998 National Sports Collectors Convention in August 1998. The card front has a color photo of

Gwynn on red and yellow rayed background. At lower-right is a gold-foil convention logo. Back has an action photo, copyright information and logos.

	NM/M
1998 Tony Gwynn	3.00

1999 Pacific Sample

This card of Pacific spokesman Tony Gwynn introduces the 1999 series. The sample card follows the format of the issued version but is overprinted "SAMPLE" on back but lacks Gwynn's 1998 season and career stats.

	NM/M
Tony Gwynn	2.00

1999 Pacific

The 450-card base set features full bleed fronts enhanced with silver foil stamping. Card backs have year-by-year statistics, a small photo and a brief career highlight caption. There are two parallels, Platinum Blues and Reds. Platinum Blues have blue foil stamping and are seeded 1:73 packs. Reds are retail exclusive with red foil stamping and are seeded one per retail pack.

	NM/M
Complete Set (500):	30.00
Common Player:	.10
Platinum Blues (1:73):	15X
Reds (1:1R):	2.5X
Pack (10):	1.00
Wax Box (36):	35.00

No.	Player	Price
1	Garret Anderson	.10
2	Jason Dickson	.10
3	Gary DiSarcina	.10
4	Jim Edmonds	.10
5	Darin Erstad	.25
6	Chuck Finley	.10
7	Shigetosi Hasegawa	.10
8	Ken Hill	.10
9	Dave Hollins	.10
10	Phil Nevin	.10
11	Troy Percival	.10
12a	Tim Salmon/Action	.10
12b	Tim Salmon/Portrait	.10
13	Brian Anderson	.10
14	Tony Batista	.10
15	Jay Bell	.10
16	Andy Benes	.10
17	Yamil Benitez	.10
18	Omar Daal	.10
19	David Dellucci	.10
20	Karim Garcia	.10
21	Bernard Gilkey	.10
22a	Travis Lee/Action	.10
22b	Travis Lee/Portrait	.10
23	Aaron Small	.10
24	Kelly Stinnett	.10
25	Devon White	.10
26	Matt Williams	.10
27a	Bruce Chen/Action	.10
27b	Bruce Chen/Portrait	.10
28a	Andres Galarraga/Action	.10
28b	Andres Galarraga/Portrait	.10
29	Tom Glavine	.35
30	Ozzie Guillen	.10
31	Andruw Jones	1.00
32a	Chipper Jones/Action	1.50
32b	Chipper Jones/Portrait	1.50
33	Ryan Klesko	.10
34	George Lombard	.10
35	Javy Lopez	.10
36a	Greg Maddux/Action	1.50
36b	Greg Maddux/Portrait	1.50
37a	Marty Malloy/Action	.10
37b	Marty Malloy/Portrait	.10
38	Dennis Martinez	.10
39	Kevin Millwood	.10
40a	Alex Rodriguez/Action	2.50
40b	Alex Rodriguez/Portrait	2.50
41	Denny Neagle	.10
42	John Smoltz	.10
43	Michael Tucker	.10
44	Walt Weiss	.10
45a	Roberto Alomar/Action	.25
45b	Roberto Alomar/Portrait	.25
46	Brady Anderson	.10
47	Harold Baines	.10
48	Mike Bordick	.10
49a	Danny Clyburn/Action	.10
49b	Danny Clyburn/Portrait	.10
50	Eric Davis	.10
51	Scott Erickson	.10
52	Chris Hoiles	.10
53	Jimmy Key	.10
54a	Ryan Minor/Action	.10
54b	Ryan Minor/Portrait	.10
55	Mike Mussina	.40
56	Jesse Orosco	.10
57a	Rafael Palmeiro/Action	.75
57b	Rafael Palmeiro/Portrait	.75
58	Sidney Ponson	.10
59	Arthur Rhodes	.10
60a	Cal Ripken Jr./Action	3.00
60b	Cal Ripken Jr./Portrait	3.00
61	B.J. Surhoff	.10
62	Steve Avery	.10
63	Darren Bragg	.10
64	Dennis Eckersley	.75
65a	Nomar Garciaparra/Action	1.50
65b	Nomar Garciaparra/Portrait	1.50
66a	Sammy Sosa/Action	1.50
66b	Sammy Sosa/Portrait	1.50
67	Tom Gordon	.10
68	Reggie Jefferson	.10
69	Darren Lewis	.10
70a	Mark McGwire/Action	2.50
70b	Mark McGwire/Portrait	2.50
71	Pedro Martinez	1.00
72	Troy O'Leary	.10
73	Bret Saberhagen	.10
74	Mike Stanley	.10
75	John Valentin	.10
76	Jason Varitek	.10
77	Mo Vaughn	.10
78	Tim Wakefield	.10
79	Manny Alexander	.10
80	Rod Beck	.10
81	Brant Brown	.10
82	Mark Clark	.10
83	Gary Gaetti	.10
84	Mark Grace	.10
85	Jose Hernandez	.10
86	Lance Johnson	.10
87a	Jason Maxwell/Action	.10
87b	Jason Maxwell/Portrait	.10
88	Mickey Morandini	.10
89	Terry Mulholland	.10
90	Henry Rodriguez	.10
91	Scott Servais	.10
92	Kevin Tapani	.10
93	Pedro Valdes	.10
94	Kerry Wood	.40
95	Jeff Abbott	.10
96	James Baldwin	.10
97	Albert Belle	.10
98	Mike Cameron	.10
99	Mike Caruso	.10
100	Wil Cordero	.10
101	Ray Durham	.10
102	Jaime Navarro	.10
103	Greg Norton	.10
104	Magglio Ordonez	.25
105	Mike Sirotka	.10
106a	Frank Thomas/Action	1.00
106b	Frank Thomas/Portrait	1.00
107	Robin Ventura	.10
108	Craig Wilson	.10
109	Aaron Boone	.10
110	Bret Boone	.10
111	Sean Casey	.15
112	Pete Harnisch	.10
113	John Hudek	.10
114	Barry Larkin	.10
115	Eduardo Perez	.10
116	Mike Remlinger	.10
117	Reggie Sanders	.10
118	Chris Stynes	.10
119	Eddie Taubensee	.10
120	Brett Tomko	.10
121	Pat Watkins	.10
122	Dmitri Young	.10
123	Sandy Alomar Jr.	.10
124	Dave Burba	.10
125	Bartolo Colon	.10
126	Joey Cora	.10
127	Brian Giles	.10
128	Dwight Gooden	.10
129	Mike Jackson	.10
130	David Justice	.10
131	Kenny Lofton	.10
132	Charles Nagy	.10
133	Chad Ogea	.10
134a	Manny Ramirez/Action	1.00
134b	Manny Ramirez/Portrait	1.00
135	Richie Sexson	.10
136a	Jim Thome/Action	.75
136b	Jim Thome/Portrait	.75
137	Omar Vizquel	.10
138	Jaret Wright	.10
139	Pedro Astacio	.10
140	Jason Bates	.10
141a	Dante Bichette/Action	.10
141b	Dante Bichette/Portrait	.10
142a	Vinny Castilla/Action	.10
142b	Vinny Castilla/Portrait	.10
143a	Edgar Clemente/Action	.10
143b	Edgar Clemente/Portrait	.10
144a	Derrick Gibson/Action	.10
144b	Derrick Gibson/Portrait	.10
145	Curtis Goodwin	.10
146a	Todd Helton/Action	1.00
146b	Todd Helton/Portrait	1.00
147	Bobby Jones	.10
148	Darryl Kile	.10
149	Mike Lansing	.10
150	Chuck McElroy	.10
151	Neifi Perez	.10
152	Jeff Reed	.10
153	John Thomson	.10
154a	Larry Walker/Action	.10
154b	Larry Walker/Portrait	.10
155	Jamey Wright	.10
156	Kimera Bartee	.10
157	Geronimo Berroa	.10
158	Raul Casanova	.10
159	Frank Catalanotto	.10
160	Tony Clark	.10
161	Deivi Cruz	.10
162	Damion Easley	.10
163	Juan Encarnacion	.10
164	Luis Gonzalez	.10
165	Seth Greisinger	.10
166	Bob Higginson	.10
167	Brian Hunter	.10
168	Todd Jones	.10
169	Justin Thompson	.10
170	Antonio Alfonseca	.10
171	Dave Berg	.10
172	John Cangelosi	.10
173	Craig Counsell	.10
174	Todd Dunwoody	.10
175	Cliff Floyd	.10
176	Alex Gonzalez	.10
177	Livan Hernandez	.10
178	Ryan Jackson	.10
179	Mark Kotsay	.10
180	Derrek Lee	.65
181	Matt Mantei	.10
182	Brian Meadows	.10
183	Edgar Renteria	.10
184a	Moises Alou/Action	.10
184b	Moises Alou/Portrait	.10
185	Brad Ausmus	.10
186a	Jeff Bagwell/Action	1.00
186b	Jeff Bagwell/Portrait	1.00
187	Derek Bell	.10
188	Sean Berry	.10
189	Craig Biggio	.10
190	Carl Everett	.10
191	Ricky Gutierrez	.10
192	Mike Hampton	.10
193	Doug Henry	.10
194	Richard Hidalgo	.10
195	Randy Johnson	1.00
196a	Russ Johnson/Action	.10
196b	Russ Johnson/Portrait	.10
197	Shane Reynolds	.10
198	Bill Spiers	.10
199	Kevin Appier	.10
200	Tim Belcher	.10
201	Jeff Conine	.10
202	Johnny Damon	.35
203	Jermaine Dye	.10
204a	Jeremy Giambi (Batting stance.)	.10
204b	Jeremy Giambi (Follow-through.)	.10
205	Jeff King	.10
206	Shane Mack	.10
207	Jeff Montgomery	.10
208	Hal Morris	.10
209	Jose Offerman	.10
210	Dean Palmer	.10
211	Jose Rosado	.10
212	Glendon Rusch	.10
213	Larry Sutton	.10
214	Mike Sweeney	.10
215	Bobby Bonilla	.10
216	Alex Cora	.10
217	Darren Dreifort	.10
218	Mark Grudzielanek	.10
219	Todd Hollandsworth	.10
220	Trenidad Hubbard	.10
221	Charles Johnson	.10
222	Eric Karros	.10
223	Matt Luke	.10
224	Ramon Martinez	.10
225	Raul Mondesi	.10
226	Chan Ho Park	.10
227	Jeff Shaw	.10
228	Gary Sheffield	.40
229	Eric Young	.10
230	Jeromy Burnitz	.10
231	Jeff Cirillo	.10
232	Marquis Grissom	.10
233	Bobby Hughes	.10
234	John Jaha	.10
235	Geoff Jenkins	.10
236	Scott Karl	.10
237	Mark Loretta	.10
238	Mike Matheny	.10
239	Mike Myers	.10
240	Dave Nilsson	.10
241	Bob Wickman	.10
242	Jose Valentin	.10
243	Fernando Vina	.10
244	Rick Aguilera	.10
245	Ron Coomer	.10
246	Marty Cordova	.10
247	Denny Hocking	.10
248	Matt Lawton	.10
249	Pat Meares	.10
250a	Paul Molitor/Action	1.00
250b	Paul Molitor/Portrait	1.00
251	Otis Nixon	.10
252	Alex Ochoa	.10
253	David Ortiz	.65
254	A.J. Pierzynski	.10
255	Brad Radke	.10
256	Terry Steinbach	.10
257	Bob Tewksbury	.10
258	Todd Walker	.10
259	Shane Andrews	.10
260	Shayne Bennett	.10
261	Orlando Cabrera	.10
262	Brad Fullmer	.10
263	Vladimir Guerrero	1.00
264	Wilton Guerrero	.10
265	Dustin Hermanson	.10
266	Terry Jones	.10
267	Steve Kline	.10
268	Carl Pavano	.10
269	F.P. Santangelo	.10
270a	Fernando Seguignol/Action	.10
270b	Fernando Seguignol/Portrait	.10
271	Ugueth Urbina	.10
272	Jose Vidro	.10
273	Chris Widger	.10
274	Edgardo Alfonzo	.10
275	Carlos Baerga	.10
276	John Franco	.10
277	Todd Hundley	.10
278	Butch Huskey	.10
279	Bobby Jones	.10
280	Al Leiter	.10
281	Greg McMichael	.10
282	Brian McRae	.10
283	Hideo Nomo	.50
284	John Olerud	.10
285	Rey Ordonez	.10
286a	Mike Piazza/Action	1.75
286b	Mike Piazza/Portrait	1.75
287	Turk Wendell	.10
288	Masato Yoshii	.10
289	David Cone	.10
290	Chad Curtis	.10
291	Joe Girardi	.10
292	Orlando Hernandez	.10
293a	Hideki Irabu/Action	.10
293b	Hideki Irabu/Portrait	.10
294a	Derek Jeter/Action	3.00
294b	Derek Jeter/Portrait	3.00
295	Chuck Knoblauch	.10
296a	Mike Lowell/Action	.10
296b	Mike Lowell/Portrait	.10
297	Tino Martinez	.10
298	Ramiro Mendoza	.10
299	Paul O'Neill	.10
300	Andy Pettitte	.25
301	Jorge Posada	.10
302	Tim Raines	.10
303	Mariano Rivera	.15
304	David Wells	.10
305a	Bernie Williams/Action	.10
305b	Bernie Williams/Portrait	.10
306	Mike Blowers	.10
307	Tom Candiotti	.10
308a	Eric Chavez/Action	.15
308b	Eric Chavez/Portrait	.15
309	Ryan Christenson	.10
310	Jason Giambi	.65
311a	Ben Grieve/Action	.10
311b	Ben Grieve/Portrait	.10
312	Rickey Henderson	1.00
313	A.J. Hinch	.10
314	Jason McDonald	.10
315	Bip Roberts	.10
316	Kenny Rogers	.10
317	Scott Spiezio	.10
318	Matt Stairs	.10
319	Miguel Tejada	.20
320	Bob Abreu	.20
321	Alex Arias	.10
322a	Gary Bennett RC/Action	.10
322b	Gary Bennett RC/Portrait	.10
323	Ricky Bottalico	.10
324	Rico Brogna	.10
325	Bobby Estalella	.10
326	Doug Glanville	.10
327	Kevin Jordan	.10
328	Mark Leiter	.10
329	Wendell Magee	.10
330	Mark Portugal	.10
331	Desi Relaford	.10
332	Scott Rolen	.65
333	Curt Schilling	.35
334	Kevin Sefcik	.10
335	Adrian Brown	.10
336	Emil Brown	.10
337	Lou Collier	.10
338	Francisco Cordova	.10
339	Freddy Garcia	.10
340	Jose Guillen	.10
341	Jason Kendall	.10
342	Al Martin	.10
343	Abraham Nunez	.10
344	Aramis Ramirez	.10
345	Ricardo Rincon	.10
346	Jason Schmidt	.10
347	Turner Ward	.10
348	Tony Womack	.10
349	Kevin Young	.10
350	Juan Acevedo	.10
351	Delino DeShields	.10
352a	J.D. Drew/Action	.40
352b	J.D. Drew/Portrait	.40
353	Ron Gant	.10
354	Brian Jordan	.10
355	Ray Lankford	.10
356	Eli Marrero	.10
357	Kent Mercker	.10
358	Matt Morris	.10
359	Luis Ordaz	.10
360	Donovan Osborne	.10
361	Placido Polanco	.10
362	Fernando Tatis	.10
363	Andy Ashby	.10
364	Kevin Brown	.10
365	Ken Caminiti	.10
366	Steve Finley	.10
367	Chris Gomez	.10
368a	Tony Gwynn/Action	1.50
368b	Tony Gwynn/Portrait	1.50
369	Joey Hamilton	.10
370	Carlos Hernandez	.10
371	Trevor Hoffman	.10
372	Wally Joyner	.10
373	Jim Leyritz	.10
374	Ruben Rivera	.10
375	Greg Vaughn	.10
376	Quilvio Veras	.10
377	Rich Aurilia	.10
378a	Barry Bonds/Action	3.00
378b	Barry Bonds/Portrait	3.00
379	Ellis Burks	.10
380	Joe Carter	.10
381	Stan Javier	.10
382	Brian Johnson	.10
383	Jeff Kent	.10
384	Jose Mesa	.10
385	Bill Mueller	.10
386	Robb Nen	.10
387a	Armando Rios/Action	.10
387b	Armando Rios/Portrait	.10
388	Kirk Rueter	.10
389	Rey Sanchez	.10
390	J.T. Snow	.10
391	David Bell	.10
392	Jay Buhner	.10
393	Ken Cloude	.10
394	Russ Davis	.10
395	Jeff Fassero	.10
396a	Ken Griffey Jr./Action	2.00
396b	Ken Griffey Jr./Portrait	2.00
397	Giomar Guevara RC	.10
398	Carlos Guillen	.10
399	Edgar Martinez	.10
400	Shane Monahan	.10
401	Jamie Moyer	.10
402	David Segui	.10
403	Makoto Suzuki	.10
404	Mike Timlin	.10
405	Dan Wilson	.10
406	Wilson Alvarez	.10
407	Rolando Arrojo	.10
408	Wade Boggs	1.50
409	Miguel Cairo	.10
410	Roberto Hernandez	.10
411	Mike Kelly	.10
412	Aaron Ledesma	.10
413	Albie Lopez	.10
414	Dave Martinez	.10
415	Quinton McCracken	.10
416	Fred McGriff	.10
417	Bryan Rekar	.10
418	Paul Sorrento	.10
419	Randy Winn	.10
420	John Burkett	.10
421	Will Clark	.10
422	Royce Clayton	.10
423a	Juan Gonzalez/Action	.50
423b	Juan Gonzalez/Portrait	.50
424	Tom Goodwin	.10
425	Rusty Greer	.10
426	Rick Helling	.10
427	Roberto Kelly	.10
428	Mark McLemore	.10
429a	Ivan Rodriguez/Action	.75
429b	Ivan Rodriguez/Portrait	.75
430	Aaron Sele	.10
431	Lee Stevens	.10
432	Todd Stottlemyre	.10
433	John Wetteland	.10

434	Todd Zeile	.10
435	Jose Canseco	.50
436a	Roger Clemens/Action	1.75
436b	Roger Clemens/Portrait	1.75
437	Felipe Crespo	.10
438a	Jose Cruz Jr./Action	.10
438b	Jose Cruz Jr./Portrait	.10
439	Carlos Delgado	.50
440a	Tom Evans/Action	.10
440b	Tom Evans/Portrait	.10
441	Tony Fernandez	.10
442	Darrin Fletcher	.10
443	Alex Gonzalez	.10
444	Shawn Green	.30
445	Roy Halladay	.10
446	Pat Hentgen	.10
447	Juan Samuel	.10
448	Benito Santiago	.10
449	Shannon Stewart	.10
450	Woody Williams	.10

Cramer's Choice

Pacific CEO Michael Cramer personally chose this 10-card set. Die-cut in a trophy shape, the cards are enhanced with silver holographic etching and gold foil stamping across the card bottom. Cards are serially numbered to 299.

		NM/M
Complete Set (10):		65.00
Common Player:		7.50
Inserted 1:721		
1	Cal Ripken Jr.	20.00
2	Nomar Garciaparra	12.50
3	Frank Thomas	10.00
4	Ken Griffey Jr.	15.00
5	Alex Rodriguez	17.50
6	Greg Maddux	12.50
7	Sammy Sosa	12.50
8	Kerry Wood	7.50
9	Mark McGwire	17.50
10	Tony Gwynn	12.50

Dynagon Diamond

Dynagon Diamond captures 20 of baseball's biggest stars in action against a mirror-patterned full-foil background. These are seeded about 1:9. A Titanium parallel with each card numbered to 99 was exclusive to hobby packs.

		NM/M
Complete Set (20):		20.00
Common Player:		.40
Inserted 1:9		
Titanium (99 Sets)		8X
1	Cal Ripken Jr.	2.50
2	Nomar Garciaparra	1.00
3	Frank Thomas	.75
4	Derek Jeter	2.50
5	Ben Grieve	.40
6	Ken Griffey Jr.	1.50
7	Alex Rodriguez	2.00
8	Juan Gonzalez	.75
9	Travis Lee	.40
10	Chipper Jones	1.00
11	Greg Maddux	1.00
12	Sammy Sosa	1.00
13	Kerry Wood	.50
14	Jeff Bagwell	.75
15	Hideo Nomo	.50
16	Mike Piazza	12.50
17	J.D. Drew	.50
18	Mark McGwire	2.00

19	Tony Gwynn	1.00
20	Barry Bonds	2.50

Gold Crown Die-Cuts

This 36-card die-cut set is shaped like a crown at the top and features dual foiling, 24-pt. stock and gold foil stamping. These are seeded 1:37 packs.

		NM/M
Complete Set (36):		75.00
Common Player:		.75
Inserted 1:37		
1	Darin Erstad	1.00
2	Cal Ripken Jr.	7.50
3	Nomar Garciaparra	4.00
4	Pedro Martinez	3.00
5	Mo Vaughn	.75
6	Frank Thomas	3.00
7	Kenny Lofton	.75
8	Manny Ramirez	3.00
9	Paul Molitor	3.00
10	Derek Jeter	7.50
11	Bernie Williams	.75
12	Ben Grieve	.75
13	Ken Griffey Jr.	5.00
14	Alex Rodriguez	6.00
15	Wade Boggs	4.00
16	Juan Gonzalez	1.50
17	Ivan Rodriguez	2.50
18	Jose Canseco	1.50
19	Roger Clemens	4.50
20	Travis Lee	.75
21	Chipper Jones	4.00
22	Greg Maddux	4.00
23	Sammy Sosa	4.00
24	Kerry Wood	1.50
25	Todd Helton	3.00
26	Larry Walker	.75
27	Jeff Bagwell	3.00
28	Craig Biggio	.75
29	Raul Mondesi	.75
30	Vladimir Guerrero	3.00
31	Mike Piazza	4.50
32	Scott Rolen	2.00
33	J.D. Drew	1.50
34	Mark McGwire	6.00
35	Tony Gwynn	4.00
36	Barry Bonds	7.50

Hot Cards

This dealer-only 10-card set was awarded to any dealer that had sold any packs/boxes that produced a card for the Pacific Hot Cards Registry Program. Fronts have a metallic foil background. Backs have a portrait photo and are serial numbered within an edition of 500 each.

		NM/M
Complete Set (10):		75.00
Common Player:		3.00
1	Alex Rodriguez	12.50
2	Tony Gwynn	7.50
3	Ken Griffey Jr.	10.00
4	Sammy Sosa	7.50
5	Ivan Rodriguez	6.00
6	Derek Jeter	15.00
7	Cal Ripken Jr.	15.00
8	Mark McGwire	15.00
9	J.D. Drew	4.50
10	Bernie Williams	3.00

Team Checklists

This 30-card horizontal insert set features a star player from each team on the card front, with each team's complete checklist on the card back. Fronts feature a holo-

graphic silver-foiled and embossed logo of the player's respective team. These are seeded 2:37 packs.

		NM/M
Complete Set (30):		30.00
Common Player:		.30
Inserted 1:18		
1	Darin Erstad	.50
2	Cal Ripken Jr.	3.00
3	Nomar Garciaparra	1.50
4	Frank Thomas	1.00
5	Manny Ramirez	1.00
6	Damion Easley	.30
7	Jeff King	.30
8	Paul Molitor	1.00
9	Derek Jeter	3.00
10	Ben Grieve	.30
11	Ken Griffey Jr.	2.00
12	Wade Boggs	1.50
13	Juan Gonzalez	.60
14	Roger Clemens	1.75
15	Travis Lee	.30
16	Chipper Jones	1.50
17	Sammy Sosa	1.50
18	Barry Larkin	.30
19	Todd Helton	1.00
20	Mark Kotsay	.30
21	Jeff Bagwell	1.00
22	Raul Mondesi	.30
23	Jeff Cirillo	.30
24	Vladimir Guerrero	1.00
25	Mike Piazza	1.75
26	Scott Rolen	.75
27	Jason Kendall	.30
28	Mark McGwire	2.50
29	Tony Gwynn	1.50
30	Barry Bonds	3.00

Timelines

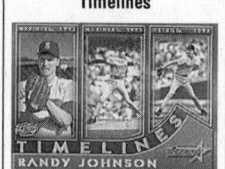

Timelines features 20 superstars, giving a chronological history of each player complete with photos from early in their careers. Three photos of the player are on the card front. Inserted exclusively in hobby packs these are limited to 199 serially numbered sets.

		NM/M
Complete Set (20):		200.00
Common Player:		6.00
Inserted 1:181 H		
1	Cal Ripken Jr.	30.00
2	Frank Thomas	12.00
3	Jim Thome	10.00
4	Paul Molitor	12.00
5	Bernie Williams	6.00
6	Derek Jeter	30.00
7	Ken Griffey Jr.	20.00
8	Alex Rodriguez	25.00
9	Wade Boggs	15.00
10	Jose Canseco	9.00
11	Roger Clemens	17.50
12	Andres Galarraga	6.00
13	Chipper Jones	15.00
14	Greg Maddux	15.00
15	Sammy Sosa	15.00
16	Larry Walker	6.00
17	Randy Johnson	12.00
18	Mike Piazza	17.50
19	Mark McGwire	25.00
20	Tony Gwynn	15.00

1999 Pacific Aurora

The 200-card set features two photos on the card front and one on the back. Card backs also have '98 and career stats along with personal information. The player's name and Aurora logo are stamped with gold foil. A parallel "Opening Day" issued is stamped with a gold foil seal and numbered within an edition of 31 each.

		NM/M
Complete Set (200):		20.00
Common Player:		.10
Opening Days:		20X
Production 31 Sets		
Reds:		2X
Retail Only (1:6)		
Pack (6):		1.50
Wax Box (36):		22.50
1	Garret Anderson	.10
2	Jim Edmonds	.10
3	Darin Erstad	.30
4	Matt Luke	.10
5	Tim Salmon	.10
6	Mo Vaughn	.10
7	Jay Bell	.10
8	David Dellucci	.10
9	Steve Finley	.10
10	Bernard Gilkey	.10
11	Randy Johnson	1.00
12	Travis Lee	.10
13	Matt Williams	.10
14	Andres Galarraga	.10
15	Tom Glavine	.35
16	Andruw Jones	1.00
17	Chipper Jones	1.50
18	Brian Jordan	.10
19	Javy Lopez	.10
20	Greg Maddux	1.50
21	Albert Belle	.10
22	Will Clark	.10
23	Scott Erickson	.10
24	Mike Mussina	.40
25	Cal Ripken Jr.	3.00
26	B.J. Surhoff	.10
27	Nomar Garciaparra	1.50
28	Reggie Jefferson	.10
29	Darren Lewis	.10
30	Pedro Martinez	1.00
31	John Valentin	.10
32	Rod Beck	.10
33	Mark Grace	.10
34	Lance Johnson	.10
35	Mickey Morandini	.10
36	Sammy Sosa	1.50
37	Kerry Wood	.40
38	James Baldwin	.10
39	Mike Caruso	.10
40	Ray Durham	.10
41	Magglio Ordonez	.25
42	Frank Thomas	1.00
43	Aaron Boone	.10
44	Sean Casey	.20
45	Barry Larkin	.10
46	Hal Morris	.10
47	Denny Neagle	.10
48	Greg Vaughn	.10
49	Pat Watkins	.10
50	Roberto Alomar	.25
51	Sandy Alomar Jr.	.10
52	David Justice	.10
53	Kenny Lofton	.10
54	Manny Ramirez	1.00
55	Richie Sexson	.10
56	Jim Thome	.75
57	Omar Vizquel	.10
58	Dante Bichette	.10
59	Vinny Castilla	.10
60	Edgard Clemente **RC**	.10
61	Derrick Gibson	.10
62	Todd Helton	1.00
63	Darryl Kile	.10
64	Larry Walker	.10
65	Tony Clark	.10
66	Damion Easley	.10
67	Bob Higginson	.10
68	Brian Hunter	.10
69	Dean Palmer	.10
70	Justin Thompson	.10
71	Craig Counsell	.10
72	Todd Dunwoody	.10
73	Cliff Floyd	.10
74	Alex Gonzalez	.10
75	Livan Hernandez	.10
76	Mark Kotsay	.10
77	Derrek Lee	.65
78	Moises Alou	.10
79	Jeff Bagwell	1.00
80	Derek Bell	.10
81	Craig Biggio	.10
82	Ken Caminiti	.10
83	Richard Hidalgo	.10
84	Shane Reynolds	.10
85	Jeff Conine	.10
86	Johnny Damon	.35
87	Jermaine Dye	.10
88	Jeff King	.10
89	Jeff Montgomery	.10
90	Mike Sweeney	.10
91	Kevin Brown	.10
92	Mark Grudzielanek	.10
93	Eric Karros	.10
94	Raul Mondesi	.10
95	Chan Ho Park	.10
96	Gary Sheffield	.40

97	Jeromy Burnitz	.10
98	Jeff Cirillo	.10
99	Marquis Grissom	.10
100	Geoff Jenkins	.10
101	Dave Nilsson	.10
102	Jose Valentin	.10
103	Fernando Vina	.10
104	Marty Cordova	.10
105	Matt Lawton	.10
106	David Ortiz	.60
107	Brad Radke	.10
108	Todd Walker	.10
109	Shane Andrews	.10
110	Orlando Cabrera	.10
111	Brad Fullmer	.10
112	Vladimir Guerrero	1.00
113	Wilton Guerrero	.10
114	Carl Pavano	.10
115	Fernando Seguignol	.10
116	Ugueth Urbina	.10
117	Edgardo Alfonzo	.10
118	Bobby Bonilla	.10
119	Rickey Henderson	1.00
120	Hideo Nomo	.60
121	John Olerud	.10
122	Rey Ordonez	.10
123	Mike Piazza	2.00
124	Masato Yoshii	.10
125	Scott Brosius	.10
126	Orlando Hernandez	.10
127	Hideki Irabu	.10
128	Derek Jeter	3.00
129	Chuck Knoblauch	.10
130	Tino Martinez	.10
131	Jorge Posada	.10
132	Bernie Williams	.10
133	Eric Chavez	.20
134	Ryan Christenson	.10
135	Jason Giambi	.65
136	Ben Grieve	.10
137	A.J. Hinch	.10
138	Matt Stairs	.10
139	Miguel Tejada	.20
140	Bob Abreu	.20
141	Gary Bennett **RC**	.10
142	Desi Relaford	.10
143	Scott Rolen	.75
144	Curt Schilling	.35
145	Kevin Sefcik	.10
146	Brian Giles	.10
147	Jose Guillen	.10
148	Jason Kendall	.10
149	Aramis Ramirez	.10
150	Tony Womack	.10
151	Kevin Young	.10
152	Eric Davis	.10
153	J.D. Drew	.50
154	Ray Lankford	.10
155	Eli Marrero	.10
156	Mark McGwire	2.50
157	Luis Ordaz	.10
158	Edgar Renteria	.10
159	Andy Ashby	.10
160	Tony Gwynn	1.50
161	Trevor Hoffman	.10
162	Wally Joyner	.10
163	Jim Leyritz	.10
164	Ruben Rivera	.10
165	Reggie Sanders	.10
166	Quilvio Veras	.10
167	Rich Aurilia	.10
168	Marvin Benard	.10
169	Barry Bonds	3.00
170	Ellis Burks	.10
171	Jeff Kent	.10
172	Bill Mueller	.10
173	J.T. Snow	.10
174	Jay Buhner	.10
175	Jeff Fassero	.10
176	Ken Griffey Jr.	2.25
177	Carlos Guillen	.10
178	Edgar Martinez	.10
179	Alex Rodriguez	2.50
180	David Segui	.10
181	Dan Wilson	.10
182	Rolando Arrojo	.10
183	Wade Boggs	1.50
184	Jose Canseco	.40
185	Aaron Ledesma	.10
186	Dave Martinez	.10
187	Quinton McCracken	.10
188	Fred McGriff	.10
189	Juan Gonzalez	.60
190	Tom Goodwin	.10
191	Rusty Greer	.10
192	Roberto Kelly	.10
193	Rafael Palmeiro	.75
194	Ivan Rodriguez	.75
195	Roger Clemens	2.00
196	Jose Cruz Jr.	.10
197	Carlos Delgado	.60
198	Alex Gonzalez	.10
199	Roy Halladay	.10
200	Pat Hentgen	.10

Complete Players

The 10 players featured in this serial numbered 20-card set each have two cards, designed to fit together. Card fronts feature a red border on the top and bottom with the rest of the card done in gold foil etching. Each card is serially numbered to 299.

	NM/M
Complete Set (10):	40.00

Common Player:		3.00
Production 299 Sets		
1	Cal Ripken Jr.	9.00
2	Nomar Garciaparra	4.50
3	Sammy Sosa	4.50
4	Kerry Wood	3.00
5	Frank Thomas	4.00
6	Mike Piazza	5.00
7	Mark McGwire	7.50
8	Tony Gwynn	4.50
9	Ken Griffey Jr.	6.00
10	Alex Rodriguez	7.50

Kings of the Major Leagues

The full foiled card fronts also utilize gold foil stamping. Pacific's crown as well as the featured player's team are shadow boxed in the background with the player's image in the foreground. These are seeded 1:361.

		NM/M
Complete Set (10):		80.00
Common Player:		5.00
Inserted 1:361		
1	Cal Ripken Jr.	17.50
2	Nomar Garciaparra	9.00
3	Sammy Sosa	9.00
4	Kerry Wood	5.00
5	Frank Thomas	7.50
6	Mike Piazza	10.00
7	Mark McGwire	15.00
8	Tony Gwynn	9.00
9	Ken Griffey Jr.	12.50
10	Alex Rodriguez	15.00

On Deck

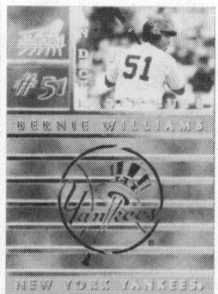

Twenty of the game's hottest players are featured in this laser-cut and silver foil stamped set. The player's team logo is laser cut into the bottom half of the card beneath the player photo.

		NM/M
Complete Set (20):		17.50
Common Player:		.50
Inserted 1:9		
1	Chipper Jones	1.00
2	Cal Ripken Jr.	3.00
3	Nomar Garciaparra	1.00
4	Sammy Sosa	1.00
5	Frank Thomas	.75
6	Manny Ramirez	.75
7	Todd Helton	.50
8	Larry Walker	.50
9	Jeff Bagwell	.75
10	Vladimir Guerrero	.75

#	Player	Price
11	Mike Piazza	1.50
12	Derek Jeter	3.00
13	Bernie Williams	.50
14	J.D. Drew	.50
15	Mark McGwire	2.50
16	Tony Gwynn	1.00
17	Ken Griffey Jr.	2.00
18	Alex Rodriguez	2.50
19	Juan Gonzalez	.50
20	Ivan Rodriguez	.65

Pennant Fever

Regular Pennant Fever inserts feature gold foil stamping of 20 of the hottest players in the hobby. These are seeded 4:37 packs. There are also three parallel versions: Platinum Blue, Silver and Copper. Platinum Blues are limited to 100 serial numbered sets, Silvers are retail exclusive and limited to 250 numbered sets and Coppers are hobby exclusive and limited to 20 numbered sets. Pacific spokesman Tony Gwynn autographed 97 regular Pennant Fever cards and one each of the Silver, Blue and Copper.

		NM/M
Complete Set (20):		30.00
Common Player:		.75
Silver (250 Sets):		2X
Platinum Blue (100):		6X
Copper (20):		20X
Tony Gwynn Autograph:		25.00
1	Chipper Jones	2.00
2	Greg Maddux	2.00
3	Cal Ripken Jr.	5.00
4	Nomar Garciaparra	2.00
5	Sammy Sosa	2.00
6	Kerry Wood	.75
7	Frank Thomas	1.50
8	Manny Ramirez	1.50
9	Todd Helton	1.50
10	Jeff Bagwell	1.50
11	Mike Piazza	2.50
12	Derek Jeter	5.00
13	Bernie Williams	.75
14	J.D. Drew	.75
15	Mark McGwire	4.00
16	Tony Gwynn	2.00
17	Ken Griffey Jr.	3.00
18	Alex Rodriguez	4.00
19	Juan Gonzalez	.75
20	Ivan Rodriguez	1.25

Styrotechs

This 20-card set features styrene stock, making the cards more resilient. Fronts have a black border highlighted with gold foil. Backs have a photo and brief career highlights. These are seeded 1:37 packs.

		NM/M
Complete Set (20):		35.00
Common Player:		1.00
Inserted 1:37		
1	Chipper Jones	3.00
2	Greg Maddux	3.00
3	Cal Ripken Jr.	6.00
4	Nomar Garciaparra	3.00
5	Sammy Sosa	3.00
6	Kerry Wood	1.25
7	Frank Thomas	2.00
8	Manny Ramirez	2.00
9	Larry Walker	1.00
10	Jeff Bagwell	2.00
11	Mike Piazza	4.00
12	Derek Jeter	6.00
13	Bernie Williams	1.00
14	J.D. Drew	1.25
15	Mark McGwire	5.00
16	Tony Gwynn	3.00
17	Ken Griffey Jr.	4.50
18	Alex Rodriguez	5.00
19	Juan Gonzalez	1.25
20	Ivan Rodriguez	1.50

1999 Pacific Crown Collection Sample

This card of Pacific spokesman Tony Gwynn introduces the 1999 Crown series. The sample card follows the format of the issued version but is overprinted "SAMPLE" on back.

	NM/M
Tony Gwynn	2.00

1999 Pacific Crown Collection

Released in one series the 300-card set has white borders and gold-foil highlights on front. Backs have a small photo along with English and Spanish narrative. A Platinum Blue parallel to the base set utilizes platinum blue holographic foil and is seeded 1:73 packs. A WalMart-exclusive red-foiled parallel is seeded 1:9 packs. Twelve-card packs had an S.R.P. of $2.49.

		NM/M
Complete Set (300):		20.00
Common Player:		.10
Red Stars:		6X
Inserted 1:9		
Platinum Blue Stars:		30X
Inserted 1:73		
Pack (12):		1.00
Wax Box (36):		22.50
1	Garret Anderson	.10
2	Gary DiSarcina	.10
3	Jim Edmonds	.10
4	Darin Erstad	.25
5	Shigetoshi Hasegawa	.10
6	Norberto Martin	.10
7	Omar Olivares	.10
8	Orlando Palmeiro	.10
9	Tim Salmon	.10
10	Randy Velarde	.10
11	Tony Batista	.10
12	Jay Bell	.10
13	Yamil Benitez	.10
14	Omar Daal	.10
15	David Dellucci	.10
16	Karim Garcia	.10
17	Travis Lee	.10
18	Felix Rodriguez	.10
19	Devon White	.10
20	Matt Williams	.10
21	Andres Galarraga	.10
22	Tom Glavine	.35
23	Ozzie Guillen	.10
24	Andruw Jones	1.00
25	Chipper Jones	1.50
26	Ryan Klesko	.10
27	Javy Lopez	.10
28	Greg Maddux	1.50
29	Dennis Martinez	.10
30	Odaliz Perez	.10
31	Rudy Seanez	.10
32	John Smoltz	.10
33	Roberto Alomar	.25
34	Armando Benitez	.10
35	Scott Erickson	.10
36	Juan Guzman	.10
37	Mike Mussina	.35
38	Jesse Orosco	.10
39	Rafael Palmeiro	.75
40	Sidney Ponson	.10
41	Cal Ripken Jr.	3.00
42	B.J. Surhoff	.10
43	Lenny Webster	.10
44	Dennis Eckersley	.75
45	Nomar Garciaparra	1.50
46	Darren Lewis	.10
47	Pedro Martinez	1.00
48	Troy O'Leary	.10
49	Bret Saberhagen	.10
50	John Valentin	.10
51	Mo Vaughn	.10
52	Tim Wakefield	.10
53	Manny Alexander	.10
54	Rod Beck	.10
55	Gary Gaetti	.10
56	Mark Grace	.10
57	Felix Heredia	.10
58	Jose Hernandez	.10
59	Henry Rodriguez	.10
60	Sammy Sosa	1.50
61	Kevin Tapani	.10
62	Kerry Wood	.45
63	James Baldwin	.10
64	Albert Belle	.10
65	Mike Caruso	.10
66	Carlos Castillo	.10
67	Wil Cordero	.10
68	Jaime Navarro	.10
69	Magglio Ordonez	.25
70	Frank Thomas	1.00
71	Robin Ventura	.10
72	Bret Boone	.10
73	Sean Casey	.20
74	Guillermo Garcia **RC**	.10
75	Barry Larkin	.10
76	Melvin Nieves	.10
77	Eduardo Perez	.10
78	Roberto Petagine	.10
79	Reggie Sanders	.10
80	Eddie Taubensee	.10
81	Brett Tomko	.10
82	Sandy Alomar Jr.	.10
83	Bartolo Colon	.10
84	Joey Cora	.10
85	Einar Diaz	.10
86	David Justice	.10
87	Kenny Lofton	.10
88	Manny Ramirez	1.00
89	Jim Thome	.75
90	Omar Vizquel	.10
91	Enrique Wilson	.10
92	Pedro Astacio	.10
93	Dante Bichette	.10
94	Vinny Castilla	.10
95	Edgard Clemente **RC**	.10
96	Todd Helton	1.00
97	Darryl Kile	.10
98	Mike Munoz	.10
99	Neifi Perez	.10
100	Jeff Reed	.10
101	Larry Walker	.10
102	Gabe Alvarez	.10
103	Kimera Bartee	.10
104	Frank Castillo	.10
105	Tony Clark	.10
106	Deivi Cruz	.10
107	Damion Easley	.10
108	Luis Gonzalez	.10
109	Marino Santana	.10
110	Justin Thompson	.10
111	Antonio Alfonseca	.10
112	Alex Fernandez	.10
113	Cliff Floyd	.10
114	Alex Gonzalez	.10
115	Livan Hernandez	.10
116	Mark Kotsay	.10
117	Derrek Lee	.65
118	Edgar Renteria	.10
119	Jesus Sanchez	.10
120	Moises Alou	.10
121	Jeff Bagwell	1.00
122	Derek Bell	.10
123	Craig Biggio	.10
124	Tony Eusebio	.10
125	Ricky Gutierrez	.10
126	Richard Hidalgo	.10
127	Randy Johnson	1.00
128	Jose Lima	.10
129	Shane Reynolds	.10
130	Johnny Damon	.40
131	Carlos Febles	.10
132	Jeff King	.10
133	Mendy Lopez	.10
134	Hal Morris	.10
135	Jose Offerman	.10
136	Jose Rosado	.10
137	Jose Santiago	.10
138	Bobby Bonilla	.10
139	Roger Cedeno	.10
140	Alex Cora	.10
141	Eric Karros	.10
142	Raul Mondesi	.10
143	Antonio Osuna	.10
144	Chan Ho Park	.10
145	Gary Sheffield	.30
146	Ismael Valdes	.10
147	Jeromy Burnitz	.10
148	Jeff Cirillo	.10
149	Valerio de los Santos	.10
150	Marquis Grissom	.10
151	Scott Karl	.10
152	Dave Nilsson	.10
153	Al Reyes	.10
154	Rafael Roque	.10
155	Jose Valentin	.10
156	Fernando Vina	.10
157	Rick Aguilera	.10
158	Hector Carrasco	.10
159	Marty Cordova	.10
160	Eddie Guardado	.10
161	Paul Molitor	1.00
162	Otis Nixon	.10
163	Alex Ochoa	.10
164	David Ortiz	.45
165	Frank Rodriguez	.10
166	Todd Walker	.10
167	Miguel Batista	.10
168	Orlando Cabrera	.10
169	Vladimir Guerrero	1.00
170	Wilton Guerrero	.10
171	Carl Pavano	.10
172	Robert Perez	.10
173	F.P. Santangelo	.10
174	Fernando Seguignol	.10
175	Ugueth Urbina	.10
176	Javier Vazquez	.10
177	Edgardo Alfonzo	.10
178	Carlos Baerga	.10
179	John Franco	.10
180	Luis Lopez	.10
181	Hideo Nomo	.50
182	John Olerud	.10
183	Rey Ordonez	.10
184	Mike Piazza	1.75
185	Armando Reynoso	.10
186	Masato Yoshii	.10
187	David Cone	.10
188	Orlando Hernandez	.10
189	Hideki Irabu	.10
190	Derek Jeter	3.00
191	Ricky Ledee	.10
192	Tino Martinez	.10
193	Ramiro Mendoza	.10
194	Paul O'Neill	.10
195	Jorge Posada	.10
196	Mariano Rivera	.15
197	Luis Sojo	.10
198	Bernie Williams	.10
199	Rafael Bournigal	.10
200	Eric Chavez	.20
201	Ryan Christenson	.10
202	Jason Giambi	.60
203	Ben Grieve	.10
204	Rickey Henderson	1.00
205	A.J. Hinch	.10
206	Kenny Rogers	.10
207	Miguel Tejada	.20
208	Jorge Velandia	.10
209	Bobby Abreu	.20
210	Marlon Anderson	.10
211	Alex Arias	.10
212	Bobby Estalella	.10
213	Doug Glanville	.10
214	Scott Rolen	.65
215	Curt Schilling	.35
216	Kevin Sefcik	.10
217	Adrian Brown	.10
218	Francisco Cordova	.10
219	Freddy Garcia	.10
220	Jose Guillen	.10
221	Jason Kendall	.10
222	Al Martin	.10
223	Abraham Nunez	.10
224	Aramis Ramirez	.10
225	Ricardo Rincon	.10
226	Kevin Young	.10
227	J.D. Drew	.40
228	Ron Gant	.10
229	Jose Jimenez	.10
230	Brian Jordan	.10
231	Ray Lankford	.10
232	Eli Marrero	.10
233	Mark McGwire	2.50
234	Luis Ordaz	.10
235	Placido Polanco	.10
236	Fernando Tatis	.10
237	Andy Ashby	.10
238	Kevin Brown	.10
239	Ken Caminiti	.10
240	Steve Finley	.10
241	Chris Gomez	.10
242	Tony Gwynn	1.50
243	Carlos Hernandez	.10
244	Trevor Hoffman	.10
245	Wally Joyner	.10
246	Ruben Rivera	.10
247	Greg Vaughn	.10
248	Quilvio Veras	.10
249	Rich Aurilia	.10
250	Barry Bonds	3.00
251	Stan Javier	.10
252	Jeff Kent	.10
253	Ramon Martinez	.10
254	Jose Mesa	.10
255	Armando Rios	.10
256	Rich Rodriguez	.10
257	Rey Sanchez	.10
258	J.T. Snow	.10
259	Julian Tavarez	.10
260	Jeff Fassero	.10
261	Ken Griffey Jr.	2.00
262	Giomar Guevara **RC**	.10
263	Carlos Guillen	.10
264	Raul Ibanez	.10
265	Edgar Martinez	.10
266	Jamie Moyer	.10
267	Alex Rodriguez	2.50
268	David Segui	.10
269	Makoto Suzuki	.10
270	Wilson Alvarez	.10
271	Rolando Arrojo	.10
272	Wade Boggs	1.50
273	Miguel Cairo	.10
274	Roberto Hernandez	.10
275	Aaron Ledesma	.10
276	Albie Lopez	.10
277	Quinton McCracken	.10
278	Fred McGriff	.10
279	Esteban Yan	.10
280	Luis Alicea	.10
281	Will Clark	.10
282	Juan Gonzalez	.50
283	Rusty Greer	.10
284	Rick Helling	.10
285	Xavier Hernandez	.10
286	Roberto Kelly	.10
287	Esteban Loaiza	.10
288	Ivan Rodriguez	.75
289	Aaron Sele	.10
290	John Wetteland	.10
291	Jose Canseco	.40
292	Roger Clemens	1.75
293	Felipe Crespo	.10
294	Jose Cruz Jr.	.10
295	Carlos Delgado	.60
296	Kelvim Escobar	.10
297	Tony Fernandez	.10
298	Alex Gonzalez	.10
299	Tomas Perez	.10
300	Juan Samuel	.10

In The Cage

These die-cut inserts have a netting like background with laser cutting, giving the look that the player is hitting in a batting cage. These are seeded 1:145 packs.

		NM/M
Complete Set (20):		80.00
Common Player:		2.00
Inserted 1:145		
1	Chipper Jones	7.50
2	Cal Ripken Jr.	15.00
3	Nomar Garciaparra	7.50
4	Sammy Sosa	7.50
5	Frank Thomas	5.00
6	Manny Ramirez	5.00
7	Todd Helton	5.00
8	Moises Alou	2.00
9	Vladimir Guerrero	5.00
10	Mike Piazza	9.00
11	Derek Jeter	15.00
12	Ben Grieve	2.00
13	J.D. Drew	3.00
14	Mark McGwire	12.00
15	Tony Gwynn	7.50
16	Ken Griffey Jr.	10.00
17	Edgar Martinez	2.00
18	Alex Rodriguez	12.00
19	Juan Gonzalez	2.50
20	Ivan Rodriguez	4.00

Latinos/Major Leagues

This 36-card set salutes the many Latino players in the major leagues.

		NM/M
Complete Set (36):		25.00
Common Player:		.30
Inserted 1:18		
1	Roberto Alomar	.60
2	Rafael Palmeiro	2.00
3	Nomar Garciaparra	3.50
4	Pedro Martinez	2.50
5	Magglio Ordonez	1.50
6	Sandy Alomar Jr.	.30
7	Bartolo Colon	.30
8	Manny Ramirez	2.50
9	Omar Vizquel	.30
10	Enrique Wilson	.30
11	David Ortiz	1.50
12	Orlando Hernandez	.30
13	Tino Martinez	.30
14	Mariano Rivera	.45
15	Bernie Williams	.30
16	Edgar Martinez	.30
17	Alex Rodriguez	5.00
18	David Segui	.30
19	Rolando Arrojo	.30
20	Juan Gonzalez	1.25
21	Ivan Rodriguez	2.00
22	Jose Canseco	1.00
23	Jose Cruz Jr.	.30
24	Andres Galarraga	.30
25	Andruw Jones	2.50
26	Javy Lopez	.30
27	Sammy Sosa	3.50
28	Vinny Castilla	.30
29	Alex Gonzalez	.30
30	Moises Alou	.30
31	Bobby Bonilla	.30
32	Raul Mondesi	.30
33	Fernando Vina	.30
34	Vladimir Guerrero	2.50
35	Carlos Baerga	.30
36	Rey Ordonez	.30

Pacific Cup

These die-cut inserts are shaped like a trophy with the featured player's photo in the foreground. These are seeded 1:721 packs.

		NM/M
Complete Set (10):		80.00
Common Player:		5.00
Inserted 1:721		
1	Cal Ripken Jr.	20.00
2	Nomar Garciaparra	8.00
3	Frank Thomas	6.00
4	Ken Griffey Jr.	12.00
5	Alex Rodriguez	16.00
6	Greg Maddux	8.00
7	Sammy Sosa	8.00
8	Kerry Wood	5.00
9	Mark McGwire	16.00
10	Tony Gwynn	8.00

Players Choice

In conjunction with the annual Players Choice Awards ceremonies, Pacific produced a special edition of the cards of some of the players involved. Cards have a "Players Choice" foil stamp on front. Quantities produced were in the range of 25-40 of each.

		NM/M
Complete Set (6):		55.00
Common Player:		5.00
10	Randy Velarde	5.00
41	Cal Ripken Jr.	30.00
47	Pedro Martinez	12.00
88	Manny Ramirez	12.00
112	Alex Fernandez	5.00
128	Jose Lima	5.00

Tape Measure

This 20-card insert set is fully foiled in platinum blue with rainbow highlights in the background of the player photo.

	NM/M
Complete Set (20):	20.00
Common Player:	.60
Inserted 1:73	

1	Andres Galarraga	.60
2	Chipper Jones	2.50
3	Nomar Garciaparra	2.50
4	Sammy Sosa	2.50
5	Frank Thomas	1.50
6	Manny Ramirez	1.50
7	Vinny Castilla	.60
8	Moises Alou	.60
9	Jeff Bagwell	1.50
10	Raul Mondesi	.60
11	Vladimir Guerrero	1.50
12	Mike Piazza	2.75
13	J.D. Drew	1.00
14	Mark McGwire	3.50
15	Greg Vaughn	.60
16	Ken Griffey Jr.	3.00
17	Alex Rodriguez	3.50
18	Juan Gonzalez	1.00
19	Ivan Rodriguez	1.25
20	Jose Canseco	.60

Team Checklists

This features holographic silver-foil stamping and a horizontal format. The backs have a complete team checklist for the featured player's team.

		NM/M
Complete Set (30):		25.00
Common Player:		.50
Inserted 1:37		
1	Darin Erstad	.60
2	Travis Lee	.50
3	Chipper Jones	2.00
4	Cal Ripken Jr.	4.00
5	Nomar Garciaparra	1.75
6	Sammy Sosa	1.75
7	Frank Thomas	1.25
8	Barry Larkin	.50
9	Manny Ramirez	1.25
10	Larry Walker	.50
11	Bob Higginson	.50
12	Livan Hernandez	.50
13	Moises Alou	.50
14	Jeff King	.50
15	Raul Mondesi	.50
16	Marquis Grissom	.50
17	David Ortiz	1.00
18	Vladimir Guerrero	1.25
19	Mike Piazza	2.00
20	Derek Jeter	4.00
21	Ben Grieve	.50
22	Scott Rolen	.75
23	Jason Kendall	.50
24	Mark McGwire	3.00
25	Tony Gwynn	1.75
26	Barry Bonds	4.00
27	Ken Griffey Jr.	2.50
28	Wade Boggs	1.75
29	Juan Gonzalez	.75
30	Jose Canseco	.60

1999 Pacific Crown Royale

The Crown Royale 144-card base set has a horizontal format die-cut around a crown design at the top. The cards are double foiled and etched. There are 18 short-printed rookies and prospects cards, which were inserted at a rate of about one per pack. There are two parallels: Limited Series and Opening Day. Limited Series is produced on 24-point stock with silver foil and limited to 99 numbered sets. Opening Day is limited to 72 numbered sets.

		NM/M
Complete Set (144):		75.00
Common Player:		.25
Common SP:		.50
Limited Series (99 Sets):		6X
SP's:		2X
Opening Day (72 Sets):		12X
SP's:		2X
Pack (6):		.25
Wax Box (24):		35.00
1	Jim Edmonds	.25
2	Darin Erstad	.50
3	Troy Glaus	2.00
4	Tim Salmon	.25
5	Mo Vaughn	.25
6	Jay Bell	.25
7	Steve Finley	.25
8	Randy Johnson	2.00
9	Travis Lee	.25
10	Matt Williams	.25
11	Andruw Jones	2.00
12	Chipper Jones	3.00
13	Brian Jordan	.25
14	Ryan Klesko	.25
15	Javy Lopez	.25
16	Greg Maddux	3.00
17	Randall Simon/SP	.50
18	Albert Belle	.25
19	Will Clark	.25
20	Delino DeShields	.25
21	Mike Mussina	.50
22	Cal Ripken Jr.	6.00
23	Nomar Garciaparra	3.00
24	Pedro Martinez	2.00
25	Jose Offerman	.25
26	John Valentin	.25
27	Mark Grace	.25
28	Lance Johnson	.25
29	Henry Rodriguez	.25
30	Sammy Sosa	3.00
31	Kerry Wood	1.00
32	Mike Caruso	.25
33	Ray Durham	.25
34	Magglio Ordonez	.40
35	Brian Simmons/SP	.50
36	Frank Thomas	2.00
37	Mike Cameron	.25
38	Barry Larkin	.25
39	Greg Vaughn	.25
40	Dmitri Young	.25
41	Roberto Alomar	.40
42	Sandy Alomar Jr.	.25
43	David Justice	.25
44	Kenny Lofton	.25
45	Manny Ramirez	2.00
46	Jim Thome	1.50
47	Dante Bichette	.25
48	Vinny Castilla	.25
49	Todd Helton	2.00
50	Larry Walker	.25
51	Tony Clark	.25
52	Damion Easley	.25
53	Bob Higginson	.25
54	Brian Hunter	.25
55	Gabe Kapler/SP	.50
56	Jeff Weaver/SP RC	2.50
57	Cliff Floyd	.25
58	Alex Gonzalez/SP	.50
59	Mark Kotsay	.25
60	Derek Lee	1.00
61	Preston Wilson/SP	.75
62	Moises Alou	.25
63	Jeff Bagwell	2.00
64	Derek Bell	.25
65	Craig Biggio	.25
66	Ken Caminiti	.25
67	Carlos Beltran/SP	2.00
68	Johnny Damon	.45
69	Carlos Febles/SP	.65
70	Jeff King	.25
71	Kevin Brown	.25
72	Todd Hundley	.25
73	Eric Karros	.25
74	Raul Mondesi	.25
75	Gary Sheffield	.75
76	Jeromy Burnitz	.25
77	Jeff Cirillo	.25
78	Marquis Grissom	.25
79	Fernando Vina	.25
80	Chad Allen/SP RC	.50
81	Matt Lawton	.25
82	Doug Mientkiewicz/SP	.75
83	Brad Radke	.25
84	Todd Walker	.25
85	Michael Barrett/SP	.25
86	Brad Fullmer	.25
87	Vladimir Guerrero	2.00
88	Wilton Guerrero	.25
89	Ugueth Urbina	.25
90	Bobby Bonilla	.25
91	Rickey Henderson	2.00
92	Rey Ordonez	.25
93	Mike Piazza	3.50
94	Robin Ventura	.25
95	Roger Clemens	3.50
96	Orlando Hernandez	.25
97	Derek Jeter	6.00
98	Chuck Knoblauch	.25
99	Tino Martinez	.25
100	Bernie Williams	.25
101	Eric Chavez/SP	1.50
102	Jason Giambi	1.00
103	Ben Grieve	.25
104	Tim Raines	.25
105	Marlon Anderson/SP	.65
106	Doug Glanville	.25
107	Scott Rolen	1.25
108	Curt Schilling	.40
109	Brian Giles	.25
110	Jose Guillen	.25
111	Jason Kendall	.25
112	Kevin Young	.25
113	J.D. Drew/SP	2.00
114	Jose Jimenez/SP	.50
115	Ray Lankford	.25
116	Mark McGwire	5.00
117	Fernando Tatis	.25
118	Matt Clement/SP	.75
119	Tony Gwynn	3.00
120	Trevor Hoffman	.25
121	Wally Joyner	.25
122	Reggie Sanders	.25
123	Barry Bonds	6.00
124	Ellis Burks	.25
125	Jeff Kent	.25
126	J.T. Snow	.25
127	Freddy Garcia/SP RC	1.00
128	Ken Griffey Jr.	4.00
129	Edgar Martinez	.25
130	Alex Rodriguez	5.00
131	David Segui	.25
132	Rolando Arrojo	.25
133	Wade Boggs	3.00
134	Jose Canseco	.65
135	Quinton McCracken	.25
136	Fred McGriff	.25
137	Juan Gonzalez	1.00
138	Rusty Greer	.25
139	Rafael Palmeiro	1.50
140	Ivan Rodriguez	1.50
141	Jose Cruz Jr.	.25
142	Carlos Delgado	.75
143	Shawn Green	.75
144	Roy Halladay/SP	1.00

Century 21

This 10-card set features some of baseball's most dominating players, on a full silver foil front. These are seeded 1:25 packs.

		NM/M
Complete Set (10):		30.00
Common Player:		2.00
Inserted 1:25		
1	Cal Ripken Jr.	7.50
2	Nomar Garciaparra	4.00
3	Sammy Sosa	4.00
4	Frank Thomas	3.00
5	Mike Piazza	4.50
6	J.D. Drew	2.00
7	Mark McGwire	6.00
8	Tony Gwynn	4.00
9	Ken Griffey Jr.	5.00
10	Alex Rodriguez	6.00

Cramer's Choice Premiums

This enlarged (about 5" x 7") 10-card set is die-cut into a trophy shape. Cards are enhanced with silver holographic fronts with silver holographic etching and gold-foil stamping across the bottom. They are found one per box. Six serially numbered parallels were randomly seeded: Dark Blue (35 each), Green (30), Red (25), Light Blue (20), Gold (10) and Purple (1).

		NM/M
Complete Set (10):		20.00
Common Player:		2.00
Inserted 1:Box		
Dark Blue (35 Sets):		5X
Green (30):		6X
Red (25):		8X
Light Blue (20):		10X
Gold (10):		15X
Purple (1):		Value Undetermined
1	Cal Ripken Jr.	6.50
2	Nomar Garciaparra	3.00
3	Sammy Sosa	3.00
4	Frank Thomas	2.50
5	Mike Piazza	3.50
6	Derek Jeter	6.50
7	J.D. Drew	2.00
8	Mark McGwire	5.00
9	Tony Gwynn	3.00
10	Ken Griffey Jr.	4.00

Gold Crown Die-Cut Premiums

This enlarged six-card set was an unannounced premium box-topper. They were limited to 1,036 numbered sets, found less than once every other box.

		NM/M
Complete Set (6):		15.00
Common Player:		2.50
Inserted 6:10 boxes.		
1	Cal Ripken Jr.	7.00
2	Mike Piazza	4.50
3	Ken Griffey Jr.	5.00
4	Tony Gwynn	3.00
5	Mark McGwire	6.00
6	J.D. Drew	2.50

Living Legends

This 10-card set spotlights baseball's top stars on a fully foiled card front. These are serial numbered to 375 sets.

		NM/M
Complete Set (10):		100.00
Common Player:		7.50
Production 375 Sets		
1	Greg Maddux	10.00
2	Cal Ripken Jr.	20.00
3	Nomar Garciaparra	10.00
4	Sammy Sosa	10.00
5	Frank Thomas	7.50
6	Mike Piazza	12.00
7	Mark McGwire	15.00
8	Tony Gwynn	10.00
9	Ken Griffey Jr.	13.50
10	Alex Rodriguez	15.00

Master Performers

This 20-card set features a full foiled front with the player photo in a frame like border. Master Performers are seeded 2:25 packs.

		NM/M
Complete Set (20):		40.00
Common Player:		1.00
Inserted 2:25		
1	Chipper Jones	2.50
2	Greg Maddux	2.50
3	Cal Ripken Jr.	5.00
4	Nomar Garciaparra	2.50
5	Sammy Sosa	2.50
6	Frank Thomas	2.00
7	Raul Mondesi	1.00
8	Vladimir Guerrero	2.00
9	Mike Piazza	3.00
10	Roger Clemens	3.00
11	Derek Jeter	5.00
12	Scott Rolen	1.75
13	J.D. Drew	1.50
14	Mark McGwire	4.00
15	Tony Gwynn	2.50
16	Barry Bonds	5.00
17	Ken Griffey Jr.	3.50
18	Alex Rodriguez	4.00
19	Juan Gonzalez	1.50
20	Ivan Rodriguez	1.75

Pillars of the Game

This 25-card set features holographic silver foil fronts on a horizontal format.

		NM/M
Complete Set (25):		30.00
Common Player:		.50
Inserted 1:1		
1	Mo Vaughn	.50
2	Chipper Jones	2.00
3	Greg Maddux	2.00
4	Albert Belle	.50
5	Cal Ripken Jr.	4.00
6	Nomar Garciaparra	2.00
7	Sammy Sosa	2.00
8	Frank Thomas	1.50
9	Manny Ramirez	1.50
10	Jeff Bagwell	.50
11	Raul Mondesi	.50
12	Vladimir Guerrero	1.50
13	Mike Piazza	2.25
14	Roger Clemens	2.25
15	Derek Jeter	4.00
16	Bernie Williams	.50
17	Ben Grieve	.50
18	J.D. Drew	1.00
19	Mark McGwire	3.00
20	Tony Gwynn	2.00
21	Barry Bonds	4.00
22	Ken Griffey Jr.	2.50
23	Alex Rodriguez	4.00
24	Juan Gonzalez	1.00
25	Ivan Rodriguez	1.25

Pivotal Players

This 25-card set features holographic silver foil fronts with a flame in the background of the player photo.

		NM/M
Complete Set (25):		20.00
Common Player:		.50
Inserted 1:1		
1	Mo Vaughn	.50
2	Chipper Jones	2.00
3	Greg Maddux	2.00
4	Albert Belle	.50
5	Cal Ripken Jr.	4.00
6	Nomar Garciaparra	2.00
7	Sammy Sosa	2.00
8	Frank Thomas	1.50
9	Manny Ramirez	1.50
10	Craig Biggio	.50
11	Raul Mondesi	.50
12	Vladimir Guerrero	1.50
13	Mike Piazza	2.25
14	Roger Clemens	2.50
15	Derek Jeter	4.00
16	Bernie Williams	.50
17	Ben Grieve	.50
18	Scott Rolen	.60
19	J.D. Drew	.75
20	Mark McGwire	3.00
21	Tony Gwynn	2.00
22	Ken Griffey Jr.	2.50
23	Alex Rodriguez	3.00
24	Juan Gonzalez	.75
25	Ivan Rodriguez	1.00

Home Run Heroes

These cards were part of an unannounced multi-manufacturer (Fleer, Upper Deck, Topps, Pacific) insert program which was exclusive to Wal-Mart. Each company produced cards of Mark McGwire and Sammy Sosa, along with two other premier sluggers. Each company's cards share a "Power Elite" logo at top and "Home Run Heroes" logo vertically at right.

		NM/M
Complete Set (4):		3.50
Common Player:		.50
13	Mark McGwire	1.50
14	Sammy Sosa	1.25
15	Juan Gonzalez	.50
16	Manny Ramirez	.50

1999 Pacific Invincible

The base set consists of 150 cards. Each features an action photo with a portrait in a cel window at bottom. There are two parallels to the base set: Opening Day and Platinum Blue. Both parallels are limited to 67 serial numbered sets.

		NM/M
Complete Set (150):		60.00
Common Player:		.25
Opening Day (69 Sets):		6X
Platinum Blues (67):		6X
Pack (3):		1.50
Wax Box (24):		35.00
1	Jim Edmonds	.25
2	Darin Erstad	.50
3	Troy Glaus	2.50
4	Tim Salmon	.25
5	Mo Vaughn	.25
6	Steve Finley	.25
7	Randy Johnson	2.50
8	Travis Lee	.25
9	Dante Powell	.25
10	Matt Williams	.25
11	Bret Boone	.25
12	Andruw Jones	2.50
13	Chipper Jones	3.00
14	Brian Jordan	.25
15	Ryan Klesko	.25
16	Javy Lopez	.25
17	Greg Maddux	3.00
18	Brady Anderson	.25
19	Albert Belle	.25
20	Will Clark	.25
21	Mike Mussina	.75
22	Cal Ripken Jr.	6.00
23	Nomar Garciaparra	3.00
24	Pedro Martinez	2.50
25	Trot Nixon	.25
26	Jose Offerman	.25
27	Donnie Sadler	.25
28	John Valentin	.25
29	Mark Grace	.25
30	Lance Johnson	.25
31	Henry Rodriguez	.25
32	Sammy Sosa	3.00
33	Kerry Wood	1.25
34	McKay Christensen	.25
35	Ray Durham	.25
36	Jeff Liefer	.25
37	Frank Thomas	2.50
38	Mike Cameron	.25
39	Barry Larkin	.25

#	Player	Price
40	Greg Vaughn	.25
41	Dmitri Young	.25
42	Roberto Alomar	.50
43	Sandy Alomar Jr.	.25
44	David Justice	.25
45	Kenny Lofton	.25
46	Manny Ramirez	2.50
47	Jim Thome	2.25
48	Dante Bichette	.25
49	Vinny Castilla	.25
50	Darryl Hamilton	.25
51	Todd Helton	2.50
52	Neifi Perez	.25
53	Larry Walker	.25
54	Tony Clark	.25
55	Damion Easley	.25
56	Bob Higginson	.25
57	Brian Hunter	.25
58	Gabe Kapler	.25
59	Cliff Floyd	.25
60	Alex Gonzalez	.25
61	Mark Kotsay	.25
62	Derrek Lee	2.00
63	Braden Looper	.25
64	Moises Alou	.25
65	Jeff Bagwell	2.50
66	Craig Biggio	.25
67	Ken Caminiti	.25
68	Scott Elarton	.25
69	Mitch Meluskey	.25
70	Carlos Beltran	.65
71	Johnny Damon	.50
72	Carlos Febles	.25
73	Jeremy Giambi	.25
74	Kevin Brown	.25
75	Todd Hundley	.25
76	Paul LoDuca	.25
77	Raul Mondesi	.25
78	Gary Sheffield	1.00
79	Geoff Jenkins	.25
80	Jeromy Burnitz	.25
81	Marquis Grissom	.25
82	Jose Valentin	.25
83	Fernando Vina	.25
84	Corey Koskie	.25
85	Matt Lawton	.25
86	Christian Guzman	.25
87	Torii Hunter	.25
88	Doug Mientkiewicz	.25
89	Michael Barrett	.25
90	Brad Fullmer	.25
91	Vladimir Guerrero	2.50
92	Fernando Seguignol	.25
93	Ugueth Urbina	.25
94	Bobby Bonilla	.25
95	Rickey Henderson	2.50
96	Rey Ordonez	.25
97	Mike Piazza	3.50
98	Robin Ventura	.25
99	Roger Clemens	3.50
100	Derek Jeter	6.00
101	Chuck Knoblauch	.25
102	Tino Martinez	.25
103	Paul O'Neill	.25
104	Bernie Williams	.25
105	Eric Chavez	.50
106	Ryan Christenson	.25
107	Jason Giambi	1.25
108	Ben Grieve	.25
109	Miguel Tejada	.25
110	Marlon Anderson	.25
111	Doug Glanville	.25
112	Scott Rolen	2.25
113	Curt Schilling	.50
114	Brian Giles	.25
115	Warren Morris	.25
116	Jason Kendall	.25
117	Kris Benson	.25
118	J.D. Drew	1.25
119	Ray Lankford	.25
120	Mark McGwire	5.00
121	Matt Clement	.25
122	Tony Gwynn	3.00
123	Trevor Hoffman	.25
124	Wally Joyner	.25
125	Reggie Sanders	.25
126	Barry Bonds	6.00
127	Ellis Burks	.25
128	Jeff Kent	.25
129	Stan Javier	.25
130	J.T. Snow	.25
131	Jay Buhner	.25
132	Freddy Garcia **RC**	2.00
133	Ken Griffey Jr.	4.00
134	Russ Davis	.25
135	Edgar Martinez	.25
136	Alex Rodriguez	5.00
137	David Segui	.25
138	Rolando Arrojo	.25
139	Wade Boggs	3.00
140	Jose Canseco	1.00
141	Quinton McCracken	.25
142	Fred McGriff	.25
143	Juan Gonzalez	1.25
144	Tom Goodwin	.25
145	Rusty Greer	.25
146	Ivan Rodriguez	2.25
147	Jose Cruz Jr.	.25
148	Carlos Delgado	1.00
149	Shawn Green	.75
150	Roy Halladay	.25

Diamond Magic

This 10-card set features a horizontal format with silver foil stamping on the front. Diamond Magic's are seeded 1:49 packs.

	NM/M
Complete Set (10):	35.00
Common Player:	3.00
Inserted 1:49	
1 Cal Ripken Jr.	7.50
2 Nomar Garciaparra	4.00
3 Sammy Sosa	4.00
4 Frank Thomas	3.50
5 Mike Piazza	4.50
6 J.D. Drew	3.00
7 Mark McGwire	6.00
8 Tony Gwynn	3.00
9 Ken Griffey Jr.	6.00
10 Alex Rodriguez	5.00

Flash Point

This 20-card set features gold etching and gold foil stamping on the card front. These were seeded 1:25 packs.

	NM/M
Complete Set (20):	50.00
Common Player:	1.25
Inserted 1:25	
1 Mo Vaughn	1.25
2 Chipper Jones	4.00
3 Greg Maddux	3.50
4 Cal Ripken Jr.	9.00
5 Nomar Garciaparra	3.50
6 Sammy Sosa	3.50
7 Frank Thomas	2.50
8 Manny Ramirez	2.50
9 Vladimir Guerrero	2.50
10 Mike Piazza	4.00
11 Roger Clemens	4.00
12 Derek Jeter	9.00
13 Ben Grieve	1.25
14 Scott Rolen	2.00
15 J.D. Drew	1.50
16 Mark McGwire	7.50
17 Tony Gwynn	3.50
18 Ken Griffey Jr.	5.00
19 Alex Rodriguez	7.50
20 Juan Gonzalez	1.50

Giants of the Game

This jumbo mail-in redemption set of baseball's top stars is limited to 10 serially numbered specimens of each card.

	NM/M
Complete Set (10):	300.00
Common Player:	25.00
Production 10 Sets	
1 Cal Ripken Jr.	75.00
2 Nomar Garciaparra	35.00
3 Sammy Sosa	35.00
4 Frank Thomas	30.00
5 Mike Piazza	40.00
6 J.D. Drew	25.00
7 Mark McGwire	60.00
8 Tony Gwynn	35.00
9 Ken Griffey Jr.	60.00
10 Alex Rodriguez	60.00

Sandlot Heroes

Sandlot Heroes salutes baseball's top players on a horizontal format with holographic silver foil stamping on front. These were inserted one per pack. Each player can be found in two versions. A special edition, serially numbered to 10 of each and overprinted with a SportsFest logo, was created for use as a redemption prize at Pacific's booth at the show.

	NM/M
Complete Set (20):	15.00
Common Player:	.50
Inserted 1:1	
SportsFest (10 Sets):	25X
1 Mo Vaughn	.50
2 Chipper Jones	1.00
3 Greg Maddux	1.00
4 Cal Ripken Jr.	3.00
5 Nomar Garciaparra	1.00
6 Sammy Sosa	1.00
7 Frank Thomas	.75
8 Manny Ramirez	.75
9 Vladimir Guerrero	.75
10 Mike Piazza	1.25
11 Roger Clemens	1.25
12 Derek Jeter	3.00
13 Eric Chavez	.50
14 Ben Grieve	.50
15 J.D. Drew	.60
16 Mark McGwire	2.00
17 Tony Gwynn	1.00
18 Ken Griffey Jr.	1.50
19 Alex Rodriguez	2.00
20 Juan Gonzalez	.60

Seismic Force

This 20-card set has a dot pattern behind the featured player with the left side and bottom of the card in a gold border. These were seeded one per pack. A specially marked SportsFest version was created for use as a redemption prize at Pacific's booth at the show. These are serially numbered to just 20 apiece.

	NM/M
Complete Set (20):	15.00
Common Player:	.50
Inserted 1:1	
SportsFest (20 Sets):	15X
1 Mo Vaughn	.50
2 Chipper Jones	1.00
3 Greg Maddux	1.00
4 Cal Ripken Jr.	3.00
5 Nomar Garciaparra	1.00
6 Sammy Sosa	1.00
7 Frank Thomas	.75
8 Manny Ramirez	.75
9 Vladimir Guerrero	.75
10 Mike Piazza	1.25
11 Bernie Williams	.50
12 Derek Jeter	3.00
13 Ben Grieve	.50
14 J.D. Drew	.60
15 Mark McGwire	2.00
16 Tony Gwynn	1.00
17 Ken Griffey Jr.	1.50
18 Alex Rodriguez	2.00
19 Juan Gonzalez	.50
20 Ivan Rodriguez	.65

Thunder Alley

Thunder Alley focuses on baseball's top power hitters. These were inserted 1:121 packs.

	NM/M
Complete Set (20):	75.00
Common Player:	2.50
Inserted 1:121	
1 Mo Vaughn	2.50
2 Chipper Jones	6.00
3 Cal Ripken Jr.	12.00
4 Nomar Garciaparra	6.00
5 Sammy Sosa	6.00
6 Frank Thomas	5.00
7 Manny Ramirez	5.00
8 Todd Helton	5.00
9 Vladimir Guerrero	5.00
10 Mike Piazza	7.50
11 Derek Jeter	12.00
12 Ben Grieve	2.50
13 Scott Rolen	4.50
14 J.D. Drew	3.00
15 Mark McGwire	10.00
16 Tony Gwynn	6.00
17 Ken Griffey Jr.	9.00
18 Alex Rodriguez	10.00
19 Juan Gonzalez	3.00
20 Ivan Rodriguez	4.50

1999 Pacific Omega Sample

The Omega brand for '99 was launched with this sample card of spokesman Tony Gwynn. The card is in the same format as the regular-issue card, except for the "SAMPLE" overprint on back and in the card-number circle at bottom-right.

	NM/M
SAMPLE Tony Gwynn	2.00

1999 Pacific Omega

This single-series product features both portrait and action photos on front in a horizontal format. Four parallel versions distinguished by the color of foil highlights were random inserts in the six-card packs. Gold parallels are serially numbered to 299 each; Copper to 99; Platinum Blue to 75 and Premiere Date to 50.

	NM/M
Complete Set (250):	20.00
Common Player:	.10
Gold (299 Sets):	4X
Copper (99):	10X
Platinum Blue (75):	15X
Premiere Date (50):	20X
Wax Pack (6):	1.50
Wax Box (36):	35.00
1 Garret Anderson	.10
2 Jim Edmonds	.10
3 Darin Erstad	.20
4 Chuck Finley	.10
5 Troy Glaus	.75
6 Troy Percival	.10
7 Chris Pritchett	.10
8 Tim Salmon	.10
9 Mo Vaughn	.10
10 Jay Bell	.10
11 Steve Finley	.10
12 Luis Gonzalez	.10
13 Randy Johnson	.75
14 Byung-Hyun Kim **RC**	.75
15 Travis Lee	.10
16 Matt Williams	.10
17 Tony Womack	.10
18 Bret Boone	.10
19 Mark DeRosa	.10
20 Tom Glavine	.35
21 Andruw Jones	.75
22 Chipper Jones	1.00
23 Brian Jordan	.10
24 Ryan Klesko	.10
25 Javy Lopez	.10
26 Greg Maddux	1.00
27 John Smoltz	.10
28 Bruce Chen, Odalis Perez	.10
29 Brady Anderson	.10
30 Harold Baines	.10
31 Albert Belle	.10
32 Will Clark	.10
33 Delino DeShields	.10
34 Jerry Hairston Jr.	.10
35 Charles Johnson	.10
36 Mike Mussina	.40
37 Cal Ripken Jr.	2.50
38 B.J. Surhoff	.10
39 Jin Ho Cho	.10
40 Nomar Garciaparra	1.00
41 Pedro Martinez	.75
42 Jose Offerman	.10
43 Troy O'Leary	.10
44 John Valentin	.10
45 Jason Varitek	.10
46 Juan Pena **RC**, Brian Rose	.10
47 Mark Grace	.10
48 Glenallen Hill	.10
49 Tyler Houston	.10
50 Mickey Morandini	.10
51 Henry Rodriguez	.10
52 Sammy Sosa	1.00
53 Kevin Tapani	.10
54 Mike Caruso	.10
55 Ray Durham	.10
56 Paul Konerko	.20
57 Carlos Lee	.10
58 Magglio Ordonez	.20
59 Mike Sirotka	.10
60 Frank Thomas	.75
61 Mark L. Johnson, Chris Singleton	.10
62 Mike Cameron	.10
63 Sean Casey	.20
64 Pete Harnisch	.10
65 Barry Larkin	.10
66 Pokey Reese	.10
67 Greg Vaughn	.10
68 Scott Williamson	.10
69 Dmitri Young	.10
70 Roberto Alomar	.25
71 Sandy Alomar Jr.	.10
72 Travis Fryman	.10
73 David Justice	.10
74 Kenny Lofton	.10
75 Manny Ramirez	.75
76 Richie Sexson	.10
77 Jim Thome	.65
78 Omar Vizquel	.10
79 Jaret Wright	.10
80 Dante Bichette	.10
81 Vinny Castilla	.10
82 Todd Helton	.75
83 Darryl Hamilton	.10
84 Darryl Kile	.10
85 Neifi Perez	.10
86 Larry Walker	.10
87 Tony Clark	.10
88 Damion Easley	.10
89 Juan Encarnacion	.10
90 Bobby Higginson	.10
91 Gabe Kapler	.10
92 Dean Palmer	.10
93 Justin Thompson	.10
94 Masao Kida **RC**, Jeff Weaver **RC**	1.00
95 Bruce Aven	.10
96 Luis Castillo	.10
97 Alex Fernandez	.10
98 Cliff Floyd	.10
99 Alex Gonzalez	.10
100 Mark Kotsay	.10
101 Preston Wilson	.10
102 Moises Alou	.10
103 Jeff Bagwell	.75
104 Derek Bell	.10
105 Craig Biggio	.10
106 Mike Hampton	.10
107 Richard Hidalgo	.10
108 Jose Lima	.10
109 Billy Wagner	.10
110 Russ Johnson, Daryle Ward	.10
111 Carlos Beltran	.50
112 Johnny Damon	.35
113 Jermaine Dye	.10
114 Carlos Febles	.10
115 Jeremy Giambi	.10
116 Joe Randa	.10
117 Mike Sweeney	.10
118 Orber Moreno **RC**, Jose Santiago	.10
119 Kevin Brown	.10
120 Todd Hundley	.10
121 Eric Karros	.10
122 Raul Mondesi	.10
123 Chan Ho Park	.10
124 Angel Pena	.10
125 Gary Sheffield	.45
126 Devon White	.10
127 Eric Young	.10
128 Ron Belliard	.10
129 Jeromy Burnitz	.10
130 Jeff Cirillo	.10
131 Marquis Grissom	.10
132 Geoff Jenkins	.10
133 David Nilsson	.10
134 Hideo Nomo	.40
135 Fernando Vina	.10
136 Ron Coomer	.10
137 Marty Cordova	.10
138 Corey Koskie	.10
139 Brad Radke	.10
140 Todd Walker	.10
141 Chad Allen **RC**, Torii Hunter	.10
142 Cristian Guzman, Jacque Jones	.10
143 Michael Barrett	.10
144 Orlando Cabrera	.10
145 Vladimir Guerrero	.75
146 Wilton Guerrero	.10
147 Ugueth Urbina	.10
148 Rondell White	.10
149 Chris Widger	.10
150 Edgardo Alfonzo	.10
151 Roger Cedeno	.10
152 Octavio Dotel	.10
153 Rickey Henderson	.75
154 John Olerud	.10
155 Rey Ordonez	.10
156 Mike Piazza	1.25
157 Robin Ventura	.10
158 Scott Brosius	.10
159 Roger Clemens	1.25
160 David Cone	.10
161 Chili Davis	.10
162 Orlando Hernandez	.10
163 Derek Jeter	2.50
164 Chuck Knoblauch	.10
165 Tino Martinez	.10
166 Paul O'Neill	.10
167 Bernie Williams	.10
168 Jason Giambi	.60
169 Ben Grieve	.10
170 Chad Harville **RC**	.10
171 Tim Hudson **RC**	2.00
172 Tony Phillips	.10
173 Kenny Rogers	.10
174 Matt Stairs	.10
175 Miguel Tejada	.25
176 Eric Chavez	.25
177 Bobby Abreu	.20
178 Ron Gant	.10
179 Doug Glanville	.10
180 Mike Lieberthal	.10
181 Desi Relaford	.10
182 Scott Rolen	.65
183 Curt Schilling	.35
184 Marlon Anderson, Randy Wolf	.10
185 Brant Brown	.10
186 Brian Giles	.10
187 Jason Kendall	.10
188 Al Martin	.10
189 Ed Sprague	.10
190 Kevin Young	.10
191 Kris Benson, Warren Morris	.10
192 Kent Bottenfield	.10
193 Eric Davis	.10
194 J.D. Drew	.45
195 Ray Lankford	.10
196 Joe McEwing **RC**	.25
197 Mark McGwire	2.00
198 Edgar Renteria	.10
199 Fernando Tatis	.10
200 Andy Ashby	.10
201 Ben Davis	.10
202 Tony Gwynn	1.00
203 Trevor Hoffman	.10
204 Wally Joyner	.10
205 Gary Matthews Jr.	.10
206 Ruben Rivera	.10
207 Reggie Sanders	.10
208 Rich Aurilia	.10
209 Marvin Benard	.10
210 Barry Bonds	2.50
211 Ellis Burks	.10
212 Stan Javier	.10
213 Jeff Kent	.10
214 Robb Nen	.10
215 J.T. Snow	.10
216 David Bell	.10
217 Jay Buhner	.10
218 Freddy Garcia **RC**	.50
219 Ken Griffey Jr.	1.50
220 Brian Hunter	.10
221 Butch Huskey	.10
222 Edgar Martinez	.10
223 Jamie Moyer	.10
224 Alex Rodriguez	2.00
225 David Segui	.10
226 Rolando Arrojo	.10
227 Wade Boggs	1.00
228 Miguel Cairo	.10
229 Jose Canseco	.60
230 Dave Martinez	.10
231 Fred McGriff	.10
232 Kevin Stocker	.10
233 Mike Duvall **RC**, David Lamb	.10
234 Royce Clayton	.10
235 Juan Gonzalez	.40
236 Rusty Greer	.10
237 Ruben Mateo	.10
238 Rafael Palmeiro	.65
239 Ivan Rodriguez	.65
240 John Wetteland	.10
241 Todd Zeile	.10
242 Jeff Zimmerman	.10
243 Homer Bush	.10
244 Jose Cruz Jr.	.10
245 Carlos Delgado	.60
246 Tony Fernandez	.10
247 Shawn Green	.35
248 Shannon Stewart	.10
249 David Wells	.10
250 Roy Halladay, Billy Koch	.10

Debut Duos

The careers of two players who made their major league debuts the same season are compared in this scarce (1:145) insert series. Fronts feature action photos of the pair, backs have portraits.

		NM/M
Complete Set (10):		45.00
Common Player:		2.50
Inserted 1:145		
1	Nomar Garciaparra, Vladimir Guerrero	6.00
2	Derek Jeter, Andy Pettitte	12.00
3	Garret Anderson, Alex Rodriguez	9.00
4	Chipper Jones, Raul Mondesi	6.00
5	Pedro Martinez, Mike Piazza	6.50
6	Mo Vaughn, Bernie Williams	2.50
7	Juan Gonzalez, Ken Griffey Jr.	7.50
8	Sammy Sosa, Larry Walker	6.00
9	Barry Bonds, Mark McGwire	12.00
10	Wade Boggs, Tony Gwynn	6.00

Diamond Masters

		NM/M
Complete Set (36):		27.50
Common Player:		.25
Inserted 1:9		
1	Darin Erstad	.35
2	Mo Vaughn	.25
3	Matt Williams	.25
4	Andruw Jones	.75
5	Chipper Jones	1.00
6	Greg Maddux	1.00
7	Cal Ripken Jr.	3.00
8	Nomar Garciaparra	1.00
9	Pedro Martinez	.75
10	Sammy Sosa	1.00
11	Frank Thomas	.75
12	Kenny Lofton	.25
13	Manny Ramirez	.75
14	Larry Walker	.25
15	Gabe Kapler	.25
16	Jeff Bagwell	.75
17	Craig Biggio	.25
18	Raul Mondesi	.25
19	Vladimir Guerrero	.75
20	Mike Piazza	1.25
21	Roger Clemens	1.25
22	Derek Jeter	3.00
23	Bernie Williams	.25
24	Scott Rolen	.65
25	J.D. Drew	.60
26	Mark McGwire	2.00
27	Fernando Tatis	.25
28	Tony Gwynn	1.00
29	Barry Bonds	3.00
30	Ken Griffey Jr.	1.50
31	Alex Rodriguez	2.00
32	Jose Canseco	.60
33	Juan Gonzalez	.40
34	Ruben Mateo	.25
35	Ivan Rodriguez	.65
36	Rusty Greer	.25

EO Portraits

		NM/M
Complete Set (20):		60.00
Common Player:		1.00
Inserted 1:73		
1-of-1 numbered parallels exist.		
1	Mo Vaughn	1.00
2	Chipper Jones	5.00
3	Greg Maddux	5.00
4	Cal Ripken Jr.	10.00
5	Nomar Garciaparra	5.00
6	Sammy Sosa	5.00
7	Frank Thomas	4.00
8	Manny Ramirez	4.00
9	Jeff Bagwell	4.00
10	Mike Piazza	5.50
11	Roger Clemens	5.50
12	Derek Jeter	10.00
13	Scott Rolen	3.00
14	Mark McGwire	8.00
15	Tony Gwynn	5.00
16	Barry Bonds	10.00
17	Ken Griffey Jr.	6.00
18	Alex Rodriguez	8.00
19	Jose Canseco	2.50
20	Juan Gonzalez	2.00

Hit Machine 3000

Within days of Tony Gwynn's 3,000 hit on August 6, Pacific had rushed into production a special insert set honoring the achievement of its long-time spokesman. A total of 3,000 serially numbered sets of 20 cards were issued as random pack inserts in Omega. Fronts feature various game-action and studio photos of Gwynn, and are highlighted in silver foil. Backs have two more color photos of Gwynn and a few sentences about the player. A serial number in printed on front.

		NM/M
Complete Set (20):		24.00
Common Card:		1.50
1	The Hitting Machine	1.50
2	The Eyes Have It	1.50
3	The Art of Hitting	1.50
4	Solid as a Rock	1.50
5	Seeing Doubles	1.50
6	Pithcer's Worst Nightmare	1.50
7	Portrait of an All-Star	1.50
8	An American Hero	1.50
9	Fan Favorite	1.50
10	Mr. Batting Title	1.50
11	4-for-5!	1.50
12	Mission Accomplished	1.50
13	One Hit Away	1.50
14	A Tip of the Hat	1.50
15	It's a Base Hit!	1.50
16	2997th - Grand Slam!	1.50
17	2998th Hit	1.50
18	2999th Hit - 2-Run Double	1.50
19	3000th Hit!	1.50
20	3000 Hits, 8874 At-Bats, 18 Years	1.50

HR '99

		NM/M
Complete Set (20):		20.00
Common Player:		.25
Inserted 1:37		
1	Mo Vaughn	.25
2	Matt Williams	.25
3	Chipper Jones	2.00
4	Albert Belle	.25
5	Nomar Garciaparra	2.00
6	Sammy Sosa	2.00
7	Frank Thomas	1.25
8	Manny Ramirez	1.25
9	Jeff Bagwell	1.25
10	Raul Mondesi	.25
11	Vladimir Guerrero	1.25
12	Mike Piazza	2.25
13	Derek Jeter	4.00
14	Mark McGwire	3.00
15	Fernando Tatis	.25
16	Barry Bonds	4.00
17	Ken Griffey Jr.	2.50
18	Alex Rodriguez	3.00
19	Jose Canseco	.75
20	Juan Gonzalez	.65

5-Tool Talents

		NM/M
Complete Set (30):		40.00
Common Player:		.40
Inserted 4:37		
1	Randy Johnson	1.50
2	Greg Maddux	2.00
3	Pedro Martinez	1.50
4	Kevin Brown	.40
5	Roger Clemens	2.50
6	Carlos Lee	.40
7	Gabe Kapler	.40
8	Carlos Beltran	.75
9	J.D. Drew	.75
10	Ruben Mateo	.40
11	Chipper Jones	2.00
12	Sammy Sosa	2.00
13	Manny Ramirez	1.50
14	Vladimir Guerrero	1.50
15	Mark McGwire	4.00
16	Ken Griffey Jr.	3.00
17	Jose Canseco	.75
18	Nomar Garciaparra	2.00
19	Frank Thomas	1.50
20	Larry Walker	.40
21	Jeff Bagwell	1.50
22	Mike Piazza	2.50
23	Tony Gwynn	2.00
24	Juan Gonzalez	.75
25	Cal Ripken Jr.	5.00
26	Derek Jeter	5.00
27	Scott Rolen	1.25
28	Barry Bonds	5.00
29	Alex Rodriguez	4.00
30	Ivan Rodriguez	1.50

5-Tool Talents Tiered

A parallel of the 5-Tool Talents inserts is fractured into five tiers of increasing scarcity, differentiated by the color of foil highlights and the serially numbered limited edition. The breakdown is: Tier 1, blue, 100 sets; Tier 2, red, 75 sets; Tier 3, green, 50 sets; Tier 4, purple, 25 sets; Tier 5, gold, one set. The unique gold cards are not priced due to their rarity.

		NM/M
1	Randy Johnson	4.00
6	Carlos Lee	2.00
18	Chipper Jones	5.00
21	Nomar Garciaparra	5.00
28	Jeff Bagwell	4.00
2	Barry Bonds	7.50
2	Greg Maddux	7.50
8	Gabe Kapler	2.00
13	Manny Ramirez	6.00
19	Ken Griffey Jr.	10.00
30	Frank Thomas	6.00
30	Ivan Rodriguez	5.00
3	Pedro Martinez	12.50
8	Carlos Beltran	6.00
16	Mark McGwire	20.00
20	Larry Walker	2.00
25	Cal Ripken Jr.	30.00
26	Derek Jeter	30.00
4	Kevin Brown	7.50
9	J.D. Drew	15.00
12	Sammy Sosa	25.00
17	Jose Canseco	20.00
23	Tony Gwynn	25.00
29	Alex Rodriguez	35.00

Paramount Sample

Pacific spokesman Tony Gwynn is featured on the sample card issued to introduce the brand for 1999. The card carries a large "SAMPLE" overprint diagonally on back.

		NM/M
Tony Gwynn		2.00

1999 Pacific Paramount

The 250-card base set is highlighted by silver foil stamping and a white border. Card backs have a small photo along with 1998 statistics and career totals and a brief career note. There are six parallels to the base set: Copper, Platinum Blue, Holographic Silver, Opening Day Issue, Gold and Holographic Gold. Each parallel is enhanced with the appropriate foil color. Coppers are found exclusively in hobby packs at a rate of one per pack. Platinum Blues are seeded one per 73 packs, Holographic Silvers are hobby only and limited to 99 serial numbered sets. Opening Day Issue is limited to 74 numbered sets. Golds are found one per retail pack. Holographic Golds are limited to 199 numbered sets.

		NM/M
Complete Set (250):		25.00
Common Player:		.10
Copper (1:1H):		2X
Red (1:1R):		2X
Gold (1:1R):		2X
Platinum Blue (1:73):		4X
Holographic Gold (199):		10X
Holographic Silver (99 Sets):		15X
Opening Day (74):		15X
Pack (6):		1.00
Wax Box (36):		25.00
1	Garret Anderson	.10
2	Gary DiSarcina	.10
3	Jim Edmonds	.10
4	Darin Erstad	.25
5	Chuck Finley	.10
6	Troy Glaus	.75
7	Troy Percival	.10
8	Tim Salmon	.10
9	Mo Vaughn	.10
10	Tony Batista	.10
11	Jay Bell	.10
12	Andy Benes	.10
13	Steve Finley	.10
14	Luis Gonzalez	.10
15	Randy Johnson	.75
16	Travis Lee	.10
17	Todd Stottlemyre	.10
18	Matt Williams	.10
19	David Dellucci	.10
20	Bret Boone	.10
21	Andres Galarraga	.10
22	Tom Glavine	.35
23	Andruw Jones	.75
24	Chipper Jones	1.50
25	Brian Jordan	.10
26	Ryan Klesko	.10
27	Javy Lopez	.10
28	Greg Maddux	1.50
29	John Smoltz	.10
30	Brady Anderson	.10
31	Albert Belle	.10
32	Will Clark	.10
33	Delino DeShields	.10
34	Charles Johnson	.10
35	Mike Mussina	.40
36	Cal Ripken Jr.	3.00
37	B.J. Surhoff	.10
38	Nomar Garciaparra	1.50
39	Reggie Jefferson	.10
40	Darren Lewis	.10
41	Pedro Martinez	.75
42	Troy O'Leary	.10
43	Jose Offerman	.10
44	Donnie Sadler	.10
45	John Valentin	.10
46	Rod Beck	.10
47	Gary Gaetti	.10
48	Mark Grace	.10
49	Lance Johnson	.10
50	Mickey Morandini	.10
51	Henry Rodriguez	.10
52	Sammy Sosa	1.50
53	Kerry Wood	.40
54	Mike Caruso	.10
55	Ray Durham	.10
56	Paul Konerko	.20
57	Jaime Navarro	.10
58	Greg Norton	.10
59	Magglio Ordonez	.30
60	Frank Thomas	.75
61	Aaron Boone	.10
62	Mike Cameron	.10
63	Barry Larkin	.20
64	Hal Morris	.10
65	Pokey Reese	.10
66	Brett Tomko	.10
67	Greg Vaughn	.10
68	Dmitri Young	.10
69	Roberto Alomar	.25
70	Sandy Alomar Jr.	.10
71	Bartolo Colon	.10
72	Travis Fryman	.10
73	David Justice	.10
74	Kenny Lofton	.10
75	Manny Ramirez	.25
76	Richie Sexson	.10
77	Jim Thome	.65
78	Omar Vizquel	.10
79	Dante Bichette	.10
80	Vinny Castilla	.10
81	Darryl Hamilton	.10
82	Todd Helton	.75
83	Darryl Kile	.10
84	Mike Lansing	.10
85	Neifi Perez	.10
86	Larry Walker	.10
87	Tony Clark	.10
88	Damion Easley	.10
89	Bob Higginson	.10
90	Brian Hunter	.10
91	Dean Palmer	.10
92	Justin Thompson	.10
93	Todd Dunwoody	.10
94	Cliff Floyd	.10
95	Alex Gonzalez	.10
96	Livan Hernandez	.10
97	Mark Kotsay	.10
98	Derrek Lee	.60
99	Kevin Orie	.10
100	Moises Alou	.10
101	Jeff Bagwell	.75
102	Derek Bell	.10
103	Craig Biggio	.10
104	Ken Caminiti	.10
105	Ricky Gutierrez	.10
106	Richard Hidalgo	.10
107	Billy Wagner	.10
108	Jeff Conine	.10
109	Johnny Damon	.35
110	Carlos Febles	.10
111	Jeremy Giambi	.10
112	Jeff King	.10
113	Jeff Montgomery	.10
114	Joe Randa	.10
115	Kevin Brown	.10
116	Mark Grudzielanek	.10
117	Todd Hundley	.10
118	Eric Karros	.10
119	Raul Mondesi	.10
120	Chan Ho Park	.10
121	Gary Sheffield	.40
122	Devon White	.10
123	Eric Young	.10
124	Jeromy Burnitz	.10
125	Jeff Cirillo	.10
126	Marquis Grissom	.10
127	Geoff Jenkins	.10
128	Dave Nilsson	.10
129	Jose Valentin	.10
130	Fernando Vina	.10
131	Rick Aguilera	.10
132	Ron Coomer	.10
133	Marty Cordova	.10
134	Matt Lawton	.10
135	David Ortiz	.50
136	Brad Radke	.10
137	Terry Steinbach	.10
138	Javier Valentin	.10
139	Todd Walker	.10
140	Orlando Cabrera	.10
141	Brad Fullmer	.10
142	Vladimir Guerrero	.75
143	Wilton Guerrero	.10
144	Carl Pavano	.10
145	Ugueth Urbina	.10
146	Rondell White	.10
147	Chris Widger	.10
148	Edgardo Alfonzo	.10
149	Bobby Bonilla	.10
150	Rickey Henderson	.75
151	Brian McRae	.10
152	Hideo Nomo	.40
153	John Olerud	.10
154	Rey Ordonez	.10
155	Mike Piazza	1.75
156	Robin Ventura	.10
157	Masato Yoshii	.10
158	Roger Clemens	1.75
159	David Cone	.10
160	Orlando Hernandez	.10
161	Hideki Irabu	.10
162	Derek Jeter	3.00
163	Chuck Knoblauch	.10
164	Tino Martinez	.10
165	Paul O'Neill	.10
166	Darryl Strawberry	.10
167	Bernie Williams	.10
168	Eric Chavez	.20
169	Ryan Christenson	.10
170	Jason Giambi	.50
171	Ben Grieve	.10
172	Tony Phillips	.10
173	Tim Raines	.10
174	Scott Spiezio	.10
175	Miguel Tejada	.20
176	Bobby Abreu	.20
177	Rico Brogna	.10
178	Ron Gant	.10
179	Doug Glanville	.10
180	Desi Relaford	.10
181	Scott Rolen	.65
182	Curt Schilling	.35
183	Brant Brown	.10
184	Brian Giles	.10
185	Jose Guillen	.10
186	Jason Kendall	.10
187	Al Martin	.10
188	Ed Sprague	.10
189	Kevin Young	.10
190	Eric Davis	.10
191	J.D. Drew	.40
192	Ray Lankford	.10
193	Eli Marrero	.10
194	Mark McGwire	2.50
195	Edgar Renteria	.10
196	Fernando Tatis	.10
197	Andy Ashby	.10
198	Tony Gwynn	1.50
199	Carlos Hernandez	.10
200	Trevor Hoffman	.10
201	Wally Joyner	.10
202	Jim Leyritz	.10
203	Ruben Rivera	.10
204	Matt Clement	.10
205	Quilvio Veras	.10
206	Rich Aurilia	.10
207	Marvin Benard	.10
208	Barry Bonds	3.00
209	Ellis Burks	.10
210	Jeff Kent	.10
211	Bill Mueller	.10
212	Robb Nen	.10
213	J.T. Snow	.10
214	Jay Buhner	.10
215	Jeff Fassero	.10
216	Ken Griffey Jr.	2.00
217	Carlos Guillen	.10
218	Butch Huskey	.10
219	Edgar Martinez	.10
220	Alex Rodriguez	2.50
221	David Segui	.10
222	Dan Wilson	.10
223	Rolando Arrojo	.10
224	Wade Boggs	1.50
225	Jose Canseco	.50
226	Roberto Hernandez	.10
227	Dave Martinez	.10
228	Quinton McCracken	.10
229	Fred McGriff	.10
230	Kevin Stocker	.10
231	Randy Winn	.10
232	Royce Clayton	.10
233	Juan Gonzalez	.40
234	Tom Goodwin	.10
235	Rusty Greer	.10
236	Rick Helling	.10
237	Rafael Palmeiro	.65
238	Ivan Rodriguez	.65
239	Aaron Sele	.10
240	John Wetteland	.10
241	Todd Zeile	.10
242	Jose Cruz Jr.	.10
243	Carlos Delgado	.50
244	Tony Fernandez	.10
245	Cecil Fielder	.10
246	Alex Gonzalez	.10
247	Shawn Green	.35
248	Roy Halladay	.10
249	Shannon Stewart	.10
250	David Wells	.10

Cooperstown Bound

This 10-card set focuses on players who seem destined for the Hall of Fame. These inserts feature silver foil stamping and are seeded 1:361 packs.

		NM/M
Complete Set (10):		35.00
Common Player:		3.00
Inserted 1:361		
1	Greg Maddux	4.00
2	Cal Ripken Jr.	10.00
3	Nomar Garciaparra	4.00
4	Sammy Sosa	4.00
5	Frank Thomas	3.00
6	Mike Piazza	5.00
7	Mark McGwire	10.00
8	Tony Gwynn	4.00
9	Ken Griffey Jr.	6.00
10	Alex Rodriguez	8.00

Fielder's Choice

Cal Ripken Jr.
BALTIMORE ORIOLES

This 20-card set is die-cut into a glove shape and enhanced with gold foil stamping. These are seeded 1:73 packs.

		NM/M
Complete Set (20):		60.00
Common Player:		2.50
Inserted 1:73		
1	Chipper Jones	5.00
2	Greg Maddux	5.00
3	Cal Ripken Jr.	10.00
4	Nomar Garciaparra	5.00
5	Sammy Sosa	5.00
6	Kerry Wood	3.00
7	Frank Thomas	4.00
8	Manny Ramirez	4.00
9	Todd Helton	4.00
10	Jeff Bagwell	4.00
11	Mike Piazza	5.50
12	Derek Jeter	10.00
13	Bernie Williams	2.50
14	J.D. Drew	3.00
15	Mark McGwire	7.50
16	Tony Gwynn	5.00
17	Ken Griffey Jr.	6.00
18	Alex Rodriguez	7.50
19	Juan Gonzalez	2.50
20	Ivan Rodriguez	3.50

Personal Bests

Ken Griffey Jr.
OF Seattle Mariners

This 36-card set features holographic silver foil stamping on the card front. Card backs include a close-up photo of the featured player and a career note. These are seeded 1:37 packs.

		NM/M
Complete Set (36):		45.00
Common Player:		.50
Inserted 1:37		
1	Darin Erstad	.65
2	Mo Vaughn	.50
3	Travis Lee	.50
4	Chipper Jones	3.00
5	Greg Maddux	3.00
6	Albert Belle	.50
7	Cal Ripken Jr.	6.00
8	Nomar Garciaparra	3.00
9	Sammy Sosa	3.00
10	Kerry Wood	1.00
11	Frank Thomas	2.00
12	Greg Vaughn	.50
13	Manny Ramirez	2.00
14	Todd Helton	2.00
15	Larry Walker	.50
16	Jeff Bagwell	2.00
17	Craig Biggio	.50
18	Raul Mondesi	.50
19	Vladimir Guerrero	2.00
20	Hideo Nomo	1.00
21	Mike Piazza	3.50
22	Roger Clemens	3.50
23	Derek Jeter	6.00
24	Bernie Williams	1.50
25	Eric Chavez	.75
26	Ben Grieve	.50
27	Scott Rolen	1.50
28	J.D. Drew	1.25
29	Mark McGwire	4.50
30	Tony Gwynn	3.00
31	Barry Bonds	6.00
32	Ken Griffey Jr.	4.00
33	Alex Rodriguez	4.50
34	Jose Canseco	1.25
35	Juan Gonzalez	1.00
36	Ivan Rodriguez	1.50

Team Checklists

MARQUIS GRISSOM

This 30-card set features gold foil etching and stamping on the card front. Card backs show the featured player's team checklist for the base set. These were seeded 2:37 packs.

		NM/M
Complete Set (30):		40.00
Common Player:		.50
Inserted 2:37		
1	Mo Vaughn	.50
2	Travis Lee	.50
3	Chipper Jones	3.00
4	Cal Ripken Jr.	6.00
5	Nomar Garciaparra	3.00
6	Sammy Sosa	3.00
7	Frank Thomas	2.50
8	Greg Vaughn	.50
9	Manny Ramirez	2.50
10	Larry Walker	.50
11	Damion Easley	.50
12	Mark Kotsay	.50
13	Jeff Bagwell	2.50
14	Jeremy Giambi	.50
15	Raul Mondesi	.50
16	Marquis Grissom	.50
17	Brad Radke	.50
18	Vladimir Guerrero	2.50
19	Mike Piazza	3.50
20	Roger Clemens	3.50
21	Ben Grieve	.50
22	Scott Rolen	2.00
23	Brian Giles	.50
24	Mark McGwire	5.00
25	Tony Gwynn	3.00
26	Barry Bonds	6.00
27	Ken Griffey Jr.	4.00
28	Jose Canseco	1.25
29	Juan Gonzalez	1.25
30	Jose Cruz Jr.	.50

1999 Pacific Prism Sample

Tony GWYNN

This card of Pacific spokesman Tony Gwynn introduces the 1999 Prism series. The sample card follows the format of the issued version but is overprinted "SAMPLE" on back.

	NM/M
Tony Gwynn	2.00

1999 Pacific Prism

Greg MADDUX
41 of 320

This 150-card base set has a full, holographic silver card front. Card backs feature two more player photos along with 1998 and career statistics. Hobby packs consist of five cards. There are also five parallels including Holographic Gold, Holographic Mirror, Holographic Blue, Holographic Purple and Red. Golds are limited to 480 serial numbered sets, Mirrors 160 sets, Blues 80 numbered sets, and, Purples 320 sets. Red parallels are a retail-only insert and are seeded at a rate of one per 12.5 packs.

		NM/M
Complete Set (150):		50.00
Common Player:		.15
Red (2:25R):		3X
HoloGold (480 Sets):		3X
HoloPurple (320):		4X
HoloMirror (160):		8X
HoloBlue (80):		15X
Retail Pack (3):		1.00
Hobby Pack (5):		1.50
1	Garret Anderson	.15
2	Jim Edmonds	.15
3	Darin Erstad	.30
4	Chuck Finley	.15
5	Tim Salmon	.15
6	Jay Bell	.15
7	David Dellucci	.15
8	Travis Lee	.15
9	Matt Williams	.15
10	Andres Galarraga	.15
11	Tom Glavine	.40
12	Andruw Jones	1.50
13	Chipper Jones	2.00
14	Ryan Klesko	.15
15	Javy Lopez	.15
16	Greg Maddux	2.00
17	Roberto Alomar	.50
18	Ryan Minor	.15
19	Mike Mussina	.40
20	Rafael Palmeiro	1.25
21	Cal Ripken Jr.	4.00
22	Nomar Garciaparra	2.00
23	Pedro Martinez	1.50
24	John Valentin	.15
25	Mo Vaughn	.15
26	Tim Wakefield	.15
27	Rod Beck	.15
28	Mark Grace	.15
29	Lance Johnson	.15
30	Sammy Sosa	2.00
31	Kerry Wood	.50
32	Albert Belle	.15
33	Mike Caruso	.15
34	Magglio Ordonez	.30
35	Frank Thomas	1.50
36	Robin Ventura	.15
37	Aaron Boone	.15
38	Barry Larkin	.15
39	Reggie Sanders	.15
40	Brett Tomko	.15
41	Sandy Alomar Jr.	.15
42	Bartolo Colon	.15
43	David Justice	.15
44	Kenny Lofton	.15
45	Manny Ramirez	1.50
46	Richie Sexson	.15
47	Jim Thome	1.00
48	Omar Vizquel	.15
49	Dante Bichette	.15
50	Vinny Castilla	.15
51	Edgard Clemente **RC**	.15
52	Todd Helton	1.50
53	Quinton McCracken	.15
54	Larry Walker	.15
55	Tony Clark	.15
56	Damion Easley	.15
57	Luis Gonzalez	.15
58	Bob Higginson	.15
59	Brian Hunter	.15
60	Cliff Floyd	.15
61	Alex Gonzalez	.15
62	Livan Hernandez	.15
63	Derrek Lee	.65
64	Edgar Renteria	.15
65	Moises Alou	.15
66	Jeff Bagwell	1.50
67	Derek Bell	.15
68	Craig Biggio	.15
69	Randy Johnson	1.50
70	Johnny Damon	.35
71	Jeff King	.15
72	Hal Morris	.15
73	Dean Palmer	.15
74	Eric Karros	.15
75	Raul Mondesi	.15
76	Chan Ho Park	.15
77	Gary Sheffield	.50
78	Jeromy Burnitz	.15
79	Jeff Cirillo	.15
80	Marquis Grissom	.15
81	Jose Valentin	.15
82	Fernando Vina	.15
83	Paul Molitor	1.50
84	Otis Nixon	.15
85	David Ortiz	.65
86	Todd Walker	.15
87	Vladimir Guerrero	1.50
88	Carl Pavano	.15
89	Fernando Seguignol	.15
90	Ugueth Urbina	.15
91	Carlos Baerga	.15
92	Bobby Bonilla	.15
93	Hideo Nomo	.75
94	John Olerud	.15
95	Rey Ordonez	.15
96	Mike Piazza	2.25
97	David Cone	.15
98	Orlando Hernandez	.15
99	Hideki Irabu	.15
100	Derek Jeter	4.00
101	Tino Martinez	.15
102	Bernie Williams	.15
103	Eric Chavez	.25
104	Jason Giambi	1.00
105	Ben Grieve	.15
106	Rickey Henderson	1.50
107	Bob Abreu	.15
108	Doug Glanville	.15
109	Scott Rolen	1.00
110	Curt Schilling	.40
111	Emil Brown	.15
112	Jose Guillen	.15
113	Jason Kendall	.15
114	Al Martin	.15
115	Aramis Ramirez	.15
116	Kevin Young	.15
117	J.D. Drew	.75
118	Ron Gant	.15
119	Brian Jordan	.15
120	Eli Marrero	.15
121	Mark McGwire	3.00
122	Kevin Brown	.15
123	Tony Gwynn	2.00
124	Trevor Hoffman	.15
125	Wally Joyner	.15
126	Greg Vaughn	.15
127	Barry Bonds	4.00
128	Ellis Burks	.15
129	Jeff Kent	.15
130	Robb Nen	.15
131	J.T. Snow	.15
132	Jay Buhner	.15
133	Ken Griffey Jr.	2.50
134	Edgar Martinez	.15
135	Alex Rodriguez	3.00
136	David Segui	.15
137	Rolando Arrojo	.15
138	Wade Boggs	2.00
139	Aaron Ledesma	.15
140	Fred McGriff	.15
141	Will Clark	.15
142	Juan Gonzalez	.75
143	Rusty Greer	.15
144	Ivan Rodriguez	1.25
145	Aaron Sele	.15
146	Jose Canseco	.40
147	Roger Clemens	2.25
148	Jose Cruz Jr.	.15
149	Carlos Delgado	.50
150	Alex Gonzalez	.15

Ahead of the Game

ST. Louis Cardinals • Outfielder

Each card features full gold foil and etching with a close-up photo of baseball's top 20 stars. These are seeded 1:49 packs.

		NM/M
Complete Set (20):		40.00
Common Player:		1.00
Inserted 1:49		
1	Darin Erstad	1.25
2	Travis Lee	1.00
3	Chipper Jones	3.00
4	Cal Ripken Jr.	6.00
5	Nomar Garciaparra	3.00
6	Sammy Sosa	3.00
7	Kerry Wood	1.25
8	Frank Thomas	2.00
9	Manny Ramirez	2.00
10	Todd Helton	2.00
11	Jeff Bagwell	2.00
12	Mike Piazza	3.50
13	Derek Jeter	6.00
14	Bernie Williams	2.00
15	J.D. Drew	1.25
16	Mark McGwire	5.00
17	Tony Gwynn	3.00
18	Ken Griffey Jr.	4.00
19	Alex Rodriguez	5.00
20	Ivan Rodriguez	1.50

Ballpark Legends

OUTFIELDER
CHICAGO CUBS

This 10 card set salutes baseball's biggest stars. These inserts feature silver foil stamping and etching with an image of a ballpark in the background of the player photo. These are seeded 1:193 packs.

		NM/M
Complete Set (10):		40.00
Common Player:		2.50
Inserted 1:193		
1	Cal Ripken Jr.	10.00
2	Nomar Garciaparra	4.00
3	Frank Thomas	4.00
4	Ken Griffey Jr.	6.00
5	Alex Rodriguez	7.50
6	Greg Maddux	5.00
7	Sammy Sosa	5.00
8	Kerry Wood	2.50
9	Mark McGwire	7.50
10	Tony Gwynn	5.00

Diamond Glory

MARINERS

Card fronts feature full copper foil stamping with a star in the background of the player's photo. The 20-card set features 20 of baseball's most exciting players including several top 1999 rookies. These are seeded 2:25 packs.

		NM/M
Complete Set (20):		25.00
Common Player:		.60
Inserted 2:25		
1	Darin Erstad	.60
2	Travis Lee	.60
3	Chipper Jones	2.00
4	Greg Maddux	2.00
5	Cal Ripken Jr.	3.50
6	Nomar Garciaparra	2.00
7	Sammy Sosa	2.00
8	Kerry Wood	.75
9	Frank Thomas	1.50
10	Todd Helton	1.50
11	Jeff Bagwell	1.50
12	Mike Piazza	2.25
13	Derek Jeter	3.50
14	Bernie Williams	.60
15	J.D. Drew	.75
16	Mark McGwire	3.00
17	Tony Gwynn	2.00
18	Ken Griffey Jr.	2.50
19	Alex Rodriguez	3.00
20	Juan Gonzalez	.75

Epic Performers

EPIC PERFORMERS

This hobby-only set features top hobby favorites and is seeded at 1:97 packs.

		NM/M
Complete Set (10):		60.00
Common Player:		4.00
Inserted 1:97 H		
1	Cal Ripken Jr.	15.00
2	Nomar Garciaparra	7.50
3	Frank Thomas	6.00
4	Ken Griffey Jr.	10.00
5	Alex Rodriguez	12.50
6	Greg Maddux	7.50
7	Sammy Sosa	7.50
8	Kerry Wood	4.00
9	Mark McGwire	12.50
10	Tony Gwynn	7.50

1999 Pacific Private Stock

The premiere issue of Private Stock base cards features holographic silver foil on 30-pt. cardboard. Card backs have selected box scores from the '98 season, with a brief commentary on the player. Packs consist of six cards.

		NM/M
Complete Set (150):		25.00
Common Player:		.10
Pack (6):		1.50
Wax Box (24):		20.00
Wax Box (36):		25.00
1	Jeff Bagwell	1.00
2	Roger Clemens	1.75
3	J.D. Drew	.60
4	Nomar Garciaparra	1.50
5	Juan Gonzalez	.50
6	Ken Griffey Jr.	2.00
7	Tony Gwynn	1.50
8	Derek Jeter	3.00
9	Chipper Jones	1.50
10	Travis Lee	.10
11	Greg Maddux	1.50
12	Mark McGwire	2.50
13	Mike Piazza	1.75
14	Manny Ramirez	1.00
15	Cal Ripken Jr.	3.00
16	Alex Rodriguez	2.50
17	Ivan Rodriguez	.75
18	Sammy Sosa	1.50
19	Frank Thomas	1.00
20	Kerry Wood	.40
21	Roberto Alomar	.25
22	Moises Alou	.10
23	Albert Belle	.10
24	Craig Biggio	.10
25	Wade Boggs	1.50
26	Barry Bonds	3.00
27	Jose Canseco	.50
28	Jim Edmonds	.10
29	Darin Erstad	.25
30	Andres Galarraga	.10
31	Tom Glavine	.35
32	Ben Grieve	.10
33	Vladimir Guerrero	1.00
34	Wilton Guerrero	.10
35	Todd Helton	1.00
36	Andruw Jones	.10
37	Ryan Klesko	.10
38	Kenny Lofton	.10
39	Javy Lopez	.10
40	Pedro Martinez	1.00
41	Paul Molitor	1.00
42	Raul Mondesi	.10
43	Rafael Palmeiro	.75
44	Tim Salmon	.10
45	Jim Thome	.75
46	Mo Vaughn	.10
47	Larry Walker	.10
48	David Wells	.10
49	Bernie Williams	.10
50	Jaret Wright	.10
51	Bobby Abreu	.15
52	Garret Anderson	.10
53	Rolando Arrojo	.10
54	Tony Batista	.10
55	Rod Beck	.10
56	Derek Bell	.10
57	Marvin Benard	.10
58	Dave Berg	.10
59	Dante Bichette	.10
60	Aaron Boone	.10
61	Bret Boone	.10
62	Scott Brosius	.10
63	Brant Brown	.10
64	Kevin Brown	.10
65	Jeromy Burnitz	.10
66	Ken Caminiti	.10
67	Mike Caruso	.10
68	Sean Casey	.20
69	Vinny Castilla	.10
70	Eric Chavez	.20
71	Ryan Christenson	.10
72	Jeff Cirillo	.10
73	Tony Clark	.10

74	Will Clark	.10
75	Edgard Clemente RC	.10
76	David Cone	.10
77	Marty Cordova	.10
78	Jose Cruz Jr.	.10
79	Eric Davis	.10
80	Carlos Delgado	.50
81	David Dellucci	.10
82	Delino DeShields	.10
83	Gary DiSarcina	.10
84	Damion Easley	.10
85	Dennis Eckersley	.65
86	Cliff Floyd	.10
87	Jason Giambi	.65
88	Doug Glanville	.10
89	Alex Gonzalez	.10
90	Mark Grace	.10
91	Rusty Greer	.10
92	Jose Guillen	.10
93	Carlos Guillen	.10
94	Jeffrey Hammonds	.10
95	Rick Helling	.10
96	Bob Henley	.10
97	Livan Hernandez	.10
98	Orlando Hernandez	.10
99	Bob Higginson	.10
100	Trevor Hoffman	.10
101	Randy Johnson	1.00
102	Brian Jordan	.10
103	Wally Joyner	.10
104	Eric Karros	.10
105	Jason Kendall	.10
106	Jeff Kent	.10
107	Jeff King	.10
108	Mark Kotsay	.10
109	Ray Lankford	.10
110	Barry Larkin	.10
111	Mark Loretta	.10
112	Edgar Martinez	.10
113	Tino Martinez	.10
114	Quinton McCracken	.10
115	Fred McGriff	.10
116	Ryan Minor	.10
117	Hal Morris	.10
118	Bill Mueller	.10
119	Mike Mussina	.40
120	Dave Nilsson	.10
121	Otis Nixon	.10
122	Hideo Nomo	.50
123	Paul O'Neill	.10
124	Jose Offerman	.10
125	John Olerud	.10
126	Rey Ordonez	.10
127	David Ortiz	.50
128	Dean Palmer	.10
129	Chan Ho Park	.10
130	Aramis Ramirez	.10
131	Edgar Renteria	.10
132	Armando Rios	.10
133	Henry Rodriguez	.10
134	Scott Rolen	.75
135	Curt Schilling	.35
136	David Segui	.10
137	Richie Sexson	.10
138	Gary Sheffield	.45
139	John Smoltz	.10
140	Matt Stairs	.10
141	Justin Thompson	.10
142	Greg Vaughn	.10
143	Omar Vizquel	.10
144	Tim Wakefield	.10
145	Todd Walker	.10
146	Devon White	.10
147	Rondell White	.10
148	Matt Williams	.10
149	Enrique Wilson RC	.25
150	Kevin Young	.10

Exclusive Series

This 20-card set is a partial parallel to the base set. Taking the first 20 cards from the set and serially numbering them to 299 sets. These are inserted exclusively in hobby packs.

		NM/M
Complete Set (20):		50.00
Common Player:		1.00
Production: 299 Sets H		
1	Jeff Bagwell	2.00
2	Roger Clemens	3.50
3	J.D. Drew	1.25
4	Nomar Garciaparra	3.00
5	Juan Gonzalez	1.25
6	Ken Griffey Jr.	4.00
7	Tony Gwynn	3.00
8	Derek Jeter	6.00
9	Chipper Jones	3.00
10	Travis Lee	1.00
11	Greg Maddux	3.00
12	Mark McGwire	5.00
13	Mike Piazza	3.50
14	Manny Ramirez	2.00
15	Cal Ripken Jr.	6.00
16	Alex Rodriguez	5.00
17	Ivan Rodriguez	1.50
18	Sammy Sosa	3.00
19	Frank Thomas	2.00
20	Kerry Wood	1.25

Platinum Series

Another partial parallel of the first 50 cards in the base set. Cards have a platinum holographic sheen to them with a Platinum stamp on the front. These are limited to 199 numbered sets.

		NM/M
Complete Set (50):		160.00
Common Player:		.75
Production 199 Sets		
1	Jeff Bagwell	5.00
2	Roger Clemens	6.50
3	J.D. Drew	3.00
4	Nomar Garciaparra	6.00
5	Juan Gonzalez	2.50
6	Ken Griffey Jr.	8.00
7	Tony Gwynn	6.00
8	Derek Jeter	12.00
9	Chipper Jones	6.00
10	Travis Lee	.75
11	Greg Maddux	6.00
12	Mark McGwire	10.00
13	Mike Piazza	6.50
14	Manny Ramirez	3.00
15	Cal Ripken Jr.	12.00
16	Alex Rodriguez	10.00
17	Ivan Rodriguez	4.00
18	Sammy Sosa	6.00
19	Frank Thomas	5.00
20	Kerry Wood	2.00
21	Roberto Alomar	1.50
22	Moises Alou	.75
23	Albert Belle	.75
24	Craig Biggio	.75
25	Wade Boggs	6.00
26	Barry Bonds	12.00
27	Jose Canseco	3.00
28	Jim Edmonds	.75
29	Darin Erstad	1.50
30	Andres Galarraga	.75
31	Tom Glavine	2.00
32	Ben Grieve	.75
33	Vladimir Guerrero	5.00
34	Wilton Guerrero	.75
35	Todd Helton	5.00
36	Andruw Jones	5.00
37	Ryan Klesko	.75
38	Kenny Lofton	.75
39	Javy Lopez	.75
40	Pedro Martinez	5.00
41	Paul Molitor	5.00
42	Raul Mondesi	.75
43	Rafael Palmeiro	4.00
44	Tim Salmon	.75
45	Jim Thome	3.50
46	Mo Vaughn	.75
47	Larry Walker	.75
48	David Wells	.75
49	Bernie Williams	.75
50	Jaret Wright	.75

Preferred Series

Another partial parallel of the first 20 base cards. Each card is stamped with a holographic Preferred logo and are numbered to 399 sets.

		NM/M
Complete Set (20):		37.50
Common Player:		.60
Production: 399 Sets		
1	Jeff Bagwell	1.50
2	Roger Clemens	2.25
3	J.D. Drew	.75
4	Nomar Garciaparra	2.00
5	Juan Gonzalez	.75
6	Ken Griffey Jr.	2.50
7	Tony Gwynn	2.00
8	Derek Jeter	5.00
9	Chipper Jones	2.00
10	Travis Lee	.60
11	Greg Maddux	2.00
12	Mark McGwire	3.50
13	Mike Piazza	2.25
14	Manny Ramirez	1.50
15	Cal Ripken Jr.	5.00
16	Alex Rodriguez	3.50
17	Ivan Rodriguez	1.25
18	Sammy Sosa	2.00
19	Frank Thomas	1.50
20	Kerry Wood	.75

Vintage Series

This insert set is a partial parallel of the first 50 cards in the base set and has a Vintage holographic stamp on the card fronts. These are limited to 99 numbered sets.

		NM/M
Complete Set (50):		375.00
Common Player:		2.50
Production: 99 Sets		
1	Jeff Bagwell	12.50
2	Roger Clemens	17.50
3	J.D. Drew	7.50
4	Nomar Garciaparra	15.00
5	Juan Gonzalez	6.00
6	Ken Griffey Jr.	20.00
7	Tony Gwynn	15.00
8	Derek Jeter	30.00
9	Chipper Jones	15.00
10	Travis Lee	2.50
11	Greg Maddux	15.00
12	Mark McGwire	25.00
13	Mike Piazza	17.50
14	Manny Ramirez	12.50
15	Cal Ripken Jr.	30.00
16	Alex Rodriguez	25.00
17	Ivan Rodriguez	10.00
18	Sammy Sosa	15.00
19	Frank Thomas	12.50
20	Kerry Wood	6.00
21	Roberto Alomar	3.50
22	Moises Alou	2.50
23	Albert Belle	2.50
24	Craig Biggio	2.50
25	Wade Boggs	15.00
26	Barry Bonds	30.00
27	Jose Canseco	2.50
28	Jim Edmonds	2.50
29	Darin Erstad	3.50
30	Andres Galarraga	2.50
31	Tom Glavine	5.00
32	Ben Grieve	2.50
33	Vladimir Guerrero	12.50
34	Wilton Guerrero	.75
35	Todd Helton	12.50
36	Andruw Jones	12.50
37	Ryan Klesko	2.50
38	Kenny Lofton	2.50
39	Javy Lopez	2.50
40	Pedro Martinez	12.50
41	Paul Molitor	12.50
42	Raul Mondesi	2.50
43	Rafael Palmeiro	10.00
44	Tim Salmon	2.50
45	Jim Thome	10.00
46	Mo Vaughn	2.50
47	Larry Walker	2.50
48	David Wells	2.50
49	Bernie Williams	2.50
50	Jaret Wright	2.50

PS-206

This 150-card set takes reverent reach back into collecting history with its smaller format (1.5" x 2.5"). Card fronts have a white border with silver foil stamping and a blue back, these are found one per pack. A parallel also exists with a red back, which are seeded 1:25 packs.

		NM/M
Complete Set (150):		20.00
Common Player:		.15
Inserted 1:1		
Red Parallels:		4X
Inserted 1:25		
1	Jeff Bagwell	.75
2	Roger Clemens	1.25
3	J.D. Drew	.50
4	Nomar Garciaparra	1.00
5	Juan Gonzalez	.40
6	Ken Griffey Jr.	1.50
7	Tony Gwynn	1.00
8	Derek Jeter	3.00
9	Chipper Jones	1.00
10	Travis Lee	.15
11	Greg Maddux	1.00
12	Mark McGwire	2.00
13	Mike Piazza	1.25
14	Manny Ramirez	.75
15	Cal Ripken Jr.	3.00
16	Alex Rodriguez	2.00
17	Ivan Rodriguez	.65
18	Sammy Sosa	1.00
19	Frank Thomas	.75
20	Kerry Wood	.40
21	Roberto Alomar	.30
22	Moises Alou	.15
23	Albert Belle	.15
24	Craig Biggio	.15
25	Wade Boggs	1.00
26	Barry Bonds	3.00
27	Jose Canseco	.50
28	Jim Edmonds	.15
29	Darin Erstad	.30
30	Andres Galarraga	.15
31	Tom Glavine	.35
32	Ben Grieve	.15
33	Vladimir Guerrero	.75
34	Wilton Guerrero	.15
35	Todd Helton	.75
36	Andruw Jones	.75
37	Ryan Klesko	.15
38	Kenny Lofton	.15
39	Javy Lopez	.15
40	Pedro Martinez	.75
41	Paul Molitor	.75
42	Raul Mondesi	.15
43	Rafael Palmeiro	.65
44	Tim Salmon	.15
45	Jim Thome	.65
46	Mo Vaughn	.15
47	Larry Walker	.15
48	David Wells	.15
49	Bernie Williams	.15
50	Jaret Wright	.15
51	Bobby Abreu	.15
52	Garret Anderson	.15
53	Rolando Arrojo	.15
54	Tony Batista	.15
55	Rod Beck	.15
56	Derek Bell	.15
57	Marvin Benard	.15
58	Dave Berg	.15
59	Dante Bichette	.15
60	Aaron Boone	.15
61	Bret Boone	.15
62	Scott Brosius	.15
63	Brant Brown	.15
64	Kevin Brown	.15
65	Jeromy Burnitz	.15
66	Ken Caminiti	.15
67	Mike Caruso	.15
68	Sean Casey	.25
69	Vinny Castilla	.15
70	Eric Chavez	.25
71	Ryan Christenson	.15
72	Jeff Cirillo	.15
73	Tony Clark	.15
74	Will Clark	.15
75	Edgard Clemente	.15
76	David Cone	.15
77	Marty Cordova	.15
78	Jose Cruz Jr.	.15
79	Eric Davis	.15
80	Carlos Delgado	.60
81	David Dellucci	.15
82	Delino DeShields	.15
83	Gary DiSarcina	.15
84	Damion Easley	.15
85	Dennis Eckersley	.65
86	Cliff Floyd	.15
87	Jason Giambi	.15
88	Doug Glanville	.15
89	Alex Gonzalez	.15
90	Mark Grace	.15
91	Rusty Greer	.15
92	Jose Guillen	.15
93	Carlos Guillen	.15
94	Jeffrey Hammonds	.15
95	Rick Helling	.15
96	Bob Henley	.15
97	Livan Hernandez	.15
98	Orlando Hernandez	.15
99	Bob Higginson	.15
100	Trevor Hoffman	.15
101	Randy Johnson	.75
102	Brian Jordan	.15
103	Wally Joyner	.15
104	Eric Karros	.15
105	Jason Kendall	.15
106	Jeff Kent	.15
107	Jeff King	.15
108	Mark Kotsay	.15
109	Ray Lankford	.15
110	Barry Larkin	.15
111	Mark Loretta	.15
112	Edgar Martinez	.15
113	Tino Martinez	.15
114	Quinton McCracken	.15
115	Fred McGriff	.15
116	Ryan Minor	.15
117	Hal Morris	.15
118	Bill Mueller	.15
119	Mike Mussina	.40
120	Dave Nilsson	.15
121	Otis Nixon	.15
122	Hideo Nomo	.40
123	Paul O'Neill	.15
124	Jose Offerman	.15
125	John Olerud	.15
126	Rey Ordonez	.15
127	David Ortiz	.50
128	Dean Palmer	.15
129	Chan Ho Park	.15
130	Aramis Ramirez	.15
131	Edgar Renteria	.15
132	Armando Rios	.15
133	Henry Rodriguez	.15
134	Scott Rolen	.60
135	Curt Schilling	.35
136	David Segui	.15
137	Richie Sexson	.15
138	Gary Sheffield	.50
139	John Smoltz	.15
140	Matt Stairs	.15
141	Justin Thompson	.15
142	Greg Vaughn	.15
143	Omar Vizquel	.15
144	Tim Wakefield	.15
145	Todd Walker	.15
146	Devon White	.15
147	Rondell White	.15
148	Matt Williams	.15
149	Enrique Wilson	.15
150	Kevin Young	.15

Homerun History

This holographic silver foiled commemorative set honors Mark McGwire and Sammy Sosa's historic '98 seasons. Two cards were added to the end of the set, which are Silver Crown Die-Cuts honoring Ripken Jr.'s consecutive games streak and McGwire's 70 home runs. These are inserted 2:25 packs.

		NM/M
Complete Set (22):		25.00
Common McGwire:		1.50
Common Sosa:		1.00
Inserted 1:12		
1	Home Run #61 (Mark McGwire)	3.00
2	Home Run #59 (Sammy Sosa)	1.00
3	Home Run #62 (Mark McGwire)	1.50
4	Home Run #60 (Sammy Sosa)	1.00
5	Home Run #63 (Mark McGwire)	1.50
6	Home Run #61 (Sammy Sosa)	3.00
7	Home Run #64 (Mark McGwire)	1.50
8	Home Run #62 (Sammy Sosa)	1.00
9	Home Run #65 (Mark McGwire)	1.50
10	Home Run #63 (Sammy Sosa)	1.00
11	Home Run #67 (Mark McGwire)	1.50
12	Home Run #64 (Sammy Sosa)	1.00
13	Home Run #68 (Mark McGwire)	1.50
14	Home Run #65 (Sammy Sosa)	1.00
15	Home Run #70 (Mark McGwire)	5.00
16	Home Run #66 (Sammy Sosa)	3.00
17	A Season of Celebration (Mark McGwire)	1.50
18	A Season of Celebration (Sammy Sosa)	1.00
19	Awesome Power (Sammy Sosa, Mark McGwire)	1.50
20	Transcending Sports (Mark McGwire, Sammy Sosa)	1.50
21	Crown Die-Cut (Mark McGwire)	1.50
22	Crown Die-Cut (Cal Ripken Jr.)	1.00

1999 Pacific Revolution

The 150-card set features dual foiled etching and embossing enhanced by gold-foil stamping. Card backs have year-by-year statistics along with a close-up photo. There are 25 short-printed rookie and prospect cards, which were inserted at a rate of about one per four packs. There are three parallels to the base set: Premiere Date, Red and Shadow. Reds are retail exclusive and are limited to 299 numbered sets. Shadows have light blue foil stamping and are limited to 99 numbered sets. Premiere Date are seeded exclusively in hobby packs at a rate of 1:25 packs.

		NM/M
Complete Set (150):		60.00
Common Player:		.15
Shadow (99 Sets H):		6X
SP:		3X
Red (299 R):		2X
SP:		1.5X
Premiere Date (49 H):		12X
SP:		6X
Wax Pack (3):		2.00
Wax Box (24):		35.00
1	Jim Edmonds	.15
2	Darin Erstad	.30
3	Troy Glaus	1.00
4	Tim Salmon	.15
5	Mo Vaughn	.15
6	Steve Finley	.15
7	Luis Gonzalez	.15
8	Randy Johnson	1.00
9	Travis Lee	.15
10	Matt Williams	.15
11	Andruw Jones	1.00
12	Chipper Jones	1.50
13	Brian Jordan	.15
14	Javy Lopez	.15
15	Greg Maddux	1.50
16	Kevin McGlinchy/SP RC	.15
17	John Smoltz	.15
18	Brady Anderson	.15
19	Albert Belle	.15
20	Will Clark	.15
21	Willis Otanez/SP RC	.25
22	Calvin Pickering/SP RC	.25
23	Cal Ripken Jr.	4.00
24	Nomar Garciaparra	1.50
25	Pedro Martinez	1.00
26	Troy O'Leary	.15
27	Jose Offerman	.15
28	Mark Grace	.15
29	Mickey Morandini	.15
30	Henry Rodriguez	.15
31	Sammy Sosa	1.50
32	Ray Durham	.15
33	Carlos Lee/SP	.50
34	Jeff Liefer/SP RC	.35
35	Magglio Ordonez	.30
36	Frank Thomas	1.50
37	Mike Cameron	.15
38	Sean Casey	.35
39	Barry Larkin	.15
40	Greg Vaughn	.15
41	Roberto Alomar	.15
42	Sandy Alomar Jr.	.15
43	David Justice	.15
44	Kenny Lofton	.15
45	Manny Ramirez	1.00
46	Richie Sexson	.15
47	Jim Thome	.65
48	Dante Bichette	.15
49	Vinny Castilla	.15
50	Darryl Hamilton	.15
51	Todd Helton	.15

#	Player	Price
52	Larry Walker	.15
53	Tony Clark	.15
54	Damion Easley	.15
55	Bob Higginson	.15
56	Gabe Kapler/SP	.25
57	Alex Gonzalez/SP **RC**	.35
58	Mark Kotsay	.15
59	Kevin Orie	.15
60	Preston Wilson/SP	1.00
61	Jeff Bagwell	1.00
62	Derek Bell	.15
63	Craig Biggio	.15
64	Ken Caminiti	.15
65	Carlos Beltran/SP	.65
66	Johnny Damon	.35
67	Jermaine Dye	.15
68	Carlos Febles/SP	.15
69	Kevin Brown	.15
70	Todd Hundley	.15
71	Eric Karros	.15
72	Raul Mondesi	.15
73	Gary Sheffield	.45
74	Jeromy Burnitz	.15
75	Jeff Cirillo	.15
76	Marquis Grissom	.15
77	Fernando Vina	.15
78	Chad Allen/SP **RC**	.25
79	Corey Koskie/SP **RC**	1.50
80	Doug Mientkiewicz/ SP **RC**	1.00
81	Brad Radke	.15
82	Todd Walker	.15
83	Michael Barrett/SP **RC**	.35
84	Vladimir Guerrero	1.00
85	Wilton Guerrero	.15
86	Guillermo Mota/SP **RC**	.35
87	Rondell White	.15
88	Edgardo Alfonzo	.15
89	Rickey Henderson	1.00
90	John Olerud	.15
91	Mike Piazza	2.00
92	Robin Ventura	.15
93	Roger Clemens	2.00
94	Chili Davis	.15
95	Derek Jeter	4.00
96	Chuck Knoblauch	.15
97	Tino Martinez	.15
98	Paul O'Neill	.15
99	Bernie Williams	.15
100	Eric Chavez/SP	.35
101	Jason Giambi	.65
102	Ben Grieve	.15
103	John Jaha	.15
104	Olmedo Saenz/SP **RC**	.15
105	Bobby Abreu	.25
106	Doug Glanville	.15
107	Desi Relaford	.15
108	Scott Rolen	.75
109	Curt Schilling	.35
110	Brian Giles	.15
111	Jason Kendall	.15
112	Pat Meares	.15
113	Kevin Young	.15
114	J.D. Drew/SP	1.00
115	Ray Lankford	.15
116	Eli Marrero	.15
117	Joe McEwing/SP **RC**	.35
118	Mark McGwire	3.00
119	Fernando Tatis	.15
120	Tony Gwynn	1.50
121	Trevor Hoffman	.15
122	Wally Joyner	.15
123	Reggie Sanders	.15
124	Barry Bonds	4.00
125	Ellis Burks	.15
126	Jeff Kent	.15
127	Ramon Martinez/SP **RC**	.25
128	Joe Nathan/SP **RC**	.25
129	Freddy Garcia/SP **RC**	1.00
130	Ken Griffey Jr.	2.50
131	Brian Hunter	.15
132	Edgar Martinez	.15
133	Alex Rodriguez	3.00
134	David Segui	.15
135	Wade Boggs	1.50
136	Jose Canseco	.45
137	Quinton McCracken	.15
138	Fred McGriff	.15
139	Kelly Dransfeldt/SP **RC**	.25
140	Juan Gonzalez	.50
141	Rusty Greer	.15
142	Rafael Palmeiro	.75
143	Ivan Rodriguez	.75
144	Lee Stevens	.15
145	Jose Cruz Jr.	.15
146	Carlos Delgado	.60
147	Shawn Green	.50
148	Roy Halladay/SP **RC**	1.50
149	Shannon Stewart	.15
150	Kevin Witt/SP **RC**	.35

Shadow

This hobby-only parallel insert features blue metallic-foil background and graphics on front. Backs are identical to the base version except they include a dot-matrix applied serial number at left within an edition of 99.

	NM/M
Common Player:	4.00
Stars:	6X
SP's:	3X

Diamond Legacy

This 36-card set features a holographic patterned foil card front. Card backs have a small close-up photo along with a career note. These were seeded 2:25 packs.

		NM/M
Complete Set (36):		60.00
Common Player:		.50
Inserted 2:25		
1	Troy Glaus	2.00
2	Mo Vaughn	.50
3	Matt Williams	.50
4	Chipper Jones	3.00
5	Andruw Jones	2.00
6	Greg Maddux	3.00
7	Albert Belle	.50
8	Cal Ripken Jr.	6.00
9	Nomar Garciaparra	3.00
10	Sammy Sosa	3.00
11	Frank Thomas	2.00
12	Manny Ramirez	2.00
13	Todd Helton	2.00
14	Larry Walker	.50
15	Gabe Kapler	.50
16	Jeff Bagwell	2.00
17	Craig Biggio	.50
18	Raul Mondesi	.50
19	Vladimir Guerrero	2.00
20	Mike Piazza	3.50
21	Roger Clemens	3.50
22	Derek Jeter	6.00
23	Bernie Williams	.50
24	Ben Grieve	.50
25	Scott Rolen	1.75
26	J.D. Drew	1.50
27	Mark McGwire	5.00
28	Fernando Tatis	.50
29	Tony Gwynn	3.00
30	Barry Bonds	6.00
31	Ken Griffey Jr.	4.00
32	Alex Rodriguez	5.00
33	Jose Canseco	1.25
34	Juan Gonzalez	1.00
35	Ivan Rodriguez	1.75
36	Shawn Green	1.50

Foul Pole

This 20-card set features netting down the right side of each card, with the player photo on the left side. The player name, position and logo are stamped with gold foil. These were seeded 1:49 packs.

		NM/M
Complete Set (20):		100.00
Common Player:		1.50
Inserted 1:49		
1	Chipper Jones	8.00
2	Andruw Jones	6.00
3	Cal Ripken Jr.	16.00
4	Nomar Garciaparra	8.00
5	Sammy Sosa	8.00
6	Frank Thomas	6.00
7	Manny Ramirez	6.00
8	Jeff Bagwell	6.00
9	Raul Mondesi	1.50
10	Vladimir Guerrero	6.00
11	Mike Piazza	9.00
12	Derek Jeter	16.00
13	Bernie Williams	1.50
14	Scott Rolen	5.00
15	J.D. Drew	3.00
16	Mark McGwire	12.00
17	Tony Gwynn	8.00
18	Ken Griffey Jr.	10.00
19	Alex Rodriguez	12.00
20	Juan Gonzalez	3.00

Icons

This 10-card set spotlights the top players, each card is die-cut in the shape of a shield with silver foil etching and stamping. These were seeded 1:121 packs.

		NM/M
Complete Set (10):		50.00
Common Player:		4.00
Inserted 1:121		
1	Cal Ripken Jr.	10.00
2	Nomar Garciaparra	5.00
3	Sammy Sosa	5.00
4	Frank Thomas	4.00
5	Mike Piazza	6.50
6	Derek Jeter	10.00
7	Mark McGwire	8.00
8	Tony Gwynn	5.00
9	Ken Griffey Jr.	7.50
10	Alex Rodriguez	8.00

Thorn in the Side

This 20-card set features full holographic silver foil and is die-cut in the upper right portion. Card backs analyzes the featured player's success against a certain opponent over the years. These were seeded 1:25 packs.

		NM/M
Complete Set (20):		35.00
Common Player:		1.00
Inserted 1:25		
1	Mo Vaughn	1.00
2	Chipper Jones	3.00
3	Greg Maddux	3.00
4	Cal Ripken Jr.	6.00
5	Nomar Garciaparra	3.00
6	Sammy Sosa	3.00
7	Frank Thomas	2.25
8	Manny Ramirez	2.25
9	Jeff Bagwell	2.25
10	Mike Piazza	3.50
11	Derek Jeter	6.00
12	Bernie Williams	1.00
13	J.D. Drew	1.50
14	Mark McGwire	4.50
15	Tony Gwynn	3.00
16	Barry Bonds	6.00
17	Ken Griffey Jr.	4.00
18	Alex Rodriguez	4.50
19	Juan Gonzalez	1.50
20	Ivan Rodriguez	2.00

Tripleheader

This 30-card set features spotted gold foil blotching around the player image with the name, postion, team and logo stamped in gold foil. These were seeded 4:25 hobby packs. The set is also broken down into three separate tiers of 10 cards. Tier 1 (cards 1-10) are limited to 99 numbered sets. Tier 2 (11-20) 199 numbered sets and Tier 3 (21-30) 299 numbered sets.

		NM/M
Complete Set (30):		30.00
Common Player:		.25
Inserted 4:25 H		
Tier 1 (1-10)		
Production 99 Sets H		
Tier 2 (11-20)		
Production 199 Sets H		
Tier 3 (21-30)		
Production 299 Sets H		
1	Greg Maddux	1.50
2	Cal Ripken Jr.	3.00
3	Nomar Garciaparra	1.50
4	Sammy Sosa	1.50
5	Frank Thomas	1.00
6	Mike Piazza	1.75
7	Mark McGwire	2.50
8	Tony Gwynn	1.50
9	Ken Griffey Jr.	2.00
10	Alex Rodriguez	2.50
11	Mo Vaughn	.25
12	Chipper Jones	1.50
13	Manny Ramirez	1.00
14	Larry Walker	.25
15	Jeff Bagwell	1.00
16	Vladimir Guerrero	1.00
17	Derek Jeter	3.00
18	J.D. Drew	.60
19	Barry Bonds	3.00
20	Juan Gonzalez	.50
21	Troy Glaus	1.00
22	Andruw Jones	1.00
23	Matt Williams	.25
24	Craig Biggio	.25
25	Raul Mondesi	.25
26	Roger Clemens	1.75
27	Bernie Williams	.25
28	Scott Rolen	.75
29	Jose Canseco	.50
30	Ivan Rodriguez	.75

2000 Pacific Sample

Tony Gwynn was once again the spokesman for Pacific's 2000 line-up of baseball cards products. To showcase its base brand for the year, Pacific produced this sample card, so overprinted and "numbered" on back, but otherwise virtually identical to the issued version.

	NM/M
SAMPLE Tony Gwynn	3.00

2000 Pacific

The base set consists of 500-cards with the Pacific logo and player name stamped in silver foil on the card front. Card backs have a small photo along with complete career statistics and a brief career highlight. 50 players in the base set also have another version and are priced equally.

		NM/M
Complete Set (500):		60.00
Common Player:		.10
Pack (12):		1.50
Wax Box (24):		25.00
1	Garret Anderson	.15
2	Tim Belcher	.10
3	Gary DiSarcina	.10
4	Trent Durrington	.10
5	Jim Edmonds	.15
6a	Darin Erstad/Action	.35
6b	Darin Erstad/Portrait	.35
7	Chuck Finley	.10
8	Troy Glaus	.75
9	Todd Greene	.10
10	Bret Hemphill	.10
11	Ken Hill	.10
12	Ramon Ortiz	.10
13	Troy Percival	.10
14	Mark Petkovsek	.10
15	Tim Salmon	.20
16a	Mo Vaughn	.15
16b	Mo Vaughn/Portrait	.15
17	Jay Bell	.10
18	Omar Daal	.10
19	Erubiel Durazo	.10
20	Steve Finley	.10
21	Bernard Gilkey	.10
22	Luis Gonzalez	.20
23	Randy Johnson	.75
24	Byung-Hyun Kim	.10
25	Travis Lee	.10
26	Matt Mantei	.10
27	Armando Reynoso	.10
28	Rob Ryan	.10
29	Kelly Stinnett	.10
30	Todd Stottlemyre	.10
31a	Matt Williams/Action	.15
31b	Matt Williams/Portrait	.15
32	Tony Womack	.10
33	Bret Boone	.10
34	Andres Galarraga	.15
35	Tom Glavine	.35
36	Ozzie Guillen	.10
37a	Andruw Jones/Action	.75
37b	Andruw Jones/Portrait	.75
38a	Chipper Jones/Action	1.00
38b	Chipper Jones/Portrait	1.00
39	Brian Jordan	.10
40	Ryan Klesko	.15
41	Javy Lopez	.15
42a	Greg Maddux/Action	1.00
42b	Greg Maddux/Portrait	1.00
43	Kevin Millwood	.15
44	John Rocker	.10
45	Randall Simon	.10
46	John Smoltz	.15
47	Gerald Williams	.10
48	Brady Anderson	.15
49a	Albert Belle/Action	.15
49b	Albert Belle/Portrait	.15
50	Mike Bordick	.10
51	Will Clark	.25
52	Jeff Conine	.10
53	Delino DeShields	.10
54	Jerry Hairston Jr.	.10
55	Charles Johnson	.10
56	Eugene Kingsale	.10
57	Ryan Minor	.10
58	Mike Mussina	.35
59	Sidney Ponson	.10
60a	Cal Ripken Jr./Action	2.50
60b	Cal Ripken Jr./Portrait	2.50
61	B.J. Surhoff	.10
62	Mike Timlin	.10
63	Rod Beck	.10
64a	Nomar Garciaparra/ Action	1.50
64b	Nomar Garciaparra/ Portrait	1.50
65	Tom Gordon	.10
66	Butch Huskey	.10
67	Derek Lowe	.10
68a	Pedro Martinez/Action	.75
68b	Pedro Martinez/Portrait	.75
69	Trot Nixon	.10
70	Jose Offerman	.10
71	Troy O'Leary	.10
72	Pat Rapp	.10
73	Donnie Sadler	.10
74	Mike Stanley	.10
75	John Valentin	.10
76	Jason Varitek	.10
77	Wilton Veras	.10
78	Tim Wakefield	.10
79	Rick Aguilera	.10
80	Manny Alexander	.10
81	Roosevelt Brown	.10
82	Mark Grace	.20
83	Glenallen Hill	.10
84	Lance Johnson	.10
85	Jon Lieber	.10
86	Cole Liniak	.10
87	Chad Meyers	.10
88	Mickey Morandini	.10
89	Jose Nieves	.10
90	Henry Rodriguez	.10
91a	Sammy Sosa/Action	1.50
91b	Sammy Sosa/Portrait	1.50
92	Kevin Tapani	.10
93	Kerry Wood	.50
94	Mike Caruso	.10
95	Ray Durham	.10
96	Brook Fordyce	.10
97	Bobby Howry	.10
98	Paul Konerko	.25
99	Carlos Lee	.10
100	Aaron Myette	.10
101	Greg Norton	.10
102	Magglio Ordonez	.25
103	Jim Parque	.10
104	Liu Rodriguez	.10
105	Chris Singleton	.10
106	Mike Sirotka	.10
107a	Frank Thomas/Action	.75
107b	Frank Thomas/Portrait	.75
108	Kip Wells	.10
109	Aaron Boone	.10
110	Mike Cameron	.10
111a	Sean Casey/Action	.20
111b	Sean Casey/Portrait	.20
112	Jeffrey Hammonds	.10
113	Pete Harnisch	.10
114a	Barry Larkin/Portrait	.15
114b	Barry Larkin/Portrait	.15
115	Jason LaRue	.10
116	Denny Neagle	.10
117	Pokey Reese	.10
118	Scott Sullivan	.10
119	Eddie Taubensee	.10
120	Greg Vaughn	.10
121	Scott Williamson	.10
122	Dmitri Young	.10
123a	Roberto Alomar/Action	.35
123b	Roberto Alomar/Portrait	.35
124	Sandy Alomar Jr.	.10
125	Harold Baines	.10
126	Russell Branyan	.10
127	Dave Burba	.10
128	Bartolo Colon	.10
129	Travis Fryman	.15
130	Mike Jackson	.10
131	David Justice	.15
132a	Kenny Lofton/Action	.15
132b	Kenny Lofton/Portrait	.15
133	Charles Nagy	.10
134a	Manny Ramirez/Action	.75
134b	Manny Ramirez/Portrait	.75
135	Dave Roberts	.10
136	Richie Sexson	.15
137	Jim Thome	.60
138	Omar Vizquel	.15
139	Jaret Wright	.10
140	Pedro Astacio	.10
141	Dante Bichette	.10
142	Brian Bohanon	.10
143a	Vinny Castilla/Action	.10
143b	Vinny Castilla/Portrait	.10
144	Edgard Clemente	.10
145	Derrick Gibson	.10
146	Todd Helton	.75
147	Darryl Kile	.10
148	Mike Lansing	.10
149	Kirt Manwaring	.10
150	Neifi Perez	.10
151	Ben Petrick	.10
152	Juan Sosa **RC**	.20
153	Dave Veres	.10
154a	Larry Walker/Action	.15
154b	Larry Walker/Portrait	.15
155	Brad Ausmus	.10
156	Dave Borkowski	.10
157	Tony Clark	.10
158	Francisco Cordero	.10
159	Deivi Cruz	.10
160	Damion Easley	.10
161	Juan Encarnacion	.10
162	Robert Fick	.10
163	Bobby Higginson	.10
164	Gabe Kapler	.15
165	Brian Moehler	.10
166	Dean Palmer	.10
167	Luis Polonia	.10
168	Justin Thompson	.10
169	Jeff Weaver	.10
170	Antonio Alfonseca	.10
171	Bruce Aven	.10
172	A.J. Burnett	.10
173	Luis Castillo	.10
174	Ramon Castro	.10
175	Ryan Dempster	.10
176	Alex Fernandez	.10
177	Cliff Floyd	.10
178	Amaury Garcia	.10
179	Alex Gonzalez	.10
180	Mark Kotsay	.10
181	Mike Lowell	.15
182	Brian Meadows	.10
183	Kevin Orie	.10
184	Julio Ramirez	.10
185	Preston Wilson	.15
186	Moises Alou	.15
187a	Jeff Bagwell/Action	.75
187b	Jeff Bagwell/Portrait	.75
188	Glen Barker	.10
189	Derek Bell	.10
190a	Craig Biggio/Action	.15
190b	Craig Biggio/Portrait	.15
191	Ken Caminiti	.10
192	Scott Elarton	.10
193	Carl Everett	.10
194	Mike Hampton	.10
195	Carlos Hernandez	.10
196	Richard Hidalgo	.10
197	Jose Lima	.10

#	Player	Price
198	Shane Reynolds	.15
199	Bill Spiers	.10
200	Billy Wagner	.15
201a	Carlos Beltran/Action	.50
201b	Carlos Beltran/Portrait	.50
202	Dermal Brown	.10
203	Johnny Damon	.25
204	Jermaine Dye	.10
205	Carlos Febles	.10
206	Jeremy Giambi	.10
207	Mark Quinn	.10
208	Joe Randa	.10
209	Dan Reichert	.10
210	Jose Rosado	.10
211	Rey Sanchez	.10
212	Jeff Suppan	.10
213	Mike Sweeney	.10
214a	Kevin Brown/Action	.15
214b	Kevin Brown/Portrait	.15
215	Darren Dreifort	.10
216	Eric Gagne	.10
217	Mark Grudzielanek	.10
218	Todd Hollandsworth	.10
219	Todd Hundley	.10
220	Eric Karros	.15
221	Raul Mondesi	.15
222	Chan Ho Park	.10
223	Jeff Shaw	.10
224a	Gary Sheffield/Action	.30
224b	Gary Sheffield/Portrait	.30
225	Ismael Valdes	.10
226	Devon White	.10
227	Eric Young	.10
228	Kevin Barker	.10
229	Ron Belliard	.10
230a	Jeromy Burnitz/Action	.10
230b	Jeromy Burnitz/Portrait	.10
231	Jeff Cirillo	.10
232	Marquis Grissom	.10
233	Geoff Jenkins	.10
234	Mark Loretta	.10
235	David Nilsson	.10
236	Hideo Nomo	.75
237	Alex Ochoa	.10
238	Kyle Peterson	.10
239	Fernando Vina	.10
240	Bob Wickman	.10
241	Steve Woodard	.10
242	Chad Allen	.10
243	Ron Coomer	.10
244	Marty Cordova	.10
245	Cristian Guzman	.10
246	Denny Hocking	.10
247	Jacque Jones	.10
248	Corey Koskie	.10
249	Matt Lawton	.10
250	Joe Mays	.10
251	Eric Milton	.10
252	Brad Radke	.10
253	Mark Redman	.10
254	Terry Steinbach	.10
255	Todd Walker	.10
256	Tony Armas Jr.	.10
257	Michael Barrett	.10
258	Peter Bergeron	.10
259	Geoff Blum	.10
260	Orlando Cabrera	.10
261	Trace Coquillette RC	.15
262	Brad Fullmer	.10
263a	Vladimir Guerrero/Action	.75
263b	Vladimir Guerrero/Portrait	.75
264	Wilton Guerrero	.10
265	Dustin Hermanson	.10
266	Manny Martinez	.10
267	Ryan McGuire	.10
268	Ugueth Urbina	.10
269	Jose Vidro	.10
270	Rondell White	.15
271	Chris Widger	.10
272	Edgardo Alfonzo	.15
273	Armando Benitez	.10
274	Roger Cedeno	.10
275	Dennis Cook	.10
276	Octavio Dotel	.10
277	John Franco	.10
278	Darryl Hamilton	.10
279	Rickey Henderson	.75
280	Orel Hershiser	.10
281	Al Leiter	.15
282a	John Olerud/Action	.15
282b	John Olerud/Portrait	.15
283	Rey Ordonez	.10
284a	Mike Piazza/Action	1.50
284b	Mike Piazza/Portrait	1.50
285	Kenny Rogers	.10
286	Jorge Toca	.10
287	Robin Ventura	.15
288	Scott Brosius	.10
289a	Roger Clemens/Action	1.25
289b	Roger Clemens/Portrait	1.25
290	David Cone	.15
291	Chili Davis	.10
292	Orlando Hernandez	.15
293	Hideki Irabu	.10
294a	Derek Jeter/Action	2.50
294b	Derek Jeter/Portrait	2.50
295	Chuck Knoblauch	.10
296	Ricky Ledee	.10
297	Jim Leyritz	.10
298	Tino Martinez	.15
299	Paul O'Neill	.15
300	Andy Pettitte	.25
301	Jorge Posada	.15
302	Mariano Rivera	.25
303	Alfonso Soriano	.75
304a	Bernie Williams/Action	.20
304b	Bernie Williams/Portrait	.20
305	Ed Yarnall	.10
306	Kevin Appier	.10
307	Rich Becker	.10
308	Eric Chavez	.25
309	Jason Giambi	.60
310	Ben Grieve	.10
311	Ramon Hernandez	.10
312	Tim Hudson	.25
313	John Jaha	.10
314	Doug Jones	.10
315	Omar Olivares	.10
316	Mike Oquist	.10
317	Matt Stairs	.10
318	Miguel Tejada	.25
319	Randy Velarde	.10
320	Bobby Abreu	.15
321	Marlon Anderson	.10
322	Alex Arias	.10
323	Rico Brogna	.10
324	Paul Byrd	.10
325	Ron Gant	.10
326	Doug Glanville	.10
327	Wayne Gomes	.10
328	Mike Lieberthal	.10
329	Robert Person	.10
330	Desi Relaford	.10
331a	Scott Rolen/Action	.60
331b	Scott Rolen/Portrait	.60
332a	Curt Schilling/Action	.35
332b	Curt Schilling/Portrait	.35
333	Kris Benson	.10
334	Adrian Brown	.10
335	Brant Brown	.10
336	Brian Giles	.15
337	Chad Hermansen	.10
338	Jason Kendall	.15
339	Al Martin	.10
340	Pat Meares	.10
341a	Warren Morris/Action	.10
341b	Warren Morris/Portrait	.10
342	Todd Ritchie	.10
343	Jason Schmidt	.10
344	Ed Sprague	.10
345	Mike Williams	.10
346	Kevin Young	.10
347	Rick Ankiel	.25
348	Ricky Bottalico	.10
349	Kent Bottenfield	.10
350	Darren Bragg	.10
351	Eric Davis	.15
352a	J.D. Drew/Action	.35
352b	J.D. Drew/Portrait	.35
353	Adam Kennedy	.15
354	Ray Lankford	.10
355	Joe McEwing	.10
356a	Mark McGwire/Action	2.00
356b	Mark McGwire/Portrait	2.00
357	Matt Morris	.10
358	Darren Oliver	.10
359	Edgar Renteria	.10
360	Fernando Tatis	.10
361	Andy Ashby	.10
362	Ben Davis	.10
363a	Tony Gwynn/Action	1.00
363b	Tony Gwynn/Portrait	1.00
364	Sterling Hitchcock	.10
365	Trevor Hoffman	.10
366	Damian Jackson	.10
367	Wally Joyner	.10
368	Dave Magadan	.10
369	Gary Matthews Jr.	.10
370	Phil Nevin	.10
371	Eric Owens	.10
372	Ruben Rivera	.10
373a	Reggie Sanders/Action	.10
373b	Reggie Sanders/Portrait	.10
374	Quilvio Veras	.10
375	Rich Aurilia	.10
376	Marvin Benard	.10
377a	Barry Bonds/Action	2.50
377b	Barry Bonds/Portrait	2.50
378	Ellis Burks	.10
379	Shawn Estes	.10
380	Livan Hernandez	.10
381a	Jeff Kent/Action	.15
381b	Jeff Kent/Portrait	.15
382	Brent Mayne	.10
383	Bill Mueller	.10
384	Calvin Murray	.10
385	Robb Nen	.10
386	Russ Ortiz	.10
387	Kirk Rueter	.10
388	J.T. Snow	.10
389	David Bell	.10
390	Jay Buhner	.15
391	Russ Davis	.10
392a	Freddy Garcia/Action	.10
392b	Freddy Garcia/Portrait	.10
393a	Ken Griffey Jr./Action	1.50
393b	Ken Griffey Jr./Portrait	1.50
394	Carlos Guillen	.10
395	John Halama	.10
396	Brian Hunter	.10
397	Ryan Jackson	.10
398	Edgar Martinez	.15
399	Gil Meche	.10
400	Jose Mesa	.10
401	Jamie Moyer	.10
402a	Alex Rodriguez/Action	2.00
402b	Alex Rodriguez/Portrait	2.00
403	Dan Wilson	.10
404	Wilson Alvarez	.10
405	Rolando Arrojo	.10
406a	Wade Boggs/Action	1.00
406b	Wade Boggs/Portrait	1.00
407	Miguel Cairo	.10
408a	Jose Canseco/Action	.40
408b	Jose Canseco/Portrait	.40
409	John Flaherty	.10
410	Jose Guillen	.10
411	Roberto Hernandez	.10
412	Terrell Lowery	.10
413	Dave Martinez	.10
414	Quinton McCracken	.10
415a	Fred McGriff/Action	.15
415b	Fred McGriff/Portrait	.15
416	Ryan Rupe	.10
417	Kevin Stocker	.10
418	Bubba Trammell	.10
419	Royce Clayton	.10
420a	Juan Gonzalez/Action	.75
420b	Juan Gonzalez/Portrait	.75
421	Tom Goodwin	.10
422	Rusty Greer	.10
423	Rick Helling	.10
424	Roberto Kelly	.10
425	Ruben Mateo	.10
426	Mark McLemore	.10
427	Mike Morgan	.10
428	Rafael Palmeiro	.65
429a	Ivan Rodriguez/Action	.65
429b	Ivan Rodriguez/Portrait	.65
430	Aaron Sele	.10
431	Lee Stevens	.10
432	John Wetteland	.10
433	Todd Zeile	.10
434	Jeff Zimmerman	.10
435	Tony Batista	.10
436	Casey Blake	.10
437	Homer Bush	.10
438	Chris Carpenter	.10
439	Jose Cruz Jr.	.10
440a	Carlos Delgado/Action	.50
440b	Carlos Delgado/Portrait	.50
441	Tony Fernandez	.10
442	Darrin Fletcher	.10
443	Alex Gonzalez	.10
444a	Shawn Green/Action	.35
444b	Shawn Green/Portrait	.35
445	Roy Halladay	.20
446	Billy Koch	.10
447	David Segui	.10
448	Shannon Stewart	.10
449	David Wells	.10
450	Vernon Wells	.15

Copper

Coppers are a parallel set to the 500-card base set and are identical to the base cards besides the copper foil stamping. Inserted exclusively in hobby packs Coppers are limited to 99 serial numbered sets.

	NM/M
Common Copper:	5.00
Stars:	4-8X
Production 99 Sets	

Platinum Blue

A parallel to the 500-card base set these have identical photos as the regular cards besides platinum blue foil stamping. A total of 75 serial numbered sets were produced.

	NM/M
Common Player:	8.00
Stars:	6-10X
Production 75 Sets	

Premiere Date

A parallel to the 500-card base set these are sequentially numbered to 37 sets.

	NM/M
Common Player:	15.00
Stars:	8X to15X
Production 37 Sets	

Ruby Red (Seven-11)

This parallel to the base set of 2000 Pacific was available only in 10-card retail "Jewel Collection" packs at Seven-11 convenience stores. Other than the use of red metallic foil for the player name and Pacific logo, the cards are identical to the regular-issue version.

	NM/M
Complete Set (500):	65.00
Common Player:	.15
Stars/Rookies	1.5X

Command Performers

		NM/M
Complete Set (20):		45.00
Common Player:		1.00
Inserted 1:24 Retail		
1	Chipper Jones	3.00
2	Greg Maddux	3.00
3	Cal Ripken Jr.	6.00
4	Nomar Garciaparra	4.00
5	Sammy Sosa	4.00
6	Sean Casey	1.00
7	Manny Ramirez	2.00
8	Larry Walker	1.00
9	Jeff Bagwell	2.00
10	Vladimir Guerrero	2.00
11	Mike Piazza	4.00
12	Roger Clemens	3.50
13	Derek Jeter	6.00
14	Mark McGwire	6.00
15	Tony Gwynn	3.00
16	Barry Bonds	6.00
17	Ken Griffey Jr.	4.00
18	Alex Rodriguez	5.00
19	Ivan Rodriguez	1.50
20	Shawn Green	1.25

Cramer's Choice Awards

This die-cut set is shaped in a trophy-like design on a holographic silver foil design. Cramer's Choice are seeded 1:721 packs.

		NM/M
Complete Set (10):		300.00
Common Player:		25.00
Inserted 1:721		
1	Chipper Jones	25.00
2	Cal Ripken Jr.	50.00
3	Nomar Garciaparra	30.00
4	Sammy Sosa	30.00
5	Mike Piazza	30.00
6	Derek Jeter	50.00
7	Mark McGwire	40.00
8	Tony Gwynn	25.00
9	Ken Griffey Jr.	30.00
10	Alex Rodriguez	40.00

Diamond Leaders

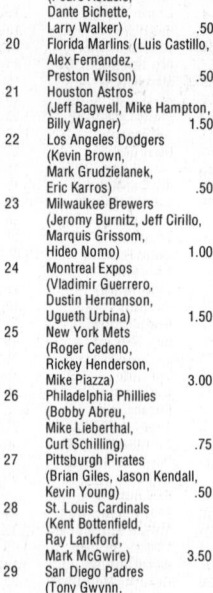

Designed on a horizontal format each card features three statistical leaders from the 1999 season for each respective team. Card fronts have gold holofoil stamping while card backs give statistical leaders for eight categories for the featured team. These were seeded 2:25 packs.

		NM/M
Complete Set (30):		25.00
Common Card:		.50
Inserted 2:25		
1	Anaheim Angels (Garret Anderson, Chuck Finley, Troy Percival, Mo Vaughn)	.50
2	Baltimore Orioles (Albert Belle, Mike Mussina, B.J. Surhoff)	.50
3	Boston Red Sox (Nomar Garciaparra, Pedro J. Martinez, Troy O'Leary)	3.00
4	Chicago White Sox (Ray Durham, Magglio Ordonez, Frank Thomas)	1.50
5	Cleveland Indians (Bartolo Colon, Manny Ramirez, Omar Vizquel)	1.50
6	Detroit Tigers (Deivi Cruz, Dave Mlicki, David Palmer)	.50
7	Kansas City Royals (Johnny Damon, Jermaine Dye, Jose Rosado, Mike Sweeney)	.50
8	Minnesota Twins (Corey Koskie, Eric Milton, Brad Radke)	.50
9	New York Yankees (Orlando Hernandez, Derek Jeter, Mariano Rivera, Bernie Williams)	4.00
10	Oakland Athletics (Jeremy Giambi, Tim Hudson, Matt Stairs)	1.00
11	Seattle Mariners (Freddy Garcia, Ken Griffey Jr., Edgar Martinez)	3.00
12	Tampa Bay Devil Rays (Jose Canseco, Roberto Hernandez, Fred McGriff)	.75
13	Texas Rangers (Rafael Palmeiro, Ivan Rodriguez, John Wetteland)	1.00
14	Toronto Blue Jays (Carlos Delgado, Shannon Stewart, David Wells)	1.00
15	Arizona Diamondbacks (Luis Gonzalez, Randy Johnson, Matt Williams)	1.50
16	Atlanta Braves (Chipper Jones, Brian Jordan, Greg Maddux)	2.00
17	Chicago Cubs (Mark Grace, Jon Lieber, Sammy Sosa)	3.00
18	Cincinnati Reds (Sean Casey, Pete Harnisch, Greg Vaughn)	.50
19	Colorado Rockies (Pedro Astacio, Dante Bichette, Larry Walker)	.50
20	Florida Marlins (Luis Castillo, Alex Fernandez, Preston Wilson)	.50
21	Houston Astros (Jeff Bagwell, Mike Hampton, Billy Wagner)	1.50
22	Los Angeles Dodgers (Kevin Brown, Mark Grudzielanek, Eric Karros)	.50
23	Milwaukee Brewers (Jeromy Burnitz, Jeff Cirillo, Marquis Grissom, Hideo Nomo)	1.00
24	Montreal Expos (Vladimir Guerrero, Dustin Hermanson, Ugueth Urbina)	1.50
25	New York Mets (Roger Cedeno, Rickey Henderson, Mike Piazza)	3.00
26	Philadelphia Phillies (Bobby Abreu, Mike Lieberthal, Curt Schilling)	.75
27	Pittsburgh Pirates (Brian Giles, Jason Kendall, Kevin Young)	.50
28	St. Louis Cardinals (Kent Bottenfield, Ray Lankford, Mark McGwire)	3.50
29	San Diego Padres (Tony Gwynn, Trevor Hoffman, Reggie Sanders)	2.00
30	San Francisco Giants (Barry Bonds, Jeff Kent, Russ Ortiz)	4.00

Gold Crown Die-Cuts

Printed on a 24-point stock this set features Pacific's classic crown shaped design on a dual foiled holographic gold and silver stock. These were seeded 1:25 packs.

		NM/M
Complete Set (36):		150.00
Common Player:		1.50
Inserted 1:25		
1	Mo Vaughn	1.50
2	Matt Williams	1.50
3	Andruw Jones	6.00
4	Chipper Jones	8.00
5	Greg Maddux	8.00
6	Cal Ripken Jr.	15.00
7	Nomar Garciaparra	10.00
8	Pedro Martinez	6.00
9	Sammy Sosa	10.00
10	Magglio Ordonez	2.50
11	Frank Thomas	6.00
12	Sean Casey	1.50
13	Roberto Alomar	2.00
14	Manny Ramirez	6.00
15	Larry Walker	1.50
16	Jeff Bagwell	6.00
17	Craig Biggio	1.50
18	Carlos Beltran	4.00
19	Vladimir Guerrero	6.00
20	Mike Piazza	10.00
21	Roger Clemens	9.00
22	Derek Jeter	15.00
23	Bernie Williams	2.00
24	Scott Rolen	5.00
25	Warren Morris	1.50
26	J.D. Drew	2.00
27	Mark McGwire	12.00
28	Tony Gwynn	8.00
29	Barry Bonds	15.00
30	Ken Griffey Jr.	10.00
31	Alex Rodriguez	12.00
32	Jose Canseco	6.00
33	Juan Gonzalez	6.00
34	Rafael Palmeiro	5.00
35	Ivan Rodriguez	5.00
36	Shawn Green	3.00

Reflections

This 20-card die-cut set features a unique sunglasses-on-cap design utilizing cel technology for added effect on the sunglasses portion of the insert. The backs have a small photo of the featured player. These were seeded 1:97 packs.

		NM/M
Common Player:		3.00
Inserted 1:97		
1	Andruw Jones	6.00
2	Chipper Jones	8.00
3	Cal Ripken Jr.	20.00
4	Nomar Garciaparra	12.00
5	Sammy Sosa	12.00
6	Frank Thomas	6.00
7	Manny Ramirez	6.00
8	Jeff Bagwell	6.00
9	Vladimir Guerrero	6.00
10	Mike Piazza	12.00
11	Derek Jeter	20.00
12	Bernie Williams	3.00
13	Scott Rolen	5.00
14	J.D. Drew	3.00
15	Mark McGwire	15.00
16	Tony Gwynn	8.00
17	Ken Griffey Jr.	12.00
18	Alex Rodriguez	15.00
19	Juan Gonzalez	6.00
20	Ivan Rodriguez	5.00

Past & Present

Inserted exclusively in hobby packs at a rate of 1:49, these inserts have a silver prism front and a cardboard textured back. The fronts have a current photo of the player while the backs have a photo taken years before.

		NM/M
Complete Set (20):		80.00
Common Player:		1.50
Inserted 1:49 H		
1	Chipper Jones	5.00
2	Greg Maddux	5.00
3	Cal Ripken Jr.	10.00
4	Nomar Garciaparra	6.00
5	Pedro Martinez	4.00
6	Sammy Sosa	6.00
7	Frank Thomas	4.00
8	Manny Ramirez	4.00
9	Larry Walker	1.50
10	Jeff Bagwell	4.00
11	Mike Piazza	6.00
12	Roger Clemens	5.50
13	Derek Jeter	10.00
14	Mark McGwire	8.00
15	Tony Gwynn	5.00
16	Barry Bonds	10.00
17	Ken Griffey Jr.	6.00
18	Alex Rodriguez	8.00
19	Wade Boggs	5.00
20	Ivan Rodriguez	3.00

Ornaments

This 20-card set features a number of different Christmas patterned die-cut shapes, including ornaments, wreaths and Christmas trees. Each card comes with a string intended to hang from a tree on a holographic foil design. These were seeded 2:25 packs.

		NM/M
Complete Set (20):		40.00
Common Player:		1.00
Inserted 2:25		
1	Mo Vaughn	1.00
2	Chipper Jones	3.00
3	Greg Maddux	3.00
4	Cal Ripken Jr.	6.00
5	Nomar Garciaparra	4.00
6	Sammy Sosa	4.00
7	Frank Thomas	2.00
8	Manny Ramirez	2.00
9	Larry Walker	1.00
10	Jeff Bagwell	2.00
11	Mike Piazza	4.00
12	Roger Clemens	3.50
13	Derek Jeter	6.00
14	Scott Rolen	1.50
15	J.D. Drew	1.25
16	Mark McGwire	5.00
17	Tony Gwynn	4.00
18	Ken Griffey Jr.	3.00
19	Alex Rodriguez	5.00
20	Ivan Rodriguez	1.50

2000 Pacific Aurora Sample

Nearly identical to the issued version of spokesman Tony Gwynn's card, this features a large white diagonal "SAMPLE" overprint on back and in the space where a card number usually appears.

	NM/M
Tony Gwynn	3.00

2000 Pacific Aurora

		NM/M
Complete Set (151):		25.00
Common Player:		.15
Pack (10):		2.00
Wax Box (24):		30.00
1	Darin Erstad	.25
2	Troy Glaus	.75
3	Tim Salmon	.25
4	Mo Vaughn	.15
5	Jay Bell	.15
6	Erubiel Durazo	.15
7	Luis Gonzalez	.25
8	Randy Johnson	.75
9	Matt Williams	.15
10	Tom Glavine	.35
11	Andruw Jones	.75
12	Chipper Jones	1.00
13	Brian Jordan	.15
14	Greg Maddux	1.00
15	Kevin Millwood	.15
16	Albert Belle	.15
17	Will Clark	.25
18	Mike Mussina	.35
19	Cal Ripken Jr.	2.50
20	B.J. Surhoff	.15
21	Nomar Garciaparra	1.50
22	Pedro Martinez	.75
23	Troy O'Leary	.15
24	Wilton Veras	.15
25	Mark Grace	.25
26	Henry Rodriguez	.15
27	Sammy Sosa	1.50
28	Kerry Wood	.50
29	Ray Durham	.15
30	Paul Konerko	.25
31	Carlos Lee	.15
32	Magglio Ordonez	.25
33	Chris Singleton	.15
34	Frank Thomas	.75
35	Mike Cameron	.15
36	Sean Casey	.25
37	Barry Larkin	.15
38	Pokey Reese	.15
39	Eddie Taubensee	.15
40	Roberto Alomar	.40
41	David Justice	.15
42	Kenny Lofton	.15
43	Manny Ramirez	.75
44	Richie Sexson	.15
45	Jim Thome	.60
46	Omar Vizquel	.15
47	Todd Helton	.75
48	Mike Lansing	.15
49	Neifi Perez	.15
50	Ben Petrick	.15
51	Larry Walker	.15
52	Tony Clark	.15
53	Damion Easley	.15
54	Juan Encarnacion	.15
55	Juan Gonzalez	.75
56	Dean Palmer	.15
57	Luis Castillo	.15
58	Cliff Floyd	.15
59	Alex Gonzalez	.15
60	Mike Lowell	.15
61	Preston Wilson	.15
62	Jeff Bagwell	.75
63	Craig Biggio	.15
64	Ken Caminiti	.15
65	Jose Lima	.15
66	Billy Wagner	.15
67	Carlos Beltran	.50
68	Johnny Damon	.25
69	Jermaine Dye	.15
70	Mark Quinn	.15
71	Mike Sweeney	.15
72	Kevin Brown	.15
73	Shawn Green	.35
74	Eric Karros	.15
75	Chan Ho Park	.15
76	Gary Sheffield	.40
77	Ron Belliard	.15
78	Jeromy Burnitz	.15
79	Marquis Grissom	.15
80	Geoff Jenkins	.15
81	David Nilsson	.15
82	Ron Coomer	.15
83	Jacque Jones	.15
84	Brad Radke	.15
85	Todd Walker	.15
86	Michael Barrett	.15
87	Peter Bergeron	.15
88	Vladimir Guerrero	.75
89	Jose Vidro	.15
90	Rondell White	.15
91	Edgardo Alfonzo	.15
92	Darryl Hamilton	.15
93	Rey Ordonez	.15
94	Mike Piazza	1.50
95	Robin Ventura	.15
96	Roger Clemens	1.25
97	Orlando Hernandez	.15
98	Derek Jeter	2.50
99	Tino Martinez	.15
100	Mariano Rivera	.25
101	Bernie Williams	.25
102	Eric Chavez	.25
103	Jason Giambi	.60
104	Ben Grieve	.15
105	Tim Hudson	.25
106	John Jaha	.15
107	Matt Stairs	.15
108	Bobby Abreu	.15
109	Doug Glanville	.15
110	Mike Lieberthal	.15
111	Scott Rolen	.60
112	Curt Schilling	.40
113	Brian Giles	.15
114	Chad Hermansen	.15
115	Jason Kendall	.15
116	Warren Morris	.15
117	Kevin Young	.15
118	Rick Ankiel	.25
119	J.D. Drew	.25
120	Ray Lankford	.15
121	Mark McGwire	2.00
122	Edgar Renteria	.15
123	Fernando Tatis	.15
124	Ben Davis	.15
125	Tony Gwynn	1.00
126	Trevor Hoffman	.15
127	Phil Nevin	.15
128	Barry Bonds	2.50
129	Ellis Burks	.15
130	Jeff Kent	.15
131	J.T. Snow	.15
132	Freddy Garcia	.15
133	Ken Griffey Jr.	1.50
133a	Ken Griffey Jr. Reds	2.00
134	Edgar Martinez	.15
135	Alex Rodriguez	2.00
136	Dan Wilson	.15
137	Jose Canseco	.40
138	Roberto Hernandez	.15
139	Dave Martinez	.15
140	Fred McGriff	.15
141	Rusty Greer	.15
142	Ruben Mateo	.15
143	Rafael Palmeiro	.65
144	Ivan Rodriguez	.65
145	Jeff Zimmerman	.15
146	Homer Bush	.15
147	Carlos Delgado	.50
148	Raul Mondesi	.15
149	Shannon Stewart	.15
150	Vernon Wells	.15

Copper

Stars: 2-4X
Production 399 Sets

Platinum Blue

Stars: 5-10X
Production 67 Sets

Silver

Stars: 3-6X
Production 199 Sets

At-Bat Styrotechs

		NM/M
Complete Set (20):		125.00
Common Player:		2.00
Production 299 Sets		
1	Chipper Jones	7.50
2	Cal Ripken Jr.	15.00
3	Nomar Garciaparra	10.00
4	Sammy Sosa	10.00
5	Frank Thomas	6.00
6	Manny Ramirez	6.00
7	Larry Walker	2.00
8	Jeff Bagwell	6.00
9	Carlos Beltran	2.00
10	Vladimir Guerrero	6.00
11	Mike Piazza	10.00
12	Derek Jeter	15.00
13	Bernie Williams	2.00
14	Mark McGwire	12.00
15	Tony Gwynn	7.50
16	Barry Bonds	15.00
17	Ken Griffey Jr.	10.00
18	Alex Rodriguez	12.00
19	Jose Canseco	3.00
20	Ivan Rodriguez	5.00

Dugout View Net-Fusions

Tony Gwynn San Diego Padres™ - OF
In 1999, Tony batted .338 to record his 17th straight season at .300 or better. His rookie year (.821) is the only time Gwynn missed the .300 mark

		NM/M
Complete Set (20):		110.00
Common Player:		2.50
Inserted 1:37		
1	Mo Vaughn	2.50
2	Chipper Jones	8.00
3	Cal Ripken Jr.	15.00
4	Nomar Garciaparra	10.00
5	Sammy Sosa	10.00
6	Manny Ramirez	6.00
7	Larry Walker	2.50
8	Juan Gonzalez	6.00
9	Jeff Bagwell	6.00
10	Craig Biggio	2.50
11	Shawn Green	3.00
12	Vladimir Guerrero	6.00
13	Mike Piazza	10.00
14	Derek Jeter	15.00
15	Scott Rolen	5.00
16	Mark McGwire	12.00
17	Tony Gwynn	8.00
18	Ken Griffey Jr.	10.00
19	Alex Rodriguez	12.00
20	Rafael Palmeiro	4.00

Pennant Fever

		NM/M
Complete Set (20):		25.00
Common Player:		1.00
T. Gwynn Auto./147		75.00
Inserted 4:37		
1	Andruw Jones	1.50
2	Chipper Jones	2.00
3	Greg Maddux	2.00
4	Cal Ripken Jr.	4.00
5	Nomar Garciaparra	2.50
6	Pedro Martinez	1.50
7	Sammy Sosa	2.50
8	Manny Ramirez	1.50
9	Jim Thome	1.50
10	Jeff Bagwell	1.50
11	Mike Piazza	2.50
12	Roger Clemens	2.25
13	Derek Jeter	4.00
14	Bernie Williams	1.00
15	Mark McGwire	3.00
16	Tony Gwynn	2.00
17	Ken Griffey Jr.	2.50
18	Alex Rodriguez	3.00
19	Rafael Palmeiro	1.00
20	Ivan Rodriguez	1.00

Pinstripes

		NM/M
Complete Set (50):		30.00
Common Player:		.25
Premiere Date:		3-6X
Production 51 Sets		
4	Mo Vaughn	1.50
8	Randy Johnson	1.50
11	Matt Williams	.25
12	Andruw Jones	1.50
13	Chipper Jones	2.00
17	Greg Maddux	2.00
19	Cal Ripken Jr.	4.00
21	Nomar Garciaparra	2.50
22	Pedro Martinez	1.50
32	Sammy Sosa	2.50
34	Magglio Ordonez	.35
36	Frank Thomas	1.50
37	Sean Casey	.35
42	Barry Larkin	.25
43	Kenny Lofton	.25
45	Manny Ramirez	1.50
47	Jim Thome	1.50
55	Todd Helton	1.50
62	Larry Walker	.25
63	Juan Gonzalez	1.50
67	Jeff Bagwell	1.50
73	Craig Biggio	.25
76	Carlos Beltran	.50
88	Shawn Green	.40
91	Gary Sheffield	.40
96	Jeromy Burnitz	.25
97	Vladimir Guerrero	1.50
98	Edgardo Alfonzo	.25
101	Mike Piazza	2.50
105	Roger Clemens	2.25
112	Orlando Hernandez	.25
113	Derek Jeter	4.00
121	Bernie Williams	.35
128	Eric Chavez	.35
130	Tim Hudson	.35
133	Scott Rolen	1.25
137	Curt Schilling	.50
140	Brian Giles	.25
144	Rick Ankiel	.25
147	Mark McGwire	3.00
	Tony Gwynn	2.00
	Barry Bonds	4.00
	Jeff Kent	.25
	Ken Griffey Jr.	2.50
	Alex Rodriguez	3.00
	Jose Canseco	.50
	Fred McGriff	.25
	Rafael Palmeiro	.75
	Ivan Rodriguez	.75
	Carlos Delgado	.25

Star Factor

		NM/M
Complete Set (10):		200.00
Common Player:		20.00
Inserted 1:361		
1	Chipper Jones	20.00
2	Cal Ripken Jr.	40.00
3	Nomar Garciaparra	25.00
4	Sammy Sosa	25.00
5	Mike Piazza	25.00
6	Derek Jeter	40.00
7	Mark McGwire	30.00
8	Tony Gwynn	20.00
9	Ken Griffey Jr.	25.00
10	Alex Rodriguez	30.00

2000 Pacific Crown Collection Sample

Nearly identical to the issued version of spokesman Tony Gwynn's card, this features a large white diagonal "SAMPLE" overprint on back and in the space where a card number usually appears.

	NM/M
Tony Gwynn	3.00

2000 Pacific Crown Collection

This 300-card base set has a white bordered design with the logo, player name and team stamped in gold foil. Card backs have a small close-up photo, a brief career highlight and 1999 statistics along with career totals.

		NM/M
Complete Set (300):		25.00
Common Player:		.10
Pack (10):		1.50
Wax Box (36):		30.00
1	Garret Anderson	.10
2	Darin Erstad	.25
3	Ben Molina	.10
4	Ramon Ortiz	.10
5	Orlando Palmeiro	.10
6	Troy Percival	.10
7	Tim Salmon	.10
8	Mo Vaughn	.10
9	Checklist (Mo Vaughn)	.10
10	Jay Bell	.10
11	Omar Daal	.10
12	Erubiel Durazo	.10
13	Steve Finley	.10
14	Hanley Frias	.10
15	Luis Gonzalez	.25
16	Randy Johnson	.75
17	Matt Williams	.10
18	Checklist (Matt Williams)	.10
19	Andres Galarraga	.10
20	Tom Glavine	.35
21	Andruw Jones	.75
22	Chipper Jones	1.00
23	Brian Jordan	.10
24	Javy Lopez	.10
25	Greg Maddux	1.00
26	Kevin Millwood	.10
27	Eddie Perez	.10
28	John Smoltz	.10
29	Checklist (Chipper Jones)	.50
30	Albert Belle	.15
31	Jesse Garcia	.10
32	Jerry Hairston Jr.	.10
33	Charles Johnson	.10
34	Mike Mussina	.30
35	Sidney Ponson	.10
36	Cal Ripken Jr.	2.50
37	B.J. Surhoff	.10
38	Checklist (Cal Ripken Jr.)	1.00
39	Nomar Garciaparra	1.50
40	Pedro Martinez	.75
41	Ramon Martinez	.10
42	Trot Nixon	.10
43	Jose Offerman	.10
44	Troy O'Leary	.10
45	John Valentin	.10
46	Wilton Veras	.10
47	Checklist (Nomar Garciaparra)	.75
48	Mark Grace	.15

#	Player	Price
49	Felix Heredia	.10
50	Jose Molina	.10
51	Jose Nieves	.10
52	Henry Rodriguez	.10
53	Sammy Sosa	1.50
54	Kerry Wood	.65
55	Checklist (Sammy Sosa)	.10
56	Mike Caruso	.10
57	Carlos Castillo	.10
58	Jason Dellaero	.10
59	Carlos Lee	.10
60	Magglio Ordonez	.25
61	Jesus Pena	.10
62	Liu Rodriguez	.10
63	Frank Thomas	.75
64	Checklist (Magglio Ordonez)	.15
65	Aaron Boone	.10
66	Mike Cameron	.10
67	Sean Casey	.20
68	Juan Guzman	.10
69	Barry Larkin	.10
70	Pokey Reese	.10
71	Eddie Taubensee	.10
72	Greg Vaughn	.10
73	Checklist (Sean Casey)	.15
74	Roberto Alomar	.25
75	Sandy Alomar Jr.	.10
76	Bartolo Colon	.10
77	Jacob Cruz	.10
78	Einar Diaz	.10
79	David Justice	.10
80	Kenny Lofton	.10
81	Manny Ramirez	.75
82	Richie Sexson	.10
83	Jim Thome	.75
84	Omar Vizquel	.10
85	Enrique Wilson	.10
86	Checklist (Manny Ramirez)	.40
87	Pedro Astacio	.10
88	Henry Blanco	.10
89	Vinny Castilla	.10
90	Edgard Clemente	.10
91	Todd Helton	.75
92	Neifi Perez	.10
93	Terry Shumpert	.10
94	Juan Sosa RC	.20
95	Larry Walker	.25
96	Checklist (Vinny Castilla)	.10
97	Tony Clark	.10
98	Deivi Cruz	.10
99	Damion Easley	.10
100	Juan Encarnacion	.10
101	Karim Garcia	.10
102	Luis Garcia	.10
103	Juan Gonzalez	.75
104	Jose Macias	.10
105	Dean Palmer	.10
106	Checklist (Juan Encarnacion)	.10
107	Antonio Alfonseca	.10
108	Armando Almanza	.10
109	Bruce Aven	.10
110	Luis Castillo	.10
111	Ramon Castro	.10
112	Alex Fernandez	.10
113	Cliff Floyd	.10
114	Alex Gonzalez	.10
115	Michael Tejera RC	.10
116	Preston Wilson	.10
117	Checklist (Luis Castillo)	.10
118	Jeff Bagwell	.75
119	Craig Biggio	.25
120	Jose Cabrera	.10
121	Tony Eusebio	.10
122	Carl Everett	.10
123	Ricky Gutierrez	.10
124	Mike Hampton	.10
125	Richard Hidalgo	.10
126	Jose Lima	.10
127	Billy Wagner	.10
128	Checklist (Jeff Bagwell)	.40
129	Carlos Beltran	.50
130	Johnny Damon	.25
131	Jermaine Dye	.10
132	Carlos Febles	.10
133	Jeremy Giambi	.10
134	Jose Rosado	.10
135	Rey Sanchez	.10
136	Jose Santiago	.10
137	Checklist (Carlos Beltran)	.10
138	Kevin Brown	.10
139	Craig Counsell	.10
140	Shawn Green	.40
141	Eric Karros	.10
142	Angel Pena	.10
143	Gary Sheffield	.25
144	Ismael Valdes	.10
145	Jose Vizcaino	.10
146	Devon White	.10
147	Checklist (Eric Karros)	.10
148	Ron Belliard	.10
149	Jeromy Burnitz	.10
150	Jeff Cirillo	.10
151	Marquis Grissom	.10
152	Geoff Jenkins	.10
153	Dave Nilsson	.10
154	Rafael Roque	.10
155	Jose Valentin	.10
156	Fernando Vina	.10
157	Jeromy Burnitz	.10
158	Chad Allen	.10
159	Ron Coomer	.10
160	Eddie Guardado	.10
161	Cristian Guzman	.10
162	Jacque Jones	.10
163	Javier Valentin	.10

#	Player	Price
164	Todd Walker	.10
165	Checklist (Ron Coomer)	.10
166	Michael Barrett	.10
167	Miguel Batista	.10
168	Vladimir Guerrero	.75
169	Wilton Guerrero	.10
170	Fernando Seguignol	.10
171	Ugueth Urbina	.10
172	Javier Vazquez	.10
173	Jose Vidro	.10
174	Rondell White	.10
175	Checklist (Vladimir Guerrero)	.25
176	Edgardo Alfonzo	.10
177	Armando Benitez	.10
178	Roger Cedeno	.10
179	Octavio Dotel	.10
180	Melvin Mora	.10
181	Rey Ordonez	.10
182	Mike Piazza	1.50
183	Jorge Toca	.10
184	Robin Ventura	.10
185	Checklist (Edgardo Alfonzo)	.10
186	Roger Clemens	1.25
187	David Cone	.10
188	Orlando Hernandez	.10
189	Derek Jeter	2.50
190	Ricky Ledee	.10
191	Tino Martinez	.10
192	Ramiro Mendoza	.10
193	Jorge Posada	.10
194	Mariano Rivera	.15
195	Alfonso Soriano	.75
196	Bernie Williams	.25
197	Checklist (Derek Jeter)	1.00
198	Eric Chavez	.15
199	Jason Giambi	.60
200	Ben Grieve	.10
201	Ramon Hernandez	.10
202	Tim Hudson	.25
203	John Jaha	.10
204	Omar Olivares	.10
205	Olmedo Saenz	.10
206	Matt Stairs	.10
207	Miguel Tejada	.20
208	Checklist (Tim Hudson)	.10
209	Rico Brogna	.10
210	Bobby Abreu	.10
211	Marlon Anderson	.10
212	Alex Arias	.10
213	Doug Glanville	.10
214	Robert Person	.10
215	Scott Rolen	.60
216	Curt Schilling	.35
217	Checklist (Scott Rolen)	.25
218	Francisco Cordova	.10
219	Brian Giles	.10
220	Jason Kendall	.10
221	Warren Morris	.10
222	Abraham Nunez	.10
223	Aramis Ramirez	.10
224	Jose Silva	.10
225	Kevin Young	.10
226	Checklist (Brian Giles)	.10
227	Rick Ankiel	.25
228	Ricky Bottalico	.10
229	J.D. Drew	.25
230	Ray Lankford	.10
231	Mark McGwire	2.00
232	Eduardo Perez	.10
233	Placido Polanco	.10
234	Edgar Renteria	.10
235	Fernando Tatis	.10
236	Checklist (Mark McGwire)	.85
237	Carlos Almanzar	.10
238	Wiki Gonzalez	.10
239	Tony Gwynn	1.00
240	Trevor Hoffman	.10
241	Damian Jackson	.10
242	Wally Joyner	.10
243	Ruben Rivera	.10
244	Reggie Sanders	.10
245	Quilvio Veras	.10
246	Checklist (Tony Gwynn)	.50
247	Rich Aurilia	.10
248	Marvin Benard	.10
249	Barry Bonds	2.50
250	Ellis Burks	.10
251	Miguel Del Toro	.10
252	Edwards Guzman	.10
253	Livan Hernandez	.10
254	Jeff Kent	.10
255	Russ Ortiz	.10
256	Armando Rios	.10
257	Checklist (Barry Bonds)	1.00
258	Rafael Bournigal	.10
259	Freddy Garcia	.10
260	Ken Griffey Jr.	15.00
261	Carlos Guillen	.10
262	Raul Ibanez	.10
263	Edgar Martinez	.10
264	Jose Mesa	.10
265	Jamie Moyer	.10
266	John Olerud	.10
267	Jose Paniagua	.10
268	Alex Rodriguez	2.00
269	Checklist (Alex Rodriguez)	1.00
270	Wilson Alvarez	.10
271	Rolando Arrojo	.10
272	Wade Boggs	1.00
273	Miguel Cairo	.10
274	Jose Canseco	.40
275	Jose Guillen	.10
276	Roberto Hernandez	.10
277	Albie Lopez	.10
278	Fred McGriff	.10

#	Player	Price
279	Esteban Yan	.10
280	Checklist (Jose Canseco)	.20
281	Rusty Greer	.10
282	Roberto Kelly	.10
283	Esteban Loaiza	.10
284	Ruben Mateo	.10
285	Rafael Palmeiro	.65
286	Ivan Rodriguez	.65
287	Aaron Sele	.10
288	John Wetteland	.10
289	Checklist (Ivan Rodriguez)	.25
290	Tony Batista	.10
291	Jose Cruz Jr.	.10
292	Carlos Delgado	.50
293	Kelvim Escobar	.10
294	Tony Fernandez	.10
295	Billy Koch	.10
296	Raul Mondesi	.10
297	Willis Otanez	.10
298	David Segui	.10
299	David Wells	.10
300	Checklist (Carlos Delgado)	.20

Holographic Purple

A parallel to the 300-card base set, holographic purple stamping replaces the gold foil to differentiate these from the base cards. These are limited to 199 numbered sets.

Stars:	4-8X
Production 199 Sets	

Platinum Blue

A parallel to the 300-card base set, these have blue foil stamping in place of gold foil and are limited to 67 serial numbered sets.

Stars:	8-15X
Production 67 Sets	

In The Cage

These inserts have a die-cut design around an image of a batting cage, with net-fusion technology used to mimic the netting in a batting cage. These were inserted 1:145 packs.

		NM/M
Complete Set (20):		250.00
Common Player:		5.00
Inserted 1:145		
1	Mo Vaughn	5.00
2	Chipper Jones	15.00
3	Cal Ripken Jr.	30.00
4	Nomar Garciaparra	20.00
5	Sammy Sosa	20.00
6	Frank Thomas	10.00
7	Roberto Alomar	6.00
8	Manny Ramirez	10.00
9	Larry Walker	5.00
10	Jeff Bagwell	10.00
11	Vladimir Guerrero	10.00
12	Mike Piazza	20.00
13	Derek Jeter	30.00
14	Bernie Williams	5.00
15	Mark McGwire	25.00
16	Tony Gwynn	15.00
17	Ken Griffey Jr.	20.00
18	Alex Rodriguez	25.00
19	Rafael Palmeiro	8.00
20	Ivan Rodriguez	8.00

Latinos of the Major Leagues

This set salutes major league's who have a latino heritage. These were seeded 2:37 packs and have a horizontal format with two images of the featured player on the card front.

		NM/M
Complete Set (36):		20.00
Common Player:		.25
Inserted 2:37		

Parallel:		2-4X
Production 99 Sets		
1	Erubiel Durazo	.25
2	Luis Gonzalez	.25
3	Andruw Jones	1.00
4	Nomar Garciaparra	2.00
5	Pedro Martinez	1.00
6	Sammy Sosa	2.00
7	Carlos Lee	.25
8	Magglio Ordonez	.25
9	Roberto Alomar	.65
10	Manny Ramirez	1.00
11	Omar Vizquel	.25
12	Vinny Castilla	.25
13	Juan Gonzalez	1.00
14	Luis Castillo	.25
15	Jose Lima	.25
16	Carlos Beltran	.75
17	Vladimir Guerrero	1.00
18	Edgardo Alfonzo	.25
19	Roger Cedeno	.25
20	Rey Ordonez	.25
21	Orlando Hernandez	.25
22	Tino Martinez	.25
23	Mariano Rivera	.35
24	Bernie Williams	.50
25	Miguel Tejada	.50
26	Bobby Abreu	.25
27	Fernando Tatis	.25
28	Freddy Garcia	.25
29	Edgar Martinez	.25
30	Alex Rodriguez	3.00
31	Jose Canseco	.65
32	Ruben Mateo	.25
33	Rafael Palmeiro	.75
34	Ivan Rodriguez	.75
35	Carlos Delgado	.65
36	Raul Mondesi	.25

Moment of Truth

These inserts feature gold foil stamping and a shadow image of the player in the background of the player photo. These were inserted 1:37 packs.

		NM/M
Complete Set (30):		50.00
Common Player:		.50
Inserted 1:37		
1	Mo Vaughn	.50
2	Chipper Jones	3.00
3	Greg Maddux	3.00
4	Albert Belle	.50
5	Cal Ripken Jr.	6.00
6	Nomar Garciaparra	4.00
7	Pedro Martinez	2.00
8	Sammy Sosa	4.00
9	Frank Thomas	2.00
10	Barry Larkin	.50
11	Kenny Lofton	.50
12	Manny Ramirez	2.00
13	Larry Walker	.50
14	Juan Gonzalez	2.00
15	Jeff Bagwell	2.00
16	Craig Biggio	.50
17	Carlos Beltran	1.00
18	Vladimir Guerrero	2.00
19	Mike Piazza	4.00
20	Roger Clemens	3.50
21	Derek Jeter	6.00
22	Bernie Williams	.75
23	Mark McGwire	5.00
24	Tony Gwynn	3.00
25	Barry Bonds	6.00
26	Ken Griffey Jr.	4.00
27	Alex Rodriguez	5.00
28	Rafael Palmeiro	1.50
29	Ivan Rodriguez	1.50
30	Carlos Delgado	1.00

Pacific Cup

Pacific Cup's have a horizontal format with gold foil stamping and an image of a trophy cup beside the player photo. These were inserted 1:721 packs.

		NM/M
Complete Set (10):		220.00
Inserted 1:721		
1	Cal Ripken Jr.	40.00
2	Nomar Garciaparra	25.00
3	Pedro Martinez	15.00
4	Sammy Sosa	25.00
5	Vladimir Guerrero	15.00
6	Derek Jeter	40.00
7	Mark McGwire	35.00
8	Tony Gwynn	20.00
9	Ken Griffey Jr.	25.00
10	Alex Rodriguez	35.00

Timber 2000

These 1:73 pack inserts have a horizontal format highlighted by gold foil stamping. A black bat is in the background of the player image with 2000 written in the bat head.

		NM/M
Complete Set (20):		100.00
Common Player:		2.00
Inserted 1:73		
1	Chipper Jones	8.00
2	Nomar Garciaparra	10.00
3	Sammy Sosa	10.00
4	Magglio Ordonez	2.00
5	Manny Ramirez	6.00
6	Vinny Castilla	2.00
7	Juan Gonzalez	6.00
8	Jeff Bagwell	6.00
9	Shawn Green	3.00
10	Vladimir Guerrero	6.00
11	Mike Piazza	10.00
12	Derek Jeter	15.00
13	Bernie Williams	2.00
14	Mark McGwire	12.00
15	Ken Griffey Jr.	10.00
16	Alex Rodriguez	12.00
17	Jose Canseco	3.00
18	Rafael Palmeiro	5.00
19	Ivan Rodriguez	5.00
20	Carlos Delgado	4.00

2000 Pacific Crown Royale

The Crown Royale 144-card base set has a horizontal format die-cut around a crown design at the top. The cards are double foiled with gold and silver foil etching.

		NM/M
Complete Set (144):		40.00
Common Player:		.25
Common SP:		1.00
Pack (6):		2.50
Box (24):		45.00
1	Darin Erstad	.40
2	Troy Glaus	1.00
3	Adam Kennedy/SP	1.00
4	Derrick Turnbow/SP RC	1.00
5	Mo Vaughn	.25
6	Erubiel Durazo	.25
7	Steve Finley	.25
8	Randy Johnson	1.00
9	Travis Lee	.25
10	Matt Williams	.25
11	Rafael Furcal/SP	1.00
12	Andres Galarraga	.25
13	Andruw Jones	1.00
14	Chipper Jones	1.50
15	Javy Lopez	.25
16	Greg Maddux	1.50
17	Albert Belle	.35
18	Will Clark	.35
19	Mike Mussina	.25
20	Cal Ripken Jr.	3.00
21	Carl Everett	.25
22	Nomar Garciaparra	2.00
23	Pedro Martinez	1.00
24	Jason Varitek	.25
25	Scott Downs/SP RC	1.00
26	Mark Grace	.35
27	Sammy Sosa	2.00
28	Kerry Wood	.65
29	Ray Durham	.25
30	Paul Konerko	.25
31	Carlos Lee	.25
32	Magglio Ordonez	.40
33	Frank Thomas	1.00
34	Rob Bell SP	1.00
35	Sean Casey	.25
36	Ken Griffey Jr.	2.00
37	Barry Larkin	.25

#	Player	Price
38	Pokey Reese	.25
39	Roberto Alomar	.40
40	David Justice	.25
41	Kenny Lofton	.25
42	Manny Ramirez	1.00
43	Richie Sexson	.25
44	Jim Thome	.75
45	Rolando Arrojo	.25
46	Jeff Cirillo	.25
47	Tom Goodwin	.25
48	Todd Helton	1.00
49	Larry Walker	.25
50	Tony Clark	.25
51	Juan Encarnacion	.25
52	Juan Gonzalez	1.00
53	Hideo Nomo	1.00
54	Dean Palmer	.25
55	Cliff Floyd	.25
56	Alex Gonzalez	.25
57	Mike Lowell	.25
58	Brad Penny/SP	1.00
59	Preston Wilson	.25
60	Moises Alou	.25
61	Jeff Bagwell	1.00
62	Craig Biggio	.25
63	Roger Cedeno	.25
64	Julio Lugo/SP	1.00
65	Carlos Beltran	.60
66	Johnny Damon	.40
67	Jermaine Dye	.25
68	Carlos Febles	.25
69	Mark Quinn/SP	1.00
70	Kevin Brown	.25
71	Shawn Green	.50
72	Eric Karros	.25
73	Gary Sheffield	.50
74	Kevin Barker/SP	1.00
75	Ron Belliard	.25
76	Jeromy Burnitz	.25
77	Geoff Jenkins	.25
78	Jacque Jones	.25
79	Corey Koskie	.25
80	Matt LeCroy/SP	1.00
81	Brad Radke	.25
82	Peter Bergeron/SP	1.00
83	Matt Blank/SP	1.00
84	Vladimir Guerrero	1.00
85	Hideki Irabu	.25
86	Rondell White	.25
87	Edgardo Alfonzo	.25
88	Mike Hampton	.25
89	Rickey Henderson	1.00
90	Rey Ordonez	.25
91	Jay Payton/SP	1.00
92	Mike Piazza	2.00
93	Roger Clemens	1.75
94	Orlando Hernandez	.25
95	Derek Jeter	3.00
96	Tino Martinez	.25
97	Alfonso Soriano/SP	2.50
98	Bernie Williams	.40
99	Eric Chavez	.40
100	Jason Giambi	.75
101	Ben Grieve	.25
102	Tim Hudson	.50
103	Terrence Long/SP	1.00
104	Mark Mulder/SP	1.00
105	Adam Piatt/SP	1.00
106	Bobby Abreu	.25
107	Doug Glanville	.25
108	Mike Lieberthal	.25
109	Scott Rolen	.75
110	Brian Giles	.25
111	Chad Hermansen/SP	1.00
112	Jason Kendall	.25
113	Warren Morris	.25
114	Rick Ankiel/SP	1.00
115	Justin Brunette/SP RC	1.00
116	J.D. Drew	.40
117	Fernando Tatis	.25
118	Mark McGwire	2.50
119	Wiki Gonzalez/SP	1.00
120	Tony Gwynn	1.50
121	Trevor Hoffman	.25
122	Ryan Klesko	.25
123	Barry Bonds	3.00
124	Ellis Burks	.25
125	Jeff Kent	.25
126	Calvin Murray/SP	1.00
127	J.T. Snow	.25
128	Freddy Garcia	.25
129	John Olerud	.25
130	Alex Rodriguez	2.50
131	Kazuhiro Sasaki/SP RC	3.00
132	Jose Canseco	.50
133	Vinny Castilla	.25
134	Fred McGriff	.25
135	Greg Vaughn	.25
136	Gabe Kapler	.25
137	Mike Lamb/SP RC	1.00
138	Ruben Mateo/SP	1.00
139	Rafael Palmeiro	.75
140	Ivan Rodriguez	.75
141	Tony Batista	.25
142	Carlos Delgado	.25
143	Raul Mondesi	.25
144	Shannon Stewart	.25

Limited Series

A parallel to the 144-card base set, silver foil replaces gold foil to differentiate these from regular cards. They are also limited to 144 serial numbered sets.

Stars:	2-4X
Production 144 Sets	

Red

Identical in design to the base set, these have red foil instead of gold foil and are the base cards in retail packaging.

All singles: 1X
Base cards in retail packs.

Platinum Blue

A parallel to the 144-card base set these have blue foil in place of gold foil to differentiate them from regular cards. They are limited to 75 serial numbered sets.

Stars: 3-6X
Production 75 Sets

Premiere Date

A parallel to the 144-card base set these are found exclusively in hobby packs and are limited to 121 serial numbered sets.

Stars: 2-4X
Production 121 Sets

Card-Supials

These inserts feature a superstar's regular sized card paired with a top prospect teammate's smaller card. The standard sized card has a horizontal format with gold foil stamping, the small prospect card has gold foil stamping on a vertical format. These were seeded 2:25 packs.

	NM/M
Complete Set (20):	40.00
Common Card:	1.00
Inserted 2:25	
1 Randy Johnson, Erubiel Durazo	2.00
2 Chipper Jones, Andruw Jones	3.00
3 Cal Ripken Jr., Matt Riley	6.00
4 Nomar Garciaparra, Jason Varitek	4.00
5 Sammy Sosa, Kerry Wood	4.00
6 Frank Thomas, Magglio Ordonez	2.00
7 Ken Griffey Jr., Sean Casey	4.00
8 Manny Ramirez, Richie Sexson	2.00
9 Larry Walker, Ben Petrick	1.00
10 Juan Gonzalez, Juan Encarnacion	2.00
11 Jeff Bagwell, Lance Berkman	
12 Shawn Green, Eric Gagne	1.00
13 Vladimir Guerrero, Peter Bergeron	2.00
14 Mike Piazza, Edgardo Alfonzo	4.00
15 Derek Jeter, Alfonso Soriano	5.00
16 Scott Rolen, Bobby Abreu	1.50
17 Mark McGwire, Rick Ankiel	5.00
18 Tony Gwynn, Ben Davis	3.00
19 Alex Rodriguez, Freddy Garcia	5.00
20 Ivan Rodriguez, Ruben Mateo	1.50

Cramer's Choice Jumbo

This enlarged 10-card set is die-cut into a trophy shape. The jumbo cards are enhanced with a silver holo-foiled front with gold foil stamping and etching across the

bottom portion. These were found one per box exclusively in hobby boxes. Six parallels also were randomly inserted with each individual color replacing the gold foil stamping. Aqua's are limited to 20 numbered sets, Blue's 35 sets, Gold's 10 sets, Green's 30 sets, Purple's one set and Red's 25 sets.

	NM/M
Complete Set (10):	35.00
Common Player:	1.00
Inserted 1:Box H	
Aqua:	5-10X
Production 20 Sets	
Blue:	2-5X
Production 35 Sets	
Gold:	10-20X
Production 10 Sets	
Green:	3-6X
Production 30 Sets	
Red:	4-8X
Production 25 Sets	
1 Cal Ripken Jr.	6.00
2 Nomar Garciaparra	4.00
3 Ken Griffey Jr.	4.00
4 Sammy Sosa	4.00
5 Mike Piazza	4.00
6 Derek Jeter	6.00
7 Rick Ankiel	1.00
8 Mark McGwire	5.00
9 Tony Gwynn	2.00
10 Alex Rodriguez	5.00

Feature Attractions

This 25-card set has a horizontal format with the featured player's achievements on a billboard in the background. These were seeded one per hobby pack and one per two retail packs. An Exclusive Showing parallel is also randomly inserted and is limited to 20 serial numbered sets.

	NM/M
Complete Set (25):	10.00
Common Player:	.25
Inserted 1:1	
Exclusive Showing:	30-50X
Production 20 Sets	
1 Erubiel Durazo	.25
2 Chipper Jones	1.00
3 Greg Maddux	1.00
4 Cal Ripken Jr.	2.50
5 Nomar Garciaparra	1.50
6 Pedro Martinez	.75
7 Sammy Sosa	1.50
8 Frank Thomas	.75
9 Ken Griffey Jr.	1.50
10 Manny Ramirez	.75
11 Larry Walker	.25
12 Juan Gonzalez	.75
13 Jeff Bagwell	.75
14 Carlos Beltran	.50
15 Shawn Green	.50
16 Vladimir Guerrero	.75
17 Mike Piazza	1.50
18 Roger Clemens	1.25
19 Derek Jeter	2.50
20 Ben Grieve	.25
21 Rick Ankiel	.35
22 Mark McGwire	2.00
23 Tony Gwynn	1.00
24 Alex Rodriguez	2.00
25 Ivan Rodriguez	.65

Final Numbers

These inserts are found one per hobby pack and one per two retail packs. The logo, player name and team are stamped in silver foil and has "Final Numbers" written down the right hand portion of the

front. A holographic parallel limited to 10 serial numbered sets is also randomly inserted.

	NM/M
Complete Set (25):	10.00
Common Player:	.25
Inserted 1:1	
1 Randy Johnson	.75
2 Andruw Jones	.75
3 Chipper Jones	1.00
4 Cal Ripken Jr.	2.50
5 Nomar Garciaparra	1.50
6 Pedro Martinez	.75
7 Sammy Sosa	1.50
8 Ken Griffey Jr.	1.50
9 Sean Casey	.35
10 Manny Ramirez	.75
11 Larry Walker	.25
12 Jeff Bagwell	.75
13 Craig Biggio	.25
14 Shawn Green	.50
15 Vladimir Guerrero	.75
16 Mike Piazza	1.50
17 Derek Jeter	2.50
18 Bernie Williams	.35
19 Scott Rolen	.65
20 Mark McGwire	2.00
21 Tony Gwynn	1.00
22 Barry Bonds	2.50
23 Alex Rodriguez	2.00
24 Jose Canseco	.40
25 Ivan Rodriguez	.65

Jumbo

These jumbo cards are identical in design to the base cards besides their enlarged size. These were found exclusively in hobby boxes and were found as a box topper in 6:10 boxes.

	NM/M
Complete Set (6):	25.00
Inserted 6:10 boxes H	
1 Cal Ripken Jr.	6.00
2 Nomar Garciaparra	4.00
3 Ken Griffey Jr.	4.00
4 Derek Jeter	6.00
5 Mark McGwire	5.00
6 Alex Rodriguez	5.00

Proofs

Proofs are the actual printer's proofs used to produce this set. The inserts are transparent and have a coal black tint. These were inserted 1:25 packs. A parallel is also randomly inserted and is limited to 50 serial numbered sets.

	NM/M
Complete Set (36):	90.00
Common Player:	1.00
Inserted 1:25	
Proofs:	2-3X
1 Erubiel Durazo	1.50
2 Randy Johnson	3.00
3 Chipper Jones	5.00
4 Greg Maddux	5.00
5 Cal Ripken Jr.	10.00
6 Nomar Garciaparra	8.00
7 Pedro Martinez	3.00
8 Sammy Sosa	5.00
9 Frank Thomas	2.50
10 Sean Casey	1.50
11 Ken Griffey Jr.	5.00
12 Manny Ramirez	2.50
13 Jim Thome	2.50
14 Larry Walker	1.50
15 Juan Gonzalez	2.50
16 Jeff Bagwell	2.50
17 Craig Biggio	1.50
18 Carlos Beltran	2.00
19 Shawn Green	2.00
20 Vladimir Guerrero	2.50
21 Edgardo Alfonzo	1.00
22 Mike Piazza	5.00
23 Roger Clemens	6.00
24 Derek Jeter	10.00
25 Alfonso Soriano	4.00
26 Bernie Williams	2.00
27 Ben Grieve	2.00
28 Rick Ankiel	1.00
29 Mark McGwire	8.00
30 Tony Gwynn	3.00
31 Barry Bonds	8.00
32 Alex Rodriguez	8.00
33 Jose Canseco	2.00
34 Vinny Castilla	1.00
35 Ivan Rodriguez	2.00
36 Rafael Palmeiro	2.00

Sweet Spot Signatures

These die-cut autographed cards are done on a horizontal format with an image of a baseball beside the player photo. The signature is on the "sweet spot" of the baseball image. Red foil stamping is used on the seams of the baseball and the player name. No insertion ratio was announced.

	NM/M
Common Player:	5.00
1 Adam Kennedy	5.00
2 Trot Nixon	8.00
3 Magglio Ordonez	10.00
4 Sean Casey	8.00
5 Travis Dawkins	5.00
6 Todd Helton	25.00
7 Ben Petrick	5.00
8 Jeff Weaver	6.00
9 Preston Wilson	5.00
10 Lance Berkman	10.00
11 Roger Cedeno	5.00
12 Eric Gagne	10.00
13 Kevin Barker	5.00
14 Kyle Peterson	5.00
15 Tony Armas Jr.	5.00
16 Peter Bergeron	5.00
17 Alfonso Soriano	40.00
18 Ben Grieve	5.00
19 Ramon Hernandez	5.00
20 Brian Giles	8.00
21 Chad Hermansen	5.00
22 Warren Morris	5.00
23 Ben Davis	5.00
24 Rick Ankiel	15.00
25 Chad Hutchinson	5.00
26 Freddy Garcia	10.00
27 Gabe Kapler	5.00
28 Ruben Mateo	5.00
29 Billy Koch	5.00
30 Vernon Wells	5.00

2000 Pacific Invincible

The base set consists of 150 cards. The player image is on an acetate stock with a blue sky background. The rest of the card is on standard UV coated stock and has the player name stamped in gold foil.

	NM/M
Complete Set (150):	75.00
Common Player:	.25
Pack (3):	2.00
Box (36):	50.00
1 Darin Erstad	.50
2 Troy Glaus	1.50
3 Ramon Ortiz	.25
4 Tim Salmon	.35
5 Mo Vaughn	.25
6 Erubiel Durazo	.25
7 Luis Gonzalez	.35
8 Randy Johnson	1.50
9 Matt Williams	.25
10 Rafael Furcal	.25
11 Andres Galarraga	.25
12 Tom Glavine	.40
13 Andruw Jones	1.50
14 Chipper Jones	2.00
15 Greg Maddux	2.00
16 Kevin Millwood	.25
17 Albert Belle	.35
18 Will Clark	.35
19 Mike Mussina	.40
20 Matt Riley	.25
21 Cal Ripken Jr.	4.00
22 Carl Everett	.25
23 Nomar Garciaparra	2.50
24 Steve Lomasney	.25
25 Pedro Martinez	1.50
26 Tomo Ohka RC	.75
27 Wilton Veras	.25
28 Mark Grace	.35

29 Sammy Sosa	2.50
30 Kerry Wood	.75
31 Eric Young	.25
32 Julio Zuleta RC	.25
33 Paul Konerko	.25
34 Carlos Lee	.25
35 Magglio Ordonez	.35
36 Josh Paul	.25
37 Frank Thomas	1.50
38 Rob Bell	.25
39 Dante Bichette	.25
40 Sean Casey	.35
41 Ken Griffey Jr.	2.50
42 Barry Larkin	.25
43 Pokey Reese	.25
44 Roberto Alomar	.40
45 Manny Ramirez	1.50
46 Richie Sexson	.25
47 Jim Thome	1.50
48 Omar Vizquel	.25
49 Jeff Cirillo	.25
50 Todd Helton	1.50
51 Neifi Perez	.25
52 Larry Walker	.25
53 Tony Clark	.25
54 Juan Encarnacion	.25
55 Juan Gonzalez	1.50
56 Hideo Nomo	1.00
57 Luis Castillo	.25
58 Alex Gonzalez	.25
59 Brad Penny	.25
60 Preston Wilson	.25
61 Moises Alou	.25
62 Jeff Bagwell	1.50
63 Lance Berkman	.25
64 Craig Biggio	.25
65 Roger Cedeno	.25
66 Jose Lima	.25
67 Carlos Beltran	.50
68 Johnny Damon	.25
69 Chad Durbin RC	.50
70 Jermaine Dye	.25
71 Carlos Febles	.25
72 Mark Quinn	.25
73 Kevin Brown	.25
74 Eric Gagne	.25
75 Shawn Green	.50
76 Eric Karros	.25
77 Gary Sheffield	.40
78 Kevin Barker	.25
79 Ron Belliard	.25
80 Jeromy Burnitz	.25
81 Geoff Jenkins	.25
82 Jacque Jones	.25
83 Corey Koskie	.25
84 Matt LeCroy	.25
85 David Ortiz	.35
86 Johan Santana RC	20.00
87 Todd Walker	.25
88 Peter Bergeron	.25
89 Vladimir Guerrero	1.50
90 Jose Vidro	.25
91 Rondell White	.25
92 Edgardo Alfonzo	.25
93 Derek Bell	.25
94 Mike Hampton	.25
95 Rey Ordonez	.25
96 Mike Piazza	2.50
97 Robin Ventura	.25
98 Roger Clemens	2.25
99 Orlando Hernandez	.25
100 Derek Jeter	4.00
101 Alfonso Soriano	.25
102 Bernie Williams	.35
103 Eric Chavez	.40
104 Jason Giambi	.75
105 Ben Grieve	.25
106 Tim Hudson	.40
107 Miguel Tejada	.40
108 Bobby Abreu	.25
109 Doug Glanville	.25
110 Mike Lieberthal	.25
111 Scott Rolen	.75
112 Brian Giles	.25
113 Chad Hermansen	.25
114 Jason Kendall	.25
115 Warren Morris	.25
116 Aramis Ramirez	.25
117 Rick Ankiel	.25
118 J.D. Drew	.40
119 Mark McGwire	3.00
120 Fernando Tatis	.25
121 Fernando Vina	.25
122 Bret Boone	.25
123 Ben Davis	.25
124 Tony Gwynn	2.00
125 Trevor Hoffman	.25
126 Ryan Klesko	.25
127 Rich Aurilia	.25
128 Barry Bonds	4.00
129 Ellis Burks	.25
130 Jeff Kent	.25
131 Freddy Garcia	.25
132 Carlos Guillen	.25
133 Edgar Martinez	.25
134 John Olerud	.25
135 Robert Ramsay	.25
136 Alex Rodriguez	3.00
137 Kazuhiro Sasaki RC	3.00
138 Jose Canseco	.50
139 Vinny Castilla	.25
140 Fred McGriff	.25
141 Greg Vaughn (Front photo is Mo Vaughn.)	.25
142 Dan Wheeler	.25
143 Gabe Kapler	.25
144 Ruben Mateo	.25
145 Rafael Palmeiro	.75

146 Ivan Rodriguez	.75
147 Tony Batista	.25
148 Carlos Delgado	.65
149 Raul Mondesi	.25
150 Vernon Wells	.25

Holographic Purple

A parallel to the 150-card set, holographic purple stamping replaces the gold foil from the base cards. These are limited to 299 serial numbered sets.

Stars: 2-3X
Production 299 Sets

Platinum Blue

A parallel to the 150-card base set these differ only from the regular cards in that blue foil stamping replaces the gold. Each card is also serially numbered on the card front in an edition of 67 sets.

Stars: 4-8X
Production 67 Sets

Diamond Aces

This insert set highlights the top pitchers in the game. Silver-foil stamping is used on the card fronts, which are designed to duplicate the look of an Ace in a deck of playing cards. These were seeded 1 per pack. A parallel limited to 399 serial numbered sets is also randomly seeded.

	NM/M
Complete Set (20):	5.00
Common Player:	.25
Inserted 1:1	
Edition of 399 Parallel:	2-3X
1 Randy Johnson	.75
2 Greg Maddux	1.00
3 Tom Glavine	.40
4 John Smoltz	.25
5 Mike Mussina	.50
6 Pedro Martinez	.75
7 Kerry Wood	.60
8 Bartolo Colon	.25
9 Brad Penny	.25
10 Billy Wagner	.25
11 Kevin Brown	.25
12 Mike Hampton	.25
13 Roger Clemens	1.50
14 David Cone	.25
15 Orlando Hernandez	.25
16 Mariano Rivera	.40
17 Tim Hudson	.40
18 Trevor Hoffman	.25
19 Rick Ankiel	.25
20 Freddy Garcia	.25

Eyes of the World

This 20-card set has a horizontal format with gold foil stamping. The background of the player photo has a partial globe with a star and the country the featured player is from stamped in gold foil. These were inserted 1:25 packs.

		NM/M
	Complete Set (20):	30.00
	Common Player:	.75
	Inserted 1:25	
1	Erubiel Durazo	.75
2	Andruw Jones	2.00
3	Cal Ripken Jr.	6.00
4	Nomar Garciaparra	2.00
5	Pedro Martinez	2.00
6	Sammy Sosa	2.00
7	Ken Griffey Jr.	4.00
8	Manny Ramirez	2.00
9	Larry Walker	.75
10	Juan Gonzalez	2.00
11	Carlos Beltran	1.25
12	Vladimir Guerrero	2.00
13	Orlando Hernandez	.75
14	Derek Jeter	6.00
15	Mark McGwire	5.00
16	Tony Gwynn	3.00
17	Freddy Garcia	.75
18	Alex Rodriguez	5.00
19	Jose Canseco	1.25
20	Ivan Rodriguez	1.50

Game Gear

		NM/M
	Common Card:	4.00
1	Jeff Bagwell/Jsy/1,000	8.00
2	Tom Glavine/Jsy/1,000	6.00
3	Mark Grace/Jsy/1,000	8.00
4	Eric Karros/Jsy/1,000	4.00
5	Edgar Martinez/Jsy/800	6.00
6	Manny Ramirez/Jsy/975	8.00
7	Cal Ripken Jr./Jsy/1,000	25.00
8	Alex Rodriguez/Jsy/900	15.00
9	Ivan Rodriguez/Jsy/675	6.00
10	Mo Vaughn Jsy/1,000	4.00
11	Edgar Martinez/Bat/200	8.00
12	Manny Ramirez/145	15.00
13	Alex Rodriguez/Bat/200	25.00
14	Ivan Rodriguez/Bat/200	10.00
15	Edgar Martinez/Bat/200	10.00
16	Manny Ramirez/Bat/200	15.00
17	Ivan Rodriguez/Bat/200	10.00
18	Alex Rodriguez/Bat/200	20.00
19	Jeff Bagwell/Patch/125	30.00
20	Tom Glavine/Patch/110	25.00
21	Mark Grace/Patch/125	15.00
22	Tony Gwynn/Patch/65	40.00
23	Chipper Jones/Patch/80	40.00
24	Eric Karros/Patch/125	15.00
25	Greg Maddux/Patch/80	50.00
26	Edgar Martinez/Patch/125	20.00
27	Manny Ramirez/Patch/125	30.00
28	Cal Ripken Jr./Patch/125	65.00
29	Alex Rodriguez/Patch/125	50.00
30	Ivan Rodriguez/Patch/125	25.00
31	Frank Thomas/Patch/125	25.00
32	Mo Vaughn/Patch/125	15.00

Kings of the Diamond

Twenty of the top hitters in the game are featured on a design intended to duplicate the look of a King card in a playing deck of cards. These were seeded one per pack. A parallel version limited to 299 serial numbered sets is also randomly seeded.

		NM/M
	Complete Set (30):	10.00
	Common Player:	.20
	Inserted 1:1	
1	Mo Vaughn	.20
2	Erubiel Durazo	.20
3	Andruw Jones	.65
4	Chipper Jones	.75
5	Cal Ripken Jr.	1.50
6	Nomar Garciaparra	1.00
7	Sammy Sosa	1.00
8	Frank Thomas	.65
9	Sean Casey	.25
10	Ken Griffey Jr.	1.00
11	Manny Ramirez	.65
12	Larry Walker	.20
13	Juan Gonzalez	.65
14	Jeff Bagwell	.65
15	Craig Biggio	.20
16	Carlos Beltran	.50
17	Shawn Green	.35
18	Vladimir Guerrero	.65
19	Mike Piazza	1.00
20	Derek Jeter	1.50
21	Bernie Williams	.40
22	Ben Grieve	.20
23	Scott Rolen	.40
24	Mark McGwire	1.25
25	Tony Gwynn	.75
26	Barry Bonds	1.50
27	Alex Rodriguez	1.25
28	Jose Canseco	.25
29	Rafael Palmeiro	.50
30	Ivan Rodriguez	.50

Lighting The Fire

These full foiled inserts are die-cut in the shape of a flame, with an image of a baseball at the core of the fiery image. These were inserted 1:49 packs.

		NM/M
	Complete Set (20):	120.00
	Common Player:	3.00
	Inserted 1:49	
1	Chipper Jones	8.00
2	Greg Maddux	8.00
3	Cal Ripken Jr.	15.00
4	Nomar Garciaparra	6.00
5	Pedro Martinez	6.00
6	Ken Griffey Jr.	10.00
7	Sammy Sosa	10.00
8	Manny Ramirez	6.00
9	Juan Gonzalez	6.00
10	Jeff Bagwell	6.00
11	Shawn Green	3.00
12	Vladimir Guerrero	6.00
13	Mike Piazza	10.00
14	Roger Clemens	9.00
15	Derek Jeter	15.00
16	Mark McGwire	12.00
17	Tony Gwynn	6.00
18	Alex Rodriguez	12.00
19	Jose Canseco	3.00
20	Ivan Rodriguez	6.00

Ticket To Stardom

These unique cards have a design intended to replicate a ticket stub. Two images of the featured player are on the front, the bigger primary photo is vertical, while the smaller photo is horizontal. Silver foil stamping is used throughout. These are found 1:121 packs.

		NM/M
	Complete Set (20):	250.00
	Common Player:	5.00
	Inserted 1:121	
1	Andruw Jones	10.00
2	Chipper Jones	15.00
3	Cal Ripken Jr.	30.00
4	Nomar Garciaparra	20.00
5	Pedro Martinez	10.00
6	Ken Griffey Jr.	20.00
7	Sammy Sosa	20.00
8	Manny Ramirez	10.00
9	Jeff Bagwell	10.00
10	Shawn Green	5.00
11	Vladimir Guerrero	10.00
12	Mike Piazza	20.00
13	Derek Jeter	30.00
14	Alfonso Soriano	8.00
15	Scott Rolen	6.00
16	Rick Ankiel	5.00
17	Mark McGwire	20.00
18	Tony Gwynn	15.00
19	Alex Rodriguez	25.00
20	Ivan Rodriguez	8.00

Wild Vinyl

This scarce 10-card insert set is serial numbered on the card front, limited to only 10 sets.

		NM/M
	Complete Set (10):	
	Common Player:	
	Production 10 Sets	

2000 Pacific Omega

		NM/M
	Complete Set (20):	
	Common Player:	.10
1	Chipper Jones	1.00
2	Brian Jordan	.10
3	Greg Maddux	.75
4	B.J. Surhoff	.10
5	Brady Anderson	.10
6	Albert Belle	.10
7	Mike Mussina	.40
8	Luis Gonzalez	.20
9	Randy Johnson	.75
10	Matt Williams	.10
11	Andres Galarraga	.10
12	Andruw Jones	.75
13	Chipper Jones	1.00
14	Brian Jordan	.10
15	Greg Maddux	.75
16	B.J. Surhoff	.10
17	Brady Anderson	.10
18	Albert Belle	.10
19	Mike Mussina	.40
20	Cal Ripken Jr.	2.50
21	Carl Everett	.10
22	Nomar Garciaparra	1.50
23	Pedro Martinez	.75
24	Jason Varitek	.10
25	Mark Grace	.20
26	Sammy Sosa	1.50
27	Rondell White	.10
28	Kerry Wood	.35
29	Eric Young	.10
30	Ray Durham	.10
31	Carlos Lee	.10
32	Magglio Ordonez	.25
33	Frank Thomas	.75
34	Sean Casey	.20
35	Ken Griffey Jr.	1.50
36	Barry Larkin	.10
37	Pokey Reese	.10
38	Roberto Alomar	.40
39	Kenny Lofton	.10

40	Manny Ramirez	.75
41	David Segui	.10
42	Jim Thome	.60
43	Omar Vizquel	.10
44	Jeff Cirillo	.10
45	Jeffrey Hammonds	.10
46	Todd Helton	.75
47	Todd Hollandsworth	.10
48	Larry Walker	.10
49	Tony Clark	.10
50	Juan Encarnacion	.10
51	Juan Gonzalez	.75
52	Bobby Higginson	.10
53	Hideo Nomo	.75
54	Dean Palmer	.10
55	Luis Castillo	.10
56	Cliff Floyd	.10
57	Derrek Lee	.10
58	Mike Lowell	.10
59	Henry Rodriguez	.10
60	Preston Wilson	.10
61	Moises Alou	.10
62	Jeff Bagwell	.75
63	Craig Biggio	.10
64	Ken Caminiti	.10
65	Richard Hidalgo	.10
66	Carlos Beltran	.40
67	Johnny Damon	.25
68	Jermaine Dye	.10
69	Joe Randa	.10
70	Mike Sweeney	.10
71	Adrian Beltre	.20
72	Kevin Brown	.10
73	Shawn Green	.35
74	Eric Karros	.10
75	Chan Ho Park	.10
76	Gary Sheffield	.30
77	Ron Belliard	.10
78	Jeromy Burnitz	.10
79	Geoff Jenkins	.10
80	Richie Sexson	.10
81	Ron Coomer	.10
82	Jacque Jones	.10
83	Corey Koskie	.10
84	Matt Lawton	.10
85	Vladimir Guerrero	.75
86	Lee Stevens	.10
87	Jose Vidro	.10
88	Edgardo Alfonzo	.10
89	Derek Bell	.10
90	Mike Bordick	.10
91	Mike Piazza	1.50
92	Robin Ventura	.10
93	Jose Canseco	.10
94	Roger Clemens	1.25
95	Orlando Hernandez	.10
96	Derek Jeter	2.50
97	David Justice	.10
98	Tino Martinez	.10
99	Jorge Posada	.10
100	Bernie Williams	.40
101	Eric Chavez	.20
102	Jason Giambi	.50
103	Ben Grieve	.10
104	Miguel Tejada	.25
105	Bobby Abreu	.10
106	Doug Glanville	.10
107	Travis Lee	.10
108	Mike Lieberthal	.10
109	Scott Rolen	.65
110	Brian S. Giles	.10
111	Jason Kendall	.10
112	Warren Morris	.10
113	Kevin Young	.10
114	Will Clark	.20
115	J.D. Drew	.20
116	Jim Edmonds	.10
117	Mark McGwire	2.00
118	Edgar Renteria	.10
119	Fernando Tatis	.10
120	Fernando Vina	.10
121	Bret Boone	.10
122	Tony Gwynn	1.00
123	Trevor Hoffman	.10
124	Phil Nevin	.10
125	Eric Owens	.10
126	Barry Bonds	2.50
127	Ellis Burks	.10
128	Jeff Kent	.10
129	J.T. Snow	.10
130	Jay Buhner	.10
131	Mike Cameron	.10
132	Rickey Henderson	.75
133	Edgar Martinez	.10
134	John Olerud	.10
135	Alex Rodriguez	2.00
136	Kazuhiro Sasaki RC	1.00
137	Fred McGriff	.10
138	Greg Vaughn	.10
139	Gerald Williams	.10
140	Rusty Greer	.10
141	Gabe Kapler	.10
142	Ricky Ledee	.10
143	Rafael Palmeiro	.65
144	Ivan Rodriguez	.65
145	Tony Batista	.10
146	Jose Cruz Jr.	.10
147	Carlos Delgado	.50
148	Brad Fullmer	.10
149	Shannon Stewart	.10
150	David Wells	.10
151	Juan Alvarez	
152	Seth Etherton, Adam Kennedy	4.00
153	Ramon Ortiz, Lou Pote	4.00
154	Derrick Turnbow RC, Eric Weaver	4.00

155	Rod Barajas, Jason Conti	4.00
156	Byung-Hyun Kim, Rob Ryan	4.00
157	David Cortes, George Lombard	4.00
158	Ivanon Coffie, Melvin Mora	4.00
159	Ryan Kohlmeier RC, Luis Matos RC	6.00
160	Willie Morales, John Parrish RC	4.00
161	Chris Richard RC, Jay Spurgeon RC	5.00
162	Israel Alcantara, Tomokazu Ohka RC	5.00
163	Paxton Crawford RC, Sang-Hoon Lee RC	4.00
164	Mike Mahoney RC, Wilton Veras	4.00
165	Daniel Garibay RC, Ross Gload RC	4.00
166	Gary Matthews Jr., Phil Norton	4.00
167	Roosevelt Brown, Ruben Quevedo	4.00
168	Lorenzo Barcelo RC, Rocky Biddle RC	4.00
169	Mark Buehrle RC, John Garland	8.00
170	Aaron Myette, Josh Paul	4.00
171	Kip Wells, Kelly Wunsch	4.00
172	Rob Bell, Travis Dawkins	4.00
173	Hector Mercado RC, John Riedling RC	4.00
174	Russell Branyan, Sean DePaula	4.00
175	Tim Drew, Mark Watson	4.00
176	Craig House RC, Ben Petrick	5.00
177	Robert Fick, Jose Macias	4.00
178	Javier Cardona RC, Brandon Villafuerte	4.00
179	Armando Almanza, A.J. Burnett	4.00
180	Ramon Castro, Pablo Ozuna	4.00
181	Lance Berkman, Jason Green	4.00
182	Julio Lugo, Tony McKnight	4.00
183	Mitch Meluskey, Wade Miller	4.00
184	Chad Durbin RC, Hector Ortiz RC	5.00
185	Dermal Brown, Mark Quinn	4.00
186	Eric Gagne, Mike Judd	4.00
187	Kane Davis RC, Valerio de los Santos	4.00
188	Santiago Perez, Paul Rigdon RC	4.00
189	Matt Kinney, Matt LeCroy	4.00
190	Jason Maxwell, A.J. Pierzynski	4.00
191	J.C. Romero RC, Johan Santana RC	50.00
192	Tony Armas Jr., Peter Bergeron	4.00
193	Matt Blank, Milton Bradley	4.00
194	Tomas De La Rossa, Scott Forster	4.00
195	Yovanny Lara RC, Talmadge Nunnari RC	4.00
196	Brian Schneider, Andy Tracy	4.00
197	Scott Strickland, T.J. Tucker	4.00
198	Eric Cammack, Jim Mann RC	4.00
199	Grant Roberts, Jorge Toca	4.00
200	Alfonso Soriano, Jay Tessmer	8.00
201	Terrence Long, Mark Mulder	8.00
202	Pat Burrell, Cliff Politte	4.00
203	Jimmy Anderson, Bronson Arroyo	4.00
204	Mike Darr, Kory DeHaan	4.00
205	Adam Eaton, Wiki Gonzalez	
206	Brandon Kolb RC, Kevin Walker	4.00
207	Damon Minor, Calvin Murray	4.00
208	Kevin Hodges, Joel Pineiro RC	40.00
209	Rob Ramsay RC, Kazuhiro Sasaki RC	8.00
210	Rick Ankiel, Mike Matthews	
211	Steve Cox, Travis Harper	4.00
212	Kenny Kelly RC, Damian Rolls RC	
213	Doug Davis, Scott Sheldon	
214	Brian Sikorski, Pedro Valdes	
215	Francisco Cordero, B.J. Waszgis	
216	Matt DeWitt, Josh Phelps RC	8.00
217	Vernon Wells, Dewayne Wise	4.00

218	Geraldo Guzman RC, Jason Marquis	4.00
219	Rafael Furcal, Steve Sisco RC	4.00
220	B.J. Ryan, Kevin Beirne	4.00
221	Matt Ginter RC, Brad Penny	4.00
222	Julio Zuleta RC, Eric Munson	5.00
223	Dan Reichert, Jeff Williams	4.00
224	Jason LaRue, Danny Ardoin	4.00
225	Ray King, Mark Redman	4.00
226	Joe Crede, Mike Bell	4.00
227	Juan Pierre RC, Jay Payton	6.00
228	Wayne Franklin, Randy Choate RC	4.00
229	Chris Truby, Adam Piatt	4.00
230	Kevin Nicholson, Chris Woodward	4.00
231	Barry Zito RC, Jason Boyd	15.00
232	Brian O'Connor RC, Miguel Del Toro	4.00
233	Carlos Guillen, Aubrey Huff	4.00
234	Chad Hermansen, Jason Tyner	4.00
235	Aaron Fultz, Ryan Vogelsong	4.00
236	Shawn Wooten, Vance Wilson	4.00
237	Danny Klassen, Mike Lamb RC	4.00
238	Chad Bradford, Gene Stechschulte RC	4.00
239	Ismael Villegas, Hector Ramirez, Matt T. Williams, Luis Vizcaino	4.00
240	Mike Garcia, Domingo Guzman, Justin Brunette RC, Pasqual Coco RC	4.00
241	Frank Charles, Keith McDonald RC	4.00
242	Carlos Casimiro RC, Morgan Burkhart RC	4.00
243	Raul Gonzalez RC, Shawn Gilbert	4.00
244	Darrell Einertson, Jeff Sparks RC	4.00
245	Augie Ojeda RC, Brady Clark, Todd Belitz, Eric Byrnes RC	6.00
246	Leo Estrella RC, Charlie Greene	4.00
247	Trace Coquillette, Pedro Feliz RC	6.00
248	Tike Redman RC, David Newhan	4.00
249	Rodrigo Lopez RC, John Bales	6.00
250	Corey Patterson, Jose Ortiz RC	6.00
251	Britt Reames RC, Oswaldo Mairena RC	4.00
252	Xavier Nady RC, Timoniel Perez RC	6.00
253	Tom Jacquez, Vicente Padilla	4.00
254	Elvis Pena RC, Adam Melhuse RC	4.00
255	Ben Weber, Alex Cabrera RC	6.00

Copper

	Stars (1-150):	8-15X
	Production 45 Sets	

Gold

Stars (1-150): 4-8X
Production 120 Sets

Platinum Blue

Stars (1-150): 6-10X
Production 55 Sets

Premiere Date

Stars (1-150): 4-8X
Production 77 Sets

AL Contenders

		NM/M
Complete Set (18):		20.00
Common Player:		.50
Inserted 2:37		
1	Darin Erstad	.75
2	Troy Glaus	1.50
3	Mo Vaughn	.50
4	Albert Belle	.50
5	Cal Ripken Jr.	4.00
6	Nomar Garciaparra	3.00
7	Pedro Martinez	1.50
8	Frank Thomas	1.50
9	Manny Ramirez	1.50
10	Jim Thome	1.25
11	Juan Gonzalez	1.50
12	Roger Clemens	2.50
13	Derek Jeter	4.00
14	Bernie Williams	.75
15	Jason Giambi	1.00
16	Alex Rodriguez	3.50
17	Edgar Martinez	.50
18	Carlos Delgado	1.00

EO Portraits

		NM/M
Complete Set (20):		125.00
Common Player:		3.00
Inserted 1:73		

1-of-1 die-cut parallels exist.

1	Chipper Jones	8.00
2	Greg Maddux	8.00
3	Cal Ripken Jr.	15.00
4	Pedro Martinez	10.00
5	Nomar Garciaparra	10.00
6	Sammy Sosa	10.00
7	Frank Thomas	6.00
8	Ken Griffey Jr.	10.00
9	Gary Sheffield	4.00
10	Vladimir Guerrero	6.00
11	Mike Piazza	10.00
12	Roger Clemens	9.00
13	Derek Jeter	15.00
14	Pat Burrell	4.00
15	Tony Gwynn	8.00
16	Barry Bonds	15.00
17	Alex Rodriguez	12.00
18	Rick Ankiel	3.00
19	Mark McGwire	12.00
20	Ivan Rodriguez	5.00

Full Court

		NM/M
Complete Set (36):		30.00
Common Player:		.50
Inserted 4:37 H		

1	Magglio Ordonez	.50
2	Manny Ramirez	1.50
3	Todd Helton	1.50
4	David Justice	.50
5	Bernie Williams	.50
6	Jason Giambi	1.00
7	Scott Rolen	1.00
8	Jeff Kent	.50
9	Edgar Martinez	.50
10	Randy Johnson	1.50
11	Greg Maddux	2.00
12	Mike Mussina	.60
13	Pedro Martinez	1.50
14	Chuck Finley	.50
15	Kevin Brown	.50
16	Roger Clemens	2.25
17	Tim Hudson	.50
18	Rick Ankiel	.50
19	Troy Glaus	1.50
20	Chipper Jones	2.00
21	Nomar Garciaparra	2.50
22	Jeff Bagwell	1.50
23	Shawn Green	.60
24	Vladimir Guerrero	1.50
25	Mike Piazza	2.50
26	Jim Edmonds	.50
27	Rafael Palmeiro	.75
28	Cal Ripken Jr.	4.00
29	Sammy Sosa	2.50
30	Frank Thomas	1.50
31	Ken Griffey Jr.	2.50
32	Gary Sheffield	.50
33	Barry Bonds	4.00
34	Alex Rodriguez	3.00
35	Mark McGwire	3.00
36	Carlos Delgado	1.00

MLB Generations

		NM/M
Complete Set (20):		100.00
Common Card:		3.00
Inserted 1:145		
1	Mark McGwire, Pat Burrell	12.00
2	Cal Ripken Jr., Alex Rodriguez	15.00
3	Randy Johnson, Rick Ankiel	6.00
4	Tony Gwynn, Darin Erstad	8.00
5	Barry Bonds, Magglio Ordonez	15.00
6	Frank Thomas, Jason Giambi	6.00
7	Roger Clemens, Kerry Wood	10.00
8	Mike Piazza, Mitch Meluskey	10.00
9	Ken Griffey Jr., Andruw Jones	10.00
10	Bernie Williams, J.D. Drew	4.00
11	Chipper Jones, Troy Glaus	8.00
12	Andres Galarraga, Todd Helton	6.00
13	Juan Gonzalez, Vladimir Guerrero	6.00
14	Craig Biggio, Rafael Furcal	3.00
15	Sammy Sosa, Jermaine Dye	10.00
16	Larry Walker, Richard Hidalgo	3.00
17	Greg Maddux, Adam Eaton	8.00
18	Barry Larkin, Derek Jeter	15.00
19	Roberto Alomar, Jose Vidro	4.00
20	Jeff Kent, Edgardo Alfonzo	3.00

NL Contenders

		NM/M
Complete Set (18):		20.00
Common Player:		.50
Inserted 2:37		
1	Randy Johnson	1.50
2	Chipper Jones	2.00
3	Greg Maddux	2.00
4	Sammy Sosa	2.50
5	Sean Casey	.50
6	Ken Griffey Jr.	2.50
7	Todd Helton	1.50
8	Jeff Bagwell	1.50
9	Shawn Green	.50
10	Gary Sheffield	.75
11	Vladimir Guerrero	1.50
12	Mike Piazza	2.50
13	Scott Rolen	1.00
14	Barry Bonds	4.00
15	Rick Ankiel	.50
16	J.D. Drew	.50
17	Jim Edmonds	.50
18	Mark McGwire	3.00

Signatures

		NM/M
Common Player:		5.00
1	Darin Erstad	10.00
2	Nomar Garciaparra	125.00
3	Cal Eldred	5.00
4	Magglio Ordonez	5.00
5	Frank Thomas	30.00
6	Brady Clark	5.00
7	Richard Hidalgo	5.00
8	Gary Sheffield	10.00
9	Pat Burrell	15.00
10	Jim Edmonds	15.00

Stellar Performers

		NM/M
Complete Set (20):		50.00
Common Player:		1.00
Inserted 1:37		
1	Darin Erstad	1.00
2	Chipper Jones	3.00
3	Greg Maddux	3.00
4	Cal Ripken Jr.	6.00
5	Pedro Martinez	2.00
6	Nomar Garciaparra	4.00
7	Sammy Sosa	4.00
8	Frank Thomas	2.00
9	Ken Griffey Jr.	4.00
10	Todd Helton	2.00
11	Jeff Bagwell	2.00
12	Vladimir Guerrero	2.00
13	Mike Piazza	4.00
14	Derek Jeter	6.00
15	Roger Clemens	3.50
16	Tony Gwynn	3.00
17	Barry Bonds	6.00
18	Alex Rodriguez	5.00
19	Mark McGwire	5.00
20	Ivan Rodriguez	1.50

Opening Day 2K

As part of a multi-manufacturer promotion, Pacific issued eight cards of an "Opening Day 2K" set. Packages containing some of the 32 cards in the issue were distributed by MLB teams early in the season. The cards were also available exclusively as inserts in Pacific Crown Collection and Pacific Aurora packs sold at K-Mart stores early in the season. The Pacific OD2K cards have gold-foil graphic highlights on front. Backs have a portrait photo and are numbered with an "OD" prefix.

		NM/M
Complete Set (8):		4.00
Common Player:		.50
25	Mo Vaughn	.50
26	Chipper Jones	1.00
27	Nomar Garciaparra	1.00
28	Larry Walker	.65
29	Corey Koskie	.50
30	Scott Rolen	.75
31	Tony Gwynn	1.00
32	Jose Canseco	.65

2000 Pacific Paramount Sample

Nearly identical to the issued version of spokesman Tony Gwynn's card, this features a large white diagonal "SAMPLE" overprint on back and in the space where a card number usually appears.

	NM/M
Tony Gwynn	3.00

2000 Pacific Paramount

		NM/M
Complete Set (250):		25.00
Common Player:		.10
Pack (6):		1.50
Wax Box (36):		40.00
1	Garret Anderson	.10
2	Jim Edmonds	.10
3	Darin Erstad	.25
4	Chuck Finley	.10
5	Troy Glaus	.75
6	Troy Percival	.10
7	Tim Salmon	.20
8	Mo Vaughn	.10
9	Jay Bell	.10
10	Erubiel Durazo	.10
11	Steve Finley	.10
12	Luis Gonzalez	.20
13	Randy Johnson	.75
14	Travis Lee	.10
15	Matt Mantei	.10
16	Matt Williams	.10
17	Tony Womack	.10
18	Bret Boone	.10
19	Tom Glavine	.35
20	Andruw Jones	.75
21	Chipper Jones	1.00
22	Brian Jordan	.10
23	Javy Lopez	.10
24	Greg Maddux	1.00
25	Kevin Millwood	.10
26	John Rocker	.10
27	John Smoltz	.10
28	Brady Anderson	.10
29	Albert Belle	.20
30	Will Clark	.20
31	Charles Johnson	.10
32	Mike Mussina	.35
33	Cal Ripken Jr.	2.00
34	B.J. Surhoff	.10
35	Nomar Garciaparra	1.25
36	Derek Lowe	.10
37	Pedro Martinez	.75
38	Trot Nixon	.10
39	Troy O'Leary	.10
40	Jose Offerman	.10
41	John Valentin	.10
42	Jason Varitek	.10
43	Mark Grace	.20
44	Glenallen Hill	.10
45	Jon Lieber	.10
46	Cole Liniak	.10
47	Jose Nieves	.10
48	Henry Rodriguez	.10
49	Sammy Sosa	1.25
50	Kerry Wood	.65
51	Jason Dellaero	.10
52	Ray Durham	.10
53	Paul Konerko	.10
54	Carlos Lee	.10
55	Greg Norton	.10
56	Magglio Ordonez	.10
57	Chris Singleton	.10
58	Frank Thomas	.75
59	Aaron Boone	.10
60	Mike Cameron	.10
61	Sean Casey	.20
62	Pete Harnisch	.10
63	Barry Larkin	.10
64	Pokey Reese	.10
65	Greg Vaughn	.10
66	Scott Williamson	.10
67	Roberto Alomar	.35
68	Sean DePaula RC	.20
69	Travis Fryman	.10
70	David Justice	.10
71	Kenny Lofton	.10
72	Manny Ramirez	.75
73	Richie Sexson	.10
74	Jim Thome	.65
75	Omar Vizquel	.10
76	Pedro Astacio	.10
77	Vinny Castilla	.10
78	Derrick Gibson	.10
79	Todd Helton	.75
80	Neifi Perez	.10
81	Ben Petrick	.10
82	Larry Walker	.10
83	Brad Ausmus	.10
84	Tony Clark	.10
85	Deivi Cruz	.10
86	Damion Easley	.10
87	Juan Encarnacion	.10
88	Juan Gonzalez	.75
89	Bobby Higginson	.10
90	Dave Mlicki	.10
91	Dean Palmer	.10
92	Bruce Aven	.10
93	Luis Castillo	.10
94	Ramon Castro	.10
95	Cliff Floyd	.10
96	Alex Gonzalez	.10
97	Mike Lowell	.10
98	Preston Wilson	.10
99	Jeff Bagwell	.75
100	Derek Bell	.10
101	Craig Biggio	.10
102	Ken Caminiti	.10
103	Carl Everett	.10
104	Mike Hampton	.10
105	Jose Lima	.10
106	Billy Wagner	.10
107	Daryle Ward	.10
108	Carlos Beltran	.40
109	Johnny Damon	.25
110	Jermaine Dye	.10
111	Carlos Febles	.10
112	Mark Quinn	.10
113	Joe Randa	.10
114	Jose Rosado	.10
115	Mike Sweeney	.10
116	Kevin Brown	.10
117	Shawn Green	.35
118	Mark Grudzielanek	.10
119	Todd Hollandsworth	.10
120	Eric Karros	.10
121	Chan Ho Park	.10
122	Gary Sheffield	.35
123	Devon White	.10
124	Eric Young	.10
125	Kevin Barker	.10
126	Ron Belliard	.10
127	Jeromy Burnitz	.10
128	Jeff Cirillo	.10
129	Marquis Grissom	.10
130	Geoff Jenkins	.10
131	David Nilsson	.10
132	Chad Allen	.10
133	Ron Coomer	.10
134	Jacque Jones	.10
135	Corey Koskie	.10
136	Matt Lawton	.10
137	Brad Radke	.10
138	Todd Walker	.10
139	Michael Barrett	.10
140	Peter Bergeron	.10
141	Brad Fullmer	.10
142	Vladimir Guerrero	.75
143	Ugueth Urbina	.10
144	Jose Vidro	.10
145	Rondell White	.10
146	Edgardo Alfonzo	.10
147	Armando Benitez	.10
148	Roger Cedeno	.10
149	Rickey Henderson	.75
150	Melvin Mora	.10
151	John Olerud	.10
152	Rey Ordonez	.10
153	Mike Piazza	1.25
154	Jorge Toca	.10
155	Robin Ventura	.10
156	Roger Clemens	1.00
157	David Cone	.10
158	Orlando Hernandez	.10
159	Derek Jeter	2.00
160	Chuck Knoblauch	.10
161	Ricky Ledee	.10
162	Tino Martinez	.10
163	Paul O'Neill	.10
164	Mariano Rivera	.20
165	Alfonso Soriano	.75
166	Bernie Williams	.25
167	Eric Chavez	.25
168	Jason Giambi	.50
169	Ben Grieve	.25
170	Tim Hudson	.25
171	John Jaha	.10
172	Matt Stairs	.10
173	Miguel Tejada	.25
174	Randy Velarde	.10
175	Bobby Abreu	.10
176	Marlon Anderson	.10
177	Rico Brogna	.10
178	Ron Gant	.10
179	Doug Glanville	.10
180	Mike Lieberthal	.10
181	Scott Rolen	.65
182	Curt Schilling	.35
183	Brian Giles	.10
184	Chad Hermansen	.10
185	Jason Kendall	.10
186	Al Martin	.10
187	Pat Meares	.10
188	Warren Morris	.10
189	Ed Sprague	.10
190	Kevin Young	.10
191	Rick Ankiel	.25
192	Kent Bottenfield	.10
193	Eric Davis	.10
194	J.D. Drew	.25
195	Adam Kennedy	.10
196	Ray Lankford	.10
197	Joe McEwing	.10
198	Mark McGwire	1.50
199	Edgar Renteria	.10
200	Fernando Tatis	.10
201	Mike Darr	.10
202	Ben Davis	.10
203	Tony Gwynn	1.00
204	Trevor Hoffman	.10
205	Damian Jackson	.10
206	Phil Nevin	.10
207	Reggie Sanders	.10
208	Quilvio Veras	.10
209	Rich Aurilia	.10
210	Marvin Benard	.10
211	Barry Bonds	2.00
212	Ellis Burks	.10
213	Livan Hernandez	.10
214	Jeff Kent	.10
215	Russ Ortiz	.10
216	J.T. Snow	.10
217	Paul Abbott	.10
218	David Bell	.10
219	Freddy Garcia	.10
220	Ken Griffey Jr.	1.50
221	Carlos Guillen	.10
222	Brian Hunter	.10
223	Edgar Martinez	.10
224	Jamie Moyer	.10
225	Alex Rodriguez	1.50
226	Wade Boggs	1.00
227	Miguel Cairo	.10
228	Jose Canseco	.40
229	Roberto Hernandez	.10
230	Dave Martinez	.10
231	Quinton McCracken	.10
232	Fred McGriff	.10
233	Kevin Stocker	.10
234	Royce Clayton	.10
235	Rusty Greer	.10
236	Ruben Mateo	.10
237	Rafael Palmeiro	.65
238	Ivan Rodriguez	.65
239	Aaron Sele	.10
240	John Wetteland	.10
241	Todd Zeile	.10
242	Tony Batista	.10
243	Homer Bush	.10
244	Carlos Delgado	.50
245	Tony Fernandez	.10
246	Billy Koch	.10
247	Raul Mondesi	.10
248	Shannon Stewart	.10
249	David Wells	.10
250	Vernon Wells	.10

Copper

Stars: 2X
Inserted 1:1 H

Emerald

Stars: 1-2X
Yng Stars & RC's: 1X
Inserted 1:1 7-11 pack.

Gold

Inserted 1:1 R
Stars: 1-2X
Yng Stars & RC's: 1X

Holographic Gold

Stars: 3-6X
Production 199 Sets

Holographic Green

Stars: 6-10X
Production 99 Sets, 7-11 insert.

Holographic Silver

18	Ivan Rodriguez	5.00
19	Chipper Jones	8.00
20	Cal Ripken Jr.	15.00
21	Nomar Garciaparra	10.00
22	Pedro Martinez	6.00
23	Sammy Sosa	10.00
24	Manny Ramirez	6.00
25	Jeff Bagwell	6.00
26	Craig Biggio	3.00
27	Vladimir Guerrero	6.00
28	Mike Piazza	10.00
29	Roger Clemens	9.00
30	Derek Jeter	15.00
31	Mark McGwire	12.00
32	Tony Gwynn	8.00
33	Ken Griffey Jr.	10.00
34	Alex Rodriguez	12.00
35	Rafael Palmeiro	5.00
36	Ivan Rodriguez	5.00

Stars: 5-10X
Production 99 Sets

Platinum Blue
Stars: 6-12X
Production 67 Sets

Premiere Date
Stars: 8-15X
Production 50 Sets

Ruby Red
Stars: 1-2X
RC's: 1X
Inserted 9 per 7-11 pack.

Cooperstown Bound

		NM/M
Complete Set (10):		220.00
Common Player:		20.00

Inserted 1:361
Proofs: 2X
Production 20 Sets, hobby only.
Canvas Proofs: Values Undetermined
Production One Set

1	Greg Maddux	20.00
2	Cal Ripken Jr.	40.00
3	Nomar Garciaparra	25.00
4	Sammy Sosa	25.00
5	Roger Clemens	30.00
6	Derek Jeter	40.00
7	Mark McGwire	30.00
8	Tony Gwynn	20.00
9	Ken Griffey Jr.	25.00
10	Alex Rodriguez	30.00

Double Vision

		NM/M
Complete Set (36):		220.00
Common Player:		3.00

Inserted 1:37

1	Chipper Jones	8.00
2	Cal Ripken Jr.	15.00
3	Nomar Garciaparra	10.00
4	Pedro Martinez	6.00
5	Sammy Sosa	10.00
6	Manny Ramirez	6.00
7	Jeff Bagwell	6.00
8	Craig Biggio	3.00
9	Vladimir Guerrero	6.00
10	Mike Piazza	10.00
11	Roger Clemens	9.00
12	Derek Jeter	15.00
13	Mark McGwire	12.00
14	Tony Gwynn	8.00
15	Ken Griffey Jr.	10.00
16	Alex Rodriguez	12.00
17	Rafael Palmeiro	5.00

Fielder's Choice

		NM/M
Complete Set (20):		150.00
Common Player:		3.00

Inserted 1:73
Gold Parallel (10 Sets issued): 6-8X

1	Andruw Jones	5.00
2	Chipper Jones	8.00
3	Greg Maddux	8.00
4	Cal Ripken Jr.	20.00
5	Nomar Garciaparra	10.00
6	Sammy Sosa	10.00
7	Sean Casey	3.00
8	Manny Ramirez	5.00
9	Larry Walker	3.00
10	Jeff Bagwell	5.00
11	Mike Piazza	10.00
12	Derek Jeter	20.00
13	Bernie Williams	3.00
14	Scott Rolen	4.00
15	Mark McGwire	15.00
16	Tony Gwynn	8.00
17	Barry Bonds	20.00
18	Ken Griffey Jr.	10.00
19	Alex Rodriguez	15.00
20	Ivan Rodriguez	4.00

Maximum Impact

		NM/M
Complete Set (20):		25.00
Common Player:		.50

Inserted 2:25 7-11 packs.

1	Chipper Jones	2.00
2	Cal Ripken Jr.	4.00
3	Nomar Garciaparra	2.50
4	Pedro Martinez	1.50
5	Sammy Sosa	2.50
6	Manny Ramirez	1.50
7	Larry Walker	.50
8	Jeff Bagwell	1.50
9	Carlos Beltran	.75
10	Vladimir Guerrero	1.50
11	Mike Piazza	2.50
12	Derek Jeter	4.00
13	Roger Clemens	2.25
14	Mark McGwire	3.00
15	Tony Gwynn	2.00
16	Barry Bonds	4.00
17	Ken Griffey Jr.	2.50
18	Alex Rodriguez	3.00
19	Ivan Rodriguez	1.00
20	Carlos Delgado	.75

Season in Review

		NM/M
Complete Set (30):		25.00
Common Player:		.50

Inserted 2:37

1	Randy Johnson	1.50
2	Matt Williams	.50
3	Chipper Jones	2.00
4	Greg Maddux	2.00
5	Cal Ripken Jr.	4.00
6	Nomar Garciaparra	2.50
7	Pedro Martinez	1.50
8	Sammy Sosa	2.50
9	Manny Ramirez	1.50
10	Larry Walker	.50
11	Jeff Bagwell	1.50
12	Craig Biggio	.50
13	Carlos Beltran	.75
14	Mark Quinn	.50
15	Vladimir Guerrero	1.50
16	Mike Piazza	2.50
17	Robin Ventura	.50
18	Roger Clemens	2.25
19	David Cone	.50
20	Derek Jeter	4.00
21	Mark McGwire	3.00
22	Fernando Tatis	.50
23	Tony Gwynn	2.00
24	Barry Bonds	4.00
25	Ken Griffey Jr.	2.50
26	Alex Rodriguez	3.00
27	Wade Boggs	2.00
28	Jose Canseco	.65
29	Rafael Palmeiro	1.00
30	Ivan Rodriguez	1.00

Update

		NM/M
Complete Set (100):		10.00
Common Player:		.10

Production 12,500 Sets; retail exclusive

1-U	Adam Kennedy	.10
2-U	Bengie Molina	.10
3-U	Derrick Turnbow	.10
4-U	Randy Johnson	.75
5-U	Danny Klassen	.10
6-U	Vicente Padilla	.10
7-U	Rafael Furcal	.10
8-U	Andres Galarraga	.10
9-U	Chipper Jones	1.00
10-U	Fernando Lunar	.10
11-U	Willie Morales	.10
12-U	Cal Ripken Jr.	2.00
13-U	B.J. Ryan	.10
14-U	Carl Everett	.10
15-U	Nomar Garciaparra	1.25
16-U	Pedro Martinez	.75
17-U	Wilton Veras	.10
18-U	Scott Downs	.10
19-U	Daniel Garibay	.10
20-U	Sammy Sosa	1.25
21-U	Julio Zuleta	.10
22-U	Josh Paul	.10
23-U	Frank Thomas	.75
24-U	Rob Bell	.10
25-U	Dante Bichette	.10
26-U	Travis Dawkins	.10
27-U	Ken Griffey Jr.	1.25
28-U	Chuck Finley	.10
29-U	Manny Ramirez	.75
30-U	Paul Rigdon	.10
31-U	Jeff Cirillo	.10
32-U	Larry Walker	.10
33-U	Masato Yoshii	.10
34-U	Robert Fick	.10
35-U	Jose Macias	.10
36-U	Juan Gonzalez	.75
37-U	Hideo Nomo	.75
38-U	Jason Grilli	.10
39-U	Pablo Ozuna	.10
40-U	Brad Penny	.10
41-U	Jeff Bagwell	.75
42-U	Lance Berkman	.10
43-U	Roger Cedeno	.10
44-U	Octavio Dotel	.10
45-U	Chad Durbin	.10
46-U	Eric Gagne	.10
47-U	Shawn Green	.35
48-U	Jose Hernandez	.10
49-U	Matt LeCroy	.10
50-U	Johan Santana	.10
51-U	Vladimir Guerrero	.75
52-U	Hideki Irabu	.10
53-U	Andrew Tracy	.10
54-U	Derek Bell	.10
55-U	Eric Cammack	.10
56-U	Mike Hampton	.10
57-U	Jay Payton	.10
58-U	Mike Piazza	1.25
59-U	Todd Zeile	.10
60-U	Roger Clemens	1.00
61-U	Darrell Einertson	.10
62-U	Derek Jeter	2.00
63-U	Jason Giambi	.60
64-U	Terrence Long	.10
65-U	Mark Mulder	.10
66-U	Adam Piatt	.10
67-U	Luis Vizcaino	.10
68-U	Pat Burrell	.35
69-U	Scott Rolen	.65
70-U	Chad Hermansen	.10
71-U	Rick Ankiel	.25
72-U	Jim Edmonds	.10
73-U	Mark McGwire	1.50
74-U	Gene Stechschulte	.10
75-U	Fernando Vina	.10
76-U	Bret Boone	.10
77-U	Tony Gwynn	1.00
78-U	Ryan Klesko	.10
79-U	David Newhan	.10
80-U	Kevin Walker	.10
81-U	Barry Bonds	2.00
82-U	Aaron Fultz	.10
83-U	Ben Weber	.10
84-U	Rickey Henderson	.75
85-U	Kevin Hodges	.10
86-U	John Olerud	.10
87-U	Robert Ramsay	.10
88-U	Alex Rodriguez	1.50
89-U	Kazuhiro Sasaki	.15
90-U	Vinny Castilla	.10
91-U	Jeff Sparks	.10
92-U	Greg Vaughn	.10
93-U	Francisco Cordero	.10
94-U	Gabe Kapler	.10
95-U	Mike Lamb	.10
96-U	Ivan Rodriguez	.65
97-U	Clayton Andrews	.10
98-U	Brad Fullmer	.10
99-U	Raul Mondesi	.10
100-U	Dewayne Wise	.10

2000 Pacific Prism

		NM/M
Complete Set (150):		10.00
Common Player:		.10
Pack (5):		1.50
Wax Box (24):		15.00

1	Jeff DaVanon RC	.50
2	Troy Glaus	.50
3	Tim Salmon	.15
4	Mo Vaughn	.25
5	Jay Bell	.10
6	Erubiel Durazo	.10
7	Luis Gonzalez	.20
8	Randy Johnson	.50
9	Matt Williams	.10
10	Andres Galarraga	.50
11	Andruw Jones	.50
12	Chipper Jones	.75
13	Brian Jordan	.10
14	Greg Maddux	.65
15	Kevin Millwood	.10
16	John Smoltz	.10
17	Albert Belle	.15
18	Mike Mussina	.25
19	Calvin Pickering	.10
20	Cal Ripken Jr.	1.50
21	B.J. Surhoff	.10
22	Nomar Garciaparra	1.25
23	Pedro Martinez	.50
24	Troy O'Leary	.10
25	John Valentin	.10
26	Jason Varitek	.10
27	Mark Grace	.15
28	Henry Rodriguez	.10
29	Sammy Sosa	1.00
30	Kerry Wood	.25
31	Ray Durham	.10
32	Carlos Lee	.10
33	Magglio Ordonez	.10
34	Chris Singleton	.10
35	Frank Thomas	.50
36	Sean Casey	.15
37	Travis Dawkins	.10
38	Barry Larkin	.10
39	Pokey Reese	.10
40	Scott Williamson	.10
41	Roberto Alomar	.20
42	Bartolo Colon	.10
43	David Justice	.10
44	Manny Ramirez	.50
45	Richie Sexson	.10
46	Jim Thome	.50
47	Omar Vizquel	.10
48	Pedro Astacio	.10
49	Todd Helton	.50
50	Neifi Perez	.10
51	Ben Petrick	.10
52	Larry Walker	.10
53	Tony Clark	.10
54	Damion Easley	.10
55	Juan Gonzalez	.50
56	Dean Palmer	.10
57	A.J. Burnett	.10
58	Luis Castillo	.10
59	Cliff Floyd	.10
60	Alex Gonzalez	.10
61	Preston Wilson	.10
62	Jeff Bagwell	.50
63	Craig Biggio	.10
64	Ken Caminiti	.10
65	Jose Lima	.10
66	Billy Wagner	.10
67	Carlos Beltran	.30
68	Johnny Damon	.25
69	Jermaine Dye	.10
70	Carlos Febles	.10
71	Mike Sweeney	.10
72	Kevin Brown	.10
73	Shawn Green	.25
74	Eric Karros	.10
75	Chan Ho Park	.10
76	Gary Sheffield	.30
77	Ron Belliard	.10
78	Jeromy Burnitz	.10
79	Marquis Grissom	.10
80	Geoff Jenkins	.10
81	Mark Loretta	.10
82	Ron Coomer	.10
83	Jacque Jones	.10
84	Corey Koskie	.10
85	Brad Radke	.10
86	Todd Walker	.10
87	Michael Barrett	.10
88	Peter Bergeron	.10
89	Vladimir Guerrero	.50
90	Jose Vidro	.10
91	Rondell White	.10
92	Edgardo Alfonzo	.10
93	Rickey Henderson	.50
94	Rey Ordonez	.10
95	Mike Piazza	1.00
96	Robin Ventura	.10
97	Roger Clemens	.75
98	Orlando Hernandez	.10
99	Derek Jeter	1.50
100	Tino Martinez	.10
101	Mariano Rivera	.15
102	Alfonso Soriano	.50
103	Bernie Williams	.25
104	Eric Chavez	.10
105	Jason Giambi	.30
106	Ben Grieve	.10
107	Tim Hudson	.20
108	John Jaha	.10
109	Bobby Abreu	.10
110	Doug Glanville	.10
111	Mike Lieberthal	.10
112	Scott Rolen	.40
113	Curt Schilling	.25
114	Brian Giles	.10
115	Jason Kendall	.10
116	Warren Morris	.10
117	Kevin Young	.10
118	Rick Ankiel	.10
119	J.D. Drew	.15
120	Chad Hutchinson	.10
121	Ray Lankford	.10
122	Mark McGwire	1.25
123	Fernando Tatis	.10
124	Bret Boone	.10
125	Ben Davis	.10
126	Tony Gwynn	.65
127	Trevor Hoffman	.10
128	Barry Bonds	1.50
129	Ellis Burks	.10
130	Jeff Kent	.10
131	J.T. Snow	.10
132	Freddy Garcia	.10
133	Ken Griffey Jr.	1.00
134	Edgar Martinez	.10
135	John Olerud	.10
136	Alex Rodriguez	1.25
137	Jose Canseco	.20
138	Vinny Castilla	.10
139	Roberto Hernandez	.10
140	Fred McGriff	.10
141	Rusty Greer	.10
142	Ruben Mateo	.10
143	Rafael Palmeiro	.50
144	Ivan Rodriguez	.40
145	Lee Stevens	.10
146	Tony Batista	.10
147	Carlos Delgado	.35
148	Shannon Stewart	.10
149	David Wells	.10
150	Vernon Wells	.10

Drops Silver

One of eight silver-foil parallels to Prism, this version features a rain-drop-like patterned background. Inserted into both hobby and retail packaging, production was reported as 799 of 100 of the cards, and 916 of the other 50 cards (indicated with a (*) in the checklist). The cards are not serially numbered.

		NM/M
Common Player:		.50
Stars:		2-4X

1	Jeff DaVanon RC	.50
2	Troy Glaus	1.00
3	Tim Salmon	.60
4	Mo Vaughn (*)	.50
5	Jay Bell	.50
6	Erubiel Durazo	.50
7	Luis Gonzalez	.60
8	Randy Johnson (*)	1.00
9	Matt Williams (*)	.50
10	Andres Galarraga	.50
11	Andruw Jones (*)	1.00
12	Chipper Jones (*)	1.50
13	Brian Jordan	.50
14	Greg Maddux (*)	1.50
15	Kevin Millwood	.50
16	John Smoltz	.50
17	Albert Belle	.50
18	Mike Mussina (*)	.60
19	Calvin Pickering	.50
20	Cal Ripken Jr. (*)	3.00
21	B.J. Surhoff	.50
22	Nomar Garciaparra (*)	2.00
23	Pedro Martinez (*)	1.00
24	Troy O'Leary	.50
25	John Valentin	.50
26	Jason Varitek	.60
27	Mark Grace	.50
28	Henry Rodriguez	.50
29	Sammy Sosa (*)	2.00
30	Kerry Wood (*)	.65
31	Ray Durham	.50
32	Carlos Lee	.50
33	Magglio Ordonez (*)	.50
34	Chris Singleton	.50
35	Frank Thomas (*)	1.00
36	Sean Casey (*)	.50
37	Travis Dawkins	.50
38	Barry Larkin	.50
39	Pokey Reese	.50
40	Scott Williamson	.50
41	Roberto Alomar (*)	.60
42	Bartolo Colon	.50
43	David Justice	.50
44	Manny Ramirez (*)	1.00
45	Richie Sexson	.50
46	Jim Thome (*)	1.00
47	Omar Vizquel	.50
48	Pedro Astacio	.50
49	Todd Helton (*)	1.00
50	Neifi Perez	.50
51	Ben Petrick	.50
52	Larry Walker (*)	.50
53	Tony Clark	.50
54	Damion Easley	.50
55	Juan Gonzalez (*)	1.00
56	Dean Palmer	.50
57	A.J. Burnett	.50
58	Luis Castillo	.50
59	Cliff Floyd	.50
60	Alex Gonzalez	.50
61	Preston Wilson (*)	.50
62	Jeff Bagwell (*)	1.00
63	Craig Biggio (*)	.50
64	Ken Caminiti	.50
65	Jose Lima	.50
66	Billy Wagner	.50
67	Carlos Beltran (*)	.65
68	Johnny Damon	.65
69	Jermaine Dye	.65
70	Carlos Febles	.50
71	Mike Sweeney	.50
72	Kevin Brown (*)	.50
73	Shawn Green (*)	.75
74	Eric Karros	.50
75	Chan Ho Park	.50
76	Gary Sheffield (*)	.60
77	Ron Belliard	.50
x8	Jeromy Burnitz (*)	.50

79	Marquis Grissom	.50
80	Geoff Jenkins	.50
81	Mark Loretta	.50
82	Ron Coomer	.50
83	Jacque Jones	.50
84	Corey Koskie	.50
85	Brad Radke	.50
86	Todd Walker	.50
87	Michael Barrett	.50
88	Peter Bergeron	.50
89	Vladimir Guerrero (*)	1.00
90	Jose Vidro	.50
91	Rondell White	.50
92	Edgardo Alfonzo (*)	.50
93	Rickey Henderson	1.00
94	Rey Ordonez	.50
95	Mike Piazza (*)	2.00
96	Robin Ventura	.50
97	Roger Clemens (*)	1.75
98	Orlando Hernandez	.50
99	Derek Jeter (*)	3.00
100	Tino Martinez	.50
101	Mariano Rivera	.50
102	Alfonso Soriano	.75
103	Bernie Williams (*)	.60
104	Eric Chavez	.50
105	Jason Giambi	.75
106	Ben Grieve	.50
107	Tim Hudson	.50
108	John Jaha	.50
109	Bobby Abreu	.50
110	Doug Glanville	.50
111	Mike Lieberthal	.50
112	Scott Rolen (*)	.75
113	Curt Schilling	.60
114	Brian Giles (*)	.50
115	Jason Kendall	.50
116	Warren Morris	.50
117	Kevin Young	.50
118	Rick Ankiel (*)	.50
119	J.D. Drew (*)	.50
120	Chad Hutchinson	.50
121	Ray Lankford	.50
122	Mark McGwire (*)	2.50
123	Fernando Tatis	.50
124	Bret Boone	.60
125	Ben Davis	.50
126	Tony Gwynn (*)	1.50
127	Trevor Hoffman	.50
128	Barry Bonds (*)	3.00
129	Ellis Burks	.50
130	Jeff Kent	.50
131	J.T. Snow	.50
132	Freddy Garcia (*)	.50
133	Ken Griffey Jr. (*)	2.00
134	Edgar Martinez	.50
135	John Olerud	.50
136	Alex Rodriguez (*)	2.50
137	Jose Canseco	.60
138	Vinny Castilla	.50
139	Roberto Hernandez	.50
140	Fred McGriff	.50
141	Rusty Greer	.50
142	Ruben Mateo (*)	.50
143	Rafael Palmeiro (*)	.75
144	Ivan Rodriguez (*)	.75
145	Lee Stevens	.50
146	Tony Batista	.50
147	Carlos Delgado (*)	.60
148	Shannon Stewart	.50
149	David Wells	.50
150	Vernon Wells	.50

Holographic Blue

	NM/M
Common Player:	1.00
Stars:	4-6X
Production 80 Sets	

Holographic Gold

	NM/M
Common Player:	.50
Stars:	2-4X
Production 480 Sets	

Holographic Mirror

	NM/M
Common Player:	1.50
Stars:	4-6X
Production 160 Sets	

Holographic Purple

	NM/M
Common Player:	1.00
Stars:	6-8X
Production 99 Sets	

Pebbly Dots

One of eight silver-foil versions of Prism, there is virtually no way to describe the silver metallic foil background of this parallel set dubbed "Pebbly Dots" by the maker to allow its differentiation from the set labeled "Texture Silver," other than perhaps the vaguely vertical orientation of the texture. Production of 100 of the cards was 691 apiece, with the other 50 cards produced in an edition of 448 each indicated with an (*) in the checklist. They were inserted into both hobby and retail packaging. The cards are not serially numbered.

		NM/M
Complete Set (150):		50.00
Common Player:		.50
1	Jeff DaVanon **RC**	.50
2	Troy Glaus	.75
3	Tim Salmon	.60
4	Mo Vaughn (*)	.50
5	Jay Bell	.50
6	Erubiel Durazo	.50
7	Luis Gonzalez	.60
8	Randy Johnson (*)	.75
9	Matt Williams (*)	.50
10	Andres Galarraga	.50
11	Andruw Jones (*)	.75
12	Chipper Jones (*)	1.00
13	Brian Jordan	.50
14	Greg Maddux (*)	1.00
15	Kevin Millwood	.50
16	John Smoltz	.50
17	Albert Belle	.50
18	Mike Mussina (*)	.60
19	Calvin Pickering	.50
20	Cal Ripken Jr. (*)	3.00
21	B.J. Surhoff	.50
22	Nomar Garciaparra (*)	2.00
23	Pedro Martinez (*)	.75
24	Troy O'Leary	.50
25	John Valentin	.50
26	Jason Varitek	.50
27	Mark Grace	.60
28	Henry Rodriguez	.50
29	Sammy Sosa (*)	2.00
30	Kerry Wood (*)	.65
31	Ray Durham	.50
32	Carlos Lee	.50
33	Magglio Ordonez (*)	.50
34	Chris Singleton	.50
35	Frank Thomas (*)	.75
36	Sean Casey (*)	.60
37	Travis Dawkins	.50
38	Barry Larkin	.50
39	Pokey Reese	.50
40	Scott Williamson	.50
41	Roberto Alomar (*)	.60
42	Bartolo Colon	.50
43	David Justice	.50
44	Manny Ramirez (*)	.75
45	Richie Sexson	.50
46	Jim Thome (*)	.75
47	Omar Vizquel	.50
48	Pedro Astacio	.50
49	Todd Helton (*)	.75
50	Neifi Perez	.50
51	Ben Petrick	.50
52	Larry Walker (*)	.50
53	Tony Clark	.50
54	Damion Easley	.50
55	Juan Gonzalez (*)	.75
56	Dean Palmer	.50
57	A.J. Burnett (*)	.50
58	Luis Castillo	.50
59	Cliff Floyd	.50
60	Alex Gonzalez	.50
61	Preston Wilson (*)	.50
62	Jeff Bagwell (*)	.75
63	Craig Biggio (*)	.50
64	Ken Caminiti	.50
65	Jose Lima	.50
66	Billy Wagner	.50
67	Carlos Beltran (*)	.65
68	Johnny Damon	.50
69	Jermaine Dye	.50
70	Carlos Febles	.50
71	Mike Sweeney	.50
72	Kevin Brown (*)	.50
73	Shawn Green (*)	.65
74	Eric Karros	.50
75	Chan Ho Park	.50

76	Gary Sheffield (*)	.60
77	Ron Belliard	.50
78	Jeromy Burnitz (*)	.50
79	Marquis Grissom	.50
80	Geoff Jenkins	.50
81	Mark Loretta	.50
82	Ron Coomer	.50
83	Jacque Jones	.50
84	Corey Koskie	.50
85	Brad Radke	.50
86	Todd Walker	.50
87	Michael Barrett	.50
88	Peter Bergeron	.50
89	Vladimir Guerrero (*)	.75
90	Jose Vidro	.50
91	Rondell White	.50
92	Edgardo Alfonzo (*)	.50
93	Rickey Henderson	.75
94	Rey Ordonez	.50
95	Mike Piazza (*)	2.00
96	Robin Ventura	.50
97	Roger Clemens (*)	1.50
98	Orlando Hernandez	.50
99	Derek Jeter (*)	3.00
100	Tino Martinez	.50
101	Mariano Rivera	.50
102	Alfonso Soriano	.65
103	Bernie Williams (*)	.60
104	Eric Chavez	.50
105	Jason Giambi	.60
106	Ben Grieve	.50
107	Tim Hudson	.50
108	John Jaha	.50
109	Bobby Abreu	.50
110	Doug Glanville	.50
111	Mike Lieberthal	.50
112	Scott Rolen (*)	.60
113	Curt Schilling	.60
114	Brian Giles (*)	.50
115	Jason Kendall	.50
116	Warren Morris	.50
117	Kevin Young	.50
118	Rick Ankiel (*)	.50
119	J.D. Drew (*)	.50
120	Chad Hutchinson	.50
121	Ray Lankford	.50
122	Mark McGwire (*)	2.50
123	Fernando Tatis	.50
124	Bret Boone	.50
125	Ben Davis	.50
126	Tony Gwynn (*)	1.00
127	Trevor Hoffman	.50
128	Barry Bonds (*)	3.00
129	Ellis Burks	.50
130	Jeff Kent	.50
131	J.T. Snow	.50
132	Freddy Garcia (*)	.50
133	Ken Griffey Jr. (*)	2.00
134	Edgar Martinez	.50
135	John Olerud	.50
136	Alex Rodriguez (*)	2.50
137	Jose Canseco (*)	.60
138	Vinny Castilla	.50
139	Roberto Hernandez	.50
140	Fred McGriff	.50
141	Rusty Greer	.50
142	Ruben Mateo (*)	.50
143	Rafael Palmeiro (*)	.65
144	Ivan Rodriguez (*)	.65
145	Lee Stevens	.50
146	Tony Batista	.50
147	Carlos Delgado (*)	.60
148	Shannon Stewart	.50
149	David Wells	.50
150	Vernon Wells	.50

Premiere Date

Sixty-one of each card in '00 Prism were embossed with a round seal at center: "PREMIERE DATE / PRISM / 2000 / APR. 12, 2000" and have a dot-matrix serial number at bottom-right on front.

		NM/M
Common Player:		1.50
Stars:		8-10X
Production 61 Sets		

Rapture Gold

This complete-set parallel to Prism, features a diagonally striped metallic gold-foil background. A retail-only insert, 565 sets were produced. The cards are not serially numbered.

		NM/M
Complete Set (150):		50.00
Common Player:		.50
Stars:		2-3X

Rapture Silver

One of eight silver-foil parallels to Prism, this version features a diagonally striped background. A hobby-only insert, 916 sets were produced. The cards are not serially numbered.

		NM/M
Complete Set (150):		50.00
Common Player:		.50
Stars:		2-3X

Sheen Silver

One of eight silver-foil versions of Prism, there is virtually no way to describe the silver metallic foil background of this partial-parallel set dubbed "Sheen Silver" by the maker, other than perhaps the diagonal orientation of the jagged-edged forms. Production was reported as 565 each for cards in the numerical range of #1-40 and #80-110, and 448 each for cards skip-numbered between #42-79 and #111-150. They were inserted into both hobby and retail packaging. The cards are not serially numbered. The 100-card partial-parallel does not include most of the top stars.

		NM/M
Complete Set (100):		40.00
Common Player:		.50
1	Jeff DaVanon **RC**	.50
2	Troy Glaus	1.50
3	Tim Salmon	.50
5	Jay Bell	.50
6	Erubiel Durazo	.50
7	Luis Gonzalez	.50
10	Andres Galarraga	.50
13	Brian Jordan	.50
15	Kevin Millwood	.50
16	John Smoltz	.50
17	Albert Belle	.50
19	Calvin Pickering	.50
21	B.J. Surhoff	.50
24	Troy O'Leary	.50
25	John Valentin	.50
26	Jason Varitek	.50
27	Mark Grace	.50

Slider Silver

One of eight silver-foil versions of Prism, there is virtually no way to describe the silver metallic foil background of this parallel set dubbed "Slider Silver" by the maker, other than perhaps noting the horizontally oriented arrowhead-shaped forms in the background. Production was reported as either 334 each, 448, or 565, depending on press sheet. The number of each card produced is

28	Henry Rodriguez	.50
31	Ray Durham	.50
32	Carlos Lee	.50
34	Chris Singleton	.50
37	Travis Dawkins	.50
38	Barry Larkin	.50
39	Pokey Reese	.50
40	Scott Williamson	.50
42	Bartolo Colon	.50
43	David Justice	.50
45	Richie Sexson	.50
47	Omar Vizquel	.50
48	Pedro Astacio	.50
50	Neifi Perez	.50
51	Ben Petrick	.50
53	Tony Clark	.50
54	Damion Easley	.50
56	Dean Palmer	.50
57	A.J. Burnett	.50
58	Luis Castillo	.50
59	Cliff Floyd	.50
60	Alex Gonzalez	.50
64	Ken Caminiti	.50
65	Jose Lima	.50
66	Billy Wagner	.50
68	Johnny Damon	.50
69	Jermaine Dye	.50
70	Carlos Febles	.50
71	Mike Sweeney	.50
74	Eric Karros	.50
75	Chan Ho Park	.50
77	Ron Belliard	.50
79	Marquis Grissom	.50
80	Geoff Jenkins	.50
81	Mark Loretta	.50
82	Ron Coomer	.50
83	Jacque Jones	.50
84	Corey Koskie	.50
85	Brad Radke	.50
86	Todd Walker	.50
87	Michael Barrett	.50
88	Peter Bergeron	.50
90	Jose Vidro	.50
91	Rondell White	.50
93	Rickey Henderson	1.50
96	Robin Ventura	.50
98	Orlando Hernandez	.50
100	Tino Martinez	.50
102	Alfonso Soriano	1.00
105	Jason Giambi	1.00
106	Ben Grieve	.50
107	Tim Hudson	.50
108	John Jaha	.50
109	Bobby Abreu	.50
110	Doug Glanville	.50
111	Mike Lieberthal	.50
113	Curt Schilling	.50
116	Jason Kendall	.50
117	Warren Morris	.50
120	Kevin Young	.50
121	Chad Hutchinson	.50
124	Ray Lankford	.50
127	Fernando Tatis	.50
129	Bret Boone	.50
130	Ben Davis	.50
131	Trevor Hoffman	.50
135	Jeff Kent	.50
139	J.T. Snow	.50
140	Edgar Martinez	.50
141	John Olerud	.50
145	Vinny Castilla	.50
146	Roberto Hernandez	.50
147	Fred McGriff	.50
148	Rusty Greer	.50
149	Lee Stevens	.50
150	Tony Batista	.50
	Shannon Stewart	.50
	David Wells	.50
	Vernon Wells	.50

noted parenthetically in this checklist. They were inserted into both hobby and retail packaging. The cards are not serially numbered.

		NM/M
Complete Set (150):		50.00
Common Player:		.50
1	Jeff DaVanon/334 **RC**	.50
2	Troy Glaus/334	.75
3	Tim Salmon/334	.60
4	Mo Vaughn/565	.50
5	Jay Bell/334	.50
6	Erubiel Durazo/334	.50
7	Luis Gonzalez/334	.60
8	Randy Johnson/565	.75
9	Matt Williams/565	.50
10	Andres Galarraga/334	.50
11	Andruw Jones/565	.75
12	Chipper Jones/565	1.00
13	Brian Jordan/334	.50
14	Greg Maddux/565	1.00
15	Kevin Millwood/334	.50
16	John Smoltz/334	.50
17	Albert Belle/334	.50
18	Mike Mussina/565	.45
19	Calvin Pickering/334	.50
20	Cal Ripken Jr./565	3.00
21	B.J. Surhoff/334	.50
22	Nomar Garciaparra/565	2.00
23	Pedro Martinez/565	.50
24	Troy O'Leary/334	.50
25	John Valentin/334	.50
26	Jason Varitek/334	.50
27	Mark Grace/334	.50
28	Henry Rodriguez/334	.50
29	Sammy Sosa/565	2.00
30	Kerry Wood/565	.50
31	Ray Durham/334	.50
32	Carlos Lee/334	.50
33	Magglio Ordonez/565	.60
34	Chris Singleton/334	.50
35	Frank Thomas/565	.75
36	Sean Casey/334	.60
37	Travis Dawkins/334	.50
38	Barry Larkin/334	.50
39	Pokey Reese/334	.50
40	Scott Williamson/334	.50
41	Roberto Alomar/565	.60
42	Bartolo Colon/448	.50
43	David Justice/448	.50
44	Manny Ramirez/565	.75
45	Richie Sexson/448	.50
46	Jim Thome/565	.65
47	Omar Vizquel/448	.50
48	Pedro Astacio/448	.50
49	Todd Helton/565	.75
50	Neifi Perez/448	.50
51	Ben Petrick/448	.50
52	Larry Walker/565	.50
53	Tony Clark/448	.50
54	Damion Easley/448	.50
55	Juan Gonzalez/565	.75
56	Dean Palmer/448	.50
57	A.J. Burnett/448	.50
58	Luis Castillo/448	.50
59	Cliff Floyd/448	.50
60	Alex Gonzalez/448	.50
61	Preston Wilson/565	.50
62	Jeff Bagwell/565	.75
63	Craig Biggio/565	.50
64	Ken Caminiti/448	.50
65	Jose Lima/448	.50
66	Billy Wagner/448	.50
67	Carlos Beltran/565	.65
68	Johnny Damon/448	.50
69	Jermaine Dye/448	.50
70	Carlos Febles/448	.50
71	Mike Sweeney/448	.50
72	Kevin Brown/565	.50
73	Shawn Green/565	.60
74	Eric Karros/448	.50
75	Chan Ho Park/448	.50
76	Gary Sheffield/565	.60
77	Ron Belliard/448	.50
78	Jeromy Burnitz/565	.50
79	Marquis Grissom/448	.50
80	Geoff Jenkins/334	.50
81	Mark Loretta/334	.50
82	Ron Coomer/334	.50
83	Jacque Jones/334	.50
84	Corey Koskie/334	.50
85	Brad Radke/334	.50
86	Todd Walker/334	.50
87	Michael Barrett/334	.50
88	Peter Bergeron/334	.50
89	Vladimir Guerrero/565	.75
90	Jose Vidro/334	.50
91	Rondell White/334	.50
92	Edgardo Alfonzo/565	.50
93	Rickey Henderson/334	.50
94	Rey Ordonez/334	.50
95	Mike Piazza/565	2.00
96	Robin Ventura/334	.50
97	Roger Clemens/565	1.50
98	Orlando Hernandez/334	.50
99	Derek Jeter/565	3.00
100	Tino Martinez/334	.50
101	Mariano Rivera/334	.50
102	Alfonso Soriano/334	.60
103	Bernie Williams/334	.50
104	Eric Chavez/334	.50
105	Jason Giambi/334	.75
106	Ben Grieve/334	.50
107	Tim Hudson/334	.50
108	John Jaha/334	.50
109	Bobby Abreu/334	.50

#	Player	
110	Doug Glanville/334	.50
111	Mike Liebenthal/448	.50
112	Scott Rolen/565	.65
113	Curt Schilling/448	.60
114	Brian Giles/565	.50
115	Jason Kendall/448	.50
116	Warren Morris/448	.50
117	Kevin Young/448	.50
118	Rick Ankiel/565	.50
119	J.D. Drew/565	.60
120	Chad Hutchinson/448	.50
121	Ray Lankford/448	.50
122	Mark McGwire/565	2.50
123	Fernando Tatis/448	.50
124	Bret Boone/448	.50
125	Ben Davis/448	.50
126	Tony Gwynn/565	1.00
127	Trevor Hoffman/448	.50
128	Barry Bonds/565	3.00
129	Ellis Burks/448	.50
130	Jeff Kent/448	.50
131	J.T. Snow/448	.50
132	Freddy Garcia/565	.50
133	Ken Griffey Jr./565	2.00
134	Edgar Martinez/448	.50
135	John Olerud/448	.50
136	Alex Rodriguez/565	2.50
137	Jose Canseco/565	.60
138	Vinny Castilla/448	.50
139	Roberto Hernandez/448	.50
140	Fred McGriff/448	.50
141	Rusty Greer/448	.50
142	Ruben Mateo/565	.50
143	Rafael Palmeiro/565	.65
144	Ivan Rodriguez/565	.65
145	Lee Stevens/448	.50
146	Tony Batista/448	.50
147	Carlos Delgado/565	.60
148	Shannon Stewart/448	.50
149	David Wells/448	.50
150	Vernon Wells/448	.50

Texture Silver

One of eight silver-foil versions of Prism, there is virtually no way to describe the silver metallic foil background of this parallel set dubbed "Texture Silver" by the maker to allow its differentiation from the set labeled "Silver Pebbly Drops," other than perhaps the vaguely diagonal orientation of the texture. Production was reported as 448 sets inserted only into retail packaging. The cards are not serially numbered.

	NM/M
Complete Set (150):	50.00
Common Player:	.50
Stars:	2-3X

Tinsel Silver

One of eight silver-foil parallels to Prism, this version features a horizontally striped background that the makers labeled "Tinsel Silver." Inserted only into hobby packaging, production was reported as 331 sets. The cards are not serially numbered.

	NM/M
Complete Set (150):	50.00
Common Player:	.50
Stars:	2-3X

Woodgrain Silver

One of eight silver-foil parallels to Prism, this version features a mottled patterned background which the makers insist resembles woodgrain. Inserted only into retail packaging, production was reported as 331 sets. The cards are not serially numbered.

	NM/M
Complete Set (150):	50.00
Common Player:	.50
Stars:	2-3X

A.L. Legends

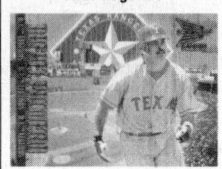

		NM/M
Complete Set (10):		15.00
Common Player:		.50
Inserted 1:25		
1	Mo Vaughn	.50
2	Cal Ripken Jr.	4.00
3	Nomar Garciaparra	2.50
4	Manny Ramirez	1.50
5	Roger Clemens	2.00
6	Derek Jeter	4.00
7	Ken Griffey Jr.	2.50
8	Alex Rodriguez	3.00
9	Jose Canseco	.75
10	Rafael Palmeiro	1.00

Center Stage

		NM/M
Complete Set (20):		40.00
Common Player:		1.00
Inserted 1:25		
1	Chipper Jones	3.00
2	Cal Ripken Jr.	6.00
3	Nomar Garciaparra	4.00
4	Pedro Martinez	2.00
5	Sammy Sosa	4.00
6	Sean Casey	1.00
7	Manny Ramirez	2.00
8	Jim Thome	1.50
9	Jeff Bagwell	2.00
10	Carlos Beltran	1.50
11	Vladimir Guerrero	2.00
12	Mike Piazza	4.00
13	Derek Jeter	6.00
14	Bernie Williams	1.00
15	Scott Rolen	1.50
16	Mark McGwire	5.00
17	Tony Gwynn	3.00
18	Ken Griffey Jr.	4.00
19	Alex Rodriguez	5.00
20	Ivan Rodriguez	1.50

Diamond Dial-A-Stats

		NM/M
Complete Set (10):		90.00
Common Player:		8.00
Inserted 1:193		
1	Chipper Jones	8.00
2	Greg Maddux	8.00
3	Cal Ripken Jr.	20.00
4	Sammy Sosa	10.00
5	Mike Piazza	10.00
6	Roger Clemens	9.00
7	Mark McGwire	15.00
8	Tony Gwynn	8.00
9	Ken Griffey Jr.	10.00
10	Alex Rodriguez	15.00

N.L. Legends

		NM/M
Complete Set (10):		15.00
Common Player:		.50
Inserted 1:25		
1	Chipper Jones	2.00
2	Greg Maddux	2.00
3	Sammy Sosa	2.50
4	Larry Walker	.50
5	Jeff Bagwell	1.00
6	Vladimir Guerrero	1.00
7	Mike Piazza	2.50
8	Mark McGwire	3.00
9	Tony Gwynn	2.00
10	Barry Bonds	4.00

Prospects

		NM/M
Complete Set (10):		12.00
Common Player:		1.00
Inserted 1:97		
1	Erubiel Durazo	1.00
2	Wilton Veras	1.00
3	Ben Petrick	1.00
4	Mark Quinn	1.00
5	Peter Bergeron	1.00
6	Alfonso Soriano	5.00
7	Tim Hudson	2.00
8	Chad Hermansen	1.00
9	Rick Ankiel	1.50
10	Ruben Mateo	1.00

2000 Pacific Private Stock

This base set consists of 150-cards, each card image uses an artist's computer generated brush strokes. Short-printed prospects are seeded 1:4 packs. The logo, player name and team are stamped in gold foil.

		NM/M
Complete Set (150):		50.00
Common Player:		.15
Common SP Prospect:		1.00
Inserted 1:4		
Pack (7):		2.00
Wax Box (24):		35.00
1	Darin Erstad	.25
2	Troy Glaus	.75
3	Tim Salmon	.25
4	Mo Vaughn	.15
5	Jay Bell	.15
6	Luis Gonzalez	.25
7	Randy Johnson	.75
8	Matt Williams	.15
9	Andruw Jones	.75
10	Chipper Jones	1.00
11	Brian Jordan	.15
12	Greg Maddux	1.00
13	Kevin Millwood	.15
14	Albert Belle	.20
15	Mike Mussina	.35
16	Cal Ripken Jr.	2.00
17	B.J. Surhoff	.15
18	Nomar Garciaparra	1.25
19	Butch Huskey	.15
20	Pedro Martinez	.75
21	Troy O'Leary	.15
22	Mark Grace	.25
23	Bo Porter/SP	1.00
24	Henry Rodriguez	.15
25	Sammy Sosa	1.25
26	Kerry Wood	.40
27	Jason Dellaero/SP	1.00
28	Ray Durham	.15
29	Paul Konerko	.15
30	Carlos Lee	.15
31	Magglio Ordonez	.25
32	Frank Thomas	.75
33	Mike Cameron	.15
34	Sean Casey	.25
35	Barry Larkin	.25
36	Greg Vaughn	.15
37	Roberto Alomar	.40
38	Russell Branyan/SP	1.00
39	Kenny Lofton	.25
40	Manny Ramirez	.75
41	Richie Sexson	.15
42	Jim Thome	.75
43	Omar Vizquel	.15
44	Dante Bichette	.15
45	Vinny Castilla	.15
46	Todd Helton	.75
47	Ben Petrick/SP	1.00
48	Juan Sosa/SP	1.00
49	Larry Walker	.15
50	Tony Clark	.15
51	Damion Easley	.15
52	Juan Encarnacion	.15
53	Robert Fick/SP	1.00
54	Dean Palmer	.15
55	A.J. Burnett/SP	1.00
56	Luis Castillo	.15
57	Alex Gonzalez	.15
58	Julio Ramirez/SP	1.00
59	Preston Wilson	.15
60	Jeff Bagwell	.15
61	Craig Biggio	.15
62	Ken Caminiti	.15
63	Carl Everett	.15
64	Mike Hampton	.15
65	Billy Wagner	.15
66	Carlos Beltran	.50
67	Dermal Brown/SP	1.00
68	Jermaine Dye	.15
69	Carlos Febles	.15
70	Mark Quinn/SP	1.00
71	Mike Sweeney	.15
72	Kevin Brown	.15
73	Eric Gagne/SP	1.50
74	Eric Karros	.15
75	Raul Mondesi	.15
76	Gary Sheffield	.40
77	Jeromy Burnitz	.15
78	Jeff Cirillo	.15
79	Geoff Jenkins	.15
80	David Nilsson	.15
81	Ron Coomer	.15
82	Jacque Jones	.15
83	Corey Koskie	.15
84	Brad Radke	.15
85	Tony Armas Jr./SP	1.00
86	Peter Bergeron/SP	1.00
87	Vladimir Guerrero	.75
88	Jose Vidro	.15
89	Rondell White	.15
90	Edgardo Alfonzo	.15
91	Roger Cedeno	.15
92	Rickey Henderson	.75
93	Jay Payton/SP	1.00
94	Mike Piazza	1.25
95	Jorge Toca/SP	1.00
96	Robin Ventura	.15
97	Roger Clemens	1.00
98	David Cone	.15
99	Derek Jeter	.15
100	D'Angelo Jimenez/SP	1.00
101	Tino Martinez	.15
102	Alfonso Soriano/SP	3.00
103	Bernie Williams	.25
104	Jason Giambi	.50
105	Ben Grieve	.15
106	Tim Hudson	.25
107	Matt Stairs	.15
108	Bobby Abreu	.15
109	Doug Glanville	.15
110	Scott Rolen	.65
111	Curt Schilling	.40
112	Brian Giles	.15
113	Chad Hermansen/SP	1.00
114	Jason Kendall	.15
115	Warren Morris	.15
116	Rick Ankiel/SP	1.00
117	J.D. Drew	.25
118	Adam Kennedy/SP	1.00
119	Ray Lankford	.15
120	Mark McGwire	1.50
121	Fernando Tatis	.15
122	Mike Darr/SP	1.00
123	Ben Davis	.15
124	Tony Gwynn	1.00
125	Trevor Hoffman	.15
126	Reggie Sanders	.15
127	Barry Bonds	2.00
128	Ellis Burks	.15
129	Jeff Kent	.15
130	J.T. Snow	.15
131	Freddy Garcia	.15
132	Ken Griffey Jr.	1.25
133	Carlos Guillen/SP	1.00
134	Edgar Martinez	.15
135	Alex Rodriguez	1.50
136	Miguel Cairo	.15
137	Jose Canseco	.40
138	Steve Cox/SP	1.00
139	Roberto Hernandez	.15
140	Fred McGriff	.15
141	Juan Gonzalez	.75
142	Rusty Greer	.15
143	Ruben Mateo/SP	1.00
144	Rafael Palmeiro	.65
145	Ivan Rodriguez	.65
146	Carlos Delgado	.15
147	Tony Fernandez	.15
148	Shawn Green	.35
149	Shannon Stewart	.15
150	Vernon Wells/SP	1.00

Gold Portraits

A parallel to the 150-card base set these have a gold foiled border. These are found exclusively in hobby packs and are limited to 99 serial numbered sets.

Stars: 5-10X
Prospects: 1-2X
Production 99 Sets

Silver Portraits

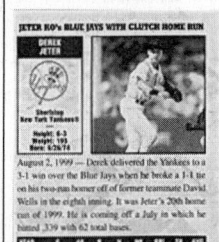

A parallel to the 150-card base set. These have a silver foiled border. Found exclusively in retail packs, these are limited to 199 serial numbered sets.

Stars: 3-6X
Prospects: 1-2X
Production 199 Sets

Premiere Date

A parallel to the 150-card base set these are limited to 34 serial numbered sets.

Stars: 5-10X
Prospects: 1-2X
Inserted 1:24

Canvas

This 20-card set is printed on real artist's canvas and has the look of a miniature piece of art.

		NM/M
Complete Set (20):		120.00
Common Player:		2.00
Inserted 1:49		
1	Chipper Jones	8.00
2	Greg Maddux	8.00
3	Cal Ripken Jr.	15.00
4	Nomar Garciaparra	10.00
5	Sammy Sosa	10.00
6	Frank Thomas	6.00
7	Manny Ramirez	6.00
8	Larry Walker	6.00
9	Jeff Bagwell	6.00
10	Vladimir Guerrero	6.00

11	Mike Piazza	10.00
12	Roger Clemens	9.00
13	Derek Jeter	15.00
14	Mark McGwire	12.00
15	Tony Gwynn	8.00
16	Barry Bonds	15.00
17	Ken Griffey Jr.	10.00
18	Alex Rodriguez	12.00
19	Juan Gonzalez	6.00
20	Ivan Rodriguez	5.00

Extreme Action

The focus of this 20-card set is the action photography, hence the name Extreme Action. They are seeded 2:25 packs.

		NM/M
Complete Set (20):		25.00
Common Player:		.50
Inserted 2:25		
1	Andruw Jones	1.50
2	Chipper Jones	2.00
3	Cal Ripken Jr.	4.00
4	Nomar Garciaparra	2.50
5	Sammy Sosa	2.50
6	Frank Thomas	1.50
7	Roberto Alomar	.60
8	Manny Ramirez	1.50
9	Larry Walker	.50
10	Jeff Bagwell	1.50
11	Vladimir Guerrero	1.50
12	Mike Piazza	2.50
13	Derek Jeter	4.00
14	Bernie Williams	.50
15	Scott Rolen	1.00
16	Mark McGwire	3.00
17	Tony Gwynn	2.00
18	Ken Griffey Jr.	2.50
19	Alex Rodriguez	3.00
20	Ivan Rodriguez	1.00

Reserve

Found exclusively in hobby packs these have a paper thin stock, enhanced with gold foil stamping. These are seeded 1:25 packs.

		NM/M
Complete Set (20):		50.00
Common Player:		1.00
Inserted 1:25		
1	Chipper Jones	3.00
2	Greg Maddux	3.00
3	Cal Ripken Jr.	6.00
4	Nomar Garciaparra	4.00
5	Sammy Sosa	3.00
6	Frank Thomas	2.00

7	Manny Ramirez	2.00
8	Larry Walker	1.00
9	Jeff Bagwell	2.00
10	Vladimir Guerrero	2.00
11	Mike Piazza	4.00
12	Roger Clemens	3.50
13	Derek Jeter	6.00
14	Mark McGwire	5.00
15	Tony Gwynn	3.00
16	Barry Bonds	6.00
17	Ken Griffey Jr.	4.00
18	Alex Rodriguez	5.00
19	Ivan Rodriguez	1.50
20	Shawn Green	1.25

PS-2000

This miniature 60-card set has a white border with gold foil stamping and are seeded two per pack.

		NM/M
Complete Set (60):		15.00
Common Player:		.15
Inserted 2:Pack		
1	Mo Vaughn	.15
2	Greg Maddux	1.00
3	Andruw Jones	.75
4	Chipper Jones	1.00
5	Cal Ripken Jr.	2.50
6	Nomar Garciaparra	1.50
7	Pedro Martinez	.75
8	Sammy Sosa	1.50
9	Jason Dellaero	.15
10	Magglio Ordonez	.15
11	Frank Thomas	.75
12	Sean Casey	.25
13	Russell Branyan	.15
14	Manny Ramirez	.75
15	Richie Sexson	.15
16	Ben Petrick	.15
17	Juan Sosa	.15
18	Larry Walker	.15
19	Robert Fick	.15
20	Craig Biggio	.15
21	Jeff Bagwell	.75
22	Carlos Beltran	.50
23	Dermal Brown	.15
24	Mark Quinn	.15
25	Eric Gagne	.15
26	Jeromy Burnitz	.15
27	Tony Armas Jr.	.15
28	Peter Bergeron	.15
29	Vladimir Guerrero	.75
30	Edgardo Alfonzo	.15
31	Mike Piazza	1.50
32	Jorge Toca	.15
33	Roger Clemens	1.25
34	Alfonso Soriano	.65
35	Bernie Williams	.25
36	Derek Jeter	2.50
37	Tim Hudson	.25
38	Bobby Abreu	.15
39	Scott Rolen	.65
40	Brian Giles	.15
41	Chad Hermansen	.15
42	Warren Morris	.15
43	Rick Ankiel	.25
44	J.D. Drew	.25
45	Adam Kennedy	.15
46	Mark McGwire	2.00
47	Mike Darr	.15
48	Tony Gwynn	1.00
49	Barry Bonds	2.50
50	Ken Griffey Jr.	1.50
51	Carlos Guillen	.15
52	Alex Rodriguez	1.50
53	Juan Gonzalez	.75
54	Ruben Mateo	.15
55	Ivan Rodriguez	.65
56	Rafael Palmeiro	.65
57	Jose Canseco	.40
58	Steve Cox	.15
59	Shawn Green	.30
60	Vernon Wells	.15

PS-2000 New Wave

This miniature 20-card set has copper foil stamping and is limited to 199 serial numbered sets.

	NM/M
Complete Set (20):	40.00
Common Player:	1.00

DEREK JETER
001/199 Shortstop

	Production 199 Sets	
1	Andruw Jones	3.50
2	Chipper Jones	5.00
3	Nomar Garciaparra	6.00
4	Magglio Ordonez	1.00
5	Sean Casey	1.00
6	Manny Ramirez	3.50
7	Richie Sexson	1.00
8	Carlos Beltran	2.00
9	Jeromy Burnitz	1.00
10	Vladimir Guerrero	3.50
11	Edgardo Alfonzo	1.00
12	Derek Jeter	10.00
13	Tim Hudson	1.00
14	Bobby Abreu	1.00
15	Scott Rolen	2.50
16	Brian Giles	1.00
17	Warren Morris	1.00
18	J.D. Drew	1.25
19	Alex Rodriguez	8.00
20	Shawn Green	1.25

PS-2000 Rookies

This miniature 20-card set has holographic silver foil stamping and is limited to 99 serial numbered sets.

		NM/M
Complete Set (20):		20.00
Common Player:		1.00
Inserted 99 Sets		
1	Jason Dellaero	1.00
2	Russell Branyan	1.00
3	Ben Petrick	1.00
4	Juan Sosa	1.00
5	Robert Fick	1.00
6	Dermal Brown	1.00
7	Mark Quinn	1.00
8	Eric Gagne	1.50
9	Tony Armas Jr.	1.00
10	Peter Bergeron	1.00
11	Jorge Toca	1.00
12	Alfonso Soriano	6.00
13	Chad Hermansen	1.00
14	Rick Ankiel	1.00
15	Adam Kennedy	1.50
16	Mike Darr	1.00
17	Carlos Guillen	1.00
18	Steve Cox	1.00
19	Ruben Mateo	1.00
20	Vernon Wells	1.50

PS-2000 Stars

This miniature 20-card set is limited to 299 serial numbered sets.

		NM/M
Complete Set (20):		40.00
Common Player:		1.00
Production 299 Sets		
1	Mo Vaughn	1.00
2	Greg Maddux	4.00
3	Cal Ripken Jr.	8.00
4	Pedro Martinez	3.00
5	Sammy Sosa	5.00
6	Frank Thomas	3.00
7	Larry Walker	1.00
8	Craig Biggio	1.00
9	Jeff Bagwell	3.00
10	Mike Piazza	5.00
11	Roger Clemens	4.50
12	Bernie Williams	1.00
13	Mark McGwire	6.00
14	Tony Gwynn	4.00
15	Barry Bonds	8.00
16	Ken Griffey Jr.	5.00
17	Juan Gonzalez	3.00
18	Ivan Rodriguez	2.00
19	Rafael Palmeiro	2.00
20	Jose Canseco	1.50

2000 Pacific Revolution

The base set consists of 150 cards with silver holofoil throughout the card front. "Revolution" is embossed on the left portion and the logo is stamped in gold foil. Twenty-five short-printed prospects are seeded 1:4 packs.

	NM/M
Complete Set (150):	60.00
Common Player:	.25
Common SP:	1.00

Pack (3):		2.00
Box:		35.00
1	Darin Erstad	.50
2	Troy Glaus	1.00
3	Adam Kennedy/SP	1.50
4	Mo Vaughn	.25
5	Erubiel Durazo	.25
6	Steve Finley	.25
7	Luis Gonzalez	.35
8	Randy Johnson	1.00
9	Travis Lee	.25
10	Vicente Padilla/SP	1.00
11	Matt Williams	.25
12	Rafael Furcal/SP	1.00
13	Andres Galarraga	1.00
14	Andruw Jones	1.00
15	Chipper Jones	1.50
16	Greg Maddux	1.50
17	Luis Rivera/SP	1.00
18	Albert Belle	.25
19	Mike Bordick	.25
20	Will Clark	.25
21	Mike Mussina	.40
22	Cal Ripken Jr.	3.00
23	B.J. Surhoff	.25
24	Carl Everett	.25
25	Nomar Garciaparra	2.00
26	Pedro Martinez	1.00
27	Jason Varitek	.25
28	Wilton Veras/SP	1.00
29	Shane Andrews	.25
30	Scott Downs/SP RC	1.00
31	Mark Grace	.35
32	Sammy Sosa	2.00
33	Kerry Wood	.50
34	Ray Durham	.25
35	Paul Konerko	.35
36	Carlos Lee	.25
37	Magglio Ordonez	.25
38	Frank Thomas	1.00
39	Rob Bell/SP	1.00
40	Sean Casey	.40
41	Ken Griffey Jr.	2.00
42	Barry Larkin	.25
43	Pokey Reese	.25
44	Roberto Alomar	.40
45	David Justice	.25
46	Kenny Lofton	.25
47	Manny Ramirez	1.00
48	Richie Sexson	.25
49	Jim Thome	.25
50	Jeff Cirillo	.25
51	Jeffrey Hammonds	.25
52	Todd Helton	1.00
53	Larry Walker	.25
54	Tony Clark	.25
55	Juan Gonzalez	1.00
56	Hideo Nomo	.25
57	Dean Palmer	.25
58	Alex Gonzalez	.25
59	Mike Lowell	.25
60	Pablo Ozuna/SP	1.00
61	Brad Penny/SP	1.00
62	Preston Wilson	.25
63	Moises Alou	.25
64	Jeff Bagwell	1.00
65	Craig Biggio	.25
66	Ken Caminiti	.25
67	Julio Lugo/SP	1.00
68	Carlos Beltran	.60
69	Johnny Damon	.40
70	Jermaine Dye	.25
71	Carlos Febles	.25
72	Mark Quinn/SP	1.00
73	Kevin Brown	.25
74	Shawn Green	.65
75	Chan Ho Park	.25
76	Gary Sheffield	.50
77	Kevin Barker/SP	1.00
78	Ron Belliard	.25
79	Jeromy Burnitz	.25
80	Geoff Jenkins	.25
81	Cristian Guzman	.25
82	Jacque Jones	.25
83	Corey Koskie	.25
84	Matt Lawton	.25
85	Peter Bergeron/SP	1.00
86	Vladimir Guerrero	1.00
87	Andy Tracy/SP	1.00
88	Jose Vidro	.25
89	Rondell White	.25
90	Edgardo Alfonzo	.25
91	Derek Bell	.25
92	Eric Cammack/SP	1.00
93	Mike Piazza	2.00
94	Robin Ventura	.25
95	Roger Clemens	1.75
96	Orlando Hernandez	.25
97	Derek Jeter	3.00
98	Tino Martinez	.25
99	Alfonso Soriano/SP	3.00
100	Bernie Williams	.35
101	Eric Chavez	.35
102	Jason Giambi	.75
103	Ben Grieve	.25
104	Terrence Long/SP	1.00
105	Mark Mulder/SP	1.00
106	Adam Piatt/SP	1.00
107	Bobby Abreu	.25
108	Rico Brogna	.25
109	Doug Glanville	.25
110	Mike Liebethal	.25
111	Scott Rolen	.75
112	Brian Giles	.25
113	Chad Hermansen/SP	1.00
114	Jason Kendall	.25
115	Warren Morris	.25
116	Rick Ankiel/SP	1.00
117	J.D. Drew	.40
118	Jim Edmonds	.25
119	Mark McGwire	2.50
120	Fernando Tatis	.25
121	Fernando Vina	.25
122	Tony Gwynn	1.50
123	Trevor Hoffman	.25
124	Ryan Klesko	.25
125	Eric Owens	.25
126	Barry Bonds	3.00
127	Ellis Burks	.25
128	Bobby Estalella	.25
129	Jeff Kent	.25
130	Scott Linebrink/SP RC	1.00
131	Jay Buhner	.25
132	Stan Javier	.25
133	Edgar Martinez	.25
134	John Olerud	.25
135	Alex Rodriguez	2.50
136	Kazuhiro Sasaki/SP RC	2.00
137	Jose Canseco	.40
138	Vinny Castilla	.25
139	Fred McGriff	.25
140	Greg Vaughn	.25
141	Gabe Kapler	.25
142	Mike Lamb/SP RC	1.00
143	Ruben Mateo	.25
144	Rafael Palmeiro	.75
145	Ivan Rodriguez	.75
146	Tony Batista	.25
147	Jose Cruz Jr.	.25
148	Carlos Delgado	.75
149	Brad Fullmer	.25
150	Raul Mondesi	.25

Red

A parallel to the 150-card base set these insert have red foil in place of the gold from the base version. These are also serial numbered on the card front, limited to 299 sets.

Stars:	1-2X
SP's:	1X
Production 299 Sets	

Shadow

Carl Everett 05

This parallel to the 150-card base set replaces the gold foil highlights with blue foil on front and has an embossed box at center which reads "SHADOW SERIES." Backs have a serial number ink-jetted from within an edition of 99 each.

Stars:	3-6X
SP's:	1-2X
Production 99 Sets	

Foul Pole Net-Fusions

These inserts utilize net-fusion technology, with netting infused in the left and right portion. The player name and logo are stamped in gold foil. These are found on the average of 1:49 packs.

		NM/M
Complete Set (20):		110.00
Common Player:		2.00
Inserted 1:49		
1	Chipper Jones	8.00
2	Cal Ripken Jr.	15.00
3	Nomar Garciaparra	10.00
4	Pedro Martinez	6.00
5	Sammy Sosa	10.00
6	Frank Thomas	6.00
7	Ken Griffey Jr.	10.00
8	Manny Ramirez	6.00
9	Jeff Bagwell	6.00
10	Shawn Green	3.00
11	Vladimir Guerrero	6.00
12	Mike Piazza	10.00
13	Derek Jeter	15.00
14	Bernie Williams	2.00
15	Rick Ankiel	4.00
16	Mark McGwire	12.00
17	Tony Gwynn	8.00
18	Barry Bonds	15.00
19	Alex Rodriguez	12.00
20	Ivan Rodriguez	5.00

Game-Ball Signatures

Travis Dawkins Shortstop

This 25-card autographed set has a piece of baseball leather embedded into the front on which the player penned his signature.

		NM/M
Common Player:		5.00
1	Randy Johnson	40.00
2	Greg Maddux	90.00
3	Rafael Furcal	7.50
4	Shane Andrews	5.00
5	Sean Casey	10.00
6	Travis Dawkins	5.00
7	Alex Gonzalez	5.00
8	Shane Reynolds	5.00
9	Eric Gagne	10.00
10	Kevin Barker	5.00
11	Eric Milton	5.00
12	Mark Quinn	5.00
13	Alfonso Soriano	40.00
14	Brian Giles	6.00
15	Mark Mulder	10.00
16	Adam Piatt	5.00
17	Warren Morris	5.00
18	Rick Ankiel	15.00
19	Adam Kennedy	6.00
20	Fernando Tatis	5.00
21	Barry Bonds	100.00
22	Alex Rodriguez	75.00
23	Ruben Mateo	5.00
24	Billy Koch	5.00
25	Brad Penny	5.00

Icons

These die-cut cards feature silver foil stamping and the player's team logo in the background. These are found on the average of 1:121 packs.

		NM/M
Complete Set (20):		250.00
Common Player:		8.00
Inserted 1:121		
1	Randy Johnson	10.00
2	Chipper Jones	15.00
3	Greg Maddux	15.00
4	Cal Ripken Jr.	30.00
5	Nomar Garciaparra	20.00
6	Pedro Martinez	10.00
7	Sammy Sosa	20.00
8	Frank Thomas	10.00
9	Ken Griffey Jr.	20.00
10	Juan Gonzalez	10.00
11	Jeff Bagwell	10.00
12	Vladimir Guerrero	10.00
13	Mike Piazza	20.00
14	Roger Clemens	17.50
15	Derek Jeter	30.00
16	Mark McGwire	25.00
17	Tony Gwynn	15.00
18	Barry Bonds	30.00
19	Alex Rodriguez	25.00
20	Ivan Rodriguez	8.00

On Deck

These inserts have a die-cut rounded bottom and feature the player in a simulated on-deck circle enhanced by green foil stamping. These are seeded 1:25 packs.

		NM/M
Complete Set (20):		40.00
Common Player:		1.00
Inserted 1:25		
1	Chipper Jones	3.00
2	Cal Ripken Jr.	6.00
3	Nomar Garciaparra	4.00
4	Sammy Sosa	4.00
5	Frank Thomas	2.00
6	Ken Griffey Jr.	4.00
7	Manny Ramirez	2.00
8	Larry Walker	1.00
9	Juan Gonzalez	2.00
10	Jeff Bagwell	2.00
11	Shawn Green	1.50
12	Vladimir Guerrero	2.00
13	Mike Piazza	4.00
14	Derek Jeter	6.00
15	Scott Rolen	1.50
16	Mark McGwire	5.00
17	Tony Gwynn	3.00
18	Alex Rodriguez	5.00
19	Jose Canseco	1.50
20	Ivan Rodriguez	1.75

Season Opener

This 36-card set has a horizontal format with the set name, team logo, player name and Revolution logo stamped in gold foil. These are seeded 2:25 packs.

		NM/M
Complete Set (36):		35.00
Common Player:		.50
Inserted 2:25		
1	Erubiel Durazo	.50
2	Randy Johnson	1.50
3	Andruw Jones	1.50
4	Chipper Jones	2.00
5	Greg Maddux	2.00
6	Cal Ripken Jr.	4.00
7	Nomar Garciaparra	3.00
8	Pedro Martinez	1.00
9	Sammy Sosa	2.50
10	Frank Thomas	1.50
11	Magglio Ordonez	.50
12	Ken Griffey Jr.	2.00
13	Barry Larkin	.50
14	Kenny Lofton	.50
15	Manny Ramirez	1.50
16	Jim Thome	1.00
17	Larry Walker	.50
18	Juan Gonzalez	1.50
19	Jeff Bagwell	1.50
20	Craig Biggio	.50
21	Carlos Beltran	.75
22	Shawn Green	.75
23	Vladimir Guerrero	1.50
24	Mike Piazza	2.50
25	Orlando Hernandez	.50
26	Derek Jeter	4.00
27	Bernie Williams	.50
28	Eric Chavez	.50
29	Scott Rolen	1.00
30	Jim Edmonds	.50
31	Tony Gwynn	2.00

32	Barry Bonds	4.00
33	Alex Rodriguez	3.00
34	Jose Canseco	.65
35	Ivan Rodriguez	1.00
36	Rafael Palmeiro	1.00

Triple Header

This 30-card set is broken down into three tiers with cards 1-10 spotlighting batting average leaders, 11-20 home run leaders and 21-30 strikeout leaders. The base versions are seeded 4:25 packs. A parallel version for each of the three groups is also inserted. Cards 1-20 are limited to 99 serial numbered sets while cards 21-30 are limited to 599 serial numbered sets.

	NM/M
Complete Set (30):	25.00
Common Player:	.25
Inserted 4:25	
Parallel (1-10):	3-6X
99 Sets Produced	
Parallel (11-20):	3-6X
99 Sets Produced	
Parallel (21-30):	1-2X
599 Sets Produced	

1	Chipper Jones	1.50
2	Cal Ripken Jr.	3.00
3	Nomar Garciaparra	2.00
4	Frank Thomas	1.00
5	Larry Walker	.25
6	Vladimir Guerrero	1.00
7	Mike Piazza	2.00
8	Derek Jeter	3.00
9	Tony Gwynn	1.50
10	Ivan Rodriguez	.75
11	Sammy Sosa	2.00
12	Ken Griffey Jr.	2.00
13	Manny Ramirez	1.00
14	Jeff Bagwell	1.00
15	Shawn Green	.40
16	Mark McGwire	2.50
17	Barry Bonds	3.00
18	Alex Rodriguez	2.50
19	Jose Canseco	.50
20	Rafael Palmeiro	.75
21	Randy Johnson	1.00
22	Tom Glavine	.40
23	Greg Maddux	1.50
24	Mike Mussina	.40
25	Pedro Martinez	1.00
26	Kerry Wood	.60
27	Chuck Finley	.25
28	Kevin Brown	.25
29	Roger Clemens	1.75
30	Rick Ankiel	.25

2000 Pacific Vanguard Sample

To introduce the hobby to its new Vanguard brand, Pacific issued this card of principal spokesman Tony Gwynn. Using the same "Vision-Glow" technology as the regular-issue cards, the sample has a large white diagonal overprint on back and "SAMPLE" instead of a card number.

	NM/M
Tony Gwynn	3.00

2000 Pacific Vanguard

RAFAEL PALMEIRO
TEXAS RANGERS®

	NM/M
Complete Set (100):	30.00
Common Player:	.15
Pack (4):	2.00
Wax Box (24):	35.00

1	Troy Glaus	1.00
2	Tim Salmon	.25
3	Mo Vaughn	.15
4	Albert Belle	.15
5	Mike Mussina	.35
6	Cal Ripken Jr.	3.00
7	Nomar Garciaparra	2.00
8	Pedro Martinez	1.00
9	Troy O'Leary	.15
10	Wilton Veras	.15
11	Magglio Ordonez	.15
12	Chris Singleton	.15
13	Frank Thomas	1.00
14	Roberto Alomar	.40
15	Russell Branyan	.15
16	Manny Ramirez	1.00
17	Jim Thome	.75
18	Omar Vizquel	.15
19	Tony Clark	.15
20	Juan Gonzalez	1.00
21	Dean Palmer	.15
22	Carlos Beltran	.15
23	Johnny Damon	.30
24	Mark Quinn	.15
25	Jacque Jones	.15
26	Jacque Jones	.15
27	Corey Koskie	.15
28	Brad Radke	.15
29	Roger Clemens	1.75
30	Derek Jeter	3.00
31	Alfonso Soriano	.75
32	Bernie Williams	.30
33	Eric Chavez	.30
34	Jason Giambi	.75
35	Ben Grieve	.15
36	Tim Hudson	.30
37	Mike Cameron	.15
38	Freddy Garcia	.15
39	Edgar Martinez	.15
40	Alex Rodriguez	2.50
41	Jose Canseco	.50
42	Vinny Castilla	.15
43	Fred McGriff	.15
44	Rusty Greer	.15
45	Ruben Mateo	.15
46	Rafael Palmeiro	.75
47	Ivan Rodriguez	.65
48	Carlos Delgado	.75
49	Shannon Stewart	.15
50	Vernon Wells	.15
51	Erubiel Durazo	.15
52	Randy Johnson	1.00
53	Matt Williams	.15
54	Andruw Jones	1.00
55	Chipper Jones	1.50
56	Greg Maddux	1.50
57	Mark Grace	.25
58	Sammy Sosa	2.00
59	Kerry Wood	.50
60	Sean Casey	.25
61	Ken Griffey Jr.	2.00
62	Barry Larkin	.15
63	Todd Helton	1.00
64	Ben Petrick	.15
65	Larry Walker	.15
66	Luis Castillo	.15
67	Alex Gonzalez	.15
68	Preston Wilson	.15
69	Jeff Bagwell	1.00
70	Craig Biggio	.15
71	Billy Wagner	.15
72	Kevin Brown	.15
73	Shawn Green	.40
74	Gary Sheffield	.40
75	Kevin Barker	.15
76	Ron Belliard	.15
77	Jeromy Burnitz	.15
78	Michael Barrett	.15
79	Peter Bergeron	.15
80	Vladimir Guerrero	1.00
81	Edgardo Alfonzo	.15
82	Rey Ordonez	.15
83	Mike Piazza	2.00
84	Robin Ventura	.15
85	Bobby Abreu	.15
86	Mike Lieberthal	.15
87	Scott Rolen	.75
88	Brian Giles	.15
89	Chad Hermansen	.15
90	Jason Kendall	.15
91	Rick Ankiel	.15

92	J.D. Drew	.25
93	Mark McGwire	2.50
94	Fernando Tatis	.15
95	Ben Davis	.15
96	Tony Gwynn	1.50
97	Trevor Hoffman	.15
98	Barry Bonds	3.00
99	Ellis Burks	.15
100	Jeff Kent	.15

Gold

A.L. (1-50):	2-4X
Production 199 Sets R	
N.L. (51-100):	3-6X
Production 99 Sets R	

Green

A.L. (1-50):	3-6X
Production 99 Sets	
N.L. (51-100):	2-4X
Production 199 Sets	

Purple

ROBERTO ALOMAR
CLEVELAND INDIANS®

04/10

Production 10 Sets
(Values Undetermined)

Premiere Date

Stars:	3-5X
Production 135 Sets H	

A.L. Vanguard Press

	NM/M
Complete Set (10):	10.00
Common Player:	.65
Inserted 2:25	

1	Cal Ripken Jr.	3.00
2	Nomar Garciaparra	2.00
3	Pedro Martinez	1.00
4	Manny Ramirez	1.00
5	Carlos Beltran	.65
6	Roger Clemens	1.50
7	Derek Jeter	3.00
8	Alex Rodriguez	2.50
9	Rafael Palmeiro	.75
10	Ivan Rodriguez	.75

Cosmic Force

TONY GWYNN

	NM/M
Complete Set (10):	30.00
Common Player:	3.00
Inserted 1:73	

1	Chipper Jones	3.00
2	Cal Ripken Jr.	6.00
3	Nomar Garciaparra	4.00
4	Sammy Sosa	4.00
5	Ken Griffey Jr.	4.00
6	Mike Piazza	4.00
7	Derek Jeter	6.00
8	Mark McGwire	5.00
9	Tony Gwynn	3.00
10	Alex Rodriguez	4.00

Diamond Architects

Diamond Architects
SCOTT ROLEN
Philadelphia Phillies

	NM/M
Complete Set (20):	25.00
Common Player:	.50
Inserted 1:25	

1	Chipper Jones	2.00
2	Greg Maddux	2.00
3	Cal Ripken Jr.	4.00
4	Nomar Garciaparra	2.50
5	Sammy Sosa	2.50
6	Ken Griffey Jr.	2.50
7	Manny Ramirez	1.50
8	Larry Walker	.50
9	Jeff Bagwell	1.50
10	Vladimir Guerrero	1.50
11	Mike Piazza	2.50

12	Roger Clemens	2.25
13	Derek Jeter	4.00
14	Bernie Williams	.50
15	Scott Rolen	1.00
16	Mark McGwire	3.00
17	Tony Gwynn	2.00
18	Alex Rodriguez	3.00
19	Rafael Palmeiro	1.00
20	Ivan Rodriguez	.75

Game Worn Jersey

	NM/M
Inserted 1:120	

1	Greg Maddux	10.00
2	Tony Gwynn	10.00
3	Alex Rodriguez	20.00
4	Frank Thomas	8.00
5	Chipper Jones	10.00

High Voltage

pitcher • NEW YORK YANKEES®
ROGER CLEMENS

	NM/M
Complete Set (36):	10.00
Common Player:	.15
Inserted 1:1	

1	Mo Vaughn	.15
2	Erubiel Durazo	.15
3	Randy Johnson	.60
4	Andruw Jones	.60
5	Chipper Jones	.75
6	Greg Maddux	.75
7	Cal Ripken Jr.	2.00
8	Nomar Garciaparra	1.25
9	Pedro Martinez	.60
10	Sammy Sosa	1.25
11	Frank Thomas	.60
12	Sean Casey	.25
13	Ken Griffey Jr.	1.25
14	Barry Larkin	.15
15	Manny Ramirez	.60
16	Jim Thome	.50
17	Larry Walker	.15
18	Jeff Bagwell	.60
19	Craig Biggio	.15
20	Carlos Beltran	.40
21	Shawn Green	.25
22	Vladimir Guerrero	.60
23	Edgardo Alfonzo	.15
24	Mike Piazza	1.50
25	Roger Clemens	1.00
26	Derek Jeter	2.00
27	Bernie Williams	.25
28	Scott Rolen	.60
29	Brian Giles	.15
30	Rick Ankiel	.15
31	Mark McGwire	1.50
32	Tony Gwynn	.75
33	Barry Bonds	2.00
34	Alex Rodriguez	1.50
35	Rafael Palmeiro	.60
36	Ivan Rodriguez	.60

N.L. Vanguard Press

Vanguard PRESS

Guerrero sets Expos' homer record

Above: The Expos result on Visitas to drive the Montreal offense

	NM/M
Complete Set (10):	10.00
Common Player:	.50
Inserted 2:37	

1	Chipper Jones	1.50
2	Greg Maddux	1.50

1991 Pacific Gas & Electric S.F. Giants

SAN FRANCISCO GIANTS

Perforated panels of six 2-3/4" x 3-3/4" Giants cards were included in each of five editions of Giants Magazine, the team's official program, for 1991. The set was sponsored by PG&E. Cards have color action photos on front with a graduated gray frame and white borders. At bottom is a team typographical logo, crossed bats and a red ribbon with player identification. A pentagon at top has the date "91." Backs are in black-and-white with a large sponsor's ad, the player's career stats, a few biographical details and uniform and card numbers.

	NM/M
Complete Set (30):	15.00
Common Player:	.50

1	Kevin Mitchell	.50
2	Robby Thompson	.50
3	John Burkett	.50
4	Kelly Downs	.50
5	Terry Kennedy	.50
6	Roger Craig	.50
7	Jeff Brantley	.50
8	Greg Litton	.50
9	Trevor Wilson	.50
10	Kevin Bass	.50
11	Matt Williams	1.00
12	Jose Uribe	.50
13	Steve Decker	.50
14	Will Clark	1.00
15	Dave Righetti	.50
16	Mike Kingery	.50
17	Mike LaCoss	.50
18	Dave Anderson	.50
19	Bud Black	.50
20	Mike Benjamin	.50
21	Don Robinson	.50
22	Mark Leonard	.50
23	Willie McGee	.50
24	Francisco Oliveras	.50
25	Kirt Manwaring	.50
26	Rick Parker	.50
27	Mike Remlinger	.50
28	Mike Felder	.50
29	Scott Garrelts	.50
30	Tony Perezchica	.50

1992 Pacific Gas & Electric S.F. Giants

Perforated panels of six 2-3/4" x 3-3/4" Giants cards were included in each of six editions of Giants Magazine, the team's official program, for 1992. The set was sponsored by PG&E. Cards have color action photos on front with a wood-look frame and white borders. At top is a gold ribbon with player name and position. At bottom is the team logo, crossed bats, uniform number and the year of issue. Horizontal backs are in black-and-white with a large sponsor's ad, the player's career stats, a few biographical details, uniform number and energy conservation tip. Cards are unnumbered and are listed here by panel.

	NM/M
Complete Set, Panels (6):	25.00
Complete Set, Singles (36):	20.00
Common Player:	.50

PANEL 1		5.00
(1)	Rod Beck	.50
(2)	Wendell Kim	.50
(3)	Gil Heredia	.50
(4)	Mike Benjamin	.50
(5)	Matt Williams	.50
(6)	Robby Thompson	.50

PANEL 2		5.00
(7)	Will Clark/AS	1.00
(8)	Bob Brenly	.50
(9)	Bryan Hickerson	.50
(10)	Bob Lillis	.50
(11)	Royce Clayton	.50
(12)	Mark Leonard (Dropping bat.)	.50

PANEL 3		5.00
(13)	Roger Craig	.50
(14)	Jeff Brantley	.50
(15)	Darren Lewis	.50
(16)	Mark Leonard/Btg	.50
(17)	John Burkett	.50
(18)	Mike Felder	.50

PANEL 4		5.00
(19)	Kelly Downs	.50
(20)	Jose Uribe	.50
(21)	Bud Black	.50
(22)	Kirt Manwaring	.50
(23)	Trevor Wilson	.50
(24)	Kevin Bass	.50

PANEL 5		5.00
(25)	Mike Jackson	.50
(26)	Will Clark	1.00
(27)	Jim McNamara	.50
(28)	Dusty Baker	.50
(29)	Scott Garrelts	.50
(30)	Chris James	.50

PANEL 6		5.00
(31)	Dave Righetti	.50
(32)	Cory Snyder	.50
(33)	Dave Burba	.50
(34)	Carlos Alfonso	.50
(35)	Bill Swift	.50
(36)	Willie McGee	.50

2000 Palm Beach Post Montreal Expos

At each of the spring training games between March 3-April 1 each copy of the newspaper sold at the ballpark contained a random insert of two Expos and two Cardinals cards. The 3-1/8" x 4-3/4" blank-back cards have action color photos on front.

	NM/M
Complete Set (20):	15.00
Common Player:	.50

(1)	Felipe Alou	.65
(2)	Michael Barrett	.50
(3)	Geoff Blum	.50
(4)	Orlando Cabrera	.75
(5)	Brad Fullmer	.65
(6)	Vladimir Guerrero	5.00
(7)	Dustin Hermanson	.75
(8)	Hideki Irabu	.50
(9)	Steve Kline	.50
(10)	Graeme Lloyd	.50
(11)	Trey Moore	.50
(12)	Mickey Morandini	.50
(13)	Mike Mordecai	.50
(14)	Carl Pavano	.75
(15)	Anthony Telford	.50
(16)	Ugueth Urbina	.50
(17)	Jose Vidro	.75
(18)	Rondell White/Btg	1.00
(19)	Rondell White/Standing	1.00
(20)	Chris Widger	.50

2000 Palm Beach Post St. Louis Cardinals

During spring training each copy of the newspaper sold at the ballpark contained a random insert of two Expos and two Cardinals cards. The 3-1/8" x 4-3/4" blank-back cards have action color photos on front.

	NM/M
Complete Set (20):	20.00
Common Player:	.50

(1)	Rick Ankiel	.50
(2)	Andy Benes	.50
(3)	Kent Bottenfield	.50
(4)	Eric Davis	.50
(5)	J.D. Drew	2.00
(6)	Pat Hentgen	.50
(7)	Chad Hutchinson	.50
(8)	Darryl Kile	.50
(9)	Ray Lankford	.50
(10)	Tony LaRussa	.50
(11)	Eli Marrero	.50
(12)	Joe McEwing	.50
(13)	Mark McGwire/Btg	5.00
(14)	Mark McGwire/Standing	5.00
(15)	Matt Morris	.50
(16)	Edgar Renteria	.50
(17)	Heathcliff Slocumb	.50
(18)	Fernando Tatis	.50
(19)	Dave Veres	.50
(20)	Fernando Vina	.50

1988 Panini Stickers

This set of 480 stickers features 312 major league players, both rookies and superstar veterans. The full-color stickers measure 2-11/16" x 1-7/8" (team emblem and uniform stickers are slightly larger). Individual players, duos and group action shots are included in the set which

BOSTON RED SOX
ROGER CLEMENS

also contains 14 stickers that depict 1987 season highlights. Panini also produced a 64-page album with Don Mattingly on the cover and two pages devoted to each team with a space marked for each sticker in the set. Individual sticker packets contained a total of six stickers; four players, one team logo and one uniform sticker. Panini offered a collectors' sticker exchange service in which up to 30 stickers could be traded or specific stickers purchased for 10 cents each. The 26 team logo/pennant stickers (numbered A-1 through Z-1) are listed as #455-480 in the following checklist.

	NM/M
Complete Set (480):	15.00
Common Player:	.05
Sticker Album:	1.00
Wax Pack (6):	.25
Wax Box (100):	7.50

No.	Player	Price
1	World Series Trophy	.05
2	Orioles Logo	.05
3	Orioles Uniform	.05
4	Eric Bell	.05
5	Mike Boddicker	.05
6	Dave Schmidt	.05
7	Terry Kennedy	.05
8	Eddie Murray	.45
9	Bill Ripken	.05
10	Orioles Action (Tony Armas, Cal Ripken Jr.)	.25
11	Orioles Action (Tony Armas, Cal Ripken Jr.)	.25
12	Ray Knight	.05
13	Cal Ripken, Jr.	1.00
14	Ken Gerhart	.05
15	Fred Lynn	.05
16	Larry Sheets	.05
17	Mike Young	.05
18	Red Sox Logo	.05
19	Red Sox Uniform	.05
20	Oil Can Boyd	.05
21	Roger Clemens	.65
22	Bruce Hurst	.05
23	Bob Stanley	.05
24	Rich Gedman	.05
25	Dwight Evans	.05
26	Red Sox Action (Marty Barrett, Tim Laudner)	.05
27	Red Sox Action (Marty Barrett, Tim Laudner)	.05
28	Marty Barrett	.05
29	Wade Boggs	.50
30	Spike Owen	.05
31	Ellis Burks	.05
32	Mike Greenwell	.05
33	Jim Rice	.10
34	Angels Logo	.05
35	Angels Uniform	.05
36	Kirk McCaskill	.05
37	Don Sutton	.40
38	Mike Witt	.05
39	Bob Boone	.05
40	Wally Joyner	.05
41	Mark McLemore	.05
42	Angels Action (Juan Bonilla, Devon White)	.05
43	Angels Action (Juan Bonilla, Devon White)	.05
44	Jack Howell	.05
45	Dick Schofield	.05
46	Brian Downing	.05
47	Ruppert Jones	.05
48	Gary Pettis	.05
49	Devon White	.05
50	White Sox Logo	.05
51	White Sox Uniform	.05
52	Floyd Bannister	.05
53	Richard Dotson	.05
54	Bob James	.05
55	Carlton Fisk	.45
56	Greg Walker	.05
57	Fred Manrique	.05
58	White Sox Action (Ozzie Guillen, Donnie Hill, Pat Sheridan)	.05
59	White Sox Action (Ozzie Guillen, Donnie Hill, Pat Sheridan)	.05
60	Steve Lyons	.05
61	Ozzie Guillen	.05
62	Harold Baines	.05
63	Ivan Calderon	.05
64	Gary Redus	.05
65	Ken Williams	.05
66	Indians Logo	.05
67	Indians Uniform	.05
68	Scott Bailes	.05
69	Tom Candiotti	.05
70	Greg Swindell	.05
71	Chris Bando	.05
72	Joe Carter	.05
73	Tommy Hinzo	.05
74	Indians Action (Juan Bonilla, Joe Carter)	.05
75	Indians Action (Juan Bonilla, Joe Carter)	.05
76	Brook Jacoby	.05
77	Julio Franco	.05
78	Brett Butler	.05
79	Mel Hall	.05
80	Cory Snyder	.05
81	Pat Tabler	.05
82	Tigers Logo	.05
83	Tigers Uniform	.05
84	Willie Hernandez	.05
85	Jack Morris	.05
86	Frank Tanana	.05
87	Walt Terrell	.05
88	Matt Nokes	.05
89	Darrell Evans	.05
90	Tigers Action (Darrell Evans, Carlton Fisk)	.05
91	Tigers Action (Darrell Evans, Carlton Fisk)	.05
92	Lou Whitaker	.05
93	Tom Brookens	.05
94	Alan Trammell	.05
95	Kirk Gibson	.05
96	Chet Lemon	.05
97	Pat Sheridan	.05
98	Royals Logo	.05
99	Royals Uniform	.05
100	Charlie Leibrandt	.05
101	Dan Quisenberry	.05
102	Bret Saberhagen	.05
103	Jamie Quirk	.05
104	George Brett	.60
105	Frank White	.05
106	Royals Action (Bret Saberhagen)	.05
107	Royals Action (Bret Saberhagen)	.05
108	Kevin Seitzer	.05
109	Angel Salazar	.05
110	Bo Jackson	.10
111	Lonnie Smith	.05
112	Danny Tartabull	.05
113	Willie Wilson	.05
114	Brewers Logo	.05
115	Brewers Uniform	.05
116	Ted Higuera	.05
117	Juan Nieves	.05
118	Dan Plesac	.05
119	Bill Wegman	.05
120	B.J. Surhoff	.05
121	Greg Brock	.05
122	Brewers Action (Jim Gantner, Lou Whitaker)	.05
123	Brewers Action (Jim Gantner, Lou Whitaker)	.05
124	Jim Gantner	.05
125	Paul Molitor	.45
126	Dale Sveum	.05
127	Glenn Braggs	.05
128	Rob Deer	.05
129	Robin Yount	.45
130	Twins Logo	.05
131	Twins Uniform	.05
132	Bert Blyleven	.05
133	Jeff Reardon	.50
134	Frank Viola	.05
135	Tim Laudner	.05
136	Kent Hrbek	.05
137	Steve Lombardozzi	.05
138	Twins Action (Steve Lombardozzi, Frank White)	.05
139	Twins Action (Steve Lombardozzi, Frank White)	.05
140	Gary Gaetti	.05
141	Greg Gagne	.05
142	Tom Brunansky	.05
143	Dan Gladden	.05
144	Kirby Puckett	.50
145	Gene Larkin	.05
146	Yankees Logo	.05
147	Yankees Uniform	.05
148	Tommy John	.05
149	Rick Rhoden	.05
150	Dave Righetti	.05
151	Rick Cerone	.05
152	Don Mattingly	.60
153	Willie Randolph	.05
154	Yankees Action (Scott Fletcher, Don Mattingly)	.25
155	Yankees Action (Scott Fletcher, Don Mattingly)	.20
156	Mike Pagliarulo	.05
157	Wayne Tolleson	.05
158	Rickey Henderson	.45
159	Dan Pasqua	.05
160	Gary Ward	.05
161	Dave Winfield	.45
162	Athletics Logo	.05
163	Athletics Uniform	.05
164	Dave Stewart	.05
165	Curt Young	.05
166	Terry Steinbach	.05
167	Mark McGwire	.75
168	Tony Phillips	.05
169	Carney Lansford	.05
170	Athletics Action (Mike Gallego, Tony Phillips)	.05
171	Athletics Action (Mike Gallego, Tony Phillips)	.05
172	Alfredo Griffin	.05
173	Jose Canseco	.30
174	Mike Davis	.05
175	Reggie Jackson	.60
176	Dwayne Murphy	.05
177	Luis Polonia	.05
178	Mariners Logo	.05
179	Mariners Uniform	.05
180	Scott Bankhead	.05
181	Mark Langston	.05
182	Edwin Nunez	.05
183	Scott Bradley	.05
184	Dave Valle	.05
185	Alvin Davis	.05
186	Mariners Action (Jack Howell, Rey Quinones)	.05
187	Mariners Action (Jack Howell, Rey Quinones)	.05
188	Harold Reynolds	.05
189	Jim Presley	.05
190	Rey Quinones	.05
191	Phil Bradley	.05
192	Mickey Brantley	.05
193	Mike Kingery	.05
194	Rangers Logo	.05
195	Rangers Uniform	.05
196	Edwin Correa	.05
197	Charlie Hough	.05
198	Bobby Witt	.05
199	Mike Stanley	.05
200	Pete O'Brien	.05
201	Jerry Browne	.05
202	Rangers Action (Steve Buechele, Eddie Murray)	.05
203	Rangers Action (Steve Buechele, Eddie Murray)	.05
204	Steve Buechele	.05
205	Larry Parrish	.05
206	Scott Fletcher	.05
207	Pete Incaviglia	.05
208	Oddibe McDowell	.05
209	Ruben Sierra	.05
210	Blue Jays Logo	.05
211	Blue Jays Uniform	.05
212	Mark Eichhorn	.05
213	Tom Henke	.05
214	Jimmy Key	.05
215	Dave Stieb	.05
216	Ernie Whitt	.05
217	Willie Upshaw	.05
218	Blue Jays Action (Harold Reynolds, Willie Upshaw)	.05
219	Blue Jays Action (Harold Reynolds, Willie Upshaw)	.05
220	Garth Iorg	.05
221	Kelly Gruber	.05
222	Tony Fernandez	.05
223	Jesse Barfield	.05
224	George Bell	.05
225	Lloyd Moseby	.05
226	National League Logo	.05
227	Terry Kennedy, Don Mattingly	.20
228	Wade Boggs, Willie Randolph	.05
229	Bret Saberhagen	
230	George Bell, Cal Ripken Jr	.45
231	Rickey Henderson, Dave Winfield	.10
232	Gary Carter, Jack Clark	.05
233	Mike Scott	.05
234	Ryne Sandberg, Mike Schmidt	.25
235	Ozzie Smith, Eric Davis	.10
236	Andre Dawson, Darryl Strawberry	.05
237	Braves Logo	.05
238	Braves Uniform	.05
239	Rick Mahler	.05
240	Zane Smith	.05
241	Ozzie Virgil	.05
242	Gerald Perry	.05
243	Glenn Hubbard	.05
244	Ken Oberkfell	.05
245	Braves Action (Glenn Hubbard, Jeffrey Leonard)	.05
246	Braves Action (Glenn Hubbard, Jeffrey Leonard)	.05
247	Rafael Ramirez	.05
248	Ken Griffey	.05
249	Albert Hall	.05
250	Dion James	.05
251	Dale Murphy	.20
252	Gary Roenicke	.05
253	Cubs Logo	.05
254	Cubs Uniform	.05
255	Jamie Moyer	.05
256	Lee Smith	.05
257	Rick Sutcliffe	.05
258	Jody Davis	.05
259	Leon Durham	.05
260	Ryne Sandberg	.50
261	Cubs Action (Jody Davis)	.05
262	Cubs Action (Jody Davis)	.05
263	Keith Moreland	.05
264	Shawon Dunston	.05
265	Andre Dawson	.25
266	Dave Martinez	.05
267	Jerry Mumphrey	.05
268	Rafael Palmeiro	.45
269	Reds Logo	.05
270	Reds Uniform	.05
271	John Franco	.05
272	Ted Power	.05
273	Bo Diaz	.05
274	Nick Esasky	.05
275	Dave Concepcion	.05
276	Kurt Stillwell	.05
277	Reds Action (Bob Melvin, Dave Parker)	.05
278	Reds Action (Bob Melvin, Dave Parker)	.05
279	Buddy Bell	.05
280	Barry Larkin	.05
281	Kal Daniels	.05
282	Eric Davis	.05
283	Tracy Jones	.05
284	Dave Parker	.05
285	Astros Logo	.05
286	Astros Uniform	.05
287	Jim Deshaies	.05
288	Nolan Ryan	1.00
289	Mike Scott	.05
290	Dave Smith	.05
291	Alan Ashby	.05
292	Glenn Davis	.05
293	Astros Action (Alan Ashby, Gary Carter)	.05
294	Astros Action (Alan Ashby, Gary Carter)	.05
295	Bill Doran	.05
296	Denny Walling	.05
297	Craig Reynolds	.05
298	Kevin Bass	.05
299	Jose Cruz	.05
300	Billy Hatcher	.05
301	Dodgers Logo	.05
302	Dodgers Uniform	.05
303	Orel Hershiser	.05
304	Fernando Valenzuela	.05
305	Bob Welch	.05
306	Matt Young	.05
307	Mike Scioscia	.05
308	Franklin Stubbs	.05
309	Dodgers Action (Mariano Duncan, Junior Ortiz)	.05
310	Dodgers Action (Mariano Duncan, Junior Ortiz)	.05
311	Steve Sax	.05
312	Jeff Hamilton	.05
313	Dave Anderson	.05
314	Pedro Guerrero	.05
315	Mike Marshall	.05
316	John Shelby	.05
317	Expos Logo	.05
318	Expos Uniform	.05
319	Neal Heaton	.05
320	Bryn Smith	.05
321	Floyd Youmans	.05
322	Mike Fitzgerald	.05
323	Andres Galarraga	.05
324	Vance Law	.05
325	Expos Action (John Kruk, Tim Raines)	.05
326	Expos Action (John Kruk, Tim Raines)	.05
327	Tim Wallach	.05
328	Hubie Brooks	.05
329	Casey Candaele	.05
330	Tim Raines	.05
331	Mitch Webster	.05
332	Herm Winningham	.05
333	Mets Logo	.05
334	Mets Uniform	.05
335	Ron Darling	.05
336	Sid Fernandez	.05
337	Dwight Gooden	.05
338	Gary Carter	.45
339	Keith Hernandez	.05
340	Wally Backman	.05
341	Mets Action (Mike Diaz, Darryl Strawberry, Tim Teufel, Mookie Wilson)	.05
342	Mets Action (Mike Diaz, Darryl Strawberry, Tim Teufel, Mookie Wilson)	.05
343	Howard Johnson	.05
344	Rafael Santana	.05
345	Lenny Dykstra	.05
346	Kevin McReynolds	.05
347	Darryl Strawberry	.05
348	Mookie Wilson	.05
349	Phillies Logo	.05
350	Phillies Uniform	.05
351	Steve Bedrosian	.05
352	Shane Rawley	.05
353	Bruce Ruffin	.05
354	Kent Tekulve	.05
355	Lance Parrish	.05
356	Von Hayes	.05
357	Phillies Action (Tony Pena, Glenn Wilson)	.05
358	Phillies Action (Tony Pena, Glenn Wilson)	.05
359	Juan Samuel	.05
360	Mike Schmidt	.60
361	Steve Jeltz	.05
362	Chris James	.05
363	Milt Thompson	.05
364	Glenn Wilson	.05
365	Pirates Logo	.05
366	Pirates Uniform	.05
367	Mike Dunne	.05
368	Brian Fisher	.05
369	Mike LaValliere	.05
370	Sid Bream	.05
371	Jose Lind	.05
372	Bobby Bonilla	.05
373	Pirates Action (Bobby Bonilla)	.05
374	Pirates Action (Bobby Bonilla)	.05
375	Al Pedrique	.05
376	Barry Bonds	1.00
377	John Cangelosi	.05
378	Mike Diaz	.05
379	R.J. Reynolds	.05
380	Andy Van Slyke	.05
381	Cardinals Logo	.05
382	Cardinals Uniform	.05
383	Danny Cox	.05
384	Bob Forsch	.05
385	Joe Magrane	.05
386	Todd Worrell	.05
387	Tony Pena	.05
388	Jack Clark	.05
389	Cardinals Action (Jody Davis, Tom Herr)	.05
390	Cardinals Action (Jody Davis, Tom Herr)	.05
391	Tom Herr	.05
392	Terry Pendleton	.05
393	Ozzie Smith	.50
394	Vince Coleman	.05
395	Curt Ford	.05
396	Willie McGee	.05
397	Padres Logo	.05
398	Padres Uniform	.05
399	Lance McCullers	.05
400	Eric Show	.05
401	Ed Whitson	.05
402	Benito Santiago	.05
403	John Kruk	.05
404	Tim Flannery	.05
405	Padres Action (Randy Ready, Benito Santiago)	.05
406	Padres Action (Randy Ready, Benito Santiago)	.05
407	Randy Ready	.05
408	Chris Brown	.05
409	Garry Templeton	.05
410	Tony Gwynn	.50
411	Stan Jefferson	.05
412	Carmelo Martinez	.05
413	Giants Logo	.05
414	Giants Uniform	.05
415	Kelly Downs	.05
416	Scott Garrelts	.05
417	Mike Krukow	.05
418	Mike LaCoss	.05
419	Bob Brenly	.05
420	Will Clark	.05
421	Giants Action (Will Clark, Mike Fitzgerald)	.05
422	Giants Action (Will Clark, Mike Fitzgerald)	.05
423	Robby Thompson	.05
424	Kevin Mitchell	.05
425	Jose Uribe	.05
426	Mike Aldrete	.05
427	Jeffrey Leonard	.05
428	Candy Maldonado	.05
429	Mike Schmidt	.40
430	Don Mattingly	.40
431	Juan Nieves	.05
432	Paul Molitor	.25
433	Benito Santiago	.05
434	Rickey Henderson	.25
435	Nolan Ryan	.65
436	Kevin Seitzer	.05
437	Tony Gwynn	.35
438	Mark McGwire	.55
439	Howard Johnson	.05
440	Steve Bedrosian	.05
441	Darrell Evans	.05
442	Eddie Murray	.25
443	1987 A.L. Championship Series (Kirby Puckett, Alan Trammell, Lou Whitaker)	.05
444	1987 A.L. Championship Series (Kirby Puckett, Alan Trammell, Lou Whitaker)	.05
445	American League Championship Series MVP (Gary Gaetti)	.05
446	National League Championship Series MVP (Jeffrey Leonard)	.05
447	1987 N.L. Championship Series (Kevin Mitchell, Tony Pena)	.05
448	1987 N.L. Championship Series (Kevin Mitchell, Tony Pena)	.05
449	1987 World Series (Tom Brunansky, Tony Pena)	.05
450	1987 World Series (Tom Brunansky, Tony Pena)	.05
451	World Series Celebration	.05
452	World Series Celebration	.05
453	World Series Celebration	.05
454	World Series Celebration	.05
(455)	Orioles Logo/Pennant	.05
(456)	Red Sox Logo/Pennant	.05
(457)	Angels Logo/Pennant	.05
(458)	White Sox Logo/Pennant	.05
(459)	Indians Logo/Pennant	.05
(460)	Tigers Logo/Pennant	.05
(461)	Royals Logo/Pennant	.05
(462)	Brewers Logo/Pennant	.05
(463)	Twins Logo/Pennant	.05
(464)	Yankees Logo/Pennant	.05
(465)	Athletics Logo/Pennant	.05
(466)	Mariners Logo/Pennant	.05
(467)	Rangers Logo/Pennant	.05
(468)	Blue Jays Logo/Pennant	.05
(469)	Braves Logo/Pennant	.05
(470)	Cubs Logo/Pennant	.05
(471)	Reds Logo/Pennant	.05
(472)	Astros Logo/Pennant	.05
(473)	Dodgers Logo/Pennant	.05
(474)	Expos Logo/Pennant	.05
(475)	Mets Logo/Pennant	.05
(476)	Phillies Logo/Pennant	.05
(477)	Pirates Logo/Pennant	.05
(478)	Cardinals Logo/Pennant	.05
(479)	Padres Logo/Pennant	.05
(480)	Giants Logo/Pennant	.05

1989 Panini Stickers

CUBS
MARK GRACE

For a second straight year, the Italian sticker manufacturer produced a 480-piece set for the American market. The 1-7/8" x 2-11/16" stickers were sold in packs of six for 30 cents. Packs contain five player stickers and a foil depicting team logos, lettering or ballparks. A 64-page album depicting Jose Canseco on the cover was offered for 69 cents. The 1989 Panini stickers used more action photos than the previous year. Color photos had banners at the bottom with team and player name. Backs had appropriate logos, sticker number and ads for Panini's sticker book.

	NM/M
Complete Set (480):	12.50
Common Player:	.05
Sticker Album:	1.00
Wax Pack (6):	.25
Wax Box (100):	7.50

No.	Player	Price
1	World Series Trophy	.05
2	World Series Trophy	.05
3	Mike Schmidt	.40
4	Tom Browning	.05
5	Doug Jones	.05
6	Wrigley Field	.05
7	Wade Boggs	.30
8	Jose Canseco	.20
9	Orel Hershiser	.05
10	Oakland A's Win ALCS	.05
11	Oakland A's Win ALCS	.05
12	Dennis Eckersley (ALCS MVP)	.20
13	Orel Hershiser (NLCS MVP)	.05
14	Dodgers Win NLCS	.05
15	Dodgers Win NLCS	.05
16	Kirk Gibson	.05
17	Kirk Gibson	.05
18	Orel Hershiser	.05
19	Orel Hershiser	.05
20	Mark McGwire	.50
21	Tim Belcher	.05
22	Jay Howell	.05
23	Mickey Hatcher	.05
24	Mike Davis	.05
25	Orel Hershiser (World Series MVP)	.05
26	Dodgers Win World Series	.05
27	Dodgers Win World Series	.05
28	Dodgers Win World Series	.05
29	Dodgers Win World Series	.05
30	Braves Logo	.05
31	Jose Alvarez	.05
32	Tommy Gregg	.05
33	Paul Assenmacher	.05
34	Tom Glavine	.25
35	Rick Mahler	.05
36	Pete Smith	.05

No.	Name	Price
37	Atlanta Stadium	.05
38	Braves Script	.05
39	Bruce Sutter	.20
40	Gerald Perry	.05
41	Jeff Blauser	.05
42	Ron Gant	.05
43	Andres Thomas	.05
44	Dion James	.05
45	Dale Murphy	.20
46	Cubs Logo	.05
47	Doug Dascenzo	.05
48	Mike Harkey	.05
49	Greg Maddux	.50
50	Jeff Pico	.05
51	Rick Sutcliffe	.05
52	Damon Berryhill	.05
53	Wrigley Field	.05
54	Cubs Script	.05
55	Mark Grace	.15
56	Ryne Sandberg	.50
57	Vance Law	.05
58	Shawon Dunston	.05
59	Andre Dawson	.25
60	Rafael Palmeiro	.40
61	Mitch Webster	.05
62	Reds Logo	.05
63	Jack Armstrong	.05
64	Chris Sabo	.05
65	Tom Browning	.05
66	John Franco	.05
67	Danny Jackson	.05
68	Jose Rijo	.05
69	Riverfront Stadium	.05
70	Reds Script	.05
71	Bo Diaz	.05
72	Nick Esasky	.05
73	Jeff Treadway	.05
74	Barry Larkin	.05
75	Kal Daniels	.05
76	Eric Davis	.05
77	Paul O'Neill	.05
78	Astros Logo	.05
79	Craig Biggio	.05
80	John Fishel	.05
81	Juan Agosto	.05
82	Bob Knepper	.05
83	Nolan Ryan	1.00
84	Mike Scott	.05
85	The Astrodome	.05
86	Astros Script	.05
87	Dave Smith	.05
88	Glenn Davis	.05
89	Bill Doran	.05
90	Rafael Ramirez	.05
91	Kevin Bass	.05
92	Billy Hatcher	.05
93	Gerald Young	.05
94	Dodgers Logo	.05
95	Tim Belcher	.05
96	Tim Crews	.05
97	Orel Hershiser	.05
98	Jay Howell	.05
99	Tim Leary	.05
100	John Tudor	.05
101	Dodgers Stadium	.05
102	Dodgers Script	.05
103	Fernando Valenzuela	.05
104	Mike Scioscia	.05
105	Mickey Hatcher	.05
106	Steve Sax	.05
107	Kirk Gibson	.05
108	Mike Marshall	.05
109	John Shelby	.05
110	Expos Logo	.05
111	Randy Johnson	.40
112	Nelson Santovenia	.05
113	Tim Burke	.05
114	Dennis Martinez	.05
115	Pascual Perez	.05
116	Bryn Smith	.05
117	Olympic Stadium	.05
118	Expos Script	.05
119	Andres Galarraga	.05
120	Wallace Johnson	.05
121	Tom Foley	.05
122	Tim Wallach	.05
123	Hubie Brooks	.05
124	Tracy Jones	.05
125	Tim Raines	.05
126	Mets Logo	.05
127	Kevin Elster	.05
128	Gregg Jefferies	.05
129	David Cone	.05
130	Ron Darling	.05
131	Dwight Gooden	.05
132	Roger McDowell	.05
133	Shea Stadium	.05
134	Mets Script	.05
135	Randy Myers	.05
136	Gary Carter	.40
137	Keith Hernandez	.05
138	Lenny Dykstra	.05
139	Kevin McReynolds	.05
140	Darryl Strawberry	.05
141	Mookie Wilson	.05
142	Phillies Logo	.05
143	Ron Jones	.05
144	Ricky Jordan	.05
145	Steve Bedrosian	.05
146	Don Carman	.05
147	Kevin Gross	.05
148	Bruce Ruffin	.05
149	Veterans Stadium	.05
150	Phillies Script	.05
151	Von Hayes	.05
152	Juan Samuel	.05
153	Mike Schmidt	.55
154	Phil Bradley	.05
155	Bob Dernier	.05
156	Chris James	.05
157	Milt Thompson	.05
158	Pirates Logo	.05
159	Randy Kramer	.05
160	Scott Medvin	.05
161	Doug Drabek	.05
162	Mike Dunne	.05
163	Jim Gott	.05
164	Jeff Robinson	.05
165	Three Rivers Stadium	.05
166	Pirates Script	.05
167	Jose Lind	.05
168	Mike LaValliere	.05
169	Sid Bream	.05
170	Jose Lind	.05
171	Bobby Bonilla	.05
172	Barry Bonds	1.00
173	Andy Van Slyke	.05
174	Cardinals Logo	.05
175	Luis Alicea	.05
176	John Costello	.05
177	Jose DeLeon	.05
178	Joe Magrane	.05
179	Todd Worrell	.05
180	Tony Pena	.05
181	Busch Stadium	.05
182	Cardinals Script	.05
183	Pedro Guerrero	.05
184	Jose Oquendo	.05
185	Terry Pendleton	.05
186	Ozzie Smith	.50
187	Tom Brunansky	.05
188	Vince Coleman	.05
189	Willie McGee	.05
190	Padres Logo	.05
191	Roberto Alomar	.15
192	Sandy Alomar, Jr.	.05
193	Mark Davis	.05
194	Andy Hawkins	.05
195	Dennis Rasmussen	.05
196	Eric Show	.05
197	Jack Murphy Stadium	.05
198	Padres Script	.05
199	Benito Santiago	.05
200	John Kruk	.05
201	Randy Ready	.05
202	Garry Templeton	.05
203	Tony Gwynn	.50
204	Carmelo Martinez	.05
205	Marvell Wynne	.05
206	Giants Logo	.05
207	Dennis Cook	.05
208	Kirt Manwaring	.05
209	Kelly Downs	.05
210	Rick Reuschel	.05
211	Don Robinson	.05
212	Will Clark	.05
213	Candlestick Park	.05
214	Giants Script	.05
215	Robby Thompson	.05
216	Kevin Mitchell	.05
217	Jose Uribe	.05
218	Matt Williams	.05
219	Mike Aldrete	.05
220	Brett Butler	.05
221	Candy Maldonado	.05
222	Tony Gwynn	.30
223	Darryl Strawberry	.05
224	Andres Galarraga	.05
225	Orel Hershiser, Danny Jackson	.05
226	Nolan Ryan	.50
227	Dwight Gooden/AS	.05
228	Gary Carter/AS	.05
229	Vince Coleman/AS	.05
230	Andre Dawson/AS	.05
231	Darryl Strawberry/AS	.05
232	Will Clark/AS	.05
233	Ryne Sandberg/AS	.25
234	Bobby Bonilla/AS	.05
235	Ozzie Smith/AS	.30
236	Terry Steinbach/AS	.05
237	Frank Viola/AS	.05
238	Jose Canseco/AS	.10
239	Rickey Henderson/AS	.20
240	Dave Winfield/AS	.20
241	Cal Ripken, Jr./AS	.50
242	Wade Boggs/AS	.25
243	Paul Molitor/AS	.20
244	Mark McGwire/AS	.40
245	Wade Boggs	.30
246	Jose Canseco	.30
247	Kirby Puckett	.30
248	Frank Viola	.05
249	Roger Clemens	.35
250	Orioles Logo	.05
251	Bob Milacki	.05
252	Craig Worthington	.05
253	Jeff Ballard	.05
254	Tom Niedenfuer	.05
255	Dave Schmidt	.05
256	Terry Kennedy	.05
257	Memorial Stadium	.05
258	Orioles Script	.05
259	Mickey Tettleton	.05
260	Eddie Murray	.40
261	Billy Ripken	.05
262	Cal Ripken, Jr.	1.00
263	Joe Orsulak	.05
264	Larry Sheets	.05
265	Pete Stanicek	.05
266	Red Sox Logo	.05
267	Steve Curry	.05
268	Jody Reed	.05
269	"Oil Can" Boyd	.05
270	Roger Clemens	.55
271	Bruce Hurst	.05
272	Lee Smith	.05
273	Fenway Park	.05
274	Red Sox Script	.05
275	Todd Benzinger	.05
276	Marty Barrett	.05
277	Wade Boggs	.50
278	Ellis Burks	.05
279	Dwight Evans	.05
280	Mike Greenwell	.05
281	Jim Rice	.10
282	Angels Logo	.05
283	Dante Bichette	.05
284	Bryan Harvey	.05
285	Kirk McCaskill	.05
286	Mike Witt	.05
287	Bob Boone	.05
288	Brian Downing	.05
289	Anaheim Stadium	.05
290	Angels Script	.05
291	Wally Joyner	.05
292	Johnny Ray	.05
293	Jack Howell	.05
294	Dick Schofield	.05
295	Tony Armas	.05
296	Chili Davis	.05
297	Devon White	.05
298	White Sox Logo	.05
299	Dave Gallagher	.05
300	Melido Perez	.05
301	Shawn Hillegas	.05
302	Jack McDowell	.05
303	Bobby Thigpen	.05
304	Carlton Fisk	.40
305	Comiskey Park	.05
306	White Sox Script	.05
307	Greg Walker	.05
308	Steve Lyons	.05
309	Ozzie Guillen	.05
310	Harold Baines	.05
311	Daryl Boston	.05
312	Lance Johnson	.05
313	Dan Pasqua	.05
314	Indians Logo	.05
315	Luis Medina	.05
316	Ron Tingley	.05
317	Tom Candiotti	.05
318	John Farrell	.05
319	Doug Jones	.05
320	Greg Swindell	.05
321	Cleveland Stadium	.05
322	Indians Script	.05
323	Andy Allanson	.05
324	Willie Upshaw	.05
325	Julio Franco	.05
326	Brook Jacoby	.05
327	Joe Carter	.05
328	Mel Hall	.05
329	Cory Snyder	.05
330	Tigers Logo	.05
331	Paul Gibson	.05
332	Torey Lovullo	.05
333	Mike Henneman	.05
334	Jack Morris	.05
335	Jeff Robinson	.05
336	Frank Tanana	.05
337	Tiger Stadium	.05
338	Tigers Script	.05
339	Matt Nokes	.05
340	Tom Brookens	.05
341	Lou Whitaker	.05
342	Luis Salazar	.05
343	Alan Trammell	.05
344	Chet Lemon	.05
345	Gary Pettis	.05
346	Royals Logo	.05
347	Luis de los Santos	.05
348	Gary Thurman	.05
349	Steve Farr	.05
350	Mark Gubicza	.05
351	Charlie Leibrandt	.05
352	Bret Saberhagen	.05
353	Royals Stadium	.05
354	Royals Script	.05
355	George Brett	.55
356	Frank White	.05
357	Kevin Seitzer	.05
358	Bo Jackson	.10
359	Pat Tabler	.05
360	Danny Tartabull	.05
361	Willie Wilson	.05
362	Brewers Logo	.05
363	Joey Meyer	.05
364	Gary Sheffield	.25
365	Don August	.05
366	Ted Higuera	.05
367	Dan Plesac	.05
368	B.J. Surhoff	.05
369	County Stadium	.05
370	Brewers Script	.05
371	Greg Brock	.05
372	Jim Gantner	.05
373	Paul Molitor	.40
374	Dale Sveum	.05
375	Glenn Braggs	.05
376	Rob Deer	.05
377	Robin Yount	.40
378	Twins Logo	.05
379	German Gonzalez	.05
380	Kelvin Torve	.05
381	Allan Anderson	.05
382	Jeff Reardon	.05
383	Frank Viola	.05
384	Tim Laudner	.05
385	HHH Metrodome	.05
386	Twins Script	.05
387	Kent Hrbek	.05
388	Gene Larkin	.05
389	Gary Gaetti	.05
390	Greg Gagne	.05
391	Randy Bush	.05
392	Dan Gladden	.05
393	Kirby Puckett	.50
394	Yankees Logo	.05
395	Roberto Kelly	.05
396	Al Leiter	.05
397	John Candelaria	.05
398	Rich Dotson	.05
399	Rick Rhoden	.05
400	Dave Righetti	.05
401	Yankee Stadium	.05
402	Yankees Script	.05
403	Don Slaught	.05
404	Don Mattingly	.55
405	Willie Randolph	.05
406	Mike Pagliarulo	.05
407	Rafael Santana	.05
408	Rickey Henderson	.40
409	Dave Winfield	.40
410	A's Logo	.05
411	Todd Burns	.05
412	Walt Weiss	.05
413	Storm Davis	.05
414	Dennis Eckersley	.35
415	Dave Stewart	.05
416	Bob Welch	.05
417	Oakland Coliseum	.05
418	A's Script	.05
419	Terry Steinbach	.05
420	Mark McGwire	.75
421	Carney Lansford	.05
422	Jose Canseco	.35
423	Dave Henderson	.05
424	Dave Parker	.05
425	Luis Polonia	.05
426	Mariners Logo	.05
427	Mario Diaz	.05
428	Edgar Martinez	.05
429	Scott Bankhead	.05
430	Mark Langston	.05
431	Mike Moore	.05
432	Scott Bradley	.05
433	The Kingdome	.05
434	Mariners Script	.05
435	Alvin Davis	.05
436	Harold Reynolds	.05
437	Jim Presley	.05
438	Rey Quinonez	.05
439	Mickey Brantley	.05
440	Jay Buhner	.05
441	Henry Cotto	.05
442	Rangers Logo	.05
443	Cecil Espy	.05
444	Chad Kreuter	.05
445	Jose Guzman	.05
446	Charlie Hough	.05
447	Jeff Russell	.05
448	Bobby Witt	.05
449	Arlington Stadium	.05
450	Rangers Script	.05
451	Geno Petralli	.05
452	Pete O'Brien	.05
453	Steve Buechele	.05
454	Scott Fletcher	.05
455	Pete Incaviglia	.05
456	Oddibe McDowell	.05
457	Ruben Sierra	.05
458	Blue Jays Logo	.05
459	Rob Ducey	.05
460	Todd Stottlemyre	.05
461	Tom Henke	.05
462	Jimmy Key	.05
463	Dave Steib	.05
464	Pat Borders	.05
465	Exhibition Stadium	.05
466	Blue Jays Script	.05
467	Fred McGriff	.05
468	Manny Lee	.05
469	Kelly Gruber	.05
470	Tony Fernandez	.05
471	Jesse Barfield	.05
472	George Bell	.05
473	Lloyd Moseby	.05
474	Orel Hershiser	.05
475	Frank Viola	.05
476	Chris Sabo	.05
477	Jose Canseco	.10
478	Walt Weiss	.05
479	Kirk Gibson	.05
480	Jose Canseco	.10

1990 Panini Stickers

and one foil sticker, the set includes 388 2-1/8" x 3" stickers. Fronts feature color action photos. Backs are printed in black-and-white and include a sticker number and appropriate logos. A 68-page album with Nolan Ryan on the cover was sold as an adjunct to the stickers. Among the foil stickers in the set are those featuring the team logo and batting helmet of each team.

	NM/M
Complete Set (388):	9.00
Common Player:	.05
English Album:	1.00
French Album:	3.00
Wax Pack (5+1):	.25
Wax Box (100):	7.50

No.	Name	Price
1	Randy Milligan	.05
2	Gregg Olson	.05
3	Bill Ripken	.05
4	Phil Bradley	.05
5	Joe Orsulak	.05
6	Bob Milacki	.05
7	Cal Ripken, Jr.	1.00
8	Mickey Tettleton	.05
9	Orioles Logo (Foil)	.05
10	Orioles Helmet (Foil)	.05
11	Craig Worthington	.05
12	Mike Devereaux	.05
13	Jeff Ballard	.05
14	Lee Smith	.05
15	Marty Barrett	.05
16	Mike Greenwell	.05
17	Dwight Evans	.05
18	John Dopson	.05
19	Wade Boggs	.50
20	Mike Boddicker	.05
21	Ellis Burks	.05
22	Red Sox Logo (Foil)	.05
23	Red Sox Helmet (Foil)	.05
24	Roger Clemens	.55
25	Jody Reed	.05
26	Nick Esasky	.05
27	Brian Downing	.05
28	Bert Blyleven	.05
29	Devon White	.05
30	Claudell Washington	.05
31	Wally Joyner	.05
32	Chuck Finley	.05
33	Johnny Ray	.05
34	Jim Abbott	.05
35	Angels Logo (Foil)	.05
36	Angels Helmet (Foil)	.05
37	Kirk McCaskill	.05
38	Lance Parrish	.05
39	Chili Davis	.05
40	Steve Lyons	.05
41	Ozzie Guillen	.05
42	Melido Perez	.05
43	Scott Fletcher	.05
44	Carlton Fisk	.40
45	Greg Walker	.05
46	Dave Gallagher	.05
47	Ivan Calderon	.05
48	White Sox Logo (Foil)	.05
49	White Sox Helmet (Foil)	.05
50	Bobby Thigpen	.05
51	Ron Kittle	.05
52	Daryl Boston	.05
53	John Farrell	.05
54	Jerry Browne	.05
55	Pete O'Brien	.05
56	Cory Snyder	.05
57	Tom Candiotti	.05
58	Brook Jacoby	.05
59	Greg Swindell	.05
60	Felix Fermin	.05
61	Indians Logo (Foil)	.05
62	Indians Helmet (Foil)	.05
63	Doug Jones	.05
64	Dion James	.05
65	Joe Carter	.05
66	Mike Heath	.05
67	Dave Bergman	.05
68	Gary Ward	.05
69	Mike Henneman	.05
70	Alan Trammell	.05
71	Lou Whitaker	.05
72	Frank Tanana	.05
73	Fred Lynn	.05
74	Tigers Logo (Foil)	.05
75	Tigers Helmet (Foil)	.05
76	Jack Morris	.05
77	Chet Lemon	.05
78	Gary Pettis	.05
79	Kurt Stillwell	.05
80	Jim Eisenreich	.05
81	Bret Saberhagen	.05
82	Mark Gubicza	.05
83	Frank White	.05
84	Bo Jackson	.10
85	Jeff Montgomery	.05
86	Kevin Seitzer	.05
87	Royals Logo (Foil)	.05
88	Royals Helmet (Foil)	.05
89	Tom Gordon	.05
90	Danny Tartabull	.05
91	George Brett	.55
92	Robin Yount	.40
93	B.J. Surhoff	.05
94	Jim Gantner	.05
95	Dan Plesac	.05
96	Ted Higuera	.05
97	Glenn Braggs	.05
98	Paul Molitor	.40
99	Chris Bosio	.05
100	Brewers Logo (Foil)	.05
101	Brewers Helmet (Foil)	.05
102	Rob Deer	.05
103	Chuck Crim	.05
104	Greg Brock	.05
105	Kirby Puckett	.50
106	Gary Gaetti	.05
107	Roy Smith	.05
108	Jeff Reardon	.05
109	Randy Bush	.05
110	Al Newman	.05
111	Dan Gladden	.05
112	Kent Hrbek	.05
113	Twins Logo (Foil)	.05
114	Twins Helmet (Foil)	.05
115	Greg Gagne	.05
116	Brian Harper	.05
117	Allan Anderson	.05
118	Lee Guetterman	.05
119	Roberto Kelly	.05
120	Jesse Barfield	.05
121	Alvaro Espinoza	.05
122	Mel Hall	.05
123	Chuck Cary	.05
124	Dave Righetti	.05
125	Don Mattingly	.55
126	Yankees Logo (Foil)	.05
127	Yankees Helmet (Foil)	.05
128	Bob Geren	.05
129	Steve Sax	.05
130	Andy Hawkins	.05
131	Bob Welch	.05
132	Mark McGwire	.75
133	Dave Henderson	.05
134	Carney Lansford	.05
135	Walt Weiss	.05
136	Mike Moore	.05
137	Dennis Eckersley	.35
138	Rickey Henderson	.40
139	A's Logo (Foil)	.05
140	A's Helmet (Foil)	.05
141	Dave Stewart	.05
142	Jose Canseco	.30
143	Terry Steinbach	.05
144	Harold Reynolds	.05
145	Darnell Coles	.05
146	Brian Holman	.05
147	Scott Bankhead	.05
148	Greg Briley	.05
149	Alvin Davis	.05
150	Jeffrey Leonard	.05
151	Mike Schooler	.05
152	Mariners Logo (Foil)	.05
153	Mariners Helmet (Foil)	.05
154	Randy Johnson	.40
155	Ken Griffey Jr.	.65
156	Dave Valle	.05
157	Pete Incaviglia	.05
158	Fred Manrique	.05
159	Jeff Russell	.05
160	Nolan Ryan	1.00
161	Geno Petralli	.05
162	Ruben Sierra	.05
163	Julio Franco	.05
164	Rafael Palmeiro	.35
165	Rangers Logo (Foil)	.05
166	Rangers Helmet (Foil)	.05
167	Harold Baines	.05
168	Kevin Brown	.05
169	Steve Buechele	.05
170	Fred McGriff	.05
171	Kelly Gruber	.05
172	Todd Stottlemyre	.05
173	Dave Steib	.05
174	Mookie Wilson	.05
175	Pat Borders	.05
176	Tony Fernandez	.05
177	John Cerutti	.05
178	Blue Jays Logo (Foil)	.05
179	Blue Jays Helmet (Foil)	.05
180	George Bell	.05
181	Jimmy Key	.05
182	Nelson Liriano	.05
183	Kirby Puckett (BA leader)	.30
184	Carney Lansford (Stats leader.)	.05
185	Nolan Ryan (K Leader)	.50
186	American League Logo (Foil)	.05
187	National League Logo (Foil)	.05
188	World's Championship Trophy (Foil)	.05
189	1988 L.A. Dodgers World Series Ring (Foil)	.05
190	1987 Minnesota Twins World Series Ring (Foil)	.05
191	1986 N.Y. Mets World Series Ring (Foil)	.05
192	1985 K.C. Royals World Series Ring (Foil)	.05
193	1984 Detroit Tigers World Series Ring (Foil)	.05
194	1983 Baltimore Orioles World Series Ring (Foil)	.05
195	1982 Cardinals World Series Ring (Foil)	.05
196	1981 L.A. Dodgers World Series Ring (Foil)	.05
197	1980 Phillies World Series Ring (Foil)	.05
198	Dave Stewart, Bo Jackson/AS	.05
199	Wade Boggs, Kirby Puckett/AS	.15
200	Harold Baines/AS	.05

BRAVES

JOHN SMOLTZ

Nearly 400 individual player and specialty stickers comprise the 1990 issue from this Italian company. Sold in packs of five regular

201 Julio Franco/AS .05
202 Cal Ripken, Jr./AS .50
203 Ruben Sierra/AS .05
204 Mark McGwire/AS .40
205 Terry Steinbach/AS .05
206 Rick Reuschel, Ozzie Smith/AS .05
207 Tony Gwynn, Will Clark/AS .05
208 Kevin Mitchell/AS .05
209 Eric Davis/AS .05
210 Howard Johnson/AS .05
211 Pedro Guerrero/AS .05
212 Ryne Sandberg/AS .25
213 Benito Santiago/AS .05
214 Kevin Mitchell (HR Leaders) .05
215 Mark Davis (Saves leader.) .05
216 Vince Coleman (SB Leader) .05
217 Jeff Blauser .05
218 Jeff Treadway .05
219 Tom Glavine .20
220 Joe Boever .05
221 Oddibe McDowell .05
222 Dale Murphy .20
223 Derek Lilliquist .05
224 Tommy Gregg .05
225 Braves Logo (Foil) .05
226 Braves Helmet (Foil) .05
227 Lonnie Smith .05
228 John Smoltz .05
229 Andres Thomas .05
230 Jerome Walton .05
231 Ryne Sandberg .50
232 Mitch Williams .05
233 Rick Sutcliffe .05
234 Damon Berryhill .05
235 Dwight Smith .05
236 Shawon Dunston .05
237 Greg Maddux .50
238 Cubs Logo (Foil) .05
239 Cubs Helmet (Foil) .05
240 Andre Dawson .25
241 Mark Grace .05
242 Mike Bielecki .05
243 Jose Rijo .05
244 John Franco .05
245 Paul O'Neill .05
246 Eric Davis .05
247 Tom Browning .05
248 Chris Sabo .05
249 Rob Dibble .05
250 Todd Benzinger .05
251 Reds Logo (Foil) .05
252 Reds Helmet (Foil) .05
253 Barry Larkin .05
254 Rolando Roomes .05
255 Danny Jackson .05
256 Terry Puhl .05
257 Dave Smith .05
258 Glenn Davis .05
259 Craig Biggio .05
260 Ken Caminiti .05
261 Kevin Bass .05
262 Mike Scott .05
263 Gerald Young .05
264 Astros Logo (Foil) .05
265 Astros Helmet (Foil) .05
266 Rafael Ramirez .05
267 Jim Deshaies .05
268 Bill Doran .05
269 Fernando Valenzuela .05
270 Alfredo Griffin .05
271 Kirk Gibson .05
272 Mike Marshall .05
273 Eddie Murray .40
274 Jay Howell .05
275 Orel Hershiser .05
276 Mike Scioscia .05
277 Dodgers Logo (Foil) .05
278 Dodgers Helmet (Foil) .05
279 Willie Randolph .05
280 Kal Daniels .05
281 Tim Belcher .05
282 Pascual Perez .05
283 Tim Raines .05
284 Andres Galarraga .05
285 Spike Owen .05
286 Tim Wallach .05
287 Mark Langston .05
288 Dennis Martinez .05
289 Nelson Santovenia .05
290 Expos Logo (Foil) .05
291 Expos Helmet (Foil) .05
292 Tom Foley .05
293 Dave Martinez .05
294 Tim Burke .05
295 Ron Darling .05
296 Kevin Elster .05
297 Dwight Gooden .05
298 Gregg Jefferies .05
299 Sid Fernandez .05
300 Dave Magadan .05
301 David Cone .05
302 Darryl Strawberry .05
303 Mets Logo (Foil) .05
304 Mets Helmet (Foil) .05
305 Kevin McReynolds .05
306 Howard Johnson .05
307 Randy Myers .05
308 Roger McDowell .05
309 Tom Herr .05
310 John Kruk .05
311 Randy Ready .05
312 Jeff Parrett .05
313 Lenny Dykstra .05
314 Ken Howell .05
315 Ricky Jordan .05

316 Phillies Logo (Foil) .05
317 Phillies Helmet (Foil) .05
318 Dickie Thon .05
319 Von Hayes .05
320 Dennis Cook .05
321 Jay Bell .05
322 Barry Bonds 1.00
323 John Smiley .05
324 Andy Van Slyke .05
325 Bobby Bonilla .05
326 Bill Landrum .05
327 Randy Kramer .05
328 Jose Lind .05
329 Pirates Logo (Foil) .05
330 Pirates Helmet (Foil) .05
331 Gary Redus .05
332 Doug Drabek .05
333 Mike LaValliere .05
334 Jose DeLeon .05
335 Pedro Guerrero .05
336 Vince Coleman .05
337 Terry Pendleton .05
338 Ozzie Smith .50
339 Willie McGee .05
340 Todd Worrell .05
341 Jose Oquendo .05
342 Cardinals Logo (Foil) .05
343 Cardinals Helmet (Foil) .05
344 Tom Brunansky .05
345 Milt Thompson .05
346 Joe Magrane .05
347 Ed Whitson .05
348 Jack Clark .05
349 Roberto Alomar .10
350 Chris James .05
351 Tony Gwynn .50
352 Mark Davis .05
353 Greg W. Harris .05
354 Garry Templeton .05
355 Padres Logo (Foil) .05
356 Padres Helmet (Foil) .05
357 Bruce Hurst .05
358 Benito Santiago .05
359 Bip Roberts .05
360 Dave Dravecky .05
361 Kevin Mitchell .05
362 Craig Lefferts .05
363 Will Clark .05
364 Steve Bedrosian .05
365 Brett Butler .05
366 Matt Williams .05
367 Scott Garrelts .05
368 Giants Logo (Foil) .05
369 Giants Helmet (Foil) .05
370 Rick Reuschel .05
371 Robby Thompson .05
372 Jose Uribe .05
373 Ben McDonald (Headliner) .05
374 Carlos Martinez (Headliner) .05
375 Steve Olin (Headliner) .05
376 Bill Spiers (Headliner) .05
377 Junior Felix (Headliner) .05
378 Joe Oliver (Headliner) .05
379 Eric Anthony (Headliner) .05
380 Ramon Martinez (Headliner) .05
381 Todd Zeile (Headliner) .05
382 Andy Benes (Headliner) .05
383 Vince Coleman (Highlight) .05
384 Bo Jackson (Highlight) .05
385 Howard Johnson (Highlight) .05
386 Dave Dravecky (Highlight) .05
387 Nolan Ryan (Highlight) .50
388 Cal Ripken, Jr. (Highlight) .50

1991 Panini Stickers

JIM PRESLEY, 3B

For 1991 the Panini stickers were considerably downsized in both the number of pieces in the set (271) and in the size of each sticker (1-1/2" x 2-9/16"). Player stickers have a color action photo at center with a few stats at bottom. There are foil pennant and team logo stickers for each team as well as 1990 season highlights kicking off the set. Backs are printed in black-and-white and have MLB and Players Association logos, along with Panini advertising. A colorful album was available to house the stickers, featuring on its cover Ken Griffey, Jr., Ryne Sandberg and Rickey Henderson.

	NM/M
Complete Set (271):	12.50
Common Player:	.05
Album:	1.00
Wax Pack (5+1):	.25
Wax Box (100):	9.00

1 Mark Langston, Mike Witt (No-hitter.) .05
2 Randy Johnson (No-hitter.) .20
3 Nolan Ryan (No-hitter.) .50
4 Dave Stewart (No-hitter.) .05
5 Fernando Valenzuela (No-hitter.) .05
6 Andy Hawkins (No-hitter.) .05
7 Melido Perez (No-hitter.) .05
8 Terry Mullholland (No-hitter.) .05
9 Dave Steib (No-hitter.) .05
10 Craig Biggio .05
11 Jim Deshaies .05
12 Dave Smith .05
13 Eric Yelding .05
14 Astros Pennant .05
15 Astros Logo .05
16 Mike Scott .05
17 Ken Caminiti .05
18 Danny Darwin .05
19 Glenn Davis .05
20 Braves Pennant .05
21 Braves Logo .05
22 Lonnie Smith .05
23 Charlie Leibrandt .05
24 Jim Presley .05
25 Greg Olson .05
26 John Smoltz .05
27 Ron Gant .05
28 Jeff Treadway .05
29 Dave Justice .05
30 Jose Oquendo .05
31 Joe Magrane .05
32 Cardinals Pennant .05
33 Cardinals Logo .05
34 Todd Zeile .05
35 Vince Coleman .05
36 Bob Tewksbury .05
37 Pedro Guerrero .05
38 Lee Smith .05
39 Ozzie Smith .50
40 Ryne Sandberg .50
41 Andre Dawson .25
42 Cubs Pennant .05
43 Greg Maddux .50
44 Jerome Walton .05
45 Cubs Logo .05
46 Mike Harkey .05
47 Shawon Dunston .05
48 Mark Grace .05
49 Joe Girardi .05
50 Ramon Martinez .05
51 Lenny Harris .05
52 Mike Morgan .05
53 Eddie Murray .40
54 Dodgers Pennant .05
55 Dodgers Logo .05
56 Hubie Brooks .05
57 Mike Scioscia .05
58 Kal Daniels .05
59 Fernando Valenzuela .05
60 Expos Pennant .05
61 Expos Logo .05
62 Spike Owen .05
63 Tim Raines .05
64 Tim Wallach .05
65 Larry Walker .05
66 Dave Martinez .05
67 Mark Gardner .05
68 Dennis Martinez .05
69 Delino DeShields .05
70 Jeff Brantley .05
71 Kevin Mitchell .05
72 Giants Pennant .05
73 Giants Logo .05
74 Don Robinson .05
75 Brett Butler .05
76 Matt Williams .05
77 Robby Thompson .05
78 John Burkett .05
79 Will Clark .05
80 David Cone .05
81 Dave Magadan .05
82 Mets Pennant .05
83 Gregg Jefferies .05
84 Frank Viola .05
85 Mets Logo .05
86 Howard Johnson .05
87 John Franco .05
88 Darryl Strawberry .05
89 Dwight Gooden .05
90 Joe Carter .05
91 Ed Whitson .05
92 Andy Benes .05
93 Benito Santiago .05
94 Padres Pennant .05
95 Padres Logo .05
96 Roberto Alomar .10
97 Bip Roberts .05
98 Jack Clark .05
99 Tony Gwynn .50
100 Phillies Pennant .05
101 Phillies Logo .05
102 Charlie Hayes .05
103 Lenny Dykstra .05
104 Dale Murphy .20
105 Von Hayes .05
106 Dickie Thon .05
107 John Kruk .05
108 Ken Howell .05
109 Darren Daulton .05
110 Jay Bell .05
111 Bobby Bonilla .05
112 Pirates Pennant .05
113 Pirates Logo .05
114 Barry Bonds 1.00
115 Neal Heaton .05
116 Doug Drabek .05
117 Jose Lind .05
118 Andy Van Slyke .05
119 Sid Bream .05
120 Paul O'Neill .05
121 Randy Myers .05
122 Reds Pennant .05
123 Mariano Duncan .05
124 Eric Davis .05
125 Red Logo .05
126 Jack Armstrong .05
127 Chris Sabo .05
128 Rob Dibble .05
129 Barry Larkin .05
130 National League Logo .05
131 American League Logo .05
132 Dave Winfield .40
133 Lance Parrish .05
134 Chili Davis .05
135 Chuck Finley .05
136 Angels Pennant .05
137 Angels Logo .05
138 Johnny Ray .05
139 Dante Bichette .05
140 Jim Abbott .05
141 Wally Joyner .05
142 A's Pennant .05
143 A's Logo .05
144 Dave Stewart .05
145 Mark McGwire .75
146 Rickey Henderson .40
147 Walt Weiss .05
148 Dennis Eckersley .35
149 Jose Canseco .30
150 Dave Henderson .05
151 Bob Welch .05
152 Tony Fernandez .05
153 David Wells .05
154 Blue Jays Pennant .05
155 Blue Jays Logo .05
156 Pat Borders .05
157 Fred McGriff .05
158 George Bell .05
159 John Olerud .05
160 Dave Steib .05
161 Kelly Gruber .05
162 Billy Spiers .05
163 Dan Plesac .05
164 Brewers Pennant .05
165 Mark Knudson .05
166 Robin Yount .40
167 Brewers Logo .05
168 Paul Molitor .40
169 B.J. Surhoff .05
170 Gary Sheffield .30
171 Dave Parker .05
172 Sandy Alomar .05
173 Doug Jones .05
174 Tom Candiotti .05
175 Mitch Webster .05
176 Indians Pennant .05
177 Indians Logo .05
178 Brook Jacoby .05
179 Candy Maldonado .05
180 Carlos Baerga .05
181 Chris James .05
182 Mariners Pennant .05
183 Mariners Logo .05
184 Mike Schooler .05
185 Alvin Davis .05
186 Erik Hanson .05
187 Edgar Martinez .05
188 Randy Johnson .40
189 Ken Griffey Jr. .60
190 Jay Buhner .05
191 Harold Reynolds .05
192 Cal Ripken Jr. 1.00
193 Gregg Olson .05
194 Orioles Pennant .05
195 Orioles Logo .05
196 Mike Devereaux .05
197 Ben McDonald .05
198 Craig Worthington .05
199 Dave Johnson .05
200 Joe Orsulak .05
201 Randy Milligan .05
202 Ruben Sierra .05
203 Bobby Witt .05
204 Rangers Pennant .05
205 Nolan Ryan 1.00
206 Jeff Huson .05
207 Rangers Logo .05
208 Steve Buechele .05
209 Julio Franco .05
210 Rafael Palmeiro .05
211 Ellis Burks .05
212 Dwight Evans .05
213 Wade Boggs .05
214 Roger Clemens .55
215 Red Sox Pennant .05
216 Red Sox Logo .05
217 Jeff Reardon .05
218 Tony Pena .05
219 Mike Greenwell .05
220 Jody Reed .05
221 Carlos Quintana .05
222 Royals Pennant .05

223 Royals Logo .05
224 George Brett .55
225 Bret Saberhagen .05
226 Bo Jackson .05
227 Kevin Seitzer .05
228 Mark Gubicza .05
229 Jim Eisenreich .05
230 Gerald Perry .05
231 Tom Gordon .05
232 Cecil Fielder .05
233 Lou Whitaker .05
234 Tigers Pennant .05
235 Tigers Logo .05
236 Mike Henneman .05
237 Mike Heath .05
238 Alan Trammell .05
239 Lloyd Moseby .05
240 Dan Petry .05
241 Dave Bergman .05
242 Brian Harper .05
243 Rick Aguilera .05
244 Twins Pennant .05
245 Greg Gagne .05
246 Gene Larkin .05
247 Twins Logo .05
248 Kirby Puckett .50
249 Kevin Tapani .05
250 Gary Gaetti .05
251 Kent Hrbek .05
252 Bobby Thigpen .05
253 Lance Johnson .05
254 Greg Hibbard .05
255 Carlton Fisk .40
256 White Sox Pennant .05
257 White Sox Logo .05
258 Ivan Calderon .05
259 Barry Jones .05
260 Robin Ventura .05
261 Ozzie Guillen .05
262 Yankees Pennant .05
263 Yankees Logo .05
264 Kevin Maas .05
265 Bob Geren .05
266 Dave Righetti .05
267 Don Mattingly .55
268 Roberto Kelly .05
269 Alvaro Espinoza .05
270 Oscar Azocar .05
271 Steve Sax .05

Canadian

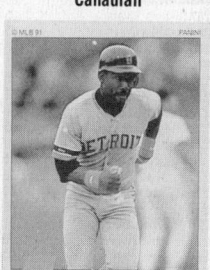

CHET LEMON
DETROIT TIGERS

While the U.S. sticker set from Panini was downsized both in physical format and number of stickers in the set, a special issue for the Canadian market was produced in the 2-1/8" x 3" size to a total of 360 pieces. The relatively simple design has a color game-action photo with a wide white border. The black player name and team at bottom are highlighted by a red (American League) or blue (National League) splash of color at lower-left. Black-and-white backs have a sticker number and a few words about the collection in English and French. Besides player stickers there are foil specialty stickers for the teams and a subset of All-Star stickers.

	NM/M
Complete Set (360):	20.00
Common Player:	.05
Album:	3.00

1 Major League Baseball Logo (foil) .05
2 MLB Players Association Logo (foil) .05
3 Panini Logo (foil) .05
4 Houston Astros Pennant (Foil) .05
5 Houston Astros Logo (Foil) .05
6 Craig Biggio .05
7 Glenn Davis .05
8 Casey Candaele .05
9 Ken Caminiti .05
10 Rafael Ramirez .05
11 Glenn Wilson .05
12 Eric Yelding .05
13 Franklin Stubbs .05
14 Mike Scott .05
15 Danny Darwin .05
16 Atlanta Braves Pennant (Foil) .05
17 Atlanta Braves Logo (Foil) .05
18 Greg Olson .05
19 Tommy Gregg .05
20 Jeff Treadway .05
21 Jim Presley .05
22 Jeff Blauser .05
23 Ron Gant .05
24 Lonnie Smith .05
25 Dave Justice .05
26 John Smoltz .05
27 Charlie Leibrandt .05
28 St. Louis Cardinals Pennant (Foil) .05
29 St. Louis Cardinals Logo (Foil) .05
30 Tom Pagnozzi .05
31 Pedro Guerrero .05
32 Jose Oquendo .05
33 Todd Zeile .05
34 Ozzie Smith .50
35 Vince Coleman .05
36 Milt Thompson .05
37 Rex Hudler .05
38 Joe Magrane .05
39 Lee Smith .05
40 Chicago Cubs Pennant (Foil) .05
41 Chicago Cubs Logo (Foil) .05
42 Joe Girardi .05
43 Mark Grace .05
44 Ryne Sandberg .50
45 Luis Salazar .05
46 Shawon Dunston .05
47 Dwight Smith .05
48 Jerome Walton .05
49 Andre Dawson .25
50 Greg Maddux .50
51 Mike Harkey .05
52 Los Angeles Dodgers Pennant (Foil) .05
53 Los Angeles Dodgers Logo (Foil) .05
54 Mike Scioscia .05
55 Eddie Murray .40
56 Juan Samuel .05
57 Lenny Harris .05
58 Alfredo Griffin .05
59 Hubie Brooks .05
60 Kal Daniels .05
61 Stan Javier .05
62 Ramon Martinez .05
63 Mike Morgan .05
64 San Francisco Giants Pennant (Foil) .05
65 San Francisco Giants Logo (Foil) .05
66 Terry Kennedy .05
67 Will Clark .05
68 Robby Thompson .05
69 Matt Williams .05
70 Jose Uribe .05
71 Kevin Mitchell .05
72 Brett Butler .05
73 Don Robinson .05
74 John Burkett .05
75 Jeff Brantley .05
76 New York Mets Pennant (Foil) .05
77 New York Mets Logo (Foil) .05
78 Mackey Sasser .05
79 Dave Magadan .05
80 Gregg Jefferies .05
81 Howard Johnson .05
82 Kevin Elster .05
83 Kevin McReynolds .05
84 Daryl Boston .05
85 Darryl Strawberry .05
86 Dwight Gooden .05
87 Frank Viola .05
88 San Diego Padres Pennant (Foil) .05
89 San Diego Padres Logo (Foil) .05
90 Benito Santiago .05
91 Jack Clark .05
92 Roberto Alomar .10
93 Mike Pagliarulo .05
94 Garry Templeton .05
95 Joe Carter .05
96 Bip Roberts .05
97 Tony Gwynn .50
98 Ed Whitson .05
99 Andy Benes .05
100 Philadelphia Phillies Pennant (Foil) .05
101 Philadelphia Phillies Logo (Foil) .05
102 Darren Daulton .05
103 Ricky Jordan .05
104 Randy Ready .05
105 Charlie Hayes .05
106 Dickie Thon .05
107 Von Hayes .05
108 Lenny Dykstra .05
109 Dale Murphy .20
110 Ken Howell .05
111 Roger McDowell .05
112 Pittsburgh Pirates Pennant (Foil) .05
113 Pittsburgh Pirates Logo (Foil) .05
114 Mike LaValliere .05
115 Sid Bream .05
116 Jose Lind .05
117 Jeff King .05
118 Jay Bell .05

119 Barry Bonds 1.00
120 Bobby Bonilla .05
121 Andy Van Slyke .05
121 Doug Drabek .05
123 Neal Heaton .05
124 Cincinnati Reds Pennant (Foil) .05
125 Cincinnati Reds Logo (Foil) .05
126 Joe Oliver .05
127 Todd Benzinger .05
128 Mariano Duncan .05
129 Chris Sabo .05
130 Barry Larkin .05
131 Eric Davis .05
132 Billy Hatcher .05
133 Paul O'Neill .05
134 Jose Rijo .05
135 Randy Myers .05
136 Montreal Expos Pennant (Foil) .05
137 Montreal Expos Logo (Foil) .05
138 Mike Fitzgerald .05
139 Andres Galarraga .05
140 Delino DeShields .05
141 Tim Wallach .05
142 Spike Owen .05
143 Tim Raines .05
144 Dave Martinez .05
145 Larry Walker .05
146 Expos batting Helmet (Foil) .05
147 Dennis Boyd .05
148 Tim Burke .05
149 Bill Sampen .05
150 Dennis Martinez .05
151 Marquis Grissom .05
152 Otis Nixon .05
153 Jerry Goff .05
154 Steve Frey .05
155 National League Logo (Foil) .05
156 American League Logo (Foil) .05
157 Benito Santiago/AS .05
158 Will Clark/AS .05
159 Ryne Sandberg/AS .25
160 Chris Sabo/AS .05
161 Ozzie Smith/AS .25
162 Kevin Mitchell/AS .05
163 Lenny Dykstra/AS .05
164 Darryl Strawberry/AS .05
165 Jack Armstrong/AS .05
166 Sandy Alomar, Jr./AS .05
167 Mark McGwire/AS .45
168 Steve Sax/AS .05
169 Wade Boggs/AS .25
170 Cal Ripken, Jr./AS .50
171 Rickey Henderson/AS .20
172 Ken Griffey Jr./AS .40
173 Jose Canseco/AS .15
174 Bob Welch/AS .05
175 All-Star Game - Wrigley Field .05
176 World's Championship Trophy (Foil) .05
177 California Angels Pennant (Foil) .05
178 California Angels Logo (Foil) .05
179 Lance Parrish .05
180 Wally Joyner .05
181 Johnny Ray .05
182 Jack Howell .05
183 Dick Schofield .05
184 Dave Winfield .40
185 Devon White .05
186 Dante Bichette .05
187 Chuck Finley .05
188 Jim Abbott .05
189 Oakland A's Pennant (Foil) .05
190 Oakland A's Logo (Foil) .05
191 Terry Steinbach .05
192 Mark McGwire .85
193 Willie Randolph .05
194 Carney Lansford .05
195 Walt Weiss .05
196 Rickey Henderson .40
197 Dave Henderson .05
198 Jose Canseco .30
199 Dave Stewart .05
200 Dennis Eckersley .35
201 Milwaukee Brewers Pennant (Foil) .05
202 Milwaukee Brewers Logo (Foil) .05
203 B.J. Surhoff .05
204 Greg Brock .05
205 Paul Molitor .40
206 Gary Sheffield .20
207 Billy Spiers .05
208 Robin Yount .40
209 Rob Deer .05
210 Dave Parker .05
211 Mark Knudson .05
212 Dan Plesac .05
213 Cleveland Indians Pennant (Foil) .05
214 Cleveland Indians Logo (Foil) .05
215 Sandy Alomar, Jr. .05
216 Brook Jacoby .05
217 Jerry Browne .05
218 Carlos Baerga .05
219 Felix Fermin .05
220 Candy Maldonado .05
221 Cory Snyder .05

222 Alex Cole, Jr. .05
223 Tom Candiotti .05
224 Doug Jones .05
225 Seattle Mariners Pennant (Foil) .05
226 Seattle Mariners Logo (Foil) .05
227 Dave Valle .05
228 Pete O'Brien .05
229 Harold Reynolds .05
230 Edgar Martinez .05
231 Omar Vizquel .05
232 Henry Cotto .05
233 Ken Griffey Jr. .75
234 Jay Buhner .05
235 Eric Hanson (Erik) .05
236 Mike Schooler .05
237 Baltimore Orioles Pennant (Foil) .05
238 Baltimore Orioles Logo (Foil) .05
239 Mickey Tettleton .05
240 Randy Milligan .05
241 Billy Ripken .05
242 Craig Worthington .05
243 Cal Ripken, Jr. 1.00
244 Steve Finley .05
245 Mike Devereaux .05
246 Joe Orsulak .05
247 Ben McDonald .05
248 Gregg Olson .05
249 Texas Rangers Pennant (Foil) .05
250 Texas Rangers Logo (Foil) .05
251 Geno Petralli .05
252 Rafael Palmeiro .40
253 Julio Franco .05
254 Steve Buechele .05
255 Jeff Huson .05
256 Gary Pettis .05
257 Ruben Sierra .05
258 Pete Incaviglia .05
259 Nolan Ryan 1.00
260 Bobby Witt .05
261 Boston Red Sox Pennant (Foil) .05
262 Boston Red Sox Logo (Foil) .05
263 Tony Pena .05
264 Carlos Quintana .05
265 Jody Reed .05
266 Wade Boggs .50
267 Luis Rivera .05
268 Mike Greenwell .05
269 Ellis Burks .05
270 Tom Brunansky .05
271 Roger Clemens .60
272 Jeff Reardon .05
273 Kansas City Royals Pennant (Foil) .05
274 Kansas City Royals Logo (Foil) .05
275 Mike Macfarlane .05
276 George Brett .60
277 Bill Pecota .05
278 Kevin Seitzer .05
279 Kurt Stillwell .05
280 Jim Eisenreich .05
281 Bo Jackson .05
282 Danny Tartabull .05
283 Bret Saberhagen .05
284 Tom Gordon .05
285 Detroit Tigers Pennant (Foil) .05
286 Detroit Tigers Logo (Foil) .05
287 Mike Heath .05
288 Cecil Fielder .05
289 Lou Whitaker .05
290 Tony Phillips .05
291 Alan Trammell .05
292 Chet Lemon .05
293 Lloyd Moseby .05
294 Gary Ward .05
295 Dan Petry .05
296 Jack Morris .05
297 Minnesota Twins Pennant (Foil) .05
298 Minnesota Twins Logo (Foil) .05
299 Brian Harper .05
300 Kent Hrbek .05
301 Al Newman .05
302 Gary Gaetti .05
303 Greg Gagne .05
304 Dan Gladden .05
305 Kirby Puckett .50
306 Gene Larkin .05
307 Kevin Tapani .05
308 Rick Aguilera .05
309 Chicago White Sox Pennant (Foil) .05
310 Chicago White Sox Logo (Foil) .05
311 Carlton Fisk .40
312 Carlos Martinez .05
313 Scott Fletcher .05
314 Robin Ventura .05
315 Ozzie Guillen .05
316 Sammy Sosa .65
317 Lance Johnson .05
318 Ivan Calderon .05
319 Greg Hibbard .05
320 Bobby Thigpen .05
321 New York Yankees Pennant (Foil) .05
322 New York Yankees Logo (Foil) .05
323 Bob Geren .05

324 Don Mattingly .60
325 Steve Sax .05
326 Jim Leyritz .05
327 Alvaro Espinoza .05
328 Roberto Kelly .05
329 Oscar Azocar .05
330 Jesse Barfield .05
331 Chuck Cary .05
332 Dave Righetti .05
333 Toronto Blue Jays Pennant (Foil) .05
334 Toronto Blue Jays Logo (Foil) .05
335 Pat Borders .05
336 Fred McGriff .05
337 Manny Lee .05
338 Kelly Gruber .05
339 Tony Fernandez .05
340 George Bell .05
341 Mookie Wilson .05
342 Junior Felix .05
343 Blue Jays Batting Helmet (Foil) .05
344 Dave Steib .05
345 Tom Henke .05
346 Greg Myers .05
347 Glenallen Hill .05
348 John Olerud .05
349 Todd Stottlemyre .05
350 David Wells .05
351 Jimmy Key .05
352 Mark Langston (No-hitter.) .05
353 Randy Johnson (No-hitter.) .20
354 Nolan Ryan (No-hitter.) .50
355 Dave Stewart (No-hitter.) .05
356 Fernando Valenzuela (No-hitter.) .05
357 Andy Hawkins (No-hitter.) .05
358 Melido Perez (No-hitter.) .05
359 Terry Mulholland (No-hitter.) .05
360 Dave Stieb (No-hitter.) .05

Top 15 Stickers (Canadian)

WILLIE McGEE
ST. LOUIS CARDINALS
BATTING AVERAGE
MOYENNE AU BÂTON
.335

The four leaders from each league in major statistical categories from the 1990 season are featured in this set of stickers marketed in Canada. The 2-1/2" x 3-1/2" stickers feature a large color photo at top. In the white border at bottom is the player's name and team, the stat in which he excelled (printed in both English and French), the number achieved, and, at lower-left, his rank among the top four. A series of team logo metallic stickers honors the teams which led in various stats. Backs are printed in black with appropriate logos and sticker number. A colorful album could be purchased to the house the sticker collection.

NM/M
Complete Set (136): 10.00
Common Player: .10
1 Willie McGee .10
2 Eddie Murray .30
3 Dave Magadan .10
4 Lenny Dykstra .10
5 George Brett .45
6 Rickey Henderson .30
7 Rafael Palmeiro .10
8 Alan Trammell .10
9 Ryne Sandberg .40
10 Darryl Strawberry .10
11 Kevin Mitchell .10
12 Barry Bonds .75
13 Cecil Fielder .10
14 Mark McGwire .65
15 Jose Canseco .15
16 Fred McGriff .10
17 Matt Williams .10
18 Bobby Bonilla .10
19 Joe Carter .10
20 Barry Bonds .75
21 Cecil Fielder .10
22 Kelly Gruber .10
23 Mark McGwire .65
24 Jose Canseco .15
25 Brett Butler .10
26 Lenny Dykstra .10
27 Ryne Sandberg .40

28 Barry Larkin .10
29 Rafael Palmeiro .30
30 Wade Boggs .40
31 Roberto Kelly .10
32 Mike Greenwell .10
33 Barry Bonds .75
34 Ryne Sandberg .40
35 Kevin Mitchell .10
36 Ron Gant .10
37 Cecil Fielder .10
38 Rickey Henderson .30
39 Jose Canseco .15
40 Fred McGriff .10
41 Vince Coleman .10
42 Eric Yelding .10
43 Barry Bonds .75
44 Brett Butler .10
45 Rickey Henderson .30
46 Steve Sax .10
47 Roberto Kelly .10
48 Alex Cole, Jr. .10
49 Ryne Sandberg .40
50 Bobby Bonilla .10
51 Brett Butler .10
52 Ron Gant .10
53 Rickey Henderson .30
54 Cecil Fielder .10
55 Harold Reynolds .10
56 Robin Yount .30
57 Doug Drabek .10
58 Ramon Martinez .10
59 Frank Viola .10
60 Dwight Gooden .10
61 Bob Welch .10
62 Dave Stewart .10
63 Roger Clemens .45
64 Dave Stieb .10
65 Danny Darwin .10
66 Zane Smith .10
67 Ed Whitson .10
68 Frank Viola .10
69 Roger Clemens .45
70 Chuck Finley .10
71 Dave Stewart .10
72 Kevin Appier .10
73 David Cone .10
74 Dwight Gooden .10
75 Ramon Martinez .10
76 Frank Viola .10
77 Nolan Ryan .75
78 Bobby Witt .10
79 Erik Hanson .10
80 Roger Clemens .45
81 John Franco .10
82 Randy Myers .10
83 Lee Smith .10
84 Craig Lefferts .10
85 Bobby Thigpen .10
86 Dennis Eckersley .25
87 Doug Jones .10
88 Gregg Olson .10
89 Mike Morgan .10
90 Bruce Hurst .10
91 Mark Gardner .10
92 Doug Drabek .10
93 Dave Stewart .10
94 Roger Clemens .45
95 Kevin Appier .10
96 Melido Perez .10
97 National League Logo .10
98 Greg Maddux .10
99 Benito Santiago .10
100 Andres Galarraga .10
101 Ryne Sandberg .40
102 Tim Wallach .10
103 Ozzie Smith .10
104 Tony Gwynn .40
105 Barry Bonds .75
106 Andy Van Slyke .10
107 American League Logo .10
108 Mike Boddicker .10
109 Sandy Alomar Jr. .10
110 Mark McGwire .65
111 Harold Reynolds .10
112 Kelly Gruber .10
113 Ozzie Guillen .10
114 Ellis Burks .10
115 Gary Pettis .10
116 Ken Griffey Jr. .50
117 Cincinnati Reds Logo .10
118 New York Mets Logo .10
119 New York Mets Script .10
120 Chicago Cubs Logo .10
121 Montreal Expos Logo .10
122 Boston Red Sox Logo .10
123 Detroit Tigers Logo .10
124 Toronto Blue Jays Logo .10
125 Boston Red Sox Script .10
126 Milwaukee Brewers Logo .10
127 Philadelphia Phillies Logo .10
128 Cincinnati Reds Logo .10
129 Montreal Expos Logo .10
130 New York Mets Logo .10
131 Cincinnati Reds Logo .10
132 California Angels Logo .10
133 Toronto Blue Jays Logo .10
134 Oakland A's Logo .10
135 Oakland A's Script .10
136 Chicago White Sox Logo .10

1992 Panini Stickers

A 288-piece set comprised Panini's annual baseball issue in 1992. Stickers were sold in packs of six for 39 cents. A colorful album for housing the stickers was also available, picturing members of the

TIM WALLACH
THIRD BASE
204

World Champion Twins. Individual stickers measured 2-1/8" x 3". Player stickers feature a color action photo at center, with a shark's tooth border at right. A colored diamond is overprinted on the first letters of the name, while a rule of the same color is printed around the photo. On American League stickers the color highlights are in magenta; teal for N.L. Stickers are numbered by position within team, and each team set includes a foil-glitter team logo stickers. Similar special stickers honor the 1991 All-Star Game starters and a few other special themes. Backs of the foils are printed in blue and promote sticker collecting. Backs of the player stickers are special themes. Backs of the foils are printed in blue and in full color and include trivia questions, "Play Ball" game situations and score cards for the game.

NM/M
Complete Set (288): 10.00
Common Player: .05
Album: 1.00
Wax Pack (5+1): .25
Wax Box (50): 5.00
1 Panini Logo (Foil) .05
2 Major League Baseball Logo (Foil) .05
3 Players Association Logo (Foil) .05
4 Lance Parrish .05
5 Wally Joyner .05
6 Luis Sojo .05
7 Gary Gaetti .05
8 Dick Schofield .05
9 Junior Felix .05
10 Luis Polonia .05
11 Mark Langston .05
12 Jim Abbott .05
13 California Angels Logo (Foil) .05
14 Terry Steinbach .05
15 Mark McGwire .75
16 Mike Gallego .05
17 Carney Lansford .05
18 Walt Weiss .05
19 Jose Canseco .30
20 Dave Henderson .05
21 Rickey Henderson .40
22 Dennis Eckersley .35
23 Oakland A's Logo (Foil) .05
24 Pat Borders .05
25 John Olerud .05
26 Roberto Alomar .20
27 Kelly Gruber .05
28 Manuel Lee .05
29 Joe Carter .05
30 Devon White .05
31 Candy Maldonado .05
32 Jimmy Key .05
33 Toronto Blue Jays Logo (Foil) .05
34 B.J. Surhoff .05
35 Franklin Stubbs .05
36 Willie Randolph .05
37 Jim Gantner .05
38 Bill Spiers .05
39 Dante Bichette .05
40 Robin Yount .40
41 Greg Vaughn .05
42 Jaime Navarro .05
43 Milwaukee Brewers Logo (Foil) .05
44 Sandy Alomar Jr. .05
45 Mike Aldrete .05
46 Mark Lewis .05
47 Carlos Baerga .05
48 Felix Fermin .05
49 Mark Whiten .05
50 Alex Cole .05
51 Albert Belle .10
52 Greg Swindell .05
53 Cleveland Indians Logo (Foil) .05
54 Dave Valle .05
55 Pete O'Brien .05
56 Harold Reynolds .05
57 Edgar Martinez .05

58 Omar Vizquel .05
59 Jay Buhner .05
60 Ken Griffey Jr. .60
61 Greg Briley .05
62 Randy Johnson .40
63 Seattle Mariners Logo (Foil) .05
64 Chris Hoiles .05
65 Randy Milligan .05
66 Billy Ripken .05
67 Leo Gomez .05
68 Cal Ripken Jr. 1.00
69 Dwight Evans .05
70 Mike Devereaux .05
71 Joe Orsulak .05
72 Gregg Olson .05
73 Baltimore Orioles Logo (Foil) .05
74 Ivan Rodriguez .40
75 Rafael Palmeiro .40
76 Julio Franco .05
77 Dean Palmer .05
78 Jeff Huson .05
79 Ruben Sierra .05
80 Gary Pettis .05
81 Juan Gonzalez .40
82 Nolan Ryan 1.00
83 Texas Rangers Logo (Foil) .05
84 Tony Pena .05
85 Carlos Quintana .05
86 Jody Reed .05
87 Wade Boggs .50
88 Luis Rivera .05
89 Tom Brunansky .05
90 Ellis Burks .05
91 Mike Greenwell .05
92 Roger Clemens .55
93 Boston Red Sox Logo (Foil) .05
94 Todd Benzinger .05
95 Terry Shumpert .05
96 Bill Pecota .05
97 Kurt Stillwell .05
98 Danny Tartabull .05
99 Mike McRae .05
100 Kirk Gibson .05
101 Bret Saberhagen .05
102 George Brett .55
103 Kansas City Royals Logo (Foil) .05
104 Mickey Tettleton .05
105 Cecil Fielder .05
106 Lou Whitaker .05
107 Travis Fryman .05
108 Alan Trammell .05
109 Rob Deer .05
110 Milt Cuyler .05
111 Lloyd Moseby .05
112 Bill Gullickson .05
113 Detroit Tigers Logo (Foil) .05
114 Brian Harper .05
115 Kent Hrbek .05
116 Chuck Knoblauch .05
117 Mike Pagliarulo .05
118 Greg Gagne .05
119 Shane Mack .05
120 Kirby Puckett .50
121 Dan Gladden .05
122 Jack Morris .05
123 Minnesota Twins Logo (Foil) .05
124 Carlton Fisk .40
125 Frank Thomas .40
126 Joey Cora .05
127 Robin Ventura .05
128 Ozzie Guillen .05
129 Sammy Sosa .60
130 Lance Johnson .05
131 Tim Raines .05
132 Bobby Thigpen .05
133 Chicago White Sox Logo (Foil) .05
134 Matt Nokes .05
135 Don Mattingly .55
136 Steve Sax .05
137 Pat Kelly .05
138 Alvaro Espinoza .05
139 Jesse Barfield .05
140 Roberto Kelly .05
141 Mel Hall .05
142 Scott Sanderson .05
143 New York Yankees Logo (Foil) .05
144 A.L. HR Leaders (Cecil Fielder, Jose Canseco) .05
145 A.L. BA Leader (Julio Franco) .05
146 A.L. ERA Leader (Roger Clemens) .25
147 N.L. HR Leader (Howard Johnson) .05
148 N.L. BA Leader (Terry Pendleton) .05
149 N.L. ERA Leader (Dennis Martinez) .05
150 Houston Astros Logo (Foil) .05
151 Craig Biggio .05
152 Jeff Bagwell .40
153 Casey Candaele .05
154 Ken Caminiti .05
155 Andujar Cedeno .05
156 Mike Simms .05
157 Steve Finley .05
158 Luis Gonzalez .05
159 Pete Harnisch .05
160 Atlanta Braves Logo (Foil) .05
161 Greg Olson .05

#	Player	Price
162	Sid Bream	.05
163	Mark Lemke	.05
164	Terry Pendleton	.05
165	Rafael Belliard	.05
166	Dave Justice	.05
167	Ron Gant	.05
168	Lonnie Smith	.05
169	Steve Avery	.05
170	St. Louis Cardinals Logo (Foil)	.05
171	Tom Pagnozzi	.05
172	Pedro Guerrero	.05
173	Jose Oquendo	.05
174	Todd Zeile	.05
175	Ozzie Smith	.50
176	Felix Jose	.05
177	Ray Lankford	.05
178	Jose DeLeon	.05
179	Lee Smith	.05
180	Chicago Cubs Logo (Foil)	.05
181	Hector Villanueva	.05
182	Mark Grace	.10
183	Ryne Sandberg	.50
184	Luis Salazar	.05
185	Shawon Dunston	.05
186	Andre Dawson	.20
187	Jerome Walton	.05
188	George Bell	.05
189	Greg Maddux	.50
190	Los Angeles Dodgers Logo (Foil)	.05
191	Mike Scioscia	.05
192	Eddie Murray	.40
193	Juan Samuel	.05
194	Lenny Harris	.05
195	Alfredo Griffin	.05
196	Darryl Strawberry	.05
197	Brett Butler	.05
198	Kal Daniels	.05
199	Orel Hershiser	.05
200	Montreal Expos Logo (Foil)	.05
201	Gilberto Reyes	.05
202	Andres Galarraga	.05
203	Delino DeShields	.05
204	Tim Wallach	.05
205	Spike Owen	.05
206	Larry Walker	.05
207	Marquis Grissom	.05
208	Ivan Calderon	.05
209	Dennis Martinez	.05
210	San Francisco Giants Logo (Foil)	.05
211	Steve Decker	.05
212	Will Clark	.10
213	Robby Thompson	.05
214	Matt Williams	.05
215	Jose Uribe	.05
216	Kevin Bass	.05
217	Willie McGee	.05
218	Kevin Mitchell	.05
219	Dave Righetti	.05
220	New York Mets Logo (Foil)	.05
221	Rick Cerone	.05
222	Dave Magadan	.05
223	Gregg Jefferies	.05
224	Howard Johnson	.05
225	Kevin Elster	.05
226	Hubie Brooks	.05
227	Vince Coleman	.05
228	Kevin McReynolds	.05
229	Frank Viola	.05
230	San Diego Padres Logo (Foil)	.05
231	Benito Santiago	.05
232	Fred McGriff	.05
233	Bip Roberts	.05
234	Jack Howell	.05
235	Tony Fernandez	.05
236	Tony Gwynn	.50
237	Darrin Jackson	.05
238	Bruce Hurst	.05
239	Craig Lefferts	.05
240	Philadelphia Phillies Logo (Foil)	.05
241	Darren Daulton	.05
242	John Kruk	.05
243	Mickey Morandini	.05
244	Charlie Hayes	.05
245	Dickie Thon	.05
246	Dale Murphy	.25
247	Lenny Dykstra	.05
248	Von Hayes	.05
249	Terry Mulholland	.05
250	Pittsburgh Pirates Logo (Foil)	.05
251	Mike LaValliere	.05
252	Orlando Merced	.05
253	Jose Lind	.05
254	Steve Buechele	.05
255	Jay Bell	.05
256	Bobby Bonilla	.05
257	Andy Van Slyke	.05
258	Barry Bonds	1.00
259	Doug Drabek	.05
260	Cincinnati Reds Logo (Foil)	.05
261	Joe Oliver	.05
262	Hal Morris	.05
263	Bill Doran	.05
264	Chris Sabo	.05
265	Barry Larkin	.05
266	Paul O'Neill	.05
267	Eric Davis	.05
268	Glenn Braggs	.05
269	Jose Rijo	.05
270	Toronto Sky Dome (Foil)	.05
271	Sandy Alomar Jr. (All-Star Foil)	.05
272	Cecil Fielder (All-Star Foil)	.05
273	Roberto Alomar (All-Star Foil)	.10
274	Wade Boggs (All-Star Foil)	.25
275	Cal Ripken Jr. (All-Star Foil)	.50
276	Dave Henderson (All-Star Foil)	.05
277	Ken Griffey Jr. (All-Star Foil)	.40
278	Rickey Henderson (All-Star Foil)	.20
279	Jack Morris (All-Star Foil)	.05
280	Benito Santiago (All-Star Foil)	.05
281	Will Clark (All-Star Foil)	.05
282	Ryne Sandberg (All-Star Foil)	.25
283	Chris Sabo (All-Star Foil)	.05
284	Ozzie Smith (All-Star Foil)	.25
285	Andre Dawson (All-Star Foil)	.05
286	Tony Gwynn (All-Star Foil)	.25
287	Ivan Calderon (All-Star Foil)	.05
288	Tom Glavine (All-Star Foil)	.05

Canadian

ROBIN VENTURA
THIRD BASE/TROISIÈME BUT

The Canadian version of the 1992 Panini stickers mirrors the U.S. set's checklist (and price guide). In the same size (2-1/8"x3") and format, the Canadian stickers differ from the U.S. version in the addition of French position on front and bilingual back.

	NM/M
Complete Set (288):	10.00
Common Player:	.05
Album:	1.00

1993 Panini Stickers

BASEBALL — ATLANTA BRAVES
DAVE JUSTICE

The 1993 issue is complete at 300 stickers. Besides 10 player stickers for each major league team, there are stickers for league leaders and major 1992-season award winners. There is a gold-foil team logo sticker for each team and one of the player stickers on each team is produced in a glitter technology. Stickers measure 2-3/8" x 3-3/8". Fronts have an action photo at center with team logo in the lower-left corner. Backs are printed in green and include the sticker number and appropriate Panini and baseball logos. A 58-page album was available to house the stickers.

	NM/M
Complete Set (300):	10.00
Common Player:	.05
Sticker Album:	1.00

#	Player	Price
1	California Angels Logo	.05
2	Mark Langston	.05
3	Ron Tingley	.05
4	Gary Gaetti	.05
5	Kelly Gruber	.05
6	Gary Disarcina	.05
7	Damion Easley (Glitter)	.05
8	Luis Polonia	.05
9	Lee Stevens	.05
10	Chad Curtis	.05
11	Rene Gonzales	.05
12	Oakland A's Logo	.05
13	Dennis Eckersley	.35
14	Terry Steinbach	.05
15	Mark McGwire	.75
16	Mike Bordick (Glitter)	.05
17	Carney Lansford	.05
18	Jerry Browne	.05
19	Rickey Henderson	.40
20	Dave Henderson	.05
21	Ruben Sierra	.05
22	Ron Darling	.05
23	Toronto Blue Jays Logo	.05
24	Jack Morris	.05
25	Pat Borders	.05
26	John Olerud	.05
27	Roberto Alomar	.10
28	Luis Sojo	.05
29	Dave Stewart	.05
30	Devon White	.05
31	Joe Carter	.05
32	Derek Bell	.05
33	Juan Guzman (Glitter)	.05
34	Milwaukee Brewers Logo	.05
35	Jaime Navarro	.05
36	B.J. Surhoff	.05
37	Franklin Stubbs	.05
38	Billy Spiers	.05
39	Pat Listach (Glitter)	.05
40	Kevin Seitzer	.05
41	Darryl Hamilton	.05
42	Robin Yount	.40
43	Kevin Reimer	.05
44	Greg Vaughn	.05
45	Cleveland Indians Logo	.05
46	Charles Nagy	.05
47	Sandy Alomar Jr.	.05
48	Reggie Jefferson	.05
49	Mark Lewis	.05
50	Felix Fermin	.05
51	Carlos Baerga	.05
52	Albert Belle	.05
53	Kenny Lofton (Glitter)	.05
54	Mark Whiten	.05
55	Paul Sorrento	.05
56	Seattle Mariners Logo	.05
57	Dave Fleming	.05
58	Dave Valle	.05
59	Pete O'Brien	.05
60	Randy Johnson	.40
61	Omar Vizquel	.05
62	Edgar Martinez	.05
63	Ken Griffey Jr. (Glitter)	.75
64	Henry Cotto	.05
65	Jay Buhner	.05
66	Tino Martinez	.05
67	Baltimore Orioles Logo	.05
68	Ben McDonald	.05
69	Mike Mussina (Glitter)	.35
70	Chris Hoiles	.05
71	Randy Milligan	.05
72	Billy Ripken	.05
73	Cal Ripken Jr.	1.00
74	Leo Gomez	.05
75	Mike Devereaux	.05
76	Brady Anderson	.05
77	Joe Orsulak	.05
78	Texas Rangers Logo	.05
79	Kevin Brown	.05
80	Ivan Rodriguez (Glitter)	.40
81	Rafael Palmeiro	.40
82	Julio Franco	.05
83	Jeff Huson	.05
84	Dean Palmer	.05
85	Jose Canseco	.30
86	Juan Gonzalez	.05
87	Nolan Ryan	1.00
88	Brian Downing	.05
89	Boston Red Sox Logo	.05
90	Roger Clemens	.55
91	Tony Pena	.05
92	Mo Vaughn	.05
93	Scott Cooper	.05
94	Luis Rivera	.05
95	Ellis Burks	.05
96	Mike Greenwell	.05
97	Andre Dawson	.20
98	Ivan Calderon	.05
99	Phil Plantier (Glitter)	.05
100	Kansas City Royals Logo	.05
101	Kevin Appier	.05
102	Mike MacFarlane	.05
103	Wally Joyner	.05
104	Jim Eisenreich	.05
105	Greg Gagne	.05
106	Gregg Jefferies	.05
107	Kevin McReynolds	.05
108	Brian McRae (Glitter)	.05
109	Keith Miller	.05
110	George Brett	.55
111	Detroit Tigers Logo	.05
112	Bill Gullickson	.05
113	Mickey Tettleton	.05
114	Cecil Fielder	.05
115	Tony Phillips	.05
116	Scott Livingstone	.05
117	Travis Fryman (Glitter)	.05
118	Dan Gladden	.05
119	Rob Deer	.05
120	Frank Tanana	.05
121	Skeeter Barnes	.05
122	Minnesota Twins Logo	.05
123	Scott Erickson	.05
124	Brian Harper	.05
125	Kent Hrbek	.05
126	Chuck Knoblauch (Glitter)	.05
127	Willie Banks	.05
128	Scott Leius	.05
129	Shane Mack	.05
130	Kirby Puckett	.50
131	Chili Davis	.05
132	Pedro Munoz	.05
133	Chicago White Sox Logo	.05
134	Jack McDowell	.05
135	Carlton Fisk	.40
136	Frank Thomas (Glitter)	.45
137	Steve Sax	.05
138	Ozzie Guillen	.05
139	Robin Ventura	.05
140	Tim Raines	.05
141	Lance Johnson	.05
142	Ron Karkovice	.05
143	George Bell	.05
144	New York Yankees Logo	.05
145	Scott Sanderson	.05
146	Matt Nokes	.05
147	Kevin Maas (Glitter)	.05
148	Randy Velarde	.05
149	Andy Stankiewicz	.05
150	Pat Kelly	.05
151	Paul O'Neill	.05
152	Wade Boggs	.50
153	Danny Tartabull	.05
154	Don Mattingly	.55
155	Edgar Martinez (B.A. Leader)	.05
156	Kevin Brown (W-L Record)	.05
157	Dennis Eckersley (Saves leader.)	.15
158	Gary Sheffield (B.A. leader.)	.05
159	Tom Glavine, Greg Maddux (W-L Leaders)	.05
160	Lee Smith (Saves leader.)	.05
161	Dennis Eckersley (Cy Young)	.05
162	Dennis Eckersley (MVP)	.15
163	Pat Listach (Rookie/Year)	.05
164	Greg Maddux (Cy Young)	.05
165	Barry Bonds (MVP)	.50
166	Eric Karros (Rookie/Year)	.05
167	Houston Astros Logo	.05
168	Pete Harnisch	.05
169	Eddie Taubensee	.05
170	Jeff Bagwell (Glitter)	.45
171	Craig Biggio	.05
172	Andujar Cedeno	.05
173	Ken Caminiti	.05
174	Steve Finley	.05
175	Luis Gonzalez	.05
176	Eric Anthony	.05
177	Casey Candaele	.05
178	Atlanta Braves Logo	.05
179	Tom Glavine	.25
180	Greg Olson	.05
181	Sid Bream	.05
182	Mark Lemke	.05
183	Jeff Blauser	.05
184	Terry Pendleton	.05
185	Ron Gant	.05
186	Otis Nixon	.05
187	Dave Justice	.05
188	Deion Sanders (Glitter)	.20
189	St. Louis Cardinals Logo	.05
190	Bob Tewksbury	.05
191	Tom Pagnozzi	.05
192	Lee Smith	.05
193	Geronimo Pena	.05
194	Ozzie Smith	.50
195	Todd Zeile	.05
196	Ray Lankford	.05
197	Bernard Gilkey	.05
198	Felix Jose	.05
199	Donovan Osborne (Glitter)	.05
200	Chicago Cubs Logo	.05
201	Mike Morgan	.05
202	Rick Wilkins	.05
203	Mark Grace (Glitter)	.05
204	Ryne Sandberg	.50
205	Shawon Dunston	.05
206	Steve Buechele	.05
207	Kal Daniels	.05
208	Sammy Sosa	.50
209	Derrick May	.05
210	Doug Dascenzo	.05
211	Los Angeles Dodgers Logo	.05
212	Ramon Martinez	.05
213	Mike Scioscia	.05
214	Eric Karros (Glitter)	.05
215	Tim Wallach	.05
216	Jose Offerman	.05
217	Mike Sharperson	.05
218	Brett Butler	.05
219	Darryl Strawberry	.05
220	Lenny Harris	.05
221	Eric Davis	.05
222	Montreal Expos Logo	.05
223	Ken Hill	.05
224	Darrin Fletcher	.05
225	Greg Colbrunn (Glitter)	.05
226	Delino DeShields	.05
227	Wil Cordero	.05
228	Dennis Martinez	.05
229	John Vander Wal	.05
230	Marquis Grissom	.05
231	Larry Walker	.05
232	Moises Alou	.05
233	San Francisco Giants Logo	.05
234	Billy Swift	.05
235	Kirt Manwaring	.05
236	Will Clark	.05
237	Robby Thompson	.05
238	Royce Clayton (Glitter)	.05
239	Matt Williams	.05
240	Willie McGee	.05
241	Mark Leonard	.05
242	Cory Snyder	.05
243	Barry Bonds	1.00
244	New York Mets Logo	.05
245	Dwight Gooden	.05
246	Todd Hundley (Glitter)	.05
247	Eddie Murray	.40
248	Sid Fernandez	.05
249	Tony Fernandez	.05
250	Dave Magadan	.05
251	Howard Johnson	.05
252	Vince Coleman	.05
253	Bobby Bonilla	.05
254	Daryl Boston	.05
255	San Diego Padres Logo	.05
256	Bruce Hurst	.05
257	Dan Walters	.05
258	Fred McGriff	.05
259	Kurt Stillwell	.05
260	Craig Shipley	.05
261	Gary Sheffield (Glitter)	.35
262	Tony Gwynn	.50
263	Oscar Azocar	.05
264	Darrin Jackson	.05
265	Andy Benes	.05
266	Philadelphia Phillies Logo	.05
267	Terry Mulholland	.05
268	Curt Schilling	.25
269	Darren Daulton	.05
270	John Kruk	.05
271	Mickey Morandini (Glitter)	.05
272	Mariano Duncan	.05
273	Dave Hollins	.05
274	Lenny Dykstra	.05
275	Wes Chamberlain	.05
276	Stan Javier	.05
277	Pittsburgh Pirates Logo	.05
278	Zane Smith	.05
279	Tim Wakefield (Glitter)	.05
280	Mike LaValliere	.05
281	Orlando Merced	.05
282	Stan Belinda	.05
283	Jay Bell	.05
284	Jeff King	.05
285	Andy Van Slyke	.05
286	Bob Walk	.05
287	Gary Varsho	.05
288	Cincinnati Reds Logo	.05
289	Jose Rijo	.05
290	Joe Oliver	.05
291	Hal Morris	.05
292	Bip Roberts	.05
293	Barry Larkin	.05
294	Chris Sabo	.05
295	Roberto Kelly	.05
296	Kevin Mitchell	.05
297	Rob Dibble	.05
298	Reggie Sanders (Glitter)	.05
299	Florida Marlins Logo	.05
300	Colorado Rockies Logo	.05

1994 Panini Stickers

Walt Weiss

With set size at the reduced count of 268, Panini retained the larger format 2-3/8" x 3-3/8" sticker size. Stickers featured green borders surrounding a color action photo on front. Below the player photo is a pennant with the team logo and player name. Backs have a sticker number at center, with appropriate licensor logos and Panini advertising in black-and-white. The set includes 16 foil stickers honoring major 1993 season award winners in the A.L. and N.L. and four World Series action stickers. The set is arranged alphabetically within-team and league. Stickers were sold in packs of six for 49 cents. A colorful album to house the stickers was also available.

	NM/M
Complete Set (268):	5.00
Common Player:	.05

#	Player	Price
1	World Series Action (Foil)	.05
2	World Series Action (Foil)	.05
3	World Series Action (Foil)	.05
4	World Series Action (Foil)	.05
5	BA Leader (John Olerud (Foil))	.05
6	HR Leader (Juan Gonzalez (Foil))	.20
7	RBI Leader (Albert Belle (Foil))	.05
8	Wins Leader (Jack McDowell (Foil))	.05
9	K Leader (Randy Johnson (Foil))	.20
10	Saves Leader (Jeff Montgomery (Foil))	.05
11	BA Leader (Andres Galarraga (Foil))	.05
12	HR Leader (Barry Bonds (Foil))	.50
13	RBI Leader (Barry Bonds (Foil))	.50
14	Wins Leaders (Tom Glavine, John Burkett (Foil))	.05
15	K Leader (Jose Rijo (Foil))	.05
16	Saves Leader (Randy Myers (Foil))	.05
17	Brady Anderson	.05
18	Harold Baines	.05
19	Mike Devereaux	.05
20	Chris Hoiles	.05
21	Mike Mussina	.30
22	Harold Reynolds	.05
23	Cal Ripken Jr.	1.00
24	David Segui	.05
25	Fernando Valenzuela	.05
26	Roger Clemens	.60
27	Scott Cooper	.05
28	Andre Dawson	.20
29	Scott Fletcher	.05
30	Mike Greenwell	.05
31	Billy Hatcher	.05
32	Tony Pena	.05
33	John Valentin	.05
34	Mo Vaughn	.05
35	Chad Curtis	.05
36	Gary DiSarcina	.05
37	Damion Easley	.05
38	Mark Langston	.05
39	Torey Lovullo	.05
40	Greg Myers	.05
41	Luis Polonia	.05
42	Tim Salmon	.05
43	J.T. Snow	.05
44	George Bell	.05
45	Ellis Burks	.05
46	Joey Cora	.05
47	Ozzie Guillen	.05
48	Roberto Hernandez	.05
49	Bo Jackson	.10
50	Jack McDowell	.05
51	Frank Thomas	.40
52	Robin Ventura	.05
53	Sandy Alomar Jr.	.05
54	Carlos Baerga	.05
55	Albert Belle	.05
56	Felix Fermin	.05
57	Wayne Kirby	.05
58	Kenny Lofton	.05
59	Charles Nagy	.05
60	Paul Sorrento	.05
61	Jeff Treadway	.05
62	Eric Davis	.05
63	Cecil Fielder	.05
64	Travis Fryman	.05
65	Bill Gullickson	.05
66	Mike Moore	.05
67	Tony Phillips	.05
68	Mickey Tettleton	.05
69	Alan Trammell	.05
70	Lou Whitaker	.05
71	Kevin Appier	.05
72	Greg Gagne	.05
73	Tom Gordon	.05
74	Felix Jose	.05
75	Wally Joyner	.05
76	Jose Lind	.05
77	Mike Macfarlane	.05
78	Brian McRae	.05
79	Kevin McReynolds	.05
80	Darryl Hamilton	.05
81	Teddy Higuera	.05
82	John Jaha	.05
83	Pat Listach	.05
84	Dave Nilsson	.05
85	Kevin Reimer	.05
86	Kevin Seitzer	.05
87	B.J. Surhoff	.05
88	Greg Vaughn	.05
89	Willie Banks	.05
90	Brian Harper	.05
91	Kent Hrbek	.05
92	Chuck Knoblauch	.05
93	Shane Mack	.05
94	Pat Meares	.05
95	Pedro Munoz	.05
96	Kirby Puckett	.50
97	Dave Winfield	.40
98	Jim Abbott	.05
99	Wade Boggs	.50
100	Mike Gallego	.05
101	Pat Kelly	.05
102	Don Mattingly	.60
103	Paul O'Neill	.05
104	Mike Stanley	.05
105	Danny Tartabull	.05
106	Bernie Williams	.05
107	Mike Bordick	.05
108	Dennis Eckersley	.35
109	Dave Henderson	.05
110	Mark McGwire	.75
111	Troy Neel	.05
112	Ruben Sierra	.05
113	Terry Steinbach	.05

#	Player	Price
114	Todd Van Poppel	.05
115	Bob Welch	.05
116	Bret Boone	.05
117	Jay Buhner	.05
118	Ken Griffey Jr.	.65
119	Randy Johnson	.40
120	Rich Amaral	.05
121	Edgar Martinez	.05
122	Tino Martinez	.05
123	Dave Valle	.05
124	Omar Vizquel	.05
125	Jose Canseco	.25
126	Julio Franco	.05
127	Juan Gonzalez	.20
128	Tom Henke	.05
129	Manuel Lee	.05
130	Rafael Palmeiro	.35
131	Dean Palmer	.05
132	Ivan Rodriguez	.35
133	Doug Strange	.05
134	Roberto Alomar	.10
135	Pat Borders	.05
136	Joe Carter	.05
137	Tony Fernandez	.05
138	Juan Guzman	.05
139	Rickey Henderson	.40
140	Paul Molitor	.40
141	John Olerud	.05
142	Devon White	.05
143	Jeff Blauser	.05
144	Ron Gant	.05
145	Tom Glavine	.20
146	Dave Justice	.05
147	Greg Maddux	.50
148	Fred McGriff	.05
149	Terry Pendleton	.05
150	Deion Sanders	.05
151	John Smoltz	.05
152	Shawon Dunston	.05
153	Mark Grace	.05
154	Derrick May	.05
155	Randy Myers	.05
156	Ryne Sandberg	.50
157	Dwight Smith	.05
158	Sammy Sosa	.50
159	Jose Vizcaino	.05
160	Rick Wilkins	.05
161	Tom Browning	.05
162	Roberto Kelly	.05
163	Barry Larkin	.05
164	Kevin Mitchell	.05
165	Hal Morris	.05
166	Joe Oliver	.05
167	Jose Rijo	.05
168	Chris Sabo	.05
169	Reggie Sanders	.05
170	Freddie Benavides	.05
171	Dante Bichette	.05
172	Vinny Castilla	.05
173	Jerald Clark	.05
174	Andres Galarraga	.05
175	Charlie Hayes	.05
176	Chris Jones	.05
177	Roberto Mejia	.05
178	Eric Young	.05
179	Bret Barberie	.05
180	Chuck Carr	.05
181	Jeff Conine	.05
182	Orestes Destrade	.05
183	Bryan Harvey	.05
184	Rich Renteria	.05
185	Benito Santiago	.05
186	Gary Sheffield	.20
187	Walt Weiss	.05
188	Eric Anthony	.05
189	Jeff Bagwell	.40
190	Craig Biggio	.05
191	Ken Caminiti	.05
192	Andujar Cedeno	.05
193	Doug Drabek	.05
194	Steve Finley	.05
195	Doug Jones	.05
196	Darryl Kile	.05
197	Brett Butler	.05
198	Tom Candiotti	.05
199	Dave Hansen	.05
200	Orel Hershiser	.05
201	Eric Karros	.05
202	Jose Offerman	.05
203	Mike Piazza	.60
204	Cory Snyder	.05
205	Darryl Strawberry	.05
206	Moises Alou	.05
207	Sean Berry	.05
208	Wil Cordero	.05
209	Delino DeShields	.05
210	Marquis Grissom	.05
211	Ken Hill	.05
212	Mike Lansing	.05
213	Larry Walker	.05
214	John Wetteland	.05
215	Bobby Bonilla	.05
216	Jeromy Burnitz	.05
217	Dwight Gooden	.05
218	Todd Hundley	.05
219	Howard Johnson	.05
220	Jeff Kent	.05
221	Eddie Murray	.40
222	Bret Saberhagen	.05
223	Ryan Thompson	.05
224	Darren Daulton	.05
225	Mariano Duncan	.05
226	Lenny Dykstra	.05
227	Jim Eisenreich	.05
228	Dave Hollins	.05
229	John Kruk	.05
230	Curt Schilling	.20
231	Kevin Stocker	.05
232	Mitch Williams	.05
233	Jay Bell	.05
234	Steve Cooke	.05
235	Carlos Garcia	.05
236	Jeff King	.05
237	Orlando Merced	.05
238	Don Slaught	.05
239	Zane Smith	.05
240	Andy Van Slyke	.05
241	Kevin Young	.05
242	Bernard Gilkey	.05
243	Gregg Jefferies	.05
244	Brian Jordan	.05
245	Ray Lankford	.05
246	Tom Pagnozzi	.05
247	Geronimo Pena	.05
248	Ozzie Smith	.50
249	Bob Tewksbury	.05
250	Mark Whiten	.05
251	Brad Ausmus	.05
252	Derek Bell	.05
253	Andy Benes	.05
254	Phil Clark	.05
255	Jeff Gardner	.05
256	Tony Gwynn	.50
257	Trevor Hoffman	.05
258	Phil Plantier	.05
259	Craig Shipley	.05
260	Rod Beck	.05
261	Barry Bonds	1.00
262	John Burkett	.05
263	Will Clark	.05
264	Royce Clayton	.05
265	Willie McGee	.05
266	Bill Swift	.05
267	Robby Thompson	.05
268	Matt Williams	.05
	Album:	1.00
	Wax Pack (5+1):	.25
	Wax Box (50):	5.00

1988 Pepsi-Cola/Kroger Tigers

(41) DARRELL EVANS, IF

Approximately 38,000 sets of cards were given to fans at Tiger Stadium on July 30th, 1988. The set, sponsored by Pepsi-Cola and Kroger, includes 25 oversized (2-7/8" x 4-1/4") cards printed on glossy white stock with blue and orange borders. The card backs include small black and white close-up photos, the players' professional records and sponsor logos. The numbers in the following checklist refer to the players' uniform.

		NM/M
Complete Set (25):		4.00
Common Player:		.25
1	Lou Whitaker	.50
2	Alan Trammell	1.00
8	Mike Heath	.25
11	Sparky Anderson	.50
12	Luis Salazar	.25
14	Dave Bergman	.25
15	Pat Sheridan	.25
16	Tom Brookens	.25
19	Doyle Alexander	.25
21	Guillermo Hernandez	.25
22	Ray Knight	.25
24	Gary Pettis	.25
25	Eric King	.25
26	Frank Tanana	.25
31	Larry Herndon	.25
32	Jim Walewander	.25
33	Matt Nokes	.25
34	Chet Lemon	.25
35	Walt Terrell	.25
39	Mike Henneman	.25
41	Darrell Evans	.50
44	Jeff Robinson	.25
47	Jack Morris	.50
48	Paul Gibson	.25
---	Coaches (Billy Consolo, Alex Grammas, Billy Muffett, Vada Pinson, Dick Tracewski)	.25

1989 Pepsi-Cola Mark McGwire

MARK McGWIRE

During the summer of 1989, selected Pepsi products in the Northern California area carried these special McGwire cards. Photos were posed with McGwire wearing a generic white uniform trimmed in A's colors and bearing his number 25 and a Pepsi logo patch. Backs have the same biographical details, recent stats and career highlights. A card number is printed at lower-right.

		NM/M
Complete Set (12):		10.00
Common Card:		1.50
1	Mark McGwire/Btg (Left foot raised.)	1.50
2	Mark McGwire/Fldg	1.50
3	Mark McGwire (Reaching for ball with glove.)	1.50
4	Mark McGwire/Btg (Foot down.)	1.50
5	Mark McGwire (Kneeling with bat.)	1.50
6	Mark McGwire (Stretching for throw at first.)	1.50
7	Mark McGwire (Bat on shoulder.)	1.50
8	Mark McGwire (Holding bat.)	1.50
9	Mark McGwire (Bat on shoulder.)	1.50
10	Mark McGwire (Holding bat.)	1.50
11	Mark McGwire (Holding bat.)	1.50
12	Mark McGwire (Batting follow-through.)	1.50

1990 Pepsi-Cola Boston Red Sox

ROGER CLEMENS

Pepsi combined with Score to produce this special 20-card Boston Red Sox team set. Cards were inserted regionally in 12-packs of Pepsi and Diet Pepsi. The card fronts feature full-color action photos with the team name across the top border and the player's name along the bottom border. The Pepsi and Diet Pepsi logos also appear on the bottom border. The card backs represent standard Score card backs, but are not numbered and also once again feature the Pepsi and Diet Pepsi logos.

		NM/M
Complete Set (20):		5.00
Common Player:		.25
(1)	Marty Barrett	.25
(2)	Mike Boddicker	.25
(3)	Wade Boggs	1.50
(4)	Bill Buckner	.35
(5)	Ellis Burks	.25
(6)	Roger Clemens	3.00
(7)	John Dopson	.25
(8)	Dwight Evans	.35
(9)	Wes Gardner	.25
(10)	Rich Gedman	.25
(11)	Mike Greenwell	.25
(12)	Dennis Lamp	.25
(13)	Rob Murphy	.25
(14)	Tony Pena	.25
(15)	Carlos Quintana	.25
(16)	Jeff Reardon	.25
(17)	Jody Reed	.25
(18)	Luis Rivera	.25
(19)	Kevin Romine	.25
(20)	Lee Smith	.25

Jose Canseco

JOSE CANSECO

Single cards from this issue were distributed in packs of Pepsi products in the San Francisco Bay area. Each card has a photo of Canseco in a generic red, white and blue uniform. Fronts have a blue border with a Pepsi logo. Backs have biographical data, recent stats and career highlights. The cards are numbered in the lower-right corner.

		NM/M
Complete Set (10):		5.00
Common Card:		1.50
1	Jose Canseco (Batting follow-through.)	.75
2	Jose Canseco (Batting follow-through.)	.75
3	Jose Canseco/Fldg	.75
4	Jose Canseco/Btg	.75
5	Jose Canseco (Holding glove.)	.75
6	Jose Canseco (Batting follow-through.)	.75
7	Jose Canseco (On dugout steps.)	.75
8	Jose Canseco/Btg	.75
9	Jose Canseco/Portrait	.75
10	Jose Canseco/Portrait	.75

1991 Pepsi-Cola Superstars

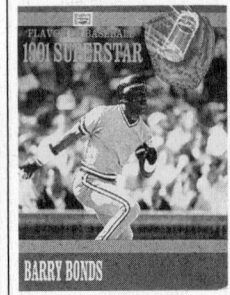

BARRY BONDS

This Florida regional issue was distributed by gluing cards inside of specially marked Pepsi products. Both front and back feature a "Flavor of Baseball" headline and logo of a glove catching a flying Pepsi can. Fronts have an action photo with colored strips at top and bottom. Player photos have uniform logos deleted. Backs have career stats, a few biographical details and a card number. The cards are slightly larger than current standards, measuring 2-5/8" x 3-1/2".

		NM/M
Complete Set (17):		18.50
Common Player:		.35
1	Dwight Gooden	.35
2	Andre Dawson	.65
3	Ryne Sandberg	2.00
4	Dave Steib	.35
5	Jose Rijo	.35
6	Roger Clemens	2.50
7	Barry Bonds	4.00
8	Cal Ripken, Jr.	4.00
9	Dave Justice	.35
10	Cecil Fielder	.35
11	Don Mattingly	2.50
12	Ozzie Smith	2.00
13	Kirby Puckett	2.00
14	Rafael Palmeiro	1.50
15	Bobby Bonilla	.35
16	Len Dykstra	.35
17	Jose Canseco	1.00

Cincinnati Reds

This team set was produced for inclusion in packages of Pepsi products in the Ohio area by Michael Schechter Assoc. Like most MSA issues, the cards have had cap and uniform logos airbrushed away because they are licensed only by the Players Union, and not MLB. Fronts have red borders with Pepsi, Diet Pepsi and MLBPA logos. Backs are in red, white and blue with the soda logos at top a few biographical notes, complete major and minor league stats and a facsimile autograph. The unnumbered cards are checklisted here alphabetically.

CHRIS SABO
CINCINNATI REDS 3RD BASE
LIMITED EDITION SERIES

		NM/M
Complete Set (20):		8.00
Common Player:		.50
(1)	Jack Armstrong	.50
(2)	Todd Benzinger	.50
(3)	Glenn Braggs	.50
(4)	Tom Browning	.50
(5)	Norm Charlton	.50
(6)	Eric Davis	.75
(7)	Rob Dibble	.50
(8)	Bill Doran	.50
(9)	Mariano Duncan	.50
(10)	Billy Hatcher	.50
(11)	Barry Larkin	.75
(12)	Hal Morris	.50
(13)	Randy Myers	.50
(14)	Joe Oliver	.50
(15)	Paul O'Neill	.75
(16)	Lou Piniella	.50
(17)	Jeff Reed	.50
(18)	Jose Rijo	.50
(19)	Chris Sabo	.50
(20)	Herm Winningham	.50

Red Sox

MIKE GREENWELL

For the second consecutive year, Pepsi/Diet Pepsi sponsored Boston Red Sox trading cards. The cards were inserted in specially marked packs of Pepsi and Diet Pepsi and were made available from July 1 through August 10. A consumer sweepstakes was also included with this promotion. Player jersey numbers are featured on the backs of the cards. Danny Darwin's jersey is incorrectly listed as #46. He actually wears #44 for the BoSox. Wade Boggs is not featured on a 1991 Pepsi-Cola Red Sox card.

		NM/M
Complete Set (20):		6.00
Common Player:		.25
2	Luis Rivera	.25
3	Jody Reed	.25
6	Tony Pena	.25
11	Tim Naehring	.25
15	Ellis Burks	.25
18	Dennis Lamp	.25
19	Carlos Quintana	.25
19	Dana Kiecker	.25
21	John Marzano	.25
21	Roger Clemens	5.00
23	Tom Brunansky	.25
27	Jack Clark	.25
29	Greg Harris	.25
30	Phil Plantier	.25
34	Matt Young	.25
38	Jeff Gray	.25
39	Mike Greenwell	.25
41	Jeff Reardon	.25
46	Danny Darwin	.25
50	Tom Bolton	.25

Griffeys

KEN GRIFFEY, JR.

This regionally released set features Ken Griffey, Sr. and Jr. and was distributed in Pepsi products. In the photos the players are shown in generic white uniforms with Pepsi logo patches. Backs are printed in black-and-white and include biographical data, recent stats and career highlights. Card numbers are in the lower-right.

		NM/M
Complete Set (8):		7.50
Common Card:		.25
1	Ken Griffey Jr. (Swinging bat.)	2.00
2	Ken Griffey Jr./Throwing	2.00
3	Ken Griffey Jr./Catching	2.00
4	Ken Griffey Jr. (Bat on shoulder.)	2.00
5	Ken Griffey Jr. (Leaning on father.)	.75
6	Ken Griffey Jr. (Standing with father.)	.75
7	Ken Griffey Sr./Btg	.25
8	Ken Griffey Sr./Fldg	.25

Rickey Henderson

RICKEY HENDERSON

A third annual issue distributed with Pepsi products in the San Francisco Bay area this set features photos of the all-time base stealing king in airbrushed uniforms. Borders are red, white and blue pinstripes. A line-art figure of a base runner appears in the lower-right. Backs have a few bits of biographical data, career stats and a career highlight. Card numbers are printed in the lower-right.

		NM/M
Complete Set (10):		9.00
Common Card:		1.00
Uncut Prize Sheet:		25.00
1	Rickey Henderson (Batting follow-through.)	1.00
2	Rickey Henderson (Base running.)	1.00
3	Rickey Henderson (Warm-up stretches.)	1.00
4	Rickey Henderson (Taking lead-off.)	1.00
5	Rickey Henderson (Bat on shoulder.)	1.00
6	Rickey Henderson (Batting follow-through.)	1.00
7	Rickey Henderson (Squatting with bat.)	1.00
8	Rickey Henderson (Throwing follow-through.)	1.00
9	Rickey Henderson (Leading off.)	1.00
10	Rickey Henderson (Warm-up swings.)	1.00

Rickey Henderson Discs

Intended as a giveaway with Pepsi fountain drinks, this four-piece set of "3-D" discs pictures Rickey Henderson in a generic Pepsi-logo uniform. Each 2-1/4" diameter disc has two pictures of Henderson which change when the disc is moved.

There is a purple border around the color photos, with "Pepsi," decorative stars and Henderson's name in white. Backs are printed in red and blue on white and are identical and unnumbered. The date and Pepsi logo are at top with 1990 season and career stats beneath.

	NM/M
Complete Set (4):	2.50
Common Disc:	1.00
(1) Rickey Henderson (Bat on shoulder/follow-through.)	1.00
(2) Rickey Henderson (Warm-up swing/batting follow-through.)	1.00
(3) Rickey Henderson (Lead-off/running for 2nd.)	1.00
(4) Rickey Henderson (Lead-off/headfirst slide.)	1.00

1996 Pepsi-Cola Cubs Convention

In conjunction with the Chicago Cubs 11th annual winter fan convention, Pepsi issued this boxed set featuring past and current Cubs with an emphasis on those appearing as convention guests. Individual cards are 4" x 5-1/2" and feature black-and-white or color photos inside a black border with white piping. The team and convention logos are printed in red, white and blue. Backs are printed in black on white and feature stats and biographical data plus the team and sponsor logos. The unnumbered cards are checklisted here in alphabetical order.

	NM/M
Complete Set (24):	8.00
Common Player:	.25
(1) Ernie Banks	3.00
(2) Glenn Beckert	.25
(3) Larry Bowa	.25
(4) Harry Caray	.25
(5) Frank Castillo	.25
(6) Jody Davis	.25
(7) Dynamic Duo (Scott Bullett, Ozzie Timmons)	.25
(8) Flashback Favorites (Milt Pappas, Tim Stoddard)	.25
(9) Golden Voices (Jack Brickhouse, Vince Lloyd)	.25
(10) Randy Hundley	.25
(11) Fergie Jenkins	.25
(12) Don Kessinger	.35
(13) Gary Matthews	.25
(14) Brian McRae	.25
(15) Jim Riggleman	.25
(16) Ron Santo	.50
(17) Sensational 70's (Jose Cardenal, Rick Monday)	.25
(18) Scott Servais	.25
(19) Rick Sutcliffe	.25
(20) Steve Trachsel	.25
(21) Billy Williams	.75
(22) Wrigleyville Sluggers (Keith Moreland, Richie Hebner)	.25
(23) Young Guns (Turk Wendell, Terry Adams)	.25
(24) Vine Line subscription offer (Ernie Banks)	.25

1998 Pepsi-Cola Arizona Diamondbacks

Pepsi-Cola and Circle K stores ran a baseball-season promotion to distribute 15 cards of Arizona Diamondback players on a regional basis. By use of a punchcard to record the purchase of five 20-oz. or one-liter Pepsi products a customer could receive a series of three players cards each month. Produced by Pinnacle, the D'back cards have action photos on front against a stylized semi-circular background. Team, Pinnacle and Pepsi logos are in three of the corners with the player name at lower-right. Backs have a red, white and blue Pepsi-style whirlpool background, another player photo, major league stats, a career highlight and licensor logos. Final production of the cards differs considerably from the player checklist provided on the punchcard and ads.

	NM/M
Complete Set (15):	6.00
Common Player:	.50
1 Andy Benes	.50
2 Willie Blair	.50
3 Jorge Fabregas	.50
4 Jay Bell	.50
5 Travis Lee	1.00
6 Matt Williams	.50
7 Devon White	.50
8 Karim Garcia	.65
9 Yamil Benitez	.50
10 Brian Anderson	.50
11 Scott Brow	.50
12 Felix Rodriguez	.50
13 Jeff Suppan	.50
14 Andy Fox	.50
15 Andy Stankiewicz	.50

Cubs Convention

In conjunction with the Chicago Cubs 13th annual winter fan convention, Pepsi issued this boxed set featuring past and current Cubs with an emphasis on those appearing as convention guests. Individual cards are 3-1/2" x 4" and feature black-and-white or color photos bordered in blue and sand. The team and convention logos are printed in red, white and blue. Backs are printed in black on white and feature stats and biographical data plus the team and sponsor logos. The unnumbered cards are checklisted here in alphabetical order.

	NM/M
Complete Set (30):	7.00
Common Card:	.25
(1) Terry Adams	.25
(2) Alumni Club (Carmen Fanzone, Paul Reuschel)	.25
(3) Alumni Club (Oscar Gamble, Larry Bowa)	.25
(4) Ernie Banks	2.00
(5) Behind the Plate (Randy Hundley, Jody Davis)	.25

(6) Booth Banter (Pat Hughes, Josh Lewin)	.25
(7) Jack Brickhouse	.25
(8) Harry Caray	.25
(9) Catching Corps (Mike Hubbard, Tyler Houston)	.25
(10) Andre Dawson	.50
(11) Flame-Throwers (Kevin Foster, Marc Pisciotta)	.25
(12) Future Stars (Kerry Wood, Pat Cline)	.50
(13) Mark Grace	.50
(14) Hot Prospects (Robin Jennings, Rodney Myers)	.25
(15) Mound Mates (Mark Clark, Jeremi Gonzalez)	.25
(16) New Cubs (Jeff Blauser, Mickey Morandini)	.25
(17) No-Hit Hurlers (Milt Pappas, Don Cardwell)	.25
(18) Kevin Orie	.25
(19) Outfield Greats (Andy Pafko, Gary Matthews)	.35
(20) Jim Riggleman	.25
(21) Ron Santo	1.00
(22) Scott Servais	.25
(23) Sammy Sosa	2.00
(24) Rick Sutcliffe	.25
(25) Steve Trachsel	.25
(26) Veteran Hurlers (Bob Patterson, Kevin Tapani)	.25
(27) Billy Williams	1.00
(28) 1969 Cubs (Dick Selma, Willie Smith)	.25
(29) 1969 Infield (Glenn Beckert, Don Kessinger)	.50
(30) 89er's (Mike Bielecki, Vance Law)	.25

1999 Pepsi-Cola Arizona Diamondbacks

Sponsored by Pepsi and produced by Fleer, this team-set promotion features action photos on front on a metallic-foil background which approximates the colors and design of the soft drink logo, which also appears at lower-left. The player's uniform is at top-left. On back is a portrait photo on a repeat of the red, white and blue background. Full Major League stats are provided, along with career highlights and biographical data. At bottom is a row of licensor and sponsor logos.

	NM/M
Complete Set (15):	9.00
Common Player:	.50
1 Jay Bell	.50
2 Andy Benes	.50
3 Randy Johnson	3.00
4 Matt Williams	.50
5 Steve Finley	.50
6 Todd Stottlemyre	.50
7 Omar Daal	.50
8 Travis Lee	.50
9 Armando Reynoso	.50
10 Gregg Olson	.50
11 Tony Batista	.50
12 Greg Swindell	.50
13 Greg Colbrunn	.50
14 Damian Miller	.50
15 Kelly Stinnett	.50
--- Checklist 1	.10
--- Checklist 2	.10
--- Checklist 3	.10
--- Checklist 4	.10

2000 Pepsi-Cola Arizona Diamondbacks

Pepsi-Cola and Circle K stores ran a baseball-season promotion to distribute 15 cards of Arizona Diamondback players on a regional basis. Produced by Upper Deck, the D'back cards have large portrait and smaller action photos in a horizontal format on a red, white and blue wave background. Team, UD and Pepsi logos appear in the corners with the player name at right. Backs have the same background, another player photo, major league stats, a career highlight and licensor logos. Cards were distributed in three five-card series, with a checklist card in each pack.

	NM/M
Complete Set (18):	9.00
Common Player:	.50
1 Jay Bell	.50
2 Matt Mantei	.50
3 Greg Swindell	.50
4 Matt Williams	.50
5 Erubiel Durazo	.50
6 Todd Stottlemyre	.50
7 Randy Johnson	3.00
8 Tony Womack	.50
9 Greg Colbrunn	.50
10 Brian Anderson	.50
11 Omar Daal	.50
12 Travis Lee	.50
13 Steve Finley	.50
14 Luis Gonzalez	.50
15 Kelly Stinnett	.50
Checklist 1	.10
Checklist 2	.10
Checklist 3	.10

Detroit Tigers

Pepsi-Cola ran a late-season promotion to distribute 15 cards of Detroit Tigers players on a regional basis. Produced by Upper Deck, the cards have large portrait and smaller action photos in a horizontal format on a red, white and blue wave background. Team, UD and Pepsi logos appear in the corners with the player name at right. Backs have the same background, another action photo, major league stats, a career highlight and licensor logos. Cards were distributed in one per 12-pack of Pepsi products.

	NM/M
Complete Set (15):	5.00
Common Player:	.50
1 Damion Easley	.50
2 Dave Mlicki	.50
3 Jeff Weaver	.50
4 Deivi Cruz	.50
5 Juan Encarnacion	.50
6 Brian Moehler	.50
7 Robert Fick	.50
8 Juan Gonzalez	1.50
9 Phil Garner	.50
10 Brad Ausmus	.50
11 Todd Jones	.50
12 Bobby Higginson	.50
13 Tony Clark	.50
14 Dean Palmer	.50
15 Doug Brocail	.50

1980-2001 Perez-Steele Hall of Fame Postcards

In 1980, Perez-Steele Galleries of Ft. Washington, Pa., produced the first in an ongoing series of limited-edition (10,000 each) postcards devoted to members of the Hall of Fame. The company updated its series regularly through 2001 to add new inductees. The 3-1/2" x 5-1/2" cards feature color portrait and smaller sepia action watercolor paintings by Dick Perez. Decorative postcard backs have a few words about the player, card and series number and individual set number from within the edition of 10,000. Cards were sold by series only, in a color-coded box which includes a checklist. To a great degree, value of

unsigned Perez-Steele cards depends on whether the player is still alive to autograph them.

	NM/M
Complete Set (270):	750.00
Common Player:	2.00
First Series, 1980	75.00
1 Ty Cobb	20.00
2 Walter Johnson	6.00
3 Christy Mathewson	7.50
4 Babe Ruth	25.00
5 Honus Wagner	7.50
6 Morgan Bulkeley	2.00
7 Ban Johnson	2.00
8 Nap Lajoie	4.00
9 Connie Mack	4.00
10 John McGraw	2.00
11 Tris Speaker	4.00
12 George Wright	2.00
13 Cy Young	7.50
14 Grover Alexander	4.00
15 Alexander Cartwright	2.00
16 Henry Chadwick	2.00
17 Cap Anson	2.00
18 Eddie Collins	2.00
19 Candy Cummings	2.00
20 Charles Comiskey	2.00
21 Buck Ewing	2.00
22 Lou Gehrig	20.00
23 Willie Keeler	2.00
24 Hoss Radbourne	2.00
25 George Sisler	2.00
26 A.G. Spalding	2.00
27 Rogers Hornsby	4.00
28 Kenesaw Landis	2.00
29 Roger Breshnahan	2.00
30 Dan Brouthers	2.00
--- First Series Checklist	1.00
Second Series, 1980	50.00
31 Fred Clarke	2.00
32 Jimmy Collins	2.00
33 Ed Delahanty	2.00
34 Hugh Duffy	2.00
35 Hughie Jennings	2.00
36 King Kelly	2.00
37 Jim O'Rourke	2.00
38 Wilbert Robinson	2.00
39 Jesse Burkett	2.00
40 Frank Chance	2.00
41 Jack Chesbro	2.00
42 Johnny Evers	2.00
43 Clark Griffith	2.00
44 Thomas McCarthy	2.00
45 Joe McGinnity	2.00
46 Eddie Plank	2.00
47 Joe Tinker	2.00
48 Rube Waddell	2.00
49 Ed Walsh	2.00
50 Mickey Cochrane	2.00
51 Frankie Frisch	2.00
52 Lefty Grove	2.00
53 Carl Hubbell	2.00
54 Herb Pennock	2.00
55 Pie Traynor	2.00
56 Mordecai Brown	2.00
57 Charlie Gehringer	2.00
58 Kid Nichols	2.00
59 Jimmie Foxx	4.00
60 Mel Ott	2.00
--- Second Series Checklist	1.00
Third Series, 1980	75.00
61 Harry Heilmann	2.00
62 Paul Waner	2.00
63 Ed Barrow	2.00
64 Chief Bender	2.00
65 Tom Connolly	2.00
66 Dizzy Dean	7.50
67 Bill Klem	2.00
68 Al Simmons	2.00
69 Bobby Wallace	2.00
70 Harry Wright	2.00
71 Bill Dickey	2.00
72 Rabbit Maranville	2.00
73 Bill Terry	2.00
74 Frank Baker	2.00
75 Joe DiMaggio	20.00
76 Gabby Hartnett	2.00
77 Ted Lyons	2.00
78 Ray Schalk	2.00
79 Dazzy Vance	2.00
80 Joe Cronin	2.00
81 Hank Greenberg	7.50
82 Sam Crawford	2.00
83 Joe McCarthy	2.00

84 Zack Wheat	2.00
85 Max Carey	2.00
86 Billy Hamilton	2.00
87 Bob Feller	6.00
88 Bill McKechnie	2.00
89 Jackie Robinson	10.00
90 Edd Roush	2.00
--- Third Series Checklist	1.00
Fourth Series, 1981	65.00
91 John Clarkson	2.00
92 Elmer Flick	2.00
93 Sam Rice	2.00
94 Eppa Rixey	2.00
95 Luke Appling	2.00
96 Red Faber	2.00
97 Burleigh Grimes	2.00
98 Miller Huggins	2.00
99 Tim Keefe	2.00
100 Heinie Manush	2.00
101 John Ward	2.00
102 Pud Galvin	2.00
103 Casey Stengel	3.00
104 Ted Williams	20.00
105 Branch Rickey	2.00
106 Red Ruffing	2.00
107 Lloyd Waner	2.00
108 Kiki Cuyler	2.00
109 Goose Goslin	2.00
110 Joe Medwick	2.00
111 Roy Campanella	7.50
112 Stan Coveleski	2.00
113 Waite Hoyt	2.00
114 Stan Musial	10.00
115 Lou Boudreau	2.00
116 Earle Combs	2.00
117 Ford Frick	2.00
118 Jesse Haines	2.00
119 David Bancroft	2.00
120 Jake Beckley	2.00
--- Fourth Series Checklist	1.00
Fifth Series, 1981	85.00
121 Chick Hafey	2.00
122 Harry Hooper	2.00
123 Joe Kelley	2.00
124 Rube Marquard	2.00
125 Satchel Paige	10.00
126 George Weiss	2.00
127 Yogi Berra	6.00
128 Josh Gibson	4.00
129 Lefty Gomez	2.00
130 William Harridge	2.00
131 Sandy Koufax	15.00
132 Buck Leonard	2.00
133 Early Wynn	2.00
134 Ross Youngs	2.00
135 Roberto Clemente	20.00
136 Billy Evans	2.00
137 Monte Irvin	4.00
138 George Kelly	2.00
139 Warren Spahn	2.00
140 Mickey Welch	2.00
141 Cool Papa Bell	2.00
142 Jim Bottomley	2.00
143 Jocko Conlan	2.00
144 Whitey Ford	5.00
145 Mickey Mantle	25.00
146 Sam Thompson	2.00
147 Earl Averill	2.00
148 Bucky Harris	2.00
149 Billy Herman	2.00
150 Judy Johnson	2.00
--- Fifth Series Checklist	1.00
Sixth Series, 1981	85.00
151 Ralph Kiner	2.00
152 Oscar Charleston	2.00
153 Roger Connor	2.00
154 Cal Hubbard	2.00
155 Bob Lemon	2.00
156 Freddie Lindstrom	2.00
157 Robin Roberts	4.00
158 Ernie Banks	6.00
159 Martin DiHigo	2.00
160 John Lloyd	2.00
161 Al Lopez	2.00
162 Amos Rusie	2.00
163 Joe Sewell	2.00
164 Addie Joss	2.00
165 Larry MacPhail	2.00
166 Eddie Mathews	4.00
167 Warren Giles	2.00
168 Willie Mays	15.00
169 Hack Wilson	2.00
170 Al Kaline	5.00
171 Chuck Klein	2.00
172 Duke Snider	5.00
173 Tom Yawkey	2.00
174 Rube Foster	2.00
175 Bob Gibson	4.00
176 Johnny Mize	2.00
A Abner Doubleday	2.00
B Stephen Clark	2.00
C Paul Kerr	2.00
D Edward W. Stack	2.00
--- Sixth Series Checklist	1.00
Seventh Series, 1983	55.00
177 Hank Aaron	20.00
178 Happy Chandler	2.00
179 Travis Jackson	3.00
180 Frank Robinson	10.00
181 Walter Alston	2.00
182 George Kell	6.00
183 Juan Marichal	7.50
184 Brooks Robinson	10.00
Eighth Series, 1985	55.00
185 Luis Aparicio	7.50
186 Don Drysdale	3.00
187 Rick Ferrell	3.00
188 Harmon Killebrew	6.00

#	Player	Price
189	Pee Wee Reese	3.00
190	Lou Brock	6.00
191	Enos Slaughter	3.00
192	Arky Vaughn	3.00
193	Hoyt Wilhelm	3.00
Ninth Series, 1987		**15.00**
194	Bobby Doerr	2.00
195	Ernie Lombardi	2.00
196	Willie McCovey	2.00
197	Ray Dandridge	2.00
198	Catfish Hunter	2.00
199	Billy Williams	4.00
E	Frank Steele, Peggy Steele, Dick Perez	2.00
Tenth Series, 1989		**20.00**
200	Willie Stargell	2.00
201	Al Barlick	2.00
202	Johnny Bench	4.00
203	Red Schoendienst	4.00
204	Carl Yastrzemski	4.00
F	George Bush, Edward Stack	4.00
Eleventh Series, 1991		**30.00**
205	Joe Morgan	4.00
206	Jim Palmer	4.00
207	Rod Carew	4.00
208	Ferguson Jenkins	4.00
209	Tony Lazzeri	2.00
210	Gaylord Perry	4.00
211	Bill Veeck	2.00
Twelfth Series, 1993		**35.00**
212	Rollie Fingers	4.00
213	Bill McGowan	3.00
214	Hal Newhouser	3.00
215	Tom Seaver	6.00
216	Reggie Jackson	7.50
217	Steve Carlton	6.00
218	Leo Durocher	3.00
219	Phil Rizzuto	6.00
Thirteenth Series, 1995		**40.00**
220	Richie Ashburn	4.00
221	Leon Day	3.00
222	William Hulbert	3.00
223	Mike Schmidt	10.00
224	Vic Willis	3.00
225	Jim Bunning	4.00
226	Andrew "Rube" Foster	3.00
227	Ned Hanlon	3.00
228	Earl Weaver	6.00
Fourteenth Series, 1997		**85.00**
229	Nellie Fox	6.00
230	Tommy Lasorda	6.00
231	Phil Niekro	4.00
232	Willie Wells	3.00
233	George Davis	3.00
234	Larry Doby	4.00
235	Lee MacPhail	3.00
236	Joe Rogan	3.00
237	Don Sutton	4.00
238	George Brett	15.00
239	Orlando Cepeda	6.00
240	Nestor Chylak	3.00
241	Nolan Ryan	20.00
242	Frank Selee	3.00
243	Joe Williams	3.00
244	Robin Yount	7.50
Fifteenth Series, 2001		**50.00**
245	Sparky Anderson	6.00
246	Carlton Fisk	7.50
247	Bid McPhee	3.00
248	Tony Perez	6.00
249	Turkey Stearnes	3.00
250	Bill Mazeroski	7.50
251	Kirby Puckett	7.50
252	Hilton Smith	3.00
253	Dave Winfield	7.50
G	Franklin A. Steele	5.00

Autographed

Because the cards are so popular with autograph collectors, a listing of Perez-Steele Hall of Fame postcards which are possible to acquire in authentically autographed form is provided here, along with current retail values. Only those players who were alive at the time of their cards' issue are included in this listings; no cards from Series 1 and very few from Series 2 are available in autographed form.

		NM/M
Common Player:		15.00
53	Carl Hubbell	80.00
57	Charlie Gehringer	80.00
71	Bill Dickey	65.00
73	Bill Terry	90.00
75	Joe DiMaggio	325.00
77	Ted Lyons	235.00
80	Joe Cronin	750.00
81	Hank Greenberg	300.00
87	Bob Feller	25.00
90	Edd Roush	75.00
95	Luke Appling	50.00
97	Burleigh Grimes	190.00
104	Ted Williams	300.00
106	Red Ruffing	450.00
107	Lloyd Waner	2,250
111	Roy Campanella	300.00
112	Stan Coveleski	300.00
113	Waite Hoyt	495.00
114	Stan Musial	75.00
115	Lou Boudreau	25.00
125	Satchel Paige	2,500
127	Yogi Berra	40.00
129	Lefty Gomez	60.00
131	Sandy Koufax	90.00
132a	Buck Leonard (Pre-stroke.)	45.00
132b	Buck Leonard (Post-stroke.)	25.00
133	Early Wynn	40.00
137	Monte Irvin	20.00
138	George Kelly	350.00
139	Warren Spahn	30.00
141	Cool Papa Bell	75.00
143	Jocko Conlan	60.00
144	Whitey Ford	40.00
145	Mickey Mantle	300.00
147	Earl Averill	450.00
149	Billy Herman	35.00
150	Judy Johnson	60.00
151	Ralph Kiner	30.00
155	Bob Lemon	30.00
157	Robin Roberts	25.00
158	Ernie Banks	30.00
161	Al Lopez	75.00
163	Joe Sewell	45.00
166	Eddie Mathews	40.00
168	Willie Mays	75.00
170	Al Kaline	25.00
172	Duke Snider	30.00
175	Bob Gibson	25.00
176	Johnny Mize	30.00
D	Edward W. Stack	15.00
177	Hank Aaron	45.00
178	Happy Chandler	50.00
179	Travis Jackson	80.00
180	Frank Robinson	35.00
181	Walter Alston	675.00
182	George Kell	20.00
183	Juan Marichal	20.00
184	Brooks Robinson	22.50
185	Luis Aparicio	22.50
186	Don Drysdale	40.00
187	Rick Ferrell	25.00
188	Harmon Killebrew	30.00
189	Pee Wee Reese	55.00
190	Lou Brock	25.00
191	Enos Slaughter	20.00
193	Hoyt Wilhelm	20.00
194	Bobby Doerr	17.50
196	Willie McCovey	35.00
197	Ray Dandridge	30.00
198	Catfish Hunter	40.00
199	Billy Williams	22.50
E	Frank Steele, Peggy Steele, Dick Perez	15.00
200	Willie Stargell	35.00
201	Al Barlick	20.00
202	Johnny Bench	45.00
203	Red Schoendienst	45.00
204	Carl Yastrzemski	65.00
F	George Bush, Edward Stack	60.00
205	Joe Morgan	35.00
206	Jim Palmer	25.00
207	Rod Carew	45.00
208	Ferguson Jenkins	30.00
210	Gaylord Perry	17.50
212	Rollie Fingers	35.00
214	Hal Newhouser	60.00
215	Tom Seaver	60.00
216	Reggie Jackson	75.00
217	Steve Carlton	45.00
219	Phil Rizzuto	40.00
220	Richie Ashburn	30.00
223	Mike Schmidt	75.00
225	Jim Bunning	35.00
228	Earl Weaver	35.00
230	Tommy Lasorda	35.00
231	Phil Niekro	35.00
234	Larry Doby	90.00
235	Lee MacPhail	35.00
237	Don Sutton	35.00
238	George Brett	100.00
239	Orlando Cepeda	40.00
241	Nolan Ryan	100.00
244	Robin Yount	100.00
245	Sparky Anderson	45.00
246	Carlton Fisk	60.00
248	Tony Perez	45.00
250	Bill Mazeroski	45.00
251	Kirby Puckett	85.00
253	Dave Winfield	85.00

1981 Perez-Steele Yankee Greats Promotional Postcard

To advertise the availability of a "Yankee Greats" lithograph by Dick Perez, the Perez-Steele Galleries issued this promotional postcard. The 3-1/2" x 5-1/2" card is printed on thin cardboard with a reproduction of the lithograph on front. Printed in blue, the postcard-style back has information on the lithograph, which was issued in a size of 19" x 24-1/2" in an edition of 1,000 signed pieces.

	NM/M
Yankee Greats (Babe Ruth, Lou Gehrig, Earle Combs)	4.00

1985-95 Perez-Steele Great Moments Postcards

Yet another collectors issue devoted solely to Hall of Fame players, the Great Moments series borrows the format of the 1911 Turkey Red cabinet cards. The 5-3/4" x 8" cards are printed on textured cardboard (which was noticeably downgraded beginning with the 1993 series). Fronts have Dick Perez paintings surrounded by a greenish-brown border; backs are in black-and-white. Each card carries a series checklist on back and an individual set serial number from within an edition of 5,000. Cards were issued in series of 12.

		NM/M
Complete Set (108):		400.00
Common Player:		3.00
1	Babe Ruth	20.00
2	Al Kaline	6.00
3	Jackie Robinson	10.00
4	Lou Gehrig	15.00
5	Whitey Ford	6.00
6	Christy Mathewson	5.00
7	Roy Campanella	7.50
8	Walter Johnson	6.00
9	Hank Aaron	6.00
10	Cy Young	5.00
11	Stan Musial	12.50
12	Ty Cobb	15.00
13	Ted Williams	15.00
14	Warren Spahn	3.00
15	Lloyd Waner, Paul Waner	3.00
16	Sandy Koufax	12.50
17	Robin Roberts	3.00
18	Dizzy Dean	4.00
19	Mickey Mantle	25.00
20	Satchel Paige	10.00
21	Ernie Banks	6.00
22	Willie McCovey	4.00
23	Johnny Mize	3.00
24	Honus Wagner	7.50
25	Willie Keeler	3.00
26	Pee Wee Reese	3.00
27	Monte Irvin	3.00
28	Eddie Mathews	3.00
29	Enos Slaughter	3.00
30	Rube Marquard	3.00
31	Charlie Gehringer	3.00
32	Roberto Clemente	15.00
33	Duke Snider	4.50
34	Ray Dandridge	3.00
35	Carl Hubbell	3.00
36	Bobby Doerr	3.00
37	Bill Dickey	3.00
38	Willie Stargell	3.00
39	Brooks Robinson	3.00
40	Joe Tinker, Johnny Evers, Frank Chance	5.00
41	Billy Herman	3.00
42	Grover Alexander	3.00
43	Luis Aparicio	3.00
44	Lefty Gomez	3.00
45	Eddie Collins	3.00
46	Judy Johnson	3.00
47	Harry Heilmann	3.00
48	Harmon Killebrew	3.00
49	Johnny Bench	4.50
51	Max Carey	3.00
52	Cool Papa Bell	3.00
53	Rube Waddell	3.00
54	Yogi Berra	6.00
55	Herb Pennock	3.00
56	Red Schoendienst	3.00
57	Juan Marichal	3.00
58	Frankie Frisch	3.00
59	Buck Leonard	3.00
60	George Kell	3.00
61	Chuck Klein	3.00
62	King Kelly	3.00
63	Jim Hunter	3.00
64	Lou Boudreau	3.00
65	Al Lopez	3.00
66	Willie Mays	12.50
67	Lou Brock	3.00
68	Bob Lemon	3.00
69	Joe Sewell	3.00
70	Billy Williams	3.00
71	Rick Ferrell	3.00
72	Arky Vaughn	3.00
73	Carl Yastrzemski	4.50
74	Tom Seaver	6.00
75	Rollie Fingers	3.00
76	Ralph Kiner	3.00
77	Frank Baker	3.00
78	Rod Carew	3.00
79	Goose Goslin	3.00
80	Gaylord Perry	3.00
81	Hack Wilson	3.00
82	Hal Newhouser	3.00
83	Early Wynn	3.00
84	Bob Feller	4.00
85	Branch Rickey (W/Jackie Robinson.)	3.00
86	Jim Palmer	3.00
87	Al Barlick	3.00
88	Willie Mays, Mickey Mantle, Duke Snider	20.00
89	Hank Greenberg	6.00
90	Joe Morgan	3.00
91	Chief Bender	3.00
92	Pee Wee Reese, Jackie Robinson	5.00
93	Jim Bottomley	3.00
94	Ferguson Jenkins	3.00
95	Frank Robinson	4.00
96	Hoyt Wilhelm	3.00
97	Cap Anson	3.00
98	Jim Bunning	3.00
99	Richie Ashburn	4.00
100	Steve Carlton	3.00
101	Mike Schmidt	6.00
102	Nellie Fox	3.00
103	Tommy Lasorda	3.00
104	Leo Durocher	3.00
105	Reggie Jackson	6.00
106	Phil Rizzuto	4.50
107	Phil Niekro	4.00
108	Earl Weaver	3.00

Autographed

Because the Perez-Steele postcards are so popular with autograph collectors, separate listings for authentically autographed examples of the cards are provided here. Those cards not listed cannot possibly have been signed because the player was deceased prior to issue.

		NM/M
Complete Set (70):		1,800
Common Player:		17.50
2	Al Kaline	30.00
5	Whitey Ford	35.00
7	Roy Campanella	400.00
9	Hank Aaron	60.00
11	Stan Musial	60.00
13	Ted Williams	300.00
14	Warren Spahn	30.00
16	Sandy Koufax	95.00
17	Robin Roberts	25.00
19	Mickey Mantle	300.00
21	Ernie Banks	55.00
22	Willie McCovey	40.00
23	Johnny Mize	40.00
26	Pee Wee Reese	60.00
27	Monte Irvin	20.00
28	Eddie Mathews	50.00
29	Enos Slaughter	27.50
31	Charlie Gehringer	65.00
33	Duke Snider	40.00
34	Ray Dandridge	45.00
35	Carl Hubbell	65.00
36	Bobby Doerr	17.50
37	Bill Dickey	65.00
38	Willie Stargell	35.00
39	Brooks Robinson	30.00
41	Billy Herman	30.00
43	Luis Aparicio	25.00
44	Lefty Gomez	25.00
48	Harmon Killebrew	35.00
49	Johnny Bench	45.00
51	Cool Papa Bell	90.00
53	Yogi Berra	35.00
55	Red Schoendienst	25.00
56	Juan Marichal	25.00
58	Buck Leonard	40.00
59	George Kell	20.00
62	Jim Hunter	55.00
63	Lou Boudreau	25.00
64	Al Lopez	60.00
65	Willie Mays	80.00
66	Lou Brock	30.00
67	Bob Lemon	35.00
68	Joe Sewell	50.00
69	Billy Williams	25.00
70	Rick Ferrell	35.00
72	Carl Yastrzemski	60.00
73	Tom Seaver	32.50
74	Rollie Fingers	32.50
75	Ralph Kiner	27.50
77	Rod Carew	35.00
79	Gaylord Perry	25.00
81	Hal Newhouser	30.00
82	Early Wynn	40.00
83	Bob Feller	25.00
85	Jim Palmer	32.50
86	Al Barlick	25.00
87	Willie Mays, Mickey Mantle, Duke Snider	325.00
89	Joe Morgan	20.00
93	Ferguson Jenkins	20.00
94	Frank Robinson	30.00
95	Hoyt Wilhelm	30.00
97	Jim Bunning	30.00
98	Richie Ashburn	25.00
99	Steve Carlton	45.00
100	Mike Schmidt	75.00
102	Tommy Lasorda	50.00
104	Reggie Jackson	50.00
105	Phil Rizzuto	35.00
106	Phil Niekro	30.00
108	Earl Weaver	30.00

1989 Perez-Steele Celebration Postcards

The Celebrations postcard issue from Perez-Steele was an attempt to offer collectors an original medium on which to obtain autographs of Hall of Famers. All 44 of the players included in the issue were alive when the set was conceived and most were still around when it was actually issued. The 3-1/2" x 5-1/2" cards have color portrait and action paintings by Dick Perez on front, which features a linen texture. Backs have postcard indicia, Perez-Steele and Hall of Fame logos, card number and individual serial number from within the edition limit of 10,000. Cards were originally sold only as complete sets.

		NM/M
Complete Set (45):		100.00
Common Player:		2.50
1	Hank Aaron	10.00
1	Luis Aparicio	2.50
3	Ernie Banks	6.00
4	Cool Papa Bell	2.50
5	Johnny Bench	2.50
6	Yogi Berra	6.00
7	Lou Boudreau	2.50
8	Roy Campanella	7.50
9	Happy Chandler	2.50
10	Jocko Conlan	2.50
11	Ray Dandridge	2.50
12	Bill Dickey	3.00
13	Bobby Doerr	2.50
14	Rick Ferrell	2.50
15	Charlie Gehringer	3.00
16	Lefty Gomez	3.00
17	Billy Herman	2.50
18	Catfish Hunter	2.50
19	Monte Irvin	2.50
20	Judy Johnson	2.50
21	Al Kaline	6.00
22	George Kell	2.50
23	Harmon Killebrew	2.50
24	Ralph Kiner	2.50
25	Bob Lemon	2.50
26	Buck Leonard	2.50
27	Al Lopez	2.50
28	Mickey Mantle	20.00
29	Juan Marichal	2.50
30	Eddie Mathews	2.50
31	Willie McCovey	2.50
32	Johnny Mize	2.50
33	Stan Musial	7.50
34	Pee Wee Reese	2.50
35	Brooks Robinson	2.50
36	Joe Sewell	2.50
37	Enos Slaughter	2.50
38	Duke Snider	6.00
39	Warren Spahn	2.50
40	Willie Stargell	2.50
41	Bill Terry	2.50
42	Billy Williams	2.50
43	Ted Williams	15.00
44	Carl Yastrzemski	2.50
---	Checklist	1.00

Autographed

Because of their popularity as an autograph vehicle, values for authentically signed examples of the Perez-Steele Celebrations postcards are presented here. Cards of Lefty Gomez (#16), Judy Johnson (#20) and Bill Terry (#41) cannot exist with genuine autographs because those players were deceased by the time the cards were issued.

		NM/M
Common Player:		15.00
1	Hank Aaron	40.00
2	Luis Aparicio	15.00
3	Ernie Banks	30.00
4	Cool Papa Bell	60.00
6	Johnny Bench	35.00
6	Yogi Berra	35.00
7	Lou Boudreau	20.00
8	Roy Campanella	400.00
9	Happy Chandler	35.00
10	Jocko Conlan	450.00
11	Ray Dandridge	30.00
12	Bill Dickey	65.00
13	Bobby Doerr	15.00
14	Rick Ferrell	20.00
15	Charlie Gehringer	45.00
17	Billy Herman	30.00
18	Catfish Hunter	40.00
19	Monte Irvin	22.50
21	Al Kaline	25.00
22	George Kell	20.00
23	Harmon Killebrew	30.00
24	Ralph Kiner	25.00
25	Bob Lemon	30.00
26	Buck Leonard	30.00
27	Al Lopez	75.00
28	Mickey Mantle	300.00
29	Juan Marichal	30.00
30	Eddie Mathews	40.00
31	Willie McCovey	30.00
32	Johnny Mize	30.00
33	Stan Musial	50.00
34	Pee Wee Reese	55.00
35	Brooks Robinson	25.00
36	Joe Sewell	40.00
37	Enos Slaughter	25.00
38	Duke Snider	30.00
39	Warren Spahn	25.00
40	Willie Stargell	30.00
42	Billy Williams	20.00
43	Ted Williams	250.00
44	Carl Yastrzemski	60.00

1990-92 Perez-Steele Master Works Postcards

A blending of the designs of classic early baseball cards with the artwork of one of today's most recognized baseball artists produced the Perez-Steele Master Works postcard series. Each of the players in the collection (living players selected for inclusion on the basis of autograph possibilities) is shown on five different cards, one of original design and four adapting the formats of the 1909 Ramly (T204), 1911 "Gold Borders" (T205) and 1908 Rose Co. postcards (PC760) and 1888 Goodwin Champions (N162). The Ramly and Rose take-offs feature gold-foil embossing. Postcard backs are printed in brown (#1-25) or dark green (#26-50). Information on back includes a description of the card set on which the design is based, card and series number and the individual set serial number from within the edition of 10,000. Series 1 (#1-25) was issued in 1990; Series 2 (#26-50) in 1992. Each was available only as a complete boxed set.

		NM/M
Complete Set (52):		150.00
Common Player:		3.00
1	Charlie Gehringer (Ramly)	3.00
2	Charlie Gehringer (Goodwin)	3.00
3	Charlie Gehringer (Rose)	3.00
4	Charlie Gehringer (Gold Border)	3.00
5	Charlie Gehringer (Perez-Steele)	3.00
6	Mickey Mantle (Ramly)	15.00
7	Mickey Mantle (Goodwin)	15.00
8	Mickey Mantle (Rose)	15.00
9	Mickey Mantle (Gold Border)	15.00
10	Mickey Mantle (Perez-Steele)	15.00
11	Willie Mays (Ramly)	9.00
12	Willie Mays (Goodwin)	9.00
13	Willie Mays (Rose)	9.00
14	Willie Mays (Gold Border)	9.00
15	Willie Mays (Perez-Steele)	9.00
16	Duke Snider (Ramly)	6.00
17	Duke Snider (Goodwin)	6.00
18	Duke Snider (Rose)	6.00
19	Duke Snider (Gold Border)	6.00
20	Duke Snider (Perez-Steele)	6.00
21	Warren Spahn (Ramly)	3.00
22	Warren Spahn (Goodwin)	3.00
23	Warren Spahn (Rose)	3.00
24	Warren Spahn (Gold Border)	3.00
25	Warren Spahn (Perez-Steele)	3.00
---	Checklist 1-25	1.00
26	Yogi Berra (Ramly)	5.00
27	Yogi Berra (Goodwin)	5.00
28	Yogi Berra (Rose)	5.00
29	Yogi Berra (Gold Border)	5.00
30	Yogi Berra (Perez-Steele)	5.00
31	Johnny Mize (Ramly)	3.00
32	Johnny Mize (Goodwin)	3.00
33	Johnny Mize (Rose)	3.00
34	Johnny Mize (Gold Border)	3.00
35	Johnny Mize (Perez-Steele)	3.00
36	Willie Stargell (Ramly)	3.00
37	Willie Stargell (Goodwin)	3.00
38	Willie Stargell (Rose)	3.00
39	Willie Stargell (Gold Border)	3.00
40	Willie Stargell (Perez-Steele)	3.00
41	Ted Williams (Ramly)	12.00
42	Ted Williams (Goodwin)	12.00
43	Ted Williams (Rose)	12.00
44	Ted Williams (Gold Border)	12.00
45	Ted Williams (Perez-Steele)	12.00
46	Carl Yastrzemski (Ramly)	4.00
47	Carl Yastrzemski (Goodwin)	4.00
48	Carl Yastrzemski (Rose)	4.00
49	Carl Yastrzemski (Gold Border)	4.00
50	Carl Yastrzemski (Perez-Steele)	4.00
---	Checklist 26-50	1.00

1985 Performance Printing Texas Rangers

A local printing company sponsored this 28-card set of the Texas Rangers. The 2-3/8" x 3-1/2" cards are in full color and are numbered on the back by uniform number. Card fronts feature full-color, game-action photos. The 25 players on the Rangers' active roster at press time are included, along with manager Bobby Valentine and unnumbered coaches and trainer cards. The black and white card backs have a smaller portrait photo of each player, as well as biographical information and career statistics.

		NM/M
Complete Set (28):		9.00
Common Player:		.25
0	Oddibe McDowell	.25
1	Scott Fletcher	.25
2	Bobby Valentine	.25
3	Ruben Sierra	.35
6	Don Slaught	.25
9	Pete O'Brien	.25
11	Toby Harrah	.25
12	Geno Petralli	.25
15	Larry Parrish	.25
16	Mike Mason	.25
17	Darrell Porter	.25
18	Edwin Correa	.25
19	Curtis Wilkerson	.25
22	Steve Buechele	.25
23	Jose Guzman	.25
24	Ricky Wright	.25
27	Greg Harris	.25
28	Mitch Williams	.25
29	Pete Incaviglia	.50
32	Gary Ward	.25
34	Dale Mohorcic	.25
40	Jeff Russell	.25
44	Tom Paciorek	.25
46	Mike Loynd	.25
48	Bobby Witt	.25
49	Charlie Hough	.25
----	Coaching Staff (Joe Ferguson, Tim Foli, Tom House, Art Howe, Tom Robson)	.25
----	Trainers (Danny Wheat, Bill Zeigler)	.25

1981 Perma-Graphics All-Star Credit Cards

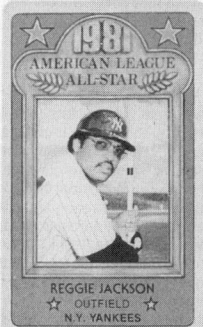

Using the same "credit card" style of its previous 1981 issue, Perma-Graphics issued an 18-card set in the fall of 1981 featuring the starting players from the 1981 All-Star Game. The front of the card contains a full-color photo, plus the player's name, position and team. The back includes personal data, career records, highlights and an "autograph panel."

		NM/M
Complete Set (18):		15.00
Common Player:		1.00
1	Gary Carter	1.50
2	Dave Concepcion	1.00
3	Andre Dawson	1.25
4	George Foster	1.00
5	Davey Lopes	1.00
6	Dave Parker	1.00
7	Pete Rose	5.00
8	Mike Schmidt	4.00
9	Fernando Valenzuela	1.00
10	George Brett	4.00
11a	Rod Carew (Outfield)	2.50
11b	Rod Carew (First base.)	2.50
11c	Rod Carew (First base, #20 on back.)	2.50
11d	Rod Carew (First base, #29 on back.)	2.50
12	Bucky Dent	1.00
13	Carlton Fisk	1.50
14	Reggie Jackson	3.00
15	Jack Morris	1.00
16	Willie Randolph	1.00
17	Ken Singleton	1.00
18	Dave Winfield	1.50

1986 Performance Printing Texas Rangers

For the second time, the Texas Rangers issued a full-color card set in conjunction with this local printing company. Fronts of the 28-card set include player name, position and team logo beneath the color photo. Backs of the 2-3/8" x 3-1/2" cards are in black and white, with a small portrait photo of each player

along with personal and professional statistics. Cards were distributed at the August 23 Rangers home game, and the set includes all of the Rangers' fine rookies such as Bobby Witt, Pete Incaviglia, Edwin Correa and Ruben Sierra.

		NM/M
Complete Set (28):		5.00
Common Player:		.25
0	Oddibe McDowell	.25
1	Scott Fletcher	.25
2	Bobby Valentine	.25
3	Ruben Sierra	.35
6	Don Slaught	.25
9	Pete O'Brien	.25
11	Toby Harrah	.25
12	Geno Petralli	.25
15	Larry Parrish	.25
16	Mike Mason	.25
17	Darrell Porter	.25
18	Edwin Correa	.25
19	Curtis Wilkerson	.25
22	Steve Buechele	.25
23	Jose Guzman	.25
24	Ricky Wright	.25
27	Greg Harris	.25
28	Mitch Williams	.25
29	Pete Incaviglia	.50
32	Gary Ward	.25
34	Dale Mohorcic	.25
40	Jeff Russell	.25
44	Tom Paciorek	.25
46	Mike Loynd	.25
48	Bobby Witt	.25
49	Charlie Hough	.25
----	Coaching Staff (Rich Donnelly, Glenn Ezell, Tom House, Art Howe, Wayne Terwilliger)	.50
----	Trainers (Danny Wheat, Bill Ziegler)	.50
----	Rangers Coaches	

Super Star Credit Cards

Issued in 1981 by Perma-Graphics of Maryland Heights, Mo., this innovative 32-card set was printed on high-impact, permanently laminated vinyl to give the appearance of a real credit card. The front of the wallet-sized cards includes career statistics and highlights, along with an "autograph panel" for obtaining the player's signature.

		NM/M
Complete Set (32):		25.00
Common Player:		1.00
1	Johnny Bench	2.00
2	Mike Schmidt	4.00
3	George Brett	4.00
4	Carl Yastrzemski	2.00
5	Pete Rose	5.00
6	Bob Horner	1.00
7	Reggie Jackson	3.00
8	Keith Hernandez	1.00
9	George Foster	1.00
10	Garry Templeton	1.00
11	Tom Seaver	2.00
12	Steve Garvey	1.25
13	Dave Parker	1.00
14	Willie Stargell	1.50
15	Cecil Cooper	1.00
16	Steve Carlton	1.50
17	Ted Simmons	1.00
18	Dave Kingman	1.00
19	Rickey Henderson	1.50
20	Fred Lynn	1.00
21	Dave Winfield	1.50
22a	Rod Carew (Uniform #20 on back.)	2.00
22b	Rod Carew (Uniform #29 on back.)	2.00
23	Jim Rice	1.25
24	Bruce Sutter	1.00
25	Cesar Cedeno	1.00
26	Nolan Ryan	6.00
27	Dusty Baker	1.00
28	Jim Palmer	1.50
29	Gorman Thomas	1.00
30	Ben Oglivie	1.00
31	Willie Wilson	1.00
32	Gary Carter	1.50

1982 Perma-Graphics All-Star Credit Cards

Perma-Graphics issued its second "All-Star Credit Card" set in the fall of 1982. Consisting of 18 cards, the set pictured the starters from both leagues in the 1982 All-Star Game. The set was also available in a more limited "gold" version.

		NM/M
Complete Set (18):		15.00
Common Player:		1.00
Gold:		3X
1	Dennis Eckersley	1.50
2	Cecil Cooper	1.00
3	Carlton Fisk	2.00
4	Robin Yount	2.00
5	Bobby Grich	1.00
6	Rickey Henderson	2.00
7	Reggie Jackson	3.00
8	Fred Lynn	1.00
9	George Brett	4.00
10	Gary Carter	2.00
11	Dave Concepcion	1.00
12	Andre Dawson	1.25
13	Tim Raines	1.00
14	Dale Murphy	1.25
15	Steve Rogers	1.00
16	Pete Rose	5.00
17	Mike Schmidt	4.00
18	Manny Trillo	1.00

Super Star Credit Cards

Perma-Graphics reduced its "Superstar Credit Card Set" to 24 players in 1982, maintaining the same basic credit card appearance. The player photos on the front of the cards are surrounded by a wood-tone border and the backs include the usual personal data, career sta-

tistics, highlights and autograph panel. The set was also issued in a limited-edition "gold" version.

		NM/M
Complete Set (24):		25.00
Common Player:		1.00
Gold:		3X
1	Johnny Bench	2.00
2	Tom Seaver	2.00
3	Mike Schmidt	4.00
4	Gary Carter	1.50
5	Willie Stargell	1.50
6	Tim Raines	1.00
7	Bill Madlock	1.00
8	Keith Hernandez	1.00
9	Pete Rose	5.00
10	Steve Carlton	1.50
11	Steve Garvey	1.25
12	Fernando Valenzuela	1.00
13	Carl Yastrzemski	2.00
14	Dave Winfield	1.50
15	Carney Lansford	1.00
16	Rollie Fingers	1.00
17	Tony Armas	1.00
18	Cecil Cooper	1.00
19	George Brett	4.00
20	Reggie Jackson	3.00
21	Rod Carew	1.50
22	Eddie Murray	1.50
23	Rickey Henderson	1.50
24	Kirk Gibson	1.00

1983 Perma-Graphics All-Star Credit Cards

The final issue from Perma-Graphics, this 18-card set was produced in the fall of 1983 and features the 18 starting players from the 1983 All-Star Game. Similar to other Perma-Graphics sets, the cards were printed on wallet-size vinyl to give the appearance of a real credit card. The set was also available in a limited-edition "gold" version.

		NM/M
Complete Set (18):		17.50
Common Player:		1.00
Gold:		3X
1	George Brett	4.00
2	Rod Carew	2.00
3	Fred Lynn	1.00
4	Jim Rice	1.50
5	Ted Simmons	1.00
6	Dave Stieb	1.00
7	Manny Trillo	1.00
8	Dave Winfield	2.00
9	Robin Yount	2.00
10	Gary Carter	2.00
11	Andre Dawson	1.50
12	Dale Murphy	1.50
13	Al Oliver	1.00
14	Tim Raines	1.00
15	Steve Sax	1.00
16	Mike Schmidt	4.00
17	Ozzie Smith	3.00
18	Mario Soto	1.00

Super Star Credit Cards

Similar in design to its previous sets, Perma-Graphics increased the number of cards in its 1983 "Superstar" set to 36, including 18 players from each league. The front of the vinyl card has a full-color photo with the player's name, team, league and position below. The backs contain career records, highlights and autograph panel. The cards were also issued in a special "gold" version, more limited than the regular edition.

		NM/M
Complete Set (36):		25.00
Common Player:		1.00
Gold:		3X
1	Bill Buckner	1.00
2	Steve Carlton	2.00
3	Gary Carter	2.00
4	Andre Dawson	1.25
5	Pedro Guerrero	1.00
6	George Hendrick	1.00
7	Keith Hernandez	1.00
8	Bill Madlock	1.00
9	Dale Murphy	1.25
10	Al Oliver	1.00
11	Dave Parker	1.00
12	Darrell Porter	1.00
13	Pete Rose	5.00
14	Mike Schmidt	4.00
15	Lonnie Smith	1.00
16	Ozzie Smith	2.50
17	Bruce Sutter	1.50
18	Fernando Valenzuela	1.00
19	George Brett	4.00
20	Rod Carew	2.00
21	Cecil Cooper	1.00
22	Doug DeCinces	1.00
23	Rollie Fingers	1.50
24	Damaso Garcia	1.00
25	Toby Harrah	1.00
26	Rickey Henderson	2.00
27	Reggie Jackson	3.00
28	Hal McRae	1.00
29	Eddie Murray	2.00
30	Lance Parrish	1.00
31	Jim Rice	1.25
32	Gorman Thomas	1.00
33	Willie Wilson	1.00
34	Dave Winfield	2.00
35	Carl Yastrzemski	2.50
36	Robin Yount	2.00

1983 Gaylord Perry Career Highlights

Although their name does not appear anywhere on the six cards in this set, Topps was the manufacturer of this career highlights issue which was distributed by Perry's own memorabilia company. In standard 2-1/2" x 3-1/2" format, card fronts feature a color photo with various colored borders and name plates. The year of the career highlight printed on back is presented in the lower-right. Backs have a card number in a peanut and a write-up of the career accomplishment, printed in brown and orange.

		NM/M
Complete Set (6):		8.00
Common Card:		1.50
1	Gaylord Perry (First win.)	1.50
2	Gaylord Perry (No-hitter.)	1.50
3	Gaylord Perry (Cy Young Award)	1.50
4	Gaylord Perry (2,500th K)	1.50
5	Gaylord Perry (Cy Young/3,000th K)	1.50
6	Gaylord Perry (300th win)	1.50

1981 Peter Pan Bakery Discs

(See 1981 MSA/Peter Pan - Sunbeam Bakery Discs.)

1991 Petro Canada All-Star FanFest Standups

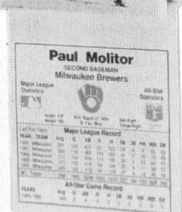

Paul Molitor — SECOND BASEMAN — Milwaukee Brewers

Petro-Canada Standups are vaguely reminiscent of the 1964 Topps Standups. The set was distributed at Fanfest in Toronto in conjunction with the All-Star Game. The folded card as issued measures 2-7/8" x 3-9/16". The card can be unfolded to reveal a die-cut action figure of the player superimposed in front of a photo of stadium surroundings. The base which the player stands on has major league and All-Star Game statistics, with career highlights on the back and a player quiz.

		NM/M
Complete Set (26):		12.50
Common Player:		.25
1	Cal Ripken, Jr.	3.00
2	Greg Olson	.25
3	Roger Clemens	2.00
4	Ryne Sandberg	1.50
5	Dave Winfield	1.00
6	Eric Davis	.25
7	Carlton Fisk	1.00
8	Mike Scott	.25
9	Sandy Alomar, Jr.	.25
10	Tim Wallach	.25
11	Cecil Fielder	.25
12	Dwight Gooden	.25
13	George Brett	2.00
14	Dale Murphy	.50
15	Paul Molitor	1.00
16	Barry Bonds	3.00
17	Kirby Puckett	1.50
18	Ozzie Smith	1.50
19	Don Mattingly	2.00
20	Will Clark	.25
21	Rickey Henderson	1.00
22	Orel Hershiser	.25
23	Ken Griffey Jr.	2.50
24	Tony Gwynn	1.50
25	Nolan Ryan	3.00
26	Kelly Gruber	.25

1998-99 Philadelphia A's Historical Society

A major undertaking by the Philadelphia A's Historical Society was the creation of this collectors card set in conjunction with the group's fourth reunion in 1998. Card designs are strongly reminiscent of the classic Topps and Bowman cards of the early 1950s.

Crash Davis — PHILADELPHIA ATHLETICS — INFIELD

Fronts have a painting of each player by Ron Joyner, noted sports artist. Backs have a cartoon, career stats with the A's and lifetime, biographical data and career highlights. Backs are printed in blue and black on white. A card of 1908-09 A's Joe Jackson has been printed in a limited edition of 500 numbered cards and is available only in those sets sold directly through the Society at its original $18.50 price. Seventy-five sets of the cards, which included a sample Joe Jackson card and a pair of large-format cards of Jimmie Foxx and Roger Cramer, were sold as uncut sheets.

		NM/M
Complete Set, W/Jackson (42):		24.00
Complete Set, No/Jackson (41):		18.50
Complete Set, uncut sheet:		60.00
Common Player:		.50
1	Connie Mack	.75
2	Sam Chapman	.50
3	Bobby Shantz	.60
4	Al Brancato	.50
5	Bob Dillinger	.50
6	Irv Hall	.50
7	Joe Hauser	.50
8	Taffy Wright	.50
9	Gus Zernial	.60
10	Ray Murray	.50
11	Skeeter Kell	.50
12	Morrie Martin	.50
13	Pete Suder	.50
14	Pinky Higgins	.50
15	Allie Clark	.50
16	Hank Wyse	.50
17	George Kell	.75
18	Hank Majeski	.50
19	Jimmie Foxx	1.00
20	Crash Davis	.50
21	Elmer Valo	.50
22	Ray Coleman	.50
23	Carl Scheib	.50
24	Billy Hitchcock	.50
25	Earle Brucker Jr.	.50
26	Dave Philley	.50
27	Joe DeMaestri	.50
28	Eddie Collins Jr.	.50
29	Eddie Joost	.50
30	Spook Jacobs	.50
31	Ferris Fain	.60
32	Eddie Robinson	.50
33	Vic Power	.60
34	Lou Brissie	.50
35	Bill Renna	.50
36	Nellie Fox	1.00
37	Lou Limmer	.50
38	Eddie Collins Sr.	1.00
39	Roger Cramer	.50
40	Joe Astroth	.50
---	Joe Jackson (# of 500)	8.00
---	Joe Jackson (Sample overprint.)	4.00
---	Roger Cramer (3-1/2" x 6")	2.00
---	Jimmie Foxx (3-1/2" x 8-1/2")	4.00
41	Bill Werber (Issued 1999)	.50

Philadelphia A's Historical Society Update

Bob Johnson — PHILADELPHIA ATHLETICS — OUTFIELD

Selected by the Society's members as "Fan Favorites" of each decade from the 1900s through the 1930s, this collectors' issue updates the group's original 1998-99 card issue. Cards are in 2-5/8" x 3-3/4" format with painted portraits on front. Black, blue and white backs have a cartoon highlight, personal data, career summary and lifetime and major league stats. The cards were also pictured on a 10-3/4" x 12-3/4" "Decades of Greatness" uncut sheet.

		NM/M
Complete Set (4):		6.00
Common Player:		2.00
Uncut Sheet:		10.00
42	Rube Oldring	2.00
43	Stuffy McInnis	2.00
44	Bing Miller	2.00
45	Bob Johnson	2.00

1985 Philadelphia Phillies Police

phillies #8 JUAN SAMUEL 2ND BASE

This is a brilliantly colored 2-5/8" x 4-1/8" set, co-sponsored by the Phillies and Cigna Corp. Card fronts include the player name, number, position and team logo. The 16 cards are numbered on the back and include biographical information and a safety tip. The cards were distributed by several Philadelphia area police departments.

		NM/M
Complete Set (16):		4.00
Common Player:		.15
1	Juan Samuel	.15
2	Von Hayes	.15
3	Ozzie Virgil	.15
4	Mike Schmidt	3.50
5	Greg Gross	.15
6	Tim Corcoran	.15
7	Jerry Koosman	.15
8	Jeff Stone	.15
9	Glenn Wilson	.15
10	Steve Jeltz	.15
11	Garry Maddox	.15
12	Steve Carlton	1.50
13	John Denny	.15
14	Kevin Gross	.15
15	Shane Rawley	.15
16	Charlie Hudson	.15

1986 Philadelphia Phillies Fire Safety

phillies #20 MIKE SCHMIDT 3RD BASE

For the second straight year, the Philadelphia Phillies issued a 16-card safety set. However, in 1986 the set was issued in conjunction with the Philadelphia Fire Department rather than the police. Cigna Corp. remained a sponsor. The cards, which measure 2-5/8" x 4-1/8" in size, feature full color photos. Along with other pertinent in-

PINNACLE — FIRST BASE — CECIL FIELDER — TIGERS

formation, the card backs contain a short player biography and a "Tips From The Dugout" fire safety hint.

		NM/M
Complete Set (16):		3.00
Common Player:		.15
1	Juan Samuel	.15
2	Don Carman	.15
3	Von Hayes	.15
4	Kent Tekulve	.15
5	Greg Gross	.15
6	Shane Rawley	.15
7	Darren Daulton	.25
8	Kevin Gross	.15
9	Steve Jeltz	.15
10	Mike Schmidt	3.00
11	Steve Bedrosian	.15
12	Gary Redus	.15
13	Charles Hudson	.15
14	John Russell	.15
15	Fred Toliver	.15
16	Glenn Wilson	.15

1989 Phoenix Holsum Super Stars Discs

(See 1989 Holsum for checklist and price guide. Distributed in Arizona.)

1992 Pinnacle

Score entered the high-end card market with the release of this 620-card set. The cards feature black borders surrounding a white frame with a full-color action photo inside. The player extends beyond the natural background. The backs are horizontal and feature a closeup photo, statistics, team logo, biographical information and career notes. Several subsets can be found within the set including "Idols, Sidelines, Grips, Shades" and "Technicians." The set was released in two 310-card series.

		NM/M
Complete Set (620):		15.00
Common Player:		.05
Foil Pack (16):		.25
Foil Box (36):		17.50
Jumbo Pack (24+3):		1.50
Jumbo Box (12):		22.50
1	Frank Thomas	.75
2	Benito Santiago	.05
3	Carlos Baerga	.05
4	Cecil Fielder	.05
5	Barry Larkin	.05
6	Ozzie Smith	1.00
7	Willie McGee	.05
8	Paul Molitor	.75
9	Andy Van Slyke	.05
10	Ryne Sandberg	1.00
11	Kevin Seitzer	.05
12	Len Dykstra	.05
13	Edgar Martinez	.05
14	Ruben Sierra	.05
15	Howard Johnson	.05
16	Dave Henderson	.05
17	Devon White	.05
18	Terry Pendleton	.05
19	Steve Finley	.05
20	Kirby Puckett	1.00
21	Orel Hershiser	.05
22	Hal Morris	.05
23	Don Mattingly	1.25
24	Delino DeShields	.05
25	Dennis Eckersley	.60
26	Ellis Burks	.05
27	Jay Buhner	.05
28	Matt Williams	.05
29	Lou Whitaker	.05
30	Alex Fernandez	.05
31	Albert Belle	.05
32	Todd Zeile	.05
33	Tony Pena	.05
34	Jay Bell	.05
35	Rafael Palmeiro	.65
36	Wes Chamberlain	.05
37	George Bell	.05
38	Robin Yount	.75
39	Vince Coleman	.05
40	Bruce Hurst	.05
41	Harold Baines	.05
42	Chuck Finley	.05
43	Ken Caminiti	.05
44	Ben McDonald	.05
45	Roberto Alomar	.15
46	Chili Davis	.05
47	Bill Doran	.05
48	Jerald Clark	.05
49	Jose Lind	.05
50	Nolan Ryan	2.00
51	Phil Plantier	.05
52	Gary DiSarcina	.05
53	Kevin Bass	.05
54	Pat Kelly	.05
55	Mark Wohlers	.05
56	Walt Weiss	.05
57	Lenny Harris	.05
58	Ivan Calderon	.05
59	Harold Reynolds	.05
60	George Brett	1.25
61	Gregg Olson	.05
62	Orlando Merced	.05
63	Steve Decker	.05
64	John Franco	.05
65	Greg Maddux	1.00
66	Alex Cole	.05
67	Dave Hollins	.05
68	Kent Hrbek	.05
69	Tom Pagnozzi	.05
70	Jeff Bagwell	.75
71	Jim Gantner	.05
72	Matt Nokes	.05
73	Brian Harper	.05
74	Andy Benes	.05
75	Tom Glavine	.35
76	Terry Steinbach	.05
77	Dennis Martinez	.05
78	John Olerud	.05
79	Ozzie Guillen	.05
80	Darryl Strawberry	.05
81	Gary Gaetti	.05
82	Dave Righetti	.05
83	Chris Hoiles	.05
84	Andujar Cedeno	.05
85	Jack Clark	.05
86	David Howard	.05
87	Bill Gullickson	.05
88	Bernard Gilkey	.05
89	Kevin Elster	.05
90	Kevin Maas	.05
91	Mark Lewis	.05
92	Greg Vaughn	.05
93	Bret Barberie	.05
94	Dave Smith	.05
95	Roger Clemens	1.25
96	Doug Drabek	.05
97	Omar Vizquel	.05
98	Jose Guzman	.05
99	Juan Samuel	.05
100	Dave Justice	.05
101	Tom Browning	.05
102	Mark Gubicza	.05
103	Mickey Morandini	.05
104	Ed Whitson	.05
105	Lance Parrish	.05
106	Scott Erickson	.05
107	Jack McDowell	.05
108	Dave Stieb	.05
109	Mike Moore	.05
110	Travis Fryman	.05
111	Dwight Gooden	.05
112	Fred McGriff	.05
113	Alan Trammell	.05
114	Roberto Kelly	.05
115	Andre Dawson	.25
116	Bill Landrum	.05
117	Brian McRae	.05
118	B.J. Surhoff	.05
119	Chuck Knoblauch	.05
120	Steve Olin	.05
121	Robin Ventura	.05
122	Will Clark	.05
123	Tino Martinez	.05
124	Dale Murphy	.25
125	Pete O'Brien	.05
126	Ray Lankford	.05
127	Juan Gonzalez	.40
128	Ron Gant	.05
129	Marquis Grissom	.05
130	Jose Canseco	.50
131	Mike Greenwell	.05
132	Mark Langston	.05
133	Brett Butler	.05
134	Kelly Gruber	.05
135	Chris Sabo	.05
136	Mark Grace	.05
137	Tony Fernandez	.05
138	Glenn Davis	.05
139	Pedro Munoz	.05
140	Craig Biggio	.05
141	Pete Schourek	.05
142	Mike Boddicker	.05
143	Robby Thompson	.05
144	Mel Hall	.05
145	Brian Harvey	.05
146	Mike LaValliere	.05
147	John Kruk	.05
148	Joe Carter	.05
149	Greg Olson	.05
150	Julio Franco	.05
151	Darryl Hamilton	.05
152	Felix Fermin	.05
153	Jose Offerman	.05
154	Paul O'Neill	.05
155	Tommy Greene	.05
156	Ivan Rodriguez	.65
157	Dave Stewart	.05
158	Jeff Reardon	.05
159	Felix Jose	.05
160	Doug Dascenzo	.05
161	Tim Wallach	.05
162	Dan Plesac	.05
163	Luis Gonzalez	.05
164	Mike Henneman	.05
165	Mike Devereaux	.05
166	Luis Polonia	.05
167	Mike Sharperson	.05
168	Chris Donnels	.05
169	Greg Harris	.05
170	Deion Sanders	.05
171	Mike Schooler	.05
172	Jose DeJesus	.05
173	Jeff Montgomery	.05
174	Milt Cuyler	.05
175	Wade Boggs	1.00
176	Kevin Tapani	.05
177	Bill Spiers	.05
178	Tim Raines	.05
179	Randy Milligan	.05
180	Rob Dibble	.05
181	Kirt Manwaring	.05
182	Pascual Perez	.05
183	Juan Guzman	.05
184	John Smiley	.05
185	David Segui	.05
186	Omar Olivares	.05
187	Joe Slusarski	.05
188	Erik Hanson	.05
189	Mark Portugal	.05
190	Walt Terrell	.05
191	John Smoltz	.05
192	Wilson Alvarez	.05
193	Jimmy Key	.05
194	Larry Walker	.05
195	Lee Smith	.05
196	Pete Harnisch	.05
197	Mike Harkey	.05
198	Frank Tanana	.05
199	Terry Mulholland	.05
200	Cal Ripken, Jr.	2.00
201	Dave Magadan	.05
202	Bud Black	.05
203	Terry Shumpert	.05
204	Mike Mussina	.40
205	Mo Vaughn	.05
206	Steve Farr	.05
207	Darrin Jackson	.05
208	Jerry Browne	.05
209	Jeff Russell	.05
210	Mike Scioscia	.05
211	Rick Aguilera	.05
212	Jaime Navarro	.05
213	Randy Tomlin	.05
214	Bobby Thigpen	.05
215	Mark Gardner	.05
216	Norm Charlton	.05
217	Mark McGwire	1.75
218	Skeeter Barnes	.05
219	Bob Tewksbury	.05
220	Junior Felix	.05
221	Sam Horn	.05
222	Jody Reed	.05
223	Luis Sojo	.05
224	Jerome Walton	.05
225	Darryl Kile	.05
226	Mickey Tettleton	.05
227	Dan Pasqua	.05
228	Jim Gott	.05
229	Bernie Williams	.05
230	Shane Mack	.05
231	Steve Avery	.05
232	Dave Valle	.05
233	Mark Leonard	.05
234	Spike Owen	.05
235	Gary Sheffield	.20
236	Steve Chitren	.05
237	Zane Smith	.05
238	Tom Gordon	.05
239	Jose Oquendo	.05
240	Todd Stottlemyre	.05
241	Darren Daulton	.05
242	Tim Naehring	.05
243	Tony Phillips	.05
244	Shawon Dunston	.05
245	Manuel Lee	.05
246	Mike Pagliarulo	.05
247	Jim Thome	.65
248	Luis Mercedes (Rookie Prospect)	.05
249	Cal Eldred (Rookie Prospect)	.05
250	Derek Bell (Rookie Prospect)	.05
251	Arthur Rhodes (Rookie Prospect)	.05
252	Scott Cooper (Rookie Prospect)	.05
253	Roberto Hernandez (Rookie Prospect)	.05
254	Mo Sanford (Rookie Prospect)	.05
255	Scott Servais (Rookie Prospect)	.05
256	Eric Karros (Rookie Prospect)	.05
257	Andy Mota (Rookie Prospect)	.05
258	Keith Mitchell (Rookie Prospect)	.05
259	Joel Johnston (Rookie Prospect)	.05
260	John Wehner (Rookie Prospect)	.05
261	Gino Minutelli (Rookie Prospect)	.05
262	Greg Gagne	.05
263	Stan Royer (Rookie Prospect)	.05

#	Player	Price
264	Carlos Garcia (Rookie Prospect)	.05
265	Andy Ashby (Rookie Prospect)	.05
266	Kim Batiste (Rookie Prospect)	.05
267	Julio Valera (Rookie Prospect)	.05
268	Royce Clayton (Rookie Prospect)	.05
269	Gary Scott (Rookie Prospect)	.05
270	Kirk Dressendorfer (Rookie Prospect)	.05
271	Sean Berry (Rookie Prospect)	.05
272	Lance Dickson (Rookie Prospect)	.05
273	Rob Maurer (Rookie Prospect)	.05
274	Scott Brosius (Rookie Prospect)	.05
275	Dave Fleming (Rookie Prospect)	.05
276	Lenny Webster (Rookie Prospect)	.05
277	Mike Humphreys	.05
278	Freddie Benavides (Rookie Prospect)	.05
279	Harvey Pulliam (Rookie Prospect)	.05
280	Jeff Carter (Rookie Prospect)	.05
281	Jim Abbott, Nolan Ryan (Idols)	.25
282	Wade Boggs, George Brett (Idols)	.25
283	Ken Griffey Jr., Rickey Henderson (Idols)	.50
284	Dale Murphy, Wally Joyner (Idols)	.10
285	Chuck Knoblauch, Ozzie Smith (Idols)	.20
286	Robin Ventura, Lou Gehrig (Idols)	.20
287	Robin Yount (Sidelines - Motocross)	.30
288	Bob Tewksbury (Sidelines - Cartoonist)	.05
289	Kirby Puckett (Sidelines - Pool Player)	.50
290	Kenny Lofton (Sidelines - Basketball Player)	.05
291	Jack McDowell (Sidelines - Guitarist)	.05
292	John Burkett (Sidelines - Bowler)	.05
293	Dwight Smith (Sidelines - Singer)	.05
294	Nolan Ryan (Sidelines - Cattle Rancher)	1.00
295	Manny Ramirez RC (1st Round Draft Pick)	2.50
296	Cliff Floyd RC (1st Round Draft Pick)	.50
297	Al Shirley RC (1st Round Draft Pick)	.05
298	Brian Barber RC (1st Round Draft Pick)	.05
299	Jon Farrell RC (1st Round Draft Pick)	.05
300	Scott Ruffcorn RC (1st Round Draft Pick)	.05
301	Tyrone Hill RC (1st Round Draft Pick)	.05
302	Benji Gil RC (1st Round Draft Pick)	.05
303	Tyler Green RC (1st Round Draft Pick)	.05
304	Allen Watson (Shades)	.05
305	Jay Buhner (Shades)	.05
306	Roberto Alomar (Shades)	.05
307	Chuck Knoblauch (Shades)	.05
308	Darryl Strawberry (Shades)	.05
309	Danny Tartabull (Shades)	.05
310	Bobby Bonilla (Shades)	.05
311	Mike Felder	.05
312	Storm Davis	.05
313	Tim Teufel	.05
314	Tom Brunansky	.05
315	Rex Hudler	.05
316	Dave Otto	.05
317	Jeff King	.05
318	Dan Gladden	.05
319	Bill Pecota	.05
320	Franklin Stubbs	.05
321	Gary Carter	.75
322	Melido Perez	.05
323	Eric Davis	.05
324	Greg Myers	.05
325	Pete Incaviglia	.05
326	Von Hayes	.05
327	Greg Swindell	.05
328	Steve Sax	.05
329	Chuck McElroy	.05
330	Gregg Jefferies	.05
331	Joe Oliver	.05
332	Paul Faries	.05
333	David West	.05
334	Craig Grebeck	.05
335	Chris Hammond	.05
336	Billy Ripken	.05
337	Scott Sanderson	.05
338	Dick Schofield	.05
339	Bob Milacki	.05
340	Kevin Reimer	.05
341	Jose DeLeon	.05
342	Henry Cotto	.05
343	Daryl Boston	.05
344	Kevin Gross	.05
345	Milt Thompson	.05
346	Luis Rivera	.05
347	Al Osuna	.05
348	Rob Deer	.05
349	Tim Leary	.05
350	Mike Stanton	.05
351	Dean Palmer	.05
352	Trevor Wilson	.05
353	Mark Eichhorn	.05
354	Scott Aldred	.05
355	Mark Whiten	.05
356	Leo Gomez	.05
357	Rafael Belliard	.05
358	Carlos Quintana	.05
359	Mark Davis	.05
360	Chris Nabholz	.05
361	Carlton Fisk	.75
362	Joe Orsulak	.05
363	Eric Anthony	.05
364	Greg Hibbard	.05
365	Scott Leius	.05
366	Hensley Meulens	.05
367	Chris Bosio	.05
368	Brian Downing	.05
369	Sammy Sosa	1.00
370	Stan Belinda	.05
371	Joe Grahe	.05
372	Luis Salazar	.05
373	Lance Johnson	.05
374	Kal Daniels	.05
375	Dave Winfield	.75
376	Brook Jacoby	.05
377	Mariano Duncan	.05
378	Ron Darling	.05
379	Randy Johnson	.75
380	Chito Martinez	.05
381	Andres Galarraga	.05
382	Willie Randolph	.05
383	Charles Nagy	.05
384	Tim Belcher	.05
385	Duane Ward	.05
386	Vicente Palacios	.05
387	Mike Gallego	.05
388	Rich DeLucia	.05
389	Scott Radinsky	.05
390	Damon Berryhill	.05
391	Kirk McCaskill	.05
392	Pedro Guerrero	.05
393	Kevin Mitchell	.05
394	Dickie Thon	.05
395	Bobby Bonilla	.05
396	Bill Wegman	.05
397	Dave Martinez	.05
398	Rick Sutcliffe	.05
399	Larry Andersen	.05
400	Tony Gwynn	1.00
401	Rickey Henderson	.75
402	Greg Cadaret	.05
403	Keith Miller	.05
404	Bip Roberts	.05
405	Kevin Brown	.05
406	Mitch Williams	.05
407	Frank Viola	.05
408	Darren Lewis	.05
409	Bob Walk	.05
410	Bob Walk	.05
411	Todd Frohwirth	.05
412	Brian Hunter	.05
413	Ron Karkovice	.05
414	Mike Morgan	.05
415	Joe Hesketh	.05
416	Don Slaught	.05
417	Tom Henke	.05
418	Kurt Stillwell	.05
419	Hector Villanueva	.05
420	Glenallen Hill	.05
421	Pat Borders	.05
422	Charlie Hough	.05
423	Charlie Leibrandt	.05
424	Eddie Murray	.75
425	Jesse Barfield	.05
426	Mark Lemke	.05
427	Kevin McReynolds	.05
428	Gilberto Reyes	.05
429	Ramon Martinez	.05
430	Steve Buechele	.05
431	David Wells	.05
432	Kyle Abbott (Rookie Prospect)	.05
433	John Habyan	.05
434	Kevin Appier	.05
435	Gene Larkin	.05
436	Sandy Alomar, Jr.	.05
437	Mike Jackson	.05
438	Todd Benzinger	.05
439	Teddy Higuera	.05
440	Reggie Sanders (Rookie Prospect)	.05
441	Mark Carreon	.05
442	Bret Saberhagen	.05
443	Gene Nelson	.05
444	Jay Howell	.05
445	Roger McDowell	.05
446	Sid Bream	.05
447	Mackey Sasser	.05
448	Bill Swift	.05
449	Hubie Brooks	.05
450	David Cone	.05
451	Bobby Witt	.05
452	Brady Anderson	.05
453	Lee Stevens	.05
454	Luis Aquino	.05
455	Carney Lansford	.05
456	Carlos Hernandez (Rookie Prospect)	.05
457	Danny Jackson	.05
458	Gerald Young	.05
459	Tom Candiotti	.05
460	Billy Hatcher	.05
461	John Wetteland	.05
462	Mike Bordick	.05
463	Don Robinson	.05
464	Jeff Johnson	.05
465	Lonnie Smith	.05
466	Paul Assenmacher	.05
467	Alvin Davis	.05
468	Jim Eisenreich	.05
469	Brent Mayne	.05
470	Jeff Brantley	.05
471	Tim Burke	.05
472	Pat Mahomes RC (Rookie Prospect)	.05
473	Ryan Bowen	.05
474	Bryn Smith	.05
475	Mike Flanagan	.05
476	Reggie Jefferson (Rookie Prospect)	.05
477	Jeff Blauser	.05
478	Craig Lefferts	.05
479	Todd Worrell	.05
480	Scott Scudder	.05
481	Kirk Gibson	.05
482	Kenny Rogers	.05
483	Jack Morris	.05
484	Russ Swan	.05
485	Mike Huff	.05
486	Ken Hill	.05
487	Geronimo Pena	.05
488	Charlie O'Brien	.05
489	Mike Maddux	.05
490	Scott Livingstone (Rookie Prospect)	.05
491	Carl Willis	.05
492	Kelly Downs	.05
493	Dennis Cook	.05
494	Joe Magrane	.05
495	Bob Kipper	.05
496	Jose Mesa	.05
497	Charlie Hayes	.05
498	Joe Girardi	.05
499	Doug Jones	.05
500	Barry Bonds	2.00
501	Bill Krueger	.05
502	Glenn Braggs	.05
503	Eric King	.05
504	Frank Castillo	.05
505	Mike Gardiner	.05
506	Cory Snyder	.05
507	Steve Howe	.05
508	Jose Rijo	.05
509	Sid Fernandez	.05
510	Archi Cianfrocco RC (Rookie Prospect)	.05
511	Mark Guthrie	.05
512	Bob Ojeda	.05
513	John Doherty (Rookie Prospect)	.05
514	Dante Bichette	.05
515	Juan Berenguer	.05
516	Jeff Robinson	.05
517	Mike MacFarlane	.05
518	Matt Young	.05
519	Otis Nixon	.05
520	Brian Holman	.05
521	Chris Haney	.05
522	Jeff Kent RC (Rookie Prospect)	.75
523	Chad Curtis RC (Rookie Prospect)	.25
524	Vince Horsman	.05
525	Rod Nichols	.05
526	Peter Hoy RC (Rookie Prospect)	.05
527	Shawn Boskie	.05
528	Alejandro Pena	.05
529	Dave Burba (Rookie Prospect)	.05
530	Ricky Jordan	.05
531	David Silvestri (Rookie Prospect)	.05
532	John Patterson	.05
533	Jeff Branson (Rookie Prospect)	.05
534	Derrick May (Rookie Prospect)	.05
535	Esteban Beltre (Rookie Prospect)	.05
536	Jose Melendez	.05
537	Wally Joyner	.05
538	Eddie Taubensee (Rookie Prospect)	.05
539	Jim Abbott	.05
540	Brian Williams RC (Rookie Prospect)	.05
541	Donovan Osborne (Rookie Prospect)	.05
542	Patrick Lennon (Rookie Prospect)	.05
543	Mike Groppuso RC (Rookie Prospect)	.05
544	Jarvis Brown (Rookie Prospect)	.05
545	Shawn Livesy RC (1st Round Draft Pick)	.05
546	Jeff Ware (1st Round Draft Pick)	.05
547	Danny Tartabull	.05
548	Bobby Jones RC (1st Round Draft Pick)	.05
549	Ken Griffey Jr.	1.50
550	Rey Sanchez RC (Rookie Prospect)	.05
551	Pedro Astacio RC (Rookie Prospect)	.10
552	Juan Guerrero RC (Rookie Prospect)	.05
553	Jacob Brumfield RC (Rookie Prospect)	.05
554	Ben Rivera RC (Rookie Prospect)	.05
555	Brian Jordan RC (Rookie Prospect)	.40
556	Denny Neagle (Rookie Prospect)	.05
557	Cliff Brantley (Rookie Prospect)	.05
558	Anthony Young (Rookie Prospect)	.05
559	John VanderWal RC (Rookie Prospect)	.05
560	Monty Fariss RC (Rookie Prospect)	.05
561	Russ Springer RC (Rookie Prospect)	.05
562	Pat Listach RC (Rookie Prospect)	.05
563	Pat Hentgen (Rookie Prospect)	.05
564	Andy Stankiewicz (Rookie Prospect)	.05
565	Mike Perez (Rookie Prospect)	.05
566	Mike Bielecki	.05
567	Butch Henry (Rookie Prospect)	.05
568	Dave Nilsson RC (Rookie Prospect)	.05
569	Scott Hatteberg RC (Rookie Prospect)	.05
570	Ruben Amaro Jr. (Rookie Prospect)	.05
571	Todd Hundley (Rookie Prospect)	.05
572	Moises Alou (Rookie Prospect)	.05
573	Hector Fajardo (Rookie Prospect)	.05
574	Todd Van Poppel (Rookie Prospect)	.05
575	Willie Banks (Rookie Prospect)	.05
576	Bob Zupcic (Rookie Prospect)	.05
577	J.J. Johnson RC (1st Round Draft Pick)	.05
578	John Burkett	.05
579	Trever Miller (1st Round Draft Pick)	.05
580	Scott Bankhead	.05
581	Rich Amaral	.05
582	Kenny Lofton (Rookie Prospect)	.05
583	Matt Stairs (Rookie Prospect)	.05
584	Don Mattingly, Rod Carew (Idols)	.25
585	Jack Morris, Steve Avery (Idols)	.05
586	Roberto Alomar, Sandy Alomar (Idols)	.10
587	Scott Sanderson, Catfish Hunter (Idols)	.05
588	Dave Justice, Willie Stargell (Idols)	.05
589	Rex Hudler, Roger Staubach (Idols)	.05
590	David Cone, Jackie Gleason (Idols)	.05
591	Willie Davis, Tony Gwynn (Idols)	.15
592	Orel Hershiser (Sidelines)	.05
593	John Wetteland (Sidelines)	.05
594	Tom Glavine (Sidelines)	.05
595	Randy Johnson (Sidelines)	.25
596	Jim Gott (Sidelines)	.05
597	Donald Harris	.05
598	Shawn Hare RC	.05
599	Chris Gardner	.05
600	Rusty Meacham	.05
601	Benito Santiago (Shades)	.05
602	Eric Davis (Shades)	.05
603	Jose Lind (Shades)	.05
604	Dave Justice (Shades)	.05
605	Tim Raines (Shades)	.05
606	Randy Tomlin (Grips)	.05
607	Jack McDowell (Grips)	.05
608	Greg Maddux (Grips)	.30
609	Charles Nagy (Grips)	.05
610	Tom Candiotti (Grips)	.05
611	David Cone (Grips)	.05
612	Steve Avery (Grips)	.05
613	Rod Beck RC	.10
614	Rickey Henderson (Technician)	.25
615	Benito Santiago (Technician)	.05
616	Ruben Sierra (Technician)	.05
617	Ryne Sandberg (Technician)	.05
618	Nolan Ryan (Technician)	1.00
619	Brett Butler (Technician)	.05
620	Dave Justice (Technician)	.05

Rookie Idols

Carrying on with the Idols subset theme in the regular issue, these Series 2 foil-pack inserts feature 18 young prospects sharing cards with their baseball heroes. Both front and back are horizontal in format and include photos of both the rookie and his idol.

		NM/M
Complete Set (18):		20.00
Common Player:		.50
1	Reggie Sanders, Eric Davis	.50
2	Hector Fajardo, Jim Abbott	.50
3	Gary Cooper, George Brett	3.50
4	Mark Wohlers, Roger Clemens	3.50
5	Luis Mercedes, Julio Franco	.50
6	Willie Banks, Dwight Gooden	.50
7	Kenny Lofton, Rickey Henderson	1.50
8	Keith Mitchell, Dave Henderson	.50
9	Kim Batiste, Barry Larkin	.50
10	Thurman Munson, Todd Hundley	1.00
11	Eddie Zosky, Cal Ripken Jr.	4.50
12	Todd Van Poppel, Nolan Ryan	4.50
13	Ryne Sandberg, Jim Thome	2.50
14	Dave Fleming, Bobby Murcer	.50
15	Royce Clayton, Ozzie Smith	2.50
16	Don Harris, Darryl Strawberry	.50
17	Alan Trammell, Chad Curtis	.50
18	Derek Bell, Dave Winfield	1.50

Rookies

Pat Listach — 1992 Rookie

Styled after the regular 1992 Pinnacle cards, this 30-card boxed set features the year's top rookies. The cards have a game-action photo which is borderless on the top and sides. Beneath the photo a team color-coded strip carries the player's name in gold foil, with a gold-bordered team logo at left. A black strip at bottom has the notation "1992 Rookie." Horizontal backs follow a similar design and include a bit of player information, Pinnacle's anti-counterfeiting strip and some gold-foil enhancements.

		NM/M
Complete Set (30):		2.00
Common Player:		.05
1	Luis Mercedes	.05
2	Scott Cooper	.05
3	Kenny Lofton	.25
4	John Doherty	.05
5	Pat Listach	.05
6	Andy Stankiewicz	.05
7	Derek Bell	.25
8	Gary DiSarcina	.05
9	Roberto Hernandez	.15
10	Joel Johnston	.05
11	Pat Mahomes	.05
12	Todd Van Poppel	.05
13	Dave Fleming	.05
14	Monty Fariss	.05
15	Gary Scott	.05
16	Moises Alou	.25
17	Todd Hundley	.25
18	Kim Batiste	.05
19	Denny Neagle	.05
20	Donovan Osborne	.05
21	Mark Wohlers	.05
22	Reggie Sanders	.10
23	Brian Williams	.05
24	Eric Karros	.25
25	Frank Seminara	.05
26	Royce Clayton	.05
27	Dave Nilsson	.05
28	Matt Stairs	.25
29	Chad Curtis	.25
30	Carlos Hernandez	.25

Slugfest

Ron Gant — Slugfest

Each specially marked Slugfest jumbo pack of '92 Pinnacle contained one of these horizontal-format cards of the game's top hitters. The player's name is printed in gold foil at the bottom of the card, along with a red and white Slugfest logo. Backs, which are vertical, have a color player photo, a career summary and a few lifetime stats.

		NM/M
Complete Set (15):		15.00
Common Player:		.30
1	Cecil Fielder	.30
2	Mark McGwire	2.50
3	Jose Canseco	.65
4	Barry Bonds	3.00
5	Dave Justice	.30
6	Bobby Bonilla	.30
7	Ken Griffey Jr.	2.00
8	Ron Gant	.30
9	Ryne Sandberg	1.50
10	Ruben Sierra	.30
11	Frank Thomas	1.00
12	Will Clark	.30
13	Kirby Puckett	1.50
14	Cal Ripken, Jr.	3.00
15	Jeff Bagwell	1.00

Team Pinnacle

Justice • RF — 10 of 12

The most sought-after of the 1992 Pinnacle inserts is this 12-piece set of "two-headed" cards. An American and a National League superstar at each position are featured on each card, with two cards each for starting and relief pitchers. The ultra-realistic artwork of Chris Greco is featured on the cards, which were inserted into Series 1 foil packs.

		NM/M
Complete Set (12):		40.00
Common Player:		1.50
1	Roger Clemens, Ramon Martinez	8.00
2	Jim Abbott, Steve Avery	1.50
3	Benito Santiago, Ivan Rodriguez	3.00
4	Frank Thomas, Will Clark	3.00
5	Roberto Alomar, Ryne Sandberg	6.00
6	Robin Ventura, Matt Williams	1.50
7	Cal Ripken, Jr., Barry Larkin	10.00
8	Danny Tartabull, Barry Bonds	8.00
9	Brett Butler, Ken Griffey Jr.	8.00
10	Ruben Sierra, Dave Justice	1.50
11	Dennis Eckersley, Rob Dibble	1.50
12	Scott Radinsky, John Franco	1.50

Team 2000

Young stars projected to be the superstars of the 2000 season were chosen for this insert set found three at a time in jumbo packs. Cards #1-40 were included in Series 1 packaging, while cards #41-80 were inserted with Series 2 Pinnacle. Cards feature gold foil highlights on both front and back.

		NM/M
Complete Set (80):		3.00
Common Player:		.05
1	Mike Mussina	.30
2	Phil Plantier	.05
3	Frank Thomas	.50
4	Travis Fryman	.05
5	Kevin Appier	.05
6	Chuck Knoblauch	.05
7	Pat Kelly	.05
8	Ivan Rodriguez	.40
9	Dave Justice	.05
10	Jeff Bagwell	.50
11	Marquis Grissom	.05
12	Andy Benes	.05
13	Gregg Olson	.05
14	Kevin Morton	.05
15	Tim Naehring	.05
16	Dave Hollins	.05
17	Sandy Alomar Jr.	.05
18	Albert Belle	.05
19	Charles Nagy	.05
20	Brian McRae	.05
21	Larry Walker	.05
22	Delino DeShields	.05
23	Jeff Johnson	.05
24	Bernie Williams	.05
25	Jose Offerman	.05
26	Juan Gonzalez	.25
27	Juan Guzman	.05
28	Eric Anthony	.05
29	Brian Hunter	.05
30	Jim Smoltz	.05
31	Deion Sanders	.05
32	Greg Maddux	.75
33	Andujar Cedeno	.05
34	Royce Clayton	.05
35	Kenny Lofton	.05
36	Cal Eldred	.05
37	Jim Thome	.50
38	Gary DiSarcina	.05
39	Brian Jordan	.05
40	Chad Curtis	.05
41	Ben McDonald	.05
42	Jim Abbott	.05
43	Robin Ventura	.05
44	Milt Cuyler	.05
45	Gregg Jefferies	.05
46	Scott Radinsky	.05
47	Ken Griffey Jr.	1.00
48	Roberto Alomar	.15
49	Ramon Martinez	.05
50	Bret Barberie	.05
51	Ray Lankford	.05
52	Leo Gomez	.05
53	Tommy Greene	.05
54	Mo Vaughn	.05
55	Sammy Sosa	.75
56	Carlos Baerga	.05
57	Mark Lewis	.05
58	Tom Gordon	.05
59	Gary Sheffield	.25
60	Scott Erickson	.05
61	Pedro Munoz	.05
62	Tino Martinez	.05
63	Darren Lewis	.05
64	Dean Palmer	.05
65	John Olerud	.05
66	Steve Avery	.05
67	Pete Harnisch	.05
68	Luis Gonzalez	.05
69	Kim Batiste	.05
70	Reggie Sanders	.05
71	Luis Mercedes	.05
72	Todd Van Poppel	.05
73	Gary Scott	.05
74	Monty Fariss	.05
75	Kyle Abbott	.05
76	Eric Karros	.05
77	Mo Vaughn	.05
78	Todd Hundley	.05
79	Reggie Jefferson	.05
80	Pat Mahomes	.05

Mickey Mantle

This boxed set highlighting the career of Mickey Mantle was issued in a reported edition of 180,000 sets. Fronts and backs feature an assortment of black-and-white, color and colorized photos. Fronts have gold-foil stamped highlights. Card backs have a few sentences about Mantle's life or career.

		NM/M
Complete Set (30):		20.00
Common Card:		1.00
1	Father and Son	1.00
2	High School	1.00
3	Commerce Comet	1.00
4	Spring Training	1.00
5	The Beginning	1.00
6	No. 6	1.00
7	The Rookie	1.00
8	Tape-Measure Shots	1.00
9	Shortstop	1.00
10	Outfield	1.00
11	Speed, Speed, Speed	1.00
12	Contracts	1.00
13	Three-time MVP	1.00
14	Triple Crown	1.00
15	Series Slam	1.00
16	Series Star	1.00
17	Switch Hitter	1.00
18	Fan Favorite	1.00
19	Milestones	1.00
20	Enthuiasm	1.00
21	Hitting	1.00
22	First Base	1.00
23	Courage	1.00
24	Mick & Stan (Musial)	1.00
25	Whitey & Yogi (Ford, Berra)	1.00
26	Mick & Billy (Martin)	1.00
27	Mick & Casey (Stengel)	1.00
28	Awards	1.00
29	Retirement	1.00
30	Cooperstown	1.00

1993 Pinnacle Promos

On six of the eight cards issued to premiere Pinnacle's '93 set, the difference between the promo version and the issued version is so slight it can easily go unnoticed - the "TM" in the upper-right corner on front is larger on the promo than on the regular card. Promo cards #3 and 5 are easier to spot because the team logos on back of the promos are the old Expos and Mariners logos, rather than the new versions found on issued cards.

		NM/M
Complete Set (8):		10.00
Common Player:		1.25
1	Gary Sheffield	3.00
2	Cal Eldred	1.25
3	Larry Walker	1.25
4	Deion Sanders	1.50
5	Dave Fleming	1.25
6	Carlos Baerga	1.25
7	Bernie Williams	1.25
8	John Kruk	1.25

1993 Pinnacle

This set offers many of the same features which made the debut Pinnacle set so popular in 1992. Subsets are titled Rookies, Now & Then (which shows the player as he looked as a rookie and in 1993), Idols (active players and their heroes on the same card), Hometown Heroes (players who are playing with their hometown team), Draft Picks and Rookies. More than 100 rookies and 10 draft picks are featured. All regular cards have an action photo, a black border and the Pinnacle name in gold foil. Series 1 cards feature portraits of players on the two new expansion teams; Series 2 cards feature action shots of them. Team Pinnacle insert cards returned, while Rookie Team Pinnacle cards made their debut. Other insert sets are titled Team 2001, Slugfest and Tribute, which features five cards each of Nolan Ryan and George Brett.

		NM/M
Complete Set (620):		17.50
Common Player:		.05
Series 1 Pack (15):		.35
Series 1 Box (36):		8.00
Series 2 Pack (15):		.75
Series 2 Box (36):		20.00
1	Gary Sheffield	.30
2	Cal Eldred	.05
3	Larry Walker	.05
4	Deion Sanders	.05
5	Dave Fleming	.05
6	Carlos Baerga	.05
7	Bernie Williams	.05
8	John Kruk	.05
9	Jimmy Key	.05
10	Jeff Bagwell	.60
11	Jim Abbott	.05
12	Terry Steinbach	.05
13	Bob Tewksbury	.05
14	Eric Karros	.05
15	Ryne Sandberg	.75
16	Will Clark	.05
17	Edgar Martinez	.05
18	Eddie Murray	.60
19	Andy Van Slyke	.05
20	Cal Ripken, Jr.	2.00
21	Ivan Rodriguez	.50
22	Barry Larkin	.05
23	Don Mattingly	.85
24	Gregg Jefferies	.05
25	Roger Clemens	.85
26	Cecil Fielder	.05
27	Kent Hrbek	.05
28	Robin Ventura	.05
29	Rickey Henderson	.60
30	Roberto Alomar	.15
31	Luis Polonia	.05
32	Andujar Cedeno	.05
33	Pat Listach	.05
34	Mark Grace	.05
35	Otis Nixon	.05
36	Felix Jose	.05
37	Mike Sharperson	.05
38	Dennis Martinez	.05
39	Willie McGee	.05
40	Kenny Lofton	.05
41	Randy Johnson	.60
42	Andy Benes	.05
43	Bobby Bonilla	.50
44	Mike Mussina	.50
45	Len Dykstra	.05
46	Ellis Burks	.05
47	Chris Sabo	.05
48	Jay Bell	.05
49	Jose Canseco	.40
50	Craig Biggio	.05
51	Wally Joyner	.05
52	Mickey Tettleton	.05
53	Tim Raines	.05
54	Brian Harper	.05
55	Rene Gonzales	.05
56	Mark Langston	.05
57	Jack Morris	.05
58	Mark McGwire	1.50
59	Ken Caminiti	.05
60	Terry Pendleton	.05

61	Dave Nilsson	.05
62	Tom Pagnozzi	.05
63	Mike Morgan	.05
64	Darryl Strawberry	.05
65	Charles Nagy	.05
66	Ken Hill	.05
67	Matt Williams	.05
68	Jay Buhner	.05
69	Vince Coleman	.05
70	Brady Anderson	.05
71	Fred McGriff	.05
72	Ben McDonald	.05
73	Terry Mulholland	.05
74	Randy Tomlin	.05
75	Nolan Ryan	2.00
76	Frank Viola	.05
77	Jose Rijo	.05
78	Shane Mack	.05
79	Travis Fryman	.05
80	Jack McDowell	.05
81	Mark Gubicza	.05
82	Matt Nokes	.05
83	Bert Blyleven	.05
84	Eric Anthony	.05
85	Mike Bordick	.05
86	John Olerud	.05
87	B.J. Surhoff	.05
88	Bernard Gilkey	.05
89	Shawon Dunston	.05
90	Tom Glavine	.30
91	Brett Butler	.05
92	Moises Alou	.05
93	Albert Belle	.05
94	Darren Lewis	.05
95	Omar Vizquel	.05
96	Dwight Gooden	.05
97	Gregg Olson	.05
98	Tony Gwynn	.75
99	Darren Daulton	.05
100	Dennis Eckersley	.50
101	Rob Dibble	.05
102	Mike Greenwell	.05
103	Jose Lind	.05
104	Julio Franco	.05
105	Tom Gordon	.05
106	Scott Livingstone	.05
107	Chuck Knoblauch	.05
108	Frank Thomas	.60
109	Melido Perez	.05
110	Ken Griffey Jr.	1.00
111	Harold Baines	.05
112	Gary Gaetti	.05
113	Pete Harnisch	.05
114	David Wells	.05
115	Charlie Leibrandt	.05
116	Ray Lankford	.05
117	Kevin Seitzer	.05
118	Robin Yount	.60
119	Lenny Harris	.05
120	Chris James	.05
121	Delino DeShields	.05
122	Kirt Manwaring	.05
123	Glenallen Hill	.05
124	Hensley Meulens	.05
125	Darrin Jackson	.05
126	Todd Hundley	.05
127	Dave Hollins	.05
128	Sam Horn	.05
129	Roberto Hernandez	.05
130	Vicente Palacios	.05
131	George Brett	.85
132	Dave Martinez	.05
133	Kevin Appier	.05
134	Pat Kelly	.05
135	Pedro Munoz	.05
136	Mark Carreon	.05
137	Lance Johnson	.05
138	Devon White	.05
139	Julio Valera	.05
140	Eddie Taubensee	.05
141	Willie Wilson	.05
142	Stan Belinda	.05
143	John Smoltz	.05
144	Darryl Hamilton	.05
145	Sammy Sosa	.75
146	Carlos Hernandez	.05
147	Tom Candiotti	.05
148	Mike Felder	.05
149	Rusty Meacham	.05
150	Ivan Calderon	.05
151	Pete O'Brien	.05
152	Erik Hanson	.05
153	Billy Ripken	.05
154	Kurt Stillwell	.05
155	Jeff Kent	.05
156	Mickey Morandini	.05
157	Randy Milligan	.05
158	Reggie Sanders	.05
159	Luis Rivera	.05
160	Orlando Merced	.05
161	Dean Palmer	.05
162	Mike Perez	.05
163	Scott Erickson	.05
164	Kevin McReynolds	.05
165	Kevin Maas	.05
166	Ozzie Guillen	.05
167	Rob Deer	.05
168	Danny Tartabull	.05
169	Lee Stevens	.05
170	Dave Henderson	.05
171	Derek Bell	.05
172	Steve Finley	.05
173	Greg Olson	.05
174	Geronimo Pena	.05
175	Paul Quantrill	.05
176	Steve Buechele	.05
177	Kevin Gross	.05
178	Tim Wallach	.05

179	Dave Valle	.05
180	Dave Silvestri	.05
181	Bud Black	.05
182	Henry Rodriguez	.05
183	Tim Teufel	.05
184	Mark McLemore	.05
185	Bret Saberhagen	.05
186	Chris Hoiles	.05
187	Ricky Jordan	.05
188	Don Slaught	.05
189	Mo Vaughn	.05
190	Joe Oliver	.05
191	Juan Gonzalez	.30
192	Scott Leius	.05
193	Milt Cuyler	.05
194	Chris Haney	.05
195	Ron Karkovice	.05
196	Steve Farr	.05
197	John Orton	.05
198	Kelly Gruber	.05
199	Ron Darling	.05
200	Ruben Sierra	.05
201	Chuck Finley	.05
202	Mike Moore	.05
203	Pat Borders	.05
204	Sid Bream	.05
205	Todd Zeile	.05
206	Rick Wilkins	.05
207	Jim Gantner	.05
208	Frank Castillo	.05
209	Dave Hansen	.05
210	Trevor Wilson	.05
211	Sandy Alomar, Jr.	.05
212	Sean Berry	.05
213	Tino Martinez	.05
214	Chito Martinez	.05
215	Dan Walters	.05
216	John Franco	.05
217	Glenn Davis	.05
218	Mariano Duncan	.05
219	Mike LaValliere	.05
220	Rafael Palmeiro	.50
221	Jack Clark	.05
222	Hal Morris	.05
223	Ed Sprague	.05
224	John Valentin	.05
225	Sam Militello	.05
226	Bob Wickman	.05
227	Damion Easley	.05
228	John Jaha	.05
229	Bob Ayrault	.05
230	Mo Sanford/ED	.05
231	Walt Weiss/ED	.05
232	Dante Bichette/ED	.05
233	Steve Decker/ED	.05
234	Jerald Clark/ED	.05
235	Bryan Harvey/ED	.05
236	Joe Girardi/ED	.05
237	Dave Magadan/ED	.05
238	David Nied (Rookie Prospect)	.05
239	Eric Wedge RC (Rookie Prospect)	.05
240	Rico Brogna (Rookie Prospect)	.05
241	J.T. Bruett (Rookie Prospect)	.05
242	Jonathan Hurst (Rookie Prospect)	.05
243	Bret Boone (Rookie Prospect)	.05
244	Manny Alexander (Rookie Prospect)	.05
245	Scooter Tucker (Rookie Prospect)	.05
246	Troy Neel (Rookie Prospect)	.05
247	Eddie Zosky (Rookie Prospect)	.05
248	Melvin Nieves (Rookie Prospect)	.05
249	Ryan Thompson (Rookie Prospect)	.05
250	Shawn Barton (Rookie Prospect)	.05
251	Ryan Klesko (Rookie Prospect)	.05
252	Mike Piazza (Rookie Prospect)	1.00
253	Steve Hosey (Rookie Prospect)	.05
254	Shane Reynolds (Rookie Prospect)	.05
255	Dan Wilson (Rookie Prospect)	.05
256	Tom Marsh (Rookie Prospect)	.05
257	Barry Manuel (Rookie Prospect)	.05
258	Paul Miller (Rookie Prospect)	.05
259	Pedro Martinez (Rookie Prospect)	.60
260	Steve Cooke (Rookie Prospect)	.05
261	Johnny Guzman (Rookie Prospect)	.05
262	Mike Butcher (Rookie Prospect)	.05
263	Bien Figueroa (Rookie Prospect)	.05
264	Rich Rowland (Rookie Prospect)	.05
265	Shawn Jeter (Rookie Prospect)	.05
266	Gerald Williams (Rookie Prospect)	.05

267	Derek Parks (Rookie Prospect)	.05
268	Henry Mercedes (Rookie Prospect)	.05
269	David Hulse RC (Rookie Prospect)	.05
270	Tim Pugh RC (Rookie Prospect)	.05
271	William Suero (Rookie Prospect)	.05
272	Ozzie Canseco (Rookie Prospect)	.05
273	Fernando Ramsey (Rookie Prospect)	.05
274	Bernardo Brito (Rookie Prospect)	.05
275	Dave Mlicki (Rookie Prospect)	.05
276	Tim Salmon (Rookie Prospect)	.05
277	Mike Raczka (Rookie Prospect)	.05
278	Ken Ryan RC (Rookie Prospect)	.05
279	Rafael Bournigal (Rookie Prospect)	.05
280	Wil Cordero (Rookie Prospect)	.05
281	Billy Ashley (Rookie Prospect)	.05
282	Paul Wagner (Rookie Prospect)	.05
283	Blas Minor (Rookie Prospect)	.05
284	Rick Trlicek (Rookie Prospect)	.05
285	Willie Greene (Rookie Prospect)	.05
286	Ted Wood (Rookie Prospect)	.05
287	Phil Clark (Rookie Prospect)	.05
288	Jesse Levis (Rookie Prospect)	.05
289	Tony Gwynn (Now & The n)	.40
290	Nolan Ryan (Now & Then)	1.00
291	Dennis Martinez (Now & Then)	.05
292	Eddie Murray (Now & Then)	.30
293	Robin Yount (Now & Then)	.30
294	George Brett (Now & Then)	.45
295	Dave Winfield (Now & Then)	.30
296	Bert Blyleven (Now & Then)	.05
297	Jeff Bagwell (Idols - Carl Yastrzemski)	.30
298	John Smoltz (Idols - Jack Morris)	.05
299	Larry Walker (Idols - Mike Bossy)	.05
300	Gary Sheffield (Idols - Barry Larkin)	.15
301	Ivan Rodriguez (Idols - Carlton Fisk)	.30
302	Delino DeShields (Idols - Malcolm X)	.05
303	Tim Salmon (Idols - Dwight Evans)	.05
304	Bernard Gilkey (Hometown Heroes)	.05
305	Cal Ripken, Jr. (Hometown Heroes)	1.00
306	Barry Larkin (Hometown Heroes)	.05
307	Kent Hrbek (Hometown Heroes)	.05
308	Rickey Henderson (Hometown Heroes)	.30
309	Darryl Strawberry (Hometown Heroes)	.05
310	John Franco (Hometown Heroes)	.05
311	Todd Stottlemyre	.05
312	Luis Gonzalez	.05
313	Tommy Greene	.05
314	Randy Velarde	.05
315	Steve Avery	.05
316	Jose Oquendo	.05
317	Rey Sanchez	.05
318	Greg Vaughn	.05
319	Orel Hershiser	.05
320	Paul Sorrento	.05
321	Royce Clayton	.05
322	John Vander Wal	.05
323	Henry Cotto	.05
324	Pete Schourek	.05
325	David Segui	.05
326	Arthur Rhodes	.05
327	Bruce Hurst	.05
328	Wes Chamberlain	.05
329	Ozzie Smith	.75
330	Scott Cooper	.05
331	Felix Fermin	.05
332	Mike Macfarlane	.05
333	Dan Gladden	.05
334	Kevin Tapani	.05
335	Steve Sax	.05
336	Jeff Montgomery	.05
337	Gary DiSarcina	.05
338	Lance Blankenship	.05
339	Brian Williams	.05
340	Duane Ward	.05

341	Chuck McElroy	.05
342	Joe Magrane	.05
343	Jaime Navarro	.05
344	Dave Justice	.05
345	Jose Offerman	.05
346	Marquis Grissom	.05
347	Bill Swift	.05
348	Jim Thome	.50
349	Archi Cianfrocco	.05
350	Anthony Young	.05
351	Leo Gomez	.05
352	Bill Gullickson	.05
353	Alan Trammell	.05
354	Dan Pasqua	.05
355	Jeff King	.05
356	Kevin Brown	.05
357	Tim Belcher	.05
358	Bip Roberts	.05
359	Brent Mayne	.05
360	Rheal Cormier	.05
361	Mark Guthrie	.05
362	Craig Grebeck	.05
363	Andy Stankiewicz	.05
364	Juan Guzman	.05
365	Bobby Witt	.05
366	Mark Portugal	.05
367	Brian McRae	.05
368	Mark Lemke	.05
369	Bill Wegman	.05
370	Donovan Osborne	.05
371	Derrick May	.05
372	Carl Willis	.05
373	Chris Nabholz	.05
374	Mark Lewis	.05
375	John Burkett	.05
376	Luis Mercedes	.05
377	Ramon Martinez	.05
378	Kyle Abbott	.05
379	Mark Wohlers	.05
380	Bob Walk	.05
381	Kenny Rogers	.05
382	Tim Naehring	.05
383	Alex Fernandez	.05
384	Keith Miller	.05
385	Mike Henneman	.05
386	Rick Aguilera	.05
387	George Bell	.05
388	Mike Gallego	.05
389	Howard Johnson	.05
390	Kim Batiste	.05
391	Jerry Browne	.05
392	Damon Berryhill	.05
393	Ricky Bones	.05
394	Omar Olivares	.05
395	Mike Harkey	.05
396	Pedro Astacio	.05
397	John Wetteland	.05
398	Rod Beck	.05
399	Thomas Howard	.05
400	Mike Devereaux	.05
401	Tim Wakefield	.05
402	Curt Schilling	.30
403	Zane Smith	.05
404	Bob Zupcic	.05
405	Tom Browning	.05
406	Tony Phillips	.05
407	John Doherty	.05
408	Pat Mahomes	.05
409	John Habyan	.05
410	Steve Olin	.05
411	Chad Curtis	.05
412	Joe Grahe	.05
413	John Patterson	.25
414	Brian Hunter	.05
415	Doug Henry	.05
416	Lee Smith	.05
417	Bob Scanlan	.05
418	Kent Mercker	.05
419	Mel Rojas	.05
420	Mark Whiten	.05
421	Carlton Fisk	.60
422	Candy Maldonado	.05
423	Doug Drabek	.05
424	Wade Boggs	.75
425	Mark Davis	.05
426	Kirby Puckett	.75
427	Joe Carter	.25
428	Paul Molitor	.60
429	Eric Davis	.05
430	Darryl Kile	.05
431	Jeff Parrett/ED	.05
432	Jeff Blauser	.05
433	Dan Plesac	.05
434	Andres Galarraga/ED	.05
435	Jim Gott	.05
436	Jose Mesa	.05
437	Ben Rivera	.05
438	Dave Winfield	.60
439	Norm Charlton	.05
440	Chris Bosio	.05
441	Wilson Alvarez	.05
442	Dave Stewart	.05
443	Doug Jones	.05
444	Jeff Russell	.05
445	Ron Gant	.05
446	Paul O'Neill	.05
447	Charlie Hayes/ED	.05
448	Joe Hesketh	.05
449	Chris Hammond	.05
450	Hipolito Pichardo	.05
451	Scott Radinsky	.05
452	Bobby Thigpen	.05
453	Xavier Hernandez	.05
454	Lonnie Smith	.05
455	Jamie Arnold **RC**	
	(1st Draft Pick)	.05
456	B.J. Wallace	
	(1st Draft Pick)	.05

457	Derek Jeter **RC**	
	(Rookie Prospect)	10.00
458	Jason Kendall **RC**	
	(Rookie Prospect)	.75
459	Rick Helling	
	(Rookie Prospect)	.05
460	Derek Wallace **RC**	
	(Rookie Prospect)	.05
461	Sean Lowe **RC**	
	(Rookie Prospect)	.05
462	Shannon Stewart **RC**	
	(Rookie Prospect)	.60
463	Benji Grigsby **RC**	
	(Rookie Prospect)	.05
464	Todd Steverson **RC**	
	(Rookie Prospect)	.05
465	Dan Serafini **RC**	
	(Rookie Prospect)	.05
466	Michael Tucker	
	(Rookie Prospect)	.05
467	Chris Roberts	
	(Rookie Prospect)	.05
468	Pete Janicki **RC**	
	(1st Draft Pick)	.05
469	Jeff Schmidt **RC**	
	(1st Draft Pick)	.05
470	Don Mattingly	
	(Now & Then)	.45
471	Cal Ripken, Jr.	
	(Now & Then)	1.00
472	Jack Morris (Now & Then)	.05
473	Terry Pendleton	
	(Now & Then)	.05
474	Dennis Eckersley	
	(Now & Then)	.25
475	Carlton Fisk (Now & Then)	.30
476	Wade Boggs	
	(Now & Then)	.35
477	Len Dykstra	
	(Idols - Ken Stabler)	.05
478	Danny Tartabull	
	(Idols - Jose Tartabull)	.05
479	Jeff Conine	
	(Idols - Dale Murphy)	.10
480	Gregg Jefferies	
	(Idols - Ron Cey)	.05
481	Paul Molitor	
	(Idols - Harmon Killebrew)	.30
482	John Valentin	
	(Idols - Dave Concepcion)	.05
483	Alex Arias	
	(Idols - Dave Winfield)	.10
484	Barry Bonds	
	(Hometown Heroes)	1.00
485	Doug Drabek	
	(Hometown Heroes)	.05
486	Dave Winfield	
	(Hometown Heroes)	.30
487	Brett Butler	
	(Hometown Heroes)	.05
488	Harold Baines	
	(Hometown Heroes)	.05
489	David Cone	
	(Hometown Heroes)	.05
490	Willie McGee	
	(Hometown Heroes)	.05
491	Robby Thompson	.05
492	Pete Incaviglia	.05
493	Manuel Lee	.05
494	Rafael Belliard	.05
495	Scott Fletcher	.05
496	Jeff Frye	.05
497	Andre Dawson	.25
498	Mike Scioscia	.05
499	Spike Owen	.05
500	Sid Fernandez	.05
501	Joe Orsulak	.05
502	Benito Santiago/ED	.05
503	Dale Murphy	.25
504	Barry Bonds	2.00
505	Jose Guzman	.05
506	Tony Pena	.05
507	Doug Swindell	.05
508	Mike Pagliarulo	.05
509	Lou Whitaker	.05
510	Greg Gagne	.05
511	Butch Henry/ED	.05
512	Jeff Brantley	.05
513	Jack Armstrong/ED	.05
514	Danny Jackson	.05
515	Junior Felix/ED	.05
516	Milt Thompson	.05
517	Greg Maddux	.75
518	Eric Young/ED	.05
519	Jody Reed	.05
520	Roberto Kelly	.05
521	Darren Holmes/ED	.05
522	Craig Lefferts	.05
523	Charlie Hough/ED	.05
524	Bo Jackson	.10
525	Bill Spiers	.05
526	Orestes Destrade/ED	.05
527	Greg Hibbard	.05
528	Roger McDowell	.05
529	Cory Snyder	.05
530	Harold Reynolds	.05
531	Kevin Reimer	.05
532	Rick Sutcliffe	.05
533	Tony Fernandez	.05
534	Tom Brunansky	.05
535	Jeff Reardon	.05
536	Chili Davis	.05
537	Bob Ojeda	.05
538	Greg Colbrunn	.05
539	Grame Lloyd **RC**	
	(Rookie Prospect)	.05
540	Brian Jordan	.05
541	Pete Smith	.05
542	Frank Tanana	.05

543	John Smiley	.05
544	David Cone	.05
545	Daryl Boston/ED	.05
546	Tom Henke	.05
547	Bill Krueger	.05
548	Freddie Benavides/ED	.05
549	Randy Myers	.05
550	Reggie Jefferson	.05
551	Kevin Mitchell	.05
552	Dave Stieb	.05
553	Bret Barberie/ED	.05
554	Tim Crews	.05
555	Doug Dascenzo	.05
556	Alex Cole/ED	.05
557	Jeff Innis	.05
558	Carlos Garcia	.05
559	Steve Howe	.05
560	Kirk McCaskill	.05
561	Frank Seminara	.05
562	Cris Carpenter/ED	.05
563	Mike Stanley	.05
564	Carlos Quintana	.05
565	Mitch Williams	.05
566	Juan Bell	.05
567	Eric Fox	.05
568	Al Leiter	.05
569	Mike Stanton	.05
570	Scott Kamieniecki	.05
571	Ryan Bowen/ED	.05
572	Andy Ashby/ED	.05
573	Bob Welch	.05
574	Scott Sanderson	.05
575	Joe Kmak	
	(Rookie Prospect)	.05
576	Scott Pose/ED	
	(Rookie Prospect)	.05
577	Ricky Gutierrez	
	(Rookie Prospect)	.05
578	Mike Trombley	
	(Rookie Prospect)	.05
579	Sterling Hitchcock **RC**	
	(Rookie Prospect)	.10
580	Rodney Bolton	
	(Rookie Prospect)	.05
581	Tyler Green	
	(Rookie Prospect)	.05
582	Tim Costo	
	(Rookie Prospect)	.05
583	Tim Laker **RC**	
	(Rookie Prospect)	.05
584	Steve Reed/ED **RC**	
	(Rookie Prospect)	.05
585	Tom Kramer **RC**	
	(Rookie Prospect)	.05
586	Robb Nen	
	(Rookie Prospect)	.05
587	Jim Tatum **RC**	
	(Rookie Prospect)	.05
588	Frank Bolick	
	(Rookie Prospect)	.05
589	Kevin Young	
	(Rookie Prospect)	.05
590	Matt Whiteside **RC**	
	(Rookie Prospect)	.05
591	Cesar Hernandez	
	(Rookie Prospect)	.05
592	Mike Mohler **RC**	
	(Rookie Prospect)	.05
593	Alan Embree	
	(Rookie Prospect)	.05
594	Terry Jorgensen	
	(Rookie Prospect)	.05
595	John Cummings **RC**	
	(Rookie Prospect)	.05
596	Domingo Martinez	
	(Rookie Prospect)	.05
597	Benji Gil	
	(Rookie Prospect)	.05
598	Todd Pratt **RC**	
	(Rookie Prospect)	.05
599	Rene Arocha **RC**	
	(Rookie Prospect)	.05
600	Dennis Moeller	
	(Rookie Prospect)	.05
601	Jeff Conine/ED	
	(Rookie Prospect)	.05
602	Trevor Hoffman/ED	
	(Rookie Prospect)	.05
603	Daniel Smith	
	(Rookie Prospect)	.05
604	Lee Tinsley	
	(Rookie Prospect)	.05
605	Dan Peltier	
	(Rookie Prospect)	.05
606	Billy Brewer	
	(Rookie Prospect)	.05
607	Matt Walbeck **RC**	
	(Rookie Prospect)	.05
608	Richie Lewis/ED	
	(Rookie Prospect)	.05
609	J.T. Snow **RC**	
	(Rookie Prospect)	.40
610	Pat Gomez **RC**	
	(Rookie Prospect)	.05
611	Phil Hiatt	
	(Rookie Prospect)	.05
612	Alex Arias/ED	
	(Rookie Prospect)	.05
613	Kevin Rogers	
	(Rookie Prospect)	.05
614	Al Martin	
	(Rookie Prospect)	.05
615	Greg Gohr	
	(Rookie Prospect)	.05
616	Grame Lloyd **RC**	
	(Rookie Prospect)	.05
617	Kent Bottenfield	
	(Rookie Prospect)	.05

618	Chuck Carr/ED	
	(Rookie Prospect)	.05
619	Darrell Sherman **RC**	
	(Rookie Prospect)	.05
620	Mike Lansing **RC**	
	(Rookie Prospect)	.15

Expansion Opening Day

This nine-card set features 18 players for the two N.L. expansion teams: Florida Marlins and Colorado Rockies. Each "two-headed" card shows a projected Opening Day starter for each team. Cards were available one per Series 2 hobby box. Complete sets were available through a special mail-in offer.

		NM/M
Complete Set (9):		2.50
Common Player:		.25
1	Charlie Hough, David Nied	.25
2	Benito Santiago, Joe Girardi	.40
3	Orestes Destrade, Andres Galarraga	.75
4	Bret Barberie, Eric Young	.25
5	Dave Magadan, Charlie Hayes	.25
6	Walt Weiss, Freddie Benavides	.25
7	Jeff Conine, Jerald Clark	.50
8	Scott Pose, Alex Cole	.25
9	Junior Felix, Dante Bichette	.40

Rookie Team Pinnacle

These 10 cards were randomly inserted into Series 2 packs. Rookie Team Pinnacle is printed in gold foil on both sides of the card. Cards are numbered 1 of 10, etc., and use the special Dufex process. Each card shows two players painted by artist Christopher Greco. Stated odds of finding a Rookie Team Pinnacle insert were one in 90 packs.

		NM/M
Complete Set (10):		20.00
Common Player:		1.50
1	Pedro Martinez, Mike Trombley	6.00
2	Kevin Rogers, Sterling Hitchcock	1.50
3	Mike Piazza, Jesse Levis	10.00
4	Ryan Klesko, J.T. Snow	1.50
5	John Patterson, Bret Boone	1.50
6	Domingo Martinez, Kevin Young	1.50
7	Wil Cordero, Manny Alexander	1.50
8	Steve Hosey, Tim Salmon	1.50
9	Ryan Thompson, Gerald Williams	1.50
10	Melvin Nieves, David Hulse	1.50

Slugfest

Baseball's top sluggers are featured in this 30-card insert set. Cards were available one per Series 2 jumbo pack. Slugfest is printed in gold foil on the card front.

		NM/M
Complete Set (30):		12.50
Common Player:		.25
1	Juan Gonzalez	.50
2	Mark McGwire	2.00
3	Cecil Fielder	.25
4	Joe Carter	.25
5	Fred McGriff	.25
6	Barry Bonds	2.50
7	Gary Sheffield	.50
8	Dave Hollins	.25
9	Frank Thomas	1.00
10	Danny Tartabull	.25
11	Albert Belle	.25
12	Ruben Sierra	.25
13	Larry Walker	.25
14	Jeff Bagwell	1.00
15	Dave Justice	.25
16	Kirby Puckett	1.25
17	John Kruk	.25
18	Howard Johnson	.25
19	Darryl Strawberry	.25
20	Will Clark	.25
21	Kevin Mitchell	.25
22	Mickey Tettleton	.25
23	Don Mattingly	1.50
24	Jose Canseco	.75
25	Sam Militello	.25
26	Andre Dawson	.50
27	Ryne Sandberg	1.25
28	Ken Griffey Jr.	1.75
29	Carlos Baerga	.25
30	Travis Fryman	.25

Team Pinnacle

These cards were randomly inserted in Series 1 at a rate of about one in every 24 packs. Each card features two players painted by artist Christopher Greco. An eleventh card, featuring relief pitchers, was available only via a mail-in offer.

		NM/M
Complete Set (11):		40.00
Common Player:		1.50
1	Greg Maddux, Mike Mussina	10.00
2	Tom Glavine, John Smiley	2.00
3	Darren Daulton, Ivan Rodriguez	3.00
4	Fred McGriff, Frank Thomas	4.00
5	Delino DeShields, Carlos Baerga	1.50
6	Gary Sheffield, Edgar Martinez	2.00
7	Ozzie Smith, Pat Listach	8.00
8	Barry Bonds, Juan Gonzalez	15.00
9	Kirby Puckett, Andy Van Slyke	8.00
10	Larry Walker, Joe Carter	1.50
11	Rick Aguilera, Rob Dibble	1.50

Team 2001

This insert set features 30 players who are expected to be stars in the year 2001. Cards were randomly inserted into 27-card jumbo packs from Series 1.

		NM/M
Complete Set (30):		5.00
Common Player:		.05
1	Wil Cordero	.05
2	Cal Eldred	.05
3	Mike Mussina	.60
4	Chuck Knoblauch	.05
5	Melvin Nieves	.05
6	Tim Wakefield	.05
7	Carlos Baerga	.05
8	Bret Boone	.05
9	Jeff Bagwell	1.00
10	Travis Fryman	.05
11	Royce Clayton	.05
12	Delino DeShields	.05
13	Juan Gonzalez	.50
14	Pedro Martinez	1.00
15	Bernie Williams	.05
16	Billy Ashley	.05
17	Marquis Grissom	.05
18	Kenny Lofton	.05
19	Ray Lankford	.05
20	Tim Salmon	.05
21	Steve Hosey	.05
22	Charles Nagy	.05
23	Dave Fleming	.05
24	Reggie Sanders	.05
25	Sam Militello	.05
26	Eric Karros	.05
27	Ryan Klesko	.05
28	Dean Palmer	.05
29	Ivan Rodriguez	.75
30	Sterling Hitchcock	.05

Tribute

These Hall of Famers each have five-card sets devoted to their career achievements. Each card commemorates a career milestone. Cards were random inserts in Series 2, about one every 24 packs. Fronts have a gold-foil stamped "Tribute" vertically at right.

		NM/M
Complete Set (10):		10.00
George Brett Card (1-5):		1.00
Nolan Ryan Card (6-10):		1.50
1	Kansas City Royalty (George Brett)	1.00
2	The Chase for .400 (George Brett)	1.00
3	Pine Tar Pandemonium - "The Bat" (George Brett)	1.00
4	MVP and a World Series, Too (George Brett)	1.00
5	3,000 or Bust (George Brett)	1.00
6	The Rookie (Nolan Ryan)	1.50
7	Angel of No Mercy (Nolan Ryan)	1.50
8	Astronomical Success (Nolan Ryan)	1.50
9	5,000 Ks (Nolan Ryan)	1.50
10	No-Hitter No. 7 (Nolan Ryan)	1.50

Cooperstown

This boxed set features "today's superstar players bound to become Cooperstown inductees." In standard 2-1/2" x 3-1/2" format, the cards feature on both front and back an action photo which is borderless at the top and sides. At bottom-center of each photo is a half-moon green and gold-foil "Cooperstown Card" logo. On front, the player's name is gold-foil stamped in a black bar at bottom. On back is a black box, again with the player's name in gold-foil, plus a few stats justifying the player's Hall of Fame potential. Pinnacle's trademark optical-variable anti-counterfeiting device is at the bottom. Cards are UV coated on both sides. A special edition of 1,000 of the Cooperstown sets was produced in Pinnacle's "Dufex" technology and distributed at the 1993 SCAI trade show. Other than being printed on foil, the cards are identical to the regular-issue Cooperstown cards. Each of the Pinnacle Cooperstown cards can also be found in a sample version which differs from the issued cards principally in the appearance on back of a large "PROMO" overprint.

		NM/M
Complete Set (30):		7.50
Common Player:		.25
Dufex:		25X
Promo:		30X
1	Nolan Ryan	2.00
2	George Brett	.85
3	Robin Yount	.65
4	Carlton Fisk	.65
5	Dale Murphy	.35
6	Dennis Eckersley	.50
7	Rickey Henderson	.65
8	Ryne Sandberg	.75
9	Ozzie Smith	.75
10	Dave Winfield	.65
11	Andre Dawson	.35
12	Kirby Puckett	.75
13	Wade Boggs	.75
14	Don Mattingly	.85
15	Barry Bonds	2.00
16	Will Clark	.25
17	Cal Ripken, Jr.	2.00
18	Roger Clemens	.85
19	Dwight Gooden	.25
20	Tony Gwynn	.75
21	Joe Carter	.25
22	Ken Griffey Jr.	1.00
23	Paul Molitor	.60
24	Frank Thomas	.60
25	Juan Gonzalez	.35
26	Barry Larkin	.25
27	Eddie Murray	.60
28	Cecil Fielder	.25
29	Roberto Alomar	.35
30	Mark McGwire	1.50

Joe DiMaggio

Sold in a special tin box in a limited edition of 200,000 sets, this set highlights the career of "The Yankee Clipper." Fronts feature black-and-white or colorized photos with a black border and gold-foil highlights. Backs feature a woodgrain center panel with a portion of DiMaggio's career recounted. The boxed set includes an "Authenticator" lens through which the

name "DiMaggio" can be seen when placed over the optical-variable printing on back. Genuine DiMaggio autographed cards were randomly inserted into 9,000 sets.

		NM/M
Complete Set (30):		7.50
Common Card:		.35
1	An American Hero	.50
2	San Francisco Seals	.35
3	Seals Farewell	.35
4	First Game	.35
5	The Rookie	.35
6	Rookie All-Star (With Dizzy Dean.)	.45
7	Fan Favorite	.35
8	Teammates' Awe	.35
9	Classic Swing	.35
10	Joltin' Power	.35
11	Rapid Robert vs. Joltin' Joe (With Bob Feller.)	.45
12	The Complete Hitter	.35
13	Makin' It Look Easy	.35
14	Extra Swings	.35
15	The Run Producer	.35
16	Quiet Confidence	.35
17	Sticks 'N' Bones	.35
18	A Link to the Past (With Lou Gehrig.)	.50
19	The Center of Attention	.35
20	The DiMaggio Mystique	.35
21	Joe McCarthy (With Joe McCarthy.)	.35
22	World War II	.35
23	Fearless Baserunner	.35
24	The Summer of '41	.50
25	Career Statistics	.50
26	No. 45	.35
27	Chasing Ruth	.35
28	The Final Season	.35
29	Retirement	.35
30	Baseball's Greatest Living Player	.50

Joe DiMaggio Autographs

Eighteen hundred of each of five different insert cards were personally autographed by the Yankee Clipper and randomly inserted into the Joe DiMaggio box set tins at a rate of about one autograph per 22 sets. Fronts of the 2-1/8" x 3-1/2" cards have sepia artwork of DiMaggio at a particular stage of his career. In the wide white border at bottom is the autograph. Backs have a photo, part of a narrative about DiMaggio's career, and a serial number. A certificate of authenticity accompanies each signed card.

		NM/M
Complete Set (5):		850.00
1-5	Joe DiMaggio	175.00

Home Run Club

Pinnacle released this boxed set produced in a special metallic-foil printing process called "Dufex." Limited to 200,000 numbered sets, the cards are UV-coated and gold-

foil stamped. The checklist includes 28 American League and 20 National League sluggers.

		NM/M
Complete Set (48):		6.00
Common Player:		.10
1	Juan Gonzalez	.40
2	Fred McGriff	.10
3	Cecil Fielder	.10
4	Barry Bonds	1.50
5	Albert Belle	.10
6	Gary Sheffield	.25
7	Joe Carter	.10
8	Mark McGwire	1.25
9	Darren Daulton	.10
10	Jose Canseco	.50
11	Dave Hollins	.10
12	Ryne Sandberg	.85
13	Ken Griffey Jr.	1.00
14	Larry Walker	.10
15	Rob Deer	.10
16	Andre Dawson	.25
17	Frank Thomas	.75
18	Mickey Tettleton	.10
19	Charlie Hayes	.10
20	Ron Gant	.10
21	Rickey Henderson	.75
22	Matt Williams	.10
23	Kevin Mitchell	.10
24	Robin Ventura	.10
25	Dean Palmer	.10
26	Mike Piazza	1.00
27	J.T. Snow	.25
28	Jeff Bagwell	.75
29	John Olerud	.10
30	Greg Vaughn	.10
31	Dave Justice	.10
32	Dave Winfield	.75
33	Danny Tartabull	.10
34	Eric Anthony	.10
35	Eddie Murray	.75
36	Jay Buhner	.10
37	Derek Bell	.10
38	Will Clark	.10
39	Carlos Baerga	.10
40	Mo Vaughn	.10
41	Bobby Bonilla	.10
42	Tim Salmon	.10
43	Bo Jackson	.10
44	Howard Johnson	.10
45	Kent Hrbek	.10
46	Ruben Sierra	.10
47	Cal Ripken, Jr.	1.50
48	Travis Fryman	.10

1994 Pinnacle Samples

Basically the same as the issued versions, these promo cards differ in the presence of a diagonal "SAMPLE" overprint on front and back. Cello-wrapped packs of hobby and retail versions were produced, with appropriate header cards.

		NM/M
Complete Set (12):		10.00
Common Player:		.50
2	Carlos Baerga	.50
3	Sammy Sosa	2.00
5	John Olerud	.75
7	Moises Alou	.50
8	Steve Avery	.50
10	Cecil Fielder	.50
11	Greg Maddux	2.00
269	Jeff Granger	.50
---	Jeff Granger (Museum) (Blank-back.)	1.00
---	Jeff Granger (Museum) (Black print on back.)	1.00
TR1	Paul Molitor (Tribute)	1.50
---	Hobby Version Header Card	.05
---	Retail Version Header Card	.05

1994 Pinnacle

Pinnacle's 1994 mid-priced brand features full bleed photos, gold-foil graphics and UV coating. On front, player and team names appear in a shield-and-bar motif in the lower-left corner. On horizontal backs, the front photo is reproduced as a subdued background photo, over which are printed recent stats

and a few biographical details. A different player photo is featured at left, while the brand's optical-variable anti-counterfeiting device is at bottom center. Subsets include major award winners, Rookie Prospects and Draft Picks which are appropriately noted with gold-foil lettering on front. The issue was produced in two series of 270 cards each.

		NM/M
Complete Set (540):		15.00
Common Player:		.05
Artist's Proofs:		20X
Museums:		6X
Series 1 or 2 Pack (14):		.75
Series 1 or 2 Box (24):		12.50
1	Frank Thomas	.65
2	Carlos Baerga	.05
3	Sammy Sosa	.75
4	Tony Gwynn	.75
5	John Olerud	.05
6	Ryne Sandberg	.75
7	Moises Alou	.05
8	Steve Avery	.05
9	Tim Salmon	.05
10	Cecil Fielder	.05
11	Greg Maddux	.75
12	Barry Larkin	.05
13	Mike Devereaux	.05
14	Charlie Hayes	.05
15	Albert Belle	.05
16	Andy Van Slyke	.05
17	Mo Vaughn	.05
18	Brian McRae	.05
19	Cal Eldred	.05
20	Craig Biggio	.05
21	Kirby Puckett	.75
22	Derek Bell	.05
23	Don Mattingly	.85
24	John Burkett	.05
25	Roger Clemens	.85
26	Barry Bonds	2.00
27	Paul Molitor	.65
28	Mike Piazza	1.00
29	Robin Ventura	.05
30	Jeff Conine	.05
31	Wade Boggs	.50
32	Dennis Eckersley	.05
33	Bobby Bonilla	.05
34	Len Dykstra	.05
35	Manny Alexander	.05
36	Ray Lankford	.05
37	Greg Vaughn	.05
38	Chuck Finley	.05
39	Todd Benzinger	.05
40	Dave Justice	.05
41	Rob Dibble	.05
42	Tom Henke	.05
43	David Nied	.05
44	Sandy Alomar Jr.	.05
45	Pete Harnisch	.05
46	Jeff Russell	.05
47	Terry Mulholland	.05
48	Kevin Appier	.05
49	Randy Tomlin	.05
50	Cal Ripken, Jr.	2.00
51	Andy Benes	.05
52	Jimmy Key	.05
53	Kirt Manwaring	.05
54	Kevin Tapani	.05
55	Jose Guzman	.05
56	Todd Stottlemyre	.05
57	Jack McDowell	.05
58	Orel Hershiser	.05
59	Chris Hammond	.05
60	Chris Nabholz	.05
61	Ruben Sierra	.05
62	Dwight Gooden	.05
63	John Kruk	.05
64	Omar Vizquel	.05
65	Tim Naehring	.05
66	Dwight Smith	.05
67	Mickey Tettleton	.05
68	J.T. Snow	.05
69	Greg McMichael	.05
70	Kevin Mitchell	.05
71	Kevin Brown	.05
72	Scott Cooper	.05
73	Jim Thome	.60
74	Joe Girardi	.05
75	Eric Anthony	.05
76	Orlando Merced	.05
77	Felix Jose	.05
78	Tommy Greene	.05

79	Bernard Gilkey	.05
80	Phil Plantier	.05
81	Danny Tartabull	.05
82	Trevor Wilson	.05
83	Chuck Knoblauch	.05
84	Rick Wilkins	.05
85	Devon White	.05
86	Lance Johnson	.05
87	Eric Karros	.05
88	Gary Sheffield	.35
89	Wil Cordero	.05
90	Ron Darling	.05
91	Darren Daulton	.05
92	Joe Orsulak	.05
93	Steve Cooke	.05
94	Darryl Hamilton	.05
95	Aaron Sele	.05
96	John Doherty	.05
97	Gary DiSarcina	.05
98	Jeff Blauser	.05
99	John Smiley	.05
100	Ken Griffey Jr.	1.00
101	Dean Palmer	.05
102	Felix Fermin	.05
103	Jerald Clark	.05
104	Doug Drabek	.05
105	Curt Schilling	.30
106	Jeff Montgomery	.05
107	Rene Arocha	.05
108	Carlos Garcia	.05
109	Wally Whitehurst	.05
110	Jim Abbott	.05
111	Royce Clayton	.05
112	Chris Hoiles	.05
113	Mike Morgan	.05
114	Joe Magrane	.05
115	Tom Candiotti	.05
116	Ron Karkovice	.05
117	Ryan Bowen	.05
118	Rod Beck	.05
119	John Wetteland	.05
120	Terry Steinbach	.05
121	Dave Hollins	.05
122	Jeff Kent	.05
123	Ricky Bones	.05
124	Brian Jordan	.05
125	Chad Kreuter	.05
126	John Valentin	.05
127	Billy Hathaway	.05
128	Wilson Alvarez	.05
129	Tino Martinez	.05
130	Rodney Bolton	.05
131	David Segui	.05
132	Wayne Kirby	.05
133	Eric Young	.05
134	Scott Servais	.05
135	Scott Radinsky	.05
136	Bret Barberie	.05
137	John Roper	.05
138	Ricky Gutierrez	.05
139	Bernie Williams	.05
140	Bud Black	.05
141	Jose Vizcaino	.05
142	Gerald Williams	.05
143	Duane Ward	.05
144	Danny Jackson	.05
145	Allen Watson	.05
146	Scott Fletcher	.05
147	Delino DeShields	.05
148	Shane Mack	.05
149	Jim Eisenreich	.05
150	Troy Neel	.05
151	Jay Bell	.05
152	B.J. Surhoff	.05
153	Mark Whiten	.05
154	Mike Henneman	.05
155	Todd Hundley	.05
156	Greg Myers	.05
157	Ryan Klesko	.05
158	Dave Fleming	.05
159	Mickey Morandini	.05
160	Blas Minor	.05
161	Reggie Jefferson	.05
162	David Hulse	.05
163	Greg Swindell	.05
164	Roberto Hernandez	.05
165	Brady Anderson	.05
166	Jack Armstrong	.05
167	Phil Clark	.05
168	Melido Perez	.05
169	Darren Lewis	.05
170	Sam Horn	.05
171	Mike Harkey	.05
172	Juan Guzman	.05
173	Bob Natal	.05
174	Deion Sanders	.05
175	Carlos Quintana	.05
176	Mel Rojas	.05
177	Willie Banks	.05
178	Ben Rivera	.05
179	Kenny Lofton	.05
180	Leo Gomez	.05
181	Roberto Mejia	.05
182	Mike Perez	.05
183	Travis Fryman	.05
184	Ben McDonald	.05
185	Steve Frey	.05
186	Kevin Young	.05
187	Dave Magadan	.05
188	Bobby Munoz	.05
189	Pat Rapp	.05
190	Jose Offerman	.05
191	Vinny Castilla	.05
192	Ivan Calderon	.05
193	Ken Caminiti	.05
194	Benji Gil	.05
195	Chuck Carr	.05
196	Derrick May	.05

197	Pat Kelly	.05
198	Jeff Brantley	.05
199	Jose Lind	.05
200	Steve Buechele	.05
201	Wes Chamberlain	.05
202	Eduardo Perez	.05
203	Bret Saberhagen	.05
204	Gregg Jefferies	.05
205	Darrin Fletcher	.05
206	Kent Hrbek	.05
207	Kim Batiste	.05
208	Jeff King	.05
209	Donovan Osborne	.05
210	Dave Nilsson	.05
211	Al Martin	.05
212	Mike Moore	.05
213	Sterling Hitchcock	.05
214	Geronimo Pena	.05
215	Kevin Higgins	.05
216	Norm Charlton	.05
217	Don Slaught	.05
218	Mitch Williams	.05
219	Derek Lilliquist	.05
220	Armando Reynoso	.05
221	Kenny Rogers	.05
222	Doug Jones	.05
223	Luis Aquino	.05
224	Mike Oquist	.05
225	Darryl Scott	.05
226	Kurt Abbott	.05
227	Andy Tomberlin	.05
228	Norberto Martin	.05
229	Pedro Castellano	.05
230	Curtis Pride **RC**	.05
231	Jeff McNeely	.05
232	Scott Lydy	.05
233	Darren Oliver	.05
234	Danny Bautista	.05
235	Butch Huskey	.05
236	Chipper Jones	.75
237	Eddie Zambrano	.05
238	Jean Domingo	.05
239	Javier Lopez	.05
240	Nigel Wilson	.05
241	Drew Denson **RC**	.05
242	Raul Mondesi	.65
243	Luis Ortiz	.05
244	Manny Ramirez	.65
245	Greg Blosser	.05
246	Rondell White	.05
247	Steve Karsay	.05
248	Scott Stahoviak	.05
249	Jose Valentin	.05
250	Marc Newfield	.05
251	Keith Kessinger	.05
252	Carl Everett	.05
253	John O'Donoghue	.05
254	Turk Wendell	.05
255	Scott Ruffcorn	.05
256	Tony Tarasco	.05
257	Andy Cook	.05
258	Matt Mieske	.05
259	Luis Lopez	.05
260	Ramon Caraballo	.05
261	Salomon Torres	.05
262	Brooks Kieschnick **RC**	.05
263	Daron Kirkreit **RC**	.05
264	Bill Wagner **RC**	.10
265	Matt Drews **RC**	.05
266	Scott Christman	.05
267	Torii Hunter **RC**	1.00
268	Jamey Wright **RC**	.05
269	Jeff Granger	.05
270	Trot Nixon **RC**	1.00
271	Randy Myers	.05
272	Trevor Hoffman	.05
273	Bob Wickman	.05
274	Willie McGee	.05
275	Hipolito Pichardo	.05
276	Bobby Witt	.05
277	Gregg Olson	.05
278	Randy Johnson	.65
279	Robb Nen	.05
280	Paul O'Neill	.05
281	Lou Whitaker	.05
282	Chad Curtis	.05
283	Doug Henry	.05
284	Tom Glavine	.30
285	Mike Greenwell	.05
286	Roberto Kelly	.05
287	Roberto Alomar	.15
288	Charlie Hough	.05
289	Alex Fernandez	.05
290	Jeff Bagwell	.65
291	Wally Joyner	.05
292	Andujar Cedeno	.05
293	Rick Aguilera	.05
294	Darryl Strawberry	.05
295	Mike Mussina	.35
296	Jeff Gardner	.05
297	Chris Gwynn	.05
298	Matt Williams	.05
299	Brent Gates	.05
300	Mark McGwire	1.50
301	Jim Deshaies	.05
302	Edgar Martinez	.05
303	Danny Darwin	.05
304	Pat Meares	.05
305	Benito Santiago	.05
306	Jose Canseco	.40
307	Jim Gott	.05
308	Paul Sorrento	.05
309	Scott Kamieniecki	.05
310	Larry Walker	.05
311	Mark Langston	.05
312	John Jaha	.05
313	Stan Javier	.05
314	Hal Morris	.05

315	Robby Thompson	.05
316	Pat Hentgen	.05
317	Tom Gordon	.05
318	Joey Cora	.05
319	Luis Alicea	.05
320	Andre Dawson	.25
321	Darryl Kile	.05
322	Jose Rijo	.05
323	Luis Gonzalez	.05
324	Billy Ashley	.05
325	David Cone	.05
326	Bill Swift	.05
327	Phil Hiatt	.05
328	Craig Paquette	.05
329	Bob Welch	.05
330	Tony Phillips	.05
331	Archi Cianfrocco	.05
332	Dave Winfield	.65
333	David McCarty	.05
334	Al Leiter	.05
335	Tom Browning	.05
336	Mark Grace	.05
337	Jose Mesa	.05
338	Mike Stanley	.05
339	Roger McDowell	.05
340	Damion Easley	.05
341	Angel Miranda	.05
342	John Smoltz	.05
343	Jay Buhner	.05
344	Bryan Harvey	.05
345	Joe Carter	.05
346	Dante Bichette	.05
347	Jason Bere	.05
348	Frank Viola	.05
349	Ivan Rodriguez	.60
350	Juan Gonzalez	.35
351	Steve Finley	.05
352	Mike Felder	.05
353	Ramon Martinez	.05
354	Greg Gagne	.05
355	Ken Hill	.05
356	Pedro Munoz	.05
357	Todd Van Poppel	.05
358	Marquis Grissom	.05
359	Milt Cuyler	.05
360	Reggie Sanders	.05
361	Scott Erickson	.05
362	Billy Hatcher	.05
363	Gene Harris	.05
364	Rene Gonzales	.05
365	Kevin Rogers	.05
366	Eric Plunk	.05
367	Todd Zeile	.05
368	John Franco	.05
369	Brett Butler	.05
370	Bill Spiers	.05
371	Terry Pendleton	.05
372	Chris Bosio	.05
373	Orestes Destrade	.05
374	Dave Stewart	.05
375	Darren Holmes	.05
376	Doug Strange	.05
377	Brian Turang	.05
378	Carl Willis	.05
379	Mark McLemore	.05
380	Bobby Jones	.05
381	Scott Sanders	.05
382	Kirk Rueter	.05
383	Randy Velarde	.05
384	Fred McGriff	.05
385	Charles Nagy	.05
386	Rich Amaral	.05
387	Geronimo Berroa	.05
388	Eric Davis	.05
389	Ozzie Smith	.75
390	Alex Arias	.05
391	Brad Ausmus	.05
392	Cliff Floyd	.05
393	Roger Salkeld	.05
394	Jim Edmonds	.05
395	Jeromy Burnitz	.05
396	Dave Staton	.05
397	Rob Butler	.05
398	Marcos Armas	.05
399	Darrell Whitmore	.05
400	Ryan Thompson	.05
401	Ross Powell RC	.05
402	Joe Oliver	.05
403	Paul Carey	.05
404	Bob Hamelin	.05
405	Chris Turner	.05
406	Nate Minchey	.05
407	Lonnie Maclin RC	.05
408	Harold Baines	.05
409	Brian Williams	.05
410	Johnny Ruffin	.05
411	Julian Tavarez RC	.05
412	Mark Hutton	.05
413	Carlos Delgado	.50
414	Chris Gomez	.05
415	Mike Hampton	.05
416	Alex Diaz	.05
417	Jeffrey Hammonds	.05
418	Jayhawk Owens	.05
419	J.R. Phillips	.05
420	Cory Bailey RC	.05
421	Denny Hocking	.05
422	Jon Shave	.05
423	Damon Buford	.05
424	Troy O'Leary	.05
425	Tripp Cromer	.05
426	Albie Lopez	.05
427	Tony Fernandez	.05
428	Ozzie Guillen	.05
429	Alan Trammell	.05
430	John Wasdin RC	.05
431	Marc Valdes	.05
432	Brian Anderson RC	.20
433	Matt Brunson RC	.05
434	Wayne Gomes RC	.05
435	Jay Powell RC	.05
436	Kirk Presley RC	.05
437	Jon Ratliff RC	.05
438	Derrek Lee RC	2.00
439	Tom Pagnozzi	.05
440	Kent Mercker	.05
441	Phil Leftwich RC	.05
442	Jamie Moyer	.05
443	John Flaherty	.05
444	Mark Wohlers	.05
445	Jose Bautista	.05
446	Andres Galarraga	.05
447	Mark Lemke	.05
448	Tim Wakefield	.05
449	Pat Listach	.05
450	Rickey Henderson	.65
451	Mike Gallego	.05
452	Bob Tewksbury	.05
453	Kirk Gibson	.05
454	Pedro Astacio	.05
455	Mike Lansing	.05
456	Sean Berry	.05
457	Bob Walk	.05
458	Chili Davis	.05
459	Ed Sprague	.05
460	Kevin Stocker	.05
461	Mike Stanton	.05
462	Tim Raines	.05
463	Mike Bordick	.05
464	David Wells	.05
465	Tim Laker	.05
466	Cory Snyder	.05
467	Alex Cole	.05
468	Pete Incaviglia	.05
469	Roger Pavlik	.05
470	Greg W. Harris	.05
471	Xavier Hernandez	.05
472	Erik Hanson	.05
473	Jesse Orosco	.05
474	Greg Colbrunn	.05
475	Harold Reynolds	.05
476	Greg Harris	.05
477	Pat Borders	.05
478	Melvin Nieves	.05
479	Mariano Duncan	.05
480	Greg Hibbard	.05
481	Tim Pugh	.05
482	Bobby Ayala	.05
483	Sid Fernandez	.05
484	Tim Wallach	.05
485	Randy Milligan	.05
486	Walt Weiss	.05
487	Matt Walbeck	.05
488	Mike Macfarlane	.05
489	Jerry Browne	.05
490	Chris Sabo	.05
491	Tim Belcher	.05
492	Spike Owen	.05
493	Rafael Palmeiro	.60
494	Brian Harper	.05
495	Eddie Murray	.65
496	Ellis Burks	.05
497	Karl Rhodes	.05
498	Otis Nixon	.05
499	Lee Smith	.05
500	Bip Roberts	.05
501	Pedro Martinez	.65
502	Brian L. Hunter	.05
503	Tyler Green	.05
504	Bruce Hurst	.05
505	Alex Gonzalez	.05
506	Mark Portugal	.05
507	Bob Ojeda	.05
508	Dave Henderson	.05
509	Bo Jackson	.10
510	Bret Boone	.05
511	Mark Eichhorn	.05
512	Luis Polonia	.05
513	Will Clark	.05
514	Dave Valle	.05
515	Dan Wilson	.05
516	Dennis Martinez	.05
517	Jim Leyritz	.05
518	Howard Johnson	.05
519	Jody Reed	.05
520	Julio Franco	.05
521	Jeff Reardon	.05
522	Willie Greene	.05
523	Shawon Dunston	.05
524	Keith Mitchell	.05
525	Rick Helling	.05
526	Mark Kiefer	.05
527	Chan Ho Park RC	.75
528	Tony Longmire	.05
529	Rich Becker	.05
530	Tim Hyers	.05
531	Darrin Jackson	.05
532	Jack Morris	.05
533	Rick White	.05
534	Mike Kelly	.05
535	James Mouton	.05
536	Steve Trachsel	.05
537	Tony Eusebio	.05
538	Kelly Stinnett	.05
539	Paul Spoljaric	.05
540	Darren Dreifort	.05

Artist's Proof

A specially designated version of the regular Pinnacle set, described as the first day's production of the first 1,000 of each card, was issued as a random pack insert. Cards feature a small gold-foil "Artist's Proof" rectangle embossed

above the player/team name shield on front. In all other respects the cards are identical to the regular-issue versions.

	NM/M
Complete Set (540):	250.00
Common Player:	1.50
Stars/Rookies:	20X

Museum Collection

Each card in the 1994 Pinnacle set was produced in a parallel "Museum Collection" version. The inserts were produced utilizing the company's Dufex foil-printing technology on front, with rays emanating from the Pinnacle logo. Backs are identical to the regular-issue version except for the substitution of a "1994 Museum Collection" logo for the optical-variable anti-counterfeiting bar at bottom-center. Museums were random package inserts, appearing at the rate of about once per four packs.

	NM/M
Complete Set (540):	225.00
Common Player:	1.00
Stars/Rookies:	6X

Rookie Team Pinnacle

The popular Rookie Team Pinnacle insert card tradition continued in 1994 with a series of nine "two-headed" cards featuring the top prospect from each league at each position. The cards again feature the ultra-realistic artwork of Chris Greco. Each side is enhanced with gold-foil presentations of the player's name, the Pinnacle logo and the Rookie Team Pinnacle logo. The inserts were packaged, on average, one per 90 packs of hobby foil only.

		NM/M
Complete Set (9):		12.00
Common Player:		.75
1	Carlos Delgado, Javier Lopez	2.50
2	Bob Hamelin, J.R. Phillips	.75
3	Jon Shave, Keith Kessinger	.75
4	Butch Huskey, Luis Ortiz	.75
5	Chipper Jones, Kurt Abbott	5.00
6	Rondell White, Manny Ramirez	3.00
7	Cliff Floyd, Jeffrey Hammonds	.75
8	Marc Newfield, Nigel Wilson	.75
9	Salomon Torres, Mark Hutton	.75

Run Creators

This insert set, exclusive to Pinnacle jumbo packaging, features the top 44 performers of the previous season in the arcane statistic of "runs created." Fronts have an action photo on which the stadium background has been muted in soft-focus red or blue. The player's last name appears at right in gold foil; the logo, "The Run Creators" is in one of the lower corners. Backs are printed in teal with a color team logo at center, beneath the stats that earned the player's inclusion in the series. The player's runs created are in gold foil above the write-up. Cards are numbered with an "RC" prefix.

		NM/M
Complete Set (44):		17.50
Common Player:		.25
1	John Olerud	.25
2	Frank Thomas	1.00
3	Ken Griffey Jr.	3.00
4	Paul Molitor	1.00
5	Rafael Palmeiro	.75
6	Roberto Alomar	.35
7	Juan Gonzalez	.50
8	Albert Belle	.25
9	Travis Fryman	.25
10	Rickey Henderson	1.00
11	Tony Phillips	.25
12	Mo Vaughn	.25
13	Tim Salmon	.25
14	Kenny Lofton	.25
15	Carlos Baerga	.25
16	Greg Vaughn	.25
17	Jay Buhner	.25
18	Chris Hoiles	.25
19	Mickey Tettleton	.25
20	Kirby Puckett	1.50
21	Danny Tartabull	.25
22	Devon White	.25
23	Barry Bonds	4.00
24	Lenny Dykstra	.25
25	John Kruk	.25
26	Fred McGriff	.25
27	Gregg Jefferies	.25
28	Mike Piazza	3.00
29	Jeff Blauser	.25
30	Andres Galarraga	.25
31	Darren Daulton	.25
32	Dave Justice	.25
33	Craig Biggio	.25
34	Mark Grace	.25
35	Tony Gwynn	1.50
36	Jeff Bagwell	1.00
37	Jay Bell	.25
38	Marquis Grissom	.25
39	Matt Williams	.25
40	Charlie Hayes	.25
41	Dante Bichette	.25
42	Bernard Gilkey	.25
43	Brett Butler	.25
44	Rick Wilkins	.25

Team Pinnacle

The double-sided Team Pinnacle insert set features 18 of the top players in the game. They were inserted into Series 2 at a rate of one every 90 packs.

		NM/M
Complete Set (9):		35.00
Common Player:		1.50
1	Jeff Bagwell, Frank Thomas	4.00
2	Carlos Baerga, Robby Thompson	1.50
3	Matt Williams, Dean Palmer	1.50
4	Cal Ripken, Jr., Jay Bell	12.00
5	Ivan Rodriguez, Mike Piazza	6.00
6	Len Dykstra, Ken Griffey Jr.	8.00
7	Juan Gonzalez, Barry Bonds	10.00
8	Tim Salmon, Dave Justice	1.50
9	Greg Maddux, Jack McDowell	8.00

Tribute

A hobby-only insert set, found approximately one per 18 foil packs, this nine-card series honors players who reached significant season or career milestones or otherwise had special achievements in 1993. Fronts feature full-bleed action photos. At left is a black strip with "TRIBUTE" in gold foil. A colored strip at bottom has the player name in gold foil and a short description of why he is being feted beneath. The Pinnacle logo is in gold foil at top. The same gold-foil enhancements are found on back, along with a portrait photo. In a black box at bottom are details of the tribute. The Pinnacle optical-variable anti-counterfeiting device is at bottom center. Card numbers are prefixed with "TR."

		NM/M
Complete Set (18):		15.00
Common Player:		.25
1	Paul Molitor	1.00
2	Jim Abbott	.25
3	Dave Winfield	1.00
4	Bo Jackson	.35
5	Dave Justice	.25
6	Len Dykstra	.25
7	Mike Piazza	2.50
8	Barry Bonds	4.50
9	Randy Johnson	1.00
10	Ozzie Smith	1.50
11	Mark Whiten	.25
12	Greg Maddux	1.50
13	Cal Ripken, Jr.	4.50
14	Frank Thomas	1.00
15	Juan Gonzalez	.45
16	Roberto Alomar	.25
17	Ken Griffey Jr.	3.00
18	Lee Smith	.25

New Generation

Baseball's hottest rookies and second-year players were featured in this boxed set. Cards are typical Pinnacle quality with full-bleed action photos, UV coating and gold-foil stamping on front and back. A total of 100,000 sets was produced, with a suggested retail price of $9.95.

		NM/M
Complete Set (25):		5.00
Common Player:		.25
1	Tim Salmon	.25
2	Mike Piazza	2.00
3	Jason Bere	.25
4	Jeffrey Hammonds	.25
5	Aaron Sele	.25
6	Salomon Torres	.25
7	Wil Cordero	.25
8	Allen Watson	.25
9	J.T. Snow	.25
10	Cliff Floyd	.25
10a	Cliff Floyd (Overprinted "SAMPLE" card.)	.50
11	Jeff McNeely	.25
12	Butch Huskey	.25
13	J.R. Phillips	.25
14	Bobby Jones	.25
15	Javier Lopez	.25
16	Scott Ruffcorn	.25
17	Manny Ramirez	1.25
18	Carlos Delgado	1.00
19	Rondell White	.25
20	Chipper Jones	1.50
21	Billy Ashley	.25
22	Nigel Wilson	.25
23	Jeromy Burnitz	.25
24	Danny Bautista	.25
25	Darrell Whitmore	.25

Power Surge

The major leagues' heaviest hitters are featured in this boxed set. Cards are typical Pinnacle quality with gold-foil stamping, on front, UV coating on both sides and high-tech graphics. Fronts feature game-action photos while backs have smaller portrait and action photos on a marbled background, along with 1993 and career stats and a description of the player's power potential. Cards are numbered with a "PS" prefix. A total of 100,000 sets was produced.

		NM/M
Complete Set (25):		4.00
Common Player:		.25
1	Dave Justice	.25
2	Chris Hoiles	.25
3	Mo Vaughn	.25
4	Tim Salmon	.25
5	J.T. Snow	.25
6	Frank Thomas	.65
7	Sammy Sosa	.75
8	Rick Wilkins	.25
9	Robin Ventura	.25
10	Reggie Sanders	.25
11	Albert Belle	.25
12	Carlos Baerga	.25
12a	Carlos Baerga (Overprinted "SAMPLE" card.)	.50
13	Manny Ramirez	.65
14	Travis Fryman	.25
15	Gary Sheffield	.35
16	Jeff Bagwell	.65
17	Mike Piazza	.25
18	Eric Karros	.25
19	Cliff Floyd	.25
20	Mark Whiten	.25
21	Phil Plantier	.25
22	Derek Bell	.25
23	Ken Griffey Jr.	1.00
24	Juan Gonzalez	.35
25	Dean Palmer	.25

The Naturals

The Naturals boxed set puts a game-action photo against a textured-foil background. Backs picture the player on a background of nature photography, including lightning, blue skies and clouds. Pinnacle produced 100,000 sets, which come in a numbered, sealed box with a certificate of authenticity.

	NM/M
Complete Set (25):	6.00
Common Player:	.15
1 Frank Thomas	.50
2 Barry Bonds	1.50
3 Ken Griffey Jr.	1.00
4 Juan Gonzalez	.25
5 Dave Justice	.15
6 Albert Belle	.15
7 Kenny Lofton	.15
8 Roberto Alomar	.35
9 Tim Salmon	.15
10 Randy Johnson	.50
11 Kirby Puckett	.65
12 Tony Gwynn	.65
13 Fred McGriff	.15
14 Ryne Sandberg	.65
15 Greg Maddux	.65
16 Matt Williams	.15
17 Lenny Dykstra	.15
18 Gary Sheffield	.35
18a Gary Sheffield (Overprinted "SAMPLE" card.)	.50
19 Mike Piazza	1.00
20 Dean Palmer	.15
21 Travis Fryman	.15
22 Carlos Baerga	.15
23 Cal Ripken, Jr.	1.50
24 John Olerud	.15
25 Roger Clemens	.75

1995 Pinnacle Series 1 Samples

This eight-card cello-wrapped sample set was sent to dealers to preview the 1995 Pinnacle Series 1 cards. The cards are identical to regular-issue Pinnacle cards except they carry a white diagonal "SAMPLE" notation on front and back.

	NM/M
Complete Set (9):	6.00
Common Player:	.50
16 Mickey Morandini	.50
22US Wil Cordero (Upstart) (Card not included in most packs.)	2.00
119 Gary Sheffield	1.00
122 Ivan Rodriguez	1.50
132 Alex Rodriguez (Rookie)	3.00
208 Bo Jackson	.75
223 Jose Rijo	.50
224 Ryan Klesko	.50
---- Header card	.05

1995 Pinnacle

The 1995 Pinnacle set was produced in two series of 225 base cards each, plus inserts. Fronts have borderless photos with a large embossed gold foil "wave" at bottom containing the player's last name and team logo. Horizontal backs

have a portrait photo at left, an action photo at right and a few sentences about the player at center. Stats at the bottom offer previous year, career and career-best numbers. Subsets with the base cards include rookie specials in both Series 1 and 2 have a design featuring a green stripe at one side or bottom with the player's name in gold and a special round gold-foil logo. A similar design, with red stripes, is used for Series 1 cards featuring Draft Picks. In Series 2, a 30-card Swing Men subset has a blue vortex background design and special gold-foil identifier. Basic pack configurations offered 12-card ($2.49) and 15-card ($2.99) counts in both retail and hobby versions, each with some unique inserts.

	NM/M
Complete Set (450):	15.00
Common Player:	.10
Artist's Proofs:	10X
Museum Collection:	4X
Hobby Pack (12):	1.00
Hobby Wax Box (24):	15.00
Retail Pack (12):	1.00
Retail Wax Box (36):	20.00
1 Jeff Bagwell	.75
2 Roger Clemens	1.25
3 Mark Whiten	.10
4 Shawon Dunston	.10
5 Bobby Bonilla	.10
6 Kevin Tapani	.10
7 Eric Karros	.10
8 Cliff Floyd	.10
9 Pat Kelly	.10
10 Jeffrey Hammonds	.10
11 Jeff Conine	.10
12 Fred McGriff	.10
13 Chris Bosio	.10
14 Mike Mussina	.40
15 Danny Bautista	.10
16 Mickey Morandini	.10
17 Chuck Finley	.10
18 Jim Thome	.65
19 Luis Ortiz	.10
20 Walt Weiss	.10
21 Don Mattingly	1.25
22 Bob Hamelin	.10
23 Melido Perez	.10
24 Kevin Mitchell	.10
25 John Smoltz	.10
26 Hector Carrasco	.10
27 Pat Hentgen	.10
28 Derrick May	.10
29 Mike Kingery	.10
30 Chuck Carr	.10
31 Billy Ashley	.10
32 Todd Hundley	.10
33 Luis Gonzalez	.10
34 Marquis Grissom	.10
35 Jeff King	.10
36 Eddie Williams	.10
37 Tom Pagnozzi	.10
38 Chris Hoiles	.10
39 Sandy Alomar	.10
40 Mike Greenwell	.10
41 Lance Johnson	.10
42 Junior Felix	.10
43 Felix Jose	.10
44 Scott Leius	.10
45 Ruben Sierra	.10
46 Kevin Seitzer	.10
47 Wade Boggs	1.00
48 Reggie Jefferson	.10
49 Jose Canseco	.40
50 Dave Justice	.10
51 John Smiley	.10
52 Joe Carter	.10
53 Rick Wilkins	.10
54 Ellis Burks	.10
55 Dave Weathers	.10
56 Pedro Astacio	.10
57 Ryan Thompson	.10
58 James Mouton	.10
59 Mel Rojas	.10
60 Orlando Merced	.10
61 Matt Williams	.10
62 Bernard Gilkey	.10
63 J.R. Phillips	.10
64 Lee Smith	.10

65 Jim Edmonds	.10
66 Darrin Jackson	.10
67 Scott Cooper	.10
68 Ron Karkovice	.10
69 Chris Gomez	.10
70 Kevin Appier	.10
71 Bobby Jones	.10
72 Doug Drabek	.10
73 Matt Mieske	.10
74 Sterling Hitchcock	.10
75 John Valentin	.10
76 Reggie Sanders	.10
77 Wally Joyner	.10
78 Turk Wendell	.10
79 Wendell Hayes	.10
80 Bret Barberie	.10
81 Troy Neel	.10
82 Ken Caminiti	.10
83 Milt Thompson	.10
84 Paul Sorrento	.10
85 Trevor Hoffman	.10
86 Jay Bell	.10
87 Mark Portugal	.10
88 Sid Fernandez	.10
89 Charles Nagy	.10
90 Jeff Montgomery	.10
91 Chuck Knoblauch	.10
92 Jeff Frye	.10
93 Tony Gwynn	1.00
94 John Olerud	.10
95 David Nied	.10
96 Chris Hammond	.10
97 Edgar Martinez	.10
98 Kevin Stocker	.10
99 Jeff Fassero	.10
100 Curt Schilling	.30
101 Dave Clark	.10
102 Delino DeShields	.10
103 Leo Gomez	.10
104 Dave Hollins	.10
105 Tim Naehring	.10
106 Otis Nixon	.10
107 Ozzie Guillen	.10
108 Jose Lind	.10
109 Stan Javier	.10
110 Greg Vaughn	.10
111 Chipper Jones	1.00
112 Ed Sprague	.10
113 Mike Macfarlane	.10
114 Steve Finley	.10
115 Ken Hill	.10
116 Carlos Garcia	.10
117 Lou Whitaker	.10
118 Todd Zeile	.10
119 Gary Sheffield	.40
120 Ben McDonald	.10
121 Pete Harnisch	.10
122 Ivan Rodriguez	.65
123 Wilson Alvarez	.10
124 Travis Fryman	.10
125 Pedro Munoz	.10
126 Mark Lemke	.10
127 Jose Valentin	.10
128 Ken Griffey Jr.	1.50
129 Omar Vizquel	.10
130 Milt Cuyler	.10
131 Steve Traschel	.10
132 Alex Rodriguez	2.00
133 Garret Anderson	.10
134 Armando Benitez	.10
135 Shawn Green	.35
136 Jorge Fabregas	.10
137 Orlando Miller	.10
138 Rikkert Faneyte	.10
139 Ismael Valdes	.10
140 Jose Oliva	.10
141 Aaron Small	.10
142 Tim Davis	.10
143 Ricky Bottalacio	.10
144 Mike Matheny	.10
145 Roberto Petagine	.10
146 Fausto Cruz	.10
147 Bryce Florie	.10
148 Jose Lima	.10
149 John Hudek	.10
150 Duane Singleton	.10
151 John Mabry	.10
152 Robert Eenhoorn	.10
153 Jon Lieber	.10
154 Garey Ingram	.10
155 Paul Shuey	.10
156 Mike Lieberthal	.10
157 Steve Dunn	.10
158 Charles Johnson	.10
159 Ernie Young	.10
160 Jose Martinez	.10
161 Kurt Miller	.10
162 Joey Eischen	.10
163 Dave Stevens	.10
164 Brian Hunter	.10
165 Jeff Cirillo	.10
166 Mark Smith	.10
167 McKay Christensen RC	.10
168 C.J. Nitkowski	.10
169 Antone Williamson RC	.10
170 Paul Konerko	.15
171 Scott Elarton RC	.15
172 Jacob Shumate	.10
173 Terrence Long	.10
174 Mark Johnson RC	.10
175 Ben Grieve	.10
176 Jayson Peterson RC	.10
177 Checklist	.10
178 Checklist	.10
179 Checklist	.10
180 Checklist	.10
181 Brian Anderson	.10
182 Steve Buechele	.10

183 Mark Clark	.10
184 Cecil Fielder	.10
185 Steve Avery	.10
186 Devon White	.10
187 Craig Shipley	.10
188 Brady Anderson	.10
189 Kenny Lofton	.10
190 Alex Cole	.10
191 Brent Gates	.10
192 Dean Palmer	.10
193 Alex Gonzalez	.10
194 Steve Cooke	.10
195 Ray Lankford	.10
196 Mark McGwire	2.00
197 Marc Newfield	.10
198 Pat Rapp	.10
199 Darren Lewis	.10
200 Carlos Baerga	.10
201 Rickey Henderson	.75
202 Kurt Abbott	.10
203 Kirt Manwaring	.10
204 Cal Ripken Jr.	2.50
205 Darren Daulton	.10
206 Greg Colbrunn	.10
207 Darryl Hamilton	.10
208 Bo Jackson	.15
209 Tony Phillips	.10
210 Geronimo Berroa	.10
211 Rich Becker	.10
212 Tony Tarasco	.10
213 Karl Rhodes	.10
214 Phil Plantier	.10
215 J.T. Snow	.10
216 Mo Vaughn	.10
217 Greg Gagne	.10
218 Rickey Bones	.10
219 Mike Bordick	.10
220 Chad Curtis	.10
221 Royce Clayton	.10
222 Roberto Alomar	.15
223 Jose Rijo	.10
224 Ryan Klesko	.10
225 Mark Langston	.10
226 Frank Thomas	.75
227 Juan Gonzalez	.40
228 Ron Gant	.10
229 Javier Lopez	.10
230 Sammy Sosa	1.00
231 Kevin Brown	.10
232 Gary DiSarcina	.10
233 Albert Belle	.10
234 Jay Buhner	.10
235 Pedro Martinez	.75
236 Bob Tewksbury	.10
237 Mike Piazza	1.50
238 Darryl Kile	.10
239 Bryan Harvey	.10
240 Andres Galarraga	.10
241 Jeff Blauser	.10
242 Jeff Kent	.10
243 Bobby Munoz	.10
244 Greg Maddux	1.00
245 Paul O'Neill	.10
246 Lenny Dykstra	.10
247 Todd Van Poppel	.10
248 Bernie Williams	.05
249 Glenallen Hill	.10
250 Duane Ward	.10
251 Dennis Eckersley	.60
252 Pat Mahomes	.10
253 Rusty Greer (Photo actually Jeff Frye.)	.10
254 Roberto Kelly	.10
255 Randy Myers	.10
256 Scott Ruffcorn	.10
257 Robin Ventura	.10
258 Eduardo Perez	.10
259 Aaron Sele	.10
260 Paul Molitor	.75
261 Juan Guzman	.10
262 Darren Oliver	.10
263 Mike Stanley	.10
264 Tom Glavine	.30
265 Rico Brogna	.10
266 Craig Biggio	.10
267 Darrell Whitmore	.10
268 Jimmy Key	.10
269 Will Clark	.10
270 David Cone	.10
271 Brian Jordan	.10
272 Barry Bonds	2.50
273 Danny Tartabull	.10
274 Ramon Martinez	.10
275 Al Martin	.10
276 Fred McGriff (Swing Men)	.10
277 Carlos Delgado (Swing Men)	.25
278 Juan Gonzalez (Swing Men)	.20
279 Shawn Green (Swing Men)	.20
280 Carlos Baerga (Swing Men)	.10
281 Cliff Floyd (Swing Men)	.10
282 Ozzie Smith (Swing Men)	.50
283 Alex Rodriguez (Swing Men)	1.00
284 Kenny Lofton (Swing Men)	.10
285 Dave Justice (Swing Men)	.10
286 Tim Salmon (Swing Men)	.10
287 Manny Ramirez (Swing Men)	.40
288 Will Clark (Swing Men)	.10
289 Garret Anderson (Swing Men)	.10
290 Billy Ashley (Swing Men)	.10
291 Tony Gwynn (Swing Men)	.50

292 Raul Mondesi (Swing Men)	.10
293 Rafael Palmeiro (Swing Men)	.30
294 Matt Williams (Swing Men)	.10
295 Don Mattingly (Swing Men)	.60
296 Kirby Puckett (Swing Men)	.50
297 Paul Molitor (Swing Men)	.40
298 Albert Belle (Swing Men)	.10
299 Barry Bonds (Swing Men)	1.25
300 Mike Piazza (Swing Men)	.85
301 Jeff Bagwell (Swing Men)	.40
302 Frank Thomas (Swing Men)	.40
303 Chipper Jones (Swing Men)	.50
304 Ken Griffey Jr. (Swing Men)	.75
305 Cal Ripken Jr. (Swing Men)	1.25
306 Eric Anthony	.10
307 Todd Benzinger	.10
308 Jacob Brumfield	.10
309 Wes Chamberlain	.10
310 Tino Martinez	.10
311 Roberto Mejia	.10
312 Jose Offerman	.10
313 David Segui	.10
314 Eric Young	.10
315 Rey Sanchez	.10
316 Raul Mondesi	.10
317 Bret Boone	.10
318 Andre Dawson	.30
319 Brian McRae	.10
320 Dave Nilsson	.10
321 Moises Alou	.10
322 Don Slaught	.10
323 Dave McCarty	.10
324 Mike Huff	.10
325 Rick Aguilera	.10
326 Rod Beck	.10
327 Kenny Rogers	.10
328 Andy Benes	.10
329 Allen Watson	.10
330 Randy Johnson	.75
331 Willie Greene	.10
332 Hal Morris	.10
333 Ozzie Smith	1.00
334 Jason Bere	.10
335 Scott Erickson	.10
336 Dante Bichette	.10
337 Willie Banks	.10
338 Eric Davis	.10
339 Rondell White	.10
340 Kirby Puckett	1.00
341 Deion Sanders	.10
342 Eddie Murray	.75
343 Mike Harkey	.10
344 Joey Hamilton	.10
345 Roger Salkeld	.10
346 Wil Cordero	.10
347 John Wetteland	.10
348 Geronimo Pena	.10
349 Kirk Gibson	.10
350 Manny Ramirez	.75
351 William Van Landingham	.10
352 B.J. Surhoff	.10
353 Ken Ryan	.10
354 Terry Steinbach	.10
355 Bret Saberhagen	.10
356 John Jaha	.10
357 Joe Girardi	.10
358 Steve Karsay	.10
359 Alex Fernandez	.10
360 Salomon Torres	.10
361 John Burkett	.10
362 Derek Bell	.10
363 Tom Henke	.10
364 Gregg Jefferies	.10
365 Jack McDowell	.10
366 Andujar Cedeno	.10
367 Dave Winfield	.75
368 Carl Everett	.10
369 Danny Jackson	.10
370 Jeromy Burnitz	.10
371 Mark Grace	.10
372 Larry Walker	.10
373 Bill Swift	.10
374 Dennis Martinez	.10
375 Mickey Tettleton	.10
376 Mel Nieves	.10
377 Cal Eldred	.10
378 Orel Hershiser	.10
379 David Wells	.10
380 Gary Gaetti	.10
381 Tim Raines	.10
382 Barry Larkin	.10
383 Jason Jacome	.10
384 Tim Wallach	.10
385 Robby Thompson	.10
386 Frank Viola	.10
387 Dave Stewart	.10
388 Bip Roberts	.10
389 Ron Darling	.10
390 Carlos Delgado	.45
391 Tim Salmon	.10
392 Alan Trammell	.10
393 Kevin Foster	.10
394 Jim Abbott	.10
395 John Kruk	.10
396 Andy Van Slyke	.10
397 Dave Magadan	.10
398 Rafael Palmeiro	.65
399 Mike Devereaux	.10

400 Benito Santiago	.10
401 Brett Butler	.10
402 John Franco	.10
403 Matt Walbeck	.10
404 Terry Pendleton	.10
405 Chris Sabo	.10
406 Andrew Lorraine	.10
407 Dan Wilson	.10
408 Mike Lansing	.10
409 Ray McDavid	.10
410 Shane Andrews	.10
411 Tom Gordon	.10
412 Chad Ogea	.10
413 James Baldwin	.10
414 Russ Davis	.10
415 Ray Holbert	.10
416 Ray Durham	.10
417 Matt Nokes	.10
418 Rodney Henderson	.10
419 Gabe White	.10
420 Todd Hollandsworth	.10
421 Midre Cummings	.10
422 Harold Baines	.10
423 Troy Percival	.10
424 Joe Vitiello	.10
425 Andy Ashby	.10
426 Michael Tucker	.10
427 Mark Gubicza	.10
428 Jim Bullinger	.10
429 Jose Malave	.10
430 Pete Schourek	.10
431 Bobby Ayala	.10
432 Marvin Freeman	.10
433 Pat Listach	.10
434 Eddie Taubensee	.10
435 Steve Howe	.10
436 Kent Mercker	.10
437 Hector Fajardo	.10
438 Scott Kamieniecki	.10
439 Robb Nen	.10
440 Mike Kelly	.10
441 Tom Candiotti	.10
442 Albie Lopez	.10
443 Jeff Granger	.10
444 Rich Aude	.10
445 Luis Polonia	.10
446 A.L. Checklist (Frank Thomas)	.40
447 A.L. Checklist (Ken Griffey Jr.)	.65
448 N.L. Checklist (Mike Piazza)	.75
449 N.L. Checklist (Jeff Bagwell)	.40
450 Insert Checklist (Frank Thomas, Ken Griffey Jr., Mike Piazza, Jeff Bagwell)	.40

Artist's Proof

Said to represent the first 1,000 of each card printed, the Artist's Proof chase set is a parallel issue with a counterpart for each of the regular-issue cards. The proofs differ in the use of silver, rather than gold foil for front graphic highlights, and the inclusion of a rectangular silver-foil "ARTIST'S PROOF" logo on front. The AP inserts were reported seeded at an average rate of one per 26 packs.

	NM/M
Complete Set (450):	300.00
Common Player:	1.00
Stars/Rookies:	10X

Museum Collection

Pinnacle's Dufex foil-printing technology on the card fronts differentiates this parallel insert from the corresponding cards in the regular issue. Backs have a rectangular "1995 Museum Collection" logo at lower-left. Museum inserts are found at an average rate of one per four packs. Because of production difficulties, trade cards had to be issued in place of seven of the rookie cards in Series 2. Those redemption cards were valid only through Dec. 31, 1995.

	NM/M
Complete Set (450):	200.00
Common Player:	.50
Stars/Rookies:	4X
Redemption Card	.25

E.T.A. '95

This hobby-only chase set identifies six players picked to arrive in the major leagues for a 1995 debut. Both sides have borderless action photos on which the background has been subdued and posterized. Gold-foil headlines on each side of the card give the player's credentials. These inserts are found on average of once per 24 packs.

	NM/M
Complete Set (6):	5.00
Common Player:	.70
1 Ben Grieve	.75
2 Alex Ochoa	.75
3 Joe Vitiello	.75
4 Johnny Damon	3.00
5 Trey Beamon	.75
6 Brooks Kieschnick	.75

Gate Attraction

Series 2 jumbo packs are the exclusive source for this chase set. Printed on metallic foil, the cards have a color photo at top and a second photo at bottom that is shown in gold tones only. A "Gate Attraction" seal is in the lower-left corner. Backs have a large portrait photo on a color-streaked background, plus a few words about the player.

	NM/M
Complete Set (18):	25.00
Common Player:	.50
1 Ken Griffey Jr.	3.50
2 Frank Thomas	1.50
3 Cal Ripken Jr.	5.00
4 Jeff Bagwell	1.50
5 Mike Piazza	3.50
6 Barry Bonds	5.00
7 Kirby Puckett	2.00
8 Albert Belle	.50
9 Tony Gwynn	2.00
10 Raul Mondesi	.50
11 Will Clark	.50
12 Don Mattingly	2.75
13 Roger Clemens	2.75
14 Paul Molitor	1.50
15 Matt Williams	.50
16 Greg Maddux	2.00
17 Kenny Lofton	.50
18 Cliff Floyd	.50

New Blood

Both hobby and retail packs of Series 2 hide this insert set of young stars, at an average rate of one card per 90 packs. A player photo appears in the red and silver foil-printed background, and there is a color action photo in the foreground. Conventionally printed backs feature the same photos, but with their prominence reversed. A few words of text describe the player's star potential.

	NM/M
Complete Set (9):	10.00
Common Player:	.75
1 Alex Rodriguez	5.00
2 Shawn Green	1.50
3 Brian Hunter	.75
4 Garret Anderson	.75
5 Charles Johnson	.75
6 Chipper Jones	3.00
7 Carlos Delgado	1.50
8 Billy Ashley	.75
9 J.R. Phillips	.75

Performers

Series 1 jumbos were the only place to find this chase set. Fronts have a deep red background with a golden pyramid at center and a silver apex, all in foil printing. A color player action photo is in the center foreground. The reverse repeats the front photo in the background, in one color, and has a second color photo, along with a few words about the player.

	NM/M
Complete Set (18):	15.00
Common Player:	.35
1 Frank Thomas	2.00
2 Albert Belle	.35
3 Barry Bonds	3.50
4 Juan Gonzalez	1.00
5 Andres Galarraga	.35
6 Raul Mondesi	.35
7 Paul Molitor	2.00
8 Tim Salmon	.35
9 Mike Piazza	2.50
10 Gregg Jefferies	.35
11 Will Clark	.35
12 Greg Maddux	2.25
13 Manny Ramirez	2.00
14 Kirby Puckett	2.25
15 Shawn Green	1.25
16 Rafael Palmeiro	1.75
17 Paul O'Neill	.35
18 Jason Bere	.35

Red Hot

These Series 2 inserts are found at an average rate of one per 16 packs and feature top veteran stars. Fronts have a large action photo on right, over a background of foil-printed red and yellow flames. A vertical strip at left of graduated red tones has a player portrait photo and the "RED HOT" flame logo, again printed on foil. Backs are conventionally printed

and have a black background with large flaming "RED HOT" letters and a color player photo.

	NM/M
Complete Set (25):	35.00
Common Player:	.75
1 Cal Ripken Jr.	5.50
2 Ken Griffey Jr.	4.00
3 Frank Thomas	1.50
4 Jeff Bagwell	1.50
5 Mike Piazza	4.00
6 Barry Bonds	5.50
7 Albert Belle	.75
8 Tony Gwynn	2.00
9 Kirby Puckett	2.00
10 Don Mattingly	2.50
11 Matt Williams	.75
12 Greg Maddux	2.00
13 Raul Mondesi	.75
14 Paul Molitor	1.50
15 Manny Ramirez	1.50
16 Joe Carter	.75
17 Will Clark	.75
18 Roger Clemens	2.50
19 Tim Salmon	.75
20 Dave Justice	.75
21 Kenny Lofton	.75
22 Deion Sanders	.75
23 Roberto Alomar	1.00
24 Cliff Floyd	.75
25 Carlos Baerga	.75

White Hot

Similar in format to the Red Hot inserts, and featuring the same players, the hobby-only White Hot cards are a chase set of a chase set. Seeded once per 36 packs on average (more than twice as scarce as the Red Hots), the White Hot cards have fronts totally printed in the Dufex process, with predominantly blue and white background colors, while the backs are highlighted by blue foil printing in the "WHITE HOT" background lettering on black background.

	NM/M
Complete Set (25):	140.00
Common Player:	2.50
1 Cal Ripken Jr.	16.00
2 Ken Griffey Jr.	13.50
3 Frank Thomas	8.00
4 Jeff Bagwell	8.00
5 Mike Piazza	13.50
6 Barry Bonds	16.00
7 Albert Belle	2.50
8 Tony Gwynn	10.00
9 Kirby Puckett	10.00
10 Don Mattingly	12.00
11 Matt Williams	2.50
12 Greg Maddux	10.00
13 Raul Mondesi	2.50
14 Paul Molitor	8.00
15 Manny Ramirez	8.00
16 Joe Carter	2.50
17 Will Clark	2.50
18 Roger Clemens	12.00
19 Tim Salmon	2.50
20 Dave Justice	2.50
21 Kenny Lofton	2.50
22 Deion Sanders	2.50
23 Roberto Alomar	3.50
24 Cliff Floyd	2.50
25 Carlos Baerga	2.50

Team Pinnacle

This nine-card Series 1 insert set becomes an 18-card challenge if the collector decides to hunt for both versions of each card. As in the past the Team Pinnacle cards picture National and American League counterparts at each position on different sides of the same card. In 1995 each card is printed with one side in Pinnacle's Dufex foil technology, and the other side conventionally printed. Thus card #1 can be found with Mike Mussina in Dufex and Greg Maddux conventionally printed, or with Maddux in Dufex and Mussina conventional. Team Pinnacle cards are found inserted at an average rate of only one per 90 packs. Card numbers have a "TP" prefix.

		NM/M
Complete Set (9):		35.00
Common Player:		1.50
1	Mike Mussina, Greg Maddux	8.00
2	Carlos Delgado, Mike Piazza	6.00
3	Frank Thomas, Jeff Bagwell	4.00
4	Roberto Alomar, Craig Biggio	3.00
5	Cal Ripken Jr., Ozzie Smith	12.00
6	Travis Fryman, Matt Williams	1.50
7	Ken Griffey Jr., Barry Bonds	10.00
8	Albert Belle, Dave Justice	1.50
9	Kirby Puckett, Tony Gwynn	8.00

Team Pinnacle Pin Trade Cards

In one of the hobby's first major attempts to cross-promote pin- and card-collecting, Series 2 Pinnacle packs offered a special insert set of cards which could be redeemed for a collector's pin of the same player. Seeded at the rate of one per 48 regular packs and one per 36 jumbo packs, the pin redemption cards were valid until Nov. 15, 1995. Payment of $2 handling fee was required for redemption.

	NM/M
Complete Set (18):	40.00
Common Player:	.75
1 Greg Maddux	4.00
2 Mike Mussina	1.50
3 Mike Piazza	5.00
4 Carlos Delgado	1.50
5 Jeff Bagwell	3.00
6 Frank Thomas	3.00
7 Craig Biggio	1.00
8 Roberto Alomar	1.00
9 Ozzie Smith	4.00
10 Cal Ripken Jr.	6.00
11 Matt Williams	.75
12 Travis Fryman	.75
13 Barry Bonds	6.00
14 Ken Griffey Jr.	5.00
15 Dave Justice	.75
16 Albert Belle	.75
17 Tony Gwynn	4.00
18 Kirby Puckett	4.00

Team Pinnacle Collector Pins

Redemption cards in Series 2 packs could be traded in (until Nov. 15, 1995) for an enameled pin of the player pictured on the trade card. Pins are about 1-3/8" x 1-1/4". A raised relief portrait of the player is at center with his name in pennants above and his team logo at bottom, along with the Pinnacle logo. Backs are gold-tone with a post-and-button style of pinback. The unnumbered pins are listed here in the same sequence as the redemption cards.

	NM/M
Complete Set (18):	135.00
Common Player:	5.00
(1) Greg Maddux	10.00
(2) Mike Mussina	6.00
(3) Mike Piazza	15.00
(4) Carlos Delgado	8.00
(5) Jeff Bagwell	8.00
(6) Frank Thomas	8.00
(7) Craig Biggio	5.00
(8) Roberto Alomar	5.00
(9) Ozzie Smith	10.00
(10) Cal Ripken Jr.	20.00
(11) Matt Williams	5.00
(12) Travis Fryman	5.00
(13) Barry Bonds	20.00
(14) Ken Griffey Jr.	15.00
(15) Dave Justice	5.00
(16) Albert Belle	5.00
(17) Tony Gwynn	10.00
(18) Kirby Puckett	10.00

Pin-Cards

Virtually nothing is known of this issue except that it is connected in some way to the Series 2 Pinnacle player pin issue. The front features portrait and action photos on a red background with gold-foil graphics. Backs have career highlights, a large color photo and a card number with "PPC" prefix. To date only a single card is known.

Upstarts

The most dominant young players in the game were featured in this insert series. Cards are printed with most of the photo's background covered by the legs of a large blue-and-gold star device, which includes the team logo at its red center. A blue circular "'95 UPSTARTS" logo at bottom-left has the player name in gold.

These cards are exclusive to Series 1, found at an average rate of one per eight packs.

	NM/M
Complete Set (30):	10.00
Common Player:	.15
1 Frank Thomas	1.50
2 Roberto Alomar	.30
3 Mike Piazza	2.50
4 Javier Lopez	.15
5 Albert Belle	.15
6 Carlos Delgado	.75
7 Rusty Greer	.15
8 Tim Salmon	.15
9 Raul Mondesi	.15
10 Juan Gonzalez	.75
11 Manny Ramirez	1.50
12 Sammy Sosa	2.00
13 Jeff Kent	.15
14 Melvin Nieves	.15
15 Rondell White	.15
16 Shawn Green	.75
17 Bernie Williams	.15
18 Aaron Sele	.15
19 Jason Bere	.15
20 Joey Hamilton	.15
21 Mike Kelly	.15
22 Wil Cordero	.15
23 Moises Alou	.15
24 Roberto Kelly	.15
25 Deion Sanders	.15
26 Steve Karsay	.15
27 Bret Boone	.15
28 Willie Greene	.15
29 Billy Ashley	.15
30 Brian Anderson	.15

FanFest

Pinnacle's sponsorship of the July 7-11 All-Star FanFest was marked with the issue of this set. Cards were distributed in two-card packs at various venues around the All-Star celebration in Arlington, Texas. Each card features the FanFest logo at lower-left on front, with the player's name and team logo in a stylized gold-foil baseball diamond diagram at lower-right. A full-bleed action photo comprises the rest of the front. Horizontal backs show a portrait photo of the player before a photo of The Ballpark at Arlington. The FanFest logo is repeated at bottom-center.

	NM/M
Complete Set (30):	7.50
Common Player:	.15
1 Cal Ripken Jr.	1.50
2 Roger Clemens	.75
3 Don Mattingly	.75
4 Albert Belle	.15
5 Kirby Puckett	.65
6 Cecil Fielder	.15
7 Kevin Appier	.15
8 Will Clark	.15
9 Juan Gonzalez	.25
10 Ivan Rodriguez	.45
11 Ken Griffey Jr.	1.00
12 Tim Salmon	.15
13 Frank Thomas	.50
14 Roberto Alomar	.20
15 Rickey Henderson	.50
16 Raul Mondesi	.15
17 Matt Williams	.15
18 Ozzie Smith	.65
19 Deion Sanders	.15
20 Tony Gwynn	.65
21 Greg Maddux	.65
22 Sammy Sosa	.15
23 Mike Piazza	1.00
24 Barry Bonds	1.50
25 Jeff Bagwell	.50
26 Len Dykstra	.15
27 Rico Brogna	.15
28 Larry Walker	.15
29 Gary Sheffield	.35
30 Wil Cordero	.15

1996 Pinnacle Samples

GREG MADDUX

Pinnacle's 1996 issue was premiered with this nine-card sample set. The cards are virtually identical in format to the regular-issue cards, but feature a large white "SAMPLE" printed diagonally on front and back. The cards were sent to dealers and hobby media in a cello pack.

		NM/M
Complete Set (9):		5.00
Common Player:		.75
1	Greg Maddux	1.50
2	Bill Pulsipher	.75
3	Dante Bichette	.75
4	Mike Piazza	2.00
5	Garret Anderson	.75
165	Ruben Rivera	.75
168	Tony Clark	.75
2	Mo Vaughn (Pinnacle Power)	1.00
---	Header Card	.10

1996 Pinnacle

RUBEN RIVERA

Pinnacle's 400-card regular-issue set has borderless front photos highlighted by prismatic gold-foil graphics in a triangle at bottom. Backs have another photo along with stats and data. Parallel Starburst and Starburst Artist's Proof sets contain only 200 of the cards in the base issue. Series 1 inserts include a Cal Ripken Jr. "Tribute" card, numbered "1 of 1," along with Team Pinnacle, Pinnacle Power, Team Tomorrow, Essence of the Game and First Rate. Series 2 inserts are Christie Brinkley Collection, Project Stardom, Skylines, Slugfest and Team Spirit. Pinnacle was sold in 10-card hobby and retail foil packs, and 18-card jumbo packs.

		NM/M
Complete Set (400):		15.00
Common Player:		.10
Series 1 or 2 Pack (10):		.75
Series 1 or 2 Box (24):		15.00
1	Greg Maddux	1.00
2	Bill Pulsipher	.10
3	Dante Bichette	.10
4	Mike Piazza	1.50
5	Garret Anderson	.10
6	Steve Finley	.10
7	Andy Benes	.10
8	Chuck Knoblauch	.10
9	Tom Gordon	.10
10	Jeff Bagwell	.75
11	Wil Cordero	.10
12	John Mabry	.10
13	Jeff Frye	.10
14	Travis Fryman	.10
15	John Wetteland	.10
16	Jason Bates	.10
17	Danny Tartabull	.10
18	Charles Nagy	.10
19	Robin Ventura	.10
20	Reggie Sanders	.10
21	Dave Clark	.10
22	Jaime Navarro	.10
23	Joey Hamilton	.10
24	Al Leiter	.10
25	Deion Sanders	.10
26	Tim Salmon	.10
27	Tino Martinez	.10
28	Mike Greenwell	.10
29	Phil Plantier	.10
30	Bobby Bonilla	.10
31	Kenny Rogers	.10
32	Chili Davis	.10
33	Joe Carter	.10
34	Mike Mussina	.40
35	Matt Mieske	.10
36	Jose Canseco	.40
37	Brad Radke	.10
38	Juan Gonzalez	.40
39	David Segui	.10
40	Alex Fernandez	.10
41	Jeff Kent	.10
42	Todd Zeile	.10
43	Darryl Strawberry	.10
44	Jose Rijo	.10
45	Ramon Martinez	.10
46	Manny Ramirez	.75
47	Gregg Jefferies	.10
48	Bryan Rekar	.10
49	Jeff King	.10
50	John Olerud	.10
51	Marc Newfield	.10
52	Charles Johnson	.10
53	Robby Thompson	.10
54	Brian Hunter	.10
55	Mike Blowers	.10
56	Keith Lockhart	.10
57	Ray Lankford	.10
58	Tim Wallach	.10
59	Ivan Rodriguez	.65
60	Ed Sprague	.10
61	Paul Molitor	.75
62	Eric Karros	.10
63	Glenallen Hill	.10
64	Jay Bell	.10
65	Tom Pagnozzi	.10
66	Greg Colbrunn	.10
67	Edgar Martinez	.10
68	Paul Sorrento	.10
69	Kirt Manwaring	.10
70	Pete Schourek	.10
71	Orlando Merced	.10
72	Shawon Dunston	.10
73	Ricky Bottalico	.10
74	Brady Anderson	.10
75	Steve Ontiveros	.10
76	Jim Abbott	.10
77	Carl Everett	.10
78	Mo Vaughn	.10
79	Pedro Martinez	.75
80	Harold Baines	.10
81	Alan Trammell	.10
82	Steve Avery	.10
83	Jeff Cirillo	.10
84	John Valentin	.10
85	Bernie Williams	.10
86	Andre Dawson	.30
87	Dave Winfield	.75
88	B.J. Surhoff	.10
89	Jeff Blauser	.10
90	Barry Larkin	.10
91	Cliff Floyd	.10
92	Sammy Sosa	1.00
93	Andres Galarraga	.10
94	Dave Nilsson	.10
95	James Mouton	.10
96	Marquis Grissom	.10
97	Matt Williams	.10
98	John Jaha	.10
99	Don Mattingly	1.25
100	Tim Naehring	.10
101	Kevin Appier	.10
102	Bobby Higginson	.10
103	Andy Pettitte	.25
104	Ozzie Smith	1.00
105	Kenny Lofton	.10
106	Ken Caminiti	.10
107	Walt Weiss	.10
108	Jack McDowell	.10
109	Brian McRae	.10
110	Gary Gaetti	.10
111	Curtis Goodwin	.10
112	Dennis Martinez	.10
113	Omar Vizquel	.10
114	Chipper Jones	1.00
115	Mark Gubicza	.10
116	Ruben Sierra	.10
117	Eddie Murray	.75
118	Chad Curtis	.10
119	Hal Morris	.10
120	Ben McDonald	.10
121	Marty Cordova	.10
122	Ken Griffey Jr.	1.50
123	Gary Sheffield	.40
124	Charlie Hayes	.10
125	Shawn Green	.40
126	Jason Giambi	.50
127	Mark Langston	.10
128	Mark Whiten	.10
129	Greg Vaughn	.10
130	Mark McGwire	1.75
131	Hideo Nomo	.40
132	Eric Karros, Raul Mondesi, Hideo Nomo, Mike Piazza	.10
133	Jason Bere	.10
134	Ken Griffey Jr. (The Naturals)	.65
135	Frank Thomas (The Naturals)	.40
136	Cal Ripken Jr. (The Naturals)	1.00
137	Albert Belle (The Naturals)	.10
138	Mike Piazza (The Naturals)	.65
139	Dante Bichette (The Naturals)	.10
140	Sammy Sosa (The Naturals)	.50
141	Mo Vaughn (The Naturals)	.10
142	Tim Salmon (The Naturals)	.10
143	Reggie Sanders (The Naturals)	.10
144	Cecil Fielder (The Naturals)	.10
145	Jim Edmonds (The Naturals)	.10
146	Rafael Palmeiro (The Naturals)	.10
147	Edgar Martinez (The Naturals)	.10
148	Barry Bonds (The Naturals)	1.00
149	Manny Ramirez (The Naturals)	.35
150	Larry Walker (The Naturals)	.10
151	Jeff Bagwell (The Naturals)	.35
152	Ron Gant (The Naturals)	.10
153	Andres Galarraga (The Naturals)	.10
154	Eddie Murray (The Naturals)	.35
155	Kirby Puckett (The Naturals)	.50
156	Will Clark (The Naturals)	.10
157	Don Mattingly (The Naturals)	.60
158	Mark McGwire (The Naturals)	.75
159	Dean Palmer (The Naturals)	.10
160	Matt Williams (The Naturals)	.10
161	Fred McGriff (The Naturals)	.10
162	Joe Carter (The Naturals)	.10
163	Juan Gonzalez (The Naturals)	.15
164	Alex Ochoa	.10
165	Ruben Rivera	.10
166	Tony Clark	.10
167	Brian Barber	.10
168	Matt Lawton	.10
169	Terrell Wade	.10
170	Johnny Damon	.30
171	Derek Jeter	2.00
172	Phil Nevin	.10
173	Robert Perez	.10
174	C.J. Nitkowski	.10
175	Joe Vitiello	.10
176	Roger Cedeno	.10
177	Ron Coomer	.10
178	Chris Widger	.10
179	Jimmy Haynes	.10
180	Mike Sweeney RC	.50
181	Howard Battle	.10
182	John Wasdin	.10
183	Jim Pittsley	.10
184	Bob Wolcott	.10
185	LaTroy Hawkins	.10
186	Nigel Wilson	.10
187	Dustin Hermanson	.10
188	Chris Snopek	.10
189	Mariano Rivera	.15
190	Jose Herrera	.10
191	Chris Stynes	.10
192	Larry Thomas	.10
193	David Bell	.10
194	Frank Thomas (Checklist)	.40
195	Ken Griffey Jr. (Checklist)	.65
196	Cal Ripken Jr. (Checklist)	.75
197	Jeff Bagwell (Checklist)	.35
198	Mike Piazza (Checklist)	.60
199	Barry Bonds (Checklist)	.75
200	Garret Anderson, Chipper Jones (Checklist)	.25
201	Frank Thomas	.75
202	Michael Tucker	.10
203	Kirby Puckett	1.00
204	Alex Gonzalez	.10
205	Tony Gwynn	1.00
206	Moises Alou	.10
207	Albert Belle	.10
208	Barry Bonds	2.00
209	Fred McGriff	.10
210	Dennis Eckersley	.65
211	Craig Biggio	.10
212	David Cone	.10
213	Will Clark	.10
214	Cal Ripken Jr.	2.00
215	Wade Boggs	1.00
216	Pete Schourek	.10
217	Darren Daulton	.10
218	Carlos Baerga	.10
219	Larry Walker	.10
220	Denny Neagle	.10
221	Jim Edmonds	.10
222	Lee Smith	.10
223	Jason Isringhausen	.10
224	Jay Buhner	.10
225	John Olerud	.10
226	Jeff Conine	.10
227	Dean Palmer	.10
228	Jim Abbott	.10
229	Raul Mondesi	.10
230	Tom Glavine	.35
231	Kevin Seitzer	.10
232	Lenny Dykstra	.10
233	Brian Jordan	.10
234	Rondell White	.10
235	Bret Boone	.10
236	Randy Johnson	.75
237	Paul O'Neill	.10
238	Jim Thome	.65
239	Edgardo Alfonzo	.10
240	Terry Pendleton	.10
241	Harold Baines	.10
242	Roberto Alomar	.20
243	Mark Grace	.10
244	Derek Bell	.10
245	Vinny Castilla	.10
246	Cecil Fielder	.10
247	Roger Clemens	1.25
248	Orel Hershiser	.10
249	J.T. Snow	.10
250	Rafael Palmeiro	.65
251	Bret Saberhagen	.10
252	Todd Hollandsworth	.10
253	Ryan Klesko	.10
254	Greg Maddux (Hardball Heroes)	.50
255	Ken Griffey Jr. (Hardball Heroes)	.65
256	Hideo Nomo (Hardball Heroes)	.15
257	Frank Thomas (Hardball Heroes)	.40
258	Cal Ripken Jr. (Hardball Heroes)	1.00
259	Jeff Bagwell (Hardball Heroes)	.35
260	Barry Bonds (Hardball Heroes)	1.00
261	Mo Vaughn (Hardball Heroes)	.10
262	Albert Belle (Hardball Heroes)	.10
263	Sammy Sosa (Hardball Heroes)	.50
264	Reggie Sanders (Hardball Heroes)	.10
265	Mike Piazza (Hardball Heroes)	.65
266	Chipper Jones (Hardball Heroes)	.50
267	Tony Gwynn (Hardball Heroes)	.50
268	Kirby Puckett (Hardball Heroes)	.50
269	Wade Boggs (Hardball Heroes)	.45
270	Will Clark (Hardball Heroes)	.10
271	Gary Sheffield (Hardball Heroes)	.10
272	Dante Bichette (Hardball Heroes)	.10
273	Randy Johnson (Hardball Heroes)	.35
274	Matt Williams (Hardball Heroes)	.10
275	Alex Rodriguez (Hardball Heroes)	.75
276	Tim Salmon (Hardball Heroes)	.10
277	Johnny Damon (Hardball Heroes)	.10
278	Manny Ramirez (Hardball Heroes)	.35
279	Derek Jeter (Hardball Heroes)	1.00
280	Eddie Murray (Hardball Heroes)	.35
281	Ozzie Smith (Hardball Heroes)	.50
282	Garret Anderson (Hardball Heroes)	.10
283	Raul Mondesi (Hardball Heroes)	.10
284	Terry Steinbach	.10
285	Carlos Garcia	.10
286	Dave Justice	.10
287	Eric Anthony	.10
288	Benji Gil	.10
289	Bob Hamelin	.10
290	Dwayne Hosey	.10
291	Andy Pettitte	.25
292	Rod Beck	.10
293	Shane Andrews	.10
294	Julian Tavarez	.10
295	Willie Greene	.10
296	Ismael Valdes	.10
297	Glenallen Hill	.10
298	Troy Percival	.10
299	Ray Durham	.10
300	Jeff Conine (.300 Series)	.10
301.8	Ken Griffey Jr. (.300 Series)	.75
302	Will Clark (.300 Series)	.10
303	Mike Greenwell (.300 Series)	.10
304.9	Carlos Baerga (.300 Series)	.10
305.3	Paul Molitor (.300 Series)	.35
305.6	Jeff Bagwell (.300 Series)	.35
306	Mark Grace (.300 Series)	.10
307	Don Mattingly (.300 Series)	.60
308	Hal Morris (.300 Series)	.10
309	Butch Huskey	.10
310	Ozzie Guillen	.10
311	Erik Hanson	.10
312	Kenny Lofton (.300 Series)	.10
313	Edgar Martinez (.300 Series)	.10
314	Kurt Abbott	.10
315	John Smoltz	.10
316	Ariel Prieto	.10
317	Mark Carreon	.10
318	Kirby Puckett (.300 Series)	.50
319	Carlos Perez	.10
320	Gary DiSarcina	.10
321	Trevor Hoffman	.10
322	Mike Piazza (.300 Series)	.65
323	Frank Thomas (.300 Series)	.40
324	Juan Acevedo	.10
325	Bip Roberts	.10
326	Javier Lopez	.10
327	Benito Santiago	.10
328	Mark Lewis	.10
329	Royce Clayton	.10
330	Tom Gordon	.10
331	Ben McDonald	.10
332	Dan Wilson	.10
333	Ron Gant	.10
334	Wade Boggs (.300 Series)	.45
335	Paul Molitor	.10
336	Tony Gwynn (.300 Series)	.50
337	Sean Berry	.10
338	Rickey Henderson	.75
339	Wil Cordero	.10
340	Kent Mercker	.10
341	Kenny Rogers	.10
342	Ryne Sandberg	1.00
343	Charlie Hayes	.10
344	Andy Benes	.10
345	Sterling Hitchcock	.10
346	Bernard Gilkey	.10
347	Julio Franco	.10
348	Ken Hill	.10
349	Russ Davis	.10
350	Mike Blowers	.10
351	B.J. Surhoff	.10
352	Lance Johnson	.10
353	Darryl Hamilton	.10
354	Shawon Dunston	.10
355	Rick Aguilera	.10
356	Danny Tartabull	.10
357	Todd Stottlemyre	.10
358	Mike Bordick	.10
359	Jack McDowell	.10
360	Todd Zeile	.10
361	Tino Martinez	.10
362	Greg Gagne	.10
363	Mike Kelly	.10
364	Tim Raines	.10
365	Ernie Young	.10
366	Mike Stanley	.10
367	Wally Joyner	.10
368	Karim Garcia	.10
369	Paul Wilson	.10
370	Sal Fasano	.10
371	Jason Schmidt	.10
372	Livan Hernandez RC	.25
373	George Arias	.10
374	Steve Gibralter	.10
375	Jermaine Dye	.10
376	Jason Kendall	.10
377	Brooks Kieschnick	.10
378	Jeff Ware	.10
379	Alan Benes	.10
380	Rey Ordonez	.10
381	Jay Powell	.10
382	Osvaldo Fernandez RC	.15
383	Wilton Guerrero RC	.10
384	Eric Owens	.10
385	George Williams	.10
386	Chan Ho Park	.10
387	Jeff Suppan	.10
388	F.P. Santangelo RC	.10
389	Terry Adams	.10
390	Bob Abreu	.10
391	Quinton McCracken RC	.10
392	Mike Busby RC	.10
393	Cal Ripken Jr. (Checklist)	.75
394	Ken Griffey Jr. (Checklist)	.60
395	Frank Thomas (Checklist)	.50
396	Chipper Jones (Checklist)	.50
397	Greg Maddux (Checklist)	.50
398	Mike Piazza (Checklist)	.65
399	Ken Griffey Jr., Frank Thomas, Cal Ripken Jr., Greg Maddux, Chipper Jones, Mike Piazza (Checklist)	.50

Artist's Proof

PHIL NEVIN

AP is a parallel to the Starburst partial parallel of '96 Pinnacle. Like Starburst, the Artist's Proof cards are printed in Dufex technology on front, with the AP cards having the words "ARTIST'S PROOF" repeated throughout the background. AP backs are identical to Starburst. Stated insertion rate for the Artist's Proofs was one per 47 packs in hobby and one per 67 retail packs.

	NM/M
Common Artist's Proof:	2.00
Stars:	3X

Starburst

PETE SCHOUREK

For 1996 Pinnacle abbreviated its parallel insert set to just half of the cards from the base issue. Only 200 select players are included in the Starburst Dufex-printed parallel set found on average of once per seven hobby packs and once per 10 retail packs.

		NM/M
Complete Set (200):		150.00
Common Player:		.40
Common Artist's Proof:		.75
Artist's Proofs:		2X
1	Greg Maddux	3.00
2	Bill Pulsipher	.40
3	Dante Bichette	.40
4	Mike Piazza	4.00
5	Garret Anderson	.40
6	Chuck Knoblauch	.40
7	Jeff Bagwell	2.25
8	Wil Cordero	.40
9	Travis Fryman	.40
10	Reggie Sanders	.40
11	Deion Sanders	.40
12	Tim Salmon	.40
13	Tino Martinez	.40
14	Bobby Bonilla	.40
15	Joe Carter	.40
16	Mike Mussina	1.25
17	Jose Canseco	1.25
18	Manny Ramirez	2.25
19	Gregg Jefferies	.40
20	Charles Johnson	.40
21	Brian Hunter	.40
22	Ray Lankford	.40
23	Ivan Rodriguez	2.00
24	Paul Molitor	2.25
25	Eric Karros	.40
26	Edgar Martinez	.40
27	Shawon Dunston	.40
28	Mo Vaughn	.40
29	Pedro Martinez	2.25
30	Marty Cordova	.40
31	Ken Caminiti	.40
32	Gary Sheffield	.75
33	Shawn Green	.75
34	Cliff Floyd	.40
35	Andres Galarraga	.40
36	Matt Williams	.40
37	Don Mattingly	3.50
38	Kevin Appier	.40
39	Ozzie Smith	3.00
40	Kenny Lofton	.40
41	Ken Griffey Jr.	4.00
42	Jack McDowell	.40
43	Gary Gaetti	.40
44	Dennis Martinez	.40
45	Chipper Jones	3.00
46	Eddie Murray	2.25
47	Bernie Williams	.40
48	Andre Dawson	.60
49	Dave Winfield	2.25
50	B.J. Surhoff	.40
51	Barry Larkin	.40
52	Alan Trammell	.40
53	Sammy Sosa	3.00
54	Hideo Nomo	1.00
55	Mark McGwire	4.50
56	Jay Bell	.40
57	Juan Gonzalez	1.00
58	Chili Davis	.40
59	Robin Ventura	.40
60	John Mabry	.40
61	Ken Griffey Jr. (Naturals)	2.00
62	Frank Thomas (Naturals)	3.00
63	Cal Ripken Jr. (Naturals)	3.00
64	Albert Belle (Naturals)	.40
65	Mike Piazza (Naturals)	2.00
66	Dante Bichette (Naturals)	.40
67	Sammy Sosa (Naturals)	1.50
68	Mo Vaughn (Naturals)	.40
69	Tim Salmon (Naturals)	.40
70	Reggie Sanders (Naturals)	.40
71	Cecil Fielder (Naturals)	.40
72	Jim Edmonds (Naturals)	.40

73 Rafael Palmeiro (Naturals) .75
74 Edgar Martinez (Naturals) .40
75 Barry Bonds (Naturals) 3.00
76 Manny Ramirez (Naturals) 1.25
77 Larry Walker (Naturals) .40
78 Jeff Bagwell (Naturals) 1.25
79 Ron Gant (Naturals) .40
80 Andres Galarraga (Naturals) .40
81 Eddie Murray (Naturals) .40
82 Kirby Puckett (Naturals) 1.50
83 Will Clark (Naturals) .40
84 Don Mattingly (Naturals) 1.75
85 Mark McGwire (Naturals) 2.25
86 Dean Palmer (Naturals) .40
87 Matt Williams (Naturals) .40
88 Fred McGriff (Naturals) .40
89 Joe Carter (Naturals) .40
90 Juan Gonzalez (Naturals) .65
91 Alex Ochoa .40
92 Ruben Rivera .40
93 Tony Clark .40
94 Pete Schourek .40
95 Terrell Wade .40
96 Johnny Damon .65
97 Derek Jeter 6.00
98 Phil Nevin .40
99 Robert Perez .40
100 Dustin Hermanson .40
101 Frank Thomas 2.25
102 Michael Tucker .40
103 Kirby Puckett 3.00
104 Alex Gonzalez .40
105 Tony Gwynn 3.00
106 Moises Alou .40
107 Albert Belle .40
108 Barry Bonds 6.00
109 Fred McGriff .40
110 Dennis Eckersley 1.50
111 Craig Biggio .40
112 David Cone .40
113 Will Clark .40
114 Cal Ripken Jr. 6.00
115 Wade Boggs 3.00
116 Pete Schourek .40
117 Darren Daulton .40
118 Carlos Baerga .40
119 Larry Walker .40
120 Denny Neagle .40
121 Jim Edmonds .40
122 Lee Smith .40
123 Jason Isringhausen .40
124 Jay Buhner .40
125 John Olerud .40
126 Jeff Conine .40
127 Dean Palmer .40
128 Jim Abbott .40
129 Raul Mondesi .40
130 Tom Glavine .60
131 Kevin Seitzer .40
132 Lenny Dykstra .40
133 Brian Jordan .40
134 Rondell White .40
135 Bret Boone .40
136 Randy Johnson 2.25
137 Paul O'Neill .40
138 Jim Thome .75
139 Edgardo Alfonzo .40
140 Terry Pendleton .40
141 Harold Baines .40
142 Roberto Alomar .45
143 Mark Grace .40
144 Derek Bell .40
145 Vinny Castilla .40
146 Cecil Fielder .40
147 Roger Clemens 3.50
148 Orel Hershiser .40
149 J.T. Snow .40
150 Rafael Palmeiro 1.75
151 Bret Saberhagen .40
152 Todd Hollandsworth .40
153 Ryan Klesko .40
154 Greg Maddux (Hardball Heroes) 1.50
155 Ken Griffey Jr. (Hardball Heroes) 2.00
156 Hideo Nomo (Hardball Heroes) .65
157 Frank Thomas (Hardball Heroes) 1.25
158 Cal Ripken Jr. (Hardball Heroes) 3.00
159 Jeff Bagwell (Hardball Heroes) 1.25
160 Barry Bonds (Hardball Heroes) 3.00
161 Mo Vaughn (Hardball Heroes) .40
162 Albert Belle (Hardball Heroes) .40
163 Sammy Sosa (Hardball Heroes) 1.50
164 Reggie Sanders (Hardball Heroes) .40
165 Mike Piazza (Hardball Heroes) 2.00
166 Chipper Jones (Hardball Heroes) 1.50
167 Tony Gwynn (Hardball Heroes) 1.50
168 Kirby Puckett (Hardball Heroes) 1.50
169 Wade Boggs (Hardball Heroes) 1.25
170 Will Clark (Hardball Heroes) .40

171 Gary Sheffield (Hardball Heroes) .45
172 Dante Bichette (Hardball Heroes) .40
173 Randy Johnson (Hardball Heroes) 1.25
174 Matt Williams (Hardball Heroes) .40
175 Alex Rodriguez (Hardball Heroes) 4.50
176 Tim Salmon (Hardball Heroes) .40
177 Johnny Damon (Hardball Heroes) .40
178 Manny Ramirez (Hardball Heroes) 1.25
179 Derek Jeter (Hardball Heroes) 3.00
180 Eddie Murray (Hardball Heroes) 1.25
181 Ozzie Smith (Hardball Heroes) 1.50
182 Garret Anderson (Hardball Heroes) .40
183 Raul Mondesi (Hardball Heroes) .40
184 Jeff Conine (.300 Series) .40
185 Ken Griffey Jr. (.300 Series) 2.00
186 Will Clark (.300 Series) .40
187 Mike Greenwell (.300 Series) .40
188 Carlos Baerga (.300 Series) .40
189 Paul Molitor (.300 Series) 1.25
190 Jeff Bagwell (.300 Series) 1.25
191 Mark Grace (.300 Series) .40
192 Don Mattingly (.300 Series) 1.75
193 Hal Morris (.300 Series) .40
194 Kenny Lofton (.300 Series) .40
195 Edgar Martinez (.300 Series) .40
196 Kirby Puckett (.300 Series) 1.50
197 Mike Piazza (.300 Series) 2.00
198 Frank Thomas (.300 Series) 1.25
199 Wade Boggs (.300 Series) 1.25
200 Tony Gwynn (.300 Series) 1.50

Foil Series 2

The 200 cards from Series 2 were paralleled in a special foil edition which was sold at retail outlets only in five-card $2.99 packs. Fronts have a metallic foil background to differentiate them from the regular-issue Series 2 version.

NM/M
Complete Set (200): 15.00
Common Player: .20
Stars: 1.5X

Christie Brinkley Collection Promo

To promote its Brinkley-photographed insert cards in Series 2 Pinnacle, the company issued a card of the celebrity photographer. In the same format as the player inserts, the promo card has a gold-foil enhanced borderless glamor photo on front. The back repeats a detail of the front photo and has details of the insert series.

NM/M
Christie Brinkley 5.00

Christie Brinkley Collection

Supermodel Christie Brinkley took the photos for these 1996 Pinnacle Series 2 inserts. The cards capture players from the 1995 World Series participants during a spring training photo session. Cards were seeded one per every 23 hobby packs or 32 retail packs.

Complete Set (16): 15.00
Common Player: .75
1 Greg Maddux 3.50
2 Ryan Klesko .75
3 Dave Justice .75
4 Tom Glavine 1.50
5 Chipper Jones 4.00
6 Fred McGriff .75
7 Javier Lopez .75
8 Marquis Grissom .75
9 Jason Schmidt .75
10 Albert Belle .75
11 Manny Ramirez 2.25
12 Carlos Baerga .75
13 Sandy Alomar .75
14 Jim Thome 2.25
15 Julio Franco .75
16 Kenny Lofton .75

Essence of the Game

Essence of the Game is an 18-card insert set found only in hobby packs at a one per 23 packs rate in Series 1. Cards are printed on clear plastic with the front photo also appearing in an inverted fashion on back. Micro-etched Dufex printing technology is utilized on the front.

NM/M
Complete Set (18): 35.00
Common Player: .75
1 Cal Ripken Jr. 6.00
2 Greg Maddux 3.00
3 Frank Thomas 2.50
4 Matt Williams .75
5 Chipper Jones 3.00
6 Reggie Sanders .75
7 Ken Griffey Jr. 4.00
8 Kirby Puckett 3.00
9 Hideo Nomo 1.50
10 Mike Piazza 4.00
11 Jeff Bagwell 2.50
12 Mo Vaughn .75
13 Albert Belle .75
14 Tim Salmon .75
15 Don Mattingly 3.50
16 Will Clark .75
17 Eddie Murray 2.50
18 Barry Bonds 6.00

First Rate

Retail-exclusive First Rate showcases former first round draft picks playing in the majors. Printed in Dufex foil throughout, a red swirl pattern covers the left 2/3 of the front. Backs show the player again, within a large numeral "1." These inserts are found at an average rate of one per 23 packs in Series 1.

NM/M
Complete Set (18): 40.00
Common Player: 1.25
1 Ken Griffey Jr. 5.00
2 Frank Thomas 2.50
3 Mo Vaughn 1.25
4 Chipper Jones 4.00
5 Alex Rodriguez 6.50
6 Kirby Puckett 3.50
7 Gary Sheffield 1.75
8 Matt Williams 1.25
9 Barry Bonds 7.50
10 Craig Biggio 1.25
11 Robin Ventura 1.25
12 Michael Tucker 1.25
13 Derek Jeter 7.50
14 Manny Ramirez 2.50
15 Barry Larkin 1.25
16 Shawn Green 1.75
17 Will Clark 1.25
18 Mark McGwire 6.50

Pinnacle Power

Pinnacle Power inserts are seeded at the rate of one per 47 packs in both hobby and retail Series 1. The sluggers are featured on a two-layered front. The bottom layer is silver Dufex foil with solid black on top; a color action photo of the player is at center, giving the card a die-cut appearance.

NM/M
Complete Set (20): 40.00
Common Player: 1.25
1 Frank Thomas 2.50
2 Mo Vaughn 1.25
2p Mo Vaughn (Promo) 1.50
3 Ken Griffey Jr. 4.50
4 Matt Williams 1.25
5 Barry Bonds 6.00
6 Reggie Sanders 1.25
7 Mike Piazza 4.50
8 Jim Edmonds 1.25
9 Dante Bichette 1.25
10 Sammy Sosa 3.50
11 Jeff Bagwell 2.50
12 Fred McGriff 1.25
13 Albert Belle 1.25
14 Tim Salmon 1.25
15 Joe Carter 1.25
16 Manny Ramirez 2.50
17 Eddie Murray 2.50
18 Cecil Fielder 1.25
19 Larry Walker 1.25
20 Juan Gonzalez 1.75

Project Stardom

These inserts feature young players on their way to stardom. The cards, which use Dufex technology, are seeded one per every 35 packs of Series 2 hobby packs.

NM/M
Complete Set (18): 35.00
Common Player: 1.00
1 Paul Wilson 1.00
2 Derek Jeter 8.50
3 Karim Garcia 1.00
4 Johnny Damon 2.75
5 Alex Rodriguez 7.50
6 Chipper Jones 8.00
7 Charles Johnson 1.00
8 Bob Abreu 1.00
9 Alan Benes 1.00
10 Richard Hidalgo 1.00
11 Brooks Kieschnick 1.00
12 Garret Anderson 1.00
13 Livan Hernandez 1.00
14 Manny Ramirez 5.00
15 Jermaine Dye 1.00
16 Todd Hollandsworth 1.00
17 Raul Mondesi 1.00
18 Ryan Klesko 1.00

Cal Ripken Tribute

A special Cal Ripken Tribute card was issued in Series 1 Pinnacle packs at a rate of 1:150. Front features an etched metallic foil background, a gold-foil facsimile autograph and a "2,131+ Consecutive Games Played" starburst. Back has a photo of the scoreboard on that historic occasion, and a photo of Ripken being driven around Camden Yards in a red Corvette. The card is numbered "1 of 1," but it is not unique.

NM/M
1 of 1 Cal Ripken Jr. 5.00

Skylines

These inserts feature player portraits looming over the city skyline where they play their home games. Printed on a clear plastic stock, the cards were seeded one per every 29 Series 2 magazine packs, and one per 50 retail packs.

NM/M
Complete Set (18): 375.00
Common Player: 10.00
1 Ken Griffey Jr. 50.00
2 Frank Thomas 30.00
3 Greg Maddux 40.00
4 Cal Ripken Jr. 65.00
5 Albert Belle 10.00
6 Mo Vaughn 10.00
7 Mike Piazza 50.00
8 Wade Boggs 40.00
9 Will Clark 10.00
10 Barry Bonds 65.00
11 Gary Sheffield 10.00
12 Hideo Nomo 25.00
13 Tony Gwynn 40.00
14 Kirby Puckett 40.00
15 Chipper Jones 40.00
16 Jeff Bagwell 30.00
17 Manny Ramirez 30.00
18 Raul Mondesi 10.00

Slugfest

These Series 2 inserts feature the game's heaviest hitters on all-foil Dufex cards. The cards were seeded one per every 35 retail packs.

NM/M
Complete Set (18): 40.00
Common Player: 1.25
1 Frank Thomas 2.75
2 Ken Griffey Jr. 4.00
3 Jeff Bagwell 2.75
4 Barry Bonds 5.00
5 Mo Vaughn 1.25
6 Albert Belle 1.25
7 Mike Piazza 4.00
8 Matt Williams 1.25
9 Dante Bichette 1.25
10 Sammy Sosa 3.00
11 Gary Sheffield 2.00
12 Reggie Sanders 1.25
13 Manny Ramirez 2.75
14 Eddie Murray 2.75
15 Juan Gonzalez 2.25
16 Dean Palmer 1.25
17 Rafael Palmeiro 2.75
18 Cecil Fielder 1.25

Team Pinnacle

Team Pinnacle inserts offer 18 players in a double-sided nine-card set. Each card can be found with Dufex printing on one side and regular gold-foil printing on the other. Inserted one per 72 packs of Series 1, Team Pinnacle pairs up an American League player and a National Leaguer at the same position on each card.

NM/M
Complete Set (9): 35.00
Common Player: 1.50
1 Frank Thomas, Jeff Bagwell 4.00
2 Chuck Knoblauch, Craig Biggio 1.50
3 Jim Thome, Matt Williams 3.00
4 Barry Larkin, Cal Ripken Jr. 12.00
5 Barry Bonds, Tim Salmon 10.00
6 Ken Griffey Jr., Reggie Sanders 8.00
7 Albert Belle, Sammy Sosa 6.00
8 Ivan Rodriguez, Mike Piazza 6.00
9 Greg Maddux, Randy Johnson 8.00

Team Spirit

One in every 72 Series 2 hobby packs or every 103 retail packs has one of these die-cut insert cards. Each card has a holographic baseball design behind an embossed glossy action photo of the player on a flat black background. Backs are conventionally printed.

NM/M
Complete Set (12): 45.00
Common Player: 1.25
1 Greg Maddux 4.00
2 Ken Griffey Jr. 5.00
3 Derek Jeter 8.00
4 Mike Piazza 5.00
5 Cal Ripken Jr. 8.00
6 Frank Thomas 2.75
7 Jeff Bagwell 2.75
8 Mo Vaughn 1.25
9 Albert Belle 1.25
10 Chipper Jones 2.75
11 Johnny Damon 1.50
12 Barry Bonds 8.00

Team Tomorrow

Team Tomorrow showcases young superstars on a horizontal Dufex design. While the player appears twice on the card front, the left side is merely a close-up of the same shot appearing on the right. These inserts are exclusive to Series 1 jumbo packs, found on average at the rate of one per 19 packs.

		NM/M
Complete Set (10):		20.00
Common Player:		.50
1	Ruben Rivera	.50
2	Johnny Damon	1.00
3	Raul Mondesi	.50
4	Manny Ramirez	3.00
5	Hideo Nomo	1.50
6	Chipper Jones	4.00
7	Garret Anderson	.50
8	Alex Rodriguez	5.00
9	Derek Jeter	6.00
10	Karim Garcia	.50

1996 Pinnacle/Aficionado

Pinnacle's 1996 Aficionado set gives every card the look of maple woodgrain. The 200 regular issue cards include 160 cards in an antique-look sepia-tone finish. The horizontal front also has a rainbow holographic foil image of the player. The back has comparison statistics that show how the player compares with the league average at that position and the league average at that position in different eras. There are also 60 four-color cards, which include 25 rookie cards, and a 10-card Global Reach subset. This subset, which honors baseball's international flavor, features Aficionado's new heliogram printing process. Artist's Proof parallel cards, seeded about one per 35 packs, were also created. These cards mirror the regular issue and use a unique gold foil stamp. There were three insert sets: Slick Picks, Rivals and Magic Numbers.

		NM/M
Complete Set (200):		20.00
Common Player:		.10
Common Artist's Proof:		.50
Artist's Proof Stars:		8X
Pack (5):		1.50
Wax Box (16):		30.00
1	Jack McDowell	.10
2	Jay Bell	.10
3	Rafael Palmeiro	1.25
4	Wally Joyner	.10
5	Ozzie Smith	2.00
6	Mark McGwire	3.00
7	Kevin Seitzer	.10
8	Fred McGriff	.10
9	Roger Clemens	2.25
9s	Roger Clemens (Marked "SAMPLE.")	4.00
10	Randy Johnson	1.50
11	Cecil Fielder	.10
12	David Cone	.10
13	Chili Davis	.10
14	Andres Galarraga	.10
15	Joe Carter	.10
16	Ryne Sandberg	2.00
17	Paul O'Neill	.10
18	Cal Ripken Jr.	4.00
19	Wade Boggs	2.00
20	Greg Gagne	.10
21	Edgar Martinez	.10
22	Greg Maddux	2.00
23	Ken Caminiti	.10
24	Kirby Puckett	2.00
25	Craig Biggio	.10
26	Will Clark	.10
27	Ron Gant	.10
28	Eddie Murray	1.50
29	Lance Johnson	.10
30	Tony Gwynn	2.00
31	Dante Bichette	.10

32	Darren Daulton	.10
33	Danny Tartabull	.10
34	Jeff King	.10
35	Tom Glavine	.40
36	Rickey Henderson	1.50
37	Jose Canseco	1.00
38	Barry Larkin	.10
39	Dennis Martinez	.10
40	Ruben Sierra	.10
41	Bobby Bonilla	.10
42	Jeff Conine	.10
43	Lee Smith	.10
44	Charlie Hayes	.10
45	Walt Weiss	.10
46	Jay Buhner	.10
47	Kenny Rogers	.10
48	Paul Molitor	1.50
49	Hal Morris	.10
50	Todd Stottlemyre	.10
51	Mike Stanley	.10
52	Mark Grace	.10
53	Lenny Dykstra	.10
54	Andre Dawson	.25
55	Dennis Eckersley	1.25
56	Ben McDonald	.10
57	Ray Lankford	.10
58	Mo Vaughn	.10
59	Frank Thomas	1.50
60	Julio Franco	.10
61	Jim Abbott	.10
62	Greg Vaughn	.10
63	Marquis Grissom	.10
64	Tino Martinez	.10
65	Kevin Appier	.10
66	Matt Williams	.10
67	Sammy Sosa	2.00
68	Larry Walker	.10
69	Ivan Rodriguez	1.25
70	Eric Karros	.10
71	Bernie Williams	.10
72	Carlos Baerga	.10
73	Jeff Bagwell	1.50
74	Pete Schourek	.10
75	Ken Griffey Jr.	2.50
76	Bernard Gilkey	.10
77	Albert Belle	.10
78	Chuck Knoblauch	.10
79	John Smoltz	.10
80	Barry Bonds	4.00
81	Vinny Castilla	.10
82	John Olerud	.10
83	Mike Mussina	1.00
84	Alex Fernandez	.10
85	Shawon Dunston	.10
86	Travis Fryman	.10
87	Moises Alou	.10
88	Dean Palmer	.10
89	Gregg Jefferies	.10
90	Jim Thome	1.25
91	Dave Justice	.10
92	B.J. Surhoff	.10
93	Ramon Martinez	.10
94	Gary Sheffield	.40
95	Andy Benes	.10
96	Reggie Sanders	.10
97	Roberto Alomar	.35
98	Omar Vizquel	.10
99	Juan Gonzalez	.75
100	Robin Ventura	.10
101	Jason Isringhausen	.10
102	Greg Colbrunn	.10
103	Brian Jordan	.10
104	Shawn Green	.40
105	Brian Hunter	.10
106	Rondell White	.10
107	Ryan Klesko	.10
107s	Ryan Klesko (Marked "SAMPLE.")	1.00
108	Sterling Hitchcock	.10
109	Manny Ramirez	1.50
110	Bret Boone	.10
111	Michael Tucker	.10
112	Julian Tavarez	.10
113	Benji Gil	.10
114	Kenny Lofton	.10
115	Mike Kelly	.10
116	Ray Durham	.10
117	Trevor Hoffman	.10
118	Butch Huskey	.10
119	Phil Nevin	.10
120	Pedro Martinez	1.50
121	Wil Cordero	.10
122	Tim Salmon	.10
123	Jim Edmonds	.10
124	Mike Piazza	2.50
125	Rico Brogna	.10
126	John Mabry	.10
127	Chipper Jones	2.00
128	Johnny Damon	.35
129	Raul Mondesi	.10
130	Denny Neagle	.10
131	Marc Newfield	.10
132	Hideo Nomo	.75
133	Joe Vitiello	.10
134	Garret Anderson	.10
135	Dave Nilsson	.10
136	Alex Rodriguez	3.00
137	Russ Davis	.10
138	Frank Rodriguez	.10
139	Royce Clayton	.10
140	John Valentin	.10
141	Marty Cordova	.10
142	Alex Gonzalez	.10
143	Carlos Delgado	.75
144	Willie Greene	.10
145	Cliff Floyd	.10
146	Bobby Higginson	.10
147	J.T. Snow	.10

148	Derek Bell	.10
149	Edgardo Alfonzo	.10
150	Charles Johnson	.10
151	Hideo Nomo (Global Reach)	.60
152	Larry Walker (Global Reach)	.10
153	Bob Abreu (Global Reach)	.10
154	Karim Garcia (Global Reach)	.10
155	Dave Nilsson (Global Reach)	.10
156	Chan Ho Park (Global Reach)	.10
157	Dennis Martinez (Global Reach)	.10
158	Sammy Sosa (Global Reach)	1.25
159	Rey Ordonez (Global Reach)	.10
160	Roberto Alomar (Global Reach)	.10
161	George Arias	.10
162	Jason Schmidt	.10
163	Derek Jeter	4.00
164	Chris Snopek	.10
165	Todd Hollandsworth	.10
166	Sal Fasano	.10
167	Jay Powell	.10
168	Paul Wilson	.10
169	Jim Pittsley	.10
170	LaTroy Hawkins	.10
171	Bob Abreu	.10
172	Mike Grace RC	.10
173	Karim Garcia	.10
174	Richard Hidalgo	.10
175	Felipe Crespo	.10
176	Terrell Wade	.10
177	Steve Gibralter	.10
178	Jermaine Dye	.10
179	Alan Benes	.10
180	Wilton Guerrero RC	.10
181	Brooks Kieschnick	.10
182	Roger Cedeno	.10
183	Osvaldo Fernandez RC	.10
184	Matt Lawton RC	.50
185	George Williams	.10
186	Jimmy Haynes	.10
187	Mike Busby RC	.10
188	Chan Ho Park	.10
189	Marc Barcelo	.10
190	Jason Kendall	.10
191	Rey Ordonez	.10
192	Tyler Houston	.10
193	John Wasdin	.10
194	Jeff Suppan	.10
195	Jeff Ware	.10
196	Checklist	.10
197	Checklist	.10
198	Checklist	.10
199	Checklist	.10
200	Checklist	.10

First Pitch Previews

This parallel set differs from the regularly issued version in that there is a "FIRST PITCH / PREVIEW" label printed on the front on the end opposite the heliogram player portrait. Also, whereas on the regular cards, the player portrait is in silver metallic composition, the First Pitch Preview cards have the portrait in gold. These cards were most often obtained by visiting Pinnacle's site on the Internet and answering a trivia question.

	NM/M
Complete Set (200):	250.00
Common Player:	2.00

Magic Numbers

This insert set focuses on 10 of the game's best players, printing them on a wooden stock which car-

ries the distinct grain and color of natural wood. The cards, seeded one every 72 packs, compares current players with others who have worn the same uniform number. Each card can also be found with a large black "SAMPLE" printed on back.

		NM/M
Complete Set (10):		15.50
Common Player:		.75
Samples:		1X
1	Ken Griffey Jr.	3.25
2	Greg Maddux	2.50
3	Frank Thomas	1.50
4	Mo Vaughn	.75
5	Jeff Bagwell	1.50
6	Chipper Jones	2.50
7	Albert Belle	.75
8	Cal Ripken Jr.	4.50
9	Matt Williams	.75
10	Sammy Sosa	2.50

Rivals

These inserts concentrate on the many matchups and rivalries that make baseball fun. Each card uses spot embossing. The cards are seeded one per every 24 packs.

		NM/M
Complete Set (24):		65.00
Common Player:		2.00
1	Ken Griffey Jr., Frank Thomas	4.00
2	Frank Thomas, Cal Ripken Jr.	4.50
3	Cal Ripken Jr., Mo Vaughn	4.00
4	Mo Vaughn, Ken Griffey Jr.	2.50
5	Ken Griffey Jr., Cal Ripken Jr.	5.00
6	Frank Thomas, Mo Vaughn	2.00
7	Cal Ripken Jr., Ken Griffey Jr.	5.00
8	Mo Vaughn, Frank Thomas	2.00
9	Ken Griffey Jr., Mo Vaughn	2.50
10	Frank Thomas, Ken Griffey Jr.	4.00
11	Cal Ripken Jr., Frank Thomas	4.50
12	Mo Vaughn, Cal Ripken Jr.	4.00
13	Mike Piazza, Jeff Bagwell	2.50
14	Jeff Bagwell, Barry Bonds	4.50
15	Jeff Bagwell, Mike Piazza	2.50
16	Tony Gwynn, Mike Piazza	3.00
17	Mike Piazza, Barry Bonds	5.00
18	Jeff Bagwell, Tony Gwynn	2.00
19	Barry Bonds, Mike Piazza	5.00
20	Tony Gwynn, Jeff Bagwell	2.00
21	Barry Bonds, Tony Gwynn	3.00
22	Barry Bonds, Jeff Bagwell	4.50
23	Tony Gwynn, Barry Bonds	4.50
24	Barry Bonds, Tony Gwynn	4.50

Slick Picks

This insert set pictures 32 of the best players in baseball on cards which use Spectroetch printing. Each card notes where that player was selected in the annual draft, emphasizing that there are numerous bargains available throughout the amateur

draft. The cards were seeded one per 10 packs, making them the easiest to obtain of the set's insert cards.

		NM/M
Complete Set (32):		40.00
Common Player:		.50
1	Mike Piazza	2.50
2	Cal Ripken Jr.	4.00
3	Ken Griffey Jr.	2.50
4	Paul Wilson	.50
5	Frank Thomas	1.50
6	Mo Vaughn	.50
7	Barry Bonds	4.00
8	Albert Belle	.50
9	Jeff Bagwell	1.50
10	Dante Bichette	.50
11	Hideo Nomo	.75
12	Raul Mondesi	.50
13	Manny Ramirez	1.50
14	Greg Maddux	1.50
15	Tony Gwynn	2.00
16	Ryne Sandberg	2.00
17	Reggie Sanders	.50
18	Derek Bell	4.00
19	Johnny Damon	.75
20	Alex Rodriguez	3.00
21	Ryan Klesko	.50
22	Jim Thome	1.50
23	Kenny Lofton	.50
24	Tino Martinez	.50
25	Randy Johnson	1.50
26	Wade Boggs	2.00
27	Juan Gonzalez	.75
28	Kirby Puckett	2.00
29	Tim Salmon	.50
30	Chipper Jones	2.00
31	Garret Anderson	.50
32	Eddie Murray	1.50

FanFest

In conjunction with its title sponsorship of baseball's All-Star FanFest, July 5-9 in Philadelphia, the company distributed two-card foil packs prior to and at the show. Fronts have a negative posterized image of Independence Hall as a backdrop for a player action photo. Textured gold-foil bottom corners hold a team logo and a Liberty Bell silhouette with the player's position. The player name appears in gold foil above the FanFest logo at bottom center. Backs repeat the negative background and have another player photo, a few words about him and all the appropriate logos. The Darren Daulton card is in Sportflix technology as a tribute to the recently retired Phillies fan favorite. Card #31, Steve Carlton, was not distributed in packs. Cards of the Phillie Phanatic team mascot, the city's mayor and several other local dignitaries were produced and given to those persons.

		NM/M
Complete Set (30, No Carlton):		25.00
Common Player:		.50
1	Cal Ripken Jr.	4.00
2	Greg Maddux	2.00
3	Ken Griffey Jr.	2.50
4	Frank Thomas	1.50
5	Jeff Bagwell	1.50
6	Hideo Nomo	.75
7	Tony Gwynn	2.00
8	Albert Belle	.50
9	Mo Vaughn	.50
10	Mike Piazza	2.50
11	Dante Bichette	.50
12	Ryne Sandberg	2.00
13	Wade Boggs	2.00
14	Kirby Puckett	2.00
15	Ozzie Smith	2.00
16	Barry Bonds	4.00
17	Gary Sheffield	.75
18	Barry Larkin	.50
19	Kevin Seitzer	.50
20	Jay Bell	.50
21	Chipper Jones	2.00
22	Ivan Rodriguez	1.25
23	Cecil Fielder	.50

24	Manny Ramirez	1.50
25	Randy Johnson	1.50
26	Moises Alou	.50
27	Mark McGwire	3.00
28	Jason Isringhausen	.50
29	Joe Carter	.50
30	Darren Daulton (Sportflix)	1.50
31	Steve Carlton	10.00
---	Benjamin Franklin	5.00
---	Phillie Phanatic (Mascot)	5.00
---	Edward G. Rendell (Mayor)	3.00

FanFest Playing Cards

A special version of Pinnacle's FanFest cards was produced for construction of a large "house of cards" at the FanFest site. Following the event, some of the cards made their way into the hobby. Similar in format to the regular cards, the special issue was produced on textured playing-card stock in a 2-1/4" x 3-1/2" format with rounded corners. The playing cards lack the gold-foil found on regular cards and thus the player's name is nowhere to be found. Backs have a large gold-and-white Pinnacle logo on a black background. Cards are listed here using the numbering found on the regular version; the playing cards are unnumbered.

		NM/M
Complete Set (29):		300.00
Common Player:		10.00
(1)	Cal Ripken Jr.	30.00
(2)	Greg Maddux	17.50
(3)	Ken Griffey Jr.	20.00
(4)	Frank Thomas	15.00
(5)	Jeff Bagwell	15.00
(6)	Hideo Nomo	12.50
(7)	Tony Gwynn	17.50
(8)	Albert Belle	10.00
(9)	Mo Vaughn	10.00
(10)	Mike Piazza	20.00
(11)	Dante Bichette	10.00
(12)	Ryne Sandberg	17.50
(13)	Wade Boggs	17.50
(14)	Kirby Puckett	17.50
(15)	Ozzie Smith	17.50
(16)	Barry Bonds	30.00
(17)	Gary Sheffield	12.50
(18)	Barry Larkin	10.00
(19)	Kevin Seitzer	10.00
(20)	Jay Bell	10.00
(21)	Chipper Jones	17.50
(22)	Ivan Rodriguez	12.50
(23)	Cecil Fielder	10.00
(24)	Manny Ramirez	15.00
(25)	Randy Johnson	15.00
(26)	Moises Alou	10.00
(27)	Mark McGwire	25.00
(28)	Jason Isringhausen	10.00
(29)	Joe Carter	10.00

1997 Pinnacle

Pinnacle baseball consists of 200 base cards. Fronts have the player's name stamped within a foil baseball-diamond shape at the bottom of each card. Backs contain summaries of the players' 1996 and lifetime statistics. Included within the base set is a 30-card Rookies subset, a 12-card Clout subset and three checklists. Inserts include two parallel sets (Artist's Proof and Museum Collection), Passport to the Majors, Shades, Team Pinnacle, Cardfrontations, and Home/Away. Cards were sold in 10-card packs for $2.49 each.

	NM/M
Complete Set (200):	10.00
Common Player:	.05
Pack (10):	1.00
Wax Box (24):	12.50
Wax Retail Box (16):	10.00

		NM/M
1	Cecil Fielder	.05
2	Garret Anderson	.05
3	Charles Nagy	.05
4	Darryl Hamilton	.05
5	Greg Myers	.05
6	Eric Davis	.05
7	Jeff Frye	.05
8	Marquis Grissom	.05
9	Curt Schilling	.35
10	Jeff Fassero	.05
11	Alan Benes	.05
12	Orlando Miller	.05
13	Alex Fernandez	.05
14	Andy Pettitte	.25
15	Andre Dawson	.25
16	Mark Grudzielanek	.05
17	Joe Vitiello	.05
18	Juan Gonzalez	.40
19	Mark Whiten	.05
20	Lance Johnson	.05
21	Trevor Hoffman	.05
22	Marc Newfield	.05
23	Jim Eisenreich	.05
24	Joe Carter	.05
25	Jose Canseco	.30
26	Bill Swift	.05
27	Ellis Burks	.05
28	Ben McDonald	.05
29	Edgar Martinez	.05
30	Jamie Moyer	.05
31	Chan Ho Park	.05
32	Carlos Delgado	.50
33	Kevin Mitchell	.05
34	Carlos Garcia	.05
35	Darryl Strawberry	.05
36	Jim Thome	.60
37	Jose Offerman	.05
38	Ryan Klesko	.05
39	Ruben Sierra	.05
40	Devon White	.05
41	Brian Jordan	.05
42	Tony Gwynn	.75
43	Rafael Palmeiro	.05
44	Dante Bichette	.05
45	Scott Stahoviak	.05
46	Roger Cedeno	.05
47	Ivan Rodriguez	.50
48	Bob Abreu	.05
49	Darryl Kile	.05
50	Darren Dreifort	.05
51	Shawon Dunston	.05
52	Mark McGwire	1.50
53	Tim Salmon	.05
54	Gene Schall	.05
55	Roger Clemens	.85
56	Rondell White	.05
57	Ed Sprague	.05
58	Craig Paquette	.05
59	David Segui	.05
60	Jaime Navarro	.05
61	Tom Glavine	.35
62	Jeff Brantley	.05
63	Kimera Bartee	.05
64	Fernando Vina	.05
65	Eddie Murray	.65
66	Lenny Dykstra	.05
67	Kevin Elster	.05
68	Vinny Castilla	.05
69	Todd Greene	.05
70	Brett Butler	.05
71	Robby Thompson	.05
72	Reggie Jefferson	.05
73	Todd Hundley	.05
74	Jeff King	.05
75	Ernie Young	.05
76	Jeff Bagwell	.65
77	Dan Wilson	.05
78	Paul Molitor	.65
79	Kevin Seitzer	.05
80	Kevin Brown	.05
81	Ron Gant	.05
82	Dwight Gooden	.05
83	Todd Stottlemyre	.05
84	Ken Caminiti	.05
85	James Baldwin	.05
86	Jermaine Dye	.05
87	Harold Baines	.05
88	Pat Hentgen	.05
89	Frank Rodriguez	.05
90	Mark Johnson	.05
91	Jason Kendall	.05
92	Alex Rodriguez	1.50
93	Alan Trammell	.05
94	Scott Brosius	.05
95	Delino DeShields	.05
96	Chipper Jones	.75
97	Barry Bonds	2.00
98	Brady Anderson	.05
99	Ryne Sandberg	.75
100	Albert Belle	.05
101	Jeff Cirillo	.05
102	Frank Thomas	.65
103	Mike Piazza	1.00
104	Rickey Henderson	.65
105	Rey Ordonez	.05
106	Mark Grace	.05
107	Terry Steinbach	.05
108	Ray Durham	.05
109	Barry Larkin	.05
110	Tony Clark	.05
111	Bernie Williams	.05
112	John Smoltz	.05
113	Moises Alou	.05
114	Alex Gonzalez	.05
115	Rico Brogna	.05
116	Eric Karros	.05
117	Jeff Conine	.05
118	Todd Hollandsworth	.05
119	Troy Percival	.05
120	Paul Wilson	.05
121	Orel Hershiser	.05
122	Ozzie Smith	.75
123	Dave Hollins	.05
124	Ken Hill	.05
125	Rick Wilkins	.05
126	Scott Servais	.05
127	Fernando Valenzuela	.05
128	Mariano Rivera	.15
129	Mark Loretta	.05
130	Shane Reynolds	.05
131	Darren Oliver	.05
132	Steve Trachsel	.05
133	Darren Bragg	.05
134	Jason Dickson	.05
135	Darren Fletcher	.05
136	Gary Gaetti	.05
137	Joey Cora	.05
138	Terry Pendleton	.05
139	Derek Jeter	2.00
140	Danny Tartabull	.05
141	John Flaherty	.05
142	B.J. Surhoff	.05
143	Mark Sweeney	.05
144	Chad Mottola	.05
145	Andujar Cedeno	.05
146	Tim Belcher	.05
147	Mark Thompson	.05
148	Rafael Bournigal	.05
149	Marty Cordova	.05
150	Osvaldo Fernandez	.05
151	Mike Stanley	.05
152	Ricky Bottalico	.05
153	Donnie Wall	.05
154	Omar Vizquel	.05
155	Mike Mussina	.30
156	Brant Brown	.05
157	F.P. Santangelo	.05
158	Ryan Hancock	.05
159	Jeff D'Amico	.05
160	Luis Castillo	.05
161	Darin Erstad	.10
162	Ugueth Urbina	.05
163	Andruw Jones	.65
164	Steve Gibralter	.05
165	Robin Jennings	.05
166	Mike Cameron	.05
167	George Arias	.05
168	Chris Stynes	.05
169	Justin Thompson	.05
170	Jamey Wright	.05
171	Todd Walker	.05
172	Nomar Garciaparra	.75
173	Jose Paniagua	.05
174	Marvin Benard	.05
175	Rocky Coppinger	.05
176	Quinton McCracken	.05
177	Amaury Telemaco	.05
178	Neifi Perez	.05
179	Todd Greene	.05
180	Jason Thompson	.05
181	Wilton Guerrero	.05
182	Edgar Renteria	.05
183	Billy Wagner	.05
184	Alex Ochoa	.05
185	Billy McMillon	.05
186	Kenny Lofton	.05
187	Andres Galarraga (Clout)	.05
188	Chuck Knoblauch (Clout)	.05
189	Greg Maddux (Clout)	.75
190	Mo Vaughn (Clout)	.05
191	Cal Ripken Jr. (Clout)	2.00
192	Hideo Nomo (Clout)	.40
193	Ken Griffey Jr. (Clout)	1.00
194	Sammy Sosa (Clout)	.75
195	Jay Buhner (Clout)	.05
196	Manny Ramirez (Clout)	.65
197	Matt Williams (Clout)	.05
198	Andruw Jones (Checklist)	.30
199	Darin Erstad (Checklist)	.05
200	Trey Beamon (Checklist)	.05

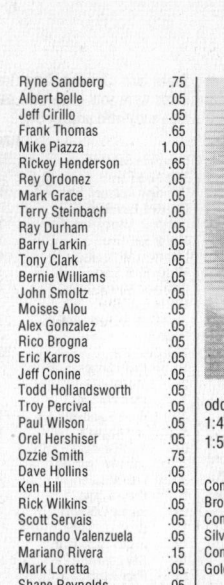

Artist's Proofs

Artist's Proofs parallels for 1997 Pinnacle were issued in a "fractured" set form. That is, three levels of scarcity were created, with each card available in only one of those levels. For 125 of the players, bronze is the scarcity level; 50 of the players have a silver-level scarcity and 25 players are found in the top-shelf gold level, with a reported production of 300 each. Stated

odds of finding an AP parallel were 1:47 in hobby and retail packs, and 1:55 in magazine packs.

	NM/M
Common Bronze (125):	1.00
Bronze Stars:	30X
Common Silver (50):	2.50
Silver Stars:	12X
Common Gold (25):	4.00
Gold Stars:	10X

Museum Collection

Each of the 200 cards in 1997 Pinnacle Series 1 was also issued in a graphically enhanced Museum Collection parallel set. The Museum cards utilize basically the same design as the regular-issue Pinnacle cards, but the front is printed in the company's Dufex gold-foil technology. On back, a small rectangular logo verifies the card's special status.

	NM/M
Complete Set (200):	100.00
Common Player:	1.00
Stars/Rookies:	6X

Cardfrontations

This hobby-only set was inserted every 23 packs of 1997 Pinnacle baseball. Fronts depict a player portrait imaged over a foil rainbow background. The same player is then pictured in action shots with the "Cardfrontation" logo in gold foil in the lower right half. The player's name appears in gold foil below the gold-foil team logo. Backs depict another player's portrait with text describing interaction between the two players. The cards are numbered as "x of 20."

	NM/M
Complete Set (20):	35.00
Common Player:	.50
1	Greg Maddux, Mike Piazza	4.00
2	Tom Glavine, Ken Caminiti	.75
3	Randy Johnson, Cal Ripken Jr.	5.00
4	Kevin Appier, Mark McGwire	4.00

	NM/M
5	Andy Pettitte, Juan Gonzalez	1.00
6	Pat Hentgen, Albert Belle	.50
7	Hideo Nomo, Chipper Jones	2.00
8	Ismael Valdes, Sammy Sosa	2.50
9	Mike Mussina, Manny Ramirez	1.50
10	David Cone, Jay Buhner	.50
11	Mark Wohlers, Gary Sheffield	.75
12	Alan Benes, Barry Bonds	5.00
13	Roger Clemens, Ivan Rodriguez	2.50
14	Mariano Rivera, Ken Griffey Jr.	3.00
15	Dwight Gooden, Frank Thomas	1.50
16	John Wetteland, Darin Erstad	.50
17	John Smoltz, Brian Jordan	.50
18	Kevin Brown, Jeff Bagwell	1.50
19	Jack McDowell, Alex Rodriguez	4.00
20	Charles Nagy, Bernie Williams	.50

Home/Away

The 24-card, shirt-shaped, die-cut set was inserted every 33 retail packs. The background on front and back is a facsimile of the player's home or road jersey. A color action photo is on front with gold-foil graphics. Backs have a few words about the player.

	NM/M
Complete Set (12):	65.00
Common Player:	2.00
1	Chipper Jones	5.00
2	Ken Griffey Jr.	6.00
3	Mike Piazza	6.00
4	Frank Thomas	4.00
5	Jeff Bagwell	4.00
6	Alex Rodriguez	8.00
7	Barry Bonds	10.00
8	Mo Vaughn	2.00
9	Derek Jeter	10.00
10	Mark McGwire	8.00
11	Cal Ripken Jr.	10.00
12	Albert Belle	2.00

Passport to the Majors

The 25-card, regular-sized set was inserted every 36 packs of 1997 Pinnacle baseball. The cards fold out and resemble a mini passport.

	NM/M
Complete Set (25):	55.00
Common Player:	1.00
1	Greg Maddux	4.00
1s	Greg Maddux ("SAMPLE" overprint.)	4.00
2	Ken Griffey Jr.	6.00
3	Frank Thomas	3.00
4	Cal Ripken Jr.	10.00
5	Mike Piazza	6.00
6	Alex Rodriguez	7.50
7	Mo Vaughn	4.00
8	Chipper Jones	4.00
9	Roberto Alomar	1.00
10	Edgar Martinez	1.00
11	Javier Lopez	1.00

		NM/M
12	Ivan Rodriguez	2.50
13	Juan Gonzalez	1.50
14	Carlos Baerga	1.00
15	Sammy Sosa	4.00
16	Manny Ramirez	3.00
17	Raul Mondesi	1.00
18	Henry Rodriguez	1.00
19	Rafael Palmeiro	2.50
20	Rey Ordonez	1.00
21	Hideo Nomo	1.50
22	Makoto Suzuki	1.00
23	Chan Ho Park	1.00
24	Larry Walker	1.00
25	Ruben Rivera	1.00

Shades

This set was inserted every 23 retail packs of Pinnacle baseball. The horizontal cards are die-cut at the top of a pair of sunglasses whose lenses contain color portrait and action pictures of the player. The player face beneath the shades is printed on silver foil stock. Backs have a mirror-image of the front photos in the lenses and a baseball diamond in the background.

	NM/M
Complete Set (10):	15.00
Common Player:	.75
1	Ken Griffey Jr.	3.00
2	Juan Gonzalez	1.50
3	John Smoltz	.75
4	Gary Sheffield	1.00
5	Cal Ripken Jr.	5.00
6	Mo Vaughn	.75
7	Brian Jordan	.75
8	Mike Piazza	3.00
9	Frank Thomas	2.25
10	Alex Rodriguez	4.00

Team Pinnacle

This insert features top National League players from a position on one side with the best American League players on the other. One side of the card is in Dufex printing and there is actually two versions of each card, as either side can feature the Dufex foil. Team Pinnacle is inserted every 90 packs.

	NM/M
Complete Set (10):	30.00
Common Player:	1.50
1	Frank Thomas, Jeff Bagwell	4.00
2	Chuck Knoblauch, Eric Young	1.50
3	Ken Caminiti, Jim Thome	3.00
4	Alex Rodriguez, Chipper Jones	6.00
5	Mike Piazza, Ivan Rodriguez	5.00
6	Albert Belle, Barry Bonds	8.00
7	Ken Griffey Jr., Ellis Burks	6.00
8	Juan Gonzalez, Gary Sheffield	3.00
9	John Smoltz, Andy Pettitte	2.00
10	All Players	2.00

1997 New Pinnacle Samples

This group of sample cards was sent to dealers to introduce the New Pinnacle brand which took the place of a second series of Pinnacle in 1997. Cards are virtually identical to the issued versions except for the large diagonal black-and-white "SAMPLE" overprint on front and back.

	NM/M
Complete Set (6):	7.50
Common Player:	.50
2	Sammy Sosa	3.00
45	Mike Piazza	3.00
57	Jeff Bagwell	1.50
81	Alex Rodriguez	5.00
127	Ryan Klesko	.50
175	Andruw Jones	2.00

1997 New Pinnacle

In lieu of a second series of Pinnacle Baseball, the company offered collectors New Pinnacle, a 200-card set sold in 10-card packs for $2.99 each. Two parallel versions of the 200-card set exist in Museum Collection and Artist's Proofs. Other inserts include Press Plates, Spellbound, Keeping the Pace and Interleague Encounter. Collectors who obtained four Press Plates of the same player's card back or front were eligible to win cash prizes.

	NM/M
Complete Set (200):	12.50
Common Player:	.05
Common Museum:	1.00
Museum Stars:	8X
Common Red Artist's Proof:	1.00
Red AP Stars:	10X
Common Blue Artist's Proof:	3.00
Blue AP Stars:	25X
Common Green Artist's Proof:	6.00
Green AP Stars:	35X
Pack (10):	1.50
Wax Box (18):	15.00
1	Ken Griffey Jr.	1.00
2	Sammy Sosa	.75
3	Greg Maddux	.75
4	Matt Williams	.05
5	Jason Isringhausen	.05
6	Gregg Jefferies	.05
7	Chili Davis	.05
8	Paul O'Neill	.05
9	Larry Walker	.05
10	Ellis Burks	.05
11	Cliff Floyd	.05
12	Albert Belle	.05
13	Javier Lopez	.05
14	David Cone	.05
15	Jose Canseco	.40
16	Todd Zeile	.05
17	Bernard Gilkey	.05
18	Andres Galarraga	.05
19	Chris Snopek	.05
20	Tim Salmon	.05
21	Roger Clemens	.85
22	Reggie Sanders	.05
23	John Jaha	.05
24	Andy Pettitte	.25
25	Kenny Lofton	.05
26	Robb Nen	.05
27	John Wetteland	.05
28	Bobby Bonilla	.05
29	Hideo Nomo	.40
30	Cecil Fielder	.05
31	Garret Anderson	.05
32	Pat Hentgen	.05
33	David Justice	.05
34	Billy Wagner	.05
35	Al Leiter	.05
36	Mark Wohlers	.05
37	Rondell White	.05
38	Charles Johnson	.05
39	Mark Grace	.05
40	Pedro Martinez	.65
41	Tom Goodwin	.05
42	Manny Ramirez	.65
43	Greg Vaughn	.05
44	Brian Jordan	.05
45	Mike Piazza	1.00
46	Roberto Hernandez	.05
47	Wade Boggs	.75
48	Scott Sanders	.05
49	Alex Gonzalez	.05

50	Kevin Brown	.05	168	Wilton Guerrero	.05
51	Bob Higginson	.05	169	Vladimir Guerrero	.65
52	Ken Caminiti	.05	170	Nomar Garciaparra	.75
53	Derek Jeter	2.00	171	Shannon Stewart	.05
54	Carlos Baerga	.05	172	Scott Rolen	.60
55	Jay Buhner	.05	173	Bob Abreu	.05
56	Tim Naehring	.05	174	Danny Patterson RC	.05
57	Jeff Bagwell	.65	175	Andruw Jones	.65
58	Steve Finley	.05	176	Brian Giles RC	.50
59	Kevin Appier	.05	177	Dmitri Young	.05
60	Jay Bell	.05	178	Cal Ripken Jr.	
61	Ivan Rodriguez	.60		(East Meets West)	1.00
62	Terrell Wade	.05	179	Chuck Knoblauch	
63	Rusty Greer	.05		(East Meets West)	.05
64	Juan Guzman	.05	180	Alex Rodriguez	
65	Fred McGriff	.05		(East Meets West)	.75
66	Tino Martinez	.05	181	Andres Galarraga	
67	Ray Lankford	.05		(East Meets West)	.05
68	Juan Gonzalez	.40	182	Pedro Martinez	
69	Ron Gant	.05		(East Meets West)	.35
70	Jack McDowell	.05	183	Brady Anderson	
71	Tony Gwynn	.75		(East Meets West)	.05
72	Joe Carter	.05	184	Barry Bonds	
73	Wilson Alvarez	.05		(East Meets West)	1.00
74	Jason Giambi	.60	185	Ivan Rodriguez	
75	Brian Hunter	.05		(East Meets West)	.30
76	Michael Tucker	.05	186	Gary Sheffield	
77	Andy Benes	.05		(East Meets West)	.05
78	Brady Anderson	.05	187	Denny Neagle	
79	Ramon Martinez	.05		(East Meets West)	.05
80	Troy Percival	.05	188	Mark McGwire (Aura)	.75
81	Alex Rodriguez	1.50	189	Ellis Burks (Aura)	.05
82	Jim Thome	.60	190	Alex Rodriguez (Aura)	.75
83	Denny Neagle	.05	191	Mike Piazza (Aura)	.65
84	Rafael Palmeiro	.60	192	Barry Bonds (Aura)	1.00
85	Jose Valentin	.05	193	Albert Belle (Aura)	.05
86	Marc Newfield	.05	194	Chipper Jones (Aura)	.40
87	Mariano Rivera	.15	195	Juan Gonzalez (Aura)	.20
88	Alan Benes	.05	196	Brady Anderson (Aura)	.05
89	Jimmy Key	.05	197	Frank Thomas (Aura)	.35
90	Joe Randa	.05	198	Checklist	
91	Cal Ripken Jr.	2.00		(Vladimir Guerrero)	.35
92	Craig Biggio	.05	199	Checklist (Todd Walker)	.05
93	Dean Palmer	.05	200	Checklist (Scott Rolen)	.30
94	Gary Sheffield	.45			
95	Ismael Valdez	.05			

Artist's Proof

96	John Valentin	.05
97	Johnny Damon	.35
98	Mo Vaughn	.05
99	Paul Sorrento	.05
100	Randy Johnson	.65
101	Raul Mondesi	.05
102	Roberto Alomar	.20
103	Royce Clayton	.05
104	Mark Grudzielanek	.05
105	Wally Joyner	.05
106	Wil Cordero	.05
107	Will Clark	.05
108	Chuck Knoblauch	.05
109	Derek Bell	.05
110	Henry Rodriguez	.05
111	Edgar Renteria	.05
112	Travis Fryman	.05
113	Eric Young	.05
114	Sandy Alomar Jr.	.05
115	Darin Erstad	.25
116	Barry Larkin	.05
117	Barry Bonds	2.00
118	Frank Thomas	.65
119	Carlos Delgado	.05
120	Jason Kendall	.05
121	Todd Hollandsworth	.05
122	Jim Edmonds	.05
123	Chipper Jones	.75
124	Jeff Fassero	.05
125	Deion Sanders	.05
126	Matt Lawton	.05
127	Ryan Klesko	.05
128	Mike Mussina	.40
129	Paul Molitor	.65
130	Dante Bichette	.05
131	Bill Pulsipher	.05
132	Todd Hundley	.05
133	J.T. Snow	.05

This 200-card parallel set features a special AP seal and foil treatment and is fractured into three levels of scarcity - Red (125 cards), Blue (50 cards) and Green (25 cards). Cards were inserted at a rate of 1:39 packs. "Artist's Proof" is stamped along the lower edge.

	NM/M
Common Red Artist's Proof:	1.00
Red Artist's Proofs:	10X
Common Blue Artist's Proof:	
Blue Artist's Proofs:	25X
Common Green Artist's Proof:	6.00
Green Artist's Proofs:	35X

Museum Collection

134	Chuck Finley	.05
135	Shawn Green	.30
136	Charles Nagy	.05
137	Willie Greene	.05
138	Marty Cordova	.05
139	Eddie Murray	.65
140	Ryne Sandberg	.75
141	Alex Fernandez	.05
142	Mark McGwire	1.50
143	Eric Davis	.05
144	Jermaine Dye	.05
145	Ruben Sierra	.05
146	Damon Buford	.05
147	John Smoltz	.05
148	Alex Ochoa	.05
149	Moises Alou	.05
150	Rico Brogna	.05
151	Terry Steinbach	.05
152	Jeff King	.05
153	Carlos Garcia	.05
154	Tom Glavine	.35
155	Edgar Martinez	.05
156	Kevin Elster	.05
157	Darryl Hamilton	.05
158	Jason Dickson	.05
159	Kevin Orie	.05
160	Bubba Trammell RC	.25
161	Jose Guillen	.05
162	Brant Brown	.05
163	Wendell Magee	.05
164	Scott Spiezio	.05
165	Todd Walker	.05
166	Rod Myers RC	.05
167	Damon Mashore	.05

Dufex printing on gold-foil backgrounds differentiates the Museum Collection parallel of New Pinnacle from the regular-issue cards. Museums were inserted at an average rate of one per nine packs.

	NM/M
Complete Set (200):	200.00
Common Player:	1.00
Stars/Rookies:	8X

Interleague Encounter

Inserted 1:240 packs, this 10-card set showcases 20 American League and National League rivals with the date of their first interleague match-up on double-sided mirror mylar cards.

		NM/M
Complete Set (10):		60.00
Common Player:		2.50
1	Albert Belle, Brian Jordan	2.50
2	Andruw Jones, Brady Anderson	4.50
3	Ken Griffey Jr., Tony Gwynn	7.50
4	Cal Ripken Jr., Chipper Jones	12.00
5	Mike Piazza, Ivan Rodriguez	7.50
6	Derek Jeter, Vladimir Guerrero	12.00
7	Greg Maddux, Mo Vaughn	6.00
8	Alex Rodriguez, Hideo Nomo	10.00
9	Juan Gonzalez, Barry Bonds	12.00
10	Frank Thomas, Jeff Bagwell	4.50

Keeping the Pace

Top sluggers who were considered candidates to break Roger Maris' single-season record of 61 home runs were featured in this insert set. Cards feature Dot Matrix holographic borders and backgrounds on front. Backs present career stats of an all-time great and project future numbers for the current player. The cards were inserted 1:89 packs.

		NM/M
Complete Set (18):		100.00
Common Player:		1.00
1	Juan Gonzalez	3.00
2	Greg Maddux	7.50
3	Ivan Rodriguez	4.50
4	Ken Griffey Jr.	12.00
5	Alex Rodriguez	13.50
6	Barry Bonds	15.00
7	Frank Thomas	6.00
8	Chuck Knoblauch	1.00
9	Derek Jeter	15.00
10	Roger Clemens	9.00
11	Kenny Lofton	1.00
12	Tony Gwynn	7.50
13	Troy Percival	1.00
14	Cal Ripken Jr.	15.00
15	Andy Pettitte	1.50
16	Hideo Nomo	3.00
17	Randy Johnson	6.00
18	Mike Piazza	12.00

Press Plates

Just when collectors thought they had seen every type of insert card imaginable, New Pinnacle proved them wrong by cutting up and inserting into packs (about one per 1,250) the metal plates used to print the set. There are black, blue, red and yellow plates for the front and back of each card. Rather than touting the collector value of the

plates, Pinnacle created a treasure hunt by offering $20,000-35,000 to anybody assembling a complete set of four plates for either the front or back of any card. The $35,000, which would have been awarded for completion prior to August 22, was unclaimed. The amount decreased to $20,000 for any set redeemed by the end of 1997.

Spellbound

Each of the 50 cards in this insert features a letter of the alphabet as the basic card design. The letters can be used to spell out the names of nine players featured in the set. Cards feature micro-etched foil and are inserted 1:19 packs. Cards of Griffey, Ripken and the Jones were inserted only in hobby packs; retail packs have cards of Belle, Thomas, Piazza and the Rodriguezes. Values shown are per card; multiply by number of cards to determine a player's set value.

		NM/M
Complete Set (50):		110.00
1-5AB	Albert Belle	1.00
1-6AJ	Andruw Jones	2.00
1-4AR	Alex Rodriguez	4.50
1-7CJ	Chipper Jones	2.00
1-6CR	Cal Ripken Jr.	6.00
1-5FT	Frank Thomas	2.00
1-5IR	Ivan Rodriguez	1.50
1-6KG	Ken Griffey Jr.	3.50
1-6MP	Mike Piazza	3.50

1997 Pinnacle Certified

This 150-card base features a mirror-like mylar finish and a peel-off protector on each card front. Backs feature the player's 1996 statistics against each opponent. There are four different parallel sets, each with varying degrees of scarcity: Certified Red (1:5), Mirror Red (1:99), Mirror Blue (1:199) and Mirror Gold (1:299). Other inserts include Lasting Impressions, Certified

Team, and Certified Gold Team. Cards were sold in six-card packs for a suggested price of $4.99.

	NM/M
Complete Set (150):	30.00
Common Player:	.15
Common Certified Red:	1.00
Certified Red Stars:	5X
Common Mirror Red:	3.00
Mirror Red Stars:	12X
Common Mirror Blue:	4.00
Mirror Blue Stars:	15X
Common Mirror Gold:	7.50
Mirror Gold Stars:	35X
Jose Cruz Jr. Redemption:	2.00
Pack (6):	2.00
Wax Box (20):	35.00

1	Barry Bonds	3.00
2	Mo Vaughn	.15
3	Matt Williams	.15
4	Ryne Sandberg	1.25
5	Jeff Bagwell	1.00
6	Alan Benes	.15
7	John Wetteland	.15
8	Fred McGriff	.15
9	Craig Biggio	.15
10	Bernie Williams	.15
11	Brian L. Hunter	.15
12	Sandy Alomar Jr.	.15
13	Ray Lankford	.15
14	Ryan Klesko	.15
15	Jermaine Dye	.15
16	Andy Benes	.15
17	Albert Belle	.15
18	Tony Clark	.15
19	Dean Palmer	.15
20	Bernard Gilkey	.15
21	Ken Caminiti	.15
22	Alex Rodriguez	2.25
23	Tim Salmon	.15
24	Larry Walker	.15
25	Barry Larkin	.15
26	Mike Piazza	1.50
27	Brady Anderson	.15
28	Cal Ripken Jr.	3.00
29	Charles Nagy	.15
30	Paul Molitor	1.00
31	Darin Erstad	.25
32	Rey Ordonez	.15
33	Wally Joyner	.15
34	David Cone	.15
35	Sammy Sosa	1.25
36	Dante Bichette	.15
37	Eric Karros	.15
38	Omar Vizquel	.15
39	Roger Clemens	1.25
40	Joe Carter	.15
41	Frank Thomas	1.00
42	Javier Lopez	.15
43	Mike Mussina	.45
44	Gary Sheffield	.60
45	Tony Gwynn	1.25
46	Jason Kendall	.15
47	Jim Thome	.75
48	Andres Galarraga	.15
49	Mark McGwire	2.25
50	Troy Percival	.15
51	Derek Jeter	3.00
52	Todd Hollandsworth	.15
53	Ken Griffey Jr.	1.50
54	Randy Johnson	1.00
55	Pat Hentgen	.15
56	Rusty Greer	.15
57	John Jaha	.15
58	Kenny Lofton	.15
59	Chipper Jones	1.25
60	Robb Nen	.15
61	Rafael Palmeiro	.75
62	Mariano Rivera	.30
63	Hideo Nomo	.50
64	Greg Vaughn	.15
65	Ron Gant	.15
66	Eddie Murray	1.00
67	John Smoltz	.15
68	Manny Ramirez	1.00
69	Juan Gonzalez	.50
70	F.P. Santangelo	.15
71	Moises Alou	.15
72	Alex Ochoa	.15
73	Chuck Knoblauch	.15
74	Raul Mondesi	.15
75	J.T. Snow	.15
76	Rickey Henderson	1.00
77	Bobby Bonilla	.15
78	Wade Boggs	1.25
79	Ivan Rodriguez	.75
80	Brian Jordan	.15
81	Al Leiter	.15
82	Jay Buhner	.15
83	Greg Maddux	1.25
84	Edgar Martinez	.15
85	Kevin Brown	.15
86	Eric Young	.15
87	Todd Hundley	.15
88	Ellis Burks	.15
89	Marquis Grissom	.15
90	Jose Canseco	.60
91	Henry Rodriguez	.15
92	Andy Pettitte	.45
93	Mark Grudzielanek	.15
94	Dwight Gooden	.15
95	Roberto Alomar	.50
96	Paul Wilson	.15
97	Will Clark	.15
98	Rondell White	.15
99	Charles Johnson	.15
100	Jim Edmonds	.15

101	Jason Giambi	.60
102	Billy Wagner	.15
103	Edgar Renteria	.15
104	Johnny Damon	.45
105	Jason Isringhausen	.15
106	Andruw Jones	1.00
107	Jose Guillen	.15
108	Kevin Orie	.15
109	Brian Giles RC	1.25
110	Danny Patterson	.15
111	Vladimir Guerrero	1.00
112	Scott Rolen	.75
113	Damon Mashore	.15
114	Nomar Garciaparra	1.25
115	Todd Walker	.15
116	Wilton Guerrero	.15
117	Bob Abreu	.25
118	Brooks Kieschnick	.15
119	Pokey Reese	.15
120	Todd Greene	.15
121	Dmitri Young	.15
122	Raul Casanova	.15
123	Glendon Rusch	.15
124	Jason Dickson	.15
125	Jorge Posada	.15
126	Rod Myers RC	.15
127	Bubba Trammell RC	.40
128	Scott Spiezio	.15
129	Hideki Irabu RC	.40
130	Wendell Magee	.15
131	Bartolo Colon	.15
132	Chris Holt	.15
133	Calvin Maduro	.15
134	Ray Montgomery	.15
135	Shannon Stewart	.15
136	Ken Griffey Jr. (Certified Stars)	1.00
137	Vladimir Guerrero (Certified Stars)	.50
138	Roger Clemens (Certified Stars)	.75
139	Mark McGwire (Certified Stars)	1.25
140	Albert Belle (Certified Stars)	.15
141	Derek Jeter (Certified Stars)	1.50
142	Juan Gonzalez (Certified Stars)	.25
143	Greg Maddux (Certified Stars)	.60
144	Alex Rodriguez (Certified Stars)	1.25
145	Jeff Bagwell (Certified Stars)	.50
146	Cal Ripken Jr. (Certified Stars)	1.50
147	Tony Gwynn (Certified Stars)	.60
148	Frank Thomas (Certified Stars)	.50
149	Hideo Nomo (Certified Stars)	.25
150	Andruw Jones (Certified Stars)	.50

Red

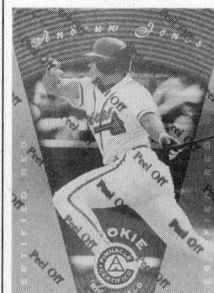

This parallel set features a red tint to the triangular mylar background left and right of the photo on front. "CERTIFIED RED" is printed vertically on both edges. Backs are identical to regular Certified cards. A peel-off protection coating is on the front of the card. Cards were inserted 1:5 packs.

	NM/M
Common Certified Red:	1.00
Certified Red Stars:	5X

Mirror Red

This parallel set features a red design element on the front of each card. Cards were inserted 1:99 packs.

NM/M
| Common Mirror Red: | 3.00 |
| Mirror Red Stars: | 12X |

Mirror Blue

This parallel set features a blue design element on the front of each card. Cards were inserted 1:199 packs.

NM/M
| Common Mirror Blue: | 4.00 |
| Mirror Blue Stars: | 15X |

Mirror Gold

This parallel set features a holographic gold design on the front of each card. Cards were inserted 1:299 packs.

NM/M
| Common Mirror Gold: | 7.50 |
| Mirror Gold Stars: | 35X |

Mirror Black

The exact nature of these cards is undetermined. They may have been intentionally created and "secretly" seeded in packs as an insert or they may have been test cards which were mistakenly inserted. They are not marked in any fashion. The cards are said to reflect in a bright green under direct light. It is commonly believed that each "Mirror Black" card exists in only a single piece, but that has not been verified. Neither is it confirmed that a Mirror Black parallel exists for each of the 151 cards in the base set. Even the most undistinguished player's card can sell for $100 or more due to the scarcity of the type.

NM/M
| Common Player: | 100.00 |

Lasting Impression

This insert features an hourglass die-cut design and a mirror mylar finish and pictures some of baseball's top veteran stars. Backs are conventionally printed and in-

clude a color portrait photo and a few words about the player. Cards were inserted 1:19 packs.

NM/M
Complete Set (20):	40.00
Common Player:	1.00
1	Cal Ripken Jr.	7.50
2	Ken Griffey Jr.	5.00
3	Mo Vaughn	1.00
4	Brian Jordan	1.00
5	Mark McGwire	6.00
6	Chuck Knoblauch	1.00
7	Sammy Sosa	3.00
8	Brady Anderson	1.00
9	Frank Thomas	2.00
10	Tony Gwynn	3.00
11	Roger Clemens	4.00
12	Alex Rodriguez	6.00
13	Paul Molitor	2.00
14	Kenny Lofton	1.00
15	John Smoltz	1.00
16	Roberto Alomar	1.50
17	Randy Johnson	2.00
18	Ryne Sandberg	3.00
19	Manny Ramirez	2.00
20	Mike Mussina	1.50

Team

The top 20 players in the game are honored on cards with frosted silver mylar printing. Cards were inserted 1:19 packs. A parallel version of this set, Certified Gold Team, has a gold mylar design with each card numbered to 500; while a super-premium parallel, Mirror Gold, is numbered to 25. Each card can also be found in a promo version overprinted "SAMPLE."

NM/M
Complete Set (20):	30.00
Common Player:	.50
Gold:	3X
Mirror Gold:	15X
Sample:	1X
1	Frank Thomas	1.50
2	Jeff Bagwell	1.50
3	Derek Jeter	4.00
4	Chipper Jones	2.00
5	Alex Rodriguez	3.00
6	Ken Caminiti	.50
7	Cal Ripken Jr.	4.00
8	Mo Vaughn	.50
9	Ivan Rodriguez	1.00
10	Mike Piazza	2.50
11	Juan Gonzalez	.75
12	Barry Bonds	4.00
13	Ken Griffey Jr.	2.50
14	Andruw Jones	1.50
15	Albert Belle	.50
16	Gary Sheffield	.75
17	Andy Pettitte	.65
18	Hideo Nomo	.75
19	Greg Maddux	2.00
20	John Smoltz	.50

1997 Totally Certified Samples

This trio of promo cards previews the high-tech, all-numbered Totally Certified issue. The samples are similar in format to the issued versions except they carry a large, black "SAMPLE" overprint diago-

nally on front and back. Also, backs have a gold-foil "PROMO" instead of the individual serial number.

NM/M
Complete Set (3):	5.00
Common Player:	1.00
18	Tony Clark (Platinum Red)	1.00
39	Roger Clemens (Platinum Blue)	3.00
41	Frank Thomas (Platinum Gold)	2.00

1997 Totally Certified Platinum Red

Totally Certified doesn't have a true base set. Instead, the product consists of three different 150-card parallel sets. Packs consisted of three cards for $6.99 each. The first of three parallels is the Platinum Red set, inserted two per pack, and featuring micro-etched holographic mylar stock with red accents and foil stamping. Each card in the Red set is sequentially-numbered to 3,999.

NM/M
Complete Set (150):	75.00
Common Player:	.25
Pack (3):	3.00
Wax Box (20):	45.00
1	Barry Bonds	4.00
2	Mo Vaughn	.25
3	Matt Williams	.25
4	Ryne Sandberg	2.00
5	Jeff Bagwell	1.25
6	Alan Benes	.25
7	John Wetteland	.25
8	Fred McGriff	.25
9	Craig Biggio	.25
10	Bernie Williams	.25
11	Brian Hunter	.25
12	Sandy Alomar Jr.	.25
13	Ray Lankford	.25
14	Ryan Klesko	.25
15	Jermaine Dye	.25
16	Andy Benes	.25
17	Albert Belle	.25
18	Tony Clark	.25
19	Dean Palmer	.25
20	Bernard Gilkey	.25
21	Ken Caminiti	.25
22	Alex Rodriguez	3.00
23	Tim Salmon	.25
24	Larry Walker	.25
25	Barry Larkin	.25
26	Mike Piazza	2.50
27	Brady Anderson	.25
28	Cal Ripken Jr.	4.00
29	Charles Nagy	.25
30	Paul Molitor	1.25
31	Darin Erstad	.35
32	Rey Ordonez	.25
33	Wally Joyner	.25
34	David Cone	.25
35	Sammy Sosa	2.00
36	Dante Bichette	.25
37	Eric Karros	.25
38	Omar Vizquel	.25
39	Roger Clemens	2.25
40	Joe Carter	.25
41	Frank Thomas	1.25
42	Javier Lopez	.25
43	Mike Mussina	.75
44	Gary Sheffield	.60
45	Tony Gwynn	2.00
46	Jason Kendall	.25
47	Jim Thome	1.00
48	Andres Galarraga	.25
49	Mark McGwire	3.00
50	Troy Percival	.25
51	Derek Jeter	4.00
52	Todd Hollandsworth	.25
53	Ken Griffey Jr.	2.50
54	Randy Johnson	1.25
55	Pat Hentgen	.25
56	Rusty Greer	.25
57	John Jaha	.25
58	Kenny Lofton	.25
59	Chipper Jones	2.00
60	Robb Nen	.25
61	Rafael Palmeiro	1.00
62	Mariano Rivera	.35
63	Hideo Nomo	.65

64	Greg Vaughn	.25
65	Ron Gant	.25
66	Eddie Murray	1.25
67	John Smoltz	.25
68	Manny Ramirez	1.25
69	Juan Gonzalez	.65
70	F.P. Santangelo	.25
71	Moises Alou	.25
72	Alex Ochoa	.25
73	Chuck Knoblauch	.25
74	Raul Mondesi	.25
75	J.T. Snow	.25
76	Rickey Henderson	.25
77	Bobby Bonilla	.25
78	Wade Boggs	2.00
79	Ivan Rodriguez	1.00
80	Brian Jordan	.25
81	Al Leiter	.25
82	Jay Buhner	.25
83	Greg Maddux	2.00
84	Edgar Martinez	.25
85	Kevin Brown	.25
86	Eric Young	.25
87	Todd Hundley	.25
88	Ellis Burks	.25
89	Marquis Grissom	.25
90	Jose Canseco	.60
91	Henry Rodriguez	.25
92	Andy Pettitte	.50
93	Mark Grudzielanek	.25
94	Dwight Gooden	.25
95	Roberto Alomar	.35
96	Paul Wilson	.25
97	Will Clark	.25
98	Rondell White	.25
99	Charles Johnson	.25
100	Jim Edmonds	.25
101	Jason Giambi	.75
102	Billy Wagner	.25
103	Edgar Renteria	.25
104	Johnny Damon	.45
105	Jason Isringhausen	.25
106	Andruw Jones	1.25
107	Jose Guillen	.25
108	Kevin Orie	.25
109	Brian Giles RC	2.00
110	Danny Patterson	.25
111	Vladimir Guerrero	1.25
112	Scott Rolen	1.00
113	Damon Mashore	.25
114	Nomar Garciaparra	2.00
115	Todd Walker	.25
116	Wilton Guerrero	.25
117	Bob Abreu	.25
118	Brooks Kieschnick	.25
119	Pokey Reese	.25
120	Todd Greene	.25
121	Dmitri Young	.25
122	Raul Casanova	.25
123	Glendon Rusch	.25
124	Jason Dickson	.25
125	Jorge Posada	.25
126	Rod Myers	.25
127	Bubba Trammell	.25
128	Scott Spiezio	.25
129	Hideki Irabu	.25
130	Wendell Magee	.25
131	Bartolo Colon	.25
132	Chris Holt	.25
133	Calvin Maduro	.25
134	Ray Montgomery	.25
135	Shannon Stewart	.25
136	Ken Griffey Jr. (Certified Stars)	1.50
137	Vladimir Guerrero (Certified Stars)	.60
138	Roger Clemens (Certified Stars)	1.25
139	Mark McGwire (Certified Stars)	1.50
140	Albert Belle (Certified Stars)	.25
141	Derek Jeter (Certified Stars)	2.00
142	Juan Gonzalez (Certified Stars)	.30
143	Greg Maddux (Certified Stars)	1.00
144	Alex Rodriguez (Certified Stars)	1.50
145	Jeff Bagwell (Certified Stars)	.60
146	Cal Ripken Jr. (Certified Stars)	2.00
147	Tony Gwynn (Certified Stars)	1.00
148	Frank Thomas (Certified Stars)	.60
149	Hideo Nomo (Certified Stars)	.30
150	Andruw Jones (Certified Stars)	.60

Platinum Blue

Featuring blue accents and foil stamping, the Platinum Blue cards are sequentially numbered on back in gold foil to 1,999 and inserted per pack.

NM/M
Complete Set (150):	200.00
Common Player:	1.00
Platinum Blue Stars:	1.5X

Platinum Gold

The most difficult to find of the Totally Certified cards, the Platinum Gold versions are sequentially-numbered to 30 per card and inserted 1:79 packs.

NM/M
| Common Player: | 25.00 |
| Platinum Gold Stars: | 30X |

1997 Pinnacle FanFest

As title sponsor for baseball's All-Star FanFest in Cleveland, July 4-8, Pinnacle issued a number of special cards including this set which was distributed in three-card cello packs both prior to and during the event. To help promote the event, six of the cards were issued with a schedule back, as well as the regular back design. Fronts have action photos highlighted at bottom by a stadium facade in gold foil. The FanFest logo is at bottom center. Backs feature a player portrait photo within a large star. Also on back are a few stats and personal data, a few words about the player and appropriate logos. Cards are numbered with an "FF" prefix and "of 21" following the number. Card #21 of the host team's Sandy Alomar, Jr., was not issued in packs. A redemption card, which could be traded in at area card shops for the Alomar card, was substituted.

NM/M
Complete Set (21):	12.50
Common Player:	.25
FF1	Frank Thomas	.65
FF2	Jeff Bagwell	.65
FF3	Chuck Knoblauch	.25
FF4	Craig Biggio	.25
FF5	Alex Rodriguez	1.50
FF6	Chipper Jones	.75
FF7	Cal Ripken Jr.	1.50
FF8	Ken Caminiti	.25
FF9	Juan Gonzalez	.45
FF10	Barry Bonds	2.00

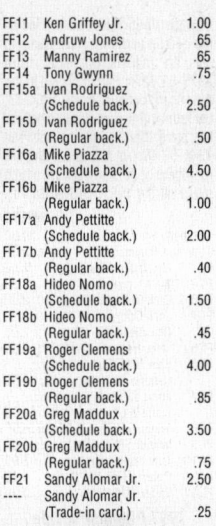

FF11	Ken Griffey Jr.	1.00
FF12	Andruw Jones	.65
FF13	Manny Ramirez	.65
FF14	Tony Gwynn	.75
FF15a	Ivan Rodriguez (Schedule back.)	2.50
FF15b	Ivan Rodriguez (Regular back.)	.50
FF16a	Mike Piazza (Schedule back.)	4.50
FF16b	Mike Piazza (Regular back.)	1.00
FF17a	Andy Pettitte (Schedule back.)	2.00
FF17b	Andy Pettitte (Regular back.)	.40
FF18a	Hideo Nomo (Schedule back.)	1.50
FF18b	Hideo Nomo (Regular back.)	.45
FF19a	Roger Clemens (Schedule back.)	4.00
FF19b	Roger Clemens (Regular back.)	.85
FF20a	Greg Maddux (Schedule back.)	3.50
FF20b	Greg Maddux (Regular back.)	.75
FF21	Sandy Alomar Jr.	2.50
----	Sandy Alomar Jr. (Trade-in card.)	.25

Larry Doby

Marking the 50th anniversary of the American League's integration, Pinnacle, title sponsor of baseball's All-Star FanFest, issued a special card of black A.L. pioneer Larry Doby, who debuted in 1947 with the Indians. FanFest and the All-Star Game were held in Cleveland in 1997, with Doby attending many of the functions. In the same format as its FanFest set of current players, the special Doby card has a black-and-white action photo on front, with gold-foil highlights at bottom. Back repeats the front photo within a star and offers some career notes and stats. The Doby card was given away to FanFest volunteer workers and laminated into identification badges for FanFest dealers.

NM/M
| Larry Doby | 4.00 |

Personal Cards

Continuing a tradition begun a year earlier, Pinnacle, the title sponsor for baseball's FanFest, produced a series of cards for various local and media celebrities. The cards are in the same format as the FanFest player cards, with color photos on front and gold-foil highlights. Backs feature a photo detail within a star design and a few words about the personality, along with stats such as Indians' games attended, popcorn consumed, etc. Cards are numbered with a PC prefix and are difficult to find because their distribution was controlled by the person pictured. Rick Manning was an Indians outfielder from 1975-83. Mike Hegan played in the American League from 1964-77; his father, Jim, was a staple behind the plate for the Indians between 1941-57. Six of the cards feature members of the Fox network which televised the 1997 All-Star Game.

		NM/M
Complete Set (12):		30.00
Common Player:		2.00
PC1	Macie McInnis (Fox)	2.00
PC2	Bill Martin (Fox)	2.00
PC3	Dick Gaddard (Fox)	2.00
PC4	Jack Corrigan (WUAB-TV)	2.00
PC5	Mike Hegan (WUAB-TV)	6.00
PC6	Rick Manning (Sports Channel)	5.00
PC7	John Sanders (Sports Channel)	
PC8	Mayor Michael R. White	4.50
PC9	Wilma Smith (Fox)	2.00
PC10	Tim Taylor (Fox)	2.00
PC11	Robin Swoboda (Fox)	2.00
PC12	Slider (Mascot)	3.00

1997 Pinnacle Inside

The first baseball card set to be sold within a sealed tin can, Inside Baseball consists of a 150-card base set featuring both a color and black-and-white photo of the player on front. Included in the base set are 20 Rookies cards and three checklists. Inserts include the Club Edition and Diamond Edition parallel sets, Dueling Dugouts and Fortysomething. In addition, 24 different cans, each featuring a different player, were available. Cans containing one pack of 10 cards were sold for $2.99 each.

		NM/M
Complete Set (150):		15.00
Common Player:		.05
Common Club Edition:		.75
Club Edition Stars:		5X
Common Diamond Edition:		5.00
Diamond Edition Stars:		25X
Unopened Can (10):		2.00
Case Cans (48):		60.00
1	David Cone	.05
2	Sammy Sosa	1.00
3	Joe Carter	.05
4	Juan Gonzalez	.40
5	Hideo Nomo	.40
6	Moises Alou	.05
7	Marc Newfield	.05
8	Alex Rodriguez	2.00
9	Kimera Bartee	.05
10	Chuck Knoblauch	.05
11	Jason Isringhausen	.05
12	Jermaine Allensworth	.05
13	Frank Thomas	.75
14	Paul Molitor	.75
15	John Mabry	.05
16	Greg Maddux	1.00
17	Rafael Palmeiro	.65
18	Brian Jordan	.05
19	Ken Griffey Jr.	1.50
20	Brady Anderson	.05
21	Ruben Sierra	.05
22	Travis Fryman	.05
23	Cal Ripken Jr.	2.50
24	Will Clark	.05
25	Todd Hollandsworth	.05
26	Kevin Brown	.05
27	Mike Piazza	1.50
28	Craig Biggio	.05
29	Paul Wilson	.05
30	Andres Galarraga	.05
31	Chipper Jones	1.00
32	Jason Giambi	.65
33	Ernie Young	.05
34	Marty Cordova	.05
35	Albert Belle	.05
36	Roger Clemens	1.25
37	Ryne Sandberg	1.00
38	Henry Rodriguez	.05
39	Jay Buhner	.05
40	Raul Mondesi	.05
41	Jeff Fassero	.05
42	Edgar Martinez	.05
43	Trey Beamon	.05
44	Mo Vaughn	.05
45	Gary Sheffield	.40
46	Ray Durham	.05
47	Brett Butler	.05
48	Ivan Rodriguez	.65
49	Fred McGriff	.05
50	Dean Palmer	.05
51	Rickey Henderson	.75
52	Andy Pettitte	.30
53	Bobby Bonilla	.05
54	Shawn Green	.50
55	Tino Martinez	.05
56	Tony Gwynn	1.00
57	Tom Glavine	.35
58	Eric Young	.05
59	Kevin Appier	.05
60	Barry Bonds	2.50
61	Wade Boggs	1.00
62	Jason Kendall	.05
63	Jeff Bagwell	.75
64	Jeff Conine	.05
65	Greg Vaughn	.05
66	Eric Karros	.05
67	Manny Ramirez	.75
68	John Smoltz	.05
69	Terrell Wade	.05
70	John Wetteland	.05
71	Kenny Lofton	.05
72	Jim Thome	.65
73	Bill Pulsipher	.05
74	Darryl Strawberry	.05
75	Roberto Alomar	.25
76	Bobby Higginson	.05
77	James Baldwin	.05
78	Mark McGwire	2.00
79	Jose Canseco	.40
80	Mark Grudzielanek	.05
81	Ryan Klesko	.05
82	Javier Lopez	.05
83	Ken Caminiti	.05
84	Dave Nilsson	.05
85	Tim Salmon	.05
86	Cecil Fielder	.05
87	Derek Jeter	2.50
88	Garret Anderson	.05
89	Dwight Gooden	.05
90	Carlos Delgado	.50
91	Ugueth Urbina	.05
92	Chan Ho Park	.05
93	Eddie Murray	.75
94	Alex Ochoa	.05
95	Rusty Greer	.05
96	Mark Grace	.05
97	Pat Hentgen	.05
98	John Jaha	.05
99	Charles Johnson	.05
100	Jermaine Dye	.05
101	Quinton McCracken	.05
102	Troy Percival	.05
103	Shane Reynolds	.05
104	Rondell White	.05
105	Charles Nagy	.05
106	Alan Benes	.05
107	Tom Goodwin	.05
108	Ron Gant	.05
109	Dan Wilson	.05
110	Darin Erstad	.10
111	Matt Williams	.05
112	Barry Larkin	.05
113	Mariano Rivera	.15
114	Larry Walker	.05
115	Jim Edmonds	.05
116	Michael Tucker	.05
117	Todd Hundley	.05
118	Alex Fernandez	.05
119	J.T. Snow	.05
120	Ellis Burks	.05
121	Steve Finley	.05
122	Mike Mussina	.40
123	Curtis Pride	.05
124	Derek Bell	.05
125	Dante Bichette	.05
126	Terry Steinbach	.05
127	Randy Johnson	.75
128	Andruw Jones	.75
129	Vladimir Guerrero	.75
130	Ruben Rivera	.05
131	Billy Wagner	.05
132	Scott Rolen	.65
133	Rey Ordonez	.05
134	Karim Garcia	.05
135	George Arias	.05
136	Todd Greene	.05
137	Robin Jennings	.05
138	Raul Casanova	.05
139	Josh Booty	.05
140	Edgar Renteria	.05
141	Chad Mottola	.05
142	Dmitri Young	.05
143	Tony Clark	.05
144	Todd Walker	.05
145	Kevin Brown	.05
146	Nomar Garciaparra	1.00
147	Neifi Perez	.05
148	Derek Jeter, Todd Hollandsworth	.50
149	Pat Hentgen, John Smoltz	.50
150	Juan Gonzalez, Ken Caminiti	.05

Club Edition

A 150-card parallel set featuring a special silver foil design and "CLUB EDITION" notation on back, these cards were inserted 1:7 can of Inside.

	NM/M
Complete Club Edition Set (150):	300.00
Common Club Edition:	.75
Stars:	5X

Diamond Edition

A second parallel set, this time featuring a special die-cut design and gold holographic stamping. Cards were inserted 1:63 packs.

	NM/M
Common Diamond Edition:	5.00
Stars:	25X

Cans

In addition to the cards, collectors had the option of collecting the 24 different player cans which are the "packs" in which the cards were sold. About the size of a can of peas (3" diameter, 4-1/2" tall), the cans feature several color and black-and-white reproductions of the player's Inside card. The package had to be opened with a can opener to access the cards. Values shown are for empty cans which have been opened from the bottom; top-opened cans have little collectible value.

		NM/M
Complete Set (24):		10.00
Common Can:		.25
Sealed Cans:		2X
1	Ken Griffey Jr.	.75
2	Juan Gonzalez	.30
3	Frank Thomas	.40
4	Cal Ripken Jr.	1.50
5	Derek Jeter	1.50
6	Andruw Jones	.40
7	Alex Rodriguez	1.00
8	Mike Piazza	.75
9	Mo Vaughn	.25
10	Jeff Bagwell	.40
11	Ken Caminiti	.25
12	Andy Pettitte	.30
13	Barry Bonds	1.50
14	Mark McGwire	1.00
15	Ryan Klesko	.25
16	Manny Ramirez	.40
17	Ivan Rodriguez	.35
18	Chipper Jones	.50
19	Albert Belle	.25
20	Tony Gwynn	.50
21	Kenny Lofton	.25
22	Greg Maddux	.50
23	Hideo Nomo	.40
24	John Smoltz	.25

Dueling Dugouts

This 20-card insert set features a veteran player on one side, a rising star on the other, and a spinning wheel that reveals their respective achievements in various statistical categories. Cards were inserted 1:23 packs.

		NM/M
Complete Set (20):		65.00
Common Player:		1.25
1	Alex Rodriguez, Cal Ripken Jr.	10.00
2	Jeff Bagwell, Ken Caminiti	3.00
3	Barry Bonds, Albert Belle	10.00
4	Mike Piazza, Ivan Rodriguez	6.00
5	Chuck Knoblauch, Roberto Alomar	1.25
6	Ken Griffey Jr., Andruw Jones	6.00
7	Chipper Jones, Jim Thome	4.00
8	Frank Thomas, Mo Vaughn	3.00
9	Fred McGriff, Mark McGwire	7.50
10	Brian Jordan, Tony Gwynn	4.00
11	Barry Larkin, Derek Jeter	10.00
12	Kenny Lofton, Bernie Williams	1.25
13	Juan Gonzalez, Manny Ramirez	3.00
14	Will Clark, Rafael Palmeiro	2.50
15	Greg Maddux, Roger Clemens	4.50
16	John Smoltz, Andy Pettitte	1.25
17	Mariano Rivera, John Wetteland	1.25
18	Hideo Nomo, Mike Mussina	2.00
19	Todd Hollandsworth, Darin Erstad	1.25
20	Vladimir Guerrero, Karim Garcia	3.00

Fortysomething

The top home run hitters in the game are pictured in this 16-card set. Cards were inserted 1:47 packs.

		NM/M
Complete Set (16):		50.00
Common Player:		1.00
1	Juan Gonzalez	3.00
2	Barry Bonds	12.00
3	Ken Caminiti	1.00
4	Mark McGwire	10.00
5	Todd Hundley	1.00
6	Albert Belle	1.00
7	Ellis Burks	1.00
8	Jay Buhner	1.00
9	Brady Anderson	1.00
10	Vinny Castilla	1.00
11	Mo Vaughn	1.00
12	Ken Griffey Jr.	7.50
13	Sammy Sosa	6.50
14	Andres Galarraga	1.00
15	Gary Sheffield	2.00
16	Frank Thomas	5.00

Mint Collection

The 30-card Mint Collection set came in three-card packs that also contained two coins. Cards come in two versions: die-cut and foil. Three foil versions appear with Bronze as the "common." Silver (1:15) and Gold (1:48) parallels also appear. The coins that come with each pack arrive in brass, silver and gold and can be matched up with the corresponding player's die-cut card. Fronts feature a player action shot on the left side with a shadowed portrait at right. On the die-cut versions, the coin-size hole is in the lower-right; the foil team stamp for the common cards is in the same location. Backs are numbered as "x of 30" and deliver a short text.

		NM/M
Complete Set (30):		100.00
Common Player:		1.25
Silver Cards:		4X
Gold Cards:		6X
Die-Cuts: 50 Percent		
Wax Box (24):		25.00
1	Ken Griffey Jr.	2.00
2	Frank Thomas	1.25
3	Alex Rodriguez	2.50
4	Cal Ripken Jr.	3.00
5	Mo Vaughn	.25
6	Juan Gonzalez	.60
7	Mike Piazza	2.00
8	Albert Belle	.25
9	Chipper Jones	1.50
10	Andruw Jones	1.25
11	Greg Maddux	1.50
12	Hideo Nomo	.60
13	Jeff Bagwell	1.25
14	Manny Ramirez	1.25
15	Mark McGwire	2.50
16	Derek Jeter	3.00
17	Sammy Sosa	1.50
18	Barry Bonds	3.00
19	Chuck Knoblauch	.25
20	Dante Bichette	.25
21	Tony Gwynn	1.50
22	Ken Caminiti	.25
23	Gary Sheffield	.60
24	Tim Salmon	.25
25	Ivan Rodriguez	1.00
26	Henry Rodriguez	.25
27	Barry Larkin	.25
28	Ryan Klesko	.25
29	Brian Jordan	.25
30	Jay Buhner	.25

Mint Collection Coins

Two coins from the 30-coin set were included in each three-card pack of 1997 Pinnacle Mint Collection. Brass coins are common while nickel-silver coins were inserted every 20 packs and gold-plated coins were inserted every 48 packs. Redemption cards for solid silver coins were found every 2,300 packs and a redemption card for a solid gold coin was inserted one per 47,200 packs. Only one of each 24K gold coin was produced. The front of the coins feature the player's portrait while the backs have a baseball diamond with "Limited Edition, Pinnacle Mint Collection 1997" printed.

		NM/M
Complete Set (30):		35.00
Common Brass Coin:		.25
Nickel Coins:		2X
Gold Plated Coins:		6X
Silver Coins:		20X
24K Gold Coins: Value Undetermined		
1	Ken Griffey Jr.	2.50
2	Frank Thomas	1.50
3	Alex Rodriguez	3.00
4	Cal Ripken Jr.	4.00
5	Mo Vaughn	.25
6	Juan Gonzalez	.75
7	Mike Piazza	2.50
8	Albert Belle	.25
9	Chipper Jones	2.00
10	Andruw Jones	1.50
11	Greg Maddux	.75
12	Hideo Nomo	.75
13	Jeff Bagwell	1.50
14	Manny Ramirez	1.50
15	Mark McGwire	3.00
16	Derek Jeter	4.00
17	Sammy Sosa	2.00
18	Barry Bonds	4.00
19	Chuck Knoblauch	.25
20	Dante Bichette	.25
21	Tony Gwynn	2.00
22	Ken Caminiti	.25
23	Gary Sheffield	.65
24	Tim Salmon	.25
25	Ivan Rodriguez	1.00
26	Henry Rodriguez	.25
27	Barry Larkin	.25
28	Ryan Klesko	.25
29	Brian Jordan	.25
30	Jay Buhner	.25

1997 Pinnacle X-Press

The 150-card set features 115 base cards, a 22-card Rookies subset, 10 Peak Performers and three checklist cards. Each of the regular cards features a horizontal design with two photos of each player on front. Inserts include Swing for the Fences (regular player cards as well as base and booster cards that can be used to accumulate points for a sweepstakes), Men of Summer, Far & Away, Melting Pot, and Metal Works Silver and Gold redemptions. Cards were sold in eight-card packs for $1.99. X-Press Metal Works boxes were also available for $14.99 and contained a regular pack, one metal card and a master deck used to play the Swing for the Fences game.

		NM/M
Complete Set (150):		7.50
Common Player:		.05
Men of Summer:		4X
Pack (8):		.75
Wax Box (24):		10.00
1	Larry Walker	.05
2	Andy Pettitte	.30
3	Matt Williams	.05
4	Juan Gonzalez	.40
5	Frank Thomas	.40
6	Kenny Lofton	.05
7	Ken Griffey Jr.	1.25
8	Andres Galarraga	.05
9	Greg Maddux	1.00
10	Hideo Nomo	.40
11	Cecil Fielder	.05
12	Jose Canseco	.40
13	Tony Gwynn	.75
14	Eddie Murray	.75
15	Alex Rodriguez	1.50
16	Mike Piazza	1.25
17	Ken Hill	.05
18	Chuck Knoblauch	.05
19	Ellis Burks	.05
20	Rafael Palmeiro	.65
21	Vinny Castilla	.05
22	Rusty Greer	.05
23	Chipper Jones	1.00
24	Rey Ordonez	.05
25	Mariano Rivera	.15
26	Garret Anderson	.05

27	Edgar Martinez	.05
28	Dante Bichette	.05
29	Todd Hundley	.05
30	Barry Bonds	2.00
31	Barry Larkin	.05
32	Derek Jeter	2.00
33	Marquis Grissom	.05
34	David Justice	.05
35	Ivan Rodriguez	.65
36	Jay Buhner	.05
37	Fred McGriff	.05
38	Brady Anderson	.05
39	Tony Clark	.05
40	Eric Young	.05
41	Charles Nagy	.05
42	Mark McGwire	1.50
43	Paul O'Neill	.05
44	Tino Martinez	.05
45	Ryne Sandberg	1.00
46	Bernie Williams	.05
47	Albert Belle	.05
48	Jeff Cirillo	.05
49	Tim Salmon	.05
50	Steve Finley	.05
51	Lance Johnson	.05
52	John Smoltz	.05
53	Javier Lopez	.05
54	Roger Clemens	1.00
55	Kevin Appier	.05
56	Ken Caminiti	.05
57	Cal Ripken Jr.	2.00
58	Moises Alou	.05
59	Marty Cordova	.05
60	David Cone	.05
61	Manny Ramirez	.75
62	Ray Durham	.05
63	Jermaine Dye	.05
64	Craig Biggio	.05
65	Will Clark	.05
66	Omar Vizquel	.05
67	Bernard Gilkey	.05
68	Greg Vaughn	.05
69	Wade Boggs	1.00
70	Dave Nilsson	.05
71	Mark Grace	.05
72	Dean Palmer	.05
73	Sammy Sosa	1.00
74	Mike Mussina	.30
75	Alex Fernandez	.05
76	Henry Rodriguez	.05
77	Travis Fryman	.05
78	Jeff Bagwell	.75
79	Pat Hentgen	.05
80	Gary Sheffield	.40
81	Jim Edmonds	.05
82	Darin Erstad	.10
83	Mark Grudzielanek	.05
84	Jim Thome	.65
85	Bobby Higginson	.05
86	Al Martin	.05
87	Jason Giambi	.50
88	Mo Vaughn	.05
89	Jeff Conine	.05
90	Edgar Renteria	.05
91	Andy Ashby	.05
92	Ryan Klesko	.05
93	John Jaha	.05
94	Paul Molitor	.75
95	Brian Hunter	.05
96	Randy Johnson	.75
97	Joey Hamilton	.05
98	Billy Wagner	.05
99	John Wetteland	.05
100	Jeff Fassero	.05
101	Rondell White	.05
102	Kevin Brown	.05
103	Andy Benes	.05
104	Raul Mondesi	.05
105	Todd Hollandsworth	.05
106	Alex Ochoa	.05
107	Bobby Bonilla	.05
108	Brian Jordan	.05
109	Tom Glavine	.35
110	Ron Gant	.05
111	Jason Kendall	.05
112	Roberto Alomar	.30
113	Troy Percival	.05
114	Michael Tucker	.05
115	Joe Carter	.05
116	Andruw Jones	.75
117	Nomar Garciaparra	1.00
118	Todd Walker	.05
119	Jose Guillen	.05
120	Bubba Trammell **RC**	.20
121	Wilton Guerrero	.05
122	Bob Abreu	.15
123	Vladimir Guerrero	.75
124	Dmitri Young	.05
125	Kevin Orie	.05
126	Glendon Rusch	.05
127	Brooks Kieschnick	.05
128	Scott Spiezio	.05
129	Brian Giles **RC**	.75
130	Jason Dickson	.05
131	Damon Mashore	.05
132	Wendell Magee	.05
133	Matt Morris	.05
134	Scott Rolen	.65
135	Shannon Stewart	.05
136	Deivi Cruz **RC**	.05
137	Hideki Irabu **RC**	.15
138	Larry Walker (Peak Performers)	.05
139	Ken Griffey Jr. (Peak Performers)	.65
140	Frank Thomas (Peak Performers)	.40

141	Ivan Rodriguez (Peak Performers)	.30
142	Randy Johnson (Peak Performers)	.40
143	Mark McGwire (Peak Performers)	.75
144	Tino Martinez (Peak Performers)	.05
145	Tony Clark (Peak Performers)	.05
146	Mike Piazza (Peak Performers)	.50
147	Alex Rodriguez (Peak Performers)	.75
148	Checklist (Roger Clemens)	
149	Checklist (Greg Maddux)	.45
150	Checklist (Hideo Nomo)	.20

Men of Summer

This parallel set of the 150 cards in the base X-Press issue differs in that the fronts are printed on foil backgrounds and the backs have a notation "MEN OF SUMMER" printed in gold vertically at top.

	NM/M
Complete Set (150):	50.00
Common Player:	.25
Stars:	3X

Far & Away

This 18-card insert highlights the top home run hitters in baseball and is printed with Dufex technology. Cards were inserted 1:19 packs.

		NM/M
Complete Set (18):		25.00
Common Player:		.50
1	Albert Belle	.50
2	Mark McGwire	4.50
3	Frank Thomas	1.75
4	Mo Vaughn	.50
5	Jeff Bagwell	1.75
6	Juan Gonzalez	1.00
7	Mike Piazza	3.50
8	Andruw Jones	1.75
9	Chipper Jones	2.50
10	Gary Sheffield	1.00
11	Sammy Sosa	2.50
12	Darin Erstad	.75
13	Jay Buhner	.50
14	Ken Griffey Jr.	3.50
15	Ken Caminiti	.50
16	Brady Anderson	.50
17	Manny Ramirez	1.75
18	Alex Rodriguez	4.50

Melting Pot

This insert showcases the talents of major leaguers from various countries. Fronts have color player photos on a background which combines shiny silver foil and textured foil in the design of the player's

native flag. Backs have another photo and are ink-jet numbered in a white stripe at bottom in an edition of 500 each. Stated insertion rate was one per 288 packs. Each card can also be found in a promo card version overprinted "SAMPLE."

		NM/M
Complete Set (20):		110.00
Common Player:		1.50
Samples:		1X
1	Jose Guillen	1.50
2	Vladimir Guerrero	8.00
3	Andruw Jones	8.00
4	Larry Walker	1.50
5	Manny Ramirez	8.00
6	Ken Griffey Jr.	10.00
7	Alex Rodriguez	12.00
8	Frank Thomas	8.00
9	Juan Gonzalez	4.00
10	Ivan Rodriguez	6.00
11	Hideo Nomo	4.00
12	Rafael Palmeiro	1.50
13	Dave Nilsson	1.50
14	Nomar Garciaparra	9.00
15	Wilton Guerrero	1.50
16	Sammy Sosa	9.00
17	Edgar Renteria	1.50
18	Cal Ripken Jr.	16.00
19	Derek Jeter	16.00
20	Rey Ordonez	1.50

Metal Works

Each Home Plate Box of X-Press contains one heavy bronze Metal Works "card." The 2-3/8" x 3-1/2" slabs have a player portrait on front. Backs have a few words about the player. Redemption cards for silver-plated parallels were inserted 1:470 packs, while a silver slab was found 1:54 Home Plate Boxes. Silver Metal Works are serially numbered to 400 each. Gold-plated Metal Works were produced in an edition of 200 each, with redemption cards inserted 1:950 packs or one per 108 Home Plate Boxes.

		NM/M
Complete Set (20):		25.00
Common Player:		.50
Silver:		3X
Gold:		6X
1	Ken Griffey Jr.	2.00
2	Frank Thomas	1.00
3	Andruw Jones	1.00
4	Alex Rodriguez	2.50
5	Derek Jeter	3.00
6	Cal Ripken Jr.	3.00
7	Mike Piazza	2.00
8	Chipper Jones	1.50
9	Juan Gonzalez	.65
10	Greg Maddux	1.50
11	Tony Gwynn	1.50
12	Jeff Bagwell	1.50
13	Albert Belle	.50
14	Mark McGwire	2.50
15	Nomar Garciaparra	1.50
16	Mo Vaughn	.50
17	Andy Pettitte	.65
18	Manny Ramirez	1.00
19	Kenny Lofton	.50
20	Roger Clemens	1.75

Swing for the Fences

These inserts allowed collectors to play an interactive game based on the number of home runs hit by the home run champion of each league. Cards feature 60 different players and were inserted 1:2 packs. Base cards feature a number between 20-42 printed on them and are found one in every master deck. Booster cards feature a plus-or-minus point total (i.e. +7, -2) that can be used to add or subtract points to get to the winning home run total. Booster cards are found 1:2 packs. Collectors who accumu-

lated the winning home run totals were eligible to win prizes ranging from autographs to a trip to the 1998 All-Star Game. The unnumbered cards are checklisted here in alphabetical order.

		NM/M
Complete Set (60):		20.00
Common Player:		.15
(1)	Sandy Alomar Jr.	.15
(2)	Moises Alou	.15
(3)	Brady Anderson	.15
(4)	Jeff Bagwell	1.00
(5)	Derek Bell	.15
(6)	Jay Bell	.15
(7)	Albert Belle	.15
(8)	Geronimo Berroa	.15
(9)	Dante Bichette	.15
(10)	Barry Bonds	2.50
(11)	Bobby Bonilla	.15
(12)	Jay Buhner	.15
(13)	Ellis Burks	.15
(14)	Ken Caminiti	.15
(15)	Jose Canseco	.40
(16)	Joe Carter	.15
(17)	Vinny Castilla	.15
(18)	Tony Clark	.15
(19)	Carlos Delgado	.50
(20)	Jim Edmonds	.15
(21)	Cecil Fielder	.15
(22)	Andres Galarraga	.15
(23)	Ron Gant	.15
(24)	Bernard Gilkey	.15
(25)	Juan Gonzalez	.50
(26)	Ken Griffey Jr. (AL WINNER)	4.00
(27)	Vladimir Guerrero	1.00
(28)	Todd Hundley	.15
(29)	John Jaha	.15
(30)	Andruw Jones	1.00
(31)	Chipper Jones	1.25
(32)	David Justice	.15
(33)	Jeff Kent	.15
(34)	Ryan Klesko	.15
(35)	Barry Larkin	.15
(36)	Mike Lieberthal	.15
(37)	Javy Lopez	.15
(38)	Edgar Martinez	.15
(39)	Tino Martinez	.15
(40)	Fred McGriff	.15
(41)	Mark McGwire (AL/NL WINNER)	4.00
(42)	Raul Mondesi	.15
(43)	Tim Naehring	.15
(44)	Dave Nillson	.15
(45)	Rafael Palmeiro	.75
(46)	Dean Palmer	.15
(47)	Mike Piazza	1.50
(48)	Cal Ripken Jr.	2.50
(49)	Henry Rodriguez	.15
(50)	Tim Salmon	.15
(51)	Gary Sheffield	.40
(52)	Sammy Sosa	1.25
(53)	Terry Steinbach	.15
(54)	Frank Thomas	1.00
(55)	Jim Thome	.75
(56)	Mo Vaughn	.50
(57)	Larry Walker (NL Winner)	1.25
(58)	Rondell White	.15
(59)	Matt Williams	.15
(60)	Todd Zeile	.15

Swing/Fences Gold

Collectors who correctly matched Swing for the Fences insert game cards of the final 1997 season American and National home run champions with proper point cards equal to the number of home runs each hit could exchange them for a random assortment of 10 upgraded cards featuring gold-foil highlights and a premium card stock. The first 1,000 redemptions received an autographed Andruw Jones gold card. The redemption period ended March 1, 1998.

	NM/M
Complete Set (60):	125.00
Common Player:	1.00
Stars:	4X
Andruw Jones Autograph:	25.00

1998 Pinnacle Samples

Six stars from its 1998 issue were issued in a promo card version with "SAMPLE" printed in large black letters diagonally on back. They were distributed in two-card cello packs.

		NM/M
Complete Set (6):		6.00
Common Player:		1.00
8	Nomar Garciaparra	2.00
9	Ken Griffey Jr.	2.00
24	Frank Thomas	1.25
33	Mike Piazza	2.00
56	Chipper Jones	1.50
72	Larry Walker	1.00

1998 Pinnacle

Pinnacle's 200-card base set features full-bleed photos on front. Three different backs were produced for each card #1-157: home stats, away stats and seasonal stats. The set also includes cards, 24 Rookies, six Field of Vision, 10 Goin' Jake cards and three checklists. Parallel sets include Artist's Proofs, Press Plates and Museum Collection. Inserts include Epix, Hit it Here, Spellbound and Uncut.

		NM/M
Complete Set (200):		12.50
Common Player:		.05
Pack (10):		.50
Wax Box (18):		12.00
1	Tony Gwynn/AS	1.00
2	Pedro Martinez/AS	.75
3	Kenny Lofton/AS	.05
4	Curt Schilling/AS	.35
5	Shawn Estes/AS	.05
6	Tom Glavine/AS	.35
7	Mike Piazza/AS	1.50
8	Ray Lankford/AS	.05
9	Barry Larkin/AS	.05
10	Tony Womack/AS	.05
11	Jeff Blauser/AS	.05
12	Rod Beck/AS	.05
13	Larry Walker/AS	.05
14	Greg Maddux/AS	1.00
15	Mark Grace/AS	.05
16	Ken Caminiti/AS	.05
17	Bobby Jones/AS	.05
18	Chipper Jones/AS	1.00*

19	Javier Lopez/AS	.05
20	Moises Alou/AS	.05
21	Royce Clayton/AS	.05
22	Darryl Kile/AS	.05
23	Barry Bonds/AS	2.50
24	Steve Finley/AS	.05
25	Andres Galarraga/AS	.05
26	Denny Neagle/AS	.05
27	Todd Hundley/AS	.05
28	Jeff Bagwell	.75
29	Andy Pettitte	.25
30	Darin Erstad	.15
31	Carlos Delgado	.50
32	Matt Williams	.05
33	Will Clark	.05
34	Vinny Castilla	.05
35	Brad Radke	.05
36	John Olerud	.05
37	Andruw Jones	.75
38	Jason Giambi	.50
39	Scott Rolen	.65
40	Gary Sheffield	.40
41	Jimmy Key	.05
42	Kevin Appier	.05
43	Wade Boggs	1.00
44	Hideo Nomo	.40
45	Manny Ramirez	.75
46	Wilton Guerrero	.05
47	Travis Fryman	.05
48	Chili Davis	.05
49	Jeromy Burnitz	.05
50	Craig Biggio	.05
51	Tim Salmon	.05
52	Jose Cruz Jr.	.05
53	Sammy Sosa	1.00
54	Hideki Irabu	.05
55	Chan Ho Park	.05
56	Robin Ventura	.05
57	Jose Guillen	.05
58	Deion Sanders	.05
59	Jose Canseco	.40
60	Jay Buhner	.05
61	Rafael Palmeiro	.65
62	Vladimir Guerrero	.75
63	Mark McGwire	2.00
64	Derek Jeter	2.50
65	Bobby Bonilla	.05
66	Raul Mondesi	.05
67	Paul Molitor	.75
68	Joe Carter	.05
69	Marquis Grissom	.05
70	Juan Gonzalez	.40
71	Kevin Orie	.05
72	Rusty Greer	.05
73	Henry Rodriguez	.05
74	Fernando Tatis	.05
75	John Valentin	.05
76	Matt Morris	.05
77	Ray Durham	.05
78	Geronimo Berroa	.05
79	Scott Brosius	.05
80	Willie Greene	.05
81	Rondell White	.05
82	Doug Drabek	.05
83	Derek Bell	.05
84	Butch Huskey	.05
85	Doug Jones	.05
86	Jeff Kent	.05
87	Jim Edmonds	.05
88	Mark McLemore	.05
89	Todd Zeile	.05
90	Edgardo Alfonzo	.05
91	Carlos Baerga	.05
92	Jorge Fabregas	.05
93	Alan Benes	.05
94	Troy Percival	.05
95	Edgar Renteria	.05
96	Jeff Fassero	.05
97	Reggie Sanders	.05
98	Dean Palmer	.05
99	J.T. Snow	.05
100	Dave Nilsson	.05
101	Dan Wilson	.05
102	Robb Nen	.05
103	Damion Easley	.05
104	Kevin Foster	.05
105	Jose Offerman	.05
106	Steve Cooke	.05
107	Matt Stairs	.05
108	Darryl Hamilton	.05
109	Steve Karsay	.05
110	Gary DiSarcina	.05
111	Dante Bichette	.05
112	Billy Wagner	.05
113	David Segui	.05
114	Bobby Higginson	.05
115	Jeffrey Hammonds	.05
116	Kevin Brown	.05
117	Paul Sorrento	.05
118	Mark Leiter	.05
119	Charles Nagy	.05
120	Danny Patterson	.05
121	Brian McRae	.05
122	Jay Bell	.05
123	Jamie Moyer	.05
124	Carl Everett	.05
125	Greg Colbrunn	.05
126	Jason Kendall	.05
127	Luis Sojo	.05
128	Mike Lieberthal	.05
129	Reggie Jefferson	.05
130	Cal Eldred	.05
131	Orel Hershiser	.05
132	Doug Glanville	.05
133	Willie Blair	.05
134	Neifi Perez	.05
135	Sean Berry	.05
136	Chuck Finley	.05

No.	Player	Price
137	Alex Gonzalez	.05
138	Dennis Eckersley	.65
139	Kenny Rogers	.05
140	Troy O'Leary	.05
141	Roger Bailey	.05
142	Yamil Benitez	.05
143	Wally Joyner	.05
144	Bobby Witt	.05
145	Pete Schourek	.05
146	Terry Steinbach	.05
147	B.J. Surhoff	.05
148	Esteban Loaiza	.05
149	Heathcliff Slocumb	.05
150	Ed Sprague	.05
151	Gregg Jefferies	.05
152	Scott Erickson	.05
153	Jaime Navarro	.05
154	David Wells	.05
155	Alex Fernandez	.05
156	Tim Belcher	.05
157	Mark Grudzielanek	.05
158	Scott Hatteberg	.05
159	Paul Konerko	.15
160	Ben Grieve	.05
161	Abraham Nunez	.05
162	Shannon Stewart	.05
163	Jaret Wright	.05
164	Derrek Lee	.50
165	Todd Dunwoody	.05
166	Steve Woodard RC	.10
167	Ryan McGuire	.05
168	Jeremi Gonzalez	.05
169	Mark Kotsay	.05
170	Brett Tomko	.05
171	Bobby Estalella	.05
172	Livan Hernandez	.05
173	Todd Helton	.75
174	Garrett Stephenson	.05
175	Pokey Reese	.05
176	Tony Saunders	.05
177	Antone Williamson	.05
178	Bartolo Colon	.05
179	Karim Garcia	.05
180	Juan Encarnacion	.05
181	Jacob Cruz	.05
182	Alex Rodriguez (Field of Vision)	2.00
183	Cal Ripken Jr., Roberto Alomar (Field of Vision)	1.00
184	Roger Clemens (Field of Vision)	1.25
185	Derek Jeter (Field of Vision)	2.00
186	Frank Thomas (Field of Vision)	.75
187	Ken Griffey Jr. (Field of Vision)	1.50
188	Mark McGwire (Goin' Jake)	1.00
189	Tino Martinez (Goin' Jake)	.05
190	Larry Walker (Goin' Jake)	.05
191	Brady Anderson (Goin' Jake)	.05
192	Jeff Bagwell (Goin' Jake)	.75
193	Ken Griffey Jr. (Goin' Jake)	1.50
194	Chipper Jones (Goin' Jake)	1.00
195	Ray Lankford (Goin' Jake)	.05
196	Jim Thome (Goin' Jake)	.65
197	Nomar Garciaparra (Goin' Jake)	1.00
198	Checklist (1997 HR Contest)	.05
199	Checklist (1997 HR Contest Winner)	.05
200	Checklist (Overall View of the Park)	.05
9	Ken Griffey Jr./AS (Overprinted "SAMPLE" on back.)	2.00
24	Frank Thomas/AS (Overprinted "SAMPLE" on back.)	1.50

Artist's Proofs

Artist's Proofs is a 100-card partial parallel of the Pinnacle base set. The gold-foil Dufex cards were renumbered with a "PP" prefix and inserted one per 39 packs. A red AP seal appears on front.

		NM/M
	Complete Set (100):	375.00
	Common Artist's Proof:	1.50
1	Tony Gwynn/AS	12.50

No.	Player	Price
2	Pedro Martinez/AS	10.00
3	Kenny Lofton/AS	1.50
4	Curt Schilling/AS	3.00
5	Shawn Estes/AS	1.50
6	Tom Glavine/AS	3.00
7	Mike Piazza/AS	16.00
8	Ray Lankford/AS	1.50
9	Barry Larkin/AS	1.50
10	Tony Womack/AS	1.50
11	Jeff Blauser/AS	1.50
12	Rod Beck/AS	1.50
13	Larry Walker/AS	1.50
14	Greg Maddux/AS	12.50
15	Mark Grace/AS	1.50
16	Ken Caminiti/AS	1.50
17	Bobby Jones/AS	1.50
18	Chipper Jones/AS	12.50
19	Javier Lopez/AS	1.50
20	Moises Alou/AS	1.50
21	Royce Clayton/AS	1.50
22	Darryl Kile/AS	1.50
23	Barry Bonds/AS	25.00
24	Steve Finley/AS	1.50
25	Andres Galarraga/AS	1.50
26	Denny Neagle/AS	1.50
27	Todd Hundley/AS	1.50
28	Jeff Bagwell	10.00
29	Andy Pettitte	2.50
30	Darin Erstad	2.00
31	Carlos Delgado	4.00
32	Matt Williams	1.50
33	Will Clark	1.50
34	Brad Radke	1.50
35	John Olerud	1.50
36	Andruw Jones	10.00
37	Scott Rolen	7.50
38	Gary Sheffield	3.00
39	Jimmy Key	1.50
40	Wade Boggs	12.50
41	Hideo Nomo	5.00
42	Manny Ramirez	10.00
43	Wilton Guerrero	1.50
44	Travis Fryman	1.50
45	Craig Biggio	1.50
46	Tim Salmon	1.50
47	Jose Cruz Jr.	1.50
48	Sammy Sosa	12.50
49	Hideki Irabu	1.50
50	Jose Guillen	1.50
51	Deion Sanders	1.50
52	Jose Canseco	4.00
53	Jay Buhner	1.50
54	Rafael Palmeiro	7.50
55	Vladimir Guerrero	10.00
56	Mark McGwire	20.00
57	Derek Jeter	25.00
58	Bobby Bonilla	1.50
59	Raul Mondesi	1.50
60	Paul Molitor	10.00
61	Joe Carter	1.50
62	Marquis Grissom	1.50
63	Juan Gonzalez	5.00
64	Dante Bichette	1.50
65	Shannon Stewart (Rookie)	1.50
66	Jaret Wright (Rookie)	1.50
67	Derrek Lee (Rookie)	6.00
68	Todd Dunwoody (Rookie)	1.50
69	Steve Woodard (Rookie)	1.50
70	Ryan McGuire (Rookie)	1.50
71	Jeremi Gonzalez (Rookie)	1.50
72	Mark Kotsay (Rookie)	1.50
73	Brett Tomko (Rookie)	1.50
74	Bobby Estalella (Rookie)	1.50
75	Livan Hernandez (Rookie)	1.50
76	Todd Helton (Rookie)	10.00
77	Garrett Stephenson (Rookie)	1.50
78	Pokey Reese (Rookie)	1.50
79	Tony Saunders (Rookie)	1.50
80	Antone Williamson (Rookie)	1.50
81	Bartolo Colon (Rookie)	1.50
82	Karim Garcia (Rookie)	1.50
83	Juan Encarnacion (Rookie)	1.50
84	Jacob Cruz (Rookie)	1.50
85	Alex Rodriguez (Field of Vision)	20.00
86	Cal Ripken Jr., Roberto Alomar (Field of Vision)	15.00
87	Roger Clemens (Field of Vision)	13.50
88	Derek Jeter (Field of Vision)	25.00
89	Frank Thomas (Field of Vision)	10.00
90	Ken Griffey Jr. (Field of Vision)	16.00
91	Mark McGwire (Goin' Jake)	20.00
92	Tino Martinez (Goin' Jake)	1.50
93	Larry Walker (Goin' Jake)	1.50
94	Brady Anderson (Goin' Jake)	1.50
95	Jeff Bagwell (Goin' Jake)	10.00
96	Ken Griffey Jr. (Goin' Jake)	16.00
97	Chipper Jones (Goin' Jake)	12.50
98	Ray Lankford (Goin' Jake)	1.50
99	Jim Thome (Goin' Jake)	7.50
100	Nomar Garciaparra (Goin' Jake)	12.50

Museum Collection

Museum Collection is a 100-card partial parallel of the Pinnacle base set. The silver-foil Dufex cards were renumbered with a "PP" prefix. Backs have a small "Musuem Collection" logo at bottom-center. The cards were inserted one per nine packs.

		NM/M
	Complete Museum Set (100):	110.00
	Common Museum:	.50
1	Tony Gwynn/AS	.50
2	Pedro Martinez/AS	2.50
3	Kenny Lofton/AS	.50
4	Curt Schilling/AS	1.50
5	Shawn Estes/AS	.50
6	Tom Glavine/AS	1.50
7	Mike Piazza/AS	4.00
8	Ray Lankford/AS	.50
9	Barry Larkin/AS	.50
10	Tony Womack/AS	.50
11	Jeff Blauser/AS	.50
12	Rod Beck/AS	.50
13	Larry Walker/AS	.50
14	Greg Maddux/AS	3.00
15	Mark Grace/AS	.50
16	Ken Caminiti/AS	.50
17	Bobby Jones/AS	.50
18	Chipper Jones/AS	3.00
19	Javier Lopez/AS	.50
20	Moises Alou/AS	.50
21	Royce Clayton/AS	.50
22	Darryl Kile/AS	.50
23	Barry Bonds/AS	6.00
24	Steve Finley/AS	.50
25	Andres Galarraga/AS	.50
26	Denny Neagle/AS	.50
27	Todd Hundley/AS	.50
28	Jeff Bagwell	2.50
29	Andy Pettitte	1.00
30	Darin Erstad	1.00
31	Carlos Delgado	1.50
32	Matt Williams	.50
33	Will Clark	.50
34	Brad Radke	.50
35	John Olerud	.50
36	Andruw Jones	2.50
37	Scott Rolen	2.00
38	Gary Sheffield	1.50
39	Jimmy Key	.50
40	Wade Boggs	3.00
41	Hideo Nomo	1.25
42	Manny Ramirez	2.50
43	Wilton Guerrero	.50
44	Travis Fryman	.50
45	Craig Biggio	.50
46	Tim Salmon	.50
47	Jose Cruz Jr.	.50
48	Sammy Sosa	3.00
49	Hideki Irabu	.50
50	Jose Guillen	.50
51	Deion Sanders	.50
52	Jose Canseco	1.50
53	Jay Buhner	.50
54	Rafael Palmeiro	2.00
55	Vladimir Guerrero	2.50
56	Mark McGwire	5.00
57	Derek Jeter	6.00
58	Bobby Bonilla	.50
59	Raul Mondesi	.50
60	Paul Molitor	2.50
61	Joe Carter	.50
62	Marquis Grissom	.50
63	Juan Gonzalez	1.25
64	Dante Bichette	.50
65	Shannon Stewart (Rookie)	.50
66	Jaret Wright (Rookie)	.50
67	Derrek Lee (Rookie)	2.00
68	Todd Dunwoody (Rookie)	.50
69	Steve Woodard (Rookie)	.50
70	Ryan McGuire (Rookie)	.50
71	Jeremi Gonzalez (Rookie)	.50
72	Mark Kotsay (Rookie)	.50
73	Brett Tomko (Rookie)	.50
74	Bobby Estalella (Rookie)	.50
75	Livan Hernandez (Rookie)	.50
76	Todd Helton (Rookie)	2.50
77	Garrett Stephenson (Rookie)	.50
78	Pokey Reese (Rookie)	.50
79	Tony Saunders (Rookie)	.50
80	Antone Williamson (Rookie)	.50
81	Bartolo Colon (Rookie)	.50
82	Karim Garcia (Rookie)	.50
83	Juan Encarnacion (Rookie)	.50
84	Jacob Cruz (Rookie)	.50
85	Alex Rodriguez (Field of Vision)	5.00
86	Cal Ripken Jr., Roberto Alomar (Field of Vision)	3.50
87	Roger Clemens (Field of Vision)	2.50
88	Derek Jeter (Field of Vision)	6.00
89	Frank Thomas (Field of Vision)	2.50
90	Ken Griffey Jr. (Field of Vision)	4.00
91	Mark McGwire (Goin' Jake)	5.00
92	Tino Martinez (Goin' Jake)	.50
93	Larry Walker (Goin' Jake)	.50
94	Brady Anderson (Goin' Jake)	.50
95	Jeff Bagwell (Goin' Jake)	2.50
96	Ken Griffey Jr. (Goin' Jake)	4.00
97	Chipper Jones (Goin' Jake)	3.00
98	Ray Lankford (Goin' Jake)	.50
99	Jim Thome (Goin' Jake)	2.00
100	Nomar Garciaparra (Goin' Jake)	3.00

Power Packs Supers

Two dozen regular and subset (Goin' Jake, Field of Vision) cards from Pinnacle are paralleled in this super-size (3-1/2" x 5") version which was included along with 21 regular cards in a $5.99 "Power Pack." Other than being four times the size of the regular card, these supers differ only in their numbering which specifies "x of 24" on back. Each card can also be found in a promo version with a large black "SAMPLE" overprinted on back.

		NM/M
	Complete Set (24):	30.00
	Common Player:	.50
	Samples:	1.5X
1	Alex Rodriguez (Field of Vision)	3.00
2	Cal Ripken Jr., Roberto Alomar (Field of Vision)	2.00
3	Roger Clemens (Field of Vision)	2.25
4	Derek Jeter (Field of Vision)	3.50
5	Frank Thomas (Field of Vision)	1.50
6	Ken Griffey Jr. Field of Vision)	2.50
7	Mark McGwire (Goin' Jake)	3.00
8	Tino Martinez (Goin' Jake)	.50
9	Larry Walker (Goin' Jake)	.50
10	Brady Anderson (Goin' Jake)	.50
11	Jeff Bagwell (Goin' Jake)	1.50
12	Ken Griffey Jr. (Goin' Jake)	2.50
13	Chipper Jones (Goin' Jake)	2.00
14	Ray Lankford (Goin' Jake)	.50
15	Jim Thome, Field of Vision)	1.00
16	Nomar Garciaparra (Goin' Jake)	2.00
17	Mike Piazza	2.50
18	Andruw Jones	1.50
19	Greg Maddux	2.00
20	Tony Gwynn	2.00
21	Larry Walker	.50
22	Jeff Bagwell	1.50
23	Chipper Jones	2.00
24	Scott Rolen	1.00

Epix

This cross-brand insert was included in Pinnacle, Score, Pinnacle Certified and Zenith. Twenty-four cards were seeded in Pinnacle packs (1:21). The four-tiered set highlights a memorable Game, Season, Mo-

-ment and Play in a player's career. The holographic foil cards came in three colors: orange, purple and emerald.

		NM/M
	Complete Set (24):	45.00
	Common Player:	1.00
	Purples:	2X
	Emeralds:	4X
1	Ken Griffey Jr./G	3.00
2	Juan Gonzalez/G	1.25
3	Jeff Bagwell/G	2.00
4	Ivan Rodriguez/G	1.50
5	Nomar Garciaparra/G	2.50
6	Ryne Sandberg/G	2.50
7	Frank Thomas/S	2.00
8	Derek Jeter/S	5.00
9	Tony Gwynn/S	2.50
10	Albert Belle/S	1.00
11	Scott Rolen/S	1.00
12	Barry Larkin/S	1.00
13	Alex Rodriguez/M	5.00
14	Cal Ripken Jr./M	5.00
15	Chipper Jones/M	3.00
16	Roger Clemens/M	2.75
17	Mo Vaughn/M	1.00
18	Mark McGwire/M	4.00
19	Mike Piazza/P	3.00
20	Andruw Jones/P	2.00
21	Greg Maddux/P	2.50
22	Barry Bonds/P	2.00
23	Paul Molitor/P	2.00
24	Eddie Murray/P	2.00

Hit It Here

Hit it Here is seeded one per 17 packs. The micro-etched silver foil cards feature a color player photo with a red "Hit it Here" target at left. Each card has a serial number. If the pictured player hit for the cycle on Opening Day 1998, the collector with the correct serially numbered card would have won $1 million. Each card was also produced in a promo version without serial number and with a large black "SAMPLE" overprint on back.

		NM/M
	Complete Set (10):	12.00
	Common Player:	.50
	Inserted 1:17	
	Samples:	1X
1	Larry Walker	.50
2	Ken Griffey Jr.	2.00
3	Mike Piazza	2.00
4	Frank Thomas	1.50
5	Barry Bonds	3.00
6	Albert Belle	1.00
7	Tino Martinez	.50
8	Mark McGwire	2.50
9	Juan Gonzalez	.75
10	Jeff Bagwell	1.00

Press Plates

Pinnacle cut up and inserted into packs (about one per 1,250) the metal plates used to print the regular and insert cards in the set. There are black, blue, magenta and yellow plates for the front and back of each card. Because of their unique nature, establishment of catalog values isn't feasible.

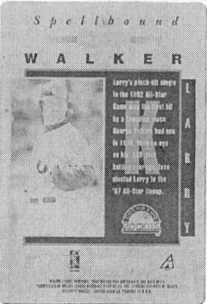

	NM/M
Common Player:	50.00

Spellbound

Spellbound is a 50-card insert seeded one per 17 packs. Nine players are featured in the set. The cards feature a photo of the player with a letter from his first or last name in the background. Each player has enough cards to spell his first or last name or a nickname. Values shown are per card and should be multiplied by the number of cards in a player name to arrive at a value for a complete-player set.

		NM/M
	Complete Set (50):	90.00
	Common Card:	.75
	Inserted 1:17	
1	Mark McGwire (M)	3.50
2	Mark McGwire (C)	3.50
3	Mark McGwire (G)	3.50
4	Mark McGwire (W)	3.50
5	Mark McGwire (I)	3.50
6	Mark McGwire (R)	3.50
7	Mark McGwire (E)	3.50
8	Roger Clemens (R)	2.50
9	Roger Clemens (O)	2.50
10	Roger Clemens (C)	2.50
11	Roger Clemens (K)	2.50
12	Roger Clemens (E)	2.50
13	Roger Clemens (T)	2.50
14	Frank Thomas (B)	1.50
15	Frank Thomas (I)	1.50
16	Frank Thomas (G)	1.50
17	Frank Thomas (H)	1.50
18	Frank Thomas (U)	1.50
19	Frank Thomas (R)	1.50
20	Frank Thomas (T)	1.50
21	Scott Rolen (R)	1.25
22	Scott Rolen (O)	1.25
23	Scott Rolen (L)	1.25
24	Scott Rolen (E)	1.25
25	Scott Rolen (N)	1.25
26	Ken Griffey Jr. (G)	3.00
27	Ken Griffey Jr. (R)	3.00
28	Ken Griffey Jr. (I)	3.00
29	Ken Griffey Jr. (F)	3.00
30	Ken Griffey Jr. (E)	3.00
31	Ken Griffey Jr. (E)	3.00
32	Ken Griffey Jr. (Y)	3.00
33	Larry Walker (W)	.75
34	Larry Walker (A)	.75
35	Larry Walker (K)	.75
36	Larry Walker (E)	.75
37	Larry Walker (R)	.75
38	Larry Walker (R)	.75
39	Nomar Garciaparra (N)	2.25
40	Nomar Garciaparra (O)	2.25
41	Nomar Garciaparra (M)	2.25
42	Nomar Garciaparra (A)	2.25
43	Nomar Garciaparra (R)	2.25
44	Cal Ripken Jr. (C)	4.50
45	Cal Ripken Jr. (A)	4.50
46	Cal Ripken Jr. (L)	4.50
47	Tony Gwynn (T)	2.25
48	Tony Gwynn (O)	2.25
49	Tony Gwynn (N)	2.25
50	Tony Gwynn (Y)	2.25

All-Star FanFest John Elway

The quarterback of the World's Champion Denver Broncos was featured on a card harkening back to his minor league baseball playing days. During the July 1998 All-Star FanFest in Denver, Pinnacle sold a special card of Elway, with proceeds benefiting the city's schools. Initial cost was $2 per card. Front has a black-and-white posed action photo with blue and white pinstriped backgrounds. Back has a ghosted photo of Elway in his Broncos uniform and provides details of his baseball career.

	NM/M
John Elway	3.00

Certified Mirrors

Among several card issues that were aborted by Pinnacle's bankruptcy in mid-1998, but that have leaked into the hobby market in dribs and drabs, are specimens of some of the intended mirror parallels for a Pinnacle Certified set. The majority of cards seen have been Mirror Reds, with a few Mirror Gold issues and even fewer Mirror Blues. Many cards are known in only a single example, and some commons have not yet been verified, though it is presumed that all cards among the first 99 numbers on the unissued Certified base set checklist will be found eventually.

	NM/M
Common Player:	15.00
1 Vladimir Guerrero	25.00
2 Andruw Jones	25.00
3 Paul Molitor	25.00
4 Jose Cruz Jr.	15.00
5 Edgar Martinez	15.00
6 Andy Pettitte	15.00
7 Darin Erstad	15.00
8 Barry Larkin	15.00
9 Derek Jeter	60.00
10 Rusty Greer	15.00
11 Brady Anderson	15.00
12 Tony Clark	15.00
13 Manny Ramirez	25.00
14 Jim Thome	20.00
15 Matt Williams	15.00
16 Ivan Rodriguez	20.00
17 Scott Rolen	20.00
18 Gary Sheffield	15.00
19 David Justice	15.00
20 Roberto Alomar	15.00
21 Ken Caminiti	15.00
22 Sammy Sosa	40.00
23 Albert Belle	15.00
24 Chuck Knoblauch	15.00
25 Mo Vaughn	15.00
26 Raul Mondesi	15.00
27 Tim Salmon	15.00
28 Bernie Williams	15.00
29 Tony Gwynn	25.00
30 Pedro Martinez	25.00
31 Roger Clemens	40.00
32 Craig Biggio	15.00
33 Randy Johnson	25.00
34 Tino Martinez	15.00
35 Chipper Jones	25.00
36 Kenny Lofton	15.00
37 Greg Maddux	25.00
38 Hideo Nomo	20.00
39 Andres Galarraga	15.00
40 Nomar Garciaparra	30.00
41 Juan Gonzalez	20.00
42 Mark McGwire	50.00
43 Mike Piazza	30.00
44 Jeff Bagwell	25.00
45 Barry Bonds	60.00
46 Larry Walker	15.00
47 Alex Rodriguez	60.00
48 Frank Thomas	30.00
49 Cal Ripken Jr.	75.00
50 Ken Griffey Jr.	50.00
51 Todd Walker	15.00
52 Jose Guillen	15.00
53 Vinny Castilla	15.00
54 Shannon Stewart	15.00
55 Jim Edmonds	15.00
56 Bobby Higginson	15.00
57 Jay Buhner	15.00
58 Mike Mussina	15.00
59 Todd Greene	15.00
60 Chan Ho Park	15.00
61 Livan Hernandez	15.00
62 Sandy Alomar Jr.	15.00
63 Fred McGriff	15.00
64 Travis Fryman	15.00
65 Jaret Wright	15.00
66 Bobby Bonilla	15.00
67 Moises Alou	15.00
68 Rafael Palmeiro	25.00
69 Charles Johnson	15.00
70 Ray Lankford	15.00
71 Kevin Brown	15.00
72 Neifi Perez	15.00
73 Rondell White	15.00
74 Bartolo Colon	15.00
75 Bob Abreu	15.00
76 Eric Young	15.00
77 Jason Giambi	20.00
78 Edgardo Alfonzo	15.00
79 Dante Bichette	15.00
80 Eric Karros	15.00
81 Matt Morris	15.00
82 Tom Glavine	15.00
83 Randy Hundley	15.00
84 Jason Dickson	15.00
85 Ryan Klesko	15.00
86 Mark Grace	15.00
87 Brett Tomko	15.00
88 Kevin Orie	15.00
89 Robin Ventura	15.00
90 Jose Canseco	15.00
91 Brian Jordan	15.00
92 Jason Kendall	15.00
93 Mike Cameron	15.00
94 Curt Schilling	20.00
95 Carlos Delgado	15.00
96 Garret Anderson	15.00
97 John Smoltz	15.00
98 Wade Boggs	25.00
99 Javy Lopez	15.00

1998 Pinnacle Inside

Pinnacle Inside features cards in a can. The 150 base cards have full-bleed photos on front with stats on the right and the player's name and position at bottom. The Club Edition parallel (1:7) is printed on silver foil board and the Diamond Edition parallel (1:67) is printed on prismatic foil board. Each pack of cards was packaged inside a collectible can. Inserts include Behind the Numbers and Stand Up Guys.

	NM/M
Complete Set (150):	12.00
Common Player:	.05
Club Edition (1:7):	4X
Diamond Edition (1:67):	10X
Can (10):	1.00
Box (48):	45.00
1 Darin Erstad	.15
2 Derek Jeter	2.50
3 Alex Rodriguez	2.00
4 Bobby Higginson	.05
5 Nomar Garciaparra	1.00
6 Kenny Lofton	.05
7 Ivan Rodriguez	.65
8 Cal Ripken Jr.	2.50
9 Todd Hundley	.05
10 Chipper Jones	1.00
11 Barry Larkin	.05
12 Roberto Alomar	.15
13 Mo Vaughn	.05
14 Sammy Sosa	1.00
15 Sandy Alomar Jr.	.05
16 Albert Belle	.05
17 Scott Rolen	.65
18 Pokey Reese	.05
19 Ryan Klesko	.05
20 Andres Galarraga	.05
21 Justin Thompson	.05
22 Gary Sheffield	.40
23 David Justice	.05
24 Ken Griffey Jr.	1.50
25 Andruw Jones	.75
26 Jeff Bagwell	.75
27 Vladimir Guerrero	.75
28 Mike Piazza	1.50
29 Chuck Knoblauch	.05
30 Rondell White	.05
31 Greg Maddux	1.00
32 Andy Pettitte	.20
33 Larry Walker	.05
34 Bobby Estalella	.05
35 Frank Thomas	.75
36 Tony Womack	.05
37 Tony Gwynn	1.00
38 Barry Bonds	2.50
39 Randy Johnson	.75
40 Mark McGwire	2.00
41 Juan Gonzalez	.40
42 Tim Salmon	.05
43 John Smoltz	.05
44 Rafael Palmeiro	.65
45 Mark Grace	.05
46 Mike Cameron	.05
47 Jim Thome	.65
48 Neifi Perez	.05
49 Kevin Brown	.05
50 Craig Biggio	.05
51 Bernie Williams	.05
52 Hideo Nomo	.40
53 Bob Abreu	.15
54 Edgardo Alfonzo	.05
55 Wade Boggs	1.00
56 Jose Guillen	.05
57 Ken Caminiti	.05
58 Paul Molitor	.75
59 Shawn Estes	.05
60 Edgar Martinez	.05
61 Livan Hernandez	.05
62 Ray Lankford	.05
63 Rusty Greer	.05
64 Jim Edmonds	.05
65 Tom Glavine	.35
66 Alan Benes	.05
67 Will Clark	.05
68 Garret Anderson	.05
69 Javier Lopez	.05
70 Mike Mussina	.35
71 Kevin Orie	.05
72 Matt Williams	.05
73 Bobby Bonilla	.05
74 Ruben Rivera	.05
75 Jason Giambi	.60
76 Todd Walker	.05
77 Tino Martinez	.05
78 Matt Morris	.05
79 Fernando Tatis	.05
80 Todd Greene	.05
81 Fred McGriff	.05
82 Brady Anderson	.05
83 Mark Kotsay	.05
84 Raul Mondesi	.05
85 Moises Alou	.05
86 Roger Clemens	1.25
87 Wilton Guerrero	.05
88 Shannon Stewart	.05
89 Chan Ho Park	.05
90 Carlos Delgado	.60
91 Jose Cruz Jr.	.05
92 Shawn Green	.35
93 Robin Ventura	.05
94 Reggie Sanders	.05
95 Orel Hershiser	.05
96 Dante Bichette	.05
97 Charles Johnson	.05
98 Pedro Martinez	.75
99 Mariano Rivera	.15
100 Joe Randa	.05
101 Jeff Kent	.05
102 Jay Buhner	.05
103 Brian Jordan	.05
104 Jason Kendall	.05
105 Scott Spiezio	.05
106 Desi Relaford	.05
107 Bernard Gilkey	.05
108 Manny Ramirez	.75
109 Tony Clark	.05
110 Eric Young	.05
111 Johnny Damon	.30
112 Glendon Rusch	.05
113 Ben Grieve	.05
114 Homer Bush	.05
115 Miguel Tejada	.25
116 Lou Collier	.05
117 Derrek Lee	.60
118 Jacob Cruz	.05
119 Raul Ibanez	.05
120 Ryan McGuire	.05
121 Antone Williamson	.05
122 Abraham Nunez	.05
123 Jeff Abbott	.05
124 Brett Tomko	.05
125 Richie Sexson	.05
126 Todd Helton	.75
127 Juan Encarnacion	.05
128 Richard Hidalgo	.05
129 Paul Konerko	.10
130 Brad Fullmer	.05
131 Jeremi Gonzalez	.05
132 Jaret Wright	.05
133 Derek Jeter (Inside Tips)	1.25
134 Frank Thomas (Inside Tips)	.40
135 Nomar Garciaparra (Inside Tips)	.50
136 Kenny Lofton (Inside Tips)	.05
137 Jeff Bagwell (Inside Tips)	.40
138 Todd Hundley (Inside Tips)	.05
139 Alex Rodriguez (Inside Tips)	1.00
140 Ken Griffey Jr. (Inside Tips)	.75
141 Sammy Sosa (Inside Tips)	.50
142 Greg Maddux (Inside Tips)	.50
143 Albert Belle (Inside Tips)	.05
144 Cal Ripken Jr. (Inside Tips)	1.25
145 Mark McGwire (Inside Tips)	1.00
146 Chipper Jones (Inside Tips)	.50
147 Charles Johnson (Inside Tips)	.05
148 Checklist (Ken Griffey Jr.)	.75
149 Checklist (Jose Cruz Jr.)	.05
150 Checklist (Larry Walker)	.05

Club Edition

This parallel set is virtually identical to the regular Inside cards, except for the addition of a "CLUB EDITION" notice to the right of the player's first name, and the use of gold foil highlights instead of silver on front.

	NM/M
Complete Set (150):	50.00
Common Player:	2.00
Stars:	4X
Inserted 1:7	

Diamond Edition

Diamond Edition cards parallel all 150 cards in Pinnacle Inside. The fronts have the insert name. These are printed on prismatic foil board and inserted one per 67 cans.

	NM/M
Common Card:	6.00
Stars:	10X
Inserted 1:67	

Behind the Numbers

Behind the Numbers is seeded one per 23 cans. Fronts feature an action photo printed in front of the player's number. The card is die-cut around the large metallic foil numerals. The back has a portrait photo and text explaining why the player wears that number.

	NM/M
Complete Set (20):	85.00
Common Player:	1.50
Inserted 1:23	
1 Ken Griffey Jr.	7.50
2 Cal Ripken Jr.	12.00
3 Alex Rodriguez	10.00
4 Jose Cruz Jr.	1.50
5 Mike Piazza	7.50
6 Nomar Garciaparra	5.50
7 Scott Rolen	2.50
8 Andruw Jones	4.00
9 Frank Thomas	4.00
10 Mark McGwire	10.00
11 Ivan Rodriguez	3.00
12 Greg Maddux	5.50
13 Roger Clemens	6.50
14 Derek Jeter	12.00
15 Tony Gwynn	5.50
16 Ben Grieve	1.50
17 Jeff Bagwell	4.00
18 Chipper Jones	6.00
19 Hideo Nomo	2.00
20 Sandy Alomar Jr.	1.50

Stand Up Guys

This 50-card insert was seeded one per can. Each card has a match; the two cards join together in the center to form a stand-up collectible featuring four Major League players. Each card can also be found in a promo edition with a large "SAMPLE" overprint.

	NM/M
Complete Set (50):	35.00
Common Card:	.25
Sample:	3X
1-A/B Ken Griffey Jr., Cal Ripken Jr.	2.00
1-C/D Tony Gwynn, Mike Piazza	1.25
2-A/B Andruw Jones, Alex Rodriguez	1.50
2-C/D Scott Rolen, Nomar Garciaparra	1.00
3-A/B Andruw Jones, Greg Maddux	1.00
3-C/D Javy Lopez, Chipper Jones	1.00
4-A/B Jay Buhner, Randy Johnson	.75
4-C/D Ken Griffey Jr., Alex Rodriguez	1.50
5-A/B Frank Thomas, Jeff Bagwell	.75
5-C/D Mark McGwire, Mo Vaughn	1.50
6-A/B Nomar Garciaparra, Derek Jeter	2.00
6-C/D Alex Rodriguez, Barry Larkin	1.50
7-A/B Mike Piazza, Ivan Rodriguez	1.25
7-C/D Charles Johnson, Javy Lopez	.25
8-A/B Cal Ripken Jr., Chipper Jones	2.00
8-C/D Ken Caminiti, Scott Rolen	.65
9-A/B Jose Cruz Jr., Vladimir Guerrero	.75
9-C/D Andruw Jones, Jose Guillen	.75
10-A/B Larry Walker, Dante Bichette	.25
10-C/D Ellis Burks, Neifi Perez	.25
11-A/B Juan Gonzalez, Sammy Sosa	1.00
11-C/D Vladimir Guerrero, Manny Ramirez	.75
12-A/B Greg Maddux, Roger Clemens	1.00
12-C/D Hideo Nomo, Randy Johnson	.75
13-A/B Ben Grieve, Paul Konerko	.40
13-C/D Jose Cruz Jr., Fernando Tatis	.25
14-A/B Ryne Sandberg, Chuck Knoblauch	1.00
14-C/D Roberto Alomar, Craig Biggio	.35
15-A/B Cal Ripken Jr., Brady Anderson	2.00
15-C/D Rafael Palmeiro, Roberto Alomar	.65
16-A/B Darin Erstad, Jim Edmonds	.35
16-C/D Tim Salmon, Garret Anderson	.25
17-A/B Mike Piazza, Hideo Nomo	1.25
17-C/D Raul Mondesi, Eric Karros	.25
18-A/B Ivan Rodriguez, Juan Gonzalez	.65
18-C/D Will Clark, Rusty Greer	.25
19-A/B Derek Jeter, Bernie Williams	2.00
19-C/D Tino Martinez, Andy Pettitte	.25
20-A/B Kenny Lofton, Ken Griffey Jr.	1.25
20-C/D Brady Anderson, Bernie Williams	.25
21-A/B Paul Molitor, Eddie Murray	.75
21-C/D Ryne Sandberg, Rickey Henderson	1.00
22-A/B Tony Clark, Frank Thomas	.75
22-C/D Jeff Bagwell, Mark McGwire	1.50
23-A/B Manny Ramirez, Jim Thome	.75
23-C/D David Justice, Sandy Alomar Jr.	.25
24-A/B Barry Bonds, Albert Belle	2.00
24-C/D Jeff Bagwell, Dante Bichette	.60
25-A/B Ken Griffey Jr., Frank Thomas	1.25
25-C/D Alex Rodriguez, Andruw Jones	1.50

Cans

Ten-card packs of Pinnacle Inside were packaged in collectible cans. The 24 cans featured a player photo or team logo. Cans were created to honor the Florida Marlins' world championship and the expansion Arizona and Tampa Bay teams. Gold parallel versions of the cans were found one every 47 cans. Values shown are for bottom-opened cans; cans opened from the top have little collectible value.

	NM/M
Complete Set (23):	15.00
Common Can:	.40
Gold Cans:	2X
1 Ken Griffey Jr.	1.25
2 Frank Thomas	.65
3 Alex Rodriguez	1.50
4 Andruw Jones	.65
5 Mike Piazza	1.25
6 Ben Grieve	.40
7 Hideo Nomo	.50
8 Vladimir Guerrero	.65
9 Roger Clemens	1.00
10 Tony Gwynn	.75
11 Mark McGwire	1.50
12 Cal Ripken Jr.	2.00
13 Jose Cruz Jr.	.40
14 Greg Maddux	.75
15 Chipper Jones	.75
16 Derek Jeter	2.00
17 Juan Gonzalez	.50
18 Nomar Garciaparra (AL ROY)	1.00
19 Scott Rolen (NL ROY)	.65
20 Florida Marlins World Series Winner	.40
21 Larry Walker (NL MVP)	.40
22 Tampa Bay Devil Rays	.40
23 Arizona Diamondbacks	.40

1998 Pinnacle Mint Collection

Mint Collection consists of 30 cards and 30 matching coins with numerous parallels of each. The cards come in four different versions. The base card features a player photo at left with a circular bronze foil team logo at right. The base cards were inserted one per hobby pack and two per retail pack. Die-cut versions removed the team logo and were inserted two per hobby and one per retail packs. Silver Mint Team (1:15 hobby, 1:23 retail) and Gold Mint Team (1:47 hobby, 1:71 retail) parallels were printed on silver foil and gold foil board, respectively.

		NM/M
Complete Set (30):		10.00
Common Die-Cut:		.25
Bronze (1:1H):		2X
Silver (1:15H):		5X
Gold (1:47):		12X
Pack (3+2):		1.00
Wax Box (24):		12.00
1	Jeff Bagwell	.65
2	Albert Belle	.25
3	Barry Bonds	2.00
4	Tony Clark	.25
5	Roger Clemens	1.00
6	Juan Gonzalez	.35
7	Ken Griffey Jr.	1.25
8	Tony Gwynn	.75
9	Derek Jeter	2.00
10	Randy Johnson	.65
11	Chipper Jones	.75
12	Greg Maddux	.75
13	Tino Martinez	.25
14	Mark McGwire	1.50
15	Hideo Nomo	.35
16	Andy Pettitte	.25
17	Mike Piazza	1.25
18	Cal Ripken Jr.	2.00
19	Alex Rodriguez	1.50
20	Ivan Rodriguez	.50
21	Sammy Sosa	.75
22	Frank Thomas	.65
23	Mo Vaughn	.25
24	Larry Walker	.25
25	Jose Cruz Jr.	.25
26	Nomar Garciaparra	.75
27	Vladimir Guerrero	.65
28	Livan Hernandez	.25
29	Andruw Jones	.65
30	Scott Rolen	.50

Coins

Two base coins were included in each pack of Mint Collection. The coins feature the player's image, name and number on the front along with his team's name and logo. The back has the Mint Collection logo. Seven parallels are included: Nickel-Silver (1:41), Brass Proof (numbered to 250), Gold Proof (numbered to 100), Gold-Plated (1:199), Solid Silver (1:288 hobby, 1:960 retail) and Solid Gold by redemption (1-of-1).

		NM/M
Complete Set (30):		20.00
Common Brass Coin:		.50
Brass Proof (500):		5X
Nickel (1:41):		3X
Nickel Proof (250):		12X
Silver:		12X
Inserted 1:288 H, 1:960 R		
Gold Plated (1:199):		15X
Gold Proof (100):		20X
1	Jeff Bagwell	.75
2	Albert Belle	.50
3	Barry Bonds	2.00
4	Tony Clark	.50
5	Roger Clemens	1.50
6	Juan Gonzalez	.50
7	Ken Griffey Jr.	1.50
8	Tony Gwynn	1.00
9	Derek Jeter	2.00
10	Randy Johnson	1.00
11	Chipper Jones	1.00
12	Greg Maddux	1.50
13	Tino Martinez	.50
14	Mark McGwire	1.50
15	Hideo Nomo	.50
16	Andy Pettitte	.75
17	Mike Piazza	1.00
18	Cal Ripken Jr.	2.00
19	Alex Rodriguez	2.00
20	Ivan Rodriguez	.75
21	Sammy Sosa	.75
22	Frank Thomas	.75
23	Mo Vaughn	.50
24	Larry Walker	.50
25	Jose Cruz Jr.	.50
26	Nomar Garciaparra	.75
27	Vladimir Guerrero	.75
28	Livan Hernandez	.50
29	Andruw Jones	.75
30	Scott Rolen	.75

Mint Gems

Mint Gems is a six-card insert printed on silver foil board. The cards were inserted 1:31 hobby packs and 1:47 retail. The oversized Mint Gems coins are twice the size of the regular coins. The six coins were inserted 1:31 hobby packs.

		NM/M
Complete Set (6):		20.00
Common Player:		2.00
Coins:		1X
1	Ken Griffey Jr.	6.00
2	Larry Walker	2.00
3	Roger Clemens	5.00
4	Pedro Martinez	4.00
5	Nomar Garciaparra	4.50
6	Scott Rolen	3.00

1998 Pinnacle Performers

Pinnacle Performers consists of a 150-card base set. The Peak Performers parallel adds silver foil to the base cards and was inserted 1:7. Inserts in the home run-themed product include Big Bang, Launching Pad, Player's Card and Power Trip.

		NM/M
Complete Set (150):		12.00
Common Player:		.05
Peak Performers (1:7):		2X
Pack (10):		1.00
Wax Box (24):		15.00
1	Ken Griffey Jr.	1.00
2	Frank Thomas	.65
3	Cal Ripken Jr.	1.50
4	Alex Rodriguez	1.25
5	Greg Maddux	.75
6	Mike Piazza	1.00
7	Chipper Jones	.75
8	Tony Gwynn	.75
9	Derek Jeter	1.50
10	Jeff Bagwell	.65
11	Juan Gonzalez	.35
12	Nomar Garciaparra	.75
13	Andruw Jones	.65
14	Hideo Nomo	.35
15	Roger Clemens	.85
16	Mark McGwire	1.25
17	Scott Rolen	.60
18	Vladimir Guerrero	.65
19	Barry Bonds	1.50
20	Darin Erstad	.15
21	Albert Belle	.05
22	Kenny Lofton	.05
23	Mo Vaughn	.05
24	Tony Clark	.05
25	Ivan Rodriguez	.60
26	Jose Cruz Jr.	.05
27	Larry Walker	.05
28	Jaret Wright	.05
29	Andy Pettitte	.25
30	Roberto Alomar	.20
31	Randy Johnson	.65
32	Manny Ramirez	.65
33	Paul Molitor	.65
34	Mike Mussina	.35
35	Jim Thome	.60
36	Tino Martinez	.05
37	Gary Sheffield	.45
38	Chuck Knoblauch	.05
39	Bernie Williams	.05
40	Tim Salmon	.05
41	Sammy Sosa	.75
42	Wade Boggs	.75
43	Will Clark	.05
44	Andres Galarraga	.05
45	Raul Mondesi	.05
46	Rickey Henderson	.65
47	Jose Canseco	.45
48	Pedro Martinez	.05
49	Jay Buhner	.05
50	Ryan Klesko	.05
51	Barry Larkin	.05
52	Charles Johnson	.05
53	Tom Glavine	.35
54	Edgar Martinez	.05
55	Fred McGriff	.05
56	Moises Alou	.05
57	Dante Bichette	.05
58	Jim Edmonds	.05
59	Mark Grace	.05
60	Chan Ho Park	.05
61	Justin Thompson	.05
62	John Smoltz	.05
63	Craig Biggio	.05
64	Ken Caminiti	.05
65	Richard Hidalgo	.05
66	Carlos Delgado	.50
67	David Justice	.05
68	J.T. Snow	.05
69	Jason Giambi	.50
70	Garret Anderson	.05
71	Rondell White	.05
72	Matt Williams	.05
73	Brady Anderson	.05
74	Eric Karros	.05
75	Javier Lopez	.05
76	Pat Hentgen	.05
77	Todd Hundley	.05
78	Ray Lankford	.05
79	Denny Neagle	.05
80	Sandy Alomar Jr.	.05
81	Jason Kendall	.05
82	Omar Vizquel	.05
83	Kevin Brown	.05
84	Kevin Appier	.05
85	Al Martin	.05
86	Rusty Greer	.05
87	Bobby Bonilla	.05
88	Shawn Estes	.05
89	Rafael Palmeiro	.60
90	Edgar Renteria	.05
91	Alan Benes	.05
92	Bobby Higginson	.05
93	Mark Grudzielanek	.05
94	Jose Guillen	.05
95	Neifi Perez	.05
96	Jeff Abbott	.05
97	Todd Walker	.05
98	Eric Young	.05
99	Brett Tomko	.05
100	Mike Cameron	.05
101	Karim Garcia	.05
102	Brian Jordan	.05
103	Jeff Suppan	.05
104	Robin Ventura	.05
105	Henry Rodriguez	.05
106	Shannon Stewart	.05
107	Kevin Orie	.05
108	Bartolo Colon	.05
109	Bob Abreu	.15
110	Vinny Castilla	.05
111	Livan Hernandez	.05
112	Derrek Lee	.50
113	Mark Kotsay	.05
114	Todd Greene	.05
115	Edgardo Alfonzo	.05
116	A.J. Hinch	.05
117	Paul Konerko	.15
118	Todd Helton	.65
119	Miguel Tejada	.20
120	Fernando Tatis	.05
121	Ben Grieve	.05
122	Travis Lee	.05
123	Kerry Wood	.25
124	Eli Marrero	.05
125	David Ortiz	.50
126	Juan Encarnacion	.05
127	Brad Fullmer	.05
128	Richie Sexson	.05
129	Aaron Boone	.05
130	Enrique Wilson	.05
131	Javier Valentin	.05
132	Abraham Nunez	.05
133	Ricky Ledee	.05
134	Carl Pavano	.05
135	Bobby Estalella	.05
136	Homer Bush	.05
137	Brian Rose	.05
138	Ken Griffey Jr. (Far and Away)	.50
139	Frank Thomas (Far and Away)	.35
140	Cal Ripken Jr. (Far and Away)	.75
141	Alex Rodriguez (Far and Away)	.65
142	Greg Maddux (Far and Away)	.40
143	Chipper Jones (Far and Away)	.40
144	Mike Piazza (Far and Away)	.50
145	Tony Gwynn (Far and Away)	.40
146	Derek Jeter (Far and Away)	.75
147	Jeff Bagwell (Far and Away)	.35
148	Checklist (Hideo Nomo)	.20
149	Checklist (Roger Clemens)	.45
150	Checklist (Greg Maddux)	.35

Peak Performers

This 150-card parallel set is printed on silver foil vs. the white cardboard stock used on regular-issue cards. The parallel set name is printed down the right side in gold letters. They were seeded one per seven packs.

	NM/M
Complete Set (150):	100.00
Common Player:	2.00
Stars:	6X
Inserted 1:7	

Big Bang

This 20-card insert features top power hitters. The micro-etched cards are sequentially numbered to 2,500. Each player has a Seasonal Outburst parallel, with a red overlay and numbered to that player's best seasonal home run total. Each card is also found in a promo edition with a large black "SAMPLE" overprinted on back.

		NM/M
Complete Set (20):		27.50
Common Player:		.50
Production 2,500 Sets		
Sample:		1X
1	Ken Griffey Jr.	2.50
2	Frank Thomas	1.50
3	Mike Piazza	2.50
4	Chipper Jones	2.00
5	Alex Rodriguez	3.00
6	Nomar Garciaparra	2.00
7	Jeff Bagwell	1.50
8	Cal Ripken Jr.	3.50
9	Albert Belle	.50
10	Mark McGwire	3.00
11	Juan Gonzalez	2.00
12	Larry Walker	.50
13	Tino Martinez	.50
14	Jim Thome	1.00
15	Manny Ramirez	1.50
16	Barry Bonds	3.50
17	Mo Vaughn	.50
18	Jose Cruz Jr.	.50
19	Tony Clark	.50
20	Andruw Jones	1.50

Big Bang Seasonal Outburst

Season Outburst parallels the Big Bang insert. The cards have a red overlay and are sequentially numbered to each player's season-high home run total. Unnumbered versions of the cards, likely leaked into the market after Pinnacle went bankrupt in mid-1998, have been seen; their value is much lower than the issued version.

		NM/M
Complete Set (20):		500.00
Common Player:		10.00
#'d to player's 1997 HR total		
Unnumbered: 25 Percent		
1	Ken Griffey Jr./56	40.00
2	Frank Thomas/35	40.00
3	Mike Piazza/40	40.00
4	Chipper Jones/21	65.00
5	Alex Rodriguez/23	75.00
6	Nomar Garciaparra/30	40.00
7	Jeff Bagwell/43	65.00
8	Cal Ripken Jr./17	80.00
9	Albert Belle/30	10.00
10	Mark McGwire/58	65.00
11	Juan Gonzalez/42	12.50
12	Larry Walker/49	10.00
13	Tino Martinez /44	10.00
14	Jim Thome/40	15.00
15	Manny Ramirez/26	25.00
16	Barry Bonds/40	75.00
17	Mo Vaughn/35	10.00
18	Jose Cruz Jr./26	10.00
19	Tony Clark/32	10.00
20	Andruw Jones/18	25.00

Launching Pad

Launching Pad is a 20-card insert seeded one per nine packs. It features top sluggers on foil-on-foil cards with an outer space background.

		NM/M
Complete Set (20):		25.00
Common Player:		.50
Inserted 1:9		
1	Ben Grieve	.50
2	Ken Griffey Jr.	2.50
3	Derek Jeter	3.50
4	Frank Thomas	1.00
5	Travis Lee	.50
6	Vladimir Guerrero	1.00
7	Tony Gwynn	2.00
8	Jose Cruz Jr.	.50
9	Cal Ripken Jr.	3.50
10	Chipper Jones	2.00
11	Scott Rolen	.75
12	Andruw Jones	1.00
13	Ivan Rodriguez	.75
14	Todd Helton	1.00
15	Nomar Garciaparra	2.00
16	Mark McGwire	3.00
17	Gary Sheffield	.50
18	Bernie Williams	.50
19	Alex Rodriguez	3.00
20	Mike Piazza	2.50

Power Trip

This 10-card insert was seeded 1:21. Printed on silver foil, each card is sequentially-numbered to 10,000. Cards backs have details about one of the player's power-hitting highlights of the previous season.

		NM/M
Complete Set (10):		16.00
Common Player:		1.00
Production 10,000 Sets		
1	Frank Thomas	1.00
2	Alex Rodriguez	3.00
3	Nomar Garciaparra	1.50
4	Jeff Bagwell	1.00
5	Cal Ripken Jr.	4.00
6	Mike Piazza	2.00
7	Chipper Jones	1.50
8	Ken Griffey Jr.	2.00
9	Mark McGwire	3.00
10	Juan Gonzalez	1.00

Swing for the Fences

Pinnacle Performers included the "Swing for the Fences" sweepstakes. Fifty players were featured on cards with numbers on an all-red background. Fifty Home Run Points cards were also inserted, with each card featuring a point total on the front. Collectors who found the player cards of the AL and NL home run leaders, as well as enough point cards to match each of their season totals, were eligible to win prizes. A player or point card was inserted in each pack.

		NM/M
Complete Set (50):		24.00
Common Player:		.25
Inserted 1:1		
1	Brady Anderson	.25
2	Albert Belle	.25
3	Jay Buhner	.25
4	Jose Canseco	.50
5	Tony Clark	.25
6	Jose Cruz Jr.	.25
7	Jim Edmonds	.25
8	Cecil Fielder	.25
9	Travis Fryman	.25
10	Nomar Garciaparra	1.00
11	Juan Gonzalez	.40
12	Ken Griffey Jr.	1.50
13	David Justice	.25
14	Travis Lee	.25
15	Edgar Martinez	.25
16	Tino Martinez	.25
17	Rafael Palmeiro	.65
18	Manny Ramirez	.75
19	Cal Ripken Jr.	2.50
20	Alex Rodriguez	2.00
21	Tim Salmon	.25
22	Frank Thomas	.75
23	Jim Thome	.65
24	Mo Vaughn	.25
25	Bernie Williams	.25
26	Fred McGriff	.25
27	Jeff Bagwell	.75
28	Dante Bichette	.25
29	Barry Bonds	2.50
30	Ellis Burks	.25
31	Ken Caminiti	.25
32	Vinny Castilla	.25
33	Andres Galarraga	.25
34	Vladimir Guerrero	.75
35	Todd Helton	.75
36	Todd Hundley	.25
37	Andruw Jones	.75
38	Chipper Jones	1.00
39	Eric Karros	.25
40	Ryan Klesko	.25
41	Ray Lankford	.25
42	Mark McGwire	2.00
43	Raul Mondesi	.25
44	Mike Piazza	1.50
45	Scott Rolen	.65
46	Gary Sheffield	.50
47	Sammy Sosa	.75
48	Larry Walker	.25
49	Matt Williams	.25
50	WILDCARD	

Swing/Fences Prize Cards

This set was evidently intended to be one of the prizes in Pinnacle's Swing for the Fences sweepstakes, but the cards were never officially distributed due to the company's midyear bankruptcy. Making their way out the back into hobby channels in later years, the cards feature action photos on a silver prismatic foil background. Unnumbered backs have the player's career home run totals versus each team.

		NM/M
Complete Set (10):		10.00
Common Player:		.50
(1)	Jeff Bagwell	1.00
(2)	Barry Bonds	3.00
(3)	Nomar Garciaparra	1.50
(4)	Juan Gonzalez	.50
(5)	Ken Griffey Jr.	2.00
(6)	Chipper Jones	1.50
(7)	Mark McGwire	2.50
(8)	Mike Piazza	1.50
(9)	Alex Rodriguez	2.50
(10)	Frank Thomas	1.00

1998 Pinnacle Plus

Pinnacle Plus consists of a 200-card base set. Five subsets are included: Field of Vision, Naturals, All-Stars, Devil Rays and Diamondbacks. Artist's Proof is a 60-card partial parallel of the base set, inserted 1:35 packs. Gold Artist's Proof cards are numbered to 100 and Mirror Artist's Proofs are 1-of-1 inserts. Inserts include Lasting Memories, Yardwork, A Piece of the Game, All-Star Epix, Team Pinnacle, Gold Team Pinnacle, Pinnabilia and Certified Souvenir.

		NM/M
Complete Set (200):		12.00
Common Player:		.05
Pack (10):		1.00
Wax Box (20):		12.00
1	Roberto Alomar/AS	.20
2	Sandy Alomar Jr./AS	.05
3	Brady Anderson/AS	.05
4	Albert Belle/AS	.05
5	Jeff Cirillo/AS	.05
6	Roger Clemens/AS	1.25
7	David Cone/AS	.05
8	Nomar Garciaparra/AS	.75
9	Ken Griffey Jr./AS	1.50
10	Jason Dickson/AS	.05
11	Edgar Martinez/AS	.05
12	Tino Martinez/AS	.05
13	Randy Johnson/AS	.75
14	Mark McGwire/AS	2.00
15	David Justice/AS	.05
16	Mike Mussina/AS	.40
17	Chuck Knoblauch/AS	.05
18	Joey Cora/AS	.05
19	Pat Hentgen/AS	.05
20	Randy Myers/AS	.05
21	Cal Ripken Jr./AS	2.50
22	Mariano Rivera/AS	.15
23	Jose Rosado/AS	.05
24	Frank Thomas/AS	.75
25	Alex Rodriguez/AS	2.00
26	Justin Thompson/AS	.05
27	Ivan Rodriguez/AS	.65

28	Bernie Williams/AS	.05
29	Pedro Martinez	.75
30	Tony Clark	.05
31	Garret Anderson	.05
32	Travis Fryman	.05
33	Mike Piazza	1.50
34	Carl Pavano	.05
35	Kevin Millwood RC	1.00
36	Miguel Tejada	.20
37	Willie Blair	.05
38	Devon White	.05
39	Andres Galarraga	.05
40	Barry Larkin	.05
41	Al Leiter	.05
42	Moises Alou	.05
43	Eric Young	.05
44	John Jaha	.05
45	Bernard Gilkey	.05
46	Freddy Garcia	.05
47	Ruben Rivera	.05
48	Robb Nen	.05
49	Ray Lankford	.05
50	Kenny Lofton	.05
51	Joe Carter	.05
52	Jason McDonald	.05
53	Quinton McCracken	.05
54	Kerry Wood	.50
55	Mike Lansing	.05
56	Chipper Jones	1.00
57	Barry Bonds	2.50
58	Brad Fullmer	.05
59	Jeff Bagwell	.75
60	Rondell White	.05
61	Geronimo Berroa	.05
62	Magglio Ordonez RC	1.50
63	Dwight Gooden	.05
64	Brian Hunter	.05
65	Todd Walker	.05
66	Frank Catalanotto RC	.05
67	Tony Saunders	.05
68	Travis Lee	.05
69	Michael Tucker	.05
70	Reggie Sanders	.05
71	Derrek Lee	.50
72	Larry Walker	.05
73	Marquis Grissom	.05
74	Craig Biggio	.05
75	Kevin Brown	.05
76	J.T. Snow	.05
77	Eric Davis	.05
78	Jeff Abbott	.05
79	Jermaine Dye	.05
80	Otis Nixon	.05
81	Curt Schilling	.35
82	Enrique Wilson	.05
83	Tony Gwynn	1.00
84	Orlando Cabrera	.05
85	Ramon Martinez	.05
86	Greg Vaughn	.05
87	Alan Benes	.05
88	Dennis Eckersley	.65
89	Jim Thome	.65
90	Juan Encarnacion	.05
91	Jeff King	.05
92	Shannon Stewart	.05
93	Roberto Hernandez	.05
94	Raul Ibanez	.05
95	Darryl Kile	.05
96	Charles Johnson	.05
97	Rich Becker	.05
98	Hal Morris	.05
99	Ismael Valdes	.05
100	Orel Hershiser	.05
101	Mo Vaughn	.05
102	Aaron Boone	.05
103	Jeff Conine	.05
104	Paul O'Neill	.05
105	Tom Candiotti	.05
106	Wilson Alvarez	.05
107	Mike Stanley	.05
108	Carlos Delgado	.50
109	Tony Batista	.05
110	Dante Bichette	.05
111	Henry Rodriguez	.05
112	Karim Garcia	.05
113	Shane Reynolds	.05
114	Ken Caminiti	.05
115	Jose Silva	.05
116	Juan Gonzalez	.40
117	Brian Jordan	.05
118	Jim Leyritz	.05
119	Manny Ramirez	.75
120	Fred McGriff	.05
121	Brooks Kieschnick	.05
122	Sean Casey	.15
123	John Smoltz	.05
124	Rusty Greer	.05
125	Cecil Fielder	.05
126	Mike Cameron	.05
127	Reggie Jefferson	.05
128	Bobby Higginson	.05
129	Kevin Appier	.05
130	Robin Ventura	.05
131	Ben Grieve	.05
132	Wade Boggs	1.00
133	Jose Cruz Jr.	.05
134	Jeff Suppan	.05
135	Vinny Castilla	.05
136	Sammy Sosa	1.00
137	Mark Wohlers	.05
138	Jay Bell	.05
139	Brett Tomko	.05
140	Gary Sheffield	.40
141	Tim Salmon	.05
142	Jaret Wright	.05
143	Kenny Rogers	.05
144	Brian Anderson	.05
145	Darrin Fletcher	.05

146	John Flaherty	.05
147	Dmitri Young	.05
148	Andruw Jones	.75
149	Matt Williams	.05
150	Bobby Bonilla	.05
151	Mike Hampton	.05
152	Al Martin	.05
153	Mark Grudzielanek	.05
154	Dave Nilsson	.05
155	Roger Cedeno	.05
156	Greg Maddux	1.00
157	Mark Kotsay	.05
158	Steve Finley	.05
159	Wilson Delgado	.05
160	Ron Gant	.05
161	Jim Edmonds	.05
162	Jeff Blauser	.05
163	Dave Burba	.05
164	Pedro Astacio	.05
165	Livan Hernandez	.05
166	Neifi Perez	.05
167	Ryan Klesko	.05
168	Fernando Tatis	.05
169	Richard Hidalgo	.05
170	Carlos Perez	.05
171	Bob Abreu	.15
172	Francisco Cordova	.05
173	Todd Helton	.75
174	Doug Glanville	.05
175	Brian Rose	.05
176	Yamil Benitez	.05
177	Darin Erstad	.15
178	Scott Rolen	.60
179	John Wetteland	.05
180	Paul Sorrento	.05
181	Walt Weiss	.05
182	Vladimir Guerrero	.75
183	Ken Griffey Jr. (The Naturals)	.75
184	Alex Rodriguez (The Naturals)	1.00
185	Cal Ripken Jr. (The Naturals)	1.25
186	Frank Thomas (The Naturals)	.40
187	Chipper Jones (The Naturals)	.50
188	Hideo Nomo (The Naturals)	.20
189	Nomar Garciaparra (The Naturals)	.60
190	Mike Piazza (The Naturals)	.50
191	Greg Maddux (The Naturals)	.50
192	Tony Gwynn (The Naturals)	.50
193	Mark McGwire (The Naturals)	1.00
194	Roger Clemens (The Naturals)	.65
195	Mike Piazza (Field of Vision)	.75
196	Mark McGwire (Field of Vision)	1.00
197	Chipper Jones (Field of Vision)	.50
198	Larry Walker (Field of Vision)	.05
199	Hideo Nomo (Field of Vision)	.20
200	Barry Bonds (Field of Vision)	1.25

Artist's Proofs

Artist's Proofs is a 60-card partial parallel of the Pinnacle Plus base set. The dot matrix hologram cards were inserted 1:35. Gold Artist's Proofs added a gold finish and are sequentially numbered to 100. Mirror Artist's Proofs are a "1-of-1" insert. Card numbers have an "AP" prefix.

		NM/M
Complete Set (60):		150.00
Common Player:		.75
Inserted 1:35		
Golds:		10X
Production 100 Sets		
1	Roberto Alomar/AS	1.50
2	Albert Belle/AS	.75
3	Roger Clemens/AS	8.00
4	Nomar Garciaparra/AS	7.50
5	Ken Griffey Jr./AS	10.00
6	Tino Martinez/AS	.75

7	Randy Johnson/AS	6.00
8	Mark McGwire/AS	12.50
9	David Justice/AS	.75
10	Chuck Knoblauch/AS	.75
11	Cal Ripken Jr./AS	15.00
12	Frank Thomas/AS	6.00
13	Alex Rodriguez/AS	12.50
14	Ivan Rodriguez/AS	5.00
15	Bernie Williams/AS	.75
16	Pedro Martinez	6.00
17	Tony Clark	.75
18	Mike Piazza	10.00
19	Miguel Tejada	1.00
20	Andres Galarraga	.75
21	Barry Larkin	.75
22	Kenny Lofton	.75
23	Chipper Jones	7.50
24	Barry Bonds	15.00
25	Brad Fullmer	.75
26	Jeff Bagwell	6.00
27	Todd Walker	.75
28	Travis Lee	.75
29	Larry Walker	.75
30	Craig Biggio	.75
31	Tony Gwynn	7.50
32	Jim Thome	5.00
33	Juan Encarnacion	.75
34	Mo Vaughn	.75
35	Karim Garcia	.75
36	Ken Caminiti	.75
37	Juan Gonzalez	3.00
38	Manny Ramirez	6.00
39	Fred McGriff	.75
40	Rusty Greer	.75
41	Bobby Higginson	.75
42	Ben Grieve	.75
43	Wade Boggs	7.50
44	Jose Cruz Jr.	.75
45	Sammy Sosa	7.50
46	Gary Sheffield	2.00
47	Tim Salmon	.75
48	Jaret Wright	.75
49	Andruw Jones	6.00
50	Matt Williams	.75
51	Greg Maddux	7.50
52	Jim Edmonds	.75
53	Livan Hernandez	.75
54	Neifi Perez	.75
55	Fernando Tatis	.75
56	Richard Hidalgo	.75
57	Todd Helton	6.00
58	Darin Erstad	1.50
59	Scott Rolen	5.00
60	Vladimir Guerrero	6.00

A Piece of the Game

Inserted 1:17 hobby packs (1:19 retail), this 10-card insert features baseball's top players on micro-etched foil cards.

		NM/M
Complete Set (10):		8.00
Common Player:		.50
Inserted 1:19		
1	Ken Griffey Jr.	1.00
2	Frank Thomas	.65
3	Alex Rodriguez	1.50
4	Chipper Jones	.75
5	Cal Ripken Jr.	2.00
6	Mike Piazza	1.00
7	Greg Maddux	.75
8	Juan Gonzalez	.50
9	Nomar Garciaparra	.75
10	Larry Walker	.50

Epix All-Star Moment

The All-Star Epix insert is part of the cross-brand Epix set. The cards honor the All-Star Game achievements of baseball's stars on cards with dot matrix holograms. All-Star Epix was seeded 1:21. Cards #1-12 were distributed in Score Rookie/Traded.

		NM/M
Complete Set (12):		25.00
Common Player:		1.00
Purples:		1.5X
Emeralds:		2.5X
Inserted 1:21		
13	Alex Rodriguez	3.50
14	Cal Ripken Jr.	5.00
15	Chipper Jones	2.50
16	Roger Clemens	2.75
17	Mo Vaughn	1.00
18	Mark McGwire	3.50
19	Mike Piazza	3.00
20	Andruw Jones	2.00
21	Greg Maddux	2.50
22	Barry Bonds	5.00
23	Paul Molitor	2.00
24	Hideo Nomo	1.50

Lasting Memories

Lasting Memories is a 30-card insert seeded 1:5. Printed on foil board, the cards feature a player photo with a sky background.

		NM/M
Complete Set (30):		16.00
Common Player:		.25
Inserted 1:5		
1	Nomar Garciaparra	.75
2	Ken Griffey Jr.	1.00
3	Livan Hernandez	.25
4	Hideo Nomo	.40
5	Ben Grieve	.25
6	Scott Rolen	.50
7	Roger Clemens	.85
8	Cal Ripken Jr.	1.00
9	Mo Vaughn	.25
10	Frank Thomas	.65
11	Mark McGwire	1.50
12	Barry Larkin	.25
13	Matt Williams	.25
14	Jose Cruz Jr.	.25
15	Andruw Jones	.65
16	Mike Piazza	1.00
17	Jeff Bagwell	.65
18	Chipper Jones	.75
19	Juan Gonzalez	.40
20	Kenny Lofton	.25
21	Greg Maddux	.75
22	Ivan Rodriguez	.50
23	Alex Rodriguez	1.50
24	Derek Jeter	2.00
25	Albert Belle	.25
26	Barry Bonds	2.00
27	Larry Walker	.25
28	Sammy Sosa	.75
29	Tony Gwynn	.75
30	Randy Johnson	.65

Team Pinnacle

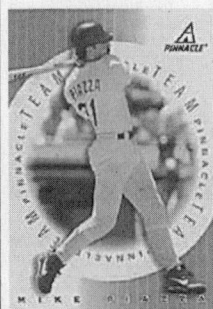

Team Pinnacle is a 15-card, double-sided insert. Printed on mirror-mylar, the cards were inserted 1:71. The hobby-only Gold Team Pinnacle parallel was inserted 1:199 packs.

		NM/M
Complete Set (15):		50.00
Common Player:		1.50
Inserted 1:71		
Golds:		2X
Inserted 1:199		
1	Mike Piazza, Ivan Rodriguez	6.00
2	Mark McGwire, Mo Vaughn	5.00
3	Roberto Alomar, Craig Biggio	2.00
4	Alex Rodriguez, Barry Larkin	8.00
5	Cal Ripken Jr., Chipper Jones	10.00
6	Ken Griffey Jr., Larry Walker	6.00
7	Juan Gonzalez, Tony Gwynn	4.00
8	Albert Belle, Barry Bonds	8.00
9	Kenny Lofton, Andruw Jones	3.00
10	Tino Martinez, Jeff Bagwell	3.00
11	Frank Thomas, Andres Galarraga	3.00
12	Roger Clemens, Greg Maddux	8.00
13	Pedro Martinez, Hideo Nomo	4.00
14	Nomar Garciaparra, Scott Rolen	5.00
15	Ben Grieve, Paul Konerko	1.50

Yardwork

Yardwork is a 15-card insert seeded one per 19 packs. It features the top home run hitters in Major League Baseball.

		NM/M
Complete Set (15):		12.50
Common Player:		.35
Inserted 1:9		
1	Mo Vaughn	.35
2	Frank Thomas	.75
3	Albert Belle	.35
4	Nomar Garciaparra	1.00
5	Tony Clark	.35
6	Tino Martinez	.35
7	Ken Griffey Jr.	1.50
8	Juan Gonzalez	.60
9	Sammy Sosa	1.00
10	Jose Cruz Jr.	.35
11	Jeff Bagwell	.75
12	Mike Piazza	1.50
13	Larry Walker	.35
14	Mark McGwire	2.00
15	Barry Bonds	2.50

1998 Pinnacle Snapshots

One of Pinnacle's last issues was a team-oriented presentation of large-format (4"x6") cards called Snapshots. Like their namesake, the focus on this issue is on candid photos rather than posed portraits or game-action pictures. The cards are printed on thin high-gloss cardboard stock resembling photo paper. Fronts, many of them horizontally formatted, are borderless and have no graphic enhancement. Backs are lightly printed with Pinnacle and licensor logos and a card number expressed as "x of 18." The player's name is nowhere to be found. Snapshots were sold regionally in single-team boxes of 25 packs with eight cards each.

Angels

		NM/M
Complete Set (18):		7.50
Common Player:		.50
1	Jason Dickson	.50
2	Gary DiSarcina	.50
3	Garret Anderson	.50
4	Shigetosi Hasegawa	.50
5	Ken Hill	.50
6	Todd Greene	.50
7	Tim Salmon	.75
8	Jim Edmonds	.60
9	Garret Anderson	.50
10	Dave Hollins	.50
11	Todd Greene	.50
12	Troy Percival	.50
13	Gary DiSarcina	.50
14	Cecil Fielder	.50
15	Darin Erstad	.75
16	Chuck Finley	.50
17	Jim Edmonds	.50
18	Jason Dickson	.50

Braves

		NM/M
Complete Set (18):		11.00
Common Player:		.50
1	Ryan Klesko	.50
2	Walt Weiss	.50
3	Tom Glavine	.75
4	Randall Simon	.50
5	John Smoltz	.50
6	Chipper Jones	1.50
7	Javier Lopez	.50
8	Greg Maddux	1.50
9	Andruw Jones	1.00
10	Michael Tucker	.50
11	Andres Galarraga	.50
12	Andres Galarraga	.50
13	Greg Maddux	1.50
14	Wes Helms	.50
15	Bruce Chen	.50
16	Denny Neagle	.50
17	Mark Wohlers	.50
18	Kevin Millwood	.60

Cardinals

		NM/M
Complete Set (18):		10.00
Common Player:		.50
1	Alan Benes	.50
2	Ron Gant	.50
3	Donovan Osborne	.50
4	Eli Marrero	.50

5	Mark McGwire	2.50
6	Delino DeShields	.50
7	Tom Pagnozzi	.50
8	Delino DeShields	.50
9	Mark McGwire	2.50
10	Royce Clayton	.50
11	Brian Jordan	.50
12	Ray Lankford	.50
13	Brian Jordan	.50
14	Matt Morris	.50
15	John Mabry	.50
16	Luis Ordaz	.50
17	Ron Gant	.50
18	Todd Stottlemyre	.50

Cubs

		NM/M
Complete Set (18):		9.00
Common Player:		.50
1	Mark Grace	.60
2	Manny Alexander	.50
3	Jeremi Gonzalez	.50
4	Brant Brown	.50
5	Mark Grace	.60
6	Lance Johnson	.50
7	Mark Clark	.50
8	Kevin Foster	.50
9	Brant Brown	.50
10	Kevin Foster	.50
11	Kevin Tapani	.50
12	Sammy Sosa	1.50
13	Sammy Sosa	1.50
14	Pat Cline	.50
15	Kevin Orie	.50
16	Steve Trachsel	.50
17	Lance Johnson	.50
18	Robin Jennings	.50

Devil Rays

		NM/M
Complete Set (18):		7.50
Common Player:		.50
1	Kevin Stocker	.50
2	Paul Sorrento	.50
3	John Flaherty	.50
4	Wade Boggs	1.50
5	Rich Butler	.50
6	Wilson Alvarez	.50
7	Bubba Trammell	.50
8	David Martinez	.50
9	Brooks Kieschnick	.50
10	Tony Saunders	.50
11	Esteban Yan	.50
12	Quinton McCracken	.50
13	Albie Lopez	.50
14	Roberto Hernandez	.50
15	Fred McGriff	.50
16	Bubba Trammell	.50
17	Brooks Kieschnick	.50
18	Fred McGriff	.50

Diamondbacks

		NM/M
Complete Set (18):		7.50
Common Player:		.50
1	Travis Lee	1.00
2	Matt Williams	.50
3	Jay Bell	.50
4	Devon White	.50
5	Andy Benes	.50
6	Tony Batista	.50
7	Jay Bell	.50
8	Edwin Diaz	.50
9	Devon White	.50
10	Bob Wolcott	.50
11	Karim Garcia	1.00
12	Yamil Benitez	.50
13	Jorge Fabregas	.50
14	Jeff Suppan	.50
15	Ben Ford	.50
16	Brian Anderson	.50
17	Travis Lee	1.00
18	Matt Williams	.50

Dodgers

		NM/M
Complete Set (18):		12.00
Common Player:		.50
1	Mike Piazza	2.50
2	Eric Karros	.50
3	Raul Mondesi	.50
4	Wilton Guerrero	.50
5	Darren Dreifort	.50
6	Roger Cedeno	.50
7	Todd Zeile	.50
8	Paul Konerko	.75
9	Todd Hollandsworth	.50

10	Ismael Valdes	.50
11	Hideo Nomo	1.00
12	Ramon Martinez	.50
13	Chan Ho Park	.75
14	Eric Young	.50
15	Dennis Reyes	.50
16	Eric Karros	.50
17	Mike Piazza	2.50
18	Raul Mondesi	.50

Indians

		NM/M
Complete Set (18):		7.50
Common Player:		.50
1	Manny Ramirez	1.50
2	Travis Fryman	.50
3	Jaret Wright	.50
4	Brian Giles	.50
5	Bartolo Colon	.50
6	Kenny Lofton	.50
7	David Justice	.50
8	Brian Giles	.50
9	Sandy Alomar Jr.	.50
10	Jose Mesa	.50
11	Jim Thome	1.00
12	Sandy Alomar Jr.	.50
13	Omar Vizquel	.50
14	Geronimo Berroa	.50
15	John Smiley	.50
16	Chad Ogea	.50
17	Charles Nagy	.50
18	Enrique Wilson	.50

Mariners

		NM/M
Complete Set (18):		12.00
Common Player:		.50
1	Alex Rodriguez	2.50
2	Jay Buhner	.50
3	Russ Davis	.50
4	Joey Cora	.50
5	Joey Cora	.50
6	Jay Buhner	.50
7	Ken Griffey Jr.	2.00
8	Raul Ibanez	.50
9	Rich Amaral	.50
10	Shane Monahan	.50
11	Alex Rodriguez	2.50
12	Dan Wilson	.50
13	Bob Wells	.50
14	Randy Johnson	1.00
15	Randy Johnson	1.00
16	Jeff Fassero	.50
17	Ken Cloude	.50
18	Edgar Martinez	.50

Mets

		NM/M
Complete Set (18):		7.50
Common Player:		.50
1	Rey Ordonez	.50
2	Todd Hundley	.50
3	Preston Wilson	.50
4	Rich Becker	.50
5	Bernard Gilkey	.50
6	Rey Ordonez	.50
7	Butch Huskey	.50
8	Carlos Baerga	.50
9	Edgardo Alfonzo	.50
10	Bill Pulsipher	.50
11	John Franco	.50
12	Todd Pratt	.50
13	Brian McRae	.50
14	Bobby Jones	.50
15	John Olerud	.50
16	Todd Hundley	.50
17	Jay Payton	.50
18	Paul Wilson	.50

Orioles

		NM/M
Complete Set (18):		12.50
Common Player:		.50
1	Cal Ripken Jr.	3.00
2	Rocky Coppinger	.50
3	Eric Davis	.50
4	Chris Hoiles	.50
5	Mike Mussina	.75
6	Joe Carter	.50
7	Rafael Palmeiro	1.00
8	B.J. Surhoff	.50
9	Jimmy Key	.50
10	Scott Erickson	.50
11	Armando Benitez	.50
12	Roberto Alomar	.65
13	Cal Ripken Jr.	3.00
14	Mike Bordick	.50
15	Roberto Alomar	.65
16	Jeffrey Hammonds	.50
17	Rafael Palmeiro	1.00
18	Brady Anderson	.50

Rangers

		NM/M
Complete Set (18):		9.00
Common Player:		.50
1	Ivan Rodriguez	1.00
2	Fernando Tatis	.50
3	Danny Patterson	.50
4	Will Clark	.66
5	Kevin Elster	.50
6	Rusty Greer	.50
7	Darren Oliver	.50
8	John Burkett	.50
9	Tom Goodwin	.50
10	Roberto Kelly	.50
11	Aaron Sele	.50
12	Rick Helling	.50
13	Mark McLemore	.50
14	Lee Stevens	.50
15	John Wetteland	.50
16	Will Clark	.65
17	Juan Gonzalez	.75
18	Roger Pavlik	.50

Red Sox

		NM/M
Complete Set (18):		9.00
Common Player:		.50
1	Tim Naehring	.50
2	Brian Rose	.50
3	Darren Bragg	.50
4	Pedro Martinez	1.00
5	Mo Vaughn	.50
6	Jim Leyritz	.50
7	Troy O'Leary	.50
8	Mo Vaughn	.50
9	Nomar Garciaparra	1.50
10	Michael Coleman	.50
11	Tom Gordon	.50
12	Tim Naehring	.50
13	Nomar Garciaparra	1.50
14	John Valentin	.50
15	Steve Avery	.50
16	Damon Buford	.50
17	Troy O'Leary	.50
18	Bret Saberhagen	.50

Rockies

		NM/M
Complete Set (18):		7.50
Common Player:		.50
1	Larry Walker	.50
2	Pedro Astacio	.50
3	Jamey Wright	.50
4	Darryl Kile	.50
5	Kirt Manwaring	.50
6	Todd Helton	1.50
7	Mike Lansing	.50
8	Neifi Perez	.50
9	Dante Bichette	.50
10	Derrick Gibson	.50
11	Neifi Perez	.50
12	Darryl Kile	.50
13	Larry Walker	.50
14	Roger Bailey	.50
15	Ellis Burks	.50
16	Dante Bichette	.50
17	Derrick Gibson	.50
18	Ellis Burks	.50

Yankees

		NM/M
Complete Set (18):		12.50
Common Player:		.75
1	Andy Pettitte	.75
2	Darryl Strawberry	.50

3	Joe Girardi	.50
4	Derek Jeter	3.00
5	Andy Pettitte	.75
6	Tim Raines	.50
7	Mariano Rivera	.75
8	Tino Martinez	.50
9	Derek Jeter	3.00
10	Hideki Irabu	.50
11	Tino Martinez	.50
12	David Cone	.50
13	Bernie Williams	.65
14	David Cone	.50
15	Bernie Williams	.65
16	Chuck Knoblauch	.50
17	Paul O'Neill	.50
18	David Wells	.50

Sport Block

By manipulating the eight cubes of which this novelty is comprised, pictures of eight popular players and the team logo can be displayed. The cube measures 2-3/4" x 2-3/4" x 2-3/4".

		NM/M
Complete Set (10):		20.00
Common Team:		3.00
(1)	Anaheim Angels (Garret Anderson, Jason Dickson, Jim Edmonds, Darin Erstad, Chuck Finley, Todd Greene, Troy Percival, Tim Salmon, Angels Logo)	3.00
(2)	Arizona Diamondbacks	3.00
(3)	Atlanta Braves (Andres Galarraga, Tom Glavine, Andruw Jones, Chipper Jones, Ryan Klesko, Javier Lopez, Greg Maddux, John Smoltz, Braves Logo)	3.00
(4)	Baltimore Orioles	3.00
(5)	Boston Red Sox (Darren Bragg, Nomar Garciaparra, Reggie Jefferson, Jim Leyritz, Pedro Martinez, Troy O'Leary, John Valentin, Mo Vaughn, Red Sox Logo)	3.00
(6)	Cleveland Indians	3.00
(7)	Los Angeles Dodgers (Eric Karros, Paul Konerko, Ramon Martinez, Raul Mondesi, Hideo Nomo, Chan Ho Park, Mike Piazza, Ismael Valdes, Dodgers Logo)	3.00
(8)	New York Yankees	3.00
(9)	Seattle Mariners (Jay Buhner, Russ Davis, Jeff Fassero, Ken Griffey Jr., Randy Johnson, Edgar Martinez, Alex Rodriguez, Dan Wilson, Mariners Logo)	3.00
(10)	Tampa Bay Devil Rays (Wilson Alvarez, Wade Boggs, Dave Martinez, Quinton McCracken, Fred McGriff, Tony Saunders, Paul Sorrento, Bubba Trammell, Devil Rays Logo)	3.00

Totally Certified Platinum Gold

Among several card issues that were aborted by Pinnacle's bankruptcy in mid-1998, but which have leaked into the hobby market in dribs and drabs, are 10 Totally Certified Platinum Gold cards that were intended to be random pack inserts in 1998 Certified. Each of the cards was produced in an edition of 30 serially numbered pieces. To date, confirmation of back-door release of the Platinum Red and Platinum Blue versions has not been made.

		NM/M
Complete Set (10):		125.00
Common Player:		7.50
1	Vladimir Guerrero	15.00
2	Andruw Jones	12.00
3	Paul Molitor	15.00
4	Jose Cruz Jr.	7.50
5	Edgar Martinez	7.50
6	Andy Pettitte	9.00
7	Darin Erstad	9.00
8	Barry Larkin	7.50
9	Derek Jeter	40.00
10	Rusty Greer	7.50

1998 Team Pinnacle Baseball

With each $30 membership in Pinnacle's collectors' club, "Team Pinnacle," the member received a litho tin box with 10 each special baseball, football and hockey cards, and a pack of unnumbered promo cards. In standard 2-1/2" x 3-1/2", cards have game-action photos on front, bordered in a dominant team color and enhanced with a gold-foil Team Pinnacle logo at bottom. Backs have portrait photos, a few personal details, career highlights and the player's uniform number ghosted in the background.

		NM/M
Complete Set (10):		16.00
Common Player:		1.00
B1	Ken Griffey Jr.	2.00
B2	Frank Thomas	1.25
B3	Cal Ripken Jr.	3.00
B4	Alex Rodriguez	2.50
B5	Mike Piazza	2.00
B6	Derek Jeter	3.00
B7	Greg Maddux	1.50
B8	Chipper Jones	1.50
B9	Mark McGwire	2.50
B10	Juan Gonzalez	1.00
---	Cal Ripken Jr. (Unmarked sample.)	2.50

Team Pinnacle (Unissued)

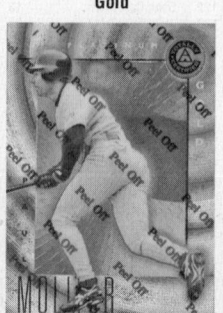

This four-card set was reportedly created for distribution to members of the card company's "Team Pinnacle" but was never officially issued due to the manufacturer's bankruptcy. The 2-1/2" x 3-1/2" cards have game-action photos on front with a wide diagonal color stripe at top and a gold-foil "98 TEAM PINNACLE" logo at bottom. Backs have a color portrait photo along with some stats and highlights. The cards are unnumbered.

NM/M

Complete Set (4): 7.50
Common Player: 3.00
(1) John Elway/Football 2.00
(2) Ken Griffey Jr. 2.00
(3) Derek Jeter 3.00
(4) Eric Lindros/Hockey 2.00

Uncut

Advertised as the "BIGGEST CARD EVER!" these 13-3/8 x 18-5/8 cards are approximately 30 times larger than standard cards. Sold in individual cello bags with a suggested retail price of around $10, the cards are super-size replicas of the same players' cards found in the Field of Vision subset in regular 1998 Pinnacle. The giant cards have an etched metallic foil front not found on the regular cards. They are packaged with a die-cut cardboard backing which tends to bruise the edges or chip off small patches of ink.

NM/M

Complete Set (6): 20.00
Common Player: 3.00
182 Alex Rodriguez 6.00
183 Cal Ripken Jr., Roberto Alomar 4.50
184 Roger Clemens 3.50
185 Derek Jeter 7.00
186 Frank Thomas 5.00
186p Frank Thomas ("SAMPLE" on back.) 4.50
187 Ken Griffey Jr. 4.50

2004 Pitt Ohio Express 1979 Pirates

The purpose for which the Pennsylvania trucking company produced this card set, and the manner of its distribution, is unclear. The set commemorates the World Champion Pittsburgh Pirates of 1979. Fronts of the approximately 4-3/4" x 3-5/8" cards have large black-and-white portrait photos. Highlighted by gold graphics, the fronts also include a team logo, player name, position and uniform number. Backs have an ad for the trucking company.

NM/M

Complete Set (18): 20.00
Common Player: 2.00
(1) Matt Alexander 2.00
(2) Tony Bartirome 2.00
(3) Jim Bibby 2.00
(4) Mike Easler 2.00
(5) Grant Jackson 2.00
(6) Bruce Kison 2.00
(7) Lee Lacy 2.00
(8) Bill Madlock 3.00
(9) Omar Moreno 2.00
(10) Steve Nicosia 2.00
(11) Ed Ott 2.00
(12) Dave Parker 4.00
(13) Dave Roberts 2.00
(14) Don Robinson 2.00
(15) Jim Rooker 2.00
(16) Manny Sanguillen 2.00
(17) Chuck Tanner 2.00
(18) Kent Tekulve 2.00

1992 Pittsburgh Brewing Co. Roberto Clemente Tribute

The first 15,000 fans at Three Rivers Stadium on September 6 at a special promotional Clemente tribute night received this perforated pair of cards honoring the Pirates superstar. The 7" square panel has a pair of two-part cards. Each side has a 3-1/2" x 5-1/2" picture portion at top and a 1-1/2" tab at bottom, perforated for easy separation. The left side has a portrait of the Pirate great with his first name; at right is his last name and an action picture. Back of the portrait card has career stats; back of the action card has career highlights. Artwork on each card is by Tom Mosser. The sponsor logo is on back of each tab along with a quotation and copyright information.

NM/M

Complete Panel: 18.00
Complete Set (2): 15.00
#21 Roberto/Portrait 7.50
#21 Clemente/Action 7.50

1985 Pittsburgh Pirates Yearbook Cards

This 18-card set was issued on two nine-card perforated panels inserted into the Bucs' 1985 yearbook. Individual cards measure 2-1/2" x 3-1/2" and feature color photos surrounded by black and gold borders. The player's name, position and uniform number are printed in a white panel at bottom. Backs are in black-and-white and offer complete major and minor league stats, along with the logos of sponsor Cameron/Coca-Cola.

NM/M

Complete Set (18): 7.50
Common Player: .50
2 Jim Morrison .50
3 Johnny Ray .50
5 Bill Madlock .60
6 Tony Pena .50
7 Chuck Tanner .50
10 Tim Foli .50
13 Steve Kemp .50
15 George Hendrick .50
25 Jose DeLeon .50
27 Kent Tekulve .50
28 Sixto Lezcano .50
29 Rick Rhoden .50
30 Jason Thompson .50
36 Marvell Wynne .50
43 Don Robinson .50
45 John Candelaria .50
49 Larry McWilliams .50
53 Doug Frobel .50

1996 Pizza Hut

In conjunction with a foam bat/ball promotion, Pizza Hut issued a small set of small cards (2-1/2" x 2-1/4") featuring players involved in the endorsement. The player portrait photos on the cards are devoid of cap logos and surrounded by a rainbow border. Player names are in yellow with a nick-

name in red. A choking hazard warning is in black-and-white on bottom. Backs are printed in red and black and have career summaries, logos and copyright notice. The unnumbered cards are checklisted here alphabetically.

NM/M

Complete Set (4): 8.00
Common Card: 1.50
(1) Jeff Bagwell (Thumper), Orel Hershiser (Bulldawg) 1.50
(2) David Cone (Controller), Mike Piazza (Crusher) 3.00
(3) Ken Griffey Jr. (Junior), Greg Maddux (Surgeon) 3.00
(4) Randy Johnson (Big Unit), Mo Vaughn (Hit Dog) 1.50

1985 Polaroid/J.C. Penney Indians

Polaroid / JCPenney — JOE CARTER, Outfielder

While the Cleveland Indians continued its four-year tradition of baseball card promotional game issues in 1985, the sponsor changed from Wheaties to Polaroid/J.C. Penney. The set features 30 player cards, a manager card and a group card of the coaching staff. Though produced in the "safety set" format - slightly oversize (2-13/16" by 4-1/8") with wide white borders - the Indians cards carry no safety message. Backs, once again numbered by uniform number, contain major and minor league stats.

NM/M

Complete Set (32): 9.00
Common Player: .50
2 Brett Butler .50
3 Tony Bernazard .50
8 Carmen Castillo .50
10 Pat Tabler .50
12 Benny Ayala .50
14 Ernie Camacho .50
16 Julio Franco .50
17 Jerry Willard .50
18 Pat Corrales .50
20 Otis Nixon .35
21 Mike Hargrove .50
22 Mike Fischlin .50
23 Chris Bando .50
24 George Vukovich .50
26 Brook Jacoby .50
27 Mel Hall .50
28 Bert Blyleven 1.00
29 Andre Thornton .30
30 Joe Carter .50
32 Rick Behenna .50
33 Roy Smith .50
35 Jerry Reed .50
36 Jamie Easterly .50
38 Dave Von Ohlen .50
43 Rich Thompson .50
43 Bryan Clark .50
44 Neal Heaton .50
48 Vern Ruhle .50
49 Jeff Barkley .50
52 Ramon Romero .50
54 Tom Waddell .50
--- Coaches (Bobby Bonds, Johnny Goryl, Don McMahon, Ed Napoleon, Dennis Sommers) .50

1999 Pop Secret Detroit Tigers

GABE KAPLER - OF

This team set was sponsored by the snack food company and distributed at a promotional game at Tiger Stadium. The 2-1/2" x 3-1/2" cards have color photos which are borderless at top, bottom and right. At left are black and blue vertical stripes with player identification. Backs have a color portrait photo, career stats and team and sponsor logos. The unnumbered cards are checklisted here alphabetically.

NM/M

Complete Set (26): 9.00
Common Player: .50
(1) Matt Anderson .50
(2) Brad Ausmus .50
(3) Willie Blair .50
(4) Doug Brocail .50
(5) Frank Catalanotto .50
(6) Tony Clark .50
(7) Deivi Cruz .50
(8) Damion Easley .50
(9) Juan Encarnacion .50
(10) Karim Garcia .50
(11) Seth Greisinger .50
(12) Bill Haselman .50
(13) Bobby Higginson .50
(14) Gregg Jefferies .50
(15) Todd Jones .50
(16) Gabe Kapler 1.00
(17) Masao Kida .50
(18) Dave Mlicki .50
(19) Brian Moehler .50
(20) C.J. Nitkowski .50
(21) Dean Palmer .50
(22) Larry Parrish .50
(23) Luis Polonia .50
(24) Justin Thompson .50
(25) Jeff Weaver .50
(26) The Corner (Tiger Stadium) .50

1990 Post Cereal

WILL CLARK — SAN FRANCISCO GIANTS — FIRST BASE

Post Cereal returned in 1990 with a 30-card set. Card fronts feature borders in white, red and blue, with the Post logo at top-left and the Major League Baseball logo at top-right. Backs show complete major league statistics; underneath is a facsimile autograph. The player photos do not display team logos. Cards were included three per box, inside Alpha-Bits cereal. An uncut sheet version of the set was also offered in a run of 5,000 serially numbered pieces.

NM/M

Complete Set (30): 4.00
Common Player: .10
Uncut Sheet: 15.00
1 Don Mattingly .75
2 Roger Clemens .75
3 Kirby Puckett .60
4 George Brett .75
5 Tony Gwynn .60
6 Ozzie Smith .60
7 Will Clark .10
8 Orel Hershiser .10
9 Ryne Sandberg .60
10 Darryl Strawberry .10
11 Nolan Ryan 1.50
12 Mark McGwire 1.00
13 Jim Abbott .10
14 Bo Jackson .20
15 Kevin Mitchell .10
16 Jose Canseco .35
17 Wade Boggs .60
18 Dale Murphy .20
19 Mark Grace .10
20 Mike Scott .10
21 Cal Ripken, Jr. 1.50
22 Pedro Guerrero .10
23 Ken Griffey Jr. .85
24 Eric Davis .10
25 Rickey Henderson .45
26 Robin Yount .45
27 Von Hayes .10
28 Alan Trammell .10
29 Dwight Gooden .10
30 Joe Carter .10

1991 Post Cereal

Post 1991 Collector Series — MARK McGWIRE, OAKLAND A's

These superstar trading cards were inserted in several brands of Post's children's cereals. The cards were produced by Mike Schechter Associates, Inc. and are authorized by the Players Association, but not MLB, so team logos have been removed from the photos. Card backs feature statistics and a facsimile autograph.

NM/M

Complete Set (30): 4.00
Common Player: .10
1 Dave Justice .10
2 Mark McGwire .75
3 Will Clark .10
4 Jose Canseco .30
5 Vince Coleman .10
6 Sandy Alomar, Jr. .10
7 Darryl Strawberry .10
8 Len Dykstra .10
9 Gregg Jefferies .10
10 Tony Gwynn .50
11 Ken Griffey Jr. .75
12 Roger Clemens .65
13 Chris Sabo .10
14 Bobby Bonilla .10
15 Gary Sheffield .30
16 Ryne Sandberg .50
17 Nolan Ryan 1.00
18 Barry Larkin .10
19 Cal Ripken, Jr. 1.00
20 Jim Abbott .10
21 Barry Bonds 1.00
22 Mark Grace .10
23 Cecil Fielder .10
24 Kevin Mitchell .10
25 Todd Zeile .10
26 George Brett .65
27 Rickey Henderson .45
28 Kirby Puckett .50
29 Don Mattingly .65
30 Kevin Maas .10

Canadian

SÉRIE DES ÉTOILES — 1991 SUPER STAR SERIES — BENITO SANTIAGO

Specially-marked Post cereal boxes sold in Canada included one of 30 cards from a 1991 Super Star series. Cards are bilingual, and include player statistics and biographical information on the backs. The major league logos are airbrushed from the players' caps and uniforms. American Leaguers' cards have blue stripes above and below the photo on front and as a back border color; National Leaguers are in red.

NM/M

Complete Set (30): 10.00
Set in Album: 12.50
Common Player: .25
1 Delino DeShields .25
2 Tim Wallach .25
3 Andres Galarraga .25
4 Dave Magadan .25
5 Barry Bonds 2.00
6 Len Dykstra .25
7 Andre Dawson .35
8 Ozzie Smith .65
9 Will Clark .25
10 Chris Sabo .25
11 Eddie Murray .60
12 Dave Justice .25
13 Benito Santiago .25
14 Glenn Davis .25
15 Kelly Gruber .25
16 Dave Stieb .25
17 John Olerud .25
18 Roger Clemens .85
19 Cecil Fielder .25
20 Kevin Maas .25
21 Robin Yount .60
22 Cal Ripken, Jr. 2.00
23 Sandy Alomar .25
24 Rickey Henderson .60
25 Bobby Thigpen .25
26 Ken Griffey Jr. 1.00
27 Nolan Ryan 2.00
28 Dave Winfield .60
29 George Brett .75
30 Kirby Puckett .65

1992 Post Cereal

Post 1992 Collector Series — Joe Carter, TORONTO BLUE JAYS

The addition of a back photo is notable on Post's 1992 set. Again packaged at the rate of three cards in specially marked boxes, a complete set was available via a mail-in offer. Front photos have a blue strip at top with the Post logo at upper-left. A red stripe at bottom has the player's name and the logo of the Major League Baseball Player's Association. The absence of a Major League Baseball logo, and the airbrushing of uniform logos on all photos identifies this set as the work of Mike Schechter Associates. Backs have a small photo at left, bordered in red. At right are biographical details, career stats and a facsimile autograph. The cards of 1991 Rookies of the Year Jeff Bagwell and Chuck Knoblauch are designated with a "Rookie Star" banner over the front photo.

NM/M

Complete Set (30): 3.00
Common Player: .10
1 Jeff Bagwell .35
2 Ryne Sandberg .45
3 Don Mattingly .50
4 Wally Joyner .10
5 Dwight Gooden .10
6 Chuck Knoblauch .45
7 Kirby Puckett .45
8 Ozzie Smith .45
9 Cal Ripken, Jr. .75
10 Darryl Strawberry .10
11 George Brett .50
12 Joe Carter .10
13 Cecil Fielder .10
14 Will Clark .10
15 Barry Bonds .75
16 Roger Clemens .50
17 Paul Molitor .35
18 Scott Erickson .10
19 Wade Boggs .45
20 Ken Griffey Jr. .85
21 Bobby Bonilla .10
22 Terry Pendleton .10
23 Barry Larkin .10
24 Frank Thomas .35
25 Jose Canseco .25

26	Tony Gwynn	.45
27	Nolan Ryan	.75
28	Howard Johnson	.10
29	Dave Justice	.10
30	Danny Tartabull	.10

Canadian

For the second year in a row Post Cereal of Canada issued a set of cards inserted in cereal boxes. The 1992 cards have a player photo on front (with airbrushed cap) and information on the reverse in both English and French. The back of the card also contains an action photo, which has a pop-up tab which when opened stands up, revealing a statistical base.

		NM/M
Complete Set (18):		9.00
Common Player:		.25
1	Dennis Martinez	.25
2	Benito Santiago	.25
3	Will Clark	.25
4	Ryne Sandberg	1.00
5	Tim Wallach	.25
6	Ozzie Smith	1.00
7	Darryl Strawberry	.25
8	Brett Butler	.25
9	Barry Bonds	2.00
10	Roger Clemens	1.25
11	Sandy Alomar	.25
12	Cecil Fielder	.25
13	Roberto Alomar	.35
14	Kelly Gruber	.25
15	Cal Ripken, Jr.	2.00
16	Jose Canseco	.50
17	Kirby Puckett	1.00
18	Rickey Henderson	.75

1993 Post Cereal

Post Cereal's 1993 Collectors Series cards feature a black border on the bottom and the right side, with the Post logo located at top right and the player's name, team and position along the bottom. Team logos have been air-brushed from the uniforms. Backs have a black background, a color player portrait photo, personal data, a career summary, 1992 and career stats, and a red strip with a white facsimile autograph. A special edition of 5,000 numbered uncut sheets was also produced.

		NM/M
Complete Set (30):		3.00
Common Player:		.10
Uncut Sheet:		10.00
1	Dave Fleming	.10
2	Will Clark	.10
3	Kirby Puckett	.60
4	Roger Clemens	.65
5	Fred McGriff	.10
6	Eric Karros	.10
7	Ken Griffey Jr.	.75
8	Tony Gwynn	.60
9	Cal Ripken, Jr.	1.25
10	Cecil Fielder	.10
11	Gary Sheffield	.25
12	Don Mattingly	.65
13	Ryne Sandberg	.60

14	Frank Thomas	.50
15	Barry Bonds	1.25
16	Paul Molitor	.50
17	Terry Pendleton	.10
18	Darren Daulton	.10
19	Mark McGwire	1.00
20	Nolan Ryan	1.25
21	Tom Glavine	.30
22	Roberto Alomar	.20
23	Juan Gonzalez	.20
24	Bobby Bonilla	.10
25	George Brett	.60
26	Ozzie Smith	.60
27	Andy Van Slyke	.10
28	Barry Larkin	.10
29	John Kruk	.10
30	Robin Yount	.50

Canadian

For the third consecutive year, Post Canada produced a set of cards. The 1993 set features a two-sided card with one side containing a special pop-up feature, much the same as their 1992 offering. There are 18 black-bordered and gold-lettered cards in the set. The cards were available in specially-marked boxes of cereal.

		NM/M
Complete Set (18):		10.00
Common Player:		.25
1	Pat Borders	.25
2	Juan Guzman	.25
3	Roger Clemens	1.25
4	Joe Carter	.25
5	Roberto Alomar	.35
6	Robin Yount	.75
7	Cal Ripken, Jr.	3.00
8	Kirby Puckett	1.00
9	Ken Griffey Jr.	2.00
10	Darren Daulton	.25
11	Andy Van Slyke	.25
12	Bobby Bonilla	.25
13	Larry Walker	.25
14	Ryne Sandberg	1.00
15	Barry Larkin	.25
16	Gary Sheffield	.40
17	Ozzie Smith	1.00
18	Terry Pendleton	.25

1994 Post Cereal

Post cereals' 1994 set was issued three cards at a time in cellophane packages in cereal boxes. A special edition of 5,000 numbered 15-1/2" x 20-1/2" uncut sheets was also produced.

		NM/M
Complete Set (30):		3.00
Common Player:		.10
Uncut Sheet:		15.00
1	Mike Piazza	.75
2	Don Mattingly	.65
3	Juan Gonzalez	.35
4	Kirby Puckett	.60
5	Gary Sheffield	.25
6	David Justice	.10
7	Jack McDowell	.10
8	Mo Vaughn	.25
9	Darren Daulton	.10
10	Bobby Bonilla	.10
11	Barry Bonds	1.00
12	Barry Larkin	.10

13	Tony Gwynn	.60
14	Mark Grace	.10
15	Ken Griffey Jr.	.75
16	Tom Glavine	.35
17	Cecil Fielder	.10
18	Roberto Alomar	.25
19	Mark Whiten	.10
20	Lenny Dykstra	.10
21	Frank Thomas	.45
22	Will Clark	.10
23	Andres Galarraga	.10
24	John Olerud	.10
25	Cal Ripken, Jr.	1.00
26	Tim Salmon	.10
27	Albert Belle	.10
28	Gregg Jefferies	.10
29	Jeff Bagwell	.45
30	Orlando Merced	.10

Canadian

The emphasis was on Expos and Blue Jays players in the 1994 Post cereal cards issued in Canada. Several of the cards featured gold-foil stamping on the fronts. Like all contemporary Post cards, the uniform logos were airbrushed from the photos due to lack of licensing from Major League Baseball.

		NM/M
Complete Set (18):		12.00
Common Player:		.25
1	Joe Carter	1.00
2	Paul Molitor	.75
3	Roberto Alomar	.40
4	John Olerud	.25
5	Dave Stewart	.25
6	Juan Guzman	.25
7	Pat Borders	.25
8	Larry Walker	.25
9	Moises Alou	.25
10	Ken Griffey Jr.	1.50
11	Barry Bonds	2.50
12	Frank Thomas	.75
13	Cal Ripken, Jr.	2.50
14	Mike Piazza	1.50
15	Juan Gonzalez	.40
16	Lenny Dykstra	.25
17	David Justice	.25
18	Kirby Puckett	1.25

1995 Post Cereal

The 1995 Post Collector Series differs dramatically in format from the company's recent cereal-box insert issues. Each card measures 5" x 3-1/2" and is vertically scored at center to allow it to be folded. When folded, the front has a player action photo against a blue marbled background. On back is another photo, with career stats and highlights and a yellow facsimile autograph. In the center of the folded piece is a large game-action photo. All pictures have had the team logos removed for lack of a license by MLB. The cards are licensed by the Players Association. Complete sets of the '95 Post cards were available in a special cardboard display folder. Large quantities of the set made their way into dealer hands by 1998, and the value plummeted.

		NM/M
Complete Set (16):		2.50
Common Player:		.10
1	Wade Boggs	.25
2	Jeff Bagwell	.45
3	Greg Maddux	.60
4	Ken Griffey Jr.	.65

5	Roberto Alomar	.20
6	Kirby Puckett	.60
7	Tony Gwynn	.60
8	Cal Ripken Jr.	1.00
9	Matt Williams	.10
10	Dave Justice	.10
11	Barry Bonds	.60
12	Mike Piazza	.65
13	Albert Belle	.10
14	Frank Thomas	.45
15	Len Dykstra	.10
16	Will Clark	.10

Canadian

Post cereals celebrated its fifth anniversary of baseball card production for the Canadian market by switching providers to Upper Deck, and issuing a high-quality album to house the 18-card set. Cards feature color action photos that are borderless at top, bottom and right. At left is a vertical black marbled panel with the player's name, team and position. An Upper Deck logo is at top-right; a Post anniversary logo at lower-left. Because the cards are licensed by the Major League Players Association, but not Major League Baseball, team logos have been airbrushed from photos. Backs have another player photo plus bilingual biographical data, career highlights and stats for the previous five seasons and lifetime. A ghost image of the front photo appears under the typography. As might be expected, the set's roster is especially rich in Expos and Blue Jays players.

		NM/M
Complete Set (18):		12.00
Common Player:		.50
Album:		6.00
1	Ken Griffey Jr.	2.00
2	Roberto Alomar	.35
3	Paul Molitor	.75
4	Devon White	.25
5	Moises Alou	.25
6	Ken Hill	.25
7	Paul O'Neill	.25
8	Joe Carter	.25
9	Kirby Puckett	1.50
10	Jimmy Key	.25
11	Frank Thomas	.75
12	David Cone	.25
13	Tony Gwynn	1.50
14	Matt Williams	.25
15	Jeff Bagwell	.75
16	Greg Maddux	1.50
17	Barry Bonds	3.00
18	Cal Ripken Jr.	3.00

2001 Post Collector's Series

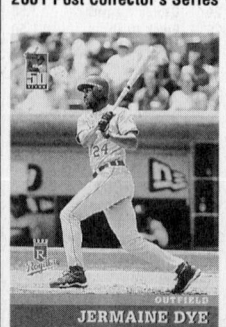

(See 2001 Topps/Post Collector's Series.)

2001 Post 500 Home Run Club

(See 2001 Topps/Post 500 Home Run Club for checklist and values.)

2002 Post Collector's Series

(See 2002 Topps/Post Collector's Series.)

2003 Post MVP Action

(See 2003 Upper Deck/Post MVP Action.)

1985 P.R.E. Pete Rose Set

This 120-card set traces the career of Pete Rose through the 1985 season. Many cards feature photos used on earlier Topps cards. Each card, and the box in which they were sold, says the set was "Designed by Topps Chewing Gum Inc." The set was distributed within the hobby by Renata Galasso and the copyright-holder is identified as "P.R.E." (Pete Rose Enterprises?). Besides the Topps photos, the cards include a number of original paintings by Ron Lewis, a few family-album type photos and some game-action shots of career highlights. Backs of the first three cards offer complete minor and major league stats through 1985. Cards #4-90 have a question and answer format on back and the final 30 cards in the set have a puzzle-back depicting many of Rose's Topps cards in full color. Single cards from the set are seldom offered in the market. A borderless version of card #1 was issued in an edition of 1,000, all cards being autographed.

	NM/M
Complete Set (120):	15.00
Single Card:	.25
Autographed #1:	35.00
1-120 Pete Rose	.25

1986 Provigo Expos

This 28-card set was issued in three-card panels of 7-1/2" x 3-3/8". Each card measures 2-1/2" x 3-3/8", and each panel includes two players

and an advertising card. Panels are perforated to allow for separation, if desired. Card fronts have high quality game-action color photos with the player's name, uniform number and Expos and Provigo logos. Card backs include biographical information in both French and English and list the card's number within the set. There are 24 player, one manager and two coaches cards, along with a card of the Expos mascot, Youppi.

		NM/M
Complete Panel Set:		3.00
Complete Singles Set:		2.50
Common Panel:		.15
Common Single Player:		.10
Album:		5.00
Panel 1		.15
1	Hubie Brooks	.10
2	Dann Bilardello	.10
----	Checklist	.02
Panel 2		.15
3	Buck Rodgers	.10
4	Andy McGaffigan	.10
----	Album Offer	.02
Panel 3		.15
5	Mitch Webster	.10
6	Jim Wohlford	.10
----	Album Offer	.02
Panel 4		1.00
7	Tim Raines	.35
8	Jay Tibbs	.10
----	Album Offer	.02
Panel 5		.75
9	Andre Dawson	.50
10	Andres Galarraga	.35
----	Album Offer	.02
Panel 6		.30
11	Tim Wallach	.10
12	Dan Schatzeder	.10
----	Checklist	.02
Panel 7		.15
13	Jeff Reardon	.10
14	Expos' Coaching Staff (Larry Bearnarth, Joe Kerrigan, Bobby Winkles)	.10
----	Album Offer	.02
Panel 8		.15
15	Jason Thompson	.10
16	Bert Roberge	.10
----	$1 Expos Ticket Coupon	.02
Panel 9		.15
17	Al Newman	.10
18	Tim Burke	.10
----	Album Offer	.02
Panel 10		.15
19	Bryn Smith	.10
20	Wayne Krenchicki	.10
----	Album Offer	.02
Panel 11		.15
21	Joe Hesketh	.10
22	Herman Winningham	.10
----	Album Offer	.02
Panel 12		.15
23	Vance Law	.10
24	Floyd Youmans	.10
----	Album Offer	.02
Panel 13		.15
25	Jeff Parrett	.10
26	Mike Fitzgerald	.10
----	Album Offer	.02
Panel 14		.15
27	Youppi (Mascot)	.10
28	Expos' Coaching Staff (Ron Hansen, Ken Macha, Rick Renick)	.10
----	Album Offer	.02

Posters

This Provigo issue is much scarcer than the smaller card panels issued the same year. These posters measure about 9" x 14-7/8". A large (9" x 12-1/2") player portrait is separated from a bottom coupon panel. Backs are blank and can be found in red, white or blue. The player pictures have facsimile autographs and a white strip at bottom with identification, uniform number, team and sponsor logos and card number. Values shown are for complete poster/coupon combinations.

		NM/M
Complete Set (12):		20.00
Common Player:		2.00
1	Tim Raines	4.00
2	Bryn Smith	2.00
3	Hubie Brooks	2.00
4	Buck Rodgers	2.00
5	Mitch Webster	2.00
6	Joe Hesketh	2.00
7	Mike Fitzgerald	2.00
8	Andy McGaffigan	2.00
9	Andre Dawson	7.50
10	Tim Wallach	2.00
11	Jeff Reardon	2.00
12	Vance Law	2.00

1994 PruCare N.Y. Mets

Top names on the 1994 Mets are featured in this issue sponsored by PruCare, a division of Prudential Insurance, whose logo appears on front and back. Cards were issued in a nine-card panel, perforated for easy separation. Individual cards are 2-1/2" x 3-1/2". Fronts have color action photos surrounded by team-color frames and white borders. Backs are printed in orange and blue with personal data, 1993 stats and highlights and career major league stats. The unnumbered cards are checklisted here in alphabetical order.

		NM/M
Complete Sheet:		3.50
Complete Set (9):		3.00
Common Player:		.50
(1)	Bobby Bonilla	.50
(2)	Jeromy Burnitz	.50
(3)	John Franco	.50
(4)	Dwight Gooden	.50
(5)	Bud Harrelson	.50
(6)	Jeff Kent	.50
(7)	Kevin McReynolds	.50
(8)	Ryan Thompson	.50
(9)	Mookie Wilson	.50

1990 Publications International Stickers

Nolan Ryan

This large set was issued in the form of an album with pages of bound-in stickers which were to be removed and placed in the appropriately numbered spots. Arranged by team, the album's spaces have a trivia question about the player whose sticker belongs there. The 1-3/8" x 1-3/4" stickers are unnumbered and are listed according to the number of their album space.

	NM/M
Complete Album:	20.00
Complete Sticker Set (648):	15.00
Common Player:	.05

#	Player	Price
(1)	Dave Anderson	.05
(2)	Tim Belcher	.05
(3)	Mike Davis	.05
(4)	Rick Dempsey	.05
(5)	Kirk Gibson	.05
(6)	Alfredo Griffin	.05
(7)	Jeff Hamilton	.05
(8)	Mickey Hatcher	.05
(9)	Orel Hershiser	.05
(10)	Ricky Horton	.05
(11)	Jay Howell	.05
(12)	Tim Leary	.05
(13)	Mike Marshall	.05
(14)	Eddie Murray	.60
(15)	Alejandro Pena	.05
(16)	Willie Randolph	.05
(17)	Mike Scioscia	.05
(18)	John Shelby	.05
(19)	Franklin Stubbs	.05
(20)	John Tudor	.05
(21)	Fernando Valenzuela	.05
(22)	Todd Benzinger	.05
(23)	Tom Browning	.05
(24)	Norm Charlton	.05
(25)	Kal Daniels	.05
(26)	Eric Davis	.05
(27)	Bo Diaz	.05
(28)	Rob Dibble	.05
(29)	John Franco	.05
(30)	Ken Griffey Sr.	.05
(31)	Lenny Harris	.05
(32)	Danny Jackson	.05
(33)	Barry Larkin	.05
(34)	Rick Mahler	.05
(35)	Ron Oester	.05
(36)	Paul O'Neill	.05
(37)	Jeff Reed	.05
(38)	Jose Rijo	.05
(39)	Chris Sabo	.05
(40)	Kent Tekulve	.05
(41)	Manny Trillo	.05
(42)	Joel Youngblood	.05
(43)	Roberto Alomar	.15
(44)	Greg Booker	.05
(45)	Jack Clark	.05
(46)	Jerald Clark	.05
(47)	Mark Davis	.05
(48)	Tim Flannery	.05
(49)	Mark Grant	.05
(50)	Tony Gwynn	.75
(51)	Bruce Hurst	.05
(52)	John Kruk	.05
(53)	Dave Leiper	.05
(54)	Carmelo Martinez	.05
(55)	Mark Parent	.05
(56)	Dennis Rasmussen	.05
(57)	Randy Ready	.05
(58)	Benito Santiago	.05
(59)	Eric Show	.05
(60)	Garry Templeton	.05
(61)	Walt Terrell	.05
(62)	Ed Whitson	.05
(63)	Marvell Wynne	.05
(64)	Brett Butler	.05
(65)	Will Clark	.05
(66)	Kelly Downs	.05
(67)	Scott Garrelts	.05
(68)	Rich "Goose" Gossage	.05
(69)	Atlee Hammaker	.05
(70)	Tracy Jones	.05
(71)	Terry Kennedy	.05
(72)	Mike Krukow	.05
(73)	Mike LaCoss	.05
(74)	Craig Lefferts	.05
(75)	Candy Maldonado	.05
(76)	Kirt Manwaring	.05
(77)	Kevin Mitchell	.05
(78)	Donell Nixon	.05
(79)	Rick Reuschel	.05
(80)	Ernest Riles	.05
(81)	Don Robinson	.05
(82)	Chris Speier	.05
(83)	Robby Thompson	.05
(84)	Jose Uribe	.05
(85)	Juan Agosto	.05
(86)	Larry Andersen	.05
(87)	Kevin Bass	.05
(88)	Craig Biggio	.05
(89)	Ken Caminiti	.05
(90)	Jim Clancy	.05
(91)	Danny Darwin	.05
(92)	Glenn Davis	.05
(93)	Jim Deshaies	.05
(94)	Bill Doran	.05
(95)	Bob Forsch	.05
(96)	Billy Hatcher	.05
(97)	Bob Knepper	.05
(98)	Terry Puhl	.05
(99)	Rafael Ramirez	.05
(100)	Craig Reynolds	.05
(101)	Rick Rhoden	.05
(102)	Mike Scott	.05
(103)	Dave Smith	.05
(104)	Alex Trevino	.05
(105)	Gerald Young	.05
(106)	Jose Alvarez	.05
(107)	Paul Assenmacher	.05
(108)	Bruce Benedict	.05
(109)	Jeff Blauser	.05
(110)	Joe Boever	.05
(111)	Jody Davis	.05
(112)	Darrell Evans	.05
(113)	Ron Gant	.05
(114)	Tommy Gregg	.05
(115)	Dion James	.05
(116)	Derek Lilliquist	.05
(117)	Dale Murphy	.20
(118)	Gerald Perry	.05
(119)	Charlie Puleo	.05
(120)	John Russell	.05
(121)	Lonnie Smith	.05
(122)	Pete Smith	.05
(123)	Zane Smith	.05
(124)	John Smoltz	.05
(125)	Bruce Sutter	.20
(126)	Andres Thomas	.05
(127)	Rick Aguilera	.05
(128)	Gary Carter	.60
(129)	David Cone	.05
(130)	Ron Darling	.05
(131)	Lenny Dykstra	.05
(132)	Kevin Elster	.05
(133)	Sid Fernandez	.05
(134)	Dwight Gooden	.05
(135)	Keith Hernandez	.05
(136)	Gregg Jefferies	.05
(137)	Howard Johnson	.05
(138)	Dave Magadan	.05
(139)	Lee Mazzilli	.05
(140)	Roger McDowell	.05
(141)	Kevin McReynolds	.05
(142)	Randy Myers	.05
(143)	Bob Ojeda	.05
(144)	Mackey Sasser	.05
(145)	Darryl Strawberry	.05
(146)	Tim Teufel	.05
(147)	Mookie Wilson	.05
(148)	Rafael Belliard	.05
(149)	Barry Bonds	1.50
(150)	Bobby Bonilla	.05
(151)	Sid Bream	.05
(152)	Benny Distefano	.05
(153)	Doug Drabek	.05
(154)	Brian Fisher	.05
(155)	Jim Gott	.05
(156)	Neal Heaton	.05
(157)	Bill Landrum	.05
(158)	Mike LaValliere	.05
(159)	Jose Lind	.05
(160)	Junior Ortiz	.05
(161)	Tom Prince	.05
(162)	Gary Redus	.05
(163)	R.J. Reynolds	.05
(164)	Jeff Robinson	.05
(165)	John Smiley	.05
(166)	Andy Van Slyke	.05
(167)	Bob Walk	.05
(168)	Glenn Wilson	.05
(169)	Hubie Brooks	.05
(170)	Tim Burke	.05
(171)	Mike Fitzgerald	.05
(172)	Tom Foley	.05
(173)	Andres Galarraga	.05
(174)	Kevin Gross	.05
(175)	Joe Hesketh	.05
(176)	Brian Holman	.05
(177)	Rex Hudler	.05
(178)	Wallace Johnson	.05
(179)	Mark Langston	.05
(180)	Dave Martinez	.05
(181)	Dennis Martinez	.05
(182)	Andy McGaffigan	.05
(183)	Otis Nixon	.05
(184)	Spike Owen	.05
(185)	Pascual Perez	.05
(186)	Tim Raines	.05
(187)	Nelson Santovenia	.05
(188)	Bryn Smith	.05
(189)	Tim Wallach	.05
(190)	Damon Berryhill	.05
(191)	Mike Bielecki	.05
(192)	Andre Dawson	.20
(193)	Shawon Dunston	.05
(194)	Mark Grace	.05
(195)	Darrin Jackson	.05
(196)	Paul Kilgus	.05
(197)	Vance Law	.05
(198)	Greg Maddux	.75
(199)	Pat Perry	.05
(200)	Jeff Pico	.05
(201)	Ryne Sandberg	.75
(202)	Scott Sanderson	.05
(203)	Calvin Schiraldi	.05
(204)	Dwight Smith	.05
(205)	Rick Sutcliffe	.05
(206)	Gary Varsho	.05
(207)	Jerome Walton	.05
(208)	Mitch Webster	.05
(209)	Curtis Wilkerson	.05
(210)	Mitch Williams	.05
(211)	Tom Brunansky	.05
(212)	Cris Carpenter	.05
(213)	Vince Coleman	.05
(214)	John Costello	.05
(215)	Danny Cox	.05
(216)	Ken Dayley	.05
(217)	Jose DeLeon	.05
(218)	Frank DiPino	.05
(219)	Pedro Guerrero	.05
(220)	Joe Magrane	.05
(221)	Greg Mathews	.05
(222)	Willie McGee	.05
(223)	Jose Oquendo	.05
(224)	Tom Pagnozzi	.05
(225)	Tony Pena	.05
(226)	Terry Pendleton	.05
(227)	Dan Quisenberry	.05
(228)	Ozzie Smith	.75
(229)	Scott Terry	.05
(230)	Milt Thompson	.05
(231)	Todd Worrell	.05
(232)	Steve Bedrosian	.05
(233)	Don Carman	.05
(234)	Darren Daulton	.05
(235)	Bob Dernier	.05
(236)	Marvin Freeman	.05
(237)	Greg Harris	.05
(238)	Von Hayes	.05
(239)	Tommy Herr	.05
(240)	Ken Howell	.05
(241)	Chris James	.05
(242)	Steve Jeltz	.05
(243)	Ron Jones	.05
(244)	Ricky Jordan	.05
(245)	Steve Lake	.05
(246)	Mike Maddux	.05
(247)	Larry McWilliams	.05
(248)	Jeff Parrett	.05
(249)	Juan Samuel	.05
(250)	Mike Schmidt	.85
(251)	Dickie Thon	.05
(252)	Floyd Youmans	.05
(253)	Bobby Bonilla/AS	.05
(254)	Will Clark/AS	.05
(255)	Eric Davis/AS	.05
(256)	Andre Dawson/AS	.05
(257)	Bill Doran/AS	.05
(258)	John Franco/AS	.05
(259)	Kirk Gibson/AS	.05
(260)	Dwight Gooden/AS	.05
(261)	Tony Gwynn/AS	.35
(262)	Keith Hernandez/AS	.05
(263)	Orel Hershiser/AS	.05
(264)	Danny Jackson/AS	.05
(265)	Howard Johnson/AS	.05
(266)	Barry Larkin/AS	.05
(267)	Joe Magrane/AS	.05
(268)	Kevin McReynolds/AS	.05
(269)	Tony Pena/AS	.05
(270)	Ryne Sandberg/AS	.35
(271)	Benito Santiago/AS	.05
(272)	Ozzie Smith/AS	.35
(273)	Darryl Strawberry/AS	.05
(274)	Todd Worrell/AS	.05
(275)	Harold Baines/AS	.05
(276)	George Bell/AS	.05
(277)	Wade Boggs/AS	.35
(278)	Bob Boone/AS	.05
(279)	Jose Canseco/AS	.20
(280)	Joe Carter/AS	.05
(281)	Roger Clemens/AS	.40
(282)	Dennis Eckersley/AS	.25
(283)	Tony Fernandez/AS	.05
(284)	Carlton Fisk/AS	.30
(285)	Julio Franco/AS	.05
(286)	Gary Gaetti/AS	.05
(287)	Mike Greenwell/AS	.05
(288)	Rickey Henderson/AS	.30
(289)	Kent Hrbek/AS	.05
(290)	Don Mattingly/AS	.40
(291)	Kirby Puckett/AS	.35
(292)	Jeff Reardon/AS	.05
(293)	Harold Reynolds/AS	.05
(294)	Dave Stewart/AS	.05
(295)	Alan Trammell/AS	.05
(296)	Frank Viola/AS	.05
(297)	Dave Winfield/AS	.30
(298)	Todd Burns	.05
(299)	Greg Cadaret	.05
(300)	Jose Canseco	.30
(301)	Storm Davis	.05
(302)	Dennis Eckersley	.45
(303)	Mike Gallego	.05
(304)	Ron Hassey	.05
(305)	Dave Henderson	.05
(306)	Rick Honeycutt	.05
(307)	Stan Javier	.05
(308)	Carney Lansford	.05
(309)	Mark McGwire	1.25
(310)	Mike Moore	.05
(311)	Dave Parker	.05
(312)	Eric Plunk	.05
(313)	Luis Polonia	.05
(314)	Terry Steinbach	.05
(315)	Dave Stewart	.05
(316)	Walt Weiss	.05
(317)	Bob Welch	.05
(318)	Curt Young	.05
(319)	Allan Anderson	.05
(320)	Wally Backman	.05
(321)	Doug Baker	.05
(322)	Juan Berenguer	.05
(323)	Randy Bush	.05
(324)	Jim Dwyer	.05
(325)	Gary Gaetti	.05
(326)	Greg Gagne	.05
(327)	Dan Gladden	.05
(328)	Brian Harper	.05
(329)	Kent Hrbek	.05
(330)	Gene Larkin	.05
(331)	Tim Laudner	.05
(332)	John Moses	.05
(333)	Al Newman	.05
(334)	Kirby Puckett	.75
(335)	Shane Rawley	.05
(336)	Jeff Reardon	.05
(337)	Steve Shields	.05
(338)	Frank Viola	.05
(339)	Gary Wayne	.05
(340)	Luis Aquino	.05
(341)	Floyd Bannister	.05
(342)	Bob Boone	.05
(343)	George Brett	.85
(344)	Bill Buckner	.05
(345)	Jim Eisenreich	.05
(346)	Steve Farr	.05
(347)	Tom Gordon	.05
(348)	Mark Gubicza	.05
(349)	Bo Jackson	.10
(350)	Charlie Leibrandt	.05
(351)	Mike Macfarlane	.05
(352)	Jeff Montgomery	.05
(353)	Bret Saberhagen	.05
(354)	Kevin Seitzer	.05
(355)	Kurt Stillwell	.05
(356)	Pat Tabler	.05
(357)	Danny Tartabull	.05
(358)	Gary Thurman	.05
(359)	Frank White	.05
(360)	Willie Wilson	.05
(361)	Jim Abbott	.05
(362)	Kent Anderson	.05
(363)	Tony Armas	.05
(364)	Dante Bichette	.05
(365)	Bert Blyleven	.05
(366)	Chili Davis	.05
(367)	Brian Downing	.05
(368)	Chuck Finley	.05
(369)	Willie Fraser	.05
(370)	Jack Howell	.05
(371)	Wally Joyner	.05
(372)	Kirk McCaskill	.05
(373)	Bob McClure	.05
(374)	Greg Minton	.05
(375)	Lance Parrish	.05
(376)	Dan Petry	.05
(377)	Johnny Ray	.05
(378)	Dick Schofield	.05
(379)	Claudell Washington	.05
(380)	Devon White	.05
(381)	Mike Witt	.05
(382)	Harold Baines	.05
(383)	Daryl Boston	.05
(384)	Ivan Calderon	.05
(385)	Carlton Fisk	.60
(386)	Dave Gallagher	.05
(387)	Ozzie Guillen	.05
(388)	Shawn Hillegas	.05
(389)	Barry Jones	.05
(390)	Ron Karkovice	.05
(391)	Eric King	.05
(392)	Ron Kittle	.05
(393)	Bill Long	.05
(394)	Steve Lyons	.05
(395)	Fred Manrique	.05
(396)	Donn Pall	.05
(397)	Dan Pasqua	.05
(398)	Melido Perez	.05
(399)	Jerry Reuss	.05
(400)	Bobby Thigpen	.05
(401)	Greg Walker	.05
(402)	Eddie Williams	.05
(403)	Buddy Bell	.05
(404)	Kevin Brown	.05
(405)	Steve Buechele	.05
(406)	Cecil Espy	.05
(407)	Scott Fletcher	.05
(408)	Julio Franco	.05
(409)	Cecilio Guante	.05
(410)	Jose Guzman	.05
(411)	Charlie Hough	.05
(412)	Pete Incaviglia	.05
(413)	Chad Kreuter	.05
(414)	Jeff Kunkel	.05
(415)	Rick Leach	.05
(416)	Jamie Moyer	.05
(417)	Rafael Palmeiro	.50
(418)	Geno Petralli	.05
(419)	Jeff Russell	.05
(420)	Nolan Ryan	1.50
(421)	Ruben Sierra	.05
(422)	Jim Sundberg	.05
(423)	Bobby Witt	.05
(424)	Steve Balboni	.05
(425)	Scott Bankhead	.05
(426)	Scott Bradley	.05
(427)	Mickey Brantley	.05
(428)	Darnell Coles	.05
(429)	Henry Cotto	.05
(430)	Alvin Davis	.05
(431)	Mario Diaz	.05
(432)	Ken Griffey Jr.	1.00
(433)	Erik Hanson	.05
(434)	Mike Jackson	.05
(435)	Jeffrey Leonard	.05
(436)	Edgar Martinez	.05
(437)	Tom Niedenfuer	.05
(438)	Jim Presley	.05
(439)	Jerry Reed	.05
(440)	Harold Reynolds	.05
(441)	Bill Swift	.05
(442)	Steve Trout	.05
(443)	Dave Valle	.05
(444)	Omar Vizquel	.05
(445)	Marty Barrett	.05
(446)	Mike Boddicker	.05
(447)	Wade Boggs	.75
(448)	Dennis "Oil Can" Boyd	.05
(449)	Ellis Burks	.05
(450)	Rick Cerone	.05
(451)	Roger Clemens	.85
(452)	Nick Esasky	.05
(453)	Dwight Evans	.05
(454)	Wes Gardner	.05
(455)	Rich Gedman	.05
(456)	Mike Greenwell	.05
(457)	Sam Horn	.05
(458)	Randy Kutcher	.05
(459)	Dennis Lamp	.05
(460)	Rob Murphy	.05
(461)	Jody Reed	.05
(462)	Jim Rice	.10
(463)	Lee Smith	.05
(464)	Mike Smithson	.05
(465)	Bob Stanley	.05
(466)	Doyle Alexander	.05
(467)	Dave Bergman	.05
(468)	Chris Brown	.05
(469)	Paul Gibson	.05
(470)	Mike Heath	.05
(471)	Mike Henneman	.05
(472)	Guillermo Hernandez	.05
(473)	Charles Hudson	.05
(474)	Chet Lemon	.05
(475)	Fred Lynn	.05
(476)	Keith Moreland	.05
(477)	Jack Morris	.05
(478)	Matt Nokes	.05
(479)	Gary Pettis	.05
(480)	Jeff Robinson	.05
(481)	Pat Sheridan	.05
(482)	Frank Tanana	.05
(483)	Alan Trammell	.05
(484)	Lou Whitaker	.05
(485)	Frank Williams	.05
(486)	Kenny Williams	.05
(487)	Don August	.05
(488)	Mike Birkbeck	.05
(489)	Chris Bosio	.05
(490)	Glenn Braggs	.05
(491)	Greg Brock	.05
(492)	Chuck Crim	.05
(493)	Rob Deer	.05
(494)	Mike Felder	.05
(495)	Jim Gantner	.05
(496)	Ted Higuera	.05
(497)	Joey Meyer	.05
(498)	Paul Mirabella	.05
(499)	Paul Molitor	.60
(500)	Juan Nieves	.05
(501)	Charlie O'Brien	.05
(502)	Dan Plesac	.05
(503)	Gary Sheffield	.30
(504)	B.J. Surhoff	.05
(505)	Dale Sveum	.05
(506)	Bill Wegman	.05
(507)	Robin Yount	.60
(508)	George Bell	.05
(509)	Pat Borders	.05
(510)	John Cerutti	.05
(511)	Rob Ducey	.05
(512)	Tony Fernandez	.05
(513)	Mike Flanagan	.05
(514)	Kelly Gruber	.05
(515)	Tom Henke	.05
(516)	Alexis Infante	.05
(517)	Jimmy Key	.05
(518)	Tom Lawless	.05
(519)	Manny Lee	.05
(520)	Al Leiter	.05
(521)	Nelson Liriano	.05
(522)	Fred McGriff	.05
(523)	Lloyd Moseby	.05
(524)	Rance Mulliniks	.05
(525)	Dave Steib	.05
(526)	Todd Stottlemyre	.05
(527)	Duane Ward	.05
(528)	Ernie Whitt	.05
(529)	Jesse Barfield	.05
(530)	Bob Brower	.05
(531)	John Candelaria	.05
(532)	Richard Dotson	.05
(533)	Lee Guetterman	.05
(534)	Mel Hall	.05
(535)	Andy Hawkins	.05
(536)	Rickey Henderson	.60
(537)	Roberto Kelly	.05
(538)	Dave LaPoint	.05
(539)	Don Mattingly	.85
(540)	Lance McCullers	.05
(541)	Mike Pagliarulo	.05
(542)	Clay Parker	.05
(543)	Ken Phelps	.05
(544)	Dave Righetti	.05
(545)	Rafael Santana	.05
(546)	Steve Sax	.05
(547)	Don Slaught	.05
(548)	Wayne Tolleson	.05
(549)	Dave Winfield	.60
(550)	Andy Allanson	.05
(551)	Keith Atherton	.05
(552)	Scott Bailes	.05
(553)	Bud Black	.05
(554)	Jerry Browne	.05
(555)	Tom Candiotti	.05
(556)	Joe Carter	.05
(557)	David Clark	.05
(558)	John Farrell	.05
(559)	Felix Fermin	.05
(560)	Brook Jacoby	.05
(561)	Doug Jones	.05
(562)	Oddibe McDowell	.05
(563)	Luis Medina	.05
(564)	Pete O'Brien	.05
(565)	Jesse Orosco	.05
(566)	Joel Skinner	.05
(567)	Cory Snyder	.05
(568)	Greg Swindell	.05
(569)	Rich Yett	.05
(570)	Mike Young	.05
(571)	Brady Anderson	.05

(573)	Jeff Ballard	.05
(574)	Jose Bautista	.05
(575)	Phil Bradley	.05
(576)	Mike Devereaux	.05
(577)	Kevin Hickey	.05
(578)	Brian Holton	.05
(579)	Bob Melvin	.05
(580)	Bob Milacki	.05
(581)	Gregg Olson	.05
(582)	Joe Orsulak	.05
(583)	Bill Ripken	.05
(584)	Cal Ripken Jr.	1.50
(585)	Dave Schmidt	.05
(586)	Larry Sheets	.05
(587)	Mickey Tettleton	.05
(588)	Mark Thurmond	.05
(589)	Jay Tibbs	.05
(590)	Jim Traber	.05
(591)	Mark Williamson	.05
(592)	Craig Worthington	.05
(593)	Allan Anderson	.05
(594)	Ellis Burks	.05
(595)	Ken Griffey Jr.	1.00
(596)	Bo Jackson	.05
(597)	Roberto Kelly	.05
(598)	Kirk McCaskill	.05
(599)	Fred McGriff	.05
(600)	Mark McGwire	1.25
(601)	Bob Milacki	.05
(602)	Melido Perez	.05
(603)	Jeff Robinson	.05
(604)	Gary Sheffield	.05
(605)	Ruben Sierra	.05
(606)	Greg Swindell	.05
(607)	Roberto Alomar	.15
(608)	Tim Belcher	.05
(609)	Vince Coleman	.05
(610)	Kal Daniels	.05
(611)	Andres Galarraga	.05
(612)	Ron Gant	.05
(613)	Mark Grace	.05
(614)	Gregg Jefferies	.05
(615)	Ricky Jordan	.05
(616)	Jose Lind	.05
(617)	Kevin Mitchell	.05
(618)	Gerald Young	.05
(619)	Base	.05
(620)	Batting Helmets	.05
(621)	Bats	.05
(622)	Batting Gloves	.05
(623)	Los Angeles Dodgers	.05
(624)	Cincinnati Reds	.05
(625)	San Diego Padres	.05
(626)	San Francisco Giants	.05
(627)	Houston Astros	.05
(628)	Atlanta Braves	.05
(629)	New York Mets	.05
(630)	Pittsburgh Pirates	.05
(631)	Montreal Expos	.05
(632)	Chicago Cubs	.05
(633)	St. Louis Cardinals	.05
(634)	Philadelphia Phillies	.05
(635)	Oakland A's	.05
(636)	Minnesota Twins	.05
(637)	Kansas City Royals	.05
(638)	California Angels	.05
(639)	Chicago White Sox	.05
(640)	Texas Rangers	.05
(641)	Seattle Mariners	.05
(642)	Boston Red Sox	.05
(643)	Detroit Tigers	.05
(644)	Milwaukee Brewers	.05
(645)	Toronto Blue Jays	.05
(646)	New York Yankees	.05
(647)	Cleveland Indians	.05
(648)	Baltimore Orioles	.05

Hottest Players Stickers

Established major league stars are featured in this set of large-format (4-1/8" x 5-7/16") blank-back stickers. The stickers are printed four per sheet and were sold with a 36-page album for mounting. The album has player data, stats and highlights for each of the stars. Stickers have color action photos with a white frame at center. There is a red stripe at top of the frame and a blue stripe at bottom, which contains the player name. The unnumbered stickers are checklisted here in alphabetical order.

		NM/M
Complete Set, W/Album (56):		4.00
Common Player:		.05

(1)	George Bell	.05
(2)	Wade Boggs	.50
(3)	Bobby Bonilla	.05
(4)	Jose Canseco	.25
(5)	Joe Carter	.05
(6)	Will Clark	.05
(7)	Roger Clemens	.60
(8)	Alvin Davis	.05
(9)	Eric Davis	.05
(10)	Glenn Davis	.05
(11)	Mark Davis	.05
(12)	Carlton Fisk	.35
(13)	John Franco	.05
(14)	Gary Gaetti	.05
(15)	Andres Galarraga	.05
(16)	Dwight Gooden	.05
(17)	Mark Grace	.05
(18)	Pedro Guerrero	.05
(19)	Tony Gwynn	.50
(20)	Rickey Henderson	.35
(21)	Orel Hershiser	.05
(22)	Bo Jackson	.05
(23)	Ricky Jordan	.05
(24)	Wally Joyner	.05
(25)	Don Mattingly	.60
(26)	Fred McGriff	.05
(27)	Kevin Mitchell	.05
(28)	Paul Molitor	.35
(29)	Dale Murphy	.25
(30)	Eddie Murray	.35
(31)	Kirby Puckett	.50
(32)	Tim Raines	.05
(33)	Harold Reynolds	.05
(34)	Cal Ripken Jr.	1.00
(35)	Nolan Ryan	1.00
(36)	Bret Saberhagen	.05
(37)	Ryne Sandberg	.50
(38)	Steve Sax	.05
(39)	Mike Scott	.05
(40)	Ruben Sierra	.05
(41)	Ozzie Smith	.50
(42)	John Smoltz	.05
(43)	Darryl Strawberry	.05
(44)	Greg Swindell	.05
(45)	Mickey Tettleton	.05
(46)	Alan Trammell	.05
(47)	Andy Van Slyke	.05
(48)	Lou Whitaker	.05
(49)	Devon White	.05
(50)	Robin Yount	.35
(51)	Dodger Stadium	.05
(52)	Jack Murphy Stadium	.05
(53)	Shea Stadium	.05
(54)	Three Rivers Stadium	.05
(55)	Tiger Stadium	.05
(56)	Yankee Stadium	.05

Hottest Rookies Stickers

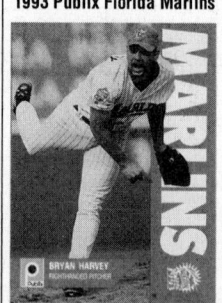

This set of large-format (4-1/8" x 5-7/16") stickers features the rookie crop of 1990 along with other young players who were not technically rookies in 1990. The stickers were sold four per sheet in complete sets which included a 36-page color album to mount the stamps. The album pages have personal data, career stats and highlights about each player. On the stickers, each action photo has a central frame in white with a blue stripe at top and a red stripe at bottom bearing the player name. Backs are, of course, blank. The set is checklisted here alphabetically.

		NM/M
Complete Set, W/Album (56):		4.00
Common Player:		.05

(1)	Jim Abbott	.05
(2)	Sandy Alomar	.05
(3)	Kent Anderson	.05
(4)	Eric Anthony	.05
(5)	Jeff Ballard	.05
(6)	Joey Belle	.15
(7)	Andy Benes	.05
(8)	Lance Blankenship	.05
(9)	Jeff Brantley	.05
(10)	Cris Carpenter	.05
(11)	Mark Carreon	.05
(12)	Dennis Cook	.05
(13)	Scott Coolbaugh	.05
(14)	Luis de los Santos	.05
(15)	Junior Felix	.05
(16)	Mark Gardner	.05
(17)	German Gonzalez	.05
(18)	Tom Gordon	.05
(19)	Ken Griffey Jr.	2.00
(20)	Marquis Grissom	.05
(21)	Charlie Hayes	.05
(22)	Gregg Jefferies	.05
(23)	Randy Johnson	1.00
(24)	Felix Jose	.05
(25)	Jeff King	.05
(26)	Randy Kramer	.05
(27)	Derek Lilliquist	.05
(28)	Greg Litton	.05
(29)	Kelly Mann	.05
(30)	Ramon Martinez	.05
(31)	Luis Medina	.05
(32)	Hal Morris	.05
(33)	Joe Oliver	.05
(34)	Gregg Olson	.05
(35)	Dean Palmer	.05
(36)	Carlos Quintana	.05
(37)	Kevin Ritz	.05
(38)	Deion Sanders	.05
(39)	Scott Scudder	.05
(40)	Steve Searcy	.05
(41)	Gary Sheffield	.05
(42)	Dwight Smith	.05
(43)	Sam Sosa	1.50
(44)	Greg Vaughn	.05
(45)	Robin Ventura	.05
(46)	Jerome Walton	.05
(47)	Dave West	.05
(48)	John Wetteland	.05
(49)	Eric Yelding	.05
(50)	Todd Zeile	.05
(51)	Dodger Stadium	.05
(52)	Jack Murphy Stadium	.05
(53)	Shea Stadium	.05
(54)	Three Rivers Stadium	.05
(55)	Tiger Stadium	.05
(56)	Yankee Stadium	.05

1993 Publix Florida Marlins

		NM/M
Complete Set (29):		10.00
Common Player:		.50

6	Rich Renteria	.50
8	Bret Barbarie	.50
09	Benito Santiago	.50
10	Gary Sheffield	1.50
11	Chris Hammond	.50
13	Bob Natal	.50
15	Rene Lachemann	.50
17	Darrell Whitmore	.50
19	Jeff Conine	.50
20	Greg Briley	.50
21	Chuck Carr	.50
22	Walt Weiss	.50
25	Richie Lewis	.50
26	Alex Arias	.50
27	Luis Aquino	.50
29	Henry Cotto	.50
30	Nigel Wilson	.50
31	Robb Nen	.50
34	Bryan Harvey	.50
39	Orestes Destrade	.50
42	Rich Rodriguez	.50
46	Ryan Bowen	.50
48	Pat Rapp	.50
49	Charlie Hough	.50
55	Matt Turner	.50
58	Joe Klink	.50
77	Jack Armstrong	.50
---	Marlins Coaches (Marcel Lachemann, Doug Rader, Vada Pinson, Frank Reberger, Cookie Rojas)	.50
---	Billy (Mascot)	.50
---	$1 Coke-Publix Coupon	.50

Q

1986 Quaker Oats

The Quaker Co., in conjunction with Topps, produced this 33-card set of current basebAll-Stars for packaging in groups of three in Chewy Granola Bars packages. The cards are noted as the "1st Annual Collectors Edition." They are numbered and measure 2-1/2" x 3-1/2." Card fronts feature full-color player photos with the product name at the top and the player name, team

and position below the photo. The complete set was offered via mail order by the Quaker Company.

		NM/M
Complete Set (33):		4.00
Common Player:		.05

1	Willie McGee	.05
2	Dwight Gooden	.05
3	Vince Coleman	.05
4	Gary Carter	.50
5	Jack Clark	.05
6	Steve Garvey	.15
7	Tony Gwynn	.65
8	Dale Murphy	.25
9	Dave Parker	.05
10	Tim Raines	.05
11	Pete Rose	1.00
12	Nolan Ryan	1.50
13	Ryne Sandberg	.65
14	Mike Schmidt	.75
15	Ozzie Smith	.65
16	Darryl Strawberry	.05
17	Fernando Valenzuela	.05
18	Don Mattingly	.75
19	Bret Saberhagen	.05
20	Ozzie Guillen	.05
21	Bert Blyleven	.05
22	Wade Boggs	.65
23	George Brett	.75
24	Darrell Evans	.05
25	Rickey Henderson	.75
26	Reggie Jackson	.75
27	Eddie Murray	.50
28	Phil Niekro	.25
29	Dan Quisenberry	.05
30	Jim Rice	.15
31	Cal Ripken, Jr.	1.50
32	Tom Seaver	.65
33	Dave Winfield	.65
----	Offer Card	.03

R

1993 Rainbow Foods Dave Winfield

Dave Winfield's return to Minnesota where he excelled in college sports was marked by the "Homecoming Collection," tracing the future Hall of Famer's career. The 2-1/2" x 3-1/2" cards have black-and-white or color photos on front and back. Each side also sports a special logo identifying the issue. Rainbow's logo appears on front, while that of a major food brand such as Kraft or Oscar Mayer appear on back, along with information about Winfield's career. Cards were sold in five-card packs with four blue-bordered cards and one gold-bordered parallel card.

		NM/M
Complete Set, Blue (10):		7.50
Common Player, Blue:		1.00
Gold:		2-3X

1	Dave Winfield (University of Minnesota Outfielder)	1.00
2	Dave Winfield (University of Minnesota Pitcher)	1.00
3	Dave Winfield (University of Minnesota BasketbAll-Star)	1.00
4	Dave Winfield (San Diego Padres 1973-1980)	1.00
5	Dave Winfield (N.Y. Yankees 1981-1990)	1.00
6	Dave Winfield (California Angels 1990-1991)	1.00
7	Dave Winfield (Toronto Blue Jays 1992)	1.00
8	Dave Winfield (Minnesota Twins 1993-)	1.00
9	Dave Winfield (7-time Gold Glove Winner)	1.00
10	Dave Winfield (Pride of Minnesota)	1.00

2001 Rainbow Foods Minnesota Twins 10th Anniversary

As part of a three-game celebration of the 10th annivsary of the Twins 1991 World's Championship, Rainbow Foods sponsored a team-card giveaway on June 29, distributing 10,000 sets. Fronts of the 2-1/2" x 3-1/2" cards have borderless game-action photos with an anniversary logo. Backs have team and sponsor logos and player career highlights on a baseball diamond design in color. The unnumbered cards are checklisted here in alphabetical order.

		NM/M
Complete Set (26):		9.00
Common Player:		.25

(1)	Rick Aguilera	.25
(2)	Steve Bedrosian	.25
(3)	Jarvis Brown	.25
(4)	Randy Bush	.25
(5)	Chili Davis	.25
(6)	Scott Erickson	.25
(7)	Greg Gagne	.25
(8)	Dan Gladden	.25
(9)	Mark Guthrie	.25
(10)	Brian Harper	.25
(11)	Kent Hrbek	.50
(12)	Tom Kelly	.25
(13)	Chuck Knoblauch	.25
(14)	Gene Larkin	.25
(15)	Terry Leach	.25
(16)	Scott Leius	.25
(17)	Shane Mack	.25
(18)	Jack Morris	.25
(19)	Al Newman	.25
(20)	Junior Ortiz	.25
(21)	Mike Pagliarulo	.25
(22)	Kirby Puckett	5.00
(23)	Paul Sorrento	.25
(24)	Kevin Tapani	.25
(25)	Dave West	.25
(26)	Carl Willis	.25

1989 Rainier Farms Super Stars Discs

This set is one of the scarcer late-1980s disc issues produced by Michael Schechter Associates for various local businesses. The bakery began distribution of the discs by placing them directly in the cello wrapper with a loaf of bread. This resulted in those cards being severely grease stained and often creased. It also resulted in problems with public health officials who halted the distribution. Since the bakery could not economically and sanitarily package the cards they dropped the promotion and sold the remainder cards into the hobby. Discs measure 2-3/4" in diameter and feature a color player photo (with team logos airbrushed away) at center with a white border. A Rainier Farms Homestyle logo is at top in red and black. Backs are printed in dark blue and feature a few stats, biographical details and a card number.

		NM/M
Complete Set (20):		15.00
Common Player:		.60

1	Wally Joyner	.60
2	Wade Boggs	2.25
3	Ozzie Smith	2.25
4	Don Mattingly	2.50
5	Jose Canseco	1.25
6	Tony Gwynn	2.25
7	Eric Davis	.60
8	Kirby Puckett	2.25
9	Kevin Seitzer	.60
10	Darryl Strawberry	.60
11	Gregg Jefferies	.60
12	Mark Grace	.60
13	Matt Nokes	.60
14	Mark McGwire	3.50
15	Bobby Bonilla	.60
16	Roger Clemens	2.50
17	Frank Viola	.60
18	Orel Hershiser	.60
19	Dave Cone	.60
20	Kirk Gibson	.60

1984 Ralston Purina

This set, produced by Topps, features the game's top players. Photos on the 2-1/2" x 3-1/2" cards are all close-up poses. Topps' logo appears only on the card fronts, and the backs are completely different from Topps' regular issue of 1984, featuring a checkerboard look, coinciding with the well-known Ralston Purina logo. Cards are numbered with odd numbers for American Leaguers and even numbered cards for National Leaguers. Four cards were packed in boxes of Cookie Crisp and Donkey Kong Junior brand cereals, and the complete set was available via a mail-in offer in panel form.

		NM/M
Complete Set, Singles (33):		4.00
Complete Set, Panel:		4.00
Common Player:		.05

1	Eddie Murray	.25
2	Ozzie Smith	.35
3	Ted Simmons	.05
4	Pete Rose	.75
5	Greg Luzinski	.05
6	Andre Dawson	.15
7	Dave Winfield	.25
8	Tom Seaver	.25
9	Jim Rice	.15
10	Fernando Valenzuela	.05
11	Wade Boggs	.35
12	Dale Murphy	.15
13	George Brett	.50
14	Nolan Ryan	1.00
15	Rickey Henderson	.25
16	Steve Carlton	.25
17	Rod Carew	.25
18	Steve Garvey	.15
19	Reggie Jackson	.50
20	Dave Concepcion	.05
21	Robin Yount	.25
22	Mike Schmidt	.50
23	Jim Palmer	.25
24	Bruce Sutter	.20
25	Dan Quisenberry	.05
26	Bill Madlock	.05
27	Cecil Cooper	.05
28	Gary Carter	.25
29	Fred Lynn	.05
30	Pedro Guerrero	.05
31	Ron Guidry	.15
32	Keith Hernandez	.05
33	Carlton Fisk	.25

1987 Ralston Purina

Ralston Purina, in conjunction with Mike Schechter Associates, issued this set in specially marked boxes of Cookie Crisp and Honey Graham Chex. Three cards, wrapped in cellophane, were inserted in each box. Fronts contain a full-color photo with the team insignia airbrushed away. Above the photo are two yellow crossed bats and a star, with the player's uniform number inside the star. Backs are gray with red printing and contain personal information and career major league statistics. As part of the promotion, the company advertised an uncut sheet of cards which was available by finding an "instant-winner" game card or sending $1 plus two non-winning cards. Cards on the uncut sheet are identical in design to the single cards, save the omission of the words "1987 Collectors' Edition" in the upper-right corner.

	NM/M
Complete Set (15):	7.50
Common Player:	.25
1 Nolan Ryan	1.50
2 Steve Garvey	.35
3 Wade Boggs	.65
4 Dave Winfield	.50
5 Don Mattingly	.75
6 Don Sutton	.35
7 Dave Parker	.25
8 Eddie Murray	.50
9 Gary Carter	.50
10 Roger Clemens	.75
11 Fernando Valenzuela	.25
12 Cal Ripken Jr.	1.50
13 Ozzie Smith	.65
14 Mike Schmidt	.75
15 Ryne Sandberg	.65

Collectors' Sheet

Cards obtained from the mail-in redemption uncut sheet offer are identical to the cereal-box insert versions except that they lack the "1987 / COLLECTORS' / EDITION" legend at top-right.

	NM/M
Complete Panel:	8.00
Complete Singles Set (15):	5.00
Common Single Player:	.15
1 Nolan Ryan	1.00
2 Steve Garvey	.25
3 Wade Boggs	.50
4 Dave Winfield	.40
5 Don Mattingly	.65
6 Don Sutton	.30
7 Dave Parker	.15
8 Eddie Murray	.40
9 Gary Carter	.40
10 Roger Clemens	.65
11 Fernando Valenzuela	.15
12 Cal Ripken Jr.	1.00
13 Ozzie Smith	.50
14 Mike Schmidt	.65
15 Ryne Sandberg	.50

1989 Ralston Purina

Ralston Purina, in conjunction with Mike Schechter Associates, issued this "Superstars" set in 1989. As part of a late-spring and early-summer promotion, the standard-size cards were inserted, two per box, in specially-marked boxes of Crisp Crunch, Honey Nut O's, Fruit Rings and Frosted Flakes in most parts of the country. Ads on cereal boxes also offered complete sets through a mail-in offer. Fronts feature player portraits flanked by stars in all four corners. Backs include stats and player data. Team logos have been removed from the photos.

	NM/M
Complete Set (12):	3.00
Common Player:	.10
1 Ozzie Smith	.75
2 Andre Dawson	.20
3 Darryl Strawberry	.10
4 Mike Schmidt	1.00
5 Orel Hershiser	.10
6 Tim Raines	.10
7 Roger Clemens	1.00
8 Kirby Puckett	.75
9 George Brett	1.00
10 Alan Trammell	.10
11 Don Mattingly	1.00
12 Jose Canseco	.35

1990 Real Milk Mike Henneman

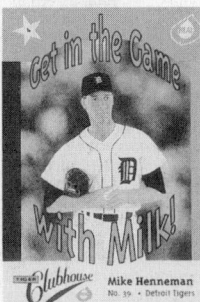

"Get in the Game" urges the headline on each of the cards in this collection featuring then-star Tiger relief pitcher Mike Henneman. The 2-1/2" x 3-1/2" cards have red, white and blue borders with a color photo at center. Backs are in red, black and white with Henneman's stats or career highlights. The set was available as a mail-in premium.

	NM/M
Complete Set (8):	6.00
Common Card:	.25
1 Mike Henneman (Drinking milk.)	2.00
2 Mike Henneman/Pitching	2.00
3 Mike Henneman (In jacket.)	2.00
4 Mike Henneman (Rubbing up ball.)	2.00
5 Milk Carton	.25
6 Hand Holding Carton	.25
-- Title Card	.25
-- Tiger Clubhouse Membership Card	.25

1990 Red Apple Mariners Pin/Cards

It is unknown whether the checklist presented here is complete. This combination promotional issue features a 2-1/2" x 3-13/16" baseball card separated by perforations from a 2-1/2" x 1-7/16" tab. The card portion has a color player photo with a large M's logo. The front of the tab is

HAROLD REYNOLDS 2B

THE NEW SEATTLE MARINERS

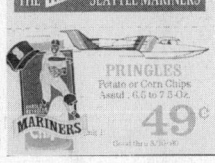

PRINGLES
Potato or Corn Chips
Asstd. 6.6 to 7.5 Oz.

49¢

a coupon for a food product. On back the card has a black-and-white portrait photo along with player data and career highlights. The back of the tab has a Red Apple Markets logo. Attached to the tab is a color enameled pin of the player in action.

	NM/M
Common Player:	5.00
(1) Alvin Davis	6.00
(2) Ken Griffey Jr.	12.00
(3) Harold Reynolds	6.00
(4) David Valle	5.00

1982 Red Lobster Cubs

#48 DICKIE NOLES RHP

This 28-card set was co-sponsored by the team and a seafood restaurant chain for distribution at a 1982 Cubs promotional game. Card fronts are unbordered color photos, with player name, number, position and a superimposed facsimile autograph. The set includes 25 players on the 2-1/4" x 3-1/2" cards, along with a card for manager Lee Elia, an unnumbered card for the coaching staff and a team picture. Card backs have complete player statistics and a Red Lobster ad. Production was reported to be 15,000 sets.

	NM/M
Complete Set (28):	60.00
Common Player:	.50
1 Larry Bowa	.50
4 Lee Elia	.50
6 Keith Moreland	.50
7 Jody Davis	.50
10 Leon Durham	.50
15 Junior Kennedy	.50
17 Bump Wills	.50
18 Scot Thompson	.50
21 Jay Johnstone	.50
22 Bill Buckner	.50
23 Ryne Sandberg	50.00
24 Jerry Morales	.50
25 Gary Woods	.50
28 Steve Henderson	.50
29 Bob Molinaro	.50
31 Fergie Jenkins	2.00
33 Al Ripley	.50
34 Randy Martz	.50
36 Mike Proly	.50
37 Ken Kravec	.50
38 Willie Hernandez	.50
39 Bill Campbell	.50
41 Dick Tidrow	.50
46 Lee Smith	1.00
47 Doug Bird	.50
48 Dickie Noles	.50
-- Team Photo	.50

1991 Retort Negro League Legends, Series 1

MAXWELL "MAX" MANNING

One of the most extensive collectors' issues featuring former Negro League players was issued over a two-year period by Robert Retort Enterprises. Sold only in a boxed set with accompanying history book, the premiere issue featured 65 individual players, plus game-action and team photos. Fronts of the 3-1/2" x 5-1/2" cards feature sepia photos with a sepia border. Player identification is in the bottom border. Postcard style backs specify the teams on which the player appeared, have a card number and a serial number from within the edition of 10,000 sets.

	NM/M
Complete Set (100):	35.00
Common Player:	.50
1 Otha Bailey	.50
2 Harry Barnes	.50
3 Gene Benson	.50
4 Bill Beverly	.50
5 Charlie Biot	.50
6 Bob Boyd	.65
7 Allen Bryant	.50
8 Marlin Carter	.50
9 Bill Cash	.50
10 Jim Cohen	.50
11 Elliott Coleman	.50
12 Johnnie Cowan	.50
13 Jimmie Crutchfield	.65
14 Saul Davis	.50
15 Piper Davis	.65
16 Leon Day	2.00
17 Lou Dials	.75
18 Mahlon Duckett	.50
19 Felix Evans	.50
20 Rudy Fernandez	.50
21 Joe Fillmore	.50
22 George Giles	.50
23 Louis Gillis	.50
24 Stanley Glenn	.50
25 Willie Grace	.50
26 Wiley Griggs	.50
27 Albert Haywood	.50
28 Jimmy Hill	.50
29 Cowan Hyde	.50
30 Monte Irvin	1.50
31 Sam Jethroe	1.00
32 Connie Johnson	.65
33 Josh Johnson	.50
34 Clinton Jones	.50
35 Larry Kimbrough	.50
36 Clarence King	.50
37 Jim LaMarque	.50
38 Buck Leonard	2.00
39 Max Manning	.50
40 Verdell Mathis	.50
41 Nath McClinic	.50
42 Clinton McCord	.50
43 Clyde McNeal	.50
44 John Miles	.50
45 Buck O'Neil	2.00
46 Frank Pearson	.50
47 Art Pennington	.75
48 Nathan Peoples	.50
49 Andy Porter	.50
50 Ted Radcliffe	.50
51 Chico Renfroe	.50
52 Bobby Robinson	.50
53 Tommy Sampson	.50
54 Joe Scott	.50
55 Joe Burt Scott	.50
56 Herb Simpson	.50
57 Lonnie Summers	.50
58 Alfred Surratt	.50
59 Bob Thurman	.50
60 Harold Tinker	.50
61 Quincy Trouppe	.75
62 Edsall Walker	.50
63 Al Wilmore	.50
64 Artie Wilson	.75

65	Jim Zapp	.50
66	Grays vs. Stars/1937	.50
67	Grays vs. Eagles/1943	.50
68	Homestead Grays/1944	.50
69	Grays vs. Cuban Stars/1944	.50
70	Grays vs. Cubans/1944	.50
71	Grays vs. Eagles/1945	.50
72	Eagles Pitching Staff/1941	.50
73	Buckeyes Infield/1945	.50
74	Homestead Grays/1948	.50
75	Chicago Murderers Row/1943	.50
76	Indianapolis Clowns/1945	.50
77	East All-Stars/1937	.50
78	East All-Stars/1938	.50
79	East All-Stars/1939	.50
80	East All-Stars/1948	.50
81	West All-Stars/1948	.50
82	Homestead Grays/1931	.50
83	Homestead Grays/1938	.50
84	Pittsburgh Crawfords/1936	.50
85	Kansas City Monarchs/1934	.50
86	Kansas City Monarchs/1949	.50
87	Chicago American Giants/1941	.50
88	Chicago American Giants/1947	.50
89	Memphis Red Sox/1940	.50
90	Memphis Red Sox/1946	.50
91	Birmingham Black Barons/1946	.50
92	Birmingham Black Barons/1948	.50
93	Birmingham Black Barons/1950	.50
94	Harlem Globetrotters/1948	.50
95	Cleveland Buckeyes/1947	.50
96	Philadelphia Stars/1944	.50
97	Newark Eagles/1939	.50
98	Baltimore Elite Giants/1949	.50
99	Indianapolis Clowns/1943	.50
100	Cincinnati Tigers/1937	.50

1993 Retort Negro League Legends, Series 2

One of the most extensive collectors' issues featuring former Negro League players was issued over a two-year period by Robert Retort Enterprises. Sold only in a boxed set, the Series 2 issue features 41 individual players, plus game-action and team photos. Fronts of the 3-1/2" x 5-1/2" cards feature sepia photos with a white border. Player identification is in the bottom border, which also has space for autographing. Postcard style backs specify the teams on which the player appeared, have a card number and a serial number from within the edition of 10,000 sets.

	NM/M
Complete Set (100):	30.00
Common Player:	.50
1 Frank Barnes	.50
2 John Bissant	.50
3 Garnett Blair	.50
4 Jim "Fireball" Bolden	.50
5 Luther Branham	.50
6 Sherwood Brewer	.50
7 Jimmy Dean	.50
8 Frank Duncan, Jr.	.50
9 Wilmer Fields	.50
10 Harold Gordon	.50
11 Bill Greason	.50
12 Acie Griggs	.50
13 Napoleon Gulley	.75
14 Ray Haggins	.50
15 Wilmer Harris	.50
16 Bob Harvey	.50
17 Jehosie Heard	.65
18 Gordon Hopkins	.50
19 Herman Horn	.50
20 James Ivory	.50
21 Henry Kimbro	.75
22 Milford Laurent	.50
23 Ernest Long	.50
24 Frank Marsh	.50
25 Francis Matthews	.50
26 Jim McCurine	.50
27 John Mitchell	.50
28 Lee Moody	.50
29 Rogers Pierre	.50
30 Nathaniel Pollard	.50
31 Merle Porter	.50
32 William Powell	.50
33 Ulysses Redd	.50
34 Harry Rhodes	.50
35 DeWitt Smallwood	.50
36 Joseph Spencer	.50
37 Riley Stewart	.50
38 Earl Taborn	.50
39 Ron Teasley	.50
40 Joe Wiley	.50
41 Buck Leonard	2.00
42 Grays vs. Giants/1945	.50
43 Grays vs. Monarchs/1945	.50
44 Homestead Grays/1948	.50

45	Pittsburgh Crawfords/1928	.50
46	Pittsburgh Crawfords/1935	.50
47	Kansas City Monarchs/1942	.50
48	Buck O'Neil, William Dismukes	.50
49	Chicago American Giants/1942	.50
50	Nashville Elite Giants/1935	.50
51	Baltimore Elite Giants/1941	.50
52	Birmingham Black Barons/1948	.50
53	Birmingham Black Barons/1959	.50
54	Memphis Red Sox/1954	.50
55	Indianapolis ABCs/1923	.50
56	Harlem Globetrotters/1948	.50
57	Harlem Globetrotters/1948	.50
58	Bismarck Barons/1955	.50
59	Culican/1952	.50
60	Santuroe/1947	.50
61	Pittsburgh Crawfords/1928	.50
62	Pittsburgh Crawfords/1932	.50
63	Pittsburgh Crawfords/1935	.50
64	Homestead Grays/1937	.50
65	Homestead Grays/1938	.50
66	Homestead Grays/1940	.50
67	Homestead Grays/1945	.50
68	Homestead Grays/1948	.50
69	Kansas City Monarchs/1932	.50
70	Kansas City Monarchs/1934	.50
71	Kansas City Monarchs/1941	.50
72	Kansas City Monarchs/1946	.50
73	Chicago American Giants/1950	.50
74	Memphis Red Sox/1949	.50
75	Birmingham Black Barons/1946	.50
76	Birmingham Black Barons/1948	.50
77	Birmingham Black Barons/1951	.50
78	Birmingham Black Barons/1954	.50
79	St. Louis Stars/1931	.50
80	Newark Dodgers/1935	.50
81	Brooklyn Eagles/1935	.50
82	Newark Eagles/1946	.50
83	Philadelphia Stars/1939	.50
84	Philadelphia Stars/1946	.50
85	Philadelphia Stars/1949	.50
86	Nashville Elite Giants/1935	.50
87	Baltimore Elite Giants/1939	.50
88	Baltimore Elite Giants/1949	.50
89	Cleveland Buckeyes/1947	.50
90	Cincinnati Tigers/1936	.50
91	Miami Ethiopian Clowns/1940	.50
92	Indianapolis Clowns/1944	.50
93	Indianapolis Clowns/1948	.50
94	New York Cubans/1943	.50
95	Harlem Globetrotters/1948	.50
96	House of David/1938	.50
97	E.T. Community/1926	.50
98	Bismarck Giants/1935	.50
99	American All-Stars/1945	.50
100	New York Stars/1949	.50

1988 Revco

KIRBY PUCKETT

This super-glossy boxed set of 33 standard-size cards was produced by Topps for exclusive distribution by Revco stores east of the Mississippi River. Card fronts feature a large blue Revco logo in the upper-left corner, opposite a yellow and black boxed "Topps League Leader" label. Player photos are framed in black and orange with a diagonal player identification banner in the lower-right corner. Backs are horizontal, printed in red and black on white stock and include the player name, biographical data, batting/pitching stats and a brief career summary.

		NM/M
Complete Set (33):		4.00
Common Player:		.05
1	Tony Gwynn	.65
2	Andre Dawson	.25
3	Vince Coleman	.05
4	Jack Clark	.05
5	Tim Raines	.05
6	Tim Wallach	.05
7	Juan Samuel	.05
8	Nolan Ryan	1.50
9	Rick Sutcliffe	.05
10	Kent Tekulve	.05
11	Steve Bedrosian	.05
12	Orel Hershiser	.05
13	Rick Rueschel	.05
14	Fernando Valenzuela	.05
15	Bob Welch	.05
16	Wade Boggs	.05
17	Mark McGwire	1.00
18	George Bell	.05
19	Harold Reynolds	.05
20	Paul Molitor	.50
21	Kirby Puckett	.65
22	Kevin Seitzer	.05
23	Brian Downing	.05
24	Dwight Evans	.05
25	Willie Wilson	.05
26	Danny Tartabull	.05
27	Jimmy Key	.05
28	Roger Clemens	.75
29	Dave Stewart	.05
30	Mark Eichhorn	.05
31	Tom Henke	.05
32	Charlie Hough	.05
33	Mark Langston	.05

1996 Revco Cleveland Indians

This set is identified by a logo on front as the "1995 Award Winner Series," but its manner of distribution is unknown. Fronts of the 2-1/2" x 3-1/2" cards have action photos with mottled border. Backs have logos of the 1995 Indians A.L. Championship and of the sponsor, Revco drug stores. Listed on back are the awards earned by the player for the 1995 season. A uniform number also appears, where applicable.

		NM/M
Complete Set (12):		12.00
Common Player:		.50
(1)	Carlos Baerga	.50
(2)	Albert Belle	1.25
(3)	Mike Hargrove	.50
(4)	John Hart (GM)	.50
(5)	Orel Hershiser	1.00
(6)	Kenny Lofton	1.00
(7)	Jose Mesa	.50
(8)	Manny Ramirez	5.00
(9)	Julian Tavares	.50
(10)	Jim Thome	2.50
(11)	Omar Vizquel	1.00
(12)	Cleveland Indians (On-field celebration.)	.50

1985-86 RGI

(See listings under Renata Galasso.)

Renata Galasso Inc.

1988 Rite Aid

This premiere edition was produced by Topps for distribution by Rite Aid discount drug stores in the Eastern U.S. The boxed set includes 33 standard-size full-color cards with at least one card for each major league team. Four cards in the set highlight MVPs from the 1987 season. Card fronts have white borders and carry a yellow "Team MVP's" header above the player photo which is bordered in red and blue. A large Rite Aid logo appears upper-left; the player's name appears bottom center. The numbered card backs are black on blue and white card stock in a horizontal layout containing the player name, biography and statistics.

		NM/M
Complete Set (33):		4.00
Common Player:		.05
1	Dale Murphy	.15
2	Andre Dawson	.15
3	Eric Davis	.05
4	Mike Scott	.05
5	Pedro Guerrero	.05
6	Tim Raines	.05
7	Darryl Strawberry	.05
8	Mike Schmidt	.05
9	Mike Dunne	.05
10	Jack Clark	.05
11	Tony Gwynn	.60
12	Will Clark	.05
13	Cal Ripken, Jr.	1.00
14	Wade Boggs	.60
15	Wally Joyner	.05
16	Harold Baines	.05
17	Joe Carter	.05
18	Alan Trammell	.05
19	Kevin Seitzer	.05
20	Paul Molitor	.50
21	Kirby Puckett	.60
22	Don Mattingly	.65
23	Mark McGwire	.75
24	Alvin Davis	.05
25	Ruben Sierra	.05
26	George Bell	.05
27	Jack Morris	.05
28	Jeff Reardon	.05
29	John Tudor	.05
30	Rick Rueschel	.05
31	Gary Gaetti	.05
32	Jeffrey Leonard	.05
33	Frank Viola	.05

1982 Roy Rogers N.Y. Yankees Lids

Members of the N.Y. Yankees (although in uniform which have the logos removed) are featured on these soft drink lids given away at Roy Rogers restaurants in the metropolitan area. Lids are 3-9/16" in diameter with a red plastic ring around a cardboard disc. At the center of the disc is a black-and-white player portrait photo. Player data appears in colored panels at the sides and in the white center section at bottom. The unnumbered lids are checklisted here in alphabetical order.

		NM/M
Complete Set (12):		35.00
Common Player:		2.50
(1)	Rick Cerone	2.50
(2)	Goose Gossage	3.50
(3)	Ken Griffey	2.50
(4)	Ron Guidry	2.50
(5)	Steve Kemp	2.50
(6)	Jerry Mumphrey	2.50
(7)	Graig Nettles	3.00
(8)	Lou Piniella	3.00
(9)	Willie Randolph	3.00
(10)	Andre Robertson	2.50
(11)	Roy Smalley	2.50
(12)	Dave Winfield	7.50

1993 Rolaids Cubs Relief Pitchers

The Chicago Cubs issued a four-card All-Time Cubs Relief Pitchers set as a giveaway at the Sept. 4, 1993 game at Wrigley Field. The four were selected by Cubs fans in a ballot conducted by Rolaids. The standard-sized cards have white borders with a color photo at center. Backs include the player's name, years he pitched for the Cubs, the Rolaids logo and an explanation of the card set's purpose.

		NM/M
Complete Set (4):		4.50
Common Player:		1.00
(1)	Randy Myers	1.00
(2)	Lee Smith	1.50
(3)	Bruce Sutter	2.50
(4)	Mitch Williams	1.00

1993 Nolan Ryan Topps Stickers

Twenty-seven of Nolan Ryan's Topps cards from 1968 through 1992 were reproduced, probably without authorization from Topps or Ryan, in a sticker format for regional distribution in Texas area grocery stores. Printed just slightly smaller than the 2-1/2" x 3-1/2" cards, the stickers were issued in strips of three. When the front picture was peeled away, the back of the sticker could be used as a coupon for specific purchases. Stores known to have participated in the program include: Brookshire Bros., Budget Chopper, Minyards and Super S. Strips of three were generally offered on a weekly basis.

		NM/M
Complete Set, Strips (9):		30.00
Common Sticker:		2.00

S

1986 Safeway Houston Astros

Though not marked, these 6" x 9" color player photo were given away over the course of several weeks by area Safeway food stores. The pictures are player portraits in uniform, but without caps because they were licensed by the Players Union, but not MLB. The white-bordered pictures have a facsimile autograph and are blank-backed. Unnumbered, the pictures are checklisted here in alphabetical order.

		NM/M
Complete Set (16):		25.00
Common Player:		1.00
(1)	Alan Ashby	1.00
(2)	Kevin Bass	1.00
(3)	Jose Cruz	1.00
(4)	Glenn Davis	1.00
(5)	Bill Doran	1.00
(6)	Phil Garner	1.00
(7)	Billy Hatcher	1.00
(8)	Charlie Kerfeld	1.00
(9)	Bob Knepper	1.00
(10)	Aurelio Lopez	1.00
(11)	Terry Puhl	1.00
(12)	Craig Reynolds	1.00
(13)	Nolan Ryan	15.00
(14)	Mike Scott	1.00
(15)	Dickie Thon	1.00
(16)	Denny Walling	1.00

2005 Ryne Sandberg Jersey Retirement Day

Stadium giveaway August 28.

		NM/M
Ryne Sandberg		6.00

1984 San Diego Padres Fire Safety

This set of 28 full-color 2-1/2" x 3-1/2" cards pictures Padres players, coaches, broadcasters and the Famous Chicken each posing with Smokey the Bear. Smokey's portrait and logo of the California and U.S. Forest Services are printed in the bottom border. Backs offer brief player information and a fire prevention tip. The cards were given away at a home game.

		NM/M
Complete Set (28):		7.00
Common Player:		.25
1	Garry Templeton	.25
2	Alan Wiggins	.25
3	Luis Salazar	.25
6	Steve Garvey	1.00
7	Kurt Bevacqua	.25
10	Doug Gwosdz	.25
11	Tim Flannery	.25
16	Terry Kennedy	.25
18	Kevin McReynolds	.25
19	Tony Gwynn	5.00
20	Bobby Brown	.25
30	Eric Show	.25
31	Ed Whitson	.25
35	Luis DeLeon	.25
38	Mark Thurmond	.25
42	Sid Monge	.25
43	Dave Dravecky	.25
48	Tim Lollar	.25
---	Smokey Logo Card	.25
---	The Chicken (Mascot)	.25
---	Dave Campbell (Broadcaster)	.25
---	Jerry Coleman (Broadcaster)	.25
---	Harry Dunlop	.25
---	Harold (Doug) Harvey (Umpire)	.25
---	Jack Krol (Coach)	.25
---	Jack McKeon (Vice President)	.25
---	Norm Sherry (Coach)	.25
---	Ozzie Virgil (Coach)	.25
---	Dick Williams (Manager)	.25

1986-87 San Diego Padres Fire Safety Flip Books

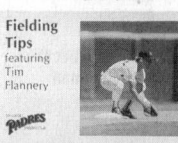

Fielding Tips featuring Tim Flannery

Differing from the contemporary fire safety issues of its time, the 1986-87 Padres promotional effort took the form of 24-page flip books, rather than cards. About 3-1/2" x 2-1/2", the multipage black-and-white books offered photographic playing tips when the pictures were rapidly thumbed. When turned over, the books showed Smokey in action preventing forest fires. The 1987 books, McCullers and Santiago, are slightly larger, at about 4-1/2" x 2-3/4".

		NM/M
Complete Set (5):		25.00
Common Player:		4.00
(1)	Dave Dravecky	4.00
(2)	Tim Flannery	4.00
(3)	Tony Gwynn	15.00
(4)	Lance McCullers	4.00
(5)	Benito Santiago	4.00

1988 San Diego Padres Fire Safety

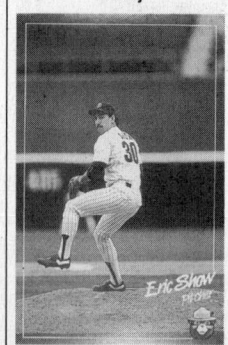

This oversized (3"x 5") set was produced in conjunction with the U.S. Forest Service as a fire prevention campaign promotion. A full-

color player photo, framed by a thin white line, fills the card face. The player number, position and Smokey Bear logo appear at lower-right. Backs are printed in horizontal postcard format, with player info and a Smokey Bear cartoon on the left half of the card back. The set was available for purchase at the Padres Gift Shop. Cards of Candy Sierra and Larry Bowa were not officially released and are quite rare.

		NM/M
Complete Set (33):		45.00
Common Player:		.50
(1)	Shawn Abner	.50
(2)	Roberto Alomar	8.00
(3)	Sandy Alomar	3.00
(4)	Greg Booker	.50
(5)	Larry Bowa	15.00
(6)	Chris Brown	.50
(7)	Mark Davis	.50
(8)	Pat Dobson	.50
(9)	Tim Flannery	.50
(10)	Mark Grant	.50
(11)	Tony Gwynn	15.00
(12)	Andy Hawkins	.50
(13)	Stan Jefferson	.50
(14)	Jimmy Jones	.50
(15)	John Kruk	.50
(16)	Dave Leiper	.50
(17)	Shane Mack	.50
(18)	Carmelo Martinez	.50
(19)	Lance McCullers	.50
(20)	Keith Moreland	.50
(21)	Eric Nolte	.50
(22)	Amos Otis	.50
(23)	Mark Parent	.50
(24)	Randy Ready	.50
(25)	Greg Riddoch	.50
(26)	Benito Santiago	1.00
(27)	Eric Show	.50
(28)	Candy Sierra	10.00
(29)	Denny Sommers	.50
(30)	Garry Templeton	.50
(31)	Dickie Thon	.50
(32)	Ed Whitson	.50
(33)	Marvell Wynne	.50

1989 San Diego Padres Magazine/S.D. Sports Inserts

During the course of the 1989 season, a 24-card set sponsored by a local baseball card dealer was offered to collectors as an insert to the team's official game program, "Padres Magazine." The cards were offered in six panels of four cards. Each panel included a former Padres star and a career highlight. To complete the set, at least six copies of the $1.50 program had to be purchased. The 2-1/2" x 3-1/2" cards have color portrait photos on front. Backs have player identification and a career stats line, along with trivia about the player.

		NM/M
Complete Set (24):		15.00
Common Player:		.50
1	Jack McKeon	.50
2	Sandy Alomar Jr.	.50
3	Tony Gwynn	6.00
4	Willie McCovey	2.00
5	John Kruk	.50
6	Jack Clark	.50
7	Eric Show	.50
8	Rollie Fingers	1.50
9	The Alomars (Sandy Alomar, Roberto Alomar, Sandy Alomar Jr.)	.65
10	Carmelo Martinez	.50
11	Benito Santiago	.50
12	Nate Colbert	.50
13	Mark Davis	.50
14	Roberto Alomar	1.50
15	Tim Flannery	.50
16	Randy Jones	.50
17	Dennis Rasmussen	.50
18	Greg Harris	.50
19	Garry Templeton	.50
20	Steve Garvey	1.50
21	Bruce Hurst	.50
22	Ed Whitson	.50
23	Chris James	.50
24	Gaylord Perry	1.50

1990 San Diego Padres Magazine/Unocal inserts

The first 24 cards in this set, sponsored by area Unocal service stations, were found in four-card panels bound into various issues of Padres Magazine, the team's official program. Sheets measure about 5" x 9" and the individual perforated cards are about 2-1/2" x 3-1/2". A coupon attached to the sheets could be redeemed at participating gas stations for cards #25-27. Fronts

Ed Whitson
Pitcher 76

have color action photos with team logo at top and sponsor logo at lower-right. Black-and-white backs have player data, a line of career stats and highlights of his time with the Padres.

		NM/M
Complete Set (27):		15.00
Common Player:		.50
1	Tony Gwynn	5.00
2	Benito Santiago	.50
3	Mike Pagliarulo	.50
4	Dennis Rasmussen	.50
5	Eric Show	.50
6	Darrin Jackson	.50
7	Mark Parent	.50
8	Jerry Coleman, Rick Monday (Announcers)	.50
9	Andy Benes	.50
10	Roberto Alomar	2.50
11	Craig Lefferts	.50
12	Ed Whitson	.50
13	Calvin Schiraldi	.50
14	Garry Templeton	.50
15	Tony Gwynn	5.00
16	Bob Chandler, Ted Leitner (Announcers)	.50
17	Fred Lynn	.50
18	Jack Clark	.50
19	Mike Dunne	.50
20	Mark Grant	.50
21	Benito Santiago	.50
22	Sandy Alomar Sr., Pat Dobson, Amos Otis, Greg Riddoch, Denny Sommers	.50
23	Bruce Hurst	.50
24	Greg Harris	.50
25	Jack McKeon	1.00
26	Bip Roberts	1.00
27	Joe Carter	4.00

1991 San Diego Padres Magazine/Rally's inserts

The first 24 cards of this set were issued as 5" x 8" perforated panels stapled into issues of "Padres Magazine." Due to substitutions dictated by player moves during the season (which also created Short-Printed cards) it would have been necessary to purchase six of the $2 programs to get the 27-card basic set. Cards #25-27 were only available at Rally's restaurants with a coupon attached to the magazine panels. Single cards measure about 2-1/2" x 3-1/2". Fronts have color portrait photos on a diamond background. Player name and position are in an orange banner at bottom. Team and sponsor logos appear in the upper corners on a dark blue background. Backs are in black-and-white with player identification, a line of career stats and highlights of his tenure in San Diego.

		NM/M
Complete Set (30):		27.50
Common Player:		.50
1	Greg Riddoch	.50
2	Dennis Rasmussen	.50

3	Thomas Howard	.50
4	Tom Lampkin	.50
5	Bruce Hurst	.50
6	Darrin Jackson	.50
7	Jerald Clark	.50
8	Shawn Abner	.50
9	Bip Roberts	.50
10	Marty Barrett	.50
11	Jim Vatcher	.50
12	Greg Gross	.50
13	Greg Harris	.50
14	Ed Whitson	.50
15a	Calvin Schiraldi/SP	1.50
15b	Jerald Clark	.50
16	Rich Rodriguez	.50
17	Larry Andersen	.50
18	Andy Benes	.50
19a	Wes Gardner/SP	1.50
19b	Bruce Hurst	.50
20	Paul Faries	.50
21	Craig Lefferts	.50
22	Tony Gwynn	8.00
23a	Jim Presley/SP	1.50
23b	Bip Roberts	.50
24	Fred McGriff	1.00
25	Gaylord Perry	2.00
26	Benito Santiago	1.50
27	Tony Fernandez	1.50

1992 San Diego Padres Fire Safety

The Padres issued a Smokey the Bear postcard set, sponsored by the U.S. Forest Service. Backs contain the usual fire safety messages, but they are also translated into Spanish. Fronts have full-bleed color photos with the player's name and position in orange in a dark blue box at bottom-center. A color Smokey logo appears in one of the upper corners. The unnumbered cards are checklisted here alphabetically.

		NM/M
Complete Set (36):		15.00
Common Player:		.25
(1)	Larry Andersen	.25
(2)	Oscar Azocar	.25
(3)	Andy Benes	.25
(4)	Dan Bilardello	.25
(5)	Jerald Clark	.25
(6)	Pat Clements	.25
(7)	Dave Eiland	.25
(8)	Tony Fernandez	.25
(9)	Tony Gwynn	6.00
(10)	Gene Harris	.25
(11)	Greg Harris	.25
(12)	Jeremy Hernandez	.25
(13)	Bruce Hurst	.25
(14)	Darrin Jackson	.25
(15)	Tom Lampkin	.25
(16)	Bruce Kimm	.25
(17)	Craig Lefferts	.25
(18)	Mike Maddux	.25
(19)	Fred McGriff	.25
(20)	Jose Melendez	.25
(21)	Randy Myers, Craig Shipley	.25
(22)	Gary Pettis	.25
(23)	Rob Picciolo	.25
(24)	Merv Rettenmund	.25
(25)	Greg Riddoch	.25
(26)	Mike Roarke	.25
(27)	Rich Rodriguez	.25
(28)	Benito Santiago	.25
(29)	Frank Seminara	.25
(30)	Gary Sheffield	2.00
(31)	Jim Snyder	.25
(32)	Dave Staton	.25
(33)	Kurt Stillwell	.25
(34)	Tim Teufel	.25
(35)	Kevin Ward	.25

Police

TONY FERNANDEZ   INF

Anti-drug messages are featured on this safety set. The 2-1/2" x 3-1/2" cards have color action photos on front with wide white borders. Backs are horizontally formatted and feature a few player biographical notes, the D.A.R.E. logo and safety message. Unnumbered cards are checklisted here in alpha-

betical order. Cards #28-30 in this checklist were not distributed with the rest of the set and are scarcer.

		NM/M
Complete Set (30):		12.00
Common Player:		.25
(1)	Oscar Azocar	.25
(2)	Andy Benes	.25
(3)	Jerald Clark	.25
(4)	Jim Deshaies	.25
(5)	Dave Eiland	.25
(6)	Tony Fernandez	.25
(7)	Tony Gwynn	6.00
(8)	Greg W. Harris	.25
(9)	Bruce Hurst	.25
(10)	Darrin Jackson	.25
(11)	Tom Lampkin	.25
(12)	Fred McGriff	.25
(13)	Merv Rettenmund	.25
(14)	Greg Riddoch	.25
(15)	Benito Santiago	.25
(16)	Frank Seminara	.25
(17)	Gary Sheffield	1.00
(18)	Craig Shipley	.25
(19)	Phil Stephenson	.25
(20)	Kurt Stillwell	.25
(21)	Tim Teufel	.25
(22)	Dan Walters	.25
(23)	Kevin Ward	.25
(24)	Padres relievers (Larry Andersen, Mike Maddux, Jose Melendez, Rich Rodriguez, Tim Scott)	.25
(25)	Coaches (Bruce Kimm, Rob Picciolo, Merv Rettenmund, Mike Roarke, Jim Snyder)	.25
(26)	Bluepper (Mascot)	.25
(27)	Jack Murphy Stadium	.25
(28)	Craig Lefferts	1.00
(29)	Rob Picciolo	1.00
(30)	Fred McGriff, Tony Fernandez, Gary Sheffield, Tony Gwynn	2.00

1991 San Francisco Examiner A's

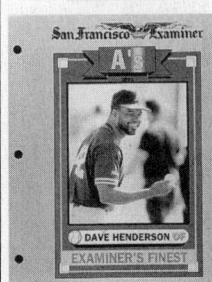

DAVE HENDERSON OF
EXAMINER'S FINEST

Evidently issued over the course of the season by the Bay Area daily newspaper, these large-format (8-3/8" x 10-7/8") cards are printed on light cardboard pre-punched for a three-ring binder. Color photos on the fronts are surrounded by team colors of green and yellow. The newspaper's logo appears in black at the top. Backs are in black-and-white with a portrait photo of the player, biographical data, major league stats and career highlights. The unnumbered cards are checklisted here alphabetically.

		NM/M
Complete Set (15):		45.00
Common Player:		2.00
(1)	Harold Baines	2.00
(2)	Jose Canseco	5.00
(3)	Dennis Eckersley	5.00
(4)	Mike Gallego	2.00
(5)	Dave Henderson	2.00
(6)	Rickey Henderson	6.00
(7)	Rick Honeycutt	2.00
(8)	Mark McGwire	10.00
(9)	Mike Moore	2.00
(10)	Gene Nelson	2.00
(11)	Eric Show	2.00
(12)	Terry Steinbach	2.00
(13)	Dave Stewart	2.00
(14)	Walt Weiss	2.00
(15)	Bob Welch	2.00

Giants

Evidently issued over the course of the season by the Bay Area daily newspaper, these large-format (8-3/8" x 10-7/8") cards are printed on light cardboard pre-punched for a three-ring binder. Color photos on the fronts are surrounded by team-color borders of orange and black on a gray background. The newspaper's logo ap-

GIANTS
STEVE DECKER C
EXAMINER'S FINEST

pears in black at the top. Backs are in black-and-white with a portrait photo of the player, biographical data, major league stats and career highlights. The unnumbered cards are checklisted here alphabetically.

1990 SCD Baseball Card Price Guide Pocket Price Guides

For its first full year of inserting repli-cards in each issue, SCD Baseball Card Price Guide Monthly magazine rendered the game's stars and hot rookies in the style of 1957 Topps cards. Black, white and red backs have a photo of one of the player's other cards, personal data, current values of selected cards and market advice. Cards were printed on panels of five stapled into each month's issue.

		NM/M
Complete Set (16):		35.00
Common Player:		2.00
(1)	Kevin Bass	2.00
(2)	Mike Benjamin	2.00
(3)	Bud Black	2.00
(4)	Jeff Brantley	2.00
(5)	John Burkett	2.00
(6)	Will Clark	4.00
(7)	Steve Decker	2.00
(8)	Scott Garrelts	2.00
(9)	Mike LaCoss	2.00
(10)	Willie McGee	2.00
(11)	Kevin Mitchell	2.00
(12)	Dave Righetti	2.00
(13)	Don Robinson	2.00
(14)	Robby Thompson	2.00
(15)	Jose Uribe	2.00
(16)	Matt Williams	4.00

2003 Ron Santo Jersey Retirement Card

SEPTEMBER 28, 2003
Ron Santo
#10

This high-gloss, 2-1/2"x3-1/2" card was a Wrigley Field giveaway on Sept. 23, 2003, on the occasion of the Cubs' retirement of the star third baseman's uniform number. The back has Santo's complete Major League stats.

	NM/M
Ron Santo	6.00

1989 SCD Baseball Card Price Guide Pocket Price Guides

ROYALS

BO JACKSON   outfield

Between its premiere issue of April 1988 and the September 1989 issue, SCD's monthly price guide magazine issued a gatefold player poster in each issue. Beginning with the October 1989 issue, panels of five (later six) repli-cards were stapled into the magazine in place of the posters. The 1989 repli-card series depicts contemporary players in the design of the 1964 Topps. Backs

are in black-and-white with a photo of the player's rookie card and market advice pertaining to the player.

		NM/M
Complete Set (15):		6.00
Common Player:		.25
1	Mark McGwire	1.50
2	Bo Jackson	.35
3	Ken Griffey	1.50
4	Kevin Mitchell	.25
5	Ryne Sandberg	1.00
6	Will Clark	.25
7	Gregg Jefferies	.25
8	Gary Sheffield	.50
9	Fred McGriff	.25
10	Don Mattingly	1.00
11	Jim Abbott	.25
12	Mitch Williams	.25
13	Glenn Davis	.25
14	Ruben Sierra	.25
15	Robin Yount	.75

1991 SCD Baseball Card Price Guide Pocket Price Guides

MARINERS
ken griffey jr. • outfield

In its third year of including insert cards with each issue, the Price Guide chose the classic 1971 Topps design to showcase the game's top stars and hot rookies. The first five cards have red backgrounds on their backs, the rest are deep green. Backs have a black-and-white photo of one of the player's other cards, along with selected card value data. Also presented are some personal data and the editors' thoughts on each player's future market value.

		NM/M
Complete Set (60):		15.00
Common Player:		.25
1	Ryne Sandberg	.75
2	Bobby Thigpen	.25
3	Rickey Henderson	.65
4	Dwight Gooden	.25
5	Kevin Maas	.25
6	Ron Gant	.25
7	Frank Thomas	.65
8	Doug Drabek	.25
9	Bobby Bonilla	.25
10	Sandy Alomar Jr.	.25
11	Bob Welch	.25
12	Joe Carter	.25
13	Cecil Fielder	.25
14	Dave Justice	.25
15	Barry Bonds	2.00
16	Barry Larkin	.25
17	Ramon Martinez	.25
18	Ben McDonald	.25
19	Roger Clemens	1.00
20	Jose Canseco	.40
21	Will Clark	.25
22	Jeff Conine	.25
23	Chris Sabo	.25
24	Alan Trammell	.25
25	Howard Johnson	.25
26	Dale Murphy	.30
27	Gregg Jefferies	.25
28	Bo Jackson	.30
29	Craig Biggio	.25
30	Delino DeShields	.25
31	Rafael Palmeiro	.50
32	Robin Yount	.65
33	Mark McGwire	1.50
34	Kevin Mitchell	.25
35	George Brett	1.00
36	Tim Wallach	.25
37	Andre Dawson	.30
38	Kirby Puckett	.75
39	Matt Williams	.25
40	Wade Boggs	.75
41	Dave Winfield	.65
42	Don Mattingly	1.00
43	Carlton Fisk	.65
44	Dave Stewart	.25
45	Ken Griffey Jr.	1.25
46	Ruben Sierra	.25
47	George Bell	.25
48	Cal Ripken	2.00
49	Ellis Burks	.25
50	Roberto Alomar	.30
51	Tim Raines	.25
52	Mike Greenwell	.25
53	Benito Santiago	.25
54	Tom Glavine	.25
55	Scott Erickson	.25
56	Chuck Finley	.25
57	Julio Franco	.25
58	Paul Molitor	.65
59	Todd Van Poppel	.25
60	Mo Vaughn	.25

Center columns (1989 SCD Baseball Card Price Guide 60-card set):

		NM/M
Complete Set (60):		20.00
Common Player:		.25
1	Darryl Strawberry	.25
2	Wade Boggs	.75
3	Roger Clemens	1.00
4	Paul Molitor	.60
5	Craig Biggio	.25
6	Ruben Sierra	.25
7	Sandy Alomar Jr.	.25
8	Rickey Henderson	.60
9	Mark Langston	.25
10	Dwight Evans	.25
11	Ben McDonald	.25
12	Bo Jackson	.35
13	Don Mattingly	1.00
14	Todd Zeile	.25
15	Mike Greenwell	.25
16	Eric Anthony	.25
17	Dennis Eckersley	.50
18	Greg Vaughn	.25
19	Kevin Mitchell	.25
20	Ryne Sandberg	.25
21	Will Clark	.25
22	Robin Yount	.60
23	Kirby Puckett	.75
24	Andy Benes	.25
25	Wally Joyner	.25
26	Ozzie Smith	.75
27	John Olerud	.25
28	Devon White	.25
29	Alan Trammell	.25
30	Bobby Bonilla	.25
31	Jose Canseco	.40
32	Fred McGriff	.25
33	Mark Grace	.25
34	Ricky Jordan	.25
35	George Brett	1.00
36	Eric Davis	.25
37	Tony Gwynn	.75
38	Cal Ripken Jr.	2.00
39	Bret Saberhagen	.25
40	Howard Johnson	.25
41	Jerome Walton	.25
42	Mark McGwire	1.50
43	A.L. East Power Hitters (Mike Greenwell, Don Mattingly)	.50
44	Ken Griffey Jr.	1.25
45	Texas' Top Twirlers (Nolan Ryan, Mike Scott)	1.00
46	Barry Larkin	.25
47	Delino DeShields	.25
48	Roberto Alomar	.35
49	Frank Viola	.25
50	Kelly Gruber	.25
51	Michael Jordan	7.50
52	Glenn Davis	.25
53	Marquis Grissom	.25
54	Joe Carter	.25
55	Gregg Jefferies	.25
56	Gary Sheffield	.45
57	Cecil Fielder	.25
58	Matt Williams	.25
59	Ramon Martinez	.25
60	Len Dykstra	.25

1992 BB Card Price Guide/ Sports Card Price Guide

New collector focus on other team sports resulted in SCD's Baseball Card Price Guide Monthly changing its name to Sports Card Price Guide Monthly with its May 1992 issue. The title change was also reflected in the annual series of repli-cards stapled into each issue. For the first time football, basketball and hockey players joined the base-bAll-Stars. That change was effective with card #19. The '92 series utilized the design of Topps' 1974 baseball cards. Backs are printed in black, white and green and, as in previous years, include a photo of one of the player's cards along with selective current values and a market forecast. Only the set's baseball players are listed here.

		NM/M
Complete (Baseball) Set (56):		20.00
Common Player:		.25
1	Will Clark	.25
2	Albert Belle	.25
3	Luis Gonzalez	.25
4	Ramon Martinez	.25
5	Frank Thomas	.65
6	Travis Fryman	.25
7	Carlton Fisk	.65
8	Bo Jackson	.35
9	Chuck Knoblauch	.25
10	Ron Gant	.25
11	Jose Canseco	.45
12	Roger Clemens	1.00
13	Darren Lewis	.25
14	Kirby Puckett	.75
15	Tom Glavine	.35
16	Royce Clayton	.25
18	Ozzie Smith	.75
20	Robin Ventura	.25
21	Derek Bell	.25
23	Ryne Sandberg	.75
25	Andy Van Slyke	.25
26	Jim Abbott	.25
27	Ken Griffey Jr.	1.25
30	Jeff Bagwell	.65
32	Dwight Gooden	.25
33	Ruben Sierra	.25
35	David Justice	.25
36	Wade Boggs	.75
38	Barry Larkin	.25
39	Felix Jose	.25
40	Howard Johnson	.25
42	Fred McGriff	.25
44	Todd Van Poppel	.25
46	Brien Taylor	.25
48	Cal Ripken Jr.	2.00
50	Dave Winfield	.65
52	Juan Gonzalez	.40
53	Reggie Sanders	.25
57	Gary Sheffield	.45
58	Roberto Alomar	.40
59	Barry Bonds	2.00
60	Tom Glavine	.35
62	Kenny Lofton	.25
63	Joe Carter	.25
66	Paul Molitor	.65
67	Phil Plantier	.25
69	Mark McGwire	1.50
70	Nolan Ryan	2.00
72	Darryl Strawberry	.25
73	Pat Listach	.25
74	Dennis Eckersley	.50
75	Bobby Bonilla	.25
78	Delino DeShields	.25
80	Doug Drabek	.25
81	Deion Sanders	.25
84	Darren Daulton	.25

1993 Sports Card Pocket Price Guide

The final year of production of an annual repli-card insert set for the SCD price guide magazine combined stars and hot rookies from all four major team sports. Cards were produced in the style of Topps' 1973 football issue, with varying colored striped pennants down the

left side of the front. Backs are printed in black, white and green (#1-8) and black, white and red (#9-104), and include a cartoon trivia question along with price guide and player data. The repli-cards were printed on sheets of eight stapled into the magazine's monthly issues. Only the baseball players are listed here.

		NM/M
Complete (Baseball) Set (54):		20.00
Common Player:		.25
1	Tyler Green	.25
3	Ozzie Smith	.75
5	Fred McGriff	.25
7	Marquis Grissom	.25
13	John Smoltz	.25
16	Ruben Sierra	.25
19	Roberto Alomar	.40
20	Gary Sheffield	.40
23	Carlos Baerga	.25
24	Robin Ventura	.25
25	Nigel Wilson	.25
26	David Nied	.25
27	Cal Ripken Jr.	2.00
28	Albert Belle	.25
34	Larry Walker	.25
37	Eric Karros	.25
38	Dwight Gooden	.25
40	Nolan Ryan	2.00
41	Juan Gonzalez	.45
43	Robin Yount	.65
44	Darryl Strawberry	.25
45	George Brett	1.00
46	Ray Lankford	.25
47	Kirby Puckett	.75
48	David Justice	.25
49	Travis Fryman	.25
51	Eddie Murray	.65
52	Tony Gwynn	.75
54	Jack McDowell	.25
57	Ryne Sandberg	.75
58	Deion Sanders	.25
61	Frank Thomas	.65
62	Carlton Fisk	.65
65	Tim Salmon	.25
66	Jeff Conine	.25
67	Benito Santiago	.25
68	Mike Piazza	1.50
70	Andres Galarraga	.25
71	Gregg Jefferies	.25
76	Joe Carter	.25
79	Rickey Henderson	.65
80	Barry Larkin	.25
82	Juan Gonzalez	.45
83	Gary Sheffield	.40
84	Will Clark	.25
89	Mark Grace	.25
90	Cliff Floyd	.25
91	Bobby Bonds Jr.	.25
92	Barry Bonds	2.00
94	Matt Williams	.25
97	Paul Molitor	.65
98	Ken Griffey Jr.	1.50
99	Steve Avery	.25
100	Kirby Puckett	.65

1989 Schafer's Bakery Super Stars Discs

(See 1989 Holsum for checklist and value information. Distributed in Michigan.)

1987 Schnucks St. Louis Cardinals

Sponsored by Schnucks food stores, and distributed at more than 50 locations around St. Louis, the company is not mentioned anywhere

on these photos. The set of 6" x 9" photocards depicts the players without caps or other visible uniform logos or color photos against a plain blue backdrop. A facsimile autograph appears in the lower-left corner, with a Players Association logo at upper-left. Backs are blank. The unnumbered cards are checklisted here alphabetically. A Schnucks spokesman said about 50,000 of each picture were produced.

		NM/M
Complete Set (16):		14.00
Common Player:		.50
(1)	Jack Clark	.50
(2)	Vince Coleman	.75
(3)	Danny Cox	.50
(4)	Curt Ford	.50
(5)	Bob Forsch	.50
(6)	Tom Herr	.50
(7)	Whitey Herzog	.50
(8)	Ricky Horton	.50
(9)	Greg Mathews	.50
(10)	Willie McGee	.75
(11)	Jose Oquendo	.50
(12)	Tony Pena	.50
(13)	Terry Pendleton	.75
(14)	Ozzie Smith	6.00
(15)	John Tudor	.50
(16)	Todd Worrell	.50

1996 Schwebel's Stars Discs

Distributed in loaves of bread in the Youngstown, Ohio, area, the players in this disc set lean heavily towards Cleveland Indians. The 2-3/4" diameter discs were inserted into a special pocket in the bread wrapper to keep them from contact with the bread. Fronts have a purple-to-red graduated color scheme around the border, with a player photo at center. Uniform logos have been removed from the photos because the discs are licensed only by the Players Union; they are a product of Mike Schechter Assoc. Backs are printed in purple with 1995 and career stats along with appropriate logos. A die-cut poster into which the discs could be inserted for display was also available.

		NM/M
Complete Set (20):		20.00
Common Player:		1.00
1	Jim Thome	1.50
2	Orel Hershiser	1.00
3	Greg Maddux	2.50
4	Charles Nagy	1.00
5	Omar Vizquel	1.00
6	Manny Ramirez	2.00
7	Dennis Martinez	1.00
8	Eddie Murray	2.00
9	Albert Belle	1.00
10	Fred McGriff	1.00
11	Jack McDowell	1.00
12	Kenny Lofton	1.00
13	Cal Ripken Jr.	4.00
14	Jose Mesa	1.00
15	Randy Johnson	2.00
16	Ken Griffey Jr.	3.00
17	Carlos Baerga	1.00
18	Frank Thomas	2.00
19	Sandy Alomar Jr.	1.00
20	Barry Bonds	4.00

1988 Score Promo Cards

While these Score promotional sample cards carry a 1988 copyright date on back, they were actually released to hobby dealers late in 1987. They can be easily differentiated from regular-issue 1988 cards by the use of zeros in the stats lines on back for 1987 and career figures. Most of the promos are otherwise identical to the issued versions of the same players. These were among the first promo cards to be widely distributed within the hobby.

		NM/M
Complete Set (6):		20.00
Common Player:		4.00
30	Mark Langston	4.00
48	Tony Pena	4.00
71	Keith Moreland	4.00
72	Barry Larkin	4.00
121	Dennis Boyd	4.00
149	Denny Walling	4.00

1988 Score Proofs

The first six cards in the eventual 1988 Score debut issue can also be found in proof versions intended to test various inks, finishes, etc. These cards are differentiated from regular issues (and promo cards) by the use of zeros in place of actual stats for 1987 and career on the backs.

		NM/M
Complete Set (6):		150.00
Common Player:		15.00
1	Don Mattingly	45.00
2	Wade Boggs	35.00
3	Tim Raines	15.00
4	Andre Dawson	25.00
5	Mark McGwire	60.00
6	Kevin Seitzer	15.00

1988 Score

A fifth member joined the group of nationally distributed baseball cards in 1988. Titled "Score," the cards are characterized by extremely sharp color photography and printing. Card backs are full-color also and carry a player portrait

along with a brief biography, player data and statistics. The 660 cards in the set are standard 2-1/2" x 3-1/2" format. The fronts come with one of six different border colors which are equally divided at 110 cards per color. The Score set was produced by Major League Marketing, the same company that marketed the "triple-action" Sportflics card sets.

		NM/M
Unopened Fact. Set (660):		9.00
Complete Set (660):		6.00
Common Player:		.05
Pack:		.35
Wax Box:		9.00
Rack Pack (54):		.75
Rack Box (24):		12.00
1	Don Mattingly	.65
2	Wade Boggs	.50
3	Tim Raines	.25
4	Andre Dawson	.25
5	Mark McGwire	.75
6	Kevin Seitzer	.05
7	Wally Joyner	.05
8	Jesse Barfield	.05
9	Pedro Guerrero	.05
10	Eric Davis	.05
11	George Brett	.65
12	Ozzie Smith	.50
13	Rickey Henderson	.40
14	Jim Rice	.15
15	Matt Nokes RC	.05
16	Mike Schmidt	.65
17	Dave Parker	.05
18	Eddie Murray	.40
19	Andres Galarraga	.05
20	Tony Fernandez	.05
21	Kevin McReynolds	.05
22	B.J. Surhoff	.05
23	Pat Tabler	.05
24	Kirby Puckett	.50
25	Benny Santiago	.05
26	Ryne Sandberg	.50
27	Kelly Downs	.05
28	Jose Cruz	.05
29	Pete O'Brien	.05
30	Mark Langston	.05
31	Lee Smith	.05
32	Juan Samuel	.05
33	Kevin Bass	.05
34	R.J. Reynolds	.05
35	Steve Sax	.05
36	John Kruk	.05
37	Alan Trammell	.05
38	Chris Bosio	.05
39	Brook Jacoby	.05
40	Willie McGee	.05
41	Dave Magadan	.05
42	Fred Lynn	.05
43	Kent Hrbek	.05
44	Brian Downing	.05
45	Jose Canseco	.30
46	Jim Presley	.05
47	Mike Stanley	.05
48	Tony Pena	.05
49	David Cone	.05
50	Rick Sutcliffe	.05
51	Doug Drabek	.05
52	Bill Doran	.05
53	Mike Scioscia	.05
54	Candy Maldonado	.05
55	Dave Winfield	.40
56	Lou Whitaker	.05
57	Tom Henke	.05
58	Ken Gerhart	.05
59	Glenn Braggs	.05
60	Julio Franco	.05
61	Charlie Leibrandt	.05
62	Gary Gaetti	.05
63	Bob Boone	.05
64	Luis Polonia RC	.05
65	Dwight Evans	.05
66	Phil Bradley	.05
67	Mike Boddicker	.05
68	Vince Coleman	.05
69	Howard Johnson	.05
70	Tim Wallach	.05
71	Keith Moreland	.05
72	Barry Larkin	.05
73	Alan Ashby	.05
74	Rick Rhoden	.05
75	Darrell Evans	.05
76	Dave Stieb	.05
77	Dan Plesac	.05
78	Will Clark	.05
79	Frank White	.05
80	Joe Carter	.05
81	Mike Witt	.05
82	Terry Steinbach	.05
83	Alvin Davis	.05
84	Tom Herr	.05
85	Vance Law	.05
86	Kal Daniels	.05
87	Rick Honeycutt	.05
88	Alfredo Griffin	.05
89	Bret Saberhagen	.05
90	Bert Blyleven	.05
91	Jeff Reardon	.05
92	Cory Snyder	.05
93	Greg Walker	.05
94	Joe Magrane RC	.10
95	Rob Deer	.05
96	Ray Knight	.05
97	Casey Candaele	.05

98	John Cerutti	.05
99	Buddy Bell	.05
100	Jack Clark	.05
101	Eric Bell	.05
102	Willie Wilson	.05
103	Dave Schmidt	.05
104	Dennis Eckersley	.35
105	Don Sutton	.35
106	Danny Tartabull	.05
107	Fred McGriff	.05
108	Les Straker RC	.05
109	Lloyd Moseby	.05
110	Roger Clemens	.65
111	Glenn Hubbard	.05
112	Ken Williams RC	.05
113	Ruben Sierra	.05
114	Stan Jefferson	.05
115	Milt Thompson	.05
116	Bobby Bonilla	.05
117	Wayne Tolleson	.05
118	Matt Williams	.05
119	Chet Lemon	.05
120	Dale Sveum	.05
121	Dennis Boyd	.05
122	Brett Butler	.05
123	Terry Kennedy	.05
124	Jack Howell	.05
125	Curt Young	.05
126a	Dale Valle (First name incorrect.)	.25
126b	Dave Valle (Correct spelling.)	.05
127	Curt Wilkerson	.05
128	Tim Teufel	.05
129	Ozzie Virgil	.05
130	Brian Fisher	.05
131	Lance Parrish	.05
132	Tom Browning	.05
133a	Larry Anderson (Incorrect spelling.)	.25
133b	Larry Andersen (Correct spelling.)	.05
134a	Bob Brenley (Incorrect spelling.)	.25
134b	Bob Brenly (Correct spelling.)	.05
135	Mike Marshall	.05
136	Gerald Perry	.05
137	Bobby Meacham	.05
138	Larry Herndon	.05
139	Fred Manrique RC	.05
140	Charlie Hough	.05
141	Ron Darling	.05
142	Herm Winningham	.05
143	Mike Diaz	.05
144	Mike Jackson RC	.05
145	Denny Walling	.05
146	Rob Thompson	.05
147	Franklin Stubbs	.05
148	Albert Hall	.05
149	Bobby Witt	.05
150	Lance McCullers	.05
151	Scott Bradley	.05
152	Mark McLemore	.05
153	Tim Laudner	.05
154	Greg Swindell	.05
155	Marty Barrett	.05
156	Mike Heath	.05
157	Gary Ward	.05
158a	Lee Mazilli (Incorrect spelling.)	.25
158b	Lee Mazzilli (Correct spelling.)	.05
159	Tom Foley	.05
160	Robin Yount	.40
161	Steve Bedrosian	.05
162	Bob Walk	.05
163	Nick Esasky	.05
164	Ken Caminiti RC	.15
165	Jose Uribe	.05
166	Dave Anderson	.05
167	Ed Whitson	.05
168	Ernie Whitt	.05
169	Cecil Cooper	.05
170	Mike Pagliarulo	.05
171	Pat Sheridan	.05
172	Chris Bando	.05
173	Lee Lacy	.05
174	Steve Lombardozzi	.05
175	Mike Greenwell	.05
176	Greg Minton	.05
177	Moose Haas	.05
178	Mike Kingery	.05
179	Greg Harris	.05
180	Bo Jackson	.10
181	Carmelo Martinez	.05
182	Alex Trevino	.05
183	Ron Oester	.05
184	Danny Darwin	.05
185	Mike Krukow	.05
186	Rafael Palmeiro	.40
187	Tim Burke	.05
188	Roger McDowell	.05
189	Garry Templeton	.05
190	Terry Pendleton	.05
191	Larry Parrish	.05
192	Rey Quinones	.05
193	Joaquin Andujar	.05
194	Tom Brunansky	.05
195	Donnie Moore	.05
196	Dan Pasqua	.05
197	Jim Gantner	.05
198	Mark Eichhorn	.05
199	John Grubb	.05
200	Bill Ripken RC	.05
201	Sam Horn RC	.05
202	Todd Worrell	.05
203	Terry Leach	.05

#	Player	Price
204	Garth Iorg	.05
205	Brian Dayett	.05
206	Bo Diaz	.05
207	Craig Reynolds	.05
208	Brian Holton	.05
209	Marvelle Wynne (Marvell)	.05
210	Dave Concepcion	.05
211	Mike Davis	.05
212	Devon White	.05
213	Mickey Brantley	.05
214	Greg Gagne	.05
215	Oddibe McDowell	.05
216	Jimmy Key	.05
217	Dave Bergman	.05
218	Calvin Schiraldi	.05
219	Larry Sheets	.05
220	Mike Easler	.05
221	Kurt Stillwell	.05
222	Chuck Jackson RC	.05
223	Dave Martinez	.05
224	Tim Leary	.05
225	Steve Garvey	.20
226	Greg Mathews	.05
227	Doug Sisk	.05
228	Dave Henderson	.05
229	Jimmy Dwyer	.05
230	Larry Owen	.05
231	Andre Thornton	.05
232	Mark Salas	.05
233	Tom Brookens	.05
234	Greg Brock	.05
235	Rance Mulliniks	.05
236	Bob Brower	.05
237	Joe Niekro	.05
238	Scott Bankhead	.05
239	Doug DeCinces	.05
240	Tommy John	.05
241	Rich Gedman	.05
242	Ted Power	.05
243	Dave Meads RC	.05
244	Jim Sundberg	.05
245	Ken Oberkfell	.05
246	Jimmy Jones	.05
247	Ken Landreaux	.05
248	Jose Oquendo	.05
249	John Mitchell RC	.05
250	Don Baylor	.05
251	Scott Fletcher	.05
252	Al Newman	.05
253	Carney Lansford	.05
254	Johnny Ray	.05
255	Gary Pettis	.05
256	Ken Phelps	.05
257	Rick Leach	.05
258	Tim Stoddard	.05
259	Ed Romero	.05
260	Sid Bream	.05
261a	Tom Neidenfuer (Incorrect spelling.)	.25
261b	Tom Niedenfuer (Correct spelling.)	.05
262	Rick Dempsey	.05
263	Lonnie Smith	.05
264	Bob Forsch	.05
265	Barry Bonds	1.00
266	Willie Randolph	.05
267	Mike Ramsey	.05
268	Don Slaught	.05
269	Mickey Tettleton	.05
270	Jerry Reuss	.05
271	Marc Sullivan	.05
272	Jim Morrison	.05
273	Steve Balboni	.05
274	Dick Schofield	.05
275	John Tudor	.05
276	Gene Larkin RC	.05
277	Harold Reynolds	.05
278	Jerry Browne	.05
279	Willie Upshaw	.05
280	Ted Higuera	.05
281	Terry McGriff	.05
282	Terry Puhl	.05
283	Mark Wasinger RC	.05
284	Luis Salazar	.05
285	Ted Simmons	.05
286	John Shelby	.05
287	John Smiley RC	.05
288	Curt Ford	.05
289	Steve Crawford	.05
290	Dan Quisenberry	.05
291	Alan Wiggins	.05
292	Randy Bush	.05
293	John Candelaria	.05
294	Tony Phillips	.05
295	Mike Morgan	.05
296	Bill Wegman	.05
297a	Terry Franconia (Incorrect spelling.)	.25
297b	Terry Francona (Correct spelling.)	.05
298	Mickey Hatcher	.05
299	Andres Thomas	.05
300	Bob Stanley	.05
301	Alfredo Pedrique RC	.05
302	Jim Lindeman	.05
303	Wally Backman	.05
304	Paul O'Neill	.05
305	Hubie Brooks	.05
306	Steve Buechele	.05
307	Bobby Thigpen	.05
308	George Hendrick	.05
309	John Moses	.05
310	Ron Guidry	.05
311	Bill Schroeder	.05
312	Jose Nunez RC	.05
313	Bud Black	.05
314	Joe Sambito	.05
315	Scott McGregor	.05
316	Rafael Santana	.05
317	Frank Williams	.05
318	Mike Fitzgerald	.05
319	Rick Mahler	.05
320	Jim Gott	.05
321	Mariano Duncan	.05
322	Jose Guzman	.05
323	Lee Guetterman	.05
324	Dan Gladden	.05
325	Gary Carter	.40
326	Tracy Jones	.05
327	Floyd Youmans	.05
328	Bill Dawley	.05
329	Bob Noce RC	.05
330	Angel Salazar	.05
331	Goose Gossage	.10
332	George Frazier	.05
333	Ruppert Jones	.05
334	Billy Jo Robidoux	.05
335	Mike Scott	.05
336	Randy Myers	.05
337	Bob Sebra	.05
338	Eric Show	.05
339	Mitch Williams	.05
340	Paul Molitor	.40
341	Gus Polidor	.05
342	Steve Trout	.05
343	Jerry Don Gleaton	.05
344	Bob Knepper	.05
345	Mitch Webster	.05
346	John Morris	.05
347	Andy Hawkins	.05
348	Dave Leiper	.05
349	Ernest Riles	.05
350	Dwight Gooden	.05
351	Dave Righetti	.05
352	Pat Dodson	.05
353	John Habyan	.05
354	Jim Deshaies	.05
355	Butch Wynegar	.05
356	Bryn Smith	.05
357	Matt Young	.05
358	Tom Pagnozzi RC	.05
359	Floyd Rayford	.05
360	Darryl Strawberry	.50
361	Sal Butera	.05
362	Domingo Ramos	.05
363	Chris Brown	.05
364	Jose Gonzalez	.05
365	Dave Smith	.05
366	Andy McGaffigan	.05
367	Stan Javier	.05
368	Henry Cotto	.05
369	Mike Birkbeck	.05
370	Len Dykstra	.05
371	Dave Collins	.05
372	Spike Owen	.05
373	Geno Petralli	.05
374	Ron Karkovice	.05
375	Shane Rawley	.05
376	DeWayne Buice RC	.05
377	Bill Pecota RC	.05
378	Leon Durham	.05
379	Ed Olwine	.05
380	Bruce Hurst	.05
381	Bob McClure	.05
382	Mark Thurmond	.05
383	Buddy Biancalana	.05
384	Tim Conroy	.05
385	Tony Gwynn	.50
386	Greg Gross	.05
387	Barry Lyons RC	.05
388	Mike Felder	.05
389	Pat Clements	.05
390	Ken Griffey	.05
391	Mark Davis	.05
392	Jose Rijo	.05
393	Mike Young	.05
394	Willie Fraser	.05
395	Dion James	.05
396	Steve Shields RC	.05
397	Randy St. Claire	.05
398	Danny Jackson	.05
399	Cecil Fielder	.05
400	Keith Hernandez	.05
401	Don Carman	.05
402	Chuck Crim RC	.05
403	Rob Woodward	.05
404	Junior Ortiz	.05
405	Glenn Wilson	.05
406	Ken Howell	.05
407	Jeff Kunkel	.05
408	Jeff Reed	.05
409	Chris James	.05
410	Zane Smith	.05
411	Ken Dixon	.05
412	Ricky Horton	.05
413	Frank DiPino	.05
414	Shane Mack RC	.05
415	Danny Cox	.05
416	Andy Van Slyke	.05
417	Danny Heep	.05
418	John Cangelosi	.05
419a	John Christiansen (Incorrect spelling.)	.25
419b	John Christensen (Correct spelling.)	.05
420	Joey Cora RC	.05
421	Mike LaValliere	.05
422	Kelly Gruber	.05
423	Bruce Benedict	.05
424	Len Matuszek	.05
425	Kent Tekulve	.05
426	Rafael Ramirez	.05
427	Mike Flanagan	.05
428	Mike Gallego	.05
429	Juan Castillo	.05
430	Neal Heaton	.05
431	Phil Garner	.05
432	Mike Dunne RC	.05
433	Wallace Johnson	.05
434	Jack O'Connor	.05
435	Steve Jeltz	.05
436	Donnell Nixon RC	.05
437	Jack Lazorko	.05
438	Keith Comstock RC	.05
439	Jeff Robinson	.05
440	Graig Nettles	.05
441	Mel Hall	.05
442	Gerald Young RC	.05
443	Gary Redus	.05
444	Charlie Moore	.05
445	Bill Madlock	.05
446	Mark Clear	.05
447	Greg Booker	.05
448	Rick Schu	.05
449	Ron Kittle	.05
450	Dale Murphy	.25
451	Bob Dernier	.05
452	Dale Mohorcic	.05
453	Rafael Belliard	.05
454	Charlie Puleo	.05
455	Dwayne Murphy	.05
456	Jim Eisenreich	.05
457	David Palmer	.05
458	Dave Stewart	.05
459	Pascual Perez	.05
460	Glenn Davis	.05
461	Dan Petry	.05
462	Jim Winn	.05
463	Darrell Miller	.05
464	Mike Moore	.05
465	Mike LaCoss	.05
466	Steve Farr	.05
467	Jerry Mumphrey	.05
468	Kevin Gross	.05
469	Bruce Bochy	.05
470	Orel Hershiser	.05
471	Eric King	.05
472	Ellis Burks RC	.25
473	Darren Daulton	.05
474	Mookie Wilson	.05
475	Frank Viola	.05
476	Ron Robinson	.05
477	Bob Melvin	.05
478	Jeff Musselman	.05
479	Charlie Kerfeld	.05
480	Richard Dotson	.05
481	Kevin Mitchell	.05
482	Gary Roenicke	.05
483	Tim Flannery	.05
484	Rich Yett	.05
485	Pete Incaviglia	.05
486	Rick Cerone	.05
487	Tony Armas	.05
488	Jerry Reed	.05
489	Davey Lopes	.05
490	Frank Tanana	.05
491	Mike Loynd	.05
492	Bruce Ruffin	.05
493	Chris Speier	.05
494	Tom Hume	.05
495	Jesse Orosco	.05
496	Robby Wine, Jr. RC	.05
497	Jeff Montgomery RC	.15
498	Jeff Dedmon	.05
499	Luis Aguayo	.05
500	Reggie Jackson (1968-75)	.15
501	Reggie Jackson (1976)	.15
502	Reggie Jackson (1977-81)	.15
503	Reggie Jackson (1982-86)	.15
504	Reggie Jackson (1987)	.15
505	Billy Hatcher	.05
506	Ed Lynch	.05
507	Willie Hernandez	.05
508	Jose DeLeon	.05
509	Joel Youngblood	.05
510	Bob Welch	.05
511	Steve Ontiveros	.05
512	Randy Ready	.05
513	Juan Nieves	.05
514	Jeff Russell	.05
515	Von Hayes	.05
516	Mark Gubicza	.05
517	Ken Dayley	.05
518	Don Aase	.05
519	Rick Reuschel	.05
520	Mike Henneman RC	.10
521	Rick Aguilera	.05
522	Jay Howell	.05
523	Ed Correa	.05
524	Manny Trillo	.05
525	Kirk Gibson	.05
526	Wally Ritchie RC	.05
527	Al Nipper	.05
528	Atlee Hammaker	.05
529	Shawon Dunston	.05
530	Jim Clancy	.05
531	Tom Paciorek	.05
532	Joel Skinner	.05
533	Scott Garrelts	.05
534	Tom O'Malley	.05
535	John Franco	.05
536	Paul Kilgus RC	.05
537	Darrell Porter	.05
538	Walt Terrell	.05
539	Bill Long RC	.05
540	George Bell	.05
541	Jeff Sellers	.05
542	Joe Boever RC	.05
543	Steve Howe	.05
544	Scott Sanderson	.05
545	Jack Morris	.05
546	Todd Benzinger RC	.05
547	Steve Henderson	.05
548	Eddie Milner	.05
549	Jeff Robinson RC	.05
550	Cal Ripken, Jr.	1.00
551	Jody Davis	.05
552	Kirk McCaskill	.05
553	Craig Lefferts	.05
554	Darnell Coles	.05
555	Phil Niekro	.35
556	Mike Aldrete	.05
557	Pat Perry	.05
558	Juan Agosto	.05
559	Rob Murphy	.05
560	Dennis Rasmussen	.05
561	Manny Lee	.05
562	Jeff Blauser RC	.10
563	Bob Ojeda	.05
564	Dave Dravecky	.05
565	Gene Garber	.05
566	Ron Roenicke	.05
567	Tommy Hinzo RC	.05
568	Eric Nolte RC	.05
569	Ed Hearn	.05
570	Mark Davidson RC	.05
571	Jim Walewander RC	.05
572	Donnie Hill	.05
573	Jamie Moyer	.05
574	Ken Schrom	.05
575	Nolan Ryan	1.00
576	Jim Acker	.05
577	Jamie Quirk	.05
578	Jay Aldrich RC	.05
579	Claudell Washington	.05
580	Jeff Leonard	.05
581	Carmen Castillo	.05
582	Daryl Boston	.05
583	Jeff DeWillis RC	.05
584	John Marzano RC	.05
585	Bill Gullickson	.05
586	Andy Allanson	.05
587	Lee Tunnell	.05
588	Gene Nelson	.05
589	Dave LaPoint	.05
590	Harold Baines	.05
591	Bill Buckner	.05
592	Carlton Fisk	.05
593	Rick Manning	.05
594	Doug Jones	.10
595	Tom Candiotti	.05
596	Steve Lake	.05
597	Jose Lind RC	.05
598	Ross Jones RC	.05
599	Gary Matthews	.05
600	Fernando Valenzuela	.05
601	Dennis Martinez	.05
602	Les Lancaster RC	.05
603	Ozzie Guillen	.05
604	Tony Bernazard	.05
605	Chili Davis	.05
606	Roy Smalley	.05
607	Ivan Calderon	.05
608	Jay Tibbs	.05
609	Guy Hoffman	.05
610	Doyle Alexander	.05
611	Mike Bielecki	.05
612	Shawn Hillegas RC	.05
613	Keith Atherton	.05
614	Eric Plunk	.05
615	Sid Fernandez	.05
616	Dennis Lamp	.05
617	Dave Engle	.05
618	Harry Spilman	.05
619	Don Robinson	.05
620	John Farrell RC	.05
621	Nelson Liriano RC	.05
622	Floyd Bannister	.05
623	Randy Milligan RC	.05
624	Kevin Elster RC	.10
625	Jody Reed RC	.05
626	Shawn Abner RC	.05
627	Kirt Manwaring RC	.10
628	Pete Stanicek RC	.05
629	Rob Ducey RC	.05
630	Steve Kiefer	.05
631	Gary Thurman RC	.05
632	Darrel Akerfelds RC	.05
633	Dave Clark	.05
634	Roberto Kelly RC	.05
635	Keith Hughes RC	.05
636	John Davis RC	.05
637	Mike Devereaux RC	.05
638	Tom Glavine RC	1.00
639	Keith Miller RC	.05
640	Chris Gwynn RC	.05
641	Tim Crews RC	.05
642	Mackey Sasser RC	.05
643	Vicente Palacios RC	.05
644	Kevin Romine	.05
645	Gregg Jefferies RC	.25
646	Jeff Treadway RC	.05
647	Ron Gant RC	.25
648	Rookie Sluggers (Mark McGwire, Matt Nokes)	.35
649	Speed and Power (Tim Raines, Eric Davis)	.05
650	Game Breakers (Jack Clark, Don Mattingly)	.25
651	Super Shortstops (Tony Fernandez, Cal Ripken, Jr., Alan Trammell)	.05
652	Vince Coleman (Highlight)	.05
653	Kirby Puckett (Highlight)	.05
654	Benito Santiago (Highlight)	.05
655	Juan Nieves (Highlight)	.05
656	Steve Bedrosian (Highlight)	.05
657	Mike Schmidt (Highlight)	.30
658	Don Mattingly (Highlight)	.30
659	Mark McGwire (Highlight)	.35
660	Paul Molitor (Highlight)	.20

Glossy

With production of a reported 5,000 sets, there is a significant premium attached to the glossy version of Score's debut baseball card issue. The specially packaged collector's edition features cards with a high-gloss front finish and was sold only as a complete set.

	NM/M
Complete Set (660):	65.00
Common Player:	.25
Stars:	15X

Box Panels

1987 ALL-STAR — ERIC DAVIS

This 18-card set, produced by Major League Marketing and manufactured by Optigraphics, is the premiere box-bottom set issued under the Score trademark. The set features 1987 major league All-star players in full-color action poses, framed by a white border. A "1987 All-Star" banner (red or purple) curves above an orange player name block beneath the player photo. Card backs are printed in red, blue, gold and black and carry the card number, player name and position and league logo. Six colorful "Great Moments in Baseball" trivia cards are also included in this set.

		NM/M
Complete Panel Set:		7.50
Complete Singles Set (18):		7.50
Common Panel:		.50
Common Single Player:		.15
Panel 1		1.00
1	Terry Kennedy	.15
3	Willie Randolph	.15
15	Eric Davis	.15
Panel 2		4.50
3	Don Mattingly	1.00
5	Cal Ripken, Jr.	2.00
11	Jack Clark	.15
Panel 3		3.00
4	Wade Boggs	.75
9	Bret Saberhagen	.25
12	Ryne Sandberg	.75
Panel 4		2.50
6	George Bell	.15
13	Mike Schmidt	1.00
18	Mike Scott	.15
Panel 5		2.00
7	Rickey Henderson	.65
16	Andre Dawson	.25
17	Darryl Strawberry	.25
Panel 6		3.50
8	Dave Winfield	.65
10	Gary Carter	.65
14	Ozzie Smith	.75

Traded/Rookie

JACK CLARK

This 110-card set featuring rookies and traded veterans is similar in design to the 1988 Score set, except for a difference in border color. Individual standard-size player cards (2-1/2" x 3-1/2") feature a bright orange border framing action photos highlighted by a thin white outline. The player name (in white) is centered in the bottom margin, flanked by three yellow stars lower left and a yellow Score logo lower right. The backs carry full-color player portraits on a cream-colored background, plus team name and logo, personal information and a purple stats chart that lists year-by-year and major league totals. A brief player profile follows the stats chart and, on some cards, information is included about the player's trade or acquisition. The boxed update set also includes 10 Magic Motion 3-D trivia cards. The cards are numbered with a "T" suffix.

	NM/M
Complete Set (110):	12.00
Common Player:	.05

#	Player	Price
1	Jack Clark	.05
2	Danny Jackson	.05
3	Brett Butler	.05
4	Kurt Stillwell	.05
5	Tom Brunansky	.05
6	Dennis Lamp	.05
7	Jose DeLeon	.05
8	Tom Herr	.05
9	Keith Moreland	.05
10	Kirk Gibson	.05
11	Bud Black	.05
12	Rafael Ramirez	.05
13	Luis Salazar	.05
14	Goose Gossage	.05
15	Bob Welch	.05
16	Vance Law	.05
17	Ray Knight	.05
18	Dan Quisenberry	.05
19	Don Slaught	.05
20	Lee Smith	.25
21	Rick Cerone	.05
22	Pat Tabler	.05
23	Larry McWilliams	.05
24	Rick Horton	.05
25	Graig Nettles	.05
26	Dan Petry	.05
27	Jose Rijo	.05
28	Chili Davis	.05
29	Dickie Thon	.05
30	Mackey Sasser	.05
31	Mickey Tettleton	.05
32	Rick Dempsey	.05
33	Ron Hassey	.05
34	Phil Bradley	.05
35	Jay Howell	.05
36	Bill Buckner	.05
37	Alfredo Griffin	.05
38	Gary Pettis	.05
39	Calvin Schiraldi	.05
40	John Candelaria	.05
41	Joe Orsulak	.05
42	Willie Upshaw	.05
43	Herm Winningham	.05
44	Ron Kittle	.05
45	Bob Dernier	.05
46	Steve Balboni	.05
47	Steve Shields	.05
48	Henry Cotto	.05
49	Dave Henderson	.05
50	Dave Parker	.05
51	Mike Young	.05
52	Mark Salas	.05
53	Mike Davis	.05
54	Rafael Santana	.05
55	Don Baylor	.05
56	Dan Pasqua	.05
57	Ernest Riles	.05
58	Glenn Hubbard	.05
59	Mike Smithson	.05
60	Richard Dotson	.05
61	Jerry Reuss	.05
62	Mike Jackson	.05
63	Floyd Bannister	.05
64	Jesse Orosco	.05
65	Larry Parrish	.05
66	Jeff Bittiger RC	.05
67	Ray Hayward RC	.05
68	Ricky Jordan RC	.05
69	Tommy Gregg RC	.05
70	Brady Anderson RC	.50
71	Jeff Montgomery	.05
72	Darryl Hamilton RC	.05
73	Cecil Espy RC	.05
74	Greg Briley RC	.05
75	Joey Meyer RC	.05
76	Mike Macfarlane RC	.05
77	Oswald Peraza RC	.05
78	Jack Armstrong RC	.05
79	Don Heinkel RC	.05
80	Mark Grace RC	1.50
81	Steve Curry RC	.05
82	Damon Berryhill RC	.05
83	Steve Ellsworth RC	.05
84	Pete Smith RC	.05
85	Jack McDowell RC	.05
86	Rob Dibble RC	.05
87	Bryan Harvey RC	.05
88	John Dopson RC	.05
89	Dave Gallagher RC	.05
90	Todd Stottlemyre RC	.25
91	Mike Schooler RC	.05

92	Don Gordon RC	.05
93	Sil Campusano RC	.05
94	Jeff Pico RC	.05
95	Jay Buhner RC	.75
96	Nelson Santovenia RC	.05
97	Al Leiter RC	.05
98	Luis Alicea RC	.05
99	Pat Borders RC	.05
100	Chris Sabo RC	.25
101	Tim Belcher RC	.05
102	Walt Weiss RC	.05
103	Craig Biggio RC	6.00
104	Don August RC	.05
105	Roberto Alomar RC	5.00
106	Todd Burns RC	.05
107	John Costello RC	.05
108	Melido Perez RC	.05
109	Darrin Jackson RC	.05
110	Orestes Destrade RC	.05

Traded/Rookie Glossy

Among the scarcest of the major card companies' high-gloss collector's editions of the late 1980s is the 1988 Score Rookie/Traded issue. Production of the regular-finish set was limited in itself and the glossy version is more so, adding a significant premium value.

	NM/M
Complete Set (110):	60.00
Common Player:	.25
Stars:	3X

Young Superstar Series 1

This 40-card set of 2-1/2" x 3-1/2" cards is divided into five separate eight-card subsets. Similar to the company's regular issue, these cards are distinguished by excellent full-color photography on both front and back. The glossy player photos are centered on a white background and framed by a vivid blue and green border. A player name banner beneath the photo includes the name, position and uniform number. The card backs feature color player portraits beneath a hot pink player name/Score logo banner. Hot pink also frames the personal stats (in green), career stats (in black) and career biography (in blue). The backs also include quotes from well-known baseball authorities discussing player performance. This set was distributed via a write-in offer printed on 1988 Score 17-card package wrappers.

	NM/M
Complete Set (40):	3.00
Common Player:	.10
1 Mark McGwire	2.50
2 Benito Santiago	.10
3 Sam Horn	.10
4 Chris Bosio	.10
5 Matt Nokes	.10
6 Ken Williams	.10
7 Dion James	.10
8 B.J. Surhoff	.10
9 Joe Margrane	.10
10 Kevin Seitzer	.10
11 Stanley Jefferson	.10
12 Devon White	.10
13 Nelson Liriano	.10
14 Chris James	.10
15 Mike Henneman	.10
16 Terry Steinbach	.10
17 John Kruk	.10
18 Matt Williams	.10
19 Kelly Downs	.10
20 Bill Ripken	.10
21 Ozzie Guillen	.10
22 Luis Polonia	.10
23 Dave Magadan	.10
24 Mike Greenwell	.10
25 Will Clark	.10
26 Mike Dunne	.10
27 Wally Joyner	.10
28 Robby Thompson	.10
29 Ken Caminiti	.10

30	Jose Canseco	.50
31	Todd Benzinger	.10
32	Pete Incaviglia	.10
33	John Farrell	.10
34	Casey Candaele	.10
35	Mike Aldrete	.10
36	Ruben Sierra	.10
37	Ellis Burks	.10
38	Tracy Jones	.10
39	Kal Daniels	.10
40	Cory Snyder	.10

Young Superstar Series 2

This set of 40 standard-size cards and five Magic trivia cards is part of a double series issued by Score. Each series is divided into five smaller sets of eight baseball cards and one trivia card. The design on both series is similar, except for border color. Series I has blue and green borders. Series II has red and blue borders framing full-color player photos. Backs carry color portrait photos and stats in a variety of colors. Young Superstar series were offered via a write-in offer on '88 Score wrappers. For each eight-card subset, collectors were instructed to send two Score wrappers and $1. Complete sets were offered by a number of hobby dealers nationwide.

	NM/M
Complete Set (40):	4.00
Common Player:	.10
1 Don Mattingly	1.00
2 Glenn Braggs	.10
3 Dwight Gooden	.10
4 Jose Lind	.10
5 Danny Tartabull	.10
6 Tony Fernandez	.10
7 Julio Franco	.10
8 Andres Galarraga	.10
9 Bobby Bonilla	.10
10 Eric Davis	.10
11 Gerald Young	.10
12 Barry Bonds	2.00
13 Jerry Browne	.10
14 Jeff Blauser	.10
15 Mickey Brantley	.10
16 Floyd Youmans	.10
17 Bret Saberhagen	.10
18 Shawon Dunston	.10
19 Len Dykstra	.10
20 Darryl Strawberry	.10
21 Rick Aguilera	.10
22 Ivan Calderon	.10
23 Roger Clemens	1.00
24 Vince Coleman	.10
25 Gary Thurman	.10
26 Jeff Treadway	.10
27 Oddibe McDowell	.10
28 Fred McGriff	.10
29 Mark McLemore	.10
30 Jeff Musselman	.10
31 Mitch Williams	.10
32 Dan Plesac	.10
33 Juan Nieves	.10
34 Barry Larkin	.10
35 Greg Mathews	.10
36 Shane Mack	.10
37 Scott Bankhead	.10
38 Eric Bell	.10
39 Greg Swindell	.10
40 Kevin Elster	.10

1989 Score

This set of 660 cards plus 56 Magic Motion trivia cards is the second annual base issue from Score. Full-color player photos highlight 651 individual players and nine season highlights, including the first Wrigley Field night game. Action photos are framed by thin brightly colored borders (green, cyan blue, purple, orange, red, royal blue) with a baseball diamond logo/player name beneath the photo. Full-color player close-ups (1-5/16" x 1-5/8") are printed on the pastel-colored

backs, along with personal information, stats and career highlights. The cards measure 2-1/2" x 3-1/2".

	NM/M
Unopened Fact. Set (660):	12.00
Complete Set (660):	9.00
Common Player:	.05
Pack (16):	.50
Wax Box (36):	10.00
1 Jose Canseco	.25
2 Andre Dawson	.25
3 Mark McGwire	.65
4 Benny Santiago	.05
5 Rick Reuschel	.05
6 Fred McGriff	.05
7 Kal Daniels	.05
8 Gary Gaetti	.05
9 Ellis Burks	.05
10 Darryl Strawberry	.05
11 Julio Franco	.05
12 Lloyd Moseby	.05
13 Jeff Pico RC	.05
14 Johnny Ray	.05
15 Cal Ripken, Jr.	.75
16 Dick Schofield	.05
17 Mel Hall	.05
18 Bill Ripken	.05
19 Brook Jacoby	.05
20 Kirby Puckett	.50
21 Bill Doran	.05
22 Pete O'Brien	.05
23 Matt Nokes	.05
24 Brian Fisher	.05
25 Jack Clark	.05
26 Gary Pettis	.05
27 Dave Valle	.05
28 Willie Wilson	.05
29 Curt Young	.05
30 Dale Murphy	.20
31 Barry Larkin	.05
32 Dave Stewart	.05
33 Mike LaValliere	.05
34 Glenn Hubbard	.05
35 Ryne Sandberg	.50
36 Tony Pena	.05
37 Greg Walker	.05
38 Von Hayes	.05
39 Kevin Mitchell	.05
40 Tim Raines	.05
41 Keith Hernandez	.05
42 Keith Moreland	.05
43 Ruben Sierra	.05
44 Chet Lemon	.05
45 Willie Randolph	.05
46 Andy Allanson	.05
47 Candy Maldonado	.05
48 Sid Bream	.05
49 Denny Walling	.05
50 Dave Winfield	.40
51 Alvin Davis	.05
52 Cory Snyder	.05
53 Hubie Brooks	.05
54 Chili Davis	.05
55 Kevin Seitzer	.05
56 Jose Uribe	.05
57 Tony Fernandez	.05
58 Tim Teufel	.05
59 Oddibe McDowell	.05
60 Les Lancaster	.05
61 Billy Hatcher	.05
62 Dan Gladden	.05
63 Marty Barrett	.05
64 Nick Esasky	.05
65 Wally Joyner	.05
66 Mike Greenwell	.05
67 Ken Williams	.05
68 Bob Horner	.05
69 Steve Sax	.05
70 Rickey Henderson	.40
71 Mitch Webster	.05
72 Rob Deer	.05
73 Jim Presley	.05
74 Albert Hall	.05
75a George Brett ("At age 33 ...")	1.00
75b George Brett ("At age 35 ...")	.50
76 Brian Downing	.05
77 Dave Martinez	.05
78 Scott Fletcher	.05
79 Phil Bradley	.05
80 Ozzie Smith	.50
81 Larry Sheets	.05
82 Mike Aldrete	.05
83 Darnell Coles	.05
84 Len Dykstra	.05

85	Jim Rice	.15
86	Jeff Treadway	.05
87	Jose Lind	.05
88	Willie McGee	.05
89	Mickey Brantley	.05
90	Tony Gwynn	.50
91	R.J. Reynolds	.05
92	Milt Thompson	.05
93	Kevin McReynolds	.05
94	Eddie Murray	.40
95	Lance Parrish	.05
96	Ron Kittle	.05
97	Gerald Young	.05
98	Ernie Whitt	.05
99	Jeff Reed	.05
100	Don Mattingly	.60
101	Gerald Perry	.05
102	Vance Law	.05
103	John Shelby	.05
104	Chris Sabo	.05
105	Danny Tartabull	.05
106	Glenn Wilson	.05
107	Mark Davidson	.05
108	Dave Parker	.05
109	Eric Davis	.05
110	Alan Trammell	.05
111	Ozzie Virgil	.05
112	Frank Tanana	.05
113	Rafael Ramirez	.05
114	Dennis Martinez	.05
115	Jose DeLeon	.05
116	Bob Ojeda	.05
117	Doug Drabek	.05
118	Andy Hawkins	.05
119	Greg Maddux	.50
120	Cecil Fielder (Reversed negative.)	.05
121	Mike Scioscia	.05
122	Dan Petry	.05
123	Terry Kennedy	.05
124	Kelly Downs	.05
125	Greg Gross	.05
126	Fred Lynn	.05
127	Barry Bonds	.75
128	Harold Baines	.05
129	Doyle Alexander	.05
130	Kevin Elster	.05
131	Mike Heath	.05
132	Teddy Higuera	.05
133	Charlie Leibrandt	.05
134	Tim Laudner	.05
135a	Ray Knight (Photo reversed.)	.40
135b	Ray Knight (Correct photo.)	.05
136	Howard Johnson	.05
137	Terry Pendleton	.05
138	Andy McGaffigan	.05
139	Ken Oberkfell	.05
140	Butch Wynegar	.05
141	Rob Murphy	.05
142	Rich Renteria RC	.05
143	Jose Guzman	.05
144	Andres Galarraga	.05
145	Rick Horton	.05
146	Frank DiPino	.05
147	Glenn Braggs	.05
148	John Kruk	.05
149	Mike Schmidt	.60
150	Lee Smith	.05
151	Robin Yount	.40
152	Mark Eichhorn	.05
153	DeWayne Buice	.05
154	B.J. Surhoff	.05
155	Vince Coleman	.05
156	Tony Phillips	.05
157	Willie Fraser	.05
158	Lance McCullers	.05
159	Greg Gagne	.05
160	Jesse Barfield	.05
161	Mark Langston	.05
162	Kurt Stillwell	.05
163	Dion James	.05
164	Glenn Davis	.05
165	Walt Weiss	.05
166	Dave Concepcion	.05
167	Alfredo Griffin	.05
168	Don Heinkel RC	.05
169	Luis Rivera RC	.05
170	Shane Rawley	.05
171	Darrell Evans	.05
172	Robby Thompson	.05
173	Jody Davis	.05
174	Andy Van Slyke	.05
175	Wade Boggs	.50
176	Garry Templeton	.05
177	Gary Redus	.05
178	Craig Lefferts	.05
179	Carney Lansford	.05
180	Ron Darling	.05
181	Kirk McCaskill	.05
182	Tony Armas	.05
183	Steve Farr	.05
184	Tom Brunansky	.05
185	Bryan Harvey RC	.05
186	Mike Marshall	.05
187	Bo Diaz	.05
188	Willie Upshaw	.05
189	Mike Pagliarulo	.05
190	Mike Krukow	.05
191	Tommy Herr	.05
192	Jim Pankovits	.05
193	Dwight Evans	.05
194	Kelly Gruber	.05
195	Bobby Bonilla	.05
196	Wallace Johnson	.05
197	Dave Stieb	.05
198	Pat Borders RC	.05

199	Rafael Palmeiro	.35
200	Dwight Gooden	.05
201	Pete Incaviglia	.05
202	Chris James	.05
203	Marvell Wynne	.05
204	Pat Sheridan	.05
205	Don Baylor	.05
206	Paul O'Neill	.05
207	Pete Smith	.05
208	Mark McLemore	.05
209	Henry Cotto	.05
210	Kirk Gibson	.05
211	Claudell Washington	.05
212	Randy Bush	.05
213	Joe Carter	.05
214	Bill Buckner	.05
215	Bert Blyleven	.05
216	Brett Butler	.05
217	Lee Mazzilli	.05
218	Spike Owen	.05
219	Bill Swift	.05
220	Tim Wallach	.05
221	David Cone	.05
222	Don Carman	.05
223	Rich Gossage	.05
224	Bob Walk	.05
225	Dave Righetti	.05
226	Kevin Bass	.05
227	Kevin Gross	.05
228	Tim Burke	.05
229	Rick Mahler	.05
230	Lou Whitaker	.05
231	Luis Alicea RC	.05
232	Roberto Alomar	.25
233	Bob Boone	.05
234	Dickie Thon	.05
235	Shawon Dunston	.05
236	Pete Stanicek	.05
237	Craig Biggio	.05
238	Dennis Boyd	.05
239	Tom Candiotti	.05
240	Gary Carter	.40
241	Mike Stanley	.05
242	Ken Phelps	.05
243	Chris Bosio	.05
244	Les Straker	.05
245	Dave Smith	.05
246	John Candelaria	.05
247	Joe Orsulak	.05
248	Storm Davis	.05
249	Floyd Bannister	.05
250	Jack Morris	.05
251	Bret Saberhagen	.05
252	Tom Niedenfuer	.05
253	Neal Heaton	.05
254	Eric Show	.05
255	Juan Samuel	.05
256	Dale Sveum	.05
257	Jim Gott	.05
258	Scott Garrelts	.05
259	Larry McWilliams	.05
260	Steve Bedrosian	.05
261	Jack Howell	.05
262	Jay Tibbs	.05
263	Jamie Moyer	.05
264	Doug Sisk	.05
265	Todd Worrell	.05
266	John Farrell	.05
267	Dave Collins	.05
268	Sid Fernandez	.05
269	Tom Brookens	.05
270	Shane Mack	.05
271	Paul Kilgus	.05
272	Chuck Crim	.05
273	Bob Knepper	.05
274	Mike Moore	.05
275	Guillermo Hernandez	.05
276	Dennis Eckersley	.35
277	Graig Nettles	.05
278	Rich Dotson	.05
279	Larry Herndon	.05
280	Gene Larkin	.05
281	Roger McDowell	.05
282	Greg Swindell	.05
283	Juan Agosto	.05
284	Jeff Robinson	.05
285	Mike Dunne	.05
286	Greg Mathews	.05
287	Kent Tekulve	.05
288	Jerry Mumphrey	.05
289	Jack McDowell	.05
290	Frank Viola	.05
291	Mark Gubicza	.05
292	Dave Schmidt	.05
293	Mike Henneman	.05
294	Jimmy Jones	.05
295	Charlie Hough	.05
296	Rafael Santana	.05
297	Chris Speier	.05
298	Mike Witt	.05
299	Pascual Perez	.05
300	Nolan Ryan	.75
301	Mitch Williams	.05
302	Mookie Wilson	.05
303	Mackey Sasser	.05
304	John Cerutti	.05
305	Jeff Reardon	.05
306	Randy Myers	.05
307	Greg Brock	.05
308	Bob Welch	.05
309	Jeff Robinson	.05
310	Harold Reynolds	.05
311	Jim Walewander	.05
312	Dave Magadan	.05
313	Jim Gantner	.05
314	Walt Terrell	.05
315	Wally Backman	.05
316	Luis Salazar	.05

317	Rick Rhoden	.05
318	Tom Henke	.05
319	Mike Macfarlane	.05
320	Dan Plesac	.05
321	Calvin Schiraldi	.05
322	Stan Javier	.05
323	Devon White	.05
324	Scott Bradley	.05
325	Bruce Hurst	.05
326	Manny Lee	.05
327	Rick Aguilera	.05
328	Bruce Ruffin	.05
329	Ed Whitson	.05
330	Bo Jackson	.10
331	Ivan Calderon	.05
332	Mickey Hatcher	.05
333	Barry Jones RC	.05
334	Ron Hassey	.05
335	Bill Wegman	.05
336	Damon Berryhill	.05
337	Steve Ontiverso	.05
338	Dan Pasqua	.05
339	Bill Pecota	.05
340	Greg Cadaret	.05
341	Scott Bankhead	.05
342	Ron Guidry	.10
343	Danny Heep	.05
344	Bob Brower	.05
345	Rich Gedman	.05
346	Nelson Santovenia RC	.05
347	George Bell	.05
348	Ted Power	.05
349	Mark Grant	.05
350a	Roger Clemens (778 Wins)	2.00
350b	Roger Clemens (78 Wins)	.60
351	Bill Long	.05
352	Jay Bell RC	.05
353	Steve Balboni	.05
354	Bob Kipper	.05
355	Steve Jeltz	.05
356	Jesse Orosco	.05
357	Bob Dernier	.05
358	Mickey Tettleton	.05
359	Duane Ward RC	.05
360	Darrin Jackson RC	.05
361	Rey Quinones	.05
362	Mark Grace	.05
363	Steve Lake	.05
364	Pat Perry	.05
365	Terry Steinbach	.05
366	Alan Ashby	.05
367	Jeff Montgomery	.05
368	Steve Buechele	.05
369	Chris Brown	.05
370	Orel Hershiser	.05
371	Todd Benzinger	.05
372	Ron Gant	.05
373	Paul Assenmacher RC	.05
374	Joey Meyer	.05
375	Neil Allen	.05
376	Mike Davis	.05
377	Jeff Parrett RC	.05
378	Jay Howell	.05
379	Rafael Belliard	.05
380	Luis Polonia	.05
381	Keith Atherton	.05
382	Kent Hrbek	.05
383	Bob Stanley	.05
384	Dave LaPoint	.05
385	Rance Mulliniks	.05
386	Melido Perez	.05
387	Doug Jones	.05
388	Steve Lyons	.05
389	Alejandro Pena	.05
390	Frank White	.05
391	Pat Tabler	.05
392	Eric Plunk RC	.05
393	Mike Maddux RC	.05
394	Allan Anderson RC	.05
395	Bob Brenly	.05
396	Rick Cerone	.05
397	Scott Terry RC	.05
398	Mike Jackson	.05
399	Bobby Thigpen	.05
400	Don Sutton	.35
401	Cecil Espy	.05
402	Junior Ortiz	.05
403	Mike Smithson	.05
404	Bud Black	.05
405	Tom Foley	.05
406	Andres Thomas	.05
407	Rick Sutcliffe	.05
408	Brian Harper	.05
409	John Smiley	.05
410	Juan Nieves	.05
411	Shawn Abner	.05
412	Wes Gardner RC	.05
413	Darren Daulton	.05
414	Juan Berenguer	.05
415	Charles Hudson	.05
416	Rick Honeycutt	.05
417	Greg Booker	.05
418	Tim Belcher	.05
419	Don August	.05
420	Dale Mohorcic	.05
421	Steve Lombardozzi	.05
422	Atlee Hammaker	.05
423	Jerry Don Gleaton	.05
424	Scott Bailes RC	.05
425	Bruce Sutter	.40
426	Randy Ready	.05
427	Jerry Reed	.05
428	Bryn Smith	.05
429	Tim Leary	.05
430	Mark Clear	.05
431	Terry Leach	.05
432	John Moses	.05

433	Ozzie Guillen	.05
434	Gene Nelson	.05
435	Gary Ward	.05
436	Luis Aguayo	.05
437	Fernando Valenzuela	.05
438	Jeff Russell	.05
439	Cecilio Guante	.05
440	Don Robinson	.05
441	Rick Anderson RC	.05
442	Tom Glavine	.35
443	Daryl Boston	.05
444	Joe Price	.05
445	Stewart Cliburn	.05
446	Manny Trillo	.05
447	Joel Skinner	.05
448	Charlie Puleo	.05
449	Carlton Fisk	.40
450	Will Clark	.05
451	Otis Nixon	.05
452	Rick Schu	.05
453	Todd Stottlemyre	.05
454	Tim Birtsas	.05
455	Dave Gallagher RC	.05
456	Barry Lyons	.05
457	Fred Manrique	.05
458	Ernest Riles	.05
459	Doug Jennings RC	.05
460	Joe Magrane	.05
461	Jamie Quirk	.05
462	Jack Armstrong RC	.05
463	Bobby Witt	.05
464	Keith Miller	.05
465	Todd Burns RC	.05
466	John Dopson RC	.05
467	Rich Yett	.05
468	Craig Reynolds	.05
469	Dave Bergman	.05
470	Rex Hudler	.05
471	Eric King	.05
472	Joaquin Andujar	.05
473	Sil Campusano RC	.05
474	Terry Mulholland RC	.05
475	Mike Flanagan	.05
476	Greg Harris	.05
477	Tommy John	.10
478	Dave Anderson	.05
479	Fred Toliver	.05
480	Jimmy Key	.05
481	Donell Nixon	.05
482	Mark Portugal RC	.05
483	Tom Pagnozzi	.05
484	Jeff Kunkel	.05
485	Frank Williams	.05
486	Jody Reed	.05
487	Roberto Kelly	.05
488	Shawn Hillegas	.05
489	Jerry Reuss	.05
490	Mark Davis	.05
491	Jeff Sellers	.05
492	Zane Smith	.05
493	Al Newman RC	.05
494	Mike Young	.05
495	Larry Parrish	.05
496	Herm Winningham	.05
497	Carmen Castillo	.05
498	Joe Hesketh	.05
499	Darrell Miller	.05
500	Mike LaCoss	.05
501	Charlie Lea	.05
502	Bruce Benedict	.05
503	Chuck Finley RC	.05
504	Brad Wellman RC	.05
505	Tim Crews	.05
506	Ken Gerhart	.05
507a	Brian Holton (Born: 1/25/65, Denver.)	.15
507b	Brian Holton (Born: 11/29/59, McKeesport.)	.05
508	Dennis Lamp	.05
509	Bobby Meacham	.05
510	Tracy Jones	.05
511	Mike Fitzgerald	.05
512	Jeff Bittiger RC	.05
513	Tim Flannery	.05
514	Ray Hayward RC	.05
515	Dave Leiper	.05
516	Rod Scurry	.05
517	Carmelo Martinez	.05
518	Curtis Wilkerson	.05
519	Stan Jefferson	.05
520	Dan Quisenberry	.05
521	Lloyd McClendon RC	.05
522	Steve Trout	.05
523	Larry Andersen	.05
524	Don Aase	.05
525	Bob Forsch	.05
526	Geno Petralli	.05
527	Angel Salazar	.05
528	Mike Schooler RC	.05
529	Jose Oquendo	.05
530	Jay Buhner	.05
531	Tom Bolton RC	.05
532	Al Nipper	.05
533	Dave Henderson	.05
534	John Costello RC	.05
535	Donnie Moore	.05
536	Mike Laga	.05
537	Mike Gallego	.05
538	Jim Clancy	.05
539	Joel Youngblood	.05
540	Rick Leach	.05
541	Kevin Romine	.05
542	Mark Salas	.05
543	Greg Minton	.05
544	Dave Palmer	.05
545	Dwayne Murphy	.05
546	Jim Deshaies	.05
547	Don Gordon RC	.05

548	Ricky Jordan	.05
549	Mike Boddicker	.05
550	Mike Scott	.05
551	Jeff Ballard RC	.05
552a	Jose Rijo (Uniform number #24 on card back.)	.15
552b	Jose Rijo (Uniform number #27 on card back.)	.10
553	Danny Darwin	.05
554	Tom Browning	.05
555	Danny Jackson	.05
556	Rick Dempsey	.05
557	Jeffrey Leonard	.05
558	Jeff Musselman	.05
559	Ron Robinson	.05
560	John Tudor	.05
561	Don Slaught	.05
562	Dennis Rasmussen	.05
563	Brady Anderson	.05
564	Pedro Guerrero	.05
565	Paul Molitor	.40
566	Terry Clark RC	.05
567	Terry Puhl	.05
568	Mike Campbell RC	.05
569	Paul Mirabella	.05
570	Jeff Hamilton RC	.05
571	Oswald Peraza RC	.05
572	Bob McClure	.05
573	Jose Bautista RC	.05
574	Alex Trevino	.05
575	John Franco	.05
576	Mark Parent RC	.05
577	Nelson Liriano	.05
578	Steve Shields	.05
579	Odell Jones	.05
580	Al Leiter	.05
581	Dave Stapleton RC	.05
582	1988 World Series (Jose Canseco, Kirk Gibson, Orel Hershiser, Dave Stewart)	.10
583	Donnie Hill	.05
584	Chuck Jackson	.05
585	Rene Gonzales RC	.05
586	Tracy Woodson RC	.05
587	Jim Adduci RC	.05
588	Mario Soto	.05
589	Jeff Blauser	.05
590	Jim Traber	.05
591	Jon Perlman RC	.05
592	Mark Williamson RC	.05
593	Dave Meads	.05
594	Jim Eisenreich	.05
595a	Paul Gibson RC (Player in background adjusting cup.)	.25
595b	Paul Gibson RC (Hand airbrushed away.)	.05
596	Mike Birkbeck	.05
597	Terry Francona	.05
598	Paul Zuvella	.05
599	Franklin Stubbs	.05
600	Gregg Jefferies	.05
601	John Cangelosi	.05
602	Mike Sharperson RC	.05
603	Mike Diaz	.05
604	Gary Varsho RC	.05
605	Terry Blocker RC	.05
606	Charlie O'Brien RC	.05
607	Jim Eppard RC	.05
608	John Davis	.05
609	Ken Griffey Sr.	.05
610	Buddy Bell	.05
611	Ted Simmons	.05
612	Matt Williams	.05
613	Danny Cox	.05
614	Al Pedrique	.05
615	Ron Oester	.05
616	John Smoltz	.05
617	Bob Melvin	.05
618	Rob Dibble RC	.10
619	Kirt Manwaring	.05
620	Felix Fermin RC	.05
621	Doug Dascenzo RC	.05
622	Bill Brennan RC	.05
623	Carlos Quintana RC	.05
624	Mike Harkey RC	.05
625	Gary Sheffield RC	1.25
626	Tom Prince RC	.05
627	Steve Searcy RC	.05
628	Charlie Hayes RC	.05
629	Felix Jose RC	.05
630	Sandy Alomar RC	.50
631	Derek Lilliquist RC	.05
632	Geronimo Berroa RC	.05
633	Luis Medina RC	.05
634	Tom Gordon RC	.05
635	Ramon Martinez RC	.25
636	Craig Worthington RC	.05
637	Edgar Martinez RC	.05
638	Chad Kreuter RC	.05
639	Ron Jones RC	.05
640	Van Snider RC	.05
641	Lance Blankenship RC	.05
642	Dwight Smith RC	.05
643	Cameron Drew RC	.05
644	Jerald Clark RC	.05
645	Randy Johnson RC	2.00
646	Norm Charlton RC	.05
647	Todd Frohwirth RC	.05
648	Luis de los Santos RC	.05
649	Tim Jones RC	.05
650	Dave West RC	.05
651	Bob Milacki RC	.05
652	1988 Highlight (Wrigley Field)	.05
653	1988 Highlight (Orel Hershiser)	.05

654a	1988 Highlight (Wade Boggs) ("...sixth consecutive seaason..." on back)	2.00
654b	1988 Highlight (Wade Boggs) ("Season" corrected.)	.10
655	1988 Highlight (Jose Canseco)	.15
656	1988 Highlight (Doug Jones)	.05
657	1988 Highlight (Rickey Henderson)	.10
658	1988 Highlight (Tom Browning)	.05
659	1988 Highlight (Mike Greenwell)	.05
660	1988 Highlight (Joe Morgan) (A.L. Win Streak)	.05

Rookie/Traded

Score issued its second consecutive traded set in 1989 to supplement and update its regular set. The 110-card traded set features the same basic card design as the regular 1989 Score set. The set consists of rookies and traded players pictured with correct teams. The set was sold by hobby dealers in a special box that included an assortment of "Magic Motion" trivia cards. Cards are numbered with a "T" suffix.

		NM/M
	Complete Set (110):	10.00
	Common Player:	.05
1	Rafael Palmeiro	.35
2	Nolan Ryan	1.00
3	Jack Clark	.05
4	Dave LaPoint	.05
5	Mike Moore	.05
6	Pete O'Brien	.05
7	Jeffrey Leonard	.05
8	Rob Murphy	.05
9	Tom Herr	.05
10	Claudell Washington	.05
11	Mike Pagliarulo	.05
12	Steve Lake	.05
13	Spike Owen	.05
14	Andy Hawkins	.05
15	Todd Benzinger	.05
16	Mookie Wilson	.05
17	Bert Blyleven	.05
18	Jeff Treadway	.05
19	Bruce Hurst	.05
20	Steve Sax	.05
21	Juan Samuel	.05
22	Jesse Barfield	.05
23	Carmelo Castillo	.05
24	Terry Leach	.05
25	Mark Langston	.05
26	Eric King	.05
27	Steve Balboni	.05
28	Len Dykstra	.05
29	Keith Moreland	.05
30	Terry Kennedy	.05
31	Eddie Murray	.45
32	Mitch Williams	.05
33	Jeff Parrett	.05
34	Wally Backman	.05
35	Julio Franco	.05
36	Lance Parrish	.05
37	Nick Esasky	.05
38	Luis Polonia	.05
39	Kevin Gross	.05
40	John Dopson	.05
41	Willie Randolph	.05
42	Jim Clancy	.05
43	Tracy Jones	.05
44	Phil Bradley	.05
45	Milt Thompson	.05
46	Chris James	.05
47	Scott Fletcher	.05
48	Kal Daniels	.05
49	Steve Bedrosian	.05
50	Rickey Henderson	.45
51	Dion James	.05
52	Tim Leary	.05
53	Roger McDowell	.05
54	Mel Hall	.05
55	Dickie Thon	.05
56	Zane Smith	.05
57	Danny Heep	.05
58	Bob McClure	.05
59	Brian Holton	.05
60	Randy Ready	.05

61	Bob Melvin	.05
62	Harold Baines	.05
63	Lance McCullers	.05
64	Jody Davis	.05
65	Darrell Evans	.05
66	Joel Youngblood	.05
67	Frank Viola	.05
68	Mike Aldrete	.05
69	Greg Cadaret	.05
70	John Kruk	.05
71	Pat Sheridan	.05
72	Oddibe McDowell	.05
73	Tom Brookens	.05
74	Bob Boone	.05
75	Walt Terrell	.05
76	Joel Skinner	.05
77	Randy Johnson	1.50
78	Felix Fermin	.05
79	Rick Mahler	.05
80	Rich Dotson	.05
81	Cris Carpenter RC	.05
82	Bill Spiers RC	.05
83	Junior Felix RC	.05
84	Joe Girardi RC	.05
85	Jerome Walton RC	.05
86	Greg Litton RC	.05
87	Greg Harris RC	.05
88	Jim Abbott RC	.05
89	Kevin Brown RC	.05
90	John Wetteland RC	.10
91	Gary Wayne RC	.05
92	Rich Monteleone RC	.05
93	Bob Geren RC	.05
94	Clay Parker RC	.05
95	Steve Finley RC	.05
96	Gregg Olson RC	.05
97	Ken Patterson RC	.05
98	Ken Hill RC	.05
99	Scott Scudder RC	.05
100	Ken Griffey Jr. RC	6.00
101	Jeff Brantley RC	.05
102	Donn Pall RC	.05
103	Carlos Martinez RC	.05
104	Joe Oliver RC	.05
105	Omar Vizquel RC	.25
106	Albert Belle RC	1.00
107	Kenny Rogers RC	.05
108	Mark Carreon RC	.05
109	Rolando Roomes RC	.05
110	Pete Harnisch RC	.05

Rising Stars

Similar in design to the Score Superstar set, this 100-card set showcased a host of rookies. Full-color action photos are surrounded by a bright blue border with a green inner highlight line. Backs display a full-color player portrait above his name and career highlights. The card number and player's rookie year are featured to the right. A "Rising Star" headline highlights the top border. The Score "Rising Star" set was marketed as a combination with a related magazine: "1988-89 Baseball's 100 Hottest Rookies." The set also includes six Magic Motion baseball trivia cards featuring "Rookies to Remember." The magazine/card sets were available at a select group of retailers.

		NM/M
	Complete Set (100):	5.00
	Common Player:	.10
1	Gregg Jefferies	.10
2	Vicente Palacios	.10
3	Cameron Drew	.10
4	Doug Dascenzo	.10
5	Luis Medina	.10
6	Craig Worthington	.10
7	Rob Ducey	.10
8	Hal Morris	.10
9	Bill Brennan	.10
10	Gary Sheffield	.25
11	Mike Devereaux	.10
12	Hensley Meulens	.10
13	Carlos Quintana	.10
14	Todd Frohwirth	.10
15	Scott Lusader	.10
16	Mark Carreon	.10
17	Torey Lovullo	.10
18	Randy Velarde	.10
19	Billy Bean	.10
20	Lance Blankenship	.10
21	Chris Gwynn	.10
22	Felix Jose	.10
23	Derek Lilliquist	.10
24	Gary Thurman	.10
25	Ron Jones	.10
26	Dave Justice	.10
27	Johnny Paredes	.10
28	Tim Jones	.10
29	Jose Gonzalez	.10
30	Geronimo Berroa	.10
31	Trevor Wilson	.10
32	Morris Madden	.10
33	Lance Johnson P	.10
34	Marvin Freeman	.10
35	Jose Cecena	.10
36	Jim Corsi	.10
37	Rolando Roomes	.10
38	Scott Medvin	.10
39	Charlie Hayes	.10
40	Edgar Martinez	.10
41	Van Snider	.10
42	John Fishel	.10
43	Bruce Fields	.10
44	Darryl Hamilton	.10
45	Tom Prince	.10
46	Kirt Manwaring	.10
47	Steve Searcy	.10
48	Mike Harkey	.10
49	German Gonzalez	.10
50	Tony Perezchica	.10
51	Chad Kreuter	.10
52	Luis de los Santos	.10
53	Steve Curry	.10
54	Greg Bailey	.10
55	Ramon Martinez	.10
56	Ron Tingley	.10
57	Randy Kramer	.10
58	Alex Madrid	.10
59	Kevin Reimer	.10
60	Dave Otto	.10
61	Ken Patterson	.10
62	Keith Miller	.10
63	Randy Johnson	2.50
64	Dwight Smith	.10
65	Eric Yelding	.10
66	Bob Geren	.10
67	Shane Turner	.10
68	Tom Gordon	.10
69	Jeff Huson	.10
70	Marty Brown	.10
71	Nelson Santovenia	.10
72	Roberto Alomar	1.00
73	Mike Schooler	.10
74	Pete Smith	.10
75	John Costello	.10
76	Chris Sabo	.10
77	Damon Berryhill	.10
78	Mark Grace	.20
79	Melido Perez	.10
80	Al Leiter	.10
81	Todd Stottlemyre	.10
82	Mackey Sasser	.10
83	Don August	.10
84	Jeff Treadway	.10
85	Jody Reed	.10
86	Mike Campbell	.10
87	Ron Gant	.10
88	Ricky Jordan	.10
89	Terry Clark	.10
90	Roberto Kelly	.10
91	Pat Borders	.10
92	Bryan Harvey	.10
93	Joey Meyer	.10
94	Tim Belcher	.10
95	Walt Weiss	.10
96	Dave Gallagher	.10
97	Mike Macfarlane	.10
98	Craig Biggio	.10
99	Jack Armstrong	.10
100	Todd Burns	.10

Superstars

This 100-card set features full-color action photos of baseball's superstars, and six Magic Motion "Rookies to Remember" baseball trivia cards. Card fronts have a bright red border with a blue line inside highlighting the photo. The player ID is displayed in overlapping triangles of white, green, and yellow. The flip side features a full-color player close-up directly beneath a bright red "Superstar" headline. The set was marketed along with the magazine "1989 Baseball's 100 Hottest Players," at select retailers.

		NM/M
	Complete Set (100):	6.00
	Common Player:	.05
1	Jose Canseco	.35
2	David Cone	.05
3	Dave Winfield	.50
4	George Brett	.75
5	Frank Viola	.05
6	Cory Snyder	.05
7	Alan Trammell	.05
8	Dwight Evans	.05
9	Tim Leary	.05
10	Don Mattingly	.75
11	Kirby Puckett	.65
12	Carney Lansford	.05
13	Dennis Martinez	.05
14	Kent Hrbek	.05
15	Doc Gooden	.05
16	Dennis Eckersley	.40
17	Kevin Seitzer	.05
18	Lee Smith	.05
19	Danny Tartabull	.05
20	Gerald Perry	.05
21	Gary Gaetti	.05
22	Rick Reuschel	.05
23	Keith Hernandez	.05
24	Jeff Reardon	.05
25	Mark McGwire	.85
26	Juan Samuel	.05
27	Jack Clark	.05
28	Robin Yount	.50
29	Steve Bedrosian	.05
30	Kirk Gibson	.05
31	Barry Bonds	1.00
32	Dan Plesac	.05
33	Steve Sax	.05
34	Jeff Robinson	.05
35	Orel Hershiser	.05
36	Julio Franco	.05
37	Dave Righetti	.05
38	Bob Knepper	.05
39	Carlton Fisk	.50
40	Tony Gwynn	.65
41	Doug Jones	.05
42	Bobby Bonilla	.05
43	Ellis Burks	.05
44	Pedro Guerrero	.05
45	Rickey Henderson	.50
46	Glenn Davis	.05
47	Benny Santiago	.05
48	Greg Maddux	.05
49	Teddy Higuera	.05
50	Darryl Strawberry	.05
51	Ozzie Guillen	.05
52	Barry Larkin	.05
53	Tony Fernandez	.05
54	Ryne Sandberg	.65
55	Joe Carter	.05
56	Rafael Palmeiro	.40
57	Paul Molitor	.50
58	Eric Davis	.05
59	Mike Henneman	.05
60	Mike Scott	.05
61	Tom Browning	.05
62	Mark Davis	.05
63	Tom Henke	.05
64	Nolan Ryan	1.00
65	Fred McGriff	.05
66	Dale Murphy	.20
67	Mark Langston	.05
68	Bobby Thigpen	.05
69	Mark Gubicza	.05
70	Mike Greenwell	.05
71	Ron Darling	.05
72	Gerald Young	.05
73	Wally Joyner	.05
74	Andres Galarraga	.05
75	Danny Jackson	.05
76	Mike Schmidt	.75
77	Cal Ripken, Jr.	1.00
78	Alvin Davis	.05
79	Bruce Hurst	.05
80	Andre Dawson	.25
81	Bob Boone	.05
82	Harold Reynolds	.05
83	Eddie Murray	.50
84	Robby Thompson	.05
85	Will Clark	.05
86	Vince Coleman	.05
87	Doug Drabek	.05
88	Ozzie Smith	.65
89	Bob Welch	.05
90	Roger Clemens	.75
91	George Bell	.05
92	Andy Van Slyke	.05
93	Willie McGee	.05
94	Todd Worrell	.05
95	Tim Raines	.05
96	Kevin McReynolds	.05
97	John Franco	.05
98	Jim Gott	.05
99	Johnny Ray	.05
100	Wade Boggs	.65

Yankees

This team set was sponsored by National Westminster Bank and produced by Score as an in-stadium promotion in 1989; distributed to fans attending the July 29 game at Yankee Stadium. The standard-size cards include a full-color player photo with a line drawing of the fa-

Dave Righetti
NEW YORK YANKEES

mous Yankee Stadium facade running along the top of the card. The player's name, "New York Yankees" and position appear below the photo. A second full-color photo is included on the back of the card, along with stats, data and a brief player profile. The set includes a special Thurman Munson commemorative card.

		NM/M
Complete Set (33):		4.00
Common Player:		.15
1	Don Mattingly	2.00
2	Steve Sax	.15
3	Alvaro Espinoza	.15
4	Luis Polonia	.15
5	Jesse Barfield	.15
6	Dave Righetti	.15
7	Dave Winfield	1.00
8	John Candelaria	.15
9	Wayne Tolleson	.15
10	Ken Phelps	.15
11	Rafael Santana	.15
12	Don Slaught	.15
13	Mike Pagliarulo	.15
14	Lance McCullers	.15
15	Dave LaPoint	.15
16	Dale Mohorcic	.15
17	Steve Balboni	.15
18	Roberto Kelly	.15
19	Andy Hawkins	.15
20	Mel Hall	.15
21	Tom Brookens	.15
22	Deion Sanders	.50
23	Richard Dotson	.15
24	Lee Guetterman	.15
25	Bob Geren	.15
26	Jimmy Jones	.15
27	Chuck Cary	.15
28	Ron Guidry	.25
29	Hal Morris	.15
30	Clay Parker	.15
31	Dallas Green	.15
32	Thurman Munson	1.00
33	Sponsor Card	.05

Young Superstars Series 1

PAT BORDERS   CATCHER 10

These standard-size cards (2-1/2" x 3-1/2") display color action photos with a high-gloss finish. Fronts feature a red and blue border surrounding the photo with the team logo in the lower right. A red band beneath the photo provides the setting for the player ID including name, position, and uniform number. Backs feature a red "Young Superstar" headline above a portrait photo. Above the headline appears the player's personal information and statistics in orange and black. To the right photo a condensed scouting report and career hightlights are revealed. The card number and related logos appear on the bottom portion. Five trivia cards featuring "A Year to Remember" accompanied the series. Each trivia card relates to a highlight from the past 56 years. This set was distributed via a write-in offer with Score card wrappers.

		NM/M
Complete Set (42):		3.00
Common Player:		.10
1	Gregg Jefferies	.10
2	Jody Reed	.10
3	Mark Grace	.10
4	Dave Gallagher	.10
5	Bo Jackson	.15
6	Jay Buhner	.10
7	Melido Perez	.10
8	Bobby Witt	.10
9	David Cone	.10
10	Chris Sabo	.10
11	Pat Borders	.10
12	Mark Grant	.10
13	Mike Macfarlane	.10
14	Mike Jackson	.10
15	Ricky Jordan	.10
16	Ron Gant	.10
17	Al Leiter	.10
18	Jeff Parrett	.10
19	Pete Smith	.10
20	Walt Weiss	.10
21	Doug Drabek	.10
22	Keith Miller	.10
23	Keith Miller	.10
24	Damon Berryhill	.10
25	Gary Sheffield	.25
26	Brady Anderson	.10
27	Mitch Williams	.10
28	Roberto Alomar	.25
29	Bobby Thigpen	.10
30	Bryan Harvey	.10
31	Jose Rijo	.10
32	Dave West	.10
33	Joey Meyer	.10
34	Allan Anderson	.10
35	Rafael Palmeiro	.75
36	Tim Belcher	.10
37	John Smiley	.10
38	Mackey Sasser	.10
39	Greg Maddux	1.00
40	Ramon Martinez	.10
41	Randy Myers	.10
42	Scott Bankhead	.10

Young Superstars Series 2

TODD BURNS

Score followed up with a second series of Young Superstars in 1989. The second series also included 42 cards and featured the same design as the first series. The set was also distributed via a write-in offer with Score card wrappers.

		NM/M
Complete Set (42):		10.00
Common Player:		.10
1	Sandy Alomar	.10
2	Tom Gordon	.10
3	Ron Jones	.10
4	Todd Burns	.10
5	Paul O'Neill	.10
6	Gene Larkin	.10
7	Eric King	.10
8	Jeff Robinson	.10
9	Bill Wegman	.10
10	Cecil Espy	.10
11	Jose Guzman	.10
12	Kelly Gruber	.10
13	Duane Ward	.10
14	Mark Gubicza	.10
15	Norm Charlton	.10
16	Jose Oquendo	.10
17	Geronimo Berroa	.10
18	Ken Griffey Jr.	9.00
19	Lance McCullers	.10
20	Todd Stottlemyre	.10
21	Craig Worthington	.10
22	Mike Devereaux	.10
23	Tom Glavine	.50
24	Dale Sveum	.10
25	Roberto Kelly	.10
26	Luis Medina	.10
27	Steve Searcy	.10
28	Don August	.10
29	Shawn Hillegas	.10
30	Mike Campbell	.10
31	Mike Harkey	.10
32	Randy Johnson	1.00
33	Craig Biggio	.10
34	Mike Schooler	.10
35	Andres Thomas	.10
36	Jerome Walton	.10
37	Cris Carpenter	.10
38	Kevin Mitchell	.10
39	Eddie Williams	.10

40	Chad Kreuter	.10
41	Danny Jackson	.10
42	Kurt Stillwell	.10

Scoremasters

This unique 42-card boxed set from Score was reproduced from original artwork done by New York artist Jeffrey Rubin. The paintings are reproduced on a standard-size, white, glossy stock, and the set includes the top stars of the game, plus selected rookies.

		NM/M
Complete Set (42):		8.00
Common Player:		.10
1	Bo Jackson	.20
2	Jerome Walton	.10
3	Cal Ripken, Jr.	2.00
4	Mike Scott	.10
5	Nolan Ryan	2.00
6	Don Mattingly	1.00
7	Tom Gordon	.10
8	Jack Morris	.10
9	Carlton Fisk	.75
10	Will Clark	.10
11	George Brett	1.00
12	Kevin Mitchell	.10
13	Mark Langston	.10
14	Dave Stewart	.10
15	Dale Murphy	.30
16	Gary Gaetti	.10
17	Wade Boggs	.85
18	Eric Davis	.10
19	Kirby Puckett	.85
20	Roger Clemens	1.00
21	Orel Hershiser	.10
22	Mark Grace	.10
23	Ryne Sandberg	.85
24	Barry Larkin	.10
25	Ellis Burks	.10
26	Dwight Gooden	.10
27	Ozzie Smith	.85
28	Andre Dawson	.30
29	Julio Franco	.10
30	Ken Griffey Jr.	1.25
31	Ruben Sierra	.50
32	Mark McGwire	1.50
33	Andres Galarraga	.10
34	Joe Carter	.10
35	Vince Coleman	.10
36	Mike Greenwell	.10
37	Tony Gwynn	.85
38	Andy Van Slyke	.10
39	Gregg Jefferies	.10
40	Jose Canseco	.50
41	Dave Winfield	.75
42	Darryl Strawberry	.10

1990 Score Promos

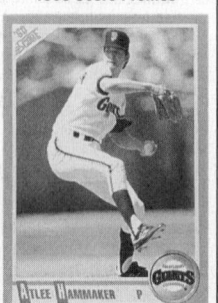

ATLEE HAMMAKER   GIANTS

To preview its 1990 baseball cards, Score pre-released the first 110 cards (#221-330) from its redbordered series as samples. Subtle differences exist on most cards between the samples and the issued version; most easily spotted is that the samples have no statistics on the 1989 season or career lines. Many cards have different versions of the career highlight write-ups on the back, as well. A handful of the sample cards were widely distributed to dealers and the hobby

press, while others from the sheet were released more sparingly, creating inequities in the number of each card available. As few as two examples are known of some of the superstar cards, making them extremely expensive among the single-player specialists.

		NM/M
Common Player:		5.00
221	Steve Buechele	5.00
222	Jesse Barfield	5.00
223	Juan Berenguer	5.00
224	Andy McGaffigan	5.00
225	Pete Smith	5.00
226	Mike Witt	5.00
227	Jay Howell	5.00
228	Scott Bradley	5.00
229	Jerome Walton	5.00
230	Greg Swindell	5.00
231	Atlee Hammaker	5.00
232	Mike Devereaux	5.00
233	Ken Hill	5.00
234	Craig Worthington	5.00
235	Scott Terry	5.00
236	Brett Butler	5.00
237	Doyle Alexander	5.00
238	Dave Anderson	5.00
239	Bob Milacki	5.00
240	Dwight Smith	5.00
241	Otis Nixon	5.00
242	Pat Tabler	5.00
243	Derek Lilliquist	5.00
244	Danny Tartabull	5.00
245	Wade Boggs	65.00
246	Scott Garrelts	5.00
247	Spike Owen	5.00
248	Norm Charlton	5.00
249	Gerald Perry	5.00
250	Nolan Ryan	150.00
251	Kevin Gross	5.00
252	Randy Milligan	5.00
253	Mike LaCoss	5.00
254	Dave Bergman	5.00
255	Tony Gwynn	65.00
256	Felix Fermin	5.00
257	Greg W. Harris	5.00
258	Junior Felix	5.00
259	Mark Davis	5.00
260	Vince Coleman	5.00
261	Paul Gibson	5.00
262	Mitch Williams	5.00
263	Jeff Russell	5.00
264	Omar Vizquel	5.00
265	Andre Dawson	20.00
266	Storm Davis	5.00
267	Guillermo Hernandez	5.00
268	Mike Felder	5.00
269	Tom Candiotti	5.00
270	Bruce Hurst	5.00
271	Fred McGriff	5.00
272	Glenn Davis	5.00
273	John Franco	5.00
274	Rich Yett	5.00
275	Craig Biggio	5.00
276	Gene Larkin	5.00
277	Rob Dibble	5.00
278	Randy Bush	5.00
279	Kevin Bass	5.00
280	Bo Jackson	12.50
281	Wally Backman	5.00
282	Larry Andersen	5.00
283	Chris Bosio	5.00
284	Juan Agosto	5.00
285	Ozzie Smith	65.00
286	George Bell	5.00
287	Rex Hudler	5.00
288	Pat Borders	5.00
289	Danny Jackson	5.00
290	Carlton Fisk	30.00
291	Tracy Jones	5.00
292	Allan Anderson	5.00
293	Johnny Ray	5.00
294	Lee Guetterman	5.00
295	Paul O'Neill	5.00
296	Carney Lansford	5.00
297	Tom Brookens	5.00
298	Claudell Washington	5.00
299	Hubie Brooks	5.00
300	Will Clark	5.00
301	Kenny Rogers	5.00
302	Darrell Evans	5.00
303	Greg Briley	5.00
304	Donn Pall	5.00
305	Teddy Higuera	5.00
306	Dan Pasqua	5.00
307	Dave Winfield	30.00
308	Dennis Powell	5.00
309	Jose DeLeon	5.00
310	Roger Clemens	90.00
311	Melido Perez	5.00
312	Devon White	5.00
313	Dwight Gooden	5.00
314	Carlos Martinez	5.00
315	Dennis Eckersley	25.00
316	Clay Parker	5.00
317	Rick Honeycutt	5.00
318	Tim Laudner	5.00
319	Joe Carter	5.00
320	Robin Yount	30.00
321	Felix Jose	5.00
322	Mickey Tettleton	5.00
323	Mike Gallego	5.00
324	Edgar Martinez	5.00
325	Dave Henderson	5.00
326	Chili Davis	5.00

327	Steve Balboni	5.00
328	Jody Davis	5.00
329	Shawn Hillegas	5.00
330	Jim Abbott	5.00

1990 Score

RANDY JOHNSON   P   M's

The regular Score set increased to 704 cards in 1990. Included were a series of cards picturing first-round draft picks, an expanded subset of rookie cards, four World Series specials, five Highlight cards, and a 13-card "Dream Team" series featuring the game's top players pictured on old tobacco-style cards. For the first time in a Score set, team logos are displayed on the card fronts Card backs include a full-color portrait photo with player data. A one-paragraph write-up of each player was again provided by former Sports Illustrated editor Les Woodcock. The Score set was again distributed with "Magic Motion" trivia cards, this year using "Baseball's Most Valuable Players" as its theme.

		NM/M
Hobby Factory Set (714):		8.00
Retail Factory Set (704):		7.00
Complete Set (704):		6.00
Common Player:		.05
Plastic Pack (16):		.40
Plastic Wax Box (36):		9.00
1	Don Mattingly	.50
2	Cal Ripken, Jr.	1.00
3	Dwight Evans	.05
4	Barry Bonds	1.00
5	Kevin McReynolds	.05
6	Ozzie Guillen	.05
7	Terry Kennedy	.05
8	Bryan Harvey	.05
9	Alan Trammell	.05
10	Cory Snyder	.05
11	Jody Reed	.05
12	Roberto Alomar	.20
13	Pedro Guerrero	.05
14	Gary Redus	.05
15	Marty Barrett	.05
16	Ricky Jordan	.05
17	Joe Magrane	.05
18	Sid Fernandez	.05
19	Rich Dotson	.05
20	Jack Clark	.05
21	Bob Walk	.05
22	Ron Karkovice	.05
23	Lenny Harris RC	.05
24	Phil Bradley	.05
25	Andres Galarraga	.05
26	Brian Downing	.05
27	Dave Martinez	.05
28	Eric King	.05
29	Barry Lyons	.05
30	Dave Schmidt	.05
31	Mike Boddicker	.05
32	Tom Foley	.05
33	Brady Anderson	.05
34	Jim Presley	.05
35	Lance Parrish	.05
36	Von Hayes	.05
37	Lee Smith	.05
38	Herm Winningham	.05
39	Alejandro Pena	.05
40	Mike Scott	.05
41	Joe Orsulak	.05
42	Rafael Ramirez	.05
43	Gerald Young	.05
44	Dick Schofield	.05
45	Dave Smith	.05
46	Dave Magadan	.05
47	Dennis Martinez	.05
48	Greg Minton	.05
49	Milt Thompson	.05
50	Orel Hershiser	.05
51	Bip Roberts	.05
52	Jerry Browne	.05
53	Bob Ojeda	.05
54	Fernando Valenzuela	.05
55	Matt Nokes	.05
56	Brook Jacoby	.05
57	Frank Tanana	.05
58	Scott Fletcher	.05
59	Ron Oester	.05
60	Bob Boone	.05

61	Dan Gladden	.05
62	Darnell Coles	.05
63	Gregg Olson	.05
64	Todd Burns	.05
65	Todd Benzinger	.05
66	Dale Murphy	.25
67	Mike Flanagan	.05
68	Jose Oquendo	.05
69	Cecil Espy	.05
70	Chris Sabo	.05
71	Shane Rawley	.05
72	Tom Brunansky	.05
73	Vance Law	.05
74	B.J. Surhoff	.05
75	Lou Whitaker	.05
76	Ken Caminiti	.05
77	Nelson Liriano	.05
78	Tommy Gregg	.05
79	Don Slaught	.05
80	Eddie Murray	.40
81	Joe Boever	.05
82	Charlie Leibrandt	.05
83	Jose Lind	.05
84	Tony Phillips	.05
85	Mitch Webster	.05
86	Dan Plesac	.05
87	Rick Mahler	.05
88	Steve Lyons	.05
89	Tony Fernandez	.05
90	Ryne Sandberg	.45
91	Nick Esasky	.05
92	Luis Salazar	.05
93	Pete Incaviglia	.05
94	Ivan Calderon	.05
95	Jeff Treadway	.05
96	Kurt Stillwell	.05
97	Gary Sheffield	.30
98	Jeffrey Leonard	.05
99	Andres Thomas	.05
100	Roberto Kelly	.05
101	Alvaro Espinoza RC	.05
102	Greg Gagne	.05
103	John Farrell	.05
104	Willie Wilson	.05
105	Glenn Braggs	.05
106	Chet Lemon	.05
107	Jamie Moyer	.05
108	Chuck Crim	.05
109	Dave Valle	.05
110	Walt Weiss	.05
111	Larry Sheets	.05
112	Don Robinson	.05
113	Danny Heep	.05
114	Carmelo Martinez	.05
115	Dave Gallagher	.05
116	Mike LaValliere	.05
117	Bob McClure	.05
118	Rene Gonzales	.05
119	Mark Parent	.05
120	Wally Joyner	.05
121	Mark Gubicza	.05
122	Tony Pena	.05
123	Carmen Castillo	.05
124	Howard Johnson	.05
125	Steve Sax	.05
126	Tim Belcher	.05
127	Tim Burke	.05
128	Al Newman	.05
129	Dennis Rasmussen	.05
130	Doug Jones	.05
131	Fred Lynn	.05
132	Jeff Hamilton	.05
133	German Gonzalez	.05
134	John Morris	.05
135	Dave Parker	.05
136	Gary Pettis	.05
137	Dennis Boyd	.05
138	Candy Maldonado	.05
139	Rick Cerone	.05
140	George Brett	.50
141	Dave Clark	.05
142	Dickie Thon	.05
143	Junior Ortiz	.05
144	Don August	.05
145	Gary Gaetti	.05
146	Kirt Manwaring	.05
147	Jeff Reed	.05
148	Jose Alvarez RC	.05
149	Mike Schooler	.05
150	Mark Grace	.05
151	Geronimo Berroa	.05
152	Barry Jones	.05
153	Geno Petralli	.05
154	Jim Deshaies	.05
155	Barry Larkin	.05
156	Alfredo Griffin	.05
157	Tom Henke	.05
158	Mike Jeffcoat RC	.05
159	Bob Welch	.05
160	Julio Franco	.05
161	Henry Cotto	.05
162	Terry Steinbach	.05
163	Damon Berryhill	.05
164	Tim Crews	.05
165	Tom Browning	.05
166	Frd Manrique	.05
167	Harold Reynolds	.05
168a	Ron Hassey	
	(Uniform #27 on back.)	
168b	Ron Hassey	
	(Uniform #24 on back.)	.50
169	Shawon Dunston	.05
170	Bobby Bonilla	.05
171	Tom Herr	.05
172	Mike Heath	.05
173	Rich Gedman	.05
174	Bill Ripken	.05
175	Pete O'Brien	.05

#	Player	Price
176a	Lloyd McClendon (Uniform number 1 on back.)	.50
176b	Lloyd McClendon (Uniform number 10 on back.)	.50
177	Brian Holton	.05
178	Jeff Blauser	.05
179	Jim Eisenreich	.05
180	Bert Blyleven	.05
181	Rob Murphy	.05
182	Bill Doran	.05
183	Curt Ford	.05
184	Mike Henneman	.05
185	Eric Davis	.05
186	Lance McCullers	.05
187	Steve Davis RC	.05
188	Bill Wegman	.05
189	Brian Harper	.05
190	Mike Moore	.05
191	Dale Mohorcic	.05
192	Tim Wallach	.05
193	Keith Hernandez	.05
194	Dave Righetti	.05
195a	Bret Saberhagen ("Joke" on card back.)	.10
195b	Bret Saberhagen ("Joker" on card back.)	.30
196	Paul Kilgus	.05
197	Bud Black	.05
198	Juan Samuel	.05
199	Kevin Seitzer	.05
200	Darryl Strawberry	.05
201	Dave Steib	.05
202	Charlie Hough	.05
203	Jack Morris	.05
204	Rance Mulliniks	.05
205	Alvin Davis	.05
206	Jack Howell	.05
207	Ken Patterson RC	.05
208	Terry Pendleton	.05
209	Craig Lefferts	.05
210	Kevin Brown RC	.05
211	Dan Petry	.05
212	Dave Leiper	.05
213	Daryl Boston	.05
214	Kevin Hickey RC	.05
215	Mike Krukow	.05
216	Terry Francona	.05
217	Kirk McCaskill	.05
218	Scott Bailes	.05
219	Bob Forsch	.05
220	Mike Aldrete	.05
221	Steve Buechele	.05
222	Jesse Barfield	.05
223	Juan Berenguer	.05
224	Andy McGaffigan	.05
225	Pete Smith	.05
226	Mike Witt	.05
227	Jay Howell	.05
228	Scott Bradley	.05
229	Jerome Walton RC	.05
230	Greg Swindell	.05
231	Atlee Hammaker	.05
232a	Mike Devereaux (RF)	.05
232b	Mike Devereaux (CF)	2.00
233	Ken Hill	.05
234	Craig Worthington	.05
235	Scott Terry	.05
236	Brett Butler	.05
237	Doyle Alexander	.05
238	Dave Anderson	.05
239	Bob Milacki	.05
240	Dwight Smith	.05
241	Otis Nixon	.05
242	Pat Tabler	.05
243	Derek Lilliquist	.05
244	Danny Tartabull	.05
245	Wade Boggs	.45
246	Scott Garrelts	.05
247	Spike Owen	.05
248	Norm Charlton	.05
249	Gerald Perry	.05
250	Nolan Ryan	1.00
251	Kevin Gross	.05
252	Randy Milligan	.05
253	Mike LaCoss	.05
254	Dave Bergman	.05
255	Tony Gwynn	.45
256	Felix Fermin	.05
257	Greg Harris	.05
258	Junior Felix RC	.05
259	Mark Davis	.05
260	Vince Coleman	.05
261	Paul Gibson	.05
262	Mitch Williams	.05
263	Jeff Russell	.05
264	Omar Vizquel	.05
265	Andre Dawson	.05
266	Storm Davis	.05
267	Guillermo Hernandez	.05
268	Mike Felder	.05
269	Tom Candiotti	.05
270	Bruce Hurst	.05
271	Fred McGriff	.05
272	Glenn Davis	.05
273	John Franco	.05
274	Rich Yett	.05
275	Craig Biggio	.05
276	Gene Larkin	.05
277	Rob Dibble	.05
278	Randy Bush	.05
279	Kevin Bass	.05
280a	Bo Jackson ("Watham" on back.)	.15
280b	Bo Jackson ("Wathan" on back.)	.50
281	Wally Backman	.05
282	Larry Andersen	.05
283	Chris Bosio	.05
284	Juan Agosto	.05
285	Ozzie Smith	.45
286	George Bell	.05
287	Rex Hudler	.05
288	Pat Borders	.05
289	Danny Jackson	.05
290	Carlton Fisk	.40
291	Tracy Jones	.05
292	Allan Anderson	.05
293	Johnny Ray	.05
294	Lee Guetterman	.05
295	Paul O'Neill	.05
296	Carney Lansford	.05
297	Tom Brookens	.05
298	Claudell Washington	.05
299	Hubie Brooks	.05
300	Will Clark	.05
301	Kenny Rogers	.05
302	Darrell Evans	.05
303	Greg Briley	.05
304	Donn Pall	.05
305	Teddy Higuera	.05
306	Dan Pasqua	.05
307	Dave Winfield	.40
308	Dennis Powell	.05
309	Jose DeLeon	.05
310	Roger Clemens	.50
311	Melido Perez	.05
312	Devon White	.05
313	Dwight Gooden	.05
314	Carlos Martinez RC	.05
315	Dennis Eckersley	.35
316	Clay Parker	.05
317	Rick Honeycutt	.05
318	Tim Laudner	.05
319	Joe Carter	.05
320	Robin Yount	.40
321	Felix Jose	.05
322	Mickey Tettleton	.05
323	Mike Gallego	.05
324	Edgar Martinez	.05
325	Dave Henderson	.05
326	Chili Davis	.05
327	Steve Balboni	.05
328	Jody Davis	.05
329	Shawn Hillegas	.05
330	Jim Abbott	.05
331	John Dopson	.05
332	Mark Williamson	.05
333	Jeff Robinson	.05
334	John Smiley	.05
335	Bobby Thigpen	.05
336	Garry Templeton	.05
337	Marvell Wynne	.05
338a	Ken Griffey Sr. (Uniform #25 on card back.)	.05
338b	Ken Griffey Sr. (Uniform #30 on card back.)	1.00
339	Steve Finley	.05
340	Ellis Burks	.05
341	Frank Williams	.05
342	Mike Morgan	.05
343	Kevin Mitchell	.05
344	Joel Youngblood	.05
345	Mike Greenwell	.05
346	Glenn Wilson	.05
347	John Costello	.05
348	Wes Gardner	.05
349	Jeff Ballard	.05
350	Mark Thurmond	.05
351	Randy Myers	.05
352	Shawn Abner	.05
353	Jesse Orosco	.05
354	Greg Walker	.05
355	Pete Harnisch	.05
356	Steve Farr	.05
357	Dave LaPoint	.05
358	Willie Fraser	.05
359	Mickey Hatcher	.05
360	Rickey Henderson	.40
361	Mike Fitzgerald	.05
362	Bill Schroeder	.05
363	Mark Carreon	.05
364	Ron Jones	.05
365	Jeff Montgomery	.05
366	Bill Krueger RC	.05
367	John Cangelosi	.05
368	Jose Gonzalez	.05
369	Greg Hibbard RC	.05
370	John Smoltz	.05
371	Jeff Brantley RC	.05
372	Frank White	.05
373	Ed Whitson	.05
374	Willie McGee	.05
375	Jose Canseco	.30
376	Randy Ready	.05
377	Don Aase	.05
378	Tony Armas	.05
379	Steve Bedrosian	.05
380	Chuck Finley	.05
381	Kent Hrbek	.05
382	Jim Gantner	.05
383	Mel Hall	.05
384	Mike Marshall	.05
385	Mark McGwire	.75
386	Wayne Tolleson	.05
387	Brian Holton	.05
388	John Wetteland	.05
389	Darren Daulton	.05
390	Rob Deer	.05
391	John Moses	.05
392	Todd Worrell	.05
393	Chuck Cary RC	.05
394	Stan Javier	.05
395	Willie Randolph	.05
396	Bill Buckner	.05
397	Robby Thompson	.05
398	Mike Scioscia	.05
399	Lonnie Smith	.05
400	Kirby Puckett	.45
401	Mark Langston	.05
402	Danny Darwin	.05
403	Greg Maddux	.45
404	Lloyd Moseby	.05
405	Rafael Palmeiro	.35
406	Chad Kreuter	.05
407	Jimmy Key	.05
408	Tim Birtsas	.05
409	Tim Raines	.05
410	Dave Stewart	.05
411	Eric Yelding RC	.05
412	Kent Anderson RC	.05
413	Les Lancaster	.05
414	Rick Dempsey	.05
415	Randy Johnson	.40
416	Gary Carter	.40
417	Rolando Roomes	.05
418	Dan Schatzeder	.05
419	Bryn Smith	.05
420	Ruben Sierra	.05
421	Steve Jeltz	.05
422	Ken Oberkfell	.05
423	Sid Bream	.05
424	Jim Clancy	.05
425	Kelly Gruber	.05
426	Rick Leach	.05
427	Len Dykstra	.05
428	Jeff Pico	.05
429	John Cerutti	.05
430	David Cone	.05
431	Jeff Kunkel	.05
432	Luis Aquino	.05
433	Ernie Whitt	.05
434	Bo Diaz	.05
435	Steve Lake	.05
436	Pat Perry	.05
437	Mike Davis	.05
438	Cecilio Guante	.05
439	Duane Ward	.05
440	Andy Van Slyke	.05
441	Gene Nelson	.05
442	Luis Polonia	.05
443	Kevin Elster	.05
444	Keith Moreland	.05
445	Roger McDowell	.05
446	Ron Darling	.05
447	Ernest Riles	.05
448	Mookie Wilson	.05
449a	Bill Spiers RC (66 missing for year of birth)	.50
449b	Bill Spiers (1966 for birth year)	.05
450	Rick Sutcliffe	.05
451	Nelson Santovenia	.05
452	Andy Allanson	.05
453	Bob Melvin	.05
454	Benny Santiago	.05
455	Jose Uribe	.05
456	Bill Landrum RC	.05
457	Bobby Witt	.05
458	Kevin Romine	.05
459	Lee Mazzilli	.05
460	Paul Molitor	.40
461	Ramon Martinez	.05
462	Frank DiPino	.05
463	Walt Terrell	.05
464	Bob Geren RC	.05
465	Rick Reuchel	.05
466	Mark Grant	.05
467	John Kruk	.05
468	Gregg Jefferies	.05
469	R.J. Reynolds	.05
470	Harold Baines	.05
471	Dennis Lamp	.05
472	Tom Gordon	.05
473	Terry Puhl	.05
474	Curtis Wilkerson	.05
475	Dan Quisenberry	.05
476	Oddibe McDowell	.05
477a	Zane Smith (Career ERA 3.93.)	.50
477b	Zane Smith	.05
478	Franklin Stubbs	.05
479	Wallace Johnson	.05
480	Jay Tibbs	.05
481	Tom Glavine	.35
482	Manny Lee	.05
483	Joe Hesketh	.05
484	Mike Bielecki	.05
485	Greg Brock	.05
486	Pascual Perez	.05
487	Kirk Gibson	.05
488	Scott Sanderson	.05
489	Domingo Ramos	.05
490	Kal Daniels	.05
491a	David Wells (Reversed negative on back photo.)	1.50
491b	David Wells (Corrected)	.05
492	Jerry Reed	.05
493	Eric Show	.05
494	Mike Pagliarulo	.05
495	Ron Robinson	.05
496	Brad Komminsk	.05
497	Greg Litton RC	.05
498	Chris James	.05
499	Luis Quinones	.05
500	Frank Viola	.05
501	Tim Teufel	.05
502	Terry Leach	.05
503	Matt Williams	.05
504	Tim Leary	.05
505	Doug Drabek	.05
506	Mariano Duncan	.05
507	Charlie Hayes	.05
508	Albert Belle	.05
509	Pat Sheridan	.05
510	Mackey Sasser	.05
511	Jose Rijo	.05
512	Mike Smithson	.05
513	Gary Ward	.05
514	Dion James	.05
515	Jim Gott	.05
516	Drew Hall RC	.05
517	Doug Bair	.05
518	Scott Scudder RC	.05
519	Rick Aguilera	.05
520	Rafael Belliard	.05
521	Jay Buhner	.05
522	Jeff Reardon	.05
523	Steve Rosenberg RC	.05
524	Randy Velarde RC	.05
525	Jeff Musselman	.05
526	Bill Long	.05
527	Gary Wayne RC	.05
528	Dave Johnson RC	.05
529	Ron Kittle	.05
530	Erik Hanson RC	.05
531	Steve Wilson RC	.05
532	Joey Meyer	.05
533	Curt Young	.05
534	Kelly Downs	.05
535	Joe Girardi	.05
536	Lance Blankenship	.05
537	Greg Mathews	.05
538	Donell Nixon	.05
539	Mark Knudson RC	.05
540	Jeff Wetherby RC	.05
541	Darrin Jackson	.05
542	Terry Mulholland	.05
543	Eric Hetzel RC	.05
544	Rick Reed RC	.05
545	Dennis Cook RC	.05
546	Mike Jackson	.05
547	Brian Fisher	.05
548	Gene Harris RC	.05
549	Jeff King RC	.05
550	Dave Dravecky (Salute)	.05
551	Randy Kutcher RC	.05
552	Mark Portugal	.05
553	Jim Corsi RC	.05
554	Todd Stottlemyre	.05
555	Scott Bankhead	.05
556	Ken Dayley	.05
557	Rick Wrona RC	.10
558	Sammy Sosa RC	3.00
559	Keith Miller	.05
560	Ken Griffey Jr.	.65
561a	Ryne Sandberg (Highlight, 3B on front.)	2.00
561b	Ryne Sandberg (Highlight, no position.)	.25
562	Billy Hatcher	.05
563	Jay Bell	.05
564	Jack Daugherty RC	.05
565	Rich Monteleone RC	.05
566	Bo Jackson (All-Star MVP)	.10
567	Tony Fossas RC	.05
568	Roy Smith RC	.05
569	Jaime Navarro RC	.05
570	Lance Johnson	.05
571	Mike Dyer RC	.05
572	Kevin Ritz RC	.05
573	Dave West	.05
574	Gary Mielke RC	.05
575	Scott Lusader RC	.05
576	Joe Oliver	.05
577	Sandy Alomar, Jr.	.05
578	Andy Benes	.05
579	Tim Jones	.05
580	Randy McCament RC	.05
581	Curt Schilling RC	.35
582	John Orton RC	.05
583a	Milt Cuyler RC (998 games)	1.00
583b	Milt Cuyler RC (98 games)	.05
584	Eric Anthony RC	.05
585	Greg Vaughn RC	.15
586	Deion Sanders	.05
587	Jose DeJesus RC	.05
588	Chip Hale RC	.05
589	John Olerud RC	.50
590	Steve Olin RC	.05
591	Marquis Grissom RC	.40
592	Moises Alou RC	.40
593	Mark Lemke RC	.05
594	Dean Palmer RC	.15
595	Robin Ventura	.05
596	Tino Martinez	.05
597	Mike Huff RC	.05
598	Scott Hemond RC	.05
599	Wally Whitehurst RC	.05
600	Todd Zeile	.15
601	Glenallen Hill RC	.05
602	Hal Morris RC	.05
603	Juan Bell RC	.05
604	Bobby Rose RC	.05
605	Matt Merullo RC	.05
606	Kevin Maas RC	.05
607	Randy Nosek RC	.05
608a	Billy Bates RC ("12 triples" mentioned in second-last line)	.05
608b	Billy Bates (Triples not mentioned.)	.75
609	Mike Stanton RC	.05
610	Goose Gozzo RC	.05
611	Charles Nagy RC	.40
612	Scott Coolbaugh RC	.05
613	Jose Vizcaino RC	.10
614	Greg Smith RC	.05
615	Jeff Huson RC	.05
616	Mickey Weston RC	.05
617	John Pawlowski RC	.05
618a	Joe Skalski RC (Uniform #27 on card back.)	.15
618b	Joe Skalski RC (Uniform #67 on card back.)	1.00
619	Bernie Williams RC	1.00
620	Shawn Holman RC	.05
621	Gary Eave RC	.05
622	Darrin Fletcher RC	.10
623	Pat Combs RC	.05
624	Mike Blowers RC	.05
625	Kevin Appier	.05
626	Pat Austin RC	.05
627	Kelly Mann RC	.05
628	Matt Kinzer RC	.05
629	Chris Hammond RC	.05
630	Dean Wilkins RC	.05
631	Larry Walker RC	.50
632	Blaine Beatty RC	.05
633a	Tom Barrett RC (Uniform #29 on card back.)	.05
633b	Tom Barrett RC (Uniform #14 on card back.)	1.00
634	Stan Belinda RC	.05
635	Tex Smith RC	.05
636	Hensley Meulens RC	.10
637	Juan Gonzalez RC	1.50
638	Lenny Webster RC	.10
639	Mark Gardner RC	.05
640	Tommy Greene RC	.05
641	Mike Hartley RC	.05
642	Phil Stephenson RC	.05
643	Kevin Mmahat RC	.05
644	Ed Whited RC	.05
645	Delino DeShields RC	.15
646	Kevin Blankenship RC	.05
647	Paul Sorrento RC	.05
648	Mike Roesler RC	.05
649	Jason Grimsley RC	.05
650	Dave Justice RC	1.00
651	Scott Cooper RC	.05
652	Dave Eiland RC	.05
653	Mike Munoz RC	.05
654	Jeff Fischer RC	.05
655	Terry Jorgenson RC	.05
656	George Canale RC	.05
657	Brian DuBois RC	.05
658	Carlos Quintana	.05
659	Luis de los Santos	.05
660	Jerald Clark	.05
661	Donald Harris RC (1st Round Pick)	.05
662	Paul Coleman RC (1st Round Pick)	.05
663	Frank Thomas RC (1st Round Pick)	2.00
664	Brent Mayne RC (1st Round Pick)	.05
665	Eddie Zosky RC (1st Round Pick)	.05
666	Steve Hosey RC (1st Round Pick)	.05
667	Scott Bryant RC (1st Round Pick)	.05
668	Tom Goodwin RC (1st Round Pick)	.10
669	Cal Eldred RC (1st Round Pick)	.10
670	Earl Cunningham RC (1st Round Pick)	.05
671	Alan Zinter RC (1st Round Pick)	.05
672	Chuck Knoblauch RC (1st Round Pick)	.40
672(a)	Chuck Knoblauch (3,000 autographed cards with a special hologram on back were inserted into 1992 rack packs)	10.00
673	Kyle Abbott RC (1st Round Pick)	.10
674	Roger Salkeld RC (1st Round Pick)	.05
675	Mo Vaughn RC (1st Round Pick)	.50
676	Kiki Jones RC (1st Round Pick)	.05
677	Tyler Houston RC (1st Round Pick)	.10
678	Jeff Jackson RC (1st Round Pick)	.05
679	Greg Gohr RC (1st Round Pick)	.05
680	Ben McDonald RC (1st Round Pick)	.15
681	Greg Blosser RC (1st Round Pick)	.05
682	Willie Green RC (Greene) (1st Round Pick)	.05
683	Wade Boggs (Dream Team)	.25
684	Will Clark (Dream Team)	.05
685	Tony Gwynn (Dream Team)	.25
686	Rickey Henderson (Dream Team)	.20
687	Bo Jackson (Dream Team)	.15
688	Mark Langston (Dream Team)	.05
689	Barry Larkin (Dream Team)	.05
690	Kirby Puckett (Dream Team)	.25
691	Ryne Sandberg (Dream Team)	.25
692	Mike Scott (Dream Team)	.05
693	Terry Steinbach (Dream Team)	.05
694	Bobby Thigpen (Dream Team)	.05
695	Mitch Williams (Dream Team)	.05
696	Nolan Ryan (Highlight)	.40
697	Bo Jackson (FB/BB)	.05
698	Rickey Henderson (ALCS MVP)	.20
699	Will Clark (NLCS MVP)	.05
700	World Series Games 1-2	.05
701	Lights Out: Candlestick	.15
702	World Series Game 3	.05
703	World Series Wrap-up	.05
704	Wade Boggs (Highlight)	.25

Rookie Dream Team

MARK LEMKE   BRAVES•2B

This 10-card "Rookie Dream Team" set, in the same format as those found in the regular-issue 1990 Score, was available only in factory sets for the hobby trade. Factory sets for general retail outlets did not include these cards, nor were they available in Score packs. Cards carry a "B" prefix to their numbers.

		NM/M
Complete Set (10):		1.00
Common Player:		.10
1	A. Bartlett Giamatti	.10
2	Pat Combs	.10
3	Todd Zeile	.10
4	Luis de los Santos	.10
5	Mark Lemke	.10
6	Robin Ventura	.10
7	Jeff Huson	.10
8	Greg Vaughn	.10
9	Marquis Grissom	.10
10	Eric Anthony	.10

Traded

ERIC LINDROS 3B

This 110-card set features players with new teams as well as 1990 Major League rookies. The cards feature full-color action photos framed in yellow with an orange border. The player's ID appears in green below the photo. The team logo is displayed next to the player's name. The card backs feature posed player photos and follow the style of the regular 1990 Score issue. The cards are numbered 1T-110T. Young hockey phenom Eric Lindros is featured trying out for the Toronto Blue Jays.

		NM/M
Complete Set (110):		4.00
Common Player:		.05
1	Dave Winfield	.75
2	Kevin Bass	.05
3	Nick Esasky	.05
4	Mitch Webster	.05
5	Pascual Perez	.05
6	Gary Pettis	.05
7	Tony Pena	.05
8	Candy Maldonado	.05
9	Cecil Fielder	.05
10	Carmelo Martinez	.05
11	Mark Langston	.05
12	Dave Parker	.05
13	Don Slaught	.05
14	Tony Phillips	.05
15	John Franco	.05
16	Randy Myers	.05

17	Jeff Reardon	.05
18	Sandy Alomar, Jr.	.05
19	Joe Carter	.05
20	Fred Lynn	.05
21	Storm Davis	.05
22	Craig Lefferts	.05
23	Pete O'Brien	.05
24	Dennis Boyd	.05
25	Lloyd Moseby	.05
26	Mark Davis	.05
27	Tim Leary	.05
28	Gerald Perry	.05
29	Don Aase	.05
30	Ernie Whitt	.05
31	Dale Murphy	.35
32	Alejandro Pena	.05
33	Juan Samuel	.05
34	Hubie Brooks	.05
35	Gary Carter	.75
36	Jim Presley	.05
37	Wally Backman	.05
38	Matt Nokes	.05
39	Dan Petry	.05
40	Franklin Stubbs	.05
41	Jeff Huson	.05
42	Billy Hatcher	.05
43	Terry Leach	.05
44	Phil Bradley	.05
45	Claudell Washington	.05
46	Luis Polonia	.05
47	Daryl Boston	.05
48	Lee Smith	.05
49	Tom Brunansky	.05
50	Mike Witt	.05
51	Willie Randolph	.05
52	Stan Javier	.05
53	Brad Komminsk	.05
54	John Candelaria	.05
55	Bryn Smith	.05
56	Glenn Braggs	.05
57	Keith Hernandez	.05
58	Ken Oberkfell	.05
59	Steve Jeltz	.05
60	Chris James	.05
61	Scott Sanderson	.05
62	Bill Long	.05
63	Rick Cerone	.05
64	Scott Bailes	.05
65	Larry Sheets	.05
66	Junior Ortiz	.05
67	Francisco Cabrera RC	.05
68	Gary DiSarcina RC	.05
69	Greg Olson RC	.05
70	Beau Allred RC	.05
71	Oscar Azocar RC	.05
72	Kent Mercker RC	.05
73	John Burkett RC	.05
74	Carlos Baerga RC	.05
75	Dave Hollins RC	.05
76	Todd Hundley RC	.25
77	Rick Parker RC	.05
78	Steve Cummings RC	.05
79	Bill Sampen RC	.05
80	Jerry Kutzler RC	.05
81	Derek Bell RC	.05
82	Kevin Tapani RC	.05
83	Jim Leyritz RC	.25
84	Ray Lankford RC	.25
85	Wayne Edwards RC	.05
86	Frank Thomas	2.00
87	Tim Naehring RC	.05
88	Willie Blair RC	.05
89	Alan Mills RC	.05
90	Scott Radinsky RC	.05
91	Howard Farmer RC	.05
92	Julio Machado RC	.05
93	Rafael Valdez RC	.05
94	Shawn Boskie RC	.05
95	David Segui RC	.05
96	Chris Hoiles RC	.05
97	D.J. Dozier RC	.05
98	Hector Villanueva RC	.05
99	Eric Gunderson RC	.05
100	Eric Lindros RC	1.00
101	Dave Otto RC	.05
102	Dana Kiecker RC	.05
103	Tim Drummond RC	.05
104	Mickey Pina RC	.05
105	Craig Grebeck RC	.05
106	Bernard Gilkey RC	.25
107	Tim Layana RC	.05
108	Scott Chiamparino RC	.05
109	Steve Avery RC	.05
110	Terry Shumpert RC	.05

Rising Stars

For the second consecutive year Score produced a 100-card "Rising Stars" set. The 1990 issue was made available as a boxed set and also marketed with a related magazine like the 1989 issue. Magic Motion trivia cards featuring past MVP's accompany the card set. The cards feature full-color action photos on the front and portrait photos on the back.

		NM/M
Complete Set (100):		5.00
Common Player:		.05
1	Tom Gordon	.05
2	Jerome Walton	.05
3	Ken Griffey Jr.	1.25
4	Dwight Smith	.05
5	Jim Abbott	.05
6	Todd Zeile	.05
7	Donn Pall	.05
8	Rick Reed	.05
9	Joey Belle	.25
10	Gregg Jefferies	.05
11	Kevin Ritz	.05
12	Charlie Hayes	.05
13	Kevin Appier	.05
14	Jeff Huson	.05
15	Gary Wayne	.05
16	Eric Yelding	.05
17	Clay Parker	.05
18	Junior Felix	.05
19	Derek Lilliquist	.05
20	Gary Sheffield	.25
21	Craig Worthington	.05
22	Jeff Brantley	.05
23	Eric Hetzel	.05
24	Greg Harris	.05
25	John Wetteland	.05
26	Joe Oliver	.05
27	Kevin Maas	.05
28	Kevin Brown	.05
29	Mike Stanton	.05
30	Greg Vaughn	.05
31	Ron Jones	.05
32	Gregg Olson	.05
33	Joe Girardi	.05
34	Ken Hill	.05
35	Sammy Sosa	3.00
36	Geronimo Berroa	.05
37	Omar Vizquel	.05
38	Dean Palmer	.05
39	John Olerud	.05
40	Deion Sanders	.05
41	Randy Kramer	.05
42	Scott Lusader	.05
43	Dave Johnson	.05
44	Jeff Wetherby	.05
45	Eric Anthony	.05
46	Kenny Rogers	.05
47	Matt Winters	.05
48	Goose Gozzo	.05
49	Carlos Quintana	.05
50	Bob Geren	.05
51	Chad Kreuter	.05
52	Randy Johnson	.75
53	Hensley Meulens	.05
54	Gene Harris	.05
55	Bill Spiers	.05
56	Kelly Mann	.05
57	Tom McCarthy	.05
58	Steve Finley	.05
59	Ramon Martinez	.05
60	Greg Briley	.05
61	Jack Daugherty	.05
62	Tim Jones	.05
63	Doug Strange	.05
64	John Orton	.05
65	Scott Scudder	.05
66	Mark Gardner (Photo on back actually Steve Frey.)	.05
67	Mark Carreon	.05
68	Bob Milacki	.05
69	Andy Benes	.05
70	Carlos Martinez	.05
71	Jeff King	.05
72	Brad Arnsberg	.05
73	Rick Wrona	.05
74	Cris Carpenter	.05
75	Dennis Cook	.05
76	Pete Harnisch	.05
77	Greg Hibbard	.05
78	Ed Whited	.05
79	Scott Coolbaugh	.05
80	Billy Bates	.05
81	German Gonzalez	.05
82	Lance Blankenship	.05
83	Lenny Harris	.05
84	Milt Cuyler	.05
85	Erik Hanson	.05
86	Kent Anderson	.05
87	Hal Morris	.05
88	Mike Brumley	.05
89	Ken Patterson	.05
90	Mike Devereaux	.05
91	Greg Litton	.05
92	Rolando Roomes	.05
93	Ben McDonald	.05
94	Curt Schilling	.35
95	Jose DeJesus	.05
96	Robin Ventura	.05
97	Steve Searcy	.05
98	Chip Hale	.05
99	Marquis Grissom	.05
100	Luis de los Santos	.05

Superstars

The game's top 100 players are featured in this set. The card fronts feature full-color action photos and are similar in style to the past Score Superstar set. The set was marketed as a boxed set and with a special magazine devoted to baseball's 100 hottest players. Each set includes a series of Magic Motion cards honoring past MVP winners. The player cards measure 2-1/2" x 3-1/2".

		NM/M
Complete Set (100):		3.00
Common Player:		.05
1	Kirby Puckett	.50
2	Steve Sax	.50
3	Tony Gwynn	.50
4	Willie Randolph	.05
5	Jose Canseco	.25
6	Ozzie Smith	.05
7	Rick Reuschel	.05
8	Bill Doran	.05
9	Mickey Tettleton	.05
10	Don Mattingly	.60
11	Greg Swindell	.05
12	Bert Blyleven	.05
13	Dave Stewart	.05
14	Andres Galarraga	.05
15	Darryl Strawberry	.05
16	Ellis Burks	.05
17	Paul O'Neill	.05
18	Bruce Hurst	.05
19	Dave Smith	.05
20	Carney Lansford	.05
21	Robby Thompson	.05
22	Gary Gaetti	.05
23	Jeff Russell	.05
24	Chuck Finley	.05
25	Mark McGwire	.65
26	Alvin Davis	.05
27	George Bell	.05
28	Cory Snyder	.05
29	Keith Hernandez	.05
30	Will Clark	.40
31	Steve Bedrosian	.05
32	Ryne Sandberg	.50
33	Tom Browning	.05
34	Tim Burke	.05
35	John Smoltz	.05
36	Phil Bradley	.05
37	Bobby Bonilla	.05
38	Kirk McCaskill	.05
39	Dave Righetti	.05
40	Bo Jackson	.10
41	Alan Trammell	.05
42	Mike Moore	.05
43	Harold Reynolds	.05
44	Nolan Ryan	.75
45	Fred McGriff	.05
46	Brian Downing	.05
47	Brett Butler	.05
48	Mike Scioscia	.05
49	John Franco	.05
50	Kevin Mitchell	.05
51	Mark Davis	.05
52	Glenn Davis	.05
53	Barry Bonds	.75
54	Dwight Evans	.05
55	Terry Steinbach	.05
56	Dave Gallagher	.05
57	Roberto Kelly	.05
58	Rafael Palmeiro	.35
59	Joe Carter	.05
60	Mark Grace	.05
61	Pedro Guerrero	.05
62	Von Hayes	.05
63	Benny Santiago	.05
64	Dale Murphy	.25
65	John Smiley	.05
66	Cal Ripken, Jr.	.75
67	Mike Greenwell	.05
68	Devon White	.05
69	Ed Whitson	.05
70	Carlton Fisk	.40
71	Lou Whitaker	.05
72	Danny Tartabull	.05
73	Vince Coleman	.05
74	Andre Dawson	.25
75	Tim Raines	.05
76	George Brett	.60
77	Tom Herr	.05
78	Andy Van Slyke	.05
79	Roger Clemens	.60
80	Wade Boggs	.50
81	Wally Joyner	.05
82	Lonnie Smith	.05
83	Howard Johnson	.05
84	Julio Franco	.05
85	Ruben Sierra	.05
86	Dan Plesac	.05
87	Bobby Thigpen	.05
88	Kevin Seitzer	.05
89	Dave Steib	.05
90	Rickey Henderson	.40
91	Jeffrey Leonard	.05
92	Robin Yount	.40
93	Mitch Williams	.05
94	Orel Hershiser	.05
95	Eric Davis	.05
96	Mark Langston	.05
97	Mike Scott	.05
98	Paul Molitor	.40
99	Dwight Gooden	.05
100	Kevin Bass	.05

Yankees

For a second year, National Westminster Bank sponsored a Score-produced team set as a stadium promotion. The set features color player photos on front and back and is graphically enhanced by the team's traditional pinstripe motif. A tribute card to former Yankees infielder and manager Billy Martin, who was killed the previous Christmas, is included in the set. The set was given to fans attending the August 18 game.

		NM/M
Complete Set (32):		4.00
Common Player:		.15
1	Stump Merrill	.15
2	Don Mattingly	2.50
3	Steve Sax	.15
4	Alvaro Espinoza	.15
5	Jesse Barfield	.15
6	Roberto Kelly	.15
7	Mel Hall	.15
8	Claudell Washington	.15
9	Bob Geren	.15
10	Jim Leyritz	.15
11	Pascual Perez	.15
12	Dave LaPoint	.15
13	Tim Leary	.15
14	Mike Witt	.15
15	Chuck Cary	.15
16	Dave Righetti	.15
17	Lee Guetterman	.15
18	Andy Hawkins	.15
19	Greg Cadaret	.15
20	Eric Plunk	.15
21	Jimmy Jones	.15
22	Deion Sanders	.75
23	Jeff Robinson	.15
24	Matt Nokes	.15
25	Steve Balboni	.15
26	Wayne Tolleson	.15
27	Randy Velarde	.15
28	Rick Cerone	.15
29	Alan Mills	.15
30	Billy Martin	.30
31	Yankee Stadium	.15
	All-Time Yankee Records	.15

Young Superstars Set 1

For the third consecutive year, Score produced Young Superstars boxed sets. The 1990 versions contain 42 player cards plus five Magic-Motion trivia cards. The cards are similar to previous Young Superstar sets, with action photography on the front and a glossy finish. Card backs have a color portrait, major league statistics and scouting reports. Besides the boxed set, cards from Set I were inserted into rack packs.

		NM/M
Complete Set (42):		2.00
Common Player:		.10
1	Bo Jackson	.25
2	Dwight Smith	.10
3	Joey Belle	.25
4	Gregg Olson	.10
5	Jim Abbott	.10
6	Felix Fermin	.10
7	Brian Holman	.10
8	Clay Parker	.10
9	Junior Felix	.10
10	Joe Oliver	.10
11	Steve Finley	.10
12	Greg Briley	.10
13	Greg Vaughn	.10
14	Bill Spiers	.10
15	Eric Yelding	.10
16	Jose Gonzalez	.10
17	Mark Carreon	.10
18	Greg Harris	.10
19	Felix Jose	.10
20	Bob Milacki	.10
21	Kenny Rogers	.10
22	Rolando Roomes	.10
23	Bip Roberts	.10
24	Jeff Brantley	.10
25	Jeff Ballard	.10
26	John Dopson	.10
27	Ken Patterson	.10
28	Omar Vizquel	.10
29	Kevin Brown	.10
30	Derek Lilliquist	.10
31	David Wells	.10
32	Ken Hill	.10
33	Greg Litton	.10
34	Rob Ducey	.10
35	Carlos Martinez	.10
36	John Smoltz	.10
37	Lenny Harris	.10
38	Charlie Hayes	.10
39	Tommy Gregg	.10
40	John Wetteland	.10
41	Jeff Huson	.10
42	Eric Anthony	.10

Young Superstars Set 2

Available only as a boxed set via a mail-order offer, Set II of 1990 Score Young Superstars is identical in format to Set I, with the exception that the graphic elements on the front of Set II cards are in red and green, while in Set I they are in blue and magenta.

		NM/M
Complete Set (42):		5.00
Common Player:		.10
1	Todd Zeile	.10
2	Ben McDonald	.10
3	Delino DeShields	.10
4	Pat Combs	.10
5	John Olerud	.10
6	Marquis Grissom	.10
7	Mike Stanton	.10
8	Robin Ventura	.10
9	Larry Walker	.10
10	Dante Bichette	.10
11	Jack Armstrong	.10
12	Jay Bell	.10
13	Andy Benes	.10
14	Joey Cora	.10
15	Rob Dibble	.10
16	Jeff King	.10
17	Jeff Hamilton	.10
18	Erik Hanson	.10
19	Pete Harnisch	.10
20	Greg Hibbard	.10
21	Stan Javier	.10
22	Mark Lemke	.10
23	Steve Olin	.10
24	Tommy Greene	.10
25	Sammy Sosa	4.00
26	Gary Wayne	.10
27	Deion Sanders	.10
28	Steve Wilson	.10
29	Joe Girardi	.10
30	John Orton	.10
31	Kevin Tapani	.10
32	Carlos Baerga	.10
33	Glenallen Hill	.10
34	Mike Blowers	.10
35	Dave Hollins	.10
36	Lance Blankenship	.10
37	Hal Morris	.10
38	Lance Johnson	.10
39	Chris Gwynn	.10
40	Doug Dascenzo	.10
41	Jerald Clark	.10
42	Carlos Quintana	.10

Sportflics 11th National Nolan Ryan

This two-fronted card is a unique souvenir given to those who participated in a special 1990 convention tour of the Optigraphics card manufacturing plant in Dallas. The card features Nolan Ryan on two of the company's best-known products, Score on one side, Sportflics on the other. Each side is similar to Ryan's regularly issued card in those sets, but carries logos or typography related to the 11th Annual National Sports Collectors Convention, held in nearby Arlington. Only 600 of the cards were reported produced.

	NM/M
Nolan Ryan	100.00

1991 Score Promos

To preview its 1991 baseball cards Score pre-released the 110 cards from its teal-bordered series (cards #111-220) as samples. The main difference on most cards between the samples and the issued version is that the samples have no statistics on the 1990 season or career lines. Many cards have different career highlight write-ups on back, as well. A handful of the sample cards were widely distributed to dealers and the hobby press, while others from the sheet were released more sparingly. As few as two specimens are known of some superstar cards, driving up their prices among single-player specialty collectors.

		NM/M
Common Player:		5.00
111	Juan Berenguer	5.00
112	Mike Heath	5.00
113	Scott Bradley	5.00
114	Jack Morris	5.00
115	Barry Jones	5.00
116	Kevin Romine	5.00
117	Garry Templeton	5.00
118	Scott Sanderson	5.00

#	Player	Price
119	Roberto Kelly	5.00
120	George Brett	60.00
121	Oddibe McDowell	5.00
122	Jim Acker	5.00
123	Bill Swift	5.00
124	Eric King	5.00
125	Jay Buhner	5.00
126	Matt Young	5.00
127	Alvaro Espinoza	5.00
128	Greg Hibbard	5.00
129	Jeff M. Robinson	5.00
130	Mike Greenwell	5.00
131	Dion James	5.00
132	Donn Pall	5.00
133	Lloyd Moseby	5.00
134	Randy Velarde	5.00
135	Allan Anderson	5.00
136	Mark Davis	5.00
137	Eric Davis	5.00
138	Phil Stephenson	5.00
139	Felix Fermin	5.00
140	Pedro Guerrero	5.00
141	Charlie Hough	5.00
142	Mike Henneman	5.00
143	Jeff Montgomery	5.00
144	Lenny Harris	5.00
145	Bruce Hurst	5.00
146	Eric Anthony	5.00
147	Paul Assenmacher	5.00
148	Jesse Barfield	5.00
149	Carlos Quintana	5.00
150	Dave Stewart	5.00
151	Roy Smith	5.00
152	Paul Gibson	5.00
153	Mickey Hatcher	5.00
154	Jim Eisenreich	5.00
155	Kenny Rogers	5.00
156	Dave Schmidt	5.00
157	Lance Johnson	5.00
158	Dave West	5.00
159	Steve Balboni	5.00
160	Craig Biggio	5.00
161	Craig Biggio	5.00
162	Brook Jacoby	5.00
163	Dan Gladden	5.00
164	Jeff Reardon	5.00
165	Mark Carreon	5.00
166	Mel Hall	5.00
167	Gary Mielke	5.00
168	Cecil Fielder	5.00
169	Darrin Jackson	5.00
170	Rick Aguilera	5.00
171	Walt Weiss	5.00
172	Steve Farr	5.00
173	Jody Reed	5.00
174	Mike Jeffcoat	5.00
175	Mark Grace	5.00
176	Larry Sheets	5.00
177	Bill Gullickson	5.00
178	Chris Gwynn	5.00
179	Melido Perez	5.00
180	Sid Fernandez	5.00
181	Tim Burke	5.00
182	Gary Pettis	5.00
183	Rob Murphy	5.00
184	Craig Lefferts	5.00
185	Howard Johnson	5.00
186	Ken Caminiti	5.00
187	Tim Belcher	5.00
188	Greg Cadaret	5.00
189	Matt Williams	5.00
190	Dave Magadan	5.00
191	Geno Petralli	5.00
192	Jeff D. Robinson	5.00
193	Jim Deshaies	5.00
194	Willie Randolph	5.00
195	George Bell	5.00
196	Hubie Brooks	5.00
197	Tom Gordon	5.00
198	Mike Fitzgerald	5.00
199	Mike Pagliarulo	5.00
200	Kirby Puckett	40.00
201	Shawon Dunston	5.00
202	Dennis Boyd	5.00
203	Junior Felix	5.00
204	Alejandro Pena	5.00
205	Pete Smith	5.00
206	Tom Glavine	20.00
207	Luis Salazar	5.00
208	John Smoltz	5.00
209	Doug Dascenzo	5.00
210	Tim Wallach	5.00
211	Greg Gagne	5.00
212	Mark Gubicza	5.00
213	Mark Parent	5.00
214	Ken Oberkfell	5.00
215	Gary Carter	30.00
216	Rafael Palmeiro	25.00
217	Tom Niedenfuer	5.00
218	Dave LaPoint	5.00
219	Jeff Treadway	5.00
220	Mitch Williams	5.00

1991 Score

Score introduced a two-series format in 1991. The first series includes cards 1-441. Score cards once again feature multiple border colors within the set, several subsets (Master Blaster, K-Man, Highlights and Riflemen), full-color action photos on the front and portraits on the flip side. Score eliminated display of the player's uniform number on the 1991 cards. Black-and-white Dream Team cards, plus Prospects and #1 Draft Picks highlight the 1991 set. The second series was released in February of 1991.

	NM/M
Unopened Fact. Set (900):	10.00
Complete Set (893):	6.00
Common Player:	.05
Series 1 or 2 Pack (16):	.25
Series 1 or 2 Box (36):	6.00

#	Player	Price
1	Jose Canseco	.25
2	Ken Griffey Jr.	.60
3	Ryne Sandberg	.50
4	Nolan Ryan	.75
5	Bo Jackson	.10
6	Bret Saberhagen	.05
7	Will Clark	.05
8	Ellis Burks	.05
9	Joe Carter	.05
10	Rickey Henderson	.40
11	Ozzie Guillen	.05
12	Wade Boggs	.50
13	Jerome Walton	.05
14	John Franco	.05
15	Ricky Jordan	.05
16	Wally Backman	.05
17	Rob Dibble	.05
18	Glenn Braggs	.05
19	Cory Snyder	.05
20	Kal Daniels	.05
21	Mark Langston	.05
22	Kevin Gross	.05
23	Don Mattingly	.55
24	Dave Righetti	.05
25	Roberto Alomar	.15
26	Robby Thompson	.05
27	Jack McDowell	.05
28	Bip Roberts	.05
29	Jay Howell	.05
30	Dave Steib	.05
31	Johnny Ray	.05
32	Steve Sax	.05
33	Terry Mulholland	.05
34	Lee Guetterman	.05
35	Tim Raines	.05
36	Scott Fletcher	.05
37	Lance Parrish	.05
38	Tony Phillips	.05
39	Todd Stottlemyre	.05
40	Alan Trammell	.05
41	Todd Burns	.05
42	Mookie Wilson	.05
43	Chris Bosio	.05
44	Jeffrey Leonard	.05
45	Doug Jones	.05
46	Mike Scott	.05
47	Andy Hawkins	.05
48	Harold Reynolds	.05
49	Paul Molitor	.40
50	John Farrell	.05
51	Danny Darwin	.05
52	Jeff Blauser	.05
53	John Tudor	.05
54	Milt Thompson	.05
55	Dave Justice	.05
56	Greg Olson RC	.05
57	Willie Blair RC	.05
58	Rick Parker RC	.05
59	Shawn Boskie	.05
60	Kevin Tapani	.05
61	Dave Hollins	.05
62	Scott Radinsky RC	.05
63	Francisco Cabrera	.05
64	Tim Layana RC	.05
65	Jim Leyritz	.05
66	Wayne Edwards	.05
67	Lee Stevens RC	.05
68	Bill Sampen RC	.05
69	Craig Grebeck RC	.05
70	John Burkett	.05
71	Hector Villanueva RC	.05
72	Oscar Azocar RC	.05
73	Alan Mills	.05
74	Carlos Baerga RC	.05
75	Charles Nagy RC	.05
76	Tim Drummond	.05
77	Dana Kiecker RC	.05
78	Tom Edens RC	.05
79	Kent Mercker	.05
80	Steve Avery	.05
81	Lee Smith	.05
82	Dave Martinez	.05
83	Dave Winfield	.40
84	Bill Spiers	.05
85	Dan Pasqua	.05
86	Randy Milligan	.05
87	Tracy Jones	.05
88	Greg Myers RC	.05
89	Keith Hernandez	.05
90	Todd Benzinger	.05
91	Mike Jackson	.05
92	Mike Stanley	.05
93	Candy Maldonado	.05
94	John Kruk	.05
95	Cal Ripken, Jr.	.75
96	Willie Fraser	.05
97	Mike Felder	.05
98	Bill Landrum	.05
99	Chuck Crim	.05
100	Chuck Finley	.05
101	Kirt Manwaring	.05
102	Jaime Navarro	.05
103	Dickie Thon	.05
104	Brian Downing	.05
105	Jim Abbott	.05
106	Tom Brookens	.05
107	Darryl Hamilton	.05
108	Bryan Harvey	.05
109	Greg Harris	.05
110	Greg Swindell	.05
111	Juan Berenguer	.05
112	Mike Heath	.05
113	Scott Bradley	.05
114	Jack Morris	.05
115	Barry Jones	.05
116	Kevin Romine	.05
117	Garry Templeton	.05
118	Scott Sanderson	.05
119	Roberto Kelly	.05
120	George Brett	.50
121	Oddibe McDowell	.05
122	Jim Acker	.05
123	Bill Swift	.05
124	Eric King	.05
125	Jay Buhner	.05
126	Matt Young	.05
127	Alvaro Espinoza	.05
128	Greg Hibbard	.05
129	Jeff Robinson	.05
130	Mike Greenwell	.05
131	Dion James	.05
132	Donn Pall	.05
133	Lloyd Moseby	.05
134	Randy Velarde	.05
135	Allan Anderson	.05
136	Mark Davis	.05
137	Eric Davis	.05
138	Phil Stephenson	.05
139	Felix Fermin	.05
140	Pedro Guerrero	.05
141	Charlie Hough	.05
142	Mike Henneman	.05
143	Jeff Montgomery	.05
144	Lenny Harris	.05
145	Bruce Hurst	.05
146	Eric Anthony	.05
147	Paul Assenmacher	.05
148	Jesse Barfield	.05
149	Carlos Quintana	.05
150	Dave Stewart	.05
151	Roy Smith	.05
152	Paul Gibson	.05
153	Mickey Hatcher	.05
154	Jim Eisenreich	.05
155	Kenny Rogers	.05
156	Dave Schmidt	.05
157	Lance Johnson	.05
158	Dave West	.05
159	Steve Balboni	.05
160	Jeff Brantley	.05
161	Craig Biggio	.05
162	Brook Jacoby	.05
163	Dan Gladden	.05
164	Jeff Reardon	.05
165	Mark Carreon	.05
166	Mel Hall	.05
167	Gary Mielke	.05
168	Cecil Fielder	.05
169	Darrin Jackson	.05
170	Rick Aguilera	.05
171	Walt Weiss	.05
172	Steve Farr	.05
173	Jody Reed	.05
174	Mike Jeffcoat	.05
175	Mark Grace	.05
176	Larry Sheets	.05
177	Bill Gullickson	.05
178	Chris Gwynn	.05
179	Melido Perez	.05
180	Sid Fernandez	.05
181	Tim Burke	.05
182	Gary Pettis	.05
183	Rob Murphy	.05
184	Craig Lefferts	.05
185	Howard Johnson	.05
186	Ken Caminiti	.05
187	Tim Belcher	.05
188	Greg Cadaret	.05
189	Matt Williams	.05
190	Dave Magadan	.05
191	Geno Petralli	.05
192	Jeff Robinson	.05
193	Jim Deshaies	.05
194	Willie Randolph	.05
195	George Bell	.05
196	Hubie Brooks	.05
197	Tom Gordon	.05
198	Mike Fitzgerald	.05
199	Mike Pagliarulo	.05
200	Kirby Puckett	.50
201	Shawon Dunston	.05
202	Dennis Boyd	.05
203	Junior Felix	.05
204	Alejandro Pena	.05
205	Pete Smith	.05
206	Tom Glavine	.35
207	Luis Salazar	.05
208	John Smoltz	.05
209	Doug Dascenzo	.05
210	Tim Wallach	.05
211	Greg Gagne	.05
212	Mark Gubicza	.05
213	Mark Parent	.05
214	Ken Oberkfell	.05
215	Gary Carter	.40
216	Rafael Palmeiro	.35
217	Tom Niedenfuer	.05
218	Dave LaPoint	.05
219	Jeff Treadway	.05
220	Mitch Williams	.05
221	Jose DeLeon	.05
222	Mike LaValliere	.05
223	Darrel Akerfelds	.05
224a	Kent Anderson ("Flachy" in first line.)	
224b	Kent Anderson ("Flashy" in first line.)	
225	Dwight Evans	.05
226	Gary Redus	.05
227	Paul O'Neill	.05
228	Marty Barrett	.05
229	Tom Browning	.05
230	Terry Pendleton	.05
231	Jack Armstrong	.05
232	Mike Boddicker	.05
233	Neal Heaton	.05
234	Marquis Grissom	.05
235	Bert Blyleven	.05
236	Curt Young	.05
237	Don Carman	.05
238	Charlie Hayes	.05
239	Mark Knudson	.05
240	Todd Zeile	.05
241	Larry Walker	.05
242	Jerald Clark	.05
243	Jeff Ballard	.05
244	Jeff King	.05
245	Tom Brunansky	.05
246	Darren Daulton	.05
247	Scott Terry	.05
248	Rob Deer	.05
249	Brady Anderson	.05
250	Len Dykstra	.05
251	Greg Harris	.05
252	Mike Hartley	.05
253	Joey Cora	.05
254	Ivan Calderon	.05
255	Ted Power	.05
256	Sammy Sosa	.50
257	Steve Buechele	.05
258	Mike Devereaux	.05
259	Brad Komminsk	.05
260	Teddy Higuera	.05
261	Shawn Abner	.05
262	Dave Valle	.05
263	Jeff Huson	.05
264	Edgar Martinez	.05
265	Carlton Fisk	.40
266	Steve Finley	.05
267	John Wetteland	.05
268	Kevin Appier	.05
269	Steve Lyons	.05
270	Mickey Tettleton	.05
271	Luis Rivera	.05
272	Steve Jeltz	.05
273	R.J. Reynolds	.05
274	Carlos Martinez	.05
275	Dan Plesac	.05
276	Mike Morgan	.05
277	Jeff Russell	.05
278	Pete Incaviglia	.05
279	Kevin Seitzer	.05
280	Bobby Thigpen	.05
281	Stan Javier	.05
282	Henry Cotto	.05
283	Gary Wayne	.05
284	Shane Mack	.05
285	Brian Holman	.05
286	Gerald Perry	.05
287	Steve Crawford	.05
288	Nelson Liriano	.05
289	Don Aase	.05
290	Randy Johnson	.40
291	Harold Baines	.05
292	Kent Hrbek	.05
293a	Les Lancaster ("Dallas Texas")	
293b	Les Lancaster ("Dallas, Texas")	
294	Jeff Musselman	.05
295	Kurt Stillwell	.05
296	Stan Belinda	.05
297	Lou Whitaker	.05
298	Glenn Wilson	.05
299	Omar Vizquel	.05
300	Ramon Martinez	.05
301	Dwight Smith	.05
302	Tim Crews	.05
303	Lance Blankenship	.05
304	Sid Bream	.05
305	Rafael Ramirez	.05
306	Steve Wilson	.05
307	Mackey Sasser	.05
308	Franklin Stubbs	.05
309	Jack Daugherty	.05
310	Eddie Murray	.40
311	Bob Welch	.05
312	Brian Harper	.05
313	Lance McCullers	.05
314	Dave Smith	.05
315	Bobby Bonilla	.05
316	Jerry Don Gleaton	.05
317	Greg Maddux	.50
318	Keith Miller	.05
319	Mark Portugal	.05
320	Robin Ventura	.05
321	Bob Ojeda	.05
322	Mike Harkey	.05
323	Jay Bell	.05
324	Mark McGwire	.65
325	Gary Gaetti	.05
326	Jeff Pico	.05
327	Kevin McReynolds	.05
328	Frank Tanana	.05
329	Eric Yelding	.05
330	Barry Bonds	.75
331	Brian McRae RC	.05
332	Pedro Munoz RC	.05
333	Daryl Irvine RC	.05
334	Chris Hoiles	.05
335	Thomas Howard RC	.05
336	Jeff Schulz RC	.05
337	Jeff Manto RC	.05
338	Beau Allred	.05
339	Mike Bordick RC	.10
340	Todd Hundley	.05
341	Jim Vatcher RC	.05
342	Luis Sojo RC	.05
343	Jose Offerman RC	.05
344	Pete Coachman RC	.05
345	Mike Benjamin RC	.05
346	Ozzie Canseco RC	.05
347	Tim McIntosh RC	.05
348	Phil Plantier RC	.05
349	Terry Shumpert RC	.05
350	Darren Lewis	.05
351	David Walsh RC	.05
352a	Scott Chiamparino RC (Bats: Left)	
352b	Scott Chiamparino RC (Bats: Right)	
353	Julio Valera RC	.05
354	Anthony Telford RC	.05
355	Kevin Wickander RC	.05
356	Tim Naehring RC	.05
357	Jim Poole RC	.05
358	Mark Whiten RC	.05
359	Terry Wells RC	.05
360	Rafael Valdez RC	.05
361	Mel Stottlemyre RC	.05
362	David Segui RC	.10
363	Paul Abbott	.05
364	Steve Howard RC	.05
365	Karl Rhodes RC	.10
366	Rafael Novoa RC	.05
367	Joe Grahe RC	.05
368	Darren Reed RC	.05
369	Jeff McKnight RC	.05
370	Scott Leius RC	.05
371	Mark Dewey RC	.05
372	Mark Lee RC	.05
373	Rosario Rodriguez RC	.05
374	Chuck McElroy RC	.05
375	Mike Bell RC	.05
376	Mickey Morandini RC	.05
377	Bill Haselman RC	.05
378	Dave Pavlas RC	.05
379	Derrick May	.05
380	Jeromy Burnitz RC (1st Draft Pick)	.25
381	Donald Peters RC (1st Draft Pick)	.05
382	Alex Fernandez RC (1st Draft Pick)	.05
383	Mike Mussina RC (1st Draft Pick)	1.00
384	Daniel Smith RC (1st Draft Pick)	.05
385	Lance Dickson RC (1st Draft Pick)	.10
386	Carl Everett RC (1st Draft Pick)	.40
387	Thomas Nevers RC (1st Draft Pick)	.05
388	Adam Hyzdu RC (1st Draft Pick)	.05
389	Todd Van Poppel RC (1st Draft Pick)	.10
390	Rondell White RC (1st Draft Pick)	.30
391	Marc Newfield RC (1st Draft Pick)	.05
392	Julio Franco/AS	.05
393	Wade Boggs/AS	.25
394	Ozzie Guillen/AS	.05
395	Cecil Fielder /AS	.05
396	Ken Griffey Jr./AS	.30
397	Rickey Henderson/AS	.20
398	Jose Canseco/AS	.15
399	Roger Clemens/AS	.30
400	Sandy Alomar, Jr./AS	.05
401	Bobby Thigpen/AS	.05
402	Bobby Bonilla (Master Blaster)	.05
403	Eric Davis (Master Blaster)	.05
404	Fred McGriff (Master Blaster)	.05
405	Glenn Davis (Master Blaster)	.05
406	Kevin Mitchell (Master Blaster)	.05
407	Rob Dibble (K-Man)	.05
408	Ramon Martinez (K-Man)	.05
409	David Cone (K-Man)	.05
410	Bobby Witt (K-Man)	.05
411	Mark Langston (K-Man)	.05
412	Bo Jackson (Rifleman)	.10
413	Shawon Dunston (Rifleman)	.05
414	Jesse Barfield (Rifleman)	.05
415	Ken Caminiti (Rifleman)	.05
416	Benito Santiago (Rifleman)	.05
417	Nolan Ryan (Highlight)	.40
418	Bobby Thigpen (HL)	.05
419	Ramon Martinez (HL)	.05
420	Bo Jackson (HL)	.10
421	Carlton Fisk (HL)	.20
422	Jimmy Key	.05
423	Junior Noboa RC	.05
424	Al Newman	.05
425	Pat Borders	.05
426	Von Hayes	.05
427	Tim Teufel	.05
428	Eric Plunk	.05
429	John Moses	.05
430	Mike Witt	.05
431	Otis Nixon	.05
432	Tony Fernandez	.05
433	Rance Mulliniks	.05
434	Dan Petry	.05
435	Bob Geren	.05
436	Steve Frey RC	.05
437	Jamie Moyer	.05
438	Junior Ortiz	.05
439	Tom O'Malley	.05
440	Pat Combs	.05
441	Jose Canseco (Dream Team)	.15
442	Alfredo Griffin	.05
443	Andres Galarraga	.05
444	Bryn Smith	.05
445	Andre Dawson	.25
446	Juan Samuel	.05
447	Mike Aldrete	.05
448	Ron Gant	.05
449	Fernando Valenzuela	.05
450	Vince Coleman	.05
451	Kevin Mitchell	.05
452	Spike Owen	.05
453	Mike Bielecki	.05
454	Dennis Martinez	.05
455	Brett Butler	.05
456	Ron Darling	.05
457	Dennis Rasmussen	.05
458	Ken Howell	.05
459	Steve Bedrosian	.05
460	Frank Viola	.05
461	Jose Lind	.05
462	Chris Sabo	.05
463	Dante Bichette	.05
464	Rick Mahler	.05
465	John Smiley	.05
466	Devon White	.05
467	John Orton	.05
468	Mike Stanton	.05
469	Billy Hatcher	.05
470	Wally Joyner	.05
471	Gene Larkin	.05
472	Doug Drabek	.05
473	Gary Sheffield	.30
474	David Wells	.05
475	Andy Van Slyke	.05
476	Mike Gallego	.05
477	B.J. Surhoff	.05
478	Gene Nelson	.05
479	Mariano Duncan	.05
480	Fred McGriff	.05
481	Jerry Browne	.05
482	Alvin Davis	.05
483	Bill Wegman	.05
484	Dave Parker	.05
485	Dennis Eckersley	.35
486	Erik Hanson	.05
487	Bill Ripken	.05
488	Tom Candiotti	.05
489	Mike Schooler	.05
490	Gregg Olson	.05
491	Chris James	.05
492	Pete Harnisch	.05
493	Julio Franco	.05
494	Greg Briley	.05
495	Ruben Sierra	.05
496	Steve Olin	.05
497	Mike Fetters	.05
498	Mark Williamson	.05
499	Bob Tewksbury	.05
500	Tony Gwynn	.50
501	Randy Myers	.05
502	Keith Comstock	.05
503	Craig Worthington	.05
504	Mark Eichhorn	.05
505	Barry Larkin	.05
506	Dave Johnson	.05
507	Bobby Witt	.05
508	Joe Orsulak	.05
509	Pete O'Brien	.05
510	Brad Arnsberg	.05
511	Storm Davis	.05
512	Bob Milacki	.05
513	Bill Pecota	.05
514	Glenallen Hill	.05
515	Danny Tartabull	.05
516	Mike Moore	.05
517	Ron Robinson	.05
518	Mark Gardner	.05
519	Rick Wrona	.05
520	Mike Scioscia	.05
521	Frank Wills	.05
522	Greg Brock	.05
523	Jack Clark	.05
524	Bruce Ruffin	.05
525	Robin Yount	.40
526	Tom Foley	.05
527	Pat Perry	.05
528	Greg Vaughn	.05
529	Wally Whitehurst	.05
530	Norm Charlton	.05
531	Marvell Wynne	.05

No.	Player	Price
532	Jim Gantner	.05
533	Greg Litton	.05
534	Manny Lee	.05
535	Scott Bailes	.05
536	Charlie Leibrandt	.05
537	Roger McDowell	.05
538	Andy Benes	.05
539	Rick Honeycutt	.05
540	Dwight Gooden	.05
541	Scott Garrelts	.05
542	Dave Clark	.05
543	Lonnie Smith	.05
544	Rick Rueschel	.05
545	Delino DeShields	.05
546	Mike Sharperson	.05
547	Mike Kingery	.05
548	Terry Kennedy	.05
549	David Cone	.05
550	Orel Hershiser	.05
551	Matt Nokes	.05
552	Eddie Williams	.05
553	Frank DiPino	.05
554	Fred Lynn	.05
555	Alex Cole RC	.05
556	Terry Leach	.05
557	Chet Lemon	.05
558	Paul Mirabella	.05
559	Bill Long	.05
560	Phil Bradley	.05
561	Duane Ward	.05
562	Dave Bergman	.05
563	Eric Show	.05
564	Xavier Hernandez RC	.05
565	Jeff Parrett	.05
566	Chuck Cary	.05
567	Ken Hill	.05
568	Bob Welch	.05
569	John Mitchell	.05
570	Travis Fryman	.05
571	Derek Lilliquist	.05
572	Steve Lake	.05
573	John Barfield RC	.05
574	Randy Bush	.05
575	Joe Magrane	.05
576	Edgar Diaz	.05
577	Casy Candaele	.05
578	Jesse Orosco	.05
579	Tom Henke	.05
580	Rick Cerone	.05
581	Drew Hall	.05
582	Tony Castillo	.05
583	Jimmy Jones	.05
584	Rick Reed	.05
585	Joe Girardi RC	.05
586	Jeff Gray RC	.05
587	Luis Polonia	.05
588	Joe Klink RC	.05
589	Rex Hudler	.05
590	Kirk McCaskill	.05
591	Juan Agosto	.05
592	Wes Gardner	.05
593	Rich Rodriguez RC	.05
594	Mitch Webster	.05
595	Kelly Gruber	.05
596	Dale Mohorcic	.05
597	Willie McGee	.05
598	Bill Krueger	.05
599	Bob Walk	.05
600	Kevin Maas	.05
601	Danny Jackson	.05
602	Craig McMurtry	.05
603	Curtis Wilkerson	.05
604	Adam Peterson	.05
605	Sam Horn	.05
606	Tommy Gregg	.05
607	Ken Dayley	.05
608	Carmelo Castillo	.05
609	John Shelby	.05
610	Don Slaught	.05
611	Calvin Schiraldi	.05
612	Dennis Lamp	.05
613	Andres Thomas	.05
614	Jose Gonzales	.05
615	Randy Ready	.05
616	Kevin Bass	.05
617	Mike Marshall	.05
618	Daryl Boston	.05
619	Andy McGaffigan	.05
620	Joe Oliver	.05
621	Jim Gott	.05
622	Jose Oquendo	.05
623	Jose DeJesus	.05
624	Mike Brumley	.05
625	John Olerud	.05
626	Ernest Riles	.05
627	Gene Harris	.05
628	Jose Uribe	.05
629	Darnell Coles	.05
630	Carney Lansford	.05
631	Tim Leary	.05
632	Tim Hulett	.05
633	Kevin Elster	.05
634	Tony Fossas	.05
635	Francisco Oliveras	.05
636	Bob Patterson	.05
637	Gary Ward	.05
638	Rene Gonzales	.05
639	Don Robinson	.05
640	Darryl Strawberry	.05
641	Dave Anderson	.05
642	Scott Scudder	.05
643	Reggie Harris RC	.05
644	Dave Henderson	.05
645	Ben McDonald	.05
646	Bob Kipper	.05
647	Hal Morris	.05
648	Tim Birtsas	.05
649	Steve Searcy	.05
650	Dale Murphy	.20
651	Ron Oester	.05
652	Mike LaCoss	.05
653	Ron Jones	.05
654	Kelly Downs	.05
655	Roger Clemens	.55
656	Herm Winningham	.05
657	Trevor Wilson	.05
658	Jose Rijo	.05
659	Dann Bilardello	.05
660	Gregg Jefferies	.05
661	Doug Drabek/AS	.05
662	Randy Myers/AS	.05
663	Benito Santiago/AS	.05
664	Will Clark/AS	.05
665	Ryne Sandberg/AS	.25
666	Barry Larkin/AS	.05
667	Matt Williams/AS	.05
668	Barry Bonds/AS	.35
669	Eric Davis/AS	.05
670	Bobby Bonilla/AS	.05
671	Chipper Jones RC (1st Draft Pick)	3.00
672	Eric Christopherson RC (1st Draft Pick)	.05
673	Robbie Beckett RC (1st Draft Pick)	.05
674	Shane Andrews RC (1st Draft Pick)	.15
675	Steve Karsay RC (1st Draft Pick)	.10
676	Aaron Holbert RC (1st Draft Pick)	.05
677	Donovan Osborne RC (1st Draft Pick)	.05
678	Todd Ritchie RC (1st Draft Pick)	.05
679	Ron Walden RC (1st Draft Pick)	.05
680	Tim Costo RC (1st Draft Pick)	.05
681	Dan Wilson RC (1st Draft Pick)	.10
682	Kurt Miller RC (1st Draft Pick)	.05
683	Mike Lieberthal RC (1st Draft Pick)	.25
684	Roger Clemens (K-Man)	.25
685	Dwight Gooden (K-Man)	.05
686	Nolan Ryan (K-Man)	.35
687	Frank Viola (K-Man)	.05
688	Erik Hanson (K-Man)	.05
689	Matt Williams (Master Blaster)	.05
690	Jose Canseco (Master Blaster)	.10
691	Darryl Strawberry (Master Blaster)	.05
692	Bo Jackson (Master Blaster)	.10
693	Cecil Fielder (Master Blaster)	.05
694	Sandy Alomar, Jr. (Rifleman)	.05
695	Cory Snyder (Rifleman)	.05
696	Eric Davis (Rifleman)	.05
697	Ken Griffey Jr. (Rifleman)	.30
698	Andy Van Slyke (Rifleman)	.05
699	Mark Langston, Mike Witt (No-hitter)	.05
700	Randy Johnson (No-hitter)	.20
701a	Nolan Ryan (No-hitter)(White background on stat box.)	2.00
701b	Nolan Ryan (No-hitter)(Blue background on stat box.)	.05
702	Dave Stewart (No-hitter)	.05
703	Fernando Valenzuela (No-hitter)	.05
704	Andy Hawkins (No-hitter)	.05
705	Melido Perez (No-hitter)	.05
706	Terry Mulholland (No-hitter)	.05
707	Dave Stieb (No-hitter)	.05
708	Brian Barnes RC	.05
709	Bernard Gilkey RC	.05
710	Steve Decker RC	.05
711	Paul Faries RC	.05
712	Paul Marak RC	.05
713	Wes Chamberlain RC	.05
714	Kevin Belcher RC	.05
715	Dan Boone RC	.05
716	Steve Adkins RC	.05
717	Geronimo Pena RC	.05
718	Howard Farmer RC	.05
719	Mark Leonard RC	.05
720	Tom Lampkin RC	.05
721	Mike Gardiner RC	.05
722	Jeff Conine RC	.25
723	Efrain Valdez RC	.05
724	Chuck Malone RC	.05
725	Leo Gomez RC	.05
726	Paul McClellan RC	.05
727	Mark Leiter RC	.05
728	Rich DeLucia RC	.05
729	Mel Rojas RC	.05
730	Hector Wagner RC	.05
731	Ray Lankford RC	.05
732	Turner Ward RC	.05
733	Gerald Alexander RC	.05
734	Scott Anderson RC	.05
735	Tony Perezchica RC	.05
736	Jimmy Kremers RC	.05
737a	American Flag (SCORE 1991 copyright, unmarked promo.)	.25
737b	American Flag (1991 SCORE in copyright)	.25
738	Mike York RC	.05
739	Mike Rochford RC	.05
740	Scott Aldred RC	.05
741	Rico Brogna RC	.05
742	Dave Burba RC	.05
743	Ray Stephens RC	.05
744	Eric Gunderson RC	.05
745	Troy Afenir RC	.05
746	Jeff Shaw RC	.05
747	Orlando Merced RC	.10
748	Omar Oliveras RC	.05
749	Jerry Kutzler RC	.05
750	Mo Vaughn	.05
751	Matt Stark RC	.05
752	Randy Hennis RC	.05
753	Andujar Cedeno RC	.05
754	Kelvin Torve RC	.05
755	Joe Kraemer RC	.05
756	Phil Clark RC	.05
757	Ed Vosberg RC	.05
758	Mike Perez RC	.05
759	Scott Lewis RC	.05
760	Steve Chitren RC	.05
761	Ray Young RC	.05
762	Andres Santana RC	.05
763	Rodney McCray RC	.05
764	Sean Berry RC	.05
765	Brent Mayne	.05
766	Mike Simms RC	.05
767	Glenn Sutko RC	.05
768	Gary Disarcina	.05
769	George Brett (HL)	.25
770	Cecil Fielder (HL)	.05
771	Jim Presley	.05
772	John Dopson	.05
773	Bo Jackson (Breaker)	.10
774	Brent Knackert RC	.05
775	Bill Doran	.05
776	Dick Schofield	.05
777	Nelson Santovenia	.05
778	Mark Guthrie RC	.05
779	Mark Lemke	.05
780	Terry Steinbach	.05
781	Tom Bolton	.05
782	Randy Tomlin RC	.05
783	Jeff Kunkel	.05
784	Felix Jose	.05
785	Rick Sutcliffe	.05
786	John Cerutti	.05
787	Jose Vizcaino	.05
788	Curt Schilling	.35
789	Ed Whitson	.05
790	Tony Pena	.05
791	John Candelaria	.05
792	Carmelo Martinez	.05
793	Sandy Alomar, Jr.	.05
794	Jim Neidlinger RC	.05
795	Red's October (Barry Larkin, Chris Sabo)	.10
796	Paul Sorrento	.05
797	Tom Pagnozzi	.05
798	Tino Martinez	.05
799	Scott Ruskin RC	.05
800	Kirk Gibson	.05
801	Walt Terrell	.05
802	John Russell	.05
803	Chili Davis	.05
804	Chris Nabholz RC	.05
805	Juan Gonzalez	.20
806	Ron Hassey	.05
807	Todd Worrell	.05
808	Tommy Greene	.05
809	Joel Skinner	.05
810	Benito Santiago	.05
811	Pat Tabler	.05
812	Scott Erickson RC	.05
813	Moises Alou	.05
814	Dale Sveum	.05
815	Ryne Sandberg (Man of the Year)	.25
816	Rick Dempsey	.05
817	Scott Bankhead	.05
818	Jason Grimsley	.05
819	Doug Jennings	.05
820	Tom Herr	.05
821	Rob Ducey	.05
822	Luis Quinones	.05
823	Greg Minton	.05
824	Mark Grant	.05
825	Ozzie Smith	.50
826	Dave Eiland	.05
827	Danny Heep	.05
828	Hensley Meulens	.05
829	Charlie O'Brien	.05
830	Glenn Davis	.05
831	John Marzano	.05
832	Steve Ontiveros	.05
833	Ron Karkovice	.05
834	Jerry Goff RC	.05
835	Ken Griffey Sr.	.05
836	Kevin Reimer RC	.05
837	Randy Kutcher	.05
838	Mike Blowers	.05
839	Mike Macfarlane	.05
840	Frank Thomas	.40
841	Ken Griffey Sr., Ken Griffey Jr.	.20
842	Jack Howell	.05
843	Mauro Gozzo RC	.05
844	Gerald Young	.05
845	Zane Smith	.05
846	Kevin Brown	.05
847	Sil Campusano	.05
848	Larry Andersen	.05
849	Cal Ripken, Jr. (Franchise)	.35
850	Roger Clemens (Franchise)	.30
851	Sandy Alomar, Jr. (Franchise)	.05
852	Alan Trammell (Franchise)	.05
853	George Brett (Franchise)	.25
854	Robin Yount (Franchise)	.25
855	Kirby Puckett (Franchise)	.25
856	Don Mattingly (Franchise)	.30
857	Rickey Henderson (Franchise)	.05
858	Ken Griffey Jr. (Franchise)	.30
859	Ruben Sierra (Franchise)	.05
860	John Olerud (Franchise)	.05
861	Dave Justice (Franchise)	.05
862	Ryne Sandberg (Franchise)	.25
863	Eric Davis (Franchise)	.05
864	Darryl Strawberry (Franchise)	.05
865	Tim Wallach (Franchise)	.05
866	Dwight Gooden (Franchise)	.05
867	Len Dykstra (Franchise)	.05
868	Barry Bonds (Franchise)	.35
869	Todd Zeile (Franchise)	.05
870	Benito Santiago (Franchise)	.05
871	Will Clark (Franchise)	.05
872	Craig Biggio (Franchise)	.05
873	Wally Joyner (Franchise)	.05
874	Frank Thomas (Franchise)	.20
875	Rickey Henderson (MVP)	.20
876	Barry Bonds (MVP)	.35
877	Bob Welch (Cy Young)	.05
878	Doug Drabek (Cy Young)	.05
879	Sandy Alomar, Jr. (ROY)	.05
880	Dave Justice (ROY)	.05
881	Damon Berryhill	.05
882	Frank Viola (Dream Team)	.05
883	Dave Stewart (Dream Team)	.05
884	Doug Jones (Dream Team)	.05
885	Randy Myers (Dream Team)	.05
886	Will Clark (Dream Team)	.05
887	Roberto Alomar (Dream Team)	.10
888	Barry Larkin (Dream Team)	.05
889	Wade Boggs (Dream Team)	.25
890	Rickey Henderson (Dream Team)	.20
891	Kirby Puckett (Dream Team)	.25
892	Ken Griffey Jr. (Dream Team)	.30
893	Benito Santiago (Dream Team)	.05

Cooperstown

NOLAN RYAN

This seven-card set was included as an insert in every factory set. The card fronts are white, with an oval-vignetted player portrait. The backs have green borders surrounding a yellow background which contains a summary of the player's career.

		NM/M
Complete Set (7):		3.50
Common Player:		.25
B1	Wade Boggs	.50
B2	Barry Larkin	.25
B3	Ken Griffey Jr.	1.00
B4	Rickey Henderson	.35
B5	George Brett	.75
B6	Will Clark	.25
B7	Nolan Ryan	1.50

Hot Rookies

HOT ROOKIE — HAL MORRIS

These standard-size cards were inserted one per every 100-card 1991 Score blister pack. Ac-tion photos with white borders are featured on the front, and "Hot Rookie" is written in yellow at the top. The background is shaded from yellow to orange. The backs are numbered and each has a color mug shot and a career summary.

		NM/M
Complete Set (10):		2.50
Common Player:		.10
1	Dave Justice	.25
2	Kevin Maas	.10
3	Hal Morris	.10
4	Frank Thomas	1.50
5	Jeff Conine	.10
6	Sandy Alomar Jr.	.10
7	Ray Lankford	.10
8	Steve Decker	.10
9	Juan Gonzalez	.50
10	Jose Offerman	.10

Mickey Mantle

This special set recalls Mickey Mantle's career as a Yankee. Card fronts are glossy and have red and white borders. The card's caption appears at the bottom in a blue stripe. The backs have a photo and a summary of the caption, plus the card number and serial number. Dealers and media members received the sets, which were limited to 5,000, in a fin-fold plastic wrapper. A total of 2,500 of the cards were numbered and autographed.

		NM/M
Complete Set (7):		35.00
Common Card:		7.50
Autographed Card:		575.00
1	The Rookie	9.00
2	Triple Crown	7.50
3	World Series	7.50
4	Going, Going, Gone	7.50
5	Speed and Grace	7.50
6	A True Yankee	7.50
7	Twilight	7.50

Traded

GEORGE BELL

This 110-card set features players with new teams as well as 1991 Major League rookies. The cards are designed in the same style as the regular 1991 Score issue. The cards once again feature a "T" designation along with the card number. The complete set was sold at hobby shops in a special box.

		NM/M
Complete Set (110):		4.00
Common Player:		.05
1	Bo Jackson	.10
2	Mike Flanagan	.05
3	Pete Incaviglia	.05
4	Jack Clark	.05
5	Hubie Brooks	.05
6	Ivan Calderon	.05
7	Glenn Davis	.05
8	Wally Backman	.05
9	Dave Smith	.05
10	Tim Raines	.05
11	Joe Carter	.05
12	Sid Bream	.05
13	George Bell	.05
14	Steve Bedrosian	.05
15	Willie Wilson	.05
16	Darryl Strawberry	.05
17	Danny Jackson	.05
18	Kirk Gibson	.05
19	Willie McGee	.05
20	Junior Felix	.05
21	Steve Farr	.05
22	Pat Tabler	.05
23	Brett Butler	.05
24	Danny Darwin	.05
25	Mickey Tettleton	.05
26	Gary Carter	.50
27	Mitch Williams	.05
28	Candy Maldonado	.05
29	Otis Nixon	.05
30	Brian Downing	.05
31	Tom Candiotti	.05
32	John Candelaria	.05
33	Rob Murphy	.05
34	Deion Sanders	.05
35	Willie Randolph	.05
36	Pete Harnisch	.05
37	Dante Bichette	.05
38	Garry Templeton	.05
39	Gary Gaetti	.05
40	John Cerutti	.05
41	Rick Cerone	.05
42	Mike Pagliarulo	.05
43	Ron Hassey	.05
44	Roberto Alomar	.20
45	Mike Boddicker	.05
46	Bud Black	.05
47	Rob Deer	.05
48	Devon White	.05
49	Luis Sojo	.05
50	Terry Pendleton	.05
51	Kevin Gross	.05
52	Mike Huff	.05
53	Dave Righetti	.05
54	Matt Young	.05
55	Ernest Riles	.05
56	Bill Gullickson	.05
57	Vince Coleman	.05
58	Fred McGriff	.05
59	Franklin Stubbs	.05
60	Eric King	.05
61	Cory Snyder	.05
62	Dwight Evans	.05
63	Gerald Perry	.05
64	Eric Show	.05
65	Shawn Hillegas	.05
66	Tony Fernandez	.05
67	Tim Teufel	.05
68	Mitch Webster	.05
69	Mike Heath	.05
70	Chili Davis	.05
71	Larry Andersen	.05
72	Gary Varsho	.05
73	Juan Berenguer	.05
74	Jack Morris	.05
75	Barry Jones	.05
76	Rafael Belliard	.05
77	Steve Buechele	.05
78	Scott Sanderson	.05
79	Bob Ojeda	.05
80	Curt Schilling	.35
81	Brian Drahman RC	.05
82	Ivan Rodriguez RC	1.00
83	David Howard RC	.05
84	Heath Slocumb RC	.05
85	Mike Timlin RC	.05
86	Darryl Kile RC	.05
87	Pete Schourek RC	.05
88	Bruce Walton RC	.05
89	Al Osuna RC	.05
90	Gary Scott RC	.05
91	Doug Simons RC	.05
92	Chris Jones RC	.05
93	Chuck Knoblauch	.05
94	Dana Allison RC	.05
95	Erik Pappas RC	.05
96	Jeff Bagwell RC	2.50
97	Kirk Dressendorfer RC	.05
98	Freddie Benavides RC	.05
99	Luis Gonzalez RC	.50
100	Wade Taylor RC	.05
101	Ed Sprague RC	.05
102	Bob Scanlan RC	.05
103	Rick Wilkins RC	.05
104	Chris Donnels RC	.05
105	Joe Slusarski RC	.05
106	Mark Lewis RC	.05
107	Pat Kelly RC	.05
108	John Briscoe RC	.05
109	Luis Lopez RC	.05
110	Jeff Johnson RC	.05

Blue Jays

Sold as a special boxed issue including 40 player cards and five trivia cards, this set features the 1991 Blue Jays and their hosting of the 1991 All-Star Game. Cards carry a super-glossy front finish that features a player action photo in a home plate-shaped frame at center. Around the photo are blue and white border designs with the player's name and position at top, and Score and Blue Jays logos at bottom. Backs repeat the blue and

DUANE WARD RP

white motif with a color player portrait, biographical notes, stats and career summary.

		NM/M
Complete Set (40):		7.00
Common Player:		.25
1	Joe Carter	.35
2	Tom Henke	.25
3	Jimmy Key	.25
4	Al Leiter	.25
5	Dave Steib	.25
6	Todd Stottlemyre	.35
7	Mike Timlin	.25
8	Duane Ward	.25
9	David Wells	.50
10	Frank Wills	.25
11	Pat Borders	.25
12	Greg Myers	.25
13	Roberto Alomar	2.50
14	Rene Gonzalez	.25
15	Kelly Gruber	.25
16	Manny Lee	.25
17	Rance Mulliniks	.25
18	John Olerud	1.00
19	Pat Tabler	.25
20	Derek Bell	.25
21	Jim Acker	.25
22	Rob Ducey	.25
23	Devon White	.35
24	Mookie Wilson	.25
25	Juan Guzman	.25
26	Ed Sprague	.25
27	Ken Dayley	.25
28	Tom Candiotti	.25
29	Candy Maldonado	.25
30	Eddie Zosky	.25
31	Steve Karsay	.25
32	Bob MacDonald	.25
33	Ray Giannelli	.25
34	Jerry Schunk	.25
35	Dave Weathers	.25
36	Cito Gaston	.25
37	Joe Carter/AS	.25
38	Jimmy Key/AS	.25
39	Roberto Alomar/AS	1.50
40	1991 All-Star Game	.25

FanFest/National

Two versions of this 10-card set were produced for distribution at the All-Star FanFest and the National Sports Collectors Convention. The appropriate venue is listed in a red stripe on back under the player career summary. Fronts have a color action photo against a background of pale green with blue ballplayer silhouettes and yellow baseballs. Backs repeat the player figure and baseball motif on a white background. A trapezoid at center has a player portrait photo, color team logo, biographical details and career highlights. At present neither version of these cards carries a premium over the other.

		NM/M
Complete Set (10):		2.00
Common Player:		.25
1	Ray Lankford	.25
2	Steve Decker	.25
3	Gary Scott	.25
4	Hensley Meulens	.25
5	Tim Naehring	.25

6	Mark Whiten	.25
7	Ed Sprague	.25
8	Charles Nagy	.25
9	Terry Shumpert	.25
10	Chuck Knoblauch	.25

"Life and Times of Nolan Ryan"

This four-card career highlights set was distributed with a series of four collector magazines. Cards feature color photos with Score and Texas Rangers logos in separate corners. A red stripe above the photo, or to its left, names the highlight; a blue stripe above or to the left of that has his name and position. Horizontally formatted backs have another color photo and a paragraph about the milestone.

		NM/M
Complete Set (4):		6.00
Common Player:		1.50
1	5,000th Career Strikeout (Nolan Ryan)	1.50
2	6th Career No-Hitter (Nolan Ryan)	1.50
3	300th Career Victory (Nolan Ryan)	1.50
4	7th Career No-Hitter (Nolan Ryan)	1.50

Rising Stars

JOSE OFFERMAN SHORTSTOP

Marketed along with 1990-91 "Baseball's Hottest Rookies" magazine, this 100-card set features top rookies and young players. The cards are similar in design to the Score Superstar set. The magazine/card sets were available to a select group of retailers.

		NM/M
Complete Set (100):		2.50
Common Player:		.05
1	Sandy Alomar, Jr.	.05
2	Tom Edens	.05
3	Terry Shumpert	.05
4	Shawn Boskie	.05
5	Steve Avery	.05
6	Deion Sanders	.05
7	John Burkett	.05
8	Stan Belinda	.05
9	Thomas Howard	.05
10	Wayne Edwards	.05
11	Rick Parker	.05
12	Randy Veres	.05
13	Alex Cole	.05
14	Scott Chiamparino	.05
15	Greg Olson	.05
16	Jose DeJesus	.05
17	Mike Blowers	.05
18	Jeff Huson	.05
19	Willie Blair	.05
20	Howard Farmer	.05
21	Larry Walker	.05
22	Scott Hemond	.05
23	Mel Stottlemyre	.05
24	Mark Whiten	.05
25	Jeff Schulz	.05
26	Gary Disarcina	.05
27	George Canale	.05
28	Dean Palmer	.05
29	Jim Leyritz	.05
30	Carlos Baerga	.05
31	Rafael Valdez	.05
32	Derek Bell	.05
33	Francisco Cabrera	.05
34	Chris Hoiles	.05
35	Craig Grebeck	.05
36	Scott Coolbaugh	.05
37	Kevin Wickander	.05
38	Marquis Grissom	.05
39	Chip Hale	.05

40	Kevin Maas	.05
41	Juan Gonzalez	.50
42	Eric Anthony	.05
43	Luis Sojo	.05
44	Paul Sorrento	.05
45	Dave Justice	.05
46	Oscar Azocar	.05
47	Charles Nagy	.05
48	Robin Ventura	.05
49	Reggie Harris	.05
50	Ben McDonald	.05
51	Hector Villanueva	.05
52	Kevin Tapani	.05
53	Brian Bohanon	.05
54	Tim Layana	.05
55	Delino DeShields	.05
56	Beau Allred	.05
57	Eric Gunderson	.05
58	Kent Mercker	.05
59	Juan Bell	.05
60	Glenallen Hill	.05
61	David Segui	.05
62	Alan Mills	.05
63	Mike Harkey	.05
64	Bill Sampen	.05
65	Greg Vaughn	.05
66	Alex Fernandez	.05
67	Mike Hartley	.05
68	Travis Fryman	.05
69	Dave Rohde	.05
70	Tom Lampkin	.05
71	Mark Gardner	.05
72	Pat Combs	.05
73	Kevin Appier	.05
74	Mike Fetters	.05
75	Greg Myers	.05
76	Steve Searcy	.05
77	Tim Naehring	.05
78	Frank Thomas	1.50
79	Todd Hundley	.05
80	Ed Vosburg	.05
81	Todd Zeile	.05
82	Lee Stevens	.05
83	Scott Radinsky	.05
84	Hensley Meulens	.05
85	Brian DuBois	.05
86	Steve Olin	.05
87	Julio Machado	.05
88	Jose Vizcaino	.05
89	Mark Lemke	.05
90	Felix Jose	.05
91	Wally Whitehurst	.05
92	Dana Kiecker	.05
93	Mike Munoz	.05
94	Adam Peterson	.05
95	Tim Drummond	.05
96	Dave Hollins	.05
97	Craig Wilson	.05
98	Hal Morris	.05
99	Jose Offerman	.05
100	John Olerud	.05

Rookies

1991 ROOKIE

This 40-card boxed set did not receive much attention in the hobby world, but features some of the top young players of 1991. The card fronts feature full-color action photos with a "Rookies" banner along the side border. The backs feature statistics and a player profile. This set was available through hobby dealers and is Score's first release of its kind.

		NM/M
Complete Set (40):		1.00
Common Player:		.05
1	Mel Rojas	.05
2	Ray Lankford	.05
3	Scott Aldred	.05
4	Turner Ward	.05
5	Omar Olivares	.05
6	Mo Vaughn	.05
7	Phil Clark	.05
8	Brent Mayne	.05
9	Scott Lewis	.05
10	Brian Barnes	.05
11	Bernard Gilkey	.05
12	Steve Decker	.05
13	Paul Marak	.05
14	Wes Chamberlain	.05
15	Kevin Belcher	.05
16	Steve Adkins	.05
17	Geronimo Pena	.05
18	Mark Leonard	.05
19	Jeff Conine	.05
20	Leo Gomez	.05

21	Chuck Malone	.05
22	Beau Allred	.05
23	Todd Hundley	.05
24	Lance Dickson	.05
25	Mike Benjamin	.05
26	Jose Offerman	.05
27	Terry Shumpert	.05
28	Darren Lewis	.05
29	Scott Chiamparino	.05
30	Tim Naehring	.05
31	David Segui	.05
32	Karl Rhodes	.05
33	Mickey Morandini	.05
34	Chuck McElroy	.05
35	Tim McIntosh	.05
36	Derrick May	.05
37	Rich DeLucia	.05
38	Tino Martinez	.05
39	Hensley Meulens	.05
40	Andujar Cedeno	.05

Superstars

NOLAN RYAN PITCHER

This 100-card set features full-color action photos on the card fronts and posed shots on the flip sides. The set was marketed along with the magazine "1991 Baseball's Hottest Players." The cards feature red, white, and blue borders. The backs contain brief career highlights. The magazine/card set combo was available to select retailers.

		NM/M
Complete Set (100):		5.00
Common Player:		.05
1	Jose Canseco	.25
2	Bo Jackson	.10
3	Wade Boggs	.50
4	Will Clark	.05
5	Ken Griffey Jr.	.65
6	Doug Drabek	.05
7	Kirby Puckett	.50
8	Joe Orsulak	.05
9	Eric Davis	.05
10	Rickey Henderson	.40
11	Lenny Dykstra	.05
12	Ruben Sierra	.05
13	Paul Molitor	.40
14	Ron Gant	.05
15	Ozzie Guillen	.05
16	Ramon Martinez	.05
17	Edgar Martinez	.05
18	Ozzie Smith	.50
19	Charlie Hayes	.05
20	Barry Larkin	.05
21	Cal Ripken, Jr.	1.00
22	Andy Van Slyke	.05
23	Don Mattingly	.60
24	Dave Stewart	.05
25	Nolan Ryan	1.00
26	Barry Bonds	1.00
27	Gregg Olson	.05
28	Chris Sabo	.05
29	John Franco	.05
30	Gary Sheffield	.25
31	Jeff Treadway	.05
32	Tom Browning	.05
33	Jose Lind	.05
34	Dave Magadan	.05
35	Dale Murphy	.20
36	Tom Candiotti	.05
37	Willie McGee	.05
38	Robin Yount	.40
39	Mark McGwire	.75
40	George Bell	.05
41	Carlton Fisk	.40
42	Bobby Bonilla	.05
43	Randy Milligan	.05
44	Dave Parker	.05
45	Shawon Dunston	.05
46	Brian Harper	.05
47	John Tudor	.05
48	Ellis Burks	.05
49	Bob Welch	.05
50	Roger Clemens	.60
51	Mike Henneman	.05
52	Eddie Murray	.40
53	Kal Daniels	.05
54	Doug Jones	.05
55	Craig Biggio	.05
56	Rafael Palmeiro	.35
57	Wally Joyner	.05
58	Tim Wallach	.05
59	Bret Saberhagen	.05
60	Ryne Sandberg	.50
61	Benito Santiago	.05

62	Darryl Strawberry	.05
63	Alan Trammell	.05
64	Kelly Gruber	.05
65	Dwight Gooden	.05
66	Dave Winfield	.40
67	Rick Aguilera	.05
68	Dave Righetti	.05
69	Jim Abbott	.05
70	Frank Viola	.05
71	Fred McGriff	.05
72	Steve Sax	.05
73	Dennis Eckersley	.35
74	Cory Snyder	.05
75	Mackey Sasser	.05
76	Candy Maldonado	.05
77	Matt Williams	.05
78	Kent Hrbek	.05
79	Randy Myers	.05
80	Gregg Jefferies	.05
81	Joe Carter	.05
82	Mike Greenwell	.05
83	Jack Armstrong	.05
84	Julio Franco	.05
85	George Brett	.60
86	Howard Johnson	.05
87	Andre Dawson	.25
88	Cecil Fielder	.05
89	Tim Raines	.05
90	Chuck Finley	.05
91	Mark Grace	.05
92	Brook Jacoby	.05
93	Dave Steib	.05
94	Tony Gwynn	.50
95	Bobby Thigpen	.05
96	Roberto Kelly	.05
97	Kevin Seitzer	.05
98	Kevin Mitchell	.05
99	Dwight Evans	.05
100	Roberto Alomar	.20

1992 Score Promos

ROBIN VENTURA

The six known Score promo cards differ from the issued versions in 1992 only in the lack of 1991 and career stats on the back and changes in the career summaries on some of the cards. The promos of Sandberg and Mack were distributed at a St. Louis baseball card show in November 1991, and are somewhat scarcer than the others.

		NM/M
Complete Set (6):		15.00
Common Player:		2.00
1	Ken Griffey Jr.	6.00
4	Dave Justice	2.00
122	Robin Ventura	2.00
200	Ryne Sandberg	5.00
241	Steve Avery	2.00
284	Shane Mack	2.00

1992 Score/Pinnacle Promo Panels

Score debuted both its base-brand (Score) and premium-brand (Pinnacle) sets at one time in 1992 with this issue of four-card panels. Each panel measures 1/16" short each way of 5" x 7" and features Score cards in the upper-left and lower-right, with Pinnacle samples at upper-right and lower-left. Backs have a very light gray overprint, "FOR PROMOTIONAL PURPOSES

ONLY NOT FOR RESALE." Cards cut from the panels would be otherwise indistinguishable from the issued versions. Panels are checklisted here alphabetically according to the lowest-numbered Score player. S prefix to the card number indicates Score, P is for Pinnacle. The prefixes do not appear on the cards.

		NM/M
Complete Set (25):		100.00
Common Panel:		3.00
(1)	S2 Nolan Ryan, S13 Lonnie Smith, P7 Willie McGee, P18 Terry Pendleton	15.00
(2)	S3 Will Clark, S12 Mark Langston, P8 Paul Molitor, P17 Devon White	4.50
(3)	S4 Dave Justice, S19 Mark Carreon, P1 Frank Thomas, P16 Dave Henderson	4.50
(4)	S5 Dave Henderson, S15 Roberto Alomar, P10 Ryne Sandberg, P20 Kirby Puckett	7.50
(5)	S9 Darryl Strawberry, S14 Jeff Montgomery, P6 Ozzie Smith, P11 Kevin Seitzer	5.00
(6)	S22 Chuck Crim, S33 Jimmy Jones, P27 Jay Buhner, P38 Robin Yount	4.50
(7)	S23 Don Mattingly, S32 Dave Winfield, P28 Matt Williams, P37 George Bell	10.00
(8)	S24 Dickie Thon, S39 Gary Gaetti, P21 Orel Hershiser, P36 Wes Chamberlain	3.00
(9)	S25 Ron Gant, S35 Andres Galarraga, P30 Alex Fernandez, P40 Bruce Hurst	3.00
(10)	S29 Melido Perez, S34 Kevin Gross, P26 Ellis Burks, P31 Albert Belle	3.00
(11)	S42 Rick Aguilera, S53 Doug Jones, P47 Bill Doran, P58 Ivan Calderon	3.00
(12)	S43 Mike Gallego, S52 Todd Zeile, P48 Jerald Clark, P57 Lenny Harris	3.00
(13)	S44 Eric Davis, S59 Randy Ready, P41 Harold Baines, P56 Walt Weiss	3.00
(14)	S45 George Bell, S55 Rafael Palmeiro, P50 Nolan Ryan, P60 George Brett	20.00
(15)	S49 David Wells, S54 Bob Walk, P46 Chili Davis, P51 Phil Plantier	3.00
(16)	S62 Jack McDowell, S73 Juan Samuel, P67 Dave Hollins, P78 John Olerud	3.00
(17)	S72 Jim Acker, S72 Carlton Fisk, P68 Kent Hrbek, P77 Dennis Martinez	3.00
(18)	S64 Jay Buhner, S79 Kirk McCaskill, P61 Gregg Olson, P76 Terry Steinbach	3.00
(19)	S65 Travis Fryman, S75 Andre Dawson, P70 Jeff Bagwell, P80 Darryl Strawberry	4.50
(20)	S69 Ken Caminiti, S74 Todd Stottlemyre, P66 Alex Cole, P71 Jim Gantner	3.00
(21)	S82 Alex Fernandez, S93 Shawn Hillegas, P87 Bill Gullickson, P98 Jose Guzman	3.00
(22)	S83 Ivan Calderon, S92 Ozzie Guillen, P88 Bernard Gilkey, P97 Omar Vizquel	3.00
(23)	S84 Brent Mayne, S99 Tom Bolton, P81 Gary Gaetti, P96 Doug Drabek	3.00
(24)	S85 Jody Reed, S95 Vince Coleman, P90 Kevin Maas, P100 Dave Justice	3.00
(25)	S89 Hensley Meulens, S94 Chili Davis, P86 David Howard, P91 Mark Lewis	3.00

1992 Score

Score used a two series format for the second consecutive year in 1992. Cards 1-442 are featured in the first series. Fronts feature full-color game action photos. Backs feature color head shots of the players, team logo and career stats. Several subsets are included in 1992, including a five-card Joe DiMaggio set. DiMaggio autographed cards were also inserted into random packs. Cards 736-772 can be found with or without a "Rookie Prospects" banner on the card front. Rack packs could be found with random inserts of 1991 Rookie of the Year Chuck Knoblauch's 1990 Score #1 Draft Pick card in a special autographed edition of 3,000. Factory sets contain 17 bonus cards not found in any other packaging.

		NM/M
	Unopened Fact. Set (910):	7.50
	Complete Set (893):	5.00
	Common Player:	.05
	Wax Pack (16):	.40
	Wax Box (36):	7.50
1	Ken Griffey Jr.	.65
2	Nolan Ryan	1.00
3	Will Clark	.05
4	Dave Justice	.05
5	Dave Henderson	.05
6	Bret Saberhagen	.05
7	Fred McGriff	.05
8	Erik Hanson	.05
9	Darryl Strawberry	.05
10	Dwight Gooden	.05
11	Juan Gonzalez	.20
12	Mark Langston	.05
13	Lonnie Smith	.05
14	Jeff Montgomery	.05
15	Roberto Alomar	.20
16	Delino DeShields	.05
17	Steve Bedrosian	.05
18	Terry Pendleton	.05
19	Mark Carreon	.05
20	Mark McGwire	.75
21	Roger Clemens	.60
22	Chuck Crim	.05
23	Don Mattingly	.60
24	Dickie Thon	.05
25	Ron Gant	.05
26	Milt Cuyler	.05
27	Mike Macfarlane	.05
28	Dan Gladden	.05
29	Melido Perez	.05
30	Willie Randolph	.05
31	Albert Belle	.05
32	Dave Winfield	.40
33	Jimmy Jones	.05
34	Kevin Gross	.05
35	Andres Galarraga	.05
36	Mike Devereaux	.05
37	Chris Bosio	.05
38	Mike LaValliere	.05
39	Gary Gaetti	.05
40	Felix Jose	.05
41	Alvaro Espinoza	.05
42	Rick Aguilera	.05
43	Mike Gallego	.05
44	Eric Davis	.05
45	George Bell	.05
46	Tom Brunansky	.05
47	Steve Farr	.05
48	Duane Ward	.05
49	David Wells	.05
50	Cecil Fielder	.25
51	Walt Weiss	.05
52	Todd Zeile	.05
53	Doug Jones	.05
54	Bob Walk	.05
55	Rafael Palmeiro	.35
56	Rob Deer	.05
57	Paul O'Neill	.05
58	Jeff Reardon	.05
59	Randy Ready	.05
60	Scott Erickson	.05
61	Paul Molitor	.40
62	Jack McDowell	.05
63	Jim Acker	.05
64	Jay Buhner	.05
65	Travis Fryman	.05
66	Marquis Grissom	.05
67	Mike Harkey	.05
68	Luis Polonia	.05
69	Ken Caminiti	.05
70	Chris Sabo	.05
71	Gregg Olson	.05
72	Carlton Fisk	.40
73	Juan Samuel	.05
74	Todd Stottlemyre	.05
75	Andre Dawson	.25
76	Alvin Davis	.05
77	Bill Doran	.05
78	B.J. Surhoff	.05
79	Kirk McCaskill	.05
80	Dale Murphy	.25
81	Jose DeLeon	.05
82	Alex Fernandez	.05
83	Ivan Calderon	.05
84	Brent Mayne	.05
85	Jody Reed	.05
86	Randy Tomlin	.05
87	Randy Milligan	.05
88	Pascual Perez	.05
89	Hensley Meulens	.05
90	Joe Carter	.05
91	Mike Moore	.05
92	Ozzie Guillen	.05
93	Shawn Hillegas	.05
94	Chili Davis	.05
95	Vince Coleman	.05
96	Jimmy Key	.05
97	Billy Ripken	.05
98	Dave Smith	.05
99	Tom Bolton	.05
100	Barry Larkin	.05
101	Kenny Rogers	.05
102	Mike Boddicker	.05
103	Kevin Elster	.05
104	Ken Hill	.05
105	Charlie Leibrandt	.05
106	Pat Combs	.05
107	Hubie Brooks	.05
108	Julio Franco	.05
109	Vicente Palacios	.05
110	Kal Daniels	.05
111	Bruce Hurst	.05
112	Willie McGee	.05
113	Ted Power	.05
114	Milt Thompson	.05
115	Doug Drabek	.05
116	Rafael Belliard	.05
117	Scott Garrelts	.05
118	Terry Mulholland	.05
119	Jay Howell	.05
120	Danny Jackson	.05
121	Scott Ruskin	.05
122	Robin Ventura	.05
123	Bip Roberts	.05
124	Jeff Russell	.05
125	Hal Morris	.05
126	Teddy Higuera	.05
127	Luis Sojo	.05
128	Carlos Baerga	.05
129	Jeff Ballard	.05
130	Tom Gordon	.05
131	Sid Bream	.05
132	Rance Mulliniks	.05
133	Andy Benes	.05
134	Mickey Tettleton	.05
135	Rich DeLucia	.05
136	Tom Pagnozzi	.05
137	Harold Baines	.05
138	Danny Darwin	.05
139	Kevin Bass	.05
140	Chris Nabholz	.05
141	Pete O'Brien	.05
142	Jeff Treadway	.05
143	Mickey Morandini	.05
144	Eric King	.05
145	Danny Tartabull	.05
146	Lance Johnson	.05
147	Casey Candaele	.05
148	Felix Fermin	.05
149	Rich Rodriguez	.05
150	Dwight Evans	.05
151	Joe Klink	.05
152	Kevin Reimer	.05
153	Orlando Merced	.05
154	Mel Hall	.05
155	Randy Myers	.05
156	Greg Harris	.05
157	Jeff Brantley	.05
158	Jim Eisenreich	.05
159	Luis Rivera	.05
160	Cris Carpenter	.05
161	Bruce Ruffin	.05
162	Omar Vizquel	.05
163	Gerald Alexander	.05
164	Mark Guthrie	.05
165	Scott Lewis	.05
166	Bill Sampen	.05
167	Dave Anderson	.05
168	Kevin McReynolds	.05
169	Jose Vizcaino	.05
170	Bob Geren	.05
171	Mike Morgan	.05
172	Jim Gott	.05
173	Mike Pagliarulo	.05
174	Mike Jeffcoat	.05
175	Craig Lefferts	.05
176	Steve Finley	.05
177	Wally Backman	.05
178	Kent Mercker	.05
179	John Cerutti	.05
180	Jay Bell	.05
181	Dale Sveum	.05
182	Greg Harris	.05
183	Donnie Hill	.05
184	Rex Hudler	.05
185	Pat Kelly	.05
186	Jeff Robinson	.05
187	Jeff Gray	.05
188	Jerry Willard	.05
189	Carlos Quintana	.05
190	Dennis Eckersley	.35
191	Kelly Downs	.05
192	Gregg Jefferies	.05
193	Darrin Fletcher	.05
194	Mike Jackson	.05
195	Eddie Murray	.40
196	Billy Landrum	.05
197	Eric Yelding	.05
198	Devon White	.05
199	Larry Walker	.05
200	Ryne Sandberg	.50
201	Dave Magadan	.05
202	Steve Chitren	.05
203	Scott Fletcher	.05
204	Dwayne Henry	.05
205	Scott Coolbaugh	.05
206	Tracy Jones	.05
207	Von Hayes	.05
208	Bob Melvin	.05
209	Scott Scudder	.05
210	Luis Gonzalez	.25
211	Scott Sanderson	.05
212	Chris Donnels	.05
213	Heath Slocumb	.05
214	Mike Timlin	.05
215	Brian Harper	.05
216	Juan Berenguer	.05
217	Mike Henneman	.05
218	Bill Spiers	.05
219	Scott Terry	.05
220	Frank Viola	.05
221	Mark Eichhorn	.05
222	Ernest Riles	.05
223	Ray Lankford	.05
224	Pete Harnisch	.05
225	Bobby Bonilla	.05
226	Mike Scioscia	.05
227	Joel Skinner	.05
228	Brian Holman	.05
229	Gilberto Reyes RC	.05
230	Matt Williams	.05
231	Jaime Navarro	.05
232	Jose Rijo	.05
233	Atlee Hammaker	.05
234	Tim Teufel	.05
235	John Kruk	.05
236	Kurt Stillwell	.05
237	Dan Pasqua	.05
238	Tim Crews	.05
239	Dave Gallagher	.05
240	Leo Gomez	.05
241	Steve Avery	.05
242	Bill Gullickson	.05
243	Mark Portugal	.05
244	Lee Guetterman	.05
245	Benny Santiago	.05
246	Jim Gantner	.05
247	Robby Thompson	.05
248	Terry Shumpert	.05
249	Mike Bell RC	.05
250	Harold Reynolds	.05
251	Mike Felder	.05
252	Bill Pecota	.05
253	Bill Krueger	.05
254	Alfredo Griffin	.05
255	Lou Whitaker	.05
256	Roy Smith	.05
257	Jerald Clark	.05
258	Sammy Sosa	.50
259	Tim Naehring	.05
260	Dave Righetti	.05
261	Paul Gibson	.05
262	Chris James	.05
263	Larry Andersen	.05
264	Storm Davis	.05
265	Jose Lind	.05
266	Greg Hibbard	.05
267	Norm Charlton	.05
268	Paul Kilgus	.05
269	Greg Maddux	.50
270	Ellis Burks	.05
271	Frank Tanana	.05
272	Gene Larkin	.05
273	Ron Hassey	.05
274	Jeff Robinson	.05
275	Steve Howe	.05
276	Daryl Boston	.05
277	Mark Lee	.05
278	Jose Segura RC	.05
279	Lance Blankenship	.05
280	Don Slaught	.05
281	Russ Swan	.05
282	Bob Tewksbury	.05
283	Geno Petralli	.05
284	Shane Mack	.05
285	Bob Scanlan	.05
286	Tim Leary	.05
287	John Smoltz	.05
288	Pat Borders	.05
289	Mark Davidson	.05
290	Sam Horn	.05
291	Lenny Harris	.05
292	Franklin Stubbs	.05
293	Thomas Howard	.05
294	Steve Lyons	.05
295	Francisco Oliveras	.05
296	Terry Leach	.05
297	Barry Jones	.05
298	Lance Parrish	.05
299	Wally Whitehurst	.05
300	Bob Welch	.05
301	Charlie Hayes	.05
302	Charlie Hough	.05
303	Gary Redus	.05
304	Scott Bradley	.05
305	Jose Oquendo	.05
306	Pete Incaviglia	.05
307	Marvin Freeman	.05
308	Gary Pettis	.05
309	Joe Slusarski	.05
310	Kevin Seitzer	.05
311	Jeff Reed	.05
312	Pat Tabler	.05
313	Mike Maddux	.05
314	Bob Milacki	.05
315	Eric Anthony	.05
316	Dante Bichette	.05
317	Steve Decker	.05
318	Jack Clark	.05
319	Doug Dascenzo	.05
320	Scott Leius	.05
321	Jim Lindeman	.05
322	Bryan Harvey	.05
323	Spike Owen	.05
324	Roberto Kelly	.05
325	Stan Belinda	.05
326	Joey Cora	.05
327	Jeff Innis	.05
328	Willie Wilson	.05
329	Juan Agosto	.05
330	Charles Nagy	.05
331	Scott Bailes	.05
332	Pete Schourek	.05
333	Mike Flanagan	.05
334	Omar Olivares	.05
335	Dennis Lamp	.05
336	Tommy Greene	.05
337	Randy Velarde	.05
338	Tom Lampkin	.05
339	John Russell	.05
340	Bob Kipper	.05
341	Todd Burns	.05
342	Ron Jones	.05
343	Dave Valle	.05
344	Mike Heath	.05
345	John Olerud	.05
346	Gerald Young	.05
347	Ken Patterson	.05
348	Les Lancaster	.05
349	Steve Crawford	.05
350	John Candelaria	.05
351	Mike Aldrete	.05
352	Mariano Duncan	.05
353	Julio Machado	.05
354	Ken Williams	.05
355	Walt Terrell	.05
356	Mitch Williams	.05
357	Al Newman	.05
358	Bud Black	.05
359	Joe Hesketh	.05
360	Paul Assenmacher	.05
361	Bo Jackson	.05
362	Jeff Blauser	.05
363	Mike Brumley	.05
364	Jim Deshaies	.05
365	Brady Anderson	.05
366	Chuck McElroy	.05
367	Matt Merullo	.05
368	Tim Belcher	.05
369	Luis Aquino	.05
370	Joe Oliver	.05
371	Greg Swindell	.05
372	Lee Stevens	.05
373	Mark Knudson	.05
374	Bill Wegman	.05
375	Jerry Don Gleaton	.05
376	Pedro Guerrero	.05
377	Randy Bush	.05
378	Greg Harris	.05
379	Eric Plunk	.05
380	Jose DeJesus	.05
381	Bobby Witt	.05
382	Curtis Wilkerson	.05
383	Gene Nelson	.05
384	Wes Chamberlain	.05
385	Tom Henke	.05
386	Mark Lemke	.05
387	Greg Briley	.05
388	Rafael Ramirez	.05
389	Tony Fossas	.05
390	Henry Cotto	.05
391	Tim Hulett	.05
392	Dean Palmer	.05
393	Glenn Braggs	.05
394	Mark Salas	.05
395	Rusty Meacham RC	.05
396	Andy Ashby RC	.10
397	Jose Melendez RC	.05
398	Warren Newson RC	.05
399	Frank Castillo RC	.05
400	Chito Martinez RC	.05
401	Bernie Williams	.05
402	Derek Bell	.05
403	Javier Ortiz RC	.05
404	Tim Sherrill RC	.05
405	Rob MacDonald RC	.05
406	Phil Plantier	.05
407	Troy Afenir	.05
408	Gino Minutelli RC	.05
409	Reggie Jefferson RC	.05
410	Mike Remlinger RC	.05
411	Carlos Rodriguez RC	.05
412	Joe Redfield RC	.05
413	Alonzo Powell RC	.05
414	Scott Livingstone RC	.05
415	Scott Kamieniecki RC	.05
416	Tim Spehr RC	.05
417	Brian Hunter RC	.05
418	Ced Landrum RC	.05
419	Bret Barberie RC	.05
420	Kevin Morton RC	.05
421	Doug Henry RC	.05
422	Doug Piatt RC	.05
423	Pat Rice RC	.05
424	Juan Guzman	.05
425	Nolan Ryan (No-Hit)	.50
426	Tommy Greene (No-Hit)	.05
427	Bob Milacki, Mike Flanagan, Mark Williamson, Gregg Olson (No-Hit)	.05
428	Wilson Alvarez (No-Hit)	.05
429	Otis Nixon (Highlight)	.05
430	Rickey Henderson (Highlight)	.20
431	Cecil Fielder/AS	.05
432	Julio Franco/AS	.05
433	Cal Ripken, Jr./AS	.50
434	Wade Boggs/AS	.25
435	Joe Carter/AS	.05
436	Ken Griffey Jr./AS	.35
437	Ruben Sierra/AS	.05
438	Scott Erickson/AS	.05
439	Tom Henke/AS	.05
440	Terry Steinbach/AS	.05
441	Rickey Henderson (Dream Team)	.20
442	Ryne Sandberg (Dream Team)	.30
443	Otis Nixon	.05
444	Scott Radinsky	.05
445	Mark Grace	.05
446	Tony Pena	.05
447	Billy Hatcher	.05
448	Glenallen Hill	.05
449	Chris Gwynn	.05
450	Tom Glavine	.35
451	John Habyan	.05
452	Al Osuna	.05
453	Tony Phillips	.05
454	Greg Cadaret	.05
455	Rob Dibble	.05
456	Rick Honeycutt	.05
457	Jerome Walton	.05
458	Mookie Wilson	.05
459	Mark Gubicza	.05
460	Craig Biggio	.05
461	Dave Cochrane	.05
462	Keith Miller	.05
463	Alex Cole	.05
464	Pete Smith	.05
465	Brett Butler	.05
466	Jeff Huson	.05
467	Steve Lake	.05
468	Lloyd Moseby	.05
469	Tim McIntosh	.05
470	Dennis Martinez	.05
471	Greg Myers	.05
472	Mackey Sasser	.05
473	Junior Ortiz	.05
474	Greg Olson	.05
475	Steve Sax	.05
476	Ricky Jordan	.05
477	Max Venable	.05
478	Brian McRae	.05
479	Doug Simons	.05
480	Rickey Henderson	.40
481	Gary Varsho	.05
482	Carl Willis	.05
483	Rick Wilkins	.05
484	Donn Pall	.05
485	Edgar Martinez	.05
486	Tom Foley	.05
487	Mark Williamson	.05
488	Jack Armstrong	.05
489	Gary Carter	.40
490	Ruben Sierra	.05
491	Gerald Perry	.05
492	Rob Murphy	.05
493	Zane Smith	.05
494	Darryl Kile	.05
495	Kelly Gruber	.05
496	Jerry Browne	.05
497	Darryl Hamilton	.05
498	Mike Stanton	.05
499	Mark Leonard	.05
500	Jose Canseco	.30
501	Dave Martinez	.05
502	Jose Guzman	.05
503	Terry Kennedy	.05
504	Ed Sprague	.05
505	Frank Thomas	.40
506	Darren Daulton	.05
507	Kevin Tapani	.05
508	Luis Salazar	.05
509	Paul Faries	.05
510	Sandy Alomar, Jr.	.05
511	Jeff King	.05
512	Gary Thurman	.05
513	Chris Hammond	.05
514	Pedro Munoz RC	.05
515	Alan Trammell	.05
516	Geronimo Pena	.05
517	Rodney McCray	.05
518	Manny Lee	.05
519	Junior Felix	.05
520	Kirk Gibson	.05
521	Darrin Jackson	.05
522	John Burkett	.05
523	Jeff Johnson	.05
524	Jim Corsi	.05
525	Robin Yount	.40
526	Jamie Quirk	.05
527	Bob Ojeda	.05
528	Mark Lewis	.05
529	Bryn Smith	.05
530	Kent Hrbek	.05
531	Dennis Boyd	.05
532	Ron Karkovice	.05
533	Don August	.05
534	Todd Frohwirth	.05
535	Wally Joyner	.05
536	Dennis Rasmussen	.05
537	Andy Allanson	.05
538	Rich Gossage	.05
539	John Marzano	.05
540	Cal Ripken, Jr.	1.00
541	Bill Swift	.05
542	Kevin Appier	.05
543	Dave Bergman	.05
544	Bernard Gilkey	.05
545	Mike Greenwell	.05
546	Jose Uribe	.05
547	Jesse Orosco	.05
548	Bob Patterson	.05
549	Mike Stanley	.05
550	Howard Johnson	.05
551	Joe Orsulak	.05
552	Dick Schofield	.05
553	Dave Hollins	.05
554	David Segui	.05
555	Barry Bonds	1.00
556	Mo Vaughn	.05
557	Craig Wilson	.05
558	Bobby Rose	.05
559	Rod Nichols	.05
560	Len Dykstra	.05
561	Craig Grebeck	.05
562	Darren Lewis	.05
563	Todd Benzinger	.05
564	Ed Whitson	.05
565	Jesse Barfield	.05
566	Lloyd McClendon	.05
567	Dan Plesac	.05
568	Danny Cox	.05
569	Skeeter Barnes	.05
570	Bobby Thigpen	.05
571	Deion Sanders	.05
572	Chuck Knoblauch	.05
573	Matt Nokes	.05
574	Herm Winningham	.05
575	Tom Candiotti	.05
576	Jeff Bagwell	.40
577	Brook Jacoby	.05
578	Chico Walker	.05
579	Brian Downing	.05
580	Dave Stewart	.05
581	Francisco Cabrera	.05
582	Rene Gonzales	.05
583	Stan Javier	.05
584	Randy Johnson	.40
585	Chuck Finley	.05
586	Mark Gardner	.05
587	Mark Whiten	.05
588	Garry Templeton	.05
589	Gary Sheffield	.30
590	Ozzie Smith	.50
591	Candy Maldonado	.05
592	Mike Sharperson	.05
593	Carlos Martinez	.05
594	Scott Bankhead	.05
595	Tim Wallach	.05
596	Tino Martinez	.05
597	Roger McDowell	.05
598	Cory Snyder	.05
599	Andujar Cedeno	.05
600	Kirby Puckett	.50
601	Rick Parker	.05
602	Todd Hundley	.05
603	Greg Litton	.05
604	Dave Johnson	.05
605	John Franco	.05
606	Mike Fetters	.05
607	Luis Alicea	.05
608	Trevor Wilson	.05
609	Rob Ducey	.05
610	Ramon Martinez	.05
611	Dave Burba	.05
612	Dwight Smith	.05
613	Kevin Maas	.05
614	John Costello	.05
615	Glenn Davis	.05
616	Shawn Abner	.05
617	Scott Hemond	.05
618	Tom Prince	.05
619	Wally Ritchie	.05
620	Jim Abbott	.05
621	Charlie O'Brien	.05
622	Jack Daugherty	.05
623	Tommy Gregg	.05
624	Jeff Shaw	.05
625	Tony Gwynn	.50
626	Mark Leiter	.05
627	Jim Clancy	.05
628	Tim Layana	.05
629	Jeff Schaefer	.05
630	Lee Smith	.05
631	Wade Taylor	.05
632	Mike Simms	.05
633	Terry Steinbach	.05
634	Shawon Dunston	.05
635	Tim Raines	.05
636	Kirt Manwaring	.05
637	Warren Cromartie	.05
638	Luis Quinones	.05
639	Greg Vaughn	.05
640	Kevin Mitchell	.05
641	Chris Hoiles	.05
642	Tom Browning	.05
643	Mitch Webster	.05
644	Steve Olin	.05
645	Tony Fernandez	.05
646	Juan Bell	.05
647	Joe Boever	.05
648	Carney Lansford	.05
649	Mike Benjamin	.05

#	Player	Price
650	George Brett	.60
651	Tim Burke	.05
652	Jack Morris	.05
653	Orel Hershiser	.05
654	Mike Schooler	.05
655	Andy Van Slyke	.05
656	Dave Stieb	.05
657	Dave Clark	.05
658	Ben McDonald	.05
659	John Smiley	.05
660	Wade Boggs	.50
661	Eric Bullock	.05
662	Eric Show	.05
663	Lenny Webster	.05
664	Mike Huff	.05
665	Rick Sutcliffe	.05
666	Jeff Manto	.05
667	Mike Fitzgerald	.05
668	Matt Young	.05
669	Dave West	.05
670	Mike Hartley	.05
671	Curt Schilling	.35
672	Brian Bohanon	.05
673	Cecil Espy	.05
674	Joe Grahe	.05
675	Sid Fernandez	.05
676	Edwin Nunez	.05
677	Hector Villanueva	.05
678	Sean Berry	.05
679	Dave Eiland	.05
680	David Cone	.05
681	Mike Bordick	.05
682	Tony Castillo	.05
683	John Barfield	.05
684	Jeff Hamilton	.05
685	Ken Dayley	.05
686	Carmelo Martinez	.05
687	Mike Capel	.05
688	Scott Chiamparino	.05
689	Rich Gedman	.05
690	Rich Monteleone	.05
691	Alejandro Pena	.05
692	Oscar Azocar	.05
693	Jim Poole	.05
694	Mike Gardiner	.05
695	Steve Buechele	.05
696	Rudy Seanez	.05
697	Paul Abbott	.05
698	Steve Searcy	.05
699	Jose Offerman	.05
700	Ivan Rodriguez	.35
701	Joe Girardi	.05
702	Tony Perezchica	.05
703	Paul McClellan	.05
704	David Howard RC	.05
705	Dan Petry	.05
706	Jack Howell	.05
707	Jose Mesa	.05
708	Randy St. Claire	.05
709	Kevin Brown	.05
710	Ron Darling	.05
711	Jason Grimsley	.05
712	John Orton	.05
713	Shawn Boskie	.05
714	Pat Clements	.05
715	Brian Barnes	.05
716	Luis Lopez RC	.05
717	Bob McClure	.05
718	Mark Davis	.05
719	Dann Billardello	.05
720	Tom Edens	.05
721	Willie Fraser	.05
722	Curt Young	.05
723	Neal Heaton	.05
724	Craig Worthington	.05
725	Mel Rojas	.05
726	Daryl Irvine	.05
727	Roger Mason	.05
728	Kirk Dressendorfer	.05
729	Scott Aldred	.05
730	Willie Blair	.05
731	Allan Anderson	.05
732	Dana Kiecker	.05
733	Jose Gonzalez	.05
734	Brian Drahman	.05
735	Brad Komminsk	.05
736	Arthur Rhodes RC	.10
737	Terry Mathews RC	.05
738	Jeff Fassero RC	.05
739	Mike Magnante RC	.05
740	Kip Gross RC	.05
741	Jim Hunter RC	.05
742	Jose Mota RC	.05
743	Joe Bitker RC	.05
744	Tim Mauser RC	.05
745	Ramon Garcia RC	.05
746	Rod Beck RC	.10
747	Jim Austin RC	.05
748	Keith Mitchell RC	.05
749	Wayne Rosenthal RC	.05
750	Bryan Hickerson RC	.05
751	Bruce Egloff RC	.05
752	John Wehner RC	.05
753	Darren Holmes RC	.05
754	Dave Hansen	.05
755	Mike Mussina	.30
756	Anthony Young RC	.05
757	Ron Tingley RC	.05
758	Ricky Bones RC	.05
759	Mark Wohlers RC	.05
760	Wilson Alvarez RC	.05
761	Harvey Pulliam RC	.05
762	Ryan Bowen RC	.05
763	Terry Bross RC	.05
764	Joel Johnston RC	.05
765	Terry McDaniel RC	.05
766	Esteban Beltre RC	.05
767	Rob Maurer RC	.05

#	Player	Price
768	Ted Wood	.05
769	Mo Sanford RC	.05
770	Jeff Carter RC	.05
771	Gil Heredia RC	.05
772	Monty Fariss RC	.05
773	Wilf Clark/AS	.05
774	Ryne Sandberg/AS	.25
775	Barry Larkin/AS	.05
776	Howard Johnson/AS	.05
777	Barry Bonds/AS	.50
778	Brett Butler /AS	.05
779	Tony Gwynn/AS	.25
780	Ramon Martinez/AS	.05
781	Lee Smith/AS	.05
782	Mike Scioscia/AS	.05
783	Dennis Martinez (Highlight)	.05
784	Dennis Martinez (No-Hit)	.05
785	Mark Gardner (No-Hit)	.05
786	Bret Saberhagen (No-Hit)	.05
787	Kent Mercker, Mark Wohlers, Alejandro Pena (No-Hit)	.05
788	Cal Ripken (MVP)	.50
789	Terry Pendleton (MVP)	.05
790	Roger Clemens (CY)	.35
791	Tom Glavine (CY)	.05
792	Chuck Knoblauch (ROY)	.05
793	Jeff Bagwell (ROY)	.20
794	Cal Ripken, Jr. (Man of the Year)	.50
795	David Cone (Highlight)	.05
796	Kirby Puckett (Highlight)	.25
797	Steve Avery (Highlight)	.05
798	Jack Morris (Highlight)	.05
799	Allen Watson RC	.05
800	Manny Ramirez RC	2.00
801	Cliff Floyd RC	.50
802	Al Shirley RC	.05
803	Brian Barber RC	.05
804	Jon Farrell RC	.05
805	Brent Gates RC	.05
806	Scott Ruffcorn RC	.05
807	Tyrone Hill RC	.05
808	Benji Gil RC	.05
809	Aaron Sele RC	.25
810	Tyler Green RC	.05
811	Chris Jones	.05
812	Steve Wilson	.05
813	Cliff Young RC	.05
814	Don Wakamatsu RC	.05
815	Mike Humphreys RC	.05
816	Scott Servais RC	.05
817	Rico Rossy RC	.05
818	John Ramos RC	.05
819	Rob Mallicoat	.05
820	Milt Hill RC	.05
821	Carlos Carcia	.05
822	Stan Royer	.05
823	Jeff Plympton RC	.05
824	Braulio Castillo RC	.05
825	David Haas RC	.05
826	Luis Mercedes RC	.05
827	Eric Karros	.05
828	Shawn Hare RC	.05
829	Reggie Sanders	.05
830	Tom Goodwin	.05
831	Dan Gakeler RC	.05
832	Stacy Jones RC	.05
833	Kim Batiste RC	.05
834	Cal Eldred	.05
835	Chris George RC	.05
836	Wayne Housie RC	.05
837	Mike Ignasiak RC	.05
838	Josias Manzanillo RC	.05
839	Jim Olander RC	.05
840	Gary Cooper RC	.05
841	Royce Clayton	.05
842	Hector Fajardo	.05
843	Blaine Beatty	.05
844	Jorge Pedre RC	.05
845	Kenny Lofton	.05
846	Scott Brosius	.05
847	Chris Cron RC	.05
848	Denis Boucher	.05
849	Kyle Abbott	.05
850	Bob Zupcic	.05
851	Rheal Cormier RC	.05
852	Jim Lewis RC	.05
853	Anthony Telford	.05
854	Cliff Brantley RC	.05
855	Kevin Campbell RC	.05
856	Craig Shipley RC	.05
857	Chuck Carr	.05
858	Tony Eusebio RC	.10
859	Jim Thome	.35
860	Vinny Castilla RC	.30
861	Dann Howitt	.05
862	Kevin Ward RC	.05
863	Steve Wapnick RC	.05
864	Rod Brewer	.05
865	Todd Van Poppel	.05
866	Jose Hernandez RC	.05
867	Amalio Carreno RC	.05
868	Calvin Jones RC	.05
869	Jeff Gardner RC	.05
870	Jarvis Brown RC	.05
871	Eddie Taubensee RC	.10
872	Andy Mota RC	.05
873	Chris Haney (Front photo actually Scott Ruskin.)	.05
874	Roberto Hernandez	.05
875	Laddie Renfroe RC	.05
876	Scott Cooper	.05
877	Armando Reynoso RC	.05
878	Ty Cobb (Memorabilia)	.40
879	Babe Ruth (Memorabilia)	.40
880	Honus Wagner (Memorabilia)	.30

#	Player	Price
881	Lou Gehrig (Memorabilia)	.30
882	Satchel Paige (Memorabilia)	.35
883	Will Clark (Dream Team)	.05
884	Cal Ripken, Jr. (Dream Team)	.50
885	Wade Boggs (Dream Team)	.25
886	Kirby Puckett (Dream Team)	.30
887	Tony Gwynn (Dream Team)	.30
888	Craig Biggio (Dream Team)	.05
889	Scott Erickson (Dream Team)	.05
890	Tom Glavine (Dream Team)	.10
891	Rob Dibble (Dream Team)	.05
892	Mitch Williams (Dream Team)	.05
893	Frank Thomas (Dream Team)	.25

Joe DiMaggio

Colorized vintage photos are featured on the front and back of each of five Joe DiMaggio tribute cards which were issued as random inserts in 1992 Score Series 1 packs. It was reported at the time that 30,000 of each card were produced. A limited number (from an edition of 2,500) of each card were autographed.

		NM/M
Complete Set (5):		25.00
Common Card:		8.00
Autographed Card:		365.00
1	Joe DiMaggio (The Minors)	8.00
2	Joe DiMaggio (The Rookie)	8.00
3	Joe DiMaggio (The MVP)	8.00
4	Joe DiMaggio (The Streak)	8.00
5	Joe DiMaggio (The Legend)	8.00

Factory Set Inserts - Cooperstown

Available exclusively in factory sets, these bonus cards have posterized color portraits vignetted on a white background. Blue-bordered backs have a yellow "tombstone" at center with career highlights and a quote or two about the player.

		NM/M
Complete Set (4):		1.50
Common Player:		.50
B8	Carlton Fisk	.50
B9	Ozzie Smith	.75
B10	Dave Winfield	.50
B11	Robin Yount	.50

Factory Set Inserts - DiMaggio

Available exclusively in factory sets, these bonus cards honor Joe DiMaggio's career. Fronts have black-and-white photos with silver borders. Color backs have quotes from the Clipper or other ballplayers, plus detailed career highlights.

		NM/M
Complete Set (3):		4.00
Common Card:		1.25
B12	Joe DiMaggio (The Hard Hitter)	1.50
B13	Joe DiMaggio (The Stylish Fielder)	1.50
B14	Joe DiMaggio (The Championship Player)	1.50

Factory Set Inserts - World Series

Available exclusively in factory sets 17 bonus cards are divided into four subsets commemorating the 1991 World Series, potential Hall of Famers, the career of Joe DiMaggio and Carl Yastrzemski's 1967 Triple Crown season. Cards carry a "B" prefix to the card number.

		NM/M
Complete Set (7):		1.00
Common Card:		.15
1	World Series Game 1 (Greg Gagne)	.15
2	World Series Game 2 (Scott Leius)	.15
3	World Series Game 3 (David Justice, Brian Harper)	.15
4	World Series Game 4 (Lonnie Smith, Brian Harper)	.15
5	World Series Game 5 (David Justice)	.15
6	World Series Game 6 (Kirby Puckett)	1.00
7	World Series Game 7 (Gene Larkin)	.15

Factory Set Inserts - Yastrzemski

Available exclusively in factory sets, these bonus cards honor Carl Yastrzemski's 1967 Triple

Crown season. Fronts have game-action photos with silver borders and a silver 25 Years logo. Color backs have quotes from Yaz or teammates, plus details of the season's highlights.

		NM/M
Complete Set (3):		2.00
Common Card:		1.00
B15	Carl Yastrzemski (The Impossible Dream)	1.00
B16	Carl Yastrzemski (The Triple Crown)	1.00
B17	Carl Yastrzemski (The World Series)	1.00

Hot Rookies

This 10-card rookie issue was produced as an insert in special blister packs of 1992 Score cards sold at retail outlets. Action photos on front and portraits on back are set against white backgrounds with orange highlights. Cards are standard 2-1/2" x 3-1/2".

		NM/M
Complete Set (10):		4.00
Common Player:		.50
1	Cal Eldred	.50
2	Royce Clayton	.50
3	Kenny Lofton	.75
4	Todd Van Poppel	.50
5	Scott Cooper	.50
6	Todd Hundley	.50
7	Tino Martinez	.75
8	Anthony Telford	.50
9	Derek Bell	.50
10	Reggie Jefferson	.50

Impact Players

Jumbo packs of 1992 Score Series 1 and 2 contained five of these special inserts labeled "90's Impact Players." Front action photos contrast with portrait photos on the backs, which are color-coded by team. Cards #1-45 were packaged with Series 1, cards #46-90 were included in Series 2 packs.

		NM/M
Complete Set (90):		3.00
Common Player:		.05
1	Chuck Knoblauch	.05
2	Jeff Bagwell	.50
3	Juan Guzman	.05
4	Milt Cuyler	.05
5	Ivan Rodriguez	.45
6	Rich DeLucia	.05
7	Orlando Merced	.05
8	Ray Lankford	.05
9	Brian Hunter	.05
10	Roberto Alomar	.25
11	Wes Chamberlain	.05
12	Steve Avery	.05
13	Scott Erickson	.05
14	Jim Abbott	.05
15	Mark Whiten	.05
16	Leo Gomez	.05
17	Doug Henry	.05
18	Brent Mayne	.05
19	Charles Nagy	.05
20	Phil Plantier	.05
21	Mo Vaughn	.05
22	Craig Biggio	.05
23	Derek Bell	.05
24	Royce Clayton	.05
25	Gary Cooper	.05
26	Scott Cooper	.05
27	Juan Gonzalez	.25
28	Ken Griffey Jr.	.75
29	Larry Walker	.05
30	John Smoltz	.05
31	Todd Hundley	.05
32	Kenny Lofton	.05
33	Andy Mota	.05
34	Todd Zeile	.05
35	Arthur Rhodes	.05
36	Jim Thome	.45
37	Todd Van Poppel	.05
38	Mark Wohlers	.05
39	Anthony Young	.05
40	Sandy Alomar Jr.	.05
41	John Olerud	.05
42	Robin Ventura	.05
43	Frank Thomas	.50
44	Dave Justice	.05
45	Hal Morris	.05
46	Ruben Sierra	.05
47	Travis Fryman	.05
48	Mike Mussina	.25
49	Tom Glavine	.35
50	Barry Larkin	.05
51	Will Clark	.05
52	Jose Canseco	.30
53	Bo Jackson	.10
54	Dwight Gooden	.05
55	Barry Bonds	1.00
56	Fred McGriff	.05
57	Roger Clemens	.65
58	Benito Santiago	.05
59	Darryl Strawberry	.05
60	Cecil Fielder	.05
61	John Franco	.05
62	Matt Williams	.05
63	Marquis Grissom	.05
64	Danny Tartabull	.05
65	Ron Gant	.05
66	Paul O'Neill	.05
67	Devon White	.05
68	Rafael Palmeiro	.45
69	Tom Gordon	.05
70	Shawon Dunston	.05
71	Rob Dibble	.05
72	Eddie Zosky	.05
73	Jack McDowell	.05
74	Len Dykstra	.05
75	Ramon Martinez	.05
76	Reggie Sanders	.05
77	Greg Maddux	.60
78	Ellis Burks	.05
79	John Smiley	.05
80	Roberto Kelly	.05
81	Ben McDonald	.05
82	Mark Lewis	.05
83	Jose Rijo	.05
84	Ozzie Guillen	.05
85	Lance Dickson	.05
86	Kim Batiste	.05
87	Gregg Olson	.05
88	Andy Benes	.05
89	Cal Eldred	.05
90	David Cone	.05

The Franchise

This four-card set, in both autographed and unautographed form, was a random insert in various premium packaging of Score's 1992 Series II cards. Each of the four cards was produced in an edition of 150,000, with 2,000 of each player's card being autographed and 500 of the triple-player card carrying the autographs of all three superstars.

		NM/M
Complete Set (4):		5.00
Common Player:		1.25
Musial Autograph:		80.00
Mantle Autograph:		450.00
Yastrzemski Autograph:		80.00
Triple Autograph:		1,100
1	Stan Musial	1.50
2	Mickey Mantle	2.50
3	Carl Yastrzemski	1.25
4	Stan Musial, Mickey Mantle, Carl Yastrzemski	1.50

Rookie & Traded

This 110-card set features traded players, free agents and top rookies from 1992. The cards are styled after the regular 1992 Score cards. Cards 80-110 feature the rookies. The set was released as a boxed set and was available only through hobby dealers.

		NM/M
Complete Set (110):		5.00
Common Player:		.05
1	Gary Sheffield	.20
2	Kevin Seitzer	.05
3	Danny Tartabull	.05
4	Steve Sax	.05
5	Bobby Bonilla	.05
6	Frank Viola	.05
7	Dave Winfield	.60
8	Rick Sutcliffe	.05
9	Jose Canseco	.45
10	Greg Swindell	.05
11	Eddie Murray	.60
12	Randy Myers	.05
13	Wally Joyner	.05
14	Kenny Lofton	.05
15	Jack Morris	.05
16	Charlie Hayes	.05
17	Pete Incaviglia	.05
18	Kevin Mitchell	.05
19	Kurt Stillwell	.05
20	Bret Saberhagen	.05
21	Steve Buechele	.05
22	John Smiley	.05
23	Sammy Sosa	3.00
24	George Bell	.05
25	Curt Schilling	.30
26	Dick Schofield	.05
27	David Cone	.05
28	Dan Gladden	.05
29	Kirk McCaskill	.05
30	Mike Gallego	.05
31	Kevin McReynolds	.05
32	Bill Swift	.05
33	Dave Martinez	.05
34	Storm Davis	.05
35	Willie Randolph	.05
36	Melido Perez	.05
37	Mark Carreon	.05
38	Doug Jones	.05
39	Gregg Jefferies	.05
40	Mike Jackson	.05
41	Dickie Thon	.05
42	Eric King	.05
43	Herm Winningham	.05
44	Derek Lilliquist	.05
45	Dave Anderson	.05
46	Jeff Reardon	.05
47	Scott Bankhead	.05
48	Cory Snyder	.05
49	Al Newman	.05
50	Keith Miller	.05
51	Dave Burba	.05
52	Bill Pecota	.05
53	Chuck Crim	.05
54	Mariano Duncan	.05
55	Dave Gallagher	.05
56	Chris Gwynn	.05
57	Scott Ruskin	.05
58	Jack Armstrong	.05
59	Gary Carter	.60
60	Andres Galarraga	.05
61	Gary Hill	.05
62	Eric Davis	.05
63	Ruben Sierra	.05
64	Darrin Fletcher	.05
65	Tim Belcher	.05
66	Mike Morgan	.05
67	Scott Scudder	.05
68	Tom Candiotti	.05
69	Hubie Brooks	.05
70	Kal Daniels	.05
71	Bruce Ruffin	.05
72	Billy Hatcher	.05
73	Bob Melvin	.05
74	Lee Guetterman	.05
75	Rene Gonzales	.05
76	Kevin Bass	.05
77	Tom Bolton	.05
78	John Wetteland	.05
79	Bip Roberts	.05
80	Pat Listach RC	.05
81	John Doherty RC	.05
82	Sam Militello RC	.05
83	Brian Jordan RC	.05
84	Jeff Kent RC	.10
85	Dave Fleming RC	.05
86	Jeff Tackett RC	.05
87	Chad Curtis RC	.05
88	Eric Fox	.05
89	Denny Neagle RC	.05
90	Donovan Osborne	.05
91	Carlos Hernandez RC	.05
92	Tim Wakefield RC	.05
93	Tim Salmon RC	.05
94	Dave Nilsson RC	.05
95	Mike Perez RC	.05
96	Pat Hentgen RC	.05
97	Frank Seminara RC	.05
98	Ruben Amaro Jr. RC	.05
99	Archi Cianfrocco RC	.05
100	Andy Stankiewicz RC	.05
101	Jim Bullinger RC	.05
102	Pat Mahomes RC	.05
103	Hipolito Pichardo RC	.05
104	Bret Boone RC	.05
105	John Vander Wal RC	.05
106	Vince Horsman RC	.05
107	James Austin RC	.05
108	Brian Williams RC	.05
109	Dan Walters RC	.05
110	Wil Cordero RC	.05

Procter & Gamble

In 1992 Score and Procter and Gamble combined to produce an 18-card All-Star set, reportedly two million cards making 101,000 sets offered to collectors originally for $1.49 along with proof of purchase from P & G products. Card fronts feature a color player action photo set against a background of blue star and pink-to-purple diagonal stripes (American Leaguers) or red star and green stripes (National Leaguers). Back designs include a color player portrait photo at upper-right, with personal data, career stats and highlights. Appropriate logos and card number complete the design, which is bordered in color striping similar to the front background.

		NM/M
Complete Set (18):		3.00
Common Player:		.10
1	Sandy Alomar Jr.	.10
2	Mark McGwire	.75
3	Roberto Alomar	.20
4	Wade Boggs	.50
5	Cal Ripken, Jr.	1.00
6	Kirby Puckett	.50
7	Ken Griffey Jr.	.65
8	Jose Canseco	.25
9	Kevin Brown	.10
10	Benito Santiago	.10
11	Fred McGriff	.10
12	Ryne Sandberg	.50
13	Terry Pendleton	.10
14	Ozzie Smith	.50
15	Barry Bonds	1.00
16	Tony Gwynn	.50
17	Andy Van Slyke	.10
18	Tom Glavine	.35

Rising Stars

CHARLES NAGY
P • CLEVELAND INDIANS

Sold in a blister pack with a book and a handful of "Magic Motion" trivia cards this 100-card set features baseball's top young play-

ers. Backs have a player portrait, a career summary and team, league and card company logos.

		NM/M
Complete Set (100):		3.00
Common Player:		.10
1	Milt Cuyler	.10
2	David Howard	.10
3	Brian Hunter	.10
4	Darryl Kile	.10
5	Pat Kelly	.10
6	Luis Gonzalez	.10
7	Mike Benjamin	.10
8	Eric Anthony	.10
9	Moises Alou	.10
10	Darren Lewis	.10
11	Chuck Knoblauch	.10
12	Geronimo Pena	.10
13	Jeff Plympton	.10
14	Bret Barberie	.10
15	Chris Haney	.10
16	Rick Wilkins	.10
17	Julio Valera	.10
18	Joe Slusarski	.10
19	Jose Melendez	.10
20	Pete Schourek	.10
21	Jeff Conine	.10
22	Paul Faries	.10
23	Scott Kamieniecki	.10
24	Bernard Gilkey	.10
25	Wes Chamberlain	.10
26	Charles Nagy	.10
27	Juan Guzman	.10
28	Heath Slocumb	.10
29	Eddie Taubensee	.10
30	Cedric Landrum	.10
31	Jose Offerman	.10
32	Andres Santana	.10
33	David Segui	.10
34	Bernie Williams	.10
35	Jeff Bagwell	1.50
36	Kevin Morton	.10
37	Kirk Dressendorfer	.10
38	Mike Fetters	.10
39	Darren Holmes	.10
40	Jeff Johnson	.10
41	Scott Aldred	.10
42	Kevin Ward	.10
43	Ray Lankford	.10
44	Terry Shumpert	.10
45	Wade Taylor	.10
46	Rob MacDonald	.10
47	Jose Mota	.10
48	Reggie Harris	.10
49	Mike Remlinger	.10
50	Mark Lewis	.10
51	Tino Martinez	.10
52	Ed Sprague	.10
53	Freddie Benavides	.10
54	Rich DeLucia	.10
55	Brian Drahman	.10
56	Steve Decker	.10
57	Scott Livingstone	.10
58	Mike Timlin	.10
59	Bob Scanlan	.10
60	Dean Palmer	.10
61	Frank Castillo	.10
62	Mark Leonard	.10
63	Chuck McElroy	.10
64	Derek Bell	.10
65	Andujar Cedeno	.10
66	Leo Gomez	.10
67	Rusty Meacham	.10
68	Dann Howitt	.10
69	Chris Jones	.10
70	Dave Cochrane	.10
71	Carlos Martinez	.10
72	Hensley Meulens	.10
73	Rich Reed	.10
74	Pedro Munoz	.10
75	Orlando Merced	.10
76	Chito Martinez	.10
77	Ivan Rodriguez	.75
78	Brian Barnes	.10
79	Chris Donnels	.10
80	Todd Hundley	.10
81	Gary Scott	.10
82	John Wehner	.10
83	Al Osuna	.10
84	Luis Lopez	.10
85	Brent Mayne	.10
86	Phil Plantier	.10
87	Joe Bitker	.10
88	Scott Cooper	.10
89	Chris Hammond	.10
90	Tim Sherrill	.10
91	Doug Simons	.10
92	Kip Gross	.10
93	Tim McIntosh	.10
94	Larry Casian	.10
95	Mike Dalton	.10
96	Lance Dickson	.10
97	Joe Grahe	.10
98	Glenn Sutko	.10
99	Gerald Alexander	.10
100	Mo Vaughn	.10

Rookies

A selection of 40 1992 rookie players is featured in this boxed set. Fronts have green borders with a red and white "1992 ROOKIE" notation printed vertically to the left of a game-action photo. Backs repeat the notation on a graduated blue background with a player portrait

photo at top, biographical details and a career summary at center and appropriate logos at bottom.

		NM/M
Complete Set (40):		1.50
Common Player:		.05
1	Todd Van Poppel	.05
2	Kyle Abbott	.05
3	Derek Bell	.05
4	Jim Thome	.50
5	Mark Wohlers	.05
6	Todd Hundley	.05
7	Arthur Rhodes	.05
8	John Ramos	.05
9	Chris George	.05
10	Kenny Lofton	.05
11	Ted Wood	.05
12	Royce Clayton	.05
13	Scott Cooper	.05
14	Anthony Young	.05
15	Joel Johnston	.05
16	Andy Mota	.05
17	Lenny Webster	.05
18	Andy Ashby	.05
19	Jose Mota	.05
20	Tim McIntosh	.05
21	Terry Bross	.05
22	Harvey Pulliam	.05
23	Hector Fajardo	.05
24	Esteban Beltre	.05
25	Gary DiSarcina	.05
26	Mike Humphreys	.05
27	Jarvis Brown	.05
28	Gary Cooper	.05
29	Chris Donnels	.05
30	Monty Fariss	.05
31	Eric Karros	.05
32	Braulio Castillo	.05
33	Cal Eldred	.05
34	Tom Goodwin	.05
35	Reggie Sanders	.05
36	Scott Servais	.05
37	Kim Batiste	.05
38	Eric Wedge	.05
39	Willie Banks	.05
40	Mo Sanford	.05

Superstars

SUPERST★R

SCOTT ERICKSON
P • MINNESOTA TWINS

Available in a blister pack with a book and six "Magic Motion" trivia cards, this 100-card set spotlights the games top veteran stars.

		NM/M
Complete Set (100):		4.00
Common Player:		.05
1	Ken Griffey Jr.	.75
2	Scott Erickson	.05
3	John Smiley	.05
4	Rick Aguilera	.05
5	Jeff Reardon	.05
6	Chuck Finley	.05
7	Kirby Puckett	.50
8	Paul Molitor	.40
9	Dave Winfield	.40
10	Mike Greenwell	.05
11	Bret Saberhagen	.05
12	Pete Harnisch	.05
13	Ozzie Guillen	.05
14	Hal Morris	.05
15	Tom Glavine	.30
16	David Cone	.05
17	Edgar Martinez	.05
18	Willie McGee	.05
19	Jim Abbott	.05
20	Mark Grace	.05
21	George Brett	.65

22	Jack McDowell	.05
23	Don Mattingly	.65
24	Will Clark	.05
25	Dwight Gooden	.05
26	Barry Bonds	1.00
27	Rafael Palmeiro	.35
28	Lee Smith	.05
29	Wally Joyner	.05
30	Wade Boggs	.50
31	Tom Henke	.05
32	Mark Langston	.05
33	Robin Ventura	.05
34	Steve Avery	.05
35	Joe Carter	.05
36	Benito Santiago	.05
37	Dave Stieb	.05
38	Julio Franco	.05
39	Albert Belle	.05
40	Dale Murphy	.25
41	Rob Dibble	.05
42	Dave Justice	.05
43	Jose Rijo	.05
44	Eric Davis	.05
45	Terry Pendleton	.05
46	Kevin Maas	.05
47	Ozzie Smith	.50
48	Andre Dawson	.25
49	Sandy Alomar, Jr.	.05
50	Nolan Ryan	1.00
51	Frank Thomas	.40
52	Craig Biggio	.05
53	Doug Drabek	.05
54	Bobby Thigpen	.05
55	Darryl Strawberry	.35
56	Dennis Eckersley	.35
57	John Franco	.05
58	Paul O'Neill	.05
59	Scott Sanderson	.05
60	Dave Stewart	.05
61	Ivan Calderon	.05
62	Frank Viola	.05
63	Mark McGwire	.75
64	Kelly Gruber	.05
65	Fred McGriff	.05
66	Cecil Fielder	.05
67	Jose Canseco	.30
68	Howard Johnson	.05
69	Juan Gonzalez	.20
70	Tim Wallach	.05
71	John Olerud	.05
72	Carlton Fisk	.40
73	Otis Nixon	.05
74	Roger Clemens	.65
75	Ramon Martinez	.05
76	Ron Gant	.05
77	Barry Larkin	.05
78	Eddie Murray	.40
79	Vince Coleman	.05
80	Bobby Bonilla	.05
81	Tony Gwynn	.50
82	Roberto Alomar	.20
83	Ellis Burks	.05
84	Robin Yount	.40
85	Ryne Sandberg	.50
86	Len Dykstra	.05
87	Ruben Sierra	.05
88	George Bell	.05
89	Cal Ripken, Jr.	1.00
90	Danny Tartabull	.05
91	Gregg Olson	.05
92	Dave Henderson	.05
93	Kevin Mitchell	.05
94	Ben McDonald	.05
95	Matt Williams	.05
96	Roberto Kelly	.05
97	Dennis Martinez	.05
98	Kent Hrbek	.05
99	Felix Jose	.05
100	Rickey Henderson	.40

1993 Score Promos

DARREN DAULTON

Only close comparison with regularly issued versions can detect these unmarked promos. The promos feature slightly different croppings of the pictures, situated higher than the normal version.

		NM/M
Complete Set (8):		15.00
Common Player:		1.00
1	Ken Griffey Jr.	4.00
3	Frank Thomas	2.00
4	Ryne Sandberg	3.00
6	Cal Ripken, Jr.	5.00
7	Roger Clemens	2.50
8	Bobby Bonilla	.05

10	Darren Daulton	1.00
11	Travis Fryman	1.00

1993 Score

CHUCK KNOBLAUCH

Score's 1993 cards have white borders surrounding color action photographs. The player's name is at the bottom of the card, while his team's name and position appears on the left side in a color band. Backs have color portraits, statistics and text. Subsets feature rookies, award winners, draft picks, highlights, World Series highlights, all-star caricatures, dream team players, and the Man of the Year (Kirby Puckett). Insert sets include: Boys of Summer, the Franchise and Stat Leaders, which feature Select's card design.

		NM/M
Complete Set (660):		15.00
Common Player:		.05
Pack (16):		.75
Wax Box (36):		17.50
1	Ken Griffey Jr.	.65
2	Gary Sheffield	.30
3	Frank Thomas	.40
4	Ryne Sandberg	.45
5	Larry Walker	.05
6	Cal Ripken, Jr.	1.00
7	Roger Clemens	.50
8	Bobby Bonilla	.05
9	Carlos Baerga	.05
10	Darren Daulton	.05
11	Travis Fryman	.05
12	Andy Van Slyke	.05
13	Jose Canseco	.30
14	Roberto Alomar	.15
15	Tom Glavine	.30
16	Barry Larkin	.05
17	Gregg Jefferies	.05
18	Craig Biggio	.05
19	Shane Mack	.05
20	Brett Butler	.05
21	Dennis Eckersley	.35
22	Will Clark	.05
23	Don Mattingly	.50
24	Tony Gwynn	.45
25	Ivan Rodriguez	.35
26	Shawon Dunston	.05
27	Mike Mussina	.30
28	Marquis Grissom	.05
29	Charles Nagy	.05
30	Len Dykstra	.05
31	Cecil Fielder	.05
32	Jay Bell	.05
33	B.J. Surhoff	.05
34	Bob Tewksbury	.05
35	Danny Tartabull	.05
36	Terry Pendleton	.05
37	Jack Morris	.05
38	Hal Morris	.05
39	Luis Polonia	.05
40	Ken Caminiti	.05
41	Robin Ventura	.05
42	Darryl Strawberry	.05
43	Wally Joyner	.05
44	Fred McGriff	.05
45	Kevin Tapani	.05
46	Matt Williams	.05
47	Robin Yount	.40
48	Ken Hill	.05
49	Edgar Martinez	.05
50	Mark Grace	.05
51	Juan Gonzalez	.20
52	Curt Schilling	.30
53	Dwight Gooden	.05
54	Chris Hoiles	.05
55	Frank Viola	.05
56	Ray Lankford	.05
57	George Brett	.50
58	Kenny Lofton	.05
59	Nolan Ryan	1.00
60	Mickey Tettleton	.05
61	John Smoltz	.05
62	Howard Johnson	.05
63	Eric Karros	.05
64	Rick Aguilera	.05
65	Steve Finley	.05
66	Mark Langston	.05
67	Bill Swift	.05
68	John Olerud	.05
69	Kevin McReynolds	.05
70	Jack McDowell	.05

No.	Player	Price
71	Rickey Henderson	.40
72	Brian Harper	.05
73	Mike Morgan	.05
74	Rafael Palmeiro	.40
75	Dennis Martinez	.05
76	Tino Martinez	.05
77	Eddie Murray	.40
78	Ellis Burks	.05
79	John Kruk	.05
80	Gregg Olson	.05
81	Bernard Gilkey	.05
82	Milt Cuyler	.05
83	Mike LaValliere	.05
84	Albert Belle	.05
85	Bip Roberts	.05
86	Melido Perez	.05
87	Otis Nixon	.05
88	Bill Spiers	.05
89	Jeff Bagwell	.40
90	Orel Hershiser	.05
91	Andy Benes	.05
92	Devon White	.05
93	Willie McGee	.05
94	Ozzie Guillen	.05
95	Ivan Calderon	.05
96	Keith Miller	.05
97	Steve Buechele	.05
98	Kent Hrbek	.05
99	Dave Hollins	.05
100	Mike Bordick	.05
101	Randy Tomlin	.05
102	Omar Vizquel	.05
103	Lee Smith	.05
104	Leo Gomez	.05
105	Jose Rijo	.05
106	Mark Whiten	.05
107	Dave Justice	.05
108	Eddie Taubensee	.05
109	Lance Johnson	.05
110	Felix Jose	.05
111	Mike Harkey	.05
112	Randy Milligan	.05
113	Anthony Young	.05
114	Rico Brogna	.05
115	Bret Saberhagen	.05
116	Sandy Alomar, Jr.	.05
117	Terry Mulholland	.05
118	Darryl Hamilton	.05
119	Todd Zeile	.05
120	Bernie Williams	.05
121	Zane Smith	.05
122	Derek Bell	.05
123	Deion Sanders	.05
124	Luis Sojo	.05
125	Joe Oliver	.05
126	Craig Grebeck	.05
127	Andujar Cedeno	.05
128	Brian McRae	.05
129	Jose Offerman	.05
130	Pedro Munoz	.05
131	Bud Black	.05
132	Mo Vaughn	.05
133	Bruce Hurst	.05
134	Dave Henderson	.05
135	Tom Pagnozzi	.05
136	Erik Hanson	.05
137	Orlando Merced	.05
138	Dean Palmer	.05
139	John Franco	.05
140	Brady Anderson	.05
141	Ricky Jordan	.05
142	Jeff Blauser	.05
143	Sammy Sosa	.45
144	Bob Walk	.05
145	Delino DeShields	.05
146	Kevin Brown	.05
147	Mark Lemke	.05
148	Chuck Knoblauch	.05
149	Chris Sabo	.05
150	Bobby Witt	.05
151	Luis Gonzalez	.05
152	Ron Karkovice	.05
153	Jeff Brantley	.05
154	Kevin Appier	.05
155	Darrin Jackson	.05
156	Kelly Gruber	.05
157	Royce Clayton	.05
158	Chuck Finley	.05
159	Jeff King	.05
160	Greg Vaughn	.05
161	Geronimo Pena	.05
162	Steve Farr	.05
163	Jose Oquendo	.05
164	Mark Lewis	.05
165	John Wetteland	.05
166	Mike Henneman	.05
167	Todd Hundley	.05
168	Wes Chamberlain	.05
169	Steve Avery	.05
170	Mike Devereaux	.05
171	Reggie Sanders	.05
172	Jay Buhner	.05
173	Eric Anthony	.05
174	John Burkett	.05
175	Tom Candiotti	.05
176	Phil Plantier	.05
177	Doug Henry	.05
178	Scott Leius	.05
179	Kirt Manwaring	.05
180	Jeff Parrett	.05
181	Don Slaught	.05
182	Scott Radinsky	.05
183	Luis Alicea	.05
184	Tom Gordon	.05
185	Rick Wilkins	.05
186	Todd Stottlemyre	.05
187	Moises Alou	.05
188	Joe Grahe	.05
189	Jeff Kent	.05
190	Bill Wegman	.05
191	Kim Batiste	.05
192	Matt Nokes	.05
193	Mark Wohlers	.05
194	Paul Sorrento	.05
195	Chris Hammond	.05
196	Scott Livingstone	.05
197	Doug Jones	.05
198	Scott Cooper	.05
199	Ramon Martinez	.05
200	Dave Valle	.05
201	Mariano Duncan	.05
202	Ben McDonald	.05
203	Darren Lewis	.05
204	Kenny Rogers	.05
205	Manuel Lee	.05
206	Scott Erickson	.05
207	Dan Gladden	.05
208	Bob Welch	.05
209	Greg Olson	.05
210	Dan Pasqua	.05
211	Tim Wallach	.05
212	Jeff Montgomery	.05
213	Derrick May	.05
214	Ed Sprague	.05
215	David Haas	.05
216	Darrin Fletcher	.05
217	Brian Jordan	.05
218	Jaime Navarro	.05
219	Randy Velarde	.05
220	Ron Gant	.05
221	Paul Quantrill	.05
222	Damion Easley	.05
223	Charlie Hough	.05
224	Brad Brink **RC**	.05
225	Barry Manual **RC**	.05
226	Kevin Koslofski **RC**	.05
227	Ryan Thompson **RC**	.05
228	Mike Munoz **RC**	.05
229	Dan Wilson **RC**	.10
230	Peter Hoy **RC**	.05
231	Pedro Astacio **RC**	.10
232	Matt Stairs **RC**	.10
233	Jeff Reboulet **RC**	.05
234	Manny Alexander **RC**	.05
235	Willie Banks **RC**	.05
236	John Jaha **RC**	.05
237	Scooter Tucker **RC**	.05
238	Russ Springer **RC**	.05
239	Paul Miller **RC**	.05
240	Dan Peltier **RC**	.05
241	Ozzie Canseco **RC**	.05
242	Ben Rivera **RC**	.05
243	John Valentin **RC**	.05
244	Henry Rodriguez **RC**	.05
245	Derek Parks **RC**	.05
246	Carlos Garcia **RC**	.10
247	Tim Pugh **RC**	.05
248	Melvin Nieves **RC**	.05
249	Rich Amaral **RC**	.05
250	Willie Greene **RC**	.05
251	Tim Scott **RC**	.05
252	Dave Silvestri **RC**	.05
253	Rob Mallicoat **RC**	.05
254	Donald Harris **RC**	.05
255	Craig Colbert **RC**	.05
256	Jose Guzman	.05
257	Domingo Martinez **RC**	.05
258	William Suero **RC**	.05
259	Juan Guerrero **RC**	.05
260	J.T. Snow **RC**	.45
261	Tony Pena	.05
262	Tim Fortugno **RC**	.05
263	Tom Marsh **RC**	.05
264	Kurt Knudsen **RC**	.05
265	Tim Costo **RC**	.05
266	Steve Shifflett **RC**	.05
267	Billy Ashley **RC**	.05
268	Jerry Nielsen **RC**	.05
269	Pete Young **RC**	.05
270	Johnny Guzman **RC**	.05
271	Greg Colbrunn **RC**	.05
272	Jeff Nelson **RC**	.05
273	Kevin Young **RC**	.05
274	Jeff Frye **RC**	.05
275	J.T. Bruett **RC**	.05
276	Todd Pratt **RC**	.05
277	Mike Butcher **RC**	.05
278	John Flaherty **RC**	.05
279	John Patterson **RC**	.05
280	Eric Hillman **RC**	.05
281	Bien Figueros **RC**	.05
282	Shane Reynolds **RC**	.05
283	Rich Rowland **RC**	.05
284	Steve Foster **RC**	.05
285	Dave Mlicki **RC**	.05
286	Mike Piazza **RC**	.05
287	Mike Trombley **RC**	.05
288	Jim Pena **RC**	.05
289	Bob Ayrault **RC**	.05
290	Henry Mercedes **RC**	.05
291	Bob Wickman **RC**	.05
292	Jacob Brumfield **RC**	.05
293	David Hulse **RC**	.05
294	Ryan Klesko **RC**	.05
295	Doug Linton **RC**	.05
296	Steve Cooke **RC**	.05
297	Eddie Zosky	.05
298	Gerald Williams **RC**	.05
299	Jonathan Hurst **RC**	.05
300	Larry Carter **RC**	.05
301	William Pennyfeather **RC**	.05
302	Cesar Hernandez **RC**	.05
303	Steve Hosey **RC**	.05
304	Blas Minor **RC**	.05
305	Jeff Grotewold **RC**	.05
306	Bernardo Brito **RC**	.05
307	Rafael Bournigal **RC**	.05
308	Jeff Branson **RC**	.05
309	Tom Quinlan **RC**	.05
310	Pat Gomez **RC**	.05
311	Sterling Hitchcock **RC**	.10
312	Kent Bottenfield **RC**	.05
313	Alan Trammell	.05
314	Cris Colon **RC**	.05
315	Paul Wagner **RC**	.05
316	Matt Maysey **RC**	.05
317	Mike Stanton	.05
318	Rick Trlicek **RC**	.05
319	Kevin Rogers **RC**	.05
320	Mark Clark **RC**	.05
321	Pedro Martinez	.40
322	Al Martin **RC**	.05
323	Mike Macfarlane	.05
324	Rey Sanchez **RC**	.10
325	Roger Pavlik **RC**	.05
326	Troy Neel	.05
327	Kerry Woodson **RC**	.05
328	Wayne Kirby **RC**	.05
329	Ken Ryan **RC**	.05
330	Jesse Levis **RC**	.05
331	James Austin	.05
332	Dan Walters	.05
333	Brian Williams	.05
334	Wil Cordero	.05
335	Bret Boone	.05
336	Hipolito Pichardo	.05
337	Pat Mahomes	.05
338	Andy Stankiewicz	.05
339	Jim Bullinger	.05
340	Archi Cianfrocco	.05
341	Ruben Amaro Jr.	.05
342	Frank Seminara	.05
343	Pat Hentgen	.05
344	Dave Nilsson	.05
345	Mike Perez	.05
346	Tim Salmon	.05
347	Tim Wakefield **RC**	.10
348	Carlos Hernandez	.05
349	Donovan Osborne	.05
350	Denny Naegle	.05
351	Sam Militello	.05
352	Eric Fox	.05
353	John Doherty	.05
354	Chad Curtis	.05
355	Jeff Tackett	.05
356	Dave Fleming	.05
357	Pat Listach	.05
358	Kevin Wickander	.05
359	John VanderWal	.05
360	Arthur Rhodes	.05
361	Bob Scanlan	.05
362	Bob Zupcic	.05
363	Mel Rojas	.05
364	Jim Thome	.35
365	Bill Pecota	.05
366	Mark Carreon	.05
367	Mitch Williams	.05
368	Cal Eldred	.05
369	Stan Belinda	.05
370	Pat Kelly	.05
371	Pheal Cormier	.05
372	Juan Guzman	.05
373	Damon Berryhill	.05
374	Gary DiSarcina	.05
375	Norm Charlton	.05
376	Roberto Hernandez	.05
377	Scott Kamieniecki	.05
378	Rusty Meacham	.05
379	Kurt Stillwell	.05
380	Lloyd McClendon	.05
381	Mark Leonard	.05
382	Jerry Browne	.05
383	Glenn Davis	.05
384	Randy Johnson	.40
385	Mike Greenwell	.05
386	Scott Chiamparino	.05
387	George Bell	.05
388	Steve Olin	.05
389	Chuck McElroy	.05
390	Mark Gardner	.05
391	Rod Beck	.05
392	Dennis Rasmussen	.05
393	Charlie Leibrandt	.05
394	Julio Franco	.05
395	Pete Harnisch	.05
396	Sid Bream	.05
397	Milt Thompson	.05
398	Glenallen Hill	.05
399	Chico Walker	.05
400	Alex Cole	.05
401	Trevor Wilson	.05
402	Jeff Conine	.05
403	Kyle Abbott	.05
404	Tom Browning	.05
405	Jerald Clark	.05
406	Vince Horsman	.05
407	Kevin Mitchell	.05
408	Pete Smith	.05
409	Jeff Innis	.05
410	Mike Timlin	.05
411	Charlie Hayes	.05
412	Alex Fernandez	.05
413	Jeff Russell	.05
414	Jody Reed	.05
415	Darnell Coles	.05
416	Xavier Hernandez	.05
417	Steve Sax	.05
418	Joe Girardi	.05
419	Mike Fetters	.05
420	Danny Jackson	.05
421	Jim Gott	.05
422	Tim Belcher	.05
423	Jose Mesa	.05
424	Jose Mesa	.05
425	Junior Felix	.05
426	Thomas Howard	.05
427	Julio Valera	.05
428	Dante Bichette	.05
429	Mike Sharperson	.05
430	Darryl Kile	.10
431	Lonnie Smith	.05
432	Monty Fariss	.05
433	Reggie Jefferson	.05
434	Bob McClure	.05
435	Craig Lefferts	.05
436	Duane Ward	.05
437	Shawn Abner	.05
438	Roberto Kelly	.05
439	Paul O'Neill	.05
440	Alan Mills	.05
441	Roger Mason	.05
442	Gary Pettis	.05
443	Steve Lake	.05
444	Gene Larkin	.05
445	Larry Anderson	.05
446	Doug Dascenzo	.05
447	Daryl Boston	.05
448	John Candelaria	.05
449	Storm Davis	.05
450	Tom Edens	.05
451	Mike Maddux	.05
452	Tim Naehring	.05
453	John Orton	.05
454	Joey Cora	.05
455	Chuck Crim	.05
456	Dan Plesac	.05
457	Mike Bielecki	.05
458	Terry Jorgensen **RC**	.05
459	John Habyan	.05
460	Pete O'Brien	.05
461	Jeff Treadway	.05
462	Frank Castillo	.05
463	Jimmy Jones	.05
464	Tommy Greene	.05
465	Tracy Woodson	.05
466	Rich Rodriguez	.05
467	Joe Hesketh	.05
468	Greg Myers	.05
469	Kirk McCaskill	.05
470	Ricky Bones	.05
471	Lenny Webster	.05
472	Francisco Cabrera	.05
473	Turner Ward	.05
474	Dwayne Henry	.05
475	Al Osuna	.05
476	Craig Wilson	.05
477	Chris Nabholz	.05
478	Rafael Belliard	.05
479	Terry Leach	.05
480	Tim Teufel	.05
481	Dennis Eckersley (Award Winner)	.15
482	Barry Bonds (Award Winner)	.50
483	Dennis Eckersley (Award Winner)	.15
484	Greg Maddux (Award Winner)	.25
485	Pat Listach (ROY)	.05
486	Eric Karros (ROY)	.05
487	Jamie Arnold **RC**	.05
488	B.J. Wallace **RC**	.05
489	Derek Jeter **RC**	8.00
490	Jason Kendall **RC**	.45
491	Rick Helling **RC**	.05
492	Derek Wallace **RC**	.05
493	Sean Lowe **RC**	.05
494	Shannon Stewart **RC**	.65
495	Benji Grigsby **RC**	.05
496	Todd Steverson **RC**	.05
497	Dan Serafini **RC**	.05
498	Michael Tucker **RC**	.05
499	Chris Roberts (Draft Pick)	.05
500	Pete Janicki (Draft Pick)	.05
501	Jeff Schmidt **RC**	.05
502	Edgar Martinez/AS	.05
503	Omar Vizquel/AS	.05
504	Ken Griffey Jr./AS	.35
505	Kirby Puckett/AS	.25
506	Joe Carter/AS	.05
507	Ivan Rodriguez/AS	.15
508	Jack Morris/AS	.05
509	Dennis Eckersley/AS	.15
510	Frank Thomas/AS	.20
511	Roberto Alomar/AS	.10
512	Mickey Morandini (Highlight)	.05
513	Dennis Eckersley (Highlight)	.05
514	Jeff Reardon (Highlight)	.05
515	Danny Tartabull (Highlight)	.05
516	Bip Roberts (Highlight)	.05
517	George Brett (Highlight)	.30
518	Robin Yount (Highlight)	.20
519	Kevin Gross (Highlight)	.05
520	Ed Sprague (World Series Highlight)	.05
521	Dave Winfield (World Series Highlight)	.20
522	Ozzie Smith/AS	.25
523	Barry Bonds/AS	.50
524	Andy Van Slyke/AS	.05
525	Tony Gwynn/AS	.25
526	Darren Daulton/AS	.05
527	Greg Maddux/AS	.25
528	Fred McGriff/AS	.05
529	Lee Smith/AS	.05
530	Ryne Sandberg/AS	.25
531	Gary Sheffield/AS	.10
532	Ozzie Smith (Dream Team)	.25
533	Kirby Puckett (Dream Team)	.25
534	Gary Sheffield (Dream Team)	.10
535	Andy Van Slyke (Dream Team)	.05
536	Ken Griffey Jr. (Dream Team)	.35
537	Ivan Rodriguez (Dream Team)	.15
538	Charles Nagy (Dream Team)	.05
539	Tom Glavine (Dream Team)	.10
540	Dennis Eckersley (Dream Team)	.15
541	Frank Thomas (Dream Team)	.20
542	Roberto Alomar (Dream Team)	.10
543	Sean Barry	.05
544	Mike Schooler	.05
545	Chuck Carr	.05
546	Lenny Harris	.05
547	Gary Scott	.05
548	Derek Lilliquist	.05
549	Brian Hunter	.05
550	Kirby Puckett (MOY)	.25
551	Jim Eisenreich	.05
552	Andre Dawson	.25
553	David Nied	.05
554	Spike Owen	.05
555	Greg Gagne	.05
556	Sid Fernandez	.05
557	Mark McGwire	.75
558	Bryan Harvey	.05
559	Harold Reynolds	.05
560	Barry Bonds	1.00
561	Eric Wedge **RC**	.05
562	Ozzie Smith	.45
563	Rick Sutcliffe	.05
564	Jeff Reardon	.05
565	Alex Arias **RC**	.05
566	Greg Swindell	.05
567	Brook Jacoby	.05
568	Pete Incaviglia	.05
569	Butch Henry **RC**	.05
570	Eric Davis	.05
571	Kevin Seitzer	.05
572	Tony Fernandez	.05
573	Steve Reed **RC**	.05
574	Cory Snyder	.05
575	Joe Carter	.05
576	Greg Maddux	.45
577	Bert Blyleven	.05
578	Kevin Bass	.05
579	Carlton Fisk	.40
580	Doug Drabek	.05
581	Mark Gubicza	.05
582	Bobby Thigpen	.05
583	Chili Davis	.05
584	Scott Bankhead	.05
585	Harold Baines	.05
586	Eric Young **RC**	.15
587	Lance Parrish	.05
588	Juan Bell	.05
589	Bob Ojeda	.05
590	Joe Orsulak	.05
591	Benito Santiago	.05
592	Wade Boggs	.45
593	Robby Thompson	.05
594	Erik Plunk	.05
595	Hensley Meulens	.05
596	Lou Whitaker	.05
597	Dale Murphy	.25
598	Paul Molitor	.40
599	Greg W. Harris	.05
600	Darren Holmes	.05
601	Dave Martinez	.05
602	Tom Henke	.05
603	Mike Benjamin	.05
604	Rene Gonzales	.05
605	Roger McDowell	.05
606	Kirby Puckett	.45
607	Randy Myers	.05
608	Ruben Sierra	.05
609	Wilson Alvarez	.05
610	Dave Segui	.05
611	Juan Samuel	.05
612	Tom Brunansky	.05
613	Willie Randolph	.05
614	Tony Phillips	.05
615	Candy Maldonado	.05
616	Chris Bosio	.05
617	Bret Barberie	.05
618	Scott Sanderson	.05
619	Ron Darling	.05
620	Dave Winfield	.40
621	Mike Felder	.05
622	Greg Hibbard	.05
623	Mike Scioscia	.05
624	John Smiley	.05
625	Alejandro Pena	.05
626	Terry Steinbach	.05
627	Freddie Benavides	.05
628	Kevin Reimer	.05
629	Braulio Castillo	.05
630	Dave Stieb	.05
631	Dave Magadan	.05
632	Scott Fletcher	.05
633	Cris Carpenter	.05
634	Kevin Maas	.05
635	Todd Worrell	.05
636	Rob Deer	.05
637	Dwight Smith	.05
638	Chito Martinez	.05
639	Jimmy Key	.05
640	Greg Harris	.05
641	Mike Moore	.05
642	Pat Borders	.05
643	Bill Gullickson	.05
644	Gary Gaetti	.05
645	David Howard	.05
646	Jim Abbott	.05
647	Willie Wilson	.05
648	David Wells	.05
649	Andres Galarraga	.05
650	Vince Coleman	.05
651	Rob Dibble	.05
652	Frank Tanana	.05
653	Steve Decker	.05
654	David Cone	.05
655	Jack Armstrong	.05
656	Dave Stewart	.05
657	Billy Hatcher	.05
658	Tim Raines	.05
659	Walt Weiss	.05
660	Jose Lind	.05

Boys of Summer

These cards were available as inserts only in Score 35-card Super Packs, about one in every four packs. Borderless fronts have a color action photo of the player superimposed over the sun. The player's name is in black script in a green strip at bottom, along with a subset logo. On back is a player portrait, again with the sun as a background. Subset, company, team and major league logos are in color on the right, and there is a short career summary on the green background at bottom.

		NM/M
Complete Set (30):		12.50
Common Player:		.25
1	Billy Ashley	.25
2	Tim Salmon	.50
3	Pedro Martinez	4.00
4	Luis Mercedes	.25
5	Mike Piazza	8.00
6	Troy Neel	.25
7	Melvin Nieves	.25
8	Ryan Klesko	.25
9	Ryan Thompson	.25
10	Kevin Young	.25
11	Gerald Williams	.25
12	Willie Greene	.25
13	John Patterson	.25
14	Carlos Garcia	.25
15	Eddie Zosky	.25
16	Sean Berry	.25
17	Rico Brogna	.25
18	Larry Carter	.25
19	Bobby Ayala	.25
20	Alan Embree	.25
21	Donald Harris	.25
22	Sterling Hitchcock	.25
23	David Nied	.25
24	Henry Mercedes	.25
25	Ozzie Canseco	.25
26	David Hulse	.25
27	Al Martin	.25
28	Dan Wilson	.25
29	Paul Miller	.25
30	Rich Rowland	.25

Dream Team

This set which features most of the players in street clothes in sepia-toned photos on a white background, has gold-foil graphics and was available only via a mail-in offer.

		NM/M
Complete Set (12):		5.00
Common Player:		.25
1	Ozzie Smith	1.00
2	Kirby Puckett	1.00
3	Gary Sheffield	.35
4	Andy Van Slyke	.25
5	Ken Griffey Jr.	2.00
6	Ivan Rodriguez	.60
7	Charles Nagy	.25
8	Tom Glavine	.35
9	Dennis Eckersley	.60
10	Frank Thomas	.75
11	Roberto Alomar	.30
---	Header Card	.05

The Franchise

These glossy inserts have full-bleed color action photos against a darkened background so that the player stands out. Cards could be found in 16-card packs only; odds of finding one are 1 in every 24 packs. The fronts have gold-foil highlights.

		NM/M
Complete Set (28):		50.00
Common Player:		.60
1	Cal Ripken, Jr.	12.00
2	Roger Clemens	6.00
3	Mark Langston	.60
4	Frank Thomas	3.50
5	Carlos Baerga	.60
6	Cecil Fielder	.60
7	Gregg Jefferies	.60
8	Robin Yount	3.50
9	Kirby Puckett	5.00
10	Don Mattingly	6.00
11	Dennis Eckersley	3.00
12	Ken Griffey Jr.	9.00
13	Juan Gonzalez	3.50
14	Roberto Alomar	1.50
15	Terry Pendleton	.60
16	Ryne Sandberg	5.00
17	Barry Larkin	.60
18	Jeff Bagwell	3.50
19	Brett Butler	.60
20	Larry Walker	.60
21	Bobby Bonilla	.60
22	Darren Daulton	.60
23	Andy Van Slyke	.60
24	Ray Lankford	.60
25	Gary Sheffield	1.50
26	Will Clark	.60
27	Bryan Harvey	.60
28	David Nied	.60

Procter & Gamble Rookies

This set was available via a mail-in offer in the summer of 1993. Ten proofs of purchase were required along with a small amount of cash for postage. Fronts feature a player action photo in a diamond at center with the name, position and team logo in a home plate device at the bottom of the photo. At bottom center is a color photo of the player's home stadium, flanked

by silver-foil stripes on a dark green background. Above the player photo are gold-foil Score and P&G logos on a dark green background. A center bar in gold foil has the word "ROOKIE" in green. Backs have a small player portrait photo at top against a dark green background. His name and position are in white at left and personal data at right. At center is a large color photo of the player's hometeam skyline, with the city name in gold type in a green stripe below. At bottom are complete major and minor league stats, MLB and MLBPA logos and the card number.

		NM/M
Complete Set (10):		3.00
Common Player:		.25
1	Wil Cordero	.25
2	Pedro Martinez	2.00
3	Bret Boone	.25
4	Melvin Nieves	.25
5	Ryan Klesko	.25
6	Ryan Thompson	.25
7	Kevin Young	.25
8	Willie Greene	.25
9	Eric Wedge	.25
10	David Nied	.25

1994 Score Samples

Regular and Gold Rush versions of the first eight cards in the 1994 Score set were produced in a special promo version to familiarize buyers with the new issue. Cards have all zeroes in place of the 1993 stats and are overprinted on front and back with a diagonal black "SAMPLE." The samples were distributed in 11-card cello packs containing eight regular sample cards, one of the Gold Rush samples, a Barry Larkin Dream Team promo card and a header.

		NM/M
Complete Set (18):		20.00
Common Player:		.40
1	Barry Bonds	2.00
1	Barry Bonds (Gold Rush)	6.00
2	John Olerud	1.00
2	John Olerud (Gold Rush)	1.00
3	Ken Griffey Jr.	1.50
3	Ken Griffey Jr. (Gold Rush)	4.50
4	Jeff Bagwell	1.00
4	Jeff Bagwell (Gold Rush)	3.00
5	John Burkett	.40
5	John Burkett (Gold Rush)	1.00
6	Jack McDowell	.40
6	Jack McDowell (Gold Rush)	1.00
7	Albert Belle	.50
7	Albert Belle (Gold Rush)	1.50
8	Andres Galarraga	.40
8	Andres Galarraga (Gold Rush)	1.00
5	Barry Larkin (Dream Team)	.50
--	Hobby Header Card	.05
--	Retail Header Card	.05

1994 Score

Score's 1994 set, with a new design and UV coating, was issued in two series of 330 cards each. The cards, which use more action photos than before, have dark blue borders with the player's name in a team color-coded strip at the bottom. A special Gold Rush card, done for each card in the set, is included in every pack. Series 1 includes American League checklists, which are printed on the backs of cards depicting panoramic views of each team's ballpark. Series 2 has the National League team

checklists. Insert sets include Dream Team players, and National (Series 1 packs) and American League Gold Stars (Series 2 packs), which use the Gold Rush process and appear once every 18 packs.

		NM/M
Complete Set (660):		15.00
Common Player:		.05
Gold Rush:		2X
Pack (14):		.75
Wax Box (36):		15.00
1	Barry Bonds	1.00
2	John Olerud	.05
3	Ken Griffey Jr.	.65
4	Jeff Bagwell	.40
5	John Burkett	.05
6	Jack McDowell	.05
7	Albert Belle	.05
8	Andres Galarraga	.05
9	Mike Mussina	.30
10	Will Clark	.05
11	Travis Fryman	.05
12	Tony Gwynn	.50
13	Robin Yount	.40
14	Dave Magadan	.05
15	Paul O'Neill	.05
16	Ray Lankford	.05
17	Damion Easley	.05
18	Andy Van Slyke	.05
19	Brian McRae	.05
20	Ryne Sandberg	.50
21	Kirby Puckett	.50
22	Dwight Gooden	.05
23	Don Mattingly	.50
24	Kevin Mitchell	.05
25	Roger Clemens	.60
26	Eric Karros	.05
27	Juan Gonzalez	.20
28	John Kruk	.05
29	Gregg Jefferies	.05
30	Tom Glavine	.30
31	Ivan Rodriguez	.35
32	Jay Bell	.05
33	Randy Johnson	.40
34	Darren Daulton	.05
35	Rickey Henderson	.40
36	Eddie Murray	.40
37	Brian Harper	.05
38	Delino DeShields	.05
39	Jose Lind	.05
40	Benito Santiago	.05
41	Frank Thomas	.40
42	Mark Grace	.05
43	Roberto Alomar	.20
44	Andy Benes	.05
45	Luis Polonia	.05
46	Brett Butler	.05
47	Terry Steinbach	.05
48	Craig Biggio	.05
49	Greg Vaughn	.05
50	Charlie Hayes	.05
51	Mickey Tettleton	.05
52	Jose Rijo	.05
53	Carlos Baerga	.05
54	Jeff Blauser	.05
55	Leo Gomez	.05
56	Bob Tewksbury	.05
57	Mo Vaughn	.05
58	Orlando Merced	.05
59	Tino Martinez	.05
60	Len Dykstra	.05
61	Jose Canseco	.25
62	Tony Fernandez	.05
63	Donovan Osborne	.05
64	Ken Hill	.05
65	Kent Hrbek	.05
66	Bryan Harvey	.05
67	Wally Joyner	.05
68	Derrick May	.05
69	Lance Johnson	.05
70	Willie McGee	.05
71	Mark Langston	.05
72	Terry Pendleton	.05
73	Joe Carter	1.00
74	Barry Larkin	.05
75	Jimmy Key	.05
76	Joe Girardi	.05
77	B.J. Surhoff	.05
78	Pete Harnisch	.05
79	Lou Whitaker	.05
80	Cory Snyder	.05
81	Kenny Lofton	.05
82	Fred McGriff	.05
83	Mike Greenwell	.05
84	Mike Perez	.05

85	Cal Ripken, Jr.	1.00
86	Don Slaught	.05
87	Omar Vizquel	.05
88	Curt Schilling	.30
89	Chuck Knoblauch	.05
90	Moises Alou	.05
91	Greg Gagne	.05
92	Bret Saberhagen	.05
93	Ozzie Guillen	.05
94	Matt Williams	.05
95	Chad Curtis	.05
96	Mike Harkey	.05
97	Devon White	.05
98	Walt Weiss	.05
99	Kevin Brown	.05
100	Gary Sheffield	.25
101	Wade Boggs	.50
102	Orel Hershiser	.05
103	Tony Phillips	.05
104	Andujar Cedeno	.05
105	Bill Spiers	.05
106	Otis Nixon	.05
107	Felix Fermin	.05
108	Bip Roberts	.05
109	Dennis Eckersley	.35
110	Dante Bichette	.05
111	Ben McDonald	.05
112	Jim Poole	.05
113	John Dopson	.05
114	Rob Dibble	.05
115	Jeff Treadway	.05
116	Ricky Jordan	.05
117	Mike Henneman	.05
118	Willie Blair	.05
119	Doug Henry	.05
120	Gerald Perry	.05
121	Greg Myers	.05
122	John Franco	.05
123	Roger Mason	.05
124	Chris Hammond	.05
125	Hubie Brooks	.05
126	Kent Mercker	.05
127	Jim Abbott	.05
128	Kevin Bass	.05
129	Rick Aguilera	.05
130	Mitch Webster	.05
131	Eric Plunk	.05
132	Mark Carreon	.05
133	Dave Stewart	.05
134	Willie Wilson	.05
135	Dave Fleming	.05
136	Jeff Tackett	.05
137	Geno Petralli	.05
138	Gene Harris	.05
139	Scott Bankhead	.05
140	Trevor Wilson	.05
141	Alvaro Espinoza	.05
142	Ryan Bowen	.05
143	Mike Moore	.05
144	Bill Pecota	.05
145	Jaime Navarro	.05
146	Jack Daugherty	.05
147	Bob Wickman	.05
148	Chris Jones	.05
149	Todd Stottlemyre	.05
150	Brian Williams	.05
151	Chuck Finley	.05
152	Lenny Harris	.05
153	Alex Fernandez	.05
154	Candy Maldonado	.05
155	Jeff Montgomery	.05
156	David West	.05
157	Mark Williamson	.05
158	Milt Thompson	.05
159	Ron Darling	.05
160	Stan Belinda	.05
161	Henry Cotto	.05
162	Mel Rojas	.05
163	Doug Strange	.05
164	Rene Arocha (1993 Rookie)	.05
165	Tim Hulett	.05
166	Steve Avery	.05
167	Jim Thome	.35
168	Tom Browning	.05
169	Mario Diaz	.05
170	Steve Reed (1993 Rookie)	.05
171	Scott Livingstone	.05
172	Chris Donnels	.05
173	John Jaha	.05
174	Carlos Hernandez	.05
175	Dion James	.05
176	Bud Black	.05
177	Tony Castillo	.05
178	Jose Guzman	.05
179	Torey Lovullo	.05
180	John Vander Wal	.05
181	Mike LaValliere	.05
182	Sid Fernandez	.05
183	Brent Mayne	.05
184	Terry Mulholland	.05
185	Willie Banks	.05
186	Steve Cooke (1993 Rookie)	.05
187	Brent Gates (1993 Rookie)	.05
188	Erik Pappas (1993 Rookie)	.05
189	Bill Haselman (1993 Rookie)	.05
190	Fernando Valenzuela	.05
191	Gary Redus	.05
192	Danny Darwin	.05
193	Mark Portugal	.05
194	Derek Lilliquist	.05
195	Charlie O'Brien	.05
196	Matt Nokes	.05
197	Danny Sheaffer	.05
198	Bill Gullickson	.05
199	Alex Arias (1993 Rookie)	.05

200	Mike Fetters	.05
201	Brian Jordan	.05
202	Joe Grahe	.05
203	Tom Candiotti	.05
204	Jeremy Stanton	.05
205	Mike Stanton	.05
206	David Howard	.05
207	Darren Holmes	.05
208	Rick Honeycutt	.05
209	Danny Jackson	.05
210	Rich Amaral (1993 Rookie)	.05
211	Blas Minor (1993 Rookie)	.05
212	Kenny Rogers	.05
213	Jim Leyritz	.05
214	Mike Morgan	.05
215	Dan Gladden	.05
216	Randy Velarde	.05
217	Mitch Williams	.05
218	Hipolito Pichardo	.05
219	Dave Burba	.05
220	Wilson Alvarez	.05
221	Bob Zupcic	.05
222	Francisco Cabrera	.05
223	Julio Valera	.05
224	Paul Assenmacher	.05
225	Jeff Branson	.05
226	Todd Frohwirth	.05
227	Armando Reynoso	.05
228	Rich Rowland (1993 Rookie)	.05
229	Freddie Benavides	.05
230	Wayne Kirby (1993 Rookie)	.05
231	Darryl Kile	.05
232	Skeeter Barnes	.05
233	Ramon Martinez	.05
234	Tom Gordon	.05
235	Dave Gallagher	.05
236	Ricky Bones	.05
237	Larry Andersen	.05
238	Pat Meares (1993 Rookie)	.05
239	Zane Smith	.05
240	Tim Leary	.05
241	Phil Clark	.05
242	Danny Cox	.05
243	Mike Jackson	.05
244	Mike Gallego	.05
245	Lee Smith	.05
246	Todd Jones (1993 Rookie)	.05
247	Steve Bedrosian	.05
248	Troy Neel	.05
249	Jose Bautista	.05
250	Steve Frey	.05
251	Jeff Reardon	.05
252	Stan Javier	.05
253	Mo Sanford (1993 Rookie)	.05
254	Steve Sax	.05
255	Luis Aquino	.05
256	Domingo Jean (1993 Rookie)	.05
257	Scott Servais	.05
258	Brad Pennington (1993 Rookie)	.05
259	Dave Hansen	.05
260	Goose Gossage	.05
261	Jeff Fassero	.05
262	Junior Ortiz	.05
263	Anthony Young	.05
264	Chris Bosio	.05
265	Ruben Amaro Jr.	.05
266	Mark Eichhorn	.05
267	Dave Clark	.05
268	Gary Thurman	.05
269	Les Lancaster	.05
270	Jamie Moyer	.05
271	Ricky Gutierrez (1993 Rookie)	.05
272	Greg Harris	.05
273	Mike Benjamin	.05
274	Gene Nelson	.05
275	Damon Berryhill	.05
276	Scott Radinsky	.05
277	Mike Aldrete	.05
278	Jerry DiPoto (1993 Rookie)	.05
279	Chris Haney	.05
280	Richie Lewis (1993 Rookie)	.05
281	Jarvis Brown	.05
282	Juan Bell	.05
283	Joe Klink	.05
284	Graeme Lloyd (1993 Rookie)	.05
285	Casey Candaele	.05
286	Bob MacDonald	.05
287	Mike Sharperson	.05
288	Gene Larkin	.05
289	Brian Barnes	.05
290	David McCarty (1993 Rookie)	.05
291	Jeff Innis	.05
292	Bob Patterson	.05
293	Ben Rivera	.05
294	John Habyan	.05
295	Rich Rodriguez	.05
296	Edwin Nunez	.05
297	Rod Brewer	.05
298	Mike Timlin	.05
299	Jesse Orosco	.05
300	Gary Gaetti	.05
301	Todd Benzinger	.05
302	Jeff Nelson	.05
303	Rafael Belliard	.05
304	Matt Whiteside	.05
305	Vinny Castilla	.05
306	Matt Turner	.05
307	Eduardo Perez	.05

308	Joel Johnston	.05
309	Chris Gomez	.05
310	Pat Rapp	.05
311	Jim Tatum	.05
312	Kirk Rueter	.05
313	John Flaherty	.05
314	Tom Kramer	.05
315	Mark Whiten (Highlights)	.05
316	Chris Bosio (Highlights)	.05
317	Orioles Checklist	.05
318	Red Sox Checklist	.05
319	Angels Checklist	.05
320	White Sox Checklist	.05
321	Indians Checklist	.05
322	Tigers Checklist	.05
323	Royals Checklist	.05
324	Brewers Checklist	.05
325	Twins Checklist	.05
326	Yankees Checklist	.05
327	Athletics Checklist	.05
328	Mariners Checklist	.05
329	Rangers Checklist	.05
330	Blue Jays Checklist	.05
331	Frank Viola	.05
332	Ron Gant	.05
333	Charles Nagy	.05
334	Roberto Kelly	.05
335	Brady Anderson	.05
336	Alex Cole	.05
337	Alan Trammell	.05
338	Derek Bell	.05
339	Bernie Williams	.05
340	Jose Offerman	.05
341	Bill Wegman	.05
342	Ken Caminiti	.05
343	Pat Borders	.05
344	Kirt Manwaring	.05
345	Chili Davis	.05
346	Steve Buechele	.05
347	Robin Ventura	.05
348	Teddy Higuera	.05
349	Jerry Browne	.05
350	Scott Kamieniecki	.05
351	Kevin Tapani	.05
352	Marquis Grissom	.05
353	Jay Buhner	.05
354	Dave Hollins	.05
355	Dan Wilson	.05
356	Bob Walk	.05
357	Chris Hoiles	.05
358	Todd Zeile	.05
359	Kevin Appier	.05
360	Chris Sabo	.05
361	David Segui	.05
362	Jerald Clark	.05
363	Tony Pena	.05
364	Steve Finley	.05
365	Roger Pavlik	.05
366	John Smoltz	.05
367	Scott Fletcher	.05
368	Jody Reed	.05
369	David Wells	.05
370	Jose Vizcaino	.05
371	Pat Listach	.05
372	Orestes Destrade	.05
373	Danny Tartabull	.05
374	Greg W. Harris	.05
375	Juan Guzman	.05
376	Larry Walker	.05
377	Gary DiSarcina	.05
378	Bobby Bonilla	.05
379	Tim Raines	.05
380	Tommy Greene	.05
381	Chris Gwynn	.05
382	Jeff King	.05
383	Shane Mack	.05
384	Ozzie Smith	.50
385	Eddie Zambrano RC	.05
386	Mike Devereaux	.05
387	Erik Hanson	.05
388	Scott Cooper	.05
389	Dean Palmer	.05
390	John Wetteland	.05
391	Reggie Jefferson	.05
392	Mark Lemke	.05
393	Cecil Fielder	.05
394	Reggie Sanders	.05
395	Darryl Hamilton	.05
396	Daryl Boston	.05
397	Pat Kelly	.05
398	Joe Orsulak	.05
399	Ed Sprague	.05
400	Eric Anthony	.05
401	Scott Sanderson	.05
402	Jim Gott	.05
403	Ron Karkovice	.05
404	Phil Plantier	.05
405	David Cone	.05
406	Robby Thompson	.05
407	Dave Winfield	.40
408	Dwight Smith	.05
409	Ruben Sierra	.05
410	Jack Armstrong	.05
411	Mike Felder	.05
412	Wil Cordero	.05
413	Julio Franco	.05
414	Howard Johnson	.05
415	Mark McLemore	.05
416	Pete Incaviglia	.05
417	John Valentin	.05
418	Tim Wakefield	.05
419	Jose Mesa	.05
420	Bernard Gilkey	.05
421	Kirk Gibson	.05
422	Dave Justice	.05
423	Tom Brunansky	.05
424	John Smiley	.05
425	Kevin Maas	.05

#	Player	Price		#	Player	Price
426	Doug Drabek	.05		544	Doug Jones	.05
427	Paul Molitor	.40		545	Scott Leius	.05
428	Darryl Strawberry	.05		546	Al Martin	.05
429	Tim Naehring	.05		547	Bob Welch	.05
430	Bill Swift	.05		548	Scott Christman RC	.05
431	Ellis Burks	.05		549	Norm Charlton	.05
432	Greg Hibbard	.05		550	Mark McGwire	.75
433	Felix Jose	.05		551	Greg McMichael	.05
434	Bret Barberie	.05		552	Tim Costo	.05
435	Pedro Munoz	.05		553	Rodney Bolton	.05
436	Darrin Fletcher	.05		554	Pedro Martinez	.40
437	Bobby Witt	.05		555	Marc Valdes	.05
438	Wes Chamberlain	.05		556	Darrell Whitmore	.05
439	Mackey Sasser	.05		557	Tim Bogar	.05
440	Mark Whiten	.05		558	Steve Karsay	.05
441	Harold Reynolds	.05		559	Danny Bautista	.05
442	Greg Olson	.05		560	Jeffrey Hammonds	.05
443	Billy Hatcher	.05		561	Aaron Sele	.05
444	Joe Oliver	.05		562	Russ Springer	.05
445	Sandy Alomar Jr.	.05		563	Jason Bere	.05
446	Tim Wallach	.05		564	Billy Brewer	.05
447	Karl Rhodes	.05		565	Sterling Hitchcock	.05
448	Royce Clayton	.05		566	Bobby Munoz	.05
449	Cal Eldred	.05		567	Craig Paquette	.05
450	Rick Wilkins	.05		568	Bret Boone	.05
451	Mike Stanley	.05		569	Dan Peltier	.05
452	Charlie Hough	.05		570	Jeromy Burnitz	.05
453	Jack Morris	.05		571	John Wasdin RC	.05
454	Jon Ratliff RC	.05		572	Chipper Jones	.50
455	Rene Gonzales	.05		573	Jamey Wright RC	.05
456	Eddie Taubensee	.05		574	Jeff Granger	.05
457	Roberto Hernandez	.05		575	Jay Powell RC	.05
458	Todd Hundley	.05		576	Ryan Thompson	.05
459	Mike MacFarlane	.05		577	Lou Frazier	.05
460	Mickey Morandini	.05		578	Paul Wagner	.05
461	Scott Erickson	.05		579	Brad Ausmus	.05
462	Lonnie Smith	.05		580	Jack Voigt	.05
463	Dave Henderson	.05		581	Kevin Rogers	.05
464	Ryan Klesko	.05		582	Damon Buford	.05
465	Edgar Martinez	.05		583	Paul Quantrill	.05
466	Tom Pagnozzi	.05		584	Marc Newfield	.05
467	Charlie Leibrandt	.05		585	Derrek Lee RC	1.00
468	Brian Anderson RC	.10		586	Shane Reynolds	.05
469	Harold Baines	.05		587	Cliff Floyd	.05
470	Tim Belcher	.05		588	Jeff Schwarz	.05
471	Andre Dawson	.25		589	Ross Powell RC	.05
472	Eric Young	.05		590	Gerald Williams	.05
473	Paul Sorrento	.05		591	Mike Trombley	.05
474	Luis Gonzalez	.05		592	Ken Ryan	.05
475	Rob Deer	.05		593	John O'Donoghue	.05
476	Mike Piazza	.65		594	Rod Correia	.05
477	Kevin Reimer	.05		595	Darrell Sherman	.05
478	Jeff Gardner	.05		596	Steve Scarsone	.05
479	Melido Perez	.05		597	Sherman Obando	.05
480	Darren Lewis	.05		598	Kurt Abbott	.05
481	Duane Ward	.05		599	Dave Telgheder	.05
482	Rey Sanchez	.05		600	Rick Trlicek	.05
483	Mark Lewis	.05		601	Carl Everett	.05
484	Jeff Conine	.05		602	Luis Ortiz	.05
485	Joey Cora	.05		603	Larry Luebbers RC	.05
486	Trot Nixon RC	.50		604	Kevin Roberson	.05
487	Kevin McReynolds	.05		605	Butch Huskey	.05
488	Mike Lansing	.05		606	Benji Gil	.05
489	Mike Pagliarulo	.05		607	Todd Van Poppel	.05
490	Mariano Duncan	.05		608	Mark Hutton	.05
491	Mike Bordick	.05		609	Chip Hale	.05
492	Kevin Young	.05		610	Matt Maysey	.05
493	Dave Valle	.05		611	Scott Ruffcorn	.05
494	Wayne Gomes RC	.05		612	Hilly Hathaway	.05
495	Rafael Palmeiro	.35		613	Allen Watson	.05
496	Deion Sanders	.05		614	Carlos Delgado	.30
497	Rick Sutcliffe	.05		615	Roberto Mejia	.05
498	Randy Milligan	.05		616	Turk Wendell	.05
499	Carlos Quintana	.05		617	Tony Tarasco	.05
500	Chris Turner	.05		618	Raul Mondesi	.05
501	Thomas Howard	.05		619	Kevin Stocker	.05
502	Greg Swindell	.05		620	Javier Lopez	.05
503	Chad Kreuter	.05		621	Keith Kessinger RC	.05
504	Eric Davis	.05		622	Bob Hamelin	.05
505	Dickie Thon	.05		623	John Roper	.05
506	Matt Drews RC	.05		624	Len Dykstra (World Series)	.05
507	Spike Owen	.05		625	Joe Carter (World Series)	.05
508	Rod Beck	.05		626	Jim Abbott (Highlight)	.05
509	Pat Hentgen	.05		627	Lee Smith (Highlight)	.05
510	Sammy Sosa	.50		628	Ken Griffey Jr. (HL)	.35
511	J.T. Snow	.05		629	Dave Winfield (Highlight)	.05
512	Chuck Carr	.05		630	Darryl Kile (Highlight)	.05
513	Bo Jackson	.10		631	Frank Thomas (MVP)	.25
514	Dennis Martinez	.05		632	Barry Bonds (MVP)	.50
515	Phil Hiatt	.05		633	Jack McDowell (Cy Young)	.05
516	Jeff Kent	.05		634	Greg Maddux (Cy Young)	.25
517	Brooks Kieschnick RC	.05		635	Tim Salmon (ROY)	.05
518	Kirk Presley RC	.05		636	Mike Piazza (ROY)	.40
519	Kevin Seitzer	.05		637	Brian Turang RC	.05
520	Carlos Garcia	.05		638	Rondell White	.05
521	Mike Blowers	.05		639	Nigel Wilson	.05
522	Luis Alicea	.05		640	Torii Hunter RC	.75
523	David Hulse	.05		641	Salomon Torres	.05
524	Greg Maddux	.50		642	Kevin Higgins	.05
525	Gregg Olson	.05		643	Eric Wedge	.05
526	Hal Morris	.05		644	Roger Salkeld	.05
527	Daron Kirkreit	.05		645	Manny Ramirez	.40
528	David Nied	.05		646	Jeff McNeely	.05
529	Jeff Russell	.05		647	Braves Checklist	.05
530	Kevin Gross	.05		648	Cubs Checklist	.05
531	John Doherty	.05		649	Reds Checklist	.05
532	Matt Brunson RC	.05		650	Rockies Checklist	.05
533	Dave Nilsson	.05		651	Marlins Checklist	.05
534	Randy Myers	.05		652	Astros Checklist	.05
535	Steve Farr	.05		653	Dodgers Checklist	.05
536	Billy Wagner RC	.10		654	Expos Checklist	.05
537	Darnell Coles	.05		655	Mets Checklist	.05
538	Frank Tanana	.05		656	Phillies Checklist	.05
539	Tim Salmon	.05		657	Pirates Checklist	.05
540	Kim Batiste	.05		658	Cardinals Checklist	.05
541	George Bell	.05		659	Padres Checklist	.05
542	Tom Henke	.05		660	Giants Checklist	.05
543	Sam Horn	.05				

Gold Rush

Opting to include one insert card in each pack of its 1994 product, Score created a "Gold Rush" version of each card in its regular set. Gold Rush cards are basically the same as their counterparts with a few enhancements. Card fronts are printed on foil with a gold border and a Score Gold Rush logo in one of the upper corners. The background of the photo has been metalized, allowing the color player portion to stand out in sharp contrast. Backs are identical to the regular cards except for the appearance of a large Gold Rush logo under the typography.

	NM/M
Complete Set (660):	40.00
Common Player:	.15
Stars:	2X

Boys of Summer

A heavy emphasis on rookies and recent rookies is noted in this insert set. Released in two series, cards #1-30 are found in Series 1, with #31-60 packaged with Series 2. Fronts feature a color action photo on which the background has been rendered in a blurred watercolor effect. A hot-color aura separates the player from the background. The player's name appears vertically in gold foil. Backs have the background in reds and orange with a portrait-style player photo on one side and a large "Boys of Summer" logo on the other. A short description of the player's talents appears at center.

		NM/M
Complete Set (60):		25.00
Common Player:		.25
1	Jeff Conine	.25
2	Aaron Sele	.25
3	Kevin Stocker	.25
4	Pat Meares	.25
5	Jeromy Burnitz	.25
6	Mike Piazza	6.00
7	Allen Watson	.25
8	Jeffrey Hammonds	.25
9	Kevin Roberson	.25
10	Hilly Hathaway	.25
11	Kirk Reuter	.25
12	Eduardo Perez	.25
13	Ricky Gutierrez	.25
14	Domingo Jean	.25
15	David Nied	.25
16	Wayne Kirby	.25
17	Mike Lansing	.25
18	Jason Bere	.25
19	Brent Gates	.25
20	Javier Lopez	.25
21	Greg McMichael	.25
22	David Hulse	.25
23	Roberto Mejia	.25
24	Tim Salmon	.50
25	Rene Arocha	.25
26	Bret Boone	.25
27	David McCarty	.25
28	Todd Van Poppel	.25
29	Lance Painter	.25
30	Erik Pappas	.25
31	Chuck Carr	.25
32	Mark Hutton	.25
33	Jeff McNeely	.25
34	Willie Greene	.25
35	Nigel Wilson	.25
36	Rondell White	.25
37	Brian Turang	.25
38	Manny Ramirez	3.00
39	Salomon Torres	.25
40	Melvin Nieves	.25
41	Ryan Klesko	.25
42	Keith Kessinger	.25
43	Eric Wedge	.25
44	Bob Hamelin	.25
45	Carlos Delgado	2.50
46	Marc Newfield	.25
47	Raul Mondesi	.25
48	Tim Costo	.25
49	Pedro Martinez	3.00
50	Steve Karsay	.25
51	Danny Bautista	.25
52	Butch Huskey	.25
53	Kurt Abbott	.25
54	Darrell Sherman	.25
55	Damon Buford	.25
56	Ross Powell	.25
57	Darrell Whitmore	.25
58	Chipper Jones	5.00
59	Jeff Granger	.25
60	Cliff Floyd	.25

Dream Team

Score's 1994 "Dream Team," one top player at each position, was featured in a 10-card insert set. The stars were decked out in vintage uniforms and equipment for the photos. Green and black bars at top and bottom frame the photo, and all printing on the front is in gold foil. Backs have a white background with green highlights. A color player portrait photo is featured, along with a brief justification for the player's selection to the squad. Cards are UV coated on both sides. Stated odds of finding a Dream Team insert were given as one per 72 packs.

		NM/M
Complete Set (10):		15.00
Common Player:		1.00
1	Mike Mussina	2.00
2	Tom Glavine	2.00
3	Don Mattingly	10.00
4	Carlos Baerga	1.00
5	Barry Larkin	1.00
6	Matt Williams	1.00
7	Juan Gonzalez	4.00
8	Andy Van Slyke	1.00
9	Larry Walker	1.00
10	Mike Stanley	1.00

Gold Stars

Limited to inclusion in hobby packs, Score's 60-card "Gold Stars" insert set features 30 National League players, found in Series I packs, and 30 American Leaguers inserted with Series II. Stated odds of finding a Gold Stars card were listed on the wrapper as one in 18 packs. A notation on the cards' back indicates that no more than 6,500 sets of Gold Stars were produced. The high-tech cards feature a color player action photo, the full-bleed background of which has been converted to metallic tones. Backs have a graduated gold background with a portrait-style color player photo.

		NM/M
Complete Set (60):		40.00
Common Player:		.25
1	Barry Bonds	6.00
2	Orlando Merced	.25
3	Mark Grace	.25
4	Darren Daulton	.25
5	Jeff Blauser	.25
6	Deion Sanders	.25
7	John Kruk	.25
8	Jeff Bagwell	2.50
9	Gregg Jefferies	.25
10	Matt Williams	.25
11	Andres Galarraga	.25
12	Jay Bell	.25
13	Mike Piazza	4.50
14	Ron Gant	.25
15	Barry Larkin	.25
16	Tom Glavine	.50
17	Len Dykstra	.25
18	Fred McGriff	.25
19	Andy Van Slyke	.25
20	Gary Sheffield	.75
21	John Burkett	.25
22	Dante Bichette	.25
23	Tony Gwynn	3.50
24	Dave Justice	.25
25	Marquis Grissom	.25
26	Bobby Bonilla	.25
27	Larry Walker	.25
28	Brett Butler	.25
29	Robby Thompson	.25
30	Jeff Conine	.25
31	Joe Carter	.25
32	Ken Griffey Jr.	4.50
33	Juan Gonzalez	1.25
34	Rickey Henderson	2.50
35	Bo Jackson	.35
36	Cal Ripken, Jr.	6.00
37	John Olerud	.25
38	Carlos Baerga	.25
39	Jack McDowell	.25
40	Cecil Fielder	.25
41	Kenny Lofton	.25
42	Roberto Alomar	1.00
43	Randy Johnson	2.50
44	Tim Salmon	.25
45	Frank Thomas	2.50
46	Albert Belle	.25
47	Greg Vaughn	.25
48	Travis Fryman	.25
49	Don Mattingly	4.00
50	Wade Boggs	3.50
51	Mo Vaughn	.25
52	Kirby Puckett	3.50
53	Devon White	.25
54	Tony Phillips	.25
55	Brian Harper	.25
56	Chad Curtis	.25
57	Paul Molitor	2.50
58	Ivan Rodriguez	2.00
59	Rafael Palmeiro	2.00
60	Brian McRae	.25

The Cycle

Leaders in the previous season's production of singles, doubles, triples and home runs are featured in this insert set which was packaged with Series II Score. Player action photos pop out of a circle at center and are surrounded by dark blue borders. "The Cycle" is printed in green at top. The player's name is in gold foil at bottom, printed over an infield diagram in a green strip. The stat which earned the player inclusion in the set is in gold foil at bottom right. On back are the rankings for the statistical category. Cards are numbered with a "TC" prefix.

		NM/M
Complete Set (20):		12.00
Common Player:		.50
1	Brett Butler	.50
2	Kenny Lofton	.50
3	Paul Molitor	2.00
4	Carlos Baerga	.50
5	Gregg Jefferies, Tony Phillips	.50
6	John Olerud	.50
7	Charlie Hayes	.50
8	Len Dykstra	.50
9	Dante Bichette	.50
10	Devon White	.50
11	Lance Johnson	.50
12	Joey Cora, Steve Finley	.50
13	Tony Fernandez	.50
14	David Hulse, Brett Butler	.50
15	Jay Bell, Brian McRae, Mickey Morandini	.50
16	Juan Gonzalez, Barry Bonds	4.00
17	Ken Griffey Jr.	4.00
18	Frank Thomas	2.50
19	Dave Justice	.50
20	Matt Williams, Albert Belle	.50

Cal Ripken, Jr.

Although the cards themselves do not indicate it, this issue was co-sponsored by Burger King and Coke, and distributed in BK restaurants in the Baltimore-Washington area. Cards were available in three-card packs for 25 cents with the purchase of a Coke product. Each pack contains two regular cards and a gold card. Each of the nine cards could be found in a regular and gold version. Cards feature color photos with a semi-circular black border at top or left. "Score '94" appears in orange in one of the upper corners, along with an Orioles logo. Cal Ripken, Jr.'s name appears at the bottom. On the gold premium version, there is a gold-foil circle around the Orioles logo and Ripken's name appears in gold, rather than white. Backs have a smaller color photo, again meeting at a semi-circular edge with the black border at left and bottom. In the black are another Score logo, a card number, an Orioles logo, a headline and a few career details and/or stats. Cards are UV coated on each side. Several hundred of the cards were personally autographed by Ripken and distributed in a drawing.

		NM/M
Complete Set (9):		3.00
Complete Set, Gold (9):		6.00
Common Player:		.50
Common Card, Gold:		.50
Autographed Card:		200.00
1	Double Honors	.50
1a	Double Honors/Gold	1.00
2	Perennial All-Star	.50
2a	Perennial All-Star/Gold	1.00
3	Peerless Power	.50
3a	Peerless Power/Gold	1.00
4	Fitness Fan	.50
4a	Fitness Fan/Gold	1.00
5	Prime Concerns	.50
5a	Prime Concerns/Gold	1.00
6	Home Run Club	.50
6a	Home Run Club/Gold	1.00
7	The Iron Man	.50
7a	The Iron Man/Gold	1.00
8	Heavy Hitter	.50
8a	Heavy Hitter/Gold	1.00
9	Gold Glover	.50
9a	Gold Glover/Gold	1.00

1994 Score Rookie/Traded Samples

To introduce the various types of card which would be included in the 1994 Score Rookie/Traded set, the company produced this sample set. Cards are virtually identical to the issued versions except for the overprint "SAMPLE" running diagonally on front and back. The Rafael Palmeiro "Changing Places" sample card does not feature the red foil logo found on issued cards.

		NM/M
Complete Set (11):		7.50
Common Player:		.50
1RT	Lee Smith	.50
2CP	Rafael Palmeiro	
	(Changing Places)	2.00
2RT	Will Clark	.50
2SU	Manny Ramirez	
	(Super Rookie)	2.50
3RT	Bo Jackson (Gold Rush)	1.00
4RT	Ellis Burks	.50
5RT	Eddie Murray	2.00
6RT	Delino DeShields	.50
102RT	Carlos Delgado	1.50
---	September Call-Up	
	Winner Card	.10
---	Hobby Header Card	.10
---	Retail Header Card	.10

1994 Score Rookie/Traded

Score Rookie & Traded completed the 1994 baseball season with a 165-card update set. These were available in both retail and hobby packs. Score issued Super Rookies and Changing Places insert sets, as well as a Traded Redemption card and a parallel Gold Rush set. Basic cards features red front borders. Team logos are in a bottom corner in a gold polygon. One of the upper corners contains a green polygon with a gold Score logo. Most cards #71-163 feature a square multi-colored "Rookie '94" logo in a lower corner. Backs of all cards have a purple background. Traded players' card backs are vertical and contain two additional photos. Backs of the rookie cards are horizontal and feature a portrait photo at left. The "Rookie '94" logo is repeated in the upper-right corner. This is in reverse of the fronts, on which traded players have a single photo and rookie cards have both portrait and action photos. Card numbers have an "RT" prefix.

		NM/M
Complete Set (165):		5.00
Common Player:		.05
Gold Rush:		2X
Pack (10):		.40
Wax Box (36):		9.00
1	Will Clark	.05
2	Lee Smith	.05
3	Bo Jackson	.10
4	Ellis Burks	.05
5	Eddie Murray	1.00
6	Delino DeShields	.05
7	Erik Hanson	.05
8	Rafael Palmeiro	.75
9	Luis Polonia	.05
10	Omar Vizquel	.05
11	Kurt Abbott	.05

12	Vince Coleman	.05
13	Rickey Henderson	1.00
14	Terry Mulholland	.05
15	Greg Hibbard	.05
16	Walt Weiss	.05
17	Chris Sabo	.05
18	Dave Henderson	.05
19	Rick Sutcliffe	.05
20	Harold Reynolds	.05
21	Jack Morris	.05
22	Dan Wilson	.05
23	Dave Magadan	.05
24	Dennis Martinez	.05
25	Wes Chamberlain	.05
26	Otis Nixon	.05
27	Eric Anthony	.05
28	Randy Milligan	.05
29	Julio Franco	.05
30	Kevin McReynolds	.05
31	Anthony Young	.05
32	Brian Harper	.05
33	Lenny Harris	.05
34	Eddie Taubensee	.05
35	David Segui	.05
36	Stan Javier	.05
37	Felix Fermin	.05
38	Darrin Jackson	.05
39	Tony Fernandez	.05
40	Jose Vizcaino	.05
41	Willie Banks	.05
42	Brian Hunter	.05
43	Reggie Jefferson	.05
44	Junior Felix	.05
45	Jack Armstrong	.05
46	Bip Roberts	.05
47	Jerry Browne	.05
48	Marvin Freeman	.05
49	Jody Reed	.05
50	Alex Cole	.05
51	Sid Fernandez	.05
52	Pete Smith	.05
53	Xavier Hernandez	.05
54	Scott Sanderson	.05
55	Turner Ward	.05
56	Rex Hudler	.05
57	Deion Sanders	.05
58	Sid Bream	.05
59	Tony Pena	.05
60	Bret Boone	.05
61	Bobby Ayala	.05
62	Pedro Martinez	1.00
63	Howard Johnson	.05
64	Mark Portugal	.05
65	Roberto Kelly	.05
66	Spike Owen	.05
67	Jeff Treadway	.05
68	Mike Harkey	.05
69	Doug Jones	.05
70	Steve Farr	.05
71	Billy Taylor	.05
72	Manny Ramirez	1.00
73	Bob Hamelin	.05
74	Steve Karsay	.05
75	Ryan Klesko	.05
76	Cliff Floyd	.05
77	Jeffrey Hammonds	.05
78	Javier Lopez	.05
79	Roger Salkeld	.05
80	Hector Carrasco	.05
81	Gerald Williams	.05
82	Raul Mondesi	.05
83	Sterling Hitchcock	.05
84	Danny Bautista	.05
85	Chris Turner	.05
86	Shane Reynolds	.05
87	Rondell White	.05
88	Salomon Torres	.05
89	Turk Wendell	.05
90	Tony Tarasco	.05
91	Shawn Green	.65
92	Greg Colbrunn	.05
93	Eddie Zambrano	.05
94	Rich Becker	.05
95	Chris Gomez	.05
96	John Patterson	.05
97	Derek Parks	.05
98	Rich Rowland	.05
99	James Mouton	.05
100	Tim Hyers	.05
101	Jose Valentin	.05
102	Carlos Delgado	.65
103	Robert Eisenhoorn	.05
104	John Hudek	.05
105	Domingo Cedeno	.05
106	Denny Hocking	.05
107	Greg Pirkl	.05
108	Mark Smith	.05
109	Paul Shuey	.05
110	Jorge Fabregas	.05
111	Rikkert Faneyte	.05
112	Rob Butler	.05
113	Darren Oliver	.05
114	Troy O'Leary	.05
115	Scott Brow	.05
116	Tony Eusebio	.05
117	Carlos Reyes	.05
118	J.R. Phillips	.05
119	Alex Diaz	.05
120	Charles Johnson	.05
121	Nate Minchey	.05
122	Scott Sanders	.05
123	Daryl Boston	.05
124	Joey Hamilton	.05
125	Brian Anderson	.05
126	Dan Miceli	.05
127	Tom Brunansky	.05
128	Dave Staton	.05
129	Mike Oquist	.05

130	John Mabry	.05
131	Norberto Martin	.05
132	Hector Fajardo	.05
133	Mark Hutton	.05
134	Fernando Vina	.05
135	Lee Tinsley	.05
136	Chan Ho Park RC	1.50
137	Paul Spoljaric	.05
138	Matias Carrillo	.05
139	Mark Kiefer	.05
140	Stan Royer	.05
141	Bryan Eversgerd	.05
143	Joe Hall	.05
144	Johnny Ruffin	.05
145	Alex Gonzalez	.05
146	Keith Lockhart	.05
147	Tom Marsh	.05
148	Tony Longmire	.05
149	Keith Mitchell	.05
150	Melvin Nieves	.05
151	Kelly Stinnett	.05
152	Miguel Jimenez	.05
153	Jeff Juden	.05
154	Matt Walbeck	.05
155	Marc Newfield	.05
156	Matt Mieske	.05
157	Marcus Moore	.05
158	Jose Lima RC	.25
159	Mike Kelly	.05
160	Jim Edmonds	.05
161	Steve Trachsel	.05
162	Greg Blosser	.05
163	Mark Acre	.05
164	AL Checklist	.05
165	NL Checklist	.05

Gold Rush

Each pack of Score Rookie and Traded cards included one Gold Rush parallel version of one of the set's cards. The insert cards feature fronts that are printed directly on gold foil and include a Gold Rush logo in an upper corner.

	NM/M
Complete Set (165):	15.00
Common Player:	.15
Stars:	2X

Changing Places

Changing Places documents the relocation of 10 veteran stars. Cards were inserted into one of every 36 retail or hobby packs. Fronts have a color photo of the player in his new uniform and are enhanced with red foil. Backs have a montage of color and black-and-white photos and a few words about the trade. Card numbers have a "CP" prefix.

		NM/M
Complete Set (10):		15.00
Common Player:		1.00
1	Will Clark	1.00
2	Rafael Palmeiro	4.00
3	Roberto Kelly	1.00
4	Bo Jackson	1.25
5	Otis Nixon	1.00
6	Rickey Henderson	5.00
7	Ellis Burks	1.00
8	Lee Smith	1.00
9	Delino DeShields	1.00
10	Deion Sanders	1.00

Super Rookies

Super Rookies is an 18-card set honoring baseball's brightest young stars. They appear only in hobby packs at a rate of one every 36 packs. Fronts are printed on foil, with a multi-colored border. Backs feature another photo, most of which is rendered in single-color blocks, along with a few words about the player and a large Super Rookie logo. Cards are numbered with an "SU" prefix.

		NM/M
Complete Set (18):		15.00
Common Player:		1.00
1	Carlos Delgado	5.00
2	Manny Ramirez	5.00
3	Ryan Klesko	1.00
4	Raul Mondesi	1.00
5	Bob Hamelin	1.00
6	Steve Karsay	1.00
7	Jeffrey Hammonds	1.00
8	Cliff Floyd	1.00
9	Kurt Abbott	1.00
10	Marc Newfield	1.00
11	Javier Lopez	1.00
12	Rich Becker	1.00
13	Greg Pirkl	1.00
14	Rondell White	1.00
15	James Mouton	1.00
16	Tony Tarasco	1.00
17	Brian Anderson	1.00
18	Jim Edmonds	1.00

Redemption Card

The Score Rookie and Traded Redemption card was inserted at a rate of one every 240 packs. It gave collectors a chance to mail in for the best rookie in the annual September call-up: Alex Rodriguez.

	NM/M
September Call-Up	
Redemption Card	
(Expired)	2.00
Alex Rodriguez	400.00

1995 Score Samples

This cello-wrapped 10-card sample set of 1995 Score cards was sent to dealers to preview the issue. Cards are identical to the reg-

ular-issue versions except they have a diagonal white "SAMPLE" printed on front and back. The SAMPLE notice can be found on each card in either black or white, with the black version appearing to be somewhat less common.

		NM/M
Complete Set (10):		6.00
Common Player:		.50
2	Roberto Alomar	.75
4	Jose Canseco	1.00
5	Matt Williams	.50
5HG	Cal Ripken, Jr.	
	(Hall of Gold)	2.50
8DP	McKay Christensen	
	('94 Draft Pick)	
221	Jeff Bagwell	1.25
223	Albert Belle	.50
224	Chuck Carr	.50
288	Jorge Fabreges (Rookie)	.50
	Header Card	.05

1995 Score

Score 1995 Baseball is composed of 605 cards, issued in two series; the first comprising 330 cards, the second, 275. Cards are identical to the regular-issue versions except they have a diagonal white "SAMPLE" printed on the front and back. The SAMPLE notice can be found on each card in either black or white, with the black version appearing to be somewhat less common. The player's name, position, and team logo is given in white letters on a blue strip across the bottom. Backs resemble the fronts, except with a smaller, portrait photo of the player, which leaves room for statistics and biographical information. Score had a parallel set of Gold Rush cards, along with several other series of inserts. Eleven players in Series 2 can be found in two team variations as a result of a redemption program for updated cards.

		NM/M
Complete Set (605):		13.50
Common Player:		.05
Gold Rush:		2X
Platinums:		3X
Series 1 or 2 Pack (12):		.75
Series 1 or 2 Box (36):		12.50
1	Frank Thomas	.50
2	Roberto Alomar	.15
3	Cal Ripken, Jr.	1.50
4	Jose Canseco	.30
5	Matt Williams	.05
6	Esteban Beltre	.05
7	Domingo Cedeno	.05
8	John Valentin	.05
9	Glenallen Hill	.05
10	Rafael Belliard	.05
11	Randy Myers	.05
12	Mo Vaughn	.05
13	Hector Carrasco	.05
14	Chili Davis	.05
15	Dante Bichette	.05
16	Darren Jackson	.05
17	Mike Piazza	.75
18	Junior Felix	.05
19	Moises Alou	.05
20	Mark Gubicza	.05
21	Bret Saberhagen	.05
22	Len Dykstra	.05
23	Steve Howe	.05
24	Mark Dewey	.05
25	Brian Harper	.05
26	Ozzie Smith	.60
27	Scott Erickson	.05
28	Tony Gwynn	.60
29	Bob Welch	.05
30	Barry Bonds	1.50
31	Leo Gomez	.05
32	Greg Maddux	.60
33	Mike Greenwell	.05
34	Sammy Sosa	.60
35	Darnell Coles	.05
36	Tommy Greene	.05

37	Will Clark	.05
38	Steve Ontiveros	.05
39	Stan Javier	.05
40	Bip Roberts	.05
41	Paul O'Neill	.05
42	Bill Haselman	.05
43	Shane Mack	.05
44	Orlando Merced	.05
45	Kevin Seitzer	.05
46	Trevor Hoffman	.05
47	Greg Gagne	.05
48	Jeff Kent	.05
49	Tony Phillips	.05
50	Ken Hill	.05
51	Carlos Baerga	.05
52	Henry Rodriguez	.05
53	Scott Sanderson	.05
54	Jeff Conine	.05
55	Chris Turner	.05
56	Ken Caminiti	.05
57	Harold Baines	.05
58	Charlie Hayes	.05
59	Roberto Kelly	.05
60	John Olerud	.05
61	Tim Davis	.05
62	Rich Rowland	.05
63	Rey Sanchez	.05
64	Junior Ortiz	.05
65	Ricky Gutierrez	.05
66	Rex Hudler	.05
67	Johnny Ruffin	.05
68	Jay Buhner	.05
69	Tom Pagnozzi	.05
70	Julio Franco	.05
71	Eric Young	.05
72	Mike Bordick	.05
73	Don Slaught	.05
74	Goose Gossage	.05
75	Lonnie Smith	.05
76	Jimmy Key	.05
77	Dave Hollins	.05
78	Mickey Tettleton	.05
79	Luis Gonzalez	.05
80	Dave Winfield	.50
81	Ryan Thompson	.05
82	Felix Jose	.05
83	Rusty Meacham	.05
84	Darryl Hamilton	.05
85	John Wetteland	.05
86	Tom Brunansky	.05
87	Mark Lemke	.05
88	Spike Owen	.05
89	Shawon Dunston	.05
90	Wilson Alvarez	.05
91	Lee Smith	.05
92	Scott Kamieniecki	.05
93	Jacob Brumfield	.05
94	Kirk Gibson	.05
95	Joe Girardi	.05
96	Mike Macfarlane	.05
97	Greg Colbrunn	.05
98	Ricky Bones	.05
99	Delino DeShields	.05
100	Pat Meares	.05
101	Jeff Fassero	.05
102	Jim Leyritz	.05
103	Gary Redus	.05
104	Terry Steinbach	.05
105	Kevin McReynolds	.05
106	Felix Fermin	.05
107	Danny Jackson	.05
108	Chris James	.05
109	Jeff King	.05
110	Pat Hentgen	.05
111	Gerald Perry	.05
112	Tim Raines	.05
113	Eddie Williams	.05
114	Jamie Moyer	.05
115	Bud Black	.05
116	Chris Gomez	.05
117	Luis Lopez	.05
118	Roger Clemens	.65
119	Javier Lopez	.05
120	Dave Nilsson	.05
121	Karl Rhodes	.05
122	Rick Aguilera	.05
123	Tony Fernandez	.05
124	Bernie Williams	.05
125	James Mouton	.05
126	Mark Langston	.05
127	Mike Lansing	.05
128	Tino Martinez	.05
129	Joe Orsulak	.05
130	David Hulse	.05
131	Pete Incaviglia	.05
132	Mark Clark	.05
133	Tony Eusebio	.05
134	Chuck Finley	.05
135	Lou Frazier	.05
136	Craig Grebeck	.05
137	Kelly Stinnett	.05
138	Paul Shuey	.05
139	David Nied	.05
140	Billy Brewer	.05
141	Dave Weathers	.05
142	Scott Leius	.05
143	Brian Jordan	.05
144	Melido Perez	.05
145	Tony Tarasco	.05
146	Dan Wilson	.05
147	Rondell White	.05
148	Mike Henneman	.05
149	Brian Johnson	.05
150	Tom Henke	.05
151	John Patterson	.05
152	Bobby Witt	.05
153	Eddie Taubensee	.05
154	Pat Borders	.05

#	Player	Price		#	Player	Price		#	Player	Price		#	Player	Price		#	Player	Price
155	Ramon Martinez	.05		272	Ismael Valdes	.05		371	Charles Nagy	.05		485	Bernard Gilkey	.05		591	Kurt Miller	.05
156	Mike Kingery	.05		273	Ben McDonald	.05		372	Kevin Bass	.05		486	John Burkett	.05		592	Aaron Small	.05
157	Zane Smith	.05		274	Darren Lewis	.05		373	Lou Whitaker	.05		487	Matt Nokes	.05		593	Troy O'Leary	.05
158	Benito Santiago	.05		275	Graeme Lloyd	.05		374	Rene Arocha	.05		488	Mel Rojas	.05		594	Phil Stidham	.05
159	Matias Carrillo	.05		276	Luis Ortiz	.05		375	Derrick Parks	.05		489	Craig Shipley	.05		595	Steve Dunn	.05
160	Scott Brosius	.05		277	Julian Tavarez	.05		376	Mark Whiten	.05		490	Chip Hale	.05		596	Cory Bailey	.05
161	Dave Clark	.05		278	Mark Dalesandro	.05		377	Mark McGwire	1.00		491	Bill Swift	.05		597	Alex Gonzalez	.05
162	Mark McLemore	.05		279	Brett Merriman	.05		378	Doug Drabek	.05		492	Pat Rapp	.05		598	Jim Bowie	.05
163	Curt Schilling	.30		280	Ricky Bottalico	.05		379	Greg Vaughn	.05		493a	Brian McRae (Royals)	.05		599	Jeff Cirillo	.05
164	J.T. Snow	.05		281	Robert Eenhoorn	.05		380	Al Martin	.05		493b	Brian McRae (Cubs)	.10		600	Mark Hutton	.05
165	Rod Beck	.05		282	Rikkert Faneyte	.05		381	Ron Darling	.05		494	Mickey Morandini	.05		601	Russ Davis	.05
166	Scott Fletcher	.05		283	Mike Kelly	.05		382	Tim Wallach	.05		495	Tony Pena	.05		602	Checklist #331-400	.05
167	Bob Tewksbury	.05		284	Mark Smith	.05		383	Alan Trammell	.05		496	Danny Bautista	.05		603	Checklist #401-469	.05
168	Mike LaValliere	.05		285	Turk Wendell	.05		384	Randy Velarde	.05		497	Armando Reynoso	.05		604	Checklist #470-537	.05
169	Dave Hansen	.05		286	Greg Blosser	.05		385	Chris Sabo	.05		498	Ken Ryan	.05		605	Checklist #538-605	.05
170	Pedro Martinez	.50		287	Garey Ingram	.05		386	Wil Cordero	.05		499	Billy Ripken	.05		----	"You Trade 'em" Redemption Card (Expired Dec. 31, 1995.)	.10
171	Kirk Rueter	.05		288	Jorge Fabregas	.05		387	Darrin Fletcher	.05		500	Pat Mahomes	.05				
172	Jose Lind	.05		289	Blaise Ilsley	.05		388	David Segui	.05		501	Mark Acre	.05				
173	Luis Alicea	.05		290	Joe Hall	.05		389	Steve Buechele	.05		502	Geronimo Berroa	.05				
174	Mike Moore	.05		291	Orlando Miller	.05		390	Otis Nixon	.05		503	Norberto Martin	.05				
175	Andy Ashby	.05		292	Jose Lima	.05		391	Jeff Brantley	.05		504	Chad Kreuter	.05				
176	Jody Reed	.05		293	Greg O'Halloran	.05		392a	Chad Curtis (Angels)	.05		505	Howard Johnson	.05				
177	Darryl Kile	.05		294	Mark Kiefer	.05		392b	Chad Curtis (Tigers)	.10		506	Eric Anthony	.05				
178	Carl Willis	.05		295	Jose Oliva	.05		393	Cal Eldred	.05		507	Mark Wohlers	.05				
179	Jeromy Burnitz	.05		296	Rich Becker	.05		394	Jason Bere	.05		508	Scott Sanders	.05				
180	Mike Gallego	.05		297	Brian Hunter	.05		395	Bret Barberie	.05		509	Pete Harnisch	.05				
181	W. Van Landingham RC	.05		298	Dave Silvestri	.05		396	Paul Sorrento	.05		510	Wes Chamberlain	.05				
182	Sid Fernandez	.05		299	Armando Benitez RC	.10		397	Steve Finley	.05		511	Tom Candiotti	.05				
183	Kim Batiste	.05		300	Darren Dreifort	.05		398	Cecil Fielder	.05		512	Albie Lopez	.05				
184	Greg Myers	.05		301	John Mabry	.05		399	Eric Karros	.05		513	Denny Neagle	.05				
185	Steve Avery	.05		302	Greg Pirkl	.05		400	Jeff Montgomery	.05		514	Sean Berry	.05				
186	Steve Farr	.05		303	J.R. Phillips	.05		401	Cliff Floyd	.05		515	Billy Hatcher	.05				
187	Robb Nen	.05		304	Shawn Green	.30		402	Matt Mieske	.05		516	Todd Jones	.05				
188	Dan Pasqua	.05		305	Roberto Petagine	.05		403	Brian Hunter	.05		517	Wayne Kirby	.05				
189	Bruce Ruffin	.05		306	Keith Lockhart	.05		404	Alex Cole	.05		518	Butch Henry	.05				
190	Jose Valentin	.05		307	Jonathon Hurst	.05		405	Kevin Stocker	.05		519	Sandy Alomar Jr.	.05				
191	Willie Banks	.05		308	Paul Spoljaric	.05		406	Eric Davis	.05		520	Kevin Appier	.05				
192	Mike Aldrete	.05		309	Mike Lieberthal	.05		407	Marvin Freeman	.05		521	Robert Mejia	.05				
193	Randy Milligan	.05		310	Garret Anderson	.05		408	Dennis Eckersley	.40		522	Steve Cooke	.05				
194	Steve Karsay	.05		311	John Johnston	.05		409	Todd Zeile	.05		523	Terry Shumpert	.05				
195	Mike Stanley	.05		312	Alex Rodriguez	1.50		410	Keith Mitchell	.05		524	Mike Jackson	.05				
196	Jose Mesa	.05		313	Kent Mercker	.05		411	Andy Benes	.05		525	Kent Mercker	.05				
197	Tom Browning	.05		314	John Valentin	.05		412	Juan Bell	.05		526	David Wells	.05				
198	John Vander Wal	.05		315	Kenny Rogers	.05		413	Royce Clayton	.05		527	Juan Samuel	.05				
199	Kevin Brown	.05		316	Fred McGriff	.05		414	Ed Sprague	.05		528	Salomon Torres	.05				
200	Mike Oquist	.05		317	Atlanta Braves,	.05		415	Mike Mussina	.30		529	Duane Ward	.05				
201	Greg Swindell	.05			Baltimore Orioles,	.05		416	Todd Hundley	.05		530a	Rob Dibble (Reds)	.05				
202	Eddie Zambrano	.05		318	Chicago Cubs,	.05		417	Pat Listach	.05		530b	Rob Dibble (White Sox)	.05				
203	Joe Boever	.05			Boston Red Sox,	.05		418	Joe Oliver	.05		531	Mike Blowers	.05				
204	Gary Varsho	.05		319	Cincinnati Reds,	.05		419	Rafael Palmeiro	.40		532	Mark Eichhorn	.05				
205	Chris Gwynn	.05			California Angels,	.05		420	Tim Salmon	.05		533	Alex Diaz	.05				
206	David Howard	.05		320	Colorado Rockies,	.05		421	Brady Anderson	.05		534	Dan Miceli	.05				
207	Jerome Walton	.05			Chicago White Sox,	.05		422	Kenny Lofton	.05		535	Jeff Branson	.05				
208	Danny Darwin	.05		321	Cleveland Indians,	.05		423	Craig Biggio	.05		536	Dave Stevens	.05				
209	Darryl Strawberry	.05			Florida Marlins,	.05		424	Bobby Bonilla	.05		537	Charlie O'Brien	.05				
210	Todd Van Poppel	.05		322	Houston Astros,	.05		425	Kenny Rogers	.05		538	Shane Reynolds	.05				
211	Scott Livingstone	.05			Detroit Tigers,	.05		426	Derek Bell	.05		539	Rich Amaral	.05				
212	Dave Fleming	.05		323	Los Angeles Dodgers,	.05		427a	Scott Cooper (Red Sox)	.05		540	Rusty Greer	.05				
213	Todd Worrell	.05			Kansas City Royals,	.05		427b	Scott Cooper (Cardinals)	.10		541	Alex Arias	.05				
214	Carlos Delgado	.40		324	Montreal Expos,	.05		428	Ozzie Guillen	.05		542	Eric Plunk	.05				
215	Bill Pecota	.05			Milwaukee Brewers,	.05		429	Omar Vizquel	.05		543	John Hudek	.05				
216	Jim Lindeman	.05		325	New York Mets,	.05		430	Phil Plantier	.05		544	Kirk McCaskill	.05				
217	Rick White	.05			Minnesota Twins,	.05		431	Chuck Knoblauch	.05		545	Jeff Reboulet	.05				
218	Jose Oquendo	.05		326	Philadelphia Phillies,	.05		432	Darren Daulton	.05		546	Sterling Hitchcock	.05				
219	Tony Castillo	.05			New York Yankees,	.05		433	Bob Hamelin	.05		547	Warren Newson	.05				
220	Fernando Vina	.05		327	Pittsburgh Pirates,	.05		434	Tom Glavine	.30		548	Bryan Harvey	.05				
221	Jeff Bagwell	.50			Oakland Athletics,	.05		435	Walt Weiss	.05		549	Mike Huff	.05				
222	Randy Johnson	.50		328	San Diego Padres,	.05		436	Jose Vizcaino	.05		550	Lance Parrish	.05				
223	Albert Belle	.05			Seattle Mariners,	.05		437	Ken Griffey Jr.	.75		551	Ken Griffey Jr. (Hitters Inc.)	.65				
224	Chuck Carr	.05		329	San Francisco Giants,	.05		438	Jay Bell	.05		552	Matt Williams (Hitters Inc.)	.05				
225	Mark Leiter	.05			Texas Rangers,	.05		439	Juan Gonzalez	.25		553	Roberto Alomar (Hitters Inc.)	.10				
226	Hal Morris	.05		330	St. Louis Cardinals,	.05		440	Jeff Blauser	.05		554	Jeff Bagwell (Hitters Inc.)	.25				
227	Robin Ventura	.05			Toronto Blue Jays,	.05		441	Rickey Henderson	.50		555	Dave Justice (Hitters Inc.)	.05				
228	Mike Munoz	.05		331	Pedro Munoz	.05		442	Bobby Ayala	.05		556	Cal Ripken Jr. (Hitters Inc.)	.75				
229	Jim Thome	.40		332	Ryan Klesko	.05		443a	David Cone (Royals)	.05		557	Albert Belle (Hitters Inc.)	.05				
230	Mario Diaz	.05		333a	Andre Dawson (Red Sox)	.25		443b	David Cone (Blue Jays)	.10		558	Mike Piazza (Hitters Inc.)	.45				
231	John Doherty	.05		333b	Andre Dawson (Marlins)	.35		444	Pedro Martinez	.05		559	Kirby Puckett (Hitters Inc.)	.35				
232	Bobby Jones	.05		334	Derrick May	.05		445	Manny Ramirez	.50		560	Wade Boggs (Hitters Inc.)	.30				
233	Raul Mondesi	.05		335	Aaron Sele	.05		446	Mark Portugal	.05		561	Tony Gwynn (Hitters Inc.)	.35				
234	Ricky Jordan	.05		336	Kevin Mitchell	.05		447	Damion Easley	.05		562	Barry Bonds (Hitters Inc.)	.75				
235	John Jaha	.05		337	Steve Traschel	.05		448	Gary DiSarcina	.05		563	Mo Vaughn (Hitters Inc.)	.05				
236	Carlos Garcia	.05		338	Andres Galarraga	.05		449	Roberto Hernandez	.05		564	Don Mattingly (Hitters Inc.)	.40				
237	Kirby Puckett	.60		339a	Terry Pendleton (Braves)	.05		450	Jeffrey Hammonds	.05		565	Carlos Baerga (Hitters Inc.)	.05				
238	Orel Hershiser	.05		339b	Terry Pendleton (Marlins)	.10		451	Jeff Treadway	.05		566	Paul Molitor (Hitters Inc.)	.25				
239	Don Mattingly	.65		340	Gary Sheffield	.30		452a	Jim Abbott (Yankees)	.05		567	Raul Mondesi (Hitters Inc.)	.05				
240	Sid Bream	.05		341	Travis Fryman	.05		452b	Jim Abbott (White Sox)	.10		568	Manny Ramirez (Hitters Inc.)	.25				
241	Brent Gates	.05		342	Bo Jackson	.10		453	Carlos Rodriguez	.05		569	Alex Rodriguez (Hitters Inc.)	.75				
242	Tony Longmire	.05		343	Gary Gaetti	.05		454	Joey Cora	.05		570	Will Clark (Hitters Inc.)	.05				
243	Robby Thompson	.05		344a	Brett Butler (Dodgers)	.05		455	Bret Boone	.05		571	Frank Thomas (Hitters Inc.)	.30				
244	Rick Sutcliffe	.05		344b	Brett Butler (Mets)	.10		456	Danny Tartabull	.05		572	Moises Alou (Hitters Inc.)	.05				
245	Dean Palmer	.05		345	B.J. Surhoff	.05		457	John Franco	.05		573	Jeff Conine (Hitters Inc.)	.05				
246	Marquis Grissom	.05		346a	Larry Walker (Expos)	.05		458	Roger Salkeld	.05		574	Joe Ausanio	.05				
247	Paul Molitor	.50		346b	Larry Walker (Rockies)	.10		459	Fred McGriff	.05		575	Charles Johnson	.05				
248	Mark Carreon	.05		347	Kevin Tapani	.05		460	Pedro Astacio	.05		576	Ernie Young	.05				
249	Jack Voight	.05		348	Rick Wilkins	.05		461	Jon Lieber	.05		577	Jeff Granger	.05				
250	Greg McMichael (Photo on front is Mike Stanton.)	.05		349	Wade Boggs	.60		462	Luis Polonia	.05		578	Robert Perez	.05				
251	Damon Berryhill	.05		350	Mariano Duncan	.05		463	Geronimo Pena	.05		579	Melvin Nieves	.05				
252	Brian Dorsett	.05		351	Ruben Sierra	.05		464	Tom Gordon	.05		580	Gar Finnvold	.05				
253	Jim Edmonds	.05		352a	Andy Van Slyke (Pirates)	.05		465	Brad Ausmus	.05		581	Duane Singleton	.05				
254	Barry Larkin	.05		352b	Andy Van Slyke (Orioles)	.10		466	Willie McGee	.05		582	Chan Ho Park	.05				
255	Jack McDowell	.05		353	Reggie Jefferson	.05		467	Doug Jones	.05		583	Fausto Cruz	.05				
256	Wally Joyner	.05		354	Gregg Jefferies	.05		468	John Smoltz	.05		584	Dave Staton	.05				
257	Eddie Murray	.50		355	Tim Naehring	.05		469	Troy Neel	.05		585	Denny Hocking	.05				
258	Lenny Webster	.05		356	John Roper	.05		470	Luis Sojo	.05		586	Nate Minchey	.05				
259	Milt Cuyler	.05		357	Joe Carter	.05		471	John Smiley	.05		587	Marc Newfield	.05				
260	Todd Benzinger	.05		358	Kurt Abbott	.05		472	Rafael Bournigal	.05		588	Jayhawk Owens	.05				
261	Vince Coleman	.05		359	Lenny Harris	.05		473	Billy Taylor	.05		589	Darren Bragg	.05				
262	Todd Stottlemyre	.05		360	Lance Johnson	.05		474	Juan Guzman	.05		590	Kevin King	.05				
263	Turner Ward	.05		361	Brian Anderson	.05		475	Dave Magadan	.05								
264	Ray Lankford	.05		362	Jim Eisenreich	.05		476	Mike Devereaux	.05								
265	Matt Walbeck	.05		363	Jerry Browne	.05		477	Andujar Cedeno	.05								
266	Deion Sanders	.05		364	Mark Grace	.05		478	Edgar Martinez	.05								
267	Gerald Williams	.05		365	Devon White	.05		479	Troy Neel	.05								
268	Jim Gott	.05		366	Reggie Sanders	.05		480	Allen Watson	.05								
269	Jeff Frye	.05		367	Ivan Rodriguez	.40		481	Ron Karkovice	.05								
270	Jose Rijo	.05		368	Kirt Manwaring	.05		482	Joey Hamilton	.05								
271	Dave Justice	.05		369	Pat Kelly	.05		483	Vinny Castilla	.05								
				370	Ellis Burks	.05		484	Kevin Gross	.05								

Airmail

Young ballplayers with a propensity for hitting the long ball are featured in this insert set found only in Series II jumbo packs. Cards have a player batting action photo set in sky-and-clouds background. A gold-foil stamp in the upper-left corner identifies the series. Backs have a background photo of sunset and dark clouds, with a player portrait photo in the foreground. A few stats and sentences describe the player's power hitting potential. Cards have an AM prefix to the number. Stated odds for insertion rate are an average of one Airmail chase card per 24 packs.

		NM/M
Complete Set (18):		8.00
Common Player:		.25
1	Bob Hamelin	.25
2	John Mabry	.25
3	Marc Newfield	.25
4	Jose Oliva	.25
5	Charles Johnson	.25
6	Russ Davis	.25
7	Ernie Young	.25
8	Billy Ashley	.25
9	Ryan Klesko	.25
10	J.R. Phillips	.25
11	Cliff Floyd	.25
12	Carlos Delgado	1.50
13	Melvin Nieves	.25
14	Raul Mondesi	2.00
15	Manny Ramirez	2.00
16	Mike Kelly	.25
17	Alex Rodriguez	5.00
18	Rusty Greer	.25

Gold Rush

Besides being collectible in their own right, the gold-foil printed parallel versions of the Score regular-issue cards could be collected into team sets and exchanged with a trade card for platinum versions. The deadline for redemption of Series I was July 1, 1995; Oct. 1, 1995, for Series II. Gold Rush cards were found either one or two per pack, depending on pack card count. Gold Rush versions exist for each card in the Score set and have fronts that are identical to the regular cards except they are printed on foil and have gold borders. Backs of the Gold Rush cards have a small rectangular "GOLD RUSH" logo overprinted.

	NM/M
Complete Set (605):	35.00
Common Player:	.10
Gold Rush Stars:	2X

Platinum Redemption Team Sets

This top of the line parallel set was only available by exchanging a complete Series 1 or Series 2 Gold Rush team set, along with a redemption card. Production of the Platinum sets was limited to 4,950 of each team in each series. Using the same photos and format as the regular issue and Gold Rush cards, the Platinum parallels have card fronts printed on silver prismatic foil. Backs are identical to the regular-issue cards. Platinum series team sets were sent to collectors in specially printed plastic cases with a certificate of authenticity.

	NM/M
Complete Set (587):	100.00
Complete Series 1 (316):	60.00
Complete Series 2 (271):	40.00
Common Player:	.25
Platinum Stars:	3X

Double Gold Champions

A dozen veteran players, who have won at least two of the game's top awards are designated as "Double Gold Champs," in this Series II hobby insert set. Fronts have horizontal action photos at top, with a speckled red border at bottom. Vertical backs have a portrait photo and a list of the major awards won by the player. Cards have a GC prefix to the number. These chase cards were reportedly inserted at an average rate of one per 36.

		NM/M
Complete Set (12):		25.00
Common Player:		.40
1	Frank Thomas	2.00
2	Ken Griffey Jr.	3.50
3	Barry Bonds	5.00
4	Tony Gwynn	2.50
5	Don Mattingly	3.00
6	Greg Maddux	2.50
7	Roger Clemens	3.00
8	Kenny Lofton	.40
9	Jeff Bagwell	2.00
10	Matt Williams	.40
11	Kirby Puckett	2.50
12	Cal Ripken Jr.	5.00

Draft Picks

These cards were randomly included in 1995 Score hobby packs at a rate of one per every 36 packs. The cards showcase 18 of baseball's potential superstars and document their professional beginnings. The card front has the player's team logo and name in the lower-right corner. "'94 Draft Pick" appears in the upper-right corner. The front also has a mug shot and an action shot of the player. The card back has a portrait and career summary and is numbered with a DP prefix.

		NM/M
Complete Set (18):		4.00
Common Player:		.50
1	McKay Christensen	.50
2	Brett Wagner	.50
3	Paul Wilson	.50
4	C.J. Nitkowski	.50
5	Josh Booty	.50
6	Antone Williamson	.50
7	Paul Konerko	1.50
8	Scott Elarton	.50
9	Jacob Shumate	.50
10	Terrence Long	.50
11	Mark Johnson	.50
12	Ben Grieve	.50
13	Doug Million	.50
14	Jayson Peterson	.50
15	Dustin Hermanson	.50
16	Matt Smith	.50
17	Kevin Witt	.50
18	Brian Buchanan	.50

Dream Team Gold

The Major Leagues' top players at each position are featured in this Series I insert set. Fronts are printed entirely on rainbow holographic foil and feature a large and a small player action photo. Backs have a single-color version of one of the front photos as well as a color portrait photo in a circle at center, all in conventional printing technology. Card numbers have a DG prefix.

		NM/M
Complete Set (12):		12.00
Common Player:		.30
1	Frank Thomas	1.25
2	Roberto Alomar	.50
3	Cal Ripken Jr.	4.00
4	Matt Williams	.30
5	Mike Piazza	2.50
6	Albert Belle	.45
7	Ken Griffey Jr.	2.50
8	Tony Gwynn	1.50
9	Paul Molitor	1.25
10	Jimmy Key	.30
11	Greg Maddux	1.50
12	Lee Smith	.30

Hall of Gold

Hall of Gold inserts picture 110 of the top players on gold foil cards. Each card front has the Hall of Gold logo in an upper corner, plus a color action photo of the player, and his name and team logo

at the bottom. The card back is numbered using an "HG" prefix and includes another color photo of the player, his team's name, his position, and a career summary. Cards were inserted one per every six regular 1995 Score packs and one per every two jumbo packs. Updated versions of five traded players were issued in Series II, available only via mail-in offer with a trade card found randomly inserted in packs.

		NM/M
Complete Set (110):		25.00
Common Player:		.10
1	Ken Griffey Jr.	1.25
2	Matt Williams	.10
3	Roberto Alomar	.25
4	Jeff Bagwell	.75
5	Dave Justice	.10
6	Cal Ripken Jr.	2.00
7	Randy Johnson	.75
8	Barry Larkin	.10
9	Albert Belle	.10
10	Mike Piazza	1.25
11	Kirby Puckett	1.00
12	Moises Alou	.10
13	Jose Canseco	.45
14	Tony Gwynn	1.00
15	Roger Clemens	1.00
16	Barry Bonds	2.00
17	Mo Vaughn	.10
18	Greg Maddux	1.00
19	Dante Bichette	.10
20	Will Clark	.10
21	Len Dykstra	.10
22	Don Mattingly	1.00
23	Carlos Baerga	.10
24	Ozzie Smith	1.00
25	Paul Molitor	.75
26	Paul O'Neill	.10
27	Deion Sanders	.10
28	Jeff Conine	.10
29	John Olerud	.10
30	Jose Rijo	.10
31	Sammy Sosa	1.00
32	Robin Ventura	.10
33	Raul Mondesi	.10
34	Eddie Murray	.75
35	Marquis Grissom	.10
36	Darryl Strawberry	.10
37	Dave Nilsson	.10
38	Manny Ramirez	.75
39	Delino DeShields	.10
40	Lee Smith	.10
41	Alex Rodriguez	1.50
42	Julio Franco	.10
43	Bret Saberhagen	.10
44	Ken Hill	.10
45	Roberto Kelly	.10
46	Hal Morris	.10
47	Jimmy Key	.10
48	Terry Steinbach	.10
49	Mickey Tettleton	.10
50	Tony Phillips	.10
51	Carlos Garcia	.10
52	Jim Edmonds	.10
53	Rod Beck	.10
54	Shane Mack	.10
55	Ken Caminiti	.10
56	Frank Thomas	.75
57	Kenny Lofton	.10
58	Jack McDowell	.10
59	Jason Bere	.10
60	Joe Carter	.10
61	Gary Sheffield	.45
62	Andres Galarraga	.10
63	Gregg Jefferies	.10
64	Bobby Bonilla	.10
65	Tom Glavine	.35
66	John Smoltz	.10
67	Fred McGriff	.10
68	Craig Biggio	.10
69	Reggie Sanders	.10
70	Kevin Mitchell	.10
71a	Larry Walker (Expos)	.10
71b	Larry Walker (Rockies)	.10
72	Carlos Delgado	.50
73	Andujar Cedeno	.10
74	Ivan Rodriguez	.65
75	Ryan Klesko	.10
76a	John Kruk (Phillies)	.10
76b	John Kruk (White Sox)	.10
77a	Brian McRae (Royals)	.10
77b	Brian McRae (Cubs)	.10
78	Tim Salmon	.10
79	Travis Fryman	.10
80	Chuck Knoblauch	.10
81	Jay Bell	.10
82	Cecil Fielder	.10
83	Cliff Floyd	.10
84	Ruben Sierra	.10
85	Mike Mussina	.45
86	Mark Grace	.10
87	Dennis Eckersley	.65
88	Dennis Martinez	.10
89	Rafael Palmeiro	.65
90	Ben McDonald	.10
91	Dave Hollins	.10
92	Steve Avery	.10
93a	David Cone (Royals)	.10
93b	David Cone (Blue Jays)	.10
94	Darren Daulton	.10
95	Bret Boone	.10
96	Wade Boggs	1.00

97	Doug Drabek	.10
98	Derek Bell	.10
99	Jim Thome	.65
100	Chili Davis	.10
101	Jeffrey Hammonds	.10
102	Rickey Henderson	.75
103	Brett Butler	.10
104	Tim Wallach	.10
105	Wil Cordero	.10
106	Mark Whiten	.10
107	Bob Hamelin	.10
108	Rondell White	.10
109	Devon White	.10
110a	Tony Tarasco (Braves)	.10
110b	Tony Tarasco (Expos)	.10
----	Redemption Trade Card (Expired Dec. 31, 1995.)	.10

Rookie Dream Team

These Series 2 inserts feature a dozen of 1995's best rookie prospects. Fronts are printed on a silver-foil background. The words "ROOKIE DREAM TEAM" are formed of sky-and-cloud images within the letters. Horizontal backs repeat the motif and include another player photo in a vignette at center. Card numbers have an RDT prefix.

		NM/M
Complete Set (12):		9.00
Common Player:		.50
1	J.R. Phillips	.50
2	Alex Gonzalez	.50
3	Alex Rodriguez	6.00
4	Jose Oliva	.50
5	Charles Johnson	.50
6	Shawn Green	1.50
7	Brian Hunter	.50
8	Garret Anderson	.50
9	Julian Tavarez	.50
10	Jose Lima	.50
11	Armando Benitez	.50
12	Ricky Bottalico	.50

Rookie Greatness

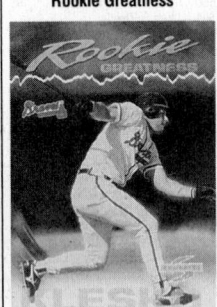

This single-card insert set is the toughest pull among the 1995 Score chase cards. Honoring slugging Braves star Ryan Klesko, the card is inserted at the rate of one per 720 retail packs. An even scarcer autographed version of the card in an edition of just over 6,000 was also created for insertion into hobby packs.

		NM/M
RG1	Ryan Klesko	1.00
SG1	Ryan Klesko/Auto.	7.50

Score Rules

Series I jumbo packs were the only sources for "Score Rules" insert set of rookie and veteran stars. A color player photo at left has a team logo toward the bottom, beneath which is a gold-foil "tie tack" device with the league initials and position. At top-right is a baseball which appears to be dripping orange and green goop down the card. The player's last name is presented vertically with a sepia photo

of the player within the letters. Backs repeat the green baseball and ooze motif, with three progressive color proof versions of the sepia front photo and a few sentences about the star. Cards are numbered with an "SR" prefix.

		NM/M
Complete Set (30):		30.00
Common Player:		.30
1	Ken Griffey Jr.	3.50
2	Frank Thomas	1.50
3	Mike Piazza	3.50
4	Jeff Bagwell	1.50
5	Alex Rodriguez	4.50
6	Albert Belle	.30
7	Matt Williams	.30
8	Roberto Alomar	.45
9	Barry Bonds	5.00
10	Raul Mondesi	.30
11	Jose Canseco	.60
12	Kirby Puckett	2.50
13	Fred McGriff	.30
14	Kenny Lofton	.30
15	Greg Maddux	2.50
16	Juan Gonzalez	.75
17	Cliff Floyd	.30
18	Cal Ripken, Jr.	5.00
19	Will Clark	.30
20	Tim Salmon	.30
21	Paul O'Neill	.30
22	Jason Bere	.30
23	Tony Gwynn	2.50
24	Manny Ramirez	1.50
25	Don Mattingly	3.00
26	Dave Justice	.30
27	Javier Lopez	.30
28	Ryan Klesko	.30
29	Carlos Delgado	.90
30	Mike Mussina	.60

Score Rules Supers

While colorful in the standard size, the Score Rules super-size cards found in special collectors kits are positively garish. The 7-1/2" x 10-1/2" cards are virtually identical to the Series 1 inserts, except that on back is a box with a serial number identifying the card from among an edition of 3,000. The Score Rules supers were available only in a collectors kit sold at large retail chains and came packaged with 26 Series 1 and 2 foil packs, a three-ring binder and 10 plastic sheets with a suggested retail price of around $25.

		NM/M
Complete Set (30):		60.00
Common Player:		.90
1	Ken Griffey Jr.	5.00
2	Frank Thomas	3.50
3	Mike Piazza	5.00
4	Jeff Bagwell	3.50
5	Alex Rodriguez	6.00
6	Albert Belle	.90
7	Matt Williams	.90
8	Roberto Alomar	1.25
9	Barry Bonds	7.50
10	Raul Mondesi	.90
11	Jose Canseco	2.50
12	Kirby Puckett	4.50
13	Fred McGriff	.90
14	Kenny Lofton	.90

15	Greg Maddux	4.50
16	Juan Gonzalez	2.00
17	Cliff Floyd	.90
18	Cal Ripken, Jr.	7.50
19	Will Clark	.90
20	Tim Salmon	.90
21	Paul O'Neill	.90
22	Jason Bere	.90
23	Tony Gwynn	4.50
24	Manny Ramirez	3.75
25	Don Mattingly	4.50
26	Dave Justice	.90
27	Javier Lopez	.90
28	Ryan Klesko	.90
29	Carlos Delgado	2.00
30	Mike Mussina	1.50

Ad Prize Cards

In a series of ads in hobby and public media, Score offered a pair of special cards as prizes in a mail-in offer. Cards feature the same basic design as 1995 Score, but are printed on platinum foil on front. Backs are conventionally printed with a portrait photo and a few words about the player.

		NM/M
Complete Set (2):		10.00
AD1	Alex Rodriguez	6.50
AD2	Ivan Rodriguez	3.50

1996 Score Samples

Score premiered its 1996 base brand offering with a cello pack of nine cards, including one of its new Dugout Collection inserts. The samples are virtually identical to the issued versions except that all 1995 and career stats are stated as zeros and the word "SAMPLE" is printed in white letters diagonally across front and back. Each of the cards can be found as a Dugout Collection version, making them eight times scarcer than the other samples.

		NM/M
Complete Set (16):		12.00
Common Player:		.50
3	Ryan Klesko	.50
3	Ryan Klesko (Dugout Collection)	1.00
4	Jim Edmonds	.50
4	Jim Edmonds (Dugout Collection)	1.00
5	Barry Larkin	.50
5	Barry Larkin (Dugout Collection)	1.00
6	Jim Thome	1.00
6	Jim Thome (Dugout Collection)	1.50
7	Raul Mondesi	.50
7	Raul Mondesi (Dugout Collection)	1.00
110	Derek Bell	.50
110	Derek Bell (Dugout Collection)	1.00
240	Derek Jeter	2.00
240	Derek Jeter (Dugout Collection)	4.50
241	Michael Tucker	.50
241	Michael Tucker (Dugout Collection)	1.00

1996 Score

Large, irregularly shaped action photos are featured on the fronts of the basic cards in the 1996 Score issue. Backs feature a portrait photo (in most cases) at left and a full slate of major and minor league stats at right, along with a few words about the player. Slightly different design details and a "ROOKIE" headline identify that subset within the regular issue. A wide variety of insert cards was produced, most of them exclusive to one type of packaging.

		NM/M
Complete Set (510):		15.00
Common Player:		.05
Wax Pack (10):		.45
Wax Box (36):		10.00
1	Will Clark	.05
2	Rich Becker	.05
3	Ryan Klesko	.05
4	Jim Edmonds	.05
5	Barry Larkin	.05
6	Jim Thome	.40
7	Raul Mondesi	.05
8	Don Mattingly	.65
9	Jeff Conine	.05
10	Rickey Henderson	.50
11	Chad Curtis	.05
12	Darren Daulton	.05
13	Larry Walker	.05
14	Carlos Garcia	.05
15	Carlos Baerga	.05
16	Tony Gwynn	.60
17	Jon Nunally	.05
18	Deion Sanders	.05
19	Mark Grace	.05
20	Alex Rodriguez	1.00
21	Frank Thomas	.50
22	Brian Jordan	.05
23	J.T. Snow	.05
24	Shawn Green	.30
25	Tim Wakefield	.05
26	Curtis Goodwin	.05
27	John Smoltz	.05
28	Devon White	.05
29	Brian Hunter	.05
30	Rusty Greer	.05
31	Rafael Palmeiro	.40
32	Bernard Gilkey	.05
33	John Valentin	.05
34	Randy Johnson	.50
35	Garret Anderson	.05
36	Rikkert Faneyte	.05
37	Ray Durham	.05
38	Bip Roberts	.05
39	Jaime Navarro	.05
40	Mark Johnson	.05
41	Darren Lewis	.05
42	Tyler Green	.05
43	Bill Pulsipher	.05
44	Jason Giambi	.40
45	Kevin Ritz	.05
46	Jack McDowell	.05
47	Felipe Lira	.05
48	Rico Brogna	.05
49	Terry Pendleton	.05
50	Rondell White	.05
51	Andre Dawson	.25
52	Kirby Puckett	.60
53	Wally Joyner	.05
54	B.J. Surhoff	.05
55	Chan Ho Park	.05
56	Greg Vaughn	.05
57	Roberto Alomar	.20
58	Dave Justice	.05
59	Kevin Seitzer	.05
60	Cal Ripken Jr.	1.50
61	Ozzie Smith	.05
62	Mo Vaughn	.05
63	Ricky Bones	.05
64	Gary DiSarcina	.05
65	Matt Williams	.05
66	Wilson Alvarez	.05
67	Lenny Dykstra	.05
68	Brian McRae	.05
69	Todd Stottlemyre	.05
70	Bret Boone	.05
71	Sterling Hitchcock	.05
72	Albert Belle	.05
73	Todd Hundley	.05
74	Vinny Castilla	.05
75	Moises Alou	.05

#	Player	Price
76	Cecil Fielder	.05
77	Brad Radke	.05
78	Quilvio Veras	.05
79	Eddie Murray	.50
80	James Mouton	.05
81	Pat Listach	.05
82	Mark Gubicza	.05
83	Dave Winfield	.50
84	Fred McGriff	.05
85	Darryl Hamilton	.05
86	Jeffrey Hammonds	.05
87	Pedro Munoz	.05
88	Craig Biggio	.05
89	Cliff Floyd	.05
90	Tim Naehring	.05
91	Brett Butler	.05
92	Kevin Foster	.05
93	Patrick Kelly	.05
94	John Smiley	.05
95	Terry Steinbach	.05
96	Orel Hershiser	.05
97	Darrin Fletcher	.05
98	Walt Weiss	.05
99	John Wetteland	.05
100	Alan Trammell	.05
101	Steve Avery	.05
102	Tony Eusebio	.05
103	Sandy Alomar	.05
104	Joe Girardi	.05
105	Rick Aguilera	.05
106	Tony Tarasco	.05
107	Chris Hammond	.05
108	Mike McFarlane	.05
109	Doug Drabek	.05
110	Derek Bell	.05
111	Ed Sprague	.05
112	Todd Hollandsworth	.05
113	Otis Nixon	.05
114	Keith Lockhart	.05
115	Donovan Osborne	.05
116	Dave Magadan	.05
117	Edgar Martinez	.05
118	Chuck Carr	.05
119	J.R. Phillips	.05
120	Sean Bergman	.05
121	Andujar Cedeno	.05
122	Eric Young	.05
123	Al Martin	.05
124	Ken Hill	.05
125	Jim Eisenreich	.05
126	Benito Santiago	.05
127	Ariel Prieto	.05
128	Jim Bullinger	.05
129	Russ Davis	.05
130	Jim Abbott	.05
131	Jason Isringhausen	.05
132	Carlos Perez	.05
133	David Segui	.05
134	Troy O'Leary	.05
135	Pat Meares	.05
136	Chris Hoiles	.05
137	Ismael Valdes	.05
138	Jose Oliva	.05
139	Carlos Delgado	.35
140	Tom Goodwin	.05
141	Bob Tewksbury	.05
142	Chris Gomez	.05
143	Jose Oquendo	.05
144	Mark Lewis	.05
145	Salomon Torres	.05
146	Luis Gonzalez	.05
147	Mark Carreon	.05
148	Lance Johnson	.05
149	Melvin Nieves	.05
150	Lee Smith	.05
151	Jacob Brumfield	.05
152	Armando Benitez	.05
153	Curt Schilling	.30
154	Javier Lopez	.05
155	Frank Rodriguez	.05
156	Alex Gonzalez	.05
157	Todd Worrell	.05
158	Benji Gil	.05
159	Greg Gagne	.05
160	Tom Henke	.05
161	Randy Myers	.05
162	Joey Cora	.05
163	Scott Ruffcorn	.05
164	William Van Landingham	.05
165	Tony Phillips	.05
166	Eddie Williams	.05
167	Bobby Bonilla	.05
168	Denny Neagle	.05
169	Troy Percival	.05
170	Billy Ashley	.05
171	Andy Van Slyke	.05
172	Jose Offerman	.05
173	Mark Parent	.05
174	Edgardo Alfonzo	.05
175	Trevor Hoffman	.05
176	David Cone	.05
177	Dan Wilson	.05
178	Steve Ontiveros	.05
179	Dean Palmer	.05
180	Mike Kelly	.05
181	Jim Leyritz	.05
182	Ron Karkovice	.05
183	Kevin Brown	.05
184	Jose Valentin RC	.05
185	Jorge Fabregas	.05
186	Jose Mesa	.05
187	Brent Mayne	.05
188	Carl Everett	.05
189	Paul Sorrento	.05
190	Pete Shourek	.05
191	Scott Kamienicki	.05
192	Roberto Hernandez	.05

#	Player	Price
193	Randy Johnson (Radar Rating)	.25
194	Greg Maddux (Radar Rating)	.35
195	Hideo Nomo (Radar Rating)	.15
196	David Cone (Radar Rating)	.05
197	Mike Mussina (Radar Rating)	.15
198	Andy Benes (Radar Rating)	.05
199	Kevin Appier (Radar Rating)	.05
200	John Smoltz (Radar Rating)	.05
201	John Wetteland (Radar Rating)	.05
202	Mark Wohlers (Radar Rating)	.05
203	Stan Belinda	.05
204	Brian Anderson	.05
205	Mike Devereaux	.05
206	Mark Wohlers	.05
207	Omar Vizquel	.05
208	Jose Rijo	.05
209	Willie Blair	.05
210	Jamie Moyer	.05
211	Craig Shipley	.05
212	Shane Reynolds	.05
213	Chad Fonville	.05
214	Jose Vizcaino	.05
215	Sid Fernandez	.05
216	Andy Ashby	.05
217	Frank Castillo	.05
218	Kevin Tapani	.05
219	Kent Mercker	.05
220	Karim Garcia	.05
221	Chris Snopek	.05
222	Tim Unroe	.05
223	Johnny Damon	.25
224	LaTroy Hawkins	.10
225	Mariano Rivera	.10
226	Jose Alberro	.05
227	Angel Martinez	.05
228	Jason Schmidt	.05
229	Tony Clark	.05
230	Kevin Jordan	.05
231	Mark Thompson	.05
232	Jim Dougherty	.05
233	Roger Cedeno	.05
234	Ugueth Urbina	.05
235	Ricky Otero	.05
236	Mark Smith	.05
237	Brian Barber	.05
238	Marc Kroon	.05
239	Joe Rosselli	.05
240	Derek Jeter	1.50
241	Michael Tucker	.05
242	Joe Borowski RC	.05
243	Joe Vitiello	.05
244	Orlando Palmeiro	.05
245	James Baldwin	.05
246	Alan Embree	.05
247	Shannon Penn	.05
248	Chris Stynes	.05
249	Oscar Munoz	.05
250	Jose Herrera	.05
251	Scott Sullivan	.05
252	Reggie Williams	.05
253	Mark Grudzielanek	.05
254	Kevin Jordan	.05
255	Terry Bradshaw	.05
256	F.P. Santangelo RC	.05
257	Doug Johns	.05
258	George Williams	.05
259	Larry Thomas	.05
260	Rudy Pemberton	.05
261	Jim Pittsley	.05
262	Les Norman	.05
263	Ruben Rivera	.05
264	Cesar Devarez RC	.05
265	Gregg Zaun	.05
266	Eric Owens	.05
267	John Frascatore	.05
268	Shannon Stewart	.05
269	Checklist	.05
270	Checklist	.05
271	Checklist	.05
272	Checklist	.05
273	Checklist	.05
274	Checklist	.05
275	Checklist	.05
276	Greg Maddux	.60
277	Pedro Martinez	.05
278	Bobby Higginson	.05
279	Ray Lankford	.05
280	Shawon Dunston	.05
281	Gary Sheffield	.35
282	Ken Griffey Jr.	.75
283	Paul Molitor	.50
284	Kevin Appier	.05
285	Chuck Knoblauch	.05
286	Alex Fernandez	.05
287	Steve Finley	.05
288	Jeff Blauser	.05
289	Charles Johnson	.05
290	John Franco	.05
291	Mark Langston	.05
292	Bret Saberhagen	.05
293	John Mabry	.05
294	Ramon Martinez	.05
295	Mike Blowers	.05
296	Paul O'Neill	.05
297	Dave Nilsson	.05
298	Dante Bichette	.05
299	Marty Cordova	.05
300	Jay Bell	.05

#	Player	Price
301	Mike Mussina	.30
302	Ivan Rodriguez	.40
303	Jose Canseco	.30
304	Jeff Bagwell	.50
305	Manny Ramirez	.50
306	Dennis Martinez	.05
307	Charlie Hayes	.05
308	Joe Carter	.05
309	Travis Fryman	.05
310	Mark McGwire	1.00
311	Reggie Sanders	.05
312	Julian Tavarez	.05
313	Jeff Montgomery	.05
314	Andy Benes	.05
315	John Jaha	.05
316	Jeff Kent	.05
317	Mike Piazza	.75
318	Erik Hanson	.05
319	Kenny Rogers	.05
320	Hideo Nomo	.25
321	Gregg Jefferies	.05
322	Chipper Jones	.75
323	Jay Buhner	.05
324	Dennis Eckersley	.40
325	Kenny Lofton	.05
326	Robin Ventura	.05
327	Tom Glavine	.35
328	Tim Salmon	.05
329	Andres Galarraga	.05
330	Hal Morris	.05
331	Brady Anderson	.05
332	Chili Davis	.05
333	Roger Clemens	.65
334	Marquis Grissom	.05
335	Jeff (Mike) Greenwell	.05
336	Sammy Sosa	.60
337	Ron Gant	.05
338	Ken Caminiti	.05
339	Danny Tartabull	.05
340	Barry Bonds	1.50
341	Ben McDonald	.05
342	Ruben Sierra	.05
343	Bernie Williams	.05
344	Wil Cordero	.05
345	Wade Boggs	.60
346	Gary Gaetti	.05
347	Greg Colbrunn	.05
348	Juan Gonzalez	.25
349	Marc Newfield	.05
350	Charles Nagy	.05
351	Robby Thompson	.05
352	Roberto Petagine	.05
353	Darryl Strawberry	.05
354	Tino Martinez	.05
355	Eric Karros	.05
356	Cal Ripken Jr. (Star Struck)	.75
357	Cecil Fielder (Star Struck)	.05
358	Kirby Puckett (Star Struck)	.35
359	Jim Edmonds (Star Struck)	.05
360	Matt Williams (Star Struck)	.05
361	Alex Rodriguez (Star Struck)	.50
362	Barry Larkin (Star Struck)	.05
363	Rafael Palmeiro (Star Struck)	.20
364	David Cone (Star Struck)	.05
365	Roberto Alomar (Star Struck)	.10
366	Eddie Murray (Star Struck)	.25
367	Randy Johnson (Star Struck)	.20
368	Ryan Klesko (Star Struck)	.05
369	Raul Mondesi (Star Struck)	.05
370	Mo Vaughn (Star Struck)	.05
371	Will Clark (Star Struck)	.05
372	Carlos Baerga (Star Struck)	.05
373	Frank Thomas (Star Struck)	.30
374	Larry Walker (Star Struck)	.05
375	Garret Anderson (Star Struck)	.05
376	Edgar Martinez (Star Struck)	.05
377	Don Mattingly (Star Struck)	.40
378	Tony Gwynn (Star Struck)	.35
379	Albert Belle (Star Struck)	.05
380	Jason Isringhausen (Star Struck)	.05
381	Ruben Rivera (Star Struck)	.05
382	Johnny Damon (Star Struck)	.05
383	Karim Garcia (Star Struck)	.05
384	Derek Jeter (Star Struck)	.75
385	David Justice (Star Struck)	.05
386	Royce Clayton	.05
387	Mark Whiten	.05
388	Mickey Tettleton	.05
389	Steve Trachsel	.05
390	Danny Bautista	.05
391	Midre Cummings	.05
392	Scott Leius	.05
393	Manny Alexander	.05
394	Brent Gates	.05
395	Rey Sanchez	.05
396	Andy Pettitte	.20
397	Jeff Cirillo	.05
398	Kurt Abbott	.05
399	Lee Tinsley	.05

#	Player	Price
400	Paul Assenmacher	.05
401	Scott Erickson	.05
402	Todd Zeile	.05
403	Tom Pagnozzi	.05
404	Ozzie Guillen	.05
405	Jeff Frye	.05
406	Kirt Manwaring	.05
407	Chad Ogea	.05
408	Harold Baines	.05
409	Jason Bere	.05
410	Chuck Finley	.05
411	Jeff Fassero	.05
412	Joey Hamilton	.05
413	John Olerud	.05
414	Kevin Stocker	.05
415	Eric Anthony	.05
416	Aaron Sele	.05
417	Chris Bosio	.05
418	Michael Mimbs	.05
419	Orlando Miller	.05
420	Stan Javier	.05
421	Matt Mieske	.05
422	Jason Bates	.05
423	Orlando Merced	.05
424	John Flaherty	.05
425	Reggie Jefferson	.05
426	Scott Stahoviak	.05
427	John Burkett	.05
428	Rod Beck	.05
429	Bill Swift	.05
430	Scott Cooper	.05
431	Mel Rojas	.05
432	Todd Van Poppel	.05
433	Bobby Jones	.05
434	Mike Harkey	.05
435	Sean Berry	.05
436	Glenallen Hill	.05
437	Ryan Thompson	.05
438	Luis Alicea	.05
439	Esteban Loaiza	.05
440	Jeff Reboulet	.05
441	Vince Coleman	.05
442	Ellis Burks	.05
443	Allen Battle	.05
444	Jimmy Key	.05
445	Ricky Bottalico	.05
446	Delino DeShields	.05
447	Albie Lopez	.05
448	Mark Petkovsek	.05
449	Tim Raines	.05
450	Bryan Harvey	.05
451	Pat Hentgen	.05
452	Tim Laker	.05
453	Tom Gordon	.05
454	Phil Plantier	.05
455	Ernie Young	.05
456	Pete Harnisch	.05
457	Roberto Kelly	.05
458	Mark Portugal	.05
459	Mark Leiter	.05
460	Tony Pena	.05
461	Roger Pavlik	.05
462	Jeff King	.05
463	Bryan Rekar	.05
464	Al Leiter	.05
465	Phil Nevin	.05
466	Jose Lima	.05
467	Mike Stanley	.05
468	David McCarty	.05
469	Herb Perry	.05
470	Geronimo Berroa	.05
471	David Wells	.05
472	Vaughn Eshelman	.05
473	Greg Swindell	.05
474	Steve Sparks	.05
475	Luis Sojo	.05
476	Derrick May	.05
477	Joe Oliver	.05
478	Alex Arias	.05
479	Brad Ausmus	.05
480	Gabe White	.05
481	Pat Rapp	.05
482	Damon Buford	.05
483	Turk Wendell	.05
484	Jeff Brantley	.05
485	Curtis Leskanic	.05
486	Robb Nen	.05
487	Lou Whitaker	.05
488	Melido Perez	.05
489	Luis Polonia	.05
490	Scott Brosius	.05
491	Robert Perez	.05
492	Mike Sweeney RC	.50
493	Mark Loretta	.05
494	Alex Ochoa	.05
495	Matt Lawton RC	.10
496	Shawn Estes	.05
497	John Wasdin	.05
498	Marc Kroon	.05
499	Chris Snopek	.05
500	Jeff Suppan	.05
501	Terrell Wade	.05
502	Marvin Benard RC	.10
503	Chris Widger	.05
504	Quinton McCracken	.05
505	Bob Wolcott	.05
506	C.J. Nitkowski	.05
507	Aaron Ledesma	.05
508	Scott Hatteberg	.05
509	Jimmy Haynes	.05
510	Howard Battle	.05

Dugout Collection

The concept of a partial parallel set, including the stars and rookies, but not the journeymen and bench warmers, was initiated with

Score's "Dugout Collection," with fewer than half of the cards from the regular series chosen for inclusion. The white borders of the regular cards are replaced with copper-foil and background printing is also done on foil in this special version. On back is a special "Dugout Collection '96" logo. Advertised insertion rate of the copper-version cards is one per three packs.

	NM/M
Complete Set (220):	60.00
Complete Series 1 (1-110):	30.00
Complete Series 2 (1-110):	30.00
Common Player:	.20
Artist's Proofs:	4X

#	Player	Price
1	Will Clark	.20
2	Rich Becker	.20
3	Ryan Klesko	.20
4	Jim Edmonds	.20
5	Barry Larkin	.20
6	Jim Thome	.65
7	Raul Mondesi	.20
8	Don Mattingly	1.25
9	Jeff Conine	.20
10	Rickey Henderson	.75
11	Chad Curtis	.20
12	Darren Daulton	.20
13	Larry Walker	.20
14	Carlos Baerga	.20
15	Tony Gwynn	1.00
16	Jon Nunnally	.20
17	Deion Sanders	.20
18	Mark Grace	.20
19	Alex Rodriguez	2.00
20	Frank Thomas	.75
21	Brian Jordan	.20
22	J.T. Snow	.20
23	Shawn Green	.50
24	Tim Wakefield	.20
25	Curtis Goodwin	.20
26	John Smoltz	.20
27	Devon White	.20
28	Brian Hunter	.20
29	Rusty Greer	.20
30	Rafael Palmeiro	.65
31	Bernard Gilkey	.20
32	John Valentin	.20
33	Randy Johnson	.75
34	Garret Anderson	.20
35	Ray Durham	.20
36	Bip Roberts	.20
37	Tyler Green	.20
38	Bill Pulsipher	.20
39	Jason Giambi	.50
40	Jack McDowell	.20
41	Rico Brogna	.20
42	Terry Pendleton	.20
43	Rondell White	.20
44	Andre Dawson	.35
45	Kirby Puckett	1.00
46	Wally Joyner	.20
47	B.J. Surhoff	.20
48	Randy Velarde	.20
49	Greg Vaughn	.20
50	Roberto Alomar	.30
51	David Justice	.20
52	Cal Ripken Jr.	3.00
53	Ozzie Smith	1.00
54	Mo Vaughn	.20
55	Gary DiSarcina	.20
56	Matt Williams	.20
57	Lenny Dykstra	.20
58	Bret Boone	.20
59	Albert Belle	.20
60	Vinny Castilla	.20
61	Moises Alou	.20
62	Cecil Fielder	.20
63	Brad Radke	.20
64	Quilvio Veras	.20
65	Eddie Murray	.75
66	Dave Winfield	.75
67	Fred McGriff	.20
68	Craig Biggio	.20
69	Cliff Floyd	.20
70	Tim Naehring	.20
71	John Wetteland	.20
72	Alan Trammell	.20
73	Steve Avery	.20
74	Rick Aguilera	.20
75	Derek Bell	.20
76	Todd Hollandsworth	.20
77	Edgar Martinez	.20
78	Mark Lemke	.20
79	Ariel Prieto	.20
80	Russ Davis	.20
81	Jim Abbott	.20
82	Jason Isringhausen	.20
83	Carlos Perez	.20
84	David Segui	.20
85	Troy O'Leary	.20
86	Ismael Valdes	.20
87	Carlos Delgado	.50
88	Lee Smith	.20
89	Javy Lopez	.20
90	Frank Rodriguez	.20
91	Alex Gonzalez	.20
92	Benji Gil	.20
93	Greg Gagne	.20
94	Randy Myers	.20
95	Bobby Bonilla	.20
96	Billy Ashley	.20
97	Andy Van Slyke	.20
98	Edgardo Alfonzo	.20
99	David Cone	.20
100	Dean Palmer	.20
101	Jose Mesa	.20
102	Karim Garcia	.20
103	Johnny Damon	.40
104	LaTroy Hawkins	.20
105	Mark Smith	.20
106	Derek Jeter	3.00
107	Michael Tucker	.20
108	Joe Vitiello	.20
109	Ruben Rivera	.20
110	Gregg Zaun	.20
1	Greg Maddux	1.00
2	Pedro Martinez	.75
3	Bobby Higginson	.20
4	Ray Lankford	.20
5	Shawon Dunston	.20
6	Gary Sheffield	.45
7	Ken Griffey Jr.	1.50
8	Paul Molitor	.75
9	Kevin Appier	.20
10	Chuck Knoblauch	.20
11	Alex Fernandez	.20
12	Steve Finley	.20
13	Jeff Blauser	.20
14	Charles Johnson	.20
15	John Franco	.20
16	Mark Langston	.20
17	Bret Saberhagen	.20
18	John Mabry	.20
19	Ramon Martinez	.20
20	Mike Blowers	.20
21	Paul O'Neill	.20
22	Dave Nilsson	.20
23	Dante Bichette	.20
24	Marty Cordova	.20
25	Jay Bell	.20
26	Mike Mussina	.40
27	Ivan Rodriguez	.65
28	Jose Canseco	.50
29	Jeff Bagwell	.75
30	Manny Ramirez	.75
31	Dennis Martinez	.20
32	Charlie Hayes	.20
33	Joe Carter	.20
34	Travis Fryman	.20
35	Mark McGwire	2.00
36	Reggie Sanders	.20
37	Julian Tavarez	.20
38	Jeff Montgomery	.20
39	Andy Benes	.20
40	John Jaha	.20
41	Jeff Kent	.20
42	Mike Piazza	1.50
43	Erik Hanson	.20
44	Kenny Rogers	.20
45	Hideo Nomo	.50
46	Gregg Jefferies	.20
47	Chipper Jones	1.00
48	Jay Buhner	.20
49	Dennis Eckersley	.65
50	Kenny Lofton	.20
51	Robin Ventura	.20
52	Tom Glavine	.30
53	Tim Salmon	.20
54	Andres Galarraga	.20
55	Hal Morris	.20
56	Brady Anderson	.20
57	Chili Davis	.20
58	Roger Clemens	1.25
59	Marquis Grissom	.20
60	Mike Greenwell	.20
61	Sammy Sosa	1.00
62	Ron Gant	.20
63	Ken Caminiti	.20
64	Danny Tartabull	.20
65	Barry Bonds	3.00
66	Ben McDonald	.20
67	Ruben Sierra	.20
68	Bernie Williams	.20
69	Wil Cordero	.20
70	Wade Boggs	1.00
71	Gary Gaetti	.20
72	Greg Colbrunn	.20
73	Juan Gonzalez	.50
74	Marc Newfield	.20
75	Charles Nagy	.20
76	Robby Thompson	.20
77	Roberto Petagine	.20
78	Darryl Strawberry	.20
79	Tino Martinez	.20
80	Eric Karros	.20
81	Cal Ripken Jr. (Star Struck)	1.50
82	Cecil Fielder (Star Struck)	.20
83	Kirby Puckett (Star Struck)	.50

84	Jim Edmonds (Star Struck)	.20
85	Matt Williams (Star Struck)	.20
86	Alex Rodriguez (Star Struck)	1.00
87	Barry Larkin (Star Struck)	.20
88	Rafael Palmeiro (Star Struck)	.40
89	David Cone (Star Struck)	.20
90	Roberto Alomar (Star Struck)	.25
91	Eddie Murray (Star Struck)	.40
92	Randy Johnson (Star Struck)	.40
93	Ryan Klesko (Star Struck)	.20
94	Raul Mondesi (Star Struck)	.20
95	Mo Vaughn (Star Struck)	.20
96	Will Clark (Star Struck)	.20
97	Carlos Baerga (Star Struck)	.20
98	Frank Thomas (Star Struck)	.45
99	Larry Walker (Star Struck)	.20
100	Garret Anderson (Star Struck)	.20
101	Edgar Martinez (Star Struck)	.20
102	Don Mattingly (Star Struck)	.60
103	Tony Gwynn (Star Struck)	.50
104	Albert Belle (Star Struck)	.20
105	Jason Isringhausen (Star Struck)	.20
106	Ruben Rivera (Star Struck)	.20
107	Johnny Damon (Star Struck)	.35
108	Karim Garcia (Star Struck)	.20
109	Derek Jeter (Star Struck)	1.50
110	David Justice (Star Struck)	.20

Dugout Collection Artist's Proofs

A parallel set within a parallel set, the Artist's Proof logo added to the copper-foil design of the Dugout Collection cards raises the odds of finding one to just once in 36 packs.

	NM/M
Complete Set (220):	300.00
Common Player:	1.00
Artist's Proof Stars:	4X

All-Stars

An exclusive insert found only in 20-card Series 2 jumbo packs at an average rate of one per nine packs, these inserts feature the game's top stars printed in a rainbow holographic-foil technology.

		NM/M
Complete Set (20):		13.50
Common Player:		.25
1	Frank Thomas	1.25
2	Albert Belle	.25
3	Ken Griffey Jr.	2.00
4	Cal Ripken Jr.	3.00
5	Mo Vaughn	.25
6	Matt Williams	.25
7	Barry Bonds	3.00
8	Dante Bichette	.25
9	Tony Gwynn	1.50
10	Greg Maddux	1.50
11	Randy Johnson	1.25
12	Hideo Nomo	.75
13	Tim Salmon	.25
14	Jeff Bagwell	1.25
15	Edgar Martinez	.25
16	Reggie Sanders	.25
17	Larry Walker	.25
18	Chipper Jones	1.50
19	Manny Ramirez	1.25
20	Eddie Murray	1.25

Big Bats

Gold-foil printing highlights cards of 20 of the game's top hitters found in this retail-packaging exclusive insert set. Stated odds of picking a Big Bats card are one in 31 packs.

		NM/M
Complete Set (20):		12.50
Common Player:		.45
1	Cal Ripken Jr.	3.00
2	Ken Griffey Jr.	2.00
3	Frank Thomas	.75
4	Jeff Bagwell	.75
5	Mike Piazza	2.00
6	Barry Bonds	3.00
7	Matt Williams	.45
8	Raul Mondesi	.45
9	Tony Gwynn	1.25
10	Albert Belle	.45
11	Manny Ramirez	.75
12	Carlos Baerga	.45
13	Mo Vaughn	.45
14	Derek Bell	.45
15	Larry Walker	.45
16	Kenny Lofton	.45
17	Edgar Martinez	.45
18	Reggie Sanders	.45
19	Eddie Murray	.75
20	Chipper Jones	1.25

Diamond Aces

Thirty of the top veterans and young stars are included in this jumbo-only insert set, seeded at a rate of one per eight packs.

		NM/M
Complete Set (30):		25.00
Common Player:		.35
1	Hideo Nomo	.60
2	Brian Hunter	.35
3	Ray Durham	.35
4	Frank Thomas	1.00
5	Cal Ripken Jr.	3.50
6	Barry Bonds	3.50
7	Greg Maddux	1.25
8	Chipper Jones	1.25
9	Raul Mondesi	.35
10	Mike Piazza	2.00
11	Derek Jeter	3.50
12	Bill Pulsipher	.35
13	Larry Walker	.35
14	Ken Griffey Jr.	2.00
15	Alex Rodriguez	3.00
16	Manny Ramirez	1.00
17	Mo Vaughn	.35
18	Reggie Sanders	.35
19	Derek Bell	.35
20	Jim Edmonds	.35
21	Albert Belle	.35
22	Eddie Murray	1.00
23	Tony Gwynn	1.25
24	Jeff Bagwell	1.00
25	Carlos Baerga	.35
26	Matt Williams	.35
27	Garret Anderson	.35
28	Todd Hollandsworth	.35
29	Johnny Damon	.75
30	Tim Salmon	.35

Dream Team

The hottest player at each position is honored in the Dream Team insert set. Once again featured on holographic foil printing technology, the cards are found in all types of Score packaging at a rate of once per 72 packs.

		NM/M
Complete Set (9):		15.00
Common Player:		.75
1	Cal Ripken Jr.	4.00
2	Frank Thomas	1.50
3	Carlos Baerga	.75
4	Matt Williams	.75
5	Mike Piazza	2.00
6	Barry Bonds	4.00
7	Ken Griffey Jr.	3.00
8	Manny Ramirez	1.50
9	Greg Maddux	2.00

Future Franchise

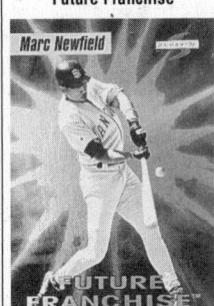

Future Franchise is the most difficult insert to pull from packs of Series 2, at the rate of once per 72 packs, on average. Sixteen young stars are showcased in holographic gold-foil printing in the set.

		NM/M
Complete Set (16):		20.00
Common Player:		.75
1	Jason Isringhausen	.75
2	Chipper Jones	2.50
3	Derek Jeter	5.00
4	Alex Rodriguez	4.00
5	Alex Ochoa	.75
6	Manny Ramirez	1.50
7	Johnny Damon	1.00
8	Ruben Rivera	.75
9	Karim Garcia	.75
10	Garret Anderson	.75
11	Marty Cordova	.75
12	Bill Pulsipher	.75
13	Hideo Nomo	1.00
14	Marc Newfield	.75
15	Charles Johnson	.75
16	Raul Mondesi	.75

Gold Stars

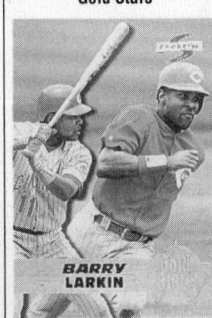

Appearing once in every 15 packs of Series 2, Gold Stars are labeled with a stamp in the upper-left corner. The set contains 30 top current stars printed on gold-foil and seeded at the average rate of one per 15 packs.

		NM/M
Complete Set (30):		20.00
Common Player:		.20
1	Ken Griffey Jr.	2.00
2	Frank Thomas	1.00
3	Reggie Sanders	.20
4	Tim Salmon	.20
5	Mike Piazza	2.00
6	Tony Gwynn	1.50
7	Gary Sheffield	.45
8	Matt Williams	.20
9	Bernie Williams	.20
10	Jason Isringhausen	.20
11	Albert Belle	.20
12	Chipper Jones	1.50
13	Edgar Martinez	.20
14	Barry Larkin	.20
15	Barry Bonds	3.00
16	Jeff Bagwell	1.00
17	Greg Maddux	1.50
18	Mo Vaughn	.20
19	Ryan Klesko	.20
20	Sammy Sosa	1.50
21	Darren Daulton	.20
22	Ivan Rodriguez	.75
23	Dante Bichette	.20
24	Hideo Nomo	.50
25	Cal Ripken Jr.	3.00
26	Rafael Palmeiro	.75
27	Larry Walker	.20
28	Carlos Baerga	.20
29	Randy Johnson	1.00
30	Manny Ramirez	1.00

Numbers Game

Some of the 1995 season's most impressive statistical accomplishments are featured in this chase set. Cards are enhanced with gold foil and found in all types of Score packs at an average rate of one per 15 packs.

		NM/M
Complete Set (30):		17.50
Common Player:		.15
1	Cal Ripken Jr.	2.50
2	Frank Thomas	.75
3	Ken Griffey Jr.	1.50
4	Mike Piazza	1.50
5	Barry Bonds	2.50
6	Greg Maddux	1.00
7	Jeff Bagwell	.75
8	Derek Bell	.15
9	Tony Gwynn	1.00
10	Hideo Nomo	.50
11	Raul Mondesi	.15
12	Manny Ramirez	.75
13	Albert Belle	.15
14	Matt Williams	.15
15	Jim Edmonds	.15
16	Edgar Martinez	.15
17	Mo Vaughn	.15
18	Reggie Sanders	.15
19	Chipper Jones	1.00
20	Larry Walker	.15
21	Juan Gonzalez	.75
22	Kenny Lofton	.15
23	Don Mattingly	1.25
24	Ivan Rodriguez	.65
25	Randy Johnson	.75
26	Derek Jeter	2.50
27	J.T. Snow	.15
28	Will Clark	.15
29	Rafael Palmeiro	.65
30	Alex Rodriguez	2.00

Power Pace

Power Pace is exclusive to retail packs in Series 2, where they are found on average every 31 packs. Eighteen top power hitters are featured in this issue in a gold-foil design.

		NM/M
Complete Set (18):		24.00
Common Player:		.50
1	Mark McGwire	4.00
2	Albert Belle	.50
3	Jay Buhner	.50
4	Frank Thomas	1.50
5	Matt Williams	.50
6	Gary Sheffield	.75
7	Mike Piazza	3.00
8	Larry Walker	.50
9	Mo Vaughn	.50
10	Rafael Palmeiro	1.25
11	Dante Bichette	.50
12	Ken Griffey Jr.	3.00
13	Barry Bonds	5.00
14	Manny Ramirez	1.50
15	Sammy Sosa	2.00
16	Tim Salmon	.50
17	Dave Justice	.50
18	Eric Karros	.50

Reflexions

Appearing only in hobby packs this insert set pairs 20 veteran stars with 20 up-and-coming players in a foil-printed format. Odds of finding a Reflexions insert are stated as one per 31 packs.

		NM/M
Complete Set (20):		35.00
Common Player:		.45
1	Cal Ripken Jr., Chipper Jones	5.00
2	Ken Griffey Jr., Alex Rodriguez	4.50
3	Frank Thomas, Mo Vaughn	2.50
4	Kenny Lofton, Brian Hunter	.45
5	Don Mattingly, J.T. Snow	3.75
6	Manny Ramirez, Raul Mondesi	2.50
7	Tony Gwynn, Garret Anderson	3.75
8	Roberto Alomar, Carlos Baerga	.50
9	Andre Dawson, Larry Walker	.45
10	Barry Larkin, Derek Jeter	5.00
11	Barry Bonds, Reggie Sanders	5.00
12	Mike Piazza, Albert Belle	4.00
13	Wade Boggs, Edgar Martinez	3.75
14	David Cone, John Smoltz	.45
15	Will Clark, Jeff Bagwell	2.50
16	Mark McGwire, Cecil Fielder	4.50
17	Greg Maddux, Mike Mussina	3.75
18	Randy Johnson, Hideo Nomo	2.50
19	Jim Thome, Dean Palmer	2.00
20	Chuck Knoblauch, Craig Biggio	.45

Cal Ripken Tribute

The toughest pick among the 1996 Score inserts is this special card marking Cal Ripken's 2,131st consecutive game. The insertion rate is one per 300 packs hobby and retail, one per 150 jumbo packs.

	NM/M
2131 Cal Ripken Jr. (Tribute)	4.00

Titanic Taters

One of the more creative names in the 1996 insert lineup, Titanic Taters are found one in every 31 packs of Series 2 hobby. Gold-foil fronts feature 18 of the game's heaviest hitters.

		NM/M
Complete Set (18):		25.00
Common Player:		.60
1	Albert Belle	.60
2	Frank Thomas	2.00
3	Mo Vaughn	.60
4	Ken Griffey Jr.	3.00
5	Matt Williams	.60
6	Mark McGwire	3.50
7	Dante Bichette	.60
8	Tim Salmon	.60
9	Jeff Bagwell	2.00
10	Rafael Palmeiro	1.50
11	Mike Piazza	3.00
12	Cecil Fielder	.60
13	Larry Walker	.60
14	Sammy Sosa	2.50
15	Manny Ramirez	2.00
16	Gary Sheffield	.90
17	Barry Bonds	5.00
18	Jay Buhner	.60

1997 Score

A total of 551 cards make up the base set, with 330 cards sold in Series I and 221 making up Series II. The basic card design features a color action photo surrounded by a white border. The player's name is above the photo, with the team name underneath. Backs feature text and statistics against a white background with the image of the team logo ghosted into the background. Two parallel insert sets - Artist's Proof and Showcase Series - were part of each series. Other inserts in Series I were Pitcher Perfect, The Franchise, The Glowing Franchise, Titanic Taters (retail exclusive), Stellar Season (magazine packs only), and The Highlight Zone (hobby exclusive). Series II inserts were Blastmasters, Heart of the Order and Stand and Deliver. Cards were sold in 10-card packs for 99 cents each.

		NM/M
Complete Set (551):		16.00
Factory Tin-Box Set (551):		17.50
Common Player:		.05
Showcase:		3X
Artist's Proofs:		10X
Premium Stocks:		3X
Wax Pack (10):		.50
Wax Box (36):		12.00
1	Jeff Bagwell	.50
2	Mickey Tettleton	.05
3	Johnny Damon	.25
4	Jeff Conine	.05
5	Bernie Williams	.05
6	Will Clark	.05
7	Ryan Klesko	.05
8	Cecil Fielder	.05
9	Paul Wilson	.05
10	Gregg Jefferies	.05
11	Chili Davis	.05
12	Albert Belle	.05
13	Ken Hill	.05
14	Cliff Floyd	.05
15	Jaime Navarro	.05
16	Ismael Valdes	.05
17	Jeff King	.05

No.	Player	Price
18	Chris Bosio	.05
19	Reggie Sanders	.05
20	Darren Daulton	.05
21	Ken Caminiti	.05
22	Mike Piazza	.75
23	Chad Mottola	.05
24	Darin Erstad	.15
25	Dante Bichette	.05
26	Frank Thomas	.50
27	Ben McDonald	.05
28	Raul Casanova	.05
29	Kevin Ritz	.05
30	Garret Anderson	.05
31	Jason Kendall	.05
32	Billy Wagner	.05
33	David Justice	.05
34	Marty Cordova	.05
35	Derek Jeter	1.50
36	Trevor Hoffman	.05
37	Geronimo Berroa	.05
38	Walt Weiss	.05
39	Kirt Manwaring	.05
40	Alex Gonzalez	.05
41	Sean Berry	.05
42	Kevin Appier	.05
43	Rusty Greer	.05
44	Pete Incaviglia	.05
45	Rafael Palmeiro	.45
46	Eddie Murray	.50
47	Moises Alou	.05
48	Mark Lewis	.05
49	Hal Morris	.05
50	Edgar Renteria	.05
51	Rickey Henderson	.50
52	Pat Listach	.05
53	John Wasdin	.05
54	James Baldwin	.05
55	Brian Jordan	.05
56	Edgar Martinez	.05
57	Wil Cordero	.05
58	Danny Tartabull	.05
59	Keith Lockhart	.05
60	Rico Brogna	.05
61	Ricky Bottalico	.05
62	Terry Pendleton	.05
63	Bret Boone	.05
64	Charlie Hayes	.05
65	Marc Newfield	.05
66	Sterling Hitchcock	.05
67	Roberto Alomar	.15
68	John Jaha	.05
69	Greg Colbrunn	.05
70	Sal Fasano	.05
71	Brooks Kieschnick	.05
72	Pedro Martinez	.50
73	Kevin Elster	.05
74	Ellis Burks	.05
75	Chuck Finley	.05
76	John Olerud	.05
77	Jay Bell	.05
78	Allen Watson	.05
79	Darryl Strawberry	.05
80	Orlando Miller	.05
81	Jose Herrera	.05
82	Andy Pettitte	.20
83	Juan Guzman	.05
84	Alan Benes	.05
85	Jack McDowell	.05
86	Ugueth Urbina	.05
87	Rocky Coppinger	.05
88	Jeff Cirillo	.05
89	Tom Glavine	.35
90	Robby Thompson	.05
91	Barry Bonds	1.50
92	Carlos Delgado	.40
93	Mo Vaughn	.05
94	Ryne Sandberg	.65
95	Alex Rodriguez	1.00
96	Brady Anderson	.05
97	Scott Brosius	.05
98	Dennis Eckersley	.45
99	Brian McRae	.05
100	Rey Ordonez	.05
101	John Valentin	.05
102	Brett Butler	.05
103	Eric Karros	.05
104	Harold Baines	.05
105	Javier Lopez	.05
106	Alan Trammell	.05
107	Jim Thome	.45
108	Frank Rodriguez	.05
109	Bernard Gilkey	.05
110	Reggie Jefferson	.05
111	Scott Stahoviak	.05
112	Steve Gibralter	.05
113	Todd Hollandsworth	.05
114	Ruben Rivera	.05
115	Dennis Martinez	.05
116	Mariano Rivera	.10
117	John Smoltz	.05
118	John Mabry	.05
119	Tom Gordon	.05
120	Alex Ochoa	.05
121	Jamey Wright	.05
122	Dave Nilsson	.05
123	Bobby Bonilla	.05
124	Al Leiter	.05
125	Rick Aguilera	.05
126	Jeff Brantley	.05
127	Kevin Brown	.05
128	George Arias	.05
129	Darren Oliver	.05
130	Bill Pulsipher	.05
131	Roberto Hernandez	.05
132	Delino DeShields	.05
133	Mark Grudzielanek	.05
134	John Wetteland	.05
135	Carlos Baerga	.05
136	Paul Sorrento	.05
137	Leo Gomez	.05
138	Andy Ashby	.05
139	Julio Franco	.05
140	Brian Hunter	.05
141	Jermaine Dye	.05
142	Tony Clark	.05
143	Ruben Sierra	.05
144	Donovan Osborne	.05
145	Mark McLemore	.05
146	Terry Steinbach	.05
147	Bob Wells	.05
148	Chan Ho Park	.05
149	Tim Salmon	.05
150	Paul O'Neill	.05
151	Cal Ripken Jr.	1.50
152	Wally Joyner	.05
153	Omar Vizquel	.05
154	Mike Mussina	.30
155	Andres Galarraga	.05
156	Ken Griffey Jr.	.75
157	Kenny Lofton	.05
158	Ray Durham	.05
159	Hideo Nomo	.25
160	Ozzie Guillen	.05
161	Roger Pavlik	.05
162	Manny Ramirez	.50
163	Mark Lemke	.05
164	Mike Stanley	.05
165	Chuck Knoblauch	.05
166	Kimera Bartee	.05
167	Wade Boggs	.65
168	Jay Buhner	.05
169	Eric Young	.05
170	Jose Canseco	.30
171	Dwight Gooden	.05
172	Fred McGriff	.05
173	Sandy Alomar Jr.	.05
174	Andy Benes	.05
175	Dean Palmer	.05
176	Larry Walker	.05
177	Charles Nagy	.05
178	David Cone	.05
179	Mark Grace	.05
180	Robin Ventura	.05
181	Roger Clemens	.70
182	Bobby Witt	.05
183	Vinny Castilla	.05
184	Gary Sheffield	.35
185	Dan Wilson	.05
186	Roger Cedeno	.05
187	Mark McGwire	1.00
188	Darren Bragg	.05
189	Quinton McCracken	.05
190	Randy Myers	.05
191	Jeromy Burnitz	.05
192	Randy Johnson	.50
193	Chipper Jones	.75
194	Greg Vaughn	.05
195	Travis Fryman	.05
196	Tim Naehring	.05
197	B.J. Surhoff	.05
198	Juan Gonzalez	.25
199	Terrell Wade	.05
200	Jeff Frye	.05
201	Joey Cora	.05
202	Raul Mondesi	.05
203	Ivan Rodriguez	.45
204	Armando Reynoso	.05
205	Jeffrey Hammonds	.05
206	Darren Dreifort	.05
207	Kevin Seitzer	.05
208	Tino Martinez	.05
209	Jim Bruske	.05
210	Jeff Suppan	.05
211	Mark Carreon	.05
212	Wilson Alvarez	.05
213	John Burkett	.05
214	Tony Phillips	.05
215	Greg Maddux	.65
216	Mark Whiten	.05
217	Curtis Pride	.05
218	Lyle Mouton	.05
219	Todd Hundley	.05
220	Greg Gagne	.05
221	Rich Amaral	.05
222	Tom Goodwin	.05
223	Chris Hoiles	.05
224	Jayhawk Owens	.05
225	Kenny Rogers	.05
226	Mike Greenwell	.05
227	Mark Wohlers	.05
228	Henry Rodriguez	.05
229	Robert Perez	.05
230	Jeff Kent	.05
231	Darryl Hamilton	.05
232	Alex Fernandez	.05
233	Ron Karkovice	.05
234	Jimmy Haynes	.05
235	Craig Biggio	.05
236	Ray Lankford	.05
237	Lance Johnson	.05
238	Matt Williams	.05
239	Chad Curtis	.05
240	Mark Thompson	.05
241	Jason Giambi	.40
242	Barry Larkin	.05
243	Paul Molitor	.50
244	Sammy Sosa	.65
245	Kevin Tapani	.05
246	Marquis Grissom	.05
247	Joe Carter	.05
248	Ramon Martinez	.05
249	Tony Gwynn	.65
250	Andy Fox	.05
251	Troy O'Leary	.05
252	Warren Newson	.05
253	Troy Percival	.05
254	Jamie Moyer	.05
255	Danny Graves	.05
256	David Wells	.05
257	Todd Zeile	.05
258	Raul Ibanez	.05
259	Tyler Houston	.05
260	LaTroy Hawkins	.05
261	Joey Hamilton	.05
262	Mike Sweeney	.05
263	Brant Brown	.05
264	Pat Hentgen	.05
265	Mark Johnson	.05
266	Robb Nen	.05
267	Justin Thompson	.05
268	Ron Gant	.05
269	Jeff D'Amico	.05
270	Shawn Estes	.05
271	Derek Bell	.05
272	Fernando Valenzuela	.05
273	Luis Castillo	.05
274	Ray Montgomery	.05
275	Ed Sprague	.05
276	F.P. Santangelo	.05
277	Todd Greene	.05
278	Butch Huskey	.05
279	Steve Finley	.05
280	Eric Davis	.05
281	Shawn Green	.30
282	Al Martin	.05
283	Michael Tucker	.05
284	Shane Reynolds	.05
285	Matt Mieske	.05
286	Jose Rosado	.05
287	Mark Langston	.05
288	Ralph Milliard	.05
289	Mike Lansing	.05
290	Scott Servais	.05
291	Royce Clayton	.05
292	Mike Grace	.05
293	James Mouton	.05
294	Charles Johnson	.05
295	Gary Gaetti	.05
296	Kevin Mitchell	.05
297	Carlos Garcia	.05
298	Desi Relaford	.05
299	Jason Thompson	.05
300	Osvaldo Fernandez	.05
301	Fernando Vina	.05
302	Jose Offerman	.05
303	Yamil Benitez	.05
304	J.T. Snow	.05
305	Rafael Bournigal	.05
306	Jason Isringhausen	.05
307	Bob Higginson	.05
308	Nerio Rodriguez RC	.05
309	Brian Giles RC	.50
310	Andruw Jones	.50
311	Billy McMillon	.05
312	Arquimedez Pozo	.05
313	Jermaine Allensworth	.05
314	Luis Andujar	.05
315	Angel Echevarria	.05
316	Karim Garcia	.05
317	Trey Beamon	.05
318	Makoto Suzuki	.05
319	Robin Jennings	.05
320	Dmitri Young	.05
321	Damon Mashore RC	.05
322	Wendell Magee	.05
323	Dax Jones RC	.05
324	Todd Walker	.05
325	Marvin Benard	.05
326	Brian Raabe RC	.05
327	Marcus Jensen	.05
328	Checklist	.05
329	Checklist	.05
330	Checklist	.05
331	Norm Charlton	.05
332	Bruce Ruffin	.05
333	John Wetteland	.05
334	Marquis Grissom	.05
335	Sterling Hitchcock	.05
336	John Olerud	.05
337	David Wells	.05
338	Chili Davis	.05
339	Mark Lewis	.05
340	Kenny Lofton	.05
341	Alex Fernandez	.05
342	Ruben Sierra	.05
343	Delino DeShields	.05
344	John Wasdin	.05
345	Dennis Martinez	.05
346	Kevin Elster	.05
347	Bobby Bonilla	.05
348	Jaime Navarro	.05
349	Chad Curtis	.05
350	Terry Steinbach	.05
351	Ariel Prieto	.05
352	Jeff Kent	.05
353	Carlos Garcia	.05
354	Mark Whiten	.05
355	Todd Zelle	.05
356	Eric Davis	.05
357	Greg Colbrunn	.05
358	Moises Alou	.05
359	Allen Watson	.05
360	Jose Canseco	.30
361	Matt Williams	.05
362	Jeff King	.05
363	Darryl Hamilton	.05
364	Mark Clark	.05
365	J.T. Snow	.05
366	Kevin Mitchell	.05
367	Orlando Miller	.05
368	Rico Brogna	.05
369	Mike James	.05
370	Brad Ausmus	.05
371	Darryl Kile	.05
372	Edgardo Alfonzo	.05
373	Julian Tavarez	.05
374	Darren Lewis	.05
375	Steve Karsay	.05
376	Lee Stevens	.05
377	Albie Lopez	.05
378	Orel Hershiser	.05
379	Lee Smith	.05
380	Rick Helling	.05
381	Carlos Perez	.05
382	Tony Tarasco	.05
383	Melvin Nieves	.05
384	Benji Gil	.05
385	Devon White	.05
386	Armando Benitez	.05
387	Bill Swift	.05
388	John Smiley	.05
389	Midre Cummings	.05
390	Tim Belcher	.05
391	Tim Raines	.05
392	Todd Worrell	.05
393	Quilvio Veras	.05
394	Matt Lawton	.05
395	Aaron Sele	.05
396	Bip Roberts	.05
397	Denny Neagle	.05
398	Tyler Green	.05
399	Hipolito Pichardo	.05
400	Scott Erickson	.05
401	Bobby Jones	.05
402	Jim Edmonds	.05
403	Chad Ogea	.05
404	Cal Eldred	.05
405	Pat Listach	.05
406	Todd Stottlemyre	.05
407	Phil Nevin	.05
408	Otis Nixon	.05
409	Billy Ashley	.05
410	Jimmy Key	.05
411	Mike Timlin	.05
412	Joe Vitiello	.05
413	Rondell White	.05
414	Jeff Fassero	.05
415	Rex Hudler	.05
416	Curt Schilling	.35
417	Rich Becker	.05
418	William Van Landingham	.05
419	Chris Snopek	.05
420	David Segui	.05
421	Eddie Murray	.50
422	Shane Andrews	.05
423	Gary DiSarcina	.05
424	Brian Hunter	.05
425	Willie Greene	.05
426	Felipe Crespo	.05
427	Jason Bates	.05
428	Albert Belle	.05
429	Rey Sanchez	.05
430	Roger Clemens	.70
431	Deion Sanders	.05
432	Ernie Young	.05
433	Jay Bell	.05
434	Jeff Blauser	.05
435	Lenny Dykstra	.05
436	Chuck Carr	.05
437	Russ Davis	.05
438	Carl Everett	.05
439	Damion Easley	.05
440	Pat Kelly	.05
441	Pat Rapp	.05
442	David Justice	.05
443	Graeme Lloyd	.05
444	Damon Buford	.05
445	Jose Valentin	.05
446	Jason Schmidt	.05
447	Dave Martinez	.05
448	Danny Tartabull	.05
449	Jose Vizcaino	.05
450	Steve Avery	.05
451	Mike Devereaux	.05
452	Jim Eisenreich	.05
453	Mark Leiter	.05
454	Roberto Kelly	.05
455	Benito Santiago	.05
456	Steve Trachsel	.05
457	Gerald Williams	.05
458	Pete Schourek	.05
459	Esteban Loaiza	.05
460	Mel Rojas	.05
461	Tim Wakefield	.05
462	Tony Fernandez	.05
463	Doug Drabek	.05
464	Joe Girardi	.05
465	Mike Bordick	.05
466	Jim Leyritz	.05
467	Erik Hanson	.05
468	Michael Tucker	.05
469	Tony Womack RC	.10
470	Doug Glanville	.05
471	Rudy Pemberton	.05
472	Keith Lockhart	.05
473	Nomar Garciaparra	.65
474	Scott Rolen	.40
475	Jason Dickson	.05
476	Glendon Rusch	.05
477	Todd Walker	.05
478	Dmitri Young	.05
479	Rod Myers RC	.05
480	Wilton Guerrero	.05
481	Jorge Posada	.05
482	Brant Brown	.05
483	Bubba Trammell RC	.10
484	Jose Guillen	.05
485	Scott Spiezio	.05
486	Bob Abreu	.10
487	Chris Holt	.05
488	Deivi Cruz RC	.15
489	Vladimir Guerrero	.50
490	Julio Santana	.05
491	Ray Montgomery	.05
492	Kevin Orie	.05
493	Todd Hundley (Goin' Yard)	.05
494	Tim Salmon (Goin' Yard)	.05
495	Albert Belle (Goin' Yard)	.05
496	Manny Ramirez (Goin' Yard)	.25
497	Rafael Palmeiro (Goin' Yard)	.20
498	Juan Gonzalez (Goin' Yard)	.15
499	Ken Griffey Jr. (Goin' Yard)	.40
500	Andruw Jones (Goin' Yard)	.25
501	Mike Piazza (Goin' Yard)	.40
502	Jeff Bagwell (Goin' Yard)	.25
503	Bernie Williams (Goin' Yard)	.05
504	Barry Bonds (Goin' Yard)	.65
505	Ken Caminiti (Goin' Yard)	.05
506	Darin Erstad (Goin' Yard)	.10
507	Alex Rodriguez (Goin' Yard)	.50
508	Frank Thomas (Goin' Yard)	.30
509	Chipper Jones (Goin' Yard)	.40
510	Mo Vaughn (Goin' Yard)	.05
511	Mark McGwire (Goin' Yard)	.50
512	Fred McGriff (Goin' Yard)	.05
513	Jay Buhner (Goin' Yard)	.05
514	Jim Thome (Goin' Yard)	.20
515	Gary Sheffield (Goin' Yard)	.20
516	Dean Palmer (Goin' Yard)	.05
517	Henry Rodriguez (Goin' Yard)	.05
518	Andy Pettitte (Rock & Fire)	.10
519	Mike Mussina (Rock & Fire)	.10
520	Greg Maddux (Rock & Fire)	.35
521	John Smoltz (Rock & Fire)	.05
522	Hideo Nomo (Rock & Fire)	.15
523	Troy Percival (Rock & Fire)	.05
524	John Wetteland (Rock & Fire)	.05
525	Roger Clemens (Rock & Fire)	.40
526	Charles Nagy (Rock & Fire)	.05
527	Mariano Rivera (Rock & Fire)	.10
528	Tom Glavine (Rock & Fire)	.15
529	Randy Johnson (Rock & Fire)	.25
530	Jason Isringhausen (Rock & Fire)	.05
531	Alex Fernandez (Rock & Fire)	.05
532	Kevin Brown (Rock & Fire)	.05
533	Chuck Knoblauch (True Grit)	.05
534	Rusty Greer (True Grit)	.05
535	Tony Gwynn (True Grit)	.35
536	Ryan Klesko (True Grit)	.05
537	Ryne Sandberg (True Grit)	.35
538	Barry Larkin (True Grit)	.05
539	Will Clark (True Grit)	.05
540	Kenny Lofton (True Grit)	.05
541	Paul Molitor (True Grit)	.30
542	Roberto Alomar (True Grit)	.10
543	Rey Ordonez (True Grit)	.05
544	Jason Giambi (True Grit)	.25
545	Derek Jeter (True Grit)	.75
546	Cal Ripken Jr. (True Grit)	.75
547	Ivan Rodriguez (True Grit)	.25
548	Checklist (Ken Griffey Jr.)	.35
549	Checklist (Frank Thomas)	.25
550	Checklist (Mike Piazza)	.40
551a	Hideki Irabu/SP RC (English on back; factory sets/retailpacks.)	.25
551b	Hideki Irabu/SP RC (Japanese back; Hobby Reserve packs.)	.35

White Border Artist's Proofs

Specially marked Artist's Proof cards were random inserts in Series 1 retail packs. Like the regular-issue cards, they have white borders, so the gold-foil "ARTIST'S PROOF" logo on front may be overlooked. Only Series 1 (#1-330) are found in this style.

	NM/M
Complete Set (330):	150.00
Common Player:	.50
Artist's Proof Stars:	10X

Hobby Reserve

This is a hobby-only parallel version of Score Series 2, similar in concept to the Series 1 Premium Stock. Cards are identical to the regular Series 2 cards except for the addition of a gold Hobby Reserve foil seal on front.

	NM/M
Complete Set (221):	35.00
Common Player:	.10
Hobby Reserve Stars:	3X

Premium Stock

This is an upscale version of Score's regular Series 1 1997 issue, designated for hobby sales only. The cards are basically the same as the regular issue, except for the use of gray borders on front and an embossed gold-foil "Premium Stock" logo.

	NM/M
Complete Set (330):	17.50
Common Player:	.10
Premium Stock Stars:	3X

Reserve Collection

This was a hobby-only parallel version of Score Series 2. Cards are similar to regular Series 2 Score except for the use of a textured ray-like silver-foil background on front and a Reserve Collection underprint on back. Cards are numbered with an "HR" prefix. Average insertion rate was one per 11 packs.

	NM/M
Complete Set (221):	250.00
Common Player:	1.00
Reserve Collection Stars:	8X

Showcase

A silver metallic-foil background distinguishes the cards in this parallel set, inserted at a rate of about one per seven packs of both hobby and retail.

	NM/M
Complete Set (551):	200.00
Common Player:	.50
Showcase Stars:	3X

Showcase Artist's Proofs

This is a parallel of the Showcase parallel set covering all 551 cards of the base '97 Score set. The Artist's Proofs cards carry over the silver foil background of the Showcase cards on front with a rainbow-wave effect, and are marked with a round red "ARTIST'S PROOF" logo.

	NM/M
Common Player:	1.00
Showcase AP Stars:	10X

All-Star Fanfest

Highlighted with red foil and featuring participants in the 1996 All-Star Game, these inserts have a 1:29 seed in special retail boxes of Series 1 Score.

	NM/M
Complete Set (20):	15.00
Common Player:	.30
1 Frank Thomas	1.00
2 Jeff Bagwell	1.00
3 Chuck Knoblauch	.30
4 Ryne Sandberg	1.50
5 Alex Rodriguez	3.00
6 Chipper Jones	1.50
7 Jim Thome	.75
8 Ken Caminiti	.30
9 Albert Belle	.50
10 Tony Gwynn	1.50
11 Ken Griffey Jr.	2.00
12 Andruw Jones	1.00
13 Juan Gonzalez	.50
14 Brian Jordan	.30
15 Ivan Rodriguez	.75
16 Mike Piazza	2.00
17 Andy Pettitte	.30
18 John Smoltz	.30
19 John Wetteland	.30
20 Mark Wohlers	.30

Blast Masters

This set was inserted one per 35 Series 2 retail packs and every 23 hobby packs. The set displays the top power hitters in the game over a prismatic gold foil background. The word "Blast" is printed across the top, while "Master" is

---

printed across the bottom, both in red. Backs are predominantly black with a color player photo at center.

	NM/M
Complete Set (18):	17.50
Common Player:	.25
1 Mo Vaughn	.25
2 Mark McGwire	2.25
3 Juan Gonzalez	.75
4 Albert Belle	.25
5 Barry Bonds	3.00
6 Ken Griffey Jr.	2.00
7 Andruw Jones	1.25
8 Chipper Jones	1.50
9 Mike Piazza	2.00
10 Jeff Bagwell	1.25
11 Dante Bichette	.25
12 Alex Rodriguez	2.25
13 Gary Sheffield	.60
14 Ken Caminiti	.25
15 Sammy Sosa	1.50
16 Vladimir Guerrero	1.25
17 Brian Jordan	.25
18 Tim Salmon	.25

Heart of the Order

This 36-card set was distributed in Series 2 retail and hobby packs, with cards 1-18 in retail (one per 23 packs) and cards 19-36 in hobby (one per 15). The cards are printed in a horizontal format, with some of the top hitters in the game included in the insert. Fronts are highlighted in red metallic foil. Backs have a color portrait photo and a few words about the player.

	NM/M
Complete Set (36):	35.00
Complete Retail Set (1-18):	20.00
Complete Hobby Set (19-36):	15.00
Common Player:	.50
1 Ivan Rodriguez	1.00
2 Will Clark	.50
3 Juan Gonzalez	.75
4 Frank Thomas	1.25
5 Albert Belle	.50
6 Robin Ventura	.50
7 Alex Rodriguez	3.00
8 Ken Griffey Jr.	2.50
9 Jay Buhner	.50
10 Roberto Alomar	.65
11 Rafael Palmeiro	.50
12 Cal Ripken Jr.	4.00
13 Manny Ramirez	1.25
14 Matt Williams	.50
15 Jim Thome	.50
16 Derek Jeter	4.00
17 Wade Boggs	2.00
18 Bernie Williams	.50
19 Chipper Jones	2.00
20 Andruw Jones	1.25
21 Ryan Klesko	.50
22 Wilton Guerrero	.50
23 Mike Piazza	2.50
24 Raul Mondesi	.50
25 Tony Gwynn	2.00
26 Ken Caminiti	.50
27 Greg Vaughn	.50
28 Brian Jordan	.50
29 Ron Gant	.50
30 Dmitri Young	.50
31 Darin Erstad	.50
32 Jim Edmonds	.50
33 Tim Salmon	.50
34 Chuck Knoblauch	.50
35 Paul Molitor	1.25
36 Todd Walker	.50

Highlight Zone

Exclusive to 1997 Score Series 1 hobby packs are these Highlight Zone inserts, seeded one per every 35 packs. Within the 18-card set, card

---

numbers 1-9 are in regular hobby packs, while numbers 10-18 are found only in premium stock packs.

	NM/M
Complete Set (18):	30.00
Common Player:	.60
1 Frank Thomas	1.50
2 Ken Griffey Jr.	3.00
3 Mo Vaughn	.60
4 Albert Belle	.60
5 Mike Piazza	3.00
6 Barry Bonds	4.50
7 Greg Maddux	2.25
8 Sammy Sosa	2.25
9 Jeff Bagwell	1.50
10 Alex Rodriguez	3.50
11 Chipper Jones	2.50
12 Brady Anderson	.60
13 Ozzie Smith	2.25
14 Edgar Martinez	.60
15 Cal Ripken Jr.	4.50
16 Ryan Klesko	.60
17 Randy Johnson	1.50
18 Eddie Murray	1.50

Andruw Jones Goin' Yard

This special card was a blister-pack topper on Series 2 jumbo retail packs. Jones' home run swing is featured on front with a background of the distances of his blasts. Back has details on Series 2 inserts and the Stand and Deliver promotion.

	NM/M
Andruw Jones	2.50

Pitcher Perfect

Seattle Mariners' star pitcher and accomplished photographer Randy Johnson makes his picks for the top talent in this 1997 Score Series 1 insert set. Fronts have player photos with a gold-foil filmstrip graphic at bottom featuring player names and a portrait of The Big Unit. Backs have additional color photos in a filmstrip design and a few words about the player.

	NM/M
Complete Set (15):	6.50
Common Player:	.15
1 Cal Ripken Jr.	2.00
2 Alex Rodriguez	1.25
3 Cal Ripken Jr.,	
Alex Rodriguez	1.25
4 Edgar Martinez	.15
5 Ivan Rodriguez	.50
6 Mark McGwire	1.25
7 Tim Salmon	.15
8 Chili Davis	.15
9 Joe Carter	.15
10 Frank Thomas	.60
11 Will Clark	.15
12 Mo Vaughn	.15
13 Wade Boggs	.75
14 Ken Griffey Jr.	1.00
15 Randy Johnson	.60

Stand & Deliver

This 24-card insert was printed on a silver foil background, with the series name and team logo in gold foil across the bottom. Cards were found in Series 2 packs at the rate of one per 71 retail, one per 41 hobby. Card numbers 21-24 (Wild Card) were the winning group in a World Series contest, allowing the first 225 collectors that mailed in those four cards to receive a gold upgrade ver-

---

sion of the set framed in glass. The gold cards have a gold foil background and red foil highlights.

	NM/M
Complete Set (24):	50.00
Common Player:	.50
Gold:	4X
1 Andruw Jones	3.00
2 Greg Maddux	4.00
3 Chipper Jones	4.00
4 John Smoltz	1.50
5 Ken Griffey Jr.	5.00
6 Alex Rodriguez	6.00
7 Jay Buhner	.50
8 Randy Johnson	3.00
9 Derek Jeter	7.50
10 Andy Pettitte	.75
11 Bernie Williams	.50
12 Mariano Rivera	.50
13 Mike Piazza	5.00
14 Hideo Nomo	.50
15 Raul Mondesi	.50
16 Todd Hollandsworth	.50
17 Manny Ramirez	3.00
18 Jim Thome	2.00
19 David Justice	.50
20 Matt Williams	.50
21 Juan Gonzalez	1.50
22 Jeff Bagwell	3.00
23 Cal Ripken Jr.	7.50
24 Frank Thomas	3.00

Stellar Season

These 1997 Score Series 1 inserts were seeded one per every 17 magazine packs.

	NM/M
Complete Set (18):	15.00
Common Player:	.50
1 Juan Gonzalez	.75
2 Chuck Knoblauch	.50
3 Jeff Bagwell	1.50
4 John Smoltz	.50
5 Mark McGwire	3.00
6 Ken Griffey Jr.	2.50
7 Frank Thomas	1.50
8 Alex Rodriguez	3.00
9 Mike Piazza	2.50
10 Albert Belle	.50
11 Roberto Alomar	.60
12 Sammy Sosa	2.00
13 Mo Vaughn	.50
14 Brady Anderson	.50
15 Henry Rodriguez	.50
16 Eric Young	.50
17 Gary Sheffield	.75
18 Ryan Klesko	.50

The Franchise

There were two versions made for these 1997 Score Series 1 inserts - regular and The Glowing Franchise, which has glow-in-the-dark highlights. The regular version

---

is seeded one per 72 packs; glow-in-the-dark cards are seeded one per 240 packs. Each regular card can also be found in a promo version with a large, black "SAMPLE" on front and back.

	NM/M
Complete Set (9):	5.00
Common Player:	.15
Glowing:	2.5X
Samples:	2.5X
1 Ken Griffey Jr.	1.00
2 John Smoltz	.15
3 Cal Ripken Jr.	2.00
4 Chipper Jones	.75
5 Mike Piazza	1.00
6 Albert Belle	.15
7 Frank Thomas	.60
8 Sammy Sosa	.75
9 Roberto Alomar	.30

Titanic Taters

Some of the game's most powerful hitters are featured on these Series 1 inserts, found on average of one per 35 retail packs.

	NM/M
Complete Set (18):	25.00
Common Player:	.35
1 Mark McGwire	4.00
2 Mike Piazza	3.50
3 Ken Griffey Jr.	3.50
4 Juan Gonzalez	1.00
5 Frank Thomas	1.50
6 Albert Belle	.35
7 Sammy Sosa	2.50
8 Jeff Bagwell	1.50
9 Todd Hundley	.35
10 Ryan Klesko	.35
11 Brady Anderson	.35
12 Mo Vaughn	.35
13 Jay Buhner	.35
14 Chipper Jones	3.00
15 Barry Bonds	6.00
16 Gary Sheffield	.75
17 Alex Rodriguez	4.00
18 Cecil Fielder	.35

Team Collection

Team sets consisting of 15 players each were produced for 10 different teams. Each card is similar in design to the regular 1997 Score set except for a special foil stamping at the bottom of the card that corresponds with team colors. In a parallel "Platinum" version, seeded one per six packs, the background and team foil on front are replaced with silver prismatic foil. A top of the line parallel set, "Premier" utilizes gold foil highlights on fronts and is found one per 31 packs. Team Collection was sold in five-card, single-team packs with a suggested retail price of about $1.29. It was reported that 100 cases of each team were issued.

	NM/M
Complete Set (150):	30.00
Common Player:	.10
Platinums:	4X
Premiers:	15X
Braves Wax Box:	7.50
Orioles Wax Box:	6.00
Red Sox Wax Box:	6.00
White Sox Wax Box:	6.00
Indians Wax Box:	6.00
Rockies Wax Box:	5.00
Dodgers Wax Box:	6.00
Yankees Wax Box:	7.50
Mariners Wax Box:	7.50

	NM/M
Rangers Wax Box:	5.00
Atlanta Braves	5.00
1 Ryan Klesko	.10
2 David Justice	.10
3 Terry Pendleton	.10
4 Tom Glavine	.35
5 Javier Lopez	.10
6 John Smoltz	.10
7 Jermaine Dye	.10
8 Mark Lemke	.10
9 Fred McGriff	.10
10 Chipper Jones	1.50
11 Terrell Wade	.10
12 Greg Maddux	1.50
13 Mark Wohlers	.10
14 Marquis Grissom	.10
15 Andruw Jones	1.00
Baltimore Orioles	4.50
1 Rafael Palmeiro	.75
2 Eddie Murray	1.00
3 Roberto Alomar	.40
4 Rocky Coppinger	.10
5 Brady Anderson	.10
6 Bobby Bonilla	.10
7 Cal Ripken Jr.	2.50
8 Mike Mussina	.45
9 Nerio Rodriguez	.10
10 Randy Myers	.10
11 B.J. Surhoff	.10
12 Jeffrey Hammonds	.10
13 Chris Hoiles	.10
14 Jimmy Haynes	.10
15 David Wells	.10
Boston Red Sox	3.00
1 Wil Cordero	.10
2 Mo Vaughn	.10
3 John Valentin	.10
4 Reggie Jefferson	.10
5 Tom Gordon	.10
6 Mike Stanley	.10
7 Jose Canseco	.45
8 Roger Clemens	1.75
9 Darren Bragg	.10
10 Jeff Frye	.10
11 Jeff Suppan	.10
12 Mike Greenwell	.10
13 Arquimedez Pozo	.10
14 Tim Naehring	.10
15 Troy O'Leary	.10
Chicago White Sox	2.25
1 Frank Thomas	1.00
2 James Baldwin	.10
3 Danny Tartabull	.10
4 Jeff Darwin	.10
5 Harold Baines	.10
6 Roberto Hernandez	.10
7 Ray Durham	.10
8 Robin Ventura	.10
9 Wilson Alvarez	.10
10 Lyle Mouton	.10
11 Alex Fernandez	.10
12 Ron Karkovice	.10
13 Kevin Tapani	.10
14 Tony Phillips	.10
15 Mike Cameron	.10
Cleveland Indians	2.25
1 Albert Belle	.10
2 Jack McDowell	.10
3 Jim Thome	.75
4 Dennis Martinez	.10
5 Julio Franco	.10
6 Omar Vizquel	.10
7 Kenny Lofton	.10
8 Manny Ramirez	1.00
9 Sandy Alomar Jr.	.10
10 Charles Nagy	.10
11 Kevin Seitzer	.10
12 Mark Carreon	.10
13 Jeff Kent	.10
14 Danny Graves	.10
15 Brian Giles	.10
Colorado Rockies	1.75
1 Dante Bichette	.10
2 Kevin Ritz	.10
3 Walt Weiss	.10
4 Ellis Burks	.10
5 Jamey Wright	.10
6 Andres Galarraga	.10
7 Eric Young	.10
8 Larry Walker	.10
9 Vinny Castilla	.10
10 Quinton McCracken	.10
11 Armando Reynoso	.10
12 Jayhawk Owens	.10
13 Mark Thompson	.10
14 John Burke	.10
15 Bruce Ruffin	.10
Los Angeles Dodgers	4.00
1 Ismael Valdez	.10
2 Mike Piazza	2.00
3 Todd Hollandsworth	.10
4 Delino DeShields	.10
5 Chan Ho Park	.10
6 Roger Cedeno	.10
7 Raul Mondesi	.10
8 Darren Dreifort	.10
9 Jim Bruske	.10
10 Greg Gagne	.10
11 Chad Curtis	.10
12 Ramon Martinez	.10
13 Brett Butler	.10
14 Eric Karros	.10
15 Hideo Nomo	.50
New York Yankees	4.50
1 Bernie Williams	.10
2 Cecil Fielder	.10
3 Derek Jeter	2.50
4 Darryl Strawberry	.10

#	Player	Price
5	Andy Pettitte	.20
6	Ruben Rivera	.10
7	Mariano Rivera	.15
8	John Wetteland	.10
9	Paul O'Neill	.10
10	Wade Boggs	1.50
11	Dwight Gooden	.10
12	David Cone	.10
13	Tino Martinez	.10
14	Kenny Rogers	.10
15	Andy Fox	.10
Seattle Mariners		**5.00**
1	Chris Bosio	.10
2	Edgar Martinez	.10
3	Alex Rodriguez	2.25
4	Paul Sorrento	.10
5	Bob Wells	.10
6	Ken Griffey Jr.	2.00
7	Jay Buhner	.10
8	Dan Wilson	.10
9	Randy Johnson	1.00
10	Joey Cora	.10
11	Mark Whiten	.10
12	Rich Amaral	.10
13	Raul Ibanez	.10
14	Jamie Moyer	.10
15	Makoto Suzuki	.10
Texas Rangers		**2.25**
1	Mickey Tettleton	.10
2	Will Clark	.10
3	Ken Hill	.10
4	Rusty Greer	.10
5	Kevin Elster	.10
6	Darren Oliver	.10
7	Mark McLemore	.10
8	Roger Pavlik	.10
9	Dean Palmer	.10
10	Bobby Witt	.10
11	Juan Gonzalez	.50
12	Ivan Rodriguez	.75
13	Darryl Hamilton	.10
14	John Burkett	.10
15	Warren Newson	.10

Team Collection Platinum Team

Team sets consisting of 15 players each were produced for 10 different teams. Each card is similar in design to the regular 1997 Score set except for a special foil stamping at the bottom of the card that corresponds with team colors. In a parallel "Platinum" version, seeded one per six packs, the background and team foil on front are replaced with silver prismatic foil. Backs are overprinted in gold script, "Platinum Team." Team Collection was sold in five-card, single-team packs with a suggested retail price of about $1.29. It was reported that 100 cases of each team were issued.

	NM/M
Common Player:	2.00
Platinum Stars:	3X

Team Collection Premier Club

Team sets consisting of 15 players each were produced for 10 different teams. Each card is similar in design to the regular 1997 Score set except for a special foil stamp-

ing at the bottom of the card that corresponds with team colors. In a top of the line parallel "Premier Club" version, seeded one per 31 packs, the background and team foil on front are replaced with gold prismatic foil, and backs are overprinted "Premier Club" in gold script. Team Collection was sold in five-card, single-team packs with a suggested retail price of about $1.29. It was reported that 100 cases of each team were issued.

	NM/M
Common Player:	5.00
Premier Club Stars:	15X

1998 Score Samples

Half a dozen top stars were picked to introduce 1998 Score in this series of promo cards. Cards are virtually identical to the issued version except for the large black overprinted "SAMPLE" on back and the use of zeroes to replace 1997 stats.

		NM/M
Complete Set (6):		7.50
Common Player:		1.00
10	Alex Rodriguez	1.50
24	Mike Piazza	1.50
34	Ken Griffey Jr.	1.50
43	Cal Ripken Jr.	2.00
51	Chipper Jones	1.25
60	Carlos Delgado	1.00

1998 Score

The cards in the 270-card base set feature a color photo inside a black and white border. The player's name is printed in the left border. The entire base set is paralleled in the silver-foil Showcase Series (1:5). The Artist's Proof partial parallel gives a prismatic foil treatment to 165 base cards and was seeded 1:23. Inserts included All-Stars, Complete Players and Epix.

		NM/M
Complete Set (270):		12.00
Common Player:		.05
Showcases:		3X
Artist's Proofs:		6X
Pack (10):		.75
Wax Box (36):		15.00
All-Star Edition Box (36/10):		10.00
Jumbo Pack (20):		1.00
Jumbo Box (24):		15.00
1	Andruw Jones	.50
2	Dan Wilson	.05
3	Hideo Nomo	.30
4	Chuck Carr	.05
5	Jack McDowell	.05
6	Albert Belle	.05
7	Francisco Cordova	.05
8	Greg Maddux	.65
9	Alex Rodriguez	1.00
10	Steve Avery	.05
11	Chuck McElroy	.05
12	Larry Walker	.05
13	Hideki Irabu	.05
14	Roberto Alomar	.20
15	Neifi Perez	.05
16	Jim Thome	.40
17	Rickey Henderson	.50
18	Andres Galarraga	.05
19	Jeff Fassero	.05
20	Kevin Young	.05
21	Derek Jeter	1.50
22	Andy Benes	.05
23	Mike Piazza	.75
24	Todd Stottlemyre	.05
25	Michael Tucker	.05
26	Denny Neagle	.05
27	Javier Lopez	.05
28	Aaron Sele	.05
29	Ryan Klesko	.05
30	Dennis Eckersley	.40
31	Quinton McCracken	.05
32	Brian Anderson	.05
33	Ken Griffey Jr.	.75
34	Shawn Estes	.05

#	Player	Price
36	Tim Wakefield	.05
37	Jimmy Key	.05
38	Jeff Bagwell	.50
39	Edgardo Alfonzo	.05
40	Mike Cameron	.05
41	Mark McGwire	1.00
42	Tino Martinez	.05
43	Cal Ripken Jr.	1.50
44	Curtis Goodwin	.05
45	Bobby Ayala	.05
46	Sandy Alomar Jr.	.05
47	Bobby Jones	.05
48	Omar Vizquel	.05
49	Roger Clemens	.70
50	Tony Gwynn	.65
51	Chipper Jones	.75
52	Ron Coomer	.05
53	Dmitri Young	.05
54	Brian Giles	.05
55	Steve Finley	.05
56	David Cone	.05
57	Andy Pettitte	.20
58	Wilton Guerrero	.05
59	Deion Sanders	.05
60	Carlos Delgado	.30
61	Jason Giambi	.30
62	Ozzie Guillen	.05
63	Jay Bell	.05
64	Barry Larkin	.05
65	Sammy Sosa	.65
66	Bernie Williams	.05
67	Terry Steinbach	.05
68	Scott Rolen	.40
69	Melvin Nieves	.05
70	Craig Biggio	.05
71	Todd Greene	.05
72	Greg Gagne	.05
73	Shigetosi Hasegawa	.05
74	Mark McLemore	.05
75	Darren Bragg	.05
76	Brett Butler	.05
77	Ron Gant	.05
78	Mike Difelice	.05
79	Charles Nagy	.05
80	Scott Hatteberg	.05
81	Brady Anderson	.05
82	Jay Buhner	.05
83	Todd Hollandsworth	.05
84	Geronimo Berroa	.05
85	Jeff Suppan	.05
86	Pedro Martinez	.05
87	Roger Cedeno	.05
88	Ivan Rodriguez	.40
89	Jaime Navarro	.05
90	Chris Hoiles	.05
91	Nomar Garciaparra	.65
92	Rafael Palmeiro	.40
93	Darin Erstad	.15
94	Kenny Lofton	.05
95	Mike Timlin	.05
96	Chris Clemons	.05
97	Vinny Castilla	.05
98	Charlie Hayes	.05
99	Lyle Mouton	.05
100	Jason Dickson	.05
101	Justin Thompson	.05
102	Pat Kelly	.05
103	Chan Ho Park	.05
104	Ray Lankford	.05
105	Frank Thomas	.50
106	Jermaine Allensworth	.05
107	Doug Drabek	.05
108	Todd Hundley	.05
109	Carl Everett	.05
110	Edgar Martinez	.05
111	Robin Ventura	.05
112	John Wetteland	.05
113	Mariano Rivera	.10
114	Jose Rosado	.05
115	Ken Caminiti	.05
116	Paul O'Neill	.05
117	Tim Salmon	.05
118	Eduardo Perez	.05
119	Mike Jackson	.05
120	John Smoltz	.05
121	Brant Brown	.05
122	John Mabry	.05
123	Chuck Knoblauch	.05
124	Reggie Sanders	.05
125	Ken Hill	.05
126	Mike Mussina	.25
127	Chad Curtis	.05
128	Todd Worrell	.05
129	Chris Widger	.05
130	Damon Mashore	.05
131	Kevin Brown	.05
132	Bip Roberts	.05
133	Tim Naehring	.05
134	Dave Martinez	.05
135	Jeff Blauser	.05
136	David Justice	.05
137	Dave Hollins	.05
138	Pat Hentgen	.05
139	Darren Daulton	.05
140	Ramon Martinez	.05
141	Raul Casanova	.05
142	Tom Glavine	.30
143	J.T. Snow	.05
144	Tony Graffanino	.05
145	Randy Johnson	.50
146	Orlando Merced	.05
147	Jeff Juden	.05
148	Darryl Kile	.05
149	Ray Durham	.05
150	Alex Fernandez	.05
151	Joey Cora	.05
152	Royce Clayton	.05
153	Randy Myers	.05

#	Player	Price
154	Charles Johnson	.05
155	Alan Benes	.05
156	Mike Bordick	.05
157	Heathcliff Slocumb	.05
158	Roger Bailey	.05
159	Reggie Jefferson	.05
160	Ricky Bottalico	.05
161	Scott Erickson	.05
162	Matt Williams	.05
163	Robb Nen	.05
164	Matt Stairs	.05
165	Ismael Valdes	.05
166	Lee Stevens	.05
167	Gary DiSarcina	.05
168	Brad Radke	.05
169	Mike Lansing	.05
170	Armando Benitez	.05
171	Mike James	.05
172	Russ Davis	.05
173	Lance Johnson	.05
174	Joey Hamilton	.05
175	John Valentin	.05
176	David Segui	.05
177	David Wells	.05
178	Delino DeShields	.05
179	Eric Karros	.05
180	Jim Leyritz	.05
181	Raul Mondesi	.05
182	Travis Fryman	.05
183	Todd Zeile	.05
184	Brian Jordan	.05
185	Rey Ordonez	.05
186	Jim Edmonds	.05
187	Terrell Wade	.05
188	Marquis Grissom	.05
189	Chris Snopek	.05
190	Shane Reynolds	.05
191	Jeff Frye	.05
192	Paul Sorrento	.05
193	James Baldwin	.05
194	Brian McRae	.05
195	Fred McGriff	.05
196	Troy Percival	.05
197	Rich Amaral	.05
198	Juan Guzman	.05
199	Cecil Fielder	.05
200	Willie Blair	.05
201	Chili Davis	.05
202	Gary Gaetti	.05
203	B.J. Surhoff	.05
204	Steve Cooke	.05
205	Chuck Finley	.05
206	Jeff Kent	.05
207	Ben McDonald	.05
208	Jeffrey Hammonds	.05
209	Tom Goodwin	.05
210	Billy Ashley	.05
211	Wil Cordero	.05
212	Shawon Dunston	.05
213	Tony Phillips	.05
214	Jamie Moyer	.05
215	John Jaha	.05
216	Troy O'Leary	.05
217	Brad Ausmus	.05
218	Garret Anderson	.05
219	Wilson Alvarez	.05
220	Kent Mercker	.05
221	Wade Boggs	.65
222	Mark Wohlers	.05
223	Kevin Appier	.05
224	Tony Fernandez	.05
225	Ugueth Urbina	.05
226	Gregg Jefferies	.05
227	Mo Vaughn	.05
228	Arthur Rhodes	.05
229	Jorge Fabregas	.05
230	Mark Gardner	.05
231	Shane Mack	.05
232	Jorge Posada	.05
233	Jose Cruz Jr.	.30
234	Paul Konerko	.15
235	Derek Lee	.05
236	Steve Woodard **RC**	.15
237	Todd Dunwoody	.05
238	Fernando Tatis	.05
239	Jacob Cruz	.05
240	Pokey Reese **RC**	.25
241	Mark Kotsay	.05
242	Matt Morris	.05
243	Antone Williamson **RC**	.05
244	Ben Grieve	.05
245	Ryan McGuire	.05
246	Lou Collier **RC**	.05
247	Shannon Stewart	.05
248	Brett Tomko **RC**	.10
249	Bobby Estalella	.05
250	Livan Hernandez **RC**	.15
251	Todd Helton	.40
252	Jaret Wright	.05
253	Darryl Hamilton (Interleague Moments)	.05
254	Stan Javier (Interleague Moments)	.05
255	Glenallen Hill (Interleague Moments)	.05
256	Mark Gardner (Interleague Moments)	.05
257	Cal Ripken Jr. (Interleague Moments)	.75
258	Mike Mussina (Interleague Moments)	.15
259	Mike Piazza (Interleague Moments)	.45
260	Sammy Sosa (Interleague Moments)	.35
261	Todd Hundley (Interleague Moments)	.05

#	Player	Price
262	Eric Karros (Interleague Moments)	.05
263	Denny Neagle (Interleague Moments)	.05
264	Jeromy Burnitz (Interleague Moments)	.05
265	Greg Maddux (Interleague Moments)	.35
266	Tony Clark (Interleague Moments)	.05
267	Vladimir Guerrero (Interleague Moments)	.25
268	Checklist	.05
269	Checklist	.05
270	Checklist	.05

Artist's Proofs

This partial parallel reprinted 160 of the 270 cards in Score Baseball on a foil background with an Artist's Proof logo on the front. The cards were renumbered within the 160-card set and inserted one per 35 packs. Cards have a "PP" prefix to the number on back.

		NM/M
Complete Set (160):		125.00
Common Player:		.50
Inserted 1:35		
1	Andruw Jones	1.25
2	Dan Wilson	.50
3	Hideo Nomo	.75
4	Neifi Perez	.50
5	Jim Thome	1.00
6	Jeff Fassero	.50
7	Derek Jeter	4.00
8	Andy Benes	.50
9	Michael Tucker	.50
10	Ryan Klesko	.50
11	Dennis Eckersley	1.00
12	Jimmy Key	.50
13	Edgardo Alfonzo	.50
14	Mike Cameron	.50
15	Omar Vizquel	.50
16	Ron Coomer	.50
17	Dmitri Young	.50
18	Brian Giles	.50
19	Steve Finley	.50
20	Andy Pettitte	.75
21	Wilton Guerrero	.50
22	Deion Sanders	.50
23	Carlos Delgado	.50
24	Jason Giambi	.75
25	David Cone	.50
26	Jay Bell	.50
27	Sammy Sosa	2.00
28	Barry Larkin	.50
29	Scott Rolen	1.00
30	Todd Greene	.50
31	Bernie Williams	.50
32	Brett Butler	.50
33	Ron Gant	.50
34	Brady Anderson	.50
35	Craig Biggio	.50
36	Charles Nagy	.50
37	Jay Buhner	.50
38	Geronimo Berroa	.50
39	Jeff Suppan	.50
40	Rafael Palmeiro	1.00
41	Darin Erstad	.65
42	Mike Timlin	.50
43	Vinny Castilla	.50
44	Carl Everett	.50
45	Robin Ventura	.50
46	John Wetteland	.50
47	Paul O'Neill	.50
48	Tim Salmon	.50
49	Mike Jackson	.50
50	John Smoltz	.50
51	Brant Brown	.50
52	Reggie Sanders	.50
53	Ken Hill	.50
54	Todd Worrell	.50
55	Bip Roberts	.50
56	Tim Naehring	.50
57	Darren Daulton	.50
58	Ramon Martinez	.50
59	Raul Casanova	.50
60	J.T. Snow	.50
61	Jeff Juden	.50
62	Royce Clayton	.50
63	Charles Johnson	.50
64	Alan Benes	.50
65	Reggie Jefferson	.50
66	Ricky Bottalico	.50
67	Scott Erickson	.50

#	Player	Price
68	Matt Williams	.50
69	Robb Nen	.50
70	Matt Stairs	.50
71	Ismael Valdes	.50
72	Brad Radke	.50
73	Armando Benitez	.50
74	Russ Davis	.50
75	Lance Johnson	.50
76	Joey Hamilton	.50
77	John Valentin	.50
78	David Segui	.50
79	David Wells	.50
80	Eric Karros	.50
81	Raul Mondesi	.50
82	Travis Fryman	.50
83	Todd Zeile	.50
84	Brian Jordan	.50
85	Rey Ordonez	.50
86	Jim Edmonds	.50
87	Marquis Grissom	.50
88	Shane Reynolds	.50
89	Paul Sorrento	.50
90	Brian McRae	.50
91	Fred McGriff	.50
92	Troy Percival	.50
93	Juan Guzman	.50
94	Cecil Fielder	.50
95	Chili Davis	.50
96	B.J. Surhoff	.50
97	Chuck Finley	.50
98	Jeff Kent	.50
99	Ben McDonald	.50
100	Jeffrey Hammonds	.50
101	Tom Goodwin	.50
102	Wil Cordero	.50
103	Tony Phillips	.50
104	John Jaha	.50
105	Garret Anderson	.50
106	Wilson Alvarez	.50
107	Wade Boggs	2.00
108	Mark Wohlers	.50
109	Kevin Appier	.50
110	Mo Vaughn	.50
111	Ray Durham	.50
112	Alex Fernandez	.50
113	Barry Bonds	4.00
114	Albert Belle	.50
115	Greg Maddux	2.00
116	Alex Rodriguez	3.00
117	Larry Walker	.50
118	Roberto Alomar	.60
119	Andres Galarraga	.50
120	Mike Piazza	2.50
121	Denny Neagle	.50
122	Javier Lopez	.50
123	Ken Griffey Jr.	2.50
124	Shawn Estes	.50
125	Jeff Bagwell	1.25
126	Mark McGwire	3.00
127	Tino Martinez	.50
128	Cal Ripken Jr.	4.00
129	Sandy Alomar Jr.	.50
130	Bobby Jones	.50
131	Roger Clemens	2.25
132	Tony Gwynn	2.00
133	Chipper Jones	2.00
134	Orlando Merced	.50
135	Todd Stottlemyre	.50
136	Delino DeShields	.50
137	Pedro Martinez	1.25
138	Ivan Rodriguez	1.00
139	Nomar Garciaparra	2.00
140	Kenny Lofton	.50
141	Jason Dickson	.50
142	Justin Thompson	.50
143	Ray Lankford	.50
144	Frank Thomas	1.25
145	Todd Hundley	.50
146	Edgar Martinez	.50
147	Mariano Rivera	.50
148	Jose Rosado	.50
149	Ken Caminiti	.50
150	Chuck Knoblauch	.50
151	Mike Mussina	.65
152	Kevin Brown	.50
153	Jeff Blauser	.50
154	David Justice	.50
155	Pat Hentgen	.50
156	Tom Glavine	.65
157	Randy Johnson	1.25
158	Darryl Kile	.50
159	Joey Cora	.50
160	Randy Myers	.50

Showcase Series

This partial parallel reprinted 160 of the 270 cards in Score Baseball on silver foil. They were marked on the back and renumbered within the 160-card set. Showcase parallels were inserted one per seven packs. All Showcase Series cards except #1 have a "PP" prefix to the number.

	NM/M
Complete Set (160):	40.00
Common Player:	.25
Inserted 1:7	
1 Andruw Jones	.75
2 Dan Wilson	.25
3 Hideo Nomo	.40
4 Neifi Perez	.25
5 Jim Thome	.60
6 Jeff Fassero	.25
7 Derek Jeter	2.00
8 Andy Benes	.25
9 Michael Tucker	.25
10 Ryan Klesko	.25
11 Dennis Eckersley	.65
12 Jimmy Key	.25
13 Edgardo Alfonzo	.25
14 Mike Cameron	.25
15 Omar Vizquel	.25
16 Ron Coomer	.25
17 Dmitri Young	.25
18 Brian Giles	.25
19 Steve Finley	.25
20 Andy Pettitte	.40
21 Wilton Guerrero	.25
22 Deion Sanders	.25
23 Carlos Delgado	.50
24 Jason Giambi	.50
25 David Cone	.25
26 Jay Bell	.25
27 Sammy Sosa	1.00
28 Barry Larkin	.25
29 Scott Rolen	.60
30 Todd Greene	.25
31 Bernie Williams	.25
32 Brett Butler	.25
33 Ron Gant	.25
34 Brady Anderson	.25
35 Craig Biggio	.25
36 Charles Nagy	.25
37 Jay Buhner	.25
38 Geronimo Berroa	.25
39 Jeff Suppan	.25
40 Rafael Palmeiro	.65
41 Darin Erstad	.35
42 Mike Timlin	.25
43 Vinny Castilla	.25
44 Carl Everett	.25
45 Robin Ventura	.25
46 John Wetteland	.25
47 Paul O'Neill	.25
48 Tim Salmon	.25
49 Mike Jackson	.25
50 John Smoltz	.25
51 Brant Brown	.25
52 Reggie Sanders	.25
53 Ken Hill	.25
54 Todd Worrell	.25
55 Bip Roberts	.25
56 Tim Naehring	.25
57 Darren Daulton	.25
58 Ramon Martinez	.25
59 Raul Casanova	.25
60 J.T. Snow	.25
61 Jeff Juden	.25
62 Royce Clayton	.25
63 Charles Johnson	.25
64 Alan Benes	.25
65 Reggie Jefferson	.25
66 Ricky Bottalico	.25
67 Scott Erickson	.25
68 Matt Williams	.25
69 Robb Nen	.25
70 Matt Stairs	.25
71 Ismael Valdes	.25
72 Brad Radke	.25
73 Armando Benitez	.25
74 Russ Davis	.25
75 Lance Johnson	.25
76 Joey Hamilton	.25
77 John Valentin	.25
78 David Segui	.25
79 David Wells	.25
80 Eric Karros	.25
81 Raul Mondesi	.25
82 Travis Fryman	.25
83 Todd Zeile	.25
84 Brian Jordan	.25
85 Rey Ordonez	.25
86 Jim Edmonds	.25
87 Marquis Grissom	.25
88 Shane Reynolds	.25
89 Paul Sorrento	.25
90 Brian McRae	.25
91 Fred McGriff	.25
92 Troy Percival	.25
93 Juan Guzman	.25
94 Cecil Fielder	.25
95 Chili Davis	.25
96 B.J. Surhoff	.25
97 Chuck Finley	.25
98 Jeff Kent	.25
99 Ben McDonald	.25
100 Jeffrey Hammonds	.25
101 Tom Goodwin	.25
102 Wil Cordero	.25
103 Tony Phillips	.25
104 John Jaha	.25

105 Garret Anderson	.25
106 Wilson Alvarez	.25
107 Wade Boggs	1.00
108 Mark Wohlers	.25
109 Kevin Appier	.25
110 Mo Vaughn	.25
111 Ray Durham	.25
112 Alex Fernandez	.25
113 Barry Bonds	2.00
114 Albert Belle	.25
115 Greg Maddux	1.00
116 Alex Rodriguez	1.50
117 Larry Walker	.25
118 Roberto Alomar	.35
119 Andres Galarraga	.25
120 Mike Piazza	1.25
121 Denny Neagle	.25
122 Javier Lopez	.25
123 Ken Griffey Jr.	1.25
124 Shawn Estes	.25
125 Jeff Bagwell	.75
126 Mark McGwire	1.50
127 Tino Martinez	.25
128 Cal Ripken Jr.	2.00
129 Sandy Alomar Jr.	.25
130 Bobby Jones	.25
131 Roger Clemens	1.00
132 Tony Gwynn	1.00
133 Chipper Jones	1.00
134 Orlando Merced	.25
135 Todd Stottlemyre	.25
136 Delino DeShields	.25
137 Pedro Martinez	.75
138 Ivan Rodriguez	.65
139 Nomar Garciaparra	.75
140 Kenny Lofton	.25
141 Jason Dickson	.25
142 Justin Thompson	.25
143 Ray Lankford	.25
144 Frank Thomas	.75
145 Todd Hundley	.25
146 Edgar Martinez	.25
147 Mariano Rivera	.25
148 Jose Rosado	.25
149 Ken Caminiti	.25
150 Chuck Knoblauch	.25
151 Mike Mussina	.40
152 Kevin Brown	.25
153 Jeff Blauser	.25
154 David Justice	.25
155 Pat Hentgen	.25
156 Tom Glavine	.40
157 Randy Johnson	.75
158 Darryl Kile	.25
159 Joey Cora	.25
160 Randy Myers	.25

All Score Team

For its 10th anniversary Score selected an all-star team and issued this insert set. Cards have player action photos on a silver-foil background with an anniversary logo at bottom. Backs have a portrait photo and a career summary. The cards were inserted one per 35 packs.

	NM/M
Complete Set (20):	15.00
Common Player:	.25
Inserted 1:35	
1 Mike Piazza	1.50
2 Ivan Rodriguez	.65
3 Frank Thomas	.75
4 Mark McGwire	2.00
5 Ryne Sandberg	1.00
6 Roberto Alomar	.35
7 Cal Ripken Jr.	2.50
8 Barry Larkin	.75
9 Paul Molitor	.75
10 Travis Fryman	.25
11 Kirby Puckett	1.00
12 Tony Gwynn	1.00
13 Ken Griffey Jr.	1.50
14 Juan Gonzalez	.45
15 Barry Bonds	2.50
16 Andruw Jones	.75
17 Roger Clemens	1.25
18 Randy Johnson	.75
19 Greg Maddux	1.00
20 Dennis Eckersley	.65

All Score Team - Gold

The purpose for which this variation of the regular All Score Team insert was created will likely remain unknown. A small number

of the Gold version have turned up in the hobby market since Score's bankruptcy in mid-1998. This apprarently premium version differs from the issued silver version only in its use of gold metallic foil background on front.

	NM/M
Complete Set (20):	115.00
Common Player:	2.00
1 Mike Piazza	10.00
2 Ivan Rodriguez	5.00
3 Frank Thomas	6.00
4 Mark McGwire	12.00
5 Ryne Sandberg	7.50
6 Roberto Alomar	2.50
7 Cal Ripken Jr.	15.00
8 Barry Larkin	2.00
9 Paul Molitor	6.00
10 Travis Fryman	2.00
11 Kirby Puckett	7.50
12 Tony Gwynn	7.50
13 Ken Griffey Jr.	10.00
14 Juan Gonzalez	3.00
15 Barry Bonds	15.00
16 Andruw Jones	6.00
17 Roger Clemens	8.00
18 Randy Johnson	6.00
19 Greg Maddux	7.50
20 Dennis Eckersley	5.00

All Score Team Andruw Jones Autograph

This special version of Jones' All Score Team was a prize in a random hobby-shop drawing. Instead of the silver foil seen on regular All Score Team inserts, this version has a gold-foil background and an "AUTHENTIC SIGNATURE" notation at right-center. Only 500 of the cards were produced.

	NM/M
16 Andruw Jones	25.00

Complete Players

Complete Players is a 30-card insert featuring 10 players who can do it all. Each player had three cards displaying their variety of skills. The cards feature holographic foil highlights on fronts. Backs form a three-piece vertical picture of the player. The cards were inserted about one per 23 packs. Cards can be found with either gold or silver holographic foil. The gold version was found in packs of Score Team Collection at a 1:11 pack ratio. Because of these looser odds, the gold cards are valued lower than the silver.

	NM/M
Complete Set (30):	75.00
Common Player:	1.00
Inserted 1:23	
75 Percent	
1A-1C Ken Griffey Jr.	3.25
2A-2C Mark McGwire	3.75
3A-3C Derek Jeter	5.00
4A-4C Cal Ripken Jr.	5.00
5A-5C Mike Piazza	3.25
6A-6C Darin Erstad	1.00
7A-7C Frank Thomas	2.00
8A-8C Andruw Jones	2.00
9A-9C Nomar Garciaparra	3.00
10A-10C Manny Ramirez	2.00

Epix

Epix is a cross-brand insert, with 24 cards appearing in Score. The cards are printed on 20-point stock with holographic foil technology. The cards honor the top Play, Game, Season and Moment in a player's career and come in Orange, Purple and Emerald versions. Game cards were inserted 1:141, Plays 1:171, Seasons 1:437 and Moments 1:757.

	NM/M
Common Card:	.50
Purple:	2X
Emeralds:	3X
1 Ken Griffey Jr./P	2.50
2 Juan Gonzalez/P	.75
3 Jeff Bagwell/P	1.00
4 Ivan Rodriguez/P	1.00
5 Nomar Garciaparra/P	.75
6 Ryne Sandberg/P	1.50
7 Frank Thomas/G	1.25
8 Derek Jeter/G	3.50
9 Tony Gwynn/G	2.00
10 Albert Belle/G	.50
11 Scott Rolen/G	1.00
12 Barry Larkin/G	.50
13 Alex Rodriguez/S	6.00
14 Cal Ripken Jr./S	7.50
15 Chipper Jones/S	4.50
16 Roger Clemens/S	4.50
17 Mo Vaughn/S	1.50
18 Mark McGwire/S	6.00
19 Mike Piazza/M	8.00
20 Andruw Jones/M	4.00
21 Greg Maddux/M	6.00
22 Barry Bonds/M	12.00
23 Paul Molitor/M	4.00
24 Eddie Murray/M	4.00

First Pitch

These inserts were a 1:11 pack find in Score's All-Star edition. Fronts have portrait photos printed in the center of textured foil background of red and silver. The basic design is repeated on back, with career highlights and team logo instead of a photo.

	NM/M
Complete Set (20):	25.00
Common Player:	.50
Inserted 1:11 All-Star Edition.	
1 Ken Griffey Jr.	2.00
2 Frank Thomas	1.25
3 Alex Rodriguez	2.50
4 Cal Ripken Jr.	3.25
5 Chipper Jones	1.50
6 Juan Gonzalez	1.25
7 Derek Jeter	3.25
8 Mike Piazza	2.00
9 Andruw Jones	1.25
10 Nomar Garciaparra	1.50
11 Barry Bonds	1.50
12 Jeff Bagwell	1.25
13 Scott Rolen	1.00
14 Hideo Nomo	.75
15 Roger Clemens	1.75

16 Mark McGwire	2.50
17 Greg Maddux	1.50
18 Albert Belle	.50
19 Ivan Rodriguez	1.00
20 Mo Vaughn	.50

Andruw Jones Icon Order Card

This special card was the pack-topper on retail 27-card blister packs of 1998 Score. The front is identical to the regular Jones card in the set, but the back carries an ad for Pinnacle's Icon card display mail-in offer.

	NM/M
Andruw Jones	2.50

Loaded Lineup

This insert series was packaged on average of one card per 45 packs of Score's All-Star edition. Fronts have action photos printed on a copper and silver textured metallic-foil background. Backs have a portrait photo, career highlights, the Loaded Lineup batting order and stats for the player's best season. Cards have an "LL" prefix to their number.

	NM/M
Complete Set (10):	20.00
Common Player:	.50
Inserted 1:45 All-Star Edition.	
LL1 Chuck Knoblauch	.50
LL2 Tony Gwynn	2.25
LL3 Frank Thomas	1.50
LL4 Ken Griffey Jr.	3.00
LL5 Mike Piazza	3.00
LL6 Barry Bonds	4.50
LL7 Cal Ripken Jr.	4.50
LL8 Paul Molitor	1.50
LL9 Nomar Garciaparra	2.25
LL10 Greg Maddux	2.25

New Season

Found only in Score All-Star Edition, at an average rate of one per 23 packs, this insert series mixes veteran stars with hot young players. Fronts have a large portrait photo. Horizontal backs have an action photo.

	NM/M
Complete Set (15):	18.00
Common Player:	.50
Inserted 1:23 All-Star Edition.	
NS1 Kenny Lofton	.50
NS2 Nomar Garciaparra	2.00
NS3 Todd Helton	1.00
NS4 Miguel Tejada	.75
NS5 Jaret Wright	.75
NS6 Alex Rodriguez	3.00
NS7 Vladimir Guerrero	1.25
NS8 Ken Griffey Jr.	2.50
NS9 Ben Grieve	.75
NS10 Travis Lee	.50
NS11 Jose Cruz Jr.	.50
NS12 Paul Konerko	.75
NS13 Frank Thomas	1.50
NS14 Chipper Jones	2.00
NS15 Cal Ripken Jr.	4.00

1998 Score Rookie & Traded

Score Rookie/Traded consists of a 270-card base set. The base cards have a white and gray border with the player's name on the left. Cards are printed on a slightly glossier stock. Cards #1-50 were short-printed and inserted at a rate of one per pack. Ten-card packs carried an SRP of 99 cents. The Showcase Series parallels 110 base cards and was inserted 1:7. Artist's Proofs is a 50-card partial parallel done on prismatic foil and inserted 1:35. Inserts included All-Star Epix, Complete Players and Star Gazing.

	NM/M
Complete Set (270):	10.00
Common SP (1-50):	.10
Common Player (51-270):	.05
Artist's Proofs:	4X
Inserted 1:35	
Paul Konerko Auto. (500):	15.00
Pack (10):	.65
Wax Box (36):	15.00
Jumbo Pack (20):	1.50
Jumbo Box (24):	25.00
1 Tony Clark	.10
2 Juan Gonzalez	.35
3 Frank Thomas	.60
4 Greg Maddux	.75
5 Barry Larkin	.10
6 Derek Jeter	1.50
7 Randy Johnson	.60
8 Roger Clemens	.85
9 Tony Gwynn	.75
10 Barry Bonds	1.50
11 Jim Edmonds	.10
12 Bernie Williams	.10
13 Ken Griffey Jr.	1.00
14 Tim Salmon	.10
15 Mo Vaughn	.10
16 David Justice	.10
17 Jose Cruz Jr.	.10
18 Andruw Jones	.60
19 Sammy Sosa	.75
20 Jeff Bagwell	.60
21 Scott Rolen	.50
22 Darin Erstad	.30
23 Andy Pettitte	.35
24 Mike Mussina	.40
25 Mark McGwire	1.25
26 Hideo Nomo	.35
27 Chipper Jones	.75
28 Cal Ripken Jr.	1.50
29 Chuck Knoblauch	.10
30 Alex Rodriguez	1.25
31 Jim Thome	.50
32 Mike Piazza	1.00
33 Ivan Rodriguez	.50
34 Roberto Alomar	.40
35 Nomar Garciaparra	.75
36 Albert Belle	.10
37 Vladimir Guerrero	.60
38 Raul Mondesi	.10
39 Larry Walker	.10
40 Manny Ramirez	.60
41 Tino Martinez	.10
42 Craig Biggio	.10
43 Jay Buhner	.10
44 Kenny Lofton	.10
45 Pedro Martinez	.60
46 Edgar Martinez	.10
47 Gary Sheffield	.45
48 Jose Guillen	.10
49 Ken Caminiti	.10
50 Bobby Higginson	.10
51 Alan Benes	.05
52 Shawn Green	.15
53 Ron Coomer	.05
54 Charles Nagy	.05
55 Steve Karsay	.05
56 Matt Morris	.05
57 Bobby Jones	.05
58 Jason Kendall	.05
59 Jeff Conine	.05
60 Joe Girardi	.05
61 Mark Kotsay	.05
62 Eric Karros	.05
63 Bartolo Colon	.05
64 Mariano Rivera	.10
65 Alex Gonzalez	.05
66 Scott Spiezio	.05
67 Luis Castillo	.05

#	Player	Price
68	Joey Cora	.05
69	Mark McLemore	.05
70	Reggie Jefferson	.05
71	Lance Johnson	.05
72	Damian Jackson	.05
73	Jeff D'Amico	.05
74	David Ortiz	.30
75	J.T. Snow	.05
76	Todd Hundley	.05
77	Billy Wagner	.05
78	Vinny Castilla	.05
79	Ismael Valdes	.05
80	Neifi Perez	.05
81	Derek Bell	.05
82	Ryan Klesko	.05
83	Rey Ordonez	.05
84	Carlos Garcia	.05
85	Curt Schilling	.30
86	Robin Ventura	.05
87	Pat Hentgen	.05
88	Glendon Rusch	.05
89	Hideki Irabu	.05
90	Antone Williamson	.05
91	Denny Neagle	.05
92	Kevin Orie	.05
93	Reggie Sanders	.05
94	Brady Anderson	.05
95	Andy Benes	.05
96	John Valentin	.05
97	Bobby Bonilla	.05
98	Walt Weiss	.05
99	Robin Jennings	.05
100	Marty Cordova	.05
101	Brad Ausmus	.05
102	Brian Rose	.05
103	Calvin Maduro	.05
104	Raul Casanova	.05
105	Jeff King	.05
106	Sandy Alomar	.05
107	Tim Naehring	.05
108	Mike Cameron	.05
109	Omar Vizquel	.05
110	Brad Radke	.05
111	Jeff Fassero	.05
112	Deivi Cruz	.05
113	Dave Hollins	.05
114	Dean Palmer	.05
115	Esteban Loaiza	.05
116	Brian Giles	.05
117	Steve Finley	.05
118	Jose Canseco	.30
119	Al Martin	.05
120	Eric Young	.05
121	Curtis Goodwin	.05
122	Ellis Burks	.05
123	Mike Hampton	.05
124	Lou Collier	.05
125	John Olerud	.05
126	Ramon Martinez	.05
127	Todd Dunwoody	.05
128	Jermaine Allensworth	.05
129	Eduardo Perez	.05
130	Dante Bichette	.05
131	Edgar Renteria	.05
132	Bob Abreu	.10
133	Rondell White	.05
134	Michael Coleman	.05
135	Jason Giambi	.30
136	Brant Brown	.05
137	Michael Tucker	.05
138	Dave Nilsson	.05
139	Benito Santiago	.05
140	Ray Durham	.05
141	Jeff Kent	.05
142	Matt Stairs	.05
143	Kevin Young	.05
144	Eric Davis	.05
145	John Wetteland	.05
146	Esteban Yan	.05
147	Wilton Guerrero	.05
148	Moises Alou	.05
149	Edgardo Alfonzo	.05
150	Andy Ashby	.05
151	Todd Walker	.05
152	Jermaine Dye	.05
153	Brian Hunter	.05
154	Shawn Estes	.05
155	Bernard Gilkey	.05
156	Tony Womack	.05
157	John Smoltz	.05
158	Delino DeShields	.05
159	Jacob Cruz	.05
160	Javier Valentin	.05
161	Chris Hoiles	.05
162	Garret Anderson	.05
163	Dan Wilson	.05
164	Paul O'Neill	.05
165	Matt Williams	.05
166	Travis Fryman	.05
167	Javier Lopez	.05
168	Ray Lankford	.05
169	Bobby Estalella	.05
170	Henry Rodriguez	.05
171	Quinton McCracken	.05
172	Jaret Wright	.05
173	Darryl Kile	.05
174	Wade Boggs	.65
175	Orel Hershiser	.05
176	B.J. Surhoff	.05
177	Fernando Tatis	.05
178	Carlos Delgado	.30
179	Jorge Fabregas	.05
180	Tony Saunders	.05
181	Devon White	.05
182	Dmitri Young	.05
183	Ryan McGuire	.05
184	Mark Bellhorn	.05
185	Joe Carter	.05
186	Kevin Stocker	.05
187	Mike Lansing	.05
188	Jason Dickson	.05
189	Charles Johnson	.05
190	Will Clark	.05
191	Shannon Stewart	.05
192	Johnny Damon	.20
193	Todd Greene	.05
194	Carlos Baerga	.05
195	David Cone	.05
196	Pokey Reese	.05
197	Livan Hernandez	.05
198	Tom Glavine	.25
199	Geronimo Berroa	.05
200	Darryl Hamilton	.05
201	Terry Steinbach	.05
202	Robb Nen	.05
203	Ron Gant	.05
204	Rafael Palmeiro	.40
205	Rickey Henderson	.40
206	Justin Thompson	.05
207	Jeff Suppan	.05
208	Kevin Brown	.05
209	Jimmy Key	.05
210	Brian Jordan	.05
211	Aaron Sele	.05
212	Fred McGriff	.05
213	Jay Bell	.05
214	Andres Galarraga	.05
215	Mark Grace	.05
216	Brett Tomko	.05
217	Francisco Cordova	.05
218	Rusty Greer	.05
219	Bubba Trammell	.05
220	Derrek Lee	.35
221	Brian Anderson	.05
222	Mark Grudzielanek	.05
223	Marquis Grissom	.05
224	Gary DiSarcina	.05
225	Jim Leyritz	.05
226	Jeffrey Hammonds	.05
227	Karim Garcia	.05
228	Chan Ho Park	.05
229	Brooks Kieschnick	.05
230	Trey Beamon	.05
231	Kevin Appier	.05
232	Wally Joyner	.05
233	Richie Sexson	.05
234	Frank Catalanotto **RC**	.05
235	Rafael Medina	.05
236	Travis Lee	.05
237	Eli Marrero	.05
238	Carl Pavano	.05
239	Enrique Wilson	.05
240	Richard Hidalgo	.05
241	Todd Helton	.40
242	Ben Grieve	.05
243	Mario Valdez	.05
244	Magglio Ordonez **RC**	.75
245	Juan Encarnacion	.05
246	Russell Branyan	.05
247	Sean Casey	.10
248	Abraham Nunez	.05
249	Brad Fullmer	.05
250	Paul Konerko	.20
251	Miguel Tejada	.15
252	Mike Lowell **RC**	.50
253	Ken Griffey Jr. (Spring Training)	.35
254	Frank Thomas (Spring Training)	.25
255	Alex Rodriguez (Spring Training)	.45
256	Jose Cruz Jr. (Spring Training)	.20
257	Jeff Bagwell (Spring Training)	.30
258	Chipper Jones (Spring Training)	.30
259	Mo Vaughn (Spring Training)	.05
260	Nomar Garciaparra (Spring Training)	.30
261	Jim Thome (Spring Training)	.05
262	Derek Jeter (Spring Training)	.50
263	Mike Piazza (Spring Training)	.45
264	Tony Gwynn (Spring Training)	.30
265	Scott Rolen (Spring Training)	.15
266	Andruw Jones (Spring Training)	.20
267	Cal Ripken Jr. (Spring Training)	.50
268	Checklist (Ken Griffey Jr.)	.30
269	Checklist (Cal Ripken Jr.)	.45
270	Checklist (Jose Cruz Jr.)	.05

Artist's Proofs

This partial parallel reprints 160 (the same cards as the Showcase Series) of the 270 cards in Score Rookie & Traded. The cards are printed on a foil surface and feature an Artist's Proof logo on front. The cards were renumbered within the 160-card set and inserted one per 35 packs.

NM/M	
Common Player:	1.00
AP Stars:	4X

Artist's Proofs 1 of 1

Printed on primatic gold metallic foil background and featuring a gold "001/001 One of One" seal on front, these were random inserts in hobby packs. More than one "1/1" from this issue are known for some players, probably having been produced for use as replacements for damaged cards pulled from packs, then entering the hobby with the company's demise in mid-1998.

NM/M	
Common Player:	40.00

Showcase Series

The Showcase Series is a partial parallel reprint of 160 of the 270 cards in Rookie & Traded. The cards are printed on a silver-foil surface, marked on the back and renumbered (with an "RTPP" prefix) within the 160-card set. Showcase parallels were inserted one per seven packs.

#	Player	NM/M
	Complete Set (160):	10.00
	Common Player:	.15
1	Tony Clark	.15
2	Juan Gonzalez	.30
3	Frank Thomas	.60
4	Greg Maddux	.75
5	Barry Larkin	.25
6	Derek Jeter	1.50
7	Randy Johnson	.60
8	Roger Clemens	.85
9	Tony Gwynn	.75
10	Barry Bonds	1.50
11	Jim Edmonds	.15
12	Bernie Williams	.15
13	Ken Griffey Jr.	1.00
14	Tim Salmon	.15
15	Mo Vaughn	.15
16	David Justice	.15
17	Jose Cruz Jr.	.15
18	Andruw Jones	.60
19	Sammy Sosa	.75
20	Jeff Bagwell	.60
21	Scott Rolen	.50
22	Darin Erstad	.25
23	Andy Pettitte	.30
24	Mike Mussina	.30
25	Mark McGwire	1.25
26	Hideo Nomo	.30
27	Chipper Jones	.75
28	Cal Ripken Jr.	1.50
29	Chuck Knoblauch	.15
30	Alex Rodriguez	1.25
31	Jim Thome	.50
32	Mike Piazza	1.00
33	Ivan Rodriguez	.50
34	Roberto Alomar	.25
35	Nomar Garciaparra	1.00
36	Albert Belle	.15
37	Vladimir Guerrero	.60
38	Raul Mondesi	.15
39	Larry Walker	.15
40	Manny Ramirez	.60
41	Tino Martinez	.15
42	Craig Biggio	.15
43	Jay Buhner	.15
44	Kenny Lofton	.15
45	Pedro Martinez	.60
46	Edgar Martinez	.15
47	Gary Sheffield	.40
48	Jose Guillen	.15
49	Ken Caminiti	.15
50	Bobby Higginson	.15
51	Alan Benes	.15
52	Shawn Green	.35
53	Matt Morris	.15
54	Jason Kendall	.15
55	Mark Kotsay	.15
56	Bartolo Colon	.15
57	Damian Jackson	.15
58	David Ortiz	.35
59	J.T. Snow	.15
60	Todd Hundley	.15
61	Neifi Perez	.15
62	Ryan Klesko	.15
63	Robin Ventura	.15
64	Pat Hentgen	.15
65	Antone Williamson	.15
66	Kevin Orie	.15
67	Brady Anderson	.15
68	Bobby Bonilla	.15
69	Brian Rose	.15
70	Sandy Alomar Jr.	.15
71	Mike Cameron	.15
72	Omar Vizquel	.15
73	Steve Finley	.15
74	Jose Canseco	.15
75	Al Martin	.15
76	Eric Young	.15
77	Ellis Burks	.15
78	Todd Dunwoody	.15
79	Dante Bichette	.15
80	Edgar Renteria	.15
81	Bobby Abreu	.15
82	Rondell White	.15
83	Michael Coleman	.15
84	Jason Giambi	.50
85	Wilton Guerrero	.15
86	Moises Alou	.15
87	Todd Walker	.15
88	Shawn Estes	.15
89	John Smoltz	.15
90	Jacob Cruz	.15
91	Javier Valentin	.15
92	Garret Anderson	.15
93	Paul O'Neill	.15
94	Matt Williams	.15
95	Travis Fryman	.15
96	Javier Lopez	.15
97	Ray Lankford	.15
98	Bobby Estalella	.15
99	Jaret Wright	.15
100	Wade Boggs	.75
101	Fernando Tatis	.15
102	Carlos Delgado	.50
103	Joe Carter	.15
104	Jason Dickson	.15
105	Charles Johnson	.15
106	Will Clark	.15
107	Shannon Stewart	.15
108	Todd Greene	.15
109	Pokey Reese	.15
110	Livan Hernandez	.15
111	Tom Glavine	.35
112	Rafael Palmeiro	.50
113	Justin Thompson	.15
114	Jeff Suppan	.15
115	Kevin Brown	.15
116	Brian Jordan	.15
117	Fred McGriff	.15
118	Andres Galarraga	.15
119	Mark Grace	.15
120	Rusty Greer	.15
121	Bubba Trammell	.15
122	Derrek Lee	.40
123	Brian Anderson	.15
124	Karim Garcia	.15
125	Chan Ho Park	.15
126	Richie Sexson	.15
127	Frank Catalanotto	.15
128	Rafael Medina	.15
129	Travis Lee	.15
130	Eli Marrero	.15
131	Carl Pavano	.15
132	Enrique Wilson	.15
133	Richard Hidalgo	.15
134	Todd Helton	.40
135	Ben Grieve	.15
136	Mario Valdez	.15
137	Magglio Ordonez	.25
138	Juan Encarnacion	.15
139	Russell Branyan	.15
140	Sean Casey	.15
141	Abraham Nunez	.15
142	Brad Fullmer	.15
143	Paul Konerko	.25
144	Miguel Tejada	.30
145	Mike Lowell	.15
146	Ken Griffey Jr. (Spring Training)	.50
147	Frank Thomas (Spring Training)	.35
148	Alex Rodriguez (Spring Training)	.65
149	Jose Cruz Jr. (Spring Training)	.15
150	Jeff Bagwell (Spring Training)	.35
151	Chipper Jones (Spring Training)	.40
152	Mo Vaughn (Spring Training)	.15
153	Nomar Garciaparra (Spring Training)	.40
154	Jim Thome (Spring Training)	.30
155	Derek Jeter (Spring Training)	.75
156	Mike Piazza (Spring Training)	.50
157	Tony Gwynn (Spring Training)	.40
158	Scott Rolen (Spring Training)	.25
159	Andruw Jones (Spring Training)	.35
160	Cal Ripken Jr. (Spring Training)	.75

Complete Players

Complete Players is a 30-card insert seeded one per 11 packs. The set highlights 10 players who can do it all on the field. Each player has three cards showcasing one of their talents. The cards feature holographic foil stamping. Each card can also be found in a promo version with a large, black "SAMPLE" overprinted on front and back.

		NM/M
	Complete Set (30):	65.00
	Common Player:	1.00
	Inserted 1:11	
	Samples:	1X
1A-1C	Ken Griffey Jr.	3.50
2A-2C	Larry Walker	1.00
3A-3C	Alex Rodriguez	4.00
4A-4C	Jose Cruz Jr.	1.00
5A-5C	Jeff Bagwell	2.00
6A-6C	Greg Maddux	2.75
7A-7C	Ivan Rodriguez	1.75
8A-8C	Roger Clemens	3.00
9A-9C	Chipper Jones	2.75
10A-10C	Hideo Nomo	1.50

Epix All-Star Moment

All-Star Epix is a 1:61 insert. The cards honor the top All-Star Game moments of 12 star players. The dot matrix hologram cards were printed in orange, purple and emerald versions. This series was continued with cards numbered 13-24 in Pinnacle Plus.

	NM/M
Complete Set (12):	25.00
Common Player:	1.00

#	Player	Price
	Purples:	1.5X
	Emeralds:	2.5X
1	Ken Griffey Jr.	4.00
2	Juan Gonzalez	1.50
3	Jeff Bagwell	2.50
4	Ivan Rodriguez	2.00
5	Nomar Garciaparra	3.00
6	Ryne Sandberg	3.00
7	Frank Thomas	2.50
8	Derek Jeter	5.00
9	Tony Gwynn	3.00
10	Albert Belle	1.00
11	Scott Rolen	2.00
12	Barry Larkin	1.00

Star Gazing

Printed on micro-etched foil board, Star Gazing features 20 top players and was seeded 1:35.

#	Player	NM/M
	Complete Set (20):	12.00
	Common Player:	.25
	Inserted 1:35	
1	Ken Griffey Jr.	1.00
2	Frank Thomas	.60
3	Chipper Jones	.75
4	Mark McGwire	1.25
5	Cal Ripken Jr.	1.50
6	Mike Piazza	1.00
7	Nomar Garciaparra	.75
8	Derek Jeter	1.50
9	Juan Gonzalez	.35
10	Vladimir Guerrero	.60
11	Alex Rodriguez	1.25
12	Tony Gwynn	.75
13	Andruw Jones	.60
14	Scott Rolen	.40
15	Jose Cruz Jr.	.25
16	Mo Vaughn	.25
17	Bernie Williams	.25
18	Greg Maddux	.75
19	Tony Clark	.25
20	Ben Grieve	.25

1998 Score Team Collection

Team sets of 15 players each were produced for 10 different teams. Each card is similar in design to the regular 1998 Score set except for a special silver-foil team logo stamped at the bottom of the card. On back, this version has a "Team Collection" underprinted and each card is numbered "_ of 15." In a parallel "Platinum" version, seeded one per six packs, the front background is replaced with silver prismatic foil. A gold highlighted version of the three-card Complete Players inserts were found one per 11 packs. Team Collection was sold in five-card, single-team packs (32 per box).

#	Player	NM/M
	Complete Set (150):	25.00
	Common Player:	.10
	ANAHEIM ANGELS TEAM SET	2.00
1	Rickey Henderson	.60
2	Todd Greene	.10
3	Shigetoshi Hasegawa	.10
4	Darin Erstad	.20
5	Jason Dickson	.10
6	Tim Salmon	.10
7	Ken Hill	.10

8	Dave Hollins	.10
9	Gary DiSarcina	.10
10	Mike James	.10
11	Jim Edmonds	.10
12	Troy Percival	.10
13	Chuck Finley	.10
14	Tony Phillips	.10
15	Garret Anderson	.10

ATLANTA BRAVES TEAM SET 2.75

1	Andruw Jones	.60
2	Greg Maddux	.75
3	Michael Tucker	.10
4	Denny Naegle	.10
5	Javier Lopez	.10
6	Ryan Klesko	.10
7	Chipper Jones	.75
8	Kenny Lofton	.10
9	John Smoltz	.10
10	Jeff Blauser	.10
11	Tom Glavine	.30
12	Tony Graffanino	.10
13	Terrell Wade	.10
14	Fred McGriff	.10
15	Mark Wohlers	.10

BALTIMORE ORIOLES TEAM SET 3.25

1	Roberto Alomar	.20
2	Jimmy Key	.10
3	Cal Ripken Jr.	1.75
4	Brady Anderson	.10
5	Geronimo Berroa	.10
6	Chris Hoiles	.10
7	Rafael Palmeiro	.50
8	Mike Mussina	.30
9	Randy Myers	.10
10	Mike Bordick	.10
11	Scott Erickson	.10
12	Armando Benitez	.10
13	B.J. Surhoff	.10
14	Jeffrey Hammonds	.10
15	Arthur Rhodes	.10

BOSTON RED SOX TEAM SET 2.25

1	Steve Avery	.10
2	Aaron Sele	.10
3	Tim Wakefield	.10
4	Darren Bragg	.10
5	Scott Hatteberg	.10
6	Jeff Suppan	.10
7	Nomar Garciaparra	.75
8	Tim Naehring	.10
9	Reggie Jefferson	.10
10	John Valentin	.10
11	Jeff Frye	.10
12	Wil Cordero	.10
13	Troy O'Leary	.10
14	Mo Vaughn	.10
15	Shane Mack	.10

CHICAGO WHITE SOX TEAM SET 2.00

1	Albert Belle	.10
2	Chuck McElroy	.10
3	Mike Cameron	.10
4	Ozzie Guillen	.10
5	Jaime Navarro	.10
6	Chris Clemons	.10
7	Lyle Mouton	.10
8	Frank Thomas	.60
9	Doug Drabek	.10
10	Robin Ventura	.10
11	Dave Martinez	.10
12	Ray Durham	.10
13	Chris Snopek	.10
14	James Baldwin	.10
15	Jorge Fabregas	.10

CLEVELAND INDIANS TEAM SET 1.25

1	Jack McDowell	.10
2	Jim Thome	.50
3	Brian Anderson	.10
4	Sandy Alomar Jr.	.10
5	Omar Vizquel	.10
6	Brian Giles	.10
7	Charles Nagy	.10
8	Mike Jackson	.10
9	David Justice	.10
10	Jeff Juden	.10
11	Matt Williams	.10
12	Marquis Grissom	.10
13	Tony Fernandez	.10
14	Bartolo Colon	.10
15	Jaret Wright	.10

LOS ANGELES DODGERS TEAM SET 2.75

1	Hideo Nomo	.30
2	Mike Piazza	1.00
3	Wilton Guerrero	.10
4	Greg Gagne	.10
5	Brett Butler	.10
6	Todd Hollandsworth	.10
7	Roger Cedeno	.10
8	Chan Ho Park	.10
9	Todd Worrell	.10
10	Ramon Martinez	.10
11	Ismael Valdes	.10
12	Eric Karros	.10
13	Raul Mondesi	.10
14	Todd Zeile	.10
15	Billy Ashley	.10

NEW YORK YANKEES TEAM SET 3.25

1	Hideki Irabu	.10
2	Derek Jeter	1.75
3	Tino Martinez	.10
4	David Cone	.10
5	Andy Pettitte	.25
6	Bernie Williams	.10
7	Charlie Hayes	.10
8	Pat Kelly	.10

9	Mariano Rivera	.15
10	Paul O'Neill	.10
11	Chad Curtis	.10
12	David Wells	.10
13	Cecil Fielder	.10
14	Wade Boggs	.75
15	Jorge Posada	.10

SEATTLE MARINERS TEAM SET 3.25

1	Dan Wilson	.10
2	Alex Rodriguez	1.25
3	Jeff Fassero	.10
4	Ken Griffey Jr.	1.00
5	Bobby Ayala	.10
6	Jay Buhner	.10
7	Mike Timlin	.10
8	Edgar Martinez	.10
9	Randy Johnson	.60
10	Joey Cora	.10
11	Heathcliff Slocumb	.10
12	Russ Davis	.10
13	Paul Sorrento	.10
14	Rich Amaral	.10
15	Jamie Moyer	.10

ST. LOUIS CARDINALS TEAM SET 2.25

1	Andy Benes	.10
2	Todd Stottlemyre	.10
3	Dennis Eckersley	.45
4	Mark McGwire	1.25
5	Dmitri Young	.10
6	Ron Gant	.10
7	Mike Difelice	.10
8	Ray Lankford	.10
9	John Mabry	.10
10	Royce Clayton	.10
11	Alan Benes	.10
12	Delino DeShields	.10
13	Brian Jordan	.10
14	Gary Gaetti	.10
15	Matt Morris	.10

Platinum

Each of the Team Collection cards was also issued in a Platinum Team version, inserted on average of one card per six packs. The front has a background of star-studded refractive silver foil and a "PLATINUM TEAM" designation at the right edge of the photo. That designation is repeated on back as an underprint.

	NM/M
Common Player:	.50
Stars:	4X

Complete Players

(See 1998 Score Complete Players.)

1996-97 Score Board All Sport PPF

Stars and prospects, Past, Present and Future (PPF), in the four major team sports are featued in this two series set whose issue spanned late 1996 and early 1997. Borderless action photos and gold-foil graphic highlights are featured on front. Another photo, stats and personal data can be found on back. Only the baseball players from the 200-card set are listed here. A gold parallel edition was also issued.

LIVAN HERNANDEZ
FLORIDA • pitcher

	NM/M
Common Player:	.10
Gold:	2X
Wax Pack (6):	.65
Wax Box (18):	7.50
Wax Box (36):	15.00
21	Ryan Minor	.10
60	Rey Ordonez	.10
61	Todd Greene	.10
62	Jermaine Dye	.10
63	Karim Garcia	.10
64	Todd Walker	.10
65	Calvin Reese	.10
66	Roger Cedeno	.10
67	Ben Davis	.10
68	Chad Hermansen	.10
69	Vladimir Guerrero	.50
70	Billy Wagner	.10
94	Barry Bonds	.50
95	Vladimir Guerrero	.50
96	Livan Hernandez	.10
160	Barry Bonds	.50
161	Jay Payton	.10
162	Jose Cruz Jr.	.10
163	Richard Hidalgo	.10
164	Bartolo Colon	.10
165	Matt Drews	.10
166	Kerry Wood	.35
167	Ben Grieve	.10
168	Wes Helms	.10
169	Livan Hernandez	.10
196	Todd Walker	.10
197	Rey Ordonez	.10
198	Todd Greene	.10

Retro

Current and potential stars in the format of classic sports cards are featured in this Series 2 insert found at an announced rate of one per 35 packs. Only a single baseball player is included among the 10 cards in the set.

	NM/M
R10	Rey Ordonez	.50

Revivals

Current and potential stars in the format of classic sports cards are featured in this Series 1 insert found at an announced rate of one per 35 packs. Only a single baseball player is included among the 10 cards in the set.

	NM/M
REV10	Barry Bonds	1.00

1997 Score Board Mickey Mantle Shoe Box Collection

MICKEY MANTLE

Yet another collectors' issue of Mickey Mantle cards, the Score Board "Shoe Box Collection" offered packs containing two of the

75 Mantle cards or seven-card insert set, along with a genuine - usually a low-grade common - Topps card from 1951-69. Several designs of Mantle cards are featured in the set, including color photos as well as blue-and-white duotones. Five of the cards are printed with gold-foil backgrounds and die-cut. Cards #51-69 are short-printed at a ratio of about 1-to-3 with cards #1-50. Suggested retail price was $6.50 per pack.

		NM/M
Complete Set (75):		60.00
Common Card:		.75
1	Summary Of The Legend (Foil die-cut.)	3.00
1p	Summary of the Legend (Promo Card)	3.00
2	Triple Crown 1956	.75
3	MVP 1956	.75
4	MVP 1957	.75
5	MVP 1962	.75
6	Uniform #6 (Foil die-cut)	3.00
6p	Uniform #6 (Promo Card)	3.00
7	Uniform #7 (Foil die-cut)	3.00
7p	Uniform #7 (Promo Card)	3.00
8	Gold Glove Winner	.75
9	17-time All-Star	.75
10	4-time HR Champion	.75
11	World Series Records	.75
12	The Dirty Dozen (Post-Seasons)	.75
13	World Champion-1951	.75
14	World Champion-1952	.75
15	World Champion-1953	.75
16	World Champion-1956	.75
17	World Champion-1958	.75
18	World Champion-1961	.75
19	World Champion-1962	.75
20	Replacing A Legend	.75
21	Casey On Mantle	.75
22	Mickey & The Media	.75
23	Family Man	.75
24	Fan Favorite	.75
25	Playing Injured	.75
26	Clubhouse Leader	.75
27	Team Leader	.75
28	M & M Boys	.75
29	Legendary Friendships	.75
30	Time Out	.75
31	Mantle Is Born	.75
32	Mutt Mantle	.75
33	Growing Up	.75
34	5-tool player-Arm	.75
35	5-tool player-Defense	.75
36	5-tool player-Average	.75
37	5-tool player-Speed	.75
38	5-tool player-Power	.75
39	First Homer	.75
40	100th Homer	.75
41	200th Homer	.75
42	300th Homer	.75
43	400th Homer	.75
44	500th Homer	.75
45	536 Career Homers	.75
46	Yankee Stadium Blasts	.75
47	Switch-hit Home Runs	.75
48	565-ft. Home Run	.75
49	Signs 1st Pro Contract	.75
50	Mickey In The Minors	.75
51	1951 Trading Card	3.00
52	1952 Trading Card	3.00
53	1953 Trading Card	3.00
54	1954 Trading Card	3.00
55	1955 Trading Card	3.00
56A	1956 Trading Card	3.00
56B	1956 Trading Card	3.00
57	1957 Trading Card	3.00
58	1958 Trading Card	3.00
59	1959 Trading Card	3.00
60	1960 Trading Card	3.00
61	1961 Trading Card	3.00
62	1962 Trading Card	3.00
63	1963 Trading Card	3.00
64	1964 Trading Card	3.00
65	1965 Trading Card	3.00
66	1966 Trading Card	3.00
67	1967 Trading Card	3.00
68	1968 Trading Card	3.00
69	1969 Trading Card	3.00
70	Number Retired By Yankees (Foil die-cut.)	3.00
70p	Number Retired By Yankees (Promo Card)	3.00
71	Mickey Mantle Day/1965	.75
72	Mickey Mantle Day/1969	.75
73	Life After Baseball	.75
74	Hall Of Fame Induction (Foil die-cut.)	3.00
74p	Hall Of Fame Induction (Promo Card)	3.00

Mickey Mantle Shoe Box Inserts

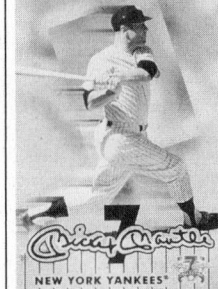

A set of seven insert cards, found on average of one per 16 packs, was part of the Mickey Mantle Shoe Box Collection. The inserts have a photo of Mantle on front, with blue metallic foil highlights. Contest rules on the back specify that the first seven persons to redeem a complete set of the seven insert cards will win a $7,000 Mantle phone card. All others redeeming the set of seven prior to July 7, 1998, received a $700 Mantle phone card. The #7 insert card was short-printed to limit the number of phone card winners.

	NM/M
Complete Set (7):	70.00
Common Card:	6.00
$700 Phone Card:	115.00
$7,000 Phone Card:	850.00
1	Mickey Mantle Insert #1	6.00
2	Mickey Mantle Insert #2	6.00
3	Mickey Mantle Insert #3	6.00
4	Mickey Mantle Insert #4	6.00
5	Mickey Mantle Insert #5	25.00
6	Mickey Mantle Insert #6	6.00
7	Mickey Mantle Insert #7 (Short-Print)	40.00

Players Club

JOSE CRUZ

Seven baseball players are among the cards in this multi-sport issue. Card fronts feature borderless action photos from which uniform logos have been removed. The player's name and the city in which he plays are in gold-foil in a baseball strip at bottom. Backs have another photo, biographical data and stats, including projected 1998 figures. Only the baseball players in the set are listed here.

		NM/M
Common Player:		.25
3	Barry Bonds	.50
7	Jose Cruz Jr.	.25
17	Matt Drews	.25
27	Wes Helms	.25
37	Richard Hidalgo	.25
48	Jay Payton	.25
69	Kerry Wood	.35

Players Club #1 Die-Cuts

Former #1 draft picks from all four major sports are included in this insert set. Highlighted in gold foil, cards are die-cut into the shape of a numeral 1. Backs have biographical information and stats. Cards are numbered with a "D" prefix. Only the baseball players are listed here. They were a 1:32 pack insert.

	NM/M
D10	Jose Cruz Jr.	1.00
D11	Barry Bonds	5.00

Talk N' Sports

Insert phone cards with talk time worth up to $1,000, along with trivia contests to win memorabilia were among the incentives to purchase this four-sport issue. The base card set features 50 stars and prospects, all of whom are also found, along with a few other superstars, in the inserts. Fronts of the base cards have action photos on which uniform logos have been airbrushed away. Backs have a couple more photos, some player bio and stats. Only the baseball players from the set are listed here.

		NM/M
Common Player:		.10
40	Barry Bonds	.50
41	Jay Payton	.10
42	Todd Walker	.10
43	Jose Cruz Jr.	.10
44	Kerry Wood	.30
45	Wes Helms	.10

Talk N' Sports Essentials

BARRY BONDS
ESSENTIALS

See-through plastic and action photos are combined on this 1:20 pack insert. Only a single baseball player is included among the four-sport stars and prospects.

	NM/M
E3	Barry Bonds	7.50

Visions Signings

JOSE CRUZ JR.

Stars and prospects from all four major team sports are included in this issue. Fronts have borderless action photos with professional logos removed as necessary to meet licensing regulations. Front graphics feature holographic foil highlights. Backs have another photo along with stats, personal data and career notes. Cards were sold in five-card packs, each of which contained either an autographed card or an insert card. Only the seven baseball players from the 50-card set are listed here.

		NM/M
Common Player:		.25
Gold Parallel:		2X
1	Barry Bonds	1.50
5	Jose Cruz Jr.	.25
6	Ben Grieve	.25
7	Kerry Wood	.75
44	Wes Helms	.25
45	Richard Hidalgo	.25
46	Jay Payton	.25

Visions Signings Autographs

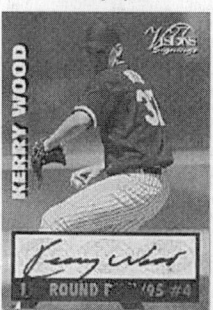

Each five-card pack of Score Board Vision Signings contained either an authentically autographed card or an insert card. Only the baseball players from the 63 autographed cards in the multi-sports set of stars and prospects are listed here. Barry Bonds autographs can be found on other companies' cards, with a Score Board authenticity seal.

		NM/M
9	Jose Cruz Jr.	2.00
20	Ben Grieve	2.00
21	Vladimir Guerrero	30.00
26	Wes Helms	2.00
27	Richard Hidalgo	2.00
34	Jason Kendall	2.00
44	Jay Payton	2.00
62	Paul Wilson	2.00
63	Kerry Wood	20.00
	Barry Bonds	45.00

Visions Signings Artistry

These specially printed cards were a one-in-six packs insert (regular version; 1:18 autographed) in five-card Visions Signings packs. Only a single baseball player is represented among the 20 cards in the set.

		NM/M
1	Jose Cruz Jr.	1.00
1	Jose Cruz Jr./Auto.	3.00

Autographed Collection

A handful of baseball players are among the four-sport stars and prospects in this set. Luring collectors was the presence of autographed cards at the rate of one per 4-1/2 packs, Blue Ribbon serially numbered autographs and memorabilia redemption cards (many of which became worthless when Score Board went bankrupt shortly after the set was issued). Because the cards

---

JOSE CRUZ JR.

are licensed only by the players, and not leagues, there are no uniform logos on the photos, nor mention of team names, only cities. Only the baseball players are listed here.

		NM/M
Common Player:		.25
3	J.D. Drew	1.50
11	Matt White	.25
12	Jay Payton	.25
23	Brandon Larson	.25
28	Jose Cruz Jr.	.25
49	Adrian Beltre	.50

Autographed Collection Strongbox

As part of a special $125 television offer, a parallel version of Score Board's Autographed Collection was offered featuring special inserts, autographs and memorabilia. The parallel cards are marked with an embossed "Strongbox" logo.

		NM/M
Common Player:		.25
3	J.D. Drew	2.00
11	Matt White	.50
12	Jay Payton	.50
23	Brandon Larson	.50
28	Jose Cruz Jr.	.50
49	Adrian Beltre	1.50

Autographed Collection Autographs

JAY PAYTON
1st Rounder

Authentically autographed cards were inserted in this issue at the rate of about four per 18-pack box. Cards have a round player photo at center with the signature in a white oval below. Backs have a congratulatory message. Only the baseball players among the four-sport stars and prospects are listed here. Cards are unnumbered.

	NM/M
Ben Grieve	2.00
Wes Helms	2.00
Jay Payton	2.00
Kerry Wood	20.00

Autographed Collection Blue Ribbon

These one-per-box inserts are similar in format to the autographed cards, but have a blue ribbon beneath the player photo on which the signature has been penned. Each card is individually serial numbered from within editions which vary from fewer than 100 to nearly 2,000. Only one baseball player was among the four-sport stars and prospects.

	NM/M
Jose Cruz Jr. /1,600	3.00

Autographed Collection Sports City USA

Players whose teams share a common city are featured in this insert series, found on average one per nine packs. A parallel version, embossed "Strongbox" was issued in special $125 television-offer packages of Autographed Collection. The parallels are individually serial numbered to 600. Only cards with baseball players are listed here.

		NM/M
Common Card:		1.00
Embossed:		2X
		NM/M
SC3	Richard Hidalgo (Olajuwan, Drexler)	1.00
SC4	Kerry Wood (Pippen, Autry)	2.50
SC6	Adrian Beltre (Bryant)	1.50
SC7	J.D. Drew (Thomas, Staley)	2.50
SC12	Wes Helms (Hanspard, Gray)	1.00
SC14	Jay Payton (Barber, Van Horn)	1.00
SC15	Matt Drews (Westbrook, Pollard)	1.00

1981 Seattle Mariners Police

FLOYD BANNISTER Pitcher
Seattle Mariners

These 2-5/8" x 4-1/8" cards were co-sponsored by the Washington State Crime Prevention Assoc., Coca-Cola, Kiwanis and Ernst Home Centers. Fronts have a color photo, player name and position and a team logo. Card backs are printed in blue and red and offer a "Tip from the Mariners" along with the four sponsor logos.

		NM/M
Complete Set (16):		3.00
Common Player:		.25
1	Jeff Burroughs	.25
2	Floyd Bannister	.25
3	Glenn Abbott	.25
4	Jim Anderson	.25
5	Danny Meyer	.25
6	Dave Edler	.25
7	Julio Cruz	.25
8	Kenny Clay	.25
9	Lenny Randle	.25
10	Mike Parrott	.25
11	Tom Paciorek	.25
12	Jerry Narron	.25
13	Richie Zisk	.25
14	Maury Wills	.50
15	Joe Simpson	.25
16	Shane Rawley	.25

1993 Select Promos

MITCH WILLIAMS

Zeroes in the career stats line on the back of the card distinguish the promo cards for Score's premiere issue of its Select brand name. The promo cards were distributed to introduce dealers and collectors to the new mid-range set.

		NM/M
Complete Set (8):		12.00
Common Player:		1.00
22	Robin Yount	3.00
24	Don Mattingly	5.00
26	Sandy Alomar Jr.	1.00
41	Gary Sheffield	2.00
56	Brady Anderson	1.00
65	Rob Dibble	1.00
75	John Smiley	1.00
79	Mitch Williams	1.00

1993 Select Dufex Proofs

DAVE FLEMING P

To test the Dufex textured foil printing technology which was used on its Stars, Rookies and Triple Crown insert sets, Select produced a very limited number of blank-back proof cards.

Select Rookies:	15X
Select Stars:	20X
Select Triple Crown:	20X

1993 Select

TIM RAINES

This 400-card set from Score is designed for the mid-priced card market. The card fronts feature green borders on two sides of the card with the photo filling the remaining portion of the card front. The backs feature an additional photo, player information and statistics. Cards numbered 271-360 are devoted to rookies and draft picks.

		NM/M
Complete Set (405):		15.00
Common Player:		.05
Wax Box (36):		22.50
1	Barry Bonds	1.50
2	Ken Griffey Jr.	1.00
3	Will Clark	.50
4	Kirby Puckett	.75
5	Tony Gwynn	.75
6	Frank Thomas	.65

7	Tom Glavine	.35
8	Roberto Alomar	.25
9	Andre Dawson	.25
10	Ron Darling	.05
11	Bobby Bonilla	.05
12	Danny Tartabull	.05
13	Darren Daulton	.05
14	Roger Clemens	.75
15	Ozzie Smith	.75
16	Mark McGwire	1.25
17	Terry Pendleton	.05
18	Cal Ripken, Jr.	1.50
19	Fred McGriff	.05
20	Cecil Fielder	.05
21	Darryl Strawberry	.05
22	Robin Yount	.65
23	Barry Larkin	.05
24	Don Mattingly	.85
25	Craig Biggio	.05
26	Sandy Alomar Jr.	.05
27	Larry Walker	.05
28	Junior Felix	.05
29	Eddie Murray	.65
30	Robin Ventura	.05
31	Greg Maddux	.75
32	Dave Winfield	.65
33	John Kruk	.05
34	Wally Joyner	.05
35	Andy Van Slyke	.05
36	Chuck Knoblauch	.05
37	Tom Pagnozzi	.05
38	Dennis Eckersley	.60
39	Dave Justice	.05
40	Juan Gonzalez	.35
41	Gary Sheffield	.40
42	Paul Molitor	.65
43	Delino DeShields	.05
44	Travis Fryman	.05
45	Hal Morris	.05
46	Gregg Olson	.05
47	Ken Caminiti	.05
48	Wade Boggs	.75
49	Orel Hershiser	.05
50	Albert Belle	.05
51	Bill Swift	.05
52	Mark Langston	.05
53	Joe Girardi	.05
54	Keith Miller	.05
55	Gary Carter	.65
56	Brady Anderson	.05
57	Dwight Gooden	.05
58	Julio Franco	.05
59	Len Dykstra	.05
60	Mickey Tettleton	.05
61	Randy Tomlin	.05
62	B.J. Surhoff	.05
63	Todd Zeile	.05
64	Roberto Kelly	.05
65	Rob Dibble	.05
66	Leo Gomez	.05
67	Doug Jones	.05
68	Ellis Burks	.05
69	Mike Scioscia	.05
70	Charles Nagy	.05
71	Cory Snyder	.05
72	Devon White	.05
73	Mark Grace	.05
74	Luis Polonia	.05
75	John Smiley	.05
76	Carlton Fisk	.65
77	Luis Sojo	.05
78	George Brett	.85
79	Mitch Williams	.05
80	Kent Hrbek	.05
81	Jay Bell	.05
82	Edgar Martinez	.05
83	Lee Smith	.05
84	Deion Sanders	.25
85	Bill Gullickson	.05
86	Paul O'Neill	.05
87	Kevin Seitzer	.05
88	Steve Finley	.05
89	Mel Hall	.05
90	Nolan Ryan	1.50
91	Eric Davis	.05
92	Mike Mussina	.35
93	Tony Fernandez	.05
94	Frank Viola	.05
95	Matt Williams	.05
96	Joe Carter	.05
97	Ryne Sandberg	.75
98	Jim Abbott	.05
99	Marquis Grissom	.05
100	George Bell	.05
101	Howard Johnson	.05
102	Kevin Appier	.05
103	Dale Murphy	.20
104	Shane Mack	.05
105	Jose Lind	.05
106	Rickey Henderson	.65
107	Bob Tewksbury	.05
108	Kevin Mitchell	.05
109	Steve Avery	.05
110	Candy Maldonado	.05
111	Bip Roberts	.05
112	Lou Whitaker	.05
113	Jeff Bagwell	.65
114	Dante Bichette	.05
115	Brett Butler	.05
116	Melido Perez	.05
117	Andy Benes	.05
118	Randy Johnson	.65
119	Willie McGee	.05
120	Jody Reed	.05
121	Shawon Dunston	.05
122	Carlos Baerga	.05
123	Bret Saberhagen	.05
124	John Olerud	.05

125	Ivan Calderon	.05
126	Bryan Harvey	.05
127	Terry Mulholland	.05
128	Ozzie Guillen	.05
129	Steve Buechele	.05
130	Kevin Tapani	.05
131	Felix Jose	.05
132	Terry Steinbach	.05
133	Ron Gant	.05
134	Harold Reynolds	.05
135	Chris Sabo	.05
136	Ivan Rodriguez	.60
137	Eric Anthony	.05
138	Mike Henneman	.05
139	Robby Thompson	.05
140	Scott Fletcher	.05
141	Bruce Hurst	.05
142	Kevin Maas	.05
143	Tom Candiotti	.05
144	Chris Hoiles	.05
145	Mike Morgan	.05
146	Mark Whiten	.05
147	Dennis Martinez	.05
148	Tony Pena	.05
149	Dave Magadan	.05
150	Mark Lewis	.05
151	Mariano Duncan	.05
152	Gregg Jefferies	.05
153	Doug Drabek	.05
154	Brian Harper	.05
155	Ray Lankford	.05
156	Carney Lansford	.05
157	Mike Sharperson	.05
158	Jack Morris	.05
159	Otis Nixon	.05
160	Steve Sax	.05
161	Mark Lemke	.05
162	Rafael Palmeiro	.60
163	Jose Rijo	.05
164	Omar Vizquel	.05
165	Sammy Sosa	.75
166	Milt Cuyler	.05
167	John Franco	.05
168	Darryl Hamilton	.05
169	Ken Hill	.05
170	Mike Devereaux	.05
171	Don Slaught	.05
172	Steve Farr	.05
173	Bernard Gilkey	.05
174	Mike Fetters	.05
175	Vince Coleman	.05
176	Kevin McReynolds	.05
177	John Smoltz	.05
178	Greg Gagne	.05
179	Greg Swindell	.05
180	Juan Guzman	.05
181	Kal Daniels	.05
182	Rick Sutcliffe	.05
183	Orlando Merced	.05
184	Bill Wegman	.05
185	Mark Gardner	.05
186	Rob Deer	.05
187	Dave Hollins	.05
188	Jack Clark	.05
189	Brian Hunter	.05
190	Tim Wallach	.05
191	Tim Belcher	.05
192	Walt Weiss	.05
193	Kurt Stillwell	.05
194	Charlie Hayes	.05
195	Willie Randolph	.05
196	Jack McDowell	.05
197	Jose Offerman	.05
198	Chuck Finley	.05
199	Darrin Jackson	.05
200	Kelly Gruber	.05
201	John Wetteland	.05
202	Jay Buhner	.05
203	Mike LaValliere	.05
204	Kevin Brown	.05
205	Luis Gonzalez	.05
206	Rick Aguilera	.05
207	Norm Charlton	.05
208	Mike Bordick	.05
209	Charlie Leibrandt	.05
210	Tom Brunansky	.05
211	Tom Henke	.05
212	Randy Milligan	.05
213	Ramon Martinez	.05
214	Mo Vaughn	.05
215	Randy Myers	.05
216	Greg Hibbard	.05
217	Wes Chamberlain	.05
218	Tony Phillips	.05
219	Pete Harnisch	.05
220	Mike Gallego	.05
221	Bud Black	.05
222	Greg Vaughn	.05
223	Milt Thompson	.05
224	Ben McDonald	.05
225	Billy Hatcher	.05
226	Paul Sorrento	.05
227	Mark Gubicza	.05
228	Mike Greenwell	.05
229	Curt Schilling	.35
230	Alan Trammell	.05
231	Zane Smith	.05
232	Bobby Thigpen	.05
233	Joe Grahe	.05
234	Joe Orsulak	.05
235	Joe Oliver	.05
236	Tim Raines	.05
237	Juan Samuel	.05
238	Chili Davis	.05
239	Spike Owen	.05
240	Dave Stewart	.05
241	Jim Eisenreich	.05
242	Phil Plantier	.05

243	Sid Fernandez	.05
244	Dan Gladden	.05
245	Mickey Morandini	.05
246	Tino Martinez	.05
247	Kirt Manwaring	.05
248	Dean Palmer	.05
249	Tom Browning	.05
250	Brian McRae	.05
251	Scott Leius	.05
252	Bert Blyleven	.05
253	Scott Erickson	.05
254	Bob Welch	.05
255	Pat Kelly	.05
256	Felix Fermin	.05
257	Harold Baines	.05
258	Duane Ward	.05
259	Bill Spiers	.05
260	Jaime Navarro	.05
261	Scott Sanderson	.05
262	Gary Gaetti	.05
263	Bob Ojeda	.05
264	Jeff Montgomery	.05
265	Scott Bankhead	.05
266	Lance Johnson	.05
267	Rafael Belliard	.05
268	Kevin Reimer	.05
269	Benito Santiago	.05
270	Mike Moore	.05
271	Dave Fleming	.05
272	Moises Alou	.05
273	Pat Listach	.05
274	Reggie Sanders	.05
275	Kenny Lofton	.05
276	Donovan Osborne	.05
277	Rusty Meacham	.05
278	Eric Karros	.05
279	Andy Stankiewicz	.05
280	Brian Jordan	.05
281	Gary DiSarcina	.05
282	Mark Wohlers	.05
283	Dave Nilsson	.05
284	Anthony Young	.05
285	Jim Bullinger	.05
286	Derek Bell	.05
287	Brian Williams	.05
288	Julio Valera	.05
289	Dan Walters	.05
290	Chad Curtis	.05
291	Michael Tucker	.05
292	Bob Zupcic	.05
293	Todd Hundley	.05
294	Jeff Tackett	.05
295	Greg Colbrunn	.05
296	Cal Eldred	.05
297	Chris Roberts	.05
298	John Doherty	.05
299	Denny Neagle	.05
300	Arthur Rhodes	.05
301	Mark Clark	.05
302	Scott Cooper	.05
303	Jamie Arnold RC	.05
304	Jim Thome	.60
305	Frank Seminara	.05
306	Kurt Knudsen	.05
307	Tim Wakefield	.05
308	John Jaha	.05
309	Pat Hentgen	.05
310	B.J. Wallace	.05
311	Roberto Hernandez	.05
312	Hipolito Pichardo	.05
313	Eric Fox	.05
314	Willie Banks	.05
315	Sam Militello	.05
316	Vince Horsman	.05
317	Carlos Hernandez	.05
318	Jeff Kent	.05
319	Mike Perez	.05
320	Scott Livingstone	.05
321	Jeff Conine	.05
322	James Austin	.05
323	John Vander Wal	.05
324	Pat Mahomes	.05
325	Pedro Astacio	.05
326	Bret Boone	.05
327	Matt Stairs	.05
328	Damion Easley	.05
329	Ben Rivera	.05
330	Reggie Jefferson	.05
331	Luis Mercedes	.05
332	Kyle Abbott	.05
333	Eddie Taubensee	.05
334	Tim McIntosh	.05
335	Phil Clark	.05
336	Wil Cordero	.05
337	Russ Springer	.05
338	Craig Colbert	.05
339	Tim Salmon	.05
340	Braulio Castillo	.05
341	Donald Harris	.05
342	Eric Young	.05
343	Bob Wickman	.05
344	John Valentin	.05
345	Dan Wilson	.05
346	Steve Hosey	.05
347	Mike Piazza	1.00
348	Willie Greene	.05
349	Tom Goodwin	.05
350	Eric Hillman	.05
351	Steve Reed RC	.05
352	Dan Serafini RC	.05
353	Todd Steverson RC	.05
354	Benji Grigsby	.05
355	Shannon Stewart RC	1.00
356	Sean Lowe	.05
357	Derek Wallace	.05
358	Rick Helling	.05
359	Jason Kendall RC	1.00
360	Derek Jeter RC	10.00

361	David Cone	.05
362	Jeff Reardon	.05
363	Bobby Witt	.05
364	Jose Canseco	.40
365	Jeff Russell	.05
366	Ruben Sierra	.05
367	Alan Mills	.05
368	Matt Nokes	.05
369	Pat Borders	.05
370	Pedro Munoz	.05
371	Danny Jackson	.05
372	Geronimo Pena	.05
373	Craig Lefferts	.05
374	Joe Grahe	.05
375	Roger McDowell	.05
376	Jimmy Key	.05
377	Steve Olin	.05
378	Glenn Davis	.05
379	Rene Gonzales	.05
380	Manuel Lee	.05
381	Ron Karkovice	.05
382	Sid Bream	.05
383	Gerald Williams	.05
384	Lenny Harris	.05
385	J.T. Snow RC	.75
386	Dave Stieb	.05
387	Kirk McCaskill	.05
388	Lance Parrish	.05
389	Craig Greback	.05
390	Rick Wilkins	.05
391	Manny Alexander	.05
392	Mike Schooler	.05
393	Bernie Williams	.05
394	Kevin Koslofski	.05
395	Willie Wilson	.05
396	Jeff Parrett	.05
397	Mike Harkey	.05
398	Frank Tanana	.05
399	Doug Henry	.05
400	Royce Clayton	.05
401	Eric Wedge	.05
402	Derrick May	.05
403	Carlos Garcia	.05
404	Henry Rodriguez	.05
405	Ryan Klesko	.05

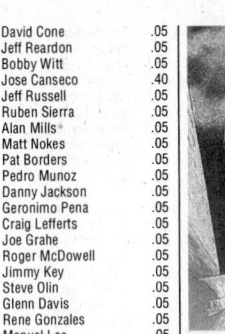

JEFF CONINE 1B-OF

2	Moises Alou	.50
3	Reggie Sanders	.50
4	Kenny Lofton	.50
5	Eric Karros	.50
6	Brian Williams	.50
7	Donovan Osborne	.50
8	Sam Militello	.50
9	Chad Curtis	.50
10	Bob Zupcic	.50
11	Tim Salmon	1.50
12	Jeff Conine	.50
13	Pedro Astacio	.50
14	Arthur Rhodes	.50
15	Cal Eldred	.50
16	Tim Wakefield	.50
17	Andy Stankiewicz	.50
18	Wil Cordero	.50
19	Todd Hundley	.50
20	Dave Fleming	.50
21	Bret Boone	1.00

Stars

FRED McGRIFF

The top 24 players from 1992 are featured in this insert set. Cards were randomly inserted in 15-card retail packs. Fronts are printed on metallic foil.

		NM/M
Complete Set (24):		40.00
Common Player:		.60
1	Fred McGriff	.60
2	Ryne Sandberg	4.00
3	Ozzie Smith	4.00
4	Gary Sheffield	1.25
5	Darren Daulton	.60
6	Andy Van Slyke	.60
7	Barry Bonds	7.50
8	Tony Gwynn	4.00
9	Greg Maddux	4.00
10	Tom Glavine	1.00
11	John Franco	.60
12	Lee Smith	.60
13	Cecil Fielder	.60
14	Roberto Alomar	1.00
15	Cal Ripken, Jr.	7.50
16	Edgar Martinez	.60
17	Ivan Rodriguez	2.50
18	Kirby Puckett	4.00
19	Ken Griffey Jr.	6.00
20	Joe Carter	.60
21	Roger Clemens	.60
22	Dave Fleming	.60
(22)	Dave Fleming (Blank-back sample card.)	1.00
23	Paul Molitor	3.00
(23)	Paul Molitor (Blank-back sample card.)	2.75
24	Dennis Eckersley	2.50

Stat Leaders

GARY SHEFFIELD
SLUGGING %

Aces

Cards from this set feature 24 of the top pitchers from 1992 and were included one per every 27-card Super Pack. The fronts have a picture of the player in action against an Ace card background. Backs have text and a portrait in the middle of a card suit for an Ace.

		NM/M
Complete Set (24):		20.00
Common Player:		1.00
1	Roger Clemens	6.00
2	Tom Glavine	3.00
3	Jack McDowell	1.00
4	Greg Maddux	4.50
5	Jack Morris	1.00
6	Dennis Martinez	1.00
7	Kevin Brown	1.00
8	Dwight Gooden	1.00
9	Kevin Appier	1.00
10	Mike Morgan	1.00
11	Juan Guzman	1.00
12	Charles Nagy	1.00
13	John Smiley	1.00
14	Ken Hill	1.00
15	Bob Tewksbury	1.00
16	Doug Drabek	1.00
17	John Smoltz	1.00
18	Greg Swindell	1.00
19	Bruce Hurst	1.00
20	Mike Mussina	2.00
21	Cal Eldred	1.00
22	Melido Perez	1.00
23	Dave Fleming	1.00
24	Kevin Tapani	1.00

Rookies

Top newcomers in 1992 are featured in this 21-card insert set. Cards were randomly inserted in 15-card hobby packs. The fronts, printed on metallic foil, have a Score Select Rookies logo on the front. The backs have text and a player portrait.

		NM/M
Complete Set (21):		4.00
Common Player:		.50
1	Pat Listach	.50

This 90-card set features 1992 American League and National League leaders in various statistical categories. Each card front indicates the league and the category in which the player finished at or near the top. The backs have a list of the leaders; the pictured player's name is in larger type size. Cards were inserted one per foil pack.

		NM/M
Complete Set (90):		8.00
Common Player:		.05
1	Edgar Martinez	.05
2	Kirby Puckett	.30
3	Frank Thomas	.25
4	Gary Sheffield	.15
5	Andy Van Slyke	.05
6	John Kruk	.05
7	Kirby Puckett	.30
8	Carlos Baerga	.05
9	Paul Molitor	.05
10	Andy Van Slyke, Terry Pendleton	.05
11	Ryne Sandberg	.30
12	Mark Grace	.05
13	Frank Thomas	.25
14	Don Mattingly	.35
15	Ken Griffey Jr.	.45
16	Andy Van Slyke	.05
17	Mariano Duncan, Jerald Clark, Ray Lankford	.05
18	Marquis Grissom, Terry Pendleton	.05
19	Lance Johnson	.05
20	Mike Devereaux	.05
21	Brady Anderson	.05
22	Deion Sanders	.05
23	Steve Finley	.05
24	Andy Van Slyke	.05
25	Juan Gonzalez	.15
26	Mark McGwire	.50
27	Cecil Fielder	.05
28	Fred McGriff	.05
29	Barry Bonds	.60
30	Gary Sheffield	.15
31	Cecil Fielder	.05
32	Joe Carter	.05
33	Frank Thomas	.25
34	Darren Daulton	.05
35	Terry Pendleton	.05
36	Fred McGriff	.05
37	Tony Phillips	.05
38	Frank Thomas	.25
39	Roberto Alomar	.15
40	Barry Bonds	.60
41	Dave Hollins	.05
42	Andy Van Slyke	.05
43	Mark McGwire	.50
44	Edgar Martinez	.05
45	Frank Thomas	.25
46	Barry Bonds	.60
47	Gary Sheffield	.15
48	Fred McGriff	.05
49	Frank Thomas	.25
50	Danny Tartabull	.05
51	Roberto Alomar	.15
52	Barry Bonds	.60
53	John Kruk	.05
54	Brett Butler	.05
55	Kenny Lofton	.05
56	Pat Listach	.05
57	Brady Anderson	.05
58	Marquis Grissom	.05
59	Delino DeShields	.05
60	Steve Finley, Bip Roberts	.05
61	Jack McDowell	.05
62	Kevin Brown	.05
63	Melido Perez	.05
64	Terry Mulholland	.05
65	Curt Schilling	.20
66	John Smoltz, Doug Drabek, Greg Maddux	.05
67	Dennis Eckersley	.20
68	Rick Aguilera	.05
69	Jeff Montgomery	.05
70	Lee Smith	.05
71	Randy Myers	.05
72	John Wetteland	.05
73	Randy Johnson	.25
74	Melido Perez	.05
75	Roger Clemens	.35
76	John Smoltz	.05
77	David Cone	.05
78	Greg Maddux	.30
79	Roger Clemens	.35
80	Kevin Appier	.05
81	Mike Mussina	.15
82	Bill Swift	.05
83	Bob Tewksbury	.05
84	Greg Maddux	.30
85	Kevin Brown	.05
86	Jack McDowell	.05
87	Roger Clemens	.35
88	Tom Glavine	.05
89	Ken Hill, Bob Tewksbury	.05
90	Dennis Martinez, Mike Morgan	.05

Triple Crown

CARL YASTRZEMSKI
Triple Crown

This three-card set commemorates the Triple Crown seasons of Hall of Famers Mickey Mantle, Frank Robinson and Carl Yastrzemski. Cards were randomly inserted in 15-card hobby packs. Card fronts have a green metallic-look textured border, with the player's name at top in gold, and "Triple Crown" in gold at bottom. There are other silver and green highlights around the photo, which feature the player set against a metallized background. Dark green backs have a player photo and information on his Triple Crown season.

		NM/M
Complete Set (3):		35.00
Common Player:		10.00
1	Mickey Mantle	22.50
2	Frank Robinson	10.00
3	Carl Yastrzemski	12.50

Rookie/Traded

EDUARDO PEREZ

Production of this 150-card set was limited to 1,950 numbered cases. Several future Hall of Famers and six dozen top rookies are featured in the set. Cards were available in packs rather than collated sets and include randomly inserted FX cards, which feature Nolan Ryan (two per 24-box case), Tim Salmon and Mike Piazza (one per 576 packs) and All-Star Rookie Team members (one per 58 packs).

		NM/M
Complete Set (150):		11.00
Common Player:		.05
Pack (12):		1.25
Wax Box (24):		20.00
1	Rickey Henderson	.75
2	Rob Deer	.05
3	Tim Belcher	.05
4	Gary Sheffield	.35
5	Fred McGriff	.05
6	Mark Whiten	.05
7	Jeff Russell	.05
8	Harold Baines	.05
9	Dave Winfield	.75
10	Ellis Burks	.05
11	Andre Dawson	.25
12	Gregg Jefferies	.05
13	Jimmy Key	.05
14	Harold Reynolds	.05
15	Tom Henke	.05
16	Paul Molitor	.75
17	Wade Boggs	1.00
18	David Cone	.05
19	Tony Fernandez	.05
20	Roberto Kelly	.05
21	Paul O'Neill	.05
22	Jose Lind	.05
23	Barry Bonds	2.00
24	Dave Stewart	.05
25	Randy Myers	.05
26	Benito Santiago	.05
27	Tim Wallach	.05
28	Greg Gagne	.05
29	Kevin Mitchell	.05
30	Jim Abbott	.05

31	Lee Smith	.05
32	Bobby Munoz RC	.05
33	Mo Sanford RC	.05
34	John Roper	.05
35	David Hulse RC	.05
36	Pedro Martinez	.75
37	Chuck Carr RC	.05
38	Armando Reynoso RC	.10
39	Ryan Thompson	.05
40	Carlos Garcia RC	.05
41	Matt Whiteside	.05
42	Benji Gil	.05
43	Rodney Bolton RC	.05
44	J.T. Snow	.05
45	David McCarty	.05
46	Paul Quantrill RC	.05
47	Al Martin	.05
48	Lance Painter	.05
49	Lou Frazier RC	.05
50	Eduardo Perez	.05
51	Kevin Young	.05
52	Mike Trombley	.05
53	Sterling Hitchcock RC	.10
54	Tim Bogar RC	.05
55	Hilly Hathaway RC	.05
56	Wayne Kirby RC	.05
57	Craig Paquette RC	.05
58	Bret Boone	.05
59	Greg McMichael RC	.05
60	Mike Lansing RC	.35
61	Brent Gates	.05
62	Rene Arocha	.05
63	Ricky Gutierrez	.05
64	Kevin Rogers RC	.05
65	Ken Ryan RC	.05
66	Phil Hiatt	.05
67	Pat Meares RC	.05
68	Troy Neel	.05
69	Steve Cooke	.05
70	Sherman Obando RC	.05
71	Blas Minor RC	.05
72	Angel Miranda RC	.05
73	Tom Kramer RC	.05
74	Chip Hale RC	.05
75	Brad Pennington RC	.05
76	Graeme Lloyd RC	.05
77	Darrell Whitmore RC	.05
78	David Nied	.05
79	Todd Van Poppel	.05
80	Chris Gomez RC	.10
81	Jason Bere	.05
82	Jeffrey Hammonds	.05
83	Brad Ausmus RC	.10
84	Kevin Stocker	.05
85	Jeromy Burnitz	.05
86	Aaron Sele	.05
87	Roberto Mejia RC	.05
88	Kirk Rueter RC	.10
89	Kevin Roberson RC	.05
90	Allen Watson RC	.05
91	Charlie Leibrandt	.05
92	Eric Davis	.05
93	Jody Reed	.05
94	Danny Jackson	.05
95	Gary Gaetti	.05
96	Norm Charlton	.05
97	Doug Drabek	.05
98	Scott Fletcher	.05
99	Greg Swindell	.05
100	John Smiley	.05
101	Kevin Reimer	.05
102	Andres Galarraga	.05
103	Greg Hibbard	.05
104	Chris Hammond	.05
105	Darnell Coles	.05
106	Mike Felder	.05
107	Jose Guzman	.05
108	Chris Bosio	.05
109	Spike Owen	.05
110	Felix Jose	.05
111	Cory Snyder	.05
112	Craig Lefferts	.05
113	David Wells	.05
114	Pete Incaviglia	.05
115	Mike Pagliarulo	.05
116	Dave Magadan	.05
117	Charlie Hough	.05
118	Ivan Calderon	.05
119	Manuel Lee	.05
120	Bob Patterson	.05
121	Bob Ojeda	.05
122	Scott Bankhead	.05
123	Greg Maddux	1.00
124	Chili Davis	.05
125	Milt Thompson	.05
126	Dave Martinez	.05
127	Frank Tanana	.05
128	Phil Plantier	.05
129	Juan Samuel	.05
130	Eric Young	.05
131	Joe Orsulak	.05
132	Derek Bell	.05
133	Darrin Jackson	.05
134	Tom Brunansky	.05
135	Jeff Reardon	.05
136	Kevin Higgins RC	.05
137	Joel Johnston RC	.05
138	Rick Trlicek RC	.05
139	Richie Lewis RC	.05
140	Jeff Gardner RC	.05
141	Jack Voigt RC	.05
142	Rod Correia RC	.05
143	Billy Brewer RC	.05
144	Terry Jorgensen RC	.05
145	Rich Amaral RC	.05
146	Sean Berry RC	.05
147	Dan Peltier RC	.05
148	Paul Wagner RC	.05

149	Damon Buford **RC**	.05
150	Wil Cordero	.05

Rookie/Traded All-Star Rookies

These cards were randomly inserted into the Score Select Rookie/Traded packs, making them among the scarcest of the year's many "chase" cards. Card fronts feature metallic foil printing. Backs have a few words about the player. Stated odds of finding an All-Star Rookie Team insert card are one per 58 packs.

		NM/M
Complete Set (10):		30.00
Common Player:		1.00
1	Jeff Conine	1.00
2	Brent Gates	1.00
3	Mike Lansing	1.00
4	Kevin Stocker	1.00
5	Mike Piazza	25.00
6	Jeffrey Hammonds	1.00
7	David Hulse	1.00
8	Tim Salmon	2.00
9	Rene Arocha	1.00
10	Greg McMichael	1.00

Rookie/Traded Inserts

Three cards honoring the 1993 Rookies of the Year and retiring superstar Nolan Ryan were issued as random inserts in the Select Rookie/Traded packs. Cards are printed with metallic foil front backgrounds. Stated odds of finding a Piazza or Salmon card are about one per 24-box case; Ryan cards are found on average two per case.

		NM/M
Complete Set (3):		60.00
Common Player:		6.00
1NR	Nolan Ryan	40.00
1ROY	Tim Salmon	6.00
2ROY	Mike Piazza	20.00

1994 Select Promos

To introduce its 1994 offering to dealers and collectors, Score Select created an eight-card promo set. Cards are identical in format to regular-issue cards with the exception of the word "SAMPLE" overprinted diagonally on front and back. The promos included five of the regular-run cards, a Rookie Prospect card and one each of its Rookie Surge '94 and Crown Contenders insert sets. The promos were cellopackaged with a header card describing the set and chase cards.

		NM/M
Complete Set (8):		7.50
Common Player:		.75
3	Paul Molitor	1.50
17	Kirby Puckett	2.50
19	Randy Johnson	1.50
24	John Kruk	.75
51	Jose Lind	.75
197	Ryan Klesko (Rookie Prospect)	1.00
1CC	Lenny Dykstra (Crown Contenders)	1.00
1RS	Cliff Floyd (Rookie Surge)	1.00
---	Header Card	.05

1994 Select

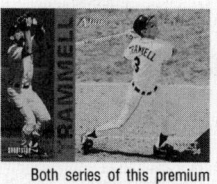

Both series of this premium brand from the Score/Pinnacle lineup offered 210 regular cards for a combined 420 cards, and seven insert sets. The announced press run for each series was 4,950 20-box cases. Cards have a horizontal format with a color action photo at right and a second photo at left done in a single team color-coded hue. The player's last name is dropped out of a vertical gold-foil strip between the two photos, with his first name in white at top-center. Backs are vertical with yet another color action photo at center. In a vertical bar at right, matching the color-coding on front and printed over the photo are 1993 and career stats, a "Select Stat," and a few sentences about the player. The appropriate logos and Pinnacle's optical-variable anti-counterfeiting device are at bottom-center. Thirty of the final 33 cards in the first series are a "1994 Rookie Prospect" subset, so noted in a special gold-foil logo on front.

		NM/M
Complete Set (420):		12.50
Common Player:		.05
Pack (12):		1.25
Wax Box (24):		16.00
1	Ken Griffey Jr.	1.50
2	Greg Maddux	1.00
3	Paul Molitor	.75
4	Mike Piazza	1.50
5	Jay Bell	.05
6	Frank Thomas	.75
7	Barry Larkin	.05
8	Paul O'Neill	.05
9	Darren Daulton	.05
10	Mike Greenwell	.05
11	Chuck Carr	.05
12	Joe Carter	.05
13	Lance Johnson	.05
14	Jeff Blauser	.05
15	Chris Hoiles	.05
16	Rick Wilkins	.05
17	Kirby Puckett	1.00
18	Larry Walker	.05
19	Randy Johnson	.75
20	Bernard Gilkey	.05
21	Devon White	.05
22	Randy Myers	.05
23	Don Mattingly	1.25
24	John Kruk	.05
25	Ozzie Guillen	.05
26	Jeff Conine	.05
27	Mike Macfarlane	.05
28	Dave Hollins	.05
29	Chuck Knoblauch	.05
30	Ozzie Smith	1.00
31	Harold Baines	.05
32	Ryne Sandberg	1.00
33	Ron Karkovice	.05
34	Terry Pendleton	.05
35	Wally Joyner	.05
36	Mike Mussina	.35
37	Felix Jose	.05
38	Derrick May	.05
39	Scott Cooper	.05
40	Jose Rijo	.05
41	Robin Ventura	.05
42	Charlie Hayes	.05
43	Jimmy Key	.05
44	Eric Karros	.05
45	Ruben Sierra	.05
46	Ryan Thompson	.05
47	Brian McRae	.05
48	Pat Hentgen	.05
49	John Valentin	.05
50	Al Martin	.05
51	Jose Lind	.05
52	Kevin Stocker	.05
53	Mike Gallego	.05

54	Dwight Gooden	.05
55	Brady Anderson	.05
56	Jeff King	.05
57	Mark McGwire	1.75
58	Sammy Sosa	1.00
59	Ryan Bowen	.05
60	Mark Lemke	.05
61	Roger Clemens	1.25
62	Brian Jordan	.05
63	Andres Galarraga	.05
64	Kevin Appier	.05
65	Don Slaught	.05
66	Mike Blowers	.05
67	Wes Chamberlain	.05
68	Troy Neel	.05
69	John Wetteland	.05
70	Joe Girardi	.05
71	Reggie Sanders	.05
72	Edgar Martinez	.05
73	Todd Hundley	.05
74	Pat Borders	.05
75	Roberto Mejia	.05
76	David Cone	.05
77	Tony Gwynn	1.00
78	Jim Abbott	.05
79	Jay Buhner	.05
80	Mark McLemore	.05
81	Wil Cordero	.05
82	Pedro Astacio	.05
83	Bob Tewksbury	.05
84	Dave Winfield	.75
85	Jeff Kent	.05
86	Todd Van Poppel	.05
87	Steve Avery	.05
88	Mike Lansing	.05
89	Len Dykstra	.05
90	Jose Guzman	.05
91	Brian Hunter	.05
92	Tim Raines	.05
93	Andre Dawson	.25
94	Joe Orsulak	.05
95	Ricky Jordan	.05
96	Billy Hatcher	.05
97	Jack McDowell	.05
98	Tom Pagnozzi	.05
99	Darryl Strawberry	.05
100	Mike Stanley	.05
101	Bret Saberhagen	.05
102	Willie Greene	.05
103	Bryan Harvey	.05
104	Tim Bogar	.05
105	Jack Voight	.05
106	Brad Ausmus	.05
107	Ramon Martinez	.05
108	Mike Perez	.05
109	Jeff Montgomery	.05
110	Danny Darwin	.05
111	Wilson Alvarez	.05
112	Kevin Mitchell	.05
113	David Nied	.05
114	Rich Amaral	.05
115	Stan Javier	.05
116	Mo Vaughn	1.25
117	Ben McDonald	.05
118	Tom Gordon	.05
119	Carlos Garcia	.05
120	Phil Plantier	.05
121	Mike Morgan	.05
122	Pat Meares	.05
123	Kevin Young	.05
124	Jeff Fassero	.05
125	Gene Harris	.05
126	Bob Welch	.05
127	Walt Weiss	.05
128	Bobby Witt	.05
129	Andy Van Slyke	.05
130	Steve Cooke	.05
131	Mike Devereaux	.05
132	Joey Cora	.05
133	Bret Barberie	.05
134	Orel Hershiser	.05
135	Ed Sprague	.05
136	Shawon Dunston	.05
137	Alex Arias	.05
138	Archi Cianfrocco	.05
139	Tim Wallach	.05
140	Bernie Williams	.05
141	Karl Rhodes	.05
142	Pat Kelly	.05
143	Dave Magadan	.05
144	Kevin Tapani	.05
145	Eric Young	.05
146	Derek Bell	.05
147	Dante Bichette	.05
148	Geronimo Pena	.05
149	Joe Oliver	.05
150	Orestes Destrade	.05
151	Tim Naehring	.05
152	Ray Lankford	.05
153	Phil Clark	.05
154	David McCarty	.05
155	Tommy Greene	.05
156	Wade Boggs	1.00
157	Kevin Gross	.05
158	Hal Morris	.05
159	Moises Alou	.05
160	Rick Aguilera	.05
161	Curt Schilling	.35
162	Chip Hale	.05
163	Tino Martinez	.05
164	Mark Whiten	.05
165	Dave Stewart	.05
166	Steve Buechele	.05
167	Bobby Jones	.05
168	Darrin Fletcher	.05
169	Jim Smiley	.05
170	Cory Snyder	.05
171	Scott Erickson	.05

172	Kirk Rueter	.05
173	Dave Fleming	.05
174	John Smoltz	.05
175	Ricky Gutierrez	.05
176	Mike Bordick	.05
177	Chan Ho Park **RC**	1.00
178	Alex Gonzalez	.05
179	Steve Karsay	.05
180	Jeffrey Hammonds	.05
181	Manny Ramirez	.75
182	Salomon Torres	.05
183	Raul Mondesi	.05
184	James Mouton	.05
185	Cliff Floyd	.05
186	Danny Bautista	.05
187	Kurt Abbott **RC**	.05
188	Javier Lopez	.05
189	John Patterson	.05
190	Greg Blosser	.05
191	Bob Hamelin	.05
192	Tony Eusebio	.05
193	Carlos Delgado	.50
194	Chris Gomez	.05
195	Kelly Stinnett	.05
196	Shane Reynolds	.05
197	Ryan Klesko	.05
198	Jim Edmonds	.05
199	James Hurst	.05
200	Dave Staton	.05
201	Rondell White	.05
202	Keith Mitchell	.05
203	Darren Oliver	.05
204	Mike Matheny	.05
205	Chris Turner	.05
206	Matt Mieske	.05
207	N.L. Team Checklist	.05
208	N.L. Team Checklist	.05
209	A.L. Team Checklist	.05
210	A.L. Team Checklist	.05
211	Barry Bonds	2.00
212	Juan Gonzalez	.40
213	Jim Eisenreich	.05
214	Ivan Rodriguez	.65
215	Tony Phillips	.05
216	John Jaha	.05
217	Lee Smith	.05
218	Bip Roberts	.05
219	Dave Hansen	.05
220	Pat Listach	.05
221	Willie McGee	.05
222	Damion Easley	.05
223	Dean Palmer	.05
224	Mike Moore	.05
225	Brian Harper	.05
226	Gary DiSarcina	.05
227	Delino DeShields	.05
228	Otis Nixon	.05
229	Roberto Alomar	.30
230	Mark Grace	.05
231	Kenny Lofton	.05
232	Gregg Jefferies	.05
233	Cecil Fielder	.05
234	Jeff Bagwell	.75
235	Albert Belle	.05
236	Dave Justice	.05
237	Tom Henke	.05
238	Bobby Bonilla	.05
239	John Olerud	.05
240	Robby Thompson	.05
241	Dave Valle	.05
242	Marquis Grissom	.05
243	Greg Swindell	.05
244	Todd Zeile	.05
245	Dennis Eckersley	.65
246	Jose Offerman	.05
247	Greg McMichael	.05
248	Tim Belcher	.05
249	Cal Ripken, Jr.	2.00
250	Tom Glavine	.05
251	Luis Polonia	.05
252	Bill Swift	.05
253	Juan Guzman	.05
254	Rickey Henderson	.75
255	Terry Mulholland	.05
256	Gary Sheffield	.40
257	Terry Steinbach	.05
258	Brett Butler	.05
259	Jason Bere	.05
260	Doug Strange	.05
261	Kent Hrbek	.05
262	Graeme Lloyd	.05
263	Lou Frazier	.05
264	Charles Nagy	.05
265	Bret Boone	.05
266	Kirk Gibson	.05
267	Kevin Brown	.05
268	Matt Williams	.05
269	Greg Gagne	.05
270	Mariano Duncan	.05
271	Jeff Russell	.05
272	Eric Davis	.05
273	Shane Mack	.05
274	Jose Vizcaino	.05
275	Jose Canseco	.45
276	Roberto Hernandez	.05
277	Royce Clayton	.05
278	Carlos Baerga	.05
279	Pete Incaviglia	.05
280	Brent Gates	.05
281	Jeromy Burnitz	.05
282	Chili Davis	.05
283	Pete Harnisch	.05
284	Alan Trammell	.05
285	Eric Anthony	.05
286	Ellis Burks	.05
287	Julio Franco	.05
288	Jack Morris	.05
289	Erik Hanson	.05

291	Chuck Finley	.05
292	Reggie Jefferson	.05
293	Kevin McReynolds	.05
294	Greg Hibbard	.05
295	Travis Fryman	.05
296	Craig Biggio	.05
297	Kenny Rogers	.05
298	Dave Henderson	.05
299	Jim Thome	.50
300	Rene Arocha	.05
301	Pedro Munoz	.05
302	David Hulse	.05
303	Greg Vaughn	.05
304	Darren Lewis	.05
305	Deion Sanders	.05
306	Danny Tartabull	.05
307	Darryl Hamilton	.05
308	Andujar Cedeno	.05
309	Tim Salmon	.05
310	Tony Fernandez	.05
311	Alex Fernandez	.05
312	Roberto Kelly	.05
313	Harold Reynolds	.05
314	Chris Sabo	.05
315	Howard Johnson	.05
316	Mark Portugal	.05
317	Rafael Palmeiro	.65
318	Pete Smith	.05
319	Will Clark	.05
320	Henry Rodriguez	.05
321	Omar Vizquel	.05
322	David Segui	.05
323	Lou Whitaker	.05
324	Felix Fermin	.05
325	Spike Owen	.05
326	Darryl Kile	.05
327	Chad Kreuter	.05
328	Rod Beck	.05
329	Eddie Murray	.75
330	B.J. Surhoff	.05
331	Mickey Tettleton	.05
332	Pedro Martinez	.75
333	Roger Pavlik	.05
334	Eddie Taubensee	.05
335	John Doherty	.05
336	Jody Reed	.05
337	Aaron Sele	.05
338	Leo Gomez	.05
339	Dave Nilsson	.05
340	Rob Dibble	.05
341	John Burkett	.05
342	Wayne Kirby	.05
343	Dan Wilson	.05
344	Armando Reynoso	.05
345	Chad Curtis	.05
346	Dennis Martinez	.05
347	Cal Eldred	.05
348	Luis Gonzalez	.05
349	Doug Drabek	.05
350	Jim Leyritz	.05
351	Mark Langston	.05
352	Darrin Jackson	.05
353	Sid Fernandez	.05
354	Benito Santiago	.05
355	Kevin Seitzer	.05
356	Bo Jackson	.10
357	David Wells	.05
358	Paul Sorrento	.05
359	Ken Caminiti	.05
360	Eduardo Perez	.05
361	Orlando Merced	.05
362	Steve Finley	.05
363	Andy Benes	.05
364	Manuel Lee	.05
365	Todd Benzinger	.05
366	Sandy Alomar Jr.	.05
367	Rex Hudler	.05
368	Mike Henneman	.05
369	Vince Coleman	.05
370	Kirt Manwaring	.05
371	Ken Hill	.05
372	Glenallen Hill	.05
373	Sean Berry	.05
374	Geronimo Berroa	.05
375	Duane Ward	.05
376	Allen Watson	.05
377	Marc Newfield	.05
378	Dan Miceli	.05
379	Denny Hocking	.05
380	Mark Kiefer	.05
381	Tony Tarasco	.05
382	Tony Longmire	.05
383	Brian Anderson **RC**	.05
384	Fernando Vina	.05
385	Hector Carrasco	.05
386	Mike Kelly	.05
387	Greg Colbrunn	.05
388	Roger Salkeld	.05
389	Steve Trachsel	.05
390	Rich Becker	.05
391	Billy Taylor **RC**	.05
392	Rich Rowland	.05
393	Carl Everett	.05
394	Johnny Ruffin	.05
395	Keith Lockhart **RC**	.05
396	J.R. Phillips	.05
397	Sterling Hitchcock	.05
398	Jorge Fabregas	.05
399	Jeff Granger	.05
400	Eddie Zambrano **RC**	.05
401	Rikkert Faneyte **RC**	.05
402	Gerald Williams	.05
403	Joey Hamilton	.05
404	Joe Hall **RC**	.05
405	John Hudek **RC**	.05
406	Roberto Petagine	.05
407	Charles Johnson	.05
408	Mark Smith	.05

409	Jeff Juden	.05
410	Carlos Pulido **RC**	.05
411	Paul Shuey	.05
412	Rob Butler	.05
413	Mark Acre	.05
414	Greg Pirkl	.05
415	Melvin Nieves	.05
416	Tim Hyers **RC**	.05
417	N.L. Checklist	.05
418	N.L. Checklist	.05
419	A.L. Checklist	.05
420	A.L. Checklist	.05

Crown Contenders

Candidates for the major baseball annual awards are featured in this subset. Horizontal-format cards have a color player photo printed on a holographic foil background. Backs are vertically oriented with a player portrait photo and justification for the player's inclusion in the set. Cards are numbered with a "CC" prefix and feature a special optical-variable anti-counterfeiting device at bottom-center. According to stated odds of one card on average in every 24 packs it has been estimated that fewer than 12,000 of each Crown Contenders card was produced.

		NM/M
Complete Set (10):		12.50
Common Player:		.50
1	Len Dykstra	.50
2	Greg Maddux	1.75
3	Roger Clemens	2.00
4	Randy Johnson	1.50
5	Frank Thomas	1.50
6	Barry Bonds	3.00
7	Juan Gonzalez	1.00
8	John Olerud	.50
9	Mike Piazza	2.50
10	Ken Griffey Jr.	2.50

MVP

Paul Molitor was the 1994 Select MVP and is featured in this one card set. Molitor is pictured in front of three distinct foil designs across the rest of the card.

		NM/M
MVP1	Paul Molitor	5.00

Rookie of the Year

Carlos Delgado was the 1994 Select Rookie of the Year. Delgado is pictured on top of a glowing foil background with his initials in large capital letters in the background and Rookie of the Year printed across the bottom.

		NM/M
RY1	Carlos Delgado	7.50

Rookie Surge

Each series of 1994 Score Select offered a chase card set of nine top rookies. Fronts feature action photos set against a rainbow-colored metallic foil background. Backs have a portrait photo and a few words about the player. Cards are numbered with an "RS" prefix and were inserted at an average rate of one per 48 packs.

		NM/M
Complete Set (18):		10.00
Common Player:		.75
1	Cliff Floyd	.75
2	Bob Hamelin	.75
3	Ryan Klesko	.75
4	Carlos Delgado	3.00
5	Jeffrey Hammonds	.75
6	Rondell White	.75
7	Salomon Torres	.75
8	Steve Karsay	.75
9	Javier Lopez	.75
10	Manny Ramirez	3.00
11	Tony Tarasco	.75
12	Kurt Abbott	.75
13	Chan Ho Park	.75
14	Rich Becker	.75
15	James Mouton	.75
16	Alex Gonzalez	.75
17	Raul Mondesi	.75
18	Steve Trachsel	.75

Salute

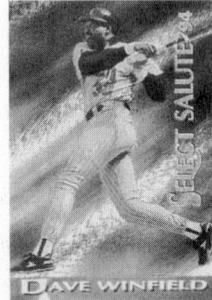

With odds of finding one of these cards stated at one per 360 packs, it is estimated that only about 4,000 of each of this two-card chase set were produced.

		NM/M
Complete Set (2):		15.00
1	Cal Ripken, Jr.	12.50
2	Dave Winfield	5.00

Skills

Select Skills is a 10-card insert that was randomly inserted into every 24 packs. Ten specific skills were designated and matched with the player whom, in the opinion of Select officials, demonstrated that particular skill the best in baseball. Each card is printed on a

foil background with the player name vertically on left side of the card and the skill they are being featured for along the bottom.

		NM/M
Complete Set (10):		15.00
Common Player:		.75
1	Randy Johnson	3.00
2	Barry Larkin	.75
3	Len Dykstra	.75
4	Kenny Lofton	.75
5	Juan Gonzalez	1.50
6	Barry Bonds	6.00
7	Marquis Grissom	.75
8	Ivan Rodriguez	2.50
9	Larry Walker	.75
10	Travis Fryman	.75

1995 Select Samples

Pinnacle's hobby-only Select brand issue for 1995 was previewed with this four-card cello-packed sample set. Three player cards are in the basic format of the regular-issue Select cards, except they have a large white "SAMPLE" printed diagonally across the front and back. The fourth card in the sample pack is a header card advertising the features of the issue.

		NM/M
Complete Set (4):		4.00
Common Player:		.50
34	Roberto Alomar	.50
37	Jeff Bagwell	.75
241	Alex Rodriguez	4.00
--	Header Card	.05

1995 Select

The 250 regular-issue cards in Pinnacle's mid-price brand feature three basic formats. Veteran players' cards are presented horizontally and feature an action photo at left. At right is a portrait in a trapezoidal gold-foil frame set against a team color-coordinated marbled background. The team logo beneath the portrait and the player's name below that are printed in gold foil. Backs feature a black-and-white photo with a few career highlights, 1994 and career stats, and a "Select Stat" printed in red. The colored marble effect is carried over from the front. The Select Rookie cards, which are grouped toward the end of the set, are vertical in format and feature a borderless player photo with a gold-foil band at bottom which includes the player name and team logo, along with waves of gold emanating from the logo. Backs have a small, narrow color photo at left, with a large sepia version of the same photo ghosted at center and overprinted with a career summary. At bottom are 1994 and career stats. Ending the set are a series of "Show Time" cards of top prospects. Cards feature large gold-foil "Show Time" and team logos at bottom, with a facsimile autograph printed above. The player photo is shown as if at a curtain raising, with spotlight effects behind. Backs repeat the curtain and spotlight motif and feature another player photo, with autograph above. Production of this hobby-only product was stated as 4,950 cases, which translates to about 110,000 of each regular-issue card. A special card (#251) of Hideo Nomo was added to the set later. It

was not issued in foil packs, but distributed to dealers who had purchased Select cases.

		NM/M
Complete Set (251):		9.00
Common Player:		.05
Artist's Proofs:		10X
Pack (12):		1.50
Wax Box (24):		17.50
1	Cal Ripken Jr.	1.50
2	Robin Ventura	.05
3	Al Martin	.05
4	Jeff Frye	.05
5	Darryl Strawberry	.05
6	Chan Ho Park	.05
7	Steve Avery	.05
8	Bret Boone	.05
9	Danny Tartabull	.05
10	Dante Bichette	.05
11	Rondell White	.05
12	Dave McCarty	.05
13	Bernard Gilkey	.05
14	Mark McGwire	1.25
15	Ruben Sierra	.05
16	Wade Boggs	.75
17	Mike Piazza	1.00
18	Jeffrey Hammonds	.05
19	Mike Mussina	.35
20	Darryl Kile	.05
21	Greg Maddux	.75
22	Frank Thomas	.65
23	Kevin Appier	.05
24	Jay Bell	.05
25	Kirk Gibson	.05
26	Pat Hentgen	.05
27	Joey Hamilton	.05
28	Bernie Williams	.05
29	Aaron Sele	.05
30	Delino DeShields	.05
31	Danny Bautista	.05
32	Jim Thome	.45
33	Rikkert Faneyte	.05
34	Roberto Alomar	.20
35	Paul Molitor	.52
36	Allen Watson	.05
37	Jeff Bagwell	.65
38	Jay Buhner	.05
39	Marquis Grissom	.05
40	Jim Edmonds	.05
41	Kevin Klesko	.05
42	Fred McGriff	.05
43	Tony Tarasco	.05
44	Darren Daulton	.05
45	Marc Newfield	.05
46	Barry Bonds	1.50
47	Bobby Bonilla	.05
48	Greg Pirkl	.05
49	Steve Karsay	.05
50	Bob Hamelin	.05
51	Javier Lopez	.05
52	Barry Larkin	.05
53	Kevin Young	.05
54	Sterling Hitchcock	.05
55	Tom Glavine	.05
56	Carlos Delgado	.40
57	Darren Oliver	.05
58	Cliff Floyd	.05
59	Tim Salmon	.05
60	Albert Belle	.05
61	Salomon Torres	.05
62	Gary Sheffield	.05
63	Ivan Rodriguez	.50
64	Charles Nagy	.05
65	Eduardo Perez	.05
66	Terry Steinbach	.05
67	Dave Justice	.05
68	Jason Bere	.05
69	Dave Nilsson	.05
70	Brian Anderson	.05
71	Billy Ashley	.05
72	Roger Clemens	.85
73	Jimmy Key	.05
74	Wally Joyner	.05
75	Andy Benes	.05
76	Ray Lankford	.05
77	Jeff Kent	.05
78	Moises Alou	.05
79	Kirby Puckett	.05
80	Joe Carter	.05
81	Manny Ramirez	.05
82	J.R. Phillips	.05
83	Matt Mieske	.05
84	John Olerud	.05
85	Andres Galarraga	.05
86	Juan Gonzalez	.35
87	Pedro Martinez	.65
88	Dean Palmer	.05
89	Ken Griffey Jr.	1.00
90	Brian Jordan	.05
91	Hal Morris	.05
92	Lenny Dykstra	.05
93	Wil Cordero	.05
94	Tony Gwynn	.75
95	Alex Gonzalez	.05
96	Cecil Fielder	.05
97	Mo Vaughn	.05
98	John Valentin	.05
99	Will Clark	.05
100	Geronimo Pena	.05
101	Don Mattingly	.85
102	Charles Johnson	.05
103	Raul Mondesi	.05
104	Reggie Sanders	.05
105	Royce Clayton	.05
106	Reggie Jefferson	.05
107	Craig Biggio	.05
108	Jack McDowell	.05
109	James Mouton	.05
110	Mike Greenwell	.05
111	David Cone	.05
112	Matt Williams	.05
113	Garret Anderson	.05
114	Carlos Garcia	.05
115	Alex Fernandez	.05
116	Deion Sanders	.05
117	Chili Davis	.05
118	Mike Kelly	.05
119	Jeff Conine	.05
120	Kenny Lofton	.05
121	Rafael Palmeiro	.50
122	Chuck Knoblauch	.05
123	Ozzie Smith	.75
124	Carlos Baerga	.05
125	Brett Butler	.05
126	Sammy Sosa	.75
127	Ellis Burks	.05
128	Bret Saberhagen	.05
129	Doug Drabek	.05
130	Dennis Martinez	.05
131	Paul O'Neill	.05
132	Travis Fryman	.05
133	Brent Gates	.05
134	Rickey Henderson	.05
135	Randy Johnson	.65
136	Mark Langston	.05
137	Greg Colbrunn	.05
138	Jose Rijo	.05
139	Bryan Harvey	.05
140	Dennis Eckersley	.50
141	Ron Gant	.05
142	Carl Everett	.05
143	Jeff Granger	.05
144	Ben McDonald	.05
145	Kurt Abbott	.05
146	Jim Abbott	.05
147	Jason Jacome	.05
148	Rico Brogna	.05
149	Cal Eldred	.05
150	Rich Becker	.05
151	Pete Harnisch	.05
152	Roberto Petagine	.05
153	Jacob Brumfield	.05
154	Todd Hundley	.05
155	Roger Cedeno	.05
156	Harold Baines	.05
157	Steve Dunn	.05
158	Tim Belk	.05
159	Marty Cardova	.05
160	Russ Davis	.05
161	Jose Malave	.05
162	Brian Hunter	.05
163	Andy Pettitte	.05
164	Brooks Kieschnick	.05
165	Midre Cummings	.05
166	Frank Rodriguez	.05
167	Chad Mottola	.05
168	Brian Barber	.05
169	Tim Unroe	.05
170	Shane Andrews	.05
171	Kevin Flora	.05
172	Ray Durham	.05
173	Chipper Jones	.75
174	Butch Huskey	.05
175	Ray McDavid	.05
176	Jeff Cirillo	.05
177	Terry Pendleton	.05
178	Scott Ruffcorn	.05
179	Ray Holbert	.05
180	Joe Randa	.05
181	Jose Oliva	.05
182	Andy Van Slyke	.05
183	Albie Lopez	.05
184	Chad Curtis	.05
185	Ozzie Guillen	.05
186	Chad Ogea	.05
187	Dan Wilson	.05
188	Tony Fernandez	.05
189	John Smoltz	.05
190	Willie Greene	.05
191	Darren Lewis	.05
192	Orlando Miller	.05
193	Kurt Miller	.05
194	Andrew Lorraine	.05
195	Ernie Young	.05
196	Jimmy Haynes	.05
197	Raul Casanova RC	.05
198	Joe Vitiello	.05
199	Brad Woodall	.05
200	Juan Acevedo	.05
201	Michael Tucker	.05
202	Shawn Green	.35
203	Alex Rodriguez	1.25
204	Julian Tavarez	.05
205	Jose Lima	.05
206	Wilson Alvarez	.05
207	Rich Aude	.05
208	Armando Benitez	.05
209	Dwayne Hosey	.05
210	Gabe White	.05
211	Joey Eischen	.05
212	Bill Pulsipher	.05
213	Robby Thompson	.05
214	Toby Borland	.05
215	Rusty Greer	.05
216	Fausto Cruz	.05
217	Luis Ortiz	.05
218	Duane Singleton	.05
219	Troy Percival	.05
220	Gregg Jefferies	.05
221	Mark Grace	.05
222	Mickey Tettleton	.05
223	Phil Plantier	.05
224	Larry Walker	.05
225	Ken Caminiti	.05
226	Dave Winfield	.65
227	Brady Anderson	.05
228	Kevin Brown	.05
229	Andujar Cedeno	.05
230	Roberto Kelly	.05
231	Jose Canseco	.35
231	Scott Ruffcorn (Showtime)	.05
232	Billy Ashley (Showtime)	.05
234	J.R. Phillips (Showtime)	.05
235	Chipper Jones (Showtime)	.40
236	Charles Johnson (Showtime)	.05
237	Midre Cummings (Showtime)	.05
238	Brian Hunter (Showtime)	.05
239	Garret Anderson (Showtime)	.05
240	Shawn Green (Showtime)	.10
241	Alex Rodriguez (Showtime)	.65
242	Checklist #1 (Frank Thomas)	.35
243	Checklist #2 (Ken Griffey Jr.)	.50
244	Checklist #3 (Albert Belle)	.05
245	Checklist #4 (Cal Ripken Jr.)	.65
246	Checklist #5 (Barry Bonds)	.75
247	Checklist #6 (Raul Mondesi)	.05
248	Checklist #7 (Mike Piazza)	.65
249	Checklist #8 (Jeff Bagwell)	.30
250	Checklist #9 (Jeff Bagwell, Frank Thomas, Ken Griffey Jr., Mike Piazza)	.25
251	Hideo Nomo	.35

Artist's Proofs

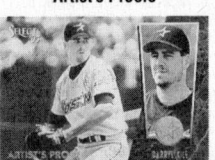

Among the scarcest and most valuable of 1995's baseball card inserts are the Select Artist's Proof parallel set. While an AP card is found on average once per 24 packs, the limited print run of the basic Select set means that only about 475 of each of the 250 regular-issue cards in the Select set were made in this edition. The AP inserts have a gold-foil "ARTIST'S PROOF" line at bottom, and other gold-foil highlights are embossed, rather than merely stamped on, as on regular Select cards.

	NM/M
Complete Set (250):	100.00
Common Player:	1.00
AP Stars:	10X

Big Sticks

With fronts printed in what Pinnacle describes as "holographic Gold Rush technology," the Big Sticks chase card issue offers a dozen of the game's big hitters in action photos superimposed over their team's logo. Conventionally printed backs have another player photo, along with a summary of career highlights and description of the player's power potential. Stated odds of pulling a Big Sticks chase card are one per 48 packs, on average. Cards are numbered with a "BS" prefix.

		NM/M
Complete Set (12):		40.00
Common Player:		1.50
1	Frank Thomas	4.00
2	Ken Griffey Jr.	7.50
3	Cal Ripken Jr.	10.00
4	Mike Piazza	7.50
5	Don Mattingly	6.00
6	Will Clark	1.50
7	Tony Gwynn	5.00
8	Jeff Bagwell	4.00
9	Barry Bonds	10.00
10	Paul Molitor	4.00
11	Matt Williams	1.50
12	Albert Belle	1.50

Can't Miss

A mix of rookies and sophomore standouts, along with a few players of slightly longer service are presented in this chase set. Cards feature color player action photos printed on a metallic red background, with their last name in gold foil at lower-left. An umpire on the "Can't Miss" logo is at upper-left. Backs repeat the logo, have a tall, narrow player photo, a few biographical details and a paragraph of career summary. Cards are numbered with a "CM" prefix.

		NM/M
Complete Set (12):		10.00
Common Player:		.35
1	Cliff Floyd	.35
2	Ryan Klesko	.35
3	Charles Johnson	.35
4	Raul Mondesi	.35
5	Manny Ramirez	2.00
6	Billy Ashley	.35
7	Alex Gonzalez	.35
8	Carlos Delgado	.75
9	Garret Anderson	.35
10	Alex Rodriguez	5.00
11	Chipper Jones	3.00
12	Shawn Green	.75

Sure Shots

Ten of Select's picks for future stardom are featured in this chase set, the toughest find of any of the 1995 Select inserts, at an average rate of one per 90 packs. Card fronts feature player action photos set against a gold "Dufex" foil printed background with a Sure Shots logo vertically at left. Backs have a blue background with a few words about the player and a portrait photo at left. Cards are numbered with a "SS" prefix.

		NM/M
Complete Set (10):		10.00
Common Player:		1.00
1	Ben Grieve	1.00
2	Kevin Witt	1.00
3	Mark Farris	1.00
4	Paul Konerko	3.00
5	Dustin Hermanson	1.00
6	Ramon Castro	1.00
7	McKay Christensen	1.00
8	Brian Buchanan	1.00
9	Paul Wilson	1.00
10	Terrence Long	1.00

Certified Samples

Pinnacle's hobby-only Select brand issue for 1995 was previewed with this four-card cello-packed sample set. Three player cards are in the basic format of the regular-issue Select cards, except they have a large "SAMPLE" printed diagonally across the front and back. The fourth card in the sample pack is a header card advertising the features of the issue.

		NM/M
Complete Set (8):		7.50
Common Player:		.50
2	Reggie Sanders	.50
10	Mo Vaughn	.50
39	Mike Piazza	2.00
50	Mark McGwire	2.50
75	Roberto Alomar	.65
89	Larry Walker	.50
110	Ray Durham	.50
3 of 12	Cal Ripken Jr. (Gold Team)	4.00

1995 Select Certified

The concepts of hobby-only distribution and limited production, which were the hallmarks of Pinnacle's Select brand, were carried a step further with the postseason release of Select Certified baseball. Printed on double-thick cardboard stock card fronts feature all metallic-foil printing protected by a double laminated gloss coat. Backs have key player stats against each team in the league. The final 44 cards in the set are distinguished with a special Rookie logo and with gold added to the silver foil in the photo background.

		NM/M
Complete Set (135):		10.00
Common Player:		.05
Mirror Gold Stars:		5X
Pack (6):		2.00
Wax Box (20):		25.00
1	Barry Bonds	2.50
2	Reggie Sanders	.05
3	Terry Steinbach	.05
4	Eduardo Perez	.05
5	Frank Thomas	.75
6	Wil Cordero	.05
7	John Olerud	.05
8	Deion Sanders	.05
9	Mike Mussina	.40
10	Mo Vaughn	.05
11	Will Clark	.05
12	Chili Davis	.05
13	Jimmy Key	.05
14	Eddie Murray	.75
15	Bernard Gilkey	.05
16	David Cone	.05
17	Tim Salmon	.05
18	Steve Ontiveros	.05
19	Andres Galarraga	.05
20	Don Mattingly	1.25
21	Kevin Appier	.05
22	Paul Molitor	.75
23	Edgar Martinez	.05
24	Andy Benes	.05

26	Rafael Palmeiro	.65
27	Barry Larkin	.05
28	Gary Sheffield	.25
29	Wally Joyner	.05
30	Wade Boggs	1.00
31	Rico Brogna	.05
32	Eddie Murray (Murray Tribute)	.40
33	Kirby Puckett	1.00
34	Bobby Bonilla	.05
35	Hal Morris	.05
36	Moises Alou	.05
37	Javier Lopez	.05
38	Chuck Knoblauch	.05
39	Mike Piazza	1.50
40	Travis Fryman	.05
41	Rickey Henderson	.75
42	Jim Thome	.60
43	Carlos Baerga	.05
44	Dean Palmer	.05
45	Kirk Gibson	.05
46	Bret Saberhagen	.05
47	Cecil Fielder	.05
48	Manny Ramirez	.75
49	Derek Bell	.05
50	Mark McGwire	2.00
51	Jim Edmonds	.05
52	Robin Ventura	.05
53	Ryan Klesko	.05
54	Jeff Bagwell	.75
55	Ozzie Smith	1.00
56	Albert Belle	.05
57	Darren Daulton	.05
58	Jeff Conine	.05
59	Greg Maddux	1.00
60	Lenny Dykstra	.05
61	Randy Johnson	.75
62	Fred McGriff	.05
63	Ray Lankford	.05
64	Dave Justice	.05
65	Paul O'Neill	.05
66	Tony Gwynn	1.00
67	Matt Williams	.05
68	Dante Bichette	.05
69	Craig Biggio	.05
70	Ken Griffey Jr.	1.50
71	J.T. Snow	.05
72	Cal Ripken Jr.	2.50
73	Jay Bell	.05
74	Joe Carter	.05
75	Roberto Alomar	.30
76	Benji Gil	.05
77	Ivan Rodriguez	.65
78	Raul Mondesi	.05
79	Cliff Floyd	.05
80	Eric Karros, Mike Piazza, Raul Mondesi (Dodger Dynasty)	.30
81	Royce Clayton	.05
82	Billy Ashley	.05
83	Joey Hamilton	.05
84	Sammy Sosa	1.00
85	Jason Bere	.05
86	Dennis Martinez	.05
87	Greg Vaughn	.05
88	Roger Clemens	1.25
89	Larry Walker	.05
90	Mark Grace	.05
91	Kenny Lofton	.05
92	Carlos Perez RC	.05
93	Roger Cedeno	.05
94	Scott Ruffcorn	.05
95	Jim Pittsley	.05
96	Andy Pettitte	.20
97	James Baldwin	.05
98	Hideo Nomo RC	1.50
99	Ismael Valdes	.05
100	Armando Benitez	.05
101	Jose Malave	.05
102	Bobby Higginson RC	.25
103	LaTroy Hawkins	.05
104	Russ Davis	.05
105	Shawn Green	.40
106	Joe Vitiello	.05
107	Chipper Jones	1.00
108	Shane Andrews	.05
109	Jose Oliva	.05
110	Ray Durham	.05
111	Jon Nunnally	.05
112	Alex Gonzalez	.05
113	Vaughn Eshelman	.05
114	Marty Cordova	.05
115	Mark Grudzielanek RC	.25
116	Brian Hunter	.05
117	Charles Johnson	.05
118	Alex Rodriguez	2.00
119	David Bell	.05
120	Todd Hollandsworth	.05
121	Joe Randa	.05
122	Derek Jeter	2.50
123	Frank Rodriguez	.05
124	Curtis Goodwin	.05
125	Bill Pulsipher	.05
126	John Mabry	.05
127	Julian Tavarez	.05
128	Edgardo Alfonzo	.05
129	Orlando Miller	.05
130	Juan Acevedo	.05
131	Jeff Cirillo	.05
132	Roberto Petagine	.05
133	Antonio Osuna	.05
134	Michael Tucker	.05
135	Garret Anderson	.05
2131	Cal Ripken Jr. (Consecutive Game Record)	1.00

Mirror Gold

Inserted at an average rate of one per nine packs, this parallel set is a gold-foil version of the regular Select Certified set. Backs have a "MIRROR GOLD" notation at bottom.

	NM/M
Complete Set (135):	150.00
Common Player:	1.00
Mirror Gold Stars:	5X

Checklists

The seven checklists issued with Select Certified are not numbered as part of the set. They are found one per foil pack and are printed on much thinner card stock than the regular-issue cards.

		NM/M
Complete Set (7):		2.00
Common Player:		.40
1	Ken Griffey Jr. (A.L. #3-41)	.50
2	Frank Thomas (A.L. #42-95)	.40
3	Cal Ripken Jr. (A.L. #96-135)	.65
4	Jeff Bagwell (N.L. #1-58)	.40
5	Mike Piazza (N.L. #59-92)	.50
6	Barry Bonds (N.L. #93-133)	.65
7	Manny Ramirez, Raul Mondesi (Chase Cards)	.40

Future

A striking new all-metal, brushed-foil printing technology was used in the production of this chase set of 10 rookie players with "unlimited future potential." Stated odds of finding a Certified Future insert card were one in 19 packs.

		NM/M
Complete Set (10):		10.00
Common Player:		.50
1	Chipper Jones	2.00
2	Curtis Goodwin	.50
3	Hideo Nomo	1.00
4	Shawn Green	1.00
5	Ray Durham	.50
6	Todd Hollandsworth	.50
7	Brian Hunter	.50
8	Carlos Delgado	1.00
9	Michael Tucker	.50
10	Alex Rodriguez	4.00

1996 Select

Gold Team

A dozen of the top position players in the league were selected for appearance in this insert set. Cards are printed in a special double-sided, all-gold Dufex technology. An action photo is featured on the front, a portrait on back. Odds of picking a Gold Team card were stated as one in 41 packs.

		NM/M
Complete Set (12):		40.00
Common Player:		2.00
1	Ken Griffey Jr.	7.50
2	Frank Thomas	4.00
3	Cal Ripken Jr.	10.00
4	Jeff Bagwell	4.00
5	Mike Piazza	7.50
6	Barry Bonds	10.00
7	Matt Williams	2.00
8	Don Mattingly	6.00
9	Will Clark	2.00
10	Tony Gwynn	5.00
11	Kirby Puckett	5.00
12	Jose Canseco	2.50

Potential Unlimited

Dufex printing with textured foil highlights and transparent inks is featured in this chase set, produced in an edition of 1,975, as witnessed by the numbering on card backs. Approximate odds of finding a Potential Unlimited card are one per 29 packs. A super-scarce edition of 903 cards each featuring "microetch" foil printing technology was issued at the rate of one per 70 packs.

		NM/M
Complete Set (20):		35.00
Common Player:		1.00
903s:		2.5X
1	Cliff Floyd	1.00
2	Manny Ramirez	4.50
3	Raul Mondesi	1.00
4	Scott Ruffcorn	1.00
5	Billy Ashley	1.00
6	Alex Gonzalez	1.00
7	Midre Cummings	1.00
8	Charles Johnson	1.00
9	Garret Anderson	1.00
10	Hideo Nomo	8.00
11	Chipper Jones	2.00
12	Curtis Goodwin	1.00
13	Frank Rodriguez	1.00
14	Shawn Green	2.00
15	Ray Durham	1.00
16	Todd Hollandsworth	1.00
17	Brian Hunter	1.00
18	Carlos Delgado	2.00
19	Michael Tucker	1.00
20	Alex Rodriguez	9.00

1996 Select

Select's 1996 baseball set has 200 cards in it, including 35 rookies, five checklists and 10 Lineup Leaders subset cards. All 200 cards are also reprinted as part of an Artist's Proof parallel set, using a holographic Artist's Proof logo. Cards were seeded one per every 35 packs; there were approximately 435 sets produced. Three insert sets were also created: Claim to Fame, En Fuego and Team Nucleus.

		NM/M
Complete Set (200):		9.00
Common Player:		.05
Artist's Proofs:		7X
Pack (10):		1.00
Wax Box (24):		16.00
1	Wade Boggs	1.00
2	Shawn Green	.35
3	Andres Galarraga	.05
4	Bill Pulsipher	.05
5	Chuck Knoblauch	.05
6	Ken Griffey Jr.	1.25
7	Greg Maddux	1.00
8	Manny Ramirez	.75
9	Ivan Rodriguez	.65
10	Tim Salmon	.05
11	Frank Thomas	.75
12	Jeff Bagwell	.75
13	Travis Fryman	.05
14	Kenny Lofton	.05
15	Matt Williams	.05
16	Jay Bell	.05
17	Ken Caminiti	.05
18	Ray Lankford	.05
19	Cal Ripken Jr.	2.00
20	Roger Clemens	1.00
21	Carlos Baerga	.05
22	Mike Piazza	1.25
23	Gregg Jefferies	.05
24	Reggie Sanders	.05
25	Rondell White	.05
26	Sammy Sosa	.05
27	Kevin Appier	.05
28	Kevin Seitzer	.05
29	Gary Sheffield	.40
30	Mike Stanley	.35
31	Mark McGwire	1.50
32	Barry Larkin	.05
33	Marc Newfield	.05
34	Ismael Valdes	.05
35	Marty Cordova	.05
36	Albert Belle	.05
37	Johnny Damon	.35
38	Garret Anderson	.05
39	Cecil Fielder	.05
40	John Mabry	.05
41	Chipper Jones	1.00
42	Omar Vizquel	.05
43	Jose Rijo	.05
44	Charles Johnson	.05
45	Alex Rodriguez	1.50
46	Rico Brogna	.05
47	Joe Carter	.05
48	Mo Vaughn	.05
49	Moises Alou	.05
50	Raul Mondesi	.05
51	Robin Ventura	.05
52	Jim Thome	.60
53	Dave Justice	.05
54	Jeff King	.05
55	Brian Hunter	.05
56	Juan Gonzalez	.40
57	John Olerud	.05
58	Rafael Palmeiro	.65
59	Tony Gwynn	1.00
60	Eddie Murray	.75
61	Jason Isringhausen	.05
62	Dante Bichette	.05
63	Randy Johnson	.75
64	Kirby Puckett	1.00
65	Jim Edmonds	.05
66	David Cone	.05
67	Ozzie Smith	1.00
68	Fred McGriff	.05
69	Darren Daulton	.05
70	Edgar Martinez	.05
71	J.T. Snow	.05
72	Butch Huskey	.05
73	Hideo Nomo	.40
74	Pedro Martinez	.75
75	Bobby Bonilla	.05
76	Jeff Conine	.05
77	Ryan Klesko	.05
78	Bernie Williams	.05
79	Andre Dawson	.25
80	Trevor Hoffman	.05
81	Mark Grace	.05
82	Benji Gil	.05
83	Eric Karros	.05
84	Edgardo Alfonzo	.05
85	Jay Buhner	.05
86	Vinny Castilla	.05
87	Bret Boone	.05
88	Brian Jordan	.05
89	Ray Durham	.05
90	Jose Canseco	.05
91	Paul O'Neill	.05
92	Chili Davis	.05
93	Tom Glavine	.30
94	Julian Tavarez	.05
95	Derek Bell	.05
96	Will Clark	.05

98	Larry Walker	.05
99	Denny Neagle	.05
100	Alex Fernandez	.05
101	Barry Bonds	2.00
102	Ben McDonald	.05
103	Andy Pettitte	.25
104	Tino Martinez	.05
105	Sterling Hitchcock	.05
106	Royce Clayton	.05
107	Jim Abbott	.05
108	Rickey Henderson	.75
109	Ramon Martinez	.05
110	Paul Molitor	.75
111	Dennis Eckersley	.65
112	Alex Gonzalez	.05
113	Marquis Grissom	.05
114	Greg Vaughn	.05
115	Lance Johnson	.05
116	Todd Stottlemyre	.05
117	Jack McDowell	.05
118	Ruben Sierra	.05
119	Brady Anderson	.05
120	Julio Franco	.05
121	Brooks Kieschnick	.05
122	Roberto Alomar	.20
123	Greg Gagne	.05
124	Wally Joyner	.05
125	John Smoltz	.05
126	John Valentin	.05
127	Russ Davis	.05
128	Joe Vitiello	.05
129	Shawon Dunston	.05
130	Frank Rodriguez	.05
131	Charlie Hayes	.05
132	Andy Benes	.05
133	B.J. Surhoff	.05
134	Dave Nilsson	.05
135	Carlos Delgado	.50
136	Walt Weiss	.05
137	Mike Stanley	.05
138	Greg Colbrunn	.05
139	Mike Kelly	.05
140	Ryne Sandberg	1.00
141	Lee Smith	.05
142	Dennis Martinez	.05
143	Bernard Gilkey	.05
144	Lenny Dykstra	.05
145	Danny Tartabull	.05
146	Dean Palmer	.05
147	Craig Biggio	.05
148	Juan Acevedo	.05
149	Michael Tucker	.05
150	Bobby Higginson	.05
151	Ken Griffey Jr. (Line Up Leaders)	.65
152	Frank Thomas (Line Up Leaders)	.45
153	Cal Ripken Jr. (Line Up Leaders)	1.00
154	Albert Belle (Line Up Leaders)	.05
155	Mike Piazza (Line Up Leaders)	.65
156	Barry Bonds (Line Up Leaders)	1.00
157	Sammy Sosa (Line Up Leaders)	.60
158	Mo Vaughn (Line Up Leaders)	.05
159	Greg Maddux (Line Up Leaders)	.50
160	Jeff Bagwell (Line Up Leaders)	.40
161	Derek Jeter	2.00
162	Paul Wilson	.05
163	Chris Snopek	.05
164	Jason Schmidt	.05
165	Jimmy Haynes	.05
166	George Arias	.05
167	Steve Gibralter	.05
168	Bob Wolcott	.05
169	Jason Kendall	.05
170	Gregg Zaun	.05
171	Quinton McCracken	.05
172	Alan Benes	.05
173	Rey Ordonez	.05
174	Ugueth Urbina	.05
175	Osvaldo Fernandez RC	.10
176	Marc Barcelo	.05
177	Sal Fasano	.05
178	Mike Grace RC	.05
179	Chan Ho Park	.05
180	Robert Perez	.05
181	Todd Hollandsworth	.05
182	Wilton Guerrero RC	.05
183	John Wasdin	.05
184	Jim Pittsley	.05
185	LaTroy Hawkins	.05
186	Jay Powell	.05
187	Felipe Crespo	.05
188	Jermaine Dye	.05
189	Bob Abreu	.05
190	Matt Luke RC	.05
191	Richard Hidalgo	.05
192	Karim Garcia	.05
193	Tavo Alvarez	.05
194	Andy Fox RC	.05
195	Terrell Wade	.05
196	Frank Thomas (Checklist)	.05
197	Ken Griffey Jr. (Checklist)	.65
198	Greg Maddux (Checklist)	.50
199	Mike Piazza (Checklist)	.50
200	Cal Ripken Jr. (Checklist)	.75

Artist's Proofs

Approximately once per 35 packs, a card from this parallel chase set is encountered among 1996 Select. Reported production was 435 sets. The Artist's Proof cards are distinguished by a holographic logo testifying to their status on the front of the card.

	NM/M
Complete Set (200):	200.00
Common Player:	1.00
AP Stars:	7X

Claim to Fame

Twenty different stars are featured on these 1996 Select insert cards. Each card is numbered "1 of 2100" and uses an external die-cut design. The cards were seeded one per every 72 packs.

		NM/M
Complete Set (20):		45.00
Common Player:		.75
1	Cal Ripken Jr.	7.50
2	Greg Maddux	4.50
3	Ken Griffey Jr.	6.00
4	Frank Thomas	3.50
5	Mo Vaughn	.75
6	Albert Belle	.75
7	Jeff Bagwell	3.50
8	Sammy Sosa	4.50
8s	Sammy Sosa (Overprinted "SAMPLE.")	2.50
9	Reggie Sanders	.75
10	Hideo Nomo	2.00
11	Chipper Jones	4.50
12	Mike Piazza	6.00
13	Matt Williams	.75
14	Tony Gwynn	4.50
15	Johnny Damon	1.50
16	Dante Bichette	.75
17	Kirby Puckett	4.50
18	Barry Bonds	7.50
19	Randy Johnson	3.50
20	Eddie Murray	3.50

En Fuego

ESPN announcer Dan Patrick is featured on his own card in this set, inspired by his Sportscenter catch phrase "en fuego," which means "on fire." Patrick's teammate, Keith Olberman, wrote the card backs. The 25 cards, printed on all-foil Dufex stock, are seeded one per every 48 packs of 1996 Select baseball.

		NM/M
Complete Set (25):		35.00
Common Player:		.75
1	Ken Griffey Jr.	3.50
2	Frank Thomas	2.00

3	Cal Ripken Jr.	5.00
4	Greg Maddux	3.00
5	Jeff Bagwell	2.00
6	Barry Bonds	5.00
7	Mo Vaughn	.75
8	Albert Belle	.75
9	Sammy Sosa	3.00
10	Reggie Sanders	.75
11	Mike Piazza	3.50
12	Chipper Jones	3.00
13	Tony Gwynn	3.00
14	Kirby Puckett	3.00
15	Wade Boggs	3.00
16	Dan Patrick	.75
17	Gary Sheffield	1.25
18	Dante Bichette	.75
19	Randy Johnson	2.00
20	Matt Williams	.75
21	Alex Rodriguez	4.00
22	Tim Salmon	.75
23	Johnny Damon	1.25
24	Manny Ramirez	2.00
25	Hideo Nomo	1.25

Team Nucleus

This 1996 Select insert set pays tribute to the three top players from each Major League Baseball team; each card features the three teammates on it. The cards are printed on a clear plastic, utilizing a holographic micro-etched design. They are seeded one per every 18 packs.

		NM/M
Complete Set (28):		20.00
Common Player:		.50
1	Albert Belle, Manny Ramirez, Carlos Baerga	1.00
2	Ray Lankford, Brian Jordan, Ozzie Smith	1.25
3	Jay Bell, Jeff King, Denny Neagle	.50
4	Dante Bichette, Andres Galarraga, Larry Walker	.50
5	Mark McGwire, Mike Bordick, Terry Steinbach	1.75
6	Bernie Williams, Wade Boggs, David Cone	1.25
7	Joe Carter, Alex Gonzalez, Shawn Green	.50
8	Roger Clemens, Mo Vaughn, Jose Canseco	1.25
9	Ken Griffey Jr., Edgar Martinez, Randy Johnson	1.50
10	Gregg Jefferies, Darren Daulton, Lenny Dykstra	.50
11	Mike Piazza, Raul Mondesi, Hideo Nomo	1.50
12	Greg Maddux, Chipper Jones, Ryan Klesko	1.25
13	Cecil Fielder, Travis Fryman, Phil Nevin	.50
14	Ivan Rodriguez, Will Clark, Juan Gonzalez	1.00
15	Ryne Sandberg, Sammy Sosa, Mark Grace	1.50
16	Gary Sheffield, Charles Johnson, Andre Dawson	.60
17	Johnny Damon, Michael Tucker, Kevin Appier	.65
18	Barry Bonds, Matt Williams, Rod Beck	2.00
19	Kirby Puckett, Chuck Knoblauch, Marty Cordova	1.25
20	Cal Ripken Jr., Bobby Bonilla, Mike Mussina	2.00
21	Jason Isringhausen, Bill Pulsipher, Rico Brogna	.50
22	Tony Gwynn, Ken Caminiti, Marc Newfield	1.25
23	Tim Salmon, Garret Anderson, Jim Edmonds	.50
24	Moises Alou, Rondell White, Cliff Floyd	.50
25	Barry Larkin, Reggie Sanders, Bret Boone	.50
26	Jeff Bagwell, Craig Biggio, Derek Bell	1.00
27	Frank Thomas, Robin Ventura, Alex Fernandez	1.00
28	John Jaha, Greg Vaughn, Kevin Seitzer	.50

1996 Select Certified

This hobby-exclusive set has 144 cards in its regular issue, plus six parallel versions and two insert sets. The parallel sets are: Certified Red (one per five packs), Certified Blue (one per 50), Artist's Proofs (one per 12), Mirror Red (one per 100), Mirror Blue (one per 200), and Mirror Gold (one per 300). Breaking down the numbers, there are 1,800 Certified Red sets, 180 Certified Blue, 500 Artist's Proofs, 90 Mirror Red 45 Mirror Blue and 30 Mirror Gold sets. The insert sets are Interleague Preview cards and Select Few. Cards #135-144 are a "Pastime Power" subset.

		NM/M
Complete Set (144):		20.00
Common Player:		.15
Pack (6):		2.50
Wax Box (20):		40.00
1	Frank Thomas	1.25
2	Tino Martinez	.15
3	Gary Sheffield	.50
4	Kenny Lofton	.15
5	Joe Carter	.15
6	Alex Rodriguez	2.50
7	Chipper Jones	1.50
8	Roger Clemens	1.75
9	Jay Bell	.15
10	Eddie Murray	1.00
11	Will Clark	.15
12	Mike Mussina	.35
13	Hideo Nomo	.50
14	Andres Galarraga	.15
15	Marc Newfield	.15
16	Jason Isringhausen	.15
17	Randy Johnson	1.00
18	Chuck Knoblauch	.15
19	J.T. Snow	.15
20	Mark McGwire	2.50
21	Tony Gwynn	1.50
22	Albert Belle	.15
23	Gregg Jefferies	.15
24	Reggie Sanders	.15
25	Bernie Williams	.15
26	Ray Lankford	.15
27	Johnny Damon	.40
28	Ryne Sandberg	1.50
29	Rondell White	.15
30	Mike Piazza	2.00
31	Barry Bonds	3.00
32	Greg Maddux	1.50
33	Craig Biggio	.15
34	John Valentin	.15
35	Ivan Rodriguez	.75
36	Rico Brogna	.15
37	Tim Salmon	.15
38	Sterling Hitchcock	.15
39	Charles Johnson	.15
40	Travis Fryman	.15
41	Barry Larkin	.15
42	Tom Glavine	.35
43	Marty Cordova	.15
44	Shawn Green	.40
45	Ben McDonald	.15
46	Robin Ventura	.15
47	Ken Griffey Jr.	2.00
48	Orlando Merced	.15
49	Paul O'Neill	.15
50	Ozzie Smith	1.50
51	Manny Ramirez	.15
52	Ismael Valdes	.15
53	Cal Ripken Jr.	3.00
54	Jeff Bagwell	1.00
55	Greg Vaughn	.15
56	Juan Gonzalez	.50
57	Raul Mondesi	.15
58	Carlos Baerga	.15
59	Sammy Sosa	1.50
60	Mike Kelly	.15
61	Edgar Martinez	.15
62	Kirby Puckett	1.50
63	Cecil Fielder	.15
64	David Cone	.15
65	Moises Alou	.15
66	Fred McGriff	.15
67	Mo Vaughn	.15
68	Edgardo Alfonzo	.15
69	Jim Thome	.15
70	Rickey Henderson	1.00
71	Dante Bichette	.15

72	Lenny Dykstra	.15
73	Benji Gil	.15
74	Wade Boggs	1.50
75	Jim Edmonds	.15
76	Michael Tucker	.15
77	Carlos Delgado	.65
78	Butch Huskey	.15
79	Billy Ashley	.15
80	Dean Palmer	.15
81	Paul Molitor	1.00
82	Ryan Klesko	.15
83	Brian Hunter	.15
84	Jay Buhner	.15
85	Larry Walker	.15
86	Mike Bordick	.15
87	Matt Williams	.15
88	Jack McDowell	.15
89	Hal Morris	.15
90	Brian Jordan	.15
91	Andy Pettitte	.35
92	Melvin Nieves	.15
93	Pedro Martinez	1.00
94	Mark Grace	.15
95	Garret Anderson	.15
96	Andre Dawson	.30
97	Ray Durham	.15
98	Jose Canseco	.50
99	Roberto Alomar	.30
100	Derek Jeter	3.00
101	Alan Benes	.15
102	Karim Garcia	.15
103	Robin Jennings RC	.15
104	Bob Abreu	.15
105	Sal Fasano (Livan Hernandez' name on front.)	.15
106	Steve Gibralter	.15
107	Jermaine Dye	.15
108	Jason Kendall	.15
109	Mike Grace RC	.15
110	Jason Schmidt	.15
111	Paul Wilson	.15
112	Rey Ordonez	.15
113	Wilton Guerrero RC	.15
114	Brooks Kieschnick	.15
115	George Arias	.15
116	Osvaldo Fernandez RC	.15
117	Todd Hollandsworth	.15
118	John Wasdin	.15
119	Eric Owens	.15
120	Chan Ho Park	.15
121	Mark Loretta	.15
122	Richard Hidalgo	.15
123	Jeff Suppan	.15
124	Jim Pittsley	.15
125	LaTroy Hawkins	.15
126	Chris Snopek	.15
127	Justin Thompson	.15
128	Jay Powell	.15
129	Alex Ochoa	.15
130	Felipe Crespo	.15
131	Matt Lawton RC	.15
132	Jimmy Haynes	.15
133	Terrell Wade	.15
134	Ruben Rivera	.15
135	Frank Thomas (Pastime Power)	.55
136	Ken Griffey Jr. (Pastime Power)	1.00
137	Greg Maddux (Pastime Power)	.65
138	Mike Piazza (Pastime Power)	.75
139	Cal Ripken Jr. (Pastime Power)	1.50
140	Albert Belle (Pastime Power)	.15
141	Mo Vaughn (Pastime Power)	.15
142	Chipper Jones (Pastime Power)	.75
143	Hideo Nomo (Pastime Power)	.25
144	Ryan Klesko (Pastime Power)	.15

Artist's Proofs

Only 500 cards each of this parallel issue were produced, seeded one in every dozen packs. The cards are identical to the regular-issue Select Certified except for the presence on front of a prismatic gold Artist's Proof logo.

	NM/M
Complete Set (144):	200.00
Common Player:	1.00
AP Stars:	7X

Red, Blue

These 1996 Select Certified insert cards were the most common of the parallel cards issued; they were seeded one per five packs. There were 1,800 Certified Red sets produced, with the number of Certified Blue sets at 180. Cards are essentially the same as regular-issue Select Certified except for the color of the foil background on front.

	NM/M
Common Red:	.50
Red Stars:	3X
Common Blue:	2.50
Blue Stars:	10X

Mirror Red, Blue, Gold

These 1996 Select Certified inserts are the scarcest of the set. Only 30 Mirror Gold sets were made, with 60 Mirror Blue sets and 90 Mirror Red. Due to the improbability of completing the collection, no complete set price is given.

	NM/M
Common Mirror Red:	6.00
Mirror Red Stars:	20X
Common Mirror Blue:	12.00
Mirror Blue Stars:	30X
Common Mirror Gold:	20.00
Mirror Gold Stars:	100X

Interleague Preview

These 1996 Select Certified insert cards feature 21 prospective matchups from interleague play's beginnings. The cards were seeded one per 42 packs. Each card can also be found in a promo version with a large, black "SAMPLE" overprint on front and back.

		NM/M
Complete Set (25):		45.00
Common Card:		.75
Promos:		1X
1	Ken Griffey Jr., Hideo Nomo	3.50
2	Greg Maddux, Mo Vaughn	3.00
3	Frank Thomas, Sammy Sosa	3.00
4	Mike Piazza, Jim Edmonds	3.50
5	Ryan Klesko, Roger Clemens	3.25
6	Derek Jeter, Rey Ordonez	4.50
7	Johnny Damon, Ray Lankford	1.00
8	Manny Ramirez, Reggie Sanders	2.50
9	Barry Bonds, Jay Buhner	4.50

10	Jason Isringhausen, Wade Boggs	3.00
11	David Cone, Chipper Jones	3.00
12	Jeff Bagwell, Will Clark	2.50
13	Tony Gwynn, Randy Johnson	3.00
14	Cal Ripken Jr., Tom Glavine	4.50
15	Kirby Puckett, Alan Benes	3.00
16	Gary Sheffield, Mike Mussina	1.00
17	Raul Mondesi, Tim Salmon	.75
18	Rondell White, Carlos Delgado	1.00
19	Cecil Fielder, Ryne Sandberg	3.00
20	Kenny Lofton, Brian Hunter	.75
21	Paul Wilson, Paul O'Neill	.75
22	Ismael Valdes, Edgar Martinez	.75
23	Matt Williams, Mark McGwire	4.00
24	Albert Belle, Barry Larkin	.75
25	Brady Anderson, Marquis Grissom	.75

Select Few

Eighteen top players are featured on these 1996 Select Certified inserts, which utilize holographic technology with a dot matrix hologram. Cards were seeded one per every 60 packs.

		NM/M
Complete Set (18):		40.00
Common Player:		1.00
1	Sammy Sosa	3.00
2	Derek Jeter	5.00
3	Ken Griffey Jr.	3.50
4	Albert Belle	1.00
5	Cal Ripken Jr.	5.00
6	Greg Maddux	3.00
7	Frank Thomas	2.50
8	Mo Vaughn	1.00
9	Chipper Jones	3.00
10	Mike Piazza	3.50
11	Ryan Klesko	1.00
12	Hideo Nomo	1.00
13	Alan Benes	1.00
14	Manny Ramirez	2.50
15	Gary Sheffield	2.00
16	Barry Bonds	5.00
17	Matt Williams	1.00
18	Johnny Damon	2.00

1997 Select Samples

The 1997 edition of Select was previewed with the issue of several regular-issue and Select Co. cards carrying a large black "SAMPLE" overprint on front and back. The Rodriguez sample, untrimmed and larger than standard size, was not distributed in three-card cello packs like the other cards. This checklist may not be complete.

		NM/M
Common Player:		1.00
3	Tony Gwynn	2.00
8	Frank Thomas	1.50
15	Paul Molitor	1.50

23	Greg Maddux	2.00
28	Javy Lopez	1.00
47	Ken Griffey Jr.	3.00
53	Alex Rodriguez	4.00
94	Will Clark	1.00

1997 Select

The Series 1 base set is made up of 150 cards printed on thick 16-point stock. Each card features a distinctive silver-foil treatment and either red (100 units) or blue (50 cards) foil accent. Blue-foiled cards were short-printed at a ratio of 1:2 compared to the red-foil cards. Blue-foil cards are indicated with a (B) in the checklist. Subsets include 40 Rookies, eight Super Stars and two checklists. Inserts include two parallel sets, (Artist's Proof and Registered Gold), Tools of the Trade, Mirror Blue Tools of the Trade, and Rookie Revolution. The cards were sold only at hobby shops in six-card packs for $2.99 each. A high-number series was issued with each card bearing a "Select Company" notation.

		NM/M
Complete Set (200):		30.00
Series 1 (#1-150):		20.00
Common Red Player:		.10
Common Blue Player:		.25
Registered Golds:		2X
Artist's Proofs:		5X
High Series (#151-200):		10.00
Common High Series:		.25
Pack (6):		1.50
Wax Box (24):		25.00
1	Juan Gonzalez (B)	2.00
2	Mo Vaughn (B)	.25
3	Tony Gwynn	1.50
4	Manny Ramirez (B)	2.00
5	Jose Canseco	.50
6	David Cone	.10
7	Chan Ho Park	.10
8	Frank Thomas	2.50
9	Todd Hollandsworth	.10
10	Marty Cordova	.10
11	Gary Sheffield (B)	.75
12	John Smoltz (B)	.25
13	Mark Grudzielanek	.10
14	Sammy Sosa (B)	3.00
15	Paul Molitor	1.00
16	Kevin Brown	.10
17	Albert Belle (B)	.25
18	Eric Young	.10
19	John Wetteland	.10
20	Ryan Klesko (B)	.25
21	Joe Carter	.10
22	Alex Ochoa	.10
23	Greg Maddux (B)	3.00
24	Roger Clemens (B)	3.00
25	Ivan Rodriguez (B)	1.50
26	Barry Bonds (B)	5.00
27	Kenny Lofton	.25
28	Javy Lopez	.10
29	Hideo Nomo (B)	1.00
30	Rusty Greer	.10
31	Rafael Palmeiro	.75
32	Mike Piazza (B)	3.50
33	Ryne Sandberg	1.50
34	Wade Boggs	1.50
35	Jim Thome (B)	1.50
36	Ken Caminiti (B)	.25
37	Mark Grace	.10
38	Brian Jordan (B)	.25
39	Craig Biggio	.10
40	Henry Rodriguez	.10
41	Dean Palmer	.10
42	Jason Kendall	.10
43	Bill Pulsipher	.10
44	Tim Salmon (B)	.25
45	Marc Newfield	.10
46	Pat Hentgen	.10
47	Ken Griffey Jr. (B)	4.00
48	Paul Wilson	.10
49	Jay Buhner	.25
50	Rickey Henderson	1.00
51	Jeff Bagwell (B)	2.00
52	Cecil Fielder	.10
53	Alex Rodriguez (B)	4.00
54	John Jaha	.10
55	Brady Anderson (B)	.25
56	Andres Galarraga	.10
57	Raul Mondesi	.10
58	Andy Pettitte	.30
59	Roberto Alomar (B)	1.00
60	Derek Jeter (B)	5.00
61	Charles Johnson	.10
62	Travis Fryman	.10
63	Chipper Jones (B)	3.00
64	Edgar Martinez	.10
65	Bobby Bonilla	.10
66	Greg Vaughn	.10
67	Bobby Higginson	.10
68	Garret Anderson	.10
69	Chuck Knoblauch (B)	.25
70	Jermaine Dye	.10
71	Cal Ripken Jr. (B)	5.00
72	Jason Giambi	.60
73	Trey Beamon	.10
74	Shawn Green	.35
75	Mark McGwire (B)	4.00
76	Carlos Delgado	.60
77	Jason Isringhausen	.10
78	Randy Johnson (B)	2.00
79	Troy Percival (B)	.25
80	Ron Gant	.10
81	Ellis Burks	.10
82	Mike Mussina (B)	1.00
83	Todd Hundley	.10
84	Jim Edmonds	.10
85	Charles Nagy	.10
86	Dante Bichette (B)	.25
87	Mariano Rivera	.20
88	Matt Williams (B)	.25
89	Rondell White	.10
90	Steve Finley	.10
91	Alex Fernandez	.10
92	Barry Larkin	.10
93	Tom Goodwin	.10
94	Will Clark	.10
95	Michael Tucker	.10
96	Derek Bell	.10
97	Larry Walker	.10
98	Alan Benes	.10
99	Tom Glavine	.35
100	Darin Erstad (B)	.35
101	Andruw Jones (B)	2.00
102	Scott Rolen	.65
103	Todd Walker (B)	.25
104	Dmitri Young	.10
105	Vladimir Guerrero (B)	2.00
106	Nomar Garciaparra	1.50
107	Danny Patterson RC	.10
108	Karim Garcia	.10
109	Todd Greene	.10
110	Ruben Rivera	.10
111	Raul Casanova	.10
112	Mike Cameron	.10
113	Bartolo Colon	.10
114	Rod Myers RC	.10
115	Todd Dunn	.10
116	Torii Hunter	.10
117	Jason Dickson	.10
118	Gene Kingsale RC	.10
119	Rafael Medina	.10
120	Raul Ibanez	.10
121	Bobby Henley RC	.10
122	Scott Spiezio	.10
123	Bobby Smith RC	.10
124	J.J. Johnson	.10
125	Bubba Trammell RC	.50
126	Jeff Abbott	.10
127	Neifi Perez	.10
128	Derrek Lee	.65
129	Kevin Brown RC	.10
130	Mendy Lopez	.10
131	Kevin Orie	.10
132	Ryan Jones	.10
133	Juan Encarnacion	.10
134	Jose Guillen (B)	.25
135	Greg Norton	.10
136	Richie Sexson	.10
137	Jay Payton	.10
138	Bob Abreu	.15
139	Ronnie Belliard RC	.10
140	Wilton Guerrero (B)	.25
141	Alex Rodriguez (Select Stars)(B)	2.00
142	Juan Gonzalez (Select Stars)(B)	.50
143	Ken Caminiti (Select Stars)(B)	.25
144	Frank Thomas (Select Stars)(B)	1.25
145	Ken Griffey Jr. (Select Stars)(B)	1.75
146	John Smoltz (Select Stars)(B)	.25
147	Mike Piazza (Select Stars)(B)	1.75
148	Derek Jeter (Select Stars)(B)	3.00
149	Frank Thomas (Checklist)	.75
150	Ken Griffey Jr. (Checklist)	1.00
151	Jose Cruz Jr. RC	1.00
152	Moises Alou	.25
153	Hideki Irabu RC	.50
154	Glendon Rusch	.25
155	Ron Coomer	.25
156	Jeremi Gonzalez RC	.25
157	Fernando Tatis RC	.40
158	John Olerud	.25
159	Rickey Henderson	1.00
160	Shannon Stewart	.25
161	Kevin Polcovich	.25
162	Jose Rosado	.25
163	Ray Lankford	.25
164	David Justice	.25
165	Mark Kotsay RC	.50
166	Deivi Cruz RC	.50
167	Billy Wagner	.25
168	Jacob Cruz	.25
169	Matt Morris	.25
170	Brian Banks	.25
171	Brett Tomko	.25
172	Todd Helton	.75
173	Eric Young	.25
174	Bernie Williams	.25
175	Jeff Fassero	.25
176	Ryan McGuire	.25
177	Darryl Kile	.25
178	Kelvim Escobar RC	.50
179	Dave Nilsson	.25
180	Geronimo Berroa	.25
181	Livan Hernandez	.25
182	Tony Womack RC	.50
183	Deion Sanders	.25
184	Jeff Kent	.25
185	Brian Hunter	.25
186	Jose Malave	.25
187	Steve Woodard RC	.50
188	Brad Radke	.25
189	Todd Dunwoody	.25
190	Joey Hamilton	.25
191	Denny Naegle	.25
192	Bobby Jones	.25
193	Tony Clark	.25
194	Jaret Wright RC	.50
195	Matt Stairs	.25
196	Francisco Cordova	.25
197	Justin Thompson	.25
198	Pokey Reese	.25
199	Garrett Stephenson	.25
200	Carl Everett	.25

Artist's Proofs

Featuring a holographic foil background and special Artist's Proof logo on front, this parallel of the 150-card Series 1 Select was a random pack insert at an average pull rate of 1:71 for reds and 1:355 for blues.

	NM/M
Complete Set (150):	450.00
Common Red:	1.25
Red Stars:	5X
Common Blue:	2.50
Blue Stars:	1.5X

Company

Select Company was intended to be a one-per-pack parallel found in '97 high series. The cards have the front background photo replaced with textured silver metallic foil and "Select Company" printed vertically at right-center. While all high-number (151-200) cards have the "Select Company" notation erroneously printed on front, only those cards with silver-foil backgrounds are true parallels. All Select Company cards can also be found in a promo version with a large black "SAMPLE" overprinted on back.

	NM/M
Complete Set (200):	150.00
Common Player:	.50
Red Stars:	3X
Blue Stars:	1.5X
High-Series Stars:	1.5X
Samples:	10X

Registered Gold

This parallel insert set, like the regular issue, can be found with 100 red-foil and 50 blue-foil enhanced cards. They differ from the regular issue in the use of gold foil instead of silver on the right side of the front. Also, the inserts have "Registered Gold" printed vertically on the right side of the photo. Backs are identical to the regular issue. Red-foil Registered Gold cards are found on average of once every 11 packs; blue-foiled cards are a 1-in-47 pick.

	NM/M
Complete Set (150):	300.00
Common Red Gold:	.75
Common Blue Gold:	1.50
Registered Gold Stars:	2X

Autographs

Four top candidates for the 1997 Rookie of the Year Award - Wilton Guerrero, Jose Guillen, Andruw Jones and Todd Walker - each signed a limited number of their Select Rookie cards. Jones signed 2,500 cards while each of the other players signed 3,000 each.

		NM/M
Complete Set (4):		15.00
Common Autograph:		3.00
AU1	Wilton Guerrero	3.00
AU2	Jose Guillen	3.00
AU3	Andruw Jones	10.00
AU4	Todd Walker	3.00

Rookie Revolution

This 20-card insert highlights some of the top young stars in the game. Cards feature a silver micro-etched mylar design on front. Backs are sequentially numbered and contain a few words about the player. Odds of finding a card are 1:56 packs.

		NM/M
Complete Set (20):		21.00
Common Player:		.50
1	Andruw Jones	2.50
2	Derek Jeter	6.00
3	Todd Hollandsworth	.50
4	Edgar Renteria	.50
5	Jason Kendall	.50
6	Rey Ordonez	.50
7	F.P. Santangelo	.50
8	Jermaine Dye	.50
9	Alex Ochoa	.50
10	Vladimir Guerrero	2.50
11	Dmitri Young	.50
12	Todd Walker	.50
13	Scott Rolen	1.50
14	Nomar Garciaparra	3.50
15	Ruben Rivera	.50
16	Darin Erstad	1.00
17	Todd Greene	.50
18	Mariano Rivera	1.00
19	Trey Beamon	.50
20	Karim Garcia	.50

Tools of the Trade

A 25-card insert featuring a double-front design salutes a top veteran player on one side and a promising youngster on the other. Cards feature a silver-foil card stock with gold-foil stamping. Cards were inserted in 1:9 packs. A parallel to this set - Blue Mirror Tools of the Trade - features blue-foil stock with an insert ratio of 1:240 packs.

		NM/M
Complete Set (25):		25.00
Common Player:		.40
Mirror Blues:		2.5X
1	Ken Griffey Jr., Andruw Jones	2.00
2	Greg Maddux, Andy Pettitte	1.50
3	Cal Ripken Jr., Chipper Jones	2.50
4	Mike Piazza, Jason Kendall	2.00
5	Albert Belle, Karim Garcia	.40
6	Mo Vaughn, Dmitri Young	.40
7	Juan Gonzalez, Vladimir Guerrero	1.50
8	Tony Gwynn, Jermaine Dye	1.50
9	Barry Bonds, Alex Ochoa	2.50
10	Jeff Bagwell, Jason Giambi	1.00
11	Kenny Lofton, Darin Erstad	.50
12	Gary Sheffield, Manny Ramirez	1.00
13	Tim Salmon, Todd Hollandsworth	.40
14	Sammy Sosa, Ruben Rivera	1.50
15	Paul Molitor, George Arias	1.00
16	Jim Thome, Todd Walker	.75
17	Wade Boggs, Scott Rolen	1.50
18	Ryne Sandberg, Chuck Knoblauch	1.50
19	Mark McGwire, Frank Thomas	2.25
20	Ivan Rodriguez, Charles Johnson	.75
21	Brian Jordan, Trey Beamon	.40
22	Roger Clemens, Troy Percival	1.75
23	John Smoltz, Mike Mussina	.65
24	Alex Rodriguez, Rey Ordonez	2.25
25	Derek Jeter, Nomar Garciaparra	2.50

1998 Select

Select was intended to be a four-tier, 100-player, 250-card base set based on the "Quasar System." One hundred players were to appear as one-star cards; two-star cards comprised a shortened checklist of 75 of those players, and so on through three- and four-star subsets. Besides an increase in player popularity, each level featured enhanced technical bells and whistles on the cards themselves. Each five-card $3.99 pack was to have three one-star cards and two two-star cards, unless one or more were replaced with three- or four-star cards or one of several insert series. The set was never officially released due to the mid-year collapse and subsequent bankruptcy of Select's parent firm, Pinnacle.

	NM/M
Common Player:	10.00

Numbers

Five players from each of four major statistical categories were selected for inclusion in this all-numbered insert issue. Each player in the chase set was intended to have cards numbered to his 1997 performance in the category for which he was chosen. While distribution of the cards was halted by Pinnacle's bankruptcy, limited quantities of these insert cards have found their way into the hobby. Those cards seen thus far do not bear sequential numbers. The number of cards intended for each player is listed, although it is unknown how many of each player were actually released.

		NM/M
Complete Set (20):		1,150
Common Player:		20.00
1	Mark McGwire/58	225.00
2	Juan Gonzalez/42	40.00
3	Ken Griffey Jr./56	225.00
4	Jeff Bagwell/43	60.00
5	Andres Galarraga/41	40.00
6	Frank Thomas/347	30.00
7	Mike Piazza/362	100.00
8	Tony Gwynn/372	35.00
9	Larry Walker/366	20.00
10	Kenny Lofton/333	20.00
11	Barry Bonds/446	50.00
12	Chuck Knoblauch/390	20.00
13	Derek Jeter/370	150.00
14	Nomar Garciaparra/342	75.00
15	Chipper Jones/371	60.00
16	Pedro Martinez/305	40.00
17	Hideo Nomo/233	65.00
18	Randy Johnson/291	30.00
19	Roger Clemens/292	75.00
20	Greg Maddux/177	75.00

Jersey Numbers

Whatever the intended scope and manner of distribution for this parallel insert may never be known because Pinnacle's bankruptcy interrupted the issue. Only a few specimens have made their way into the hobby. The gold-foil highlighted cards were intended to be serially numbered on back to the extent of the player's uniform number.

		NM/M
116	Ken Griffey Jr./24	65.00

1998 Select Selected Samples

Selected promos were released in two-card cello packs prior to Pinnacle's bankruptcy. Fronts have color action photos on bright metallic-foil backgrounds was a large "S." Backs have a smaller version of the front photo along with career highlights and a large overprinted "SAMPLE."

	NM/M
Complete Set (10):	30.00
Common Player:	2.50
1 Vladimir Guerrero	4.00
2 Nomar Garciaparra	5.00
3 Ben Grieve	2.50
4 Travis Lee	2.50
5 Jose Cruz Jr.	2.50
6 Alex Rodriguez	6.00
7 Todd Helton	3.50
8 Derek Jeter	7.00
9 Scott Rolen	3.50
10 Jaret Wright	2.50

1998 Select Selected

Intended as a 1:23 pack insert for a set which was never released due to Pinnacle's bankruptcy, Selected cards later leaked out into the hobby market. Fronts have color action photos on bright metallic-foil backgrounds with a large "S." Backs have a smaller version of the front photo along with career highlights.

	NM/M
Complete Set (10):	135.00
Common Player:	10.00
1 Vladimir Guerrero	15.00
2 Nomar Garciaparra	20.00
3 Ben Grieve	10.00
4 Travis Lee	10.00
5 Jose Cruz Jr.	10.00
6 Alex Rodriguez	22.50
7 Todd Helton	12.50
8 Derek Jeter	25.00
9 Scott Rolen	12.50
10 Jaret Wright	10.00

2002 Select Rookies & Prospects Autographs

	NM/M
Common Player:	3.00
Retail-Exclusive	

1	Abraham Nunez	5.00
2	Adam Bernero	3.00
3	Adam Pettyjohn	3.00
4	Alex Escobar	4.00
5	Allan Simpson	4.00
6	Andres Torres	3.00
7	Andy Pratt	4.00
8	Bert Snow	3.00
9	Bill Ortega	3.00
10	Billy Sylvester	3.00
11	Brad Voyles	3.00
12	Brandon Backe	3.00
13	Brent Abernathy	3.00
14	Brian Mallette	3.00
15	Brian Rogers	3.00
16	Cam Esslinger	3.00
17	Carlos Garcia	3.00
18	Carlos Valderrama	3.00
19	Cesar Izturis	6.00
20	Chad Durbin	3.00
21	Chris Baker	3.00
22	Claudio Vargas	3.00
23	Cory Aldridge	3.00
24	Craig Monroe	5.00
25	David Elder	3.00
26	David Brous	3.00
27	David Espinosa	3.00
28	Derrick Lewis	3.00
29	Elio Serrano	3.00
30	Elpidio Guzman	3.00
31	Eric Cyr	3.00
32	Eric Valent	4.00
33	Erik Bedard	5.00
34	Esix Snead	3.00
35	Francis Beltran	3.00
36	George Perez	3.00
37	Gene Altman	3.00
38	Greg Miller	4.00
39	Horacio Ramirez	3.00
40	Jason Hart	4.50
41	Jason Karnuth	3.00
42	Jason Romano	3.00
43	Jeff Deardorff	3.00
44	Jeremy Affeldt	3.00
45	Jeremy Lambert	3.00
46	John Ennis	3.00
47	John Grabow	3.00
48	Jose Cueto	3.00
49	Jose Mieses	3.00
50	Jose Ortiz	3.00
51	Josh Pearce	3.00
52	Josue Perez	3.00
53	Juan Diaz	3.00
54	Juan Pena	3.00
55	Keith Ginter	3.00
56	Kevin Frederick	3.00
57	Kevin Joseph	3.00
58	Kevin Olsen	3.00
59	Kris Keller	3.00
60	Larry Bigbie	3.00
61	Les Walrond	3.00
62	Luis Pineda	3.00
63	Luis Rivas	3.00
64	Luis Rivera	4.50
65	Luke Hudson	3.00
66	Marcus Giles	8.00
67	Mark Ellis	3.00
68	Martin Vargas	3.00
69	Matt Childers	3.00
70	Matt Guerrier	3.00
71	Matt Thornton	3.00
72	Matt White	3.00
73	Mike Penney	3.00
74	Nate Teut	3.00
75	Nick Maness	3.00
76	Orlando Woodards	3.00
77	Paul Phillips	3.00
78	Pedro Feliz	3.00
79	Ramon Vazquez	3.00
80	Raul Chavez	3.00
81	Reed Johnson	3.00
82	Ryan Freel	4.50
83	Ryan Jamison	3.00
84	Ryan Ludwick	10.00
85	Saul Rivera	3.00
86	Steve Bechler	3.00
87	Steve Green	3.00
88	Steve Smyth	3.00
89	Tike Redman	3.00
90	Tom Shearn	3.00
91	Tomas de la Rosa	3.00
92	Tony Cogan	3.00
93	Travis Hafner	25.00
94	Travis Hughes	3.00
95	Wilkin Ruan	3.00
96	Will Ohman	3.00
97	Wilmy Caceres	3.00
98	Wilson Guzman	3.00
99	Winston Abreu	3.00

1992 Sentry Robin Yount

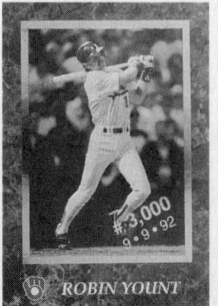

	NM/M
Common Player:	3.00

At the Sept. 25, 1992, Brewers home game, the first 25,000 fans through the turnstile received a four-card set commemorating Robin Yount's 3,000th career hit. The 2-1/2" x 3-1/2" cards feature on front a gold-foil framed action photo set against a purple marbled border. Backs have a write-up about the career milestone hit and include the grocery store logo at bottom. The cards are unnumbered and were issued in a heavy paper wrapper.

	NM/M
Complete Set (4):	15.00
Common Card:	5.00
(1) Hit #1, April 12, 1974 (Robin Yount)	5.00
(2) Hit #1,000, Aug. 16, 1980 (Robin Yount)	5.00
(3) Hit #2,000, Sept. 6, 1986 (Robin Yount)	5.00
(4) Hit #3,000, Sept. 9, 1992 (Robin Yount)	5.00

1993 Sentry Brewers Memorable Moments

Fans at a special Brewer home game were given this set of team highlight cards. Fronts have a color photo of the highlight with a brief description and date printed in gold foil. The photo is framed in dark blue, which is also used for the border of the card. The territory between the photo and border is printed in light blue and includes the Brewers logo and "Memorable Moments" headline. Backs have a description of the action shown on front, and the sponsor's logo. Cards are numbered according to player uniform number printed on back.

	NM/M
Complete Set (4):	8.00
Common Card:	1.00
4 Paul Molitor	3.50
7 Dale Sveum	1.00
19 Robin Yount	3.50
20 Juan Nieves	1.00

1993 Sentry Milwaukee Brewers

This set of a dozen coupon/card combos was distributed at Milwaukee area Sentry grocery stores during the 1993 season. A new card was issued every week or two between April 27 and September 28. Each piece measures 12-1/2" x 7" and has a 5" x 7" Brewer player photo attached to six perforated coupons, each of which has a postage stamp-size Brewer photo at lower-right. Backs are blank. Cards #11 and 12 were never officially issued and have blank coupons.

	NM/M
Complete Set (12):	7.00
Common Player:	.60
1 Pat Listach	.50

2	Tom Brunansky	.50
3	B.J. Surhoff	.50
4	Kevin Reimer	.50
5	Darryl Hamilton	.50
6	Greg Vaughn	.50
7	Robin Yount	4.00
8	Phil Garner	.50
9	Bill Spiers	.50
10	Dave Nilsson	.50
11	Bill Wegman	.50
12	Cal Eldred	.50

1994 Sentry Brewer Highlights

This eight-card set featuring highlights from Brewers history was issued in the team's 25th anniversary season. Sponsored by Sentry Foods, the cards were available on a one-per-week basis, attached to an 8-1/2" x 11" sheet of coupons, from May through August. (The last two cards were never officially issued due to the strike.) In standard 2-1/2" x 3-1/2", cards feature wide violet borders highlighted by green and gold geometric shapes. The team's 25th anniversary logo is at top-left, with the featured highlight at upper-right in gold. The player's name appears in white in a black ribbon beneath the color photo. Backs describe the highlight and are printed in blue and black. There is no sponsor's logo or card number. Cards are checklisted here alphabetically.

	NM/M
Complete Set (8):	14.00
Common Player:	1.00
(1) Hank Aaron (Final Home Run)	5.00
(2) Rollie Fingers (Cy Young/MVP Season)	1.50
(3) Pat Listach (Rookie of the Year)	1.00
(4) Paul Molitor (39-game Hitting Streak)	3.50
(5) Juan Nieves (No-hitter)	1.00
(6) Don Sutton (3,000th Strikeout)	1.00
(7) Robin Yount (3,000 Hit)	3.50
(8) Triumphant Trio (Jim Gantner, Paul Molitor, Robin Yount)	2.50

1983 7-11 Slurpee Coins

This first production of player coins by 7-Eleven stores was distributed only in the Los Angeles area. The test promotion, which awarded a coin to every purchaser of a large Slurpee drink, must have proved successful, as it was expanded nationally in subsequent years. Six California Angels and six Los Angeles Dodgers are included in the full-color set, with Angels players in red backgrounds and the Dodgers in blue. The 1-3/4" diameter plastic coins feature both an action and a portrait photo of the player, which can be alternately seen by moving the coin slightly

from side to side. The 12 coin backs are numbered and include brief statistics and the company logo.

	NM/M
Complete Set (12):	6.00
Common Player:	.50
1 Rod Carew	2.00
2 Steve Sax	.50
3 Fred Lynn	.50
4 Pedro Guerrero	.50
5 Reggie Jackson	3.00
6 Dusty Baker	.50
7 Doug DeCinces	.50
8 Fernando Valenzuela	.50
9 Tommy John	.50
10 Rick Monday	.50
11 Bobby Grich	.50
12 Greg Brock	.50

1984 7-11 Slurpee Coins Central Region

The 7-Eleven/Slurpee coins were distributed nationally in 1984 with 60 different players in three regional issues of 24 pieces each. Coins of Brett, Dawson, Murphy, Murray, Schmidt and Yount were common to all three regions. The 1-3/4" diameter plastic coins feature an action and a portrait photo on front which change when the viewing angle is altered. Statistics and coin numbers are found on the backs, along with the 7-Eleven logo.

	NM/M
Complete Set (24):	7.50
Common Player:	.25
1 Andre Dawson	.40
2 Robin Yount	.75
3 Dale Murphy	.50
4 Mike Schmidt	1.25
5 George Brett	1.25
6 Eddie Murray	.75
7 Bruce Sutter	.65
8 Cecil Cooper	.25
9 Willie McGee	.25
10 Mike Hargrove	.25
11 Kent Hrbek	.25
12 Carlton Fisk	.75
13 Mario Soto	.25
14 Lonnie Smith	.25
15 Gary Carter	.75
16 Lou Whitaker	.25
17 Ron Kittle	.25
18 Paul Molitor	.75
19 Ozzie Smith	1.00
20 Fergie Jenkins	.40
21 Ted Simmons	.25
22 Pete Rose	1.50
23 LaMarr Hoyt	.25
24 Dan Quisenberry	.25

Eastern Region

	NM/M
Complete Set (24):	10.00
Common Player:	.25
1 Andre Dawson	.40
2 Robin Yount	.75
3 Dale Murphy	.50
4 Mike Schmidt	1.25
5 George Brett	1.25
6 Eddie Murray	.75
7 Dave Winfield	.75
8 Tom Seaver	.75
9 Mike Boddicker	.25
10 Wade Boggs	1.00
11 Bill Madlock	.25
12 Steve Carlton	.50
13 Dave Stieb	.25
14 Cal Ripken, Jr.	3.00
15 Jim Rice	.40
16 Ron Guidry	.25
17 Darryl Strawberry	.25
18 Tony Pena	.25
19 John Denny	.25
20 Tim Raines	.25
21 Rick Dempsey	.25
22 Rich Gossage	.25
23 Gary Matthews	.25
24 Keith Hernandez	.25

Western Region

	NM/M
Complete Set (24):	9.00
Common Player:	.25
1 Andre Dawson	.40
2 Robin Yount	.75
3 Dale Murphy	.50
4 Mike Schmidt	1.25

5	George Brett	1.25
6	Eddie Murray	.75
7	Steve Garvey	.35
8	Rod Carew	.75
9	Fernando Valenzuela	.25
10	Bob Horner	.25
11	Buddy Bell	.25
12	Reggie Jackson	1.00
13	Nolan Ryan	2.00
14	Pedro Guerrero	.25
15	Atlee Hammaker	.25
16	Fred Lynn	.25
17	Terry Kennedy	.25
18	Dusty Baker	.25
19	Jose Cruz	.25
20	Steve Rogers	.25
21	Rickey Henderson	.75
22	Steve Sax	.25
23	Dickie Thon	.25
24	Matt Young	.25

Jumbo Coin

Dale Murphy, the MVP of the National League in 1983 was featured on a jumbo-format (4-1/2" diameter) "3D" disc distributed by 7-11 stores in conjunction with their Slurpee fountain drink. Like the smaller Slurpee coins, the photos on the disc change as the viewing angle is changed.

	NM/M
Dale Murphy	15.00

1985 7-11 Slurpee Coins Eastern Region

In 1985, the "Slurpee Disc" promotion was further expanded to a total of 94 full-color coins. The formats were very similar to the previous two years, but there were six different regional sets. Five of these regional series contain 16 coins, with a Detroit series totaling 14. The other five regions are: East, West, Great Lakes, Central and Southeast. The coins are again 1-1/4" in diameter, printed on plastic with double-image photos. All coins are numbered. No player appears in all regions, although several are in two or more.

	NM/M
Complete Set (16):	10.00
Common Player:	.25
1 Eddie Murray	1.00
2 George Brett	2.50
3 Steve Carlton	1.00
4 Jim Rice	.45
5 Dave Winfield	1.00
6 Mike Boddicker	.25
7 Wade Boggs	2.00
8 Dwight Evans	.25
9 Dwight Gooden	.25
10 Keith Hernandez	.25
11 Bill Madlock	.25
12 Don Mattingly	2.50
13 Dave Righetti	.25
14 Cal Ripken, Jr.	4.00
15 Juan Samuel	.25
16 Mike Schmidt	2.50

Great Lakes Region

	NM/M
Complete Set (16):	10.00
Common Player:	.25
1 Willie Hernandez	.25
2 George Brett	2.50
3 Dave Winfield	1.00
4 Eddie Murray	1.00
5 Bruce Sutter	.75
6 Harold Baines	.25
7 Bert Blyleven	.25
8 Leon Durham	.25
9 Chet Lemon	.25
10 Pete Rose	3.00
11 Ryne Sandberg	2.00
12 Tom Seaver	1.00
13 Mario Soto	.25
14 Rick Sutcliffe	.25
15 Alan Trammell	.25
16 Robin Yount	1.00

Southeastern Region

	NM/M
Complete Set (16):	7.50
Common Player:	.25
1 Dale Murphy	.75
2 Steve Carlton	1.00

#	Player	NM/M
3	Nolan Ryan	4.00
4	Bruce Sutter	.75
5	Dave Winfield	1.00
6	Steve Bedrosian	.50
7	Andre Dawson	.50
8	Kirk Gibson	.25
9	Fred Lynn	.25
10	Gary Matthews	.25
11	Phil Niekro	1.00
12	Tim Raines	.25
13	Darryl Strawberry	.25
14	Dave Stieb	.25
15	Willie Upshaw	.25
16	Lou Whitaker	.25

Southwest/Central Region

#	Player	NM/M
	Complete Set (16):	10.00
	Common Player:	.25
1	Nolan Ryan	4.00
2	George Brett	2.50
3	Dave Winfield	1.00
4	Mike Schmidt	2.50
5	Bruce Sutter	.75
6	Joaquin Andujar	.25
7	Willie Hernandez	.25
8	Wade Boggs	1.50
9	Gary Carter	1.00
10	Jose Cruz	.25
11	Kent Hrbek	.25
12	Reggie Jackson	1.50
13	Lance Parrish	.25
14	Terry Puhl	.25
15	Dan Quisenberry	.25
16	Ozzie Smith	1.50

Western Region

#	Player	NM/M
	Complete Set (16):	7.50
	Common Player:	.25
1	Mike Schmidt	2.50
2	Jim Rice	.45
3	Dale Murphy	.50
4	Eddie Murray	1.00
5	Dave Winfield	1.00
6	Rod Carew	1.00
7	Alvin Davis	.35
8	Steve Garvey	.35
9	Rich Gossage	.25
10	Pedro Guerrero	.25
11	Tony Gwynn	1.50
12	Rickey Henderson	1.00
13	Reggie Jackson	2.00
14	Jeff Leonard	.25
15	Alejandro Pena	.25
16	Fernando Valenzuela	.25

Tigers

#	Player	NM/M
	Complete Set (14):	7.50
	Common Player:	.75
1	Sparky Anderson	1.00
2	Darrell Evans	.75
3	Kirk Gibson	1.00
4	Willie Hernandez	.75
5	Larry Herndon	.75
6	Chet Lemon	.75
7	Aurelio Lopez	.75
8	Jack Morris	1.00
9	Lance Parrish	.75
10	Dan Petry	.75
11	Dave Rozema	.75
12	Alan Trammell	1.00
13	Lou Whitaker	1.00
14	Milt Wilcox	.75

Test Coins

These 3-D "Magic Motion" coins are identical to the regional issues in all aspects except size. These test coins are 2-1/4" diameter, an inch bigger than the issued versions.

#	Player	NM/M
	Complete Set (3):	4.00
	Common Player:	1.00
1	Mike Schmidt	2.50
2	Bruce Sutter	1.00
3	Dave Winfield	1.50

Jumbo Coins

World Series MVP Alan Trammell and Yankees slugger Dave Winfield were featured on jumbo-format (4-1/2" diameter) "3D" discs distributed by 7-11 stores in conjunction with their Slurpee fountain drink. Like the smaller Slurpee coins, the photos on the disc change as the viewing angle is changed.

#	Player	NM/M
	Complete Set (2):	15.00
(1)	Alan Trammell	5.00
(2)	Dave Winfield	10.00

Twins

The Minnesota Twins, in co-operation with 7-Eleven and the Fire Marshall's Association, issued this set of 13 baseball fire safety cards. The card fronts feature full-color pictures of Twins players. A fire safety tip and short player history appear on the back. The cards were given out at all 7-Eleven stores in the state and at the Twins June 3 baseball game. Each fan received one baseball card with a poster which told how to collect the other cards in the set. Twelve cards feature players and the 13th card has an artist's rendering of Twins players on the front and a checklist of the set on the back. A group of 50,000 cards was distributed to fifth graders throughout the state by the fire departments.

#	Player	NM/M
	Complete Set (13):	6.00
	Common Player:	.35
1	Kirby Puckett	5.00
2	Frank Viola	.35
3	Mickey Hatcher	.35
4	Kent Hrbek	.35
5	John Butcher	.35
6	Roy Smalley	.35
7	Tom Brunansky	.35
8	Ron Davis	.35
9	Gary Gaetti	.35
10	Tim Teufel	.35
11	Mike Smithson	.35
12	Tim Laudner	.35
---	Checklist	.10

1986 7-11 Slurpee Coins Eastern Region

This marked the fourth year of production for these coins, issued with the purchase of a large Slurpee drink at 7-Eleven stores. Once again, there are several regional issues, with 16 coins issued for four different regions in 1986. The 1-3/4" diameter plastic coins each feature three different players' pictures, which can be seen alternately by tilting from side to side. Eight of the coins are the same in every region. Each coin is numbered on the back, along with brief player information.

#	Coin	NM/M
	Complete Set (16):	7.50
	Common Coin:	.25
1	Dwight Gooden	.25
2	Batting Champs (Wade Boggs, George Brett, Pete Rose)	2.50
3	MVP's (Keith Hernandez, Don Mattingly, Cal Ripken, Jr.)	2.50
4	Slugging Champs (Harold Baines, Pedro Guerrero, Dave Parker)	.25
5	Home Run Champs (Dale Murphy, Jim Rice, Mike Schmidt)	2.00
6	Cy Young Winners (Ron Guidry, Bret Saberhagen, Fernando Valenzuela)	.25
7	Bullpen Aces (Rich Gossage, Dan Quisenberry, Bruce Sutter)	.50
8	Strikeout Kings (Steve Carlton, Nolan Ryan, Tom Seaver)	2.50
9	1985 Rookies (Steve Lyons, Rick Schu, Larry Sheets)	.25
10	Bullpen Aces (Jeff Reardon, Dave Righetti, Bob Stanley)	.25
11	Power Hitters (George Bell, Darryl Strawberry, Dave Winfield)	.75
12	Base Stealers (Rickey Henderson, Tim Raines, Juan Samuel)	.75
13	Home Run Hitters (Andre Dawson, Dwight Evans, Eddie Murray)	.75
14	Ace Pitchers (Mike Boddicker, Ron Darling, Dave Stieb)	.25
15	1985 Bullpen Rookies (Tim Burke, Brian Fisher, Roger McDowell)	.25
16	Sluggers (Jesse Barfield, Gary Carter, Fred Lynn)	.75

Mideastern Region

#	Coin	NM/M
	Complete Set (16):	7.50
	Common Coin:	.25
1	Dwight Gooden	.25
2	Batting Champs (Wade Boggs, George Brett, Pete Rose)	2.50
3	MVP's (Keith Hernandez, Don Mattingly, Cal Ripken)	2.50
4	Slugging Champs (Harold Baines, Pedro Guerrero, Dave Parker)	.25
5	Home Run Champs (Dale Murphy, Jim Rice, Mike Schmidt)	2.00
6	Cy Young Winners (Ron Guidry, Bret Saberhagen, Fernando Valenzuela)	.25
7	Bullpen Aces (Rich Gossage, Dan Quisenberry, Bruce Sutter)	.50
8	Strikeout Kings (Steve Carlton, Nolan Ryan, Tom Seaver)	2.50
9	MVP's (Willie Hernandez, Ryne Sandberg, Robin Yount)	1.50
10	Ace Pitchers (Bert Blyleven, Jack Morris, Rick Sutcliffe)	.25
11	Bullpen Aces (Rollie Fingers, Bob James, Lee Smith)	.50
12	All-Star Catchers (Carlton Fisk, Lance Parrish, Tony Pena)	.75
13	1985 Rookies (Shawon Dunston, Ozzie Guillen, Ernest Riles)	.25
14	Star Outfielders (Brett Butler, Chet Lemon, Willie Wilson)	.25
15	Home Run Hitters (Tom Brunansky, Cecil Cooper, Darrell Evans)	.25
16	Big Hitters (Kirk Gibson, Paul Molitor, Greg Walker)	.75

Midwestern Region

#	Coin	NM/M
	Complete Set (16)	7.50
	Common Coin:	.25
1	Dwight Gooden	.25
2	Batting Champs (Wade Boggs, George Brett, Pete Rose)	2.50
3	MVP's (Keith Hernandez, Don Mattingly, Cal Ripken, Jr.)	2.50
4	Slugging Champs (Harold Baines, Pedro Guerrero, Dave Parker)	.25
5	Home Run Champs (Dale Murphy, Jim Rice, Mike Schmidt)	2.00
6	Cy Young Winners (Ron Guidry, Bret Saberhagen, Fernando Valenzuela)	.25
7	Bullpen Aces (Rich Gossage, Dan Quisenberry, Bruce Sutter)	.50
8	Strikeout Kings (Steve Carlton, Nolan Ryan, Tom Seaver)	2.50
9	1985 Rookies (Vince Coleman, Glenn Davis, Oddibe McDowell)	.25
10	Gold Glovers (Buddy Bell, Ozzie Smith, Lou Whitaker)	1.00
11	Ace Pitchers (Mike Scott, Mario Soto, John Tudor)	.25
12	Bullpen Aces (Jeff Lahti, Ted Power, Dave Smith)	.25
13	Big Hitters (Jack Clark, Jose Cruz, Bob Horner)	.25
14	Star Second Basemen (Bill Doran, Tommy Herr, Ron Oester)	.25
15	1985 Rookie Pitchers (Tom Browning, Joe Hesketh, Todd Worrell)	.25
16	Top Switch-Hitters (Willie McGee, Jerry Mumphrey, Pete Rose)	2.00

Western Region

#	Coin	NM/M
	Complete Set (16)	7.50
	Common Coin:	.25
1	Dwight Gooden	.25
2	Batting Champs (Wade Boggs, George Brett, Pete Rose)	2.50
3	MVP's (Keith Hernandez, Don Mattingly, Cal Ripken, Jr.)	2.50
4	Slugging Champs (Harold Baines, Pedro Guerrero, Dave Parker)	.25
5	Home Run Champs (Dale Murphy, Jim Rice, Mike Schmidt)	2.00
6	Cy Young Winners (Ron Guidry, Bret Saberhagen, Fernando Valenzuela)	.25
7	Bullpen Aces (Rich Gossage, Dan Quisenberry, Bruce Sutter)	.50
8	Strikeout Kings (Steve Carlton, Nolan Ryan, Tom Seaver)	2.50
9	Home Run Champs (Reggie Jackson, Dave Kingman, Gorman Thomas)	1.00
10	Batting Champs (Rod Carew, Tony Gwynn, Carney Lansford)	1.00
11	Sluggers (Phil Bradley, Mike Marshall, Graig Nettles)	.25
12	Ace Pitchers (Andy Hawkins, Orel Hershiser, Mike Witt)	.25
13	1985 Rookies (Chris Brown, Ivan Calderon, Mariano Duncan)	.25
14	Big Hitters (Steve Garvey, Bill Madlock, Jim Presley)	.25
15	Bullpen Aces (Jay Howell, Donnie Moore, Ed Nunez)	.25
16	1985 Bullpen Rookies (Karl Best, Stewart Cliburn, Steve Ontiveros)	.25

Jumbo Coin

Three of the game's top stars were featured on a jumbo-format (4-1/2" diameter) "3D" disc distributed by 7-11 stores in conjunction with their Slurpee fountain drink. Like the smaller Slurpee coins, the photos on the disc change as the viewing angle is changed.

Coin	NM/M
Wade Boggs, George Brett, Pete Rose	10.00

1987 7-11 Slurpee Coins Eastern Region

Continuing with a tradition started in 1983, 7-Eleven stores offered a free "Super Star Sports Coin" with the purchase of a Slurpee drink. Five different regional sets of Slurpee coins were issued for 1987, a total of 75 coins. Each coin measures 1-3/4" in diameter and features a multiple image effect which allows three different pictures to be seen, depending on how the coin is tilted. The coin reverses contain career records and personal player information.

#	Player	NM/M
	Complete Set (15):	7.50
	Common Player:	.25
1	Gary Carter	1.00
2	Don Baylor	.25
3	Rickey Henderson	1.00
4	Lenny Dykstra	.25
5	Wade Boggs	1.50
6	Mike Pagliarulo	.25
7	Dwight Gooden	.25
8	Roger Clemens	2.00
9	Dave Righetti	.25
10	Keith Hernandez	.25
11	Pat Dodson	.25
12	Don Mattingly	2.00
13	Darryl Strawberry	.25
14	Jim Rice	.45
15	Dave Winfield	1.00

Great Lakes Region

#	Player	NM/M
	Complete Set (16):	6.00
	Common Player:	.25
1	Harold Baines	.25
2	Jody Davis	.25
3	John Cangelosi	.25
4	Shawon Dunston	.25
5	Dave Cochrane	.25
6	Leon Durham	.25
7	Carlton Fisk	1.50
8	Dennis Eckersley	1.00
9	Ozzie Guillen	.25
10	Gary Matthews	.25
11	Ron Karkovice	.25
12	Keith Moreland	.25
13	Bobby Thigpen	.25
14	Ryne Sandberg	2.50
15	Greg Walker	.25
16	Lee Smith	.25

Mideastern Region

#	Player	NM/M
	Complete Set (16):	7.50
	Common Player:	.25
1	Gary Carter	1.00
2	Marty Barrett	.25
3	Jody Davis	.25
4	Don Aase	.25
5	Lenny Dykstra	.25
6	Wade Boggs	1.50
7	Keith Moreland	.25
8	Mike Boddicker	.25
9	Dwight Gooden	.25
10	Roger Clemens	2.00
11	Ryne Sandberg	1.50
12	Eddie Murray	1.00
13	Keith Hernandez	.25
14	Jim Rice	.45
15	Lee Smith	.25
16	Cal Ripken, Jr.	4.00

Western Region

#	Player	NM/M
	Complete Set (16):	2.00
	Common Player:	.25
1	Doug DeCinces	.25
2	Mariano Duncan	.25
3	Wally Joyner	.25
4	Pedro Guerrero	.25
5	Kirk McCaskill	.25
6	Orel Hershiser	.25
7	Gary Pettis	.25
8	Mike Marshall	.25
9	Dick Schofield	.25
10	Steve Sax	.25
11	Don Sutton	.25
12	Mike Scioscia	.25
13	Devon White	.25
14	Franklin Stubbs	.25
15	Mike Witt	.25
16	Fernando Valenzuela	.25

Tigers Coins

#	Player	NM/M
	Complete Set (12):	6.00
	Common Player:	.50
1	Darnell Coles	.50
2	Darrell Evans	.60
3	Kirk Gibson	.60
4	Willie Hernandez	.50
5	Larry Herndon	.50
6	Chet Lemon	.50
7	Dwight Lowry	.50
8	Jack Morris	.60
9	Dan Petry	.50
10	Frank Tanana	.50
11	Alan Trammell	.75
12	Lou Whitaker	.65

1991 7-11 Slurpee Coins Atlantic Region

After a three-year hiatus, "3-D" magic-motion coins returned to 7-11 stores in the form of regional sets produced by Score under the name Superstar Sports Coins and given away with the purchase of Slurpee fountain drinks. In the familiar 1-3/4" diameter, the discs have alternating portrait and action images on the front with the player name at top, the team at bottom, the uniform number at left and position at right. Each regional set has a different border color. Backs have 7-11 and Score logos along with career stats and a short career summary. The 120 coins in the sets feature 81 different major leaguers.

#	Player	NM/M
	Complete Set (15):	7.50
	Common Player:	.25
1	Glenn Davis	.25
2	Dwight Evans	.25
3	Leo Gomez	.25
4	Ken Griffey Jr.	1.50
5	Rickey Henderson	.75
6	Jose Canseco	.60
7	Dave Justice	.25
8	Ben McDonald	.25
9	Randy Milligan	.25
10	Gregg Olson	.25
11	Kirby Puckett	1.00
12	Bill Ripken	.25
13	Cal Ripken Jr.	2.50
14	Nolan Ryan	2.50
15	David Segui	.25

Florida Region

#	Player	NM/M
	Complete Set (15):	10.00
	Common Player:	.25
1	Barry Bonds	2.50
2	George Brett	1.50
3	Roger Clemens	1.50
4	Glenn Davis	.25
5	Alex Fernandez	.25
6	Cecil Fielder	.25
7	Ken Griffey Jr.	2.00
8	Dwight Gooden	.25
9	Dave Justice	.25
10	Barry Larkin	.25
11	Ramon Martinez	.25
12	Jose Offerman	.25
13	Kirby Puckett	1.00
14	Nolan Ryan	2.50
15	Terry Schumpert	.25

Metro Northeast Region

#	Player	NM/M
	Complete Set (15):	9.00
	Common Player:	.25
1	Wade Boggs	1.00
2	Barry Bonds	2.50
3	Roger Clemens	1.50
4	Len Dykstra	.25
5	Dwight Gooden	.25
6	Ken Griffey Jr.	2.00
7	Rickey Henderson	.75
8	Gregg Jefferies	.25
9	Roberto Kelly	.25
10	Kevin Maas	.25
11	Don Mattingly	1.50
12	Mickey Morandini	.25
13	Dale Murphy	.50
14	Darryl Strawberry	.25
15	Frank Viola	.25

Midwest

#	Player	NM/M
	Complete Set (15):	6.00
	Common Player:	.25
1	George Brett	1.50
2	Andre Dawson	.40
3	Cecil Fielder	.25
4	Carlton Fisk	.75
5	Travis Fryman	.25
6	Mark Grace	.25
7	Ken Griffey Jr.	2.00
8	Ozzie Guillen	.25
9	Alex Fernandez	.25
10	Ray Lankford	.25
11	Ryne Sandberg	1.00
12	Ozzie Smith	1.00
13	Bobby Thigpen	.25
14	Frank Thomas	.75
15	Alan Trammell	.25

Northern California Region

		NM/M
Complete Set (15):		9.00
Common Player:		.25
1	John Burkett	.25
2	Jose Canseco	.65
3	Will Clark	.25
4	Steve Decker	.25
5	Dennis Eckersley	.25
6	Ken Griffey Jr.	2.00
7	Rickey Henderson	.75
8	Nolan Ryan	3.00
9	Mark McGwire	2.50
10	Kevin Mitchell	.25
11	Terry Steinbach	.25
12	Dave Stewart	.25
13	Todd Van Poppel	.25
14	Bob Welch	.25
15	Matt Williams	.25

Northwest Region

		NM/M
Complete Set (15):		9.00
Common Player:		.25
1	George Brett	1.50
2	Jose Canseco	.60
3	Alvin Davis	.25
4	Ken Griffey Jr., Ken Griffey Sr.	1.00
5	Ken Griffey Jr.	2.00
6	Erik Hanson	.25
7	Rickey Henderson	.75
8	Ryne Sandberg	1.00
9	Randy Johnson	.75
10	Dave Justice	.25
11	Edgar Martinez	.25
12	Tino Martinez	.25
13	Harold Reynolds	.25
14	Nolan Ryan	3.00
15	Mike Schooler	.25

Southern California Region

		NM/M
Complete Set (15):		7.00
Common Player:		.25
1	Jim Abbott	.25
2	Jose Canseco	.60
3	Ken Griffey Jr.	2.00
4	Tony Gwynn	1.00
5	Orel Hershiser	.25
6	Eric Davis	.25
7	Wally Joyner	.25
8	Ramon Martinez	.25
9	Fred McGriff	.25
10	Eddie Murray	.75
11	Jose Offerman	.25
12	Nolan Ryan	3.00
13	Benito Santiago	.25
14	Darryl Strawberry	.25
15	Fernando Valenzuela	.25

Texas Region

		NM/M
Complete Set (15):		10.00
Common Player:		.25
1	Craig Biggio	.25
2	Barry Bonds	3.00
3	Jose Canseco	.50
4	Roger Clemens	1.50
5	Glenn Davis	.25
6	Julio Franco	.25
7	Juan Gonzalez	.50
8	Ken Griffey Jr.	2.00
9	Mike Scott	.25
10	Rafael Palmeiro	.75
11	Nolan Ryan	3.00
12	Ryne Sandberg	1.00
13	Ruben Sierra	.25
14	Todd Van Poppel	.25
15	Bobby Witt	.25

1992 7-11 Slurpee Superstar Action Coins

Score baseball 3-D coins returned to 7-11 stores on a very limited basis in 1992. A 26-piece set of the plastic coins (one for each major league team) was produced by Score in the familiar 1-3/4" diameter format. The coins feature a maroon border on which is printed in white the player's name, team, position and uniform number. At center is a 1-1/4" circle with "flasher" portrait and action photos of the player. Backs have a black border with the player name in yellow at the top, a few career stats, 7-11 and Score

logos and a coin number in a pale yellow center circle. At bottom in green is "Superstar Action Coin."

		NM/M
Complete Set (26):		10.00
Common Player:		.25
1	Dwight Gooden	.25
2	Don Mattingly	1.00
3	Roger Clemens	1.00
4	Ivan Calderon	.25
5	Roberto Alomar	.40
6	Sandy Alomar, Jr.	.25
7	Andy Van Slyke	.25
8	Lenny Dykstra	.25
9	Cal Ripken, Jr.	2.00
10	Dave Justice	.25
11	Nolan Ryan	2.00
12	Craig Biggio	.25
13	Barry Larkin	.25
14	Ozzie Smith	.75
15	Ryne Sandberg	.75
16	Frank Thomas	.60
17	Robin Yount	.60
18	Kirby Puckett	.75
19	Cecil Fielder	.25
20	Will Clark	.25
21	Jose Canseco	.45
22	Jim Abbott	.25
23	Tony Gwynn	.75
24	Darryl Strawberry	.25
25	George Brett	1.00
26	Ken Griffey Jr.	1.50

2000 7-11 Slurpee Coins

Returning after a long hiatus, lenticular-motion player discs were once again affixed to the bottoms of Super Big Gulp and 32-oz. Slurpee cups at 20,000 convenience stores nationwide. A step up in quality from the "flicker image" coins of the 1980s, this generation was produced by Pacific Trading Cards and licensed by MLB and the Players Union. The 1-3/4" plastic discs have three photos at center with player identification at top and bottom; uniform numbers and logos are at the sides. On back, conventionally printed, is a color portrait photo, a few stats and vital data and appropriate copyright and licensing notices. There is one player coin from each major league team. An album was available to house the set.

		NM/M
Complete Set (30):		10.00
Common Player:		.25
	Album:	3.00
	In-Store Ad Sheet:	6.00
1	Tim Salmon	.25
2	Erubiel Durazo	.25
3	Chipper Jones	.65
4	Cal Ripken Jr.	2.00
5	Nomar Garciaparra	.65
6	Mark Grace	.25
7	Frank Thomas	.50
8	Sean Casey	.25
9	Manny Ramirez	.50
10	Larry Walker	.25
11	Dean Palmer	.25
12	Alex Gonzalez	.25
13	Jeff Bagwell	.50
14	Carlos Beltran	.45
15	Gary Sheffield	.40
16	Jeromy Burnitz	.25
17	Corey Koskie	.25
18	Vladimir Guerrero	.50
19	Mike Piazza	1.00
20	Roger Clemens	.75
21	Ben Grieve	.25
22	Scott Rolen	.45
23	Jason Kendall	.25
24	Mark McGwire	1.50
25	Tony Gwynn	.65
26	Jeff Kent	.25
27	Jay Buhner	.25
28	Jose Canseco	.40
29	Ivan Rodriguez	.45
30	Carlos Delgado	.45

1981 7-Up

These 5-1/2" x 8-1/2" color photocards are part of a multi-sport series. Fronts have a borderless photo, a facsimile autograph and, at lower-right, a 7-Up logo and slogan. Back is printed in black, red and green on white and features a

career summary through the 1980 season, and a large version of the soda logo. Posters in 19" x 25" size were also issued.

		NM/M
Common Player:		3.00
(1)	George Brett	6.00
(3)	Dave Parker	3.00
(5)	Mike Schmidt	6.00

1984 7-Up Cubs

The Chicago Cubs and 7-Up issued this 28-card set featuring full-color game-action photos on a 2-1/4" x 3-1/2" borderless front. The backs have the player's stats and personal information. This was the third consecutive year the Cubs issued this type of set as a giveaway at a "Baseball Card Day" promotional game.

		NM/M
Complete Set (28):		13.50
Common Player:		.25
1	Larry Bowa	.25
6	Keith Moreland	.25
7	Jody Davis	.25
11	Leon Durham	.25
15	Ron Hassey	.25
16	Richie Hebner	.25
19	Dave Owen	.25
20	Bob Dernier	.25
21	Jay Johnstone	.25
23	Ryne Sandberg	9.00
24	Scott Sanderson	.25
25	Gary Woods	.25
28	Thad Bosley	.25
29	Henry Cotto	.25
34	Steve Trout	.25
36	Gary Matthews	.25
39	George Frazier	.25
40	Rick Sutcliffe	.25
41	Warren Brusstar	.25
42	Rich Bordi	.25
43	Dennis Eckersley	3.00
44	Dick Ruthven	.25
46	Lee Smith	.25
47	Rick Reuschel	.25
49	Tim Stoddard	.25
---	Jim Frey	.25
---	Cubs Coaches (Ruben Amaro, Billy Connors, Johnny Oates, John Vukovich, Don Zimmer)	.25

1985 7-Up Cubs

This was the second year a Chicago Cubs card set was released with 7-Up as the sponsor. The set was 28 unnumbered cards in the standard 2-1/2" x 3-1/2" size. They were distributed to fans attending the Cubs game on August 14 at Wrigley Field. They feature full-color game-action photos of the players. Card backs contain the player's professional stats.

(7) JODY DAVIS C

		NM/M
Complete Set (28):		10.00
Common Player:		.25
1	Larry Bowa	.25
6	Keith Moreland	.25
7	Jody Davis	.25
11	Leon Durham	.25
11	Ron Cey	.25
15	Davey Lopes	.25
16	Steve Lake	.25
18	Richie Hebner	.25
20	Bob Dernier	.25
21	Scott Sanderson	.25
22	Billy Hatcher	.25
23	Ryne Sandberg	7.50
24	Brian Dayett	.25
25	Gary Woods	.25
27	Thad Bosley	.25
28	Chris Speier	.25
31	Ray Fontenot	.25
34	Steve Trout	.25
36	Gary Matthews	.25
39	George Frazier	.25
40	Rick Sutcliffe	.25
41	Warren Brusstar	.25
42	Lary Sorensen	.25
43	Dennis Eckersley	2.00
44	Dick Ruthven	.25
46	Lee Smith	.25
---	Jim Frey	.25
---	Coaching Staff (Ruben Amaro, Billy Connors, Johnny Oates, John Vukovich, Don Zimmer)	.25

1995 Skin Bracer

BILL MAZEROSKI

This three-card set was included in several packagings of Mennen skin care products for men. Three sepia-toned 3-1/2" x 2-1/2" cards feature great moments in post-season play. Fronts are trimmed in gold ink and feature the player's name in a green box. Backs are printed in black, green and gold and describe the highlight. Logos of the sponsor and Major League Baseball Players Alumni Association are also included on back. A related offer allowed collectors to purchase autographed 8" x 10" photos of the events for $7.99 each via a coupon.

		NM/M
Complete Set (3):		6.00
Common Player:		2.00
(1)	The Perfect Game (Don Larsen)	2.00
(2)	The Series Ender (Bill Mazeroski)	2.00
(3)	The Shot Heard 'Round the World (Bobby Thomson)	2.00

2001 Skippy Peanut Butter Derek Jeter

Specially marked jars Skippy Peanut Butter had a Derek Jeter "Digital Card" under the cap, enclosed in protective plastic. The 2-1/2" diame-

ter discs are printed on thin cardboard and have portrait and action photos of the spokesman on front (Yankees team logos have been removed) along with a facsimile autograph and logos of Skippy and CyberAction. Backs are in red and blue with information on the company's website and a card title.

		NM/M
Complete Set (4):		6.00
Common Card:		2.00
1	1,000 Hits Club/Btg (Derek Jeter)	2.00
2	1998 Runs Leader/Running (Derek Jeter)	2.00
3	Three Time All-Star/Leaping (Derek Jeter)	2.00
4	World Champion MVP/Throwing (Derek Jeter)	2.00

1995 SkyBox E-Motion Promo

To introduce its new super-premium baseball card line, SkyBox debuted a Cal Ripken promo card at the 1995 National Sports Collectors Convention. The card is virtually identical to Ripken's card in the regular issue, except for diagonal overprinting on each side which reads, "Promotional Sample."

		NM/M
8	Cal Ripken Jr. (Class)	2.50

1995 SkyBox E-Motion

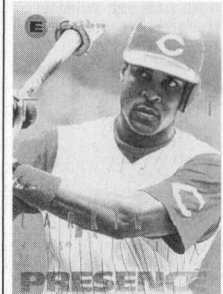

This is a super-premium debut issue from the newly merged Fleer/SkyBox company. Printed on double-thick cardboard, card fronts have borderless photos marred by the presence of four gold-foil "view-finder" corner marks. The player's last name and team are printed in gold foil near the bottom. On each card there is a large silver-foil word printed in block letters; either a nickname or an emotion or attribute associated with the player. Backs have two more player photos, 1994 and career stats and a few biographical bits. Eight-cards packs were issued with a suggested retail price of $4.99.

		NM/M
Complete Set (200):		15.00
Common Player:		.05
Pack (8):		1.00
Wax Box (36):		20.00
1	Brady Anderson	.05
2	Kevin Brown	.05
3	Curtis Goodwin	.05
4	Jeffrey Hammonds	.05
5	Ben McDonald	.05
6	Mike Mussina	.35
7	Rafael Palmeiro	.65
8	Cal Ripken Jr.	2.00
9	Jose Canseco	.45
10	Roger Clemens	1.00
11	Vaughn Eshelman	.05
12	Mike Greenwell	.05
13	Erik Hanson	.05
14	Tim Naehring	.05
15	Aaron Sele	.05
16	John Valentin	.05
17	Mo Vaughn	.05
18	Chili Davis	.05
19	Gary DiSarcina	.05
20	Chuck Finley	.05
21	Tim Salmon	.05
22	Lee Smith	.05
23	J.T. Snow	.05
24	Jim Abbott	.05
25	Jason Bere	.05
26	Ray Durham	.05
27	Ozzie Guillen	.05
28	Tim Raines	.05
29	Frank Thomas	.75
30	Robin Ventura	.05
31	Carlos Baerga	.05
32	Albert Belle	.05
33	Orel Hershiser	.05
34	Kenny Lofton	.05
35	Dennis Martinez	.05
36	Eddie Murray	.75
37	Manny Ramirez	.75
38	Julian Tavarez	.05
39	Jim Thome	.60
40	Dave Winfield	.75
41	Chad Curtis	.05
42	Cecil Fielder	.05
43	Travis Fryman	.05
44	Kirk Gibson	.05
45	Bob Higginson RC	.25
46	Alan Trammell	.05
47	Lou Whitaker	.05
48	Kevin Appier	.05
49	Gary Gaetti	.05
50	Jeff Montgomery	.05
51	Jon Nunnally	.05
52	Ricky Bones	.05
53	Cal Eldred	.05
54	Joe Oliver	.05
55	Kevin Seitzer	.05
56	Marty Cordova	.05
57	Chuck Knoblauch	.05
58	Kirby Puckett	1.00
59	Wade Boggs	1.00
60	Derek Jeter	2.00
61	Jimmy Key	.05
62	Don Mattingly	1.00
63	Jack McDowell	.05
64	Paul O'Neill	.05
65	Andy Pettitte	.30
66	Ruben Rivera	.05
67	Mike Stanley	.05
68	John Wetteland	.05
69	Geronimo Berroa	.05
70	Dennis Eckersley	.65
71	Rickey Henderson	.75
72	Mark McGwire	1.50
73	Steve Ontiveros	.05
74	Ruben Sierra	.05
75	Terry Steinbach	.05
76	Jay Buhner	.05
77	Ken Griffey Jr.	1.25
78	Randy Johnson	.75
79	Edgar Martinez	.05
80	Tino Martinez	.05
81	Marc Newfield	.05
82	Alex Rodriguez	1.50
83	Will Clark	.05
84	Benji Gil	.05
85	Juan Gonzalez	.40
86	Rusty Greer	.05
87	Dean Palmer	.05
88	Ivan Rodriguez	.65
89	Kenny Rogers	.05
90	Roberto Alomar	.30
91	Joe Carter	.05
92	David Cone	.05
93	Alex Gonzalez	.05
94	Shawn Green	.40
95	Pat Hentgen	.05
96	Paul Molitor	.75
97	John Olerud	.05
98	Devon White	.05
99	Steve Avery	.05
100	Tom Glavine	.35
101	Marquis Grissom	.05
102	Chipper Jones	1.00
103	Dave Justice	.05
104	Ryan Klesko	.05
105	Javier Lopez	.05
106	Greg Maddux	1.00
107	Fred McGriff	.05
108	John Smoltz	.05
109	Shawon Dunston	.05
110	Mark Grace	.05
111	Brian McRae	.05
112	Randy Myers	.05
113	Sammy Sosa	1.00
114	Steve Trachsel	.05
115	Bret Boone	.05
116	Ron Gant	.05
117	Barry Larkin	.05
118	Deion Sanders	.05
119	Reggie Sanders	.05
120	Pete Schourek	.05
121	John Smiley	.05
122	Jason Bates	.05
123	Dante Bichette	.05
124	Vinny Castilla	.05
125	Andres Galarraga	.05
126	Larry Walker	.05
127	Greg Colbrunn	.05
128	Jeff Conine	.05
129	Andre Dawson	.30
130	Chris Hammond	.05
131	Charles Johnson	.05
132	Gary Sheffield	.45

133	Quilvio Veras	.05
134	Jeff Bagwell	.75
135	Derek Bell	.05
136	Craig Biggio	.05
137	Jim Dougherty	.05
138	John Hudek	.05
139	Orlando Miller	.05
140	Phil Plantier	.05
141	Eric Karros *	.05
142	Ramon Martinez	.05
143	Raul Mondesi	.05
144	Hideo Nomo RC	2.00
145	Mike Piazza	1.25
146	Ismael Valdes	.05
147	Todd Worrell	.05
148	Moises Alou	.05
149	Yamil Benitez RC	.05
150	Wil Cordero	.05
151	Jeff Fassero	.05
152	Cliff Floyd	.05
153	Pedro Martinez	.75
154	Carlos Perez RC	.05
155	Tony Tarasco	.05
156	Rondell White	.05
157	Edgardo Alfonzo	.05
158	Bobby Bonilla	.05
159	Rico Brogna	.05
160	Bobby Jones	.05
161	Bill Pulsipher	.05
162	Bret Saberhagen	.05
163	Ricky Bottalico	.05
164	Darren Daulton	.05
165	Lenny Dykstra	.05
166	Charlie Hayes	.05
167	Dave Hollins	.05
168	Gregg Jefferies	.05
169	Michael Mimbs RC	.05
170	Curt Schilling	.35
171	Heathcliff Slocumb	.05
172	Jay Bell	.05
173	Micah Franklin RC	.05
174	Mark Johnson RC	.05
175	Jeff King	.05
176	Al Martin	.05
177	Dan Miceli	.05
178	Denny Neagle	.05
179	Bernard Gilkey	.05
180	Ken Hill	.05
181	Brian Jordan	.05
182	Ray Lankford	.05
183	Ozzie Smith	1.00
184	Andy Benes	.05
185	Ken Caminiti	.05
186	Steve Finley	.05
187	Tony Gwynn	1.00
188	Joey Hamilton	.05
189	Melvin Nieves	.05
190	Scott Sanders	.05
191	Rod Beck	.05
192	Barry Bonds	2.00
193	Royce Clayton	.05
194	Glenallen Hill	.05
195	Darren Lewis	.05
196	Mark Portugal	.05
197	Matt Williams	.05
198	Checklist	.05
199	Checklist	.05
200	Checklist	.05

Masters

Ten of the game's top veterans are featured in this chase card set. A large close-up photo in a single team-related color in the background, with a color action photo in the foreground. Backs have a borderless color photo and a top to bottom color bar with some good words about the player. The Masters inserts are found at an average rate of one per eight packs.

		NM/M
Complete Set (10):		12.00
Common Player:		.50
1	Barry Bonds	2.50
2	Juan Gonzalez	.65
3	Ken Griffey Jr.	2.00
4	Tony Gwynn	1.50
5	Kenny Lofton	.50
6	Greg Maddux	1.50
7	Raul Mondesi	.50
8	Cal Ripken Jr.	2.50
9	Frank Thomas	1.00
10	Matt Williams	.50

N-Tense

A colored wave-pattern printed on metallic foil is the background for the action photo of one of baseball's top sluggers in this chase card set. A huge rainbow prismatic foil "N" appears in an upper corner. The player's name and team are at lower-right in gold foil. Backs are conventionally printed and repeat the front's patterned background, with another color player photo and a shaded box with a few career highlights.

		NM/M
Complete Set (12):		16.00
Common Player:		.50
1	Jeff Bagwell	2.00
2	Albert Belle	.50
3	Barry Bonds	4.00
4	Cecil Fielder	.50
5	Ron Gant	.50
6	Ken Griffey Jr.	2.50
7	Mark McGwire	3.00
8	Mike Piazza	2.50
9	Manny Ramirez	2.00
10	Frank Thomas	2.00
11	Mo Vaughn	.50
12	Matt Williams	.50

Cal Ripken Jr. Timeless

A white background with a clockface and gold-foil "TIMELESS" logo are the standard elements of this insert tribute to Cal Ripken, Jr. Fronts also feature a large color photo and a smaller sepia photo contemporary to some phase of his career. The first 10 cards in the set chronicle Ripken's career through 1994. A special mail-in offer provided five more cards featuring highlights of his 1995 season.

		NM/M
Complete Set (15):		20.00
Common Card:		1.50
1	High School Pitcher	1.50
2	Role Model	1.50
3	Rookie of the Year	1.50
4	1st MVP Season	1.50
5	95 Consecutive Errorless Games	1.50
6	All-Star MVP	1.50
7	Conditioning	1.50
8	Shortstop HR Record	1.50
9	Literacy Work	1.50
10	2000th Consecutive Game	1.50
11	All-Star Selection	2.25
12	Record-tying Game	2.25
13	Record-breaking Game	2.25
14	2,153 and Counting	2.25
15	Birthday	2.25

Rookies

A bold colored background with outline white letters repeating the word "ROOKIE" is the frame for the central action photo in this insert series. The top of the photo is vignetted with a white circle that

has the player's name in gold at left, and his team in white at right. Backs repeat the front background and include a player portrait photo and a few sentences about his potential. Rookie inserts are found at an average rate of one per five packs.

		NM/M
Complete Set (10):		6.50
Common Player:		.25
1	Edgardo Alfonzo	.25
2	Jason Bates	.25
3	Marty Cordova	.25
4	Ray Durham	.25
5	Alex Gonzalez	.25
6	Shawn Green	.75
7	Charles Johnson	.25
8	Chipper Jones	1.50
9	Hideo Nomo	1.00
10	Alex Rodriguez	3.00

1996 SkyBox E-Motion XL

Each card in SkyBox's 1996 E-Motion XL Baseball arrives on two layers of stock - a die-cut matte frame over a UV-coated card. The frames come in three colors - blue, green and maroon (but each player has only one color version). The 300-card set also includes four insert sets: Legion of Boom, D-Fense, N-Tense and Rare Breed.

		NM/M
Complete Set (300):		10.00
Common Player:		.05
Pack (7):		1.00
Wax Box (24):		20.00
1	Roberto Alomar	.15
2	Brady Anderson	.05
3	Bobby Bonilla	.05
4	Jeffrey Hammonds	.05
5	Chris Hoiles	.05
6	Mike Mussina	.30
7	Randy Myers	.05
8	Rafael Palmeiro	.50
9	Cal Ripken Jr.	2.00
10	B.J. Surhoff	.05
11	Jose Canseco	.25
12	Roger Clemens	1.00
13	Wil Cordero	.05
14	Mike Greenwell	.05
15	Dwayne Hosey	.05
16	Tim Naehring	.05
17	Troy O'Leary	.05
18	Mike Stanley	.05
19	John Valentin	.05
20	Mo Vaughn	.50
21	Jim Abbott	.05
22	Garret Anderson	.05
23	George Arias	.05
24	Chili Davis	.05
25	Jim Edmonds	.05
26	Chuck Finley	.05
27	Todd Greene	.05
28	Mark Langston	.05
29	Troy Percival	.05
30	Tim Salmon	.05
31	Lee Smith	.05
32	J.T. Snow	.05
33	Harold Baines	.05
34	Jason Bere	.05
35	Ray Durham	.05
36	Alex Fernandez	.05
37	Ozzie Guillen	.05
38	Darren Lewis	.05
39	Lyle Mouton	.05
40	Tony Phillips	.05
41	Danny Tartabull	.05
42	Frank Thomas	.60
43	Robin Ventura	.05
44	Sandy Alomar	.05
45	Carlos Baerga	.05
46	Albert Belle	.25
47	Julio Franco	.05
48	Orel Hershiser	.05
49	Kenny Lofton	.25
50	Dennis Martinez	.05
51	Jack McDowell	.05
52	Jose Mesa	.05
53	Eddie Murray	.60
54	Charles Nagy	.05
55	Manny Ramirez	.60
55p	Manny Ramirez/OPS	
56	Jim Thome	.45
57	Omar Vizquel	.05
58	Chad Curtis	.05
59	Cecil Fielder	.05
60	Travis Fryman	.05
61	Chris Gomez	.05
62	Felipe Lira	.05
63	Alan Trammell	.05
64	Kevin Appier	.05
65	Johnny Damon	.35
66	Tom Goodwin	.05
67	Mark Gubicza	.05
68	Jeff Montgomery	.05
69	Jon Nunnally	.05
70	Bip Roberts	.05
71	Ricky Bones	.05
72	Chuck Carr	.05
73	John Jaha	.05
74	Ben McDonald	.05
75	Matt Mieske	.05
76	Dave Nilsson	.05
77	Kevin Seitzer	.05
78	Greg Vaughn	.05
79	Rick Aguilera	.05
80	Marty Cordova	.05
81	Roberto Kelly	.05
82	Chuck Knoblauch	.05
83	Pat Meares	.05
84	Paul Molitor	.60
85	Kirby Puckett	.75
86	Brad Radke	.05
87	Wade Boggs	.75
88	David Cone	.05
89	Dwight Gooden	.05
90	Derek Jeter	2.00
91	Tino Martinez	.05
92	Paul O'Neill	.05
93	Andy Pettitte	.15
94	Tim Raines	.05
95	Ruben Rivera	.05
96	Kenny Rogers	.05
97	Ruben Sierra	.05
98	John Wetteland	.05
99	Bernie Williams	.05
100	Allen Battle	.05
101	Geronimo Berroa	.05
102	Brent Gates	.05
103	Doug Johns	.05
104	Mark McGwire	1.50
105	Pedro Munoz	.05
106	Ariel Prieto	.05
107	Terry Steinbach	.05
108	Todd Van Poppel	.05
109	Chris Bosio	.05
110	Jay Buhner	.05
111	Joey Cora	.05
112	Russ Davis	.05
113	Ken Griffey Jr.	1.25
114	Sterling Hitchcock	.05
115	Randy Johnson	.60
116	Edgar Martinez	.05
117	Alex Rodriguez	1.50
118	Paul Sorrento	.05
119	Dan Wilson	.05
120	Will Clark	.05
121	Juan Gonzalez	.30
122	Rusty Greer	.05
123	Kevin Gross	.05
124	Ken Hill	.05
125	Dean Palmer	.05
126	Roger Pavlik	.05
127	Ivan Rodriguez	.50
128	Mickey Tettleton	.05
129	Joe Carter	.05
130	Carlos Delgado	.40
131	Alex Gonzalez	.05
132	Shawn Green	.25
133	Erik Hanson	.05
134	Pat Hentgen	.05
135	Otis Nixon	.05
136	John Olerud	.05
137	Ed Sprague	.05
138	Steve Avery	.05
139	Jermaine Dye	.05
140	Tom Glavine	.35
141	Marquis Grissom	.05
142	Chipper Jones	.75
143	David Justice	.05
144	Ryan Klesko	.05
145	Javier Lopez	.05
146	Greg Maddux	.75
147	Fred McGriff	.05
148	Jason Schmidt	.05
149	John Smoltz	.05
150	Mark Wohlers	.05
151	Jim Bullinger	.05
152	Frank Castillo	.05
153	Kevin Foster	.05
154	Luis Gonzalez	.05
155	Mark Grace	.05
156	Brian McRae	.05
157	Jaime Navarro	.05
158	Rey Sanchez	.05
159	Ryne Sandberg	.75
160	Sammy Sosa	.75
161	Bret Boone	.05
162	Jeff Brantley	.05
163	Vince Coleman	.05
164	Steve Gibralter	.05
165	Barry Larkin	.05
166	Hal Morris	.05
167	Mark Portugal	.05
168	Reggie Sanders	.05
169	Pete Schourek	.05
170	John Smiley	.05
171	Jason Bates	.05
172	Dante Bichette	.05
173	Ellis Burks	.05
174	Vinny Castilla	.05
175	Andres Galarraga	.05
176	Kevin Ritz	.05
177	Bill Swift	.05
178	Larry Walker	.05
179	Walt Weiss	.05
180	Eric Young	.05
181	Kurt Abbott	.05
182	Kevin Brown	.05
183	John Burkett	.05
184	Greg Colbrunn	.05
185	Jeff Conine	.05
186	Chris Hammond	.05
187	Charles Johnson	.05
188	Terry Pendleton	.05
189	Pat Rapp	.05
190	Gary Sheffield	.25
191	Quilvio Veras	.05
192	Devon White	.05
193	Jeff Bagwell	.60
194	Derek Bell	.05
195	Sean Berry	.05
196	Craig Biggio	.05
197	Doug Drabek	.05
198	Tony Eusebio	.05
199	Mike Hampton	.05
200	Brian Hunter	.05
201	Derrick May	.05
202	Orlando Miller	.05
203	Shane Reynolds	.05
204	Mike Blowers	.05
205	Tom Candiotti	.05
206	Delino DeShields	.05
207	Greg Gagne	.05
208	Karim Garcia	.05
209	Todd Hollandsworth	.05
210	Eric Karros	.05
211	Ramon Martinez	.05
212	Raul Mondesi	.05
213	Hideo Nomo	.30
214	Chan Ho Park	.05
215	Mike Piazza	1.25
216	Ismael Valdes	.05
217	Todd Worrell	.05
218	Moises Alou	.05
219	Yamil Benitez	.05
220	Jeff Fassero	.05
221	Darrin Fletcher	.05
222	Cliff Floyd	.05
223	Pedro Martinez	.60
224	Carlos Perez	.05
225	Mel Rojas	.05
226	David Segui	.05
227	Rondell White	.05
228	Rico Brogna	.05
229	Carl Everett	.05
230	John Franco	.05
231	Bernard Gilkey	.05
232	Todd Hundley	.05
233	Jason Isringhausen	.05
234	Lance Johnson	.05
235	Bobby Jones	.05
236	Jeff Kent	.05
237	Rey Ordonez	.05
238	Bill Pulsipher	.05
239	Jose Vizcaino	.05
240	Paul Wilson	.05
241	Ricky Bottalico	.05
242	Darren Daulton	.05
243	Lenny Dykstra	.05
244	Jim Eisenreich	.05
245	Sid Fernandez	.05
246	Gregg Jefferies	.05
247	Mickey Morandini	.05
248	Benito Santiago	.05
249	Curt Schilling	.35
250	Mark Whiten	.05
251	Todd Zeile	.05
252	Jay Bell	.05
253	Carlos Garcia	.05
254	Charlie Hayes	.05
255	Jason Kendall	.05
256	Jeff King	.05
257	Al Martin	.05
258	Orlando Merced	.05
259	Dan Miceli	.05
260	Denny Neagle	.05
261	Alan Benes	.05
262	Andy Benes	.05
263	Royce Clayton	.05
264	Dennis Eckersley	.50
265	Gary Gaetti	.05
266	Ron Gant	.05
267	Brian Jordan	.05
268	Ray Lankford	.05
269	John Mabry	.05
270	Tom Pagnozzi	.05
271	Ozzie Smith	.75
272	Todd Stottlemyre	.05
273	Andy Ashby	.05
274	Brad Ausmus	.05
275	Ken Caminiti	.05
276	Steve Finley	.05
277	Tony Gwynn	.75
278	Joey Hamilton	.05
279	Rickey Henderson	.60
280	Trevor Hoffman	.05
281	Wally Joyner	.05
282	Jody Reed	.05
283	Bob Tewksbury	.05
284	Fernando Valenzuela	.05
285	Rod Beck	.05
286	Barry Bonds	2.00
287	Mark Carreon	.05
288	Shawon Dunston	.05
289	Osvaldo Fernandez RC	.10
290	Glenallen Hill	.05
291	Stan Javier	.05
292	Mark Leiter	.05
293	Kirt Manwaring	.05
294	Robby Thompson	.05
295	William Van Landingham	.05
296	Allen Watson	.05
297	Matt Williams	.05
298	Checklist	.05
299	Checklist	.05
300	Checklist	.05

XL D-Fense

Ten top defensive players are featured on these 1996 SkyBox E-Motion XL insert cards. The cards were seeded at a rate of one per every four packs.

		NM/M
Complete Set (10):		9.00
Common Player:		.50
1	Roberto Alomar	.65
2	Barry Bonds	3.50
3	Mark Grace	.50
4	Ken Griffey Jr.	2.50
5	Kenny Lofton	.50
6	Greg Maddux	1.50
7	Raul Mondesi	.50
8	Cal Ripken Jr.	3.50
9	Ivan Rodriguez	1.00
10	Matt Williams	.50

XL Legion of Boom

The top power hitters in baseball are featured on these 1996 SkyBox E-Motion XL insert cards. The cards, exclusive to hobby packs at a ratio of one per every 36 packs, have translucent card backs.

		NM/M
Complete Set (12):		27.50
Common Player:		2.00
1	Albert Belle	2.00
2	Barry Bonds	6.00
3	Juan Gonzalez	2.50
4	Ken Griffey Jr.	4.00
5	Mark McGwire	5.00
6	Mike Piazza	4.00
7	Manny Ramirez	3.00
8	Tim Salmon	2.00
9	Sammy Sosa	3.50
10	Frank Thomas	3.00
11	Mo Vaughn	2.00
12	Matt Williams	2.00

XL N-Tense

Ten top clutch performers are featured on these 1996 SkyBox E-Motion XL insert cards. The cards, which use an N-shaped die-cut design, were included one per every 12 packs.

		NM/M
Complete Set (10):		17.50
Common Player:		.50
1	Albert Belle	.50
2	Barry Bonds	3.50
3	Jose Canseco	1.00
4	Ken Griffey Jr.	3.00
5	Tony Gwynn	2.50
6	Randy Johnson	2.00
7	Greg Maddux	2.50
8	Cal Ripken Jr.	3.50
9	Frank Thomas	2.00
10	Matt Williams	.50

XL Rare Breed

These 1996 E-Motion XL inserts are the most difficult to find; they are seeded one per every 100 packs. The cards showcase top young stars on a 3-D lenticular-motion design.

		NM/M
Complete Set (10):		50.00
Common Player:		3.00
1	Garret Anderson	3.00
2	Marty Cordova	3.00
3	Brian Hunter	3.00
4	Jason Isringhausen	3.00
5	Charles Johnson	3.00
6	Chipper Jones	16.00
7	Raul Mondesi	3.00
8	Hideo Nomo	6.00
9	Manny Ramirez	12.00
10	Rondell White	3.00

E-X2000 Sample

To introduce its innovative high-tech premium brand, SkyBox released this promo card. It is identical in format to the issued version, except it carries a "SAMPLE" notation instead of a card number on back.

	NM/M
Alex Rodriguez	4.00

1997 SkyBox E-X2000

The premiere issue of E-X2000 consists of 100 base cards designed with "SkyView" technology, utilizing a die-cut holofoil border and the player silhouetted in front of a transparent "window" featuring a variety of sky patterns. Inserts include two sequentially-numbered parallel sets - Credentials (1:50 packs) and Essential Credentials (1:200 packs) - as well as Emerald Autograph Exchange Cards, A Cut Above, Hall of Nothing, and Star Date. Cards were sold in two-card packs for $3.99 each.

		NM/M
Complete Set (100):		20.00
Common Player:		.15
Credentials Stars:		6X
Essential Credentials:		10X
Pack (2):		1.25
Wax Box (24):		20.00
1	Jim Edmonds	.15
2	Darin Erstad	.25
3	Eddie Murray	1.00
4	Roberto Alomar	.25
5	Brady Anderson	.15
6	Mike Mussina	.45
7	Rafael Palmeiro	.75
8	Cal Ripken Jr.	3.00
9	Steve Avery	.15
10	Nomar Garciaparra	1.50
11	Mo Vaughn	.15
12	Albert Belle	.15
13	Mike Cameron	.15
14	Ray Durham	.15
15	Frank Thomas	1.00
16	Robin Ventura	.15
17	Manny Ramirez	1.00
18	Jim Thome	.65
19	Matt Williams	.15
20	Tony Clark	.15
21	Travis Fryman	.15
22	Bob Higginson	.15
23	Kevin Appier	.15
24	Johnny Damon	.45
25	Jermaine Dye	.15
26	Jeff Cirillo	.15
27	Ben McDonald	.15
28	Chuck Knoblauch	.15
29	Paul Molitor	1.00
30	Todd Walker	.15
31	Wade Boggs	1.50
32	Cecil Fielder	.15
33	Derek Jeter	3.00
34	Andy Pettitte	.25
35	Ruben Rivera	.15
36	Bernie Williams	.15
37	Jose Canseco	.50
38	Mark McGwire	2.50
39	Jay Buhner	.15
40	Ken Griffey Jr.	2.00
41	Randy Johnson	1.00
42	Edgar Martinez	.15
43	Alex Rodriguez	2.50
44	Dan Wilson	.15
45	Will Clark	.40
46	Juan Gonzalez	.50
47	Ivan Rodriguez	.75
48	Joe Carter	.15
49	Roger Clemens	1.75
50	Juan Guzman	.15
51	Pat Hentgen	.15
52	Tom Glavine	.35
53	Andruw Jones	1.00
54	Chipper Jones	1.50
55	Ryan Klesko	.15
56	Kenny Lofton	.15
57	Greg Maddux	1.50
58	Fred McGriff	.15
59	John Smoltz	.15
60	Mark Wohlers	.15
61	Mark Grace	.15
62	Ryne Sandberg	1.50
63	Sammy Sosa	1.50
64	Barry Larkin	.15
65	Deion Sanders	.15
66	Reggie Sanders	.15
67	Dante Bichette	.15
68	Ellis Burks	.15
69	Andres Galarraga	.15
70	Moises Alou	.15
71	Kevin Brown	.15
72	Cliff Floyd	.15
73	Edgar Renteria	.15
74	Gary Sheffield	.50
75	Bob Abreu	.15
76	Jeff Bagwell	1.00
77	Craig Biggio	.15
78	Todd Hollandsworth	.15
79	Eric Karros	.15
80	Raul Mondesi	.15
81	Hideo Nomo	.50
82	Mike Piazza	2.00
83	Vladimir Guerrero	1.00
84	Henry Rodriguez	.15
85	Todd Hundley	.15
86	Rey Ordonez	.15
87	Alex Ochoa	.15
88	Gregg Jefferies	.15
89	Scott Rolen	.65
90	Jermaine Allensworth	.15
91	Jason Kendall	.15
92	Ken Caminiti	.15
93	Tony Gwynn	1.50
94	Rickey Henderson	1.00
95	Barry Bonds	3.00
96	J.T. Snow	.15
97	Dennis Eckersley	.75
98	Ron Gant	.15
99	Brian Jordan	.15
100	Ray Lankford	.15

Credentials

This parallel set features different colored foils from the base cards, as well as different images on the "window." Cards are sequentially numbered on back within an issue of 299. Cards were inserted 1:50 packs.

	NM/M
Common Player:	1.00
Credentials Stars:	6X

Essential Credentials

A sequentially-numbered parallel set, found one per 200 packs, and limited to 99 total sets.

	NM/M
Common Player:	3.00
Essential Credentials Stars:	10X

A Cut Above

Some of the game's elite players are featured in this 1:288 pack insert that features a die-cut design resembling a saw blade. Printed on silver-foil stock, the player's name and Cut Above logo are embossed on front. On back is another color photo and a few words about the player.

		NM/M
Complete Set (10):		55.00
Common Player:		2.00
1	Frank Thomas	7.50
2	Ken Griffey Jr.	9.00
3	Alex Rodriguez	12.00
4	Albert Belle	2.00
5	Juan Gonzalez	4.00
6	Mark McGwire	10.00
7	Mo Vaughn	2.00
8	Manny Ramirez	7.50
9	Barry Bonds	12.00
10	Fred McGriff	2.00

Emerald Autograph Redemptions

Inserted 1:480 packs, these cards could be exchanged by mail prior to May 1, 1998 for autographed cards or memorabilia from one of six major leaguers.

		NM/M
Complete Set (6):		17.50
Common Player:		1.00
(1)	Darin Erstad	2.50
(2)	Todd Hollandsworth	1.00
(3)	Alex Ochoa	1.00
(4)	Alex Rodriguez	10.00
(5)	Scott Rolen	3.00
(6)	Todd Walker	1.00

Emerald Autographs

These authentically autographed versions of the players' E-X2000 cards were available (until May 1, 1998) by a mail-in exchange of redemption cards. The autographed cards are authenticated by the presence of an embossed SkyBox logo seal.

		NM/M
Complete Set (6):		75.00
Common Player:		3.00
2	Darin Erstad	12.00
30	Todd Walker	5.00
43	Alex Rodriguez	60.00
78	Todd Hollandsworth	3.00
86	Alex Ochoa	3.00
89	Scott Rolen	25.00

Hall or Nothing

This 20-card insert, featuring players who are candidates for the Hall of Fame, utilizes a die-cut design on plastic stock. Stately architectural details and brush bronze highlights frame the player picture on front. The player silhouette on back contains career information. Cards were inserted 1:20 packs.

		NM/M
Complete Set (20):		55.00
Common Player:		1.00
1	Frank Thomas	2.50
2	Ken Griffey Jr.	5.00
3	Eddie Murray	2.50
4	Cal Ripken Jr.	7.00
5	Ryne Sandberg	4.00
6	Wade Boggs	1.50
7	Roger Clemens	4.50
8	Tony Gwynn	4.00
9	Alex Rodriguez	6.00
10	Mark McGwire	6.00
11	Barry Bonds	7.00
12	Greg Maddux	4.00
13	Juan Gonzalez	1.25
14	Albert Belle	1.00
15	Mike Piazza	5.00
16	Jeff Bagwell	2.50
17	Dennis Eckersley	1.50
18	Mo Vaughn	1.00
19	Roberto Alomar	1.00
20	Kenny Lofton	1.00

Alex Rodriguez Jumbo

This 8" x 10" version of A-Rod's SkyBox E-X2000 card was given to dealers who ordered case quantities of the new product. The card is identical in design to the standard-sized issued version, but is numbered on back from within an edition of 3,000.

	NM/M
Alex Rodriguez	12.00

Star Date 2000

A 15-card set highlighting young stars that are likely to be the game's top players in the year 2000. Cards were inserted 1:9 packs.

		NM/M
Complete Set (15):		10.00
Common Player:		.40
1	Alex Rodriguez	2.00
2	Andruw Jones	1.25
3	Andy Pettitte	.60
4	Brooks Kieschnick	.40
5	Chipper Jones	1.50
6	Darin Erstad	.60
7	Derek Jeter	2.50
8	Jason Kendall	.40
9	Jermaine Dye	.40
10	Neifi Perez	.40
11	Scott Rolen	.90
12	Todd Hollandsworth	.40
13	Todd Walker	.40
14	Tony Clark	.40
15	Vladimir Guerrero	1.25

1998 SkyBox E-X2001 Sample

To preview its high-tech E-X2001 brand for 1998, SkyBox issued this sample card of A-Rod. Similar in format to the issued version, it is numbered "SAMPLE" on back and has a "PROMOTIONAL SAMPLE" overprint on back.

	NM/M
Alex Rodriguez	2.00

1998 SkyBox E-X2001

This super-premium set featured 100 players on a layered, die-cut design utilizing a mirror-image silhouetted photography and etched holofoil treatment over a clear, 20-point plastic card.

		NM/M
Complete Set (100):		25.00
Common Player:		.15
Pack (2):		1.50
Wax Box (24):		25.00
1	Alex Rodriguez	2.50
2	Barry Bonds	3.00
3	Greg Maddux	1.50
4	Roger Clemens	1.75
5	Juan Gonzalez	.50
6	Chipper Jones	1.50
7	Derek Jeter	3.00
8	Frank Thomas	1.00
9	Cal Ripken Jr.	3.00
10	Ken Griffey Jr.	2.00
11	Mark McGwire	2.50
12	Hideo Nomo	.50
13	Tony Gwynn	1.50
14	Ivan Rodriguez	.75
15	Mike Piazza	2.00
16	Roberto Alomar	.30
17	Jeff Bagwell	1.00
18	Andruw Jones	1.00
19	Albert Belle	.15
20	Mo Vaughn	.15
21	Kenny Lofton	.15
22	Gary Sheffield	.40
23	Tony Clark	.15
24	Mike Mussina	.30
25	Barry Larkin	.15
26	Moises Alou	.15
27	Brady Anderson	.15
28	Andy Pettitte	.25
29	Sammy Sosa	1.50
30	Raul Mondesi	.15
31	Andres Galarraga	.15
32	Chuck Knoblauch	.15
33	Jim Thome	.65
34	Craig Biggio	.15
35	Jay Buhner	.15
36	Rafael Palmeiro	.75
37	Curt Schilling	.35
38	Tino Martinez	.15
39	Pedro Martinez	1.00
40	Jose Canseco	.50
41	Jeff Cirillo	.15
42	Dean Palmer	.15
43	Tim Salmon	.15
44	Jason Giambi	.50
45	Bobby Higginson	.15
46	Jim Edmonds	.15
47	David Justice	.15
48	John Olerud	.15
49	Ray Lankford	.15
50	Al Martin	.15
51	Mike Lieberthal	.15
52	Henry Rodriguez	.15
53	Edgar Renteria	.15
54	Eric Karros	.15
55	Marquis Grissom	.15
56	Wilson Alvarez	.15
57	Darryl Kile	.15
58	Jeff King	.15
59	Shawn Estes	.15
60	Tony Womack	.15
61	Willie Greene	.15
62	Ken Caminiti	.15
63	Vinny Castilla	.15
64	Mark Grace	.15
65	Ryan Klesko	.15
66	Robin Ventura	.15
67	Todd Hundley	.15
68	Travis Fryman	.15
69	Edgar Martinez	.15
70	Matt Williams	.15
71	Paul Molitor	1.00
72	Kevin Brown	.15
73	Randy Johnson	1.00
74	Bernie Williams	.10
75	Manny Ramirez	1.00
76	Fred McGriff	.15
77	Tom Glavine	.35
78	Carlos Delgado	.60
79	Larry Walker	.15
80	Hideki Irabu	.15
81	Ryan McGuire	.15
82	Justin Thompson	.15
83	Kevin Orie	.15
84	Jon Nunnally	.15
85	Mark Kotsay	.15
86	Todd Walker	.15
87	Jason Dickson	.15
88	Fernando Tatis	.15
89	Karim Garcia	.15
90	Ricky Ledee	.15
91	Paul Konerko	.15
92	Jaret Wright	.15
93	Darin Erstad	.30
94	Livan Hernandez	.15
95	Nomar Garciaparra	1.50
96	Jose Cruz Jr.	.15
97	Scott Rolen	.65
98	Ben Grieve	.15

99	Vladimir Guerrero	1.00
100	Travis Lee	.15

Essential Credentials Future

Essential Credentials Future, along with Essential Credentials Now, paralleled all 100 cards in the base set. Production varied depending on the card number, with the exact production number of each player determined by subtracting his card number from 101. Number issued for each card is shown in parentheses.

		NM/M
	Common Player:	5.00
1	Alex Rodriguez/100	55.00
2	Barry Bonds/99	60.00
3	Greg Maddux/98	40.00
4	Roger Clemens/97	45.00
5	Juan Gonzalez/96	15.00
6	Chipper Jones/95	40.00
7	Derek Jeter/94	55.00
8	Frank Thomas/93	35.00
9	Cal Ripken Jr./92	65.00
10	Ken Griffey Jr./91	45.00
11	Mark McGwire/90	55.00
12	Hideo Nomo/89	15.00
13	Tony Gwynn/88	25.00
14	Ivan Rodriguez/87	25.00
15	Mike Piazza/86	40.00
16	Roberto Alomar/85	15.00
17	Jeff Bagwell/84	25.00
18	Andruw Jones/83	25.00
19	Albert Belle/82	5.00
20	Mo Vaughn/81	5.00
21	Kenny Lofton/80	5.00
22	Gary Sheffield/79	12.00
23	Tony Clark/78	5.00
24	Mike Mussina/77	25.00
25	Barry Larkin/76	5.00
26	Moises Alou/75	5.00
27	Brady Anderson/74	5.00
28	Andy Pettitte/73	7.50
29	Sammy Sosa/72	40.00
30	Raul Mondesi/71	5.00
31	Andres Galarraga/70	6.00
32	Chuck Knoblauch/69	6.00
33	Jim Thome/68	20.00
34	Craig Biggio/67	6.00
35	Jay Buhner/66	6.00
36	Rafael Palmeiro/65	30.00
37	Curt Schilling/64	20.00
38	Tino Martinez/63	6.00
39	Pedro Martinez/62	32.50
40	Jose Canseco/61	30.00
41	Jeff Cirillo/60	6.00
42	Dean Palmer/59	6.00
43	Tim Salmon/58	7.50
44	Jason Giambi/57	25.00
45	Bobby Higginson/56	6.00
46	Jim Edmonds/55	6.00
47	David Justice/54	6.00
48	John Olerud/53	6.00
49	Ray Lankford/52	6.00
50	Al Martin/51	6.00
51	Mike Lieberthal/50	6.00
52	Henry Rodriguez/49	6.00
53	Edgar Renteria/48	6.00
54	Eric Karros/47	6.00
55	Marquis Grissom/46	6.00
56	Wilson Alvarez/45	6.00
57	Darryl Kile/44	6.00
58	Jeff King/43	6.00
59	Shawn Estes/42	6.00
60	Tony Womack/41	6.00
61	Willie Greene/40	6.00
62	Ken Caminiti/39	6.00
63	Vinny Castilla/38	6.00
64	Mark Grace/37	6.00
65	Ryan Klesko/36	6.00
66	Robin Ventura/35	6.00
67	Todd Hundley/34	6.00
68	Travis Fryman/33	6.00
69	Edgar Martinez/32	7.50
70	Matt Williams/31	7.50
71	Paul Molitor/30	45.00
72	Kevin Brown/29	7.50
73	Randy Johnson/28	40.00
74	Bernie Williams/27	20.00
75	Manny Ramirez/26	45.00
76	Fred McGriff/25	20.00
77	Tom Glavine/24	35.00
78	Carlos Delgado/23	35.00
79	Larry Walker/22	9.00
80	Hideki Irabu/21	9.00

81	Ryan McGuire/20	9.00
82	Justin Thompson/19	9.00
83	Kevin Orie/18	9.00
84	Jon Nunnally/17	9.00
85	Mark Kotsay/16	9.00

Essential Credentials Now

Essential Credentials Now parallels all 100 cards in the E-X2001 base set. Production for each card was limited to that player's card number, as shown in parentheses.

		NM/M
	Common Player:	5.00
21	Kenny Lofton/21	10.00
22	Gary Sheffield/22	20.00
23	Tony Clark/23	10.00
24	Mike Mussina/24	30.00
25	Barry Larkin/25	10.00
26	Moises Alou/26	10.00
27	Brady Anderson/27	10.00
28	Andy Pettitte/28	15.00
29	Sammy Sosa/29	30.00
30	Raul Mondesi/30	10.00
31	Andres Galarraga/31	10.00
32	Chuck Knoblauch/32	10.00
33	Jim Thome/33	25.00
34	Craig Biggio/34	10.00
35	Jay Buhner/35	10.00
36	Rafael Palmeiro/36	25.00
37	Curt Schilling/37	20.00
38	Tino Martinez/38	10.00
39	Pedro Martinez/39	30.00
40	Jose Canseco/40	20.00
41	Jeff Cirillo/41	5.00
42	Dean Palmer/42	5.00
43	Tim Salmon/43	5.00
44	Jason Giambi/44	15.00
45	Bobby Higginson/45	5.00
46	Jim Edmonds/46	5.00
47	David Justice/47	5.00
48	John Olerud/48	5.00
49	Ray Lankford/49	5.00
50	Al Martin/50	5.00
51	Mike Lieberthal/51	5.00
52	Henry Rodriguez/52	5.00
53	Edgar Renteria/53	5.00
54	Eric Karros/54	5.00
55	Marquis Grissom/55	5.00
56	Wilson Alvarez/56	5.00
57	Darryl Kile/57	5.00
58	Jeff King/58	5.00
59	Shawn Estes/59	5.00
60	Tony Womack/60	5.00
61	Willie Greene/61	5.00
62	Ken Caminiti/62	5.00
63	Vinny Castilla/63	5.00
64	Mark Grace/64	5.00
65	Ryan Klesko/65	5.00
66	Robin Ventura/66	5.00
67	Todd Hundley/67	5.00
68	Travis Fryman/68	5.00
69	Edgar Martinez/69	5.00
70	Matt Williams/70	5.00
71	Paul Molitor/71	15.00
72	Kevin Brown/72	5.00
73	Randy Johnson/73	20.00
74	Bernie Williams/74	5.00
75	Manny Ramirez/75	20.00
76	Fred McGriff/76	5.00
77	Tom Glavine/77	12.00
78	Carlos Delgado/78	10.00
79	Larry Walker/79	5.00
80	Hideki Irabu/80	5.00
81	Ryan McGuire/81	5.00
82	Justin Thompson/82	5.00
83	Kevin Orie/83	5.00
84	Jon Nunnally/84	5.00
85	Mark Kotsay/85	5.00
86	Todd Walker/86	5.00
87	Jason Dickson/87	5.00
88	Fernando Tatis/88	5.00
89	Karim Garcia/89	5.00
90	Ricky Ledee/90	5.00
91	Paul Konerko/91	7.50
92	Jaret Wright/92	5.00
93	Darin Erstad/93	5.00
94	Livan Hernandez/94	5.00
95	Nomar Garciaparra/95	20.00
96	Jose Cruz Jr./96	5.00
97	Scott Rolen/97	10.00
98	Ben Grieve/98	5.00
99	Vladimir Guerrero/99	12.00
100	Travis Lee/100	5.00

Cheap Seat Treats

This 20-card die-cut insert arrived in the shape of a stadium seat. Inserted at one per 24 packs, Cheap Seat Treats included some of the top home run hitters and were numbered with a "CS" prefix.

		NM/M
	Complete Set (20):	30.00
	Common Player:	1.00
	Inserted 1:24	
1	Frank Thomas	2.00
2	Ken Griffey Jr.	3.00
3	Mark McGwire	4.00
4	Tino Martinez	1.00
5	Larry Walker	1.00
6	Juan Gonzalez	1.50
7	Mike Piazza	3.00
8	Jeff Bagwell	2.00
9	Tony Clark	1.00
10	Albert Belle	1.00
11	Andres Galarraga	1.00
12	Jim Thome	1.50
13	Mo Vaughn	1.00
14	Barry Bonds	5.00
15	Vladimir Guerrero	2.00
16	Scott Rolen	1.25
17	Travis Lee	1.00
18	David Justice	1.00
19	Jose Cruz Jr.	1.00
20	Andruw Jones	2.00

Destination: Cooperstown

Destination: Cooperstown captures a mixture of rising young stars and top veterans on die-cut cards that were inserted one per 720 packs. Cards resemble a luggage tag and have a string through a hole at top. Fronts have an action photo, backs have a portrait. Cards are numbered with a "DC" prefix.

		NM/M
	Complete Set (15):	375.00
	Common Player:	8.00
	Inserted 1:720	
1	Alex Rodriguez	40.00
2	Frank Thomas	20.00
3	Cal Ripken Jr.	50.00
4	Roger Clemens	30.00
5	Greg Maddux	25.00
6	Chipper Jones	25.00
7	Ken Griffey Jr.	35.00
8	Mark McGwire	40.00
9	Tony Gwynn	25.00
10	Mike Piazza	35.00
11	Jeff Bagwell	20.00
12	Jose Cruz Jr.	8.00
13	Derek Jeter	50.00
14	Hideo Nomo	10.00
15	Ivan Rodriguez	15.00

Signature 2001

Seventeen top young and future stars signed cards for Signature 2001 inserts in E-X2001. The cards featured the player over a blue and white, sky-like background, with an embossed SkyBox seal of authenticity. Backs were horizontal and also included a Cer-

tificate of Authenticity. These cards were unnumbered and inserted one per 60 packs.

		NM/M
	Complete Set (17):	100.00
	Common Player:	3.00
	Inserted 1:60	
1	Ricky Ledee	3.00
2	Derrick Gibson	3.00
3	Mark Kotsay	3.00
4	Kevin Millwood	10.00
5	Brad Fullmer	3.00
6	Todd Walker	4.00
7	Ben Grieve	3.00
8	Tony Clark	3.00
9	Jaret Wright	4.00
10	Randall Simon	3.00
11	Paul Konerko	15.00
12	Todd Helton	15.00
13	David Ortiz	30.00
14	Alex Gonzalez	4.00
15	Bobby Estalella	3.00
16	Alex Rodriguez	50.00
17	Mike Lowell	10.00

Star Date 2001

Star Date 2001 displays 15 of the top rising stars on an acetate space/planet background with gold-foil printing on front. This insert was seeded one per 12 packs and was numbered with a "SD" suffix.

		NM/M
	Complete Set (15):	5.00
	Common Player:	.25
	Inserted 1:12	
1	Travis Lee	.25
2	Jose Cruz Jr.	.25
3	Paul Konerko	1.00
4	Bobby Estalella	.25
5	Magglio Ordonez	1.00
6	Juan Encarnacion	.25
7	Richard Hidalgo	.25
8	Abraham Nunez	.25
9	Sean Casey	.50
10	Todd Helton	1.50
11	Brad Fullmer	.25
12	Ben Grieve	.25
13	Livan Hernandez	.25
14	Jaret Wright	.25
15	Todd Dunwoody	.25

Kerry Wood

In an effort to get rookie pitching phenom Kerry Wood into its E-X2001 set, SkyBox created a cardboard, rather than plastic, trade card and inserted it at a rate of one per 50 packs. The trade card could be exchanged by mail for a plastic version.

		NM/M
	Complete Set (2):	2.00
---	Kerry Wood (Cardboard trade card.)	1.00
101	Kerry Wood (Plastic redemption card.)	4.00

1998 SkyBox Dugout Axcess Promo

This introduction to SkyBox's new brand is labeled front and back as a "PROMOTIONAL SAMPLE."

		NM/M
15	Alex Rodriguez	3.00

1998 SkyBox Dugout Axcess

Dugout Axcess was a 150-card set that attempted to provide collectors with an inside look at baseball. The cards were printed on "playing card" quality stock and used unique information and photography. The product arrived in 12-card packs with an Inside Axcess parallel set that was individually numbered to 50 sets. Six different inserts sets were available, including Double Header, Frequent Flyers, Dishwashers, Superheroes, Gronks and Autograph Redemptions.

		NM/M
	Complete Set (150):	12.00
	Common Player:	.05
	Inside Axcess Stars:	25X
	Production 50 Sets	
	Pack (12):	1.00
	Wax Box (36):	20.00
1	Travis Lee	.05
2	Matt Williams	.05
3	Andy Benes	.05
4	Chipper Jones	.75
5	Ryan Klesko	.05
6	Greg Maddux	.75
7	Sammy Sosa	.75
8	Henry Rodriguez	.05
9	Mark Grace	.05
10	Barry Larkin	.05
11	Bret Boone	.05
12	Reggie Sanders	.05
13	Vinny Castilla	.05
14	Larry Walker	.05
15	Darryl Kile	.05
16	Charles Johnson	.05
17	Edgar Renteria	.05
18	Gary Sheffield	.40
19	Jeff Bagwell	.65
20	Craig Biggio	.05
21	Moises Alou	.05
22	Mike Piazza	1.00
23	Hideo Nomo	.35
24	Raul Mondesi	.05
25	John Jaha	.05
26	Jeff Cirillo	.05
27	Jeromy Burnitz	.05
28	Mark Grudzielanek	.05
29	Vladimir Guerrero	.65
30	Rondell White	.05
31	Edgardo Alfonzo	.05
32	Rey Ordonez	.05
33	Bernard Gilkey	.05
34	Scott Rolen	.50
35	Curt Schilling	.35
36	Ricky Bottalico	.05
37	Tony Womack	.05
38	Al Martin	.05
39	Jason Kendall	.05
40	Ron Gant	.05
41	Mark McGwire	1.25
42	Ray Lankford	.05
43	Tony Gwynn	.65
44	Ken Caminiti	.05
45	Kevin Brown	.05
46	Barry Bonds	1.50
47	J.T. Snow	.05
48	Shawn Estes	.05
49	Jim Edmonds	.05
50	Tim Salmon	.05

51	Jason Dickson	.05
52	Cal Ripken Jr.	1.50
53	Mike Mussina	.35
54	Roberto Alomar	.20
55	Mo Vaughn	.05
56	Pedro Martinez	.65
57	Nomar Garciaparra	.75
58	Albert Belle	.05
59	Frank Thomas	.65
60	Robin Ventura	.05
61	Jim Thome	.60
62	Sandy Alomar Jr.	.05
63	Jaret Wright	.05
64	Bobby Higginson	.05
65	Tony Clark	.05
66	Justin Thompson	.05
67	Dean Palmer	.05
68	Kevin Appier	.05
69	Johnny Damon	.35
70	Paul Molitor	.65
71	Marty Cordova	.05
72	Brad Radke	.05
73	Derek Jeter	1.50
74	Bernie Williams	.05
75	Andy Pettitte	.25
76	Matt Stairs	.05
77	Ben Grieve	.05
78	Jason Giambi	.50
79	Randy Johnson	.65
80	Ken Griffey Jr.	1.00
81	Alex Rodriguez	1.25
82	Fred McGriff	.05
83	Wade Boggs	.75
84	Wilson Alvarez	.05
85	Juan Gonzalez	.35
86	Ivan Rodriguez	.50
87	Fernando Tatis	.05
88	Roger Clemens	.85
89	Jose Cruz Jr.	.05
90	Shawn Green	.30
91	Jeff Suppan (Little Dawgs)	.05
92	Eli Marrero (Little Dawgs)	.05
93	Mike Lowell RC (Little Dawgs)	1.00
94	Ben Grieve (Little Dawgs)	.05
95	Cliff Politte (Little Dawgs)	.05
96	Rolando Arrojo RC (Little Dawgs)	.25
97	Mike Caruso (Little Dawgs)	.05
98	Miguel Tejada (Little Dawgs)	.15
99	Rod Myers (Little Dawgs)	.05
100	Juan Encarnacion (Little Dawgs)	.05
101	Enrique Wilson (Little Dawgs)	.05
102	Brian Giles (Little Dawgs)	.05
103	Magglio Ordonez RC (Little Dawgs)	1.00
104	Brian Rose (Little Dawgs)	.05
105	Ryan Jackson RC (Little Dawgs)	.25
106	Mark Kotsay (Little Dawgs)	.05
107	Desi Relaford (Little Dawgs)	.05
108	A.J. Hinch (Little Dawgs)	.05
109	Eric Milton (Little Dawgs)	.05
110	Ricky Ledee (Little Dawgs)	.05
111	Karim Garcia (Little Dawgs)	.05
112	Derrek Lee (Little Dawgs)	.60
113	Brad Fullmer (Little Dawgs)	.05
114	Travis Lee (Little Dawgs)	.05
115	Greg Norton (Little Dawgs)	.05
116	Rich Butler (Little Dawgs)	.05
117	Masato Yoshii RC (Little Dawgs)	.25
118	Paul Konerko (Little Dawgs)	.20
119	Richard Hidalgo (Little Dawgs)	.05
120	Todd Helton (Little Dawgs)	.60
121	Nomar Garciaparra (7th Inning Sketch)	.40
122	Scott Rolen (7th Inning Sketch)	.20
123	Cal Ripken Jr. (7th Inning Sketch)	.75
124	Derek Jeter (7th Inning Sketch)	.75
125	Mike Piazza (7th Inning Sketch)	.45
126	Tony Gwynn (7th Inning Sketch)	.40
127	Mark McGwire (7th Inning Sketch)	.65
128	Kenny Lofton (7th Inning Sketch)	.05
129	Greg Maddux (7th Inning Sketch)	.05
130	Jeff Bagwell (7th Inning Sketch)	.30
131	Randy Johnson (7th Inning Sketch)	.30
132	Alex Rodriguez (7th Inning Sketch)	.65
133	Mo Vaughn (Name Plates)	.05
134	Chipper Jones (Name Plates)	.40
135	Juan Gonzalez (Name Plates)	.15
136	Tony Clark (Name Plates)	.05

		NM/M
137	Fred McGriff (Name Plates)	.05
138	Roger Clemens (Name Plates)	.45
139	Ken Griffey Jr. (Name Plates)	.65
140	Ivan Rodriguez (Name Plates)	.25
141	Vinny Castilla (Trivia Card)	.05
142	Livan Hernandez (Trivia Card)	.05
143	Jose Cruz Jr. (Trivia Card)	.05
144	Andruw Jones (Trivia Card)	.30
145	Rafael Palmeiro (Trivia Card)	.50
146	Chuck Knoblauch (Trivia Card)	.05
147	Jay Buhner (Trivia Card)	.05
148	Andres Galarraga (Trivia Card)	.05
149	Frank Thomas (Trivia Card)	.35
150	Todd Hundley (Trivia Card)	.05

Inside Axcess

This 150-card parallel set was sequentially numbered to 50 sets, with each card containing a stamped logo on the front and serial numbering on the back.

	NM/M
Common Player:	4.00
Inside Axcess Stars:	25X

Autograph Redemption Cards

These scarce - one per 96 packs - inserts were redeemable (until March 31, 1999) for autographed baseballs or gloves from more than a dozen established stars and promising youngsters. Because the cards do not picture the player involved, having a generic photo of a person's arm signing an autograph, the exchange cards don't have tremendous collector value now that the redemption period has expired. The autographed balls and gloves would be valued according to supply and demand in the memorabilia marketplace.

		NM/M
Complete Set (15):		37.00
Common Card:		1.50
(1)	Jay Buhner/Ball	1.50
(2)	Roger Clemens/Ball	3.00
(3)	Jose Cruz Jr./Ball	2.25
(4)	Darin Erstad/Glv	4.50
(5)	Nomar Garciaparra/Ball	3.00
(6)	Tony Gwynn/Ball	2.75
(7)	Roberto Hernandez/Ball	1.50
(8)	Todd Hollandsworth/Glv	3.00
(9)	Greg Maddux/Ball	3.00
(10)	Alex Ochoa/Glv	1.50
(11)	Alex Rodriguez/Ball	4.00
(12)	Scott Rolen/Glv	4.50
(13)	Scott Rolen/Ball	2.50
(14)	Todd Walker/Ball	3.00
(15)	Tony Womack/Ball	1.50

Dishwashers

This 10-card set was a tribute to the game's best pitchers who "clean the home plate of opposing batters." Cards were inserted one per eight packs.

		NM/M
Complete Set (10):		7.00
Common Player:		.50
Inserted 1:8		
D1	Greg Maddux	2.00
D2	Kevin Brown	.50
D3	Pedro Martinez	1.00
D4	Randy Johnson	1.00
D5	Curt Schilling	.75
D6	John Smoltz	.50
D7	Darryl Kile	.50
D8	Roger Clemens	2.25
D9	Andy Pettitte	.60
D10	Mike Mussina	.65

Double Header

Double Header featured 20 players on cards that doubled as game pieces. The game instructions were on the card and required two dice to play. These were inserted at a rate of two per pack.

		NM/M
Complete Set (20):		2.00
Common Player:		.05
Inserted 2:1		
DH1	Jeff Bagwell	.15
DH2	Albert Belle	.05
DH3	Barry Bonds	.40
DH4	Derek Jeter	.40
DH5	Tony Clark	.05
DH6	Nomar Garciaparra	.20
DH7	Juan Gonzalez	.10
DH8	Ken Griffey Jr.	.25
DH9	Chipper Jones	.20
DH10	Kenny Lofton	.05
DH11	Mark McGwire	.30
DH12	Mo Vaughn	.05
DH13	Mike Piazza	.25
DH14	Cal Ripken Jr.	.40
DH15	Ivan Rodriguez	.10
DH16	Scott Rolen	.10
DH17	Frank Thomas	.15
DH18	Tony Gwynn	.20
DH19	Travis Lee	.05
DH20	Jose Cruz Jr.	.05

Frequent Flyers

The game's top 10 base stealers were included in Frequent Flyers. This insert was designed to look like airline frequent flyer cards and was inserted one per four packs. Fronts have player action photos on a metallic-foil background of a cloudy sky. Backs have a portrait photo and a few words about the player's base-stealing ability. Cards are numbered with an "FF" prefix.

		NM/M
Complete Set (10):		2.50
Common Player:		.25
Inserted 1:4		
FF1	Brian Hunter	.25
FF2	Kenny Lofton	.25
FF3	Chuck Knoblauch	.25
FF4	Tony Womack	.25
FF5	Marquis Grissom	.25
FF6	Craig Biggio	.25
FF7	Barry Bonds	2.00
FF8	Tom Goodwin	.25
FF9	Delino DeShields	.25
FF10	Eric Young	.25

Gronks

Gronks featured 10 of the top home run hitters and was a hobby exclusive insert. The name of the insert originated from shortstop Greg Gagne, and the cards were inserted in one per 72 packs.

		NM/M
Complete Set (10):		30.00
Common Player:		1.50
Inserted 1:72		
G1	Jeff Bagwell	3.50
G2	Albert Belle	1.50
G3	Juan Gonzalez	1.50
G4	Ken Griffey Jr.	6.00
G5	Mark McGwire	7.50
G6	Mike Piazza	6.00
G7	Frank Thomas	3.50
G8	Mo Vaughn	1.50
G9	Ken Caminiti	1.50
G10	Tony Clark	1.50

SuperHeroes

SuperHeroes combined 10 top superstars with the Marvel Comics superhero with whom they share a common trait in this 10-card insert set. Cards were inserted at a rate of one per 20 packs.

		NM/M
Complete Set (10):		10.00
Common Player:		.50
Inserted 1:20		
SH1	Barry Bonds	3.00
SH2	Andres Galarraga	.50
SH3	Ken Griffey Jr.	1.00
SH4	Chipper Jones	1.00
SH5	Andruw Jones	.75
SH6	Hideo Nomo	.60
SH7	Cal Ripken Jr.	2.00
SH8	Alex Rodriguez	3.00
SH9	Frank Thomas	.75
SH10	Mo Vaughn	.50

Todd Helton Autograph

For use in various promotions, Fleer arranged to have Todd Helton autograph 800 of his SkyBox Dugout Axcess Little Dawgs subset cards. Besides the signature, the cards feature an embossed authentication logo.

		NM/M
120	Todd Helton	15.00

Gronks

SportsFest

As part of its participation at SportsFest in Philadelphia in May 1998, SkyBox issued a special card of hometown hero Scott Rolen. The card was available only as a wrapper redemption at the show and was limited to 5,000. Front has an action photo of Rolen on a colorful background with the team and show logos at bottom. Back has a portrait photo and stats.

		NM/M
SF1	Scott Rolen	3.00

1999 SkyBox E-X Century

The 120-card base set features a clear plastic stock with the player name, logo and position stamped in holographic foil. Card backs have the featured player's vital information along with his '98 statistics and his major league totals. Cards 91-120 are part of a prospects subset and are short-printed seeded 1:2 packs. Three-card packs have a SRP of $5.99.

		NM/M
Complete Set (120):		35.00
Common Player:		.15
Common SP (91-120):		.60
Inserted 1:2		
Pack (3):		3.00
Wax Box (18):		40.00
1	Scott Rolen	.75
2	Nomar Garciaparra	1.50
3	Mike Piazza	2.00
4	Tony Gwynn	1.50
5	Sammy Sosa	1.50
6	Alex Rodriguez	2.50
7	Vladimir Guerrero	1.00
8	Chipper Jones	1.50
9	Derek Jeter	3.00
10	Kerry Wood	.50
11	Juan Gonzalez	.50
12	Frank Thomas	1.00
13	Mo Vaughn	.15
14	Greg Maddux	1.50
15	Jeff Bagwell	1.00
16	Mark McGwire	2.50
17	Ken Griffey Jr.	2.00
18	Roger Clemens	1.75
19	Cal Ripken Jr.	3.00
20	Travis Lee	.15
21	Todd Helton	.75
22	Darin Erstad	.30
23	Pedro Martinez	1.00
24	Barry Bonds	3.00
25	Andruw Jones	1.00
26	Larry Walker	.15
27	Albert Belle	.15
28	Ivan Rodriguez	.75
29	Magglio Ordonez	.25
30	Andres Galarraga	.25
31	Mike Mussina	.50
32	Randy Johnson	1.00
33	Tom Glavine	.35
34	Barry Larkin	.25
35	Jim Thome	.25
36	Gary Sheffield	.25
37	Bernie Williams	.45
38	Carlos Delgado	.60
39	Rafael Palmeiro	.75
40	Edgar Renteria	.15

		NM/M
41	Brad Fullmer	.15
42	David Wells	.15
43	Dante Bichette	.15
44	Jaret Wright	.15
45	Ricky Ledee	.15
46	Ray Lankford	.15
47	Mark Grace	.15
48	Jeff Cirillo	.15
49	Rondell White	.15
50	Jeromy Burnitz	.15
51	Sean Casey	.25
52	Rolando Arrojo	.15
53	Jason Giambi	.65
54	John Olerud	.15
55	Will Clark	.15
56	Raul Mondesi	.15
57	Scott Brosius	.15
58	Bartolo Colon	.15
59	Steve Finley	.15
60	Javy Lopez	.15
61	Tim Salmon	.15
62	Roberto Alomar	.30
63	Vinny Castilla	.15
64	Craig Biggio	.15
65	Jose Guillen	.15
66	Greg Vaughn	.15
67	Jose Canseco	.40
68	Shawn Green	.50
69	Curt Schilling	.35
70	Orlando Hernandez	.15
71	Jose Cruz Jr.	.15
72	Alex Gonzalez	.15
73	Tino Martinez	.15
74	Todd Hundley	.15
75	Brian Giles	.15
76	Cliff Floyd	.15
77	Paul O'Neill	.15
78	Ken Caminiti	.15
79	Ron Gant	.15
80	Juan Encarnacion	.15
81	Ben Grieve	.15
82	Brian Jordan	.15
83	Rickey Henderson	1.00
84	Tony Clark	.15
85	Shannon Stewart	.15
86	Robin Ventura	.15
87	Todd Walker	.15
88	Kevin Brown	.15
89	Moises Alou	.15
90	Manny Ramirez	1.00
91	Gabe Alvarez	.60
92	Jeremy Giambi	.60
93	Adrian Beltre	.75
94	George Lombard	.60
95	Ryan Minor	.60
96	Kevin Witt	.60
97	Scott Hunter RC	.60
98	Carlos Guillen	.60
99	Derrick Gibson	.60
100	Trot Nixon	.75
101	Troy Glaus	3.00
102	Armando Rios	.60
103	Preston Wilson	.60
104	Pat Burrell RC	3.00
105	J.D. Drew	1.50
106	Bruce Chen	.60
107	Matt Clement	.60
108	Carlos Beltran	1.50
109	Carlos Febles	.60
110	Rob Fick	.60
111	Russell Branyan	.60
112	Roosevelt Brown RC	.60
113	Corey Koskie	.60
114	Mario Encarnacion	.60
115	Peter Tucci RC	.60
116	Eric Chavez	.75
117	Gabe Kapler	.60
118	Marlon Anderson	.60
119	A.J. Burnett RC	.75
120	Ryan Bradley	.60
---	Checklist 1-96	.05
---	Checklist 97-120/Inserts	.05

Essential Credentials Future

A glossy silver design replaces the clear plastic portions seen on the base cards. Production varied depending on the card number, with the exact production number of each player determined by subtracting his card number from 121. Quantity issued is listed in parentheses.

		NM/M
Common Player:		5.00
1	Scott Rolen/120	10.00
2	Nomar Garciaparra/119	15.00

		NM/M
3	Mike Piazza/118	25.00
4	Tony Gwynn/117	20.00
5	Sammy Sosa/116	15.00
6	Alex Rodriguez/115	25.00
7	Vladimir Guerrero/114	15.00
8	Chipper Jones/113	25.00
9	Derek Jeter/112	50.00
10	Kerry Wood/111	10.00
11	Juan Gonzalez/110	10.00
12	Frank Thomas/109	25.00
13	Mo Vaughn/108	5.00
14	Greg Maddux/107	25.00
15	Jeff Bagwell/106	15.00
16	Mark McGwire/105	20.00
17	Ken Griffey Jr./104	25.00
18	Roger Clemens/103	15.00
19	Cal Ripken Jr./102	40.00
20	Travis Lee/101	5.00
21	Todd Helton/100	15.00
22	Darin Erstad/99	5.00
23	Pedro Martinez/98	15.00
24	Barry Bonds/97	40.00
25	Andruw Jones/96	10.00
26	Larry Walker/95	5.00
27	Albert Belle/94	5.00
28	Ivan Rodriguez/93	15.00
29	Magglio Ordonez/92	10.00
30	Andres Galarraga/91	5.00
31	Mike Mussina/90	10.00
32	Randy Johnson/89	20.00
33	Tom Glavine/88	15.00
34	Barry Larkin/87	8.00
35	Jim Thome/86	15.00
36	Gary Sheffield/85	15.00
37	Bernie Williams/84	5.00
38	Carlos Delgado/83	15.00
39	Rafael Palmeiro/82	10.00
40	Edgar Renteria/81	5.00
41	Brad Fullmer/80	5.00
42	David Wells/79	5.00
43	Dante Bichette/78	5.00
44	Jaret Wright/77	5.00
45	Ricky Ledee/76	5.00
46	Ray Lankford/75	5.00
47	Mark Grace/74	8.00
48	Jeff Cirillo/73	5.00
49	Rondell White/72	5.00
50	Jeromy Burnitz/71	5.00
51	Sean Casey/70	5.00
52	Rolando Arrojo/69	5.00
53	Jason Giambi/68	10.00
54	John Olerud/67	5.00
55	Will Clark/66	8.00
56	Raul Mondesi/65	5.00
57	Scott Brosius/64	5.00
58	Bartolo Colon/63	5.00
59	Steve Finley/62	5.00
60	Javy Lopez/61	5.00
61	Tim Salmon/60	5.00
62	Roberto Alomar/59	10.00
63	Vinny Castilla/58	5.00
64	Craig Biggio/57	8.00
65	Jose Guillen/56	5.00
66	Greg Vaughn/55	5.00
67	Jose Canseco/54	10.00
68	Shawn Green/53	5.00
69	Curt Schilling/52	15.00
70	Orlando Hernandez/51	5.00
71	Jose Cruz Jr./50	5.00
72	Alex Gonzalez/49	5.00
73	Tino Martinez/48	8.00
74	Todd Hundley/47	5.00
75	Brian Giles/46	5.00
76	Cliff Floyd/45	5.00
77	Paul O'Neill/44	10.00
78	Ken Caminiti/43	5.00
79	Ron Gant/42	5.00
80	Juan Encarnacion/41	8.00
81	Ben Grieve/40	5.00
82	Brian Jordan/39	5.00
83	Rickey Henderson/38	15.00
84	Tony Clark/37	5.00
85	Shannon Stewart/36	5.00
86	Robin Ventura /35	5.00
87	Todd Walker/34	5.00
88	Kevin Brown/33	5.00
89	Moises Alou/32	10.00
90	Manny Ramirez/31	25.00
91	Gabe Alvarez/30	5.00
92	Jeremy Giambi/29	5.00
93	Adrian Beltre/28	8.00
94	George Lombard/27	5.00
95	Ryan Minor/26	5.00
96	Kevin Witt/25	5.00
97	Scott Hunter/24	5.00
98	Carlos Guillen/23	10.00
99	Derrick Gibson/22	5.00
100	Trot Nixon/21	10.00

Essential Credentials Now

Like Future, this is a parallel of the base set, with production of each card limited to that player's card number. These cards have a glossy gold look.

		NM/M
Common Player:		5.00
21	Todd Helton/21	15.00
22	Darin Erstad/22	8.00
23	Pedro Martinez/23	20.00
24	Barry Bonds/24	50.00
25	Andruw Jones/25	10.00
26	Larry Walker/26	8.00
27	Albert Belle/27	5.00
28	Ivan Rodriguez/28	10.00
29	Magglio Ordonez/29	10.00

30	Andres Galarraga/30	5.00
31	Mike Mussina/31	10.00
32	Randy Johnson/32	15.00
33	Tom Glavine/33	10.00
34	Barry Larkin/34	10.00
35	Jim Thome/35	10.00
36	Gary Sheffield/36	10.00
37	Bernie Williams/37	10.00
38	Carlos Delgado/38	10.00
39	Rafael Palmeiro/39	10.00
40	Edgar Renteria/40	10.00
41	Brad Fullmer/41	5.00
42	David Wells/42	5.00
43	Dante Bichette/43	5.00
44	Jaret Wright/44	5.00
45	Ricky Ledee/45	5.00
46	Ray Lankford/46	5.00
47	Mark Grace/47	8.00
48	Jeff Cirillo/48	5.00
49	Rondell White/49	5.00
50	Jeromy Burnitz/50	5.00
51	Sean Casey/51	5.00
52	Rolando Arrojo/52	5.00
53	Jason Giambi/53	10.00
54	John Olerud/54	5.00
55	Will Clark/55	8.00
56	Raul Mondesi/56	5.00
57	Scott Brosius/57	5.00
58	Bartolo Colon/58	5.00
59	Steve Finley/59	5.00
60	Javy Lopez/60	5.00
61	Tim Salmon/61	5.00
62	Roberto Alomar/62	8.00
63	Vinny Castilla/63	5.00
64	Craig Biggio/64	8.00
65	Jose Guillen/65	5.00
66	Greg Vaughn/66	5.00
67	Jose Canseco/67	10.00
68	Shawn Green/68	5.00
69	Curt Schilling/69	15.00
70	Orlando Hernandez/70	5.00
71	Jose Cruz Jr./71	5.00
72	Alex Gonzalez/72	5.00
73	Tino Martinez/73	8.00
74	Todd Hundley/74	5.00
75	Brian Giles/75	5.00
76	Cliff Floyd/76	5.00
77	Paul O'Neill/77	8.00
78	Ken Caminiti/78	5.00
79	Ron Gant/79	5.00
80	Juan Encarnacion/80	5.00
81	Ben Grieve/81	5.00
82	Brian Jordan/82	5.00
83	Rickey Henderson/83	10.00
84	Tony Clark/84	5.00
85	Shannon Stewart/85	5.00
86	Robin Ventura/86	5.00
87	Todd Walker/87	5.00
88	Kevin Brown/88	5.00
89	Moises Alou/89	8.00
90	Manny Ramirez/90	15.00
91	Gabe Alvarez/91	5.00
92	Jeremy Giambi/92	5.00
93	Adrian Beltre/93	5.00
94	George Lombard/94	5.00
95	Ryan Minor/95	5.00
96	Kevin Witt/96	5.00
97	Scott Hunter/97	5.00
98	Carlos Guillen/98	5.00
99	Derrick Gibson/99	5.00
100	Trot Nixon/100	5.00
101	Troy Glaus/101	8.00
102	Armando Rios/102	5.00
103	Preston Wilson/103	5.00
104	Pat Burrell/104	5.00
105	J.D. Drew/105	5.00
106	Bruce Chen/106	5.00
107	Matt Clement/107	5.00
108	Carlos Beltran/108	10.00
109	Carlos Febles/109	5.00
110	Rob Fick/110	5.00
111	Russell Branyan/111	5.00
112	Roosevelt Brown/112	5.00
113	Corey Koskie/113	5.00
114	Mario Encarnacion/114	5.00
115	Peter Tucci/115	5.00
116	Eric Chavez/116	8.00
117	Gabe Kapler/117	5.00
118	Marlon Anderson/118	5.00
119	A.J. Burnett/119	5.00
120	Ryan Bradley/120	5.00

Authen-Kicks

Authen-Kicks is a game-used insert that embeds game-worn shoe swatches from the featured player.

Each is done in a horizontal format and is sequentially hand-numbered. The number of swatch cards differs from player to player, and is indicated here in parentheses. Autographed versions of two colors of J.D. Drew shoes were also produced.

		NM/M
Common Player:		4.00
(1)	J.D. Drew/160	8.00
(1ab)	J.D. Drew/8	
	(Autographed black.)	75.00
(1ar)	J.D. Drew/8	
	(Autographed red.)	75.00
(2)	Travis Lee/175	4.00
(3)	Kevin Millwood/160	6.00
(4)	Bruce Chen/205	4.00
(5)	Troy Glaus/205	10.00
(6)	Todd Helton/205	15.00
(7)	Ricky Ledee/180	4.00
(8)	Scott Rolen/205	15.00
(9)	Jeremy Giambi/205	4.00

E-X Quisite

15 of baseball's top young players are showcased, with a black background and interior die-cutting around the player image. These are seeded 1:18 packs.

		NM/M
Complete Set (15):		15.00
Common Player:		.50
Inserted 1:18		
1	Troy Glaus	3.00
2	J.D. Drew	2.00
3	Pat Burrell	2.00
4	Russell Branyan	.50
5	Kerry Wood	1.50
6	Eric Chavez	1.00
7	Ben Grieve	.50
8	Gabe Kapler	.50
9	Adrian Beltre	1.00
10	Todd Helton	4.00
11	Roosevelt Brown	.50
12	Marlon Anderson	.50
13	Jeremy Giambi	.50
14	Magglio Ordonez	1.50
15	Travis Lee	.50

Favorites for Fenway

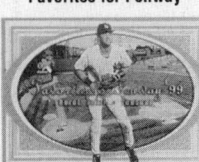

This 20-card set pays tribute to one of baseball's favorite ballparks, Fenway Park the venue for the 1999 All-Star Game. These have a photo of the featured player with an image of Fenway Park in the background on a horizontal format. These are seeded 1:36 packs.

		NM/M
Complete Set (20):		45.00
Common Player:		1.00
Inserted 1:36		
1	Mo Vaughn	1.00
2	Nomar Garciaparra	2.00
3	Frank Thomas	2.00
4	Ken Griffey Jr.	3.00
5	Roger Clemens	2.50
6	Alex Rodriguez	4.00
7	Derek Jeter	5.00
8	Juan Gonzalez	1.50
9	Cal Ripken Jr.	5.00
10	Ivan Rodriguez	1.50

11	J.D. Drew	1.50
12	Barry Bonds	5.00
13	Tony Gwynn	2.00
14	Vladimir Guerrero	2.00
15	Chipper Jones	2.00
16	Kerry Wood	1.50
17	Mike Piazza	3.00
18	Sammy Sosa	2.00
19	Scott Rolen	1.50
20	Mark McGwire	4.00

Milestones of the Century

This 10-card set spotlights the top statistical performances from the 1998 season, sequentially numbered to that performance in a multi-layered design.

		NM/M
Common Player:		5.00
Numbered to featured milestone.		
1	Kerry Wood/20	15.00
2	Mark McGwire/70	20.00
3	Sammy Sosa/66	15.00
4	Ken Griffey Jr./350	15.00
5	Roger Clemens/98	25.00
6	Cal Ripken Jr./17	100.00
7	Alex Rodriguez/40	40.00
8	Barry Bonds/400	25.00
9	N.Y. Yankees/114	15.00
10	Travis Lee/98	5.00

1999 SkyBox Molten Metal

Distributed exclusively to the hobby, the 150-card set consists of three subsets: Metal Smiths, Heavy Metal and Supernatural. Metal Smiths (1-100) show baseball's top players, Heavy Metal (101-130) focus on power hitters and Supernatural (131-150) focus on rookies. Base cards feature silver foil stamping on a 24-point stock with holofoil and wet-laminate overlays. Molten Metal was released in six-card packs with a SRP of $4.99. A special version of the issue was sold only at the 20th Nat'l Sports Collectors Convention in Atlanta, July 19-24. The show version includes autograph redemption cards for show guests and a die-cut series of 30 current and former Braves favorites. Each of the show version cards has a small National Convention logo printed on back; they currently carry no premium.

		NM/M
Complete Set (150):		35.00
Common Metalsmiths (1-100):		.15
Inserted 4:1		
Common Heavy Metal (101-130):		.25
Inserted 1:1		
Common Supernatural (131-150):		.50
Inserted 1:2		
Pack (6):		1.00
Wax Box (24):		20.00
1	Larry Walker	.15
2	Jose Canseco	.50
3	Brian Jordan	.15
4	Rafael Palmeiro	.65
5	Edgar Renteria	.15
6	Dante Bichette	.15
7	Mark Kotsay	.15

8	Denny Neagle	.15
9	Ellis Burks	.15
10	Paul O'Neill	.15
11	Miguel Tejada	.30
12	Ken Caminiti	.15
13	David Cone	.15
14	Jason Kendall	.15
15	Ruben Rivera	.15
16	Todd Walker	.15
17	Bobby Higginson	.15
18	Derrek Lee	.60
19	Rondell White	.15
20	Pedro J. Martinez	.75
21	Jeff Kent	.15
22	Randy Johnson	.75
23	Matt Williams	.15
24	Sean Casey	.25
25	Eric Davis	.15
26	Ryan Klesko	.15
27	Curt Schilling	.35
28	Geoff Jenkins	.15
29	Armand Abreu	.15
30	Vinny Castilla	.15
31	Will Clark	.25
32	Ray Durham	.15
33	Ray Lankford	.15
34	Richie Sexson	.15
35	Derrick Gibson	.15
36	Mark Grace	.15
37	Greg Vaughn	.15
38	Bartolo Colon	.15
39	Steve Finley	.15
40	Chuck Knoblauch	.15
41	Ricky Ledee	.15
42	John Smoltz	.15
43	Moises Alou	.15
44	Jim Edmonds	.15
45	Cliff Floyd	.15
46	Javy Lopez	.15
47	Jim Thome	.65
48	J.T. Snow	.15
49	Sandy Alomar Jr.	.15
50	Andy Pettitte	.25
51	Juan Encarnacion	.15
52	Travis Fryman	.15
53	Eli Marrero	.15
54	Jeff Cirillo	.15
55	Brady Anderson	.15
56	Jose Cruz Jr.	.15
57	Edgar Martinez	.15
58	Garret Anderson	.15
59	Paul Konerko	.30
60	Eric Milton	.15
61	Jason Giambi	.45
62	Tom Glavine	.35
63	Justin Thompson	.15
64	Brad Fullmer	.15
65	Marquis Grissom	.15
66	Fernando Tatis	.15
67	Carlos Beltran	.45
68	Charles Johnson	.15
69	Raul Mondesi	.15
70	Richard Hildalgo	.15
71	Barry Larkin	.15
72	David Wells	.15
73	Jay Buhner	.15
74	Matt Clement	.15
75	Eric Karros	.15
76	Carl Pavano	.15
77	Mariano Rivera	.25
78	Livan Hernandez	.15
79	A.J. Hinch	.15
80	Tino Martinez	.15
81	Rusty Greer	.15
82	Jose Guillen	.15
83	Robin Ventura	.15
84	Kevin Brown	.15
85	Chan Ho Park	.15
86	John Olerud	.15
87	Johnny Damon	.35
88	Todd Hundley	.15
89	Fred McGriff	.15
90	Wade Boggs	1.00
91	Mike Cameron	.15
92	Gary Sheffield	.50
93	Rickey Henderson	.15
94	Pat Hentgen	.15
95	Omar Vizquel	.15
96	Craig Biggio	.15
97	Mike Caruso	.15
98	Neifi Perez	.15
99	Mike Mussina	.50
100	Carlos Delgado	.45
101	Andruw Jones	
	(Heavy Metal)	1.00
102	Pat Burrell RC	
	(Heavy Metal)	3.00
103	Orlando Hernandez	
	(Heavy Metal)	.25
104	Darin Erstad	
	(Heavy Metal)	.40
105	Roberto Alomar	
	(Heavy Metal)	.35
106	Tim Salmon (Heavy Metal)	.25
107	Albert Belle (Heavy Metal)	.25
108	Chad Allen RC	
	(Heavy Metal)	.25
109	Travis Lee (Heavy Metal)	.25
110	Jesse Garcia RC	
	(Heavy Metal)	.25
111	Tony Clark (Heavy Metal)	.25
112	Ivan Rodriguez	
	(Heavy Metal)	.75
113	Troy Glaus (Heavy Metal)	1.00
114	A.J. Burnett RC	
	(Heavy Metal)	1.50
115	David Justice	
	(Heavy Metal)	.25

116	Adrian Beltre	
	(Heavy Metal)	.50
117	Eric Chavez (Heavy Metal)	.35
118	Kenny Lofton	
	(Heavy Metal)	.25
119	Michael Barrett	
	(Heavy Metal)	.25
120	Jeff Weaver RC	
	(Heavy Metal)	1.50
121	Manny Ramirez	
	(Heavy Metal)	1.00
122	Barry Bonds	
	(Heavy Metal)	2.00
123	Bernie Williams	
	(Heavy Metal)	.25
124	Freddy Garcia RC	
	(Heavy Metal)	1.50
125	Scott Hunter RC	
	(Heavy Metal)	.25
126	Jeremy Giambi	
	(Heavy Metal)	.25
127	Masao Kida RC	
	(Heavy Metal)	.25
128	Todd Helton	
	(Heavy Metal)	1.00
129	Mike Figga (Heavy Metal)	.25
130	Mo Vaughn (Heavy Metal)	.25
131	J.D. Drew (Supernaturals)	.65
132	Cal Ripken Jr.	
	(Supernaturals)	3.00
133	Ken Griffey Jr.	
	(Supernaturals)	1.50
134	Mark McGwire	
	(Supernaturals)	2.00
135	Nomar Garciaparra	
	(Supernaturals)	1.00
136	Greg Maddux	
	(Supernaturals)	1.00
137	Mike Piazza	
	(Supernaturals)	1.50
138	Alex Rodriguez	
	(Supernaturals)	2.00
139	Frank Thomas	
	(Supernaturals)	.85
140	Juan Gonzalez	
	(Supernaturals)	.65
141	Tony Gwynn	
	(Supernaturals)	1.00
142	Derek Jeter	
	(Supernaturals)	3.00
143	Chipper Jones	
	(Supernaturals)	1.00
144	Scott Rolen	
	(Supernaturals)	.65
145	Sammy Sosa	
	(Supernaturals)	1.00
146	Kerry Wood	
	(Supernaturals)	.50
147	Roger Clemens	
	(Supernaturals)	1.25
148	Jeff Bagwell	
	(Supernaturals)	.75
149	Vladimir Guerrero	
	(Supernaturals)	.75
150	Ben Grieve	
	(Supernaturals)	.50

Fusion

Fusion is a 50-card partial parallel that is paralleled three times: Fusion, Sterling Fusion and Titanium Fusion. The three parallels consist of the two subsets Heavy Metal and Supernatural. Fusion Heavy Metals (1-30) are seeded 1:12 packs and Supernatural Fusions are seeded 1:24 packs. Fusions are laser die-cut with additional silverfoil stamping. Sterling Fusions are limited to 500 numbered sets with each card laser die-cut on a blue background with blue foil stamping. Titanium Fusions are limited to 50 sequentially numbered sets with gold background and enhanced with gold foil highlights.

	NM/M
Complete Set (50):	100.00
Common Heavy Metal (1-30):	1.00
Inserted 1:12	
Common Supernatural (31-50):	2.50
Inserted 1:24	
Sterling (31-50):	1.5X
Production 500 Sets	
Titanium (31-50):	6X

Production 50 Sets

1	Andruw Jones	4.00
2	Pat Burrell	2.00
3	Orlando Hernandez	1.50
4	Darin Erstad	1.50
5	Roberto Alomar	1.50
6	Tim Salmon	1.00
7	Albert Belle	1.00
8	Chad Allen	1.00
9	Travis Lee	1.00
10	Jesse Garcia	1.00
11	Tony Clark	1.00
12	Ivan Rodriguez	3.00
13	Troy Glaus	3.00
14	A.J. Burnett	1.00
15	David Justice	1.00
16	Adrian Beltre	1.50
17	Eric Chavez	1.50
18	Kenny Lofton	1.00
19	Michael Barrett	1.00
20	Jeff Weaver	1.00
21	Manny Ramirez	4.00
22	Barry Bonds	10.00
23	Bernie Williams	1.00
24	Freddy Garcia	1.00
25	Scott Hunter	1.00
26	Jeremy Giambi	1.00
27	Masao Kida	1.00
28	Todd Helton	3.00
29	Mike Figga	1.00
30	Mo Vaughn	1.00
31	J.D. Drew	2.00
32	Cal Ripken Jr.	10.00
33	Ken Griffey Jr.	6.00
34	Mark McGwire	7.50
35	Nomar Garciaparra	5.00
36	Greg Maddux	5.00
37	Mike Piazza	6.00
38	Alex Rodriguez	7.50
39	Frank Thomas	4.00
40	Juan Gonzalez	1.50
41	Tony Gwynn	5.00
42	Derek Jeter	10.00
43	Chipper Jones	5.00
44	Scott Rolen	3.00
45	Sammy Sosa	5.00
46	Kerry Wood	2.00
47	Roger Clemens	5.50
48	Jeff Bagwell	4.00
49	Vladimir Guerrero	4.00
50	Ben Grieve	1.00

Fusion - Sterling

Sterling Fusions are limited to 500 numbered sets with each card laser die-cut on a blue background with blue foil graphic highlights. A special version of the issue was sold only at the 20th Nat'l Sports Collectors Convention in Atlanta, July 19-24. Each of the show-version cards has a small National Convention logo printed on back; they currently carry no premium.

	NM/M
Common Player:	1.50
Sterling Stars:	1.5X

Fusion - Titanium

Titanium Fusions are limited to 50 sequentially numbered sets with gold background and enhanced with gold foil highlights. A special version of the issue was sold only at the 20th Nat'l Sports

Collectors Convention in Atlanta, July 19-24. Each of the show-version cards has a small National Convention logo printed on back; they currently carry no premium.

	NM/M
Common Player:	4.00
Titanium Stars:	6X

Oh Atlanta!

This 30-card set features players who are either current or former Atlanta Braves like Chipper Jones and Dave Justice. These inserts are seeded one per pack and was produced in conjunction with the 20th annual National Sports Collectors Convention in Atlanta.

	NM/M
Complete Set (30):	30.00
Common Player:	.60
Inserted 1:1	

1	Kenny Lofton	.60
2	Kevin Millwood	.60
3	Bret Boone	.60
4	Otis Nixon	.60
5	Vinny Castilla	.60
6	Brian Jordan	.60
7	Chipper Jones	8.00
8	Dave Justice	.60
9	Micah Bowie	.60
10	Fred McGriff	.60
11	Ron Gant	.60
12	Andruw Jones	4.00
13	Kent Mercker	.60
14	Greg McMichael	.60
15	Steve Avery	.60
16	Marquis Grissom	.60
17	Jason Schmidt	.60
18	Ryan Klesko	.60
19	Charlie O'Brien	.60
20	Terry Pendleton	.60
21	Denny Neagle	.60
22	Greg Maddux	8.00
23	Tom Glavine	1.50
24	Javy Lopez	.60
25	John Rocker	.60
26	Walt Weiss	.60
27	John Smoltz	.60
28	Michael Tucker	.60
29	Odalis Perez	.60
30	Andres Galarraga	.60

Xplosion Sample

This sample card was issued to preview SkyBox's Xplosion metal inserts. Etched and printed on metal stock, the card is identical in format to the issued versions, except for sample notations on back.

	NM/M
Kerry Wood	3.00

Xplosion

This is a 150-card parallel set, which is seeded 1:2 packs. These are made of actual metal that have added etching and some foil stamping.

	NM/M
Complete Set (150):	300.00
Common Player:	1.00
Stars:	3X
Inserted 1:2	

1999 SkyBox Premium

The base set consists of 300 cards, base cards feature full bleed fronts with gold-foil stamped player and team names. Card backs have complete year-by-year stats along with a close-up photo. The Rookie subset (223-272) also have a short-printed parallel version as well. Different photos are used but they have the same card number and card back. The short-print versions are seeded 1:8 packs and have an action photo front while the non-seeded cards have a close-up photo.

	NM/M
Complete Set (300):	20.00
Complete Set w/SP's (350):	40.00
Common Player:	.10
Common SP (223-272):	.60
SP's inserted 1:8	
Star Rubies: 50X	
Production 50 Sets	
SP Star Rubies:	15X
Production 15 Sets	
Pack (8):	1.50
Wax Box (24):	25.00

1	Alex Rodriguez	2.00
2	Sidney Ponson	.10
3	Shawn Green	.35
4	Dan Wilson	.10
5	Rolando Arrojo	.10
6	Roberto Alomar	.30
7	Matt Anderson	.10
8	David Segui	.10
9	Alex Gonzalez	.10
10	Edgar Renteria	.10
11	Benito Santiago	.10
12	Todd Stottlemyre	.10
13	Rico Brogna	.10
14	Troy Glaus	.65
15	Al Leiter	.10
16	Pedro J. Martinez	.75
17	Paul O'Neill	.10
18	Manny Ramirez	.75
19	Scott Rolen	.65
20	Curt Schilling	.35
21	Bobby Abreu	.15
22	Robb Nen	.10
23	Andy Pettitte	.25
24	John Wetteland	.10
25	Bobby Bonilla	.10
26	Darin Erstad	.20
27	Shawn Estes	.10
28	John Franco	.10
29	Nomar Garciaparra	1.00
30	Rick Helling	.10
31	David Justice	.10
32	Chuck Knoblauch	.10
33	Quinton McCracken	.10
34	Kenny Rogers	.10
35	Brian Giles	.10
36	Armando Benitez	.10
37	Trevor Hoffman	.10
38	Charles Johnson	.10
39	Travis Lee	.10
40	Tom Glavine	.35
41	Rondell White	.10
42	Orlando Hernandez	.10

43	Mickey Morandini	.10
44	Darryl Kile	.10
45	Greg Vaughn	.10
46	Gregg Jefferies	.10
47	Mark McGwire	2.00
48	Kerry Wood	.40
49	Jeromy Burnitz	.10
50	Ron Gant	.10
51	Vinny Castilla	.10
52	Doug Glanville	.10
53	Juan Guzman	.10
54	Dustin Hermanson	.10
55	Jose Hernandez	.10
56	Bob Higginson	.10
57	A.J. Hinch	.10
58	Randy Johnson	.75
59	Eli Marrero	.10
60	Rafael Palmeiro	.65
61	Carl Pavano	.10
62	Brett Tomko	.10
63	Jose Guillen	.10
64	Mike Lieberthal	.10
65	Jim Abbott	.10
66	Dante Bichette	.10
67	Jeff Cirillo	.10
68	Eric Davis	.10
69	Delino DeShields	.10
70	Steve Finley	.10
71	Mark Grace	.10
72	Jason Kendall	.10
73	Jeff Kent	.10
74	Desi Relaford	.10
75	Ivan Rodriguez	.65
76	Shannon Stewart	.10
77	Geoff Jenkins	.10
78	Ben Grieve	.10
79	Cliff Floyd	.10
80	Jason Giambi	.50
81	Rod Beck	.10
82	Derek Bell	.10
83	Will Clark	.10
84	David Dellucci	.10
85	Joey Hamilton	.10
86	Livan Hernandez	.10
87	Barry Larkin	.10
88	Matt Mantei	.10
89	Dean Palmer	.10
90	Chan Ho Park	.10
91	Jim Thome	.65
92	Miguel Tejada	.20
93	Justin Thompson	.10
94	David Wells	.10
95	Bernie Williams	.10
96	Jeff Bagwell	.75
97	Derek Lee	.50
98	Devon White	.10
99	Jeff Shaw	.10
100	Brad Radke	.10
101	Mark Grudzielanek	.10
102	Javy Lopez	.10
103	Mike Sirotka	.10
104	Robin Ventura	.10
105	Andy Ashby	.10
106	Juan Gonzalez	.40
107	Albert Belle	.10
108	Andy Benes	.10
109	Jay Buhner	.10
110	Ken Caminiti	.10
111	Roger Clemens	1.25
112	Mike Hampton	.10
113	Pete Harnisch	.10
114	Mike Piazza	1.50
115	J.T. Snow	.10
116	John Olerud	.10
117	Tony Womack	.10
118	Todd Zeile	.10
119	Tony Gwynn	1.00
120	Brady Anderson	.10
121	Sean Casey	.20
122	Jose Cruz Jr.	.10
123	Carlos Delgado	.50
124	Edgar Martinez	.10
125	Jose Mesa	.10
126	Shane Reynolds	.10
127	John Valentin	.10
128	Mo Vaughn	.10
129	Kevin Young	.10
130	Jay Bell	.10
131	Aaron Boone	.10
132	John Smoltz	.10
133	Mike Stanley	.10
134	Bret Saberhagen	.10
135	Tim Salmon	.10
136	Mariano Rivera	.15
137	Ken Griffey Jr.	1.50
138	Jose Offerman	.10
139	Troy Percival	.10
140	Greg Maddux	1.00
141	Frank Thomas	.75
142	Steve Avery	.10
143	Kevin Millwood	.10
144	Sammy Sosa	1.00
145	Larry Walker	.10
146	Matt Williams	.10
147	Mike Caruso	.10
148	Todd Helton	.65
149	Andruw Jones	.75
150	Ray Lankford	.10
151	Craig Biggio	.10
152	Ugueth Urbina	.10
153	Wade Boggs	1.00
154	Derek Jeter	2.50
155	Wally Joyner	.10
156	Mike Mussina	.30
157	Gregg Olson	.10
158	Henry Rodriguez	.10
159	Reggie Sanders	.10
160	Fernando Tatis	.10

161	Dmitri Young	.10
162	Rick Aguilera	.10
163	Marty Cordova	.10
164	Johnny Damon	.30
165	Ray Durham	.10
166	Brad Fullmer	.10
167	Chipper Jones	1.00
168	Bobby Smith	.10
169	Omar Vizquel	.10
170	Todd Hundley	.10
171	David Cone	.10
172	Royce Clayton	.10
173	Ryan Klesko	.10
174	Jeff Montgomery	.10
175	Magglio Ordonez	.10
176	Billy Wagner	.10
177	Masato Yoshii	.10
178	Jason Christiansen	.10
179	Chuck Finley	.10
180	Tom Gordon	.10
181	Wilton Guerrero	.10
182	Rickey Henderson	.75
183	Sterling Hitchcock	.10
184	Kenny Lofton	.10
185	Tino Martinez	.10
186	Fred McGriff	.10
187	Matt Stairs	.10
188	Neifi Perez	.10
189	Bob Wickman	.10
190	Barry Bonds	2.50
191	Jose Canseco	.40
192	Damion Easley	.10
193	Jim Edmonds	.10
194	Juan Encarnacion	.50
195	Travis Fryman	.10
196	Tom Goodwin	.10
197	Rusty Greer	.10
198	Roberto Hernandez	.10
199	B.J. Surhoff	.10
200	Scott Brosius	.10
201	Brian Jordan	.10
202	Paul Konerko	.20
203	Ismael Valdes	.10
204	Eric Milton	.10
205	Adrian Beltre	.25
206	Tony Clark	.10
207	Bartolo Colon	.10
208	Cal Ripken Jr.	2.50
209	Moises Alou	.10
210	Wilson Alvarez	.10
211	Kevin Brown	.10
212	Orlando Cabrera	.10
213	Vladimir Guerrero	.75
214	Jose Rosado	.10
215	Raul Mondesi	.10
216	Dave Nilsson	.10
217	Carlos Perez	.10
218	Jason Schmidt	.10
219	Richie Sexson	.10
220	Gary Sheffield	.40
221	Fernando Vina	.10
222	Todd Walker	.10
223	Scott Sauerbeck RC	.10
223	Scott Sauerbeck/SP RC	.60
224	Pascual Matos RC	.10
224	Pascual Matos/SP RC	.60
225	Kyle Farnsworth RC	.15
225	Kyle Farnsworth/SP RC	.60
226	Freddy Garcia RC	.75
226	Freddy Garcia/SP RC	1.50
227	David Lundquist RC	.10
227	David Lundquist/SP RC	.60
228	Jolbert Cabrera RC	.10
228	Jolbert Cabrera/SP RC	.60
229	Dan Perkins RC	.10
229	Dan Perkins/SP RC	.60
230	Warren Morris	.10
230	Warren Morris/SP	.60
231	Carlos Febles	.10
231	Carlos Febles/SP	.60
232	Brett Hinchliffe RC	.10
232	Brett Hinchliffe/SP RC	.60
233	Jason Phillips RC	.10
233	Jason Phillips/SP RC	.60
234	Glen Barker RC	.10
234	Glen Barker/SP RC	.60
235	Jose Macias RC	.25
235	Jose Macias/SP RC	1.00
236	Joe Mays RC	.10
236	Joe Mays/SP RC	.60
237	Chad Allen RC	.10
237	Chad Allen/SP RC	.60
238	Miguel Del Toro RC	.10
238	Miguel Del Toro/SP RC	.60
239	Chris Singleton RC	.10
239	Chris Singleton/SP	.60
240	Jesse Garcia RC	.10
240	Jesse Garcia/SP RC	.60
241	Kris Benson	.10
241	Kris Benson/SP	.60
242	Clay Bellinger RC	.10
242	Clay Bellinger/SP RC	.60
243	Scott Williamson	.10
243	Scott Williamson/SP	.60
244	Masao Kida RC	.10
244	Masao Kida/SP RC	.60
245	Guillermo Garcia RC	.10
245	Guillermo Garcia/SP RC	.60
246	A.J. Burnett RC	.25
246	A.J. Burnett/SP RC	1.50
247	Bo Porter RC	.10
247	Bo Porter/SP RC	.60
248	Pat Burrell RC	1.50
248	Pat Burrell/SP RC	4.00
249	Carlos Lee	.10
249	Carlos Lee/SP	1.50
250	Jeff Weaver RC	.50
250	Jeff Weaver/SP RC	1.50

251	Ruben Mateo	.10
251	Ruben Mateo/SP	.60
252	J.D. Drew	.40
252	J.D. Drew/SP	2.00
253	Jeremy Giambi	.10
253	Jeremy Giambi/SP	.60
254	Gary Bennett RC	.10
254	Gary Bennett/SP RC	.60
255	Edwards Guzman RC	.10
255	Edwards Guzman/SP RC	.60
256	Ramon Martinez	.10
256	Ramon Martinez/SP	.60
257	Giomar Guevara RC	.10
257	Giomar Guevara/SP RC	.60
258	Joe McEwing RC	.10
258	Joe McEwing/SP RC	.60
259	Tom Davey RC	.10
259	Tom Davey/SP RC	.60
260	Gabe Kapler	.10
260	Gabe Kapler/SP	.60
261	Ryan Rupe RC	.10
261	Ryan Rupe/SP RC	.60
262	Kelly Dransfeldt RC	.10
262	Kelly Dransfeldt/SP RC	.60
263	Michael Barrett	.10
263	Michael Barrett/SP	.60
264	Eric Chavez	.25
264	Eric Chavez/SP	1.00
265	Orber Moreno RC	.10
265	Orber Moreno/SP RC	.60
266	Marlon Anderson	.10
266	Marlon Anderson/SP	.60
267	Carlos Beltran	.50
267	Carlos Beltran/SP	1.50
268	Doug Mientkiewicz	.10
268	Doug Mientkiewicz/SP	.60
269	Roy Halladay	.10
269	Roy Halladay/SP	.60
270	Torii Hunter	.10
270	Torii Hunter/SP	.60
271	Stan Spencer	.10
271	Stan Spencer/SP	.60
272	Alex Gonzalez	.10
272	Alex Gonzalez/SP	.60
273	Mark McGwire (Spring Fling)	1.00
274	Scott Rolen (Spring Fling)	.30
275	Jeff Bagwell (Spring Fling)	.40
276	Derek Jeter (Spring Fling)	1.50
277	Tony Gwynn (Spring Fling)	.50
278	Frank Thomas (Spring Fling)	.40
279	Sammy Sosa (Spring Fling)	.50
280	Nomar Garciaparra (Spring Fling)	.50
281	Cal Ripken Jr. (Spring Fling)	1.50
282	Albert Belle (Spring Fling)	.10
283	Kerry Wood (Spring Fling)	.20
284	Greg Maddux (Spring Fling)	.50
285	Barry Bonds (Spring Fling)	1.50
286	Juan Gonzalez (Spring Fling)	.25
287	Ken Griffey Jr. (Spring Fling)	.75
288	Alex Rodriguez (Spring Fling)	1.00
289	Ben Grieve (Spring Fling)	.10
290	Travis Lee (Spring Fling)	.10
291	Mo Vaughn (Spring Fling)	.10
292	Mike Piazza (Spring Fling)	.85
293	Roger Clemens (Spring Fling)	.60
294	J.D. Drew (Spring Fling)	.20
295	Randy Johnson (Spring Fling)	.40
296	Chipper Jones (Spring Fling)	.50
297	Vladimir Guerrero (Spring Fling)	.40
298	Checklist (Nomar Garciaparra)	.40
299	Checklist (Ken Griffey Jr.)	.50
300	Checklist (Mark McGwire)	.60

Star Rubies

Star Rubies are a parallel of the base set and are limited to 50 sequentially numbered sets. SP Rookie parallels are limited to 15

numbered sets. Rubies feature a complete prism foil front with red-foil stamping.

Star Rubies:	50X
Production 50 Sets	
SP Star Rubies:	15X
Production 15 Sets	

Autographics

This 54-card autographed set feature an embossed SkyBox Seal of Authenticity stamp and are seeded 1:68 packs. Cards are commonly found signed in black ink. Blue-ink versions, serially numbered to 50 each, were also produced.

	NM/M
Common Player:	3.00
Inserted 1:68	
Blue Ink:	1.5X
Production 50 Sets	

Roberto Alomar	15.00
Paul Bako	3.00
Michael Barrett	8.00
Kris Benson	8.00
Micah Bowie	3.00
Roosevelt Brown	3.00
A.J. Burnett	8.00
Pat Burrell	15.00
Ken Caminiti	15.00
Royce Clayton	3.00
Edgard Clemente	3.00
Bartolo Colon	10.00
J.D. Drew	15.00
Damion Easley	5.00
Derrin Ebert	3.00
Mario Encarnacion	4.00
Juan Encarnacion	5.00
Troy Glaus	15.00
Tom Glavine	20.00
Juan Gonzalez	15.00
Juan Gonzalez/SP	50.00
Shawn Green	10.00
Wilton Guerrero	3.00
Jose Guillen	8.00
Tony Gwynn	30.00
Mark Harriger	3.00
Bobby Higginson	3.00
Todd Hollandsworth	3.00
Scott Hunter	3.00
Gabe Kapler	3.00
Scott Karl	3.00
Mike Kinkade	3.00
Ray Lankford	3.00
Barry Larkin	15.00
Matt Lawton	5.00
Ricky Ledee	3.00
Travis Lee	5.00
Eli Marrero	5.00
Ruben Mateo	3.00
Joe McEwing	3.00
Doug Mientkiewicz	4.00
Russ Ortiz	5.00
Jim Parque	3.00
Robert Person	3.00
Alex Rodriguez	80.00
Scott Rolen	20.00
Benj Sampson	3.00
Luis Saturria	3.00
Curt Schilling	35.00
David Segui	3.00
Fernando Tatis	3.00
Peter Tucci	3.00
Javier Vasquez	6.00
Robin Ventura	10.00
Checklist	.05

Diamond Debuts

JEFF WEAVER

This 15-card set features the best rookies of 1999 on a silver rainbow holo-foil card stock. These are seeded 1:49 packs. Card backs are numbered with a "DD" suffix.

		NM/M
Complete Set (15):		17.50
Common Player:		2.00
Inserted 1:49		
1	Eric Chavez	3.00
2	Kyle Farnsworth	2.00
3	Ryan Rupe	2.00
4	Jeremy Giambi	2.00
5	Marlon Anderson	2.00
6	J.D. Drew	4.00
7	Carlos Febles	2.00
8	Joe McEwing	2.00
9	Jeff Weaver	2.00
10	Alex Gonzalez	2.00
11	Chad Allen	2.00
12	Michael Barrett	2.00
13	Gabe Kapler	2.00
14	Carlos Lee	2.00
15	Edwards Guzman	2.00

Intimidation Nation

This 15-card set highlights the top performers in baseball and features gold rainbow holo-foil stamping. These are limited to 99 sequentially numbered sets. Card backs are numbered with a "IN" suffix.

		NM/M
Complete Set (15):		280.00
Common Player:		12.00
Production 99 Sets		
1	Cal Ripken Jr.	40.00
2	Tony Gwynn	20.00
3	Nomar Garciaparra	20.00
4	Frank Thomas	15.00
5	Mike Piazza	25.00
6	Mark McGwire	30.00
7	Scott Rolen	12.00
8	Chipper Jones	20.00
9	Greg Maddux	20.00
10	Ken Griffey Jr.	25.00
11	Juan Gonzalez	12.00
12	Derek Jeter	40.00
13	J.D. Drew	12.00
14	Roger Clemens	22.50
15	Alex Rodriguez	30.00

Live Bats

This 15-card set spotlights baseball's top hitters and feature red foil stamping. Card backs are numbered with a "LB" suffix and are seeded 1:7 packs.

		NM/M
Complete Set (15):		10.00
Common Player:		.25
Inserted 1:7		
1	Juan Gonzalez	.35
2	Mark McGwire	1.50
3	Jeff Bagwell	.50
4	Frank Thomas	.50
5	Mike Piazza	1.00
6	Nomar Garciaparra	.75
7	Alex Rodriguez	1.50
8	Scott Rolen	.40
9	Travis Lee	.25
10	Tony Gwynn	.75
11	Derek Jeter	2.00
12	Ben Grieve	.25
13	Chipper Jones	.75
14	Ken Griffey Jr.	1.00
15	Cal Ripken Jr.	1.50

Show Business

This 15-card set features some of the best players in the "show" on double foil-stamped card fronts. Card backs are numbered with a "SB" suffix and are seeded 1:70 packs.

		NM/M
Complete Set (15):		60.00
Common Player:		2.00
Inserted 1:70		
1	Mark McGwire	7.50
2	Tony Gwynn	5.00
3	Nomar Garciaparra	5.00
4	Juan Gonzalez	2.50

5	Roger Clemens	5.00
6	Chipper Jones	5.00
7	Cal Ripken Jr.	10.00
8	Alex Rodriguez	7.50
9	Orlando Hernandez	2.00
10	Greg Maddux	5.00
11	Mike Piazza	6.00
12	Frank Thomas	4.00
13	Ken Griffey Jr.	6.00
14	Scott Rolen	3.00
15	Derek Jeter	10.00

Soul Of The Game

This 15-card set features rainbow foil stamping and the name Soul of the Game prominently stamped, covering the entire card behind the player photo. Card backs are numbered with a "SG" suffix and are seeded 1:14 packs.

		NM/M
Complete Set (15):		15.00
Common Player:		.60
Inserted 1:14		
1	Alex Rodriguez	2.00
2	Vladimir Guerrero	.90
3	Chipper Jones	1.25
4	Derek Jeter	2.50
5	Tony Gwynn	1.25
6	Scott Rolen	.60
7	Juan Gonzalez	.60
8	Mark McGwire	2.00
9	Ken Griffey Jr.	1.50
10	Jeff Bagwell	.90
11	Cal Ripken Jr.	2.50
12	Frank Thomas	.90
13	Mike Piazza	1.50
14	Nomar Garciaparra	1.25
15	Sammy Sosa	1.25

1999 SkyBox Thunder

Skybox Thunder consists of a 300-card base set with three parallels and six inserts. The base set is inserted at varying odds. In hobby packs, regular-player cards #1-140 come 4-5 per pack, veteran stars on cards #141-240 come two per pack, and superstars on cards #241-300 are seeded one per pack. For retail packs the odds were: #1-141 (3-4 per pack), #141-240 (two per pack), and #241-300 (one per pack). Parallels include Rave (numbered to 150 sets) and Super Rave

(25 sets), which are both hobby exclusive. The Rant parallel set is retail exclusive (1:2).

		NM/M
Complete Set (300):		15.00
Common Player (1-240):		.05
Common Player (241-300):		.15
Raves:		15X
Production 150 Sets		
SuperRaves:		45X
Production 25 Sets		
Rants:		8X
Inserted 1:2 R		
Pack (8):		1.50
Wax Box (36):		25.00
1	John Smoltz	.05
2	Garret Anderson	.05
3	Matt Williams	.05
4	Daryle Ward	.05
5	Andy Ashby	.05
6	Miguel Tejada	.15
7	Dmitri Young	.05
8	Roberto Alomar	.25
9	Kevin Brown	.05
10	Eric Young	.05
11	Odalis Perez	.05
12	Preston Wilson	.05
13	Jeff Abbott	.05
14	Bret Boone	.05
15	Mendy Lopez	.05
16	B.J. Surhoff	.05
17	Steve Woodard	.05
18	Ron Coomer	.05
19	Rondell White	.05
20	Edgardo Alfonzo	.05
21	Kevin Millwood	.05
22	Jose Canseco	.45
23	Blake Stein	.05
24	Quilvio Veras	.05
25	Chuck Knoblauch	.05
26	David Segui	.05
27	Eric Davis	.05
28	Francisco Cordova	.05
29	Randy Winn	.05
30	Will Clark	.05
31	Billy Wagner	.05
32	Kevin Witt	.05
33	Jim Edmonds	.05
34	Todd Stottlemyre	.05
35	Shane Andrews	.05
36	Michael Tucker	.05
37	Sandy Alomar Jr.	.05
38	Neifi Perez	.05
39	Jaret Wright	.05
40	Devon White	.05
41	Edgar Renteria	.05
42	Shane Reynolds	.05
43	Jeff King	.05
44	Darren Dreifort	.05
45	Fernando Vina	.05
46	Marty Cordova	.05
47	Ugueth Urbina	.05
48	Bobby Bonilla	.05
49	Omar Vizquel	.05
50	Tom Gordon	.05
51	Ryan Christenson	.05
52	Aaron Boone	.05
53	Jamie Moyer	.05
54	Brian Giles	.05
55	Kevin Tapani	.05
56	Scott Brosius	.05
57	Ellis Burks	.05
58	Al Leiter	.05
59	Royce Clayton	.05
60	Chris Carpenter	.05
61	Bubba Trammell	.05
62	Tom Glavine	.35
63	Shannon Stewart	.05
64	Todd Zeile	.05
65	J.T. Snow	.05
66	Matt Clement	.05
67	Matt Stairs	.05
68	Ismael Valdes	.05
69	Todd Walker	.05
70	Jose Lima	.05
71	Mike Caruso	.05
72	Brett Tomko	.05
73	Mike Lansing	.05
74	Justin Thompson	.05
75	Damion Easley	.05
76	Derrek Lee	.50
77	Derek Bell	.05
78	Brady Anderson	.05
79	Charles Johnson	.05
80	Rafael Roque **RC**	.05
81	Corey Koskie	.05
82	Fernando Seguignol	.05
83	Jay Tessmer	.05
84	Jason Giambi	.50
85	Mike Lieberthal	.05
86	Jose Guillen	.05
87	Jim Leyritz	.05
88	Shawn Estes	.05
89	Ray Lankford	.05
90	Paul Sorrento	.05
91	Javy Lopez	.05
92	John Wetteland	.05
93	Sean Casey	.15
94	Chuck Finley	.05
95	Trot Nixon	.05
96	Ray Durham	.05
97	Reggie Sanders	.05
98	Bartolo Colon	.05
99	Henry Rodriguez	.05
100	Rolando Arrojo	.05
101	Geoff Jenkins	.05
102	Darryl Kile	.05

103	Mark Kotsay	.05
104	Craig Biggio	.05
105	Omar Daal	.05
106	Carlos Febles	.05
107	Eric Karros	.05
108	Matt Lawton	.05
109	Carl Pavano	.05
110	Brian McRae	.05
111	Mariano Rivera	.15
112	Jay Buhner	.05
113	Doug Glanville	.05
114	Jason Kendall	.05
115	Wally Joyner	.05
116	Jeff Kent	.05
117	Shane Monahan	.05
118	Eli Marrero	.05
119	Bobby Smith	.05
120	Shawn Green	.20
121	Kirk Rueter	.05
122	Tom Goodwin	.05
123	Andy Benes	.05
124	Ed Sprague	.05
125	Mike Mussina	.25
126	Jose Offerman	.05
127	Mickey Morandini	.05
128	Paul Konerko	.20
129	Denny Neagle	.05
130	Travis Fryman	.05
131	John Rocker	.05
132	Rob Fick **RC**	.05
133	Livan Hernandez	.05
134	Ken Caminiti	.05
135	Johnny Damon	.30
136	Jeff Kubenka	.05
137	Marquis Grissom	.05
138	Doug Mientkiewicz	.05
139	Dustin Hermanson	.05
140	Carl Everett	.05
141	Hideo Nomo	.40
142	Jorge Posada	.05
143	Rickey Henderson	.75
144	Robb Nen	.05
145	Ron Gant	.05
146	Aramis Ramirez	.05
147	Trevor Hoffman	.05
148	Bill Mueller	.05
149	Edgar Martinez	.05
150	Fred McGriff	.05
151	Rusty Greer	.05
152	Tom Evans	.05
153	Todd Greene	.05
154	Jay Bell	.05
155	Mike Lowell	.05
156	Orlando Cabrera	.05
157	Troy O'Leary	.05
158	Jose Hernandez	.05
159	Magglio Ordonez	.05
160	Barry Larkin	.05
161	David Justice	.05
162	Derrick Gibson	.05
163	Luis Gonzalez	.05
164	Alex Gonzalez	.05
165	Scott Elarton	.05
166	Dermal Brown	.05
167	Eric Milton	.05
168	Raul Mondesi	.05
169	Jeff Cirillo	.05
170	Benj Sampson	.05
171	John Olerud	.05
172	Andy Pettitte	.20
173	A.J. Hinch	.05
174	Rico Brogna	.05
175	Jason Schmidt	.05
176	Dean Palmer	.05
177	Matt Morris	.05
178	Quinton McCracken	.05
179	Rick Helling	.05
180	Walt Weiss	.05
181	Troy Percival	.05
182	Tony Batista	.05
183	Brian Jordan	.05
184	Jerry Hairston Jr.	.05
185	Bret Saberhagen	.05
186	Mark Grace	.05
187	Brian Simmons	.05
188	Pete Harnisch	.05
189	Kenny Lofton	.05
190	Vinny Castilla	.05
191	Bobby Higginson	.05
192	Joey Hamilton	.05
193	Cliff Floyd	.05
194	Andres Galarraga	.05
195	Chan Ho Park	.05
196	Jeromy Burnitz	.05
197	David Ortiz	.35
198	Wilton Guerrero	.05
199	Rey Ordonez	.05
200	Paul O'Neill	.05
201	Kenny Rogers	.05
202	Marlon Anderson	.05
203	Tony Womack	.05
204	Robin Ventura	.05
205	Russ Ortiz	.05
206	Mike Frank	.05
207	Fernando Tatis	.05
208	Miguel Cairo	.05
209	Ivan Rodriguez	.65
210	Carlos Delgado	.05
211	Tim Salmon	.15
212	Brian Anderson	.05
213	Ryan Klesko	.05
214	Scott Erickson	.05
215	Mike Stanley	.05
216	Brant Brown	.05
217	Rod Beck	.05
218	Guillermo Garcia **RC**	.05
219	David Wells	.05
220	Dante Bichette	.05

221	Armando Benitez	.05
222	Todd Dunwoody	.05
223	Kelvim Escobar	.05
224	Richard Hidalgo	.05
225	Angel Pena	.05
226	Ronnie Belliard	.05
227	Brad Radke	.05
228	Brad Fullmer	.05
229	Jay Payton	.05
230	Tino Martinez	.05
231	Scott Spiezio	.05
232	Bobby Abreu	.05
233	John Valentin	.05
234	Kevin Young	.05
235	Steve Finley	.05
236	David Cone	.05
237	Armando Rios	.05
238	Russ Davis	.05
239	Wade Boggs	1.00
240	Aaron Sele	.05
241	Jose Cruz Jr.	.15
242	George Lombard	.15
243	Todd Helton	.65
244	Andruw Jones	.75
245	Troy Glaus	.65
246	Manny Ramirez	.75
247	Ben Grieve	.15
247p	Ben Grieve ("PROMOTIONAL SAMPLE")	1.00
248	Richie Sexson	.15
249	Juan Encarnacion	.15
250	Randy Johnson	.75
251	Gary Sheffield	.45
252	Rafael Palmeiro	.65
253	Roy Halladay	.15
254	Mike Piazza	1.50
255	Tony Gwynn	1.00
256	Juan Gonzalez	.40
257	Jeremy Giambi	.15
258	Ben Davis	.15
259	Russ Branyan	.15
260	Pedro Martinez	.75
261	Frank Thomas	.75
262	Calvin Pickering	.15
263	Chipper Jones	1.00
264	Ryan Minor	.15
265	Roger Clemens	1.25
266	Sammy Sosa	1.00
267	Mo Vaughn	.15
268	Carlos Beltran	.50
269	Jim Thome	.65
270	Mark McGwire	2.00
271	Travis Lee	.15
272	Darin Erstad	.30
273	Derek Jeter	2.50
274	Greg Maddux	1.00
275	Ricky Ledee	.15
276	Alex Rodriguez	2.00
277	Vladimir Guerrero	.75
278	Greg Vaughn	.15
279	Scott Rolen	.60
280	Carlos Guillen	.15
281	Jeff Bagwell	.75
282	Bruce Chen	.15
283	Tony Clark	.15
284	Albert Belle	.05
285	Cal Ripken Jr.	2.50
286	Barry Bonds	2.50
287	Curt Schilling	.35
288	Eric Chavez	.30
289	Larry Walker	.15
290	Orlando Hernandez	.15
291	Moises Alou	.15
292	Ken Griffey Jr.	1.50
293	Kerry Wood	.50
294	Nomar Garciaparra	1.00
295	Gabe Kapler	.15
296	Bernie Williams	.05
297	Matt Anderson	.15
298	Adrian Beltre	.35
299	J.D. Drew	.40
300	Ryan Bradley	.15
---	Checklist 1-230	.05
---	Checklist 231-300 and Inserts	.05
---	Video Game Sweepstakes Form (Derek Jeter)	.05

Dial 1

Designed to look like a mobile phone, this insert set features 10 cards of long distance hitters. The format consists of black plastic cards with rounded corners.

	NM/M
Complete Set (10):	70.00

		NM/M
Common Player:		2.50
Inserted 1:300		
1D	Nomar Garciaparra	7.50
2D	Juan Gonzalez	3.40
3D	Ken Griffey Jr.	10.00
4D	Chipper Jones	7.50
5D	Mark McGwire	12.50
6D	Mike Piazza	10.00
7D	Manny Ramirez	6.00
8D	Alex Rodriguez	12.50
9D	Sammy Sosa	7.50
10D	Mo Vaughn	2.50

Rant

A retail-only parallel of the 300-card base set, Rant substitutes purple metallic foil highlights for the regular-issue's silver on front, and a has a "RANT" notation at upper-right on back, also in purple. The stated insertion rate for the parallel is one per two retail packs.

	NM/M
Common Player:	.50
Rant Stars:	8X

Todd Helton Autograph

An unknown number of Helton's regular card (#243) were autographed and received an embossed seal of authenticity for use in various promotional endeavors.

		NM/M
243	Todd Helton	15.00

Hip-No-Tized

This insert set consisted of 15 cards, featuring both hitters and pitchers. The cards were seeded one card in every 36 packs, and consist of mesmerizing patterned holo-foil stamping.

		NM/M
Complete Set (15):		20.00
Common Player:		1.25
Inserted 1:36		
1H	J.D. Drew	1.25
2H	Nomar Garciaparra	2.00
3H	Juan Gonzalez	1.25
4H	Ken Griffey Jr.	2.50
5H	Derek Jeter	4.00
6H	Randy Johnson	1.50
7H	Chipper Jones	2.00
8H	Mark McGwire	3.00

9H	Mike Piazza	2.50
10H	Cal Ripken Jr.	4.00
11H	Alex Rodriguez	3.00
12H	Sammy Sosa	2.00
13H	Frank Thomas	1.50
14H	Jim Thome	1.25
15H	Kerry Wood	1.25

In Depth

This insert set consists of 10 cards, featuring baseball's elite players. The cards are highlighted with gold rainbow holo-foil and gold metallic ink. The insertion rate for this insert was one card in every 24 packs.

		NM/M
Complete Set (10):		17.50
Common Player:		1.00
Inserted 1:24		
1ID	Albert Belle	1.00
2ID	Barry Bonds	5.00
3ID	Roger Clemens	1.50
4ID	Juan Gonzalez	1.25
5ID	Ken Griffey Jr.	3.00
6ID	Mark McGwire	4.00
7ID	Mike Piazza	3.00
8ID	Sammy Sosa	2.50
9ID	Mo Vaughn	1.00
10ID	Kerry Wood	1.25

Turbo Charged

This 10-card insert set consisted of the top home run hitters. The players were featured on plastic see-through cards with rainbow holofoil.

		NM/M
Complete Set (10):		35.00
Common Player:		2.00
Inserted 1:72		
1TC	Jose Canseco	2.50
2TC	Juan Gonzalez	2.00
3TC	Ken Griffey Jr.	5.00
4TC	Vladimir Guerrero	3.00
5TC	Mark McGwire	6.00
6TC	Mike Piazza	5.00
7TC	Manny Ramirez	3.00
8TC	Alex Rodriguez	6.00
9TC	Sammy Sosa	4.00
10TC	Mo Vaughn	2.00

Unleashed

This insert set contained 15 cards designed to resemble a cereal box. The players featured included the best young talent in baseball. The cards were silver-foil stamped, and offered facsimile signatures of each player. One card was included with every six packs.

		NM/M
Complete Set (15):		10.00
Common Player:		.50
Inserted 1:6		
1U	Carlos Beltran	1.50
2U	Adrian Beltre	1.00
3U	Eric Chavez	.75
4U	J.D. Drew	1.00
5U	Juan Encarnacion	.50
6U	Jeremy Giambi	.50
7U	Troy Glaus	2.00
8U	Ben Grieve	.50
9U	Todd Helton	1.00
10U	Orlando Hernandez	.50
11U	Gabe Kapler	.50
12U	Travis Lee	.50
13U	Calvin Pickering	.50
14U	Richie Sexson	.50
15U	Kerry Wood	1.00

www.Batterz.com

www.batterz.com is a 10-card insert set that was seeded one card per every 18 packs. The game's best hitters are in their own home site in this computer-inspired set.

		NM/M
Complete Set (10):		12.00
Common Player:		.50
Inserted 1:18		
1WB	J.D. Drew	.60
2WB	Nomar Garciaparra	1.00
3WB	Ken Griffey Jr.	1.50
4WB	Tony Gwynn	1.00
5WB	Derek Jeter	3.00
6WB	Mark McGwire	2.00
7WB	Alex Rodriguez	2.00
8WB	Scott Rolen	.65
9WB	Sammy Sosa	1.00
10WB	Bernie Williams	.50

2000 SkyBox National Covention Promos

Six-card cello packs of specially marked (printed logo in top corner) cards were distributed at the 2000 National Sports Collectors Convention in Anaheim, Calif., to promote Fleer's SkyBox brand. Cards are numbered "X of 6" on back.

		NM/M
Complete Set (6):		8.00
Common Player:		1.25
1	Cal Ripken Jr.	2.00
2	Ken Griffey Jr.	1.25
3	Derek Jeter	2.00
4	Alex Rodriguez	1.50
5	Mark McGwire	1.50
6	Mike Piazza	1.25

2000 SkyBox

		NM/M
Complete Set (250):		25.00
Comp. Set w/SPs (300):		60.00
Common Player:		.10
Common SP (201-240):		1.00
Inserted 1:8		
Common SP (241-250):		.50
Inserted 1:12		
Pack (10):		1.50
Wax Box (24):		30.00
1	Cal Ripken Jr.	2.00

2	Ivan Rodriguez	.65
3	Chipper Jones	1.00
4	Dean Palmer	.10
5	Devon White	.10
6	Ugueth Urbina	.10
7	Doug Glanville	.10
8	Damian Jackson	.10
9	Jose Canseco	.40
10	Billy Koch	.10
11	Brady Anderson	.10
12	Vladimir Guerrero	.75
13	Dan Wilson	.10
14	Kevin Brown	.10
15	Eddie Taubensee	.10
16	Jose Lima	.10
17	Greg Maddux	1.00
18	Manny Ramirez	.75
19	Brad Fullmer	.10
20	Ron Gant	.10
21	Edgar Martinez	.10
22	Pokey Reese	.10
23	Jason Varitek	.10
24	Neifi Perez	.10
25	Shane Reynolds	.10
26	Robin Ventura	.10
27	Scott Rolen	.65
28	Trevor Hoffman	.10
29	John Valentin	.10
30	Shannon Stewart	.10
31	Troy Glaus	.75
32	Kerry Wood	.65
33	Jim Thome	.65
34	Rafael Roque	.10
35	Tino Martinez	.10
36	Jeffrey Hammonds	.10
37	Orlando Hernandez	.10
38	Kris Benson	.10
39	Fred McGriff	.10
40	Brian Jordan	.10
41	Trot Nixon	.10
42	Matt Clement	.10
43	Ray Durham	.10
44	Johnny Damon	.30
45	Todd Hollandsworth	.10
46	Edgardo Alfonzo	.10
47	Tim Hudson	.25
48	Tony Gwynn	1.00
49	Barry Bonds	2.00
50	Andruw Jones	.75
51	Pedro Martinez	.75
52	Mike Hampton	.10
53	Miguel Tejada	.25
54	Kevin Young	.10
55	J.T. Snow	.10
56	Carlos Delgado	.50
57	Bobby Howry	.10
58	Andres Galarraga	.10
59	Paul Konerko	.20
60	Mike Cameron	.10
61	Jeremy Giambi	.10
62	Todd Hundley	.10
63	Al Leiter	.10
64	Matt Stairs	.10
65	Edgar Renteria	.10
66	Jeff Kent	.10
67	John Wetteland	.10
68	Nomar Garciaparra	1.25
69	Jeff Weaver	.10
70	Matt Williams	.10
71	Kyle Farnsworth	.10
72	Brad Radke	.10
73	Eric Chavez	.25
74	J.D. Drew	.25
75	Steve Finley	.10
76	Pete Harnisch	.10
77	Chad Kreuter	.10
78	Todd Pratt	.10
79	John Jaha	.10
80	Armando Rios	.10
81	Luis Gonzalez	.25
82	Ryan Minor	.10
83	Juan Gonzalez	.75
84	Rickey Henderson	.75
85	Jason Giambi	.50
86	Shawn Estes	.10
87	Chad Curtis	.10
88	Jeff Cirillo	.10
89	Juan Encarnacion	.10
90	Tony Womack	.10
91	Mike Mussina	.35
92	Jeff Bagwell	.75
93	Rey Ordonez	.10
94	Joe McEwing	.10
95	Robb Nen	.10
96	Will Clark	.10
97	Chris Singleton	.10
98	Jason Kendall	.10
99	Ken Griffey Jr.	1.25

100	Rusty Greer	.10
101	Charles Johnson	.10
102	Carlos Lee	.10
103	Brad Ausmus	.10
104	Preston Wilson	.10
105	Ronnie Belliard	.10
106	Mike Lieberthal	.10
107	Alex Rodriguez	1.50
108	Jay Bell	.10
109	Frank Thomas	.75
110	Adrian Beltre	.30
111	Ron Coomer	.10
112	Ben Grieve	.10
113	Darryl Kile	.10
114	Erubiel Durazo	.10
115	Magglio Ordonez	.10
116	Gary Sheffield	.40
117	Joe Mays	.10
118	Fernando Tatis	.10
119	David Wells	.10
120	Tim Salmon	.20
121	Troy O'Leary	.10
122	Roberto Alomar	.40
123	Damion Easley	.10
124	Brant Brown	.10
125	Carlos Beltran	.45
126	Eric Karros	.10
127	Geoff Jenkins	.10
128	Roger Clemens	1.00
129	Warren Morris	.10
130	Eric Owens	.10
131	Jose Cruz Jr.	.10
132	Mo Vaughn	.10
133	Eric Young	.10
134	Kenny Lofton	.10
135	Marquis Grissom	.10
136	A.J. Burnett	.10
137	Bernie Williams	.25
138	Javy Lopez	.10
139	Jose Offerman	.10
140	Sean Casey	.25
141	Alex Gonzalez	.10
142	Carlos Febles	.10
143	Mike Piazza	1.25
144	Curt Schilling	.35
145	Ben Davis	.10
146	Rafael Palmeiro	.65
147	Scott Williamson	.10
148	Darin Erstad	.25
149	Joe Girardi	.10
150	Gerald Williams	.10
151	Richie Sexson	.10
152	Corey Koskie	.10
153	Paul O'Neill	.10
154	Chad Hermansen	.10
155	Randy Johnson	.75
156	Henry Rodriguez	.10
157	Bartolo Colon	.10
158	Tony Clark	.10
159	Mike Lowell	.10
160	Moises Alou	.10
161	Todd Walker	.10
162	Mariano Rivera	.20
163	Mark McGwire	1.50
164	Roberto Hernandez	.10
165	Larry Walker	.10
166	Albert Belle	.15
167	Barry Larkin	.10
168	Rolando Arrojo	.10
169	Mark Kotsay	.10
170	Ken Caminiti	.10
171	Dermal Brown	.10
172	Michael Barrett	.10
173	Jay Buhner	.10
174	Ruben Mateo	.10
175	Jim Edmonds	.10
176	Sammy Sosa	1.25
177	Omar Vizquel	.10
178	Todd Helton	.75
179	Kevin Barker	.10
180	Derek Jeter	2.00
181	Brian Giles	.10
182	Greg Vaughn	.10
183	Roy Halladay	.10
184	Tom Glavine	.35
185	Craig Biggio	.10
186	Jose Vidro	.10
187	Andy Ashby	.10
188	Freddy Garcia	.10
189	Garret Anderson	.10
190	Mark Grace	.20
191	Travis Fryman	.10
192	Jeromy Burnitz	.10
193	Jacque Jones	.10
194	David Cone	.10
195	Ryan Rupe	.10
196	John Smoltz	.10
197	Daryle Ward	.10
198	Rondell White	.10
199	Bobby Abreu	.10
200	Justin Thompson	.10
201	Norm Hutchins (Prospect)	.10
201	Norm Hutchins/SP	1.00
202	Ramon Ortiz (Prospect)	.10
202	Ramon Ortiz/SP	1.00
203	Dan Wheeler (Prospect)	.10
203	Dan Wheeler/SP	1.00
204	Matt Riley (Prospect)	.10
204	Matt Riley/SP	1.00
205	Steve Lomasney (Prospect)	.10
205	Steve Lomasney/SP	1.00
206	Chad Meyers (Prospect)	.10
206	Chad Meyers/SP	1.00
207	Gary Glover RC (Prospect)	.20
207	Gary Glover/SP	.15
208	Joe Crede (Prospect)	.10
208	Joe Crede/SP	1.00

209	Kip Wells (Prospect)	.10
209	Kip Wells/SP	1.00
210	Travis Dawkins (Prospect)	.10
210	Travis Dawkins/SP	1.00
211	Denny Stark RC (Prospect)	.20
211	Denny Stark/SP	1.00
212	Ben Petrick (Prospect)	.10
212	Ben Petrick/SP	1.00
213	Eric Munson (Prospect)	.10
213	Eric Munson/SP	1.00
214	Josh Beckett (Prospect)	.25
214	Josh Beckett/SP	1.50
215	Pablo Ozuna (Prospect)	.10
215	Pablo Ozuna/SP	1.00
216	Brad Penny (Prospect)	.10
216	Brad Penny/SP	1.00
217	Julio Ramirez (Prospect)	.10
217	Julio Ramirez/SP	1.00
218	Danny Peoples (Prospect)	.10
218	Danny Peoples/SP	1.00
219	Wilfredo Rodriguez RC (Prospect)	.10
219	Wilfredo Rodriguez/SP RC	1.00
220	Julio Lugo (Prospect)	.10
220	Julio Lugo/SP	1.00
221	Mark Quinn (Prospect)	.10
221	Mark Quinn/SP	1.00
222	Eric Gagne (Prospect)	.10
222	Eric Gagne/SP	1.00
223	Chad Green (Prospect)	.10
223	Chad Green/SP	1.00
224	Tony Armas Jr. (Prospect)	.10
224	Tony Armas Jr./SP	1.00
225	Milton Bradley (Prospect)	.10
225	Milton Bradley/SP	1.00
226	Rob Bell (Prospect)	.10
226	Rob Bell/SP	1.00
227	Alfonso Soriano (Prospect)	
227	Alfonso Soriano/SP	4.00
228	Wily Pena (Prospect)	.10
228	Wily Pena/SP	1.00
229	Nick Johnson (Prospect)	.10
229	Nick Johnson/SP	1.50
230	Ed Yarnall (Prospect)	.10
230	Ed Yarnall/SP	1.00
231	Ryan Bradley (Prospect)	.10
231	Ryan Bradley/SP	1.00
232	Adam Piatt (Prospect)	.10
232	Adam Piatt/SP	1.00
233	Chad Harville (Prospect)	.10
233	Chad Harville/SP	1.00
234	Alex Sanchez (Prospect)	.10
234	Alex Sanchez/SP	1.00
235	Michael Coleman (Prospect)	.10
235	Michael Coleman/SP	1.00
236	Pat Burrell (Prospect)	.25
236	Pat Burrell/SP	1.50
237	Wascar Serrano RC (Prospect)	.10
237	Wascar Serrano/SP RC	1.00
238	Rick Ankiel (Prospect)	.25
238	Rick Ankiel/SP	1.00
239	Mike Lamb RC (Prospect)	.10
239	Mike Lamb/SP RC	1.00
240	Vernon Wells (Prospect)	.10
240	Vernon Wells/SP	1.00
241	Jorge Toca, Goefrey Tomlinson (Premium Pairs)	.10
241	Jorge Toca, Goefrey Tomlinson/SP	.50
242	Shea Hillenbrand, Josh Phelps RC (Premium Pairs)	2.00
242	Shea Hillenbrand, Josh Phelps/SP RC	4.00
243	Aaron Myette, Doug Davis (Premium Pairs)	.10
243	Aaron Myette, Doug Davis/SP	.50
244	Brett Laxton, Robert Ramsay (Premium Pairs)	.10
244	Brett Laxton, Robert Ramsay/SP	.50
245	B.J. Ryan, Corey Lee (Premium Pairs)	.10
245	B.J. Ryan, Corey Lee/SP	.50
246	Chris Haas, Wilton Veras (Premium Pairs)	.10
246	Chris Haas, Wilton Veras/SP	.50
247	Jimmy Anderson, Kyle Peterson (Premium Pairs)	.10
247	Jimmy Anderson, Kyle Peterson/SP	.50
248	Jason Dewey, Giuseppe Chiaramonte (Premium Pairs)	.10
248	Jason Dewey, Giuseppe Chiaramonte/SP	.50
249	Guillermo Mota, Orber Moreno (Premium Pairs)	.10
249	Guillermo Mota, Orber Moreno/SP	.50
250	Steve Cox, Julio Zuleta RC (Premium Pairs)	.15
250	Steve Cox, Julio Zuleta/SP RC	.50

Star Rubies

This parallel of the 250-card SkyBox base set shares the same format and photos. On front, however, the player identification and SkyBox logo are in red foil. On back, an SR has been added beneath the card number. Insertion rate was one per 12 packs.

	NM/M
Complete Set (250):	200.00
Common Player (1-200):	.50
Common SP Prospect (201-250):	3.00
Stars:	6X
Star SP's:	3X

Star Rubies Extreme

This parallel of the 250-card SkyBox base set shares the same format and photos. On front, however, the player identification and SkyBox logo are in red foil, and the metallic-foil background has an optical variable layer of stars. On back, an SRE has been added beneath the card number, as well as a strip with a red-foil serial number from within an edition of 50 cards each.

	NM/M
Common Player (1-200):	3.00
Common SP Prospect (201-250):	4.50
Stars:	25X
Star SP's:	15X

Autographics

	NM/M
Common Player:	5.00
Rick Ankiel	15.00
Michael Barrett	5.00
Josh Beckett	25.00
Rob Bell	5.00
Adrian Beltre	15.00
Peter Bergeron	5.00
Lance Berkman	20.00
Rico Brogna	5.00
Pat Burrell	20.00
Orlando Cabrera	15.00
Mike Cameron	8.00
Roger Cedeno	5.00
Eric Chavez	15.00
Bruce Chen	5.00
Johnny Damon	20.00
Ben Davis	5.00
Jason Dewey	5.00
Octavio Dotel	5.00
J.D. Drew	15.00
Erubiel Durazo	8.00
Jason Giambi	20.00
Doug Glanville	5.00
Troy Glaus	20.00
Alex Gonzalez	8.00
Shawn Green	15.00
Jason Grilli	5.00
Tony Gwynn	40.00
Mike Hampton	8.00
Tim Hudson	15.00
Norm Hutchins	5.00
John Jaha	5.00
Derek Jeter	100.00
D'Angelo Jimenez	5.00
Randy Johnson	60.00
Andruw Jones	20.00

Gabe Kapler	8.00
Jason Kendall	10.00
Adam Kennedy	8.00
Cesar King	5.00
Paul Konerko	8.00
Mark Kotsay	6.00
Carlos Lee	8.00
Mike Lieberthal	8.00
Steve Lomasney	5.00
Greg Maddux	60.00
Edgar Martinez	15.00
Aaron McNeal	5.00
Kevin Millwood	10.00
Raul Mondesi	8.00
Joe Nathan	5.00
Magglio Ordonez	15.00
Eric Owens	5.00
Rafael Palmeiro	25.00
Angel Pena	5.00
Wily Pena	15.00
Cal Ripken Jr.	85.00
Scott Rolen	20.00
Jimmy Rollins	15.00
B.J. Ryan	5.00
Tim Salmon	10.00
Chris Singleton	5.00
J.T. Snow	6.00
Mike Sweeney	8.00
Jose Vidro	8.00
Rondell White	8.00
Jaret Wright	5.00

E-Ticket

NM/M
Complete Set (14): 15.00
Common Player: .50
Inserted 1:4
Star Ruby: 4-8X
Production 100 Sets

1	Alex Rodriguez	2.50
2	Derek Jeter	3.00
3	Nomar Garciaparra	1.50
4	Cal Ripken Jr.	3.00
5	Sean Casey	.50
6	Mark McGwire	2.50
7	Sammy Sosa	1.50
8	Ken Griffey Jr.	2.00
9	Tony Gwynn	1.50
10	Pedro Martinez	1.00
11	Chipper Jones	1.50
12	Vladimir Guerrero	1.00
13	Roger Clemens	1.75
14	Mike Piazza	2.00

Genuine Coverage

NM/M
Common Player: 8.00
Inserted 1:399

1	Troy Glaus	15.00
2	Cal Ripken Jr.	40.00
3	Alex Rodriguez	25.00
4	Mike Mussina	10.00
5	J.D. Drew	8.00
6	Robin Ventura	8.00
7	Matt Williams	8.00

Genuine Coverage HOBBY

NM/M
Common Player: 10.00
Inserted 1:144

1	Ivan Rodriguez	12.00
2	Jose Canseco	10.00
3	Frank Thomas	15.00
4	Manny Ramirez	15.00

Higher Level

NM/M
Complete Set (10): 20.00
Common Player: 1.00
Inserted 1:24
Star Ruby: 5-10X
Production 50 Sets

1	Cal Ripken Jr.	4.00
2	Derek Jeter	3.00
3	Nomar Garciaparra	2.00
4	Chipper Jones	2.00

5	Mike Piazza	2.50
6	Ivan Rodriguez	1.00
7	Ken Griffey Jr.	2.50
8	Sammy Sosa	2.00
9	Alex Rodriguez	3.00
10	Mark McGwire	3.00

Preeminence

NM/M
Complete Set (10): 15.00
Common Player: .50
Inserted 1:24
Star Ruby: 5-10X
Production 50 Sets

1	Pedro Martinez	1.25
2	Derek Jeter	4.00
3	Nomar Garciaparra	1.50
4	Alex Rodriguez	3.00
5	Mark McGwire	3.00
6	Sammy Sosa	1.50
7	Sean Casey	.50
8	Mike Piazza	2.00
9	Chipper Jones	1.50
10	Ivan Rodriguez	1.00

SkyLines

NM/M
Complete Set (10): 10.00
Common Player: .50
Inserted 1:11
Star Ruby: 10-20X
Production 50 Sets

1	Cal Ripken Jr.	2.00
2	Mark McGwire	1.50
3	Alex Rodriguez	1.50
4	Sammy Sosa	.75
5	Derek Jeter	2.00
6	Mike Piazza	1.00
7	Nomar Garciaparra	.75
8	Chipper Jones	.75
9	Ken Griffey Jr.	1.00
10	Manny Ramirez	.50

Speed Merchants

NM/M
Complete Set (10): 12.00
Common Player: .50
Inserted 1:8
Star Ruby: 3-6X
Production 100 Sets

1	Derek Jeter	3.00
2	Sammy Sosa	1.25
3	Nomar Garciaparra	1.25
4	Alex Rodriguez	2.50
5	Randy Johnson	1.00
6	Ken Griffey Jr.	1.50
7	Pedro Martinez	1.00
8	Pat Burrell	.50
9	Barry Bonds	3.00
10	Mark McGwire	2.50

The Technique

NM/M
Complete Set (15): 20.00
Common Player: .50
Inserted 1:11
Star Ruby: 3-6X
Production 50 Sets

1	Alex Rodriguez	3.00
2	Tony Gwynn	1.50
3	Sean Casey	.50
4	Mark McGwire	3.00
5	Sammy Sosa	1.50
6	Ken Griffey Jr.	2.00
7	Mike Piazza	2.00
8	Nomar Garciaparra	1.50
9	Derek Jeter	4.00
10	Vladimir Guerrero	1.00
11	Cal Ripken Jr.	4.00
12	Chipper Jones	1.50
13	Frank Thomas	1.00
14	Manny Ramirez	1.00
15	Jeff Bagwell	1.00

2000 SkyBox Dominion

NM/M
Complete Set (300): 20.00
Common Player: .10
Pack (10): 1.50
Wax Box (36): 30.00

1	Mark McGwire, Ken Griffey Jr. (League Leaders)	.40
2	Mark McGwire, Manny Ramirez (League Leaders)	.40
3	Larry Walker, Nomar Garciaparra (League Leaders)	.25
4	Tony Womack, Brian Hunter (League Leaders)	.10
5	Mike Hampton, Pedro Martinez (League Leaders)	.20
6	Randy Johnson, Pedro Martinez (League Leaders)	.20
7	Randy Johnson, Pedro Martinez (League Leaders)	.20
8	Uegeth Urbina, Mariano Rivera (League Leaders)	.10
9	Vinny Castilla (Highlights)	.10
10	Orioles host Cuban National Team (Highlights)	.10
11	Jose Canseco (Highlights)	.10
12	Fernando Tatis (Highlights)	.10
13	Robin Ventura (Highlights)	.10
14	Roger Clemens (Highlights)	.10
15	Jose Jimenez (Highlights)	.10
16	David Cone (Highlights)	.10
17	Mark McGwire (Highlights)	.65
18	Cal Ripken Jr. (Highlights)	.75
19	Tony Gwynn (Highlights)	.30
20	Wade Boggs (Highlights)	.25
21	Ivan Rodriguez (Highlights)	.20
22	Chuck Finley (Highlights)	.10
23	Eric Milton (Highlights)	.10
24	Adrian Beltre (Highlights)	.10
25	Brad Radke	.10
26	Derek Bell	.10
27	Garret Anderson	.10
28	Ivan Rodriguez	.40
29	Jeff Kent	.10
30	Jeremy Giambi	.10
31	John Franco	.10
32	Jose Hernandez	.10
33	Jose Offerman	.10
34	Jose Rosado	.10
35	Kevin Appier	.10
36	Kris Benson	.10
37	Mark McGwire	1.00
38	Matt Williams	.10
39	Paul O'Neill	.10
40	Rickey Henderson	.50
41	Todd Greene	.10
42	Russ Ortiz	.10
43	Sean Casey	.20
44	Tony Womack	.10
45	Troy O'Leary	.10
46	Ugueth Urbina	.10
47	Tom Glavine	.25
48	Mike Mussina	.30
49	Carlos Febles	.10
50	Jon Lieber	.10
51	Juan Gonzalez	.30
52	Matt Clement	.10
53	Moises Alou	.10
54	Ray Durham	.10
55	Robb Nen	.10
56	Tino Martinez	.10
57	Troy Glaus	.40
58	Curt Schilling	.30
59	Mike Sweeney	.10
60	Steve Finley	.10
61	Roger Cedeno	.10
62	Bobby Jones	.10
63	John Smoltz	.10
64	Darin Erstad	.20
65	Carlos Delgado	.35
66	Ray Lankford	.10
67	Todd Stottlemyre	.10
68	Andy Ashby	.10
69	Bobby Abreu	.15
70	Chuck Finley	.10
71	Damion Easley	.10
72	Dustin Hermanson	.10
73	Frank Thomas	.50
74	Kevin Brown	.10
75	Kevin Millwood	.10
76	Mark Grace	.10
77	Matt Stairs	.10
78	Mike Hampton	.10
79	Omar Vizquel	.10
80	Preston Wilson	.10
81	Robin Ventura	.10
82	Todd Helton	.40
83	Tony Clark	.10
84	Al Leiter	.10
85	Alex Fernandez	.10
86	Bernie Williams	.10
87	Edgar Martinez	.10
88	Edgar Renteria	.10
89	Fred McGriff	.10
90	Jermaine Dye	.10
91	Joe McEwing	.10
92	John Halama	.10
93	Lee Stevens	.10
94	Matt Lawton	.10
95	Mike Piazza	.75
96	Pete Harnisch	.10
97	Scott Karl	.10
98	Tony Fernandez	.10
99	Sammy Sosa	.60
100	Bobby Higginson	.10
101	Tony Gwynn	.60
102	J.D. Drew	.20
103	Roberto Hernandez	.10
104	Rondell White	.10
105	David Nilsson	.10
106	Shane Reynolds	.10
107	Jaret Wright	.10
108	Jeff Bagwell	.50
109	Jay Bell	.10
110	Kevin Tapani	.10
111	Michael Barrett	.10
112	Neifi Perez	.10
113	Pat Hentgen	.10
114	Roger Clemens	.65
115	Travis Fryman	.10
116	Aaron Sele	.10
117	Eric Davis	.10
118	Trevor Hoffman	.10
119	Chris Singleton	.10
120	Ryan Klesko	.10
121	Scott Rolen	.40
122	Jorge Posada	.10
123	Abraham Nunez	.10
124	Alex Gonzalez	.10
125	B.J. Surhoff	.10
126	Barry Bonds	1.50
127	Billy Koch	.10
128	Billy Wagner	.10
129	Brad Ausmus	.10
130	Bret Boone	.10
131	Cal Ripken Jr.	1.50
132	Chad Allen	.10
133	Chris Carpenter	.10
134	Craig Biggio	.10
135	Dante Bichette	.10
136	Dean Palmer	.10
137	Derek Jeter	1.50
138	Ellis Burks	.10
139	Freddy Garcia	.10
140	Gabe Kapler	.10
141	Greg Maddux	.60
142	Greg Vaughn	.10
143	Jason Kendall	.10
144	Jim Parque	.10
145	John Valentin	.10
146	Jose Vidro	.10
147	Ken Griffey Jr.	.75
148	Kenny Lofton	.10
149	Kenny Rogers	.10
150	Kent Bottenfield	.10
151	Chuck Knoblauch	.10
152	Larry Walker	.10
153	Manny Ramirez	.50
154	Mickey Morandini	.10
155	Mike Cameron	.10
156	Mike Lieberthal	.10
157	Mo Vaughn	.10
158	Randy Johnson	.50
159	Rey Ordonez	.10
160	Roberto Alomar	.20
161	Scott Williamson	.10
162	Shawn Estes	.10
163	Tim Wakefield	.10
164	Tony Batista	.10
165	Will Clark	.10
166	Wade Boggs	.60
167	David Cone	.10
168	Doug Glanville	.10
169	Jeff Cirillo	.10
170	John Jaha	.10
171	Mariano Rivera	.20
172	Tom Gordon	.10
173	Wally Joyner	.10
174	Alex Gonzalez	.10
175	Andruw Jones	.50
176	Barry Larkin	.10
177	Bartolo Colon	.10
178	Brian Giles	.10
179	Carlos Lee	.10
180	Darren Dreifort	.10
181	Eric Chavez	.20
182	Henry Rodriguez	.10
183	Ismael Valdes	.10
184	Jason Giambi	.40
185	John Wetteland	.10
186	Juan Encarnacion	.10
187	Luis Gonzalez	.10
188	Reggie Sanders	.10
189	Richard Hidalgo	.10
190	Ryan Rupe	.10
191	Sean Berry	.10
192	Rick Helling	.10
193	Randy Wolf	.10
194	Cliff Floyd	.10
195	Jose Lima	.10
196	Chipper Jones	.60
197	Charles Johnson	.10
198	Nomar Garciaparra	.60
199	Magglio Ordonez	.10
200	Shawn Green	.25
201	Travis Lee	.10
202	Jose Canseco	.35
203	Fernando Tatis	.10
204	Bruce Aven	.10
205	Johnny Damon	.35
206	Gary Sheffield	.25
207	Ken Caminiti	.10
208	Ben Grieve	.10
209	Sidney Ponson	.10
210	Vinny Castilla	.10
211	Alex Rodriguez	1.00
212	Chris Widger	.10
213	Carl Pavano	.10
214	J.T. Snow	.10
215	Jim Thome	.40
216	Kevin Young	.10
217	Mike Sirotka	.10
218	Rafael Palmeiro	.40
219	Rico Brogna	.10
220	Todd Walker	.10
221	Todd Zelle	.10
222	Brian Rose	.10
223	Chris Fussell	.10
224	Corey Koskie	.10
225	Rich Aurilia	.10
226	Geoff Jenkins	.10
227	Pedro Martinez	.50
228	Todd Hundley	.10
229	Brian Jordan	.10
230	Cristian Guzman	.10
231	Raul Mondesi	.10
232	Tim Hudson	.10
233	Albert Belle	.10
234	Andy Pettitte	.25
235	Brady Anderson	.10
236	Brian Bohannon	.10
237	Carlos Beltran	.35
238	Doug Mientkiewicz	.10
239	Jason Schmidt	.10
240	Jeff Zimmerman	.10
241	John Olerud	.10
242	Paul Byrd	.10
243	Vladimir Guerrero	.50
244	Warren Morris	.10
245	Eric Karros	.10
246	Jeff Weaver	.10
247	Jeromy Burnitz	.10
248	David Bell	.10
249	Rusty Greer	.10
250	Kevin Stocker	.10
251	Shea Hillenbrand (Prospect)	.15
252	Alfonso Soriano (Prospect)	.50
253	Micah Bowie (Prospect)	.10
254	Gary Matthews Jr. (Prospect)	.10
255	Lance Berkman (Prospect)	.10
256	Pat Burrell (Prospect)	.25
257	Ruben Mateo (Prospect)	.10
258	Kip Wells (Prospect)	.10
259	Wilton Veras (Prospect)	.10
260	Ben Davis (Prospect)	.10
261	Eric Munson (Prospect)	.10
262	Ramon Hernandez (Prospect)	.10
263	Tony Armas Jr. (Prospect)	.10
264	Erubiel Durazo (Prospect)	.10
265	Chad Meyers (Prospect)	.10
266	Rick Ankiel (Prospect)	.10
267	Ramon Ortiz (Prospect)	.10
268	Adam Kennedy (Prospect)	.10
269	Vernon Wells (Prospect)	.10
270	Chad Hermansen	.10
271	Norm Hutchins, Trent Durrington (Prospects)	.10
272	Gabe Molina, B.J. Ryan (Prospects)	.10
273	Juan Pena, Tomokazu Ohka **RC** (Prospects)	.25
274	Pat Daneker, Aaron Myette (Prospects)	.15
275	Jason Rakers, Russell Branyan (Prospects)	.10
276	Beiker Graterol, Dave Borkowski (Prospects)	.10
277	Mark Quinn, Dan Reichert (Prospects)	.15
278	Mark Redman, Jacque Jones (Prospects)	.15
279	Ed Yarnall, Wily Pena (Prospects)	.10
280	Chad Harville, Brett Laxton (Prospects)	.10
281	Aaron Scheffer, Gil Meche (Prospects)	.10
282	Jim Morris, Dan Wheeler (Prospects)	.10
283	Danny Kolb, Kelly Dransfeldt (Prospects)	.10
284	Peter Munro, Casey Blake (Prospects)	.10
285	Rob Ryan, Byung-Hyun Kim (Prospects)	.10
286	Derrin Ebert, Pascual Matos (Prospects)	.10
287	Richard Barker, Kyle Farnsworth (Prospects)	.10
288	Jason LaRue, Travis Dawkins (Prospects)	.10
289	Chris Sexton, Edgard Clemente (Prospects)	.10
290	Amaury Garcia, A.J. Burnett (Prospects)	.10
291	Carlos Hernandez, Daryle Ward (Prospects)	.10
292	Eric Gagne, Jeff Williams (Prospects)	.10
293	Kyle Peterson, Kevin Barker (Prospects)	.10
294	Fernando Seguignol, Guillermo Mota (Prospects)	.10
295	Melvin Mora, Octavio Dotel (Prospects)	.10
296	Anthony Shumaker, Cliff Politte (Prospects)	.10
297	Yamid Haad, Jimmy Anderson (Prospects)	.10
298	Rick Heiserman, Chad Hutchinson (Prospects)	.10
299	Mike Darr, Wiki Gonzalez (Prospects)	.10
300	Joe Nathan, Calvin Murray (Prospects)	.10

Autographs

NM/M
Common Player: 5.00
Inserted 1:144

1	Rick Ankiel	15.00
2	Peter Bergeron	5.00
3	Wade Boggs	25.00
4	Barry Bonds	200.00
5	Pat Burrell	5.00
6	Miguel Cairo	5.00
7	Mike Cameron	8.00
8	Ben Davis	5.00
9	Russ Davis	5.00
10	Einar Diaz	5.00
11	Scott Elarton	5.00
12	Jeremy Giambi	5.00
13	Todd Greene	5.00
14	Vladimir Guerrero	25.00
15	Tony Gwynn	30.00
16	Bobby Howry	5.00
17	Tim Hudson	15.00
18	Randy Johnson	50.00
19	Andruw Jones	20.00
20	Jacque Jones	8.00
21	Jason LaRue	5.00
22	Matt Lawton	5.00
23	Greg Maddux	50.00
24	Pedro Martinez	50.00
25	Pokey Reese	5.00
26	Alex Rodriguez	75.00
27	Ryan Rupe	5.00
28	J.T. Snow	6.00
29	Jose Vidro	6.00
30	Tony Womack	5.00
31	Ed Yarnall	5.00
32	Kevin Young	5.00

Double Play

	NM/M
Complete Set (10):	10.00
Common Player:	1.00
Inserted 1:9	
Plus:	2-4X
Inserted 1:90	
WarpTek:	10-20X
Inserted 1:900	
1 Nomar Garciaparra	1.50
2 Pedro Martinez	1.25
3 Chipper Jones	1.50
4 Mark McGwire	2.50
5 Cal Ripken Jr.	3.00
6 Roger Clemens	1.75
7 Juan Gonzalez	1.00
8 Tony Gwynn	1.50
9 Sammy Sosa	1.50
10 Mike Piazza	2.00

Eye on October

	NM/M
Complete Set (15):	25.00
Common Player:	1.00
Inserted 1:24	
Plus:	2-4X
Inserted 1:240	
1 Ken Griffey Jr.	2.50
2 Mark McGwire	3.00
3 Derek Jeter	4.00
4 Juan Gonzalez	1.00
5 Chipper Jones	2.00
6 Sammy Sosa	1.50
7 Greg Maddux	2.00
8 Frank Thomas	1.50
9 Nomar Garciaparra	2.00
10 Shawn Green	1.00
11 Cal Ripken Jr.	4.00
12 Manny Ramirez	1.50
13 Scott Rolen	1.25
14 Mike Piazza	2.50
15 Alex Rodriguez	3.00

Hats Off

	NM/M
Common Player:	15.00
Inserted 1:468 H	
1 Wade Boggs	25.00
2 Barry Bonds	75.00
3 J.D. Drew	15.00
4 Shawn Green	15.00
5 Vladimir Guerrero	25.00
6 Randy Johnson	30.00
7 Andruw Jones	20.00
8 Greg Maddux	40.00
9 Pedro Martinez	25.00
10 Mike Mussina	15.00
11 Rafael Palmeiro	20.00
12 Alex Rodriguez	50.00
13 Scott Rolen	15.00
14 Tim Salmon	15.00
15 Robin Ventura	15.00

Milestones

	NM/M
Common Player:	15.00
Inserted 1:1,999	
1 Mark McGwire	60.00
2 Roger Clemens	40.00
3 Tony Gwynn	25.00
4 Wade Boggs	25.00
5 Cal Ripken Jr.	75.00
6 Jose Canseco	15.00

New Era

	NM/M
Complete Set (20):	5.00
Common Player:	.25
Inserted 1:3	
Plus:	2-4X
Inserted 1:30	
WarpTek:	5-10X
Inserted 1:300	
1 Pat Burrell	.75
2 Ruben Mateo	.25
3 Wilton Veras	.25
4 Eric Munson	.25
5 Jeff Weaver	.25
6 Tim Hudson	.50
7 Carlos Beltran	1.00
8 Chris Singleton	.25
9 Lance Berkman	.25
10 Freddy Garcia	.25
11 Erubiel Durazo	.25
12 Randy Wolf	.25
13 Shea Hillenbrand	.25
14 Kip Wells	.25
15 Alfonso Soriano	1.50
16 Rick Ankiel	.25
17 Ramon Ortiz	.25
18 Adam Kennedy	.25
19 Vernon Wells	.25
20 Chad Hermansen	.25

2000 E-X

Released as a 90-card set the card fronts have a holo-foil card front, with the E-X logo and player name stamped in silver foil. Card backs have a player image, 1999 stats and the featured player's career totals.

	NM/M
Complete Set (90):	80.00
Common Player:	.25
Common Prospect (61-90):	3.00
Production 3,499 Sets	
Pack:	2.75
Box:	50.00
1 Alex Rodriguez	2.50
2 Jeff Bagwell	1.00
3 Mike Piazza	2.00
4 Tony Gwynn	1.50
5 Ken Griffey Jr.	2.00
6 Juan Gonzalez	.40
7 Vladimir Guerrero	1.00
8 Cal Ripken Jr.	3.00
9 Mo Vaughn	.25
10 Chipper Jones	1.50
11 Derek Jeter	3.00
12 Nomar Garciaparra	1.50
13 Mark McGwire	2.50
14 Sammy Sosa	1.50
15 Pedro Martinez	1.00
16 Greg Maddux	1.50
17 Frank Thomas	.75
18 Shawn Green	.50
19 Carlos Beltran	.50
20 Roger Clemens	1.75
21 Randy Johnson	1.00
22 Bernie Williams	.25
23 Carlos Delgado	.50
24 Manny Ramirez	.75
25 Freddy Garcia	.25
26 Barry Bonds	3.00
27 Tim Hudson	.40
28 Larry Walker	.25
29 Raul Mondesi	.65
30 Ivan Rodriguez	.65
31 Magglio Ordonez	.25
32 Scott Rolen	.65
33 Mike Mussina	.40
34 J.D. Drew	.40
35 Tom Glavine	.50
36 Barry Larkin	.25
37 Jim Thome	.65
38 Erubiel Durazo	.50
39 Curt Schilling	.50
40 Orlando Hernandez	.65
41 Rafael Palmeiro	.65
42 Gabe Kapler	.25
43 Mark Grace	.25
44 Jeff Cirillo	.25
45 Jeromy Burnitz	.25
46 Sean Casey	.35
47 Kevin Millwood	.25
48 Vinny Castilla	.25
49 Jose Canseco	.50
50 Roberto Alomar	.30
51 Craig Biggio	.25
52 Preston Wilson	.25
53 Jeff Weaver	.25
54 Robin Ventura	.25
55 Ben Grieve	.25
56 Troy Glaus	.65
57 Jacque Jones	.25
58 Brian Giles	.25
59 Kevin Brown	.25
60 Todd Helton	.65
61 Ben Petrick (Prospects)	3.00
62 Chad Hermansen (Prospects)	3.00
63 Kevin Barker (Prospects)	3.00
64 Matt LeCroy (Prospects)	3.00
65 Brad Penny (Prospects)	4.00
66 D.T. Cromer (Prospects)	3.00
67 Steve Lomasney (Prospects)	3.00
68 Cole Liniak (Prospects)	3.00
69 B.J. Ryan (Prospects)	3.00
70 Wilton Veras (Prospects)	3.00
71 Aaron McNeal RC (Prospects)	4.00
72 Nick Johnson (Prospects)	4.00
73 Adam Piatt (Prospects)	3.00
74 Adam Kennedy (Prospects)	3.00
75 Cesar King (Prospects)	3.00
76 Peter Bergeron (Prospects)	3.00
77 Rob Bell (Prospects)	3.00
78 Wily Pena (Prospects)	4.00
79 Ruben Mateo (Prospects)	3.00
80 Kip Wells (Prospects)	3.00
81 Alex Escobar (Prospects)	3.00
82 Danys Baez RC	5.00
83 Travis Dawkins (Prospects)	3.00
84 Mark Quinn (Prospects)	3.00
85 Jimmy Anderson (Prospects)	3.00
86 Rick Ankiel (Prospects)	4.00
87 Alfonso Soriano (Prospects)	5.00
88 Pat Burrell (Prospects)	4.00
89 Eric Munson (Prospects)	3.00
90 Josh Beckett (Prospects)	4.00

Autographics

	NM/M
Common Player:	5.00
Inserted 1:24	
Bob Abreu	15.00
Moises Alou	15.00
Rick Ankiel	20.00
Michael Barrett	5.00
Josh Beckett	25.00
Rob Bell	5.00
Adrian Beltre	15.00
Carlos Beltran	15.00
Wade Boggs	25.00
Barry Bonds	150.00
Kent Bottenfield	5.00
Milton Bradley	10.00
Pat Burrell	15.00
Chris Carpenter	20.00
Sean Casey	8.00
Eric Chavez	15.00
Will Clark	25.00
Johnny Damon	20.00
Mike Darr	5.00
Ben Davis	5.00
Russ Davis	5.00
Carlos Delgado	20.00
Jason Dewey	5.00
Octavio Dotel	5.00
J.D. Drew	10.00
Ray Durham	8.00
Damion Easley	5.00
Kelvim Escobar	6.00
Carlos Febles	5.00
Freddy Garcia	5.00
Jeremy Giambi	5.00
Todd Greene	5.00
Jason Grilli	5.00
Vladimir Guerrero	30.00

Tony Gwynn	40.00
Jerry Hairston Jr.	5.00
Mike Hampton	8.00
Todd Helton	20.00
Trevor Hoffman	10.00
Tim Hudson	15.00
John Jaha	5.00
Derek Jeter	100.00
D'Angelo Jimenez	5.00
Randy Johnson	60.00
Jason Kendall	8.00
Adam Kennedy	8.00
Cesar King	5.00
Paul Konerko	10.00
Mark Kotsay	6.00
Ray Lankford	6.00
Jason LaRue	6.00
Matt Lawton	8.00
Carlos Lee	8.00
Mike Lieberthal	8.00
Cole Liniak	5.00
Steve Lomasney	5.00
Jose Macias	5.00
Greg Maddux	60.00
Edgar Martinez	15.00
Pedro Martinez	60.00
Ruben Mateo	5.00
Gary Matthews Jr.	8.00
Aaron McNeal	5.00
Raul Mondesi	8.00
Orber Moreno	5.00
Warren Morris	5.00
Eric Munson	5.00
Heath Murray	5.00
Mike Mussina	30.00
Joe Nathan	5.00
Rafael Palmeiro	25.00
Jim Parque	6.00
Angel Pena	5.00
Wily Pena	8.00
Pokey Reese	6.00
Matt Riley	5.00
Cal Ripken Jr.	85.00
Alex Rodriguez	75.00
Scott Rolen	20.00
Jimmy Rollins	20.00
B.J. Ryan	5.00
Randall Simon	5.00
Chris Singleton	5.00
Alfonso Soriano	30.00
Shannon Stewart	8.00
Mike Sweeney	8.00
Miguel Tejada	20.00
Frank Thomas	25.00
Wilton Veras	5.00
Billy Wagner	8.00
Jeff Weaver	5.00
Rondell White	5.00
Scott Williamson	8.00
Randy Wolf	8.00
Jaret Wright	5.00
Ed Yarnall	5.00
Kevin Young	5.00

Essential Credentials Future

Production varied for these parallel inserts depending on the card number, with the exact production number for cards 1-60 determined by subtracting the card number from 61. Cards 61-90 are determined by subtracting the card number from 91. Quantity issued is listed in parantheses.

	NM/M
Common Player:	10.00
1 Alex Rodriguez/60	75.00
2 Jeff Bagwell/59	30.00
3 Mike Piazza/58	50.00
4 Tony Gwynn/57	50.00
5 Ken Griffey Jr./56	50.00
6 Juan Gonzalez/55	15.00
7 Vladimir Guerrero/54	20.00
8 Cal Ripken Jr./53	85.00
9 Mo Vaughn/52	10.00
10 Chipper Jones/51	30.00
11 Derek Jeter/50	85.00
12 Nomar Garciaparra/49	45.00
13 Mark McGwire/48	50.00
14 Sammy Sosa/47	50.00
15 Pedro Martinez/46	50.00
16 Greg Maddux/45	50.00
17 Frank Thomas/44	20.00
18 Shawn Green/43	10.00
19 Carlos Beltran/42	10.00
20 Roger Clemens/41	60.00
21 Randy Johnson/40	30.00
22 Bernie Williams/39	15.00
23 Carlos Delgado/38	15.00
24 Manny Ramirez/37	20.00
25 Freddy Garcia/36	5.00
26 Barry Bonds/35	90.00
27 Tim Hudson/34	5.00
28 Larry Walker/33	10.00
29 Raul Mondesi/32	5.00
30 Ivan Rodriguez/31	15.00
31 Magglio Ordonez/30	10.00
32 Scott Rolen/29	15.00
33 Mike Mussina/28	25.00
34 J.D. Drew/27	5.00
35 Tom Glavine/26	25.00
36 Barry Larkin/25	15.00
37 Jim Thome/24	30.00
38 Erubiel Durazo/23	15.00
39 Curt Schilling/22	25.00
40 Orlando Hernandez/21	15.00
41 Rafael Palmeiro/20	40.00
42 Gabe Kapler/19	15.00
43 Mark Grace/18	15.00
44 Jeff Cirillo/17	15.00
45 Jeromy Burnitz/16	15.00
46 Sean Casey/15	15.00
47 Kevin Millwood/14	20.00
48 Vinny Castilla/13	20.00
49 Jose Canseco/12	40.00
50 Roberto Alomar/11	50.00
51 Craig Biggio/10	50.00
61 Ben Petrick/30 (Prospects)	10.00
62 Chad Hermansen/29 (Prospects)	10.00
63 Kevin Barker/28 (Prospects)	10.00
64 Matt LeCroy/27 (Prospects)	10.00
65 Brad Penny/26 (Prospects)	10.00
66 D.T. Cromer/25 (Prospects)	10.00
67 Steve Lomasney/24 (Prospects)	10.00
68 Cole Liniak/23 (Prospects)	10.00
69 B.J. Ryan/22 (Prospects)	10.00
70 Wilton Veras/21 (Prospects)	10.00
71 Aaron McNeal/20 (Prospects)	15.00
72 Nick Johnson/19 (Prospects)	25.00
73 Adam Piatt/18 (Prospects)	15.00
74 Adam Kennedy/17 (Prospects)	15.00
75 Cesar King/16 (Prospects)	15.00
76 Peter Bergeron/15 (Prospects)	15.00
77 Rob Bell/14 (Prospects)	15.00
78 Wily Pena/13 (Prospects)	15.00
79 Ruben Mateo/12 (Prospects)	15.00
80 Kip Wells/11 (Prospects)	15.00
81 Alex Escobar/10 (Prospects)	20.00

Essential Credentials Now

Like Future, this is a parallel of the base set, with the production of cards 1-60 limited to that player's card number. Production for cards 61-90 can be determined by subtracting 60 from the card number. Quantity issued is listed in parantheses.

	NM/M
Common Player:	8.00
20 Roger Clemens/20	50.00
21 Randy Johnson/21	30.00
22 Bernie Williams/22	10.00
23 Carlos Delgado/23	25.00
24 Manny Ramirez/24	30.00
25 Freddy Garcia/25	10.00
26 Barry Bonds/26	75.00
27 Tim Hudson/27	15.00
28 Larry Walker/28	10.00
29 Raul Mondesi/29	10.00
30 Ivan Rodriguez/30	15.00
31 Magglio Ordonez/31	10.00
32 Scott Rolen/32	20.00
33 Mike Mussina/33	15.00
34 J.D. Drew/34	15.00
35 Tom Glavine/35	20.00
36 Barry Larkin/36	15.00
37 Jim Thome/37	25.00
38 Erubiel Durazo/38	8.00
39 Curt Schilling/39	20.00
40 Orlando Hernandez/40	8.00
41 Rafael Palmeiro/41	15.00
42 Gabe Kapler/42	8.00
43 Mark Grace/43	8.00
44 Jeff Cirillo/44	8.00
45 Jeromy Burnitz/45	8.00
46 Sean Casey/46	8.00
47 Kevin Millwood/47	8.00
48 Vinny Castilla/48	8.00
49 Jose Canseco/49	15.00
50 Roberto Alomar/50	12.00
51 Craig Biggio/51	8.00
52 Preston Wilson/52	8.00
53 Jeff Weaver/53	8.00
54 Robin Ventura/54	8.00
55 Ben Grieve/55	8.00
56 Troy Glaus/56	15.00
57 Jacque Jones/57	12.00
58 Brian Giles/58	8.00
59 Kevin Brown/59	8.00
60 Todd Helton/60	20.00
74 Adam Kennedy/14 (Prospects)	15.00
75 Cesar King/15 (Prospects)	15.00
76 Peter Bergeron/16 (Prospects)	15.00
77 Rob Bell/17 (Prospects)	15.00
78 Wily Pena/18 (Prospects)	15.00
79 Ruben Mateo/19 (Prospects)	15.00
80 Kip Wells/20 (Prospects)	15.00
81 Alex Escobar/21 (Prospects)	15.00
82 Danys Baez/22 (Prospects)	15.00
83 Travis Dawkins/23 (Prospects)	15.00
84 Mark Quinn/24 (Prospects)	15.00
85 Jimmy Anderson/25 (Prospects)	15.00
86 Rick Ankiel/26 (Prospects)	15.00
87 Alfonso Soriano/27 (Prospects)	60.00
88 Pat Burrell/28 (Prospects)	30.00
89 Eric Munson/29 (Prospects)	15.00
90 Josh Beckett/30 (Prospects)	20.00

E-Xceptional Red

Die-cut in a shape similar to an oval, these inserts have a cloth like feel with silver foil stamping with a red background. Card backs are numbered consecutively "1 Of 15XC" and so on. These are seeded 1:14 packs. Two parallels are also inserted: Blues are seeded 1:288 packs and Greens are limited to 999 serial numbered sets.

	NM/M
Complete Set (15):	100.00
Common Player:	4.00
Inserted 1:14	
Blue:	2-3X
Inserted 1:288	
Green:	1-1.5X
Production 999 Sets	
1 Ken Griffey Jr.	
2 Derek Jeter	15.00
3 Nomar Garciaparra	6.00
4 Mark McGwire	10.00
5 Sammy Sosa	6.00
6 Mike Piazza	8.00
7 Alex Rodriguez	10.00
8 Cal Ripken Jr.	15.00
9 Chipper Jones	6.00
10 Pedro Martinez	4.00
11 Jeff Bagwell	4.00
12 Greg Maddux	6.00
13 Roger Clemens	7.00
14 Tony Gwynn	5.00
15 Frank Thomas	4.00

E-Xciting

Die-cut in the shape of a jersey card fronts have a holograpic appearance with silver foil stamping. These were seeded 1:24 packs. Card backs are numbered with an "XT" suffix.

		NM/M
Complete Set (10):		25.00
Common Player:		1.00
Inserted 1:24		
1	Mark McGwire	6.00
2	Ken Griffey Jr.	4.00
3	Randy Johnson	2.00
4	Sammy Sosa	3.00
5	Manny Ramirez	2.00
6	Jose Canseco	1.00
7	Derek Jeter	6.00
8	Scott Rolen	1.50
9	Juan Gonzalez	1.25
10	Barry Bonds	6.00

E-Xplosive

These inserts have a traditional format, with a holographic star like image in the background and "explosive" running down the top left side. Card backs are numbered with an "XP" suffix and are serial numbered on the bottom portion in an edition of 2,499 sets.

		NM/M
Complete Set (20):		90.00
Common Player:		2.00
Production 2,499 Sets		
1	Tony Gwynn	6.00
2	Alex Rodriguez	10.00
3	Pedro Martinez	5.00
4	Sammy Sosa	6.00
5	Cal Ripken Jr.	15.00
6	Adam Piatt	2.50
7	Pat Burrell	2.50
8	J.D. Drew	2.50
9	Mike Piazza	6.00
10	Shawn Green	2.50
11	Troy Glaus	4.00
12	Randy Johnson	5.00
13	Juan Gonzalez	6.00
14	Chipper Jones	6.00
15	Ivan Rodriguez	4.00
16	Nomar Garciaparra	8.00
17	Ken Griffey Jr.	8.00
18	Nick Johnson	2.50
19	Mark McGwire	10.00
20	Frank Thomas	10.00

Generation E-X

This 15-card set spotlights the top young players in the game and were seeded 1:8 packs. Card fronts have silver foil stamping over a background resembling a sky. These were seeded 1:8 packs. Card backs are numbered with a "GX" suffix.

		NM/M
Complete Set (15):		20.00
Common Player:		1.00
Inserted 1:8		
1	Rick Ankiel	1.00
2	Josh Beckett	1.50
3	Carlos Beltran	2.00
4	Pat Burrell	2.00
5	Freddy Garcia	1.00
6	Alex Rodriguez	5.00
7	Derek Jeter	6.00
8	Tim Hudson	1.50
9	Shawn Green	1.50
10	Eric Munson	1.00
11	Adam Piatt	1.00
12	Adam Kennedy	1.00
13	Nick Johnson	1.00
14	Alfonso Soriano	2.00
15	Nomar Garciaparra	4.00

Genuine Coverage

		NM/M
Common Player:		5.00
Inserted 1:144		
1	Alex Rodriguez	40.00
2	Tom Glavine	10.00
3	Cal Ripken Jr.	50.00
4	Edgar Martinez	5.00
5	Raul Mondesi	5.00
6	Carlos Beltran	5.00
7	Chipper Jones	25.00
8	Barry Bonds	50.00
9	Heath Murray	5.00
10	Tim Hudson	10.00
11	Mike Mussina	10.00
12	Derek Jeter	50.00

1992 Snyder's Bread Washington Sports Heroes

This set was sponsored by Snyder's, a Northwest baker, and produced by Little Sun, which had earlier done a number of amateur baseball card sets. Two baseball players are included in the set: Ryne Sandberg (in a high school football jersey) and John Olerud (pitching for WSU). Cards picture the athletes against a pine tree border photo. Backs are printed in blue and yellow on white and feature a summary of the athlete's days in Washington.

		NM/M
Complete Set (8):		15.00
1	Ryne Sandberg	12.00
6	John Olerud	3.00

1995 Sonic/Coke Heroes of Baseball

In a promotion with the Sonic chain of Southern drive-in restaurants, Upper Deck issued a 20-card set of baseball greats. Cards featured vintage sepia photos on the front, with player biographies and stats on the back. The Coca-Cola and Sonic logos also appear on back.

		NM/M
Complete Set (20):		5.00
Common Player:		.25
1	Whitey Ford	.25
2	Cy Young	.25
3	Babe Ruth	1.50
4	Lou Gehrig	1.00
5	Mike Schmidt	.35
6	Nolan Ryan	1.00
7	Robin Yount	.25
8	Gary Carter	.25
9	Tom Seaver	.25
10	Reggie Jackson	.25
11	Bob Gibson	.25
12	Gil Hodges	.25
13	Monte Irvin	.25
14	Minnie Minoso	.25
15	Willie Stargell	.25
16	Al Kaline	.25
17	Joe Jackson	1.50
18	Walter Johnson	.25
19	Ty Cobb	.50
20	Satchel Paige	.25

1995 Sonic/Pepsi Baseball Greats

While some Sonic drive-in restaurants (basically a Southern chain) featured a baseball card promotion using Upper Deck cards with a Coca-Cola logo on back, other drive-ins in the chain featured a 12-card set sponsored by Pepsi. Cards have a red border on front and a color photo of a player on which team logos have been airbrushed away. Backs have career data and the Pepsi logo, along with that of the Major League Baseball Players Alumni, and are printed in red and blue. The cards were issued in three-card cello packs with a meal purchase. The unnumbered cards are checklisted here in alphabetical order.

		NM/M
Complete Set (12):		4.00
Common Player:		.25
(1)	Bert Campaneris	.25
(2)	George Foster	.25
(3)	Steve Garvey	.40
(4)	Fergie Jenkins	.25
(5)	Tommy John	.25
(6)	Harmon Killebrew	.75
(7)	Sparky Lyle	.25
(8)	Fred Lynn	.25
(9)	Joe Morgan	.60
(10)	Graig Nettles	.25
(11)	Warren Spahn	.75
(12)	Maury Wills	.25

1987 Sonshine Industries 19th Century Baseball

There is no indication of the origins of this collectors' issue on the cards themselves. Fronts feature black-and-white reproductions of vintage woodcuts of the players with an ornate orange framework. Backs of the 2-1/2" x 3-1/2" cards are printed in black on blue-gray with lengthy biographical information. The unnumbered cards are checklisted here in alphabetical order.

		NM/M
Complete Set (20):		20.00
Common Player:		1.00
(1)	A.C. Anson	2.00
(2)	Cap Anson	2.00
(3)	D. Brouthers	1.00
(4)	Alexander Cartwright	1.50
(5)	Alexander Cartwright	1.50
(6)	L.N. David	1.00
(7)	Wes Fisler	1.00
(8)	F.E. Goldsmith	1.00
(9)	T.J. Keefe	1.00
(10)	M.J. Kelly	2.00
(11)	Robert T. Mathews	1.00
(12)	Wm. McLean	1.00
(13)	C.A. McVey	1.00
(14)	James Mutrie	1.00
(15)	Lipman Pike	1.50
(16)	John J. Smith	1.00
(17)	A.G. Spalding	1.50
(18)	M. Welch	1.50
(19)	N.E. Young	1.00
(20)	Going to the game	1.00

1995 South Carolina Athletic Hall of Fame

Sports stars from around the state were honored in this 108-card issue. Fronts feature borderless color or sepia photos with the S.C. Athletic Hall of Fame logo in an upper corner and a gold-foil seal at bottom-right. A colored stripe has the athlete's name in gold foil. On back are a few personal and career stats and highlights. Only the baseball players are listed here. Issue price of the set was $40.

		NM/M
Complete Set (108):		40.00
Common (Baseball) Player:		.50
5	Frank Howard	.75
6	Bobby Richardson	1.00
13	Shoeless Joe Jackson	4.00
27	Van Lingle Mungo	.50
53	Earl Wooten	.50
54	Marty Marion	.50
55	Frank Howard	.75
72	Jim Rice	.75
74	Danny Ford	.50
83	Lou Brissie	.50
84	Billy O'Dell	.50
100	Frank Howard	.75

1993 SP

Upper Deck's first super-premium baseball card issue features 290 cards in the single-series set; 252 are individual player cards, while the remainder includes a Premier Prospects subset featuring top prospects (20 cards), 18 All-Stars and a Platinum Power insert set of 20 top home run hitters. Cards, which were available in 12-card foil packs, feature borderless color photos and UV coating on the front, plus a special logo using lenticular printing. Foil is also used intricately in the design. Backs have a large color photo and statistics. Cards are numbered and color-coded by team.

		NM/M
Complete Set (290):		75.00
Common Player:		.10
Pack (12):		10.00
Wax Box (24):		220.00
1	Roberto Alomar	.30
2	Wade Boggs	2.00
3	Joe Carter	.10
4	Ken Griffey Jr.	2.50
5	Mark Langston	.10
6	John Olerud	.10
7	Kirby Puckett	2.00
8	Cal Ripken, Jr.	4.00
9	Ivan Rodriguez	1.25
10	Barry Bonds	4.00
11	Darren Daulton	.10
12	Marquis Grissom	.10
13	Dave Justice	.10
14	John Kruk	.10
15	Barry Larkin	.10
16	Terry Mulholland	.10
17	Ryne Sandberg	2.00
18	Gary Sheffield	.10
19	Chad Curtis	.10
20	Chili Davis	.10
21	Gary DiSarcina	.10
22	Damion Easley	.10
23	Chuck Finley	.10
24	Luis Polonia	.10
25	Tim Salmon	.10
26	J.T. Snow RC	1.00
27	Russ Springer	.10
28	Jeff Bagwell	1.50
29	Craig Biggio	.10
30	Ken Caminiti	.10
31	Andujar Cedeno	.10
32	Doug Drabek	.10
33	Steve Finley	.10
34	Luis Gonzalez	.10
35	Pete Harnisch	.10
36	Darryl Kile	.10
37	Mike Bordick	.10
38	Dennis Eckersley	1.25
39	Brent Gates	.10
40	Rickey Henderson	1.50
41	Mark McGwire	3.00
42	Craig Paquette	.10
43	Ruben Sierra	.10
44	Terry Steinbach	.10
45	Todd Van Poppel	.10
46	Pat Borders	.10
47	Tony Fernandez	.10
48	Juan Guzman	.10
49	Pat Hentgen	.10
50	Paul Molitor	1.50
51	Jack Morris	.10
52	Ed Sprague	.10
53	Duane Ward	.10
54	Devon White	.10
55	Steve Avery	.10
56	Jeff Blauser	.10
57	Ron Gant	.10
58	Tom Glavine	.40
59	Greg Maddux	2.00
60	Fred McGriff	.10
61	Terry Pendleton	.10
62	Deion Sanders	.10
63	John Smoltz	.10
64	Cal Eldred	.10
65	Darryl Hamilton	.10
66	John Jaha	.10
67	Pat Listach	.10
68	Jaime Navarro	.10
69	Kevin Reimer	.10
70	B.J. Surhoff	.10
71	Greg Vaughn	.10
72	Robin Yount	1.50
73	Rene Arocha RC	.10
74	Bernard Gilkey	.10
75	Gregg Jefferies	.10
76	Ray Lankford	.10
77	Tom Pagnozzi	.10
78	Lee Smith	.10
79	Ozzie Smith	2.00
80	Bob Tewksbury	.10
81	Mark Whiten	.10
82	Steve Buechele	.10
83	Mark Grace	.10
84	Jose Guzman	.10
85	Derrick May	.10
86	Mike Morgan	.10
87	Randy Myers	.10
88	Kevin Roberson RC	.10
89	Sammy Sosa	2.00
90	Rick Wilkins	.10
91	Brett Butler	.10
92	Eric Davis	.10
93	Orel Hershiser	.10
94	Eric Karros	.10
95	Ramon Martinez	.10
96	Raul Mondesi	.10
97	Jose Offerman	.10
98	Mike Piazza	2.50
99	Darryl Strawberry	.10
100	Moises Alou	.10
101	Wil Cordero	.10
102	Delino DeShields	.10
103	Darrin Fletcher	.10
104	Ken Hill	.10
105	Mike Lansing RC	.40
106	Dennis Martinez	.10
107	Larry Walker	.10
108	John Wetteland	.10
109	Rod Beck	.10
110	John Burkett	.10
111	Will Clark	.10
112	Royce Clayton	.10
113	Darren Lewis	.10
114	Willie McGee	.10
115	Bill Swift	.10
116	Robby Thompson	.10
117	Matt Williams	.10
118	Sandy Alomar Jr.	.10
119	Carlos Baerga	.10
120	Albert Belle	.10
121	Reggie Jefferson	.10
122	Kenny Lofton	.10
123	Wayne Kirby	.10
124	Carlos Martinez	.10
125	Charles Nagy	.10
126	Paul Sorrento	.10
127	Rich Amaral	.10
128	Jay Buhner	.10
129	Norm Charlton	.10
130	Dave Fleming	.10
131	Erik Hanson	.10
132	Randy Johnson	1.50
133	Edgar Martinez	.10
134	Tino Martinez	.10
135	Omar Vizquel	.10
136	Bret Barberie	.10
137	Chuck Carr	.10
138	Jeff Conine	.10
139	Orestes Destrade	.10
140	Chris Hammond	.10
141	Bryan Harvey	.10
142	Benito Santiago	.10
143	Walt Weiss	.10
144	Darrell Whitmore RC	.10
145	Tim Bolger RC	.10
146	Bobby Bonilla	.10
147	Jeromy Burnitz	.10
148	Vince Coleman	.10
149	Dwight Gooden	.10
150	Todd Hundley	.10
151	Howard Johnson	.10
152	Eddie Murray	1.50
153	Bret Saberhagen	.10
154	Brady Anderson	.10
155	Mike Devereaux	.10
156	Jeffrey Hammonds	.10
157	Chris Hoiles	.10
158	Ben McDonald	.10
159	Mark McLemore	.10
160	Mike Mussina	.50
161	Gregg Olson	.10
162	David Segui	.10
163	Derek Bell	.10
164	Andy Benes	.10
165	Archi Cianfrocco	.10
166	Ricky Gutierrez	.10
167	Tony Gwynn	2.00
168	Gene Harris	.10
169	Trevor Hoffman	.10
170	Ray McDavid RC	.10
171	Phil Plantier	.10
172	Mariano Duncan	.10
173	Len Dykstra	.10
174	Tommy Greene	.10
175	Dave Hollins	.10
176	Pete Incaviglia	.10
177	Mickey Morandini	.10
178	Curt Schilling	.40
179	Kevin Stocker	.10
180	Mitch Williams	.10
181	Stan Belinda	.10
182	Jay Bell	.10
183	Steve Cooke	.10
184	Carlos Garcia	.10
185	Jeff King	.10
186	Orlando Merced	.10
187	Don Slaught	.10
188	Andy Van Slyke	.10
189	Kevin Young	.10
190	Kevin Brown	.10
191	Jose Canseco	.60
192	Julio Franco	.10
193	Benji Gil	.10
194	Juan Gonzalez	.75
195	Tom Henke	.10
196	Rafael Palmeiro	1.25
197	Dean Palmer	.10
198	Nolan Ryan	4.00
199	Roger Clemens	2.25
200	Scott Cooper	.10
201	Andre Dawson	.35
202	Mike Greenwell	.10
203	Carlos Quintana	.10
204	Jeff Russell	.10
205	Aaron Sele	.10
206	Mo Vaughn	.10
207	Frank Viola	.10
208	Rob Dibble	.10
209	Roberto Kelly	.10
210	Kevin Mitchell	.10
211	Hal Morris	.10
212	Joe Oliver	.10
213	Jose Rijo	.10
214	Bip Roberts	.10
215	Chris Sabo	.10
216	Reggie Sanders	.10
217	Dante Bichette	.10
218	Jerald Clark	.10
219	Alex Cole	.10
220	Andres Galarraga	.10
221	Joe Girardi	.10
222	Charlie Hayes	.10
223	Robert Mejia RC	.10
224	Armando Reynoso	.10
225	Eric Young	.10
226	Kevin Appier	.10
227	George Brett	2.25
228	David Cone	.10
229	Phil Hiatt	.10
230	Felix Jose	.10
231	Wally Joyner	.10
232	Mike Macfarlane	.10
233	Brian McRae	.10
234	Jeff Montgomery	.10
235	Rob Deer	.10

236	Cecil Fielder	.10
237	Travis Fryman	.10
238	Mike Henneman	.10
239	Tony Phillips	.10
240	Mickey Tettleton	.10
241	Alan Trammell	.10
242	David Wells	.10
243	Lou Whitaker	.10
244	Rick Aguilera	.10
245	Scott Erickson	.10
246	Brian Harper	.10
247	Kent Hrbek	.10
248	Chuck Knoblauch	.10
249	Shane Mack	.10
250	David McCarty	.10
251	Pedro Munoz	.10
252	Dave Winfield	1.50
253	Alex Fernandez	.10
254	Ozzie Guillen	.10
255	Bo Jackson	.20
256	Lance Johnson	.10
257	Ron Karkovice	.10
258	Jack McDowell	.10
259	Tim Raines	.10
260	Frank Thomas	1.50
261	Robin Ventura	.10
262	Jim Abbott	.10
263	Steve Farr	.10
264	Jimmy Key	.10
265	Don Mattingly	2.25
266	Paul O'Neill	.10
267	Mike Stanley	.10
268	Danny Tartabull	.10
269	Bob Wickman	.10
270	Bernie Williams	.10
271	Jason Bere	.10
272	Roger Cedeno RC	.50
273	Johnny Damon RC	12.00
274	Russ Davis RC	.25
275	Carlos Delgado	.75
276	Carl Everett	.10
277	Cliff Floyd	.10
278	Alex Gonzalez	.10
279	Derek Jeter RC	75.00
280	Chipper Jones	2.00
281	Javier Lopez	.10
282	Chad Mottola RC	.10
283	Marc Newfield	.10
284	Eduardo Perez	.10
285	Manny Ramirez	1.50
286	Todd Steverson RC	.10
287	Michael Tucker	.10
288	Allen Watson	.10
289	Rondell White	.10
290	Dmitri Young	.10

Platinum Power

This 20-card insert set features 20 of the game's top home run hitters. The top of each insert card features a special die cut treatment. Backs are numbered with a PP prefix.

		NM/M
Complete Set (20):		27.50
Common Player:		.50
1	Albert Belle	.50
2	Barry Bonds	5.00
3	Joe Carter	.50
4	Will Clark	.50
5	Darren Daulton	.50
6	Cecil Fielder	.50
7	Ron Gant	.50
8	Juan Gonzalez	1.00
9	Ken Griffey Jr.	3.00
10	Dave Hollins	.50
11	Dave Justice	.50
12	Fred McGriff	.50
13	Mark McGwire	5.00
14	Dean Palmer	.50
15	Mike Piazza	3.00
16	Tim Salmon	.50
17	Ryne Sandberg	2.50
18	Gary Sheffield	.75
19	Frank Thomas	2.00
20	Matt Williams	.50

Jumbos

These jumbo-size (8-1/2" x 11") versions of the players' 1993 SP cards were sold through Upper Deck Authenticated. Each player's jumbo card was produced in a limited edition of 1,000, except for Frank Thomas, whose jumbo card was an edition of 1,993. The jumbos were sold in heavy plastic screwdown holders.

		NM/M
Complete Set (5):		35.00
Common Player:		5.00
10	Barry Bonds	12.50
58	Tom Glavine	6.00
173	Lenny Dykstra	5.00
199	Roger Clemens	10.00
260	Frank Thomas	7.50

1994 SP Promo

Virtually identical to the issued version of Ken Griffey, Jr.'s card in the regular SP set (#105) this differs in the card number on the back (#24) and the inclusion on front and back of the notice, "For Promotional Use Only."

		NM/M
24	Ken Griffey Jr.	3.00

1994 SP

The second edition of Upper Deck's top-shelf SP brand features each card with a front background printed on metallic foil; the first 20 cards in the set, a series of "Prospects," have front backgrounds of textured metallic foil. Backs are printed with standard processes and include a color player photo a few stats and typical copyright notice and logos. Each foil pack contains one card featuring a special die-cut treatment at top.

		NM/M
Complete Set (200):		125.00
Common Player:		.10
Die-Cut:		1-2X
Pack (8):		15.00
Wax Box (32):		450.00
1	Mike Bell RC	.10
2	D.J. Boston	.10
3	Johnny Damon	.45
4	Brad Fullmer RC	.75
5	Joey Hamilton	.10
6	Todd Hollandsworth	.10
7	Brian Hunter	.10
8	LaTroy Hawkins RC	.25
9	Brooks Kieschnick RC	.10
10	Derrek Lee RC	15.00
11	Trot Nixon RC	3.00
12	Alex Ochoa	.10
13	Chan Ho Park RC	1.50
14	Kirk Presley RC	.10
15	Alex Rodriguez RC	100.00
16	Jose Silva RC	.10
17	Terrell Wade RC	.10
18	Billy Wagner RC	1.00
19	Glenn Williams RC	.10
20	Preston Wilson	.10
21	Brian Anderson	.10
22	Chad Curtis	.10
23	Chili Davis	.10
24	Bo Jackson	.25
25	Mark Langston	.10
26	Tim Salmon	.50
27	Jeff Bagwell	1.00
28	Craig Biggio	.50
29	Ken Caminiti	.10
30	Doug Drabek	.10
31	John Hudek	.10
32	Greg Swindell	.10
33	Brent Gates	.10
34	Rickey Henderson	1.00

35	Steve Karsay	.10
36	Mark McGwire	2.50
37	Ruben Sierra	.10
38	Terry Steinbach	.10
39	Roberto Alomar	.30
40	Joe Carter	.10
41	Carlos Delgado	.50
42	Alex Gonzalez	.10
43	Juan Guzman	.10
44	Paul Molitor	1.00
45	John Olerud	.10
46	Devon White	.10
47	Steve Avery	.10
48	Jeff Blauser	.10
49	Tom Glavine	.35
50	Dave Justice	.10
51	Roberto Kelly	.10
52	Ryan Klesko	.10
53	Javier Lopez	.10
54	Greg Maddux	1.25
55	Fred McGriff	.10
56	Ricky Bones	.10
57	Cal Eldred	.10
58	Brian Harper	.10
59	Pat Listach	.10
60	B.J. Surhoff	.10
61	Greg Vaughn	.10
62	Bernard Gilkey	.10
63	Gregg Jefferies	.10
64	Ray Lankford	.10
65	Ozzie Smith	1.25
66	Bob Tewksbury	.10
67	Mark Whiten	.10
68	Todd Zeile	.10
69	Mark Grace	.10
70	Randy Myers	.10
71	Ryne Sandberg	1.25
72	Sammy Sosa	1.25
73	Steve Trachsel	.10
74	Rick Wilkins	.10
75	Brett Butler	.10
76	Delino DeShields	.10
77	Orel Hershiser	.10
78	Eric Karros	.10
79	Raul Mondesi	.10
80	Mike Piazza	2.00
81	Tim Wallach	.10
82	Moises Alou	.10
83	Cliff Floyd	.10
84	Marquis Grissom	.10
85	Pedro Martinez	1.00
86	Larry Walker	.10
87	John Wetteland	.10
88	Rondell White	.10
89	Rod Beck	.10
90	Barry Bonds	3.00
91	John Burkett	.10
92	Royce Clayton	.10
93	Billy Swift	.10
94	Robby Thompson	.10
95	Matt Williams	.10
96	Carlos Baerga	.10
97	Albert Belle	.10
98	Kenny Lofton	.10
99	Dennis Martinez	.10
100	Eddie Murray	1.00
101	Manny Ramirez	1.00
102	Eric Anthony	.10
103	Chris Bosio	.10
104	Jay Buhner	.10
105	Ken Griffey Jr.	2.00
106	Randy Johnson	1.00
107	Edgar Martinez	.10
108	Chuck Carr	.10
109	Jeff Conine	.10
110	Carl Everett	.10
111	Chris Hammond	.10
112	Bryan Harvey	.10
113	Charles Johnson	.10
114	Gary Sheffield	.45
115	Bobby Bonilla	.10
116	Dwight Gooden	.10
117	Todd Hundley	.10
118	Bobby Jones	.10
119	Jeff Kent	.10
120	Bret Saberhagen	.10
121	Jeffrey Hammonds	.10
122	Chris Hoiles	.10
123	Ben McDonald	.10
124	Mike Mussina	.40
125	Rafael Palmeiro	.75
126	Cal Ripken, Jr.	3.00
127	Lee Smith	.10
128	Derek Bell	.10
129	Andy Benes	.10
130	Tony Gwynn	1.25
131	Trevor Hoffman	.10
132	Phil Plantier	.10
133	Bip Roberts	.10
134	Darren Daulton	.10
135	Len Dykstra	.10
136	Dave Hollins	.10
137	Danny Jackson	.10
138	John Kruk	.10
139	Kevin Stocker	.10
140	Jay Bell	.10
141	Carlos Garcia	.10
142	Jeff King	.10
143	Orlando Merced	.10
144	Andy Van Slyke	.10
145	Paul Wagner	.10
146	Jose Canseco	.50
147	Will Clark	.10
148	Juan Gonzalez	.50
149	Rick Helling	.10
150	Dean Palmer	.10
151	Ivan Rodriguez	.75
152	Roger Clemens	1.50

153	Scott Cooper	.10
154	Andre Dawson	.30
155	Mike Greenwell	.10
156	Aaron Sele	.10
157	Mo Vaughn	.10
158	Bret Boone	.10
159	Barry Larkin	.10
160	Kevin Mitchell	.10
161	Jose Rijo	.10
162	Deion Sanders	.10
163	Reggie Sanders	.10
164	Dante Bichette	.10
165	Ellis Burks	.10
166	Andres Galarraga	.10
167	Charlie Hayes	.10
168	David Nied	.10
169	Walt Weiss	.10
170	Kevin Appier	.10
171	David Cone	.10
172	Jeff Granger	.10
173	Felix Jose	.10
174	Wally Joyner	.10
175	Brian McRae	.10
176	Cecil Fielder	.10
177	Travis Fryman	.10
178	Mike Henneman	.10
179	Tony Phillips	.10
180	Mickey Tettleton	.10
181	Alan Trammell	.10
182	Rick Aguilera	.10
183	Rich Becker	.10
184	Scott Erickson	.10
185	Chuck Knoblauch	.10
186	Kirby Puckett	1.25
187	Dave Winfield	1.00
188	Wilson Alvarez	.10
189	Jason Bere	.10
190	Alex Fernandez	.10
191	Julio Franco	.10
192	Jack McDowell	.10
193	Frank Thomas	1.00
194	Robin Ventura	.10
195	Jim Abbott	.10
196	Wade Boggs	1.25
197	Jimmy Key	.10
198	Don Mattingly	1.50
199	Paul O'Neill	.10
200	Danny Tartabull	.10

Die-Cut

Upper Deck SP Die-cuts are a 200-card parallel set inserted at the rate of one per foil pack. Each card has a die-cut top instead of the flat-top found on regular SP cards. Die-cuts also have a silver-foil Upper Deck hologram logo on back, in contrast to the gold-tone hologram found on regular SP; this is an effort to prevent fraudulent replication by any crook with a pair of scissors.

Holoview Blue

Holoview F/X Blue is a 38-card set utilizing Holoview printing technology, which uses 200 frames of video to produce a three-dimensional image on the bottom third of each card. The hologram is bordered in blue and there is a blue stripe running down the right side of the card. Backs are done with a blue background and feature a player photo over top of bold

letters reading "Holoview FX." This insert could be found in one per five packs of SP baseball.

		NM/M
Common Player:		1.50
1	Roberto Alomar	2.00
2	Kevin Appier	1.50
3	Jeff Bagwell	3.00
4	Jose Canseco	3.00
5	Roger Clemens	6.00
6	Carlos Delgado	2.00
7	Cecil Fielder	1.50
8	Cliff Floyd	1.50
9	Travis Fryman	1.50
10	Andres Galarraga	1.50
11	Juan Gonzalez	2.00
12	Ken Griffey Jr.	6.00
13	Tony Gwynn	4.00
14	Jeffrey Hammonds	1.50
15	Bo Jackson	3.00
16	Michael Jordan	15.00
17	Dave Justice	1.50
18	Steve Karsay	1.50
19	Jeff Kent	2.00
20	Brooks Kieschnick	1.50
21	Ryan Klesko	1.50
22	John Kruk	1.50
23	Barry Larkin	2.00
24	Pat Listach	1.50
25	Don Mattingly	5.00
26	Mark McGwire	8.00
27	Raul Mondesi	1.50
28	Trot Nixon	2.00
29	Mike Piazza	6.00
30	Kirby Puckett	4.00
31	Manny Ramirez	3.00
32	Cal Ripken, Jr.	10.00
33	Alex Rodriguez	75.00
34	Tim Salmon	1.50
35	Gary Sheffield	2.00
36	Ozzie Smith	4.00
37	Sammy Sosa	4.00
38	Andy Van Slyke	1.50

Holoview Blue Mismatches

Some Holoview Blue inserts are known on which the player photograph and data do not match the player shown in the horizontal hologram at bottom front.

Holoview Red

Holoview F/X Red is a parallel set to the Blue insert. Once again, this 38-card set utilizes Holoview printing technology. However, these cards have a red border surrounding the hologram and along the right side, as well as a red background on the back and a large "SPECIAL FX" under the player photo. Holoview red cards also have die-cut tops. Red cards are much scarcer than blue; the red being inserted once per 75 packs of SP baseball.

		NM/M
Common Player:		12.00
1	Roberto Alomar	15.00
2	Kevin Appier	12.00
3	Jeff Bagwell	30.00
4	Jose Canseco	20.00
5	Roger Clemens	50.00
6	Carlos Delgado	20.00
7	Cecil Fielder	12.00
8	Cliff Floyd	12.00
9	Travis Fryman	12.00
10	Andres Galarraga	20.00
11	Juan Gonzalez	20.00
12	Ken Griffey Jr.	50.00
13	Tony Gwynn	40.00
14	Jeffrey Hammonds	12.00
15	Bo Jackson	20.00
16	Michael Jordan	120.00
17	Dave Justice	12.00
18	Steve Karsay	12.00
19	Jeff Kent	12.00
20	Brooks Kieschnick	12.00
21	Ryan Klesko	12.00
22	John Kruk	12.00
23	Barry Larkin	12.00
24	Pat Listach	12.00
25	Don Mattingly	45.00
26	Mark McGwire	60.00
27	Raul Mondesi	12.00
28	Trot Nixon	20.00
29	Mike Piazza	50.00
30	Kirby Puckett	40.00
31	Manny Ramirez	30.00
32	Cal Ripken, Jr.	80.00
33	Alex Rodriguez	1,200
34	Tim Salmon	12.00
35	Gary Sheffield	15.00
36	Ozzie Smith	40.00
37	Sammy Sosa	40.00
38	Andy Van Slyke	12.00

Alex Rodriguez Autographed Jumbo

This 3-1/2" x 5" version of A-Rod's SP rookie card was produced in an authentically autographed edition of 500. The card has serial numbers on front and back and a numbered UD Authenticated hologram sticker on front. The card was sold sealed in a heavy plastic holder and velour drawstring bag.

		NM/M
15	Alex Rodriguez	250.00

1995 SP

Foil highlights and die-cut specialty cards are once again featured in Upper Deck's premium-brand SP baseball card issue. The 207-card set opens with four die-cut tribute cards, followed by 20 Premier Prospect die-cuts printed on metallic foil backgrounds with copper-foil highlights. Three checklists follow, also die-cut. The regular player cards in the set are arranged in team-alphabetical order within league. Card fronts feature photos which are borderless at top, bottom and right. On the left is a gold-highlighted metallic foil border of blue for N.L., red for A.L. Backs have a large photo at top, with a few stats and career highlights at bottom, along with a gold infield-shaped hologram. The SP insert program consists of a "SuperbaFoil" parallel set, in which each card's normal foil highlights are replaced with silver foil; a 48-card Special F/X set utilizing holographic portraits, and, a 20-card Platinum Power set. The hobby-only SP was issued in eight-card foil packs with a $3.99 suggested retail price.

		NM/M
Complete Set (207):		12.50
Common Player:		.05
Pack (8):		1.25
Wax Box (32):		25.00
1	Cal Ripken Jr. (Salute)	2.00
2	Nolan Ryan (Salute)	2.00
3	George Brett (Salute)	1.25
4	Mike Schmidt (Salute)	1.25
5	Dustin Hermanson (Premier Prospects)	.05
6	Antonio Osuna (Premier Prospects)	.05
7	Mark Grudzielanek RC (Premier Prospects)	.35
8	Ray Durham (Premier Prospects)	.05
9	Ugueth Urbina (Premier Prospects)	.05
10	Ruben Rivera (Premier Prospects)	.05
11	Curtis Goodwin (Premier Prospects)	.05
12	Jimmy Hurst (Premier Prospects)	.05
13	Jose Malave (Premier Prospects)	.05
14	Hideo Nomo RC (Premier Prospects)	1.50
15	Juan Acevedo (Premier Prospects)	.05
16	Tony Clark (Premier Prospects)	.05
17	Jim Pittsley (Premier Prospects)	.05
18	Freddy Garcia RC (Premier Prospects)	.50
19	Carlos Perez RC (Premier Prospects)	.05
20	Raul Casanova RC (Premier Prospects)	.05
21	Quilvio Veras (Premier Prospects)	.05
22	Edgardo Alfonzo (Premier Prospects)	.05
23	Marty Cordova (Premier Prospects)	.05
24	C.J. Nitkowski (Premier Prospects)	.05
25	Checklist 1-69 (Wade Boggs)	.30
26	Checklist 70-138 (Dave Winfield)	.25
27	Checklist 139-207 (Eddie Murray)	.25
28	Dave Justice	.05
29	Marquis Grissom	.05
30	Fred McGriff	.05
31	Greg Maddux	1.00
32	Tom Glavine	.35
33	Steve Avery	.05
34	Chipper Jones	1.00
35	Sammy Sosa	1.00
36	Jaime Navarro	.05
37	Randy Myers	.05
38	Mark Grace	.05
39	Todd Zeile	.05
40	Brian McRae	.05
41	Reggie Sanders	.05
42	Ron Gant	.05
43	Deion Sanders	.05
44	Barry Larkin	.05
45	Bret Boone	.05
46	Jose Rijo	.05
47	Jason Bates	.05
48	Andres Galarraga	.05
49	Bill Swift	.05
50	Larry Walker	.05
51	Vinny Castilla	.05
52	Dante Bichette	.05
53	Jeff Conine	.05
54	John Burkett	.05
55	Gary Sheffield	.40
56	Andre Dawson	.30
57	Terry Pendleton	.05
58	Charles Johnson	.05
59	Brian L. Hunter	.05
60	Jeff Bagwell	.75
61	Craig Biggio	.05
62	Phil Nevin	.05
63	Doug Drabek	.05
64	Derek Bell	.05
65	Raul Mondesi	.05
66	Eric Karros	.05
67	Roger Cedeno	.05
68	Delino DeShields	.05
69	Ramon Martinez	.05
70	Mike Piazza	1.50
71	Billy Ashley	.05
72	Jeff Fassero	.05
73	Shane Andrews	.05
74	Wil Cordero	.05
75	Tony Tarasco	.05
76	Rondell White	.05
77	Pedro Martinez	.75
78	Moises Alou	.05
79	Rico Brogna	.05
80	Bobby Bonilla	.05
81	Jeff Kent	.05
82	Brett Butler	.05
83	Bobby Jones	.05
84	Bill Pulsipher	.05
85	Bret Saberhagen	.05
86	Gregg Jefferies	.05
87	Lenny Dykstra	.05

88	Dave Hollins	.05
89	Charlie Hayes	.05
90	Darren Daulton	.05
91	Curt Schilling	.35
92	Heathcliff Slocumb	.05
93	Carlos Garcia	.05
94	Denny Neagle	.05
95	Jay Bell	.05
96	Orlando Merced	.05
97	Dave Clark	.05
98	Bernard Gilkey	.05
99	Scott Cooper	.05
100	Ozzie Smith	1.00
100	Ken Griffey Jr. (Promo Card)	2.00
101	Tom Henke	.05
102	Ken Hill	.05
103	Brian Jordan	.05
104	Ray Lankford	.05
105	Tony Gwynn	1.00
106	Andy Benes	.05
107	Ken Caminiti	.05
108	Steve Finley	.05
109	Joey Hamilton	.05
110	Bip Roberts	.05
111	Eddie Williams	.05
112	Rod Beck	.05
113	Matt Williams	.05
114	Glenallen Hill	.05
115	Barry Bonds	2.50
116	Robby Thompson	.05
117	Mark Portugal	.05
118	Brady Anderson	.35
119	Mike Mussina	.35
120	Rafael Palmeiro	.65
121	Chris Hoiles	.05
122	Harold Baines	.05
123	Jeffrey Hammonds	.05
124	Tim Naehring	.05
125	Mo Vaughn	.05
126	Mike Macfarlane	.05
127	Roger Clemens	1.25
128	John Valentin	.05
129	Aaron Sele	.05
130	Jose Canseco	.50
131	J.T. Snow	.05
132	Mark Langston	.05
133	Chili Davis	.05
134	Chuck Finley	.05
135	Tim Salmon	.05
136	Tony Phillips	.05
137	Jason Bere	.05
138	Robin Ventura	.05
139	Tim Raines	.05
140a	Frank Thomas (5-yr. BA .326)	.75
140b	Frank Thomas (5-yr. BA .303)	.75
141	Alex Fernandez	.05
142	Jim Abbott	.05
143	Wilson Alvarez	.05
144	Carlos Baerga	.05
145	Albert Belle	.05
146	Jim Thome	.65
147	Dennis Martinez	.05
148	Eddie Murray	.75
149	Dave Winfield	.75
150	Kenny Lofton	.05
151	Manny Ramirez	.75
152	Chad Curtis	.05
153	Lou Whitaker	.05
154	Alan Trammell	.05
155	Cecil Fielder	.05
156	Kirk Gibson	.05
157	Michael Tucker	.05
158	Jon Nunnally	.05
159	Wally Joyner	.05
160	Kevin Appier	.05
161	Jeff Montgomery	.05
162	Greg Gagne	.05
163	Ricky Bones	.05
164	Cal Eldred	.05
165	Greg Vaughn	.05
166	Kevin Seitzer	.05
167	Jose Valentin	.05
168	Joe Oliver	.05
169	Rick Aguilera	.05
170	Kirby Puckett	1.00
171	Scott Stahoviak	.05
172	Kevin Tapani	.05
173	Chuck Knoblauch	.05
174	Rich Becker	.05
175	Don Mattingly	1.25
176	Jack McDowell	.05
177	Jimmy Key	.05
178	Paul O'Neill	.05
179	John Wetteland	.05
180	Wade Boggs	1.00
181	Derek Jeter	2.50
182	Rickey Henderson	.75
183	Terry Steinbach	.05
184	Ruben Sierra	.05
185	Mark McGwire	2.00
186	Todd Stottlemyre	.05
187	Dennis Eckersley	.65
188	Alex Rodriguez	2.00
189	Randy Johnson	.75
190	Ken Griffey Jr.	1.50
191	Tino Martinez	.05
192	Jay Buhner	.05
193	Edgar Martinez	.05
194	Mickey Tettleton	.05
195	Juan Gonzalez	.40
196	Benji Gil	.05
197	Dean Palmer	.05
198	Ivan Rodriguez	.65
199	Kenny Rogers	.05
200	Will Clark	.05
201	Roberto Alomar	.20
202	David Cone	.05
203	Paul Molitor	.75

204	Shawn Green	.40
205	Joe Carter	.05
206	Alex Gonzalez	.05
207	Pat Hentgen	.05

SuperbaFoil

This chase set parallels the 207 regular cards in the SP issue. Cards were found at the rate of one per eight-card foil pack. SuperbaFoil cards feature a silver-rainbow metallic foil in place of the gold, copper, red or blue foil highlights on regular-issue SP cards. On back, the SuperbaFoil inserts have a silver hologram instead of the gold version found on standard cards.

	NM/M
Complete Set (207):	30.00
Common Player:	.10
SuperbaFoil Stars:	1.5X

Platinum Power

This die-cut insert set features the game's top power hitters in color action photos set against a background of two-toned gold rays emanating from the SP logo at lower-right. Player name, team and position are printed in white in a black band at bottom. Backs repeat the golden ray effect in the background and have a color photo at center. Career and 1994 stats are presented. An infield-shaped gold foil hologram is at lower-right. Cards have a "PP" prefix. Stated odds of finding one of the 20 Platinum Power inserts are one per five packs.

		NM/M
Complete Set (20):		10.00
Common Player:		.20
1	Jeff Bagwell	.75
2	Barry Bonds	2.00
3	Ron Gant	.20
4	Fred McGriff	.20
5	Raul Mondesi	.20
6	Mike Piazza	1.25
7	Larry Walker	.20
8	Matt Williams	.20
9	Albert Belle	.20
10	Cecil Fielder	.20
11	Juan Gonzalez	.40
12	Ken Griffey Jr.	1.25
13	Mark McGwire	1.50
14	Eddie Murray	.75
15	Manny Ramirez	.75
16	Cal Ripken Jr.	2.00
17	Tim Salmon	.20
18	Frank Thomas	.75
19	Jim Thome	.65
20	Mo Vaughn	.20

Special F/X

By far the preferred pick of the '95 SP insert program is the Special F/X set of 48. The cards have a color action photo on front, printed on a metallic foil background. A 3/4" square holographic portrait is printed on the front. Backs are printed in standard technology and include an-

other photo and a few stats and career highlights. Stated odds of finding a Special F/X card are 1 per 75 packs, or about one per two boxes.

		NM/M
Complete Set (48):		200.00
Common Player:		2.00
1	Jose Canseco	6.00
2	Roger Clemens	20.00
3	Mo Vaughn	2.00
4	Tim Salmon	2.00
5	Chuck Finley	2.00
6	Robin Ventura	2.00
7	Jason Bere	2.00
8	Carlos Baerga	2.00
9	Albert Belle	8.00
10	Kenny Lofton	3.00
11	Manny Ramirez	8.00
12	Jeff Montgomery	2.00
13	Kirby Puckett	15.00
14	Wade Boggs	5.00
15	Don Mattingly	15.00
16	Cal Ripken Jr.	25.00
17	Ruben Sierra	2.00
18	Ken Griffey Jr.	20.00
19	Randy Johnson	8.00
20	Alex Rodriguez	25.00
21	Will Clark	5.00
22	Juan Gonzalez	4.00
23	Roberto Alomar	4.00
24	Joe Carter	3.00
25	Alex Gonzalez	2.00
26	Paul Molitor	6.00
27	Ryan Klesko	2.00
28	Fred McGriff	3.00
29	Greg Maddux	15.00
30	Sammy Sosa	10.00
31	Bret Boone	2.00
32	Barry Larkin	5.00
33	Reggie Sanders	2.00
34	Dante Bichette	2.00
35	Andres Galarraga	2.00
36	Charles Johnson	2.00
37	Gary Sheffield	5.00
38	Jeff Bagwell	6.00
39	Craig Biggio	4.00
40	Eric Karros	2.00
41	Billy Ashley	2.00
42	Raul Mondesi	2.00
43	Mike Piazza	10.00
44	Rondell White	2.00
45	Bret Saberhagen	2.00
46	Tony Gwynn	8.00
47	Melvin Nieves	2.00
48	Matt Williams	2.00

Griffey Gold Signature

A specially autographed version of Griffey's card from 1995 SP was made available from Upper Deck Authenticated. These cards are signed and numbered in gold ink from within an edition of 1,000.

		NM/M
190	Ken Griffey Jr.	65.00

1995 SP/Championship

Championship was a version of Upper Deck's popular SP line designed for sale in retail outlets. The first 20 cards in the set are a "Diamond in the Rough" subset featuring hot rookies printed on textured metallic foil background. Regular player cards are arranged by team within

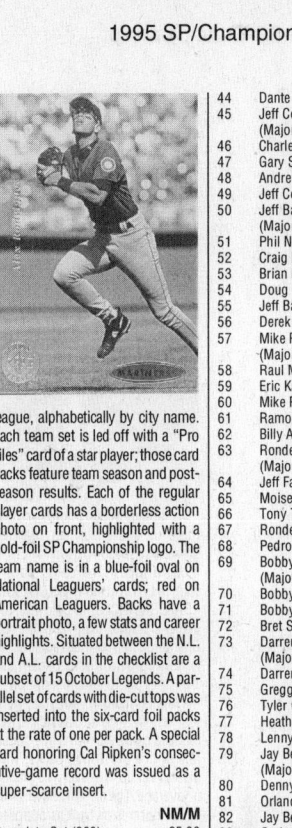

league, alphabetically by city name. Each team set is led off with a "Pro Files" card of a star player; those card backs feature team season and post-season results. Each of the regular player cards has a borderless action photo on front, highlighted with a gold-foil SP Championship logo. The team name is in a blue-foil oval on National Leaguers' cards; red on American Leaguers. Backs have a portrait photo, a few stats and career highlights. Situated between the N.L. and A.L. cards in the checklist are a subset of 15 October Legends. A parallel set of cards with die-cut tops was inserted into the six-card foil packs at the rate of one per pack. A special card honoring Cal Ripken's consecutive-game record was issued as a super-scarce insert.

		NM/M
Complete Set (200):		25.00
Common Player:		.05
Die-Cuts		1.5X
Wax Pack (6):		1.00
Wax Box (44):		30.00
1	Hideo Nomo RC (Diamonds in the Rough)	1.50
2	Roger Cedeno (Diamonds in the Rough)	.05
3	Curtis Goodwin (Diamonds in the Rough)	.05
4	Jon Nunnally (Diamonds in the Rough)	.05
5	Bill Pulsipher (Diamonds in the Rough)	.05
6	C.J. Nitkowski (Diamonds in the Rough)	.05
7	Dustin Hermanson (Diamonds in the Rough)	.05
8	Marty Cordova (Diamonds in the Rough)	.05
9	Ruben Rivera (Diamonds in the Rough)	.05
10	Ariel Prieto RC (Diamonds in the Rough)	.05
11	Edgardo Alfonzo (Diamonds in the Rough)	.05
12	Ray Durham (Diamonds in the Rough)	.05
13	Quilvio Veras (Diamonds in the Rough)	.05
14	Ugueth Urbina (Diamonds in the Rough)	.05
15	Carlos Perez RC (Diamonds in the Rough)	.05
16	Glenn Dishman RC (Diamonds in the Rough)	.05
17	Jeff Suppan (Diamonds in the Rough)	.05
18	Jason Bates (Diamonds in the Rough)	.05
19	Jason Isringhausen (Diamonds in the Rough)	.05
20	Derek Jeter (Diamonds in the Rough)	2.00
21	Fred McGriff (Major League ProFiles)	.05
22	Marquis Grissom	.05
23	Fred McGriff	.05
24	Tom Glavine	.35
25	Greg Maddux	1.00
26	Chipper Jones	1.00
27	Sammy Sosa (Major League ProFiles)	.50
28	Randy Myers	.05
29	Mark Grace	.05
30	Sammy Sosa	1.00
31	Todd Zeile	.05
32	Brian McRae	.05
33	Ron Gant (Major League ProFiles)	.05
34	Reggie Sanders	.05
35	Ron Gant	.05
36	Barry Larkin	.05
37	Bret Boone	.05
38	John Smiley	.05
39	Larry Walker (Major League ProFiles)	.05
40	Andres Galarraga	.05
41	Bill Swift	.05
42	Larry Walker	.05
43	Vinny Castilla	.05

44	Dante Bichette	.05
45	Jeff Conine (Major League ProFiles)	.05
46	Charles Johnson	.05
47	Gary Sheffield	.45
48	Andre Dawson	.25
49	Jeff Conine	.05
50	Jeff Bagwell (Major League ProFiles)	.40
51	Phil Nevin	.05
52	Craig Biggio	.05
53	Brian L. Hunter	.05
54	Doug Drabek	.05
55	Jeff Bagwell	.75
57	Mike Piazza (Major League ProFiles)	.65
58	Raul Mondesi	.05
59	Eric Karros	.05
60	Mike Piazza	1.25
61	Ramon Martinez	.05
62	Billy Ashley	.05
63	Rondell White (Major League ProFiles)	.05
64	Jeff Fassero	.05
65	Moises Alou	.05
66	Tony Tarasco	.05
67	Rondell White	.05
68	Pedro Martinez	.75
69	Bobby Jones (Major League ProFiles)	.05
70	Bobby Bonilla	.05
71	Bobby Jones	.05
72	Bret Saberhagen	.05
73	Darren Daulton (Major League ProFiles)	.05
74	Darren Daulton	.05
75	Gregg Jefferies	.05
76	Tyler Green	.05
77	Heathcliff Slocumb	.05
78	Lenny Dykstra	.05
79	Jay Bell (Major League ProFiles)	.05
80	Denny Neagle	.05
81	Orlando Merced	.05
82	Jay Bell	.05
83	Ozzie Smith (Major League ProFiles)	.50
84	Ken Hill	.05
85	Ozzie Smith	1.00
86	Bernard Gilkey	.05
87	Ray Lankford	.05
88	Tony Gwynn (Major League ProFiles)	.50
89	Ken Caminiti	.05
90	Tony Gwynn	1.00
91	Joey Hamilton	.05
92	Bip Roberts	.05
93	Deion Sanders (Major League ProFiles)	.05
94	Glenallen Hill	.05
95	Matt Williams	.05
96	Barry Bonds	2.00
97	Rod Beck	.05
98	Eddie Murray (Checklist)	.35
99	Cal Ripken Jr. (Checklist)	1.00
100	Roberto Alomar (October Legends)	.10
101	George Brett (October Legends)	.60
102	Joe Carter (Ocober Legends)	.05
103	Will Clark (October Legends)	.05
104	Dennis Eckersley (October Legends)	.40
105	Whitey Ford (October Legends)	.40
106	Steve Garvey (October Legends)	.05
107	Kirk Gibson (October Legends)	.05
108	Orel Hershiser (October Legends)	.05
109	Reggie Jackson (October Legends)	.50
110	Paul Molitor (October Legends)	.40
111	Kirby Puckett (October Legends)	.50
112	Mike Schmidt (October Legends)	.60
113	Dave Stewart (October Legends)	.05
114	Alan Trammell (October Legends)	.05
115	Cal Ripken Jr. (Major League ProFiles)	1.00
116	Brady Anderson	.05
117	Mike Mussina	.30
118	Rafael Palmeiro	.65
119	Chris Hoiles	.05
120	Cal Ripken Jr.	2.00
121	Mo Vaughn (Major League ProFiles)	.05
122	Roger Clemens	1.25
123	Tim Naehring	.05
124	John Valentin	.05
125	Mo Vaughn	.05
126	Tim Wakefield	.05
127	Jose Canseco	.40
128	Rick Aguilera	.05
129	Chili Davis (Major League ProFiles)	.05
130	Lee Smith	.05
131	Jim Edmonds	.05
132	Chuck Finley	.05
133	Chili Davis	.05

#	Player	Price
134	J.T. Snow	.05
135	Tim Salmon	.05
136	Frank Thomas	.05
	(Major League ProFiles)	.45
137	Jason Bere	.05
138	Robin Ventura	.05
139	Tim Raines	.05
140	Frank Thomas	.75
141	Alex Fernandez	.05
142	Eddie Murray	.05
	(Major League ProFiles)	.40
143	Carlos Baerga	.05
144	Eddie Murray	.75
145	Albert Belle	.05
146	Jim Thome	.65
147	Dennis Martinez	.05
148	Dave Winfield	.75
149	Kenny Lofton	.05
150	Manny Ramirez	.75
151	Cecil Fielder	.05
	(Major League ProFiles)	.05
152	Lou Whitaker	.05
153	Alan Trammell	.05
154	Kirk Gibson	.05
155	Cecil Fielder	.05
156	Bobby Higginson RC	.25
157	Kevin Appier	.05
	(Major League ProFiles)	.05
158	Wally Joyner	.05
159	Jeff Montgomery	.05
160	Kevin Appier	.05
161	Gary Gaetti	.05
162	Greg Gagne	.05
163	Ricky Bones	.05
	(Major League ProFiles)	.05
164	Greg Vaughn	.05
165	Kevin Seitzer	.05
166	Ricky Bones	.05
167	Kirby Puckett	.05
	(Major League ProFiles)	.50
168	Pedro Munoz	.05
169	Chuck Knoblauch	.05
170	Kirby Puckett	1.00
171	Don Mattingly	.05
	(Major League ProFiles)	.60
172	Wade Boggs	1.00
173	Paul O'Neill	.05
174	John Wetteland	.05
175	Don Mattingly	1.25
176	Jack McDowell	.05
177	Mark McGwire	.05
	(Major League ProFiles)	.75
178	Rickey Henderson	.75
179	Terry Steinbach	.05
180	Ruben Sierra	.05
181	Mark McGwire	1.50
182	Dennis Eckersley	.05
183	Ken Griffey Jr.	.05
	(Major League ProFiles)	.65
184	Alex Rodriguez	1.50
185	Ken Griffey Jr.	1.25
186	Randy Johnson	.75
187	Jay Buhner	.05
188	Edgar Martinez	.05
189	Will Clark	.05
	(Major League ProFiles)	.05
190	Juan Gonzalez	.40
191	Benji Gil	.05
192	Ivan Rodriguez	.65
193	Kenny Rogers	.05
194	Will Clark	.05
195	Paul Molitor	.05
	(Major League ProFiles)	.40
196	Roberto Alomar	.20
197	David Cone	.05
198	Paul Molitor	.75
199	Shawn Green	.30
200	Joe Carter	.05
CR1	Cal Ripken Jr. (2,131 games tribute)	5.00
CR1	Cal Ripken Jr. Die-Cut	7.50

Die-Cuts

Each of the 200 cards in the regular SP championship issue, plus the 20 insert cards, can also be found in a parallel chase card set with die-cut tops. One die-cut card was found in each six-card foil pack, making them five times scarcer than the regular cards. To prevent regular cards from being fraudulently cut, factory-issue die-cuts have the Upper Deck hologram on back in silver tone, rather than the gold holograms found on regular cards.

	NM/M
Complete Set (200):	50.00
Common Player:	.25
Die-Cut Stars:	1.5X

Classic Performances

Vintage action photos are featured in this chase set marking great post-season performances of modern times. The cards have a wide red strip at top with "CLASSIC PERFORMANCES" in gold-foil; the player's name, team and the SP Championship embossed logo at bottom are also in gold. Backs have a portrait photo and description of the highlight along with stats from that series. Regular Classic Performances cards are found at a stated rate of one per 15 foil packs, with die-cut versions in every 75 packs, on average. The die-cuts have silver UD holograms on back as opposed to the gold hologram found on regular versions of the chase cards.

	NM/M
Complete Set (10):	8.00
Common Player:	.50
Complete Die-Cut Set (10):	16.00
Common Die-Cuts:	1.00
CP1 Reggie Jackson (Game 6 of '77 WS)	.60
CP1 Reggie Jackson (Die-Cut)	2.00
CP2 Nolan Ryan (Game 3 of '69 WS)	4.00
CP2 Nolan Ryan (Die-Cut)	8.00
CP3 Kirk Gibson (Game 1 of '88 WS)	.50
CP3 Kirk Gibson (Die-Cut)	1.00
CP4 Joe Carter (Game 6 of '93 WS)	.50
CP4 Joe Carter (Die-Cut)	1.00
CP5 George Brett (Game 3 of '80 ALCS)	1.25
CP5 George Brett (Die-Cut)	2.50
CP6 Roberto Alomar (Game 4 of '92 ALCS)	.50
CP6 Roberto Alomar (Die-Cut)	1.00
CP7 Ozzie Smith (Game 5 of '85 NLCS)	.75
CP7 Ozzie Smith (Die-Cut)	1.50
CP8 Kirby Puckett (Game 6 of '91 WS)	1.25
CP8 Kirby Puckett (Die-Cut)	2.00
CP9 Bret Saberhagen (Game 7 of '85 WS)	.50
CP9 Bret Saberhagen (Die-Cut)	1.00
CP10 Steve Garvey (Game 4 of '84 NLCS)	.50
CP10 Steve Garvey (Die-Cut)	1.00

Destination: Fall Classic

Colored foil background printing and copper-foil graphic highlights are featured on this insert set picturing players who, for the most part, had yet to make a post-season appearance prior to 1995's expanded playoffs. Found at a stated average rate of one per 40 foil packs, the cards have short career summaries and another photo on back. A die-cut version of the cards was also issued, with a silver UD hologram on back rather than the gold found on the standard chase cards. The die-cut Fall Classic cards were inserted at a rate of one per 75 packs.

	NM/M
Complete Set (9):	18.00
Common Player:	1.00
Complete Die-Cut Set (9):	36.00
Common Die-Cut:	2.00
1 Ken Griffey Jr.	3.00
1 Ken Griffey Jr. (Die-Cut)	6.00
2 Frank Thomas	2.00
2 Frank Thomas (Die-Cut)	4.00
3 Albert Belle	1.00
3 Albert Belle (Die-Cut)	2.00
4 Mike Piazza	3.00
4 Mike Piazza (Die-Cut)	6.00
5 Don Mattingly	2.75
5 Don Mattingly (Die-Cut)	5.50
6 Hideo Nomo	1.50
6 Hideo Nomo (Die-Cut)	2.00
7 Greg Maddux	2.50
7 Greg Maddux (Die-Cut)	5.00
8 Fred McGriff	1.00
8 Fred McGriff (Die-Cut)	2.00
9 Barry Bonds	5.00
9 Barry Bonds (Die-Cut)	8.00

Ripken Tribute Jumbo

A special super-size (3" x 5") version of the SP/Championship edition Cal Ripken Jr. 2,131 Games tribute card insert was created for sale by Upper Deck Authentic on home shopping programs. The card is die-cut and serially numbered on back from within an edition of 2,131 pieces.

	NM/M
CR1 Cal Ripken Jr.	12.00

1996 SP FanFest Promos

To introduce its SP product, Upper Deck prepared an eight-card promo set for distribution at the All-Star FanFest in Philadelphia. The promos are identical in format to the issued versions except for the presence of a bright silver-foil FanFest logo in the lower-left corner of each card's front. The cards lack the overprint which has become standard on promo cards in the recent years.

	NM/M
Complete Set (8):	8.00
Common Player:	.60
1 Ken Griffey Jr.	1.50
2 Frank Thomas	1.00
3 Albert Belle	.60
4 Mo Vaughn	.60
5 Barry Bonds	2.50
6 Mike Piazza	1.50
7 Matt Williams	.60
8 Sammy Sosa	1.25

1996 SP

This 188-card set, distributed through hobby-only channels, features tremendous photography, including two photos on the front, and six insert sets. The inserts sets are Heroes, Marquee Matchups Blue and Die-Cut Marquee Matchups Red, Holoview Special F/X Blue and Die-Cut Holoview Special F/X Red, and the continuation of the Cal Ripken Collection.

#	Player	Price
	Complete Set (188):	12.50
	Common Player:	.05
	Pack (8):	1.25
	Wax Box (30):	25.00
1	Rey Ordonez (Premier Prospects)	.05
2	George Arias (Premier Prospects)	.05
3	Osvaldo Fernandez RC (Premier Prospects)	.25
4	Darin Erstad RC (Premier Prospects)	2.00
5	Paul Wilson (Premier Prospects)	.05
6	Richard Hidalgo (Premier Prospects)	.05
7	Bob Wolcott (Premier Prospects)	.05
8	Jimmy Haynes (Premier Prospects)	.05
9	Edgar Renteria (Premier Prospects)	.05
10	Alan Benes (Premier Prospects)	.05
11	Chris Snopek (Premier Prospects)	.05
12	Billy Wagner (Premier Prospects)	.05
13	Mike Grace RC (Premier Prospects)	.05
14	Todd Greene (Premier Prospects)	.05
15	Karim Garcia (Premier Prospects)	.05
16	John Wasdin (Premier Prospects)	.05
17	Jason Kendall (Premier Prospects)	.05
18	Bob Abreu (Premier Prospects)	.15
19	Jermaine Dye (Premier Prospects)	.05
20	Jason Schmidt (Premier Prospects)	.05
21	Javy Lopez	.05
22	Ryan Klesko	.05
23	Tom Glavine	.35
24	John Smoltz	.05
25	Greg Maddux	1.00
26	Chipper Jones	1.00
27	Fred McGriff	.05
28	David Justice	.05
29	Roberto Alomar	.20
30	Cal Ripken Jr.	2.00
31	Jeffrey Hammonds	.05
32	Bobby Bonilla	.05
33	Mike Mussina	.30
34	Randy Myers	.05
35	Rafael Palmeiro	.65
36	Brady Anderson	.05
37	Tim Naehring	.05
38	Jose Canseco	.40
39	Roger Clemens	1.00
40	Mo Vaughn	.05
41	Jose Valentin RC	.05
42	Kevin Mitchell	.05
43	Chili Davis	.05
44	Garret Anderson	.05
45	Tim Salmon	.05
46	Chuck Finley	.05
47	Mark Langston	.05
48	Jim Abbott	.05
49	J.T. Snow	.05
50	Jim Edmonds	.05
51	Sammy Sosa	.05
52	Brian McRae	.05
53	Ryne Sandberg	1.00
54	Mark Grace	.05
55	Jaime Navarro	.05
56	Harold Baines	.05
57	Robin Ventura	.05
58	Tony Phillips	.05
59	Alex Fernandez	.05
60	Frank Thomas	.75
61	Ray Durham	.05
62	Bret Boone	.05
63	Barry Larkin	.05
64	Pete Schourek	.05
65	Reggie Sanders	.05
66	John Smiley	.05
67	Carlos Baerga	.05
68	Jim Thome	.65
69	Eddie Murray	.75
70	Albert Belle	.05
71	Dennis Martinez	.05
72	Jack McDowell	.05
73	Kenny Lofton	.05
74	Manny Ramirez	.75
75	Dante Bichette	.05
76	Vinny Castilla	.05
77	Andres Galarraga	.05
78	Walt Weiss	.05
79	Ellis Burks	.05
80	Larry Walker	.05
81	Cecil Fielder	.05
82	Melvin Nieves	.05
83	Travis Fryman	.05
84	Chad Curtis	.05
85	Alan Trammell	.05
86	Gary Sheffield	.45
87	Charles Johnson	.05
88	Andre Dawson	.30
89	Jeff Conine	.05
90	Greg Colbrunn	.05
91	Derek Bell	.05
92	Brian Hunter	.05
93	Doug Drabek	.05
94	Craig Biggio	.05
95	Jeff Bagwell	.75
96	Kevin Appier	.05
97	Jeff Montgomery	.05
98	Michael Tucker	.05
99	Bip Roberts	.05
100	Johnny Damon	.35
101	Eric Karros	.05
102	Raul Mondesi	.05
103	Ramon Martinez	.05
104	Ismael Valdes	.05
105	Mike Piazza	1.25
106	Hideo Nomo	.40
107	Chan Ho Park	.05
108	Ben McDonald	.05
109	Kevin Seitzer	.05
110	Greg Vaughn	.05
111	Jose Valentin	.05
112	Rick Aguilera	.05
113	Marty Cordova	.05
114	Brad Radke	.05
115	Kirby Puckett	1.00
116	Chuck Knoblauch	.05
117	Paul Molitor	.75
118	Pedro Martinez	.75
119	Mike Lansing	.05
120	Rondell White	.05
121	Moises Alou	.05
122	Mark Grudzielanek	.05
123	Jeff Fassero	.05
124	Rico Brogna	.05
125	Jason Isringhausen	.05
126	Jeff Kent	.05
127	Bernard Gilkey	.05
128	Todd Hundley	.05
129	David Cone	.05
130	Andy Pettitte	.25
131	Wade Boggs	1.00
132	Paul O'Neill	.05
133	Ruben Sierra	.05
134	John Wetteland	.05
135	Derek Jeter	2.00
136	Geronimo Pena	.05
137	Terry Steinbach	.05
138	Ariel Prieto	.05
139	Scott Brosius	.05
140	Mark McGwire	1.50
141	Lenny Dykstra	.05
142	Todd Zeile	.05
143	Benito Santiago	.05
144	Mickey Morandini	.05
145	Gregg Jefferies	.05
146	Denny Neagle	.05
147	Orlando Merced	.05
148	Charlie Hayes	.05
149	Carlos Garcia	.05
150	Jay Bell	.05
151	Ray Lankford	.05
152	Alan Benes	.05
153	Dennis Eckersley	.65
154	Gary Gaetti	.05
155	Ozzie Smith	1.00
156	Ron Gant	.05
157	Brian Jordan	.05
158	Ken Caminiti	.05
159	Rickey Henderson	.75
160	Tony Gwynn	1.00
161	Wally Joyner	.05
162	Andy Ashby	.05
163	Steve Finley	.05
164	Glenallen Hill	.05
165	Matt Williams	.05
166	Barry Bonds	2.00
167	William Van Landingham	.05
168	Rod Beck	.05
169	Randy Johnson	.75
170	Ken Griffey Jr.	1.25
170p	Ken Griffey Jr. (Unmarked promo; bio on backs says, ". . .against Cleveland" as opposed to ". . . against the Indians.")	4.00
171	Alex Rodriguez	1.50
172	Edgar Martinez	.05
173	Jay Buhner	.05
174	Russ Davis	.05
175	Juan Gonzalez	.40
176	Mickey Tettleton	.05
177	Will Clark	.05
178	Ken Hill	.05
179	Dean Palmer	.05
180	Ivan Rodriguez	.65
181	Carlos Delgado	.50
182	Alex Gonzalez	.05
183	Shawn Green	.30
184	Erik Hanson	.05
185	Joe Carter	.05
186	Checklist (Hideo Nomo)	.20
187	Checklist (Cal Ripken Jr.)	1.00
188	Checklist (Ken Griffey Jr.)	.65

Baseball Heroes

This 1996 insert set is a continuation of the series which began in 1990. These cards, numbered 81-90, feature nine of today's top stars, plus a Ken Griffey Jr. header card (#81). The cards were seeded one per every 96 packs.

	NM/M
Complete Set (10):	65.00
Common Player:	4.00
81 Ken Griffey Jr. Header	8.00
82 Frank Thomas	6.50
83 Albert Belle	4.00
84 Barry Bonds	12.00
85 Chipper Jones	8.00
86 Hideo Nomo	5.00
87 Mike Piazza	10.00
88 Manny Ramirez	6.50
89 Greg Maddux	8.00
90 Ken Griffey Jr.	10.00

Marquee Matchups Blue

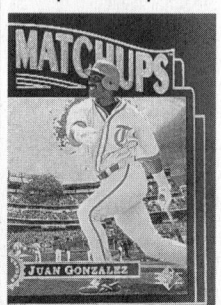

This 20-card Upper Deck SP insert set contains cards that allow collectors to match up the game's top players against each other, such as Greg Maddux against Cal Ripken Jr. The design and stadiums in the background match together when the two cards are next to each other. Blue versions are seeded one per five packs. Cards are numbered with a "MM" prefix.

	NM/M
Complete Set (20):	15.00
Common Player:	.50
1 Ken Griffey Jr.	2.00
2 Hideo Nomo	.50
3 Derek Jeter	3.00
4 Rey Ordonez	.50
5 Tim Salmon	.50
6 Mike Piazza	1.50
7 Mark McGwire	1.50
8 Barry Bonds	.50
9 Cal Ripken Jr.	3.00
10 Greg Maddux	1.50
11 Albert Belle	.50
12 Barry Larkin	1.00
13 Jeff Bagwell	.75
14 Juan Gonzalez	.75
15 Frank Thomas	1.00
16 Sammy Sosa	1.00
17 Mike Mussina	.75
18 Chipper Jones	1.00

19 Roger Clemens 2.00
20 Fred McGriff .50

Marquee Matchups Red

A parallel set to the blue Marquee Matchups, the red cards are found on average of one per 61 packs. Besides the red background printing, this version is distinguished from the more common blue version by the die-cutting around the top. Cards are numbered with a "MM" prefix.

		NM/M
Common Player:		1.50
1	Ken Griffey Jr.	10.00
2	Hideo Nomo	2.00
3	Derek Jeter	15.00
4	Rey Ordonez	1.50
5	Tim Salmon	1.50
6	Mike Piazza	8.00
7	Mark McGwire	8.00
8	Barry Bonds	15.00
9	Cal Ripken Jr.	15.00
10	Greg Maddux	10.00
11	Albert Belle	1.50
12	Barry Larkin	4.00
13	Jeff Bagwell	4.00
14	Juan Gonzalez	3.00
15	Frank Thomas	5.00
16	Sammy Sosa	5.00
17	Mike Mussina	4.00
18	Chipper Jones	5.00
19	Roger Clemens	10.00
20	Fred McGriff	3.00

Ripken Collection

The last five cards of the Cal Ripken Jr. Collection, which began in Collector's Choice Series I, are featured in this Upper Deck SP product. These five cards, numbered 18-22, cover Ripken's early days, including his 1982 Rookie of the Year Award, his Major League debut, and photos of him playing third base. Ripken Collection inserts are found one per every 45 packs.

	NM/M
Complete Set (5):	25.00
Common Card:	5.00
18-22 Cal Ripken Jr.	5.00

SpecialFX

These 48 cards capture Upper Deck Holoview technology. Blue versions were seeded one per every five packs of 1996 Upper Deck SP baseball.

		NM/M
Complete Set (48):		50.00
Common Player:		.60
1	Greg Maddux	2.50
2	Eric Karros	.60
3	Mike Piazza	3.00
4	Raul Mondesi	.60
5	Hideo Nomo	1.00
6	Jim Edmonds	.60
7	Jason Isringhausen	.60
8	Jay Buhner	.60
9	Barry Larkin	.60
10	Ken Griffey Jr.	3.00
11	Gary Sheffield	1.25
12	Craig Biggio	.60
13	Paul Wilson	.60
14	Rondell White	.60
15	Chipper Jones	2.50
16	Kirby Puckett	2.50
17	Ron Gant	.60
18	Wade Boggs	2.50
19	Fred McGriff	.60
20	Cal Ripken Jr.	5.00
21	Jason Kendall	.60
22	Johnny Damon	.90
23	Kenny Lofton	.60
24	Roberto Alomar	1.00
25	Barry Bonds	5.00
26	Dante Bichette	.60
27	Mark McGwire	4.00
28	Rafael Palmeiro	1.50
29	Juan Gonzalez	1.00
30	Albert Belle	.60
31	Randy Johnson	1.75
32	Jose Canseco	1.25
33	Sammy Sosa	2.50
34	Eddie Murray	1.75
35	Frank Thomas	1.75
36	Tom Glavine	.90
37	Matt Williams	.60
38	Roger Clemens	2.75
39	Paul Molitor	1.75
40	Tony Gwynn	2.50
41	Mo Vaughn	.60
42	Tim Salmon	.60
43	Manny Ramirez	1.75
44	Jeff Bagwell	1.75
45	Edgar Martinez	.60
46	Rey Ordonez	.60
47	Osvaldo Fernandez	.60
48	Derek Jeter	5.00

SpecialFX Red

These 1996 Upper Deck SP red die-cut cards use Upper Deck's Holoview technology. They are scarcer than the blue versions; these being seeded one per every 75 packs.

		NM/M
Common Player:		3.00
Inserted 1:75		
1	Greg Maddux	20.00
2	Eric Karros	3.00
3	Mike Piazza	10.00
4	Raul Mondesi	3.00
5	Hideo Nomo	4.00
6	Jim Edmonds	4.00
7	Jason Isringhausen	4.00
8	Jay Buhner	3.00
9	Barry Larkin	5.00
10	Ken Griffey Jr.	20.00
11	Gary Sheffield	8.00
12	Craig Biggio	5.00
13	Paul Wilson	3.00
14	Rondell White	3.00
15	Chipper Jones	15.00
16	Kirby Puckett	20.00
17	Ron Gant	3.00
18	Wade Boggs	6.00
19	Fred McGriff	4.00
20	Cal Ripken Jr.	25.00
21	Jason Kendall	3.00
22	Johnny Damon	8.00
23	Kenny Lofton	4.00
24	Roberto Alomar	5.00
25	Barry Bonds	25.00
26	Dante Bichette	3.00
27	Mark McGwire	15.00
28	Rafael Palmeiro	6.00
29	Juan Gonzalez	5.00
30	Albert Belle	3.00
31	Randy Johnson	10.00
32	Jose Canseco	5.00
33	Sammy Sosa	10.00
34	Eddie Murray	8.00
35	Frank Thomas	10.00
36	Tom Glavine	10.00
37	Matt Williams	4.00
38	Roger Clemens	20.00
39	Paul Molitor	8.00
40	Tony Gwynn	10.00
41	Mo Vaughn	5.00
42	Tim Salmon	4.00
43	Manny Ramirez	10.00
44	Jeff Bagwell	8.00
45	Edgar Martinez	3.00
46	Rey Ordonez	3.00
47	Osvaldo Fernandez	3.00
48	Derek Jeter	25.00

1996 SPx

Upper Deck's 1996 SPx set has 60 players in it, which are each paralleled as a Gold version (one per every seven packs). Base cards feature a new look with a different perimeter die-cut design from those used in the past for basketball and football sets. A 10-card insert set, Bound for Glory, was also produced. Tribute cards were also made for Ken Griffey Jr. and Mike Piazza, with scarcer autographed versions also produced for each player.

		NM/M
Complete Set (60):		17.50
Common Player:		.15
Golds:		1.5X
Pack (1):		1.25
Wax Box (36):		25.00
1	Greg Maddux	1.50
2	Chipper Jones	1.50
3	Fred McGriff	.15
4	Tom Glavine	.50
5	Cal Ripken Jr.	3.00
6	Roberto Alomar	.50
7	Rafael Palmeiro	1.00
8	Jose Canseco	.65
9	Roger Clemens	1.75
10	Mo Vaughn	.15
11	Jim Edmonds	.15
12	Tim Salmon	.15
13	Sammy Sosa	1.50
14	Ryne Sandberg	1.50
15	Mark Grace	.15
16	Frank Thomas	1.25
17	Barry Larkin	.15
18	Kenny Lofton	.15
19	Albert Belle	.15
20	Eddie Murray	1.25
21	Manny Ramirez	1.25
22	Dante Bichette	.15
23	Larry Walker	.15
24	Vinny Castilla	.15
25	Andres Galarraga	.15
26	Cecil Fielder	.15
27	Gary Sheffield	.75
28	Craig Biggio	.15
29	Jeff Bagwell	1.25
30	Derek Bell	.15
31	Johnny Damon	.60
32	Eric Karros	.15
33	Mike Piazza	2.00
34	Raul Mondesi	.15
35	Hideo Nomo	.65
36	Kirby Puckett	1.50
37	Paul Molitor	1.25
38	Marty Cordova	.15
39	Rondell White	.15
40	Jason Isringhausen	.15
41	Paul Wilson	.15
42	Rey Ordonez	.15
43	Derek Jeter	3.00
44	Wade Boggs	1.50
45	Mark McGwire	2.50
46	Jason Kendall	.15
47	Ron Gant	.15
48	Ozzie Smith	1.50
49	Tony Gwynn	1.50
50	Ken Caminiti	.15
51	Barry Bonds	3.00
52	Matt Williams	.15
53	Osvaldo Fernandez RC	.15
54	Jay Buhner	.15
55	Ken Griffey Jr.	2.00
55p	Ken Griffey Jr./OPS	
56	Randy Johnson	1.25
57	Alex Rodriguez	2.50
58	Juan Gonzalez	.65
59	Joe Carter	.15
60	Carlos Delgado	.75

Bound for Glory

Some of baseball's best players are highlighted on these 1996 Upper Deck SPx insert cards. The cards were seeded one per every 24 packs. Fronts of the die-cut cards feature a color photograph on a background of silver-foil holographic portrait and action photos. Backs have another portrait photo, stats, career highlights and logos.

		NM/M
Complete Set (10):		18.00
Common Player:		1.00
1	Ken Griffey Jr.	3.00
2	Frank Thomas	1.50
3	Barry Bonds	4.00
4	Cal Ripken Jr.	4.00
5	Greg Maddux	2.00
6	Chipper Jones	2.00
7	Roberto Alomar	1.00
8	Manny Ramirez	1.50
9	Tony Gwynn	2.00
10	Mike Piazza	3.00

Ken Griffey Jr. Commemorative

Seattle Mariners' star Ken Griffey Jr. has this tribute card in Upper Deck's 1996 SPx set. The card was seeded one per every 75 packs. Autographed versions were also produced; these cards were seeded one per every 2,000 packs.

		NM/M
KG1	Ken Griffey Jr.	2.50
KGA1	Ken Griffey Jr./Auto.	100.00

Mike Piazza Tribute

Los Angeles Dodgers' star catcher Mike Piazza is featured on this 1996 Upper Deck SPx insert card. Normal versions of the card are found one per every 95 packs, making it scarcer than the Ken Griffey Jr. inserts. Autographed Piazza cards are seeded one per every 2,000 packs.

		NM/M
MP1	Mike Piazza	2.00
MP1	Mike Piazza/Auto.	125.00

1997 SP Sample

To preview its SP brand for 1997, Upper Deck issued a sample card of Ken Griffey Jr. Similar in format to the issued cards, the promo bears card number 1 and is overprinted "SAMPLE" on back.

		NM/M
1	Ken Griffey Jr.	3.00

1997 SP

The fifth anniversary edition of SP Baseball features 184 regular cards sold in eight-card packs for $4.39. Card fronts feature the player's name in gold foil-stamping at bottom. Team name and position are vertically at one edge. Backs have two more photos along with "Best Year" and career stats. Inserts include Marquee Matchups, Special FX, Inside Info, Baseball Heroes, Game Film, SPx Force, and Autographed Vintage SP cards.

		NM/M
Complete Set (184):		12.00
Common Player:		.05
Pack (8):		2.00
Wax Box (30):		45.00
1	Andruw Jones (Great Futures)	.75
2	Kevin Orie (Great Futures)	.05
3	Nomar Garciaparra (Great Futures)	1.00
4	Jose Guillen (Great Futures)	.05
5	Todd Walker (Great Futures)	.05
6	Derrick Gibson (Great Futures)	.05
7	Aaron Boone (Great Futures)	.05
8	Bartolo Colon (Great Futures)	.05
9	Derrek Lee (Great Futures)	.50
10	Vladimir Guerrero (Great Futures)	.75
11	Wilton Guerrero (Great Futures)	.05
12	Luis Castillo (Great Futures)	.05
13	Jason Dickson (Great Futures)	.05
14	Bubba Trammell RC (Great Futures)	.25
15	Jose Cruz Jr. RC (Great Futures)	.50
16	Eddie Murray	.75
17	Darin Erstad	.20
18	Garret Anderson	.05
19	Jim Edmonds	.05
20	Tim Salmon	.05
21	Chuck Finley	.05
22	John Smoltz	.05
23	Greg Maddux	1.00
24	Kenny Lofton	.05
25	Chipper Jones	1.00
26	Ryan Klesko	.05
27	Javier Lopez	.05
28	Fred McGriff	.20
29	Roberto Alomar	.20
30	Rafael Palmeiro	.05
31	Mike Mussina	.30
32	Brady Anderson	.05
33	Rocky Coppinger	.05
34	Cal Ripken Jr.	2.00
35	Mo Vaughn	.05
36	Steve Avery	.05
37	Tom Gordon	.05
38	Tim Naehring	.05
39	Troy O'Leary	.05
40	Sammy Sosa	1.00
41	Brian McRae	.05
42	Mel Rojas	.05
43	Ryne Sandberg	1.00
44	Mark Grace	.05
45	Albert Belle	.05
46	Robin Ventura	.05
47	Roberto Hernandez	.05
48	Ray Durham	.05
49	Harold Baines	.05
50	Frank Thomas	.75
51	Bret Boone	.05
52	Reggie Sanders	.05
53	Deion Sanders	.05
54	Hal Morris	.05
55	Barry Larkin	.05
56	Jim Thome	.65
57	Marquis Grissom	.05
58	David Justice	.05
59	Charles Nagy	.05
60	Manny Ramirez	.75
61	Matt Williams	.05
62	Jack McDowell	.05
63	Vinny Castilla	.05
64	Dante Bichette	.05
65	Andres Galarraga	.05
66	Ellis Burks	.05
67	Larry Walker	.05
68	Eric Young	.05
69	Brian L. Hunter	.05
70	Travis Fryman	.05
71	Tony Clark	.05
72	Bobby Higginson	.05
73	Melvin Nieves	.05
74	Jeff Conine	.05
75	Gary Sheffield	.40
76	Moises Alou	.05
77	Edgar Renteria	.05
78	Alex Fernandez	.05
79	Charles Johnson	.05
80	Bobby Bonilla	.05
81	Darryl Kile	.05
82	Derek Bell	.05
83	Shane Reynolds	.05
84	Craig Biggio	.05
85	Jeff Bagwell	.75
86	Billy Wagner	.05
87	Chili Davis	.05
88	Kevin Appier	.05
89	Jay Bell	.05
90	Johnny Damon	.35
91	Jeff King	.05
92	Hideo Nomo	.40
93	Todd Hollandsworth	.05
94	Eric Karros	.05
95	Mike Piazza	1.25
96	Ramon Martinez	.05
97	Todd Worrell	.05
98	Raul Mondesi	.05
99	Dave Nilsson	.05
100	John Jaha	.05
101	Jose Valentin	.05
102	Jeff Cirillo	.05
103	Jeff D'Amico	.05
104	Ben McDonald	.05
105	Paul Molitor	.75
106	Rich Becker	.05
107	Frank Rodriguez	.05
108	Marty Cordova	.05
109	Terry Steinbach	.05
110	Chuck Knoblauch	.05
111	Mark Grudzielanek	.05
112	Mike Lansing	.05
113	Pedro Martinez	.75
114	Henry Rodriguez	.05
115	Rondell White	.05
116	Rey Ordonez	.05
117	Carlos Baerga	.05
118	Lance Johnson	.05
119	Bernard Gilkey	.05
120	Todd Hundley	.05
121	John Franco	.05
122	Bernie Williams	.05
123	David Cone	.05
124	Cecil Fielder	.05
125	Derek Jeter	2.00
126	Tino Martinez	.05
127	Mariano Rivera	.15
128	Andy Pettitte	.15
129	Wade Boggs	1.00
130	Mark McGwire	1.50
131	Jose Canseco	.50
132	Geronimo Berroa	.05
133	Jason Giambi	.45
134	Ernie Young	.05
135	Scott Rolen	.65
136	Ricky Bottalico	.05
137	Curt Schilling	.35
138	Gregg Jefferies	.05
139	Mickey Morandini	.05
140	Jason Kendall	.05
141	Kevin Elster	.05
142	Al Martin	.05
143	Joe Randa	.05
144	Jason Schmidt	.05
145	Ray Lankford	.05
146	Brian Jordan	.05
147	Andy Benes	.05
148	Alan Benes	.05
149	Gary Gaetti	.05
150	Ron Gant	.05
151	Dennis Eckersley	.05
152	Rickey Henderson	.75
153	Joey Hamilton	.05
154	Ken Caminiti	.05
155	Tony Gwynn	1.00
156	Steve Finley	.05
157	Trevor Hoffman	.05
158	Greg Vaughn	.05
159	J.T. Snow	.05
160	Barry Bonds	2.00
161	Glenallen Hill	.05
162	William Van Landingham	.05
163	Jeff Kent	.05
164	Jay Buhner	.05
165	Ken Griffey Jr.	1.25
166	Alex Rodriguez	1.50
167	Randy Johnson	.75
168	Edgar Martinez	.05
169	Dan Wilson	.05
170	Ivan Rodriguez	.65
171	Roger Pavlik	.05
172	Will Clark	.05
173	Dean Palmer	.05
174	Rusty Greer	.05
175	Juan Gonzalez	.40
176	John Wetteland	.05
177	Joe Carter	.05
178	Ed Sprague	.05

179	Carlos Delgado	.45
180	Roger Clemens	1.00
181	Juan Guzman	.05
182	Pat Hentgen	.05
183	Ken Griffey Jr. (Checklist)	.65
184	Hideki Irabu RC	.25

Buy-Back Autographed Inserts

To celebrate the fifth anniversary of its premium SP brand, Upper Deck went into the hobby market to buy nearly 3,000 previous years' cards for a special insert program in 1997 SP packs. Various SP cards from 1993-96 issues and inserts were autographed by star players and a numbered holographic seal added on back. The number of each particular card signed ranged widely from fewer than 10 to more than 100. Numbers in parentheses in the checklist are the quantity reported signed for that card. All cards were inserted into foil packs except those of Mo Vaughn, which were a mail-in redemption.

		NM/M
Common Autograph:		7.50
4	Ken Griffey Jr./16	600.00
28	Jeff Bagwell/7	100.00
167	Tony Gwynn/17	250.00
280	Chipper Jones/34	110.00
PP9	Ken Griffey Jr./5	800.00
6	Todd Hollandsworth/167	7.50
15	Alex Rodriguez/94	1,200
105	Ken Griffey Jr./103	125.00
114	Gary Sheffield/130	25.00
130	Tony Gwynn/367	25.00
13	Tony Gwynn/31	150.00
35	Gary Sheffield/4	60.00
34	Chipper Jones/60	125.00
60	Jeff Bagwell/173	40.00
75	Gary Sheffield/221	20.00
105	Tony Gwynn/64	60.00
188	Alex Rodriguez/63	200.00
190	Ken Griffey Jr./38	200.00
195	Jay Buhner/57	15.00
1	Rey Ordonez/111	7.50
18	Gary Sheffield/58	30.00
26	Chipper Jones/102	50.00
40	Mo Vaughn/250	15.00
95	Jeff Bagwell/292	20.00
160	Tony Gwynn/20	200.00
170	Ken Griffey Jr./312	65.00
171	Alex Rodriguez/125	75.00
173	Jay Buhner/79	30.00
MM13	Jeff Bagwell/23	65.00
MM4	Rey Ordonez/40	15.00
8	Jay Buhner/27	30.00

Game Film

A 10-card insert utilizing pieces of actual game footage to highlight the top stars in the game. Only 500 of each card were available. Cards are numbered with a "GF" prefix.

		NM/M
Complete Set (10):		175.00
Common Player:		12.00
1	Alex Rodriguez	25.00
2	Frank Thomas	12.00
3	Andruw Jones	10.00
4	Cal Ripken Jr.	30.00
5	Mike Piazza	15.00
6	Derek Jeter	30.00
7	Mark McGwire	20.00
8	Chipper Jones	15.00
9	Barry Bonds	30.00
10	Ken Griffey Jr.	20.00

Griffey Baseball Heroes

First started in 1990, this single-player insert continues with a salute to Ken Griffey Jr. Each card in the set is numbered to 2,000.

	NM/M
Complete Set (10):	75.00
Common Griffey Jr.:	10.00
91-100 Ken Griffey Jr.	10.00

Inside Info

Each of the 25 cards in this insert feature a pull-out panel describing the player's major accomplishments. Both front and back are printed on metallic-foil stock. Cards were inserted one per box.

		NM/M
Complete Set (25):		75.00
Common Player:		1.00
1	Ken Griffey Jr.	5.00
2	Mark McGwire	6.00
3	Kenny Lofton	1.00
4	Paul Molitor	3.00
5	Frank Thomas	4.00
6	Greg Maddux	3.50
7	Mo Vaughn	1.00
8	Cal Ripken Jr.	7.50
9	Jeff Bagwell	3.00
10	Alex Rodriguez	6.00
11	John Smoltz	1.00
12	Manny Ramirez	3.00
13	Sammy Sosa	3.50
14	Vladimir Guerrero	3.00
15	Albert Belle	4.00
16	Mike Piazza	5.00
17	Derek Jeter	7.50
18	Scott Rolen	2.00
19	Tony Gwynn	3.50
20	Barry Bonds	7.50
21	Ken Caminiti	1.00
22	Chipper Jones	4.00
23	Juan Gonzalez	1.50
24	Roger Clemens	4.00
25	Andruw Jones	3.00

Marquee Matchups

A 20-card die-cut set designed to highlight top interleague matchups, when the matching cards are put together, a third player is highlighted in the background. Cards were inserted 1:5 packs and have an "MM" card-number prefix.

		NM/M
Complete Set (20):		20.00
Common Player:		.25
1	Ken Griffey Jr.	1.50
2	Andres Galarraga	.25
3	Barry Bonds	3.00
4	Mark McGwire	2.00
5	Mike Piazza	1.50
6	Tim Salmon	.25
7	Tony Gwynn	1.00
8	Alex Rodriguez	2.00
9	Chipper Jones	1.00
10	Derek Jeter	3.00
11	Manny Ramirez	.75
12	Jeff Bagwell	.75
13	Greg Maddux	1.00
14	Cal Ripken Jr.	3.00
15	Mo Vaughn	.25
16	Gary Sheffield	.45
17	Jim Thome	.65
18	Barry Larkin	.25
19	Frank Thomas	.75
20	Sammy Sosa	1.00

Special FX

Color 3-D motion portraits are front and center on these cards that also feature a die-cut design. The rest of the front includes color action photos printed on silver-foil stock. Backs have another color photo. One of the Alex Rodriguez cards (#49) features the 1996 die-cut design. Special FX were inserted 1:9 packs.

		NM/M
Common Player:		.75
1	Ken Griffey Jr.	6.00
2	Frank Thomas	3.00
3	Barry Bonds	8.00
4	Albert Belle	.75
5	Mike Piazza	4.00
6	Greg Maddux	5.00
7	Chipper Jones	4.00
8	Cal Ripken Jr.	8.00
9	Jeff Bagwell	2.00
10	Alex Rodriguez	8.00
11	Mark McGwire	5.00
12	Kenny Lofton	.75
13	Juan Gonzalez	1.50
14	Mo Vaughn	.75
15	John Smoltz	1.00
16	Derek Jeter	8.00
17	Tony Gwynn	4.00
18	Ivan Rodriguez	2.00
19	Barry Larkin	1.00
20	Sammy Sosa	3.00
21	Mike Mussina	1.50
22	Gary Sheffield	2.00
23	Brady Anderson	.75
24	Roger Clemens	6.00
25	Ken Caminiti	.75
26	Roberto Alomar	1.50
27	Hideo Nomo	1.00
28	Bernie Williams	1.00
29	Todd Hundley	.75
30	Manny Ramirez	3.00
31	Eric Karros	.75
32	Tim Salmon	.75
33	Jay Buhner	.75
34	Andy Pettitte	1.50
35	Jim Thome	2.00
36	Ryne Sandberg	3.00
37	Matt Williams	1.00
38	Ryan Klesko	.75
39	Jose Canseco	1.50
40	Paul Molitor	2.00
41	Eddie Murray	2.00
42	Darin Erstad	.75
43	Todd Walker	.75
44	Wade Boggs	2.50
45	Andruw Jones	2.00
46	Scott Rolen	2.00
47	Vladimir Guerrero	3.00
49	Alex Rodriguez	
	(1996 design)	8.00

SPx Force

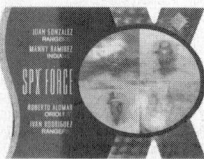

Each of the 10 cards in this set feature four different players. Cards are individually numbered to 500. In addition, a number of players signed 100 versions of their SPx Force cards that are also randomly inserted into packs.

		NM/M
Complete Set (10):		60.00
Common Player:		6.00
1	Ken Griffey Jr., Jay Buhner, Andres Galarraga, Dante Bichette	7.50
2	Albert Belle, Brady Anderson, Mark McGwire, Cecil Fielder	9.00
3	Mo Vaughn, Ken Caminiti, Frank Thomas, Jeff Bagwell	6.00
4	Gary Sheffield, Sammy Sosa, Barry Bonds, Jose Canseco	12.00
5	Greg Maddux, Roger Clemens, John Smoltz, Randy Johnson	6.00
6	Alex Rodriguez, Derek Jeter, Chipper Jones, Rey Ordonez	12.00
7	Todd Hollandsworth, Mike Piazza, Raul Mondesi, Hideo Nomo	7.50
8	Juan Gonzalez, Manny Ramirez, Roberto Alomar, Ivan Rodriguez	6.00
9	Tony Gwynn, Wade Boggs, Eddie Murray, Paul Molitor	6.00
10	Andruw Jones, Vladimir Guerrero, Todd Walker, Scott Rolen	6.00

SPx Force Autographs

Ten players signed cards for this insert, which was serially numbered to 100. The cards were randomly seeded in packs except the Mo Vaughn card which was available by redemption.

		NM/M
Common Player:		20.00
1	Ken Griffey Jr.	125.00
2	Albert Belle	25.00
3	Mo Vaughn	20.00
4	Gary Sheffield	25.00
5	Greg Maddux	100.00
6	Alex Rodriguez	160.00
7	Todd Hollandsworth	20.00
8	Roberto Alomar	30.00
9	Tony Gwynn	75.00
10	Andruw Jones	40.00

1997 SPx

Fifty cards, each featuring a perimeter die-cut design and a 3-D holoview photo, make up the SPx base set. Five different parallel sets - Steel (1:1 pack), Bronze (1:1), Silver (1:1), Gold (1:17) and Grand Finale (50 per card) - are found as inserts, as are Cornerstones of the Game, Bound for Glory and Bound for Glory Signature cards. Packs contain three cards and carried a suggested retail price of $5.99.

		NM/M
Complete Set (50):		20.00
Common Player:		.15
Steel:		1.5X
Bronze:		1.5X
Silver:		1.5X
Gold:		3X
Grand Finale:		4X
Pack (3):		2.00
Wax Box (18):		30.00
1	Eddie Murray	1.00
2	Darin Erstad	.35
3	Tim Salmon	.15
4	Andruw Jones	1.00
5	Chipper Jones	1.50
6	John Smoltz	.15
7	Greg Maddux	1.50
8	Kenny Lofton	.15
9	Roberto Alomar	.30
10	Rafael Palmeiro	.75
11	Brady Anderson	.15
12	Cal Ripken Jr.	3.00
13	Nomar Garciaparra	1.50
14	Mo Vaughn	.15
15	Ryne Sandberg	1.50
16	Sammy Sosa	1.50
17	Frank Thomas	1.00
18	Albert Belle	.15
19	Barry Larkin	.15
20	Deion Sanders	.15
21	Manny Ramirez	1.00
22	Jim Thome	.65
23	Dante Bichette	.15
24	Andres Galarraga	.15
25	Larry Walker	.15
26	Gary Sheffield	.50
27	Jeff Bagwell	1.00
28	Raul Mondesi	.15
29	Hideo Nomo	.50
30	Mike Piazza	2.00
31	Paul Molitor	1.00
32	Todd Walker	.15
33	Vladimir Guerrero	1.00
34	Todd Hundley	.15
35	Andy Pettitte	.25
36	Derek Jeter	3.00
37	Jose Canseco	.50
38	Mark McGwire	2.50
39	Scott Rolen	.65
40	Ron Gant	.15
41	Ken Caminiti	.15
42	Tony Gwynn	1.50
43	Barry Bonds	3.00
44	Jay Buhner	.15
45	Ken Griffey Jr.	2.00
45s	Ken Griffey Jr. (Overprinted "SAMPLE" on back.)	2.00
46	Alex Rodriguez	2.50
47	Jose Cruz Jr. RC	4.00
48	Juan Gonzalez	.50
49	Ivan Rodriguez	.75
50	Roger Clemens	1.75

SPx Bound for Glory

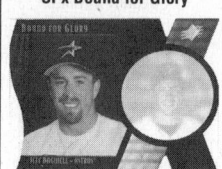

This 20-card insert utilizes holoview technology and is sequentially numbered to 1,500 per card.

		NM/M
Complete Set (20):		60.00
Common Player:		1.00
1	Andruw Jones	3.00
2	Chipper Jones	4.00
3	Greg Maddux	4.00
4	Kenny Lofton	1.00
5	Cal Ripken Jr.	7.50
6	Mo Vaughn	1.00
7	Frank Thomas	3.00
8	Albert Belle	1.00
9	Manny Ramirez	3.00
10	Gary Sheffield	1.50
11	Jeff Bagwell	3.00
12	Mike Piazza	5.00
13	Derek Jeter	7.50
14	Mark McGwire	6.00
15	Tony Gwynn	4.00
16	Ken Caminiti	1.00
17	Barry Bonds	7.50
18	Alex Rodriguez	6.00
19	Ken Griffey Jr.	5.00
20	Juan Gonzalez	1.50

SPx Bound for Glory Supreme Signatures

This five-card set featured autographs from the players and was sequentially numbered to 250.

		NM/M
Complete Set (5):		250.00
Common Player:		30.00

SPx Cornerstones of the Game

A 20-card insert utilizing a double-front design highlighting 40 of the top players in the game. Each card is sequentially numbered to 500.

		NM/M
Complete Set (10):		150.00
Common Player:		12.00
1	Ken Griffey Jr., Barry Bonds	25.00
2	Frank Thomas, Albert Belle	12.00
3	Chipper Jones, Greg Maddux	15.00
4	Tony Gwynn, Paul Molitor	15.00
5	Andruw Jones, Vladimir Guerrero	12.00
6	Jeff Bagwell, Ryne Sandberg	15.00
7	Mike Piazza, Ivan Rodriguez	20.00
8	Cal Ripken Jr., Eddie Murray	25.00
9	Mo Vaughn, Mark McGwire	20.00
10	Alex Rodriguez, Derek Jeter	25.00

1998 SP Authentic Sample

This card of Upper Deck spokesman Ken Griffey, Jr., was issued to preview the new SP Authentic line. Design is similar to the issued version but the sample displays different photos, a different the card number and the word "SAMPLE" printed in large letters on back.

	NM/M
Ken Griffey Jr.	3.00

1998 SP Authentic

The SP Authentic base set consists of 198 cards, including the 30-card Future Watch subset and one checklist card. The base cards have a color photo inside a thick white border. Inserts include Chirography, Sheer Dominance and SP Authentics.

		NM/M
Complete Set (198):		15.00
Common Player:		.05
Pack (5):		2.00
Wax Box (24):		35.00
1	Travis Lee (Future Watch)	.10

(Right-hand column, SP Authentic Sample/prices)

1	Jeff Bagwell	40.00
2	Ken Griffey Jr.	120.00
3	Andruw Jones	40.00
4	Alex Rodriguez	160.00
5	Gary Sheffield	30.00

#	Player	Price
2	Mike Caruso (Future Watch)	.05
3	Kerry Wood (Future Watch)	.65
4	Mark Kotsay (Future Watch)	.05
5	Magglio Ordonez RC (Future Watch)	5.00
6	Scott Elarton (Future Watch)	.05
7	Carl Pavano (Future Watch)	.10
8	A.J. Hinch (Future Watch)	.05
9	Rolando Arrojo RC (Future Watch)	.40
10	Ben Grieve (Future Watch)	.05
11	Gabe Alvarez (Future Watch)	.05
12	Mike Kinkade RC (Future Watch)	.40
13	Bruce Chen (Future Watch)	.05
14	Juan Encarnacion (Future Watch)	.05
15	Todd Helton (Future Watch)	.75
16	Aaron Boone (Future Watch)	.05
17	Sean Casey (Future Watch)	.15
18	Ramon Hernandez (Future Watch)	.05
19	Daryle Ward (Future Watch)	.05
20	Paul Konerko (Future Watch)	.15
21	David Ortiz (Future Watch)	.50
22	Derrek Lee (Future Watch)	.50
23	Brad Fullmer (Future Watch)	.05
24	Javier Vazquez (Future Watch)	.05
25	Miguel Tejada (Future Watch)	.15
26	David Dellucci (Future Watch)	.05
27	Alex Gonzalez (Future Watch)	.05
28	Matt Clement (Future Watch)	.05
29	Eric Milton (Future Watch)	.05
30	Russell Branyan (Future Watch)	.05
31	Chuck Finley	.05
32	Jim Edmonds	.05
33	Darin Erstad	.20
34	Jason Dickson	.05
35	Tim Salmon	.05
36	Cecil Fielder	.05
37	Todd Greene	.05
38	Andy Benes	.05
39	Jay Bell	.05
40	Matt Williams	.05
41	Brian Anderson	.05
42	Karim Garcia	.05
43	Javy Lopez	.05
44	Tom Glavine	.35
45	Greg Maddux	1.50
46	Andruw Jones	1.00
47	Chipper Jones	1.50
48	Ryan Klesko	.05
49	John Smoltz	.05
50	Andres Galarraga	.05
51	Rafael Palmeiro	.75
52	Mike Mussina	.30
53	Roberto Alomar	.20
54	Joe Carter	.05
55	Cal Ripken Jr.	3.00
56	Brady Anderson	.05
57	Mo Vaughn	.05
58	John Valentin	.05
59	Dennis Eckersley	.75
60	Nomar Garciaparra	1.50
61	Pedro J. Martinez	1.00
62	Jeff Blauser	.05
63	Kevin Orie	.05
64	Henry Rodriguez	.05
65	Mark Grace	.05
66	Albert Belle	.05
67	Mike Cameron	.05
68	Robin Ventura	.05
69	Frank Thomas	1.00
70	Barry Larkin	.05
71	Brett Tomko	.05
72	Willie Greene	.05
73	Reggie Sanders	.05
74	Sandy Alomar Jr.	.05
75	Kenny Lofton	.05
76	Jaret Wright	.05
77	David Justice	.05
78	Omar Vizquel	.05
79	Manny Ramirez	1.00
80	Jim Thome	.75
81	Travis Fryman	.05
82	Neifi Perez	.05
83	Mike Lansing	.05
84	Vinny Castilla	.05
85	Larry Walker	.05
86	Dante Bichette	.05
87	Darryl Kile	.05
88	Justin Thompson	.05
89	Damion Easley	.05
90	Tony Clark	.05
91	Bobby Higginson	.05
92	Brian L. Hunter	.05
93	Edgar Renteria	.05
94	Craig Counsell	.05
95	Mike Piazza	2.00

#	Player	Price
96	Livan Hernandez	.05
97	Todd Zeile	.05
98	Richard Hidalgo	.05
99	Moises Alou	.05
100	Jeff Bagwell	1.00
101	Mike Hampton	.05
102	Craig Biggio	.05
103	Dean Palmer	.05
104	Tim Belcher	.05
105	Jeff King	.05
106	Jeff Conine	.05
107	Johnny Damon	.30
108	Hideo Nomo	.50
109	Raul Mondesi	.05
110	Gary Sheffield	.45
111	Ramon Martinez	.05
112	Chan Ho Park	.05
113	Eric Young	.05
114	Charles Johnson	.05
115	Eric Karros	.05
116	Bobby Bonilla	.05
117	Jeromy Burnitz	.05
118	Carl Eldred	.05
119	Jeff D'Amico	.05
120	Marquis Grissom	.05
121	Dave Nilsson	.05
122	Brad Radke	.05
123	Marty Cordova	.05
124	Ron Coomer	.05
125	Paul Molitor	1.00
126	Todd Walker	.05
127	Rondell White	.05
128	Mark Grudzielanek	.05
129	Carlos Perez	.05
130	Vladimir Guerrero	1.00
131	Dustin Hermanson	.05
132	Butch Huskey	.05
133	John Franco	.05
134	Rey Ordonez	.05
135	Todd Hundley	.05
136	Edgardo Alfonzo	.05
137	Bobby Jones	.05
138	John Olerud	.05
139	Chili Davis	.05
140	Tino Martinez	.05
141	Andy Pettitte	.15
142	Chuck Knoblauch	.05
143	Bernie Williams	.05
144	David Cone	.05
145	Derek Jeter	3.00
146	Paul O'Neill	.05
147	Rickey Henderson	1.00
148	Jason Giambi	.50
149	Kenny Rogers	.05
150	Scott Brosius	.75
151	Curt Schilling	.35
152	Ricky Bottalico	.05
153	Mike Lieberthal	.05
154	Francisco Cordova	.05
155	Jose Guillen	.05
156	Jason Schmidt	.05
157	Jason Kendall	.05
158	Kevin Young	.05
159	Delino DeShields	.05
160	Mark McGwire	2.50
161	Ray Lankford	.05
162	Brian Jordan	.05
163	Ron Gant	.05
164	Todd Stottlemyre	.05
165	Ken Caminiti	.05
166	Kevin Brown	.05
167	Trevor Hoffman	.05
168	Steve Finley	.05
169	Wally Joyner	.05
170	Tony Gwynn	1.50
171	Shawn Estes	.05
172	J.T. Snow	.05
173	Jeff Kent	.05
174	Robb Nen	.05
175	Barry Bonds	3.00
176	Randy Johnson	1.00
177	Edgar Martinez	.05
178	Jay Buhner	.05
179	Alex Rodriguez	2.50
180	Ken Griffey Jr.	2.00
181	Ken Cloude	.05
182	Wade Boggs	1.50
183	Tony Saunders	.05
184	Wilson Alvarez	.05
185	Fred McGriff	.05
186	Roberto Hernandez	.05
187	Kevin Stocker	.05
188	Fernando Tatis	.05
189	Will Clark	.05
190	Juan Gonzalez	.50
191	Rusty Greer	.05
192	Ivan Rodriguez	.75
193	Jose Canseco	.45
194	Carlos Delgado	.50
195	Roger Clemens	1.75
196	Pat Hentgen	.05
197	Randy Myers	.05
198	Checklist (Ken Griffey Jr.)	.85

Chirography

Chirography insert are seeded one per 25 packs. The featured player signed his cards in the white border at the bottom.

		NM/M
Common Card:		4.00
Inserted 1:25		
RA	Roberto Alomar	15.00
RB	Russell Branyan	4.00
SC	Sean Casey	10.00
TC	Tony Clark	5.00
RC	Roger Clemens/SP/400	80.00

JC	Jose Cruz Jr.	4.00
DE	Darin Erstad	7.50
NG	Nomar Garciaparra/SP/400	30.00
BG	Ben Grieve	4.00
KG	Ken Griffey Jr./SP/400	60.00
VG	Vladimir Guerrero	30.00
TG	Tony Gwynn/SP/850	30.00
TH	Todd Helton	15.00
LH	Livan Hernandez	6.00
CJ	Charles Johnson	6.00
AJ	Andruw Jones	17.50
CHIP	Chipper Jones/SP/800	40.00
PK	Paul Konerko	15.00
MK	Mark Kotsay	6.00
KG	Ray Lankford	6.00
TL	Travis Lee	6.00
PM	Paul Molitor/SP/800	20.00
MM	Mike Mussina	20.00
AR	Alex Rodriguez/SP/800	80.00
IR	Ivan Rodriguez	30.00
SR	Scott Rolen	20.00
GS	Gary Sheffield	15.00
MT	Miguel Tejada	20.00
JW	Jaret Wright	6.00
MV	Mo Vaughn/SP/800	12.50

Ken Griffey Jr. 300th HR Redemption

This 5" x 7" version of Ken Griffey Jr.'s SP Authentic card was issued as a redemption for one of the 1000 Trade Cards which were foil-pack inserts.

		NM/M
KG300	Ken Griffey Jr.	30.00

Jersey Swatch

These 5" x 7" redemption cards were issued in exchange for Trade Cards found as random foil-packs inserts. Fronts have a player action photo on a white background. Backs have a congratulatory message of authenticity. Sandwiched between is a swatch of that player's uniform jersey. The large-format jersey cards were available in limited editions which are listed in parentheses, though all might not have been redeemed prior to the August 1, 1999, cut-off date.

		NM/M
Complete Set (6):		130.00
Common Player:		7.50
(1)	Jay Buhner/125	7.50
(2)	Ken Griffey Jr./125	50.00
(3)	Tony Gwynn/415	10.00
(4)	Greg Maddux/125	30.00
(5)	Alex Rodriguez/125	60.00
(6)	Gary Sheffield/125	12.00

Trade Cards

Cards which could be traded (prior to the Aug. 1, 1999 cut-off) for special cards and autographed memorabilia were inserted into SP Authentic foil packs at an announced rate of one per 291 packs. Trade cards have a white background on front with a color player action photo and the name of the

redemption item. Backs gives details for redemption. In some cases, because of their insertion-rate rarity, the cards are worth more than the redemption items. The un-numbered cards are listed here alphabetically.

		NM/M
Common Card:		5.00
(1)	Roberto Alomar/ Auto. Ball/100	15.00
(2)	Albert Belle/ Auto. Ball/100	7.50
(3)	Jay Buhner/ Jersey Card 125	5.00
(4)	Ken Griffey Jr./ Auto. Glv/30	200.00
(5)	Ken Griffey Jr./ Auto. Jsy/30	200.00
(6)	Ken Griffey Jr./ Jsy Card 125	25.00
(7)	Ken Griffey Jr./ Standee/200	15.00
(8)	Ken Griffey Jr./ 300th HR Card 1000	5.00
(9)	Tony Gwynn/ Jsy Card 415	5.00
(10)	Brian Jordan/ Auto. Ball/50	10.00
(11)	Greg Maddux/ Jsy Card/125	20.00
(12)	Raul Mondesi/ Auto. Ball/100	5.00
(13)	Alex Rodriguez/ Jsy Card/125	40.00
(14)	Gary Sheffield/ Jsy Card/125	5.00
(15)	Robin Ventura/ Auto. Ball/50	10.00

Sheer Dominance

Sheer Dominance is a 42-card insert. The base set is inserted one per three packs. The Sheer Dominance Gold parallel is sequentially numbered to 2,000 and the Titanium parallel is numbered to 100. The cards feature a player photo inside a white border. The background color corresponds to the level of the insert.

	NM/M
Complete Set (42):	32.50
Common Player:	.25
Inserted 1:3	
Gold (2,000 Sets):	2X
Titanium (100 Sets):	12X
SD1 Ken Griffey Jr.	1.75
SD2 Rickey Henderson	1.00
SD3 Jaret Wright	.25
SD4 Craig Biggio	.25
SD5 Travis Lee	.25
SD6 Kenny Lofton	.25
SD7 Raul Mondesi	.25
SD8 Cal Ripken Jr.	2.50
SD9 Matt Williams	.25
SD10 Mark McGwire	2.00
SD11 Alex Rodriguez	2.00
SD12 Fred McGriff	.25
SD13 Scott Rolen	.75
SD14 Paul Molitor	1.00
SD15 Nomar Garciaparra	1.50
SD16 Vladimir Guerrero	1.00
SD17 Andruw Jones	1.00
SD18 Manny Ramirez	1.00
SD19 Tony Gwynn	1.50
SD20 Barry Bonds	2.50
SD21 Ben Grieve	.25
SD22 Ivan Rodriguez	.75
SD23 Jose Cruz Jr.	.25
SD24 Pedro J. Martinez	1.00
SD25 Chipper Jones	1.50
SD26 Albert Belle	.25
SD27 Todd Helton	.75
SD28 Paul Konerko	.35
SD29 Sammy Sosa	1.50
SD30 Frank Thomas	1.50
SD31 Greg Maddux	1.50
SD32 Randy Johnson	.75
SD33 Larry Walker	.25
SD34 Roberto Alomar	.45
SD35 Roger Clemens	1.50
SD36 Mo Vaughn	.25
SD37 Jim Thome	.75
SD38 Jeff Bagwell	1.00
SD39 Tino Martinez	.25
SD40 Mike Piazza	1.75
SD41 Derek Jeter	2.50
SD42 Juan Gonzalez	.50

Sheer Dominance Gold

Identical in format and using the same photos as the Silver version, the scarcer Sheer Dominance Gold card differs on front in its use of a gold-metallic foil background within the white border. Backs of the gold version are individually serial numbered within an edition of 2,000 each.

	NM/M
Common Player:	.50
Gold Stars:	2X

Sheer Dominance Titanium

Sheer Dominance Titanium is a parallel of the 42-card Sheer Dominance insert. The cards are numbered to 100 and have a gray background with "Titanium" printed across it.

	NM/M
Common Player:	4.00
Titanium Stars:	12X

1998 SPx Finite Sample

This card was issued to promote SPx's all-numbered Finite issue. The serial number on the card's back is "0000/0000." The card is overprinted "SAMPLE" on back.

		NM/M
1	Ken Griffey Jr.	3.00

1998 SPx Finite

SPx Finite is an all-sequentially numbered set issued in two 180-card series. The Series 1 base set consists of five subsets: 90 regular cards (numbered to 9,000), 30 Star Focus (7,000), 30 Youth Movement (5,000), 20 Power Explosion (4,000) and 10 Heroes of the Game (2,000). The set is paralleled in the Radiance and Spectrum sets. Radiance regular cards are numbered to 4,500, Star Focus to 3,500, Youth Movement to 2,500, Power Explosion to 1,000 and Heroes of the Game to 100. Spectrum regular cards are numbered to 2,250, Star Focus to 1,750, Youth Movement to 1,250, Power Explosion to 50 and Heroes of the Game to 1. The Series 2 base set has 90 regular cards (numbered to 9,000), 30 Power Passion (7,000), 30 Youth Movement (5,000), 20 Tradewinds (4,000) and 10 Cornerstones of the Game (2,000). Series 2 also has Radiance and Spectrum parallels. Radiance regular cards are numbered to 4,500, Power Passion to 3,500, Youth Movement to 2,500, Tradewinds to 1,000 and Cornerstones of the Game to 100. Spectrum regular cards are numbered to 2,250, Power Passion to 1,750, Youth Movement to 1,250, Tradewinds to 50 and Cornerstones of the Game to 1. The 1-of-1 cards are not valued due to scarcity and fluctuating demand. The only insert is Home Run Hysteria.

	NM/M
Complete Set (360):	200.00

	Player	Price
	Common Youth Movement: (#1-30, 181-210):	.50
	Radiance YM (2,500):	1.5X
	Spectrum YM (1,250):	2X
	Common Power Explosion: (#31-50):	.50
	Radiance PE (1,000):	2X
	Spectrum PE (50):	25X
	Common Base Card (#51-140, 241-330):	.15
	Radiance Base Card (4,500):	1X
	Spectrum Base Card (2,250):	2X
	Common Star Focus: (#141-170):	.35
	Radiance SF (3,500):	1X
	Spectrum SF (1,750):	2X
	Common Heroes of the Game: (#171-180):	2.50
	Radiance HG (100):	15X
	Common Power Passion: (#211-240):	.50
	Radiance PP (3,500):	1X
	Spectrum PP (1,750):	2X
	Common Tradewinds: (#331-350):	.75
	Radiance TW (1,000):	2X
	Spectrum TW (50):	25X
	Common Cornerstones/Game: (#351-360):	2.50
	Radiance CG (100):	15X
	Pack (3):	2.00
	Wax Box:	25.00
1	Nomar Garciaparra (Youth Movement)	3.00
2	Miguel Tejada (Youth Movement)	.75
3	Mike Cameron (Youth Movement)	.50
4	Ken Cloude (Youth Movement)	.50
5	Jaret Wright (Youth Movement)	.50
6	Mark Kotsay (Youth Movement)	.50
7	Craig Counsell (Youth Movement)	.50
8	Jose Guillen (Youth Movement)	.50
9	Neifi Perez (Youth Movement)	.50
10	Jose Cruz Jr. (Youth Movement)	.50
11	Brett Tomko (Youth Movement)	.50
12	Matt Morris (Youth Movement)	.50
13	Justin Thompson (Youth Movement)	.50
14	Jeremi Gonzalez (Youth Movement)	.50
15	Scott Rolen (Youth Movement)	1.50
16	Vladimir Guerrero (Youth Movement)	2.00
17	Brad Fullmer (Youth Movement)	.50
18	Brian Giles (Youth Movement)	.50
19	Todd Dunwoody (Youth Movement)	.50
20	Ben Grieve (Youth Movement)	.50
21	Juan Encarnacion (Youth Movement)	.50
22	Aaron Boone (Youth Movement)	.50
23	Richie Sexson (Youth Movement)	.50
24	Richard Hidalgo (Youth Movement)	.50
25	Andruw Jones (Youth Movement)	2.00
26	Todd Helton (Youth Movement)	1.50
27	Paul Konerko (Youth Movement)	.75
28	Dante Powell (Youth Movement)	.50
29	Elieser Marrero (Youth Movement)	.50
30	Derek Jeter (Youth Movement)	5.00
31	Mike Piazza (Power Explosion)	3.00
32	Tony Clark (Power Explosion)	.50
33	Larry Walker (Power Explosion)	.50
34	Jim Thome (Power Explosion)	1.50
35	Juan Gonzalez (Power Explosion)	1.00
36	Jeff Bagwell (Power Explosion)	2.00
37	Jay Buhner (Power Explosion)	.50
38	Tim Salmon (Power Explosion)	.50
39	Albert Belle (Power Explosion)	.50
40	Mark McGwire (Power Explosion)	4.00
41	Sammy Sosa (Power Explosion)	2.50
42	Mo Vaughn (Power Explosion)	.50
43	Manny Ramirez (Power Explosion)	2.00

44 Tino Martinez (Power Explosion) .50
45 Frank Thomas (Power Explosion) 2.00
46 Nomar Garciaparra (Power Explosion) 2.50
47 Alex Rodriguez (Power Explosion) 4.00
48 Chipper Jones (Power Explosion) 2.50
49 Barry Bonds (Power Explosion) 5.00
50 Ken Griffey Jr. (Power Explosion) 3.00
51 Jason Dickson .15
52 Jim Edmonds .15
53 Darin Erstad .35
54 Tim Salmon .15
55 Chipper Jones 2.00
56 Ryan Klesko .15
57 Tom Glavine .35
58 Denny Neagle .15
59 John Smoltz .15
60 Javy Lopez .15
61 Roberto Alomar .30
62 Rafael Palmeiro 1.25
63 Mike Mussina .35
64 Cal Ripken Jr. 4.00
65 Mo Vaughn .15
66 Tim Naehring .15
67 John Valentin .15
68 Mark Grace .15
69 Kevin Orie .15
70 Sammy Sosa 2.50
71 Albert Belle .15
72 Frank Thomas 1.50
73 Robin Ventura .15
74 David Justice .15
75 Kenny Lofton .15
76 Omar Vizquel .15
77 Manny Ramirez 1.50
78 Jim Thome .65
79 Dante Bichette .15
80 Larry Walker .15
81 Vinny Castilla .15
82 Ellis Burks .15
83 Bobby Higginson .15
84 Brian L. Hunter .15
85 Tony Clark .15
86 Mike Hampton .15
87 Jeff Bagwell 1.50
88 Craig Biggio .15
89 Derek Bell .15
90 Mike Piazza 3.00
91 Ramon Martinez .15
92 Raul Mondesi .15
93 Hideo Nomo .75
94 Eric Karros .15
95 Paul Molitor 1.50
96 Marty Cordova .15
97 Brad Radke .15
98 Mark Grudzielanek .15
99 Carlos Perez .15
100 Rondell White .15
101 Todd Hundley .15
102 Edgardo Alfonzo .15
103 John Franco .15
104 John Olerud .15
105 Tino Martinez .15
106 David Cone .15
107 Paul O'Neill .25
108 Andy Pettitte .15
109 Bernie Williams .15
110 Rickey Henderson 1.50
111 Jason Giambi .75
112 Matt Stairs .15
113 Gregg Jefferies .15
114 Rico Brogna .15
115 Curt Schilling .35
116 Jason Schmidt .15
117 Jose Guillen .15
118 Kevin Young .15
119 Ray Lankford .15
120 Mark McGwire 3.00
121 Delino DeShields .15
122 Ken Caminiti .15
123 Tony Gwynn 2.00
124 Trevor Hoffman .15
125 Barry Bonds 4.00
126 Jeff Kent .15
127 Shawn Estes .15
128 J.T. Snow .15
129 Jay Buhner .15
130 Ken Griffey Jr. 2.50
131 Dan Wilson .15
132 Edgar Martinez .15
133 Alex Rodriguez 3.00
134 Rusty Greer .15
135 Juan Gonzalez .75
136 Fernando Tatis .15
137 Ivan Rodriguez 1.00
138 Carlos Delgado .75
139 Pat Hentgen .15
140 Roger Clemens 2.25
141 Chipper Jones (Star Focus) 2.00
142 Greg Maddux (Star Focus) 2.00
143 Rafael Palmeiro (Star Focus) 1.25
144 Mike Mussina (Star Focus) .65
145 Cal Ripken Jr. (Star Focus) 4.00
146 Nomar Garciaparra (Star Focus) 2.00
147 Mo Vaughn (Star Focus) .35
148 Sammy Sosa (Star Focus) 2.00
149 Albert Belle (Star Focus) .35
150 Frank Thomas (Star Focus) 2.00
151 Jim Thome (Star Focus) 1.25
152 Kenny Lofton (Star Focus) .35
153 Manny Ramirez (Star Focus) 1.50
154 Larry Walker (Star Focus) .35
155 Jeff Bagwell (Star Focus) 1.50
156 Craig Biggio (Star Focus) .35
157 Mike Piazza (Star Focus) 2.50
158 Paul Molitor (Star Focus) 1.50
159 Derek Jeter (Star Focus) 4.00
160 Tino Martinez (Star Focus) .35
161 Curt Schilling (Star Focus) .50
162 Mark McGwire (Star Focus) 3.00
163 Tony Gwynn (Star Focus) 2.00
164 Barry Bonds (Star Focus) 4.00
165 Ken Griffey Jr. (Star Focus) 2.50
166 Randy Johnson (Star Focus) 1.50
167 Alex Rodriguez (Star Focus) 3.00
168 Juan Gonzalez (Star Focus) .75
169 Ivan Rodriguez (Star Focus) 1.25
170 Roger Clemens (Star Focus) 2.25
171 Greg Maddux (Heroes of the Game) 3.00
172 Cal Ripken Jr. (Heroes of the Game) 6.50
173 Frank Thomas (Heroes of the Game) 2.00
174 Jeff Bagwell (Heroes of the Game) 2.00
175 Mike Piazza (Heroes of the Game) 4.00
176 Mark McGwire (Heroes of the Game) 5.00
177 Barry Bonds (Heroes of the Game) 6.50
178 Ken Griffey Jr. (Heroes of the Game) 4.00
179 Alex Rodriguez (Heroes of the Game) 5.00
180 Roger Clemens (Heroes of the Game) 3.25
181 Mike Caruso (Youth Movement) .50
182 David Ortiz (Youth Movement) 1.00
183 Gabe Alvarez (Youth Movement) .50
184 Gary Matthews Jr. (Youth Movement) .50
185 Kerry Wood (Youth Movement) 1.25
186 Carl Pavano (Youth Movement) .50
187 Alex Gonzalez (Youth Movement) .50
188 Masato Yoshii (Youth Movement) .50
189 Larry Sutton (Youth Movement) .50
190 Russell Branyan (Youth Movement) .50
191 Bruce Chen (Youth Movement) .50
192 Rolando Arrojo (Youth Movement) .50
193 Ryan Christenson (Youth Movement) .50
194 Cliff Politte (Youth Movement) .50
195 A.J. Hinch (Youth Movement) .50
196 Kevin Witt (Youth Movement) .50
197 Daryle Ward (Youth Movement) .50
198 Corey Koskie (Youth Movement) .50
199 Mike Lowell RC (Youth Movement) 3.00
200 Travis Lee (Youth Movement) .50
201 Kevin Millwood RC (Youth Movement) .50
202 Robert Smith (Youth Movement) .50
203 Magglio Ordonez RC (Youth Movement) 10.00
204 Eric Milton (Youth Movement) .50
205 Geoff Jenkins (Youth Movement) .50
206 Rich Butler (Youth Movement) .50
207 Mike Kinkade RC (Youth Movement) .75
208 Braden Looper (Youth Movement) .50
209 Matt Clement (Youth Movement) .50
210 Derrek Lee (Youth Movement) 1.50
211 Randy Johnson (Power Passion) 1.50
212 John Smoltz (Power Passion) .50
213 Roger Clemens (Power Passion) 2.25
214 Curt Schilling (Power Passion) .75
215 Pedro J. Martinez (Power Passion) 1.50
216 Vinny Castilla (Power Passion) .50
217 Jose Cruz Jr. (Power Passion) .50
218 Jim Thome (Power Passion) 1.20
219 Alex Rodriguez (Power Passion) 3.00
220 Frank Thomas (Power Passion) 1.50
221 Tim Salmon (Power Passion) .50
222 Larry Walker (Power Passion) .50
223 Albert Belle (Power Passion) .50
224 Manny Ramirez (Power Passion) 1.50
225 Mark McGwire (Power Passion) 3.00
226 Mo Vaughn (Power Passion) .50
227 Andres Galarraga (Power Passion) .50
228 Scott Rolen (Power Passion) 1.25
229 Travis Lee (Power Passion) .50
230 Mike Piazza (Power Passion) 2.50
231 Nomar Garciaparra (Power Passion) 2.50
232 Andruw Jones (Power Passion) 1.50
233 Barry Bonds (Power Passion) 4.00
234 Jeff Bagwell (Power Passion) 1.50
235 Juan Gonzalez (Power Passion) .75
236 Tino Martinez (Power Passion) .50
237 Vladimir Guerrero (Power Passion) 1.50
238 Rafael Palmeiro (Power Passion) 1.25
239 Russell Branyan (Power Passion) .50
240 Ken Griffey Jr. (Power Passion) 2.50
241 Cecil Fielder .15
242 Chuck Finley .15
243 Jay Bell .15
244 Andy Benes .15
245 Matt Williams .15
246 Brian Anderson .15
247 David Dellucci .15
248 Andres Galarraga .15
249 Andruw Jones 1.50
250 Greg Maddux 2.00
251 Brady Anderson .15
252 Joe Carter .15
253 Eric Davis .15
254 Pedro J. Martinez 1.50
255 Nomar Garciaparra 2.00
256 Dennis Eckersley 1.25
257 Henry Rodriguez .15
258 Jeff Blauser .15
259 Jaime Navarro .15
260 Ray Durham .15
261 Chris Stynes .15
262 Willie Greene .15
263 Reggie Sanders .15
264 Bret Boone .15
265 Barry Larkin .15
266 Travis Fryman .15
267 Charles Nagy .15
268 Sandy Alomar Jr. .15
269 Darryl Kile .15
270 Mike Lansing .15
271 Pedro Astacio .15
272 Damion Easley .15
273 Joe Randa .15
274 Luis Gonzalez .15
275 Mike Piazza 2.50
276 Todd Zeile .15
277 Edgar Renteria .15
278 Livan Hernandez .15
279 Cliff Floyd .15
280 Moises Alou .15
281 Billy Wagner .15
282 Jeff King .15
283 Hal Morris .15
284 Johnny Damon .35
285 Dean Palmer .15
286 Tim Belcher .15
287 Eric Young .15
288 Bobby Bonilla .15
289 Gary Sheffield .60
290 Chan Ho Park .15
291 Charles Johnson .15
292 Jeff Cirillo .15
293 Jeromy Burnitz .15
294 Jose Valentin .15
295 Marquis Grissom .15
296 Todd Walker .15
297 Terry Steinbach .15
298 Rick Aguilera .15
299 Vladimir Guerrero 1.50
300 Rey Ordonez .15
301 Butch Huskey .15
302 Bernard Gilkey .15
303 Mariano Rivera .25
304 Chuck Knoblauch .15
305 Derek Jeter 4.00
306 Ricky Bottalico .15
307 Bob Abreu .15
308 Scott Rolen 1.25
309 Al Martin .15
310 Jason Kendall .15
311 Brian Jordan .15
312 Ron Gant .15
313 Todd Stottlemyre .15
314 Greg Vaughn .15
315 J. Kevin Brown .15
316 Wally Joyner .15
317 Robb Nen .15
318 Orel Hershiser .15
319 Russ Davis .15
320 Randy Johnson 1.50
321 Quinton McCracken .15
322 Tony Saunders .15
323 Wilson Alvarez .15
324 Wade Boggs 2.00
325 Fred McGriff .15
326 Lee Stevens .15
327 John Wetteland .15
328 Jose Canseco .60
329 Randy Myers .15
330 Jose Cruz Jr. .15
331 Matt Williams (Tradewinds) .50
332 Andres Galarraga (Tradewinds) .50
333 Walt Weiss (Tradewinds) .50
334 Joe Carter (Tradewinds) .50
335 Pedro J. Martinez (Tradewinds) 2.00
336 Henry Rodriguez (Tradewinds) .50
337 Travis Fryman (Tradewinds) .50
338 Darryl Kile (Tradewinds) .50
339 Mike Lansing (Tradewinds) .50
340 Mike Piazza (Tradewinds) 4.00
341 Moises Alou (Tradewinds) .50
342 Charles Johnson (Tradewinds) .50
343 Chuck Knoblauch (Tradewinds) .50
344 Rickey Henderson (Tradewinds) 2.00
345 J. Kevin Brown (Tradewinds) .50
346 Orel Hershiser (Tradewinds) .50
347 Wade Boggs (Tradewinds) 3.00
348 Fred McGriff (Tradewinds) .50
349 Jose Canseco (Tradewinds) 1.00
350 Gary Sheffield (Tradewinds) 1.00
351 Travis Lee (Cornerstones) 2.50
352 Nomar Garciaparra (Cornerstones) 5.00
353 Frank Thomas (Cornerstones) 4.00
354 Cal Ripken Jr. (Cornerstones) 10.00
355 Mark McGwire (Cornerstones) 8.00
356 Mike Piazza (Cornerstones) 6.00
357 Alex Rodriguez (Cornerstones) 8.00
358 Barry Bonds (Cornerstones) 10.00
359 Tony Gwynn (Cornerstones) 5.00
360 Ken Griffey Jr. (Cornerstones) 6.00

Home Run Hysteria

Home Run Hysteria is a 10-card insert in SPx Finite Series Two. The cards were sequentially numbered to 62.

	NM/M
Complete Set (10):	400.00
Common Player:	15.00
Production 62 Sets	
HR1 Ken Griffey Jr.	75.00
HR2 Mark McGwire	100.00
HR3 Sammy Sosa	60.00
HR4 Albert Belle	15.00
HR5 Alex Rodriguez	100.00
HR6 Greg Vaughn	15.00
HR7 Andres Galarraga	15.00
HR8 Vinny Castilla	15.00
HR9 Juan Gonzalez	25.00
HR10 Chipper Jones	60.00

1999 SP Authentic Sample

UD spokesman Ken Griffey Jr. is featured on the promo card for '99 SP Authentic. In the same format as the issued version, the sample card has different photos on front and back, a different season summary on back and a large, black "SAMPLE" overprint on back.

		NM/M
1	Ken Griffey Jr.	3.00

1999 SP Authentic

SP Authentic was a 135-card set that sold in packs of five cards for $4.99. The set includes a 30-card Future Watch subset and a 15-card Season to Remember subset. Both subsets were shorted-printed, with each card sequentially numbered to 2,700. The insert lineup included Ernie Banks 500 Club "Piece of History" bat cards. Other insert sets included SP Chirography, The Home Run Chronicles, Epic Figures, Reflections, and SP Authentics.

	NM/M
Complete Set (135):	100.00
Common Player (1-90):	.10
Common Future Watch (91-120):	2.00
Production: (2,700)	
Common Season to Remember (121-135):	2.00
Production: (2,700)	
Pack (5):	3.50
Wax Box (75):	75.00

1 Mo Vaughn .10
2 Jim Edmonds .10
3 Darin Erstad .25
4 Travis Lee .10
5 Matt Williams .10
6 Randy Johnson 1.50
7 Chipper Jones 1.75
8 Greg Maddux 1.75
9 Andruw Jones .75
10 Andres Galarraga .10
11 Tom Glavine .35
12 Cal Ripken Jr. 3.00
13 Brady Anderson .10
14 Albert Belle .10
15 Nomar Garciaparra 1.75
16 Donnie Sadler .10
17 Pedro Martinez 1.50
18 Sammy Sosa 1.75
19 Kerry Wood .60
20 Mark Grace .15
21 Mike Caruso .10
22 Frank Thomas 1.50
23 Paul Konerko .20
24 Sean Casey .15
25 Barry Larkin .10
26 Kenny Lofton .15
27 Manny Ramirez 1.50
28 Jim Thome 1.25
29 Bartolo Colon .10
30 Jaret Wright .10
31 Larry Walker .10
32 Todd Helton 1.25
33 Tony Clark .10
34 Dean Palmer .10
35 Mark Kotsay .10
36 Cliff Floyd .10
37 Ken Caminiti .10
38 Craig Biggio .15
39 Jeff Bagwell 1.50
40 Moises Alou .10
41 Johnny Damon .35
42 Larry Sutton .10
43 Kevin Brown .10
44 Gary Sheffield .40
45 Raul Mondesi .10
46 Jeromy Burnitz .10
47 Jeff Cirillo .10
48 Todd Walker .10
49 David Ortiz .50
50 Brad Radtke .10
51 Vladimir Guerrero 1.50
52 Rondell White .10
53 Brad Fullmer .10
54 Mike Piazza 2.00
55 Robin Ventura .10
56 John Olerud .10
57 Derek Jeter 3.00
58 Tino Martinez .10
59 Bernie Williams .10
60 Roger Clemens 1.75
61 Ben Grieve .10
62 Miguel Tejada .20
63 A.J. Hinch .10
64 Scott Rolen 1.00
65 Curt Schilling .35
66 Doug Glanville .10
67 Aramis Ramirez .10
68 Tony Womack .10
69 Jason Kendall .10
70 Tony Gwynn 1.75
71 Wally Joyner .10
72 Greg Vaughn .10
73 Barry Bonds 3.00
74 Ellis Burks .10
75 Jeff Kent .10
76 Ken Griffey Jr. 2.00
77 Alex Rodriguez 2.50
78 Edgar Martinez .10
79 Mark McGwire 2.50
80 Eli Marrero .10
81 Matt Morris .10
82 Rolando Arrojo .10
83 Quinton McCracken .10
84 Jose Canseco .50
85 Ivan Rodriguez 1.25
86 Juan Gonzalez .75
87 Royce Clayton .10
88 Shawn Green .30
89 Jose Cruz Jr. .10
90 Carlos Delgado .60
91 Troy Glaus/Future Watch 6.00
92 George Lombard/Future Watch 2.00
93 Ryan Minor/Future Watch 2.00
94 Calvin Pickering/Future Watch 2.00
95 Jin Ho Cho (Future Watch) 2.00
96 Russ Branyan (Future Watch) 2.00
97 Derrick Gibson (Future Watch) 2.00
98 Gabe Kapler (Future Watch) 2.00
99 Matt Anderson (Future Watch) 2.00
100 Preston Wilson (Future Watch) 2.00
101 Alex Gonzalez (Future Watch) 2.00
102 Carlos Beltran (Future Watch) 6.00
103 Dee Brown (Future Watch) 2.00
104 Jeremy Giambi (Future Watch) 2.00
105 Angel Pena (Future Watch) 2.00
106 Geoff Jenkins (Future Watch) 2.00
107 Corey Koskie (Future Watch) 2.00
108 A.J. Pierzynski (Future Watch) 2.00
109 Michael Barrett (Future Watch) 2.00
110 Fernando Seguignol (Future Watch) 2.00
111 Mike Kinkade (Future Watch) 2.00
112 Ricky Ledee (Future Watch) 2.00
113 Mike Lowell (Future Watch) 2.00
114 Eric Chavez (Future Watch) 2.50
115 Matt Clement (Future Watch) 2.00
116 Shane Monahan (Future Watch) 2.00
117 J.D. Drew (Future Watch) 4.00
118 Bubba Trammell (Future Watch) 2.00
119 Kevin Witt (Future Watch) 2.00
120 Roy Halladay (Future Watch) 2.50

		NM/M
121	Mark McGwire (Season to Remember)	5.00
122	Mark McGwire, Sammy Sosa (Season to Remember)	4.00
123	Sammy Sosa (Season to Remember)	2.50
124	Ken Griffey Jr. (Season to Remember)	3.00
125	Cal Ripken Jr. (Season to Remember)	6.00
126	Juan Gonzalez (Season to Remember)	2.50
127	Kerry Wood (Season to Remember)	2.50
128	Trevor Hoffman (Season to Remember)	2.00
129	Barry Bonds (Season to Remember)	5.00
130	Alex Rodriguez (Season to Remember)	4.00
131	Ben Grieve (Season to Remember)	2.00
132	Tom Glavine (Season to Remember)	2.00
133	David Wells (Season to Remember)	2.00
134	Mike Piazza (Season to Remember)	3.00
135	Scott Brosius (Season to Remember)	2.00

Chirography

Baseball's top players and future stars are included in this 39-card autograph insert set. The set was split into Level 1 and Level 2 versions. Level 1 cards are not numbered and were inserted one card per 24 packs. Level 2 (gold) cards are sequentially numbered to the featured player's jersey number.

		NM/M
	Common Player:	4.00
	Inserted 1:24	
EC	Eric Chavez	8.00
GK	Gabe Kapler	4.00
GMj	Gary Matthews Jr.	4.00
CP	Calvin Pickering	4.00
CK	Corey Koskie	6.00
SM	Shane Monahan	4.00
RH	Richard Hidalgo	4.00
MK	Mike Kinkade	4.00
CB	Carlos Beltran	35.00
AG	Alex Gonzalez	4.00
BC	Bruce Chen	4.00
MA	Matt Anderson	4.00
RM	Ryan Minor	4.00
RL	Ricky Ledee	4.00
RR	Ruben Rivera	4.00
BF	Brad Fullmer	4.00
RB	Russ Branyan	4.00
ML	Mike Lowell	15.00
JG	Jeremy Giambi	4.00
GL	George Lombard	4.00
KW	Kevin Witt	4.00
TW	Todd Walker	4.00
SR	Scott Rolen	20.00
KW	Kerry Wood	25.00
BG	Ben Grieve	4.00
JR	Ken Griffey Jr.	75.00
CJ	Chipper Jones	40.00
IR	Ivan Rodriguez	25.00
TGI	Troy Glaus	15.00
TL	Travis Lee	4.00
VG	Vladimir Guerrero	30.00
GV	Greg Vaughn	4.00
JT	Jim Thome	25.00
JD	J.D. Drew	15.00
TH	Todd Helton	15.00
GM	Greg Maddux	75.00
NG	Nomar Garciaparra	75.00
TG	Tony Gwynn	30.00
CR	Cal Ripken Jr.	125.00

Chirography Gold

These Chirography parallels can be identified by the gold tint on the card front and their sequential numbering; each featured player signed to his jersey number.

		NM/M
	Common Player:	5.00
	Inserted 1:24	
EC	Eric Chavez/30	40.00
GK	Gabe Kapler/51	10.00

16/24

GMj	Gary Matthews Jr./68	5.00
CP	Calvin Pickering/6	40.00
CK	Corey Koskie/47	15.00
SM	Shane Monahan/12	20.00
RH	Richard Hidalgo/15	30.00
MK	Mike Kinkade/33	10.00
CB	Carlos Beltran/36	75.00
AG	Alex Gonzalez/22	20.00
BC	Bruce Chen/48	10.00
MA	Matt Anderson/14	20.00
RM	Ryan Minor/10	35.00
RL	Ricky Ledee/38	10.00
RR	Ruben Rivera/28	10.00
BF	Brad Fullmer/20	10.00
RB	Russ Branyon/66	10.00
ML	Mike Lowell/60	15.00
JG	Jeremy Giambi/15	20.00
GL	George Lombard/26	10.00
KW	Kevin Witt/6	20.00
TW	Todd Walker/12	40.00
SR	Scott Rolen/17	75.00
KW	Kerry Wood/34	60.00
BG	Ben Grieve/14	35.00
JR	Ken Griffey Jr./24	250.00
CJ	Chipper Jones/10	200.00
IR	Ivan Rodriguez/7	125.00
TGI	Troy Glaus/14	90.00
TL	Travis Lee/16	35.00
VG	Vladimir Guerrero/27	75.00
GV	Greg Vaughn/23	10.00
JT	Jim Thome/25	40.00
JD	J.D. Drew/8	125.00
TH	Todd Helton/17	75.00
GM	Greg Maddux/31	150.00
NG	Nomar Garciaparra/5	375.00
TG	Tony Gwynn/19	125.00
CR	Cal Ripken Jr./8	650.00

Epic Figures

This 30-card set highlights baseball's biggest talents, including Mark McGwire and Derek Jeter. The card fronts have two photos, with the larger photo done with a shadow look in the background. Fronts also feature a holographic look, while the card backs feature the player's career highlights. These are seeded one per seven packs.

		NM/M
	Complete Set (30):	30.00
	Common Player:	.50
	Inserted 1:7	
E01	Mo Vaughn	.50
E02	Travis Lee	.50
E03	Andres Galarraga	.50
E04	Andruw Jones	1.00
E05	Chipper Jones	1.50
E06	Greg Maddux	1.25
E07	Cal Ripken Jr.	3.00
E08	Nomar Garciaparra	1.25
E09	Sammy Sosa	1.25
E10	Frank Thomas	1.00
E11	Kerry Wood	.60
E12	Kenny Lofton	.50
E13	Manny Ramirez	1.00
E14	Larry Walker	.50
E15	Jeff Bagwell	1.00
E16	Paul Molitor	1.00
E17	Vladimir Guerrero	1.00
E18	Derek Jeter	3.00
E19	Tino Martinez	.50
E20	Mike Piazza	1.50
E21	Ben Grieve	.50
E22	Scott Rolen	.75
E23	Mark McGwire	2.00
E24	Tony Gwynn	1.25
E25	Barry Bonds	3.00
E26	Ken Griffey Jr.	1.50
E27	Alex Rodriguez	2.00
E28	J.D. Drew	.65
E29	Juan Gonzalez	.60
E30	Kevin Brown	.50

Home Run Chronicles

This two-tiered 70-card set focuses on the amazing seasons of McGwire and Sammy Sosa. Other players help round out the 70-card set, but special emphasis has been placed on the duo. These are seeded one per pack. A die-cut version also exists, with each card serially numbered to 70.

		NM/M
	Complete Set (70):	50.00
	Common Player:	.15
	Inserted 1:1	
	Die-Cuts:	10X
	Production 70 Sets	
HR01	Mark McGwire	1.50
HR02	Sammy Sosa	1.25
HR03	Ken Griffey Jr.	1.00
HR04	Mark McGwire	1.50
HR05	Mark McGwire	1.50
HR06	Albert Belle	.15
HR07	Jose Canseco	.30
HR08	Juan Gonzalez	.45
HR09	Manny Ramirez	.65
HR10	Rafael Palmeiro	.50
HR11	Mo Vaughn	.15
HR12	Carlos Delgado	.45
HR13	Nomar Garciaparra	.75
HR14	Barry Bonds	1.50
HR15	Alex Rodriguez	1.25
HR16	Tony Clark	.15
HR17	Jim Thome	.50
HR18	Edgar Martinez	.15
HR19	Frank Thomas	.65
HR20	Greg Vaughn	.15
HR21	Vinny Castilla	.15
HR22	Andres Galarraga	.15
HR23	Moises Alou	.15
HR24	Jeromy Burnitz	.15
HR25	Vladimir Guerrero	.65
HR26	Jeff Bagwell	.65
HR27	Chipper Jones	.75
HR28	Javier Lopez	.15
HR29	Mike Piazza	1.00
HR30	Andruw Jones	.65
HR31	Henry Rodriguez	.15
HR32	Jeff Kent	.15
HR33	Ray Lankford	.15
HR34	Scott Rolen	.50
HR35	Raul Mondesi	.15
HR36	Ken Caminiti	.15
HR37	J.D. Drew	.40
HR38	Troy Glaus	.50
HR39	Gabe Kapler	.15
HR40	Alex Rodriguez	1.25
HR41	Ken Griffey Jr.	1.00
HR42	Sammy Sosa	1.25
HR43	Mark McGwire	1.50
HR44	Sammy Sosa	1.25
HR45	Mark McGwire	1.50
HR46	Vinny Castilla	.15
HR47	Sammy Sosa	1.25
HR48	Mark McGwire	1.50
HR49	Sammy Sosa	1.25
HR50	Greg Vaughn	.15
HR51	Sammy Sosa	1.25
HR52	Mark McGwire	1.50
HR53	Sammy Sosa	1.25
HR54	Mark McGwire	1.50
HR55	Sammy Sosa	1.25
HR56	Ken Griffey Jr.	1.00
HR57	Mark McGwire	1.50
HR58	Mark McGwire	1.50
HR59	Sammy Sosa	1.25
HR60	Mark McGwire	1.50
HR61	Mark McGwire	2.50
HR62	Mark McGwire	2.50
HR63	Mark McGwire	1.50
HR64	Mark McGwire	1.50
HR65	Mark McGwire	1.50
HR66	Sammy Sosa	2.50
HR67	Mark McGwire	1.50
HR68	Mark McGwire	1.50
HR69	Mark McGwire	1.50
HR70	Mark McGwire	4.00

Home Run Chronicles Die-Cuts

Each of the 70 cards in the Home Run Chronicles insert set was also issued in a die-cut version. The die-cuts share the basic front and back design of the regular HR Chronicle cards but have portions of the upper-left and lower-right cut away. On back, each of the die-cuts features an ink-jetted serial number from within an edition of 70.

HR Chronicle Die-Cuts:		10X

Reflections

Dot Matrix technology is utilized to provide a unique look at 30 of the best players in the game. Card fronts are horizontal with two small and one large photo. These are seeded 1:23 packs.

		NM/M
	Complete Set (30):	60.00
	Common Player:	.75
	Inserted 1:23	
R01	Mo Vaughn	.75
R02	Travis Lee	.75
R03	Andres Galarraga	.75
R04	Andruw Jones	2.50
R05	Chipper Jones	3.00
R06	Greg Maddux	3.00
R07	Cal Ripken Jr.	6.00
R08	Nomar Garciaparra	3.00
R09	Sammy Sosa	3.00
R10	Frank Thomas	2.50
R11	Kerry Wood	1.50
R12	Kenny Lofton	.75
R13	Manny Ramirez	2.50
R14	Larry Walker	.75
R15	Jeff Bagwell	2.50
R16	Paul Molitor	2.50
R17	Vladimir Guerrero	2.50
R18	Derek Jeter	6.00
R19	Tino Martinez	.75
R20	Mike Piazza	3.50
R21	Ben Grieve	.75
R22	Scott Rolen	2.00
R23	Mark McGwire	4.50
R24	Tony Gwynn	3.00
R25	Barry Bonds	6.00
R26	Ken Griffey Jr.	3.50
R27	Alex Rodriguez	4.50
R28	J.D. Drew	1.25
R29	Juan Gonzalez	1.25
R30	Roger Clemens	3.25

SP Authentics

These 1:864 pack inserts are redemption cards that could be redeemed for special pieces of memorabilia from either Ken Griffey Jr. or Mark McGwire. The redemption period ended March 1, 2000. Because of rarity any surviving unredeemed McGwire home run-game autographed tickets cannot be valued.

		NM/M
	Common Card:	10.00
(1)	K.Griffey Jr./ Auto. Ball/75	60.00
(2)	Ken Griffey Jr./Glv/200	20.00
(3)	K. Griffey Jr./ HR Cel Card/346	10.00
(4)	Ken Griffey Jr./ Auto. Jsy/25	125.00
(5)	K. Griffey Jr./ Auto. Mini Helmet/75	80.00
(6)	K. Griffey Jr./ SI Cover/200	15.00
(7)	K. Griffey Jr./ SI Cover Auto./75	75.00
(8)	Ken Griffey Jr./ Standee/300	10.00

500 Club Piece of History

These cards feature a piece of game-used bat once swung by Ernie Banks. Approximately 350 cards exist. An autographed version of this card also exists, only 14 were produced.

		NM/M
EB	Ernie Banks	120.00
EB	Ernie Banks/Auto./14	325.00

1999 SP Signature Edition

Even with one autograph per three-card pack, this single-series issue's price of $19.99 per pack shocked the hobby when it was introduced. Horizontal cards have a color or black-and-white photo at the left end with foil highlights and airbrushed geometric designs on a white background. Backs repeat the portrait portion of the front photo and add player data and some stats.

		NM/M
	Complete Set (180):	60.00
	Common Player:	.15
	Pack (3):	15.00
	Wax Box (12):	150.00
1	Nomar Garciaparra	2.00
2	Ken Griffey Jr.	2.50
3	J.D. Drew	.50
4	Alex Rodriguez	3.00
5	Juan Gonzalez	.60
6	Mo Vaughn	.15
7	Greg Maddux	2.00
8	Chipper Jones	2.00
9	Frank Thomas	1.50
10	Vladimir Guerrero	1.50
11	Mike Piazza	2.50
12	Eric Chavez	.25
13	Tony Gwynn	2.00
14	Orlando Hernandez	.15
15	Pat Burrell RC	6.00
16	Darin Erstad	.30
17	Greg Vaughn	.15
18	Russ Branyan	.15
19	Gabe Kapler	.15
20	Craig Biggio	.15
21	Troy Glaus	1.25
22	Pedro J. Martinez	1.50
23	Carlos Beltran	.50
24	Derrek Lee	.50
25	Manny Ramirez	1.50
26	Shea Hillenbrand RC	1.00
27	Carlos Lee	.15
28	Angel Pena	.15
29	Rafael Roque	.15
30	Octavio Dotel	.15
31	Jeromy Burnitz	.15
32	Jeremy Giambi	.15
33	Andruw Jones	1.50
34	Todd Helton	1.25
35	Scott Rolen	1.25
36	Jason Kendall	.15
37	Trevor Hoffman	.15
38	Barry Bonds	4.00
39	Ivan Rodriguez	1.25
40	Roy Halladay	.15
41	Rickey Henderson	1.50
42	Ryan Minor	.15
43	Brian Jordan	.15
44	Alex Gonzalez	.15
45	Raul Mondesi	.15
46	Corey Koskie	.15
47	Paul O'Neill	.15
48	Todd Walker	.15
49	Carlos Febles	.15
50	Travis Fryman	.15
51	Albert Belle	.15
52	Travis Lee	.15
53	Bruce Chen	.15
54	Reggie Sanders	.15
55	Jerry Hairston Jr.	.15
56	Carlos Guillen	.15
57	Michael Barrett	.15
58	Jason Conti	.15
59	Joe Lawrence	.15
60	Jeff Cirillo	.15
61	Juan Melo	.15
62	Chad Hermansen	.15
63	Ruben Mateo	.15
64	Ben Davis	.15
65	Mike Caruso	.15
66	Jason Giambi	.50
67	Jose Canseco	.50
68	Chad Hutchinson RC	.15
69	Mitch Meluskey	.15
70	Adrian Beltre	.25
71	Mark Kotsay	.15
72	Juan Encarnacion	.15
73	Dermal Brown	.15
74	Kevin Witt	.15
75	Vinny Castilla	.15
76	Aramis Ramirez	.15
77	Marlon Anderson	.15
78	Mike Kinkade	.15
79	Kevin Barker	.15
80	Ron Belliard	.15
81	Chris Haas	.15
82	Bob Henley	.15
83	Fernando Seguignol	.15
84	Damon Minor	.15
85	A.J. Burnett RC	1.00
86	Calvin Pickering	.15
87	Mike Darr	.15
88	Cesar King	.15
89	Rob Bell	.15
90	Derrick Gibson	.15
91	Ober Moreno RC	.15
92	Robert Fick	.15
93	Doug Mientkiewicz RC	.75
94	A.J. Pierzynski	.15
95	Orlando Palmeiro	.15
96	Sidney Ponson	.15
97	Ivanon Coffie RC	.15
98	Juan Pena RC	1.00
99	Mark Karchner	.15
100	Carlos Castillo	.15
101	Bryan Ward	.15
102	Mario Valdez	.15
103	Billy Wagner	.15
104	Miguel Tejada	.25
105	Jose Cruz Jr.	.15
106	George Lombard	.15
107	Geoff Jenkins	.15
108	Ray Lankford	.15
109	Todd Stottlemyre	.15
110	Mike Lowell	.15
111	Matt Clement	.15
112	Scott Brosius	.15
113	Preston Wilson	.15
114	Bartolo Colon	.15
115	Rolando Arrojo	.15
116	Jose Guillen	.15
117	Ron Gant	.15
118	Ricky Ledee	.15
119	Carlos Delgado	.50
120	Abraham Nunez	.15
121	John Olerud	.15
122	Chan Ho Park	.15
123	Brad Radke	.15
124	Al Leiter	.15
125	Gary Matthews Jr.	.15
126	F.P. Santangelo	.15
127	Brad Fullmer	.15
128	Matt Anderson	.15
129	A.J. Hinch	.15
130	Sterling Hitchcock	.15
131	Edgar Martinez	.15
132	Fernando Tatis	.15
133	Bobby Smith	.15
134	Paul Konerko	.25
135	Sean Casey	.15
136	Donnie Sadler	.15
137	Denny Neagle	.15
138	Sandy Alomar	.15
139	Mariano Rivera	.25
140	Emil Brown	.15
141	J.T. Snow	.15
142	Eli Marrero	.15
143	Rusty Greer	.15
144	Johnny Damon	.35
145	Damion Easley	.15
146	Eric Milton	.15
147	Rico Brogna	.15
148	Ray Durham	.15
149	Wally Joyner	.15
150	Royce Clayton	.15
151	David Ortiz	.50
152	Wade Boggs	2.00
153	Ugueth Urbina	.15
154	Richard Hidalgo	.15
155	Bobby Abreu	.15
156	Robb Nen	.15
157	David Segui	.15
158	Sean Berry	.15
159	Kevin Tapani	.15
160	Jason Varitek	.15
161	Fernando Vina	.15
162	Jim Leyritz	.15
163	Enrique Wilson	.15
164	Jim Parque	.15
165	Doug Glanville	.15
166	Jesus Sanchez	.15
167	Nolan Ryan	4.00
168	Robin Yount	.50
169	Stan Musial	1.00
170	Tom Seaver	.50
171	Mike Schmidt	1.00
172	Willie Stargell	.50
173	Rollie Fingers	.45
174	Willie McCovey	.50
175	Harmon Killebrew	.50
176	Eddie Mathews	.50
177	Reggie Jackson	1.00
178	Frank Robinson	.50
179	Ken Griffey Sr.	.15
180	Eddie Murray	1.50

Autographs

Authentically autographed cards of nearly 100 current stars, top prospects and Hall of Famers were featured as one-per-pack inserts in SP Signature Edition. Some players did not return their signed cards in time for pack inclusion and had to be obtained by returning an exchange card prior to the May 12, 2000, deadline.

		NM/M
Common Player:		3.00
Inserted 1:1		
BA	Bobby Abreu	15.00
SA	Sandy Alomar	5.00
MA	Marlon Anderson	4.00
KB	Kevin Barker	3.00
MB	Michael Barrett	4.00
RoB	Rob Bell	3.00
AB	Albert Belle	15.00
RBe	Ron Belliard	3.00
CBe	Carlos Beltran	50.00
ABe	Adrian Beltre	25.00
BB	Barry Bonds	180.00
RB	Russ Branyan	3.00
SB	Scott Brosius/SP	30.00
DB	Dermal Brown	3.00
EB	Emil Brown	3.00
AJB	A.J. Burnett (Exchange Card)	3.00
AJB	A.J. Burnett/Auto.	20.00
PB	Pat Burrell	25.00
JoC	Jose Canseco	30.00
MC	Mike Caruso	3.00
SC	Sean Casey (Exchange Card)	3.00
SC	Sean Casey/Auto.	15.00
VC	Vinny Castilla (Exchange Card)	3.00
VC	Vinny Castilla/Auto.	8.00
CC	Carlos Castillo	3.00
EC	Eric Chavez	10.00
BC	Bruce Chen	3.00
JCi	Jeff Cirillo	3.00
RC	Royce Clayton	3.00
MCl	Matt Clement	6.00
IC	Ivanon Coffie	3.00
BCo	Bartolo Colon (Exchange Card)	3.00
BCo	Bartolo Colon/Auto.	8.00
JC	Jason Conti	3.00
JDa	Johnny Damon	25.00
BD	Ben Davis	3.00
CD	Carlos Delgado	20.00
OD	Octavio Dotel	3.00
JD	J.D. Drew	15.00
RD	Ray Durham	3.00
DEa	Damion Easley	3.00
JE	Juan Encarnacion	3.00
DE	Darin Erstad	8.00
CF	Carlos Febles	3.00
Rob	Robert Fick	3.00
Rol	Rollie Fingers	8.00
BF	Brad Fullmer	3.00
RGa	Ron Gant	8.00
NG	Nomar Garciaparra	30.00
JaG	Jason Giambi	20.00
DG	Derrick Gibson	3.00
DGl	Doug Glanville	3.00
TGl	Troy Glaus	15.00
AG	Alex Gonzalez	5.00
RGr	Rusty Greer	3.00
Jr.	Ken Griffey Jr.	80.00
1	Ken Griffey Jr. (Facsimile autographed "SAMPLE.")	15.00
Sr.	Ken Griffey Sr.	8.00
VG	Vladimir Guerrero	30.00
JG	Jose Guillen	10.00
TG	Tony Gwynn	35.00
CHa	Chris Haas	3.00
JHj	Jerry Hairston Jr.	4.00
RH	Roy Halladay	15.00
THe	Todd Helton	20.00
BH	Bob Henley	3.00
ED	Orlando Hernandez	40.00
CH	Chad Hermansen	3.00
ShH	Shea Hillenbrand	8.00
StH	Sterling Hitchcock	3.00
THo	Trevor Hoffman	8.00
CHu	Chad Hutchinson	3.00
RJ	Reggie Jackson/SP	40.00
GJ	Geoff Jenkins	5.00
AJ	Andruw Jones	20.00
CJ	Chipper Jones	50.00
WJ	Wally Joyner	8.00
GK	Gabe Kapler	3.00
MKa	Mark Karchner	3.00
JK	Jason Kendall	6.00
HK	Harmon Killebrew	40.00
CKi	Cesar King	3.00
MKi	Mike Kinkade	3.00
PK	Paul Konerko	15.00
CK	Corey Koskie	6.00

MK	Mark Kotsay	4.00
RL	Ray Lankford	5.00
JLa	Joe Lawrence	3.00
CL	Carlos Lee	20.00
DL	Derrek Lee	25.00
AL	Al Leiter	6.00
JLe	Jim Leyritz	6.00
GL	George Lombard	3.00
GM	Greg Maddux	80.00
Eli	Eli Marrero	3.00
EM	Edgar Martinez	20.00
PM	Pedro J. Martinez (Exchange Card)	5.00
PM	Pedro J. Martinez (Autographed)	100.00
RMa	Ruben Mateo (Exchange Card)	3.00
RMa	Ruben Mateo/Auto.	8.00
EMa	Eddie Mathews	60.00
GMj	Gary Matthews Jr.	3.00
WMc	Willie McCovey	35.00
JM	Juan Melo	3.00
MMe	Mitch Meluskey	3.00
DoM	Doug Mientkiewicz	6.00
EMi	Eric Milton	3.00
DaM	Damon Minor	3.00
RM	Ryan Minor	3.00
EMu	Eddie Murray	20.00
SM	Stan Musial	50.00
RN	Robb Nen	3.00
JO	John Olerud	10.00
PO	Paul O'Neill	20.00
DO	David Ortiz	40.00
OP	Orlando Palmeiro	3.00
JP	Jim Parque	3.00
AP	Angel Pena	3.00
MP	Mike Piazza (Exchange Card)	6.00
MP	Mike Piazza/Auto.	150.00
CP	Calvin Pickering	3.00
AJP	A.J. Pierzynski	5.00
SP	Sidney Ponson	8.00
BR	Brad Radke	4.00
ARa	Aramis Ramirez	20.00
MR	Manny Ramirez	50.00
MRi	Mariano Rivera	25.00
FR	Frank Robinson	25.00
AR	Alex Rodriguez	120.00
PG	Ivan Rodriguez	25.00
SR	Scott Rolen (Exchange Card)	3.00
SR	Scott Rolen/Auto.	25.00
RR	Rafael Roque	3.00
NR	Nolan Ryan	120.00
DS	Donnie Sadler	3.00
JS	Jesus Sanchez	3.00
MS	Mike Schmidt	60.00
TSe	Tom Seaver	35.00
DSe	David Segui	3.00
FS	Fernando Seguignol	3.00
BS	Bobby Smith	3.00
JT	J.T. Snow (Exchange Card)	3.00
JT	J.T. Snow/Auto.	6.00
POP	Willie Stargell (Exchange Card)	3.00
POP	Willie Stargell/Auto.	60.00
TSt	Todd Stottlemyre	3.00
RT	Reggie Taylor	3.00
MT	Miguel Tejada	20.00
FT	Frank Thomas	50.00
MV	Mario Valdez	3.00
JV	Jason Varitek	30.00
GV	Greg Vaughn	3.00
MO	Mo Vaughn	8.00
FV	Fernando Vina	3.00
BWa	Billy Wagner	10.00
TW	Todd Walker	3.00
BW	Bryan Ward	3.00
EW	Enrique Wilson	3.00
KW	Kevin Witt	3.00
RY	Robin Yount	40.00

Autographs Gold

This parallel edition of the Signature Series Autographs features special gold graphic highlights on front and cards serially numbered within an edition of 50 each (except A.J. Burnett). Cards of 11 players were never signed, while cards of several others had to be obtained by sending in an exchange card, valid through May 12, 2000.

		NM/M
Common Player:		12.00
Production 50 Sets		
MA	Marlon Anderson	12.00
KB	Kevin Barker	12.00
MB	Michael Barrett	12.00
RoB	Rob Bell	12.00
AB	Albert Belle	20.00
RBe	Ron Belliard	12.00

CBe	Carlos Beltran	75.00
ABe	Adrian Beltre	40.00
CB	Craig Biggio (Unsigned)	3.00
BB	Barry Bonds	250.00
RB	Russ Branyan	12.00
DB	Dermal Brown	12.00
AJB	A.J. Burnett (Exchange Card)	4.00
AJB	A.J. Burnett (Autographed edition of 20.)	40.00
JB	Jeromy Burnitz (Unsigned)	3.00
PB	Pat Burrell	40.00
JoC	Jose Canseco	50.00
MC	Mike Caruso	12.00
VC	Vinny Castilla (Exchange Card)	3.00
VC	Vinny Castilla/Auto.	20.00
CC	Carlos Castillo	12.00
EC	Eric Chavez	20.00
BC	Bruce Chen	12.00
JCi	Jeff Cirillo	12.00
JC	Jason Conti	12.00
MD	Mike Darr (Unsigned)	3.00
BD	Ben Davis	12.00
OD	Octavio Dotel	12.00
JD	J.D. Drew	30.00
JE	Juan Encarnacion	12.00
DE	Darin Erstad	20.00
CF	Carlos Febles	12.00
TF	Travis Fryman (Unsigned)	3.00
BF	Brad Fullmer	12.00
NG	Nomar Garciaparra	100.00
JaG	Jason Giambi	40.00
JeG	Jeremy Giambi (Unsigned)	3.00
DG	Derrick Gibson	12.00
DGl	Doug Glanville	12.00
TGl	Troy Glaus	30.00
AG	Alex Gonzalez	12.00
JG	Juan Gonzalez (Unsigned)	6.00
Jr.	Ken Griffey Jr.	150.00
Sr.	Ken Griffey Sr.	12.00
VG	Vladimir Guerrero	75.00
JG	Jose Guillen (Unsigned)	3.00
TG	Tony Gwynn	60.00
CHa	Chris Haas	12.00
JHj	Jerry Hairston Jr.	12.00
RH	Roy Halladay	25.00
THe	Todd Helton	30.00
RH	Rickey Henderson (Unsigned)	6.00
BH	Bob Henley	12.00
ED	Orlando Hernandez	25.00
CH	Chad Hermansen	12.00
ShH	Shea Hillenbrand	20.00
StH	Sterling Hitchcock	12.00
THo	Trevor Hoffman	30.00
CHu	Chad Hutchinson	12.00
GJ	Geoff Jenkins	12.00
AJ	Andruw Jones	40.00
CJ	Chipper Jones	80.00
BJ	Brian Jordan (Unsigned)	3.00
WJ	Wally Joyner	25.00
GK	Gabe Kapler	12.00
MKa	Mark Karchner	12.00
JK	Jason Kendall	20.00
CKi	Cesar King	12.00
MKi	Mike Kinkade	12.00
PK	Paul Konerko	15.00
CK	Corey Koskie	20.00
MK	Mark Kotsay	12.00
RL	Ray Lankford	12.00
JLa	Joe Lawrence	12.00
CL	Carlos Lee	25.00
DL	Derrek Lee	50.00
TL	Travis Lee (Unsigned)	4.00
AL	Al Leiter	12.00
JLe	Jim Leyritz	12.00
GL	George Lombard	12.00
GM	Greg Maddux	150.00
PM	Pedro Martinez (Exchange Card)	6.00
PM	Pedro Martinez/Auto.	200.00
RMa	Ruben Mateo (Exchange Card)	3.00
RMa	Ruben Mateo/Auto.	15.00
GMj	Gary Matthews Jr.	12.00
JM	Juan Melo	12.00
MMe	Mitch Meluskey	12.00
DoM	Doug Mientkiewicz	12.00
EMi	Eric Milton	12.00
DaM	Damon Minor	12.00
RM	Ryan Minor	12.00
PO	Paul O'Neill	30.00
DO	David Ortiz	75.00
OP	Orlando Palmeiro	12.00
AP	Angel Pena	12.00
MP	Mike Piazza (Exchange Card)	10.00
MP	Mike Piazza/Auto.	250.00
CP	Calvin Pickering	12.00
ARa	Aramis Ramirez	30.00
MR	Manny Ramirez	80.00
AR	Alex Rodriguez	185.00
PG	Ivan Rodriguez	45.00
SR	Scott Rolen (Exchange Card)	4.00
SR	Scott Rolen/Auto.	75.00
RR	Rafael Roque	12.00
DSe	David Segui	12.00
FS	Fernando Seguignol	12.00
RT	Reggie Taylor	12.00
FT	Frank Thomas	70.00
MV	Mario Valdez	12.00

CBe	Carlos Beltran	75.00
ABe	Adrian Beltre	40.00
CB	Craig Biggio (Unsigned)	3.00
BB	Barry Bonds	250.00
RB	Russ Branyan	12.00
DB	Dermal Brown	12.00

Legendary Cuts

Each of the cards in this one-of-one insert series is unique, thus catalog values are impossible to assign.

No Pricing
Production One Set

500 Club Piece of History

		NM/M
MO	Mel Ott/350	100.00

1999 SPx

Formerly SPx Finite, this super-premium product showcases 80 of baseball's veteran players on regular cards and a 40-card rookie subset, which are serially numbered to 1,999. Two top rookies, J.D. Drew and Gabe Kapler autographed all 1,999 of their rookie subset cards. There are two parallels, SPx Radiance and SPx Spectrum. Radiance are serially numbered to 100 with Drew and Kapler signing all 100 of their cards. They are exclusive to Finite Radiance Hot Packs. Spectrums are limited to only one set and available only in Finite Spectrum Hot Packs. Packs consist of three cards with a S.R.P. of $5.99.

	NM/M
Complete Set (120):	100.00
Common Player:	.50
Common SPx Rookie (81-120):	2.00
Production 1,999 Sets	
Radiance (1-80):	7X
Radiance SP (81-120):	1.5X
Spectrum (1-of-1):	Value Undetermined
Pack (3):	3.00
Wax Box (18):	40.00

1	Mark McGwire #61	2.50
2	Mark McGwire #62	1.00
3	Mark McGwire #63	1.00
4	Mark McGwire #64	1.00
5	Mark McGwire #65	1.00
6	Mark McGwire #66	1.00
7	Mark McGwire #67	1.00
8	Mark McGwire #68	1.00
9	Mark McGwire #69	1.00
10	Mark McGwire #70	2.50
11	Mo Vaughn	.50
12	Darin Erstad	.75
13	Travis Lee	.50
14	Randy Johnson	1.50
15	Matt Williams	.50
16	Chipper Jones	.50
17	Greg Maddux	2.00
18	Andruw Jones	1.50
19	Andres Galarraga	.50
20	Cal Ripken Jr.	4.00
21	Albert Belle	.50
22	Mike Mussina	.75
23	Nomar Garciaparra	2.00
24	Pedro Martinez	1.50
25	John Valentin	.50
26	Kerry Wood	1.00
27	Sammy Sosa	2.00
28	Mark Grace	.50
29	Frank Thomas	1.50
30	Mike Caruso	.50
31	Barry Larkin	.50
32	Sean Casey	.50
33	Jim Thome	1.25
34	Kenny Lofton	.50
35	Manny Ramirez	1.50
36	Larry Walker	.50
37	Todd Helton	1.25
38	Vinny Castilla	.50

39	Tony Clark	.50
40	Derrek Lee	1.00
41	Mark Kotsay	.50
43	Jeff Bagwell	1.50
43	Craig Biggio	.50
44	Moises Alou	.50
45	Larry Sutton	.50
46	Johnny Damon	1.00
47	Gary Sheffield	1.00
48	Raul Mondesi	.50
49	Jeromy Burnitz	.50
50	Todd Walker	.50
51	David Ortiz	1.00
52	Vladimir Guerrero	1.50
53	Rondell White	.50
54	Mike Piazza	2.50
55	Derek Jeter	4.00
56	Tino Martinez	.50
57	David Wells	.50
58	Ben Grieve	.50
59	A.J. Hinch	.50
60	Scott Rolen	1.25
61	Doug Glanville	.50
62	Aramis Ramirez	.50
63	Jose Guillen	.50
64	Tony Gwynn	2.00
65	Greg Vaughn	.50
66	Ruben Rivera	.50
67	Barry Bonds	4.00
68	J.T. Snow	.50
69	Alex Rodriguez	2.00
70	Ken Griffey Jr.	2.50
71	Jay Buhner	.50
72	Mark McGwire	3.00
73	Fernando Tatis	.50
74	Quinton McCracken	.50
75	Wade Boggs	2.00
76	Ivan Rodriguez	1.25
77	Juan Gonzalez	1.00
78	Rafael Palmeiro	1.25
79	Jose Cruz Jr.	1.00
80	Carlos Delgado	1.00
81	Troy Glaus	5.00
82	Vladimir Nunez	2.00
83	George Lombard	2.00
84	Bruce Chen	2.00
85	Ryan Minor	2.00
86	Calvin Pickering	2.00
87	Jin Ho Cho	2.00
88	Russ Branyan	2.00
89	Derrick Gibson	2.00
90	Gabe Kapler/Auto.	6.00
91	Matt Anderson	2.00
92	Robert Fick	2.00
93	Juan Encarnacion	2.00
94	Preston Wilson	2.00
95	Alex Gonzalez	2.00
96	Carlos Beltran	5.00
97	Jeremy Giambi	2.00
98	Dee Brown	2.00
99	Adrian Beltre	4.00
100	Alex Cora	2.00
101	Angel Pena	2.00
102	Geoff Jenkins	2.00
103	Ronnie Belliard	2.00
104	Corey Koskie	2.00
105	A.J. Pierzynski	2.00
106	Michael Barrett	2.00
107	Fernando Seguignol	2.00
108	Mike Kinkade	2.00
109	Mike Lowell	2.00
110	Ricky Ledee	2.00
111	Eric Chavez	3.00
112	Abraham Nunez	2.00
113	Matt Clement	2.00
114	Ben Davis	2.00
115	Mike Darr	2.00
116	Ramon Martinez	2.00
117	Carlos Guillen	2.00
118	Shane Monahan	2.00
119	J.D. Drew/Auto.	15.00
120	Kevin Witt	2.00

Dominance

This 20-card set showcases the most dominant MLB superstars, including Derek Jeter and Alex Rodriguez. These are seeded in 1:17 packs and numbered with a FB prefix.

	NM/M
Complete Set (20):	35.00
Common Player:	1.00
Inserted 1:17	
1	Chipper Jones	2.00
2	Greg Maddux	2.00
3	Cal Ripken Jr.	4.00
4	Nomar Garciaparra	2.00

Power Explosion

This 30-card set salutes the top power hitters in the game today, including Mark McGwire and Sammy Sosa. These are numbered with a PE prefix.

	NM/M
Complete Set (30):	15.00
Common Player:	.20
Inserted 1:3	
1	Troy Glaus	.65
2	Mo Vaughn	.20
3	Travis Lee	.20
4	Chipper Jones	1.00
5	Andres Galarraga	.20
6	Brady Anderson	.20
7	Albert Belle	.20
8	Nomar Garciaparra	1.00
9	Sammy Sosa	1.00
10	Frank Thomas	.75
11	Jim Thome	.65
12	Manny Ramirez	.75
13	Larry Walker	.20
14	Tony Clark	.20
15	Jeff Bagwell	.75
16	Moises Alou	.20
17	Ken Caminiti	.20
18	Vladimir Guerrero	.75
19	Mike Piazza	1.25
20	Tino Martinez	.20
21	Ben Grieve	.20
22	Scott Rolen	.60
23	Greg Vaughn	.20
24	Barry Bonds	2.00
25	Ken Griffey Jr.	1.25
26	Alex Rodriguez	1.50
27	Mark McGwire	1.50
28	J.D. Drew	.35
29	Juan Gonzalez	.45
30	Ivan Rodriguez	.60

Premier Stars

This 30-card set captures baseball's most dominant players, including Randy Johnson and Ken Griffey Jr. Featured on a rainbow-foil design, these are numbered with a PS prefix.

	NM/M
Complete Set (30):	45.00
Common Player:	1.00
Inserted 1:17	
1	Mark McGwire	3.00
2	Sammy Sosa	1.50
3	Frank Thomas	1.50
4	J.D. Drew	1.25
5	Kerry Wood	1.25
6	Moises Alou	1.00
7	Kenny Lofton	1.00
8	Jeff Bagwell	1.50
9	Tony Clark	1.00
10	Roberto Alomar	1.00
11	Cal Ripken Jr.	4.00
12	Derek Jeter	4.00
13	Mike Piazza	2.50
14	Jose Cruz Jr.	1.00
15	Chipper Jones	2.00
16	Nomar Garciaparra	2.00

5	Mo Vaughn	1.00
6	Sammy Sosa	2.00
7	Albert Belle	1.00
8	Frank Thomas	1.50
9	Jim Thome	1.25
10	Jeff Bagwell	1.50
11	Vladimir Guerrero	1.50
12	Mike Piazza	2.50
13	Derek Jeter	4.00
14	Tony Gwynn	2.00
15	Barry Bonds	4.00
16	Ken Griffey Jr.	2.50
17	Alex Rodriguez	3.00
18	Mark McGwire	3.00
19	J.D. Drew	1.25
20	Juan Gonzalez	1.25

17	Greg Maddux	2.00
18	Scott Rolen	1.25
19	Vladimir Guerrero	1.50
20	Albert Belle	1.00
21	Ken Griffey Jr.	2.50
22	Alex Rodriguez	3.00
23	Ben Grieve	1.00
24	Juan Gonzalez	1.25
25	Barry Bonds	4.00
26	Larry Walker	1.00
27	Tony Gwynn	2.00
28	Randy Johnson	1.50
29	Travis Lee	1.00
30	Mo Vaughn	1.00

Star Focus

This 30-card set focuses on the 30 brightest stars in the game. These are numbered with a SF prefix.

		NM/M
Complete Set (30):		50.00
Common Player:		.75
Inserted 1:8		
1	Chipper Jones	2.25
2	Greg Maddux	2.25
3	Cal Ripken Jr.	4.50
4	Nomar Garciaparra	2.25
5	Mo Vaughn	.75
6	Sammy Sosa	2.25
7	Albert Belle	.75
8	Frank Thomas	1.50
9	Jim Thome	1.25
10	Kenny Lofton	.75
11	Manny Ramirez	1.50
12	Larry Walker	.75
13	Jeff Bagwell	1.50
14	Craig Biggio	.75
15	Randy Johnson	1.50
16	Vladimir Guerrero	1.50
17	Mike Piazza	3.00
18	Derek Jeter	4.50
19	Tino Martinez	.75
20	Bernie Williams	.75
21	Curt Schilling	1.00
22	Tony Gwynn	2.25
23	Barry Bonds	4.50
24	Ken Griffey Jr.	3.00
25	Alex Rodriguez	4.00
26	Mark McGwire	4.00
27	J.D. Drew	1.00
28	Juan Gonzalez	1.00
29	Ivan Rodriguez	1.25
30	Ben Grieve	.75

Winning Materials

This eight-card set includes a piece of the featured player's game-worn jersey and game-used bat on each card. These are seeded 1:251 packs.

		NM/M
Complete Set (8):		90.00
Common Player:		5.00
Inserted 1:251		
VC	Vinny Castilla	5.00
JD	J.D. Drew	7.50
JR	Ken Griffey Jr.	20.00
VG	Vladimir Guerrero	12.00
TG	Tony Gwynn	15.00
TH	Todd Helton	10.00
TL	Travis Lee	5.00
IR	Ivan Rodriguez	10.00

500 Club Piece of History

Each of these approximately 350 cards include a piece of game-used Louisville Slugger once swung by Willie Mays. Mays also signed 24 of his Piece of History cards.

		NM/M
WM	Willie Mays/350	275.00
WM	Willie Mays/Auto./24	1,700

2000 SP Authentic

The 135-card base set is composed of 90 regular cards, 30 Future Watch subset cards (serial numbered to 2,500) and 15 SP Superstars (serial numbered to 2,500). The regular cards have a gold foiled stamped line around the player image with a matte finished white border around the player image. The player name is stamped in gold foil in the top portion and the SP Authentic logo is stamped in silver foil. Card backs have a small photo, a brief career note and up to the past five seasons of complete statistics. Five-card packs carried a $4.99 SRP.

		NM/M
Complete Set (135):		150.00
Common Player:		.15
Common (91-105):		2.00
Production 2,500 Sets		
Common (106-135):		2.00
Production 2,500 Sets		
Pack (5):		3.00
Box (24):		60.00
1	Mo Vaughn	.15
2	Troy Glaus	.50
3	Jason Giambi	.75
4	Tim Hudson	.40
5	Eric Chavez	.25
6	Shannon Stewart	.15
7	Raul Mondesi	.15
8	Carlos Delgado	.50
9	Jose Canseco	.50
10	Vinny Castilla	.15
11	Greg Vaughn	.15
12	Manny Ramirez	1.00
13	Roberto Alomar	.40
14	Jim Thome	.75
15	Richie Sexson	.40
16	Alex Rodriguez	2.50
17	Fred Garcia	.15
18	John Olerud	.15
19	Albert Belle	.25
20	Cal Ripken Jr.	3.00
21	Mike Mussina	.50
22	Ivan Rodriguez	.75
23	Gabe Kapler	.15
24	Rafael Palmeiro	.75
25	Nomar Garciaparra	1.00
26	Pedro Martinez	1.00
27	Carl Everett	.15
28	Carlos Beltran	.50
29	Jermaine Dye	.15
30	Juan Gonzalez	.50
31	Dean Palmer	.15
32	Corey Koskie	.15
33	Jacque Jones	.15
34	Frank Thomas	.75
35	Paul Konerko	.40
36	Magglio Ordonez	.25
37	Bernie Williams	.40
38	Derek Jeter	2.50
39	Roger Clemens	2.00
40	Mariano Rivera	.40
41	Jeff Bagwell	.50
42	Craig Biggio	.40
43	Jose Lima	.15
44	Moises Alou	.25
45	Chipper Jones	1.00
46	Greg Maddux	1.50
47	Andruw Jones	1.00
48	Kevin Millwood	.15
49	Jeromy Burnitz	.15
50	Geoff Jenkins	.15
51	Mark McGwire	1.50
52	Fernando Tatis	.15
53	J.D. Drew	.25
54	Sammy Sosa	1.00
55	Kerry Wood	.50
56	Mark Grace	.25
57	Matt Williams	.15
58	Randy Johnson	1.00
59	Erubiel Durazo	.15
60	Gary Sheffield	.50
61	Kevin Brown	.15
62	Shawn Green	.40
63	Vladimir Guerrero	1.00
64	Michael Barrett	.15
65	Barry Bonds	2.50
66	Jeff Kent	.25
67	Russ Ortiz	.15
68	Preston Wilson	.15
69	Mike Lowell	.15
70	Mike Piazza	1.00
71	Mike Hampton	.15
72	Robin Ventura	.15
73	Edgardo Alfonzo	.15
74	Tony Gwynn	1.50
75	Ryan Klesko	.15
76	Trevor Hoffman	.15
77	Scott Rolen	1.00
78	Bob Abreu	.40
79	Mike Lieberthal	.15
80	Curt Schilling	.75
81	Jason Kendall	.15
82	Brian Giles	.15
83	Kris Benson	.15
84	Ken Griffey Jr.	2.00
85	Sean Casey	.25
86	Pokey Reese	.15
87	Barry Larkin	.40
88	Larry Walker	.25
89	Todd Helton	.75
90	Jeff Cirillo	.15
91	Ken Griffey Jr. (SP Superstars)	4.00
92	Mark McGwire (SP Superstars)	4.00
93	Chipper Jones (SP Superstars)	3.00
94	Derek Jeter (SP Superstars)	6.00
95	Shawn Green (SP Superstars)	2.00
96	Pedro Martinez (SP Superstars)	4.00
97	Mike Piazza (SP Superstars)	4.00
98	Alex Rodriguez (SP Superstars)	5.00
99	Jeff Bagwell (SP Superstars)	2.50
100	Cal Ripken Jr. (SP Superstars)	6.00
101	Sammy Sosa (SP Superstars)	3.00
102	Barry Bonds (SP Superstars)	5.00
103	Jose Canseco (SP Superstars)	2.00
104	Nomar Garciaparra (SP Superstars)	4.00
105	Ivan Rodriguez (SP Superstars)	2.50
106	Rick Ankiel (Future Watch)	2.00
107	Pat Burrell (Future Watch)	2.50
108	Vernon Wells (Future Watch)	2.50
109	Nick Johnson (Future Watch)	2.50
110	Kip Wells (Future Watch)	2.00
111	Matt Riley (Future Watch)	2.00
112	Alfonso Soriano (Future Watch)	8.00
113	Josh Beckett (Future Watch)	4.00
114	Danys Baez RC (Future Watch)	6.00
115	Travis Dawkins (Future Watch)	2.50
116	Eric Gagne (Future Watch)	4.00
117	Mike Lamb RC (Future Watch)	4.00
118	Eric Munson (Future Watch)	2.50
119	Wilfredo Rodriguez RC (Future Watch)	2.00
120	Kazuhiro Sasaki RC (Future Watch)	3.00
121	Chad Hutchinson (Future Watch)	2.00
122	Peter Bergeron (Future Watch)	2.00
123	Wascar Serrano RC (Future Watch)	2.00
124	Tony Armas Jr. (Future Watch)	2.00
125	Ramon Ortiz (Future Watch)	2.00
126	Adam Kennedy (Future Watch)	2.00
127	Joe Crede (Future Watch)	5.00
128	Roosevelt Brown (Future Watch)	2.00
129	Mark Mulder (Future Watch)	2.50
130	Brad Penny (Future Watch)	2.00
131	Terrence Long (Future Watch)	2.00
132	Ruben Mateo (Future Watch)	2.00
133	Wily Mo Pena (Future Watch)	2.00
134	Rafael Furcal (Future Watch)	2.00
135	Mario Encarnacion (Future Watch)	2.00

Limited

A parallel to the 135-card base set these have "SP Limited" printed down the right side of the front and are serial numbered on the card front in an edition of 100 sets.

Cards (1-90):	4-8X
Cards (91-105):	2-3X
Cards (106-135):	1-2X
Production 100 Sets	

Chirography

This autographed insert set has a horizontal format with two player images on the card front. The player signature appears in the top right portion over a silver, checkered background. The insert name and logo have a silver tint. Card backs are numbered with the featured players first and last initial. Chirographies are seeded 1:23 packs.

		NM/M
Common Player:		5.00
Inserted 1:23		
RA	Rick Ankiel	25.00
CBe	Carlos Beltran	30.00
BB	Barry Bonds	200.00
PB	Pat Burrell	15.00
JC	Jose Canseco	25.00
SC	Sean Casey	8.00
RC	Roger Clemens	80.00
ED	Erubiel Durazo	5.00
TGl	Troy Glaus	20.00
VG	Vladimir Guerrero	30.00
TG	Tony Gwynn	40.00
DJ	Derek Jeter	120.00
NJ	Nick Johnson	10.00
CJ	Chipper Jones	40.00
AJ	Andruw Jones	20.00
SK	Sandy Koufax	250.00
BP	Ben Petrick	5.00
MQ	Mark Quinn	5.00
MR	Manny Ramirez	40.00
CR	Cal Ripken Jr.	100.00
AR	Alex Rodriguez	90.00
IR	Ivan Rodriguez	25.00
SR	Scott Rolen	25.00
AS	Alfonso Soriano	30.00
MV	Mo Vaughn	8.00
EY	Ed Yarnall	5.00

Chirography Gold

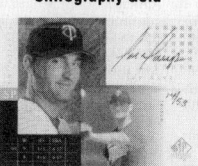

Golds use the same photos as the regular Chirography inserts and can be differentiated by the gold checkered background of the player signature in the upper right portion as well as the gold tint in the insert name and logo. Golds are also hand-numbered to the player's jersey number on the card front and are numbered with a "G" prefix on the card back before the players initials.

		NM/M
Common Player:		25.00
RA	Rick Ankiel/66 EXCH	50.00
CBe	Carlos Beltran/15	65.00
BB	Barry Bonds/25	300.00
PB	Pat Burrell/33 EXCH	50.00
JC	Jose Canseco/33	75.00
SC	Sean Casey/21	65.00
RC	Roger Clemens/22	300.00
ED	Erubiel Durazo/44	25.00
VG	Vladimir Guerrero/27	100.00
TG	Tony Gwynn/19	200.00
NJ	Nick Johnson/63	15.00
BP	Ben Petrick/15	30.00
MR	Manny Ramirez/24 EXCH	100.00
AS	Alfonso Soriano/53	60.00
MV	Mo Vaughn/42	25.00
EY	Ed Yarnall/41	15.00

Joe DiMaggio Game Jersey

This is DiMaggio's first Game Jersey insert and has three different versions. The first is limited to 500 total cards, the second version is Gold and numbered to 56. The rarest version has a DiMaggio cut signature along with a piece of his game-used jersey and is limited to only five total cards.

		NM/M
DiMaggio Jersey Card		
JD	Joe DiMaggio/Jsy/500	120.00
JD	Joe DiMaggio/Jsy Gold/56	200.00

Midsummer Classics

This 10-card set spotlights perennial All-Stars and has a silver holo-foiled front with gold foil etching and stamping. These are found 1:12 packs and are numbered on the card back with an "MC" prefix.

		NM/M
Complete Set (10):		10.00
Common Player:		.50
Inserted 1:12		
1	Cal Ripken Jr.	3.00
2	Roger Clemens	1.75
3	Jeff Bagwell	.75
4	Barry Bonds	3.00
5	Jose Canseco	.50
6	Frank Thomas	.75
7	Mike Piazza	2.00
8	Tony Gwynn	1.50
9	Juan Gonzalez	.75
10	Greg Maddux	1.50

Premier Performers

This 10-card set spotlights baseball's best on a silver holo-foiled card front with the player name, insert name and logo stamped in gold foil. Card backs are numbered with a "PP" prefix and are found 1:12 packs.

		NM/M
Complete Set (10):		10.00
Common Player:		.75
Inserted 1:12		
1	Mark McGwire	2.00
2	Alex Rodriguez	2.50
3	Cal Ripken Jr.	3.00
4	Nomar Garciaparra	1.50
5	Ken Griffey Jr.	1.50
6	Chipper Jones	1.50
7	Derek Jeter	3.00
8	Ivan Rodriguez	.75
9	Vladimir Guerrero	.75
10	Sammy Sosa	1.50

SP Buyback

This autographed set features previously issued SP cards that were re-purchased by Upper Deck. The cards are autographed by the featured player and hand-numbered on the card front. The number autographed and released by Upper Deck is listed after the player name. Buybacks are found 1:95 packs.

		NM/M
Common Player:		50.00
1	Jeff Bagwell Exch.	50.00
2	Craig Biggio '93/59	50.00
3	Craig Biggio '94/69	50.00
4	Craig Biggio '95/171	40.00
5	Craig Biggio '96/71	50.00
6	Craig Biggio '97/46	50.00
7	Craig Biggio '98/40	50.00
8	Craig Biggio '99/125	40.00
15	Barry Bonds '99/520	150.00
16	Jose Canseco '93/29	60.00
17	Jose Canseco '94/20	60.00
19	Jose Canseco '96/23	60.00
20	Jose Canseco '97/23	60.00
21	Jose Canseco '98/24	60.00
22	Jose Canseco '99/502	30.00
24	Sean Casey '99/139	20.00
25	Roger Clemens '93/68	85.00
26	Roger Clemens '94/60	85.00
27	Roger Clemens '95/68	85.00
28	Roger Clemens '96/68	85.00
30	Roger Clemens '98/25	200.00
31	Roger Clemens '99/134	75.00
32	Jason Giambi '97/34	50.00
33	Jason Giambi '98/25	50.00
34	Tom Glavine '93/99	40.00
35	Tom Glavine '94/107	40.00
36	Tom Glavine '95/97	40.00
37	Tom Glavine '96/42	50.00
38	Tom Glavine '98/40	50.00
39	Tom Glavine '99/138	40.00
40	Shawn Green '96/55	50.00
41	Shawn Green '99/530	20.00
42	Ken Griffey Jr. '96/12	275.00
47	Tony Gwynn '97/24	150.00
48	Tony Gwynn '99/129	50.00
50	Tony Gwynn '99/369	40.00
56	Derek Jeter '99/119	200.00
57	Randy Johnson '93/60	75.00
58	Randy Johnson '94/45	80.00
59	Randy Johnson '95/70	75.00
60	Randy Johnson '96/60	75.00
63	Randy Johnson '99/113	75.00
64	Andruw Jones Exch.	40.00
65	Chipper Jones Exch.	75.00
66	Kenny Lofton '94/100	25.00
67	Kenny Lofton '95/84	25.00
68	Kenny Lofton '96/34	40.00
69	Kenny Lofton '97/82	40.00
70	Kenny Lofton '98/21	40.00
71	Kenny Lofton '99/99	20.00
72	Javy Lopez '93/106	15.00
73	Javy Lopez '94/160	20.00
74	Javy Lopez '96/99	15.00
75	Javy Lopez '97/61	20.00
77	Greg Maddux '93/22	275.00
78	Greg Maddux '94/19	275.00
83	Greg Maddux '99/504	75.00
84	Paul O'Neill '93/110	25.00
85	Paul O'Neill '94/97	30.00
86	Paul O'Neill '95/142	25.00
87	Paul O'Neill '96/70	30.00
88	Paul O'Neill '98/23	40.00
89	Manny Ramirez Redemp	
91	Cal Ripken Jr. '94/22	300.00
96	Cal Ripken Jr. '99/510	125.00
97	Alex Rodriguez Exch.	125.00
98	Ivan Rodriguez '93/29	100.00
100	Ivan Rodriguez '95/18	125.00
101	Ivan Rodriguez '96/22	125.00
103	Ivan Rodriguez '98/27	125.00
109	Frank Thomas '97/20	75.00
111	Frank Thomas '99/100	50.00
112	Greg Vaughn '93/79	20.00

113	Greg Vaughn '94/75	20.00
114	Greg Vaughn '95/155	15.00
115	Greg Vaughn '96/113	15.00
117	Greg Vaughn '99/527	10.00
118	Mo Vaughn '93/119	20.00
119	Mo Vaughn '94/96	20.00
120	Mo Vaughn '95/121	20.00
121	Mo Vaughn '96/114	20.00
122	Mo Vaughn '97/61	25.00
124	Mo Vaughn '99/537	15.00
125	Robin Ventura '93/59	25.00
126	Robin Ventura '94/49	25.00
127	Robin Ventura '95/125	20.00
128	Robin Ventura '96/55	25.00
129	Robin Ventura '97/44	30.00
130	Robin Ventura '98/28	35.00
131	Robin Ventura '99/370	15.00
133	Matt Williams '94/50	40.00
134	Matt Williams '95/137	40.00
135	Matt Williams '96/77	40.00
136	Matt Williams '97/54	40.00
137	Matt Williams '98/29	60.00
138	Matt Williams '99/529	15.00
139	Preston Wilson '94/249	15.00
140	Preston Wilson '99/195	15.00

SP Cornerstones

Printed on a silver holo-foiled card front a close-up image of the player appears in a baseball diamond shaped enclosed by gold foil etching. Another shadow image of the featured player appears in the background. The player name, insert name and logo are stamped in gold foil. These are seeded 1:23 packs and are numbered with a "C" prefix on the card back.

		NM/M
Complete Set (7):		15.00
Common Player:		2.00
Inserted 1:23		
1	Ken Griffey Jr.	2.00
2	Cal Ripken Jr.	4.00
3	Mike Piazza	2.00
4	Derek Jeter	4.00
5	Mark McGwire	3.00
6	Nomar Garciaparra	2.00
7	Sammy Sosa	2.00

SP Supremacy

This seven-card set has a silver foiled card front with the insert name and logo stamped in gold foil. The inserts are found on the average of 1:23 packs and are numbered with a "S" prefix.

		NM/M
Complete Set (7):		8.00
Common Player:		.75
Inserted 1:23		
1	Alex Rodriguez	3.00
2	Shawn Green	.75
3	Pedro Martinez	1.00
4	Chipper Jones	2.00
5	Tony Gwynn	2.00
6	Ivan Rodriguez	1.00
7	Jeff Bagwell	1.00

United Nations

Done on a horizontal format this 10-card set salutes the top international stars of the game. The featured player's country of origin flag is in the background of the player image. The card design features silver holofoil and silver foil etching and stamping. These are seeded 1:4 packs and are numbered with an "UN" prefix on the card back.

		NM/M
Complete Set (10):		5.00
Common Player:		.50
Inserted 1:4		
1	Sammy Sosa (Dominican Rep.)	1.50
2	Ken Griffey Jr. (USA)	2.00
3	Orlando Hernandez (Cuba)	.50
4	Andres Galarraga (Venezuela)	.50
5	Kazuhiro Sasaki (Japan)	.50
6	Larry Walker (Canada)	.50
7	Vinny Castilla (Mexico)	.50
8	Andruw Jones (Neth. Antilles)	.75
9	Ivan Rodriguez (Puerto Rico)	.75
10	Chan Ho Park (So. Korea)	.50

3,000 Hit Club

A continuation of Upper Deck's cross brand salute to players who have reached the magical 3,000 hit milestone. 350 game-used bat cards and five bat/cut signature combos were issued for each player.

		NM/M
PW	Paul Waner/Bat/350	50.00
TS	Tris Speaker/Bat/350	100.00

2000 SPx

The base set consists of 120-cards including 30 Rookie/ Young Star subset cards which has three tiers. The first five are numbered to 1,000, the next 22 autographed and numbered to 1,500 and the final three are autographed and numbered to 500. Each base card has a holo-foiled front with the SPx logo, player name, team name stamped in gold foil.

		NM/M
Complete Set (120):		400.00
Common Player:		.15
Common Rookie (91-120):		10.00
Pack (4):		6.00
Box (18):		80.00
1	Troy Glaus	.50
2	Mo Vaughn	.15
3	Ramon Ortiz	.15
4	Jeff Bagwell	.75
5	Moises Alou	.25
6	Craig Biggio	.40
7	Jose Lima	.15
8	Jason Giambi	.75
9	John Jaha	.15
10	Matt Stairs	.15
11	Chipper Jones	1.00
12	Greg Maddux	1.50
13	Andres Galarraga	.15

14	Andruw Jones	1.00
15	Jeromy Burnitz	.15
16	Ron Belliard	.15
17	Carlos Delgado	.75
18	David Wells	.15
19	Tony Batista	.15
20	Shannon Stewart	.15
21	Sammy Sosa	1.00
22	Mark Grace	.50
23	Henry Rodriguez	.15
24	Mark McGwire	2.00
25	J.D. Drew	.25
26	Luis Gonzalez	.25
27	Randy Johnson	1.00
28	Matt Williams	.15
29	Steve Finley	.15
30	Shawn Green	.25
31	Kevin Brown	.15
32	Gary Sheffield	.50
33	Jose Canseco	.50
34	Greg Vaughn	.15
35	Vladimir Guerrero	1.00
36	Michael Barrett	.15
37	Russ Ortiz	.15
38	Barry Bonds	3.00
39	Jeff Kent	.25
40	Richie Sexson	.40
41	Manny Ramirez	1.00
42	Jim Thome	1.00
43	Roberto Alomar	.50
44	Edgar Martinez	.15
45	Alex Rodriguez	2.50
46	John Olerud	.15
47	Alex Gonzalez	.15
48	Cliff Floyd	.15
49	Mike Piazza	1.50
50	Al Leiter	.15
51	Robin Ventura	.15
52	Edgardo Alfonzo	.15
53	Albert Belle	.15
54	Cal Ripken Jr.	3.00
55	B.J. Surhoff	.15
56	Tony Gwynn	1.50
57	Trevor Hoffman	.15
58	Brian Giles	.15
59	Jason Kendall	.15
60	Kris Benson	.15
61	Bob Abreu	.50
62	Scott Rolen	1.00
63	Curt Schilling	.75
64	Mike Lieberthal	.15
65	Sean Casey	.25
66	Dante Bichette	.15
67	Ken Griffey Jr.	2.00
68	Pokey Reese	.15
69	Mike Sweeney	.15
70	Carlos Febles	.15
71	Ivan Rodriguez	1.00
72	Ruben Mateo	.15
73	Rafael Palmeiro	1.00
74	Larry Walker	.40
75	Todd Helton	.75
76	Nomar Garciaparra	1.00
77	Pedro Martinez	1.00
78	Troy O'Leary	.15
79	Jacque Jones	.15
80	Corey Koskie	.15
81	Juan Gonzalez	.50
82	Dean Palmer	.15
83	Juan Encarnacion	.15
84	Frank Thomas	1.00
85	Magglio Ordonez	.25
86	Paul Konerko	.50
87	Bernie Williams	.50
88	Derek Jeter	3.00
89	Roger Clemens	2.50
90	Orlando Hernandez	.15
91	Vernon Wells AU-1,000	25.00
92	Rick Ankiel AU-1,000	60.00
93	Eric Chavez AU-1,000	20.00
94	Alfonso Soriano AU-1,000	50.00
95	Eric Gagne AU-1,000	25.00
96	Rob Bell AU-1,000	10.00
97	Matt Riley AU-1,500	10.00
98	Josh Beckett AU-1,500	80.00
99	Ben Petrick AU-1,500	10.00
100	Rob Ramsay AU-1,500 RC	10.00
101	Scott Williamson AU-1,500	10.00
102	Doug Davis AU-1,500	15.00
103	Eric Munson AU-1,500	10.00
104	Pat Burrell AU-500	30.00
105	Jim Morris AU-1,500	20.00
106	Gabe Kapler AU-500	15.00
107	Lance Berkman 1,500	35.00
108	Erubiel Durazo AU-1,500	15.00
109	Tim Hudson AU-1,500	30.00
110	Ben Davis AU-1,500	10.00
111	Nick Johnson AU-1,500	20.00
112	Octavio Dotel AU-1,500	10.00
113	Jerry Hairston Jr. 1,500	10.00
114	Ruben Mateo 1,500	10.00
115	Chris Singleton 1,500	10.00
116	Bruce Chen 1,500	10.00
117	Derrick Gibson AU-1,500	10.00
118	Carlos Beltran AU-500	80.00
119	Fred Garcia AU-500	10.00
120	Preston Wilson AU-500	15.00

Radiance

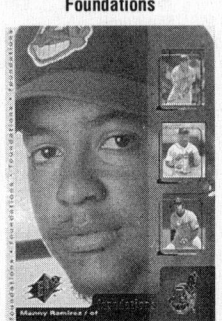

A parallel to the 120-card base set these are serially numbered to 100. A one-of-one Spectrum parallel of each base card is also randomly seeded.

	NM/M
Stars (1-90):	4-8X
Common Young Star (91-120):	10.00
Production 100 Sets	

Foundations

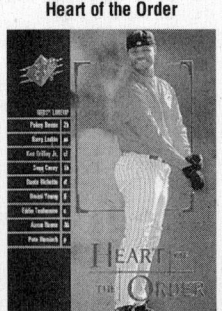

This 10-card set features a holo-foiled front with gold foil stamping. Three miniature action shots appear to the right of a close-up shot of the featured player. Card backs are numbered with an "F" prefix and inserted 1:32 packs.

		NM/M
Complete Set (10):		15.00
Common Player:		.50
Inserted 1:32		
1	Ken Griffey Jr.	3.00
2	Nomar Garciaparra	3.00
3	Cal Ripken Jr.	4.00
4	Chipper Jones	2.00
5	Mike Piazza	3.00
6	Derek Jeter	4.00
7	Manny Ramirez	1.00
8	Jeff Bagwell	1.00
9	Tony Gwynn	2.00
10	Larry Walker	.50

Heart of the Order

This 20-card set features a top hitter with his teams batting order to the left of his photo. The SPx logo and insert name are stamped in gold foil. Card backs are numbered with an "H" prefix and seeded 1:8 packs.

		NM/M
Complete Set (20):		10.00
Common Player:		.40
Inserted 1:8		
1	Bernie Williams	.50
2	Mike Piazza	2.00
3	Ivan Rodriguez	.75
4	Mark McGwire	2.50
5	Manny Ramirez	1.00
6	Ken Griffey Jr.	2.00
7	Matt Williams	.40
8	Sammy Sosa	2.00
9	Mo Vaughn	.40
10	Carlos Delgado	.75

Highlight Heroes

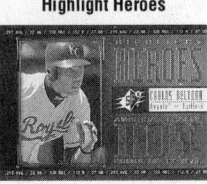

This 10-card set has a horizontal format on a holo-foiled front with gold foil stamping. Card backs are numbered with an "HH" prefix and inserted 1:16 packs.

		NM/M
Complete Set (10):		10.00
Common Player:		.50
Inserted 1:16		
1	Pedro Martinez	1.00
2	Ivan Rodriguez	.75
3	Carlos Beltran	.65
4	Nomar Garciaparra	2.00
5	Ken Griffey Jr.	2.00
6	Randy Johnson	1.00
7	Chipper Jones	1.50
8	Scott Williamson	.50
9	Larry Walker	.50
10	Mark McGwire	2.50

Power Brokers

This 20-card set has a horizontal format with the background of the player photo having a kaleidoscope effect. The SPx logo is stamped in gold foil. Card backs are numbered with an "PB" prefix and are inserted 1:8 packs.

		NM/M
Complete Set (20):		10.00
Common Player:		.25
Inserted 1:8		
1	Rafael Palmeiro	.75
2	Carlos Delgado	.65
3	Ken Griffey Jr.	2.00
4	Matt Stairs	.25
5	Mike Piazza	2.00
6	Vladimir Guerrero	1.00
7	Chipper Jones	1.50
8	Mark McGwire	2.50
9	Matt Williams	.25
10	Juan Gonzalez	1.00
11	Shawn Green	.50
12	Sammy Sosa	2.00
13	Brian Giles	.25
14	Jeff Bagwell	1.00
15	Alex Rodriguez	2.50
16	Frank Thomas	1.00
17	Larry Walker	.25
18	Albert Belle	.25
19	Dean Palmer	.25
20	Mo Vaughn	.25

SPxcitement

This 20-card set features a holo-foiled front with gold foil stamping. Card backs are numbered with an "XC" prefix and are inserted 1:4 packs.

	NM/M
Complete Set (20):	15.00

11	Brian Giles	.40
12	Chipper Jones	1.50
13	Sean Casey	.40
14	Tony Gwynn	1.50
15	Barry Bonds	3.00
16	Carlos Beltran	.65
17	Scott Rolen	.75
18	Juan Gonzalez	1.00
19	Larry Walker	.40
20	Vladimir Guerrero	1.00

Common Player: .25
Inserted 1:4

1	Nomar Garciaparra	1.25
2	Mark McGwire	1.50
3	Derek Jeter	2.00
4	Cal Ripken Jr.	2.00
5	Barry Bonds	2.00
6	Alex Rodriguez	1.50
7	Scott Rolen	.75
8	Pedro Martinez	.75
9	Sean Casey	.25
10	Sammy Sosa	1.25
11	Randy Johnson	.75
12	Ivan Rodriguez	.75
13	Frank Thomas	.75
14	Greg Maddux	1.00
15	Tony Gwynn	1.00
16	Ken Griffey Jr.	1.25
17	Carlos Beltran	.50
18	Mike Piazza	1.25
19	Chipper Jones	1.00
20	Craig Biggio	.25

SPx Signatures

These autographed inserts are seeded 1:112 packs.

		NM/M
Common Player:		10.00
Inserted 1:179		
JB	Jeff Bagwell	25.00
BB	Barry Bonds	150.00
JC	Jose Canseco	25.00
SC	Sean Casey	15.00
RC	Roger Clemens	125.00
KG	Ken Griffey Jr.	100.00
VG	Vladimir Guerrero	35.00
TG	Tony Gwynn	40.00
OH	Orlando Hernandez	40.00
DJ	Derek Jeter	125.00
CJ	Chipper Jones	50.00
MR	Manny Ramirez	40.00
CR	Cal Ripken Jr.	125.00
IR	Ivan Rodriguez	25.00
SR	Scott Rolen	30.00

Untouchable Talents

These inserts have a holo-foiled front and are numbered with an "UT" prefix. They are found on the average of 1:96 packs.

		NM/M
Complete Set (10):		30.00
Common Player:		1.50
Inserted 1:96		
1	Mark McGwire	8.00
2	Ken Griffey Jr.	6.00
3	Shawn Green	2.00
4	Ivan Rodriguez	2.50
5	Sammy Sosa	5.00
6	Derek Jeter	10.00
7	Sean Casey	1.50
8	Chipper Jones	5.00
9	Pedro Martinez	3.00
10	Vladimir Guerrero	3.00

Winning Materials

Five different tiers make up this memorabilia insert set with players having varying levels of their inserts in the set. Each insert has two pieces of memorabilia, combinations include Jersey/Bat, Jersey/Bat numbered to player's jersey number, Jersey/Cap, Jersey/Ball and Ball/Bat.

		NM/M
Common Bat/Jsy		6.00
AR	Alex Rodriguez/Bat/Jsy	25.00
AR	Alex Rodriguez/Cap/Jsy/100	40.00
AR	Alex Rodriguez/Ball/Jsy/50	50.00
DJ	Derek Jeter/Bat/Jsy	40.00
DJ	Derek Jeter/Bat/Jsy/50	75.00
BB	Barry Bonds/Bat/Jsy	30.00
BB	Barry Bonds/Cap/Jsy/100	50.00
BB	Barry Bonds/Ball/Jsy/Auto./25	350.00
JB	Jeff Bagwell/Bat/Jsy	8.00
JB	Jeff Bagwell/Cap/Jsy/100	15.00
JB	Jeff Bagwell/Bat/Jsy/50	25.00
KG	Ken Griffey Jr./Bat/Jsy	20.00
KG	Ken Griffey Jr./Ball/Jsy/50	50.00
KG	Ken Griffey Jr./Jsy/Bat/Auto./24	225.00
TG	Tony Gwynn/Bat/Jsy	10.00
TG	Tony Gwynn/Ball/Jsy/50	40.00
TG	Tony Gwynn/Cap/Jsy/100	30.00
BW	Bernie Williams/Bat/Jsy	8.00
EC	Eric Chavez/Bat/Jsy	8.00
EC	Eric Chavez/Cap/Jsy/100	15.00
GM	Greg Maddux/Bat/Jsy	25.00
IR	Ivan Rodriguez/Bat/Jsy	8.00
JC	Jose Canseco/Bat/Jsy	8.00
JL	Javy Lopez/Bat/Jsy	6.00
JL	Javy Lopez/Cap/Jsy/100	8.00
MM	Mark McGwire/Base/Bat/500	50.00
MR	Manny Ramirez/Bat/Jsy	10.00
MW	Matt Williams/Bat/Jsy	6.00
PM	Pedro Martinez/Cap/Jsy/100	25.00
PO	Paul O'Neill/Bat/Jsy	6.00
VG	Vladimir Guerrero/Bat/Jsy	10.00
VG	Vladimir Guerrero/Cap/Jsy/100	20.00
VG	Vladimir Guerrero/Ball/Jsy/50	30.00
TG	Troy Glaus/Bat/Jsy	8.00

3,000 Hit Club

A continuation of Upper Deck's cross-brand insert program, this set pays tribute to Ty Cobb with three variations. The collection includes 350 bat cards, three cut signatures and one bat/cut signature card.

	NM/M
TC-B Ty Cobb/Bat/350	130.00

1993 Spectrum Diamond Club Promo Set

Ten Hall of Famers are featured in this promo card set. Fronts of the 2-1/2" x 3-1/2" cards have borderless player action or posed photos. The issuer's logo, player's name and striping are printed in gold. Backs have a color ghost-image photo of the player along with personal data and career summary. A box near the bottom indicates the set's serial number from within an edition of 10,000. A "Pure Gold" parallel edition of 5,000 each was also produced.

		NM/M
Complete Set (10):		8.00
Common Player:		1.00
Pure Gold:		2X
1	Carl Yastrzemski	1.50
2	Johnny Bench (Numbered promo.)	1.00
--	Johnny Bench ("For Promotional Use Only" on back.)	1.00
3	Al Kaline	1.00
4	Ernie Banks	2.00
5	Catfish Hunter	1.00
6	Rod Carew	1.00
7	Mike Schmidt	2.00
8	Harmon Killebrew	1.00
9	Frank Robinson	1.50
10	Rollie Fingers	1.00

Diamond Club Red Sox

This collectors' issue features five stars of the Boston Red Sox from the 1940s-1970s. Fronts have action photos on which uniform logos are eliminated. A pinstripe around the photo, the issuer's logo and player name are printed in gold. Size is standard 2-1/2" x 3-1/2". Horizontal backs have a color Fenway Park photo ghosted in the background. Player career highlights and stats are overprinted.

		NM/M
Complete Set (5):		1.00
Common Player:		.25
1	Carl Yastrzemski	.50
2	Bobby Doerr	.25
3	Dwight Evans	.25
4	Fred Lynn	.25
5	Luis Tiant	.25

Legends of Baseball

This collectors' edition of 10 of baseball's greatest players was issued in two versions, with and without a gold facsimile autograph on the cards' fronts. The gold-signature cards were limited to an edition of 5,000 numbered cards of each player. Fronts have black-and-white photos with gold-foil graphic highlights. Backs have another photo subdued in the background with career history and stats and personal data overprinted in black. Copyright information is at bottom. Cards were issued in two series of five each and are checklisted here alphabetically.

		NM/M
Complete Set (10):		7.50
Common Player:		.50
Gold Signature:		2X
(1)	Grover Alexander	.50
(2)	Ty Cobb	.75
(3)	Dizzy Dean	.50
(4)	Lou Gehrig	1.00
(5)	Rogers Hornsby	.50
(6)	Satchel Paige	.75
(7)	Babe Ruth	2.00
(8)	Casey Stengel	.50
(9)	Honus Wagner	.75
(10)	Cy Young	.50

Nolan Ryan

Produced in the same format as its Legends of Baseball 10-card sets, this issue honors the career of Nolan Ryan. Each set comes with a numbered certificate of authenticity. There were 5,000 regular sets produced and 5,000 with gold-foil facsimile autographs on fronts. Each card can also be found in a promotional overprinted version.

	NM/M
Complete Set (10):	3.00
Common Card:	.50
Gold:	2X
Promo:	2X

Nolan Ryan 23K

A "pure gold" background on front offsets the color action photo of Ryan in action (team logos have been removed for licensing reasons). Backs of the 2-1/2" x 3-1/2" cards have career highlights and stats. Each set was issued with a certificate of authenticity numbered from an edition of 10,000.

	NM/M
Complete Set (3):	3.00
Common Card:	1.00
1-3 Nolan Ryan	1.00

1994 Spectrum 1969 Miracle Mets

The 1969 Miracle Mets card set, produced by Spectrum Holdings Group of Birmingham, Mich., was part of what the company called "an integrated memorabilia program," with the 1969 Mets card set as the centerpiece." The 70-card set measures the standard 2-1/2" x 3-1/2", with UV coating on both sides and gold foil on fronts. It was sold complete at $24.95, and limited to 25,000 sets. A reported 1,000 numbered sets were signed by all 25 living play-ers, including Hall of Famer Tom Seaver and future Cooperstown resident Nolan Ryan.

		NM/M
Complete Set (70):		20.00
Common Player:		.25
Autographed Set:		500.00
1	Commemorative Card	.25
2	Team Photo	.25
3	Tom Seaver	4.00
4	Jerry Koosman	.35
5	Tommie Agee	.25
6	Bud Harrelson	.25
7	Nolan Ryan	6.00
8	Jerry Grote	.25
9	Ron Swoboda	.25
10	Donn Clendenon	.25
11	Art Shamsky	.25
12	Tug McGraw	.25
13	Ed Kranepool	.25
14	Cleon Jones	.25
15	Ron Taylor	.25
16	Gary Gentry	.25
17	Ken Boswell	.25
18	Ed Charles	.25
19	J.C. Martin	.25
20	Al Weis	.25
21	Jack DiLauro	.25
22	Duffy Dyer	.25
23	Wayne Garrett	.25
24	Jim McAndrew	.25
25	Rod Gaspar	.25
26	Don Cardwell	.25
27	Bob Pfeil	.25
28	Cal Koonce	.25
29	Gil Hodges	1.50
30	Yogi Berra	2.00
31	Joe Pignatano	.25
32	Rube Walker	.25
33	Eddie Yost	.25
34	First-ever Met Game	.25
35	Opening Day 1969	.25
36	Kranepool Breaks Home Run Record	.25
37	Koosman Sets Club Strikeout Record	.25
38	Mets Trade for Clendenon	.25
39	Koosman's 23 Scoreless Innings	.25
40	Mets Begin 7-Game Winning Streak	.25
41	Mets vs. Division Leading Cubs	.25
42	Seaver's Near Perfect Game	.25
43	Mets Trail by 3-1/2	.25
44	All-Star Break	.25
45	All-Star Game	.25
46	Mets Sweep Atlanta	.25
47	Mets Sweep Padres	.25
48	Mets Defeat Cubs, Koosman Strikes Out 1	.25
49	Mets Defeat Cubs 1/2 Game Back	.25
50	First Place!	.25
51	Mets Continue Nine Game Winning Streak	.25
52	Seaver Earns 22nd Victory	.25
53	Mets Win, Carlton Strikes Out 19	.25
54	Koosman Pitches 15th Complete Game	.25
55	Eastern Division Champs!	.25
56	100th Victory	.25
57	Final Game, Mets Prepare for Braves	.25
58	N.L. Championship Series, Game 1	.25
59	N.L. Championship Series, Game 2	.25
60	N.L. Championship Series, Game 3	.25
61	World Series, Game 1	.25
62	World Series, Game 2	.25
63	World Series, Game 3	.25
64	World Series, Game 4	.25
65	World Series, Game 5	.25
66	World Champions	.25
67	World Champions	.25
68	World Champions	.25
69	World Champions	.25
----	Checklist	.25

1986 Sportflics Prototype Cards

This six-card set was apparently produced as a prototype as part of the licensing process. Similar in format to the 1986 Sportflics issue the cards have stats through the 1984 season. The prototype cards are much rarer than the promo cards. The Schmidt, Sutter and Winfield cards are standard 2-1/2" x 3-1/2" in size while the DiMaggio card is 1-5/16" square and the MLB logo card is 1-3/4" x 2".

		NM/M
Complete Set (7):		175.00
Common Card:		2.00
(1)	Joe DiMaggio (Black-and-white.)	100.00
(2)	Mike Schmidt	20.00
(3)	Bruce Sutter	5.00
(4)	Dave Winfield (Biographical back.)	50.00
(5)	Dave Winfield (Statistical back.)	37.50
(6)	Mike Schmidt, Bruce Sutter, Dave Winfield (Blank-back.)	10.00
(7)	Major League Baseball Logo	2.00

1986 Sportflics Promo Cards

Though they carry stats only through 1984, and have a 1986 copyright date, these promo cards were issued late in 1985 to preview the "Triple Action Sportflics" concept. They were the first really widely distributed promo cards. Each of the promo cards differs slightly from the issued version. The RBI Sluggers card in the issued set, for instance, was #126 and pictured Gary Carter, George Foster and Al Oliver. In the regular set, Pete Rose's card was #50 while Tom Seaver was #25. The regular-issue 1986 Sportflics cards, of course, include complete 1985 stats on back. Promo cards were distributed in three-card cello packs.

		NM/M
Complete Set (3):		12.50
Common Player:		3.00
1	RBI Sluggers (Dale Murphy, Jim Rice, Mike Schmidt)	3.00
43	Pete Rose	10.00
45	Tom Seaver	4.00

1986 Sportflics

The premiere issue from Sportflics was distributed nationally by Amurol Division of Wrigley Gum Co. The three-phase "Magic Motion" cards depict three different photos per card, with each visible separately as the card is tilted. The 1986 issue features 200 full-color baseball cards plus 133 trivia cards. The cards are in the standard 2-1/2" x 3-1/2" size with the backs containing player stats and personal information. There are three different types of picture cards: 1) Tri-Star cards - 50 cards feature three players on one card; 2) Big Six cards - 10 cards which have six players in special categories; and 3) the Big Twelve card of 12 World Series players from the Kansas City Royals. The trivia cards are 1-3/4" x 2" and do not have player photos.

		NM/M
Unopened Factory Set (200):		10.00
Complete Set (200):		7.50
Common Player:		.10
Foil Pack (3+2):		.50
Foil Box (36):		9.00
1	George Brett	2.25
2	Don Mattingly	2.25
3	Wade Boggs	2.00
4	Eddie Murray	1.00
5	Dale Murphy	.65
6	Rickey Henderson	.10
7	Harold Baines	.10
8	Cal Ripken, Jr.	3.00
9	Orel Hershiser	.10
10	Bret Saberhagen	.10
11	Tim Raines	.10
12	Fernando Valenzuela	.10
13	Tony Gwynn	2.00
14	Pedro Guerrero	.10
15	Keith Hernandez	.10
16	Ernest Riles	.10
17	Jim Rice	.20
18	Ron Guidry	.10
19	Willie McGee	.10
20	Ryne Sandberg	2.00
21	Kirk Gibson	.10
22	Ozzie Guillen	.10
23	Dave Parker	.10
24	Vince Coleman	.10
25	Tom Seaver	1.00
26	Brett Butler	.10
27	Steve Carlton	1.00
28	Gary Carter	1.00
29	Cecil Cooper	.10
30	Jose Cruz	.10
31	Alvin Davis	.10
32	Dwight Evans	.10
33	Julio Franco	.10
34	Damaso Garcia	.10
35	Steve Garvey	.60
36	Kent Hrbek	.10
37	Reggie Jackson	2.25
38	Fred Lynn	.10
39	Paul Molitor	1.00
40	Jim Presley	.10
41	Dave Righetti	.10
42a	Robin Yount (Yankees logo on back.)	85.00
42b	Robin Yount (Brewers logo.)	2.00
43	Nolan Ryan	3.00
44	Mike Schmidt	2.25
45	Lee Smith	.10
46	Rick Sutcliffe	.10
47	Bruce Sutter	.75
48	Lou Whitaker	.10
49	Dave Winfield	1.00
50	Pete Rose	2.50
51	N.L. MVPs (Steve Garvey, Pete Rose, Ryne Sandberg)	1.00
52	Slugging Stars (Harold Baines, George Brett, Jim Rice)	.35
53	No-Hitters (Phil Niekro, Jerry Reuss, Mike Witt)	.25
54	Big Hitters (Don Mattingly, Cal Ripken, Jr., Robin Yount)	2.00
55	Bullpen Aces (Goose Gossage, Dan Quisenberry, Lee Smith)	.10
56	Rookies of the Year (Pete Rose, Steve Sax, Darryl Strawberry)	1.00
57	A.L. MVPs (Don Baylor, Reggie Jackson, Cal Ripken, Jr.)	.50
58	Repeat Batting Champs (Bill Madlock, Dave Parker, Pete Rose)	.45
59	Cy Young Winners (Mike Flanagan, Ron Guidry, LaMarr Hoyt)	.10
60	Double Award Winners (Tom Seaver, Rick Sutcliffe, Fernando Valenzuela)	.20
61	Home Run Champs (Tony Armas, Reggie Jackson, Jim Rice)	.25
62	N.L. MVPs (Keith Hernandez, Dale Murphy, Mike Schmidt)	.40
63	A.L. MVPs (George Brett, Fred Lynn, Robin Yount)	.30
64	Comeback Players (Bert Blyleven, John Denny, Jerry Koosman)	.10
65	Cy Young Relievers (Rollie Fingers, Willie Hernandez, Bruce Sutter)	.10
66	Rookies of the Year (Andre Dawson, Bob Horner, Gary Matthews)	.20

67 Rookies of the Year (Carlton Fisk, Ron Kittle, Tom Seaver) .25
68 Home Run Champs (George Foster, Dave Kingman, Mike Schmidt) .25
69 Double Award Winners (Rod Carew, Cal Ripken, Jr., Pete Rose) 2.00
70 Cy Young Winners (Steve Carlton, Tom Seaver, Rick Sutcliffe) .25
71 Top Sluggers (Reggie Jackson, Fred Lynn, Robin Yount) .30
72 Rookies of the Year (Dave Righetti, Rick Sutcliffe, Fernando Valenzuela) .10
73 Rookies of the Year (Fred Lynn, Eddie Murray, Cal Ripken, Jr.) .50
74 Rookies of the Year (Rod Carew, Alvin Davis, Lou Whitaker) .20
75 Batting Champs (Wade Boggs, Carney Lansford, Don Mattingly) 1.00
76 Jesse Barfield .10
77 Phil Bradley .10
78 Chris Brown .10
79 Tom Browning .10
80 Tom Brunansky .10
81 Bill Buckner .10
82 Chili Davis .10
83 Mike Davis .10
84 Rich Gedman .10
85 Willie Hernandez .10
86 Ron Kittle .10
87 Lee Lacy .10
88 Bill Madlock .10
89 Mike Marshall .10
90 Keith Moreland .10
91 Graig Nettles .10
92 Lance Parrish .10
93 Kirby Puckett 2.00
94 Juan Samuel .10
95 Steve Sax .10
96 Dave Stieb .10
97 Darryl Strawberry .10
98 Willie Upshaw .10
99 Frank Viola .10
100 Dwight Gooden .10
101 Joaquin Andujar .10
102 George Bell .10
103 Bert Blyleven .10
104 Mike Boddicker .10
105 Britt Burns .10
106 Rod Carew 1.00
107 Jack Clark .10
108 Danny Cox .10
109 Ron Darling .10
110 Andre Dawson .45
111 Leon Durham .10
112 Tony Fernandez .10
113 Tom Herr .10
114 Teddy Higuera .10
115 Bob Horner .10
116 Dave Kingman .10
117 Jack Morris .10
118 Dan Quisenberry .10
119 Jeff Reardon .10
120 Bryn Smith .10
121 Ozzie Smith 2.00
122 John Tudor .10
123 Tim Wallach .10
124 Willie Wilson .10
125 Carlton Fisk 1.00
126 RBI Sluggers (Gary Carter, George Foster, Al Oliver) .10
127 Run Scorers (Keith Hernandez, Tim Raines, Ryne Sandberg) .25
128 Run Scorers (Paul Molitor, Cal Ripken, Jr., Willie Wilson) .50
129 No-Hitters (John Candelaria, Dennis Eckersley, Bob Forsch) .25
130 World Series MVPs (Ron Cey, Rollie Fingers, Pete Rose) .35
131 All-Star Game MVPs (Dave Concepcion, George Foster, Bill Madlock) .10
132 Cy Young Winners (Vida Blue, John Denny, Fernando Valenzuela) .10
133 Comeback Players (Doyle Alexander, Joaquin Andujar, Richard Dotson) .10
134 Big Winners (John Denny, Tom Seaver, Rick Sutcliffe) .10
135 Veteran Pitchers (Phil Niekro, Tom Seaver, Don Sutton) .25
136 Rookies of the Year (Vince Coleman, Dwight Gooden, Alfredo Griffin) .20
137 All-Star Game MVPs (Gary Carter, Steve Garvey, Fred Lynn) .20
138 Veteran Hitters (Tony Perez, Pete Rose, Rusty Staub) .50

139 Power Hitters (George Foster, Jim Rice, Mike Schmidt) .30
140 Batting Champs (Bill Buckner, Tony Gwynn, Al Oliver) .25
141 No-Hitters (Jack Morris, Dave Righetti, Nolan Ryan) .50
142 No-Hitters (Vida Blue, Bert Blyleven, Tom Seaver) .10
143 Strikeout Kings (Dwight Gooden, Nolan Ryan, Fernando Valenzuela) 1.25
144 Base Stealers (Dave Lopes, Tim Raines, Willie Wilson) .10
145 RBI Sluggers (Tony Armas, Cecil Cooper, Eddie Murray) .15
146 A.L. MVPs (Rod Carew, Rollie Fingers, Jim Rice) .15
147 World Series MVPs (Rick Dempsey, Reggie Jackson, Alan Trammell) .25
148 World Series MVPs (Pedro Guerrero, Darrell Porter, Mike Schmidt) .20
149 ERA Leaders (Mike Boddicker, Ron Guidry, Rick Sutcliffe) .10
150 Comeback Players (Reggie Jackson, Dave Kingman, Fred Lynn) .20
151 Buddy Bell .10
152 Dennis Boyd .10
153 Dave Concepcion .10
154 Brian Downing .10
155 Shawon Dunston .10
156 John Franco .10
157 Scott Garrelts .10
158 Bob James .10
159 Charlie Leibrandt .10
160 Oddibe McDowell .10
161 Roger McDowell .10
162 Mike Moore .10
163 Phil Niekro .75
164 Al Oliver .10
165 Tony Pena .10
166 Ted Power .10
167 Mike Scioscia .10
168 Mario Soto .10
169 Bob Stanley .10
170 Garry Templeton .10
171 Andre Thornton .10
172 Alan Trammell .10
173 Doug DeCinces .10
174 Greg Walker .10
175 Don Sutton .75
176 1985 Award Winners (Vince Coleman, Dwight Gooden, Ozzie Guillen, Don Mattingly, Willie McGee, Bret Saberhagen) .50
177 1985 Hot Rookies (Stewart Cliburn, Brian Fisher, Joe Hesketh, Joe Orsulak, Mark Salas, Larry Sheets) .10
178a Future Stars (Jose Canseco RC, Mark Funderburk, Mike Greenwell, Steve Lombardozzi, Billy Joe Robidoux, Danny Tartabull) 2.00
178b Future Stars (Jose Canseco, Mike Greenwell, Steve Lombardozzi, Billy Jo Robidoux, Danny Tartabull, Jim Wilson) 30.00
179 Gold Glove (George Brett, Ron Guidry, Keith Hernandez, Don Mattingly, Willie McGee, Dale Murphy) 1.00
180 .300 (Wade Boggs, George Brett, Rod Carew, Cecil Cooper, Don Mattingly, Willie Wilson) 1.00
181 .300 (Pedro Guerrero, Tony Gwynn, Keith Hernandez, Bill Madlock, Dave Parker, Pete Rose) .50
182 1985 Milestones (Rod Carew, Phil Niekro, Pete Rose, Nolan Ryan, Tom Seaver, Matt Tallman) 1.50
183 1985 Triple Crown (Wade Boggs, Darrell Evans, Don Mattingly, Willie McGee, Dale Murphy, Dave Parker) 1.00
184 1985 HL (Wade Boggs, Dwight Gooden, Rickey Henderson, Don Mattingly, Willie McGee, John Tudor) 1.00
185 1985 20-Game Winners (Joaquin Andujar, Tom Browning, Dwight Gooden, Ron Guidry, Bret Saberhagen, John Tudor) .10
186 World Series Champs (Steve Balboni, George Brett, Dane Iorg, Danny Jackson, Charlie Leibrandt,

Darryl Motley, Dan Quisenberry, Bret Saberhagen, Lonnie Smith, Jim Sundberg, Frank White, Willie Wilson) .40
187 Hubie Brooks .10
188 Glenn Davis .10
189 Darrell Evans .10
190 Rich Gossage .10
191 Andy Hawkins .10
192 Jay Howell .10
193 LaMarr Hoyt .10
194 Davey Lopes .10
195 Mike Scott .10
196 Ted Simmons .10
197 Gary Ward .10
198 Bob Welch .10
199 Mike Young .10
200 Buddy Biancalana .10

Decade Greats Sample Cards

To promote its Decade Greats set of current and former cards, Sportflics issued this two-card promo set. Card fronts are identical to the issued versions. Backs are printed in blue on white: "DECADE GREATS / SAMPLE CARD." The players are not identified on the cards.

		NM/M
Complete Set (2):		2.00
(1)	Dwight Gooden	1.00
(2)	Mel Ott	1.00

Decade Greats

This set, produced by Sportflics, features outstanding players, by position, from the 1930s to the 1980s by decades. The card fronts are printed in sepia-toned photos or full-color with the Sportflics three-phase "Magic Motion" animation. The complete set contains 75 cards with 59 single player cards and 16 multi-player cards. Biographies appear on the card backs which are printed in full-color and color-coded by decade. The set was distributed only through hobby dealers and is in the popular 2-1/2" x 3-1/2" size.

NM/M
Complete Set (75): 9.00
Common Player: .10
1 Babe Ruth 2.00
2 Jimmie Foxx .15
3 Lefty Grove .10
4 Hank Greenberg .25
5 Al Simmons .10
6 Carl Hubbell .10
7 Joe Cronin .10
8 Mel Ott .10
9 Lefty Gomez .10
10 Lou Gehrig 1.25
11 Pie Traynor .10
12 Charlie Gehringer .10
13 Catchers (Mickey Cochrane, Bill Dickey, Gabby Hartnett) .10
14 Pitchers (Dizzy Dean, Paul Derringer, Red Ruffing) .10

15 Outfielders (Earl Averill, Joe Medwick, Paul Waner) .10
16 Bob Feller .40
17 Lou Boudreau .15
18 Enos Slaughter .15
19 Hal Newhouser .10
20 Joe DiMaggio 1.25
21 Pee Wee Reese .25
22 Phil Rizzuto .15
23 Ernie Lombardi .10
24 Infielders (Joe Cronin, George Kell, Johnny Mize) .10
25 Ted Williams 1.25
26 Mickey Mantle 3.00
27 Warren Spahn .15
28 Jackie Robinson 1.00
29 Ernie Banks .20
30 Stan Musial .75
31 Yogi Berra .40
32 Duke Snider .50
33 Roy Campanella .50
34 Eddie Mathews .15
35 Ralph Kiner .15
36 Early Wynn .10
37 Double Play Duo (Luis Aparicio, Nellie Fox) .35
38 First Basemen (Gil Hodges, Ted Kluszewski, Mickey Vernon) .25
40 Henry Aaron .75
41 Frank Robinson .20
42 Bob Gibson .20
43 Roberto Clemente 1.75
44 Whitey Ford .25
45 Brooks Robinson .35
46 Juan Marichal .15
47 Carl Yastrzemski .40
48 First Basemen (Orlando Cepeda, Harmon Killebrew, Willie McCovey) .15
49 Catchers (Bill Freehan, Elston Howard, Joe Torre) .15
50 Willie Mays .75
51 Outfielders (Al Kaline, Tony Oliva, Billy Williams) .15
52 Tom Seaver .40
53 Reggie Jackson .50
54 Steve Carlton .25
55 Mike Schmidt .50
56 Joe Morgan .15
57 Jim Rice .15
58 Jim Palmer .20
59 Lou Brock .20
60 Pete Rose 1.00
61 Steve Garvey .25
62 Catchers (Carlton Fisk, Thurman Munson, Ted Simmons) .15
63 Pitchers (Vida Blue, Catfish Hunter, Nolan Ryan) .20
64 George Brett .50
65 Don Mattingly 1.00
66 Fernando Valenzuela .10
67 Dale Murphy .25
68 Wade Boggs .40
69 Rickey Henderson .40
70 Eddie Murray .25
71 Ron Guidry .10
72 Catchers (Gary Carter, Lance Parrish, Tony Pena) .15
73 Infielders (Cal Ripken, Jr., Lou Whitaker, Robin Yount) .35
74 Outfielders (Pedro Guerrero, Tim Raines, Dave Winfield) .15
75 Dwight Gooden .10

Rookies

The 1986 Rookies set offers 50 cards and features 47 individual rookie players. In addition, there are two Tri-Star cards; one highlights former Rookies of the Year and the other features three prominent players. There is one "Big Six" card featuring six superstars. The full-color photos on the 2-1/2" x 3-1/2" cards use Sportflics three-phase "Magic Motion" animation. The set was packaged in a collector box which also contained 34 trivia cards that measure 1-3/4" x 2". The set was distributed only by hobby dealers.

NM/M
Complete Set (50): 17.50
Common Player: .10
1 John Kruk .10
2 Edwin Correa .10
3 Pete Incaviglia .10
4 Dale Sveum .10
5 Juan Nieves .10
6 Will Clark .25
7 Wally Joyner .25
8 Lance McCullers .10
9 Scott Bailes .10
10 Dan Plesac .10
11 Jose Canseco 1.50
12 Bobby Witt .10
13 Barry Bonds 15.00
14 Andres Thomas .10
15 Jim Deshaies .10
16 Ruben Sierra .10
17 Steve Lombardozzi .10
18 Cory Snyder .10
19 Reggie Williams .10
20 Mitch Williams .10
21 Glenn Braggs .10
22 Danny Tartabull .10
23 Charlie Kerfeld .10
24 Paul Assenmacher .10
25 Robby Thompson .10
26 Bobby Bonilla .10
27 Andres Galarraga .10
28 Billy Jo Robidoux .10
29 Bruce Ruffin .10
30 Greg Swindell .10
31 John Cangelosi .10
32 Jim Traber .10
33 Russ Morman .10
34 Barry Larkin .10
35 Todd Worrell .10
36 John Cerutti .10
37 Mike Kingery .10
38 Mark Eichhorn .10
39 Scott Bankhead .10
40 Bo Jackson .25
41 Greg Mathews .10
42 Eric King .10
43 Kal Daniels .10
44 Calvin Schiraldi .10
45 Mickey Brantley .10
46 Outstanding Rookie Seasons (Fred Lynn, Willie Mays, Pete Rose) .60
47 Outstanding Rookie Seasons (Dwight Gooden, Tom Seaver, Fernando Valenzuela) .25
48 Outstanding Rookie Seasons (Eddie Murray, Dave Righetti, Cal Ripken, Jr., Steve Sax, Darryl Strawberry, Lou Whitaker) .25
49 Kevin Mitchell .10
50 Mike Diaz .10

Dwight Gooden Discs

As the viewing angle changes on these 3-D simulated motion plastic discs, three different pictures of "Dr. K" can be seen, two action and one portrait. The discs are found in two diameters, 2-1/4" and 4-1/2". Fronts have team-color borders of blue with orange lettering. Backs are blank.

NM/M
Complete Set (2): 3.00
(1) Dwight Gooden (2-1/4") 1.00
(2) Dwight Gooden (4-1/2") 2.00

Jumbo Discs

A portrait and two action pictures of the players are featured in these large-format (4-1/2" diameter) "Magic Motion" discs. Fronts have the player's name below the photos, with a title above. Backs are printed in purple, red, black and white. Discs were available for $5 each with a paper coupon found in Sportflics packs.

NM/M
Complete Set (6): 13.50
Common Player: 1.50
(1) Wade Boggs 4.00
(2) Roger Clemens 5.00
(3) Wally Joyner 1.50
(4) Mickey Mantle 6.00
(5) Don Mattingly 5.00
(6) Dave Winfield 3.00
(1) Wade Boggs 1.00
(2) Roger Clemens 1.25
(3) Wally Joyner .40
(4) Mickey Mantle 2.00
(5) Don Mattingly 1.25
(6) Dave Winfield .75

1987 Sportflics

In its second year in the national market, Sportflics' basic issue was again a 200-card set of 2-1/2" x 3-1/2" "Magic Motion" cards, which offer three different photos on the same card, each visible in turn as the card is moved from top to bottom or side to side. Besides single-player cards, the '87 Sportflics set includes several three- and six-player cards, though not as many as in the 1986 set. The card backs feature a small player portrait photo on the single-player cards, an innovation for 1987. The cards were issued with a series of 136 team logo trivia cards. Most cards exist in two variations, carrying 1986 or 1987 copyright dates on back.

NM/M
Factory Set (200+136): 12.00
Complete Set (200): 7.50
Common Player: .10
Foil Pack (3+2): .50
Foil Box (36): 10.00
1 Don Mattingly 1.25
2 Wade Boggs 1.00
3 Dale Murphy .50
4 Rickey Henderson .75
5 George Brett 1.25
6 Eddie Murray .75
7 Kirby Puckett 1.00
8 Ryne Sandberg 1.00
9 Cal Ripken, Jr. 2.00
10 Roger Clemens 1.25
11 Ted Higuera .10
12 Steve Sax .10
13 Chris Brown .10
14 Jesse Barfield .10
15 Kent Hrbek .10
16 Robin Yount .75
17 Glenn Davis .10
18 Hubie Brooks .10
19 Mike Scott .10
20 Darryl Strawberry .10
21 Alvin Davis .10
22 Eric Davis .10
23 Danny Tartabull .10
24a Cory Snyder (Pat Tabler photo on back.) 1.50
24b Cory Snyder (Pat Tabler photo on back.)(Facing front, 1/4 swing on front.) 1.50
24c Cory Snyder (Snyder photo on back.)(Facing to side.) .50
25 Pete Rose 1.50
26 Wally Joyner .75
27 Pedro Guerrero .25
28 Tom Seaver .75
29 Bob Knepper .10
30 Mike Schmidt 1.25
31 Tony Gwynn 1.00
32 Don Slaught .10
33 Todd Worrell .10
34 Tim Raines .10
35 Dave Parker .10
36 Bob Ojeda .10
37 Pete Incaviglia .10
38 Bruce Hurst .10
39 Bobby Witt .10
40 Steve Garvey .40
41 Dave Winfield .75
42 Jose Cruz .10
43 Orel Hershiser .10
44 Reggie Jackson .75

45	Chili Davis	.10
46	Robby Thompson	.10
47	Dennis Boyd	.10
48	Kirk Gibson	.10
49	Fred Lynn	.10
50	Gary Carter	.75
51	George Bell	.10
52	Pete O'Brien	.10
53	Ron Darling	.10
54	Paul Molitor	.75
55	Mike Pagliarulo	.10
56	Mike Boddicker	.10
57	Dave Righetti	.10
58	Len Dykstra **RC**	.10
59	Mike Witt	.10
60	Tony Bernazard	.10
61	John Kruk	.10
62	Mike Krukow	.10
63	Sid Fernandez	.10
64	Gary Gaetti	.10
65	Vince Coleman	.10
66	Pat Tabler	.10
67	Mike Scioscia	.10
68	Scott Garrelts	.10
69	Brett Butler	.10
70	Bill Buckner	.10
71a	Dennis Rasmussen (John Montefusco photo on back; mustache.)	.25
71b	Dennis Rasmussen (Correct photo on back, no mustache.)	.10
72	Tim Wallach	.10
73	Bob Horner	.10
74	Willie McGee	.10
75	A.L. First Basemen (Wally Joyner, Don Mattingly, Eddie Murray)	.50
76	Jesse Orosco	.10
77	N.L. Relief Pitchers (Jeff Reardon, Dave Smith, Todd Worrell)	.10
78	Candy Maldonado	.10
79	N.L. Shortstops (Hubie Brooks, Shawon Dunston, Ozzie Smith)	.10
80	A.L. Left Fielders (George Bell, Jose Canseco, Jim Rice)	.25
81	Bert Blyleven	.10
82	Mike Marshall	.10
83	Ron Guidry	.10
84	Julio Franco	.10
85	Willie Wilson	.10
86	Lee Lacy	.10
87	Jack Morris	.10
88	Ray Knight	.10
89	Phil Bradley	.10
90	Jose Canseco	.60
91	Gary Ward	.10
92	Mike Easler	.10
93	Tony Pena	.10
94	Dave Smith	.10
95	Will Clark	.10
96	Lloyd Moseby	.10
97	Jim Rice	.25
98	Shawon Dunston	.10
99	Don Sutton	.50
100	Dwight Gooden	.10
101	Lance Parrish	.10
102	Mark Langston	.10
103	Floyd Youmans	.10
104	Lee Smith	.10
105	Willie Hernandez	.10
106	Doug DeCinces	.10
107	Ken Schrom	.10
108	Don Carman	.10
109	Brook Jacoby	.10
110	Steve Bedrosian	.10
111	A.L. Pitchers (Roger Clemens, Teddy Higuera, Jack Morris)	.25
112	A.L. Second Basemen (Marty Barrett, Tony Bernazard, Lou Whitaker)	.10
113	A.L. Shortstops (Tony Fernandez, Scott Fletcher, Cal Ripken, Jr.)	.10
114	A.L. Third Basemen (Wade Boggs, George Brett, Gary Gaetti)	.25
115	N.L. Third Basemen (Chris Brown, Mike Schmidt, Tim Wallach)	.20
116	N.L. Second Basemen (Bill Doran, Johnny Ray, Ryne Sandberg)	.10
117	N.L. Right Fielders (Kevin Bass, Tony Gwynn, Dave Parker)	.10
118	Hot Rookie Prospects (David Clark, Pat Dodson, Ty Gainey, Phil Lombardi, Benito Santiago, Terry Steinbach **RC**)	.25
119	1986 Season Highlights (Dave Righetti, Mike Scott, Fernando Valenzuela)	.10
120	N.L. Pitchers (Dwight Gooden, Mike Scott, Fernando Valenzuela)	.10
121	Johnny Ray	.10
122	Keith Moreland	.10
123	Juan Samuel	.10
124	Wally Backman	.10
125	Nolan Ryan	2.00
126	Greg Harris	.10
127	Kirk McCaskill	.10
128	Dwight Evans	.10
129	Rick Rhoden	.10
130	Bill Madlock	.10
131	Oddibe McDowell	.10
132	Darrell Evans	.10
133	Keith Hernandez	.10
134	Tom Brunansky	.10
135	Kevin McReynolds	.10
136	Scott Fletcher	.10
137	Lou Whitaker	.10
138	Carney Lansford	.10
139	Andre Dawson	.45
140	Carlton Fisk	.75
141	Buddy Bell	.10
142	Ozzie Smith	1.00
143	Dan Pasqua	.10
144	Kevin Mitchell	.10
145	Bret Saberhagen	.10
146	Charlie Kerfeld	.10
147	Phil Niekro	.50
148	John Candelaria	.10
149	Rich Gedman	.10
150	Fernando Valenzuela	.10
151	N.L. Catchers (Gary Carter, Tony Pena, Mike Scioscia)	.10
152	N.L. Left Fielders (Vince Coleman, Jose Cruz, Tim Raines)	.10
153	A.L. Right Fielders (Harold Baines, Jesse Barfield, Dave Winfield)	.10
154	A.L. Catchers (Rich Gedman, Lance Parrish, Don Slaught)	.10
155	N.L. Center Fielders (Kevin McReynolds, Dale Murphy, Eric Davis)	.10
156	'86 Highlights (Jim Deshaies, Mike Schmidt, Don Sutton)	.10
157	A.L. Speedburners (John Cangelosi, Rickey Henderson, Gary Pettis)	.10
158	Hot Rookie Prospects (Randy Asadoor, Casey Candaele, Dave Cochrane, Rafael Palmeiro, Tim Pyznarski, Kevin Seitzer)	.75
159	The Best of the Best (Roger Clemens, Dwight Gooden, Rickey Henderson, Don Mattingly, Dale Murphy, Eddie Murray)	.75
160	Roger McDowell	.10
161	Brian Downing	.10
162	Bill Doran	.10
163	Don Baylor	.10
164	Alfredo Griffin	.10
165	Don Aase	.10
166	Glenn Wilson	.10
167	Dan Quisenberry	.10
168	Frank White	.10
169	Cecil Cooper	.10
170	Jody Davis	.10
171	Harold Baines	.10
172	Rob Deer	.10
173	John Tudor	.10
174	Larry Parrish	.10
175	Kevin Bass	.10
176	Joe Carter	.10
177	Mitch Webster	.10
178	Dave Kingman	.10
179	Jim Presley	.10
180	Mel Hall	.10
181	Shane Rawley	.10
182	Marty Barrett	.10
183	Damaso Garcia	.10
184	Bobby Grich	.10
185	Leon Durham	.10
186	Ozzie Guillen	.10
187	Tony Fernandez	.10
188	Alan Trammell	.10
189	Jim Clancy	.10
190	Bo Jackson	.15
191	Bob Forsch	.10
192	John Franco	.10
193	Von Hayes	.10
194	A.L. Relief Pitchers (Don Aase, Mark Eichhorn, Dave Righetti)	.10
195	N.L. First Basemen (Will Clark, Glenn Davis, Keith Hernandez)	.10
196	'86 Highlights (Roger Clemens, Joe Cowley, Bob Horner)	.10
197	The Best of the Best (Wade Boggs, George Brett, Hubie Brooks, Tony Gwynn, Tim Raines, Ryne Sandberg)	.75
198	A.L. Center Fielders (Rickey Henderson, Fred Lynn, Kirby Puckett)	.50
199	N.L. Speedburners (Vince Coleman, Tim Raines, Eric Davis)	.10
200	Steve Carlton	.75

Rookie Discs

The 1987 Sportflics Rookie Discs set consists of seven discs which measure 4" in diameter. The front of the discs offer three "Magic Motion" photos in full color, encompassed by a blue border. The disc backs are printed in color and include the team logo, player statistics, biography and the disc number. The set was issued with Cooperstown Timeless Trivia Cards.

		NM/M
Complete Set (7):		8.00
Common Player:		1.00
1	Casey Candaele	1.00
2	Mark McGwire	6.00
3	Kevin Seitzer	1.00
4	Joe Magrane	1.00
5	Benito Santiago	1.00
6	Dave Magadan	1.00
7	Devon White	1.00

Rookie Prospects

The Rookie Prospects set consists of 10 cards in standard 2-1/2" x 3-1/2" size. The card fronts feature Sportflics' "Magic Motion" process. Card backs contain a player photo plus a short biography and player personal and statistical information. The set was offered in two separately wrapped mylar packs of five cards to hobby dealers purchasing cases of Sportflics' Team Preview set. Twenty-four packs of "Rookie Prospects" cards were included with each case.

		NM/M
Complete Set (10):		4.00
Common Player:		.25
1	Terry Steinbach	.25
2	Rafael Palmeiro	3.00
3	Dave Magadan	.25
4	Marvin Freeman	.25
5	Brick Smith	.25
6	B.J. Surhoff	.25
7	John Smiley	.25
8	Alonzo Powell	.25
9	Benny Santiago	.25
10	Devon White	.25

Rookies

The Rookies set was issued in two boxed series of 25 cards. The first was released in July with the second series following in October. The cards, which are the standard 2-1/2" x 3-1/2", feature Sportflics' special "Magic Motion" process. The card fronts contain a full-color photo and present three different pictures, depending on how the card is held. The backs also contain a full-color photo along with player statistics and a biography.

		NM/M
Complete Set One (1-25):		4.00
Complete Set Two (26-50):		2.00
Common Player:		.10
1	Eric Bell	.10
2	Chris Bosio	.10
3	Bob Brower	.10
4	Jerry Browne	.10
5	Ellis Burks	.10
6	Casey Candaele	.10
7	Ken Gerhart	.10
8	Mike Greenwell	.10
9	Stan Jefferson	.10
10	Dave Magadan	.10
11	Joe Magrane	.10
12	Fred McGriff	.25
13	Mark McGwire	3.00
14	Mark McLemore	.10
15	Jeff Musselman	.10
16	Matt Nokes	.10
17	Paul O'Neill	.10
18	Luis Polonia	.10
19	Benny Santiago	.10
20	Kevin Seitzer	.10
21	John Smiley	.10
22	Terry Steinbach	.10
23	B.J. Surhoff	.10
24	Devon White	.10
25	Matt Williams	.25
26	DeWayne Buice	.10
27	Willie Fraser	.10
28	Bill Ripken	.10
29	Mike Henneman	.10
30	Shawn Hillegas	.10
31	Shane Mack	.10
32	Rafael Palmeiro	1.50
33	Mike Jackson	.10
34	Gene Larkin	.10
35	Jimmy Jones	.10
36	Gerald Young	.10
37	Ken Caminiti	.10
38	Sam Horn	.10
39	David Cone	.10
40	Mike Dunne	.10
41	Ken Williams	.10
42	John Morris	.10
43	Jim Lindeman	.10
44	Mike Stanley	.10
45	Les Straker	.10
46	Jeff Robinson	.10
47	Todd Benzinger	.10
48	Jeff Blauser	.10
49	John Marzano	.10
50	Keith Miller	.10

Superstar Discs

Released in three series of six discs, the Superstar Disc set features the special "Magic Motion" process. Each disc, which measures 4-1/2" in diameter, contains three different player photos, depending which way it is tilted. A red border, containing 11 stars, the player's name and uniform number, surrounds the photo. The backs feature a turquoise border which carries the words "Superstar Disc Collector Series." The backs also include the team logo, player statistics, biography and the disc number. The discs were issued with 18 1-3/4" x 2-1/2" Cooperstown Timeless Trivia Cards.

		NM/M
Complete Set (18):		35.00
Common Player:		1.50
1	Jose Canseco	2.50
2	Mike Scott	1.50
3	Ryne Sandberg	3.50
4	Mike Schmidt	4.00
5	Dale Murphy	2.00
6	Fernando Valenzuela	1.50
7	Tony Gwynn	3.50
8	Cal Ripken, Jr.	6.00
9	Gary Carter	3.00
10	Cory Snyder	1.50
11	Kirby Puckett	3.50
12	George Brett	3.50
13	Keith Hernandez	1.50
14	Rickey Henderson	3.00
15	Tim Raines	1.50
16	Bo Jackson	2.00
17	Pete Rose	4.50
18	Eric Davis	1.50

Team Previews

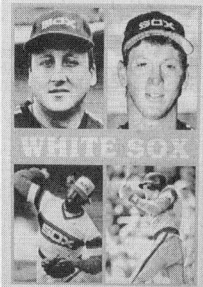

The 1987 Sportflics Team Preview set appeared to be a good idea, but never caught on with collectors. The intent of the set is to provide a pre-season look at each of the 26 major league clubs. The card backs contain three categories of the team preview: Outlook, Newcomers to Watch and Summary. Using the "Magic Motion" process, 12 different players are featured on the card fronts. Four of the different player photos can be made visible at once. The cards, which measure 2-1/2" x 3-1/2", were issued with team logo/trivia cards in a specially designed box.

		NM/M
Complete Set (26):		15.00
Common Team:		.50
1	Texas Rangers (Scott Fletcher, Greg Harris, Charlie Hough, Pete Incaviglia, Mike Loynd, Oddibe McDowell, Pete O'Brien, Larry Parrish, Ruben Sierra, Don Slaught, Mitch Williams, Bobby Witt)	.50
2	New York Mets (Wally Backman, Gary Carter, Ron Darling, Lenny Dykstra, Sid Fernandez, Dwight Gooden, Keith Hernandez, Dave Magadan, Kevin McReynolds, Randy Myers, Bob Ojeda, Darryl Strawberry)	.75
3	Cleveland Indians (Tony Bernazard, Brett Butler, Tom Candiotti, Joe Carter, Julio Franco, Mel Hall, Brook Jacoby, Phil Niekro, Ken Schrom, Cory Snyder, Greg Swindell, Pat Tabler)	.50
4	Cincinnati Reds (Buddy Bell, Tom Browning, Kal Daniels, John Franco, Bill Gullickson, Tracy Jones, Barry Larkin, Rob Murphy, Dave Parker, Pete Rose, Eric Davis)	1.00
5	Toronto Blue Jays (Jesse Barfield, George Bell, John Cerutti, Mark Eichhorn, Tony Fernandez, Tom Henke, Glenallen Hill, Jimmy Key, Fred McGriff, Lloyd Moseby, Dave Stieb, Willie Upshaw)	.50
6	Philadelphia Phillies (Steve Bedrosian, Don Carman, Marvin Freeman, Kevin Gross, Von Hayes, Shane Rawley, Bruce Ruffin, Juan Samuel, Mike Schmidt, Kent Tekulve, Milt Thompson, Glenn Wilson)	.75
7	New York Yankees (Rickey Henderson, Phil Lombardi, Don Mattingly, Mike Pagliarulo, Dan Pasqua, Willie Randolph, Dennis Rasmussen, Rick Rhoden, Dave Righetti, Joel Skinner, Bob Tewksbury, Dave Winfield)	1.25
8	Houston Astros (Kevin Bass, Jose Cruz, Glenn Davis, Jim Deshaies, Bill Doran, Ty Gainey, Charlie Kerfeld, Bob Knepper, Nolan Ryan, Mike Scott, Dave Smith, Robby Wine)	1.50
9	Boston Red Sox (Marty Barrett, Don Baylor, Wade Boggs, Dennis Boyd, Roger Clemens, Pat Dodson, Dwight Evans, Mike Greenwell, Dave Henderson, Bruce Hurst, Jim Rice, Calvin Schiraldi)	1.00
10	San Francisco Giants (Bob Brenly, Chris Brown, Will Clark, Chili Davis, Kelly Downs, Scott Garrelts, Mark Grant, Mike Krukow, Jeff Leonard, Candy Maldonado, Terry Mulholland, Robby Thompson)	.50
11	California Angels (John Candelaria, Doug DeCinces, Brian Downing, Ruppert Jones, Wally Joyner, Kirk McCaskill, Darrell Miller, Donnie Moore, Gary Pettis, Don Sutton, Devon White, Mike Witt)	.50
12	St. Louis Cardinals (Jack Clark, Vince Coleman, Danny Cox, Bob Forsch, Tom Herr, Joe Magrane, Willie McGee, Terry Pendleton, Ozzie Smith, John Tudor, Andy Van Slyke, Todd Worrell)	.75
13	Kansas City Royals (George Brett, Mark Gubicza, Bo Jackson, Charlie Leibrandt, Hal McRae, Dan Quisenberry, Bret Saberhagen, Kevin Seitzer, Lonnie Smith, Danny Tartabull, Frank White, Willie Wilson)	.75
14	Los Angeles Dodgers (Ralph Bryant, Mariano Duncan, Jose Gonzalez, Pedro Guerrero, Orel Hershiser, Mike Marshall, Steve Sax, Mike Scioscia, Franklin Stubbs, Fernando Valenzuela, Reggie Williams, Matt Young)	.50
15	Detroit Tigers (Darnell Coles, Darrell Evans, Kirk Gibson, Willie Hernandez, Eric King, Chet Lemon, Dwight Lowry, Jack Morris, Dan Petry, Frank Tanana, Alan Trammell, Lou Whitaker)	.50
16	San Diego Padres (Randy Asadoor, Steve Garvey, Tony Gwynn, Andy Hawkins, Jim Jones, John Kruk, Craig Lefferts, Shane Mack, Lance McCullers, Kevin Mitchell, Benny Santiago, Ed Wojna)	.75
17	Minnesota Twins (Bert Blyleven, Tom Brunansky, Gary Gaetti, Greg Gagne, Kent Hrbek, Joe Klink, Steve Lombardozzi, Kirby Puckett, Jeff Reardon, Mark Salas, Roy Smalley, Frank Viola)	.75
18	Pittsburgh Pirates (Barry Bonds, Bobby Bonilla, Sid Bream, Mike Diaz, Brian Fisher, Jim Morrison, Joe Orsulak, Bob Patterson, Tony Pena, Johnny Ray, R.J. Reynolds, John Smiley)	1.50
19	Milwaukee Brewers (Glenn Braggs, Rob Deer, Teddy Higuera, Paul Molitor, Juan Nieves, Dan Plesac, Tim Pyznarski, Ernest Riles, Billy Jo Robidoux, B.J. Surhoff, Dale Sveum, Robin Yount)	.75
20	Montreal Expos (Hubie Brooks, Tim Burke, Casey Candaele, Dave Collins, Mike Fitzgerald, Andres Galarraga, Billy Moore, Alonzo Powell, Randy St. Claire, Tim Wallach, Mitch Webster, Floyd Youmans)	.50
21	Baltimore Orioles (Don Aase, Eric Bell, Mike Boddicker, Ken Gerhardt, Terry Kennedy, Ray Knight, Lee Lacy, Fred Lynn, Eddie Murray, Cal Ripken, Jr., Larry Sheets, Jim Traber)	1.50
22	Chicago Cubs (Jody Davis, Shawon Dunston, Leon Durham, Dennis Eckersley, Greg Maddux, Dave Martinez, Keith Moreland, Jerry Mumphrey, Rafael Palmeiro,

Ryne Sandberg,
Scott Sanderson,
Lee Smith) 1.00
23 Oakland Athletics
(Jose Canseco, Mike Davis,
Alfredo Griffin,
Reggie Jackson,
Carney Lansford,
Mark McGwire,
Dwayne Murphy, Rob Nelson,
Tony Phillips, Jose Rijo,
Terry Steinbach,
Curt Young) 1.50
24 Atlanta Braves
(Paul Assenmacher,
Gene Garber, Tom Glavine,
Ken Griffey, Glenn Hubbard,
Dion James, Rick Mahler,
Dale Murphy, Ken Oberkfell,
David Palmer, Zane Smith,
Andres Thomas) .50
25 Seattle Mariners
(Scott Bankhead,
Phil Bradley, Scott Bradley,
Mickey Brantley, Alvin Davis,
Steve Fireovid,
Mark Langston, Mike Moore,
Donell Nixon, Ken Phelps,
Jim Presley, Dave Valle) .50
26 Chicago White Sox
(Harold Baines,
John Cangelosi,
Dave Cochrane, Joe Cowley,
Carlton Fisk, Ozzie Guillen,
Ron Hassey, Bob James,
Ron Karkovice,
Russ Mormon,
Bobby Thigpen,
Greg Walker) .50

4-in-1 Panels

These 4-in-1 player and team logo panels were given to dealers who made quantity purchases of Sportflics products. The player panels measure 4-7/8" x 6-7/8", making each of the four cards slightly smaller than the regular-issue versions. Otherwise the cards are identical to the standard version, right down to the card numbers. The team-logo panels correspond to the players on the player panels, but they are smaller, at 3-3/8"x3-7/8". The logo cards have two views of each logo on front and on back display various team stats. Each of the panels carries a 1986 copyright.

	NM/M
Complete Set (8):	15.00
Common Panel:	1.00

(1) 1 Don Mattingly,
10 Roger Clemens,
30 Mike Schmidt,
34 Tim Raines 5.00
(2) 2 Wade Boggs,
6 Eddie Murray,
26 Wally Joyner,
150 Fernando Valenzuela 2.50
(3) 3 Dale Murphy,
31 Tony Gwynn, 97 Jim Rice,
133 Keith Hernandez 2.50
(4) 4 Rickey Henderson,
5 George Brett,
9 Cal Ripken Jr.,
100 Dwight Gooden 6.50
(5) Yankees, Expos, Red Sox,
Phillies 1.00
(6) Red Sox, Dodgers, Angels,
Orioles 1.00
(7) Braves, Mets, Red Sox,
Padres 1.00
(8) Mets, Orioles, Yankees,
Royals 1.00

1988 Sportflics

RYNE SANDBERG 23 — SECOND BASE

The design of the 1988 Sportflics set differs greatly from the previous two years. Besides increasing the number of cards in the set to 225, Sportflics included the player name, team and uniform number on the card front. The triple-action color photos are surrounded by a red border. The backs are re-designed, also. Full-color action photos, plus extensive statistics and informative biographies are utilized. Three highlights cards and three rookie prospects card are included in the set. The cards are the standard 2-1/2" x 3-1/2".

	NM/M
Factory Set (225+136):	17.50
Complete Set (225):	10.00
Common Player:	.10
Foil Pack (3+2):	.50
Foil Box (36):	9.00

1 Don Mattingly 1.25
2 Tim Raines .10
3 Andre Dawson .25
4 George Bell .10
5 Joe Carter .10
6 Matt Nokes .10
7 Dave Winfield .75
8 Kirby Puckett 1.00
9 Will Clark .10
10 Eric Davis .10
11 Rickey Henderson .75
12 Ryne Sandberg 1.00
13 Jesse Barfield .10
14 Ozzie Guillen .10
15 Bret Saberhagen .10
16 Tony Gwynn 1.00
17 Kevin Seitzer .10
18 Jack Clark .10
19 Danny Tartabull .10
20 Ted Higuera .10
21 Charlie Leibrandt, Jr. .10
22 Benny Santiago .10
23 Fred Lynn .10
24 Rob Thompson .10
25 Alan Trammell .10
26 Tony Fernandez .10
27 Rick Sutcliffe .10
28 Gary Carter .75
29 Cory Snyder .10
30 Lou Whitaker .10
31 Keith Hernandez .10
32 Mike Witt .10
33 Harold Baines .10
34 Robin Yount .75
35 Mike Schmidt 1.25
36 Dion James .10
37 Tom Candiotti .10
38 Tracy Jones .10
39 Nolan Ryan 2.00
40 Fernando Valenzuela .10
41 Vance Law .10
42 Roger McDowell .10
43 Carlton Fisk .75
44 Scott Garrelts .10
45 Lee Guetterman .10
46 Mark Langston .10
47 Willie Randolph .10
48 Bill Doran .10
49 Larry Parrish .10
50 Wade Boggs 1.00
51 Shane Rawley .10
52 Alvin Davis .10
53 Jeff Reardon .10
54 Jim Presley .10
55 Kevin Bass .10
56 Kevin McReynolds .10
57 B.J. Surhoff .10
58 Julio Franco .10
59 Eddie Murray .75
60 Jody Davis .10
61 Todd Worrell .10
62 Von Hayes .10
63 Billy Hatcher .10
64 John Kruk .10
65 Tom Henke .10
66 Mike Scott .10
67 Vince Coleman .10
68 Ozzie Smith 1.00
69 Ken Williams .10
70 Steve Bedrosian .10
71 Luis Polonia .10
72 Brook Jacoby .10
73 Ron Darling .10
74 Lloyd Moseby .10
75 Wally Joyner .10
76 Dan Quisenberry .10
77 Scott Fletcher .10
78 Kirk McCaskill .10
79 Paul Molitor .75
80 Mike Aldrete .10
81 Neal Heaton .10
82 Jeffrey Leonard .10
83 Dave Magadan .10
84 Danny Cox .10
85 Lance McCullers .10
86 Jay Howell .10
87 Charlie Hough .10
88 Gene Garber .10
89 Jesse Orosco .10
90 Don Robinson .10
91 Willie McGee .10
92 Bert Blyleven .10
93 Phil Bradley .10
94 Terry Kennedy .10
95 Kent Hrbek .10
96 Juan Samuel .10
97 Pedro Guerrero .10
98 Sid Bream .10
99 Devon White .10
100 Mark McGwire 1.50
101 Dave Parker .10
102 Glenn Davis .10
103 Greg Walker .10
104 Rick Rhoden .10
105 Mitch Webster .10
106 Lenny Dykstra .10
107 Gene Larkin .10
108 Floyd Youmans .10
109 Andy Van Slyke .10
110 Mike Scioscia .10
111 Kirk Gibson .10
112 Kal Daniels .10
113 Ruben Sierra .10
114 Sam Horn .10
115 Ray Knight .10
116 Jimmy Key .10
117 Bo Diaz .10
118 Mike Greenwell .10
119 Barry Bonds 2.00
120 Reggie Jackson 1.25
121 Mike Pagliarulo .10
122 Tommy John .10
123 Bill Madlock .10
124 Ken Caminiti .10
125 Gary Ward .10
126 Candy Maldonado .10
127 Harold Reynolds .10
128 Joe Magrane .10
129 Mike Henneman .10
130 Jim Gantner .10
131 Bobby Bonilla .10
132 John Farrell .10
133 Frank Tanana .10
134 Zane Smith .10
135 Dave Righetti .10
136 Rick Reuschel .10
137 Dwight Evans .10
138 Howard Johnson .10
139 Terry Leach .10
140 Casey Candaele .10
141 Tom Herr .10
142 Tony Pena .10
143 Lance Parrish .10
144 Ellis Burks .10
145 Pete O'Brien .10
146 Mike Boddicker .10
147 Buddy Bell .10
148 Bo Jackson .15
149 Frank White .10
150 George Brett 1.25
151 Tim Wallach .10
152 Cal Ripken, Jr. 2.00
153 Brett Butler .10
154 Gary Gaetti .10
155 Darryl Strawberry .20
156 Alfredo Griffin .10
157 Marty Barrett .10
158 Jim Rice .25
159 Terry Pendleton .10
160 Orel Hershiser .10
161 Larry Sheets .10
162 Dave Stewart .10
163 Shawon Dunston .10
164 Keith Moreland .10
165 Ken Oberkfell .10
166 Ivan Calderon .10
167 Bob Welch .10
168 Fred McGriff .10
169 Pete Incaviglia .10
170 Dale Murphy .25
171 Mike Dunne .10
172 Chili Davis .10
173 Milt Thompson .10
174 Terry Steinbach .10
175 Oddibe McDowell .10
176 Jack Morris .10
177 Sid Fernandez .10
178 Ken Griffey .10
179 Lee Smith .10
180 1987 Highlights
(Juan Nieves, Kirby Puckett,
Mike Schmidt) .25
181 Brian Downing .10
182 Andres Galarraga .10
183 Rob Deer .10
184 Greg Brock .10
185 Doug DeCinces .10
186 Johnny Ray .10
187 Hubie Brooks .10
188 Darrell Evans .10
189 Mel Hall .10
190 Jim Deshaies .10
191 Dan Plesac .10
192 Willie Wilson .10
193 Mike LaValliere .10
194 Tom Brunansky .10
195 John Franco .10
196 Frank Viola .10
197 Bruce Hurst .10
198 John Tudor .10
199 Bob Forsch .10
200 Dwight Gooden .10
201 Jose Canseco .65
202 Carney Lansford .10
203 Kelly Downs .10
204 Glenn Wilson .10
205 Pat Tabler .10
206 Mike Davis .10
207 Roger Clemens 1.25
208 Dave Smith .10
209 Curt Young .10
210 Mark Eichhorn .10
211 Juan Nieves .10
212 Bob Boone .10
213 Don Sutton .50
214 Willie Upshaw .10
215 Jim Clancy .10
216 Bill Ripken .10
217 Ozzie Virgil .10
218 Dave Concepcion .10
219 Alan Ashby .10
220 Mike Marshall .10
221 '87 Highlights
(Vince Coleman,
Mark McGwire,
Paul Molitor) .75
222 '87 Highlights
(Steve Bedrosian,
Don Mattingly,
Benito Santiago) .40
223 Hot Rookie Prospects
(Shawn Abner,
Jay Buhner RC,
Gary Thurman) .25
224 Hot Rookie Prospects
(Tim Crews, John Davis,
Vincente Palacios) .10
225 Hot Rookie Prospects
(Keith Miller, Jody Reed,
Jeff Treadway) .10

Gamewinners

GAMEWINNERS — 23 DON MATTINGLY 13

This set of 25 standard-size cards (2-1/2" x 3-1/2"), featuring star players in the Sportflics patented 3-D Magic Motion design, was issued by Weiser Card Co. of Plainsboro, N.J., for use as a youth organizational fundraiser. (Weiser's president was former Yankees outfielder Bobby Murcer.) A limited number of sets was produced for test marketing in the Northwestern U.S., with plans for a 1989 set to be marketed nationwide. A green-and-yellow Gamewinners logo banner spans the upper border of the cards face, with a matching player name (with uniform number and position) below the full-color triple photo. The card backs carry large full-color player photos along with stats, personal information and career highlights.

	NM/M
Complete Set (25):	7.50
Common Player:	.25

1 Don Mattingly 1.50
2 Mark McGwire 3.50
3 Wade Boggs 1.25
4 Will Clark .25
5 Eric Davis .25
6 Willie Randolph .25
7 Dave Winfield .75
8 Rickey Henderson .75
9 Dwight Gooden .25
10 Benny Santiago .25
11 Keith Hernandez .25
12 Juan Samuel .25
13 Kevin Seitzer .25
14 Gary Carter .75
15 Darryl Strawberry .25
16 Rick Rhoden .25
17 Howard Johnson .25
18 Matt Nokes .25
19 Dave Righetti .25
20 Roger Clemens 1.50
21 Mike Schmidt 1.50
22 Kevin McReynolds .25
23 Mike Pagliarulo .25
24 Kevin Elster .25
25 Jack Clark .25

1989 Sportflics

GEORGE BRETT — KANSAS CITY ROYALS

This basic issue includes 225 standard-size player cards (2-1/2" x 3-1/2") and 153 trivia cards, all featuring the patented Magic Motion design. A five-card sub-set of "Tri-Star" cards features a mix of veterans and rookies. The card fronts feature a white outer border and double color inner border in one of six color schemes. The inner border color changes when the card is tilted and the bottom border carries a double stripe of colors. The player name appears in the top border, player postition and uniform number appear, alternately, in the bottom border. The card backs contain crisp 1-7/8 by 1-3/4 player action shots, along with personal information, stats and career highlights. "The Unforgettables" trivia cards in this set salute members of the Hall of Fame.

	NM/M
Factory Set (225+153):	17.50
Complete Set (225):	12.00
Common Player:	.10
Foil Pack (3+2):	.50
Foil Box (36):	10.00

1 Jose Canseco .60
2 Wally Joyner .10
3 Roger Clemens 1.25
4 Greg Swindell .10
5 Jack Morris .10
6 Mickey Brantley .10
7 Jim Presley .10
8 Pete O'Brien .10
9 Jesse Barfield .10
10 Frank Viola .10
11 Kevin Bass .10
12 Glenn Wilson .10
13 Chris Sabo .10
14 Fred McGriff .10
15 Mark Grace .20
16 Devon White .10
17 Juan Samuel .10
18 Lou Whitaker .10
19 Greg Walker .10
20 Roberto Alomar .20
21 Mike Schmidt 1.25
22 Benny Santiago .10
23 Dave Stewart .10
24 Dave Winfield .75
25 George Bell .10
26 Jack Clark .10
27 Doug Drabek .10
28 Ron Gant .10
29 Glenn Braggs .10
30 Rafael Palmeiro .65
31 Brett Butler .10
32 Ron Darling .10
33 Alvin Davis .10
34 Bob Walk .10
35 Dave Stieb .10
36 Orel Hershiser .10
37 John Farrell .10
38 Doug Jones .10
39 Kelly Downs .10
40 Bob Boone .10
41 Gary Sheffield .35
42 Doug Dascenzo .10
43 Chad Krueter .10
44 Ricky Jordan .10
45 Dave West .10
46 Danny Tartabull .10
47 Teddy Higuera .10
48 Gary Gaetti .10
49 Dave Parker .10
50 Don Mattingly 1.25
51 David Cone .10
52 Kal Daniels .10
53 Carney Lansford .10
54 Mike Marshall .10
55 Kevin Seitzer .10
56 Mike Henneman .10
57 Bill Doran .10
58 Steve Sax .10
59 Lance Parrish .10
60 Keith Hernandez .10
61 Jose Uribe .10
62 Jose Lind .10
63 Steve Bedrosian .10
64 George Brett 1.25
65 Kirk Gibson .10
66 Cal Ripken, Jr. 2.00
67 Mitch Webster .10
68 Fred Lynn .10
69 Eric Davis .10
70 Bo Jackson .15
71 Kevin Elster .10
72 Rick Reuschel .10
73 Tim Burke .10
74 Mark Davis .10
75 Claudell Washington .10
76 Lance McCullers .10
77 Mike Moore .10
78 Robby Thompson .10
79 Roger McDowell .10
80 Danny Jackson .10
81 Tim Leary .10
82 Bobby Witt .10
83 Jim Gott .10
84 Andy Hawkins .10
85 Ozzie Guillen .10
86 John Tudor .10
87 Todd Burns .10
88 Dave Gallagher .10
89 Jay Buhner .10
90 Gregg Jefferies .10
91 Bob Welch .10
92 Charlie Hough .10
93 Tony Fernandez .10
94 Ozzie Virgil .10
95 Andre Dawson .25
96 Hubie Brooks .10
97 Kevin McReynolds .10
98 Mike LaValliere .10
99 Terry Pendleton .10
100 Wade Boggs 1.00
101 Dennis Eckersley .65
102 Mark Gubicza .10
103 Frank Tanana .10
104 Joe Carter .10
105 Ozzie Smith 1.00
106 Dennis Martinez .10
107 Jeff Treadway .10
108 Greg Maddux 1.00
109 Bret Saberhagen .10
110 Dale Murphy .20
111 Rob Deer .10
112 Pete Incaviglia .10
113 Vince Coleman .10
114 Tim Wallach .10
115 Nolan Ryan 2.00
116 Walt Weiss .10
117 Brian Downing .10
118 Melido Perez .10
119 Terry Steinbach .10
120 Mike Scott .10
121 Tim Belcher .10
122 Mike Boddicker .10
123 Len Dykstra .10
124 Fernando Valenzuela .10
125 Gerald Young .10
126 Tom Henke .10
127 Dave Henderson .10
128 Dan Plesac .10
129 Chili Davis .10
130 Bryan Harvey .10
131 Don August .10
132 Mike Harkey .10
133 Luis Polonia .10
134 Craig Worthington .10
135 Joey Meyer .10
136 Barry Larkin .10
137 Glenn Davis .10
138 Mike Scioscia .10
139 Andres Galarraga .10
140 Doc Gooden .10
141 Keith Moreland .10
142 Kevin Mitchell .10
143 Mike Greenwell .10
144 Mel Hall .10
145 Rickey Henderson .75
146 Barry Bonds 2.00
147 Eddie Murray .75
148 Lee Smith .10
149 Julio Franco .10
150 Tim Raines .10
151 Mitch Williams .10
152 Tim Laudner .10
153 Mike Pagliarulo .10
154 Floyd Bannister .10
155 Gary Carter .75
156 Kirby Puckett 1.00
157 Harold Baines .10
158 Dave Righetti .10
159 Mark Langston .10
160 Tony Gwynn 1.00
161 Tom Brunansky .10
162 Vance Law .10
163 Kelly Gruber .10
164 Gerald Perry .10
165 Harold Reynolds .10
166 Andy Van Slyke .10
167 Jimmy Key .10
168 Jeff Reardon .10
169 Milt Thompson .10
170 Will Clark .10
171 Chet Lemon .10
172 Pat Tabler .10
173 Jim Rice .25
174 Billy Hatcher .10
175 Bruce Hurst .10
176 John Franco .10
177 Van Snider .10
178 Ron Jones .10
179 Jerald Clark .10
180 Tom Browning .10
181 Von Hayes .10
182 Bobby Bonilla .10
183 Todd Worrell .10
184 John Kruk .10
185 Scott Fletcher .10
186 Willie Wilson .10
187 Jody Davis .10
188 Kent Hrbek .10
189 Ruben Sierra .10
190 Shawon Dunston .10
191 Ellis Burks .10
192 Brook Jacoby .10
193 Jeff Robinson .10
194 Rich Dotson .10
195 Johnny Ray .10
196 Cory Snyder .10
197 Mike Witt .10
198 Marty Barrett .10
199 Robin Yount .75
200 Mark McGwire 1.50
201 Ryne Sandberg 1.00
202 John Candelaria .10

#	Player	Price
203	Matt Nokes	.10
204	Dwight Evans	.10
205	Darryl Strawberry	.10
206	Willie McGee	.10
207	Bobby Thigpen	.10
208	B.J. Surhoff	.10
209	Paul Molitor	.75
210	Jody Reed	.10
211	Doyle Alexander	.10
212	Dennis Rasmussen	.10
213	Kevin Gross	.10
214	Kirk McCaskill	.10
215	Alan Trammell	.10
216	Damon Berryhill	.10
217	Rick Sutcliffe	.10
218	Don Slaught	.10
219	Carlton Fisk	.75
220	Allan Anderson	.10
221	'88 Highlights (Wade Boggs, Jose Canseco, Mike Greenwell)	.15
222	'88 Highlights (Tom Browning, Dennis Eckersley, Orel Hershiser)	.20
223	Hot Rookie Prospects (Sandy Alomar, Gregg Jefferies, Gary Sheffield)	.50
224	Hot Rookie Prospects (Randy Johnson, Ramon Martinez, Bob Milacki)	.75
225	Hot Rookie Prospects (Geronimo Berroa, Cameron Drew, Ron Jones)	.10

1990 Sportflics

The Sportflics set for 1990 again contains 225 cards. The cards feature the unique "Magic Motion" effect which displays either of two different photos depending on how the card is tilted. (Previous years' sets had used three photos per card.) The two-photo "Magic Motion" sequence is designed to depict sequential game-action, showing a batter following through on his swing, a pitcher completing his motion, etc. Sportflics also added a moving red and yellow "marquee" border on the cards to complement the animation effect. The player's name, which appears below the animation, remains stationary. The set includes 19 special rookie cards. The backs contain a color player photo, team logo, player information and stats. The cards were distributed in non-transparent mylar packs with small MVP trivia cards.

	NM/M
Factory Set (225+153):	15.00
Complete Set (225):	12.00
Common Player:	.10
Foil Pack (3+2):	.75
Foil Box (36):	20.00

#	Player	Price
1	Kevin Mitchell	.10
2	Wade Boggs	1.00
3	Cory Snyder	.10
4	Paul O'Neill	.10
5	Will Clark	.10
6	Tony Fernandez	.10
7	Ken Griffey Jr.	1.50
8	Nolan Ryan	2.00
9	Rafael Palmeiro	.65
10	Jesse Barfield	.10
11	Kirby Puckett	1.00
12	Steve Sax	.10
13	Fred McGriff	.10
14	Gregg Jefferies	.10
15	Mark Grace	.10
16	Devon White	.10
17	Juan Samuel	.10
18	Robin Yount	.75
19	Glenn Davis	.10
20	Jeffrey Leonard	.10
21	Chili Davis	.10
22	Craig Biggio	.10
23	Jose Canseco	.50
24	Derek Lilliquist	.10
25	Chris Bosio	.10
26	Dave Steib	.10
27	Bobby Thigpen	.10
28	Jack Clark	.10
29	Kevin Ritz	.10
30	Tom Gordon	.10
31	Bryan Harvey	.10
32	Jim Deshaies	.10
33	Terry Steinbach	.10
34	Tom Glavine	.35
35	Bob Welch	.10
36	Charlie Hayes	.10
37	Jeff Reardon	.10
38	Joe Orsulak	.10
39	Scott Garrelts	.10
40	Bob Boone	.10
41	Scott Bankhead	.10
42	Tom Henke	.10
43	Greg Briley	.10
44	Teddy Higuera	.10
45	Pat Borders	.10
46	Kevin Seitzer	.10
47	Bruce Hurst	.10
48	Ozzie Guillen	.10
49	Wally Joyner	.10
50	Mike Greenwell	.10
51	Gary Gaetti	.10
52	Gary Sheffield	.30
53	Dennis Martinez	.10
54	Ryne Sandberg	1.00
55	Mike Scott	.10
56	Todd Benzinger	.10
57	Kelly Gruber	.10
58	Jose Lind	.10
59	Allan Anderson	.10
60	Robby Thompson	.10
61	John Smoltz	.10
62	Mark Davis	.10
63	Tom Herr	.10
64	Randy Johnson	.75
65	Lonnie Smith	.10
66	Pedro Guerrero	.10
67	Jerome Walton	.10
68	Ramon Martinez	.10
69	Tim Raines	.10
70	Matt Williams	.10
71	Joe Oliver	.10
72	Nick Esasky	.10
73	Kevin Brown	.10
74	Walt Weiss	.10
75	Roger McDowell	.10
76	Jose DeLeon	.10
77	Brian Downing	.10
78	Jay Howell	.10
79	Jose Uribe	.10
80	Ellis Burks	.10
81	Sammy Sosa	7.50
82	Johnny Ray	.10
83	Danny Darwin	.10
84	Carney Lansford	.10
85	Jose Oquendo	.10
86	John Cerutti	.10
87	Dave Winfield	.75
88	Dave Righetti	.10
89	Danny Jackson	.10
90	Andy Benes	.10
91	Tom Browning	.10
92	Pete O'Brien	.10
93	Roberto Alomar	.20
94	Bret Saberhagen	.10
95	Phil Bradley	.10
96	Doug Jones	.10
97	Eric Davis	.10
98	Tony Gwynn	1.00
99	Jim Abbott	.10
100	Cal Ripken, Jr.	2.00
101	Andy Van Slyke	.10
102	Dan Plesac	.10
103	Lou Whitaker	.10
104	Steve Bedrosian	.10
105	Dave Gallagher	.10
106	Keith Hernandez	.10
107	Duane Ward	.10
108	Andre Dawson	.35
109	Howard Johnson	.10
110	Mark Langston	.10
111	Jerry Browne	.10
112	Alvin Davis	.10
113	Sid Fernandez	.10
114	Mike Devereaux	.10
115	Benny Santiago	.10
116	Bip Roberts	.10
117	Craig Worthington	.10
118	Kevin Elster	.10
119	Harold Reynolds	.10
120	Joe Carter	.10
121	Brian Harper	.10
122	Frank Viola	.10
123	Jeff Ballard	.10
124	John Kruk	.10
125	Harold Baines	.10
126	Tom Candiotti	.10
127	Kevin McReynolds	.10
128	Mookie Wilson	.10
129	Danny Tartabull	.10
130	Craig Lefferts	.10
131	Jose DeJesus	.10
132	John Orton	.10
133	Curt Schilling	.35
134	Marquis Grissom	.10
135	Greg Vaughn	.10
136	Brett Butler	.10
137	Rob Deer	.10
138	John Franco	.10
139	Keith Moreland	.10
140	Dave Smith	.10
141	Mark McGwire	1.50
142	Vince Coleman	.10
143	Barry Bonds	2.00
144	Mike Henneman	.10
145	Doc Gooden	.10
146	Darryl Strawberry	.10
147	Von Hayes	.10
148	Andres Galarraga	.10
149	Roger Clemens	1.25
150	Don Mattingly	1.25
151	Joe Magrane	.10
152	Dwight Smith	.10
153	Ricky Jordan	.10
154	Alan Trammell	.10
155	Brook Jacoby	.10
156	Lenny Dykstra	.10
157	Mike LaValliere	.10
158	Julio Franco	.10
159	Joey Belle	.25
160	Barry Larkin	.10
161	Rick Reuschel	.10
162	Nelson Santovenia	.10
163	Mike Scioscia	.10
164	Damon Berryhill	.10
165	Todd Worrell	.10
166	Jim Eisenreich	.10
167	Ivan Calderon	.10
168	Goose Gozzo	.10
169	Kirk McCaskill	.10
170	Dennis Eckersley	.65
171	Mickey Tettleton	.10
172	Chuck Finley	.10
173	Dave Magadan	.10
174	Terry Pendleton	.10
175	Willie Randolph	.10
176	Jeff Huson	.10
177	Todd Zeile	.10
178	Steve Olin	.10
179	Eric Anthony	.10
180	Scott Coolbaugh	.10
181	Rick Sutcliffe	.10
182	Tim Wallach	.10
183	Paul Molitor	.75
184	Roberto Kelly	.10
185	Mike Moore	.10
186	Junior Felix	.10
187	Mike Schooler	.10
188	Ruben Sierra	.10
189	Dale Murphy	.30
190	Dan Gladden	.10
191	John Smiley	.10
192	Jeff Russell	.10
193	Bert Blyleven	.10
194	Dave Stewart	.10
195	Bobby Bonilla	.10
196	Mitch Williams	.10
197	Orel Hershiser	.10
198	Kevin Bass	.10
199	Tim Burke	.10
200	Bo Jackson	.15
201	David Cone	.10
202	Gary Pettis	.10
203	Kent Hrbek	.10
204	Carlton Fisk	.75
205	Bob Geren	.10
206	Bill Spiers	.10
207	Oddibe McDowell	.10
208	Rickey Henderson	.75
209	Ken Caminiti	.10
210	Devon White	.10
211	Greg Maddux	1.00
212	Ed Whitson	.10
213	Carlos Martinez	.10
214	George Brett	1.25
215	Gregg Olson	.10
216	Kenny Rogers	.10
217	Dwight Evans	.10
218	Pat Tabler	.10
219	Jeff Treadway	.10
220	Scott Fletcher	.10
221	Deion Sanders	.15
222	Robin Ventura	.10
223	Chip Hale	.10
224	Tommy Greene	.10
225	Dean Palmer	.10

1994 Sportflics 2000 Promos

To reintroduce its "Magic Motion" baseball cards to the hobby (last produced by Score in 1990), Pinnacle Brands produced a three-card promo set which it sent to dealers along with a header card explaining the issue. In the same format as the regular issue, though some different photos were used, the promos feature on front what Sportflics calls "state-of-the-art lenticular technology" to create an action effect when the card is moved. Backs are produced by standard printing techniques and are gold-foil highlighted and UV-coated. Each of the promo cards has a large black "SAMPLE" overprinted diagonally across front and back.

	NM/M
Complete Set (4):	5.00
Common Player:	1.00

#	Player	Price
1a	Lenny Dykstra ("SAMPLE" front only.)	1.00
1b	Lenny Dykstra ("SAMPLE" back and front.)	1.00
7	Javy Lopez (Shakers)	1.00
193	Greg Maddux (Starflics)	3.00
	Header Card	.25

1994 Sportflics 2000

The concept of "Magic Motion" baseball cards returned to the hobby in 1994 after a three-year hiatus. Pinnacle refined its "state-of-the-art lenticular technology" to produce cards which show alternating pictures when viewed from different angles on the basic cards, and to create a striking 3-D effect on its "Starflics" A.L. and N.L. All-Star team subset. Backs are conventionally printed, UV-coated and gold-foil highlighted, featuring a player photo and recent stats. Cards were sold in eight-card foil packs with a suggested retail price of $2.49.

	NM/M
Complete Set (193):	15.00
Common Player:	.10
Pack (8):	.50
Wax Box (36):	15.00

#	Player	Price
1	Len Dykstra	.10
2	Mike Stanley	.10
3	Alex Fernandez	.10
4	Mark McGuire (McGwire)	1.50
5	Eric Karros	.10
6	Dave Justice	.10
7	Jeff Bagwell	.65
8	Darren Lewis	.10
9	David McCarty	.10
10	Albert Belle	.10
11	Ben McDonald	.10
12	Joe Carter	.10
13	Benito Santiago	.10
14	Rob Dibble	.10
15	Roger Clemens	.85
16	Travis Fryman	.10
17	Doug Drabek	.10
18	Jay Buhner	.10
19	Orlando Merced	.10
20	Ryan Klesko	.10
21	Chuck Finley	.10
22	Dante Bichette	.10
23	Wally Joyner	.10
24	Robin Yount	.65
25	Tony Gwynn	.75
26	Allen Watson	.10
27	Rick Wilkins	.10
28	Gary Sheffield	.40
29	John Burkett	.10
30	Randy Johnson	.65
31	Roberto Alomar	.25
32	Fred McGriff	.10
33	Ozzie Guillen	.10
34	Jimmy Key	.10
35	Juan Gonzalez	.35
36	Wil Cordero	.10
37	Aaron Sele	.10
38	Mark Langston	.10
39	David Cone	.10
40	John Jaha	.10
41	Ozzie Smith	.75
42	Kirby Puckett	.75
43	Kenny Lofton	.10
44	Mike Mussina	.40
45	Ryne Sandberg	.75
46	Robby Thompson	.10
47	Bryan Harvey	.10
48	Marquis Grissom	.10
49	Bobby Bonilla	.10
50	Dennis Eckersley	.60
51	Curt Schilling	.35
52	Andy Benes	.10
53	Greg Maddux	.75
54	Bill Swift	.10
55	Andres Galarraga	.10
56	Tony Phillips	.10
57	Darryl Hamilton	.10
58	Duane Ward	.10
59	Bernie Williams	.10
60	Steve Avery	.10
61	Eduardo Perez	.10
62	Jeff Conine	.10
63	Dave Winfield	.65
64	Phil Plantier	.10
65	Ray Lankford	.10
66	Robin Ventura	.10
67	Mike Piazza	1.00
68	Jason Bere	.10
69	Cal Ripken, Jr.	2.00
70	Frank Thomas	.65
71	Carlos Baerga	.10
72	Darryl Kile	.10
73	Ruben Sierra	.10
74	Gregg Jefferies	.10
75	John Olerud	.10
76	Andy Van Slyke	.10
77	Larry Walker	.10
78	Cecil Fielder	.10
79	Andre Dawson	.25
80	Tom Glavine	.35
81	Sammy Sosa	.10
82	Charlie Hayes	.10
83	Chuck Knoblauch	.10
84	Kevin Appier	.10
85	Dean Palmer	.10
86	Royce Clayton	.10
87	Moises Alou	.10
88	Ivan Rodriguez	.60
89	Tim Salmon	.10
90	Ron Gant	.10
91	Barry Bonds	2.00
92	Jack McDowell	.10
93	Alan Trammell	.10
94	Dwight Gooden	.10
95	Jay Bell	.10
96	Devon White	.10
97	Wilson Alvarez	.10
98	Jim Thome	.60
99	Ramon Martinez	.10
100	Kent Hrbek	.10
101	John Kruk	.10
102	Wade Boggs	.75
103	Greg Vaughn	.10
104	Tom Henke	.10
105	Brian Jordan	.10
106	Paul Molitor	.65
107	Cal Eldred	.10
108	Deion Sanders	.10
109	Barry Larkin	.10
110	Mike Greenwell	.10
111	Jeff Blauser	.10
112	Jose Rijo	.10
113	Pete Harnisch	.10
114	Chris Hoiles	.10
115	Edgar Martinez	.10
116	Juan Guzman	.10
117	Todd Zeile	.10
118	Danny Tartabull	.10
119	Chad Curtis	.10
120	Mark Grace	.10
121	J.T. Snow	.10
122	Mo Vaughn	.10
123	Lance Johnson	.10
124	Eric Davis	.10
125	Orel Hershiser	.10
126	Kevin Mitchell	.10
127	Don Mattingly	.85
128	Darren Daulton	.10
129	Rod Beck	.10
130	Charles Nagy	.10
131	Mickey Tettleton	.10
132	Kevin Brown	.10
133	Pat Hentgen	.10
134	Terry Mulholland	.10
135	Steve Finley	.10
136	John Smoltz	.10
137	Frank Viola	.10
138	Jim Abbott	.10
139	Matt Williams	.10
140	Bernard Gilkey	.10
141	Jose Canseco	.45
142	Mark Whiten	.10
143	Ken Griffey Jr.	1.00
144	Rafael Palmeiro	.10
145	Dave Hollins	.10
146	Will Clark	.10
147	Paul O'Neill	.10
148	Bobby Jones	.10
149	Butch Huskey	.10
150	Jeffrey Hammonds	.10
151	Manny Ramirez	.65
152	Bob Hamelin	.10
153	Kurt Abbott	.10
154	Scott Stahoviak	.10
155	Steve Hosey	.10
156	Salomon Torres	.10
157	Sterling Hitchcock	.10
158	Nigel Wilson	.10
159	Luis Lopez	.10
160	Chipper Jones	.75
161	Norberto Martin	.10
162	Raul Mondesi	.10
163	Steve Karsay	.10
164	J.R. Phillips	.10
165	Marc Newfield	.10
166	Mark Hutton	.10
167	Curtis Pride	.10
168	Carl Everett	.10
169	Scott Ruffcorn	.10
170	Turk Wendell	.10
171	Jeff McNeely	.10
172	Javier Lopez	.10
173	Cliff Floyd	.10
174	Rondell White	.10
175	Scott Lydy	.10
176	Frank Thomas/AS	.35
177	Roberto Alomar/AS	.20
178	Travis Fryman/AS	.10
179	Cal Ripken, Jr./AS	1.00
180	Chris Hoiles/AS	.10
181	Ken Griffey Jr./AS	.60
182	Juan Gonzalez/AS	.20
183	Joe Carter/AS	.10
184	Jack McDowell/AS	.10
185	Fred McGriff/AS	.10
186	Robby Thompson/AS	.10
187	Matt Williams/AS	.10
188	Jay Bell/AS	.10
189	Mike Piazza/AS	.60
190	Barry Bonds/AS	1.00
191	Len Dykstra/AS	.10
192	Dave Justice/AS	.10
193	Greg Maddux/AS	.45

Commemoratives

A pair of extra-rare commemorative chase cards was produced for the Sportflics 2000 set honoring Canada's veteran superstar Paul Molitor and its hottest rookie, Cliff Floyd. Cards, utilizing Magic Motion technology to alternate card-front pictures when the viewing angle changes, were inserted on average once in every 360 packs.

	NM/M
Complete Set (2):	5.00
1 Paul Molitor	4.50
2 Cliff Floyd	1.25

Movers

A dozen top veteran ballplayers were featured in the "Movers" insert set produced for inclusion in retail packaging of Sportflics 2000. The inserts feature the same Magic Motion features as the regular cards, showing different images on the card front when the card is viewed from different angles. The UV-coated, gold-foil highlighted backs are printed conventionally. A special "Movers" logo is found on both front and back. Stated odds of finding a Movers card are one in 24 packs.

	NM/M
Complete Set (12):	12.00
Common Player:	.60

#	Player	Price
1	Gregg Jefferies	.60
2	Ryne Sandberg	2.00
3	Cecil Fielder	.60
4	Kirby Puckett	2.00
5	Tony Gwynn	2.00
6	Andres Galarraga	.60
7	Sammy Sosa	.60
8	Rickey Henderson	1.00
9	Don Mattingly	2.50
10	Joe Carter	.60
11	Carlos Baerga	.60
12	Len Dykstra	.60

Shakers

Hobby packs are the exclusive source for this 12-card insert set of top rookies, found on average once every 24 packs. The chase cards utilize the Sportflics Magic Motion technology to create two different images on the card front when the card is viewed from different angles. Backs are printed conventionally but feature UV-coating and gold-foil highlights. The "Shakers" logo appears on both front and back.

		NM/M
Complete Set (12):		12.00
Common Player:		.60
1	Kenny Lofton	.60
2	Tim Salmon	.60
3	Jeff Bagwell	2.50
4	Jason Bere	.60
5	Salomon Torres	.60
6	Rondell White	.60
7	Javier Lopez	.60
8	Dean Palmer	.60
9	Jim Thome	2.00
10	J.T. Snow	.60
11	Mike Piazza	4.00
12	Manny Ramirez	2.50

1994 Sportflics 2000 Rookie/Traded Promos

This nine-card set was issued to promote the Sportflics Rookie/Traded update set which was released as a hobby-only product. Cards are virtually identical to the corresponding cards in the R/T set except for the overprinted "SAMPLE" in white on front and back.

		NM/M
Complete Set (9):		5.00
Common Player:		1.00
1	Will Clark	1.00
14	Bret Boone	1.00
20	Ellis Burks	1.00
25	Deion Sanders	1.00
62	Chris Turner	1.00
82	Tony Tarasco	1.00
102	Rich Becker	1.00
GG1	Gary Sheffield (Going, Going, Gone)	2.00
---	Header Card	.25

1994 Sportflics 2000 Rookie/Traded

Each of the 150 regular cards in the Sportflics 2000 Rookie & Traded issue was also produced in a parallel chase card set designated on front with a black and gold "Artist's Proof" logo. Stated odds of finding an AP cards were one per 24 packs. Fewer than 1,000 or each AP card were reportedly produced.

		NM/M
Complete Set (150):		20.00
Common Player:		.10
Pack (5):		3.00
Wax Box (24):		60.00
1	Will Clark	.10
2	Sid Fernandez	.10
3	Joe Magrane	.10
4	Pete Smith	.10

5	Roberto Kelly	.10
6	Delino DeShields	.10
7	Brian Harper	.10
8	Darrin Jackson	.10
9	Omar Vizquel	.10
10	Luis Polonia	.10
11	Reggie Jefferson	.10
12	Geronimo Berroa	.10
13	Mike Harkey	.10
14	Bret Boone	.10
15	Dave Henderson	.10
16	Pedro Martinez	.75
17	Jose Vizcaino	.10
18	Xavier Hernandez	.10
19	Eddie Taubensee	.10
20	Ellis Burks	.10
21	Turner Ward	.10
22	Terry Mulholland	.10
23	Howard Johnson	.10
24	Vince Coleman	.10
25	Deion Sanders	.60
26	Rafael Palmeiro	.65
27	Dave Weathers	.10
28	Kent Mercker	.10
29	Gregg Olson	.10
30	Cory Bailey	.10
31	Brian Hunter	.10
32	Garey Ingram	.10
33	Daniel Smith	.10
34	Denny Hocking	.10
35	Charles Johnson	.10
36	Otis Nixon	.10
37	Hector Fajardo	.10
38	Lee Smith	.10
39	Phil Stidham	.10
40	Melvin Nieves	.10
41	Julio Franco	.10
42	Greg Gohr	.10
43	Steve Dunn	.10
44	Tony Fernandez	.10
45	Toby Borland	.10
46	Paul Shuey	.10
47	Shawn Hare	.10
48	Shawn Green	.50
49	Julian Tavarez RC	.10
50	Ernie Young	.10
51	Chris Sabo	.10
52	Greg O'Halloran	.10
53	Donnie Elliott	.10
54	Jim Converse	.10
55	Ray Holbert	.10
56	Keith Lockhart	.10
57	Tony Longmire	.10
58	Jorge Fabregas	.10
59	Ravelo Manzanillo	.10
60	Marcus Moore	.10
61	Carlos Rodriguez	.10
62	Mark Portugal	.10
63	Yorkis Perez	.10
64	Dan Miceli	.10
65	Chris Turner	.10
66	Mike Oquist	.10
67	Tom Quinlan	.10
68	Matt Walbeck	.10
69	Dave Staton	.10
70	Bill Van Landingham RC	.10
71	Dave Stevens	.10
72	Domingo Cedeno	.10
73	Alex Diaz	.10
74	Darren Bragg	.10
75	James Hurst	.10
76	Alex Gonzalez	.10
77	Steve Dreyer	.10
78	Robert Eenhoorn	.10
79	Derek Parks	.10
80	Jose Valentin	.10
81	Wes Chamberlain	.10
82	Tony Tarasco	.10
83	Steve Trachsel	.10
84	Willie Banks	.10
85	Rob Butler	.10
86	Miguel Jimenez	.10
87	Gerald Williams	.10
88	Aaron Small	.10
89	Matt Mieske	.10
90	Tim Hyers	.10
91	Eddie Murray	.75
92	Dennis Martinez	.10
93	Tony Eusebio	.10
94	Brian Anderson RC	.25
95	Blaise Ilsley	.10
96	Johnny Ruffin	.10
97	Carlos Reyes	.10
98	Greg Pirkl	.10
99	Jack Morris	.10
100	John Mabry	.10
101	Mike Kelly	.10
102	Rich Becker	.10
103	Chris Gomez	.10
104	Jim Edmonds	.10
105	Rich Rowland	.10
106	Damon Buford	.10
107	Mark Kiefer	.10
108	Matias Carrillo	.10
109	James Mouton	.10
110	Kelly Stinnett	.10
111	Billy Ashley	.10
112	Fausto Cruz RC	.10
113	Roberto Petagine	.10
114	Joe Hall	.10
115	Brian Johnson RC	.10
116	Kevin Jarvis	.10
117	Tim Davis	.10
118	John Patterson	.10
119	Stan Royer	.10
120	Jeff Juden	.10
121	Bryan Eversgerd	.10
122	Chan Ho Park RC	1.00

123	Shane Reynolds	.10
124	Danny Bautista	.10
125	Rikkert Faneyte	.10
126	Carlos Pulido	.10
127	Mike Matheny	.10
128	Hector Carrasco	.10
129	Eddie Zambrano	.10
130	Lee Tinsley	.10
131	Roger Salkeld	.10
132	Carlos Delgado	1.00
133	Troy O'Leary	.10
134	Keith Mitchell	.10
135	Lance Painter	.10
136	Nate Minchey	.10
137	Eric Anthony	.10
138	Rafael Bournigal	.10
139	Joey Hamilton	.10
140	Bobby Munoz	.10
141	Rex Hudler	.10
142	Alex Cole	.10
143	Stan Javier	.10
144	Jose Oliva	.10
145	Tom Brunansky	.10
146	Greg Colbrunn	.10
147	Luis Lopez	.10
148	Alex Rodriguez RC	10.00
149	Darryl Strawberry	.10
150	Bo Jackson	.15

Artist's Proof

Each of the 150 regular cards in the Sportflics 2000 Rookie & Traded issue was also produced in a parallel chase set designated on front with a black and gold "Artist's Proof" logo. Stated odds of finding an AP card were one per 24 packs. Fewer than 1,000 of each AP card were reportedly produced.

		NM/M
Complete Set (150):		300.00
Common Player:		1.00
Stars:		25X
148 Alex Rodriguez:		

Going, Going, Gone

A dozen of the game's top home run hitters are featured in this insert set. On front, simulated 3-D action photos depict the player's swing for the fences. Backs have a portrait photo and information about the player's home run prowess. A crossed bats and "Going, Going Gone" logo appear on both front and back. Cards are numbered with a "GG" prefix. Stated odds of finding one of these inserts were once in 18 packs.

		NM/M
Complete Set (12):		10.00
Common Player:		.50
1	Gary Sheffield	.75
2	Matt Williams	.50
3	Juan Gonzalez	.90
4	Ken Griffey Jr.	2.00
5	Mike Piazza	2.00
6	Frank Thomas	1.50
7	Tim Salmon	.50
8	Barry Bonds	3.00
9	Fred McGriff	.50
10	Cecil Fielder	.50
11	Albert Belle	.50
12	Joe Carter	.50

Rookies of the Year

Sportflics' choices for Rookies of the Year were featured on this one-card insert set. Ryan Klesko (National League) and Manny Ramirez (American League) are shown on the card when viewed from different angles. Sportflics batted .000 in their guesses, however, as Raul Mondesi and Bob Hamelin were the actual R.O.Y. selections. This card was inserted at the average rate of once per 360 packs.

		NM/M
Complete Set (1):		
RO1	Ryan Klesko, Manny Ramirez	3.00

3-D Rookies

Eighteen of 1994's premier rookies are featured in this insert set. Combining a 3-D look and Sportflics' "Magic Motion" technology, the horizontal-format Starflics rookie cards present a striking appearance. Backs feature a full-bleed color photo overprinted with gold foil. A notice on back gives the production run of the chase cards as "No more than 5,000 sets." Stated odds of finding a Starflics Rookie card were given as one per 36 packs. Cards are numbered with a "TR" prefix.

		NM/M
Complete Set (18):		65.00
Common Player:		2.00
1	John Hudek	2.00
2	Manny Ramirez	15.00
3	Jeffrey Hammonds	2.00
4	Carlos Delgado	7.50
5	Javier Lopez	2.00
6	Alex Gonzalez	2.00
7	Raul Mondesi	2.00
8	Bob Hamelin	2.00
9	Ryan Klesko	2.00
10	Brian Anderson	2.00
11	Alex Rodriguez	40.00
12	Cliff Floyd	2.00
13	Chan Ho Park	2.00
14	Steve Karsay	2.00
15	Rondell White	2.00
16	Shawn Green	6.00
17	Rich Becker	2.00
18	Charles Johnson	2.00

FanFest All-Stars

An American and a National League player at each position share the fronts of these "Magic Motion" cards. Cards were available by redeeming coupons acquired at various locations around the Pittsburgh All-Star FanFest celebration in July, 1994. Action photos of the players alternate on the fronts of the cards when the viewing angle is changed. The N.L. player's name appears at upper-left; the A.L. All-Star at lower-right. Backs have portrait photos of the players and a few stats and com-

ments. The players' names, teams, position and card number are printed in gold foil, along with the notation "1 of 10,000." Cards are numbered with an "AS" prefix.

		NM/M
Complete Set (9):		25.00
Common Card:		2.50
1	Fred McGriff, Frank Thomas	3.00
2	Ryne Sandberg, Roberto Alomar	3.50
3	Matt Williams, Travis Fryman	2.50
4	Ozzie Smith, Cal Ripken Jr.	5.00
5	Mike Piazza, Ivan Rodriguez	4.00
6	Barry Bonds, Juan Gonzalez	5.00
7	Len Dykstra, Ken Griffey Jr.	4.00
8	Gary Sheffield, Kirby Puckett	3.50
9	Greg Maddux, Mike Mussina	3.50

1995 Sportflix Samples

This nine-card promo pack was sent to Pinnacle's dealer network to introduce its revamped (new logo, spelling) magic-motion card set for 1995. The sample cards are identical in format to the regular-issue Sportflix cards except that a large white "SAMPLE" is printed diagonally on front and back of the promos.

		NM/M
Complete Set (9):		20.00
Common Player:		2.00
3	Fred McGriff	2.00
20	Frank Thomas	3.50
105	Manny Ramirez	3.00
122	Cal Ripken Jr.	5.00
128	Roberto Alomar	2.25
152	Russ Davis (Rookie)	2.00
162	Chipper Jones (Rookie)	4.00
DE2	Matt Williams (Detonators)	2.00
----	Advertising Card	.10

1995 Sportflix

With only 170 cards in the set, only the biggest stars and hottest rookies (25 of them in a specially designed subset) are included in this simulated 3-D issue. Fronts feature two borderless action photos which are alternately visible as the card's viewing angle is changed. Backs are conventionally printed and have a portrait photo, a few career stats and a couple of sentences about the player. The basic packaging options for '95 Sportflix were five- and eight card foils at $1.89 and $2.99, respectively.

		NM/M
Complete Set (170):		13.50
Common Player:		.10
Artist's Proofs:		12X
Pack (5):		1.50
Wax Box (36):		30.00

1	Ken Griffey Jr.	1.25
2	Jeffrey Hammonds	.10
3	Fred McGriff	.10
4	Rickey Henderson	.75
5	Derrick May	.10
6	Robin Ventura	.10
7	Royce Clayton	.10
8	Paul Molitor	.75
9	Charlie Hayes	.10
10	David Nied	.10
11	Ellis Burks	.10
12	Bernard Gilkey	.10
13	Don Mattingly	1.00
14	Albert Belle	.10
15	Doug Drabek	.10
16	Tony Gwynn	1.00
17	Delino DeShields	.10
18	Bobby Bonilla	.10
19	Cliff Floyd	.10
20	Frank Thomas	.75
21	Raul Mondesi	.10
22	Dave Nilsson	.10
23	Todd Zeile	.10
24	Bernie Williams	.10
25	Kirby Puckett	1.00
26	David Cone	.10
27	Darren Daulton	.10
28	Marquis Grissom	.10
29	Randy Johnson	.75
30	Jeff Kent	.10
31	Orlando Merced	.10
32	Dave Justice	.10
33	Ivan Rodriguez	.65
34	Kirk Gibson	.10
35	Alex Fernandez	.10
36	Rick Wilkins	.10
37	Andy Benes	.10
38	Bret Saberhagen	.10
39	Billy Ashley	.10
40	Jose Rijo	.10
41	Matt Williams	.10
42	Lenny Dykstra	.10
43	Jay Bell	.10
44	Reggie Jefferson	.10
45	Greg Maddux	1.00
46	Gary Sheffield	.35
47	Bret Boone	.10
48	Jeff Bagwell	.75
49	Ben McDonald	.10
50	Eric Karros	.10
51	Roger Clemens	1.00
52	Sammy Sosa	1.00
53	Barry Bonds	2.00
54	Joey Hamilton	.10
55	Brian Jordan	.10
56	Wil Cordero	.10
57	Aaron Sele	.10
58	Paul O'Neill	.10
59	Carlos Garcia	.10
60	Mike Mussina	.40
61	John Olerud	.10
62	Kevin Appier	.10
63	Matt Mieske	.10
64	Carlos Baerga	.10
65	Ryan Klesko	.10
66	Jimmy Key	.10
67	James Mouton	.10
68	Tim Salmon	.10
69	Hal Morris	.10
70	Albie Lopez	.10
71	Dave Hollins	.10
72	Greg Colbrunn	.10
73	Juan Gonzalez	.40
74	Wally Joyner	.10
75	Bob Hamelin	.10
76	Brady Anderson	.10
77	Deion Sanders	.10
78	Javier Lopez	.10
79	Brian McRae	.10
80	Craig Biggio	.10
81	Kenny Lofton	.10
82	Cecil Fielder	.10
83	Mike Piazza	1.25
84	Rafael Palmeiro	.65
85	Jim Thome	.65
86	Ruben Sierra	.10
87	Mark Langston	.10
88	John Valentin	.10
89	Shawon Dunston	.10
90	Travis Fryman	.10
91	Chuck Knoblauch	.10
92	Dean Palmer	.10
93	Robby Thompson	.10
94	Barry Larkin	.10
95	Darren Lewis	.10
96	Andres Galarraga	.10
97	Tony Phillips	.10
98	Mo Vaughn	.10
99	Pedro Martinez	.75
100	Chad Curtis	.10
101	Brent Gates	.10
102	Pat Hentgen	.10
103	Rico Brogna	.10
104	Carlos Delgado	.50
105	Manny Ramirez	.75
106	Mike Greenwell	.10
107	Wade Boggs	1.00
108	Ozzie Smith	1.00
109	Rusty Greer	.10
110	Willie Greene	.10
111	Chili Davis	.10
112	Reggie Sanders	.10
113	Roberto Kelly	.10
114	Tom Glavine	.35
115	Moises Alou	.10
116	Dennis Eckersley	.65
117	Danny Tartabull	.10
118	Jeff Conine	.10

119	Will Clark	.10
120	Joe Carter	.10
121	Mark McGwire	1.50
122	Cal Ripken Jr.	2.00
123	Danny Jackson	.10
124	Phil Plantier	.10
125	Dante Bichette	.10
126	Jack McDowell	.10
127	Jose Canseco	.40
128	Roberto Alomar	.20
129	Rondell White	.10
130	Ray Lankford	.10
131	Ryan Thompson	.10
132	Ken Caminiti	.10
133	Gregg Jefferies	.10
134	Omar Vizquel	.10
135	Mark Grace	.10
136	Derek Bell	.10
137	Mickey Tettleton	.10
138	Wilson Alvarez	.10
139	Larry Walker	.10
140	Bo Jackson	.15
141	Alex Rodriguez	1.50
142	Orlando Miller	.10
143	Shawn Green	.35
144	Steve Dunn	.10
145	Midre Cummings	.10
146	Chan Ho Park	.10
147	Jose Oliva	.10
148	Armando Benitez	.10
149	J.R. Phillips	.10
150	Charles Johnson	.10
151	Garret Anderson	.10
152	Russ Davis	.10
153	Brian Hunter	.10
154	Ernie Young	.10
155	Marc Newfield	.10
156	Greg Pirkl	.10
157	Scott Ruffcorn	.10
158	Rikkert Faneyte	.10
159	Duane Singleton	.10
160	Gabe White	.10
161	Alex Gonzalez	.10
162	Chipper Jones	1.00
163	Mike Kelly	.10
164	Kurt Miller	.10
165	Roberto Petagine	.10
166	Checklist (Jeff Bagwell)	.40
167	Checklist (Mike Piazza)	.65
168	Checklist (Ken Griffey Jr.)	.65
169	Checklist (Frank Thomas)	.40
170	Checklist (Barry Bonds, Cal Ripken Jr.)	.75

Artist's Proofs

Each of the 170 cards in the regular Sportflix set can be found with a special tombstone shaped black-and-gold "Artist's Proof" seal designating it as one of a parallel edition of 700 cards each. Cards are otherwise identical to the regular-issue version. AP cards were inserted at an average rate of one per 36 packs.

	NM/M
Complete Set (170):	200.00
Common Player:	.75
Stars:	12X

Double Take

A see-through plastic background and A.L. and N.L. stars at the same position sharing the card with their shadows marks this chase set as the top of the line for '95 Sportflix. Found at an average rate of one per 48 packs, the Double Take inserts represent a new level in "magic motion" card technology.

		NM/M
Complete Set (12):		25.00
Common Player:		1.00
1	Frank Thomas, Jeff Bagwell	1.50
2	Will Clark, Fred McGriff	1.00
3	Roberto Alomar, Jeff Kent	1.00
4	Wade Boggs, Matt Williams	2.00
5	Cal Ripken Jr., Ozzie Smith	6.00
6	Alex Rodriguez, Wil Cordero	4.00
7	Carlos Delgado, Mike Piazza	3.00
8	Kenny Lofton, Dave Justice	1.00
9	Ken Griffey Jr., Barry Bonds	6.00
10	Albert Belle, Raul Mondesi	1.00
11	Kirby Puckett, Tony Gwynn	2.50
12	Jimmy Key, Greg Maddux	2.00

ProMotion

Twelve of baseball's biggest stars morph into team logos on a bright team-color background in this chase series. Backs have a portrait photo and a few words about the players. The ProMotion inserts are a one per 18 pack pick in jumbo packs only.

		NM/M
Complete Set (12):		30.00
Common Player:		1.50
1	Ken Griffey Jr.	4.00
2	Frank Thomas	2.50
3	Cal Ripken Jr.	5.00
4	Jeff Bagwell	2.50
5	Mike Piazza	4.00
6	Matt Williams	1.50
7	Albert Belle	1.50
8	Jose Canseco	2.00
9	Don Mattingly	3.50
10	Barry Bonds	5.00
11	Will Clark	1.50
12	Kirby Puckett	3.00

3D Detonators

With the players on a pedestal and fireworks in the background, this chase set lives up to its name, "Detonators." The cards feature a deep 3-D look on front. Backs have a close-up photo of the player in the pedestal's column. Detonator cards are pulled at an average rate of one per 16 packs.

		NM/M
Complete Set (9):		8.00
Common Player:		.40
1	Jeff Bagwell	1.00
2	Matt Williams	.40
3	Ken Griffey Jr.	1.50

4	Frank Thomas	1.25
5	Mike Piazza	1.50
6	Barry Bonds	2.00
7	Albert Belle	.40
8	Cliff Floyd	.40
9	Juan Gonzalez	.60

3D Hammer Team

Sledge hammers flying in formation through a cloud-studded sky are the background for this insert set featuring the game's heavy hitters. Backs have a portrait photo and a few words about the player's power hitting prowess. Hammer Team cards are picked on an average of once per four packs.

		NM/M
Complete Set (18):		7.50
Common Player:		.20
1	Ken Griffey Jr.	1.50
2	Frank Thomas	.65
3	Jeff Bagwell	.65
4	Mike Piazza	1.50
5	Cal Ripken Jr.	2.00
6	Albert Belle	.20
7	Barry Bonds	2.00
8	Don Mattingly	1.00
9	Will Clark	.20
10	Tony Gwynn	.75
11	Matt Williams	.20
12	Kirby Puckett	.75
13	Manny Ramirez	.65
14	Fred McGriff	.20
15	Juan Gonzalez	.35
16	Kenny Lofton	.20
17	Raul Mondesi	.20
18	Tim Salmon	.20

1995 Sportflix/UC3 Samples

To introduce the new technology it was bringing to the insert cards in the Sportflix UC3 issue, the company sent a sample of the Clear Shots insert, along with a header card describing the entire UC3 issue, to card dealers and the media in June 1995. A large, black, "SAMPLE" is overprinted diagonally on the front. A similarly marked Fred McGriff previewed the set's regular cards.

		NM/M
Complete Set (3):		5.00
3	Fred McGriff	2.00
CS8	Cliff Floyd	2.00
CS10	Alex Gonzalez	2.00
--	Header Card	.05

1995 Sportflix/UC3

Using advanced technology to create a premium 3-D card brand and inserts, UC3 offers three distinctly different card formats in the base 147-card set, plus a parallel set and three insert sets. All cards have borderless fronts and feature a heavy ribbed plastic top layer. The first 95 cards are veteran players in a horizontal format. A central action photo is flanked at left by a large gold glove (National Leaguers) or baseball (A.L.), and at right by a blue and green vista from which flies one (N.L.) or three (A.L.) baseballs. Player identification is in red at upper-left, the UC3 logo at lower-left. Backs have another color photo and a few stats set against a background of the team logo. Cards #96-122 are a vertical-format Rookie subset. Player photos are set against a purple and green vista with a large bat, ball and glove behind the player. His name is at upper-right; team logo at lower-right. Horizontal backs are similar to the other cards. The final 25 cards of the set are a subset titled, "In-Depth." These vertically formatted cards feature eye-popping graphics on front in which the main player photo almost jumps from the background. The only graphics are the player's name at left and the UC3 logo at upper-left. Backs have a portrait photo at top, bathed in golden rays. A team logo is at center and an outer space design at bottom. There is a short paragraph describing the player at right.

		NM/M
Complete Set (147):		12.50
Common Player:		.10
Artist's Proofs		12X
Pack (5):		1.00
Wax Box (36):		25.00
1	Frank Thomas	.75
2	Wil Cordero	.10
3	John Olerud	.10
4	Deion Sanders	.10
5	Mike Mussina	.30
6	Mo Vaughn	.10
7	Will Clark	.10
8	Chili Davis	.10
9	Jimmy Key	.10
10	John Valentin	.10
11	Tony Tarasco	.10
12	Alan Trammell	.10
13	David Cone	.10
14	Tim Salmon	.10
15	Danny Tartabull	.10
16	Aaron Sele	.10
17	Alex Fernandez	.10
18	Barry Bonds	2.00
19	Andres Galarraga	.10
20	Don Mattingly	1.00
21	Kevin Appier	.10
22	Paul Molitor	.75
23	Omar Vizquel	.10
24	Andy Benes	.10
25	Rafael Palmeiro	.65
26	Barry Larkin	.10
27	Bernie Williams	.10
28	Gary Sheffield	.40
29	Wally Joyner	.10
30	Wade Boggs	1.00
31	Rico Brogna	.10
32	Ken Caminiti	.10
33	Kirby Puckett	1.00
34	Bobby Bonilla	.10
35	Hal Morris	.10
36	Moises Alou	.10
37	Jim Thome	.65
38	Chuck Knoblauch	.10
39	Mike Piazza	1.25
40	Travis Fryman	.10
41	Rickey Henderson	.75
42	Jack McDowell	.10
43	Carlos Baerga	.10
44	Gregg Jeffries	.10
45	Kirk Gibson	.10
46	Bret Saberhagen	.10
47	Cecil Fielder	.10
48	Manny Ramirez	.75
49	Marquis Grissom	.10
50	Dave Winfield	.75
51	Mark McGwire	1.50
52	Dennis Eckersley	.65
53	Robin Ventura	.10
54	Ryan Klesko	.10
55	Jeff Bagwell	.75
56	Ozzie Smith	1.00
57	Brian McRae	.10
58	Albert Belle	.10
59	Darren Daulton	.10
60	Jose Canseco	.40
61	Greg Maddux	1.00
62	Ben McDonald	.10
63	Lenny Dykstra	.10
64	Randy Johnson	.75
65	Fred McGriff	.65
66	Ray Lankford	.10
67	Dave Justice	.40
68	Paul O'Neill	.10

69	Tony Gwynn	1.00
70	Matt Williams	.10
71	Dante Bichette	.10
72	Craig Biggio	.10
73	Ken Griffey Jr.	1.25
74	Juan Gonzalez	.40
75	Cal Ripken Jr.	2.00
76	Jay Bell	.10
77	Joe Carter	.10
78	Roberto Alomar	.20
79	Mark Langston	.10
80	Dave Hollins	.10
81	Tom Glavine	.35
82	Ivan Rodriguez	.65
83	Mark Whiten	.10
84	Raul Mondesi	.10
85	Kenny Lofton	.10
86	Ruben Sierra	.10
87	Mark Grace	.10
88	Royce Clayton	.10
89	Billy Ashley	.10
90	Larry Walker	.10
91	Sammy Sosa	1.00
92	Jason Bere	.10
93	Bob Hamelin	.10
94	Greg Vaughn	.10
95	Roger Clemens	1.00
96	Scott Ruffcorn	.10
97	Hideo Nomo RC	1.50
98	Michael Tucker	.10
99	J.R. Phillips	.10
100	Roberto Petagine	.10
101	Chipper Jones	1.00
102	Armando Benitez	.10
103	Orlando Miller	.10
104	Carlos Delgado	.50
105	Jeff Cirillo	.10
106	Shawn Green	.30
107	Joe Rando	.10
108	Vaughn Eshelman	.10
109	Frank Rodriguez	.10
110	Russ Davis	.10
111	Todd Hollandsworth	.10
112	Mark Grudzielanek	.10
113	Jose Oliva	.10
114	Ray Durham	.10
115	Alex Rodriguez	1.50
116	Alex Gonzalez	.10
117	Midre Cummings	.10
118	Marty Cordova	.10
119	John Mabry	.10
120	Jason Jacome	.10
121	Joe Vitiello	.10
122	Charles Johnson	.10
123	Cal Ripken Jr. (In Depth)	1.00
124	Ken Griffey Jr. (In Depth)	.65
125	Frank Thomas (In Depth)	.40
126	Mike Piazza (In Depth)	.65
127	Matt Williams (In Depth)	.10
128	Barry Bonds (In Depth)	1.00
129	Greg Maddux (In Depth)	.50
130	Randy Johnson (In Depth)	.40
131	Albert Belle (In Depth)	.10
132	Will Clark (In Depth)	.10
133	Tony Gwynn (In Depth)	.50
134	Manny Ramirez (In Depth)	.40
135	Raul Mondesi (In Depth)	.10
136	Mo Vaughn (In Depth)	.10
137	Mark McGwire (In Depth)	.75
138	Kirby Puckett (In Depth)	.50
139	Don Mattingly (In Depth)	.60
140	Carlos Baerga (In Depth)	.10
141	Roger Clemens (In Depth)	.60
142	Fred McGriff (In Depth)	.10
143	Kenny Lofton (In Depth)	.10
144	Jeff Bagwell (In Depth)	.40
145	Larry Walker (In Depth)	.10
146	Joe Carter (In Depth)	.10
147	Rafael Palmeiro (In Depth)	.30

UC3 Artist's Proof

This chase set parallels the 147 regular cards in the UC3 set with a version on which a round, gold "ARTIST'S PROOF" seal is printed on the front of the card. The AP cards are found on the average of one per box (36 packs).

	NM/M
Complete Set (147):	200.00
Common Player:	.75
Stars:	12X

Clear Shots

Seeded at the rate of about one per 24 packs, the 12 cards in this chase set feature top rookies in a technologically advanced format. The left two-thirds of the card are clear plastic, the right third is blue (American League) or red-purple (N.L.). At center is a circle which features the player photos, portrait and action, depending on the viewing angle. Also changing with the viewpoint are the words "CLEAR" and "SHOT" at top-right, and team and UC3 logos at bottom-right. The player's last name is in black at lower-left and appears to change size as the card is moved. Backs have a gray strip vertically at left with the card number, manufacturer and licensor logos and copyright information. Card numbers have a "CS" prefix.

		NM/M
Complete Set (12):		12.00
Common Player:		.25
1	Alex Rodriguez	5.00
2	Shawn Green	.75
3	Hideo Nomo	1.25
4	Charles Johnson	.25
5	Orlando Miller	.25
6	Billy Ashley	.25
7	Carlos Delgado	1.50
8	Cliff Floyd	.25
9	Chipper Jones	4.00
10	Alex Gonzalez	.25
11	J.R. Phillips	.25
12	Michael Tucker	.25

Cyclone Squad

The most commonly encountered (one per four packs, on average) of the UC3 chase cards are the 20-card Cyclone Squad, featuring the game's top batsmen. Cards have a player in a batting pose set against a dark copper background with two golden pinwheels behind him which appear to spin when the card is moved. Horizontal backs have a green toned photo of the player in his follow-through swing, with shock waves radiating from the lower-left corner. Cards have a CS prefix.

		NM/M
Complete Set (20):		10.00
Common Player:		.25
1	Frank Thomas	.65
2	Ken Griffey Jr.	1.00
3	Jeff Bagwell	.65
4	Cal Ripken Jr.	2.00
5	Barry Bonds	2.00
6	Mike Piazza	1.00
7	Matt Williams	.25
8	Kirby Puckett	.75
9	Jose Canseco	.45
10	Will Clark	.25
11	Don Mattingly	.85
12	Albert Belle	.25
13	Tony Gwynn	.75
14	Raul Mondesi	.25

15 Bobby Bonilla .25
16 Rafael Palmeiro .60
17 Fred McGriff .25
18 Tim Salmon .25
19 Kenny Lofton .25
20 Joe Carter .25

In Motion

Found on an average of once per 18 packs, the cards in this chase set feature maximim motion. When the card is held almost vertically a small eight-piece jigsaw puzzle photo of the player is visible against a light blue background. As the card is moved toward a horizontal position, the pieces appear to become large and move together until the picture fills most of the card. The player's name is in orange at lower-left, with manufacturer's logos at top. Horizontal backs have a green background, two color player photos and a few words of career highlights. The In Motion card numbers are preceded by an "IM" prefix.

	NM/M
Complete Set (10):	7.00
Common Player:	.25
1 Cal Ripken Jr.	1.50
2 Ken Griffey Jr.	1.00
3 Frank Thomas	.50
4 Mike Piazza	1.50
5 Barry Bonds	1.50
6 Matt Williams	.25
7 Kirby Puckett	.75
8 Greg Maddux	.75
9 Don Mattingly	.85
10 Will Clark	.25

1996 Sportflix

Distributed in only retail locations, this 1996 Sportflix set has 144 cards, including 24-card UC3 and 21-card Rookies subsets. The set also has a parallel set, Artist's Proof; these cards are seeded one per every 48 packs. Four insert sets were also produced: Double Take, Hit Parade, Power Surge and Pro-Motion.

	NM/M
Complete Set (144):	17.50
Common Player:	.10
Common Artist's Proof:	1.00
AP Stars:	12X
Pack (5):	
Wax Box (36):	30.00
1 Wade Boggs	1.00
2 Tim Salmon	.10
3 Will Clark	.10
4 Dante Bichette	.10
5 Barry Bonds	2.00
6 Kirby Puckett	1.00
7 Albert Belle	.10
8 Greg Maddux	1.00
9 Tony Gwynn	1.00
10 Mike Piazza	1.25
11 Ivan Rodriguez	.65
12 Marty Cordova	.10
13 Frank Thomas	.75
14 Raul Mondesi	.10
15 Johnny Damon	.35
16 Mark McGwire	1.50
17 Lenny Dykstra	.10
18 Ken Griffey Jr.	1.25
19 Chipper Jones	1.00
20 Alex Rodriguez	1.50
21 Jeff Bagwell	.75
22 Jim Edmonds	.10
23 Edgar Martinez	.10
24 David Cone	.10
25 Tom Glavine	.35
26 Eddie Murray	.75
27 Paul Molitor	.75
28 Ryan Klesko	.10
29 Rafael Palmeiro	.65
30 Manny Ramirez	.75
31 Mo Vaughn	.10
32 Rico Brogna	.10
33 Marc Newfield	.10
34 J.T. Snow	.10
35 Reggie Sanders	.10
36 Fred McGriff	.10
37 Craig Biggio	.10
38 Jeff King	.10
39 Kenny Lofton	.10
40 Gary Gaetti	.10
41 Eric Karros	.10
42 Jason Isringhausen	.10
43 B.J. Surhoff	.10
44 Michael Tucker	.10
45 Gary Sheffield	.45
46 Chili Davis	.10
47 Bobby Bonilla	.10
48 Hideo Nomo	.40
49 Ray Durham	.10
50 Phil Nevin	.10
51 Randy Johnson	.75
52 Bill Pulsipher	.10
53 Ozzie Smith	1.00
54 Cal Ripken Jr.	2.00
55 Cecil Fielder	.10
56 Matt Williams	.10
57 Sammy Sosa	1.00
58 Roger Clemens	1.00
59 Brian Hunter	.10
60 Barry Larkin	.10
61 Charles Johnson	.10
62 Dave Justice	.10
63 Garret Anderson	.10
64 Rondell White	.10
65 Derek Bell	.10
66 Andres Galarraga	.10
67 Moises Alou	.10
68 Travis Fryman	.10
69 Pedro Martinez	.75
70 Carlos Baerga	.10
71 John Valentin	.10
72 Larry Walker	.10
73 Roberto Alomar	.20
74 Mike Mussina	.30
75 Kevin Appier	.10
76 Bernie Williams	.10
77 Ray Lankford	.10
78 Gregg Jefferies	.10
79 Robin Ventura	.10
80 Kenny Rogers	.10
81 Paul O'Neill	.10
82 Mark Grace	.10
83 Deion Sanders	.10
84 Tino Martinez	.10
85 Joe Carter	.10
86 Pete Schourek	.10
87 Jack McDowell	.10
88 John Mabry	.10
89 Darren Daulton	.10
90 Jim Thome	.65
91 Jay Buhner	.10
92 Jay Bell	.10
93 Kevin Seitzer	.10
94 Jose Canseco	.40
95 Juan Gonzalez	.40
96 Jeff Conine	.10
97 Chipper Jones (UC3)	.50
98 Ken Griffey Jr. (UC3)	.65
99 Frank Thomas (UC3)	.40
100 Cal Ripken Jr. (UC3)	1.00
101 Albert Belle (UC3)	.10
102 Mike Piazza (UC3)	.65
103 Dante Bichette (UC3)	.10
104 Sammy Sosa (UC3)	.50
105 Mo Vaughn (UC3)	.10
106 Tim Salmon (UC3)	.10
107 Reggie Sanders (UC3)	.10
108 Gary Sheffield (UC3)	.25
109 Ruben Rivera (UC3)	.10
110 Rafael Palmeiro (UC3)	.35
111 Edgar Martinez (UC3)	.10
112 Barry Bonds (UC3)	1.00
113 Manny Ramirez (UC3)	.40
114 Larry Walker (UC3)	.10
115 Jeff Bagwell (UC3)	.40
116 Matt Williams (UC3)	.10
117 Mark McGwire (UC3)	.75
118 Johnny Damon (UC3)	.30
119 Eddie Murray (UC3)	.40
120 Jay Buhner (UC3)	.10
121 Tim Unroe (Rookie)	.10
122 Todd Hollandsworth (Rookie)	.10
123 Tony Clark (Rookie)	.10
124 Roger Cedeno (Rookie)	.10
125 Jim Pittsley (Rookie)	.10
126 Ruben Rivera (Rookie)	.10
127 Bob Wolcott (Rookie)	.10
128 Chan Ho Park (Rookie)	.10
129 Chris Snopek (Rookie)	.10
130 Alex Ochoa (Rookie)	.10
131 Yamil Benitez (Rookie)	.10
132 Jimmy Haynes (Rookie)	.10
133 Dustin Hermanson (Rookie)	.10
134 Shawn Estes (Rookie)	.10
135 Howard Battle (Rookie)	.10
136 Matt Lawton RC (Rookie)	.25
137 Terrell Wade (Rookie)	.10
138 Jason Schmidt (Rookie)	.10
139 Derek Jeter (Rookie)	2.50
140 Shannon Stewart (Rookie)	.10
141 Chris Stynes (Rookie)	.10
142 Ken Griffey Jr. (Checklist)	.65
143 Greg Maddux (Checklist)	.50
144 Cal Ripken Jr. (Checklist)	1.00

Artist's Proofs

Artist's Proof parallels to 1996 Sportflix are a 1:48 find and are distinctively marked with an AP seal on front.

	NM/M
Complete Set (144):	200.00
Common Player:	1.00
AP Stars:	12X

Double Take

These 1996 Sportflix insert cards each feature two players who are tops at a particular position. Tilting the card to change the angle of view brings each player into focus. The cards were seeded one per 22 packs.

	NM/M
Complete Set (12):	30.00
Common Player:	1.50
1 Barry Larkin, Cal Ripken Jr.	6.00
2 Roberto Alomar, Craig Biggio	1.50
3 Chipper Jones, Matt Williams	2.50
4 Ken Griffey Jr., Ruben Rivera	3.50
5 Greg Maddux, Hideo Nomo	3.00
6 Frank Thomas, Mo Vaughn	2.00
7 Mike Piazza, Ivan Rodriguez	3.50
8 Albert Belle, Barry Bonds	6.00
9 Alex Rodriguez, Derek Jeter	8.00
10 Kirby Puckett, Tony Gwynn	3.00
11 Manny Ramirez, Sammy Sosa	3.00
12 Jeff Bagwell, Rico Brogna	2.00

Hit Parade

Sixteen of baseball's most productive hitters are featured on these inserts. Horizontal fronts have a player portrait at right. In the background is a lenticular-motion scene of a generic player swinging the bat. Backs have an action photo and a few career highlights. The cards were seeded one per every 35 packs.

	NM/M
Complete Set (16):	24.00
Common Player:	.50
1 Ken Griffey Jr.	2.50
2 Cal Ripken Jr.	4.00
3 Frank Thomas	1.50
4 Mike Piazza	2.50
5 Mo Vaughn	.50
6 Albert Belle	.50
7 Jeff Bagwell	1.50
8 Matt Williams	.50
9 Sammy Sosa	2.00
9p Sammy Sosa (Overprinted "SAMPLE.")	2.00
10 Kirby Puckett	2.00
11 Dante Bichette	.50
12 Gary Sheffield	1.00
13 Tony Gwynn	2.00
14 Wade Boggs	2.00
15 Chipper Jones	2.00
16 Barry Bonds	4.00

Power Surge

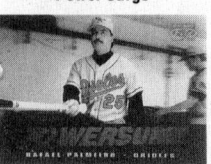

This 1996 Sportflix insert set showcases 24 sluggers on a clear 3-D parallel rendition of the UC3 subset in the main issue. These cards are seeded one per every 35 packs.

	NM/M
Complete Set (24):	30.00
Common Player:	.50
1 Chipper Jones	2.00
2 Ken Griffey Jr.	2.50
3 Frank Thomas	1.50
4 Cal Ripken Jr.	4.00
5 Albert Belle	.50
6 Mike Piazza	2.50
7 Dante Bichette	.50
8 Sammy Sosa	.50
9 Mo Vaughn	.50
10 Tim Salmon	.50
11 Reggie Sanders	.50
12 Gary Sheffield	1.00
13 Ruben Rivera	.50
14 Rafael Palmeiro	1.25
15 Edgar Martinez	.50
16 Barry Bonds	4.00
17 Manny Ramirez	1.50
18 Larry Walker	.50
19 Jeff Bagwell	1.50
20 Matt Williams	.50
21 Mark McGwire	3.00
22 Johnny Damon	.90
23 Eddie Murray	1.50
24 Jay Buhner	.50

ProMotion

Frank Thomas

These 1996 Sportflix inserts were seeded one per every 17 packs. The cards' "morphing" technology turns baseball equipment, such as bats, balls and gloves, into 20 of the top veteran superstars using multi-phase animation.

	NM/M
Complete Set (20):	22.50
Common Player:	.50
1 Cal Ripken Jr.	5.00
2 Greg Maddux	2.00
3 Mo Vaughn	.50
4 Albert Belle	.50
5 Mike Piazza	3.00
6 Ken Griffey Jr.	3.00
7 Frank Thomas	1.50
8 Jeff Bagwell	1.50
9 Hideo Nomo	1.00
10 Chipper Jones	2.00
11 Tony Gwynn	1.00
12 Don Mattingly	2.50
13 Dante Bichette	.50
14 Matt Williams	.50
15 Manny Ramirez	1.50
16 Barry Bonds	5.00
17 Reggie Sanders	.50
18 Tim Salmon	.50
19 Ruben Rivera	.50
20 Garret Anderson	.50

Rookie Supers

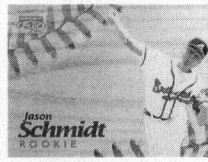

Eight of the young players included in the Sportflix Rookies subset are featured in an enlarged version which was issued one per retail box. The cards measure 3" x 5" and are numbered "X of 8," on back, but are otherwise identical to the smaller version.

	NM/M
Complete Set (8):	12.50
Common player:	1.00
1 Jason Schmidt	1.00
2 Chris Snopek	1.00
3 Tony Clark	1.00
4 Todd Hollandsworth	1.00
5 Alex Ochoa	1.00
6 Derek Jeter	10.00
7 Howard Battle	1.00
8 Bob Wolcott	1.00

1981 Sporting News Conlon Collection

This set of 100 cards was sold directly into the hobby by The Sporting News in a slip-cover case for $50. The blank-backed cards measure 4" x 5" and feature a sepia-toned photo surrounded by a 1/4" white border. The photos were the first of several uses on baseball cards of TSN's archives of ballplayer photos taken by Charles Martin Conlon between 1915-1935. The paper's logo appears at the top of the card. At bottom are the player's or players' names(s), team at the time the photo was taken, and position or positions played for the season indicated. A card number appears at lower-right.

	NM/M
Complete Set (100):	90.00
Common Player:	1.00
1 Ty Cobb	10.00
2 Hughie Jennings	1.00
3 Miller Huggins	1.00
4 Babe Ruth	12.50
5 Lou Gehrig	10.00
6 John McGraw	1.00
7 Bill Terry	1.00
8 Stan Baumgartner	1.00
9 Christy Mathewson	5.00
10 Grover Alexander	2.00
11 Tony Lazzeri	1.00
12 Frank Chance, Joe Tinker	2.00
13 Johnny Evers	1.00
14 Tris Speaker	2.00
15 Harry Hooper	1.00
16 Duffy Lewis	1.00
17 Joe Wood	1.00
18 Hugh Duffy	1.00
19 Rogers Hornsby	4.00
20 Earl Averill	1.00
21 Dizzy Dean	2.00
22 Daffy Dean	1.00
23 Frankie Frisch	2.00
24 Pepper Martin	1.00
25 Blondie Ryan	1.00
26 Hank Gowdy	1.00
27 Fred Merkle	1.00
28 Ernie Lombardi	1.00
29 Greasy Neale	1.00
30 Morris "Red" Badgro	1.00
31 Jim Thorpe	9.00
32 Roy Johnson	1.00
33 Bob Johnson	1.00
34 Mule Solters	1.00
35 Specs Toporcer	1.00
36 Jackie Hayes	1.00
37 Walter Johnson	5.00
38 Lefty Grove	2.00
39 Eddie Collins	2.00
40 Buck Weaver	7.50
41 Cozy Dolan	1.00
42 Emil Meusel	1.00
43 Bob Meusel	1.00
44 Lefty Gomez	1.00
45 Rube Marquard	1.00
46 Jeff Tesreau	1.00
47 Joe Heving	1.00
48 John Heving	1.00
49 Rick Ferrell	1.00
50 Wes Ferrell	1.00
51 Bill Wambsganss	1.00
52 Ben Chapman	1.00
53 Joe Sewell	1.00
54 Luke Sewell	1.00
55 Odell Hale	1.00
56 Sammy Hale	1.00
57 Earle Mack	1.00
58 Connie Mack	1.00
59 Rube Walberg	1.00
60 Mule Haas	1.00
61 Paul Waner	1.00
62 Lloyd Waner	1.00
63 Pie Traynor	1.00
64 Honus Wagner	2.00
65 Joe Cronin	1.00
66 Joe Harris	1.00
67 Dave Harris	1.00
68 Bucky Harris	1.00
69 Alex Gaston	1.00
70 Milt Gaston	1.00
71 Casey Stengel	2.00
72 Amos Rusie	1.00
73 Mickey Welch	1.00
74 Roger Bresnahan	1.00
75 Jesse Burkett	1.00
76 Harry Heilmann	1.00
77 Heinie Manush	1.00
78 Charlie Gehringer	1.00
79 Hank Greenberg	2.00
80 Jimmie Foxx	4.00
81 Al Simmons	1.00
82 Eddie Plank	1.00
83 George Sisler	1.00
84 Joe Medwick	1.00
85 Mel Ott	1.00
86 Hack Wilson	1.00
87 Jimmy Wilson	1.00
88 Chuck Klein	1.00
89 Gabby Hartnett	1.00
90 Henie Groh	1.00
91 Ping Bodie	1.00
92 Ted Lyons	1.00
93 Jack Quinn	1.00
94 Oscar Roettger	1.00
95 Wally Roettger	1.00
96 Bubbles Hargrave	1.00
97 Pinky Hargrave	1.00
98 Sam Crawford	1.00
99 Gee Walker	1.00
100 Homer Summa	1.00

1983 Sporting News Conlon Collection Prototypes

Walter (Barney) Johnson
Pitcher, Senators 1926

Unlike the issued cards which were in a large format, these prototypes are in standard 2-1/2" x 3-1/2" size. Fronts are printed in sepia. Black-and-white backs have player data, career summary and stats up to the date the photo was taken. Backs also have the TSN Conlon Collection logo and a Marketcom copyright.

	NM/M
Complete Set (5):	7.50
Common Player:	2.00
83-1 Lewis (Hack) Wilson	2.00
83-2 Joe Cronin	2.00
83-3 Walter (Barney) Johnson	3.00
83-4 Paul (Daffy) Dean	2.00
83-5 Connie Mack	2.00

1983 Sporting News Conlon Collection

This set was issued to mark the 50th anniversary of the first All-Star game in 1933. Besides the American and National League players who made up those teams, the set includes a group of all-stars from the Negro Leagues. The oversize (4-1/2" x 6-1/8") cards were sold only as complete sets. The cards feature sepia player photos on front, with a facsimile autograph and appropriate commemorative labeling. Black-and-white backs feature 1933 stats, an anecdote about the player, and the logos of appropriate parties in the set's marketing. The major leaguers' photos were the work of Charles M. Conlon, while the Black ballplayers' pictures were garnered from a variety of sources.

	NM/M
Complete Set (60):	20.00
Common Player:	.25
1 Jimmie Foxx	.50
2 Heinie Manush	.25
3 Lou Gehrig	2.50
4 Al Simmons	.25
5 Charlie Gehringer	.25
6 Luke Appling	.25
7 Mickey Cochrane	.25
8 Joe Kuhel	.25
9 Bill Dickey	.40
10 Pinky Higgins	.25
11 Roy Johnson	.25
12 Ben Chapman	.25
13 Johnny Hodapp	.25
14 Joe Cronin	.25
15 Evar Swanson	.25
16 Earl Averill	.25
17 Babe Ruth	4.00
18 Tony Lazzeri	.40
19 Alvin Crowder	.25
20 Lefty Grove	.25
21 Earl Whitehill	.25
22 Lefty Gomez	.25
23 Mel Harder	.25
24 Tommy Bridges	.25
25 Chuck Klein	.25
26 Spud Davis	.25
27 Riggs Stephenson	.25
28 Tony Piet	.25
29 Bill Terry	.25
30 Wes Schulmerich	.25
31a Pepper Martin (Teeth don't show.)	.25
31b Pepper Martin (Teeth show.)	.25
32 Arky Vaughan	.25
33 Wally Berger	.25
34 Rip Collins	.25
35 Fred Lindstrom	.25
36 Chick Fullis	.25
37 Paul Waner	.25
38 Johnny Frederick	.25
39 Joe Medwick	.25
40 Pie Traynor	.25
41 Frank Frisch	.25
42 Chick Hafey	.25
43 Carl Hubbell	.25
44 Guy Bush	.25
45 Dizzy Dean	.40
46 Hal Schumacher	.25
47 Larry French	.25
48 Lon Warneke	.25
49 Cool Papa Bell	.25
50 Oscar Charleston	.25
51 Josh Gibson	.50
52 Satchel Paige	1.00
53 Dave Malarcher	.25
54 Pop Lloyd	.25
55 Rube Foster	.25
56 Buck Leonard	.40
57 Smoky Joe Williams	.40
58 Willie Wells	.40
59 Judy Johnson	.25
60 Martin DiHigo	.25

1984 Sporting News Conlon Collection

This 60-card set, mostly Hall of Famers, was produced in conjunction with the Smithsonian Institution's "Baseball Immortals" photo exhibition of the work of Charles Martin Conlon. The oversize (4-1/2" x 6-1/8") cards have sepia-toned photos on front; backs are printed in black-and-white. The issue was initially sold only as a complete set.

	NM/M
Complete Set (60):	35.00
Common Player:	.25
1 Grover Cleveland Alexander	.60
2 Chief Bender	.25
3a Fred Clarke (Jack Coombs front.)	1.50
3b Fred Clarke (Correct front.)	.40
4-7 Ty Cobb	1.25
8 Mickey Cochrane	.25
9a Jack Coombs (Fred Clarke front.)	1.50
9b Jack Coombs (Correct front.)	.40
10 Charles & Margie Conlon	.25
11 Charles Conlon	.25
12 Joe Cronin	.25
13 Dizzy Dean	.60
14 Leo Durocher	.25
15 Jimmie Foxx	.40
16 The Gashouse Gang (Frank Frisch, Mike Gonzalez, Buzzy Wares)	.25
17 Lou Gehrig	1.75
18 Lou Gehrig	1.75
19 Lou Gehrig	1.75
20 Lou Gehrig	1.75
21 Charlie Gehringer	.25
22 Lefty Gomez	.25
23 Lefty Grove	.25
24 Bucky Harris	.25
25 Harry Heilmann	.25
26 Rogers Hornsby	.40
27 Waite Hoyt	.25
28 Carl Hubbell	.25
29 Miller Huggins	.25
30 Walter Johnson	.60
31 Bill Klem	.25
32 Connie Mack	.25
33 Heinie Manush	.25
34 Rube Marquard	.25
35 Pepper Martin	.25
36 Christy Mathewson	.60
37 Christy Mathewson	.60
38 Christy Mathewson	.60
39 Joe McCarthy	.25
40 John McGraw	.25
41 Fred Merkle	.25
42 Mel Ott	.25
43 Roger Peckinpaugh	.25
44 Herb Pennock	.25
45-50 Babe Ruth	2.25
51 Al Simmons	.25
52 Tris Speaker	.40
53 Casey Stengel	.25
54 Bill Terry	.25
55 Pie Traynor	.25
56 Rube Waddell	.25
57 Honus Wagner	1.00
58 Lloyd Waner, Paul Waner	.25
59 Paul Waner	.25
60 Hack Wilson	.25

1981 Sportrait Hall of Fame

This collectors' issue feature portrait art by Stan Sypulski in a blank-back 3-1/2" x 5" format. Portraits have a color frame line and are numbered.

	NM/M
Complete Set (25):	55.00
Common Player:	2.00
1 Honus Wagner	4.00
2 Miller Huggins	2.00
3 Babe Ruth	6.00
4 Connie Mack	2.00
5 Ty Cobb	5.00
6 Lou Gehrig	5.00
7 Eddie Collins	2.00
8 Chuck Klein	2.00
9 Ted Williams	5.00
10 Jimmy Foxx	3.00
11 Frank Baker	2.00
12 Nap Lajoie	2.00
13 Casey Stengel	2.00
14 Joe DiMaggio	5.00
15 Mickey Mantle	6.00
16 Frank Frisch	2.00
17 Bill Terry	2.00
18 Jackie Robinson	5.00
19 Sam Rice	2.00
20 Mickey Cochrane	2.00
21 George Sisler	2.00
22 Bob Feller	3.00
23 Walter Johnson	3.00
24 Tris Speaker	3.00
--- Checklist	2.00

1984 Sports Design Products Doug West

The art of Doug West is featured in portrait and action pictures on each card in this collectors set. The player art is on a blue background. In the white border at bottom a red box displays the player name and position in white. The producer's logo is in black at bottom-right. Backs are printed in red and blue on white with personal data, career summary and stats. Production was reported as 5,000 sets, including 250 uncut sheets. Issue price was about $10.

	NM/M
Complete Set (24):	15.00
Common Player:	.50
1 Jackie Robinson	1.25
2 Luis Aparicio	.50
3 Roberto Clemente	3.00
4 Mickey Mantle	5.00
5 Joe DiMaggio	3.00
6 Willie Stargell	.50
7 Brooks Robinson	.60
8 Ty Cobb	1.50
9 Don Drysdale	.50
10 Bob Feller	.50
11 Stan Musial	1.00
12 Al Kaline	.50
13 Willie Mays	1.75
14 Willie McCovey	.50
15 Thurman Munson	.75
16 Charlie Gehringer	.50
17 Eddie Mathews	.50
18 Carl Yastrzemski	.50
19 Warren Spahn	.50
20 Ted Williams	2.00
21 Ernie Banks	.60
22 Roy Campanella	.75
23 Harmon Killebrew	.50
24 Duke Snider	.75

1985 Sports Design Products Doug West

The art of Doug West is featured in portrait and action pictures on each card in this collectors' set. In the white border at bottom a blue box displays the player name and position in white. The producer's logo is in black at bottom-right. Backs are printed in red and blue on white with personal data, career summary and stats. Cards are numbered sequentially from the previous year's issue. Besides 5,000 complete sets (issued at $8), 250 uncut sheets were also sold.

	NM/M
Complete Set (24):	7.50
Common Player:	.25
25 Lou Gehrig	1.00
26 Hoyt Wilhelm	.25
27 Enos Slaughter	.25
28 Lou Brock	.25
29 Mickey Cochrane	.25
30 Gil Hodges	.50
31 Yogi Berra	.50
32 Carl Hubbell	.25
33 Hank Greenberg	.50

34 Casey Stengel	.25
35 Pee Wee Reese	.35
36 Ralph Kiner	.25
37 Satchel Paige	.50
38 Richie Ashburn	.35
39 Connie Mack	.25
40 Dick Groat	.25
41 Tony Oliva	.25
42 Honus Wagner	.40
43 Denny McLain	.25
44 Johnny Mize	.25
45 Bob Lemon	.25
46 Fergie Jenkins	.25
47 Babe Ruth	2.00
48 Ted Kluszewski	.35

1997 Sports Illustrated

Fleer teamed up with Sports Illustrated to produce a 180-card World Series Fever set. The regular set is divided into six different sub-sets: 96 Player Cards, 27 Fresh Faces, 18 Inside Baseball, 18 SIber Vision, 12 covers and 9 Newsmakers. Inserts included the Extra Edition parallel set, Great Shots, Cooperstown Collection and Autographed Mini-Cover Redemption Cards. Cards were sold in six-card packs for $1.99 each.

	NM/M
Complete Set (180):	20.00
Common Player:	.05
Extra Edition Stars:	8X
Pack (6):	1.25
Wax Box (24):	20.00
1 Bob Abreu (Fresh Faces)	.10
2 Jaime Bluma (Fresh Faces)	.05
3 Emil Brown (Fresh Faces)	.05
4 Jose Cruz, Jr. (Fresh Faces)	.05
5 Jason Dickson (Fresh Faces)	.05
6 Nomar Garciaparra (Fresh Faces)	1.00
7 Todd Greene (Fresh Faces)	.05
8 Vladimir Guerrero (Fresh Faces)	.75
9 Wilton Guerrero (Fresh Faces)	.05
10 Jose Guillen (Fresh Faces)	.05
11 Hideki Irabu (Fresh Faces)	.05
12 Russ Johnson (Fresh Faces)	.05
13 Andruw Jones (Fresh Faces)	.75
14 Damon Mashore (Fresh Faces)	.05
15 Jason McDonald (Fresh Faces)	.05
16 Ryan McGuire (Fresh Faces)	.05
17 Matt Morris (Fresh Faces)	.05
18 Kevin Orie (Fresh Faces)	.05
19 Dante Powell (Fresh Faces)	.05
20 Pokey Reese (Fresh Faces)	.05
21 Joe Roa (Fresh Faces)	.05
22 Scott Rolen (Fresh Faces)	.65
23 Glendon Rusch (Fresh Faces)	.05
24 Scott Spiezio (Fresh Faces)	.05
25 Bubba Trammell (Fresh Faces)	.05
26 Todd Walker (Fresh Faces)	.05
27 Jamey Wright (Fresh Faces)	.05
28 Ken Griffey Jr. (Season Highlights)	.75
29 Tino Martinez (Season Highlights)	.05
30 Roger Clemens (Season Highlights)	.65
31 Hideki Irabu (Season Highlights)	.05
32 Kevin Brown (Season Highlights)	.05
33 Chipper Jones, Cal Ripken Jr. (Season Highlights)	.65
34 Sandy Alomar (Season Highlights)	.05
35 Ken Caminiti (Season Highlights)	.05
36 Randy Johnson (Season Highlights)	.40
37 Andy Ashby (Inside Baseball)	.05
38 Jay Buhner (Inside Baseball)	.05
39 Joe Carter (Inside Baseball)	.05
40 Darren Daulton (Inside Baseball)	.05
41 Jeff Fassero (Inside Baseball)	.05
42 Andres Galarraga (Inside Baseball)	.05
43 Rusty Greer (Inside Baseball)	.05
44 Marquis Grissom (Inside Baseball)	.05
45 Joey Hamilton (Inside Baseball)	.05
46 Jimmy Key (Inside Baseball)	.05
47 Ryan Klesko (Inside Baseball)	.05
48 Eddie Murray (Inside Baseball)	.75
49 Charles Nagy (Inside Baseball)	.05
50 Dave Nilsson (Inside Baseball)	.05
51 Ricardo Rincon (Inside Baseball)	.05
52 Billy Wagner (Inside Baseball)	.05
53 Dan Wilson (Inside Baseball)	.05
54 Dmitri Young (Inside Baseball)	.05
55 Roberto Alomar (S.I.BER Vision)	.30
56 Sandy Alomar Jr. (S.I.BER Vision)	.05
57 Scott Brosius (S.I.BER Vision)	.05
58 Tony Clark (S.I.BER Vision)	.05
59 Carlos Delgado (S.I.BER Vision)	.05
60 Jermaine Dye (S.I.BER Vision)	.05
61 Darin Erstad (S.I.BER Vision)	.20
62 Derek Jeter (S.I.BER Vision)	1.00
63 Jason Kendall (S.I.BER Vision)	.05
64 Hideo Nomo (S.I.BER Vision)	.20
65 Rey Ordonez (S.I.BER Vision)	.05
66 Andy Pettitte (S.I.BER Vision)	.10
67 Manny Ramirez (S.I.BER Vision)	.75
68 Edgar Renteria (S.I.BER Vision)	.05
69 Shane Reynolds (S.I.BER Vision)	.05
70 Alex Rodriguez (S.I.BER Vision)	1.00
71 Ivan Rodriguez (S.I.BER Vision)	.65
72 Jose Rosado (S.I.BER Vision)	.05
73 John Smoltz	.05
74 Tom Glavine	.35
75 Greg Maddux	1.00
76 Chipper Jones	1.00
77 Kenny Lofton	.05
78 Fred McGriff	.05
79 Kevin Brown	.05
80 Alex Fernandez	.05
81 Al Leiter	.05
82 Bobby Bonilla	.05
83 Gary Sheffield	.40
84 Moises Alou	.05
85 Henry Rodriguez	.05
86 Mark Grudzielanek	.05
87 Pedro Martinez	.75
88 Todd Hundley	.05
89 Bernard Gilkey	.05
90 Bobby Jones	.05
91 Curt Schilling	.35
92 Ricky Bottalico	.05
93 Mike Lieberthal	.05
94 Sammy Sosa	1.00
95 Ryne Sandberg	1.00
96 Mark Grace	.05
97 Deion Sanders	.05
98 Reggie Sanders	.05
99 Barry Larkin	.05
100 Craig Biggio	.05
101 Jeff Bagwell	.75
102 Derek Bell	.05
103 Brian Jordan	.05
104 Ray Lankford	.05
105 Ron Gant	.05
106 Al Martin	.05
107 Kevin Elster	.05
108 Jermaine Allensworth	.05
109 Vinny Castilla	.05
110 Dante Bichette	.05
111 Larry Walker	.05
112 Mike Piazza	1.25
113 Eric Karros	.05
114 Todd Hollandsworth	.05
115 Raul Mondesi	.05
116 Hideo Nomo	.40

117 Ramon Martinez	.05
118 Ken Caminiti	.05
119 Tony Gwynn	1.00
120 Steve Finley	.05
121 Barry Bonds	2.00
122 J.T. Snow	.05
123 Rod Beck	.05
124 Cal Ripken Jr.	2.00
125 Mike Mussina	.30
126 Brady Anderson	.05
127 Bernie Williams	.05
128 Derek Jeter	2.00
129 Tino Martinez	.05
130 Andy Pettitte	.30
131 David Cone	.05
132 Mariano Rivera	.15
133 Roger Clemens	1.00
134 Pat Hentgen	.05
135 Juan Guzman	.05
136 Bob Higginson	.05
137 Tony Clark	.05
138 Travis Fryman	.05
139 Mo Vaughn	.05
140 Tim Naehring	.05
141 John Valentin	.05
142 Matt Williams	.05
143 David Justice	.05
144 Jim Thome	.65
145 Chuck Knoblauch	.05
146 Paul Molitor	.75
147 Marty Cordova	.05
148 Frank Thomas	.85
149 Albert Belle	.05
150 Robin Ventura	.05
151 John Jaha	.05
152 Jeff Cirillo	.05
153 Jose Valentin	.05
154 Jay Bell	.05
155 Jeff King	.05
156 Kevin Appier	.05
157 Ken Griffey Jr.	1.25
158 Alex Rodriguez	1.50
158p Alex Rodriguez/OPS	1.50
159 Randy Johnson	.75
160 Juan Gonzalez	.40
161 Will Clark	.05
162 Dean Palmer	.05
163 Tim Salmon	.05
164 Jim Edmonds	.05
165 Jim Leyritz	.05
166 Jose Canseco	.40
167 Jason Giambi	.05
168 Mark McGwire	1.50
169 Barry Bonds (Classic Covers)	1.00
170 Alex Rodriguez (Classic Covers)	.75
171 Roger Clemens (Classic Covers)	.65
172 Ken Griffey Jr. (Classic Covers)	.65
173 Greg Maddux (Classic Covers)	.50
174 Mike Piazza (Classic Covers)	.65
175 Will Clark, Mark McGwire (Classic Covers)	1.00
176 Hideo Nomo (Classic Covers)	.20
177 Cal Ripken Jr. (Classic Covers)	1.00
178 Ken Griffey Jr., Frank Thomas (Classic Covers)	.50
179 Alex Rodriguez, Derek Jeter (Classic Covers)	1.50
180 John Wetteland (Classic Covers)	.05
--- Checklist (Jose Cruz Jr.)	.05

Extra Edition

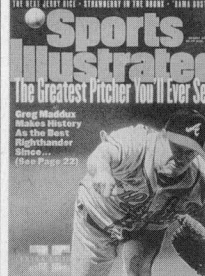

Each of the regular cards in the premiere Fleer SI issue is also found in a parallel set designated on front in gold holographic foil as "Extra Edition." Backs of the cards carry a serial number from within a production of 500 of each card.

	NM/M
Complete Set (180):	150.00
Common Player:	1.00
Extra Edition Stars:	8X

Autographed Mini-Covers

Six different players autographed 250 magazine mini-covers that were available through randomly seeded redemption cards. The players who autographed cards were Hank Aaron, Willie Mays, Frank Robinson, Kirby Puckett, Cal Ripken Jr., and Alex Rodriguez.

	NM/M
Complete Set (6):	300.00
Common Player:	30.00
Alex Rodriguez	100.00
Cal Ripken Jr.	100.00
Kirby Puckett	80.00
Willie Mays	125.00
Frank Robinson	30.00
Hank Aaron	200.00

Box Topper

This special version of A-Rod's card was packaged one per box of foil packs. It was intended to be inserted into die-cuts on the box to create a sample display for the new issue. The card measures 2-1/2" x 4-1/16". The back is in black-and-white with instructions on how to insert the card into the box.

	NM/M
Alex Rodriguez	4.50

Cooperstown Collection

This 12-card insert (found 1:12 packs) lets collectors relive classic SI baseball covers with a description of each issue on the back.

		NM/M
Complete Set (12):		27.50
Common Player:		2.00
1	Hank Aaron	6.00
2	Yogi Berra	3.00
3	Lou Brock	2.00
4	Rod Carew	2.00
5	Juan Marichal	2.00
6	Al Kaline	2.50
7	Joe Morgan	2.00
8	Brooks Robinson	3.00
9	Willie Stargell	2.00
10	Kirby Puckett	4.00
11	Willie Mays	6.00
12	Frank Robinson	3.00

Great Shots

A 25-card insert, found one per pack, designed to highlight Sports Illustrated's classic photography. Each card in the set folds out to a 5" x 7" format to showcase a larger photo.

		NM/M
Complete Set (25):		10.00
Common Player:		.20
(1)	Roberto Alomar	.30
(2)	Andy Ashby	.20
(3)	Albert Belle	.20
(4)	Barry Bonds	2.00
(5)	Jay Buhner	.20
(6)	Vinny Castilla, Andres Galarraga	.20
(7)	Darren Daulton	.20
(8)	Juan Gonzalez	.40
(9)	Ken Griffey Jr.	1.25
(10)	Derek Jeter	2.00
(11)	Randy Johnson	.75
(12)	Chipper Jones	1.00
(13)	Eric Karros	.20
(14)	Ryan Klesko	.20
(15)	Kenny Lofton	.20
(16)	Greg Maddux	1.00
(17)	Mark McGwire	1.50
(18)	Mike Piazza	1.25
(19)	Cal Ripken Jr.	2.00
(20)	Alex Rodriguez	1.50
(21)	Ryne Sandberg	1.00
(22)	Deion Sanders	.30
(23)	John Smoltz	.20
(24)	Frank Thomas	.75
(25)	Mo Vaughn	.20

1998 Sports Illustrated Promo

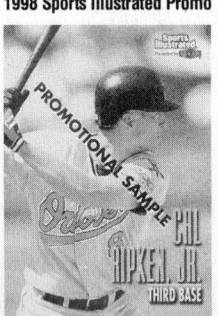

This sample card was issued to preview the 1998 Sports Illustrated set presented by Fleer. The card is in the same format as the regular issue, but has a different card number and is overprinted "PROMOTIONAL SAMPLE" on front and back.

		NM/M
8	Cal Ripken Jr.	3.00

1998 Sports Illustrated

The second of three Sports Illustrated releases of 1998 from Fleer contained 200 cards and featured exclusive Sports Illustrated photography and commentary. Cards arrived in six-card packs and carried a Sports Illustrated logo in a top corner. The set included a Travis Lee One to Watch cards (#201) that was inserted just before going to press. Subsets included: Baseball's Best (129-148), One to Watch (149-176), and '97 in Review (177-200). Inserts sets include: Extra Edition and First Edition parallels, Autographs, Covers, Editor's Choice and Opening Day Mini Posters.

		NM/M
Complete Set (201):		20.00
Common Player:		.05
Pack (6):		1.50
Wax Box (24):		25.00
1	Edgardo Alfonzo	.05
2	Roberto Alomar	.20
3	Sandy Alomar	.05
4	Moises Alou	.05
5	Brady Anderson	.05
6	Garret Anderson	.05
7	Kevin Appier	.05
8	Jeff Bagwell	.75
9	Jay Bell	.05
10	Albert Belle	.05
11	Dante Bichette	.05
12	Craig Biggio	.05
13	Barry Bonds	2.00
14	Bobby Bonilla	.05
15	Kevin Brown	.05
16	Jay Buhner	.05
17	Ellis Burks	.05
18	Mike Cameron	.05
19	Ken Caminiti	.05
20	Jose Canseco	.45
21	Joe Carter	.05
22	Vinny Castilla	.05
23	Jeff Cirillo	.05
24	Tony Clark	.05
25	Will Clark	.05
26	Roger Clemens	1.00
27	David Cone	.05
28	Jose Cruz Jr.	.05
29	Carlos Delgado	.50
30	Jason Dickson	.05
31	Dennis Eckersley	.65
32	Jim Edmonds	.05
33	Scott Erickson	.05
34	Darin Erstad	.20
35	Shawn Estes	.05
36	Jeff Fassero	.05
37	Alex Fernandez	.05
38	Chuck Finley	.05
39	Steve Finley	.05
40	Travis Fryman	.05
41	Andres Galarraga	.05
42	Ron Gant	.05
43	Nomar Garciaparra	1.00
44	Jason Giambi	.50
45	Tom Glavine	.35
46	Juan Gonzalez	.40
47	Mark Grace	.05
48	Willie Green	.05
49	Rusty Greer	.05
50	Ben Grieve	.05
51	Ken Griffey Jr.	1.25
52	Mark Grudzielanek	.05
53	Vladimir Guerrero	.75
54	Juan Guzman	.05
55	Tony Gwynn	1.00
56	Joey Hamilton	.05
57	Rickey Henderson	.75
58	Pat Hentgen	.05
59	Livan Hernandez	.05
60	Bobby Higginson	.05
61	Todd Hundley	.05
62	Hideki Irabu	.05
63	John Jaha	.05
64	Derek Jeter	2.00
65	Charles Johnson	.05
66	Randy Johnson	.75
67	Andruw Jones	.05
68	Bobby Jones	.05
69	Chipper Jones	1.00
70	Brian Jordan	.05
71	David Justice	.05
72	Eric Karros	.05
73	Jeff Kent	.05
74	Jimmy Key	.05
75	Darryl Kile	.05
76	Jeff King	.05
77	Ryan Klesko	.05
78	Chuck Knoblauch	.05
79	Ray Lankford	.05
80	Barry Larkin	.05
81	Kenny Lofton	.05
82	Greg Maddux	1.00
83	Al Martin	.05
84	Edgar Martinez	.05
85	Pedro Martinez	.75
86	Tino Martinez	.05
87	Mark McGwire	1.50
88	Paul Molitor	.75
89	Raul Mondesi	.05
90	Jamie Moyer	.05
91	Mike Mussina	.30
92	Tim Naehring	.05
93	Charles Nagy	.05
94	Denny Neagle	.05
95	Dave Nilsson	.05
96	Hideo Nomo	.40
97	Rey Ordonez	.05
98	Dean Palmer	.05
99	Rafael Palmeiro	.65
100	Andy Pettitte	.30
101	Mike Piazza	1.25
102	Brad Radke	.05
103	Manny Ramirez	.75
104	Edgar Renteria	.05
105	Cal Ripken Jr.	2.00
106	Alex Rodriguez	1.50
106p	Alex Rodriguez ("PROMOTIONAL SAMPLE")	1.50
107	Henry Rodriguez	.05
108	Ivan Rodriguez	.65
109	Scott Rolen	.65
110	Tim Salmon	.05
111	Curt Schilling	.35
112	Gary Sheffield	.45
113	John Smoltz	.05
114	J.T. Snow	.05
115	Sammy Sosa	1.00
116	Matt Stairs	.05
117	Shannon Stewart	.05
118	Frank Thomas	.75
119	Jim Thome	.65
120	Justin Thompson	.05
121	Mo Vaughn	.05
122	Robin Ventura	.05
123	Larry Walker	.05
124	Rondell White	.05
125	Bernie Williams	.05
126	Matt Williams	.05
127	Tony Womack	.05
128	Jaret Wright	.05
129	Edgar Renteria (Baseball's Best)	.05
130	Kenny Lofton (Baseball's Best)	.05
131	Tony Gwynn (Baseball's Best)	.50
132	Mark McGwire (Baseball's Best)	.75
133	Craig Biggio (Baseball's Best)	.05
134	Charles Johnson (Baseball's Best)	.05
135	J.T. Snow (Baseball's Best)	.05
136	Ken Caminiti (Baseball's Best)	.05
137	Vladimir Guerrero (Baseball's Best)	.40
138	Jim Edmonds (Baseball's Best)	.05
139	Randy Johnson (Baseball's Best)	.40
140	Darryl Kile (Baseball's Best)	.05
141	John Smoltz (Baseball's Best)	.05
142	Greg Maddux (Baseball's Best)	.50
143	Andy Pettitte (Baseball's Best)	.05
144	Ken Griffey Jr. (Baseball's Best)	.65
145	Mike Piazza (Baseball's Best)	.65
146	Todd Greene (Baseball's Best)	.05
147	Vinny Castilla (Baseball's Best)	.05
148	Derek Jeter (Baseball's Best)	1.00
149	Robert Machado (One to Watch)	.05
150	Mike Gulan (One to Watch)	.05
151	Randall Simon (One to Watch)	.05
152	Michael Coleman (One to Watch)	.05
153	Brian Rose (One to Watch)	.05
154	Scott Eyre RC (One to Watch)	.05
155	Magglio Ordonez RC (One to Watch)	1.50
156	Todd Helton (One to Watch)	.65
157	Juan Encarnacion (One to Watch)	.05
158	Mark Kotsay (One to Watch)	.05
159	Josh Booty (One to Watch)	.05
160	Melvin Rosario RC (One to Watch)	.05
161	Shane Halter (One to Watch)	.05
162	Paul Konerko (One to Watch)	.25
163	Henry Blanco RC (One to Watch)	.05
164	Antone Williamson (One to Watch)	.05
165	Brad Fullmer (One to Watch)	.05
166	Ricky Ledee (One to Watch)	.05
167	Ben Grieve (One to Watch)	.05
168	Frank Catalanotto RC (One to Watch)	.25
169	Bobby Estalella (One to Watch)	.05
170	Dennis Reyes (One to Watch)	.05
171	Kevin Polcovich (One to Watch)	.05
172	Jacob Cruz (One to Watch)	.05
173	Ken Cloude (One to Watch)	.05
174	Eli Marrero (One to Watch)	.05
175	Fernando Tatis (One to Watch)	.05
176	Tom Evans (One to Watch)	.05
177	Carl Everett, Nomar Garciaparra (97 in Review)	.35
178	Eric Davis (97 in Review)	.05
179	Roger Clemens (97 in Review)	.60
180	Brett Butler, Eddie Murray (97 in Review)	.30
181	Frank Thomas (97 in Review)	.45
182	Curt Schilling (97 in Review)	.15
183	Jeff Bagwell (97 in Review)	.40
184	Mark McGwire, Ken Griffey Jr. (97 in Review)	.75
185	Kevin Brown (97 in Review)	.05
186	Marty Cordova, Ricardo Rincon (97 in Review)	.05
187	Charles Johnson (97 in Review)	.05
188	Hideki Irabu (97 in Review)	.05
189	Tony Gwynn (97 in Review)	.50
190	Sandy Alomar (97 in Review)	.05
191	Ken Griffey Jr. (97 in Review)	.65
192	Larry Walker (97 in Review)	.05
193	Roger Clemens (97 in Review)	.60
194	Pedro Martinez (97 in Review)	.40
195	Nomar Garciaparra (97 in Review)	.60
196	Scott Rolen (97 in Review)	.40
197	Brian Anderson (97 in Review)	.05
198	Tony Saunders (97 in Review)	.05
199	Florida Celebration (97 in Review)	.05
200	Livan Hernandez (97 in Review)	.05
201	Travis Lee/SP (One to Watch)	2.00

Extra Edition

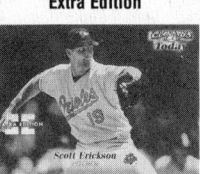

Extra Edition is a 201-card parallel set that includes a holofoil stamp on the front and sequential numbering to 250 on the back. There is also a First Edition version of these that was identical on the front, but contains the text "The Only 1 of 1 First Edition" in purple lettering on the card back.

	NM/M
Common Player:	2.00
Extra Edition Stars:	8X

Autographs

This six-card insert features autographs of players. The Konerko and Grieve cards were available through redemptions until Nov. 1, 1999.

	NM/M
Common Player:	7.50
Lou Brock/500	40.00
Jose Cruz Jr./250	10.00
Rollie Fingers/500	10.00
Ben Grieve/250 (Exchange Card)	3.00
Ben Grieve (Signed Card)	7.50
Paul Konerko/250 (Exchange Card)	3.00
Paul Konerko (Signed Card)	20.00
Brooks Robinson/250	50.00

Covers

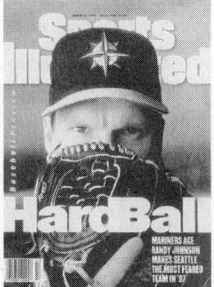

This 10-card insert set pictures actual Sports Illustrated covers on trading cards. The cards are numbered with a "C" prefix and inserted one per nine packs.

		NM/M
Complete Set (10):		15.00
Common Player:		1.00
Inserted 1:9		
1	Ken Griffey Jr., Mike Piazza	2.00
2	Derek Jeter	3.00
3	Ken Griffey Jr.	2.50
4	Cal Ripken Jr.	3.00
5	Manny Ramirez	1.50
6	Jay Buhner	1.00
7	Matt Williams	1.00
8	Randy Johnson	1.50
9	Deion Sanders	1.00
10	Jose Canseco	1.50

Editor's Choice

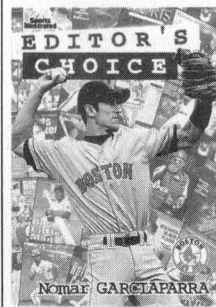

Editor's Choice includes 10 top players in 1998 as profiled by the editors of Sports Illustrated. Cards are numbered with an "EC" prefix and seeded one per 24 packs.

		NM/M
Complete Set (10):		20.00
Common Player:		1.00
Inserted 1:24		
1	Ken Griffey Jr.	3.00
2	Alex Rodriguez	4.00
3	Frank Thomas	1.50
4	Mark McGwire	4.00
5	Greg Maddux	2.00
6	Derek Jeter	5.00
7	Cal Ripken Jr.	5.00
8	Nomar Garciaparra	2.50
9	Jeff Bagwell	1.50
10	Jose Cruz Jr.	1.00

Mini-Posters

Thirty 5" x 7" mini-posters were available at a rate of one per pack. The posters took the top player or two from each team and added their 1998 schedule. Backs were blank so the cards are numbered on the front with an "OD" prefix.

	NM/M
Complete Set (30):	8.00
Common Player:	.10
Inserted 1:1	

1	Tim Salmon	.10
2	Travis Lee	.10
3	John Smoltz, Greg Maddux	.50
4	Cal Ripken Jr.	1.00
5	Nomar Garciaparra	.50
6	Sammy Sosa	.50
7	Frank Thomas	.45
8	Barry Larkin	.10
9	David Justice	.10
10	Larry Walker	.10
11	Tony Clark	.10
12	Livan Hernandez	.10
13	Jeff Bagwell	.45
14	Kevin Appier	.10
15	Mike Piazza	.65
16	Fernando Vina	.10
17	Chuck Knoblauch	.10
18	Vladimir Guerrero	.45
19	Rey Ordonez	.10
20	Bernie Williams	.10
21	Matt Stairs	.10
22	Curt Schilling	.30
23	Tony Womack	.10
24	Mark McGwire	.75
25	Tony Gwynn	.50
26	Barry Bonds	1.00
27	Ken Griffey Jr.	.65
28	Fred McGriff	.10
29	Juan Gonzalez, Alex Rodriguez	.50
30	Roger Clemens	.60

1998 Sports Illustrated Then & Now

Then and Now was the first of three Sports Illustrated baseball releases in 1998. It contained 150 cards and sold in six-card packs, with five cards and a mini-poster. Fronts carried photos of active and retired players, as well as rookies. There was only one subset - A Place in History (#37-53) - which compares statistics between current players and retired greats. The product arrived with an Extra Edition parallel set, Art of the Game, Autograph Redemptions, Covers and Great Shots inserts. There was also an Alex Rodriguez checklist / mini-poster seeded every 12th pack.

	NM/M
Complete Set (150):	15.00
Common Player:	.05
Extra Edition Stars:	6X
Production 500 Sets	
Pack (5):	1.00
Wax Box (24):	16.00

1	Luis Aparicio (Legends of the Game)	.05
2	Richie Ashburn (Legends of the Game)	.05
3	Ernie Banks (Legends of the Game)	.50
4	Yogi Berra (Legends of the Game)	.50
5	Lou Boudreau (Legends of the Game)	.05
6	Lou Brock (Legends of the Game)	.15
7	Jim Bunning (Legends of the Game)	.05
8	Rod Carew (Legends of the Game)	.15
9	Bob Feller (Legends of the Game)	.25
10	Rollie Fingers (Legends of the Game)	.05
11	Bob Gibson (Legends of the Game)	.15
12	Fergie Jenkins (Legends of the Game)	.05
13	Al Kaline (Legends of the Game)	.25
14	George Kell (Legends of the Game)	.05
15	Harmon Killebrew (Legends of the Game)	.25
16	Ralph Kiner (Legends of the Game)	.05
17	Tommy Lasorda (Legends of the Game)	.05
18	Juan Marichal (Legends of the Game)	.05
19	Eddie Mathews (Legends of the Game)	.25
20	Willie Mays (Legends of the Game)	1.00
21	Willie McCovey (Legends of the Game)	.05
22	Joe Morgan (Legends of the Game)	.15
23	Gaylord Perry (Legends of the Game)	.05
24	Kirby Puckett (Legends of the Game)	1.00
25	Pee Wee Reese (Legends of the Game)	.25
26	Phil Rizzuto (Legends of the Game)	.25
27	Robin Roberts (Legends of the Game)	.05
28	Brooks Robinson (Legends of the Game)	.35
29	Frank Robinson (Legends of the Game)	.35
30	Red Schoendienst (Legends of the Game)	.05
31	Enos Slaughter (Legends of the Game)	.05
32	Warren Spahn (Legends of the Game)	.25
33	Willie Stargell (Legends of the Game)	.15
34	Earl Weaver (Legends of the Game)	.05
35	Billy Williams (Legends of the Game)	.15
36	Early Wynn (Legends of the Game)	.05
37	Rickey Henderson (A Place in History)	.75
38	Greg Maddux (A Place in History)	1.00
39	Mike Mussina (A Place in History)	.40
40	Cal Ripken Jr. (A Place in History)	2.00
41	Albert Belle (A Place in History)	.05
42	Frank Thomas (A Place in History)	.75
43	Jeff Bagwell (A Place in History)	.75
44	Paul Molitor (A Place in History)	.75
45	Chuck Knoblauch (A Place in History)	.05
46	Todd Hundley (A Place in History)	.05
47	Bernie Williams (A Place in History)	.05
48	Tony Gwynn (A Place in History)	1.00
49	Barry Bonds (A Place in History)	2.00
50	Ken Griffey Jr. (A Place in History)	1.25
51	Randy Johnson (A Place in History)	.75
52	Mark McGwire (A Place in History)	1.50
53	Roger Clemens (A Place in History)	1.00
54	Jose Cruz Jr. (A Place in History)	1.00
55	Roberto Alomar (Legends of Today)	.20
56	Sandy Alomar (Legends of Today)	.05
57	Brady Anderson (Legends of Today)	.05
58	Kevin Appier (Legends of Today)	.05
59	Jeff Bagwell (Legends of Today)	.75
60	Albert Belle (Legends of Today)	.05
61	Dante Bichette (Legends of Today)	.05
62	Craig Biggio (Legends of Today)	.05
63	Barry Bonds (Legends of Today)	2.00
64	Kevin Brown (Legends of Today)	.05
65	Jay Buhner (Legends of Today)	.05
66	Ellis Burks (Legends of Today)	.05
67	Ken Caminiti (Legends of Today)	.05
68	Jose Canseco (Legends of Today)	.50
69	Joe Carter (Legends of Today)	.05
70	Vinny Castilla (Legends of Today)	.05
71	Tony Clark (Legends of Today)	.05
72	Roger Clemens (Legends of Today)	1.00
73	David Cone (Legends of Today)	.05
74	Jose Cruz Jr. (Legends of Today)	.05
75	Jason Dickson (Legends of Today)	.05
76	Jim Edmonds (Legends of Today)	.05
77	Scott Erickson (Legends of Today)	.05
78	Darin Erstad (Legends of Today)	.20
79	Alex Fernandez (Legends of Today)	.05
80	Steve Finley (Legends of Today)	.05
81	Travis Fryman (Legends of Today)	.05
82	Andres Galarraga (Legends of Today)	.05
83	Nomar Garciaparra (Legends of Today)	1.00
84	Tom Glavine (Legends of Today)	.35
85	Juan Gonzalez (Legends of Today)	.40
86	Mark Grace (Legends of Today)	.05
87	Willie Greene (Legends of Today)	.05
88	Ken Griffey Jr. (Legends of Today)	1.25
89	Vladimir Guerrero (Legends of Today)	.75
90	Tony Gwynn (Legends of Today)	1.00
91	Livan Hernandez (Legends of Today)	.05
92	Bobby Higginson (Legends of Today)	.05
93	Derek Jeter (Legends of Today)	2.00
94	Charles Johnson (Legends of Today)	.05
95	Randy Johnson (Legends of Today)	.75
96	Andruw Jones (Legends of Today)	.75
97	Chipper Jones (Legends of Today)	1.00
98	David Justice (Legends of Today)	.05
99	Eric Karros (Legends of Today)	.05
100	Jason Kendall (Legends of Today)	.05
101	Jimmy Key (Legends of Today)	.05
102	Darryl Kile (Legends of Today)	.05
103	Chuck Knoblauch (Legends of Today)	.05
104	Ray Lankford (Legends of Today)	.05
105	Barry Larkin (Legends of Today)	.05
106	Kenny Lofton (Legends of Today)	.05
107	Greg Maddux (Legends of Today)	1.00
108	Al Martin (Legends of Today)	.05
109	Edgar Martinez (Legends of Today)	.05
110	Pedro Martinez (Legends of Today)	.75
111	Ramon Martinez (Legends of Today)	.05
112	Tino Martinez (Legends of Today)	.05
113	Mark McGwire (Legends of Today)	1.50
114	Raul Mondesi (Legends of Today)	.05
115	Matt Morris (Legends of Today)	.05
116	Charles Nagy (Legends of Today)	.05
117	Denny Neagle (Legends of Today)	.05
118	Hideo Nomo (Legends of Today)	.40
119	Dean Palmer (Legends of Today)	.05
120	Andy Pettitte (Legends of Today)	.25
121	Mike Piazza (Legends of Today)	1.25
122	Manny Ramirez (Legends of Today)	.75
123	Edgar Renteria (Legends of Today)	.05
124	Cal Ripken Jr. (Legends of Today)	2.00
125	Alex Rodriguez (Legends of Today)	1.50
126	Henry Rodriguez (Legends of Today)	.05
127	Ivan Rodriguez (Legends of Today)	.65
128	Scott Rolen (Legends of Today)	.65
129	Tim Salmon (Legends of Today)	.05
130	Curt Schilling (Legends of Today)	.35
131	Gary Sheffield (Legends of Today)	.45
132	John Smoltz (Legends of Today)	.05
133	Sammy Sosa (Legends of Today)	1.00
134	Frank Thomas (Legends of Today)	.75
135	Jim Thome (Legends of Today)	.65
136	Mo Vaughn (Legends of Today)	.05
137	Robin Ventura (Legends of Today)	.05
138	Larry Walker (Legends of Today)	.05
139	Bernie Williams (Legends of Today)	.05
140	Matt Williams (Legends of Today)	.05
141	Jaret Wright (Legends of Today)	.05
142	Michael Coleman (Legends of the Future)	.05
143	Juan Encarnacion (Legends of the Future)	.05
144	Brad Fullmer (Legends of the Future)	.05
145	Ben Grieve (Legends of the Future)	.75
146	Todd Helton (Legends of the Future)	.75
147	Paul Konerko (Legends of the Future)	.20
148	Derrek Lee (Legends of the Future)	.50
149	Magglio Ordonez RC (Legends of the Future)	1.50
150	Enrique Wilson (Legends of the Future)	.05
---	Alex Rodriguez (Checklist)	1.00

Then & Now Extra Edition

This 150-card set paralleled the base set and was distinguished by an "Extra Edition" foil stamp on the front. There were 500 sets of Extra Edition and the cards were individually numbered on the back.

	NM/M
Common Extra Edition:	1.00
Extra Edition Stars:	6X
Production 500 Sets	

Then & Now Art of the Game

"Brooks"

Art of the Game was an eight-card insert featuring reproductions of original artwork of current and retired baseAll-Stars done by eight popular sports artists. Cards are numbered with a "AG" prefix and inserted one per nine packs.

	NM/M
Complete Set (8):	11.00
Common Player:	1.00
Inserted 1:9	
1 It's Gone (Ken Griffey Jr.)	1.50
2 Alex Rodriguez	2.00
3 Mike Piazza	1.50
4 Brooks Robinson	1.00
5 David Justice/AS	1.00
6 Cal Ripken Jr.	3.00
7 The Prospect and the Prospector	1.00
8 Barry Bonds	3.00

Then & Now Autographs

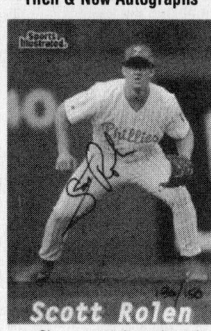

Scott Rolen

Six autograph redemption cards were randomly inserted into packs of Then & Now and could be exchanged prior to Nov. 1, 1999. The signed cards were produced in the following quantities: Clemens 250, Gibson 500, Gwynn 250, Killebrew 500, Mays 250 and Rolen 150. Four of the six cards use the same fronts as the Covers insert; Gibson and Rolen cards each feature unique card fronts.

	NM/M
Common Autograph:	15.00
Redemption Cards: 10 Percent	
Bob Gibson/500	15.00
Tony Gwynn/250	35.00
Roger Clemens/250	120.00
Scott Rolen/150	20.00
Willie Mays/250	90.00
Harmon Killebrew/500	25.00

Then & Now Covers

This 12-card insert features color shots of six actual Sports Illustrated covers, including six current players and six retired players. The cards are numbered with a "C" prefix and were seeded one per 18 packs.

	NM/M
Complete Set (12):	22.00
Common Player:	1.00
Inserted 1:18	
1 Lou Brock (10/16/67)	1.00
2 Kirby Puckett (4/6/92)	2.50
3 Harmon Killebrew (4/8/63 - inside)	1.00
4 Eddie Mathews (8/16/54)	1.00
5 Willie Mays (5/22/72)	2.00
6 Frank Robinson (10/6/69)	1.00
7 Cal Ripken Jr. (9/11/95)	5.00
8 Roger Clemens (5/12/86)	2.50
9 Ken Griffey Jr. (10/16/95)	3.00
10 Mark McGwire (6/1/92)	3.00
11 Tony Gwynn (7/28/97)	2.50
12 Ivan Rodriguez (8/11/97)	1.50

Then & Now Great Shots!

This 25-card set featured 5" x 7" fold-out mini-posters using Sports Illustrated photos. Great Shots were inserted one per pack and contained a mix of retired and current players.

	NM/M
Complete Set (25):	7.50
Common Player:	.10
Inserted 1:1	
1 Ken Griffey Jr.	.65
2 Frank Thomas	.45
3 Alex Rodriguez	.75
4 Andruw Jones	.45

Nomar Garciaparra — Boston Red Sox

5	Chipper Jones	.50
6	Cal Ripken Jr.	1.00
7	Mark McGwire	.75
8	Derek Jeter	1.00
9	Greg Maddux	.50
10	Jeff Bagwell	.45
11	Mike Piazza	.65
12	Scott Rolen	.35
13	Nomar Garciaparra	.50
14	Jose Cruz Jr.	.10
15	Charles Johnson	.10
16	Lou Brock	.10
17	Lou Brock	.10
18	Bob Gibson	.10
19	Harmon Killebrew	.10
20	Juan Marichal	.10
21	Brooks Robinson	.10
22	Rod Carew	.10
23	Yogi Berra	.25
24	Willie Mays	.50
25	Kirby Puckett	.50

Then & Now Road to Cooperstown

ROAD TO COOPERSTOWN — KEN GRIFFEY, JR.

Road to Cooperstown features 10 current players who are having Hall of Fame careers. The insert name is printed across the back in bold, gold letters. Cards are numbered with a "RC" prefix and were inserted one per 24 packs.

	NM/M
Complete Set (10):	10.00
Common Player:	.75
Inserted 1:24	
1 Barry Bonds	2.50
2 Roger Clemens	1.25
3 Ken Griffey Jr.	1.50
4 Tony Gwynn	1.00
5 Rickey Henderson	.75
6 Greg Maddux	1.00
7 Paul Molitor	.75
8 Mike Piazza	1.50
9 Cal Ripken Jr.	2.50
10 Frank Thomas	.75

World Series Fever

ANDRUW JONES — OUTFIELD

The third and final Sports Illustrated release of 1998 contained 150 cards and focused on the World Series while recapping memorable moments from the season. The set also included many stars of tomorrow, like Kerry Wood, Orlando Hernandez, Ben Grieve and Travis Lee. Once again, all the photos were taken from Sports Illustrated archives. The set has two subsets - 10 Magnificent Moments and 20 Cover Collection. The set is paralleled twice in Extra and First Edition parallel sets, and has three insert sets - MVP Collection, Reggie Jackson's Picks and Autumn Excellence.

	NM/M
Complete Set (150):	10.00
Common Player:	.05
Pack (6):	1.00
Wax Box (24):	17.50

1	Mickey Mantle (Covers)	1.50
2	1957 World Series Preview (Covers)	.15
3	1958 World Series Preview (Covers)	.15
4	1959 World Series Preview (Covers)	.15
5	1962 World Series (Covers)	.10
6	Lou Brock (Covers)	.25
7	Brooks Robinson (Covers)	.25
8	Frank Robinson (Covers)	.25
9	1974 World Series (Covers)	.10
10	Reggie Jackson (Covers)	.60
11	1985 World Series (Covers)	.10
12	1987 World Series (Covers)	.10
13	Orel Hershiser (Covers)	.05
14	Rickey Henderson (Covers)	.40
15	1991 World Series (Covers)	.10
16	1992 World Series (Covers)	.05
17	Joe Carter (Covers)	.05
18	1995 World Series (Covers)	.10
19	1996 World Series (Covers)	.15
20	Edgar Renteria (Covers)	.05
21	Bill Mazeroski (Magnificent Moments)	.15
22	Joe Carter (Magnificent Moments)	.05
23	Carlton Fisk (Magnificent Moments)	.40
24	Bucky Dent (Magnificent Moments)	.15
25	Mookie Wilson (Magnificent Moments)	.05
26	Enos Slaughter (Magnificent Moments)	.05
27	Mickey Lolich (Magnificent Moments)	.05
28	Bobby Richardson (Magnificent Moments)	.05
29	Kirk Gibson (Magnificent Moments)	.05
30	Edgar Renteria (Magnificent Moments)	.05
31	Albert Belle	.05
32	Kevin Brown	.05
33	Brian Rose	.05
34	Ron Gant	.05
35	Jeromy Burnitz	.05
36	Andres Galarraga	.05
37	Jim Edmonds	.05
38	Jose Cruz Jr.	.05
39	Mark Grudzielanek	.05
40	Shawn Estes	.05
41	Mark Grace	.05
42	Nomar Garciaparra	.50
43	Juan Gonzalez	.20
44	Tom Glavine	.25
45	Brady Anderson	.05
46	Tony Clark	.05
47	Jeff Cirillo	.05
48	Dante Bichette	.05
49	Ben Grieve	.05
50	Ken Griffey Jr.	.65
51	Edgardo Alfonzo	.05
52	Roger Clemens	.60
53	Pat Hentgen	.05
54	Todd Helton	.30
55	Andy Benes	.05
56	Tony Gwynn	.50
57	Andruw Jones	.40
58	Bobby Higginson	.05
59	Bobby Jones	.05
60	Darryl Kile	.05
61	Chan Ho Park	.05
62	Charles Johnson	.05
63	Rusty Greer	.05
64	Travis Fryman	.05
65	Derek Jeter	1.00
66	Jay Buhner	.05
67	Chuck Knoblauch	.05
68	David Justice	.05
69	Brian Hunter	.05
70	Eric Karros	.05
71	Edgar Martinez	.05
72	Chipper Jones	.50
73	Barry Larkin	.05
74	Mike Lansing	.05
75	Craig Biggio	.05
76	Al Martin	.05
77	Barry Bonds	1.00
78	Randy Johnson	.40
79	Ryan Klesko	.05
80	Mark McGwire	.75
81	Fred McGriff	.05

82	Javy Lopez	.05
83	Kenny Lofton	.05
84	Sandy Alomar Jr.	.05
85	Matt Morris	.05
86	Paul Konerko	.10
87	Ray Lankford	.05
88	Kerry Wood	.30
89	Roberto Alomar	.20
90	Greg Maddux	.50
91	Travis Lee	.05
92	Moises Alou	.05
93	Dean Palmer	.05
94	Hideo Nomo	.20
95	Ken Caminiti	.05
96	Pedro Martinez	.40
97	Raul Mondesi	.05
98	Denny Neagle	.05
99	Tino Martinez	.05
100	Mike Mussina	.20
101	Kevin Appier	.05
102	Vinny Castilla	.05
103	Jeff Bagwell	.40
104	Paul O'Neill	.05
105	Rey Ordonez	.05
106	Vladimir Guerrero	.40
107	Rafael Palmeiro	.05
108	Alex Rodriguez	.75
109	Andy Pettitte	.15
110	Carl Pavano	.05
111	Henry Rodriguez	.05
112	Gary Sheffield	.40
113	Curt Schilling	.25
114	John Smoltz	.05
115	Reggie Sanders	.05
116	Scott Rolen	.35
117	Mike Piazza	.65
118	Manny Ramirez	.40
119	Cal Ripken Jr.	1.00
120	Brad Radke	.05
121	Tim Salmon	.05
122	Brett Tomko	.05
123	Robin Ventura	.05
124	Mo Vaughn	.05
125	A.J. Hinch	.05
126	Derrek Lee	.45
127	Orlando Hernandez RC	.40
128	Aramis Ramirez	.05
129	Frank Thomas	.40
130	J.T. Snow	.05
131	Magglio Ordonez RC	1.00
132	Bobby Bonilla	.05
133	Marquis Grissom	.05
134	Jim Thome	.45
135	Justin Thompson	.05
136	Matt Williams	.05
137	Matt Stairs	.05
138	Wade Boggs	.50
139	Chuck Finley	.05
140	Jaret Wright	.05
141	Ivan Rodriguez	.35
142	Brad Fullmer	.05
143	Bernie Williams	.05
144	Jason Giambi	.30
145	Larry Walker	.15
146	Tony Womack	.05
147	Sammy Sosa	.05
148	Rondell White	.05
149	Todd Stottlemyre	.05
150	Shane Reynolds	.05

WS Fever Extra Edition

Extra Edition parallels the entire 150-card base set and is identified by a gold-foil stamp on the card front and sequential numbering to 98 sets on the back. World Series Fever also includes one-of-one parallel versions called First Edition. These have a purple-foil identifier on front, with the legend on back, "THE ONLY 1 OF 1 FIRST EDITION," also in purple foil.

	NM/M
Common EE Player:	2.00
EE Stars:	15X
Production: 98 Sets	
Common FE Player:	100.00
FE Stars: Values Undetermined	
1 of 1	

WS Fever Autumn Excellence

Autumn Excellence honors players with the most select World Series records. The 10-card set was seeded one per 24 packs, while rarer Gold versions were seeded one per 240 packs.

	NM/M
Complete Set (10):	15.00
Common Player:	.50
Inserted 1:24	
Golds:	2X
Inserted 1:240	

AE1	Willie Mays	2.50
AE2	Kirby Puckett	2.00
AE3	Babe Ruth	4.00
AE4	Reggie Jackson	1.50
AE5	Whitey Ford	.50
AE6	Lou Brock	.50
AE7	Mickey Mantle	4.00
AE8	Yogi Berra	.75
AE9	Bob Gibson	.50
AE10	Don Larsen	1.00

WS Fever Reggie Jackson Picks

Reggie Jackson's Picks contains top players that Jackson believes have what it takes to perform on center stage in the World Series. Fronts have a shot of the player with his name in the background, and a head shot of Reggie Jackson in the bottom right corner. These were numbered with a "RP" prefix and inserted one per 12 packs.

	NM/M
Complete Set (15):	12.50
Common Player:	.25
Inserted 1:12	

1	Paul O'Neill	.25
2	Barry Bonds	2.50
3	Ken Griffey Jr.	1.50
4	Juan Gonzalez	.40
5	Greg Maddux	1.00
6	Mike Piazza	1.50
7	Larry Walker	.25
8	Mo Vaughn	.25
9	Roger Clemens	1.25
10	John Smoltz	.25
11	Alex Rodriguez	2.00
12	Frank Thomas	.75
13	Mark McGwire	2.00
14	Jeff Bagwell	.75
15	Randy Johnson	.75

WS Fever MVP Collection

This 10-card insert set features select MVPs from the World Series. Card fronts contain a shot of the player over a white border with the year in black letters and the insert and player's name in blue foil. MVP Collection inserts were seeded one per four packs and numbered with a "MC" prefix.

	NM/M
Complete Set (10):	1.00
Common Player:	.10
Inserted 1:4	

1	Frank Robinson	.25

2	Brooks Robinson	.25
3	Willie Stargell	.10
4	Bret Saberhagen	.10
5	Rollie Fingers	.10
6	Orel Hershiser	.10
7	Paul Molitor	.50
8	Tom Glavine	.15
9	John Wetteland	.10
10	Livan Hernandez	.10

1999 Sports Illustrated

The Sports Illustrated set from Fleer consists of 180 base cards composed of 107 player cards, and four subsets. They include Team 2000, Postseason Review, Award Winners, and Season Highlights. Cards came in six-card packs with an SRP of $1.99. The set also includes five insert sets, along with hobby exclusive autographed J.D. Drew cards numbered to 250.

	NM/M
Complete Set (180):	15.00
Common Player:	.05
Wax Pack (6):	1.00
Hobby Box (24):	15.00
Retail Box (16):	10.00

1	Yankees (Postseason Review)	.25
2	Scott Brosius (Postseason Review)	.05
3	David Wells (Postseason Review)	.05
4	Sterling Hitchcock (Postseason Review)	.05
5	David Justice (Postseason Review)	.05
6	David Cone (Postseason Review)	.05
7	Greg Maddux (Postseason Review)	.50
8	Jim Leyritz (Postseason Review)	.05
9	Gary Gaetti (Postseason Review)	.05
10	Mark McGwire (Award Winners)	.75
11	Sammy Sosa (Award Winners)	.50
12	Larry Walker (Award Winners)	.05
13	Tony Womack (Award Winners)	.05
14	Tom Glavine (Award Winners)	.10
15	Curt Schilling (Award Winners)	.10
16	Greg Maddux (Award Winners)	.50
17	Trevor Hoffman (Award Winners)	.05
18	Kerry Wood (Award Winners)	.20
19	Tom Glavine (Award Winners)	.10
20	Sammy Sosa (Award Winners)	.50
21	Travis Lee (Season Highlights)	.05
22	Roberto Alomar (Season Highlights)	.05
23	Roger Clemens (Season Highlights)	.60
24	Barry Bonds (Season Highlights)	1.00

25	Paul Molitor (Season Highlights)	.45
26	Todd Stottlemyre (Season Highlights)	.05
27	Chris Hoiles (Season Highlights)	.05
28	Albert Belle (Season Highlights)	.05
29	Tony Clark (Season Highlights)	.05
30	Kerry Wood (Season Highlights)	.20
31	David Wells (Season Highlights)	.05
32	Dennis Eckersley (Season Highlights)	.05
33	Mark McGwire (Season Highlights)	.75
34	Cal Ripken Jr. (Season Highlights)	1.00
35	Ken Griffey Jr. (Season Highlights)	.65
36	Alex Rodriguez (Season Highlights)	.75
37	Craig Biggio (Season Highlights)	.05
38	Sammy Sosa (Season Highlights)	.50
39	Dennis Martinez (Season Highlights)	.05
40	Curt Schilling (Season Highlights)	.10
41	Orlando Hernandez (Season Highlights)	.05
42	Troy Glaus, Ben Molina RC, Todd Greene ("Team" 2000)	.45
43	Mitch Meluskey, Daryle Ward, Mike Grzanich ("Team" 2000)	.05
44	Eric Chavez, Mike Neill, Steve Connelly RC ("Team" 2000)	.10
45	Roy Halladay, Tom Evans, Kevin Witt ("Team" 2000)	.05
46	George Lombard, Adam Butler, Bruce Chen ("Team" 2000)	.05
47	Ronnie Belliard, Valerio de los Santos, Rafael Roque RC ("Team" 2000)	.05
48	J.D. Drew, Placido Polanco, Mark Little RC ("Team" 2000)	.50
49	Jason Maxwell, Jose Nieves RC, Jeremi Gonzalez ("Team" 2000)	.05
50	Scott McClain, Kerry Robinson, Mike Duvall RC ("Team" 2000)	.05
51	Ben Ford, Bryan Corey RC, Danny Klassen ("Team" 2000)	.05
52	Angel Pena, Jeff Kubenka, Paul LoDuca ("Team" 2000)	.05
53	Kirk Bullinger, Fernando Seguignol, Tim Young ("Team" 2000)	.05
54	Ramon Martinez, Wilson Delgado, Armando Rios ("Team" 2000)	.05
55	Russ Branyon, Jolbert Cabrera RC, Jason Rakers ("Team" 2000)	.05
56	Carlos Guillen RC, David Holdridge RC, Giomar Guevara RC ("Team" 2000)	.10
57	Alex Gonzalez, Joe Fontenot, Preston Wilson ("Team" 2000)	.05
58	Mike Kinkade, Jay Payton, Masato Yoshii ("Team" 2000)	.05
59	Willis Otanez, Ryan Minor, Calvin Pickering ("Team" 2000)	.05
60	Ben Davis, Matt Clement, Stan Spencer ("Team" 2000)	.05
61	Marlon Anderson, Mike Welch, Gary Bennett RC ("Team" 2000)	.05
62	Abraham Nunez, Sean Lawrence RC, Aramis Ramirez ("Team" 2000)	.05
63	Jonathan Johnson, Rob Sasser RC, Scott Sheldon RC ("Team" 2000)	.05
64	Keith Glauber RC, Guillermo Garcia RC, Eddie Priest ("Team" 2000)	.05
65	Brian Barkley, Jin Ho Cho, Donnie Sadler ("Team" 2000)	.05
66	Derrick Gibson, Mark Strittmatter, Edgard Clemente RC ("Team" 2000)	.05

67	Jeremy Giambi, Dermal Brown, Chris Hatcher RC ("Team" 2000)	.05
68	Rob Fick RC, Gabe Kapler, Marino Santana ("Team" 2000)	.10
69	Corey Koskie, A.J. Pierzynski, Benj Sampson ("Team" 2000)	.05
70	Brian Simmons, Mark Johnson, Craig Wilson ("Team" 2000)	.05
71	Ryan Bradley, Mike Lowell, Jay Tessmer ("Team" 2000)	.05
72	Ben Grieve	.05
73	Shawn Green	.45
74	Rafael Palmeiro	.65
75	Juan Gonzalez	.40
76	Mike Piazza	1.25
77	Devon White	.05
78	Jim Thome	.65
79	Barry Larkin	.05
80	Scott Rolen	.65
81	Raul Mondesi	.05
82	Jason Giambi	.05
83	Jose Canseco	.45
84	Tony Gwynn	1.00
85	Cal Ripken Jr.	2.00
86	Andy Pettitte	.15
87	Carlos Delgado	.05
88	Jeff Cirillo	.05
89	Bret Saberhagen	.05
90	John Olerud	.05
91	Ron Coomer	.05
92	Todd Helton	.65
93	Ray Lankford	.05
94	Tim Salmon	.05
95	Fred McGriff	.05
96	Matt Stairs	.05
97	Ken Griffey Jr.	1.25
98	Chipper Jones	1.00
99	Mark Grace	.05
100	Ivan Rodriguez	.65
101	Jeromy Burnitz	.05
102	Kenny Rogers	.05
103	Kevin Millwood	.05
104	Vinny Castilla	.05
105	Jim Edmonds	.05
106	Craig Biggio	.05
107	Andres Galarraga	.05
108	Sammy Sosa	1.00
109	Juan Encarnacion	.05
110	Larry Walker	.05
111	John Smoltz	.05
112	Randy Johnson	.75
113	Bobby Higginson	.05
114	Albert Belle	.05
115	Jaret Wright	.05
116	Edgar Renteria	.05
117	Andruw Jones	.75
118	Barry Bonds	2.00
119	Rondell White	.05
120	Jamie Moyer	.05
121	Darin Erstad	.20
122	Al Leiter	.05
123	Mark McGwire	1.50
124	Mo Vaughn	.05
125	Livan Hernandez	.05
126	Jason Kendall	.05
127	Frank Thomas	.75
128	Denny Neagle	.05
129	Johnny Damon	.35
130	Derek Bell	.05
131	Jeff Kent	.05
132	Tony Womack	.05
133	Trevor Hoffman	.05
134	Gary Sheffield	.40
135	Tino Martinez	.05
136	Travis Fryman	.05
137	Rolando Arrojo	.05
138	Dante Bichette	.05
139	Nomar Garciaparra	1.00
140	Moises Alou	.05
141	Chuck Knoblauch	.05
142	Robin Ventura	.05
143	Scott Erickson	.05
144	David Cone	.05
145	Greg Vaughn	.05
146	Wade Boggs	1.00
147	Mike Mussina	.30
148	Tony Clark	.05
149	Alex Rodriguez	1.50
150	Javy Lopez	.05
151	Bartolo Colon	.05
152	Derek Jeter	2.00
153	Greg Maddux	1.00
154	Kevin Brown	.05
155	Curt Schilling	.35
156	Jeff King	.05
157	Bernie Williams	.05
158	Roberto Alomar	.20
159	Travis Lee	.05
160	Kerry Wood	.50
160p	Kerry Wood ("PROMOTIONAL SAMPLE")	1.00
161	Jeff Bagwell	1.00
162	Roger Clemens	1.00
163	Matt Williams	.05
164	Chan Ho Park	.05
165	Damion Easley	.05
166	Manny Ramirez	.75
167	Quinton McCracken	.05
168	Todd Walker	.05
169	Eric Karros	.05
170	Will Clark	.05

171	Edgar Martinez	.05
172	Cliff Floyd	.05
173	Vladimir Guerrero	.75
174	Tom Glavine	.35
175	Pedro Martinez	.75
176	Chuck Finley	.05
177	Dean Palmer	.05
178	Omar Vizquel	.05
179	Checklist	.05
180	Checklist	.05

Diamond Dominators

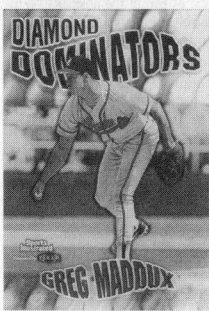

This 10-card insert set features five hitters and five pitchers on embossed cards. The hitters are seeded 1 in every 180 packs, while the pitchers are seeded 1 in every 90 packs.

		NM/M
Complete Set (10):		30.00
Common Player:		1.50
Pitchers inserted 1:90		
Hitters inserted 1:180		
1DD	Kerry Wood	1.50
2DD	Roger Clemens	3.00
3DD	Randy Johnson	2.00
4DD	Greg Maddux	2.50
5DD	Pedro Martinez	2.00
6DD	Ken Griffey Jr.	5.00
7DD	Sammy Sosa	2.50
8DD	Nomar Garciaparra	2.50
9DD	Mark McGwire	6.00
10DD	Alex Rodriguez	6.00

Fabulous 40s

This 13-card insert set consists of the players that hit 40 or more homers during the 1998 season. The cards are sculpture embossed and foil-stamped, with the player's home run total also on the card. One card comes with every 20 packs.

		NM/M
Complete Set (13):		9.00
Common Player:		.25
Inserted 1:20		
1FF	Mark McGwire	2.00
2FF	Sammy Sosa	1.25
3FF	Ken Griffey Jr.	1.50
4FF	Greg Vaughn	.25
5FF	Albert Belle	.25
6FF	Jose Canseco	.50
7FF	Vinny Castilla	.25
8FF	Juan Gonzalez	.50
9FF	Manny Ramirez	1.00
10FF	Andres Galarraga	.25
11FF	Rafael Palmeiro	.75
12FF	Alex Rodriguez	2.00
13FF	Mo Vaughn	.25

Fabulous 40s Extra

The insert set parallels the 13 cards in the Fabulous 40s set. The cards are hobby exclusive, highlighted with silver patterned holofoil. Each player's cards are hand-numbered to the total number of home runs he hit in 1998.

		NM/M
Common Player:		12.00
Numbered to amount of HRs.		
1FF	Mark McGwire/70	60.00
2FF	Sammy Sosa/66	40.00
3FF	Ken Griffey Jr./56	35.00

Inserted 1:12		
10W	J.D. Drew	.65
20W	Marlon Anderson	.25
30W	Roy Halladay	.35
40W	Ben Grieve	.25
50W	Todd Helton	.75
60W	Gabe Kapler	.25
70W	Troy Glaus	.75
80W	Ben Davis	.25
90W	Eric Chavez	.35
100W	Richie Sexson	.25
110W	Fernando Seguignol	.25
120W	Kerry Wood	.50
130W	Bobby Smith	.25
140W	Ryan Minor	.25
150W	Jeremy Giambi	.25
	J.D. Drew autograph/250	15.00

1999 Sports Illustrated Greats of the Game

The 90-card base set includes many legendary major-leaguers including Babe Ruth and Cy Young. Card fronts feature a full bleed photo with the player name across the bottom and Greats of the Game printed on the bottom left portion of the card. Card backs have the player's vital information, along with career statistics and a few career highlights. Seven-card packs were issued with an SRP of $15.

		NM/M
Complete Set (90):		12.00
Common Player:		.05
Pack (7):		15.00
Wax Box (12):		150.00
1	Jimmie Foxx	.25
2	Red Schoendienst	.05
3	Babe Ruth	3.00
4	Lou Gehrig	2.00
5	Mel Ott	.25
6	Stan Musial	.25
7	Mickey Mantle	3.00
8	Carl Yastrzemski	.15
9	Enos Slaughter	.05
10	Andre Dawson	.05
11	Luis Aparicio	.05
12	Ferguson Jenkins	.05
13	Christy Mathewson	.25
14	Ernie Banks	.15
15	Johnny Podres	.05
16	George Foster	.05
17	Jerry Koosman	.05
18	Curt Simmons	.05
19	Bob Feller	.05
20	Frank Robinson	.05
21	Gary Carter	.05
22	Frank Thomas	.05
23	Bill Lee	.05
24	Willie Mays	1.00
25	Tommie Agee	.05
26	Boog Powell	.05
27	Jimmy Wynn	.05
28	Sparky Lyle	.05
29	Bo Belinsky	.05
30	Maury Wills	.05
31	Bill Buckner	.05
32	Steve Carlton	.05
33	Harmon Killebrew	.05
34	Nolan Ryan	1.00
35	Randy Jones	.05
36	Robin Roberts	.05
37	Al Oliver	.05
38	Rico Petrocelli	.05
39	Dave Parker	.05
40	Eddie Mathews	.05
41	Earl Weaver	.05
42	Jackie Robinson	1.50
43	Lou Brock	.15
44	Reggie Jackson	.15
45	Bob Gibson	.05
46	Jeff Burroughs	.05
47	Jim Bouton	.05
48	Bob Forsch	.05
49	Ron Guidry	.05
50	Ty Cobb	2.00
51	Roy White	.05
52	Joe Rudi	.05
53	Moose Skowron	.05
54	Goose Gossage	.05
55	Ed Kranepool	.05
56	Paul Blair	.05
57	Kent Hrbek	.05
58	Orlando Cepeda	.05
59	Buck O'Neil	.05

60	Al Kaline	.05
61	Vida Blue	.05
62	Sam McDowell	.05
63	Jesse Barfield	.05
64	Dave Kingman	.05
65	Ron Santo	.05
66	Steve Garvey	.05
67	Gaylord Perry	.05
68	Darrell Evans	.05
69	Rollie Fingers	.05
70	Walter Johnson	.25
71	Al Hrabosky	.05
72	Mickey Rivers	.05
73	Mike Torrez	.05
74	Hank Bauer	.05
75	Tug McGraw	.05
76	David Clyde	.05
77	Jim Lonborg	.05
78	Clete Boyer	.05
79	Harry Walker	.05
80	Cy Young	.25
81	Bud Harrelson	.05
82	Paul Splittorff	.05
83	Bert Campaneris	.05
84	Joe Niekro	.05
85	Bob Horner	.05
86	Jerry Royster	.05
87	Tommy John	.05
88	Mark Fidrych	.05
89	Dick Williams	.05
90	Graig Nettles	.05

Greats/Game Autographs

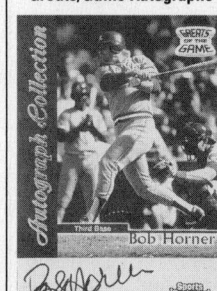

Each Greats of the Game pack has one autograph from the 80 card autograph checklist. Each card is autographed on the white portion on the bottom of the card, and is stamped "seal of authenticity." Card backs certify the autograph is authentic and "has been embossed with the Fleer Mark of Authenticity." The unnumbered cards are checklisted here in alphabetical order.

		NM/M
Common Player:		4.00
Inserted 1:1		
(1)	Tommie Agee	8.00
(2)	Luis Aparicio	12.00
(3)	Ernie Banks	25.00
(4)	Jesse Barfield	6.00
(5)	Hank Bauer	10.00
(6)	Bo Belinsky	6.00
(7)	Paul Blair	6.00
(8)	Vida Blue	10.00
(9)	Jim Bouton	10.00
(10)	Clete Boyer	10.00
(11)	Lou Brock	15.00
(12)	Bill Buckner	10.00
(13)	Jeff Burroughs	5.00
(14)	Bert Campaneris	8.00
(15)	Steve Carlton	20.00
(16)	Gary Carter	10.00
(17)	Orlando Cepeda	12.00
(18)	David Clyde	5.00
(19)	Andre Dawson	10.00
(20)	Darrell Evans	8.00
(21)	Bob Feller	15.00
(22)	Mark Fidrych	15.00
(23)	Rollie Fingers	10.00
(24)	Bob Forsch	6.00
(25)	George Foster	10.00
(26)	Steve Garvey	10.00
(27)	Bob Gibson	15.00
(28)	Goose Gossage	10.00
(29)	Ron Guidry	20.00
(30)	Bud Harrelson	10.00
(31)	Bob Horner	10.00
(32)	Al Hrabosky	8.00
(33)	Kent Hrbek	10.00
(34a)	Reggie Jackson	150.00
(34b)	Reggie Jackson ("Mr. October")	200.00
(34c)	Reggie Jackson ("HoF 93")	200.00
(35)	Ferguson Jenkins	10.00
(36)	Tommy John	8.00
(37)	Randy Jones	4.00
(38)	Al Kaline	25.00
(39)	Harmon Killebrew	25.00
(40)	Dave Kingman	8.00
(41)	Jerry Koosman	8.00
(42)	Ed Kranepool	8.00
(43)	Bill Lee	10.00
(44)	Jim Lonborg	5.00
(45)	Sparky Lyle	8.00

(46)	Eddie Mathews	60.00
(47)	Willie Mays	125.00
(48)	Sam McDowell	8.00
(49)	Tug McGraw	25.00
(50)	Stan Musial	100.00
(51)	Graig Nettles	10.00
(52)	Joe Niekro	8.00
(53)	Buck O'Neil	20.00
(54)	Al Oliver	10.00
(55)	Dave Parker	10.00
(56)	Gaylord Perry	10.00
(57)	Rico Petrocelli	10.00
(58)	Johnny Podres	20.00
(59)	Boog Powell	10.00
(60)	Mickey Rivers	8.00
(61)	Robin Roberts	20.00
(62)	Frank Robinson	20.00
(63)	Jerry Royster	4.00
(64)	Joe Rudi	8.00
(65)	Nolan Ryan	200.00
(66)	Ron Santo	15.00
(67)	Red Schoendienst	12.00
(68)	Curt Simmons	6.00
(69)	Moose Skowron	15.00
(70)	Enos Slaughter	20.00
(71)	Paul Splittorff	6.00
(72)	Frank Thomas	8.00
(73)	Mike Torrez	4.00
(74)	Harry Walker	4.00
(75)	Earl Weaver	10.00
(76)	Roy White	8.00
(77)	Dick Williams	10.00
(78)	Maury Wills	10.00
(79)	Jimmy Wynn	10.00
(80)	Carl Yastrzemski	50.00

Greats/ Game Cover Collection

Each pack features one of the 50 chosen baseball covers from the Sports Illustrated archives. Card fronts are a reprint of the actual cover, while the backs give a brief description of the cover article and date of the magazine cover. Each card is numbered with a "C" suffix.

		NM/M
Complete Set (50):		25.00
Common Player:		.50
Inserted 1:1		
1	Johnny Podres	.50
2	Mickey Mantle	5.00
3	Stan Musial	.50
4	Eddie Mathews	.50
5	Frank Thomas	.50
6	Willie Mays	1.00
7	Red Schoendienst	.50
8	Luis Aparicio	.50
9	Mickey Mantle	3.00
10	Al Kaline	.50
11	Maury Wills	.50
12	Sam McDowell	.50
13	Harry Walker	.50
14	Carl Yastrzemski	.50
15	Carl Yastrzemski	.50
16	Lou Brock	.50
17	Ron Santo	.50
18	Reggie Jackson	.50
19	Frank Robinson	.50
20	Jerry Koosman	.50
21	Bud Harrelson	.50
22	Vida Blue	.50
23	Ferguson Jenkins	.50
24	Sparky Lyle	.50
25	Steve Carlton	.50
26	Bert Campaneris	.50
27	Jimmy Wynn	.50
28	Steve Garvey	.50
29	Nolan Ryan	1.00
30	Randy Jones	.50
31	Reggie Jackson	.50
32	Joe Rudi	.50
33	Reggie Jackson	.50
34	Dave Parker	.50
35	Mark Fidrych	.50
36	Earl Weaver	.50
37	Nolan Ryan	1.00
38	Steve Carlton	.50
39	Reggie Jackson	.50
40	Rollie Fingers	.50
41	Gary Carter	.50
42	Graig Nettles	.50
43	Gaylord Perry	.50
44	Kent Hrbek	.50
45	Gary Carter	.50
46	Steve Garvey	.50

47	Steve Carlton	.50
48	Nolan Ryan	1.00
49	Nolan Ryan	1.00
50	Mickey Mantle	3.00

Greats/ Game Record Breakers

This 10-card set spotlights the top record breakers in the past century from Christy Mathewson to Nolan Ryan. Card fronts are full foiled with a oblong stamp on the bottom portion detailing the player's respective record. Card backs are numbered with a "RB" suffix and gives more detail on the featured player's record. These are seeded 1:12 packs. A Gold parallel is also randomly seeded 1:120 packs and have gold holo-foil.

		NM/M
Complete Set (10):		40.00
Common Player:		2.00
Inserted 1:12		
Golds:		6X
Inserted 1:120		
1	Mickey Mantle	8.00
2	Stan Musial	3.50
3	Babe Ruth	8.00
4	Christy Mathewson	2.00
5	Cy Young	2.00
6	Nolan Ryan	7.50
7	Jackie Robinson	6.00
8	Lou Gehrig	7.00
9	Ty Cobb	3.50
10	Walter Johnson	2.00

1989-91 Sports Illustrated For Kids

Beginning with its January 1989 issue and continuing for three years, the magazine "Sports Illustrated For Kids" produced a set of sportscards featuring many professional and amateur stars in more than a dozen sports. Generally issued in a nine-card panel, cards were perforated so they could be removed from the magazine and separated from each other. A variety of designs and formats were used in that period. Only the pro baseball cards from the series are checklisted here.

		NM/M
Complete Set (60):		55.00
Common Player:		.50
5	Orel Hershiser	.50
11	Jose Canseco	1.00
20	Darryl Strawberry	.50
31	Mike Greenwell	.50
33	Tony Gwynn	2.00
35	Frank Viola	.50
37	Don Mattingly	2.25
43	Ozzie Smith	2.00
46	Rickey Henderson	1.50
48	Chris Sabo	.50
52	Andre Dawson	.75
56	Alan Trammell	.50
60	Roger Clemens	2.25
63	Andres Galarraga	.50
64	John Franco	.50

Headliners

Headliners is a 25-card insert set that features silver foil stamped, team-color coded cards. One card comes with every four packs.

		NM/M
Complete Set (25):		10.00
Common Player:		.25
Inserted 1:4		
1H	Vladimir Guerrero	.40
2H	Randy Johnson	.40
3H	Mo Vaughn	.25
4H	Chipper Jones	.50
5H	Jeff Bagwell	.40
6H	Juan Gonzalez	.30
7H	Mark McGwire	.75
8H	Cal Ripken Jr.	1.00
9H	Frank Thomas	.40
10H	Manny Ramirez	.40
11H	Ken Griffey Jr.	.65
12H	Scott Rolen	.35
13H	Alex Rodriguez	.75
14H	Barry Bonds	1.00
15H	Roger Clemens	.55
16H	Darin Erstad	.30
17H	Nomar Garciaparra	.50
18H	Mike Piazza	.65
19H	Greg Maddux	.50
20H	Ivan Rodriguez	.35
21H	Derek Jeter	1.00
22H	Sammy Sosa	.50
23H	Andruw Jones	.40
24H	Pedro Martinez	.40
25H	Kerry Wood	.35

Ones To Watch

This 15-card insert set features the game's top rookies and young stars. The cards have 100 percent foil background and are team-color coded. One card was inserted in every 12 packs.

		NM/M
Complete Set (15):		5.00
Common Player:		.25

4FF Greg Vaughn/50 12.00
5FF Albert Belle/49 12.00
6FF Jose Canseco/46 25.00
7FF Vinny Castilla/46 12.00
8FF Juan Gonzalez/45 20.00
9FF Manny Ramirez/45 30.00
10FF Andres Galarraga/44 12.00
11FF Rafael Palmeiro/43 25.00
12FF Alex Rodriguez/42 45.00
13FF Mo Vaughn/40 12.00

#	Player	NM/M
69	Cal Ripken Jr.	4.00
70	Will Clark	.50
75	Bo Jackson	.75
81	Nolan Ryan	4.00
90	Mike Schmidt	2.25
112	Kevin Mitchell	.50
121	Ryne Sandberg	2.00
127	Robin Yount	1.50
133	Dave Stewart	.50
140	Eric Davis	.50
144	Mike Scott	.50
146	Mark McGwire	3.00
151	Dwight Gooden	.50
158	Ken Griffey Jr.	2.50
162	George Brett	2.25
165	Ruben Sierra	.50
167	Kirby Puckett	2.00
171	Carlton Fisk	1.50
172	Fred McGriff	.50
176	Wade Boggs	2.00
178	Tim Raines	.50
181	Bobby Bonilla	.50
189	Kelly Gruber	.25
197	Dennis Eckersley	1.00
205	Cecil Fielder	.50
212	Jackie Robinson	2.00
216	Babe Ruth	3.00
229	Barry Bonds	4.00
240	Jose Rijo	.50
248	Sandy Alomar Jr.	.50
251	Ron Gant	.50
259	David Justice	.50
261	Bob Welch	.50
266	Doug Drabek	.50
268	Rafael Palmeiro	1.25
271	Paul Molitor	1.50
275	Bobby Thigpen	.50
279	Edgar Martinez	.50
282	Dave Winfield	1.50
283	Mark Grace	.50
288	Dwight Evans	.50
289	Dave Henderson	.50
294	Lee Smith	.50
303	Ramon Martinez	.50
321	Ty Cobb	1.50

1992-2000 Sports Illustrated For Kids

A new series, with cards numbered consecutively from #1, of magazine insert cards was begun with SI For Kids' in its January 1992 issue. Like the earlier series, cards are 2-1/2" x 3-1/2" inches and most often found as a nine-card panel, with each card perforated for removal from the magazine and separation from the other cards. As before, the cards feature a number of different designs, formats and back treatments. Backs usually include a few personal details and a trivia question. Only the cards of pro baseball players are checklisted here.

#	Player	NM/M
	Complete Set (157):	150.00
	Common Player:	.25
24	Terry Pendleton	.25
29	Kirby Puckett	2.00
36	Roger Clemens	2.25
40	Tom Glavine	.45
45	Frank Thomas	1.50
50	Jim Abbott	.25
54	Roberto Alomar	.25
64	Matt Williams	.25
68	Bobby Bonilla	.25
72	Chuck Finley	.25
75	Danny Tartabull	.25
81	Jack Morris	.25
86	Will Clark	.25
108	Lou Gehrig	2.50
121	Juan Gonzalez	.75
132	Cal Ripken Jr.	4.00
136	Jack McDowell	.25
144	Marquis Grissom	.25
145	Andy Van Slyke	.25
152	Dennis Eckersley	1.00
157	Barry Bonds	4.00
162	Greg Maddux	2.00
168	Nolan Ryan	4.00
170	Dave Winfield	1.50
173	Ken Griffey Jr.	2.50
178	Wade Boggs	2.00
185	Kirk Gibson	.25
187	Albert Belle	.25
190	John Burkett	.25
196	John Kruk	.25
199	Randy Johnson	1.50
204	Lou Whitaker	.25
212	Yogi Berra	.50
236	Lenny Dykstra	.25
244	Carlos Baerga	.25
254	Joe Carter	.25
266	Chuck Carr	.25
268	Julie Croteau (Colorado Silver Bullets)	.25
270	Michael Jordan	3.00
274	Andres Galarraga	.25
278	Jeff Bagwell	1.50
281	John Olerud	.25
288	Tony Gwynn	2.00
292	Gregg Jefferies	.25
297	Mo Vaughn	.25
298	Moises Alou	.25
305	Jimmy Key	.40
311	Mike Mussina	.40
313	Mike Piazza	2.50
320	Stan Musial	2.00
327	Matt Williams	.25
343	Frank Thomas (Boyhood photo.)	1.00
349	Michael Jordan (Boyhood photo.)	2.00
359	Kenny Lofton	.25
362	Raul Mondesi	.25
381	David Cone	.25
386	Brady Anderson	.25
390	Eric Karros	.25
391	Paul O'Neill	.25
398	Eddie Murray	1.50
402	Barry Larkin	.25
407	Edgar Martinez	.25
412	Mark McGwire	3.00
416	Albert Belle (Cartoon)	.25
430	Mark Grace	.25
433	Chuck Knoblauch	.25
447	Chipper Jones	2.00
451	Tom Glavine (Boyhood photo.)	.25
455	Cal Ripken Jr. (Boyhood photo.)	3.00
462	Jeff Conine	.25
470	Hideo Nomo	.75
475	Bernie Williams	.25
478	Craig Biggio	.25
485	Jose Mesa	.25
497	Roberto Alomar	.35
503	John Smoltz	.25
505	Henry Rodriguez	.25
513	Rey Ordonez	.25
516	Ellis Burks	.25
518	Ivan Rodriguez	1.25
543	Alex Rodriguez	3.00
553	Mo Vaughn	.25
561	Andy Pettitte	.35
562	Barry Bonds	4.00
582	Andruw Jones	1.50
570	Randy Johnson (April Fool card as L.A. Laker.)	1.50
572	Ken Griffey Jr. (April Fool card as Orlando Magic.)	2.50
588	Brian Jordan	.25
589	Derek Jeter	4.00
596	Juan Gonzalez	.75
598	Andres Galarraga	.25
608	Mark McGwire	3.00
611	Pat Hentgen	.25
627	Cal Ripken Jr. (Cartoon as Tin Man.)	4.00
634	Sandy Alomar Jr.	.25
641	Brady Anderson	.25
652	Jeff Bagwell	1.50
669	Larry Walker	.25
673	Roger Clemens	2.25
685	Frank Thomas	1.50
693	Denny Neagle	.25
695	Tony Gwynn	2.00
697	Mike Piazza	2.50
703	Kenny Lofton	.25
708	Moises Alou	.25
712	Dante Bichette	.25
720	John Wetteland	.25
721	Curt Schilling	.45
725	Nomar Garciaparra	2.00
734	Ken Griffey Jr. (Cartoon as The Cat in the Hat.)	2.50
737	Greg Maddux (Cartoon as Encyclopedia Brown.)	2.00
743	Sammy Sosa	2.00
749	David Wells	.25
No#	Mark McGwire (The Best of 1998)	2.50
758	Pedro Martinez	1.50
768	Ila Borders	.25
770	David Cone	.25
784	Mike Piazza (April Fool's - hockey player.)	2.50
790	Mark McGwire (April Fool's - Chicago Cub.)	3.00
795	Craig Biggio	.25
796	Tom Glavine	.25
802	Alex Rodriguez	3.00
804	Trevor Hoffman	.25
813	Rickey Henderson	1.50
815	Mo Vaughn	.25
817	Vinny Castilla	.25
820	John Smoltz	.25
825	Jose Canseco	.65
833	Matt Williams	.25
835	Derek Jeter	4.00
840	Ivan Rodriguez (As Darth Vader.)	1.25
841	Roger Clemens (As lion.)	2.25
846	Ken Caminiti (As Ghoul.)	.25
849	Roberto Alomar	.35
No#	Greg Maddux (Fall/Winter 1999)	2.00
No#	Ken Griffey Jr. (Fall/Winter 1999)	2.50
856	Randy Johnson	1.50
866	Babe Ruth	3.00
869	Mickey Mantle	5.00
870	Jackie Robinson	5.00
882	Mark McGwire (Kid photo.)	3.00
884	Mariano Rivera	.35
892	Billy the Marlin (Mascot)	.25
896	The Phillie Phanatic (Mascot)	.25
901	Kevin Millwood	.25
906	Manny Ramirez	1.50
910	Bernie Williams	.25
914	Larry Walker	.25
918	Ken Griffey Jr.	2.50
922	David Wells	.25
929	Chipper Jones	2.00
935	Carlos Beltran	.50
941	Vladimir Guerrero	1.50
945	Andres Galarraga	.25
953	Jason Kendall (As Pokemon's Ash Ketchum.)	.40
955	Pedro Martinez	1.50
962	Todd Helton	1.25

1996-98 Sports Illustrated For Kids Legends

Unlike the nine-card panels which appear in every issue of SI For Kids, the Legends series appeared sporadically as a four-card panel honoring the past greats of many sports. While designs vary from issue to issue, the format of the cards has remained a consistent 2-9/16" x 4". Only the baseball players are listed here.

#	Player	NM/M
	Complete Set (7):	9.00
	Common Player:	.25
45	Sadaharu Oh	1.00
52	Willie Mays	2.00
66	Mike Schmidt	1.50
(1)	Mickey Mantle	3.00
(2)	Bob Feller	.50
(3)	Lou Brock	.50
(4)	Honus Wagner	.50

1999 SI for Kids 10th Anniversary Sheet

Saluting Sports Illustrated for Kids on its 10th anniversary, Major League Baseball, the Players' Association and the four card licensees created a a special eight-card insert sheet which appears in the magazine's July 1999 issue. The sheet consists of nine 2-1/2" x 3-1/2" cards printed on thin cardboard and perforated for easy separation. The Fleer and Upper Deck cards are very similar to those companies' regular 1999 issues, except for the absence of foil printing and UV coating. The Topps and Pacific offerings are new designs. All player cards feature action photos on front along with card company and SI for Kids logos. Backs have another photo plus stats, biographical data and copyright notice.

#	Player	NM/M
	Complete Sheet:	6.00
	Complete Set (9):	5.00
	Common Player:	.50
7	J.D. Drew (Fleer Tradition)	.50
49	Cal Ripken Jr. (Upper Deck)	1.00
205	Ken Griffey Jr. (Upper Deck)	.65
266	Sammy Sosa (SkyBox Thunder)	.65
---	Roger Clemens (Topps)	.50
---	Tony Gwynn (Pacific)	.50
---	Mark McGwire (Pacific)	.75
---	Mike Piazza (Topps)	.65
---	Sponsors' card	.10

1981 Spot-Bilt George Brett

This one-card set was released in both 1981 and 1982 (see stats on back to differentiate) in boxes of turf baseball shoes, for which Brett served on the athletic advisory staff. Cards are standard 2-1/2" x 3-1/2". Despite the card number 5 on the back, there are no other players in the series. Brett wore uniform #5.

#	Player	NM/M
5	George Brett	2.50

1981 Squirt

These cards, issued in conjunction with Topps, were issued as two-card panels in eight-pack cartons of the soft drink. Individual cards measure the standard 2-1/2" x 3-1/2", while the vertical panels measure 2-1/2" x 10-1/2", with a promotional card reading "Free Topps 1981 Baseball Cards" attached. The promotional card is blank-backed, while the player card backs are similar to Topps' regular issue, though re-numbered for inclusion in this 33-card set. Most of the game's top players are included. There are only 22 different two-card panels, as card numbers 1-11 appear in two different bottom panel combinations. Card fronts feature a color player portrait photo within a baseball design, team and position designation, and the Squirt logo.

#	Player	NM/M
	Complete Panel Set (22):	20.00
	Complete Singles Set (33):	20.00
	Common Panel:	.50
	Common Player:	.15
	Panel (1)	2.00
1	George Brett	1.50
12	Garry Templeton	.15
	Panel (2)	2.00
1	George Brett	1.50
23	Jerry Mumphrey	.15
	Panel (3)	.50
2	George Foster	.15
13	Rick Burleson	.15
	Panel (4)	.50
2	George Foster	.15
24	Tony Armas	.15
	Panel (5)	.50
3	Ben Oglivie	.15
14	Dave Kingman	.15
	Panel (6)	.50
3	Ben Oglivie	.15
25	Fred Lynn	.15
	Panel (7)	1.50
4	Steve Garvey	.50
15	Eddie Murray	.75
	Panel (8)	.75
4	Steve Garvey	.50
26	Ron LeFlore	.15
	Panel (9)	2.00
5	Reggie Jackson	1.50
16	Don Sutton	.50
	Panel (10)	2.00
5	Reggie Jackson	1.50
27	Steve Kemp	.15
	Panel (11)	.75
6	Bill Buckner	.15
17	Dusty Baker	.15
	Panel (12)	1.50
6	Bill Buckner	.15
28	Rickey Henderson	1.50
	Panel (13)	.50
7	Jim Rice	.25
18	Jack Clark	.15
	Panel (14)	.50
7	Jim Rice	.25
29	John Castino	.15
	Panel (15)	3.00
8	Mike Schmidt	1.50
19	Dave Winfield	.75
	Panel (16)	2.00
8	Mike Schmidt	1.50
30	Cecil Cooper	.15
	Panel (17)	2.50
9	Rod Carew	1.00
20	Johnny Bench	1.00
	Panel (18)	1.00
9	Rod Carew	1.00
31	Bruce Bochte	.15
	Panel (19)	.50
10	Dave Parker	.15
21	Lee Mazzilli	.15
	Panel (20)	.65
10	Dave Parker	.15
32	Joe Charboneau	.25
	Panel (21)	3.00
11	Pete Rose	2.00
22	Al Oliver	.15
	Panel (22)	3.00
11	Pete Rose	2.00
33	Chet Lemon	.15

1982 Squirt

This set was again prepared in conjunction with Topps, but the 1982 Squirt cards are completely different from Topps' regular issue. Only 22 players are included in the full-color set, with the 2-1/2" x 3-1/2" player cards available on one- or two-player panels. Card panels come in four variations, with free grocery contest and scratch-off game cards taking one or two of the positions on the three-card panels. Card backs are numbered and list player statistics.

#	Player	NM/M
	Complete Set (22):	12.00
	Common Player:	.15
1	Cecil Cooper	.15
2	Jerry Remy	.15
3	George Brett	2.00
4	Alan Trammell	.15
5	Reggie Jackson	2.00
6	Kirk Gibson	.75
7	Dave Winfield	.75
8	Carlton Fisk	.75
9	Ron Guidry	.15
10	Dennis Leonard	.15
11	Rollie Fingers	.60
12	Pete Rose	2.50
13	Phil Garner	.15
14	Mike Schmidt	2.00
15	Dave Concepcion	.15
16	George Hendrick	.15
17	Andre Dawson	.35
18	George Foster	.75
19	Gary Carter	.75
20	Fernando Valenzuela	.15
21	Tom Seaver	1.00
22	Bruce Sutter	.60

1996 St. Louis Browns Historical Society

This collectors issue honoring the 1944 American League Champion St. Louis Browns was issued in conjunction with a reunion of that team in 1996, sponsored by the St. Louis Browns Historical Society. Every player on the '44 team is included in the set, representing the first-ever baseball card for some of them. Fronts of the 2-5/8" x 3-3/4" cards feature color portraits by artist Ronnie Joyner. Shades of brown form the border. Backs are also printed in brown tones and include a cartoon, 1944 season and World Series stats, lifetime stats, personal data, a career summary and part of a team "Timeline" of the 1944 season. It was reported 2,500 sets were issued at $10 retail.

#	Player	NM/M
	Complete Set (36):	10.00
	Common Player:	.50
1	Team Logo Card	.50
2	Don Gutteridge	.50
3	Milt Byrnes	.50
4	Al Hollingsworth	.50
5	Willis Hudlin	.50
6	Sig Jakucki	.50
7	Nelson Potter	.50
8	Len Schulte	.50
9	Vern Stephens	.50
10	Frank Demaree	.50
11	Al Zarilla	.50
12	Bob Muncrief	.50
13	Steve Sundra	.50
14	Jack Kramer	.50
15	Lefty West	.50
16	Denny Galehouse	.50
17	Luke Sewell	.50
18	Joe Schultz	.50
19	George McQuinn	.50
20	Ellis Clary	.50
21	Babe Martin	.50
22	Red Hayworth	.50
23	Frank Mancuso	.50
24	Tex Shirley	.50
25	Mike Chartak	.50
26	Mark Christman	.50

27	Tom Hafey	.50
28	Tom Turner	.50
29	Floyd Baker	.50
30	Mike Kreevich	.50
31	George Caster	.50
32	Gene Moore	.50
33	Chet Laabs	.50
34	Sam Zoldak	.50
35	Hal Epps	.50
36	Team Composite/ Checklist Card	.50

1987 St. Louis Cardinals Fire Safety

Approximately 25,000 fans in attendance at Busch Stadium on August 24 received this set produced by the U.S. Forestry Service. The cards measure 4" x 6". Fronts feature a full-color photo set inside an oval frame. Only the player's last name appears on front. Backs carry the player's name, position and personal data plus a Smokey Bear cartoon fire prevention message.

		NM/M
	Complete Set (25):	6.00
	Common Player:	.25
1	Ray Soff	.25
2	Todd Worrell	.25
3	John Tudor	.25
4	Pat Perry	.25
5	Rick Horton	.25
6	Dan Cox	.25
7	Bob Forsch	.25
8	Greg Mathews	.25
9	Bill Dawley	.25
10	Steve Lake	.25
11	Tony Pena	.25
12	Tom Pagnozzi	.25
13	Jack Clark	.25
14	Jim Lindeman	.25
15	Mike Laga	.25
16	Terry Pendleton	.25
17	Ozzie Smith	3.50
18	Jose Oquendo	.25
19	Tom Lawless	.25
20	Tom Herr	.25
21	Curt Ford	.25
22	Willie McGee	.25
23	Tito Landrum	.25
24	Vince Coleman	.25
25	Whitey Herzog	.25

1988 St. Louis Cardinals Fire Safety

This set of oversized (3" x 5") cards features full-color action photos that fill the entire front. A thin white line frames the player photo. The player name, team logo and Smokey Bear picture logo are printed in the lower-right corner. Black-and-white backs contain player information and a Smokey Bear fire prevention cartoon. The sets were distributed to young St. Louis fans as part of a U.S. Forest

Service fire prevention campaign. The National Association of State Foresters co-sponsored this set.

		NM/M
	0omplete Set (25):	6.00
	Common Player:	.25
1	Whitey Herzog	.25
2	Danny Cox	.25
3	Ken Dayley	.25
4	Jose DeLeon	.25
5	Bob Forsch	.25
6	Joe Magrane	.25
7	Greg Mathews	.25
8	Scott Terry	.25
9	John Tudor	.25
10	Todd Worrell	.25
11	Steve Lake	.25
12	Tom Pagnozzi	.25
13	Tony Pena	.25
14	Bob Horner	.25
15	Tom Lawless	.25
16	Jose Oquendo	.25
17	Terry Pendleton	.25
18	Ozzie Smith	3.50
19	Vince Coleman	.25
20	Curt Ford	.25
21	Willie McGee	.25
22	Larry McWilliams	.25
23	Steve Peters	.25
24	Luis Alicea	.25
25	Tom Brunansky	.25

1989 St. Louis Cardinals Fire Safety

This set featuring action player photos was issued by the U.S. Forest Service to promote fire safety. The cards measure 4" x 6" and include the player's name, team logo and a small picture of Smokey Bear beneath the player photo.

		NM/M
	Complete Set (25):	6.00
	Common Player:	.25
(1)	Tom Brunansky	.25
(2)	Cris Carpenter	.25
(3)	Vince Coleman	.25
(4)	John Costello	.25
(5)	Ken Dayley	.25
(6)	Jose DeLeon	.25
(7)	Frank DiPino	.25
(8)	Whitey Herzog	.25
(9)	Ken Hill	.25
(10)	Pedro Guerrero	.25
(11)	Tim Jones	.25
(12)	Jim Lindeman	.25
(13)	Joe Magrane	.25
(14)	Willie McGee	.25
(15)	John Morris	.25
(16)	Jose Oquendo	.25
(17)	Tom Pagnozzi	.25
(18)	Tony Pena	.25
(19)	Terry Pendleton	.25
(20)	Dan Quisenberry	.25
(21)	Ozzie Smith	3.50
(22)	Scott Terry	.25
(23)	Milt Thompson	.25
(24)	Denny Walling	.25
(25)	Todd Worrell	.25

1990 St. Louis Cardinals Fire Safety

Player photos dominate the fronts of this large-format (3" x 5") set sponsored by the U.S. Forest Service. Backs have a cartoon fire safety tip plus a few stats and personal data. The unnumbered cards are checklisted here in alphabetical order.

		NM/M
	Complete Set (27):	6.00
	Common Player:	.25
(1)	Vince Coleman	.25
(2)	Dave Collins	.25
(3)	Danny Cox	.25
(4)	Ken Dayley	.25
(5)	Frank DiPino	.25
(6)	Jose DeLeon	.25
(7)	Pedro Guerrero	.25
(8)	Whitey Herzog	.25
(9)	Rick Horton	.25
(10)	Rex Hudler	.25
(11)	Tim Jones	.25
(12)	Joe Magrane	.25
(13)	Greg Mathews	.25
(14)	Willie McGee	.25
(15)	John Morris	.25
(16)	Tom Niedenfuer	.25
(17)	Jose Oquendo	.25
(18)	Tom Pagnozzi	.25
(19)	Terry Pendleton	.25
(20)	Bryn Smith	.25
(21)	Lee Smith	.35
(22)	Ozzie Smith	3.50
(23)	Scott Terry	.25
(24)	Milt Thompson	.25
(25)	John Tudor	.25
(26)	Denny Walling	.25
(27)	Todd Zeile	.25

1991 St. Louis Cardinals Police

Cardinals. #34 Felix Jose

Color action photos are featured prominently on these large-format (2-5/8" x 4-1/16") cards. In the white border at bottom, the team name is printed in red, with the player name and uniform number printed in black. Backs feature a large cartoon safety message, career stats, some biographical data and the logos of the set's sponsors, Kansas City Life Insurance and the Greater St. Louis Law Enforcement Agencies. Backs are printed in red on white.

		NM/M
	Complete Set (24):	7.50
	Common Player:	.15
1	Ozzie Smith	5.00
7	Geronimo Pena	.15
9	Joe Torre	.50
10	Rex Hudler	.15
11	Jose Oquendo	.15
12	Craig Wilson	.15
16	Ray Lankford	.25
19	Tom Pagnozzi	.15
21	Gerald Perry	.15
23	Bernard Gilkey	.15
25	Milt Thompson	.15
27	Todd Zeile	.25
28	Pedro Guerrero	.15
29	Rich Gedman	.15
34	Felix Jose	.15
35	Frank DiPino	.15
36	Bryn Smith	.15
37	Scott Terry	.15
38	Todd Worrell	.15
39	Bob Tewksbury	.15
43	Ken Hill	.15
47	Lee Smith	.25
48	Jose DeLeon	.15
49	Juan Agosto	.15

1992 St. Louis Cardinals Police

Cardinals. #1 Ozzie Smith

The Cardinals were the subject of this set given out at Busch Stadium on April 25. Sponsored by Kansas City Life Insurance and distributed by Greater St. Louis law enforcement agencies, the cards are 2-1/2" x 4", and contain a special logo on the front which commemorates the team's 100th anniversary.

		NM/M
	Complete Set (27):	7.50
	Common Player:	.25
1	Ozzie Smith	5.00
7	Geronimo Pena	.25
9	Joe Torre	.50
10	Rex Hudler	.25
11	Jose Oquendo	.25
12	Craig Wilson	.25
16	Ray Lankford	.25
19	Tom Pagnozzi	.25
21	Gerald Perry	.25
23	Bernard Gilkey	.25
25	Milt Thompson	.25

1993 St. Louis Cardinals Police

BERNARD GILKEY OF • 23

This Cardinals/Kansas City Life police set features 2-5/8" x 4" cards with a blue border and "Cardinals" printed in red at top. The team logo appears in the lower-left corner, while the player's name, position and number appear lower-right. Backs are printed in red on a white background with the player's biography and statistics listed above a safety message.

		NM/M
	Complete Set (25):	7.50
	Common Player:	.25
1	Ozzie Smith	5.00
3	Brian Jordan	.35
5	Stan Royer	.25
9	Joe Torre	.50
11	Jose Oquendo	.25
16	Ray Lankford	.25
19	Luis Alicea	.25
21	Tom Pagnozzi	.25
22	Geronimo Pena	.25
23	Bernard Gilkey	.25
25	Gregg Jefferies	.25
26	Rob Murphy	.25
27	Todd Zeile	.25
28	Gerald Perry	.25
29	Hector Villanueva	.25
31	Donovan Osborne	.25
33	Rod Brewer	.25
39	Bob Tewksbury	.25
42	Mike Perez	.25
43	Rene Arocha	.25
46	Ozzie Canseco	.25
47	Lee Smith	.25
54	Rheal Cormier	.25
54	Tracy Woodson	.25
---	Checklist	.25

1994 St. Louis Cardinals Police

Cardinals

Gregg Jefferies 1st Base 25

An emphasis on border graphics marks the perennial Cardinals safety set for 1994. The 2-5/8" x 4" cards have a cream colored border. Near the left edge is a vertical red stripe with a team logo at top. Above the color photo at center is the team name. The player name and position are at lower-left. A baseball zooms out of the photo at lower-right car-

rying the uniform number. Backs are printed in red on white and feature a large cartoon safety message at center. Career stats and biographical data are at top. At bottom are sponsors' logos for the Kansas City Life Insurance Co., and Greater St. Louis Law Enforcement Agencies.

		NM/M
	Complete Set (26):	7.50
	Common Player:	.15
1	Ozzie Smith	5.00
3	Brian Jordan	.25
5	Stan Royer	.15
9	Joe Torre	.50
11	Jose Oquendo	.15
12	Erik Pappas	.15
16	Ray Lankford	.15
18	Luis Alicea	.15
19	Tom Pagnozzi	.15
21	Geronimo Pena	.15
22	Mark Whiten	.15
23	Bernard Gilkey	.15
25	Gregg Jefferies	.15
26	Omar Olivares	.15
27	Todd Zeile	.15
28	Gerald Perry	.15
34	Tom Urbani	.15
36	Paul Kilgus	.15
38	Allen Watson	.15
39	Bob Tewksbury	.15
40	Rick Sutcliffe	.15
42	Mike Perez	.15
43	Rene Arocha	.15
46	Rob Murphy	.15
48	Rich Batchelor	.15
52	Rheal Cormier	.15

1995 St. Louis Cardinals Police

In 1995, the Cardinals safety set was sponsored by Kansas City Life Insurance Co., and distributed by law enforcement agencies in the greater St. Louis area. The cards measure about 2-5/8" x 4" and feature action photos on front. The team name is scripted at bottom and the player's last name and "1995" are vertically at right. Backs have a few vital data, a career stats line, a safety message and sponsor's logo. Cards are listed here in alphabetical order.

		NM/M
	Complete Set (12):	7.50
	Common Player:	.50
(1)	Rene Arocha	.50
(2)	Scott Cooper	.50
(3)	Tripp Cromer	.50
(4)	Bernard Gilkey	.50
(5)	Tom Henke	.50
(6)	Ken Hill	.50
(7)	Danny Jackson	.50
(8)	Brian Jordan	.50
(9)	Ray Lankford	.50
(10)	Jose Oquendo	.50
(11)	Tom Pagnozzi	.50
(12)	Ozzie Smith	5.00

1996 St. Louis Cardinals Police

Once again for 1996, the Cardinals safety set was sponsored by Kansas City Life Insurance Co., and distributed by law enforcement agencies in the greater St. Louis area. The cards measure about 2-5/8" x 4" and feature action photos on front. The team name is vertically in a ghosted strip at left. At bottom, beneath a "torn" photo edge are the player's last name, uniform number and the team logo. Backs have a few vital data, a career stats line, a safety message and sponsor's logo.

		NM/M
	Complete Set (26):	10.00
	Common Player:	.25
1	Ozzie Smith	5.00
3	Brian Jordan	.25
5	Ron Gant	.25
8	Gary Gaetti	.25
12	Tony LaRussa	.25
12	Royce Clayton	.25
16	Ray Lankford	.25
19	Tom Pagnozzi	.25
22	Mike Gallego	.25
23	Mark Sweeney	.25
24	Tom Urbani	.25
29	Danny Jackson	.25
30	Todd Stottlemyre	.25
31	Donovan Osborne	.25
32	Rick Honeycutt	.25
37	T.J. Mathews	.25
38	Mike Morgan	.25
38	Pat Borders	.25
40	Andy Benes	.25
41	Alan Benes	.25
43	Dennis Eckersley	3.00

1998 St. Louis Cardinals Police

Similar in format to those used in the preceding years, this safety issue is printed on a 2-1/4" x 4" format. Fronts have color action photos surrounded by busy borders in predominantly yellow and green. A blue strip at bottom has player name and uniform number and team logo. Backs are in red-and-white with a few biographical details and stats, a cartoon baseball figure, safety message and sponsors' credits. Cards are checklisted here by uniform number.

		NM/M
	Complete Set (26):	8.00
	Common Player:	.25
3	Brian Jordan	.25
5	Ron Gant	.25
7	Delino DeShields	.25
8	Gary Gaetti	.25
10	Tony LaRussa	.25
11	Royce Clayton	.25
13	David Howard	.25
16	Ray Lankford	.25
19	Tom Pagnozzi	.25
25	Mark McGwire	6.00
26	Eli Marrero	.25
28	Lance Painter	.25
30	Todd Stottlemyre	.25
35	Matt Morris	.25
37	Kent Bottenfield	.25
38	Manny Aybar	.25
41	Alan Benes	.25
43	Kent Mercker	.25
45	Jeff Brantley	.25
46	Mark Petkovsek	.25
47	John Mabry	.25
49	Tom Lampkin	.25
50	John Frascatore	.25
54	Willie McGee	.25
57	Curtis King	.25
---	Fredbird (Mascot)	.25

46	Mark Petkovsek	.25
47	John Mabry	.25
48	Tony Fossas	.25
51	Willie McGee	.25
---	Fredbird/Checklist (Mascot)	.25

2000 St. Louis Cardinals Police

ST. LOUIS 2000

The Cardinals issued this safety set to fans 15 and under at the April 22 game in Busch Stadium. The 2-5/8" x 4" cards have game-action color photos bordered in white. Backs are in red on white with a few bits of personal data, a cartoon safety message and the logo of sponsoring Kansas City Life Insurance, which provided the cards for distribution by the Metropolitan Chiefs and Sheriffs Assn. Cards are checklisted here by uniform number. The checklist of actually-issued cards does not correspond with the checklist on the Fredbird card due to the trades which sent away Kent Bottenfield, Joe McEwing, Brian McRae and Paul Spoljaric.

		NM/M
Complete Set (23):		6.00
Common Player:		.25
3	Edgar Renteria	.45
4	Fernando Vina	.25
5	Thomas Howard	.25
7	J.D. Drew	1.50
10	Tony LaRussa	.25
12	Shawon Dunston	.25
16	Ray Lankford	.25
21	Craig Paquette	.25
22	Mike Matheny	.25
23	Fernando Tatis	.25
24	Eric Davis	.25
25	Mark McGwire	3.00
26	Eli Marrero	.25
31	Alan Benes	.25
36	Scott Radinsky	.25
40	Andy Benes	.25
41	Pat Hentgen	.25
43	Dave Veres	.25
55	Garrett Stephenson	.25
57	Darryl Kile	.25
58	Heathcliff Slocumb	.25
66	Rick Ankiel	.25
	Fredbird/Checklist	.25

1991 Stadium Club Promos

Topps' response to the upscale Leaf baseball card issue was a new brand labeled Stadium Club. To introduce the premium cards, a set of 50 promo cards was produced with single cards distributed to employees and candy companies. Production has been reported in the area of 600 of each card. The promos differ from the issued cards on front in that there are four horizontal gold-foil stripes on the promos, instead of three. The back of each promo card is identical, showing a 1986 Topps Traded Jose Canseco card. The unnumbered cards are checklisted here in alphabetical order.

		NM/M
Complete Set (50):		150.00
Common Player:		2.50
(1)	Allan Anderson	2.50
(2)	Steve Balboni	2.50
(3)	Jeff Ballard	2.50
(4)	Jesse Barfield	2.50
(5)	Andy Benes	2.50
(6)	Bobby Bonilla	2.50
(7)	Chris Bosio	2.50
(8)	Daryl Boston	2.50
(9)	Chuck Cary	2.50
(10)	Pat Combs	2.50
(11)	Delino DeShields	2.50
(12)	Shawon Dunston	2.50
(13)	Alvaro Espinoza	2.50
(14)	Sid Fernandez	2.50
(15)	Bob Geren	2.50
(16)	Brian Holman	2.50
(17)	Jay Howell	2.50
(18)	Stan Javier	2.50
(19)	Dave Johnson	2.50
(20)	Howard Johnson	2.50
(21)	Kevin Maas	2.50
(22)	Shane Mack	2.50
(23)	Joe Magrane	2.50
(24)	Denny Martinez	2.50
(25)	Don Mattingly	30.00
(26)	Ben McDonald	15.00
(27)	Eddie Murray	15.00
(28)	Matt Nokes	2.50
(29)	Greg Olson	2.50
(30)	Gregg Olson	2.50
(31)	Jose Oquendo	2.50
(32)	Tony Phillips	2.50
(33)	Rafael Ramirez	2.50
(34)	Dennis Rasmussen	2.50
(35)	Billy Ripken	2.50
(36)	Nolan Ryan	65.00
(37)	Bill Sampen	2.50
(38)	Steve Sax	2.50
(39)	Mike Scioscia	2.50
(40)	David Segui	2.50
(41)	Zane Smith	2.50
(42)	B.J. Surhoff	2.50
(43)	Bobby Thigpen	2.50
(44)	Alan Trammell	2.50
(45)	Fernando Valenzuela	2.50
(46)	Andy Van Slyke	2.50
(47)	Hector Villanueva	2.50
(48)	Larry Walker	2.50
(49)	Walt Weiss	2.50
(50)	Bob Welch	2.50

1991 Stadium Club

One of the most popular sets of 1991, this 600-card issue was released in two 300-card series. The cards were available in foil packs only. No factory sets were available. The cards feature borderless high gloss photos on the front and a player evaluation and card photo on the back. Each card can be found with two different letters preceding the copyright cymbol on back. A special Stadium Club membership package was made available for $29.95 with 10 proof of purchase seals from wrappers.

		NM/M
Complete Set (600):		20.00
Common Player:		.05
Series 1 or 2 Pack (13):		.60
Series 1 or 2 Box (36):		15.00
1	Dave Stewart	.05
2	Wally Joyner	.05
3	Shawon Dunston	.05
4	Darren Daulton	.05
5	Will Clark	.05
6	Sammy Sosa	1.00
7	Dan Plesac	.05
8	Marquis Grissom	.05
9	Erik Hanson	.05
10	Geno Petralli	.05
11	Jose Rijo	.05
12	Carlos Quintana	.05
13	Junior Ortiz	.05
14	Bob Walk	.05
15	Mike Macfarlane	.05
16	Eric Yelding	.05
17	Bryn Smith	.05
18	Bip Roberts	.05
19	Mike Scioscia	.05
20	Mark Williamson	.05
21	Don Mattingly	1.00
22	John Franco	.05
23	Chet Lemon	.05
24	Tom Henke	.05
25	Jerry Browne	.05
26	Dave Justice	.05
27	Mark Langston	.05
28	Damon Berryhill	.05
29	Kevin Bass	.05
30	Scott Fletcher	.05
31	Moises Alou	.05
32	Dave Valle	.05
33	Jody Reed	.05
34	Dave West	.05
35	Kevin McReynolds	.05
36	Pat Combs	.05
37	Eric Davis	.05
38	Bret Saberhagen	.05
39	Stan Javier	.05
40	Chuck Cary	.05
41	Tony Phillips	.05
42	Lee Smith	.05
43	Tim Teufel	.05
44	Lance Dickson	.05
45	Greg Litton	.05
46	Teddy Higuera	.05
47	Edgar Martinez	.05
48	Steve Avery	.05
49	Walt Weiss	.05
50	David Segui	.05
51	Andy Benes	.05
52	Karl Rhodes	.05
53	Neal Heaton	.05
54	Dan Gladden	.05
55	Luis Rivera	.05
56	Kevin Brown	.05
57	Frank Thomas	.75
58	Terry Mulholland	.05
59	Dick Schofield	.05
60	Ron Darling	.05
61	Sandy Alomar, Jr.	.05
62	Dave Stieb	.05
63	Alan Trammell	.05
64	Matt Nokes	.05
65	Lenny Harris	.05
66	Milt Thompson	.05
67	Storm Davis	.05
68	Joe Oliver	.05
69	Andres Galarraga	.05
70	Ozzie Guillen	.05
71	Ken Howell	.05
72	Garry Templeton	.05
73	Derrick May	.05
74	Xavier Hernandez	.05
75	Dave Parker	.05
76	Rick Aguilera	.05
77	Robby Thompson	.05
78	Pete Incaviglia	.05
79	Bob Welch	.05
80	Randy Milligan	.05
81	Chuck Finley	.05
82	Alvin Davis	.05
83	Tim Naehring	.05
84	Jay Bell	.05
85	Joe Magrane	.05
86	Howard Johnson	.05
87	Jack McDowell	.05
88	Kevin Seitzer	.05
89	Bruce Ruffin	.05
90	Fernando Valenzuela	.05
91	Terry Kennedy	.05
92	Barry Larkin	.05
93	Larry Walker	.05
94	Luis Salazar	.05
95	Gary Sheffield	.45
96	Bobby Witt	.05
97	Lonnie Smith	.05
98	Bryan Harvey	.05
99	Mookie Wilson	.05
100	Dwight Gooden	.05
101	Lou Whitaker	.05
102	Ron Karkovice	.05
103	Jesse Barfield	.05
104	Jose DeJesus	.05
105	Benito Santiago	.05
106	Brian Holman	.05
107	Rafael Ramirez	.05
108	Ellis Burks	.05
109	Mike Bielecki	.05
110	Kirby Puckett	1.00
111	Terry Shumpert	.05
112	Chuck Crim	.05
113	Todd Benzinger	.05
114	Brian Barnes	.05
115	Carlos Baerga	.05
116	Kal Daniels	.05
117	Dave Johnson	.05
118	Andy Van Slyke	.05
119	John Burkett	.05
120	Rickey Henderson	.75
121	Tim Jones	.05
122	Daryl Irvine	.05
123	Ruben Sierra	.05
124	Jim Abbott	.05
125	Daryl Boston	.05
126	Greg Maddux	1.00
127	Von Hayes	.05
128	Mike Fitzgerald	.05
129	Wayne Edwards	.05
130	Greg Briley	.05
131	Rob Dibble	.05
132	Gene Larkin	.05
133	David Wells	.05
134	Steve Balboni	.05
135	Greg Vaughn	.05
136	Mark Davis	.05
137	Dave Rohde	.05
138	Eric Show	.05
139	Bobby Bonilla	.05
140	Dana Kiecker	.05
141	Gary Pettis	.05
142	Dennis Boyd	.05
143	Mike Benjamin	.05
144	Luis Polonia	.05
145	Doug Jones	.05
146	Al Newman	.05
147	Alex Fernandez	.05
148	Bill Doran	.05
149	Kevin Elster	.05
150	Len Dykstra	.05
151	Mike Gallego	.05
152	Tim Belcher	.05
153	Jay Buhner	.05
154	Ozzie Smith	1.00
155	Jose Canseco	.50
156	Gregg Olson	.05
157	Charlie O'Brien	.05
158	Frank Tanana	.05
159	George Brett	1.00
160	Jeff Huson	.05
161	Kevin Tapani	.05
162	Jerome Walton	.05
163	Charlie Hayes	.05
164	Chris Bosio	.05
165	Chris Sabo	.05
166	Lance Parrish	.05
167	Don Robinson	.05
168	Manuel Lee	.05
169	Dennis Rasmussen	.05
170	Wade Boggs	1.00
171	Bob Geren	.05
172	Mackey Sasser	.05
173	Julio Franco	.05
174	Otis Nixon	.05
175	Bert Blyleven	.05
176	Craig Biggio	.05
177	Eddie Murray	.75
178	Randy Tomlin	.05
179	Tino Martinez	.05
180	Carlton Fisk	.75
181	Dwight Smith	.05
182	Scott Garrelts	.05
183	Jim Gantner	.05
184	Dickie Thon	.05
185	John Farrell	.05
186	Cecil Fielder	.05
187	Glenn Braggs	.05
188	Allan Anderson	.05
189	Kurt Stillwell	.05
190	Jose Oquendo	.05
191	Joe Orsulak	.05
192	Ricky Jordan	.05
193	Kelly Downs	.05
194	Delino DeShields	.05
195	Omar Vizquel	.05
196	Mark Carreon	.05
197	Mike Harkey	.05
198	Jack Howell	.05
199	Lance Johnson	.05
200	Nolan Ryan	2.00
201	John Marzano	.05
202	Doug Drabek	.05
203	Mark Lemke	.05
204	Steve Sax	.05
205	Greg Harris	.05
206	B.J. Surhoff	.05
207	Todd Burns	.05
208	Jose Gonzalez	.05
209	Mike Scott	.05
210	Dave Magadan	.05
211	Dante Bichette	.05
212	Trevor Wilson	.05
213	Hector Villanueva	.05
214	Dan Pasqua	.05
215	Greg Colbrunn	.05
216	Mike Jeffcoat	.05
217	Harold Reynolds	.05
218	Paul O'Neill	.05
219	Mark Guthrie	.05
220	Barry Bonds	2.00
221	Jimmy Key	.05
222	Billy Ripken	.05
223	Tom Pagnozzi	.05
224	Bo Jackson	.10
225	Sid Fernandez	.05
226	Mike Marshall	.05
227	John Kruk	.05
228	Mike Fetters	.05
229	Eric Anthony	.05
230	Ryne Sandberg	1.00
231	Carney Lansford	.05
232	Jose Lind	.05
233	Darryl Hamilton	.05
234	Tom Browning	.05
235	Spike Owen	.05
236	Juan Gonzalez	.40
237	Felix Fermin	.05
238	Felix Fermin	.05
239	Keith Miller	.05
240	Mark Gubicza	.05
241	Kent Anderson	.05
242	Alvaro Espinoza	.05
243	Dale Murphy	.20
244	Orel Hershiser	.05
245	Paul Molitor	.75
246	Eddie Whitson	.05
247	Joe Girardi	.05
248	Kent Hrbek	.05
249	Bill Sampen	.05
250	Kevin Mitchell	.05
251	Mariano Duncan	.05
252	Scott Bradley	.05
253	Mike Greenwell	.05
254	Tom Gordon	.05
255	Todd Zeile	.05
256	Bobby Thigpen	.05
257	Gregg Jefferies	.05
258	Kenny Rogers	.05
259	Shane Mack	.05
260	Zane Smith	.05
261	Mitch Williams	.05
262	Jim DeShaies	.05
263	Dave Winfield	.75
264	Ben McDonald	.05
265	Randy Ready	.05
266	Pat Borders	.05
267	Jose Uribe	.05
268	Derek Lilliquist	.05
269	Greg Brock	.05
270	Ken Griffey Jr.	1.25
271	Jeff Gray	.05
272	Danny Tartabull	.05
273	Dennis Martinez	.05
274	Robin Ventura	.05
275	Randy Myers	.05
276	Jack Daugherty	.05
277	Greg Gagne	.05
278	Jay Howell	.05
279	Mike LaValliere	.05
280	Rex Hudler	.05
281	Mike Simms	.05
282	Kevin Maas	.05
283	Jeff Ballard	.05
284	Dave Henderson	.05
285	Pete O'Brien	.05
286	Brook Jacoby	.05
287	Mike Henneman	.05
288	Greg Olson	.05
289	Greg Myers	.05
290	Mark Grace	.05
291	Shawn Abner	.05
292	Frank Viola	.05
293	Lee Stevens	.05
294	Jason Grimsley	.05
295	Matt Williams	.05
296	Ron Robinson	.05
297	Tom Brunansky	.05
298	Checklist	.05
299	Checklist	.05
300	Checklist	.05
301	Darryl Strawberry	.05
302	Bud Black	.05
303	Harold Baines	.05
304	Roberto Alomar	.20
305	Norm Charlton	.05
306	Gary Thurman	.05
307	Mike Felder	.05
308	Tony Gwynn	1.00
309	Roger Clemens	1.00
310	Andre Dawson	.25
311	Scott Radinsky	.05
312	Bob Melvin	.05
313	Kirk McCaskill	.05
314	Pedro Guerrero	.05
315	Walt Terrell	.05
316	Sam Horn	.05
317	Wes Chamberlain RC	.05
318	Pedro Munoz RC	.05
319	Roberto Kelly	.05
320	Mark Portugal	.05
321	Tim McIntosh	.05
322	Jesse Orosco	.05
323	Gary Green	.05
324	Greg Harris	.05
325	Hubie Brooks	.05
326	Chris Nabholz	.05
327	Terry Pendleton	.05
328	Eric King	.05
329	Chili Davis	.05
330	Anthony Telford	.05
331	Kelly Gruber	.05
332	Dennis Eckersley	.65
333	Mel Hall	.05
334	Bob Kipper	.05
335	Willie McGee	.05
336	Steve Olin	.05
337	Steve Buechele	.05
338	Scott Leius	.05
339	Hal Morris	.05
340	Jose Offerman	.05
341	Kent Mercker	.05
342	Ken Griffey	.05
343	Pete Harnisch	.05
344	Kirk Gibson	.05
345	Dave Smith	.05
346	Dave Martinez	.05
347	Atlee Hammaker	.05
348	Brian Downing	.05
349	Todd Hundley	.05
350	Candy Maldonado	.05
351	Dwight Evans	.05
352	Gary Searcy	.05
353	Gary Gaetti	.05
354	Jeff Reardon	.05
355	Travis Fryman	.05
356	Dave Righetti	.05
357	Fred McGriff	.05
358	Don Slaught	.05
359	Gene Nelson	.05
360	Billy Spiers	.05
361	Lee Guetterman	.05
362	Darren Lewis	.05
363	Duane Ward	.05
364	Lloyd Moseby	.05
365	John Smoltz	.05
366	Felix Jose	.05
367	David Cone	.05
368	Wally Backman	.05
369	Rich Garces	.05
370	Jeff Montgomery	.05
371	Billy Hatcher	.05
372	Bill Swift	.05
373	Jim Eisenreich	.05
374	Rob Ducey	.05
375	Tim Crews	.05
376	Steve Finley	.05
377	Jeff Blauser	.05
378	Willie Wilson	.05
379	Gerald Perry	.05
380	Jose Mesa	.05
381	Pat Kelly	.05
382	Matt Merullo	.05
383	Ivan Calderon	.05
384	Scott Chiamparino	.05
385	Lloyd McClendon	.05
386	Dave Bergman	.05
387	Ed Sprague	.05
388	Jeff Bagwell RC	3.00
389	Brett Butler	.05
390	Larry Andersen	.05
391	Alex Cole	.05
392	Alex Cole (Photo is Otis Nixon.)	.05
393	Mike Heath	.05
394	Danny Darwin	.05
395	Steve Lake	.05
396	Tim Layana	.05
397	Terry Leach	.05
398	Bill Wegman	.05
399	Mark McGwire	1.50
400	Mike Boddicker	.05
401	Steve Howe	.05
402	Bernard Gilkey	.05
403	Thomas Howard	.05
404	Rafael Belliard	.05
405	Tom Candiotti	.05
406	Rene Gonzalez	.05
407	Chuck McElroy	.05
408	Paul Sorrento	.05
409	Randy Johnson	.75
410	Brady Anderson	.05
411	Dennis Cook	.05
412	Mickey Tettleton	.05
413	Mike Stanton	.05
414	Ken Oberkfell	.05
415	Rick Honeycutt	.05
416	Nelson Santovenia	.05
417	Bob Tewksbury	.05
418	Brent Mayne	.05
419	Steve Farr	.05
420	Phil Stephenson	.05
421	Jeff Russell	.05
422	Chris James	.05
423	Tim Leary	.05
424	Gary Carter	.75
425	Glenallen Hill	.05
426	Matt Young	.05
427	Sid Bream	.05
428	Greg Swindell	.05
429	Scott Aldred	.05
430	Cal Ripken, Jr.	2.00
431	Bill Landrum	.05
432	Ernie Riles	.05
433	Danny Jackson	.05
434	Casey Candaele	.05
435	Ken Hill	.05
436	Jaime Navarro	.05
437	Lance Blankenship	.05
438	Randy Velarde	.05
439	Frank DiPino	.05
440	Carl Nichols	.05
441	Jeff Robinson	.05
442	Deion Sanders	.05
443	Vincente Palacios	.05
444	Devon White	.05
445	John Cerutti	.05
446	Tracy Jones	.05
447	Jack Morris	.05
448	Mitch Webster	.05
449	Bob Ojeda	.05
450	Oscar Azocar	.05
451	Luis Aquino	.05
452	Mark Whiten	.05
453	Stan Belinda	.05
454	Ron Gant	.05
455	Jose DeLeon	.05
456	Mark Salas	.05
457	Junior Felix	.05
458	Wally Whitehurst	.05
459	Phil Plantier RC	.05
460	Juan Berenguer	.05
461	Franklin Stubbs	.05
462	Joe Boever	.05
463	Tim Wallach	.05
464	Mike Moore	.05
465	Albert Belle	.05
466	Mike Witt	.05
467	Craig Worthington	.05
468	Jerald Clark	.05
469	Scott Terry	.05
470	Milt Cuyler	.05
471	John Smiley	.05
472	Charles Nagy	.05
473	Alan Mills	.05
474	John Russell	.05
475	Bruce Hurst	.05
476	Andujar Cedeno	.05
477	Dave Eiland	.05
478	Brian McRae RC	.10
479	Mike LaCoss	.05
480	Chris Gwynn	.05
481	Jamie Moyer	.05
482	John Olerud	.05
483	Efrain Valdez	.05
484	Sil Campusano	.05
485	Pascual Perez	.05
486	Gary Redus	.05
487	Andy Hawkins	.05
488	Cory Snyder	.05
489	Chris Hoiles	.05
490	Ron Hassey	.05
491	Gary Wayne	.05
492	Mark Lewis	.05
493	Scott Coolbaugh	.05
494	Gerald Young	.05
495	Juan Samuel	.05
496	Willie Fraser	.05
497	Jeff Treadway	.05
498	Vince Coleman	.05
499	Cris Carpenter	.05
500	Jack Clark	.05
501	Kevin Appier	.05
502	Rafael Palmeiro	.65
503	Hensley Meulens	.05
504	George Bell	.05
505	Tony Pena	.05
506	Roger McDowell	.05
507	Luis Sojo	.05
508	Mike Schooler	.05
509	Robin Yount	.75
510	Jack Armstrong	.05
511	Rick Cerone	.05
512	Curt Wilkerson	.05
513	Joe Carter	.05
514	Tim Burke	.05
515	Tony Fernandez	.05
516	Ramon Martinez	.05
517	Tim Hulett	.05
518	Terry Steinbach	.05
519	Pete Smith	.05
520	Ken Caminiti	.05
521	Shawn Boskie	.05
522	Mike Pagliarulo	.05
523	Tim Raines	.05
524	Alfredo Griffin	.05
525	Henry Cotto	.05
526	Mike Stanley	.05
527	Charlie Leibrandt	.05
528	Jeff King	.05
529	Eric Plunk	.05
530	Tom Lampkin	.05
531	Steve Bedrosian	.05
532	Tom Herr	.05
533	Craig Lefferts	.05
534	Jeff Reed	.05

535	Mickey Morandini	.05
536	Greg Cadaret	.05
537	Ray Lankford	.05
538	John Candelaria	.05
539	Rob Deer	.05
540	Brad Arnsberg	.05
541	Mike Sharperson	.05
542	Jeff Robinson	.05
543	Mo Vaughn	.05
544	Jeff Parrett	.05
545	Willie Randolph	.05
546	Herm Winningham	.05
547	Jeff Innis	.05
548	Chuck Knoblauch	.05
549	Tommy Greene	.05
550	Jeff Hamilton	.05
551	Barry Jones	.05
552	Ken Dayley	.05
553	Rick Dempsey	.05
554	Greg Smith	.05
555	Mike Devereaux	.05
556	Keith Comstock	.05
557	Paul Faries	.05
558	Tom Glavine	.35
559	Craig Grebeck	.05
560	Scott Erickson	.05
561	Joel Skinner	.05
562	Mike Morgan	.05
563	Dave Gallagher	.05
564	Todd Stottlemyre	.05
565	Rich Rodriguez	.05
566	Craig Wilson RC	.05
567	Jeff Brantley	.05
568	Scott Kamieniecki	.05
569	Steve Decker	.05
570	Juan Agosto	.05
571	Tommy Gregg	.05
572	Kevin Wickander	.05
573	Jamie Quirk	.05
574	Jerry Don Gleaton	.05
575	Chris Hammond	.05
576	Luis Gonzalez RC	1.00
577	Russ Swan	.05
578	Jeff Conine RC	.50
579	Charlie Hough	.05
580	Jeff Kunkel	.05
581	Darrel Akerfelds	.05
582	Jeff Manto	.05
583	Alejandro Pena	.05
584	Mark Davidson	.05
585	Bob MacDonald	.05
586	Paul Assenmacher	.05
587	Dan Wilson	.05
588	Tom Bolton	.05
589	Brian Harper	.05
590	John Habyan	.05
591	John Orton	.05
592	Mark Gardner	.05
593	Turner Ward	.05
594	Bob Patterson	.05
595	Edwin Nunez	.05
596	Gary Scott	.05
597	Scott Bankhead	.05
598	Checklist	
599	Checklist	
600	Checklist	.05

Charter Members

Charter members of Topps Stadium Club received a package which included a 50-card multi-sport set unavailable in any other fashion. Cards are similar in format to S.C. regular issues, with full-bleed photos on front, UV coating and gold-foil highlights. This special edition has a gold foil "Charter Member" notation at the bottom of each card front. Backs have a simulated newspaper page describing a career highlight. The cards are unnumbered and the checklist here includes only the baseball cards from the set.

		NM/M
Complete Set (50):		12.50
Common Player:		.15
(1)	Sandy Alomar, Jr.	.15
(2)	George Brett	1.00
(3)	Barry Bonds	2.50
(4)	Ellis Burks	.15
(5)	Eric Davis	.15
(6)	Delino DeShields	.15
(7)	Doug Drabek	.15
(8)	Cecil Fielder	.15
(9)	Carlton Fisk	.50

(10)	Ken Griffey Jr., Ken Griffey Sr.	1.50
(11)	Billy Hatcher	.15
(12)	Andy Hawkins	.15
(13)	Rickey Henderson (A.L. MVP)	.50
(14)	Rickey Henderson (A.L. base-stealing leader.)	.50
(15)	Randy Johnson	.50
(16)	Dave Justice	.15
(17)	Mark Langston, Mike Witt	.15
(18)	Kevin Maas	.15
(19)	Ramon Martinez	.15
(20)	Willie McGee	.15
(21)	Terry Mulholland	.15
(22)	Jose Offerman	.15
(23)	Melido Perez	.15
(24)	Nolan Ryan (No-hitter.)	2.50
(25)	Nolan Ryan (300th win)	2.50
(26)	Ryne Sandberg	.75
(27)	Dave Stewart	.15
(28)	Dave Stieb	.15
(29)	Bobby Thigpen	.15
(30)	Fernando Valenzuela	.15
(31)	Frank Viola	.15
(32)	Bob Welch	.15

Members Only

Each member of Topps Stadium Club during 1991 received three packages of multi-sport cards bearing a special design and stamped "Members Only" in gold foil on the front. Cards followed the basic Stadium Club format of full-bleed action photos on front. Backs have a facsimile newspaper page - the "Stadium Club Herald" - which gives details of a career highlight. Cards are unnumbered and the baseball-only checklist here is arranged alphabetically.

		NM/M
Complete Set (30):		9.00
Common Player:		.15
(1)	A.L. Home Run Leaders (Jose Canseco, Cecil Fielder)	.15
(2)	Wilson Alvarez	.15
(3)	Andy Ashby	.15
(4)	Jeff Bagwell	1.00
(5)	Braves no-hitter (Kent Mercker, Mark Wohlers, Alejandro Pena)	.15
(6)	Roger Clemens	.75
(7)	David Cone	.15
(8)	Carlton Fisk	.50
(9)	Julio Franco	.15
(10)	Tom Glavine	.35
(11)	Tommy Greene	.15
(12)	Pete Harnisch	.15
(13)	Rickey Henderson (All-time theft leader.)	.50
(14)	Rickey Henderson (11th time A.L. theft leader)	.50
(15)	Howard Johnson	.15
(16)	Chuck Knoblauch	.15
(17)	Ray Lankford	.15
(18)	Denny Martinez	.15
(19)	Paul Molitor	.50
(20)	Jack Morris	.15
(21)	Orioles No-Hitter (Bob Milacki, Mike Flanagan, Mark Williamson, Gregg Olson, Chris Hoiles)	.15
(22)	Terry Pendleton (N.L. leading hitter)	.15
(23)	Terry Pendleton (MVP)	.15
(24)	Jeff Reardon	.15
(25)	Cal Ripken, Jr.	2.50
(26)	Nolan Ryan (7th no-hitter)	2.50
(27)	Nolan Ryan (22nd 100-K season)	2.50
(28)	Bret Saberhagen	.15
(29)	Robby Thompson	.15
(30)	Dave Winfield	.50

Nolan Ryan Bronze

One of the premiums included with charter membership in the Topps Stadium Club was a bronze replica of the Nolan Ryan card from the Charter Member's card set. The

replica measures 2-1/2" x 3-1/2" and reproduces both front and back of the Ryan card on a 10-oz. metal slab.

		NM/M
Nolan Ryan (Bronze)		15.00

1992 Stadium Club

This 900-card set was released in three 100-card series. Like the 1991 issue, the cards feature borderless high-gloss photos on the front. The flip sides feature the player's first Topps card and a player evaluation. Topps released updated cards in the third series for traded player and free agents. Several players appear on two cards. Special Members Choice cards are included in the set. Series III features special inserts of the last three number one draft picks: Phil Nevin, Brien Taylor and Chipper Jones.

		NM/M
Complete Set (900):		20.00
Common Player:		.05
Series 1, 2, 3 Pack (15):		.75
Series 1, 2, 3 Box (36):		15.00
1	Cal Ripken, Jr.	1.50
2	Eric Yelding	.05
3	Geno Petralli	.05
4	Wally Backman	.05
5	Milt Cuyler	.05
6	Kevin Bass	.05
7	Dante Bichette	.05
8	Ray Lankford	.05
9	Mel Hall	.05
10	Joe Carter	.05
11	Juan Samuel	.05
12	Jeff Montgomery	.05
13	Glenn Braggs	.05
14	Henry Cotto	.05
15	Deion Sanders	.05
16	Dick Schofield	.05
17	David Cone	.05
18	Chili Davis	.05
19	Tom Foley	.05
20	Ozzie Guillen	.05
21	Luis Salazar	.05
22	Terry Steinbach	.05
23	Chris James	.05
24	Jeff King	.05
25	Carlos Quintana	.05
26	Mike Maddux	.05
27	Tommy Greene	.05
28	Jeff Russell	.05
29	Steve Finley	.05
30	Mike Flanagan	.05
31	Darren Lewis	.05
32	Mark Lee	.05
33	Willie Fraser	.05
34	Mike Henneman	.05
35	Kevin Maas	.05
36	Dave Hansen	.05
37	Erik Hanson	.05
38	Bill Doran	.05
39	Mike Boddicker	.05
40	Vince Coleman	.05
41	Devon White	.05
42	Mark Gardner	.05
43	Scott Lewis	.05
44	Juan Berenguer	.05
45	Carney Lansford	.05
46	Curt Wilkerson	.05
47	Shane Mack	.05

48	Bip Roberts	.05
49	Greg Harris	.05
50	Ryne Sandberg	.75
51	Mark Whiten	.05
52	Jack McDowell	.05
53	Jimmy Jones	.05
54	Steve Lake	.05
55	Bud Black	.05
56	Dave Valle	.05
57	Kevin Reimer	.05
58	Rich Gedman	.05
59	Travis Fryman	.05
60	Steve Avery	.05
61	Francisco de la Rosa	.05
62	Scott Hemond	.05
63	Hal Morris	.05
64	Hensley Meulens	.05
65	Frank Castillo	.05
66	Gene Larkin	.05
67	Jose DeLeon	.05
68	Al Osuna	.05
69	Dave Cochrane	.05
70	Robin Ventura	.05
71	John Cerutti	.05
72	Kevin Gross	.05
73	Ivan Calderon	.05
74	Mike Macfarlane	.05
75	Stan Belinda	.05
76	Shawn Hillegas	.05
77	Pat Borders	.05
78	Jim Vatcher	.05
79	Bobby Rose	.05
80	Roger Clemens	.85
81	Craig Worthington	.05
82	Jeff Treadway	.05
83	Jamie Quirk	.05
84	Randy Bush	.05
85	Anthony Young	.05
86	Trevor Wilson	.05
87	Jaime Navarro	.05
88	Les Lancaster	.05
89	Pat Kelly	.05
90	Alvin Davis	.05
91	Larry Andersen	.05
92	Rob Deer	.05
93	Mike Sharperson	.05
94	Lance Parrish	.05
95	Cecil Espy	.05
96	Tim Spehr	.05
97	Dave Stieb	.05
98	Terry Mulholland	.05
99	Dennis Boyd	.05
100	Barry Larkin	.05
101	Ryan Bowen	.05
102	Felix Fermin	.05
103	Luis Alicea	.05
104	Tim Hulett	.05
105	Rafael Belliard	.05
106	Mike Gallego	.05
107	Dave Righetti	.05
108	Jeff Schaefer	.05
109	Ricky Bones	.05
110	Scott Erickson	.05
111	Matt Nokes	.05
112	Bob Scanlan	.05
113	Tom Candiotti	.05
114	Sean Berry	.05
115	Kevin Morton	.05
116	Scott Fletcher	.05
117	B.J. Surhoff	.05
118	Dave Magadan	.05
119	Bill Gullickson	.05
120	Marquis Grissom	.05
121	Lenny Harris	.05
122	Wally Joyner	.05
123	Kevin Brown	.05
124	Braulio Castillo	.05
125	Eric King	.05
126	Mark Portugal	.05
127	Calvin Jones	.05
128	Mike Heath	.05
129	Todd Van Poppel	.05
130	Benny Santiago	.05
131	Gary Thurman	.05
132	Joe Girardi	.05
133	Dave Eiland	.05
134	Orlando Merced	.05
135	Joe Orsulak	.05
136	John Burkett	.05
137	Ken Dayley	.05
138	Ken Hill	.05
139	Walt Terrell	.05
140	Mike Scioscia	.05
141	Junior Felix	.05
142	Ken Caminiti	.05
143	Carlos Baerga	.05
144	Tony Fossas	.05
145	Craig Grebeck	.05
146	Scott Bradley	.05
147	Kent Mercker	.05
148	Derrick May	.05
149	Jerald Clark	.05
150	George Brett	.85
151	Luis Quinones	.05
152	Mike Pagliarulo	.05
153	Jose Guzman	.05
154	Charlie O'Brien	.05
155	Darren Holmes	.05
156	Joe Boever	.05
157	Rich Monteleone	.05
158	Reggie Harris	.05
159	Roberto Alomar	.20
160	Robby Thompson	.05
161	Chris Hoiles	.05
162	Tom Pagnozzi	.05
163	Omar Vizquel	.05
164	John Candelaria	.05
165	Terry Shumpert	.05

166	Andy Mota	.05
167	Scott Bailes	.05
168	Jeff Blauser	.05
169	Steve Olin	.05
170	Doug Drabek	.05
171	Dave Bergman	.05
172	Eddie Whitson	.05
173	Gilberto Reyes	.05
174	Mark Grace	.05
175	Paul O'Neill	.05
176	Greg Cadaret	.05
177	Mark Williamson	.05
178	Casey Candaele	.05
179	Candy Maldonado	.05
180	Lee Smith	.05
181	Harold Reynolds	.05
182	Dave Justice	.05
183	Lenny Webster	.05
184	Donn Pall	.05
185	Gerald Alexander	.05
186	Jack Clark	.05
187	Stan Javier	.05
188	Ricky Jordan	.05
189	Franklin Stubbs	.05
190	Dennis Eckersley	.60
191	Danny Tartabull	.05
192	Pete O'Brien	.05
193	Mark Lewis	.05
194	Mike Felder	.05
195	Mickey Tettleton	.05
196	Dwight Smith	.05
197	Shawn Abner	.05
198	Jim Leyritz	.05
199	Mike Devereaux	.05
200	Craig Biggio	.05
201	Kevin Elster	.05
202	Rance Mulliniks	.05
203	Tony Fernandez	.05
204	Allan Anderson	.05
205	Herm Winningham	.05
206	Tim Jones	.05
207	Ramon Martinez	.05
208	Teddy Higuera	.05
209	John Kruk	.05
210	Jim Abbott	.05
211	Dean Palmer	.05
212	Mark Davis	.05
213	Jay Buhner	.05
214	Jesse Barfield	.05
215	Kevin Mitchell	.05
216	Mike LaValliere	.05
217	Mark Wohlers	.05
218	Dave Henderson	.05
219	Dave Smith	.05
220	Albert Belle	.05
221	Spike Owen	.05
222	Jeff Gray	.05
223	Paul Gibson	.05
224	Bobby Thigpen	.05
225	Mike Mussina	.30
226	Darrin Jackson	.05
227	Luis Gonzalez	.05
228	Greg Briley	.05
229	Brent Mayne	.05
230	Paul Molitor	.05
231	Al Leiter	.05
232	Andy Van Slyke	.05
233	Ron Tingley	.05
234	Bernard Gilkey	.05
235	Kent Hrbek	.05
236	Eric Karros	.05
237	Randy Velarde	.05
238	Andy Allanson	.05
239	Willie McGee	.05
240	Juan Gonzalez	.35
241	Karl Rhodes	.05
242	Luis Mercedes	.05
243	Billy Swift	.05
244	Tommy Gregg	.05
245	David Howard	.05
246	Dave Hollins	.05
247	Kip Gross	.05
248	Walt Weiss	.05
249	Mackey Sasser	.05
250	Cecil Fielder	.05
251	Jerry Browne	.05
252	Doug Dascenzo	.05
253	Darryl Hamilton	.05
254	Dann Bilardello	.05
255	Luis Rivera	.05
256	Larry Walker	.05
257	Ron Karkovice	.05
258	Bob Tewksbury	.05
259	Jimmy Key	.05
260	Bernie Williams	.05
261	Gary Wayne	.05
262	Mike Simms	.05
263	John Orton	.05
264	Marvin Freeman	.05
265	Mike Jeffcoat	.05
266	Roger Mason	.05
267	Edgar Martinez	.05
268	Henry Rodriguez	.05
269	Sam Horn	.05
270	Brian McRae	.05
271	Kirt Manwaring	.05
272	Mike Bordick	.05
273	Chris Sabo	.05
274	Jim Olander	.05
275	Greg Harris	.05
276	Dan Gakeler	.05
277	Bill Sampen	.05
278	Joel Skinner	.05
279	Curt Schilling	.05
280	Dale Murphy	.25
281	Lee Stevens	.05
282	Lonnie Smith	.05
283	Manuel Lee	.05

284	Shawn Boskie	.05
285	Kevin Seitzer	.05
286	Stan Royer	.05
287	John Dopson	.05
288	Scott Bullett	.05
289	Ken Patterson	.05
290	Todd Hundley	.05
291	Tim Leary	.05
292	Brett Butler	.05
293	Gregg Olson	.05
294	Jeff Brantley	.05
295	Brian Holman	.05
296	Brian Harper	.05
297	Brian Bohanon	.05
298	Checklist 1-100	.05
299	Checklist 101-200	.05
300	Checklist 201-300	.05
301	Frank Thomas	.65
302	Lloyd McClendon	.05
303	Brady Anderson	.05
304	Julio Valera	.05
305	Mike Aldrete	.05
306	Joe Oliver	.05
307	Todd Stottlemyre	.05
308	Rey Sanchez	.05
309	Gary Sheffield	.35
310	Andujar Cedeno	.05
311	Kenny Rogers	.05
312	Bruce Hurst	.05
313	Mike Schooler	.05
314	Mike Benjamin	.05
315	Chuck Finley	.05
316	Mark Lemke	.05
317	Scott Livingstone	.05
318	Chris Nabholz	.05
319	Mike Humphreys	.05
320	Pedro Guerrero	.05
321	Willie Banks	.05
322	Tom Goodwin	.05
323	Hector Wagner	.05
324	Wally Ritchie	.05
325	Mo Vaughn	.05
326	Joe Klink	.05
327	Cal Eldred	.05
328	Daryl Boston	.05
329	Mike Huff	.05
330	Jeff Bagwell	.65
331	Bob Milacki	.05
332	Tom Prince	.05
333	Pat Tabler	.05
334	Ced Landrum	.05
335	Reggie Jefferson	.05
336	Mo Sanford	.05
337	Kevin Ritz	.05
338	Gerald Perry	.05
339	Jeff Hamilton	.05
340	Tim Wallach	.05
341	Jeff Huson	.05
342	Jose Melendez	.05
343	Willie Wilson	.05
344	Mike Stanton	.05
345	Joel Johnston	.05
346	Lee Guetterman	.05
347	Francisco Olivares	.05
348	Dave Burba	.05
349	Tim Crews	.05
350	Scott Leius	.05
351	Danny Cox	.05
352	Wayne Housie	.05
353	Chris Donnels	.05
354	Chris George	.05
355	Gerald Young	.05
356	Roberto Hernandez	.05
357	Neal Heaton	.05
358	Todd Frohwirth	.05
359	Jose Vizcaino	.05
360	Jim Thome	.60
361	Craig Wilson	.05
362	Dave Haas	.05
363	Billy Hatcher	.05
364	John Barfield	.05
365	Luis Aquino	.05
366	Charlie Leibrandt	.05
367	Howard Farmer	.05
368	Bryn Smith	.05
369	Mickey Morandini	.05
370	Jose Canseco (Members Choice, should have been #597.)	.35
371	Jose Uribe	.05
372	Bob MacDonald	.05
373	Luis Sojo	.05
374	Craig Shipley	.05
375	Scott Bankhead	.05
376	Greg Gagne	.05
377	Scott Cooper	.05
378	Jose Offerman	.05
379	Billy Spiers	.05
380	John Smiley	.05
381	Jeff Carter	.05
382	Heathcliff Slocumb	.05
383	Jeff Tackett	.05
384	John Kiely	.05
385	John Vander Wal	.05
386	Omar Olivares	.05
387	Ruben Sierra	.05
388	Tom Gordon	.05
389	Charles Nagy	.05
390	Dave Stewart	.05
391	Pete Harnisch	.05
392	Tim Burke	.05
393	Roberto Kelly	.05
394	Freddie Benavides	.05
395	Tom Glavine	.35
396	Wes Chamberlain	.05
397	Eric Gunderson	.05
398	Dave West	.05
399	Ellis Burks	.05

400 Ken Griffey Jr.	1.00	518 Steve Chitren	.05	617 Alvin Davis	.05	735 Ken Hill	.05
401 Thomas Howard	.05	519 Moises Alou	.05	618 Craig Lefferts	.05	736 Xavier Hernandez	.05
402 Juan Guzman	.05	520 Wade Boggs	.75	619 Kevin McReynolds	.05	737 Gregg Jefferies	.05
403 Mitch Webster	.05	521 Pete Schourek	.05	620 Barry Bonds	1.50	738 Dick Schofield	.05
404 Matt Merullo	.05	522 Scott Terry	.05	621 Turner Ward	.05	739 Ron Robinson	.05
405 Steve Buechele	.05	523 Kevin Appier	.05	622 Joe Magrane	.05	740 Sandy Alomar	.05
406 Danny Jackson	.05	524 Gary Redus	.05	623 Mark Parent	.05	741 Mike Stanley	.05
407 Felix Jose	.05	525 George Bell	.05	624 Tom Browning	.05	742 Butch Henry	.05
408 Doug Piatt	.05	526 Jeff Kaiser	.05	625 John Smiley	.05	743 Floyd Bannister	.05
409 Jim Eisenreich	.05	527 Alvaro Espinoza	.05	626 Steve Wilson	.05	744 Brian Drahman	.05
410 Bryan Harvey	.05	528 Luis Polonia	.05	627 Mike Gallego	.05	745 Dave Winfield	.65
411 Jim Austin	.05	529 Darren Daulton	.05	628 Sammy Sosa	.75	746 Bob Walk	.05
412 Jim Poole	.05	530 Norm Charlton	.05	629 Rico Rossy	.05	747 Chris James	.05
413 Glenallen Hill	.05	531 John Olerud	.05	630 Royce Clayton	.05	748 Don Prybylinski	.05
414 Gene Nelson	.05	532 Dan Plesac	.05	631 Clay Parker	.05	749 Dennis Rasmussen	.05
415 Ivan Rodriguez	.60	533 Billy Ripken	.05	632 Pete Smith	.05	750 Rickey Henderson	.65
416 Frank Tanana	.05	534 Rod Nichols	.05	633 Jeff McKnight	.05	751 Chris Hammond	.05
417 Steve Decker	.05	535 Joey Cora	.05	634 Jack Daugherty	.05	752 Bob Kipper	.05
418 Jason Grimsley	.05	536 Harold Baines	.05	635 Steve Sax	.05	753 Dave Rohde	.05
419 Tim Layana	.05	537 Bob Ojeda	.05	636 Joe Hesketh	.05	754 Hubie Brooks	.05
420 Don Mattingly	.85	538 Mark Leonard	.05	637 Vince Horsman	.05	755 Bret Saberhagen	.05
421 Jerome Walton	.05	539 Danny Darwin	.05	638 Eric King	.05	756 Jeff Robinson	.05
422 Rob Ducey	.05	540 Shawon Dunston	.05	639 Joe Boever	.05	757 Pat Listach RC	.05
423 Andy Benes	.05	541 Pedro Munoz	.05	640 Jack Morris	.05	758 Bill Wegman	.05
424 John Marzano	.05	542 Mark Gubicza	.05	641 Arthur Rhodes	.05	759 John Wetteland	.05
425 Gene Harris	.05	543 Kevin Baez	.05	642 Bob Melvin	.05	760 Phil Plantier	.05
426 Tim Raines	.05	544 Todd Zeile	.05	643 Rick Wilkins	.05	761 Wilson Alvarez	.05
427 Bret Barberie	.05	545 Don Slaught	.05	644 Scott Scudder	.05	762 Scott Aldred	.05
428 Harvey Pulliam	.05	546 Tony Eusebio	.05	645 Bip Roberts	.05	763 Armando Reynoso RC	.05
429 Cris Carpenter	.05	547 Alonzo Powell	.05	646 Julio Valera	.05	764 Todd Benzinger	.05
430 Howard Johnson	.05	548 Gary Pettis	.05	647 Kevin Campbell	.05	765 Kevin Mitchell	.05
431 Orel Hershiser	.05	549 Brian Barnes	.05	648 Steve Searcy	.05	766 Gary Sheffield	.35
432 Brian Hunter	.05	550 Lou Whitaker	.05	649 Scott Kamieniecki	.05	767 Allan Anderson	.05
433 Kevin Tapani	.05	551 Keith Mitchell	.05	650 Kurt Stillwell	.05	768 Rusty Meacham	.05
434 Rick Reed	.05	552 Oscar Azocar	.05	651 Bob Welch	.05	769 Rick Parker	.05
435 Ron Witmeyer	.05	553 Stu Cole	.05	652 Andres Galarraga	.05	770 Nolan Ryan	1.50
436 Gary Gaetti	.05	554 Steve Wapnick	.05	653 Mike Jackson	.05	771 Jeff Ballard	.05
437 Alex Cole	.05	555 Derek Bell	.05	654 Bo Jackson	.10	772 Cory Snyder	.05
438 Chito Martinez	.05	556 Luis Lopez	.05	655 Sid Fernandez	.05	773 Denis Boucher	.05
439 Greg Litton	.05	557 Anthony Telford	.05	656 Mike Bielecki	.05	774 Jose Gonzales	.05
440 Julio Franco	.05	558 Tim Mauser	.05	657 Jeff Reardon	.05	775 Juan Guerrero	.05
441 Mike Munoz	.05	559 Glenn Sutko	.05	658 Wayne Rosenthal	.05	776 Ed Nunez	.05
442 Erik Pappas	.05	560 Darryl Strawberry	.05	659 Eric Bullock	.05	777 Scott Ruskin	.05
443 Pat Combs	.05	561 Tom Bolton	.05	660 Eric Davis	.05	778 Terry Leach	.05
444 Lance Johnson	.05	562 Cliff Young	.05	661 Randy Tomlin	.05	779 Carl Willis	.05
445 Ed Sprague	.05	563 Bruce Walton	.05	662 Tom Edens	.05	780 Bobby Bonilla	.05
446 Mike Greenwell	.05	564 Chico Walker	.05	663 Rob Murphy	.05	781 Duane Ward	.05
447 Milt Thompson	.05	565 John Franco	.05	664 Leo Gomez	.05	782 Joe Slusarski	.05
448 Mike Magnante	.05	566 Paul McClellan	.05	665 Greg Maddux	.75	783 David Segui	.05
449 Chris Haney	.05	567 Paul Abbott	.05	666 Greg Vaughn	.05	784 Kirk Gibson	.05
450 Robin Yount	.65	568 Gary Varsho	.05	667 Wade Taylor	.05	785 Frank Viola	.05
451 Rafael Ramirez	.05	569 Carlos Maldonado	.05	668 Brad Arnsberg	.05	786 Keith Miller	.05
452 Gino Minutelli	.05	570 Kelly Gruber	.05	669 Mike Moore	.05	787 Mike Morgan	.05
453 Tom Lampkin	.05	571 Jose Oquendo	.05	670 Mark Langston	.05	788 Kim Batiste	.05
454 Tony Perezchica	.05	572 Steve Frey	.05	671 Barry Jones	.05	789 Sergio Valdez	.05
455 Dwight Gooden	.05	573 Tino Martinez	.05	672 Bill Landrum	.05	790 Eddie Taubensee	.05
456 Mark Guthrie	.05	574 Bill Haselman	.05	673 Greg Swindell	.05	791 Jack Armstrong	.05
457 Jay Howell	.05	575 Eric Anthony	.05	674 Wayne Edwards	.05	792 Scott Fletcher	.05
458 Gary DiSarcina	.05	576 John Habyan	.05	675 Greg Olson	.05	793 Steve Farr	.05
459 John Smoltz	.05	577 Jeffrey McNeely	.05	676 Bill Pulsipher RC	.05	794 Dan Pasqua	.05
460 Will Clark	.05	578 Chris Bosio	.05	677 Bobby Witt	.05	795 Eddie Murray	.65
461 Dave Otto	.05	579 Joe Grahe	.05	678 Mark Carreon	.05	796 John Morris	.05
462 Rob Maurer	.05	580 Fred McGriff	.05	679 Patrick Lennon	.05	797 Francisco Cabrera	.05
463 Dwight Evans	.05	581 Rick Honeycutt	.05	680 Ozzie Smith	.75	798 Mike Perez	.05
464 Tom Brunansky	.05	582 Matt Williams	.05	681 John Briscoe	.05	799 Ted Wood	.05
465 Shawn Hare RC	.05	583 Cliff Brantley	.05	682 Matt Young	.05	800 Jose Rijo	.05
466 Geronimo Pena	.05	584 Rob Dibble	.05	683 Jeff Conine	.05	801 Danny Gladden	.05
467 Alex Fernandez	.05	585 Skeeter Barnes	.05	684 Phil Stephenson	.05	802 Arci Cianfrocco	.05
468 Greg Myers	.05	586 Greg Hibbard	.05	685 Ron Darling	.05	803 Monty Fariss	.05
469 Jeff Fassero	.05	587 Randy Milligan	.05	686 Bryan Hickerson	.05	804 Roger McDowell	.05
470 Len Dykstra	.05	588 Checklist 301-400	.05	687 Dale Sveum	.05	805 Randy Myers	.05
471 Jeff Johnson	.05	589 Checklist 401-500	.05	688 Kirk McCaskill	.05	806 Kirk Dressendorfer	.05
472 Russ Swan	.05	590 Checklist 501-600	.05	689 Rich Amaral	.05	807 Zane Smith	.05
473 Archie Corbin	.05	591 Frank Thomas		690 Danny Tartabull	.05	808 Glenn Davis	.05
474 Chuck McElroy	.05	(Members Choice)	.35	691 Donald Harris	.05	809 Torey Lovullo	.05
475 Mark McGwire	1.25	592 Dave Justice		692 Doug Davis	.05	810 Andre Dawson	.25
476 Wally Whitehurst	.05	(Members Choice)	.05	693 John Farrell	.05	811 Bill Pecota	.05
477 Tim McIntosh	.05	593 Roger Clemens		694 Paul Gibson	.05	812 Ted Power	.05
478 Sid Bream	.05	(Members Choice)	.45	695 Kenny Lofton	.05	813 Willie Blair	.05
479 Jeff Juden	.05	594 Steve Avery		696 Mike Fetters	.05	814 Dave Fleming	.05
480 Carlton Fisk	.65	(Members Choice)	.05	697 Rosario Rodriguez	.05	815 Chris Gwynn	.05
481 Jeff Plympton	.05	595 Cal Ripken, Jr.		698 Chris Jones	.05	816 Jody Reed	.05
482 Carlos Martinez	.05	(Members Choice)	.75	699 Jeff Manto	.05	817 Mark Dewey	.05
483 Jim Gott	.05	596 Barry Larkin		700 Rick Sutcliffe	.05	818 Kyle Abbott	.05
484 Bob McClure	.05	(Members Choice)	.05	701 Scott Bankhead	.05	819 Tom Henke	.05
485 Tim Teufel	.05	597 Not issued (See #370)	.05	702 Donnie Hill	.05	820 Kevin Seitzer	.05
486 Vicente Palacios	.05	598 Will Clark		703 Todd Worrell	.05	821 Al Newman	.05
487 Jeff Reed	.05	(Members Choice)	.05	704 Rene Gonzales	.05	822 Tim Sherrill	.05
488 Tony Phillips	.05	599 Cecil Fielder		705 Rick Cerone	.05	823 Chuck Crim	.05
489 Mel Rojas	.05	(Members Choice)	.05	706 Tony Pena	.05	824 Darren Reed	.05
490 Ben McDonald	.05	600 Ryne Sandberg		707 Paul Sorrento	.05	825 Tony Gwynn	.75
491 Andres Santana	.05	(Members Choice)	.40	708 Gary Scott	.05	826 Steve Foster	.05
492 Chris Beasley	.05	601 Chuck Knoblauch		709 Junior Noboa	.05	827 Steve Howe	.05
493 Mike Timlin	.05	(Members Choice)	.05	710 Wally Joyner	.05	828 Brook Jacoby	.05
494 Brian Downing	.05	602 Dwight Gooden		711 Charlie Hayes	.05	829 Rodney McCray	.05
495 Kirk Gibson	.05	(Members Choice)	.05	712 Rich Rodriguez	.05	830 Chuck Knoblauch	.05
496 Scott Sanderson	.05	603 Ken Griffey Jr.		713 Rudy Seanez	.05	831 John Wehner	.05
497 Nick Esasky	.05	(Members Choice)	.65	714 Jim Bullinger	.05	832 Scott Garrelts	.05
498 Johnny Guzman RC	.05	604 Barry Bonds		715 Jeff Robinson	.05	833 Alejandro Pena	.05
499 Mitch Williams	.05	(Members Choice)	.75	716 Jeff Branson	.05	834 Jeff Parrett	.05
500 Kirby Puckett	.75	605 Nolan Ryan		717 Andy Ashby	.05	835 Juan Bell	.05
501 Mike Harkey	.05	(Members Choice)	.75	718 Dave Burba	.05	836 Lance Dickson	.05
502 Jim Gantner	.05	606 Jeff Bagwell		719 Rich Gossage	.05	837 Darryl Kile	.05
503 Bruce Egloff	.05	(Members Choice)	.35	720 Randy Johnson	.65	838 Efrain Valdez	.05
504 Josias Manzanillo	.05	607 Robin Yount		721 David Wells	.05	839 Bob Zupcic RC	.05
505 Delino DeShields	.05	(Members Choice)	.30	722 Paul Kilgus	.05	840 George Bell	.05
506 Rheal Cormier	.05	608 Bobby Bonilla		723 Dave Martinez	.05	841 Dave Gallagher	.05
507 Jay Bell	.05	(Members Choice)	.05	724 Denny Neagle	.05	842 Tim Belcher	.05
508 Rich Rowland	.05	609 George Brett		725 Andy Stankiewicz	.05	843 Jeff Shaw	.05
509 Scott Servais	.05	(Members Choice)	.50	726 Rick Aguilera	.05	844 Mike Fitzgerald	.05
510 Terry Pendleton	.05	610 Howard Johnson		727 Junior Ortiz	.05	845 Gary Carter	.65
511 Rich DeLucia	.05	(Members Choice)	.05	728 Storm Davis	.05	846 John Russell	.05
512 Warren Newson	.05	611 Esteban Beltre	.05	729 Don Robinson	.05	847 Eric Hillman RC	.05
513 Paul Faries	.05	612 Mike Christopher	.05	730 Ron Gant	.05	848 Mike Witt	.05
514 Kal Daniels	.05	613 Troy Afenir	.05	731 Paul Assenmacher	.05	849 Curt Wilkerson	.05
515 Jarvis Brown	.05	614 Mariano Duncan	.05	732 Mark Gardiner	.05	850 Alan Trammell	.05
516 Rafael Palmeiro	.60	615 Doug Henry	.05	733 Milt Hill	.05	851 Rex Hudler	.05
517 Kelly Downs	.05	616 Doug Jones	.05	734 Jeremy Hernandez	.05	852 Michael Walkden RC	.05

853 Kevin Ward	.05
854 Tim Naehring	.05
855 Bill Swift	.05
856 Damon Berryhill	.05
857 Mark Eichhorn	.05
858 Hector Villanueva	.05
859 Jose Lind	.05
860 Denny Martinez	.05
861 Bill Krueger	.05
862 Mike Kingery	.05
863 Jeff Innis	.05
864 Derek Lilliquist	.05
865 Reggie Sanders	.05
866 Ramon Garcia	.05
867 Bruce Ruffin	.05
868 Dickie Thon	.05
869 Melido Perez	.05
870 Ruben Amaro	.05
871 Alan Mills	.05
872 Matt Sinatro	.05
873 Eddie Zosky	.05
874 Pete Incaviglia	.05
875 Tom Candiotti	.05
876 Bob Patterson	.05
877 Neal Heaton	.05
878 Terrel Hansen RC	.05
879 Dave Eiland	.05
880 Von Hayes	.05
881 Tim Scott	.05
882 Otis Nixon	.05
883 Herm Winningham	.05
884 Dion James	.05
885 Dave Wainhouse	.05
886 Frank DiPino	.05
887 Dennis Cook	.05
888 Jose Mesa	.05
889 Mark Leiter	.05
890 Willie Randolph	.05
891 Craig Colbert	.05
892 Dwayne Henry	.05
893 Jim Lindeman	.05
894 Charlie Hough	.05
895 Gil Heredia	.05
896 Scott Chiamparino	.05
897 Lance Blankenship	.05
898 Checklist 601-700	.05
899 Checklist 701-800	.05
900 Checklist 801-900	.05

First Draft Picks

Issued as inserts with Stadium Club Series 3, this three-card set features the No. 1 draft picks of 1990-92. Fronts have a full-bleed photo with S.C. logo and player name in the lower-right corner. At bottom-left in a red strip is a gold-foil stamping, "#1 Draft Pick of the '90's." An orange circle at upper-right has the year the player was the No. 1 choice. The basic red-and-black back has a color photo, a few biographical and draft details and a gold facsimile autograph among other gold-foil highlights.

	NM/M
Complete Set (3):	4.50
Common Player:	.60
1 Chipper Jones	4.00
2 Brien Taylor	.25
3 Phil Nevin	.25

Master Photos

Uncropped versions of the photos which appear on regular Stadium Club cards are featured on these large-format (5" x 7") cards. The photos are set against a white background and trimmed with holographic foil. Backs are blank and the cards are unnumbered. Members of Topps' Stadium Club received a Master Photo in their members' packs for 1992. The cards were also available as inserts in special boxes of Stadium Club cards sold at Wal-Mart stores.

	NM/M
Complete Set (15):	20.00
Common Player:	.50
(1) Wade Boggs	2.25
(2) Barry Bonds	4.00
(3) Jose Canseco	1.00
(4) Will Clark	.50
(5) Cecil Fielder	.50
(6) Dwight Gooden	.50
(7) Ken Griffey Jr.	3.00
(8) Rickey Henderson	2.00
(9) Lance Johnson	.50
(10) Cal Ripken, Jr.	4.00
(11) Nolan Ryan	4.00
(12) Deion Sanders	.50
(13) Darryl Strawberry	.50
(14) Danny Tartabull	.50
(15) Frank Thomas	2.00

East Coast National

In conjunction with its appearance at the August 1992 East Coast National card show, Topps distributed 22,000 five-card cello packs of its 1992 Stadium Club series bearing a special gold-foil show commemorative overprint. The cards are in all other respects identical to regular issue '92 S.C. Only 100 cards from Series III can be found with the overprint. Production of each card thus totals 1,100.

		NM/M
Complete Set (100):		40.00
Common Player:		.60
601	Chuck Knoblauch	
	(Members Choice)	.60
602	Dwight Gooden	
	(Members Choice)	.60
603	Ken Griffey Jr.	
	(Members Choice)	6.00
604	Barry Bonds	
	(Members Choice)	6.50
605	Nolan Ryan	
	(Members Choice)	7.50
606	Jeff Bagwell	
	(Members Choice)	2.50
607	Robin Yount	
	(Members Choice)	2.50
608	Bobby Bonilla	
	(Members Choice)	.60
609	George Brett	
	(Members Choice)	5.50
610	Howard Johnson	
	(Members Choice)	.60
611	Esteban Beltre	.60
612	Mike Christopher	.60
613	Troy Afenir	.60
619	Kevin McReynolds	.60
620	Barry Bonds	7.50
622	Joe Magrane	.60
623	Mark Parent	.60
626	Steve Wilson	.60
629	Rico Rossy	.60
631	Clay Parker	.60
633	Jeff McKnight	.60
637	Vince Horsman	.60
638	Eric King	.60
639	Joe Boever	.60
641	Arthur Rhodes	.60
647	Kevin Campbell	.60
653	Mike Jackson	.60
661	Randy Tomlin	.60
665	Greg Maddux	3.00
668	Brad Arnsberg	.60
671	Barry Jones	.60
672	Bill Landrum	.60
673	Greg Swindell	.60
676	Bill Pulsipher	.60

679	Patrick Lennon	.60
681	John Briscoe	.60
684	Phil Stephenson	.60
685	Ron Darling	.60
686	Bryan Hickerson	.60
688	Kirk McCaskill	.60
689	Rich Amaral	.60
692	Doug Davis	.60
693	John Farrell	.60
700	Rick Sutcliffe	.60
704	Rene Gonzalez	.60
713	Rudy Seanez	.60
714	Jim Bullinger	.60
716	Jeff Branson	.60
717	Andy Ashby	.60
725	Andy Stankiewicz	.60
733	Milt Hill	.60
739	Ron Robinson	.60
742	Butch Henry	.60
747	Chris James	.60
749	Dennis Rasmussen	.60
753	Dave Rohde	.60
757	Pat Listach	.60
758	Bill Wegman	.60
763	Armando Reynoso	.60
765	Kevin Mitchell	.60
766	Gary Sheffield	.90
769	Rick Parker	.60
771	Jeff Ballard	.60
772	Cory Snyder	.60
774	Jose Gonzalez	.60
775	Juan Guerrero	.60
776	Edwin Nunez	.60
778	Terry Leach	.60
782	Joe Slusarski	.60
784	Kirk Gibson	.60
788	Kim Batiste	.60
802	Arci Cianfrocco	.60
806	Kirk Dressendorfer	.60
807	Zane Smith	.60
814	Dave Fleming	.60
815	Chris Gwynn	.60
817	Mark Dewey	.60
819	Tom Henke	.60
822	Tim Sherrill	.60
826	Steve Foster	.60
831	John Wehner	.60
832	Scott Garrelts	.60
840	George Bell	.60
841	Dave Gallagher	.60
846	John Russell	.60
847	Eric Hillman	.60
852	Michael Walkden	.60
855	Bill Swift	.60
864	Derek Lilliquist	.60
876	Bob Patterson	.60
878	Terrel Hansen	.60
881	Tim Scott	.60
886	Frank DiPino	.60
891	Craig Colbert	.60
892	Dwayne Henry	.60
893	Jim Lindeman	.60
895	Gil Heredia	.60
898	Checklist 601-700	.05
899	Checklist 701-800	.05
900	Checklist 801-900	.05

National Convention

To promote its Stadium Club baseball card brand to dealers, Topps distributed sample cards during the National Sports Collectors Convention in Atlanta, Ga. The sample cards are regular-issue S.C. cards which had received a gold-foil overprint of the 1992 National logo. Only 100 cards from the third series can be found with the overprint. Only 5,000 four-card packs were distributed, thus only 200 of each card were made.

		NM/M
Complete Set (100):		135.00
Common Player:		1.50
616	Doug Jones	1.50
617	Alvin Davis	1.50
618	Craig Lefferts	1.50
621	Turner Ward	1.50
625	John Smiley	1.50
627	Mike Gallego	1.50
630	Royce Clayton	1.50
634	Jack Daugherty	1.50
635	Steve Sax	1.50
636	Joe Hesketh	1.50
643	Rick Wilkins	1.50
644	Scott Scudder	1.50
645	Bip Roberts	1.50
650	Kurt Stillwell	1.50
652	Andres Galarraga	1.50
657	Jeff Reardon	1.50
660	Eric Davis	1.50
662	Tom Edens	1.50
669	Greg Olson	1.50
678	Mark Carreon	1.50
680	Ozzie Smith	15.00

682	Matt Young	1.50
690	Danny Tartabull	1.50
691	Donald Harris	1.50
695	Kenny Lofton	1.50
697	Rosario Rodriguez	1.50
701	Scott Bankhead	1.50
705	Rick Cerone	1.50
706	Tony Pena	1.50
710	Junior Noboa	1.50
711	Wally Joyner	1.50
712	Charlie Hayes	1.50
713	Rich Rodriguez	1.50
721	David Wells	1.50
723	Dave Martinez	1.50
726	Rick Aguilera	1.50
727	Junior Ortiz	1.50
729	Don Robinson	1.50
730	Ron Gant	1.50
731	Paul Assenmacher	1.50
732	Mark Gardiner	1.50
735	Ken Hill	1.50
736	Xavier Hernandez	1.50
737	Gregg Jefferies	1.50
740	Sandy Alomar, Jr.	1.50
741	Mike Stanley	1.50
744	Brian Drahman	1.50
746	Bob Walk	1.50
751	Chris Hammond	1.50
759	John Wetteland	1.50
760	Phil Plantier	1.50
761	Wilson Alvarez	1.50
773	Denis Boucher	1.50
777	Scott Ruskin	1.50
779	Carl Willis	1.50
783	David Segui	1.50
786	Keith Miller	1.50
790	Eddie Taubensee	1.50
791	Jack Armstrong	1.50
792	Scott Fletcher	1.50
793	Steve Farr	1.50
794	Dan Pasqua	1.50
797	Francisco Cabrera	1.50
798	Mike Perez	1.50
801	Danny Gladden	1.50
803	Monty Fariss	1.50
804	Roger McDowell	1.50
805	Randy Myers	1.50
808	Glenn Davis	1.50
809	Torey Lovullo	1.50
816	Jody Reed	1.50
825	Tony Gwynn	15.00
827	Steve Howe	1.50
828	Brook Jacoby	1.50
829	Rodney McCray	1.50
830	Chuck Knoblauch	1.50
835	Juan Bell	1.50
836	Lance Dickson	1.50
837	Darryl Kile	1.50
842	Tim Belcher	1.50
843	Jeff Shaw	1.50
844	Mike Fitzgerald	1.50
845	Gary Carter	6.00
850	Alan Trammell	1.50
851	Rex Hudler	1.50
855	Damon Berryhill	1.50
857	Mark Eichhorn	1.50
859	Hector Villanueva	1.50
860	Denny Martinez	1.50
865	Reggie Sanders	1.50
869	Melido Perez	1.50
874	Pete Incaviglia	1.50
875	Tom Candiotti	1.50
877	Neal Heaton	1.50
879	Dave Eiland	1.50
882	Otis Nixon	1.50
884	Herm Winningham	1.50
885	Dion James	1.50
887	Dennis Cook	1.50
894	Charlie Hough	1.50

Members Only

A multi-sport set of 50 cards was sent in four installments to members of Topps' Stadium Club as part of their 1992 benefits package. Cards are similar in format to regular Stadium Club cards, 2-1/2" x 3-1/2", UV coated on front. Fronts have a special gold foil "Members Only" logo on front. Backs have a stadium scoreboard design with details of a career highlight. The un-numbered cards (baseball only) are checklisted here alphabetically.

		NM/M
Complete Set (36):		18.00
Common Player:		.15
(1)	Carlos Baerga	.15
(2)	Wade Boggs	1.00
(3)	Barry Bonds	2.50
(4)	Bret Boone	.15
(5)	Pat Borders	.15
(6)	George Brett	1.00
(7)	George Brett (3,000 hits)	1.00
(8)	Jim Bullinger	.15
(9)	Gary Carter	.15
(10)	Andujar Cedeno	.15
(11)	Roger Clemens, Matt Young	.45
(12)	Dennis Eckersley (Cy Young Award)	.60
(13)	Dennis Eckersley (MVP)	.60
(14)	Dave Eiland	.15
(15)	Dwight Gooden, Gary Sheffield	.25
(16)	Ken Griffey Jr.	1.50
(17)	Kevin Gross	.15
(18)	Bo Jackson	.25
(19)	Eric Karros	.15
(20)	Pat Listach	.15
(21)	Greg Maddux	1.00
(22)	Fred McGriff, Gary Sheffield	.25
(23)	Mickey Morandini	.15
(24)	Jack Morris	.15
(25)	Eddie Murray	.75
(26)	Eddie Murray	.75
(27)	Bip Roberts	.15
(28)	Nolan Ryan (27 seasons)	2.50
(29)	Nolan Ryan (1993 finale)	2.50
(30)	Lee Smith	.15
(31)	Ozzie Smith (2,000 hits)	1.00
(32)	Ozzie Smith (7,000 assists)	1.00
(33)	Ozzie Smith (Stolen base record.)	1.00
(34)	Bobby Thigpen	.15
(35)	Dave Winfield	.75
(36)	Robin Yount	.75

1992 Stadium Club SkyDome

This 200-card special Stadium Club set from Topps was uniquely packaged in a plastic replica of the Toronto SkyDome, the home of the 1991 All-Star Game. Featured in the set are members of Team USA, All-Stars, draft picks, top prospects and eight cards from the World Series between the Twins and Braves. The cards are styled much like the regular Stadium Club cards. Some cards have been found with incorrect gold-foil identifiers as well as the correct version.

		NM/M
Unopened Factory Set (200):		15.00
Complete Set (200):		10.00
Common Player:		.05
1	Terry Adams RC	.05
2	Tommy Adams	.05
3	Rick Aguilera	.05
4	Ron Allen	.05
5	Roberto Alomar/AS	.20
6	Sandy Alomar	.05
7	Greg Anthony	.05
8	James Austin	.05
9	Steve Avery	.05
10	Harold Baines	.05
11	Brian Barber RC	.05
12	Jon Barnes	.05
13	George Bell	.05
14	Doug Bennett	.05
15	Sean Bergman	.05
16	Craig Biggio	.05
17	Bill Bliss	.05
18	Wade Boggs/AS	.60
19	Bobby Bonilla/AS	.15
20	Russell Brock	.05
21	Tarrik Brock	.05
22	Tom Browning	.05
23	Brett Butler	.05
24	Ivan Calderon	.05
25	Joe Carter	.05
26	Joe Caruso	.05
27	Dan Cholowsky	.05
28	Will Clark/AS	.05
29	Roger Clemens/AS	.65
30	Shawn Curran	.05
31	Chris Curtis	.05
32	Chili Davis	.05
33	Andre Dawson	.25
34	Joe DeBerry	.05
35	John Dettmer	.05
36	Rob Dibble	.05
37	John Donati RC	.05
38	Dave Doorneweerd	.05
39	Darren Dreifort	.05
40	Mike Durant	.05
41	Chris Durkin	.05
42	Dennis Eckersley	.40
43	Brian Edmondson RC	.05
44	Vaughn Eshelman RC	.05
45	Shawn Estes RC	.50
46	Jorge Fabregas RC	.10
47	Jon Farrell	.05
48	Cecil Fielder/AS	.05
49	Carlton Fisk	.50
50	Tim Flannelly	.05
51	Cliff Floyd RC	.50
52	Julio Franco	.05
53	Greg Gagne	.05
54	Chris Gambs RC	.05
55	Ron Gant	.05
56	Brent Gates	.05
57	Dwayne Gerald	.05
58	Jason Giambi	1.50
59	Benji Gil RC	.05
60	Mark Gipner	.05
61	Danny Gladden	.05
62	Tom Glavine	.35
63	Jimmy Gonzalez	.05
64	Jeff Granger	.05
65	Dan Grapenthien	.05
66	Dennis Gray	.05
67	Shawn Green RC	2.00
68	Tyler Green	.05
69	Todd Greene	.05
70	Ken Griffey Jr./AS	.75
71	Kelly Gruber	.05
72	Ozzie Guillen	.05
73	Tony Gwynn/AS	.60
74	Shane Halter	.05
75	Jeffrey Hammonds	.75
76	Larry Hanlon	.05
77	Pete Harnisch	.05
78	Mike Harrison	.05
79	Bryan Harvey	.05
80	Scott Hatteberg	.05
81	Rick Helling	.05
82	Dave Henderson	.05
83	Rickey Henderson/AS	.50
84	Tyrone Hill	.05
85	Todd Hollandsworth RC	.10
86	Brian Holliday	.05
87	Terry Horn	.05
88	Jeff Hostetler	.05
89	Kent Hrbek	.05
90	Mark Hubbard	.05
91	Charles Johnson	.05
92	Howard Johnson	.05
93	Todd Johnson	.05
94	Bobby Jones RC	.10
95	Dan Jones	.05
96	Felix Jose	.05
97	Dave Justice	.05
98	Jimmy Key	.05
99	Marc Kroom RC	.05
100	John Kruk	.05
101	Mark Langston	.05
102	Barry Larkin	.05
103	Mike LaValliere	.05
104a	Scott Leius (1991 N.L. All-Star - Error)	.05
104b	Scott Leius (1991 World Series - Correct)	.25
105	Mark Lemke	.05
106	Donnie Leshnock	.05
107	Jimmy Lewis	.05
108	Shawn Livesy	.05
109	Ryan Long	.05
110	Trevor Mallory	.05
111	Denny Martinez	.05
112	Justin Mashore	.05
113	Jason McDonald	.05
114	Jack McDowell	.05
115	Tom McKinnon	.05
116	Billy McKinnon	.05
117	Buck McNabb RC	.05
118	Jim Mecir	.05
119	Dan Melendez	.05
120	Shawn Miller RC	.05
121	Trever Miller	.05
122	Paul Molitor	.50
123	Vincent Moore	.05
124	Mike Morgan	.05
125	Jack Morris (World Series)	.05
126	Jack Morris/AS	.05
127	Sean Mulligan	.05
128	Eddie Murray	.50
129	Mike Neill	.05
130	Phil Nevin	.05
131	Mark O'Brien	.05
132	Alex Ochoa RC	.05
133	Chad Ogea RC	.05
134	Greg Olson	.05
135	Paul O'Neill	.05
136a	Jared Osentowski (1991 World Series - Error)	.05
136b	Jared Osentowski (Draft Pick - Correct)	.25
137	Mike Pagliarulo	.05
138	Rafael Palmeiro	.40
139	Rodney Pedraza	.05
140	Tony Phillips	.05
141	Scott Pisciotta RC	.05
142	Chris Pritchett	.05
143	Jason Pruitt	.05
144a	Kirby Puckett (1991 N.L. All-Star - Error)	.60
144b	Kirby Puckett (1991 World Series - Correct)	3.00
145	Kirby Puckett/AS	.60
146	Manny Ramirez RC	5.00
147	Eddie Ramos	.05
148	Mark Ratekin	.05
149	Jeff Reardon	.05
150	Sean Rees	.05
151	Calvin Reese RC	.50
152	Desmond Relaford RC	.10
153	Eric Richardson	.05
154	Cal Ripken, Jr./AS	1.50
155	Chris Roberts	.05
156	Mike Robertson	.05
157	Steve Rodriguez	.05
158	Mike Rossiter	.05
159	Scott Ruffcorn	.05
160a	Chris Sabo (1991 World Series - Error)	.05
160b	Chris Sabo (1991 N.L. All-Star - Correct)	.25
161	Juan Samuel	.05
162	Ryne Sandberg/AS	.60
163	Scott Sanderson	.05
164	Benito Santiago	.05
165	Gene Schall RC	.05
166	Chad Schoenvogel	.05
167	Chris Seelbach RC	.05
168	Aaron Sele RC	.50
169	Basil Shabazz	.05
170	Al Shirley RC	.05
171	Paul Shuey	.05
172	Ruben Sierra	.05
173	John Smiley	.05
174	Lee Smith	.05
175	Ozzie Smith	.60
176	Tim Smith	.05
177	Zane Smith	.05
178	John Smoltz	.05
179	Scott Stahoviak	.05
180	Kennie Steenstra	.05
181	Kevin Stocker	.05
182	Chris Stynes RC	.05
183	Danny Tartabull	.05
184	Brien Taylor	.05
185	Todd Taylor	.05
186	Larry Thomas	.05
187a	Ozzie Timmons RC	.05
187b	David Tuttle (Should be #188.)	.05
188	Not issued	
189	Andy Van Slyke	.05
190a	Frank Viola (1991 World Series - Error)	.05
190b	Frank Viola (1991 N.L. All-Star - Correct)	.25
191	Michael Walkden	.05
192	Jeff Ware	.05
193	Allen Watson RC	.05
194	Steve Whitaker	.05
195a	Jerry Willard (1991 Draft Pick - Error)	.05
195b	Jerry Willard (1991 World Series - Correct)	.25
196	Craig Wilson	.05
197	Chris Wimmer	.05
198	Steve Wojciechowski RC	.05
199	Joel Wolfe	.05
200	Ivan Zweig	.05

1993 Stadium Club

Topps' premium set for 1993 was issued in three series, two 300-card series and a final series of 150. Boxes contained 24 packs this year, compared to 36 in the past. Packs had 14 cards and an insert card. Each box had a 5" x 7" Master Photo card.

		NM/M
Complete Set (750):		25.00
Common Player:		.05
First Day:		8X
Pack (15):		.75
Wax Box (24):		10.00
1	Pat Borders	.05
2	Greg Maddux	.85
3	Daryl Boston	.05
4	Bob Ayrault	.05
5	Tony Phillips	.05
6	Damion Easley	.05
7	Kip Gross	.05
8	Jim Thome	.65
9	Tim Belcher	.05
10	Gary Wayne	.05
11	Sam Militello	.05
12	Mike Magnante	.05
13	Tim Wakefield	.05
14	Tim Hulett	.05
15	Rheal Cormier	.05
16	Juan Guerrero	.05
17	Rich Gossage	.05
18	Tim Laker	.05
19	Darrin Jackson	.05
20	Jack Clark	.05
21	Roberto Hernandez	.05
22	Dean Palmer	.05
23	Harold Reynolds	.05
24	Dan Plesac	.05
25	Brent Mayne	.05
26	Pat Hentgen	.05
27	Luis Sojo	.05
28	Ron Gant	.05
29	Paul Gibson	.05
30	Bip Roberts	.05
31	Mickey Tettleton	.05
32	Randy Velarde	.05
33	Brian McRae	.05
34	Wes Chamberlain	.05
35	Wayne Kirby	.05
36	Rey Sanchez	.05
37	Jesse Orosco	.05
38	Mike Stanton	.05
39	Royce Clayton	.05
40	Cal Ripken, Jr.	2.50
41	John Dopson	.05
42	Gene Larkin	.05
43	Tim Raines	.05
44	Randy Myers	.05
45	Clay Parker	.05
46	Mike Scioscia	.05
47	Pete Incaviglia	.05
48	Todd Van Poppel	.05
49	Ray Lankford	.05
50	Eddie Murray	.75
51	Barry Bonds	2.50
52	Gary Thurman	.05
53	Bob Wickman	.05
54	Joey Cora	.05
55	Kenny Rogers	.05
56	Mike Devereaux	.05
57	Kevin Seitzer	.05
58	Rafael Belliard	.05
59	David Wells	.05
60	Mark Clark	.05
61	Carlos Baerga	.05
62	Scott Brosius	.05
63	Jeff Grotewold	.05
64	Rick Wrona	.05
65	Kurt Knudsen	.05
66	Lloyd McClendon	.05
67	Omar Vizquel	.05
68	Jose Vizcaino	.05
69	Rob Ducey	.05
70	Casey Candaele	.05
71	Ramon Martinez	.05
72	Todd Hundley	.05
73	John Marzano	.05
74	Derek Parks	.05
75	Jack McDowell	.05
76	Tim Scott	.05
77	Mike Mussina	.40
78	Delino DeShields	.05
79	Chris Bosio	.05
80	Mike Bordick	.05
81	Rod Beck	.05
82	Ted Power	.05
83	John Kruk	.05
84	Steve Shifflett	.05
85	Danny Tartabull	.05
86	Mike Greenwell	.05
87	Jose Melendez	.05
88	Craig Wilson	.05
89	Melvin Nieves	.05
90	Ed Sprague	.05
91	Willie McGee	.05
92	Joe Orsulak	.05
93	Jeff King	.05
94	Dan Pasqua	.05
95	Brian Harper	.05
96	Joe Oliver	.05
97	Shane Turner	.05
98	Lenny Harris	.05
99	Jeff Parrett	.05
100	Luis Polonia	.05
101	Kent Bottenfield	.05
102	Albert Belle	.05
103	Mike Maddux	.05
104	Randy Tomlin	.05
105	Andy Stankiewicz	.05
106	Rico Rossy	.05
107	Joe Hesketh	.05
108	Dennis Powell	.05
109	Derrick May	.05
110	Pete Harnisch	.05
111	Kent Mercker	.05
112	Scott Fletcher	.05
113	Rex Hudler	.05
114	Chico Walker	.05
115	Rafael Palmeiro	.65
116	Mark Leiter	.05
117	Pedro Munoz	.05
118	Jim Bullinger	.05
119	Ivan Calderon	.05
120	Mike Timlin	.05
121	Rene Gonzales	.05
122	Greg Vaughn	.05
123	Mike Flanagan	.05
124	Mike Hartley	.05
125	Jeff Montgomery	.05
126	Mike Gallego	.05

No.	Player	Price
127	Don Slaught	.05
128	Charlie O'Brien	.05
129a	Jose Offerman (Home: (Blank))	2.00
129b	Jose Offerman (Home: S.P. de MACORIS, D.R.)	.05
130	Mark Wohlers	.05
131	Eric Fox	.05
132	Doug Strange	.05
133	Jeff Frye	.05
134	Wade Boggs	.85
135	Lou Whitaker	.05
136	Craig Grebeck	.05
137	Rich Rodriguez	.05
138	Jay Bell	.05
139	Felix Fermin	.05
140	Denny Martinez	.05
141	Eric Anthony	.05
142	Roberto Alomar	.20
143	Darren Lewis	.05
144	Mike Blowers	.05
145	Scott Bankhead	.05
146	Jeff Reboulet	.05
147	Frank Viola	.05
148	Bill Pecota	.05
149	Carlos Hernandez	.05
150	Bobby Witt	.05
151	Sid Bream	.05
152	Todd Zeile	.05
153	Dennis Cook	.05
154	Brian Bohanon	.05
155	Pat Kelly	.05
156	Milt Cuyler	.05
157	Juan Bell	.05
158	Randy Milligan	.05
159	Mark Gardner	.05
160	Pat Tabler	.05
161	Jeff Reardon	.05
162	Ken Patterson	.05
163	Bobby Bonilla	.05
164	Tony Pena	.05
165	Greg Swindell	.05
166	Kirk McCaskill	.05
167	Doug Drabek	.05
168	Franklin Stubbs	.05
169	Ron Tingley	.05
170	Willie Banks	.05
171	Sergio Valdez	.05
172	Mark Lemke	.05
173	Robin Yount	.75
174	Storm Davis	.05
175	Dan Walters	.05
176	Steve Farr	.05
177	Curt Wilkerson	.05
178	Luis Alicea	.05
179	Russ Swan	.05
180	Mitch Williams	.05
181	Wilson Alvarez	.05
182	Carl Willis	.05
183	Craig Biggio	.05
184	Sean Berry	.05
185	Trevor Wilson	.05
186	Jeff Tackett	.05
187	Ellis Burks	.05
188	Jeff Branson	.05
189	Matt Nokes	.05
190	John Smiley	.05
191	Danny Gladden	.05
192	Mike Boddicker	.05
193	Roger Pavlik	.05
194	Paul Sorrento	.05
195	Vince Coleman	.05
196	Gary DiSarcina	.05
197	Rafael Bournigal	.05
198	Mike Schooler	.05
199	Scott Ruskin	.05
200	Frank Thomas	.75
201	Kyle Abbott	.05
202	Mike Perez	.05
203	Andre Dawson	.25
204	Bill Swift	.05
205	Alejandro Pena	.05
206	Dave Winfield	.75
207	Andujar Cedeno	.05
208	Terry Steinbach	.05
209	Chris Hammond	.05
210	Todd Burns	.05
211	Hipolito Pichardo	.05
212	John Kiely	.05
213	Tim Teufel	.05
214	Lee Guetterman	.05
215	Geronimo Pena	.05
216	Brett Butler	.05
217	Bryan Hickerson	.05
218	Rick Trlicek	.05
219	Lee Stevens	.05
220	Roger Clemens	1.25
221	Carlton Fisk	.75
222	Chili Davis	.05
223	Walt Terrell	.05
224	Jim Eisenreich	.05
225	Ricky Bones	.05
226	Henry Rodriguez	.05
227	Ken Hill	.05
228	Rick Wilkins	.05
229	Ricky Jordan	.05
230	Bernard Gilkey	.05
231	Tim Fortugno	.05
232	Geno Petralli	.05
233	Jose Rijo	.05
234	Jim Leyritz	.05
235	Kevin Campbell	.05
236	Al Osuna	.05
237	Pete Smith	.05
238	Pete Schourek	.05
239	Moises Alou	.05
240	Donn Pall	.05
241	Denny Neagle	.05
242	Dan Peltier	.05
243	Scott Scudder	.05
244	Juan Guzman	.05
245	Dave Burba	.05
246	Rick Sutcliffe	.05
247	Tony Fossas	.05
248	Mike Munoz	.05
249	Tim Salmon	.05
250	Rob Murphy	.05
251	Roger McDowell	.05
252	Lance Parrish	.05
253	Cliff Brantley	.05
254	Scott Leius	.05
255	Carlos Martinez	.05
256	Vince Horsman	.05
257	Oscar Azocar	.05
258	Craig Shipley	.05
259	Ben McDonald	.05
260	Jeff Brantley	.05
261	Damon Berryhill	.05
262	Joe Grahe	.05
263	Dave Hansen	.05
264	Rich Amaral	.05
265	Tim Pugh RC	.05
266	Dion James	.05
267	Frank Tanana	.05
268	Stan Belinda	.05
269	Jeff Kent	.05
270	Bruce Ruffin	.05
271	Xavier Hernandez	.05
272	Darrin Fletcher	.05
273	Tino Martinez	.05
274	Benny Santiago	.05
275	Scott Radinsky	.05
276	Mariano Duncan	.05
277	Kenny Lofton	.05
278	Dwight Smith	.05
279	Joe Carter	.05
280	Tim Jones	.05
281	Jeff Huson	.05
282	Phil Plantier	.05
283	Kirby Puckett	.85
284	Johnny Guzman	.05
285	Mike Morgan	.05
286	Chris Sabo	.05
287	Matt Williams	.05
288	Checklist 1-100	.05
289	Checklist 101-200	.05
290	Checklist 201-300	.05
291	Dennis Eckersley (Members Choice)	.30
292	Eric Karros (Members Choice)	.05
293	Pat Listach (Members Choice)	.05
294	Andy Van Slyke (Members Choice)	.05
295	Robin Ventura (Members Choice)	.05
296	Tom Glavine (Members Choice)	.05
297	Juan Gonzalez (Members Choice)	.20
298	Travis Fryman (Members Choice)	.05
299	Larry Walker (Members Choice)	.05
300	Gary Sheffield (Members Choice)	.20
301	Chuck Finley	.05
302	Luis Gonzalez	.05
303	Darryl Hamilton	.05
304	Bien Figueroa	.05
305	Ron Darling	.05
306	Jonathan Hurst	.05
307	Mike Sharperson	.05
308	Mike Christopher	.05
309	Marvin Freeman	.05
310	Jay Buhner	.05
311	Butch Henry	.05
312	Greg Harris	.05
313	Darren Daulton	.05
314	Chuck Knoblauch	.05
315	Greg Harris	.05
316	John Franco	.05
317	John Wehner	.05
318	Donald Harris	.05
319	Benny Santiago	.05
320	Larry Walker	.05
321	Randy Knorr	.05
322	Ramon D. Martinez RC	.05
323	Mike Stanley	.05
324	Bill Wegman	.05
325	Tom Candiotti	.05
326	Glenn Davis	.05
327	Chuck Crim	.05
328	Scott Livingstone	.05
329	Eddie Taubensee	.05
330	George Bell	.05
331	Edgar Martinez	.05
332	Paul Assenmacher	.05
333	Steve Hosey	.05
334	Mo Vaughn	.05
335	Bret Saberhagen	.05
336	Mike Trombley	.05
337	Mark Lewis	.05
338	Terry Pendleton	.05
339	Dave Hollins	.05
340	Jeff Conine	.05
341	Bob Tewksbury	.05
342	Zane Smith	.05
343	John Wetteland	.05
344	John Wetteland	.05
345	Chris Hoiles	.05
346	Frank Castillo	.05
347	Bruce Hurst	.05
348	Kevin McReynolds	.05
349	Dave Henderson	.05
350	Ryan Bowen	.05
351	Sid Fernandez	.05
352	Mark Whiten	.05
353	Nolan Ryan	2.50
354	Rick Aguilera	.05
355	Mark Langston	.05
356	Jack Morris	.05
357	Rob Deer	.05
358	Dave Fleming	.05
359	Lance Johnson	.05
360	Joe Millette	.05
361	Wil Cordero	.05
362	Chito Martinez	.05
363	Scott Servais	.05
364	Bernie Williams	.05
365	Pedro Martinez	.75
366	Ryne Sandberg	.85
367	Brad Ausmus	.05
368	Scott Cooper	.05
369	Rob Dibble	.05
370	Walt Weiss	.05
371	Mark Davis	.05
372	Orlando Merced	.05
373	Mike Jackson	.05
374	Kevin Appier	.05
375	Esteban Beltre	.05
376	Joe Slusarski	.05
377	William Suero	.05
378	Pete O'Brien	.05
379	Alan Embree	.05
380	Lenny Webster	.05
381	Eric Davis	.05
382	Duane Ward	.05
383	John Habyan	.05
384	Jeff Bagwell	.75
385	Ruben Amaro	.05
386	Julio Valera	.05
387	Robin Ventura	.05
388	Archi Cianfrocco	.05
389	Skeeter Barnes	.05
390	Tim Costo	.05
391	Luis Mercedes	.05
392	Jeremy Hernandez	.05
393	Shawon Dunston	.05
394	Andy Van Slyke	.05
395	Kevin Maas	.05
396	Kevin Brown	.05
397	J.T. Bruett	.05
398	Darryl Strawberry	.05
399	Tom Pagnozzi	.05
400	Sandy Alomar	.05
401	Keith Miller	.05
402	Rich DeLucia	.05
403	Shawn Abner	.05
404	Howard Johnson	.05
405	Mike Benjamin	.05
406	Roberto Mejia RC	.05
407	Mike Butcher	.05
408	Deion Sanders	.05
409	Todd Stottlemyre	.05
410	Scott Kamieniecki	.05
411	Doug Jones	.05
412	John Burkett	.05
413	Lance Blankenship	.05
414	Jeff Parrett	.05
415	Barry Larkin	.05
416	Alan Trammell	.05
417	Mark Kiefer	.05
418	Gregg Olson	.05
419	Mark Grace	.05
420	Shane Mack	.05
421	Bob Walk	.05
422	Curt Schilling	.25
423	Erik Hanson	.05
424	George Brett	1.25
425	Reggie Jefferson	.05
426	Mark Portugal	.05
427	Ron Karkovice	.05
428	Matt Young	.05
429	Troy Neel	.05
430	Hector Fajardo	.05
431	Dave Righetti	.05
432	Pat Listach	.05
433	Jeff Innis	.05
434	Bob MacDonald	.05
435	Brian Jordan	.05
436	Jeff Blauser	.05
437	Mike Myers RC	.05
438	Frank Seminara	.05
439	Rusty Meacham	.05
440	Greg Briley	.05
441	Derek Lilliquist	.05
442	John Vander Wal	.05
443	Scott Erickson	.05
444	Bob Scanlan	.05
445	Todd Frohwirth	.05
446	Tom Goodwin	.05
447	William Pennyfeather	.05
448	Travis Fryman	.05
449	Mickey Morandini	.05
450	Greg Olson	.05
451	Trevor Hoffman	.05
452	Dave Magadan	.05
453	Shawn Jeter	.05
454	Andres Galarraga	.05
455	Ted Wood	.05
456	Freddie Benavides	.05
457	Junior Felix	.05
458	Alex Cole	.05
459	John Orton	.05
460	Eddie Zosky	.05
461	Dennis Eckersley	.65
462	Lee Smith	.05
463	John Smoltz	.05
464	Ken Caminiti	.05
465	Melido Perez	.05
466	Tom Marsh	.05
467	Jeff Nelson	.05
468	Jesse Levis	.05
469	Chris Nabholz	.05
470	Mike Mcfarlane	.05
471	Reggie Sanders	.05
472	Chuck McElroy	.05
473	Kevin Gross	.05
474	Matt Whiteside RC	.05
475	Cal Eldred	.05
476	Dave Gallagher	.05
477	Len Dykstra	.05
478	Mark McGwire	2.00
479	David Segui	.05
480	Mike Henneman	.05
481	Bret Barberie	.05
482	Steve Sax	.05
483	Dave Valle	.05
484	Danny Darwin	.05
485	Devon White	.05
486	Eric Plunk	.05
487	Jim Gott	.05
488	Scooter Tucker	.05
489	Omar Oliveres	.05
490	Greg Myers	.05
491	Brian Hunter	.05
492	Kevin Tapani	.05
493	Rich Monteleone	.05
494	Steve Buechele	.05
495	Bo Jackson	.10
496	Mike LaValliere	.05
497	Mark Leonard	.05
498	Daryl Boston	.05
499	Jose Canseco	.45
500	Brian Barnes	.05
501	Randy Johnson	.75
502	Tim McIntosh	.05
503	Cecil Fielder	.05
504	Derek Bell	.05
505	Kevin Koslofski	.05
506	Darren Holmes	.05
507	Brady Anderson	.05
508	John Valentin	.05
509	Jerry Browne	.05
510	Fred McGriff	.05
511	Pedro Astacio	.05
512	Gary Gaetti	.05
513	John Burke RC	.05
514	Dwight Gooden	.05
515	Thomas Howard	.05
516	Darrell Whitmore RC	.05
517	Ozzie Guillen	.05
518	Darryl Kile	.05
519	Rich Rowland	.05
520	Carlos Delgado	.50
521	Doug Henry	.05
522	Greg Colbrunn	.05
523	Tom Gordon	.05
524	Ivan Rodriguez	.65
525	Kent Hrbek	.05
526	Eric Young	.05
527	Rod Brewer	.05
528	Eric Karros	.05
529	Marquis Grissom	.05
530	Rico Brogna	.05
531	Sammy Sosa	1.00
532	Bret Boone	.05
533	Luis Rivera	.05
534	Hal Morris	.05
535	Monty Fariss	.05
536	Leo Gomez	.05
537	Wally Joyner	.05
538	Tony Gwynn	.85
539	Mike Williams	.05
540	Juan Gonzalez	.40
541	Ryan Klesko	.05
542	Ryan Thompson	.05
543	Chad Curtis	.05
544	Orel Hershiser	.05
545	Carlos Garcia	.05
546	Bob Welch	.05
547	Vinny Castilla	.05
548	Ozzie Smith	.85
549	Luis Salazar	.05
550	Mark Guthrie	.05
551	Charles Nagy	.05
552	Alex Fernandez	.05
553	Mel Rojas	.05
554	Orestes Destrade	.05
555	Mark Gubicza	.05
556	Steve Finley	.05
557	Don Mattingly	1.25
558	Rickey Henderson	.75
559	Tommy Greene	.05
560	Arthur Rhodes	.05
561	Alfredo Griffin	.05
562	Will Clark	.05
563	Bob Zupcic	.05
564	Chuck Carr	.05
565	Henry Cotto	.05
566	Billy Spiers	.05
567	Jack Armstrong	.05
568	Kurt Stillwell	.05
569	David McCarty	.05
570	Joe Vitiello	.05
571	Gerald Williams	.05
572	Dale Murphy	.25
573	Scott Aldred	.05
574	Bill Gullickson	.05
575	Bobby Thigpen	.05
576	Glenallen Hill	.05
577	Dwayne Henry	.05
578	Calvin Jones	.05
579	Al Martin	.05
580	Ruben Sierra	.05
581	Anthony Young	.05
582	Shawn Boskie	.05
583	Scott Pose RC	.05
584	[illegible]	.05
585	Mike Piazza	1.50
586	Donovan Osborne	.05
587	James Austin	.05
588	Checklist 301-400	.05
589	Checklist 401-500	.05
590	Checklist 501-600	.05
591	Ken Griffey Jr. (Members Choice)	.75
592	Ivan Rodriguez (Members Choice)	.40
593	Carlos Baerga (Members Choice)	.05
594	Fred McGriff (Members Choice)	.05
595	Mark McGwire (Members Choice)	1.00
596	Roberto Alomar (Members Choice)	.10
597	Kirby Puckett (Members Choice)	.45
598	Marquis Grissom (Members Choice)	.05
599	John Smoltz (Members Choice)	.05
600	Ryne Sandberg (Members Choice)	.45
601	Wade Boggs	.85
602	Jeff Reardon	.05
603	Billy Ripken	.05
604	Bryan Harvey	.05
605	Carlos Quintana	.05
606	Greg Hibbard	.05
607	Ellis Burks	.05
608	Greg Swindell	.05
609	Dave Winfield	.75
610	Charlie Hough	.05
611	Chili Davis	.05
612	Jody Reed	.05
613	Mark Williamson	.05
614	Phil Plantier	.05
615	Jim Abbott	.05
616	Dante Bichette	.05
617	Mark Eichhorn	.05
618	Gary Sheffield	.45
619	Richie Lewis RC	.05
620	Joe Girardi	.05
621	Jaime Navarro	.05
622	Willie Wilson	.05
623	Scott Fletcher	.05
624	Bud Black	.05
625	Tom Brunansky	.05
626	Steve Avery	.05
627	Paul Molitor	.75
628	Gregg Jefferies	.05
629	Dave Stewart	.05
630	Javier Lopez	.05
631	Greg Gagne	.05
632	Bobby Kelly	.05
633	Mike Fetters	.05
634	Ozzie Canseco	.05
635	Jeff Russell	.05
636	Pete Incaviglia	.05
637	Tom Henke	.05
638	Chipper Jones	1.00
639	Jimmy Key	.05
640	Dave Martinez	.05
641	Dave Stieb	.05
642	Milt Thompson	.05
643	Alan Mills	.05
644	Tony Fernandez	.05
645	Randy Bush	.05
646	Joe Magrane	.05
647	Ivan Calderon	.05
648	Jose Guzman	.05
649	John Olerud	.05
650	Tom Glavine	.25
651	Julio Franco	.05
652	Armando Reynoso	.05
653	Felix Jose	.05
654	Ben Rivera	.05
655	Andre Dawson	.25
656	Mike Harkey	.05
657	Kevin Seitzer	.05
658	Lonnie Smith	.05
659	Norm Charlton	.05
660	Dave Justice	.05
661	Fernando Valenzuela	.05
662	Dan Wilson	.05
663	Mark Gardner	.05
664	Doug Dascenzo	.05
665	Greg Maddux	.85
666	Harold Baines	.05
667	Randy Myers	.05
668	Harold Reynolds	.05
669	Candy Maldonado	.05
670	Al Leiter	.05
671	Jerald Clark	.05
672	Doug Drabek	.05
673	Kirk Gibson	.05
674	Steve Reed RC	.05
675	Mike Felder	.05
676	Ricky Gutierrez	.05
677	Spike Owen	.05
678	Otis Nixon	.05
679	Scott Sanderson	.05
680	Mark Carreon	.05
681	Troy Percival	.05
682	Kevin Stocker	.05
683	Jim Converse RC	.05
684	Barry Bonds	2.50
685	Greg Gohr	.05
686	Tim Wallach	.05
687	Matt Mieske	.05
688	Robby Thompson	.05
689	Brien Taylor	.05
690	Kirt Manwaring	.05
691	Mike Lansing RC	.25
692	Steve Decker	.05
693	Mike Moore	.05
694	Kevin Mitchell	.05
695	Phil Hiatt	.05
696	Tony Tarasco RC	.05
697	Benji Gil	.05
698	Jeff Juden	.05
699	Kevin Reimer	.05
700	Andy Ashby	.05
701	John Jaha	.05
702	Tim Bogar RC	.05
703	David Cone	.05
704	Willie Greene	.05
705	David Hulse RC	.05
706	Cris Carpenter	.05
707	Ken Griffey Jr.	1.50
708	Steve Bedrosian	.05
709	Dave Nilsson	.05
710	Paul Wagner	.05
711	B.J. Surhoff	.05
712	Rene Arocha RC	.05
713	Manny Lee	.05
714	Brian Williams	.05
715	Sherman Obando RC	.05
716	Terry Mulholland	.05
717	Paul O'Neill	.05
718	David Nied	.05
719	J.T. Snow RC	.50
720	Nigel Wilson	.05
721	Mike Bielecki	.05
722	Kevin Young	.05
723	Charlie Leibrandt	.05
724	Frank Bolick	.05
725	Jon Shave RC	.05
726	Steve Cooke	.05
727	Domingo Martinez RC	.05
728	Todd Worrell	.05
729	Jose Lind	.05
730	Jim Tatum RC	.05
731	Mike Hampton	.05
732	Mike Draper	.05
733	Henry Mercedes	.05
734	John Johnstone RC	.05
735	Mitch Webster	.05
736	Russ Springer	.05
737	Rob Natal	.05
738	Steve Howe	.05
739	Darrell Sherman RC	.05
740	Pat Mahomes	.05
741	Alex Arias	.05
742	Damon Buford	.05
743	Charlie Hayes	.05
744	Guillermo Velasquez	.05
745	Checklist 601-750	.05
746	Frank Thomas (Members Choice)	.40
747	Barry Bonds (Members Choice)	1.50
748	Roger Clemens (Members Choice)	.50
749	Joe Carter (Members Choice)	.05
750	Greg Maddux (Members Choice)	.45

1st Day Production

Inserted at the rate of about one per box, with an estimated production of 2,000 apiece, 1st Day Production cards are a parallel of 1993 TSC on which an embossed silver holographic foil logo has been added. Because of the considerably higher value of the 1st Day parallels, collectors should be aware that fakes can be created by cutting the logo off a common player's card and attaching it to a superstar card.

	NM/M
Common Player:	1.00
1st Day Stars:	8X

Series 1 Inserts

Four bonus cards were produced as special inserts in Series I Stadium Club packs. Two of the full-bleed, gold-foil enhanced cards honor Robin Yount and George Brett for achieving the 3,000-hit mark, while the other two commemorate the first picks in the 1993 expansion draft by the Colorado Rockies (David Nied) and Marlins (Nigel Wilson).

	NM/M
Complete Set (4):	3.00
Common Player:	.25
1 Robin Yount (3,000 hits)	1.00
2 George Brett (3,000 hits)	2.00
3 David Nied (#1 pick)	.25
4 Nigel Wilson (#1 pick)	.25

Series 2 Inserts

Cross-town and regional rivals were featured in this four-card insert set found, on average, one per 24 packs of Series II Stadium Club. Each of the two-faced cards is typical S.C. quality with gold-foil stamping and UV coating front and back.

	NM/M
Complete Set (4):	5.00
Common Card:	1.50
1 Pacific Terrific (Will Clark, Mark McGwire)	2.00
2 Broadway Stars (Dwight Gooden, Don Mattingly)	1.50
3 Second City Sluggers (Ryne Sandberg, Frank Thomas)	1.50
4 Pacific Terrific (Ken Griffey Jr., Darryl Strawberry)	1.50

Series 3 Inserts

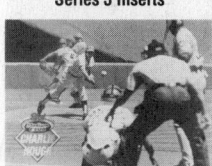

Team "firsts" - first game, first pitch, first batter, etc. - for the 1993 expansion Florida Marlins and Colorado Rockies are featured on this pair of inserts found in Series III Stadium Club packs. Fronts featured game-action photos with the player's name in gold foil. On back is a stadium scene with the team first overprinted in black. At top the team name and Stadium Club logo are in gold foil.

	NM/M
Complete Set (2):	.50
Common Player:	.25
1 David Nied	.25
2 Charlie Hough	.25

Master Photos

Each box of 1993 Stadium Club packs included one Master Photo premium insert. Prize cards good for three Master Photos in a mail-in offer were also included in each of the three series. The 5" x 7" Master Photos feature wide white borders and a large Stadium Club logo at top, highlighted by prismatic foil. The same foil is used as a border for a larger-format version of the player's regular S.C. card at the center of the Master

Photo. A "Members Only" version of each of the 1993 Master Photos was available as a premium with the purchase of a Members Only Stadium Club set. the Members Only Master Photos have a gold-foil seal in the upper-right corner.

	NM/M
Complete Set (30):	15.00
Common Player:	.20
Series 1	
(1) Carlos Baerga	.20
(2) Delino DeShields	.20
(3) Brian McRae	.20
(4) Sam Militello	.20
(5) Joe Oliver	.20
(6) Kirby Puckett	1.50
(7) Cal Ripken Jr.	4.00
(8) Bip Roberts	.20
(9) Mike Scioscia	.20
(10) Rick Sutcliffe	.20
(11) Danny Tartabull	.20
(12) Tim Wakefield	.20
Series 2	
(13) George Brett	3.00
(14) Jose Canseco	.50
(15) Will Clark	.20
(16) Travis Fryman	.20
(17) Dwight Gooden	.20
(18) Mark Grace	.30
(19) Rickey Henderson	1.00
(20) Mark McGwire	2.50
(21) Nolan Ryan	4.00
(22) Ruben Sierra	.20
(23) Darryl Strawberry	.20
(24) Larry Walker	.20
Series 3	
(25) Barry Bonds	5.00
(26) Ken Griffey Jr.	2.50
(27) Greg Maddux	2.00
(28) David Nied	.20
(29) J.T. Snow	.20
(30) Brien Taylor	.20
Redemption Card:	3X

Members Only

A special version of the Topps' 1993 Stadium Club set was made available exclusively to members of the company's Stadium Club program. The set is a parallel of the regular-issue SC set (plus insert) on which a gold-foil "Members Only" shield logo has been added to the card front. In all other respects the cards are identical to the regular SC issue. Production was a reported 12,000 sets.

	NM/M
Complete Set (750):	100.00
Common Player:	.50
Members Only Stars:	8X

Members Only Baseball

As a benefit of membership in Topps' Stadium Club, each member received a 59-card set in four separate shipments. The cards featured highlights of the 1993 baseball, hockey, football and basketball seasons. Besides the 28 baseball player cards checklisted here there were nine football cards, six hockey

card and 16 basketball cards. Each sport's cards came separately in a heat-sealed cello wrap in a special box. Cards were typical S.C. quality, featuring full-bleed action photos on the front, with the Stadium Club log and player name enhanced with gold-foil stamping and a gold-foil "Members Only" notice beneath the player's name. Backs feature a parti-color background with a colorized, stylized player figure at right. At left is the story of the player's season or career highlight. The cards are unnumbered and are checklisted alphabetically.

	NM/M
Complete Set (28):	9.00
Common Player:	.10
(1) Jim Abbott	.10
(2) Barry Bonds	2.50
(3) Chris Bosio	.10
(4) George Brett	.75
(5) Jay Buhner	.10
(6) Joe Carter (3 HR in game 5th time)	.10
(7) Joe Carter (World Series-winning HR)	.10
(8) Carlton Fisk	.60
(9) Travis Fryman	.10
(10) Mark Grace	.20
(11) Ken Griffey Jr.	1.50
(12) Darryl Kile	.10
(13) Darren Lewis	.10
(14) Greg Maddux	.65
(15) Jack McDowell	.10
(16) Paul Molitor	.60
(17) Eddie Murray	.60
(18) Mike Piazza (Rookie catcher HR record)	1.50
(19) Mike Piazza (N.L. Rookie of the Year)	1.50
(20) Kirby Puckett	.65
(21) Jeff Reardon	.10
(22) Tim Salmon	.20
(23) Curt Schilling	.35
(24) Lee Smith	.10
(25) Dave Stewart	.10
(26) Frank Thomas	.60
(27) Mark Whiten	.10
(28) Dave Winfield	.60

1993 Stadium Club Special

Though the packaging and the cards themselves identify this 200-card set as a 1992 issue, it was not released until 1993 and is thought of by the hobby at large as a 1993 set. The set is sold in a plastic replica of Jack Murphy Stadium in San Diego, venue for the 1993 All-Star Game. Fifty-six of the cards feature players from that contest and are so identified by a line of gold-foil on the card front and an All-Star logo on back. Twenty-five members of the 1992 Team U.S.A. Olympic baseball squad are also included in the set, with appropriate logos and notations front and back. There are 19 cards depicting action and stars of the the 1992 League Cham-

pionships and World Series. The other 100 cards in the set are 1992 draft picks. All cards have the same basic format as the regular-issue 1992 Topps Stadium Club cards, full-bleed photos on front and back, UV coating on both sides and gold-foil highlights on front. Besides the 200 standard-size cards, the Special Edition set included a dozen "Master Photos," 5" x 7" white-bordered premium cards.

	NM/M
Unopened Set (200):	45.00
Complete Set (200):	40.00
Common Player:	.05
1 Dave Winfield	.75
2 Juan Guzman	.05
3 Tony Gwynn	.85
4 Chris Roberts	.05
5 Benny Santiago	.05
6 Sherard Clinkscales	.05
7 Jonathan Nunnally **RC**	.05
8 Chuck Knoblauch	.05
9 Bob Wolcott **RC**	.05
10 Steve Rodriguez	.05
11 Mark Williams **RC**	.05
12 Danny Clyburn **RC**	.05
13 Darren Dreifort	.05
14 Andy Van Slyke	.05
15 Wade Boggs	.85
16 Scott Patton	.05
17 Gary Sheffield	.45
18 Ron Villone	.05
19 Roberto Alomar	.20
20 Marc Valdes	.05
21 Daron Kirkreit	.05
22 Jeff Granger	.05
23 Levon Largusa	.05
24 Jimmy Key	.05
25 Kevin Pearson	.05
26 Michael Moore	.05
27 Preston Wilson **RC**	1.00
28 Kirby Puckett	.85
29 Tim Crabtree **RC**	.05
30 Bip Roberts	.05
31 Kelly Gruber	.05
32 Tony Fernandez	.05
33 Jason Angel	.05
34 Calvin Murray	.05
35 Chad McConnell	.05
36 Jason Moler	.05
37 Mark Lemke	.05
38 Tom Knauss	.05
39 Larry Mitchell	.05
40 Doug Mirabelli	.05
41 Everett Stull II	.05
42 Chris Wimmer	.05
43 Dan Serafini **RC**	.05
44 Ryne Sandberg	.85
45 Steve Lyons	.05
46 Ryan Freeburg	.05
47 Ruben Sierra	.05
48 David Mysel	.05
49 Joe Hamilton	.05
50 Steve Rodriguez	.05
51 Tim Wakefield	.05
52 Scott Gentile	.05
53 Doug Jones	.05
54 Willie Brown	.05
55 Chad Mottola **RC**	.05
56 Ken Griffey Jr.	1.50
57 Jon Lieber **RC**	.50
58 Denny Martinez	.05
59 Joe Petcka	.05
60 Benji Simonton	.05
61 Brett Backlund	.05
62 Damon Berryhill	.05
63 Juan Guzman	.05
64 Doug Hecker	.05
65 Jamie Arnold	.05
66 Bob Tewksbury	.05
67 Tim Leger	.05
68 Todd Etler	.05
69 Lloyd McClendon	.05
70 Kurt Ehmann	.05
71 Rick Magdaleno	.05
72 Tom Pagnozzi	.05
73 Jeffrey Hammonds	.05
74 Joe Carter	.05
75 Chris Holt	.05
76 Charles Johnson	.05
77 Bob Walk	.05
78 Fred McGriff	.05
79 Tom Evans	.05
80 Scott Klingenbeck	.05
81 Chad McConnell	.05
82 Chris Eddy	.05
83 Phil Nevin	.05
84 John Kruk	.05
85 Tony Sheffield	.05
86 John Smoltz	.05
87 Trevor Humphry	.05
88 Charles Nagy	.05
89 Sean Runyan	.05
90 Mike Gulan	.05
91 Darren Daulton	.05
92 Otis Nixon	.05
93 Nomar Garciaparra	8.00
94 Larry Walker	.05
95 Hut Smith	.05
96 Rick Helling	.05
97 Roger Clemens	1.00
98 Ron Gant	.05
99 Kenny Felder	.05
100 Steve Murphy	.05
101 Mike Smith	.05
102 Terry Pendleton	.05
103 Tim Davis	.05
104 Jeff Patzke	.05
105 Craig Wilson	.05
106 Tom Glavine	.35
107 Mark Langston	.05
108 Mark Thompson	.05
109 Eric Owens **RC**	.05
110 Keith Johnson	.05
111 Robin Ventura	.05
112 Ed Sprague	.05
113 Jeff Schmidt **RC**	.05
114 Don Wengert	.05
115 Craig Biggio	.05
116 Kenny Carlyle	.05
117 Derek Jeter **RC**	30.00
118 Manuel Lee	.05
119 Jeff Haas	.05
120 Roger Bailey	.05
121 Sean Lowe	.05
122 Rick Aguilera	.05
123 Sandy Alomar	.05
124 Derek Wallace	.05
125 B.J. Wallace	.05
126 Greg Maddux	.85
127 Tim Moore	.05
128 Lee Smith	.05
129 Todd Steverson	.05
130 Chris Widger	.05
131 Paul Molitor	.75
132 Chris Smith	.05
133 Chris Gomez **RC**	.05
134 Jimmy Baron	.05
135 John Smoltz	.05
136 Pat Borders	.05
137 Donnie Leshnock	.05
138 Gus Gandarillos	.05
139 Will Clark	.05
140 Ryan Luzinski **RC**	.05
141 Cal Ripken, Jr.	2.50
142 B.J. Wallace	.05
143 Trey Beamon **RC**	.05
144 Norm Charlton	.05
145 Mike Mussina	.30
146 Billy Owens	.05
147 Ozzie Smith	.85
148 Jason Kendall **RC**	1.00
149 Mike Matthews **RC**	.05
150 David Spykstra	.05
151 Benji Grigsby	.05
152 Sean Smith	.05
153 Mark McGwire	2.00
154 David Cone	.05
155 Shon Walker **RC**	.05
156 Jason Giambi	.50
157 Jack McDowell	.05
158 Paxton Briley	.05
159 Edgar Martinez	.05
160 Brian Sackinsky	.05
161 Barry Bonds	2.50
162 Roberto Kelly	.05
163 Jeff Alkire	.05
164 Mike Sharperson	.05
165 Jamie Taylor	.05
166 John Saffer	.05
167 Jerry Browne	.05
168 Travis Fryman	.05
169 Brady Anderson	.05
170 Chris Roberts	.05
171 Lloyd Peever	.05
172 Francisco Cabrera	.05
173 Ramiro Martinez	.05
174 Jeff Alkire	.05
175 Ivan Rodriguez	.65
176 Kevin Brown	.05
177 Chad Roper	.05
178 Rod Henderson	.05
179 Dennis Eckersley	.05
180 Shannon Stewart **RC**	1.00
181 DeShawn Warren	.05
182 Lonnie Smith	.05
183 Willie Adams	.05
184 Jeff Montgomery	.05
185 Damon Hollins	.05
186 Byron Matthews	.05
187 Harold Baines	.05
188 Rick Greene	.05
189 Carlos Baerga	.05
190 Brandon Cromer	.05
191 Roberto Alomar	.20
192 Rich Ireland	.05
193 Steve Montgomery	.05
194 Brant Brown	.05
195 Ritchie Moody	.05
196 Michael Tucker	.05
197 Jason Varitek **RC**	6.00
198 David Manning	.05
199 Marquis Riley	.05
200 Jason Giambi	.60

Special Master Photos

Each 1993 Stadium Club Special (Jack Murphy Stadium) set included 12 Master Photos replicating cards from the set. There were nine All-Stars, two '92 rookies and a Team USA player among the Master Photos. Gold-tone prismatic foil highlights the 5" x 7" cards, decorating the large logo at top and separating the card photo from the wide white border. Backs have Stadium Club and MLB logos and copyright

information printed in black. The unnumbered cards are checklisted here in alphabetical order.

	NM/M
Complete Set (12):	5.00
Common Player:	.20
(1) Sandy Alomar	.20
(2) Tom Glavine	.65
(3) Ken Griffey Jr.	2.00
(4) Tony Gwynn	1.50
(5) Chuck Knoblauch	.20
(6) Chad Mottola	.20
(7) Kirby Puckett	1.50
(8) Chris Roberts	.20
(9) Ryne Sandberg	1.50
(10) Gary Sheffield	.40
(11) Larry Walker	.20
(12) Preston Wilson	.20

Team Sets

This special edition of Stadium Club cards consists of 16 separate team sets of 30 cards each. Each blister-packed team set was priced around $6 and sold exclusively at Wal-Mart. Fronts of the UV coated cards have a player photo that is borderless at the top, bottom and left. At right is a green stripe, at top of which is a partial baseball design and some other striping in gold-foil. Backs are basically green, with a light blue box at lower-right containing personal information and stats, along with the S.C. logo. A player photo is at upper-left, with his name superimposed on a bat. Cards are checklisted here within team set. Several of the Braves cards were authentically autographed as pack-toppers on specially marked sets.

	NM/M
Complete Set (480):	30.00
Common Player:	.10
ATLANTA BRAVES	
Team Set:	3.00
1 Tom Glavine	.35
2 Bill Pecota	.10
3 David Justice	.10
4 Mark Lemke	.10
5 Jeff Blauser	.10
6 Ron Gant	.10
7 Greg Olson	.10
8 Francisco Cabrera	.10
9 Chipper Jones	1.00
9a Chipper Jones/Auto.	20.00
10 Steve Avery	.10
11 Kent Mercker	.10
12 John Smoltz	.10
12a John Smoltz/Auto.	6.00
13 Pete Smith	.10
14 Damon Berryhill	.10
15 Sid Bream	.10
16 Otis Nixon	.10
17 Mike Stanton	.10
18 Greg Maddux	1.00
19 Jay Howell	.10
20 Rafael Belliard	.10
21 Terry Pendleton	.10
22 Deion Sanders	.15
23 Brian Hunter	.10
24 Marvin Freeman	.10

#	Player	Price
25	Mark Wohlers	.10
26	Ryan Klesko	.10
26a	Ryan Klesko/Auto.	4.00
27a	Javy Lopez/Auto.	4.00
27	Javy Lopez	.10
28	Melvin Nieves	.10
29	Tony Tarasco	.10
30	Ramon Caraballo	.10

CHICAGO CUBS
Team Set: 2.50

1	Ryne Sandberg	1.50
2	Sammy Sosa	1.50
3	Greg Hibbard	.25
4	Candy Maldonado	.10
5	Willie Wilson	.10
6	Dan Plesac	.10
7	Steve Buechele	.10
8	Mark Grace	.25
9	Shawon Dunston	.10
10	Steve Lake	.10
11	Dwight Smith	.10
12	Derrick May	.10
13	Paul Assenmacher	.10
14	Mike Harkey	.10
15	Lance Dickson	.10
16	Randy Myers	.10
17	Mike Morgan	.10
18	Chuck McElroy	.10
19	Jose Guzman	.10
20	Jose Vizcaino	.10
21	Frank Castillo	.10
22	Bob Scanlon	.10
23	Rick Wilkins	.10
24	Rey Sanchez	.10
25	Phil Dauphin	.10
26	Jim Bullinger	.10
27	Jessie Hollins	.10
28	Matt Walbeck	.10
29	Fernando Ramsey	.10
30	Jose Bautista	.10

CALIFORNIA ANGELS
Team Set: 1.50

1	J.T. Snow	.25
2	Chuck Crim	.10
3	Chili Davis	.10
4	Mark Langston	.10
5	Ron Tingley	.10
6	Eduardo Perez	.10
7	Scott Sanderson	.10
8	Jorge Fabregas	.10
9	Troy Percival	.10
10	Rod Correia	.10
11	Greg Myers	.10
12	Steve Frey	.10
13	Tim Salmon	.25
14	Scott Lewis	.10
15	Rene Gonzales	.10
16	Chuck Finley	.10
17	John Orton	.10
18	Joe Grahe	.10
19	Luis Polonia	.10
20	John Farrell	.10
21	Damion Easley	.10
22	Gene Nelson	.10
23	Chad Curtis	.10
24	Russ Springer	.10
25	De Shawn Warren	.10
26	Darryl Scott	.10
27	Gary DiSarcina	.10
28	Jerry Nielson	.10
29	Torey Lovullo	.10
30	Julio Valera	.10

CHICAGO WHITE SOX
Team Set: 2.50

1	Frank Thomas	1.00
2	Bo Jackson	.25
3	Rod Bolton	.10
4	Dave Stieb	.10
5	Tim Raines	.10
6	Joey Cora	.10
7	Warren Newson	.10
8	Roberto Hernandez	.10
9	Brandon Wilson	.10
10	Wilson Alvarez	.10
11	Dan Pasqua	.10
12	Ozzie Guillen	.10
13	Robin Ventura	.25
14	Craig Grebeck	.10
15	Lance Johnson	.10
16	Carlton Fisk	.75
17	Ron Karkovice	.10
18	Jack McDowell	.10
19	Scott Radinsky	.10
20	Bobby Thigpen	.10
21	Donn Pall	.10
22	George Bell	.10
23	Alex Fernandez	.10
24	Mike Huff	.10
25	Jason Bere	.10
26	Johnny Ruffin	.10
27	Ellis Burks	.10
28	Kirk McCaskill	.10
29	Terry Leach	.10
30	Shawn Gilbert	.10

COLORADO ROCKIES
Team Set: 1.50

1	David Nied	.10
2	Quinton McCracken	.10
3	Charlie Hayes	.10
4	Bryn Smith	.10
5	Dante Bichette	.10
6	Alex Cole	.10
7	Scott Aldred	.10
8	Roberto Mejia	.10
9	Jeff Parrett	.10
10	Joe Girardi	.10
11	Andres Galarraga	.10
12	Daryl Boston	.10
13	Jerald Clark	.10
14	Gerald Young	.10
15	Bruce Ruffin	.10
16	Rudy Seanez	.10
17	Darren Holmes	.10
18	Andy Ashby	.10
19	Chris Jones	.10
20	Mark Thompson	.10
21	Freddie Benavides	.10
22	Eric Wedge	.10
23	Vinny Castilla	.10
24	Butch Henry	.10
25	Jim Tatum	.10
26	Steve Reed	.10
27	Eric Young	.10
28	Danny Sheaffer	.10
29	Roger Bailey	.10
30	Brad Ausmus	.10

FLORIDA MARLINS
Team Set: 1.50

1	Nigel Wilson	.10
2	Bryan Harvey	.10
3	Bob McClure	.10
4	Alex Arias	.10
5	Walt Weiss	.10
6	Charlie Hough	.10
7	Scott Chiamparino	.10
8	Junior Felix	.10
9	Jack Armstrong	.10
10	Dave Magadan	.10
11	Cris Carpenter	.10
12	Benny Santiago	.10
13	Jeff Conine	.10
14	Jerry Don Gleaton	.10
15	Steve Decker	.10
16	Ryan Bowen	.10
17	Ramon Martinez	.10
18	Bret Barberie	.10
19	Monty Fariss	.10
20	Trevor Hoffman	.25
21	Scott Pose	.10
22	Mike Myers	.10
23	Geronimo Berroa	.10
24	Darrell Whitmore	.10
25	Chuck Carr	.10
26	Dave Weathers	.10
27	Matt Turner	.10
28	Jose Martinez	.10
29	Orestes Destrade	.10
30	Carl Everett	.10

HOUSTON ASTROS
Team Set: 1.50

1	Doug Drabek	.10
2	Eddie Taubensee	.10
3	James Mouton	.10
4	Ken Caminiti	.10
5	Chris James	.10
6	Jeff Juden	.10
7	Eric Anthony	.10
8	Jeff Bagwell	1.00
9	Greg Swindell	.10
10	Steve Finley	.10
11	Al Osuna	.10
12	Gary Mota	.10
13	Scott Servais	.10
14	Craig Biggio	.50
15	Doug James	.10
16	Rob Mallicoat	.10
17	Darryl Kile	.10
18	Kevin Bass	.10
19	Pete Harnisch	.10
20	Andujar Cedeno	.10
21	Brian Hunter	.10
22	Brian Williams	.10
23	Chris Donnels	.10
24	Xavier Hernandez	.10
25	Todd Jones	.10
26	Luis Gonzalez	.10
27	Rick Parker	.10
28	Casey Candaele	.10
29	Tony Eusebio	.10
30	Mark Portugal	.10

KANSAS CITY ROYALS
Team Set: 1.50

1	George Brett	1.00
2	Mike MacFarlane	.10
3	Tom Gordon	.15
4	Wally Joyner	.10
5	Kevin Appier	.10
6	Phil Hiatt	.10
7	Keith Miller	.10
8	Hipolito Pichardo	.10
9	Chris Gwynn	.10
10	Jose Lind	.10
11	Mark Gubicza	.10
12	Dennis Rasmussen	.10
13	Mike Magnante	.10
14	Joe Vitiello	.10
15	Kevin McReynolds	.10
16	Greg Gagne	.10
17	David Cone	.15
18	Brent Mayne	.10
19	Jeff Montgomery	.10
20	Joe Randa	.10
21	Felix Jose	.10
22	Bill Sampen	.10
23	Curt Wilkerson	.10
24	Mark Gardner	.10
25	Brian McRae	.10
26	Hubie Brooks	.10
27	Chris Eddy	.10
28	Harvey Pulliam	.10
29	Rusty Meacham	.10
30	Danny Miceli	.10

LOS ANGELES DODGERS
Team Set: 3.00

1	Darryl Strawberry	.25
2	Pedro Martinez	.75
3	Jody Reed	.10
4	Carlos Hernandez	.10
5	Kevin Gross	.10
6	Mike Piazza	1.50
7	Jim Gott	.10
8	Eric Karros	.10
9	Mike Sharperson	.10
10	Ramon Martinez	.10
11	Tim Wallach	.10
12	Pedro Astacio	.10
13	Lenny Harris	.10
14	Brett Butler	.10
15	Raul Mondesi	.10
16	Todd Worrell	.10
17	Jose Offerman	.10
18	Mitch Webster	.10
19	Tom Candiotti	.10
20	Eric Davis	.10
21	Michael Moore	.10
22	Billy Ashley	.10
23	Orel Hershiser	.15
24	Roger Cedeno	.10
25	Roger McDowell	.10
26	Mike James	.10
27	Steve Wilson	.10
28	Todd Hollandsworth	.10
29	Cory Snyder	.10
30	Todd Williams	.10

NEW YORK YANKEES
Team Set: 2.50

1	Don Mattingly	1.25
2	Jim Abbott	.10
3	Matt Nokes	.10
4	Danny Tartabull	.10
5	Wade Boggs	1.00
6	Melido Perez	.10
7	Steve Farr	.10
8	Kevin Maas	.10
9	Randy Velarde	.10
10	Mike Humphreys	.10
11	Mike Gallego	.10
12	Mike Stanley	.10
13	Jimmy Key	.10
14	Paul O'Neill	.10
15	Spike Owen	.10
16	Pat Kelly	.10
17	Sterling Hitchcock	.10
18	Mike Witt	.10
19	Scott Kamieniecki	.10
20	John Habyan	.10
21	Bernie Williams	.20
22	Brien Taylor	.10
23	Rich Monteleone	.10
24	Mark Hutton	.10
25	Robert Eenhoorn	.10
26	Gerald Williams	.10
27	Sam Militello	.10
28	Bob Wickman	.10
29	Andy Stankiewicz	.10
30	Domingo Jean	.10

OAKLAND A'S
Team Set: 3.00

1	Dennis Eckersley	.75
2	Lance Blankenship	.10
3	Mike Mohler	.10
4	Jerry Browne	.10
5	Kevin Seitzer	.10
6	Storm Davis	.10
7	Mark McGwire	2.00
8	Rickey Henderson	.75
9	Terry Steinbach	.10
10	Ruben Sierra	.10
11	Dave Henderson	.10
12	Bob Welch	.10
13	Rick Honeycutt	.10
14	Ron Darling	.10
15	Joe Boever	.10
16	Bobby Witt	.10
17	Izzy Molina	.10
18	Mike Bordick	.10
19	Brent Gates	.10
20	Shawn Hillegas	.10
21	Scott Hammond	.10
22	Todd Van Poppel	.10
23	Johnny Guzman	.10
24	Scott Lydy	.10
25	Scott Baker	.10
26	Todd Revenig	.10
27	Scott Brosius	.10
28	Troy Neel	.10
29	Dale Sveum	.10
30	Mike Neill	.10

PHILADELPHIA PHILLIES
Team Set: 1.50

1	Darren Daulton	.10
2	Larry Anderson	.10
3	Kyle Abbott	.10
4	Chad McConnell	.10
5	Danny Jackson	.10
6	Kevin Stocker	.10
7	Jim Eisenreich	.10
8	Mickey Morandini	.10
9	Bob Ayrault	.10
10	Doug Lindsey	.10
11	Dave Hollins	.10
12	Dave West	.10
13	Wes Chamberlain	.10
14	Curt Schilling	.35
15	Len Dykstra	.10
16	Trevor Humphry	.10
17	Terry Mulholland	.10
18	Gene Schall	.10
19	Mike Lieberthal	.15
20	Ben Rivera	.10
21	Mariano Duncan	.10
22	Pete Incaviglia	.10
23	Ron Blazier	.10
24	Jeff Jackson	.10
25	Jose DeLeon	.10
26	Ron Lockett	.10
27	Tommy Greene	.10
28	Milt Thompson	.10
29	Mitch Williams	.10
30	John Kruk	.10

ST. LOUIS CARDINALS
Team Set: 1.50

1	Ozzie Smith	1.00
2	Rene Arocha	.10
3	Bernard Gilkey	.10
4	Jose Oquendo	.10
5	Mike Perez	.10
6	Tom Pagnozzi	.10
7	Rod Brewer	.10
8	Joe Magrane	.10
9	Todd Zeile	.10
10	Bob Tewksbury	.10
11	Darrel Deak	.10
12	Gregg Jefferies	.10
13	Lee Smith	.25
14	Ozzie Canseco	.10
15	Tom Urbani	.10
16	Donovan Osborne	.10
17	Ray Lankford	.10
18	Rheal Cormier	.10
19	Allen Watson	.10
20	Geronimo Pena	.10
21	Rob Murphy	.10
22	Tracy Woodson	.10
23	Basil Shabazz	.10
24	Omar Olivares	.10
25	Les Lancaster	.10
26	Sean Lowe	.10
27	Hector Villanueva	.10
28	Brian Barber	.10
29	Aaron Holbert	.10

SAN FRANCISCO GIANTS
Team Set: 2.50

1	Barry Bonds	2.00
2	Dave Righetti	.10
3	Matt Williams	.10
3a	Matt Williams/Auto.	10.00
4	Royce Clayton	.10
5	Salomon Torres	.10
6	Kirt Manwaring	.10
7	J.R. Phillips	.10
8	Kevin Rogers	.10
9	Will Clark	.10
10	John Burkett	.10
11	Willie McGee	.10
12	Rod Beck	.10
13	Jeff Reed	.10
14	Jeff Brantley	.10
15	Steve Hosey	.10
16	Chris Hancock	.10
17	Adell Davenport	.10
18	Mike Jackson	.10
19	Dave Martinez	.10
20	Bill Swift	.10
21	Steve Scarsone	.10
22	Trevor Wilson	.10
23	Mark Carreon	.10
24	Bud Black	.10
25	Darren Lewis	.10
26	Dan Carlson	.10
27	Craig Colbert	.10
28	Greg Brummet	.10
29	Bryan Hickerson	.10
30	Robby Thompson	.10

SEATTLE MARINERS
Team Set: 3.00

1	Ken Griffey Jr.	1.50
2	Desi Realford	.10
3	Dave Weinhouse	.10
4	Rich Amaral	.10
5	Brian Deak	.10
6	Bret Boone	.10
7	Bill Haselman	.10
8	Dave Fleming	.10
9	Fernando Vina	.10
10	Greg Litton	.10
11	Mackey Sasser	.10
12	Lee Tinsley	.10
13	Norm Charlton	.10
14	Russ Swan	.10
15	Brian Holman	.10
16	Randy Johnson	.75
17	Erik Hanson	.10
18	Tino Martinez	.10
19	Marc Newfield	.10
20	Dave Valle	.10
21	John Cummings	.10
22	Mike Hampton	.10
23	Jay Buhner	.10
24	Edgar Martinez	.10
25	Omar Vizquel	.10
26	Pete O'Brien	.10
27	Brian Turang	.10
28	Chris Bosio	.10
29	Mike Felder	.10
30	Shawn Estes	.10

TEXAS RANGERS
Team Set: 5.00

1	Nolan Ryan	2.50
2	Ritchie Moody	.10
3	Matt Whiteside	.10
4	David Hulse	.10
5	Roger Pavlik	.10
6	Dan Smith	.10
7	Donald Harris	.10
8	Butch Davis	.10
9	Benji Gil	.10
10	Ivan Rodriguez	.65
11	Dean Palmer	.10
12	Jeff Huson	.10
13	Rob Mauer	.10
14	Gary Redus	.10
15	Doug Dascenzo	.10
16	Charlie Liebrandt	.10
17	Tom Henke	.10
18	Manuel Lee	.10
19	Kenny Rogers	.10
20	Kevin Brown	.10
21	Juan Gonzalez	.50
22	Geno Petralli	.10
23	John Russell	.10
24	Robb Nen	.10
25	Julio Franco	.10
26	Rafael Palmeiro	.65
27	Todd Burns	.10
28	Jose Canseco	.50
29	Billy Ripken	.10
30	Dan Peltier	.10

cecil FIELDER

Ultra Pro

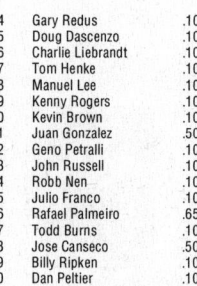

feature a borderless photo with the player's name presented in a unique typewriter/label maker style at bottom. The player's last name and Topps Stadium Club logo at top are in red foil. Backs feature another player photo, some personal data and a headlined career summary. Various stats and skills rankings complete the data. Subsets within the issue include cards annotated with Major League debut dates, 1993 awards won, home run club cards, cards featuring two or three players, and Final Tribute cards for George Brett and Nolan Ryan.

Special packages of plastic sheets and sleeves carrying the "Topps Stadium Club UltraPro" brand name included one of 10 special Stadium Club cards of Barry Bonds, Bobby Bonds and/or Willie Mays. Cards are typical UV coated, gold-foil quality, but because the cards were not licensed by Major League Baseball, team logos were removed from the photos.

NM/M
Complete Set (10): 7.00
Common Card: .50

1	Barry Bonds, Willie Mays, Bobby Bonds	.50
2	Willie Mays	1.00
3	Bobby Bonds	.50
4	Barry Bonds	1.00
5	Barry Bonds, Bobby Bonds	.50
6	Willie Mays	1.00
7	Barry Bonds (Business suit.)	1.00
8	Willie Mays, Bobby Bonds	1.00
9	Willie Mays	1.00
10	Barry Bonds (Tuxedo)	1.00

1994 Stadium Club Pre-Production

jose LIND

These sample cards introducing the 1994 Stadium Club set differ from their regular-issue counterparts only in the inclusion of a line of type vertically on the back-right, "Pre-Production Sample."

NM/M
Complete Set (9): 5.00
Common Player: .50

6	Al Martin	.50
15	Junior Ortiz	.50
36	Tim Salmon	.75
56	Jerry Spradlin	.50
122	Tom Pagnozzi	.50
123	Ron Gant	.50
125	Dennis Eckersley	1.50
135	Jose Lind	.50
238	Barry Bonds	4.00

1994 Stadium Club

Issued in three series to a total of 720 cards, Topps' mid-price brand features a hip look and a wide range of insert specials. The regular cards

NM/M
Complete Set (720): 20.00
Common Player: .05
1st Day: 8X
Golden Rainbow: 2X
Series 1, 2, 3 Pack (12): 1.00
Series 1, 2, 3 Wax Box (24): 15.00

1	Robin Yount	.65
2	Rick Wilkins	.05
3	Steve Scarsone	.05
4	Gary Sheffield	.40
5	George Brett	1.00
6	Al Martin	.05
7	Joe Oliver	.05
8	Stan Belinda	.05
9	Denny Hocking	.05
10	Roberto Alomar	.20
11	Luis Polonia	.05
12	Scott Hemond	.05
13	Joey Reed	.05
14	Mel Rojas	.05
15	Junior Ortiz	.05
16	Harold Baines	.05
17	Brad Pennington	.05
18	Jay Bell	.05
19	Tom Henke	.05
20	Jeff Branson	.05
21	Roberto Mejia	.05
22	Pedro Munoz	.05
23	Matt Nokes	.05
24	Jack McDowell	.05
25	Cecil Fielder	.05
26	Tony Fossas	.05
27	Jim Eisenreich	.05
28	Anthony Young	.05
29	Chuck Carr	.05
30	Jeff Treadway	.05
31	Chris Nabholz	.05
32	Tom Candiotti	.05
33	Mike Maddux	.05
34	Nolan Ryan	2.00
35	Luis Gonzalez	.05
36	Tim Salmon	.05
37	Mark Whiten	.05
38	Roger McDowell	.05
39	Royce Clayton	.05
40	Troy Neel	.05
41	Mike Harkey	.05
42	Darrin Fletcher	.05
43	Wayne Kirby	.05
44	Rich Amaral	.05
45	Robb Nen	.05
46	Tim Teufel	.05
47	Steve Cooke	.05
48	Jeff McNeely	.05
49	Jeff Montgomery	.05
50	Skeeter Barnes	.05
51	Scott Stahoviak	.05
52	Pat Kelly	.05
53	Brady Anderson	.05
54	Mariano Duncan	.05
55	Brian Bohanon	.05
56	Jerry Spradlin	.05
57	Ron Karkovice	.05
58	Jeff Gardner	.05
59	Bobby Bonilla	.05
60	Tino Martinez	.05
61	Todd Benzinger	.05
62	Steve Trachsel RC	.25
63	Brian Jordan	.05
64	Steve Bedrosian	.05
65	Brent Gates	.05
66	Shawn Green	.35
67	Sean Berry	.05
68	Joe Klink	.05
69	Fernando Valenzuela	.05
70	Andy Tomberlin	.05
71	Tony Pena	.05
72	Eric Young	.05

No.	Player	Price
73	Chris Gomez	.05
74	Paul O'Neill	.05
75	Ricky Gutierrez	.05
76	Brad Holman	.05
77	Lance Painter	.05
78	Mike Butcher	.05
79	Sid Bream	.05
80	Sammy Sosa	.75
81	Felix Fermin	.05
82	Todd Hundley	.05
83	Kevin Higgins	.05
84	Todd Pratt	.05
85	Ken Griffey Jr.	1.25
86	John O'Donoghue	.05
87	Rick Renteria	.05
88	John Burkett	.05
89	Jose Vizcaino	.05
90	Kevin Seitzer	.05
91	Bobby Witt	.05
92	Chris Turner	.05
93	Omar Vizquel	.05
94	Dave Justice	.05
95	David Segui	.05
96	Dave Hollins	.05
97	Doug Strange	.05
98	Jerald Clark	.05
99	Mike Moore	.05
100	Joey Cora	.05
101	Scott Kamieniecki	.05
102	Andy Benes	.05
103	Chris Bosio	.05
104	Rey Sanchez	.05
105	John Jaha	.05
106	Otis Nixon	.05
107	Rickey Henderson	.65
108	Jeff Bagwell	.65
109	Gregg Jefferies	.05
110	Topps Trios (Roberto Alomar, Paul Molitor, John Olerud)	.25
111	Topps Trios (Ron Gant, David Justice, Fred McGriff)	.05
112	Topps Trios (Juan Gonzalez, Rafael Palmeiro, Dean Palmer)	.25
113	Greg Swindell	.05
114	Bill Hasleman	.05
115	Phil Plantier	.05
116	Ivan Rodriguez	.60
117	Kevin Tapani	.05
118	Mike LaValliere	.05
119	Tim Costo	.05
120	Mickey Morandini	.05
121	Brett Butler	.05
122	Tom Pagnozzi	.05
123	Ron Gant	.05
124	Damion Easley	.05
125	Dennis Eckersley	.60
126	Matt Mieske	.05
127	Cliff Floyd	.05
128	Julian Tavarez RC	.05
129	Arthur Rhodes	.05
130	Dave West	.05
131	Tim Naehring	.05
132	Freddie Benavides	.05
133	Paul Assenmacher	.05
134	David McCarty	.05
135	Jose Lind	.05
136	Reggie Sanders	.05
137	Don Slaught	.05
138	Andujar Cedeno	.05
139	Rob Deer	.05
140	Mike Piazza	1.25
141	Moises Alou	.05
142	Tom Foley	.05
143	Benny Santiago	.05
144	Sandy Alomar	.05
145	Carlos Hernandez	.05
146	Luis Alicea	.05
147	Tom Lampkin	.05
148	Ryan Klesko	.05
149	Juan Guzman	.05
150	Scott Servais	.05
151	Tony Gwynn	.75
152	Tim Wakefield	.05
153	David Nied	.05
154	Chris Haney	.05
155	Danny Bautista	.05
156	Randy Velarde	.05
157	Darrin Jackson	.05
158	J.R. Phillips RC	.05
159	Greg Gagne	.05
160	Luis Aquino	.05
161	John Vander Wal	.05
162	Randy Myers	.05
163	Ted Power	.05
164	Scott Brosius	.05
165	Len Dykstra	.05
166	Jacob Brumfield	.05
167	Bo Jackson	.10
168	Eddie Taubensee	.05
169	Carlos Baerga	.05
170	Tim Bogar	.05
171	Jose Canseco	.50
172	Greg Blosser	.05
173	Chili Davis	.05
174	Randy Knorr	.05
175	Mike Perez	.05
176	Henry Rodriguez	.05
177	Brian Turang RC	.05
178	Roger Pavlik	.05
179	Aaron Sele	.05
180	Tale of 2 Players (Fred McGriff, Gary Sheffield)	.05
181	Tale of 2 Players (J.T. Snow, Tim Salmon)	.05
182	Roberto Hernandez	.05
183	Jeff Reboulet	.05
184	John Doherty	.05
185	Danny Sheaffer	.05
186	Bip Roberts	.05
187	Denny Martinez	.05
188	Darryl Hamilton	.05
189	Eduardo Perez	.05
190	Pete Harnisch	.05
191	Rick Gossage	.05
192	Mickey Tettleton	.05
193	Lenny Webster	.05
194	Lance Johnson	.05
195	Don Mattingly	1.00
196	Gregg Olson	.05
197	Mark Gubicza	.05
198	Scott Fletcher	.05
199	Jon Shave	.05
200	Tim Mauser	.05
201	Jeromy Burnitz	.05
202	Rob Dibble	.05
203	Will Clark	.05
204	Steve Buechele	.05
205	Brian Williams	.05
206	Carlos Garcia	.05
207	Mark Clark	.05
208	Rafael Palmeiro	.60
209	Eric Davis	.05
210	Pat Meares	.05
211	Chuck Finley	.05
212	Jason Bere	.05
213	Gary DiSarcina	.05
214	Tony Fernandez	.05
215	B.J. Surhoff	.05
216	Lee Guetterman	.05
217	Tim Wallach	.05
218	Kirt Manwaring	.05
219	Albert Belle	.05
220	Dwight Gooden	.05
221	Archi Cianfrocco	.05
222	Terry Mulholland	.05
223	Hipolito Pichardo	.05
224	Kent Hrbek	.05
225	Criag Grebeck	.05
226	Todd Jones	.05
227	Mike Bordick	.05
228	John Olerud	.05
229	Jeff Blauser	.05
230	Alex Arias	.05
231	Bernard Gilkey	.05
232	Denny Neagle	.05
233	Pedro Borbon RC	.05
234	Dick Schofield	.05
235	Matias Carrillo	.05
236	Juan Bell	.05
237	Mike Hampton	.05
238	Barry Bonds	2.00
239	Cris Carpenter	.05
240	Eric Karros	.05
241	Greg McMichael	.05
242	Pat Hentgen	.05
243	Tim Pugh	.05
244	Vinny Castilla	.05
245	Charlie Hough	.05
246	Bobby Munoz	.05
247	Kevin Baez	.05
248	Todd Frohwirth	.05
249	Charlie Hayes	.05
250	Mike Macfarlane	.05
251	Danny Darwin	.05
252	Ben Rivera	.05
253	Dave Henderson	.05
254	Steve Avery	.05
255	Tim Belcher	.05
256	Dan Plesac	.05
257	Jim Thome	.60
258	Albert Belle (35+ HR Hitter)	.05
259	Barry Bonds (35+ HR Hitter)	1.00
260	Ron Gant (35+ HR Hitter)	.05
261	Juan Gonzalez (35+ HR Hitter)	.20
262	Ken Griffey Jr. (35+ HR Hitter)	.65
263	Dave Justice (35+ HR Hitter)	.05
264	Fred McGriff (35+ HR Hitter)	.05
265	Rafael Palmeiro (35+ HR Hitter)	.20
266	Mike Piazza (35+ HR Hitter)	.65
267	Frank Thomas (35+ HR Hitter)	.35
268	Matt Williams (35+ HR Hitter)	.05
269a	Checklist 1-135	.05
269b	Checklist 271-408	.05
270a	Checklist 136-270	.05
270b	Checklist 409-540	.05
271	Mike Stanley	.05
272	Tony Tarasco	.05
273	Teddy Higuera	.05
274	Ryan Thompson	.05
275	Rick Aguilera	.05
276	Ramon Martinez	.05
277	Orlando Merced	.05
278	Guillermo Velasquez	.05
279	Mark Hutton	.05
280	Larry Walker	.05
281	Kevin Gross	.05
282	Jose Offerman	.05
283	Jim Leyritz	.05
284	Jamie Moyer	.05
285	Frank Thomas	.65
286	Derek Bell	.05
287	Derrick May	.05
288	Dave Winfield	.65
289	Curt Schilling	.35
290	Carlos Quintana	.05
291	Bob Natal	.05
292	David Cone	.05
293	Al Osuna	.05
294	Bob Hamelin	.05
295	Chad Curtis	.05
296	Danny Jackson	.05
297	Bob Welch	.05
298	Felix Jose	.05
299	Jay Buhner	.05
300	Joe Carter	.05
301	Kenny Lofton	.05
302	Kirk Rueter RC	.15
303	Kim Batiste	.05
304	Mike Morgan	.05
305	Pat Borders	.05
306	Rene Arocha	.05
307	Ruben Sierra	.05
308	Steve Finley	.05
309	Travis Fryman	.05
310	Zane Smith	.05
311	Willie Wilson	.05
312	Trevor Hoffman	.05
313	Terry Pendleton	.05
314	Salomon Torres	.05
315	Robin Ventura	.05
316	Randy Tomlin	.05
317	Dave Stewart	.05
318	Mike Benjamin	.05
319	Matt Turner	.05
320	Manny Ramirez	.65
321	Kevin Young	.05
322	Ken Caminiti	.05
323	Joe Girardi	.05
324	Jeff McKnight	.05
325	Gene Harris	.05
326	Devon White	.05
327	Darryl Kile	.05
328	Craig Paquette	.05
329	Cal Eldred	.05
330	Bill Swift	.05
331	Alan Trammell	.05
332	Armando Reynoso	.05
333	Brent Mayne	.05
334	Chris Donnels	.05
335	Darryl Strawberry	.05
336	Dean Palmer	.05
337	Frank Castillo	.05
338	Jeff King	.05
339	John Franco	.05
340	Kevin Appier	.05
341	Lance Blankenship	.05
342	Mark McLemore	.05
343	Pedro Astacio	.05
344	Rich Batchelor	.05
345	Ryan Bowen	.05
346	Terry Steinbach	.05
347	Troy O'Leary	.05
348	Willie Blair	.05
349	Wade Boggs	.75
350	Tim Raines	.05
351	Scott Livingstone	.05
352	Rod Correia	.05
353	Ray Lankford	.05
354	Pat Listach	.05
355	Milt Thompson	.05
356	Miguel Jimenez	.05
357	Marc Newfield	.05
358	Mark McGwire	1.50
359	Kirby Puckett	.75
360	Kent Mercker	.05
361	John Kruk	.05
362	Jeff Kent	.05
363	Hal Morris	.05
364	Edgar Martinez	.05
365	Dave Magadan	.05
366	Dante Bichette	.05
367	Chris Hammond	.05
368	Bret Saberhagen	.05
369	Billy Ripken	.05
370	Bill Gullickson	.05
371	Andre Dawson	.35
372	Bobby Kelly	.05
373	Cal Ripken, Jr.	2.00
374	Craig Biggio	.05
375	Dan Pasqua	.05
376	Dave Nilsson	.05
377	Duane Ward	.05
378	Greg Vaughn	.05
379	Jeff Fassero	.05
380	Jerry Dipoto	.05
381	John Patterson	.05
382	Kevin Brown	.05
383	Kevin Roberson	.05
384	Joe Orsulak	.05
385	Hilly Hathaway	.05
386	Mike Greenwell	.05
387	Orestes Destrade	.05
388	Mike Gallego	.05
389	Ozzie Guillen	.05
390	Raul Mondesi	.05
391	Scott Lydy	.05
392	Tom Urbani	.05
393	Wil Cordero	.05
394	Tony Longmire	.05
395	Todd Zeile	.05
396	Scott Cooper	.05
397	Ryne Sandberg	.75
398	Ricky Bones	.05
399	Phil Clark	.05
400	Orel Hershiser	.05
401	Mike Henneman	.05
402	Mark Lemke	.05
403	Mark Grace	.65
404	Ken Ryan	.05
405	John Smoltz	.05
406	Jeff Conine	.05
407	Greg Harris	.05
408	Doug Drabek	.05
409	Dave Fleming	.05
410	Danny Tartabull	.05
411	Chad Kreuter	.05
412	Brad Ausmus	.05
413	Ben McDonald	.05
414	Barry Larkin	.05
415	Bret Barberie	.05
416	Chuck Knoblauch	.05
417	Ozzie Smith	.75
418	Ed Sprague	.05
419	Matt Williams	.05
420	Jeremy Hernandez	.05
421	Jose Bautista	.05
422	Kevin Mitchell	.05
423	Manuel Lee	.05
424	Mike Devereaux	.05
425	Omar Olivares	.05
426	Rafael Belliard	.05
427	Richie Lewis	.05
428	Ron Darling	.05
429	Shane Mack	.05
430	Tim Hulett	.05
431	Wally Joyner	.05
432	Wes Chamberlain	.05
433	Tom Browning	.05
434	Scott Radinsky	.05
435	Rondell White	.05
436	Rod Beck	.05
437	Rheal Cormier	.05
438	Randy Johnson	.65
439	Pete Schourek	.05
440	Mo Vaughn	.05
441	Mike Timlin	.05
442	Mark Langston	.05
443	Lou Whitaker	.05
444	Kevin Stocker	.05
445	Ken Hill	.05
446	John Wetteland	.05
447	J.T. Snow	.05
448	Erik Pappas	.05
449	David Hulse	.05
450	Darren Daulton	.05
451	Chris Hoiles	.05
452	Bryan Harvey	.05
453	Darren Lewis	.05
454	Andres Galarraga	.05
455	Joe Hesketh	.05
456	Vince Coleman	.05
457	Dan Peltier	.05
458	Joe Boever	.05
459	Kevin Rogers	.05
460	Craig Shipley	.05
461	Alvaro Espinoza	.05
462	Wilson Alvarez	.05
463	Guy Snyder	.05
464	Candy Maldonado	.05
465	Blas Minor	.05
466	Rod Bolton	.05
467	Kenny Rogers	.05
468	Greg Myers	.05
469	Jimmy Key	.05
470	Tony Castillo	.05
471	Mike Stanton	.05
472	Deion Sanders	.05
473	Tito Navarro	.05
474	Mike Gardiner	.05
475	Steve Reed	.05
476	John Roper	.05
477	Mike Trombley	.05
478	Charles Nagy	.05
479	Larry Casian	.05
480	Eric Hillman	.05
481	Bill Wertz	.05
482	Jeff Schwarz	.05
483	John Valentin	.05
484	Carl Willis	.05
485	Gary Gaetti	.05
486	Bill Pecota	.05
487	John Smiley	.05
488	Mike Mussina	.35
489	Mike Ignasiak RC	.05
490	Billy Brewer	.05
491	Jack Voigt	.05
492	Mike Munoz	.05
493	Lee Tinsley	.05
494	Bob Wickman	.05
495	Roger Salkeld	.05
496	Thomas Howard	.05
497	Mark Davis	.05
498	Dave Clark	.05
499	Turk Wendell	.05
500	Rafael Bournigal	.05
501	Chip Hale	.05
502	Matt Whiteside	.05
503	Brian Koelling	.05
504	Jeff Reed	.05
505	Paul Wagner	.05
506	Torey Lovullo	.05
507	Curtis Leskanic	.05
508	Derek Lilliquist	.05
509	Joe Magrane	.05
510	Mackey Sasser	.05
511	Lloyd McClendon	.05
512	Jayhawk Owens RC	.05
513	Woody Williams RC	.05
514	Gary Redus	.05
515	Tim Spehr	.05
516	Jim Abbott	.05
517	Lou Frazier	.05
518	Erik Plantenberg	.05
519	Tim Worrell	.05
520	Brian McRae	.05
521	Chan Ho Park RC	1.00
522	Mark Wohlers	.05
523	Geronimo Pena	.05
524	Andy Ashby	.05
525	Tale of 2 Players (Tim Raines, Andre Dawson)	.05
526	Tale of 2 Players (Paul Molitor, Dave Winfield)	.40
527	Joe Carter (RBI Leader)	.05
528	Frank Thomas (HR Leader)	.35
529	Ken Griffey Jr. (TB Leader)	.65
530	Dave Justice (HR Leader)	.05
531	Gregg Jefferies (AVG Leader)	.05
532	Barry Bonds (HR Leader)	1.00
533	John Kruk (Quick Start)	.05
534	Roger Clemens (Quick Start)	.50
535	Cecil Fielder (Quick Start)	.05
536	Ruben Sierra (Quick Start)	.05
537	Tom Gwynn (Quick Start)	.40
538	Tom Glavine (Quick Start)	.10
541	Ozzie Smith (Career Leader)	.40
542	Eddie Murray (Career Leader)	.30
543a	Lee Smith (Career Leader)	.05
543b	Lonnie Smith (Should be #643.)	.05
544	Greg Maddux	.75
545	Denis Boucher	.05
546	Mark Gardner	.05
547	Bo Jackson	.10
548	Eric Anthony	.05
549	Delino DeShields	.05
550	Turner Ward	.05
551	Scott Sanderson	.05
552	Hector Carrasco	.05
553	Tony Phillips	.05
554	Melido Perez	.05
555	Mike Felder	.05
556	Jack Morris	.05
557	Rafael Palmeiro	.60
558	Shane Reynolds	.05
559	Pete Incaviglia	.05
560	Greg Harris	.05
561	Matt Walbeck	.05
562	Todd Van Poppel	.05
563	Todd Stottlemyre	.05
564	Ricky Bones	.05
565	Mike Jackson	.05
566	Kevin McReynolds	.05
567	Melvin Nieves	.05
568	Juan Gonzalez	.35
569	Frank Viola	.05
570	Vince Coleman	.05
571	Brian Anderson RC	.25
572	Omar Vizquel	.05
573	Bernie Williams	.05
574	Tom Glavine	.35
575	Mitch Williams	.05
576	Shawon Dunston	.05
577	Mike Lansing	.05
578	Greg Pirkl	.05
579	Sid Fernandez	.05
580	Doug Jones	.05
581	Walt Weiss	.05
582	Tim Belcher	.05
583	Alex Fernandez	.05
584	Alex Cole	.05
585	Greg Cadaret	.05
586	Bob Tewksbury	.05
587	Dave Hansen	.05
588	Kurt Abbott RC	.25
589	Rick White RC	.05
590	Kevin Bass	.05
591	Geronimo Berroa	.05
592	Jaime Navarro	.05
593	Steve Farr	.05
594	Jack Armstrong	.05
595	Steve Howe	.05
596	Jose Rijo	.05
597	Otis Nixon	.05
598	Robby Thompson	.05
599	Kelly Stinnett	.05
600	Carlos Delgado	.50
601	Brian Johnson RC	.05
602	Gregg Olson	.05
603	Jim Edmonds	.05
604	Mike Blowers	.05
605	Lee Smith	.05
606	Pat Rapp	.05
607	Mike Magnante	.05
608	Karl Rhodes	.05
609	Jeff Juden	.05
610	Rusty Meacham	.05
611	Pedro Martinez	.65
612	Todd Worrell	.05
613	Stan Javier	.05
614	Mike Hampton	.05
615	Jose Guzman	.05
616	Xavier Hernandez	.05
617	David Wells	.05
618	John Habyan	.05
619	Chris Nabholz	.05
620	Bobby Jones	.05
621	Chris James	.05
622	Ellis Burks	.05
623	Erik Hanson	.05
624	Pat Meares	.05
625	Harold Reynolds	.05
626	Bob Hamelin (Rookie Rocker)	.05
627	Manny Ramirez (Rookie Rocker)	.30
628	Ryan Klesko (Rookie Rocker)	.05
629	Carlos Delgado (Rookie Rocker)	.30
630	Javier Lopez (Rookie Rocker)	.05
631	Steve Karsay (Rookie Rocker)	.05
632	Rick Helling (Rookie Rocket)	.05
633	Steve Trachsel (Rookie Rocket)	.05
634	Hector Carrasco (Rookie Rocket)	.05
635	Andy Stankiewicz	.05
636	Paul Sorrento	.05
637	Scott Erickson	.05
638	Chipper Jones	.75
639	Luis Polonia	.05
640	Howard Johnson	.05
641	John Dopson	.05
642	Jody Reed	.05
644	Mark Portugal	.05
645	Paul Molitor	.65
646	Paul Assenmacher	.05
647	Hubie Brooks	.05
648	Gary Wayne	.05
649	Sean Berry	.05
650	Roger Clemens	1.00
651	Brian Hunter	.05
652	Wally Whitehurst	.05
653	Allen Watson	.05
654	Rickey Henderson	.65
655	Sid Bream	.05
656	Dan Wilson	.05
657	Ricky Jordan	.05
658	Sterling Hitchcock	.05
659	Darrin Jackson	.05
660	Junior Felix	.05
661	Tom Brunansky	.05
662	Jose Vizcaino	.05
663	Mark Leiter	.05
664	Gil Heredia	.05
665	Fred McGriff	.65
666	Will Clark	.05
667	Al Leiter	.05
668	James Mouton	.05
669	Billy Bean	.05
670	Scott Leius	.05
671	Bret Boone	.05
672	Darren Holmes	.05
673	Dave Weathers	.05
674	Eddie Murray	.65
675	Felix Fermin	.05
676	Chris Sabo	.05
677	Billy Spiers	.05
678	Aaron Sele	.05
679	Juan Samuel	.05
680	Julio Franco	.05
681	Heathcliff Slocumb	.05
682	Denny Martinez	.05
683	Jerry Browne	.05
684	Pedro A. Martinez RC	.05
685	Rex Hudler	.05
686	Willie McGee	.05
687	Andy Van Slyke	.05
688	Pat Mahomes	.05
689	Dave Henderson	.05
690	Tony Eusebio	.05
691	Rick Sutcliffe	.05
692	Willie Banks	.05
693	Alan Mills	.05
694	Jeff Treadway	.05
695	Alex Gonzalez	.05
696	David Segui	.05
697	Rick Helling	.05
698	Bip Roberts	.05
699	Jeff Cirillo RC	.25
700	Terry Mulholland	.05
701	Marvin Freeman	.05
702	Jason Bere	.05
703	Javier Lopez	.05
704	Greg Hibbard	.05
705	Tommy Greene	.05
706	Marquis Grissom	.05
707	Brian Harper	.05
708	Steve Karsay	.05
709	Jeff Brantley	.05
710	Jeff Russell	.05
711	Bryan Hickerson	.05
712	Jim Pittsley RC	.05
713	Bobby Ayala	.05
714	John Smoltz (Fantastic Finisher)	.05
715	Jose Rijo (Fantastic Finisher)	.05
716	Greg Maddux (Fantastic Finisher)	.40
717	Matt Williams (Fantastic Finisher)	.05
718	Frank Thomas (Fantastic Finisher)	.35
719	Ryne Sandberg (Fantastic Finisher)	.40
720	Checklist	.05

Golden Rainbow

Found at the rate of one per pack, Stadium Club "Golden Rainbow" cards were issued for each of the 720 cards in the regular set. These inserts are distinguished by the use of gold prismatic foil highlights for the S.C. logo and box with the player's last name, instead of the red foil found on regular S.C. cards.

	NM/M
Complete Set (720):	60.00
Common Player:	.25
Stars:	2X

1st Day Issue

A special silver-foil emboss-ment designating "1st Day Issue" was placed on fewer than 2,000 of each of the 720 regular cards in the '94 Stadium Club set. Inserted at the rate of one per 24 foil packs and one per 15 jumbo packs, the cards are otherwise identical to the regular TSC cards.

	NM/M
Common Player:	1.00
Stars:	8X

Dugout Dirt

Cartoons of some of baseball's top stars are featured on the backs of this 12-card insert set. Fronts are virtually identical in format to regular S.C. cards, except the logo and box with the player's last name are in gold-foil, rather than red. Stated odds of finding a Dugout Dirt insert card were one per six packs, on average. Cards can also be found with a gold "Members Only" seal on front.

		NM/M
Complete Set (12):		5.00
Common Player:		.25
1	Mike Piazza (Catch of the Day)	1.00
2	Dave Winfield (The Road to 3,000)	.65
3	John Kruk (From Coal Mine to Gold Mine)	.65
4	Cal Ripken, Jr. (On Track)	2.00
5	Jack McDowell (Chin Music)	.25
6	Barry Bonds (The Bonds Market)	2.00
7	Ken Griffey Jr./AS (Gold Gloves)	1.00
8	Tim Salmon (The Salmon Run)	.25
9	Frank Thomas (Big Hurt)	.65
10	Jeff Kent (Super Kent)	.25
11	Randy Johnson (High Heat)	.65
12	Darren Daulton (Daulton's Gym)	.25

Finest

This insert set was included only in Series III packs of Topps Stadium Club, at the rate of one card per six packs, on average. Cards utilize Topps Finest technology and feature a player action photo on front, set against a red-and-gold sunburst background. Backs have a player portrait photo, a few stats and appropriate logos. Cards can also be found with a "Members Only" logo on front.

		NM/M
Complete Set (10):		11.00
Common Player:		.50
1	Jeff Bagwell	1.25
2	Albert Belle	.50
3	Barry Bonds	3.00
4	Juan Gonzalez	.75
5	Ken Griffey Jr.	2.00
6	Marquis Grissom	.50
7	David Justice	.50
8	Mike Piazza	2.00
9	Tim Salmon	.50
10	Frank Thomas	1.50

Finest Jumbo

Found only as a one per tub insert in special Wal-Mart repackaging of baseball packs, these 5" x 7" versions of the Series III Stadium Club inserts are identical to the smaller version. Cards utilize Topps Finest technology and feature a player action photo on front, set against a red-and-gold sunburst background. Backs have a player portrait photo, a few stats and appropriate logos.

		NM/M
Complete Set (10):		30.00
Common Player:		2.00
1	Jeff Bagwell	4.00
2	Albert Belle	2.00
3	Barry Bonds	6.50
4	Juan Gonzalez	3.00
5	Ken Griffey Jr.	5.00
6	Marquis Grissom	2.00
7	David Justice	2.00
8	Mike Piazza	5.00
9	Tim Salmon	2.00
10	Frank Thomas	4.00

Super Teams

Super Team cards were issued for each of the 28 major league teams and inserted at the rate of one per 24 regular packs and one per 15 jumbo packs. At the end of the 1995 season the promotion was carried over when the 1994 season was ended prematurely by the players' strike, persons holding Super Team cards of the division winners, league champions and World Champions could redeem the cards for prizes. Division winning team cards could be redeemed for a set of 10 S.C. cards of that team with a special division winner embossed logo. League champion cards could be redeemed for a set of 10 Master Photos of the team with a special league logo embossed. Persons with a Super Team card of the eventual World Series champion could trade the card in for a complete set of Stadium Club cards embossed with a World's Champion logo. Each of the Super Team cards features a small group of players on the front with the Super Team Card and S.C. logos in gold foil, and the team name in prismatic foil. Backs contain redemption rules. A version of the Super Team cards was distributed with "Members Only" sets containing such an indicia on front and team roster on back.

		NM/M
Complete Set (28):		25.00
Common Team:		.70
Expired Jan. 31, 1996.		
1	Atlanta Braves	5.00
2	Chicago Cubs	.70
3	Cincinnati Reds	1.25
4	Colorado Rockies	1.00
5	Florida Marlins	.70
6	Houston Astros	1.00
7	Los Angeles Dodgers	1.75
8	Montreal Expos	1.00
9	New York Mets	.70
10	Philadelphia Phillies	.70
11	Pittsburgh Pirates	.70
12	St. Louis Cardinals	.70
13	San Diego Padres	.70
14	San Francisco Giants	1.25
15	Baltimore Orioles	1.25
16	Boston Red Sox	1.00
17	California Angels	.70
18	Chicago White Sox	1.50
19	Cleveland Indians	2.00
20	Detroit Tigers	.70
21	Kansas City Royals	1.00
22	Milwaukee Brewers	.70
23	Minnesota Twins	1.00
24	New York Yankees	1.00
25	Oakland Athletics	1.00
26	Seattle Mariners	1.00
27	Texas Rangers	1.00
28	Toronto Blue Jays	1.00

Members Only

This special gold-seal embossed version of the 1994 Topps Stadium Club set was available by a mail-in offer to club members for $230. The set includes all regular Stadium Club cards from Series I, II and III, along with the Dugout Dirt, Finest, and Super Teams insert cards. The Super Team cards, which were not eligible for the contest, have team rosters on back, rather than contest rules. All other cards are identical to the regular-issue S.C. cards except for the present of the 1/2" round gold-foil "Members Only" seal beneath or alongside of the red-foil Topps Stadium Club logo on front. There are two different checklists each numbered 269 and 270. Only 5,000 sets were produced.

	NM/M
Complete Set (770):	150.00
Common Player:	.50
Stars:	8X

Members Only Baseball

Available for purchase by Topps Stadium Club members as a 50-card boxed set (football and basketball sets were also available), this issue features top stars, performances and career highlights from the 1993 season. Cards feature borderless action photos on front with the Topps logo and player's last name in gold-foil. Backs are horizontal and feature a black background on which the player's achievement is detailed in blue and gold. A second player photo appears on the card back. Cards #46-50 were produced in the Topps Finest-style foil-printing technology.

		NM/M
Complete Set (50):		6.00
Common Player:		.10
1	Juan Gonzalez	.25
2	Tom Henke	.10
3	John Kruk	.10
4	Paul Molitor	.50
5	Dave Justice	.10
6	Rafael Palmeiro	.45
7	John Smoltz	.10
8	Matt Williams	.10
9	John Olerud	.10
10	Mark Grace	.10
11	Joe Carter	.10
12	Wilson Alvarez	.10
13	Lenny Dykstra	.10
14	Kevin Appier	.10
15	Andres Galarraga	.10
16	Mark Langston	.10
17	Ken Griffey Jr.	.75
18	Albert Belle	.10
19	Gregg Jefferies	.10
20	Duane Ward	.10
21	Jack McDowell	.10
22	Randy Johnson	.50
23	Tom Glavine	.35
24	Barry Bonds	1.50
25	Chuck Carr	.10
26	Ron Gant	.10
27	Kenny Lofton	.10
28	Mike Piazza	.75
29	Frank Thomas	.55
30	Fred McGriff	.10
31	Bryan Harvey	.10
32	John Burkett	.10
33	Roberto Alomar	.20
34	Cecil Fielder	.10
35	Marquis Grissom	.10
36	Randy Myers	.10
37	Tony Phillips	.10
38	Rickey Henderson	.50
39	Luis Polonia	.10
40	Jose Rijo	.10
41	Jeff Montgomery	.10
42	Greg Maddux	.60
43	Tony Gwynn	.60
44	Rod Beck	.10
45	Carlos Baerga	.10
46	Wil Cordero	.10
47	Tim Salmon	.10
48	Mike Lansing	.10
49	J.T. Snow	.10
50	Jeff Conine	.10

Superstar Sampler

A small, round black-and-white "Topps Superstar Sampler" logo printed on the back is all that distinguishes these cards from regular-issue S.C. cards. This version of 45 of the top stars from the Stadium Club set was issued only in three-card cello packs inserted into 1994 Topps retail factory sets. The packs also contained the same player's cards from the Bowman and Finest sets, similarly marked.

		NM/M
Complete Set (45):		275.00
Common Player:		2.00
4	Gary Sheffield	3.00
10	Roberto Alomar	4.00
24	Jack McDowell	2.00
25	Cecil Fielder	2.00
36	Tim Salmon	2.00
59	Bobby Bonilla	2.00
85	Ken Griffey Jr.	20.00
94	Dave Justice	2.00
108	Jeff Bagwell	12.00
109	Gregg Jefferies	2.00
127	Cliff Floyd	2.00
140	Mike Piazza	20.00
151	Tony Gwynn	12.50
165	Len Dykstra	2.00
169	Carlos Baerga	2.00
171	Jose Canseco	8.00
195	Don Mattingly	15.00
203	Will Clark	2.00
208	Rafael Palmeiro	10.00
219	Albert Belle	2.00
228	John Olerud	2.00
238	Barry Bonds	30.00
280	Larry Walker	2.00
285	Frank Thomas	12.00
300	Joe Carter	2.00
320	Manny Ramirez	12.00
359	Kirby Puckett	12.50
373	Cal Ripken Jr.	30.00
390	Raul Mondesi	2.00
397	Ryne Sandberg	12.50
403	Mark Grace	2.00
414	Barry Larkin	2.00
419	Matt Williams	2.00
438	Randy Johnson	12.00
440	Mo Vaughn	2.00
450	Darren Daulton	2.00
454	Andres Galarraga	2.00
544	Greg Maddux	12.50
568	Juan Gonzalez	6.00
574	Tom Glavine	2.00
645	Paul Molitor	12.00
650	Roger Clemens	15.00
665	Fred McGriff	2.00
687	Andy Van Slyke	2.00
706	Marquis Grissom	2.00

Team Series

Only 12 of the 28 major league teams are included in this special issue marketed in both team-set blister packs and foil packs at Wal-Mart stores around the country. Card fronts feature a player action photo bordered in the lower-right corner by a dark green mottled effect. The player's name, team and "Team Stadium Club" logo are in gold foil. Backs have a second player photo set against a background in mottled shades of green. There are a few stats and player biographical details.

		NM/M
Complete Set (360):		25.00
Wax Box (24):		15.00
1	Barry Bonds	3.50
2	Royce Clayton	.10
3	Kirt Manwaring	.10
4	J.R. Phillips	.10
5	Robby Thompson	.10
6	Willie McGee	.10
7	Steve Hosey	.10
8	Dave Burba	.10
9	Steve Scarsone	.10
10	Salomon Torres	.10
11	Bryan Hickerson	.10
12	Mike Benjamin	.10
13	Mark Carreon	.10
14	Rich Monteleone	.10
15	Dave Martinez	.10
16	Bill Swift	.10
17	Jeff Reed	.10
18	John Patterson	.10
19	Darren Lewis	.10
20	Mark Portugal	.10
21	Trevor Wilson	.10
22	Matt Williams	.10
23	Kevin Rogers	.10
24	Luis Mercedes	.10
25	Mike Jackson	.10
26	Steve Frey	.10
27	Tony Menendez	.10
28	John Burkett	.10
29	Todd Benzinger	.10
30	Rod Beck	.10
31	Greg Maddux	1.50
32	Steve Avery	.10
33	Milt Hill	.10
34	Charlie O'Brien	.10
35	John Smoltz	.10
36	Jarvis Brown	.10
37	Dave Gallagher	.10
38	Ryan Klesko	.10
39	Kent Mercker	.10
40	Terry Pendleton	.10
41	Ron Gant	.10
42	Pedro Borbon	.10
43	Steve Bedrosian	.10
44	Ramon Caraballo	.10
45	Tyler Houston	.10
46	Mark Lemke	.10
47	Fred McGriff	.10
48	Jose Oliva	.10
49	David Justice	.10
50	Chipper Jones	1.50
51	Tony Tarasco	.10
52	Javy Lopez	.10
53	Mark Wohlers	.10
54	Deion Sanders	.10
55	Greg McMichael	.10
56	Tom Glavine	.35
57	Bill Pecota	.10
58	Mike Stanton	.10
59	Rafael Belliard	.10
60	Jeff Blauser	.10
61	Bryan Harvey	.10
62	Bret Barberie	.10
63	Rick Renteria	.10
64	Chris Hammond	.10
65	Pat Rapp	.10
66	Nigel Wilson	.10
67	Gary Sheffield	.30
68	Jerry Browne	.10
69	Charlie Hough	.10
70	Orestes Destrade	.10
71	Mario Diaz	.10
72	Ryan Bowen	.10
73	Carl Everett	.10
74	Richie Lewis	.10
75	Bob Natal	.10
76	Rich Rodriguez	.10
77	Darrell Whitmore	.10
78	Matt Turner	.10
79	Benny Santiago	.10
80	Robb Nen	.10
81	Dave Magadan	.10
82	Brian Drahman	.10
83	Mark Gardner	.10
84	Chuck Carr	.10
85	Alex Arias	.10
86	Kurt Abbott	.10
87	Joe Klink	.10
88	Jeff Mutis	.10
89	Dave Weathers	.10
90	Jeff Conine	.10
91	Andres Galarraga	.10
92	Vinny Castilla	.10
93	Roberto Mejia	.10
94	Darrell Sherman	.10
95	Mike Harkey	.10
96	Danny Sheaffer	.10
97	Pedro Castellano	.10
98	Walt Weiss	.10
99	Greg Harris	.10
100	Jayhawk Owens	.10
101	Bruce Ruffin	.10
102	Mike Munoz	.10
103	Armando Reynoso	.10
104	Eric Young	.10
105	Dante Bichette	.10
106	Marvin Freeman	.10
107	Joe Girardi	.10
108	Kent Bottenfield	.10
109	Howard Johnson	.10
110	Nelson Liriano	.10
111	David Nied	.10
112	Steve Reed	.10
113	Eric Wedge	.10
114	Charlie Hayes	.10
115	Ellis Burks	.10
116	Willie Blair	.10
117	Darren Holmes	.10
118	Curtis Leskanic	.10
119	Lance Painter	.10
120	Jim Tatum	.10
121	Frank Thomas	1.00
122	Jack McDowell	.10
123	Ron Karkovice	.10
124	Mike LaValliere	.10
125	Scott Radinsky	.10
126	Robin Ventura	.10

No.	Player	Price
127	Scott Ruffcorn	.10
128	Steve Sax	.10
129	Roberto Hernandez	.10
130	Jose DeLeon	.10
131	Rod Bolton	.10
132	Wilson Alvarez	.10
133	Craig Grebeck	.10
134	Lance Johnson	.10
135	Kirk McCaskill	.10
136	Tim Raines	.10
137	Jeff Schwarz	.10
138	Warren Newson	.10
139	Norberto Martin	.10
140	Mike Huff	.10
141	Ozzie Guillen	.10
142	Alex Fernandez	.10
143	Joey Cora	.10
144	Jason Bere	.10
145	James Baldwin	.10
146	Esteban Beltre	.10
147	Julio Franco	.10
148	Matt Merullo	.10
149	Dan Pasqua	.10
150	Darrin Jackson	.10
151	Joe Carter	.10
152	Danny Cox	.10
153	Roberto Alomar	.20
154	Woody Williams	.10
155	Duane Ward	.10
156	Ed Sprague	.10
157	Domingo Martinez	.10
158	Pat Hentgen	.10
159	Shawn Green	.30
160	Dick Schofield	.10
161	Paul Molitor	1.00
162	Darnell Coles	.10
163	Willie Canate	.10
164	Domingo Cedeno	.10
165	Pat Borders	.10
166	Greg Cadaret	.10
167	Tony Castillo	.10
168	Carlos Delgado	.45
169	Scott Brow	.10
170	Juan Guzman	.10
171	Al Leiter	.10
172	John Olerud	.10
173	Todd Stottlemyre	.10
174	Devon White	.10
175	Paul Spoljaric	.10
176	Randy Knorr	.10
177	Huck Flener RC	.10
178	Rob Butler	.10
179	Dave Stewart	.10
180	Mike Timlin	.10
181	Don Mattingly	2.00
182	Mark Hutton	.10
183	Mike Gallego	.10
184	Jim Abbott	.10
185	Paul Gibson	.10
186	Scott Kamieniecki	.10
187	Sam Horn	.10
188	Melido Perez	.10
189	Randy Velarde	.10
190	Gerald Williams	.10
191	Dave Silvestri	.10
192	Jim Leyritz	.10
193	Steve Howe	.10
194	Russ Davis	.10
195	Paul Assenmacher	.10
196	Pat Kelly	.10
197	Mike Stanley	.10
198	Bernie Williams	.10
199	Paul O'Neill	.10
200	Donn Pall	.10
201	Xavier Hernandez	.10
202	James Austin	.10
203	Sterling Hitchcock	.10
204	Wade Boggs	1.50
205	Jimmy Key	.10
206	Matt Nokes	.10
207	Terry Mulholland	.10
208	Luis Polonia	.10
209	Danny Tartabull	.10
210	Bob Wickman	.10
211	Len Dykstra	.10
212	Kim Batiste	.10
213	Tony Longmire	.10
214	Bobby Munoz	.10
215	Pete Incaviglia	.10
216	Doug Jones	.10
217	Mariano Duncan	.10
218	Jeff Juden	.10
219	Milt Thompson	.10
220	Dave West	.10
221	Roger Mason	.10
222	Tommy Greene	.10
223	Larry Andersen	.10
224	Jim Eisenreich	.10
225	Dave Hollins	.10
226	John Kruk	.10
227	Todd Pratt	.10
228	Ricky Jordan	.10
229	Curt Schilling	.35
230	Mike Williams	.10
231	Heathcliff Slocumb	.10
232	Ben Rivera	.10
233	Mike Lieberthal	.10
234	Mickey Morandini	.10
235	Danny Jackson	.10
236	Kevin Foster	.10
237	Darren Daulton	.10
238	Wes Chamberlain	.10
239	Tyler Green	.10
240	Kevin Stocker	.10
241	Juan Gonzalez	.50
242	Rick Honeycutt	.10
243	Bruce Hurst	.10
244	Steve Dreyer	.10
245	Brian Bohanon	.10
246	Benji Gil	.10
247	Jon Shave	.10
248	Manuel Lee	.10
249	Donald Harris	.10
250	Jose Canseco	.50
251	David Hulse	.10
252	Kenny Rogers	.10
253	Jeff Huson	.10
254	Dan Peltier	.10
255	Mike Scioscia	.10
256	Jack Armstrong	.10
257	Rob Ducey	.10
258	Will Clark	.10
259	Cris Carpenter	.10
260	Kevin Brown	.10
261	Jeff Frye	.10
262	Jay Howell	.10
263	Roger Pavlik	.10
264	Gary Redus	.10
265	Ivan Rodriguez	.75
266	Matt Whiteside	.10
267	Doug Strange	.10
268	Billy Ripken	.10
269	Dean Palmer	.10
270	Tom Henke	.10
271	Cal Ripken Jr.	3.50
272	Mark McLemore	.10
273	Sid Fernandez	.10
274	Sherman Obando	.10
275	Paul Carey	.10
276	Mike Oquist	.10
277	Alan Mills	.10
278	Harold Baines	.10
279	Mike Mussina	.30
280	Arthur Rhodes	.10
281	Kevin McGehee	.10
282	Mark Eichhorn	.10
283	Damon Buford	.10
284	Ben McDonald	.10
285	David Segui	.10
286	Brad Pennington	.10
287	Jamie Moyer	.10
288	Chris Hoiles	.10
289	Mike Cook	.10
290	Brady Anderson	.10
291	Chris Sabo	.10
292	Jack Voigt	.10
293	Jim Poole	.10
294	Jeff Tackett	.10
295	Rafael Palmeiro	.75
296	Alex Ochoa	.10
297	John O'Donoghue	.10
298	Tim Hulett	.10
299	Mike Devereaux	.10
300	Manny Alexander	.10
301	Ozzie Smith	1.50
302	Omar Olivares	.10
303	Rheal Cormier	.10
304	Donovan Osborne	.10
305	Mark Whiten	.10
306	Todd Zeile	.10
307	Geronimo Pena	.10
308	Brian Jordan	.10
309	Luis Alicea	.10
310	Ray Lankford	.10
311	Stan Royer	.10
312	Bob Tewksbury	.10
313	Jose Oquendo	.10
314	Steve Dixon	.10
315	Rene Arocha	.10
316	Bernard Gilkey	.10
317	Gregg Jefferies	.10
318	Rob Murphy	.10
319	Tom Pagnozzi	.10
320	Mike Perez	.10
321	Tom Urbani	.10
322	Allen Watson	.10
323	Erik Pappas	.10
324	Paul Kilgus	.10
325	John Habyan	.10
326	Rod Brewer	.10
327	Rich Batchelor	.10
328	Tripp Cromer	.10
329	Gerald Perry	.10
330	Les Lancaster	.10
331	Ryne Sandberg	1.50
332	Derrick May	.10
333	Steve Buechele	.10
334	Willie Banks	.10
335	Larry Luebbers	.10
336	Tommy Shields	.10
337	Eric Yelding	.10
338	Rey Sanchez	.10
339	Mark Grace	.10
340	Jose Bautista	.10
341	Frank Castillo	.10
342	Jose Guzman	.10
343	Rafael Novoa	.10
344	Karl Rhodes	.10
345	Steve Trachsel	.10
346	Rick Wilkins	.10
347	Sammy Sosa	1.50
348	Kevin Roberson	.10
349	Mark Parent	.10
350	Randy Myers	.10
351	Glenallen Hill	.10
352	Lance Dickson	.10
353	Shawn Boskie	.10
354	Shawon Dunston	.10
355	Dan Plesac	.10
356	Jose Vizcaino	.10
357	Willie Wilson	.10
358	Turk Wendell	.10
359	Mike Morgan	.10
360	Jim Bullinger	.10

Team Series 1st Day Issue

Each of the cards in the Stadium Club Team Series can be found with a speial embossed silver-foil "1st Day Issue" seal on front. Cards are otherwise identical to the regular issue.

	NM/M
Complete Set (360):	200.00
Common Player:	.50
Stars:	8X

Team Series Finest

One player from each of the 12 teams in the Stadium Club Team Series issue was printed in a chromium-metallic technology reminiscent of Topps Finest cards. These special cards are labeled "Team Stadium Club Finest." Other than the printing, the cards are in the same format as the rest of the issue.

	NM/M
Complete Set (12):	12.00
Common Player:	.50
1 Roberto Alomar	.50
2 Barry Bonds	3.00
3 Len Dykstra	.50
4 Andres Galarraga	.50
5 Juan Gonzalez	.50
6 Dave Justice	.50
7 Don Mattingly	2.00
8 Cal Ripken Jr.	3.00
9 Ryne Sandberg	1.50
10 Gary Sheffield	.65
11 Ozzie Smith	1.50
12 Frank Thomas	1.00

1995 Stadium Club

Topps' upscale brand was issued for 1995 in three series of, respectively, 270, 225 and 135 cards. Fronts have borderless color photos with a gold-foil device at bottom holding the team logo. Also in gold are the player's name at bottom and the Stadium Club logo at top. Backs have another player photo at left with a pair of computer-enhanced close-ups above it. At right are bar graphs detailing the player's '94 stats and his skills rankings. A number of specially designed subsets - "Best Seat in the House, Cover Story, MLB Debut," etc., are spread throughout the issue, which also includes a full slate of chase cards depending on the series and packaging.

	NM/M
Complete Set (630):	25.00
Common Player:	.05
Common First Day Production:	.50
First Day Stars:	7X

No.	Player	Price
	Series 1 or 2 Pack (14):	1.25
	Series 1 or 2 Wax Box (24):	20.00
	Series 3 Pack (13):	1.25
	Series 3 Wax Box (24):	20.00
1	Cal Ripken Jr.	2.50
2	Bo Jackson	.10
3	Bryan Harvey	.05
4	Curt Schilling	.35
5	Bruce Ruffin	.05
6	Travis Fryman	.05
7	Jim Abbott	.05
8	David McCarty	.05
9	Gary Gaetti	.05
10	Roger Clemens	1.25
11	Carlos Garcia	.05
12	Lee Smith	.05
13	Bobby Ayala	.05
14	Charles Nagy	.05
15	Lou Frazier	.05
16	Rene Arocha	.05
17	Carlos Delgado	.50
18	Steve Finley	.05
19	Ryan Klesko	.05
20	Cal Eldred	.05
21	Rey Sanchez	.05
22	Ken Hill	.05
23	Benny Santiago	.05
24	Julian Tavarez	.05
25	Jose Vizcaino	.05
26	Andy Benes	.05
27	Mariano Duncan	.05
28	Checklist A	.05
29	Shawon Dunston	.05
30	Rafael Palmeiro	.65
31	Dean Palmer	.05
32	Andres Galarraga	.05
33	Joey Cora	.05
34	Mickey Tettleton	.05
35	Barry Larkin	.05
36	Carlos Baerga	.05
37	Orel Hershiser	.05
38	Jody Reed	.05
39	Paul Molitor	.75
40	Jim Edmonds	.05
41	Bob Tewksbury	.05
42	John Patterson	.05
43	Ray McDavid	.05
44	Zane Smith	.05
45	Bret Saberhagen	.05
46	Greg Maddux	1.00
47	Frank Thomas	.75
48	Carlos Baerga	.05
49	Billy Spiers	.05
50	Stan Javier	.05
51	Rex Hudler	.05
52	Denny Hocking	.05
53	Todd Worrell	.05
54	Mark Clark	.05
55	Hipilito Pichardo	.05
56	Bob Wickman	.05
57	Raul Mondesi	.05
58	Steve Cooke	.05
59	Rod Beck	.05
60	Tim Davis	.05
61	Jeff Kent	.05
62	John Valentin	.05
63	Alex Arias	.05
64	Steve Reed	.05
65	Ozzie Smith	1.00
66	Terry Pendleton	.05
67	Kenny Rogers	.05
68	Vince Coleman	.05
69	Tom Pagnozzi	.05
70	Roberto Alomar	.20
71	Darrin Jackson	.05
72	Dennis Eckersley	.65
73	Jay Buhner	.05
74	Darren Lewis	.05
75	Dave Weathers	.05
76	Matt Walbeck	.05
77	Brad Ausmus	.05
78	Danny Bautista	.05
79	Bob Hamelin	.05
80	Steve Traschel	.05
81	Ken Ryan	.05
82	Chris Turner	.05
83	David Segui	.05
84	Ben McDonald	.05
85	Wade Boggs	1.00
86	John Vander Wal	.05
87	Sandy Alomar	.05
88	Ron Karkovice	.05
89	Doug Jones	.05
90	Gary Sheffield	.40
91	Ken Caminiti	.05
92	Chris Bosio	.05
93	Kevin Tapani	.05
94	Walt Weiss	.05
95	Erik Hanson	.05
96	Ruben Sierra	.05
97	Nomar Garciaparra	1.00
98	Terrence Long	.05
99	Jacob Shumate	.05
100	Paul Wilson	.05
101	Kevin Witt	.05
102	Paul Konerko	.15
103	Ben Grieve	.05
104	Mark Johnson RC	.05
105	Cade Gaspar RC	.05
106	Mark Farris	.05
107	Dustin Hermanson	.05
108	Scott Elarton RC	.15
109	Doug Million	.05
110	Matt Smith	.05
111	Brian Buchanan RC	.05
112	Jayson Peterson RC	.05
113	Bret Wagner	.05
114	C.J. Nitkowski	.05
115	Ramon Castro RC	.05
116	Rafael Bournigal	.05
117	Jeff Fassero	.05
118	Bobby Bonilla	.05
119	Ricky Gutierrez	.05
120	Roger Pavlik	.05
121	Mike Greenwell	.05
122	Deion Sanders	.05
123	Charlie Hayes	.05
124	Paul O'Neill	.05
125	Jay Bell	.05
126	Royce Clayton	.05
127	Willie Banks	.05
128	Mark Wohlers	.05
129	Todd Jones	.05
130	Todd Stottlemyre	.05
131	Will Clark	.05
132	Wilson Alvarez	.05
133	Chili Davis	.05
134	Dave Burba	.05
135	Chris Hoiles	.05
136	Jeff Blauser	.05
137	Jeff Reboulet	.05
138	Bret Saberhagen	.05
139	Kirk Rueter	.05
140	Dave Nilsson	.05
141	Pat Borders	.05
142	Ron Darling	.05
143	Derek Bell	.05
144	Dave Hollins	.05
145	Juan Gonzalez	.40
146	Andre Dawson	.25
147	Jim Thome	.65
148	Larry Walker	.05
149	Mike Piazza	1.50
150	Mike Perez	.05
151	Steve Avery	.05
152	Dan Wilson	.05
153	Andy Van Slyke	.05
154	Junior Felix	.05
155	Jack McDowell	.05
156	Danny Tartabull	.05
157	Willie Blair	.05
158	William Van Landingham	.05
159	Robb Nen	.05
160	Lee Tinsley	.05
161	Ismael Valdes	.05
162	Juan Guzman	.05
163	Scott Servais	.05
164	Cliff Floyd	.05
165	Allen Watson	.05
166	Eddie Taubensee	.05
167	Scott Hemond	.05
168	Jeff Tackett	.05
169	Chad Curtis	.05
170	Rico Brogna	.05
171	Luis Polonia	.05
172	Checklist B	.05
173	Lance Johnson	.05
174	Sammy Sosa	1.00
175	Mike MacFarlane	.05
176	Darryl Hamilton	.05
177	Rick Aguilera	.05
178	Dave West	.05
179	Mike Gallego	.05
180	Marc Newfield	.05
181	Steve Buechele	.05
182	David Wells	.05
183	Tom Glavine	.35
184	Joe Girardi	.05
185	Craig Biggio	.05
186	Eddie Murray	.75
187	Kevin Gross	.05
188	Sid Fernandez	.05
189	John Franco	.05
190	Bernard Gilkey	.05
191	Matt Williams	.05
192	Darrin Fletcher	.05
193	Jeff Conine	.05
194	Ed Sprague	.05
195	Eduardo Perez	.05
196	Scott Livingstone	.05
197	Ivan Rodriguez	.65
198	Orlando Merced	.05
199	Ricky Bones	.05
200	Javier Lopez	.05
201	Miguel Jimenez	.05
202	Terry McGriff	.05
203	Mike Lieberthal	.05
204	David Cone	.05
205	Todd Hundley	.05
206	Ozzie Guillen	.05
207	Alex Cole	.05
208	Tony Phillips	.05
209	Jim Eisenreich	.05
210	Greg Vaughn	.05
211	Barry Larkin	.05
212	Don Mattingly	1.00
213	Mark Grace	.05
214	Jose Canseco	.50
215	Joe Carter	.05
216	David Cone	.05
217	Sandy Alomar	.05
218	Al Martin	.05
219	Roberto Kelly	.05
220	Paul Sorrento	.05
221	Tony Fernandez	.05
222	Stan Belinda	.05
223	Mike Stanley	.05
224	Doug Drabek	.05
225	Todd Van Poppel	.05
226	Matt Mieske	.05
227	Tino Martinez	.05
228	Andy Ashby	.05
229	Midre Cummings	.05
230	Jeff Frye	.05
231	Hal Morris	.05
232	Jose Lind	.05
233	Shawn Green	.30
234	Rafael Belliard	.05
235	Randy Myers	.05
236	Frank Thomas	.45
237	Darren Daulton	.05
238	Sammy Sosa	.65
239	Cal Ripken Jr.	1.00
240	Jeff Bagwell	.40
241	Ken Griffey Jr.	1.50
242	Brett Butler	.05
243	Derrick May	.05
244	Pat Listach	.05
245	Mike Bordick	.05
246	Mark Langston	.05
247	Randy Velarde	.05
248	Julio Franco	.05
249	Chuck Knoblauch	.05
250	Bill Gullickson	.05
251	Dave Henderson	.05
252	Bret Boone	.05
253	Al Martin	.05
254	Armando Benitez	.05
255	Wil Cordero	.05
256	Al Leiter	.05
257	Luis Gonzalez	.05
258	Charlie O'Brien	.05
259	Tim Wallach	.05
260	Scott Sanders	.05
261	Tom Henke	.05
262	Otis Nixon	.05
263	Darren Daulton	.05
264	Manny Ramirez	.75
265	Bret Barberie	.05
266	Mel Rojas	.05
267	John Burkett	.05
268	Brady Anderson	.05
269	John Roper	.05
270	Shane Reynolds	.05
271	Barry Bonds	2.50
272	Alex Fernandez	.05
273	Brian McRae	.05
274	Todd Zeile	.05
275	Greg Swindell	.05
276	Johnny Ruffin	.05
277	Troy Neel	.05
278	Eric Karros	.05
279	John Hudek	.05
280	Thomas Howard	.05
281	Joe Carter	.05
282	Mike Devereaux	.05
283	Butch Henry	.05
284	Reggie Jefferson	.05
285	Mark Lemke	.05
286	Jeff Montgomery	.05
287	Ryan Thompson	.05
288	Paul Shuey	.05
289	Mark McGwire	2.00
290	Bernie Williams	.05
291	Mickey Morandini	.05
292	Scott Leius	.05
293	David Hulse	.05
294	Greg Gagne	.05
295	Moises Alou	.05
296	Geronimo Berroa	.05
297	Eddie Zambrano	.05
298	Alan Trammell	.05
299	Don Slaught	.05
300	Jose Rijo	.05
301	Joe Ausanio	.05
302	Tim Raines	.05
303	Melido Perez	.05
304	Kent Mercker	.05
305	James Mouton	.05
306	Luis Lopez	.05
307	Mike Kingery	.05
308	Willie Greene	.05
309	Cecil Fielder	.05
310	Scott Kamieniecki	.05
311	Mike Greenwell	.05
	(Best Seat in the House)	.05
312	Bobby Bonilla	.05
	(Best Seat in the House)	.05
313	Andres Galarraga	.05
	(Best Seat in the House)	.05
314	Cal Ripken Jr.	.05
	(Best Seat in the House)	1.25
315	Matt Williams	.05
	(Best Seat in the House)	.05
316	Tom Pagnozzi	.05
	(Best Seat in the House)	.05
317	Len Dykstra	.05
	(Best Seat in the House)	.05
318	Frank Thomas	.40
	(Best Seat in the House)	.40
319	Kirby Puckett	.05
	(Best Seat in the House)	.50
320	Mike Piazza	.05
	(Best Seat in the House)	1.00
321	Jason Jacome	.05
322	Brian Hunter	.05
323	Brent Gates	.05
324	Jim Converse	.05
325	Damion Easley	.05
326	Dante Bichette	.05
327	Kurt Abbott	.05
328	Scott Cooper	.05
329	Mike Henneman	.05
330	Orlando Miller	.05
331	John Kruk	.05
332	Jose Oliva	.05
333	Reggie Sanders	.05
334	Omar Vizquel	.05
335	Devon White	.05
336	Mike Morgan	.05
337	J.R. Phillips	.05
338	Gary DiSarcina	.05
339	Joey Hamilton	.05
340	Randy Johnson	.75

#	Player	Price
341	Jim Leyritz	.05
342	Bobby Jones	.05
343	Jaime Navarro	.05
344	Bip Roberts	.05
345	Steve Karsay	.05
346	Kevin Stocker	.05
347	Jose Canseco	.50
348	Bill Wegman	.05
349	Rondell White	.05
350	Mo Vaughn	.05
351	Joe Orsulak	.05
352	Pat Meares	.05
353	Albie Lopez	.05
354	Edgar Martinez	.05
355	Brian Jordan	.05
356	Tommy Greene	.05
357	Chuck Carr	.05
358	Pedro Astacio	.05
359	Russ Davis	.05
360	Chris Hammond	.05
361	Gregg Jefferies	.05
362	Shane Mack	.05
363	Fred McGriff	.05
364	Pat Rapp	.05
365	Bill Swift	.05
366	Checklist	.05
367	Robin Ventura	.05
368	Bobby Witt	.05
369	Karl Rhodes	.05
370	Eddie Williams	.05
371	John Jaha	.05
372	Steve Howe	.05
373	Leo Gomez	.05
374	Hector Fajardo	.05
375	Jeff Bagwell	.75
376	Mark Acre	.05
377	Wayne Kirby	.05
378	Mark Portugal	.05
379	Jesus Tavarez	.05
380	Jim Lindeman	.05
381	Don Mattingly	1.25
382	Trevor Hoffman	.05
383	Chris Gomez	.05
384	Garret Anderson	.05
385	Bobby Munoz	.05
386	Jon Lieber	.05
387	Rick Helling	.05
388	Marvin Freeman	.05
389	Juan Castillo	.05
390	Jeff Cirillo	.05
391	Sean Berry	.05
392	Hector Carrasco	.05
393	Mark Grace	.05
394	Pat Kelly	.05
395	Tim Naehring	.05
396	Greg Pirkl	.05
397	John Smoltz	.05
398	Robby Thompson	.05
399	Rick White	.05
400	Frank Thomas	.75
401	Jeff Conine (Cover Story)	.05
402	Jose Valentin (Cover Story)	.05
403	Carlos Baerga (Cover Story)	.05
404	Rick Aguilera (Cover Story)	.05
405	Wilson Alvarez (Cover Story)	.05
406	Juan Gonzalez (Cover Story)	.20
407	Barry Larkin (Cover Story)	.05
408	Ken Hill (Cover Story)	.05
409	Chuck Carr (Cover Story)	.05
410	Tim Raines (Cover Story)	.05
411	Bryan Eversgerd	.05
412	Phil Plantier	.05
413	Josias Manzanillo	.05
414	Roberto Kelly	.05
415	Rickey Henderson	.75
416	John Smiley	.05
417	Kevin Brown	.05
418	Jimmy Key	.05
419	Wally Joyner	.05
420	Roberto Hernandez	.05
421	Felix Fermin	.05
422	Checklist	.05
423	Greg Vaughn	.05
424	Ray Lankford	.05
425	Greg Maddux	1.00
426	Mike Mussina	.30
427	Geronimo Pena	.05
428	David Nied	.05
429	Scott Erickson	.05
430	Kevin Mitchell	.05
431	Mike Lansing	.05
432	Brian Anderson	.05
433	Jeff King	.05
434	Ramon Martinez	.05
435	Kevin Seitzer	.05
436	Salomon Torres	.05
437	Brian Hunter	.05
438	Melvin Nieves	.05
439	Mike Kelly	.05
440	Marquis Grissom	.05
441	Chuck Finley	.05
442	Len Dykstra	.05
443	Ellis Burks	.05
444	Harold Baines	.05
445	Kevin Appier	.05
446	Dave Justice	.05
447	Darryl Kile	.05
448	John Olerud	.05
449	Greg McMichael	.05
450	Kirby Puckett	1.00
451	Jose Valentin	.05
452	Rick Wilkins	.05
453	Arthur Rhodes	.05
454	Pat Hentgen	.05
455	Tom Gordon	.05
456	Tom Candiotti	.05
457	Jason Bere	.05
458	Wes Chamberlain	.05
459	Greg Colbrunn	.05
460	John Doherty	.05
461	Kevin Foster	.05
462	Mark Whiten	.05
463	Terry Steinbach	.05
464	Aaron Sele	.05
465	Kirt Manwaring	.05
466	Darren Hall	.05
467	Delino DeShields	.05
468	Andujar Cedeno	.05
469	Billy Ashley	.05
470	Kenny Lofton	.05
471	Pedro Munoz	.05
472	John Wetteland	.05
473	Tim Salmon	.05
474	Denny Neagle	.05
475	Tony Gwynn	1.00
476	Vinny Castilla	.05
477	Steve Dreyer	.05
478	Jeff Shaw	.05
479	Chad Ogea	.05
480	Scott Ruffcorn	.05
481	Lou Whitaker	.05
482	J.T. Snow	.05
483	Rich Rowland	.05
484	Dennis Martinez	.05
485	Pedro Martinez	.75
486	Rusty Greer	.05
487	Dave Fleming	.05
488	John Dettmer	.05
489	Albert Belle	.05
490	Ravelo Manzanillo	.05
491	Henry Rodriguez	.05
492	Andrew Lorraine	.05
493	Dwayne Hosey	.05
494	Mike Blowers	.05
495	Turner Ward	.05
496	Fred McGriff (Extreme Corps)	.05
497	Sammy Sosa (Extreme Corps)	.50
498	Barry Larkin (Extreme Corps)	.05
499	Andres Galarraga (Extreme Corps)	.05
500	Gary Sheffield (Extreme Corps)	.15
501	Jeff Bagwell (Extreme Corps)	.40
502	Mike Piazza (Extreme Corps)	1.00
503	Moises Alou (Extreme Corps)	.05
504	Bobby Bonilla (Extreme Corps)	.05
505	Darren Daulton (Extreme Corps)	.05
506	Jeff King (Extreme Corps)	.05
507	Ray Lankford (Extreme Corps)	.05
508	Tony Gwynn (Extreme Corps)	.50
509	Barry Bonds (Extreme Corps)	1.25
510	Cal Ripken Jr. (Extreme Corps)	1.25
511	Mo Vaughn (Extreme Corps)	.05
512	Tim Salmon (Extreme Corps)	.05
513	Frank Thomas (Extreme Corps)	.45
514	Albert Belle (Extreme Corps)	.05
515	Cecil Fielder (Extreme Corps)	.05
516	Kevin Appier (Extreme Corps)	.05
517	Greg Vaughn (Extreme Corps)	.05
518	Kirby Puckett (Extreme Corps)	.50
519	Paul O'Neill (Extreme Corps)	.05
520	Ruben Sierra (Extreme Corps)	.05
521	Ken Griffey Jr. (Extreme Corps)	.75
522	Will Clark (Extreme Corps)	.05
523	Joe Carter (Extreme Corps)	.05
524	Antonio Osuna	.05
525	Glenallen Hill	.05
526	Alex Gonzalez	.05
527	Dave Stewart	.05
528	Ron Gant	.05
529	Jason Bates	.05
530	Mike Macfarlane	.05
531	Esteban Loaiza	.05
532	Joe Randa	.05
533	Dave Winfield	.75
534	Danny Darwin	.05
535	Pete Harnisch	.05
536	Joey Cora	.05
537	Jaime Navarro	.05
538	Marty Cordova	.05
539	Andujar Cedeno	.05
540	Mickey Tettleton	.05
541	Andy Van Slyke	.05
542	Carlos Perez RC	.05
543	Chipper Jones	1.00
544	Tony Fernandez	.05
545	Tom Henke	.05
546	Pat Borders	.05
547	Chad Curtis	.05
548	Ray Durham	.05
549	Joe Oliver	.05
550	Jose Mesa	.05
551	Steve Finley	.05
552	Otis Nixon	.05
553	Jacob Brumfield	.05
554	Bill Swift	.05
555	Quilvio Veras	.05
556	Hideo Nomo RC	1.50
557	Joe Vitiello	.05
558	Mike Perez	.05
559	Charlie Hayes	.05
560	Brad Radke RC	.25
561	Darren Bragg	.05
562	Orel Hershiser	.05
563	Edgardo Alfonzo	.05
564	Doug Jones	.05
565	Andy Pettitte	.25
566	Benito Santiago	.05
567	John Burkett	.05
568	Brad Clontz	.05
569	Jim Abbott	.05
570	Joe Rosselli	.05
571	Mark Grudzielanek RC	.25
572	Dustin Hermanson	.05
573	Benji Gil	.05
574	Mark Whiten	.05
575	Mike Ignasiak	.05
576	Kevin Ritz	.05
577	Paul Quantrill	.05
578	Andre Dawson	.25
579	Jerald Clark	.05
580	Frank Rodriguez	.05
581	Mark Kiefer	.05
582	Trevor Wilson	.05
583	Gary Wilson RC	.05
584	Andy Stankiewicz	.05
585	Felipe Lira	.05
586	Mike Mimbs RC	.05
587	Jon Nunnally	.05
588	Tomas Perez RC	.05
589	Checklist	.05
590	Todd Hollandsworth	.05
591	Roberto Petagine	.05
592	Mariano Rivera	.15
593	Mark McLemore	.05
594	Bobby Witt	.05
595	Jose Offerman	.05
596	Jason Christiansen	.05
597	Jeff Manto	.05
598	Jim Dougherty	.05
599	Juan Acevedo	.05
600	Troy O'Leary	.05
601	Ron Villone	.05
602	Tripp Cromer	.05
603	Steve Scarsone	.05
604	Lance Parrish	.05
605	Ozzie Timmons	.05
606	Ray Holbert	.05
607	Tony Phillips	.05
608	Phil Plantier	.05
609	Shane Andrews	.05
610	Heathcliff Slocumb	.05
611	Bobby Higginson RC	.25
612	Bob Tewksbury	.05
613	Terry Pendleton	.05
614	Scott Cooper (Trans-Action)	.05
615	John Wetteland (Trans-Action)	.05
616	Ken Hill (Trans-Action)	.05
617	Marquis Grissom (Trans-Action)	.05
618	Larry Walker (Trans-Action)	.05
619	Derek Bell (Trans-Action)	.05
620	David Cone (Trans-Action)	.05
621	Ken Caminiti (Trans-Action)	.05
622	Jack McDowell (Trans-Action)	.05
623	Vaughn Eshelman (Trans-Action)	.05
624	Brian McRae (Trans-Action)	.05
625	Gregg Jefferies (Trans-Action)	.05
626	Kevin Brown (Trans-Action)	.05
627	Lee Smith (Trans-Action)	.05
628	Tony Tarasco (Trans-Action)	.05
629	Brett Butler (Trans-Action)	.05
630	Jose Canseco (Trans-Action)	.35

1st Day Pre-Production

Stadium Club 1st Day Pre-production cards were randomly packed into one every 36 packs of Topps Series I baseball. The set of nine cards is only found in hobby packs.

		NM/M
Complete Set (9):		7.50
Common Player:		.50
29	Shawon Dunston	.50
39	Paul Molitor	1.50
79	Bob Hamelin	.50
96	Ruben Sierra	.50
131	Will Clark	.50
149	Mike Piazza	3.00
153	Andy Van Slyke	.50
166	Jeff Tackett	.50
197	Ivan Rodriguez	1.00

1st Day Issue

Series II hobby packs of Topps baseball featured a chase set of Stadium Club 1st Day Issue cards, #1-270. The FDI cards have a small gold embossed seal on front. Cards were seeded on an average of one per six packs. Ten FDI cards were also randomly inserted in each Factory set.

	NM/M
Common Player:	.50
Stars:	7X

Clear Cut

Among the most technically advanced of 1995's insert cards is the Clear Cut chase set found in Series I and II packs. Cards feature a color player action photo printed on see-through plastic. There is a rainbow-hued trapezoid behind the player with an overall background tinted in blue, green and gold. The player's name is in white in a vertical blue bar at right. Backs have a few stats and data in a blue bar vertically at left. Each of the cards can also be found in a version with the round Members Only seal embossed into the plastic at lower-left.

		NM/M
Complete Set (28):		20.00
Common Player:		.65
1	Mike Piazza	3.00
2	Ruben Sierra	.65
3	Tony Gwynn	2.50
4	Frank Thomas	2.00
5	Fred McGriff	.65
6	Rafael Palmeiro	1.50
7	Bobby Bonilla	.65
8	Chili Davis	.65
9	Hal Morris	.65
10	Jose Canseco	1.00
11	Jay Bell	.65
12	Kirby Puckett	2.50
13	Gary Sheffield	1.00
14	Bob Hamelin	.65
15	Jeff Bagwell	2.00
16	Albert Belle	.65
17	Sammy Sosa	2.50
18	Ken Griffey Jr.	3.00
19	Todd Zeile	.65
20	Mo Vaughn	.65
21	Moises Alou	.65
22	Paul O'Neill	.65
23	Andres Galarraga	.65
24	Greg Vaughn	.65
25	Len Dykstra	.65
26	Joe Carter	.65
27	Barry Bonds	4.50
28	Cecil Fielder	.65

Crunch Time

Series 1 rack packs were the exclusive provenance of these cards featuring baseball's top run creators. Fronts are printed on rainbow prismatic foil. The central color action photo is repeated as an enlarged background photo, along with a team logo. At bottom in gold foil are the player name and Crunch Time logo. Backs have a positive and a negative image of the same photo as background to a pie chart and stats relative to the player's runs-created stats.

		NM/M
Complete Set (20):		15.00
Common Player:		1.00
1	Jeff Bagwell	2.50
2	Kirby Puckett	3.00
3	Frank Thomas	2.50
4	Albert Belle	1.00
5	Julio Franco	1.00
6	Jose Canseco	1.50
7	Paul Molitor	2.50
8	Joe Carter	1.00
9	Ken Griffey Jr.	4.00
10	Larry Walker	1.00
11	Dante Bichette	1.00
12	Carlos Baerga	1.00
13	Fred McGriff	1.00
14	Ruben Sierra	1.00
15	Will Clark	1.00
16	Moises Alou	1.00
17	Rafael Palmeiro	2.00
18	Travis Fryman	1.00
19	Barry Bonds	5.00
20	Cal Ripken Jr.	5.00

Crystal Ball

Multi-colored swirls around a clear central circle with the player's photo, all printed on foil, are the front design for this Series 3 insert. Backs have a portrait photo in a floating crystal ball image at one side. At the other end are year-by-year minor league stats and a few words about each of the player's seasons. This insert was also produced in an edition of 4,000 bearing a gold-foil "Members Only" seal, sold in complete Stadium Club Members Only factory sets.

		NM/M
Complete Set (15):		15.00
Common Player:		.75
1	Chipper Jones	5.00
2	Dustin Hermanson	.75
3	Ray Durham	.75
4	Phil Nevin	.75
5	Billy Ashley	.75
6	Shawn Green	2.50
7	Jason Bates	.75
8	Benji Gil	.75
9	Marty Cordova	.75
10	Quilvio Veras	.75
11	Mark Grudzielanek	.75
12	Ruben Rivera	.75
13	Bill Pulsipher	.75
14	Derek Jeter	7.50
15	LaTroy Hawkins	.75

Power Zone

The performance in several parks around the league is chronicled on the back of these Series 3 inserts. Fronts are printed on foil and feature a player swinging into an exploding asteroid. His name is printed vertically down one side in prismatic glitter foil. Backs also have a portrait photo and a baseball with a weird red and green vapor trail. A special edition of 4,000 each of these inserts was included with the purchase of Stadium Club Members Only factory sets; those cards have an embossed gold-foil seal on front.

		NM/M
Complete Set (12):		9.00
Common Player:		.50
1	Jeff Bagwell	1.00
2	Albert Belle	.50
3	Barry Bonds	3.00
4	Joe Carter	.50
5	Cecil Fielder	.50
6	Andres Galarraga	.50
7	Ken Griffey Jr.	2.00
8	Paul Molitor	1.00
9	Fred McGriff	.50
10	Rafael Palmeiro	.75
11	Frank Thomas	1.00
12	Matt Williams	.50

Ring Leaders

With a background that looks like an explosion at a jewelry factory, these cards feature players who have won championship, All-Star or other award rings. Fronts are foil-printed with a player action photo on a background of flying rings and stars, and, - for some reason - an attacking eagle. Backs repeat the background motif, have a player portrait in an oval frame at top-left, photos of some of his rings and a list of rings won. Cards were random inserts in both Series 1 and 2; complete sets could also be won in Stadium Club's phone card insert contest. A version with the Members Only gold seal was also issued for each.

		NM/M
Complete Set (40):		70.00
Common Player:		.75
1	Jeff Bagwell	3.00
2	Mark McGwire	7.50
3	Ozzie Smith	4.00
4	Paul Molitor	3.00
5	Darryl Strawberry	.75
6	Eddie Murray	3.00
7	Tony Gwynn	4.00
8	Jose Canseco	2.00
9	Howard Johnson	.75
10	Andre Dawson	1.25
11	Matt Williams	.75
12	Tim Raines	.75
13	Fred McGriff	.75
14	Ken Griffey Jr.	6.00
15	Gary Sheffield	2.00
16	Dennis Eckersley	2.50
17	Kevin Mitchell	.75
18	Will Clark	.75
19	Darren Daulton	.75
20	Paul O'Neill	.75
21	Julio Franco	.75
22	Albert Belle	.75
23	Juan Gonzalez	1.50
24	Kirby Puckett	4.00
25	Joe Carter	.75
26	Frank Thomas	3.00
27	Cal Ripken Jr.	9.00
28	John Olerud	.75
29	Ruben Sierra	.75
30	Barry Bonds	9.00
31	Cecil Fielder	.75
32	Roger Clemens	5.00
33	Don Mattingly	5.00
34	Terry Pendleton	.75
35	Rickey Henderson	.75
36	Dave Winfield	3.00
37	Edgar Martinez	.75
38	Wade Boggs	4.00
39	Willie McGee	.75
40	Andres Galarraga	.75

Ring Leaders Phone Cards

An interactive contest carrying through the "Ring Leaders" insert card set theme featured randomly inserted phone cards picturing All-

Star Game players' rings. The 2-1/8" x 3-3/8" plastic cards could be found in regular, silver and gold editions. By using the card for a long distance call, the holder could determine if it was a further winner. Regular card winners received a set of Stadium Club Ring Leaders insert cards. Winners on a silver card received a complete set of the 13 different phone cards in all three versions. Gold card winners received the genuine All-Star ring pictured on the card. Approximately 217,000 phone cards were inserted in the program; odds of finding a regular card were about one per 40 packs; silver, one per 237 packs; and, gold, one per 2,955 packs. Cards picturing the 1988 and 1989 All-Star rings were not issued. Phone cards with the number panel on back scratched off are worth 50 percent of the values quoted.

		NM/M
Complete Set, Regular (13):		10.00
Complete Set, Silver (13):		25.00
Complete Set, Gold (13):		50.00
Common Card, Regular:		1.00
Common Card, Silver:		2.50
Common Card, Gold:		5.00
(1)	1980 All-Star Game, Los Angeles	1.00
(1s)	1980 All-Star Game, Los Angeles/Silver	2.50
(1g)	1980 All-Star Game, Los Angeles/Gold	5.00
(2)	1981 All-Star Game, Cleveland	1.00
(2s)	1981 All-Star Game, Cleveland/Silver	2.50
(2g)	1981 All-Star Game, Cleveland/Gold	5.00
(3)	1982 All-Star Game, Montreal	1.00
(3s)	1982 All-Star Game, Montreal/Silver	2.50
(3g)	1982 All-Star Game, Montreal/Gold	5.00
(4)	1983 All-Star Game, Chicago A.L.	1.00
(4s)	1983 All-Star Game, Chicago A.L./Silver	2.50
(4g)	1983 All-Star Game, Chicago/Gold	5.00
(5)	1984 All-Star Game, San Francisco	1.00
(5s)	1984 All-Star Game, San Francisco/Silver	2.50
(5g)	1984 All-Star Game, San Francisco/Gold	5.00
(6)	1985 All-Star Game, Minneapolis	1.00
(6s)	1985 All-Star Game, Minneapolis (Silver)	2.50
(6g)	1985 All-Star Game, Minneapolis/Gold	5.00
(7)	1986 All-Star Game, Houston	1.00
(7s)	1986 All-Star Game, Houston/Silver	2.50
(7g)	1986 All-Star Game, Houston/Gold	5.00
(8)	1987 All-Star Game, Oakland	1.00
(8s)	1987 All-Star Game, Oakland/Silver	2.50
(8g)	1987 All-Star Game, Oakland/Gold	5.00
(9)	1990 All-Star Game, Chicago N.L.	1.00
(9s)	1990 All-Star Game, Chicago N.L./Silver	2.50
(9g)	1990 All-Star Game, Chicago N.L./Gold	5.00
(10)	1991 All-Star Game, Toronto	1.00
(10s)	1991 All-Star Game, Toronto/Silver	2.50
(10g)	1991 All-Star Game, Toronto/Gold	5.00
(11)	1992 All-Star Game, San Diego	1.00
(11s)	1992 All-Star Game, San Diego/Silver	2.50
(11g)	1992 All-Star Game, San Diego/Gold	5.00
(12)	1993 All-Star Game, Baltimore	1.00
(12s)	1993 All-Star Game, Baltimore/Silver	2.50
(12g)	1993 All-Star Game, Baltimore/Gold	5.00
(13)	1994 All-Star Game, Pittsburgh	1.00
(13s)	1994 All-Star Game, Pittsburgh/Silver	2.50
(13g)	1994 All-Star Game, Pittsburgh/Gold	5.00

Super Skills

These random hobby pack inserts in both Series 1 and 2 are printed on rainbow prismatic foil which features as a background an enlarged version of the front photo. The S.C. and Super Skills logos are printed in gold foil in opposite corners, while the player's name is in blue at bottom-right. Backs repeat the enlarged background image of a close-up foreground photo, while a few words about the player's particular specialties are in white at left. Each card can also be found in a version featuring the Members Only gold-foil seal on front.

		NM/M
Complete Set (20):		30.00
Common Player:		.75
1	Roberto Alomar	1.00
2	Barry Bonds	10.00
3	Jay Buhner	.75
4	Chuck Carr	.75
5	Don Mattingly	5.00
6	Raul Mondesi	.75
7	Tim Salmon	.75
8	Deion Sanders	.75
9	Devon White	.75
10	Mark Whiten	.75
11	Ken Griffey Jr.	7.50
12	Marquis Grissom	.75
13	Paul O'Neill	.75
14	Kenny Lofton	.75
15	Larry Walker	.75
16	Scott Cooper	.75
17	Barry Larkin	.75
18	Matt Williams	.75
19	John Wetteland	.75
20	Randy Johnson	2.50

Virtual Reality

A partial parallel set found one per foil pack, two per rack pack, these cards share the basic front and back with the corresponding card in the regular S.C. issue. On front, however, is a "Virtual Reality" seal bearing the team logo at bottom (gold foil in Series 1, silver-foil in Series 2). Backs differ in that instead of actual 1994 season stats, they present a bar graph of computer projected stats representing a full 162-game season instead of the strike-shortened reality. Each of these inserts can also be found in a version bearing the round gold-(Series 1) or silver-foil (Series 2) Members Only seal on the front.

		NM/M
Complete Set (270):		35.00
Common Player:		.10
1	Cal Ripken Jr.	2.50
2	Travis Fryman	.10
3	Jim Abbott	.10
4	Gary Gaetti	.10
5	Roger Clemens	1.25
6	Carlos Garcia	.10
7	Lee Smith	.10
8	Bobby Ayala	.10
9	Charles Nagy	.10
10	Rene Arocha	.10
11	Carlos Delgado	.50
12	Steve Finley	.10
13	Ryan Klesko	.10
14	Cal Eldred	.10
15	Rey Sanchez	.10
16	Ken Hill	.10
17	Jose Vizcaino	.10
18	Andy Benes	.10
19	Shawon Dunston	.10
20	Rafael Palmeiro	.65
21	Dean Palmer	.10
22	Joey Cora	.10
23	Mickey Tettleton	.10
24	Barry Larkin	.10
25	Carlos Baerga	.10
26	Orel Hershiser	.10
27	Jody Reed	.10
28	Paul Molitor	.75
29	Jim Edmonds	.10
30	Bob Tewksbury	.10
31	Ray McDavid	.10
32	Stan Javier	.10
33	Todd Worrell	.10
34	Bob Wickman	.10
35	Raul Mondesi	.10
36	Rod Beck	.10
37	Jeff Kent	.10
38	John Valentin	.10
39	Ozzie Smith	1.00
40	Terry Pendleton	.10
41	Kenny Rogers	.10
42	Vince Coleman	.10
43	Roberto Alomar	.20
44	Darrin Jackson	.10
45	Dennis Eckersley	.65
46	Jay Buhner	.10
47	Dave Weathers	.10
48	Danny Bautista	.10
49	Bob Hamelin	.10
50	Steve Trachsel	.10
51	Ben McDonald	.10
52	Wade Boggs	1.00
53	Sandy Alomar	.10
54	Ron Karkovice	.10
55	Doug Jones	.10
56	Gary Sheffield	.40
57	Ken Caminiti	.10
58	Kevin Tapani	.10
59	Ruben Sierra	.10
60	Bobby Bonilla	.10
61	Deion Sanders	.10
62	Charlie Hayes	.10
63	Paul O'Neill	.10
64	Jay Bell	.10
65	Todd Jones	.10
66	Todd Stottlemyre	.10
67	Will Clark	.10
68	Wilson Alvarez	.10
69	Chili Davis	.10
70	Chris Hoiles	.10
71	Bret Saberhagen	.10
72	Dave Nilsson	.10
73	Derek Bell	.10
74	Juan Gonzalez	.40
75	Andre Dawson	.30
76	Jim Thome	.65
77	Larry Walker	.10
78	Mike Piazza	1.50
79	Dan Wilson	.10
80	Junior Felix	.10
81	Jack McDowell	.10
82	Danny Tartabull	.10
83	William Van Landingham	.10
84	Robb Nen	.10
85	Ismael Valdes	.10
86	Juan Guzman	.10
87	Cliff Floyd	.10
88	Rico Brogna	.10
89	Luis Polonia	.10
90	Lance Johnson	.10
91	Sammy Sosa	1.00
92	Dave West	.10
93	Tom Glavine	.35
94	Joe Girardi	.10
95	Craig Biggio	.10
96	Eddie Murray	.75
97	Kevin Gross	.10
98	John Franco	.10
99	Matt Williams	.10
100	Darrin Fletcher	.10
101	Jeff Conine	.10
102	Ed Sprague	.10
103	Ivan Rodriguez	.65
104	Orlando Merced	.10
105	Ricky Bones	.10
106	David Cone	.10
107	Todd Hundley	.10
108	Alex Cole	.10
109	Tony Phillips	.10
110	Jim Eisenreich	.10
111	Paul Sorrento	.10
112	Mike Stanley	.10
113	Doug Drabek	.10
114	Matt Mieske	.10
115	Tino Martinez	.10
116	Midre Cummings	.10
117	Hal Morris	.10
118	Shawn Green	.40
119	Randy Myers	.10
120	Ken Griffey Jr.	1.50
121	Brett Butler	.10
122	Julio Franco	.10
123	Chuck Knoblauch	.10
124	Bret Boone	.10
125	Wil Cordero	.10
126	Luis Gonzalez	.10
127	Tim Wallach	.10
128	Scott Sanders	.10
129	Tom Henke	.10
130	Otis Nixon	.10
131	Darren Daulton	.10
132	Manny Ramirez	.75
133	Bret Barberie	.10
134	Brady Anderson	.10
135	Shane Reynolds	.10
136	Barry Bonds	2.50
137	Alex Fernandez	.10
138	Brian McRae	.10
139	Todd Zeile	.10
140	Greg Swindell	.10
141	Troy Neel	.10
142	Eric Karros	.10
143	John Hudek	.10
144	Joe Carter	.10
145	Mike Devereaux	.10
146	Butch Henry	.10
147	Mark Lemke	.10
148	Jeff Montgomery	.10
149	Ryan Thompson	.10
150	Bernie Williams	.10
151	Scott Leius	.10
152	Greg Gagne	.10
153	Moises Alou	.10
154	Geronimo Berroa	.10
155	Alan Trammell	.10
156	Don Slaught	.10
157	Jose Rijo	.10
158	Tim Raines	.10
159	Melido Perez	.10
160	Kent Mercker	.10
161	James Mouton	.10
162	Luis Lopez	.10
163	Mike Kingery	.10
164	Cecil Fielder	.10
165	Scott Kamieniecki	.10
166	Brent Gates	.10
167	Jason Jacome	.10
168	Dante Bichette	.10
169	Kurt Abbott	.10
170	Mike Henneman	.10
171	John Kruk	.10
172	Jose Oliva	.10
173	Reggie Sanders	.10
174	Omar Vizquel	.10
175	Devon White	.10
176	Mark McGwire	2.00
177	Gary DiSarcina	.10
178	Joey Hamilton	.10
179	Randy Johnson	.75
180	Jim Leyritz	.10
181	Bobby Jones	.10
182	Bip Roberts	.10
183	Jose Canseco	.40
184	Mo Vaughn	.10
185	Edgar Martinez	.10
186	Tommy Greene	.10
187	Chuck Carr	.10
188	Pedro Astacio	.10
189	Shane Mack	.10
190	Fred McGriff	.10
191	Pat Rapp	.10
192	Bill Swift	.10
193	Robin Ventura	.10
194	Bobby Witt	.10
195	Steve Howe	.10
196	Leo Gomez	.10
197	Hector Fajardo	.10
198	Jeff Bagwell	.75
199	Rondell White	.10
200	Don Mattingly	1.25
201	Trevor Hoffman	.10
202	Chris Gomez	.10
203	Bobby Munoz	.10
204	Marvin Freeman	.10
205	Sean Berry	.10
206	Mark Grace	.10
207	Pat Kelly	.10
208	Eddie Williams	.10
209	Frank Thomas	.75
210	Bryan Eversgerd	.10
211	Phil Plantier	.10
212	Roberto Kelly	.10
213	Rickey Henderson	.75
214	John Smiley	.10
215	Kevin Brown	.10
216	Jimmy Key	.10
217	Wally Joyner	.10
218	Roberto Hernandez	.10
219	Felix Fermin	.10
220	Greg Vaughn	.10
221	Ray Lankford	.10
222	Greg Maddux	1.00
223	Mike Mussina	.30
224	David Nied	.10
225	Scott Erickson	.10
226	Kevin Mitchell	.10
227	Brian Anderson	.10
228	Jeff King	.10
229	Ramon Martinez	.10
230	Kevin Seitzer	.10
231	Marquis Grissom	.10
232	Chuck Finley	.10
233	Len Dykstra	.10
234	Ellis Burks	.10
235	Harold Baines	.10
236	Kevin Appier	.10
237	Dave Justice	.10
238	Darryl Kile	.10
239	John Olerud	.10
240	Greg McMichael	.10
241	Kirby Puckett	1.00
242	Jose Valentin	.10
243	Rick Wilkins	.10
244	Pat Hentgen	.10
245	Tom Gordon	.10
246	Tom Candiotti	.10
247	Jason Bere	.10
248	Wes Chamberlain	.10
249	Jeff Cirillo	.10
250	Kevin Foster	.10
251	Mark Whiten	.10
252	Terry Steinbach	.10
253	Aaron Sele	.10
254	Kirt Manwaring	.10
255	Delino DeShields	.10
256	Andujar Cedeno	.10
257	Kenny Lofton	.10
258	John Wetteland	.10
259	Tim Salmon	.10
260	Denny Neagle	.10
261	Tony Gwynn	1.00
262	Lou Whitaker	.10
263	J.T. Snow	.10
264	Dennis Martinez	.10
265	Pedro Martinez	.75
266	Rusty Greer	.10
267	Dave Fleming	.10
268	John Dettmer	.10
269	Albert Belle	.10
270	Henry Rodriguez	.10

VR Extremist

A huge silver-blue metallic baseball separates the player from the background of the photo in this Series 2 insert found only in rack packs. A blue sky and clouds provides the front border. The player rises out of the clouds in a back photo in the foreground of which are some pie-in-the-sky stats. The metallic baseball is also repeated on the back, with the player's name in orange script onto the sweet spot. Each card was also issued in the Members Only boxed set in a version with a round silver-foil Members Only seal on front. Cards are numbered with a "VRE" prefix.

		NM/M
Complete Set (10):		25.00
Common Player:		1.50
1	Barry Bonds	7.50
2	Ken Griffey Jr.	6.00
3	Jeff Bagwell	3.50
4	Albert Belle	1.50
5	Frank Thomas	3.50
6	Tony Gwynn	4.50
7	Kenny Lofton	1.50
8	Deion Sanders	1.50
9	Ken Hill	1.50
10	Jimmy Key	1.50

Super Team Division Winners

Persons who saved 1994 Topps Stadium Club Super Team cards for the 1995 divisional winners in Major League Baseball's new playoff format were able to redeem them for a set of 10 SC cards of that team's players with a special gold-foil division series logo on front. The cards are otherwise identical to the regular-issue '95 SC versions. Included in the cello-wrapped team set was a Super Team card with the gold logo on front and a white "REDEEMED" across the back.

		NM/M
Complete Set (66):		25.00
Common Player:		.15
	Atlanta Braves Team Set	7.00
1	Atlanta Braves Super Team	.30
19	Ryan Klesko	.15
128	Mark Wohlers	.15
151	Steve Avery	.15
183	Tom Glavine	.60
200	Javy Lopez	.15
393	Fred McGriff	.15
397	John Smoltz	.15
425	Greg Maddux	3.00
446	David Justice	.15
543	Chipper Jones	3.00
	Boston Red Sox Team Set	4.50
16	Boston Red Sox Super Team	.30
10	Roger Clemens	3.25
62	John Valentin	.15
121	Mike Greenwell	.15
160	Lee Tinsley	.15
347	Jose Canseco	1.25
350	Mo Vaughn	.15
395	Tim Naehring	.15
464	Aaron Sele	.15
530	Mike MacFarlane	.15
600	Troy O;Leary	.15
	Cincinnati Red Team Set	1.50
3	Cincinnati Reds Super Team	.30
35	Barry Larkin	.15
231	Hal Morris	.15
252	Bret Boone	.15
280	Thomas Howard	.15
300	Jose Rijo	.15
333	Reggie Sanders	.15
392	Hector Carrasco	.15
416	John Smiley	.15
528	Ron Gant	.15
566	Benito Santiago	.15
	Cleveland Indians Team Set	4.50
19	Cleveland Indians Super Team	2.00
36	Carlos Baerga	.15
147	Jim Thome	1.50
186	Eddie Murray	2.00
264	Manny Ramirez	2.00
334	Omar Vizquel	.15
470	Kenny Lofton	.15
484	Dennis Martinez	.15
489	Albert Belle	.15
550	Jose Mesa	.15
562	Orel Hershiser	.15
	Los Angeles Dodgers Team Set	7.00
7	Los Angeles Dodgers Super Team	.30
57	Raul Mondesi	.15
149	Mike Piazza	4.00
161	Ismael Valdez	.15
242	Brett Butler	.15
259	Tim Wallach	.15
265	Eric Karros	.15
434	Ramon Martinez	.15
456	Tom Candiotti	.15
475	Delino DeShields	.15
556	Hideo Nomo	1.00
	Seattle Mariners Team Set	6.50
26	Seattle Mariners Super Team	.30
73	Jay Buhner	.15
92	Chris Bosio	.15
152	Dan Wilson	.15
227	Tino Martinez	.15
241	Ken Griffey Jr.	4.00
340	Randy Johnson	2.00
354	Edgar Martinez	.15
421	Felix Fermin	.15
494	Mike Blowers	.15
536	Joey Cora	.15

League Champion Master Photos

Persons who held onto Braves and Indians Super Team insert cards from the 1994 Stadium Club issue could redeem them following the 1995 season for special Master Photos team sets of the League Champions. Each team set included 10 player cards and a Super

Team card with special gold-foil League Champion logos on the fronts. The player cards are in 5" x 7" format with the player's 1995 SC card in the center of a blue background. Backs are in black-and-white with a card number and appropriate logos and copyright. The Super Team card is 2-1/2" x 3-1/2" with a white "REDEEMED" notice overprinted on back.

	NM/M
Complete Set (22):	15.00
Common Player:	.35
Atlanta Braves Team Set	9.00
1 Steve Avery	.40
2 Tom Glavine	.75
3 Chipper Jones	3.00
4 David Justice	.40
5 Ryan Klesko	.40
6 Javy Lopez	.40
7 Greg Maddux	3.00
8 Fred McGriff	.40
9 John Smoltz	.40
10 Mark Wohlers	.40
1 Atlanta Braves Super Team	.40
Cleveland Indians Team Set	7.50
11 Carlos Baerga	.40
12 Albert Belle	.40
13 Orel Hershiser	.40
14 Kenny Lofton	.40
15 Dennis Martinez	.40
16 Jose Mesa	.40
17 Eddie Murray	2.50
18 Manny Ramirez	2.50
19 Jim Thome	2.00
20 Omar Vizquel	.40
19 Cleveland Indians Super Team	.40

World Series Winners

Persons who redeemed a 1994 Stadium Club Atlanta Braves Super Team insert following the Tribe's 1995 World Series victory received a set of 1995 Stadium Club cards, each of which bears a gold-foil World Series logo on front. The cards are otherwise identical to the regular-issue SC cards. The prize "set" contains only 585 cards, a note sent with the set explains 45 of the TSC cards - #496-523 (the Extreme Corps subset) and cards #614-630 (the Trans-Action subset) were not printed in the parallel version.

	NM/M
Complete Set (585):	40.00
Common Player:	.25
Stars:	3X

Members Only

A special version of all of the regular cards from Stadium Club Series I-III, as well as many of the insert sets was offered to members of Topps' Stadium Club. Virtually identical to the regular S.C. cards, the specially boxed set differs in the presence on each card front of an embossed round 1/2" gold-foil "Members Only" seal. Even the plastic Clear Cut inserts have the members' seal embossed directly into the plastic. The edition was limited to 4,000 sets.

	NM/M
Complete Set (630):	150.00
Common Player:	.25
Stars:	6X
Inserts: 50-100 Percent	

Members Only Baseball

This boxed set was sold exclusively through the newsletter for Topps Stadium Club members. Cards feature noteworthy performances and achievements of the 1994 baseball season. Borderless card fronts have a player action photo on which the background has been quartered in colors of blue, green, orange and magenta. The Members Only logo, and player name and position are presented in gold foil. Backs have another player photo at left and a description of the highlight printed in white on a blue background at right. Both front and back of each card are UV coated. The final five cards in the set are printed in Topps Finest technology and feature the company's choice of the top rookies of 1994.

	NM/M
Complete Set (50):	9.00
Common Player:	.20
1 Moises Alou	.20
2 Jeff Bagwell	.75
3 Albert Belle	.20
4 Andy Benes	.20
5 Dante Bichette	.20
6 Craig Biggio	.20
7 Wade Boggs	1.00
8 Barry Bonds	3.00
9 Brett Butler	.20
10 Jose Canseco	.50
11 Joe Carter	.20
12 Vince Coleman	.20
13 Jeff Conine	.20
14 Cecil Fielder	.20
15 John Franco	.20
16 Julio Franco	.20
17 Travis Fryman	.20
18 Andres Galarraga	.20
19 Ken Griffey Jr.	1.50
20 Marquis Grissom	.20
21 Tony Gwynn	1.00
22 Ken Hill	.20
23 Randy Johnson	.75
24 Lance Johnson	.20
25 Jimmy Key	.20
26 Chuck Knoblauch	.20
27 Ray Lankford	.20
28 Darren Lewis	.20
29 Kenny Lofton	.20
30 Greg Maddux	1.00
31 Fred McGriff	.20
32 Kevin Mitchell	.20
33 Paul Molitor	.75
34 Hal Morris	.20
35 Paul O'Neill	.20
36 Rafael Palmeiro	.65
37 Tony Phillips	.20
38 Mike Piazza	1.50
39 Kirby Puckett	1.00
40 Cal Ripken Jr.	3.00
41 Deion Sanders	.20
42 Lee Smith	.20
43 Frank Thomas	.75
44 Larry Walker	.20
45 Matt Williams	.20
46 Manny Ramirez (Rookie Picks)	1.00
47 Joey Hamilton (Rookie Picks)	.20
48 Raul Mondesi (Rookie Picks)	.20
49 Bob Hamelin (Rookie Picks)	.20
50 Ryan Klesko (Rookie Picks)	.20

1996 Stadium Club

Consisting of 450 cards in a pair of 225-card series, Stadium Club continued Topps' 1996 tribute to Mickey Mantle with 19 Retrospective inserts. Cards feature full-bleed photos with gold-foil graphic highlights. Backs offer a TSC Skills Matrix along with another player photo, some biographical data and stats. Team TSC is the only subset with 45 cards each in Series 1 and 2. Stadium Club was issued in retail and hobby packs, with inserts found at differing ratios in each type of packaging.

	NM/M
Complete Set (450):	25.00
Common Player:	.05
Series 1 or 2 Pack (10):	1.00
Series 1 or 2 Wax Box (24):	20.00
1 Hideo Nomo (Extreme Player)	.40
2 Paul Molitor	.75
3 Garret Anderson (Extreme Player)	.05
4 Jose Mesa (Extreme Player)	.05
5 Vinny Castilla (Extreme Player)	.05
6 Mike Mussina (Extreme Player)	.30
7 Ray Durham (Extreme Player)	.05
8 Jack McDowell (Extreme Player)	.05
9 Juan Gonzalez (Extreme Player)	.40
10 Chipper Jones (Extreme Player)	1.00
11 Deion Sanders (Extreme Player)	.05
12 Rondell White (Extreme Player)	.05
13 Tom Henke (Extreme Player)	.05
14 Derek Bell (Extreme Player)	.05
15 Randy Myers (Extreme Player)	.05
16 Randy Johnson (Extreme Player)	.75
17 Len Dykstra (Extreme Player)	.05
18 Bill Pulsipher (Extreme Player)	.05
19 Greg Colbrunn (Extreme Player)	.05
20 David Wells (Extreme Player)	.05
21 Chad Curtis (Extreme Player)	.05
22 Roberto Hernandez (Extreme Player)	.05
23 Kirby Puckett (Extreme Player)	1.00
24 Joe Vitiello (Extreme Player)	.05
25 Roger Clemens (Extreme Player)	1.25
26 Al Martin	.05
27 Chad Ogea	.05
28 David Segui	.05
29 Joey Hamilton	.05
30 Dan Wilson	.05
31 Chad Fonville (Extreme Player)	.05
32 Bernard Gilkey (Extreme Player)	.05
33 Kevin Seitzer	.05
34 Shawn Green (Extreme Player)	.35
35 Rick Aguilera (Extreme Player)	.05
36 Gary DiSarcina	.05
37 Jaime Navarro	.05
38 Doug Jones	.05
39 Brent Gates	.05
40 Dean Palmer (Extreme Player)	.05
41 Pat Rapp	.05
42 Tony Clark	.05
43 Bill Swift	.05
44 Randy Velarde	.05
45 Matt Williams	.05
46 John Mabry	.05
47 Mike Fetters	.05
48 Orlando Miller	.05
49 Tom Glavine (Extreme Player)	.35
50 Delino DeShields (Extreme Player)	.05
51 Scott Erickson	.05
52 Andy Van Slyke	.05
53 Jim Bullinger	.05
54 Lyle Mouton	.05
55 Bret Saberhagen	.05
56 Benito Santiago (Extreme Player)	.05
57 Dan Miceli	.05
58 Carl Everett	.05
59 Rod Beck (Extreme Player)	.05
60 Phil Nevin	.05
61 Jason Giambi	.50
62 Paul Menhart	.05
63 Eric Karros (Extreme Player)	.05
64 Allen Watson	.05
65 Jeff Cirillo	.05
66 Lee Smith (Extreme Player)	.05
67 Sean Berry	.05
68 Luis Sojo	.05
69 Jeff Montgomery (Extreme Player)	.05
70 Todd Hundley (Extreme Player)	.05
71 John Burkett	.05
72 Mark Gubicza	.05
73 Don Mattingly (Extreme Player)	1.25
74 Jeff Brantley	.05
75 Matt Walbeck	.05
76 Steve Parris	.05
77 Ken Caminiti (Extreme Player)	.05
78 Kirt Manwaring	.05
79 Greg Vaughn	.05
80 Pedro Martinez (Extreme Player)	.75
81 Benji Gil	.05
82 Heathcliff Slocumb (Extreme Player)	.05
83 Joe Girardi (Extreme Player)	.05
84 Sean Bergman	.05
85 Matt Karchner	.05
86 Butch Huskey	.05
87 Mike Morgan	.05
88 Todd Worrell (Extreme Player)	.05
89 Mike Bordick	.05
90 Bip Roberts (Extreme Player)	.05
91 Mike Hampton	.05
92 Troy O'Leary	.05
93 Wally Joyner	.05
94 Dave Stevens	.05
95 Cecil Fielder (Extreme Player)	.05
96 Wade Boggs (Extreme Player)	1.00
97 Hal Morris	.05
98 Mickey Tettleton (Extreme Player)	.05
99 Jeff Kent (Extreme Player)	.05
100 Denny Martinez	.05
101 Luis Gonzalez	.05
102 John Jaha	.05
103 Javy Lopez (Extreme Player)	.05
104 Mark McGwire (Extreme Player)	2.00
105 Ken Griffey Jr. (Extreme Player)	1.50
106 Darren Daulton (Extreme Player)	.05
107 Bryan Rekar	.05
108 Mike Macfarlane (Extreme Player)	.05
109 Gary Gaetti (Extreme Player)	.05
110 Shane Reynolds (Extreme Player)	.05
111 Pat Meares	.05
112 Jason Schmidt	.05
113 Otis Nixon	.05
114 John Franco (Extreme Player)	.05
115 Marc Newfield	.05
116 Andy Benes (Extreme Player)	.05
117 Ozzie Guillen	.05
118 Brian Jordan (Extreme Player)	.05
119 Terry Pendleton (Extreme Player)	.05
120 Chuck Finley (Extreme Player)	.05
121 Scott Stahoviak	.05
122 Sid Fernandez	.05
123 Derek Jeter (Extreme Player)	3.00
124 John Smiley (Extreme Player)	.05
125 David Bell	.05
126 Brett Butler (Extreme Player)	.05
127 Doug Drabek (Extreme Player)	.05
128 J.T. Snow (Team TSC)	.05
129 Joe Carter (Extreme Player)	.05
130 Dennis Eckersley (Extreme Player)	.65
131 Marty Cordova (Extreme Player)	1.00
132 Greg Maddux (Extreme Player)	1.00
133 Tom Goodwin	.05
134 Andy Ashby	.05
135 Paul Sorrento (Extreme Player)	.05
136 Ricky Bones	.05
137 Shawon Dunston (Extreme Player)	.05
138 Moises Alou (Extreme Player)	.05
139 Mickey Morandini	.05
140 Ramon Martinez (Extreme Player)	.05
141 Royce Clayton (Extreme Player)	.05
142 Brad Ausmus	.05
143 Kenny Rogers (Extreme Player)	.05
144 Tim Naehring	.05
145 Chris Gomez	.05
146 Bobby Bonilla (Extreme Player)	.05
147 Wilson Alvarez	.05
148 Johnny Damon (Extreme Player)	.35
149 Pat Hentgen	.05
150 Andres Galarraga (Extreme Player)	.05
151 David Cone (Extreme Player)	.05
152 Lance Johnson (Extreme Player)	.05
153 Carlos Garcia	.05
154 Doug Johns	.05
155 Midre Cummings	.05
156 Steve Sparks	.05
157 Sandy Martinez RC	.05
158 William Van Landingham	.05
159 Dave Justice (Extreme Player)	.05
160 Mark Grace (Extreme Player)	.05
161 Robb Nen (Extreme Player)	.05
162 Mike Greenwell (Extreme Player)	.05
163 Brad Radke	.05
164 Edgardo Alfonzo	.05
165 Mark Leiter	.05
166 Walt Weiss	.05
167 Mel Rojas (Extreme Player)	.05
168 Bret Boone	.05
169 Ricky Bottalico	.05
170 Bobby Higginson	.05
171 Trevor Hoffman	.05
172 Jay Bell (Extreme Player)	.05
173 Gabe White	.05
174 Curtis Goodwin	.05
175 Tyler Green	.05
176 Roberto Alomar (Extreme Player)	.20
177 Sterling Hitchcock	.05
178 Ryan Klesko (Extreme Player)	.05
179 Donne Wall RC	.05
180 Brian McRae	.05
181 Will Clark (Team TSC)	.05
182 Frank Thomas (Team TSC)	.60
183 Jeff Bagwell (Team TSC)	.60
184 Mo Vaughn (Team TSC)	.05
185 Tino Martinez (Team TSC)	.05
186 Craig Biggio (Team TSC)	.05
187 Chuck Knoblauch (Team TSC)	.05
188 Carlos Baerga (Team TSC)	.05
189 Quilvio Veras (Team TSC)	.05
190 Luis Alicea (Team TSC)	.05
191 Jim Thome (Team TSC)	.40
192 Mike Blowers (Team TSC)	.05
193 Robin Ventura (Team TSC)	.05
194 Jeff King (Team TSC)	.05
195 Tony Phillips (Team TSC)	.05
196 John Valentin (Team TSC)	.05
197 Barry Larkin (Team TSC)	.05
198 Cal Ripken Jr. (Team TSC)	2.00
199 Omar Vizquel (Team TSC)	.05
200 Kurt Abbott (Team TSC)	.05
201 Albert Belle (Team TSC)	.05
202 Barry Bonds (Team TSC)	2.00
203 Ron Gant (Team TSC)	.05
204 Dante Bichette (Team TSC)	.05
205 John Conine (Team TSC)	.05
206 Jim Edmonds (Team TSC)	.05
207 Stan Javier (Team TSC)	.05
208 Kenny Lofton (Team TSC)	.05
209 Ray Lankford (Team TSC)	.05
210 Bernie Williams (Team TSC)	.05
211 Jay Buhner (Team TSC)	.05
212 Paul O'Neill (Team TSC)	.05
213 Tim Salmon (Team TSC)	.05
214 Reggie Sanders (Team TSC)	.05
215 Manny Ramirez (Team TSC)	.60
216 Mike Piazza (Team TSC)	1.50
217 Mike Stanley (Team TSC)	.05
218 Tony Eusebio (Team TSC)	.05
219 Chris Hoiles (Team TSC)	.05
220 Ron Karkovice (Team TSC)	.05
221 Edgar Martinez (Team TSC)	.05
222 Chili Davis (Team TSC)	.05
223 Jose Canseco (Team TSC)	.35
224 Eddie Murray (Team TSC)	.60
225 Geronimo Berroa (Team TSC)	.05
226 Chipper Jones (Team TSC)	.75
227 Garret Anderson (Team TSC)	.05
228 Marty Cordova (Team TSC)	.05
229 Jon Nunnally (Team TSC)	.05
230 Brian Hunter (Team TSC)	.05
231 Shawn Green (Team TSC)	.20
232 Ray Durham (Team TSC)	.05
233 Alex Gonzalez (Team TSC)	.05
234 Bobby Higginson (Team TSC)	.05
235 Randy Johnson (Team TSC)	.60
236 Al Leiter (Team TSC)	.05
237 Tom Glavine (Team TSC)	.10
238 Kenny Rogers (Team TSC)	.05
239 Mike Hampton (Team TSC)	.05
240 David Wells (Team TSC)	.05
241 Jim Abbott (Team TSC)	.05
242 Denny Neagle (Team TSC)	.05
243 Wilson Alvarez (Team TSC)	.05
244 John Smiley (Team TSC)	.05
245 Greg Maddux (Team TSC)	.75
246 Andy Ashby (Team TSC)	.05
247 Hideo Nomo (Team TSC)	.30
248 Pat Rapp (Team TSC)	.05
249 Tim Wakefield (Team TSC)	.05
250 John Smoltz (Team TSC)	.05
251 Joey Hamilton (Team TSC)	.05
252 Frank Castillo (Team TSC)	.05
253 Denny Martinez (Team TSC)	.05
254 Jaime Navarro (Team TSC)	.05
255 Karim Garcia (Team TSC)	.05
256 Bob Abreu (Team TSC)	.05
257 Butch Huskey (Team TSC)	.05
258 Ruben Rivera (Team TSC)	.05
259 Johnny Damon (Team TSC)	.20
260 Derek Jeter (Team TSC)	2.00
261 Dennis Eckersley (Team TSC)	.50
262 Jose Mesa (Team TSC)	.05
263 Tom Henke (Team TSC)	.05
264 Rick Aguilera (Team TSC)	.05
265 Randy Myers (Team TSC)	.05
266 John Franco (Team TSC)	.05
267 Jeff Brantley (Team TSC)	.05
268 John Wetteland (Team TSC)	.05
269 Mark Wohlers (Team TSC)	.05
270 Rod Beck (Team TSC)	.05
271 Barry Larkin	.05
272 Paul O'Neill	.05
273 Bobby Jones	.05
274 Will Clark	.05
275 Steve Avery	.05
276 Jim Edmonds	.05
277 John Olerud	.05
278 Carlos Perez	.05
279 Chris Hoiles	.05
280 Jeff Conine	.05
281 Jim Eisenreich	.05
282 Jason Jacome	.05
283 Ray Lankford	.05
284 John Wasdin	.05
285 Frank Thomas	.75
286 Jason Isringhausen	.05
287 Glenallen Hill	.05
288 Esteban Loaiza	.05
289 Bernie Williams	.05
290 Curtis Leskanic	.05
291 Scott Cooper	.05
292 Curt Schilling	.35
293 Eddie Murray	.75
294 Rick Krivda	.05
295 Domingo Cedeno	.05
296 Jeff Fassero	.05
297 Albert Belle	.05
298 Craig Biggio	.05
299 Fernando Vina	.05
300 Edgar Martinez	.05
301 Tony Gwynn	1.00
302 Felipe Lira	.05
303 Mo Vaughn	.05
304 Alex Fernandez	.05
305 Keith Lockhart	.05
306 Roger Pavlik	.05
307 Lee Tinsley	.05
308 Omar Vizquel	.05
309 Scott Servais	.05
310 Danny Tartabull	.05
311 Chili Davis	.05
312 Cal Eldred	.05
313 Roger Cedeno	.05
314 Chris Hammond	.05
315 Rusty Greer	.05
316 Brady Anderson	.05
317 Ron Villone	.05
318 Mark Carreon	.05

#	Player	Price
319	Larry Walker	.05
320	Pete Harnisch	.05
321	Robin Ventura	.05
322	Tim Belcher	.05
323	Tony Tarasco	.05
324	Juan Guzman	.05
325	Kenny Lofton	.05
326	Kevin Foster	.05
327	Wil Cordero	.05
328	Troy Percival	.05
329	Turk Wendell	.05
330	Thomas Howard	.05
331	Carlos Baerga	.05
332	B.J. Surhoff	.05
333	Jay Buhner	.05
334	Andujar Cedeno	.05
335	Jeff King	.05
336	Dante Bichette	.05
337	Alan Trammell	.05
338	Scott Leius	.05
339	Chris Snopek	.05
340	Roger Bailey	.05
341	Jacob Brumfield	.05
342	Jose Canseco	.50
343	Rafael Palmeiro	.65
344	Quilvio Veras	.05
345	Darrin Fletcher	.05
346	Carlos Delgado	.50
347	Tony Eusebio	.05
348	Ismael Valdes	.05
349	Terry Steinbach	.05
350	Orel Hershiser	.05
351	Kurt Abbott	.05
352	Jody Reed	.05
353	David Howard	.05
354	Ruben Sierra	.05
355	John Ericks	.05
356	Buck Showalter	.05
357	Jim Thome	.65
358	Geronimo Berroa	.05
359	Robby Thompson	.05
360	Jose Vizcaino	.05
361	Jeff Frye	.05
362	Kevin Appier	.05
363	Pat Kelly	.05
364	Ron Gant	.05
365	Luis Alicea	.05
366	Armando Benitez	.05
367	Rico Brogna	.05
368	Manny Ramirez	.75
369	Mike Lansing	.05
370	Sammy Sosa	1.00
371	Don Wengert	.05
372	Dave Nilsson	.05
373	Sandy Alomar	.05
374	Joey Cora	.05
375	Larry Thomas	.05
376	John Valentin	.05
377	Kevin Ritz	.05
378	Steve Finley	.05
379	Frank Rodriguez	.05
380	Ivan Rodriguez	.65
381	Alex Ochoa	.05
382	Mark Lemke	.05
383	Scott Brosius	.05
384	James Mouton	.05
385	Mark Langston	.05
386	Ed Sprague	.05
387	Joe Oliver	.05
388	Steve Ontiveros	.05
389	Rey Sanchez	.05
390	Mike Henneman	.05
391	Jose Valentin RC	.05
392	Tom Candiotti	.05
393	Damon Buford	.05
394	Erik Hanson	.05
395	Mark Smith	.05
396	Pete Schourek	.05
397	John Flaherty	.05
398	Dave Martinez	.05
399	Tommy Greene	.05
400	Gary Sheffield	.45
401	Glenn Dishman	.05
402	Barry Bonds	3.00
403	Tom Pagnozzi	.05
404	Todd Stottlemyre	.05
405	Tim Salmon	.05
406	John Hudek	.05
407	Fred McGriff	.05
408	Orlando Merced	.05
409	Brian Barber	.05
410	Ryan Thompson	.05
411	Mariano Rivera	.10
412	Eric Young	.05
413	Chris Bosio	.05
414	Chuck Knoblauch	.05
415	Jamie Moyer	.05
416	Chan Ho Park	.05
417	Mark Portugal	.05
418	Tim Raines	.05
419	Antonio Osuna	.05
420	Todd Zeile	.05
421	Steve Wojciechowski	.05
422	Marquis Grissom	.05
423	Norm Charlton	.05
424	Cal Ripken Jr.	3.00
425	Gregg Jefferies	.05
426	Mike Stanton	.05
427	Tony Fernandez	.05
428	Jose Rijo	.05
429	Jeff Bagwell	.75
430	Raul Mondesi	.05
431	Travis Fryman	.05
432	Ron Karkovice	.05
433	Alan Benes	.05
434	Tony Phillips	.05
435	Reggie Sanders	.05
436	Andy Pettitte	.25

#	Player	Price
437	Matt Lawton RC	.25
438	Jeff Blauser	.05
439	Michael Tucker	.05
440	Mark Loretta	.05
441	Charlie Hayes	.05
442	Mike Piazza	1.50
443	Shane Andrews	.05
444	Jeff Suppan	.05
445	Steve Rodriguez	.05
446	Mike Matheny	.05
447	Trenidad Hubbard	.05
448	Denny Hocking	.05
449	Mark Grudzielanek	.05
450	Joe Randa	.05

Mickey Mantle "Cereal Box" Set

This factory-set version of TSC was packaged in boxes which resembled single-serving cereal boxes. The cards are identical to the regular TSC version except for the use of silver-foil, rather than gold-foil, highlights on front.

	NM/M
Unopened Set:	30.00
Common Player:	.10

Extreme Player

A special interactive version of 179 players' cards in 1996 Stadium Club was issued as an insert set across Series 1 and 2. Specially stamped with an "Extreme Player" logo in bronze (1 per 12 packs average), silver (1:24) or gold (1:48), the cards have backs which detail a contest by which the player's on-field performance was used to rank each by position. At season's end, cards of the winning players at each position could be redeemed for special prizes. The contest cards do not have card numbers on back and are numbered here based on the regular version.

	NM/M
Complete Bronze Set (179):	40.00
Common Bronze:	.10
Silvers:	1.5X
Golds:	2.5X
1	Hideo Nomo	.50
3	Garret Anderson	.10
4	Jose Mesa	.10
5	Vinny Castilla	.10
6	Mike Mussina	.30
7	Ray Durham	.10
8	Jack McDowell	.10
9	Juan Gonzalez	.50
11	Chipper Jones	1.50
12	Deion Sanders	.10
13	Rondell White	.10
13	Tom Henke	.10
14	Derek Bell	.10
15	Randy Myers	.10
16	Randy Johnson	1.00
17	Len Dykstra	.10
18	Bill Pulsipher	.10
21	Chad Curtis	.10
22	Roberto Hernandez	.10
24	Kirby Puckett	1.50
25	Roger Clemens	1.75
31	Chad Fonville	.10
32	Bernard Gilkey	.10
34	Shawn Green	.35
35	Rick Aguilera	.10
40	Dean Palmer	.10
41	Matt Williams	.10
49	Tom Glavine	.35
50	Delino DeShields	.10
58	Benito Santiago	.10
59	Rod Beck	.10
63	Eric Karros	.10
66	Lee Smith	.10
69	Jeff Montgomery	.10
70	Todd Hundley	.10
73	Don Mattingly	1.75
80	Ken Caminiti	.10
80	Pedro Martinez	1.00
82	Heathcliff Slocumb	.10
83	Joe Girardi	.10
88	Todd Worrell	.10
90	Bip Roberts	.10

#	Player	Price
95	Cecil Fielder	.10
96	Wade Boggs	1.50
98	Mickey Tettleton	.10
99	Jeff Kent	.10
101	Luis Gonzalez	.10
103	Javier Lopez	.10
104	Mark McGwire	3.00
106	Ken Griffey Jr.	2.00
107	Darren Daulton	.10
108	Mike Macfarlane	.10
109	Gary Gaetti	.10
110	Shane Reynolds	.10
114	John Franco	.10
116	Andy Benes	.10
118	Brian Jordan	.10
119	Terry Pendleton	.10
120	Chuck Finley	.10
123	Derek Jeter	4.00
124	John Smiley	.10
126	Brett Butler	.10
127	Doug Drabek	.10
128	J.T. Snow	.10
129	Joe Carter	.10
130	Dennis Eckersley	.75
131	Marty Cordova	.10
132	Greg Maddux	1.50
135	Paul Sorrento	.10
137	Shawon Dunston	.10
138	Moises Alou	.10
140	Ramon Martinez	.10
141	Royce Clayton	.10
143	Kenny Rogers	.10
144	Tim Naehring	.10
145	Chris Gomez	.10
146	Bobby Bonilla	.10
148	Johnny Damon	.40
150	Andres Galarraga	.10
151	David Cone	.10
152	Lance Johnson	.10
159	Dave Justice	.10
160	Mark Grace	.10
161	Robb Nen	.10
162	Mike Greenwell	.10
167	Mel Rojas	.10
168	Bret Boone	.10
172	Jay Bell	.10
176	Roberto Alomar	.25
178	Ryan Klesko	.10
271	Barry Larkin	.10
272	Paul O'Neill	.10
273	Will Clark	.10
275	Steve Avery	.10
276	Jim Edmonds	.10
277	John Olerud	.10
279	Chris Hoiles	.10
280	Jeff Conine	.10
283	Ray Lankford	.10
285	Frank Thomas	1.00
286	Jason Isringhausen	.10
287	Glenallen Hill	.10
289	Bernie Williams	.10
296	Eddie Murray	1.00
296	Jeff Fassero	.10
297	Albert Belle	.10
298	Craig Biggio	.10
300	Edgar Martinez	.10
301	Tony Gwynn	1.50
303	Mo Vaughn	.10
304	Alex Fernandez	.10
308	Omar Vizquel	.10
310	Danny Tartabull	.10
316	Brady Anderson	.10
319	Larry Walker	.10
321	Robin Ventura	.10
325	Kenny Lofton	.10
327	Wil Cordero	.10
328	Troy Percival	.10
331	Carlos Baerga	.10
333	Jay Buhner	.10
335	Jeff King	.10
336	Dante Bichette	.10
337	Alan Trammell	.10
342	Jose Canseco	.50
343	Rafael Palmeiro	.75
344	Quilvio Veras	.10
345	Darrin Fletcher	.10
347	Tony Eusebio	.10
348	Ismael Valdes	.10
349	Terry Steinbach	.10
350	Orel Hershiser	.10
351	Kurt Abbott	.10
354	Ruben Sierra	.10
357	Jim Thome	.75
358	Geronimo Berroa	.10
359	Robby Thompson	.10
360	Jose Vizcaino	.10
362	Kevin Appier	.10
364	Ron Gant	.10
367	Rico Brogna	.10
368	Manny Ramirez	1.00
370	Sammy Sosa	1.50
373	Sandy Alomar	.10
378	Steve Finley	.10
380	Ivan Rodriguez	.75
382	Mark Lemke	.10
385	Mark Langston	.10
386	Ed Sprague	.10
388	Steve Ontiveros	.10
392	Tom Candiotti	.10
394	Erik Hanson	.10
396	Pete Schourek	.10
400	Gary Sheffield	.35
402	Barry Bonds	4.00
403	Tom Pagnozzi	.10
404	Todd Stottlemyre	.10
405	Tim Salmon	.10
407	Fred McGriff	.10
408	Orlando Merced	.10

#	Player	Price
412	Eric Young	.10
414	Chuck Knoblauch	.10
417	Mark Portugal	.10
419	Tim Raines	.10
420	Todd Zeile	.10
422	Marquis Grissom	.10
423	Norm Charlton	.10
424	Cal Ripken Jr.	4.00
428	Gregg Jefferies	.10
428	Jose Rijo	.10
429	Jeff Bagwell	1.00
430	Raul Mondesi	.10
431	Travis Fryman	.10
434	Tony Phillips	.10
435	Reggie Sanders	.10
436	Andy Pettitte	.25
438	Jeff Blauser	.10
441	Charlie Hayes	.10
442	Mike Piazza	2.00

Extreme Player - Bronze Winner

Ten-card sets of these special bronze-foil highlighted cards were the prize for those who redeemed bronze statistical winners' cards from the Stadium Club Extreme Player interactive series. Backs have statistical ratings pertinent to the game and scoring rules. Cards have an "EW" prefix to the number. The same photos and back design were used in different technologies in the bronze, silver and gold winners cards.

	NM/M
Complete Set (10):	6.00
Common Player:	.40
1	Greg Maddux	1.50
2	Mike Piazza	2.00
3	Andres Galarraga	.40
4	Chuck Knoblauch	.40
5	Ken Caminiti	.40
6	Barry Larkin	.40
7	Barry Bonds	3.00
8	Ken Griffey Jr.	2.00
9	Gary Sheffield	.75
10	Todd Worrell	.40

Extreme Player - Silver Winner

Ten-card sets of these Finest technology cards were the prize for those who redeemed statistical winners' cards from the Stadium Club Extreme Player interactive series. Backs have statistical ratings pertinent to the game and scoring rules. Cards have an "EW" prefix to the number.

	NM/M
Complete Set (10):	17.50
Common Player:	.75
1	Greg Maddux	3.00
2	Mike Piazza	4.00
3	Andres Galarraga	.75
4	Chuck Knoblauch	.75
5	Ken Caminiti	.75
6	Barry Larkin	.75
7	Barry Bonds	5.00
8	Ken Griffey Jr.	4.00
9	Gary Sheffield	1.50
10	Todd Worrell	.75

Extreme Player - Gold Winner

One of these large (2-3/4" x 3-3/4"), heavy, acrylic-coated bronze refractor cards was the prize for those who redeemed the same player's gold statistical winners' card from the Stadium Club Extreme Player interactive series. Backs have statistical ratings pertinent to the game and scoring rules. Cards have an "EW" prefix to the number. The same photos and back design were used in different technologies in the bronze, silver and gold winners cards.

	NM/M
Complete Set (10):	45.00
Common Player:	2.00
1	Greg Maddux	8.00
2	Mike Piazza	10.00
3	Andres Galarraga	2.00
4	Chuck Knoblauch	2.00
5	Ken Caminiti	2.00
6	Barry Larkin	2.00
7	Barry Bonds	15.00
8	Ken Griffey Jr.	10.00
9	Gary Sheffield	3.50
10	Todd Worrell	2.00

Bash & Burn

Inserted in one per 24 retail packs and one per 48 hobby packs of Series II, Bash & Burn includes 10 players on double-fronted cards. Both sides are foil-etched with the Bash side highlighting home runs and runs batted in for 1995 and career, and the Burn side featured stolen base and runs scored leaders for 1995 and career. Cards are numbered with a "B&B" prefix.

	NM/M
Complete Set (10):	10.00
Common Player:	.75
1	Sammy Sosa	3.50
2	Barry Bonds	6.00
3	Reggie Sanders	.75
4	Craig Biggio	.75
5	Raul Mondesi	.75
6	Ron Gant	.75
7	Ray Lankford	.75
8	Glenallen Hill	.75
9	Chad Curtis	.75
10	John Valentin	.75

Mickey Mantle Retrospective

Following the success of the Mantle reprints in Topps baseball, Stadium Club produced a series of 19 Mickey Mantle Retrospective inserts; nine black-and-white cards in Series 1 and 10 color cards in Series 2. The cards chronicle Mantle's career and provide insights from baseball contemporaries. The Mantle cards are found on an average of once per 24 Series 1 packs and once per 12 Series 2 packs. Cards are numbered with an "MM" prefix.

	NM/M
Complete Set (19):	35.00
Common Series 1:	4.00

	NM/M
Common Series 2:	2.00
1	Mickey Mantle/1950 (Minor league)	4.00
2	Mickey Mantle/1951	4.00
3	Mickey Mantle/1951	4.00
4	Mickey Mantle/1953	4.00
5	Mickey Mantle/1954 (W/Yogi Berra.)	4.00
6	Mickey Mantle/1956	4.00
7	Mickey Mantle/1957	4.00
8	Mickey Mantle/1958 (W/Casey Stengel.)	4.00
9	Mickey Mantle/1959	4.00
10	Mickey Mantle/1960 (W/Elston Howard.)	2.00
11	Mickey Mantle/1961	2.00
12	Mickey Mantle/1961 (W/Roger Maris.)	4.00
13	Mickey Mantle/1962	2.00
14	Mickey Mantle/1963	2.00
15	Mickey Mantle/1964	2.00
16	Mickey Mantle	2.00
17	Mickey Mantle/1968	2.00
18	Mickey Mantle/1969	2.00
19	Mickey Mantle (In Memoriam)	3.50

Mega Heroes

Ten heroic players are matched with a comic book-style illustration depicting their nicknames in the Mega Heroes insert set. Printed on foilboard in a defraction technology, the cards are found, on average, once per 48 Series 1 hobby packs and twice as often in retail packs.

	NM/M
Complete Set (10):	10.00
Common Player:	1.00
1	Frank Thomas	1.50
2	Ken Griffey Jr.	3.00
3	Hideo Nomo	1.25
5	Ozzie Smith	1.75
5	Will Clark	1.00
6	Jack McDowell	1.00
7	Andres Galarraga	1.00
8	Roger Clemens	2.00
9	Deion Sanders	1.00
10	Mo Vaughn	1.00

Metalists

Eight players who have won two or more major awards in their careers are featured in this Series II insert. Cards are printed on foilboard and feature intricate laser-cut designs that depict the player's face. Metalist inserts are found one per 96 retail and one per 48 hobby packs, on average. Cards are numbered with a "M" prefix.

		NM/M
Complete Set (8):		12.00
Common Player:		1.00
1	Jeff Bagwell	1.25
2	Barry Bonds	3.50
3	Jose Canseco	1.00
4	Roger Clemens	2.50
5	Dennis Eckersley	1.00
6	Greg Maddux	2.00
7	Cal Ripken Jr.	3.50
8	Frank Thomas	1.25

Midsummer Matchups

These inserts salute 1995 National League and American League All-Stars on back-to-back etched-foil cards. Players are matched by position in the 10-card set. Average insertion rate is one per 48 hobby packs and one per 24 retail packs in Series 1. Cards are numbered with an "M" prefix.

		NM/M
Complete Set (10):		20.00
Common Player:		1.00
1	Hideo Nomo, Randy Johnson	2.00
2	Mike Piazza, Ivan Rodriguez	4.00
3	Fred McGriff, Frank Thomas	2.00
4	Craig Biggio, Carlos Baerga	1.00
5	Vinny Castilla, Wade Boggs	2.50
6	Barry Larkin, Cal Ripken Jr.	5.00
7	Barry Bonds, Albert Belle	5.00
8	Len Dykstra, Kenny Lofton	1.00
9	Tony Gwynn, Kirby Puckett	3.00
10	Ron Gant, Edgar Martinez	1.00

Power Packed

Topps' Power Matrix technology is used to showcase 15 of the biggest, strongest players in this Series 2 insert set. Card backs feature a diagram of the player's home park with baseball graphics measuring his home runs during the 1995 season. The inserts are a one in 48 packs pick, on average, both hobby and retail. Cards are numbered with a "PP" prefix.

		NM/M
Complete Set (15):		15.00
Common Player:		1.00
1	Albert Belle	1.00
2	Mark McGwire	4.00
3	Jose Canseco	1.75
4	Mike Piazza	3.00
5	Ron Gant	1.00
6	Ken Griffey Jr.	3.00
7	Mo Vaughn	1.00
8	Cecil Fielder	1.00
9	Tim Salmon	1.00
10	Frank Thomas	2.50
11	Juan Gonzalez	1.50
12	Andres Galarraga	1.00
13	Fred McGriff	1.00
14	Jay Buhner	1.00
15	Dante Bichette	1.00

Power Streak

The best power hitters in baseball are featured in Power Matrix technology on these Series I inserts. Average insertion rate is one per 24 hobby and 48 retail packs. Cards are numbered with a "PS" prefix.

		NM/M
Complete Set (15):		20.00
Common Player:		1.00
1	Randy Johnson	2.00
2	Hideo Nomo	1.25
3	Albert Belle	1.00
4	Dante Bichette	1.00
5	Jay Buhner	1.00
6	Frank Thomas	2.00
7	Mark McGwire	4.00
8	Rafael Palmeiro	1.50
9	Mo Vaughn	1.00
10	Sammy Sosa	3.00
11	Larry Walker	1.00
12	Gary Gaetti	1.00
13	Tim Salmon	1.00
14	Barry Bonds	5.00
15	Jim Edmonds	1.00

Prime Cuts

The purest swings in baseball are the focus on these laser-cut, de-fraction-foil inserts found in Series 1 packs at an average rate of one per 36 hobby and 72 retail packs. Cards are numbered with a "PC" prefix.

		NM/M
Complete Set (8):		20.00
Common Player:		1.50
1	Albert Belle	1.50
2	Barry Bonds	6.00
3	Ken Griffey Jr.	4.00
4	Tony Gwynn	3.00
5	Edgar Martinez	1.00
6	Rafael Palmeiro	2.00
7	Mike Piazza	4.00
8	Frank Thomas	2.50

TSC Awards

TSC Awards insert cards allowed Topps' experts to honor best performances, newcomer, comeback, etc. The cards are found in Series 2 packs at an average rate of one per 24 retail and 48 hobby packs.

		NM/M
Complete Set (10):		15.00
Common Player:		.50
1	Cal Ripken Jr.	5.00
2	Albert Belle	.60
3	Tom Glavine	1.00
4	Jeff Conine	.50
5	Ken Griffey Jr.	4.00
6	Hideo Nomo	1.25
7	Greg Maddux	3.00
8	Chipper Jones	3.00
9	Randy Johnson	2.00
10	Jose Mesa	.50

Members Only

For the fourth year Topps offered a special edition of its high-end Stadium Club issue to members of its mail-order family. Each of the regular and insert cards was stamped with a gold- or silver-foil "MEMBERS ONLY" seal. The '96 edition was the scarcest ever produced, with only 750 sets offered at $200. Single "Members Only" cards paralleling the regular-issue Stadium Club cards sell for a premium while the M.O. versions of the inserts usually sell at par or even a discount from the issued cards.

	NM/M
Complete Set (660):	150.00
Common Player:	.50
Stars:	6X
Inserts:	50-100 Percent

Members Only Baseball

This 50-card boxed set was offered to members of Topps Stadium Club at about $15 retail. The first 45 cards in the set represent Topps' choice of 1995's top players in each league. The final five cards, printed in Topps Finest technology, honor hot rookies. The basic cards feature borderless action photos on which the background has been posterized and darkened to make the color photo stand out in the foreground. A gold-foil strip at bottom has the player name and position; a "Members Only" logo is in gold foil in an upper corner. Horizontal backs once again have much of the photo background darkened with a close-up photo at right and a few sentences about the player at left. "Member's Choice" Finest rookie cards have a stylized baseball diamond in red tones as background to the action photos. Backs have a large red-shaded baseball with player write-up at bottom and - honest - a pea-green portrait photo at upper-left. Each of the Finest cards has a peel-off protective layer on front.

		NM/M
Complete Set (50):		6.00
Common Player:		.10
1	Carlos Baerga	.10
2	Derek Bell	.10
3	Albert Belle	.10
4	Dante Bichette	.10
5	Craig Biggio	.10
6	Wade Boggs	.65
7	Barry Bonds	1.50
8	Jay Buhner	.10
9	Vinny Castilla	.10
10	Jeff Conine	.10
11	Jim Edmonds	.10
12	Steve Finley	.10
13	Andres Galarraga	.10
14	Mark Grace	.10
15	Tony Gwynn	.65
16	Lance Johnson	.10
17	Randy Johnson	.50
18	Eric Karros	.10
19	Chuck Knoblauch	.10
20	Barry Larkin	.10
21	Kenny Lofton	.10
22	Greg Maddux	.65
23	Edgar Martinez	.10
24	Tino Martinez	.10
25	Mark McGwire	1.00
26	Brian McRae	.10
27	Jose Mesa	.10
28	Eddie Murray	.50
29	Mike Mussina	.30
30	Randy Myers	.10
31	Hideo Nomo	.25
32	Rafael Palmeiro	.50
33	Tony Phillips	.10
34	Mike Piazza	.75
35	Kirby Puckett	.65
36	Manny Ramirez	.50
37	Tim Salmon	.10
38	Reggie Sanders	.10
39	Sammy Sosa	.65
40	Frank Thomas	.50
41	Jim Thome	.45
42	John Valentin	.10
43	Mo Vaughn	.10
44	Quilvio Veras	.10
45	Larry Walker	.10
46	Hideo Nomo (Finest)	.50
47	Marty Cordova (Finest)	.50
48	Chipper Jones (Finest)	1.50
49	Garret Anderson (Finest)	.50
50	Andy Pettitte (Finest)	.50

1997 Stadium Club Pre-Production

These specially marked promo cards were issued in a cello wrapper.

		NM/M
Complete Set (3):		4.00
Common Player:		1.00
PP1	Chipper Jones	3.00
PP2	Kenny Lofton	1.00
PP3	Gary Sheffield	1.50

1997 Stadium Club

Stadium Club totaled 390 cards in 1997, issued in two series of 195 cards each. In Series 1 (Feb.), cards #181-195 are a rookie subset called TSC 2000. In Series 2 (April), cards #376-390 form a subset called Stadium Slugger. Each of these subsets was short-printed and inserted about one per two packs. TSC is printed on an improved 20-point stock with Topps' Super Color process.

		NM/M
Complete Set (390):		35.00
Common Player:		.05
Series 1 or 2 Pack (9):		1.50
Series 1 or 2 Wax Box (24):		27.50
1	Chipper Jones	1.50
2	Gary Sheffield	.50
3	Kenny Lofton	.05
4	Brian Jordan	.05
5	Mark McGwire	2.50
6	Charles Nagy	.05
7	Tim Salmon	.05
8	Cal Ripken Jr.	3.00
9	Jeff Conine	.05
10	Paul Molitor	1.00
11	Mariano Rivera	.15
12	Pedro Martinez	1.00
13	Jeff Bagwell	1.00
14	Bobby Bonilla	.05
15	Barry Bonds	3.00
16	Ryan Klesko	.05
17	Barry Larkin	.05
18	Jim Thome	.65
19	Jay Buhner	.05
20	Juan Gonzalez	.50
21	Mike Mussina	.30
22	Kevin Appier	.05
23	Eric Karros	.05
24	Steve Finley	.05
25	Ed Sprague	.05
26	Bernard Gilkey	.05
27	Tony Phillips	.05
28	Henry Rodriguez	.05
29	John Smoltz	.05
30	Dante Bichette	.05
31	Mike Piazza	2.00
32	Paul O'Neill	.05
33	Billy Wagner	.05
34	Reggie Sanders	.05
35	John Jaha	.05
36	Eddie Murray	1.00
37	Eric Young	.05
38	Roberto Hernandez	.05
39	Pat Hentgen	.05
40	Sammy Sosa	1.50
41	Todd Hundley	.05
42	Mo Vaughn	.05
43	Robin Ventura	.05
44	Mark Grudzielanek	.05
45	Shane Reynolds	.05
46	Andy Pettitte	.25
47	Fred McGriff	.05
48	Rey Ordonez	.05
49	Will Clark	.05
50	Ken Griffey Jr.	2.00
51	Todd Worrell	.05
52	Rusty Greer	.05
53	Mark Grace	.05
54	Tom Glavine	.35
55	Derek Jeter	3.00
56	Rafael Palmeiro	.75
57	Bernie Williams	.05
58	Marty Cordova	.05
59	Andres Galarraga	.05
60	Ken Caminiti	.05
61	Garret Anderson	.05
62	Denny Martinez	.05
63	Mike Greenwell	.05
64	David Segui	.05
65	Julio Franco	.05
66	Rickey Henderson	1.00
67	Ozzie Guillen	.05
68	Pete Harnisch	.05
69	Chan Ho Park	.05
70	Harold Baines	.05
71	Mark Clark	.05
72	Steve Avery	.05
73	Brian Hunter	.05
74	Pedro Astacio	.05
75	Jack McDowell	.05
76	Gregg Jefferies	.05
77	Jason Kendall	.05
78	Todd Walker	.05
79	B.J. Surhoff	.05
80	Moises Alou	.05
81	Fernando Vina	.05
82	Darryl Strawberry	.05
83	Jose Rosado	.05
84	Chris Gomez	.05
85	Chili Davis	.05
86	Alan Benes	.05
87	Todd Hollandsworth	.05
88	Jose Vizcaino	.05
89	Edgardo Alfonzo	.05
90	Ruben Rivera	.05
91	Donovan Osborne	.05
92	Doug Glanville	.05
93	Gary DiSarcina	.05
94	Brooks Kieschnick	.05
95	Bobby Jones	.05
96	Raul Casanova	.05
97	Jermaine Allensworth	.05
98	Kenny Rogers	.05
99	Mark McLemore	.05
100	Jeff Fassero	.05
101	Sandy Alomar	.05
102	Chuck Finley	.05
103	Eric Owens	.05
104	Billy McMillon	.05
105	Dwight Gooden	.05
106	Sterling Hitchcock	.05
107	Doug Drabek	.05
108	Paul Wilson	.05
109	Chris Snopek	.05
110	Al Leiter	.05
111	Bob Tewksbury	.05
112	Todd Greene	.05
113	Jose Valentin	.05
114	Delino DeShields	.05
115	Mike Bordick	.05
116	Pat Meares	.05
117	Mariano Duncan	.05
118	Steve Trachsel	.05
119	Luis Castillo	.05
120	Andy Benes	.05
121	Donne Wall	.05
122	Alex Gonzalez	.05
123	Dan Wilson	.05
124	Omar Vizquel	.05
125	Devon White	.05
126	Darryl Hamilton	.05
127	Orlando Merced	.05
128	Royce Clayton	.05
129	William Van Landingham	.05
130	Terry Steinbach	.05
131	Jeff Blauser	.05
132	Jeff Cirillo	.05
133	Roger Pavlik	.05
134	Danny Tartabull	.05
135	Jeff Montgomery	.05
136	Bobby Higginson	.05
137	Mike Grace	.05
138	Kevin Elster	.05
139	Brian Giles RC	1.00
140	Rod Beck	.05
141	Ismael Valdes	.05
142	Scott Brosius	.05
143	Mike Fetters	.05
144	Gary Gaetti	.05
145	Mike Lansing	.05
146	Glenallen Hill	.05
147	Shawn Green	.35
148	Mel Rojas	.05
149	Joey Cora	.05
150	John Smiley	.05
151	Marvin Benard	.05
152	Curt Schilling	.35
153	Dave Nilsson	.05
154	Edgar Renteria	.05
155	Joey Hamilton	.05
156	Carlos Garcia	.05
157	Nomar Garciaparra	2.00
158	Kevin Ritz	.05
159	Keith Lockhart	.05
160	Justin Thompson	.05
161	Terry Adams	.05
162	Jamey Wright	.05
163	Otis Nixon	.05
164	Michael Tucker	.05
165	Mike Stanley	.05
166	Ben McDonald	.05
167	John Mabry	.05
168	Troy O'Leary	.05
169	Mel Nieves	.05
170	Bret Boone	.05
171	Mike Timlin	.05
172	Scott Rolen	.75
173	Reggie Jefferson	.05
174	Neifi Perez	.05
175	Brian McRae	.05
176	Tom Goodwin	.05
177	Aaron Sele	.05
178	Benny Santiago	.05
179	Frank Rodriguez	.05
180	Eric Davis	.05
181	Andruw Jones (TSC 2000)	.75
182	Todd Walker (TSC 2000)	.15
183	Wes Helms (TSC 2000)	.15
184	Nelson Figueroa RC (TSC 2000)	.15
185	Vladimir Guerrero (TSC 2000)	.75
186	Billy McMillon (TSC 2000)	.15
187	Todd Helton (TSC 2000)	.65
188	Nomar Garciaparra (TSC 2000)	2.00
189	Katsuhiro Maeda (TSC 2000)	.15
190	Russell Branyan (TSC 2000)	.15
191	Glendon Rusch (TSC 2000)	.15
192	Bartolo Colon (TSC 2000)	.15
193	Scott Rolen (TSC 2000)	.50
194	Angel Echevarria (TSC 2000)	.15
195	Bob Abreu (TSC 2000)	.20
196	Greg Maddux	1.50
197	Joe Carter	.05
198	Alex Ochoa	.05
199	Ellis Burks	.05
200	Ivan Rodriguez	.75
201	Marquis Grissom	.05
202	Trevor Hoffman	.05
203	Matt Williams	.05
204	Carlos Delgado	.50
205	Ramon Martinez	.05
206	Chuck Knoblauch	.05
207	Juan Guzman	.05
208	Derek Bell	.05
209	Roger Clemens	1.75
210	Vladimir Guerrero	.05
211	Cecil Fielder	.05
212	Hideo Nomo	.50
213	Frank Thomas	1.00
214	Greg Vaughn	.05
215	Javy Lopez	.05
216	Raul Mondesi	.05
217	Wade Boggs	1.50
218	Carlos Baerga	.05
219	Tony Gwynn	1.50
220	Tino Martinez	.05
221	Vinny Castilla	.05
222	Lance Johnson	.05
223	David Justice	.05
224	Rondell White	.05
225	Dean Palmer	.05
226	Jim Edmonds	.05
227	Albert Belle	.05
228	Alex Fernandez	.05
229	Ryne Sandberg	1.50
230	Jose Mesa	.05
231	David Cone	.05
232	Troy Percival	.05
233	Edgar Martinez	.05
234	Jose Canseco	.50
235	Kevin Brown	.05
236	Ray Lankford	.05
237	Karim Garcia	.05
238	J.T. Snow	.05

#	Player	Price
239	Dennis Eckersley	.75
240	Roberto Alomar	.35
241	John Valentin	.05
242	Ron Gant	.05
243	Geronimo Berroa	.05
244	Manny Ramirez	1.00
245	Travis Fryman	.05
246	Denny Neagle	.05
247	Randy Johnson	1.00
248	Darin Erstad	.15
249	Mark Wohlers	.05
250	Ken Hill	.05
251	Larry Walker	.05
252	Craig Biggio	.05
253	Brady Anderson	.05
254	John Wetteland	.05
255	Andruw Jones	1.00
256	Turk Wendell	.05
257	Jason Isringhausen	.05
258	Jaime Navarro	.05
259	Sean Berry	.05
260	Albie Lopez	.05
261	Jay Bell	.05
262	Bobby Witt	.05
263	Tony Clark	.05
264	Tim Wakefield	.05
265	Brad Radke	.05
266	Tim Belcher	.05
267	Mark Lewis	.05
268	Roger Cedeno	.05
269	Tim Naehring	.05
270	Kevin Tapani	.05
271	Joe Randa	.05
272	Randy Myers	.05
273	Dave Burba	.05
274a	Mike Sweeney	.05
274b	Tom Pagnozzi (Should be #374.)	.05
275	Danny Graves	.05
276	Chad Mottola	.05
277	Ruben Sierra	.05
278	Norm Charlton	.05
279	Scott Servais	.05
280	Jacob Cruz	.05
281	Mike Macfarlane	.05
282	Rich Becker	.05
283	Shannon Stewart	.05
284	Gerald Williams	.05
285	Jody Reed	.05
286	Jeff D'Amico	.05
287	Walt Weiss	.05
288	Jim Leyritz	.05
289	Francisco Cordova	.05
290	F.P. Santangelo	.05
291	Scott Erickson	.05
292	Hal Morris	.05
293	Ray Durham	.05
294	Andy Ashby	.05
295	Darryl Kile	.05
296	Jose Paniagua	.05
297	Mickey Tettleton	.05
298	Joe Girardi	.05
299	Rocky Coppinger	.05
300	Bob Abreu	.05
301	John Olerud	.05
302	Paul Shuey	.05
303	Jeff Brantley	.05
304	Bob Wells	.05
305	Kevin Seitzer	.05
306	Shawon Dunston	.05
307	Jose Herrera	.05
308	Butch Huskey	.05
309	Jose Offerman	.05
310	Rick Aguilera	.05
311	Greg Gagne	.05
312	John Burkett	.05
313	Mark Thompson	.05
314	Alvaro Alvarez	.05
315	Todd Stottlemyre	.05
316	Al Martin	.05
317	James Baldwin	.05
318	Cal Eldred	.05
319	Sid Fernandez	.05
320	Mickey Morandini	.05
321	Robb Nen	.05
322	Mark Lemke	.05
323	Pete Schourek	.05
324	Marcus Jensen	.05
325	Rich Aurilia	.05
326	Jeff King	.05
327	Scott Stahoviak	.05
328	Ricky Otero	.05
329	Antonio Osuna	.05
330	Chris Hoiles	.05
331	Luis Gonzalez	.05
332	Wil Cordero	.05
333	Johnny Damon	.35
334	Mark Langston	.05
335	Orlando Miller	.05
336	Jason Giambi	.50
337	Damian Jackson	.05
338	David Wells	.05
339	Bip Roberts	.05
340	Matt Ruebel	.05
341	Tom Candiotti	.05
342	Wally Joyner	.05
343	Jimmy Key	.05
344	Tony Batista	.05
345	Paul Sorrento	.05
346	Ron Karkovice	.05
347	Wilson Alvarez	.05
348	John Flaherty	.05
349	Rey Sanchez	.05
350	John Vander Wal	.05
351a	Jermaine Dye	.05
351b	Brant Brown (Should be #361.)	.05
352	Mike Hampton	.05
353	Greg Colbrunn	.05
354	Heathcliff Slocumb	.05
355	Ricky Bottalico	.05
356	Marty Janzen	.05
357	Orel Hershiser	.05
358	Rex Hudler	.05
359	Amaury Telemaco	.05
360	Darrin Fletcher	.05
361	Not Issued - See #351	
362	Russ Davis	.05
363	Allen Watson	.05
364	Mike Lieberthal	.05
365	Dave Stevens	.05
366	Jay Powell	.05
367	Tony Fossas	.05
368	Bob Wolcott	.05
369	Mark Loretta	.05
370	Shawn Estes	.05
371	Sandy Martinez	.05
372	Wendell Magee Jr.	.05
373	John Franco	.05
374	Not Issued - See #274	
375	Willie Adams	.05
376	Chipper Jones (Stadium Sluggers)	2.00
377	Mo Vaughn (Stadium Sluggers)	.15
378	Frank Thomas (Stadium Sluggers)	1.50
379	Albert Belle (Stadium Sluggers)	.15
380	Andres Galarraga (Stadium Sluggers)	.15
381	Gary Sheffield (Stadium Sluggers)	.85
382	Jeff Bagwell (Stadium Sluggers)	1.50
383	Mike Piazza (Stadium Sluggers)	3.00
384	Mark McGwire (Stadium Sluggers)	3.00
385	Ken Griffey Jr. (Stadium Sluggers)	2.50
386	Barry Bonds (Stadium Sluggers)	3.50
387	Juan Gonzalez (Stadium Sluggers)	.40
388	Brady Anderson (Stadium Sluggers)	.15
389	Ken Caminiti (Stadium Sluggers)	.15
390	Jay Buhner (Stadium Sluggers)	.15

Co-Signers

Each series of Stadium Club included five different Co-Signers, with an insertion ratio of one per 168 hobby packs. These double-sided cards featured authentic autographs from each star, one per side.

		NM/M
Complete Set (10):		200.00
Common Card:		5.00
CO1	Andy Pettitte, Derek Jeter	100.00
CO2	Paul Wilson, Todd Hundley	5.00
CO3	Jermaine Dye, Mark Wohlers	6.00
CO4	Scott Rolen, Gregg Jefferies	15.00
CO5	Todd Hollandsworth, Jason Kendall	8.00
CO6	Alan Benes, Robin Ventura	8.00
CO7	Eric Karros, Raul Mondesi	15.00
CO8	Rey Ordonez, Nomar Garciaparra	45.00
CO9	Rondell White, Marty Cordova	6.00
CO10	Tony Gwynn, Karim Garcia	30.00

Firebrand Redemption

Because of production problems with its "Laser-Etched Wood" technology, Stadium Club was unable to package the Firebrand insert cards with the rest of the issue. Instead, a redemption card was substituted. The redemption card pictures the Firebrand card on its horizontal front; the back has details for exchanging the redemption card for the actual wood-printed, die-cut version. The exchange offer ended Sept. 30, 1997.

		NM/M
Complete Set (12):		15.00
Common Player:		.60
F1	Jeff Bagwell	1.25
F2	Albert Belle	.60
F3	Barry Bonds	4.00
F4	Andres Galarraga	.60
F5	Ken Griffey Jr.	2.50
F6	Brady Anderson	.60
F7	Mark McGwire	3.25
F8	Chipper Jones	2.00
F9	Frank Thomas	1.25
F10	Mike Piazza	2.50
F11	Mo Vaughn	.60
F12	Juan Gonzalez	.85

Firebrand

This 12-card insert was found only in packs sold at retail chains. Cards were inserted 1:36 packs. The horizontal format cards are printed on thin wood stock, die-cut at top. Fronts are trimmed in gold foil. Cards are numbered with a "F" prefix.

		NM/M
Complete Set (12):		25.00
Common Player:		1.00
1	Jeff Bagwell	2.50
2	Albert Belle	1.00
3	Barry Bonds	6.50
4	Andres Galarraga	1.00
5	Ken Griffey Jr.	4.50
6	Brady Anderson	1.00
7	Mark McGwire	5.50
8	Chipper Jones	4.00
9	Frank Thomas	2.50
10	Mike Piazza	4.50
11	Mo Vaughn	1.00
12	Juan Gonzalez	1.50

Instavision

Instavision features holographic cards with exciting moments from the 1996 playoffs and World Series. Inserted one per 24 hobby packs and one per 36 retail packs, these cards are printed horizontally on plastic stock. Cards carry an "I" prefix, with the first 10 found in Series 1 and the final 12 in Series 2.

		NM/M
Complete Set (22):		10.00
Common Player:		.35
I1	Eddie Murray	.75
I2	Paul Molitor	.75
I3	Todd Hundley	.35
I4	Roger Clemens	1.50
I5	Barry Bonds	3.00
I6	Mark McGwire	2.00
I7	Brady Anderson	.35
I8	Barry Larkin	.35
I9	Ken Caminiti	.35
I10	Hideo Nomo	.45
I11	Bernie Williams	.35
I12	Juan Gonzalez	.45
I13	Andy Pettitte	.45
I14	Albert Belle	.35
I15	John Smoltz	.35
I16	Brian Jordan	.35
I17	Derek Jeter	3.00
I18	Ken Caminiti	.35
I19	John Wetteland	.35
I20	Brady Anderson	.35
I21	Andruw Jones	.75
I22	Jim Leyritz	.35

Millennium

Millennium was a 40-card insert that was released with 20 cards in Series I and Series II. The set featured 40 top prospects and rookies on a silver foil, holographic front, with a Future Forecast section on the back. Cards carried an "M" prefix and were numbered consecutively M1-M40. Millennium inserts were found every 24 hobby packs and every 36 retail packs.

		NM/M
Complete Set (40):		12.50
Common Player:		.25
1	Derek Jeter	5.00
2	Mark Grudzielanek	.25
3	Jacob Cruz	.25
4	Ray Durham	.25
5	Tony Clark	.25
6	Chipper Jones	2.50
7	Luis Castillo	.25
8	Carlos Delgado	.50
9	Brant Brown	.25
10	Jason Kendall	.25
11	Alan Benes	.25
12	Rey Ordonez	.25
13	Justin Thompson	.25
14	Jermaine Allensworth	.25
15	Brian Hunter	.25
16	Marty Cordova	.25
17	Edgar Renteria	.25
18	Karim Garcia	.25
19	Todd Greene	.25
20	Paul Wilson	.25
21	Andruw Jones	1.50
22	Todd Walker	.25
23	Alex Ochoa	.25
24	Bartolo Colon	.25
25	Wendell Magee Jr.	.25
26	Jose Rosado	.25
27	Katsuhiro Maeda	.25
28	Bob Abreu	.25
29	Brooks Kieschnick	.25
30	Derrick Gibson	.25
31	Mike Sweeney	.25
32	Jeff D'Amico	.25
33	Chad Mottola	.25
34	Chris Snopek	.25
35	Jaime Bluma	.25
36	Vladimir Guerrero	1.50
37	Nomar Garciaparra	2.50
38	Scott Rolen	1.25
39	Dmitri Young	.25
40	Neifi Perez	.25

Patent Leather

Patent Leather featured 13 of the top gloves in baseball on a leather, die-cut card. The cards carry a "PL" prefix and are inerted one per 36 retail packs.

		NM/M
Complete Set (13):		25.00
Common Player:		1.00
1	Ivan Rodriguez	3.00
2	Ken Caminiti	1.00
3	Barry Bonds	6.00
4	Ken Griffey Jr.	5.00
5	Greg Maddux	4.00
6	Craig Biggio	1.00
7	Andres Galarraga	1.00
8	Kenny Lofton	1.00
9	Barry Larkin	1.00
10	Mark Grace	1.00
11	Rey Ordonez	1.00
12	Roberto Alomar	1.25
13	Derek Jeter	6.00

Pure Gold

Pure Gold featured 20 of the top players in baseball, embossed foil cards. Cards carry a "PG" prefix and were inserted every 72 hobby packs and every 108 retail packs. The first 10 cards were in Series I packs, while the final 10 cards are exclusive to Series II.

		NM/M
Complete Set (20):		60.00
Common Player:		1.25
1	Brady Anderson	1.25
2	Albert Belle	1.25
3	Dante Bichette	1.25
4	Barry Bonds	12.00
5	Jay Buhner	1.25
6	Tony Gwynn	6.00
7	Chipper Jones	6.00
8	Mark McGwire	9.00
9	Gary Sheffield	2.25
10	Frank Thomas	4.50
11	Juan Gonzalez	2.50
12	Ken Caminiti	1.25
13	Kenny Lofton	1.25
14	Jeff Bagwell	4.50
15	Ken Griffey Jr.	7.50
16	Cal Ripken Jr.	12.00
17	Mo Vaughn	1.25
18	Mike Piazza	7.50
19	Derek Jeter	12.00
20	Andres Galarraga	1.25

TSC Matrix

TSC Matrix consists of 120 cards from Series I and II reprinted with Power Matrix technology. In each Series, 60 of the 190 cards were selected for inclusion in TSC Matrix and inserted every 12 hobby packs and every 18 retail packs. Each insert carries the TSC Matrix logo in a top corner of the card.

		NM/M
Complete Set (120):		70.00
Common Player:		.50
1	Chipper Jones	2.50
2	Gary Sheffield	1.00
3	Kenny Lofton	.50
4	Brian Jordan	.50
5	Mark McGwire	4.25
6	Charles Nagy	.50
7	Tim Salmon	.50
8	Cal Ripken Jr.	5.00
9	Jeff Conine	.50
10	Paul Molitor	1.75
11	Mariano Rivera	.65
12	Pedro Martinez	1.75
13	Jeff Bagwell	1.75
14	Bobby Bonilla	.50
15	Barry Bonds	5.00
16	Ryan Klesko	.50
17	Barry Larkin	.50
18	Jim Thome	1.50
19	Jay Buhner	.50
20	Juan Gonzalez	2.50
21	Mike Mussina	.75
22	Kevin Appier	.50
23	Eric Karros	.50
24	Steve Finley	.50
25	Ed Sprague	.50
26	Bernard Gilkey	.50
27	Tony Phillips	.50
28	Henry Rodriguez	.50
29	John Smoltz	.50
30	Dante Bichette	.50
31	Mike Piazza	3.25
32	Paul O'Neill	.50
33	Billy Wagner	.50
34	Reggie Sanders	.50
35	John Jaha	.50
36	Eddie Murray	1.75
37	Eric Young	.50
38	Roberto Hernandez	.50
39	Pat Hentgen	.50
40	Sammy Sosa	2.50
41	Todd Hundley	.50
42	Mo Vaughn	.50
43	Robin Ventura	.50
44	Mark Grudzielanek	.50
45	Shane Reynolds	.50
46	Andy Pettitte	.65
47	Fred McGriff	.50
48	Rey Ordonez	.50
49	Will Clark	.50
50	Ken Griffey Jr.	3.25
51	Todd Worrell	.50
52	Rusty Greer	.50
53	Mark Grace	.75
54	Tom Glavine	.50
55	Derek Jeter	5.00
56	Rafael Palmeiro	1.50
57	Bernie Williams	.50
58	Marty Cordova	.50
59	Andres Galarraga	.50
60	Ken Caminiti	.50
196	Greg Maddux	2.50
197	Joe Carter	.50
198	Alex Ochoa	.50
199	Ellis Burks	.50
200	Ivan Rodriguez	1.50
201	Marquis Grissom	.50
202	Trevor Hoffman	.50
203	Matt Williams	.50
204	Carlos Delgado	1.25
205	Ramon Martinez	.50
206	Chuck Knoblauch	.50
207	Juan Guzman	.50
208	Derek Bell	.50
209	Roger Clemens	3.00
210	Vladimir Guerrero	1.75
211	Cecil Fielder	.50
212	Hideo Nomo	1.00
213	Frank Thomas	1.75
214	Greg Vaughn	.50
215	Javy Lopez	.50
216	Raul Mondesi	.50
217	Wade Boggs	2.50
218	Carlos Baerga	.50
219	Tony Gwynn	2.50
220	Tino Martinez	.50
221	Vinny Castilla	.50
222	Lance Johnson	.50
223	David Justice	.50
224	Rondell White	.50
225	Dean Palmer	.50
226	Jim Edmonds	.50
227	Albert Belle	.50
228	Alex Fernandez	.50
229	Ryne Sandberg	2.50
230	Jose Mesa	.50
231	David Cone	.50
232	Troy Percival	.50
233	Edgar Martinez	.50
234	Jose Canseco	1.25
235	Kevin Brown	.50
236	Ray Lankford	.50
237	Karim Garcia	.50
238	J.T. Snow	.50
239	Dennis Eckersley	1.50
240	Roberto Alomar	.75
241	John Valentin	.50
242	Ron Gant	.50
243	Geronimo Berroa	.50
244	Manny Ramirez	1.75
245	Travis Fryman	.50
246	Denny Neagle	.50
247	Randy Johnson	1.75
248	Darin Erstad	.65
249	Mark Wohlers	.50
250	Ken Hill	.50
251	Larry Walker	.50
252	Craig Biggio	.50
253	Brady Anderson	.50
254	John Wetteland	.50
255	Andruw Jones	1.75

Members Only

Production was reported at just 750 complete sets of these specially marked Stadium Club cards and inserts. Sold only as complete sets through Topps' Stadium Club program, each card differs from the regular-issue TSC version only in the presence of a subdued "MEMBERS ONLY" repeated all across the cards' backs. Star players' cards sell for a significant premium over regular-issue TSC version; inserts, depending on the scarcity of the regular version, usually sell for a significant discount in the Members Only version.

	NM/M
Complete Set:	250.00
Common Player:	.50
Stars:	5X
Inserts: 50-100 Percent	

Members Only Baseball

This boxed set was available only to members of Topps' Stadium Club for a price of $15, which included a year's membership in the club. Fronts feature action photos with a 2-1/2" circle behind the player, a gold-foil Members Only seal and the player's name, also in gold-foil. Backs feature another photo and a career summary on a red background which has the Members Only seal in a repeating pattern. Cards #51-55 are rookie stars and are printed in Topps Finest technologies.

	NM/M
Complete Set (55):	12.00
Common Player:	.10
1 Brady Anderson	.10
2 Carlos Baerga	.10
3 Jeff Bagwell	.75
4 Albert Belle	.10
5 Dante Bichette	.10
6 Craig Biggio	.10
7 Wade Boggs	1.00
8 Barry Bonds	2.50
9 Jay Buhner	.10
10 Ellis Burks	.10
11 Ken Caminiti	.10
12 Jose Canseco	.50
13 Joe Carter	.10
14 Roger Clemens	1.25
15 Jeff Conine	.10
16 Andres Galarraga	.10
17 Ron Gant	.10
18 Juan Gonzalez	.40
19 Mark Grace	.10
20 Ken Griffey Jr.	1.50
21 Tony Gwynn	1.00
22 Pat Hentgen	.10
23 Todd Hollandsworth	.10
24 Todd Hundley	.10
25 Derek Jeter	2.50
26 Randy Johnson	.75
27 Chipper Jones	1.00
28 Ryan Klesko	.10
29 Chuck Knoblauch	.10
30 Barry Larkin	.10
31 Kenny Lofton	.10
32 Greg Maddux	1.00
33 Mark McGwire	2.00
34 Paul Molitor	.75
35 Raul Mondesi	.10
36 Hideo Nomo	.40
37 Rafael Palmeiro	.65
38 Mike Piazza	1.50
39 Manny Ramirez	.75
40 Cal Ripken Jr.	2.50
41 Ivan Rodriguez	.65
42 Tim Salmon	.10
43 Gary Sheffield	.45
44 John Smoltz	.10
45 Sammy Sosa	1.00
46 Frank Thomas	.75
47 Jim Thome	.65
48 Mo Vaughn	.10
49 Bernie Williams	.10
50 Matt Williams	.10
51 Darin Erstad (Finest)	.50
52 Vladimir Guerrero (Finest)	2.50
53 Andruw Jones (Finest)	2.00
54 Scott Rolen (Finest)	1.00
55 Todd Walker (Finest)	1.00

1998 Stadium Club

Stadium Club was issued in two series for 1998, with 200 odd-numbered cards in Series 1 and 200 even-numbered cards in Series 2. Retail packs contain six cards and carried an SRP of $2; hobby packs have nine cards and an SRP of $3 and HTA packs offered 15 cards at an SRP of $5. Three subsets were included: Future Stars (361-379) and Draft Picks (381-399), both being odd-numbered, and Traded (356-400) being even-numbered. Inserts in Series 1 include: First Day Issue parallels (retail), One of a Kind parallels (hobby), Printing Plates parallels (HTA), Bowman Previews, Co-Signers (hobby), In the Wings, Never Comprimise, and Triumvirates (retail). Inserts in Series 2 include: First Day Issue parallels (retail), One of a Kind parallels (hobby), Printing Plates parallels (HTA), Bowman Prospect Previews, Co-Signers (hobby), Playing with Passion, Royal Court and Triumvirates (retail).

	NM/M
Complete Set (400):	30.00
Common Player:	.05
Hobby Pack (10):	1.50
Retail Pack (7):	1.50
Home Team Adv. Pack (16):	4.00
Hobby Box (24):	30.00
1 Chipper Jones	1.00
2 Frank Thomas	.75
3 Vladimir Guerrero	.75
4 Ellis Burks	.05
5 John Franco	.05
6 Paul Molitor	.75
7 Rusty Greer	.05
8 Todd Hundley	.05
9 Brett Tomko	.05
10 Eric Karros	.05
11 Mike Cameron	.05
12 Jim Edmonds	.05
13 Bernie Williams	.05
14 Denny Neagle	.05
15 Jason Dickson	.05
16 Sammy Sosa	1.00
17 Brian Jordan	.05
18 Jose Vidro	.05
19 Scott Spiezio	.05
20 Jay Buhner	.05
21 Jim Thome	.65
22 Sandy Alomar	.05
23 Devon White	.05
24 Roberto Alomar	.20
25 John Flaherty	.05
26 John Wetteland	.05
27 Willie Greene	.05
28 Gregg Jefferies	.05
29 Johnny Damon	.05
30 Barry Larkin	.05
31 Chuck Knoblauch	.05
32 Mo Vaughn	.05
33 Tony Clark	.05
34 Marty Cordova	.05
35 Vinny Castilla	.05
36 Jeff King	.05
37 Reggie Jefferson	.05
38 Mariano Rivera	.15
39 Jermaine Allensworth	.05
40 Livan Hernandez	.05
41 Heathcliff Slocumb	.05
42 Jacob Cruz	.05
43 Barry Bonds	2.50
44 Dave Magadan	.05
45 Chan Ho Park	.05
46 Jeremi Gonzalez	.05
47 Jeff Cirillo	.05
48 Delino DeShields	.05
49 Craig Biggio	.05
50 Benito Santiago	.05
51 Mark Clark	.05
52 Fernando Vina	.05
53 F.P. Santangelo	.05
54 Pep Harris RC	.05
55 Edgar Renteria	.05
56 Jeff Bagwell	.75
57 Jimmy Key	.05
58 Bartolo Colon	.05
59 Curt Schilling	.35
60 Steve Finley	.05
61 Andy Ashby	.05
62 John Burkett	.05
63 Orel Hershiser	.05
64 Pokey Reese	.05
65 Scott Servais	.05
66 Todd Jones	.05
67 Javy Lopez	.05
68 Robin Ventura	.05
69 Miguel Tejada	.15
70 Raul Casanova	.05
71 Reggie Sanders	.05
72 Edgardo Alfonzo	.05
73 Dean Palmer	.05
74 Todd Stottlemyre	.05
75 David Wells	.05
76 Troy Percival	.05
77 Albert Belle	.05
78 Pat Hentgen	.05
79 Brian Hunter	.05
80 Richard Hidalgo	.05
81 Darren Oliver	.05
82 Mark Wohlers	.05
83 Cal Ripken Jr.	2.50
84 Hideo Nomo	.40
85 Derrek Lee	.50
86 Stan Javier	.05
87 Rey Ordonez	.05
88 Randy Johnson	.75
89 Jeff Kent	.05
90 Brian McRae	.05
91 Manny Ramirez	.75
92 Trevor Hoffman	.05
93 Doug Glanville	.05
94 Todd Walker	.05
95 Andy Benes	.05
96 Jason Schmidt	.05
97 Mike Matheny	.05
98 Tim Naehring	.05
99 Jeff Blauser	.05
100 Jose Rosado	.05
101 Roger Clemens	1.25
102 Pedro Astacio	.05
103 Mark Bellhorn	.05
104 Paul O'Neill	.05
105 Darin Erstad	.15
106 Mike Lieberthal	.05
107 Wilson Alvarez	.05
108 Mike Mussina	.30
109 George Williams	.05
110 Cliff Floyd	.05
111 Shawn Estes	.05
112 Mark Grudzielanek	.05
113 Tony Gwynn	1.00
114 Alan Benes	.05
115 Terry Steinbach	.05
116 Greg Maddux	1.00
117 Andy Pettitte	.25
118 Dave Nilsson	.05
119 Deivi Cruz	.05
120 Carlos Delgado	.50
121 Scott Hatteberg	.05
122 John Olerud	.05
123 Moises Alou	.05
124 Garret Anderson	.05
125 Royce Clayton	.05
126 Dante Powell	.05
127 Tom Glavine	.35
128 Gary DiSarcina	.05
129 Terry Adams	.05
130 Raul Mondesi	.05
131 Dan Wilson	.05
132 Al Martin	.05
133 Mickey Morandini	.05
134 Rafael Palmeiro	.65
135 Juan Encarnacion	.05
136 Jim Pittsley	.05
137 Magglio Ordonez RC	1.00
138 Will Clark	.05
139 Todd Helton	.65
140 Kelvim Escobar	.05
141 Esteban Loaiza	.05
142 John Jaha	.05
143 Jeff Fassero	.05
144 Harold Baines	.05
145 Butch Huskey	.05
146 Pat Meares	.05
147 Brian Giles	.05
148 Ramiro Mendoza	.05
149 John Smoltz	.05
150 Felix Martinez	.05
151 Jose Valentin	.05
152 Brad Rigby	.05
153 Ed Sprague	.05
154 Mike Hampton	.05
155 Mike Lansing	.05
156 Ray Lankford	.05
157 Bobby Bonilla	.05
158 Bill Mueller	.05
159 Jeffrey Hammonds	.05
160 Charles Nagy	.05
161 Rich Loiselle	.05
162 Al Leiter	.05
163 Larry Walker	.05
164 Chris Hoiles	.05
165 Jeff Montgomery	.05
166 Francisco Cordova	.05
167 James Baldwin	.05
168 Mark McLemore	.05
169 Kevin Appier	.05
170 Jamey Wright	.05
171 Nomar Garciaparra	1.00
172 Matt Franco	.05
173 Armando Benitez	.05
174 Jeromy Burnitz	.05
175 Ismael Valdes	.05
176 Lance Johnson	.05
177 Paul Sorrento	.05
178 Rondell White	.05
179 Kevin Elster	.05
180 Jason Giambi	.50
181 Carlos Baerga	.05
182 Russ Davis	.05
183 Ryan McGuire	.05
184 Eric Young	.05
185 Ron Gant	.05
186 Manny Alexander	.05
187 Scott Karl	.05
188 Brady Anderson	.05
189 Randall Simon	.05
190 Tim Belcher	.05
191 Jaret Wright	.05
192 Dante Bichette	.05
193 John Valentin	.05
194 Darren Bragg	.05
195 Mike Sweeney	.05
196 Craig Counsell	.05
197 Jaime Navarro	.05
198 Todd Dunn	.05
199 Ken Griffey Jr.	1.50
200 Juan Gonzalez	.40
201 Billy Wagner	.05
202 Tino Martinez	.05
203 Mark McGwire	2.00
204 Jeff D'Amico	.05
205 Rico Brogna	.05
206 Todd Hollandsworth	.05
207 Chad Curtis	.05
208 Tom Goodwin	.05
209 Neifi Perez	.05
210 Derek Bell	.05
211 Quilvio Veras	.05
212 Greg Vaughn	.05
213 Roberto Hernandez	.05
214 Arthur Rhodes	.05
215 Cal Eldred	.05
216 Bill Taylor	.05
217 Todd Greene	.05
218 Mario Valdez	.05
219 Ricky Bottalico	.05
220 Frank Rodriguez	.05
221 Rich Becker	.05
222 Roberto Duran	.05
223 Ivan Rodriguez	.65
224 Mike Jackson	.05
225 Deion Sanders	.05
226 Tony Womack	.05
227 Mark Kotsay	.05
228 Steve Trachsel	.05
229 Ryan Klesko	.05
230 Ken Cloude	.05
231 Luis Gonzalez	.05
232 Gary Gaetti	.05
233 Michael Tucker	.05
234 Shawn Green	.35
235 Ariel Prieto	.05
236 Kirt Manwaring	.05
237 Omar Vizquel	.05
238 Matt Beech	.05
239 Justin Thompson	.05
240 Bret Boone	.05
241 Derek Jeter	2.50
242 Ken Caminiti	.05
243 Jay Bell	.05
244 Kevin Tapani	.05
245 Jason Kendall	.05
246 Jose Guillen	.05
247 Mike Bordick	.05
248 Dustin Hermanson	.05
249 Darrin Fletcher	.05
250 Dave Hollins	.05
251 Ramon Martinez	.05
252 Hideki Irabu	.05
253 Mark Grace	.05
254 Jason Isringhausen	.05
255 Jose Cruz Jr.	.05
256 Brian Johnson	.05
257 Brad Ausmus	.05
258 Andruw Jones	.75
259 Doug Jones	.05
260 Jeff Shaw	.05
261 Chuck Finley	.05
262 Gary Sheffield	.45
263 David Segui	.05
264 John Smiley	.05
265 Tim Salmon	.05
266 J.T. Snow Jr.	.05
267 Alex Fernandez	.05
268 Matt Stairs	.05
269 B.J. Surhoff	.05
270 Keith Foulke	.05
271 Edgar Martinez	.05
272 Shannon Stewart	.05
273 Eduardo Perez	.05
274 Wally Joyner	.05
275 Kevin Young	.05
276 Eli Marrero	.05
277 Brad Radke	.05
278 Jamie Moyer	.05
279 Joe Girardi	.05
280 Troy O'Leary	.05
281 Aaron Sele	.05
282 Jose Offerman	.05
283 Scott Erickson	.05
284 Sean Berry	.05
285 Shigetosi Hasegawa	.05
286 Felix Heredia	.05
287 Willie McGee	.05
288 Alex Rodriguez	2.00
289 Ugueth Urbina	.05
290 Jon Lieber	.05
291 Fernando Tatis	.05
292 Chris Stynes	.05
293 Bernard Gilkey	.05
294 Joey Hamilton	.05
295 Matt Karchner	.05
296 Paul Wilson	.05
297 Mel Nieves	.05
298 Kevin Millwood RC	.75
299 Quinton McCracken	.05
300 Jerry DiPoto	.05
301 Jermaine Dye	.05
302 Travis Lee	.05
303 Ron Coomer	.05
304 Matt Williams	.05
305 Bobby Higginson	.05
306 Jorge Fabregas	.05
307 Hal Morris	.05
308 Jay Bell	.05
309 Joe Randa	.05
310 Andy Benes	.05
311 Sterling Hitchcock	.05
312 Jeff Suppan	.05
313 Shane Reynolds	.05
314 Willie Blair	.05
315 Scott Rolen	.65
316 Wilson Alvarez	.05
317 David Justice	.05
318 Fred McGriff	.05
319 Bobby Jones	.05
320 Wade Boggs	1.00
321 Tim Wakefield	.05
322 Tony Saunders	.05
323 David Cone	.05
324 Roberto Hernandez	.05
325 Jose Canseco	.45
326 Kevin Stocker	.05
327 Gerald Williams	.05
328 Quinton McCracken	.05
329 Mark Gardner	.05
330 Ben Grieve (Prime Rookie)	.05
331 Kevin Brown	.05
332 Mike Lowell RC (Prime Rookie)	1.00
333 Jed Hansen	.05
334 Abraham Nunez (Prime Rookie)	.05
335 John Thomson	.05
336 Derrek Lee (Prime Rookie)	.05
337 Mike Piazza	1.50
338 Brad Fullmer (Prime Rookie)	.05
339 Ray Durham	.05
340 Kerry Wood (Prime Rookie)	.50
341 Mike Polcovich RC	.05
342 Russ Johnson (Prime Rookie)	.05
343 Darryl Hamilton	.05
344 David Ortiz (Prime Rookie)	.45
345 Kevin Orie	.05
346 Sean Casey (Prime Rookie)	.25
347 Juan Guzman	.05
348 Ruben Rivera (Prime Rookie)	.05
349 Rick Aguilera	.05
350 Bobby Estalella (Prime Rookie)	.05
351 Bobby Witt	.05
352 Paul Konerko (Prime Rookie)	.25
353 Matt Morris	.05
354 Carl Pavano (Prime Rookie)	.05
355 Todd Zeile	.05
356 Kevin Brown (Transaction)	.05
357 Alex Gonzalez	.05
358 Chuck Knoblauch (Transaction)	.05
359 Joey Cora	.05
360 Mike Lansing (Transaction)	.05
361 Adrian Beltre (Future Stars)	.45
362 Dennis Eckersley (Transaction)	.65
363 A.J. Hinch (Future Stars)	.05
364 Kenny Lofton (Transaction)	.05
365 Alex Gonzalez (Future Stars)	.05
366 Henry Rodriguez (Transaction)	.05
367 Mike Stoner RC (Future Stars)	.05
368 Darryl Kile (Transaction)	.05
369 Carl Pavano (Future Stars)	.05
370 Walt Weiss (Transaction)	.05
371 Kris Benson (Future Stars)	.05
372 Cecil Fielder (Transaction)	.05
373 Dermal Brown (Future Stars)	.05
374 Rod Beck (Transaction)	.05
375 Eric Milton (Future Stars)	.05
376 Travis Fryman (Transaction)	.05
377 Preston Wilson (Future Stars)	.10
378 Chili Davis (Transaction)	.05
379 Travis Lee (Future Stars)	.10
380 Jim Leyritz (Transaction)	.05
381 Vernon Wells (Draft Picks)	.05
382 Joe Carter (Transaction)	.05
383 J.J. Davis (Draft Picks)	.05
384 Marquis Grissom (Transaction)	.05
385 Mike Cuddyer RC (Draft Picks)	.50
386 Rickey Henderson (Transaction)	.75
387 Chris Enochs RC (Draft Picks)	.10
388 Andres Galarraga (Transaction)	.05
389 Jason Dellaero (Draft Picks)	.05
390 Robb Nen (Transaction)	.05
391 Mark Mangum (Draft Picks)	.05
392 Jeff Blauser (Transaction)	.05
393 Adam Kennedy (Draft Picks)	.05
394 Bob Abreu (Transaction)	.05
395 Jack Cust RC (Draft Picks)	1.00
396 Jose Vizcaino (Transaction)	.05
397 Jon Garland (Draft Picks)	.05
398 Pedro Martinez (Transaction)	.75
399 Aaron Akin (Draft Picks)	.05
400 Jeff Conine (Transaction)	.05

First Day Issue

	NM/M
Common Player:	2.00
Stars:	10X
Production 200 Sets	

One of a Kind

This hobby-only parallel set includes all 400 cards from Series 1 and 2 printed on a silver mirror-board stock. Cards are sequentially numbered to 150 and inserted one per 21 Series 1 packs and one per 24 Series 2 packs.

	NM/M
Common Player:	2.00
Stars:	12X
Production 150 Sets	

Bowman Preview

This Series I insert gave collectors a sneak peak at Bowman's 50th anniversary set, with 10 top veterans displayed on the 1998 Bowman design. The cards were inserted one per 12 packs and numbered with a "BP" prefix.

	NM/M
Complete Set (10):	10.00
Common Player:	.25
Inserted 1:12	
BP1 Nomar Garciaparra	1.00
BP2 Scott Rolen	.65
BP3 Ken Griffey Jr.	1.50
BP4 Frank Thomas	.75
BP5 Larry Walker	.25
BP6 Mike Piazza	1.50
BP7 Chipper Jones	1.00

BP8 Tino Martinez .25
BP9 Mark McGwire 2.00
BP10 Barry Bonds 2.50

Bowman Prospect Preview

Bowman Prospect Previews were inserted into Series 2 retail and hobby packs at a rate of one per 12 and HTA packs at one per four. The 10-card insert previews the upcoming 1998 Bowman set and includes top prospects that were expected to make an impact in 1998.

	NM/M
Complete Set (10):	3.00
Common Player:	.25
Inserted 1:12	
BP1 Ben Grieve	.25
BP2 Brad Fullmer	.25
BP3 Ryan Anderson	.25
BP4 Mark Kotsay	.25
BP5 Bobby Estalella	.25
BP6 Juan Encarnacion	.25
BP7 Todd Helton	2.00
BP8 Mike Lowell	.50
BP9 A.J. Hinch	.25
BP10 Richard Hidalgo	.25

Co-Signers

Co-Signers were inserted into both Series 1 and 2 hobby and HTA packs. The complete set is 36 cards, each featuring two top players along with both autographs. They were available in three levels of scarcity: Series 1 Group A 1:4,372 hobby and 1:2,623 HTA; Series 1 Group B 1:1,457 hobby and HTA 1:874; Series 1 Group C 1:121 hobby and 1:73 HTA; Series 2 Group A 1:4,702 hobby and 1:2,821 HTA; Series 2 Group B 1:1,567 hobby and 1:940 HTA, Series 2 Group C 1:1,131 hobby and 1:78 HTA. Some cards are known to bear fake autographs, despite having the Topps seal of authenticity. Those cards are believed to have been released in unsigned form in an unauthorized manner, and then signed with counterfeit signatures.

	NM/M
Common Card:	10.00
Group A 1:4,372	
Group B 1:1,457	
Group C 1:121	
CS1 Nomar Garciaparra, Scott Rolen (A)	120.00
CS2 Nomar Garciaparra, Derek Jeter (B)	250.00
CS3 Nomar Garciaparra, Eric Karros (C)	60.00
CS4 Scott Rolen, Derek Jeter (C)	100.00
CS5 Scott Rolen, Eric Karros (B)	40.00
CS6 Derek Jeter, Eric Karros (A)	150.00
CS7 Travis Lee, Jose Cruz Jr. (B)	15.00
CS8 Travis Lee, Mark Kotsay (C)	10.00
CS9 Travis Lee, Paul Konerko (A)	25.00
CS10 Jose Cruz Jr., Mark Kotsay (A)	25.00
CS11 Jose Cruz Jr., Paul Konerko (C)	12.00
CS12 Mark Kotsay, Paul Konerko (B)	20.00
CS13 Tony Gwynn, Larry Walker (A)	120.00
CS14 Tony Gwynn, Mark Grudzielanek (A)	30.00
CS15 Tony Gwynn, Andres Galarraga (B)	60.00
CS16 Larry Walker, Mark Grudzielanek (B)	40.00
CS17 Larry Walker, Andres Galarraga (C)	30.00
CS18 Mark Grudzielanek, Andres Galarraga (A)	25.00
CS19 Sandy Alomar, Roberto Alomar (A)	75.00
CS20 Sandy Alomar, Andy Pettitte (C)	20.00
CS21 Sandy Alomar, Tino Martinez (B)	40.00
CS22 Roberto Alomar, Andy Pettitte (B)	50.00
CS23 Roberto Alomar, Tino Martinez (C)	25.00
CS24 Andy Pettitte, Tino Martinez (A)	75.00
CS25 Tony Clark, Todd Hundley (A)	25.00
CS26 Tony Clark, Tim Salmon (B)	30.00
CS27 Tony Clark, Robin Ventura (C)	10.00
CS28 Todd Hundley, Tim Salmon (C)	15.00
CS29 Todd Hundley, Robin Ventura (B)	12.00
CS30 Tim Salmon, Robin Ventura (A)	50.00
CS31 Roger Clemens, Randy Johnson (B)	175.00
CS32 Roger Clemens, Jaret Wright (A)	140.00
CS33 Roger Clemens, Matt Morris (C)	100.00
CS34 Randy Johnson, Jaret Wright (C)	50.00
CS35 Randy Johnson, Matt Morris (A)	85.00
CS36 Jaret Wright, Matt Morris (B)	20.00

In the Wings

ELI MARRERO

In the Wings was a Series I insert found every 36 packs. It included 15 future stars on uniluster technology.

	NM/M
Complete Set (15):	6.00
Common Player:	.50
Inserted 1:36	
W1 Juan Encarnacion	.50
W2 Brad Fullmer	.50
W3 Ben Grieve	.50
W4 Todd Helton	3.00
W5 Richard Hidalgo	.50
W6 Russ Johnson	.50
W7 Paul Konerko	.75
W8 Mark Kotsay	.50
W9 Derrek Lee	1.00
W10 Travis Lee	.50
W11 Eli Marrero	.50
W12 David Ortiz	.75
W13 Randall Simon	.50
W14 Shannon Stewart	.50
W15 Fernando Tatis	.50

Never Compromise

Never Compromise was a 20-card insert found in packs of Series I. Cards were inserted one per 12 packs and numbered with a "NC" prefix.

	NM/M
Complete Set (20):	10.00
Common Player:	.15
Inserted 1:12	
NC1 Cal Ripken Jr.	2.00
NC2 Ivan Rodriguez	.50
NC3 Ken Griffey Jr.	1.00
NC4 Frank Thomas	.60
NC5 Tony Gwynn	.75
NC6 Mike Piazza	1.00
NC7 Randy Johnson	.60
NC8 Greg Maddux	.75
NC9 Roger Clemens	.85
NC10 Derek Jeter	2.00
NC11 Chipper Jones	.75
NC12 Barry Bonds	2.00
NC13 Larry Walker	.15
NC14 Jeff Bagwell	.60
NC15 Barry Larkin	.15
NC16 Ken Caminiti	.15
NC17 Mark McGwire	1.50
NC18 Manny Ramirez	.60
NC19 Tim Salmon	.15
NC20 Paul Molitor	.60

Playing with Passion

This Series II insert displayed 10 players with a strong desire to win. The cards are numbered with a "P" prefix.

	NM/M
Complete Set (10):	10.00
Common Player:	.35
Inserted 1:12	
P1 Bernie Williams	.35
P2 Jim Edmonds	.35
P3 Chipper Jones	1.00
P4 Cal Ripken Jr.	3.00
P5 Craig Biggio	.35
P6 Juan Gonzalez	.45
P7 Alex Rodriguez	2.25
P8 Tino Martinez	.35
P9 Mike Piazza	1.50
P10 Ken Griffey Jr.	1.50

Printing Plates

Inserted only in Home Team Advantage boxes at a rate of approximately one per 90 packs were the actual aluminum plates used to print the fronts of the base cards. Unlike some printing plate issues, the plates used for the card backs were not inserted. Each card's plate can be found in four different colors: Cyan, magenta, yellow and black. Because of their unique nature, pricing of individual player's plates cannot be provided.

	NM/M
Common Player:	25.00

Royal Court

Frank Thomas

Fifteen players were showcased on uniluster technology for this Series II insert. The set is broken up into 10 Kings (veterans) and five Princes (rookies) and inserted one per 36 packs.

	NM/M
Complete Set (15):	15.00
Common Player:	.50
Inserted 1:36	
RC1 Ken Griffey Jr.	2.00
RC2 Frank Thomas	1.25
RC3 Mike Piazza	2.00
RC4 Chipper Jones	1.50
RC5 Mark McGwire	2.50
RC6 Cal Ripken Jr.	3.00
RC7 Jeff Bagwell	1.25
RC8 Barry Bonds	3.00
RC9 Juan Gonzalez	.85
RC10 Alex Rodriguez	2.50
RC11 Travis Lee	.50
RC12 Paul Konerko	.75
RC13 Todd Helton	1.00
RC14 Ben Grieve	.50
RC15 Mark Kotsay	.50

Screen Plays Sound Chips

One of the packs in each Home Team Advantage box of TSC "Odd Series" cards contained this special "card" commemorating the home run hit by Cal Ripken, Jr. in his historic 2,131st game on Sept. 6, 1995. The item is 3-1/2" x 2-1/2" x 3/8" deep. Glued to the top is a magic motion card showing Ripken hitting the blast. When a corner of the card is squeezed, a sound chip replays the radio call of the home run by Jon Miller and President Bill Clinton. The top of the package opens to reveal a newspaper-like presentation with a picture of Ripken, details of his home run and the technology used to produce the item.

	NM/M
SC1 Cal Ripken Jr.	5.00

Triumvirate

Triumvirates were included in both series of Stadium Club and were available only in retail packs. Series 1 has 24 players, with three players from eight different teams, while Series 2 has 30 players, with three players from 10 different positions. The cards are all die-cut and fit together to form three-card panels. Three different versions of each card were available - Luminous (regular) versions were seeded one per 48 packs, Luminescent versions were seeded one per 192 packs and Illuminator versions were seeded one per 384 packs.

	NM/M
Complete Set (54):	70.00
Complete Series 1 (24):	30.00
Complete Series 2 (30):	40.00
Common Player:	.50
Luminous 1:48	
Luminescents 1:192:	1.5X
Illuminators 1:384:	2.5X
T1a Chipper Jones	2.50
T1b Andruw Jones	2.00
T1c Kenny Lofton	.50
T2a Derek Jeter	5.00
T2b Bernie Williams	.50
T2c Tino Martinez	.50
T3a Jay Buhner	.50
T3b Edgar Martinez	.50
T3c Ken Griffey Jr.	3.00
T4a Albert Belle	.50
T4b Robin Ventura	.50
T4c Frank Thomas	2.00
T5a Brady Anderson	.50
T5b Cal Ripken Jr.	5.00
T5c Rafael Palmeiro	1.50
T6a Mike Piazza	3.00
T6b Raul Mondesi	.50
T6c Eric Karros	.50
T7a Vinny Castilla	.50
T7b Andres Galarraga	.50
T7c Larry Walker	.50
T8a Jim Thome	1.50
T8b Manny Ramirez	2.00
T8c David Justice	.50
T9a Mike Mussina	.75
T9b Greg Maddux	2.50
T9c Randy Johnson	2.00
T10a Mike Piazza	3.00
T10b Sandy Alomar	.50
T10c Ivan Rodriguez	1.50
T11a Mark McGwire	4.00
T11b Tino Martinez	.50
T11c Frank Thomas	2.00
T12a Roberto Alomar	.75
T12b Chuck Knoblauch	.50
T12c Craig Biggio	.50
T13a Cal Ripken Jr.	5.00
T13b Chipper Jones	2.50
T13c Ken Caminiti	.50
T14a Derek Jeter	5.00
T14b Nomar Garciaparra	2.50
T14c Alex Rodriguez	4.00
T15a Barry Bonds	5.00
T15b David Justice	.50
T15c Albert Belle	.50
T16a Bernie Williams	.50
T16b Ken Griffey Jr.	3.00
T16c Ray Lankford	.50
T17a Tim Salmon	.50
T17b Larry Walker	.50
T17c Tony Gwynn	2.50
T18a Paul Molitor	2.00
T18b Edgar Martinez	.50
T18c Juan Gonzalez	1.00

1999 Stadium Club

Released in two series, base cards feature a full bleed design on 20-pt. stock with an embossed holographic logo. Draft Pick, Prospect and Series 2 Future Star subset cards are short-printed, seeded in every three packs. Card backs have 1998 statistics and personal information. Hobby packs consist of six cards with an S.R.P. of $2.

	NM/M
Complete Set (355):	40.00
Complete Series 1 (170):	20.00
Complete Series 2 (185):	20.00
Common Player:	.05
Common SP (141-160; 336-355):	.50
Inserted 1:3	
Pack (6):	1.25
Wax Box (24):	25.00
1 Alex Rodriguez	2.00
2 Chipper Jones	1.50
3 Rusty Greer	.05
4 Jim Edmonds	.05
5 Ron Gant	.05
6 Kevin Polcovich	.05
7 Darryl Strawberry	.05
8 Bill Mueller	.05
9 Vinny Castilla	.05
10 Wade Boggs	1.50
11 Jose Lima	.05
12 Darren Dreifort	.05
13 Jay Bell	.05
14 Ben Grieve	.05
15 Shawn Green	.35
16 Andres Galarraga	.05
17 Bartolo Colon	.05
18 Francisco Cordova	.05
19 Paul O'Neill	.05
20 Trevor Hoffman	.05
21 Darren Oliver	.05
22 John Franco	.05
23 Eli Marrero	.05
24 Roberto Hernandez	.05
25 Craig Biggio	.05
26 Brad Fullmer	.05
27 Scott Erickson	.05
28 Tom Gordon	.05
29 Brian Hunter	.05
30 Raul Mondesi	.05
31 Rick Reed	.05
32 Jose Canseco	.50
33 Robb Nen	.05
34 Turner Ward	.05
35 Bret Boone	.05
36 Jose Offerman	.05
37 Matt Lawton	.05
38 David Wells	.05
39 Bob Abreu	.10
40 Jeromy Burnitz	.05
41 Deivi Cruz	.05
42 Mike Cameron	.05
43 Rico Brogna	.05
44 Dmitri Young	.05
45 Chuck Knoblauch	.05
46 Johnny Damon	.35
47 Brian Meadows	.05
48 Jeremi Gonzalez	.05
49 Gary DiSarcina	.05
50 Frank Thomas	1.00
51 F.P. Santangelo	.05
52 Tom Candiotti	.05
53 Shane Reynolds	.05
54 Rod Beck	.05
55 Rey Ordonez	.05
56 Todd Helton	.75
57 Mickey Morandini	.05
58 Jorge Posada	.05
59 Mike Mussina	.30
60 Bobby Bonilla	.05
61 David Segui	.05
62 Brian McRae	.05
63 Fred McGriff	.05
64 Brett Tomko	.05
65 Derek Jeter	2.50
66 Sammy Sosa	1.50
67 Kenny Rogers	.05
68 Dave Nilsson	.05
69 Eric Young	.05
70 Mark McGwire	2.00
71 Kenny Lofton	.05
72 Tom Glavine	.35
73 Joey Hamilton	.05
74 John Valentin	.05
75 Mariano Rivera	.15
76 Ray Durham	.05
77 Tony Clark	.05
78 Livan Hernandez	.05
79 Rickey Henderson	1.00
80 Vladimir Guerrero	1.00
81 J.T. Snow Jr.	.05
82 Juan Guzman	.05
83 Darryl Hamilton	.05
84 Matt Anderson	.05
85 Travis Lee	.05
86 Joe Randa	.05
87 Dave Dellucci	.05
88 Moises Alou	.05
89 Alex Gonzalez	.05
90 Tony Womack	.05
91 Neifi Perez	.05
92 Travis Fryman	.05
93 Masato Yoshii	.05
94 Woody Williams	.05
95 Ray Lankford	.05
96 Roger Clemens	1.50
97 Dustin Hermanson	.05
98 Joe Carter	.05
99 Jason Schmidt	.05
100 Greg Maddux	1.50
101 Kevin Tapani	.05
102 Charles Johnson	.05
103 Derrek Lee	.50
104 Pete Harnisch	.05
105 Dante Bichette	.05
106 Scott Brosius	.05
107 Mike Caruso	.05
108 Eddie Taubensee	.05
109 Jeff Fassero	.05
110 Marquis Grissom	.05
111 Jose Hernandez	.05
112 Chan Ho Park	.05
113 Wally Joyner	.05
114 Bobby Estalella	.05
115 Pedro Martinez	1.00
116 Shawn Estes	.05
117 Walt Weiss	.05
118 John Mabry	.05
119 Brian Johnson	.05
120 Jim Thome	.65
121 Bill Spiers	.05
122 John Olerud	.05
123 Jeff King	.05
124 Tim Belcher	.05
125 John Wetteland	.05
126 Tony Gwynn	1.50
127 Brady Anderson	.05
128 Randy Winn	.05
129 Devon White	.05
130 Eric Karros	.05
131 Kevin Millwood	.05
132 Andy Benes	.05
133 Andy Ashby	.05
134 Ron Coomer	.05
135 Juan Gonzalez	.50
136 Randy Johnson	1.00
137 Aaron Sele	.05
138 Edgardo Alfonzo	.05
139 B.J. Surhoff	.05
140 Jose Vizcaino	.05
141 Chad Moeller RC (Prospect)	.75
142 Mike Zwicka RC (Prospect)	.50
143 Angel Pena (Prospect)	.50
144 Nick Johnson RC (Prospect)	2.00
145 Giuseppe Chiaramonte RC (Prospect)	.50
146 Kit Pellow RC (Prospect)	.50
147 Clayton Andrews RC (Prospect)	.50
148 Jerry Hairston Jr. RC (Prospect)	.75
149 Jason Tyner RC (Draft Pick)	.50

#	Player	Price
150	Chip Ambres RC (Draft Pick)	.50
151	Pat Burrell RC (Draft Pick)	2.00
152	Josh McKinley RC (Draft Pick)	.75
153	Choo Freeman RC (Draft Pick)	.75
154	Rick Elder RC (Draft Pick)	.50
155	Eric Valent RC (Draft Pick)	.75
156	Jeff Winchester RC (Draft Pick)	.50
157	Mike Nannini RC (Draft Pick)	.50
158	Mamon Tucker RC (Draft Pick)	.50
159	Nate Bump RC (Draft Pick)	.50
160	Andy Brown RC (Draft Pick)	.50
161	Troy Glaus (Future Star)	1.00
162	Adrian Beltre (Future Star)	.45
163	Mitch Meluskey (Future Star)	.05
164	Alex Gonzalez (Future Star)	.05
165	George Lombard (Future Star)	.05
166	Eric Chavez (Future Star)	.25
167	Ruben Mateo (Future Star)	.05
168	Calvin Pickering (Future Star)	.05
169	Gabe Kapler (Future Star)	.05
170	Bruce Chen (Future Star)	.05
171	Darin Erstad	.15
172	Sandy Alomar	.05
173	Miguel Cairo	.05
174	Jason Kendall	.05
175	Cal Ripken Jr.	2.50
176	Darryl Kile	.05
177	David Cone	.05
178	Mike Sweeney	.05
179	Royce Clayton	.05
180	Curt Schilling	.25
181	Barry Larkin	.05
182	Eric Milton	.05
183	Ellis Burks	.05
184	A.J. Hinch	.05
185	Garret Anderson	.05
186	Sean Bergman	.05
187	Shannon Stewart	.05
188	Bernard Gilkey	.05
189	Jeff Blauser	.05
190	Andruw Jones	1.00
191	Omar Daal	.05
192	Jeff Kent	.05
193	Mark Kotsay	.05
194	Dave Burba	.05
195	Bobby Higginson	.05
196	Hideki Irabu	.05
197	Jamie Moyer	.05
198	Doug Glanville	.05
199	Quinton McCracken	.05
200	Ken Griffey Jr.	1.75
201	Mike Lieberthal	.05
202	Carl Everett	.05
203	Omar Vizquel	.05
204	Mike Lansing	.05
205	Manny Ramirez	1.00
206	Ryan Klesko	.05
207	Jeff Montgomery	.05
208	Chad Curtis	.05
209	Rick Helling	.05
210	Justin Thompson	.05
211	Tom Goodwin	.05
212	Todd Dunwoody	.05
213	Kevin Young	.05
214	Tony Saunders	.05
215	Gary Sheffield	.45
216	Jaret Wright	.05
217	Quilvio Veras	.05
218	Marty Cordova	.05
219	Tino Martinez	.05
220	Scott Rolen	.75
221	Fernando Tatis	.05
222	Damion Easley	.05
223	Aramis Ramirez	.05
224	Brad Radke	.05
225	Nomar Garciaparra	1.50
226	Magglio Ordonez	.05
227	Andy Pettitte	.20
228	David Ortiz	.45
229	Todd Jones	.05
230	Larry Walker	.05
231	Tim Wakefield	.05
232	Jose Guillen	.05
233	Gregg Olson	.05
234	Ricky Gutierrez	.05
235	Todd Walker	.05
236	Abraham Nunez	.05
237	Sean Casey	.15
238	Greg Norton	.05
239	Bret Saberhagen	.05
240	Bernie Williams	.05
241	Tim Salmon	.05
242	Jason Giambi	.50
243	Fernando Vina	.05
244	Darrin Fletcher	.05
245	Greg Vaughn	.05
246	Dennis Reyes	.05
247	Hideo Nomo	.50
248	Reggie Sanders	.05
249	Mike Hampton	.05
250	Kerry Wood	.50
251	Ismael Valdes	.05
252	Pat Hentgen	.05
253	Scott Spiezio	.05
254	Chuck Finley	.05
255	Troy Glaus	.75
256	Bobby Jones	.05
257	Wayne Gomes	.05
258	Rondell White	.05
259	Todd Zeile	.05
260	Matt Williams	.05
261	Henry Rodriguez	.05
262	Matt Stairs	.05
263	Jose Valentin	.05
264	David Justice	.05
265	Javy Lopez	.05
266	Matt Morris	.05
267	Steve Trachsel	.05
268	Edgar Martinez	.05
269	Al Martin	.05
270	Ivan Rodriguez	.75
271	Carlos Delgado	.05
272	Mark Grace	.05
273	Ugueth Urbina	.05
274	Jay Buhner	.05
275	Mike Piazza	1.75
276	Rick Aguilera	.05
277	Javier Valentin	.05
278	Brian Anderson	.05
279	Cliff Floyd	.05
280	Barry Bonds	2.50
281	Troy O'Leary	.05
282	Seth Greisinger	.05
283	Mark Grudzielanek	.05
284	Jose Cruz Jr.	.05
285	Jeff Bagwell	1.00
286	John Smoltz	.05
287	Jeff Cirillo	.05
288	Richie Sexson	.05
289	Charles Nagy	.05
290	Pedro Martinez	1.00
291	Juan Encarnacion	.05
292	Phil Nevin	.05
293	Terry Steinbach	.05
294	Miguel Tejada	.15
295	Dan Wilson	.05
296	Chris Peters	.05
297	Brian Moehler	.05
298	Jason Christiansen	.05
299	Kelly Stinnett	.05
300	Dwight Gooden	.05
301	Randy Velarde	.05
302	Kirt Manwaring	.05
303	Jeff Abbott	.05
304	Dave Hollins	.05
305	Kerry Ligtenberg	.05
306	Aaron Boone	.05
307	Carlos Hernandez	.05
308	Mike DiFelice	.05
309	Brian Meadows	.05
310	Tim Bogar	.05
311	Greg Vaughn (Transaction)	.05
312	Brant Brown (Transaction)	.05
313	Steve Finley (Transaction)	.05
314	Bret Boone (Transaction)	.05
315	Albert Belle (Transaction)	.05
316	Robin Ventura (Transaction)	.05
317	Eric Davis (Transaction)	.05
318	Todd Hundley (Transaction)	.05
319	Jose Offerman (Transaction)	.05
320	Kevin Brown (Transaction)	.05
321	Denny Neagle (Transaction)	.05
322	Brian Jordan (Transaction)	.05
323	Brian Giles (Transaction)	.05
324	Bobby Bonilla (Transaction)	.05
325	Roberto Alomar (Transaction)	.20
326	Ken Caminiti (Transaction)	.05
327	Todd Stottlemyre (Transaction)	.05
328	Randy Johnson (Transaction)	1.00
329	Luis Gonzalez (Transaction)	.05
330	Rafael Palmeiro (Transaction)	.75
331	Devon White (Transaction)	.05
332	Will Clark (Transaction)	.05
333	Dean Palmer (Transaction)	.05
334	Gregg Jefferies (Transaction)	.05
335	Mo Vaughn (Transaction)	.05
336	Brad Lidge RC (Draft Pick)	2.00
337	Chris George RC (Draft Pick)	.75
338	Austin Kearns RC (Draft Pick)	1.50
339	Matt Belisle RC (Draft Pick)	.75
340	Nate Cornejo RC (Draft Pick)	.75
341	Matt Holliday RC (Draft Pick)	5.00
342	J.M. Gold RC (Draft Pick)	.50
343	Matt Roney RC (Draft Pick)	.75
344	Seth Etherton RC (Draft Pick)	.75
345	Adam Everett RC (Draft Pick)	.75
346	Marlon Anderson (Future Star)	.50
347	Ron Belliard (Future Star)	.50
348	Fernando Seguignol (Future Star)	.50
349	Michael Barrett (Future Star)	.50
350	Dernell Stenson (Future Star)	.50
351	Ryan Anderson (Future Star)	.50
352	Ramon Hernandez (Future Star)	.50
353	Jeremy Giambi (Future Star)	.50
354	Ricky Ledee (Future Star)	.50
355	Carlos Lee (Future Star)	1.00

First Day Issue

A parallel of the 355-card set inserted exclusively in retail packs, Series I (1-170) are serially numbered to 170 at a rate of 1:75 packs. Series 2 (171-355) are serially numbered to 200 and inserted at a rate of 1:60 packs.

	NM/M
Common Player:	2.00
Stars:	8X
SP Stars:	4X

One of a Kind

This insert set parallels the 355-card base set. Cards feature a mirrorboard look and are serially numbered to 150. Inserted exclusively in hobby packs, insertion rate for Series 1 is 1:53 and Series 2 is 1:48 packs.

	NM/M
Common Player:	2.00
Stars:	8X
SP Stars:	4X

Autographs

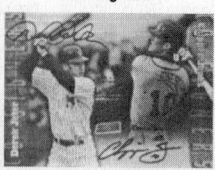

This 10-card autographed set was issued in Series 1 and 2 with five players signing in each series. Available exclusively in retail chains, Series 1 autographs were seeded 1:1,107 packs, while series 2 were inserted in every 877 packs. Each autograph is marked with the Topps Certified Autograph Issue stamp. Card numbers have an "SCA" prefix.

	NM/M
Common Player:	10.00
Inserted 1:1,107	
1 Alex Rodriguez	75.00
2 Chipper Jones	30.00
3 Barry Bonds	150.00
4 Tino Martinez	25.00
5 Ben Grieve	10.00
6 Juan Gonzalez	15.00
7 Vladimir Guerrero	30.00
8 Albert Belle	15.00
9 Kerry Wood	25.00
10 Todd Helton	20.00

Chrome

This 40-card set was inserted in Series 1 and 2 packs, with 1-20 in first series packs and 21-40 in Series 2. Chrome appropriately utilizes chromium technology. Card numbers have an "SCC" prefix.

	NM/M
Complete Set (40):	45.00
Common Player:	.50
Inserted 1:24	
Refractors:	2X
Inserted 1:96	
1 Nomar Garciaparra	2.00
2 Kerry Wood	1.00
3 Jeff Bagwell	1.50
4 Ivan Rodriguez	1.25
5 Albert Belle	.50
6 Gary Sheffield	1.00
7 Andruw Jones	1.50
8 Kevin Brown	.50
9 David Cone	.50
10 Darin Erstad	.75
11 Manny Ramirez	1.50
12 Larry Walker	.50
13 Mike Piazza	2.50
14 Cal Ripken Jr.	4.00
15 Pedro Martinez	1.50
16 Greg Vaughn	.50
17 Barry Bonds	4.00
18 Mo Vaughn	.50
19 Bernie Williams	.50
20 Ken Griffey Jr.	2.50
21 Alex Rodriguez	3.00
22 Chipper Jones	2.00
23 Ben Grieve	.50
24 Frank Thomas	1.50
25 Derek Jeter	4.00
26 Sammy Sosa	2.00
27 Mark McGwire	3.00
28 Vladimir Guerrero	1.50
29 Greg Maddux	2.00
30 Juan Gonzalez	.75
31 Troy Glaus	1.25
32 Adrian Beltre	1.25
33 Mitch Meluskey	.50
34 Alex Gonzalez	.50
35 George Lombard	.50
36 Eric Chavez	.75
37 Ruben Mateo	.50
38 Calvin Pickering	.50
39 Gabe Kapler	.50
40 Bruce Chen	.50

Co-Signers

Co-Signers feature two autographs on each card and also for the first time includes one level of four autographs per card. Co-Signers are grouped into categories A, B, C and D. Group A Co-Signers are autographed by four players, while B-D are signed by two players. Each card features the Topps Certified Autograph Issue stamp.

	NM/M
Common Group A:	90.00
Inserted 1:18,085	
Common Group B:	20.00
Inserted 1:9043	
Common Group C:	9.00
Inserted 1:3014	
Common Group D:	6.00
Inserted 1:254	
CS1 Ben Grieve, Richie Sexson (D)	15.00
CS2 Todd Helton, Troy Glaus (D)	50.00
CS3 Alex Rodriguez, Scott Rolen (D)	85.00
CS4 Derek Jeter, Chipper Jones (D)	150.00
CS5 Cliff Floyd, Eli Marrero (D)	6.00
CS6 Jay Buhner, Kevin Young (D)	8.00
CS7 Ben Grieve, Troy Glaus (C)	40.00
CS8 Todd Helton, Richie Sexson (C)	40.00
CS9 Alex Rodriguez, Chipper Jones (C)	125.00
CS10 Derek Jeter, Scott Rolen (C)	125.00
CS11 Cliff Floyd, Kevin Young (C)	10.00
CS12 Jay Buhner, Eli Marrero (B)	10.00
CS13 Ben Grieve, Todd Helton (B)	50.00
CS14 Richie Sexson, Troy Glaus (B)	40.00
CS15 Alex Rodriguez, Derek Jeter (B)	350.00
CS16 Chipper Jones, Scott Rolen (B)	150.00
CS17 Cliff Floyd, Jay Buhner (B)	15.00
CS18 Eli Marrero, Kevin Young (B)	20.00
CS19 Ben Grieve, Todd Helton, Richie Sexson, Troy Glaus (A)	180.00
CS20 Alex Rodriguez, Derek Jeter, Chipper Jones, Scott Rolen (A)	2,500
CS21 Cliff Floyd, Jay Buhner, Eli Marrero, Kevin Young (A)	100.00
CS22 Edgardo Alfonzo, Jose Guillen (D)	15.00
CS23 Mike Lowell, Ricardo Rincon (D)	10.00
CS24 Juan Gonzalez, Vinny Castilla (D)	20.00
CS25 Moises Alou, Roger Clemens (D)	60.00
CS26 Scott Spezio, Tony Womack (D)	10.00
CS27 Fernando Vina, Quilvio Veras (D)	10.00
CS28 Edgardo Alfonzo, Ricardo Rincon (C)	10.00
CS29 Jose Guillen, Mike Lowell (C)	10.00
CS30 Juan Gonzalez, Moises Alou (C)	25.00
CS31 Roger Clemens, Vinny Castilla (C)	85.00
CS32 Scott Spezio, Fernando Vina (C)	10.00
CS33 Tony Womack, Quilvio Veras (B)	20.00
CS34 Edgardo Alfonzo, Mike Lowell (B)	30.00
CS35 Jose Guillen, Ricardo Rincon (B)	30.00
CS36 Juan Gonzalez, Roger Clemens (B)	135.00
CS37 Moises Alou, Vinny Castilla (B)	30.00
CS38 Scott Spezio, Quilvio Veras (B)	20.00
CS39 Tony Womack, Fernando Vina (B)	20.00
CS40 Edgardo Alfonzo, Jose Guillen, Mike Lowell, Ricardo Rincon (A)	90.00
CS41 Juan Gonzalez, Moises Alou, Roger Clemens, Vinny Castilla (A)	900.00
CS42 Scott Spezio, Tony Womack, Fernando Vina, Quilvio Veras (A)	90.00

Never Compromise

Topps selected players who bring hard work and devotion to the field every game. The first 10 cards in the set are inserted in Series 1 packs while the remaining 10 are seeded in Series 2 at a rate of 1:12 packs.

	NM/M
Complete Set (20):	10.00
Common Player:	.25
Inserted 1:12	
NC1 Mark McGwire	1.00
NC2 Sammy Sosa	.65
NC3 Ken Griffey Jr.	.75
NC4 Greg Maddux	.65
NC5 Barry Bonds	1.50
NC6 Alex Rodriguez	1.00
NC7 Darin Erstad	.35
NC8 Roger Clemens	.65
NC9 Nomar Garciaparra	.65
NC10 Derek Jeter	1.50
NC11 Cal Ripken Jr.	1.50
NC12 Mike Piazza	.75
NC13 Greg Vaughn	.25
NC14 Andres Galarraga	.25
NC15 Vinny Castilla	.25
NC16 Jeff Bagwell	.50
NC17 Chipper Jones	.75
NC18 Eric Chavez	.35
NC19 Orlando Hernandez	.25
NC20 Troy Glaus	.40

Printing Plates

Inserted only in Home Team Advantage boxes at a rate of approximately one per 175 packs were the actual aluminum plates used to print the fronts of the base cards. Unlike some printing plate issues, the plates used for the card backs were not inserted. Each card's plate can be found in four different colors: Cyan, magenta, yellow and black. Because of their unique nature, pricing of individual player's plates cannot be provided.

	NM/M
Common Player:	25.00

Triumvirate

Three of these inserts "fuse" together to form a set of three cards, forming a Triumvirate. 48 players, 24 from each series, are available in three different technologies, Luminous, Luminescent and Illuminator.

	NM/M
Complete Set (48):	75.00
Common Player:	.50
Inserted 1:36	
Luminescents:	1.5X
Inserted 1:144	
Illuminators:	2.5X
Inserted 1:288	
T1A Greg Vaughn	.50
T1B Ken Caminiti	.50
T1C Tony Gwynn	2.50
T2A Andruw Jones	2.00
T2B Chipper Jones	2.50
T2C Andres Galarraga	.50
T3A Jay Buhner	.50
T3B Ken Griffey Jr.	3.00
T3C Alex Rodriguez	4.00
T4A Derek Jeter	6.00
T4B Tino Martinez	.50
T4C Bernie Williams	.50
T5A Brian Jordan	.50
T5B Ray Lankford	.50
T5C Mark McGwire	4.00
T6A Jeff Bagwell	2.00
T6B Craig Biggio	.50
T6C Randy Johnson	2.00

T7A	Nomar Garciaparra	2.50
T7B	Pedro Martinez	2.00
T7C	Mo Vaughn	.50
T8A	Mark Grace	.50
T8B	Sammy Sosa	2.50
T8C	Kerry Wood	1.00
T9A	Alex Rodriguez	4.00
T9B	Nomar Garciaparra	2.50
T9C	Derek Jeter	6.00
T10A	Todd Helton	1.50
T10B	Travis Lee	.50
T10C	Pat Burrell	1.50
T11A	Greg Maddux	2.50
T11B	Kerry Wood	1.00
T11C	Tom Glavine	.75
T12A	Chipper Jones	2.50
T12B	Vinny Castilla	.50
T12C	Scott Rolen	1.50
T13A	Juan Gonzalez	1.00
T13B	Ken Griffey Jr.	3.00
T13C	Ben Grieve	.50
T14A	Sammy Sosa	3.00
T14B	Vladimir Guerrero	2.00
T14C	Barry Bonds	6.00
T15A	Frank Thomas	2.00
T15B	Jim Thome	1.50
T15C	Tino Martinez	.50
T16A	Mark McGwire	4.00
T16B	Andres Galarraga	.50
T16C	Jeff Bagwell	2.00

Video Replay

Utilizing lenticular technology, these inserts capture highlights, such as McGwire's 70th home run, from the '98 season. By tilting the card, successive images show the selected highlight almost come to life. Video Replays are in inserted in Series 2 packs at a rate of 1:12.

NM/M
Complete Set (5): 4.50
Common Player: .75
Inserted 1:12

VR1	Mark McGwire	1.50
VR2	Sammy Sosa	1.00
VR3	Ken Griffey Jr.	1.25
VR4	Kerry Wood	.75
VR5	Alex Rodriguez	1.50

Photography

The photos used on some Stadium Club Series 1 cards was available as a special issue in the format of a framed 11" x 14" color photo. The borderless action photos could be ordered from a form found in TSC packs. With a $4 shipping charge, the initial cost per picture was $23.99. The numbers here are as given on the order form.

NM/M
Complete Set (10): 200.00
Common Player: 20.00

1	Alex Rodriguez	20.00
65	Derek Jeter	20.00
66	Sammy Sosa	20.00
135	Juan Gonzalez	20.00
NC1	Mark McGwire	20.00
NC3	Ken Griffey Jr.	20.00
SCA5	Ben Grieve	20.00
SCC1	Nomar Garciaparra	20.00
SCC2	Kerry Wood	20.00
SCC13	Mike Piazza	20.00

2000 Stadium Club

Released in one series, the base set consists of 250 cards, embossed and printed on 20-pt. stock with silver holo-foil stamping. Card backs have a small photo, with the player's vital information and 1999 season statistical breakdown. The 20-card Draft Pick subset (#231-250) are short-printed, seeded 1:5 packs.

NM/M
Complete Set (250): 80.00
Common Player: .15
Common SP (201-250): 2.00
Inserted 1:5
Pack (6): 1.50
Wax Box (24): 30.00

1	Nomar Garciaparra	1.25
2	Brian Jordan	.15
3	Mark Grace	.25
4	Jeromy Burnitz	.15
5	Shane Reynolds	.15
6	Alex Gonzalez	.15
7	Jose Offerman	.15
8	Orlando Hernandez	.15
9	Mike Caruso	.15
10	Tony Clark	.15
11	Sean Casey	.25
12	Johnny Damon	.25
13	Dante Bichette	.15
14	Kevin Young	.15
15	Juan Gonzalez	.75
16	Chipper Jones	1.00
17	Quilvio Veras	.15
18	Trevor Hoffman	.15
19	Roger Cedeno	.15
20	Ellis Burks	.15
21	Richie Sexson	.15
22	Gary Sheffield	.40
23	Delino DeShields	.15
24	Wade Boggs	1.00
25	Ray Lankford	.15
26	Kevin Appier	.15
27	Roy Halladay	.15
28	Harold Baines	.15
29	Todd Zeile	.15
30	Barry Larkin	.15
31	Ron Coomer	.15
32	Jorge Posada	.15
33	Magglio Ordonez	.15
34	Brian Giles	.15
35	Jeff Kent	.15
36	Henry Rodriguez	.15
37	Fred McGriff	.15
38	Shawn Green	.50
39	Derek Bell	.15
40	Ben Grieve	.15
41	Dave Nilsson	.15
42	Mo Vaughn	.15
43	Rondell White	.15
44	Doug Glanville	.15
45	Paul O'Neill	.15
46	Carlos Lee	.15
47	Vinny Castilla	.15
48	Mike Sweeney	.15
49	Rico Brogna	.15
50	Alex Rodriguez	1.50
51	Luis Castillo	.15
52	Kevin Brown	.15
53	Jose Vidro	.15
54	John Smoltz	.15
55	Garret Anderson	.15
56	Matt Stairs	.15
57	Omar Vizquel	.15
58	Tom Goodwin	.15
59	Scott Brosius	.15
60	Robin Ventura	.15
61	B.J. Surhoff	.15
62	Andy Ashby	.15
63	Chris Widger	.15
64	Tim Hudson	.40
65	Javy Lopez	.15
66	Tim Salmon	.25
67	Warren Morris	.15
68	John Wetteland	.15
69	Gabe Kapler	.15
70	Bernie Williams	.30
71	Rickey Henderson	.75
72	Andruw Jones	.75
73	Eric Young	.15
74	Bob Abreu	.15
75	David Cone	.15
76	Rusty Greer	.15
77	Ron Belliard	.15
78	Troy Glaus	.15
79	Mike Hampton	.15
80	Miguel Tejada	.30
81	Jeff Cirillo	.15
82	Todd Hundley	.15
83	Roberto Alomar	.40
84	Charles Johnson	.15
85	Rafael Palmeiro	.65
86	Doug Mientkiewicz	.15
87	Mariano Rivera	.25
88	Neifi Perez	.15
89	Jermaine Dye	.15
90	Ivan Rodriguez	.65
91	Jay Buhner	.15
92	Pokey Reese	.15
93	John Olerud	.15
94	Brady Anderson	.15
95	Manny Ramirez	.75
96	Keith Osik	.15
97	Mickey Morandini	.15
98	Matt Williams	.15
99	Eric Karros	.15
100	Ken Griffey Jr.	1.25
101	Bret Boone	.15
102	Ryan Klesko	.15
103	Craig Biggio	.15
104	John Jaha	.15
105	Vladimir Guerrero	.75
106	Devon White	.15
107	Tony Womack	.15
108	Marvin Benard	.15
109	Kenny Lofton	.15
110	Preston Wilson	.15
111	Al Leiter	.15
112	Reggie Sanders	.15
113	Scott Williamson	.15
114	Deivi Cruz	.15
115	Carlos Beltran	.50
116	Ray Durham	.15
117	Ricky Ledee	.15
118	Torii Hunter	.15
119	John Valentin	.15
120	Scott Rolen	.65
121	Jason Kendall	.15
122	Dave Martinez	.15
123	Jim Thome	.65
124	David Bell	.15
125	Jose Canseco	.45
126	Jose Lima	.15
127	Carl Everett	.15
128	Kevin Millwood	.15
129	Bill Spiers	.15
130	Omar Daal	.15
131	Miguel Cairo	.15
132	Mark Grudzielanek	.15
133	David Justice	.15
134	Russ Ortiz	.15
135	Mike Piazza	1.25
136	Brian Meadows	.15
137	Tony Gwynn	1.00
138	Cal Ripken Jr.	2.00
139	Kris Benson	.15
140	Larry Walker	.15
141	Cristian Guzman	.15
142	Tino Martinez	.25
143	Chris Singleton	.15
144	Lee Stevens	.15
145	Rey Ordonez	.15
146	Russ Davis	.15
147	J.T. Snow Jr.	.15
148	Luis Gonzalez	.25
149	Marquis Grissom	.15
150	Greg Maddux	1.00
151	Fernando Tatis	.15
152	Jason Giambi	.50
153	Carlos Delgado	.50
154	Joe McEwing	.15
155	Raul Mondesi	.15
156	Rich Aurilia	.15
157	Alex Fernandez	.15
158	Albert Belle	.25
159	Pat Meares	.15
160	Mike Lieberthal	.15
161	Mike Cameron	.15
162	Juan Encarnacion	.15
163	Chuck Knoblauch	.15
164	Pedro Martinez	.75
165	Randy Johnson	.75
166	Shannon Stewart	.15
167	Jeff Bagwell	.75
168	Edgar Renteria	.15
169	Barry Bonds	2.00
170	Steve Finley	.15
171	Brian Hunter	.15
172	Tom Glavine	.35
173	Mark Kotsay	.15
174	Tony Fernandez	.15
175	Sammy Sosa	1.25
176	Geoff Jenkins	.15
177	Adrian Beltre	.15
178	Jay Bell	.15
179	Mike Bordick	.15
180	Ed Sprague	.15
181	Dave Roberts	.15
182	Greg Vaughn	.15
183	Brian Daubach	.15
184	Damion Easley	.15
185	Carlos Febles	.15
186	Kevin Tapani	.15
187	Frank Thomas	.75
188	Roger Clemens	1.00
189	Mike Benjamin	.15
190	Curt Schilling	.40
191	Edgardo Alfonzo	.15
192	Mike Mussina	.40
193	Todd Helton	.75
194	Todd Jones	.15
195	Dean Palmer	.15
196	John Flaherty	.15
197	Derek Jeter	2.00
198	Todd Walker	.15
199	Brad Ausmus	.15
200	Mark McGwire	1.50
201	Erubiel Durazo (Future Stars)	2.00
202	Nick Johnson (Future Stars)	2.50
203	Ruben Mateo (Future Stars)	2.00
204	Lance Berkman (Future Stars)	2.50
205	Pat Burrell (Future Stars)	3.00
206	Pablo Ozuna (Future Stars)	2.00
207	Roosevelt Brown (Future Stars)	2.00
208	Alfonso Soriano (Future Stars)	4.00
209	A.J. Burnett (Future Stars)	2.00
210	Rafael Furcal (Future Stars)	2.00
211	Scott Morgan (Future Stars)	2.00
212	Adam Piatt (Future Stars)	2.00
213	Dee Brown (Future Stars)	2.00
214	Corey Patterson (Future Stars)	2.50
215	Mickey Lopez (Future Stars)	2.00
216	Rob Ryan (Future Stars)	2.00
217	Sean Burroughs (Future Stars)	2.00
218	Jack Cust (Future Stars)	2.00
219	John Patterson (Future Stars)	2.00
220	Kit Pellow (Future Stars)	2.00
221	Chad Hermansen (Future Stars)	2.00
222	Daryle Ward (Future Stars)	2.00
223	Jayson Werth (Future Stars)	2.00
224	Jason Standridge (Future Stars)	2.00
225	Mark Mulder (Future Stars)	2.50
226	Peter Bergeron (Future Stars)	2.00
227	Willi Mo Pena (Future Stars)	2.00
228	Aramis Ramirez (Future Stars)	2.00
229	John Sneed RC (Future Stars)	2.00
230	Wilton Veras (Future Stars)	2.00
231	Josh Hamilton (Draft Picks)	2.00
232	Eric Munson (Draft Picks)	2.00
233	Bobby Bradley RC (Draft Picks)	2.00
234	Larry Bigbie RC (Draft Picks)	2.00
235	B.J. Garbe RC (Draft Picks)	2.00
236	Brett Myers RC (Draft Picks)	6.00
237	Jason Stumm RC (Draft Picks)	2.00
238	Corey Myers RC (Draft Picks)	2.00
239	Ryan Christianson RC (Draft Picks)	2.00
240	David Walling (Draft Picks)	2.00
241	Josh Girdley (Draft Picks)	2.00
242	Omar Ortiz (Draft Picks)	2.00
243	Jason Jennings (Draft Picks)	2.00
244	Kyle Snyder RC (Draft Picks)	2.00
245	Jay Gehrke (Draft Picks)	2.00
246	Mike Paradis RC (Draft Picks)	2.00
247	Chance Caple RC (Draft Picks)	2.00
248	Ben Christiansen RC (Draft Picks)	2.00
249	Brad Baker RC (Draft Picks)	2.00
250	Rick Asadoorian RC (Draft Picks)	2.00
---	Checklist (Nomar Garciaparra)	.25

First Day Issue

Identifiable by the "First Day Issue" stamp, this retail exclusive parallel set is limited to 150 sequentially numbered sets.

Stars: 5-10X
Short-Prints: 2-3X
Production 150 Sets R

One of a Kind

This 250-card set is a parallel to the base set, is hobby exclusive and limited to 150 serially numbered sets.

Stars: 5-10X
Short-prints: 2-3X
Production 150 Sets H

Bats of Brilliance

This insert set focused on 10 of baseball's top hitters. Card fronts have a silver foil border over a black backdrop. Backs highlight the player's statistics from 1999 and his career statistics. They are numbered with a "BB" prefix and are seeded 1:12 packs. A die-cut parallel is also randomly seeded 1:60 packs.

NM/M
Complete Set (10): 10.00
Common Player: .50
Inserted 1:12

1	Mark McGwire	2.50
2	Sammy Sosa	1.50
3	Jose Canseco	.50
4	Jeff Bagwell	.75
5	Ken Griffey Jr.	1.50
6	Nomar Garciaparra	1.50
7	Mike Piazza	1.50
8	Alex Rodriguez	2.50
9	Vladimir Guerrero	.75
10	Chipper Jones	1.50

Capture The Action

This 20-card set is divided into categories of Rookies, Stars, and Legends. These were seeded 1:12 packs and have the insert title, player name and logo stamped in silver foil. They are numbered with a "CA" prefix on the backs. A hobby-exclusive parallel version was also available, serially numbered to 100 and featuring a replica of the actual photo slide used to create the card.

NM/M
Complete Set (20): 20.00
Common Player: .50
Inserted 1:12
Game View Stars: 3-6X
Production 100 Sets H

1	Josh Hamilton	.50
2	Pat Burrell	.75
3	Erubiel Durazo	.50
4	Alfonso Soriano	1.00
5	A.J. Burnett	.50
6	Alex Rodriguez	3.00
7	Sean Casey	.50
8	Derek Jeter	4.00
9	Vladimir Guerrero	.75
10	Nomar Garciaparra	2.00
11	Mike Piazza	2.00
12	Ken Griffey Jr.	2.00
13	Sammy Sosa	2.00
14	Juan Gonzalez	1.00
15	Mark McGwire	3.00
16	Ivan Rodriguez	.75
17	Barry Bonds	4.00
18	Wade Boggs	1.50
19	Tony Gwynn	1.50
20	Cal Ripken Jr.	4.00

Co-Signers

This 15-card hobby exclusive set features two signatures on the card front, with the Topps "Certified Autograph Issue" stamp as well as the Topps 3M sticker to ensure its authenticity. The cards are divided into three groupings with the following odds: Group A - 1:10,184; Group B - 1:5,092; and Group C - 1:508.

NM/M
Common Card: 15.00
Group A 1:10,184
Group B 1:5,092
Group C 1:508

1	Alex Rodriguez, Derek Jeter	400.00
2	Derek Jeter, Omar Vizquel	150.00
3	Alex Rodriguez, Rey Ordonez	100.00
4	Derek Jeter, Rey Ordonez	150.00
5	Omar Vizquel, Alex Rodriguez	100.00
6	Alex Rodriguez, Rey Ordonez, Omar Vizquel	15.00
7	Wade Boggs, Robin Ventura	30.00
8	Randy Johnson, Mike Mussina	90.00
9	Pat Burrell, Magglio Ordonez	40.00
10	Chad Hermansen, Pat Burrell	20.00
11	Magglio Ordonez, Chad Hermansen	20.00
12	Josh Hamilton, Corey Myers	25.00
13	B.J. Garbe, Josh Hamilton	25.00
14	Corey Myers, B.J. Garbe	15.00
15	Tino Martinez, Fred McGriff	60.00

Lone Star Signatures

This 16-card autographed set features the Topps "Certified Autograph Issue" stamp to verify its authenticity. The cards are divided into four groupings with the following odds: Group 1, 1:1,979 hobby; Group 2, 1:2,374 hobby; Group 3, 1:1,979; and Group 4, 1:424 hobby.

NM/M
Common Player: 8.00
Group 1 1:1,979
Group 2 1:2,374
Group 3 1:1,979
Group 4 1:424

1	Derek Jeter	100.00
2	Alex Rodriguez	100.00
3	Wade Boggs	25.00
4	Robin Ventura	15.00
5	Randy Johnson	60.00
6	Mike Mussina	25.00
7	Tino Martinez	35.00
8	Fred McGriff	25.00
9	Omar Vizquel	15.00
10	Rey Ordonez	8.00
11	Pat Burrell	15.00
12	Chad Hermansen	8.00
13	Magglio Ordonez	10.00
14	Josh Hamilton	35.00
15	Corey Myers	8.00
16	B.J. Garbe	8.00

Onyx Extreme

This 10-card set features black styrene technology with silver foil stamping and are seeded 1:12 packs. A die-cut parallel is also randomly inserted 1:60 hobby packs.

NM/M
Complete Set (10): 10.00
Common Player: .40
Inserted 1:12
Die-Cuts: 2-3X
Inserted 1:60

1	Ken Griffey Jr.	1.50

2	Derek Jeter	3.00
3	Vladimir Guerrero	1.00
4	Nomar Garciaparra	1.50
5	Barry Bonds	3.00
6	Alex Rodriguez	2.50
7	Sammy Sosa	1.50
8	Ivan Rodriguez	.75
9	Larry Walker	.40
10	Andruw Jones	1.00

Printing Plates

Inserted only in Home Team boxes at a rate of approximately one per 100 packs were the actual aluminum plates used to print the fronts of the base cards. Unlike some printing plate issues, the plates used for the card backs were not inserted. Each card's plate can be found in four different colors: Cyan, magenta, yellow and black. Because of their unique nature, pricing of individual player's plates cannot be provided.

	NM/M
Common Player:	60.00

Scenes

Available only in hobby and Home Team Advantage boxes, these broaden the view of the featured player and have a format sized 2-1/2" x 4-11/16". These are boxtoppers, seeded one per box.

		NM/M
Complete Set (9):		10.00
Common Player:		.50
Inserted 1:Box		
1	Mark McGwire	2.50
2	Alex Rodriguez	2.50
3	Cal Ripken Jr.	3.00
4	Sammy Sosa	2.00
5	Derek Jeter	3.00
6	Ken Griffey Jr.	2.00
7	Raul Mondesi	.50
8	Chipper Jones	2.00
9	Nomar Garciaparra	2.00

Souvenirs

These memorabilia inserts feature die-cut technology that incorporates an actual piece of a game-used uniform. Each card back contains the Topps 3M sticker to ensure its authenticity. The insert rate is 2:339 hobby packs and 2:136 HTA packs.

		NM/M
Complete Set (3):		35.00
Common Player:		8.00
Inserted 2:339		
1	Wade Boggs	20.00
2	Randy Johnson	20.00
3	Robin Ventura	8.00

3 X 3

Ten groups of three top-notch players are arranged by position on three different laser-cut technologies. The three players can be "fused" together to form one oversize card. The three versions are Luminous (1:18), Luminescent (1:72) and Illuminator (1:144).

		NM/M
Complete Set (30):		40.00
Common Player:		.75
Inserted 1:18		
Luminescent		2X
Inserted 1:72		
Illuminator		3-4X
Inserted 1:144		

1A	Randy Johnson	1.50
1B	Pedro Martinez	1.50
1C	Greg Maddux	2.00
2A	Mike Piazza	3.00
2B	Ivan Rodriguez	1.25
2C	Mike Lieberthal	1.50
3A	Mark McGwire	4.50
3B	Jeff Bagwell	1.50
3C	Sean Casey	.75
4A	Craig Biggio	.75
4B	Roberto Alomar	1.00
4C	Jay Bell	.75
5A	Chipper Jones	2.00
5B	Matt Williams	.75
5C	Robin Ventura	.75
6A	Alex Rodriguez	4.50
6B	Derek Jeter	6.00
6C	Nomar Garciaparra	3.00
7A	Barry Bonds	6.00
7B	Luis Gonzalez	1.00
7C	Dante Bichette	.75
8A	Ken Griffey Jr.	3.00
8B	Bernie Williams	1.00
8C	Andruw Jones	1.50
9A	Manny Ramirez	1.50
9B	Sammy Sosa	3.00
9C	Juan Gonzalez	1.50
10A	Jose Canseco	1.50
10B	Frank Thomas	1.50
10C	Rafael Palmeiro	1.00

2000 Stadium Club Chrome Preview

This 20-card set features Topps Chromium technology, previewing the debut of Stadium Club Chrome, a later release. The insertion odds are 1:24 packs. A Refractor parallel version is also available seeded 1:120 packs.

		NM/M
Complete Set (20):		40.00
Common Player:		1.00
Inserted 1:24		
Refractors:		2-3X
Inserted 1:120		
1	Nomar Garciaparra	3.00
2	Juan Gonzalez	1.50
3	Chipper Jones	2.00
4	Alex Rodriguez	4.50
5	Ivan Rodriguez	1.25
6	Manny Ramirez	1.50
7	Ken Griffey Jr.	3.00
8	Vladimir Guerrero	1.50
9	Mike Piazza	3.00
10	Pedro Martinez	2.00
11	Jeff Bagwell	1.50
12	Barry Bonds	6.00
13	Sammy Sosa	3.00
14	Derek Jeter	6.00
15	Mark McGwire	4.50
16	Erubiel Durazo	1.00
17	Nick Johnson	1.00
18	Pat Burrell	1.00
19	Alfonso Soriano	1.50
20	Adam Piatt	1.00

2000 Stadium Club Chrome

The 250-card base set uses the same photography and is identical to 2000 Stadium Club besides the utilization of Chromium technology. Five-card packs had a $4 SRP.

	NM/M
Complete Set (250):	40.00

96	Keith Osik	.15
97	Mickey Morandini	.15
98	Matt Williams	.15
99	Eric Karros	.15
100	Ken Griffey Jr.	1.50
101	Bret Boone	.15
102	Ryan Klesko	.15
103	Craig Biggio	.15
104	John Jaha	.15
105	Vladimir Guerrero	.75
106	Devon White	.15
107	Tony Womack	.15
108	Marvin Benard	.15
109	Kenny Lofton	.15
110	Preston Wilson	.15
111	Al Leiter	.15
112	Reggie Sanders	.15
113	Scott Williamson	.15
114	Deivi Cruz	.15
115	Carlos Beltran	.50
116	Ray Durham	.15
117	Ricky Ledee	.15
118	Torii Hunter	.15
119	John Valentin	.15
120	Scott Rolen	.65
121	Jason Kendall	.15
122	Dave Martinez	.15
123	Jim Thome	.65
124	David Bell	.15
125	Jose Canseco	.50
126	Jose Lima	.15
127	Carl Everett	.15
128	Kevin Millwood	.15
129	Bill Spiers	.15
130	Omar Daal	.15
131	Miguel Cairo	.15
132	Mark Grudzielanek	.15
133	David Justice	.15
134	Russ Ortiz	.15
135	Mike Piazza	1.50
136	Brian Meadows	.15
137	Tony Gwynn	1.00
138	Cal Ripken Jr.	3.00
139	Kris Benson	.15
140	Larry Walker	.15
141	Cristian Guzman	.15
142	Tino Martinez	.15
143	Chris Singleton	.15
144	Lee Stevens	.15
145	Rey Ordonez	.15
146	Russ Davis	.15
147	J.T. Snow Jr.	.15
148	Luis Gonzalez	.25
149	Marquis Grissom	.15
150	Greg Maddux	1.00
151	Fernando Tatis	.15
152	Jason Giambi	.50
153	Carlos Delgado	.50
154	Joe McEwing	.15
155	Raul Mondesi	.15
156	Rich Aurilia	.15
157	Alex Fernandez	.15
158	Albert Belle	.25
159	Pat Meares	.15
160	Mike Lieberthal	.15
161	Mike Cameron	.15
162	Juan Encarnacion	.15
163	Chuck Knoblauch	.15
164	Pedro Martinez	.75
165	Randy Johnson	.75
166	Shannon Stewart	.15
167	Jeff Bagwell	.75
168	Edgar Renteria	.15
169	Barry Bonds	3.00
170	Steve Finley	.15
171	Brian Hunter	.15
172	Tom Glavine	.40
173	Mark Kotsay	.15
174	Tony Fernandez	.15
175	Sammy Sosa	1.50
176	Geoff Jenkins	.15
177	Adrian Beltre	.45
178	Jay Bell	.15
179	Mike Bordick	.15
180	Ed Sprague	.15
181	Dave Roberts	.15
182	Greg Vaughn	.15
183	Brian Daubach	.15
184	Damion Easley	.15
185	Carlos Febles	.15
186	Kevin Tapani	.15
187	Frank Thomas	.75
188	Roger Clemens	1.25
189	Mike Benjamin	.15
190	Curt Schilling	.40
191	Edgardo Alfonzo	.15
192	Mike Mussina	.45
193	Todd Helton	.75
194	Todd Jones	.15
195	Dean Palmer	.15
196	John Flaherty	.15
197	Derek Jeter	3.00
198	Todd Walker	.15
199	Brad Ausmus	.15
200	Mark McGwire	2.50
201	Erubiel Durazo (Future Stars)	.15
202	Nick Johnson (Future Stars)	.15
203	Ruben Mateo (Future Stars)	.15
204	Lance Berkman (Future Stars)	.15
205	Pat Burrell (Future Stars)	.65
206	Pablo Ozuna (Future Stars)	.15
207	Roosevelt Brown (Future Stars)	.15

Common Player:		.15
Pack (11):		1.50
Wax Box (36):		40.00
1	Nomar Garciaparra	1.50
2	Brian Jordan	.15
3	Mark Grace	.25
4	Jeromy Burnitz	.15
5	Shane Reynolds	.15
6	Alex Gonzalez	.15
7	Jose Offerman	.15
8	Orlando Hernandez	.15
9	Mike Caruso	.15
10	Tony Clark	.15
11	Sean Casey	.25
12	Johnny Damon	.25
13	Dante Bichette	.15
14	Kevin Young	.15
15	Juan Gonzalez	.75
16	Chipper Jones	1.00
17	Quilvio Veras	.15
18	Trevor Hoffman	.15
19	Roger Cedeno	.15
20	Ellis Burks	.15
21	Richie Sexson	.15
22	Gary Sheffield	.45
23	Delino DeShields	.15
24	Wade Boggs	1.00
25	Ray Lankford	.15
26	Kevin Appier	.15
27	Roy Halladay	.15
28	Harold Baines	.15
29	Todd Zeile	.15
30	Barry Larkin	.15
31	Ron Coomer	.15
32	Jorge Posada	.15
33	Magglio Ordonez	.15
34	Brian Giles	.15
35	Jeff Kent	.15
36	Henry Rodriguez	.15
37	Fred McGriff	.15
38	Shawn Green	.50
39	Derek Bell	.15
40	Ben Grieve	.15
41	Dave Nilsson	.15
42	Mo Vaughn	.15
43	Rondell White	.15
44	Doug Glanville	.15
45	Paul O'Neill	.15
46	Carlos Lee	.15
47	Vinny Castilla	.15
48	Mike Sweeney	.15
49	Rico Brogna	.15
50	Alex Rodriguez	2.50
51	Luis Castillo	.15
52	Kevin Brown	.15
53	Jose Vidro	.15
54	John Smoltz	.15
55	Garret Anderson	.15
56	Matt Stairs	.15
57	Omar Vizquel	.15
58	Tom Goodwin	.15
59	Scott Brosius	.15
60	Robin Ventura	.15
61	B.J. Surhoff	.15
62	Andy Ashby	.15
63	Chris Widger	.15
64	Tim Hudson	.40
65	Javy Lopez	.15
66	Tim Salmon	.25
67	Warren Morris	.15
68	John Wetteland	.15
69	Gabe Kapler	.15
70	Bernie Williams	.25
71	Rickey Henderson	.75
72	Andruw Jones	.75
73	Eric Young	.15
74	Bobby Abreu	.15
75	David Cone	.15
76	Rusty Greer	.15
77	Ron Belliard	.15
78	Troy Glaus	.75
79	Mike Hampton	.15
80	Miguel Tejada	.30
81	Jeff Cirillo	.15
82	Todd Hundley	.15
83	Roberto Alomar	.35
84	Charles Johnson	.15
85	Rafael Palmeiro	.65
86	Doug Mientkiewicz	.15
87	Mariano Rivera	.25
88	Neifi Perez	.15
89	Jermaine Dye	.15
90	Ivan Rodriguez	.65
91	Jay Buhner	.15
92	Pokey Reese	.15
93	John Olerud	.15
94	Brady Anderson	.15
95	Manny Ramirez	.75

208	Alfonso Soriano (Future Stars)	1.00
209	A.J. Burnett (Future Stars)	.15
210	Rafael Furcal (Future Stars)	.15
211	Scott Morgan (Future Stars)	.15
212	Adam Piatt (Future Stars)	.15
213	Dee Brown (Future Stars)	.15
214	Corey Patterson (Future Stars)	.15
215	Mickey Lopez (Future Stars)	.15
216	Rob Ryan (Future Stars)	.15
217	Sean Burroughs (Future Stars)	.15
218	Jack Cust (Future Stars)	.15
219	John Patterson (Future Stars)	.15
220	Kit Pellow (Future Stars)	.15
221	Chad Hermansen (Future Stars)	.15
222	Daryle Ward (Future Stars)	.15
223	Jayson Werth (Future Stars)	.15
224	Jason Standridge (Future Stars)	.15
225	Mark Mulder (Future Stars)	.15
226	Peter Bergeron (Future Stars)	.15
227	Willi Mo Pena (Future Stars)	.15
228	Aramis Ramirez (Future Stars)	.15
229	John Sneed (Future Stars)	.15
230	Wilton Veras (Future Stars)	.15
231	Josh Hamilton (Draft Picks)	.50
232	Eric Munson (Draft Picks)	.15
233	Bobby Bradley RC (Draft Picks)	1.00
234	Larry Bigbie RC (Draft Picks)	1.00
235	B.J. Garbe RC (Draft Picks)	1.00
236	Brett Myers RC (Draft Picks)	4.00
237	Jason Stumm RC (Draft Picks)	1.00
238	Corey Myers RC (Draft Picks)	1.00
239	Ryan Christianson RC (Draft Picks)	1.00
240	David Walling (Draft Picks)	.15
241	Josh Girdley (Draft Picks)	.15
242	Omar Ortiz (Draft Picks)	.15
243	Jason Jennings (Draft Picks)	.15
244	Kyle Snyder (Draft Picks)	.15
245	Jay Gehrke (Draft Picks)	.15
246	Mike Paradis (Draft Picks)	.15
247	Chance Caple RC (Draft Picks)	1.00
248	Ben Christensen RC (Draft Picks)	1.00
249	Brad Baker RC (Draft Picks)	1.00
250	Rick Asadoorian RC (Draft Picks)	1.00

Refractor

A parallel to the 250-card base set these utilize Refractor technology and have a mirror sheen to them when held up to a light source. "Refractor" is also written under the card number on the card back. Refractors are seeded 1:12 packs.

Stars:	2-4X
Rookies:	1-2X
Inserted 1:12	

First Day Issue

A parallel to the 250-card base set. Card fronts are identical besides "First Day Issue" printed three times over the player name and Stadium Club Chrome logo. Card backs are serial numbered in an edition of 100.

A Refractor First Day Issue parallel is also randomly inserted, limited to 25 serial-numbered sets.

Stars:	4-8X
Rookies:	1-30X
Production 100 Sets	
Refractor:	25-40X
Rookies:	5-10X
Production 25 Sets	

Capture The Action

This 20-card set is divided into three groups: Rookies, Stars and Legends. Card backs are numbered with a "CA" prefix. These are found 1:18 packs. A Refractor parallel version is also randomly seeded 1:90 packs and also have "Refractor" written under the card number on the back.

		NM/M
Complete Set (20):		40.00
Common Player:		1.00
Inserted 1:18		
Refractors:		2-3X
Inserted 1:90		
1	Josh Hamilton	1.00
2	Pat Burrell	1.50
3	Erubiel Durazo	1.00
4	Alfonso Soriano	1.50
5	A.J. Burnett	1.00
6	Alex Rodriguez	5.00
7	Sean Casey	1.00
8	Derek Jeter	6.00
9	Vladimir Guerrero	1.50
10	Nomar Garciaparra	3.00
11	Mike Piazza	3.00
12	Ken Griffey Jr.	3.00
13	Sammy Sosa	3.00
14	Juan Gonzalez	1.50
15	Mark McGwire	5.00
16	Ivan Rodriguez	1.50
17	Barry Bonds	6.00
18	Wade Boggs	2.00
19	Tony Gwynn	2.00
20	Cal Ripken Jr.	6.00

Clear Shots

Printed on a clear, acetate stock this 10-card insert set will depict the front of the player on the card front and the back on the card back. Card backs are numbered with a "CS" prefix. Clear Shots are inserted 1:24 packs. A die-cut Refractor parallel version is also randomly seeded 1:120 packs.

		NM/M
Complete Set (10):		10.00
Common Player:		.50
Inserted 1:24		
Refractor:		2-3X
Inserted 1:120		
1	Derek Jeter	4.00
2	Bernie Williams	.50
3	Roger Clemens	2.50
4	Chipper Jones	2.00
5	Greg Maddux	2.00
6	Andruw Jones	1.00
7	Juan Gonzalez	1.00
8	Manny Ramirez	1.00
9	Ken Griffey Jr.	3.00
10	Josh Hamilton	.50

Eyes of the Game

Printed on a clear, acetate stock this 10-card set focuses on the facial expression of the featured player. Two images are on the front with the background image a close-up shot of the player's facial expression. These were seeded 1:16. Card backs are numbered with an "EG" prefix. A Refractor parallel is randomly inserted in 1:80 packs and has "Refractor" written under the card number on the back.

		NM/M
Complete Set (10):		10.00
Common Player:		.50
Inserted 1:16		
Refractors:		2-3X
Inserted 1:80		
1	Randy Johnson	1.00
2	Mike Piazza	1.50
3	Nomar Garciaparra	1.50
4	Mark McGwire	2.50
5	Alex Rodriguez	2.50
6	Derek Jeter	3.00
7	Tony Gwynn	1.00
8	Sammy Sosa	1.50
9	Larry Walker	.50
10	Ken Griffey Jr.	1.50

True Colors

This 10-card set focuses on players Topps deemed that performed best when the game's on the line. These were inserted 1:32 and are numbered with a "TC" prefix on the card back. A Refractor parallel is randomly inserted 1:160 packs.

		NM/M
Complete Set (10):		15.00
Common Player:		1.00
Inserted 1:32		
Refractors:		2-3X
Inserted 1:160		
1	Sammy Sosa	2.00
2	Nomar Garciaparra	2.00
3	Alex Rodriguez	2.00
4	Derek Jeter	4.00
5	Mark McGwire	3.00
6	Chipper Jones	1.50
7	Mike Piazza	2.00
8	Ken Griffey Jr.	2.00
9	Manny Ramirez	1.00
10	Vladimir Guerrero	1.00

Visionaries

This 20-card set spotlights young prospects who are deemed destined for stardom. Card backs are numbered with a "V" prefix. These are found 1:18 packs. A Refractor parallel version is also seeded 1:90 packs. "Refractor" is written under the card number on the back.

		NM/M
Complete Set (20):		17.50
Common Player:		1.00
Inserted 1:18		
Refractors:		2X
Inserted 1:90		
1	Alfonso Soriano	3.00
2	Josh Hamilton	1.00
3	A.J. Burnett	1.50
4	Pat Burrell	2.50
5	Ruben Salazar	1.00
6	Aaron Rowand	1.00
7	Adam Piatt	1.00
8	Nick Johnson	1.00
9	Rafael Furcal	1.00
10	Jack Cust	1.00
11	Corey Patterson	1.00
12	Sean Burroughs	1.50
13	Pablo Ozuna	1.00
14	Dee Brown	1.00
15	John Patterson	1.00
16	Willi Mo Pena	1.00
17	Mark Mulder	1.00
18	Eric Munson	1.00
19	Alex Escobar	1.00
20	Rob Ryan	1.00

1983 Star '83

Star's first baseball card issue was a 15-card tribute to Mike Schmidt, subtitled "Ten Years of Excellence." On the cards' fronts, Schmidt is shown in various posed and game-action photos, surrounded by a red border. Backs tell his story in words and numbers. The cards are the standard 2-1/2" x 3-1/2" and were sold only as complete sets through hobby dealers. Single cards are not listed because the sets are seldom broken for individual card sales.

	NM/M
Complete Set:	6.00

1984 Star '84

Star broadened the selection of its single-player collectors' issues in 1984 and adopted a new design which it used with little variation for several years. Most cards were issued in panels of three, perforated for easy separation. Each set has posed and game-action photos surrounded by colorful borders. Team logos are in a circle at lower-left; "Star '84" is in an inset at the photo's upper-right. Backs within a set feature stats, career highlights personal information and, sometimes, puzzle pieces.

YAZ CHECKLIST

		NM/M
1-24	George Brett	7.50
1-24	Steve Carlton	6.00
1-36	Steve Garvey (7,500 Sets)	3.50
1-36	Darryl Strawberry	2.00
1-24	Carl Yastrzemski (Not issued in panels.)	4.00
1-24	Carl Yastrzemski (First card autographed, edition of 500.)	20.00

1985 Star Nolan Ryan Promo

NOLAN RYAN "Baseball's K-King"

Issued to promote a set that was never issued, this promo card has on back logos and copyright information for an NBA issue.

	NM/M
Nolan Ryan	15.00

1985 Star '85

WORLD SERIES RECORDS I

Star maintained the basic format of 1984 for its sole single-player issue of 1985. The 36-card set of Reggie Jackson has portrait and action photos surrounded by colorful borders. The logo of the A's, Orioles or Yankees appears in a circle at lower-left on front, with a "Star '85" logo at upper-right. Backs have a mix of stats, personal data and career highlights. Cards were issued in a dozen three-card panels, perforated between the cards. Production was reported as 6,000 sets, with 500 of them signed and numbered by Jackson.

	NM/M
Complete Set (36):	5.00

1986 Star Promos

Several of the 1986 Star single-player series were introduced with the issue of a promo cards, different on their backs, but otherwise similar in appearance to the regular cards.

		NM/M
Complete Set (7):		55.00
Common Player:		2.50
(1)	Rod Carew (Ad back.)	1.50
(2)	Don Mattingly (White card.) (Blank back.)	2.50
(3)	Don Mattingly (Yellow sticker.) (Blank back.)	3.00

(4)	Dale Murphy (Ad back.)	3.50
(5)	Jim Rice (Blank back.)	2.50
(6)	Nolan Ryan (Ad back.)	15.00
(7)	Tom Seaver (Name on back.)	2.00

1986 Star '86

WALLY JOYNER CHECKLIST

The basic format of previous years' issues was retained for Star's single-player sets of 1986. Player poses and game-action photos are presented on the front, bordered in a bright color usually associated with the player's team. In standard 2-1/2" x 3-1/2" size, the cards have a circle at lower-left with the player's name - first only or first and last. At top-right, infringing on the photo is the notation, "Star '86." Backs have stats, career highlights, personal data or puzzle pieces. Most sets were issued in three-card perforated panels. Some of the player sets can also be found in a glossy edition and/or blank-back sticker version. Single cards are seldom offered and are not listed here.

		NM/M
1-24	Wade Boggs	2.00
1-24	Wade Boggs (Glossy set.)	2.00
(1-24)	Wade Boggs (Sticker set.)	2.00
1-15	Jose Canseco (Not issued in panels.)	3.00
1-15	Jose Canseco/Auto. (Edition of 500.)	17.50
1-15	Jose Canseco (Glossy set.)	3.00
(1-15)	Jose Canseco (Sticker set.)	1.50
1-24	Rod Carew	1.50
1-15	Wally Joyner (Not issued in panels.)	1.00
1-15	Wally Joyner/Auto. (Edition of 500.)	15.00
1-15	Wally Joyner (Glossy set.)	1.50
(1-15)	Wally Joyner (Sticker set.)	2.50
1-24	Don Mattingly	5.00
1-24	Don Mattingly (Glossy set.)	7.50
(1-24)	Don Mattingly (Sticker set.)	5.00
1-24	Dale Murphy	5.00
1-20	Jim Rice (Four-card panels.)	1.00
1-20	Jim Rice/Auto. (Edition of 500.)	40.00
1-20	Jim Rice (Glossy set.)	1.50
(1-20)	Jim Rice (Sticker set.)	1.50
1-24	Nolan Ryan (4,000 Sets)	9.00
1-24	Tom Seaver (8,000 Sets)	3.50

1987 Star Promos

Most of Star's single-player sets issued for 1987 were preceded by the issue of blank-backed promo cards in a nearly identical format to the issued version.

		NM/M
Complete Set (6):		8.75
Common Player:		1.00
(1)	Steve Carlton	2.50
(2)	Gary Carter	2.00
(3)	Roger Clemens	4.00
(4)	Keith Hernandez	1.00
(5)	Tim Raines	1.00
(6)	Fernando Valenzuela	1.00

1987 Star '87

The single-player sets issued by Star in 1987 retain the basic format used since 1984. Standard size (2-1/2" x 3-1/2") cards were printed singly, rather than in panels, but the design remained virtually unchanged. Posed and action photos are surrounded by a colorful border which protrudes into the photo at upper-right with the logo "Star

ROGER WALLY CLEMENS COMPLETE 1986 STATS

'87." At lower-left is a circle with the player's first name, or, in the case of Fernando Valenzuela, the team logo. Backs have stats, personal data or career highlights. Sets were also issued in a limited glossy version and/or as blank-back stickers. Single cards are usually not sold, so are not listed here.

		NM/M
		17.50
(1-5)	Wade Boggs, Jose Canseco (Unnumbered)	3.00
(1-5)	Wade Boggs, Jose Canseco (Glossy set.)	4.50
1-14	Steve Carlton (Glossy version only.)	3.50
1-14	Gary Carter	2.00
1-14	Gary Carter (Glossy set.)	2.25
(1-10)	Gary Carter (Sticker set.) (Different photos.)	2.50
1-12	Roger Clemens (8,500 Regular Sets; 500 Autographed)	2.00
1-12	Roger Clemens (Glossy; 1,000 Sets)	2.50
(1-5)	Roger Clemens (Update)(Unnumbered)	3.00
(1-5)	Roger Clemens (Update, glossy.) (Unnumbered)	4.50
1-13	Keith Hernandez (8,500 Regular Sets, 500 Autographed)	1.25
1-13	Keith Hernandez (Glossy; 1,000 Sets)	2.25
(1-6)	Don Mattingly (Unnumbered, five blank-back cards, one w/1986 stats.)	3.00
(1-6)	Don Mattingly (Glossy) (Unnumbered, five cards blank-back, one w/1986 stats.)	4.50
1-12	Tim Raines (8,500 Regular Sets; 500 Autographed)	1.00
1-12	Tim Raines (Glossy; 1,000 Sets)	1.50
1-13	Fernando Valenzuela (8,500 Regular Sets, 500 Autographed)	1.50
1-13	Fernando Valenzuela (Glossy; 1,000 Sets)	2.25
(1-10)	Fernando Valenzuela (Sticker set.) (Different photos.)	2.50

1988-89 Star Promos

NOLAN RYAN Promo · TEXAS

The lengthy series of 11-card sets issued by Star in 1988-89 in the company's "new" format included one promo card for nearly every player's set. The promos are blank-backed but otherwise similar in design to the regular cards.

		NM/M
Complete Set (40):		32.50
Common Player:		.75
(1)	Alomar Brothers (Roberto Alomar)	.75
(2)	Sandy Alomar Jr. (Alomar Brothers)	.75
(3)	Sandy Alomar Jr.	.75
(4)	Wade Boggs	2.00
(5)	Jose Canseco (Blue borders.)	1.50

(6)	Jose Conseco (Canseco) (Yellow borders.)	1.50
(7)	Jose Canseco (Bay Bombers Series)	1.50
(8)	Will Clark (Purple/Yellow)	1.50
(9)	Will Clark (Clark/Mitchell set, gold borders.)	.75
(10)	Will Clark (Bay Bombers Series)	1.50
(11)	David Cone	.75
(12)	Dwight Gooden	.75
(13)	Tom Gordon	.75
(14)	Mark Grace (1,300 Issued)	1.00
(15)	Mike Greenwell (Blue borders.)	.75
(16)	Mike Greenwell (Pink borders.)	.75
(17)	Ken Griffey Jr. (White-back set, blue/white borders.)	2.50
(18)	Ken Griffey Jr. (Yellow-back set, yellow borders.)	3.50
(19)	Orel Hershiser	.75
(20)	Sam Horn	.75
(21)	Bo Jackson	.75
(22)	Gregg Jefferies (Blue-border set, orange borders.)	.75
(23)	Gregg Jefferies (Orange-border set, dark blue borders, misspelled Greg.)	.75
(24)	Gregg Jefferies (Pink-border set, light blue borders, misspelled Greg.)	.75
(25)	Ricky Jordan	.75
(26)	Don Mattingly	2.00
(27)	Kevin McReynolds	.75
(28)	Kevin Mitchell (Clark/Mitchell set, gold borders.)	.75
(29)	Kevin Mitchell (Orange borders.)	.75
(30)	Matt Nokes (Yellow borders, glossy.)	.75
(31)	Kirby Puckett	1.75
(32)	Nolan Ryan	2.50
(33)	Benito Santiago	.75
(34)	Gary Sheffield	.75
(35)	Darryl Strawberry (Blue-border set, pink borders.)	.75
(36)	Darryl Strawberry (Purple-border set, orange borders.)	.75
(37)	Alan Trammell	.75
(38)	Robin Ventura	.75
(39)	Jerome Walton (Regular set, borders in two shades of blue.)	.75
(40)	Jerome Walton/Portrait (Glossy set, solid blue borders.)	.75

1988-1989 Star

KIRBY PUCKETT HIT MACHINE

Late in 1988 Star introduced a new format for its single-player card sets, which it carried forward into 1989. Sets were standardized at 11 cards in the 2-1/2" x 3-1/2" format. Fronts feature posed and game-action photos that are bordered by graduating shades of a particular color, or two different colors, going from dark at top to light at bottom, or vice versa. (The first Gregg Jefferies set is an exception, having the same shade of blue on all borders.) Backs may be printed in any of a variety of colors on white, yellow, pink or green backgrounds. Stats, personal data, career highlights and team logos are found on back. Sets may carry either a 1988 or 1989 copyright date. Because the sets are seldom broken up for singles sales, individual cards are not listed here. The number of player sets for which glossy versions were issued is uncertain. Existing glossy sets should retail for 2-5X the regular version, depending on player popularity.

NM/M

1-11	Alomar Brothers (Roberto Alomar, Sandy Alomar Jr.)	1.50
1-11	Sandy Alomar Jr.	1.50
1-11	Bay Bombers Series (Jose Canseco) (Solid green borders.)	3.00
1-11	Bay Bombers Series (Will Clark) (Solid orange borders.)	1.75
1-11	Wade Boggs (Solid red borders.)	4.00
1-11	Jose Canseco (Error set - "Conseco.")	5.00
1-11	Jose Canseco (Correct, dark green borders, white name.)	3.00
1-11	Jose Canseco (Correct, light green borders, green name.)	3.00
1-11	Will Clark	1.50
1-11	Will Clark, Kevin Mitchell	1.50
1-11	David Cone	1.50
1-11	Dwight Gooden	1.50
1-11	Tom Gordon	1.50
1-11	Mark Grace (Solid orange borders; 6,500 sets.)	1.00
1-11	Mark Grace/Auto. (500 sets.)	5.00
1-11	Mike Greenwell (Purple borders.)	1.50
1-11	Mike Greenwell (Red borders.)	1.50
1-11	Ken Griffey Jr. (White backs.)	7.50
1-11	Ken Griffey Jr. (Yellow backs, different photos.)	7.50
1-11	Orel Hershiser (8,000 Regular Sets.)	1.50
1-11	Orel Hershiser (Glossy - 250 sets.)	2.25
1-11	Sam Horn (Solid blue borders; 4,000 sets.)	1.00
1-11	Sam Horn (Glossy - 1,000 sets.)	1.50
1-11	Bo Jackson	1.50
1-11	Gregg Jefferies (Blue borders; 8,000 sets.)	1.50
1-11	Gregg Jefferies (Orange borders.)	1.50
1-11	Gregg Jefferies (Pink borders.)	1.50
1-11	Ron Jones	1.00
1-11	Ricky Jordan (8,000 Sets.)	1.00
1-11	Ricky Jordan (Glossy - 250 sets.)	2.00
1-11	Ricky Jones/Auto. (500 sets.)	3.00
1-11	Kevin McReynolds (8,000 sets.)	1.50
1-11	Kevin McReynolds (Glossy - 250 sets.)	2.25
1-11	Kevin Mitchell	1.50
1-11	Matt Nokes (3,500 sets, each bag serial numbered)	1.25
1-11	Kirby Puckett	4.50
---	Pete Rose (Blank-back, Reds.)	15.00
1-11	Nolan Ryan (Pink backs only.)	6.00
1-11	Benito Santiago	1.50
1-11	Gary Sheffield	1.50
1-11	Darryl Strawberry (Blue borders.)	1.00
1-11	Darryl Strawberry (Purple borders.)	1.00
1-11	Alan Trammell (#4 Misspelled Trammel)	1.50
1-11	Robin Ventura	1.50
1-11	Jerome Walton	1.50
1-11	Jerome Walton (Glossy, borders one shade of blue.)	1.50

1988-92 Star Ad Cards

KEVIN MAAS — NEW YORK — Ad Card

These cards were distributed to give dealers and collectors basic information about Star's baseball issues. Fronts look like contemporary Star cards, but most (not all) have the notation "Ad Card" beneath the city name at lower-right. Backs have an advertising message with general information except for Horn and Jefferies, whose ads are specific to ordering those player sets. Some cards exist in both regular and glossy finish. Except for the 1992s, the Ad Cards are undated and some of the dates on this possibly incomplete checklist are only best estimates. The unnumbered cards are checklisted here alphabetically.

		NM/M
	Complete Set (45):	70.00
	Common Player:	1.50
(1)	Sandy Alomar Jr./1989 (Regular gray.)	1.50
(1g)	Sandy Alomar Jr./1989 (Glossy gray.)	1.50
(2)	Steve Avery/1992 (Plastic red/blue.)	1.50
(3)	Jeff Bagwell/1992 (Plastic orange/green.)	1.50
(4)	Wade Boggs/1989 (Regular pink.)	3.25
(5)	Bobby Bonilla/1991 (Regular purple.)	1.50
(5g)	Bobby Bonilla/1991 (Glossy purple.)	1.50
(6)	Will Clark/1988 (Regular green.)	1.50
(6g)	Will Clark/1988 (Glossy green.)	1.50
(7)	Roger Clemens/1988 (Regular)	2.50
(8)	Eric Davis/1989 (Glossy red.)	1.50
(9)	Ken Griffey Jr./1989 (Regular green.)	3.50
(10)	Ken Griffey Jr./1990 (Regular green.)	2.50
(10g)	Ken Griffey Jr./1990 (Glossy green.)	3.50
(11)	Rickey Henderson/1991 (Regular green/yellow.)	1.50
(11g)	Rickey Henderson/1991 (Glossy green/yellow.)	1.50
(12)	Keith Hernandez/1989 (Regular orange.)	1.50
(13)	Orel Hershiser/1989 (Regular purple.)	1.50
(14)	Sam Horn/1988 (Regular purple.)	1.50
(15)	Bo Jackson/1990 (Regular blue.)	1.50
(16)	Bo Jackson/1992 (Regular green.)	1.50
(17)	Gregg Jefferies/1988 (Regular blue.)	1.50
(18)	Howard Johnson/1990 (Regular orange.)	1.50
(19)	David Justice/1992 (Plastic blue/yellow.)	1.50
(20)	Eric Karros/1992 (Glossy white.)	1.50
(21)	Barry Larkin/1990 (Regular red.)	1.50
(22)	Kevin Maas/1990 (Regular white.)	1.50
(23)	Don Mattingly/1988 (Regular green.)	3.50
(24)	Don Mattingly/1989 (Regular blue.)	3.50
(25)	Don Mattingly/1989 (Regular gray.)	3.50
(26)	Kevin Mitchell/1990 (Regular white/black.)	1.50
(27)	Phil Plantier/1992 (Plastic blue/purple.)	1.50
(28)	Kirby Puckett/1989 (Regular red.)	6.50
(29)	Kirby Puckett/1992 (Plastic purple/blue.)	3.25
(30)	Cal Ripken Jr./1992 (Regular black/orange.)	3.50
(31)	Reggie Sanders/1992 (Glossy white.)	1.50
(32)	Benito Santiago/1990 (Regular purple.)	1.50
(33)	Mike Scott/1989 (Regular green.)	1.50
(34)	Darryl Strawberry/1991 (Regular red.)	1.50
(35g)	Frank Thomas/1991 (Glossy blue/red.)	3.25
(35p)	Frank Thomas/1991 (Plastic blue/red.)	3.25
(36)	Frank Thomas/1992 (Plastic red/yellow.)	3.25
(37)	Alan Trammell/1989 (Glossy blue.)	1.50
(38)	Robin Ventura/1990 (Glossy gold.)	3.25
(39)	Jerome Walton/1990 (Regular blue/red.)	1.50

STAR — KIRBY PUCKETT — GOLD EDITION

the corresponding listings. Single cards are not checklisted because the issue is usually sold only as complete single-player sets. Fifteen hundred of each set were produced, plus 300 black-bordered, blank-back "promo" cards of each player.

		NM/M
	Complete Set (180):	22.50
	Common Player Set (10):	1.00
	Complete Promo Set:	32.50
	Common Promo Card:	1.50
1-10	Gregg Jefferies	1.00
	Gregg Jefferies (Promo card.)	1.50
11-20	Sam Horn	1.00
	Sam Horn (Promo card.)	1.50
21-30	Don Mattingly	6.00
	Don Mattingly (Promo card.)	7.50
31-40	Matt Nokes	1.00
	Matt Nokes (Promo card.)	1.50
41-50	Darryl Strawberry	1.00
	Darryl Strawberry (Promo card.)	1.50
51-60	Will Clark	2.00
	Will Clark (Promo card.)	3.00
61-70	Wade Boggs	3.00
	Wade Boggs (Promo card.)	3.00
71-80	Mark Grace	1.50
	Mark Grace (Promo card.)	2.00
81-90	Bo Jackson	1.00
	Bo Jackson (Promo card.)	1.50
91-100	Jose Canseco	2.00
	Jose Canseco (Promo card.)	3.00
101-110	Eric Davis	1.00
	Eric Davis (Promo card.)	1.50
110-119	Orel Hershiser (#120 Misnumbered #110)	1.00
	Orel Hershiser (Promo card.)	1.50
121-130	Mike Greenwell	1.00
	Mike Greenwell (Promo card.)	1.50
131-140	Dave Winfield	2.00
	Dave Winfield (Promo card.)	3.00
141-150	Alan Trammell	1.00
	Alan Trammell (Promo card.)	1.50
151-160	Roger Clemens	4.00
	Roger Clemens (Promo card.)	3.50
161-170	Kirby Puckett	2.50
	Kirby Puckett (Promo card.)	3.50
171-180	Kevin Seitzer	1.00
	Kevin Seitzer (Promo card.)	1.50

1988-89 Star Nova Edition

NOVA — JOSE CANSECO — Major League Stats

With production limited to just 500 sets and 40 promo cards of each player, these are the most limited of the regular Star issues of 1989. Cards follow the format of the regular-issue Star single-player sets of the 1988-

89 issue. Each of the nine-card player sets is listed here in alphabetical order. Single cards are not listed because complete player sets are seldom broken for individual card sales. The Nova promo cards have blue borders at the top and red at bottom. Cards #109-117 were not issued. Ryne Sandberg cards #154-161 have his name misspelled Sanberg on front and back.

		NM/M
	Complete Set (153):	85.00
	Common Player Set (9):	3.00
	Complete Promo Card Set (17):	225.00
	Common Promo Card:	7.50
1-9	Mike Greenwell	3.00
	Mike Greenwell (Promo card.)	7.50
10-18	Darryl Strawberry	
	Darryl Strawberry (Promo card.)	7.50
19-27	Don Mattingly	11.00
	Don Mattingly (Promo card.)	30.00
28-36	Eric Davis	3.00
	Eric Davis (Promo)	7.50
37-45	Jose Canseco	7.50
	Jose Canseco (Promo card.)	22.50
46-54	Sandy Alomar Jr.	3.00
	Sandy Alomar Jr. (Promo card.)	7.50
55-63	Kirby Puckett	9.00
	Kirby Puckett (Promo card.)	25.00
64-72	Orel Hershiser	3.00
	Orel Hershiser (Promo card.)	7.50
73-81	Wade Boggs	7.50
	Wade Boggs (Promo card.)	17.50
82-90	Rickey Henderson	5.00
	Rickey Henderson (Promo card.)	9.00
91-99	Will Clark	3.50
	Will Clark (Promo card.)	15.00
100-108	Bo Jackson	3.50
	Bo Jackson (Promo card.)	12.50
118-126	Ken Griffey Jr.	15.00
	Ken Griffey Jr. (Promo card.)	30.00
127-135	Mike Schmidt	11.00
	Mike Schmidt (Promo card.)	30.00
136-144	Gary Sheffield	3.50
	Gary Sheffield (Promo card.)	9.00
145-153	Cal Ripken Jr.	12.50
	Cal Ripken Jr. (Promo card.)	35.00
154-162	Ryne Sandberg	7.50
	Ryne Sandberg (Promo card.)	20.00

1988 Star Platinum Edition

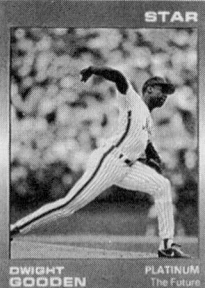

STAR — DWIGHT GOODEN — PLATINUM — The Future

Twelve single-player sets make up the 1988 Star Platinum series. Ten cards were devoted to each player. While the cards were sold as individual player sets, they were numbered continuously. Fronts feature color photos with various colorful borders (by player), highlighted in silver foil. No single card prices are quoted because the cards are usually sold only as complete player sets. One thousand sets of each player were issued, along with 200 gold-bordered promo cards per player.

		NM/M
	Complete Set (120):	27.50
	Common Player Set (10):	1.50
	Complete Promo Set (12):	32.50
	Common Promo Player:	2.00
1-10	Don Mattingly	6.00
	Don Mattingly (Promo card.)	10.00
11-20	Dwight Gooden	1.50

	Dwight Gooden (Promo card.)	2.00
21-30	Roger Clemens	3.50
	Roger Clemens (Promo card.)	3.50
31-40	Mike Schmidt	3.50
	Mike Schmidt (Promo card.)	4.00
41-50	Wade Boggs	2.50
	Wade Boggs (Promo card.)	3.00
51-60	Mark McGwire	6.00
	Mark McGwire (Promo card.)	5.00
61-70	Andre Dawson	1.50
	Andre Dawson (Promo card.)	2.50
71-80	Jose Canseco	2.50
	Jose Canseco (Promo card.)	4.00
81-90	Eric Davis	1.50
	Eric Davis (Promo card.)	2.00
91-100	George Brett	5.00
	George Brett/Throwing (Promo card.)	4.00
101-110	Darryl Strawberry	1.50
	Darryl Strawberry (Promo card.)	
	(Blue uniform.)	2.00
111-120	Dale Murphy	1.50
	Dale Murphy (Promo card.)	2.00

1988-89 Star Platinum

STAR — GEORGE BRETT — PLATINUM — 1980 MVP

Fourteen of baseball's top players are featured in 10-card single-player sets within this issue. Cards #21-30 were devoted to Gregg Jefferies, but a contract dispute prevented their release. While sold as single-player sets, the cards are numbered contiguously. Card numbers are provided for each player in the checklist below. Single cards are not checklisted because the issue is generally sold only as complete player sets. A thousand sets of each player were produced, along with 200 promo cards of each player. The cards follow the format of the regular-issue Star 1988-89 player sets.

		NM/M
	Complete Set (140):	17.50
	Common Player Set (10):	1.00
	Complete Promo Set (14):	22.50
	Common Promo Card:	1.50
1-10	Jose Canseco	2.00
	Jose Canseco (Promo card.)	2.00
11-20	Mike Greenwell	1.00
	Mike Greenwell (Promo card.)	1.50
31-40	Wade Boggs	2.50
	Wade Boggs (Promo card.)	3.00
41-50	Don Mattingly	3.25
	Don Mattingly (Promo card.)	3.75
51-60	Kirby Puckett	2.50
	Kirby Puckett (Promo card.)	3.00
61-70	Dwight Gooden	1.00
	Dwight Gooden (Promo card.)	1.50
71-80	Alan Trammell	1.00
	Alan Trammell (Promo card.)	1.50
81-90	Darryl Strawberry	1.00
	Darryl Strawberry (Promo card.)	
	(White uniform.)	1.50
91-100	Orel Hershiser	1.00
	Orel Hershiser (Promo card.)	1.50
101-110	Will Clark	1.50
	Will Clark (Promo card.)	2.50
111-120	Roger Clemens	2.00
	Roger Clemens (Promo card.)	3.50
121-130	Eric Davis	1.00
	Eric Davis (Promo card.)	1.50
131-140	George Brett	3.00

	George Brett/Btg (Promo card.)	3.50
141-150	Frank Viola	1.00
	Frank Viola (Promo card.)	1.50

1988-89 Star Silver Edition

STAR — RICKY JORDAN — SILVER SERIES — Career Stats

This 90-card issue features 10 single-player sets. Only Only 2,000 serial numbered sets were printed (plus 400 "promo" cards of each player, featuring black borders fading to white at the middle). Single-card values are not quoted because the player sets are seldom broken for individual card sales. Cards follow the format of the regular-issue 1988-89 Star player sets.

		NM/M
	Complete Set (90):	35.00
	Common Player Set:	1.50
	Complete Promo Card Set (10):	37.50
	Common Promo Card:	3.00
1-9	Ken Griffey Jr.	17.50
	Ken Griffey Jr. (Promo card.)	9.00
10-18	Wade Boggs	5.00
	Wade Boggs (Promo card.)	6.00
19-27	Ricky Jordan	1.50
	Ricky Jordan (Promo card.)	3.00
28-36	Mike Greenwell	1.50
	Mike Greenwell (Promo card.)	3.00
37-45	Sandy Alomar Jr.	1.50
	Sandy Alomar Jr. (Promo card.)	3.00
46-54	Mike Schmidt	6.00
	Mike Schmidt (Promo card.)	7.50
55-63	Gary Sheffield	2.25
	Gary Sheffield (Promo card.)	3.00
64-72	Will Clark	2.25
	Will Clark (Promo card.)	3.50
73-81	Ron Jones	1.50
	Ron Jones (Promo card.)	3.00
82-90	Kirby Puckett	6.00
	Kirby Puckett (Promo card.)	6.00

1988 Star '88 Promos

Most of the Star '88 single- and dual-player card sets also had a promo card issued; blank-backed but otherwise nearly identical to the regular cards.

		NM/M
	Complete Set (23):	35.00
	Common Player:	1.00
(1)	George Bell	1.00
(2)	Wade Boggs	2.00
(3)	Wade Boggs, Tony Gwynn	1.50
(4)	Gary Carter	1.50
(5)	Will Clark	1.50
(6)	Roger Clemens, Dwight Gooden	1.50
(7)	Eric Davis	1.00
(8)	Andre Dawson	1.50
(9)	Dwight Gooden	1.00
(10)	Tony Gwynn	2.00
(11)	Bo Jackson	3.00
(12)	Don Mattingly	1.75
(13)	Don Mattingly, Mike Schmidt	
(14)	Mark McGwire (Yellow-border set, green-border promo.)	4.00
(15)	Mark McGwire (Aqua-border set, yellow-border promo.)	2.50
(16)	Mark McGwire (Green-border set, white-border promo.)	4.00
(17)	Eddie Murray	2.00
(18)	Cal Ripken Jr.	3.50
(19)	Mike Schmidt	2.50
(20)	Mike Scott	1.00
(21)	Kevin Seitzer	1.00
(22)	Cory Snyder	1.00
(23)	Dave Winfield	2.50

1988-89 Star Gold Edition

This 180-card set was released from late 1988 into 1989 (though all cards bear 1988 copyright date) in a format matching the regular-issue player sets of the 1988-89 issue. Eighteen single-player sets of 10 cards each are included. The high quality photographs on front feature a special gold embossing. The cards devoted to each player are noted by number in

1988 Star '88

STAR '88

ANDRE DAWSON
THE HAWK

For the fifth straight year Star utilized the same basic format for its single-player card sets of 1988. Fronts have player posed and game-action photos surrounded by a brightly colored border. Pushing into the top-right of the photo is a "Star '88" logo. A circle at the lower-left contains the player name or logo. Backs have stats, personal data, career highlights or a checklist. Single cards are not listed here because sets are seldom broken. Many player sets were also issued in a more limited glossy edition, and some sets were produced with the first card authentically autographed.

NM/M

1-11	George Bell (7,500 Sets)	1.50
(1-10)	George Bell (Sticker set.)	2.00
1-11	Wade Boggs (10,000 Sets)	2.50
1-11	Wade Boggs (#1 Autographed)	25.00
1-11	Wade Boggs (Glossy - 1,000 sets.)	4.00
1-11	Wade Boggs, Tony Gwynn	2.50
1-11	Gary Carter (6,000 Sets)	2.00
1-11	Gary Carter (Glossy - 1,000 sets.)	3.00
1-11	Will Clark (7,500 Sets)	1.75
1-11	Will Clark (#1 Autographed)	15.00
1-11	Roger Clemens, Dwight Gooden	2.00
1-12	Eric Davis	1.50
1-12	Eric Davis (Glossy - 1,000 sets.)	1.50
1-11	Eric Davis, Mark McGwire	2.25
1-11	Andre Dawson (4,500 Sets)	1.50
1-11	Andre Dawson (Glossy - 1,000 sets.)	2.50
1-11	Andre Dawson (Autographed - 500 sets.)	12.50
1-12	Dwight Gooden (5,600 Sets)	1.50
1-12	Dwight Gooden (Glossy - 1,000 sets.)	2.25
1-12	Dwight Gooden (Autographed - 400 sets.)	10.00
1-11	Tony Gwynn (5,000 Sets)	2.50
1-11	Tony Gwynn (Glossy - 1,000 sets.)	4.50
1-11	Tony Gwynn (Autographed - 500 sets.)	15.00
1-16	Bo Jackson (Set includes four blank-back cards as Auburn football player; 6,000 sets.)	3.00
1-16	Bo Jackson (Glossy - 1,000 sets.)	4.50
1-11	Don Mattingly (Card #3 exists with fielding or batting pose, 10,000 sets.)	6.00
1-11	Don Mattingly (Glossy - 1,000 sets.)	7.00
1-11	Don Mattingly, Mike Schmidt (2,000 Sets)	4.00
1-11	Don Mattingly, Mike Schmidt (Glossy - 1,000 sets.)	4.50
1-12	Mark McGwire (Yellow borders; 12,000 sets.)	3.50
1-12	Mark McGwire (Yellow borders; glossy - 1,000 sets.)	4.50
1-12	Mark McGwire (Yellow borders; autographed - 500 sets.)	50.00
1-11	Mark McGwire (Aqua borders)	7.50
1-11	Mark McGwire (Green borders; 6,000 sets.)	3.50
1-11	Mark McGwire (Green borders; glossy - 1,000 sets.)	5.00
1-12	Eddie Murray (Glossy version only.)	2.00
1-12	Cal Ripken Jr.	6.00
1-12	Mike Schmidt (Glossy version only.)	4.00

1-11	Mike Scott	1.50
1-11	Kevin Seitzer (6,000 Sets)	1.50
1-11	Kevin Seitzer (Glossy - 1,000 sets.)	2.25
1-11	Cory Snyder (8,500 Sets)	1.50
1-11	Cory Snyder (Glossy - 1,000 sets.)	2.25
1-11	Cory Snyder (Autographed - 500 sets.)	5.00
(1-8)	Cory Snyder (Sticker set; 4,000 sets.)	2.00
1-12	Dave Winfield (5,000 Sets)	2.00
1-12	Dave Winfield (Glossy - 1,000 sets.)	3.00
1-12	Dave Winfield (Autographed - 500 sets.)	16.00
(1-10)	Dave Winfield (Sticker set; 3,000.)	2.00

1989-90 Star Rookies

STAR

Two-card "sets" of each of 12 promising players were produced in an edition of 10,000 each as an exclusive for a New York comic book dealer. Cards have player photos on front with a few stats on back. Cards #1-12 have borders of red and gold and backs printed in red and tan. The 1990 cards, #13-24, are bordered in purple and yellow with backs printed in purple on yellow. All cards have 1989 copyright dates. Unlike most other contemporary Star sets, no glossy or promo cards were made.

NM/M

Complete Set (24):		2.50
Common Player:		.15
1	Eric Anthony	.15
2	Eric Anthony	.15
3	Mark Lewis	.15
4	Mark Lewis	.15
5	Pete Rose, Jr.	.25
6	Pete Rose, Jr.	.25
7	Robin Ventura	.40
8	Robin Ventura	.40
9	Beau Allred	.15
10	Beau Allred	.15
11	Pat Combs	.15
12	Pat Combs	.15
13	Deion Sanders	.25
14	Deion Sanders	.25
15	Bob Hamelin	.15
16	Bob Hamelin	.15
17	Andy Benes	.20
18	Andy Benes	.20
19	Bam Bam Muelens	.15
20	Bam Bam Muelens	.15
21	Trey McCoy	.15
22	Trey McCoy	.15
23	Sandy Alomar Jr.	.25
24	Sandy Alomar Jr.	.25

1990-91 Star Promos

STAR

FRANK THOMAS — CHICAGO — Promo

Most of the 1990-91 series of Star player sets feature a promo card in the same format. They are blank-backed and have the word "Promo" on front beneath the city name. Regular and glossy promos exist for most cards.

Complete Set (44):		75.00
Common Player:		1.50
(1)	Jim Abbott	1.50
(2)	Andy Benes	1.50
(3)	Barry Bonds (Correct)	6.00
(4)	Bobby Bonds (Photo actually Barry.)	6.00
(5)	Bobby Bonilla	1.50
(6)	Jose Canseco (Blue borders, from purple set.)	1.50
(7)	Jose Canseco (Orange borders, from yellow set.)	1.50
(8)	Jose Canseco (Green borders, from yellow set.)	1.50
(9)	Will Clark (Black borders.)	1.50
(10)	Will Clark (Purple)	1.50
(11)	Will Clark (Orange, from Clark/Grace set.)	1.50
(12)	Mark Davis	1.50
(13)	Cecil Fielder (Purple, from blue set.)	1.50
(14)	Cecil Fielder (Yellow glossy, from blue set.)	12.50
(15)	Ken Griffey Jr. (Purple, from blue set.)	2.25
(16)	Ken Griffey Jr. (Blue on yellow, from blue set.)	1.50
(17)	Ken Griffey Jr. (Red, batting with "S" on helmet, from yellow set.)	1.50
(18)	Ken Griffey Jr. (Red, no "S" on helmet, from aqua Jr./Sr. set.)	2.25
(19)	Ken Griffey Jr. (Red on yellow, from red Jr./Sr. set.)	2.25
(20)	Ken Griffey Sr. (Blue, from aqua set.)	1.50
(21)	Ken Griffey Sr. (Yellow, from red set.)	1.50
(22)	Rickey Henderson/1990/Blue	1.50
(23)	Rickey Henderson/Running/1990 (Green)	1.50
(24)	Rickey Henderson/Btg/1991 (Green)	1.50
(25)	Bo Jackson/Running	1.50
(26)	Bo Jackson/Portrait	1.50
(27)	Bo Jackson (Diamond Terror, yellow.)	1.50
(28)	David Justice	1.50
(29)	Barry Larkin	1.50
(30)	Kevin Maas	1.50
(31)	Ben McDonald	1.50
(32)	Kevin Mitchell	1.50
(33)	Gregg Olson	1.50
(34)	Cal Ripken Jr.	3.00
(35)	Nolan Ryan (Blue, from Rangers set.)	4.00
(36)	Nolan Ryan (Yellow, from all-team set.)	3.00
(37)	Bret Saberhagen	1.50
(38)	Ryne Sandberg	1.50
(39)	Darryl Strawberry	1.50
(40)	Frank Thomas	1.50
(41)	Jerome Walton	1.50
(42)	Matt Williams	1.50
(43)	Robin Yount (Brown on yellow, from Mitchell/Yount set.)	1.50
(44)	Robin Yount (Blue on yellow.)	1.50

1990-91 Star

STAR

NOLAN RYAN — TEXAS — Minor League Stats

Issued as single-player sets over the two-year span these sets maintain a design continuity despite the fact some have a 1990 copyright line on back and some have a 1991 date. Fronts of all cards have posed and game-action photos which are bordered in a single bright color, by player. That border color is darkest at top and bottom and fades to white at the center. Backs are printed in one of several colors on white cardboard and feature personal data, stats, career highlights, checklists and team logos. Single cards are not listed because sets are seldom broken for

Complete Set (26):		65.00
Common Player:		1.50
(1)	Ken Griffey Jr./1990	3.50
(2)	Barry Bonds/1991	3.00
(3)	Barry Bonds/1991/Auto.	15.00
(4)	Bobby Bonilla/1991	1.50
(4)	Scott Erickson/1991	1.50
(4a)	Scott Erickson/1991/Auto.	3.00
(5)	Chuck Knoblauch/1991	1.50
(5a)	Chuck Knoblauch/1991/Auto	3.00
(6)	Frank Thomas/1991	3.00
(6a)	Frank Thomas/1991/Auto.	10.00
(6g)	Frank Thomas/1991 (Glossy)	3.00

---

individual card sales. Glossy versions are known for most, but not all, player sets.

		NM/M
1-11	Jim Abbott	1.50
1-11	Andy Benes	1.50
1-11	Barry Bonds (Error, cards #2-11 say "Bobby Bonds.")	9.00
1-11	Barry Bonds (Corrected)	9.00
1-11	Bobby Bonilla	1.50
1-11	Jose Canseco (Purple borders.)	1.50
1-11	Jose Canseco (Yellow borders.)	1.50
1-11	Will Clark	1.50
1-11	Will Clark, Mark Grace	1.50
1-11	Cecil Fielder (Blue borders.)	1.50
1-11	Cecil Fielder (Orange borders.)	1.50
1-11	Ken Griffey Jr. (Blue borders.)	3.00
1-11	Ken Griffey Jr. (Yellow borders.)	2.00
1-11	Ken Griffey Jr., Ken Griffey Sr. (Aqua borders.)	2.00
1-11	Ken Griffey Jr., Ken Griffey Sr. (Red borders.)	2.00
1-11	Rickey Henderson/1990	4.00
1-11	Rickey Henderson (Glossy - 250 sets.)	4.50
1-11	Rickey Henderson/1991	1.50
1-11	Bo Jackson	1.50
1-11	Bo Jackson, Barry Larkin (Diamond Terror)	1.50
1	Howard Johnson (Autographed card numbered to 400.)	5.00
1-11	Dave Justice	1.50
1-11	Dave Justice, Kevin Maas	1.50
1-11	Barry Larkin	1.50
1-11	Kevin Maas	1.50
1-11	Ben McDonald	1.50
1-11	Kevin Mitchell, Robin Yount	1.50
1-11	Cal Ripken Jr.	6.00
1-11	Nolan Ryan (Card #1 pitching, all Rangers photos.)	2.50
1-11	Nolan Ryan (Card #1 portrait, all four teams.)	2.50
1-11	Bret Saberhagen, Mark Davis	1.50
1-11	Ryne Sandberg	2.00
1-11	Ryne Sandberg (Glossy)	10.00
1-11	Darryl Strawberry	1.50
1-11	Frank Thomas	1.50
1-11	Jerome Walton, Gregg Olson	1.50
1-11	Matt Williams	1.50
1-11	Robin Yount	1.50

1990-93 Star "Career Stats"

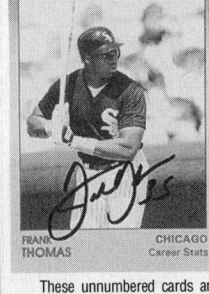

STAR

FRANK THOMAS — CHICAGO — Career Stats

These unnumbered cards are not part of any Star sets. They share a common design of two-color graduated borders on front, with color photos both front and back. The words "Career Stats" are prominently displayed on both front and back. Some players were sold in both autographed and unautographed versions, while some are known only in one version or the other.

		NM/M
(7)	Matt Williams/1991	1.50
(7a)	Matt Williams/1991/Auto.	3.00
(8)	Jeff Bagwell/1992	2.00
(9a)	Pat Kelly/1992/Auto.	3.00
(10a)	Mark Lewis/1992/Auto.	3.00
(11a)	John Olerud/1992/Auto.	3.00
(12)	Jim Abbott/1993	1.50
(12a)	Jim Abbott/1993/Auto.	3.00
(13)	Bret Barberie/1993	1.50
(13a)	Bret Barberie/1993/Auto.	3.00
(14)	Andy Benes/1993	1.50
(14a)	Andy Benes/1993/Auto.	3.00
(15)	Rickey Henderson/1993	2.00
(16a)	Eric Karros/1993/Auto.	3.00
(17)	Ryan Klesko/1993	1.50
(18)	Kevin Mass/1993 (Maas)	1.50
(19)	Dean Palmer/1993	1.50

1990-91 Star Gold Edition

STAR

GOLD — HOWARD JOHNSON — New York Mets

Only 1,500 of each nine-card, single-player set was produced in Star's 1990-91 Gold Edition. Single cards are not listed or priced because the same issue is almost exclusively traded in complete player sets. Cards are numbered contiguously as noted in the alphabetical checklist presented here. Suggested retail price at issue was $15-20 per set. An addition of 300 gray-bordered promo cards was issued for each player.

		NM/M
Complete Set (180):		40.00
Common Player Set:		1.50
Complete Promo Set (20):		50.00
Common Promo Card:		2.00
(1)	Wade Boggs (#136-144)	2.25
(1)	Wade Boggs (Promo card.)	4.00
(2)	Bobby Bonilla (#145-153)	1.50
(2)	Bobby Bonilla (Promo card.)	2.00
(3)	Jose Canseco (#19-27)	2.25
(3)	Jose Canseco (Promo card.)	3.00
(4)	Will Clark (#64-72)	2.25
(4)	Will Clark (Promo card.)	3.00
(5)	Dwight Gooden (#109-117)	1.50
(5)	Dwight Gooden (Promo card.)	2.00
(6a)	Mark Grace (#154-162)	1.50
(6)	Mark Grace (Promo card.)	2.00
(7)	Ken Griffey Jr. (#10-18)	7.50
(7)	Ken Griffey Jr. (Promo card.)	10.00
(8)	Rickey Henderson (#82-90)	3.00
(8)	Rickey Henderson (Promo card.)	2.00
(9)	Bo Jackson (#1-9)	1.50
(9)	Bo Jackson (Promo card.)	2.00
(10)	Howard Johnson (#163-171)	1.50
(11)	David Justice (#118-126)	1.50
(11)	David Justice (Promo card.)	2.00
(12)	Barry Larkin (#91-99)	1.50
(12)	Barry Larkin (Promo card.)	2.00
(13)	Kevin Maas (#127-135)	1.50
(13)	Kevin Maas (Promo card.)	2.00
(14)	Don Mattingly (#100-108)	4.50
(14)	Don Mattingly (Promo card.)	6.00
(15)	Kirby Puckett (#55-63)	4.00
(15)	Kirby Puckett (Promo card.)	6.00
(16)	Tim Raines (#37-45)	1.50
(16)	Tim Raines (Promo card.)	2.00
(17)	Cal Ripken Jr. (#73-81)	7.50
(17)	Cal Ripken Jr. (Promo card.)	10.00
(18)	Ryne Sandberg (#46-54)	3.00
(18)	Ryne Sandberg (Promo card.)	4.00

1990-91 Star Nova Edition

With just 500 of each nine-card single-player set produced, the Nova Edition was Star's top of the line in 1990. Player sets are listed alphabetically. Single cards are not listed because sets are seldom broken. Each set is also represented by an issue of 100 promo cards, featuring black borders at top and yellow at bottom.

		NM/M
Complete Set (180):		50.00
Common Player Set:		2.25
Complete Promo Set (20):		65.00
Common Promo Card:		3.00
(1)	Wade Boggs (#28-36)	5.00
(1)	Wade Boggs (Promo card.)	6.00
(2)	Jose Canseco (#55-63)	3.75
(2)	Jose Canseco (Promo card.)	5.00
(3)	Joe Carter (#118-126)	2.25
(3)	Joe Carter (Promo card.)	3.00
(4)	Will Clark (#46-54)	3.00
(4)	Will Clark (Promo card.)	4.00
(5)	Roger Clemens (#109-117)	6.50
(5)	Roger Clemens (Promo card.)	7.50
(6)	Glenn Davis (#127-135)	2.25
(6)	Glenn Davis (Promo card.)	3.00
(7)	Len Dykstra (#163-171)	2.25
(7)	Len Dykstra (Promo card.)	3.00
(8)	Cecil Fielder (#154-162)	2.25
(8)	Cecil Fielder (Promo card.)	3.00
(9)	Ken Griffey Jr. (#172-180)	7.50
(9)	Ken Griffey Jr. (Promo card.)	10.00
(10)	Rickey Henderson (#73-81)	3.00
(10)	Rickey Henderson (Promo card.)	4.00
(11)	Bo Jackson (#64-72)	2.25
(11)	Bo Jackson (Promo card.)	3.00
(12)	Howard Johnson (#37-45)	2.25
(12)	Howard Johnson (Promo card.)	3.00
(13)	Barry Larkin (#100-108)	2.25
(13)	Barry Larkin (Promo card.)	3.00
(14)	Don Mattingly (#1-9)	6.50
(14)	Don Mattingly (Promo card.)	9.00
(15)	Kevin Mitchell (#145-153)	2.25
(15)	Kevin Mitchell (Promo card.)	3.00
(16)	Nolan Ryan (#19-27)	7.50
(16)	Nolan Ryan (Promo card.)	10.00
(17)	Ryne Sandberg (#136-144)	5.00
(17)	Ryne Sandberg (Promo card.)	6.00
(18)	Dave Stewart (#91-99)	2.25
(18)	Dave Stewart (Promo card.)	3.00
(19)	Darryl Strawberry (#82-90)	2.25
(19)	Darryl Strawberry (Promo card.)	3.00
(20)	Robin Yount (#10-18)	2.25
(20)	Robin Yount (Promo card.)	3.00

1990-91 Star Platinum Edition

STAR

PLATINUM — Personal Data — BO JACKSON

The stars in Star's Platinum Edition were featured in nine-card sets with production of 1,000 each (plus 200 black-bordered promo cards of each player). Suggested retail price

at the time of issue was about $20. The player sets are checklisted here in alphabetical order. Single cards are not listed because the sets are almost never broken up. Cards are numbered contiguously as noted in the alphabetical checklist.

		NM/M
Complete Set (180):		40.00
Common Player Set:		1.50
Complete Promo Set (21):		50.00
Common Promo Card:		2.00
(1)	Jim Abbott (#19-27)	1.50
(1)	Jim Abbott (Promo card.)	2.00
(2)	Wade Boggs (#145-153)	3.00
(2)	Wade Boggs (Promo card.)	4.00
(3)	Jose Canseco (#91-99)	3.50
(3)	Jose Canseco (Promo card.)	4.00
(4)	Will Clark (#1-9)	2.50
(4)	Will Clark (Promo card.)	4.00
(5)	Roger Clemens (#46-54)	3.50
(5)	Roger Clemens (Promo card.)	7.50
(6)	Eric Davis (#55-63)	1.50
(6)	Eric Davis (Promo card.)	2.00
(7)	Dwight Gooden (#82-90)	1.50
(7)	Dwight Gooden (Promo card.)	2.00
(8)	Mark Grace (#172-180) (#172 says "Silver Series")	2.25
(8)	Mark Grace (Promo card.)	3.00
(9)	Mike Greenwell (#64-72)	1.50
(9)	Mike Greenwell (Promo card.)	2.00
(10)	Ken Griffey Jr. (#100-108)	7.00
(10)	Ken Griffey Jr. (Promo card.)	8.00
(11)	Tony Gwynn (#28-36)	4.50
(11)	Tony Gwynn (Promo card.)	6.00
(12)	Bo Jackson (#136-144)	1.50
(12)	Bo Jackson (Promo card.)	2.00
(13)	Howard Johnson (#109-117)	1.50
(13)	Howard Johnson (Promo card.)	2.00
(14)	Don Mattingly (#73-81)	5.00
(14)	Don Mattingly (Promo card.)	7.00
(15)	Kevin Mitchell (#10-18)	1.50
(15)	Kevin Mitchell/Btg (Promo card.)	2.00
(16)	Kevin Mitchell (#154-162)	1.50
(16)	Kevin Mitchell/Running (Promo card.)	2.00
(17)	Kirby Puckett (#37-45)	4.50
(17)	Kirby Puckett (Promo card.)	6.00
(18)	Ryne Sandberg (#163-171)	3.00
(18)	Ryne Sandberg (Promo card.)	4.00
(19)	Darryl Strawberry (#118-126)	1.50
(19)	Darryl Strawberry (Promo card.)	2.00
(20)	Matt Williams (#127-135)	1.50
(20)	Matt Williams (Promo card.)	2.00

1990-91 Star Silver Edition

Many of 1990's biggest stars are represented in nine-card single-player sets within Star Co.'s Silver Edition. Production of each silver-foil trimmed set was limited to 2,000. Because single cards are seldom offered, only complete player sets are priced. Cards are numbered contiguously as noted in the alphabetical checklist presented here. Retail price at issue was $10-15. Each player is also represented by an issue of 400 black-bordered promo cards.

		NM/M
Complete Set (180):		17.50
Common Player Set:		.75
Complete Promo Set:		22.50
Common Promo Card:		1.00
(1)	Jim Abbott (#1-9)	.75
(1)	Jim Abbott (Promo card.)	1.00
(2)	Sandy Alomar Jr. (#55-63)	.75
(2)	Sandy Alomar Jr. (Promo card.)	1.00
(3)	Andy Benes (#19-27)	.75
(3)	Andy Benes (Promo card.)	1.00
(4)	Barry Bonds (#172-180)	3.00
(4)	Barry Bonds (Promo card.)	4.00
(5)	Bobby Bonilla (#154-162)	.75
(5)	Bobby Bonilla (Promo card.)	1.00
(6)	Jose Canseco (#127-135)	1.25
(6)	Jose Canseco (Promo card.)	1.50
(7)	Will Clark (#73-81)	1.25
(7)	Will Clark (Promo card.)	1.50
(8)	Delino DeShields (#145-153)	.75
(8)	Delino DeShields (Promo card.)	1.00
(9)	Tom Gordon (#37-45)	.75
(9)	Tom Gordon (Promo card.)	1.00
(10)	Mark Grace (#10-18)	1.25
(10)	Mark Grace (Promo card.)	1.50
(11)	Ken Griffey Jr. (#91-99)	3.50
(11)	Ken Griffey Jr. (Promo card.)	5.00
(12)	Mike Harkey (#163-171)	.75
(12)	Mike Harkey (Promo card.)	1.00
(13)	Wally Joyner (#28-36)	.75
(13)	Wally Joyner (Promo card.)	1.00
(14)	David Justice (#118-126)	.75
(14)	David Justice (Promo card.)	1.00
(15)	Kevin Maas (#109-117)	.75
(15)	Kevin Maas (Promo card.)	1.00
(16)	Don Mattingly (#136-144)	2.50
(16)	Don Mattingly (Promo card.)	3.00
(17)	Ben McDonald (#100-108)	.75
(17)	Ben McDonald (Promo card.)	1.00
(18)	Benito Santiago (#64-72)	.75
(18)	Benito Santiago (Promo card.)	1.00
(19)	Alan Trammell (#46-54) (All cards misspelled "Allan.")	.75
(19)	Alan Trammell (Promo card.)	1.00
(20)	Jerome Walton (#82-90)	.75
(20)	Jerome Walton (Promo card.)	1.00

1990 Star Sophomore Stars

This special six-card set was distributed only at the 1990 Arlington 11th National Sports Collectors Convention. The set came polybagged with a DC comic book in exchange for a $2 donation to the Arthritis Foundation. The 2-1/2" x 3-1/2" cards feature a border that changes from dark blue at the top to red at the bottom. Backs are printed in blue-on-white and include team and MLB logos along with major and minor league career stats. Production was reported as 10,000 sets.

		NM/M
Complete Set (6):		4.50
Common Player:		.15
1	Ken Griffey Jr. (Batting cage.)	2.00
2	Ken Griffey Jr./Sitting	2.00
3	Gary Sheffield/Portrait	.30
4	Gary Sheffield/Btg	.30
5	Jerome Walton/Portrait	.15
5	Jerome Walton/Btg	.15

1991 Star

A common design is again shared by the single-player card sets released by Star for 1991. Cards feature posed and action photos on front with borders that graduate from one color at top to another at bottom (yellow to blue; green to gray, etc.). The player name is at left beneath the photo, his city at right and the card name beneath that. Backs are printed in one of several colors on white stock and feature personal data, stats, career highlights, checklist or team logo. Each set was also produced in a high-gloss version, which carries a 4-5X premium today. Single cards are not listed here because player sets are seldom broken for individual card sales. All promo cards except Clemens have a solid-color border.

		NM/M
Complete Set (88):		10.00
Common Player Set:		1.25
Complete Promo Set (6):		11.00
Common Promo Card:		1.50
1-11	Roger Clemens	1.50
1-11	Roger Clemens (Promo card.)	2.50
1-11	Rickey Henderson	1.50
1-11	Bo Jackson	1.25
1-11	Bo Jackson (Promo card.)	1.50
1-11	Pat Kelly (Glossy version only.)	1.25
	Pat Kelly (Promo card.)	1.50
1-11	Cal Ripken Jr.	2.50
1-11	Cal Ripken Jr. (Promo card.)	3.25
1-11	Nolan Ryan	2.00
1-11	Nolan Ryan (Promo card.)	3.25
1-11	Darryl Strawberry	1.25
1-11	Frank Thomas (Glossy version only.)	2.50
	Frank Thomas (Promo card.)	3.00

All-Stars

This Star issue is comprised of 500 sets and 100 promo cards of each player. (Except Jackson who has 200.) The checklist is arranged alphabetically.

		NM/M
Complete Set (135):		80.00
Common Player Set:		3.75
Complete Promo Set (15):		110.00
Common Promo Card:		5.00
(1)	Wade Boggs (#109-117)	7.50
(1)	Wade Boggs (Promo card.)	10.00
(2)	Jose Canseco (#37-45)	7.50
(2)	Jose Canseco (Promo card.)	10.00
(3)	Roger Clemens (#64-72)	7.50
(3)	Roger Clemens (Promo card.)	10.00
(4)	Lenny Dykstra (#91-99)	3.75
(4)	Lenny Dykstra (Promo card.)	5.00
(5)	Cecil Fielder (#118-126)	3.75
(5)	Cecil Fielder (Promo card.)	5.00
(6)	Dwight Gooden (#82-90)	3.75
(6)	Dwight Gooden (Promo card.)	5.00
(7)	Ken Griffey Jr. (#1-9)	10.00
(7)	Ken Griffey Jr. (Promo card.)	15.00
(8)	Rickey Henderson (#19-27)	7.50
(8)	Rickey Henderson (Promo card.)	10.00
(9)	Bo Jackson (#46-54)	3.75
(9)	Bo Jackson (Promo card.)	5.00
(10)	Don Mattingly (#73-81)	9.00
(10)	Don Mattingly (Promo card.)	12.00
(11)	Kirby Puckett (#100-108)	7.50
(11)	Kirby Puckett (Promo card.)	12.00

		NM/M
(12)	Cal Ripken Jr. (#55-63)	9.00
(12p)	Cal Ripken Jr. (#55-63) (Plastic test issue.)	12.00
(12)	Cal Ripken Jr. (Promo card.)	12.00
(12p)	Cal Ripken Jr. (Promo card.) (Plastic)	16.00
(13)	Nolan Ryan (#10-18)	9.00
(13)	Nolan Ryan (Promo card.)	12.00
(14)	Ryne Sandberg (#28-36)	7.50
(14)	Ryne Sandberg (Promo card.)	10.00

Diamond Series

Production of these nine-card, single-player sets was limited to 2,000 of each (plus 400 promo cards each), with a suggested retail price at issue of $25. Players in the edition are listed here in alphabetical order. Cards are numbered contiguously throughout the issue, as noted in the alpha-order listings here. Single cards are not priced because the sets are seldom broken up.

		NM/M
Complete Set (126):		22.50
Common Player Set:		1.00
Complete Promo Set:		27.50
Common Promo Card:		1.50
(1)	Barry Bonds (#10-18)	5.00
(1)	Barry Bonds (Promo card.)	5.00
(2)	Bobby Bonilla (#46-54)	1.50
(2)	Bobby Bonilla (Promo card.)	1.50
(3)	Jose Canseco (#37-45)	2.00
(3)	Jose Canseco (Promo card.)	2.50
(4)	Roger Clemens (#64-72)	2.50
(4)	Roger Clemens (Promo card.)	2.50
(5)	Cecil Fielder (#118-126)	1.00
(5)	Cecil Fielder (Promo card.)	1.50
(6)	Ken Griffey Jr. (#55-63)	3.50
(6)	Ken Griffey Jr. (Promo card.)	5.00
(7)	Tony Gwynn (#100-108)	1.75
(7)	Tony Gwynn (Promo card.)	2.50
(8)	Bo Jackson (#1-9)	1.00
(8)	Bo Jackson (Promo card.)	1.50
(9)	Don Mattingly (#19-27)	5.00
(9)	Don Mattingly (Promo card.)	6.00
(10)	Kirby Puckett (#82-90)	2.50
(10)	Kirby Puckett (Promo card.)	6.00
(11)	Cal Ripken Jr. (#28-36)	7.50
(11)	Cal Ripken Jr. (Promo card.)	3.50
(12)	Nolan Ryan (#109-117)	6.00
(12)	Nolan Ryan (Promo card.)	7.50
(13)	Darryl Strawberry (#73-81)	1.00
(13)	Darryl Strawberry (Promo card.)	1.50
(14)	Frank Thomas (#91-99)	2.25
(14)	Frank Thomas (Promo card.)	3.00

Gold Edition

Only 1,500 of each nine-card, single-player set was produced - along with 300 promo cards of each player - in Star's 1991 Gold Edition. Cards are numbered contiguously throughout the issue, as noted in the alphabetical checklist shown here. Single cards are not listed or priced because the issue is almost exclusively traded in complete-player sets.

		NM/M
Complete Set (144):		40.00
Common Player Set:		1.50
Complete Promo Set (16):		40.00
Common Promo Card:		2.00
(1)	Albert Belle (#118-126)	2.00
(1)	Albert Belle (Promo card.)	2.00

		NM/M
(2)	Barry Bonds (#73-81)	7.00
(2)	Barry Bonds (Promo card.)	7.00
(3)	Bobby Bonilla (#127-135)	2.00
(3)	Bobby Bonilla (Promo card.)	2.00
(4)	Jose Canseco (#55-63)	3.00
(4)	Jose Canseco (Promo card.)	2.00
(5)	Will Clark (#28-36)	2.00
(5)	Will Clark (Promo card.)	2.00
(6)	Roger Clemens (#64-72)	6.00
(6)	Roger Clemens (Promo card.)	6.00
(7)	Ken Griffey Jr. (#19-27)	5.00
(7)	Ken Griffey Jr. (Promo card.)	5.00
(8)	Bo Jackson (#37-45)	2.00
(8)	Bo Jackson (Promo card.)	2.00
(9)	David Justice (#82-90)	2.00
(9)	David Justice (Promo card.)	2.00
(10)	Don Mattingly (#91-99)	6.00
(10)	Don Mattingly (Promo card.)	6.00
(11)	Fred McGriff (#136-144)	2.00
(11)	Fred McGriff (Promo card.)	2.00
(12)	Kirby Puckett (#1-9)	4.50
(12)	Kirby Puckett (Promo card.)	4.50
(13)	Nolan Ryan (#109-117)	6.00
(13)	Nolan Ryan (Promo card.)	6.00
(14)	Ryne Sandberg (#10-18)	4.00
(14)	Ryne Sandberg (Promo card.)	4.00
(15)	Darryl Strawberry (#46-54)	2.00
(15)	Darryl Strawberry (Promo card.)	2.00
(16)	Frank Thomas (#100-108)	3.00
(16)	Frank Thomas (Promo card.)	.3.00

Home Run Series

With a suggested retail price at issue of $25 or so, and an edition limit of 1,500 each of the single-player, nine-card sets (plus 300 promo cards of each player), these are among the scarcer of the 1991 Star issues. Numbers on individual player cards run contiguously throughout the issue and are noted in the alphabetical checklist. Because sets are seldom available as singles, individual cards are not listed here.

		NM/M
Complete Set (126):		65.00
Common Player Set:		3.75
Complete Promo Set (14):		85.00
Common Promo Card:		5.00
(1)	Wade Boggs (#91-99)	5.50
(1)	Wade Boggs (Promo card.)	7.50
(2)	Barry Bonds (#64-72)	9.00
(2)	Barry Bonds (Promo card.)	12.00
(3)	Bobby Bonilla (#10-18)	3.75
(3)	Bobby Bonilla (Promo card.)	5.00
(4)	Jose Canseco (#1-9)	5.50
(4)	Jose Canseco (Promo card.)	7.50
(5)	Dwight Gooden (#73-81)	3.75
(5)	Dwight Gooden (Promo card.)	5.00
(6)	Ken Griffey Jr. (#37-45)	5.00
(6)	Ken Griffey Jr. (Promo card.)	7.50
(7)	Rickey Henderson (#19-27)	5.00
(7)	Rickey Henderson (Promo card.)	6.00
(8)	Bo Jackson (#82-90)	3.00
(8)	Bo Jackson (Promo card.)	4.50
(9)	Don Mattingly (#46-54)	9.00
(9)	Don Mattingly (Promo card.)	10.00
(10)	Cal Ripken Jr. (#109-117)	9.00

		NM/M
(10)	Cal Ripken Jr. (Promo card.)	12.00
(11)	Nolan Ryan (#55-63)	9.00
(11)	Nolan Ryan (Promo card.)	12.00
(12)	Ryne Sandberg (#100-108)	7.50
(12)	Ryne Sandberg (Promo card.)	7.50
(13)	Darryl Strawberry (#28-36)	3.75
(13)	Darryl Strawberry (Promo card.)	5.00
(14)	Frank Thomas (#118-126)	7.50
(14)	Frank Thomas (Promo card.)	10.00

Millennium Edition

As the name suggests, production of each of these nine-card, single-player sets was pegged at 1,000 (plus 200 promo cards of each player). Suggested retail price at issue was about $30. Cards are numbered contiguously throughout the issue, as noted in the alphabetical checklist (part of each Ripken and Gooden set are misnumbered). Individual cards are not listed or priced because the sets are almost never broken down for singles sales.

		NM/M
Complete Set (126):		50.00
Common Player Set:		1.50
Complete Promo Set (14):		50.00
Common Promo Card:		1.50
(1)	Wade Boggs (#55-63)	7.50
(1)	Wade Boggs (Promo card.)	7.50
(2)	Will Clark (#46-54)	3.00
(2)	Will Clark (Promo card.)	3.00
(3)	Cecil Fielder (#109-117)	1.50
(3)	Cecil Fielder (Promo card.)	1.50
(4)	Dwight Gooden (#10-14, 78-81)	1.50
(4)	Dwight Gooden (Promo card.)	1.50
(5)	Ken Griffey Jr. (#91-99)	6.00
(5)	Ken Griffey Jr. (Promo card.)	6.00
(6)	Howard Johnson (#64-72)	1.50
(6)	Howard Johnson (Promo card.)	1.50
(7)	Dave Justice (#100-108)	1.50
(7)	David Justice (Promo card.)	1.50
(8)	Kevin Maas (#82-90)	1.50
(8)	Kevin Maas (Promo card.)	1.50
(9)	Don Mattingly (#37-45)	7.50
(9)	Don Mattingly (Promo card.)	7.50
(10)	Kirby Puckett (#19-27)	7.50
(10)	Kirby Puckett (Promo card.)	7.50
(11)	Cal Ripken Jr. (#15-18, 73-77)	7.50
(11)	Cal Ripken Jr. (Promo card.)	7.50
(12)	Ryne Sandberg (#28-36)	6.00
(12)	Ryne Sandberg (Promo card.)	6.00
(13)	Frank Thomas (#118-126)	6.00
(13)	Frank Thomas (Promo card.)	6.00
(14)	Robin Yount (#1-9)	3.00
(14)	Robin Yount (Promo card.)	3.00

Nova Edition

Production of these nine-card, single-player sets was limited to 500 of each (plus 100 promo cards of each player). Sets are checklisted here in alphabetical order. Individual cards are numbered contiguously throughout the issue, as noted. Single cards are not priced because sets are seldom broken up for sale of individual cards.

Rickey Henderson — OAKLAND — Minor League Stats

	NM/M
Complete Set (144):	60.00
Common Player Set:	2.50
Complete Promo Set (16):	60.00
Common Promo Card:	2.50
(1) Wade Boggs (#82-90)	6.00
(1) Wade Boggs (Promo card.)	6.00
(2) Jose Canseco (#55-63)	5.00
(2) Jose Canseco (Promo card.)	5.00
(3) Vince Coleman (#127-135)	2.50
(3) Vince Coleman (Promo card.)	2.50
(4) Cecil Fielder (#136-144)	2.50
(4) Cecil Fielder (Promo card.)	2.50
(5) Dwight Gooden (#10-18)	2.50
(5) Dwight Gooden (Promo card.)	2.50
(6) Ken Griffey Jr. (#91-99)	7.50
(6) Ken Griffey Jr. (Promo card.)	7.50
(7) Tony Gwynn (#100-108)	5.00
(7) Tony Gwynn (Promo card.)	5.00
(8) Rickey Henderson (#1-9)	5.00
(8) Rickey Henderson (Promo card.)	5.00
(9) Bo Jackson (#28-36)	2.50
(9) Bo Jackson (Promo card.)	2.50
(10) Howard Johnson (#118-126)	2.50
(10) Howard Johnson (Promo card.)	2.50
(11) Don Mattingly (#64-72)	7.50
(11) Don Mattingly (Promo card.)	7.50
(12) Kirby Puckett (#109-117)	5.00
(12) Kirby Puckett (Promo card.)	5.00
(13) Cal Ripken Jr. (#46-54)	9.00
(13) Cal Ripken Jr. (Promo card.)	9.00
(14) Nolan Ryan (#19-27)	10.00
(14) Nolan Ryan (Promo card.)	10.00
(15) Ryne Sandberg (#73-81)	6.00
(15) Ryne Sandberg (Promo card.)	6.00
(16) Darryl Strawberry (#37-45)	2.50
(16) Darryl Strawberry (Promo card.)	2.50

Platinum Edition

These nine-card, single-player sets were produced in an edition of 1,000 each (plus 200 promo cards per player). Sets are checklisted here alphabetically, with individual card numbers shown for each player. Single cards are not listed because the sets are seldom offered as singles.

	NM/M
Complete Set (108):	45.00
Common Player Set:	2.00
Complete Promo Set (14):	60.00
Common Promo Card:	2.50
(1) Wade Boggs (#109-117)	5.00
(1) Wade Boggs (Promo card.)	5.00
(2) Barry Bonds (#28-36)	5.00

(2) Barry Bonds (Promo card.)	7.50
(3) Bobby Bonilla (#73-81)	2.00
(3) Bobby Bonilla (Promo card.)	2.50
(4) Jose Canseco (#19-27)	5.00
(4) Jose Canseco (Promo card.)	6.00
(5) Will Clark (#118-126)	3.75
(5) Will Clark (Promo card.)	5.00
(6) Roger Clemens (#10-18)	6.00
(6) Roger Clemens (Promo card.)	8.00
(7) Mark Grace (#1-9)	2.00
(7) Mark Grace (Promo card.)	2.50
(8) Ken Griffey Jr. (#55-63)	3.75
(8) Ken Griffey Jr. (Promo card.)	6.00
(9) Rickey Henderson (#46-54)	3.75
(9) Rickey Henderson (Promo card.)	5.00
(10) Kevin Maas (#37-45)	2.00
(10) Kevin Maas (Promo card.)	2.50
(11) Don Mattingly (#82-90)	6.00
(11) Don Mattingly (Promo card.)	6.50
(12) Cal Ripken Jr. (#91-99)	7.50
(12) Cal Ripken Jr. (Promo card.)	10.00
(13) Nolan Ryan (#64-72)	7.50
(13) Nolan Ryan (Promo card.)	10.00
(14) Frank Thomas (#100-108)	3.75
(14) Frank Thomas (Promo card.)	5.00

Cal Ripken Promo Set

This unusual Star set has five solid orange-bordered cards of Ripken. Unlike the other Star promo cards, which are blank-backed, the backs of these glossy-finish cards says "1 of 1,000 Promo Sets," and include stats and other information.

	NM/M
1-5 Cal Ripken Jr.	10.00

Rookie Guild Prototypes

MARK LEWIS — CLEVELAND — Prototype

Labeled as "Prototype" cards, these unnumbered blank-back cards can be found in a confusing variety of regular, glossy and plastic finish for the six players in the Rookie Guild set. Only those cards confirmed to exist are listed here.

	NM/M
Complete Set, Regular (3):	4.00
Complete Set, Glossy (3):	6.00
Complete Set, Plastic (4):	8.00
(1g) Jeff Bagwell/Glossy	2.00
(1p) Jeff Bagwell/Plastic	2.50
(2) Albert Belle	1.50
(3g) Juan Gonzalez/Glossy	2.00
(3p) Juan Gonzalez/Plastic	2.50
(4a) Chris Knoblauch (Chuck)	2.50
(4bp) Chuck Knoblauch/Plastic	2.50
(5) Mark Lewis	1.00
(6g) Frank Thomas/Glossy	3.75
(6p) Frank Thomas/Plastic	4.50

Rookie Guild Promos

A confusing variety of regular, glossy and plastic finish promo cards were issued in different combinations for the six players in Star's 1991 Rookie Guild issue. The blank-back, unnumbered cards are checklisted here in alphabetical order. Only those cards confirmed to have been issued are listed.

	NM/M
Complete Set, Regular (3):	4.00
Complete Set, Glossy (6):	12.50
Complete Set, Plastic (4):	9.00
(1g) Jeff Bagwell/Glossy	2.25
(1p) Jeff Bagwell/Plastic	2.50
(2) Albert Belle	1.50
(2g) Albert Belle/Glossy	3.00

(3g) Juan Gonzalez/Glossy	2.25
(3p) Juan Gonzalez/Plastic	2.50
(4a) Chris Knoblauch (Chuck)	1.75
(4ag) Chris Knoblauch (Chuck)/Glossy	3.25
(4bp) Chuck Knoblauch/Plastic	2.00
(5g) Mark Lewis	.70
(5g) Mark Lewis/Glossy	1.50
(6g) Frank Thomas/Glossy	2.50
(6p) Frank Thomas/Plastic	3.25

Rookie Guild

ALBERT BELLE — CLEVELAND — Career Info - 1

Late in the 1991 baseball season, Star introduced yet another series of single-player card sets. The emphasis was on young stars in 11-card sets. Most player sets were produced in some combination of regular and glossy finish, or glossy and plastic finish. Each player was also represented with some combination of 1,000 each promotional (border other than white) and prototype cards and 50 glossy and/or plastic promo cards. Single cards are not listed because sets are seldom broken for individual card sales.

	NM/M
Common Player Set, Regular:	1.00
Common Player Set, Glossy:	1.50
Common Player Set, Plastic:	4.00
(1) Albert Belle (#1-11)	1.00
(1g) Albert Belle/Glossy	3.00
(2a) Chris Knoblauch (Chuck)	3.00
(2ag) Chris Knoblauch (Chuck)/Glossy	4.50
(2bg) Chuck Knoblauch (#12-22)(Glossy only.)	1.50
(3) Mark Lewis (#23-33)	1.00
(3g) Mark Lewis/Glossy	3.00
(4g) Frank Thomas (#33-44)/Glossy	1.75
(4p) Frank Thomas/Plastic	5.00
(5g) Juan Gonzalez (#45-55)/Glossy	1.50
(5p) Juan Gonzalez/Plastic	4.00
(6g) Jeff Bagwell (#56-66)/Glossy	1.50
(6p) Jeff Bagwell/Plastic	4.00

1991 Star Silver Edition

VINCE COLEMAN — NEW YORK — Career Highlights

Two thousand of each nine-card player set was produced in Star's silver-enhanced set, along with 400 promo cards of each player. Players are listed here in alphabetical order. Individual cards are not listed because the sets are seldom offered as singles.

	NM/M
Complete Set (126):	35.00
Common Player Set:	1.50
Complete Promo Set (15):	45.00
Common Promo Card:	2.00
(1) Wade Boggs (#10-18)	4.00
(1) Wade Boggs (Promo card.)	4.00
(2) Bobby Bonilla (#37-45)	1.50
(2) Bobby Bonilla (Promo card.)	2.00
(3) Jose Canseco (#109-117)	3.00
(3) Jose Canseco (Promo card.)	4.00

(3g) Juan Gonzalez/Glossy	2.25
(3p) Juan Gonzalez/Plastic	2.50
(4a) Chris Knoblauch (Chuck)	1.75
(4ag) Chris Knoblauch (Chuck)/Glossy	3.25
(4bp) Chuck Knoblauch/Plastic	2.00
(5g) Mark Lewis	.70
(5g) Mark Lewis/Glossy	1.50
(6g) Frank Thomas/Glossy	2.50
(6p) Frank Thomas/Glossy	3.25

Stellar Edition

The same players who appear in other Star sets for 1991 are repackaged into this edition of 500 sets of each player. One hundred promo cards of each player were also issued.

	NM/M
Complete Set (126):	50.00
Common Player Set:	2.00
Complete Promo Set (14):	65.00
Common Promo Card:	2.50
(1) Bobby Bonilla (#55-63)	2.00
(1) Bobby Bonilla (Promo card.)	2.50
(2) Will Clark (#37-45)	3.00
(2) Will Clark (Promo card.)	5.00
(3) Roger Clemens (#10-18)	6.50
(3) Roger Clemens (Promo card.)	8.00
(4) Vince Coleman (#73-81)	2.00
(4) Vince Coleman (Promo card.)	2.50
(5) Ken Griffey Jr. (#1-9)	7.50
(5) Ken Griffey Jr. (Promo card.)	10.00
(6) Tony Gwynn (#46-54)	5.00
(6) Tony Gwynn (Promo card.)	6.50
(7) Rickey Henderson (#118-126)	5.00
(7) Rickey Henderson (Promo card.)	6.50
(8) Howard Johnson (#100-108)	2.00
(8) Rickey Henderson (Promo card.)	2.50
(9) Don Mattingly (#109-117)	6.00
(9) Don Mattingly (Promo card.)	8.00
(10) Kirby Puckett (#64-72)	6.00
(10) Kirby Puckett (Promo card.)	6.00
(11) Cal Ripken Jr. (#82-90)	7.50
(11) Cal Ripken Jr. (Promo card.)	8.00
(12) Nolan Ryan (#19-27)	7.50
(12) Nolan Ryan (Promo card.)	8.00
(13) Ryne Sandberg (#91-99)	6.00
(13) Ryne Sandberg (Promo card.)	6.50
(14) Robin Yount (#28-36)	4.50
(14) Robin Yount (Promo card.)	5.00

1991 Star The Future

TODD VAN POPPEL — OAKLAND — A's

1991 Star '92

Though labeled "Star '92" on front, these single-player 11-card sets were produced in 1991. Fronts feature borders which fade from one color at top to gray at the bottom. The photos at center are a mix of poses and game-action shots. Backs have a small color portrait photo - the same on all cards within a set - at upper-left. Stats, personal data, highlights, checklists and team logos are printed in color on yellow cardboard. The cards carry a 1991 copyright line at bottom center. Each set can be found in a glossy version, which carries a premium of 2X.

	NM/M
Complete Set (22):	5.00
Common Player Set:	2.50
Complete Promo Set (2):	4.00
Common Promo Card:	2.00
1-11 Scott Erickson	1.50
Scott Erickson (Promo card.)	2.00
1-11 Todd Van Poppel	1.50
Todd Van Poppel (Promo card.)	2.00

1992 Star '92

Utilizing a design introduced the previous year, the Star '92 single-player card sets produced in 1992 are printed on cardboard laminated with thin high-gloss plastic surfaces front and back. Each player's cards are bordered with a single bright color at top which fades to gray at bottom. Photos are a mix of poses and game-action shots. Backs have a yellow background with a small color portrait (the same throughout the player's set) at upper-left. Stats, personal data,

A few players who had not yet been included among the flood of 1991 Star issues joined the others in this post-season issue. Production was put at 1,000 nine-card sets per player, plus 200 promo cards of each. Players are listed here in alphabetical order. Individual cards are not listed because the sets are usually never sold as singles.

	NM/M
Complete Set (90):	15.00
Common Player Set:	1.50
Complete Promo Set (10):	20.00
Common Promo Card:	2.00
(1) Jeff Bagwell (#28-36)	3.00
(1) Jeff Bagwell (Promo card.)	4.00
(2) Albert Belle (#55-63)	2.00
(2) Albert Belle (Promo card.)	2.75
(3) Scott Erickson (#82-90)	1.50
(3) Scott Erickson (Promo card.)	2.00
(4) Juan Gonzalez (#1-9)	2.25
(4) Juan Gonzalez (Promo card.)	3.50
(5) Pat Kelly (#10-18)	1.50
(5) Pat Kelly (Promo card.)	2.00
(6) Mark Lewis (#73-81)	1.50
(6) Mark Lewis (Promo card.)	2.00
(7) Ramon Martinez (#46-54)	1.50
(7) Ramon Martinez (Promo card.)	2.00
(8) Brian McRae (#64-72)	1.50
(8) Brian McRae (Promo card.)	2.00
(9) Frank Thomas (#37-45)	3.50
(9) Frank Thomas (Promo card.)	5.00
(10) Mo Vaughn (#19-27)	1.50
(10) Mo Vaughn (Promo card.)	2.00

STAR '92 — DAVE JUSTICE — ATLANTA — Career Stats

career highlights, checklist or team logo are printed in colored ink. The cards carry a 1992 copyright date and each set has a large capital letter in the lower-right corner. It is not known whether sets were issued for the letters missing in the checklist below, though prototype cards are known for some. Production was reported as 4,000 of each player set and 800 of each promo and prototype card. Only confirmed cards are listed. Single cards are not listed because sets are seldom broken for individual card sales.

	NM/M
Common Player Set:	1.00
Common Promo Card:	1.75
Common Prototype Card:	1.75
A1-11 Jeff Bagwell	2.00
Jeff Bagwell (Promo card.)	3.00
Jeff Bagwell (Prototype)	3.00
B1-11 Albert Belle	1.50
Albert Belle (Promo)	2.00
C1-11 Ron Gant	1.00
Ron Gant (Promo card.)	1.75
Ron Gant (Prototype)	1.75
D1-11 Bo Jackson	1.00
Bo Jackson (Promo card.)	1.75
Bo Jackson (Prototype)	1.75
E1-11 Dave Justice	1.00
Dave Justice (Promo card.)	1.75
David Justice (Prototype)	1.75
F1-11 Chuck Knoblauch	1.00
Chuck Knoblauch (Promo card.)	1.75
Chuck Knoblauch (Prototype)	1.75
G1-11 Kirby Puckett	2.50
Kirby Puckett (Promo card.)	3.25
Kirby Puckett (Prototype)	3.25
H1-11 Ryne Sandberg	2.50
Ryne Sandberg (Promo)	3.25
Ryne Sandberg (Prototype)	3.25
I1-11 Steve Avery	1.00
Steve Avery (Promo)	1.75
Steve Avery (Prototype)	1.75
J1-11 Phil Plantier	1.00
Phil Plantier (Promo)	1.75
K Wade Boggs (Prototype)	3.25
M1-11 Will Clark	1.50
Will Clark (Promo card.)	3.25
N1-11 Ken Griffey Jr.	5.00
Ken Griffey Jr. (Promo card.)	6.25
Ken Griffey Jr. (Prototype)	6.25
O Cal Ripken Jr. (Prototype)	3.75
P Nolan Ryan (Prototype, regular finish.)	4.50
Nolan Ryan (Plastic prototype.)	6.00
R Frank Thomas (Prototype)	4.50
S Bobby Bonilla (Prototype)	1.75
T Kevin Mitchell (Prototype)	1.00
U1-11 Danny Tartabull	1.00
Danny Tartabull (Promo card.)	1.75
V1-11 Dean Palmer	1.00
Dean Palmer (Promo)	1.75
Dean Palmer (Prototype)	1.75

Gold Edition

The 12 players in Star's 1992 Gold Edition are represented in an issue of 750 sets each, plus 150 promo cards each. The checklist is arranged alphabetically. Single cards are not listed because sets are not often broken up for individual card sales.

	NM/M
Complete Set (108):	55.00
Common Player Set:	3.00

GOLD '92 by STAR

DON MATTINGLY — NEW YORK Yankees Captain

		NM/M
Complete Promo Set (12):		75.00
Common Promo Card:		5.00
(1)	Steve Avery (#91-99)	3.00
(1)	Steve Avery (Promo card.)	5.00
(2)	Jose Canseco (#19-27)	6.00
(2)	Jose Canseco (Promo card.)	8.00
(3)	Will Clark (#28-36)	5.00
(3)	Will Clark (Promo card.)	8.00
(4)	Ken Griffey Jr. (#82-90)	9.00
(4)	Ken Griffey Jr. (Promo card.)	12.00
(5)	Bo Jackson (#46-54)	3.00
(5)	Bo Jackson (Promo card.)	4.00
(6)	David Justice (#10-18)	3.50
(6)	David Justice (Promo card.)	5.00
(7)	Don Mattingly (#1-9)	7.50
(7)	Don Mattingly (Promo card.)	10.00
(8)	Cal Ripken Jr. (#64-72)	8.00
(8)	Cal Ripken Jr. (Promo card.)	12.00
(9)	Nolan Ryan (#37-45)	9.00
(9)	Nolan Ryan (Promo card.)	12.00
(10)	Ryne Sandberg (#55-63)	6.00
(10)	Ryne Sandberg (Promo card.)	8.00
(11)	Darryl Strawberry (#100-108)	3.50
(11)	Darryl Strawberry (Promo card.)	5.00
(12)	Frank Thomas (#73-81)	7.50
(12)	Frank Thomas (Promo card.)	10.00

Millenium Edition

Star's Millenium Edition for 1992 included an issue of 750 sets and 150 promo cards for each of 12 players, listed alphabetically in the checklist here. Single cards are not listed because player sets are seldom broken for individual card sales.

		NM/M
Complete Set (108):		70.00
Common Player Set:		4.00
Complete Promo Set (12):		95.00
Common Promo Card:		5.00
(1)	Wade Boggs (#100-108)	7.50
(1)	Wade Boggs (Promo card.)	10.00
(2)	Jose Canseco (#10-18)	7.50
(2)	Jose Canseco (Promo card.)	10.00
(3)	Roger Clemens (#28-36)	7.50
(3)	Roger Clemens (Promo card.)	10.00
(4)	Ken Griffey Jr. (#1-9)	10.00
(4)	Ken Griffey Jr. (Promo card.)	12.50
(5)	Bo Jackson (#82-90)	4.00
(5)	Bo Jackson (Promo card.)	5.00
(6)	David Justice (#73-81)	4.00
(6)	David Justice (Promo card.)	5.00
(7)	Don Mattingly (#37-45)	9.00
(7)	Don Mattingly (Promo card.)	12.00
(8)	Kirby Puckett (#91-99)	9.00
(8)	Kirby Puckett (Promo card.)	12.00
(9)	Cal Ripken Jr. (#19-27)	10.00
(9)	Cal Ripken Jr. (Promo card.)	12.50
(10)	Nolan Ryan (#55-63)	10.00
(10)	Nolan Ryan (Promo card.)	12.50
(11)	Ryne Sandberg (#46-54)	7.50
(11)	Ryne Sandberg (Promo card.)	10.00
(12)	Frank Thomas (#64-72)	9.00
(12)	Frank Thomas (Promo card.)	12.00

Nova Edition

These nine-card, single-player sets were limited to an edition of 500 for each player, plus 100 promo cards. Numbering errors occurred

---

on the Avery and Strawberry cards. The former were supposed to be numbered 10-18; the latter 64-72.

		NM/M
Complete Set (108):		75.00
Common Player:		4.50
Complete Promo Set:		100.00
Common Promo Card:		6.00
(1)	Nolan Ryan (#1-9)	12.50
(1)	Nolan Ryan (Promo card.)	15.00
(2)	Steve Avery (#10-14, 69-72)	4.50
(2)	Steve Avery (Promo card.)	6.00
(3)	Frank Thomas (#19-27)	9.00
(3)	Frank Thomas (Promo card.)	12.00
(4)	Don Mattingly (#28-36)	12.50
(4)	Don Mattingly (Promo card.)	15.00
(5)	Ken Griffey Jr. (#37-45)	12.50
(5)	Ken Griffey Jr. (Promo card.)	15.00
(6)	David Justice (#46-54)	4.50
(6)	David Justice (Promo card.)	6.00
(7)	Ryne Sandberg (#55-63)	9.00
(7)	Ryne Sandberg (Promo card.)	12.00
(8)	Darryl Strawberry (#64-68, 15-18)	4.50
(8)	Darryl Strawberry (Promo card.)	6.00
(9)	Cal Ripken Jr. (#73-81)	12.50
(9)	Cal Ripken Jr. (Promo card.)	15.00
(10)	Bo Jackson (#82-90)	4.50
(10)	Bo Jackson (Promo card.)	6.00
(11)	Jose Canseco (#91-99)	7.50
(11)	Jose Canseco (Promo card.)	10.00
(12)	Roger Clemens (#100-108)	9.00
(12)	Roger Clemens (Promo card.)	12.00

Platinum Edition

A dozen established stars are featured in the '92 Star Platinum issue, each in nine-card sets, contiguously numbered. One thousand sets of each player were issued, along with 200 promo cards. The cards are listed here in alphabetical order. Single cards are not listed because the player sets are not often broken up for individual sales.

		NM/M
Complete Set (108):		50.00
Common Player Set:		2.50
Complete Promo Set (12):		65.00
Common Promo Card:		3.00
(1)	Jeff Bagwell (#55-63)	5.00
(1)	Jeff Bagwell (Promo card.)	6.00
(2)	Jose Canseco (#73-81)	5.00
(2)	Jose Canseco (Promo card.)	6.50
(3)	Will Clark (#100-108)	5.00
(3)	Will Clark (Promo card.)	6.50
(4)	Roger Clemens (#91-99)	5.00
(4)	Roger Clemens (Promo card.)	6.50
(5)	Ken Griffey Jr. (#37-45)	7.50
(5)	Ken Griffey Jr. (Promo card.)	10.00
(6)	Bo Jackson (#28-36)	2.50
(6)	Bo Jackson (Promo card.)	3.00
(7)	David Justice (#10-18)	2.50
(7)	David Justice (Promo card.)	3.00
(8)	Don Mattingly (#64-72)	7.50
(8)	Don Mattingly (Promo card.)	10.00
(9)	Cal Ripken Jr. (#46-54)	7.50
(9)	Cal Ripken Jr. (Promo card.)	10.00
(10)	Nolan Ryan (#82-90)	7.50
(10)	Nolan Ryan (Promo card.)	10.00
(11)	Ryne Sandberg (#1-9)	5.00
(11)	Ryne Sandberg (Promo card.)	6.50
(12)	Frank Thomas (#19-27)	6.00
(12)	Frank Thomas (Promo card.)	8.00

Rookie Guild

Each of the four players in the '92 Rookie Guild issue is represented by an 11-card set, a promo card and a gold preview card. The first 10 cards in each player's set have blue borders, while the last card has white borders. Cards are seldom available as singles since the sets are rarely broken up.

	NM/M
Complete Set (44):	6.00
Complete Promo Set:	8.00

ROOKIE GUILD '92

LOS ANGELES — Ad Card — ERIC KARROS

		NM/M
Complete Preview Set:		12.00
1-11	Reggie Sanders	1.50
	Reggie Sanders (Promo card.)	2.00
	Reggie Sanders (Gold preview.)	3.00
12-22	Phil Plantier	1.50
	Phil Plantier (Promo card.)	2.00
	Phil Plantier (Gold preview.)	3.00
23-33	Dean Palmer	1.50
	Dean Palmer (Promo card.)	2.00
	Dean Palmer (Gold preview.)	3.00
34-44	Eric Karros	1.50
	Eric Karros (Promo card.)	2.00
	Eric Karros (Gold preview.)	3.00
	Eric Karros (Ad card.)	3.00

Silver Edition

Nearly the same line-up as found in other special edition Star nine-card player sets is found in the silver version. Announced production was 1,000 sets of each player along with 200 promo cards. The cards are listed here in alphabetical order. Single cards are not listed because the player sets are not often broken up for individual sales.

		NM/M
Complete Set (108):		40.00
Common Player Set:		3.00
Complete Promo Set (12):		55.00
Common Promo Card:		4.00
(1)	Jeff Bagwell (#46-54)	4.50
(1)	Jeff Bagwell (Promo card.)	6.00
(2)	Jose Canseco (#64-72)	4.50
(2)	Jose Canseco (Promo card.)	5.00
(3)	Will Clark (#1-9)	4.50
(3)	Will Clark (Promo card.)	4.00
(4)	Ken Griffey Jr. (#28-36)	6.00
(4)	Ken Griffey Jr. (Promo card.)	8.00
(5)	Bo Jackson (#37-45)	3.00
(5)	Bo Jackson (Promo card.)	4.00
(6)	David Justice (#19-27)	3.00
(6)	David Justice (Promo card.)	4.00
(7)	Don Mattingly (#100-108)	6.00
(7)	Don Mattingly (Promo card.)	8.00
(8)	Cal Ripken Jr. (#82-90)	6.00
(8)	Cal Ripken Jr. (Promo card.)	8.00
(9)	Nolan Ryan (#73-81)	6.00
(9)	Nolan Ryan (Promo card.)	8.00
(10)	Ryne Sandberg (#10-18)	6.00
(10)	Ryne Sandberg (Promo card.)	7.50
(11)	Darryl Strawberry (#91-99)	3.00
(11)	Darryl Strawberry (Promo card.)	4.00
(12)	Frank Thomas (#55-63)	5.00
(12)	Frank Thomas (Promo card.)	6.00

Stellar Edition

Among the scarcer of Star's 1992 single-player, nine-card sets, the Stellar Edition was produced in an issue of 500 sets and 100 promo cards of each player, contiguously numbered. The cards are listed here in alphabetical order. Single cards are not listed because the player sets are not often broken up for individual sales.

		NM/M
Complete Set (108):		65.00
Common Player Set:		4.50
Complete Promo Set (12):		90.00
Common Promo Card:		6.00
(1)	Jeff Bagwell (#19-27)	6.00

---

(1)	Jeff Bagwell (Promo card.)	10.00
(2)	Jose Canseco (#100-108)	7.50
(2)	Jose Canseco (Promo card.)	7.50
(3)	Will Clark (#37-45)	6.00
(3)	Will Clark (Promo card.)	6.00
(4)	Roger Clemens (#10-18)	7.50
(4)	Roger Clemens (Promo card.)	10.00
(5)	Ken Griffey Jr. (#55-63)	7.50
(5)	Ken Griffey Jr. (Promo card.)	12.00
(6)	Bo Jackson (#73-81)	4.50
(6)	Bo Jackson (Promo card.)	6.00
(7)	David Justice (#64-72)	4.50
(7)	David Justice (Promo card.)	6.00
(8)	Don Mattingly (#91-99)	7.50
(8)	Don Mattingly (Promo card.)	12.00
(9)	Cal Ripken Jr. (#46-54)	9.00
(9)	Cal Ripken Jr. (Promo card.)	12.00
(10)	Nolan Ryan (#82-90)	9.00
(10)	Nolan Ryan (Promo card.)	12.00
(11)	Ryne Sandberg (#28-36)	7.50
(11)	Ryne Sandberg (Promo card.)	10.00
(12)	Frank Thomas (#1-9)	7.50
(12)	Frank Thomas (Promo card.)	10.00

The Kid

This five-card set was reportedly produced in an edition of 1,000 as a value-added with Star's porcelain statue of Ken Griffey, Jr. One card set was given with the purchase of five statues at $125 each. No promo cards or glossy version were issued.

		NM/M
Complete Set (5):		50.00
1-5	Ken Griffey Jr.	10.00

1993 Star '93 Andy Benes

STAR '93 — ANDY BENES

It is unknown whether the usual 11-card set was produced for this continuation of the Star single-player series, or whether this represents a promotional card. In format similar to the Star '92 issues, the card has a red top border which morphs to yellow at bottom. Back repeats a detail of the front photo and has career stats printed in red on a yellow background. There is a 1993 copyright date, but no card number. The card does not have the high-gloss plastic coating found on the earlier series.

	NM/M
Andy Benes	2.00
Andy Benes (Auto. w/COA.)	3.00

1995 Star Cal Ripken, Jr.

Cal, Ripken, Jr. — They Pinch hit for Cal

A major design fault apparently prevented this issue from being widely circulated. Each of the 80 cards in the boxed set has an extraneous comma between "Cal" and "Ripken." That fatal flaw aside, the set does a creditable job of detailing Ripken's major league career through his record 2,131st consecutive game in 1995. Glossy card fronts have color photos at center with orange and brown graphic highlights. Each card has him identified as "Cal, Ripken, Jr." at bottom, below which there is a card title. Backs have a baseball at center with career highlights, stats, personal information or trivia. The name error is repeated in orange script at bottom. The set was fully licensed by Ripken and Major League Baseball.

	NM/M
Complete Boxed Set (80):	10.00
Common Card:	.25

1989 Starline Prototypes

MARK GRACE

Prior to its first major baseball card issue, Starline produced six variations of a prototype issue. The seven-card sets feature game-action photos on the front, surrounded by colorful borders and with a combination of up to three logos in the bottom border. Cards were produced with just the Starline logo, with the Starline and Coca-Cola logos and with the card company and soft drink logos in conjunction with those of McDonald's, 7-11, Burger King or Dominos pizza. Backs repeat the logos at bottom, along with that of Major League Baseball. At top is a color player photo, along with biographical data, complete major and minor league stats and career highlights. The unnumbered cards are checklisted here alphabetically.

		NM/M
Complete Set (7):		45.00
Common Player:		6.00
(1)	Eric Davis	6.00
(2)	Mark Grace	6.00
(3)	Tony Gwynn	10.00
(4)	Gregg Jefferies	6.00
(5)	Don Mattingly	12.00
(6)	Mark McGwire	13.50
(7)	Darryl Strawberry	6.00

1990 Starline

MARK GRACE

Five-card cello packs of this Coca-Cola sponsored issue were given away with the purchase of dinner and a soft drink at Long John Silver fish restaurants. Cards feature game-action photos on front, bordered in team colors. Backs repeat the team-color scheme and feature a portrait photo along with

---

major league stats and career highlights. Most of the players had two or more cards in the 40-card issue. A header card in each pack offered a 2' x 3' poster of one of 18 players in set for $3.99.

		NM/M
Complete Set (40):		3.00
Common Player:		.10
1	Don Mattingly	.40
2	Mark Grace	.10
3	Eric Davis	.10
4	Tony Gwynn	.30
5	Bobby Bonilla	.10
6	Wade Boggs	.30
7	Frank Viola	.10
8	Ruben Sierra	.10
9	Mark McGwire	.50
10	Alan Trammell	.10
11	Mark McGwire	.50
12	Gregg Jefferies	.10
13	Nolan Ryan	.60
14	John Smoltz	.10
15	Glenn Davis	.10
16	Mark Grace	.10
17	Wade Boggs	.30
18	Frank Viola	.10
19	Bret Saberhagen	.10
20	Chris Sabo	.10
21	Darryl Strawberry	.10
22	Wade Boggs	.30
23	Tim Raines	.10
24	Alan Trammell	.10
25	Chris Sabo	.10
26	Nolan Ryan	.60
27	Mark McGwire	.50
28	Don Mattingly	.40
29	Tony Gwynn	.10
30	Glenn Davis	.10
31	Bobby Bonilla	.10
32	Gregg Jefferies	.10
33	Ruben Sierra	.10
34	John Smoltz	.10
35	Don Mattingly	.40
36	Bret Saberhagen	.10
37	Darryl Strawberry	.10
38	Eric Davis	.10
39	Tim Raines	.10
40	Mark Grace	.10
---	Header Card/Poster Offer	.05

1990 Starline Americana

Americana — Babe Ruth

Several baseball players were among the subjects featured in a set of "Americana" quiz cards. The 2-1/2" x 3-1/2" cards are printed in full-color front and back. Backs repeat the front photo in miniature and provide "Historical Highlights" along with a trivia question and the answer to the question on another card.

		NM/M
237	Jackie Robinson	2.00
245	Babe Ruth	2.00

1991 Starline Prototypes

GEORGE BELL

These sample cards were produced for submission to baseball licensing authorities for approval, and to prospective sponsors. Only 60 of each card were reported produced. Card fronts have color action photos and a team logo set against a black background. The player's name appears in white and red at top and along the side. Backs have a smaller player photo at upper-right. All of the prototypes have back stats and biography of Nolan Ryan, with a gray diagonal "PROTOTYPE" across them. The Starline, MLB and Players' Associations logo appear across the bottom.

		NM/M
Complete Set (5):		50.00
Common Player:		10.00
(1)	George Bell	10.00
(2)	Bobby Bonilla	10.00
(3)	Roger Clemens	20.00
(4)	Tim Raines	10.00
(5)	Darryl Strawberry	10.00

1983 Starliner Stickers

This unauthorized collector's issue is based on 16 of the cards issued by Dexter Press in 1967 as Coca-Cola premiums. In July 1983, a Midwestern card dealer produced these stickers by reprinting the 5-1/2" x 7" Dexter Press cards in 2-7/16" x 3-1/4" format and eliminating the white border. The stickers can be found with either white ("Mactac Starliner") or tan ("Tuchdown Splitless") paper on back. By the early 1990s, the story of the true origins of these stickers had been largely forgotten within the hobby and some dealers were charging between $10-50 apiece for them. The unnumbered stickers are checklisted here in alphabetical order. Production of the white-back stickers was reported at 2,000 sets, with Mantle and Rose double printed.

		NM/M
Complete Set (16):		40.00
Common Player:		1.00
(1)	Hank Aaron	7.50
(2)	Ernie Banks	1.50
(3)	Roberto Clemente	10.00
(4)	Rocky Colavito	1.00
(5)	Al Kaline	1.50
(6)	Harmon Killebrew	1.00
(7)	Mickey Mantle/DP	20.00
(8)	Willie Mays	7.50
(9)	Willie McCovey	1.00
(10)	Joe Morgan	1.00
(11)	Jim Palmer	1.00
(12)	Brooks Robinson	1.00
(13)	Frank Robinson	1.00
(14)	Pete Rose/DP	7.50
(15)	Willie Stargell	1.00
(16)	Carl Yastrzemski	1.50

1988 Starting Lineup Talking Baseball

Measuring 2-5/8" x 3", these cards were part of the Starting Lineup Talking Baseball game produced by Kenner Parker Toys Inc. The electronic game, with a computer memory and keyboard to respond to a particular baseball game situation, retailed for more than $100. However, several hobby dealers sold the cards separately from the game. The set includes seven instruction cards that do not picture players.

		NM/M
Complete Set (42):		25.00
Common Player:		.25
11a	Terry Kennedy	.25
11b	Gary Carter	1.25
12a	Carlton Fisk	1.25
12b	Steve Sax	.25
13a	Eddie Murray	1.25
13b	Jack Clark	.25
14a	Don Mattingly	2.50
14b	Keith Hernandez	.25
15a	Willie Randolph	.25
15b	Buddy Bell	.25
16a	Cal Ripken	4.00
16b	Ryne Sandberg	2.00
17a	Lou Whitaker	.25
17b	Ozzie Smith	2.00
18a	Wade Boggs	2.00
18b	Dale Murphy	.75
19a	George Brett	2.50
19b	Mike Schmidt	2.50
20a	Alan Trammell	.25
20b	Eric Davis	.25
21a	Kirby Puckett	2.00
21b	Tony Gwynn	2.00
22a	George Bell	.25
22b	Darryl Strawberry	.25
23a	Rickey Henderson	1.25
23b	Tim Raines	.25
24a	Dave Winfield	1.25
24b	Andre Dawson	.75
25a	Jack Morris	.25
25b	Mike Scott	.25
26a	Robin Yount	1.25
26b	Jody Davis	.25
27a	Roger Clemens	2.50
27b	Todd Worrell	.25
28a	Bret Saberhagen	.25
28b	Fernando Valenzuela	.25
29a	Dave Righetti	.25
29b	Dwight Gooden	.25
30a	Dan Quisenberry	.25
30b	Nolan Ryan	4.00
---	American League Checklist	.25
---	National League Checklist	.25

Team Sets

Similar in format to the cards issued with the Parker Brothers game, these accessory cards could be purchased in groups of three team sets. The team-set cards share the format (2-5/8" x 3") and design of the boxed-set cards, but differ in that the player portraits are presented as colored drawings rather than photos. Because the issue was licensed by the Players Union, and not MLB, the caps have no team logos. Backs are in black-and-white. Each team set has 20 player cards (the Indians have only 19) plus a batting order/checklist card. Several players appear in more than one set as a result of trades. The cards are checklisted here alphabetically within team.

		NM/M
Complete Set (545):		60.00
Common Player:		.10
Atlanta Braves Team Set:		4.00
(1)	Jim Acker	.10
(2)	Paul Assenmacher	.10
(3)	Jeff Blauser	.10
(4)	Jeff Dedmon	.10
(5)	Ron Gant	.10
(6)	Tom Glavine	.75
(7)	Ken Griffey	.10
(8)	Albert Hall	.10
(9)	Glenn Hubbard	.10
(10)	Dion James	.10
(11)	Rick Mahler	.10
(12)	Dale Murphy	1.00
(13)	Ken Oberkfell	.10
(14)	Gerald Perry	.10
(15)	Gary Roenicke	.10
(16)	Paul Runge	.10
(17)	Ted Simmons	.10
(18)	Pete Smith	.10
(19)	Andres Thomas	.10
(20)	Ozzie Virgil	.10
(21)	Batting Order/Checklist	.05
Baltimore Orioles Team Set:		12.00
(1)	Eric Bell	.10
(2)	Mike Boddicker	.10
(3)	Jim Dwyer	.10
(4)	Ken Gerhart	.10
(5)	Rene Gonzalez	.10
(6)	Terry Kennedy	.10
(7)	Ray Knight	.10
(8)	Lee Lacy	.10
(9)	Fred Lynn	.10
(10)	Eddie Murray	3.00
(11)	Tom Niedenfuer	.10
(12)	Billy Ripkin (Ripken)	.10
(13)	Cal Ripken Jr.	7.50
(14)	Dave Schmidt	.10
(15)	Larry Sheets	.10
(16)	Pete Stanicek	.10
(17)	Mark Thurmond	.10
(18)	Ron Washington	.10
(19)	Mark Williamson	.10
(20)	Mike Young	.10
(21)	Batting Order/Checklist	.05
Boston Red Sox Team Set:		7.50
(1)	Marty Barrett	.10
(2)	Todd Benzinger	.10
(3)	Wade Boggs	4.00
(4)	Dennis Boyd	.10
(5)	Ellis Burks	.10
(6)	Roger Clemens	4.50
(7)	Dwight Evans	.10
(8)	Wes Gardner	.10
(9)	Rich Gedman	.10
(10)	Mike Greenwell	.10
(11)	Sam Horn	.10
(12)	Bruce Hurst	.10
(13)	John Marzano	.10
(14)	Spike Owen	.10
(15)	Jody Reed	.10
(16)	Jim Rice	.35
(17)	Ed Romero	.10
(18)	Kevin Romine	.10
(19)	Lee Smith	.10
(20)	Bob Stanley	.10
(21)	Batting Order/Checklist	.05
California Angels Team Set:		2.25
(1)	Tony Armas	.10
(2)	Bob Boone	.10
(3)	Bill Buckner	.10
(4)	DeWayne Buice	.10
(5)	Brian Downing	.10
(6)	Chuck Finley	.10
(7)	Willie Fraser	.10
(8)	George Hendrick	.10
(9)	Jack Howell	.10
(10)	Ruppert Jones	.10
(11)	Wally Joyner	.10
(12)	Kirk McCaskill	.10
(13)	Mark McLemore	.10
(14)	Darrell Miller	.10
(15)	Greg Minton	.10
(16)	Gary Pettis	.10
(17)	Johnny Ray	.10
(18)	Dick Schofield	.10
(19)	Devon White	.10
(20)	Mike Witt	.10
(21)	Batting Order/Checklist	.05
Chicago Cubs Team Set:		6.00
(1)	Jody Davis	.10
(2)	Andre Dawson	.35
(3)	Bob Dernier	.10
(4)	Frank DiPino	.10
(5)	Shawon Dunston	.10
(6)	Leon Durham	.10
(7)	Dave Martinez	.10
(8)	Keith Moreland	.10
(9)	Jamie Moyer	.10
(10)	Jerry Mumphrey	.10
(11)	Paul Noce	.10
(12)	Rafael Palmeiro	2.50
(13)	Luis Quinones	.10
(14)	Ryne Sandberg	4.00
(15)	Scott Sanderson	.10
(16)	Calvin Schiraldi	.10
(17)	Lee Smith	.10
(18)	Jim Sundberg	.10
(19)	Rick Sutcliffe	.10
(20)	Manny Trillo	.10
(21)	Batting Order/Checklist	.05
Chicago White Sox Team Set:		4.00
(1)	Harold Baines	.10
(2)	Floyd Bannister	.10
(3)	Daryl Boston	.10
(4)	Ivan Calderon	.10
(5)	Jose DeLeon	.10
(6)	Rich Dotson	.10
(7)	Carlton Fisk	3.00
(8)	Ozzie Guillen	.10
(9)	Jerry Hairston Sr.	.10
(10)	Donnie Hill	.10
(11)	Dave LaPoint	.10
(12)	Steve Lyons	.10
(13)	Fred Manrique	.10
(14)	Dan Pasqua	.10
(15)	Gary Redus	.10
(16)	Mark Salas	.10
(17)	Ray Searage	.10
(18)	Bobby Thigpen	.10
(19)	Greg Walker	.10
(20)	Ken Williams	.10
(21)	Batting Order/Checklist	.05
Cincinnati Reds Team Set:		2.25
(1)	Buddy Bell	.10
(2)	Tom Browning	.10
(3)	Dave Collins	.10
(4)	Dave Concepcion	.10
(5)	Kal Daniels	.10
(6)	Eric Davis	.10
(7)	Bo Diaz	.10
(8)	Nick Esasky	.10
(9)	John Franco	.10
(10)	Terry Francona	.10
(11)	Tracy Jones	.10
(12)	Barry Larkin	.10
(13)	Rob Murphy	.10
(14)	Paul O'Neill	.10
(15)	Dave Parker	.10
(16)	Ted Power	.10
(17)	Dennis Rasmussen	.10
(18)	Kurt Stillwell	.10
(19)	Jeff Treadway	.10
(20)	Frank Williams	.10
(21)	Batting Order/Checklist	.05
Cleveland Indians Team Set:		2.25
(1)	Andy Allanson	.10
(2)	Scott Bailes	.10
(3)	Chris Bando	.10
(4)	Jay Bell	.10
(5)	Brett Butler	.10
(6)	Tom Candiotti	.10
(7)	Joe Carter	.10
(8)	Carmen Castillo	.10
(9)	Dave Clark	.10
(10)	John Farrell	.10
(11)	Julio Franco	.10
(12)	Mel Hall	.10
(13)	Tom Hinzo	.10
(14)	Brook Jacoby	.10
(15)	Doug Jones	.10
(16)	Junior Noboa	.10
(17)	Ken Schrom	.10
(18)	Cory Snyder	.10
(19)	Pat Tabler	.10
(20)	Batting Order/Checklist	.05
Detroit Tigers Team Set:		2.25
(1)	Doyle Alexander	.10
(2)	Dave Bergman	.10
(3)	Tom Brookens	.10
(4)	Darrell Evans	.10
(5)	Kirk Gibson	.10
(6)	Mike Heath	.10
(7)	Mike Henneman	.10
(8)	Willie Hernandez	.10
(9)	Larry Herndon	.10
(10)	Eric King	.10
(11)	Ray Knight	.10
(12)	Chet Lemon	.10
(13)	Bill Madlock	.10
(14)	Jack Morris	.10
(15)	Jim Morrison	.10
(16)	Matt Nokes	.10
(17)	Pat Sheridan	.10
(18)	Frank Tanana	.10
(19)	Alan Trammell	.10
(20)	Lou Whitaker	.10
(21)	Batting Order/Checklist	.05
Houston Astros Team Set:		6.00
(1)	Juan Agosto	.10
(2)	Larry Anderson	.10
(3)	Alan Ashby	.10
(4)	Kevin Bass	.10
(5)	Ken Caminiti	.10
(6)	Jose Cruz	.10
(7)	Danny Darwin	.10
(8)	Glenn Davis	.10
(9)	Bill Doran	.10
(10)	Billy Hatcher	.10
(11)	Jim Pankovits	.10
(12)	Terry Puhl	.10
(13)	Rafael Ramirez	.10
(14)	Craig Reynolds	.10
(15)	Nolan Ryan	7.50
(16)	Mike Scott	.10
(17)	Dave Smith	.10
(18)	Marc Sullivan	.10
(19)	Dennis Walling	.10
(20)	Eric Young	.10
(21)	Batting Order/Checklist	.05
Kansas City Royals Team Set:		6.00
(1)	Steve Balboni	.10
(2)	George Brett	4.50
(3)	Jim Eisenreich	.10
(4)	Gene Garber	.10
(5)	Jerry Don Gleaton	.10
(6)	Mark Gubicza	.10
(7)	Bo Jackson	.50
(8)	Charlie Leibrandt	.10
(9)	Mike Macfarlane	.10
(10)	Larry Owen	.10
(11)	Bill Pecota	.10
(12)	Jamie Quirk	.10
(13)	Dan Quisenberry	.10
(14)	Bret Saberhagen	.10
(15)	Kevin Seitzer	.10
(16)	Kurt Stillwell	.10
(17)	Danny Tartabull	.10
(18)	Gary Thurman	.10
(19)	Frank White	.10
(20)	Willie Wilson	.10
(21)	Batting Order/Checklist	.05
Los Angeles Dodgers Team Set:		2.50
(1)	Dave Anderson	.10
(2)	Mike Davis	.10
(3)	Mariano Duncan	.10
(4)	Kirk Gibson	.10
(5)	Alfredo Griffin	.10
(6)	Pedro Guerrero	.10
(7)	Mickey Hatcher	.10
(8)	Orel Hershiser	.10
(9)	Glenn Hoffman	.10
(10)	Brian Holton	.10
(11)	Mike Marshall	.10
(12)	Jesse Orosco	.10
(13)	Alejandro Pena	.10
(14)	Steve Sax	.10
(15)	Mike Scioscia	.10
(16)	John Shelby	.10
(17)	Franklin Stubbs	.10
(18)	Don Sutton	2.00
(19)	Alex Trevino	.10
(20)	Fernando Valenzuela	.10
(21)	Batting Order/Checklist	.05
Milwaukee Brewers Team Set:		6.00
(1)	Chris Bosio	.10
(2)	Glenn Braggs	.10
(3)	Greg Brock	.10
(4)	Juan Castillo	.10
(5)	Chuck Crim	.10
(6)	Rob Deer	.10
(7)	Mike Felder	.10
(8)	Jim Gantner	.10
(9)	Teddy Higuera	.10
(10)	Steve Kiefer	.10
(11)	Paul Molitor	3.00
(12)	Juan Nieves	.10
(13)	Dan Plesac	.10
(14)	Ernie Riles	.10
(15)	Billy Jo Robidoux	.10
(16)	Bill Schroeder	.10
(17)	B.J. Surhoff	.10
(18)	Dale Sveum	.10
(19)	Bill Wegman	.10
(20)	Robin Yount	3.00
(21)	Batting Order/Checklist	.05
Minnesota Twins Team Set:		6.00
(1)	Don Baylor	.10
(2)	Juan Berenguer	.10
(3)	Bert Blyleven	.10
(4)	Tom Brunansky	.10
(5)	Randy Bush	.10
(6)	Mark Davidson	.10
(7)	Gary Gaetti	.10
(8)	Greg Gagne	.10
(9)	Dan Gladden	.10
(10)	Kent Hrbek	.10
(11)	Gene Larkin	.10
(12)	Tim Laudner	.10
(13)	Steve Lombardozzi	.10
(14)	Al Newman	.10
(15)	Kirby Puckett	4.00
(16)	Jeff Reardon	.10
(17)	Dan Schatzeder	.10
(18)	Roy Smalley	.10
(19)	Les Straker	.10
(20)	Frank Viola	.10
(21)	Batting Order/Checklist	.05
Montreal Expos Team Set:		9.00
(1)	Hubie Brooks	.10
(2)	Tim Burke	.10
(3)	Casey Candaele	.10
(4)	Mike Fitzgerald	.10
(5)	Tom Foley	.10
(6)	Andres Galarraga	.10
(7)	Neal Heaton	.10
(8)	Randy Johnson	7.50
(9)	Vance Law	.10
(10)	Bob McClure	.10
(11)	Andy McGaffigan	.10
(12)	Dennis Powell	.10
(13)	Tim Raines	.10
(14)	Jeff Reed	.10
(15)	Luis Rivera	.10
(16)	Bryn Smith	.10
(17)	Tim Wallach	.10
(18)	Mitch Webster	.10
(19)	Herm Winningham	.10
(20)	Floyd Youmans	.10
(21)	Batting Order/Checklist	.05
New York Mets Team Issue:		4.00
(1)	Bill Almon	.10
(2)	Wally Backman	.10
(3)	Gary Carter	3.00
(4)	David Cone	.10
(5)	Ron Darling	.10
(6)	Lenny Dykstra	.10
(7)	Sid Fernandez	.10
(8)	Dwight Gooden	.10
(9)	Keith Hernandez	.10
(10)	Howard Johnson	.10
(11)	Barry Lyons	.10
(12)	Dave Magadan	.10
(13)	Lee Mazzilli	.10
(14)	Roger McDowell	.10
(15)	Kevin McReynolds	.10
(16)	Jesse Orosco	.10
(17)	Rafael Santana	.10
(18)	Darryl Strawberry	.10
(19)	Tim Teufel	.10
(20)	Mookie Wilson	.10
(21)	Batting Order/Checklist	.05
New York Yankees Team Set:		9.00
(1)	Rick Cerone	.10
(2)	Jack Clark	.10
(3)	Pat Clements	.10
(4)	Mike Easler	.10
(5)	Ron Guidry	.10
(6)	Rickey Henderson	3.00
(7)	Tommy John	.10
(8)	Don Mattingly	4.50
(9)	Bobby Meacham	.10
(10)	Mike Pagliarulo	.10
(11)	Willie Randolph	.10
(12)	Rick Rhoden	.10
(13)	Dave Righetti	.10
(14)	Jerry Royster	.10
(15)	Don Slaught	.10
(16)	Tim Stoddard	.10
(17)	Wayne Tolleson	.10
(18)	Gary Ward	.10
(19)	Claudell Washington	.10
(20)	Dave Winfield	3.00
(21)	Batting Order/Checklist	.05
Oakland A's Team Set:		15.00
(1)	Tony Bernazard	.10
(2)	Jose Canseco	1.50
(3)	Mike Davis	.10
(4)	Dennis Eckersley	2.00
(5)	Mike Gallego	.10
(6)	Alfredo Griffin	.10
(7)	Rickey Henderson	3.00
(8)	Reggie Jackson	4.50
(9)	Carney Lansford	.10
(10)	Mark McGwire	6.00
(11)	Gene Nelson	.10
(12)	Steve Ontiveros	.10
(13)	Dave Parker	.10
(14)	Tony Phillips	.10
(15)	Luis Polonia	.10
(16)	Terry Steinbach	.10
(17)	Dave Stewart	.10
(18)	Mickey Tettleton	.10
(19)	Bob Welch	.10
(20)	Curt Young	.10
(21)	Batting Order/Checklist	.05
Philadelphia Phillies Team Set:		5.00
(1)	Luis Aguayo	.10
(2)	Steve Bedrosian	.10
(3)	Phil Bradley	.10
(4)	Jeff Calhoun	.10
(5)	Don Carman	.10
(6)	Darren Daulton	.10
(7)	Bob Dernier	.10
(8)	Greg Gross	.10
(9)	Von Hayes	.10
(10)	Chris James	.10
(11)	Steve Jeltz	.10
(12)	Lance Parrish	.10
(13)	Shane Rawley	.10
(14)	Bruce Ruffin	.10
(15)	Juan Samuel	.10
(16)	Mike Schmidt	4.50
(17)	Rick Schu	.10
(18)	Kent Tekulve	.10
(19)	Milt Thompson	.10
(20)	Glenn Wilson	.10
(21)	Batting Order/Checklist	.05
Pittsburgh Pirates Team Set:		9.00
(1)	Rafael Belliard	.10
(2)	Barry Bonds	7.50
(3)	Bobby Bonilla	.10
(4)	Sid Bream	.10
(5)	John Cangelosi	.10
(6)	Darnell Coles	.10
(7)	Mike Diaz	.10
(8)	Doug Drabek	.10
(9)	Mike Dunne	.10
(10)	Felix Fermin	.10
(11)	Brian Fisher	.10
(12)	Jim Gott	.10
(13)	Mike LaValliere	.10
(14)	Jose Lind	.10
(15)	Junior Ortiz	.10
(16)	Al Pedreque	.10
(17)	R.J. Reynolds	.10
(18)	Jeff Robinson	.10
(19)	John Smiley	.10
(20)	Andy Van Slyke	.10
(21)	Batting Order/Checklist	.05
San Diego Padres Team Set:		5.00
(1)	Shawn Abner	.10
(2)	Roberto Alomar	.25
(3)	Bobby Brown	.10
(4)	Joey Cora	.10
(5)	Mark Davis	.10
(6)	Tim Flannery	.10
(7)	Goose Gossage	.10
(8)	Mark Grant	.10
(9)	Tony Gwynn	4.00
(10)	Stan Jefferson	.10
(11)	John Kruk	.10
(12)	Shane Mack	.10
(13)	Carmelo Martinez	.10
(14)	Lance McCullers	.10
(15)	Randy Ready	.10
(16)	Benito Santiago	.10
(17)	Eric Show	.10
(18)	Garry Templeton	.10
(19)	Ed Whitson	.10
(20)	Marvell Wynne	.10
(21)	Batting Order/Checklist	.05
San Francisco Giants Team Set:		2.50
(1)	Mike Aldrete	.10
(2)	Bob Brenly	.10
(3)	Brett Butler	.10
(4)	Will Clark	.10
(5)	Chili Davis	.10
(6)	Dave Dravecky	.10
(7)	Scott Garrelts	.10
(8)	Atlee Hammaker	.10
(9)	Craig Lefferts	.10
(10)	Jeffrey Leonard	.10
(11)	Candy Maldonado	.10
(12)	Bob Melvin	.10
(13)	Kevin Mitchell	.10
(14)	Rick Reuschel	.10
(15)	Don Robinson	.10
(16)	Chris Speier	.10
(17)	Chris Spielman	.10
(18)	Robby Thompson	.10
(19)	Jose Uribe	.10
(20)	Matt Williams	.10
(21)	Batting Order/Checklist	.05
Seattle Mariners Team Set:		2.25
(1)	Phil Bradley	.10
(2)	Scott Bradley	.10
(3)	Mickey Brantley	.10
(4)	Mike Campbell	.10
(5)	Henry Cotto	.10
(6)	Alvin Davis	.10
(7)	Mike Kingery	.10
(8)	Mark Langston	.10
(9)	Mike Moore	.10
(10)	John Moses	.10
(11)	Donell Nixon	.10
(12)	Ed Nunez	.10
(13)	Ken Phelps	.10
(14)	Jim Presley	.10
(15)	Rey Quinones	.10

(16)	Jerry Reed	.10
(17)	Harold Reynolds	.10
(18)	Dave Valle	.10
(19)	Bill Wilkinson	.10
(20)	Glenn Wilson	.10
(21)	Batting Order/Checklist	.05
St. Louis Cardinals Team Set:		**4.50**
(1)	Greg Booker	.10
(2)	Jack Clark	.10
(3)	Vince Coleman	.10
(4)	Danny Cox	.10
(5)	Ken Dayley	.10
(6)	Curt Ford	.10
(7)	Tom Herr	.10
(8)	Bob Horner	.10
(9)	Ricky Horton	.10
(10)	Lance Johnson	.10
(11)	Steve Lake	.10
(12)	Jim Lindeman	.10
(13)	Greg Mathews	.10
(14)	Willie McGee	.10
(15)	Jose Oquendo	.10
(16)	Tony Pena	.10
(17)	Terry Pendleton	.10
(18)	Ozzie Smith	4.00
(19)	John Tudor	.10
(20)	Todd Worrell	.10
(21)	Batting Order/Checklist	.05
Texas Rangers Team Set:		**2.25**
(1)	Jerry Browne	.10
(2)	Bob Brower	.10
(3)	Steve Buechele	.10
(4)	Scott Fletcher	.10
(5)	Juan Guzman	.10
(6)	Charlie Hough	.10
(7)	Pete Incaviglia	.10
(8)	Oddibe McDowell	.10
(9)	Dale Mohorcic	.10
(10)	Pete O'Brien	.10
(11)	Tom O'Malley	.10
(12)	Larry Parrish	.10
(13)	Geno Petralli	.10
(14)	Jeff Russell	.10
(15)	Ruben Sierra	.10
(16)	Don Slaught	.10
(17)	Mike Stanley	.10
(18)	Curt Wilkerson	.10
(19)	Mitch Williams	.10
(20)	Bobby Witt	.10
(21)	Batting Order/Checklist	.05
Toronto Blue Jays Team Set:		**2.25**
(1)	Jesse Barfield	.10
(2)	George Bell	.10
(3)	Juan Beniquez	.10
(4)	Jim Clancy	.10
(5)	Mark Eichhorn	.10
(6)	Tony Fernandez	.10
(7)	Cecil Fielder	.10
(8)	Tom Henke	.10
(9)	Garth Iorg	.10
(10)	Jimmy Key	.10
(11)	Rick Leach	.10
(12)	Manny Lee	.10
(13)	Nelson Liriano	.10
(14)	Fred McGriff	.10
(15)	Lloyd Moseby	.10
(16)	Rance Mulliniks	.10
(17)	Jeff Musselman	.10
(18)	Dave Steib	.10
(19)	Willie Upshaw	.10
(20)	Ernie Whitt	.10
(21)	Batting Order/Checklist	.05

1995 Stouffer's Legends of Baseball

To promote its French bread frozen pizza, this Nestle's subsidiary issued a series of five three-dimensional cards featuring current and future Hall of Famers. The 2-1/2" x 3-1/2" cards have a die-cut action photo on front connected to a tab at the card top. When the tab is pulled, the player figure stands up. The back of the card has another player photo and a few career highlights. Because the promotion was licensed only by individuals, and not Major League Baseball, uniform and cap logos have been airbrushed off the photos.

	NM/M
Complete Set (6):	4.00
Common Player:	1.00

1	Yogi Berra	2.00
1a	Yogi Berra/Auto.	20.00
2	Gary Carter	1.50
3	Don Drysdale	2.00
4	Bob Feller	2.00
5	Willie Stargell	2.00

1983 Stuart Expos

AL OLIVER

This set of Montreal Expos players and coaches was issued by a Montreal area baking company for inclusion in packages of snack cakes. The 30 cards feature full-color player photos, with the player name, number and team logo also on the card fronts. The backs list brief player biographies in both English and French. Twenty-five players are pictured on the 2-1/2" x 3-1/2" cards.

		NM/M
Complete Set (30):		10.00
Common Player:		.25
1	Bill Virdon	.25
2	Woodie Fryman	.25
3	Vern Rapp	.25
4	Andre Dawson	2.00
5	Jeff Reardon	.35
6	Al Oliver	.50
7	Doug Flynn	.25
8	Gary Carter	5.00
9	Tim Raines	1.00
10	Steve Rogers	.25
11	Billy DeMars	.25
12	Tim Wallach	.25
13	Galen Cisco	.25
14	Terry Francona	.25
15	Bill Gullickson	.25
16	Ray Burris	.25
17	Scott Sanderson	.25
18	Warren Cromartie	.25
19	Jerry White	.25
20	Bobby Ramos	.25
21	Jim Wohlford	.25
22	Dan Schatzeder	.25
23	Charlie Lea	.25
24	Bryan Little	.25
25	Mel Wright	.25
26	Tim Blackwell	.25
27	Chris Speier	.25
28	Randy Lerch	.25
29	Bryn Smith	.25
30	Brad Mills	.25

1984 Stuart Expos

8 GARY CARTER

For the second year in a row, Stuart Cakes issued a full-color card set of the Montreal Expos. The 2-1/2" x 3-1/2" cards again list the player name and number along with the team and company logos on the card fronts. The backs are bilingual with biographical information in both English and French. The 40-card set was issued in two series. Card numbers 21-40, issued late in the summer, are more difficult to find than the first 20 cards. The 40 cards include players, the manager, coaches and team mascot.

	NM/M
Complete Set (40):	15.00
Common Player (1-20):	.25
Common Player (21-40):	.35

Album:		6.00
1	Youppi! (Mascot)	.25
2	Bill Virdon	.25
3	Billy DeMars	.25
4	Galen Cisco	.25
5	Russ Nixon	.25
6	Felipe Alou	.75
7	Dan Schatzeder	.25
8	Charlie Lea	.25
9	Bobby Ramos	.25
10	Bob James	.25
11	Andre Dawson	2.00
12	Gary Lucas	.25
13	Jeff Reardon	.35
14	Tim Wallach	.35
15	Gary Carter	5.00
16	Bill Gullickson	.25
17	Pete Rose	6.00
18	Terry Francona	.25
19	Steve Rogers	.25
20	Tim Raines	1.00
21	Bryn Smith	.25
22	Greg Harris	.35
23	David Palmer	.35
24	Jim Wohlford	.35
25	Miguel Dilone	.35
26	Mike Stenhouse	.35
27	Chris Speier	.35
28	Derrel Thomas	.35
29	Doug Flynn	.35
30	Bryan Little	.35
31	Argenis Salazar	.35
32	Mike Fuentes	.35
33	Joe Kerrigan	.35
34	Andy McGaffigan	.35
35	Fred Breining	.35
36	Expos 1983 All-Stars (Gary Carter, Andre Dawson, Tim Raines, Steve Rogers)	.75
37	Co-Players Of The Year (Andre Dawson, Tim Raines)	.75
38	Expos' Coaching Staff (Felipe Alou, Galen Cisco, Billy DeMars, Joe Kerrigan, Russ Nixon, Bill Virdon)	.35
39	Team Photo	.50
40	Checklist	.10

1987 Stuart

Joueurs étoiles • Super Stars

ROBBY THOMPSON
Les Géants de San Francisco
San Francisco Giants
2nd but / 2nd base

Twenty-eight four-part folding panels make up the 1987 Stuart Super Stars set, which was issued only in Canada. Three player cards and a sweepstakes entry form card comprise each panel. All 26 major league teams are included with the Montreal Expos and Toronto Blue Jays being represented twice. The cards, which are full color and measure 2-1/2" x 3-1/2", are written in both English and French. The card backs contain the player's previous year's statistics. All team insignias have been airbrushed away.

		NM/M
Complete Panel Set (28):		15.00
Complete Singles Set (84):		10.00
Common Panel:		.35
Common Single Player:		.05
Panel (New York Mets)		.60
1a	Gary Carter	.50
1b	Keith Hernandez	.05
1c	Darryl Strawberry	.05
Panel (Atlanta Braves)		.60
2a	Bruce Benedict	.05
2b	Ken Griffey	.05
2c	Dale Murphy	.25
Panel (Chicago Cubs)		.50
3a	Jody Davis	.05
3b	Andre Dawson	.35
3c	Leon Durham	.05
Panel (Cincinnati Reds)		.50
4a	Buddy Bell	.05
4b	Eric Davis	.05
4c	Dave Parker	.05
Panel (Houston Astros)		1.75
5a	Glenn Davis	.05
5b	Nolan Ryan	.75
5c	Mike Scott	.05
Panel (Los Angeles Dodgers)		.35
6a	Pedro Guerrero	.05
6b	Mike Marshall	.05
6c	Fernando Valenzuela	.05
Panel (Montreal Expos)		1.00
7a	Tim Raines	.50
7b	Tim Wallach	.10
7c	Mitch Webster	.10
Panel (Montreal Expos)		.75
8a	Hubie Brooks	.10
8b	Bryn Smith	.05
8c	Floyd Youmans	.10
Panel (Philadelphia Phillies)		1.25
9a	Shane Rawley	.05
9b	Juan Samuel	.05
9c	Mike Schmidt	.60
Panel (Pittsburgh Pirates)		.35
10a	Jim Morrison	.05
10b	Johnny Ray	.05
10c	R.J. Reynolds	.05
Panel (St. Louis Cardinals)		1.00
11a	Jack Clark	.05
11b	Vince Coleman	.05
11c	Ozzie Smith	.50
Panel (San Diego Padres)		1.00
12a	Steve Garvey	.15
12b	Tony Gwynn	.50
12c	John Kruk	.05
Panel (San Francisco Giants)		.35
13a	Chili Davis	.05
13b	Jeffrey Leonard	.05
13c	Robbie Thompson	.05
Panel (Baltimore Orioles)		2.50
14a	Fred Lynn	.05
14b	Eddie Murray	.05
14c	Cal Ripken, Jr.	1.00
Panel (Boston Red Sox)		1.75
15a	Don Baylor	.05
15b	Wade Boggs	.05
15c	Roger Clemens	.60
Panel (California Angels)		.40
16a	Doug DeCinces	.05
16b	Wally Joyner	.05
16c	Mike Witt	.05
Panel (Chicago White Sox)		.70
17a	Harold Baines	.05
17b	Carlton Fisk	.50
17c	Ozzie Guillen	.05
Panel (Cleveland Indians)		.35
18a	Joe Carter	.05
18b	Julio Franco	.05
18c	Pat Tabler	.05
Panel (Detroit Tigers)		.35
19a	Kirk Gibson	.05
19b	Jack Morris	.05
19c	Alan Trammell	.05
Panel (Kansas City Royals)		1.25
20a	George Brett	.50
20b	Bret Saberhagen	.05
20c	Willie Wilson	.05
Panel (Milwaukee Brewers)		1.50
21a	Cecil Cooper	.05
21b	Paul Molitor	.40
21c	Robin Yount	.40
Panel (Minnesota Twins)		.70
22a	Tom Brunansky	.05
22b	Kent Hrbek	.05
22c	Kirby Puckett	.50
Panel (New York Yankees)		2.50
23a	Rickey Henderson	.40
23b	Don Mattingly	.60
23c	Dave Winfield	.40
Panel (Oakland A's)		1.00
24a	Jose Canseco	.35
24b	Alfredo Griffin	.05
24c	Carney Lansford	.05
Panel (Seattle Mariners)		.35
25a	Phil Bradley	.05
25b	Alvin Davis	.05
25c	Mark Langston	.05
Panel (Texas Rangers)		.35
26a	Pete Incaviglia	.05
26b	Pete O'Brien	.05
26c	Larry Parrish	.05
Panel (Toronto Blue Jays)		.75
27a	Jesse Barfield	.10
27b	George Bell	.10
27c	Tony Fernandez	.05
Panel (Toronto Blue Jays)		.75
28a	Lloyd Moseby	.10
28b	Dave Steib	.10
28c	Ernie Whitt	.10

1991 Studio Preview

GARY PETTIS, CF

Each 1991 Donruss set packaged for the retail trade included a pack of four cards previewing the debut Studio set. The cards are in the same format as the regular set, 2-1/2" x 3-1/2" with evocative black-and-white photos bordered in maroon on front, and a biographical write-up on the back.

		NM/M
Complete Set (18):		5.00
Common Player:		.50
1	Juan Bell	.50
2	Roger Clemens	3.00
3	Dave Parker	.50
4	Tim Raines	.50
5	Kevin Seitzer	.50
6	Teddy Higuera	.50
7	Bernie Williams	.50
8	Harold Baines	.50
9	Gary Pettis	.50
10	Dave Justice	.50
11	Eric Davis	.50
12	Andujar Cedeno	.50
13	Tom Foley	.50
14	Dwight Gooden	.50
15	Doug Drabek	.50
16	Steve Decker	.50
17	Joe Torre	.75
18	Header Card	.10

1991 Studio

IVAN CALDERON, LF

Donruss introduced this 264-card set in 1991. The cards feature maroon borders surrounding black and white posed player photos. The card backs are printed in black and white and feature personal data, career highlights, hobbies and interests and the player's hero. The cards were released in foil packs only and feature a special Rod Carew puzzle.

		NM/M
Complete Set (264):		7.50
Common Player:		.05
Foil Pack (10):		.50
Foil Box (48):		12.50
1	Glenn Davis	.05
2	Dwight Evans	.05
3	Leo Gomez	.05
4	Chris Hoiles	.05
5	Sam Horn	.05
6	Ben McDonald	.05
7	Randy Milligan	.05
8	Gregg Olson	.05
9	Cal Ripken, Jr.	1.00
10	David Segui	.05
11	Wade Boggs	.40
12	Ellis Burks	.05
13	Jack Clark	.05
14	Roger Clemens	.45
15	Mike Greenwell	.05
16	Tim Naehring	.05
17	Tony Pena	.05
18	Phil Plantier RC	.05
19	Jeff Reardon	.05
20	Mo Vaughn	.05
21	Jimmy Reese	.05
22	Jim Abbott	.05
23	Bert Blyleven	.05
24	Chuck Finley	.05
25	Gary Gaetti	.05
26	Wally Joyner	.05
27	Mark Langston	.05
28	Kirk McCaskill	.05
29	Lance Parrish	.05
30	Dave Winfield	.30
31	Alex Fernandez	.05
32	Carlton Fisk	.30
33	Scott Fletcher	.05
34	Greg Hibbard	.05
35	Charlie Hough	.05
36	Jack McDowell	.05
37	Tim Raines	.05
38	Sammy Sosa	.40
39	Bobby Thigpen	.05
40	Frank Thomas	.30
41	Sandy Alomar	.05
42	John Farrell	.05
43	Glenallen Hill	.05
44	Brook Jacoby	.05
45	Chris James	.05
46	Doug Jones	.05
47	Eric King	.05
48	Mark Lewis	.05
49	Greg Swindell	.05
50	Mark Whiten	.05
51	Milt Cuyler	.05
52	Rob Deer	.05
53	Cecil Fielder	.05
54	Travis Fryman	.05
55	Bill Gullickson	.05
56	Lloyd Moseby	.05
57	Frank Tanana	.05

		NM/M
58	Mickey Tettleton	.05
59	Alan Trammell	.05
60	Lou Whitaker	.05
61	Mike Boddicker	.05
62	George Brett	.45
63	Jeff Conine	.05
64	Warren Cromartie	.05
65	Storm Davis	.05
66	Kirk Gibson	.05
67	Mark Gubicza	.05
68	Brian McRae RC	.05
69	Bret Saberhagen	.05
70	Kurt Stillwell	.05
71	Tim McIntosh	.05
72	Candy Maldonado	.05
73	Paul Molitor	.30
74	Willie Randolph	.05
75	Ron Robinson	.05
76	Gary Sheffield	.20
77	Franklin Stubbs	.05
78	B.J. Surhoff	.05
79	Greg Vaughn	.05
80	Robin Yount	.30
81	Rick Aguilera	.05
82	Steve Bedrosian	.05
83	Scott Erickson	.05
84	Greg Gagne	.05
85	Dan Gladden	.05
86	Brian Harper	.05
87	Kent Hrbek	.05
88	Shane Mack	.05
89	Jack Morris	.05
90	Kirby Puckett	.40
91	Jesse Barfield	.05
92	Steve Farr	.05
93	Steve Howe	.05
94	Roberto Kelly	.05
95	Tim Leary	.05
96	Kevin Maas	.05
97	Don Mattingly	.45
98	Hensley Meulens	.05
99	Scott Sanderson	.05
100	Steve Sax	.05
101	Jose Canseco	.20
102	Dennis Eckersley	.25
103	Dave Henderson	.05
104	Rickey Henderson	.30
105	Rick Honeycutt	.05
106	Mark McGwire	.75
107	Dave Stewart	.05
108	Eric Show	.05
109	Todd Van Poppel RC	.05
110	Bob Welch	.05
111	Alvin Davis	.05
112	Ken Griffey Jr.	.50
113	Ken Griffey Sr.	.05
114	Erik Hanson	.05
115	Brian Holman	.05
116	Randy Johnson	.30
117	Edgar Martinez	.05
118	Tino Martinez	.05
119	Harold Reynolds	.05
120	David Valle	.05
121	Kevin Belcher	.05
122	Scott Chiamparino	.05
123	Julio Franco	.05
124	Juan Gonzalez	.20
125	Rich Gossage	.05
126	Jeff Kunkel	.05
127	Rafael Palmeiro	.25
128	Nolan Ryan	1.00
129	Ruben Sierra	.05
130	Bobby Witt	.05
131	Roberto Alomar	.10
132	Tom Candiotti	.05
133	Joe Carter	.05
134	Ken Dayley	.05
135	Kelly Gruber	.05
136	John Olerud	.05
137	Dave Stieb	.05
138	Turner Ward	.05
139	Devon White	.05
140	Mookie Wilson	.05
141	Steve Avery	.05
142	Sid Bream	.05
143	Nick Esasky	.05
144	Ron Gant	.05
145	Tom Glavine	.20
146	Dave Justice	.05
147	Kelly Mann	.05
148	Terry Pendleton	.05
149	John Smoltz	.05
150	Jeff Treadway	.05
151	George Bell	.05
152	Shawn Boskie	.05
153	Andre Dawson	.20
154	Lance Dickson	.05
155	Shawon Dunston	.05
156	Joe Girardi	.05
157	Mark Grace	.05
158	Ryne Sandberg	.40
159	Gary Scott	.05
160	Dave Smith	.05
161	Tom Browning	.05
162	Eric Davis	.05
163	Rob Dibble	.05
164	Mariano Duncan	.05
165	Chris Hammond	.05
166	Billy Hatcher	.05
167	Barry Larkin	.05
168	Hal Morris	.05
169	Paul O'Neill	.05
170	Chris Sabo	.05
171	Eric Anthony	.05
172	Jeff Bagwell RC	1.50
173	Craig Biggio	.05
174	Ken Caminiti	.05
175	Jim Deshaies	.05

#	Player	Price
176	Steve Finley	.05
177	Pete Harnisch	.05
178	Darryl Kile	.05
179	Curt Schilling	.20
180	Mike Scott	.05
181	Brett Butler	.05
182	Gary Carter	.30
183	Orel Hershiser	.05
184	Ramon Martinez	.05
185	Eddie Murray	.30
186	Jose Offerman	.05
187	Bob Ojeda	.05
188	Juan Samuel	.05
189	Mike Scioscia	.05
190	Darryl Strawberry	.05
191	Moises Alou	.05
192	Brian Barnes	.05
193	Oil Can Boyd	.05
194	Ivan Calderon	.05
195	Delino DeShields	.05
196	Mike Fitzgerald	.05
197	Andres Galarraga	.05
198	Marquis Grissom	.05
199	Bill Sampen	.05
200	Tim Wallach	.05
201	Daryl Boston	.05
202	Vince Coleman	.05
203	John Franco	.05
204	Dwight Gooden	.05
205	Tom Herr	.05
206	Gregg Jefferies	.05
207	Howard Johnson	.05
208	Dave Magadan	.05
209	Kevin McReynolds	.05
210	Frank Viola	.05
211	Wes Chamberlain	.05
212	Darren Daulton	.05
213	Len Dykstra	.05
214	Charlie Hayes	.05
215	Ricky Jordan	.05
216	Steve Lake	.05
217	Roger McDowell	.05
218	Mickey Morandini	.05
219	Terry Mulholland	.05
220	Dale Murphy	.15
221	Jay Bell	.05
222	Barry Bonds	1.00
223	Bobby Bonilla	.05
224	Doug Drabek	.05
225	Bill Landrum	.05
226	Mike LaValliere	.05
227	Jose Lind	.05
228	Don Slaught	.05
229	John Smiley	.05
230	Andy Van Slyke	.05
231	Bernard Gilkey	.05
232	Pedro Guerrero	.05
233	Rex Hudler	.05
234	Ray Lankford	.05
235	Joe Magrane	.05
236	Jose Oquendo	.05
237	Lee Smith	.05
238	Ozzie Smith	.40
239	Milt Thompson	.05
240	Todd Zeile	.05
241	Larry Andersen	.05
242	Andy Benes	.05
243	Paul Faries	.05
244	Tony Fernandez	.05
245	Tony Gwynn	.40
246	Atlee Hammaker	.05
247	Fred McGriff	.05
248	Bip Roberts	.05
249	Benito Santiago	.05
250	Ed Whitson	.05
251	Dave Anderson	.05
252	Mike Benjamin	.05
253	John Burkett	.05
254	Will Clark	.05
255	Scott Garrelts	.05
256	Willie McGee	.05
257	Kevin Mitchell	.05
258	Dave Righetti	.05
259	Matt Williams	.05
260	Black & Decker (Bud Black, Steve Decker)	.10
261	Checklist	.03
262	Checklist	.03
263	Checklist	.03
---	Header Card	

1992 Studio Preview

CAL RIPKEN, JR. PREVIEW
Baltimore Orioles

To introduce its 1992 Studio brand, Leaf produced 22 preview cards in format virtually identical to the issued versions of the same cards. The only differences are the appearance of the word "PRE-VIEW" in the lower-right corner of the card front, in place of the player's position, and the number "X of 22 / Preview Card" on the back where regular cards have the card number in the upper-right corner. The cards were distributed on a very limited basis to members of the Donruss dealers' network.

		NM/M
Complete Set (22):		75.00
Common Player:		1.50
1	Ruben Sierra	1.50
2	Kirby Puckett	6.00
3	Ryne Sandberg	6.00
4	John Kruk	1.50
5	Cal Ripken, Jr.	12.00
6	Robin Yount	4.50
7	Dwight Gooden	1.50
8	David Justice	1.50
9	Don Mattingly	7.50
10	Wally Joyner	1.50
11	Will Clark	1.50
12	Rob Dibble	1.50
13	Roberto Alomar	2.50
14	Wade Boggs	6.00
15	Barry Bonds	12.00
16	Jeff Bagwell	4.50
17	Mark McGwire	9.00
18	Frank Thomas	6.00
19	Brett Butler	1.50
20	Ozzie Smith	6.00
21	Jim Abbott	1.50
22	Tony Gwynn	6.00

1992 Studio

PETE HARNISCH RHP
Houston Astros

Donruss introduced the Studio line in 1991 and released another 264-card set entitled Leaf Studio for 1992. The cards feature a color player closeup with a large, rough-textured black-and-white photo of the player in the background. Tan borders surround the photos. The cards were only released in foil packs. Special Heritage insert cards featuring top players in vintage uniforms could be found in foil and jumbo packs.

		NM/M
Complete Set (264):		8.00
Common Player:		.05
Pack (10):		.65
Wax Box (48):		15.00
1	Steve Avery	.05
2	Sid Bream	.05
3	Ron Gant	.05
4	Tom Glavine	.25
5	Dave Justice	.05
6	Mark Lemke	.05
7	Greg Olson	.05
8	Terry Pendleton	.05
9	Deion Sanders	.05
10	John Smoltz	.05
11	Doug Dascenzo	.05
12	Andre Dawson	.25
13	Joe Girardi	.05
14	Mark Grace	.05
15	Greg Maddux	.50
16	Chuck McElroy	.05
17	Mike Morgan	.05
18	Ryne Sandberg	.50
19	Gary Scott	.05
20	Sammy Sosa	.50
21	Norm Charlton	.05
22	Rob Dibble	.05
23	Barry Larkin	.05
24	Hal Morris	.05
25	Paul O'Neill	.05
26	Jose Rijo	.05
27	Bip Roberts	.05
28	Chris Sabo	.05
29	Reggie Sanders	.05
30	Greg Swindell	.05
31	Jeff Bagwell	.45
32	Craig Biggio	.05
33	Ken Caminiti	.05
34	Andujar Cedeno	.05
35	Steve Finley	.05
36	Pete Harnisch	.05
37	Butch Henry	.05
38	Doug Jones	.05
39	Darryl Kile	.05
40	Eddie Taubensee	.05
41	Brett Butler	.05
42	Tom Candiotti	.05
43	Eric Davis	.05
44	Orel Hershiser	.05
45	Eric Karros	.05
46	Ramon Martinez	.05
47	Jose Offerman	.05
48	Mike Scioscia	.05
49	Mike Sharperson	.05
50	Darryl Strawberry	.05
51	Bret Barbarie	.05
52	Ivan Calderon	.05
53	Gary Carter	.45
54	Delino DeShields	.05
55	Marquis Grissom	.05
56	Ken Hill	.05
57	Dennis Martinez	.05
58	Spike Owen	.05
59	Larry Walker	.05
60	Tim Wallach	.05
61	Bobby Bonilla	.05
62	Tim Burke	.05
63	Vince Coleman	.05
64	John Franco	.05
65	Dwight Gooden	.05
66	Todd Hundley	.05
67	Howard Johnson	.05
68	Eddie Murray	.45
69	Bret Saberhagen	.05
70	Anthony Young	.05
71	Kim Batiste	.05
72	Wes Chamberlain	.05
73	Darren Daulton	.05
74	Mariano Duncan	.05
75	Len Dykstra	.05
76	John Kruk	.05
77	Mickey Morandini	.05
78	Terry Mulholland	.05
79	Dale Murphy	.20
80	Mitch Williams	.05
81	Jay Bell	.05
82	Barry Bonds	1.00
83	Steve Buechele	.05
84	Doug Drabek	.05
85	Mike LaValliere	.05
86	Jose Lind	.05
87	Denny Neagle	.05
88	Randy Tomlin	.05
89	Andy Van Slyke	.05
90	Gary Varsho	.05
91	Pedro Guerrero	.05
92	Rex Hudler	.05
93	Brian Jordan	.05
94	Felix Jose	.05
95	Donovan Osborne	.05
96	Tom Pagnozzi	.05
97	Lee Smith	.05
98	Ozzie Smith	.50
99	Todd Worrell	.05
100	Todd Zeile	.05
101	Andy Benes	.05
102	Jerald Clark	.05
103	Tony Fernandez	.05
104	Tony Gwynn	.50
105	Greg Harris	.05
106	Fred McGriff	.05
107	Benito Santiago	.05
108	Gary Sheffield	.30
109	Kurt Stillwell	.05
110	Tim Teufel	.05
111	Kevin Bass	.05
112	Jeff Brantley	.05
113	John Burkett	.05
114	Will Clark	.05
115	Royce Clayton	.05
116	Mike Jackson	.05
117	Darren Lewis	.05
118	Bill Swift	.05
119	Robby Thompson	.05
120	Matt Williams	.05
121	Brady Anderson	.05
122	Glenn Davis	.05
123	Mike Devereaux	.05
124	Chris Hoiles	.05
125	Sam Horn	.05
126	Ben McDonald	.05
127	Mike Mussina	.25
128	Gregg Olson	.05
129	Cal Ripken, Jr.	1.00
130	Rick Sutcliffe	.05
131	Wade Boggs	.50
132	Roger Clemens	.60
133	Greg Harris	.05
134	Tim Naehring	.05
135	Tony Pena	.05
136	Phil Plantier	.05
137	Jeff Reardon	.05
138	Jody Reed	.05
139	Mo Vaughn	.05
140	Frank Viola	.05
141	Jim Abbott	.05
142	Hubie Brooks	.05
143	Chad Curtis RC	.05
144	Gary DiSarcina	.05
145	Chuck Finley	.05
146	Bryan Harvey	.05
147	Von Hayes	.05
148	Mark Langston	.05
149	Lance Parrish	.05
150	Lee Stevens	.05
151	George Bell	.05
152	Alex Fernandez	.05
153	Greg Hibbard	.05
154	Lance Johnson	.05
155	Kirk McCaskill	.05
156	Tim Raines	.05
157	Steve Sax	.05
158	Bobby Thigpen	.05
159	Frank Thomas	.45
160	Robin Ventura	.05
161	Sandy Alomar, Jr.	.05
162	Jack Armstrong	.05
163	Carlos Baerga	.05
164	Albert Belle	.05
165	Alex Cole	.05
166	Glenallen Hill	.05
167	Mark Lewis	.05
168	Kenny Lofton	.05
169	Paul Sorrento	.05
170	Mark Whiten	.05
171	Milt Cuyler (Color photo is Lou Whitaker.)	.05
172	Rob Deer	.05
173	Cecil Fielder	.05
174	Travis Fryman	.05
175	Mike Henneman	.05
176	Tony Phillips	.05
177	Frank Tanana	.05
178	Mickey Tettleton	.05
179	Alan Trammell	.05
180	Lou Whitaker	.05
181	George Brett	.60
182	Tom Gordon	.05
183	Mark Gubicza	.05
184	Gregg Jefferies	.05
185	Wally Joyner	.05
186	Brent Mayne	.05
187	Brian McRae	.05
188	Kevin McReynolds	.05
189	Keith Miller	.05
190	Jeff Montgomery	.05
191	Dante Bichette	.05
192	Ricky Bones	.05
193	Scott Fletcher	.05
194	Paul Molitor	.45
195	Jaime Navarro	.05
196	Franklin Stubbs	.05
197	B.J. Surhoff	.05
198	Greg Vaughn	.05
199	Bill Wegman	.05
200	Robin Yount	.45
201	Rick Aguilera	.05
202	Scott Erickson	.05
203	Greg Gagne	.05
204	Brian Harper	.05
205	Kent Hrbek	.05
206	Scott Leius	.05
207	Shane Mack	.05
208	Pat Mahomes	.05
209	Kirby Puckett	.50
210	John Smiley	.05
211	Mike Gallego	.05
212	Charlie Hayes	.05
213	Pat Kelly	.05
214	Roberto Kelly	.05
215	Kevin Maas	.05
216	Don Mattingly	.60
217	Matt Nokes	.05
218	Melido Perez	.05
219	Scott Sanderson	.05
220	Danny Tartabull	.05
221	Harold Baines	.05
222	Jose Canseco	.30
223	Dennis Eckersley	.35
224	Dave Henderson	.05
225	Carney Lansford	.05
226	Mark McGwire	.75
227	Mike Moore	.05
228	Randy Ready	.05
229	Terry Steinbach	.05
230	Dave Stewart	.05
231	Jay Buhner	.05
232	Ken Griffey Jr.	.65
233	Erik Hanson	.05
234	Randy Johnson	.45
235	Edgar Martinez	.05
236	Tino Martinez	.05
237	Kevin Mitchell	.05
238	Pete O'Brien	.05
239	Harold Reynolds	.05
240	David Valle	.05
241	Julio Franco	.05
242	Juan Gonzalez	.25
243	Jose Guzman	.05
244	Rafael Palmeiro	.35
245	Dean Palmer	.05
246	Ivan Rodriguez	.35
247	Jeff Russell	.05
248	Nolan Ryan	1.00
249	Ruben Sierra	.05
250	Dickie Thon	.05
251	Roberto Alomar	.20
252	Derek Bell	.05
253	Pat Borders	.05
254	Joe Carter	.05
255	Kelly Gruber	.05
256	Juan Guzman	.05
257	Jack Morris	.05
258	John Olerud	.05
259	Devon White	.05
260	Dave Winfield	.05
261	Checklist	.05
262	Checklist	.05
263	Checklist	.05
264	History Card	.05

Heritage

HERITAGE SERIES
RYNE SANDBERG

Superstars of 1992 were photographed in vintage-style uniforms in this 14-card insert set found in packages of Studio's 1992 issue. Cards #1-8 could be found in standard foil packs while #9-14 were inserted in Studio jumbos. Cards featured a sepia-tone photo bordered in turquoise and highlighted with copper foil. Cards carry a "BC" prefix to the card number on back.

		NM/M
Complete Set (14):		6.00
Common Player:		.50
1	Ryne Sandberg	1.00
2	Carlton Fisk	.75
3	Wade Boggs	1.00
4	Jose Canseco	.65
5	Don Mattingly	1.25
6	Darryl Strawberry	.50
7	Cal Ripken, Jr.	1.50
8	Will Clark	.50
9	Andre Dawson	.50
10	Andy Van Slyke	.50
11	Paul Molitor	.75
12	Jeff Bagwell	.75
13	Darren Daulton	.50
14	Kirby Puckett	1.00

1993 Studio Promos

Though unmarked as such, a pair of promo cards was produced in advance of '93 Studio. At first glance the cards appear identical to the same players' issued versions, but there are noticeable cropping differences. On the back of the Thomas card, the promo has a smaller projection of his face, with much more of his hair showing at top and the last line of type about even with the bottom of his nose. The issued card shows almost no hair at top and has the last line even with his top lip. The Sandberg cropping difference appears on front. On the promo his ear is well clear of the left border; on the issued version his ear touches the border.

		NM/M
Complete Set (2):		6.00
Common Player:		2.00
139	Frank Thomas	2.00
176	Ryne Sandberg	5.00

1993 Studio

This 220-card set features full-bleed photos. The player's portrait appears against one of several backgrounds featuring his team's uniform. His signature and the Studio logo are printed in gold foil. Backs have an extreme closeup partial portrait of the player and insights into his personality.

		NM/M
Complete Set (220):		15.00
Common Player:		.05
Pack (12):		.75

#	Player	Price
	Wax Box (36):	12.50
1	Dennis Eckersley	.35
2	Chad Curtis	.05
3	Eric Anthony	.05
4	Roberto Alomar	.20
5	Steve Avery	.05
6	Cal Eldred	.05
7	Bernard Gilkey	.05
8	Steve Buechele	.05
9	Brett Butler	.05
10	Terry Mulholland	.05
11	Moises Alou	.05
12	Barry Bonds	1.00
13	Sandy Alomar Jr.	.05
14	Chris Bosio	.05
15	Scott Sanderson	.05
16	Bobby Bonilla	.05
17	Brady Anderson	.05
18	Derek Bell	.05
19	Wes Chamberlain	.05
20	Jay Bell	.05
21	Kevin Brown	.05
22	Roger Clemens	.60
23	Roberto Kelly	.05
24	Dante Bichette	.05
25	George Brett	.60
26	Rob Deer	.05
27	Brian Harper	.05
28	George Bell	.05
29	Jim Abbott	.05
30	Dave Henderson	.05
31	Wade Boggs	.50
32	Chili Davis	.05
33	Ellis Burks	.05
34	Jeff Bagwell	.40
35	Kent Hrbek	.05
36	Pat Borders	.05
37	Cecil Fielder	.05
38	Sid Bream	.05
39	Greg Gagne	.05
40	Darryl Hamilton	.05
41	Jerald Clark	.05
42	Mark Grace	.05
43	Barry Larkin	.05
44	John Burkett	.05
45	Scott Cooper	.05
46	Mike Lansing RC	.25
47	Jose Canseco	.30
48	Will Clark	.05
49	Carlos Garcia	.05
50	Carlos Baerga	.05
51	Darren Daulton	.05
52	Jay Buhner	.05
53	Andy Benes	.05
54	Jeff Conine	.05
55	Mike Devereaux	.05
56	Vince Coleman	.05
57	Terry Steinbach	.05
58	J.T. Snow RC	.40
59	Greg Swindell	.05
60	Devon White	.05
61	John Smoltz	.05
62	Todd Zeile	.05
63	Rick Wilkins	.05
64	Tim Wallach	.05
65	John Wetteland	.05
66	Matt Williams	.05
67	Paul Sorrento	.05
68	David Valle	.05
69	Walt Weiss	.05
70	John Franco	.05
71	Nolan Ryan	1.00
72	Frank Viola	.05
73	Chris Sabo	.05
74	David Nied	.05
75	Kevin McReynolds	.05
76	Lou Whitaker	.05
77	Dave Winfield	.40
78	Robin Ventura	.05
79	Spike Owen	.05
80	Cal Ripken, Jr.	1.00
81	Dan Walter	.05
82	Mitch Williams	.05
83	Tim Wakefield	.05
84	Rickey Henderson	.40
85	Gary DiSarcina	.05
86	Craig Biggio	.05
87	Joe Carter	.05
88	Ron Gant	.05
89	John Jaha	.05
90	Gregg Jefferies	.05
91	Jose Guzman	.05
92	Eric Karros	.05
93	Wil Cordero	.05
94	Royce Clayton	.05
95	Albert Belle	.05
96	Ken Griffey Jr.	.65
97	Orestes Destrade	.05
98	Tony Fernandez	.05
99	Leo Gomez	.05
100	Tony Gwynn	.50
101	Len Dykstra	.05
102	Jeff King	.05
103	Julio Franco	.05
104	Andre Dawson	.25
105	Randy Milligan	.05
106	Alex Cole	.05
107	Phil Hiatt	.05
108	Travis Fryman	.05
109	Chuck Knoblauch	.05
110	Bo Jackson	.10
111	Pat Kelly	.05
112	Bret Saberhagen	.05
113	Ruben Sierra	.05
114	Tim Salmon	.05
115	Doug Jones	.05
116	Ed Sprague	.05
117	Terry Pendleton	.05

118	Robin Yount	.40
119	Mark Whiten	.05
120	Checklist	.05
121	Sammy Sosa	.50
122	Darryl Strawberry	.05
123	Larry Walker	.05
124	Robby Thompson	.05
125	Carlos Martinez	.05
126	Edgar Martinez	.05
127	Benito Santiago	.05
128	Howard Johnson	.05
129	Harold Reynolds	.05
130	Craig Shipley	.05
131	Curt Schilling	.30
132	Andy Van Slyke	.05
133	Ivan Rodriguez	.35
134	Mo Vaughn	.05
135	Bip Roberts	.05
136	Charlie Hayes	.05
137	Brian McRae	.05
138	Mickey Tettleton	.05
139	Frank Thomas	.40
140	Paul O'Neill	.05
141	Mark McGwire	.75
142	Damion Easley	.05
143	Ken Caminiti	.05
144	Juan Guzman	.05
145	Tom Glavine	.25
146	Pat Listach	.05
147	Lee Smith	.05
148	Derrick May	.05
149	Ramon Martinez	.05
150	Delino DeShields	.05
151	Kirt Manwaring	.05
152	Reggie Jefferson	.05
153	Randy Johnson	.40
154	Dave Magadan	.05
155	Dwight Gooden	.05
156	Chris Hoiles	.05
157	Fred McGriff	.05
158	Dave Hollins	.05
159	Al Martin	.05
160	Juan Gonzalez	.20
161	Mike Greenwell	.05
162	Kevin Mitchell	.05
163	Andres Galarraga	.05
164	Wally Joyner	.05
165	Kirk Gibson	.05
166	Pedro Munoz	.05
167	Ozzie Guillen	.05
168	Jimmy Key	.05
169	Kevin Seitzer	.05
170	Luis Polonia	.05
171	Luis Gonzalez	.05
172	Paul Molitor	.40
173	Dave Justice	.05
174	B.J. Surhoff	.05
175	Ray Lankford	.05
176	Ryne Sandberg	.50
177	Jody Reed	.05
178	Marquis Grissom	.05
179	Willie McGee	.05
180	Kenny Lofton	.05
181	Junior Felix	.05
182	Jose Offerman	.05
183	John Kruk	.05
184	Orlando Merced	.05
185	Rafael Palmeiro	.35
186	Billy Hatcher	.05
187	Joe Oliver	.05
188	Joe Girardi	.05
189	Jose Lind	.05
190	Harold Baines	.05
191	Mike Pagliarulo	.05
192	Lance Johnson	.05
193	Don Mattingly	.60
194	Doug Drabek	.05
195	John Olerud	.05
196	Greg Maddux	.50
197	Greg Vaughn	.05
198	Tom Pagnozzi	.05
199	Willie Wilson	.05
200	Jack McDowell	.05
201	Mike Piazza	.65
202	Mike Mussina	.30
203	Charles Nagy	.05
204	Tino Martinez	.05
205	Charlie Hough	.05
206	Todd Hundley	.05
207	Gary Sheffield	.30
208	Mickey Morandini	.05
209	Don Slaught	.05
210	Dean Palmer	.05
211	Jose Rijo	.05
212	Vinny Castilla	.05
213	Tony Phillips	.05
214	Kirby Puckett	.50
215	Tim Raines	.05
216	Otis Nixon	.05
217	Ozzie Smith	.50
218	Jose Vizcaino	.05
220	Checklist	.05

Heritage

All types of 1993 Leaf Studio packs were candidates for having one of 12 Heritage cards inserted in them. The fronts feature the player posing in an old-time uniform, framed in turquoise with copper highlights. The backs have a mug shot surrounded by an ornate frame and describe the uniform on the front. Team trivia is also included.

		NM/M
Complete Set (12):		12.00
Common Player:		.50
1	George Brett	2.00
2	Juan Gonzalez	.75
3	Roger Clemens	2.00
4	Mark McGwire	4.00
5	Mark Grace	.50
6	Ozzie Smith	1.50
7	Barry Larkin	.50
8	Frank Thomas	.50
9	Carlos Baerga	.50
10	Eric Karros	.50
11	J.T. Snow	.50
12	John Kruk	.50

Silhouettes

These insert cards were randomly included in jumbo packs only. The card fronts feature a ghosted image of the player against an action silhouette on a gray background. The player's name is in bronze foil at bottom. Backs have a player action photo and description of career highlights.

		NM/M
Complete Set (10):		7.00
Common Player:		.15
1	Frank Thomas	.65
2	Barry Bonds	3.00
3	Jeff Bagwell	.65
4	Juan Gonzalez	.40
5	Travis Fryman	.15
6	J.T. Snow	.15
7	John Kruk	.15
8	Jeff Blauser	.15
9	Mike Piazza	2.00
10	Nolan Ryan	3.00

Superstars on Canvas

Ten players are featured on these insert cards, which were available in hobby and retail packs. The cards show player portraits which mix photography and artwork.

		NM/M
Complete Set (10):		8.00
Common Player:		.25
1	Ken Griffey Jr.	1.50
2	Jose Canseco	.60
3	Mark McGwire	1.00
4	Mike Mussina	.50
5	Joe Carter	.25
6	Frank Thomas	

7	Darren Daulton	.25
8	Mark Grace	.25
9	Andres Galarraga	.25
10	Barry Bonds	2.50

Frank Thomas

This five-card set is devoted to Frank Thomas. Cards were randomly included in all types of 1993 Leaf Studio packs. Topics covered on the cards include Thomas' childhood, his baseball memories, his family, his performance and being a role model.

		NM/M
Complete Set (5):		5.00
Common Card:		1.00
1	Childhood	1.00
2	Baseball Memories	1.00
3	Importance of Family	1.00
4	Performance	1.00
5	On Being a Role Model	1.00

1994 Studio Samples

To introduce its "locker-room look" issue for 1994, Leaf's Studio brand produced this three-star sample set and distributed it to its hobby dealer network. The cards are basically the same as the regular-issue cards of those players except for the addition of a "Promotional Sample" overprinted diagonally on front and back. The "Up Close" biographies on the cards' backs are different between the promos and the regular cards and there is a slight difference in front photo cropping on the Gonzalez card.

		NM/M
Complete Set (3):		6.00
83	Barry Bonds	3.00
154	Juan Gonzalez	1.00
209	Frank Thomas	2.00

1994 Studio

Studio baseball from Donruss returned in mid-August, 1994, with a three-time MVP spokesman, several jazzy and short-printed inserts subsets and a reduced overall production figure that represents a sharp drop from 1993. Barry Bonds is the MVP whose mug adorns Stu-

dio counter boxes and advertisements. According to Donruss officials, production was limited to 8,000 cases of 20 boxes each, which represents a 35 percent decrease from 1993 and works out to about 315,000 of each card. Only 2,000 cases were earmarked for retail distribution and no jumbo packs were produced. Studio 1994 features 220 cards issued in one series, once again with close-up personal portraits of the top stars in the game. Each card is foil-stamped with a borderless design and UV coating front and back. The front of the card features the player in the foreground with his locker in the background. As in the previous three Studio offerings, the backs of the cards contain personal information about the players.

		NM/M
Complete Set (220):		7.50
Common Player:		.05
Pack (12):		.45
Wax Box (36):		10.00
1	Dennis Eckersley	.45
2	Brent Gates	.05
3	Rickey Henderson	.55
4	Mark McGwire	1.00
5	Troy Neel	.05
6	Ruben Sierra	.05
7	Terry Steinbach	.05
8	Chad Curtis	.05
9	Chili Davis	.05
10	Gary DiSarcina	.05
11	Damion Easley	.05
12	Bo Jackson	.10
13	Mark Langston	.05
14	Eduardo Perez	.05
15	Tim Salmon	.05
16	Jeff Bagwell	.55
17	Craig Biggio	.05
18	Ken Caminiti	.05
19	Andujar Cedeno	.05
20	Doug Drabek	.05
21	Steve Finley	.05
22	Luis Gonzalez	.05
23	Darryl Kile	.05
24	Roberto Alomar	.20
25	Pat Borders	.05
26	Joe Carter	.05
27	Carlos Delgado	.40
28	Pat Hentgen	.05
29	Paul Molitor	.55
30	John Olerud	.05
31	Ed Sprague	.05
32	Devon White	.05
33	Steve Avery	.05
34	Tom Glavine	.25
35	David Justice	.05
36	Roberto Kelly	.05
37	Ryan Klesko	.05
38	Javier Lopez	.05
39	Greg Maddux	.60
40	Fred McGriff	.05
41	Terry Pendleton	.05
42	Ricky Bones	.05
43	Darryl Hamilton	.05
44	Brian Harper	.05
45	John Jaha	.05
46	Dave Nilsson	.05
47	Kevin Seitzer	.05
48	Greg Vaughn	.05
49	Turner Ward	.05
50	Bernard Gilkey	.05
51	Gregg Jefferies	.05
52	Ray Lankford	.05
53	Tom Pagnozzi	.05
54	Ozzie Smith	.60
55	Bob Tewksbury	.05
56	Mark Whiten	.05
57	Todd Zeile	.05
58	Steve Buechele	.05
59	Shawon Dunston	.05
60	Mark Grace	.05
61	Derrick May	.05
62	Tuffy Rhodes	.05
63	Ryne Sandberg	.60
64	Sammy Sosa	.05
65	Rick Wilkins	.05
66	Brett Butler	.05
67	Delino DeShields	.05
68	Orel Hershiser	.05
69	Eric Karros	.05
70	Raul Mondesi	.05
71	Jose Offerman	.05
72	Mike Piazza	.75
73	Tim Wallach	.05
74	Moises Alou	.05
75	Sean Berry	.05
76	Wil Cordero	.05
77	Cliff Floyd	.05
78	Marquis Grissom	.05
79	Ken Hill	.05
80	Larry Walker	.05
81	John Wetteland	.05
82	Rod Beck	.05
83	Barry Bonds	1.50
84	Royce Clayton	.05
85	Darren Lewis	.05
86	Willie McGee	.05

87	Bill Swift	.05
88	Robby Thompson	.05
89	Matt Williams	.05
90	Sandy Alomar Jr.	.05
91	Carlos Baerga	.05
92	Albert Belle	.05
93	Kenny Lofton	.05
94	Eddie Murray	.05
95	Manny Ramirez	.55
96	Paul Sorrento	.05
97	Jim Thome	.45
98	Rich Amaral	.05
99	Eric Anthony	.05
100	Jay Buhner	.05
101	Ken Griffey Jr.	.75
102	Randy Johnson	.55
103	Edgar Martinez	.05
104	Tino Martinez	.05
105	Kurt Abbott **RC**	.05
106	Bret Barberie	.05
107	Chuck Carr	.05
108	Jeff Conine	.05
109	Chris Hammond	.05
110	Bryan Harvey	.05
111	Benito Santiago	.05
112	Gary Sheffield	.30
113	Bobby Bonilla	.05
114	Dwight Gooden	.05
115	Todd Hundley	.05
116	Bobby Jones	.05
117	Jeff Kent	.05
118	Kevin McReynolds	.05
119	Bret Saberhagen	.05
120	Ryan Thompson	.05
121	Harold Baines	.05
122	Mike Devereaux	.05
123	Jeffrey Hammonds	.05
124	Ben McDonald	.05
125	Mike Mussina	.25
126	Rafael Palmeiro	.45
127	Cal Ripken, Jr.	1.50
128	Lee Smith	.05
129	Brad Ausmus	.05
130	Derek Bell	.05
131	Andy Benes	.05
132	Tony Gwynn	.60
133	Trevor Hoffman	.05
134	Scott Livingstone	.05
135	Phil Plantier	.05
136	Darren Daulton	.05
137	Mariano Duncan	.05
138	Len Dykstra	.05
139	Dave Hollins	.05
140	Pete Incaviglia	.05
141	Danny Jackson	.05
142	John Kruk	.05
143	Kevin Stocker	.05
144	Jay Bell	.05
145	Carlos Garcia	.05
146	Jeff King	.05
147	Al Martin	.05
148	Orlando Merced	.05
149	Don Slaught	.05
150	Andy Van Slyke	.05
151	Kevin Brown	.05
152	Jose Canseco	.40
153	Will Clark	.05
154	Juan Gonzalez	.30
155	David Hulse	.05
156	Dean Palmer	.05
157	Ivan Rodriguez	.45
158	Kenny Rogers	.05
159	Roger Clemens	.65
160	Scott Cooper	.05
161	Andre Dawson	.25
162	Mike Greenwell	.05
163	Otis Nixon	.05
164	Aaron Sele	.05
165	John Valentin	.05
166	Mo Vaughn	.05
167	Bret Boone	.05
168	Barry Larkin	.05
169	Kevin Mitchell	.05
170	Hal Morris	.05
171	Jose Rijo	.05
172	Deion Sanders	.05
173	Reggie Sanders	.05
174	John Smiley	.05
175	Dante Bichette	.05
176	Ellis Burks	.05
177	Andres Galarraga	.05
178	Joe Girardi	.05
179	Charlie Hayes	.05
180	Roberto Mejia	.05
181	Walt Weiss	.05
182	David Cone	.05
183	Gary Gaetti	.05
184	Greg Gagne	.05
185	Felix Jose	.05
186	Wally Joyner	.05
187	Mike Macfarlane	.05
188	Brian McRae	.05
189	Eric Davis	.05
190	Cecil Fielder	.05
191	Travis Fryman	.05
192	Tony Phillips	.05
193	Mickey Tettleton	.05
194	Alan Trammell	.05
195	Lou Whitaker	.05
196	Kent Hrbek	.05
197	Chuck Knoblauch	.05
198	Shane Mack	.05
199	Pat Meares	.05
200	Kirby Puckett	.60
201	Matt Walbeck	.05
202	Dave Winfield	.55
203	Wilson Alvarez	.05
204	Alex Fernandez	.05

205	Julio Franco	.05
206	Ozzie Guillen	.05
207	Jack McDowell	.05
208	Tim Raines	.05
209	Frank Thomas	.55
210	Robin Ventura	.05
211	Jim Abbott	.05
212	Wade Boggs	.60
213	Pat Kelly	.05
214	Jimmy Key	.05
215	Don Mattingly	.65
216	Paul O'Neill	.05
217	Mike Stanley	.05
218	Danny Tartabull	.05
219	Checklist	.05
220	Checklist	.05

Editor's Choice

Printed in similitude to a strip of color slide film, each of the cards in this insert set feature a complete player photo at center, with partial "frames" at top and bottom. Printed on acetate, the back of the card shows a reversed image of the front. Stated odds of finding an Editor's Choice insert card are about one per box of 36 packs.

		NM/M
Complete Set (8):		12.00
Common Player:		.50
1	Barry Bonds	3.00
2	Frank Thomas	1.50
3	Ken Griffey Jr.	2.50
4	Andres Galarraga	.50
5	Juan Gonzalez	.75
6	Tim Salmon	.50
7	Paul O'Neill	.50
8	Mike Piazza	2.50

Heritage

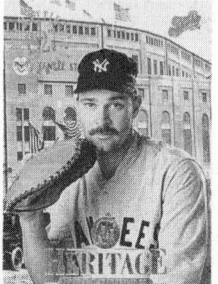

Besides picturing today's players in vintage uniforms, the 1994 Studio Heritage inserts have the player portraits set against sepia-toned photos of old ballparks. Fronts are enhanced by copper-foil logos and by a round device at upper-left containing the player's name, team and year represented. Backs have a second color player photo and a short write-up about the team represented. Unlike the other cards in the set, the Heritage cards are printed on a porous cardboard stock to enhance the image of antiquity. Stated odds of finding a Heritage Collection insert card are one in nine packs.

		NM/M
Complete Set (8):		9.00
Common Player:		.50
1	Barry Bonds	4.00
2	Frank Thomas	1.50
3	Joe Carter	.50
4	Don Mattingly	3.00
5	Ryne Sandberg	2.00
6	Javier Lopez	.50
7	Gregg Jefferies	.50
8	Mike Mussina	.65

Silver Stars

Each of the 10 players in this insert set was produced in an edition of 10,000 cards. Printed on acetate, fronts feature action photos set against a clear plastic background with a silver-foil seal at bottom. Within the player silhouette on back, a second photo is printed. The back also features a black-and-white version of the seal, including the card's unique serial number. Stated odds of picking a Silver Series Star are one per 60 packs, on average.

		NM/M
Complete Set (10):		35.00
Common Player:		1.50
1	Tony Gwynn	3.50
2	Barry Bonds	7.50
3	Frank Thomas	2.50
4	Ken Griffey Jr.	4.50
5	Joe Carter	1.50
6	Mike Piazza	4.50
7	Cal Ripken, Jr.	7.50
8	Greg Maddux	3.50
9	Juan Gonzalez	2.00
10	Don Mattingly	4.00

Gold Stars

The scarcest of the 1994 Studio chase cards, only 5,000 cards of each of the 10 players were produced. Printed on acetate, fronts feature an action photo set against a clear plastic background. At bottom is a large gold-foil seal. Backs have another player photo, within the silhouette of the front photo, and a black-and-white version of the seal, including the card's unique serial number. According to the series wrapper, odds of finding a Gold Series Star card are one in 120 packs.

		NM/M
Complete Set (10):		80.00
Common Player:		4.50
1	Tony Gwynn	9.00
2	Barry Bonds	16.00
3	Frank Thomas	7.50
4	Ken Griffey Jr.	12.50
5	Joe Carter	4.50
6	Mike Piazza	12.50
7	Cal Ripken, Jr.	16.00
8	Greg Maddux	5.00
9	Juan Gonzalez	5.00
10	Don Mattingly	10.00

1995 Studio

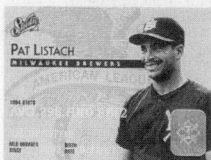

Known since its inception as a brand name for its innovative design, Studio did not disappoint in 1995,

unveiling a baseball card with a credit card look. In horizontal format the cards feature embossed stats and data on front, plus a team logo hologram. Backs have a color player photo, facsimile autograph and simulated magnetic data strip to carry through the credit card impression.

		NM/M
Complete Set (200):		25.00
Common Player:		.05
Pack (5):		1.00
Wax Box (36):		20.00
1	Frank Thomas	.75
2	Jeff Bagwell	.75
3	Don Mattingly	1.25
4	Mike Piazza	1.50
5	Ken Griffey Jr.	1.50
6	Greg Maddux	1.00
7	Barry Bonds	2.50
8	Cal Ripken Jr.	2.50
9	Jose Canseco	.40
10	Paul Molitor	.75
11	Kenny Lofton	.05
12	Will Clark	.05
13	Tim Salmon	.05
14	Joe Carter	.05
15	Albert Belle	.05
16	Roger Clemens	1.25
17	Roberto Alomar	.30
18	Alex Rodriguez	2.00
19	Raul Mondesi	.05
20	Deion Sanders	.05
21	Juan Gonzalez	.40
22	Kirby Puckett	1.00
23	Fred McGriff	.05
24	Matt Williams	.05
25	Tony Gwynn	1.00
26	Cliff Floyd	.05
27	Travis Fryman	.05
28	Shawn Green	.30
29	Mike Mussina	.35
30	Bob Hamelin	.05
31	Dave Justice	.05
32	Manny Ramirez	.75
33	David Cone	.05
34	Marquis Grissom	.05
35	Moises Alou	.05
36	Carlos Baerga	.05
37	Barry Larkin	.05
38	Robin Ventura	.05
39	Mo Vaughn	.05
40	Jeffrey Hammonds	.05
41	Ozzie Smith	1.00
42	Andres Galarraga	.05
43	Carlos Delgado	.50
44	Lenny Dykstra	.05
45	Cecil Fielder	.05
46	Wade Boggs	1.00
47	Gregg Jefferies	.05
48	Randy Johnson	.75
49	Rafael Palmeiro	.65
50	Craig Biggio	.05
51	Steve Avery	.05
52	Ricky Bottalico	.05
53	Chris Gomez	.05
54	Carlos Garcia	.05
55	Brian Anderson	.05
56	Wilson Alvarez	.05
57	Roberto Kelly	.05
58	Larry Walker	.05
59	Dean Palmer	.05
60	Rick Aguilera	.05
61	Javy Lopez	.05
62	Shawon Dunston	.05
63	William Van Landingham	.05
64	Jeff Kent	.05
65	David McCarty	.05
66	Armando Benitez	.05
67	Brett Butler	.05
68	Bernard Gilkey	.05
69	Joey Hamilton	.05
70	Chad Curtis	.05
71	Dante Bichette	.05
72	Chuck Carr	.05
73	Pedro Martinez	.75
74	Ramon Martinez	.05
75	Rondell White	.05
76	Alex Fernandez	.05
77	Dennis Martinez	.05
78	Sammy Sosa	1.00
79	Bernie Williams	.05
80	Lou Whitaker	.05
81	Kurt Abbott	.05
82	Tino Martinez	.05
83	Willie Greene	.05
84	Garret Anderson	.05
85	Jose Rijo	.05
86	Jeff Montgomery	.05
87	Mark Langston	.05
88	Reggie Sanders	.05
89	Rusty Greer	.05
90	Delino DeShields	.05
91	Jason Bere	.05
92	Lee Smith	.05
93	Devon White	.05
94	John Wetteland	.05
95	Luis Gonzalez	.05
96	Greg Vaughn	.05
97	Lance Johnson	.05
98	Alan Trammell	.05
99	Bret Saberhagen	.05
100	Jack McDowell	.05
101	Trevor Hoffman	.05
102	Dave Nilsson	.05
103	Bryan Harvey	.05

104	Chuck Knoblauch	.05
105	Bobby Bonilla	.05
106	Hal Morris	.05
107	Mark Whiten	.05
108	Phil Plantier	.05
109	Ryan Klesko	.05
110	Greg Gagne	.05
111	Ruben Sierra	.05
112	J.R. Phillips	.05
113	Terry Steinbach	.05
114	Jay Buhner	.05
115	Ken Caminiti	.05
116	Gary DiSarcina	.05
117	Ivan Rodriguez	.65
118	Bip Roberts	.05
119	Jay Bell	.05
120	Ken Hill	.05
121	Mike Greenwell	.05
122	Rick Wilkins	.05
123	Rickey Henderson	.75
124	Dave Hollins	.05
125	Terry Pendleton	.05
126	Rich Becker	.05
127	Billy Ashley	.05
128	Derek Bell	.05
129	Dennis Eckersley	.65
130	Andujar Cedeno	.05
131	John Jaha	.05
132	Chuck Finley	.05
133	Steve Finley	.05
134	Danny Tartabull	.05
135	Jeff Conine	.05
136	Jon Lieber	.05
137	Jim Abbott	.05
138	Steve Traschel	.05
139	Bret Boone	.05
140	Charles Johnson	.05
141	Mark McGwire	2.00
142	Eddie Murray	.75
143	Doug Drabek	.05
144	Steve Cooke	.05
145	Kevin Seitzer	.05
146	Rod Beck	.05
147	Eric Karros	.05
148	Tim Raines	.05
149	Joe Girardi	.05
150	Aaron Sele	.05
151	Robby Thompson	.05
152	Chan Ho Park	.05
153	Ellis Burks	.05
154	Brian McRae	.05
155	Jimmy Key	.05
156	Rico Brogna	.05
157	Ozzie Guillen	.05
158	Chili Davis	.05
159	Darren Daulton	.05
160	Chipper Jones	1.00
161	Walt Weiss	.05
162	Paul O'Neill	.05
163	Al Martin	.05
164	John Valentin	.05
165	Tim Wallach	.05
166	Scott Erickson	.05
167	Ryan Thompson	.05
168	Todd Zeile	.05
169	Scott Cooper	.05
170	Matt Mieske	.05
171	Allen Watson	.05
172	Brian Hunter	.05
173	Kevin Stocker	.05
174	Cal Eldred	.05
175	Tony Phillips	.05
176	Ben McDonald	.05
177	Mark Grace	.05
178	Midre Cummings	.05
179	Orlando Merced	.05
180	Jeff King	.05
181	Gary Sheffield	.40
182	Tom Glavine	.35
183	Edgar Martinez	.05
184	Steve Karsay	.05
185	Pat Listach	.05
186	Wil Cordero	.05
187	Brady Anderson	.05
188	Bobby Jones	.05
189	Andy Benes	.05
190	Ray Lankford	.05
191	John Doherty	.05
192	Wally Joyner	.05
193	Jim Thome	.65
194	Royce Clayton	.05
195	John Olerud	.05
196	Steve Buechele	.05
197	Harold Baines	.05
198	Geronimo Berroa	.05
199	Checklist	.05
200	Checklist	.05

Gold

The chase cards in 1995 Studio are plastic versions of some of the regular cards. The round-cornered plastic format of the inserts gives them an even greater similitude to credit cards. The first 50 numbers in the regular set are re-

produced in a parallel Studio Gold plastic version, found one per pack, except for those packs which have a platinum card.

		NM/M
Complete Set (50):		25.00
Common Player:		.15
1	Frank Thomas	1.00
2	Jeff Bagwell	1.00
3	Don Mattingly	1.75
4	Mike Piazza	2.00
5	Ken Griffey Jr.	2.00
6	Greg Maddux	1.50
7	Barry Bonds	3.00
8	Cal Ripken Jr.	3.00
9	Jose Canseco	.50
10	Paul Molitor	1.00
11	Kenny Lofton	.15
12	Will Clark	.15
13	Tim Salmon	.15
14	Joe Carter	.15
15	Albert Belle	.15
16	Roger Clemens	1.75
17	Roberto Alomar	.35
18	Alex Rodriguez	2.50
19	Raul Mondesi	.15
20	Deion Sanders	.15
21	Juan Gonzalez	.50
22	Kirby Puckett	1.50
23	Fred McGriff	.15
24	Matt Williams	.15
25	Tony Gwynn	1.50
26	Cliff Floyd	.15
27	Travis Fryman	.15
28	Shawn Green	.40
29	Mike Mussina	.35
30	Bob Hamelin	.15
31	Dave Justice	.15
32	Manny Ramirez	1.00
33	David Cone	.15
34	Marquis Grissom	.15
35	Moises Alou	.15
36	Carlos Baerga	.15
37	Barry Larkin	.15
38	Robin Ventura	.15
39	Mo Vaughn	.15
40	Jeffrey Hammonds	.15
41	Ozzie Smith	1.50
42	Andres Galarraga	.15
43	Carlos Delgado	.50
44	Lenny Dykstra	.15
45	Cecil Fielder	.15
46	Wade Boggs	1.50
47	Gregg Jefferies	.15
48	Randy Johnson	1.00
49	Rafael Palmeiro	.75
50	Craig Biggio	.15

Platinum

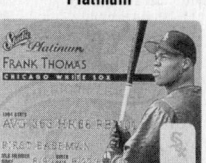

Found at the rate of one per 10 packs, Studio Platinum cards are silver-toned plastic versions of the first 25 cards from the regular set.

		NM/M
Complete Set (25):		25.00
Common Player:		.50
1	Frank Thomas	2.00
2	Jeff Bagwell	2.00
3	Don Mattingly	3.25
4	Mike Piazza	3.50
5	Ken Griffey Jr.	3.50
6	Greg Maddux	3.00
7	Barry Bonds	5.00
8	Cal Ripken Jr.	5.00
9	Jose Canseco	1.00
10	Paul Molitor	2.00
11	Kenny Lofton	.50
12	Will Clark	.50
13	Tim Salmon	.50
14	Joe Carter	.50
15	Albert Belle	.50
16	Roger Clemens	3.25
17	Roberto Alomar	.75
18	Alex Rodriguez	4.00
19	Raul Mondesi	.50
20	Deion Sanders	.50
21	Juan Gonzalez	1.00
22	Kirby Puckett	3.00
23	Fred McGriff	.50
24	Matt Williams	.50
25	Tony Gwynn	3.00

1996 Studio

The 1996 Studio set is the first Donruss product to be released under the Pinnacle Brands flagship. The 150-card set has three parallel sets - Bronze Press Proofs (2,000 sets), Silver Press Proofs (found only in magazine packs, 100 sets), and Gold Press Proofs (500 sets).

Three insert sets were also made - Hit Parade, Masterstrokes and Stained Glass Stars.

		NM/M
Complete Set (150):		9.00
Common Player:		.05
Bronze Press Proofs:		3X
Gold Press Proofs:		7X
Silver Press Proofs:		25X
Pack (7):		1.25
Wax Box (24):		20.00
1	Cal Ripken Jr.	1.50
2	Alex Gonzalez	.05
3	Roger Cedeno	.05
4	Todd Hollandsworth	.05
5	Gregg Jefferies	.05
6	Ryne Sandberg	.65
7	Eric Karros	.05
8	Jeff Conine	.05
9	Rafael Palmeiro	.45
10	Bip Roberts	.05
11	Roger Clemens	.70
12	Tom Glavine	.30
13	Jason Giambi	.40
14	Rey Ordonez	.05
15	Chan Ho Park	.05
16	Vinny Castilla	.05
17	Butch Huskey	.05
18	Greg Maddux	.65
19	Bernard Gilkey	.05
20	Marquis Grissom	.05
21	Chuck Knoblauch	.05
22	Ozzie Smith	.65
23	Garret Anderson	.05
24	J.T. Snow	.05
25	John Valentin	.05
26	Barry Larkin	.05
27	Bobby Bonilla	.05
28	Todd Zeile	.05
29	Roberto Alomar	.20
30	Ramon Martinez	.05
31	Jeff King	.05
32	Dennis Eckersley	.45
33	Derek Jeter	1.50
34	Edgar Martinez	.05
35	Geronimo Berroa	.05
36	Hal Morris	.05
37	Troy Percival	.05
38	Jason Isringhausen	.05
39	Greg Vaughn	.05
40	Robin Ventura	.05
41	Craig Biggio	.05
42	Will Clark	.05
43	Sammy Sosa	.65
44	Bernie Williams	.05
45	Kenny Lofton	.05
46	Wade Boggs	.65
47	Javy Lopez	.05
48	Reggie Sanders	.05
49	Jeff Bagwell	.55
50	Fred McGriff	.05
51	Charles Johnson	.05
52	Darren Daulton	.05
53	Jose Canseco	.40
54	Cecil Fielder	.05
55	Hideo Nomo	.30
56	Tim Salmon	.05
57	Carlos Delgado	.40
58	David Cone	.05
59	Tim Raines	.05
60	Lyle Mouton	.05
61	Wally Joyner	.05
62	Bret Boone	.05
63	Raul Mondesi	.05
64	Gary Sheffield	.35
65	Alex Rodriguez	1.00
66	Russ Davis	.05
67	Checklist	.05
68	Marty Cordova	.05
69	Ruben Sierra	.05
70	Jose Mesa	.05
71	Matt Williams	.05
72	Chipper Jones	.75
73	Randy Johnson	.55
74	Kirby Puckett	.65
75	Jim Edmonds	.05
76	Barry Bonds	1.50
77	David Segui	.05
78	Larry Walker	.05
79	Jason Kendall	.05
80	Mike Piazza	.75
81	Brian Hunter	.05
82	Julio Franco	.05
83	Jay Bell	.05
84	Kevin Seitzer	.05
85	John Smoltz	.05
86	Joe Carter	.05

87	Ray Durham	.05
88	Carlos Baerga	.05
89	Ron Gant	.05
90	Orlando Merced	.05
91	Lee Smith	.05
92	Pedro Martinez	.55
93	Frank Thomas	.55
94	Al Martin	.05
95	Chad Curtis	.05
96	Eddie Murray	.55
97	Rusty Greer	.05
98	Jay Buhner	.05
99	Rico Brogna	.05
100	Todd Hundley	.05
101	Moises Alou	.05
102	Chili Davis	.05
103	Ismael Valdes	.05
104	Mo Vaughn	.05
105	Juan Gonzalez	.30
106	Mark Grudzielanek	.05
107	Derek Bell	.05
108	Shawn Green	.30
109	David Justice	.05
110	Paul O'Neill	.05
111	Kevin Appier	.05
112	Ray Lankford	.05
113	Travis Fryman	.05
114	Manny Ramirez	.55
115	Brooks Kieschnick	.05
116	Ken Griffey Jr.	.75
117	Jeffrey Hammonds	.05
118	Mark McGwire	1.00
119	Denny Neagle	.05
120	Quivio Veras	.05
121	Alan Benes	.05
122	Rondell White	.05
123	Osvaldo Fernandez **RC**	.20
124	Andres Galarraga	.05
125	Johnny Damon	.35
126	Lenny Dykstra	.05
127	Jason Schmidt	.05
128	Mike Mussina	.30
129	Ken Caminiti	.05
130	Michael Tucker	.05
131	LaTroy Hawkins	.05
132	Checklist	.05
133	Delino DeShields	.05
134	Dave Nilsson	.05
135	Jack McDowell	.05
136	Joey Hamilton	.05
137	Dante Bichette	.05
138	Paul Molitor	.55
139	Ivan Rodriguez	.45
140	Mark Grace	.05
141	Paul Wilson	.05
142	Orel Hershiser	.05
143	Albert Belle	.05
144	Tino Martinez	.05
145	Tony Gwynn	.65
146	George Arias	.05
147	Brian Jordan	.05
148	Brian McRae	.05
149	Rickey Henderson	.55
150	Ryan Klesko	.05

Press Proofs

The basic 150-card 1996 Studio set was also produced in three parallel press proof versions. Each is basically identical to the regular-issue cards except for appropriately colored foil highlights on front and a notation of edition size in the circle around the portrait photo on back. Bronze press proofs were issued in an edition of 2,000 each and were inserted at an average rate of one per six packs. Gold press proofs were an edition of 500 with an average insertion rate of one per 24 packs. The silver press proofs were inserted only into magazine packs and limited to just 100 cards of each.

	NM/M
Common Player, Bronze:	.50
Bronze Stars:	3X
Common Player, Gold:	1.00
Gold Stars:	7X
Common Player, Silver:	4.00
Silver Stars:	25X

Hit Parade

These die-cut inserts resemble an album with half of the record pulled out of the sleeve. Hit Parade cards, which feature top long ball hitters, were seeded one per every 36 packs. The cards were individually numbered up to 7,500. Each card can also be found in a sample version which has a "XXXX/5000" serial number on back.

		NM/M
Complete Set (10):		10.00
Common Player:		.75
1	Tony Gwynn	1.50
2	Ken Griffey Jr.	2.00
3	Frank Thomas	1.00
4	Jeff Bagwell	1.00
5	Kirby Puckett	1.50
6	Mike Piazza	2.00
7	Barry Bonds	2.50
8	Albert Belle	.75
9	Tim Salmon	.75
10	Mo Vaughn	.75

Masterstrokes

Only 5,000 each of these 1996 Studio insert cards were made. The cards simulate oil painting detail on an embossed canvas-feel front. Backs are glossy and individually serial numbered. They are found on average of once per 70 packs. Sample versions of each card overprinted as such on the back and numbered "PROMO/5000" were also issued.

		NM/M
Complete Set (8):		30.00
Common Player:		4.00
Samples: 75 Percent		
1	Tony Gwynn	6.00
2	Mike Piazza	8.00
3	Jeff Bagwell	4.00
4	Manny Ramirez	4.00
5	Cal Ripken Jr.	12.00
6	Frank Thomas	4.00
7	Ken Griffey Jr.	8.00
8	Greg Maddux	6.00

Glass Stars

Twelve superstars are featured on these clear, die-cut plastic cards which resemble stained glass windows. These 1996 Studio inserts were seeded one per every 30 packs.

		NM/M
Complete Set (12):		24.00
Common Player:		1.00
1	Cal Ripken Jr.	5.00
2	Ken Griffey Jr.	3.50
3	Frank Thomas	2.00
4	Greg Maddux	2.50

5	Chipper Jones	2.50
6	Mike Piazza	3.50
7	Albert Belle	1.00
8	Jeff Bagwell	1.00
9	Hideo Nomo	1.50
10	Barry Bonds	5.00
11	Manny Ramirez	2.00
12	Kenny Lofton	1.00

1997 Studio

Innovations in both product and packaging marked the seventh annual issue of Donruss' Studio brand. As in the past, the 165 cards in the base set rely on high-quality front photos to bring out the players' personalities. For '97, the photos are set against a background of variously shaded gray horizontal stripes. Backs have a second player photo, often an action shot, along with a short career summary. The "pack" for '97 Studio is something totally new to the hobby. An 8-1/2" x 12" cardboard envelope, complete with a zip strip opener in the style of an express-mail envelope, contains a cello pack of five standard-size cards plus either an 8" x 10" Studio Portrait card or an 8" x 10" version of the Master Strokes insert. Suggested retail price at issue was $2.49 per pack. Regular-size Master Strokes cards are one of several insert series which includes silver and gold press proofs and die-cut plastic Hard Hats.

		NM/M
Complete Set (165):		17.50
Common Player:		.05
Silver Press Proofs:		4X
Gold Press Proofs:		8X
Pack (5):		3.00
Wax Box (18):		40.00
1	Frank Thomas	.65
2	Gary Sheffield	.45
3	Jason Isringhausen	.05
4	Ron Gant	.05
5	Andy Pettitte	.25
6	Todd Hollandsworth	.05
7	Troy Percival	.05
8	Mark McGwire	1.50
9	Barry Larkin	.05
10	Ken Caminiti	.05
11	Paul Molitor	.65
12	Travis Fryman	.05
13	Kevin Brown	.05
14	Robin Ventura	.05
15	Andres Galarraga	.05
16	Ken Griffey Jr.	1.00
17	Roger Clemens	.85
18	Alan Benes	.05
19	David Justice	.05
20	Damon Buford	.05
21	Mike Piazza	1.00
22	Ray Durham	.05
23	Billy Wagner	.05
24	Dean Palmer	.05
25	David Cone	.05
26	Ruben Sierra	.05
27	Henry Rodriguez	.05
28	Ray Lankford	.05
29	Jamey Wright	.05
30	Brady Anderson	.05
31	Tino Martinez	.05
32	Manny Ramirez	.65
33	Jeff Conine	.05
34	Dante Bichette	.05
35	Jose Canseco	.50
36	Mo Vaughn	.05
37	Sammy Sosa	.75
38	Mark Grudzielanek	.05
39	Mike Mussina	.35
40	Bill Pulsipher	.05
41	Ryne Sandberg	.75
42	Rickey Henderson	.65
43	Alex Rodriguez	1.50
44	Eddie Murray	.65
45	Ernie Young	.05
46	Joey Hamilton	.05
47	Wade Boggs	.75
48	Rusty Greer	.05
49	Carlos Delgado	.50

50	Ellis Burks	.05
51	Cal Ripken Jr.	2.00
52	Alex Fernandez	.05
53	Wally Joyner	.05
54	James Baldwin	.05
55	Juan Gonzalez	.35
56	John Smoltz	.05
57	Omar Vizquel	.05
58	Shane Reynolds	.05
59	Barry Bonds	2.00
60	Jason Kendall	.05
61	Marty Cordova	.05
62	Charles Johnson	.05
63	John Jaha	.05
64	Chan Ho Park	.05
65	Jermaine Allensworth	.05
66	Mark Grace	.05
67	Tim Salmon	.05
68	Edgar Martinez	.05
69	Marquis Grissom	.05
70	Craig Biggio	.05
71	Bobby Higginson	.05
72	Kevin Seitzer	.05
73	Hideo Nomo	.35
74	Dennis Eckersley	.60
75	Bobby Bonilla	.05
76	Dwight Gooden	.05
77	Jeff Cirillo	.05
78	Brian McRae	.05
79	Chipper Jones	.75
80	Jeff Fassero	.05
81	Fred McGriff	.05
82	Garret Anderson	.05
83	Eric Karros	.05
84	Derek Bell	.05
85	Kenny Lofton	.05
86	John Mabry	.05
87	Pat Hentgen	.05
88	Greg Maddux	.75
89	Jason Giambi	.45
90	Al Martin	.05
91	Derek Jeter	2.00
92	Rey Ordonez	.05
93	Will Clark	.05
94	Kevin Appier	.05
95	Roberto Alomar	.30
96	Joe Carter	.05
97	Bernie Williams	.05
98	Albert Belle	.05
99	Greg Vaughn	.05
100	Tony Clark	.05
101	Matt Williams	.05
102	Jeff Bagwell	.65
103	Reggie Sanders	.05
104	Mariano Rivera	.15
105	Larry Walker	.05
106	Shawn Green	.30
107	Alex Ochoa	.05
108	Ivan Rodriguez	.60
109	Eric Young	.05
110	Javier Lopez	.05
111	Brian Hunter	.05
112	Raul Mondesi	.05
113	Randy Johnson	.65
114	Tony Phillips	.05
115	Carlos Garcia	.05
116	Moises Alou	.05
117	Paul O'Neill	.05
118	Jim Thome	.60
119	Jermaine Dye	.05
120	Wilson Alvarez	.05
121	Rondell White	.05
122	Michael Tucker	.05
123	Mike Lansing	.05
124	Tony Gwynn	.75
125	Ryan Klesko	.05
126	Jim Edmonds	.05
127	Chuck Knoblauch	.05
128	Rafael Palmeiro	.60
129	Jay Buhner	.05
130	Tom Glavine	.35
131	Julio Franco	.05
132	Cecil Fielder	.05
133	Paul Wilson	.05
134	Deion Sanders	.05
135	Alex Gonzalez	.05
136	Charles Nagy	.05
137	Andy Ashby	.05
138	Edgar Renteria	.05
139	Pedro Martinez	.65
140	Brian Jordan	.05
141	Todd Hundley	.05
142	Marc Newfield	.05
143	Darryl Strawberry	.05
144	Dan Wilson	.05
145	Brian Giles **RC**	.50
146	Bartolo Colon	.05
147	Shannon Stewart	.05
148	Scott Spiezio	.05
149	Andruw Jones	.65
150	Karim Garcia	.05
151	Vladimir Guerrero	.65
152	George Arias	.05
153	Brooks Kieschnick	.05
154	Todd Walker	.05
155	Scott Rolen	.60
156	Todd Greene	.05
157	Dmitri Young	.05
158	Ruben Rivera	.05
159	Trey Beamon	.05
160	Nomar Garciaparra	.75
161	Bob Abreu	.05
162	Darin Erstad	.15
163	Ken Griffey Jr. (Checklist)	.50
164	Frank Thomas (Checklist)	.35
165	Alex Rodriguez (Checklist)	.75

Press Proofs

Each of the 165 cards in the base set of '97 Studio was also produced in a pair of Press Proof versions as random pack inserts. Fronts of the Press Proofs have either silver or gold holographic foil replacing the silver foil graphics found on regular cards, as well as foil strips down each side. Backs are identical to the regular issue. The silver Press Proofs were issued in an edition of 1,500 of each player; the golds are limited to 500 of each.

	NM/M
Common Player, Silver:	.50
Silver Stars:	4X
Common Player, Gold:	1.00
Gold Stars:	8X

Hard Hats

Die-cut plastic is used to represent a player's batting helmet in this set of '97 Studio inserts. A player action photo appears in the foreground with his name and other graphic elements in silver foil. Backs feature a small portrait photo, short career summary and a serial number from within the edition of 5,000 of each card.

		NM/M
Complete Set (24):		50.00
Common Player:		1.50
1	Ivan Rodriguez	3.00
2	Albert Belle	1.50
3	Ken Griffey Jr.	6.00
4	Chuck Knoblauch	1.50
5	Frank Thomas	4.00
6	Cal Ripken Jr.	8.00
7	Todd Walker	1.50
8	Alex Rodriguez	7.00
9	Jim Thome	3.00
10	Mike Piazza	6.00
11	Barry Larkin	1.50
12	Chipper Jones	5.00
13	Derek Jeter	8.00
14	Jermaine Dye	1.50
15	Jason Giambi	2.00
16	Tim Salmon	1.50
17	Brady Anderson	1.50
18	Rondell White	1.50
19	Bernie Williams	1.50
20	Juan Gonzalez	2.00
21	Karim Garcia	1.50
22	Scott Rolen	3.00
23	Darin Erstad	2.00
24	Brian Jordan	1.50

Master Strokes

The look and feel of a painting on canvas is the effect presented by '97 Studio's Master Strokes inserts.

Master Strokes 8x10

The look and feel of a painting on canvas is the effect presented by the 8" x 10" version of '97 Studio's Master Strokes inserts. Card fronts feature unique player action art and are highlighted by gold-foil graphics. Each card has a facsimile autograph on front. UV-coated backs are team-color coordinated and have a few sentences about the player. Gold-foil serial numbering identifies the card from an edition of 5,000 of each player - making the super-size version more than twice as common as the 2-1/2" x 3-1/2" version.

		NM/M
Complete Set (24):		45.00
Common Player:		.75
1	Derek Jeter	5.00
2	Jeff Bagwell	2.00
3	Ken Griffey Jr.	3.00
4	Barry Bonds	5.00
5	Frank Thomas	2.00
6	Andy Pettitte	1.00
7	Mo Vaughn	.75
8	Alex Rodriguez	4.00
9	Andruw Jones	2.00
10	Kenny Lofton	.75
11	Cal Ripken Jr.	5.00
12	Greg Maddux	2.50
13	Manny Ramirez	2.00
14	Mike Piazza	3.00
15	Vladimir Guerrero	2.00
16	Albert Belle	.75
17	Chipper Jones	2.50
18	Hideo Nomo	1.50
19	Sammy Sosa	2.50
20	Tony Gwynn	2.50
21	Gary Sheffield	1.50
22	Mark McGwire	4.00
23	Juan Gonzalez	1.50
24	Paul Molitor	2.00

Portraits

Perhaps the most innovative feature of '97 Studio is the 8" x 10" Portrait cards which come one per pack (except when a pack contains a Master Strokes 8x10). Virtually identical to the player's regular-size Studio card, the jumbo version has the word "PORTRAIT" in black beneath the team name on front. Backs have different card numbers than the same player's card in the

Card fronts feature unique player action art and are highlighted by gold-foil graphics. Each card has a facsimile autograph on front. UV-coated backs are team-color coordinated and have a few sentences about the player. Gold-foil serial numbering identifies the card from an edition of 2,000 of each player.

		NM/M
Complete Set (24):		120.00
Common Player:		2.00
1	Derek Jeter	12.00
2	Jeff Bagwell	4.50
3	Ken Griffey Jr.	8.00
4	Barry Bonds	12.00
5	Frank Thomas	4.50
6	Andy Pettitte	2.25
7	Mo Vaughn	2.00
8	Alex Rodriguez	10.00
9	Andruw Jones	4.50
10	Kenny Lofton	2.00
11	Cal Ripken Jr.	12.00
12	Greg Maddux	6.00
13	Manny Ramirez	4.50
14	Mike Piazza	8.00
14p	Mike Piazza (Promo)	3.50
15	Vladimir Guerrero	4.50
16	Albert Belle	2.00
17	Chipper Jones	6.00
18	Hideo Nomo	2.50
19	Sammy Sosa	6.00
20	Tony Gwynn	6.00
21	Gary Sheffield	2.50
22	Mark McGwire	10.00
23	Juan Gonzalez	2.50
24	Paul Molitor	4.50

regular set. The Portrait cards are produced with a special UV coating on front to facilitate autographing. Pre-autographed cards of three youngsters in the series were included as random pack inserts.

		NM/M
Complete Set (24):		10.00
Common Player:		.25
1	Ken Griffey Jr.	1.00
1s	Frank Thomas (Overprinted "SAMPLE.")	.75
2	Frank Thomas	.65
3	Alex Rodriguez	1.50
4	Andruw Jones	.65
5	Cal Ripken Jr.	2.00
6	Greg Maddux	.75
7	Mike Piazza	1.00
8	Chipper Jones	.75
9	Albert Belle	.25
10	Derek Jeter	2.00
11	Juan Gonzalez	.45
12	Todd Walker	.25
12a	Todd Walker (Autographed edition of 1,250.)	10.00
13	Mark McGwire	1.50
14	Barry Bonds	2.00
15	Jeff Bagwell	.65
16	Manny Ramirez	.65
17	Kenny Lofton	.25
18	Mo Vaughn	.25
19	Hideo Nomo	.45
20	Tony Gwynn	.75
21	Vladimir Guerrero	.65
21a	Vladimir Guerrero (Autographed edition of 500.)	30.00
22	Gary Sheffield	.45
23	Ryne Sandberg	.75
24	Scott Rolen	.50
24a	Scott Rolen (Autographed edition of 1,000.)	12.00

Portrait Collection

In a departure from traditional sportscard marketing, the 1997 Studio program offered a pair of specially framed editions directly to consumers. The offer was made in a color brochure found in about half the packs advertising the "Portrait Collection." The offer includes one standard-size card and an 8" x 10" Portrait or Master card similar to those in the regular issue. These cards differ from the regular issue in that they are trimmed in platinum holographic foil, individually hand-numbered and signed by the photographer. The cards were sold framed with a metal plaque, also numbered, attesting to the limited-edition status. The framed Studio Portrait piece was produced in an edition of 500 of each player; the Master Strokes piece was limited to 100 for each player on the checklist. The former was issued at $159; the latter at $299.

	NM/M
Complete Set, Studio Portrait (24):	2,850
Complete Set, Master Strokes (24):	5,250
Common Plaque, Studio Portrait:	125.00
Common Plaque, Master Strokes:	225.00
P1 Ken Griffey Jr.	125.00
P2 Frank Thomas	125.00
P3 Alex Rodriguez	125.00
P4 Andruw Jones	125.00
P5 Cal Ripken Jr.	125.00
P6 Greg Maddux	125.00
P7 Mike Piazza	125.00
P8 Chipper Jones	125.00
P9 Albert Belle	125.00
P10 Derek Jeter	125.00
P11 Juan Gonzalez	125.00
P12 Todd Walker	125.00
P13 Mark McGwire	125.00
P14 Barry Bonds	125.00
P15 Jeff Bagwell	125.00

P16	Manny	125.00
P17	Kenny Lofton	125.00
P18	Mo Vaughn	125.00
P19	Hideo Nomo	125.00
P20	Tony Gwynn	125.00
P21	Vladimir Guerrero	125.00
P22	Gary Sheffield	125.00
P23	Ryne Sandberg	125.00
P24	Scott Rolen	125.00
M1	Derek Jeter	225.00
M2	Jeff Bagwell	225.00
M3	Ken Griffey Jr.	225.00
M4	Barry Bonds	225.00
M5	Frank Thomas	225.00
M6	Andy Pettitte	225.00
M7	Mo Vaughn	225.00
M8	Alex Rodriguez	225.00
M9	Andruw Jones	225.00
M10	Kenny Lofton	225.00
M11	Cal Ripken Jr.	225.00
M12	Greg Maddux	225.00
M13	Manny Ramirez	225.00
M14	Mike Piazza	225.00
M15	Vladimir Guerrero	225.00
M16	Albert Belle	225.00
M17	Chipper Jones	225.00
M18	Hideo Nomo	225.00
M19	Sammy Sosa	225.00
M20	Tony Gwynn	225.00
M21	Gary Sheffield	225.00
M22	Mark McGwire	225.00
M23	Juan Gonzalez	225.00
M24	Paul Molitor	225.00

1998 Studio

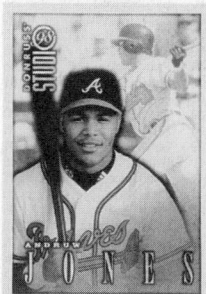

The Donruss Studio base set consists of 220 regular-sized cards and 36 8-x-10 portraits. The base cards feature a posed photo with an action shot in the background, surrounded by a white border. Silver Studio Proofs (numbered to 1,000) and Gold Studio Proofs (300) parallel the regular-size base set. Inserts included Freeze Frame, Hit Parade and Masterstrokes.

		NM/M
	Complete Set (220):	25.00
	Common Player:	.05
	Silver Proofs:	3X
	Gold Proofs:	6X
	Pack (7 Cards+8x10):	2.00
	Wax Box (18):	20.00
1	Tony Clark	.05
2	Jose Cruz Jr.	.05
3	Ivan Rodriguez	.65
4	Mo Vaughn	.05
5	Kenny Lofton	.05
6	Will Clark	.05
7	Barry Larkin	.05
8	Jay Bell	.05
9	Kevin Young	.05
10	Francisco Cordova	.05
11	Justin Thompson	.05
12	Paul Molitor	.75
13	Jeff Bagwell	.75
14	Jose Canseco	.45
15	Scott Rolen	.65
16	Wilton Guerrero	.05
17	Shannon Stewart	.05
18	Hideki Irabu	.05
19	Michael Tucker	.05
20	Joe Carter	.05
21	Gabe Alvarez	.05
22	Ricky Ledee	.05
23	Karim Garcia	.05
24	Eli Marrero	.05
25	Scott Elarton	.05
26	Mario Valdez	.05
27	Ben Grieve	.15
28	Paul Konerko	.15
29	Esteban Yan RC	.05
30	Esteban Loaiza	.05
31	Delino DeShields	.05
32	Bernie Williams	.05
33	Joe Randa	.05
34	Randy Johnson	.75
35	Brett Tomko	.05
36	Todd Erdos RC	.05
37	Bobby Higginson	.05
38	Jason Kendall	.05
39	Ray Lankford	.05
40	Mark Grace	.05
41	Andy Pettitte	.25
42	Alex Rodriguez	2.00
43	Hideo Nomo	.45
44	Sammy Sosa	1.00
45	J.T. Snow	.05
46	Jason Varitek	.05
47	Vinny Castilla	.05
48	Neifi Perez	.05
49	Todd Walker	.05
50	Mike Cameron	.05
51	Jeffrey Hammonds	.05
52	Deivi Cruz	.05
53	Brian Hunter	.05
54	Al Martin	.05
55	Ron Coomer	.05
56	Chan Ho Park	.05
57	Pedro Martinez	.75
58	Darin Erstad	.15
59	Albert Belle	.05
60	Nomar Garciaparra	1.00
61	Tony Gwynn	1.00
62	Mike Piazza	1.50
63	Todd Helton	.65
64	David Ortiz	.45
65	Todd Dunwoody	.05
66	Orlando Cabrera	.05
67	Ken Cloude	.05
68	Andy Benes	.05
69	Mariano Rivera	.15
70	Cecil Fielder	.05
71	Brian Jordan	.05
72	Darryl Kile	.05
73	Reggie Jefferson	.05
74	Shawn Estes	.05
75	Bobby Bonilla	.05
76	Denny Neagle	.05
77	Robin Ventura	.05
78	Omar Vizquel	.05
79	Craig Biggio	.05
80	Moises Alou	.05
81	Garret Anderson	.05
82	Eric Karros	.05
83	Dante Bichette	.05
84	Charles Johnson	.05
85	Rusty Greer	.05
86	Travis Fryman	.05
87	Fernando Tatis	.05
88	Wilson Alvarez	.05
89	Carl Pavano	.05
90	Brian Rose	.05
91	Geoff Jenkins	.05
92	Magglio Ordonez RC	1.50
93	David Segui	.05
94	David Cone	.05
95	John Smoltz	.05
96	Jim Thome	.65
97	Gary Sheffield	.45
98	Barry Bonds	2.50
99	Andres Galarraga	.05
100	Brad Fullmer	.05
101	Bobby Estalella	.05
102	Enrique Wilson	.05
103	Frank Catalanotto RC	.25
104	Mike Lowell RC	1.00
105	Kevin Orie	.05
106	Matt Morris	.05
107	Pokey Reese	.05
108	Shawn Green	.35
109	Tony Womack	.05
110	Ken Caminiti	.20
111	Roberto Alomar	.05
112	Ken Griffey Jr.	1.50
113	Cal Ripken Jr.	2.50
114	Lou Collier	.05
115	Larry Walker	.05
116	Fred McGriff	.05
117	Jim Edmonds	.05
118	Edgar Martinez	.05
119	Matt Williams	.05
120	Ismael Valdes	.05
121	Bartolo Colon	.05
122	Jeff Cirillo	.05
123	Steve Woodard RC	.25
124	Kevin Millwood RC	1.00
125	Derrick Gibson	.05
126	Jacob Cruz	.05
127	Russell Branyan	.05
128	Sean Casey	.15
129	Derrek Lee	.50
130	Paul O'Neill	.05
131	Brad Radke	.05
132	Kevin Appier	.05
133	John Olerud	.05
134	Alan Benes	.05
135	Todd Greene	.05
136	Carlos Mendoza RC	.05
137	Wade Boggs	1.00
138	Jose Guillen	.05
139	Tino Martinez	.05
140	Aaron Boone	.05
141	Abraham Nunez	.05
142	Preston Wilson	.05
143	Randall Simon	.05
144	Dennis Reyes	.05
145	Mark Kotsay	.05
146	Richard Hidalgo	.05
147	Travis Lee	.05
148	Hanley Frias RC	.05
149	Ruben Rivera	.05
150	Rafael Medina	.05
151	Dave Nilsson	.05
152	Curt Schilling	.35
153	Brady Anderson	.05
154	Carlos Delgado	.50
155	Jason Giambi	.45
156	Pat Hentgen	.05
157	Tom Glavine	.35
158	Ryan Klesko	.05
159	Chipper Jones	1.00
160	Juan Gonzalez	.45
161	Mark McGwire	2.00
162	Vladimir Guerrero	.75
163	Derek Jeter	2.50
164	Manny Ramirez	.75
165	Mike Mussina	.30
166	Rafael Palmeiro	.65
167	Henry Rodriguez	.05
168	Jeff Suppan	.05
169	Eric Milton	.05
170	Scott Spiezio	.05
171	Wilson Delgado	.05
172	Bubba Trammell	.05
173	Ellis Burks	.05
174	Jason Dickson	.05
175	Butch Huskey	.05
176	Edgardo Alfonzo	.05
177	Eric Young	.05
178	Marquis Grissom	.05
179	Lance Johnson	.05
180	Kevin Brown	.05
181	Sandy Alomar Jr.	.05
182	Todd Hundley	.05
183	Rondell White	.05
184	Javier Lopez	.05
185	Damian Jackson	.05
186	Raul Mondesi	.05
187	Rickey Henderson	.75
188	David Justice	.05
189	Jay Buhner	.05
190	Jaret Wright	.05
191	Miguel Tejada	.25
192	Ron Wright	.05
193	Livan Hernandez	.05
194	A.J. Hinch	.05
195	Richie Sexson	.05
196	Bob Abreu	.05
197	Luis Castillo	.05
198	Michael Coleman	.05
199	Greg Maddux	1.00
200	Frank Thomas	.75
201	Andruw Jones	.75
202	Roger Clemens	1.25
203	Tim Salmon	.05
204	Chuck Knoblauch	.05
205	Wes Helms	.05
206	Juan Encarnacion	.05
207	Russ Davis	.05
208	John Valentin	.05
209	Tony Saunders	.05
210	Mike Sweeney	.05
211	Steve Finley	.05
212	David Dellucci RC	.25
213	Edgar Renteria	.05
214	Jeremi Gonzalez	.05
215	Checklist (Jeff Bagwell)	.40
216	Checklist (Mike Piazza)	1.00
217	Checklist (Greg Maddux)	.50
218	Checklist (Cal Ripken Jr.)	1.25
219	Checklist (Frank Thomas)	.45
220	Checklist (Ken Griffey Jr.)	.75

Silver Proofs

This parallel set includes all 220 cards in Studio baseball. Cards are identified by a silver holographic strip around the borders. Silver versions are limited to 1,000 sets.

	NM/M
Common Player:	1.00
Silver Stars:	3X

Gold Proofs

Gold proofs is a parallel of the 220-card base set. Card fronts feature gold holo-foil highlights. Backs are sequentially numbered to 300 each.

	NM/M
Common Player:	3.00
Stars:	6X

Autographs

Three top rookies signed a number of 8x10s for this product. Cards have a Donruss "Authentic Signature" stamp on front.

		NM/M
1	Travis Lee/500	20.00
2	Todd Helton/1,000	20.00
3	Ben Grieve/1,000	10.00

Freeze Frame

Freeze Frame is a 30-card insert sequentially numbered to 5,000. The cards are designed to look like a piece of film with a color action photo. The first 500 of each card are die-cut.

		NM/M
	Complete Set (30):	75.00
	Common Player:	1.25
	Production 4,500 Sets	
	Die-Cuts:	1.5X
	Production 500 Sets	
1	Ken Griffey Jr.	5.00
2	Derek Jeter	7.50
3	Ben Grieve	1.25
4	Cal Ripken Jr.	7.50
5	Alex Rodriguez	6.00
6	Greg Maddux	4.00
7	David Justice	1.25
8	Mike Piazza	5.00
9	Chipper Jones	4.00
10	Randy Johnson	3.00
11	Jeff Bagwell	4.00
12	Nomar Garciaparra	4.00
13	Andruw Jones	3.00
14	Frank Thomas	3.00
15	Scott Rolen	2.50
16	Barry Bonds	7.50
17	Kenny Lofton	1.25
18	Ivan Rodriguez	2.50
19	Chuck Knoblauch	1.25
20	Jose Cruz Jr.	1.25
21	Bernie Williams	1.25
22	Tony Gwynn	4.00
23	Juan Gonzalez	2.00
24	Gary Sheffield	2.25
25	Roger Clemens	4.50
26	Travis Lee	1.25
27	Brad Fullmer	1.25
28	Tim Salmon	1.25
29	Raul Mondesi	1.25
30	Roberto Alomar	2.00

Hit Parade

These 20 cards are printed on micro-etched foil board. This set honors baseball's top hitters and is sequentially numbered to 5,000.

		NM/M
	Complete Set (20):	30.00
	Common Player:	1.00
	Production 5,000 Sets	
1	Tony Gwynn	2.50
2	Larry Walker	1.00
3	Mike Piazza	3.00
4	Frank Thomas	2.00
5	Manny Ramirez	2.00
6	Ken Griffey Jr.	3.00
7	Todd Helton	1.50
8	Vladimir Guerrero	2.00
9	Albert Belle	1.00
10	Jeff Bagwell	2.00
11	Juan Gonzalez	1.50
12	Jim Thome	1.50
13	Scott Rolen	1.50
14	Tino Martinez	4.00
15	Mark McGwire	4.00
16	Barry Bonds	5.00
17	Tony Clark	1.00
18	Mo Vaughn	1.00
19	Darin Erstad	1.25
20	Paul Konerko	1.25

Masterstrokes

Printed on a canvas-like material, these 20 cards are numbered to 1,000.

		NM/M
	Complete Set (20):	95.00
	Common Player:	2.00
	Production 1,000 Sets	
	Samples:	3X
1	Travis Lee	2.00
2	Kenny Lofton	2.00
3	Mo Vaughn	2.00
4	Ivan Rodriguez	3.50
5	Roger Clemens	6.50
6	Mark McGwire	10.00
7	Hideo Nomo	2.50
8	Andruw Jones	4.50
9	Nomar Garciaparra	6.00
10	Juan Gonzalez	2.50
11	Jeff Bagwell	4.50
12	Derek Jeter	12.50
13	Tony Gwynn	6.00
14	Chipper Jones	5.00
15	Mike Piazza	7.50
16	Greg Maddux	6.00
17	Alex Rodriguez	10.00
18	Cal Ripken Jr.	12.50
19	Frank Thomas	4.50
20	Ken Griffey Jr.	7.50

Sony MLB 99

Twenty Sony MLB '99 sweepstakes cards were inserted one per two Studio packs. The fronts feature a color action shot and the backs have sweepstakes rules and a MLB '99 tip.

		NM/M
	Complete Set (20):	8.00
	Common Player:	.15
1	Cal Ripken Jr.	1.50
2	Nomar Garciaparra	.75
3	Barry Bonds	.75
4	Mike Mussina	.35
5	Pedro Martinez	.35
6	Derek Jeter	1.50
7	Andruw Jones	.60
8	Kenny Lofton	.15
9	Gary Sheffield	.45
10	Raul Mondesi	.15
11	Jeff Bagwell	.60
12	Tim Salmon	.15
13	Tom Glavine	.35
14	Ben Grieve	.15
15	Matt Williams	.15
16	Juan Gonzalez	.35
17	Mark McGwire	1.00
18	Bernie Williams	.15
19	Andres Galarraga	.15
20	Jose Cruz Jr.	.15

8x10 Portraits Samples

Sample versions of the 8x10 cards which would be found in '98 Studio packs were also issued. They are identical in format to the issued cards, with UV coating and silver-foil graphics on fronts. Backs have a large black "SAMPLE" over-printed diagonally.

		NM/M
001	Travis Lee	2.00
002	Todd Helton	3.00

8x10 Portraits

One Studio 8-x-10 was included in each pack. The cards were blown-up versions of the regular-size base cards, which were inserted seven per pack. The large portraits are paralleled in the Gold Proofs set, which adds gold holo-foil to the cards. Gold Proofs are numbered to 300.

		NM/M
	Complete Set (36):	65.00
	Common Player:	.50
	Inserted 1:1	
1	Travis Lee	.50
2	Todd Helton	1.50
3	Ben Grieve	.50
4	Paul Konerko	.65
5	Jeff Bagwell	2.00
6	Derek Jeter	7.00
7	Ivan Rodriguez	1.50
8	Cal Ripken Jr.	7.00
9	Mike Piazza	4.00
10	Chipper Jones	3.00
11	Frank Thomas	3.00
12	Tony Gwynn	3.00
13	Nomar Garciaparra	1.00
14	Juan Gonzalez	1.00
15	Greg Maddux	3.00
16	Hideo Nomo	1.00
17	Scott Rolen	1.50
18	Barry Bonds	7.00
19	Ken Griffey Jr.	4.00
20	Alex Rodriguez	5.00
21	Roger Clemens	5.00
22	Mark McGwire	5.00
23	Jose Cruz Jr.	.50
24	Andruw Jones	.50
25	Tino Martinez	.50
26	Mo Vaughn	.50
27	Vladimir Guerrero	2.00
28	Tony Clark	.50
29	Andy Pettitte	.65
30	Jaret Wright	.50
31	Paul Molitor	2.00
32	Darin Erstad	.65
33	Larry Walker	.50
34	Chuck Knoblauch	.50
35	Barry Larkin	.50
36	Kenny Lofton	.50

Portraits Gold Proofs

This parallel of the 8x10 base set adds gold holo-foil treatments to the 36 cards, which are sequentially numbered to 300 and randomly inserted in packs.

	NM/M
Common Player:	5.00
Stars:	6X

1995 Summit Samples

Nine-card cello packs of Summit cards, including "Big Bang" inserts, were released to dealers to debut the new Score brand. Cards are specially marked as promotional samples.

		NM/M
Complete Set (9):		5.00
Common Player:		.50
10	Barry Larkin	.50
11	Albert Belle	.50
79	Cal Ripken Jr.	3.00
80	David Cone	.50
125	Alex Gonzalez (Rookie)	.50
130	Charles Johnson (Rookie)	.50
BB12	Jose Canseco (Big Bang)	1.00
BB17	Fred McGriff (Big Bang)	.50
---	Information Card	.05

1995 Summit

A late-season release, Summit introduced the Score label to a premium brand card. The rookie cards (#1-111) feature horizontal or vertical action photos with the player's name and team logo printed in gold-foil on front. Backs have a player portrait photo along with his 1994 stats in monthly charted form. The rookie cards subset (#112-173) have a large black "ROOKIE" on top-front while the back has a short career summary instead of stats. Other subsets include "BAT SPEED" (#174-188), honoring top hitters, and "SPECIAL DELIVERY" (#189-193), featuring top pitchers. Each are designated on front with special gold-foil logos. Seven checklists close out the regular 200-card set. The Summit issued featured a four-tiered chase card program, including a parallel "Nth Degree" set. Summit was a hobby-only issue sold in 7-card foil packs.

		NM/M
Complete Set (200):		10.00
Common Player:		.05
Pack (7):		1.00
Wax Box (24):		12.50
1	Ken Griffey Jr.	1.00
2	Alex Fernandez	.05
3	Fred McGriff	.05
4	Ben McDonald	.05
5	Rafael Palmeiro	.60
6	Tony Gwynn	.75
7	Jim Thome	.60
8	Ken Hill	.05
9	Barry Bonds	2.00
10	Barry Larkin	.05
11	Albert Belle	.05
12	Billy Ashley	.05
13	Matt Williams	.05
14	Andy Benes	.05
15	Midre Cummings	.05
16	J.R. Phillips	.05
17	Edgar Martinez	.05

18	Manny Ramirez	.65
19	Jose Canseco	.40
20	Chili Davis	.05
21	Don Mattingly	.85
22	Bernie Williams	.05
23	Tom Glavine	.35
24	Robin Ventura	.05
25	Jeff Conine	.05
26	Mark Grace	.05
27	Mark McGwire	1.50
28	Carlos Delgado	.45
29	Greg Colbrunn	.05
30	Greg Maddux	.75
31	Craig Biggio	.05
32	Kirby Puckett	.75
33	Derek Bell	.05
34	Lenny Dykstra	.05
35	Tim Salmon	.05
36	Deion Sanders	.05
37	Moises Alou	.05
38	Ray Lankford	.05
39	Willie Greene	.05
40	Ozzie Smith	.75
41	Roger Clemens	.85
42	Andres Galarraga	.35
43	Gary Sheffield	.35
44	Sammy Sosa	.75
45	Larry Walker	.05
46	Kevin Appier	.05
47	Raul Mondesi	.05
48	Kenny Lofton	.05
49	Darryl Hamilton	.05
50	Roberto Alomar	.20
51	Hal Morris	.05
52	Cliff Floyd	.05
53	Brent Gates	.05
54	Rickey Henderson	.65
55	John Olerud	.05
56	Gregg Jefferies	.05
57	Cecil Fielder	.05
58	Paul Molitor	.65
59	Bret Boone	.05
60	Greg Vaughn	.05
61	Wally Joyner	.05
62	Jeffrey Hammonds	.05
63	James Mouton	.05
64	Omar Vizquel	.05
65	Wade Boggs	.75
66	Terry Steinbach	.05
67	Wil Cordero	.05
68	Joey Hamilton	.05
69	Rico Brogna	.05
70	Darren Daulton	.05
71	Chuck Knoblauch	.05
72	Bob Hamelin	.05
73	Carl Everett	.05
74	Joe Carter	.05
75	Dave Winfield	.65
76	Bobby Bonilla	.05
77	Paul O'Neill	.05
78	Javier Lopez	.05
79	Cal Ripken Jr.	2.00
80	David Cone	.05
81	Bernard Gilkey	.05
82	Ivan Rodriguez	.60
83	Dean Palmer	.05
84	Jason Bere	.05
85	Will Clark	.05
86	Scott Cooper	.05
87	Royce Clayton	.05
88	Mike Piazza	1.00
89	Ryan Klesko	.05
90	Juan Gonzalez	.35
91	Travis Fryman	.05
92	Frank Thomas	.65
93	Eduardo Perez	.05
94	Mo Vaughn	.05
95	Jay Bell	.05
96	Jeff Bagwell	.65
97	Randy Johnson	.05
98	Jimmy Key	.05
99	Dennis Eckersley	.60
100	Carlos Baerga	.05
101	Eddie Murray	.65
102	Mike Mussina	.30
103	Brian Anderson	.05
104	Jeff Cirillo	.05
105	Dante Bichette	.05
106	Bret Saberhagen	.05
107	Jeff Kent	.05
108	Ruben Sierra	.05
109	Kirk Gibson	.05
110	Reggie Sanders	.05
111	Dave Justice	.05
112	Benji Gil	.05
113	Vaughn Eshelman	.05
114	Carlos Perez RC	.05
115	Chipper Jones	.75
116	Shane Andrews	.05
117	Orlando Miller	.05
118	Scott Ruffcorn	.05
119	Jose Oliva	.05
120	Joe Vitiello	.05
121	Jon Nunnally	.05
122	Garret Anderson	.05
123	Curtis Goodwin	.05
124	Mark Grudzielanek RC	.25
125	Alex Gonzalez	.05
126	David Bell	.05
127	Dustin Hermanson	.05
128	Dave Nilsson	.05
129	Wilson Heredia	.05
130	Charles Johnson	.05
131	Frank Rodriguez	.05
132	Alex Ochoa	.05
133	Alex Rodriguez	1.50
134	Bobby Higginson RC	.25
135	Edgardo Alfonso	.05

136	Armando Benitez	.05
137	Rich Aude	.05
138	Tim Naehring	.05
139	Joe Randa	.05
140	Quivlio Veras	.05
141	Hideo Nomo RC	1.00
142	Ray Holbert	.05
143	Michael Tucker	.05
144	Chad Mottola	.05
145	John Valentin	.05
146	James Baldwin	.05
147	Esteban Loaiza	.05
148	Marty Cordova	.05
149	Juan Acevedo RC	.05
150	Tim Unroe RC	.05
151	Brad Clontz	.05
152	Steve Rodriguez	.05
153	Rudy Pemberton	.05
154	Ozzie Timmons	.05
155	Ricky Otero	.05
156	Allen Battle	.05
157	Joe Roselli	.05
158	Roberto Petagine	.05
159	Todd Hollandsworth	.05
160	Shannon Penn	.05
161	Antonio Osuna	.05
162	Russ Davis	.05
163	Jason Giambi	.40
164	Terry Bradshaw	.05
165	Ray Durham	.05
166	Todd Steverson	.05
167	Tim Belk	.05
168	Andy Pettitte	.25
169	Roger Cedeno	.05
170	Jose Parra	.05
171	Scott Sullivan	.05
172	LaTroy Hawkins	.05
173	Jeff McCurry	.05
174	Ken Griffey Jr. (Bat Speed)	.50
175	Frank Thomas (Bat Speed)	.30
176	Cal Ripken Jr. (Bat Speed)	1.00
177	Jeff Bagwell (Bat Speed)	.30
178	Mike Piazza (Bat Speed)	.50
179	Barry Bonds (Bat Speed)	1.00
180	Matt Williams (Bat Speed)	.05
181	Don Mattingly (Bat Speed)	.45
182	Will Clark (Bat Speed)	.05
183	Tony Gwynn (Bat Speed)	.40
184	Kirby Puckett (Bat Speed)	.40
185	Jose Canseco (Bat Speed)	.25
186	Paul Molitor (Bat Speed)	.30
187	Albert Belle (Bat Speed)	.05
188	Joe Carter (Bat Speed)	.05
189	Greg Maddux (Special Delivery)	.40
190	Roger Clemens (Special Delivery)	.45
191	David Cone (Special Delivery)	.05
192	Mike Mussina (Special Delivery)	.15
193	Randy Johnson (Special Delivery)	.05
194	Checklist (Frank Thomas)	.30
195	Checklist (Ken Griffey Jr.)	.50
196	Checklist (Cal Ripken Jr.)	.75
197	Checklist (Jeff Bagwell)	.30
198	Checklist (Mike Piazza)	.50
199	Checklist (Barry Bonds)	.75
200	Checklist (Mo Vaughn, Matt Williams)	.05

Big Bang

The game's top sluggers are featured in this insert set. The front is printed on prismatic metallic foil, a process which Score calls "Spectroetch," with large and small action photos. Backs are conventionally printed and have a large photo with a career highlight printed beneath. The toughest of the Summit chase cards, these are found on the average of once every two boxes (72 packs). Cards are numbered with a "BB" prefix.

		NM/M
Complete Set (20):		45.00
Common Player:		1.00
1	Ken Griffey Jr.	6.00
2	Frank Thomas	3.25
3	Cal Ripken Jr.	8.00
4	Jeff Bagwell	3.25
5	Mike Piazza	6.00

6	Barry Bonds	8.00
7	Matt Williams	1.00
8	Don Mattingly	4.50
9	Will Clark	1.00
10	Tony Gwynn	4.00
11	Kirby Puckett	4.00
12	Jose Canseco	2.00
13	Paul Molitor	3.25
14	Albert Belle	1.00
15	Joe Carter	1.00
16	Rafael Palmeiro	3.00
17	Fred McGriff	1.00
18	Dave Justice	1.00
19	Tim Salmon	1.00
20	Mo Vaughn	1.00

New Age

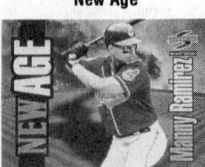

Printed on metallic foil in a horizontal format, the New Age inserts were seeded at a rate of about one per 18 packs. Red and silver colors predominate on front, while the backs are printed in standard technology and feature a second photo and career summary.

		NM/M
Complete Set (15):		10.00
Common Player:		.25
1	Cliff Floyd	.25
2	Manny Ramirez	2.00
3	Raul Mondesi	.25
4	Alex Rodriguez	5.00
5	Billy Ashley	.25
6	Alex Gonzalez	.25
7	Michael Tucker	.25
8	Charles Johnson	.25
9	Carlos Delgado	1.00
10	Benji Gil	.25
11	Chipper Jones	3.00
12	Todd Hollandsworth	.25
13	Frank Rodriguez	.25
14	Shawn Green	.60
15	Ray Durham	.25

Nth Degree

A prismatic foil background differentiates the Nth Degree parallel inserts from the Summit base cards. Nth Degree inserts are found on a 1:4 pack ratio.

		NM/M
Complete Set (200):		50.00
Common Player:		.25
Stars:		2X

21 Club

Metallic foil printing on front and back distinguishes this set of chase cards. A large red-foil "21 / CLUB" logo on each side identifies the theme of this set as players who professed to be that age during the 1955 baseball season. The players are pictured in action pose on front and a portrait on back. On average the 21 Club cards are seeded one per box (36 packs). Cards are numbered with a "TC" prefix.

		NM/M
Complete Set (9):		4.00
Common Player:		.50
1	Bob Abreu	.65

2	Pokey Reese	.50
3	Edgardo Alfonzo	.50
4	Jim Pittsley	.50
5	Ruben Rivera	.50
6	Chan Ho Park	.50
7	Julian Tavarez	.50
8	Ismael Valdes	.50
9	Dmitri Young	.50

1996 Summit

Pinnacle's 1996 Summit baseball has 200 cards, including 35 rookies, four checklists and 10 Deja Vu subset cards. Each card is also reprinted in three parallel versions - Above and Beyond (one per seven packs), Artist's Proofs (one in 36) and a retail-only silver foil-bordered version. Above and Beyond cards use an all-prismatic foil design; Artist's Proof cards have holographic foil stamping. Five insert sets were produced: Big Bang; Mirage (a parallel set to Big Bang); Hitters, Inc.; Ballparks; and Positions (found one per every 50 magazine packs).

		NM/M
Complete Set (200):		10.00
Common Player:		.05
Pack (7):		1.25
Wax Box (18):		15.00
1	Mike Piazza	1.25
2	Matt Williams	.05
3	Tino Martinez	.05
4	Reggie Sanders	.05
5	Ray Durham	.05
6	Brad Radke	.05
7	Jeff Bagwell	.65
8	Ron Gant	.05
9	Lance Johnson	.05
10	Kevin Seitzer	.05
11	Dante Bichette	.05
12	Ivan Rodriguez	.60
13	Jim Abbott	.05
14	Greg Colbrunn	.05
15	Rondell White	.05
16	Shawn Green	.40
17	Gregg Jefferies	.05
18	Omar Vizquel	.05
19	Cal Ripken Jr.	2.00
20	Mark McGwire	1.50
21	Wally Joyner	.05
22	Chili Davis	.05
23	Jose Canseco	.40
24	Royce Clayton	.05
25	Jay Bell	.05
26	Travis Fryman	.05
27	Jeff King	.05
28	Todd Hundley	.05
29	Joe Vitiello	.05
30	Russ Davis	.05
31	Mo Vaughn	.05
32	Raul Mondesi	.05
33	Ray Lankford	.05
34	Mike Stanley	.05
35	B.J. Surhoff	.05
36	Greg Vaughn	.05
37	Todd Stottlemyre	.05
38	Carlos Delgado	.50
39	Kenny Lofton	.05
40	Hideo Nomo	.35
41	Sterling Hitchcock	.05
42	Pete Schourek	.05
43	Edgardo Alfonzo	.05
44	Ken Hill	.05
45	Ken Caminiti	.05
46	Bobby Higginson	.05
47	Michael Tucker	.05
48	David Cone	.05
49	Cecil Fielder	.05
50	Brian Hunter	.05
51	Charles Johnson	.05
52	Bobby Bonilla	.05
53	Eddie Murray	.65
54	Kenny Rogers	.05
55	Jim Edmonds	.05
56	Trevor Hoffman	.05
57	Kevin Mitchell	.05
58	Ruben Sierra	.05
59	Benji Gil	.05
60	Juan Gonzalez	.35
61	Larry Walker	.05
62	Jack McDowell	.05
63	Shawon Dunston	.05
64	Andy Benes	.05

65	Jay Buhner	.05
66	Rickey Henderson	.65
67	Alex Gonzalez	.05
68	Mike Kelly	.05
69	Fred McGriff	.05
70	Ryne Sandberg	.75
71	Ernie Young	.05
72	Kevin Appier	.05
73	Moises Alou	.05
74	John Jaha	.05
75	J.T. Snow	.05
76	Jim Thome	.60
77	Kirby Puckett	.75
78	Hal Morris	.05
79	Robin Ventura	.05
80	Ben McDonald	.05
81	Tim Salmon	.05
82	Albert Belle	.05
83	Marquis Grissom	.05
84	Alex Rodriguez	1.50
85	Manny Ramirez	.65
86	Ken Griffey Jr.	1.25
87	Sammy Sosa	.75
88	Frank Thomas	.65
89	Lee Smith	.05
90	Marty Cordova	.05
91	Greg Maddux	.75
92	Lenny Dykstra	.05
93	Butch Huskey	.05
94	Garret Anderson	.05
95	Mike Bordick	.05
96	Dave Justice	.05
97	Chad Curtis	.05
98	Carlos Baerga	.05
99	Jason Isringhausen	.05
100	Gary Sheffield	.35
101	Roger Clemens	1.00
102	Ozzie Smith	.75
103	Ramon Martinez	.05
104	Paul O'Neill	.05
105	Will Clark	.05
106	Tom Glavine	.35
107	Barry Bonds	2.00
108	Barry Larkin	.05
109	Derek Bell	.05
110	Randy Johnson	.65
111	Jeff Conine	.05
112	John Mabry	.05
113	Julian Tavarez	.05
114	Gary DiSarcina	.05
115	Marc Newfield	.05
116	Frank Rodriguez	.05
117	Brady Anderson	.05
118	Mike Mussina	.30
119	Orlando Merced	.05
120	Melvin Nieves	.05
121	Brian Jordan	.05
122	Rafael Palmeiro	.30
123	Johnny Damon	.05
124	Wil Cordero	.05
125	Chipper Jones	.75
126	Eric Karros	.05
127	Darren Daulton	.05
128	Vinny Castilla	.05
129	Joe Carter	.05
130	Bernie Williams	.05
131	Bernard Gilkey	.05
132	Bret Boone	.05
133	Tony Gwynn	.75
134	Dave Nilsson	.05
135	Ryan Klesko	.05
136	Paul Molitor	.65
137	John Olerud	.05
138	Craig Biggio	.05
139	John Valentin	.05
140	Chuck Knoblauch	.05
141	Edgar Martinez	.05
142	Rico Brogna	.05
143	Dean Palmer	.05
144	Mark Grace	.05
145	Roberto Alomar	.20
146	Alex Fernandez	.05
147	Andre Dawson	.25
148	Wade Boggs	.75
149	Mark Lewis	.05
150	Gary Gaetti	.05
151	Paul Wilson, Roger Clemens (Deja Vu)	.45
152	Rey Ordonez, Ozzie Smith (Deja Vu)	.35
153	Derek Jeter, Cal Ripken Jr. (Deja Vu)	1.00
154	Alan Benes, Andy Benes (Deja Vu)	.05
155	Jason Kendall, Mike Piazza (Deja Vu)	.75
156	Ryan Klesko, Frank Thomas (Deja Vu)	.30
157	Johnny Damon, Ken Griffey Jr. (Deja Vu)	.65
158	Karim Garcia, Sammy Sosa (Deja Vu)	.40
159	Raul Mondesi, Tim Salmon (Deja Vu)	.05
160	Chipper Jones, Matt Williams (Deja Vu)	.40
161	Rey Ordonez	.05
162	Bob Wolcott	.05
163	Brooks Kieschnick	.05
164	Steve Gibralter	.05
165	Bob Abreu	.05
166	Gregg Zaun	.05
167	Tavo Alvarez	.05
168	Sal Fasano	.05
169	George Arias	.05
170	Derek Jeter	2.00
171	Livan Hernandez RC	.05

173	Alan Benes	.05
174	George Williams	.05
175	John Wasdin	.05
176	Chan Ho Park	.05
177	Paul Wilson	.05
178	Jeff Suppan	.05
179	Quinton McCracken	.05
180	Wilton Guerrero RC	.05
181	Eric Owens	.05
182	Felipe Crespo	.05
183	LaTroy Hawkins	.05
184	Jason Schmidt	.05
185	Terrell Wade	.05
186	Mike Grace RC	.05
187	Chris Snopek	.05
188	Jason Kendall	.05
189	Todd Hollandsworth	.05
190	Jim Pittsley	.05
191	Jermaine Dye	.05
192	Mike Busby RC	.05
193	Richard Hidalgo	.05
194	Tyler Houston	.05
195	Jimmy Haynes	.05
196	Karim Garcia	.05
197	Ken Griffey Jr. (Checklist)	.05
198	Frank Thomas (Checklist)	.30
199	Greg Maddux (Checklist)	.40
200	Cal Ripken Jr. (Checklist)	1.00

Artist's Proof

Holographic-foil highlights and an "ARTIST'S PROOF" notation on the front photo distinguish the cards in this parallel edition. The AP cards are found once per 36 packs.

	NM/M
Complete Set (200):	100.00
Common Player:	1.00
Stars:	8X

Foil

This parallel issue was an exclusive in Summit seven-card magazine retail packaging. The black borders of the regular Summit versions have been replaced on these cards by silver foil.

	NM/M
Complete Set (200):	30.00
Common Player:	.25
Stars:	3X

Above & Beyond

These 200 insert cards parallel Pinnacle's 1996 Summit set, using all-prismatic foil for each card. The cards were seeded one per every four packs.

	NM/M
Complete Set (200):	50.00
Common Player:	.25
Stars:	3X

Ballparks

These 18 cards feature images of players superimposed over their respective teams' ballparks. The cards were seeded one per every 18 packs of 1996 Pinnacle Summit baseball and are serially numbered within an edition of 8,000 each.

		NM/M
Complete Set (18):		45.00
Common Player:		1.00
1	Cal Ripken Jr.	7.50
2	Albert Belle	1.00
3	Dante Bichette	1.00
4	Mo Vaughn	1.00
5	Ken Griffey Jr.	6.00
6	Derek Jeter	7.50
7	Juan Gonzalez	1.50
8	Greg Maddux	4.00
9	Frank Thomas	3.00
10	Ryne Sandberg	4.00
11	Mike Piazza	4.00
12	Johnny Damon	1.50
13	Barry Bonds	7.50
14	Jeff Bagwell	3.00
15	Paul Wilson	1.00
16	Tim Salmon	1.00
17	Kirby Puckett	4.00
18	Tony Gwynn	4.00

Big Bang

Sixteen of the biggest hitters are featured on these 1996 Pinnacle Summit insert cards. The cards, seeded one per every 72 packs, use Spectroetched backgrounds with foil highlights.

		NM/M
Complete Set (16):		60.00
Common Player:		1.50
1	Frank Thomas	4.00
2	Ken Griffey Jr.	7.50
3	Albert Belle	1.50
4	Mo Vaughn	1.50
5	Barry Bonds	12.00
6	Cal Ripken Jr.	12.00
7	Jeff Bagwell	4.00
8	Mike Piazza	7.50
9	Ryan Klesko	1.50
10	Manny Ramirez	4.00
11	Tim Salmon	1.50
12	Dante Bichette	1.50
13	Sammy Sosa	6.00
14	Raul Mondesi	1.50
15	Chipper Jones	6.00
16	Garret Anderson	1.50

Big Bang Mirage

These 16 cards form a parallel version to Summit's Big Bang inserts. The cards use an innovative technology that creates a floating background behind the player's image. By holding the card in direct sunlight or under an incandescent bulb, a collector can see three dimensions and a floating baseball that seems to levitate in the background. Mirage cards are serially numbered in an edition of 600 each.

		NM/M
Complete Set (16):		115.00
Common Player:		3.50
1	Frank Thomas	10.00
2	Ken Griffey Jr.	15.00
3	Albert Belle	3.50
4	Mo Vaughn	3.50
5	Barry Bonds	20.00
6	Cal Ripken Jr.	20.00
7	Jeff Bagwell	10.00
8	Mike Piazza	15.00
9	Ryan Klesko	3.50
10	Manny Ramirez	10.00
11	Tim Salmon	3.50
12	Dante Bichette	3.50
13	Sammy Sosa	12.50
14	Raul Mondesi	3.50
15	Chipper Jones	12.50
16	Garret Anderson	3.50

Hitters, Inc.

This 1996 Pinnacle Summit set honors 16 top hitters. The cards, seeded one per 36 packs, put an embossed highlight on an enlarged photo of the player's eyes. Backs are serially numbered within an edition of 4,000 each.

		NM/M
Complete Set (16):		40.00
Common Player:		1.25
1	Tony Gwynn	4.00
2	Mo Vaughn	1.25
3	Tim Salmon	1.25
4	Ken Griffey Jr.	5.00
5	Sammy Sosa	4.00
6	Frank Thomas	3.00
7	Wade Boggs	4.00
8	Albert Belle	1.25
9	Cal Ripken Jr.	8.00
10	Manny Ramirez	3.00
11	Ryan Klesko	1.25
11p	Ryan Klesko (Overprinted "SAMPLE.")	1.25
12	Dante Bichette	1.25
13	Mike Piazza	5.00
14	Chipper Jones	4.00
15	Ryne Sandberg	4.00
16	Matt Williams	1.25

Positions

This insert issue features top players at each position. It is an exclusive magazine pack find, seeded about one per 50 packs. Fronts have action photos of three top players at the position on a baseball infield background at top. Close-ups of those photos appear at bottom, separated by a gold-foil strip. Backs have narrow action photos of each player, a few stats and a serial number from within an edition of 1,500 each.

		NM/M
Complete Set (9):		100.00
Common Card:		6.00
1	Jeff Bagwell, Mo Vaughn, Frank Thomas (First Base)	10.00
2	Roberto Alomar, Craig Biggio, Chuck Knoblauch (Second Base)	6.00
3	Matt Williams, Jim Thome, Chipper Jones (Third Base)	12.50
4	Barry Larkin, Cal Ripken Jr., Alex Rodriguez (Short Stop)	20.00
5	Mike Piazza, Ivan Rodriguez, Charles Johnson (Catcher)	15.00
6	Hideo Nomo, Greg Maddux, Randy Johnson (Pitcher)	12.50
7	Barry Bonds, Albert Belle, Ryan Klesko (Left Field)	20.00
8	Johnny Damon, Jim Edmonds, Ken Griffey Jr. (Center Field)	15.00
9	Manny Ramirez, Gary Sheffield, Sammy Sosa (Right Field)	12.50

1987 Sun Foods Milwaukee Brewers

Though they are nowhere identified on the cards, Sun Foods was the sponsor of this team set, issuing four cards per week. Measuring 6" x 9", the cards were licensed only by the Players' Association and so do not feature team uniform logos. Bare-headed players are photographed against a blue background with a black facsimile autograph at bottom. An MLBPA logo appears in the upper-left. Backs are blank. The unnumbered cards are checklisted here in alphabetical order.

		NM/M
Complete Set (16):		15.00
Common Player:		.50
(1)	Glenn Braggs	.50
(2)	Greg Brock	.50
(3)	Mark Clear	.50
(4)	Cecil Cooper	.50
(5)	Rob Deer	.50
(6)	Jim Gantner	.50
(7)	Ted Higuera	.50
(8)	Paul Molitor	5.00
(9)	Juan Nieves	.50
(10)	Dan Plesac	.50
(11)	Billy Jo Robidoux	.50
(12)	Bill Schroeder	.50
(13)	B.J. Surhoff	.50
(14)	Dale Sveum	.50
(15)	Bill Wegman	.50
(16)	Robin Yount	5.00

1994 SuperSlam

An innovative issued felled by the 1994 baseball strike, SuperSlams are a 5-1/2" x 7-1/2" tent-fold display card. Front and back have a gridded silver metallic background. At center

on front is a 3-3/4" x 5-1/4" color photo on which is superimposed a 3-D action pose of the player. Backs have extensive "This is my life" biographical information about the player. The cards are skip-numbered. Promo cards of Jack McDowell were issued with either silver or gold background. Cards were sold for $7.95 apiece with reported production between 2,000 and 50,000, depending on player.

		NM/M
Complete Set (18):		60.00
Common Player:		2.50
3	Greg Maddux	5.00
4	Fred McGriff	2.50
5	Moises Alou	2.50
19	Roberto Alomar	3.00
27	Cal Ripken Jr.	8.00
28	Roger Clemens	5.50
40	Mike Piazza	6.00
42	Barry Bonds	8.00
47	Tony Gwynn	5.00
53	Rickey Henderson	4.00
57	Tim Salmon	2.50
60	Ken Griffey Jr.	6.00
65	Juan Gonzalez	3.00
67	Jeff Bagwell	4.00
83	Albert Belle	2.50
84	Kenny Lofton	2.50
90	Kirby Puckett	5.00
95	Frank Thomas	2.50
P1	Jack McDowell/Gold	2.50
P2	Jack McDowell/Silver	2.50

1982 Superstar

A second series of Superstar collector cards was produced in 1982. Similar in format to the 1980 issue, they also feature black-and-white photos. Surrounding graphics on the second series are in red, white and blue. Backs are numbered from 45-90 in continuation of the first series and contain career narratives. Many players are again featured on multiple cards, and the second series contains sports stars other than baseball players. Issue price was again $3.50.

		NM/M
Complete Set (45):		10.00
Common Player:		.40
46	Duke Snider	.40
47	Al Kaline	.40
48	Stan Musial	.60
49	Frank Robinson	.40
50	Jim Brown	.80
51	Bobby Orr	.60
52	Roger Staubach	.40
53	Honus Wagner	.40
54	Willie Mays	.80
55	Roy Campanella	.40
56	Mickey Mantle	2.50
57	Hank Aaron	.80
58	Ernie Banks	.40
59	Babe Ruth, Lou Gehrig	1.50
60	Ted Williams	.80
61	Babe Ruth	1.50
62	Lou Gehrig	.80
63	Sandy Koufax	.40
64	Fran Tarkenton	.40
65	Gordie Howe	.60
66	Roberto Clemente	1.25
67	Ty Cobb	.60
68	Lou Brock	.40
69	Joe Namath	.60
70	O.J. Simpson	.60
71	Whitey Ford	.40
72	Jackie Robinson	.80
73	Bill Russell	.60
74	Johnny Unitas	.60
75	Bobby Hull	.60
76	Bob Cousy	.60
77	Walter Johnson	.60
78	Satchel Paige	.50
79	Joe DiMaggio	1.25
80	Yogi Berra	.40
81	Jerry West	.60
82	Rod Gilbert	.40
83	Sadaharu Oh	.40
84	Wilt Chamberlain	.60
85	Frank Gifford	.40
86	Casey Stengel	.40
87	Eddie Mathews	.40
88	Hank Aaron, Sandy Koufax	.80
89	Ted Williams, Mickey Mantle	1.25
90	Casey Stengel, Mickey Mantle	1.50

1987 Super Stars Discs

Produced by Mike Schecter Associates, the Super Stars disc set was released as part of a promotion for various brands of iced tea mixes in many parts of the country. Among the brands participating in the promotion were Acme, Alpha Beta, Bustelo, Key, King Kullen, Lady Lee, Our Own, and Weis. The discs were issued in three-part folding panels with each disc measuring 2-1/2" in diameter. Fronts feature a full-color photo inside a bright yellow border. Two player discs were included in each panel along with a coupon disc offering either an uncut press sheet of the set or a facsimile autographed ball. Because the series was licensed only by the players' union, and not MLB, cap logos were removed.

		NM/M
Complete Panel Set (10):		7.50
Complete Singles Set (20):		4.50
Common Panel:		.25
Common Single Player:		.10
Panel (1)		1.00
1	Darryl Strawberry	.10
2	Roger Clemens	.50
Panel (2)		.25
3	Ron Darling	.10
4	Keith Hernandez	.10
Panel (3)		1.00
5	Tony Pena	.10
6	Don Mattingly	.50
Panel (4)		.75
7	Eric Davis	.10
8	Gary Carter	.25
Panel (5)		.25
9	Dave Winfield	.25
10	Wally Joyner	.10
Panel (6)		1.00
11	Mike Schmidt	.50
12	Robby Thompson	.10
Panel (7)		2.00
13	Wade Boggs	.35
14	Cal Ripken Jr.	.75
Panel (8)		1.00
15	Dale Murphy	.25
16	Tony Gwynn	.35
Panel (9)		1.00
17	Jose Canseco	.20
18	Rickey Henderson	.25
Panel (10)		.25
19	Lance Parrish	.10
20	Leo Righetti	.10

1988 Super Stars Discs

The "Second Annual Collector's Edition" of Super Stars discs is similar to the 1987 issue. A set of 20 discs (2-1/2" diameter) featuring full-color player photos was inserted in specially marked cannisters of iced tea and fruit drinks. Each triple-fold insert consists of two player discs and one redemption card. Player discs are bright blue, yellow, red and green with a diamond design framing the player portrait. The player name appears upper left, the set logo appears upper right. Personalized disc series were issued for Tetley, Weis, Key Food and A&P supermarkets (untitled series were also sold at Lucky, Skaggs, Alpha Beta, Acme King Kullen, Laneco and Krasdale stores). The series name (i.e. Weis Winners) is printed below the player photo. Backs are in red with a few personal data and stats. Because the discs are licensed only through the players' union, cap logos have been airbrushed off the photos.

	NM/M
Complete Panel Set (10):	7.50

Complete Singles Set (20): 4.50
Common Panel: .25
Common Single Player: .10
Panel (1) 2.00
1 Wade Boggs .50
9 Roger Clemens .60
Panel (2) 1.25
3 Don Mattingly .60
13 Dave Magadan .10
Panel (3) 1.50
4 Mark McGwire .65
10 Will Clark .10
Panel (4) .25
5 Matt Nokes .10
11 Vince Coleman .10
Panel (5) .25
8 Kevin Seitzer .10
2 Ellis Burks .10
Panel (6) 1.25
12 Eric Davis .10
6 Kirby Puckett .50
Panel (7) .25
15 Benito Santiago .10
20 Fernando Valenzuela .10
Panel (8) 1.50
16 Mike Schmidt .60
14 Dale Murphy .25
Panel (9) .25
17 Darryl Strawberry .10
10 Dwight Gooden .10
Panel (10) .25
18 Steve Bedrosian .10
7 Billy Ripken .10

1989 Super Stars Discs

SUPER STARS
MARK McGWIRE
OAKLAND ATHLETICS

The third annual series of Super Stars perforated disc folders again offered two players and an offer for a a facsimile autographed baseball or an uncut sheet of discs. The 2-3/4" diameter discs have a yellow border with a red star at center. A player portrait photo is in the star. Backs are printed in black and have a few previous season stats and biographical bits. As in previous years, the discs were produced by Michael Schechter Associates, which does business only with the Players Union, precluding the use of MLB logos on the player photos.

NM/M
Complete Panel Set (10): 9.00
Complete Singles Set (20): 5.00
Common Panel: .25
Common Player: .10
Panel (1) 1.25
1 Don Mattingly .50
2 David Cone .10
Panel (2) 2.00
3 Mark McGwire .65
4 Will Clark .50
Panel (3) .25
5 Darryl Strawberry .10
6 Dwight Gooden .10
Panel (4) 2.00
7 Wade Boggs .45
8 Roger Clemens .50
Panel (5) .25
9 Benito Santiago .10
10 Orel Hershiser .10
Panel (6) 1.25
11 Eric Davis .10
12 Kirby Puckett .45
Panel (7) 1.25
13 Dave Winfield .40
14 Andre Dawson .25
Panel (8) 2.00
15 Steve Bedrosian .10
16 Cal Ripken Jr. .75
Panel (9) 1.00
17 Andy Van Slyke .40
18 Jose Canseco .35
Panel (10) .75
19 Jose Oquendo .10
20 Dale Murphy .25

1990 Super Stars Discs

SUPER STARS
BO JACKSON
KANSAS CITY ROYALS

In its fourth annual edition the Super Stars discs continued the three-piece perforated folder format. Each panel consists of two player discs and a disc offering a 1990-1991 calendar at the center of an uncut sheet of the discs. Discs have a red border with a player portrait photo in the center of a tombstone-shaped yellow frame. A few 1989 stats and biographical notes are printed in black on the back. Because the discs are licensed only by the players' union, and not Major League Baseball, the player photos have had team logos excised.

NM/M
Complete Panel Set (10): 9.00
Complete Set, Singles (20): 4.50
Common Panel: .25
Common Player: .10
Panel (1) .50
1 Will Clark .10
2 Howard Johnson .10
Panel (2) 1.00
3 Chris Sabo .10
4 Jose Canseco .40
Panel (3) .50
5 Bo Jackson .15
6 Kevin Mitchell .10
Panel (4) 2.25
7 Wade Boggs .50
8 Ken Griffey Jr. .65
Panel (5) .25
9 George Bell .10
10 Dwight Gooden .10
Panel (6) 1.00
11 Bobby Bonilla .10
12 Ryne Sandberg .50
Panel (7) 2.00
13 Kirby Puckett .50
14 Don Mattingly .60
Panel (8) 1.50
15 Mark McGwire .75
16 Frank Viola .10
Panel (9) .25
17 Bret Saberhagen .10
18 Mike Greenwell .10
Panel (10) 2.00
19 Steve Sax .10
20 Nolan Ryan 1.00

1989 Swell Baseball Greats

TED WILLIAMS
OUTFIELD
SWELL
HALL OF FAME

Collectors Marketing Corp. handled the distribution of Philadelphia Gum Company's debut "old-timers" set. Most cards featured color photos, though some of the older players were represented in sepia shots. Red-and-white backs featured career stats, a baseball biography and a few vital statistics.

NM/M
Complete Set (135): 12.00
Common Player: .15
Wax Pack (10): .65
Wax Box (36): 15.00
1 Babe Ruth 3.50
2 Ty Cobb 1.50
3 Walter Johnson .75
4 Honus Wagner .75
5 Cy Young .75
6 Joe Adcock .15
7 Jim Bunning .15
8 Orlando Cepeda .15
9 Harvey Kuenn .15
10 Catfish Hunter .15
11 Johnny VanderMeer .15
12 Tony Oliva .15
13 Harvey Haddix (Reversed negative.) .15
14 Dick McAuliffe .15
15 Lefty Grove .15
16 Bo Belinski .15
17 Claude Osteen .15
18 Doc Medich .15
19 Del Ennis .15
20 Rogers Hornsby .40
21 Bob Buhl .15
22 Phil Niekro .15
23 Don Zimmer .15
24 Greg Luzinski .15
25 Lou Gehrig 2.50
26 Ken Singleton .15
27 Bob Allison .15
28 Ed Kranepool .15
29 Manny Sanguillen .15
30 Luke Appling .15
31 Ralph Terry .15
32 Smoky Burgess .15
33 Gil Hodges .40
34 Harry Walker .15
35 Edd Roush .15
36 Ron Santo .15
37 Jim Perry .15
38 Jose Morales .15
39 Stan Bahnsen .15
40 Al Kaline .40
41 Mel Harder .15
42 Ralph Houk .15
43 Jack Billingham .15
44 Carl Erskine .15
45 Hoyt Wilhelm .15
46 Dick Radatz .15
47 Roy Sievers .15
48 Jim Lonborg .15
49 Bobby Richardson .25
50 Whitey Ford .40
51 Roy Face .15
52 Tom Tresh .15
53 Joe Nuxhall .15
54 Mickey Vernon .15
55 Johnny Mize .15
56 Scott McGregor .15
57 Billy Pierce .15
58 Dave Giusti .15
59 Minnie Minoso .15
60 Early Wynn .15
61 Jose Cardenal .15
62 Sam Jethroe .15
63 Sal Bando .15
64 Elrod Hendricks .15
65 Enos Slaughter .15
66 Jim Bouton .15
67 Bill Mazeroski .25
68 Tony Kubek .25
69 Joe Black .15
70 Harmon Killebrew .40
71 Sam McDowell .15
72 Bucky Dent .15
73 Virgil Trucks .15
74 Andy Pafko .15
75 Bob Feller .40
76 Tito Francona .15
77 Al Dark .15
78 Larry Dierker .15
79 Nellie Briles .15
80 Lou Boudreau .15
81 Wally Moon .15
82 Hank Bauer .15
83 Jim Piersall .15
84 Jim Grant .15
85 Richie Ashburn .15
86 Bob Friend .15
87 Ken Keltner .15
88 Jim Kaat .15
89 Dean Chance .15
90 Al Lopez .15
91 Dick Groat .15
92 Johnny Blanchard .15
93 Chuck Hinton .15
94 Clete Boyer .15
95 Steve Carlton .40
96 Tug McGraw .15
97 Mickey Lolich .15
98 Earl Weaver .15
99 Sal Maglie .15
100 Ted Williams 2.25
101 Allie Reynolds (Photo actually Marius Russo.) .15
102 Gene Woodling (Photo actually Irv Noren.) .15
103 Moe Drabowsky .15
104 Mickey Stanley .15
105 Jim Palmer .15
106 Bill Freehan .15
107 Bob Robertson .15
108 Walt Dropo .15
109 Jerry Koosman .15
110 Bobby Doerr .15
111 Phil Rizzuto .40
112 Don Kessinger .15
113 Milt Pappas .15
114 Herb Score .15
115 Larry Doby .15
116 Glenn Beckert .15
117 Andre Thornton .15
118 Gary Matthews .15
119 Bill Virdon .15
120 Billy Williams .15
121 Johnny Sain .15
122 Don Newcombe .15
123 Rico Petrocelli .15
124 Dick Bosman .15
125 Roberto Clemente 3.00
126 Rocky Colavito .15
127 Wilbur Wood .15
128 Duke Sims .15
129 Ken Holtzman .15
130 Casey Stengel .15
131 Bobby Shantz .15
132 Del Crandall .15
133 Bobby Thomson .15
134 Brooks Robinson .40
135 Checklist

1990 Swell Baseball Greats

BASEBALL GREATS
SWELL
BILL ROBINSON
OUTFIELD/1ST BASE

In its second year of "old-timers" set production, Swell moved its "Baseball Greats" banner to the card front, above a color player photo. Where color photos were unavailable, sepia pictures were used. Backs were virtually identical to the previous year, with a line of lifetime stats, a career highlights write-up and a few bits of personal data. Also nearly identical is player selection within the 135-card set.

NM/M
Complete Set (135): 12.00
Common Player: .15
Wax Pack (10): .75
Wax Box (36): 12.50
1 Tom Seaver .50
2 Hank Aaron 2.50
3 Mickey Cochrane .15
4 Rod Carew .15
5 Carl Yastrzemski .40
6 Dizzy Dean .50
7 Sal Bando .15
8 Whitey Ford .40
9 Bill White .15
10 Babe Ruth 3.50
11 Robin Roberts .15
12 Warren Spahn .15
13 Billy Williams .15
14 Joe Garagiola .15
15 Ty Cobb 1.50
16 Boog Powell .15
17 Tom Tresh .15
18 Luke Appling .15
19 Tommie Agee .15
20 Roberto Clemente 3.00
21 Bobby Thomson .15
22 Charlie Keller .15
23 George Bamberger .15
24 Eddie Lopat .15
25 Lou Gehrig 2.50
26 Manny Mota .15
27 Steve Stone .15
28 Orlando Cepeda .15
29 Al Bumbry .15
30 Grover Alexander .15
31 Lou Boudreau .15
32 Herb Score .15
33 Harry Walker .15
34 Deron Johnson .15
35 Edd Roush .15
36 Carl Erskine .15
37 Ken Forsch .15
38 Sal Maglie .15
39 Al Rosen .15
40 Casey Stengel .15
41 Cesar Cedeno .15
42 Roy White .15
43 Larry Doby .15
44 Rod Kanehl .15
45 Tris Speaker .40
46 Ralph Garr .15
47 Andre Thornton .15
48 Frankie Crosetti .15
49 Dick Groat .15
50 Honus Wagner .75
51 Rogers Hornsby .40
52 Ken Brett .15
53 Lenny Randle .15
54 Enos Slaughter .15
55 Mel Ott .15
56 Rico Petrocelli .15
57 Walt Dropo .15
58 Bob Grich .15
59 Billy Herman .15
60 Bob Feller .40
61 Davey Johnson .15
62 Don Drysdale .15
63 Larry Sorensen .15
64 Ron Santo .15
65 Eddie Mathews .15
66 Gaylord Perry .15
67 Lee May .15
68 Johnnie LeMaster .15
69 Don Kessinger .15
70 Lefty Grove .15
71 Lou Brock .15
72 Don Cardwell .15
73 Harvey Haddix .15
74 Frank Torre .15
75 Walter Johnson .75
76 Don Newcombe .15
77 Marv Throneberry .15
78 Jim Northrup .15
79 Fritz Peterson .15
80 Ralph Kiner .15
81 Mickey Lolich .15
82 Donn Clendenon .15
83 Pete Vuckovich .15
84 Lefty Gomez .15
85 Monte Irvin .15
86 Rick Ferrell .15
87 Tommy Hutton .15
88 Julio Cruz .15
89 Vida Blue .15
90 Johnny Mize .15
91 Rusty Staub .15
92 Jimmy Piersall .15
93 Bill Mazeroski .15
94 Lee Lacy .15
95 Ernie Banks .40
96 Bobby Doerr .15
97 George Foster .15
98 Eric Soderholm .15
99 Johnny VanderMeer .15
100 Cy Young .75
101 Jimmie Foxx .40
102 Clete Boyer .15
103 Steve Garvey .15
104 Johnny Podres .15
105 Yogi Berra .40
106 Bill Monbouquette .15
107 Milt Pappas .15
108 Dave LaRoche .15
109 Elliott Maddox .15
110 Steve Carlton .15
111 Bud Harrelson .15
112 Mark Littell .15
113 Frank J. Thomas .15
114 Bill Robinson .15
115 Satchel Paige .75
116 John Denny .15
117 Clyde King .15
118 Billy Sample .15
119 Rocky Colavito .15
120 Bob Gibson .15
121 Bert Campaneris .15
122 Mark Fidrych .15
123 Ed Charles .15
124 Jim Lonborg .15
125 Ted Williams 2.50
126 Manny Sanguillen .15
127 Matt Keough .15
128 Vern Ruhle .15
129 Bob Skinner .15
130 Joe Torre .15
131 Ralph Houk .15
132 Gil Hodges .40
133 Ralph Branca .15
134 Christy Mathewson .75
135 Checklist

1991 Swell Baseball Greats

GREATS
BASEBALL
Dodgers
DON DRYSDALE Pitcher

The last of three "old-timers" sets issued by Philadelphia Gum Co., this 150-card set was marketed by Impel. Cards are 2-1/2" x 3-1/2" and feature red and yellow borders around color player photos. In the case of some older players, sepia-toned photos are used instead of color. Backs are printed in red and black and include career stats and a few vital statistics.

NM/M
Complete Set (150): 17.50
Common Player: .15
Wax Pack (10): .75
Wax Box (36): 15.00
1 Tommie Agee .15
2 Matty Alou .15
3 Luke Appling .15
4 Richie Ashburn .15
5 Ernie Banks .40
6 Don Baylor .15
7 Buddy Bell .15
8 Yogi Berra .40
9 Joe Black .15
10 Vida Blue .15
11 Bobby Bonds .15
12 Lou Boudreau .15
13 Lou Brock .15
14 Ralph Branca .15
15 Bobby Brown .15
16 Lew Burdette .15
17 Steve Carlton .25
18 Rico Carty .15
19 Jerry Coleman .15
20 Frankie Crosetti .15
21 Julio Cruz .15
22 Alvin Dark .15
23 Doug DeCinces .15
24 Larry Doby .15
25 Bobby Doerr .15
26 Don Drysdale .15
27 Carl Erskine .15
28 Elroy Face .15
29 Rick Ferrell .15
30 Rollie Fingers .15
31 Joe Garagiola .40
32 Steve Garvey .15
33 Bob Gibson .15
34 Mudcat Grant .15
35 Dick Groat .15
36 Jerry Grote .15
37 Toby Harrah .15
38 Bud Harrelson .15
39 Billy Herman .15
40 Ken Holtzman .15
41 Willie Horton .15
42 Ralph Houk .15
43 Al Hrabosky .15
44 Monte Irvin .15
45 Fergie Jenkins .40
46 Davey Johnson .15
47 George Kell .15
48 Charlie Keller .15
49 Harmon Killebrew .25
50 Ralph Kiner .15
51 Clyde King .15
52 Dave Kingman .15
53 Al Kaline .40
54 Clem Labine .15
55 Vern Law .15
56 Mickey Lolich .15
57 Jim Lonborg .15
58 Eddie Lopat .15
59 Sal Maglie .15
60 Bill Mazeroski .25
61 Johnny VanderMeer .15
62 Johnny Mize .15
63 Manny Mota .15
64 Wally Moon .15
65 Rick Monday .15
66 Tom Tresh .15
67 Graig Nettles .15
68 Don Newcombe .15
69 Milt Pappas .15
70 Gaylord Perry .15
71 Rico Petrocelli .15
72 Jimmy Piersall .15
73 Johnny Podres .15
74 Boog Powell .15
75 Bobby Richardson .25
76 Vern Ruhle .15
77 Robin Roberts .15
78 Al Rosen .15
79 Billy Sample .15
80 Manny Sanguillen .15
81 Ron Santo .15
82 Herb Score .15
83 Bobby Shantz .15
84 Enos Slaughter .15
85 Eric Soderholm .15
86 Warren Spahn .15
87 Rusty Staub .15
88 Bobby Thomson .15
89 Marv Throneberry .15
90 Luis Tiant .15
91 Frank Torre .15
92 Joe Torre .25
93 Bill Virdon .15
94 Harry Walker .15
95 Earl Weaver .15
96 Bill White .15
97 Roy White .15
98 Billy Williams .15
99 Dick Williams .15
100 Ted Williams 2.50
101 Gene Woodling .15
102 Hank Aaron 2.50
103 Rod Carew .15
104 Cesar Cedeno .15
105 Orlando Cepeda .15
106 Willie Mays 2.50
107 Tom Seaver .40
108 Carl Yastrzemski .40
109 Clete Boyer .15
110 Bert Campaneris .15
111 Walt Dropo .15
112 George Foster .15
113 Phil Garner .15
114 Harvey Kuenn .15
115 Don Kessinger .15
116 Rocky Colavito .15
117 Bobby Murcer .15
118 Mel Parnell .15
119 Ken Reitz .15
120 Earl Wilson .15
121 Wilbur Wood .15
122 Ed Yost .15
123 Jim Bouton .15
124 Babe Ruth 3.50
125 Lou Gehrig 2.50
126 Honus Wagner .75
127 Ty Cobb 1.50
128 Grover C. Alexander .15

129	Lefty Gomez	.15
130	Walter Johnson	.75
131	Gil Hodges	.40
132	Roberto Clemente	3.00
133	Satchel Paige	.75
134	Edd Roush	.15
135	Cy Young	.75
136	Casey Stengel	.15
137	Rogers Hornsby	.40
138	Dizzy Dean	.50
139	Lefty Grove	.15
140	Tris Speaker	.40
141	Christy Mathewson	.75
142	Mickey Cochrane	.15
143	Jimmie Foxx	.40
144	Mel Ott	.25
145	Bob Feller	.25
146	Brooks Robinson	.40
147	Eddie Mathews	.15
148	Pie Traynor	.15
149	Thurman Munson	.25
150	Checklist	.15

T

1988 T & M Sports Umpires

8 DOUG HARVEY

The first umpires to be featured on baseball cards since the 1955 Bowman set are the arbiters included in this boxed set issued T & M and licensed by the umps' union. Cards have posed photos framed in red (American League) green (National League) with a black border on front. The correct league logo is in a lower corner. The umpire's uniform number and name are in white at bottom. The back has a blue background with personal data, career summary, service record and card number, along with licensor logos.

		NM/M
Complete Set (64):		5.00
Common Card:		.15
1	Doug Harvey	.15
2	Lee Weyer	.15
3	Billy Williams	.15
4	John Kibler	.15
5	Bob Engel	.15
6	Harry Wendelstedt	.15
7	Larry Barnett	.15
8	Don Denkinger	.15
9	Dave Phillips	.15
10	Larry McCoy	.15
11	Bruce Froemming	.15
12	John McSherry	.15
13	Jim Evans	.15
14	Frank Pulli	.15
15	Joe Brinkman	.15
16	Terry Tata	.15
17	Paul Runge	.15
18	Dutch Rennert	.15
19	Nick Bremigan	.15
20	Jim McKean	.15
21	Terry Cooney	.15
22	Rich Garcia	.15
23	Dale Ford	.15
24	Al Clark	.15
25	Greg Kosc	.15
26	Jim Quick	.15
27	Ed Montague	.15
28	Jerry Crawford	.15
29	Steve Palermo	.15
30	Durwood Merrill	.15
31	Ken Kaiser	.15
32	Vic Voltaggio	.15
33	Mike Reilly	.15
34	Eric Gregg	.15
35	Ted Hendry	.15
36	Joe West	.15
37	Dave Pallone	.15
38	Fred Brocklander	.15
39	John Shulock	.15
40	Derryl Cousins	.15
41	Charlie Williams	.15
42	Rocky Roe	.15
43	Randy Marsh	.15
44	Bob Davidson	.15
45	Drew Coble	.15

46	Tim McClelland	.15
47	Dan Morrison	.15
48	Rick Reed	.15
49	Steve Rippley	.15
50	John Hirschbeck	.15
51	Mark Johnson	.15
52	Gerry Davis	.15
53	Dana DeMuth	.15
54	Larry Young	.15
55	Tim Welke	.15
56	Greg Bonin	.15
57	Tom Hallion	.15
58	Dale Scott	.15
59	Tim Tschida	.15
60	Dick Stello	.15
61	1987 All-Star Game (Derryl Cousins, Bob Davidson, Don Denkinger, Dick Stello, Vic Voltaggio, Joe West)	.15
62	1987 World Series (Ken Kaiser, Greg Kosc, John McSherry, Dave Phillips, Terry Tata, Lee Weyer)	.15
63	Jocko Conlan	.30
64	Checklist	.15

1989 T & M Sports Senior League

ROLLIE FINGERS
PITCHER

The 120-card 1989-90 T&M Sports Senior League set features a full-color photo of the player on the front on a borderless card. A red stripe separates the photo from the black bottom with the player's name, team logo and position. The cards are printed on heavy, white cardboard stock and sold as a boxed set. The backs have a red border across the top and bio and career notes, along with a summary of the player's career. Included in the set are eight static-cling puzzle pieces which, when put together, show a drawing of a prominent player from each team.

		NM/M
Complete Set (120):		4.00
Common Player:		.05
1	Curt Flood (Commissioner)	.10
2	Willie Aikens	.05
3	Gary Allenson	.05
4	Stan Bahnsen	.05
5	Alan Bannister	.05
6	Juan Beniquez	.05
7	Jim Bibby	.05
8	Paul Blair	.05
9	Vida Blue	.10
10	Bobby Bonds	.15
11	Pedro Borbon	.05
12	Clete Boyer	.05
13	Gates Brown	.05
14	Al Bumbry	.05
15	Sal Butera	.05
16	Bert Campaneris	.10
17	Bill Campbell	.05
18	Bernie Carbo	.05
19	Dave Cash	.05
20	Cesar Cedeno	.05
21	Gene Clines	.05
22	Dave Collins	.05
23	Cecil Cooper	.05
24	Doug Corbett	.05
25	Al Cowens	.05
26	Jose Cruz	.05
27	Mike Cuellar	.10
28	Pat Dobson	.05
29	Dick Drago	.05
30	Dan Driessen	.05
31	Jamie Easterly	.05
32	Juan Eichelberger	.05
33	Dock Ellis	.05
34	Ed Figueroa	.05
35	Rollie Fingers	.50
36	George Foster	.10
37	Oscar Gamble	.05
38	Wayne Garland	.05
39	Wayne Garrett	.05
40	Ross Grimsley	.05
41	Jerry Grote	.05
42	Johnny Grubb	.05
43	Mario Guerrero	.05
44	Toby Harrah	.05

45	Steve Henderson	.05
46	George Hendrick	.05
47	Butch Hobson	.05
48	Roy Howell	.05
49	Al Hrabosky	.05
50	Clint Hurdle	.05
51	Garth Iorg	.05
52	Tim Ireland	.05
53	Grant Jackson	.05
54	Ron Jackson	.05
55	Ferguson Jenkins	.50
56	Odell Jones	.05
57	Mike Kekich	.05
58	Steve Kemp	.05
59	Dave Kingman	.10
60	Bruce Kison	.05
61	Lee Lacy	.05
62	Rafael Landestoy	.05
63	Ken Landreaux	.05
64	Tito Landrum	.05
65	Dave LaRoche	.05
66	Bill Lee	.05
67	Ron LeFlore	.05
68	Dennis Leonard	.05
69	Bill Madlock	.10
70	Mickey Mahler	.05
71	Rick Manning	.05
72	Tippy Martinez	.05
73	Jon Matlack	.05
74	Bake McBride	.05
75	Steve McCarty	.05
76	Hal McRae	.10
77	Dan Meyer	.05
78	Felix Millan	.05
79	Paul Mirabella	.05
80	Omar Moreno	.05
81	Jim Morrison	.05
82	Graig Nettles	.15
83	Al Oliver	.10
84	Amos Otis	.05
85	Tom Paciorek	.05
86	Lowell Plamer	.05
87	Pat Putnam	.05
88	Lenny Randle	.05
89	Ken Reitz	.05
90	Gene Richards	.05
91	Mickey Rivers	.05
92	Leon Roberts	.05
93	Joe Sambito	.05
94	Rodney Scott	.05
95	Bob Shirley	.05
96	Jim Slaton	.05
97	Elias Sosa	.05
98	Fred Stanley	.05
99	Bill Stein	.05
100	Rennie Stennett	.05
101	Sammy Stewart	.05
102	Tim Stoddard	.05
103	Champ Summers	.05
104	Derrell Thomas	.05
105	Luis Tiant	.10
106	Bobby Tolan	.05
107	Bill Travers	.05
108	Tom Underwood	.05
109	Rick Waits	.05
110	Ron Washington	.05
111	U.L. Washington	.05
112	Earl Weaver	.25
113	Jerry White	.05
114	Milt Wilcox	.05
115	Dick Williams	.05
116	Walt Williams	.05
117	Rick Wise	.05
118	Favorite Suns (Luis Tiant, Cesar Cedeno)	.05
119	Home Run Legends (George Foster, Bobby Bonds)	.05
120	Sunshine Skippers (Earl Weaver, Dick Williams)	.25

Umpires

LARRY McCOY

A second edition of umpires' cards from T & M was also sold as a boxed set. Fronts of the 2-1/2" x 3-1/2" cards have color photos which are borderless at top and sides. At bottom is a strip with the ump's name and uniform number at right and league logo at left. Backs have personal data and a career summary, along with logos of MLB and the Umpires' Association.

		NM/M
Complete Set (63):		7.50

Common Card:		
1	Doug Harvey	.25
2	John Kibler	.15
3	Bob Engel	.15
4	Harry Wendelstedt	.15
5	Larry Barnett	.15
6	Don Denkinger	.15
7	Dave Phillips	.15
8	Larry McCoy	.15
9	Bruce Froemming	.15
10	John McSherry	.20
11	Jim Evans	.15
12	Frank Pulli	.15
13	Joe Brinkman	.15
14	Terry Tata	.15
15	Nick Bremigan	.15
16	Jim McKean	.15
17	Paul Runge	.15
18	Dutch Rennert	.15
19	Terry Cooney	.15
20	Rich Garcia	.15
21	Dale Ford	.15
22	Al Clark	.15
23	Greg Kosc	.15
24	Jim Quick	.15
25	Ed Montague	.15
26	Jerry Crawford	.15
27	Steve Palermo	.35
28	Durwood Merrill	.15
29	Ken Kaiser	.20
30	Vic Voltaggio	.15
31	Mike Reilly	.15
32	Eric Gregg	.25
33	Ted Hendry	.15
34	Joe West	.15
35	Dave Pallone	.25
36	Fred Brocklander	.15
37	John Shulock	.15
38	Derryl Cousins	.15
39	Charlie Williams	.15
40	Rocky Roe	.15
41	Randy Marsh	.15
42	Bob Davidson	.15
43	Drew Coble	.15
44	Tim McClelland	.15
45	Dan Morrison	.15
46	Rick Reed	.15
47	Steve Rippley	.15
48	John Hirschbeck	.15
49	Mark Johnson	.15
50	Gerry Davis	.15
51	Dana DeMuth	.15
52	Larry Young	.15
53	Tim Welke	.15
54	Greg Bonin	.15
55	Tom Hallion	.15
56	Dale Scott	.15
57	Tim Tschida	.15
58	Gary Darling	.15
59	Mark Hirschbeck	.15
60	All-Star Crew	.15
61	World Series Crew	.15
62	Lee Weyer	.15
63	Tom Connolly, Bill Klem	.25

1990 T & M Sports Umpires

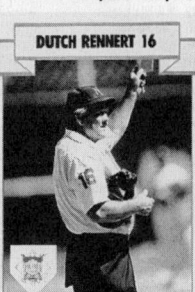

DUTCH RENNERT 16

Puzzle piece inserts and a send-away premium card offer are featured in the 1990 umpires set. Card fronts have action photos of the arbiters with league insignia in a home plate-shaped frame in a lower corner. Above the photo, the umpire's name and uniform number are printed in a banner. Backs have biographical data, a baseball rules trivia question and the logos of MLB and the Major League Umpires Association. Card #71, Hall of Fame umpire Al Barlick, was only available by sending in the four puzzle pieces overprinted with the National League logo.

		NM/M
Complete Set (70, No Barlick):		6.00
Common Card:		.10
1	Doug Harvey	.10
2	John Kibler	.10
3	Bob Engel	.10
4	Harry Wendelstedt	.10
5	Larry Barnett	.10
6	Don Denkinger	.10
7	Dave Phillips	.10
8	Larry McCoy	.10
9	Bruce Froemming	.10

10	John McSherry	.10
11	Jim Evans	.10
12	Frank Pulli	.10
13	Joe Brinkman	.10
14	Terry Tata	.10
15	Jim McKean	.10
16	Dutch Rennert	.10
17	Paul Runge	.10
18	Terry Cooney	.10
19	Rich Garcia	.10
20	Dale Ford	.10
21	Al Clark	.10
22	Greg Kosc	.10
23	Jim Quick	.10
24	Eddie Montague	.10
25	Jerry Crawford	.10
26	Steve Palermo	.10
27	Durwood Merrill	.10
28	Ken Kaiser	.10
29	Vic Voltaggio	.10
30	Mike Reilly	.10
31	Eric Gregg	.10
32	Ted Hendry	.10
33	Joe West	.10
34	Fred Brocklander	.10
35	John Shulock	.10
36	Derryl Cousins	.10
37	Charlie Williams	.10
38	Rocky Roe	.10
39	Randy Marsh	.10
40	Bob Davidson	.10
41	Drew Coble	.10
42	Tim McClelland	.10
43	Dan Morrison	.10
44	Rick Reed	.10
45	Steve Rippley	.10
46	John Hirschbeck	.10
47	Mark Johnson	.10
48	Gerry Davis	.10
49	Dana DeMuth	.10
50	Larry Young	.10
51	Tim Welke	.10
52	Greg Bonin	.10
53	Tom Hallion	.10
54	Dale Scott	.10
55	Tim Tschida	.10
56	Gary Darling	.10
57	Mark Hirschbeck	.10
58	Jerry Layne	.10
59	Jim Joyce	.10
60	Bill Hohn	.10
61	All-Star Game	.10
62	World Series	.10
63	Nick Bremigan	.10
64	The Runges (Ed Runge, Paul Runge)	.10
65	A. Bartlett Giamatti	.10
66	Puzzle Piece #1	.10
66a	Puzzle Piece #1 (W/N.L. logo on back.)	
67	Puzzle Piece #2	.10
67a	Puzzle Piece #3 (N.L. logo.)	.10
68	Puzzle Piece #3	.10
68a	Puzzle Piece #3 (N.L. logo.)	.10
69	Puzzle Piece #4	.10
69a	Puzzle piece #4 (N.L. logo.)	.10
70	Checklist	.05
71	Al Barlick	4.00

1990 Target Dodgers

CASEY STENGEL — MGR

TARGET

Virtually every player who appeared in the uniform of the Brooklyn or Los Angeles Dodgers between 1890-1990 was included in this 1,100-card issue. Quality of the photo varies wildly from sharp to barely identifiable. Cards measure 2-1/16" x 3" and are perforated on two, three or four sides, depending where they were positioned on the 15-card perforated sheets in which the cards were distributed at various Dodgers home games. Player photos are dark blue and white, bordered in speckled blue. Name and position appear in black in a light blue banner at top. At lower-left is the Dodgers 100th anniversary logo, with the Target stores logo at lower-right. On the back the

player's name and position reappear at top, with the logos below and the card number in a banner at bottom. Cards were numbered roughly alphabetically, though many are out of order. Some cards have duplicated numbers and there were some numbers skipped in the issue. All back printing is in blue on white. Career major league stats and the years in which the player was with the Dodgers are also noted on back. According to figures released by the team, production was to be about 50,000 sets.

		NM/M
Complete Set (1,103):		150.00
Common Player:		.25
1	Bert Abbey	.25
2	Cal Abrams	.50
3	Hank Aguirre	.25
4	Eddie Ainsmith	.25
5	Ed Albosta	.25
6	Luis Alcaraz	.25
7	Doyle Alexander	.25
8	Dick Allen	2.50
9	Frank Allen	.25
10	Johnny Allen	.25
11	Mel Almada	1.25
12	Walter Alston	1.25
13	Ed Amelung	.25
14	Sandy Amoros	1.25
15	Dave Anderson	.25
16	Ferrell Anderson	.25
17	John Anderson	.25
18	Stan Andrews	.25
19	Bill Antonello	.25
20	Jimmy Archer	.25
21	Bob Aspromonte	.25
22	Rick Auerbach	.25
23	Charlie Babb	.25
24	Johnny Babich	.25
25	Bob Bailey	.25
26	Bob Bailor	.25
27	Dusty Baker	1.25
28	Tom Baker	.25
29	Dave Bancroft	.25
30	Dan Bankhead	.75
31	Jack Banta	.25
32	Jim Barbieri	.25
33	Red Barkley	.25
34	Jesse Barnes	.25
35	Rex Barney	.75
36	Billy Barnie	.25
37	Bob Barrett	.25
38	Jim Baxes	.25
39	Billy Bean	.25
40	Boom Boom Beck	.25
41	Joe Beckwith	.25
42	Hank Behrman	.25
43	Mark Belanger	.25
44	Wayne Belardi	.25
45	Tim Belcher	.25
46	George Bell	.25
47	Ray Benge	.25
48	Moe Berg	4.00
49	Bill Bergen	.25
50	Ray Berres	.25
51	Don Bessent	.25
52	Steve Bilko	.25
53	Jack Billingham	.25
54	Babe Birrer	.25
55	Del Bissonette	.25
56	Joe Black	1.25
57	Lu Blue	.25
58	George Boehler	.25
59	Sammy Bohne	1.50
60	John Boiling	.25
61	Ike Boone	.25
62	Frenchy Bordagaray	.25
63	Ken Boyer	1.25
64	Buzz Boyle	.25
65	Mark Bradley	.25
66	Bobby Bragan	.25
67	Ralph Branca	1.25
68	Ed Brandt	.25
69	Sid Bream	.25
70	Marv Breeding	.25
71	Tom Brennan	.25
72	William Brennan	.25
73	Rube Bressler	.25
74	Ken Brett	.25
75	Jim Brewer	.25
76	Tony Brewer	.25
77	Rocky Bridges	.25
78	Greg Brock	.25
79	Dan Brouthers	.25
80	Eddie Brown	.25
81	Elmer Brown	.25
82	Lindsay Brown	.25
83	Lloyd Brown	.25
84	Mace Brown	.25
85	Tommy Brown	.25
86	Pete Browning	.25
87	Ralph Bryant	.25
88	Jim Bucher	.25
89	Bill Buckner	1.25
90	Jim Bunning	1.25
91	Jack Burdock	.25
92	Glenn Burke	.25
93	Buster Burrell	.25
94	Larry Burright	.25
95	Doc Bushong	.25
96	Max Butcher	.25
97	Johnny Butler	.25

No.	Player	Price
98	Enos Cabell	.25
99	Leon Cadore	.25
100	Bruce Caldwell	.25
101	Dick Calmus	.25
102	Dolf Camilli	.25
103	Doug Camilli	.25
104	Roy Campanella	9.00
105	Al Campanis	.25
106	Jim Campanis	.25
107A	Leo Callahan	.25
107B	Gilly Campbell	.25
108	Jimmy Canavan	.25
109	Chris Cannizzaro	.25
110	Guy Cantrell	.25
111	Ben Cantwell	.25
112	Andy Carey	.25
113	Max Carey	.25
114	Tex Carleton	.25
115	Ownie Carroll	.25
116	Bob Caruthers	.25
117	Doc Casey	.25
118	Hugh Casey	.25
119	Bobby Castillo	.25
120	Cesar Cedeno	.25
121	Ron Cey	1.25
122	Ed Chandler	.25
123	Ben Chapman	.25
124	Larry Cheney	.25
125	Bob Chipman	.25
126	Chuck Churn	.25
127	Gino Cimoli	.50
128	Moose Clabaugh	.25
129	Bud Clancy	.25
130	Bob Clark	.25
131	Watty Clark	.25
132	Alta Cohen	.25
133	Rocky Colavito	5.00
134	Jackie Collum	.25
135	Chuck Connors	5.00
136	Jack Coombs	.25
137	Johnny Cooney	.25
138	Tommy Corcoran	.25
139	Pop Corkhill	.25
140	John Corriden	.25
141	Pete Coscarart	.25
142	Wes Covington	.25
143	Billy Cox	1.25
144	Roger Craig	.75
145	Cannonball Crane	.25
146	Willie Crawford	.25
147	Tim Crews	.25
148	John Cronin	.25
149	Lave Cross	.25
150	Bill Crouch	.25
151	Don Crow	.25
152	Henry Cruz	.25
153	Tony Cuccinello	.25
154	Roy Cullenbine	.25
155	George Culver	.25
156	Nick Cullop	.25
157	George Cutshaw	.25
158	Kiki Cuyler	.25
159	Bill Dahlen	.25
160	Babe Dahlgren	.25
161	Jack Dalton	.25
162	Tom Daly	.25
163	Cliff Dapper	.25
164	Bob Darnell	.25
165	Bobby Darwin	.25
166	Jake Daubert	.25
167	Vic Davalillo	.25
168	Curt Davis	.25
169	Mike Davis	.25
170	Ron Davis	.25
171	Tommy Davis	1.25
172	Willie Davis	1.25
173	Pea Ridge Day	.25
174	Tommy Dean	.25
175	Hank DeBerry	9.00
176	Art Decatur	.25
177	Raoul Dedeaux	.25
178	Ivan DeJesus	.25
179	Don Demeter	.25
180	Gene DeMontreville	.25
181	Rick Dempsey	.25
182	Eddie Dent	.25
183	Mike Devereaux	.25
184	Carlos Diaz	.25
185	Dick Dietz	.25
186	Pop Dillon	.25
187	Bill Doak	.25
188	John Dobbs	.25
189	George Dockins	.25
190	Cozy Dolan	.25
191	Patsy Donovan	.25
192	Wild Bill Donovan	.25
193	Mickey Doolan	.25
194	Jack Doscher	.25
195	Phil Douglas	.25
196	Snooks Dowd	.25
197	Al Downing	.25
198	Red Downs	.25
199	Jack Doyle	.25
200	Solly Drake	.25
201	Tom Drake	.25
202	Chuck Dressen	.25
203	Don Drysdale	5.00
204	Clise Dudley	.25
205	Mariano Duncan	.25
206	Jack Dunn	.25
207	Bull Durham	.25
208	Leo Durocher	1.25
209	Billy Earle	.25
210	George Earnshaw	.25
211	Ox Eckhardt	.25
212	Bruce Edwards	.25
213	Hank Edwards	.25
214	Dick W. Egan	.25
215	Harry Eisenstat	.25
216	Kid Elberfeld	.25
217	Jumbo Elliot	.25
218	Don Elston	.25
219	Gil English	.25
220	Johnny Enzmann	.25
221	Al Epperly	.25
222	Carl Erskine	1.25
223	Tex Erwin	.25
224	Cecil Espy	.25
225	Chuck Essegian	.25
226	Dude Esterbrook	.25
227	Red Evans	.25
228	Bunny Fabrique	.25
229	Jim Fairey	.25
230	Ron Fairly	1.25
231	George Fallon	.25
232	Turk Farrell	.25
233	Duke Farrel	.25
234	Jim Faulkner	.25
235	Alex Ferguson	.25
236	Joe Ferguson	.25
237	Chico Fernandez	.25
238	Sid Fernandez	.25
239	Al Ferrara	.25
240	Wes Ferrell	.25
241	Lou Fette	.25
242	Chick Fewster	.25
243	Jack Fimple	.25
244	Neal "Mickey" Finn	.25
245	Bob Fisher	.25
246	Freddie Fitzsimmons	.25
247	Tim Flood	.25
248	Jake Flowers	.25
249	Hod Ford	.25
250	Terry Forster	.75
251	Alan Foster	.25
252	Jack Fournier	.25
253	Dave Foutz	.25
254	Art Fowler	.25
255	Fred Frankhouse	.25
256	Herman Franks	.25
257	Johnny Frederick	.25
258	Larry French	.25
259	Lonny Frey	.25
260	Pepe Frias	.25
261	Charlie Fuchs	.25
262	Carl Furillo	4.00
263	Len Gabrielson	.25
264	Augie Galan	.25
265	Joe Gallagher	.25
266	Phil Gallivan	.25
267	Balvino Galvez	.25
268	Mike Garman	.25
269	Phil Garner	.25
270	Steve Garvey	2.50
271	Ned Garvin	.25
272	Hank Gastright	.25
273	Sid Gautreaux	.25
274	Jim Gentile	.25
275	Greek George	.25
276	Ben Geraghty	.25
277	Gus Getz	.25
278	Bob Giallombardo	.25
279	Kirk Gibson	1.25
280	Charlie Gilbert	.25
281	Jim Gilliam	1.25
282	Al Gionfriddo	.50
283	Tony Giuliani	.25
284	Al Glossop	.25
285	John Gochnaur	.25
286	Jim Golden	.25
287	Dave Goltz	.25
288	Jose Gonzalez	.25
289	Johnny Gooch	.25
290	Ed Goodson	.25
291	Bill Grabarkewitz	.25
292	Jack Graham	.25
293	Mudcat Grant	.25
294	Dick Gray	.25
295	Kent Greenfield	.25
296	Hal Gregg	.25
297	Alfredo Griffin	.25
298	Mike Griffin	.25
299	Derrell Griffith	.25
300	Tommy Griffith	.25
301	Burleigh Grimes	.25
302	Lee Grissom	.25
303	Jerry Grote	.25
304	Pedro Guerrero	.75
305	Brad Gulden	.25
306	Ad Gumbert	.25
307	Chris Gwynn	.25
308	Bert Haas	.25
309	John Hale	.25
310	Tom Haller	.25
311	Bill Hallman	.25
312	Jeff Hamilton	.25
313	Luke Hamlin	.25
314	Ned Hanlon	.25
315	Gerald Hannahs	.25
316	Charlie Hargreaves	.25
317	Tim Harkness	.25
318	Harry Harper	.25
319	Joe Harris	.25
320	Lenny Harris	.25
321	Bill F. Hart	.25
322	Buddy Hassett	.25
323	Mickey Hatcher	.25
324	Joe Hatten	.25
325	Phil Haugstad	.25
326	Brad Havens	.25
327	Ray Hayworth	.25
328	Ed Head	.25
329	Danny Heep	.25
330	Fred Heimach	.25
331	Harvey Hendrick	.25
332	Weldon Henley	.25
333	Butch Henline	.25
334	Dutch Henry	.25
335	Roy Henshaw	.25
336	Babe Herman	.75
337	Billy Herman	.75
338	Gene Hermanski	.25
339	Enzo Hernandez	.25
340	Art Herring	.25
341	Orel Hershiser	1.25
342	Dave J. Hickman	.25
343	Jim Hickman	.25
344	Kirby Higbe	.25
345	Andy High	.25
346	George Hildebrand	.25
347	Hunkey Hines	.25
348	Don Hoak	.75
349	Oris Hockett	.25
350	Gil Hodges	5.00
351	Glenn Hoffman	.25
352	Al Hollingsworth	.25
353	Tommy Holmes	.25
354	Brian Holton	.25
355	Rick Honeycutt	.25
356	Burt Hooton	.25
357	Gail Hopkins	.25
358	Johnny Hopp	.25
359	Charlie Hough	.75
360	Frank Howard	1.25
361	Steve Howe	.75
362	Dixie Howell	.25
363	Harry Howell	.25
364	Jay Howell	.75
365	Ken Howell	.25
366	Waite Hoyt	.25
367	Johnny Hudson	.25
368	Jim J. Hughes	.25
369	Jim R. Hughes	.25
370	Mickey Hughes	.25
371	John Hummel	.25
372	Ron Hunt	.25
373	Willard Hunter	.25
374	Ira Hutchinson	.25
375	Tom Hutton	.25
376	Charlie Irwin	.25
377	Fred Jacklitsch	.25
378	Randy Jackson	.25
379	Merwin Jacobson	.25
380	Cleo James	.25
381	Hal Janvrin	.25
382	Roy Jarvis	.25
383	George Jeffcoat	.25
384	Jack Jenkins	.25
385	Hughie Jennings	.25
386	Tommy John	1.25
387	Lou Johnson	.25
388	Fred Ivy Johnston	.25
389	Jimmy Johnston	.25
390	Jay Johnstone	.75
391	Fielder Jones	.25
392	Oscar Jones	.25
393	Tim Jordan	.25
394	Spider Jorgensen	.25
395	Von Joshua	.25
396	Bill Joyce	.25
397	Joe Judge	.25
398	Alex Kampouris	.25
399	Willie Keeler	.25
400	Mike Kekich	.25
401	John Kelleher	.25
402	Frank Kellert	.25
403	Joe Kelley	.25
404	George Kelly	.25
405	Bob Kennedy	.25
406	Brickyard Kennedy	.25
407	John Kennedy	.25
408	Newt Kimball	.25
409	Clyde King	.25
410	Enos Kirkpatrick	.25
411	Frank Kitson	.25
412	Johnny Klippstein	.25
413	Elmer Klumpp	.25
414	Len Koenecke	.25
415	Ed Konetchy	.25
416	Andy Kosco	.25
417	Sandy Koufax	15.00
418	Ernie Koy	.25
419	Charlie Kress	.25
420	Bill Krueger	.25
421	Ernie Krueger	.25
422	Clem Labine	.75
423	Candy LaChance	.25
424	Lee Lacy	.25
425	Lerrin LaGrow	.25
426	Bill Lamar	.25
427	Wayne LaMaster	.25
428	Ray Lamb	.25
429	Rafael Landestoy	.25
430	Ken Landreaux	.25
431	Tito Landrum	.25
432	Norm Larker	.25
433	Lyn Lary	.25
434	Tom Lasorda	1.25
435	Cookie Lavagetto	.25
436	Rudy Law	.25
437	Tony Lazzeri	.25
438	Tim Leary	.25
439	Bob Lee	.25
440	Hal Lee	.25
441	Leron Lee	.25
442	Jim Lefebvre	.25
443	Ken Lehman	.25
444	Don LeJohn	.25
445	Steve Lembo	.25
446	Ed Lennox	.25
447	Dutch Leonard	.25
448	Jeffery Leonard	.25
449	Sam Leslie	.25
450	Dennis Lewallyn	.25
451	Dennis Lewallyn	.25
452	Bob Lillis	.25
453	Jim Lindsey	.25
454	Fred Lindstrom	.25
455	Billy Loes	.50
456	Bob Logan	.25
457	Bill Lohrman	.25
459	Vic Lombardi	.25
460	Davey Lopes	.75
461	Al Lopez	.25
462	Ray Lucas	.25
464	Harry Lumley	.25
465	Don Lund	.25
466	Dolf Luque	.25
467	Jim Lyttle	.25
468	Max Macon	.25
469	Bill Madlock	.75
470	Lee Magee	.25
471	Sal Maglie	.25
472	George Magoon	.25
473	Duster Mails	.25
474	Candy Maldonado	.25
475	Tony Malinosky	.25
476	Lew Malone	.25
477	Al Mamaux	.25
478	Gus Mancuso	.25
479	Charlie Manuel	.25
480	Heinie Manush	.25
481	Rabbit Maranville	.25
482	Juan Marichal	2.50
483	Rube Marquard	.25
484	Bill Marriott	.25
485	Buck Marrow	.25
486	Mike A. Marshall	.75
487	Mike G. Marshall	.75
488	Morrie Martin	.25
489	Ramon Martinez	1.25
490	Teddy Martinez	.25
491	Earl Mattingly	.25
492	Len Matuszek	.25
493	Gene Mauch	.25
494	Al Maul	.25
495	Carmen Mauro	.25
496	Alvin McBean	.25
497	Bill McCarren	.25
498	Jack McCarthy	.25
499	Tommy McCarthy	.25
500	Lew McCarty	.25
501	Mike J. McCormick	.25
502	Judge McCreedie	.25
503	Tom McCreery	.25
504	Danny McDevitt	.25
505	Chappie McFarland	.25
506	Joe McGinnity	.25
507	Bob McGraw	.25
508	Deacon McGuire	.25
509	Bill McGunnigle	.25
510	Harry McIntyre	.25
511	Cal McLish	.25
512	Ken McMullen	.25
513	Dough McWeeny	.25
514	Joe Medwick	.25
515	Rube Melton	.25
516	Fred Merkle	.25
517	Orlando Mercado	.25
518	Andy Messersmith	.25
519	Irish Meusel	.25
520	Benny Meyer	.25
521	Russ Meyer	.25
522	Chief Meyers	.25
523	Gene Michael	.25
524	Pete Mikkelsen	.25
525	Eddie Miksis	.25
526	Johnny Miljus	.25
527	Bob Miller	.25
528	Larry Miller	.25
529	Otto Miller	.25
530	Ralph Miller	.25
531	Walt Miller	.25
532	Wally Millies	.25
533	Bob Milliken	.25
534	Buster Mills	.25
535	Paul Minner	.25
536	Bobby Mitchell	.25
537	Clarence Mitchell	.25
538	Dale Mitchell	.25
539	Fred Mitchell	.25
540	Johnny Mitchell	.25
541	Joe Moeller	.25
542	Rick Monday	.75
543	Wally Moon	.75
544	Cy Moore	.25
545	Dee Moore	.25
546	Eddie Moore	.25
547	Gene Moore	.25
548	Randy Moore	.25
549	Ray Moore	.25
550	Jose Morales	.25
551	Bobby Morgan	.25
552	Eddie Morgan	.25
553	Mike Morgan	.25
554	Johnny Morrison	.25
555	Walt Moryn	.25
556	Ray Moss	.25
557	Manny Mota	.75
558	Joe Mulvey	.25
559	Van Lingle Mungo	.25
560	Les Munns	.25
561	Mike Munoz	.25
562	Simmy Murch	.25
563	Eddie Murray	4.00
564	Hy Myers	.25
565	Sam Nahem	.25
566	Earl Naylor	.25
567	Charlie Neal	.75
568	Ron Negray	.25
569	Bernie Neis	.25
570	Rocky Nelson	.25
571	Dick Nen	.25
572	Don Newcombe	2.50
573	Bobo Newsom	.25
574	Doc Newton	.25
575	Tom Niedenfuer	.25
576	Otho Nicholas	.25
577	Al Nixon	.25
578	Jerry Nops	.25
579	Irv Noren	.25
580	Fred Norman	.25
581	Bill North	.25
582	Johnny Oates	.25
583	Bob O'Brien	.25
584	John O'Brien	.25
585	Lefty O'Doul	.25
586	Joe Oeschger	.25
587	Al Oliver	.75
588	Nate Oliver	.25
589	Luis Olmo	.25
590	Ivy Olson	.25
591	Mickey O'Neil	.25
592	Joe Orengo	.25
593	Jesse Orosco	.25
594	Frank O'Rourke	.25
595	Jorge Orta	.25
596	Phil Ortega	.25
597	Claude Osteen	.25
598	Fritz Ostermueller	.25
599	Mickey Owen	.25
600	Tom Paciorek	.25
601	Don Padgett	.25
602	Andy Pafko	.75
603	Erv Palica	.25
604	Ed Palmquist	.25
605	Wes Parker	.25
606	Jay Partridge	.25
607	Camilo Pascual	.25
608	Kevin Pasley	.25
609	Dave Patterson	.25
610	Harley Payne	.25
611	Johnny Peacock	.25
612	Hal Peck	.25
613	Stu Pederson	.25
614	Alejandro Pena	.25
615	Jose Pena	.25
616	Jack Perconte	.25
617	Charlie Perkins	.25
618	Ron Perranoski	.50
619	Jim Peterson	.25
620	Jesse Petty	.25
621	Jeff Pfeffer	.25
622	Babe Phelps	.25
623	Val Picinich	.25
624	Joe Pignatano	.25
625	George Pinckney	.25
626	Ed Pipgras	.25
627	Bud Podbielan	.25
628	Johnny Podres	.75
629	Boots Poffenberger	.25
630	Nick Polly	.25
631	Paul Popovich	.25
632	Bill Posedel	.25
633	Boog Powell	.50
634	Dennis Powell	.25
635	Paul Ray Powell	.25
636	Ted Power	.25
637	Tot Pressnell	.25
638	John Purdin	.25
639	Jack Quinn	.25
640	Marv Rackley	.25
641	Jack Radtke	.25
642	Pat Ragan	.25
643	Ed Rakow	.25
644	Bob Ramazzotti	.25
645	Willie Ramsdell	.25
646	Mike James Ramsey	.25
647	Mike Jeffery Ramsey	.25
648	Willie Randolph	.25
649	Doug Rau	.25
650	Lance Rautzhan	.25
651	Howie Reed	.25
652	Pee Wee Reese	9.00
653	Phil Regan	.25
654	Bill Reidy	.25
655	Bobby Reis	.25
656	Pete Reiser	.75
657	Rip Repulski	.25
658	Ed Reulbach	.25
659	Jerry Reuss	.50
660	R.J. Reynolds	.25
661	Billy Rhiel	.25
662	Rick Rhoden	.25
663	Paul Richards	.25
664	Danny Richardson	.25
665	Pete Richert	.25
666	Harry Riconda	.25
667	Joe Riggert	.25
668	Lew Riggs	.25
669	Jimmy Ripple	.25
670	Lou Ritter	.25
671	German Rivera	.25
672	Johnny Rizzo	.25
673	Jim Roberts	.25
674	Earl Robinson	.25
675	Frank Robinson	5.00
676	Jackie Robinson	15.00
677a	Wilbert Robinson	.25
677b	Sergio Robles	.25
678	Rich Rodas	.25
679	Ellie Rodriguez	.25
680	Preacher Roe	.25
681	Ed Roebuck	.25
682	Ron Roenicke	.25
683	Oscar Roettger	.25
684	Lee Rogers	.25
685	Packy Rogers	.25
686	Stan Rojek	.25
687	Vicente Romo	.25
688	Johnny Roseboro	.75
689	Goody Rosen	.25
690	Don Ross	.25
691	Ken Rowe	.25
692	Schoolboy Rowe	.25
693	Luther Roy	.25
694	Jerry Royster	.50
695	Nap Rucker	.25
696	Dutch Ruether	.25
697	Bill Russell	.75
698	Jim Russell	.25
699	John Russell	.25
700	Johnny Rutherford	.25
701	John Ryan	.25
702	Rosy Ryan	.25
703	Mike Sandlock	.25
704	Ted Savage	.25
705	Dave Sax	.25
706	Steve Sax	.75
707	Bill Sayles	.25
708	Bill Schardt	.25
709	Johnny Schmitz	.25
710	Dick Schofield	.25
711	Howie Schultz	.25
712	Ferdie Schupp	.25
713	Mike Scioscia	.75
714	Dick Scott	.25
715	Tom Seats	.25
716	Jimmy Sebring	.25
717	Larry See	.25
718	Dave Sells	.25
719	Greg Shanahan	.25
720	Mike Sharperson	.25
721	Joe Shaute	.25
722	Merv Shea	.25
723	Jimmy Sheckard	.25
724	Jack Sheehan	.25
725	John Shelby	.25
726	Vince Sherlock	.25
727	Larry Sherry	.75
728	Norm Sherry	.75
729	Bill Shindle	.25
730	Craig Shipley	.25
731	Bart Shirley	.25
732	Steve Shirley	.25
733	Burt Shotton	.25
734	George Shuba	.50
735	Dick Siebert	.25
736	Joe Simpson	.25
737	Duke Sims	.25
738	Bill Singer	.25
739	Fred Sington	.25
740	Ted Sizemore	.25
741	Frank Skaff	.25
742	Bill Skowron	1.25
743	Gordon Slade	.25
744	Dwain Lefty Sloat	.25
745	Charley Smith	.25
746	Dick Smith	.25
747	George Smith	.25
748	Germany Smith	.25
749	Jack Smith	.25
750	Reggie Smith	.75
751	Sherry Smith	.25
752	Harry Smythe	.25
753	Duke Snider	9.00
754	Eddie Solomon	.25
755	Elias Sosa	.25
756	Daryl Spencer	.25
757	Roy Spencer	.25
758	Karl Spooner	.50
759	Eddie Stack	.25
760	Tuck Stainback	.25
761	George Stallings	.25
762	Jerry Standaert	.25
763	Don Stanhouse	.25
764	Eddie Stanky	.25
765	Dolly Stark	.25
766	Jigger Statz	.25
767	Casey Stengel	1.25
768	Jerry Stephenson	.25
769	Ed Stevens	.25
770	Dave Stewart	.75
771	Stuffy Stewart	.25
772	Bob Stinson	.25
773	Milt Stock	.25
774	Harry Stovey	.25
775	Mike Strahler	.25
776	Sammy Strang	.25
777	Elmer Stricklett	.25
778	Joe Stripp	.25
779	Dick Stuart	.50
780	Franklin Stubbs	.25
781	Bill Sudakis	.25
782	Clyde Sukeforth	.25
783	Billy Sullivan	.25
784	Tom Sunkel	.25
785	Rick Sutcliffe	.75
786	Don Sutton	4.00
787	Bill Swift	.25
788	Vito Tamulis	.25
789	Danny Taylor	.25
790	Harry Taylor	.25
791	Zack Taylor	.25
792	Chuck Templeton	.25
793	Wayne Terwilliger	.25
794	Derrel Thomas	.25
795	Fay Thomas	.25
796	Gary Thomas	.25
797	Don Thompson	.25
798	Tim Thompson	.25
799	Hank Thormahlen	.25
800	Sloppy Thurston	.25
801	Cotton Tierney	.25
802	Al Todd	.25
805	Bert Tooley	.25
806	Jeff Torborg	.25
807	Dick Tracewski	.25

#	Player	
808	Nick Tremark	.25
809	Alex Trevino	.25
810	Tommy Tucker	.25
811	John Tudor	.25
812	Mike Vail	.25
813	Rene Valdes (Valdez)	.25
814	Bobby Valentine	.75
815	Fernando Valenzuela	.75
816	Elmer Valo	.75
817	Dazzy Vance	.75
818	Sandy Vance	.25
819	Chris Van Cuyk	.25
820	Ed VandeBerg	.25
821	Arky Vaughan	.25
822	Zoilo Versalles	.25
823	Joe Vosmik	.25
824	Ben Wade	.25
825	Dixie Walker	.50
826	Rube Walker	.50
827	Stan Wall	.25
828	Lee Walls	.25
829	Danny Walton	.25
830	Lloyd Waner	.25
831	Paul Waner	.25
832	Chuck Ward	.25
833	John Monte Ward	.25
834	Preston Ward	.25
835	Jack Warner	.25
836	Tommy Warren	.25
837	Carl Warwick	.25
838	Jimmy Wasdell	.25
839	Ron Washington	.25
840	George Watkins	.25
841	Hank Webb	.25
842	Les Webber	.25
843	Gary Weiss	.75
844	Bob Welch	.25
845	Brad Wellman	.25
846	John Werhas	.25
847	Max West	.25
848	Gus Weyhing	.25
849	Mack Wheat	.25
850	Zack Wheat	.25
851	Ed Wheeler	.25
852	Larry White	.25
853	Myron White	.25
854	Terry Whitfield	.25
855	Dick Whitman	.25
856	Possum Whitted	.25
857	Kemp Wicker	.25
858	Hoyt Wilhelm	.75
859	Kaiser Wilhelm	.25
860	Nick Willhite	.75
861	Dick Williams	.75
862	Reggie Williams	.25
863	Stan Williams	.25
864	Woody Williams	.25
865	Maury Wills	.75
866	Hack Wilson	.75
867	Robert Wilson	.25
868	Gordon Windhorn	.25
869	Jim Winford	.25
870	Lave Winham	.25
871	Tom Winsett	.25
872	Hank Winston	.25
873	Whitey Witt	.25
874	Pete Wojey	.25
875	Tracy Woodson	.25
876	Clarence Wright	.25
877	Glenn Wright	.25
878	Ricky Wright	.25
879	Whit Wyatt	.25
880	Jimmy Wynn	.25
881	Joe Yeager	.25
882	Steve Yeager	.25
883	Matt Young	.25
884	Tom Zachary	.25
885	Pat Zachry	.25
886	Geoff Zahn	.25
887	Don Zimmer	.75
888	Morrie Aderholt	.25
889	Raleigh Aitchison	.25
890	Whitey Alperman	.25
891	Orlando Alvarez	.25
892	Pat Ankenman	.25
893	Ed Appleton	.25
894	Doug Baird	.25
895	Lady Baldwin	.25
896	Win Ballou	.25
897	Bob Barr	.25
898	Boyd Bartley	.25
899	Eddie Basinski	.25
900	Erve Beck	.25
901	Ralph Birkofer	.25
903	Joe Bradshaw	.25
904	Bruce Brubaker	.25
905	Oyster Burns	.25
906	John Butler	.25
908	Kid Carsey	.25
909	Pete Cassidy	.25
910	Tom Catterson	.25
911	Glenn Chapman	.25
912	Paul Chervinko	.25
913	George Cisar	.25
914	Wally Clement	.25
915	Bill Collins	.25
916	Chuck Corgan	.25
917	Dick Cox	.25
918	George Crable	.25
919	Sam Crane	.25
920	Cliff Curtis	.25
921	Fats Dantonio	.25
922	Con Daily	.25
923	Jud Daley	.25
924	Jake Daniel	.25
925	Kal Daniels	.25
926	Dan Daub	.25
927	Lindsay Deal	.25

#	Player	
928	Artie Dede	.25
929	Pat Deisel	.25
930	Bert Delmas	.25
931	Rube Dessau	.25
932	Leo Dickerman	.25
933	John Douglas	.25
934	Red Downey	.25
935	Carl Doyle	.25
936	John Duffie	.25
937	Dick Durning	.25
938	Red Durrett	.25
939	Mal Eason	.25
940	Charlie Ebbetts	.75
941	Rube Ehardt	.25
942	Rowdy Elliot	.25
943	Bones Ely	.25
944	Woody English	.25
945	Roy Evans	.25
946	Gus Felix	.25
947	Bill Fischer	.25
948	Jeff Fischer	.25
949	Chauncey Fisher	.25
950	Tom Fitzsimmons	.25
951	Darrin Fletcher	.25
952	Wes Flowers	.25
953	Howard Freigau	.25
954	Nig Fuller	.25
955	John Gaddy	.25
956	Welcome Gaston	.25
957	Frank Gatins	.25
958	Pete Gilbert	.25
959	Wally Wilbert	.25
960	Carden Gillenwater	.25
961	Roy Gleason	.25
962	Harvey Green	.25
963	Nelson Greene	.25
964	John Grim	.25
965	Dan Griner	.25
966	Bill Hall	.25
967	Johnny Hall	.25
968	Pat Hanifin	.25
970	Bill Harris	.25
971	Bill Harris	.25
972	Bill W. Hart	.25
973	Chris Hartje	.25
974	Mike Hartley	.25
975	Gil Hatfield	.25
976	Chris Haughey	.25
977	Hugh Hearne	.25
978	Mike Hechinger	.25
979	Jake Hehl	.25
980	Bob Higgins	.25
981	Still Bill Hill	.25
982	Shawn Hillegas	.25
983	Wally Hood	.25
984	Lefty Hopper	.25
985	Ricky Horton	.25
986	Ed Householder	.25
987	Bill Hubbell	.25
988	Al Humphrey	.25
989	Bernie Hungling	.25
990	George Hunter	.25
991	Pat Hurley	.25
992	Joe Hutcheson	.25
993	Bert Hutson	.25
994	Bert Inks	.25
995	Dutch Jordan	.25
997	Frank Kane	.25
998	Chet Kehn	.25
999	Maury Kent	.25
1000	Tom Kinslow	.25
1001	Fred Kipp	.25
1002	Joe Klugman	.25
1003	Elmer Knetzer	.25
1004	Barney Koch	.25
1005	Jim Korwan	.25
1006	Joe Koukalik	.25
1007	Lou Koupal	.25
1008	Joe Kustus	.25
1009	Frank Lamanske	.25
1010	Tacks Latimer	.25
1011	Bill Leard	.25
1012	Phil Lewis	.25
1013	Mickey Livingston	.25
1014	Dick Loftus	.25
1015	Charlie Loudenslager	.25
1016	Tom Lovett	.25
1017	Charlie Malay	.25
1018	Mal Mallett	.25
1019	Ralph Mauriello	.25
1020	Bill McCabe	.25
1021	Gene McCann	.25
1022	Mike McCormick	.25
1023	Terry McDermott	.25
1024	John McDougal	.25
1025	Pryor McElveen	.25
1026	Dan McGann	.25
1027	Pat McGlothin	.25
1028	Doc McJames	.25
1029	Kit McKenna	.25
1030	Sadie McMahon	.25
1032	Tommy McMillan	.25
1033	Glenn Mickens	.25
1034	Don Miles	.25
1035	Hack Miller	.25
1036	John Miller	.25
1037	Lemmie Miller	.25
1038	George Mohart	.25
1039	Gary Moore	.25
1040	Herbie Moran	.25
1041	Earl Mossor	.25
1042	Glen Moulder	.25
1043	Billy Mullen	.25
1044	Hub Northen	.25
1045	Curly Onis	.25
1046	Jim Pastorius	.25
1047	Art Parks	.25
1049	Chink Outen	.25

#	Player	
1050	Jimmy Pattison	.25
1051	Norman Pitt	.25
1052	Doc Reisling	.25
1053	Gilberto Reyes	.25
1055	Lou Rochelli	.25
1056	Jim Romano	.25
1057	Max Rosenfeld	.25
1058	Andy Rush	.25
1059	Jack Ryan	.25
1060	Jack Savage	.25
1062	Ray Schmandt	.25
1063	Henry Schmidt	.25
1064	Charlie Schmutz	.25
1065	Joe Schultz	.25
1066	Ray Searage	.25
1067	Elmer Sexauer	.25
1068	George Sharrott	.25
1069	Tommy Sheehan	.25
1071	George Shoch	.25
1072	Broadway Aleck Smith	.25
1073	Hap Smith	.25
1074	Red Smith	.25
1075	Tony Smith	.25
1076	Gene Snyder	.25
1077	Denny Sothern	.25
1078	Bill Steele	.25
1080	Farmer Steelman	.25
1081	Dutch Stryker	.25
1082	Tommy Tatum	.25
1084	Adonis Terry	.25
1085	Ray Thomas	.25
1086	George Treadway	.25
1087	Overton Tremper	.25
1088	Ty Tyson	.25
1089	Rube Vickers	.25
1090	Jose Vizcaino	.25
1091	Bull Wagner	.25
1092	Butts Wagner	.25
1093	Rube Ward	.25
1094	John Wetteland	.25
1095	Eddie Wilson	.25
1096	Tex Wilson	.25
1097	Zeke Wrigley	.25
1099	Rube Yarrison	.25
1100	Earl Yingling	.25
1101	Chink Zachary	.25
1102	Lefty Davis	.25
1103	Bob Hall	.25
1104	Darby O'Brien	.25
1105	Larry LeJeune	.25

1989 Taystee Kansas City Royals

The 1989 Royals are featured on this set of discs distributed by a K.C. area bakery. The 2-3/4" discs have color player photos at center. The team logo has been airbrushed off the caps because the issue was licensed only by the players, and not by Major League Baseball. In the white border is the issuer's logo in red at top, player identification at bottom in a yellow banner and "AL STARS" in blue stars at each side. Backs are printed in blue with player data, 1988 stats and copyright information.

		NM/M
Complete Set (12):		9.00
Common Player:		.50
1	George Brett	4.00
2	Kevin Seitzer	.50
3	Pat Tabler	.50
4	Danny Tartabull	.50
5	Willie Wilson	.50
6	Bo Jackson	1.00
7	Frank White	.50
8	Kurt Stillwell	.50
9	Mark Gubicza	.50
10	Charlie Leibrandt	.50
11	Bret Saberhagen	.75
12	Steve Farr	.50

1981 TCMA The 1960's, Series 2

A second series of cards depicting major and minor league players of the 1960s was produced by TCMA in 1981. The cards continued in the same 2-1/2" x 3-1/2" format as the earlier series. Fronts are unadorned color photos, backs have player identification, data and career summary printed in green on white. The numbering of the cards continues at #294, where the first series concluded, but only about one-third the quantity was produced of this series, compared with the first series.

		NM/M
Complete Set (189):		75.00
Common Player:		.50
294	Fritzie Brickell	.50
295	Craig Anderson	.50
296	Cliff Cook	.50
297	Pumpsie Green	.50
298	Choo Choo Coleman	.50
299	Don Buford	.50
300	Sparky Anderson	1.00
301	John Anderson	.50
302	Ted Beard	.50
303	Mickey Mantle, Roger Maris	15.00
304	Gene Freese	.50
305	Don Wilkinson	.50
306	Walter Alston	1.00
307	George Bamberger	.50
308	Nelson Briles	.50
309	Dave Baldwin	.50
310	Bob Bailey	.50
311	Paul Blair	.50
312	Ken Boswell	.50
313	Sam Bowens	.50
314	Ray Barker	.50
315	Tommie Agee, Gil Hodges	.50
316	Elmer Valo	.50
317	Ken Walters	.50
319	Joel Horlen	.50
320	Charlie Maxwell	.50
321	Joe Foy	.50
322	Tommie Agee, Cleon Jones, Ron Swoboda	.50
323	Paul Foytack	.50
324	Ron Fairly	.50
325	Wilbur Wood	.50
327	Felix Mantilla	.50
328a	Ed Bouchee	.50
328b	Don Wilson	.50
329	Sandy Valdespino	.50
330	Al Ferrera	.50
331	Jose Tartabull	.50
332	Dick Kenworthy	.50
333	Don Pavletich	.50
334	Jim Fairey	.50
335	Rico Petrocelli	.50
336	Gary Roggenburk	.50
337	Rick Reichardt	.50
338	Ken McMullen	.50
339	Dooley Womack	.50
340	Joe Moock	.50
341	Lou Brock	1.00
342	Hector Torres	.50
343	Ted Savage	.50
344	Hobie Landrith	.50
345	Ed Lopat	.50
346	Mel Nelson	.50
347	Mickey Lolich	.50
348	Al Lopez	1.00
349	Frederico Olivo	.50
350	Bob Moose	.50
351	Bill McCool	.50
352	Ernie Bowman	.50
353	Tom McCraw	.50
354	Sam Mele	.50
355	Len Boehmer	.50
356	Hank Aaron	9.00
357	Ron Hunt	.50
358	Luis Aparicio	1.00
359	Gene Mauch	.50
360	Barry Moore	.50
361	John Buzhardt	.50
362	Spring Training (St. Louis Cardinals)	.50
363	Duke Snider	3.00
364	Billy Martin	1.00
365	Wes Parker	.50
366	Dick Stuart	.50
367	Glenn Beckert	.50
368	Ollie Brown	.50
369	Stan Bahnsen	.50
370	Lee Bales	.50
371	Johnny Keane	.50
372	Wally Moon	.50
373	Larry Miller	.50
374	Fred Newman	.50
375	John Orsino	.50
376	Joe Pactwa	.50
377	John O'Donoghue	.50
378	Jim Ollom	.50
379	Ray Oyler	.50
380	Ron Nischwitz	.50
381	Ron Paul	.50
382	Yogi Berra, John Blanchard, Roger Maris	2.00
383	Jim McKnight	.50
384	Gene Michael	.50
385	Dave May	.50
386	Tim McCarver	1.00
387	Larry Mason	.50
388	Don Hoak	.50
389	Nate Oliver	.50
390	Phil Ortega	.50
391	Billy Madden	.50
392	John Miller	.50
393	Danny Murtaugh	.50
394	Nelson Mathews	.50
395	Red Schoendienst	1.00
396	Roger Nelson	.50
397	Tom Matchick	.50
398	Dennis Musgraves	.50
399	Tommy Harper	.50
400	Fracis Peters	.50
401	Tony Pierce	.50
402	Billy Williams	1.00
403	Dave Boswell	.50
404	Ray Washburn	.50
405	Al Worthington	.50
406	Jesus Alou	.50
407	Yogi Berra, Gil Hodges, Joe Pignatano, Eddie Yost	1.00
408	Wally Bunker	.50
409	Jim Brenneman	.50
410	Bobby Bragan	.50
411	Cal McLish	.50
412	Curt Blefary	.50
413	Jim Bethke	.50
414	Infield 1964 (St. Louis Cardinals)	.50
415	Richie Allen	1.00
416	Larry Brown	.50
417	Mike Andrews	.50
418	Don Mossi	.50
419	J.C. Martin	.50
420	Dick Rusteck	.50
421	Elly Rodriguez	.50
422	Casey Stengel	1.00
423	Gil Hodges, Ed Vargo	.50
424	Johnny Briggs	.50
425	Bud Harrelson, Al Weis	.50
426	Doc Edwards	.50
427	Joe Hague	.50
428	Lee Elia	.50
429	Billy Moran	.50
431	Pete Mikkelsen	.50
432a	Al Moran (Should be #430.)	.50
432b	Aurelio Monteagudo	.50
433	Ken MacKenzie	.50
434	Dick Egan	.50
435	Al McBean	.50
436	Mike Ferraro	.50
437	Gary Wagner	.50
438	Jerry Grote, J.C. Martin	.50
439	Ted Kluszewski	1.00
440	Jerry Johnson	.50
441	Ross Moschitto	.50
442	Zoilo Versalles	.50
443	Dennis Ribant	.50
444	Ted Williams	9.00
445	Steve Whitaker	.50
446	Frank Bertaina	.50
447	Bo Belinsky	.50
448	Joe Moeller	.50
449	Don Shaw, Ron Taylor	.50
450	Al Downing, Whitey Ford, Fritz Peterson, Mel Stottlemyre	1.00
451	Jack Tracy	.50
452	Tony Curry	.50
453	Roy White	.50
454	Jim Bunning	1.00
455	Ralph Houk	.50
456	Bobby Shantz	.50
457	Bill Rigney	.50
458	Roger Repoz	.50
459	Robin Roberts, Bob Turley	.50
460	Gordon Richardson	.50
461	Dick Tracewski	.50
462	Thad Tillotson	.50
463	Larry Osborne	.50
464	Larry Burright	.50
465	Alan Foster	.50
466	Ron Taylor	.50
467	Fred Talbot	.50
468	Bob Miller	.50
469	Frank Tepedino	.50
470	Danny Frisella	.50
471	Cecil Perkins	.50
472	Danny Napoleon	.50
473	John Upham	.50
474	Yogi Berra, Elston Howard, Mickey Mantle, Roger Maris, Bill Skowron	6.00
475	Al Weis	.50
476	Rich Beck	.50
477	Clete Boyer, Tony Kubek, Joe Pepitone, Bobby Richardson	3.00
478	Jack Fisher	.50
479	Archie Moore	.50
480	Roger Craig	.50
481	Frank Crosetti, Mike Hegan, Ralph Houk, Wally Moses	.50
482	Roger Craig, Gil Hodges, Clem Labine, Cookie Lavagetto	.50

1981 TCMA 1959 Chicago White Sox

The A.L. Champion Chicago White Sox are featured in this collectors' issue. The 2-1/2" x 3-1/2" cards have black-and-white player photos with dark blue borders. Backs are in black-and-white with a few bits of player data, career information, 1959 and lifetime stats, along with a TCMA copyright line.

		NM/M
Complete Set (45):		45.00
Common Player:		1.00
1	Earl Torgeson	1.00
2	Nellie Fox	5.00
3	Luis Aparicio	5.00
4	Bubba Phillips	1.00
5	Jim McAnany	1.00
6	Jim Landis	1.00
7	Al Smith	1.00
8	Sherman Lollar	1.00
9	Billy Goodman	1.00
10	Jim Rivera	1.00
11	Sammy Esposito	1.00
12	Norm Cash	2.50
13	Johnny Romano	1.00
14	Johnny Callison	1.00
15	Harry Simpson	1.00
16	Ted Kluszewski	4.00
17	Del Ennis	1.00
18	Earl Battey	1.00
19	Larry Doby	4.00
20	Ron Jackson	1.00
21	Ray Boone	1.00
22	Lou Skizas	1.00
23	Joe Hicks	1.00
24	Don Mueller	1.00
25	J.C. Martin	1.00
26	Cam Carreon	1.00
27	Early Wynn	3.00
28	Bob Shaw	1.00
29	Billy Pierce	1.50
30	Turk Lown	1.00
31	Dick Donovan	1.00
32	Gerry Staley	1.00
33	Barry Latman	1.00
34	Ray Moore	1.00
35	Rudy Arias	1.00
36	Joe Stanka	1.00
37	Ken McBride	1.00
38	Don Rudolph	1.00
39	Claude Raymond	1.00
40	Gary Peters	1.00
41	Al Lopez	1.50
42	Don Gutteridge	1.00
43	Ray Berres	1.00
44	Tony Cuccinello	1.00
45	John Cooney	1.00

1981 TCMA 1962 San Francisco Giants

The National League Champions for 1962 are featured in this collector's edition card set. The 2-1/2" x 3-1/2" cards have orange borders on front, around black-and-white player photos. Backs are in black-and-white with personal data, career information and 1982 stats.

	NM/M
Complete Set (35):	45.00
Common Player:	1.00

No.	Player	NM/M
1	Alvin Dark	1.00
2	Whitey Lockman	1.00
3	Larry Jansen	1.00
4	Wes Westrum	1.00
5	Ed Bailey	1.00
6	Tom Haller	1.00
7	Harvey Kuenn	1.00
8	Willie Mays	15.00
9	Felipe Alou	1.50
10	Orlando Cepeda	4.00
11	Chuck Hiller	1.00
12	Jose Pagan	1.00
13	Jim Davenport	1.00
14	Willie McCovey	4.00
15	Matty Alou	1.00
16	Manny Mota	1.50
17	Ernie Bowman	1.00
18	Carl Boles	1.00
19	John Orsino	1.00
20	Joe Pignatano	1.00
21	Gaylord Perry	2.50
22	Jim Duffalo	1.00
23	Dick LeMay	1.00
24	Bob Garibaldi	1.00
25	Bobby Bolin	1.00
26	Don Larsen	1.25
27	Mike McCormick	1.00
28	Stu Miller	1.00
29	Jack Sanford	1.00
30	Billy O'Dell	1.00
31	Juan Marichal	2.50
32	Billy Pierce	1.00
33	Dick Phillips	1.00
34	Cap Peterson	1.00
35	Bob Nieman	1.00

1982 TCMA Baseball's Greatest Hitters

HITTERS   JOE DiMAGGIO

Baseball's hit kings of the past are featured in this collectors set. Fronts of the 2-1/2" x 3-1/2" cards have a color or black-and-white photo surrounded by a colored frame. Backs are in black-and-white with a career summary, lifetime stats and Major League Baseball licensee logo.

No.	Player	NM/M
	Complete Set (45):	8.00
	Common Player:	.25
1	Ted Williams	1.00
2	Stan Musial	1.00
3	Joe DiMaggio	2.00
4	Roberto Clemente	2.00
5	Jackie Robinson	1.00
6	Willie Mays	1.00
7	Lou Brock	.25
8	Al Kaline	.25
9	Richie Ashburn	.25
10	Tony Oliva	.25
11	Harvey Kuenn	.25
12	Mickey Vernon	.25
13	Tommy Davis	.25
14	Ty Cobb	.75
15	Rogers Hornsby	.25
16	Joe Jackson	2.00
17	Willie Keeler	.25
18	Tris Speaker	.25
19	Babe Ruth	2.50
20	Harry Heilmann	.25
21	Bill Terry	.25
22	George Sisler	.25
23	Lou Gehrig	1.00
24	Nap Lajoie	.25
25	Riggs Stephenson	.25
26	Al Simmons	.25
27	Cap Anson	.25
28	Paul Waner	.25
29	Eddie Collins	.25
30	Heinie Manush	.25
31	Honus Wagner	.50
32	Earle Combs	.25
33	Sam Rice	.25
34	Charlie Gehringer	.25
35	Chick Hafey	.25
36	Zack Wheat	.25
37	Frank Frisch	.25
38	Bill Dickey	.25
39	Ernie Lombardi	.25
40	Joe Cronin	.25
41	Lefty O'Doul	.25
42	Luke Appling	.25
43	Ferris Fain	.25
44	Arky Vaughan	.25
45	Joe Medwick	.25

1982 TCMA Baseball's Greatest Pitchers

PITCHERS   DON DRYSDALE

The best pitchers who were no longer active are featured in this collectors issue. Color or black-and-white photos are presented at center of 2-1/2" x 3-1/2" cards, with a colored frame surrounding the title, name and position. Backs are printed in dark blue and have a career summary and lifetime stats.

No.	Player	NM/M
	Complete Set (45):	6.00
	Common Player:	.25
1	Bob Feller	.35
2	Bob Lemon	.25
3	Whitey Ford	.75
4	Joe Page	.25
5	Wilbur Wood	.25
6	Robin Roberts	.25
7	Warren Spahn	.25
8	Sandy Koufax	3.00
9	Juan Marichal	.25
10	Don Newcombe	.25
11	Hoyt Wilhelm	.25
12	Roy Face	.25
13	Allie Reynolds	.25
14	Don Drysdale	.25
15	Bob Gibson	.25
16	Cy Young	.25
17	Walter Johnson	.25
18	Grover Alexander	.25
19	Jack Chesbro	.25
20	Lefty Gomez	.25
21	Wes Ferrell	.25
22	Hal Newhouser	.25
23	Early Wynn	.25
24	Denny McLain	.25
25	Catfish Hunter	.25
26	Jim Lonborg	.25
27	Frank Lary	.25
28	Red Ruffing	.25
29	Lefty Grove	.25
30	Herb Pennock	.25
31	Satchel Paige	1.50
32	Iron Man McGinnity	.25
33	Christy Mathewson	.50
34	Mordecai Brown	.25
35	Eppa Rixey	.25
36	Dizzy Dean	.40
37	Carl Hubbell	.25
38	Dazzy Vance	.25
39	Jim Bunning	.25
40	Smokey Joe Wood	.25
41	Freddie Fitzsimmons	.25
42	Rube Waddell	.25
43	Addie Joss	.25
44	Burleigh Grimes	.25
45	Chief Bender	.25

Baseball's Greatest Sluggers

SLUGGERS   BABE RUTH

The heaviest hitters in baseball history are featured in this collectors issue. The 2-1/2" x 3-1/2" cards have color or black-and-white photos on front framed in red or green and bordered in white. Backs have a few personal data, career stats and career summary along with a logo indicating licensing by Major League Baseball, all in black-and-white, or blue-and-white. Cards can be found printed on either white or gray cardboard.

No.	Player	NM/M
	Complete Set (45):	8.00
	Common Player:	.25
1	Harmon Killebrew	.25
2	Roger Maris	.50
3	Mickey Mantle	3.00
4	Hank Aaron	1.50
5	Ralph Kiner	.25
6	Willie McCovey	.25
7	Eddie Mathews	.25
8	Ernie Banks	.50
9	Duke Snider	.50
10	Frank Howard	.25
11	Ted Kluszewski	.25
12	Frank Robinson	.25
13	Billy Williams	.25
14	Gil Hodges	.50
15	Yogi Berra	.50
16	Richie Allen	.25
17	Joe Adcock	.25
18	Babe Ruth	2.50
19	Lou Gehrig	2.00
20	Jimmie Foxx	.25
21	Rogers Hornsby	.25
22	Ted Williams	1.50
23	Hack Wilson	.25
24	Al Simmons	.25
25	John Mize	.25
26	Chuck Klein	.25
27	Hank Greenberg	.25
28	Babe Herman	.25
29	Norm Cash	.25
30	Rudy York	.25
31	Gavvy Cravath	.25
32	Mel Ott	.25
33	Orlando Cepeda	.25
34	Dolf Camilli	.25
35	Frank Baker	.25
36	Larry Doby	.25
37	Jim Gentile	.25
38	Harry Davis	.25
39	Rocco Colavito	.25
40	Cy Williams	.25
41	Roy Sievers	.25
42	Boog Powell	.25
43	Willie Mays	1.50
44	Joe DiMaggio	2.00
45	Earl Averill	.25

1982 TCMA Great Players of the 1950's & 60's: Series #1

These large-format (3-3/4" x 5-3/4") cards have white-bordered color poses on front, with no extraneous graphics. Backs have a black-and-white head shot of the player with lifetime stats, career highlights and personal data in a red border.

No.	Player	NM/M
	Complete Set (20):	15.00
	Common Player:	.60
1	Roberto Clemente	3.00
2	Sandy Koufax	2.50
3	Phil Rizzuto	1.00
4	Bob Feller	.60
5	Duke Snider	1.00
6	Hank Aaron	2.50
7	Eddie Mathews	.60
8	Roy Campanella	1.50
9	Willie Mays	2.50
10	Robin Roberts	.60
11	Nelson Fox	.60
12	Early Wynn	.60
13	Ted Williams	2.50
14	Warren Spahn	.60
15	Jackie Robinson	2.00
16	Joe DiMaggio	2.50
17	Frank Robinson	.60
18	Yogi Berra	1.25
19	Mickey Mantle	3.50
20	Stan Musial	2.00

1982 TCMA "1952" Bowman

A find of player paintings evidently intended for use in Bowman's 1952 baseball card set allowed TCMA to produce this collectors' issue of 15 Bowman "high numbers" that never were." The 2-1/8" x 3-1/8" cards approximate the size of the originals; Fronts have only the color picture with a white border around; the facsimile signatures found on original 1952 Bowmans are not present. Backs are printed in red and black and have layout and style similar to the 1952 cards, along with a 1982 TCMA copyright. The issue was numbered consecutively from #253, beginning where the original issue ended.

No.	Player	NM/M
	Complete Set (15):	12.00
	Common Player:	1.00
253	Bob Kennedy	1.00
254	Barney McCosky	1.00
255	Chris Van Cuyk	1.00
256	Morrie Martin	1.00
257	Jim Wilson	1.00
258	Bob Thorpe	1.00
259	Bill Henry	1.00
260	Bob Addis	1.00
261	Terry Moore	1.00
262	Joe Dobson	1.00
263	Jack Merson	1.00
264	Virgil Trucks	1.00
265	Johnny Hopp	1.00
266	Cookie Lavagetto	1.00
267	George Shuba	1.00

1983 TCMA All-Time Athletics

Mule Haas   OF
ALL-TIME ATHLETICS

This was one of several early 1980s collectors issues from TCMA depicting an All-Time team. The 2-1/2" x 3-1/2" cards have black-and-white photos on front with red graphics. Backs are printed in blue and offer personal data, a career summary and lifetime stats.

No.	Player	NM/M
	Complete Set (12):	12.00
	Common Player:	.75
1	Jimmie Foxx	1.50
2	Eddie Collins	1.25
3	Frank Baker	1.25
4	Jack Barry	.75
5	Al Simmons	1.25
6	Mule Haas	.75
7	Bing Miller	.75
8	Mickey Cochrane	1.25
9	Chief Bender	1.25
10	Lefty Grove	1.25
11	John Wyatt	.75
12	Connie Mack	1.25

All-Time Cardinals

A picked team of Cardinal greats through the 1970s is featured on this collectors' issue. The 2-1/2" x 3-1/2" cards have black-and-white photos on front, with the title printed in red in the white bottom border. Backs have player data and a career summary printed in purple on gray or blue on white.

Jim Bottomley   1B
ALL-TIME CARDINALS

No.	Player	NM/M
	Complete Set (12):	18.00
	Common Player:	1.00
1	Jim Bottomley	1.00
2	Rogers Hornsby	1.25
3	Ken Boyer	1.50
4	Marty Marion	1.00
5	Ducky Medwick	1.00
6	Chick Hafey	1.00
7	Stan Musial	6.00
8	Tim McCarver	1.25
9	Robert "Bob" Gibson	1.50
10	Harry Brecheen	1.00
11	Alpha Brazle	1.00
12	Red Schoendienst	1.25

All-Time Pirates

DEACON PHILLIPPE   P

This was one of several early 1980s collectors' issues from TCMA depicting an All-Time team. The 2-1/2" x 3-1/2" cards have black-and-white photos on front with blue graphics. Backs are printed in blue and offer personal data, a career summary and lifetime stats.

No.	Player	NM/M
	Complete Set (12):	12.00
	Common Player:	1.00
1	Willie Stargell	2.00
2	Bill Mazeroski	2.00
3	Pie Traynor	1.00
4	Honus Wagner	2.00
5	Roberto Clemente	6.00
6	Lloyd Waner, Paul Waner	1.50
7	Ralph Kiner	1.00
8	Manny Sanguillen	1.00
9	Deacon Phillippe	1.00
10	Bob Veale	1.00
11	Elroy Face	1.00
12	Danny Murtaugh	1.00

Play Ball Postcards

These 5-1/2" x 3-1/2" postcards have vintage photos in sepia with white borders and player identification on front. The postcard-style backs have a write-up about the team represented.

No.	Card	NM/M
	Complete Set (18):	25.00
	Common Card:	2.00
1	1949 Indians (Lou Boudreau, Joe Gordon)	2.00
2	1948 Red Sox (Murrell Jones, Bobby Doerr, Junior Stephens, Johnny Pesky)	2.00
3	1948 Red Sox (Sam Mele, Ted Williams, Stan Spence, Dom DiMaggio)	4.00
4	1948 Yankees (Joe DiMaggio, Johnny Lindell, Charlie Keller, Tommy Henrich)	5.00
5	Pittsburgh 1947 (Happy Chandler, Hank Greenberg)	2.00
6	1948 Phillies (Eddie Miller, Emil Verban)	2.00
7	1948 Cardinals (Howie Pollett, Red Munger, Murry Dickson, Harry Brecheen, Ken Burkhart)	2.00
8	1948 Braves (Warren Spahn, Johnny Sain)	2.50
9	1948 Braves (Alvin Dark, Eddie Stanky)	2.00
10	1948 Braves (Bob Elliott, Tommy Holmes)	2.00
11	1941 Yankees Team Photo	3.00
12	1943 Yankees Team Photo	3.00
13	1947 Yankees Team Photo	3.00
14	1948 Spring Training (Yankees) (Eddie Lopat, Spec Shea, Vic Raschi, Red Embree, Bill Bevens)	3.00
15	1948 A's (Lou Brissie, Connie Mack)	2.00
16	1948 Tigers (Ted Gray, Hal Newhouser, Virgil Trucks, Art Houtteman, Fred Hutchinson, Dizzy Trout)	2.00
17	Yankees (Phil Rizzuto, Joe Gordon)	3.00
18	1944 Browns (Ellis Clary, Floyd Baker, Vern Stephens, Mark Christman, Don Gutteridge, George McQuinn)	2.00

50 Years of Yankees All-Stars

Yankees' players who participated in the first 50 years of All-Star Games (1933-1983) are featured in this collectors' issue. The 2-3/4" x 3-1/2" cards feature on front the art of Robert Stephen Simon.

No.	Player	NM/M
	Complete Set (50):	12.50
	Common Player:	.40
1	Checklist (Mickey Mantle)	1.25
2	Luis Arroyo	.40
3	Hank Bauer	.40
4	Yogi Berra	.75
5	Tommy Byrne	.40
6	Spud Chandler	.40
7	Ben Chapman	.40
8	Jim Coates	.40
9	Bill Dickey	.50
10	Joe DiMaggio	3.00
11	Al Downing	.40
12	Ryne Duren	.40
13	Whitey Ford	.75
14	Whitey Ford	.75
15	Lou Gehrig	3.00
16	Lefty Gomez	.40
17	Bob Grim	.40
18	Tommy Henrich	.40
19	Elston Howard	.40
20	Catfish Hunter	.40
21	Billy Johnson	.40
22	Charlie Keller	.40
23	Johnny Kucks	.40
24	Ed Lopat	.40
25	Sparky Lyle	.40
26	Mickey Mantle	4.00
27	Roger Maris	.75
28	Billy Martin	.40
29	Johnny Mize	.50
30	Bobby Murcer	.40
31	Irv Noren	.40
32	Joe Pepitone	.40
33	Fritz Peterson	.40
34	Vic Raschi	.40
35	Allie Reynolds	.40

36	Bobby Richardson	.40
37	Phil Rizzuto	.75
38	Marius Russo	.40
39	Babe Ruth	3.50
40	Johnny Sain	.40
41	George Selkirk	.40
42	Bobby Shantz	.40
43	Spec Shea	.40
44	Moose Skowron	.40
45	Casey Stengel	.60
46	Mel Stottlemyre	.40
47	Ralph Terry	.40
48	Tom Tresh	.40
49	Bob Turley	.40
50	Roy White	.40

1936-1939 Yankee Dynasty

Many of the players who participated in one or more of the Yankees' four consecutive World Champion seasons in the late 1930s are included in this collectors' edition. Cards are 2-3/4" x 4" and feature black-and-white photos on front. In the white borders at top and bottom, the set name and player identification are printed in blue. Backs have stats for each season and are printed in black-and-white on a brown background. This set is a virtual reprint of the set made in 1974, with two player cards added. The unnumbered cards are checklisted here alphabetically.

		NM/M
Complete Set (56):		45.00
Common Player:		1.00
(1)	"Poison Ivy" Andrews	1.00
(2)	Joe Beggs	1.00
(3)	Marv Breuer	1.00
(4)	Johnny Broaca	1.00
(5)	"Jumbo" Brown	1.00
(6)	"Spud" Chandler	1.00
(7)	Ben Chapman	1.00
(8)	Earle Combs	1.00
(9)	Frankie Crosetti	1.00
(10)	"Babe" Dahlgren	1.00
(11)	Bill Dickey	1.00
(12)	Joe DiMaggio	8.00
(13)	Atley Donald	1.00
(14)	Wes Ferrell	1.00
(15)	Artie Fletcher	1.00
(16)	Joe Gallagher	1.00
(17)	Lou Gehrig	8.00
(18)	Joe Glenn	1.00
(19)	"Lefty" Gomez	1.00
(20)	Joe Gordon	1.00
(21)	"Bump" Hadley	1.00
(22)	Don Heffner	1.00
(23)	Tommy Henrich	1.00
(24)	Oral Hildebrand	1.00
(25)	Myril Hoag	1.00
(26)	Roy Johnson	1.00
(27)	Arndt Jorgens	1.00
(28)	Charlie Keller	1.00
(29)	Ted Kleinhans	1.00
(30)	Billy Knickerbocker	1.00
(31)	Tony Lazzeri	1.00
(32)	Frank Makosky	1.00
(33)	"Pat" Malone	1.00
(34)	Johnny Murphy	1.00
(35)	"Monty" Pearson	1.00
(36)	"Jake" Powell	1.00
(37)	"Red" Rolfe	1.00
(38)	"Buddy" Rosar	1.00
(39)	"Red" Ruffing	1.00
(40)	Marius Russo	1.00
(41)	"Jack" Saltzgaver	1.00
(42)	Paul Schreiber	1.00
(43)	Johnny Schulte	1.00
(44)	Bob Seeds	1.00
(45)	"Twinkletoes" Selkirk	1.00
(46)	Lee Stine	1.00
(47)	Steve Sundra	1.00
(48)	"Sandy" Vance	1.00
(49)	Dixie Walker	1.00
(50)	Kemp Wicker	1.00
(51)	Joe McCarthy, Jacob Ruppert	1.00
(52)	Joe DiMaggio, Frank Crosetti, Tony Lazzeri, Bill Dickey, Lou Gehrig, Jake Powell, George Selkirk	3.00
(53)	Lou Gehrig, Joe DiMaggio	5.00
(54)	Gehrig Hits Another	5.00
(55)	Red Rolfe, Tony Lazzeri, Lou Gehrig, Frank Crosetti	3.00
(56)	World Champions/1936	3.00

942-46 St. Louis Cardinals

This set is a virtual re-issue of the 1975 set, except for some minor changes in player selection, the use of a slightly smaller (2-1/2" x 3-1/2") format, gray cardboard backs instead of white and which include biographical information as well as stats and the appearance on a black line around the black-and-white player photos. Highlight printing on front is again in red. This version of the set includes card numbers.

		NM/M
Complete Set (68):		24.00
Common Player:		.25
1	Jimmy Brown	.25
2	Jeff Cross	.25
3	Lou Klein	.25
4	Danny Litwhiler	.25
5	Sam Narron	.25
6	Estel Crabtree	.25
7	Buzzy Wares	.25
8	Ken O'Dea	.25
9	Buddy Blattner	.25
10	Erv Dusak	.25
11	Ray Sanders	.25
12	Harry Walker	.25
13	Coaker Triplett	.25
14	Stan Musial	4.00
15	Walker Cooper	.25
16	Whitey Kurowski	.25
17	Enos Slaughter	1.50
18	Terry Moore	.35
19	Johnny Hopp	.25
20	Creepy Crespi	.25
21	Marty Marion	.50
22	Debs Garms	.25
23	Frank Demaree	.25
24	George Fallon	.25
25	Buster Adams	.25
26	Emil Verban	.50
27	Augie Bergamo	.50
28	Pepper Martin	.50
29	Mike Gonzalez	.50
30	Leo Durocher, Eddie Dyer	.50
31	Red Schoendienst	1.50
32	Del Rice	.25
33	Joe Garagiola	2.00
34	Dick Sisler	.25
35	Clyde Kluttz	.25
36	Bill Endicott	.25
37	Nippy Jones	.25
38	Walt Sessi	.25
39	Del Wilber	.25
40	Mort Cooper	.25
41	John Beazley	.25
42	Howie Krist	.25
43	Max Lanier	.25
44	Harry Grumbert (Gumbert)	.25
45	Howie Pollet	.25
46	Ernie White	.25
47	Murray Dickson (Murry)	.25
48	Lon Warneke	.25
49	Bill Lohrman	.25
50	Clyde Shoun	.25
51	Red Munger	.25
52	Harry Brecheen	.25
53	Al Brazle	.25
54	Bud Byerly	.25
55	Ted Wilks	.25
56	Fred Schmidt	.25
57	Al Jurisich	.25
58	Red Barrett	.25
59	Ken Burkhart	.25
60	Blix Donnelly	.25
61	Johnny Grodzicki	.25
62	Billy Southworth	.25
63	Eddie Dyer	.25
64	Red Ruffing, Johnny Beazley	.25
65	Stan Musial, Billy Southworth, Johnny Hopp	1.00
66	Sportsman's Park (5' x 3-1/2")	2.00
67	1942 St. Louis Cardinals (5' x 3-1/2")	2.00
68	Stan Musial, Billy Southworth, Ray Sanders	1.00

1942 Play Ball

Between 1983-85, TCMA produced eight sets of collectors' cards resurrecting the Play Ball brand name which had been active in the field from 1939-41. The TCMA sets attempt to replicate the style and substance of the earlier Play Ball cards as if the company had continued production through World War II and the end of the 1940s. The "1942" set features sepia-toned photos on front, with black graphics. Backs are printed on gray stock in blue ink. Size approximates the original Play Balls at 2-1/2" x 3-1/4".

		NM/M
Complete Set (45):		30.00
Common Player:		1.50
1	Joe Gordon	1.50
2	Joe DiMaggio	6.50
3	Bill Dickey	2.00
4	Joe McCarthy	1.50
5	Tex Hughson	1.50
6	Ted Williams	5.00
7	Walt Judnich	1.50
8	Vern Stephens	1.50
9	Denny Galehouse	1.50
10	Lou Boudreau	1.50
11	Ken Keltner	1.50
12	Jim Bagby	1.50
13	Rudy York	1.50
14	Barney McCosky	1.50
15	Schoolboy Rowe	1.50
16	Luke Appling	1.50
17	Taft Wright	1.50
18	Ted Lyons	1.50
19	Mickey Vernon	1.50
20	George Case	1.50
21	Bobo Newsom	1.50
22	Bob Johnson	1.50
23	Buddy Blair	1.50
24	Pete Suder	1.50
25	Terry Moore	1.50
26	Stan Musial	5.00
27	Marty Marion	1.50
28	Pee Wee Reese	3.50
29	Arky Vaughan	1.50
30	Larry French	1.50
31	Johnny Mize	2.00
32	Mel Ott	2.00
33	Willard Marshall	1.50
34	Carl Hubbell	2.00
35	Frank McCormick	1.50
36	Linus Frey	1.50
37	Bob Elliott	1.50
38	Vince DiMaggio	1.50
39	Al Lopez	1.50
40	Stan Hack	1.50
41	Lou Novikoff	1.50
42	Casey Stengel	2.00
43	Tommy Holmes	1.50
44	Ron Northey	1.50
45	Rube Melton	1.50

1943 Play Ball

JOE MEDWICK

Between 1983-85, TCMA produced eight sets of collectors' cards resurrecting the Play Ball brand name which had been active in the field from 1939-41. The TCMA sets attempt to replicate the style and substance of the earlier Play Ball cards as if the company had continued production through World War II and the end of the 1940s. The "1943" set features sepia-toned photos on front, with black graphics. Backs are printed on gray stock in purple ink. Size approximates the original Play Balls at 2-1/2" x 3-1/4".

		NM/M
Complete Set (45):		25.00
Common Player:		1.50
1	Spud Chandler	1.50
2	Frank Crosetti	1.50
3	Johnny Lindell	1.50
4	Emil "Dutch" Leonard	1.50
5	Stan Spence	1.50
6	Ray Mack	1.50
7	Hank Edwards	1.50
8	Al Smith	1.50
9	Mike Tresh	1.50
10	Don Kolloway	1.50
11	Orval Grove	1.50
12	Doc Cramer	1.50
13	Pinky Higgins	1.50
14	Dick Wakefield	1.50
15	Harland Clift (Harland)	1.50
16	Chet Laabs	1.50
17	George McQuinn	1.50
18	Tony Lupien	1.50
19	Oscar Judd	1.50
20	Roy Partee	1.50
21	Lum Harris	1.50
22	Roger Wolf	1.50
23	Dick Siebert	1.50
24	Walker Cooper	1.50
25	Mort Cooper	1.50
26	Whitey Kurowski	1.50
27	Eddie Miller	1.50
28	Elmer Riddle	1.50
29	Bucky Walters	1.50
30	Whitlow Wyatt	1.50
31	Dolf Camilli	1.50
32	Elbie Fletcher	1.50
33	Frank Gustine	1.50
34	Rip Sewell	1.50
35	Phil Cavarretta	1.50
36	Bill "Swish" Nicholson	1.50
37	Peanuts Lowrey	1.50
38	Phil Masi	1.50
39	Al Javery	1.50
40	Jim Tobin	1.50
41	Glen Stewart	1.50
42	Mickey Livingston	1.50
43	Ace Adams	1.50
44	Joe Medwick	2.50
45	Sid Gordon	1.50

1944 Play Ball

BOB CHIPMAN

Between 1983-85, TCMA produced eight sets of collectors' cards resurrecting the Play Ball brand name which had been active in the field from 1939-41. The TCMA sets attempt to replicate the style and substance of the earlier Play Ball cards as if the company had continued production through World War II and the end of the 1940s. The "1944" set features black-and-white photos on front, with blue graphics. Backs are printed on gray stock in black ink. Size approximates the original Play Balls at 2-1/2" x 3-1/4".

		NM/M
Complete Set (45):		25.00
Common Player:		1.50
1	Don Gutteridge	1.50
2	Mark Christman	1.50
3	Mike Kreevich	1.50
4	Jimmy Outlaw	1.50
5	Paul Richards	1.50
6	Hal Newhouser	2.50
7	Bud Metheny	1.50
8	Mike Garbark	1.50
9	Hersh Martin	1.50
10	Bob Johnson	1.50
11	Mike Ryba	1.50
12	Oris Hockett	1.50
13	Ed Klieman	1.50
14	Ford Garrison	1.50
15	Irv Hall	1.50
16	Ed Busch	1.50
17	Ralph Hodgin	1.50
18	Thurman Tucker	1.50
19	Bill Dietrich	1.50
20	Rick Ferrell	2.00
21	John Sullivan	1.50
22	Mickey Haefner	1.50
23	Ray Sanders	1.50
24	Johnny Hopp	1.50
25	Ted Wilks	1.50
26	John Barrett	1.50
27	Jim Russell	1.50
28	Nick Strincevich	1.50
29	Eric Tipton	1.50
30	Jim Konstanty	1.50
31	Gee Walker	1.50
32	Dom Dellessandro	1.50
33	Bob Chipman	1.50
34	Hank Wyse	1.50
35	Phil Weintraub	1.50
36	George Hausmann	1.50
37	Bill Voiselle	1.50
38	Whitey Wietelmann	1.50
39	Clyde Kluttz	1.50
40	Connie Ryan	1.50
41	Eddie Stanky	1.50
42	Augie Galan	1.50
43	Mickey Owen	1.50
44	Charlie Schanz	1.50
45	Bob Finley	1.50

1945 Play Ball

JOHNNY DICKSHOT

Between 1983-85, TCMA produced eight sets of collectors' cards resurrecting the Play Ball brand name which had been active in the field from 1939-41. The TCMA sets attempt to replicate the style and substance of the earlier Play Ball cards as if the company had continued production through World War II and the end of the 1940s. The "1945" set features black-and-white photos on front, with blue graphics. Backs are printed on gray stock in black ink. Size approximates the original Play Balls at 2-1/2" x 3-1/4".

		NM/M
Complete Set (45):		25.00
Common Player:		1.50
1	Eddie Mayo	1.50
2	Dizzy Trout	1.50
3	Roy Cullenbine	1.50
4	Joe Kuhel	1.50
5	George Binks	1.50
6	Roger Wolff	1.50
7	Gene Moore	1.50
8	Frank Mancuso	1.50
9	Bob Muncrief	1.50
10	Tuck Stainback	1.50
11	Bill Bevens	1.50
12	Snuffy Stirnweiss	1.50
13	Don Ross	1.50
14	Felix Mackiewicz	1.50
15	Jeff Heath	1.50
16	John Dickshot	1.50
17	Ed Lopat	2.00
18	Skeeter Newsom (Newsome)	1.50
19	Eddie Lake	1.50
20	John Lazor	1.50
21	Hal Peck	1.50
22	Al Brancato	1.50
23	Paul Derringer	1.50
24	Stan Hack	1.50
25	Len Merullo	1.50
26	Emil Verban	1.50
27	Ken O'Dea	1.50
28	Red Barrett	1.50
29	Eddie Basinski	1.50
30	Dixie Walker	1.50
31	Goody Rosen	1.50
32	Preacher Roe	1.50
33	Pete Coscarat	1.50
34	Frankie Frisch	2.50
35	Napoleon Reyes	1.50
36	Dan Gardella	1.50
37	Buddy Kerr	1.50
38	Dick Culler	1.50
39	Tommy Holmes	1.50
40	Al Libke	1.50
41	Howie Fox	1.50
42	Johnny Riddle	1.50
43	Andy Seminick	1.50
44	Andy Karl	1.50
45	Rene Monteguedo	1.50

1984 TCMA American League All-Stars

LOU BOUDREAU

The American League "players who compiled the greatest All-Star Game Records" are included in this collectors' edition - one at each position. In standard 2-1/2" x 3-1/2" size, the cards have black-and-white photos with blue frames. Backs have career All-Star Game stats and a copyright line. The unnumbered cards are listed here in alphabetical order.

		NM/M
Complete Set (9):		6.00
Common Player:		.25
(1)	Lou Boudreau	.25
(2)	Rocky Colavito	.50
(3)	Bill Dickey	.50
(4)	Nellie Fox	.50
(5)	Jimmie Foxx	1.00
(6)	Mel Harder	.25
(7)	Al Kaline	1.00
(8)	Brooks Robinson	1.00
(9)	Ted Williams	2.50

Roberto Clemente

This one-card set was produced in the same format as the four-card 1984 Hall of Fame Induction set and was probably printed on the same sheet in the same quantity (fewer than 500). Front has a black-and-white photo, back has lifetime stats.

	NM/M
Roberto Clemente	7.50

Great Players of the 1950's & 60's: Series #2

AL KALINE

These large-format (3-3/4" x 5-3/4") cards have color photos bordered in white with a green stripe at bottom bearing the player (or team) name. Backs have a black-and-white head shot of the player, his identification, personal data, career stats and a short biography, all framed in blue with decorative top corners.

		NM/M
Complete Set (33):		75.00
Common Player:		2.00
1	Brooks Robinson	6.00
2	Al Kaline	6.00
3	Tony Oliva	2.00
4	Frank Howard	2.00
5	Richie Ashburn	6.00
6	Harmon Killebrew	6.00
7	George Kell	6.00
8	Larry Doby	6.00
9	Ernie Banks	7.50
10	Maury Wills	4.00
11	Roger Maris	10.00
12	Al Rosen	2.00
13	Willie McCovey	6.00
14	Luis Aparicio	6.00
15	Ron Santo	4.00
16	Harvey Kuenn	2.00
17	Lou Brock	6.00
18	1960 Pittsburgh Pirates (Murtaugh on back)	7.50
19	1966 N.Y. Yankees (Westrum on back)	7.50
20	1950 Philadelphia Phillies (Sawyer on back)	6.00
21	1955 Brooklyn Dodgers (Alston on back)	7.50
22	1957 Milwaukee Braves (Haney on back)	7.50
23	Bob Gibson	6.00
24	Don Drysdale	6.00
25	Whitey Ford	6.00
26	Mickey Mantle, Roger Maris, Mrs. Babe Ruth	7.50
27	Harmon Killebrew, Willie Mays, Mickey Mantle	10.00
28	Willie Mays, Don Drysdale	7.50
29	1961 Yankees, Manager and Coaches	7.50
30	1964 Mets, Manager and Coaches	6.00
31	Ken Boyer, Stan Musial, Red Schoendienst	3.50
32	1952 Giants Pitching Staff	2.00
33	Vada Pinson	2.00

Hall of Fame Induction

While the production of Induction cards in the larger format continued for several years, TCMA's issue of standard 2-1/2" x 3-1/2" format cards was exclusive to 1984. The black-and-white cards have lifetime stats on back. It is reported that fewer than 500 sets were made.

		NM/M
Complete Set (4):		20.00
Common Player:		4.00
(1)	Luis Aparicio	6.00
(2)	Don Drysdale	8.00
(3)	Rick Ferrell	4.00
(4)	Harmon Killebrew	8.00

Hall of Fame Induction 8x10s

For four years TCMA produced 8" x 10" cards for the current inductees to the Baseball Hall of Fame. There are no TCMA markings on the cards, which were distributed by Baseball Nostalgia of Cooperstown, N.Y. The cards are blank-backed and unnumbered. They were printed in black-and-white in

1984, 1986-1987; the 1985 cards are blue-and-white. Only 500 of each card were issued.

		NM/M
Complete Set (18):		250.00
Common Player:		15.00
(1)	Luis Aparicio	15.00
(2)	Don Drysdale	15.00
(3)	Rick Ferrell	15.00
(4)	Harmon Killebrew	15.00
(5)	Pee Wee Reese	20.00
(6)	Composite (Luis Aparicio, Don Drysdale, Rick Ferrell, Harmon Killebrew, Pee Wee Reese)	20.00
(7)	Lou Brock	15.00
(8)	Enos Slaughter	15.00
(9)	Hoyt Wilhelm	15.00
(10)	Composite (Lou Brock, Enos Slaughter, Arky Vaughn (Vaughan), Hoyt Wilhelm)	20.00
(11)	Bobby Doerr	15.00
(12)	Willie McCovey	15.00
(13)	Composite (Bobby Doerr, Ernie Lombardi, Willie McCovey)	20.00
(14)	50th Anniversary Composite (Ty Cobb, Walter Johnson, Christy Mathewson, Babe Ruth, Honus Wagner (edition of 300))	75.00
(15)	Ray Dandridge	15.00
(16)	Jim "Catfish" Hunter	15.00
(17)	Billy Williams	15.00
(18)	Composite (Ray Dandridge, Jim "Catfish" Hunter, Billy Williams)	15.00

National League All-Stars

DICK GROAT

The National League "players who compiled the greatest All-Star Game Records" are included in this collectors' edition - one at each position. In standard 2-1/2" x 3-1/2" size, the cards have black-and-white photos with red frames. Backs have career All-Star Game stats and a copyright line. The unnumbered cards are listed here in alphabetical order.

		NM/M
Complete Set (9):		6.00
Common Player:		.25
(1)	Ernie Banks	1.00
(2)	Ken Boyer	.25
(3)	Roberto Clemente	2.50
(4)	Dick Groat	.25
(5)	Billy Herman	.25
(6)	Ernie Lombardi	.25
(7)	Juan Marichal	.25
(8)	Willie Mays	2.00
(9)	Stan Musial	1.00

Bruce Stark Postcards

JOE DI MAGGIO

Color artwork by Bruce Stark is featured on these 3-3/4" x 5-3/4" postcards.

		NM/M
Complete Set (5):		9.00
Common Player:		1.25
BS1	Joe DiMaggio	4.50
BS2	Ted Williams	3.00
BS3	Ted Kluzewski (Kluszewski)	1.75
BS4	Mickey Vernon	1.25
BS5	Stan Musial	2.50

1946 Play Ball

HANK GREENBERG

Between 1983-85, TCMA produced eight sets of collectors' cards resurrecting the Play Ball brand name which had been active in the field from 1939-41. The TCMA sets attempt to replicate the style and substance of the earlier Play Ball cards as if the company had continued production through World War II and the end of the 1940s. The "1946" set features black-and-white photos on front, with green graphics. Backs are printed on white stock in black ink. Size approximates the originals at 2-1/2" x 3-1/4".

		NM/M
Complete Set (45):		20.00
Common Player:		1.00
1	Dom DiMaggio	1.25
2	Boo Ferriss	1.00
3	Johnny Pesky	1.00
4	Hank Greenberg	2.00
5	George Kell	1.00
6	Virgil Trucks	1.00
7	Phil Rizzuto	1.75
8	Charlie Keller	1.25
9	Tommy Henrich	1.25
10	Cecil Travis	1.00
11	Al Evans	1.00
12	Buddy Lewis	1.00
13	Edgar Smith	1.00
14	Dario Lodigiani	1.00
15	Earl Caldwell	1.00
16	Jim Hegan	1.00
17	Bob Feller	1.75
18	John Berardino	1.25
19	Jack Kramer	1.00
20	John Lucadello	1.00
21	Hank Majeski	1.00
22	Elmer Valo	1.00
23	Buddy Rosar	1.00
24	Red Schoendienst	1.25
25	Dick Sisler	1.00
26	John Beazley	1.00
27	Vic Lombardi	1.00
28	Dick Whitman	1.00
29	Carl Furillo	1.75
30	Bill Jurges	1.00
31	Marv Rickert	1.00
32	Clyde McCullough	1.00
33	Johnny Hopp	1.00
34	Mort Cooper	1.00
35	Johnny Sain	1.25
36	Del Ennis	1.00
37	Roy Hughes	1.00
38	Bert Haas	1.00
39	Grady Hatton	1.00
40	Ed Bahr	1.00
41	Billy Cox	1.00
42	Lee Handley	1.00
43	Bill Rigney	1.00
44	Babe Young	1.00
45	Buddy Blattner	1.00

1985 TCMA Cy Young Award Winners

This polybagged set of 2-1/2" x 3-1/2" cards is formatted on two perforated strips. Fronts have color photos with orange borders while backs detail the player's CY season(s). The header card presents the history of the award. The unnumbered cards are listed here alphabetically.

		NM/M
Complete Set (10):		6.00
Common Player:		.25
(1)	Don Drysdale	.75
(2)	Whitey Ford	1.50
(3)	Bob Gibson	.50
(4)	Catfish Hunter	.40
(5)	Sandy Koufax	4.00
(6)	Vern Law	.25
(7)	Sparky Lyle	.25
(8)	Denny McLain	.35
(9)	Jim Palmer	.50
(10a)	Warren Spahn (Boston Braves)	.50
(10b)	Warren Spahn (Milwaukee Braves)	.50

Home Run Champs

This polybagged set of 2-1/2" x 3-1/2" cards is formatted on two perforated strips. Fronts have color photos with reddish-brown borders while backs detail the player's slugging prowess. The header card presents the history of the award. The unnumbered cards are listed here alphabetically.

		NM/M
Complete Set (10):		6.00
Common Player:		.30
(1)	Hank Aaron	1.50
(2)	Orlando Cepeda	.60
(3)	Joe DiMaggio	2.00
(4)	Larry Doby	.60
(5)	Ralph Kiner	.60
(6)	Eddie Mathews	.60
(7)	Willie McCovey	.60
(8)	Al Rosen	.30
(9)	Duke Snider	.60
(10)	Ted Williams	1.50

Most Valuable Players - A.L.

This polybagged set of 2-1/2" x 3-1/2" cards is formatted on two perforated strips. Fronts have color photos with green borders while backs detail the player's MVP season(s). The header card presents the history of the award. The unnumbered cards are listed here alphabetically.

		NM/M
Complete Set (10):		9.00
Common Player:		.40
(1)	Richie Allen	.40
(2)	Yogi Berra	.75
(3)	Elston Howard	.40
(4)	Jackie Jensen	.40
(5)	Harmon Killebrew	.75
(6)	Mickey Mantle	4.00
(7)	Roger Maris	1.50
(8)	Boog Powell	.40
(9)	Brooks Robinson	.75
(10)	Carl Yastrzemski	1.25

Most Valuable Players - N.L.

This polybagged set of 2-1/2" x 3-1/2" cards is formatted on two perforated strips. Fronts have color photos with blue borders while backs detail the player's MVP season(s). The header card presents the history of the award. The unnumbered cards are listed here alphabetically.

		NM/M
Complete Set (10):		9.00
Common Player:		.40
(1)	Ernie Banks	1.00
(2)	Johnny Bench	1.00
(3)	Roy Campanella	.90
(4)	Roberto Clemente	3.00
(5)	Dick Groat	.40
(6)	Willie Mays	2.50
(7)	Stan Musial	1.50
(8)	Frank Robinson	1.00
(9)	Willie Stargell	.75
(10)	Maury Wills	.40

N.Y. Yankees Postcards

In 1985-86, TCMA produced color player postcard sets for the two New York teams. The 1985 Yankees set is 3-1/2" x 5-1/2" with borderless color poses on front. Backs have a light blue Yankees logo at left. Player identification and data is at top-left with 1984 stats at bottom. A TCMA copyright lines is vertically at center. Cards are numbered in the stamp box NYY85-1 through NYY85-40.

		NM/M
Complete Set (40):		12.50
Common Player:		.50
1	Yogi Berra	1.75
2	Mark Connor	.50
3	Stump Merrill	.50
4	Gene Michael	.50
5	Lou Piniella	.75
6	Jeff Torborg	.50
7	Mike Armstrong	.50
8	Rich Bordi	.50
9	Clay Christensen	.50
10	Joe Cowley	.50
11	Jim Deshaies	.50
12	Ron Guidry	.75
13	John Montefusco	.50
14	Dale Murray	.50
15	Phil Niekro	1.00
16	Alfonso Pulido	.50
17	Dennis Rasmussen	.50
18	Dave Righetti	.50
19	Bob Shirley	.50
20	Ed Whitson	.50
21	Scott Bradley	.50
22	Ron Hassey	.50
23	Butch Wynegar	.50
24	Dale Berra	.50
25	Billy Sample	.50
26	Rex Hudler	.50
27	Don Mattingly	3.00
28	Bobby Meacham	.50
29	Mike Pagliarulo	.50
30	Willie Randolph	.75
31	Andre Robertson	.50
32	Henry Cotto	.50
33	Don Baylor	.75

N.Y. Mets Postcards

A certain sameness of poses, generally belt-to-cap, marks the cards in this color player postcard issue produced by TCMA for team issue. The 3-1/2" x 5-1/2" cards have borderless color photos with a glossy finish and no extraneous graphics. Backs have a large, light blue team logo at left, with player ID at top and a line of 1984 stats at bottom. A TCMA copyright line is vertically at center. The postcard indicia at right includes a card number at the bottom of the stamp box; the number is preceded by an "NYM85-" prefix.

		NM/M
Complete Set (40):		12.50
Common Player:		.50
1	Davey Johnson	.75
2	Vern Hoscheit	.50
3	Bill Robinson	.50
4	Mel Stottlemyre	.75
5	Bobby Valentine	.50
6	Bruce Berenyi	.50
7	Jeff Bettendorf	.50
8	Ron Darling	.50
9	Sid Fernandez	.50
10	Brent Gaff	.50
11	Wes Gardner	.50
12	Dwight Gooden	1.50
13	Tom Gorman	.50
14	Ed Lynch	.50
15	Jesse Orosco	.50
16	Calvin Schiraldi	.50
17	Doug Sisk	.50
18	Gary Carter	2.00
19	John Gibbons	.50
20	Ronn Reynolds	.50
21	Wally Backman	.50
22	Kelvin Chapman	.50
23	Ron Gardenhire	.50
24	Keith Hernandez	1.00
25	Howard Johnson	.75
26	Ray Knight	.75
27	Kevin Mitchell	.50
28	Terry Blocker	.50
29	Rafael Santana	.50
30	Billy Beane	.50
31	John Christensen	.50
32	Len Dykstra	1.00
33	George Foster	1.00
34	Danny Heep	.50
35	Darryl Strawberry	1.00
36	Mookie Wilson	.75
37	Jeff Bittiger	.50
38	Clint Hurdle	.50
39	Laschelle Tarver	.50
40	Roger McDowell	.50

Photo Classics Postcards

Teammate pairings and other groupings are featured in this collector's issue set of black-and-white postcards. In 3-1/2" x 5-1/2" format, the postcard-style backs identify the players on front.

		NM/M
Complete Set (40):		45.00
Common Card:		1.00
1	Warren Spahn, Johnny Sain	1.50
2	Jackie Robinson	3.00
3	President Eisenhower w/Yankees	1.50
4	Babe Ruth	4.00
5	Joe McCarthy, Lou Gehrig, Joe DiMaggio	2.00
6	Bob Feller	1.50
7	Johnny Lindell, Johnny Murphy	1.00
8	Babe Ruth, Claire Ruth	1.50
9	Babe Ruth, Joe Cook	1.50
10	Bobo Newsom	1.00
11	Johnny Antonelli, Robin Roberts	1.00
12	Joe Adcock, Eddie Mathews	1.50
13	Al Lopez, Mike Garcia, Bob Lemon, Early Wynn	2.00
14	Gil McDougald, Roy Campanella	1.50
15	Ralph Branca, Bobby Thomson	2.00
16	Lou Gehrig	2.50
17	Johnny Mize, Bill Rigney, Mel Ott	1.50
18	Spider Jorgensen, Pee Wee Reese, Eddie Stanky, Jackie Robinson	2.00
19	Tommy Holmes, Earl Torgeson, Jeff Heath, Connie Ryan, Billy Southworth	1.00
20	Ted Williams, Bobby Doerr, Dom DiMaggio, Vern Stephens	1.50
21	Chuck Schilling, Carl Yastrzemski	1.50
22	Roger Maris, Mickey Mantle	3.00
23	Rogers Hornsby, Gil McDougald	1.00
24	Jim Gentile, Gus Triandos	1.00
25	Bobby Avila, Willie Mays	1.50
26	Joe Garagiola, Ralph Kiner	1.00
27	Jim Gentile, Willie Mays	1.50
28	Red Schoendienst, Marty Marion	1.00
29	Charlie Keller	1.00
30	House of David Team	1.00
31	Harvey Kuenn, Al Kaline	1.50
32	Hank Sauer	1.00
33	Enos Slaughter	1.00
34	Stan Musial	2.00
35	Willie Mays	2.00
36	William Bendix, Babe Ruth	1.50
37	Whitey Lockman, Davey Williams, Hank Thompson, Alvin Dark, Don Mueller, Willie Mays, Monte Irvin, Wes Westrum	1.00
38	Pete Runnels, Vic Wertz	1.00
39	Stan Musial	2.00
40	Dom DiMaggio	1.00

Rookies of the Year

This polybagged set of 2-1/2" x 3-1/2" cards is formatted on two perforated strips. Fronts have color photos while backs detail the play-

34	Ken Griffey	.50
35	Rickey Henderson	2.00
36	Vic Mata	.50
37	Omar Moreno	.50
38	Dan Pasqua	.50
39	Dave Winfield	2.00
40	Brian Fisher	.50

ROOKIE OF THE YEAR

THURMAN MUNSON

er's ROY season. The header card presents the history of the award. The unnumbered cards are listed here alphabetically.

		NM/M
Complete Set (10):		6.00
Common Player:		.25
(1)	Tommy Agee	.25
(2)	Luis Aparicio	.50
(3)	Frank Howard	.25
(4)	Harvey Kuenn	.25
(5)	Thurman Munson	3.00
(6)	Don Newcombe	.25
(7)	Tony Oliva	.25
(8)	Jackie Robinson	3.00
(9)	Herb Score	.25
(10)	Billy Williams	.50

1947 Play Ball

JACKIE ROBINSON

Between 1983-85, TCMA produced eight sets of collectors' cards resurrecting the Play Ball brand name which had been active in the field from 1939-41. The TCMA sets attempt to replicate the style and substance of the earlier Play Ball cards as if the company had continued production through World War II and the end of the 1940s. The "1947" set features black-and-white photos on front, with green graphics. Backs are printed on white stock in black ink. Size approximates the originals at 2-1/2" x 3-1/4".

		NM/M
Complete Set (45):		30.00
Common Player:		1.00
1	Hal Wagner	1.00
2	Jake Jones	1.00
3	Bobby Doerr	1.00
4	Fred Hutchinson	1.00
5	Bob Swift	1.00
6	Pat Mullin	1.00
7	Joe Page	1.00
8	Allie Reynolds	1.00
9	Billy Johnson	1.00
10	Early Wynn	1.00
11	Eddie Yost	1.00
12	Floyd Baker	1.00
13	Dave Philley	1.00
14	George Dickey	1.00
15	Dale Mitchell	1.00
16	Bob Lemon	1.00
17	Jerry Witte	1.00
18	Paul Lehner	1.00
19	Sam Zoldak	1.00
20	Sam Chapman	1.00
21	Eddie Joost	1.00
22	Ferris Fain	1.00
23	Erv Dusak	1.00
24	Joe Garagiola	1.00
25	Vernal "Nippy" Jones	1.00
26	Bobby Bragan	1.00
27	Jackie Robinson	6.00
28	Spider Jorgensen	1.00
29	Bob Scheffing	1.00
30	Johnny Schmitz	1.00
31	Doyle Lade	1.00
32	Earl Torgeson	1.00
33	Warren Spahn	1.00
34	Walt Lanfranconi	1.00
35	Johnny Wyrostek	1.00
36	Oscar Judd	1.00
37	Ewell Blackwell	1.00
38	Ed Lukon	1.00
39	Benny Zientara	1.00
40	Gene Woodling	1.00

41	Ernie Bonham	1.00
42	Hank Greenberg	3.00
43	Bobby Thomson	1.00
44	Jack "Lucky" Lohrke	1.00
45	Dave Koslo	1.00

1948 Play Ball

GIL HODGES

Between 1983-85, TCMA produced eight sets of collectors' cards resurrecting the Play Ball brand name which had been active in the field from 1939-41. The TCMA sets attempt to replicate the style and substance of the earlier Play Ball cards as if the company had continued production through World War II and the end of the 1940s. The "1948" set features black-and-white photos on front, with red graphics. Backs are printed on white stock in black ink. Size approximates the originals at 2-1/2" x 3-1/4".

		NM/M
Complete Set (45):		50.00
Common Player:		1.00
1	Murry Dickson	1.00
2	Enos Slaughter	1.50
3	Don Lang	1.00
4	Joe Hatten	1.00
5	Gil Hodges	2.00
6	Gene Hermanski	1.00
7	Eddie Waitkus	1.00
8	Jess Dobernic	1.00
9	Andy Pafko	1.00
10	Vern Bickford	1.00
11	Mike McCormick	1.00
12	Harry Walker	1.00
13	Putsy Caballero	1.00
14	Hubert "Dutch" Leonard	1.00
15	Frankie Baumholtz	1.00
16	Ted Kluszewski	1.50
17	Virgil Stallcup	1.00
18	Bob Chesnes	1.00
19	Ted Beard	1.00
20	Wes Westrum	1.00
21	Clint Hartung	1.00
22	Whitey Lockman	1.00
23	Billy Goodman	1.00
24	Jack Kramer	1.00
25	Mel Parnell	1.00
26	George Vico	1.00
27	Walter "Hoot" Evers	1.00
28	Vic Wertz	1.00
29	Yogi Berra	2.00
30	Joe DiMaggio	8.00
31	Tommy Byrne	1.00
32	Al Kozar	1.00
33	Jake Early	1.00
34	Gil Coan	1.00
35	Pat Seerey	1.00
36	Ralph Hodgin	1.00
37	Allie Clark	1.00
38	Gene Bearden	1.00
39	Steve Gromek	1.00
40	Al Zarilla	1.00
41	Fred Sanford	1.00
42	Les Moss	1.00
43	Don White	1.00
44	Carl Scheib	1.00
45	Lou Brissie	1.00

1949 Play Ball

LARRY DOBY

Between 1983-85, TCMA produced eight sets of collectors' cards resurrecting the Play Ball brand name which had been active in the field from 1939-41. The TCMA sets attempt to replicate the style and substance of the earlier Play Ball cards as if the company had contin-

ued production through World War II and the end of the 1940s. The "1949" set features black-and-white photos on front, with red graphics. Backs are printed on white stock in black ink. Size approximates the originals at 2-1/2" x 3-1/4".

		NM/M
Complete Set (45):		40.00
Common Player:		1.00
1	Al Brazle	1.00
2	Harry Brecheen	1.00
3	Howie Pollett	1.00
4	Cal Abrams	1.00
5	Ralph Branca	1.00
6	Duke Snider	2.50
7	Charlie Grimm	1.00
8	Clarence Maddern	1.00
9	Hal Jeffcoat	1.00
10	Johnny Antonelli	1.00
11	Alvin Dark	1.00
12	Nelson Potter	1.00
13	Granny Hamner	1.00
14	Willie Jones	1.00
15	Robin Roberts	1.50
16	Lloyd Merriman	1.00
17	Bobby Adams	1.00
18	Herman Wehmeier	1.00
19	Ralph Kiner	1.00
20	Dino Restelli	1.00
21	Larry Jansen	1.00
22	Sheldon Jones	1.00
23	Red Webb	1.00
24	Vern Stephens	1.00
25	Tex Hughson	1.00
26	Ellis Kinder	1.00
27	Neil Berry	1.00
28	Johnny Groth	1.00
29	Art Houtteman	1.00
30	Hank Bauer	1.00
31	Vic Raschi	1.00
32	Bobby Brown	1.00
33	Joe Haynes	1.00
34	Eddie Robinson	1.00
35	Sam Dente	1.00
36	Herb Adams	1.00
37	Don Wheeler	1.00
38	Randy Gumpert	1.00
39	Ray Boone	1.00
40	Larry Doby	1.50
41	Jack Graham	1.00
42	Bob Dillinger	1.00
43	Dick Kokos	1.00
44	Wally Moses	1.00
45	Mike Guerra	1.00

1986 TCMA All Time Teams

Similar to TCMA sets of 1980-83, these sets feature 11 all-time great players and a manager from each team. In standard 2-1/2" x 3-1/2" format, most of the cards utilize black-and-white player photos, though some more recent stars are pictured in color. Several decorative borders, varying by team, surround the front photos. On most team sets there is an "All Time" designation at top, with the player name and (usually) position at bottom. Backs are fairly uniform, printed in blue, and offering a few biographical details and career highlights. Besides hobby sales, these old-timers' sets were also sold in several major retails chains, originally priced at about $4.

All Time Angels

		NM/M
Complete Set (12):		4.50
Common Player:		.50
1-ANG	Rod Carew	2.00
2-ANG	Sandy Alomar	.50
3-ANG	Jim Fregosi	.50
4-ANG	Dave Chalk	.50
5-ANG	Leon Wagner	.50
6-ANG	Albie Pearson	.50
7-ANG	Rick Reichardt	.50
8-ANG	Bob Rodgers	.50
9-ANG	Dean Chance	.50
10-ANG	Clyde Wright	.50
11-ANG	Bob Lee	.50
12-ANG	Bill Rigney	.50

All Time Astros

		NM/M
Complete Set (12):		6.00
Common Player:		.50
1-AST	Bob Watson	.50
2-AST	Joe Morgan	1.75
3-AST	Roger Metzger	.50
4-AST	Doug Rader	.50
5-AST	Jimmy Wynn	.70
6-AST	Cesar Cedeno	.70
7-AST	Rusty Staub	.70
8-AST	Johnny Edwards	.50
9-AST	J.R. Richard	.80
10-AST	Dave Roberts	.50
11-AST	Fred Gladding	.50
12-AST	Bill Virdon	.50

All Time Blue Jays

	NM/M
Complete Set (12):	5.00

All Time Boston/Milwaukee Braves

DEL CRANDALL   C

		NM/M
Complete Set (12):		7.50
Common Player:		.50
1B	Joe Adcock	.70
2B	Felix Millan	.50
3B	Rabbit Maranville	.50
4B	Eddie Mathews	2.00
5B	Hank Aaron	6.00
6B	Wally Berger	.50
7B	Tommy Holmes	.50
8B	Del Crandall	.50
9B	Warren Spahn	2.00
10B	Charles "Kid" Nichols	.50
11B	Cecil Upshaw	.50
12B	Fred Haney	.50

All Time Brewers

HARVEY KUENN   M

		NM/M
Complete Set (12):		6.00
Common Player:		.50
1-BRE	George Scott	.75
2-BRE	Pedro Garcia	.50
3-BRE	Tim Johnson	.50
4-BRE	Don Money	.50
5-BRE	Sixto Lezcano	.50
6-BRE	John Briggs	.50
7-BRE	Dave May	.50
8-BRE	Darrell Porter	.50
9-BRE	Jim Colborn	.50
10-BRE	Mike Caldwell	.50
11-BRE	Rollie Fingers	1.50
12-BRE	Harvey Kuenn	.50

All Time Expos

JIM FANNING   M

		NM/M
Complete Set (12):		5.00
Common Player:		.50
1-EXP	Ron Fairly	.50
2-EXP	Dave Cash	.50
3-EXP	Tim Foley	.50
4-EXP	Bob Bailey	.50
5-EXP	Ken Singleton	.75
6-EXP	Ellis Valentine	.50
7-EXP	Rusty Staub	.75
8-EXP	John Bateman	.50
9-EXP	Steve Rogers	.50
10-EXP	Woodie Fryman	.50
11-EXP	Mike Marshall	.50
12-EXP	Jim Fanning	.50

All Time Indians

JOE JACKSON   OF

		NM/M
Complete Set (12):		7.00
Common Player:		.50
1-IND	Hal Trosky	.50
2-IND	Nap Lajoie	.50
3-IND	Lou Boudreau	.50
4-IND	Al Rosen	.50
5-IND	Joe Jackson	6.00
6-IND	Tris Speaker	.75
7-IND	Larry Doby	1.00
8-IND	Jim Hegan	.50
9-IND	Cy Young	.50
10-IND	Sam McDowell	.60
11-IND	Ray Narleski	.50
12-IND	Al Lopez	.50

All Time Mariners

		NM/M
Complete Set (12):		5.00
Common Player:		.50
1-MAR	Pat Putnam	.50
2-MAR	Larry Milbourne	.50
3-MAR	Todd Cruz	.50
4-MAR	Bill Stein	.50
5-MAR	Leon Roberts	.50
6-MAR	Leroy Stanton	.50
7-MAR	Dan Meyer	.50
8-MAR	Bob Stinson	.50
9-MAR	Glenn Abbott	.50
10-MAR	John Montague	.50
11-MAR	Bryan Clark	.50
12-MAR	Rene Lachemann	.50

All Time Mets

		NM/M
Complete Set (12):		7.50
Common Player:		.50
1M	Ed Kranepool	.50
2M	Ron Hunt	.50
3M	Bud Harrelson	.75
4M	Wayne Garrett	.50
5M	Cleon Jones	.75
6M	Tommie Agee	.75
7M	Rusty Staub	1.00
8M	Jerry Grote	.50
9M	Gary Gentry	.50
10M	Jerry Koosman	.75
11M	Tug McGraw	.75
12M	Gil Hodges	2.00

All Time Oakland A's

JIM "CATFISH" HUNTER   P

		NM/M
Complete Set (12):		7.00
Common Player:		.50
1-ATH	Gene Tenace	.50
2-ATH	Dick Green	.50
3-ATH	Bert Campaneris	.75
4-ATH	Sal Bando	.50
5-ATH	Joe Rudi	.75
6-ATH	Rick Monday	.50
7-ATH	Bill North	.50
8-ATH	Dave Duncan	.50
9-ATH	Jim "Catfish" Hunter	1.50
10-ATH	Ken Holtzman	.50
11-ATH	Rollie Fingers	1.50
12-ATH	Alvin Dark	.50

All Time Orioles

FRANK ROBINSON   OF

		NM/M
Complete Set (12):		14.00
Common Player:		.50
1BA	Hoyt Wilhelm	.50
2BA	Hank Bauer	.50
3BA	Jim Palmer	2.00
4BA	Dave McNally	.50
5BA	Paul Blair	.50
6BA	Gus Triandos	.50
7BA	Frank Robinson	3.00
8BA	Ken Singleton	.50
9BA	Luis Aparicio	2.50
10BA	Brooks Robinson	4.00
11BA	John "Boog" Powell	.50
12BA	Dave Johnson	.50

All Time Padres

		NM/M
Complete Set (12):		6.00
Common Player:		.50
1-PAD	Nate Colbert	.50
2-PAD	Tito Fuentes	.50
3-PAD	Enzo Hernandez	.50
4-PAD	Dave Roberts	.50
5-PAD	Gene Richards	.50
6-PAD	Ollie Brown	.50
7-PAD	Clarence Gaston	.50
8-PAD	Fred Kendall	.50
9-PAD	Gaylord Perry	1.50
10-PAD	Randy Jones	.50
11-PAD	Rollie Fingers	1.50
12-PAD	Preston Gomez	.50

All Time Phillies

RICHIE ALLEN   3B

		NM/M
Complete Set (12):		7.00
Common Player:		.35
1PP	Chuck Klein	.50
2PP	Richie Ashburn	3.00
3PP	Del Ennis	.35
4PP	Spud Davis	.35
5PP	Grover Alexander	.50
6PP	Chris Short	.35
7PP	Jim Konstanty	.35
8PP	Danny Ozark	.35
9PP	Larry Bowa	.50
10PP	Richie Allen	1.00
11PP	Don Hurst	.35
12PP	Tony Taylor	.35

All Time Pirates

		NM/M
Complete Set (12):		14.00
Common Player:		.50
1-PIR	Willie Stargell	2.50
2-PIR	Bill Mazeroski	2.50
3-PIR	Honus Wagner	2.50
4-PIR	Pie Traynor	.50
5-PIR	Ralph Kiner	.75
6-PIR	Paul Waner	.50
7-PIR	Roberto Clemente	5.00
8-PIR	Manny Sanguillen	.50
9-PIR	Vic Willis	.50
10-PIR	Wilbur Cooper	.50
11-PIR	Roy Face	.50
12-PIR	Danny Murtaugh	.50

All Time Rangers

		NM/M
Complete Set (12):		6.00
Common Player:		.50
1-RAN	Gaylord Perry	2.00
2-RAN	Jon Matlack	.50
3-RAN	Jim Kern	.50
4-RAN	Billy Hunter	.50
5-RAN	Mike Hargrove	.50
6-RAN	Bump Wills	.50
7-RAN	Toby Harrah	.75
8-RAN	Lenny Randle	.50
9-RAN	Al Oliver	.75
10-RAN	Mickey Rivers	.50
11-RAN	Jeff Burroughs	.50
12-RAN	Dick Billings	.50

All Time Reds

		NM/M
Complete Set (12):		9.00
Common Player:		.50
1CR	Clay Carroll	.50
2CR	Bill McKechnie	.50
3CR	Paul Derringer	.50
4CR	Eppa Rixey	.50
5CR	Frank Robinson	2.50
6CR	Vada Pinson	1.00
7CR	Leo Cardenas	.50
8CR	Heinie Groh	.50
9CR	Ted Kluszewski	2.00
10CR	Joe Morgan	1.50
11CR	Edd Roush	.50
12CR	Johnny Bench	3.00

All Time Red Sox

JIMMIE FOXX   1B

		NM/M
Complete Set (12):		10.00
Common Player:		.50
1BRS	Sammy White	.50
2BRS	Lefty Grove	.50
3BRS	Cy Young	1.00
4BRS	Jimmie Foxx	1.00
5BRS	Bobby Doerr	.50
6BRS	Joe Cronin	.50
7BRS	Frank Malzone	.50
8BRS	Ted Williams	6.00
9BRS	Carl Yastrzemski	4.00
10BRS	Tris Speaker	1.00
11BRS	Dick Radatz	.50
12BRS	Dick Williams	.50

All Time Royals

		NM/M
Complete Set (12):		5.00
Common Player:		.50
1-ROY	John Mayberry	.50
2-ROY	Cookie Rojas	.50
3-ROY	Fred Patek	.50
4-ROY	Paul Schall	.50
5-ROY	Lou Piniella	1.00
6-ROY	Amos Otis	.50
7-ROY	Tom Poquette	.50
8-ROY	Ed Kirkpatrick	.50
9-ROY	Steve Busby	.50
10-ROY	Paul Splittorff	.50
11-ROY	Mark Littell	.50
12-ROY	Jim Frey	.50

All Time Twins

		NM/M
Complete Set (12):		9.00
Common Player:		.50
1-TWI	Harmon Killebrew	2.50
2-TWI	Rod Carew	4.00
3-TWI	Zoilo Versalles	.50
4-TWI	Cesar Tovar	.50
5-TWI	Bob Allison	.50
6-TWI	Larry Hisle	.50
7-TWI	Tony Oliva	.50
8-TWI	Earl Battey	.50
9-TWI	Jim Perry	.50
10-TWI	Jim Kaat	.75
11-TWI	Allan Worthington	.50
12-TWI	Sam Mele	.50

N.Y. Mets Postcards

For a second, and final, year TCMA produced a set of color player postcards for the Mets. The 3-1/2" x

5-1/2" cards have borderless player poses on their glossy fronts; there are no other graphic elements. Backs have a large, light blue team 25th anniversary logo at left, with player ID above and a line of 1985 stats below. There is a TCMA copyright line vertically at center. Among the postcard indicia at right, a card number prefixed with "NYM86-" appears within the stamp box. Cards were sold only as complete sets, for $7.95.

		NM/M
Complete Set (40):		7.50
Common Player:		.50
1	Rick Aguilera	.50
2	Bruce Berenyi	.50
3	Ron Darling	.50
4	Sid Fernandez	.50
5	Dwight Gooden	.75
6	Tom Gorman	.50
7	Ed Lynch	.50
8	Roger McDowell	.50
9	Randy Myers	.60
10	Bob Ojeda	.50
11	Jesse Orosco	.50
12	Doug Sisk	.50
13	Gary Carter	2.00
14	John Gibbons	.50
15	Barry Lyons	.50
16	Wally Backman	.50
17	Ron Gardenhire	.50
18	Keith Hernandez	.75
19	Howard Johnson	.75
20	Ray Knight	.75
21	Kevin Mitchell	.75
22	Rafael Santana	.50
23	Tim Teufel	.50
24	Lenny Dykstra	.75
25	George Foster	.75
26	Danny Heep	.50
27	Mel Stottlemyre	.50
28	Darryl Strawberry	.75
29	Mookie Wilson	.50
30	Randy Nieman	.50
31	Randy Nieman	.50
32	Ed Hearn	.50
33	Stan Jefferson	.50
34	Bill Robinson	.50
35	Shawn Abner	.50
36	Terry Blocker	.50
37	Davey Johnson	.50
38	Bud Harrelson	.50
39	Vern Hoscheit	.50
40	Greg Pavlick	.50
43	Tim Corcoran	.50

N.Y. Yankees Postcards

For a second consecutive year, TCMA produced a set of color player postcards for team issue. Similar in format to the 1985 cards, the 1986 version is in 3-1/2" x 5-1/2" format. Fronts have borderless color poses with no other graphics and a high-gloss finish. Backs have a Yankee logo in light blue at left and (usually) a line of 1985 stats at lower-left. Player ID is at upper left. A TCMA copyright line is vertically at center. Among the postcard indicia at right is a card number within the stamp box; cards are skip-numbered with an "NYY86-" prefix; there are two #18. The cards were sold only as complete sets, for $7.95.

		NM/M
Complete Set (40):		9.00
Common Player:		.50
1	Tommy John	1.00
2	Brad Arnsburg (Arnsberg)	.50
3	Al Holland (Al)	.50
4	Mike Armstrong	.50
5	Marty Bystrom	.50
6	Doug Drabek	.75
7	Brian Fisher	.50
8	Stump Merrill	.50
9	Ron Guidry	.75
10	Joe Niekro	.75
12	Dennis Rasmussen	.50
13	Dave Righetti	.50

14	Rod Scurry	.50
15	Bob Shirley	.50
16	Bob Tewksbury	.50
17	Ed Whitson	.50
18a	Britt Burns	.50
18b	Gene Michael	.50
19	Butch Wynegar	.50
20	Ron Hassey	.50
21	Dale Berra	.50
22	Jeff Torborg	.50
23	Mike Fischlin	.50
24	Don Mattingly	3.00
25	Bobby Meacham	.50
26	Mike Pagliarulo	.50
27	Willie Randolph	.75
28	Andre Robertson	.50
29	Roy White	.75
31	Henry Cotto	.50
32	Ken Griffey	.50
33	Rickey Henderson	2.00
34	Vic Mata	.50
35	Dan Pasqua	.50
36	Dave Winfield	2.00
37	Gary Roenicke	.50
38	Lou Piniella	.75
39	Joe Altobelli	.50
40	Sammy Ellis	.50
45	Mike Easler	.50

Premium Autographs

This three-card set was made available with the purchase of other items from TCMA. The 2-1/2" x 3-1/2" cards have a glossy front finish and each card is personally autographed by the player depicted. Backs have a message about card collecting from the player and 1985 stats, along with TCMA advertising.

		NM/M
Complete Set (3):		175.00
Common Player:		45.00
(1)	Gary Carter	60.00
(2)	Tony Gwynn	90.00
(3)	Bret Saberhagen	30.00

Simon's Super Stars

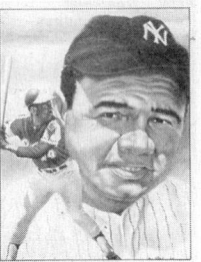

The paintings of sports artist Robert Stephen Simon are reproduced in an unusually sized (2-13/16" x 3-1/2") card issue marketed to collectors. Fronts have color pictures with no extraneous graphics, bordered in white. Backs, printed in blue and white, have biographical and career information.

		NM/M
Complete Set (50):		35.00
Common Player:		.50
1	Carl Erskine	.50
2	Babe Ruth, Henry Aaron	1.50
3	Ted Williams	1.50
4	Mickey Mantle	2.00
5	Gil Hodges	.75
6	Roberto Clemente	1.50
7	Mickey Mantle	2.00
8	Walter Johnson	.50
9	N.Y. Yankees Stars	1.50
10	Carl Yastrzemski, Ted Williams	1.50
11	Mickey Mantle	2.00
12	Harmon Killebrew	.50
13	Warren Spahn	.50
14	Ralph Kiner, Babe Ruth	1.00
15	Bob Gibson	.50
16	Pee Wee Reese	.50
17	Billy Martin	.50
18	Joe DiMaggio, Mickey Mantle	2.00
19	Phil Rizzuto	.50
20	Sandy Koufax	1.00
21	Jackie Robinson	1.00
22	Don Drysdale	.50
23	Mickey Mantle	2.00
24	Mickey Mantle	2.00
25	Joe DiMaggio	1.50
26	Robin Roberts	.50
27	Lou Brock	.50
28	Lou Gehrig	1.50
29	Willie Mays	1.50
30	Brooks Robinson	.50
31	Thurman Munson	1.00
32	Roger Maris	1.00
33	Jim Palmer	.50
34	Stan Musial	.75
35	Roy Campanella	.50

36	Joe Pepitone	.50
37	Ebbetts Field	.50
38	Honus Wagner	.50
39	Yogi Berra	.50
40	Eddie Mathews	.50
41	Carl Yastrzemski	.50
42	Babe Ruth	1.50
43	Babe Ruth	1.50
44	Pete Reiser	.50
45	Don Larsen	.50
46	Ernie Banks	.50
47	Casey Stengel	.50
48	Jackie Robinson	1.00
49	Duke Snider	.50
50	Checklist (Duke Snider)	.50

1987 TCMA All Time N.Y. Yankees

Mickey Mantle

Essentially a reprint of its 1980 team set, this TCMA collectors issue can be distinguished by the presence on back of a Major League Baseball logo. The earlier set has a TCMA date line on back. Fronts of the 2-1/2" x 3-1/2" cards have black-and-white player photos with an ornate blue frame and white border. Backs are in black-and-white and include the All Time team roster.

		NM/M
Complete Set (12):		33.00
Common Player:		.35
1	Lou Gehrig	7.00
2	Tony Lazzeri	.50
3	Red Rolfe	.40
4	Phil Rizzuto	1.25
5	Babe Ruth	7.50
6	Mickey Mantle	9.00
7	Joe DiMaggio	7.00
8	Bill Dickey	.70
9	Red Ruffing	.40
10	Whitey Ford	1.25
11	Johnny Murphy	.40
12	Casey Stengel	.60

Baseball's Greatest Teams

'69 Mets

TUG McGRAW P

Ten of the greatest line-ups in baseball history are featured in this collectors' series. Each of the nine-card team sets features a different front design while backs share a common format offering player biographical details. The earlier teams picture players in black-and-white photos, while the later sets have color photos. Original issue price was about $1 per set, retail.

		NM/M
Complete Set (90):		70.00
Common Team Set (9):		4.50
Common Player:		.25

1907 Chicago Cubs Team Set: 4.50

1	Harry Steinfeldt	.25
2	Three-Finger Brown	.25
3	Ed Reulbach	.25
4	Johnny Kling	.25
5	Orvie Overall	.25
6	Joe Tinker	.75
7	Wildfire Schulte	.25
8	Frank Chance	.75
9	Johnny Evers	.75

1927 N.Y. Yankees Team Set: 20.00

1	Miller Huggins	.25
2	Herb Pennock	.25

3	Tony Lazzeri	.25
4	Waite Hoyt	.25
5	Wilcy Moore	.25
6	Earle Combs	.25
7	Bob Meusel	.25
8	Lou Gehrig	6.00
9	Babe Ruth	9.00

1934 St. Louis Cardinals Team Set: 4.50

1	Dizzy Dean	1.50
2	Daffy Dean	.25
3	Pepper Martin	.25
4	Rip Collins	.25
5	Frank Frisch	.50
6	Leo Durocher	.25
7	Ducky Medwick	.25
8	Tex Carleton	.25
9	Spud Davis	.25

1946 Boston Red Sox Team Set: 7.50

1	Joe Cronin	.25
2	Rudy York	.25
3	Bobby Doerr	.25
4	Johnny Pesky	.25
5	Dom DiMaggio	.60
6	Ted Williams	4.50
7	Boo Ferriss	.25
8	Tex Hughson	.25
9	Mickey Harris	.25

1950 Philadelphia Phillies Team Set: 4.50

1	Eddie Sawyer	.25
2	Curt Simmons	.25
3	Jim Konstanty	.50
4	Eddie Waitkus	.25
5	Granny Hamner	.25
6	Del Ennis	.25
7	Richie Ashburn	.60
8	Dick Sisler	.25
9	Robin Roberts	.60

1955 Brooklyn Dodgers Team Set: 7.50

1	Duke Snider, Walt Alston	.75
2	Roy Campanella	1.50
3	Jackie Robinson	3.00
4	Carl Furillo	.60
5	Gil Hodges	.75
6	Pee Wee Reese, Jim Gilliam	.75
7	Don Newcombe	.25
8	Ed Roebuck, Clem Labine	.50
9	Carl Erskine	.25

1957 Milwaukee Braves Team Set: 7.50

1	Hank Aaron	4.50
2	Eddie Mathews	.60
3	Bob Hazle	.25
4	Johnny Logan	.25
5	Red Schoendienst	.50
6	Wes Covington	.25
7	Lew Burdette	.25
8	Warren Spahn	.60
9	Bob Buhl	.25

1960 Pittsburgh Pirates Team Set: 7.50

1	Dick Stuart	.25
2	Bill Mazeroski	.75
3	Dick Groat	.35
4	Roberto Clemente	6.00
5	Bob Skinner	.25
6	Smoky Burgess	.35
7	Roy Face	.25
8	Bob Friend	.25
9	Vernon Law	.25

1961 N.Y. Yankees Team Set: 20.00

1	Bill Skowron	.50
2	Mickey Mantle	10.00
3	Bobby Richardson	.50
4	Tony Kubek	.50
5	Elston Howard	.50
6	Yogi Berra	2.25
7	Whitey Ford	2.25
8	Roger Maris	4.50
9	Ralph Houk	.25

1969 N.Y. Mets Team Set: 4.50

1	Ed Kranepool	.35
2	Bud Harrelson	.35
3	Cleon Jones, Tommie Agee, Ron Swoboda	.25
4	Jerry Koosman	.25
5	Gary Gentry	.25
6	Tug McGraw	.35
7	Ron Taylor	.25
8	Jerry Grote	.25
9	Ken Boswell	.25

1996 Team Metal Ken Griffey Jr.

GRIFFEY

CUI, the parent firm of the company that produces Metallic Images sports and non-sports cards, created this set of metal cards for sale in large retail chains. The four cards come packaged in a lithographed steel box about the size and shape of a Band-aid tin. The 2-5/8" x 3-9/16" cards have a blue and teal background with a color game-action photo at center. Backs have rolled metal edges with a photo at left. A few sentences about the player are printed at right. Logos and copyright data are at bottom. Issue price of the four-card set was just under $10.

		NM/M
Complete Set (4):		7.50
Common Card:		2.00
1	Ken Griffey Jr. (Home run front.)	2.00
2	Ken Griffey Jr./Sliding	2.00
3	Ken Griffey Jr. (Batting follow-through.)	2.00
4	Ken Griffey Jr. (Batting follow-through.)	2.00

Cal Ripken, Jr.

RIPKEN
Cal Ripken Jr.

CUI, the parent firm of the company that produces Metallic Impressions sports and non-sports cards, created this set of metal cards for sale in large retail chains. The four cards come packaged in a lithographed steel box about the size and shape of a Band-aid tin. The 2-5/8" x 3-9/16" cards have a green and orange background with a color game-action photo at center. Backs have rolled metal edges with a photo at left. A few sentences about the player are printed at right. Logos and copyright data are at bottom. Issue price of the four-card set was just under $10.

		NM/M
Complete Set (4):		7.50
Common Card:		2.00
1	Cal Ripken Jr./Btg (Black jersey.)	2.00
2	Cal Ripken Jr. (Batting follow-through.)	2.00
3	Cal Ripken Jr./Fldng	2.00
4	Cal Ripken Jr./Btg (White jersey.)	2.00

1996 Team Out! Game

3RD BASE
BOGGS
NEW YORK YANKEES
3RD BASE

This baseball card game is sold as a boxed set containing 37 of the 91 different player cards, plus an assortment of 23 of the 10 cartoon "action" cards used to play the game. Cards are 2-1/4" x 3-1/2" with rounded corners and glossy surfaces. Backs have a close-up photo of a baseball with product and licensor logos and copyright information. Fronts of the player photo cards are

bordered in black; the cartoon action cards have red or blue borders. The unnumbered cards are checklisted here in alphabetical order.

		NM/M
Complete Set (101):		40.00
Common Player:		.25
(1)	Roberto Alomar	.35
(2)	Brady Anderson	.25
(3)	Kevin Appier	.25
(4)	Carlos Baerga	.25
(5)	Jeff Bagwell	1.50
(6)	Albert Belle	.25
(7)	Dante Bichette	.25
(8)	Craig Biggio	.25
(9)	Wade Boggs	2.00
(10)	Barry Bonds	3.00
(11)	Kevin Brown	.25
(12)	Jay Buhner	.25
(13)	Ellis Burks	.25
(14)	Ken Caminiti	.25
(15)	Joe Carter	.25
(16)	Vinny Castilla	.25
(17)	Jeff Cirillo	.25
(18)	Will Clark	.25
(19)	Jeff Conine	.25
(20)	Joey Cora	.25
(21)	Marty Cordova	.25
(22)	Eric Davis	.25
(23)	Ray Durham	.25
(24)	Jim Edmonds	.25
(25)	Cecil Fielder	.25
(26)	Travis Fryman	.25
(27)	Jason Giambi	.60
(28)	Bernard Gilkey	.25
(29)	Tom Glavine	.45
(30)	Juan Gonzalez	.75
(31)	Mark Grace	.25
(32)	Ken Griffey Jr.	2.25
(33)	Marquis Grissom	.25
(34)	Mark Grudzielanek	.25
(35)	Ozzie Guillen	.25
(36)	Tony Gwynn	2.00
(37)	Bobby Higginson	.25
(38)	Todd Hundley	.25
(39)	Derek Jeter	3.00
(40)	Lance Johnson	.25
(41)	Randy Johnson	1.50
(42)	Chipper Jones	2.00
(43)	Brian Jordan	.25
(44)	Wally Joyner	.25
(45)	Jason Kendall	.25
(46)	Chuck Knoblauch	.25
(47)	Ray Lankford	.25
(48)	Mike Lansing	.25
(49)	Barry Larkin	.25
(50)	Kenny Lofton	.25
(51)	Javier Lopez	.25
(52)	Mike MacFarlane	.25
(53)	Greg Maddux	2.00
(54)	Al Martin	.25
(55)	Brian McRae	.25
(56)	Mark McGwire	2.50
(57)	Raul Mondesi	.25
(58)	Denny Neagle	.25
(59)	Hideo Nomo	.75
(60)	John Olerud	.25
(61)	Rey Ordonez	.25
(62)	Troy Percival	.25
(63)	Mike Piazza	2.25
(64)	Andy Pettitte	.35
(65)	Manny Ramirez	1.50
(66)	Cal Ripken Jr.	3.00
(67)	Alex Rodriguez	2.50
(68)	Ivan Rodriguez	1.00
(69)	Ryne Sandberg	2.00
(70)	Tim Salmon	.25
(71)	Benito Santiago	.25
(72)	Kevin Seitzer	.25
(73)	Scott Servais	.25
(74)	Gary Sheffield	.60
(75)	Ozzie Smith	2.00
(76)	John Smoltz	.25
(77)	Sammy Sosa	2.00
(78)	Mike Stanley	.25
(79)	Terry Steinbach	.25
(80)	Frank Thomas	1.50
(81)	Steve Trachsel	.25
(82)	Jose Valentin	.25
(83)	Mo Vaughn	.25
(84)	Jose Vizcaino	.25
(85)	Robin Ventura	.25
(86)	Larry Walker	.25
(87)	Walt Weiss	.25
(88)	Bernie Williams	.25
(89)	Matt Williams	.25
(90)	Eric Young	.25
(91)	Todd Zeile	.25
(92)	Double Play (Roberto Alomar (Cartoon))	.25
(93)	Free Agent Acquisition (Barry Bonds (Cartoon))	1.50
(94)	No Trade - Infield (Mark McGwire, Ozzie Smith, Mo Vaughn (Cartoon))	.75
(95)	No Trade - Outfield (Albert Belle, Raul Mondesi (Cartoon))	.25
(96)	Out! (Mike Piazza, Matt Williams (Cartoon))	.75
(97)	Pitcher Bombed (Cartoon)	.25
(98)	Pitcher Stays (Greg Maddux (Cartoon))	1.00
(99)	Safe! (Frank Thomas (Cartoon))	.75

(100) Trade - Infield (Cal Ripken Jr., Alex Rodriguez (Cartoon)) .75
(101) Trade - Outfield (Ken Griffey Jr., Sammy Sosa (Cartoon)) .65

1988 Tetley Tea Discs

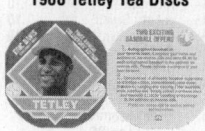

The Tetley iced tea discs are virtually identical in format to the 1988 Baseball Super Stars discs, but are labeled "FIRST ANNUAL COLLECTORS' EDITION," rather than Second and appear to have slight differences in the player pairs which make up each folder. Values for these can be extrapolated by combining the values of individual discs shown under the 1988 Baseball Super Stars listing.

1989 Tetley Tea Discs

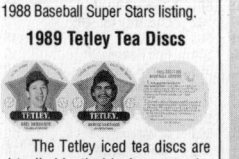

The Tetley iced tea discs are virtually identical in format to the 1989 Baseball Super Stars discs, but are labeled "SECOND ANNUAL COLLECTORS' EDITION." The trifold panels were distributed in canisters of iced tea mix in the East.

1990 Tetley Tea Discs

The Tetley iced tea discs are virtually identical in format to the 1990 Baseball Super Stars discs, but are labeled "THIRD ANNUAL COLLECTORS' EDITION." The trifold panels were distributed in canisters of iced tea mix in the East.

1986 Texas Gold Ice Cream Reds

One of the last regional baseball card sets produced during the 1986 season was a 28-card team set sponsored by a Cincinnati-area ice cream company and given to fans attending the September 19 game. Photos on the 2-1/2" x 3-1/2" cards are game-action shots, and include three different cards of playing manager Pete Rose. The set is also notable for the inclusion of first cards of some of the Reds' young prospects.

	NM/M
Complete Set (28):	16.00
Common Player:	.50
6 Bo Diaz	.50
9 Max Venable	.50
11 Kurt Stillwell	.50
12 Nick Esasky	.50
13 Dave Concepcion	.75
14a Pete Rose (Commemorative)	4.00
14b Pete Rose (Infield)	6.00
14c Pete Rose (Manager)	4.00
16 Ron Oester	.50
20 Eddie Milner	.50
22 Sal Butera	.50
24 Tony Perez	1.50
25 Buddy Bell	.75
28 Kal Daniels	.50
29 Tracy Jones	.50
31 John Franco	.50
32 Tom Browning	.50
33 Ron Robinson	.50
34 Bill Gullickson	.50
36 Mario Soto	.50
39 Dave Parker	.75
40 John Denny	.50
44 Eric Davis	1.00
45 Chris Welsh	.50
48 Ted Power	.50
49 Joe Price	.50
--- Reds Coaches (Scott Breeden, Billy Demars, Tommy Helms, Bruce Kimm, Jim Lett, George Scherger)	.50
--- Logo/Coupon Card	.20

1987 Texas Rangers Fire Safety

Co-sponsored by the team, U.S. and Texas Forest Services, the set was given out to fans at special promotions at Arlington Stadium. Cards measure 4-1/4" x 6" and feature color action photos. Backs contain brief player personal information along with a Smokey Bear wildfire prevention message. Cards of Mike Mason and Tom Paciorek were withdrawn from the sets given out by the Rangers and are quite scarce.

	NM/M
Complete Set (32):	45.00
Common Player:	.30
1 Charlie Hough	.30
2 Greg Harris	.30
3 Jose Guzman	.30
4 Mike Mason	20.00
5 Dale Mohorcic	.30
6 Bobby Witt	.30
7 Mitch Williams	.30
8 Geno Petralli	.30
9 Don Slaught	.30
10 Darrell Porter	.30
11 Steve Beuchele	.30
12 Pete O'Brien	.30
13 Scott Fletcher	.30
14 Tom Paciorek	20.00
15 Pete Incaviglia	.30
16 Oddibe McDowell	.30
17 Ruben Sierra	.30
18 Larry Parrish	.30
19 Bobby Valentine	.30
20 Tom House	.30
21 Tom Robson	.30
22 Edwin Correa	.30
23 Mike Stanley	.30
24 Joe Ferguson	.30
25 Art Howe	.30
26 Bob Brower	.30
27 Mike Loynd	.30
28 Curtis Wilkerson	.30
29 Tim Foli	.30
30 Dave Oliver	.30
31 Jerry Browne	.30
32 Jeff Russell	.30

1988 Texas Rangers Fire Safety

This oversized (3-1/2" x 5") set was distributed to Rangers' fans at Smokey Bear Game Day on August 7. Fronts feature full-color action photos framed in an oval blue and red border on a white background. A nameplate above the photo identifies the player and a "Wildfire Prevention" logo is printed beneath the photo. Rangers (left) and Smokey (right) logos fill the upper corners of the card face. The card backs are black-and-white and include player info, U.S. and Texas Forest Service logos, and fire prevention tips.

	NM/M
Complete Set (21):	5.00
Common Player:	.30
1 Tom O'Malley	.30
2 Pete O'Brien	.30
3 Geno Petralli	.30
4 Pete Incaviglia	.30
5 Oddibe McDowell	.30
6 Dale Mohorcic	.30
7 Bobby Witt	.30
8 Bobby Valentine	.30
9 Ruben Sierra	.30
10 Scott Fletcher	.30
11 Mike Stanley	.30
12 Steve Buechele	.30
13 Charlie Hough	.30
14 Larry Parrish	.30
15 Jerry Browne	.30
16 Bob Brower	.30
17 Jeff Russell	.30
18 Edwin Correa	.30
19 Mitch Williams	.30
20 Jose Guzman	.30
21 Curtis Wilkerson	.30

1989 Texas Rangers Fire Safety

Given away at a Rangers home game in 1989, this large-format (4-1/4" x 6") set features player portrait photos within an oval frame on a white border. The team logo is at upper-left; Smokey the Bear at upper-right. Backs have minimal biographical data and stats and a cartoon fire prevention tip. The un-numbered cards are checklisted here alphabetically.

	NM/M
Complete Set (34):	20.00
Common Player:	.25
(1) Darrel Akerfelds	.25
(2) Brad Arnsberg	.25
(3) Buddy Bell	.25
(4) Kevin Brown	.25
(5) Steve Buechele	.25
(6) Dick Egan	.25
(7) Cecil Espy	.25
(8) Scott Fletcher	.25
(9) Julio Franco	.25
(10) Cecilio Guante	.25
(11) Jose Guzman	.25
(12) Drew Hall	.25
(13) Toby Harrah	.25
(14) Charlie Hough	.25
(15) Tom House	.25
(16) Pete Incaviglia	.25
(17) Chad Kreuter	.25
(18) Jeff Kunkel	.25
(19) Rick Leach	.25
(20) Davey Lopes	.25
(21) Craig McMurtry	.25
(22) Jamie Moyer	.25
(23) Dave Oliver	.25
(24) Rafael Palmeiro	2.00
(25) Geno Petralli	.25
(26) Tom Robson	.25
(27) Kenny Rogers	.25
(28) Jeff Russell	.25
(29) Nolan Ryan	15.00
(30) Ruben Sierra	.25
(31) Mike Stanley	.25
(32) Jim Sundberg	.25
(33) Bobby Valentine	.25
(34) Bobby Witt	.25

1990 Texas Rangers Fire Safety

This stadium giveaway set is identical in design to the 1989 issue, but at 3-1/2" x 5", is slightly smaller. Backs have a cartoon fire safety tip and a bit of player personal data.

	NM/M
Complete Set (24):	30.00
Common Player:	.50
(1) Harold Baines	.50
(2) Brian Bohannon	.50
(3) Thad Bosley	.50
(4) Kevin Brown	.75
(5) Cecil Espy	.50
(6) Jack Daugherty	.50
(7) Julio Franco	.75
(8) Jeff Huson	.50
(9) Pete Incaviglia	.50
(10) Mike Jeffcoat	.50
(11) Chad Kreuter	.50
(12) Jeff Kunkel	.50
(13) Gary Mielke	.50
(14) Jamie Moyer	.50
(15) Rafael Palmeiro	3.00
(16) Gary Pettis	.50
(17) Kenny Rogers	.50
(18) Jeff Russell	.50
(19) John Russell	.50
(20) Nolan Ryan	25.00
(21) Ruben Sierra	.50
(22) Bobby Valentine	.50
(23) Bobby Witt	.50
(24) Arlington Stadium	1.00
46 Lee Smith	1.50
48 Dickie Noles	.50
--- Coaching Staff (Ruben Amaro, Billy Connors, Duffy Dyer, Lee Elia, Fred Koenig, John Vukovich)	.50
--- Team Photo	.50

1983 Thorn Apple Valley Cubs

#33 JOE CARTER OF

This set of 27 cards was issued in conjuction with a "Baseball Card Day" promotion at Wrigley Field in 1983. Thorn Apple Valley was the meat company which produced the hot dogs sold at the ballpark. The cards feature borderless color photos with the player's name, uniform number (also the card's number in the checklist) and an abbreviation for their position. Card backs feature annual statistics. Of the 27 cards, which measure 2-1/4" x 3-1/2", 25 feature players, one is a team card, and one features the manager and coaches.

	NM/M
Complete Set (27):	25.00
Common Player:	.50
1 Larry Bowa	.50
6 Keith Moreland	.50
9 Jody Davis	.50
10 Leon Durham	.50
11 Ron Cey	.50
16 Steve Lake	.50
20 Thad Bosley	.50
21 Jay Johnstone	.50
22 Bill Buckner	1.00
23 Ryne Sandberg	15.00
24 Jerry Morales	.50
27 Gary Woods	.50
27 Mel Hall	.50
30 Tom Veryzer	.50
30 Chuck Rainey	.50
31 Fergie Jenkins	4.00
32 Craig Lefferts	.50
33 Joe Carter	2.00
34 Steve Trout	.50
36 Mike Proly	.50
39 Bill Campbell	.50
40 Warren Brusstar	.50
44 Dick Ruthven	.50

1994 Tombstone Pizza

Score produced a special 30-card set which could be obtained by eating a lot of frozen pizzas (one card per pizza) or by sending in a dollar and five proofs of purchase. Titled "'94 Tombstone Super-Pro Series," the cards are black-bordered and UV coated on front and back. Because the set is licensed only by the Players Union and not by Major League Baseball, the uniform logos on the front action photos and back portraits have been airbrushed away. Cards feature the Tombstone logo on both front and back. Backs have recent and career stats, a facsimile autograph and a card number.

	NM/M
Complete Set (30):	4.00
Common Player:	.25
1 Jeff Bagwell	.50
2 Jay Bell	.25
3 Barry Bonds	1.50
4 Bobby Bonilla	.25
5 Andres Galarraga	.25
6 Mark Grace	.25
7 Marquis Grissom	.25
8 Tony Gwynn	.65
9 Bryan Harvey	.25
10 Gregg Jefferies	.25
11 David Justice	.25
12 John Kruk	.25
13 Barry Larkin	.25
14 Greg Maddux	.65
15 Mike Piazza	.75
16 Jim Abbott	.25
17 Albert Belle	.25
18 Cecil Fielder	.25
19 Juan Gonzalez	.35
20 Mike Greenwell	.25
21 Ken Griffey Jr.	.75
22 Jack McDowell	.25
23 Jeff Montgomery	.25
24 John Olerud	.25
25 Kirby Puckett	.65
26 Cal Ripken, Jr.	1.50
27 Tim Salmon	.25
28 Ruben Sierra	.25
29 Frank Thomas	1.50
30 Robin Yount	.50

1995 Tombstone Pizza

Tombstone's second annual baseball card issue was available either singly in frozen pizza packages, or as a 30-card boxed set via a mail-in offer. Cards feature action player photos on front and portrait photos on back; both have had uniform logos airbrushed for lack of a MLB license. There is a graduated red to black border on each side. On front at lower-right are the player and team name and the Tombstone logo. Backs have biographical data, recent stats and career highlights. At bottom is a card number and the Players Association logo.

	NM/M
Complete Set (30):	4.00
Common Player:	.25
1 Frank Thomas	.50
2 David Cone	.25
3 Bob Hamelin	.25
4 Jeff Bagwell	.50
5 Greg Maddux	.65
6 Raul Mondesi	.25
7 Chili Davis	.25
8 Cecil Fielder	.25
9 Ken Griffey Jr.	.75
10 Jimmy Key	.25
11 Kenny Lofton	.25
12 Paul Molitor	.50
13 Kirby Puckett	.65
14 Cal Ripken Jr.	1.50
15 Ivan Rodriguez	.40
16 Kevin Seitzer	.25
17 Ruben Sierra	.25
18 Mo Vaughn	.25
19 Moises Alou	.25
20 Barry Bonds	1.50
21 Jeff Conine	.25
22 Lenny Dykstra	.25
23 Andres Galarraga	.25
24 Tony Gwynn	.65
25 Barry Larkin	.25
26 Fred McGriff	.25
27 Orlando Merced	.25
28 Bret Saberhagen	.25
29 Ozzie Smith	.65
30 Sammy Sosa	.65

1981 Topps

This is another 726-card set of 2-1/2" x 3-1/2" cards from Topps. The cards have the usual color photo with all cards from the same team sharing the same color borders. Player names appear under the photo with team and position on a baseball cap at lower-left. The Topps logo returned in a small baseball in the lower-right. Card backs include the usual stats along with a headline and a cartoon if there was room. Specialty cards include previous season record-breakers, highlights of the playoffs and World Series, along with the final appearance of team cards. Eleven cards on each of the six press sheets were double-printed.

	NM/M
Complete Set (726):	45.00
Common Player:	.10
Wax Pack (15):	3.00
Wax Box (36):	85.00
Cello Pack (28):	3.00
Cello Box (24):	75.00
Rack Pack (48):	6.00
Rack Box (24):	120.00
Vending Box (500):	40.00
1 Batting Leaders (George Brett, Bill Buckner)	.75
2 Home Run Leaders (Reggie Jackson, Ben Oglivie, Mike Schmidt)	.75
3 RBI Leaders (Cecil Cooper, Mike Schmidt)	.25
4 Stolen Base Leaders (Rickey Henderson, Ron LeFlore)	.50
5 Victory Leaders (Steve Carlton, Steve Stone)	.15
6 Strikeout Leaders (Len Barker, Steve Carlton)	.15
7 ERA Leaders (Rudy May, Don Sutton)	.10
8 Leading Firemen (Rollie Fingers, Tom Hume, Dan Quisenberry)	.10
9 Pete LaCock/DP	.10
10 Mike Flanagan	.10

No.	Player	Price
11	Jim Wohlford/DP	.10
12	Mark Clear	.10
13	Joe Charboneau RC	.50
14	John Tudor RC	.20
15	Larry Parrish	.10
16	Ron Davis	.10
17	Cliff Johnson	.10
18	Glenn Adams	.10
19	Jim Clancy	.10
20	Jeff Burroughs	.10
21	Ron Oester	.10
22	Danny Darwin	.10
23	Alex Trevino	.10
24	Don Stanhouse	.10
25	Sixto Lezcano	.10
26	U.L. Washington	.10
27	Champ Summers/DP	.10
28	Enrique Romo	.10
29	Gene Tenace	.10
30	Jack Clark	.10
31	Checklist 1-121/DP	.10
32	Ken Oberkfell	.10
33	Rick Honeycutt	.10
34	Aurelio Rodriguez	.10
35	Mitchell Page	.10
36	Ed Farmer	.10
37	Gary Roenicke	.10
38	Win Remmerswaal	.10
39	Tom Veryzer	.10
40	Tug McGraw	.10
41	Rangers Future Stars (Bob Babcock, John Butcher, Jerry Don Gleaton)	.10
42	Jerry White/DP	.10
43	Jose Morales	.10
44	Larry McWilliams	.10
45	Enos Cabell	.10
46	Rick Bosetti	.10
47	Ken Brett	.10
48	Dave Skaggs	.10
49	Bob Shirley	.10
50	Dave Lopes	.10
51	Bill Robinson/DP	.10
52	Hector Cruz	.10
53	Kevin Saucier	.10
54	Ivan DeJesus	.10
55	Mike Norris	.10
56	Buck Martinez	.10
57	Dave Roberts	.10
58	Joel Youngblood	.10
59	Dan Petry	.10
60	Willie Randolph	.10
61	Butch Wynegar	.10
62	Joe Pettini	.10
63	Steve Renko/DP	.10
64	Brian Asselstine	.10
65	Scott McGregor	.10
66	Royals Future Stars (Manny Castillo, Tim Ireland, Mike Jones)	.10
67	Ken Kravec	.10
68	Matt Alexander/DP	.10
69	Ed Halicki	.10
70	Al Oliver/DP	.10
71	Hal Dues	.10
72	Barry Evans/DP	.10
73	Doug Bair	.10
74	Mike Hargrove	.10
75	Reggie Smith	.10
76	Mario Mendoza	.10
77	Mike Barlow	.10
78	Steve Dillard	.10
79	Bruce Robbins	.10
80	Rusty Staub	.15
81	Dave Stapleton	.10
82	Astros Future Stars (Danny Heep, Alan Knicely, Bobby Sprowl/DP)	.10
83	Mike Proly	.10
84	Johnnie LeMaster	.10
85	Mike Caldwell	.10
86	Wayne Gross	.10
87	Rick Camp	.10
88	Joe Lefebvre	.10
89	Darrell Jackson	.10
90	Bake McBride	.10
91	Tim Stoddard/DP	.10
92	Mike Easler	.10
93	Ed Glynn/DP	.10
94	Harry Spilman/DP	.10
95	Jim Sundberg	.10
96	A's Future Stars (Dave Beard, Ernie Camacho RC, Pat Dempsey)	.10
97	Chris Speier	.10
98	Clint Hurdle	.10
99	Eric Wilkins	.10
100	Rod Carew	2.00
101	Benny Ayala	.10
102	Dave Tobik	.10
103	Jerry Martin	.10
104	Terry Forster	.10
105	Jose Cruz	.10
106	Don Money	.10
107	Rich Wortham	.10
108	Bruce Benedict	.10
109	Mike Scott	.10
110	Carl Yastrzemski	2.00
111	Greg Minton	.10
112	White Sox Future Stars (Rusty Kuntz, Fran Mullins, Leo Sutherland)	.10
113	Mike Phillips	.10
114	Tom Underwood	.10
115	Roy Smalley	.10
116	Joe Simpson	.10
117	Pete Falcone	.10
118	Kurt Bevacqua	.10
119	Tippy Martinez	.10
120	Larry Bowa	.10
121	Larry Harlow	.10
122	John Denny	.10
123	Al Cowens	.10
124	Jerry Garvin	.10
125	Andre Dawson	1.50
126	Charlie Leibrandt RC	.40
127	Rudy Law	.10
128	Gary Allenson/DP	.10
129	Art Howe	.10
130	Larry Gura	.10
131	Keith Moreland RC	.20
132	Tommy Boggs	.10
133	Jeff Cox	.10
134	Steve Mura	.10
135	Gorman Thomas	.10
136	Doug Capilla	.10
137	Hosken Powell	.10
138	Rich Dotson/DP RC	.20
139	Oscar Gamble	.10
140	Bob Forsch	.10
141	Miguel Dilone	.10
142	Jackson Todd	.10
143	Dan Meyer	.10
144	Allen Ripley	.10
145	Mickey Rivers	.10
146	Bobby Castillo	.10
147	Dale Berra	.10
148	Randy Niemann	.10
149	Joe Nolan	.10
150	Mark Fidrych	.15
151	Claudell Washington/DP	.10
152	John Urrea	.10
153	Tom Poquette	.10
154	Rick Langford	.10
155	Chris Chambliss	.10
156	Bob McClure	.10
157	John Wathan	.10
158	Fergie Jenkins	1.00
159	Brian Doyle	.10
160	Garry Maddox	.10
161	Dan Graham	.10
162	Doug Corbett	.10
163	Billy Almon	.10
164	Lamarr Hoyt (LaMarr) RC	.15
165	Tony Scott	.10
166	Floyd Bannister	.10
167	Terry Whitfield	.10
168	Don Robinson/DP	.10
169	John Mayberry	.10
170	Ross Grimsley	.10
171	Gene Richards	.10
172	Gary Woods	.10
173	Bump Wills	.10
174	Doug Rau	.10
175	Dave Collins	.10
176	Mike Krukow	.10
177	Rick Peters	.10
178	Jim Essian/DP	.10
179	Rudy May	.10
180	Pete Rose	5.00
181	Elias Sosa	.10
182	Bob Grich	.10
183	Dick Davis/DP	.10
184	Jim Dwyer	.10
185	Dennis Leonard	.10
186	Wayne Nordhagen	.10
187	Mike Parrott	.10
188	Doug DeCinces	.10
189	Craig Swan	.10
190	Cesar Cedeno	.10
191	Rick Sutcliffe	.10
192	Braves Future Stars (Terry Harper RC, Ed Miller, Rafael Ramirez RC)	.10
193	Pete Vuckovich	.10
194	Rod Scurry RC	.10
195	Rich Murray	.10
196	Duffy Dyer	.10
197	Jim Kern	.10
198	Jerry Dybzinski	.10
199	Chuck Rainey	.10
200	George Foster	.10
201	Johnny Bench (Record Breaker)	.45
202	Steve Carlton (Record Breaker)	.25
203	Bill Gullickson (Record Breaker)	.10
204	Ron LeFlore, Rodney Scott (Record Breaker)	.10
205	Pete Rose (Record Breaker)	1.50
206	Mike Schmidt (Record Breaker)	1.00
207	Ozzie Smith (Record Breaker)	1.00
208	Willie Wilson (Record Breaker)	.10
209	Dickie Thon/DP	.10
210	Jim Palmer	1.50
211	Derrel Thomas	.10
212	Steve Nicosia	.10
213	Al Holland RC	.10
214	Angels Future Stars (Ralph Botting, Jim Dorsey, John Harris)	.10
215	Larry Hisle	.10
216	John Henry Johnson	.10
217	Rich Hebner	.10
218	Paul Splittorff	.10
219	Ken Landreaux	.10
220	Tom Seaver	2.00
221	Bob Davis	.10
222	Jorge Orta	.10
223	Roy Lee Jackson	.10
224	Pat Zachry	.10
225	Ruppert Jones	.10
226	Manny Sanguillen/DP	.10
227	Fred Martinez	.10
228	Tom Paciorek	.10
229	Rollie Fingers	1.00
230	George Hendrick	.10
231	Joe Beckwith	.10
232	Mickey Klutts	.10
233	Skip Lockwood	.10
234	Lou Whitaker	.10
235	Scott Sanderson	.10
236	Mike Ivie	.10
237	Charlie Moore	.10
238	Willie Hernandez	.10
239	Rick Miller/DP	.10
240	Nolan Ryan	5.00
241	Checklist 122-242/DP	.10
242	Chet Lemon	.10
243	Sal Butera	.10
244	Cardinals Future Stars (Tito Landrum RC, Al Olmsted, Andy Rincon)	.10
245	Ed Figueroa	.10
246	Ed Ott/DP	.10
247	Glenn Hubbard/DP	.10
248	Joey McLaughlin	.10
249	Larry Cox	.10
250	Ron Guidry	.15
251	Tom Brookens	.10
252	Victor Cruz	.10
253	Dave Bergman	.10
254	Ozzie Smith	3.00
255	Mark Littell	.10
256	Bombo Rivera	.10
257	Rennie Stennett	.10
258	Joe Price RC	.10
259	Mets Future Stars (Juan Berenguer, Hubie Brooks RC, Mookie Wilson RC)	.75
260	Ron Cey	.10
261	Rickey Henderson	4.50
262	Sammy Stewart	.10
263	Brian Downing	.10
264	Jim Norris	.10
265	John Candelaria	.10
266	Tom Herr	.10
267	Stan Bahnsen	.10
268	Jerry Royster	.10
269	Ken Forsch	.10
270	Greg Luzinski	.10
271	Bill Castro	.10
272	Bruce Kimm	.10
273	Stan Papi	.10
274	Craig Chamberlain	.10
275	Dwight Evans	.10
276	Dan Spillner	.10
277	Alfredo Griffin	.10
278	Rick Sofield	.10
279	Bob Knepper	.10
280	Ken Griffey	.10
281	Fred Stanley	.10
282	Mariners Future Stars (Rick Anderson, Greg Biercevicz, Rodney Craig)	.10
283	Billy Sample	.10
284	Brian Kingman	.10
285	Jerry Turner	.10
286	Dave Frost	.10
287	Lenn Sakata	.10
288	Bob Clark	.10
289	Mickey Hatcher	.10
290	Bob Boone/DP	.10
291	Aurelio Lopez	.10
292	Mike Squires	.10
293	Charlie Lea RC	.15
294	Mike Tyson/DP	.10
295	Hal McRae	.10
296	Bill Nahorodny/DP	.10
297	Bob Bailor	.10
298	Buddy Solomon	.10
299	Elliott Maddox	.10
300	Paul Molitor	2.00
301	Matt Keough	.10
302	Dodgers Future Stars (Jack Perconte RC, Mike Scioscia RC, Fernando Valenzuela RC)	2.00
303	Johnny Oates	.10
304	John Castino	.10
305	Ken Clay	.10
306	Juan Beniquez/DP	.10
307	Gene Garber	.10
308	Rick Manning	.10
309	Luis Salazar RC	.10
310	Vida Blue/DP	.10
311	Freddie Patek	.10
312	Rick Rhoden	.10
313	Luis Pujols	.10
314	Rich Dauer	.10
315	Kirk Gibson RC	5.00
316	Craig Minetto	.10
317	Lonnie Smith	.10
318	Steve Yeager	.10
319	Rowland Office	.10
320	Tom Burgmeier	.10
321	Leon Durham RC	.15
322	Neil Allen	.10
323	Jim Morrison/DP	.10
324	Mike Willis	.10
325	Ray Knight	.10
326	Biff Pocoroba	.10
327	Moose Haas	.10
328	Twins Future Stars (Dave Engle RC, Greg Johnston, Gary Ward)	.15
329	Joaquin Andujar	.10
330	Frank White	.10
331	Dennis Lamp	.10
332	Lee Lacy/DP	.10
333	Sid Monge	.10
334	Dane Iorg	.10
335	Rick Cerone	.10
336	Eddie Whitson	.10
337	Lynn Jones	.10
338	Checklist 243-363	.10
339	John Ellis	.10
340	Bruce Kison	.10
341	Dwayne Murphy	.10
342	Eric Rasmussen/DP	.10
343	Frank Taveras	.10
344	Byron McLaughlin	.10
345	Warren Cromartie	.10
346	Larry Christenson/DP	.10
347	Harold Baines RC	4.00
348	Bob Sykes	.10
349	Glenn Hoffman	.10
350	J.R. Richard	.10
351	Otto Velez	.10
352	Dick Tidrow/DP	.10
353	Terry Kennedy	.10
354	Mario Soto	.10
355	Bob Horner	.10
356	Padres Future Stars (George Stablein, Craig Stimac, Tom Tellmann)	.10
357	Jim Slaton	.10
358	Mark Wagner	.10
359	Tom Hausman	.10
360	Willie Wilson	.10
361	Joe Strain	.10
362	Bo Diaz	.10
363	Geoff Zahn	.10
364	Mike Davis RC	.10
365	Graig Nettles/DP	.15
366	Mike Ramsey	.10
367	Denny Martinez	.10
368	Leon Roberts	.10
369	Frank Tanana	.10
370	Dave Winfield	2.00
371	Charlie Hough	.10
372	Jay Johnstone	.10
373	Pat Underwood	.10
374	Tom Hutton	.10
375	Dave Concepcion	.10
376	Ron Reed	.10
377	Jerry Morales	.10
378	Dave Rader	.10
379	Lary Sorensen	.10
380	Willie Stargell	2.00
381	Cubs Future Stars (Carlos Lezcano, Steve Macko, Randy Martz)	.10
382	Paul Mirabella RC	.10
383	Eric Soderholm/DP	.10
384	Mike Sadek	.10
385	Joe Sambito	.10
386	Dave Edwards	.10
387	Phil Niekro	1.00
388	Andre Thornton	.10
389	Marty Pattin	.10
390	Cesar Geronimo	.10
391	Dave Lemanczyk/DP	.10
392	Lance Parrish	.10
393	Broderick Perkins	.10
394	Woodie Fryman	.10
395	Scot Thompson	.10
396	Bill Campbell	.10
397	Julio Cruz	.10
398	Ross Baumgarten	.10
399	Orioles Future Stars (Mike Boddicker RC, Mark Corey, Floyd Rayford RC)	.20
400	Reggie Jackson	3.00
401	A.L. Championships (Royals Sweep Yankees)	.50
402	N.L. Championships (Phillies Squeak Past Astros)	.25
403	World Series (Phillies Beat Royals In 6)	.25
404	World Series Summary (Phillies Win First World Series)	.25
405	Nino Espinosa	.10
406	Dickie Noles	.10
407	Ernie Whitt	.10
408	Fernando Arroyo	.10
409	Larry Herndon	.10
410	Bert Campaneris	.10
411	Terry Puhl	.10
412	Britt Burns RC	.10
413	Tony Bernazard	.10
414	John Pacella/DP	.10
415	Ben Oglivie	.10
416	Gary Alexander	.10
417	Dan Schatzeder	.10
418	Bobby Brown	.10
419	Tom Hume	.10
420	Keith Hernandez	.10
421	Bob Stanley	.10
422	Dan Ford	.10
423	Shane Rawley	.10
424	Yankees Future Stars (Tim Lollar, Bruce Robinson, Dennis Werth)	.10
425	Al Bumbry	.10
426	Warren Brusstar	.10
427	John D'Acquisto	.10
428	John Stearns	.10
429	Mick Kelleher	.10
430	Jim Bibby	.10
431	Dave Roberts	.10
432	Len Barker	.10
433	Rance Mulliniks	.10
434	Roger Erickson	.10
435	Jim Spencer	.10
436	Gary Lucas	.10
437	Mike Heath/DP	.10
438	John Montefusco	.10
439	Denny Walling	.10
440	Jerry Reuss	.10
441	Ken Reitz	.10
442	Ron Pruitt	.10
443	Jim Beattie/DP	.10
444	Garth Iorg	.10
445	Ellis Valentine	.10
446	Checklist 364-484	.10
447	Junior Kennedy/DP	.10
448	Tim Corcoran	.10
449	Paul Mitchell	.10
450	Dave Kingman/DP	.10
451	Indians Future Stars (Chris Bando, Tom Brennan, Sandy Wihtol)	.10
452	Renie Martin	.10
453	Rob Wilfong/DP	.10
454	Andy Hassler	.10
455	Rick Burleson	.10
456	Jeff Reardon RC	1.50
457	Mike Lum	.10
458	Randy Jones	.10
459	Greg Gross	.10
460	Rich Gossage	.10
461	Dave McKay	.10
462	Jack Brohamer	.10
463	Milt May	.10
464	Adrian Devine	.10
465	Bill Russell	.10
466	Bob Molinaro	.10
467	Dave Stieb	.10
468	Johnny Wockenfuss	.10
469	Jeff Leonard	.10
470	Manny Trillo	.10
471	Mike Vail	.10
472	Dyar Miller/DP	.10
473	Jose Cardenal	.10
474	Mike LaCoss	.10
475	Buddy Bell	.10
476	Jerry Koosman	.10
477	Luis Gomez	.10
478	Juan Eichelberger	.10
479	Expos Future Stars (Bobby Pate RC, Tim Raines RC, Roberto Ramos RC)	3.00
480	Carlton Fisk	2.00
481	Bob Lacey/DP	.10
482	Jim Gantner	.10
483	Mike Griffin	.10
484	Max Venable/DP	.10
485	Garry Templeton	.10
486	Marc Hill	.10
487	Dewey Robinson	.10
488	Damaso Garcia RC	.10
489	John Littlefield (Photo actually Mark Riggins.)	.10
490	Eddie Murray	2.00
491	Gordy Pladson	.10
492	Barry Foote	.10
493	Dan Quisenberry	.10
494	Bob Walk RC	.20
495	Dusty Baker	.10
496	Paul Dade	.10
497	Fred Norman	.10
498	Pat Putnam	.10
499	Frank Pastore	.10
500	Jim Rice	.25
501	Tim Foli/DP	.10
502	Giants Future Stars (Chris Bourjos, Al Hargesheimer, Mike Rowland)	.10
503	Steve McCatty	.10
504	Dale Murphy	.75
505	Jason Thompson	.10
506	Phil Huffman	.10
507	Jamie Quirk	.10
508	Rob Dressler	.10
509	Pete Mackanin	.10
510	Lee Mazzilli	.10
511	Wayne Garland	.10
512	Gary Thomasson	.10
513	Frank LaCorte	.10
514	George Riley	.10
515	Robin Yount	2.00
516	Doug Bird	.10
517	Richie Zisk	.10
518	Grant Jackson	.10
519	John Tamargo/DP	.10
520	Steve Stone	.10
521	Sam Mejias	.10
522	Mike Colbern	.10
523	John Fulgham	.10
524	Willie Aikens	.10
525	Mike Torrez	.10
526	Phillies Future Stars (Marty Bystrom, Jay Loviglio, Jim Wright)	.10
527	Danny Goodwin	.10
528	Gary Matthews	.10
529	Dave LaRoche	.10
530	Steve Garvey	.75
531	John Curtis	.10
532	Bill Stein	.10
533	Jesus Figueroa	.10
534	Dave Smith RC	.10
535	Omar Moreno	.10
536	Bob Owchinko/DP	.10
537	Ron Hodges	.10
538	Tom Griffin	.10
539	Rodney Scott	.10
540	Mike Schmidt/DP	3.00
541	Steve Swisher	.10
542	Larry Bradford/DP	.10
543	Terry Crowley	.10
544	Rich Gale	.10
545	Johnny Grubb	.10
546	Paul Moskau	.10
547	Mario Guerrero	.10
548	Dave Goltz	.10
549	Jerry Remy	.10
550	Tommy John	.20
551	Pirates Future Stars (Vance Law RC, Tony Pena RC, Pascual Perez RC)	.75
552	Steve Trout	.10
553	Tim Blackwell	.10
554	Bert Blyleven	.10
555	Cecil Cooper	.10
556	Jerry Mumphrey	.10
557	Chris Knapp	.10
558	Barry Bonnell	.10
559	Willie Montanez	.10
560	Joe Morgan	2.00
561	Dennis Littlejohn	.10
562	Checklist 485-605	.10
563	Jim Kaat	.15
564	Ron Hassey/DP	.10
565	Burt Hooton	.10
566	Del Unser	.10
567	Mark Bomback	.10
568	Dave Revering	.10
569	Al Williams/DP	.10
570	Ken Singleton	.10
571	Todd Cruz	.10
572	Jack Morris	.10
573	Phil Garner	.10
574	Bill Caudill	.10
575	Tony Perez	1.00
576	Reggie Cleveland	.10
577	Blue Jays Future Stars (Luis Leal, Brian Milner, Ken Schrom RC)	.10
578	Bill Gullickson RC	.20
579	Tim Flannery	.10
580	Don Baylor	.15
581	Roy Howell	.10
582	Gaylord Perry	1.00
583	Larry Milbourne	.10
584	Randy Lerch	.10
585	Amos Otis	.10
586	Silvio Martinez	.10
587	Jeff Newman	.10
588	Gary Lavelle	.10
589	Lamar Johnson	.10
590	Bruce Sutter	1.00
591	John Lowenstein	.10
592	Steve Comer	.10
593	Steve Kemp	.10
594	Preston Hanna/DP	.10
595	Butch Hobson	.10
596	Jerry Augustine	.10
597	Rafael Landestoy	.10
598	George Vukovich/DP	.10
599	Dennis Kinney	.10
600	Johnny Bench	2.00
601	Don Aase	.10
602	Bobby Murcer	.10
603	John Verhoeven	.10
604	Rob Picciolo	.10
605	Don Sutton	1.00
606	Reds Future Stars (Bruce Berenyi, Geoff Combe, Paul Householder/DP)	.10
607	Dave Palmer	.10
608	Greg Pryor	.10
609	Lynn McGlothen	.10
610	Darrell Porter	.10
611	Rick Matula/DP	.10
612	Duane Kuiper	.10
613	Jim Anderson	.10
614	Dave Rozema	.10
615	Rick Dempsey	.10
616	Rick Wise	.10
617	Craig Reynolds	.10
618	John Milner	.10
619	Steve Henderson	.10
620	Dennis Eckersley	1.00
621	Tom Donohue	.10
622	Randy Moffitt	.10
623	Sal Bando	.10
624	Bob Welch	.10
625	Bill Buckner	.10
626	Tigers Future Stars (Dave Steffen, Jerry Ujdur, Roger Weaver)	.10
627	Luis Tiant	.10
628	Vic Correll	.10
629	Tony Armas	.10
630	Steve Carlton	2.00
631	Ron Jackson	.10
632	Alan Bannister	.10
633	Bill Lee	.10
634	Doug Flynn	.10
635	Bobby Bonds	.10
636	Al Hrabosky	.10
637	Jerry Narron	.10
638	Checklist 606	.10
639	Carney Lansford	.10
640	Dave Parker	.10
641	Mark Belanger	.10
642	Vern Ruhle	.10
643	Lloyd Moseby RC	.20
644	Ramon Aviles/DP	.10
645	Rick Reuschel	.10
646	Marvis Foley	.10

647	Dick Drago	.10
648	Darrell Evans	.10
649	Manny Sarmiento	.10
650	Bucky Dent	.10
651	Pedro Guerrero	.10
652	John Montague	.10
653	Bill Fahey	.10
654	Ray Burris	.10
655	Dan Driessen	.10
656	Jon Matlack	.10
657	Mike Cubbage/DP	.10
658	Milt Wilcox	.10
659	Brewers Future Stars (John Flinn, Ed Romero, Ned Yost)	.10
660	Gary Carter	2.00
661	Orioles Team (Earl Weaver)	.25
662	Red Sox Team (Ralph Houk)	.20
663	Angels Team (Jim Fregosi)	.10
664	White Sox Team (Tony LaRussa)	.25
665	Indians Team (Dave Garcia)	.10
666	Tigers Team (Sparky Anderson)	.25
667	Royals Team (Jim Frey)	.10
668	Brewers Team (Bob Rodgers)	.10
669	Twins Team (John Goryl)	.10
670	Yankees Team (Gene Michael)	.15
671	A's Team (Billy Martin)	.25
672	Mariners Team (Maury Wills)	.20
673	Rangers Team (Don Zimmer)	.20
674	Blue Jays Team (Bobby Mattick)	.15
675	Braves Team (Bobby Cox)	.25
676	Cubs Team (Joe Amalfitano)	.10
677	Reds Team (John McNamara)	.10
678	Astros Team (Bill Virdon)	.10
679	Dodgers Team (Tom Lasorda)	.25
680	Expos Team (Dick Williams)	.20
681	Mets Team (Joe Torre)	.15
682	Phillies Team (Dallas Green)	.15
683	Pirates Team (Chuck Tanner)	.10
684	Cardinals Team (Whitey Herzog)	.15
685	Padres Team (Frank Howard)	.20
686	Giants Team (Dave Bristol)	.10
687	Jeff Jones	.10
688	Kiko Garcia	.10
689	Red Sox Future Stars (Bruce Hurst RC, Keith MacWhorter, Reid Nichols RC)	.30
690	Bob Watson	.10
691	Dick Ruthven	.10
692	Lenny Randle	.10
693	Steve Howe RC	.20
694	Bud Harrelson/DP	.10
695	Kent Tekulve	.10
696	Alan Ashby	.10
697	Rick Waits	.10
698	Mike Jorgensen	.10
699	Glenn Abbott	.10
700	George Brett	3.50
701	Joe Rudi	.10
702	George Medich	.10
703	Alvis Woods	.10
704	Bill Travers/DP	.10
705	Ted Simmons	.10
706	Dave Ford	.10
707	Dave Cash	.10
708	Doyle Alexander	.10
709	Alan Trammell/DP	.10
710	Ron LeFlore/DP	.10
711	Joe Ferguson	.10
712	Bill Bonham	.10
713	Bill North	.10
714	Pete Redfern	.10
715	Bill Madlock	.15
716	Glenn Borgmann	.10
717	Jim Barr/DP	.10
718	Larry Biittner	.10
719	Sparky Lyle	.10
720	Fred Lynn	.10
721	Toby Harrah	.10
722	Joe Niekro	.10
723	Bruce Bochte	.10
724	Lou Piniella	.15
725	Steve Rogers	.10
726	Rick Monday	.10

Traded

The 132 cards in this extension set are numbered from 727 to 858, technically making them a high-numbered series of the regular Topps set. The set was not packaged in gum packs, but rather sold in a specially designed red box through baseball card dealers only. The set features not only mid-season trades, but also

single-player rookie cards of some of the hottest prospects. The cards measure 2-1/2" x 3-1/2".

		NM/M
Complete Set (132):		15.00
Common Player:		.10
727	Danny Ainge RC	2.00
728	Doyle Alexander	.10
729	Gary Alexander	.10
730	Billy Almon	.10
731	Joaquin Andujar	.10
732	Bob Bailor	.10
733	Juan Beniquez	.10
734	Dave Bergman	.10
735	Tony Bernazard	.10
736	Larry Biittner	.10
737	Doug Bird	.10
738	Bert Blyleven	.25
739	Mark Bomback	.10
740	Bobby Bonds	.15
741	Rick Bosetti	.10
742	Hubie Brooks	.10
743	Rick Burleson	.10
744	Ray Burris	.10
745	Jeff Burroughs	.10
746	Enos Cabell	.10
747	Ken Clay	.10
748	Mark Clear	.10
749	Larry Cox	.10
750	Hector Cruz	.10
751	Victor Cruz	.10
752	Mike Cubbage	.10
753	Dick Davis	.10
754	Brian Doyle	.10
755	Dick Drago	.10
756	Leon Durham	.10
757	Jim Dwyer	.10
758	Dave Edwards	.10
759	Jim Essian	.10
760	Bill Fahey	.10
761	Rollie Fingers	1.00
762	Carlton Fisk	2.00
763	Barry Foote	.10
764	Ken Forsch	.10
765	Kiko Garcia	.10
766	Cesar Geronimo	.10
767	Gary Gray	.10
768	Mickey Hatcher	.10
769	Steve Henderson	.10
770	Marc Hill	.10
771	Butch Hobson	.10
772	Rick Honeycutt	.10
773	Roy Howell	.10
774	Mike Ivie	.10
775	Roy Lee Jackson	.10
776	Cliff Johnson	.10
777	Randy Jones	.10
778	Ruppert Jones	.10
779	Mick Kelleher	.10
780	Terry Kennedy	.10
781	Dave Kingman	.10
782	Bob Knepper	.10
783	Ken Kravec	.10
784	Bob Lacey	.10
785	Dennis Lamp	.10
786	Rafael Landestoy	.10
787	Ken Landreaux	.10
788	Carney Lansford	.10
789	Dave LaRoche	.10
790	Joe Lefebvre	.10
791	Ron LeFlore	.10
792	Randy Lerch	.10
793	Sixto Lezcano	.10
794	John Littlefield	.10
795	Mike Lum	.10
796	Greg Luzinski	.10
797	Fred Lynn	.10
798	Jerry Martin	.10
799	Buck Martinez	.10
800	Gary Matthews	.10
801	Mario Mendoza	.10
802	Larry Milbourne	.10
803	Rick Miller	.10
804	John Montefusco	.10
805	Jerry Morales	.10
806	Jose Morales	.10
807	Joe Morgan	2.00
808	Jerry Mumphrey	.10
809	Gene Nelson RC	.10
810	Ed Ott	.10
811	Bob Owchinko	.10
812	Gaylord Perry	1.00
813	Mike Phillips	.10
814	Darrell Porter	.10
815	Mike Proly	.10
816	Tim Raines	3.00
817	Lenny Randle	.10

818	Doug Rau	.10
819	Jeff Reardon	.10
820	Ken Reitz	.10
821	Steve Renko	.10
822	Rick Reuschel	.10
823	Dave Revering	.10
824	Dave Roberts	.10
825	Leon Roberts	.10
826	Joe Rudi	.10
827	Kevin Saucier	.10
828	Tony Scott	.10
829	Bob Shirley	.10
830	Ted Simmons	.10
831	Lary Sorensen	.10
832	Jim Spencer	.10
833	Harry Spilman	.10
834	Fred Stanley	.10
835	Rusty Staub	.25
836	Bill Stein	.10
837	Joe Strain	.10
838	Bruce Sutter	1.00
839	Don Sutton	1.00
840	Steve Swisher	.10
841	Frank Tanana	.10
842	Gene Tenace	.10
843	Jason Thompson	.10
844	Dickie Thon	.10
845	Bill Travers	.10
846	Tom Underwood	.10
847	John Urrea	.10
848	Mike Vail	.10
849	Ellis Valentine	.10
850	Fernando Valenzuela	2.00
851	Pete Vuckovich	.10
852	Mark Wagner	.10
853	Bob Walk	.10
854	Claudell Washington	.10
855	Dave Winfield	4.00
856	Geoff Zahn	.10
857	Richie Zisk	.10
858	Checklist 727-858	.05

Team Card Sheet

Via a special mail-in offer, uncut sheets of team cards from the 1981 Topps issue were made available to collectors.

	NM/M
Team Card Sheet	20.00

Giant Photo Cards

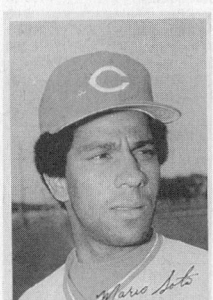

Once again testing the popularity of large-format cards, Topps issued 4-7/8" x 6-7/8" cards in two different sets. The team-set cards feature a large color photo, facsimile autograph and white border on the front. Backs have the player's name, team, position and a checklist at the bottom. The 102 cards were sold in limited areas corresponding to the teams' geographic home. Cards were sold in one-card wax packs with 36 packs per box. Boxes contained either the cards of a single team, or of two teams from the same city or state. It was also possible to order the whole set by mail. Ten teams are involved in the issue, with the number of players from each team ranging from 6 to 12.

	NM/M
Complete Set (102):	25.00
Common Player:	.25
Angels-Dodgers Wax Box:	6.00
Astros-Rangers Wax Box:	7.50
Cubs-White Sox Wax Box:	6.00
Mets-Yankees Wax Box:	9.00
Phillies Wax Box:	9.00
Reds Wax Box:	7.50
Red Sox Wax Box:	7.50
(1) Tom Burgmeier	.25
(2) Dennis Eckersley	1.00
(3) Dwight Evans	.35
(4) Carlton Fisk	1.00
(5) Glenn Hoffman	.25
(6) Carney Lansford	.25
(7) Tony Perez	1.00
(8) Jim Rice	.75
(9) Bob Stanley	.25
(10) Dave Stapleton	.25
(11) Frank Tanana	.25
(12) Carl Yastrzemski	1.50

(1) Don Baylor	.35
(2) Rick Burleson	.25
(3) Rod Carew	1.00
(4) Bobby Grich	.35
(5) Butch Hobson	.25
(1) Fred Lynn	.35
(2) Tim Blackwell	.25
(3) Bill Buckner	.25
(4) Ivan DeJesus	.25
(5) Leon Durham	.25
(6) Dave Kingman	.40
(7) Mike Krukow	.25
(8) Ken Reitz	.25
(9) Rick Reuschel	.25
(1) Mike Tyson	.25
(2) Britt Burns	.25
(3) Rich Dotson	.25
(4) Ed Farmer	.25
(5) Lamar Johnson	.25
(6) Ron LeFlore	.25
(7) Chet Lemon	.25
(8) Bob Molinaro	.25
(9) Jim Morrison	.25
(9) Wayne Nordhagen	.25
(1) Johnny Bench	1.00
(2) Dave Collins	.25
(3) Dave Concepcion	.25
(4) Dan Driessen	.25
(5) George Foster	.35
(6) Ken Griffey	.35
(7) Tom Hume	.25
(8) Ray Knight	.25
(9) Joe Nolan	.25
(10) Ron Oester	.25
(11) Tom Seaver	1.00
(12) Mario Soto	.25
(1) Cesar Cedeno	.25
(2) Jose Cruz	.25
(3) Art Howe	.25
(4) Terry Puhl	.25
(5) Nolan Ryan	3.00
(6) Don Sutton	1.00
(1) Dusty Baker	.35
(2) Ron Cey	.25
(3) Steve Garvey	.75
(4) Burt Hooton	.25
(5) Steve Howe	.25
(6) Davey Lopes	.25
(7) Rick Monday	.25
(8) Jerry Reuss	.25
(9) Bill Russell	.25
(10) Reggie Smith	.25
(11) Bob Welch	.25
(12) Steve Yeager	.25
(1) Neil Allen	.25
(2) Doug Flynn	.25
(3) Lee Mazzilli	.25
(4) Rusty Staub	.40
(5) Alex Taveras	.25
(6) Alex Trevino	.25
(1) Rick Cerone	.25
(2) Bucky Dent	.35
(3) Rich Gossage	.50
(4) Ron Guidry	.35
(5) Reggie Jackson	1.50
(6) Tommy John	.35
(7) Ruppert Jones	.25
(8) Rudy May	.25
(9) Graig Nettles	.25
(10) Willie Randolph	.25
(11) Bob Watson	.25
(12) Dave Winfield	1.00
(1) Bob Boone	.35
(2) Larry Bowa	.25
(3) Steve Carlton	1.00
(4) Greg Luzinski	.25
(5) Garry Maddox	.25
(6) Bake McBride	.25
(7) Tug McGraw	.25
(8) Pete Rose	3.00
(9) Dick Ruthven	.25
(10) Mike Schmidt	2.00
(11) Manny Trillo	.25
(12) Del Unser	.25
(1) Buddy Bell	.25
(2) Jon Matlack	.25
(3) Al Oliver	.35
(4) Mickey Rivers	.25
(5) Jim Sundberg	.25
(6) Bump Wills	.25

National 5x7 Photos

This set is the other half of Topps' efforts with large cards in 1981. Measuring 4-7/8" x 6-7/8", the National photo issue was limited to 15 cards. They were sold in areas not covered by the team-set issues. The set includes 10 cards which carry the same photos found in the team sets, but with no checklist on the backs. Five cards are unique to the National set: Brett, Cooper, Palmer, Parker and Simmons.

	NM/M
Complete Set (15):	4.00
Common Player:	.15
(1) Buddy Bell	.15
(2) Johnny Bench	.50
(3) George Brett	.75
(4) Rod Carew	.50
(5) Cecil Cooper	.15
(6) Steve Garvey	.35
(7) Rich Gossage	.15
(8) Reggie Jackson	.60
(9) Jim Palmer	.50
(10) Dave Parker	.15
(11) Jim Rice	.30
(12) Pete Rose	1.00
(13) Mike Schmidt	.75
(14) Tom Seaver	.50
(15) Ted Simmons	.15

Mets Magic Memories

Celebrating 20 years of N.Y. Mets baseball, the team issued a set of "Magic Memories" cards. Topps produced 20,000 each of the 6-7/8" x 4-7/8" cards. The cards were individually cello wrapped. Cards #1-2 were distributed at the team's August 27 game; cards #3-4 at the September 22 contest. The first card is a sepia team photo of the 1962 Mets. Card #2-3 are color team photos from 1969 and 1973. The team photo cards have player stats on back. The fourth card depicts four of the Mets managers on front, with biographies on back.

	NM/M
Complete Set (4):	24.00
Common Player:	6.00
1 1962 Mets Team Photo	6.00
2 1969 Mets Team Photo	6.00
3 1973 Mets Team Photo	6.00
4 New York Mets Managers (Casey Stengel, Gil Hodges, Yogi Berra, Joe Torre)	12.00

Scratchoffs

Sold as a separate issue with bubble gum, this 108-card set was issued in three-card panels that measure 3-1/4" x 5-1/4". Each individual card measures 1-13/16" x 3-1/4" and contains a small player photo alongside a series of black dots designed to be scratched off as part of a baseball game. Cards of National League players have a green background, while American League players have a red background. While there are 108 different players in the set, there are 144 possible panel combinations. An intact panel of three cards is valued approximately 20-25 percent more than the sum of the individual cards.

	NM/M
Complete Set (108):	10.00
Common Player:	.15
Wax Pack:	.75
Wax Box (36):	15.00

1	George Brett	1.00
2	Cecil Cooper	.15
3	Reggie Jackson	.50
4	Al Oliver	.15
5	Fred Lynn	.15
6	Tony Armas	.15
7	Ben Oglivie	.15
8	Tony Perez	.25
9	Eddie Murray	.25
10	Robin Yount	.25
11	Steve Kemp	.15
12	Joe Charboneau	.15
13	Jim Rice	.20
14	Lance Parrish	.15
15	John Mayberry	.15
16	Richie Zisk	.15
17	Ken Singleton	.15
18	Rod Carew	.15
19	Rick Manning	.15
20	Willie Wilson	.15
21	Buddy Bell	.15
22	Dave Revering	.15
23	Tom Paciorek	.15
24	Champ Summers	.15
25	Carney Lansford	.15
26	Lamar Johnson	.15
27	Willie Aikens	.15
28	Rick Cerone	.15
29	Al Bumbry	.15
30	Bruce Bochte	.15
31	Mickey Rivers	.15
32	Mike Hargrove	.15
33	John Castino	.15
34	Chet Lemon	.15
35	Paul Molitor	.25
36	Willie Randolph	.15
37	Rick Burleson	.15
38	Alan Trammell	.15
39	Rickey Henderson	.25
40	Dan Meyer	.15
41	Ken Landreaux	.15
42	Damaso Garcia	.15
43	Roy Smalley	.15
44	Otto Velez	.15
45	Sixto Lezcano	.15
46	Toby Harrah	.15
47	Frank White	.15
48	Dave Stapleton	.15
49	Steve Stone	.15
50	Jim Palmer	.25
51	Larry Gura	.15
52	Tommy John	.15
53	Mike Norris	.15
54	Ed Farmer	.15
55	Bill Buckner	.15
56	Steve Garvey	.25
57	Reggie Smith	.15
58	Bake McBride	.15
59	Dave Parker	.15
60	Mike Schmidt	1.00
61	Bob Horner	.15
62	Pete Rose	2.00
63	Ted Simmons	.15
64	Johnny Bench	.25
65	George Foster	.15
66	Gary Carter	.25
67	Keith Hernandez	.15
68	Ozzie Smith	.35
69	Dave Kingman	.15
70	Jack Clark	.15
71	Dusty Baker	.15
72	Dale Murphy	.20
73	Ron Cey	.15
74	Greg Luzinski	.15
75	Lee Mazzilli	.15
76	Gary Matthews	.15
77	Cesar Cedeno	.15
78	Warren Cromartie	.15
79	Steve Henderson	.15
80	Ellis Valentine	.15
81	Mike Easler	.15
82	Garry Templeton	.15
83	Jose Cruz	.15
84	Dave Collins	.15
85	George Hendrick	.15
86	Gene Richards	.15
87	Terry Whitfield	.15
88	Terry Puhl	.15
89	Larry Parrish	.15
90	Andre Dawson	.20
91	Ken Griffey	.15
92	Dave Lopes	.15
93	Doug Flynn	.15
94	Ivan DeJesus	.15
95	Dave Concepcion	.15
96	John Stearns	.15
97	Jerry Mumphrey	.15
98	Jerry Martin	.15
99	Art Howe	.15
100	Omar Moreno	.15
101	Ken Reitz	.15
102	Phil Garner	.15
103	Jerry Reuss	.15
104	Steve Carlton	.25
105	Jim Bibby	.15
106	Steve Rogers	.15
107	Tom Seaver	.25
108	Vida Blue	.15

Stickers

The 262 stickers in this full-color set measure 1-15/16" x 2-9/16" and are numbered on both the front and back. They were produced for Topps by the Panini Co. of Italy. The set includes a series of "All-Star...

1981 Topps

stickers printed on silver or gold "foil." An album to house the stickers was also available.

	NM/M
Complete Set (262):	9.00
Common Player:	.05
Sticker Album:	2.00
Wax Pack (5):	.40
Wax Box (100):	15.00

#	Player	Price
1	Steve Stone	.05
2	Tommy John, Mike Norris	.05
3	Rudy May	.05
4	Mike Norris	.05
5	Len Barker	.05
6	Mike Norris	.05
7	Dan Quisenberry	.05
8	Rich Gossage	.05
9	George Brett	.30
10	Cecil Cooper	.05
11	Reggie Jackson, Ben Oglivie	.05
12	Gorman Thomas	.05
13	Cecil Cooper	.05
14	George Brett, Ben Oglivie	.05
15	Rickey Henderson	.25
16	Willie Wilson	.05
17	Bill Buckner	.05
18	Keith Hernandez	.05
19	Mike Schmidt	.30
20	Bob Horner	.05
21	Mike Schmidt	.30
22	George Hendrick	.05
23	Ron LeFlore	.05
24	Omar Moreno	.05
25	Steve Carlton	.20
26	Joe Niekro	.05
27	Don Sutton	.20
28	Steve Carlton	.20
29	Steve Carlton	.20
30	Nolan Ryan	.50
31	Rollie Fingers, Tom Hume	.05
32	Bruce Sutter	.20
33	Ken Singleton	.05
34	Eddie Murray	.25
35	Al Bumbry	.05
36	Rich Dauer	.05
37	Scott McGregor	.05
38	Rick Dempsey	.05
39	Jim Palmer	.25
40	Steve Stone	.05
41	Jim Rice	.15
42	Fred Lynn	.05
43	Carney Lansford	.05
44	Tony Perez	.25
45	Carl Yastrzemski	.25
46	Carlton Fisk	.25
47	Dave Stapleton	.05
48	Dennis Eckersley	.20
49	Rod Carew	.25
50	Brian Downing	.05
51	Don Baylor	.05
52	Rick Burleson	.05
53	Bobby Grich	.05
54	Butch Hobson	.05
55	Andy Hassler	.05
56	Frank Tanana	.05
57	Chet Lemon	.05
58	Lamar Johnson	.05
59	Wayne Nordhagen	.05
60	Jim Morrison	.05
61	Bob Molinaro	.05
62	Rich Dotson	.05
63	Britt Burns	.05
64	Ed Farmer	.05
65	Toby Harrah	.05
66	Joe Charboneau	.25
67	Miguel Dilone	.05
68	Mike Hargrove	.05
69	Rick Manning	.05
70	Andre Thornton	.05
71	Ron Hassey	.05
72	Len Barker	.05
73	Lance Parrish	.05
74	Steve Kemp	.05
75	Alan Trammell	.05
76	Champ Summers	.05
77	Rick Peters	.05
78	Kirk Gibson	.05
79	Johnny Wockenfuss	.05
80	Jack Morris	.05
81	Willie Wilson	.05
82	George Brett	.30
83	Frank White	.05
84	Willie Aikens	.05
85	Clint Hurdle	.05
86	Hal McRae	.05
87	Dennis Leonard	.05
88	Larry Gura	.05
89	American League Pennant Winner (Kansas City Royals Team)	.05
90	American League Pennant Winner (Kansas City Royals Team)	.05
91	Paul Molitor	.25
92	Ben Oglivie	.05
93	Cecil Cooper	.05
94	Ted Simmons	.05
95	Robin Yount	.25
96	Gorman Thomas	.05
97	Mike Caldwell	.05
98	Moose Haas	.05
99	John Castino	.05
100	Roy Smalley	.05
101	Ken Landreaux	.05
102	Butch Wynegar	.05
103	Ron Jackson	.05
104	Jerry Koosman	.05
105	Roger Erickson	.05
106	Doug Corbett	.05
107	Reggie Jackson	.30
108	Willie Randolph	.05
109	Rick Cerone	.05
110	Bucky Dent	.05
111	Dave Winfield	.25
112	Ron Guidry	.10
113	Rich Gossage	.05
114	Tommy John	.10
115	Rickey Henderson	.25
116	Tony Armas	.05
117	Dave Revering	.05
118	Wayne Gross	.05
119	Dwayne Murphy	.05
120	Jeff Newman	.05
121	Rick Langford	.05
122	Mike Norris	.05
123	Bruce Bochte	.05
124	Tom Paciorek	.05
125	Dan Meyer	.05
126	Julio Cruz	.05
127	Richie Zisk	.05
128	Floyd Bannister	.05
129	Shane Rawley	.05
130	Buddy Bell	.05
131	Al Oliver	.05
132	Mickey Rivers	.05
133	Jim Sundberg	.05
134	Bump Wills	.05
135	Jon Matlack	.05
136	Danny Darwin	.05
137	Damaso Garcia	.05
138	Otto Velez	.05
139	John Mayberry	.05
140	Alfredo Griffin	.05
141	Alvis Woods	.05
142	Dave Stieb	.05
143	Jim Clancy	.05
144	Gary Matthews	.05
145	Bob Horner	.05
146	Dale Murphy	.25
147	Chris Chambliss	.05
148	Phil Niekro	.20
149	Glenn Hubbard	.05
150	Rick Camp	.05
151	Dave Kingman	.05
152	Bill Caudill	.05
153	Bill Buckner	.05
154	Barry Foote	.05
155	Mike Tyson	.05
156	Ivan DeJesus	.05
157	Rick Reuschel	.05
158	Ken Reitz	.05
159	George Foster	.05
160	Johnny Bench	.25
161	Dave Concepcion	.05
162	Dave Collins	.05
163	Ken Griffey	.05
164	Dan Driessen	.05
165	Tom Seaver	.25
166	Tom Hume	.05
167	Cesar Cedeno	.05
168	Rafael Landestoy	.05
169	Jose Cruz	.05
170	Art Howe	.05
171	Terry Puhl	.05
172	Joe Sambito	.05
173	Nolan Ryan	.50
174	Joe Niekro	.05
175	Dave Lopes	.05
176	Steve Garvey	.15
177	Ron Cey	.05
178	Reggie Smith	.05
179	Bill Russell	.05
180	Burt Hooton	.05
181	Jerry Reuss	.05
182	Dusty Baker	.05
183	Larry Parrish	.05
184	Gary Carter	.25
185	Rodney Scott	.05
186	Ellis Valentine	.05
187	Andre Dawson	.20
188	Warren Cromartie	.05
189	Chris Speier	.05
190	Steve Rogers	.05
191	Lee Mazzilli	.05
192	Doug Flynn	.05
193	Steve Henderson	.05
194	John Stearns	.05
195	Joel Youngblood	.05
196	Frank Taveras	.05
197	Pat Zachry	.05
198	Neil Allen	.05
199	Mike Schmidt	.30
200	Pete Rose	.50
201	Larry Bowa	.05
202	Bake McBride	.05
203	Bob Boone	.05
204	Garry Maddox	.05
205	Tug McGraw	.05
206	Steve Carlton	.20
207	National League Pennant Winner (Philadelphia Phillies Team)	.05
208	National League Pennant Winner (Philadelphia Phillies Team)	.05
209	Phil Garner	.05
210	Dave Parker	.05
211	Omar Moreno	.05
212	Mike Easler	.05
213	Bill Madlock	.05
214	Ed Ott	.05
215	Willie Stargell	.25
216	Jim Bibby	.05
217	Garry Templeton	.05
218	Sixto Lezcano	.05
219	Keith Hernandez	.05
220	George Hendrick	.05
221	Bruce Sutter	.20
222	Ken Oberkfell	.05
223	Tony Scott	.05
224	Darrell Porter	.05
225	Gene Richards	.05
226	Broderick Perkins	.05
227	Jerry Mumphrey	.05
228	Luis Salazar	.05
229	Jerry Turner	.05
230	Ozzie Smith	.30
231	John Curtis	.05
232	Rick Wise	.05
233	Terry Whitfield	.05
234	Jack Clark	.05
235	Darrell Evans	.05
236	Larry Herndon	.05
237	Milt May	.05
238	Greg Minton	.05
239	Vida Blue	.05
240	Eddie Whitson	.05
241	Cecil Cooper	.05
242	Willie Randolph	.05
243	George Brett	.30
244	Robin Yount	.25
245	Reggie Jackson	.30
246	Al Oliver	.05
247	Willie Wilson	.05
248	Rick Cerone	.05
249	Steve Stone	.05
250	Tommy John	.10
251	Rich Gossage	.05
252	Steve Garvey	.15
253	Phil Garner	.05
254	Mike Schmidt	.30
255	Garry Templeton	.05
256	George Hendrick	.05
257	Dave Parker	.05
258	Cesar Cedeno	.05
259	Gary Carter	.25
260	Jim Bibby	.05
261	Steve Carlton	.20
262	Tug McGraw	.05

Thirst Break Comics

These 2-1/2" x 1-5/8" wax paper comics were the wrapper for Thirst Break Gum, a Topps test issue distributed to parts of Ohio and Pennsylvania. Each orange foil pack contained five comics (labeled as "Sport Facts") which were folded and wrapped around five soft gum pieces. A total of 56 different comics were produced, 20 of which were baseball players. The great majority of comics found today are slightly wrinkled and stained by the gum, but are usually considered to be in Near Mint condition.

	NM/M
Complete (Baseball) Set (20):	1.00
Common Player:	1.00
Wax Pack (1):	4.00
Wax Box (48):	110.00

#		Price
1	Shortest Game	.50
2	Lefty Gomez	1.00
3	Bob Gibson	1.00
4	Hoyt Wilhelm	1.00
5	Babe Ruth	5.00
6	Toby Harrah	1.00
7	Carl Hubbell	1.00
8	Harvey Haddix	1.00
9	Steve Carlton	1.00
10	Nolan Ryan, Tom Seaver, Steve Carlton	3.50
11	Lou Brock	1.00
12	Mickey Mantle	6.00
13	Tom Seaver	2.50
14	Don Drysdale	1.00
15	Billy Williams	1.00
16	Christy Mathewson	1.00
17	Hank Aaron	4.00
18	Ron Blomberg	1.00
22	Ron Blomberg	1.00
23	Joe Nuxhall	1.00
24	Reggie Jackson	3.00

1982 Topps

At 792 cards, this was the largest issue produced up to that time, eliminating the need for double-printed cards. The 2-1/2" x 3-1/2" cards feature a front color photo with a pair of stripes down the left side. Under the player's photo are found his name, team and position. A facsimile autograph runs across the front of the picture. Specialty cards include great performances of the previous season, All-Stars, statistical leaders and "In Action" cards (indicated by "IA" in listings below). Managers and hitting/pitching leaders have cards, while rookies are shown as "Future Stars" on group cards.

	NM/M
Unopened Fact. Set (792):	180.00
Complete Set (792):	70.00
Common Player:	.10
Wax Pack (15):	5.00
Wax Box (36):	140.00
Cello Pack (28):	6.00
Cello Box (24):	130.00
Rack Pack (51):	8.00
Rack Box (24):	210.00
Vending Box (500):	60.00

#	Player	Price
1	Steve Carlton (1981 Highlight)	.25
2	Ron Davis (1981 Highlight)	.10
3	Tim Raines (1981 Highlight)	.10
4	Pete Rose (1981 Highlight)	.75
5	Nolan Ryan (1981 Highlight)	3.00
6	Fernando Valenzuela (1981 Highlight)	.10
7	Scott Sanderson	.10
8	Rich Dauer	.10
9	Ron Guidry	.15
10	Ron Guidry/IA	.10
11	Gary Alexander	.10
12	Moose Haas	.10
13	Lamar Johnson	.10
14	Steve Howe	.10
15	Ellis Valentine	.10
16	Steve Comer	.10
17	Darrell Evans	.10
18	Fernando Arroyo	.10
19	Ernie Whitt	.10
20	Garry Maddox	.10
21	Orioles Future Stars (Bob Bonner RC, Cal Ripken, Jr. RC, Jeff Schneider RC)	50.00
22	Jim Beattie	.10
23	Willie Hernandez	.10
24	Dave Frost	.10
25	Jerry Remy	.10
26	Jorge Orta	.10
27	Tom Herr	.10
28	John Urrea	.10
29	Dwayne Murphy	.10
30	Tom Seaver	1.50
31	Tom Seaver/IA	1.00
32	Gene Garber	.10
33	Jerry Morales	.10
34	Joe Sambito	.10
35	Willie Aikens	.10
36	Rangers Batting/Pitching Leaders (George Medich, Al Oliver)	.10
37	Dan Graham	.10
38	Charlie Lea	.10
39	Lou Whitaker	.10
40	Dave Parker	.10
41	Dave Parker/IA	.10
42	Rick Sofield	.10
43	Mike Cubbage	.10
44	Britt Burns	.10
45	Rick Cerone	.10
46	Jerry Augustine	.10
47	Jeff Leonard	.10
48	Bobby Castillo	.10
49	Alvis Woods	.10
50	Buddy Bell	.10
51	Chicago Cubs Future Stars (Jay Howell RC, Carlos Lezcano RC, Ty Waller RC)	.40
52	Larry Andersen	.10
53	Greg Gross	.10
54	Ron Hassey	.10
55	Rick Burleson	.10
56	Mark Littell	.10
57	Craig Reynolds	.10
58	John D'Acquisto	.10
59	Rich Gedman RC	.10
60	Tony Armas	.10
61	Tommy Boggs	.10
62	Mike Tyson	.10
63	Mario Soto	.10
64	Lynn Jones	.10
65	Terry Kennedy	.10
66	Astros Batting/Pitching Leaders (Art Howe, Nolan Ryan)	.75
67	Rich Gale	.10
68	Roy Howell	.10
69	Al Williams	.10
70	Tim Raines	.50
71	Roy Lee Jackson	.10
72	Rick Auerbach	.10
73	Buddy Solomon	.10
74	Bob Clark	.10
75	Tommy John	.20
76	Greg Pryor	.10
77	Miguel Dilone	.10
78	George Medich	.10
79	Bob Bailor	.10
80	Jim Palmer	1.00
81	Jim Palmer/IA	.30
82	Bob Welch	.10
83	Yankees Future Stars (Steve Balboni RC, Andy McGaffigan RC, Andre Robertson RC)	.15
84	Rennie Stennett	.10
85	Lynn McGlothen	.10
86	Dane Iorg	.10
87	Matt Keough	.10
88	Biff Pocoroba	.10
89	Steve Henderson	.10
90	Nolan Ryan	4.00
91	Carney Lansford	.10
92	Brad Havens	.10
93	Larry Hisle	.10
94	Andy Hassler	.10
95	Ozzie Smith	2.00
96	Royals Batting/Pitching Leaders (George Brett, Larry Gura)	.35
97	Paul Moskau	.10
98	Terry Bulling	.10
99	Barry Bonnell	.10
100	Mike Schmidt	3.00
101	Mike Schmidt/IA	1.50
102	Dan Briggs	.10
103	Bob Lacey	.10
104	Rance Mulliniks	.10
105	Kirk Gibson	.10
106	Enrique Romo	.10
107	Wayne Krenchicki	.10
108	Bob Sykes	.10
109	Dave Revering	.10
110	Carlton Fisk	1.50
111	Carlton Fisk/IA	.65
112	Billy Sample	.10
113	Steve McCatty	.10
114	Ken Landreaux	.10
115	Gaylord Perry	1.00
116	Jim Wohlford	.10
117	Rawly Eastwick	.10
118	Expos Future Stars (Terry Francona RC, Brad Mills RC, Bryn Smith RC)	.20
119	Joe Pittman	.10
120	Gary Lucas	.10
121	Ed Lynch	.10
122	Jamie Easterly	.10
123	Danny Goodwin	.10
124	Reid Nichols	.10
125	Danny Ainge	1.00
126	Braves Batting/Pitching Leaders (Rick Mahler, Claudell Washington)	.10
127	Lonnie Smith	.10
128	Frank Pastore	.10
129	Checklist 1-132	.10
130	Julio Cruz	.10
131	Stan Bahnsen	.10
132	Lee May	.10
133	Pat Underwood	.10
134	Dan Ford	.10
135	Andy Rincon	.10
136	Lenn Sakata	.10
137	George Cappuzzello	.10
138	Tony Pena	.10
139	Jeff Jones	.10
140	Ron LeFlore	.10
141	Indians Future Stars (Chris Bando, Tom Brennan, Von Hayes RC)	.20
142	Dave LaRoche	.10
143	Mookie Wilson	.10
144	Fred Breining	.10
145	Bob Horner	.10
146	Mike Griffin	.10
147	Denny Walling	.10
148	Mickey Klutts	.10
149	Pat Putnam	.10
150	Ted Simmons	.10
151	Dave Edwards	.10
152	Ramon Aviles	.10
153	Roger Erickson	.10
154	Dennis Werth	.10
155	Otto Velez	.10
156	A's Batting/Pitching Leaders (Rickey Henderson, Steve McCatty)	.10
157	Steve Crawford	.10
158	Brian Downing	.10
159	Larry Biittner	.10
160	Luis Tiant	.10
161	Batting Leaders (Carney Lansford, Bill Madlock)	.10
162	Home Run Leaders (Tony Armas, Dwight Evans, Bobby Grich, Eddie Murray, Mike Schmidt)	.25
163	RBI Leaders (Eddie Murray, Mike Schmidt)	.40
164	Stolen Base Leaders (Rickey Henderson, Tim Raines)	.35
165	Victory Leaders (Denny Martinez, Steve McCatty, Jack Morris, Tom Seaver, Pete Vuckovich)	.10
166	Strikeout Leaders (Len Barker, Fernando Valenzuela)	.10
167	ERA Leaders (Steve McCatty, Nolan Ryan)	1.50
168	Leading Relievers (Rollie Fingers, Bruce Sutter)	.15
169	Charlie Leibrandt	.10
170	Jim Bibby	.10
171	Giants Future Stars (Bob Brenly RC, Chili Davis RC, Bob Tufts RC)	2.00
172	Bill Gullickson	.10
173	Jamie Quirk	.10
174	Dave Ford	.10
175	Jerry Mumphrey	.10
176	Dewey Robinson	.10
177	John Ellis	.10
178	Dyar Miller	.10
179	Steve Garvey	.75
180	Steve Garvey/IA	.30
181	Silvio Martinez	.10
182	Larry Herndon	.10
183	Mike Proly	.10
184	Mick Kelleher	.10
185	Phil Niekro	1.00
186	Cardinals Batting/Pitching Leaders (Bob Forsch, Keith Hernandez)	.10
187	Jeff Newman	.10
188	Randy Martz	.10
189	Glenn Hoffman	.10
190	J.R. Richard	.05
191	Tim Wallach RC	2.00
192	Broderick Perkins	.10
193	Darrell Jackson	.10
194	Mike Vail	.10
195	Paul Molitor	1.50
196	Willie Upshaw	.10
197	Shane Rawley	.10
198	Chris Speier	.10
199	Don Aase	.10
200	George Brett	3.00
201	George Brett/IA	1.50
202	Rick Manning	.10
203	Blue Jays Future Stars (Jesse Barfield RC, Brian Milner, Boomer Wells)	.50
204	Gary Roenicke	.10
205	Neil Allen	.10
206	Tony Bernazard	.10
207	Rod Scurry	.10
208	Bobby Murcer	.10
209	Gary Lavelle	.10
210	Keith Hernandez	.10
211	Dan Petry	.10
212	Mario Mendoza	.10
213	Dave Stewart RC	4.00
214	Brian Asselstine	.10
215	Mike Krukow	.10
216	White Sox Batting/Pitching Leaders (Dennis Lamp, Chet Lemon)	.10
217	Bo McLaughlin	.10
218	Dave Roberts	.10
219	John Curtis	.10
220	Manny Trillo	.10
221	Jim Slaton	.10
222	Butch Wynegar	.10
223	Lloyd Moseby	.10
224	Bruce Bochte	.10
225	Mike Torrez	.10
226	Checklist 133-264	.10
227	Ray Burris	.10
228	Sam Mejias	.10
229	Geoff Zahn	.10
230	Willie Wilson	.10
231	Phillies Future Stars (Mark Davis RC, Bob Dernier RC, Ozzie Virgil RC)	.20
232	Terry Crowley	.10
233	Duane Kuiper	.10
234	Ron Hodges	.10
235	Mike Easler	.10
236	John Martin	.10
237	Rusty Kuntz	.10

238 Kevin Saucier .10
239 Jon Matlack .10
240 Bucky Dent .10
241 Bucky Dent/IA .10
242 Milt May .10
243 Bob Owchinko .10
244 Rufino Linares .10
245 Ken Reitz .10
246 Mets Batting/Pitching Leaders
(Hubie Brooks,
Mike Scott) .10
247 Pedro Guerrero .10
248 Frank LaCorte .10
249 Tim Flannery .10
250 Tug McGraw .10
251 Fred Lynn .10
252 Fred Lynn/IA .10
253 Chuck Baker .10
254 George Bell RC 1.00
255 Tony Perez 1.00
256 Tony Perez/IA .10
257 Larry Harlow .10
258 Bo Diaz .10
259 Rodney Scott .10
260 Bruce Sutter 1.00
261 Tigers Future Stars
(Howard Bailey,
Marty Castillo,
Dave Rucker) .10
262 Doug Bair .10
263 Victor Cruz .10
264 Dan Quisenberry .10
265 Al Bumbry .10
266 Rick Leach .10
267 Kurt Bevacqua .10
268 Rickey Keeton .10
269 Jim Essian .10
270 Rusty Staub .15
271 Larry Bradford .10
272 Bump Wills .10
273 Doug Bird .10
274 Bob Ojeda RC .50
275 Bob Watson .10
276 Angels Batting/Pitching
Leaders (Rod Carew,
Ken Forsch) .25
277 Terry Puhl .10
278 John Littlefield .10
279 Bill Russell .10
280 Ben Oglivie .10
281 John Verhoeven .10
282 Ken Macha .10
283 Brian Allard .10
284 Bob Grich .10
285 Sparky Lyle .10
286 Bill Fahey .10
287 Alan Bannister .10
288 Garry Templeton .10
289 Bob Stanley .10
290 Ken Singleton .10
291 Pirates Future Stars
(Vance Law, Bob Long,
Johnny Ray RC) .15
292 Dave Palmer .10
293 Rob Picciolo .10
294 Mike LaCoss .10
295 Jason Thompson .10
296 Bob Walk .10
297 Clint Hurdle .10
298 Danny Darwin .10
299 Steve Trout .10
300 Reggie Jackson 2.00
301 Reggie Jackson/IA 1.50
302 Doug Flynn .10
303 Bill Caudill .10
304 Johnnie LeMaster .10
305 Don Sutton 1.00
306 Don Sutton/IA .20
307 Randy Bass .10
308 Charlie Moore .10
309 Pete Redfern .10
310 Mike Hargrove .10
311 Dodgers Batting/Pitching
Leaders (Dusty Baker,
Burt Hooton) .10
312 Lenny Randle .10
313 John Harris .10
314 Buck Martinez .10
315 Burt Hooton .10
316 Steve Braun .10
317 Dick Ruthven .10
318 Mike Heath .10
319 Dave Rozema .10
320 Chris Chambliss .10
321 Chris Chambliss/IA .10
322 Garry Hancock .10
323 Bill Lee .10
324 Steve Dillard .10
325 Jose Cruz .10
326 Pete Falcone .10
327 Joe Nolan .10
328 Ed Farmer .10
329 U.L. Washington .10
330 Rick Wise .10
331 Benny Ayala .10
332 Don Robinson .10
333 Brewers Future Stars
(Frank DiPino RC,
Marshall Edwards,
Chuck Porter) .10
334 Aurelio Rodriguez .10
335 Jim Sundberg .10
336 Mariners Batting/Pitching
Leaders (Glenn Abbott,
Tom Paciorek) .10
337 Pete Rose/AS 1.50
338 Dave Lopes/AS .10
339 Mike Schmidt/AS 1.00

340 Dave Concepcion/AS .10
341 Andre Dawson/AS .25
342a George Foster/AS
(No autograph.) 2.00
342b George Foster/AS
(Autograph on front.) .10
343 Dave Parker/AS .10
344 Gary Carter/AS .60
345 Fernando Valenzuela/AS .10
346 Tom Seaver/AS .75
347 Bruce Sutter/AS .50
348 Derrel Thomas .10
349 George Frazier .10
350 Thad Bosley .10
351 Reds Future Stars
(Scott Brown, Geoff Combe,
Paul Householder) .10
352 Dick Davis .10
353 Jack O'Connor .10
354 Roberto Ramos .10
355 Dwight Evans .10
356 Denny Lewallyn .10
357 Butch Hobson .10
358 Mike Parrott .10
359 Jim Dwyer .10
360 Len Barker .10
361 Rafael Landestoy .10
362 Jim Wright .10
363 Bob Molinaro .10
364 Doyle Alexander .10
365 Bill Madlock .10
366 Padres Batting/Pitching
Leaders (Juan Eichelberger,
Luis Salazar) .10
367 Jim Kaat .10
368 Alex Trevino .10
369 Champ Summers .10
370 Mike Norris .10
371 Jerry Don Gleaton .10
372 Luis Gomez .10
373 Gene Nelson RC .10
374 Tim Blackwell .10
375 Dusty Baker .15
376 Chris Welsh .10
377 Kiko Garcia .10
378 Mike Caldwell .10
379 Rob Wilfong .10
380 Dave Stieb .10
381 Red Sox Future Stars
(Bruce Hurst, Dave Schmidt,
Julio Valdez) .25
382 Joe Simpson .10
383a Pascual Perez
(No position on front.) 20.00
383b Pascual Perez
("Pitcher" on front.) .10
384 Keith Moreland .10
385 Ken Forsch .10
386 Jerry White .10
387 Tom Veryzer .10
388 Joe Rudi .10
389 George Vukovich .10
390 Eddie Murray 1.50
391 Dave Tobik .10
392 Rick Bosetti .10
393 Al Hrabosky .10
394 Checklist 265-396 .10
395 Omar Moreno .10
396 Twins Batting/Pitching
Leaders (Fernando Arroyo,
John Castino) .10
397 Ken Brett .10
398 Mike Squires .10
399 Pat Zachry .10
400 Johnny Bench 1.50
401 Johnny Bench/IA .45
402 Bill Stein .10
403 Jim Tracy .10
404 Dickie Thon .10
405 Rick Reuschel .10
406 Al Holland .10
407 Danny Boone .10
408 Ed Romero .10
409 Don Cooper .10
410 Ron Cey .10
411 Ron Cey/IA .10
412 Luis Leal .10
413 Dan Meyer .10
414 Elias Sosa .10
415 Don Baylor .15
416 Marty Bystrom .10
417 Pat Kelly .10
418 Rangers Future Stars
(John Butcher,
Bobby Johnson,
Dave Schmidt RC) .10
419 Steve Stone .10
420 George Hendrick .10
421 Mark Clear .10
422 Cliff Johnson .10
423 Stan Papi .10
424 Bruce Benedict .10
425 John Candelaria .10
426 Orioles Batting/Pitching
Leaders (Eddie Murray,
Sammy Stewart) .25
427 Ron Oester .10
428 Lamarr Hoyt (LaMarr) .10
429 John Wathan .10
430 Vida Blue .10
431 Vida Blue/IA .10
432 Mike Scott .10
433 Alan Ashby .10
434 Joe Lefebvre .10
435 Robin Yount 1.50
436 Joe Strain .10
437 Juan Berenguer .10
438 Pete Mackanin .10

439 Dave Righetti RC .75
440 Jeff Burroughs .10
441 Astros Future Stars
(Danny Heep, Billy Smith,
Bobby Sprowl) .10
442 Bruce Kison .10
443 Mark Wagner .10
444 Terry Forster .10
445 Larry Parrish .10
446 Wayne Garland .10
447 Darrell Porter .10
448 Darrell Porter/IA .10
449 Luis Aguayo RC .10
450 Jack Morris .10
451 Ed Miller .10
452 Lee Smith RC 4.00
453 Art Howe .10
454 Rick Langford .10
455 Tom Burgmeier .10
456 Cubs Batting & Pitching Ldrs.
(Bill Buckner,
Randy Martz) .10
457 Tim Stoddard .10
458 Willie Montanez .10
459 Bruce Berenyi .10
460 Jack Clark .10
461 Rich Dotson .10
462 Dave Chalk .10
463 Jim Kern .10
464 Juan Bonilla .10
465 Lee Mazzilli .10
466 Randy Lerch .10
467 Mickey Hatcher .10
468 Floyd Bannister .10
469 Ed Ott .10
470 John Mayberry .10
471 Royals Future Stars
(Atlee Hammaker RC,
Mike Jones,
Darryl Motley) .15
472 Oscar Gamble .10
473 Mike Stanton .10
474 Ken Oberkfell .10
475 Alan Trammell .10
476 Brian Kingman .10
477 Steve Yeager .10
478 Ray Searage .10
479 Rowland Office .10
480 Steve Carlton 1.50
481 Steve Carlton/IA .40
482 Glenn Hubbard .10
483 Gary Woods .10
484 Ivan DeJesus .10
485 Kent Tekulve .10
486 Yankees Batting & Pitching
Ldrs. (Tommy John,
Jerry Mumphrey) .10
487 Bob McClure .10
488 Ron Jackson .10
489 Rick Dempsey .10
490 Dennis Eckersley 1.00
491 Checklist 397-528 .10
492 Joe Price .10
493 Chet Lemon .10
494 Hubie Brooks .10
495 Dennis Leonard .10
496 Johnny Grubb .10
497 Jim Anderson .10
498 Dave Bergman .10
499 Paul Mirabella .10
500 Rod Carew 1.50
501 Rod Carew/IA .40
502 Braves Future Stars
(Steve Bedrosian RC,
Brett Butler RC,
Larry Owen) 2.00
503 Julio Gonzalez .10
504 Rick Peters .10
505 Graig Nettles .10
506 Graig Nettles/IA .10
507 Terry Harper .10
508 Jody Davis RC .15
509 Harry Spilman .10
510 Fernando Valenzuela .10
511 Ruppert Jones .10
512 Jerry Dybzinski .10
513 Rick Rhoden .10
514 Joe Ferguson .10
515 Larry Bowa .10
516 Larry Bowa/IA .10
517 Mark Brouhard .10
518 Garth Iorg .10
519 Glenn Adams .10
520 Mike Flanagan .10
521 Billy Almon .10
522 Chuck Rainey .10
523 Gary Gray .10
524 Tom Hausman .10
525 Ray Knight .10
526 Expos Batting & Pitching
Ldrs. (Warren Cromartie,
Bill Gullickson) .10
527 John Henry Johnson .10
528 Matt Alexander .10
529 Allen Ripley .10
530 Dickie Noles .10
531 A's Future Stars
(Rich Bordi, Mark Budaska,
Kelvin Moore) .10
532 Toby Harrah .10
533 Joaquin Andujar .10
534 Dave McKay .10
535 Lance Parrish .10
536 Rafael Ramirez .10
537 Doug Capilla .10
538 Lou Piniella .10
539 Vern Ruhle .10
540 Andre Dawson .75

541 Barry Evans .10
542 Ned Yost .10
543 Bill Robinson .10
544 Larry Christenson .10
545 Reggie Smith .10
546 Reggie Smith/IA .10
547 Rod Carew/AS .25
548 Willie Randolph/AS .10
549 George Brett/AS 1.50
550 Bucky Dent/AS .10
551 Reggie Jackson/AS .75
552 Ken Singleton/AS .10
553 Dave Winfield/AS .60
554 Carlton Fisk/AS .25
555 Scott McGregor/AS .10
556 Jack Morris/AS .10
557 Rich Gossage/AS .10
558 John Tudor .10
559 Indians Batting & Pitching
Ldrs. (Bert Blyleven,
Mike Hargrove) .10
560 Doug Corbett .10
561 Cardinals Future Stars
(Glenn Brummer,
Luis DeLeon, Gene Roof) .10
562 Mike O'Berry .10
563 Ross Baumgarten .10
564 Doug DeCinces .10
565 Jackson Todd .10
566 Mike Jorgensen .10
567 Bob Babcock .10
568 Joe Pettini .10
569 Willie Randolph .10
570 Willie Randolph/IA .10
571 Glenn Abbott .10
572 Juan Beniquez .10
573 Rick Waits .10
574 Mike Ramsey .10
575 Al Cowens .10
576 Giants Batting & Pitching
Ldrs. (Vida Blue, Milt May) .10
577 Rick Monday .10
578 Shooty Babitt .10
579 Rick Mahler RC .10
580 Bobby Bonds .10
581 Ron Reed .10
582 Luis Pujols .10
583 Tippy Martinez .10
584 Hosken Powell .10
585 Rollie Fingers 1.00
586 Rollie Fingers/IA .15
587 Tim Lollar .10
588 Dale Berra .10
589 Dave Stapleton .10
590 Al Oliver .10
591 Al Oliver/IA .10
592 Craig Swan .10
593 Billy Smith .10
594 Renie Martin .10
595 Dave Collins .10
596 Damaso Garcia .10
597 Wayne Nordhagen .10
598 Bob Galasso .10
599 White Sox Future Stars
(Jay Loviglio,
Reggie Patterson,
Leo Sutherland) .10
600 Dave Winfield 1.50
601 Sid Monge .10
602 Freddie Patek .10
603 Rich Hebner .10
604 Orlando Sanchez .10
605 Steve Rogers .10
606 Blue Jays Batting & Pitching
Ldrs. (John Mayberry,
Dave Stieb) .10
607 Leon Durham .10
608 Jerry Royster .10
609 Rick Sutcliffe .10
610 Rickey Henderson 1.50
611 Joe Niekro .10
612 Gary Ward .10
613 Jim Gantner .10
614 Juan Eichelberger .10
615 Bob Boone .10
616 Bob Boone/IA .10
617 Scott McGregor .10
618 Tim Foli .10
619 Bill Campbell .10
620 Ken Griffey .10
621 Ken Griffey/IA .10
622 Dennis Lamp .10
623 Mets Future Stars
(Ron Gardenhire,
Terry Leach RC,
Tim Leary RC) .20
624 Fergie Jenkins 1.00
625 Hal McRae .10
626 Randy Jones .10
627 Enos Cabell .10
628 Bill Travers .10
629 Johnny Wockenfuss .10
630 Joe Charboneau .10
631 Gene Tenace .10
632 Bryan Clark .10
633 Mitchell Page .10
634 Checklist 529-660 .10
635 Ron Davis .10
636 Phillies Batting & Pitching
Ldrs. (Steve Carlton,
Pete Rose) .50
637 Rick Camp .10
638 John Milner .10
639 Ken Kravec .10
640 Cesar Cedeno .10
641 Steve Mura .10
642 Mike Scioscia .10
643 Pete Vuckovich .10

644 John Castino .10
645 Frank White .10
646 Frank White/IA .10
647 Warren Brusstar .10
648 Jose Morales .10
649 Ken Clay .10
650 Carl Yastrzemski 1.50
651 Carl Yastrzemski/IA .65
652 Steve Nicosia .10
653 Angels Future Stars
(Tom Brunansky RC,
Luis Sanchez RC,
Daryl Sconiers RC) .40
654 Jim Morrison .10
655 Joel Youngblood .10
656 Eddie Whitson .10
657 Tom Poquette .10
658 Tito Landrum .10
659 Fred Martinez .10
660 Dave Concepcion .10
661 Dave Concepcion/IA .10
662 Luis Salazar .10
663 Hector Cruz .10
664 Dan Spillner .10
665 Jim Clancy .10
666 Tigers Batting & Pitching
Ldrs. (Steve Kemp,
Dan Petry) .10
667 Jeff Reardon .15
668 Dale Murphy .75
669 Larry Milbourne .10
670 Steve Kemp .10
671 Mike Davis .10
672 Bob Knepper .10
673 Keith Drumright .10
674 Dave Goltz .10
675 Cecil Cooper .10
676 Sal Butera .10
677 Alfredo Griffin .10
678 Dave Paciorek .10
679 Sammy Stewart .10
680 Gary Matthews .10
681 Dodgers Future Stars
(Mike Marshall RC,
Ron Roenicke RC,
Dave Sax RC) .75
682 Jesse Jefferson .10
683 Phil Garner .10
684 Harold Baines .05
685 Bert Blyleven .10
686 Gary Allenson .10
687 Greg Minton .10
688 Leon Roberts .10
689 Lary Sorensen .10
690 Dave Kingman .10
691 Dan Schatzeder .10
692 Wayne Gross .10
693 Cesar Geronimo .10
694 Dave Wehrmeister .10
695 Warren Cromartie .10
696 Pirates Batting & Pitching
Ldrs. (Bill Madlock,
Buddy Solomon) .10
697 John Montefusco .10
698 Tony Scott .10
699 Dick Tidrow .10
700 George Foster .10
701 George Foster/IA .10
702 Steve Renko .10
703 Brewers Batting & Pitching
Ldrs. (Cecil Cooper,
Pete Vuckovich) .10
704 Mickey Rivers .10
705 Mickey Rivers/IA .10
706 Barry Foote .10
707 Mark Bomback .10
708 Gene Richards .10
709 Don Money .10
710 Jerry Reuss .10
711 Mariners Future Stars
(Dave Edler RC,
Dave Henderson RC,
Reggie Walton RC) .25
712 Denny Martinez .10
713 Del Unser .10
714 Jerry Koosman .10
715 Willie Stargell 1.50
716 Willie Stargell/IA .30
717 Rick Miller .10
718 Charlie Hough .10
719 Jerry Narron .10
720 Greg Luzinski .10
721 Greg Luzinski/IA .10
722 Jerry Martin .10
723 Junior Kennedy .10
724 Dave Rosello .10
725 Amos Otis .10
726 Amos Otis/IA .10
727 Sixto Lezcano .10
728 Aurelio Lopez .10
729 Jim Spencer .10
730 Gary Carter 1.50
731 Padres Future Stars
(Mike Armstrong,
Doug Gwosdz,
Fred Kuhaulua) .10
732 Mike Lum .10
733 Larry McWilliams .10
734 Mike Ivie .10
735 Rudy May .10
736 Jerry Turner .10
737 Reggie Cleveland .10
738 Dave Engle .10
739 Joey McLaughlin .10
740 Dave Lopes .10
741 Dave Lopes/IA .10
742 Dick Drago .10
743 John Stearns .10

744 Mike Witt RC .25
745 Bake McBride .10
746 Andre Thornton .10
747 John Lowenstein .10
748 Marc Hill .10
749 Bob Shirley .10
750 Jim Rice .20
751 Rick Honeycutt .10
752 Lee Lacy .10
753 Tom Brookens .10
754 Joe Morgan 1.50
755 Joe Morgan/IA .25
756 Reds Batting & Pitching Ldrs.
(Ken Griffey, Tom Seaver) .25
757 Tom Underwood .10
758 Claudell Washington .10
759 Paul Splittorff .10
760 Bill Buckner .10
761 Dave Smith .10
762 Mike Phillips .10
763 Tom Hume .10
764 Steve Swisher .10
765 Gorman Thomas .10
766 Twins Future Stars
(Lenny Faedo RC,
Kent Hrbek RC,
Tim Laudner RC) 2.00
767 Roy Smalley .10
768 Jerry Garvin .10
769 Richie Zisk .10
770 Rich Gossage .10
771 Rich Gossage/IA .10
772 Bert Campaneris .10
773 John Denny .10
774 Jay Johnstone .10
775 Bob Forsch .10
776 Mark Belanger .10
777 Tom Griffin .10
778 Kevin Hickey .10
779 Grant Jackson .10
780 Pete Rose 3.50
781 Pete Rose/IA 2.00
782 Frank Taveras .10
783 Greg Harris RC .10
784 Milt Wilcox .10
785 Dan Driessen .10
786 Red Sox Batting & Pitching
Ldrs. (Carney Lansford,
Mike Torrez) .10
787 Fred Stanley .10
788 Woodie Fryman .10
789 Checklist 661-792 .10
790 Larry Gura .10
791 Bobby Brown .10
792 Frank Tanana .10

"Blackless"

Whether through faulty pre-production work or the simple fact that the black ink may have run dry during printing, exactly half of the 1982 Topps cards can be found in a "blackless" version. All cards on the set's A, B and C press sheets can be found blackless. On regular player's cards the lack of black printing is most obvious in the absence of the facsimile autograph on front. The thin black pinstripe around the player photo is also missing on these cards. On cards in which the position was supposed to be printed in black, it will be missing on these variations. All-Star cards affected by this error will be missing the player's name. It is estimated fewer than 100 of each "blackless" card were released. Originally cards from the A and B sheets were found in metro New York, while the C cards turned up most often in the Midwest. Cards from the C sheet are much scarcer than those from the A and B sheets, although limited collector demand for full sets has kept prices in relative parity.

	NM/M
Complete Set (396):	5,500
Common Player:	12.50
8 Rich Dauer	12.50
9 Ron Guidry	20.00
10 Ron Guidry/IA	12.50
11 Gary Alexander	12.50
12 Moose Haas	12.50

No.	Player	NM/M
13	Lamar Johnson	12.50
14	Steve Howe	12.50
17	Darrell Evans	12.50
18	Fernando Arroyo	12.50
20	Garry Maddox	12.50
24	Dave Frost	12.50
26	Jorge Orta	12.50
28	John Urrea	12.50
31	Tom Seaver/IA	22.50
35	Willie Aikens	12.50
37	Dan Graham	12.50
38	Charlie Lea	12.50
39	Lou Whitaker	12.50
40	Dave Parker	12.50
42	Rick Sofield	12.50
48	Bobby Castillo	12.50
49	Alvis Woods	12.50
50	Buddy Bell	12.50
52	Larry Andersen	12.50
54	Ron Hassey	12.50
55	Rick Burleson	12.50
60	Tony Armas	12.50
64	Lynn Jones	12.50
65	Terry Kennedy	12.50
67	Rich Gale	12.50
68	Roy Howell	12.50
70	Tim Raines	12.50
71	Roy Lee Jackson	12.50
72	Rick Auerbach	12.50
73	Buddy Solomon	12.50
74	Bob Clark	12.50
77	Miguel Dilone	12.50
78	George Medich	12.50
80	Jim Palmer	40.00
81	Jim Palmer/IA	15.00
84	Rennie Stennett	12.50
87	Matt Keough	12.50
88	Biff Pocoroba	12.50
89	Steve Henderson	12.50
90	Nolan Ryan	425.00
91	Carney Lansford	12.50
92	Brad Havens	12.50
94	Andy Hassler	12.50
95	Ozzie Smith	60.00
98	Terry Bulling	12.50
99	Barry Bonnell	12.50
100	Mike Schmidt	185.00
101	Mike Schmidt/IA	130.00
105	Kirk Gibson	12.50
107	Wayne Krenchicki	12.50
109	Dave Revering	12.50
110	Carlton Fisk	45.00
112	Billy Sample	12.50
113	Steve McCatty	12.50
114	Ken Landreaux	12.50
115	Gaylord Perry	35.00
116	Jim Wohlford	12.50
117	Rawly Eastwick	12.50
119	Joe Pittman	12.50
120	Gary Lucas	12.50
122	Jamie Easterley	12.50
123	Danny Goodwin	12.50
125	Danny Ainge	22.50
127	Lonnie Smith	12.50
128	Frank Pastore	12.50
130	Julio Cruz	12.50
131	Stan Bahnsen	12.50
132	Lee May	12.50
134	Dan Ford	12.50
135	Andy Rincon	12.50
136	Lenn Sakata	12.50
137	George Cappuzzello	12.50
138	Tony Pena	12.50
140	Ron LeFlore	12.50
143	Mookie Wilson	12.50
147	Denny Walling	12.50
150	Ted Simmons	12.50
155	Otto Velez	12.50
157	Steve Crawford	12.50
158	Brian Downing	12.50
159	Larry Biittner	12.50
160	Luis Tiant	12.50
170	Jim Bibby	12.50
172	Bill Gullickson	12.50
173	Jamie Quirk	12.50
174	Dave Ford	12.50
175	Jerry Mumphrey	12.50
177	John Ellis	12.50
178	Dyar Miller	12.50
179	Steve Garvey	30.00
181	Silvio Martinez	12.50
183	Mike Proly	12.50
185	Phil Niekro	35.00
189	Glenn Hoffman	12.50
190	J.R. Richard	12.50
192	Broderick Perkins	12.50
198	Chris Speier	12.50
200	George Brett	150.00
201	George Brett/IA	55.00
204	Gary Roenicke	12.50
209	Gary Lavelle	12.50
210	Keith Hernandez	12.50
211	Dan Petry	12.50
212	Mario Mendoza	12.50
215	Mike Krukow	12.50
220	Manny Trillo	12.50
221	Jim Slaton	12.50
222	Butch Wynegar	12.50
223	Lloyd Moseby	12.50
224	Bruce Bochte	12.50
225	Mike Torrez	12.50
228	Sam Mejias	12.50
230	Willie Wilson	12.50
232	Terry Crowley	12.50
233	Duane Kuiper	12.50
234	Ron Hodges	12.50
235	Mike Easler	12.50
237	Rusty Kuntz	12.50
238	Kevin Saucier	12.50
239	Jon Matlack	12.50
240	Bucky Dent	12.50
241	Bucky Dent/IA	12.50
245	Ken Reitz	12.50
247	Pedro Guerrero	12.50
251	Fred Lynn	12.50
255	Tony Perez	35.00
256	Tony Perez/IA	12.50
257	Larry Harlow	12.50
258	Bo Diaz	12.50
259	Rodney Scott	12.50
260	Bruce Sutter	35.00
262	Doug Bair	12.50
264	Dan Quisenberry	12.50
265	Al Bumbry	12.50
267	Kurt Bevacqua	12.50
270	Rusty Staub	15.00
272	Bump Wills	12.50
275	Bob Watson	12.50
278	John Littlefield	12.50
280	Ben Oglivie	12.50
281	John Verhoeven	12.50
282	Ken Macha	12.50
283	Brian Allard	12.50
285	Sparky Lyle	12.50
287	Alan Bannister	12.50
288	Garry Templeton	12.50
289	Bob Stanley	12.50
290	Ken Singleton	12.50
297	Clint Hurdle	12.50
299	Steve Trout	12.50
300	Reggie Jackson	65.00
302	Doug Flynn	12.50
305	Don Sutton	30.00
307	Randy Bass	12.50
308	Charlie Moore	12.50
310	Mike Hargrove	12.50
312	Lenny Randle	12.50
313	John Harris	12.50
315	Burt Hooton	12.50
317	Dick Ruthven	12.50
323	Bill Lee	12.50
324	Steve Dillard	12.50
325	Jose Cruz	12.50
328	Ed Farmer	12.50
329	U.L. Washington	12.50
330	Rick Wise	12.50
332	Don Robinson	12.50
334	Aurelio Rodriguez	12.50
335	Jim Sundberg	12.50
339	Mike Schmidt/AS	130.00
340	Dave Concepcion/AS	12.50
341	Andre Dawson/AS	15.00
342	George Foster/AS	12.50
343	Dave Parker/AS	12.50
344	Gary Carter/AS	15.00
345	Fernando Valenzuela/AS	12.50
349	George Frazier	12.50
352	Dick Davis	12.50
354	Roberto Ramos	12.50
355	Dwight Evans	12.50
357	Butch Hobson	12.50
359	Jim Dwyer	12.50
360	Len Barker	12.50
363	Bob Molinaro	12.50
365	Bill Madlock	12.50
370	Mike Norris	12.50
380	Dave Stieb	12.50
382	Joe Simpson	12.50
385	Ken Forsch	12.50
387	Tom Veryzer	12.50
388	Joe Rudi	12.50
390	Eddie Murray	45.00
397	Ken Brett	12.50
398	Mike Squires	12.50
399	Pat Zachry	12.50
400	Johnny Bench	50.00
406	Al Holland	12.50
409	Don Cooper	12.50
412	Luis Leal	12.50
413	Dan Meyer	12.50
415	Don Baylor	12.50
417	Pat Kelly	12.50
419	Steve Stone	12.50
420	George Hendrick	12.50
421	Mark Clear	12.50
422	Cliff Johnson	12.50
423	Stan Papi	12.50
424	Bruce Benedict	12.50
425	John Candelaria	12.50
430	Vida Blue	12.50
440	Jeff Burroughs	12.50
442	Bruce Kison	12.50
443	Mark Wagner	12.50
445	Larry Parrish	12.50
446	Wayne Garland	12.50
448	Darrell Porter/IA	12.50
450	Jack Morris	12.50
451	Ed Miller	12.50
459	Bruce Berenyi	12.50
460	Jack Clark	12.50
461	Rich Dotson	12.50
462	Dave Chalk	12.50
463	Jim Kern	12.50
464	Juan Bonilla	12.50
465	Lee Mazzilli	12.50
467	Mickey Hatcher	12.50
468	Floyd Bannister	12.50
472	Oscar Gamble	12.50
475	Alan Trammell	12.50
476	Brian Kingman	12.50
477	Steve Yeager	12.50
480	Steve Carlton	35.00
481	Steve Carlton/IA	15.00
484	Ivan DeJesus	12.50
490	Dennis Eckersley	35.00
492	Joe Price	12.50
493	Chet Lemon	12.50
494	Hubie Brooks	12.50
495	Dennis Leonard	12.50
496	Johnny Grubb	12.50
498	Dave Bergman	12.50
499	Paul Mirabella	12.50
500	Rod Carew	45.00
501	Rod Carew/IA	15.00
503	Julio Gonzalez	12.50
507	Terry Harper	12.50
510	Fernando Valenzuela	17.50
511	Ruppert Jones	12.50
512	Jerry Dybzinski	12.50
515	Larry Bowa	12.50
518	Garth Iorg	12.50
519	Glenn Adams	12.50
520	Mike Flanagan	12.50
521	Bill Almon	12.50
523	Gary Gray	12.50
524	Tom Hausman	12.50
532	Toby Harrah	12.50
534	Dave McKay	12.50
536	Rafael Ramirez	12.50
540	Andre Dawson	30.00
541	Barry Evans	12.50
542	Ned Yost	12.50
543	Bill Robinson	12.50
547	Rod Carew/AS	25.00
548	Willie Randolph/AS	12.50
549	George Brett/AS	150.00
550	Bucky Dent/AS	15.00
551	Reggie Jackson/AS	30.00
552	Ken Singleton/AS	12.50
553	Dave Winfield/AS	25.00
554	Carlton Fisk/AS	25.00
555	Scott McGregor/AS	12.50
556	Jack Morris/AS	12.50
557	Rich Gossage/AS	12.50
560	Doug Corbett	12.50
563	Ross Baumgarten	12.50
564	Doug DeCinces	12.50
565	Jackson Todd	12.50
567	Bob Babcock	12.50
568	Joe Pettini	12.50
569	Willie Randolph	12.50
573	Rick Waits	12.50
574	Mike Ramsey	12.50
575	Al Cowens	12.50
579	Rick Mahler	12.50
580	Bobby Bonds	12.50
581	Ron Reed	12.50
582	Luis Pujols	12.50
585	Rollie Fingers	35.00
588	Dale Berra	12.50
590	Al Oliver	12.50
594	Renie Martin	12.50
600	Dave Winfield	50.00
601	Sid Monge	12.50
602	Freddie Patek	12.50
603	Richie Hebner	12.50
608	Jerry Royster	12.50
610	Rickey Henderson	150.00
611	Joe Niekro	12.50
612	Gary Ward	12.50
613	Jim Gantner	12.50
615	Bob Boone	12.50
616	Bob Boone/IA	12.50
622	Dennis Lamp	12.50
624	Fergie Jenkins	35.00
625	Hal McRae	12.50
626	Randy Jones	12.50
627	Enos Cabell	12.50
629	Johnny Wockenfuss	12.50
630	Joe Charboneau	25.00
632	Bryan Clark	12.50
635	Ron Davis	12.50
637	Rick Camp	12.50
640	Cesar Cedeno	12.50
645	Frank White	12.50
646	Frank White/IA	12.50
648	Jose Morales	12.50
649	Ken Clay	12.50
654	Jim Morrison	12.50
655	Joel Youngblood	12.50
656	Eddie Whitson	12.50
661	Dave Concepcion/IA	12.50
663	Hector Cruz	12.50
664	Dan Spillner	12.50
665	Jim Clancy	12.50
668	Dale Murphy	35.00
669	Larry Milbourne	12.50
670	Steve Kemp	12.50
672	Bob Knepper	12.50
675	Cecil Cooper	12.50
677	Alfredo Griffin	12.50
678	Tom Paciorek	12.50
684	Harold Baines	12.50
685	Bert Blyleven	12.50
686	Gary Allenson	12.50
690	Dave Kingman	12.50
691	Dan Schatzeder	12.50
694	Dave Wehrmeister	12.50
695	Warren Cromartie	12.50
700	George Foster	12.50
702	Steve Renko	12.50
704	Mickey Rivers	12.50
705	Mickey Rivers/IA	12.50
706	Barry Foote	12.50
707	Mark Bomback	12.50
708	Gene Richards	12.50
710	Jerry Reuss	12.50
713	Del Unser	12.50
715	Willie Stargell	45.00
716	Willie Stargell/IA	15.00
718	Charlie Hough	12.50
721	Greg Luzinski	12.50
721	Greg Luzinski/IA	12.50
722	Jerry Martin	12.50
724	Dave Rosello	12.50
725	Amos Otis	12.50
730	Gary Carter	45.00
735	Rudy May	12.50
737	Reggie Cleveland	12.50
738	Dave Engle	12.50
739	Joey McLaughlin	12.50
740	Dave Lopes	12.50
741	Dave Lopes/IA	12.50
742	Dick Drago	12.50
743	John Stearns	12.50
745	Bake McBride	12.50
747	John Lowenstein	12.50
748	Marc Hill	12.50
751	Rick Honeycutt	12.50
753	Tom Brookens	12.50
754	Joe Morgan	45.00
757	Tom Underwood	12.50
760	Bill Buckner	12.50
761	Dave Smith	12.50
764	Steve Swisher	12.50
765	Gorman Thomas	12.50
767	Roy Smalley	12.50
768	Jerry Garvin	12.50
769	Richie Zisk	12.50
771	Rich Gossage/IA	12.50
775	Bob Forsch	12.50
776	Mark Belanger	12.50
777	Tom Griffin	12.50
778	Kevin Hickey	12.50
780	Pete Rose	225.00
781	Pete Rose/IA	100.00
782	Frank Taveras	12.50
784	Milt Wilcox	12.50
788	Woodie Fryman	12.50
790	Larry Gura	12.50
792	Frank Tanana	12.50

Traded

CARDINALS
SHORTSTOP OZZIE SMITH

Topps released its second straight 132-card Traded set in September of 1982. Again, the 2-1/2" x 3-1/2" cards feature not only players who had been traded during the season, but also promising rookies who were given their first individual cards. The cards follow the basic design of the regular issues, but have their backs printed in red rather than the regular-issue green. As in 1981, the cards were not available in normal retail outlets and could only be purchased through regular baseball card dealers. Unlike the previous year, the cards are numbered 1-132 with the letter "T" following the number.

		NM/M
Complete Set (132):		175.00
Common Player:		.10
1T	Doyle Alexander	.10
2T	Jesse Barfield	.10
3T	Ross Baumgarten	.10
4T	Steve Bedrosian	.10
5T	Mark Belanger	.10
6T	Kurt Bevacqua	.10
7T	Tim Blackwell	.10
8T	Vida Blue	.10
9T	Bob Boone	.30
10T	Larry Bowa	.10
11T	Dan Briggs	.10
12T	Bobby Brown	.10
13T	Tom Brunansky	.10
14T	Jeff Burroughs	.10
15T	Enos Cabell	.10
16T	Bill Campbell	.10
17T	Bobby Castillo	.10
18T	Bill Caudill	.10
19T	Cesar Cedeno	.10
20T	Dave Collins	.10
21T	Doug Corbett	.10
22T	Al Cowens	.10
23T	Chili Davis	.50
24T	Dick Davis	.10
25T	Ron Davis	.10
26T	Doug DeCinces	.10
27T	Ivan DeJesus	.10
28T	Bob Dernier	.10
29T	Bo Diaz	.10
30T	Roger Erickson	.10
31T	Jim Essian	.10
32T	Ed Farmer	.10
33T	Doug Flynn	.10
34T	Tim Foli	.10
35T	Dan Ford	.10
36T	George Foster	.10
37T	Dave Frost	.10
38T	Rich Gale	.10
39T	Ron Gardenhire	.10
40T	Ken Griffey	.10
41T	Greg Harris	.10
42T	Von Hayes	.10
43T	Larry Herndon	.10
44T	Kent Hrbek	2.00
45T	Mike Ivie	.10
46T	Grant Jackson	.10
47T	Reggie Jackson	5.00
48T	Ron Jackson	.10
49T	Fergie Jenkins	2.00
50T	Lamar Johnson	.10
51T	Randy Johnson	.10
52T	Jay Johnstone	.10
53T	Mick Kelleher	.10
54T	Steve Kemp	.10
55T	Junior Kennedy	.10
56T	Jim Kern	.10
57T	Ray Knight	.10
58T	Wayne Krenchicki	.10
59T	Mike Krukow	.10
60T	Duane Kuiper	.10
61T	Mike LaCoss	.10
62T	Chet Lemon	.10
63T	Sixto Lezcano	.10
64T	Dave Lopes	.10
65T	Jerry Martin	.10
66T	Renie Martin	.10
67T	John Mayberry	.10
68T	Lee Mazzilli	.10
69T	Bake McBride	.10
70T	Dan Meyer	.10
71T	Larry Milbourne	.10
72T	Eddie Milner RC	.10
73T	Sid Monge	.10
74T	John Montefusco	.10
75T	Jose Morales	.10
76T	Keith Moreland	.10
77T	Jim Morrison	.10
78T	Rance Mulliniks	.10
79T	Steve Mura	.10
80T	Gene Nelson	.10
81T	Joe Nolan	.10
82T	Dickie Noles	.10
83T	Al Oliver	.10
84T	Jorge Orta	.10
85T	Tom Paciorek	.10
86T	Larry Parrish	.10
87T	Jack Perconte	.10
88T	Gaylord Perry	2.00
89T	Rob Picciolo	.10
90T	Joe Pittman	.10
91T	Hosken Powell	.10
92T	Mike Proly	.10
93T	Greg Pryor	.10
94T	Charlie Puleo RC	.10
95T	Shane Rawley	.10
96T	Johnny Ray	.10
97T	Dave Revering	.10
98T	Cal Ripken, Jr.	140.00
99T	Allen Ripley	.10
100T	Bill Robinson	.10
101T	Aurelio Rodriguez	.10
102T	Joe Rudi	.10
103T	Steve Sax	.50
104T	Dan Schatzeder	.10
105T	Bob Shirley	.10
106T	Eric Show RC	.10
107T	Roy Smalley	.10
108T	Lonnie Smith	.10
109T	Ozzie Smith	20.00
110T	Reggie Smith	.10
111T	Lary Sorensen	.10
112T	Elias Sosa	.10
113T	Mike Stanton	.10
114T	Steve Stroughter	.10
115T	Champ Summers	.10
116T	Rick Sutcliffe	.10
117T	Frank Tanana	.10
118T	Frank Taveras	.10
119T	Garry Templeton	.10
120T	Alex Trevino	.10
121T	Jerry Turner	.10
122T	Ed Vande Berg RC	.10
123T	Tom Veryzer	.10
124T	Ron Washington	.10
125T	Bob Watson	.10
126T	Dennis Werth	.10
127T	Eddie Whitson	.10
128T	Rob Wilfong	.10
129T	Bump Wills	.10
130T	Gary Woods	.10
131T	Butch Wynegar	.10
132T	Checklist 1-132	.10

Team Leaders Sheet

Available via a special mail-in offer, this 10-1/2" x 23" uncut sheet contained the 26 team batting and pitching leaders cards plus a card offering Topps collectors boxes. The team leader cards are identical to those issued in packs.

		NM/M
Team Leaders Sheet		10.00

Insert Stickers

85
WILLIE STARGELL
1st Base

ALBUMS COMING SOON!
SAVE THIS STICKER . . . and place it in your own 1982 Topps Baseball Sticker Album. Albums and ALL stickers are sold where Topps Baseball cards are available.

IT'S **Topps** FOR SPORTS
© 1982 Topps Chewing Gum, Inc.

This 48-player set is actually an abbreviated version of the regular 1982 Topps sticker set with different backs. Used to promote the 1982 sticker set, Topps inserted these stickers in its baseball card wax packs. They are identical to the regular 1982 stickers, except for the backs, which advertise that the Topps sticker album will be "Coming Soon." The 48 stickers retain the same numbers used in the regular sticker set, resulting in the smaller set being skip-numbered.

		NM/M
Complete Set (48):		3.00
Common Player:		.05
17	Chris Chambliss	.05
21	Bruce Benedict	.05
25	Leon Durham	.05
29	Bill Buckner	.05
33	Dave Collins	.05
37	Dave Concepcion	.05
41	Nolan Ryan	1.00
45	Bob Knepper	.05
49	Ken Landreaux	.05
53	Burt Hooton	.05
57	Andre Dawson	.15
61	Gary Carter	.25
65	Joel Youngblood	.05
69	Ellis Valentine	.05
73	Garry Maddox	.05
77	Bob Boone	.05
81	Omar Moreno	.05
85	Willie Stargell	.25
89	Ken Oberkfell	.05
93	Darrell Porter	.05
97	Juan Eichelberger	.05
101	Luis Salazar	.05
105	Enos Cabell	.05
109	Larry Herndon	.05
143	Scott McGregor	.05
148	Mike Flanagan	.05
151	Mike Torrez	.05
161	Carney Lansford	.05
161	Fred Lynn	.05
166	Rich Dotson	.05
171	Tony Bernazard	.05
176	Bo Diaz	.05
181	Alan Trammell	.05
186	Milt Wilcox	.05
191	Dennis Leonard	.05
196	Willie Aikens	.05
201	Ted Simmons	.05
206	Hosken Powell	.05
211	Roger Erickson	.05
215	Graig Nettles	.05
216	Reggie Jackson	.45
221	Rickey Henderson	.25
226	Cliff Johnson	.05
231	Jeff Burroughs	.05
236	Tom Paciorek	.05
241	Pat Putnam	.05
246	Lloyd Moseby	.05
251	Barry Bonnell	.05

Stickers

The 1982 Topps sticker set is complete at 260 stickers and includes another series of "foil" All-Stars. The stickers measure 1-15/16" x 2-9/16" and feature full-color photos surrounded by a red border for

American League players or a blue border for National League players. They are numbered on both the front and back and were designed to be mounted in a special album.

	NM/M
Complete Set (260):	7.50
Common Player:	.05
Sticker Album:	2.00
Wax Pack (5):	.25
Wax Box (100):	15.00

#	Player	Price
1	Bill Madlock	.05
2	Carney Lansford	.05
3	Mike Schmidt	.30
4	Tony Armas, Dwight Evans, Bobby Grich, Eddie Murray	.05
5	Mike Schmidt	.30
6	Eddie Murray	.25
7	Tim Raines	.05
8	Rickey Henderson	.25
9	Tom Seaver	.25
10	Denny Martinez, Steve McCatty, Jack Morris, Pete Vuckovich	.05
11	Fernando Valenzuela	.05
12	Len Barker	.05
13	Nolan Ryan	.50
14	Steve McCatty	.05
15	Bruce Sutter	.20
16	Rollie Fingers	.20
17	Chris Chambliss	.05
18	Bob Horner	.05
19	Dale Murphy	.15
20	Phil Niekro	.20
21	Bruce Benedict	.05
22	Claudell Washington	.05
23	Glenn Hubbard	.05
24	Rick Camp	.05
25	Leon Durham	.05
26	Ken Reitz	.05
27	Dick Tidrow	.05
28	Tim Blackwell	.05
29	Bill Buckner	.05
30	Steve Henderson	.05
31	Mike Krukow	.05
32	Ivan DeJesus	.05
33	Dave Collins	.05
34	Ron Oester	.05
35	Johnny Bench	.25
36	Tom Seaver	.25
37	Dave Concepcion	.05
38	Ken Griffey	.05
39	Ray Knight	.05
40	George Foster	.05
41	Nolan Ryan	.50
42	Terry Puhl	.05
43	Art Howe	.05
44	Jose Cruz	.05
45	Bob Knepper	.05
46	Craig Reynolds	.05
47	Cesar Cedeno	.05
48	Alan Ashby	.05
49	Ken Landreaux	.05
50	Fernando Valenzuela	.05
51	Ron Cey	.05
52	Dusty Baker	.05
53	Burt Hooton	.05
54	Steve Garvey	.15
55	Pedro Guerrero	.05
56	Jerry Reuss	.05
57	Andre Dawson	.20
58	Chris Speier	.05
59	Steve Rogers	.05
60	Warren Cromartie	.05
61	Gary Carter	.25
62	Tim Raines	.05
63	Scott Sanderson	.05
64	Larry Parrish	.05
65	Joel Youngblood	.05
66	Neil Allen	.05
67	Lee Mazzilli	.05
68	Hubie Brooks	.05
69	Ellis Valentine	.05
70	Doug Flynn	.05
71	Pat Zachry	.05
72	Dave Kingman	.05
73	Garry Maddox	.05
74	Mike Schmidt	.30
75	Steve Carlton	.25
76	Manny Trillo	.05
77	Bob Boone	.05
78	Pete Rose	.40
79	Gary Matthews	.05
80	Larry Bowa	.05
81	Omar Moreno	.05
82	Rick Rhoden	.05
83	Bill Madlock	.05
84	Mike Easler	.05
85	Willie Stargell	.25
86	Jim Bibby	.05
87	Dave Parker	.05
88	Tim Foli	.05
89	Ken Oberkfell	.05
90	Bob Forsch	.05
91	George Hendrick	.05
92	Keith Hernandez	.05
93	Darrell Porter	.05
94	Bruce Sutter	.20
95	Sixto Lezcano	.05
96	Garry Templeton	.05
97	Juan Eichelberger	.05
98	Broderick Perkins	.05
99	Ruppert Jones	.05
100	Terry Kennedy	.05
101	Luis Salazar	.05

#	Player	Price
102	Gary Lucas	.05
103	Gene Richards	.05
104	Ozzie Smith	.30
105	Enos Cabell	.05
106	Jack Clark	.05
107	Greg Minton	.05
108	Johnnie LeMaster	.05
109	Larry Herndon	.05
110	Milt May	.05
111	Vida Blue	.05
112	Darrell Evans	.05
113	Len Barker	.05
114	Julio Cruz	.05
115	Billy Martin	.05
116	Tim Raines	.05
117	Pete Rose	.40
118	Bill Stein	.05
119	Fernando Valenzuela	.05
120	Carl Yastrzemski	.25
121	Pete Rose	.40
122	Manny Trillo	.05
123	Mike Schmidt	.30
124	Dave Concepcion	.05
125	Andre Dawson	.20
126	George Foster	.05
127	Dave Parker	.05
128	Gary Carter	.25
129	Steve Carlton	.25
130	Bruce Sutter	.20
131	Rod Carew	.25
132	Jerry Remy	.05
133	George Brett	.30
134	Rick Burleson	.05
135	Dwight Evans	.05
136	Ken Singleton	.05
137	Dave Winfield	.25
138	Carlton Fisk	.25
139	Jack Morris	.05
140	Rich Gossage	.05
141	Al Bumbry	.05
142	Doug DeCinces	.05
143	Scott McGregor	.05
144	Ken Singleton	.05
145	Eddie Murray	.25
146	Jim Palmer	.20
147	Rich Dauer	.05
148	Mike Flanagan	.05
149	Jerry Remy	.05
150	Jim Rice	.15
151	Mike Torrez	.05
152	Tony Perez	.25
153	Dwight Evans	.05
154	Mark Clear	.05
155	Carl Yastrzemski	.25
156	Carney Lansford	.05
157	Rick Burleson	.05
158	Don Baylor	.10
159	Ken Forsch	.05
160	Rod Carew	.25
161	Fred Lynn	.05
162	Bob Grich	.05
163	Dan Ford	.05
164	Butch Hobson	.05
165	Greg Luzinski	.05
166	Rich Dotson	.05
167	Billy Almon	.05
168	Chet Lemon	.05
169	Steve Trout	.05
170	Carlton Fisk	.25
171	Tony Bernazard	.05
172	Ron LeFlore	.05
173	Bert Blyleven	.05
174	Andre Thornton	.05
175	Jorge Orta	.05
176	Bo Diaz	.05
177	Toby Harrah	.05
178	Len Barker	.05
179	Rick Manning	.05
180	Mike Hargrove	.05
181	Alan Trammell	.05
182	Al Cowens	.05
183	Jack Morris	.05
184	Kirk Gibson	.05
185	Steve Kemp	.05
186	Milt Wilcox	.05
187	Lou Whitaker	.05
188	Lance Parrish	.05
189	Willie Wilson	.05
190	George Brett	.30
191	Dennis Leonard	.05
192	John Wathan	.05
193	Frank White	.05
194	Amos Otis	.05
195	Larry Gura	.05
196	Willie Aikens	.05
197	Ben Oglivie	.05
198	Rollie Fingers	.20
199	Cecil Cooper	.05
200	Paul Molitor	.20
201	Ted Simmons	.05
202	Pete Vuckovich	.05
203	Robin Yount	.25
204	Gorman Thomas	.05
205	Rob Wilfong	.05
206	Hosken Powell	.05
207	Roy Smalley	.05
208	Butch Wynegar	.05
209	John Castino	.05
210	Doug Corbett	.05
211	Roger Erickson	.05
212	Mickey Hatcher	.05
213	Dave Winfield	.25
214	Tommy John	.10
215	Graig Nettles	.25
216	Reggie Jackson	.25
217	Rich Gossage	.05
218	Rick Cerone	.05
219	Willie Randolph	.05

#	Player	Price
220	Jerry Mumphrey	.05
221	Rickey Henderson	.25
222	Mike Norris	.05
223	Jim Spencer	.05
224	Tony Armas	.05
225	Matt Keough	.05
226	Cliff Johnson	.05
227	Dwayne Murphy	.05
228	Steve McCatty	.05
229	Richie Zisk	.05
230	Lenny Randle	.05
231	Jeff Burroughs	.05
232	Bruce Bochte	.05
233	Gary Gray	.05
234	Floyd Bannister	.05
235	Julio Cruz	.05
236	Tom Paciorek	.05
237	Danny Darwin	.05
238	Buddy Bell	.05
239	Al Oliver	.05
240	Jim Sundberg	.05
241	Pat Putnam	.05
242	Steve Comer	.05
243	Mickey Rivers	.05
244	Bump Wills	.05
245	Damaso Garcia	.05
246	Lloyd Moseby	.05
247	Ernie Whitt	.05
248	John Mayberry	.05
249	Otto Velez	.05
250	Dave Stieb	.05
251	Barry Bonnell	.05
252	Alfredo Griffin	.05
253	1981 N.L. Championship (Gary Carter)	.10
254	1981 A.L. Championship (Mike Heath, Larry Milbourne)	.05
255	1981 World Champions (Los Angeles Dodgers Team)	.05
256	1981 World Champions (Los Angeles Dodgers Team)	.05
257	1981 World Series - Game 3 (Fernando Valenzuela)	.05
258	1981 World Series - Game 4 (Steve Garvey)	.10
259	1981 World Series - Game 5 (Jerry Reuss, Steve Yeager)	.05
260	1981 World Series - Game 6 (Pedro Guerrero)	.05

1983 Topps

The 1983 Topps set totals 792 cards. Missing among the regular 2-1/2" x 3-1/2" cards are some form of future stars cards, as Topps was saving for the now-established late season "Traded" set. The 1983 cards carry a large color photo as well as a smaller color photo on the front, quite similar in design to the 1963 set. Team colors frame the card, which, at the bottom, have the player's name, position and team. At the upper right-hand corner is a Topps Logo. The backs are horizontal and include statistics, personal information and 1982 highlights. Specialty cards include record-breaking performances, league leaders, All-Stars, numbered checklists "Team Leaders" and "Super Veteran" cards which are horizontal with a current and first-season picture of the honored player.

	NM/M
Complete Set (792):	60.00
Common Player:	.05
Wax Pack (15):	3.00
Wax Box (36):	110.00
Crimp-End Test Pack (15):	4.00
Crimp-end Test Box (36):	110.00
Cello Pack (28):	5.00
Cello Box (24):	125.00
Rack Pack (51):	7.50
Rack Box (24):	175.00
Vending Box (500):	65.00

#	Player	Price
1	Tony Armas (Record Breaker)	.05
2	Rickey Henderson (Record Breaker)	.75
3	Greg Minton (Record Breaker)	.05
4	Lance Parrish (Record Breaker)	.05
5	Manny Trillo (Record Breaker)	.05
6	John Wathan (Record Breaker)	.05
7	Gene Richards	.05
8	Steve Balboni	.05
9	Joey McLaughlin	.05
10	Gorman Thomas	.05
11	Billy Gardner	.05
12	Paul Mirabella	.05
13	Larry Herndon	.05
14	Frank LaCorte	.05
15	Ron Cey	.05
16	George Vukovich	.05
17	Kent Tekulve	.05
18	Kent Tekulve (Super Veteran)	.05
19	Oscar Gamble	.05
20	Carlton Fisk	2.00
21	Orioles Batting & Pitching Ldrs. (Eddie Murray, Jim Palmer)	.25
22	Randy Martz	.05
23	Mike Heath	.05
24	Steve Mura	.05
25	Hal McRae	.05
26	Jerry Royster	.05
27	Doug Corbett	.05
28	Bruce Bochte	.05
29	Randy Jones	.05
30	Jim Rice	.15
31	Bill Gullickson	.05
32	Dave Bergman	.05
33	Jack O'Connor	.05
34	Paul Householder	.05
35	Rollie Fingers	.75
36	Rollie Fingers (Super Veteran)	.15
37	Darrell Johnson	.05
38	Tim Flannery	.05
39	Terry Puhl	.05
40	Fernando Valenzuela	.05
41	Jerry Turner	.05
42	Dale Murray	.05
43	Bob Dernier	.05
44	Don Robinson	.05
45	John Mayberry	.05
46	Richard Dotson	.05
47	Dave McKay	.05
48	Lary Sorensen	.05
49	Willie McGee RC	1.50
50	Bob Horner	.05
51	Cubs Batting & Pitching Ldrs. (Leon Durham, Fergie Jenkins)	.05
52	Onix Concepcion RC	.05
53	Mike Witt	.05
54	Jim Maler	.05
55	Mookie Wilson	.05
56	Chuck Rainey	.05
57	Tim Blackwell	.05
58	Al Holland	.05
59	Benny Ayala	.05
60	Johnny Bench	2.00
61	Johnny Bench (Super Veteran)	.75
62	Bob McClure	.05
63	Rick Monday	.05
64	Bill Stein	.05
65	Jack Morris	.05
66	Bob Lillis	.05
67	Sal Butera	.05
68	Eric Show RC	.15
69	Lee Lacy	.05
70	Steve Carlton	2.00
71	Steve Carlton (Super Veteran)	.30
72	Tom Paciorek	.05
73	Allen Ripley	.05
74	Julio Gonzalez	.05
75	Amos Otis	.05
76	Rick Mahler	.05
77	Hosken Powell	.05
78	Bill Caudill	.05
79	Mick Kelleher	.05
80	George Foster	.05
81	Yankees Batting & Pitching Ldrs. (Jerry Mumphrey, Dave Righetti)	.05
82	Bruce Hurst	.05
83	Ryne Sandberg RC	15.00
84	Milt May	.05
85	Ken Singleton	.05
86	Tom Hume	.05
87	Joe Rudi	.05
88	Jim Gantner	.05
89	Leon Roberts	.05
90	Jerry Reuss	.05
91	Larry Milbourne	.05
92	Mike LaCoss	.05
93	John Castino	.05
94	Dave Edwards	.05
95	Alan Trammell	.05
96	Dick Howser	.05
97	Ross Baumgarten	.05
98	Vance Law	.05
99	Dickie Noles	.05
100	Pete Rose	4.00
101	Pete Rose (Super Veteran)	2.00
102	Dave Beard	.05
103	Darrell Porter	.05
104	Bob Walk	.05
105	Don Baylor	.05
106	Gene Nelson	.05
107	Mike Jorgensen	.05

#	Player	Price
108	Glenn Hoffman	.05
109	Luis Leal	.05
110	Ken Griffey	.05
111	Expos Batting & Pitching Ldrs. (Al Oliver, Steve Rogers)	.05
112	Bob Shirley	.05
113	Ron Roenicke	.05
114	Jim Slaton	.05
115	Chili Davis	.05
116	Dave Schmidt	.05
117	Alan Knicely	.05
118	Chris Welsh	.05
119	Tom Brookens	.05
120	Len Barker	.05
121	Mickey Hatcher	.05
122	Jimmy Smith	.05
123	George Frazier	.05
124	Marc Hill	.05
125	Leon Durham	.05
126	Joe Torre	.25
127	Preston Hanna	.05
128	Mike Ramsey	.05
129	Checklist 1-132	.05
130	Dave Stieb	.05
131	Ed Ott	.05
132	Todd Cruz	.05
133	Jim Barr	.05
134	Hubie Brooks	.05
135	Dwight Evans	.05
136	Willie Aikens	.05
137	Woodie Fryman	.05
138	Rick Dempsey	.05
139	Bruce Berenyi	.05
140	Willie Randolph	.05
141	Indians Batting & Pitching Ldrs. (Toby Harrah, Rick Sutcliffe)	.05
142	Mike Caldwell	.05
143	Joe Pettini	.05
144	Mark Wagner	.05
145	Don Sutton	.75
146	Don Sutton (Super Veteran)	.20
147	Rick Leach	.05
148	Dave Roberts	.05
149	Johnny Ray	.05
150	Bruce Sutter	.75
151	Bruce Sutter (Super Veteran)	.50
152	Jay Johnstone	.05
153	Jerry Koosman	.05
154	Johnnie LeMaster	.05
155	Dan Quisenberry	.05
156	Billy Martin	.15
157	Steve Bedrosian	.05
158	Rob Wilfong	.05
159	Mike Stanton	.05
160	Dave Kingman	.05
161	Dave Kingman (Super Veteran)	.05
162	Mark Clear	.05
163	Cal Ripken, Jr.	6.00
164	Dave Palmer	.05
165	Dan Driessen	.05
166	John Pacella	.05
167	Mark Brouhard	.05
168	Juan Eichelberger	.05
169	Doug Flynn	.05
170	Steve Howe	.05
171	Giants Batting & Pitching Ldrs. (Bill Laskey, Joe Morgan)	.05
172	Vern Ruhle	.05
173	Jim Morrison	.05
174	Jerry Ujdur	.05
175	Bo Diaz	.05
176	Dave Righetti	.05
177	Harold Baines	.05
178	Luis Tiant	.05
179	Luis Tiant (Super Veteran)	.05
180	Rickey Henderson	2.00
181	Terry Felton	.05
182	Mike Fischlin	.05
183	Ed Vande Berg RC	.05
184	Bob Clark	.05
185	Tim Lollar	.05
186	Whitey Herzog	.05
187	Terry Leach	.05
188	Rick Miller	.05
189	Dan Schatzeder	.05
190	Cecil Cooper	.05
191	Joe Price	.05
192	Floyd Rayford	.05
193	Harry Spilman	.05
194	Cesar Geronimo	.05
195	Bob Stoddard	.05
196	Bill Fahey	.05
197	Jim Eisenreich RC	.50
198	Kiko Garcia	.05
199	Marty Bystrom	.05
200	Rod Carew	2.00
201	Rod Carew (Super Veteran)	.35
202	Blue Jays Batting & Pitching Ldrs. (Damaso Garcia, Dave Stieb)	.05
203	Mike Morgan	.05
204	Junior Kennedy	.05
205	Dave Parker	.05
206	Ken Oberkfell	.05
207	Rick Camp	.05
208	Dan Meyer	.05
209	Mike Moore RC	.15
210	Jack Clark	.05
211	John Denny	.05
212	John Stearns	.05
213	Tom Burgmeier	.05

#	Player	Price
214	Jerry White	.05
215	Mario Soto	.05
216	Tony LaRussa	.05
217	Tim Stoddard	.05
218	Roy Howell	.05
219	Mike Armstrong	.05
220	Dusty Baker	.05
221	Joe Niekro	.05
222	Damaso Garcia	.05
223	John Montefusco	.05
224	Mickey Rivers	.05
225	Enos Cabell	.05
226	Enrique Romo	.05
227	Chris Bando	.05
228	Joaquin Andujar	.05
229	Phillies Batting & Pitching Leaders (Steve Carlton, Bo Diaz)	.15
230	Fergie Jenkins	.75
231	Fergie Jenkins (Super Veteran)	.20
232	Tom Brunansky	.05
233	Wayne Gross	.05
234	Larry Andersen	.05
235	Claudell Washington	.05
236	Steve Renko	.05
237	Dan Norman	.05
238	Bud Black RC	.25
239	Dave Stapleton	.05
240	Rich Gossage	.05
241	Rich Gossage (Super Veteran)	.05
242	Joe Nolan	.05
243	Duane Walker	.05
244	Dwight Bernard	.05
245	Steve Sax	.05
246	George Bamberger	.05
247	Dave Smith	.05
248	Bake McBride	.05
249	Checklist 133-264	.05
250	Bill Buckner	.05
251	Alan Wiggins RC	.05
252	Luis Aguayo	.05
253	Larry McWilliams	.05
254	Rick Cerone	.05
255	Gene Garber	.05
256	Gene Garber (Super Veteran)	.05
257	Jesse Barfield	.05
258	Manny Castillo	.05
259	Jeff Jones	.05
260	Steve Kemp	.05
261	Tigers Batting & Pitching Ldrs. (Larry Herndon, Dan Petry)	.05
262	Ron Jackson	.05
263	Renie Martin	.05
264	Jamie Quirk	.05
265	Joel Youngblood	.05
266	Paul Boris	.05
267	Terry Francona	.05
268	Storm Davis RC	.05
269	Ron Oester	.05
270	Dennis Eckersley	.75
271	Ed Romero	.05
272	Frank Tanana	.05
273	Mark Belanger	.05
274	Terry Kennedy	.05
275	Ray Knight	.05
276	Gene Mauch	.05
277	Rance Mulliniks	.05
278	Kevin Hickey	.05
279	Greg Gross	.05
280	Bert Blyleven	.05
281	Andre Robertson	.05
282	Reggie Smith	.05
283	Reggie Smith (Super Veteran)	.05
284	Jeff Lahti	.05
285	Lance Parrish	.05
286	Rick Langford	.05
287	Bobby Brown	.05
288	Joe Cowley RC	.05
289	Jerry Dybzinski	.05
290	Jeff Reardon	.05
291	Pirates Batting & Pitching Ldrs. (John Candelaria, Bill Madlock)	.05
292	Craig Swan	.05
293	Glenn Gulliver	.05
294	Dave Engle	.05
295	Jerry Remy	.05
296	Greg Harris	.05
297	Ned Yost	.05
298	Floyd Chiffer	.05
299	George Wright	.05
300	Mike Schmidt	3.00
301	Mike Schmidt (Super Veteran)	1.50
302	Ernie Whitt	.05
303	Miguel Dilone	.05
304	Dave Rucker	.05
305	Larry Bowa	.05
306	Tom Lasorda	.25
307	Lou Piniella	.05
308	Jesus Vega	.05
309	Jeff Leonard	.05
310	Greg Luzinski	.05
311	Glenn Brummer	.05
312	Brian Kingman	.05
313	Gary Gray	.05
314	Ken Dayley RC	.05
315	Rick Burleson	.05
316	Paul Splittorff	.05
317	Gary Rajsich	.05
318	John Tudor	.05
319	Lenn Sakata	.05
320	Steve Rogers	.05

No.	Player	Price
321	Brewers Batting & Pitching Ldrs. (Pete Vuckovich, Robin Yount)	.10
322	Dave Van Gorder	.05
323	Luis DeLeon	.05
324	Mike Marshall	.05
325	Von Hayes	.05
326	Garth Iorg	.05
327	Bobby Castillo	.05
328	Craig Reynolds	.05
329	Randy Niemann	.05
330	Buddy Bell	.05
331	Mike Krukow	.05
332	Glenn Wilson **RC**	.05
333	Dave LaRoche	.05
334	Dave LaRoche (Super Veteran)	.05
335	Steve Henderson	.05
336	Rene Lachemann	.05
337	Tito Landrum	.05
338	Bob Owchinko	.05
339	Terry Harper	.05
340	Larry Gura	.05
341	Doug DeCinces	.05
342	Atlee Hammaker	.05
343	Bob Bailor	.05
344	Roger LaFrancois	.05
345	Jim Clancy	.05
346	Joe Pittman	.05
347	Sammy Stewart	.05
348	Alan Bannister	.05
349	Checklist 265-396	.05
350	Robin Yount	2.00
351	Reds Batting & Pitching Ldrs. (Cesar Cedeno, Mario Soto)	.05
352	Mike Scioscia	.05
353	Steve Comer	.05
354	Randy S. Johnson	.05
355	Jim Bibby	.05
356	Gary Woods	.05
357	Len Matuszek **RC**	.05
358	Jerry Garvin	.05
359	Dave Collins	.05
360	Nolan Ryan	5.00
361	Nolan Ryan (Super Veteran)	4.00
362	Bill Almon	.05
363	John Stuper **RC**	.05
364	Brett Butler	.05
365	Dave Lopes	.05
366	Dick Williams	.05
367	Bud Anderson	.05
368	Richie Zisk	.05
369	Jesse Orosco	.05
370	Gary Carter	2.00
371	Mike Richardt	.05
372	Terry Crowley	.05
373	Kevin Saucier	.05
374	Wayne Krenchicki	.05
375	Pete Vuckovich	.05
376	Ken Landreaux	.05
377	Lee May	.05
378	Lee May (Super Veteran)	.05
379	Guy Sularz	.05
380	Ron Davis	.05
381	Red Sox Batting & Pitching Ldrs. (Jim Rice, Bob Stanley)	.05
382	Bob Knepper	.05
383	Ozzie Virgil	.05
384	Dave Dravecky **RC**	.50
385	Mike Easler	.05
386	Rod Carew/AS	.35
387	Bob Grich/AS	.05
388	George Brett/AS	1.50
389	Robin Yount/AS	.60
390	Reggie Jackson/AS	1.00
391	Rickey Henderson/AS	.50
392	Fred Lynn/AS	.05
393	Carlton Fisk/AS	.35
394	Pete Vuckovich/AS	.05
395	Larry Gura/AS	.05
396	Dan Quisenberry/AS	.05
397	Pete Rose/AS	2.00
398	Manny Trillo/AS	.05
399	Mike Schmidt/AS	1.50
400	Dave Concepcion/AS	.05
401	Dale Murphy/AS	.20
402	Andre Dawson/AS	.35
403	Tim Raines/AS	.05
404	Gary Carter/AS	.35
405	Steve Rogers/AS	.05
406	Steve Carlton/AS	.30
407	Bruce Sutter/AS	.25
408	Rudy May	.05
409	Marvis Foley	.05
410	Phil Niekro	.75
411	Phil Niekro (Super Veteran)	.25
412	Rangers Batting & Pitching Ldrs. (Buddy Bell, Charlie Hough)	.05
413	Matt Keough	.05
414	Julio Cruz	.05
415	Bob Forsch	.05
416	Joe Ferguson	.05
417	Tom Hausman	.05
418	Greg Pryor	.05
419	Steve Crawford	.05
420	Al Oliver	.05
421	Al Oliver (Super Veteran)	.05
422	George Cappuzzello	.05
423	Tom Lawless **RC**	.05
424	Jerry Augustine	.05
425	Pedro Guerrero	.05
426	Earl Weaver	.25
427	Roy Lee Jackson	.05
428	Champ Summers	.05
429	Eddie Whitson	.05
430	Kirk Gibson	.05
431	Gary Gaetti **RC**	.75
432	Porfirio Altamirano	.05
433	Dale Berra	.05
434	Dennis Lamp	.05
435	Tony Armas	.05
436	Bill Campbell	.05
437	Rick Sweet	.05
438	Dave LaPoint **RC**	.05
439	Rafael Ramirez	.05
440	Ron Guidry	.20
441	Astros Batting & Pitching Ldrs. (Ray Knight, Joe Niekro)	.05
442	Brian Downing	.05
443	Don Hood	.05
444	Wally Backman **RC**	.05
445	Mike Flanagan	.05
446	Reid Nichols	.05
447	Bryn Smith	.05
448	Darrell Evans	.05
449	Eddie Milner **RC**	.05
450	Ted Simmons	.05
451	Ted Simmons (Super Veteran)	.05
452	Lloyd Moseby	.05
453	Lamar Johnson	.05
454	Bob Welch	.05
455	Sixto Lezcano	.05
456	Lee Elia	.05
457	Milt Wilcox	.05
458	Ron Washington	.05
459	Ed Farmer	.05
460	Roy Smalley	.05
461	Steve Trout	.05
462	Steve Nicosia	.05
463	Gaylord Perry	.75
464	Gaylord Perry (Super Veteran)	.20
465	Lonnie Smith	.05
466	Tom Underwood	.05
467	Rufino Linares	.05
468	Dave Goltz	.05
469	Ron Gardenhire	.05
470	Greg Minton	.05
471	Royals Batting & Pitching Ldrs. (Vida Blue, Willie Wilson)	.05
472	Gary Allenson	.05
473	John Lowenstein	.05
474	Ray Burris	.05
475	Cesar Cedeno	.05
476	Rob Picciolo	.05
477	Tom Niedenfuer **RC**	.05
478	Phil Garner	.05
479	Charlie Hough	.05
480	Toby Harrah	.05
481	Scot Thompson	.05
482	Tony Gwynn **RC**	25.00
483	Lynn Jones	.05
484	Dick Ruthven	.05
485	Omar Moreno	.05
486	Clyde King	.05
487	Jerry Hairston Sr.	.05
488	Alfredo Griffin	.05
489	Tom Herr	.05
490	Jim Palmer	1.50
491	Jim Palmer (Super Veteran)	.20
492	Paul Serna	.05
493	Steve McCatty	.05
494	Bob Brenly	.05
495	Warren Cromartie	.05
496	Tom Veryzer	.05
497	Rick Sutcliffe	.05
498	Wade Boggs **RC**	15.00
499	Jeff Little	.05
500	Reggie Jackson	2.00
501	Reggie Jackson (Super Veteran)	.75
502	Braves Batting & Pitching Ldrs. (Dale Murphy, Phil Niekro)	.20
503	Moose Haas	.05
504	Don Werner	.05
505	Garry Templeton	.05
506	Jim Gott **RC**	.25
507	Tony Scott	.05
508	Tom Filer	.05
509	Lou Whitaker	.05
510	Tug McGraw	.05
511	Tug McGraw (Super Veteran)	.20
512	Doyle Alexander	.05
513	Fred Stanley	.05
514	Rudy Law	.05
515	Gene Tenace	.05
516	Bill Virdon	.05
517	Gary Ward	.05
518	Bill Laskey	.05
519	Terry Bulling	.05
520	Fred Lynn	.05
521	Bruce Benedict	.05
522	Pat Zachry	.05
523	Carney Lansford	.05
524	Tom Brennan	.05
525	Frank White	.05
526	Checklist 397-528	.05
527	Larry Biittner	.05
528	Jamie Easterly	.05
529	Tim Laudner	.05
530	Eddie Murray	2.00
531	Athletics Batting & Pitching Ldrs. (Rickey Henderson, Rick Langford)	.15
532	Dave Stewart	.05
533	Luis Salazar	.05
534	John Butcher	.05
535	Manny Trillo	.05
536	Johnny Wockenfuss	.05
537	Rod Scurry	.05
538	Danny Heep	.05
539	Roger Erickson	.05
540	Ozzie Smith	2.00
541	Britt Burns	.05
542	Jody Davis	.05
543	Alan Fowlkes	.05
544	Larry Whisenton	.05
545	Floyd Bannister	.05
546	Dave Garcia	.05
547	Geoff Zahn	.05
548	Brian Giles	.05
549	Charlie Puleo **RC**	.05
550	Carl Yastrzemski	2.00
551	Carl Yastrzemski (Super Veteran)	.50
552	Tim Wallach	.05
553	Denny Martinez	.05
554	Mike Vail	.05
555	Steve Yeager	.05
556	Willie Upshaw	.05
557	Rick Honeycutt	.05
558	Dickie Thon	.05
559	Pete Redfern	.05
560	Ron LeFlore	.05
561	Cardinals Batting & Pitching Ldrs. (Joaquin Andujar, Lonnie Smith)	.05
562	Dave Rozema	.05
563	Juan Bonilla	.05
564	Sid Monge	.05
565	Bucky Dent	.05
566	Manny Sarmiento	.05
567	Joe Simpson	.05
568	Willie Hernandez	.05
569	Jack Perconte	.05
570	Vida Blue	.05
571	Mickey Klutts	.05
572	Bob Watson	.05
573	Andy Hassler	.05
574	Glenn Adams	.05
575	Neil Allen	.05
576	Frank Robinson	.25
577	Luis Aponte	.05
578	David Green	.05
579	Rich Dauer	.05
580	Tom Seaver	2.00
581	Tom Seaver (Super Veteran)	.50
582	Marshall Edwards	.05
583	Terry Forster	.05
584	Dave Hostetler	.05
585	Jose Cruz	.05
586	Frank Viola **RC**	1.50
587	Ivan DeJesus	.05
588	Pat Underwood	.05
589	Alvis Woods	.05
590	Tony Pena	.05
591	White Sox Batting & Pitching Ldrs. (LaMarr Hoyt, Greg Luzinski)	.05
592	Shane Rawley	.05
593	Broderick Perkins	.05
594	Eric Rasmussen	.05
595	Tim Raines	.05
596	Randy S. Johnson	.05
597	Mike Proly	.05
598	Dwayne Murphy	.05
599	Don Aase	.05
600	George Brett	3.00
601	Ed Lynch	.05
602	Rich Gedman	.05
603	Joe Morgan	2.00
604	Joe Morgan (Super Veteran)	.35
605	Gary Roenicke	.05
606	Bobby Cox	.05
607	Charlie Leibrandt	.05
608	Don Money	.05
609	Danny Darwin	.05
610	Steve Garvey	.50
611	Bert Roberge	.05
612	Steve Swisher	.05
613	Mike Ivie	.05
614	Ed Glynn	.05
615	Garry Maddox	.05
616	Bill Nahorodny	.05
617	Butch Wynegar	.05
618	LaMarr Hoyt	.05
619	Keith Moreland	.05
620	Mike Norris	.05
621	Mets Batting & Pitching Ldrs. (Craig Swan, Mookie Wilson)	.05
622	Dave Edler	.05
623	Luis Sanchez	.05
624	Glenn Hubbard	.05
625	Ken Forsch	.05
626	Jerry Martin	.05
627	Doug Bair	.05
628	Julio Valdez	.05
629	Charlie Lea	.05
630	Paul Molitor	2.00
631	Tippy Martinez	.05
632	Alex Trevino	.05
633	Vicente Romo	.05
634	Max Venable	.05
635	Graig Nettles	.05
636	Graig Nettles (Super Veteran)	.05
637	Pat Corrales	.05
638	Dan Petry	.05
639	Art Howe	.05
640	Andre Thornton	.05
641	Billy Sample	.05
642	Checklist 529-660	.05
643	Bump Wills	.05
644	Joe Lefebvre	.05
645	Bill Madlock	.05
646	Jim Essian	.05
647	Bobby Mitchell	.05
648	Jeff Burroughs	.05
649	Tommy Boggs	.05
650	George Hendrick	.05
651	Angels Batting & Pitching Ldrs. (Rod Carew, Mike Witt)	.05
652	Butch Hobson	.05
653	Ellis Valentine	.05
654	Bob Ojeda	.05
655	Al Bumbry	.05
656	Dave Frost	.05
657	Mike Gates	.05
658	Frank Pastore	.05
659	Charlie Moore	.05
660	Mike Hargrove	.05
661	Bill Russell	.05
662	Joe Sambito	.05
663	Tom O'Malley	.05
664	Bob Molinaro	.05
665	Jim Sundberg	.05
666	Sparky Anderson	.25
667	Dick Davis	.05
668	Larry Christenson	.05
669	Mike Squires	.05
670	Jerry Mumphrey	.05
671	Lenny Faedo	.05
672	Jim Kaat	.10
673	Jim Kaat (Super Veteran)	.05
674	Kurt Bevacqua	.05
675	Jim Beattie	.05
676	Biff Pocoroba	.05
677	Dave Revering	.05
678	Juan Beniquez	.05
679	Mike Scott	.05
680	Andre Dawson	.60
681	Dodgers Batting & Pitching Ldrs. (Pedro Guerrero, Fernando Valenzuela)	.05
682	Bob Stanley	.05
683	Dan Ford	.05
684	Rafael Landestoy	.05
685	Lee Mazzilli	.05
686	Randy Lerch	.05
687	U.L. Washington	.05
688	Jim Wohlford	.05
689	Ron Hassey	.05
690	Kent Hrbek	.05
691	Dave Tobik	.05
692	Denny Walling	.05
693	Sparky Lyle	.05
694	Sparky Lyle (Super Veteran)	.05
695	Ruppert Jones	.05
696	Chuck Tanner	.05
697	Barry Foote	.05
698	Tony Bernazard	.05
699	Lee Smith	.05
700	Keith Hernandez	.05
701	Batting Leaders (Al Oliver, Willie Wilson)	.05
702	Home Run Leaders (Reggie Jackson, Dave Kingman, Gorman Thomas)	.15
703	Runs Batted In Leaders (Hal McRae, Dale Murphy, Al Oliver)	.05
704	Stolen Base Leaders (Rickey Henderson, Tim Raines)	.10
705	Victory Leaders (Steve Carlton, LaMarr Hoyt)	.05
706	Strikeout Leaders (Floyd Bannister, Steve Carlton)	.05
707	Earned Run Average Leaders (Steve Rogers, Rick Sutcliffe)	.05
708	Leading Firemen (Dan Quisenberry, Bruce Sutter)	.10
709	Jimmy Sexton	.05
710	Willie Wilson	.05
711	Mariners Batting & Pitching Ldrs. (Jim Beattie, Bruce Bochte)	.05
712	Bruce Kison	.05
713	Ron Hodges	.05
714	Wayne Nordhagen	.05
715	Tony Perez	1.50
716	Tony Perez (Super Veteran)	.05
717	Scott Sanderson	.05
718	Jim Dwyer	.05
719	Rich Gale	.05
720	Dave Concepcion	.05
721	John Martin	.05
722	Jorge Orta	.05
723	Randy Moffitt	.05
724	Johnny Grubb	.05
725	Dan Spillner	.05
726	Harvey Kuenn	.05
727	Chet Lemon	.05
728	Ron Reed	.05
729	Jerry Morales	.05
730	Jason Thompson	.05
731	Al Williams	.05
732	Dave Henderson	.05
733	Buck Martinez	.05
734	Steve Braun	.05
735	Tommy John	.20
736	Tommy John (Super Veteran)	.05
737	Mitchell Page	.05
738	Tim Foli	.05
739	Rick Ownbey	.05
740	Rusty Staub	.05
741	Rusty Staub (Super Veteran)	.05
742	Padres Batting & Pitching Ldrs. (Terry Kennedy, Tim Lollar)	.05
743	Mike Torrez	.05
744	Brad Mills	.05
745	Scott McGregor	.05
746	John Wathan	.05
747	Fred Breining	.05
748	Derrel Thomas	.05
749	Jon Matlack	.05
750	Ben Oglivie	.05
751	Brad Havens	.05
752	Luis Pujols	.05
753	Elias Sosa	.05
754	Bill Robinson	.05
755	John Candelaria	.05
756	Russ Nixon	.05
757	Rick Manning	.05
758	Aurelio Rodriguez	.05
759	Doug Bird	.05
760	Dale Murphy	.60
761	Gary Lucas	.05
762	Cliff Johnson	.05
763	Al Cowens	.05
764	Pete Falcone	.05
765	Bob Boone	.05
766	Barry Bonnell	.05
767	Duane Kuiper	.05
768	Chris Speier	.05
769	Checklist 661-792	.05
770	Dave Winfield	2.00
771	Twins Batting & Pitching Ldrs. (Bobby Castillo, Kent Hrbek)	.05
772	Jim Kern	.05
773	Larry Hisle	.05
774	Alan Ashby	.05
775	Burt Hooton	.05
776	Larry Parrish	.05
777	John Curtis	.05
778	Rich Hebner	.05
779	Rick Waits	.05
780	Gary Matthews	.05
781	Rick Rhoden	.05
782	Bobby Murcer	.05
783	Bobby Murcer (Super Veteran)	.05
784	Jeff Newman	.05
785	Dennis Leonard	.05
786	Ralph Houk	.05
787	Dick Tidrow	.05
788	Dane Iorg	.05
789	Bryan Clark	.05
790	Bob Grich	.05
791	Gary Lavelle	.05
792	Chris Chambliss	.05

Traded

These 2-1/2" x 3-1/2" cards mark a continuation of the traded set introduced in 1981. The 132 cards retain the basic design of the year's regular issue, with their numbering being 1-132 with the "T" suffix. Cards in the set include traded players, new managers and promising rookies. Sold only through dealers, the set was in heavy demand as it contained the first cards of Darryl Strawberry, Ron Kittle, Julio Franco, and Mel Hall. While some of those cards were very hot in 1983, it seems likely that some of the rookies may not live up to their initial promise.

No.	Player	NM/M
	Complete Set (132):	20.00
	Common Player:	.05
1T	Neil Allen	.05
2T	Bill Almon	.05
3T	Joe Altobelli	.05
4T	Tony Armas	.05
5T	Doug Bair	.05
6T	Steve Baker	.05
7T	Floyd Bannister	.05
8T	Don Baylor	.25
9T	Tony Bernazard	.05
10T	Larry Biittner	.05
11T	Dann Bilardello	.05
12T	Doug Bird	.05
13T	Steve Boros	.05
14T	Greg Brock **RC**	.05
15T	Mike Brown	.05
16T	Tom Burgmeier	.05
17T	Randy Bush **RC**	.05
18T	Bert Campaneris	.05
19T	Ron Cey	.05
20T	Chris Codiroli **RC**	.05
21T	Dave Collins	.05
22T	Terry Crowley	.05
23T	Julio Cruz	.05
24T	Mike Davis	.05
25T	Frank DiPino	.05
26T	Bill Doran **RC**	.05
27T	Jerry Dybzinski	.05
28T	Jamie Easterly	.05
29T	Juan Eichelberger	.05
30T	Jim Essian	.05
31T	Pete Falcone	.05
32T	Mike Ferraro	.05
33T	Terry Forster	.05
34T	Julio Franco **RC**	3.00
35T	Rich Gale	.05
36T	Kiko Garcia	.05
37T	Steve Garvey	1.00
38T	Johnny Grubb	.05
39T	Mel Hall **RC**	.05
40T	Von Hayes	.05
41T	Danny Heep	.05
42T	Steve Henderson	.05
43T	Keith Hernandez	.15
44T	Leo Hernandez	.05
45T	Willie Hernandez	.05
46T	Al Holland	.05
47T	Frank Howard	.05
48T	Bobby Johnson	.05
49T	Cliff Johnson	.05
50T	Odell Jones	.05
51T	Mike Jorgensen	.05
52T	Bob Kearney	.05
53T	Steve Kemp	.05
54T	Matt Keough	.05
55T	Ron Kittle **RC**	.05
56T	Mickey Klutts	.05
57T	Alan Knicely	.05
58T	Mike Krukow	.05
59T	Rafael Landestoy	.05
60T	Carney Lansford	.05
61T	Joe Lefebvre	.05
62T	Bryan Little	.05
63T	Aurelio Lopez	.05
64T	Mike Madden	.05
65T	Rick Manning	.05
66T	Billy Martin	.25
67T	Lee Mazzilli	.05
68T	Andy McGaffigan	.05
69T	Craig McMurtry **RC**	.05
70T	John McNamara	.05
71T	Orlando Mercado	.05
72T	Larry Milbourne	.05
73T	Randy Moffitt	.05
74T	Sid Monge	.05
75T	Jose Morales	.05
76T	Omar Moreno	.05
77T	Joe Morgan	4.00
78T	Mike Morgan	.05
79T	Dale Murray	.05
80T	Jeff Newman	.05
81T	Pete O'Brien **RC**	.05
82T	Jorge Orta	.05
83T	Alejandro Pena **RC**	.05
84T	Pascual Perez	.05
85T	Tony Perez	1.00
86T	Broderick Perkins	.05
87T	Tony Phillips **RC**	.15
88T	Charlie Puleo	.05
89T	Pat Putnam	.05
90T	Jamie Quirk	.05
91T	Doug Rader	.05
92T	Chuck Rainey	.05
93T	Bobby Ramos	.05
94T	Gary Redus	.05
95T	Steve Renko	.05
96T	Leon Roberts	.05
97T	Aurelio Rodriguez	.05
98T	Dick Ruthven	.05
99T	Daryl Sconiers	.05
100T	Mike Scott	.05
101T	Tom Seaver	6.00
102T	John Shelby **RC**	.05
103T	Bob Shirley	.05
104T	Joe Simpson	.05
105T	Doug Sisk **RC**	.05
106T	Mike Smithson **RC**	.05
107T	Elias Sosa	.05
108T	Darryl Strawberry **RC**	10.00
109T	Tom Tellmann	.05
110T	Gene Tenace	.05
111T	Gorman Thomas	.05
112T	Dick Tidrow	.05
113T	Dave Tobik	.05
114T	Wayne Tolleson **RC**	.05
115T	Mike Torrez	.05
116T	Manny Trillo	.05
117T	Steve Trout	.05
118T	Lee Tunnell **RC**	.05
119T	Mike Vail	.05
120T	Ellis Valentine	.05
121T	Tom Veryzer	.05
122T	George Vukovich	.05
123T	Rick Waits	.05
124T	Greg Walker **RC**	.05
125T	Chris Welsh	.05
126T	Len Whitehouse	.05

127T	Eddie Whitson	.05
128T	Jim Wohlford	.05
129T	Matt Young **RC**	.05
130T	Joel Youngblood	.05
131T	Pat Zachry	.05
132T	Checklist 1-132	.05

Traded Steve Carlton Bronze

The first in a series of 1/4-size metal replicas of Topps star cards was issued to dealers who purchased cases of 1983 Topps Traded sets. Each detail of the 1983 Steve Carlton card is reproduced on the 1-1/4" x 1-3/4" bronze metal mini-card, right down to the stats.

		NM/M
70	Steve Carlton	6.00

1982 League Leaders Sheet

The leaders in various major statistical categories in 1982 are featured on this 7-1/2" x 10-1/2" blank-back sheet. Most of the cards on the sheet are identical to the players' regular 1983 Topps cards except for a white strip at upper-left identifying their statistical accomplishment. Reggie Jackson and Gorman Thomas who shared the A.L. home run record for 1982 share a card on this sheet. Available via a mail-in offer, huge quantities of these sheets are readily available.

	NM/M
Uncut Sheet:	
Willie Wilson,	
Reggie Jackson,	
Gorman Thomas, Al Oliver,	
LaMarr Hoyt, Steve Carlton,	
Dan Quisenberry,	
Dave Kingman,	
Bruce Sutter	1.00

All-Star Glossy Set of 40

This set was a "consolation prize" in a scratch-off contest in regular packs of 1983 cards. The 2-1/2" x 3-1/2" cards have a large color photo surrounded by a yellow frame on the front. In very small type on a white border is printed the player's name. Backs carry the player's name,

team, position and the card number along with a Topps identification. A major feature is that the surface of the front is glossy, which most collectors find very attractive. With many top stars, the set is a popular one, but the price has not moved too far above the issue price.

		NM/M
Complete Set (40):		3.00
Common Player:		.05
1	Carl Yastrzemski	.25
2	Mookie Wilson	.05
3	Andre Thornton	.05
4	Keith Hernandez	.05
5	Robin Yount	.25
6	Terry Kennedy	.05
7	Dave Winfield	.25
8	Mike Schmidt	.50
9	Buddy Bell	.05
10	Fernando Valenzuela	.05
11	Rich Gossage	.05
12	Bob Horner	.05
13	Toby Harrah	.05
14	Pete Rose	.75
15	Cecil Cooper	.05
16	Dale Murphy	.15
17	Carlton Fisk	.25
18	Ray Knight	.05
19	Jim Palmer	.25
20	Gary Carter	.25
21	Richard Zisk	.05
22	Dusty Baker	.05
23	Willie Wilson	.05
24	Bill Buckner	.05
25	Dave Stieb	.05
26	Bill Madlock	.05
27	Lance Parrish	.05
28	Nolan Ryan	1.00
29	Rod Carew	.25
30	Al Oliver	.05
31	George Brett	.50
32	Jack Clark	.05
33	Rickey Henderson	.25
34	Dave Concepcion	.05
35	Kent Hrbek	.05
36	Steve Carlton	.25
37	Eddie Murray	.25
38	Ruppert Jones	.05
39	Reggie Jackson	.30
40	Bruce Sutter	.20

Foldouts

Another Topps test issue, these 3-1/2" x 5-5/16" cards were printed in booklets like souvenir postcards. Each of the booklets have a theme of currently playing statistical leaders in a specific category such as home runs. The cards feature a color player photo on each side. A black strip at the bottom gives the player's name, position and team along with statistics in the particular category. A facsimile autograph crosses the photograph. Booklets carry nine cards, with eight having players on both sides and one doubling as the back cover, for a total of 17 cards per booklet. There are 85 cards in the set, although some players appear in more than one category. Naturally, most of the players pictured are stars. Even so, the set is a problem as it seems to be most valuable when complete and unseparated, so the cards are difficult to display.

		NM/M
Complete Set (5):		9.00
Common Folder:		3.00
1	Pitching Leaders (Vida Blue, Bert Blyleven, Steve Carlton, Fergie Jenkins, Tommy John, Jim Kaat, Jerry Koosman, Joe Niekro, Phil Niekro, Jim Palmer, Gaylord Perry,	

	Jerry Reuss, Nolan Ryan, Tom Seaver, Paul Splittorff, Don Sutton, Mike Torrez)	6.00
2	Home Run Leaders (Johnny Bench, Ron Cey, Darrell Evans, George Foster, Reggie Jackson, Dave Kingman, Greg Luzinski, John Mayberry, Rick Monday, Joe Morgan, Bobby Murcer, Graig Nettles, Tony Perez, Jim Rice, Mike Schmidt, Rusty Staub, Carl Yastrzemski	4.50
3	Batting Leaders (George Brett, Rod Carew, Cecil Cooper, Steve Garvey, Ken Griffey, Pedro Guerrero, Keith Hernandez, Dane Iorg, Fred Lynn, Bill Madlock, Bake McBride, Al Oliver, Dave Parker, Jim Rice, Pete Rose, Lonnie Smith, Willie Wilson)	4.50
4	Relief Aces (Tom Burgmeier, Bill Campbell, Ed Farmer, Rollie Fingers, Terry Forster, Gene Garber, Rich Gossage, Jim Kern, Gary Lavelle, Tug McGraw, Greg Minton, Randy Moffitt, Dan Quisenberry, Ron Reed, Elias Sosa, Bruce Sutter, Kent Tekulve)	3.00
5	Stolen Base Leaders (Don Baylor, Larry Bowa, Al Bumbry, Rod Carew, Cesar Cedeno, Dave Concepcion, Jose Cruz, Julio Cruz, Rickey Henderson, Ron LeFlore, Davey Lopes, Garry Maddox, Omar Moreno, Joe Morgan, Amos Otis, Mickey Rivers, Willie Wilson)	3.00

Stickers

Topps increased the number of stickers in its set to 330 in 1983, but retained the same 1-15/16" x 2-9/16" size. The stickers are again numbered on both the front and back. Similar in style to previous sticker issues, the set includes 28 "foil" stickers, and various special stickers highlighting the 1982 season, playoffs and World Series. An album was also available.

		NM/M
Complete Set (330):		15.00
Common Player:		.05
Sticker Album:		2.00
Wax Pack (5):		.25
Wax Box (100):		16.00
1	Hank Aaron	1.00
2	Babe Ruth	2.00
3	Willie Mays	1.00
4	Frank Robinson	.15
5	Reggie Jackson	.50
6	Carl Yastrzemski	.25
7	Johnny Bench	.25
8	Tony Perez	.25
9	Lee May	.05
10	Mike Schmidt	.50
11	Dave Kingman	.05
12	Reggie Smith	.05
13	Graig Nettles	.05
14	Rusty Staub	.05
15	Willie Wilson	.05
16	LaMarr Hoyt	.05
17	Reggie Jackson, Gorman Thomas	.10
18	Floyd Bannister	.05
19	Hal McRae	.05
20	Rick Sutcliffe	.05
21	Rickey Henderson	.25
22	Dan Quisenberry	.05
23	Jim Palmer	.25
24	John Lowenstein	.05
25	Mike Flanagan	.05
26	Cal Ripken, Jr.	1.00
27	Rich Dauer	.05
28	Ken Singleton	.05
29	Eddie Murray	.25
30	Rick Dempsey	.05
31	Carl Yastrzemski	.25
32	Carney Lansford	.05

33	Jerry Remy	.05
34	Dennis Eckersley	.20
35	Dave Stapleton	.05
36	Mark Clear	.05
37	Jim Rice	.15
38	Dwight Evans	.05
39	Rod Carew	.25
40	Don Baylor	.10
41	Reggie Jackson	.50
42	Geoff Zahn	.05
43	Bobby Grich	.05
44	Fred Lynn	.05
45	Bob Boone	.05
46	Doug DeCinces	.05
47	Tom Paciorek	.05
48	Britt Burns	.05
49	Tony Bernazard	.05
50	Steve Kemp	.05
51	Greg Luzinski	.05
52	Harold Baines	.05
53	LaMarr Hoyt	.05
54	Carlton Fisk	.25
55	Andre Thornton	.05
56	Mike Hargrove	.05
57	Len Barker	.05
58	Toby Harrah	.05
59	Dan Spillner	.05
60	Rick Manning	.05
61	Rick Sutcliffe	.05
62	Ron Hassey	.05
63	Lance Parrish	.05
64	John Wockenfuss	.05
65	Lou Whitaker	.05
66	Alan Trammell	.05
67	Kirk Gibson	.05
68	Larry Herndon	.05
69	Jack Morris	.05
70	Dan Petry	.05
71	Frank White	.05
72	Amos Otis	.05
73	Willie Wilson	.05
74	Dan Quisenberry	.05
75	Hal McRae	.05
76	George Brett	.60
77	Larry Gura	.05
78	John Wathan	.05
79	Rollie Fingers	.20
80	Cecil Cooper	.05
81	Robin Yount	.25
82	Ben Oglivie	.05
83	Paul Molitor	.25
84	Gorman Thomas	.05
85	Ted Simmons	.05
86	Pete Vuckovich	.05
87	Gary Gaetti	.05
88	Kent Hrbek	.05
89	John Castino	.05
90	Tom Brunansky	.05
91	Bobby Mitchell	.05
92	Gary Ward	.05
93	Tim Laudner	.05
94	Ron Davis	.05
95	Willie Randolph	.05
96	Roy Smalley	.05
97	Jerry Mumphrey	.05
98	Ken Griffey	.05
99	Dave Winfield	.25
100	Rich Gossage	.05
101	Butch Wynegar	.05
102	Ron Guidry	.05
103	Rickey Henderson	.25
104	Mike Heath	.05
105	Dave Lopes	.05
106	Rick Langford	.05
107	Dwayne Murphy	.05
108	Tony Armas	.05
109	Matt Keough	.05
110	Dan Meyer	.05
111	Bruce Bochte	.05
112	Julio Cruz	.05
113	Floyd Bannister	.05
114	Gaylord Perry	.20
115	Al Cowens	.05
116	Richie Zisk	.05
117	Jim Essian	.05
118	Bill Caudill	.05
119	Buddy Bell	.05
120	Larry Parrish	.05
121	Danny Darwin	.05
122	Bucky Dent	.05
123	Johnny Grubb	.05
124	George Wright	.05
125	Charlie Hough	.05
126	Jim Sundberg	.05
127	Dave Stieb	.05
128	Willie Upshaw	.05
129	Alfredo Griffin	.05
130	Lloyd Moseby	.05
131	Ernie Whitt	.05
132	Jim Clancy	.05
133	Barry Bonnell	.05
134	Damaso Garcia	.05
135	Jim Kaat	.05
136	Jim Kaat	.05
137	Greg Minton	.05
138	Greg Minton	.05
139	Paul Molitor	.20
140	Paul Molitor	.20
141	Manny Trillo	.05
142	Manny Trillo	.05
143	Joel Youngblood	.05
144	Joel Youngblood	.05
145	Robin Yount	.20
146	Robin Yount	.20
147	Willie McGee	.20
148	Darrell Porter	.05
149	Darrell Porter	.05
150	Robin Yount	.20

151	Bruce Benedict	.05
152	Bruce Benedict	.05
153	George Hendrick	.05
154	Bruce Benedict	.05
155	Doug DeCinces	.05
156	Paul Molitor	.05
157	Charlie Moore	.05
158	Fred Lynn	.05
159	Rickey Henderson	.25
160	Dale Murphy	.15
161	Willie Wilson	.05
162	Jack Clark	.05
163	Reggie Jackson	.50
164	Andre Dawson	.15
165	Dan Quisenberry	.05
166	Bruce Sutter	.20
167	Robin Yount	.25
168	Ozzie Smith	.05
169	Frank White	.05
170	Phil Garner	.05
171	Doug DeCinces	.05
172	Mike Schmidt	.50
173	Cecil Cooper	.05
174	Al Oliver	.05
175	Jim Palmer	.25
176	Steve Carlton	.25
177	Carlton Fisk	.05
178	Gary Carter	.25
179	Joaquin Andujar	.05
180	Ozzie Smith	.25
181	Cecil Cooper	.05
182	Darrell Porter	.05
183	Darrell Porter	.05
184	Mike Caldwell	.05
185	Mike Caldwell	.05
186	Ozzie Smith	.25
187	Bruce Sutter	.20
188	Keith Hernandez	.05
189	Dane Iorg	.05
190	Dane Iorg	.05
191	Tony Armas	.05
192	Tony Armas	.05
193	Lance Parrish	.05
194	Lance Parrish	.05
195	John Wathan	.05
196	John Wathan	.05
197	Rickey Henderson	.20
198	Rickey Henderson	.20
199	Rickey Henderson	.20
200	Rickey Henderson	.20
201	Rickey Henderson	.20
202	Rickey Henderson	.20
203	Steve Carlton	.20
204	Steve Carlton	.20
205	Al Oliver	.05
206	Dale Murphy, Al Oliver	.05
207	Dave Kingman	.05
208	Steve Rogers	.05
209	Bruce Sutter	.20
210	Tim Raines	.05
211	Dale Murphy	.15
212	Chris Chambliss	.05
213	Gene Garber	.05
214	Bob Horner	.05
215	Glenn Hubbard	.05
216	Claudell Washington	.05
217	Bruce Benedict	.05
218	Phil Niekro	.20
219	Leon Durham	.05
220	Jay Johnstone	.05
221	Larry Bowa	.05
222	Keith Moreland	.05
223	Bill Buckner	.05
224	Fergie Jenkins	.20
225	Dick Tidrow	.05
226	Jody Davis	.05
227	Dave Concepcion	.05
228	Dan Driessen	.05
229	Johnny Bench	.25
230	Ron Oester	.05
231	Cesar Cedeno	.05
232	Alex Trevino	.05
233	Tom Seaver	.25
234	Mario Soto	.05
235	Nolan Ryan	1.00
236	Art Howe	.05
237	Phil Garner	.05
238	Ray Knight	.05
239	Terry Puhl	.05
240	Joe Niekro	.05
241	Alan Ashby	.05
242	Jose Cruz	.05
243	Steve Garvey	.15
244	Ron Cey	.05
245	Dusty Baker	.05
246	Ken Landreaux	.05
247	Jerry Reuss	.05
248	Pedro Guerrero	.05
249	Bill Russell	.05
250	Fernando Valenzuela	.05
251	Al Oliver	.05
252	Andre Dawson	.15
253	Tim Raines	.05
254	Jeff Reardon	.05
255	Gary Carter	.25
256	Steve Rogers	.05
257	Tim Wallach	.05
258	Chris Speier	.05
259	Dave Kingman	.05
260	Bob Bailor	.05
261	Hubie Brooks	.05
262	Craig Swan	.05
263	George Foster	.05
264	John Stearns	.05
265	Neil Allen	.05
266	Mookie Wilson	.05
267	Steve Carlton	.20
268	Manny Trillo	.05

269	Gary Matthews	.05
270	Mike Schmidt	.50
271	Ivan DeJesus	.05
272	Pete Rose	.75
273	Bo Diaz	.05
274	Sid Monge	.05
275	Bill Madlock	.05
276	Jason Thompson	.05
277	Don Robinson	.05
278	Omar Moreno	.05
279	Dale Berra	.05
280	Dave Parker	.05
281	Tony Pena	.05
282	John Candelaria	.05
283	Lonnie Smith	.05
284	Bruce Sutter	.20
285	George Hendrick	.05
286	Tom Herr	.05
287	Ken Oberkfell	.05
288	Ozzie Smith	.25
289	Bob Forsch	.05
290	Keith Hernandez	.05
291	Garry Templeton	.05
292	Broderick Perkins	.05
293	Terry Kennedy	.05
294	Gene Richards	.05
295	Ruppert Jones	.05
296	Tim Lollar	.05
297	John Montefusco	.05
298	Sixto Lezcano	.05
299	Greg Minton	.05
300	Jack Clark	.05
301	Milt May	.05
302	Reggie Smith	.05
303	Joe Morgan	.05
304	John LeMaster	.05
305	Darrell Evans	.05
306	Al Holland	.05
307	Jesse Barfield	.05
308	Wade Boggs	.60
309	Tom Brunansky	.05
310	Storm Davis	.05
311	Von Hayes	.05
312	Dave Hostetler	.05
313	Kent Hrbek	.05
314	Tim Laudner	.05
315	Cal Ripken, Jr.	1.00
316	Andre Robertson	.05
317	Ed Vande Berg	.05
318	Glenn Wilson	.05
319	Chili Davis	.05
320	Bob Dernier	.05
321	Terry Francona	.05
322	Brian Giles	.05
323	David Green	.05
324	Atlee Hammaker	.05
325	Bill Laskey	.05
326	Willie McGee	.05
327	Johnny Ray	.05
328	Ryne Sandberg	.75
329	Steve Sax	.05
330	Eric Show	.05

Stickers Boxes

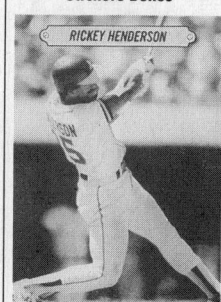

These eight cards were printed on the back panels of 1983 Topps sticker boxes, one card per box. The blank- backed cards measure the standard 2-1/2" x 3-1/2" and feature a full-color photo with the player's name at the top. The rest of the back panel advertises the sticker album, while the front of the box has an action photo of Reggie Jackson. The boxes are numbered on the front. Prices in the checklist that follows are for complete boxes.

		NM/M
Complete Set (8):		6.50
Common Player:		.75
1	Fernando Valenzuela	.75
2	Gary Carter	1.00
3	Mike Schmidt	1.50
4	Reggie Jackson	1.25
5	Jim Palmer	.75
6	Rollie Fingers	.75
7	Pete Rose	2.00
8	Rickey Henderson	1.00

1952 Reprint Set

The first of several reprint/retro sets in different sports issued by Topps, the 402-card reprinting of its classic 1952 baseball card set was controversial at the time of issue, but has since gained hobby acceptance and market value. To avoid possible confusion of the reprints for originals, the reprints were done in the now-standard 2-1/2" x 3-1/2" format instead of the original 2-5/8" x 3-3/4". Backs, printed in red, carry a line "Topps 1952 Reprint Series" at bottom, though there is no indication of the year of reprinting. Fronts have a semi-gloss finish, which also differs from the originals. Because of inability to come to terms with five of the players from the original 1952 Topps set, they were not included in the re-print series. Those cards which weren't issued are: #20 Billy Loes, #22 Dom DiMaggio, #159 Saul Rogovin, #196 Solly Hemus, and #289 Tommy Holmes. The '52 reprints were available only as a complete boxed set with a retail price of about $40 at issue.

	NM/M
Complete Sealed Boxed Set:	175.00
Complete Set (402):	150.00
Common Player:	.25
Minor Stars:	.35
Typical Hall of Famers:	2.00
Superstar Hall of Famers:	8.00
311 Mickey Mantle	30.00
407 Eddie Mathews (Sample card.)	8.00

1984 Topps

Another 792-card regular set from Topps. For the second straight year, the 2-1/2" x 3-1/2" cards featured a color action photo on the front along with a small portrait photo in the lower-left. The team name runs in big letters down the left side, while the player's name and position appear under the action photo. Backs have a team logo in the upper-right, along with statistics, personal information and a few highlights, all in a hard-to-read red and purple coloring. Specialty cards include past season highlights, team leaders, statistical leaders, All-Stars, active career leaders and numbered checklists. Again, promising rookies were saved for the traded set. The six 132-card uncut sheets which comprise the set were made available to collectors at about $30 for the set.

	NM/M
Complete Set (792):	40.00
Common Player:	.05
Wax Pack (15):	2.00
Wax Box (36):	50.00
Cello Pack (28):	2.50
Cello Box (24):	50.00
Rack Pack (54+1):	3.50
Rack Box (24):	60.00
Vending Box (500):	20.00
1 Steve Carlton (1983 Highlight)	.25

2	Rickey Henderson (1983 Highlight)	.25
3	Dan Quisenberry (1983 Highlight)	.05
4	Steve Carlton, Gaylord Perry, Nolan Ryan (1983 Highlight)	.50
5	Bob Forsch, Dave Righetti, Mike Warren (1983 Highlight)	.05
6	Johnny Bench, Gaylord Perry, Carl Yastrzemski (1983 Highlight)	.25
7	Gary Lucas	.05
8	Don Mattingly **RC**	15.00
9	Jim Gott	.05
10	Robin Yount	1.00
11	Twins Batting & Pitching Leaders (Kent Hrbek, Ken Schrom)	.05
12	Billy Sample	.05
13	Scott Holman	.05
14	Tom Brookens	.05
15	Burt Hooton	.05
16	Omar Moreno	.05
17	John Denny	.05
18	Dale Berra	.05
19	Ray Fontenot **RC**	.05
20	Greg Luzinski	.05
21	Joe Altobelli	.05
22	Bryan Clark	.05
23	Keith Moreland	.05
24	John Martin	.05
25	Glenn Hubbard	.05
26	Bud Black	.05
27	Daryl Sconiers	.05
28	Frank Viola	.05
29	Danny Heep	.05
30	Wade Boggs	3.00
31	Andy McGaffigan	.05
32	Bobby Ramos	.05
33	Tom Burgmeier	.05
34	Eddie Milner	.05
35	Don Sutton	.65
36	Denny Walling	.05
37	Rangers Batting & Pitching Leaders (Buddy Bell, Rick Honeycutt)	.05
38	Luis DeLeon	.05
39	Garth Iorg	.05
40	Dusty Baker	.05
41	Tony Bernazard	.05
42	Johnny Grubb	.05
43	Ron Reed	.05
44	Jim Morrison	.05
45	Jerry Mumphrey	.05
46	Ray Smith	.05
47	Rudy Law	.05
48	Julio Franco	.05
49	John Stuper	.05
50	Chris Chambliss	.05
51	Jim Frey	.05
52	Paul Splittorff	.05
53	Juan Beniquez	.05
54	Jesse Orosco	.05
55	Dave Concepcion	.05
56	Gary Allenson	.05
57	Dan Schatzeder	.05
58	Max Venable	.05
59	Sammy Stewart	.05
60	Paul Molitor	1.00
61	Chris Codiroli **RC**	.05
62	Dave Hostetler	.05
63	Ed Vande Berg	.05
64	Mike Scioscia	.05
65	Kirk Gibson	.05
66	Astros Batting & Pitching Leaders (Jose Cruz, Nolan Ryan)	.25
67	Gary Ward	.05
68	Luis Salazar	.05
69	Rod Scurry	.05
70	Gary Matthews	.05
71	Leo Hernandez	.05
72	Mike Squires	.05
73	Jody Davis	.05
74	Jerry Martin	.05
75	Bob Forsch	.05
76	Alfredo Griffin	.05
77	Brett Butler	.05
78	Mike Torrez	.05
79	Rob Wilfong	.05
80	Steve Rogers	.05
81	Billy Martin	.15
82	Doug Bird	.05
83	Richie Zisk	.05
84	Lenny Faedo	.05
85	Atlee Hammaker	.05
86	John Shelby **RC**	.05
87	Frank Pastore	.05
88	Rob Picciolo	.05
89	Mike Smithson **RC**	.05
90	Pedro Guerrero	.05
91	Dan Spillner	.05
92	Lloyd Moseby	.05
93	Bob Knepper	.05
94	Mario Ramirez	.05
95	Aurelio Lopez	.05
96	Royals Batting & Pitching Leaders (Larry Gura, Hal McRae)	.05
97	LaMarr Hoyt	.05
98	Steve Nicosia	.05
99	Craig Lefferts **RC**	.25
100	Reggie Jackson	1.50
101	Porfirio Altamirano	.05
102	Ken Oberkfell	.05
103	Dwayne Murphy	.05

104	Ken Dayley	.05
105	Tony Armas	.05
106	Tim Stoddard	.05
107	Ned Yost	.05
108	Randy Moffitt	.05
109	Brad Wellman	.05
110	Ron Guidry	.05
111	Bill Virdon	.05
112	Tom Niedenfuer	.05
113	Kelly Paris	.05
114	Checklist 1-132	.05
115	Andre Thornton	.05
116	George Bjorkman	.05
117	Tom Veryzer	.05
118	Charlie Hough	.05
119	Johnny Wockenfuss	.05
120	Keith Hernandez	.05
121	Pat Sheridan **RC**	.05
122	Cecilio Guante **RC**	.05
123	Butch Wynegar	.05
124	Damaso Garcia	.05
125	Britt Burns	.05
126	Braves Batting & Pitching Leaders (Craig McMurtry, Dale Murphy)	.05
127	Mike Madden	.05
128	Rick Manning	.05
129	Bill Laskey	.05
130	Ozzie Smith	2.00
131	Batting Leaders (Wade Boggs, Bill Madlock)	.25
132	Home Run Leaders (Jim Rice, Mike Schmidt)	.25
133	RBI Leaders (Cecil Cooper, Dale Murphy, Jim Rice)	.10
134	Stolen Base Leaders (Rickey Henderson, Tim Raines)	.25
135	Victory Leaders (John Denny, LaMarr Hoyt)	.05
136	Strikeout Leaders (Steve Carlton, Jack Morris)	.05
137	Earned Run Average Leaders (Atlee Hammaker, Rick Honeycutt)	.05
138	Leading Firemen (Al Holland, Dan Quisenberry)	.05
139	Bert Campaneris	.05
140	Storm Davis	.05
141	Pat Corrales	.05
142	Rich Gale	.05
143	Jose Morales	.05
144	Brian Harper **RC**	.20
145	Gary Lavelle	.05
146	Ed Romero	.05
147	Dan Petry	.05
148	Joe Lefebvre	.05
149	Jon Matlack	.05
150	Dale Murphy	.50
151	Steve Trout	.05
152	Glenn Brummer	.05
153	Dick Tidrow	.05
154	Dave Henderson	.05
155	Frank White	.05
156	Athletics Batting & Pitching Leaders (Tim Conroy, Rickey Henderson)	.15
157	Gary Gaetti	.05
158	John Curtis	.05
159	Darryl Cias	.05
160	Mario Soto	.05
161	Junior Ortiz **RC**	.05
162	Bob Ojeda	.05
163	Lorenzo Gray	.05
164	Scott Sanderson	.05
165	Ken Singleton	.05
166	Jamie Nelson	.05
167	Marshall Edwards	.05
168	Juan Bonilla	.05
169	Larry Parrish	.05
170	Jerry Reuss	.05
171	Frank Robinson	.25
172	Frank DiPino	.05
173	Marvell Wynne **RC**	.05
174	Juan Berenguer	.05
175	Graig Nettles	.05
176	Lee Smith	.05
177	Jerry Hairston Sr.	.05
178	Bill Krueger	.05
179	Buck Martinez	.05
180	Manny Trillo	.05
181	Roy Thomas	.05
182	Darryl Strawberry	.25
183	Al Williams	.05
184	Mike O'Berry	.05
185	Sixto Lezcano	.05
186	Cardinals Batting & Pitching Leaders (Lonnie Smith, John Stuper)	.05
187	Luis Aponte	.05
188	Bryan Little	.05
189	Tim Conroy **RC**	.05
190	Ben Oglivie	.05
191	Mike Boddicker	.05
192	Nick Esasky **RC**	.05
193	Darrell Brown	.05
194	Domingo Ramos	.05
195	Jack Morris	.05
196	Don Slaught **RC**	.05
197	Garry Hancock	.05
198	Bill Doran **RC**	.05
199	Willie Hernandez	.05
200	Andre Dawson	.60
201	Bruce Kison	.05
202	Bobby Cox	.05
203	Matt Keough	.05

204	Bobby Meacham **RC**	.05
205	Greg Minton	.05
206	Andy Van Slyke **RC**	.75
207	Donnie Moore	.05
208	Jose Oquendo **RC**	.05
209	Manny Sarmiento	.05
210	Joe Morgan	1.00
211	Rick Sweet	.05
212	Broderick Perkins	.05
213	Bruce Hurst	.05
214	Paul Householder	.05
215	Tippy Martinez	.05
216	White Sox Batting & Pitching Leaders (Richard Dotson, Carlton Fisk)	.05
217	Alan Ashby	.05
218	Rick Waits	.05
219	Joe Simpson	.05
220	Fernando Valenzuela	.05
221	Cliff Johnson	.05
222	Rick Honeycutt	.05
223	Wayne Krenchicki	.05
224	Sid Monge	.05
225	Lee Mazzilli	.05
226	Juan Eichelberger	.05
227	Steve Braun	.05
228	John Rabb	.05
229	Paul Owens	.05
230	Rickey Henderson	1.00
231	Gary Woods	.05
232	Tim Wallach	.05
233	Checklist 133-264	.05
234	Rafael Ramirez	.05
235	Matt Young **RC**	.05
236	Ellis Valentine	.05
237	John Castino	.05
238	Reid Nichols	.05
239	Jay Howell	.05
240	Eddie Murray	1.00
241	Billy Almon	.05
242	Alex Trevino	.05
243	Pete Ladd	.05
244	Candy Maldonado **RC**	.05
245	Rick Sutcliffe	.05
246	Mets Batting & Pitching Leaders (Tom Seaver, Mookie Wilson)	.25
247	Onix Concepcion	.05
248	Bill Dawley	.05
249	Jay Johnstone	.05
250	Bill Madlock	.05
251	Tony Gwynn	4.00
252	Larry Christenson	.05
253	Jim Wohlford	.05
254	Shane Rawley	.05
255	Bruce Benedict	.05
256	Dave Geisel	.05
257	Julio Cruz	.05
258	Luis Sanchez	.05
259	Sparky Anderson	.15
260	Scott McGregor	.05
261	Bobby Brown	.05
262	Tom Candiotti **RC**	.25
263	Jack Fimple	.05
264	Doug Frobel	.05
265	Donnie Hill **RC**	.05
266	Steve Lubratich	.05
267	Carmelo Martinez **RC**	.05
268	Jack O'Connor	.05
269	Aurelio Rodriguez	.05
270	Jeff Russell **RC**	.05
271	Moose Haas	.05
272	Rick Dempsey	.05
273	Charlie Puleo	.05
274	Rick Monday	.05
275	Len Matuszek	.05
276	Angels Batting & Pitching Leaders (Rod Carew, Geoff Zahn)	.10
277	Eddie Whitson	.05
278	Jorge Bell	.05
279	Ivan DeJesus	.05
280	Floyd Bannister	.05
281	Larry Milbourne	.05
282	Jim Barr	.05
283	Larry Biittner	.05
284	Howard Bailey	.05
285	Darrell Porter	.05
286	Lary Sorensen	.05
287	Warren Cromartie	.05
288	Jim Beattie	.05
289	Randy S. Johnson	.05
290	Dave Dravecky	.05
291	Chuck Tanner	.05
292	Tony Scott	.05
293	Ed Lynch	.05
294	U.L. Washington	.05
295	Mike Flanagan	.05
296	Jeff Newman	.05
297	Bruce Berenyi	.05
298	Jim Gantner	.05
299	John Butcher	.05
300	Pete Rose	5.00
301	Frank LaCorte	.05
302	Barry Bonnell	.05
303	Marty Castillo	.05
304	Warren Brusstar	.05
305	Roy Smalley	.05
306	Dodgers Batting & Pitching Leaders (Pedro Guerrero, Bob Welch)	.05
307	Bobby Mitchell	.05
308	Ron Hassey	.05
309	Tony Phillips	.05
310	Willie McGee	.05
311	Jerry Koosman	.05
312	Jorge Orta	.05
313	Mike Jorgensen	.05

314	Orlando Mercado	.05
315	Bob Grich	.05
316	Mark Bradley	.05
317	Greg Pryor	.05
318	Bill Gullickson	.05
319	Al Bumbry	.05
320	Bob Stanley	.05
321	Harvey Kuenn	.05
322	Ken Schrom	.05
323	Alan Knicely	.05
324	Alejandro Pena **RC**	.05
325	Darrell Evans	.05
326	Bob Kearney	.05
327	Ruppert Jones	.05
328	Vern Ruhle	.05
329	Pat Tabler **RC**	.05
330	John Candelaria	.05
331	Bucky Dent	.05
332	Kevin Gross **RC**	.05
333	Larry Herndon	.05
334	Chuck Rainey	.05
335	Don Baylor	.15
336	Mariners Batting & Pitching Leaders (Pat Putnam, Matt Young)	.05
337	Kevin Hagen	.05
338	Mike Warren	.05
339	Roy Lee Jackson	.05
340	Hal McRae	.05
341	Dave Tobik	.05
342	Tim Foli	.05
343	Mark Davis	.05
344	Rick Miller	.05
345	Kent Hrbek	.05
346	Kurt Bevacqua	.05
347	Allan Ramirez	.05
348	Toby Harrah	.05
349	Bob L. Gibson	.05
350	George Foster	.05
351	Russ Nixon	.05
352	Dave Stewart	.05
353	Jim Anderson	.05
354	Jeff Burroughs	.05
355	Jason Thompson	.05
356	Glenn Abbott	.05
357	Ron Cey	.05
358	Bob Dernier	.05
359	Jim Acker **RC**	.05
360	Willie Randolph	.05
361	Dave Smith	.05
362	David Green	.05
363	Tim Laudner	.05
364	Scott Fletcher **RC**	.05
365	Steve Bedrosian	.05
366	Padres Batting & Pitching Leaders (Dave Dravecky, Terry Kennedy)	.05
367	Jamie Easterly	.05
368	Hubie Brooks	.05
369	Steve McCatty	.05
370	Tim Raines	.05
371	Dave Gumpert	.05
372	Gary Roenicke	.05
373	Bill Scherrer	.05
374	Don Money	.05
375	Dennis Leonard	.05
376	Dave Anderson **RC**	.05
377	Danny Darwin	.05
378	Bob Brenly	.05
379	Checklist 265-396	.05
380	Steve Garvey	.45
381	Ralph Houk	.05
382	Chris Nyman	.05
383	Terry Puhl	.05
384	Lee Tunnell **RC**	.05
385	Tony Perez	1.00
386	George Hendrick/AS	.05
387	Johnny Ray/AS	.05
388	Mike Schmidt/AS	.75
389	Ozzie Smith/AS	.50
390	Tim Raines/AS	.20
391	Dale Murphy/AS	.20
392	Andre Dawson/AS	.25
393	Gary Carter/AS	.30
394	Steve Rogers/AS	.05
395	Steve Carlton/AS	.25
396	Jesse Orosco/AS	.05
397	Eddie Murray/AS	.40
398	Lou Whitaker/AS	.05
399	George Brett/AS	.75
400	Cal Ripken, Jr./AS	4.00
401	Jim Rice/AS	.05
402	Dave Winfield/AS	.30
403	Lloyd Moseby/AS	.05
404	Ted Simmons/AS	.05
405	LaMarr Hoyt/AS	.05
406	Ron Guidry/AS	.05
407	Dan Quisenberry/AS	.05
408	Lou Piniella	.05
409	Juan Agosto **RC**	.05
410	Claudell Washington	.05
411	Houston Jimenez	.05
412	Doug Rader	.05
413	Spike Owen **RC**	.05
414	Mitchell Page	.05
415	Tommy John	.15
416	Dane Iorg	.05
417	Mike Armstrong	.05
418	Ron Hodges	.05
419	John Henry Johnson	.05
420	Cecil Cooper	.05
421	Charlie Lea	.05
422	Jose Cruz	.05
423	Mike Morgan	.05
424	Dann Bilardello	.05
425	Steve Howe	.05

426	Orioles Batting & Pitching Leaders (Mike Boddicker, Cal Ripken, Jr.)	.50
427	Rick Leach	.05
428	Fred Breining	.05
429	Randy Bush **RC**	.05
430	Rusty Staub	.05
431	Chris Bando	.05
432	Charlie Hudson **RC**	.05
433	Rich Hebner	.05
434	Harold Baines	.05
435	Neil Allen	.05
436	Rick Peters	.05
437	Mike Proly	.05
438	Biff Pocoroba	.05
439	Bob Stoddard	.05
440	Steve Kemp	.05
441	Bob Lillis	.05
442	Byron McLaughlin	.05
443	Benny Ayala	.05
444	Steve Renko	.05
445	Jerry Remy	.05
446	Luis Pujols	.05
447	Tom Brunansky	.05
448	Ben Hayes	.05
449	Joe Pettini	.05
450	Gary Carter	1.00
451	Bob Jones	.05
452	Chuck Porter	.05
453	Willie Upshaw	.05
454	Joe Beckwith	.05
455	Terry Kennedy	.05
456	Cubs Batting & Pitching Leaders (Fergie Jenkins, Keith Moreland)	.05
457	Dave Rozema	.05
458	Kiko Garcia	.05
459	Kevin Hickey	.05
460	Dave Winfield	1.00
461	Jim Maler	.05
462	Lee Lacy	.05
463	Dave Engle	.05
464	Jeff Jones	.05
465	Mookie Wilson	.05
466	Gene Garber	.05
467	Mike Ramsey	.05
468	Geoff Zahn	.05
469	Tom O'Malley	.05
470	Nolan Ryan	6.00
471	Dick Howser	.05
472	Mike Brown	.05
473	Jim Dwyer	.05
474	Greg Bargar	.05
475	Gary Redus **RC**	.05
476	Tom Tellmann	.05
477	Rafael Landestoy	.05
478	Alan Bannister	.05
479	Frank Tanana	.05
480	Ron Kittle **RC**	.05
481	Mark Thurmond **RC**	.05
482	Enos Cabell	.05
483	Fergie Jenkins	.65
484	Ozzie Virgil	.05
485	Rick Rhoden	.05
486	Yankees Batting & Pitching Leaders (Don Baylor, Ron Guidry)	.05
487	Ricky Adams	.05
488	Jesse Barfield	.05
489	Dave Von Ohlen	.05
490	Cal Ripken, Jr.	6.00
491	Bobby Castillo	.05
492	Tucker Ashford	.05
493	Mike Norris	.05
494	Chili Davis	.05
495	Rollie Fingers	.65
496	Terry Francona	.05
497	Bud Anderson	.05
498	Rich Gedman	.05
499	Mike Witt	.05
500	George Brett	2.00
501	Steve Henderson	.05
502	Joe Torre	.05
503	Elias Sosa	.05
504	Mickey Rivers	.05
505	Pete Vuckovich	.05
506	Ernie Whitt	.05
507	Mike LaCoss	.05
508	Mel Hall	.05
509	Brad Havens	.05
510	Alan Trammell	.05
511	Marty Bystrom	.05
512	Oscar Gamble	.05
513	Dave Beard	.05
514	Floyd Rayford	.05
515	Gorman Thomas	.05
516	Expos Batting & Pitching Leaders (Charlie Lea, Al Oliver)	.05
517	John Moses	.05
518	Greg Walker **RC**	.05
519	Ron Davis	.05
520	Bob Boone	.05
521	Pete Falcone	.05
522	Dave Bergman	.05
523	Glenn Hoffman	.05
524	Carlos Diaz	.05
525	Willie Wilson	.05
526	Ron Oester	.05
527	Checklist 397-528	.05
528	Mark Brouhard	.05
529	Keith Atherton **RC**	.05
530	Dan Ford	.05
531	Steve Boros	.05
532	Eric Show	.05
533	Ken Landreaux	.05
534	Pete O'Brien	.05
535	Bo Diaz	.05

536	Doug Bair	.05
537	Johnny Ray	.05
538	Kevin Bass	.05
539	George Frazier	.05
540	George Hendrick	.05
541	Dennis Lamp	.05
542	Duane Kuiper	.05
543	Craig McMurtry **RC**	.05
544	Cesar Geronimo	.05
545	Bill Buckner	.05
546	Indians Batting & Pitching Leaders (Mike Hargrove, Lary Sorensen)	.05
547	Mike Moore	.05
548	Ron Jackson	.05
549	Walt Terrell **RC**	.05
550	Jim Rice	.15
551	Scott Ullger	.05
552	Ray Burris	.05
553	Joe Nolan	.05
554	Ted Power **RC**	.05
555	Greg Brock	.05
556	Joey McLaughlin	.05
557	Wayne Tolleson	.05
558	Mike Davis	.05
559	Mike Scott	.05
560	Carlton Fisk	1.00
561	Whitey Herzog	.05
562	Manny Castillo	.05
563	Glenn Wilson	.05
564	Al Holland	.05
565	Leon Durham	.05
566	Jim Bibby	.05
567	Mike Heath	.05
568	Pete Filson	.05
569	Bake McBride	.05
570	Dan Quisenberry	.05
571	Bruce Bochy	.05
572	Jerry Royster	.05
573	Dave Kingman	.05
574	Brian Downing	.05
575	Jim Clancy	.05
576	Giants Batting & Pitching Leaders (Atlee Hammaker, Jeff Leonard)	.05
577	Mark Clear	.05
578	Lenn Sakata	.05
579	Bob James	.05
580	Lonnie Smith	.05
581	Jose DeLeon **RC**	.05
582	Bob McClure	.05
583	Derrel Thomas	.05
584	Dave Schmidt	.05
585	Dan Driessen	.05
586	Joe Niekro	.05
587	Von Hayes	.05
588	Milt Wilcox	.05
589	Mike Easler	.05
590	Dave Stieb	.05
591	Tony LaRussa	.05
592	Andre Robertson	.05
593	Jeff Lahti	.05
594	Gene Richards	.05
595	Jeff Reardon	.05
596	Ryne Sandberg	3.00
597	Rick Camp	.05
598	Rusty Kuntz	.05
599	Doug Sisk **RC**	.05
600	Rod Carew	1.00
601	John Tudor	.05
602	John Wathan	.05
603	Renie Martin	.05
604	John Lowenstein	.05
605	Mike Caldwell	.05
606	Blue Jays Batting & Pitching Leaders (Lloyd Moseby, Dave Stieb)	.05
607	Tom Hume	.05
608	Bobby Johnson	.05
609	Dan Meyer	.05
610	Steve Sax	.05
611	Chet Lemon	.05
612	Harry Spilman	.05
613	Greg Gross	.05
614	Len Barker	.05
615	Garry Templeton	.05
616	Don Robinson	.05
617	Rick Cerone	.05
618	Dickie Noles	.05
619	Jerry Dybzinski	.05
620	Al Oliver	.05
621	Frank Howard	.05
622	Al Cowens	.05
623	Ron Washington	.05
624	Terry Harper	.05
625	Larry Gura	.05
626	Bob Clark	.05
627	Dave LaPoint	.05
628	Ed Jurak	.05
629	Rick Langford	.05
630	Ted Simmons	.05
631	Denny Martinez	.05
632	Tom Foley	.05
633	Mike Krukow	.05
634	Mike Marshall	.05
635	Dave Righetti	.05
636	Pat Putnam	.05
637	Phillies Batting & Pitching Leaders (John Denny, Gary Matthews)	.05
638	George Vukovich	.05
639	Rick Lysander	.05
640	Lance Parrish	.05
641	Mike Richardt	.05
642	Tom Underwood	.05
643	Mike Brown	.05
644	Tim Lollar	.05
645	Tony Pena	.05

646	Checklist 529-660	.05
647	Ron Roenicke	.05
648	Len Whitehouse	.05
649	Tom Herr	.05
650	Phil Niekro	.65
651	John McNamara	.05
652	Rudy May	.05
653	Dave Stapleton	.05
654	Bob Bailor	.05
655	Amos Otis	.05
656	Bryn Smith	.05
657	Thad Bosley	.05
658	Jerry Augustine	.05
659	Duane Walker	.05
660	Ray Knight	.05
661	Steve Yeager	.05
662	Tom Brennan	.05
663	Johnnie LeMaster	.05
664	Dave Stegman	.05
665	Buddy Bell	.05
666	Tigers Batting & Pitching Leaders (Jack Morris, Lou Whitaker)	.05
667	Vance Law	.05
668	Larry McWilliams	.05
669	Dave Lopes	.05
670	Rich Gossage	.05
671	Jamie Quirk	.05
672	Ricky Nelson	.05
673	Mike Walters	.05
674	Tim Flannery	.05
675	Pascual Perez	.05
676	Brian Giles	.05
677	Doyle Alexander	.05
678	Chris Speier	.05
679	Art Howe	.05
680	Fred Lynn	.05
681	Tom Lasorda	.15
682	Dan Morogiello	.05
683	Marty Barrett **RC**	.05
684	Bob Shirley	.05
685	Willie Aikens	.05
686	Joe Price	.05
687	Roy Howell	.05
688	George Wright	.05
689	Mike Fischlin	.05
690	Jack Clark	.05
691	Steve Lake **RC**	.05
692	Dickie Thon	.05
693	Alan Wiggins	.05
694	Mike Stanton	.05
695	Lou Whitaker	.05
696	Pirates Batting & Pitching Leaders (Bill Madlock, Rick Rhoden)	.05
697	Dale Murray	.05
698	Marc Hill	.05
699	Dave Rucker	.05
700	Mike Schmidt	2.00
701	NL Active Career Batting Leaders (Bill Madlock, Dave Parker, Pete Rose)	.25
702	NL Active Career Hit Leaders (Tony Perez, Pete Rose, Rusty Staub)	.25
703	NL Active Career Home Run Leaders (Dave Kingman, Tony Perez, Mike Schmidt)	.15
704	NL Active Career RBI Leaders (Al Oliver, Tony Perez, Rusty Staub)	.15
705	NL Active Career Stolen Bases Leaders (Larry Bowa, Cesar Cedeno, Joe Morgan)	.15
706	NL Active Career Victory Leaders (Steve Carlton, Fergie Jenkins, Tom Seaver)	.05
707	NL Active Career Strikeout Leaders (Steve Carlton, Nolan Ryan, Tom Seaver)	.35
708	NL Active Career ERA Leaders (Steve Carlton, Steve Rogers, Tom Seaver)	.05
709	NL Active Career Save Leaders (Gene Garber, Tug McGraw, Bruce Sutter)	.10
710	AL Active Career Batting Leaders (George Brett, Rod Carew, Cecil Cooper)	.25
711	AL Active Career Hit Leaders (Bert Campaneris, Rod Carew, Reggie Jackson)	.15
712	AL Active Career Home Run Leaders (Reggie Jackson, Greg Luzinski, Graig Nettles)	.15
713	AL Active Career RBI Leaders (Reggie Jackson, Graig Nettles, Ted Simmons)	.15
714	AL Active Career Stolen Bases Leaders (Bert Campaneris, Dave Lopes, Omar Moreno)	.05
715	AL Active Career Victory Leaders (Tommy John, Jim Palmer, Don Sutton)	.05
716	AL Active Strikeout Leaders (Bert Blyleven, Jerry Koosman, Don Sutton)	.05
717	AL Active Career ERA Leaders (Rollie Fingers, Ron Guidry, Jim Palmer)	.05

718	AL Active Career Save Leaders (Rollie Fingers, Rich Gossage, Dan Quisenberry)	.05
719	Andy Hassler	.05
720	Dwight Evans	.05
721	Del Crandall	.05
722	Bob Welch	.05
723	Rich Dauer	.05
724	Eric Rasmussen	.05
725	Cesar Cedeno	.05
726	Brewers Batting & Pitching Leaders (Moose Haas, Ted Simmons)	.05
727	Joel Youngblood	.05
728	Tug McGraw	.05
729	Gene Tenace	.05
730	Bruce Sutter	.75
731	Lynn Jones	.05
732	Terry Crowley	.05
733	Dave Collins	.05
734	Odell Jones	.05
735	Rick Burleson	.05
736	Dick Ruthven	.05
737	Jim Essian	.05
738	Bill Schroeder **RC**	.05
739	Bob Watson	.05
740	Tom Seaver	1.00
741	Wayne Gross	.05
742	Dick Williams	.05
743	Don Hood	.05
744	Jamie Allen	.05
745	Dennis Eckersley	.65
746	Mickey Hatcher	.05
747	Pat Zachry	.05
748	Jeff Leonard	.05
749	Doug Flynn	.05
750a	Jim Palmer	1.00
750b	Jim Palmer (Missing 1980-82 losses on back.)	3.00
750c	Jim Palmer (Missing 1979-83 losses on back.)	4.00
751	Charlie Moore	.05
752	Phil Garner	.05
753	Doug Gwosdz	.05
754	Kent Tekulve	.05
755	Garry Maddox	.05
756	Reds Batting & Pitching Leaders (Ron Oester, Mario Soto)	.05
757	Larry Bowa	.05
758	Bill Stein	.05
759	Richard Dotson	.05
760	Bob Horner	.05
761	John Montefusco	.05
762	Rance Mulliniks	.05
763	Craig Swan	.05
764	Mike Hargrove	.05
765	Ken Forsch	.05
766	Mike Vail	.05
767	Carney Lansford	.05
768	Champ Summers	.05
769	Bill Caudill	.05
770	Ken Griffey	.05
771	Billy Gardner	.05
772	Jim Slaton	.05
773	Todd Cruz	.05
774	Tom Gorman	.05
775	Dave Parker	.05
776	Craig Reynolds	.05
777	Tom Paciorek	.05
778	Andy Hawkins **RC**	.05
779	Jim Sundberg	.05
780	Steve Carlton	1.00
781	Checklist 661-792	.05
782	Steve Balboni	.05
783	Luis Leal	.05
784	Leon Roberts	.05
785	Joaquin Andujar	.05
786	Red Sox Batting & Pitching Leaders (Wade Boggs, Bob Ojeda)	.25
787	Bill Campbell	.05
788	Milt May	.05
789	Bert Blyleven	.05
790	Doug DeCinces	.05
791	Terry Forster	.05
792	Bill Russell	.05

Tiffany

In 1984 Topps introduced a specially boxed, limited edition version of its baseball card set. Sold only through hobby dealers, the cards differed from regular-issue 1984 Topps cards in their use of white cardboard stock and the application of a high-gloss finish to the front of the card. Production was limited to a reported 10,000 sets. The nickname "Tiffany" was coined by collectors to identify the glossy collectors edition.

	NM/M
Unopened Set (792):	175.00
Complete Set (792):	95.00
Common Player:	.15
Stars:	6X
8 Don Mattingly	80.00

Traded

The popular Topps Traded set returned for its fourth year in 1984 with another 132-card set. The 2-1/2" x 3-1/2" cards have an identical design to the regular Topps cards ex-

BRET SABERHAGEN P

cept that the back cardboard is white and card numbers carry a "T" suffix. As before, the set was sold only through hobby dealers. Also as before, players who changed teams, new managers and promising rookies are included in the set. A glossy-finish "Tiffany" version of the set was also issued.

	NM/M
Complete Set (132):	17.50
Common Player:	.05
1T	Willie Aikens	.05
2T	Luis Aponte	.05
3T	Mike Armstrong	.05
4T	Bob Bailor	.05
5T	Dusty Baker	.15
6T	Steve Balboni	.05
7T	Alan Bannister	.05
8T	Dave Beard	.05
9T	Joe Beckwith	.05
10T	Bruce Berenyi	.05
11T	Dave Bergman	.05
12T	Tony Bernazard	.05
13T	Yogi Berra	.25
14T	Barry Bonnell	.05
15T	Phil Bradley	.05
16T	Fred Breining	.05
17T	Bill Buckner	.05
18T	Ray Burris	.05
19T	John Butcher	.05
20T	Brett Butler	.05
21T	Enos Cabell	.05
22T	Bill Campbell	.05
23T	Bill Caudill	.05
24T	Bob Clark	.05
25T	Bryan Clark	.05
26T	Jaime Cocanower	.05
27T	Ron Darling **RC**	.50
28T	Alvin Davis **RC**	.05
29T	Ken Dayley	.05
30T	Jeff Dedmon	.05
31T	Bob Dernier	.05
32T	Carlos Diaz	.05
33T	Mike Easler	.05
34T	Dennis Eckersley	1.50
35T	Jim Essian	.05
36T	Darrell Evans	.05
37T	Mike Fitzgerald **RC**	.05
38T	Tim Foli	.05
39T	George Frazier	.05
40T	Rich Gale	.05
41T	Barbaro Garbey	.05
42T	Dwight Gooden **RC**	3.00
43T	Rich Gossage	.05
44T	Wayne Gross	.05
45T	Mark Gubicza **RC**	.25
46T	Jackie Gutierrez	.05
47T	Mel Hall	.05
48T	Toby Harrah	.05
49T	Ron Hassey	.05
50T	Rich Hebner	.05
51T	Willie Hernandez	.05
52T	Ricky Horton **RC**	.05
53T	Art Howe	.05
54T	Dane Iorg	.05
55T	Brook Jacoby **RC**	.05
56T	Mike Jeffcoat **RC**	.05
57T	Dave Johnson	.05
58T	Lynn Jones	.05
59T	Ruppert Jones	.05
60T	Mike Jorgensen	.05
61T	Bob Kearney	.05
62T	Jimmy Key **RC**	.50
63T	Dave Kingman	.05
64T	Jerry Koosman	.05
65T	Wayne Krenchicki	.05
66T	Rusty Kuntz	.05
67T	Rene Lachemann	.05
68T	Frank LaCorte	.05
69T	Dennis Lamp	.05
70T	Mark Langston **RC**	.05
71T	Rick Leach	.05
72T	Craig Lefferts	.05
73T	Gary Lucas	.05
74T	Jerry Martin	.05
75T	Carmelo Martinez	.05
76T	Mike Mason **RC**	.05
77T	Gary Matthews	.05
78T	Andy McGaffigan	.05
79T	Larry Milbourne	.05
80T	Sid Monge	.05
81T	Jackie Moore	.05
82T	Joe Morgan	2.00
83T	Graig Nettles	.05
84T	Phil Niekro	1.00

85T	Ken Oberkfell	.05
86T	Mike O'Berry	.05
87T	Al Oliver	.05
88T	Jorge Orta	.05
89T	Amos Otis	.05
90T	Dave Parker	.05
91T	Tony Perez	1.00
92T	Gerald Perry **RC**	.05
93T	Gary Pettis **RC**	.05
94T	Rob Picciolo	.05
95T	Vern Rapp	.05
96T	Floyd Rayford	.05
97T	Randy Ready **RC**	.05
98T	Ron Reed	.05
99T	Gene Richards	.05
100T	Jose Rijo **RC**	.25
101T	Jeff Robinson **RC**	.05
102T	Ron Romanick **RC**	.05
103T	Pete Rose	7.50
104T	Bret Saberhagen **RC**	3.00
105T	Juan Samuel **RC**	.05
106T	Scott Sanderson	.05
107T	Dick Schofield **RC**	.05
108T	Tom Seaver	3.00
109T	Jim Slaton	.05
110T	Mike Smithson	.05
111T	Lary Sorensen	.05
112T	Tim Stoddard	.05
113T	Champ Summers	.05
114T	Jim Sundberg	.05
115T	Rick Sutcliffe	.05
116T	Craig Swan	.05
117T	Tim Teufel **RC**	.05
118T	Derrel Thomas	.05
119T	Gorman Thomas	.05
120T	Alex Trevino	.05
121T	Manny Trillo	.05
122T	John Tudor	.05
123T	Tom Underwood	.05
124T	Mike Vail	.05
125T	Tom Waddell	.05
126T	Gary Ward	.05
127T	Curt Wilkerson	.05
128T	Frank Williams **RC**	.05
129T	Glenn Wilson	.05
130T	Johnny Wockenfuss	.05
131T	Ned Yost	.05
132T	Checklist 1-132	.05

Traded Tiffany

Following up on its inaugural Tiffany collectors'edition, Topps produced a special glossy version of its Traded set for 1984, as well. Cards in this special boxed set differ from regular Traded cards only in the use of white cardboard stock and a high-gloss finish coat on front.

	NM/M
Complete Set (132):	35.00
Common Player:	.25
Stars:	2X

Traded Darryl Strawberry Bronze

This 1/4-size metal replica of Strawberry's first-ever Topps card was issued to dealers who purchased cases of 1984 Topps Traded sets. Each detail of the 1983 Topps Traded Strawberry card is reproduced on the 1-1/4" x 1-3/4" bronze metal mini-card, right down to the stats.

	NM/M
108T Darryl Strawberry	3.00

Proofs

STEVE CARLTON P

Though still small in terms of actual numbers, the quantity of 1984 Topps proofs from the "A" sheet which have made their way into the hobby is relatively large. More precisely, 66 cards (half a production press sheet) are frequently seen in proof version. Like other true proofs, they are blank-backed but these have a very discernible difference from the issued 1984 Topps cards. On the proofs, the portrait photo at lower-left is completely within the black frame of the box. On issued cards, the cap extends above the box border. On the

proofs, portrait photos of Steve Carlton and Gary Matthews are found on each other's cards and Manny Trillo is pictured in an Indians uniform, rather than the Expos livery on which he appears in the regularly issued version. Single proofs in the market have been cut from half-sheets.

	NM/M
Uncut Sheet (66):	650.00
Complete Set, Singles (66):	800.00
Common Player:	10.00
(1)	Buddy Bell	10.00
(2)	Wade Boggs	50.00
(3)	Bob Boone	12.50
(4)	Greg Brock	10.00
(5)	Hubie Brooks	10.00
(6)	Steve Carlton (Inset photo Gary Matthews.)	150.00
(7)	Gary Carter	20.00
(8)	Cecil Cooper	10.00
(9)	Andre Dawson	20.00
(10)	Storm Davis	10.00
(11)	Doug DeCinces	10.00
(12)	Ivan DeJesus	10.00
(13)	Rick Dempsey	10.00
(14)	Dwight Evans	10.00
(15)	Rollie Fingers	20.00
(16)	Carlton Fisk	50.00
(17)	Ken Forsch	10.00
(18)	George Foster	10.00
(19)	Julio Franco	10.00
(20)	Jim Gantner	10.00
(21)	Damaso Garcia	10.00
(22)	Ken Griffey	12.50
(23)	Alfredo Griffin	10.00
(24)	Bill Gullickson	10.00
(25)	Moose Haas	10.00
(26)	Rickey Henderson	50.00
(27)	Kent Hrbek	12.50
(28)	Reggie Jackson	50.00
(29)	Roy Lee Jackson	10.00
(30)	Cliff Johnson	10.00
(31)	Ron Kittle	10.00
(32)	Charlie Lea	10.00
(33)	Luis Leal	10.00
(34)	Bill Madlock	10.00
(35)	Buck Martinez	10.00
(36)	Gary Matthews (Inset photo is Steve Carlton.)	75.00
(37)	Willie McGee	12.50
(38)	Greg Minton	10.00
(39)	Paul Molitor	30.00
(40)	Joe Morgan	30.00
(41)	Lloyd Moseby	10.00
(42)	Rance Mulliniks	10.00
(43)	Graig Nettles	15.00
(44)	Al Oliver	15.00
(45)	Lou Piniella	15.00
(46)	Bobby Ramos	10.00
(47)	Johnny Ray	10.00
(48)	Jeff Reardon	15.00
(49)	Jim Rice	20.00
(50)	Andre Robertson	10.00
(51)	Nolan Ryan	300.00
(52)	Scott Sanderson	10.00
(53)	Steve Sax	10.00
(54)	Dan Schatzeder	10.00
(55)	Tom Seaver	60.00
(56)	Lee Smith	15.00
(57)	Don Sutton	20.00
(58)	Jason Thompson	10.00
(59)	Alan Trammell	15.00
(60)	Manny Trillo (Indians)	100.00
(61)	Willie Upshaw	10.00
(62)	Fernando Valenzuela	15.00
(63)	Tim Wallach	10.00
(64)	Ernie Whitt	10.00
(65)	Glenn Wilson	10.00
(66)	Robin Yount	30.00

All-Star Glossy Set of 22

AL OLIVER

These 2-1/2" x 3-1/2" cards were a result of the success of Topps' efforts the previous year with glossy cards on a mail-in basis. The set is divided evenly between the two leagues. Each All-Star Game starter for both leagues, the managers and the honorary team captains have an All-Star Glossy card. Cards feature a large color photo on the front with an All-Star banner across the top and the league emblem in the lower-left. Player identification appears below the photo. Backs have a name, team, position and card number along with the phrase "1983 All-Star Game Commemorative Set." The '84 Glossy All-Stars were distributed one card per rack pack.

		NM/M
Complete Set (22):		4.00
Common Player:		.10
1	Harvey Kuenn	.10
2	Rod Carew	.50
3	Manny Trillo	.10
4	George Brett	1.00
5	Robin Yount	.50
6	Jim Rice	.25
7	Fred Lynn	.10
8	Dave Winfield	.50
9	Ted Simmons	.10
10	Dave Stieb	.10
11	Carl Yastrzemski	.50
12	Whitey Herzog	.10
13	Al Oliver	.10
14	Steve Sax	.10
15	Mike Schmidt	1.00
16	Ozzie Smith	.50
17	Tim Raines	.10
18	Andre Dawson	.25
19	Dale Murphy	.25
20	Gary Carter	.50
21	Mario Soto	.10
22	Johnny Bench	.50

All-Star Glossy Set of 40

For the second straight year in 1984, Topps produced a 40-card All-Star "Collector's Edition" set as a "consolation prize" for its sweepstakes game. By collecting game cards and sending them in with a bit of cash, the collector could receive one of eight different five-card series. As the previous year, the 2-1/2" x 3-1/2" cards feature a nearly full-frame color photo on its glossy finish front. Backs are printed in red and blue.

		NM/M
Complete Set (40):		6.00
Common Player:		.10
1	Pete Rose	1.00
2	Lance Parrish	.10
3	Steve Rogers	.10
4	Eddie Murray	.40
5	Johnny Ray	.10
6	Rickey Henderson	.40
7	Atlee Hammaker	.10
8	Wade Boggs	.50
9	Gary Carter	.40
10	Jack Morris	.10
11	Darrell Evans	.10
12	George Brett	1.00
13	Bob Horner	.10
14	Ron Guidry	.10
15	Nolan Ryan	1.50
16	Dave Winfield	.40
17	Ozzie Smith	.50
18	Ted Simmons	.10
19	Bill Madlock	.10
20	Tony Armas	.10
21	Al Oliver	.10
22	Jim Rice	.25
23	George Hendrick	.10
24	Dave Stieb	.10
25	Pedro Guerrero	.10
26	Rod Carew	.40
27	Steve Carlton	.40
28	Dave Righetti	.10
29	Darryl Strawberry	.10
30	Lou Whitaker	.10
31	Dale Murphy	.25
32	LaMarr Hoyt	.10
33	Jesse Orosco	.10
34	Cecil Cooper	.10
35	Andre Dawson	.25
36	Robin Yount	.40
37	Tim Raines	.10
38	Dan Quisenberry	.10
39	Mike Schmidt	1.00
40	Carlton Fisk	.40

Cereal Series

The Topps-produced 1984 Cereal Series set is identical to the Ralston Purina set from the same year in nearly all aspects. On the card fronts the words "Ralston Purina Company" were replaced by "Cereal Series" and Topps logos were substituted for Ralston checkerboard logos. The set is comprised of 33 cards, each measuring 2-1/2" x 3-1/2." The cards were inserted in unmarked boxes of Chex brand cereals.

		NM/M
Complete Set (33):		4.00
Common Player:		.05
1	Eddie Murray	.25
2	Ozzie Smith	.30
3	Ted Simmons	.05
4	Pete Rose	.75
5	Greg Luzinski	.05
6	Andre Dawson	.15
7	Dave Winfield	.25
8	Tom Seaver	.25
9	Jim Rice	.15
10	Fernando Valenzuela	.05
11	Wade Boggs	.30
12	Dale Murphy	.15
13	George Brett	.50
14	Nolan Ryan	1.00
15	Rickey Henderson	.25
16	Steve Carlton	.25
17	Rod Carew	.25
18	Steve Garvey	.15
19	Reggie Jackson	.35
20	Dave Concepcion	.05
21	Robin Yount	.25
22	Mike Schmidt	.50
23	Jim Palmer	.25
24	Bruce Sutter	.20
25	Dan Quisenberry	.05
26	Bill Madlock	.05
27	Cecil Cooper	.05
28	Gary Carter	.25
29	Fred Lynn	.05
30	Pedro Guerrero	.05
31	Ron Guidry	.05
32	Keith Hernandez	.05
33	Carlton Fisk	.25

"Darryl Palmer"

For use as a prop in the 1985 movie "The Slugger's Wife," Topps produced this 1984-style card of actor Michael O'Keefe as Darryl Palmer. (O'Keefe is better remembered as caddy Danny Noonan in "Caddyshack.") Front and back are in the '84T format, complete with personal data, stats and Topps copyrights.

		NM/M
801	Darryl Palmer	15.00

Gallery of Immortals

The Gallery of Immortals bronze and silver replicas were the first metal miniature set from Topps and the start of an annual tradition (in 1985, the name was changed to Gallery of Champions). Each mini is an exact one-quarter scale replica of the featured player's

1984 Topps baseball card, both front and back, in minute detail. The three-dimensional metal cards were packaged in a velvet-lined case that bears the title of the set in gold-embossed letters. A certificate of authenticity is included with each set. A Tom Seaver pewter metal mini-card was given as a premium to dealers who purchsed sets. Issue price was about $100 for the cased bronze set, $500 for the silver edition of 1,000.

		NM/M
Complete Bronze Set (12):		40.00
Complete Silver Set (12):		190.00
(1b)	George Brett/Bronze	12.50
(1s)	George Brett/Silver	45.00
(2b)	Rod Carew/Bronze	6.00
(2s)	Rod Carew/Silver	15.00
(3b)	Steve Carlton/Bronze	6.00
(3s)	Steve Carlton/Silver	15.00
(4b)	Rollie Fingers/Bronze	4.00
(4s)	Rollie Fingers/Silver	12.50
(5b)	Steve Garvey/Bronze	4.00
(5s)	Steve Garvey/Silver	12.50
(6b)	Reggie Jackson/Bronze	7.50
(6s)	Reggie Jackson/Silver	17.50
(7b)	Joe Morgan/Bronze	5.00
(7s)	Joe Morgan/Silver	12.50
(8b)	Jim Palmer/Bronze	5.00
(8s)	Jim Palmer/Silver	15.00
(9b)	Pete Rose/Bronze	20.00
(9s)	Pete Rose/Silver	50.00
(10b)	Nolan Ryan/Bronze	25.00
(10s)	Nolan Ryan/Silver	60.00
(11b)	Mike Schmidt/Bronze	12.50
(11s)	Mike Schmidt/Silver	45.00
(12b)	Tom Seaver/Bronze	6.00
(12s)	Tom Seaver/Silver	15.00
(12p)	Tom Seaver/Pewter	15.00

"Pewter" Gallery Ingots

All of the Topps Gallery of Immortals (1984) and Gallery of Champions (1985-1989) miniature ingots have been counterfeited in a pewter or pot metal alloy designed to look like the genuine silver pieces. The fakes are cast, rather than die-struck, have a porous surface upon magnification and sometimes the casting seam is visible despite the filing done to remove it. These are often sold on eBay as "pewter." Topps did did make one genuine pewter piece each year 1984-1991, as an ordering incentive; they are listed within each year's Gallery checklist.

Rub Downs

This set consists of 32 "Rub Down" sheets featuring 112 different players. Each sheet measures 2-3/8" x 3-15/16" and includes small, color baseball player figures along with bats, balls and gloves. The pictures can be transferred to another surface by rubbing the paper backing. The sheets, which were sold as a separate issue, are

somewhat reminiscent of earlier tattoo sets issued by Topps. The sheets are not numbered.

		NM/M
Complete Set (32):		7.50
Common Sheet:		.50
Pack (2):		.50
Box (36):		9.00
(1)	Steve Bedrosian, Bruce Benedict, Tony Armas, Harold Baines, Lonnie Smith	.50
(2)	Chris Chambliss, Bob Horner, Don Baylor, George Hendrick, Ron Kittle, Johnnie LeMaster	.50
(3)	Glenn Hubbard, Rafael Ramirez, Buddy Bell, Ray Knight, Lloyd Moseby	.50
(4)	Craig McMurtry, Bruce Benedict, Atlee Hammaker, Frank White	.50
(5)	Wade Boggs, Rick Dempsey, Keith Hernandez	.75
(6)	George Brett, Andre Dawson, Paul Molitor, Alan Wiggins	1.00
(7)	Tom Brunansky, Pedro Guerrero, Darryl Strawberry	.50
(8)	Bill Buckner, Rich Gossage, Dave Stieb, Rick Sutcliffe	.50
(9)	Rod Carew, Carlton Fisk, Johnny Ray, Matt Young	.60
(10)	Steve Carlton, Bob Horner, Dan Quisenberry	.60
(11)	Gary Carter, Phil Garner, Ron Guidry	.50
(12)	Ron Cey, Steve Kemp, Greg Luzinski, Kent Tekulve	.50
(13)	Chris Chambliss, Dwight Evans, Julio Franco	.50
(14)	Jack Clark, Damaso Garcia, Hal McRae, Lance Parrish	.50
(15)	Dave Concepcion, Cecil Cooper, Fred Lynn, Jesse Orosco	.50
(16)	Jose Cruz, Gary Matthews, Jack Morris, Jim Rice	.50
(17)	Ron Davis, Kent Hrbek, Tom Seaver	.60
(18)	John Denny, Carney Lansford, Mario Soto, Lou Whitaker	.50
(19)	Leon Durham, Dave Lopes, Steve Sax	.50
(20)	George Foster, Gary Gaetti, Bobby Grich, Gary Redus	.50
(21)	Steve Garvey, Bill Russell, Jerry Remy, George Wright	.50
(22)	Moose Haas, Bruce Sutter, Dickie Thon, Andre Thornton	.50
(23)	Toby Harrah, Pat Putnam, Tim Raines, Mike Schmidt	1.00
(24)	Rickey Henderson, Dave Righetti, Pete Rose	1.00
(25)	Steve Henderson, Bill Madlock, Alan Trammell	.50
(26)	LaMarr Hoyt, Larry Parrish, Nolan Ryan	1.50
(27)	Reggie Jackson, Eric Show, Jason Thompson	.50
(28)	Tommy John, Terry Kennedy, Eddie Murray, Ozzie Smith	.60
(29)	Jeff Leonard, Dale Murphy, Ken Singleton, Dave Winfield	.60
(30)	Craig McMurtry, Cal Ripken, Steve Rogers, Willie Upshaw	1.50
(31)	Ben Oglivie, Jim Palmer, Darrell Porter	.50
(32)	Tony Pena, Fernando Valenzuela, Robin Yount	.60

Stickers

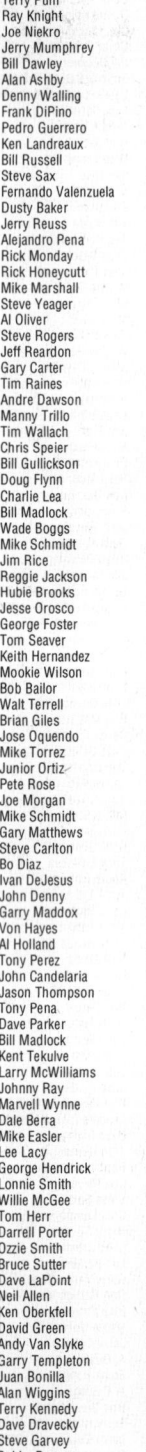

The largest sticker set issued by Topps, the 1984 set consists of 386 stickers, each measuring 1-15/16" x 2-9/16". The full color photos have stars in each of the corners and are numbered on both the front and the back. The back includes information about the sticker album and a promotion to order stickers through the mail. The back of the album is a tribute to Carl Yastrzemski, including a large photo and reproductions of his 1960-1983 cards in miniature.

		NM/M
Complete Set (386):		12.00
Common Player:		.05
Sticker Album:		3.00
Box (35):		6.00
1	Steve Carlton	.25
2	Steve Carlton	.25
3	Rickey Henderson	.25
4	Rickey Henderson	.25
5	Fred Lynn	.05
6	Fred Lynn	.05
7	Greg Luzinski	.05
8	Greg Luzinski	.05
9	Dan Quisenberry	.05
10	Dan Quisenberry	.05
11	1983 Championship (LaMarr Hoyt)	.05
12	1983 Championship (Mike Flanagan)	.05
13	1983 Championship (Mike Boddicker)	.05
14	1983 Championship (Tito Landrum)	.05
15	1983 Championship (Steve Carlton)	.10
16	1983 Championship (Fernando Valenzuela)	.05
17	1983 Championship (Charlie Hudson)	.05
18	1983 Championship (Gary Matthews)	.05
19	1983 World Series (John Denny)	.05
20	1983 World Series (John Lowenstein)	.05
21	1983 World Series (Jim Palmer)	.10
22	1983 World Series (Benny Ayala)	.05
23	1983 World Series (Rick Dempsey)	.05
24	1983 World Series (Cal Ripken)	.50
25	1983 World Series (Sammy Stewart)	.05
26	1983 World Series (Eddie Murray)	.10
27	Dale Murphy	.15
28	Chris Chambliss	.05
29	Glenn Hubbard	.05
30	Bob Horner	.05
31	Phil Niekro	.20
32	Claudell Washington	.05
33	Rafael Ramirez	.05
34	Bruce Benedict	.05
35	Gene Garber	.05
36	Pascual Perez	.05
37	Jerry Royster	.05
38	Steve Bedrosian	.05
39	Keith Moreland	.05
40	Leon Durham	.05
41	Ron Cey	.05
42	Bill Buckner	.05
43	Jody Davis	.05
44	Lee Smith	.05
45	Ryne Sandberg	.30
46	Larry Bowa	.05
47	Chuck Rainey	.05
48	Fergie Jenkins	.20
49	Dick Ruthven	.05
50	Jay Johnstone	.05
51	Mario Soto	.05
52	Gary Redus	.05
53	Ron Oester	.05
54	Cesar Cedeno	.05
55	Dan Driessen	.05
56	Dave Concepcion	.05
57	Dann Bilardello	.05
58	Joe Price	.05
59	Tom Hume	.05
60	Eddie Milner	.05
61	Paul Householder	.05
62	Bill Scherrer	.05
63	Phil Garner	.05
64	Dickie Thon	.05
65	Jose Cruz	.05
66	Nolan Ryan	.60
67	Terry Puhl	.05
68	Ray Knight	.05
69	Joe Niekro	.05
70	Jerry Mumphrey	.05
71	Bill Dawley	.05
72	Alan Ashby	.05
73	Denny Walling	.05
74	Frank DiPino	.05
75	Pedro Guerrero	.05
76	Ken Landreaux	.05
77	Bill Russell	.05
78	Steve Sax	.05
79	Fernando Valenzuela	.05
80	Dusty Baker	.05
81	Jerry Reuss	.05
82	Alejandro Pena	.05
83	Rick Monday	.05
84	Rick Honeycutt	.05
85	Mike Marshall	.05
86	Steve Yeager	.05
87	Al Oliver	.05
88	Steve Rogers	.05
89	Jeff Reardon	.05
90	Gary Carter	.25
91	Tim Raines	.15
92	Andre Dawson	.15
93	Manny Trillo	.05
94	Tim Wallach	.05
95	Chris Speier	.05
96	Bill Gullickson	.05
97	Doug Flynn	.05
98	Charlie Lea	.05
99	Bill Madlock	.05
100	Wade Boggs	.40
101	Mike Schmidt	.40
102a	Jim Rice	.15
102b	Reggie Jackson	.25
103	Hubie Brooks	.05
104	Jesse Orosco	.05
105	George Foster	.05
106	Tom Seaver	.25
107	Keith Hernandez	.05
108	Mookie Wilson	.05
109	Bob Bailor	.05
110	Walt Terrell	.05
111	Brian Giles	.05
112	Jose Oquendo	.05
113	Mike Torrez	.05
114	Junior Ortiz	.05
115	Pete Rose	.50
116	Joe Morgan	.25
117	Mike Schmidt	.40
118	Gary Matthews	.05
119	Steve Carlton	.20
120	Bo Diaz	.05
121	Ivan DeJesus	.05
122	John Denny	.05
123	Garry Maddox	.05
124	Von Hayes	.05
125	Al Holland	.05
126	Tony Perez	.25
127	John Candelaria	.05
128	Jason Thompson	.05
129	Tony Pena	.05
130	Dave Parker	.25
131	Bill Madlock	.05
132	Kent Tekulve	.05
133	Larry McWilliams	.05
134	Johnny Ray	.05
135	Marvell Wynne	.05
136	Dale Berra	.05
137	Mike Easler	.05
138	Lee Lacy	.05
139	George Hendrick	.05
140	Lonnie Smith	.05
141	Willie McGee	.05
142	Tom Herr	.05
143	Darrell Porter	.05
144	Ozzie Smith	.40
145	Bruce Sutter	.20
146	Dave LaPoint	.05
147	Neil Allen	.05
148	Ken Oberkfell	.05
149	David Green	.05
150	Andy Van Slyke	.05
151	Garry Templeton	.05
152	Juan Bonilla	.05
153	Alan Wiggins	.05
154	Terry Kennedy	.05
155	Dave Dravecky	.05
156	Steve Garvey	.10
157	Bobby Brown	.05
158	Ruppert Jones	.05
159	Luis Salazar	.05
160	Tony Gwynn	.40
161	Gary Lucas	.05
162	Eric Show	.05
163	Darrell Evans	.05
164	Gary Lavelle	.05
165	Atlee Hammaker	.05
166	Jeff Leonard	.05
167	Jack Clark	.05
168	Johnny LeMaster	.05
169	Duane Kuiper	.05
170	Tom O'Malley	.05
171	Chili Davis	.05
172	Bill Laskey	.05
173	Joel Youngblood	.05
174	Bob Brenly	.05
175	Atlee Hammaker	.05
176	Rick Honeycutt	.05
177	John Denny	.05
178	LaMarr Hoyt	.05

No.	Player	Price
179	Tim Raines	.05
180	Dale Murphy	.15
181	Andre Dawson	.15
182	Steve Rogers	.05
183	Gary Carter	.25
184	Steve Carlton	.25
185	George Hendrick	.05
186	Johnny Ray	.05
187	Ozzie Smith	.40
188	Mike Schmidt	.40
189	Jim Rice	.15
190	Dave Winfield	.25
191	Lloyd Moseby	.05
192	LaMarr Hoyt	.05
193	Ted Simmons	.05
194	Ron Guidry	.05
195	Eddie Murray	.25
196	Lou Whitaker	.05
197	Cal Ripken, Jr.	.60
198	George Brett	.40
199	Dale Murphy	.15
200a	Cecil Cooper	.05
200b	Jim Rice	.15
201	Tim Raines	.05
202	Rickey Henderson	.25
203	Eddie Murray	.25
204	Cal Ripken	.60
205	Gary Roenicke	.05
206	Ken Singleton	.05
207	Scott McGregor	.05
208	Tippy Martinez	.05
209	John Lowenstein	.05
210	Mike Flanagan	.05
211	Jim Palmer	.20
212	Dan Ford	.05
213	Rick Dempsey	.05
214	Rich Dauer	.05
215	Jerry Remy	.05
216	Wade Boggs	.25
217	Jim Rice	.15
218	Tony Armas	.05
219	Dwight Evans	.05
220	Bob Stanley	.05
221	Dave Stapleton	.05
222	Rich Gedman	.05
223	Glenn Hoffman	.05
224	Dennis Eckersley	.20
225	John Tudor	.05
226	Bruce Hurst	.05
227	Rod Carew	.25
228	Bobby Grich	.05
229	Doug DeCinces	.05
230	Fred Lynn	.05
231	Reggie Jackson	.25
232	Tommy John	.05
233	Luis Sanchez	.05
234	Bob Boone	.05
235	Bruce Kison	.05
236	Brian Downing	.05
237	Ken Forsch	.05
238	Rick Burleson	.05
239	Dennis Lamp	.05
240	LaMarr Hoyt	.05
241	Richard Dotson	.05
242	Harold Baines	.05
243	Carlton Fisk	.25
244	Greg Luzinski	.05
245	Rudy Law	.05
246	Tom Paciorek	.05
247	Floyd Bannister	.05
248	Julio Cruz	.05
249	Vance Law	.05
250	Scott Fletcher	.05
251	Toby Harrah	.05
252	Pat Tabler	.05
253	Gorman Thomas	.05
254	Rick Sutcliffe	.05
255	Andre Thornton	.05
256	Bake McBride	.05
257	Alan Bannister	.05
258	Jamie Easterly	.05
259	Lary Sorensen	.05
260	Mike Hargrove	.05
261	Bert Blyleven	.05
262	Ron Hassey	.05
263	Jack Morris	.05
264	Larry Herndon	.05
265	Lance Parrish	.05
266	Alan Trammell	.05
267	Lou Whitaker	.05
268	Aurelio Lopez	.05
269	Dan Petry	.05
270	Glenn Wilson	.05
271	Chet Lemon	.05
272	Kirk Gibson	.05
273	Enos Cabell	.05
274	Johnny Wockenfuss	.05
275	George Brett	.40
276	Willie Aikens	.05
277	Frank White	.05
278	Hal McRae	.05
279	Dan Quisenberry	.05
280	Willie Wilson	.05
281	Paul Splittorff	.05
282	U.L. Washington	.05
283	Bud Black	.05
284	John Wathan	.05
285	Larry Gura	.05
286	Pat Sheridan	.05
287a	Rusty Staub	.05
287b	Dave Righetti	.05
288a	Bob Forsch	.05
288b	Mike Warren	.05
289	Al Holland	.05
290	Dan Quisenberry	.05
291	Cecil Cooper	.05
292	Moose Haas	.05
293	Ted Simmons	.05
294	Paul Molitor	.25
295	Robin Yount	.25
296	Ben Oglivie	.05
297	Tom Tellmann	.05
298	Jim Gantner	.05
299	Rick Manning	.05
300	Don Sutton	.20
301	Charlie Moore	.05
302	Jim Slaton	.05
303	Gary Ward	.05
304	Tom Brunansky	.05
305	Kent Hrbek	.05
306	Gary Gaetti	.05
307	John Castino	.05
308	Ken Schrom	.05
309	Ron Davis	.05
310	Lenny Faedo	.05
311	Darrell Brown	.05
312	Frank Viola	.05
313	Dave Engle	.05
314	Randy Bush	.05
315	Dave Righetti	.05
316	Rich Gossage	.05
317	Ken Griffey	.05
318	Ron Guidry	.05
319	Dave Winfield	.25
320	Don Baylor	.10
321	Butch Wynegar	.05
322	Omar Moreno	.05
323	Andre Robertson	.05
324	Willie Randolph	.05
325	Don Mattingly	.60
326	Graig Nettles	.05
327	Rickey Henderson	.25
328	Carney Lansford	.05
329	Jeff Burroughs	.05
330	Chris Codiroli	.05
331	Dave Lopes	.05
332	Dwayne Murphy	.05
333	Wayne Gross	.05
334	Bill Almon	.05
335	Tom Underwood	.05
336	Dave Beard	.05
337	Mike Heath	.05
338	Mike Davis	.05
339	Pat Putnam	.05
340	Tony Bernazard	.05
341	Steve Henderson	.05
342	Richie Zisk	.05
343	Dave Henderson	.05
344	Al Cowens	.05
345	Bill Caudill	.05
346	Jim Beattie	.05
347	Ricky Nelson	.05
348	Roy Thomas	.05
349	Spike Owen	.05
350	Jamie Allen	.05
351	Buddy Bell	.05
352	Billy Sample	.05
353	George Wright	.05
354	Larry Parrish	.05
355	Jim Sundberg	.05
356	Charlie Hough	.05
357	Pete O'Brien	.05
358	Wayne Tolleson	.05
359	Danny Darwin	.05
360	Dave Stewart	.05
361	Mickey Rivers	.05
362	Bucky Dent	.05
363	Willie Upshaw	.05
364	Damaso Garcia	.05
365	Lloyd Moseby	.05
366	Cliff Johnson	.05
367	Jim Clancy	.05
368	Dave Stieb	.05
369	Alfredo Griffin	.05
370	Barry Bonnell	.05
371	Luis Leal	.05
372	Jesse Barfield	.05
373	Ernie Whitt	.05
374	Rance Mulliniks	.05
375	Mike Boddicker	.05
376	Greg Brock	.05
377	Bill Doran	.05
378	Nick Esasky	.05
379	Julio Franco	.05
380	Mel Hall	.05
381	Bob Kearney	.05
382	Ron Kittle	.05
383	Carmelo Martinez	.05
384	Craig McMurtry	.05
385	Darryl Strawberry	.05
386	Matt Young	.05

Stickers Boxes

For the second straight year, Topps printed baseball cards on the back of its sticker boxes. The 1984 set, titled "The Super Bats" features 24 hitting leaders. The cards are blank-backed and measure 2-1/2" x 3-1/2". Two cards were printed on each of 12 different boxes. The player's name appears inside a bat above his photo. Prices listed are for complete boxes.

	NM/M
Complete Set (12):	8.50
Common Player:	.75
1 Al Oliver, Lou Whitaker	.75
2 Ken Oberkfell, Ted Simmons	.75
3 Hal McRae, Alan Wiggins	.75
4 Lloyd Moseby, Tim Raines	.75

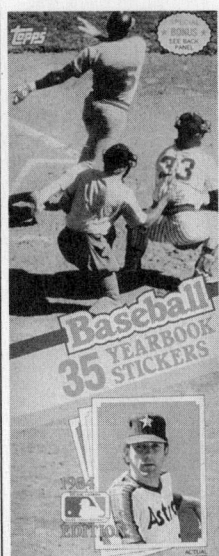

5 Lonnie Smith, Willie Wilson	.75
6 Keith Hernandez, Robin Yount	1.00
7 Wade Boggs, Johnny Ray	1.00
8 Willie McGee, Ken Singleton	.75
9 Ray Knight, Alan Trammell	.75
11 Rod Carew, George Hendrick	1.00
12 Bill Madlock, Eddie Murray	1.00
13 Jose Cruz, Cal Ripken, Jr.	3.00

Super

A new generation in Topps' experiments to market large-format cards, these 4-7/8" x 6-7/8" cards were sold in single-card plastic-wrap packs with a complete set being 30 cards. Other than their size and the change in card number on the back, there is nothing to distinguish the Supers from the regular 1984 Topps cards of the same players. One plus is that the players are all big name stars, and are likely to remain in demand.

	NM/M
Complete Set (30):	10.00
Common Player:	.25
Wax Pack (1):	.50
Wax Box (36):	9.00
1 Cal Ripken, Jr.	3.00
2 Dale Murphy	.40
3 LaMarr Hoyt	.25
4 John Denny	.25
5 Jim Rice	.40
6 Mike Schmidt	1.00
7 Wade Boggs	.60
8 Bill Madlock	.25
9 Dan Quisenberry	.25
10 Al Holland	.25
11 Ron Kittle	.25
12 Darryl Strawberry	.35
13 George Brett	1.00
14 Bill Buckner	.25
15 Carlton Fisk	.50
16 Steve Carlton	.50
17 Ron Guidry	.25
18 Gary Carter	.50
19 Rickey Henderson	.50
20 Andre Dawson	.50
21 Reggie Jackson	.75
22 Steve Garvey	.30
23 Fred Lynn	.25
24 Pedro Guerrero	.25
25 Eddie Murray	.50
26 Keith Hernandez	.25
27 Dave Winfield	.50
28 Nolan Ryan	3.00
29 Robin Yount	.50
30 Fernando Valenzuela	.25

"1977" Topps Dale Murphy Aluminum

Authorized by Topps to be issued in 1984 as a fund raiser for Huntington's Disease research, this aluminum card is a full size replica of 1977 Topps card #476, Dale Murphy's rookie card. Front features rather crude black etchings of the player portraits found on the cardboard version, while back reproduces the biographical data and includes a serial number. The cards were originally sold for $10.

	NM/M
476 Rookie Catchers (Gary Alexander, Rick Cerone, Dale Murphy, Kevin Pasley)	10.00

7-Eleven/Pepsi Sheets

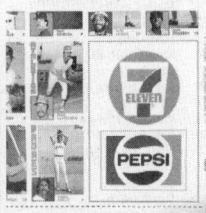

This test issue was reportedly limited to locations in the Midwest. About 28-1/2" x 43" the sheets have 128 regular '84 Topps cards and a 5" x 7" panel at lower-right with the sponsors' logos.

	NM/M
	10.00

1985 Topps

Holding the line at 792 cards, Topps initiated major design changes in its 2-1/2" x 3-1/2" cards in 1985. The use of two photos on the front was discontinued in favor of one large photo. The Topps logo appears in the upper-left corner. At bottom is a diagonal box with the team name. It joins a team logo, and below that point runs the player's position and name. The backs feature statistics, biographical information and a trivia question. Some interesting specialty sets were introduced in 1985, including the revival of the father/son theme from 1976, a subset of the 1984 U.S. Olympic Baseball Team members and a set featuring #1 draft choices since the inception of the baseball draft in 1965. Large numbers of uncut sheets were made available within the hobby, originally selling around $60 for a set of six.

	NM/M
Unopened Fact. Set (792):	140.00
Complete Set (792):	70.00
Common Player:	.05
Wax Pack (15):	4.50
Wax Box (36):	150.00
Cello Pack (28):	6.50
Cello Box (24):	150.00
Rack Pack (51+1):	9.00
Rack Box (24):	180.00
Vending Box (500):	60.00
1 Carlton Fisk (Record Breaker)	.25
2 Steve Garvey (Record Breaker)	.05
3 Dwight Gooden (Record Breaker)	.05
4 Cliff Johnson (Record Breaker)	.05
5 Joe Morgan (Record Breaker)	.10
6 Pete Rose (Record Breaker)	.50
7 Nolan Ryan (Record Breaker)	1.50
8 Juan Samuel RC (Record Breaker)	.05
9 Bruce Sutter (Record Breaker)	.10
10 Don Sutton (Record Breaker)	.05
11 Ralph Houk	.05
12 Dave Lopes	.05
13 Tim Lollar	.05
14 Chris Bando	.05
15 Jerry Koosman	.05
16 Bobby Meacham	.05
17 Mike Scott	.05
18 Mickey Hatcher	.05
19 George Frazier	.05
20 Chet Lemon	.05
21 Lee Tunnell	.05
22 Duane Kuiper	.05
23 Bret Saberhagen	.05
24 Jesse Barfield	.05
25 Steve Bedrosian	.05
26 Roy Smalley	.05
27 Bruce Berenyi	.05
28 Dann Bilardello	.05
29 Odell Jones	.05
30 Cal Ripken, Jr.	4.00
31 Terry Whitfield	.05
32 Chuck Porter	.05
33 Tito Landrum	.05
34 Ed Nunez RC	.05
35 Graig Nettles	.05
36 Fred Breining	.05
37 Reid Nichols	.05
38 Jackie Moore	.05
39 Johnny Wockenfuss	.05
40 Phil Niekro	.60
41 Mike Fischlin	.05
42 Luis Sanchez	.05
43 Andre David	.05
44 Dickie Thon	.05
45 Greg Minton	.05
46 Gary Woods	.05
47 Dave Rozema	.05
48 Tony Fernandez RC	.05
49 Butch Davis	.05
50 John Candelaria	.05
51 Bob Watson	.05
52 Jerry Dybzinski	.05
53 Tom Gorman	.05
54 Cesar Cedeno	.05
55 Frank Tanana	.05
56 Jim Dwyer	.05
57 Pat Zachry	.05
58 Orlando Mercado	.05
59 Rick Waits	.05
60 George Hendrick	.05
61 Curt Kaufman	.05
62 Mike Ramsey	.05
63 Steve McCatty	.05
64 Mark Bailey RC	.05
65 Bill Buckner	.05
66 Dick Williams	.05
67 Rafael Santana RC	.05
68 Von Hayes	.05
69 Jim Winn RC	.05
70 Don Baylor	.10
71 Tim Laudner	.05
72 Rick Sutcliffe	.05
73 Rusty Kuntz	.05
74 Mike Krukow	.05
75 Willie Upshaw	.05
76 Alan Bannister	.05
77 Joe Beckwith	.05
78 Scott Fletcher	.05
79 Rick Mahler	.05
80 Keith Hernandez	.05
81 Lenn Sakata	.05
82 Joe Price	.05
83 Charlie Moore	.05
84 Spike Owen	.05
85 Mike Marshall	.05
86 Don Aase	.05
87 David Green	.05
88 Bryn Smith	.05
89 Jackie Gutierrez	.05
90 Rich Gossage	.05
91 Jeff Burroughs	.05
92 Paul Owens	.05
93 Don Schulze RC	.05
94 Toby Harrah	.05
95 Jose Cruz	.05
96 Johnny Ray	.05
97 Pete Filson	.05
98 Steve Lake	.05
99 Milt Wilcox	.05
100 George Brett	3.00
101 Jim Acker	.05
102 Tommy Dunbar	.05
103 Randy Lerch	.05
104 Mike Fitzgerald	.05
105 Ron Kittle	.05
106 Pascual Perez	.05
107 Tom Foley	.05
108 Darnell Coles RC	.05
109 Gary Roenicke	.05
110 Alejandro Pena	.05
111 Doug DeCinces	.05
112 Tom Tellmann	.05
113 Tom Herr	.05
114 Bob James	.05
115 Rickey Henderson	.75
116 Dennis Boyd RC	.05
117 Greg Gross	.05
118 Eric Show	.05
119 Pat Corrales	.05
120 Steve Kemp	.05
121 Checklist 1-132	.05
122 Tom Brunansky	.05
123 Dave Smith	.05
124 Rich Hebner	.05
125 Kent Tekulve	.05
126 Ruppert Jones	.05
127 Mark Gubicza	.05
128 Ernie Whitt	.05
129 Gene Garber	.05
130 Al Oliver	.05
131 Father - Son (Buddy Bell, Gus Bell)	.05
132 Father - Son (Dale Berra, Yogi Berra)	.10
133 Father - Son (Bob Boone, Ray Boone)	.05
134 Father - Son (Terry Francona, Tito Francona)	.05
135 Father - Son (Bob Kennedy, Terry Kennedy)	.05
136 Father - Son (Bill Kunkel, Jeff Kunkel RC)	.05
137 Father - Son (Vance Law, Vern Law)	.05
138 Father - Son (Dick Schofield, Dick Schofield, Jr.)	.05
139 Father - Son (Bob Skinner, Joel Skinner)	.05
140 Father - Son (Roy Smalley, Jr., Roy Smalley III)	.05
141 Father - Son (Dave Stenhouse, Mike Stenhouse)	.05
142 Father - Son (Dizzy Trout, Steve Trout)	.05
143 Father - Son (Ozzie Virgil, Ozzie Virgil)	.05
144 Ron Gardenhire	.05
145 Alvin Davis	.05
146 Gary Redus	.05
147 Bill Swaggerty	.05
148 Steve Yeager	.05
149 Dickie Noles	.05
150 Jim Rice	.15
151 Moose Haas	.05
152 Steve Braun	.05
153 Frank LaCorte	.05
154 Argenis Salazar RC	.05
155 Yogi Berra	.10
156 Craig Reynolds	.05
157 Tug McGraw	.05
158 Pat Tabler	.05
159 Carlos Diaz	.05
160 Lance Parrish	.05
161 Ken Schrom	.05
162 Benny Distefano RC	.05
163 Dennis Eckersley	.60
164 Jorge Orta	.05
165 Dusty Baker	.05
166 Keith Atherton	.05
167 Rufino Linares	.05
168 Garth Iorg	.05
169 Dan Spillner	.05
170 George Foster	.05
171 Bill Stein	.05
172 Jack Perconte	.05
173 Mike Young RC	.05
174 Rick Honeycutt	.05
175 Dave Parker	.05
176 Bill Schroeder	.05
177 Dave Von Ohlen	.05
178 Miguel Dilone	.05
179 Tommy John	.10
180 Dave Winfield	.75
181 Roger Clemens	20.00
182 Tim Flannery	.05
183 Larry McWilliams	.05
184 Carmen Castillo RC	.05
185 Al Holland	.05
186 Bob Lillis	.05
187 Mike Walters	.05
188 Greg Pryor	.05
189 Warren Brusstar	.05
190 Rusty Staub	.05
191 Steve Nicosia	.05
192 Howard Johnson	.05
193 Jimmy Key	.05

No.	Player	Price
194	Dave Stegman	.05
195	Glenn Hubbard	.05
196	Pete O'Brien	.05
197	Mike Warren	.05
198	Eddie Milner	.05
199	Denny Martinez	.05
200	Reggie Jackson	2.00
201	Burt Hooton	.05
202	Gorman Thomas	.05
203	Bob McClure	.05
204	Art Howe	.05
205	Steve Rogers	.05
206	Phil Garner	.05
207	Mark Clear	.05
208	Champ Summers	.05
209	Bill Campbell	.05
210	Gary Matthews	.05
211	Clay Christiansen	.05
212	George Vukovich	.05
213	Billy Gardner	.05
214	John Tudor	.05
215	Bob Brenly	.05
216	Jerry Don Gleaton	.05
217	Leon Roberts	.05
218	Doyle Alexander	.05
219	Gerald Perry	.05
220	Fred Lynn	.05
221	Ron Reed	.05
222	Hubie Brooks	.05
223	Tom Hume	.05
224	Al Cowens	.05
225	Mike Boddicker	.05
226	Juan Beniquez	.05
227	Danny Darwin	.05
228	Dion James RC	.05
229	Dave LaPoint	.05
230	Gary Carter	.75
231	Dwayne Murphy	.05
232	Dave Beard	.05
233	Ed Jurak	.05
234	Jerry Narron	.05
235	Garry Maddox	.05
236	Mark Thurmond	.05
237	Julio Franco	.45
238	Jose Rijo	.05
239	Tim Teufel	.05
240	Dave Stieb	.05
241	Jim Frey	.05
242	Greg Harris	.05
243	Barbaro Garbey	.05
244	Mike Jones	.05
245	Chili Davis	.05
246	Mike Norris	.05
247	Wayne Tolleson	.05
248	Terry Forster	.05
249	Harold Baines	.05
250	Jesse Orosco	.05
251	Brad Gulden	.05
252	Dan Ford	.05
253	Sid Bream RC	.10
254	Pete Vuckovich	.05
255	Lonnie Smith	.05
256	Mike Stanton	.05
257	Brian Little (Bryan)	.05
258	Mike Brown	.05
259	Gary Allenson	.05
260	Dave Righetti	.05
261	Checklist 133-264	.05
262	Greg Booker RC	.05
263	Mel Hall	.05
264	Joe Sambito	.05
265	Juan Samuel RC	.05
266	Frank Viola	.05
267	Henry Cotto RC	.05
268	Chuck Tanner	.05
269	Doug Baker RC	.05
270	Dan Quisenberry	.05
271	Tim Foli (#1 Draft Pick)	.05
272	Jeff Burroughs (#1 Draft Pick)	.05
273	Bill Almon (#1 Draft Pick)	.05
274	Floyd Bannister (#1 Draft Pick)	.05
275	Harold Baines (#1 Draft Pick)	.10
276	Bob Horner (#1 Draft Pick)	.10
277	Al Chambers (#1 Draft Pick)	.05
278	Darryl Strawberry (#1 Draft Pick)	.30
279	Mike Moore RC (#1 Draft Pick)	.05
280	Shawon Dunston RC (#1 Draft Pick)	.40
281	Tim Belcher RC (#1 Draft Pick)	.30
282	Shawn Abner RC (#1 Draft Pick)	.05
283	Fran Mullins	.05
284	Marty Bystrom	.05
285	Dan Driessen	.05
286	Rudy Law	.05
287	Walt Terrell	.05
288	Jeff Kunkel RC	.05
289	Tom Underwood	.05
290	Cecil Cooper	.05
291	Bob Welch	.05
292	Brad Komminsk RC	.05
293	Curt Young RC	.05
294	Tom Nieto	.05
295	Joe Niekro	.05
296	Ricky Nelson	.05
297	Gary Lucas	.05
298	Marty Barrett	.05
299	Andy Hawkins	.05
300	Rod Carew	.75
301	John Montefusco	.05
302	Tim Corcoran	.05
303	Mike Jeffcoat RC	.05
304	Gary Gaetti	.05
305	Dale Berra	.05
306	Rick Reuschel	.05
307	Sparky Anderson	.10
308	John Wathan	.05
309	Mike Witt	.05
310	Manny Trillo	.05
311	Jim Gott	.05
312	Marc Hill	.05
313	Dave Schmidt	.05
314	Ron Oester	.05
315	Doug Sisk	.05
316	John Lowenstein	.05
317	Jack Lazorko RC	.05
318	Ted Simmons	.05
319	Jeff Jones	.05
320	Dale Murphy	.35
321	Ricky Horton RC	.05
322	Dave Stapleton	.05
323	Andy McGaffigan	.05
324	Bruce Bochy	.05
325	John Denny	.05
326	Kevin Bass	.05
327	Brook Jacoby	.05
328	Bob Shirley	.05
329	Ron Washington	.05
330	Leon Durham	.05
331	Bill Laskey	.05
332	Brian Harper	.05
333	Willie Hernandez	.05
334	Dick Howser	.05
335	Bruce Benedict	.05
336	Rance Mulliniks	.05
337	Billy Sample	.05
338	Britt Burns	.05
339	Danny Heep	.05
340	Robin Yount	.75
341	Floyd Rayford	.05
342	Ted Power	.05
343	Bill Russell	.05
344	Dave Henderson	.05
345	Charlie Lea	.05
346	Terry Pendleton RC	.75
347	Rick Langford	.05
348	Bob Boone	.05
349	Domingo Ramos	.05
350	Wade Boggs	1.00
351	Juan Agosto	.05
352	Joe Morgan	.75
353	Julio Solano	.05
354	Andre Robertson	.05
355	Bert Blyleven	.05
356	Dave Meier	.05
357	Rich Bordi	.05
358	Tony Pena	.05
359	Pat Sheridan	.05
360	Steve Carlton	.75
361	Alfredo Griffin	.05
362	Craig McMurtry	.05
363	Ron Hodges	.05
364	Richard Dotson	.05
365	Danny Ozark	.05
366	Todd Cruz	.05
367	Keefe Cato	.05
368	Dave Bergman	.05
369	R.J. Reynolds RC	.05
370	Bruce Sutter	.65
371	Mickey Rivers	.05
372	Roy Howell	.05
373	Mike Moore	.05
374	Brian Downing	.05
375	Jeff Reardon	.75
376	Jeff Newman	.05
377	Checklist 265-396	.05
378	Alan Wiggins	.05
379	Charles Hudson	.05
380	Ken Griffey	.05
381	Roy Smith	.05
382	Denny Walling	.05
383	Rick Lysander	.05
384	Jody Davis	.05
385	Jose DeLeon	.05
386	Dan Gladden RC	.30
387	Buddy Biancalana RC	.05
388	Bert Roberge	.05
389	Rod Dedeaux (Team USA)	.05
390	Sid Akins RC (Team USA)	.05
391	Flavio Alfaro (Team USA)	.05
392	Don August RC (Team USA)	.05
393	Scott Bankhead RC (Team USA)	.10
394	Bob Caffrey RC (Team USA)	.05
395	Mike Dunne RC (Team USA)	.05
396	Gary Green RC (Team USA)	.05
397	John Hoover (Team USA)	.05
398	Shane Mack RC (Team USA)	.10
399	John Marzano RC (Team USA)	.05
400	Oddibe McDowell RC (Team USA)	.05
401	Mark McGwire RC (Team USA)	20.00
402	Pat Pacillo RC (Team USA)	.05
403	Cory Snyder RC (Team USA)	.30
404	Billy Swift RC (Team USA)	.40
405	Tom Veryzer	.05
406	Len Whitehouse	.05
407	Bobby Ramos	.05
408	Sid Monge	.05
409	Brad Wellman	.05
410	Bob Horner	.05
411	Bobby Cox	.05
412	Bud Black	.05
413	Vance Law	.05
414	Gary Ward	.05
415	Ron Darling	.05
416	Wayne Gross	.05
417	John Franco RC	.50
418	Ken Landreaux	.05
419	Mike Caldwell	.05
420	Andre Dawson	.50
421	Dave Rucker	.05
422	Carney Lansford	.05
423	Barry Bonnell	.05
424	Al Nipper RC	.05
425	Mike Hargrove	.05
426	Verne Ruhle	.05
427	Mario Ramirez	.05
428	Larry Andersen	.05
429	Rick Cerone	.05
430	Ron Davis	.05
431	U.L. Washington	.05
432	Thad Bosley	.05
433	Jim Morrison	.05
434	Gene Richards	.05
435	Dan Petry	.05
436	Willie Aikens	.05
437	Al Jones	.05
438	Joe Torre	.10
439	Junior Ortiz	.05
440	Fernando Valenzuela	.05
441	Duane Walker	.05
442	Ken Forsch	.05
443	George Wright	.05
444	Tony Phillips	.05
445	Tippy Martinez	.05
446	Jim Sundberg	.05
447	Jeff Lahti	.05
448	Derrel Thomas	.05
449	Phil Bradley RC	.10
450	Steve Garvey	.25
451	Bruce Hurst	.05
452	John Castino	.05
453	Tom Waddell	.05
454	Glenn Wilson	.05
455	Bob Knepper	.05
456	Tim Foli	.05
457	Cecilio Guante	.05
458	Randy S. Johnson	.05
459	Charlie Leibrandt	.05
460	Ryne Sandberg	1.00
461	Marty Castillo	.05
462	Gary Lavelle	.05
463	Dave Collins	.05
464	Mike Mason RC	.05
465	Bob Grich	.05
466	Tony LaRussa	.10
467	Ed Lynch	.05
468	Wayne Krenchicki	.05
469	Sammy Stewart	.05
470	Steve Sax	.05
471	Pete Ladd	.05
472	Jim Essian	.05
473	Tim Wallach	.05
474	Kurt Kepshire	.05
475	Andre Thornton	.05
476	Jeff Stone RC	.05
477	Bob Ojeda	.05
478	Kurt Bevacqua	.05
479	Mike Madden	.05
480	Lou Whitaker	.05
481	Dale Murray	.05
482	Harry Spilman	.05
483	Mike Smithson	.05
484	Larry Bowa	.05
485	Matt Young	.05
486	Steve Balboni	.05
487	Frank Williams RC	.05
488	Joel Skinner RC	.05
489	Bryan Clark	.05
490	Jason Thompson	.05
491	Rick Camp	.05
492	Dave Johnson	.05
493	Orel Hershiser RC	2.00
494	Rich Dauer	.05
495	Mario Soto	.05
496	Donnie Scott	.05
497	Gary Pettis	.05
498	Ed Romero	.05
499	Danny Cox RC	.05
500	Mike Schmidt	2.00
501	Dan Schatzeder	.05
502	Rick Miller	.05
503	Tim Conroy	.05
504	Jerry Willard	.05
505	Jim Beattie	.05
506	Franklin Stubbs RC	.05
507	Ray Fontenot	.05
508	John Shelby	.05
509	Milt May	.05
510	Kent Hrbek	.05
511	Lee Smith	.05
512	Tom Brookens	.05
513	Lynn Jones	.05
514	Jeff Cornell	.05
515	Dave Concepcion	.05
516	Roy Lee Jackson	.05
517	Jerry Martin	.05
518	Chris Chambliss	.05
519	Doug Rader	.05
520	LaMarr Hoyt	.05
521	Rick Dempsey	.05
522	Paul Molitor	.75
523	Candy Maldonado	.05
524	Rob Wilfong	.05
525	Darrell Porter	.05
526	Dave Palmer	.05
527	Checklist 397-528	.05
528	Bill Krueger	.05
529	Rich Gedman	.05
530	Dave Dravecky	.05
531	Joe Lefebvre	.05
532	Frank DiPino	.05
533	Tony Bernazard	.05
534	Brian Dayett RC	.05
535	Pat Putnam	.05
536	Kirby Puckett	10.00
537	Don Robinson	.05
538	Keith Moreland	.05
539	Aurelio Lopez	.05
540	Claudell Washington	.05
541	Mark Davis	.05
542	Don Slaught	.05
543	Mike Squires	.05
544	Bruce Kison	.05
545	Lloyd Moseby	.05
546	Brent Gaff	.05
547	Pete Rose	1.50
548	Larry Parrish	.05
549	Mike Scioscia	.05
550	Scott McGregor	.05
551	Andy Van Slyke	.05
552	Chris Codiroli	.05
553	Bob Clark	.05
554	Doug Flynn	.05
555	Bob Stanley	.05
556	Sixto Lezcano	.05
557	Len Barker	.05
558	Carmelo Martinez	.05
559	Jay Howell	.05
560	Bill Madlock	.05
561	Darryl Motley	.05
562	Houston Jimenez	.05
563	Dick Ruthven	.05
564	Alan Ashby	.05
565	Kirk Gibson	.05
566	Ed Vande Berg	.05
567	Joel Youngblood	.05
568	Cliff Johnson	.05
569	Ken Oberkfell	.05
570	Darryl Strawberry	.10
571	Charlie Hough	.05
572	Tom Paciorek	.05
573	Jay Tibbs RC	.05
574	Joe Altobelli	.05
575	Pedro Guerrero	.05
576	Jaime Cocanower	.05
577	Chris Speier	.05
578	Terry Francona	.05
579	Ron Romanick RC	.05
580	Dwight Evans	.05
581	Mark Wagner	.05
582	Ken Phelps RC	.05
583	Bobby Brown	.05
584	Kevin Gross	.05
585	Butch Wynegar	.05
586	Bill Scherrer	.05
587	Doug Frobel	.05
588	Bobby Castillo	.05
589	Bob Dernier	.05
590	Ray Knight	.05
591	Larry Herndon	.05
592	Jeff Robinson RC	.05
593	Rick Leach	.05
594	Curt Wilkerson RC	.05
595	Larry Gura	.05
596	Jerry Hairston Sr.	.05
597	Brad Lesley	.05
598	Jose Oquendo	.05
599	Storm Davis	.05
600	Pete Rose	3.00
601	Tom Lasorda	.10
602	Jeff Dedmon RC	.05
603	Rick Manning	.05
604	Daryl Sconiers	.05
605	Ozzie Smith	1.00
606	Rich Gale	.05
607	Bill Almon	.05
608	Craig Lefferts	.05
609	Broderick Perkins	.05
610	Jack Morris	.05
611	Ozzie Virgil	.05
612	Mike Armstrong	.05
613	Terry Puhl	.05
614	Al Williams	.05
615	Marvell Wynne	.05
616	Scott Sanderson	.05
617	Willie Wilson	.05
618	Pete Falcone	.05
619	Jeff Leonard	.05
620	Dwight Gooden	.50
621	Marvis Foley	.05
622	Luis Leal	.05
623	Greg Walker	.05
624	Benny Ayala	.05
625	Mark Langston	.05
626	German Rivera	.05
627	Eric Davis RC	1.00
628	Rene Lachemann	.05
629	Dick Schofield	.05
630	Tim Raines	.05
631	Bob Forsch	.05
632	Bruce Bochte	.05
633	Glenn Hoffman	.05
634	Bill Dawley	.05
635	Terry Kennedy	.05
636	Shane Rawley	.05
637	Brett Butler	.05
638	Mike Pagliarulo RC	.10
639	Ed Hodge	.05
640	Steve Henderson	.05
641	Rod Scurry	.05
642	Dave Owen	.05
643	Johnny Grubb	.05
644	Mark Huismann RC	.05
645	Damaso Garcia	.05
646	Scot Thompson	.05
647	Rafael Ramirez	.05
648	Bob Jones	.05
649	Sid Fernandez RC	.05
650	Greg Luzinski	.05
651	Jeff Russell	.05
652	Joe Nolan	.05
653	Mark Brouhard	.05
654	Dave Anderson	.05
655	Joaquin Andujar	.05
656	Chuck Cottier	.05
657	Jim Slaton	.05
658	Mike Stenhouse	.05
659	Checklist 529-660	.05
660	Tony Gwynn	1.00
661	Steve Crawford	.05
662	Mike Heath	.05
663	Luis Aguayo	.05
664	Steve Farr RC	.05
665	Don Mattingly	3.00
666	Mike LaCoss	.05
667	Dave Engle	.05
668	Steve Trout	.05
669	Lee Lacy	.05
670	Tom Seaver	.75
671	Dane Iorg	.05
672	Juan Berenguer	.05
673	Buck Martinez	.05
674	Atlee Hammaker	.05
675	Tony Perez	.75
676	Albert Hall RC	.05
677	Wally Backman	.05
678	Joey McLaughlin	.05
679	Bob Kearney	.05
680	Jerry Reuss	.05
681	Ben Oglivie	.05
682	Doug Corbett	.05
683	Whitey Herzog	.05
684	Bill Doran	.05
685	Bill Caudill	.05
686	Mike Easler	.05
687	Bill Gullickson	.05
688	Len Matuszek	.05
689	Luis DeLeon	.05
690	Alan Trammell	.05
691	Dennis Rasmussen RC	.05
692	Randy Bush	.05
693	Tim Stoddard	.05
694	Joe Carter	.05
695	Rick Rhoden	.05
696	John Rabb	.05
697	Onix Concepcion	.05
698	Jorge Bell	.05
699	Donnie Moore	.05
700	Eddie Murray	.75
701	Eddie Murray/AS	.40
702	Damaso Garcia/AS	.05
703	George Brett/AS	.50
704	Cal Ripken, Jr./AS	1.50
705	Dave Winfield/AS	.40
706	Rickey Henderson/AS	.40
707	Tony Armas/AS	.05
708	Lance Parrish/AS	.05
709	Mike Boddicker/AS	.05
710	Frank Viola/AS	.05
711	Dan Quisenberry/AS	.05
712	Keith Hernandez/AS	.05
713	Ryne Sandberg/AS	.40
714	Mike Schmidt/AS	.75
715	Ozzie Smith/AS	.50
716	Dale Murphy/AS	.15
717	Tony Gwynn/AS	.75
718	Jeff Leonard/AS	.05
719	Gary Carter/AS	.40
720	Rick Sutcliffe/AS	.05
721	Bob Knepper/AS	.05
722	Bruce Sutter/AS	.30
723	Dave Stewart	.05
724	Oscar Gamble	.05
725	Floyd Bannister	.05
726	Al Bumbry	.05
727	Frank Pastore	.05
728	Bob Bailor	.05
729	Don Sutton	.60
730	Dave Kingman	.05
731	Neil Allen	.05
732	John McNamara	.05
733	Tony Scott	.05
734	John Henry Johnson	.05
735	Garry Templeton	.05
736	Jerry Mumphrey	.05
737	Bo Diaz	.05
738	Omar Moreno	.05
739	Ernie Camacho	.05
740	Jack Clark	.05
741	John Butcher	.05
742	Ron Hassey	.05
743	Frank White	.05
744	Doug Bair	.05
745	Buddy Bell	.05
746	Jim Clancy	.05
747	Alex Trevino	.05
748	Lee Mazzilli	.05
749	Julio Cruz	.05
750	Rollie Fingers	.60
751	Kelvin Chapman	.05
752	Bob Owchinko	.05
753	Greg Brock	.05
754	Larry Milbourne	.05
755	Ken Singleton	.05
756	Rob Picciolo	.05
757	Willie McGee	.05
758	Ray Burris	.05
759	Jim Fanning	.05
760	Nolan Ryan	4.00
761	Jerry Remy	.05
762	Eddie Whitson	.05
763	Kiko Garcia	.05
764	Jamie Easterly	.05
765	Willie Randolph	.05
766	Paul Mirabella	.05
767	Darrell Brown	.05
768	Ron Cey	.05
769	Joe Cowley	.05
770	Carlton Fisk	.75
771	Geoff Zahn	.05
772	Johnnie LeMaster	.05
773	Hal McRae	.05
774	Dennis Lamp	.05
775	Mookie Wilson	.05
776	Jerry Royster	.05
777	Ned Yost	.05
778	Mike Davis	.05
779	Nick Esasky	.05
780	Mike Flanagan	.05
781	Jim Gantner	.05
782	Tom Niedenfuer	.05
783	Mike Jorgensen	.05
784	Checklist 661-792	.05
785	Tony Armas	.05
786	Enos Cabell	.05
787	Jim Wohlford	.05
788	Steve Comer	.05
789	Luis Salazar	.05
790	Ron Guidry	.10
791	Ivan DeJesus	.05
792	Darrell Evans	.05

Tiffany

In its second year of producing a high-gloss collectors' edition of its regular baseball card set, Topps cut production to a reported 5,000 sets. Other than the use of white cardboard stock and the glossy front coating, the cards in this specially boxed set are identical to regular 1985 Topps cards.

	NM/M
Complete Unopened Set (792):	500.00
Complete Set, Opened (792):	325.00
Common Player:	.25
Stars:	4X
181 Roger Clemens	150.00
401 Mark McGwire	80.00

Traded

Topps continued the annual Traded set tradition with another 132-card set. The 2-1/2" x 3-1/2" cards follow the pattern of being virtually identical in design to the regular cards of that year. Sold only through hobby dealers, the set features traded veterans and promising rookies. A glossy-finish "Tiffany" edition of the set was also issued. Cards are numbered with a "T" suffix.

	NM/M
Complete Set (132):	10.00
Common Player:	.05
Wax Test Pack (8):	10.00
Wax Test Wax Box (36):	150.00
1 Don Aase	.05
2 Bill Almon	.05
3 Benny Ayala	.05
4 Dusty Baker	.25
5 George Bamberger	.05
6 Dale Berra	.05
7 Rich Bordi	.05
8 Daryl Boston RC	.05
9 Hubie Brooks	.05
10 Chris Brown RC	.05
11 Tom Browning RC	.05
12 Al Bumbry	.05
13 Ray Burris	.05
14 Jeff Burroughs	.05
15 Bill Campbell	.05
16 Don Carman RC	.05
17 Gary Carter	1.50
18 Bobby Castillo	.05
19 Bill Caudill	.05
20 Rick Cerone	.05
21 Bryan Clark	.05
22 Jack Clark	.05
23 Pat Clements RC	.05
24 Vince Coleman RC	.50
25 Dave Collins	.05
26 Danny Darwin	.05
27 Jim Davenport	.05

28	Jerry Davis	.05
29	Brian Dayett	.05
30	Ivan DeJesus	.05
31	Ken Dixon	.05
32	Mariano Duncan **RC**	.05
33	John Felske	.05
34	Mike Fitzgerald	.05
35	Ray Fontenot	.05
36	Greg Gagne **RC**	.05
37	Oscar Gamble	.05
38	Scott Garrelts **RC**	.05
39	Bob L. Gibson	.05
40	Jim Gott	.05
41	David Green	.05
42	Alfredo Griffin	.05
43	Ozzie Guillen **RC**	3.00
44	Eddie Haas	.05
45	Terry Harper	.05
46	Toby Harrah	.05
47	Greg Harris	.05
48	Ron Hassey	.05
49	Rickey Henderson	2.50
50	Steve Henderson	.05
51	George Hendrick	.05
52	Joe Hesketh **RC**	.05
53	Teddy Higuera **RC**	.05
54	Donnie Hill	.05
55	Al Holland	.05
56	Burt Hooton	.05
57	Jay Howell	.05
58	Ken Howell **RC**	.05
59	LaMarr Hoyt	.05
60	Tim Hulett **RC**	.05
61	Bob James	.05
62	Steve Jeltz **RC**	.05
63	Cliff Johnson	.05
64	Howard Johnson	.05
65	Ruppert Jones	.05
66	Steve Kemp	.05
67	Bruce Kison	.05
68	Alan Knicely	.05
69	Mike LaCoss	.05
70	Lee Lacy	.05
71	Dave LaPoint	.05
72	Gary Lavelle	.05
73	Vance Law	.05
74	Johnnie LeMaster	.05
75	Sixto Lezcano	.05
76	Tim Lollar	.05
77	Fred Lynn	.25
78	Billy Martin	.25
79	Ron Mathis	.05
80	Len Matuszek	.05
81	Gene Mauch	.05
82	Oddibe McDowell	.05
83	Roger McDowell **RC**	.05
84	John McNamara	.05
85	Donnie Moore	.05
86	Gene Nelson	.05
87	Steve Nicosia	.05
88	Al Oliver	.05
89	Joe Orsulak **RC**	.05
90	Rob Picciolo	.05
91	Chris Pittaro	.05
92	Jim Presley **RC**	.05
93	Rick Reuschel	.05
94	Bert Roberge	.05
95	Bob Rodgers	.05
96	Jerry Royster	.05
97	Dave Rozema	.05
98	Dave Rucker	.05
99	Vern Ruhle	.05
100	Paul Runge **RC**	.05
101	Mark Salas **RC**	.05
102	Luis Salazar	.05
103	Joe Sambito	.05
104	Rick Schu **RC**	.05
105	Donnie Scott	.05
106	Larry Sheets **RC**	.05
107	Don Slaught	.05
108	Roy Smalley	.05
109	Lonnie Smith	.05
110	Nate Snell	.05
111	Chris Speier	.05
112	Mike Stenhouse	.05
113	Tim Stoddard	.05
114	Jim Sundberg	.05
115	Bruce Sutter	1.00
116	Don Sutton	.50
117	Kent Tekulve	.05
118	Tom Tellmann	.05
119	Walt Terrell	.05
120	Mickey Tettleton **RC**	1.00
121	Derrel Thomas	.05
122	Rich Thompson	.05
123	Alex Trevino	.05
124	John Tudor	.05
125	Jose Uribe **RC**	.05
126	Bobby Valentine	.05
127	Dave Von Ohlen	.05
128	U.L. Washington	.05
129	Earl Weaver	.30
130	Eddie Whitson	.05
131	Herm Winningham **RC**	.05
132	Checklist 1-132	

Traded Pete Rose Bronze

This 1/4-size metal replica was issued to dealers who purchased cases of 1985 Topps Traded sets. Each detail of the 1985 Topps Pete Rose card is reproduced on the 1-3/4" x 1-3/4" bronze metal mini-card, right down to the stats.

		NM/M
600	Pete Rose	10.00

All-Star Glossy Set of 22

This was the second straight year for this set of 22 cards featuring the starting players, honorary captains and managers in the All-Star Game. The set is virtually identical to that of the previous year in design with a color photo, All-Star banner, league emblem, and player ID on the front. Fronts have a high-gloss finish. The cards were available as inserts in Topps rack packs.

		NM/M
Complete Set (22):		5.00
Common Player:		.10
1	Paul Owens	.10
2	Steve Garvey	.30
3	Ryne Sandberg	.50
4	Mike Schmidt	1.00
5	Ozzie Smith	.50
6	Tony Gwynn	.50
7	Dale Murphy	.30
8	Darryl Strawberry	.10
9	Gary Carter	.40
10	Charlie Lea	.10
11	Willie McCovey	.30
12	Joe Altobelli	.10
13	Rod Carew	.40
14	Lou Whitaker	.10
15	George Brett	1.00
16	Cal Ripken, Jr.	1.50
17	Dave Winfield	.40
18	Chet Lemon	.10
19	Reggie Jackson	.50
20	Lance Parrish	.10
21	Dave Stieb	.10
22	Hank Greenberg	.25

All-Star Glossy Set of 40

Traded Tiffany

This specially boxed collectors version of the Topps Traded sets features cards that differ only in the use of a high-gloss finish coat on the fronts.

	NM/M
Complete Set (132):	35.00
Common Player:	.25
Stars:	4X

Similar to previous years' glossy sets, the 1985 All-Star "Collector's Edition" set of 40 could be obtained through the mail in eight five-card

subsets. To obtain the 2-1/2" x 3-1/2" cards, collectors had to accumulate sweepstakes insert cards from Topps packs, and pay 75¢ postage and handling. Under the circumstances, the complete set of 40 cards was not inexpensive.

		NM/M
Complete Set (40):		8.00
Common Player:		.10
1	Dale Murphy	.30
2	Jesse Orosco	.10
3	Bob Brenly	.10
4	Mike Boddicker	.10
5	Dave Kingman	.10
6	Jim Rice	.20
7	Frank Viola	.10
8	Alvin Davis	.10
9	Rick Sutcliffe	.10
10	Pete Rose	2.00
11	Leon Durham	.10
12	Joaquin Andujar	.10
13	Keith Hernandez	.10
14	Dave Winfield	.40
15	Reggie Jackson	.50
16	Alan Trammell	.10
17	Bert Blyleven	.10
18	Tony Armas	.10
19	Rich Gossage	.10
20	Jose Cruz	.10
21	Ryne Sandberg	.50
22	Bruce Sutter	.30
23	Mike Schmidt	1.00
24	Cal Ripken, Jr.	3.00
25	Dan Petry	.10
26	Jack Morris	.10
27	Don Mattingly	1.00
28	Eddie Murray	.40
29	Tony Gwynn	.50
30	Charlie Lea	.10
31	Juan Samuel	.10
32	Phil Niekro	.30
33	Alejandro Pena	.10
34	Harold Baines	.10
35	Dan Quisenberry	.10
36	Gary Carter	.40
37	Mario Soto	.10
38	Dwight Gooden	.10
39	Tom Brunansky	.10
40	Dave Stieb	.10

All-Time Record Holders

No Pricing

Gallery of Champions

This second annual metallic miniatures issue honors 12 award winners from the previous season (MVP, Cy Young, Rookie of Year, Fireman, etc.). Each mini is an exact reproduction at one-quarter scale of the player's 1985 Topps card, both front and back. The sets (editions of 1,000) were issued in a specially-designed velvet-like case. A Dwight Gooden pewter replica was given as a premium to dealers who bought the sets.

		NM/M
Complete Bronze Set (12):		60.00
Complete Silver Set (12):		280.00
(1b)	Tony Armas/Bronze	3.00
(1s)	Tony Armas/Silver	10.00
(2b)	Alvin Davis/Bronze	3.00
(2s)	Alvin Davis/Silver	10.00
(3b)	Dwight Gooden/Bronze	5.00
(3s)	Dwight Gooden/Silver	15.00
(3p)	Dwight Gooden/Pewter	6.00
(4b)	Tony Gwynn/Bronze	15.00
(4s)	Tony Gwynn/Silver	50.00
(5b)	Willie Hernandez/Bronze	3.00
(5s)	Willie Hernandez/Silver	10.00
(6b)	Don Mattingly/Bronze	30.00
(6s)	Don Mattingly/Silver	75.00
(7b)	Dale Murphy/Bronze	10.00
(7s)	Dale Murphy/Silver	45.00
(8b)	Dan Quisenberry/Bronze	3.00
(8s)	Dan Quisenberry/Silver	10.00
(9b)	Ryne Sandberg/Bronze	15.00
(9s)	Ryne Sandberg/Silver	50.00
(10b)	Mike Schmidt/Bronze	25.00
(10s)	Mike Schmidt/Silver	60.00
(11b)	Rick Sutcliffe/Bronze	3.00
(11s)	Rick Sutcliffe/Silver	10.00
(12b)	Bruce Sutter/Bronze	6.00
(12s)	Bruce Sutter/Silver	20.00

Minis

Never released for public sale, quantities of these enigmatic cards nevertheless reached the hobby market. Smaller than the standard 2-1/2" x 3-1/2" Topps cards, the "mini" version measures 2-3/8" x 3-9/32", 10% smaller than regular cards. Printed in Canada, the minis use a whiter cardboard stock than the regular '85 Topps, making the color printing more vibrant. The minis were the result of a test of new printing equipment by O-Pee-Chee, Topps; Canadian licensee. Only 132 of the 792 cards in the '85 Topps set are found in mini version. Only about 100 of each mini card are known, including about 15% blank-backs.

		NM/M
Complete Set (132):		1,500
Common Player:		5.00
Blank-backs: 50 Percent		
12	Dave Lopes	5.00
14	Jerry Koosman	5.00
17	Mike Scott	5.00
23	Steve Bedrosian	5.00
44	Dickie Thon	5.00
65	Bill Buckner	5.00
68	Von Hayes	5.00
72	Rick Sutcliffe	5.00
75	Willie Upshaw	5.00
82	Joe Price	5.00
88	Bryn Smith	5.00
91	Jeff Burroughs	5.00
95	Jose Cruz	5.00
96	Johnny Ray	5.00
109	Gary Roenicke	5.00
113	Tom Herr	5.00
114	Bob James	5.00
119	Greg Gross	5.00
120	Steve Kemp	5.00
121	Checklist 1-132	3.00
128	Ernie Whitt	5.00
148	Steve Yeager	5.00
150	Jim Rice	15.00
151	Moose Haas	5.00
154	Argenis Salazar	5.00
158	Craig Reynolds	5.00
160	Lance Parrish	5.00
165	Dusty Baker	5.00
170	George Foster	5.00
178	Miguel Dilone	5.00
185	Al Holland	5.00
190	Rusty Staub	5.00
198	Eddie Milner	5.00
201	Burt Hooton	5.00
205	Steve Rogers	5.00
209	Bill Campbell	5.00
210	Gary Matthews	5.00
218	Doyle Alexander	5.00
222	Hubie Brooks	5.00
225	Tom Hume	5.00
225	Mike Boddicker	5.00
229	Dave LaPoint	5.00
230	Gary Carter	45.00
236	Garry Maddox	5.00
236	Mark Thurmond	5.00
237	Julio Franco	5.00
239	Tim Teufel	5.00
248	Terry Forster	5.00
250	Jesse Orosco	5.00

251	Brad Gulden	5.00
255	Lonnie Smith	5.00
261	Checklist 133-264	3.00
263	Mel Hall	5.00
266	Frank Viola	5.00
287	Walt Terrell	5.00
306	Rick Reuschel	5.00
310	Manny Trillo	5.00
313	Dave Schmidt	5.00
325	John Denny	5.00
333	Leon Durham	5.00
333	Willie Hernandez	5.00
340	Robin Yount	45.00
343	Bill Russell	5.00
345	Charlie Lea	5.00
352	Joe Morgan	45.00
355	Bert Blyleven	5.00
358	Tony Pena	5.00
360	Steve Carlton	45.00
362	Craig McMurtry	5.00
375	Jeff Reardon	5.00
379	Charles Hudson	5.00
415	Ron Darling	5.00
442	Tippy Martinez	5.00
445	Jim Sundberg	5.00
450	Steve Garvey	7.50
452	John Castino	5.00
464	Mike Mason	5.00
474	Steve Sax	5.00
485	Matt Young	5.00
487	Frank Williams	5.00
489	Bryan Clark	5.00
491	Rick Camp	5.00
495	Mario Soto	5.00
500	Mike Schmidt	250.00
501	Dan Schatzeder	5.00
504	Jerry Willard	5.00
511	Lee Smith	5.00
515	Dave Concepcion	5.00
520	LaMarr Hoyt	5.00
526	Dave Palmer	5.00
530	Dave Dravecky	5.00
538	Keith Moreland	5.00
545	Lloyd Moseby	5.00
551	Andy Van Slyke	5.00
554	Doug Flynn	5.00
556	Sixto Lezcano	5.00
560	Bill Madlock	5.00
563	Dick Ruthven	5.00
566	Ed Vande Berg	5.00
568	Cliff Johnson	5.00
569	Ken Oberkfell	5.00
575	Pedro Guerrero	5.00
587	Dwight Evans	5.00
589	Bob Bernier	5.00
592	Jeff Robinson	5.00
603	Rick Manning	5.00
608	Craig Lefferts	5.00
610	Jack Morris	5.00
613	Terry Puhl	5.00
615	Marvell Wynne	5.00
619	Jeff Leonard	5.00
625	Mark Langston	5.00
630	Tim Raines	5.00
634	Bill Dawley	5.00
670	Tom Seaver	45.00
673	Buck Martinez	5.00
674	Atlee Hammaker	5.00
685	Bill Caudill	5.00
700	Eddie Murray	45.00
725	Floyd Bannister	5.00
729	Don Sutton	10.00
731	Neil Allen	5.00
736	Jerry Mumphrey	5.00
748	Lee Mazzilli	5.00
753	Greg Brock	5.00
755	Ken Singleton	5.00
757	Willie McGee	5.00
760	Nolan Ryan	650.00
762	Eddie Whitson	5.00
775	Mookie Wilson	5.00
780	Mike Flanagan	5.00
782	Tom Niedenfuer	5.00

Rub Downs

Similar in size and design to the Rub Downs of the previous year, the 1985 set again consisted of 32 unnumbered sheets featuring 112 different players. The set was sold by Topps as a separate issue.

	NM/M
Complete Set (32):	5.00
Common Sheet:	.25
Pack (2):	.50
Wax Box (36):	7.50

(1)	Tony Armas, Harold Baines, Lonnie Smith	.25
(2)	Don Baylor, George Hendrick, Ron Kittle, Johnnie LeMaster	.25
(3)	Buddy Bell, Tony Gwynn, Lloyd Moseby	.75
(4)	Bruce Benedict, Atlee Hammaker, Frank White	.25
(5)	Mike Boddicker, Rod Carew, Carlton Fisk, Johnny Ray	.60
(6)	Wade Boggs, Rick Dempsey, Keith Hernandez	.60
(7)	George Brett, Andre Dawson, Paul Molitor, Alan Wiggins	1.00
(8)	Tom Brunansky, Pedro Guerrero, Darryl Strawberry	.25
(9)	Bill Buckner, Tim Raines, Ryne Sandberg, Mike Schmidt	1.00
(10)	Steve Carlton, Bob Horner, Dan Quisenberry	.60
(11)	Gary Carter, Phil Garner, Ron Guidry	.60
(12)	Jack Clark, Damaso Garcia, Hal McRae, Lance Parrish	.25
(13)	Dave Concepcion, Cecil Cooper, Fred Lynn, Jesse Orosco	.25
(14)	Jose Cruz, Jack Morris, Jim Rice, Rick Sutcliffe	.25
(15)	Alvin Davis, Steve Kemp, Greg Luzinski, Kent Tekulve	.25
(16)	Ron Davis, Kent Hrbek, Juan Samuel	.25
(17)	John Denny, Carney Lansford, Mario Soto, Lou Whitaker	.25
(18)	Leon Durham, Willie Hernandez, Steve Sax	.25
(19)	Dwight Evans, Julio Franco, Dwight Gooden	.25
(20)	George Foster, Gary Gaetti, Bobby Grich, Gary Redus	.25
(21)	Steve Garvey, Jerry Remy, Bill Russell, George Wright	.25
(22)	Kirk Gibson, Rich Gossage, Don Mattingly, Dave Stieb	1.00
(23)	Moose Haas, Bruce Sutter, Dickie Thon, Andre Thornton	.25
(24)	Rickey Henderson, Dave Righetti, Pete Rose	1.50
(25)	Steve Henderson, Bill Madlock, Alan Trammell	.25
(26)	LaMarr Hoyt, Larry Parrish, Nolan Ryan	2.00
(27)	Reggie Jackson, Eric Show, Jason Thompson	.75
(28)	Terry Kennedy, Eddie Murray, Tom Seaver, Ozzie Smith	.75
(29)	Mark Langston, Ben Oglivie, Darrell Porter	.25
(30)	Jeff Leonard, Gary Matthews, Dale Murphy, Dave Winfield	.60
(31)	Craig McMurtry, Cal Ripken, Jr., Steve Rogers, Willie Upshaw	2.00
(32)	Tony Pena, Fernando Valenzuela, Robin Yount	.60

Stickers

Topps went to a larger size for its stickers in 1985. Produced by Panini, each of the 376 stickers measures 2-1/8" x 3" and is numbered on both the front and the back. The backs contain either an offer to obtain an autographed team ball or a poster. An album was also available.

	NM/M
Complete Set (376):	12.50
Common Player:	.05
Sticker Album:	2.00
Pack (5):	.25
Box (100):	15.00

#	Player	Price
1	Steve Garvey	.15
2	Steve Garvey	.15
3	Dwight Gooden	.05
4	Dwight Gooden	.05
5	Joe Morgan	.30
6	Joe Morgan	.30
7	Don Sutton	.30
8	Don Sutton	.30
9	1984 A.L. Championships (Jack Morris)	.05
10	1984 A.L. Championships (Milt Wilcox)	.05
11	1984 A.L. Championships (Kirk Gibson)	.05
12	1984 N.L. Championships (Gary Matthews)	.05
13	1984 N.L. Championships (Steve Garvey)	.05
14	1984 N.L. Championships (Steve Garvey)	.05
15	1984 World Series (Jack Morris)	.05
16	1984 World Series (Kurt Bevacqua)	.05
17	1984 World Series (Milt Wilcox)	.05
18	1984 World Series (Alan Trammell)	.05
19	1984 World Series (Kirk Gibson)	.05
20	1984 World Series (Alan Trammell)	.05
21	1984 World Series (Chet Lemon)	.05
22	Dale Murphy	.25
23	Steve Bedrosian	.05
24	Bob Horner	.05
25	Claudell Washington	.05
26	Rick Mahler	.05
27	Rafael Ramirez	.05
28	Craig McMurtry	.05
29	Chris Chambliss	.05
30	Alex Trevino	.05
31	Bruce Benedict	.05
32	Ken Oberkfell	.05
33	Glenn Hubbard	.05
34	Ryne Sandberg	.40
35	Rick Sutcliffe	.05
36	Leon Durham	.05
37	Jody Davis	.05
38	Bob Dernier	.05
39	Keith Moreland	.05
40	Scott Sanderson	.05
41	Lee Smith	.05
42	Ron Cey	.05
43	Steve Trout	.05
44	Gary Matthews	.05
45	Larry Bowa	.05
46	Mario Soto	.05
47	Dave Parker	.05
48	Dave Concepcion	.05
49	Gary Redus	.05
50	Ted Power	.05
51	Nick Esasky	.05
52	Duane Walker	.05
53	Eddie Milner	.05
54	Ron Oester	.05
55	Cesar Cedeno	.05
56	Joe Price	.05
57	Pete Rose	.65
58	Nolan Ryan	.75
59	Jose Cruz	.15
60	Jerry Mumphrey	.05
61	Enos Cabell	.05
62	Bob Knepper	.05
63	Dickie Thon	.05
64	Phil Garner	.05
65	Craig Reynolds	.05
66	Frank DiPino	.05
67	Terry Puhl	.05
68	Bill Doran	.05
69	Joe Niekro	.05
70	Pedro Guerrero	.05
71	Fernando Valenzuela	.05
72	Mike Marshall	.05
73	Alejandro Pena	.05
74	Orel Hershiser	.10
75	Ken Landreaux	.05
76	Bill Russell	.05
77	Steve Sax	.05
78	Rick Honeycutt	.05
79	Mike Scioscia	.05
80	Tom Niedenfuer	.05
81	Candy Maldonado	.05
82	Tim Raines	.05
83	Gary Carter	.30
84	Charlie Lea	.05
85	Jeff Reardon	.05
86	Andre Dawson	.15
87	Tim Wallach	.05
88	Terry Francona	.05
89	Steve Rogers	.05
90	Bryn Smith	.05
91	Bill Gullickson	.05
92	Dan Driessen	.05
93	Doug Flynn	.05
94	Mike Schmidt	.50
95	Tony Armas	.05
96	Dale Murphy	.15
97	Rick Sutcliffe	.05
98	Keith Hernandez	.05
99	George Foster	.05
100	Darryl Strawberry	.05
101	Jesse Orosco	.05
102	Mookie Wilson	.05
103	Doug Sisk	.05
104	Hubie Brooks	.05
105	Ron Darling	.05
106	Wally Backman	.05
107	Dwight Gooden	.05
108	Mike Fitzgerald	.05
109	Walt Terrell	.05
110	Ozzie Virgil	.05
111	Mike Schmidt	.50
112	Steve Carlton	.30
113	Al Holland	.05
114	Juan Samuel	.05
115	Von Hayes	.05
116	Jeff Stone	.05
117	Jerry Koosman	.05
118	Al Oliver	.05
119	John Denny	.05
120	Charles Hudson	.05
121	Garry Maddox	.05
122	Bill Madlock	.05
123	John Candelaria	.05
124	Tony Pena	.05
125	Jason Thompson	.05
126	Lee Lacy	.05
127	Rick Rhoden	.05
128	Doug Frobel	.05
129	Kent Tekulve	.05
130	Johnny Ray	.05
131	Marvell Wynne	.05
132	Larry McWilliams	.05
133	Dale Berra	.05
134	George Hendrick	.05
135	Bruce Sutter	.20
136	Joaquin Andujar	.05
137	Ozzie Smith	.50
138	Andy Van Slyke	.05
139	Lonnie Smith	.05
140	Darrell Porter	.05
141	Willie McGee	.05
142	Tom Herr	.05
143	Dave LaPoint	.05
144	Neil Allen	.05
145	David Green	.05
146	Tony Gwynn	.50
147	Rich Gossage	.05
148	Terry Kennedy	.05
149	Steve Garvey	.15
150	Alan Wiggins	.05
151	Garry Templeton	.05
152	Ed Whitson	.05
153	Tim Lollar	.05
154	Dave Dravecky	.05
155	Graig Nettles	.05
156	Eric Show	.05
157	Carmelo Martinez	.05
158	Bob Brenly	.05
159	Gary Lavelle	.05
160	Jack Clark	.05
161	Jeff Leonard	.05
162	Chili Davis	.05
163	Mike Krukow	.05
164	Johnnie LeMaster	.05
165	Atlee Hammaker	.05
166	Dan Gladden	.05
167	Greg Minton	.05
168	Joel Youngblood	.05
169	Frank Williams	.05
170	Tony Gwynn	.50
171	Don Mattingly	.60
172	Bruce Sutter	.05
173	Dan Quisenberry	.05
174	Tony Gwynn	.50
175	Ryne Sandberg	.40
176	Steve Garvey	.15
177	Dale Murphy	.50
178	Mike Schmidt	.50
179	Darryl Strawberry	.05
180	Gary Carter	.30
181	Ozzie Smith	.50
182	Charlie Lea	.05
183	Lou Whitaker	.05
184	Rod Carew	.05
185	Cal Ripken, Jr.	.75
186	Dave Winfield	.05
187	Reggie Jackson	.40
188	George Brett	.05
189	Lance Parrish	.05
190	Chet Lemon	.05
191	Dave Stieb	.05
192	Gary Carter	.30
193	Mike Schmidt	.50
194	Tony Armas	.05
195	Mike Witt	.05
196	Eddie Murray	.25
197	Cal Ripken, Jr.	.75
198	Scott McGregor	.05
199	Rick Dempsey	.05
200	Tippy Martinez	.05
201	Ken Singleton	.05
202	Mike Boddicker	.05
203	Rich Dauer	.05
204	John Shelby	.05
205	Al Bumbry	.05
206	John Lowenstein	.05
207	Mike Flanagan	.05
208	Jim Rice	.10
209	Tony Armas	.05
210	Wade Boggs	.40
211	Bruce Hurst	.05
212	Dwight Evans	.05
213	Mike Easler	.05
214	Bill Buckner	.05
215	Bob Stanley	.05
216	Jackie Gutierrez	.05
217	Rich Gedman	.05
218	Jerry Remy	.05
219	Marty Barrett	.05
220	Reggie Jackson	.40
221	Geoff Zahn	.05
222	Doug DeCinces	.05
223	Rod Carew	.30
224	Brian Downing	.05
225	Fred Lynn	.05
226	Gary Pettis	.05
227	Mike Witt	.05
228	Bob Boone	.05
229	Tommy John	.05
230	Bobby Grich	.05
231	Ron Romanick	.05
232	Ron Kittle	.05
233	Richard Dotson	.05
234	Harold Baines	.05
235	Tom Seaver	.40
236	Greg Walker	.05
237	Roy Smalley	.05
238	Greg Luzinski	.05
239	Julio Cruz	.05
240	Scott Fletcher	.05
241	Rudy Law	.05
242	Vance Law	.05
243	Carlton Fisk	.30
244	Andre Thornton	.05
245	Julio Franco	.05
246	Brett Butler	.05
247	Bert Blyleven	.05
248	Mike Hargrove	.05
249	George Vukovich	.05
250	Pat Tabler	.05
251	Brook Jacoby	.05
252	Tony Bernazard	.05
253	Ernie Camacho	.05
254	Mel Hall	.05
255	Carmen Castillo	.05
256	Jack Morris	.05
257	Willie Hernandez	.05
258	Alan Trammell	.05
259	Lance Parrish	.05
260	Chet Lemon	.05
261	Lou Whitaker	.05
262	Howard Johnson	.05
263	Barbaro Garbey	.05
264	Dan Petry	.05
265	Aurelio Lopez	.05
266	Larry Herndon	.05
267	Kirk Gibson	.05
268	George Brett	.50
269	Dan Quisenberry	.05
270	Hal McRae	.05
271	Steve Balboni	.05
272	Pat Sheridan	.05
273	Jorge Orta	.05
274	Frank White	.05
275	Bud Black	.05
276	Darryl Motley	.05
277	Willie Wilson	.05
278	Larry Gura	.05
279	Don Slaught	.05
280	Dwight Gooden	.05
281	Mark Langston	.05
282	Tim Raines	.05
283	Rickey Henderson	.30
284	Robin Yount	.30
285	Rollie Fingers	.05
286	Jim Sundberg	.05
287	Cecil Cooper	.05
288	Jaime Cocanower	.05
289	Mike Caldwell	.05
290	Don Sutton	.05
291	Rick Manning	.05
292	Ben Oglivie	.05
293	Moose Haas	.05
294	Ted Simmons	.05
295	Jim Gantner	.05
296	Kent Hrbek	.05
297	Ron Davis	.05
298	Dave Engle	.05
299	Tom Brunansky	.05
300	Frank Viola	.05
301	Mike Smithson	.05
302	Gary Gaetti	.05
303	Tim Teufel	.05
304	Mickey Hatcher	.05
305	John Butcher	.05
306	Darrell Brown	.05
307	Kirby Puckett	.50
308	Dave Winfield	.40
309	Phil Niekro	.05
310	Don Mattingly	.60
311	Don Baylor	.05
312	Willie Randolph	.05
313	Ron Guidry	.05
314	Dave Righetti	.05
315	Bobby Meacham	.05
316	Butch Wynegar	.05
317	Mike Pagliarulo	.05
318	Joe Cowley	.05
319	John Montefusco	.05
320	Dave Kingman	.05
321	Rickey Henderson	.30
322	Bill Caudill	.05
323	Dwayne Murphy	.05
324	Steve McCatty	.05
325	Joe Morgan	.30
326	Mike Heath	.05
327	Chris Codiroli	.05
328	Ray Burris	.05
329	Tony Phillips	.05
330	Carney Lansford	.05
331	Bruce Bochte	.05
332	Alvin Davis	.05
333	Al Cowens	.05
334	Jim Beattie	.05
335	Bob Kearney	.05
336	Ed Vande Berg	.05
337	Mark Langston	.05
338	Dave Henderson	.05
339	Spike Owen	.05
340	Matt Young	.05
341	Jack Perconte	.05
342	Barry Bonnell	.05
343	Mike Stanton	.05
344	Pete O'Brien	.05
345	Charlie Hough	.05
346	Larry Parrish	.05
347	Buddy Bell	.05
348	Frank Tanana	.05
349	Curt Wilkerson	.05
350	Jeff Kunkel	.05
351	Billy Sample	.05
352	Danny Darwin	.05
353	Gary Ward	.05
354	Mike Mason	.05
355	Mickey Rivers	.05
356	Dave Stieb	.05
357	Damaso Garcia	.05
358	Willie Upshaw	.05
359	Lloyd Moseby	.05
360	George Bell	.05
361	Luis Leal	.05
362	Jesse Barfield	.05
363	Dave Collins	.05
364	Roy Lee Jackson	.05
365	Doyle Alexander	.05
366	Alfredo Griffin	.05
367	Cliff Johnson	.05
368	Alvin Davis	.05
369	Juan Samuel	.05
370	Brook Jacoby	.05
371	Dwight Gooden, Mark Langston	.05
372	Mike Fitzgerald	.05
373	Jackie Gutierrez	.05
374	Dan Gladden	.05
375	Carmelo Martinez	.05
376	Kirby Puckett	.50

Super

Still trying to sell collectors on the idea of jumbo-sized cards, Topps returned for a second year with its 4-7/8" x 6-7/8" "Super" set. In fact, the set size was doubled from the previous year, to 60 cards. The Supers are identical to the regular-issue 1985 cards of the same players, only the card numbers on back were changed. The cards were sold three per pack for 50 cents.

		NM/M
Complete Set (60):		12.00
Common Player:		.25
Wax Pack (1):		.25
Wax Box (24):		6.00
1	Ryne Sandberg	1.00
2	Willie Hernandez	.25
3	Rick Sutcliffe	.25
4	Don Mattingly	1.50
5	Tony Gwynn	1.00
6	Alvin Davis	.25
7	Dwight Gooden	.50
8	Dan Quisenberry	.25
9	Bruce Sutter	.65
10	Tony Armas	.25
11	Dale Murphy	.50
12	Mike Schmidt	1.50
13	Gary Carter	.75
14	Rickey Henderson	.75
15	Tim Raines	.25
16	Mike Boddicker	.25
17	Alejandro Pena	.25
18	Eddie Murray	.75
19	Gary Matthews	.25
20	Mark Langston	.25
21	Mario Soto	.25
22	Dave Stieb	.25
23	Nolan Ryan	3.00
24	Steve Carlton	.75
25	Alan Trammell	.75
26	Steve Garvey	.40
27	Kirk Gibson	.25
28	Juan Samuel	.25
29	Reggie Jackson	1.00
30	Darryl Strawberry	.25
31	Tom Seaver	.75
32	Pete Rose	2.00
33	Dwight Evans	.25
34	Jose Cruz	.25
35	Bert Blyleven	.25
36	Keith Hernandez	.25
37	Robin Yount	.75
38	Joaquin Andujar	.25
39	Lloyd Moseby	.25
40	Chili Davis	.25
41	Kent Hrbek	.25
42	Dave Parker	.25
43	Jack Morris	.25
44	Pedro Guerrero	.25
45	Mike Witt	.05
46	George Brett	1.50
47	Ozzie Smith	1.00
48	Cal Ripken, Jr.	3.00
49	Rich Gossage	.25
50	Jim Rice	.35
51	Harold Baines	.25
52	Fernando Valenzuela	.25
53	Buddy Bell	.25
54	Jesse Orosco	.25
55	Lance Parrish	.25
56	Jason Thompson	.25
57	Tom Brunansky	.25
58	Dave Righetti	.25
59	Dave Kingman	.25
60	Dave Winfield	.75

3-D

MIKE SCHMIDT

These 4-1/4" x 6" cards were something new. Printed on plastic, rather than paper, the player picture on the card is actually raised above the surface much like might be found on a relief map; a true 3-D baseball card. The plastic cards include the player's name, a Topps logo and card number across the top, and a team logo on the side. The backs are blank but have two peel-off adhesive strips so that the card may be attached to a flat surface. There are 30 cards in the set, mostly stars. Cards were sold one per pack for 50 cents.

		NM/M
Complete Set (30):		12.00
Common Player:		.25
Wax Pack (1):		.50
Wax Box (24):		12.50
1	Mike Schmidt	2.00
2	Eddie Murray	.75
3	Dale Murphy	.50
4	George Brett	2.00
5	Pete Rose	2.50
6	Jim Rice	.35
7	Ryne Sandberg	1.50
8	Don Mattingly	2.00
9	Darryl Strawberry	.25
10	Rickey Henderson	.75
11	Keith Hernandez	.25
12	Dave Kingman	.25
13	Tony Gwynn	1.50
14	Reggie Jackson	1.50
15	Gary Carter	.25
16	Cal Ripken, Jr.	3.00
17	Tim Raines	.25
18	Dave Winfield	.75
19	Dwight Gooden	.35
20	Dave Stieb	.25
21	Fernando Valenzuela	.25
22	Mark Langston	.25
23	Bruce Sutter	.65
24	Dan Quisenberry	.25
25	Steve Carlton	.75
26	Mike Boddicker	.25
27	Goose Gossage	.25
28	Jack Morris	.25
29	Rick Sutcliffe	.25
30	Tom Seaver	.75

1986 Topps

METS — GARY CARTER

The 1986 Topps set consists of 792 cards. Fronts of the 2-1/2" x 3-1/2" cards feature color photos with the Topps logo in the upper right-hand corner while the player's position is in the lower left-hand corner. Above the picture is the team name, while below it is the player's name. The borders are a departure from previous practice, as the top 7/8" is black, while the remainder is white. Once again, a 5,000-set glossy-finish "Tiffany" edition was produced.

		NM/M
Unopened Fact. Set, Retail (792):		65.00
Unopened Fact. Set, Hobby (792):		30.00
Complete Set (792):		25.00
Common Player:		.05
Wax Pack (15):		.75
Wax Box (36):		20.00
Cello Pack (28):		1.00
Cello Box (24):		20.00
Rack Pack (51):		1.25
Rack Box (24):		25.00
Vending Box (500):		10.00
1	Pete Rose	1.50
2	Pete Rose (Special 1963-66)	.50
3	Pete Rose (Special 1967-70)	.50
4	Pete Rose (Special 1971-74)	.50
5	Pete Rose (Special 1975-78)	.50
6	Pete Rose (Special 1972-82)	.50
7	Pete Rose (Special 1983-85)	.50
8	Dwayne Murphy	.05
9	Roy Smith	.05
10	Tony Gwynn	.75
11	Bob Ojeda	.05
12	Jose Uribe RC	.05
13	Bob Kearney	.05
14	Julio Cruz	.05
15	Eddie Whitson	.05
16	Rick Schu RC	.05
17	Mike Stenhouse	.05
18	Brent Gaff	.05
19	Rich Hebner	.05
20	Lou Whitaker	.05
21	George Bamberger	.05
22	Duane Walker	.05
23	Manny Lee RC	.05
24	Len Barker	.05
25	Willie Wilson	.05
26	Frank DiPino	.05
27	Ray Knight	.05
28	Eric Davis	.05
29	Tony Phillips	.05
30	Eddie Murray	.50
31	Jamie Easterly	.05
32	Steve Yeager	.05
33	Jeff Lahti	.05
34	Ken Phelps RC	.05
35	Jeff Reardon	.05
36	Tigers Leaders (Lance Parrish)	.05
37	Mark Thurmond	.05
38	Glenn Hoffman	.05
39	Dave Rucker	.05
40	Ken Griffey	.05
41	Brad Wellman	.05
42	Geoff Zahn	.05
43	Dave Engle	.05
44	Lance McCullers RC	.05
45	Damaso Garcia	.05
46	Billy Hatcher RC	.05
47	Juan Berenguer	.05
48	Bill Almon	.05
49	Rick Manning	.05
50	Dan Quisenberry	.05
51	Chris Welsh	.05
52	Len Dykstra RC	.50
53	John Franco	.05
54	Fred Lynn	.05
55	Tom Niedenfuer	.05
56	Tom Niedenfuer	.05
57a	Bill Doran	.05
57b	Bobby Wine (Supposed to be #51.)	.05
58	Bill Krueger	.05
59	Andre Thornton	.05
60	Dwight Evans	.05
61	Karl Best	.05
62	Bob Boone	.05
63	Ron Roenicke	.05
64	Floyd Bannister	.05
65	Dan Driessen	.05
66	Cardinals Leaders (Bob Forsch)	.05
67	Carmelo Martinez	.05
68	Ed Lynch	.05
69	Luis Aguayo	.05
70	Dave Winfield	.50
71	Ken Schrom	.05
72	Shawon Dunston	.05
73	Randy O'Neal RC	.05
74	Rance Mulliniks	.05
75	Jose DeLeon	.05
76	Dion James	.05
77	Charlie Leibrandt	.05
78	Bruce Benedict	.05
79	Dave Schmidt	.05
80	Darryl Strawberry	.05
81	Gene Mauch	

No.	Player	Price
82	Tippy Martinez	.05
83	Phil Garner	.05
84	Curt Young	.05
85	Tony Perez	.40
86	Tom Waddell	.05
87	Candy Maldonado	.05
88	Tom Nieto	.05
89	Randy St. Claire RC	.05
90	Garry Templeton	.05
91	Steve Crawford	.05
92	Al Cowens	.05
93	Scot Thompson	.05
94	Rich Bordi	.05
95	Ozzie Virgil	.05
96	Blue Jay Leaders (Jim Clancy)	.05
97	Gary Gaetti	.05
98	Dick Ruthven	.05
99	Buddy Biancalana	.05
100	Nolan Ryan	2.00
101	Dave Bergman	.05
102	Joe Orsulak RC	.15
103	Luis Salazar	.05
104	Sid Fernandez	.05
105	Gary Ward	.05
106	Ray Burris	.05
107	Rafael Ramirez	.05
108	Ted Power	.05
109	Len Matuszek	.05
110	Scott McGregor	.05
111	Roger Craig	.05
112	Bill Campbell	.05
113	U.L. Washington	.05
114	Mike Brown	.05
115	Jay Howell	.05
116	Brook Jacoby	.05
117	Bruce Kison	.05
118	Jerry Royster	.05
119	Barry Bonnell	.05
120	Steve Carlton	.50
121	Nelson Simmons	.05
122	Pete Filson	.05
123	Greg Walker	.05
124	Luis Sanchez	.05
125	Dave Lopes	.05
126	Mets Leaders (Mookie Wilson)	.05
127	Jack Howell RC	.05
128	John Wathan	.05
129	Jeff Dedmon RC	.05
130	Alan Trammell	.05
131	Checklist 1-132	.05
132	Razor Shines	.05
133	Andy McGaffigan	.05
134	Carney Lansford	.05
135	Joe Niekro	.05
136	Mike Hargrove	.05
137	Charlie Moore	.05
138	Mark Davis	.05
139	Daryl Boston	.05
140	John Candelaria	.05
141a	Chuck Cottier	.05
141b	Bob Rodgers (Supposed to be #171.)	.05
142	Bob Jones	.05
143	Dave Van Gorder	.05
144	Doug Sisk	.05
145	Pedro Guerrero	.05
146	Jack Perconte	.05
147	Larry Sheets	.05
148	Mike Heath	.05
149	Brett Butler	.05
150	Joaquin Andujar	.05
151	Dave Stapleton	.05
152	Mike Morgan	.05
153	Ricky Adams	.05
154	Bert Roberge	.05
155	Bob Grich	.05
156	White Sox Leaders (Richard Dotson)	.05
157	Ron Hassey	.05
158	Derrel Thomas	.05
159	Orel Hershiser	.05
160	Chet Lemon	.05
161	Lee Tunnell	.05
162	Greg Gagne	.05
163	Pete Ladd	.05
164	Steve Balboni	.05
165	Mike Davis	.05
166	Dickie Thon	.05
167	Zane Smith RC	.05
168	Jeff Burroughs	.05
169	George Wright	.05
170	Gary Carter	.50
172	Jerry Reed	.05
173	Wayne Gross	.05
174	Brian Snyder	.05
175	Steve Sax	.05
176	Jay Tibbs	.05
177	Joel Youngblood	.05
178	Ivan DeJesus	.05
179	Stu Cliburn RC	.05
180	Don Mattingly	1.00
181	Al Nipper	.05
182	Bobby Brown	.05
183	Larry Andersen	.05
184	Tim Laudner	.05
185	Rollie Fingers	.40
186	Astros Leaders (Jose Cruz)	.05
187	Scott Fletcher	.05
188	Bob Dernier	.05
189	Mike Mason	.05
190	George Hendrick	.05
191	Wally Backman	.05
192	Milt Wilcox	.05
193	Daryl Sconiers	.05
194	Craig McMurtry	.05
195	Dave Concepcion	.05
196	Doyle Alexander	.05
197	Enos Cabell	.05
198	Ken Dixon	.05
199	Dick Howser	.05
200	Mike Schmidt	1.00
201	Vince Coleman (Record Breaker)	.05
202	Dwight Gooden (Record Breaker)	.05
203	Keith Hernandez (Record Breaker)	.05
204	Phil Niekro (Record Breaker)	.05
205	Tony Perez (Record Breaker)	.05
206	Pete Rose (Record Breaker)	.25
207	Fernando Valenzuela (Record Breaker)	.05
208	Ramon Romero	.05
209	Randy Ready	.05
210	Calvin Schiraldi RC	.05
211	Ed Wojna	.05
212	Chris Speier	.05
213	Bob Shirley	.05
214	Randy Bush	.05
215	Frank White	.05
216	A's Leaders (Dwayne Murphy)	.05
217	Bill Scherrer	.05
218	Randy Hunt	.05
219	Dennis Lamp	.05
220	Bob Horner	.05
221	Dave Henderson	.05
222	Craig Gerber	.05
223	Atlee Hammaker	.05
224	Cesar Cedeno	.05
225	Ron Darling	.05
226	Lee Lacy	.05
227	Al Jones	.05
228	Tom Lawless	.05
229	Bill Gullickson	.05
230	Terry Kennedy	.05
231	Jim Frey	.05
232	Rick Rhoden	.05
233	Steve Lyons RC	.05
234	Doug Corbett	.05
235	Butch Wynegar	.05
236	Frank Eufemia	.05
237	Ted Simmons	.05
238	Larry Parrish	.05
239	Joel Skinner	.05
240	Tommy John	.10
241	Tony Fernandez	.05
242	Rich Thompson	.05
243	Johnny Grubb	.05
244	Craig Lefferts	.05
245	Jim Sundberg	.05
246	Phillies Leaders (Steve Carlton)	.10
247	Terry Harper	.05
248	Spike Owen	.05
249	Rob Deer RC	.05
250	Dwight Gooden	.05
251	Rich Dauer	.05
252	Bobby Castillo	.05
253	Dann Bilardello	.05
254	Ozzie Guillen RC	.30
255	Tony Armas	.05
256	Kurt Kepshire	.05
257	Doug DeCinces	.05
258	Tim Burke RC	.05
259	Dan Pasqua RC	.05
260	Tony Pena	.05
261	Bobby Valentine	.05
262	Mario Ramirez	.05
263	Checklist 133-264	.05
264	Darren Daulton	.05
265	Ron Davis	.05
266	Keith Moreland	.05
267	Paul Molitor	.50
268	Mike Scott	.05
269	Dane Iorg	.05
270	Jack Morris	.05
271	Dave Collins	.05
272	Tim Tolman	.05
273	Jerry Willard	.05
274	Ron Gardenhire	.05
275	Charlie Hough	.05
276	Yankees Leaders (Willie Randolph)	.05
277	Jaime Cocanower	.05
278	Sixto Lezcano	.05
279	Al Pardo	.05
280	Tim Raines	.05
281	Steve Mura	.05
282	Jerry Mumphrey	.05
283	Mike Fischlin	.05
284	Brian Dayett	.05
285	Buddy Bell	.05
286	Luis DeLeon	.05
287	John Christensen RC	.05
288	Don Aase	.05
289	Johnnie LeMaster	.05
290	Carlton Fisk	.50
291	Tom Lasorda	.10
292	Chuck Porter	.05
293	Chris Chambliss	.05
294	Danny Cox	.05
295	Kirk Gibson	.05
296	Geno Petralli RC	.05
297	Tim Lollar	.05
298	Craig Reynolds	.05
299	Bryn Smith	.05
300	George Brett	1.00
301	Dennis Rasmussen	.05
302	Greg Gross	.05
303	Curt Wardle	.05
304	Mike Gallego RC	.10
305	Phil Bradley	.05
306	Padres Leaders (Terry Kennedy)	.05
307	Dave Sax	.05
308	Ray Fontenot	.05
309	John Shelby	.05
310	Greg Minton	.05
311	Dick Schofield	.05
312	Tom Filer	.05
313	Joe DeSa	.05
314	Frank Pastore	.05
315	Mookie Wilson	.05
316	Sammy Khalifa	.05
317	Ed Romero	.05
318	Terry Whitfield	.05
319	Rick Camp	.05
320	Jim Rice	.15
321	Earl Weaver	.10
322	Bob Forsch	.05
323	Jerry Davis	.05
324	Dan Schatzeder	.05
325	Juan Beniquez	.05
326	Kent Tekulve	.05
327	Mike Pagliarulo	.05
328	Pete O'Brien	.05
329	Kirby Puckett	.75
330	Rick Sutcliffe	.05
331	Alan Ashby	.05
332	Darryl Motley	.05
333	Tom Henke RC	.05
334	Ken Oberkfell	.05
335	Don Sutton	.40
336	Indians Leaders (Andre Thornton)	.05
337	Darnell Coles	.05
338	Jorge Bell	.05
339	Bruce Berenyi	.05
340	Cal Ripken, Jr.	2.00
341	Frank Williams	.05
342	Gary Redus	.05
343	Carlos Diaz	.05
344	Jim Wohlford	.05
345	Donnie Moore	.05
346	Bryan Little	.05
347	Teddy Higuera RC	.10
348	Cliff Johnson	.05
349	Mark Clear	.05
350	Jack Clark	.05
351	Chuck Tanner	.05
352	Harry Spilman	.05
353	Keith Atherton	.05
354	Tony Bernazard	.05
355	Lee Smith	.05
356	Mickey Hatcher	.05
357	Ed Vande Berg	.05
358	Rick Dempsey	.05
359	Mike LaCoss	.05
360	Lloyd Moseby	.05
361	Shane Rawley	.05
362	Tom Paciorek	.05
363	Terry Forster	.05
364	Reid Nichols	.05
365	Mike Flanagan	.05
366	Reds Leaders (Dave Concepcion)	.05
367	Aurelio Lopez	.05
368	Greg Brock	.05
369	Al Holland	.05
370	Vince Coleman RC	.35
371	Bill Stein	.05
372	Ben Oglivie	.05
373	Urbano Lugo RC	.05
374	Terry Francona	.05
375	Rich Gedman	.05
376	Bill Dawley	.05
377	Joe Carter	.05
378	Bruce Bochte	.05
379	Bobby Meacham	.05
380	LaMarr Hoyt	.05
381	Ray Miller	.05
382	Ivan Calderon RC	.05
383	Chris Brown RC	.05
384	Steve Trout	.05
385	Cecil Cooper	.05
386	Cecil Fielder RC	.75
387	Steve Kemp	.05
388	Dickie Noles	.05
389	Glenn Davis RC	.05
390	Tom Seaver	.60
391	Julio Franco	.05
392	John Russell RC	.05
393	Sixto Pittaro	.05
394	Checklist 265-396	.05
395	Scott Garrelts	.05
396	Red Sox Leaders (Dwight Evans)	.05
397	Steve Buechele RC	.10
398	Earnie Riles RC	.05
399	Bill Swift	.05
400	Rod Carew	.50
401	Fernando Valenzuela (Turn Back the Clock)	.05
402	Tom Seaver (Turn Back the Clock)	.25
403	Willie Mays (Turn Back the Clock)	.35
404	Frank Robinson (Turn Back the Clock)	.10
405	Roger Maris (Turn Back the Clock)	.30
406	Scott Sanderson	.05
407	Sal Butera	.05
408	Dave Smith	.05
409	Paul Runge RC	.05
410	Dave Kingman	.05
411	Sparky Anderson	.10
412	Jim Clancy	.05
413	Tim Flannery	.05
414	Tom Gorman	.05
415	Hal McRae	.05
416	Denny Martinez	.05
417	R.J. Reynolds	.05
418	Alan Knicely	.05
419	Frank Wills	.05
420	Von Hayes	.05
421	Dave Palmer	.05
422	Mike Jorgensen	.05
423	Dan Spillner	.05
424	Rick Miller	.05
425	Larry McWilliams	.05
426	Brewers Leaders (Charlie Moore)	.05
427	Joe Cowley	.05
428	Max Venable	.05
429	Greg Booker	.05
430	Kent Hrbek	.05
431	George Frazier	.05
432	Mark Bailey	.05
433	Chris Codiroli	.05
434	Curt Wilkerson	.05
435	Bill Caudill	.05
436	Doug Flynn	.05
437	Rick Mahler	.05
438	Clint Hurdle	.05
439	Rick Honeycutt	.05
440	Alvin Davis	.05
441	Whitey Herzog	.05
442	Ron Robinson RC	.05
443	Bill Buckner	.05
444	Alex Trevino	.05
445	Bert Blyleven	.05
446	Lenn Sakata	.05
447	Jerry Don Gleaton	.05
448	Herm Winningham RC	.05
449	Rod Scurry	.05
450	Graig Nettles	.05
451	Mark Brown	.05
452	Bob Clark	.05
453	Steve Jeltz	.05
454	Burt Hooton	.05
455	Willie Randolph	.05
456	Braves Leaders (Dale Murphy)	.10
457	Mickey Tettleton	.05
458	Kevin Bass	.05
459	Luis Leal	.05
460	Leon Durham	.05
461	Walt Terrell	.05
462	Domingo Ramos	.05
463	Jim Gott	.05
464	Ruppert Jones	.05
465	Jesse Orosco	.05
466	Tom Foley	.05
467	Bob James	.05
468	Mike Scioscia	.05
469	Storm Davis	.05
470	Bill Madlock	.05
471	Bobby Cox	.05
472	Joe Hesketh	.05
473	Mark Brouhard	.05
474	John Tudor	.05
475	Juan Samuel	.05
476	Mike Easler	.05
477	Andy Hawkins	.05
478	Bob Melvin RC	.05
479	Oddibe McDowell RC	.05
480	Scott Bradley RC	.05
481	Rick Lysander	.05
482	George Vukovich	.05
483	Donnie Hill	.05
484	Gary Matthews	.05
485	Angels Leaders (Bob Grich)	.05
486		
487	Bret Saberhagen	.05
488	Lou Thornton	.05
489	Jim Winn	.05
490	Jeff Leonard	.05
491	Pascual Perez	.05
492	Kelvin Chapman	.05
493	Gene Nelson	.05
494	Gary Roenicke	.05
495	Mark Langston	.05
496	Jay Johnstone	.05
497	John Stuper	.05
498	Tito Landrum	.05
499	Bob L. Gibson	.05
500	Rickey Henderson	.50
501	Dave Johnson	.05
502	Glen Cook	.05
503	Mike Fitzgerald	.05
504	Denny Walling	.05
505	Jerry Koosman	.05
506	Bill Russell	.05
507	Steve Ontiveros RC	.05
508	Alan Wiggins	.05
509	Ernie Camacho	.05
510	Wade Boggs	.75
511	Ed Nunez	.05
512	Thad Bosley	.05
513	Ron Washington	.05
514	Mike Jones	.05
515	Darrell Evans	.05
516	Giants Leaders (Greg Minton)	.05
517	Milt Thompson RC	.05
518	Buck Martinez	.05
519	Danny Darwin	.05
520	Keith Hernandez	.05
521	Nate Snell	.05
522	Bob Bailor	.05
523	Joe Price	.05
524	Darrell Miller RC	.05
525	Marvell Wynne	.05
526	Charlie Lea	.05
527	Checklist 397-528	.05
528	Terry Pendleton	.05
529	Marc Sullivan	.05
530	Rich Gossage	.05
531	Tony LaRussa	.05
532	Don Carman RC	.05
533	Billy Sample	.05
534	Jeff Calhoun	.05
535	Toby Harrah	.05
536	Jose Rijo	.05
537	Mark Salas	.05
538	Dennis Eckersley	.40
539	Glenn Hubbard	.05
540	Dan Petry	.05
541	Jorge Orta	.05
542	Don Schulze	.05
543	Jerry Narron	.05
544	Eddie Milner	.05
545	Jimmy Key	.05
546	Mariner's Leaders (Dave Henderson)	.05
547	Roger McDowell	.05
548	Mike Young	.05
549	Bob Welch	.05
550	Tom Herr	.05
551	Dave LaPoint	.05
552	Marc Hill	.05
553	Jim Morrison	.05
554	Paul Householder	.05
555	Hubie Brooks	.05
556	John Denny	.05
557	Gerald Perry	.05
558	Tim Stoddard	.05
559	Tommy Dunbar	.05
560	Dave Righetti	.05
561	Bob Lillis	.05
562	Joe Beckwith	.05
563	Alejandro Sanchez	.05
564	Warren Brusstar	.05
565	Tom Brunansky	.05
566	Alfredo Griffin	.05
567	Jeff Barkley	.05
568	Donnie Scott	.05
569	Jim Acker	.05
570	Rusty Staub	.10
571	Mike Jeffcoat	.05
572	Paul Zuvella	.05
573	Tom Hume	.05
574	Ron Kittle	.05
575	Mike Boddicker	.05
576	Expos Leaders (Andre Dawson)	.05
577	Jerry Reuss	.05
578	Lee Mazzilli	.05
579	Jim Slaton	.05
580	Willie McGee	.05
581	Bruce Hurst	.05
582	Jim Gantner	.05
583	Al Bumbry	.05
584	Brian Fisher RC	.05
585	Garry Maddox	.05
586	Greg Harris	.05
587	Rafael Santana	.05
588	Steve Lake	.05
589	Sid Bream	.05
590	Bob Knepper	.05
591	Jackie Moore	.05
592	Frank Tanana	.05
593	Jesse Barfield	.05
594	Chris Bando	.05
595	Dave Parker	.05
596	Onix Concepcion	.05
597	Sammy Stewart	.05
598	Jim Presley	.05
599	Rick Aguilera RC	.25
600	Dale Murphy	.25
601	Gary Lucas	.05
602	Mariano Duncan	.05
603	Bill Laskey	.05
604	Gary Pettis	.05
605	Dennis Boyd	.05
606	Royals Leaders (Hal McRae)	.05
607	Ken Dayley	.05
608	Bruce Bochy	.05
609	Barbaro Garbey	.05
610	Ron Guidry	.05
611	Gary Woods	.05
612	Richard Dotson	.05
613	Roy Smalley	.05
614	Rick Waits	.05
615	Johnny Ray	.05
616	Glenn Brummer	.05
617	Lonnie Smith	.05
618	Jim Pankovits	.05
619	Danny Heep	.05
620	Bruce Sutter	.40
621	John Felske	.05
622	Gary Lavelle	.05
623	Floyd Rayford	.05
624	Steve McCatty	.05
625	Bob Brenly	.05
626	Roy Thomas	.05
627	Ron Oester	.05
628	Kirk McCaskill RC	.15
629	Mitch Webster RC	.05
630	Fernando Valenzuela	.05
631	Steve Braun	.05
632	Dave Von Ohlen	.05
633	Jackie Gutierrez	.05
634	Roy Lee Jackson	.05
635	Jason Thompson	.05
636	Cubs Leaders (Lee Smith)	.05
637	Rudy Law	.05
638	John Butcher	.05
639	Bo Diaz	.05
640	Jose Cruz	.05
641	Wayne Tolleson	.05
642	Ray Searage	.05
643	Tom Brookens	.05
644	Mark Gubicza	.05
645	Dusty Baker	.05
646	Mike Moore	.05
647	Mel Hall	.05
648	Steve Bedrosian	.05
649	Ronn Reynolds	.05
650	Dave Stieb	.05
651	Billy Martin	.10
652	Tom Browning	.05
653	Jim Dwyer	.05
654	Ken Howell	.05
655	Manny Trillo	.05
656	Brian Harper	.05
657	Juan Agosto	.05
658	Rob Wilfong	.05
659	Checklist 529-660	.05
660	Steve Garvey	.20
661	Roger Clemens	3.00
661	Roger Clemens (Blue streak upper-right.)	7.50
662	Bill Schroeder	.05
663	Neil Allen	.05
664	Tim Corcoran	.05
665	Alejandro Pena	.05
666	Rangers Leaders (Charlie Hough)	.05
667	Tim Teufel	.05
668	Cecilio Guante	.05
669	Ron Cey	.05
670	Willie Hernandez	.05
671	Lynn Jones	.05
672	Rob Picciolo	.05
673	Ernie Whitt	.05
674	Pat Tabler	.05
675	Claudell Washington	.05
676	Matt Young	.05
677	Nick Esasky	.05
678	Dan Gladden	.05
679	Britt Burns	.05
680	George Foster	.05
681	Dick Williams	.05
682	Junior Ortiz	.05
683	Andy Van Slyke	.05
684	Bob McClure	.05
685	Tim Wallach	.05
686	Jeff Stone	.05
687	Mike Trujillo	.05
688	Larry Herndon	.05
689	Dave Stewart	.05
690	Ryne Sandberg	.75
691	Mike Madden	.05
692	Dale Berra	.05
693	Tom Tellmann	.05
694	Garth Iorg	.05
695	Mike Smithson	.05
696	Dodgers Leaders (Bill Russell)	.05
697	Bud Black	.05
698	Brad Komminsk	.05
699	Pat Corrales	.05
700	Reggie Jackson	.75
701	Keith Hernandez/AS	.05
702	Tom Herr/AS	.05
703	Tim Wallach/AS	.05
704	Ozzie Smith/AS	.35
705	Dale Murphy/AS	.10
706	Pedro Guerrero/AS	.05
707	Willie McGee/AS	.05
708	Gary Carter/AS	.25
709	Dwight Gooden/AS	.05
710	John Tudor/AS	.05
711	Jeff Reardon/AS	.05
712	Don Mattingly/AS	.50
713	Damaso Garcia/AS	.05
714	George Brett/AS	.45
715	Cal Ripken, Jr./AS	1.00
716	Rickey Henderson/AS	.25
717	Dave Winfield/AS	.25
718	George Bell/AS	.20
719	Carlton Fisk/AS	.20
720	Bret Saberhagen/AS	.05
721	Ron Guidry/AS	.05
722	Dan Quisenberry/AS	.05
723	Marty Bystrom	.05
724	Tim Hulett	.05
725	Mario Soto	.05
726	Orioles Leaders (Rick Dempsey)	.05
727	David Green	.05
728	Mike Marshall	.05
729	Jim Beattie	.05
730	Ozzie Smith	.75
731	Don Robinson	.05
732	Floyd Youmans RC	.05
733	Ron Romanick	.05
734	Marty Barrett	.05
735	Dave Dravecky	.05
736	Glenn Wilson	.05
737	Pete Vuckovich	.05
738	Andre Robertson	.05
739	Dave Rozema	.05
740	Lance Parrish	.05
741	Pete Rose	1.00
742	Frank Viola	.05
743	Pat Sheridan	.05
744	Lary Sorensen	.05
745	Willie Upshaw	.05
746	Denny Gonzalez	.05
747	Rick Cerone	.05
748	Steve Henderson	.05
749	Ed Jurak	.05
750	Gorman Thomas	.05
751	Howard Johnson	.05
752	Mike Krukow	.05
753	Dan Ford	.05

754	Pat Clements **RC**	.05
755	Harold Baines	.05
756	Pirates Leaders	
	(Rick Rhoden)	.05
757	Darrell Porter	.05
758	Dave Anderson	.05
759	Moose Haas	.05
760	Andre Dawson	.30
761	Don Slaught	.05
762	Eric Show	.05
763	Terry Puhl	.05
764	Kevin Gross	.05
765	Don Baylor	.05
766	Rick Langford	.05
767	Jody Davis	.05
768	Vern Ruhle	.05
769	Harold Reynolds **RC**	.25
770	Vida Blue	.05
771	John McNamara	.05
772	Brian Downing	.05
773	Greg Pryor	.05
774	Terry Leach	.05
775	Al Oliver	.05
776	Gene Garber	.05
777	Wayne Krenchicki	.05
778	Jerry Hairston Sr.	.05
779	Rick Reuschel	.05
780	Robin Yount	.50
781	Joe Nolan	.05
782	Ken Landreaux	.05
783	Ricky Horton	.05
784	Alan Bannister	.05
785	Bob Stanley	.05
786	Twins Leaders	
	(Mickey Hatcher)	.05
787	Vance Law	.05
788	Marty Castillo	.05
789	Kurt Bevacqua	.05
790	Phil Niekro	.40
791	Checklist 661-792	.05
792	Charles Hudson	.05

Tiffany

A total of only 5,000 of these specially boxed collectors' edition sets was reported produced. Sold only through hobby dealers' the cards differ from the regular-issue 1986 Topps cards only in the use of white cardboard stock and the application of a high-gloss finish on the cards' fronts.

	NM/M
Unopened Set (792):	100.00
Complete Set (792):	45.00
Common Player:	.25

Traded

JOSE CANSECO

This 132-card set of 2-1/2" x 3-1/2" cards was, at issue, one of the most popular sets of recent times. As always, the set features traded veterans, and a better than usual crop of rookies. As in the previous two years, a glossy-finish "Tiffany" edition of 5,000 Traded sets was produced.

	NM/M
Unopened Set (132):	30.00
Complete Set (132):	25.00
Common Player:	.05
1T	Andy Allanson **RC**	.05
2T	Neil Allen	.05
3T	Joaquin Andujar	.05
4T	Paul Assenmacher **RC**	.05
5T	Scott Bailes **RC**	.05
6T	Don Baylor	.15
7T	Steve Bedrosian	.05
8T	Juan Beniquez	.05
9T	Juan Berenguer	.05
10T	Mike Bielecki **RC**	.05
11T	Barry Bonds **RC**	20.00
12T	Bobby Bonilla **RC**	.50
13T	Juan Bonilla	.05
14T	Rich Bordi	.05
15T	Steve Boros	.05
16T	Rick Burleson	.05
17T	Bill Campbell	.05
18T	Tom Candiotti	.05
19T	John Cangelosi **RC**	.05
20T	Jose Canseco **RC**	4.00
21T	Carmen Castillo	.05
22T	Rick Cerone	.05
23T	John Cerutti **RC**	.05

24T	Will Clark **RC**	1.50
25T	Mark Clear	.05
26T	Darnell Coles	.05
27T	Dave Collins	.05
28T	Tim Conroy	.05
29T	Joe Cowley	.05
30T	Joel Davis **RC**	.05
31T	Rob Deer	.05
32T	John Denny	.05
33T	Mike Easler	.05
34T	Mark Eichhorn **RC**	.05
35T	Steve Farr	.05
36T	Scott Fletcher	.05
37T	Terry Forster	.05
38T	Terry Francona	.05
39T	Jim Fregosi	.05
40T	Andres Galarraga **RC**	.35
41T	Ken Griffey	.05
42T	Bill Gullickson	.05
43T	Jose Guzman **RC**	.05
44T	Moose Haas	.05
45T	Billy Hatcher	.05
46T	Mike Heath	.05
47T	Tom Hume	.05
48T	Pete Incaviglia **RC**	.20
49T	Dane Iorg	.05
50T	Bo Jackson **RC**	3.00
51T	Wally Joyner **RC**	.40
52T	Charlie Kerfeld **RC**	.05
53T	Eric King **RC**	.05
54T	Bob Kipper **RC**	.05
55T	Wayne Krenchicki	.05
56T	John Kruk **RC**	.35
57T	Mike LaCoss	.05
58T	Pete Ladd	.05
59T	Mike Laga	.05
60T	Hal Lanier	.05
61T	Dave LaPoint	.05
62T	Rudy Law	.05
63T	Rick Leach	.05
64T	Tim Leary	.05
65T	Dennis Leonard	.05
66T	Jim Leyland	.05
67T	Steve Lyons	.05
68T	Mickey Mahler	.05
69T	Candy Maldonado	.05
70T	Roger Mason **RC**	.05
71T	Bob McClure	.05
72T	Andy McGaffigan	.05
73T	Gene Michael	.05
74T	Kevin Mitchell **RC**	.25
75T	Omar Moreno	.05
76T	Jerry Mumphrey	.05
77T	Phil Niekro	.25
78T	Randy Niemann	.05
79T	Juan Nieves **RC**	.05
80T	Otis Nixon **RC**	.05
81T	Bob Ojeda	.05
82T	Jose Oquendo	.05
83T	Tom Paciorek	.05
84T	Dave Palmer	.05
85T	Frank Pastore	.05
86T	Lou Piniella	.05
87T	Dan Plesac **RC**	.05
88T	Darrell Porter	.05
89T	Rey Quinones **RC**	.05
90T	Gary Redus	.05
91T	Bip Roberts	.05
92T	Billy Jo Robidoux **RC**	.05
93T	Jeff Robinson	.05
94T	Gary Roenicke	.05
95T	Ed Romero	.05
96T	Argenis Salazar	.05
97T	Joe Sambito	.05
98T	Billy Sample	.05
99T	Dave Schmidt	.05
100T	Ken Schrom	.05
101T	Tom Seaver	.50
102T	Ted Simmons	.05
103T	Sammy Stewart	.05
104T	Kurt Stillwell **RC**	.05
105T	Franklin Stubbs	.05
106T	Dale Sveum **RC**	.05
107T	Chuck Tanner	.05
108T	Danny Tartabull **RC**	.05
109T	Tim Teufel	.05
110T	Bob Tewksbury **RC**	.05
111T	Andres Thomas **RC**	.05
112T	Milt Thompson	.05
113T	Robby Thompson **RC**	.05
114T	Jay Tibbs	.05
115T	Wayne Tolleson	.05
116T	Alex Trevino	.05
117T	Manny Trillo	.05
118T	Ed Vande Berg	.05
119T	Ozzie Virgil	.05
120T	Bob Walk	.05
121T	Gene Walter **RC**	.05
122T	Claudell Washington	.05
123T	Bill Wegman **RC**	.05
124T	Dick Williams	.05
125T	Mitch Williams **RC**	.05
126T	Bobby Witt **RC**	.05
127T	Todd Worrell **RC**	.05
128T	George Wright	.05
129T	Ricky Wright	.05
130T	Steve Yeager	.05
131T	Paul Zuvella	.05
132T	Checklist	.05

Traded Tiffany

This collectors' edition differs from the regular 1986 Topps Traded set only in the use of a high-gloss front finish. The set was sold only through hobby channels in a specially design box.

	NM/M
Unopened Set (132):	700.00
Complete Set (132):	450.00
Common Player:	.25
11T	Barry Bonds	200.00

Traded Mickey Mantle Bronze

This 1/4-size metal replica of Mantle's first-ever Topps card was issued to dealers who purchased cases of 1986 Topps Traded sets. Each detail of the 1952 Topps Mantle card is reproduced on the 1-1/4" x 1-3/4" bronze metal mini-card, right down to the stats.

		NM/M
311	Mickey Mantle	9.00

Box Panels

Following the lead of Donruss, which introduced the concept in 1985, Topps produced special cards on the bottom panels of wax boxes. Individual cards measure 2-1/2" x 3-1/2", the same as regular cards. Design of the cards is virtually identical with regular '86 Topps, though the top border is in red, rather than black. The cards are lettered "A" through "P," rather than numbered on the back.

		NM/M
Complete Panel Set:		7.00
Complete Singles Set:		6.00
Common Panel:		1.00
Common Single Player:		.10
Panel		2.00
A	Jorge Bell	.10
B	Wade Boggs	.75
C	George Brett	1.00
D	Vince Coleman	.25
Panel		1.00
E	Carlton Fisk	.50
F	Dwight Gooden	1.00
G	Pedro Guerrero	.10
H	Ron Guidry	.10
Panel		2.00
I	Reggie Jackson	.75
J	Don Mattingly	1.00
K	Oddibe McDowell	.10
L	Willie McGee	.10
Panel		2.50
M	Dale Murphy	.35
N	Pete Rose	1.50
O	Bret Saberhagen	.10
P	Fernando Valenzuela	.10

All-Star Glossy Set of 22

As in previous years, Topps continued to make the popular glossy-surfaced cards as an insert in rack packs. The All-Star Glossy set of 2-1/2" x 3-1/2" cards shows little design change from previous years. Cards feature a front color photo and All-Star banner at the top. The bottom has the player's name and position. The set includes the All-Star starting teams as well as the managers and honorary captains.

1985

TONY GWYNN OF

	NM/M
Complete Set (22):	2.50
Common Player:	.05
1	Sparky Anderson	.05
2	Eddie Murray	.35
3	Lou Whitaker	.05
4	George Brett	.50
5	Cal Ripken, Jr.	.65
6	Jim Rice	.25
7	Rickey Henderson	.35
8	Dave Winfield	.35
9	Carlton Fisk	.35
10	Jack Morris	.05
11	A.L. All-Star Team	.05
12	Dick Williams	.05
13	Steve Garvey	.15
14	Tom Herr	.05
15	Graig Nettles	.05
16	Ozzie Smith	.45
17	Tony Gwynn	.45
18	Dale Murphy	.25
19	Darryl Strawberry	.05
20	Terry Kennedy	.05
21	LaMarr Hoyt	.05
22	N.L. All-Star Team	.05

All-Star Glossy Set of 60

The Topps All-Star & Hot Prospects glossy set of 60 cards represents an expansion of a good idea. The 2-1/2" x 3-1/2" cards had a good following when they were limited to stars, but Topps realized that the addition of top young players would spice up the set even further, so in 1986 it was expanded from 40 to 60 cards. The cards themselves are basically all color glossy pictures with the player's name in very small print in the lower left-hand corner. To obtain the set, it was necessary to send $1 plus six special offer cards from wax packs to Topps for each series. At 60 cards, that meant the process had to be repeated six times as there were 10 cards in each series, making the set quite expensive from the outset.

	NM/M
Complete Set (60):	8.00
Common Player:	.10
1	Oddibe McDowell	.10
2	Reggie Jackson	.50
3	Fernando Valenzuela	.10
4	Jack Clark	.10
5	Rickey Henderson	.40
6	Steve Balboni	.10
7	Keith Hernandez	.10
8	Lance Parrish	.10
9	Willie McGee	.10
10	Chris Brown	.10
11	Darryl Strawberry	.10
12	Ron Guidry	.10
13	Dave Parker	.10
14	Cal Ripken	1.00
15	Tim Raines	.10
16	Rod Carew	.50
17	Mike Schmidt	.75
18	George Brett	.75
19	Joe Hesketh	.10
20	Dan Pasqua	.10
21	Vince Coleman	.10
22	Tom Seaver	.40

23	Gary Carter	.40
24	Orel Hershiser	.10
25	Pedro Guerrero	.10
26	Wade Boggs	.50
27	Bret Saberhagen	.10
28	Carlton Fisk	.40
29	Kirk Gibson	.10
30	Brian Fisher	.10
31	Don Mattingly	.75
32	Tom Herr	.10
33	Eddie Murray	.40
34	Ryne Sandberg	.50
35	Dan Quisenberry	.10
36	Jim Rice	.30
37	Dale Murphy	.30
38	Steve Garvey	.25
39	Roger McDowell	.10
40	Earnie Riles	.10
41	Dwight Gooden	.10
42	Dave Winfield	.40
43	Dave Stieb	.10
44	Bob Horner	.10
45	Nolan Ryan	1.00
46	Ozzie Smith	.50
47	Jorge Bell	.10
48	Gorman Thomas	.10
49	Tom Browning	.10
50	Larry Sheets	.10
51	Pete Rose	.90
52	Brett Butler	.10
53	John Tudor	.10
54	Phil Bradley	.10
55	Jeff Reardon	.10
56	Rich Gossage	.10
57	Tony Gwynn	.50
58	Ozzie Guillen	.10
59	Glenn Davis	.10
60	Darrell Evans	.10

Gallery of Champions

EXPOS

JEFF REARDON

For the third consecutive year Topps issued 12 metal "mini cards," adding an alumium version to the bronze and silver. The metal replicas were minted 1/4-size (approximately 1-1/4" x 1-3/4") of the regular cards. The bronze and silver sets were issued in leather-like velvet-lined display cases, the alumnium in individual cello packs. A pewter Don Mattingly was issued as a premium to those ordering the sets.

	NM/M
Complete Aluminum Set:	15.00
Complete Bronze Set:	50.00
Complete Silver Set:	200.00
(1a)	Wade Boggs/Aluminum	2.00
(1b)	Wade Boggs/Bronze	15.00
(1s)	Wade Boggs/Silver	35.00
(2a)	Vince Coleman/	
	Aluminum	1.50
(2b)	Vince Coleman/Bronze	4.00
(2s)	Vince Coleman/Silver	12.00
(3a)	Darrell Evans/Aluminum	1.00
(3b)	Darrell Evans/Bronze	4.00
(3s)	Darrell Evans/Silver	12.00
(4a)	Dwight Gooden/	
	Aluminum	1.00
(4b)	Dwight Gooden/Bronze	4.00
(4s)	Dwight Gooden/Silver	12.00
(5a)	Ozzie Guillen/Aluminum	1.00
(5b)	Ozzie Guillen/Bronze	4.00
(5s)	Ozzie Guillen/Silver	12.00
(6a)	Don Mattingly/Aluminum	4.00
(6b)	Don Mattingly/Bronze	20.00
(6s)	Don Mattingly/Silver	75.00
(6p)	Don Mattingly/Pewter	45.00
(7a)	Willie McGee/Aluminum	1.00
(7b)	Willie McGee/Bronze	4.00
(7s)	Willie McGee/Silver	12.00
(8a)	Dale Murphy/Aluminum	1.50
(8b)	Dale Murphy/Bronze	7.50
(8s)	Dale Murphy/Silver	30.00
(9a)	Dan Quisenberry/	
	Aluminum	1.00
(9b)	Dan Quisenberry/Bronze	4.00
(9s)	Dan Quisenberry/Silver	12.00
(10a)	Jeff Reardon/Aluminum	1.00
(10b)	Jeff Reardon/Bronze	4.00
(10s)	Jeff Reardon/Silver	12.00
(11a)	Pete Rose/Aluminum	5.00
(11b)	Pete Rose/Bronze	25.00
(11s)	Pete Rose/Silver	90.00
(12a)	Bret Saberhagen/	
	Aluminum	1.00
(12b)	Bret Saberhagen/Bronze	4.00
(12s)	Bret Saberhagen/Silver	12.00

Mini League Leaders

MIKE SCHMIDT

Topps had long experimented with bigger cards, but in 1986, they also decided to try smaller ones. These 2-1/8" x 2-15/16" cards feature top players in a number of categories. Sold in plastic packs as a regular Topps issue, the 66-card set is attractive as well as innovative. The cards feature color photos and a minimum of added information on the fronts where only the player's name and Topps logo appear. Backs limited information as well, but do feature enough to justify the player's inclusion in a set of league leaders.

	NM/M
Complete Set (66):	5.00
Common Player:	.05
Wax Pack (6):	.50
Wax Box (36):	10.00
Vend Box (500):	15.00
1	Eddie Murray	.35
2	Cal Ripken, Jr.	1.00
3	Wade Boggs	.45
4	Dennis Boyd	.05
5	Dwight Evans	.05
6	Bruce Hurst	.05
7	Gary Pettis	.05
8	Harold Baines	.05
9	Floyd Bannister	.05
10	Britt Burns	.05
11	Carlton Fisk	.35
12	Brett Butler	.05
13	Darrell Evans	.05
14	Jack Morris	.05
15	Lance Parrish	.05
16	Walt Terrell	.05
17	Steve Balboni	.05
18	George Brett	.75
19	Charlie Leibrandt	.05
20	Bret Saberhagen	.05
21	Lonnie Smith	.05
22	Willie Wilson	.05
23	Bert Blyleven	.05
24	Mike Smithson	.05
25	Frank Viola	.05
26	Ron Guidry	.05
27	Rickey Henderson	.35
28	Don Mattingly	.75
29	Dave Winfield	.35
30	Mike Moore	.05
31	Gorman Thomas	.05
32	Toby Harrah	.05
33	Charlie Hough	.05
34	Doyle Alexander	.05
35	Jimmy Key	.05
36	Dave Stieb	.05
37	Dale Murphy	.20
38	Keith Moreland	.05
39	Ryne Sandberg	.45
40	Tom Browning	.05
41	Dave Parker	.05
42	Mario Soto	.05
43	Nolan Ryan	1.00
44	Pedro Guerrero	.05
45	Orel Hershiser	.05
46	Mike Scioscia	.05
47	Fernando Valenzuela	.05
48	Bob Welch	.05
49	Tim Raines	.05
50	Gary Carter	.35
51	Sid Fernandez	.05
52	Dwight Gooden	.05
53	Keith Hernandez	.05
54	Juan Samuel	.05
55	Mike Schmidt	.75
56	Glenn Wilson	.05
57	Rick Reuschel	.05
58	Joaquin Andujar	.05
59	Jack Clark	.05
60	Vince Coleman	.05
61	Danny Cox	.05
62	Tom Herr	.05
63	Willie McGee	.05
64	John Tudor	.05
65	Tony Gwynn	.45
66	Checklist	.05

Stickers

The 1986 Topps stickers are 2-1/8" x 3". The 200-piece set features 316 different subjects, with some stickers including two or three players. Numbers run only to 315, however. The set includes some specialty stickers such as League Championships and World Series themes. Stickers are numbered both front and back and included a chance to win a trip to spring training as well as an offer to buy a complete 1986 Topps regular set. An album for the stickers was available in stores. It feautres Pete Rose in action on the front cover and reproductions of his Topps cards on back.

		NM/M
Complete Set (315):		6.00
Common Player:		.05
Sticker Album:		1.50
Wax Pack (5):		.30
Wax Box (100):		11.00
1	Pete Rose	.60
2	Pete Rose	.60
3	George Brett	.50
4	Rod Carew	.40
5	Vince Coleman	.05
6	Dwight Gooden	.05
7	Phil Niekro	.30
8	Tony Perez	.05
9	Nolan Ryan	.75
10	Tom Seaver	.40
11	N.L. Championship Series (Ozzie Smith)	.10
12	N.L. Championship Series (Bill Madlock)	.05
13	N.L. Championship Series (Cardinals Celebrate)	.05
14	A.L. Championship Series (Al Oliver)	.05
15	A.L. Championship Series (Jim Sundberg)	.05
16	A.L. Championship Series (George Brett)	.10
17	World Series (Bret Saberhagen)	.05
18	World Series (Dane Iorg)	.05
19	World Series (Tito Landrum)	.05
20	World Series (John Tudor)	.05
21	World Series (Buddy Biancalana)	.05
22	World Series (Darryl Motley, Darrell Porter)	.05
23	World Series (George Brett, Frank White)	.05
24	Nolan Ryan	.75
25	Bill Doran	.05
26	Jose Cruz	.05
27	Mike Scott	.05
28	Kevin Bass	.05
29	Glenn Davis	.05
30	Mark Bailey	.05
31	Dave Smith	.05
32	Phil Garner	.05
33	Dickie Thon	.05
34	Bob Horner	.05
35	Dale Murphy	.25
36	Glenn Hubbard	.05
37	Bruce Sutter	.05
38	Ken Oberkfell	.05
39	Claudell Washington	.05
40	Steve Bedrosian	.05
41	Terry Harper	.05
42	Rafael Ramirez	.05
43	Rick Mahler	.05
44	Joaquin Andujar	.05
45	Willie McGee	.40
46	Ozzie Smith	.50
47	Vince Coleman	.05
48	Danny Cox	.05
49	Tom Herr	.05
50	Jack Clark	.05
51	Andy Van Slyke	.05
52	John Tudor	.05
53	Terry Pendleton	.05
54	Keith Moreland	.05
55	Ryne Sandberg	.40
56	Lee Smith	.05
57	Steve Trout	.05
58	Jody Davis	.05
59	Gary Matthews	.05
60	Leon Durham	.05
61	Rick Sutcliffe	.05
62	Dennis Eckersley	.30
63	Bob Dernier	.05
64	Fernando Valenzuela	.05
65	Pedro Guerrero	.05
66	Jerry Reuss	.05
67	Greg Brock	.05

68	Mike Scioscia	.05
69	Ken Howell	.05
70	Bill Madlock	.05
71	Mike Marshall	.05
72	Steve Sax	.05
73	Orel Hershiser	.05
74	Andre Dawson	.25
75	Tim Raines	.05
76	Jeff Reardon	.05
77	Hubie Brooks	.05
78	Bill Gullickson	.05
79	Bryn Smith	.05
80	Terry Francona	.05
81	Vance Law	.05
82	Tim Wallach	.05
83	Herm Winningham	.05
84	Jeff Leonard	.05
85	Chris Brown	.05
86	Scott Garrelts	.05
87	Jose Uribe	.05
88	Manny Trillo	.05
89	Dan Driessen	.05
90	Dan Gladden	.05
91	Mark Davis	.05
92	Bob Brenly	.05
93	Mike Krukow	.05
94	Dwight Gooden	.05
95	Darryl Strawberry	.05
96	Gary Carter	.40
97	Wally Backman	.05
98	Ron Darling	.05
99	Keith Hernandez	.05
100	George Foster	.05
101	Howard Johnson	.05
102	Rafael Santana	.05
103	Roger McDowell	.05
104	Steve Garvey	.15
105	Tony Gwynn	.50
106	Graig Nettles	.05
107	Rich Gossage	.05
108	Andy Hawkins	.05
109	Carmelo Martinez	.05
110	Garry Templeton	.05
111	Terry Kennedy	.05
112	Tim Flannery	.05
113	LaMarr Hoyt	.05
114	Mike Schmidt	.50
115	Ozzie Virgil	.05
116	Steve Carlton	.40
117	Garry Maddox	.05
118	Glenn Wilson	.05
119	Kevin Gross	.05
120	Von Hayes	.05
121	Juan Samuel	.05
122	Rick Schu	.05
123	Shane Rawley	.05
124	Johnny Ray	.05
125	Tony Pena	.05
126	Rick Reuschel	.05
127	Sammy Khalifa	.05
128	Marvell Wynne	.05
129	Jason Thompson	.05
130	Rick Rhoden	.05
131	Bill Almon	.05
132	Joe Orsulak	.05
133	Jim Morrison	.05
134	Pete Rose	.60
135	Dave Parker	.05
136	Mario Soto	.05
137	Dave Concepcion	.05
138	Ron Oester	.05
139	Buddy Bell	.05
140	Ted Power	.05
141	Tom Browning	.05
142	John Franco	.05
143	Tony Perez	.30
144	Willie McGee	.05
145	Dale Murphy	.25
146	Tony Gwynn	.50
147	Tom Herr	.05
148	Steve Garvey	.15
149	Dale Murphy	.25
150	Darryl Strawberry	.05
151	Graig Nettles	.05
152	Terry Kennedy	.05
153	Ozzie Smith	.50
154	LaMarr Hoyt	.05
155	Rickey Henderson	.40
156	Lou Whitaker	.05
157	George Brett	.50
158	Eddie Murray	.40
159	Cal Ripken, Jr.	.75
160	Dave Winfield	.40
161	Jim Rice	.15
162	Carlton Fisk	.40
163	Jack Morris	.05
164	Wade Boggs	.40
165	Darrell Evans	.05
166	Mike Davis	.05
167	Dave Kingman	.05
168	Alfredo Griffin	.05
169	Carney Lansford	.05
170	Bruce Bochte	.05
171	Dwayne Murphy	.05
172	Dave Collins	.05
173	Chris Codiroli	.05
174	Mike Heath	.05
175	Jay Howell	.05
176	Rod Carew	.40
177	Reggie Jackson	.05
178	Doug DeCinces	.05
179	Bob Boone	.05
180	Ron Romanick	.05
181	Bob Grich	.05
182	Donnie Moore	.05
183	Brian Downing	.05
184	Ruppert Jones	.05
185	Juan Beniquez	.05

186	Dave Stieb	.05
187	Jorge Bell	.05
188	Willie Upshaw	.05
189	Tom Henke	.05
190	Damaso Garcia	.05
191	Jimmy Key	.05
192	Jesse Barfield	.05
193	Dennis Lamp	.05
194	Tony Fernandez	.05
195	Lloyd Moseby	.05
196	Cecil Cooper	.05
197	Robin Yount	.40
198	Rollie Fingers	.20
199	Ted Simmons	.05
200	Ben Oglivie	.05
201	Moose Haas	.05
202	Jim Gantner	.05
203	Paul Molitor	.40
204	Charlie Moore	.05
205	Danny Darwin	.05
206	Brett Butler	.05
207	Brook Jacoby	.05
208	Andre Thornton	.05
209	Tom Waddell	.05
210	Tony Bernazard	.05
211	Julio Franco	.05
212	Pat Tabler	.05
213	Joe Carter	.05
214	George Vukovich	.05
215	Rich Thompson	.05
216	Gorman Thomas	.05
217	Phil Bradley	.05
218	Alvin Davis	.05
219	Jim Presley	.05
220	Matt Young	.05
221	Mike Moore	.05
222	Dave Henderson	.05
223	Ed Nunez	.05
224	Spike Owen	.05
225	Mark Langston	.05
226	Cal Ripken, Jr.	.75
227	Eddie Murray	.40
228	Fred Lynn	.05
229	Lee Lacy	.05
230	Scott McGregor	.05
231	Storm Davis	.05
232	Rick Dempsey	.05
233	Mike Boddicker	.05
234	Mike Young	.05
235	Sammy Stewart	.05
236	Pete O'Brien	.05
237	Oddibe McDowell	.05
238	Toby Harrah	.05
239	Gary Ward	.05
240	Larry Parrish	.05
241	Charlie Hough	.05
242	Burt Hooton	.05
243	Don Slaught	.05
244	Curt Wilkerson	.05
245	Greg Harris	.05
246	Jim Rice	.15
247	Wade Boggs	.40
248	Rich Gedman	.05
249	Dennis Boyd	.05
250	Marty Barrett	.05
251	Dwight Evans	.05
252	Bill Buckner	.05
253	Bob Stanley	.05
254	Tony Armas	.05
255	Mike Easler	.05
256	George Brett	.50
257	Dan Quisenberry	.05
258	Willie Wilson	.05
259	Jim Sundberg	.05
260	Bret Saberhagen	.05
261	Bud Black	.05
262	Charlie Leibrandt	.05
263	Frank White	.05
264	Lonnie Smith	.05
265	Steve Balboni	.05
266	Kirk Gibson	.05
267	Alan Trammell	.05
268	Jack Morris	.05
269	Darrell Evans	.05
270	Dan Petry	.05
271	Larry Herndon	.05
272	Lou Whitaker	.05
273	Lance Parrish	.05
274	Chet Lemon	.05
275	Willie Hernandez	.05
276	Tom Brunansky	.05
277	Kent Hrbek	.05
278	Mark Salas	.05
279	Bert Blyleven	.05
280	Tim Teufel	.05
281	Ron Davis	.05
282	Mike Smithson	.05
283	Gary Gaetti	.05
284	Frank Viola	.05
285	Kirby Puckett	.50
286	Carlton Fisk	.40
287	Tom Seaver	.40
288	Harold Baines	.05
289	Ron Kittle	.05
290	Bob James	.05
291	Rudy Law	.05
292	Britt Burns	.05
293	Greg Walker	.05
294	Ozzie Guillen	.05
295	Tim Hulett	.05
296	Don Mattingly	.50
297	Rickey Henderson	.40
298	Dave Winfield	.40
299	Butch Wynegar	.05
300	Don Baylor	.05
301	Eddie Whitson	.05
302	Ron Guidry	.05
303	Dave Righetti	.05

304	Bobby Meacham	.05
305	Willie Randolph	.05
306	Vince Coleman	.05
307	Oddibe McDowell	.05
308	Larry Sheets	.05
309	Ozzie Guillen	.05
310	Earnie Riles	.05
311	Chris Brown	.05
312	Brian Fisher, Roger McDowell	.05
313	Tom Browning	.05
314	Glenn Davis	.05
315	Mark Salas	.05

Super Sample

EDDIE MURRAY

To preview its oversize Super set for 1986, Topps issued a sample card of Eddie Murray. Front of the 4-7/8" x 6-7/8" card is the same as the issued version. On back, however, is this message: "topps / SPECIAL / COLLECTOR / SAMPLE / ACTUAL PRODUCT TO HAVE / STATISTICS PRINTED ON / WHITE-BOARD CARD BACK."

		NM/M
Eddie Murray		6.00

Super

REGGIE JACKSON

A third year of oversize (4-7/8" x 6-7/8") versions of Topps' regular issue cards saw the set once again hit the 60-card mark. Besides being four times that of a normal card, the Supers differ only in the number on the back of the card.

		NM/M
Complete Set (60):		9.00
Common Player:		.25
1	Don Mattingly	1.00
2	Willie McGee	.25
3	Bret Saberhagen	.25
4	Dwight Gooden	.25
5	Dan Quisenberry	.25
6	Jeff Reardon	.25
7	Ozzie Guillen	.25
8	Vince Coleman	.25
9	Harold Baines	.25
10	Jorge Bell	.25
11	Bert Blyleven	.25
12	Wade Boggs	.60
13	Phil Bradley	.25
14	George Brett	1.00
15	Hubie Brooks	.25
16	Tom Browning	.25
17	Bill Buckner	.25
18	Brett Butler	.25
19	Gary Carter	.45
20	Cecil Cooper	.25
21	Darrell Evans	.25
22	Dwight Evans	.25
23	Carlton Fisk	.45
24	Steve Garvey	.35
25	Kirk Gibson	.25
26	Rich Gossage	.25
27	Pedro Guerrero	.25
28	Ron Guidry	.25
29	Tony Gwynn	.60
30	Rickey Henderson	.25
31	Keith Hernandez	.25
32	Tom Herr	.25
33	Orel Hershiser	.25
34	Jay Howell	.25
35	Reggie Jackson	.75

36	Bob James	.25
37	Charlie Leibrandt	.25
38	Jack Morris	.25
39	Dale Murphy	.35
40	Eddie Murray	.45
41	Dave Parker	.25
42	Tim Raines	.25
43	Jim Rice	.35
44	Dave Righetti	.25
45	Cal Ripken, Jr.	2.00
46	Pete Rose	1.50
47	Nolan Ryan	2.00
48	Ryne Sandberg	.60
49	Mike Schmidt	1.00
50	Tom Seaver	.45
51	Bryn Smith	.25
52	Lee Smith	.25
53	Ozzie Smith	.60
54	Dave Stieb	.25
55	Darryl Strawberry	.25
56	Gorman Thomas	.25
57	John Tudor	.25
58	Fernando Valenzuela	.25
59	Willie Wilson	.25
60	Dave Winfield	.45

Super Star

(See 1986 Woolworth.)

Tattoos

Topps returned to tattoos in 1986, marketing a set of 24 different tattoo sheets. Each sheet of tattoos measures 3-7/16" x 14" and includes both player and smaller action tattoos. As the action tattoos were uniform and not of any particular player, they add little value to the sheet. The player tattoos measure 1-1/2" x 2-1/2". With 24 sheets, eight players per sheet, there are 192 players represented in the set. The sheets are numbered.

		NM/M
Complete Set (24):		9.00
Common Sheet:		.40
Pack (1):		.60
Wax Box (36):		13.50
1	Julio Franco, Rich Gossage, Keith Hernandez, Charlie Leibrandt, Jack Perconte, Lee Smith, Dickie Thon, Dave Winfield	.60

2	Jesse Barfield, Shawon Dunston, Dennis Eckersley, Brian Fisher, Moose Haas, Mike Moore, Dale Murphy, Bret Saberhagen	.50
3	George Bell, Bob Brenly, Steve Carlton, Jose DeLeon, Bob Horner, Bob James, Dan Quisenberry, Andre Thornton	.60
4	Mike Davis, Leon Durham, Darrell Evans, Glenn Hubbard, Johnny Ray, Cal Ripken, Ted Simmons	1.50
5	John Candelaria, Rick Dempsey, Steve Garvey, Ozzie Guillen, Gary Matthews, Jesse Orosco, Tony Pena	.45
6	Bruce Bochte, George Brett, Cecil Cooper, Sammy Khalifa, Ron Kittle, Scott McGregor, Pete Rose, Mookie Wilson	1.25
7	John Franco, Carney Lansford, Don Mattingly, Graig Nettles, Rick Reuschel, Mike Schmidt, Larry Sheets, Don Sutton	1.50
8	Cecilio Guante, Willie Hernandez, Mike Krukow, Fred Lynn, Phil Niekro, Ed Nunez, Ryne Sandberg, Pat Tabler	.75
9	Brett Butler, Chris Codiroli, Jim Gantner, Charlie Hough, Dave Parker, Rick Rhoden, Glenn Wilson, Robin Yount	.50
10	Tom Browning, Ron Darling, Von Hayes, Chet Lemon, Tom Seaver, Mike Smithson, Bruce Sutter, Alan Trammell	.60
11	Tony Armas, Jose Cruz, Jay Howell, Rick Mahler, Jack Morris, Rafael Ramirez, Dave Righetti, Mike Young	.40
12	Alvin Davis, Doug DeCinces, Andy Hawkins, Dennis Lamp, Keith Moreland, Jim Presley, Mario Soto, John Tudor	.40
13	Hubie Brooks, Jody Davis, Dwight Evans, Ron Hassey, Charles Hudson, Kirby Puckett, Jose Uribe	1.00
14	Tony Bernazard, Phil Bradley, Bill Buckner, Brian Downing, Dan Driessen, Ron Guidry, LaMarr Hoyt, Garry Maddox	.40
15	Buddy Bell, Joe Carter, Tony Fernandez, Tito Landrum, Jeff Leonard, Hal McRae, Willie Randolph, Juan Samuel	.40
16	Dennis Boyd, Vince Coleman, Scott Garrelts, Alfredo Griffin, Donnie Moore, Tony Perez, Ozzie Smith, Frank White	1.00
17	Rich Gedman, Kent Hrbek, Reggie Jackson, Mike Marshall, Terry Pendleton, Tim Raines, Mark Salas, Claudell Washington	1.00
18	Chris Brown, Tom Brunansky, Glenn Davis, Ron Davis, Burt Hooton, Darryl Strawberry, Frank Viola, Tim Wallach	.40
19	Jack Clark, Bill Doran, Toby Harrah, Bill Madlock, Pete O'Brien, Larry Parrish, Mike Scioscia, Garry Templeton	.40
20	Gary Carter, Andre Dawson, Dwight Gooden, Orel Hershiser, Oddibe McDowell, Roger McDowell, Dwayne Murphy, Jim Rice	.60
21	Steve Balboni, Mike Easler, Charlie Lea, Lloyd Moseby, Steve Sax, Rick Sutcliffe, Gary Ward, Willie Wilson	.40
22	Wade Boggs, Dave Concepcion, Kirk Gibson, Tom Herr, Lance Parrish, Jeff Reardon, Bryn Smith, Gorman Thomas	.75
23	Carlton Fisk, Bob Grich, Pedro Guerrero, Willie McGee, Paul Molitor, Mike Scott, Dave Stieb, Lou Whitaker	.60
24	Bert Blyleven, Damaso Garcia, Phil Garner, Tony Gwynn, Rickey Henderson, Ben Oglivie, Nolan Ryan, Fernando Valenzuela	1.50

3-D

DON MATTINGLY

This set is a second effort in the production of over-size (4-1/2" x 6") plastic cards on which the player figure is embossed. Cards were sold one per pack for 50¢. The 30 players in the set are among the game's top stars. The embossed color photo is bordered at bottom by a strip of contrasting color on which the player name appears. At the top, a row of white baseballs each contain a letter of the team nickname. Backs have no printing, and contain two self-adhesive strips with which the cards can be attached to a hard surface.

		NM/M
Complete Set (30):		9.00
Common Player:		.25
Wax Pack (1):		1.00
Wax Box (24):		15.00
1	Bert Blyleven	.25
2	Gary Carter	.60
3	Wade Boggs	.75
4	Dwight Gooden	.25
5	George Brett	1.50
6	Rich Gossage	.25
7	Darrell Evans	.25
8	Pedro Guerrero	.25
9	Ron Guidry	.25
10	Keith Hernandez	.25
11	Rickey Henderson	.60
12	Orel Hershiser	.25
13	Reggie Jackson	1.00
14	Willie McGee	.25
15	Don Mattingly	1.50
16	Dale Murphy	.45
17	Jack Morris	.25
18	Dave Parker	.25
19	Eddie Murray	.60
20	Jeff Reardon	.25
21	Dan Quisenberry	.25
22	Pete Rose	2.00
23	Jim Rice	.45
24	Mike Schmidt	1.50
25	Bret Saberhagen	.25
26	Darryl Strawberry	.25
27	Dave Stieb	.25
28	John Tudor	.25
29	Dave Winfield	.60
30	Fernando Valenzuela	.25

1987 Topps

MARIANO DUNCAN

The design of Topps' set of 792 2-1/2" x 3-1/2" cards is closely akin to the 1962 set in that the player photo is set against a woodgrain border. Instead of a rolling corner, as in 1962, the player photos in '87 feature a couple of clipped corners at top left and bottom right, where the team logo and player name appear. The player's position is not given on the front of the card. For the first time in several years, the trophy which designates members of Topps All-Star Rookie Team returned to the card design. As in the previous three years, Topps issued a glossy-finish "Tiffany" edition of their 792-card set. However, it was speculated that as many as 30,000 sets were produced as opposed to the 5,000 sets printed in 1985 and 1986.

		NM/M
Unopened Factory Set, Retail (792):		30.00
Unopened Factory Set, Hobby (792):		25.00
Complete Set (792):		20.00
Uncut Sheet Set (6):		45.00
Common Player:		.05
Wax Pack (15):		.75
Wax Box (36):		20.00
Cello Pack (31):		1.00
Cello Box (24):		20.00
Rack Pack (49):		1.50
Rack Box (24):		25.00
Vending Box (500):		12.00
1	Roger Clemens (Record Breaker)	.45
2	Jim Deshaies (Record Breaker)	.05
3	Dwight Evans (Record Breaker)	.05
4	Dave Lopes (Record Breaker)	.05
5	Dave Righetti (Record Breaker)	.05
6	Ruben Sierra (Record Breaker)	.05
7	Todd Worrell (Record Breaker)	.05
8	Terry Pendleton	.05
9	Jay Tibbs	.05
10	Cecil Cooper	.05
11	Indians Leaders (Jack Aker, Chris Bando, Phil Niekro)	.05
12	Jeff Sellers RC	.05
13	Nick Esasky	.05
14	Dave Stewart	.05
15	Claudell Washington	.05
16	Pat Clements	.05
17	Pete O'Brien	.05
18	Dick Howser	.05
19	Matt Young	.05
20	Gary Carter	.40
21	Mark Davis	.05
22	Doug DeCinces	.05
23	Lee Smith	.05
24	Tony Walker	.05
25	Bert Blyleven	.05
26	Greg Brock	.05
27	Joe Cowley	.05
28	Rick Dempsey	.05
29	Jimmy Key	.05
30	Tim Raines	.05
31	Braves Leaders (Glenn Hubbard, Rafael Ramirez)	.05
32	Tim Leary	.05
33	Andy Van Slyke	.05
34	Jose Rijo	.05
35	Sid Bream	.05
36	Eric King RC	.05
37	Marvell Wynne	.05
38	Dennis Leonard	.05
39	Marty Barrett	.05
40	Dave Righetti	.05
41	Bo Diaz	.05
42	Gary Redus	.05
43	Gene Michael	.05
44	Greg Harris	.05
45	Jim Presley	.05
46	Danny Gladden	.05
47	Dennis Powell	.05
48	Wally Backman	.05
49	Terry Harper	.05
50	Dave Smith	.05
51	Mel Hall	.05
52	Keith Atherton	.05
53	Ruppert Jones	.05
54	Bill Dawley	.05
55	Tim Wallach	.05
56	Brewers Leaders (Jamie Cocanower, Paul Molitor, Charlie Moore, Herm Starrette)	.10
57	Scott Nielsen RC	.05
58	Thad Bosley	.05
59	Ken Dayley	.05
60	Tony Pena	.05
61	Bobby Thigpen RC	.05
62	Bobby Meacham	.05
63	Fred Toliver RC	.05
64	Harry Spilman	.05
65	Tom Browning	.05
66	Marc Sullivan	.05
67	Bill Swift	.05
68	Tony LaRussa	.05
69	Lonnie Smith	.05
70	Charlie Hough	.05
71	Mike Aldrete RC	.05
72	Walt Terrell	.05
73	Dave Anderson	.05
74	Dan Pasqua	.05
75	Ron Darling	.05
76	Rafael Ramirez	.05
77	Bryan Oelkers	.05
78	Tom Foley	.05
79	Juan Nieves	.05
80	Wally Joyner RC	.35
81	Padres Leaders (Andy Hawkins, Terry Kennedy)	.05
82	Rob Murphy RC	.05
83	Mike Davis	.05
84	Steve Lake	.05
85	Kevin Bass	.05
86	Nate Snell	.05
87	Mark Salas	.05
88	Ed Wojna	.05
89	Ozzie Guillen	.05
90	Dave Stieb	.05
91	Harold Reynolds	.05
92a	Urbano Lugo (No trademark on front.)	.10
92b	Urbano Lugo (Trademark on front.)	.05
93	Jim Leyland	.05
94	Calvin Schiraldi	.05
95	Oddibe McDowell	.05
96	Frank Williams	.05
97	Glenn Wilson	.05
98	Bill Scherrer	.05
99	Darryl Motley	.05
100	Steve Garvey	.15
101	Carl Willis RC	.05
102	Paul Zuvella	.05
103	Rick Aguilera	.05
104	Billy Sample	.05
105	Floyd Youmans	.05
106	Blue Jays Leaders (George Bell, Willie Upshaw)	.05
107	John Butcher	.05
108	Jim Gantner (Photo reversed.)	.05
109	R.J. Reynolds	.05
110	John Tudor	.05
111	Alfredo Griffin	.05
112	Alan Ashby	.05
113	Neil Allen	.05
114	Billy Beane	.05
115	Donnie Moore	.05
116	Mike Stanley RC	.05
117	Jim Beattie	.05
118	Bobby Valentine	.05
119	Ron Robinson	.05
120	Eddie Murray	.40
121	Kevin Romine RC	.05
122	Jim Clancy	.05
123	John Kruk RC	.05
124	Ray Fontenot	.05
125	Bob Brenly	.05
126	Mike Loynd RC	.05
127	Vance Law	.05
128	Checklist 1-132	.05
129	Rick Cerone	.05
130	Dwight Gooden	.05
131	Pirates Leaders (Sid Bream, Tony Pena)	.05
132	Paul Assenmacher RC	.05
133	Jose Oquendo	.05
134	Rich Yett RC	.05
135	Mike Easler	.05
136	Ron Romanick	.05
137	Jerry Willard	.05
138	Roy Lee Jackson	.05
139	Devon White RC	.40
140	Bret Saberhagen	.05
141	Herm Winningham	.05
142	Rick Sutcliffe	.05
143	Steve Boros	.05
144	Mike Scioscia	.05
145	Charlie Kerfeld	.05
146	Tracy Jones RC	.05
147	Randy Niemann	.05
148	Dave Collins	.05
149	Ray Searage	.05
150	Wade Boggs	.45
151	Mike LaCoss	.05
152	Toby Harrah	.05
153	Duane Ward RC	.05
154	Tom O'Malley	.05
155	Eddie Whitson	.05
156	Mariners Leaders (Bob Kearney, Phil Regan, Matt Young)	.05
157	Danny Darwin	.05
158	Tim Teufel	.05
159	Ed Olwine	.05
160	Julio Franco	.05
161	Steve Ontiveros	.05
162	Mike LaValliere RC	.10
163	Kevin Gross	.05
164	Sammy Khalifa	.05
165	Jeff Reardon	.05
166	Bob Boone	.05
167	Jim Deshaies RC	.10
168	Lou Piniella	.05
169	Ron Washington	.05
170	Bo Jackson (Future Stars)	1.50
171	Chuck Cary RC	.05
172	Ron Oester	.05
173	Alex Trevino	.05
174	Henry Cotto	.05
175	Bob Stanley	.05
176	Steve Buechele	.05
177	Keith Moreland	.05
178	Cecil Fielder	.05
179	Bill Wegman	.05
180	Chris Brown	.05
181	Cardinals Leaders (Mike LaValliere, Ozzie Smith, Ray Soff)	.10
182	Lee Lacy	.05
183	Andy Hawkins	.05
184	Bobby Bonilla	.05
185	Roger McDowell	.05
186	Bruce Benedict	.05
187	Mark Huismann	.05
188	Tony Phillips	.05
189	Joe Hesketh	.05
190	Jim Sundberg	.05
191	Charles Hudson	.05
192	Cory Snyder RC	.05
193	Roger Craig	.05
194	Kirk McCaskill	.05
195	Mike Pagliarulo	.05
196	Randy O'Neal	.05
197	Mark Bailey	.05
198	Lee Mazzilli	.05
199	Mariano Duncan	.05
200	Pete Rose	.75
201	John Cangelosi RC	.05
202	Ricky Wright	.05
203	Mike Kingery RC	.05
204	Sammy Stewart	.05
205	Graig Nettles	.05
206	Twins Leaders (Tim Laudner, Frank Viola)	.05
207	George Frazier	.05
208	John Shelby	.05
209	Rick Schu	.05
210	Lloyd Moseby	.05
211	John Morris RC	.05
212	Mike Fitzgerald	.05
213	Randy Myers RC	.20
214	Omar Moreno	.05
215	Mark Langston	.05
216	B.J. Surhoff RC (Future Stars)	.20
217	Chris Codiroli	.05
218	Sparky Anderson	.10
219	Cecilio Guante	.05
220	Joe Carter	.05
221	Vern Ruhle	.05
222	Denny Walling	.05
223	Charlie Leibrandt	.05
224	Wayne Tolleson	.05
225	Mike Smithson	.05
226	Max Venable	.05
227	Jamie Moyer RC	.05
228	Curt Wilkerson	.05
229	Mike Birkbeck RC	.05
230	Don Baylor	.05
231	Giants Leaders (Bob Brenly, Mike Krukow)	.05
232	Reggie Williams RC	.05
233	Russ Morman RC	.05
234	Pat Sheridan	.05
235	Alvin Davis	.05
236	Tommy John	.10
237	Jim Morrison	.05
238	Bill Krueger	.05
239	Juan Espino	.05
240	Steve Balboni	.05
241	Danny Heep	.05
242	Rick Mahler	.05
243	Whitey Herzog	.05
244	Dickie Noles	.05
245	Willie Upshaw	.05
246	Jim Dwyer	.05
247	Jeff Reed RC	.05
248	Gene Walter	.05
249	Jim Pankovits	.05
250	Teddy Higuera	.05
251	Rob Wilfong	.05
252	Denny Martinez	.05
253	Eddie Milner	.05
254	Bob Tewksbury RC	.20
255	Juan Samuel	.05
256	Royals Leaders (George Brett, Frank White)	.15
257	Bob Forsch	.05
258	Steve Yeager	.05
259	Mike Greenwell RC	.25
260	Vida Blue	.05
261	Ruben Sierra	.05
262	Jim Winn	.05
263	Stan Javier RC	.05
264	Checklist 133-264	.05
265	Darrell Evans	.05
266	Jeff Hamilton RC	.05
267	Howard Johnson	.05
268	Pat Corrales	.05
269	Cliff Speck	.05
270	Jody Davis	.05
271	Mike Brown	.05
272	Andres Galarraga	.05
273	Gene Nelson	.05
274	Jeff Hearron RC	.05
275	LaMarr Hoyt	.05
276	Jackie Gutierrez	.05
277	Juan Agosto	.05
278	Gary Pettis	.05
279	Dan Plesac RC	.05
280	Jeffrey Leonard	.05
281	Reds Leaders (Bo Diaz, Bill Gullickson, Pete Rose)	.10
282	Jeff Calhoun	.05
283	Doug Drabek RC	.25
284	John Moses	.05
285	Dennis Boyd	.05
286	Mike Woodard RC	.05
287	Dave Von Ohlen	.05
288	Tito Landrum	.05
289	Bob Kipper	.05
290	Leon Durham	.05
291	Mitch Williams	.05
292	Franklin Stubbs	.05
293	Bob Rodgers	.05
294	Steve Jeltz	.05
295	Len Dykstra	.05
296	Andres Thomas RC	.05
297	Don Schulze	.05
298	Larry Herndon	.05
299	Joel Davis	.05
300	Reggie Jackson	.50
301	Luis Aquino RC	.05
302	Bill Schroeder	.05
303	Juan Berenguer	.05
304	Phil Garner	.05
305	John Franco	.05
306	Red Sox Leaders (Rich Gedman, John McNamara, Tom Seaver)	.10
307	Lee Guetterman RC	.05
308	Don Slaught	.05
309	Mike Young	.05
310	Frank Viola	.05
311	Rickey Henderson (Turn Back the Clock)	.10
312	Reggie Jackson (Turn Back the Clock)	.10
313	Roberto Clemente (Turn Back the Clock)	.50
314	Carl Yastrzemski (Turn Back the Clock)	.10
315	Maury Wills (Turn Back the Clock)	.05
316	Brian Fisher	.05
317	Clint Hurdle	.05
318	Jim Fregosi	.05
319	Greg Swindell RC	.10
320	Barry Bonds	8.00
321	Mark Laga	.05
322	Chris Bando	.05
323	Al Newman RC	.05
324	Dave Palmer	.05
325	Garry Templeton	.05
326	Mark Gubicza	.05
327	Dale Sveum RC	.05
328	Bob Welch	.05
329	Ron Roenicke	.05
330	Mike Scott	.05
331	Mets Leaders (Gary Carter, Keith Hernandez, Dave Johnson, Darryl Strawberry)	.10
332	Joe Price	.05
333	Ken Phelps	.05
334	Ed Correa RC	.05
335	Candy Maldonado	.05
336	Allan Anderson RC	.05
337	Darrell Miller	.05
338	Tim Conroy	.05
339	Donnie Hill	.05
340	Roger Clemens	.65
341	Mike Brown	.05
342	Bob James	.05
343	Hal Lanier	.05
344a	Joe Niekro (Copyright outside yellow on back.)	.25
344b	Joe Niekro (Copyright inside yellow on back.)	.05
345	Andre Dawson	.25
346	Shawon Dunston	.05
347	Mickey Brantley RC	.05
348	Carmelo Martinez	.05
349	Storm Davis	.05
350	Keith Hernandez	.05
351	Gene Garber	.05
352	Mike Felder RC	.05
353	Ernie Camacho	.05
354	Jamie Quirk	.05
355	Don Carman	.05
356	White Sox Leaders (Ed Brinkman, Julio Cruz)	.05
357	Steve Fireovid RC	.05
358	Sal Butera	.05
359	Doug Corbett	.05
360	Pedro Guerrero	.05
361	Mark Thurmond	.05
362	Luis Quinones RC	.05
363	Jose Guzman	.05
364	Randy Bush	.05
365	Rick Rhoden	.05
366	Mark McGwire	3.00
367	Jeff Lahti	.05
368	John McNamara	.05
369	Brian Dayett	.05
370	Fred Lynn	.05
371	Mark Eichhorn RC	.05
372	Jerry Mumphrey	.05
373	Jeff Dedmon	.05
374	Glenn Hoffman	.05
375	Ron Guidry	.10
376	Scott Bradley	.05
377	John Henry Johnson	.05
378	Rafael Santana	.05
379	John Russell	.05
380	Rich Gossage	.05
381	Expos Leaders (Mike Fitzgerald, Bob Rodgers)	.05
382	Rudy Law	.05
383	Ron Davis	.05
384	Johnny Grubb	.05
385	Orel Hershiser	.05
386	Dickie Thon	.05
387	T.R. Bryden RC	.05
388	Geno Petralli	.05
389	Jeff Robinson	.05
390	Gary Matthews	.05
391	Jay Howell	.05
392	Checklist 265-396	.05
393	Pete Rose	.60
394	Mike Bielecki	.05
395	Damaso Garcia	.05
396	Tim Lollar	.05
397	Greg Walker	.05
398	Brad Havens	.05
399	Curt Ford RC	.05
400	George Brett	.50
401	Billy Jo Robidoux	.05
402	Mike Trujillo	.05
403	Jerry Royster	.05
404	Doug Sisk	.05
405	Brook Jacoby	.05
406	Yankees Leaders (Rickey Henderson, Don Mattingly)	.25
407	Jim Acker	.05
408	John Mizerock	.05
409	Milt Thompson	.05
410	Fernando Valenzuela	.05
411	Darnell Coles	.05
412	Eric Davis	.05
413	Moose Haas	.05
414	Joe Orsulak	.05
415	Bobby Witt RC	.05
416	Tom Nieto	.05
417	Pat Perry RC	.05
418	Dick Williams	.05
419	Mark Portugal RC	.10
420	Will Clark	.40
421	Jose DeLeon	.05
422	Jack Howell	.05
423	Jaime Cocanower	.05
424	Chris Speier	.05
425	Tom Seaver	.40
426	Floyd Rayford	.05
427	Ed Nunez	.05
428	Bruce Bochy	.05
429	Tim Pyznarski RC (Future Stars)	.05
430	Mike Schmidt	.50
431	Dodgers Leaders (Tom Niedenfuer, Ron Perranoski, Alex Trevino)	.05
432	Jim Slaton	.05
433	Ed Hearn RC	.05
434	Mike Fischlin	.05
435	Bruce Sutter	.35
436	Andy Allanson RC	.05
437	Ted Power	.05
438	Kelly Downs RC	.05
439	Karl Best	.05
440	Willie McGee	.05
441	Dave Leiper RC	.05
442	Mitch Webster	.05
443	John Felske	.05
444	Jeff Russell	.05
445	Dave Lopes	.05
446	Chuck Finley RC	.05
447	Bill Almon	.05
448	Chris Bosio RC	.10
449	Pat Dodson RC (Future Stars)	.05
450	Kirby Puckett	.45
451	Joe Sambito	.05
452	Dave Henderson	.05
453	Scott Terry RC	.05
454	Luis Salazar	.05
455	Mike Boddicker	.05
456	A's Leaders (Carney Lansford, Tony LaRussa, Mickey Tettleton, Dave Von Ohlen)	.05
457	Len Matuszek	.05
458	Kelly Gruber RC	.05
459	Dennis Eckersley	.35
460	Darryl Strawberry	.05
461	Craig McMurtry	.05
462	Scott Fletcher	.05
463	Tom Candiotti	.05
464	Butch Wynegar	.05
465	Todd Worrell	.05
466	Kal Daniels RC	.05
467	Randy St. Claire	.05
468	George Bamberger	.05
469	Mike Diaz RC	.05
470	Dave Dravecky	.05
471	Ronn Reynolds	.05
472	Bill Doran	.05
473	Steve Farr	.05
474	Jerry Narron	.05
475	Scott Garrelts	.05
476	Danny Tartabull	.05
477	Ken Howell	.05
478	Tim Laudner	.05
479	Bob Sebra RC	.05
480	Jim Rice	.15
481	Phillies Leaders (Von Hayes, Juan Samuel, Glenn Wilson)	.05
482	Daryl Boston	.05
483	Dwight Lowry	.05
484	Jim Traber RC	.05
485	Tony Fernandez	.05
486	Otis Nixon	.05
487	Dave Gumpert	.05
488	Ray Knight	.05
489	Bill Gullickson	.05
490	Dale Murphy	.20
491	Ron Karkovice RC	.05
492	Mike Heath	.05
493	Tom Lasorda	.10
494	Barry Jones RC	.05
495	Gorman Thomas	.05
496	Bruce Bochte	.05
497	Dale Mohorcic RC	.05
498	Bob Kearney	.05
499	Bruce Ruffin RC	.05
500	Don Mattingly	.65
501	Craig Lefferts	.05
502	Dick Schofield	.05
503	Larry Andersen	.05
504	Mickey Hatcher	.05
505	Bryn Smith	.05
506	Orioles Leaders (Rich Bordi, Rick Dempsey, Earl Weaver)	.05
507	Dave Stapleton	.05
508	Scott Bankhead RC	.05

509	Enos Cabell	.05	
510	Tom Henke	.05	
511	Steve Lyons	.05	
512	Dave Magadan RC (Future Stars)	.20	
513	Carmen Castillo	.05	
514	Orlando Mercado	.05	
515	Willie Hernandez	.05	
516	Ted Simmons	.05	
517	Mario Soto	.05	
518	Gene Mauch	.05	
519	Curt Young	.05	
520	Jack Clark	.05	
521	Rick Reuschel	.05	
522	Checklist 397-528	.05	
523	Earnie Riles	.05	
524	Bob Shirley	.05	
525	Phil Bradley	.05	
526	Roger Mason	.05	
527	Jim Wohlford	.05	
528	Ken Dixon	.05	
529	Alvaro Espinoza RC	.05	
530	Tony Gwynn	.45	
531	Astros Leaders (Yogi Berra, Hal Lanier, Denis Menke, Gene Tenace)	.05	
532	Jeff Stone	.05	
533	Argenis Salazar	.05	
534	Scott Sanderson	.05	
535	Tony Armas	.05	
536	Terry Mulholland RC	.15	
537	Rance Mulliniks	.05	
538	Tom Niedenfuer	.05	
539	Reid Nichols	.05	
540	Terry Kennedy	.05	
541	Rafael Belliard RC	.05	
542	Ricky Horton	.05	
543	Dave Johnson	.05	
544	Zane Smith	.05	
545	Buddy Bell	.05	
546	Mike Morgan	.05	
547	Rob Deer	.05	
548	Bill Mooneyham RC	.05	
549	Bob Melvin	.05	
550	Pete Incaviglia	.05	
551	Frank Wills	.05	
552	Larry Sheets	.05	
553	Mike Maddux RC	.05	
554	Buddy Biancalana	.05	
555	Dennis Rasmussen	.05	
556	Angels Leaders (Bob Boone, Marcel Lachemann, Mike Witt)	.05	
557	John Cerutti RC	.05	
558	Greg Gagne	.05	
559	Lance McCullers	.05	
560	Glenn Davis	.05	
561	Rey Quinones RC	.05	
562	Bryan Clutterbuck RC	.05	
563	John Stefero	.05	
564	Larry McWilliams	.05	
565	Dusty Baker	.05	
566	Tim Hulett	.05	
567	Greg Mathews RC	.05	
568	Earl Weaver	.10	
569	Wade Rowdon RC	.05	
570	Sid Fernandez	.05	
571	Ozzie Virgil	.05	
572	Pete Ladd	.05	
573	Hal McRae	.05	
574	Manny Lee	.05	
575	Pat Tabler	.05	
576	Frank Pastore	.05	
577	Dann Bilardello	.05	
578	Billy Hatcher	.05	
579	Rick Burleson	.05	
580	Mike Krukow	.05	
581	Cubs Leaders (Ron Cey, Steve Trout)	.05	
582	Bruce Berenyi	.05	
583	Junior Ortiz	.05	
584	Ron Kittle	.05	
585	Scott Bailes RC	.05	
586	Ben Oglivie	.05	
587	Eric Plunk RC	.05	
588	Wallace Johnson	.05	
589	Steve Crawford	.05	
590	Vince Coleman	.05	
591	Spike Owen	.05	
592	Chris Welsh	.05	
593	Chuck Tanner	.05	
594	Rick Anderson	.05	
595	Keith Hernandez/AS	.05	
596	Steve Sax/AS	.05	
597	Mike Schmidt/AS	.35	
598	Ozzie Smith/AS	.30	
599	Tony Gwynn/AS	.30	
600	Dave Parker/AS	.05	
601	Darryl Strawberry/AS	.05	
602	Gary Carter/AS	.25	
603a	Dwight Gooden/AS (No trademark on front.)	.25	
603b	Dwight Gooden/AS (Trademark on front.)	.05	
604	Fernando Valenzuela/AS	.05	
605	Todd Worrell/AS	.05	
606a	Don Mattingly/AS (No trademark on front.)	.75	
606b	Don Mattingly/AS (Trademark on front.)	.35	
607	Tony Bernazard/AS	.05	
608	Wade Boggs/AS	.30	
609	Cal Ripken, Jr./AS	.45	
610	Jim Rice/AS	.05	
611	Kirby Puckett/AS	.30	
612	George Bell/AS	.05	
613	Lance Parrish/AS	.05	
614	Roger Clemens/AS	.35	

615	Teddy Higuera/AS	.05
616	Dave Righetti/AS	.05
617	Al Nipper	.05
618	Tom Kelly	.05
619	Jerry Reed	.05
620	Jose Canseco	.60
621	Danny Cox	.05
622	Glenn Braggs RC	.05
623	Kurt Stillwell RC	.05
624	Tim Burke	.05
625	Mookie Wilson	.05
626	Joel Skinner	.05
627	Ken Oberkfell	.05
628	Bob Walk	.05
629	Larry Parrish	.05
630	John Candelaria	.05
631	Tigers Leaders (Sparky Anderson, Mike Heath, Willie Hernandez)	.05
632	Rob Woodward RC	.05
633	Jose Uribe	.05
634	Rafael Palmeiro RC	2.00
635	Ken Schrom	.05
636	Darren Daulton	.05
637	Bip Roberts RC	.10
638	Rich Bordi	.05
639	Gerald Perry	.05
640	Mark Clear	.05
641	Domingo Ramos	.05
642	Al Pulido	.05
643	Ron Shepherd	.05
644	John Denny	.05
645	Dwight Evans	.05
646	Mike Mason	.05
647	Tom Lawless	.05
648	Barry Larkin RC	.60
649	Mickey Tettleton	.05
650	Hubie Brooks	.05
651	Benny Distefano	.05
652	Terry Forster	.05
653	Kevin Mitchell	.05
654	Checklist 529-660	.05
655	Jesse Barfield	.05
656	Rangers Leaders (Bobby Valentine, Rickey Wright)	.05
657	Tom Waddell	.05
658	Robby Thompson RC	.05
659	Aurelio Lopez	.05
660	Bob Horner	.05
661	Lou Whitaker	.05
662	Frank DiPino	.05
663	Cliff Johnson	.05
664	Mike Marshall	.05
665	Rod Scurry	.05
666	Von Hayes	.05
667	Ron Hassey	.05
668	Juan Bonilla	.05
669	Bud Black	.05
670	Jose Cruz	.05
671a	Ray Soff (No "D*" before copyright line.)	.20
671b	Ray Soff ("D*" before copyright line.)	.05
672	Chili Davis	.05
673	Don Sutton	.35
674	Bill Campbell	.05
675	Ed Romero	.05
676	Charlie Moore	.05
677	Bob Grich	.05
678	Carney Lansford	.05
679	Kent Hrbek	.05
680	Ryne Sandberg	.45
681	George Bell	.05
682	Jerry Reuss	.05
683	Gary Roenicke	.05
684	Kent Tekulve	.05
685	Jerry Hairston Sr.	.05
686	Doyle Alexander	.05
687	Alan Trammell	.05
688	Juan Beniquez	.05
689	Darrell Porter	.05
690	Dane Iorg	.05
691	Dave Parker	.05
692	Frank White	.05
693	Terry Puhl	.05
694	Phil Niekro	.35
695	Chico Walker	.05
696	Gary Lucas	.05
697	Ed Lynch	.05
698	Ernie Whitt	.05
699	Ken Landreaux	.05
700	Dave Bergman	.05
701	Willie Randolph	.05
702	Greg Gross	.05
703	Dave Schmidt	.05
704	Jesse Orosco	.05
705	Bruce Hurst	.05
706	Rick Manning	.05
707	Bob McClure	.05
708	Scott McGregor	.05
709	Dave Kingman	.05
710	Gary Gaetti	.05
711	Ken Griffey	.05
712	Don Robinson	.05
713	Tom Brookens	.05
714	Dan Quisenberry	.05
715	Bob Dernier	.05
716	Rick Leach	.05
717	Ed Vande Berg	.05
718	Steve Carlton	.40
719	Tom Hume	.05
720	Richard Dotson	.05
721	Tom Herr	.05
722	Bob Knepper	.05
723	Brett Butler	.05
724	Greg Minton	.05

725	George Hendrick	.05
726	Frank Tanana	.05
727	Mike Moore	.05
728	Tippy Martinez	.05
729	Tom Paciorek	.05
730	Eric Show	.05
731	Dave Concepcion	.05
732	Manny Trillo	.05
733	Bill Caudill	.05
734	Bill Madlock	.05
735	Rickey Henderson	.40
736	Steve Bedrosian	.05
737	Floyd Bannister	.05
738	Jorge Orta	.05
739	Chet Lemon	.05
740	Rich Gedman	.05
741	Paul Molitor	.40
742	Andy McGaffigan	.05
743	Dwayne Murphy	.05
744	Roy Smalley	.05
745	Glenn Hubbard	.05
746	Bob Ojeda	.05
747	Johnny Ray	.05
748	Mike Flanagan	.05
749	Ozzie Smith	.45
750	Steve Trout	.05
751	Garth Iorg	.05
752	Dan Petry	.05
753	Rick Honeycutt	.05
754	Dave LaPoint	.05
755	Luis Aguayo	.05
756	Carlton Fisk	.40
757	Nolan Ryan	.75
758	Tony Bernazard	.05
759	Joel Youngblood	.05
760	Mike Witt	.05
761	Greg Pryor	.05
762	Gary Ward	.05
763	Tim Flannery	.05
764	Bill Buckner	.05
765	Kirk Gibson	.05
766	Don Aase	.05
767	Ron Cey	.05
768	Dennis Lamp	.05
769	Steve Sax	.05
770	Dave Winfield	.40
771	Shane Rawley	.05
772	Harold Baines	.05
773	Robin Yount	.40
774	Wayne Krenchicki	.05
775	Joaquin Andujar	.05
776	Tom Brunansky	.05
777	Chris Chambliss	.05
778	Jack Morris	.05
779	Craig Reynolds	.05
780	Andre Thornton	.05
781	Atlee Hammaker	.05
782	Brian Downing	.05
783	Willie Wilson	.05
784	Cal Ripken, Jr.	.75
785	Terry Francona	.05
786	Jimy Williams	.05
787	Alejandro Pena	.05
788	Tim Stoddard	.05
789	Dan Schatzeder	.05
790	Julio Cruz	.05
791	Lance Parrish	.05
792	Checklist 661-792	.05

Tiffany

Produced in much greater quantity (reportedly 30,000 sets) than the previous years' sets, this specially boxed collectors' edition differs from the regular 1987 Topps cards only in its use of white cardboard stock and a high-gloss finish on the cards' fronts.

		NM/M
Unopened Set (792):		90.00
Complete Set (792):		50.00
Common Player:		.15
320	Barry Bonds	35.00

Traded

The Topps Traded set consists of 132 cards as did all Traded sets issued by Topps since 1981. Cards measure the standard 2-1/2" x 3-1/2" and are identical in design to the regular edition set. The purpose of the set is to update player trades and feature rookies not included in the regular issue. As they had done the previous three years, Topps produced a

glossy-coated "Tiffany" edition of the Traded set. Cards are numbered with a "T" suffix.

		NM/M
Complete Set (132):		4.00
Common Player:		.05
1	Bill Almon	.05
2	Scott Bankhead	.05
3	Eric Bell RC	.05
4	Juan Beniquez	.05
5	Juan Berenguer	.05
6	Greg Booker	.05
7	Thad Bosley	.05
8	Larry Bowa	.05
9	Greg Brock	.05
10	Bob Brower RC	.05
11	Jerry Browne RC	.05
12	Ralph Bryant RC	.05
13	DeWayne Buice RC	.05
14	Ellis Burks RC	.50
15	Ivan Calderon	.05
16	Jeff Calhoun	.05
17	Casey Candaele RC	.05
18	John Cangelosi	.05
19	Steve Carlton	.25
20	Juan Castillo RC	.05
21	Rick Cerone	.05
22	Ron Cey	.05
23	John Christensen	.05
24	Dave Cone RC	.15
25	Chuck Crim RC	.05
26	Storm Davis	.05
27	Andre Dawson	.25
28	Rick Dempsey	.05
29	Doug Drabek RC	.05
30	Mike Dunne	.05
31	Dennis Eckersley	.25
32	Lee Elia	.05
33	Brian Fisher	.05
34	Terry Francona	.05
35	Willie Fraser RC	.05
36	Billy Gardner	.05
37	Ken Gerhart RC	.05
38	Danny Gladden	.05
39	Jim Gott	.05
40	Cecilio Guante	.05
41	Albert Hall	.05
42	Terry Harper	.05
43	Mickey Hatcher	.05
44	Brad Havens	.05
45	Neal Heaton	.05
46	Mike Henneman RC	.20
47	Donnie Hill	.05
48	Guy Hoffman	.05
49	Brian Holton RC	.05
50	Charles Hudson	.05
51	Danny Jackson RC	.05
52	Reggie Jackson	.40
53	Chris James RC	.05
54	Dion James	.05
55	Stan Jefferson RC	.05
56	Joe Johnson RC	.05
57	Terry Kennedy	.05
58	Mike Kingery	.05
59	Ray Knight	.05
60	Gene Larkin RC	.05
61	Mike LaValliere	.05
62	Jack Lazorko	.05
63	Terry Leach	.05
64	Tim Leary	.05
65	Jim Lindeman RC	.05
66	Steve Lombardozzi RC	.05
67	Bill Long RC	.05
68	Barry Lyons RC	.05
69	Shane Mack RC	.05
70	Greg Maddux RC	3.00
71	Bill Madlock	.05
72	Joe Magrane RC	.05
73	Dave Martinez RC	.05
74	Fred McGriff RC	.25
75	Mark McLemore RC	.05
76	Kevin McReynolds RC	.05
77	Dave Meads RC	.05
78	Eddie Milner	.05
79	Greg Minton	.05
80	John Mitchell RC	.05
81	Kevin Mitchell	.05
82	Charlie Moore	.05
83	Jeff Musselman RC	.05
84	Gene Nelson	.05
85	Graig Nettles	.05
86	Al Newman	.05
87	Reid Nichols	.05
88	Tom Niedenfuer	.05
89	Joe Niekro	.05
90	Tom Nieto	.05
91	Matt Nokes RC	.10
92	Dickie Noles	.05
93	Pat Pacillo	.05
94	Lance Parrish	.05
95	Tony Pena	.05
96	Luis Polonia RC	.05
97	Randy Ready	.05
98	Jeff Reardon	.05
99	Gary Redus	.05
100	Jeff Reed	.05
101	Rick Rhoden	.05
102	Cal Ripken, Sr.	.05
103	Wally Ritchie RC	.05
104	Jeff Robinson RC	.05
105	Gary Roenicke	.05
106	Jerry Royster	.05
107	Mark Salas	.05
108	Luis Salazar	.05
109	Benny Santiago RC	.15
110	Dave Schmidt	.05
111	Kevin Seitzer RC	.05

112	John Shelby	.05
113	Steve Shields RC	.05
114	John Smiley RC	.20
115	Chris Speier	.05
116	Mike Stanley RC	.05
117	Terry Steinbach RC	.15
118	Les Straker RC	.05
119	Jim Sundberg	.05
120	Danny Tartabull	.05
121	Tom Trebelhorn	.05
122	Dave Valle	.05
123	Ed Vande Berg	.05
124	Andy Van Slyke	.05
125	Gary Ward	.05
126	Alan Wiggins	.05
127	Bill Wilkinson RC	.05
128	Frank Williams	.05
129	Matt Williams RC	.75
130	Jim Winn	.05
131	Matt Young	.05
132	Checklist 1T-132T	.05

Traded Tiffany

The cards in this specially boxed limited edition version of the Traded set differ from the regular-issue cards only in the application of a high-gloss finish to the cards' fronts. Production was reported as 30,000 sets.

	NM/M
Complete Set (132):	30.00
Common Player:	.15

Traded Willie Mays Bronze

This 1/4-size metal replica was issued to dealers who purchased cases of 1987 Topps Traded sets. Each detail of the 1953 Topps Mays card is reproduced on the 1-1/4" x 1-3/4" bronze metal mini-card, right down to the stats.

		NM/M
244	Willie Mays	10.00

Box Panels

Offering baseball cards on retail boxes for a second straight year, Topps reduced the size of the cards to 2-1/8" x 3". Four different wax pack boxes were available, each featuring two cards that were placed on the sides of the boxes. The card fronts are identical in design to the regular issue cards. The backs are printed in blue and red and carry a commentary imitating a newspaper format. The cards are numbered A through H.

		NM/M
Complete Singles Set (8):		2.00
Complete Panel Set (4):		2.50
Common Panel:		.50
Common Single Player:		.15
Panel		.50
A	Don Baylor	.15
B	Steve Carlton	.30
Panel		
C	Ron Cey	.15
D	Cecil Cooper	.15
Panel		.75
E	Rickey Henderson	.75
F	Jim Rice	.20
Panel		.75
G	Don Sutton	.15
H	Dave Winfield	.40

All-Star Glossy Set of 22

For the fourth consecutive year, Topps produced an All-Star Game commemorative set of 22 cards. The glossy cards, 2-1/2" x 3-1/2", were included in rack packs. Using the same basic design as in previous efforts

with a few minor changes, the 1987 edition features American and National League logos on the card fronts. Cards #1-12 feature representatives from the American League, while #13-22 are National Leaguers.

		NM/M
Complete Set (22):		2.50
Common Player:		.05
1	Whitey Herzog	.05
2	Keith Hernandez	.05
3	Ryne Sandberg	.35
4	Mike Schmidt	.50
5	Ozzie Smith	.35
6	Tony Gwynn	.35
7	Dale Murphy	.20
8	Darryl Strawberry	.05
9	Gary Carter	.30
10	Dwight Gooden	.05
11	Fernando Valenzuela	.05
12	Dick Howser	.05
13	Wally Joyner	.05
14	Lou Whitaker	.05
15	Wade Boggs	.35
16	Cal Ripken, Jr.	.60
17	Dave Winfield	.30
18	Rickey Henderson	.30
19	Kirby Puckett	.35
20	Lance Parrish	.05
21	Roger Clemens	.40
22	Teddy Higuera	.05

All-Star Glossy Set of 60

Using the same design as the previous year, the 1987 Topps All-Star glossy set includes 48 All-Star performers plus 12 potential superstars branded as "Hot Prospects." The card fronts are uncluttered, save the player's name found in very small print at the bottom. The set was available via a mail-in offer. Six subsets make up the 60-card set, with each subset being available for $1.00 plus six special offer cards that were found in wax packs.

		NM/M
Complete Set (60):		15.00
Common Player:		.10
1	Don Mattingly	.75
2	Tony Gwynn	.50
3	Gary Gaetti	.10
4	Glenn Davis	.10
5	Roger Clemens	.65
6	Dale Murphy	.25
7	Lou Whitaker	.10
8	Roger McDowell	.10
9	Cory Snyder	.10
10	Todd Worrell	.10
11	Gary Carter	.40
12	Eddie Murray	.40
13	Bob Knepper	.10
14	Harold Baines	.10
15	Jeff Reardon	.10
16	Joe Carter	.10
17	Dave Parker	.10
18	Wade Boggs	.50
19	Danny Tartabull	.10
20	Jim Deshaies	.10
21	Rickey Henderson	.40
22	Rob Deer	.10
23	Ozzie Smith	.50
24	Dave Righetti	.10
25	Kent Hrbek	.10

26	Keith Hernandez	.10
27	Don Baylor	.10
28	Mike Schmidt	.85
29	Pete Incaviglia	.10
30	Barry Bonds	9.00
31	George Brett	.85
32	Darryl Strawberry	.10
33	Mike Witt	.10
34	Kevin Bass	.10
35	Jesse Barfield	.10
36	Bob Ojeda	.10
37	Cal Ripken, Jr.	2.00
38	Vince Coleman	.10
39	Wally Joyner	.10
40	Robby Thompson	.10
41	Pete Rose	1.00
42	Jim Rice	.25
43	Tony Bernazard	.10
44	Eric Davis	.10
45	George Bell	.10
46	Hubie Brooks	.10
47	Jack Morris	.10
48	Tim Raines	.10
49	Mark Eichhorn	.10
50	Kevin Mitchell	.10
51	Dwight Gooden	.10
52	Doug DeCinces	.10
53	Fernando Valenzuela	.10
54	Reggie Jackson	.50
55	Johnny Ray	.10
56	Mike Pagliarulo	.10
57	Kirby Puckett	.50
58	Lance Parrish	.10
59	Jose Canseco	.50
60	Greg Mathews	.10

Baseball Highlights

The "Baseball Highlights" boxed set of 33 cards was prepared by Topps for distribution at stores in the Woolworth's chain, although the retailer's name does not appear on the cards. Each card measures 2-1/2" x 3-1/2" in size and features a memorable baseball event that occurred during the 1986 season. The glossy set sold for $1.99.

Coins

For the first time since 1971, Topps issued a set of baseball "coins." Similar in design to the 1964 edition, the metal discs measure 1-1/2" in diameter. The aluminum coins were sold on a limited basis in retail outlets. Three coins and three sticks of gum were found in a pack. The coin fronts feature a full-color photo along with the player's name, team and position in a white band at the bottom. Gold-colored rims are found for American League players; National League players have silver-colored rims. Backs are silvered and carry the coin number, player's name and personal and statistical information.

		NM/M
Complete Set (48):		7.50
Common Player:		.10
Wax Pack (3):		1.00
Wax Box (24):		15.00
1	Harold Baines	.10
2	Jesse Barfield	.10
3	George Bell	.10
4	Wade Boggs	.45
5	George Brett	1.00
6	Jose Canseco	.25
7	Joe Carter	.10

8	Roger Clemens	.60
9	Alvin Davis	.10
10	Rob Deer	.10
11	Kirk Gibson	.10
12	Rickey Henderson	.35
13	Kent Hrbek	.10
14	Pete Incaviglia	.10
15	Reggie Jackson	.60
16	Wally Joyner	.10
17	Don Mattingly	.75
18	Jack Morris	.10
19	Eddie Murray	.35
20	Kirby Puckett	.45
21	Jim Rice	.25
22	Dave Righetti	.10
23	Cal Ripken, Jr.	1.50
24	Cory Snyder	.10
25	Danny Tartabull	.10
26	Dave Winfield	.35
27	Hubie Brooks	.10
28	Gary Carter	.35
29	Vince Coleman	.10
30	Eric Davis	.10
31	Glenn Davis	.10
32	Steve Garvey	.15
33	Dwight Gooden	.10
34	Tony Gwynn	.45
35	Von Hayes	.10
36	Keith Hernandez	.10
37	Dale Murphy	.20
38	Dave Parker	.10
39	Tony Pena	.10
40	Nolan Ryan	1.50
41	Ryne Sandberg	.45
42	Steve Sax	.10
43	Mike Schmidt	1.00
44	Mike Scott	.10
45	Ozzie Smith	.45
46	Darryl Strawberry	.10
47	Fernando Valenzuela	.10
48	Todd Worrell	.10

Gallery of Champions

Designed as a tribute to 1986's winners of baseball's most prestigious awards, the Gallery of Champions are metal "cards" that are one-quarter size replicas of the regular issue Topps cards. The bronze and silver sets were issued in leather-like velvet-lined display cases; the aluminum sets came cello-wrapped. Hobby dealers who purchased one bronze set or a 16-set case of aluminum "cards" received one free Jose Canseco pewter metal mini-card. The purchase of a silver set included five Canseco pewters.

	NM/M
Complete Aluminum Set (12):	17.50
Complete Bronze Set (12):	75.00
Complete Silver Set (12):	250.00
(1a) Jesse Barfield/Aluminum	2.00
(1b) Jesse Barfield/Bronze	6.00
(1s) Jesse Barfield/Silver	15.00
(2a) Wade Boggs/Aluminum	4.50
(2b) Wade Boggs/Bronze	15.00
(2s) Wade Boggs/Silver	30.00
(3a) Jose Canseco/Aluminum	3.50
(3b) Jose Canseco/Bronze	10.00
(3s) Jose Canseco/Silver	25.00
(3p) Jose Canseco/Pewter	12.50
(4a) Joe Carter/Aluminum	2.00
(4b) Joe Carter/Bronze	6.00
(4s) Joe Carter/Silver	15.00
(5a) Roger Clemens/ Aluminum	5.00
(5b) Roger Clemens/Bronze	16.00
(5s) Roger Clemens/Silver	40.00
(6a) Tony Gwynn/Aluminum	4.50
(6b) Tony Gwynn/Bronze	15.00
(6s) Tony Gwynn/Silver	30.00
(7a) Don Mattingly/Aluminum	6.00
(7b) Don Mattingly/Bronze	17.50
(7s) Don Mattingly/Silver	45.00
(8a) Tim Raines/Aluminum	2.00
(8b) Tim Raines/Bronze	6.00
(8s) Tim Raines/Silver	15.00
(9a) Dave Righetti/Aluminum	2.00
(9b) Dave Righetti/Bronze	6.00
(9s) Dave Righetti/Silver	15.00
(10a) Mike Schmidt/Aluminum	6.00
(10b) Mike Schmidt/Bronze	20.00
(10s) Mike Schmidt/Silver	50.00
(11a) Mike Scott/Aluminum	2.00

(11b)	Mike Scott/Bronze	6.00
(11s)	Mike Scott/Silver	15.00
(12a)	Todd Worrell/Aluminum	2.00
(12b)	Todd Worrell/Bronze	6.00
(12s)	Todd Worrell/Silver	15.00

Glossy Rookies

The 1987 Topps Glossy Rookies set of 22 cards was introduced with Topps' new 100-card "Jumbo Packs." Intended for sale in supermarkets, the jumbo packs contained one glossy card. Measuring the standard 2-1/2" x 3-1/2" size, the special insert cards feature the top rookies from the previous season.

		NM/M
Complete Set (22):		3.00
Common Player:		.05
1	Andy Allanson	.05
2	John Cangelosi	.05
3	Jose Canseco	1.00
4	Will Clark	.25
5	Mark Eichhorn	.05
6	Pete Incaviglia	.05
7	Wally Joyner	.05
8	Eric King	.05
9	Dave Magadan	.05
10	John Morris	.05
11	Juan Nieves	.05
12	Rafael Palmeiro	2.50
13	Billy Jo Robidoux	.05
14	Bruce Ruffin	.05
15	Ruben Sierra	.05
16	Cory Snyder	.05
17	Kurt Stillwell	.05
18	Dale Sveum	.05
19	Danny Tartabull	.05
20	Andres Thomas	.05
21	Robby Thompson	.05
22	Todd Worrell	.05

Bobby Grich Night Sheet

In conjunction with a Bobby Grich Night sponsored by the California Angels on May 1, 1987, Sheraton Hotels of Los Angeles and radio station KLAC issued this sheet bearing reproductions of each of Grich's regular issue Topps cards from 1971-1987. The sheet measures 10" x 17-1/2", while the perforated cards, if removed from the sheet, measure the standard 2-1/2" x 3-1/2".

		NM/M
Complete Sheet:		10.00
Common Card:		.75
1971	Bob Grich #193	1.50
1972	Bob Grich #338	.75
1973	Bob Grich #418	.75
1974	Bob Grich #109	.75
1975	Bob Grich #225	.75
1976	Bob Grich #335	.75
1977	Bob Grich #521	.75
1978	Bob Grich #18	.75
1979	Bob Grich #477	.75
1980	Bob Grich #621	.75
1981	Bob Grich #182	.75
1982	Bob Grich #284	.75
1983	Bob Grich #790	.75
1984	Bob Grich #315	.75
1985	Bob Grich #465	.75
1986	Bob Grich #155	.75
1987	Bob Grich #677	.75

Mini League Leaders

Returning for 1987, the Topps "Major League Leaders" set was increased in size from 66 to 76 cards. The 2-1/8" x 3" cards feature woodgrain borders that encompass a white-bordered color photo. Backs are printed in yellow, orange and brown and list the player's official ranking based on his 1986 American or National League statistics. The players featured are those who finished the top five in their leagues' various batting and pitching catego-

ries. The cards were sold in plastic-wrapped packs, seven cards plus a game card per pack.

DENNIS RASMUSSEN

		NM/M
Complete Set (77):		4.00
Common Player:		.05
Wax Pack (7):		.50
Wax Box (36):		10.00
1	Bob Horner	.05
2	Dale Murphy	.15
3	Lee Smith	.05
4	Eric Davis	.05
5	John Franco	.05
6	Dave Parker	.05
7	Kevin Bass	.05
8	Glenn Davis	.05
9	Bill Doran	.05
10	Bob Knepper	.05
11	Mike Scott	.05
12	Dave Smith	.05
13	Mariano Duncan	.05
14	Orel Hershiser	.05
15	Steve Sax	.05
16	Fernando Valenzuela	.05
17	Tim Raines	.05
18	Jeff Reardon	.05
19	Floyd Youmans	.05
20	Gary Carter	.25
21	Ron Darling	.05
22	Sid Fernandez	.05
23	Dwight Gooden	.05
24	Keith Hernandez	.05
25	Bob Ojeda	.05
26	Darryl Strawberry	.05
27	Steve Bedrosian	.05
28	Von Hayes	.05
29	Juan Samuel	.05
30	Mike Schmidt	.75
31	Rick Rhoden	.05
32	Vince Coleman	.05
33	Danny Cox	.05
34	Todd Worrell	.05
35	Tony Gwynn	.35
36	Mike Krukow	.05
37	Candy Maldonado	.05
38	Don Aase	.05
39	Eddie Murray	.25
40	Cal Ripken, Jr.	1.00
41	Wade Boggs	.35
42	Roger Clemens	.40
43	Bruce Hurst	.15
44	Jim Rice	.15
45	Wally Joyner	.05
46	Donnie Moore	.05
47	Gary Pettis	.05
48	Mike Witt	.05
49	John Cangelosi	.05
50	Tom Candiotti	.05
51	Joe Carter	.05
52	Pat Tabler	.05
53	Kirk Gibson	.05
54	Willie Hernandez	.05
55	Jack Morris	.05
56	Alan Trammell	.05
57	George Brett	.75
58	Willie Wilson	.05
59	Rob Deer	.05
60	Teddy Higuera	.05
61	Bert Blyleven	.05
62	Gary Gaetti	.05
63	Kirby Puckett	.35
64	Rickey Henderson	.25
65	Don Mattingly	.50
66	Dennis Rasmussen	.05
67	Dave Righetti	.05
68	Jose Canseco	.20
69	Dave Kingman	.05
70	Phil Bradley	.05
71	Mark Langston	.05
72	Pete O'Brien	.05
73	Jesse Barfield	.05
74	George Bell	.05
75	Tony Fernandez	.05
76	Tom Henke	.05
77	Checklist	.05

Stickers - Hardback Test

In addition to its regular issue of Panini-produced paper-backed stickers, Topps in 1987 produced a very limited version of the same issue with a hard cardboard back. The Topps hard-back version is virtually identical to the more common Panini version except for the copyright line

printed on back. Production of the hard-back version was reported to be 1/10 of 1% of the Panini version.

	NM/M
Complete Set (313):	75.00
Common Player:	.50
Wax Pack (5):	1.00
Wax Box (48):	25.00

Stickers - Panini

For the seventh consecutive year, Topps issued stickers produced by Panini in Italy for use in a special album or yearbook. The 2-1/8" x 3" stickers offer a full-color front with a peel-off paper back. Fronts feature either one full-size player picture or two half-size individual stickers. The yearbook contains 36 glossy, magazine-style pages, all printed in full color. Mike Schmidt, 1986 N.L. MVP, is featured on the covers. The yearbook sold in retail outlets for $.35, while stickers were sold five in a pack for $.25. The number in parentheses in this checklist is the sticker number the player shares the sticker with. Besides the common soft-back sticker made for Topps by Panini, there was a test issue of hard-back stickercards.

	NM/M
Complete Set (313):	15.00
Common Player:	.05
Sticker Album:	1.50
Wax Pack (5):	
Wax Box (100):	15.00

1	1986 Highlights (Jim Deshaies/172)		.05
2	1986 Highlights (Roger Clemens/175)		.25
3	1986 Highlights (Roger Clemens/176)		.25
4	1986 Highlights (Dwight Evans/177)		.05
5	1986 Highlights (Dwight Gooden/178)		.05
6	1986 Highlights (Dwight Gooden/180)		.05
7	1986 Highlights (Dave Lopes/181)		.05
8	1986 Highlights (Dave Righetti/182)		.05
9	1986 Highlights (Dave Righetti/183)		.05
10	1986 Highlights (Ruben Sierra/185)		.05
11	1986 Highlights (Todd Worrell/186)		.05
12	1986 Highlights (Todd Worrell/187)		.05
13	N.L. Championship Series (Lenny Dykstra)		.05
14	N.L. Championship Series (Gary Carter)		.15
15	N.L. Championship Series (Mike Scott)		.05
16	A.L. Championship Series (Gary Pettis)		.05
17	A.L. Championship Series (Jim Rice)		.05
18	A.L. Championship Series (Bruce Hurst)		.05

19	1986 World Series (Bruce Hurst)		.05
20	1986 World Series (Wade Boggs)		.15
21	1986 World Series (Lenny Dykstra)		
22	1986 World Series (Gary Carter)		.15
23	1986 World Series (Dave Henderson)		.05
24	1986 World Series (Howard Johnson)		.05
25	1986 World Series (Mets Celebrate)		.05
26	Glenn Davis		.05
27	Nolan Ryan/188		.60
28	Charlie Kerfeld/189		.05
29	Jose Cruz/190		.05
30	Phil Garner/191		.05
31	Bill Doran/192		.05
32	Bob Knepper/195		.05
33	Denny Walling/196		.05
34	Kevin Bass/197		.05
35	Mike Scott		
36	Dale Murphy		.20
37	Paul Assenmacher/198		.05
38	Ken Oberkfell/200		.05
39	Andres Thomas/201		.05
40	Gene Garber/202		.05
41	Bob Horner		.05
42	Rafael Ramirez/203		.05
43	Rick Mahler/204		.05
44	Omar Moreno/205		.05
45	Dave Palmer/206		.05
46	Ozzie Smith		.35
47	Bob Forsch/207		.05
48	Willie McGee/209		.05
49	Tom Herr/210		.05
50	Vince Coleman/211		.05
51	Andy Van Slyke/212		.05
52	Jack Clark/215		.05
53	John Tudor/216		.05
54	Terry Pendleton/217		.05
55	Todd Worrell		.05
56	Lee Smith		.05
57	Leon Durham/218		.05
58	Jerry Mumphrey/219		.05
59	Shawon Dunston/220		.05
60	Scott Sanderson/221		.05
61	Ryne Sandberg		.35
62	Gary Matthews/222		.05
63	Dennis Eckersley/225		.25
64	Jody Davis/226		.05
65	Keith Moreland/227		.05
66	Mike Marshall/228		.05
67	Bill Madlock/229		.05
68	Greg Brock/230		.05
69	Pedro Guerrero/231		.05
70	Steve Sax		.05
71	Rick Honeycutt/232		.05
72	Franklin Stubbs/235		.05
73	Mike Scioscia/236		.05
74	Mariano Duncan/237		.05
75	Fernando Valenzuela		.05
76	Hubie Brooks		.05
77	Andre Dawson/238		.20
78	Tim Burke/240		.05
79	Floyd Youmans/241		.05
80	Tim Wallach/242		.05
81	Jeff Reardon/243		.05
82	Mitch Webster/244		.05
83	Bryn Smith/245		.05
84	Andres Galarraga/246		.05
85	Tim Raines		.05
86	Chris Brown		.05
87	Bob Brenly/247		.05
88	Will Clark/249		.10
89	Scott Garrelts/250		.05
90	Jeffrey Leonard/251		.05
91	Robby Thompson/252		.05
92	Mike Krukow/255		.05
93	Danny Gladden/256		.05
94	Candy Maldonado/257		.05
95	Chili Davis		.05
96	Dwight Gooden		.05
97	Sid Fernandez/258		.05
98	Len Dykstra/259		.05
99	Bob Ojeda/260		.05
100	Wally Backman/261		.05
101	Gary Carter		.30
102	Keith Hernandez/262		.05
103	Darryl Strawberry/265		.05
104	Roger McDowell/266		.05
105	Ron Darling/267		.05
106	Tony Gwynn		.35
107	Dave Dravecky/268		.05
108	Terry Kennedy/269		.05
109	Rich Gossage/270		.05
110	Garry Templeton/271		.05
111	Lance McCullers/272		.05
112	Eric Show/275		.05
113	John Kruk/276		.05
114	Tim Flannery/277		.05
115	Steve Garvey		.15
116	Mike Schmidt		.45
117	Glenn Wilson/278		.05
118	Kent Tekulve/280		.05
119	Gary Redus/281		.05
120	Shane Rawley/282		.05
121	Von Hayes		.05
122	Don Carman/283		.05
123	Bruce Ruffin/285		.05
124	Steve Bedrosian/286		.05
125	Juan Samuel/287		.05
126	Sid Bream/288		.05
127	Cecilio Guante/289		.05
128	Rick Reuschel/290		.05
129	Tony Pena/291		.05

130 Rick Rhoden .05
131 Barry Bonds/292 5.00
132 Joe Orsulak/295 .05
133 Jim Morrison/296 .05
134 R.J. Reynolds/297 .05
135 Johnny Ray .05
136 Eric Davis .05
137 Tom Browning/298 .05
138 John Franco/300 .05
139 Pete Rose/301 .35
140 Bill Gullickson/302 .05
141 Ron Oester/303 .05
142 Bo Diaz/304 .05
143 Buddy Bell /305 .05
144 Eddie Milner/306 .05
145 Dave Parker .05
146 Kirby Puckett .35
147 Rickey Henderson .30
148 Wade Boggs .35
149 Lance Parrish .05
150 Wally Joyner .05
151 Cal Ripken, Jr. .75
152 Dave Winfield .30
153 Lou Whitaker .05
154 Roger Clemens .40
155 Tony Gwynn .35
156 Ryne Sandberg .35
157 Keith Hernandez .05
158 Gary Carter .30
159 Darryl Strawberry .05
160 Mike Schmidt .45
161 Dale Murphy .15
162 Ozzie Smith .35
163 Dwight Gooden .05
164 Jose Canseco .25
165 Curt Young/307 .05
166 Alfredo Griffin/30 8 .05
167 Dave Stewart/309 .05
168 Mike Davis/310 .05
169 Bruce Bochte/311 .05
170 Dwayne Murphy/312 .05
171 Carney Lansford/313 .05
172 Joaquin Andujar/1 .05
173 Dave Kingman .05
174 Wally Joyner .05
175 Gary Pettis/2 .05
176 Dick Schofield/3 .05
177 Donnie Moore/4 .05
178 Brian Downing/5 .05
179 Mike Witt .05
180 Bob Boone/6 .05
181 Kirk McCaskill/7 .05
182 Doug DeCinces/8 .05
183 Don Sutton/9 .25
184 Jessie Barfield .05
185 Tom Henke/10 .05
186 Willie Upshaw/11 .05
187 Mark Eichhorn/12 .05
188 Damaso Garcia/27 .05
189 Jim Clancy/28 .05
190 Lloyd Moseby/29 .05
191 Tony Fernandez/30 .05
192 Jimmy Key/31 .05
193 George Bell .05
194 Rob Deer .05
195 Mark Clear/32 .05
196 Robin Yount/33 .20
197 Jim Gantner/34 .05
198 Cecil Cooper/(37) .05
199 Teddy Higuera .05
200 Paul Molitor/(38) .25
201 Dan Plesac/(39) .05
202 Billy Jo Robidoux/40 .05
203 Earnie Riles/42 .05
204 Ken Schrom/43 .05
205 Pat Tabler/44 .05
206 Mel Hall/45 .05
207 Tony Bernazard/47 .05
208 Joe Carter .05
209 Ernie Camacho/48 .05
210 Julio Franco/49 .05
211 Tom Candiotti/50 .05
212 Brook Jacoby/51 .05
213 Cory Snyder .05
214 Jim Presley .05
215 Mike Moore/52 .05
216 Harold Reynolds/53 .05
217 Scott Bradley/54 .05
218 Matt Young/57 .05
219 Mark Langston/58 .05
220 Alvin Davis/59 .05
221 Phil Bradley/60 .05
222 Ken Phelps/62 .05
223 Danny Tartabull .05
224 Eddie Murray .30
225 Rick Dempsey/63 .05
226 Fred Lynn/64 .05
227 Mike Boddicker/65 .05
228 Don Aase/66 .05
229 Larry Sheets/67 .05
230 Storm Davis/68 .05
231 Lee Lacy/69 .05
232 Jim Traber/71 .05
233 Cal Ripken, Jr. .75
234 Larry Parrish .05
235 Gary Ward/72 .05
236 Pete Incaviglia/73 .05
237 Scott Fletcher/77 .05
238 Greg Harris/77 .05
239 Pete O'Brien .05
240 Charlie Hough/78 .05
241 Don Slaught/79 .05
242 Steve Buechele/80 .05
243 Oddibe McDowell/81 .05
244 Roger Clemens/82 .30
245 Bob Stanley/83 .05
246 Tom Seaver/84 .20
247 Rich Gedman/87 .05

248 Jim Rice .15
249 Dennis Boyd/88 .05
250 Bill Buckner/89 .05
251 Dwight Evans/90 .05
252 Don Baylor/91 .05
253 Wade Boggs .35
254 George Brett .45
255 Steve Farr/92 .05
256 Jim Sundberg/93 .05
257 Dan Quisenberry/94 .05
258 Charlie Leibrandt/97 .05
259 Argenis Salazar/98 .05
260 Frank White/99 .05
261 Willie Wilson/100 .05
262 Lonnie Smith/102 .05
263 Steve Balboni .05
264 Darrell Evans .05
265 Johnny Grubb/103 .05
266 Jack Morris/104 .05
267 Lou Whitaker/105 .05
268 Chet Lemon/107 .05
269 Larry Parrish/108 .05
270 Alan Trammell/109 .05
271 Darnell Coles/110 .05
272 Willie Hernandez/111 .05
273 Kirk Gibson .05
274 Kirby Puckett .35
275 Mike Smithson/112 .05
276 Mickey Hatcher/113 .05
277 Frank Viola/114 .05
278 Bert Blyleven/117 .05
279 Gary Gaetti .05
280 Tom Brunansky/118 .05
281 Kent Hrbek/119 .05
282 Roy Smalley/120 .05
283 Greg Gagne/122 .05
284 Harold Baines .05
285 Ron Hassey/123 .05
286 Floyd Bannister/124 .05
287 Ozzie Guillen/125 .05
288 Carlton Fisk/126 .25
289 Tim Hulett/127 .05
290 Joe Cowley/128 .05
291 Greg Walker/129 .05
292 Neil Allen/131 .05
293 John Cangelosi/130 .05
294 Don Mattingly .45
295 Mike Easler/132 .05
296 Rickey Henderson/133 .20
297 Dan Pasqua/134 .05
298 Dave Winfield/137 .20
299 Dave Righetti .05
300 Mike Pagliarulo/138 .05
301 Ron Guidry/139 .05
302 Willie Randolph/140 .05
303 Dennis Rasmussen/141 .05
304 Jose Canseco/142 .20
305 Andres Thomas/143 .05
306 Danny Tartabull/144 .05
307 Robby Thompson/165 .05
308 Pete Incaviglia, Cory Snyder/166 .05
309 Dale Sveum/167 .05
310 Todd Worrell/168 .05
311 Andy Allanson/169 .05
312 Bruce Ruffin/170 .05
313 Wally Joyner/171 .05

1988 Topps

The 1988 Topps set features a clean, attractive design of a player photo surrounded by a thin colored frame which is encompassed by a white border. The player's name appears in the lower-right corner in a diagonal colored strip. The team nickname is in large letters at the top of the card. Backs feature black print on orange and gray stock and include the usual player personal and career statistics. Many of the cards contain a new feature titled "This Way To The Clubhouse," which explains how the player joined his current team. The 792-card set includes a number of special subsets including "Future Stars," "Turn Back The Clock," All-Star teams, All-Star rookie selections, and Record Breakers.

NM/M
Unopened Factory Set, Retail (792): 15.00
Unopened Factory Set, Hobby (792): 15.00

Complete Set (792): 12.00
Common Player: .05
Wax Pack (15): .40
Wax Box (36): 15.00
Cello Pack (28): .70
Cello Box (24): 13.50
Rack Pack (43): .75
Rack Box (24): 15.00
Vending Box (500): 7.50
1 Vince Coleman (Record Breakers) .05
2 Don Mattingly (Record Breakers) .25
3a Mark McGwire (Record Breakers, white triangle by left foot.) 1.00
3b Mark McGwire (Record Breakers, no white triangle.) .40
4a Eddie Murray (Record Breakers, no mention of record on front.) .25
4b Eddie Murray (Record Breakers, record in box on front.) .20
5 Joe Niekro, Phil Niekro (Record Breakers) .05
6 Nolan Ryan (Record Breakers) .40
7 Benito Santiago (Record Breakers) .05
8 Kevin Elster RC (Future Stars) .05
9 Andy Hawkins .05
10 Ryne Sandberg .50
11 Mike Young .05
12 Bill Schroeder .05
13 Andres Thomas .05
14 Sparky Anderson .10
15 Chili Davis .05
16 Kirk McCaskill .05
17 Ron Oester .05
18a Al Leiter RC (Future Stars, no "NY" on shirt, photo actually Steve George.) .40
18b Al Leiter RC (Future Stars, "NY" on shirt, correct photo.) .20
19 Mark Davidson RC .05
20 Kevin Gross .05
21 Red Sox Leaders (Wade Boggs, Spike Owen) .10
22 Greg Swindell .05
23 Ken Landreaux .05
24 Jim Deshaies .05
25 Andres Galarraga .25
26 Mitch Williams .05
27 R.J. Reynolds .05
28 Jose Nunez RC .05
29 Argenis Salazar .05
30 Sid Fernandez .05
31 Bruce Bochy .05
32 Mike Morgan .05
33 Rob Deer .05
34 Ricky Horton .05
35 Harold Baines .05
36 Jamie Moyer .05
37 Ed Romero .05
38 Jeff Calhoun .05
39 Gerald Perry .05
40 Orel Hershiser .05
41 Bob Melvin .05
42 Bill Landrum RC .05
43 Dick Schofield .05
44 Lou Piniella .05
45 Kent Hrbek .05
46 Darnell Coles .05
47 Joaquin Andujar .05
48 Alan Ashby .05
49 Dave Clark RC .05
50 Hubie Brooks .05
51 Orioles Leaders (Eddie Murray, Cal Ripken, Jr.) .25
52 Don Robinson .05
53 Curt Wilkerson .05
54 Jim Clancy .05
55 Phil Bradley .05
56 Ed Hearn .05
57 Tim Crews RC .05
58 Dave Magadan .05
59 Danny Cox .05
60 Rickey Henderson .40
61 Mark Knudson RC .05
62 Jeff Hamilton .05
63 Jimmy Jones RC .05
64 Ken Caminiti RC .25
65 Leon Durham .05
66 Shane Rawley .05
67 Ken Oberkfell .05
68 Dave Dravecky .05
69 Mike Hart RC .05
70 Roger Clemens .60
71 Gary Pettis .05
72 Dennis Eckersley .30
73 Randy Bush .05
74 Tom Lasorda .05
75 Joe Carter .05
76 Denny Martinez .05
77 Tom O'Malley .05
78 Dan Petry .05
79 Ernie Whitt .05
80 Mark Langston .05
81 Reds Leaders (John Franco, Ron Robinson) .05
82 Darrel Akerfelds RC .05
83 Jose Oquendo .05

84 Cecilio Guante .05
85 Howard Johnson .05
86 Ron Karkovice .05
87 Mike Mason .05
88 Earnie Riles .05
89 Gary Thurman RC .05
90 Dale Murphy .05
91 Joey Cora RC .10
92 Len Matuszek .05
93 Bob Sebra .05
94 Chuck Jackson RC .05
95 Lance Parrish .05
96 Todd Benzinger RC .05
97 Scott Garrelts .05
98 Rene Gonzales RC .05
99 Chuck Finley .05
100 Jack Clark .05
101 Allan Anderson .05
102 Barry Larkin .25
103 Curt Young .05
104 Dick Williams .05
105 Jesse Orosco .05
106 Jim Walewander RC .05
107 Scott Bailes .05
108 Steve Lyons .05
109 Joel Skinner .05
110 Teddy Higuera .05
111 Expos Leaders (Hubie Brooks, Vance Law) .05
112 Les Lancaster RC .05
113 Kelly Gruber .05
114 Jeff Russell .05
115 Johnny Ray .05
116 Jerry Don Gleaton .05
117 James Steels RC .05
118 Bob Welch .05
119 Robbie Wine RC .05
120 Kirby Puckett .50
121 Checklist 1-132 .05
122 Tony Bernazard .05
123 Tom Candiotti .05
124 Ray Knight .05
125 Bruce Hurst .05
126 Steve Jeltz .05
127 Jim Gott .05
128 Johnny Grubb .05
129 Greg Minton .05
130 Buddy Bell .05
131 Don Schulze .05
132 Donnie Hill .05
133 Greg Mathews .05
134 Chuck Tanner .05
135 Dennis Rasmussen .05
136 Brian Dayett .05
137 Chris Bosio .05
138 Mitch Webster .05
139 Jerry Browne .25
140 Jesse Barfield .05
141 Royals Leaders (George Brett, Bret Saberhagen) .20
142 Andy Van Slyke .05
143 Mickey Tettleton .05
144 Don Gordon RC .05
145 Bill Madlock .05
146 Donell Nixon RC .05
147 Bill Buckner .05
148 Carmelo Martinez .05
149 Ken Howell .05
150 Eric Davis .05
151 Bob Knepper .05
152 Jody Reed RC .10
153 John Habyan .05
154 Jeff Stone .05
155 Bruce Sutter .30
156 Gary Matthews .05
157 Atlee Hammaker .05
158 Tim Hulett .05
159 Brad Arnsberg RC .05
160 Willie McGee .05
161 Bryn Smith .05
162 Mark McLemore .05
163 Dale Mohorcic .05
164 Dave Johnson .05
165 Robin Yount .40
166 Rick Rodriguez RC .05
167 Rance Mulliniks .05
168 Barry Jones .05
169 Ross Jones RC .05
170 Rich Gossage .05
171 Cubs Leaders (Shawon Dunston, Manny Trillo) .05
172 Lloyd McClendon RC .05
173 Eric Plunk .05
174 Phil Garner .05
175 Kevin Bass .05
176 Jeff Reed .05
177 Frank Tanana .05
178 Dwayne Henry RC .05
179 Charlie Puleo .05
180 Terry Kennedy .05
181 Dave Cone .05
182 Ken Phelps .05
183 Tom Lawless .05
184 Ivan Calderon .05
185 Rick Rhoden .05
186 Rafael Palmeiro .35
187 Steve Kiefer RC .05
188 John Russell .05
189 Wes Gardner RC .05
190 Candy Maldonado .05
191 John Cerutti .05
192 Devon White .05
193 Brian Fisher .05
194 Tom Kelly .05
195 Dan Quisenberry .05
196 Dave Engle .05
197 Lance McCullers .05

198 Franklin Stubbs .05
199 Dave Meads RC .05
200 Wade Boggs .50
201 Rangers Leaders (Steve Buechele, Pete Incaviglia, Pete O'Brien, Bobby Valentine) .05
202 Glenn Hoffman .05
203 Fred Toliver .05
204 Paul O'Neill RC .05
205 Nelson Liriano RC .05
206 Domingo Ramos .05
207 John Mitchell RC .05
208 Steve Lake .05
209 Richard Dotson .05
210 Willie Randolph .05
211 Frank DiPino .05
212 Greg Brock .05
213 Albert Hall .05
214 Dave Schmidt .05
215 Von Hayes .05
216 Jerry Reuss .05
217 Harry Spilman .05
218 Dan Schatzeder .05
219 Mike Stanley .05
220 Tom Henke .05
221 Rafael Belliard .05
222 Steve Farr .05
223 Stan Jefferson .05
224 Tom Trebelhorn .05
225 Mike Scioscia .05
226 Dave Lopes .05
227 Ed Correa .05
228 Wallace Johnson .05
229 Jeff Musselman .05
230 Pat Tabler .05
231 Pirates Leaders (Barry Bonds, Bobby Bonilla) .50
232 Bob James .05
233 Rafael Santana .05
234 Ken Dayley .05
235 Gary Ward .05
236 Ted Power .05
237 Mike Heath .05
238 Luis Polonia RC .10
239 Roy Smalley .05
240 Lee Smith .05
241 Damaso Garcia .05
242 Tom Niedenfuer .05
243 Mark Ryal RC .05
244 Jeff Robinson .05
245 Rich Gedman .05
246 Mike Campbell RC (Future Stars) .05
247 Thad Bosley .05
248 Storm Davis .05
249 Mike Marshall .05
250 Nolan Ryan .75
251 Tom Foley .05
252 Bob Brower .05
253 Checklist 133-264 .05
254 Lee Elia .05
255 Mookie Wilson .05
256 Ken Schrom .05
257 Jerry Royster .05
258 Ed Nunez .05
259 Ron Kittle .05
260 Vince Coleman .05
261 Giants Leaders (Will Clark, Candy Maldonado, Kevin Mitchell, Robby Thompson, Jose Uribe) .05
262 Drew Hall .05
263 Glenn Braggs .05
264 Les Straker RC .05
265 Bo Diaz .05
266 Paul Assenmacher .05
267 Billy Bean RC .05
268 Bruce Ruffin .05
269 Ellis Burks .05
270 Mike Witt .05
271 Ken Gerhart .05
272 Steve Ontiveros .05
273 Garth Iorg .05
274 Junior Ortiz .05
275 Kevin Seitzer .05
276 Luis Salazar .05
277 Alejandro Pena .05
278 Jose Cruz .05
279 Randy St. Claire .05
280 Pete Incaviglia .05
281 Jerry Hairston Sr. .05
282 Pat Perry .05
283 Phil Lombardi RC .05
284 Larry Bowa .05
285 Jim Presley .05
286 Chuck Crim RC .05
287 Manny Trillo .05
288 Pat Pacillo RC .05
289 Dave Bergman .05
290 Tony Fernandez .05
291 Astros Leaders (Kevin Bass, Billy Hatcher) .05
292 Carney Lansford .05
293 Doug Jones RC .05
294 Al Pedrique RC .05
295 Wes Gardner .05
296 Floyd Rayford .05
297 Zane Smith .05
298 Milt Thompson .05
299 Steve Crawford .05
300 Don Mattingly .60
301 Bud Black .05
302 Jose Uribe .05
303 Eric Show .05
304 George Hendrick .05
305 Steve Sax .05

306 Billy Hatcher .05
307 Mike Trujillo .05
308 Lee Mazzilli .05
309 Bill Long RC .05
310 Tom Herr .05
311 Scott Sanderson .05
312 Joey Meyer RC (Future Stars) .05
313 Bob McClure .05
314 Jimy Williams .05
315 Dave Parker .05
316 Jose Rijo .05
317 Tom Nieto .05
318 Mel Hall .05
319 Mike Loynd .05
320 Alan Trammell .05
321 White Sox Leaders (Harold Baines, Carlton Fisk) .05
322 Vicente Palacios RC .05
323 Rick Leach .05
324 Danny Jackson .05
325 Glenn Hubbard .05
326 Al Nipper .05
327 Larry Sheets .05
328 Greg Cadaret RC .05
329 Chris Speier .05
330 Eddie Whitson .05
331 Brian Downing .05
332 Jerry Reed .05
333 Wally Backman .05
334 Dave LaPoint .05
335 Claudell Washington .05
336 Ed Lynch .05
337 Jim Gantner .05
338 Brian Holton .05
339 Kurt Stillwell .05
340 Jack Morris .05
341 Carmen Castillo .05
342 Larry Andersen .05
343 Greg Gagne .05
344 Tony LaRussa .05
345 Scott Fletcher .05
346 Vance Law .05
347 Joe Johnson .05
348 Jim Eisenreich .05
349 Bob Walk .05
350 Will Clark .05
351 Cardinals Leaders (Tony Pena, Red Schoendienst) .05
352 Billy Ripken RC .05
353 Ed Olwine .05
354 Marc Sullivan .05
355 Roger McDowell .05
356 Luis Aguayo .05
357 Floyd Bannister .05
358 Rey Quinones .05
359 Tim Stoddard .05
360 Tony Gwynn .50
361 Greg Maddux .50
362 Juan Castillo .05
363 Willie Fraser .05
364 Nick Esasky .05
365 Floyd Youmans .05
366 Chet Lemon .05
367 Tim Leary .05
368 Gerald Young RC .05
369 Greg Harris .05
370 Jose Canseco .25
371 Joe Hesketh .05
372 Matt Williams .05
373 Checklist 265-396 .05
374 Doc Edwards .05
375 Tom Brunansky .05
376 Bill Wilkinson RC .05
377 Sam Horn RC .05
378 Todd Frohwirth RC .05
379 Rafael Ramirez .05
380 Joe Magrane RC .05
381 Angels Leaders (Jack Howell, Wally Joyner) .05
382 Keith Miller RC .05
383 Eric Bell .05
384 Neil Allen .05
385 Carlton Fisk .40
386 Don Mattingly/AS .30
387 Willie Randolph/AS .05
388 Wade Boggs/AS .20
389 Alan Trammell/AS .05
390 George Bell/AS .05
391 Kirby Puckett/AS .25
392 Dave Winfield/AS .20
393 Matt Nokes/AS .05
394 Roger Clemens/AS .35
395 Jimmy Key/AS .05
396 Tom Henke/AS .05
397 Jack Clark/AS .05
398 Juan Samuel/AS .05
399 Tim Wallach/AS .05
400 Ozzie Smith/AS .25
401 Andre Dawson/AS .15
402 Tony Gwynn/AS .25
403 Tim Raines/AS .05
404 Benny Santiago/AS .05
405 Dwight Gooden/AS .05
406 Shane Rawley/AS .05
407 Steve Bedrosian/AS .05
408 Dion James .05
409 Joel McKeon RC .05
410 Tony Pena .05
411 Wayne Tolleson .05
412 Randy Myers .05
413 John Christensen .05
414 John McNamara .05
415 Don Carman .05
416 Keith Moreland .05
417 Mark Ciardi RC .05

No.	Player	Price
418	Joel Youngblood	.05
419	Scott McGregor	.05
420	Wally Joyner	.05
421	Ed Vande Berg	.05
422	Dave Concepcion	.05
423	John Smiley	.05
424	Dwayne Murphy	.05
425	Jeff Reardon	.05
426	Randy Ready	.05
427	Paul Kilgus RC	.05
428	John Shelby	.05
429	Tigers Leaders (Kirk Gibson, Alan Trammell)	.05
430	Glenn Davis	.05
431	Casey Candaele	.05
432	Mike Moore	.05
433	Bill Pecota RC	.05
434	Rick Aguilera	.05
435	Mike Pagliarulo	.05
436	Mike Bielecki	.05
437	Fred Manrique RC	.05
438	Rob Ducey RC	.05
439	Dave Martinez	.05
440	Steve Bedrosian	.05
441	Rick Manning	.05
442	Tom Bolton RC	.05
443	Ken Griffey	.05
444	Cal Ripken, Sr.	.05
445	Mike Krukow	.05
446	Doug DeCinces	.05
447	Jeff Montgomery RC	.20
448	Mike Davis	.05
449	Jeff Robinson RC	.05
450	Barry Bonds	.75
451	Keith Atherton	.05
452	Willie Wilson	.05
453	Dennis Powell	.05
454	Marvell Wynne	.05
455	Shawn Hillegas RC	.05
456	Dave Anderson	.05
457	Terry Leach	.05
458	Ron Hassey	.05
459	Yankees Leaders (Willie Randolph, Dave Winfield)	.05
460	Ozzie Smith	.50
461	Danny Darwin	.05
462	Don Slaught	.05
463	Fred McGriff	.05
464	Jay Tibbs	.05
465	Paul Molitor	.40
466	Jerry Mumphrey	.05
467	Don Aase	.05
468	Darren Daulton	.05
469	Jeff Dedmon	.05
470	Dwight Evans	.05
471	Donnie Moore	.05
472	Robby Thompson	.05
473	Joe Niekro	.05
474	Tom Brookens	.05
475	Pete Rose	.65
476	Dave Stewart	.05
477	Jamie Quirk	.05
478	Sid Bream	.05
479	Brett Butler	.05
480	Dwight Gooden	.05
481	Mariano Duncan	.05
482	Mark Davis	.05
483	Rod Booker RC	.05
484	Pat Clements	.05
485	Harold Reynolds	.05
486	Pat Keedy RC	.05
487	Jim Pankovits	.05
488	Andy McGaffigan	.05
489	Dodgers Leaders (Pedro Guerrero, Fernando Valenzuela)	.05
490	Larry Parrish	.05
491	B.J. Surhoff	.05
492	Doyle Alexander	.05
493	Mike Greenwell	.05
494	Wally Ritchie RC	.05
495	Eddie Murray	.40
496	Guy Hoffman	.05
497	Kevin Mitchell	.05
498	Bob Boone	.05
499	Eric King	.05
500	Andre Dawson	.25
501	Tim Birtsas RC	.05
502	Danny Gladden	.05
503	Junior Noboa RC	.05
504	Bob Rodgers	.05
505	Willie Upshaw	.05
506	John Cangelosi	.05
507	Mark Gubicza	.05
508	Tim Teufel	.05
509	Bill Dawley	.05
510	Dave Winfield	.40
511	Joel Davis	.05
512	Alex Trevino	.05
513	Tim Flannery	.05
514	Pat Sheridan	.05
515	Juan Nieves	.05
516	Jim Sundberg	.05
517	Ron Robinson	.05
518	Greg Gross	.05
519	Mariners Leaders (Phil Bradley, Harold Reynolds)	.05
520	Dave Smith	.05
521	Jim Dwyer	.05
522	Bob Patterson RC	.05
523	Gary Roenicke	.05
524	Gary Lucas	.05
525	Marty Barrett	.05
526	Juan Berenguer	.05
527	Steve Henderson	.05

No.	Player	Price
528a	Checklist 397-528 (#455 is Steve Carlton)	.05
528b	Checklist 397-528 (#455 is Shawn Hillegas)	.05
529	Tim Burke	.05
530	Gary Carter	.40
531	Rich Yett	.05
532	Mike Kingery	.05
533	John Farrell RC	.05
534	John Wathan	.05
535	Ron Guidry	.05
536	John Morris	.05
537	Steve Buechele	.05
538	Bill Wegman	.05
539	Mike LaValliere	.05
540	Bret Saberhagen	.05
541	Juan Beniquez	.05
542	Paul Noce RC	.05
543	Kent Tekulve	.05
544	Jim Traber	.05
545	Don Baylor	.05
546	John Candelaria	.05
547	Felix Fermin RC	.05
548	Shane Mack	.05
549	Braves Leaders (Ken Griffey, Dion James, Dale Murphy, Gerald Perry)	.05
550	Pedro Guerrero	.05
551	Terry Steinbach	.05
552	Mark Thurmond	.05
553	Tracy Jones	.05
554	Mike Smithson	.05
555	Brook Jacoby	.05
556	Stan Clarke RC	.05
557	Craig Reynolds	.05
558	Bob Ojeda	.05
559	Ken Williams RC	.05
560	Tim Wallach	.05
561	Rick Cerone	.05
562	Jim Lindeman	.05
563	Jose Guzman	.05
564	Frank Lucchesi	.05
565	Lloyd Moseby	.05
566	Charlie O'Brien RC	.05
567	Mike Diaz	.05
568	Chris Brown	.05
569	Charlie Leibrandt	.05
570	Jeffrey Leonard	.05
571	Mark Williamson RC	.05
572	Chris James	.05
573	Bob Stanley	.05
574	Graig Nettles	.05
575	Don Sutton	.30
576	Tommy Hinzo RC	.05
577	Tom Browning	.05
578	Gary Gaetti	.05
579	Mets Leaders (Gary Carter, Kevin McReynolds)	.05
580	Mark McGwire	.65
581	Tito Landrum	.05
582	Mike Henneman	.05
583	Dave Valle RC	.05
584	Steve Trout	.05
585	Ozzie Guillen	.05
586	Bob Forsch	.05
587	Terry Puhl	.05
588	Jeff Parrett RC	.05
589	Geno Petralli	.05
590	George Bell	.05
591	Doug Drabek	.05
592	Dale Sveum	.05
593	Bob Tewksbury	.05
594	Bobby Valentine	.05
595	Frank White	.05
596	John Kruk	.05
597	Gene Garber	.05
598	Lee Lacy	.05
599	Calvin Schiraldi	.05
600	Mike Schmidt	.60
601	Jack Lazorko	.05
602	Mike Aldrete	.05
603	Rob Murphy	.05
604	Chris Bando	.05
605	Kirk Gibson	.05
606	Moose Haas	.05
607	Mickey Hatcher	.05
608	Charlie Kerfeld	.05
609	Twins Leaders (Gary Gaetti, Kent Hrbek)	.05
610	Keith Hernandez	.05
611	Tommy John	.05
612	Curt Ford	.05
613	Bobby Thigpen	.05
614	Herm Winningham	.05
615	Jody Davis	.05
616	Jay Aldrich RC	.05
617	Oddibe McDowell	.05
618	Cecil Fielder	.05
619	Mike Dunne RC	.05
620	Cory Snyder	.05
621	Gene Nelson	.05
622	Kal Daniels	.05
623	Mike Flanagan	.05
624	Jim Leyland	.05
625	Frank Viola	.05
626	Glenn Wilson	.05
627	Joe Boever RC	.05
628	Dave Henderson	.05
629	Kelly Downs	.05
630	Darrell Evans	.05
631	Jack Howell	.05
632	Steve Shields RC	.05
633	Barry Lyons RC	.05
634	Jose DeLeon	.05
635	Terry Pendleton	.05
636	Charles Hudson	.05
637	Jay Bell RC	.25
638	Steve Balboni	.05

No.	Player	Price
639	Brewers Leaders (Glenn Braggs, Tony Muser)	.05
640	Garry Templeton	.05
641	Rick Honeycutt	.05
642	Bob Dernier	.05
643	Rocky Childress RC	.05
644	Terry McGriff RC	.05
645	Matt Nokes	.05
646	Checklist 529-660	.05
647	Pascual Perez	.05
648	Al Newman	.05
649	DeWayne Buice RC	.05
650	Cal Ripken, Jr.	.75
651	Mike Jackson RC	.05
652	Bruce Benedict	.05
653	Jeff Sellers	.05
654	Roger Craig	.05
655	Len Dykstra	.05
656	Lee Guetterman	.05
657	Gary Redus	.05
658	Tim Conroy	.05
659	Bobby Meacham	.05
660	Rick Reuschel	.05
661	Nolan Ryan (Turn Back the Clock)	.35
662	Jim Rice (Turn Back the Clock)	.05
663	Ron Blomberg (Turn Back the Clock)	.05
664	Bob Gibson (Turn Back the Clock)	.10
665	Stan Musial (Turn Back the Clock)	.20
666	Mario Soto	.05
667	Luis Quinones	.05
668	Walt Terrell	.05
669	Phillies Leaders (Lance Parrish, Mike Ryan)	.05
670	Dan Plesac	.05
671	Tim Laudner	.05
672	John Davis RC	.05
673	Tony Phillips	.05
674	Mike Fitzgerald	.05
675	Jim Rice	.20
676	Ken Dixon	.05
677	Eddie Milner	.05
678	Jim Acker	.05
679	Darrell Miller	.05
680	Charlie Hough	.05
681	Bobby Bonilla	.05
682	Jimmy Key	.05
683	Julio Franco	.05
684	Hal Lanier	.05
685	Ron Darling	.05
686	Terry Francona	.05
687	Mickey Brantley	.05
688	Jim Winn	.05
689	Tom Pagnozzi RC	.05
690	Jay Howell	.05
691	Dan Pasqua	.05
692	Mike Birkbeck	.05
693	Benny Santiago	.05
694	Eric Nolte RC	.05
695	Shawon Dunston	.05
696	Duane Ward	.05
697	Steve Lombardozzi	.05
698	Brad Havens	.05
699	Padres Leaders (Tony Gwynn, Benny Santiago)	.15
700	George Brett	.60
701	Sammy Stewart	.05
702	Mike Gallego	.05
703	Bob Brenly	.05
704	Dennis Boyd	.05
705	Juan Samuel	.05
706	Rick Mahler	.05
707	Fred Lynn	.05
708	Gus Polidor RC	.05
709	George Frazier	.05
710	Darryl Strawberry	.05
711	Bill Gullickson	.05
712	John Moses	.05
713	Willie Hernandez	.05
714	Jim Fregosi	.05
715	Todd Worrell	.05
716	Lenn Sakata	.05
717	Jay Baller RC	.05
718	Mike Felder	.05
719	Denny Walling	.05
720	Tim Raines	.05
721	Pete O'Brien	.05
722	Manny Lee	.05
723	Bob Kipper	.05
724	Danny Tartabull	.05
725	Mike Boddicker	.05
726	Alfredo Griffin	.05
727	Greg Booker	.05
728	Andy Allanson	.05
729	Blue Jays Leaders (George Bell, Fred McGriff)	.05
730	John Franco	.05
731	Rick Schu	.05
732	Dave Palmer	.05
733	Spike Owen	.05
734	Craig Lefferts	.05
735	Kevin McReynolds	.05
736	Matt Young	.05
737	Butch Wynegar	.05
738	Scott Bankhead	.05
739	Daryl Boston	.05
740	Rick Sutcliffe	.05
741	Mike Easler	.05
742	Mark Clear	.05
743	Larry Herndon	.05
744	Whitey Herzog	.05

No.	Player	Price
745	Bill Doran	.05
746	Gene Larkin RC	.05
747	Bobby Witt	.05
748	Reid Nichols	.05
749	Mark Eichhorn	.05
750	Bo Jackson	.10
751	Jim Morrison	.05
752	Mark Grant	.05
753	Danny Heep	.05
754	Mike LaCoss	.05
755	Ozzie Virgil	.05
756	Mike Maddux	.05
757	John Marzano RC	.05
758	Eddie Williams RC	.05
759	A's Leaders (Jose Canseco, Mark McGwire)	.35
760	Mike Scott	.05
761	Tony Armas	.05
762	Scott Bradley	.05
763	Doug Sisk	.05
764	Greg Walker	.05
765	Neal Heaton	.05
766	Henry Cotto	.05
767	Jose Lind RC (Future Stars)	.10
768	Dickie Noles	.05
769	Cecil Cooper	.05
770	Lou Whitaker	.05
771	Ruben Sierra	.05
772	Sal Butera	.05
773	Frank Williams	.05
774	Gene Mauch	.05
775	Dave Stieb	.05
776	Checklist 661-792	.05
777	Lonnie Smith	.05
778a	Keith Comstock RC (White team letters.)	.40
778b	Keith Comstock RC (Blue team letters, white name.)	.10
778c	Keith Comstock RC (Blue team letters, yellow name.)	2.00
779	Tom Glavine RC	1.50
780	Fernando Valenzuela	.05
781	Keith Hughes RC	.05
782	Jeff Ballard RC	.05
783	Ron Roenicke	.05
784	Joe Sambito	.05
785	Alvin Davis	.05
786	Joe Price	.05
787	Bill Almon	.05
788	Ray Searage	.05
789	Indians Leaders (Joe Carter, Cory Snyder)	.05
790	Dave Righetti	.05
791	Ted Simmons	.05
792	John Tudor	.05

Tiffany

Sharing a checklist with the regular issue 1988 Topps baseball set, this specially boxed, limited-edition (25,000 sets) features cards printed on white cardboard stock with high-gloss front finish. Topps offered the sets directly to the public in ads in USA Today and Sporing News at a price of $99.

	NM/M
Complete Set (792):	40.00
Common Player:	.15

Traded

In addition to new players and traded veterans, 21 members of the U.S.A. Olympic Baseball team are showcased in this 132-card set, numbered 1T-132T. The 2-1/2" x 3-1/2" cards follow the same design as the basic Topps issue - white borders, large full-color photos, team name (or U.S.A.) in large bold letters at the top of the card face, player name on a diagonal stripe across the lower-right corner. Topps had issued its traded series each year since 1981 in boxed complete sets available only through hobby dealers.

	NM/M
Complete Set (132):	5.00
Common Player:	.05

No.	Player	Price
1	Jim Abbott RC (USA)	.25
2	Juan Agosto	.05
3	Luis Alicea RC	.05
4	Roberto Alomar RC	1.50
5	Brady Anderson RC	.25
6	Jack Armstrong	.05
7	Don August	.05
8	Floyd Bannister	.05
9	Bret Barberie (USA)	.05
10	Jose Bautista RC	.05
11	Don Baylor	.05
12	Tim Belcher	.05
13	Buddy Bell	.05
14	Andy Benes RC (USA)	.25
15	Damon Berryhill	.05
16	Bud Black	.05
17	Pat Borders	.05
18	Phil Bradley	.05
19	Jeff Branson RC (USA)	.05
20	Tom Brunansky	.05
21	Jay Buhner RC	.75
22	Brett Butler	.05
23	Jim Campanis RC (USA)	.05
24	Sil Campusano RC	.05
25	John Candelaria	.05
26	Jose Cecena RC	.05
27	Rick Cerone	.05
28	Jack Clark	.05
29	Kevin Coffman RC	.05
30	Pat Combs (USA)	.05
31	Henry Cotto	.05
32	Chili Davis	.05
33	Mike Davis	.05
34	Jose DeLeon	.05
35	Richard Dotson	.05
36	Cecil Espy	.05
37	Tom Filer	.05
38	Mike Fiore RC (USA)	.05
39	Ron Gant RC	.25
40	Kirk Gibson	.05
41	Rich Gossage	.05
42	Mark Grace RC	1.00
43	Alfredo Griffin	.05
44	Ty Griffin RC (USA)	.05
45	Bryan Harvey	.05
46	Ron Hassey	.05
47	Ray Hayward RC	.05
48	Dave Henderson	.05
49	Tom Herr	.05
50	Bob Horner	.05
51	Ricky Horton	.05
52	Jay Howell	.05
53	Glenn Hubbard	.05
54	Jeff Innis RC	.05
55	Danny Jackson	.05
56	Darrin Jackson	.05
57	Roberto Kelly	.05
58	Ron Kittle	.05
59	Ray Knight	.05
60	Vance Law	.05
61	Jeffrey Leonard	.05
62	Mike Macfarlane RC	.05
63	Scotti Madison RC	.05
64	Kirt Manwaring RC	.05
65	Mark Marquess (USA)	.05
66	Tino Martinez RC (USA)	.75
67	Billy Masse RC (USA)	.05
68	Jack McDowell RC	.25
69	Jack McKeon	.05
70	Larry McWilliams	.05
71	Mickey Morandini (USA)	.05
72	Keith Moreland	.05
73	Mike Morgan	.05
74	Charles Nagy (USA)	.10
75	Al Nipper	.05
76	Russ Nixon	.05
77	Jesse Orosco	.05
78	Joe Orsulak	.05
79	Dave Palmer	.05
80	Mark Parent RC	.05
81	Dave Parker	.05
82	Dan Pasqua	.05
83	Melido Perez RC	.05
84	Steve Peters RC	.05
85	Dan Petry	.05
86	Gary Pettis	.05
87	Jeff Pico RC	.05
88	Jim Poole (USA)	.05
89	Ted Power	.05
90	Rafael Ramirez	.05
91	Dennis Rasmussen	.05
92	Jose Rijo	.05
93	Earnie Riles	.05
94	Luis Rivera RC	.05
95	Doug Robbins RC (USA)	.05
96	Frank Robinson	.15
97	Cookie Rojas	.05
98	Chris Sabo RC	.10
99	Mark Salas	.05
100	Luis Salazar	.05
101	Rafael Santana	.05
102	Nelson Santovenia RC	.05
103	Mackey Sasser RC	.05
104	Calvin Schiraldi	.05
105	Mike Schooler RC	.05
106	Scott Servais RC (USA)	.05
107	Dave Silvestri (USA)	.05
108	Don Slaught	.05
109	Joe Slusarski RC (USA)	.05
110	Lee Smith	.05
111	Pete Smith RC	.40
112	Jim Snyder	.05
113	Ed Sprague (USA)	.05
114	Pete Stanicek RC	.05
115	Kurt Stillwell	.05
116	Todd Stottlemyre	.05
117	Bill Swift	.05
118	Pat Tabler	.05
119	Scott Terry RC	.05
120	Mickey Tettleton	.05
121	Dickie Thon	.05
122	Jeff Treadway	.05
123	Willie Upshaw	.05
124	Robin Ventura RC	.25
125	Ron Washington	.05
126	Walt Weiss RC	.05
127	Bob Welch	.05
128	David Wells RC	.25
129	Glenn Wilson	.05
130	Ted Wood RC (USA)	.05
131	Don Zimmer	.05
132	Checklist 1T-132T	.05

Traded Tiffany

The high-gloss front surface is all that distinguishes this limited-edition, hobby-only collectors version from the regular Topps Traded boxed set.

	NM/M
Complete Set (132):	25.00
Common Player:	.15

Traded Duke Snider Bronze

This 1/4-size metal replica was issued to dealers who purchased cases of 1988 Topps Traded sets. Each detail of the 1955 Topps Snider card is reproduced on the 1-3/4" x 1-1/4" bronze metal mini-card, right down to the stats.

		NM/M
210	Duke Snider	7.50

Box Panels

After a one-year hiatus during which they appeared on the sides of Topps wax pack display boxes, Topps retail box cards returned to box bottoms in 1988. The series includes 16 standard-size baseball cards, four cards per each of four different display boxes. Card fronts follow the same design as the 1988 Topps basic issue; full-color player photos, framed in yellow, surrounded by a white border; diagonal player name lower-right; team name in large letters at the top. Card backs are "numbered" A through P and are printed in black and orange.

	NM/M
Complete Panel Set (4):	3.00
Complete Singles Set (16):	3.00
Common Panel:	.50
Common Single Player:	.50

	Player	Price
Panel		.50
A	Don Baylor	.10
B	Steve Bedrosian	.10
C	Juan Beniquez	.10
D	Bob Boone	.10
Panel		.75
E	Darrell Evans	.10
F	Tony Gwynn	.50
G	John Kruk	.10
H	Marvell Wynne	.10
Panel		.60
I	Joe Carter	.10
J	Eric Davis	.10
K	Howard Johnson	.10
L	Darryl Strawberry	.10
Panel		2.00
M	Rickey Henderson	.40
N	Nolan Ryan	1.00
O	Mike Schmidt	.75
P	Kent Tekulve	.10

All-Star Glossy Set of 22

The fifth edition of Topps' special All-Star inserts was included in the company's 1988 rack packs.

The 1987 American and National League All-Star lineup, plus honorary captains Jim Hunter and Billy Williams, are featured on the 2-1/2" x 3-1/2" cards. The glossy full-color fronts contain player photos centered between a red and yellow "1987 All-Star" logo at top and the player name (also red and yellow) which is printed in the bottom margin. A league logo is in the lower-left corner. Card backs are printed in red and blue on a white background, with the title and All-Star logo emblem printed above the player name and card number.

		NM/M
Complete Set (22):		3.00
Common Player:		.05
1	John McNamara	.05
2	Don Mattingly	.75
3	Willie Randolph	.05
4	Wade Boggs	.65
5	Cal Ripken, Jr.	1.00
6	George Bell	.05
7	Rickey Henderson	.50
8	Dave Winfield	.50
9	Terry Kennedy	.05
10	Bret Saberhagen	.05
11	Catfish Hunter	.05
12	Davey Johnson	.05
13	Jack Clark	.05
14	Ryne Sandberg	.65
15	Mike Schmidt	.75
16	Ozzie Smith	.65
17	Eric Davis	.05
18	Andre Dawson	.20
19	Darryl Strawberry	.50
20	Gary Carter	.50
21	Mike Scott	.05
22	Billy Williams	.05

All-Star Glossy Set of 60

This collectors' set includes 60 full-color glossy cards featuring All-Stars and Prospects in six separate 10-card sets. Card fronts have a white border and a thin red line framing the player photo, with the player's name in the lower-left corner. Backs, in red and blue, include basic player identification along with the set logo and card number. Sets were marketed via a special offer printed on a card packaged in all Topps wax packs. For six special offer cards and $1.25, collectors received one of the six 10-card sets; 18 special offer cards and $7.50 earned the entire 60-card collection.

		NM/M
Complete Set (60):		4.00
Common Player:		.10
1	Andre Dawson	.20
2	Jesse Barfield	.10
3	Mike Schmidt	.75
4	Ruben Sierra	.10
5	Mike Scott	.10
6	Cal Ripken, Jr.	1.00
7	Gary Carter	.50
8	Kent Hrbek	.10
9	Kevin Seitzer	.10
10	Mike Henneman	.10
11	Don Mattingly	.65
12	Tim Raines	.10
13	Roger Clemens	.65
14	Ryne Sandberg	.60
15	Tony Fernandez	.10
16	Eric Davis	.10
17	Jack Morris	.10
18	Tim Wallach	.10
19	Mike Dunne	.10
20	Mike Greenwell	.10
21	Dwight Evans	.10
22	Darryl Strawberry	.10
23	Cory Snyder	.10
24	Pedro Guerrero	.10
25	Rickey Henderson	.50
26	Dale Murphy	.20
27	Kirby Puckett	.60
28	Steve Bedrosian	.10
29	Devon White	.10
30	Benny Santiago	.10
31	George Bell	.10
32	Keith Hernandez	.10
33	Dave Stewart	.10
34	Dave Parker	.10
35	Tom Henke	.10
36	Willie McGee	.10
37	Alan Trammell	.10
38	Tony Gwynn	.60
39	Mark McGwire	.85
40	Joe Magrane	.10
41	Jack Clark	.10
42	Willie Randolph	.10
43	Juan Samuel	.10
44	Joe Carter	.10
45	Shane Rawley	.10
46	Dave Winfield	.50
47	Ozzie Smith	.60
48	Wally Joyner	.10
49	B.J. Surhoff	.10
50	Ellis Burks	.10
51	Wade Boggs	.50
52	Howard Johnson	.10
53	George Brett	.75
54	Dwight Gooden	.10
55	Jose Canseco	.35
56	Lee Smith	.10
57	Paul Molitor	.50
58	Andres Galarraga	.10
59	Matt Nokes	.10
60	Casey Candaele	.10

American Baseball

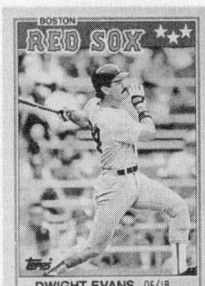

This set, ostensibly issued for sale in the United Kingdom, was also made available for distribution by U.S. hobby dealers. Cards were packaged in checklist-backed boxes with an American flag on the top flap. The 2-1/4" x 3" cards feature full-color photos printed on white stock. The team name, printed in team colors, intersects the red frame at the top of the card. A yellow name banner appears below the photo. Backs have blue borders and cartoon-style horizontal layouts which include a team logo, stats, caricature of the player and a one-line caption. Below the cartoon, a short "Talkin' Baseball" paragraph provides elementary information, designed to acquaint soccer-playing European collectors with baseball rules and terminology. Uncut sheets of all 88 cards are not uncommon.

		NM/M
Complete Set (88):		6.00
Common Player:		.05
Uncut Sheet:		12.00
Wax Box (48):		7.50
1	Harold Baines	.05
2	Steve Bedrosian	.05
3	George Bell	.05
4	Wade Boggs	.60
5	Barry Bonds	1.00
6	Bob Boone	.05
7	George Brett	.75
8	Hubie Brooks	.05
9	Ivan Calderon	.05
10	Jose Canseco	.35
11	Gary Carter	.50
12	Joe Carter	.50
13	Jack Clark	.05
14	Will Clark	.50
15	Roger Clemens	.75
16	Vince Coleman	.05
17	Alvin Davis	.05
18	Eric Davis	.05
19	Glenn Davis	.05
20	Andre Dawson	.20
21	Mike Dunne	.05
22	Dwight Evans	.05
23	Tony Fernandez	.05
24	John Franco	.05
25	Gary Gaetti	.05
26	Kirk Gibson	.05
27	Dwight Gooden	.05
28	Pedro Guerrero	.05
29	Tony Gwynn	.60
30	Billy Hatcher	.05
31	Rickey Henderson	.50
32	Tom Henke	.05
33	Keith Hernandez	.05
34	Orel Hershiser	.05
35	Teddy Higuera	.05
36	Charlie Hough	.05
37	Kent Hrbek	.05
38	Brook Jacoby	.05
39	Dion James	.05
40	Wally Joyner	.05
41	John Kruk	.05
42	Mark Langston	.05
43	Jeffrey Leonard	.05
44	Candy Maldonaldo	.05
45	Don Mattingly	.75
46	Willie McGee	.05
47	Mark McGwire	.85
48	Kevin Mitchell	.05
49	Paul Molitor	.50
50	Jack Morris	.05
51	Lloyd Moseby	.05
52	Dale Murphy	.20
53	Eddie Murray	.50
54	Matt Nokes	.05
55	Dave Parker	.05
56	Larry Parrish	.05
57	Kirby Puckett	.60
58	Tim Raines	.05
59	Willie Randolph	.05
60	Harold Reynolds	.05
61	Cal Ripken, Jr.	1.00
62	Nolan Ryan	1.00
63	Bret Saberhagen	.05
64	Juan Samuel	.05
65	Ryne Sandberg	.60
66	Benny Santiago	.05
67	Mike Schmidt	.75
68	Mike Scott	.05
69	Kevin Seitzer	.05
70	Larry Sheets	.05
71	Ruben Sierra	.05
72	Ozzie Smith	.60
73	Zane Smith	.05
74	Cory Snyder	.05
75	Dave Stewart	.05
76	Darryl Strawberry	.05
77	Rick Sutcliffe	.05
78	Danny Tartabull	.05
79	Alan Trammell	.05
80	Fernando Valenzuela	.05
81	Andy Van Slyke	.05
82	Frank Viola	.05
83	Greg Walker	.05
84	Tim Wallach	.05
85	Dave Winfield	.50
86	Mike Witt	.05
87	Robin Yount	.50
88	Checklist	.05

American Baseball Tiffany

This glossy "Tiffany" edition of the Topps American Baseball set is a complete parallel of the regular-issue.

	NM/M
Complete Set (88):	15.00
Common Player:	.40

Big Baseball

Topps Big Baseball cards (2-5/8" x 3-3/4") were issued in three series, 88 cards per series (a total set of 264 cards) sold in seven-card packs. The glossy cards are similar in format, both front and back, to the 1956 Topps set. Each card features a portrait and a game-action photo on the front, framed by a wide white border. A white outline highlights the portrait. The player's name appears at bottom on a splash of color that fades from yellow to orange to red to pink. On the card back, the player's name is printed in large red letters across the top, followed by his team name and position in black. Personal info is printed in a red rectangle beside a Topps baseball logo bearing the card number. A triple cartoon strip, in full-color, illustrates career highlights, performance, personal background, etc. A red, white and blue statistics box (pitching, batting, fielding) is printed across the bottom.

		NM/M
Complete Set (264):		9.00
Common Player:		.05
Wax Pack (7):		.50
Wax Box, Series 1-3 (36):		9.00
1	Paul Molitor	.45
2	Milt Thompson	.05
3	Billy Hatcher	.05
4	Mike Witt	.05
5	Vince Coleman	.05
6	Dwight Evans	.05
7	Tim Wallach	.05
8	Alan Trammell	.05
9	Will Clark	.05
10	Jeff Reardon	.05
11	Dwight Gooden	.05
12	Benny Santiago	.05
13	Jose Canseco	.35
14	Dale Murphy	.20
15	George Bell	.05
16	Ryne Sandberg	.60
17	Brook Jacoby	.05
18	Fernando Valenzuela	.05
19	Scott Fletcher	.05
20	Eric Davis	.05
21	Willie Wilson	.05
22	B.J. Surhoff	.05
23	Steve Bedrosian	.05
24	Dave Winfield	.45
25	Bobby Bonilla	.05
26	Larry Sheets	.05
27	Ozzie Guillen	.05
28	Checklist 1-88	.05
29	Nolan Ryan	1.50
30	Bob Boone	.05
31	Tom Herr	.05
32	Wade Boggs	.60
33	Neal Heaton	.05
34	Doyle Alexander	.05
35	Candy Maldonado	.05
36	Kirby Puckett	.60
37	Gary Carter	.45
38	Lance McCullers	.05
39a	Terry Steinbach (Black Topps logo on front.)	.10
39b	Terry Steinbach (White Topps logo on front.)	.10
40	Gerald Perry	.05
41	Tom Henke	.05
42	Leon Durham	.05
43	Cory Snyder	.05
44	Dale Sveum	.05
45	Lance Parrish	.05
46	Steve Sax	.05
47	Charlie Hough	.05
48	Kal Daniels	.05
49	Bo Jackson	.10
50	Ron Guidry	.05
51	Bill Doran	.05
52	Wally Joyner	.05
53	Terry Pendleton	.05
54	Marty Barrett	.05
55	Andres Galarraga	.05
56	Larry Herndon	.05
57	Kevin Mitchell	.05
58	Greg Gagne	.05
59	Keith Hernandez	.05
60	John Kruk	.05
61	Mike LaValliere	.05
62	Cal Ripken, Jr.	1.50
63	Ivan Calderon	.05
64	Alvin Davis	.05
65	Luis Polonia	.05
66	Robin Yount	.45
67	Juan Samuel	.05
68	Andres Thomas	.05
69	Jeff Musselman	.05
70	Jerry Mumphrey	.05
71	Joe Carter	.05
72	Mike Scioscia	.05
73	Pete Incaviglia	.05
74	Barry Larkin	.05
75	Frank White	.05
76	Willie Randolph	.05
77	Kevin Bass	.05
78	Brian Downing	.05
79	Willie McGee	.05
80	Ellis Burks	.05
81	Hubie Brooks	.05
82	Darrell Evans	.05
83	Robby Thompson	.05
84	Kent Hrbek	.05
85	Ron Darling	.05
86	Stan Jefferson	.05
87	Teddy Higuera	.05
88	Mike Schmidt	.75
89	Barry Bonds	1.50
90	Jim Presley	.05
91	Orel Hershiser	.05
92	Jesse Barfield	.05
93	Tom Candiotti	.05
94	Bret Saberhagen	.05
95	Jose Uribe	.05
96	Tom Browning	.05
97	Johnny Ray	.05
98	Mike Morgan	.05
99	Jim Sundberg	.05
100	Roger McDowell	.05
101	Randy Ready	.05
102	Mike Gallego	.05
103	Carney Lansford	.05
104	Steve Buechele	.05
105	Greg Walker	.05
106	Jose Lind	.05
107	Steve Trout	.05
108	Rick Rhoden	.05
109	Jim Pankovits	.05
110	Ken Griffey	.05
111	Danny Cox	.05
112	Franklin Stubbs	.05
113	Lloyd Moseby	.05
114	Mel Hall	.05
115	Kevin Seitzer	.05
116	Tim Raines	.05
117	Juan Castillo	.05
118	Roger Clemens	.75
119	Mike Aldrete	.05
120	Mario Soto	.05
121	Jack Howell	.05
122	Rick Schu	.05
123	Jeff Robinson	.05
124	Doug Drabek	.05
125	Henry Cotto	.05
126	Checklist 89-176	.05
127	Gary Gaetti	.05
128	Rick Sutcliffe	.05
129	Howard Johnson	.05
130	Chris Brown	.05
131	Dave Henderson	.05
132	Curt Wilkerson	.05
133	Mike Marshall	.05
134	Kelly Gruber	.05
135	Julio Franco	.05
136	Kurt Stillwell	.05
137	Donnie Hill	.05
138	Mike Pagliarulo	.05
139	Von Hayes	.05
140	Mike Scott	.05
141	Bob Kipper	.05
142	Harold Reynolds	.05
143	Bob Brenly	.05
144	Dave Concepcion	.05
145	Devon White	.05
146	Jeff Stone	.05
147	Chet Lemon	.05
148	Ozzie Virgil	.05
149	Todd Worrell	.05
150	Mitch Webster	.05
151	Rob Deer	.05
152	Rich Gedman	.05
153	Andre Dawson	.20
154	Mike Davis	.05
155	Nelson Liriano	.05
156	Greg Swindell	.05
157	George Brett	.75
158	Kevin McReynolds	.05
159	Brian Fisher	.05
160	Mike Kingery	.05
161	Tony Gwynn	.60
162	Don Baylor	.05
163	Jerry Browne	.05
164	Dan Pasqua	.05
165	Rickey Henderson	.45
166	Brett Butler	.05
167	Nick Esasky	.05
168	Kirk McCaskill	.05
169	Fred Lynn	.05
170	Jack Morris	.05
171	Pedro Guerrero	.05
172	Dave Stieb	.05
173	Pat Tabler	.05
174	Floyd Bannister	.05
175	Rafael Belliard	.05
176	Mark Langston	.05
177	Greg Mathews	.05
178	Claudell Washington	.05
179	Mark McGwire	1.00
180	Bert Blyleven	.05
181	Jim Rice	.15
182	Mookie Wilson	.05
183	Willie Fraser	.05
184	Andy Van Slyke	.05
185	Matt Nokes	.05
186	Eddie Whitson	.05
187	Tony Fernandez	.05
188	Rick Reuschel	.05
189	Ken Phelps	.05
190	Juan Nieves	.05
191	Kirk Gibson	.05
192	Kevin Davis	.05
193	Zane Smith	.05
194	Jose DeLeon	.05
195	Gary Ward	.05
196	Pascual Perez	.05
197	Carlton Fisk	.45
198	Oddibe McDowell	.05
199	Mark Gubicza	.05
200	Glenn Hubbard	.05
201	Frank Viola	.05
202	Jody Reed	.05
203	Len Dykstra	.05
204	Dick Schofield	.05
205	Sid Bream	.05
206	Guillermo Hernandez	.05
207	Keith Moreland	.05
208	Mark Eichhorn	.05
209	Rene Gonzales	.05
210	Dave Valle	.05
211	Tom Brunansky	.05
212	Charles Hudson	.05
213	John Farrell	.05
214	Jeff Treadway	.05
215	Eddie Murray	.45
216	Checklist 177-264	.05
217	Greg Brock	.05
218	John Shelby	.05
219	Craig Reynolds	.05
220	Dion James	.05
221	Carney Lansford	.05
222	Juan Berenguer	.05
223	Luis Rivera	.05
224	Harold Baines	.05
225	Shawon Dunston	.05
226	Luis Aguayo	.05
227	Pete O'Brien	.05
228	Ozzie Smith	.60
229	Don Mattingly	.75
230	Danny Tartabull	.05
231	Andy Allanson	.05
232	John Franco	.05
233	Mike Greenwell	.05
234	Bob Ojeda	.05
235	Chili Davis	.05
236	Mike Dunne	.05
237	Jim Morrison	.05
238	Carmelo Martinez	.05
239	Ernie Whitt	.05
240	Scott Garrelts	.05
241	Mike Moore	.05
242	Dave Parker	.05
243	Tim Laudner	.05
244	Bill Wegman	.05
245	Bob Horner	.05
246	Rafael Santana	.05
247	Alfredo Griffin	.05
248	Mark Bailey	.05
249	Ron Gant	.05
250	Bryn Smith	.05
251	Lance Johnson	.05
252	Sam Horn	.05
253	Darryl Strawberry	.05
254	Chuck Finley	.05
255	Darnell Coles	.05
256	Mike Henneman	.05
257	Andy Hawkins	.05
258	Jim Clancy	.05
259	Atlee Hammaker	.05
260	Glenn Wilson	.05
261	Larry McWilliams	.05
262	Jack Clark	.05
263	Walt Weiss	.05
264	Gene Larkin	.05

Cloth Experimental

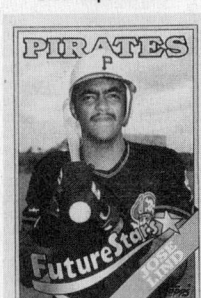

This is a true experimental issue from Topps: Baseball cards printed on heavy textured paper, much like high-quality paper towels. The cloth cards are the standard 2-1/2" x 3-1/2" in size and feature the fronts as used on Topps' regular '88 baseball card issue. Overprinted across the fronts of some cards are parts of the legend, "SAMPLE ONLY NOT FOR SALE." Backs are blank, and unlike earlier Topps cloth issues, are not gummed for use as stickers. The checklist is presented here in alphabetical order.

		NM/M
Complete Set (121):		600.00
Uncut Sheet (121):		500.00
Common Player:		8.00
(1)	A's Team Leaders (Jose Canseco, Mark McGwire)	30.00
(2)	Rick Aguilera	8.00
(3)	Andy Allanson	8.00
(4)	Tony Armas	8.00
(5)	Keith Atherton	8.00
(6)	Steve Balboni	8.00
(7)	Billy Bean	8.00
(8)	Steve Bedrosian/AS	8.00
(9)	George Bell/AS	8.00
(10)	Bruce Benedict	8.00
(11)	Dave Bergman	8.00
(12)	Mike Bielecki	8.00
(13)	Tim Birtsas	8.00
(14)	Bruce Bochy	8.00
(15)	Wade Boggs/AS	40.00
(16)	Rod Booker	8.00
(17)	Dennis Boyd	8.00
(18)	Braves Leaders (Ken Griffey, Dion James, Dale Murphy, Gerald Perry)	15.00
(19)	Tom Browning	8.00
(20)	Carmen Castillo	8.00
(21)	Rick Cerone	8.00
(22)	Jack Clark/AS	8.00
(23)	Mark Clear	8.00
(24)	Roger Clemens/AS	75.00
(25)	Pat Clements	8.00
(26)	Keith Comstock	8.00
(27)	Cecil Cooper	8.00
(28)	Joey Cora	8.00

(29)	Ed Correa	8.00
(30)	Mark Davidson	8.00
(31)	Mark Davis	8.00
(32)	Jeff Dedmon	8.00
(33)	Jim Dwyer	8.00
(34)	Doc Edwards	8.00
(35)	John Farrell	8.00
(36)	Mike Felder	8.00
(37)	Curt Ford	8.00
(38)	Bob Forsch	8.00
(39)	Damaso Garcia	8.00
(40)	Tom Glavine	45.00
(41)	Mark Grant	8.00
(42)	Tony Gwynn/AS	40.00
(43)	Drew Hall	8.00
(44)	Jeff Hamilton	8.00
(45)	Mike Hart	8.00
(46)	Andy Hawkins	8.00
(47)	Ed Hearn	8.00
(48)	Tom Henke/AS	8.00
(49)	Whitey Herzog	8.00
(50)	Shawn Hillegas	8.00
(51)	Charles Hudson	8.00
(52)	Dave Johnson	8.00
(53)	Ron Karkovice	8.00
(54)	Pat Keedy	8.00
(55)	Jimmy Key/AS	8.00
(56)	Mark Kiefer	8.00
(57)	Bob Kipper	8.00
(58)	Les Lancaster	8.00
(59)	Ken Landreaux	8.00
(60)	Craig Lefferts	8.00
(61)	Jim Leyland	8.00
(62)	Jose Lind	8.00
(63)	Gary Lucas	8.00
(64)	Frank Lucchesi	8.00
(65)	Barry Lyons	8.00
(66)	John Marzano	8.00
(67)	Greg Mathews	8.00
(68)	Don Mattingly/AS	75.00
(69)	Len Matuszek	8.00
(70)	Kirk McCaskill	8.00
(71)	Terry McGriff	8.00
(72)	Joey Meyer	8.00
(73)	John Mitchell	8.00
(74)	Jeff Montgomery	8.00
(75)	John Morris	8.00
(76)	John Moses	8.00
(77)	Tom Nieto	8.00
(78)	Matt Nokes/AS	8.00
(79)	Charlie O'Brien	8.00
(80)	Ed Olwine	8.00
(81)	Paul O'Neill	8.00
(82)	Steve Ontiveros	8.00
(83)	Pat Pacillo	8.00
(84)	Tom Pagnozzi	8.00
(85)	Jim Pankovits	8.00
(86)	Bill Pecota	8.00
(87)	Geno Petralli	8.00
(88)	Eric Plunk	8.00
(89)	Gus Polidor	8.00
(90)	Dennis Powell	8.00
(91)	Terry Puhl	8.00
(92)	Charlie Puleo	8.00
(93)	Shane Rawley/AS	8.00
(94)	Rick Rodriguez	8.00
(95)	Ron Roenicke	8.00
(96)	Pete Rose	200.00
(97)	Lenn Sakata	8.00
(98)	Joe Sambito	8.00
(99)	Juan Samuel/AS	8.00
(100)	Rafael Santana	8.00
(101)	Dan Schatzeder	8.00
(102)	Pat Sheridan	8.00
(103)	Steve Shields	8.00
(104)	Ted Simmons	8.00
(105)	Doug Sisk	8.00
(106)	Joel Skinner	8.00
(107)	Ozzie Smith/AS	40.00
(108)	Chris Speier	8.00
(109)	Jim Sundberg	8.00
(110)	Don Sutton	15.00
(111)	Chuck Tanner	8.00
(112)	Mickey Tettleton	8.00
(113)	Tim Teufel	8.00
(114)	Gary Thurman	8.00
(115)	Alex Trevino	8.00
(116)	Mike Trujillo	8.00
(117)	Twins Leaders (Gary Gaetti, Kent Hrbek)	20.00
(118)	Tim Wallach/AS	8.00
(119)	Frank Williams	8.00
(120)	Dave Winfield/AS	25.00
(121)	Butch Wynegar	8.00

Coins

This edition of 60 lightweight metal coins is similar in design to Topps' 1964 set. The 1988 coins are 1-1/2" in diameter and feature full-color player portraits under crimped edges in silver, gold and pink. Curved under the photo is a red and white player name banner pinned by two gold stars. Coin backs list the coin number, player name, personal information and career summary in black letters on a silver background.

	NM/M
Factory Boxed Set (60):	20.00
Complete Set (60):	10.00
Common Player:	.15
Wax Pack (3):	.45
Wax Box (36):	10.00
1 George Bell	.15
2 Roger Clemens	1.00
3 Mark McGwire	1.25
4 Wade Boggs	.75
5 Harold Baines	.15
6 Ivan Calderon	.15
7 Jose Canseco	.45
8 Joe Carter	.15
9 Jack Clark	.15
10 Alvin Davis	.15
11 Dwight Evans	.15
12 Tony Fernandez	.15
13 Gary Gaetti	.15
14 Mike Greenwell	.15
15 Charlie Hough	.15
16 Wally Joyner	.15
17 Jimmy Key	.15
18 Mark Langston	.15
19 Don Mattingly	1.00
20 Paul Molitor	.60
21 Jack Morris	.15
22 Eddie Murray	.60
23 Kirby Puckett	.75
24 Cal Ripken, Jr.	1.50
25 Bret Saberhagen	.15
26 Ruben Sierra	.15
27 Cory Snyder	.15
28 Terry Steinbach	.15
29 Danny Tartabull	.15
30 Alan Trammell	.15
31 Devon White	.15
32 Robin Yount	.60
33 Andre Dawson	.30
34 Steve Bedrosian	.15
35 Benny Santiago	.15
36 Tony Gwynn	.75
37 Bobby Bonilla	.15
38 Will Clark	.15
39 Eric Davis	.15
40 Mike Dunne	.15
41 John Franco	.15
42 Dwight Gooden	.15
43 Pedro Guerrero	.15
44 Dion James	.15
45 John Kruk	.15
46 Jeffrey Leonard	.15
47 Carmelo Martinez	.15
48 Dale Murphy	.30
49 Tim Raines	.15
50 Nolan Ryan	1.50
51 Juan Samuel	.15
52 Ryne Sandberg	.75
53 Mike Schmidt	1.00
54 Mike Scott	.15
55 Ozzie Smith	.75
56 Darryl Strawberry	.15
57 Rick Sutcliffe	.15
58 Fernando Valenzuela	.15
59 Tim Wallach	.15
60 Todd Worrell	.15

Glossy Rookies

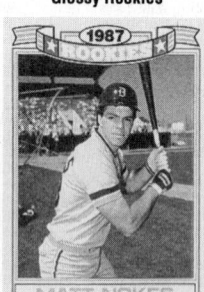

The Topps 1988 Rookies special insert cards follow the same basic design as the All-Star inserts. The set consists of 22 standard-size cards found one per pack in 100-card jumbo cellos. Large, glossy color player photos are printed on a white background below a red, yellow and blue "1987 Rookies" banner. A red and yellow player name appears beneath the photo. Red, white and blue card backs bear the title of the special insert set, the Rookies logo emblem, player name and card number.

		NM/M
Complete Set (22):		3.00
Common Player:		.05
1	Billy Ripken	.05
2	Ellis Burks	.05
3	Mike Greenwell	.05
4	DeWayne Buice	.05
5	Devon White	.05
6	Fred Manrique	.05
7	Mike Henneman	.05
8	Matt Nokes	.05
9	Kevin Seitzer	.05
10	B.J. Surhoff	.05
11	Casey Candaele	.05
12	Randy Myers	.05
13	Mark McGwire	2.50
14	Luis Polonia	.05
15	Terry Steinbach	.05
16	Mike Dunne	.05
17	Al Pedrique	.05
18	Benny Santiago	.05
19	Kelly Downs	.05
20	Joe Magrane	.05
21	Jerry Browne	.05
22	Jeff Musselman	.05

Gallery of Champions

These metal replicas are exact reproductions at one-quarter scale of Topps 1988 cards, both front and back. The set includes 12 three-dimensional raised metal cards packaged in a velvet-lined case that bears the title of the set in gold embossed letters. A deluxe limited edition of the set (1,000) was produced in sterling silver and an economy version in aluminum. A Mark McGwire pewter replica was given as a premium to dealers ordering the aluminum, bronze and silver sets. The special pewter card is distinguished from the regular issue by a diagonal name banner in the lower-right corner; regular replicas have a rectangular name banner parallel to the lower edge of the card.

	NM/M
Complete Aluminum Set (12):	10.00
Complete Bronze Set (12):	60.00
Complete Silver Set (12):	140.00
(1a) Steve Bedrosian/Aluminum	.50
(1s) Steve Bedrosian/Bronze	1.50
(1s) Steve Bedrosian/Silver	6.00
(2a) George Bell/Aluminum	.50
(2b) George Bell/Bronze	1.50
(2s) George Bell/Silver	6.00
(3a) Wade Boggs/Aluminum	1.50
(3b) Wade Boggs/Bronze	6.00
(3s) Wade Boggs/Silver	20.00
(4a) Jack Clark/Aluminum	.50
(4b) Jack Clark/Bronze	1.50
(4s) Jack Clark/Silver	6.00
(5a) Roger Clemens/ Aluminum	2.00
(5b) Roger Clemens/Bronze	10.00
(5s) Roger Clemens/Silver	25.00
(6a) Andre Dawson/Aluminum	1.00
(6b) Andre Dawson/Bronze	2.50
(6s) Andre Dawson/Silver	9.00
(7a) Tony Gwynn/Aluminum	1.50
(7b) Tony Gwynn/Bronze	6.00
(7s) Tony Gwynn/Silver	20.00
(8a) Mark Langston/Aluminum	.50
(8b) Mark Langston/Bronze	1.50
(8s) Mark Langston/Silver	6.00
(9a) Mark McGwire/Aluminum	2.50
(9b) Mark McGwire/Bronze	12.50
(9s) Mark McGwire/Silver	25.00
(9p) Mark McGwire/Pewter	13.50
(10a) Dave Righetti/Aluminum	.50
(10b) Dave Righetti/Bronze	1.50
(10s) Dave Righetti/Silver	6.00
(11a) Nolan Ryan/Aluminum	3.00
(11b) Nolan Ryan/Bronze	15.00
(11s) Nolan Ryan/Silver	30.00
(12a) Benny Santiago/Aluminum	.50
(12b) Benny Santiago/Bronze	1.50
(12s) Benny Santiago/Silver	6.00

Mini League Leaders

This third consecutive issue of Topps mini-cards (2-1/8" x 3") includes 77 cards spotlighting the top five ranked pitchers and batters. This set is unique in that it was the first time Topps included full-color player photos on both the front and back. Glossy action shots on the card fronts fade into a white border with a Topps logo in an upper corner. The player's name is printed in bold black letters beneath the photo. Horizontal reverses feature circular player photos on a blue and white background with the card number, player name, personal information, 1987 ranking and lifetime/1987 stats printed in red, black and yellow lettering.

WADE BOGGS

		NM/M
Complete Set (77):		3.00
Common Player:		.05
Wax Pack (7):		.30
Wax Box (36):		6.00
1	Wade Boggs	.60
2	Roger Clemens	.65
3	Dwight Evans	.05
4	DeWayne Buice	.05
5	Brian Downing	.05
6	Wally Joyner	.05
7	Ivan Calderon	.05
8	Carlton Fisk	.50
9	Gary Redus	.05
10	Darrell Evans	.05
11	Jack Morris	.05
12	Alan Trammell	.05
13	Lou Whitaker	.05
14	Bret Saberhagen	.05
15	Kevin Seitzer	.05
16	Danny Tartabull	.05
17	Willie Wilson	.05
18	Teddy Higuera	.05
19	Paul Molitor	.50
20	Dan Plesac	.05
21	Robin Yount	.50
22	Kent Hrbek	.05
23	Kirby Puckett	.60
24	Jeff Reardon	.05
25	Frank Viola	.05
26	Rickey Henderson	.50
27	Don Mattingly	.65
28	Willie Randolph	.05
29	Dave Righetti	.05
30	Jose Canseco	.35
31	Mark McGwire	.75
32	Dave Stewart	.05
33	Phil Bradley	.05
34	Mark Langston	.05
35	Harold Reynolds	.05
36	Charlie Hough	.05
37	George Bell	.05
38	Tom Henke	.05
39	Jimmy Key	.05
40	Dion James	.05
41	Dale Murphy	.20
42	Zane Smith	.05
43	Andre Dawson	.20
44	Lee Smith	.05
45	Rick Sutcliffe	.05
46	Eric Davis	.05
47	John Franco	.05
48	Dave Parker	.05
49	Billy Hatcher	.05
50	Nolan Ryan	1.00
51	Mike Scott	.05
52	Pedro Guerrero	.05
53	Orel Hershiser	.05
54	Fernando Valenzuela	.05
55	Bob Welch	.05
56	Andres Galarraga	.05
57	Tim Raines	.05
58	Tim Wallach	.05
59	Len Dykstra	.05
60	Dwight Gooden	.05
61	Howard Johnson	.05
62	Roger McDowell	.05
63	Darryl Strawberry	.05
64	Steve Bedrosian	.05
65	Shane Rawley	.05
66	Juan Samuel	.05
67	Mike Schmidt	.65
68	Mike Dunne	.05
69	Jack Clark	.05
70	Vince Coleman	.05
71	Willie McGee	.05
72	Ozzie Smith	.50
73	Todd Worrell	.05
74	Tony Gwynn	.60
75	John Kruk	.05
76	Rick Rueschel	.05
77	Checklist	.05

Stickercards

SUPER STAR
TONY GWYNN

Actually a part of the 1988 Topps Stickers issue, this set consists of 67 cards. The cards are the backs of the peel-off stickers and measure 2-1/8" x 3". To determine total value, combine the prices of the stickers (found in the 1988 Topps Stickers checklist) on the stickercard front with the value assigned to the stickercard in the following checklist.

		NM/M
Complete Set (67):		3.00
Common Player:		.05
1	Jack Clark	.05
2	Andres Galarraga	.05
3	Keith Hernandez	.05
4	Tom Herr	.05
5	Juan Samuel	.05
6	Ryne Sandberg	.50
7	Terry Pendleton	.05
8	Mike Schmidt	.60
9	Tim Wallach	.05
10	Hubie Brooks	.05
11	Shawon Dunston	.05
12	Ozzie Smith	.20
13	Andre Dawson	.20
14	Eric Davis	.05
15	Pedro Guerrero	.05
16	Tony Gwynn	.50
17	Jeffrey Leonard	.05
18	Dale Murphy	.20
19	Dave Parker	.05
20	Tim Raines	.05
21	Darryl Strawberry	.05
22	Gary Carter	.40
23	Jody Davis	.05
24	Ozzie Virgil	.05
25	Dwight Gooden	.05
26	Mike Scott	.05
27	Rick Sutcliffe	.05
28	Sid Fernandez	.05
29	Neal Heaton	.05
30	Fernando Valenzuela	.05
31	Steve Bedrosian	.05
32	John Franco	.05
33	Lee Smith	.05
34	Wally Joyner	.05
35	Don Mattingly	.65
36	Mark McGwire	.65
37	Willie Randolph	.05
38	Lou Whitaker	.05
39	Frank White	.05
40	Wade Boggs	.50
41	George Brett	.60
42	Paul Molitor	.40
43	Tony Fernandez	.05
44	Cal Ripken, Jr.	.75
45	Alan Trammell	.05
46	Jesse Barfield	.05
47	George Bell	.05
48	Jose Canseco	.35
49	Joe Carter	.05
50	Dwight Evans	.05
51	Rickey Henderson	.40
52	Kirby Puckett	.50
53	Cory Snyder	.05
54	Dave Winfield	.40
55	Terry Kennedy	.05
56	Matt Nokes	.05
57	B.J. Surhoff	.05
58	Roger Clemens	.60
59	Jack Morris	.05
60	Bret Saberhagen	.05
61	Ron Guidry	.05
62	Bruce Hurst	.05
63	Mark Langston	.05
64	Tom Henke	.05
65	Dan Plesac	.05
66	Dave Righetti	.05
67	Checklist	.05

Stickers

This set of 313 stickers (on 198 cards) offers an addition for 1988 - 66 different players are pictured on the backs of the sticker cards. The stickers come in two sizes (2-1/8" x 3" or 1-1/2" x 2-1/8"). Larger stickers fill an entire card, smaller ones are attached in pairs. A 36-page sticker yearbook with Mark McGwire on the cover has a designated space inside for each sticker, with one page per team and special pages of 1987 Highlights, World Series, All-Stars and Future Stars. No printing appears on the full-color action shot stickers except for a small black number in the lower left corner. Stickers were sold in packs of five (with gum) for 25 cents per pack. Unlike the 1987 Topps Stickers set, different pairings can be found, rather than the same two players/numbers always sharing the same sticker. To determine total value, combine the value of the stickercard (found in the 1988 Topps Stickercard checklist) with the values assigned the stickers in the following checklist.

		NM/M
Complete Set (313):		10.00
Common Player:		.05
Sticker Album:		1.50
Wax Pack (5):		.25
Wax Box (48):		7.00
1-263	1987 Highlights (Mark McGwire, Willie Wilson)	.25
2-304	1987 Highlights (Benny Santiago, Al Pedrique (Future Star))	.05
3-187	1987 Highlights (Don Mattingly, Ernie Whitt)	.20
4-223	1987 Highlights (Vince Coleman, Gary Matthews)	.05
5-272	1987 Highlights (Bob Boone, Jim Morrison)	.05
6-278	1987 Highlights (Steve Bedrosian, Tim Laudner)	.05
7-276	1987 Highlights (Nolan Ryan, Bert Blyleven)	.30
8-306	1987 Highlights (Darrell Evans, Kevin Seitzer (Future Star))	.05
9-255	1987 Highlights (Mike Schmidt, Frank White)	.15
10-256	1987 Highlights (Don Baylor, Dan Quisenberry)	.05
11-145	1987 Highlights (Eddie Murray, Dennis Rasmussen)	.10
12-237	1987 Highlights (Juan Beniquez, Oddibe McDowell)	.05
13	1987 Championship Series (John Tudor)	.05
14	1987 Championship Series (Jeff Reardon)	.05
15	1987 Championship Series (Tom Brunansky)	.05
16	1987 Championship Series (Jeffrey Leonard)	.05
17	1987 Championship Series (Gary Gaetti)	.05
18	1987 Championship Series (Cardinals Celebrate)	.05
19	1987 World Series (Danny Gladden)	.05
20	1987 World Series (Bert Blyleven)	.05
21	1987 World Series (John Tudor)	.05
22	1987 World Series (Tom Lawless)	.05
23	1987 World Series (Curt Ford)	.05
24	1987 World Series (Kent Hrbek)	.05
25	1987 World Series (Frank Viola)	.05
26-216	Dave Smith, Edwin Nunez	.05
27-240	Jim Deshaies, Pete O'Brien	.05
28-171	Billy Hatcher, Mike Davis	.05
29-196	Kevin Bass, Teddy Higuera	

30 Mike Scott .05
31-224 Danny Walling, Eric Bell .05
32-185 Alan Ashby, Willie Upshaw .05
33-292 Ken Caminiti, Greg Walker .05
34-245 Bill Doran, Dwight Evans .05
35 Glenn Davis .05
36 Ozzie Virgil .05
37-260 Ken Oberkfell, Charlie Leibrandt .05
38-183 Ken Griffey, Devon White .05
39-287 Albert Hall, Ken Williams .05
40-310 Zane Smith, Ellis Burks (Future Star) .05
41-207 Andres Thomas, Julio Franco .05
42-178 Don James, Gary Pettis .05
43-249 Jim Acker, Mike Greenwell .05
44-226 Tom Glavine, Dave Schmidt .20
45 Dale Murphy .20
46 Jack Clark .05
47-269 Vince Coleman, Matt Nokes .05
48-221 Ricky Horton, Harold Reynolds .05
49-303 Terry Pendleton, Gary Ward .05
50-271 Tom Herr, Eric King .05
51-265 Joe Magrane, Darrell Evans .05
52-211 Tony Pena, Brook Jacoby .05
53-298 Ozzie Smith, Rick Rhoden .40
54-169 Todd Worrell, Alfredo Griffin .05
55 Willie McGee .05
56 Andre Dawson .05
57-225 Ryne Sandberg, Terry Kennedy .35
58-291 Keith Moreland, Richard Dotson .05
59-198 Greg Maddux, Rob Deer .40
60-290 Jody Davis, Carlton Fisk .25
61 Rick Sutcliffe .05
62-295 Jamie Moyer, Mike Pagliarulo .05
63-172 Leon Durham, Luis Polonia .05
64-313 Lee Smith, Devon White (Future Star) .05
65-250 Shawon Dunston, Ellis Burks .05
66-257 Franklin Stubbs, Danny Tartabull .05
67-235 Mike Scioscia, Steve Buechele .05
68-177 Orel Hershiser, Dick Schofield .05
69-289 Mike Marshall, Bob James .05
70 Fernando Valenzuela .05
71-281 Mickey Hatcher, Danny Gladden .05
72-166 Matt Young, Jay Howell .05
73-236 Bob Welch, Charlie Hough .05
74-170 Steve Sax, Dennis Eckersley .25
75 Pedro Guerrero .05
76 Tim Raines .05
77-252 Casey Candaele, Rich Gedman .05
78-248 Mike Fitzgerald, Marty Barrett .05
79-301 Andres Galarraga, Claudell Washington .05
80-212 Neal Heaton, Brett Butler .05
81-296 Hubie Brooks, Ron Guidry .05
82-258 Floyd Youmans, Bo Jackson .10
83-201 Herm Winningham, Robin Yount .25
84-307 Denny Martinez, Mike Dunne (Future Star) .05
85 Tim Wallach .05
86 Jeffrey Leonard .05
87-251 Will Clark, Roger Clemens .05
88-288 Kevin Mitchell, Jim Winn .05
89-267 Mike Aldrete, Kirk Gibson .05
90-191 Scott Garrelts, Dave Steib .05
91-231 Jose Uribe, Mike Boddicker .05
92-246 Bob Brenly, Sam Horn .05
93-189 Robby Thompson, Lloyd Moseby .05
94-217 Don Robinson, Jim Presley .05
95 Candy Maldonado .05
96 Darryl Strawberry .05
97-192 Keith Hernandez, Jesse Barfield .05
98-220 Ron Darling, Dave Valle .05
99-218 Howard Johnson, Phil Bradley .05
100-190 Roger McDowell, Jimmy Key .05
101 Dwight Gooden .05

102-165 Kevin McReynolds, Tony Phillips .05
103-275 Sid Fernandez, Tom Brunansky .05
104-241 Dave Magadan, Scott Fletcher .05
105-167 Gary Carter, Carney Lansford .05
106-302 Carmelo Martinez, Dave Winfield .25
107-205 Eddie Whitson, Mel Hall .05
108-180 Tim Flannery, DeWayne Buice .05
109-266 Stan Jefferson, Bill Madlock .05
110 John Kruk .05
111-168 Chris Brown, Dave Stewart .05
112-215 Benny Santiago, Rey Quinones .05
113-270 Garry Templeton, Lou Whitaker .05
114-186 Lance McCullers, Tom Henke .05
115 Tony Gwynn .50
116 Steve Bedrosian .05
117-247 Von Hayes, Jim Rice .10
118-279 Kevin Gross, Gene Larkin .05
119-238 Bruce Ruffin, Mike Stanley .05
120-184 Juan Samuel, Jim Clancy .05
121-182 Shane Rawley, Bob Boone .05
122-222 Chris James, Scott Bradley .05
123-199 Lance Parrish, Dale Sveum .05
124-181 Glenn Wilson, Brian Downing .05
125 Mike Schmidt .60
126 Andy Van Slyke .05
127-297 Jose Lind, Rickey Henderson .05
128-176 Al Pedrique, Greg Minton .05
129-277 Bobby Bonilla, Gary Gaetti .05
130-175 Sid Bream, Jack Howell .05
131-230 Mike LaValliere, Larry Sheets .05
132-197 Mike Dunne, Glenn Braggs .05
133-232 Jeff Robinson, Tom Niedenfuer .05
134-195 Doug Drabek, Jim Gantner .05
135 Barry Bonds .75
136 Dave Parker .05
137-208 Nick Esasky, Cory Snyder .05
138-280 Buddy Bell, Jeff Reardon .05
139-239 Kal Daniels, Pete Incaviglia .05
140-285 Barry Larkin, Ivan Calderon .05
141 Eric Davis .05
142-227 John Franco, Billy Ripken .05
143-229 Bo Diaz, Ray Knight .05
144-261 Ron Oester, Kevin Seitzer .05
146 Eric Davis/AS .05
147 Ryne Sandberg/AS .30
148 Andre Dawson/AS .15
149 Mike Schmidt/AS .40
150 Jack Clark/AS .05
151 Darryl Strawberry/AS .05
152 Gary Carter/AS .35
153 Ozzie Smith/AS .35
154 Mike Scott/AS .05
155 Rickey Henderson/AS .35
156 Don Mattingly/AS .40
157 Wade Boggs/AS .30
158 George Bell/AS .05
159 Dave Winfield/AS .05
160 Cal Ripken, Jr./AS .50
161 Terry Kennedy/AS .05
162 Willie Randolph/AS .05
163 Bret Saberhagen/AS .05
164 Mark McGwire .65
173 Jose Canseco .35
174 Mike Witt .05
179 Wally Joyner .05
188 George Bell .05
193 Tony Fernández .05
194 Paul Molitor .40
200-308 Bill Wegman, Jeff Musselman (Future Star) .05
202-309 B.J. Surhoff, Mark McGwire (Future Star) .50
203 Dan Plesac .05
204 Pat Tabler .05
206-305 Scott Bailes, Casey Candaele (Future Star) .05
209-312 Chris Bando, Mike Greenwell (Future Star) .05
210-311 Greg Swindell, Matt Nokes (Future Star) .05
213 Joe Carter .05
214 Mark Langston .05
219 Alvin Davis .05
228 Cal Ripken, Jr. .75

233 Eddie Murray .40
234 Ruben Sierra .05
242-300 Dave Mohorcic, Dave Righetti .05
243 Larry Parrish .05
244 Wade Boggs .40
253 Bruce Hurst .05
254 Bret Saberhagen .05
259 George Brett .50
262-282 Mark Gubicza, Frank Viola .05
264-286 Frank Tanana, Donnie Hill .05
268 Jack Morris .05
273 Alan Trammell .05
274 Kent Hrbek .05
283 Kirby Puckett .50
284 Ozzie Guillen .05
293 Harold Baines .05
294 Willie Randolph .05
299 Don Mattingly .50

Campbell's Richie Ashburn Tribute Sheet

Longtime Phillies star, Hall of Famer and broadcaster Richie Ashburn was honored for his 40 years in baseball by the issue of a commemorative card set in the form of a 10" x 14" poster given away as a stadium promotion. A 5" x 7" card picturing the 61-year old Ashburn was at center, with his complete major league stats on back. Surrounding the center card and separated by perforations are reproductions of 12 of Ashburn's baseball cards. The cards are reduced to about 75 percent of actual size and shown on an American flag background. The back of each card is also reproduced, with a cartoon figure of the Campbell's Kid baseball player included on front and back.

	NM/M
Complete Set (Sheet):	25.00
Complete Set, Singles (13):	20.00
Common Card:	2.00
1952 Bowman	2.00
1952 Topps	2.00
1954 Topps	2.00
1956 Topps	2.00
1957 Topps	2.00
1958 Topps	2.00
1959 Topps	2.00
1959 Topps (N.L. Hitting Kings)	2.00
1960 Topps	2.00
1961 Topps	2.00
1962 Topps	2.00
1963 Topps	2.00
Richie Ashburn (1988 Portrait)	2.00

Sports Shots Portfolios

One hundred and thirty of the biggest names from Topps' 1988 baseball card set were reproduced in the form of 9-1/2" x 11-3/4" cardboard folders. The folders reproduce both front and back of the '88 Topps cards and open to offer two pockets for storage. Various manufacturer and licensor logos are the only printing inside. The folders carried a suggested retail price of $1 apiece and were distributed in either team packs or all-star assortments of 50 pieces each. By 1992, the folders were being wholesaled within the hobby at less than 30 cents apiece.

	NM/M
Complete Set (130):	60.00
Common Player:	.50
10 Ryne Sandberg	2.50
15 Chili Davis	.50
25 Andres Galarraga	.50
35 Harold Baines	.50
39 Gerald Perry	.50
40 Orel Hershiser	.50
45 Kent Hrbek	.50
55 Hubie Brooks	.50
55 Phil Bradley	.50
60 Rickey Henderson	2.00
70 Roger Clemens	3.00
75 Joe Carter	.50
90 Mark Langston	.50
90 Dale Murphy	1.00
95 Lance Parrish	.50
100 Jack Clark	.50
102 Barry Larkin	.50
111 Teddy Higuera	.50
118 Bob Welch	.50
120 Kirby Puckett	2.50
130 Buddy Bell	.50
138 Mitch Webster	.50
140 Jesse Barfield	.50
142 Andy Van Slyke	.50
150 Eric Davis	.50
165 Robin Yount	2.00
170 Goose Gossage	.50
180 Terry Kennedy	.50
192 Ivan Calderon	.50
193 Devon White	.50
193 Brian Fisher	.50
197 Dan Quisenberry	.50
197 Lance McCullers	.50
200 Wade Boggs	2.50
210 Willie Randolph	.50
215 Von Hayes	.50
230 Pat Tabler	.50
238 Luis Polonia	.50
240 Lee Smith	.50
250 Nolan Ryan	4.00
260 Vince Coleman	.50
260 Bo Diaz	.50
270 Mike Witt	.50
280 Pete Incaviglia	.50
285 Jim Presley	.50
297 Zane Smith	.50
300 Don Mattingly	3.00
305 Steve Sax	.50
305 Billy Hatcher	.50
320 Alan Trammell	.50
327 Larry Sheets	.50
331 Brian Downing	.50
340 Jack Morris	.50
343 Greg Gagne	.50
350 Will Clark	.50
360 Tony Gwynn	2.50
370 Jose Canseco	1.00
385 Carlton Fisk	2.00
408 Dion James	.50
410 Tony Pena	.50
420 Wally Joyner	.50
424 Dwayne Murphy	.50
430 Glenn Davis	.50
440 Steve Bedrosian	.50
450 Barry Bonds	4.00
452 Willie Wilson	.50
460 Ozzie Smith	2.50
465 Paul Molitor	2.00
470 Dwight Evans	.50
479 Dave Stewart	.50
479 Brett Butler	.50
485 Dwight Gooden	.50
485 Harold Reynolds	.50
490 Larry Parrish	.50
491 B.J. Surhoff	.50
495 Eddie Murray	2.00
497 Kevin Mitchell	.50
500 Andre Dawson	1.00
510 Dave Winfield	2.00
525 Marty Barrett	.50
530 Gary Carter	2.00
540 Bret Saberhagen	.50
550 Pedro Guerrero	.50
555 Brook Jacoby	.50
560 Tim Wallach	.50
565 Lloyd Moseby	.50
570 Jeffrey Leonard	.50
578 Gary Gaetti	.50
580 Mark McGwire	3.50
590 George Bell	.50
596 John Kruk	.50
600 Mike Schmidt	3.00
605 Kirk Gibson	.50
610 Keith Hernandez	.50
613 Bobby Thigpen	.50
615 Jody Davis	.50
619 Mike Dunne	.50
620 Cory Snyder	.50
625 Frank Viola	.50
645 Matt Nokes	.50
649 De Wayne Buice	.50
650 Cal Ripken Jr.	4.00
660 Rick Reuschel	.50
670 Dan Plesac	.50
675 Jim Rice	1.00
680 Charlie Hough	.50
681 Bobby Bonilla	.50
682 Jimmy Key	.50
685 Ron Darling	.50
693 Benito Santiago	.50
700 George Brett	3.00
705 Juan Samuel	.50
710 Darryl Strawberry	.50
715 Todd Worrell	.50
720 Tim Raines	.50
721 Pete O'Brien	.50
725 Mike Boddicker	.50
730 John Franco	.50
740 Rick Sutcliffe	.50
745 Bill Doran	.50
750 Bo Jackson	1.00
755 Ozzie Virgil	.50
760 Mike Scott	.50
764 Greg Walker	.50
770 Lou Whitaker	.50
771 Ruben Sierra	.50
775 Dave Steib	.50
780 Fernando Valenzuela	.50
785 Alvin Davis	.50
790 Dave Righetti	.50

1989 Topps

Ten top young players from the June 1988 draft are featured on "#1 Draft Pick" cards in this full-color basic set of 792 standard-size baseball cards. An additional five cards salute 1989 Future Stars, 22 cards highlight All-Stars, seven contain Record Breakers, five are designated Turn Back The Clock, and six contain checklists. This set features the familiar white borders, but upper-left and lower-right photo corners have been rounded off. A curved name banner in bright red or blue is beneath the team name in large script in the lower-right corner. The card backs are printed in black on a red background and include personal information and complete minor and major league stats. Another new addition in this set is the special Monthly Scoreboard chart that lists monthly stats (April through September) in two of several categories (hits, run, home runs, stolen bases, RBIs, wins, strikeouts, games or saves).

	NM/M
Unopened Factory Set, Retail (792):	25.00
Unopened Factory Set, Hobby (792):	25.00
Complete Set (792):	15.00
Common Player:	.05
Wax Pack (15):	.75
Wax Box (36):	12.00
Cello Pack (29):	1.00
Cello Box (24):	18.00
Rack Pack (43):	.75
Rack Box (24):	15.00
Vending Box (500):	6.00

1 George Bell (Record Breaker) .05
2 Wade Boggs (Record Breaker) .25
3 Gary Carter (Record Breaker) .20
4 Andre Dawson (Record Breaker) .10
5 Orel Hershiser (Record Breaker) .05
6 Doug Jones (Record Breaker) .05
7 Kevin McReynolds (Record Breaker) .05
8 Dave Eiland RC .05
9 Tim Teufel .05
10 Andre Dawson .25
11 Bruce Sutter .05
12 Dale Sveum .05
13 Doug Sisk .05
14 Tom Kelly .05
15 Robby Thompson .05
16 Ron Robinson .05
17 Brian Downing .05
18 Rick Rhoden .05
19 Greg Gagne .05
20 Steve Bedrosian .05
21 White Sox Leaders (Greg Walker) .05
22 Tim Crews .05
23 Mike Fitzgerald .05
24 Larry Andersen .05
25 Frank White .05
26 Dale Mohorcic .05
27 Orestes Destrade RC .05
28 Mike Moore .05
29 Kelly Gruber .05
30 Dwight Gooden .05
31 Terry Francona .05
32 Dennis Rasmussen .05
33 B.J. Surhoff .05
34 Ken Williams .05
35 John Tudor .05
36 Mitch Webster .05
37 Bob Stanley .05
38 Paul Runge .05
39 Mike Maddux .05
40 Steve Sax .05
41 Terry Mulholland .05
42 Jim Eppard RC .05
43 Guillermo Hernandez .05
44 Jim Snyder .05
45 Kal Daniels .05
46 Mark Portugal .05
47 Carney Lansford .05
48 Tim Burke .05
49 Craig Biggio .05
50 George Bell .05
51 Angels Leaders (Mark McLemore) .05
52 Bob Brenly .05
53 Ruben Sierra .05
54 Steve Trout .05
55 Julio Franco .05
56 Pat Tabler .05
57 Alejandro Pena .05
58 Lee Mazzilli .05
59 Mark Davis .05
60 Tom Brunansky .05
61 Neil Allen .05
62 Alfredo Griffin .05
63 Mark Clear .05
64 Alex Trevino .05
65 Rick Reuschel .05
66 Manny Trillo .05
67 Dave Palmer .05
68 Darrell Miller .05
69 Jeff Ballard .05
70 Mark McGwire .65
71 Mike Boddicker .05
72 John Moses .05
73 Pascual Perez .05
74 Nick Leyva .05
75 Tom Henke .05
76 Terry Blocker RC .05
77 Doyle Alexander .05
78 Jim Sundberg .05
79 Scott Bankhead .05
80 Cory Snyder .05
81 Expos Leaders (Tim Raines) .05
82 Dave Leiper .05
83 Jeff Blauser RC .05
84 Bill Bene RC (#1 Draft Pick) .05
85 Kevin McReynolds .05
86 Al Nipper .05
87 Larry Owen .05
88 Darryl Hamilton RC .05
89 Dave LaPoint .05
90 Vince Coleman .05
91 Floyd Youmans .05
92 Jeff Kunkel .05
93 Ken Howell .05
94 Chris Speier .05
95 Gerald Young .05
96 Rick Cerone .05
97 Greg Mathews .05
98 Larry Sheets .05
99 Sherman Corbett RC .05
100 Mike Schmidt .50
101 Les Straker .05
102 Mike Gallego .05
103 Tim Birtsas .05
104 Dallas Green .05
105 Ron Darling .05
106 Willie Upshaw .05
107 Jose DeLeon .05
108 Fred Manrique .05
109 Hipolito Pena RC .05
110 Paul Molitor .40
111 Reds Leaders (Eric Davis) .05
112 Jim Presley .05
113 Lloyd Moseby .05
114 Bob Kipper .05
115 Jody Davis .05
116 Jeff Montgomery .05
117 Dave Anderson .05
118 Checklist 1-132 .05
119 Terry Puhl .05
120 Frank Viola .05
121 Garry Templeton .05
122 Lance Johnson RC .05
123 Spike Owen .05
124 Jim Traber .05
125 Mike Krukow .05
126 Sid Bream .05
127 Walt Terrell .05
128 Milt Thompson .05
129 Terry Clark RC .05
130 Gerald Perry .05
131 Dave Otto RC .05
132 Curt Ford .05
133 Bill Long .05

No.	Player	Price	No.	Player	Price	No.	Player	Price	No.	Player	Price	No.	Player	Price	No.	Player	Price
134	Don Zimmer	.05	243	Bob Boone	.05	356	Kevin Elster	.05	470	Lance Parrish	.05	584	Randy Velarde RC	.05	685	Jeff Treadway	.05
135	Jose Rijo	.05	244	Jim Acker	.05	357	Jerry Reuss	.05	471	Steve Curry RC	.05	585	Harold Baines	.05	686	Scott Terry	.05
136	Joey Meyer	.05	245	Jim Rice	.15	358	Ricky Jordan RC	.05	472	Brian Harper	.05	586	Joe Boever	.05	687	Alvin Davis	.05
137	Geno Petralli	.05	246	Rey Quinones	.05	359	Tommy John	.10	473	Don Robinson	.05	587	Mike Stanley	.05	688	Zane Smith	.05
138	Wallace Johnson	.05	247	Shawn Hillegas	.05	360	Ryne Sandberg	.45	474	Bob Rodgers	.05	588	Luis Alicea RC	.05	689a	Stan Jefferson (Pink triangle at bottom-left photo.)	.05
139	Mike Flanagan	.05	248	Tony Phillips	.05	361	Kelly Downs	.05	475	Dave Parker	.05	589	Dave Meads	.05	689b	Stan Jefferson (Pink/purple triangle.)	.05
140	Shawon Dunston	.05	249	Tim Leary	.05	362	Jack Lazorko	.05	476	Jon Perlman RC	.05	590	Andres Galarraga	.05	689c	Stan Jefferson (Purple triangle.)	.05
141	Indians Leaders (Brook Jacoby)	.05	250	Cal Ripken, Jr.	.75	363	Rich Yett	.05	477	Dick Schofield	.05	591	Jeff Musselman	.05	690	Doug Jones	.05
142	Mike Diaz	.05	251	John Dopson RC	.05	364	Rob Deer	.05	478	Doug Drabek	.05	592	John Cangelosi	.05	691	Roberto Kelly	.05
143	Mike Campbell	.05	252	Billy Hatcher	.05	365	Mike Henneman	.05	479	Mike Macfarlane	.05	593	Drew Hall	.05	692	Steve Ontiveros	.05
144	Jay Bell	.05	253	Jose Alvarez RC	.05	366	Herm Winningham	.05	480	Keith Hernandez	.05	594	Jimy Williams	.05	693	Pat Borders RC	.05
145	Dave Stewart	.05	254	Tom LaSorda	.05	367	Johnny Paredes RC	.05	481	Chris Brown	.05	595	Teddy Higuera	.05	694	Les Lancaster	.05
146	Gary Pettis	.05	255	Ron Guidry	.10	368	Brian Holton	.05	482	Steve Peters RC	.05	596	Kurt Stillwell	.05	695	Carlton Fisk	.40
147	DeWayne Buice	.05	256	Benny Santiago	.05	369	Ken Caminiti	.05	483	Mickey Hatcher	.05	597	Terry Taylor RC	.05	696	Don August	.05
148	Bill Pecota	.05	257	Rick Aguilera	.05	370	Dennis Eckersley	.35	484	Steve Shields	.05	598	Ken Gerhart	.05	697	Franklin Stubbs	.05
149	Doug Dascenzo RC	.05	258	Checklist 133-264	.05	371	Manny Lee	.05	485	Hubie Brooks	.05	599	Tom Candiotti	.05	698	Keith Atherton	.05
150	Fernando Valenzuela	.05	259	Larry McWilliams	.05	372	Craig Lefferts	.05	486	Jack McDowell	.05	600	Wade Boggs	.45	699	Pirates Leaders (Al Pedrique)	.05
151	Terry McGriff	.05	260	Dave Winfield	.40	373	Tracy Jones	.05	487	Scott Lusader RC	.05	601	Dave Dravecky	.05	700	Don Mattingly	.50
152	Mark Thurmond	.05	261	Cardinals Leaders (Tom Brunansky)	.05	374	John Wathan	.05	488	Kevin Coffman	.05	602	Devon White	.05	701	Storm Davis	.05
153	Jim Pankovits	.05	262	Jeff Pico RC	.05	375	Terry Pendleton	.05	489	Phillies Leaders (Mike Schmidt)	.15	603	Frank Tanana	.05	702	Jamie Quirk	.05
154	Don Carman	.05	263	Mike Felder	.05	376	Steve Lombardozzi	.05	490	Chris Sabo	.05	604	Paul O'Neill	.05	703	Scott Garrelts	.05
155	Marty Barrett	.05	264	Rob Dibble RC	.10	377	Mike Smithson	.05	491	Mike Birkbeck	.05	605a	Bob Welch (Missing Complete Major League Pitching Record line.)	3.00	704	Carlos Quintana RC	.05
156	Dave Gallagher RC	.05	265	Kent Hrbek	.05	378	Checklist 265-396	.05	492	Alan Ashby	.05				705	Terry Kennedy	.05
157	Tom Glavine	.05	266	Luis Aquino	.05	379	Tim Flannery	.05	493	Todd Benzinger	.05	605b	Bob Welch (Contains Complete Major League Pitching Record line.)	.05	706	Pete Incaviglia	.05
158	Mike Aldrete	.05	267	Jeff Robinson	.05	380	Rickey Henderson	.40	494	Shane Rawley	.05				707	Steve Jeltz	.05
159	Pat Clements	.05	268	Keith Miller	.05	381	Orioles Leaders (Larry Sheets)	.05	495	Candy Maldonado	.05	606	Rick Dempsey	.05	708	Chuck Finley	.05
160	Jeffrey Leonard	.05	269	Tom Bolton	.05	382	John Smoltz	.50	496	Dwayne Henry	.05	607	Willie Ansley RC (#1 Draft Pick)	.05	709	Tom Herr	.05
161	Gregg Olson RC (#1 Draft Pick)	.05	270	Wally Joyner	.05	383	Howard Johnson	.05	497	Pete Stanicek	.05	608	Phil Bradley	.05	710	Dave Cone	.05
162	John Davis	.05	271	Jay Tibbs	.05	384	Mark Salas	.05	498	Dave Valle	.05	609	Tigers Leaders (Frank Tanana)	.05	711	Candy Sierra RC	.05
163	Bob Forsch	.05	272	Ron Hassey	.05	385	Von Hayes	.05	499	Don Heinkel RC	.05	610	Randy Myers	.05	712	Bill Swift	.05
164	Hal Lanier	.05	273	Jose Lind	.05	386	Andres Galarraga/AS	.05	500	Jose Canseco	.35	611	Don Slaught	.05	713	Ty Griffin RC (#1 Draft Pick)	.05
165	Mike Dunne	.05	274	Mark Eichhorn	.05	387	Ryne Sandberg/AS	.20	501	Vance Law	.05	612	Dan Quisenberry	.05	714	Joe M. Morgan	.05
166	Doug Jennings RC	.05	275	Danny Tartabull	.05	388	Bobby Bonilla/AS	.05	502	Duane Ward	.05	613	Gary Varsho RC	.05	715	Tony Pena	.05
167	Steve Searcy RC (Future Star)	.05	276	Paul Kilgus	.05	389	Ozzie Smith/AS	.25	503	Al Newman	.05	614	Joe Hesketh	.05	716	Wayne Tolleson	.05
168	Willie Wilson	.05	277	Mike Davis	.05	390	Darryl Strawberry/AS	.05	504	Bob Walk	.05	615	Robin Yount	.40	717	Jamie Moyer	.05
169	Mike Jackson	.05	278	Andy McGaffigan	.05	391	Andre Dawson/AS	.05	505	Pete Rose	.75	616	Steve Rosenberg RC	.05	718	Glenn Braggs	.05
170	Tony Fernandez	.05	279	Scott Bradley	.05	392	Andy Van Slyke/AS	.05	506	Kirt Manwaring	.05	617	Mark Parent RC	.05	719	Danny Darwin	.05
171	Braves Leaders (Andres Thomas)	.05	280	Bob Knepper	.05	393	Gary Carter/AS	.05	507	Steve Farr	.05	618	Rance Mulliniks	.05	720	Tim Wallach	.05
172	Frank Williams	.05	281	Gary Redus	.05	394	Orel Hershiser/AS	.05	508	Wally Backman	.05	619	Checklist 529-660	.05	721	Ron Tingley RC	.05
173	Mel Hall	.05	282	Cris Carpenter RC	.05	395	Danny Jackson/AS	.05	509	Bud Black	.05	620	Barry Bonds	.75	722	Todd Stottlemyre	.05
174	Todd Burns RC	.05	283	Andy Allanson	.05	396	Kirk Gibson/AS	.05	510	Bob Horner	.05	621	Rick Mahler	.05	723	Rafael Belliard	.05
175	John Shelby	.05	284	Jim Leyland	.05	397	Don Mattingly/AS	.30	511	Richard Dotson	.05	622	Stan Javier	.05	724	Jerry Don Gleaton	.05
176	Jeff Parrett	.05	285	John Candelaria	.05	398	Julio Franco/AS	.05	512	Donnie Hill	.05	623	Fred Toliver	.05	725	Terry Steinbach	.05
177	Monty Fariss RC (#1 Draft Pick)	.05	286	Darrin Jackson	.05	399	Wade Boggs/AS	.20	513	Jesse Orosco	.05	624	Jack McKeon	.05	726	Dickie Thon	.05
178	Mark Grant	.05	287	Juan Nieves	.05	400	Alan Trammell/AS	.05	514	Chet Lemon	.05	625	Eddie Murray	.40	727	Joe Orsulak	.05
179	Ozzie Virgil	.05	288	Pat Sheridan	.05	401	Jose Canseco/AS	.15	515	Barry Larkin	.05	626	Jeff Reed	.05	728	Charlie Puleo	.05
180	Mike Scott	.05	289	Ernie Whitt	.05	402	Mike Greenwell/AS	.05	516	Eddie Whitson	.05	627	Greg Harris	.05	729	Rangers Leaders (Steve Buechele)	.05
181	Craig Worthington RC	.05	290	John Franco	.05	403	Kirby Puckett/AS	.25	517	Greg Brock	.05	628	Matt Williams	.05	730	Danny Jackson	.05
182	Bob McClure	.05	291	Mets Leaders (Darryl Strawberry)	.05	404	Bob Boone/AS	.05	518	Bruce Ruffin	.05	629	Pete O'Brien	.05	731	Mike Young	.05
183	Oddibe McDowell	.05	292	Jim Corsi RC	.05	405	Roger Clemens/AS	.30	519	Yankees Leaders (Willie Randolph)	.05	630	Mike Greenwell	.05	732	Steve Buechele	.05
184	John Costello RC	.05	293	Glenn Wilson	.05	406	Frank Viola/AS	.05	520	Rick Sutcliffe	.05	631	Dave Bergman	.05	733	Randy Bockus RC	.05
185	Claudell Washington	.05	294	Juan Berenguer	.05	407	Dave Winfield/AS	.20	521	Mickey Tettleton	.05	632	Bryan Harvey RC	.10	734	Jody Reed	.05
186	Pat Perry	.05	295	Scott Fletcher	.05	408	Greg Walker	.05	522	Randy Kramer RC	.05	633	Daryl Boston	.05	735	Roger McDowell	.05
187	Darren Daulton	.05	296	Ron Gant	.05	409	Ken Dayley	.05	523	Andres Thomas	.05	634	Marvin Freeman RC	.05	736	Jeff Hamilton	.05
188	Dennis Lamp	.05	297	Oswald Peraza RC	.05	410	Jack Clark	.05	524	Checklist 397-528	.05	635	Willie Randolph	.05	737	Norm Charlton RC	.05
189	Kevin Mitchell	.05	298	Chris James	.05	411	Mitch Williams	.05	525	Chili Davis	.05	636	Bill Wilkinson	.05	738	Darnell Coles	.05
190	Mike Witt	.05	299	Steve Ellsworth RC	.05	412	Barry Lyons	.05	526	Wes Gardner	.05	637	Carmen Castillo	.05	739	Brook Jacoby	.05
191	Sil Campusano RC	.05	300	Darryl Strawberry	.05	413	Mike Kingery	.05	527	Dave Henderson	.05	638	Floyd Bannister	.05	740	Dan Plesac	.05
192	Paul Mirabella	.05	301	Charlie Leibrandt	.05	414	Jim Fregosi	.05	528	Luis Medina RC	.05	639	Athletics Leaders (Walt Weiss)	.05	741	Ken Phelps	.05
193	Sparky Anderson	.10	302	Gary Ward	.05	415	Rich Gossage	.05	529	Tom Foley	.05	640	Willie McGee	.05	742	Mike Harkey RC (Future Star)	.05
194	Greg Harris	.05	303	Felix Fermin	.05	416	Fred Lynn	.05	530	Nolan Ryan	.75	641	Curt Young	.05	743	Mike Heath	.05
195	Ozzie Guillen	.05	304	Joel Youngblood	.05	417	Mike LaCoss	.05	531	Dave Hengel RC	.05	642	Argenis Salazar	.05	744	Roger Craig	.05
196	Denny Walling	.05	305	Dave Smith	.05	418	Bob Dernier	.05	532	Jerry Browne	.05	643	Louie Meadows RC	.05	745	Fred McGriff	.05
197	Neal Heaton	.05	306	Tracy Woodson RC	.05	419	Tom Filer	.05	533	Andy Hawkins	.05	644	Lloyd McClendon	.05	746	German Gonzalez RC	.05
198	Danny Heep	.05	307	Lance McCullers	.05	420	Joe Carter	.05	534	Doc Edwards	.05	645	Jack Morris	.05	747	Wil Tejada RC	.05
199	Mike Schooler RC	.05	308	Ron Karkovice	.05	421	Kirk McCaskill	.05	535	Todd Worrell	.05	646	Kevin Bass	.05	748	Jimmy Jones	.05
200	George Brett	.50	309	Mario Diaz RC	.05	422	Bo Diaz	.05	536	Joel Skinner	.05	647	Randy Johnson RC	3.00	749	Rafael Ramirez	.05
201	Blue Jays Leaders (Kelly Gruber)	.05	310	Rafael Palmeiro	.35	423	Brian Fisher	.05	537	Pete Smith	.05	648	Sandy Alomar (Future Star)	.25	750	Bret Saberhagen	.05
202	Brad Moore RC	.05	311	Chris Bosio	.05	424	Luis Polonia	.05	538	Juan Castillo	.05	649	Stewart Cliburn	.05	751	Ken Oberkfell	.05
203	Rob Ducey	.05	312	Tom Lawless	.05	425	Jay Howell	.05	539	Barry Jones	.05	650	Kirby Puckett	.45	752	Jim Gott	.05
204	Brad Havens	.05	313	Denny Martinez	.05	426	Danny Gladden	.05	540	Bo Jackson	.10	651	Tom Niedenfuer	.05	753	Jose Uribe	.05
205	Dwight Evans	.05	314	Bobby Valentine	.05	427	Eric Show	.05	541	Cecil Fielder	.05	652	Rich Gedman	.05	754	Bob Brower	.05
206	Roberto Alomar	.35	315	Greg Swindell	.05	428	Craig Reynolds	.05	542	Todd Frohwirth	.05	653	Tommy Barrett RC	.05	755	Mike Scioscia	.05
207	Terry Leach	.05	316	Walt Weiss	.05	429	Twins Leaders (Greg Gagne)	.05	543	Damon Berryhill	.05	654	Whitey Herzog	.05	756	Scott Medvin RC	.05
208	Tom Pagnozzi	.05	317	Jack Armstrong RC	.05	430	Mark Gubicza	.05	544	Jeff Sellers	.05	655	Dave Magadan	.05	757	Brady Anderson	.05
209	Jeff Bittiger RC	.05	318	Gene Larkin	.05	431	Luis Rivera	.05	545	Mookie Wilson	.05	656	Ivan Calderon	.05	758	Gene Walter	.05
210	Dale Murphy	.15	319	Greg Booker	.05	432	Chad Kreuter RC	.10	546	Mark Williamson	.05	657	Joe Magrane	.05	759	Brewers Leaders (Rob Deer)	.05
211	Mike Pagliarulo	.05	320	Lou Whitaker	.05	433	Albert Hall	.05	547	Mark McLemore	.05	658	R.J. Reynolds	.05	760	Lee Smith	.05
212	Scott Sanderson	.05	321	Red Sox Leaders (Jody Reed)	.05	434	Ken Patterson RC	.05	548	Bobby Witt	.05	659	Al Leiter	.05	761	Dante Bichette RC	.25
213	Rene Gonzales	.05	322	John Smiley	.05	435	Len Dykstra	.05	549	Cubs Leaders (Jamie Moyer)	.05	660	Will Clark	.05	762	Bobby Thigpen	.05
214	Charlie O'Brien	.05	323	Gary Thurman	.05	436	Bobby Meacham	.05	550	Orel Hershiser	.05	661	Dwight Gooden (Turn Back the Clock)	.05	763	Dave Martinez	.05
215	Kevin Gross	.05	324	Bob Milacki RC	.05	437	Andy Benes (#1 Draft Pick)	.05	551	Randy Ready	.05	662	Lou Brock (Turn Back the Clock)	.05	764	Robin Ventura (#1 Draft Pick)	.25
216	Jack Howell	.05	325	Jesse Barfield	.05	438	Greg Gross	.05	552	Greg Cadaret	.05	663	Hank Aaron (Turn Back the Clock)	.15	765	Glenn Davis	.05
217	Joe Price	.05	326	Dennis Boyd	.05	439	Frank DiPino	.05	553	Luis Salazar	.05	664	Gil Hodges (Turn Back the Clock)	.05	766	Cecilio Guante	.05
218	Mike LaValliere	.05	327	Mark Lemke RC	.05	440	Bobby Bonilla	.05	554	Nick Esasky	.05	665a	Tony Oliva (No copyright line.)	12.50	767	Mike Capel RC	.05
219	Jim Clancy	.05	328	Rick Honeycutt	.05	441	Jerry Reed	.05	555	Bert Blyleven	.05	665b	Tony Oliva (With copyright line.)	.05	768	Bill Wegman	.05
220	Gary Gaetti	.05	329	Bob Melvin	.05	442	Jose Oquendo	.05	556	Bruce Fields RC	.05	666	Randy St. Claire	.05	769	Junior Ortiz	.05
221	Cecil Espy	.05	330	Eric Davis	.05	443	Rod Nichols RC	.05	557	Keith Miller RC	.05	667	Dwayne Murphy	.05	770	Alan Trammell	.05
222	Mark Lewis RC (#1 Draft Pick)	.05	331	Curt Wilkerson	.05	444	Moose Stubing	.05	558	Dan Pasqua	.05	668	Mike Bielecki	.05	771	Ron Kittle	.05
223	Jay Buhner	.05	332	Tony Armas	.05	445	Matt Nokes	.05	559	Juan Agosto	.05	669	Dodgers Leaders (Orel Hershiser)	.05	772	Ron Oester	.05
224	Tony LaRussa	.05	333	Bob Ojeda	.05	446	Rob Murphy	.05	560	Tim Raines	.05	670	Kevin Seitzer	.05	773	Keith Moreland	.05
225	Ramon Martinez RC	.05	334	Steve Lyons	.05	447	Donell Nixon	.05	561	Luis Aguayo	.05	671	Jim Gantner	.05	774	Frank Robinson	.15
226	Bill Doran	.05	335	Dave Righetti	.05	448	Eric Plunk	.05	562	Danny Cox	.05	672	Allan Anderson	.05	775	Jeff Reardon	.05
227	John Farrell	.05	336	Steve Balboni	.05	449	Carmelo Martinez	.05	563	Bill Schroeder	.05	673	Don Baylor	.05	776	Nelson Liriano	.05
228	Nelson Santovenia RC	.05	337	Calvin Schiraldi	.05	450	Roger Clemens	.50	564	Russ Nixon	.05	674	Otis Nixon	.05	777	Ted Power	.05
229	Jimmy Key	.05	338	Jim Adduci RC	.05	451	Mark Davidson	.05	565	Jeff Russell	.05	675	Bruce Hurst	.05	778	Bruce Benedict	.05
230	Ozzie Smith	.45	339	Scott Bailes	.05	452	Israel Sanchez RC	.05	566	Al Pedrique	.05	676	Ernie Riles	.05	779	Craig McMurtry	.05
231	Padres Leaders (Roberto Alomar)	1.50	340	Kirk Gibson	.05	453	Tom Prince RC	.05	567	David Wells	.05	677	Dave Schmidt	.05	780	Pedro Guerrero	.05
232	Ricky Horton	.05	341	Jim Deshaies	.05	454	Paul Assenmacher	.05	568	Mickey Brantley	.05	678	Dion James	.05	781	Greg Briley RC	.05
233	Gregg Jefferies (Future Star)	.20	342	Tom Brookens	.05	455	Johnny Ray	.05	569	German Jimenez RC	.05	679	Willie Fraser	.05	782	Checklist 661-792	.05
234	Tom Browning	.05	343	Gary Sheffield RC (Future Star)	1.50	456	Tim Belcher	.05	570	Tony Gwynn	.45	680	Gary Carter	.40	783	Trevor Wilson RC	.05
235	John Kruk	.05	344	Tom Trebelhorn	.05	457	Mackey Sasser	.05	571	Billy Ripken	.05	681	Jeff Robinson	.05	784	Steve Avery RC (#1 Draft Pick)	.15
236	Charles Hudson	.05	345	Charlie Hough	.05	458	Donn Pall RC	.05	572	Atlee Hammaker	.05	682	Rick Leach	.05	785	Ellis Burks	.05
237	Glenn Hubbard	.05	346	Rex Hudler RC	.05	459	Mariners Leaders (Dave Valle)	.05	573	Jim Abbott (#1 Draft Pick)	.10	683	Jose Cecena RC	.05	786	Melido Perez	.05
238	Eric King	.05	347	John Cerutti	.05	460	Dave Stieb	.05	574	Dave Clark	.05	684	Dave Johnson	.05	787	Dave West RC	.05
239	Tim Laudner	.05	348	Ed Hearn	.05	461	Buddy Bell	.05	575	Juan Samuel	.05				788	Mike Morgan	.05
240	Greg Maddux	.45	349	Ron Jones RC	.05	462	Jose Guzman	.05	576	Greg Minton	.05				789	Royals Leaders (Bo Jackson)	.05
241	Brett Butler	.05	350	Andy Van Slyke	.05	463	Steve Lake	.05	577	Randy Bush	.05						
242	Ed Vande Berg	.05	351	Giants Leaders (Bob Melvin)	.05	464	Bryn Smith	.05	578	John Morris	.05						
			352	Rick Schu	.05	465	Mark Grace	.05	579	Astros Leaders (Glenn Davis)	.05						
			353	Marvell Wynne	.05	466	Chuck Crim	.05	580	Harold Reynolds	.05						
			354	Larry Parrish	.05	467	Jim Walewander	.05	581	Gene Nelson	.05						
			355	Mark Langston	.05	468	Henry Cotto	.05	582	Mike Marshall	.05						
						469	Jose Bautista RC	.05	583	Paul Gibson RC	.05						

790	Sid Fernandez	.05
791	Jim Lindeman	.05
792	Rafael Santana	.05

Tiffany

This special hobby-only edition shares the checklist with the regular 1989 Topps set. Cards are identical except for the use of white cardboard stock and the high-gloss front coating. Production has been reported as 25,000 sets.

	NM/M
Unopened Set (792):	75.00
Complete Set (792):	40.00
Common Player:	.10

Traded

For the ninth straight year, Topps issued its annual 132-card "Traded" set at the end of the 1989 baseball season. The set, which was packaged in a special box and sold by hobby dealers, includes traded players and rookies who were not in the regular 1989 Topps set.

		NM/M
Unopened Set, Retail (132):		12.50
Unopened Set, Hobby (132):		10.00
Complete Set (132):		7.50
Common Player:		.05
1T	Don Aase	.05
2T	Jim Abbott	.05
3T	Kent Anderson RC	.05
4T	Keith Atherton	.05
5T	Wally Backman	.05
6T	Steve Balboni	.05
7T	Jesse Barfield	.05
8T	Steve Bedrosian	.05
9T	Todd Benzinger	.05
10T	Geronimo Berroa	.05
11T	Bert Blyleven	.05
12T	Bob Boone	.05
13T	Phil Bradley	.05
14T	Jeff Brantley RC	.05
15T	Kevin Brown RC	.05
16T	Jerry Browne	.05
17T	Chuck Cary	.05
18T	Carmen Castillo	.05
19T	Jim Clancy	.05
20T	Jack Clark	.05
21T	Bryan Clutterbuck	.05
22T	Jody Davis	.05
23T	Mike Devereaux	.05
24T	Frank DiPino	.05
25T	Benny Distefano	.05
26T	John Dopson	.05
27T	Len Dykstra	.05
28T	Jim Eisenreich	.05
29T	Nick Esasky	.05
30T	Alvaro Espinoza	.05
31T	Darrell Evans	.05
32T	Junior Felix	.05
33T	Felix Fermin	.05
34T	Julio Franco	.05
35T	Terry Francona	.05
36T	Cito Gaston	.05
37T	Bob Geren RC (Photo actually Mike Fennell.)	.05
38T	Tom Gordon RC	.10
39T	Tommy Gregg RC	.05
40T	Ken Griffey	.05
41T	Ken Griffey Jr. RC	6.00
42T	Kevin Gross	.05
43T	Lee Guetterman	.05
44T	Mel Hall	.05
45T	Erik Hanson RC	.05
46T	Gene Harris RC	.05
47T	Andy Hawkins	.05
48T	Rickey Henderson	.40
49T	Tom Herr	.05
50T	Ken Hill RC	.05
51T	Brian Holman RC	.05
52T	Brian Holton	.05
53T	Art Howe	.05
54T	Ken Howell	.05
55T	Bruce Hurst	.05
56T	Chris James	.05
57T	Randy Johnson	1.50
58T	Jimmy Jones	.05
59T	Terry Kennedy	.05
60T	Paul Kilgus	.05
61T	Eric King	.05
62T	Ron Kittle	.05
63T	John Kruk	.05
64T	Randy Kutcher RC	.05
65T	Steve Lake	.05
66T	Mark Langston	.05
67T	Dave LaPoint	.05
68T	Rick Leach	.05
69T	Terry Leach	.05
70T	Jim Levebvre	.05
71T	Al Leiter	.05
72T	Jeffrey Leonard	.05
73T	Derek Lilliquist RC	.05
74T	Rick Mahler	.05
75T	Tom McCarthy RC	.05
76T	Lloyd McClendon	.05
77T	Lance McCullers	.05
78T	Oddibe McDowell	.05
79T	Roger McDowell	.05
80T	Larry McWilliams	.05
81T	Randy Milligan	.05
82T	Mike Moore	.05
83T	Keith Moreland	.05
84T	Mike Morgan	.05
85T	Jamie Moyer	.05
86T	Rob Murphy	.05
87T	Eddie Murray	.40
88T	Pete O'Brien	.05
89T	Gregg Olson	.05
90T	Steve Ontiveros	.05
91T	Jesse Orosco	.05
92T	Spike Owen	.05
93T	Rafael Palmeiro	.35
94T	Clay Parker RC	.05
95T	Jeff Parrett	.05
96T	Lance Parrish	.05
97T	Dennis Powell	.05
98T	Rey Quinones	.05
99T	Doug Rader	.05
100T	Willie Randolph	.05
101T	Shane Rawley	.05
102T	Randy Ready	.05
103T	Bip Roberts	.05
104T	Kenny Rogers RC	.10
105T	Ed Romero	.05
106T	Nolan Ryan	1.00
107T	Luis Salazar	.05
108T	Juan Samuel	.05
109T	Alex Sanchez RC	.05
110T	Deion Sanders RC	.50
111T	Steve Sax	.05
112T	Rick Schu	.05
113T	Dwight Smith RC	.05
114T	Lonnie Smith	.05
115T	Billy Spiers RC	.05
116T	Kent Tekulve	.05
117T	Walt Terrell	.05
118T	Milt Thompson	.05
119T	Dickie Thon	.05
120T	Jeff Torborg	.05
121T	Jeff Treadway	.05
122T	Omar Vizquel RC	.50
123T	Jerome Walton RC	.05
124T	Gary Ward	.05
125T	Claudell Washington	.05
126T	Curt Wilkerson	.05
127T	Eddie Williams	.05
128T	Frank Williams	.05
129T	Ken Williams	.05
130T	Mitch Williams	.05
131T	Steve Wilson RC	.05
---	Topps Magazine Subscription Offer Card	.05

Traded Tiffany

The Topps Traded set was issued in a separately boxed, hobby-only edition. Cards are identical to the regular-issue Topps Traded cards except for the application of a high-gloss to the fronts. Production has been reported as 15,000 sets.

	NM/M
Unopened Set (132):	85.00
Complete Set (132):	50.00
Common Player:	.10

Traded Jackie Robinson Bronze

This 1/4-size metal replica of Robinson's first-ever Topps card was issued to dealers who purchased cases of 1989 Topps Traded sets. Each detail of the 1952 Topps Robinson card is reproduced on the 1-1/4" x 1-3/4" bronze metal mini-card, right down to the stats.

		NM/M
312	Jackie Robinson	10.00

Box Panels

Continuing its practice of printing baseball cards on the bottom panels of its wax pack boxes, Topps in 1989 issued a special 16-card set, printing four cards on each of four different box-bottom panels. The cards are identical in design to the regular 1989 Topps cards. They are designated by letter (from A through P) rather than by number.

		NM/M
Complete Panel Set (4):		7.50
Complete Singles Set: (16):		7.50
Common Panel:		1.50
Common Single Player:		.10
PANEL		1.50
A	George Bell	.10
B	Bill Buckner	.10
C	Darrell Evans	.10
D	Goose Gossage	.10
PANEL		1.50
E	Greg Gross	.10
F	Rickey Henderson	.60
G	Keith Hernandez	.10
H	Tommy Lasorda	.10
PANEL		7.50
I	Jim Rice	.20
J	Cal Ripken Jr.	2.00
K	Nolan Ryan	2.00
L	Mike Schmidt	.75
PANEL		2.00
M	Bruce Sutter	.30
N	Don Sutton	.30
O	Kent Tekulve	.10
P	Dave Winfield	.60

All-Star Glossy Set of 22

The glossy All-Stars were included in the Topps 1989 rack packs. Format was very similar to the sets produced since 1984. Besides the starting lineups of the 1988 All-Star Game, the set included the managers and honorary team captains, Bobby Doerr and Willie Stargell.

		NM/M
Complete Set (22):		3.00
Common Player:		.05
1	Tom Kelly	.05
2	Mark McGwire	.75
3	Paul Molitor	.40
4	Wade Boggs	.50
5	Cal Ripken, Jr.	1.00
6	Jose Canseco	.40
7	Rickey Henderson	.40
8	Dave Winfield	.40
9	Terry Steinbach	.05
10	Frank Viola	.05
11	Bobby Doerr	.05
12	Whitey Herzog	.05
13	Will Clark	.50
14	Ryne Sandberg	.50
15	Bobby Bonilla	.05
16	Ozzie Smith	.40
17	Vince Coleman	.05
18	Andre Dawson	.25
19	Darryl Strawberry	.40
20	Gary Carter	.40
21	Dwight Gooden	.40
22	Willie Stargell	.10

All-Star Glossy Set of 60

For the seventh straight year Topps issued this "send-away" glossy set. Divided into six 10-card sets, it was available only by sending in special offer cards from wax packs. The 2-1/2" x 3-1/2" cards feature full-color photos bordered in white with a thin yellow frame. The player's name appears in small print in the lower-right corner. Red-and-blue-printed flip sides provide basic information. Any of the six 10-card sets were available for $1.25 and six special offer cards. The set was also made available in its complete 60-card set form for $7.50 and 18 special offer cards.

		NM/M
Complete Set (60):		6.00
Common Player:		.05
1	Kirby Puckett	.60
2	Eric Davis	.05
3	Joe Carter	.05
4	Andy Van Slyke	.05
5	Wade Boggs	.60
6	Dave Cone	.05
7	Kent Hrbek	.05
8	Darryl Strawberry	.05
9	Jay Buhner	.05
10	Ron Gant	.05
11	Will Clark	.05
12	Jose Canseco	.35
13	Juan Samuel	.05
14	George Brett	.75
15	Benny Santiago	.05
16	Dennis Eckersley	.40
17	Gary Carter	.50
18	Frank Viola	.05
19	Roberto Alomar	.15
20	Paul Gibson	.05
21	Dave Winfield	.50
22	Howard Johnson	.05
23	Roger Clemens	.65
24	Bobby Bonilla	.05
25	Alan Trammell	.05
26	Kevin McReynolds	.05
27	George Bell	.05
28	Bruce Hurst	.05
29	Mark Grace	.05
30	Tim Belcher	.05
31	Mike Greenwell	.05
32	Glenn Davis	.05
33	Gary Gaetti	.05
34	Ryne Sandberg	.60
35	Rickey Henderson	.50
36	Dwight Evans	.05
37	Doc Gooden	.05
38	Robin Yount	.50
39	Damon Berryhill	.05
40	Chris Sabo	.05
41	Mark McGwire	1.00
42	Ozzie Smith	.60
43	Paul Molitor	.50
44	Andres Galarraga	.05
45	Dave Stewart	.05
46	Tom Browning	.05
47	Cal Ripken, Jr.	1.50
48	Orel Hershiser	.05
49	Dave Gallagher	.05
50	Walt Weiss	.05
51	Don Mattingly	.65
52	Tony Fernandez	.05
53	Tim Raines	.05
54	Jeff Reardon	.05
55	Kirk Gibson	.05
56	Jack Clark	.05
57	Danny Jackson	.05
58	Tony Gwynn	.60
59	Cecil Espy	.05
60	Jody Reed	.05

American Baseball

For the second consecutive year Topps released an 88-card set of baseball cards available in both the United States and the United Kingdom. The mini-sized cards (2-1/4" x 3") are printed on white stock with a low-gloss finish. The game-action color player photo is outlined in red, white and blue and framed in white. Backs are horizontal and include a characterization cartoon along with biographical information and statistics. The cards were sold in packs of five with a stick of bubble gum for 12 pence.

		NM/M
Complete Set (88):		6.00
Common Player:		.05
Wax Pack (5):		.50
Wax Box (48):		8.00
1	Brady Anderson	.05
2	Harold Baines	.05
3	George Bell	.05
4	Wade Boggs	.60
5	Barry Bonds	1.50
6	Bobby Bonilla	.05
7	George Brett	.75
8	Hubie Brooks	.05
9	Tom Brunansky	.05
10	Jay Buhner	.05
11	Brett Butler	.05
12	Jose Canseco	.30
13	Joe Carter	.05
14	Jack Clark	.05
15	Will Clark	.05
16	Roger Clemens	.65
17	Dave Cone	.05
18	Alvin Davis	.05
19	Eric Davis	.05
20	Glenn Davis	.05
21	Andre Dawson	.25
22	Bill Doran	.05
23	Dennis Eckersley	.35
24	Dwight Evans	.05
25	Tony Fernandez	.05
26	Carlton Fisk	.45
27	John Franco	.05
28	Andres Galarraga	.05
29	Ron Gant	.05
30	Kirk Gibson	.05
31	Dwight Gooden	.05
32	Mike Greenwell	.05
33	Mark Gubicza	.05
34	Pedro Guerrero	.05
35	Ozzie Guillen	.05
36	Tony Gwynn	.60
37	Rickey Henderson	.45
38	Orel Hershiser	.05
39	Teddy Higuera	.05
40	Charlie Hough	.05
41	Kent Hrbek	.05
42	Bruce Hurst	.05
43	Bo Jackson	.10
44	Gregg Jefferies	.05
45	Ricky Jordan	.05
46	Wally Joyner	.05
47	Mark Langston	.05
48	Mike Marshall	.05
49	Don Mattingly	.75
50	Fred McGriff	.05
51	Mark McGwire	1.00
52	Kevin McReynolds	.05
53	Paul Molitor	.45
54	Jack Morris	.05
55	Dale Murphy	.20
56	Eddie Murray	.45
57	Pete O'Brien	.05
58	Rafael Palmeiro	.35
59	Gerald Perry	.05
60	Kirby Puckett	.60
61	Tim Raines	.05
62	Johnny Ray	.05
63	Rick Reuschel	.05
64	Cal Ripken	1.50
65	Chris Sabo	.05
66	Juan Samuel	.05
67	Ryne Sandberg	.60
68	Benny Santiago	.05
69	Steve Sax	.05
70	Mike Schmidt	.75
71	Ruben Sierra	.60
72	Ozzie Smith	.60
73	Cory Snyder	.05
74	Dave Stewart	.05
75	Darryl Strawberry	.05
76	Greg Swindell	.05
77	Alan Trammell	.05
78	Fernando Valenzuela	.05
79	Andy Van Slyke	.05
80	Frank Viola	.05
81	Claudell Washington	.05
82	Walt Weiss	.05
83	Lou Whitaker	.05
84	Dave Winfield	.45
85	Mike Witt	.05
86	Gerald Young	.05
87	Robin Yount	.45
88	Checklist	.05

Batting Leaders

The active career batting leaders are showcased in this 22-card set. The 2-1/2" x 3-1/2" cards are printed on super glossy stock with full-color photos and bright red borders. A "Top Active Career Batting Leaders" cup is displayed in a lower corner. The player's name appears above the photo. This set is specially numbered in accordance to career batting average. Wade Boggs is featured on card #1 as the top active career batting leader. The flip sides present batting statistics. One batting leader card was included in each K-Mart blister pack, which also includes 100 cards from the 1989 regular Topps set.

		NM/M
Complete Set (22):		90.00
Common Player:		1.50
1	Wade Boggs	12.00
2	Tony Gwynn	12.00
3	Don Mattingly	16.00
4	Kirby Puckett	12.00
5	George Brett	16.00
6	Pedro Guerrero	1.50
7	Tim Raines	1.50
8	Keith Hernandez	1.50
9	Jim Rice	3.00
10	Paul Molitor	8.00
11	Eddie Murray	8.00
12	Willie McGee	1.50
13	Dave Parker	1.50
14	Julio Franco	1.50
15	Rickey Henderson	8.00
16	Kent Hrbek	1.50
17	Willie Wilson	1.50
18	Johnny Ray	1.50
19	Pat Tabler	1.50
20	Carney Lansford	1.50
21	Robin Yount	8.00
22	Alan Trammell	1.50

Big Baseball

Known by collectors as Topps "Big Baseball," the cards in this 330-card set measure 2-5/8" x 3-3/4" and are patterned after the 1956 Topps cards. The glossy card fronts are horizontally-designed and include two photos of each player, a portrait alongside an action photo. The backs include 1988 and career stats, but are dominated by a color cartoon featuring the player. Members of the 1988 Team U.S.A. Olympic baseball team are included in the set, which was issued in three series of 110 cards each.

		NM/M
Complete Set (330):		9.00
Common Player:		.05
Wax Pack:		.40
Wax Box (36):		7.50
1	Orel Hershiser	.05
2	Harold Reynolds	.05
3	Jody Davis	.05
4	Greg Walker	.05
5	Barry Bonds	1.00
6	Bret Saberhagen	.05
7	Johnny Ray	.05
8	Mike Fiore	.05
9	Juan Castillo	.05
10	Todd Burns	.05
11	Carmelo Martinez	.05
12	Geno Petralli	.05
13	Mel Hall	.05

#	Player	Price
14	Tom Browning	.05
15	Fred McGriff	.05
16	Kevin Elster	.05
17	Tim Leary	.05
18	Jim Rice	.20
19	Bret Barberie	.05
20	Jay Buhner	.05
21	Atlee Hammaker	.05
22	Lou Whitaker	.05
23	Paul Runge	.05
24	Carlton Fisk	.40
25	Jose Lind	.05
26	Mark Gubicza	.05
27	Billy Ripken	.05
28	Mike Pagliarulo	.05
29	Jim Deshaies	.05
30	Mark McLemore	.05
31	Scott Terry	.05
32	Franklin Stubbs	.05
33	Don August	.05
34	Mark McGwire	.75
35	Eric Show	.05
36	Cecil Espy	.05
37	Ron Tingley	.05
38	Mickey Brantley	.05
39	Paul O'Neill	.05
40	Ed Sprague	.05
41	Len Dykstra	.05
42	Roger Clemens	.60
43	Ron Gant	.05
44	Dan Pasqua	.05
45	Jeff Robinson	.05
46	George Brett	.65
47	Bryn Smith	.05
48	Mike Marshall	.05
49	Doug Robbins	.05
50	Don Mattingly	.65
51	Mike Scott	.05
52	Steve Jeltz	.05
53	Dick Schofield	.05
54	Tom Brunansky	.05
55	Gary Sheffield	.45
56	Dave Valle	.05
57	Carney Lansford	.05
58	Tony Gwynn	.50
59	Checklist	.05
60	Damon Berryhill	.05
61	Jack Morris	.05
62	Brett Butler	.05
63	Mickey Hatcher	.05
64	Bruce Sutter	.35
65	Robin Ventura	.05
66	Junior Ortiz	.05
67	Pat Tabler	.05
68	Greg Swindell	.05
69	Jeff Branson	.05
70	Manny Lee	.05
71	Dave Magadan	.05
72	Rich Gedman	.05
73	Tim Raines	.05
74	Mike Maddux	.05
75	Jim Presley	.05
76	Chuck Finley	.05
77	Jose Oquendo	.05
78	Rob Deer	.05
79	Jay Howell	.05
80	Terry Steinbach	.05
81	Eddie Whitson	.05
82	Ruben Sierra	.05
83	Bruce Benedict	.05
84	Fred Manrique	.05
85	John Smiley	.05
86	Mike Macfarlane	.05
87	Rene Gonzales	.05
88	Charles Hudson	.05
89	Les Straker	.05
90	Carmen Castillo	.05
91	Tracy Woodson	.05
92	Tino Martinez	.15
93	Herm Winningham	.05
94	Kelly Gruber	.05
95	Terry Leach	.05
96	Jody Reed	.05
97	Nelson Santovenia	.05
98	Tony Armas	.05
99	Greg Brock	.05
100	Dave Stewart	.05
101	Roberto Alomar	.20
102	Jim Sundberg	.05
103	Albert Hall	.05
104	Steve Lyons	.05
105	Sid Bream	.05
106	Danny Tartabull	.05
107	Rick Dempsey	.05
108	Rich Renteria	.05
109	Ozzie Smith	.50
110	Steve Sax	.05
111	Kelly Downs	.05
112	Larry Sheets	.05
113	Andy Benes	.05
114	Pete O'Brien	.05
115	Kevin McReynolds	.05
116	Juan Berenguer	.05
117	Billy Hatcher	.05
118	Rick Cerone	.05
119	Andre Dawson	.15
120	Storm Davis	.05
121	Devon White	.05
122	Alan Trammell	.05
123	Vince Coleman	.05
124	Al Leiter	.05
125	Dale Sveum	.05
126	Pete Incaviglia	.05
127	Dave Stieb	.05
128	Kevin Mitchell	.05
129	Dave Schmidt	.05
130	Gary Redus	.05
131	Ron Robinson	.05

#	Player	Price
132	Ron Robinson	.05
133	Darnell Coles	.05
134	Benny Santiago	.05
135	John Farrell	.05
136	Willie Wilson	.05
137	Steve Bedrosian	.05
138	Don Slaught	.05
139	Darryl Strawberry	.05
140	Frank Viola	.05
141	Dave Silvestri	.05
142	Carlos Quintana	.05
143	Vance Law	.05
144	Dave Parker	.05
145	Tim Belcher	.05
146	Will Clark	.05
147	Mark Williamson	.05
148	Ozzie Guillen	.05
149	Kirk McCaskill	.05
150	Pat Sheridan	.05
151	Terry Pendleton	.05
152	Roberto Kelly	.05
153	Joey Meyer	.05
154	Mark Grant	.05
155	Joe Carter	.05
156	Steve Buechele	.05
157	Tony Fernandez	.05
158	Jeff Reed	.05
159	Bobby Bonilla	.05
160	Henry Cotto	.05
161	Kurt Stillwell	.05
162	Mickey Morandini	.05
163	Robby Thompson	.05
164	Rick Schu	.05
165	Stan Jefferson	.05
166	Ron Darling	.05
167	Kirby Puckett	.50
168	Bill Doran	.05
169	Dennis Lamp	.05
170	Ty Griffin	.05
171	Ron Hassey	.05
172	Dale Murphy	.15
173	Andres Galarraga	.05
174	Tim Flannery	.05
175	Cory Snyder	.05
176	Checklist	.05
177	Tommy Barrett	.05
178	Dan Petry	.05
179	Billy Masse	.05
180	Terry Kennedy	.05
181	Joe Orsulak	.05
182	Doyle Alexander	.05
183	Willie McGee	.05
184	Jim Gantner	.05
185	Keith Hernandez	.05
186	Greg Gagne	.05
187	Kevin Bass	.05
188	Mark Eichhorn	.05
189	Mark Grace	.15
190	Jose Canseco	.35
191	Bobby Witt	.05
192	Rafael Santana	.05
193	Dwight Evans	.05
194	Greg Booker	.05
195	Brook Jacoby	.05
196	Rafael Belliard	.05
197	Candy Maldonado	.05
198	Mickey Tettleton	.05
199	Barry Larkin	.05
200	Frank White	.05
201	Wally Joyner	.05
202	Chet Lemon	.05
203	Joe Magrane	.05
204	Glenn Braggs	.05
205	Scott Fletcher	.05
206	Gary Ward	.05
207	Nelson Liriano	.05
208	Howard Johnson	.05
209	Kent Hrbek	.05
210	Ken Caminiti	.05
211	Mike Greenwell	.05
212	Ryne Sandberg	.50
213	Joe Slusarski	.05
214	Donnell Nixon	.05
215	Tim Wallach	.05
216	John Kruk	.05
217	Charles Nagy	.05
218	Alvin Davis	.05
219	Oswald Peraza	.05
220	Mike Schmidt	.65
221	Spike Owen	.05
222	Mike Smithson	.05
223	Dion James	.05
224	Ernie Whitt	.05
225	Mike Davis	.05
226	Gene Larkin	.05
227	Pat Combs	.05
228	Jack Howell	.05
229	Ron Oester	.05
230	Paul Gibson	.05
231	Mookie Wilson	.05
232	Glenn Hubbard	.05
233	Shawon Dunston	.05
234	Otis Nixon	.05
235	Melido Perez	.05
236	Jerry Browne	.05
237	Rick Rhoden	.05
238	Bo Jackson	.10
239	Randy Velarde	.05
240	Jack Clark	.05
241	Wade Boggs	.50
242	Lonnie Smith	.05
243	Mike Flanagan	.05
244	Willie Randolph	.05
245	Oddibe McDowell	.05
246	Ricky Jordan	.05
247	Greg Briley	.05
248	Rex Hudler	.05
249	Robin Yount	.40
250	Lance Parrish	.05

#	Player	Price
251	Chris Sabo	.05
252	Mike Henneman	.05
253	Gregg Jefferies	.05
254	Curt Young	.05
255	Andy Van Slyke	.05
256	Rod Booker	.05
257	Rafael Palmeiro	.35
258	Jose Uribe	.05
259	Ellis Burks	.05
260	John Smoltz	.05
261	Tom Foley	.05
262	Lloyd Moseby	.05
263	Jim Poole	.05
264	Gary Gaetti	.05
265	Bob Dernier	.05
266	Harold Baines	.05
267	Tom Candiotti	.05
268	Rafael Ramirez	.05
269	Bob Boone	.05
270	Buddy Bell	.05
271	Rickey Henderson	.40
272	Willie Fraser	.05
273	Eric Davis	.05
274	Jeff Robinson	.05
275	Damaso Garcia	.05
276	Sid Fernandez	.05
277	Stan Javier	.05
278	Marty Barrett	.05
279	Gerald Perry	.05
280	Rob Ducey	.05
281	Mike Scioscia	.05
282	Randy Bush	.05
283	Tom Herr	.05
284	Glenn Wilson	.05
285	Pedro Guerrero	.05
286	Cal Ripken, Jr.	1.00
287	Randy Johnson	.50
288	Julio Franco	.05
289	Ivan Calderon	.05
290	Rich Yett	.05
291	Scott Servais	.05
292	Bill Pecota	.05
293	Ken Phelps	.05
294	Chili Davis	.05
295	Manny Trillo	.05
296	Mike Boddicker	.05
297	Geronimo Berroa	.05
298	Todd Stottlemyre	.05
299	Kirk Gibson	.05
300	Wally Backman	.05
301	Hubie Brooks	.05
302	Von Hayes	.05
303	Matt Nokes	.05
304	Dwight Gooden	.05
305	Walt Weiss	.05
306	Mike LaValliere	.05
307	Cris Carpenter	.05
308	Ted Wood	.05
309	Jeff Russell	.05
310	Dave Gallagher	.05
311	Andy Allanson	.05
312	Craig Reynolds	.05
313	Kevin Seitzer	.05
314	Dave Winfield	.40
315	Andy McGaffigan	.05
316	Nick Esasky	.05
317	Jeff Blauser	.05
318	George Bell	.05
319	Eddie Murray	.40
320	Mark Davidson	.05
321	Juan Samuel	.05
322	Jim Abbott	.05
323	Kal Daniels	.05
324	Mike Brumley	.05
325	Gary Carter	.05
326	Dave Henderson	.40
327	Checklist	.05
328	Garry Templeton	.05
329	Pat Perry	.05
330	Paul Molitor	.40

Coins

Similar in format to previous Topps coins, this 60-piece set features 1-1/2" diameter coins with rolled colored edges. A shooting star device printed over the player photo gives his name, team and position. Backs have a few biographical details and a summary of the player's previous season performance printed in black on silver. The coins were sold three per pack, with each pack including an offer card for an album to house the pieces.

	NM/M
Factory Boxed Set (60):	15.00
Complete Set (60):	7.50
Common Player:	.10
Wax Pack (3):	.50
Wax Box (36):	8.00

#	Player	Price
1	Kirk Gibson	.10
2	Orel Hershiser	.10
3	Chris Sabo	.50
4	Tony Gwynn	.50
5	Brett Butler	.10
6	Bobby Bonilla	.10
7	Jack Clark	.10
8	Will Clark	.10
9	Eric Davis	.10
10	Glenn Davis	.10
11	Andre Dawson	.15
12	John Franco	.10
13	Andres Galarraga	.10
14	Dwight Gooden	.10
15	Mark Grace	.10
16	Pedro Guerrero	.10
17	Ricky Jordan	.10
18	Mike Marshall	.10
19	Dale Murphy	.15
20	Eddie Murray	.40
21	Gerald Perry	.10
22	Tim Raines	.10
23	Juan Samuel	.10
24	Benito Santiago	.10
25	Ozzie Smith	.50
26	Darryl Strawberry	.10
27	Andy Van Slyke	.10
28	Gerald Young	.10
29	Jose Canseco	.35
30	Frank Viola	.10
31	Walt Weiss	.10
32	Wade Boggs	.50
33	Harold Baines	.10
34	George Brett	.75
35	Jay Buhner	.10
36	Joe Carter	.10
37	Roger Clemens	.60
38	Alvin Davis	.10
39	Tony Fernandez	.10
40	Carlton Fisk	.40
41	Mike Greenwell	.10
42	Kent Hrbek	.10
43	Don Mattingly	.75
44	Fred McGriff	.10
45	Mark McGwire	1.00
46	Paul Molitor	.40
47	Rafael Palmeiro	.35
48	Kirby Puckett	.50
49	Johnny Ray	.10
50	Cal Ripken, Jr.	1.50
51	Ruben Sierra	.10
52	Pete Stanicek	.10
53	Dave Stewart	.10
54	Greg Swindell	.10
55	Danny Tartabull	.10
56	Alan Trammell	.10
57	Lou Whitaker	.10
58	Dave Winfield	.40
59	Mike Witt	.10
60	Robin Yount	.40

Double Headers All-Stars

This scarce test issue was produced in two versions, an All-Stars set and a set of exclusively Mets and Yankees players. The "cards" are two-sided miniature (1-5/8" x 2-1/4") reproductions of the player's 1989 Topps card and his Topps rookie card, encased in a clear plastic stand.

	NM/M
Complete Set (24):	9.00
Common Player:	.50
Wax Pack (1):	.50
Wax Box (24):	9.00
(1) Alan Ashby	.50
(2) Wade Boggs	1.00
(3) Bobby Bonilla	.50
(4) Jose Canseco	.65
(5) Will Clark	.50
(6) Roger Clemens	1.25
(7) Andre Dawson	.65
(8) Dennis Eckersley	.65
(9) Carlton Fisk	.75
(10) John Franco	.50
(11) Julio Franco	.50
(12) Kirk Gibson	.50
(13) Mike Greenwell	.50
(14) Orel Hershiser	.50
(15) Danny Jackson	.50
(16) Don Mattingly	1.25
(17) Mark McGwire	2.00
(18) Kirby Puckett	1.00
(19) Ryne Sandberg	1.00
(20) Ozzie Smith	1.00
(21) Darryl Strawberry	.50
(22) Alan Trammell	.50
(23) Andy Van Slyke	.50
(24) Frank Viola	.50

Double Headers Mets/Yankees Proofs

In advance of its special Mets/Yankees Double Headers novelty issue, Topps prepared a series of proof versions featuring four players from each of the New York teams. Like the later issues, these Double Headers feature miniature versions of the players' Topps rookie cards in a small plastic stand-up frame. However, the proof versions have the rookie cards back-to-back with the players' 1988 Topps cards, rather than 1989 as on the regularly issued pieces. Two different types of wrappers are found for the proofs, an opaque paper envelope picturing Gary Carter's piece and a cellophane wrapper with the proof issue's checklist.

	NM/M
Complete Set (8):	425.00
Common Player:	50.00
(1) Gary Carter	125.00
(2) Ron Darling	50.00
(3) Dwight Gooden	50.00
(4) Darryl Strawberry	50.00
(1) Rickey Henderson	125.00
(2) Don Mattingly	200.00
(3) Dave Righetti	50.00
(4) Dave Winfield	125.00

Double Headers Mets/Yankees

This was a regionally issued test for the concept of two "mini" baseball cards of a player encapsulated in clear plastic. Only New York players are represented in the set. Each double header plastic frame holds miniature (1-5/8" x 2-1/4") versions of the player's 1989 Topps card, and his first Topps card, printed on thin paper. The Double Headers of players who also appeared in the All-Star issue are indistinguishable in this version. The stand-ups were sold in boxes of 24 paper-wrapped pieces. It is reported that each box contains a full set. The un-numbered pieces are checklisted here in alphabetical order by team.

	NM/M
Complete Set (24):	150.00
Common Player:	10.00
New York Mets Team Set:	85.00
(1) Gary Carter	25.00
(2) David Cone	10.00
(3) Ron Darling	10.00
(4) Len Dykstra	10.00
(5) Doc Gooden	10.00
(6) Keith Hernandez	10.00
(7) Gregg Jefferies	10.00
(8) Howard Johnson	10.00
(9) Kevin McReynolds	10.00
(10) Randy Myers	10.00
(11) Darryl Strawberry	.50
(12) Tim Teufel	10.00
(13) Mookie Wilson	10.00
New York Yankees Team Set:	65.00
(14) Richard Dotson	10.00
(15) Rickey Henderson	25.00
(16) Don Mattingly	3.00
(17) Mike Pagliarulo	10.00
(18) Ken Phelps	10.00
(19) Rick Rhoden	10.00
(20) Dave Righetti	10.00
(21) Rafael Santana	10.00
(22) Steve Sax	10.00
(23) Claudell Washington	10.00
(24) Dave Winfield	10.00

Gallery of Champions

Topps continued its issue of 1/4-size metallic ingot reproductions of current-year baseball cards with aluminum, bronze and sterling silver sets in 1989. Again the players represented major award winners from the previous season. The

metal mini-cards were sold only as complete sets. Dealers who ordered bronze and silver sets could receive as a bonus a pewter version of the Jose Canseco ingot.

	NM/M
Complete Aluminum Set (12):	12.50
Complete Bronze Set (12):	50.00
Complete Silver Set (12):	120.00
(1a) Wade Boggs/Aluminum	3.50
(1b) Wade Boggs/Bronze	10.00
(1s) Wade Boggs/Silver	25.00
(2a) Jose Canseco/Aluminum	2.00
(2b) Jose Canseco/Bronze	5.00
(2s) Jose Canseco/Silver	15.00
(2p) Jose Canseco/Pewter	7.50
(3a) Will Clark/Aluminum	1.00
(3b) Will Clark/Bronze	3.50
(3s) Will Clark/Silver	7.50
(4a) Dennis Eckersley/Aluminum	1.50
(4b) Dennis Eckersley/Bronze	5.00
(4s) Dennis Eckersley/Silver	10.00
(5a) John Franco/Aluminum	1.00
(5b) John Franco/Bronze	3.50
(5s) John Franco/Silver	7.50
(6a) Kirk Gibson/Aluminum	1.00
(6b) Kirk Gibson/Bronze	3.50
(6s) Kirk Gibson/Silver	7.50
(7a) Tony Gwynn/Aluminum	3.50
(7b) Tony Gwynn/Bronze	10.00
(7s) Tony Gwynn/Silver	25.00
(8a) Orel Hershiser/Aluminum	1.00
(8b) Orel Hershiser/Bronze	3.50
(8s) Orel Hershiser/Silver	7.50
(9a) Chris Sabo/Aluminum	1.00
(9b) Chris Sabo/Bronze	3.50
(9s) Chris Sabo/Silver	7.50
(10a) Darryl Strawberry/Aluminum	1.00
(10b) Darryl Strawberry/Bronze	3.50
(10s) Darryl Strawberry/Silver	7.50
(11a) Frank Viola/Aluminum	1.00
(11b) Frank Viola/Bronze	3.50
(11s) Frank Viola/Silver	7.50
(12a) Walt Weiss/Aluminum	1.00
(12b) Walt Weiss/Bronze	3.50
(12s) Walt Weiss/Silver	7.50

Glossy Rookies Set of 22

Bearing the same design and style of the past two years, Topps featured the top first-year players from the 1988 season in this glossy set. The full-color player photo appears beneath the "1988 Rookies" banner. The player's name is displayed beneath the photo. The flip side features the "1988 Rookies Commemorative Set" logo followed by the player ID and card number. Glossy rookies were found only in 100-card jumbo cello packs.

	NM/M
Complete Set (22):	5.00
Common Player:	.10
1 Roberto Alomar	.50
2 Brady Anderson	.15
3 Tim Belcher	.15
4 Damon Berryhill	.15
5 Jay Buhner	.15
6 Kevin Elster	.15
7 Cecil Espy	.15
8 Dave Gallagher	.15

9	Ron Gant	.25
10	Paul Gibson	.15
11	Mark Grace	.50
12	Darrin Jackson	.15
13	Gregg Jefferies	.25
14	Ricky Jordan	.15
15	Al Leiter	.15
16	Melido Perez	.15
17	Chris Sabo	.15
18	Nelson Santovenia	.15
19	Mackey Sasser	.15
20	Gary Sheffield	2.00
21	Walt Weiss	.15
22	David Wells	.15

Heads Up! Test Issue

Much rarer than the 1990 issue, this 24-card test set debuted the bizarre "shrunken head" format of a die-cut player's head and cap printed on heavy cardboard, approximately 4-1/2" x 6-1/2" in size and sold one per pack. Backs feature both a small plastic suction cup and an adhesive strip for hanging the card. The player's name and team are printed in black on the back. Except for the copyright date on back, the cards of players from the 1989 test set which were repeated in the 1990 regular issue are virtually identical and often sell for much less than those players who were unique to the 1989 set.

		NM/M
Complete Set (24):		600.00
Common Player:		12.00
1	Tony Gwynn	65.00
2	Will Clark	17.50
3	Dwight Gooden	12.00
4	Ricky Jordan	12.00
5	Ken Griffey Jr.	150.00
6	Darryl Strawberry	17.50
7	Frank Viola	17.50
8	Bo Jackson	15.00
9	Ryne Sandberg	65.00
10	Gregg Jefferies	17.50
11	Wade Boggs	65.00
12	Ellis Burks	17.50
13	Gary Sheffield	25.00
14	Mark McGwire	150.00
15	Mark Grace	17.50
16	Jim Abbott	12.00
17	Ozzie Smith	65.00
18	Jose Canseco	25.00
19	Don Mattingly	75.00
20	Kirby Puckett	65.00
21	Eric Davis	17.50
22	Mike Greenwell	17.50
23	Dale Murphy	30.00
24	Mike Schmidt	125.00

Mini League Leaders

This 77-card set features baseball's statistical leaders from the 1988 season. It is referred to as a "mini" set because of the cards' small (2-1/8" x 3") size. The glossy cards feature action photos that have a soft focus on all edges. The player's team and name appear along the bottom of the card. The back features a head-shot of the player along with his 1988 season ranking and stats.

		NM/M
Complete Set (77):		3.00
Common Player:		.05
Wax Pack (7):		.25
Wax Box (36):		6.00
1	Dale Murphy	.20
2	Gerald Perry	.05
3	Andre Dawson	.25
4	Greg Maddux	.65
5	Rafael Palmeiro	.45
6	Tom Browning	.05
7	Kal Daniels	.05
8	Eric Davis	.05
9	John Franco	.05
10	Danny Jackson	.05
11	Barry Larkin	.05
12	Jose Rijo	.05
13	Chris Sabo	.05
14	Nolan Ryan	1.00
15	Mike Scott	.05
16	Gerald Young	.05
17	Kirk Gibson	.05
18	Orel Hershiser	.05
19	Steve Sax	.05
20	John Tudor	.05
21	Hubie Brooks	.05
22	Andres Galarraga	.05
23	Otis Nixon	.05
24	Dave Cone	.05
25	Sid Fernandez	.05
26	Dwight Gooden	.05
27	Kevin McReynolds	.05
28	Darryl Strawberry	.05
29	Juan Samuel	.05
30	Bobby Bonilla	.05
31	Sid Bream	.05
32	Jim Gott	.05
33	Andy Van Slyke	.05
34	Vince Coleman	.05
35	Jose DeLeon	.05
36	Joe Magrane	.05
37	Ozzie Smith	.65
38	Todd Worrell	.05
39	Tony Gwynn	.65
40	Brett Butler	.05
41	Will Clark	.65
42	Rick Reuschel	.05
43	Checklist	.05
44	Eddie Murray	.50
45	Wade Boggs	.65
46	Roger Clemens	.70
47	Dwight Evans	.05
48	Mike Greenwell	.65
49	Bruce Hurst	.05
50	Johnny Ray	.05
51	Doug Jones	.05
52	Greg Swindell	.05
53	Gary Pettis	.05
54	George Brett	.70
55	Mark Gubicza	.05
56	Willie Wilson	.05
57	Teddy Higuera	.05
58	Paul Molitor	.50
59	Allan Anderson	.05
60	Gary Gaetti	.05
61	Kirby Puckett	.50
62	Jeff Reardon	.05
63	Frank Viola	.05
64	Jack Clark	.05
65	Rickey Henderson	.50
66	Dave Winfield	.50
67	Jose Canseco	.35
68	Dennis Eckersley	.45
69	Mark McGwire	.75
70	Dave Stewart	.05
71	Alvin Davis	.05
72	Mark Langston	.05
73	Harold Reynolds	.05
74	George Bell	.05
75	Tony Fernandez	.05
76	Fred McGriff	.05

Stickercards

Once again in 1989 Topps used a stickercard as cardboard backing for its paper sticker issue. Measuring 2-1/8"x3", the cards are found with either one or two player stickers on back. The stickercards have a player photo on a background of graduated color. Minimal stats and biographic data are presented at the bottom. Values shown are for complete stickercard/sticker(s), without regard to which stickers are on back.

		NM/M
Complete Set (66):		5.00
Common Player:		.05
Wax Pack (5):		.25
Wax Box (48):		6.00
1	George Brett	.65
2	Don Mattingly	.65
3	Mark McGwire	.75
4	Julio Franco	.05
5	Harold Reynolds	.05
6	Lou Whitaker	.05
7	Wade Boggs	.50
8	Gary Gaetti	.05
9	Paul Molitor	.45
10	Tony Fernandez	.05
11	Cal Ripken Jr.	1.00
12	Alan Trammell	.05
13	Jose Canseco	.30
14	Joe Carter	.05
15	Dwight Evans	.05
16	Mike Greenwell	.05
17	Dave Henderson	.05
18	Rickey Henderson	.45
19	Kirby Puckett	.50
20	Dave Winfield	.45
21	Robin Yount	.45
22	Bob Boone	.05
23	Carlton Fisk	.45
24	Geno Petralli	.05
25	Roger Clemens	.65
26	Mark Gubicza	.05
27	Dave Stewart	.05
28	Teddy Higuera	.05
29	Bruce Hurst	.05
30	Frank Viola	.05
31	Dennis Eckersley	.40
32	Doug Jones	.05
33	Jeff Reardon	.05
34	Will Clark	.05
35	Glenn Davis	.05
36	Andres Galarraga	.05
37	Juan Samuel	.05
38	Ryne Sandberg	.50
39	Steve Sax	.05
40	Bobby Bonilla	.05
41	Howard Johnson	.05
42	Vance Law	.05
43	Shawon Dunston	.05
44	Barry Larkin	.05
45	Ozzie Smith	.05
46	Barry Bonds	1.00
47	Eric Davis	.05
48	Andre Dawson	.25
49	Kirk Gibson	.05
50	Tony Gwynn	.50
51	Kevin McReynolds	.05
52	Rafael Palmeiro	.40
53	Darryl Strawberry	.05
54	Andy Van Slyke	.05
55	Gary Carter	.45
56	Mike LaValliere	.05
57	Benito Santiago	.05
58	David Cone	.05
59	Dwight Gooden	.05
60	Orel Hershiser	.05
61	Tom Browning	.05
62	Danny Jackson	.05
63	Bob Knepper	.05
64	Mark Davis	.05
65	John Franco	.05
66	Randy Myers	.05

Stickers

Topps' 1989 stickers were produced in two formats. Some measure 2-1/8" x 3" while there were 128 pairs of half-size (1-1/2" x 2-1/8") stickers. All stickers are attached to Super Star stickercards from which they can be peeled and affixed in a special Yearbook which was sold separately for 50 cents. Stickers have large center photos with white borders. Above and below are zipping fastball graphics trailing graduated color bars (blues for N.L., reds for A.L.). A tiny black sticker number is in the lower-right corner. There is no player name on the stickers; the albums have a box under each space with player data. The half-size stickers are printed in pairs and are checklisted in that fashion. Values given are for complete sticker(s)/stickercard combinations, but without regard to which stickercard is on back.

		NM/M
Complete Set (326):		11.00
Common Player/Pair:		.05

Album:		2.00
1-230	George Bell, Jeff Ballard	.05
2-272	Gary Carter, Steve Farr	.25
3-324	Doug Jones, Mark Grace	.05
4-320	John Franco, Cecil Espy	.05
5-322	Andre Dawson, Ron Gant	.15
6-326	Pat Tabler, Walt Weiss	.05
7-317	Tom Browning, Tim Belcher	.05
8-239	Jeff Reardon, Larry Sheets	.05
9-325	Wade Boggs, Chris Sabo	.30
10-319	Kevin McReynolds, Jay Buhner	.05
11-323	Jose Canseco, Paul Gibson	.20
12-318	Orel Hershiser, Damon Berryhill	.05
13-231	Dave Smith, Mickey Tettleton	.05
14-302	Kevin Bass, Jack McDowell	.05
15-232	Mike Scott, Pete Stanicek	.05
16-256	Bill Doran, Jim Rice	.10
17-207	Rafael Ramirez, Andy Allanson	.05
18-181	Buddy Bell, Jack Howell	.05
19-214	Billy Hatcher, John Farrell	.05
20-275	Nolan Ryan, Frank Tanana	.50
21	Glenn Davis	.05
22	Bob Knepper	.05
23-211	Gerald Young, Tom Candiotti	.05
24-208	Dion James, Julio Franco	.05
25-243	Bruce Sutter, Jeff Russell	.20
26-310	Andres Thomas, Tommy John	.05
27-200	Zane Smith, B.J. Surhoff	.05
28-198	Ozzie Virgil, Teddy Higuera	.05
29-269	Rick Mahler, Floyd Bannister	.05
30-219	Albert Hall, Mickey Brantley	.05
31-203	Pete Smith, Jim Gantner	.05
32	Dale Murphy	.20
33	Gerald Perry	.05
34-177	Ron Gant, Chili Davis	.05
35-244	Bob Horner, Mike Stanley	.05
36-313	Willie McGee, Rafael Santana	.05
37-288	Luis Alicea, Greg Gagne	.05
38-279	Tony Pena, Gary Pettis	.05
39-184	Todd Worrell, Kirk McCaskill	.05
40-228	Pedro Guerrero, Bill Swift	.05
41-174	Tom Brunansky, Dick Schofield	.05
42-262	Terry Pendleton, Frank White	.05
43	Vince Coleman	.05
44	Ozzie Smith	.60
45-240	Jose Oquendo, Cecil Espy	.05
46-191	Vance Law, Pat Borders	.05
47-258	Rafael Palmeiro, Bob Stanley	.25
48-213	Greg Maddux, Greg Swindell	.30
49-229	Shawon Dunston, Jose Bautista	.05
50-210	Mark Grace, Cory Snyder	.05
51-187	Damon Berryhill, Kelly Gruber	.05
52-192	Rick Sutcliffe, Rance Mulliniks	.05
53-291	Jamie Moyer, Juan Berenguer	.05
54	Andre Dawson	.25
55	Ryne Sandberg	.60
56-284	Calvin Schiraldi, Jeff Reardon	.05
57-308	Steve Sax, Jack Clark	.05
58-263	Mike Scioscia, Bret Saberhagen	.05
59-298	Alfredo Griffin, Steve Lyons	.05
60-202	Fernando Valenzuela, Rob Deer	.05
61-286	Jay Howell, Dan Gladden	.05
62-305	Tim Leary, Bobby Thigpen	.05
63-212	John Shelby, Brook Jacoby	.05
64-306	John Tudor, John Candelaria	.05
65	Orel Hershiser	.05
66	Kirk Gibson	.05
67-223	Mike Marshall, Jim Presley	.05
68-206	Luis Rivera, Dale Sveum	.05
69-311	Tim Burke, Mike Pagliarulo	.05
70-253	Tim Wallach, Rich Gedman	.05
71-265	Pascual Perez, Bo Jackson	.05
72-185	Hubie Brooks, Fred McGriff	.05
73-250	Jeff Parrett, Steve Buechele	.05
74-316	Dennis Martinez, Rich Dotson	.05
75-285	Andy McGaffigan, Bert Blyleven	.05
76	Andres Galarraga	.05
77	Rock Raines	.05
78-287	Nelson Santovenia, Kent Hrbek	.05
79-261	Rick Reuschel, Mike Boddicker	.05
80-276	Mike Aldrete, Luis Salazar	.05
81-247	Kelly Downs, Mitch Williams	.05
82-283	Jose Uribe, Chet Lemon	.05
83-190	Mike Krukow, Mike Flanagan	.05
84-179	Kevin Mitchell, Devon White	.05
85-195	Brett Butler, Tom Henke	.05
86-252	Don Robinson, Dwight Evans	.05
87	Robby Thompson	.05
88	Will Clark	.05
89-188	Candy Maldonado, Lloyd Moseby	.05
90-180	Len Dykstra, Bryan Harvey	.05
91-234	Howard Johnson, Rene Gonzalez	.05
92-266	Roger McDowell, Kurt Stillwell	.05
93-222	Keith Hernandez, Steve Balboni	.05
94-178	Gary Carter, Brian Downing	.05
95-277	Kevin McReynolds, Jack Morris	.05
96-307	David Cone, Dave Righetti	.05
97-175	Randy Myers, Bob Boone	.05
98	Darryl Strawberry	.05
99	Doc Gooden	.05
100-257	Ron Darling, Marty Barrett	.05
101-201	Benny Santiago, Greg Brock	.05
102-273	John Kruk, Mike Henneman	.05
103-242	Chris Brown, Ruben Sierra	.05
104-255	Roberto Alomar, Mike Greenwell	.10
105-290	Keith Moreland, Tim Laudner	.05
106-217	Randy Ready, Scott Bailes	.05
107-267	Marvell Wynne, Danny Tartabull	.05
108-176	Lance McCullers, Mike Witt	.05
109	Tony Gwynn	.60
110	Mark Davis	.05
111-236	Andy Hawkins, Tom Niedenfuer	.05
112-233	Steve Bedrosian, Jim Traber	.05
113-196	Phil Bradley, Glenn Braggs	.05
114-189	Steve Jeltz, Tony Fernandez	.05
115-209	Von Hayes, Bud Black	.05
116-245	Kevin Gross, Charlie Hough	.05
117-218	Juan Samuel, Henry Cotto	.05
118-274	Shane Rawley, Doyle Alexander	.05
119-186	Chris James, Jimmy Key	.05
120	Mike Schmidt	.65
121	Don Carman	.05
122-280	Bruce Ruffin, Matt Nokes	.05
123-246	Bob Walk, Scott Fletcher	.05
124-278	John Smiley, Tom Brookens	.05
125-301	Sid Bream, Dan Pasqua	.05
126-251	Jose Lind, Lee Smith	.05
127-309	Barry Bonds, Willie Randolph	.40
128-294	Mike LaValliere, Gene Larkin	.05
129-225	Jeff D. Robinson, Scott Bradley	.05
130-295	Mike Dunne, Dave Gallagher	.05
131	Bobby Bonilla	.05
132	Andy Van Slyke	.05
133-241	Rafael Belliard, Jose Guzman	.05
134	Nick Esasky, Dan Plesac	.05
135-300	Bo Diaz, Fred Manrique	.05
136-221	John Franco, Mark Langston	.05
137-312	Barry Larkin, Rickey Henderson	.25
138-173	Eric Davis, Ron Hassey	.05
139-299	Jeff Treadway, Carlton Fisk	.05
140-254	Jose Rijo, Ellis Burks	.05
141-220	Tom Browning, Mike Moore	.05
142	Chris Sabo	.05
143	Danny Jackson	.05
144-199	Kal Daniels, Jeffrey Leonard	.05
145	Rickey Henderson/AS	.50
146	Paul Molitor/AS	.25
147	Wade Boggs/AS	.35
148	Jose Canseco/AS	.20
149	Dave Winfield/AS	.05
150	Cal Ripken Jr./AS	.50
151	Mark McGwire/AS	.40
152	Terry Steinbach/AS	.05
153	Frank Viola/AS	.05
154	Vince Coleman/AS	.05
155	Ryne Sandberg/AS	.35
156	Andre Dawson/AS	.15
157	Darryl Strawberry/AS	.05
158	Bobby Bonilla/AS	.05
159	Will Clark/AS	.05
160	Gary Carter/AS	.05
161	Ozzie Smith/AS	.35
162	Doc Gooden/AS	.05
163-268	Dave Stewart, Willie Wilson	.05
164-297	Dave Henderson, Ivan Calderon	.05
165-321	Terry Steinbach, Dave Gallagher	.05
166-264	Bob Welch, Kevin Seitzer	.05
167-224	Dennis Eckersley, Rey Quinones	.30
168-235	Walt Weiss, Terry Kennedy	.05
169-296	Dave Parker, Melido Perez	.05
170-289	Carney Lansford, Gary Gaetti	.05
171	Jose Canseco	.35
172	Mark McGwire	.75
182	Johnny Ray	.05
183	Wally Joyner	.05
193	George Bell	.05
194	Dave Steib	.05
204	Paul Molitor	.05
205	Robin Yount	.50
215	Doug Jones	.05
216	Joe Carter	.05
226	Harold Reynolds	.05
237	Alvin Davis	.05
247	Cal Ripken Jr.	1.00
238	Eddie Murray	.50
248	Pete O'Brien	.05
249	Pete Incaviglia	.05
259	Roger Clemens	.65
260	Wade Boggs	.60
270	George Brett	.65
271	Mark Gubicza	.05
281	Alan Trammell	.05
282	Lou Whitaker	.05
292	Frank Viola	.05
293	Kirby Puckett	.60
303	Ozzie Guillen	.05
304	Harold Baines	.05
314	Don Mattingly	.65
315	Dave Winfield	.50

LJN Baseball Talk

Another generation of "talking baseball cards" was produced by Topps and the LJN Toy Co. in 1989. After purchasing a hand-held player, collectors could buy sets of four "Baseball Talk Collection" cards for about $4. The 3-1/4" x 5-1/4" cards have a plastic sheet laminated on their backs containing information about the player which could be heard by inserting the card into the player. Fronts of the cards of players active in 1989 reproduce their 1989 Topps cards. The cards of earlier stars reproduce various older Topps cards of those players. Narrators on the cards were Don Drysdale, Joe Torre and Mel Allen.

1989 Topps

	NM/M
Complete Set (164):	125.00
Common Player:	1.00
Record Player:	30.00

1 1975 World Series Game 6 ... 1.00
2 1986 World Series Game 6 ... 1.00
3 1986 ALCS Game 6 1.00
4 1956 World Series Game 5 ... 1.00
5 1986 NLCS Game 6 1.00
6 1969 World Series Game 5 ... 1.00
7 1984 World Series Game 5 ... 1.00
8 1988 World Series Game 1 ... 1.00
9 Reggie Jackson 4.00
10 Brooks Robinson 1.50
11 Billy Williams 1.50
12 Bobby Thomson 1.50
13 Harmon Killebrew 1.50
14 Johnny Bench 2.00
15 Tom Seaver 2.00
16 Willie Stargell 1.50
17 Ernie Banks 4.00
18 Gaylord Perry 1.50
19 Bill Mazeroski 1.50
20 Babe Ruth 7.50
21 Lou Gehrig 6.00
22 Ty Cobb 5.00
23 Bob Gibson 1.50
24 Al Kaline 1.50
25 Rod Carew 1.50
26 Lou Brock 1.50
27 Stan Musial 4.00
28 Joe Morgan 1.50
29 Willie McCovey 1.50
30 Duke Snider 4.00
31 Whitey Ford 4.00
32 Eddie Mathews 1.50
33 Carl Yastrzemski 2.00
34 Pete Rose 7.50
35 Hank Aaron (1976) 6.00
36 Ralph Kiner 1.50
37 Steve Carlton 1.50
38 Roberto Clemente 7.50
39 Don Drysdale 1.50
40 Robin Roberts 1.50
41 Hank Aaron (1954) 6.00
42 Dave Winfield 2.00
43 Alan Trammell 1.00
44 Darryl Strawberry 1.00
45 Ozzie Smith 3.00
46 Kirby Puckett 3.00
47 Will Clark 1.00
48 Keith Hernandez 1.00
49 Wally Joyner 1.00
50 Mike Scott 1.00
51 Eric Davis 1.00
52 George Brett 4.00
53 George Bell 1.00
54 Tommy Lasorda 1.00
55 Rickey Henderson 2.00
56 Robin Yount 2.00
57 Wade Boggs 3.00
58 Roger Clemens 1.00
59 Vince Coleman 1.00
60 Jose Canseco 1.50
61 Fernando Valenzuela 1.00
62 Tony Gwynn 3.00
63 Dwight Gooden 1.00
64 Mark McGwire 6.00
65 Jack Clark 1.00
66 Dale Murphy 1.25
67 Kirk Gibson 1.00
68 Jack Morris 1.00
69 Ryne Sandberg 3.00
70 Nolan Ryan 9.00
71 John Tudor 1.00
72 Mike Schmidt 4.00
73 Dave Righetti 1.00
74 Pedro Guerrero 1.00
75 Rick Sutcliffe 1.00
76 Gary Carter 2.00
77 Cal Ripken Jr. 9.00
78 Andre Dawson 1.25
79 Andy Van Slyke 1.00
80 Tim Raines 1.00
81 Frank Viola 1.00
82 Don Mattingly 4.00
83 Rick Reuschel 1.00
84 Willie McGee 1.00
85 Mark Langston 1.00
86 Ron Darling 1.00
87 Gregg Jefferies 1.00
88 Harold Baines 1.00
89 Eddie Murray 1.00
90 Barry Larkin 1.00
91 Gary Gaetti 1.00
92 Bret Saberhagen 1.00
93 Roger McDowell 1.00
94 Joe Magrane 1.00
95 Juan Samuel 1.00
96 Bert Blyleven 1.00
97 Kal Daniels 1.00
98 Kevin Bass 1.00
99 Glenn Davis 1.00
100 Steve Sax 1.00
101 Rich Gossage 1.00
102 Roger Craig 1.00
103 Carney Lansford 1.00
104 Joe Carter 1.00
105 Bruce Sutter 2.00
106 Barry Bonds 9.00
107 Danny Jackson 1.00
108 Mike Flanagan 1.00
109 Dwight Evans 1.00
110 Ron Guidry 1.00
111 Bruce Hurst 1.00
112 Jim Rice 1.25
113 Oddibe McDowell 1.00
114 Bobby Bonilla 1.00
115 Bob Welch 1.00
116 Dave Parker 1.00
117 Tim Wallach 1.00
118 Tom Henke 1.00
119 Mike Greenwell 1.00
120 Kevin Seitzer 1.00
121 Randy Myers 1.00
122 Andres Galarraga 1.00
123 Orel Hershiser 1.00
124 Cory Snyder 1.00
125 Mike Witt 1.00
126 Mike LaValliere 1.00
127 Pete Incaviglia 1.00
128 Dennis Eckersley 2.00
129 Jimmy Key 1.00
130 John Franco 1.00
131 Dan Plesac 1.00
132 Tony LaRussa 1.00
133 Hubie Brooks 1.00
134 Chili Davis 1.00
135 Bob Boone 1.00
136 Jeff Reardon 1.00
137 Candy Maldonado 1.00
138 Mike Marshall 1.00
139 Tommy John 1.00
140 Chris Sabo 1.00
141 Alvin Davis 1.00
142 Frank White 1.00
143 Harold Reynolds 1.00
144 Lee Smith 1.00
145 John Kruk 1.00
146 Tony Fernandez 1.00
147 Steve Bedrosian 1.00
148 Benito Santiago 1.00
149 Ozzie Guillen 1.00
150 Gerald Perry 1.00
151 Carlton Fisk 2.00
152 Tom Brunansky 1.00
153 Paul Molitor 2.00
154 Todd Worrell 1.00
155 Brett Butler 1.00
156 Sparky Anderson 1.00
157 Kent Hrbek 1.00
158 Frank Tanana 1.00
159 Kevin Mitchell 1.00
160 Charlie Hough 1.00
161 Doug Jones 1.00
162 Lou Whitaker 1.00
163 Fred Lynn 1.00
--- Checklist .50

Sport Shots Portfolios

In its second year, the number of baseball card folders produced by Shaeffer Eaton reproducing current Topps baseball cards was drastically reduced, from 130 to 39. The format remains the same, a 9-1/2" x 11-3/4" cardboard two-pocket folder. The 1989 portfolios are considerably scarcer than the 1988s.

	NM/M
Complete Set (39):	40.00
Common Player:	1.00

10 Andre Dawson 1.25
30 Doc Gooden 1.00
70 Mark McGwire 4.00
85 Kevin McReynolds 1.00
110 Paul Molitor 1.50
120 Frank Viola 1.00
145 Dave Stewart 1.00
180 Mike Scott 1.00
200 George Brett 2.50
205 Dwight Evans 1.00
230 Ozzie Smith 2.00
233 Gregg Jefferies 1.00
260 Dave Winfield 1.50
300 Darryl Strawberry 1.00
330 Eric Davis 1.00
335 Dave Righetti 1.00
340 Kirk Gibson 1.00
370 Dennis Eckersley 1.25
380 Rickey Henderson 1.50
425 Jay Howell 1.00
450 Roger Clemens 2.50
480 Keith Hernandez 1.00
500 Jose Canseco 1.25
527 Dave Henderson 1.00
550 Orel Hershiser 1.00
570 Tony Gwynn 2.00
582 Mike A. Marshall 1.00
590 Andres Galarraga 1.00
600 Wade Boggs 2.00
630 Mike Greenwell 1.00
650 Kirby Puckett 2.00
660 Will Clark 1.00
700 Don Mattingly 2.50
710 David Cone 1.00
725 Terry Steinbach 1.00
730 Danny Jackson 1.00
755 Mike Scioscia 1.00
770 Alan Trammell 1.00
785 Ellis Burks 1.00

1990 Topps

The 1990 Topps set again included 792 cards, and sported a newly-designed front that featured six different color schemes. The set led off with a special four-card salute to Nolan Ryan, and features other specials including All-Stars, Number 1 Draft Picks, Record Breakers, managers, rookies, and "Turn Back the Clock" cards. The set also includes a special card commemorating A. Bartlett Giamatti, the late baseball commissioner. Backs are printed in black on a chartreuse background. The set features 725 different individual player cards, the most ever, including 138 players' first appearance in a regular Topps set.

	NM/M
Unopened Factory Set, Retail (792):	25.00
Unopened Factory Set, Hobby (792):	20.00
Complete Set (792):	15.00
Common Player:	.05
Wax Pack (16):	.60
Wax Box (36):	12.00
Cello Pack (31):	1.00
Cello Box (24):	15.00
Rack Pack (45):	1.00
Rack Box (24):	16.00
Vending Box (500):	7.50

1 Nolan Ryan .75
2 Nolan Ryan (Mets) .35
3 Nolan Ryan (Angels) .25
4 Nolan Ryan (Astros) .25
5 Nolan Ryan (Rangers) .25
6 Vince Coleman (Record Breaker) .05
7 Rickey Henderson (Record Breaker) .20
8 Cal Ripken, Jr. (Record Breaker) .40
9 Eric Plunk .05
10 Barry Larkin .05
11 Paul Gibson .05
12 Joe Girardi RC .05
13 Mark Williamson .05
14 Mike Fetters RC .05
15 Teddy Higuera .05
16 Kent Anderson RC .05
17 Kelly Downs .05
18 Carlos Quintana .05
19 Al Newman .05
20 Mark Gubicza .05
21 Jeff Torborg .05
22 Bruce Ruffin .05
23 Randy Velarde .05
24 Joe Hesketh .05
25 Willie Randolph .05
26 Don Slaught .05
27 Rick Leach .05
28 Duane Ward .05
29 John Cangelosi .05
30 David Cone .05
31 Henry Cotto .05
32 John Farrell .05
33 Greg Walker .05
34 Tony Fossas RC .05
35 Benito Santiago .05
36 John Costello .05
37 Domingo Ramos .05
38 Wes Gardner .05
39 Curt Ford .05
40 Jay Howell .05
41 Matt Williams .05
42 Jeff Robinson .05
43 Dante Bichette .05
44 Roger Salkeld RC (#1 Draft Pick) .10
45 Dave Parker .05
46 Rob Dibble .05
47 Brian Harper .05
48 Zane Smith .05
49 Tom Lawless .05
50 Glenn Davis .05
51 Doug Rader .05
52 Jack Daugherty RC .05
53 Mike LaCoss .05
54 Joel Skinner .05
55 Darrell Evans .05
56 Franklin Stubbs .05
57 Greg Vaughn .05
58 Keith Miller .05
59 Ted Power .05
60 George Brett .50
61 Deion Sanders .10
62 Ramon Martinez .05
63 Mike Pagliarulo .05
64 Danny Darwin .05
65 Devon White .05
66 Greg Litton RC .05
67 Scott Sanderson .05
68 Dave Henderson .05
69 Todd Frohwirth .05
70 Mike Greenwell .05
71 Allan Anderson .05
72 Jeff Huson RC .05
73 Bob Milacki .05
74 Jeff Jackson RC (#1 Draft Pick) .05
75 Doug Jones .05
76 Dave Valle .05
77 Dave Bergman .05
78 Mike Flanagan .05
79 Ron Kittle .05
80 Jeff Russell .05
81 Bob Rodgers .05
82 Scott Terry .05
83 Hensley Meulens .05
84 Ray Searage .05
85 Juan Samuel .05
86 Paul Kilgus .05
87 Rick Luecken RC .05
88 Glenn Braggs .05
89 Clint Zavaras RC .05
90 Jack Clark .05
91 Steve Frey RC .05
92 Mike Stanley .05
93 Shawn Hillegas .05
94 Herm Winningham .05
95 Todd Worrell .05
96 Jody Reed .05
97 Curt Schilling .25
98 Jose Gonzalez RC .05
99 Rich Monteleone RC .05
100 Will Clark .25
101 Shane Rawley .05
102 Stan Javier .05
103 Marvin Freeman .05
104 Bob Knepper .05
105 Randy Myers .05
106 Charlie O'Brien .05
107 Fred Lynn .05
108 Rod Nichols .05
109 Roberto Kelly .05
110 Tommy Helms .05
111 Ed Whited .05
112 Glenn Wilson .05
113 Manny Lee .05
114 Mike Bielecki .05
115 Tony Pena .05
116 Floyd Bannister .05
117 Mike Sharperson RC .05
118 Erik Hanson .05
119 Billy Hatcher .05
120 John Franco .05
121 Robin Ventura .05
122 Shawn Abner .05
123 Rich Gedman .05
124 Dave Dravecky .05
125 Kent Hrbek .05
126 Randy Kramer .05
127 Mike Devereaux .05
128 Checklist 1-132 .05
129 Ron Jones .05
130 Bert Blyleven .05
131 Matt Nokes .05
132 Lance Blankenship RC .05
133 Ricky Horton .05
134 Earl Cunningham RC (#1 Draft Pick) .05
135 Dave Magadan .05
136 Kevin Brown .05
137 Marty Pevey RC .05
138 Al Leiter .05
139 Greg Brock .05
140 Andre Dawson .25
141 John Hart .05
141 John Hart (No black top-left corner.) 8.00
142 Jeff Wetherby RC .05
143 Rafael Belliard .05
144 Bud Black .05
145 Terry Steinbach .05
146 Rob Richie RC .05
147 Chuck Finley .05
148 Edgar Martinez RC .05
149 Steve Farr .05
150 Kirk Gibson .05
151 Rick Mahler .05
152 Lonnie Smith .05
153 Randy Milligan .05
154 Mike Maddux .05
155 Ellis Burks .05
156 Ken Patterson .05
157 Craig Biggio .05
158 Craig Lefferts .05
159 Mike Felder .05
160 Dave Righetti .05
161 Harold Reynolds .05
162 Todd Zeile RC .20
163 Phil Bradley .05
164 Jeff Juden RC (#1 Draft Pick) .05
165 Walt Weiss .05
166 Bobby Witt .05
167 Kevin Appier RC .05
168 Jose Lind .05
169 Richard Dotson .05
170 George Bell .05
171 Russ Nixon .05
172 Tom Lampkin RC .05
173 Tim Belcher .05
174 Jeff Kunkel .05
175 Mike Moore .05
176 Luis Quinones .05
177 Mike Henneman .05
178 Chris James .05
179 Brian Holton .05
180 Rock Raines .05
181 Juan Agosto .05
182 Mookie Wilson .05
183 Steve Lake .05
184 Danny Cox .05
185 Ruben Sierra .05
186 Dave LaPoint .05
187 Rick Wrona RC .05
188 Mike Smithson .05
189 Dick Schofield .05
190 Rick Reuschel .05
191 Pat Borders .05
192 Don August .05
193 Andy Benes .05
194 Glenallen Hill RC .05
195 Tim Burke .05
196 Gerald Young .05
197 Doug Drabek .05
198 Mike Marshall .05
199 Sergio Valdez RC .05
200 Don Mattingly .50
201 Cito Gaston .05
202 Mike Macfarlane .05
203 Mike Roesler RC .05
204 Bob Dernier .05
205 Mark Davis .05
206 Nick Esasky .05
207 Bob Ojeda .05
208 Brook Jacoby .05
209 Greg Mathews .05
210 Ryne Sandberg .45
211 John Cerutti .05
212 Joe Orsulak .05
213 Scott Bankhead .05
214 Terry Francona .05
215 Kirk McCaskill .05
216 Ricky Jordan .05
217 Don Robinson .05
218 Wally Backman .05
219 Donn Pall .05
220 Barry Bonds .75
221 Gary Mielke RC .05
222 Kurt Stillwell .05
223 Tommy Gregg .05
224 Delino DeShields RC .15
225 Jim Deshaies .05
226 Mickey Hatcher .05
227 Kevin Tapani RC .15
228 Dave Martinez .05
229 David Wells .05
230 Keith Hernandez .05
231 Jack McKeon .05
232 Darnell Coles .05
233 Ken Hill RC .05
234 Mariano Duncan .05
235 Jeff Reardon .05
236 Hal Morris .05
237 Kevin Ritz RC .05
238 Felix Jose RC .05
239 Eric Show .05
240 Mark Grace .05
241 Mike Krukow .05
242 Fred Manrique .05
243 Barry Jones .05
244 Bill Schroeder .05
245 Roger Clemens .50
246 Jim Eisenreich .05
247 Jerry Reed .05
248 Dave Anderson .05
249 Mike Smith RC .05
250 Jose Canseco .25
251 Jeff Blauser .05
252 Otis Nixon .05
253 Mark Portugal .05
254 Francisco Cabrera .05
255 Bobby Thigpen .05
256 Marvell Wynne .05
257 Jose DeLeon .05
258 Barry Lyons .05
259 Lance McCullers .05
260 Eric Davis .05
261 Whitey Herzog .05
262 Checklist 133-264 .05
263 Mel Stottlemyre, Jr. RC .10
264 Bryan Clutterbuck .05
265 Pete O'Brien .05
266 German Gonzalez .05
267 Mark Davidson .05
268 Rob Murphy .05
269 Dickie Thon .05
270 Dave Stewart .05
271 Chet Lemon .05
272 Bryan Harvey .05
273 Bobby Bonilla .05
274 Goose Gozzo RC .05
275 Mickey Tettleton .05
276 Gary Thurman .05
277 Lenny Harris RC .05
278 Pascual Perez .05
279 Steve Buechele .05
280 Lou Whitaker .05
281 Kevin Bass .05
282 Derek Lilliquist .05
283 Albert Belle .15
284 Mark Gardner RC .05
285 Willie McGee .05
286 Lee Guetterman .05
287 Vance Law .05
288 Greg Briley .05
289 Norm Charlton .05
290 Robin Yount .35
291 Dave Johnson .05
292 Jim Gott .05
293 Mike Gallego .05
294 Craig McMurtry .05
295 Fred McGriff .05
296 Jeff Ballard .05
297 Tom Herr .05
298 Danny Gladden .05
299 Adam Peterson RC .05
300 Bo Jackson .10
301 Don Aase .05
302 Marcus Lawton RC .05
303 Rick Cerone .05
304 Marty Clary RC .05
305 Eddie Murray .35
306 Tom Niedenfuer .05
307 Bip Roberts .05
308 Jose Guzman .05
309 Eric Yelding RC .05
310 Steve Bedrosian .05
311 Dwight Smith .05
312 Dan Quisenberry .05
313 Gus Polidor .05
314 Donald Harris RC (#1 Draft Pick) .05
315 Bruce Hurst .05
316 Carney Lansford .05
317 Mark Guthrie RC .05
318 Wallace Johnson .05
319 Dion James .05
320 Dave Steib .05
321 Joe M. Morgan .05
322 Junior Ortiz .05
323 Willie Wilson .05
324 Pete Harnisch RC .05
325 Robby Thompson .05
326 Tom McCarthy RC .05
327 Ken Williams .05
328 Curt Young .05
329 Oddibe McDowell .05
330 Ron Darling .05
331 Juan Gonzalez RC 1.50
332 Paul O'Neill .05
333 Bill Wegman .05
334 Johnny Ray .05
335 Andy Hawkins .05
336 Ken Griffey Jr. .75
337 Lloyd McClendon .05
338 Dennis Lamp .05
339 Dave Clark .05
340 Fernando Valenzuela .05
341 Tom Foley .05
342 Alex Trevino .05
343 Frank Tanana .05
344 George Canale RC .05
345 Harold Baines .05
346 Jim Presley .05
347 Junior Felix RC .05
348 Gary Wayne RC .05
349 Steve Finley RC .15
350 Bret Saberhagen .05
351 Roger Craig .05
352 Bryn Smith .05
353 Sandy Alomar .05
354 Stan Belinda RC .05
355 Marty Barrett .05
356 Randy Ready .05
357 Dave West .05
358 Andres Thomas .05
359 Jimmy Jones .05
360 Paul Molitor .35
361 Randy McCament RC .05
362 Damon Berryhill .05
363 Dan Petry .05
364 Rolando Roomes RC .05
365 Ozzie Guillen .05
366 Mike Heath .05
367 Mike Morgan .05
368 Bill Doran .05
369 Todd Burns .05
370 Tim Wallach .05
371 Jimmy Key .05
372 Terry Kennedy .05
373 Alvin Davis .05
374 Steve Cummings RC .05
375 Dwight Evans .05
376 Checklist 265-396 .05
377 Mickey Weston RC .05
378 Luis Salazar .05
379 Steve Rosenberg .05
380 Dave Winfield .35
381 Frank Robinson .10
382 Jeff Musselman .05
383 John Morris .05
383 John Morris (No black top-right corner.) 8.00
384 Pat Combs RC .05
385 Fred McGriff/AS .05
386 Julio Franco/AS .05
387 Wade Boggs/AS .20
388 Cal Ripken, Jr./AS .40
389 Robin Yount/AS .20
390 Ruben Sierra/AS .05
391 Kirby Puckett/AS .25
392 Carlton Fisk/AS .20
393 Bret Saberhagen/AS .05
394 Jeff Ballard/AS .05
395 Jeff Russell/AS .05
396 A. Bartlett Giamatti .20
397 Will Clark/AS .20
398 Ryne Sandberg/AS .20
399 Howard Johnson/AS .05
400 Ozzie Smith/AS .20
401 Kevin Mitchell/AS .05
402 Eric Davis/AS .05
403 Tony Gwynn/AS .25

#	Player	Price
404	Craig Biggio/AS	.05
405	Mike Scott/AS	.05
406	Joe Magrane/AS	.05
407	Mark Davis/AS	.05
408	Trevor Wilson	.05
409	Tom Brunansky	.05
410	Joe Boever	.05
411	Ken Phelps	.05
412	Jamie Moyer	.05
413	Brian DuBois RC	.05
414a	Frank Thomas No Name RC	
	(No name on front.)	500.00
414b	Frank Thomas RC	
	(Name on front.)	3.00
415	Shawon Dunston	.05
416	Dave Johnson RC	.05
417	Jim Gantner	.05
418	Tom Browning	.05
419	Beau Allred RC	.05
420	Carlton Fisk	.35
421	Greg Minton	.05
422	Pat Sheridan	.05
423	Fred Toliver	.05
424	Jerry Reuss	.05
425	Bill Landrum	.05
426	Jeff Hamilton	.05
427	Carmem Castillo	.05
428	Steve Davis RC	.05
429	Tom Kelly	.05
430	Pete Incaviglia	.05
431	Randy Johnson	.35
432	Damaso Garcia	.05
433	Steve Olin RC	.05
434	Mark Carreon RC	.05
435	Kevin Seitzer	.05
436	Mel Hall	.05
437	Les Lancaster	.05
438	Greg Myers RC	.05
439	Jeff Parrett	.05
440	Alan Trammell	.05
441	Bob Kipper	.05
442	Jerry Browne	.05
443	Cris Carpenter	.05
444	Kyle Abbott RC (FDP)	.10
445	Danny Jackson	.05
446	Dan Pasqua	.05
447	Atlee Hammaker	.05
448	Greg Gagne	.05
449	Dennis Rasmussen	.05
450	Rickey Henderson	.35
451	Mark Lemke	.05
452	Luis de los Santos RC	.05
453	Jody Davis	.05
454a	Jeff King RC	
	(No white on back.)	100.00
454b	Jeff King	
	(Correct use of white.)	.05
455	Jeffrey Leonard	.05
456	Chris Gwynn RC	.05
457	Gregg Jefferies	.05
458	Bob McClure	.05
459	Jim Lefebvre	.05
460	Mike Scott	.05
461	Carlos Martinez RC	.05
462	Denny Walling	.05
463	Drew Hall	.05
464	Jerome Walton RC	.05
465	Kevin Gross	.05
466	Rance Mulliniks	.05
467	Juan Nieves	.05
468	Billy Ripken	.05
469	John Kruk	.05
470	Frank Viola	.05
471	Mike Brumley	.05
472	Jose Uribe	.05
473	Joe Price	.05
474	Rich Thompson	.05
475	Bob Welch	.05
476	Brad Komminsk	.05
477	Willie Fraser	.05
478	Mike LaValliere	.05
479	Frank White	.05
480	Sid Fernandez	.05
481	Garry Templeton	.05
482	Steve Carter RC	.05
483	Alejandro Pena	.05
484	Mike Fitzgerald	.05
485	John Candelaria	.05
486	Jeff Treadway	.05
487	Steve Searcy	.05
488	Ken Oberkfell	.05
489	Nick Leyva	.05
490	Dan Plesac	.05
491	Dave Cochrane RC	.10
492	Ron Oester	.10
493	Jason Grimsley RC	.05
494	Terry Puhl	.05
495	Lee Smith	.05
496	Cecil Espy	.05
497	Dave Schmidt	.05
498	Rick Schu	.05
499	Bill Long	.05
500	Kevin Mitchell	.05
501	Matt Young	.05
502	Mitch Webster	.05
503	Randy St. Claire	.05
504	Tom O'Malley	.05
505	Kelly Gruber	.05
506	Tom Glavine	.25
507	Gary Redus	.05
508	Terry Leach	.05
509	Tom Pagnozzi	.05
510	Dwight Gooden	.05
511	Clay Parker	.05
512	Gary Pettis	.05
513	Mark Eichhorn	.05
514	Andy Allanson	.05
515	Len Dykstra	.05

#	Player	Price
516	Tim Leary	.05
517	Roberto Alomar	.15
518	Bill Krueger	.05
519	Bucky Dent	.05
520	Mitch Williams	.05
521	Craig Worthington	.05
522	Mike Dunne	.05
523	Jay Bell	.05
524	Daryl Boston	.05
525	Wally Joyner	.05
526	Checklist 397-528	.05
527	Ron Hassey	.05
528	Kevin Wickander RC	.05
529	Greg Harris	.05
530	Mark Langston	.05
531	Ken Caminiti	.05
532	Cecilio Guante	.05
533	Tim Jones RC	.05
534	Louie Meadows	.05
535	John Smoltz	.05
536	Bob Geren RC	.05
537	Mark Grant	.05
538	Billy Spiers RC	.05
539	Neal Heaton	.05
540	Danny Tartabull	.05
541	Pat Perry	.05
542	Darren Daulton	.05
543	Nelson Liriano	.05
544	Dennis Boyd	.05
545	Kevin McReynolds	.05
546	Kevin Hickey	.05
547	Jack Howell	.05
548	Pat Clements	.05
549	Don Zimmer	.05
550	Julio Franco	.05
551	Tim Crews	.05
552	Mike Smith RC	.05
553	Scott Scudder RC	.05
554	Jay Buhner	.05
555	Jack Morris	.05
556	Gene Larkin	.05
557	Jeff Innis RC	.05
558	Rafael Ramirez	.05
559	Andy McGaffigan	.05
560	Steve Sax	.05
561	Ken Dayley	.05
562	Chad Kreuter	.05
563	Alex Sanchez	.05
564	Tyler Houston RC	
	(#1 Draft Pick)	.10
565	Scott Fletcher	.05
566	Mark Knudson	.05
567	Ron Gant	.05
568	John Smiley	.05
569	Ivan Calderon	.05
570	Cal Ripken, Jr.	.75
571	Brett Butler	.05
572	Greg Harris	.05
573	Danny Heep	.05
574	Bill Swift	.05
575	Lance Parrish	.05
576	Mike Dyer RC	.05
577	Charlie Hayes RC	.05
578	Joe Magrane	.05
579	Art Howe	.05
580	Joe Carter	.05
581	Ken Griffey	.05
582	Rick Honeycutt	.05
583	Bruce Benedict	.05
584	Phil Stephenson RC	.05
585	Kal Daniels	.05
586	Ed Nunez	.05
587	Lance Johnson	.05
588	Rick Rhoden	.05
589	Mike Aldrete	.05
590	Ozzie Smith	.45
591	Todd Stottlemyre	.05
592	R.J. Reynolds	.05
593	Scott Bradley	.05
594	Luis Sojo RC	.05
595	Greg Swindell	.05
596	Jose DeJesus RC	.05
597	Chris Bosio	.05
598	Brady Anderson	.05
599	Frank Williams	.05
600	Darryl Strawberry	.05
601	Luis Rivera	.05
602	Scott Garrelts	.05
603	Tony Armas	.05
604	Ron Robinson	.05
605	Mike Scioscia	.05
606	Storm Davis	.05
607	Steve Jeltz	.05
608	Eric Anthony RC	.10
609	Sparky Anderson	.10
610	Pedro Guerrero	.05
611	Walt Terrell	.05
612	Dave Gallagher	.05
613	Jeff Pico	.05
614	Nelson Santovenia	.05
615	Rob Deer	.05
616	Brian Holman	.05
617	Geronimo Berroa	.05
618	Eddie Whitson	.05
619	Rob Ducey	.05
620	Tony Castillo RC	.05
621	Melido Perez	.05
622	Sid Bream	.05
623	Jim Corsi	.05
624	Darrin Jackson	.05
625	Roger McDowell	.05
626	Bob Melvin	.05
627	Jose Rijo	.05
628	Candy Maldonado	.05
629	Eric Hetzel RC	.05
630	Gary Gaetti	.05
631	John Wetteland RC	.15
632	Scott Lusader	.05

#	Player	Price
633	Dennis Cook RC	.05
634	Luis Polonia	.05
635	Brian Downing	.05
636	Jesse Orosco	.05
637	Craig Reynolds	.05
638	Jeff Montgomery	.05
639	Tony LaRussa	.05
640	Rick Sutcliffe	.05
641	Doug Strange RC	.05
642	Jack Armstrong	.05
643	Alfredo Griffin	.05
644	Paul Assenmacher	.05
645	Jose Oquendo	.05
646	Checklist 529-660	.05
647	Rex Hudler	.05
648	Jim Clancy	.05
649	Dan Murphy RC	.05
650	Mike Witt	.05
651	Rafael Santana	.05
652	Mike Boddicker	.05
653	John Moses	.05
654	Paul Coleman RC	
	(#1 Draft Pick)	.05
655	Gregg Olson	.05
656	Mackey Sasser	.05
657	Terry Mulholland	.05
658	Donell Nixon	.05
659	Greg Cadaret	.05
660	Vince Coleman	.05
661	Dick Howser	
	(Turn Back the Clock)	.05
662	Mike Schmidt	
	(Turn Back the Clock)	.10
663	Fred Lynn	
	(Turn Back the Clock)	.05
664	Johnny Bench	
	(Turn Back the Clock)	.05
665	Sandy Koufax	
	(Turn Back the Clock)	.15
666	Brian Fisher	.05
667	Curt Wilkerson	.05
668	Joe Oliver RC	.05
669	Tom Lasorda	.05
670	Dennis Eckersley	.30
671	Bob Boone	.05
672	Roy Smith	.05
673	Joey Meyer	.05
674	Spike Owen	.05
675	Jim Abbott	.05
676	Randy Kutcher RC	.05
677	Jay Tibbs	.05
678	Kirt Manwaring	.05
679	Gary Ward	.05
680	Howard Johnson	.05
681	Mike Schooler	.05
682	Dann Bilardello	.05
683	Kenny Rogers	.05
684	Julio Machado RC	.05
685	Tony Fernandez	.05
686	Carmelo Martinez	.05
687	Tim Birtsas	.05
688	Milt Thompson	.05
689	Rich Yett	.05
690	Mark McGwire	.65
691	Chuck Cary	.05
692	Sammy Sosa RC	4.00
693	Calvin Schiraldi	.05
694	Mike Stanton RC	.05
695	Tom Henke	.05
696	B.J. Surhoff	.05
697	Mike Davis	.05
698	Omar Vizquel	.05
699	Jim Leyland	.05
700	Kirby Puckett	.45
701	Bernie Williams RC	1.00
702	Tony Phillips	.05
703	Jeff Brantley	.05
704	Chip Hale RC	.05
705	Claudell Washington	.05
706	Geno Petralli	.05
707	Luis Aquino	.05
708	Larry Sheets	.05
709	Juan Berneguer	.05
710	Von Hayes	.05
711	Rick Aguilera	.05
712	Todd Benzinger	.05
713	Tim Drummond RC	.05
714	Marquis Grissom RC	.25
715	Greg Maddux	.45
716	Steve Balboni	.05
717	Ron Kakovice	.05
718	Gary Sheffield	.30
719	Wally Whitehurst RC	.05
720	Andres Galarraga	.05
721	Lee Mazzilli	.05
722	Felix Fermin	.05
723	Jeff Robinson	.05
724	Juan Bell RC	.05
725	Terry Pendleton	.05
726	Gene Nelson	.05
727	Pat Tabler	.05
728	Jim Acker	.05
729	Bobby Valentine	.05
730	Tony Gwynn	.45
731	Don Carman	.05
732	Ernie Riles	.05
733	John Dopson	.05
734	Kevin Elster	.05
735	Charlie Hough	.05
736	Rick Dempsey	.05
737	Chris Sabo	.05
738	Gene Harris RC	.05
739	Dale Sveum	.05
740	Jesse Barfield	.05
741	Steve Wilson	.05
742	Ernie Whitt	.05
743	Tom Candiotti	.05
744	Kelly Mann RC	.05

#	Player	Price
745	Hubie Brooks	.05
746	Dave Smith	.05
747	Randy Bush	.05
748	Doyle Alexander	.05
749	Mark Parent	.05
750	Dale Murphy	.15
751	Steve Lyons	.05
752	Tom Gordon	.05
753	Chris Speier	.05
754	Bob Walk	.05
755	Rafael Palmeiro	.30
756	Ken Howell	.05
757	Larry Walker RC	.75
758	Mark Thurmond	.05
759	Tom Trebelhorn	.05
760	Wade Boggs	.45
761	Mike Jackson	.05
762	Doug Dascenzo	.05
763	Denny Martinez	.05
764	Tim Teufel	.05
765	Chili Davis	.05
766	Brian Meyer RC	.05
767	Tracy Jones	.05
768	Chuck Crim	.05
769	Greg Hibbard RC	.05
770	Cory Snyder	.05
771	Pete Smith	.05
772	Jeff Reed	.05
773	Dave Leiper	.05
774	Ben McDonald RC	.20
775	Andy Van Slyke	.05
776	Charlie Leibrandt	.05
777	Tim Laudner	.05
778	Mike Jeffcoat	.05
779	Lloyd Moseby	.05
780	Orel Hershiser	.05
781	Mario Diaz	.05
782	Jose Alvarez	.05
783	Checklist 661-792	.05
784	Scott Bailes	.05
785	Jim Rice	.15
786	Eric King	.05
787	Rene Gonzales	.05
788	Frank DiPino	.05
789	John Wathan	.05
790	Gary Carter	.35
791	Alvaro Espinoza	.05
792	Gerald Perry	.05

Tiffany

This specially boxed version of Topps' 1990 baseball card set was sold through hobby channels only. The checklist is identical to the regular-issue Topps set and the cards are nearly so. The Tiffany version features white cardboard stock and a high-gloss finish on the fronts.

	NM/M
Unopened Set (792):	115.00
Complete Set (792):	90.00
Common Player:	.10

Traded

TRAVIS FRYMAN

For the first time, Topps "Traded" series cards were made available nationwide in retail wax packs. The 132-card set was also sold in complete boxed form as it has been in recent years. The wax pack traded cards feature gray backs, while the boxed set cards feature white backs. Each of the gray-back wax-pack cards can be found with copyright lines preceded by one or two asterisks. The cards are numbered 1T-132T, and showcase rookies, players who changed teams and new managers.

	NM/M
Complete Set, Retail (132):	6.00
Complete Set, Hobby (132):	4.00
Common Player:	.05
Wax Pack (7):	.75
Wax Box (36):	9.00

#	Player	Price
1	Darrel Akerfelds	.05
2	Sandy Alomar, Jr.	.05
3	Brad Arnsberg	.05
4	Steve Avery	.05
5	Wally Backman	.05
6	Carlos Baerga RC	.10
7	Kevin Bass	.05
8	Willie Blair RC	.05
9	Mike Blowers RC	.05

#	Player	Price
10	Shawn Boskie RC	.05
11	Daryl Boston	.05
12	Dennis Boyd	.05
13	Glenn Braggs	.05
14	Hubie Brooks	.05
15	Tom Brunansky	.05
16	John Burkett RC	.05
17	Casey Candaele	.05
18	John Candelaria	.05
19	Gary Carter	.75
20	Joe Carter	.05
21	Rick Cerone	.05
22	Scott Coolbaugh RC	.05
23	Bobby Cox	.05
24	Mark Davis	.05
25	Storm Davis	.05
26	Edgar Diaz RC	.05
27	Wayne Edwards RC	.05
28	Mark Eichhorn	.05
29	Scott Erickson RC	.05
30	Nick Esasky	.05
31	Cecil Fielder	.05
32	John Franco	.05
33	Travis Fryman RC	.25
34	Bill Gullickson	.05
35	Darryl Hamilton	.05
36	Mike Harkey	.05
37	Bud Harrelson	.05
38	Billy Hatcher	.05
39	Keith Hernandez	.05
40	Joe Hesketh	.05
41	Dave Hollins RC	.05
42	Sam Horn	.05
43	Steve Howard RC	.05
44	Todd Hundley RC	.15
45	Jeff Huson	.05
46	Chris James	.05
47	Stan Javier	.05
48	Dave Justice RC	.75
49	Jeff Kaiser RC	.05
50	Dana Kiecker RC	.05
51	Joe Klink RC	.05
52	Brent Knackert RC	.05
53	Brad Komminsk	.05
54	Mark Langston	.05
55	Tim Layana RC	.05
56	Rick Leach	.05
57	Terry Leach	.05
58	Tim Leary	.05
59	Craig Lefferts	.05
60	Charlie Leibrandt	.05
61	Jim Leyritz RC	.05
62	Fred Lynn	.05
63	Kevin Maas RC	.05
64	Shane Mack	.05
65	Candy Maldonado	.05
66	Fred Manrique	.05
67	Mike Marshall	.05
68	Carmelo Martinez	.05
69	John Marzano	.05
70	Ben McDonald	.05
71	Jack McDowell	.05
72	John McNamara	.05
73	Orlando Mercado	.05
74	Stump Merrill	.05
75	Alan Mills RC	.05
76	Hal Morris	.05
77	Lloyd Moseby	.05
78	Randy Myers	.05
79	Tim Naehring RC	.05
80	Junior Noboa	.05
81	Matt Nokes	.05
82	Pete O'Brien	.05
83	John Olerud RC	.75
84	Greg Olson RC	.05
85	Junior Ortiz	.05
86	Dave Parker	.05
87	Rick Parker RC	.05
88	Bob Patterson	.05
89	Alejandro Pena	.05
90	Tony Pena	.05
91	Pascual Perez	.05
92	Gerald Perry	.05
93	Dan Petry	.05
94	Gary Pettis	.05
95	Tony Phillips	.05
96	Lou Pinella	.05
97	Luis Polonia	.05
98	Jim Presley	.05
99	Scott Radinsky RC	.05
100	Willie Randolph	.05
101	Jeff Reardon	.05
102	Greg Riddoch	.05
103	Jeff Robinson	.05
104	Ron Robinson	.05
105	Kevin Romine	.05
106	Scott Ruskin RC	.05
107	John Russell	.05
108	Bill Sampen RC	.05
109	Juan Samuel	.05
110	Scott Sanderson	.05
111	Jack Savage RC	.05
112	Dave Schmidt	.05
113	Red Schoendienst	.10
114	Terry Shumpert RC	.05
115	Matt Sinatro	.05
116	Don Slaught	.05
117	Bryn Smith	.05
118	Lee Smith	.05
119	Paul Sorrento RC	.05
120	Franklin Stubbs	.05
121	Russ Swan RC	.05
122	Bob Tewksbury	.05
123	Wayne Tolleson	.05
124	John Tudor	.05
125	Randy Veres RC	.05
126	Hector Villanueva RC	.05
127	Mitch Webster	.05

#	Player	Price
128	Ernie Whitt	.05
129	Frank Wills	.05
130	Dave Winfield	.75
131	Matt Young	.05
132	Checklist	.05

Traded Tiffany

Identical to the regular Topps Traded issue except for the glossy front surface, this special hobby-only boxed set shares the same checklist.

	NM/M
Complete Set (132):	25.00
Common Player:	.15

Traded Hank Aaron Bronze

This 1/4-size metal replica of Aaron's first-ever Topps card was issued to dealers who purchased cases of 1990 Topps Traded sets. Each detail of the 1954 Topps Aaron card is reproduced on the 1-1/4" x 1-3/4" bronze metal mini-card, right down to the stats.

	NM/M
128	Hank Aaron	15.00

Box Panels

This special 16-card set features four cards on four different box-bottom panels. The cards are identical in design to the regular 1990 Topps cards. The cards are designated by letter.

	NM/M
Complete Panel Set (4):	7.00
Complete Singles Set (16):	6.00
Common Panel:	1.00
Common Player:	.10
Panel		2.00
A	Wade Boggs	.60
B	George Brett	.75
C	Andre Dawson	.15
D	Darrell Evans	.10
Panel		1.00
E	Dwight Gooden	.10
F	Rickey Henderson	.45
G	Tom Lasorda	.10
H	Fred Lynn	.10
Panel		1.50
I	Mark McGwire	1.00
J	Dave Parker	.10
K	Jeff Reardon	.10
L	Rick Reuschel	.10
Panel		4.00
M	Jim Rice	.10
N	Cal Ripken, Jr.	1.50
O	Nolan Ryan	1.50
P	Ryne Sandberg	.60

All-Star Glossy Set of 22

One glossy All-Star card was included in each 1990 Topps rack pack. The cards measure 2-1/2" x 3-1/2" and feature a similar style to past glossy All-Star cards. Special cards of All-Star team captains Carl Yastrzemski and Don Drysdale are included in the set.

	NM/M
Complete Set (22):	4.00
Common Player:	.05

1989 ALL-STAR

CAL RIPKEN SS — Orioles

41	Andre Dawson	.10
42	Mark McGwire	1.50
43	Howard Johnson	.10
44	Bo Jackson	.20
45	Shawon Dunston	.10
46	Carlton Fisk	.60
47	Mitch Williams	.10
48	Kirby Puckett	.75
49	Craig Worthington	.10
50	Jim Abbott	.10
51	Cal Ripken, Jr.	2.00
52	Will Clark	.10
53	Dennis Eckersley	.55
54	Craig Biggio	.10
55	Fred McGriff	.10
56	Tony Gwynn	.75
57	Mickey Tettleton	.10
58	Mark Davis	.10
59	Omar Vizquel	.10
60	Gregg Jefferies	.10

1	Tom Lasorda	.05
2	Will Clark	.05
3	Ryne Sandberg	.50
4	Howard Johnson	.05
5	Ozzie Smith	.40
6	Kevin Mitchell	.05
7	Eric Davis	.05
8	Tony Gwynn	.50
9	Benny Santiago	.05
10	Rick Rueschel	.05
11	Don Drysdale	.10
12	Tony LaRussa	.05
13	Mark McGwire	.75
14	Julio Franco	.05
15	Wade Boggs	.50
16	Cal Ripken, Jr.	1.00
17	Bo Jackson	.10
18	Kirby Puckett	.50
19	Ruben Sierra	.05
20	Terry Steinbach	.05
21	Dave Stewart	.05
22	Carl Yastrzemski	.10

All-Star Glossy Set of 60

Sharp color photographs and a clutter-free design are features of the cards in this 60-card send away set. Topps initiated the redemption series in 1983. Six special offer cards, included in Topps baseball wax packs, were necessary to obtain each of the six 10-card sets in the series.

		NM/M
Complete Set (60):		9.00
Common Player:		.10
1	Ryne Sandberg	.75
2	Nolan Ryan	2.00
3	Glenn Davis	.10
4	Dave Stewart	.10
5	Barry Larkin	.10
6	Carney Lansford	.10
7	Darryl Strawberry	.10
8	Steve Sax	.10
9	Carlos Martinez	.10
10	Gary Sheffield	.50
11	Don Mattingly	1.00
12	Mark Grace	.10
13	Bret Saberhagen	.10
14	Mike Scott	.10
15	Robin Yount	.60
16	Ozzie Smith	.75
17	Jeff Ballard	.10
18	Rick Reuschel	.10
19	Greg Briley	.10
20	Ken Griffey Jr.	1.25
21	Kevin Mitchell	.10
22	Wade Boggs	.75
23	Dwight Gooden	.10
24	George Bell	.10
25	Eric Davis	.10
26	Ruben Sierra	.10
27	Roberto Alomar	.20
28	Gary Gaetti	.10
29	Gregg Olson	.10
30	Tom Gordon	.10
31	Jose Canseco	.45
32	Pedro Guerrero	.10
33	Joe Carter	.10
34	Mike Scioscia	.10
35	Julio Franco	.10
36	Joe Magrane	.10
37	Rickey Henderson	.60
38	Tim Raines	.10
39	Jerome Walton	.10
40	Bob Geren	.10

Glossy Rookies

1989 ROOKIES

KEN GRIFFEY, JR.

While the size of the annual glossy rookies set increased to 33 cards from previous years' issues of 22, the format remained identical in 1990. Above the player photo is a colored banner with "1989 Rookies." The player's name appears in red in a yellow bar beneath the photo. Backs are printed in red and blue and contain a shield design with the notation, "1989 Rookies Commemorative Set." The player's name, position and team are listed below, along with a card number. Cards are numbered alphabetically in the set. The glossy rookies were found one per pack in jumbo (100-card) cello packs.

		NM/M
Complete Set (33):		6.00
Common Player:		.10
1	Jim Abbott	.10
2	Joey Belle	.50
3	Andy Benes	.10
4	Greg Briley	.10
5	Kevin Brown	.10
6	Mark Carreon	.10
7	Mike Devereaux	.10
8	Junior Felix	.10
9	Bob Geren	.10
10	Tom Gordon	.10
11	Ken Griffey Jr.	5.00
12	Pete Harnisch	.10
13	Greg W. Harris	.10
14	Greg Hibbard	.10
15	Ken Hill	.10
16	Gregg Jefferies	.10
17	Jeff King	.10
18	Derek Lilliquist	.10
19	Carlos Martinez	.10
20	Ramon Martinez	.10
21	Bob Milacki	.10
22	Gregg Olson	.10
23	Donn Pall	.10
24	Kenny Rogers	.10
25	Gary Sheffield	1.50
26	Dwight Smith	.10
27	Billy Spiers	.10
28	Omar Vizquel	.10
29	Jerome Walton	.10
30	Dave West	.10
31	John Wetteland	.10
32	Steve Wilson	.10
33	Craig Worthington	.10

Glossy Rookies Foil-Test Cards

To test the use of metallic-foil highlights which it would debut on its 1991 Stadium Club and Desert Shield cards, Topps made a test run using as base cards the 33-piece "1989 Rookies Commemorative Set." The test consists of a 2-1/4" x 1/4" metallic strip with a "topps" logotype punched out of the center. Cards can be found with the strip in many different locations horizontally on the cards' fronts, and in many colors including silver, gold, red, green, blue and purple. Color

1989 ROOKIES

KEN GRIFFEY, JR.

of foil does not affect values, though a complete set in matching color might command a premium.

		NM/M
Complete Set (33):		40.00
Common Player:		1.00
1	Jim Abbott	1.00
2	Joey Belle	2.00
3	Andy Benes	1.00
4	Greg Briley	1.00
5	Kevin Brown	1.00
6	Mark Carreon	1.00
7	Mike Devereaux	1.00
8	Junior Felix	1.00
9	Bob Geren	1.00
10	Tom Gordon	1.00
11	Ken Griffey Jr.	20.00
12	Pete Harnisch	1.00
13	Greg W. Harris	1.00
14	Greg Hibbard	1.00
15	Ken Hill	1.00
16	Gregg Jefferies	1.00
17	Jeff King	1.00
18	Derek Lilliquist	1.00
19	Carlos Martinez	1.00
20	Ramon Martinez	1.00
21	Bob Milacki	1.00
22	Gregg Olson	1.00
23	Donn Pall	1.00
24	Kenny Rogers	1.00
25	Gary Sheffield	5.00
26	Dwight Smith	1.00
27	Billy Spiers	1.00
28	Omar Vizquel	1.00
29	Jerome Walton	1.00
30	Dave West	1.00
31	John Wetteland	1.00
32	Steve Wilson	1.00
33	Craig Worthington	1.00

Award Winners Commemorative Sheet

AWARD WINNERS COMMEMORATIVE SHEET

Six of 1989's top award winners are pictured in the style of 1990 Topps baseball cards on this sheet issued with blister packed sets of Topps baseball stickers. The cards are blank-backed and use photos which are different from those found on the same players' regular 1990 cards. Each player's award is noted in the panel beneath his name. The sheet measures 8-3/4" x 8-1/8" with individual cards measuring the standard 2-1/2" x 3-1/2".

		NM/M
Complete Set, Sheet:		3.00
Complete Set, Singles (6):		2.00
Common Player:		.10
(1)	Mark Davis	
	(N.L. Cy Young)	.10
(2)	Kevin Mitchell (N.L. MVP)	.10
(3)	Gregg Olson (A.L. R.O.Y.)	.10
(4)	Bret Saberhagen	
	(A.L. Cy Young)	.10
(5)	Jerome Walton	
	(N.L. R.O.Y.)	.10
(6)	Robin Yount (A.L. MVP)	1.50

Batting Leaders

Once again produced as an exclusive insert in jumbo blister packs for K-Mart stores, the 1990 career batting leaders cards are similar in concept and design to the previous year's issue; in fact, some of the same player photos were used. The 22 cards in the set are arranged roughly in order of the players'

RICKEY HENDERSON

standings in lifetime batting average. Cards fronts are bordered in bright green; backs are printed in red, white and dark green.

		NM/M
Complete Set (22):		110.00
Common Player:		1.50
1	Wade Boggs	12.50
2	Tony Gwynn	15.00
3	Kirby Puckett	15.00
4	Don Mattingly	20.00
5	George Brett	20.00
6	Pedro Guerrero	1.50
7	Tim Raines	1.50
8	Paul Molitor	12.50
9	Jim Rice	3.00
10	Keith Hernandez	1.50
11	Julio Franco	1.50
12	Carney Lansford	1.50
13	Dave Parker	1.50
14	Willie McGee	1.50
15	Robin Yount	12.50
16	Tony Fernandez	1.50
17	Eddie Murray	12.50
18	Johnny Ray	1.50
19	Lonnie Smith	1.50
20	Phil Bradley	1.50
21	Rickey Henderson	12.50
22	Kent Hrbek	1.50

Big Baseball

ANDRES GALARRAGA

For the third consecutive year, Topps issued a 330-card set of oversized cards (2-5/8" x 3-3/4") in three 110-card series. The cards are reminiscent of Topps cards from the mid-1950s, featuring players in portrait and action shots. As in previous years, the cards are printed on white stock with a glossy front finish. Backs include 1989 and career hitting, fielding and pitching stats and a player cartoon. Series 3 cards (#221-330) are believed to have been somewhat scarcer than the first two series.

		NM/M
Complete Set (330):		15.00
Common Player:		.05
Wax Pack (8):		.50
Wax Box, Series 1-2 (36):		7.50
Wax Box, Series 3 (36):		20.00
1	Dwight Evans	.05
2	Kirby Puckett	.60
3	Kevin Gross	.05
4	Ron Hassey	.05
5	Lloyd McClendon	.05
6	Bo Jackson	.10
7	Lonnie Smith	.05
8	Alvaro Espinoza	.05
9	Roberto Alomar	.15
10	Glenn Braggs	.05
11	David Cone	.05
12	Claudell Washington	.05
13	Pedro Guerrero	.05
14	Todd Benzinger	.05
15	Jeff Russell	.05
16	Terry Kennedy	.05
17	Kelly Gruber	.05
18	Alfredo Griffin	.05
19	Mark Grace	.05
20	Dave Winfield	.50
21	Bret Saberhagen	.05
22	Roger Clemens	.65
23	Bob Walk	.05
24	Dave Magadan	.05
25	Spike Owen	.05
26	Jody Davis	.05
27	Kent Hrbek	.05
28	Mark McGwire	1.00
29	Eddie Murray	.50
30	Paul O'Neill	.05
31	Jose DeLeon	.05

32	Steve Lyons	.05
33	Dan Plesac	.05
34	Jack Howell	.05
35	Greg Briley	.05
36	Andy Hawkins	.05
37	Cecil Espy	.05
38	Rick Sutcliffe	.05
39	Jack Clark	.05
40	Dale Murphy	.15
41	Mike Henneman	.05
42	Rick Honeycutt	.05
43	Willie Randolph	.05
44	Marty Barrett	.05
45	Willie Wilson	.05
46	Wallace Johnson	.05
47	Greg Brock	.05
48	Tom Browning	.05
49	Gerald Young	.05
50	Dennis Eckersley	.40
51	Scott Garrelts	.05
52	Gary Redus	.05
53	Al Newman	.05
54	Darryl Boston	.05
55	Ron Oester	.05
56	Danny Tartabull	.05
57	Gregg Jefferies	.05
58	Tom Foley	.05
59	Robin Yount	.50
60	Pat Borders	.05
61	Mike Greenwell	.05
62	Shawon Dunston	.05
63	Steve Buechele	.05
64	Dave Stewart	.05
65	Jose Oquendo	.05
66	Ron Gant	.05
67	Mike Scioscia	.05
68	Randy Velarde	.05
69	Charlie Hayes	.05
70	Tim Wallach	.05
71	Eric Show	.05
72	Eric Davis	.05
73	Mike Gallego	.05
74	Rob Deer	.05
75	Ryne Sandberg	.60
76	Kevin Seitzer	.05
77	Wade Boggs	.60
78	Greg Gagne	.05
79	John Smiley	.05
80	Ivan Calderon	.05
81	Pete Incaviglia	.05
82	Orel Hershiser	.05
83	Carney Lansford	.05
84	Mike Fitzgerald	.05
85	Don Mattingly	.65
86	Chet Lemon	.05
87	Rolando Roomes	.05
88	Bill Spiers	.05
89	Pat Tabler	.05
90	Danny Heep	.05
91	Andre Dawson	.25
92	Randy Bush	.05
93	Tony Gwynn	.60
94	Tom Brunansky	.05
95	Johnny Ray	.05
96	Matt Williams	.05
97	Barry Lyons	.05
98	Jeff Hamilton	.05
99	Tom Glavine	.20
100	Ken Griffey Sr.	.05
101	Ron Henke	.05
102	Dave Righetti	.05
103	Paul Molitor	.50
104	Mike LaValliere	.05
105	Frank White	.05
106	Bob Welch	.05
107	Ellis Burks	.05
108	Andres Galarraga	.05
109	Mitch Williams	.05
110	Checklist	.05
111	Craig Biggio	.05
112	Dave Steib	.05
113	Ron Darling	.05
114	Bert Blyleven	.05
115	Dickie Thon	.05
116	Carlos Martinez	.05
117	Jeff King	.05
118	Terry Steinbach	.05
119	Frank Tanana	.05
120	Mark Lemke	.05
121	Chris Sabo	.05
122	Glenn Davis	.05
123	Mel Hall	.05
124	Jim Gantner	.05
125	Benito Santiago	.05
126	Milt Thompson	.05
127	Rafael Palmeiro	.40
128	Barry Bonds	1.50
129	Mike Bielecki	.05
130	Lou Whitaker	.05
131	Bob Ojeda	.05
132	Dion James	.05
133	Denny Martinez	.05
134	Fred McGriff	.05
135	Terry Pendleton	.05
136	Pat Combs	.05
137	Kevin Mitchell	.05
138	Marquis Grissom	.05
139	Chris Bosio	.05
140	Omar Vizquel	.05
141	Steve Sax	.05
142	Nelson Liriano	.05
143	Kevin Elster	.05
144	Dan Pasqua	.05
145	Dave Smith	.05
146	Craig Worthington	.05
147	Dan Gladden	.05
148	Oddibe McDowell	.05
149	Bip Roberts	.05

150	Randy Ready	.05
151	Dwight Smith	.05
152	Ed Whitson	.05
153	George Bell	.05
154	Tim Raines	.05
155	Sid Fernandez	.05
156	Henry Cotto	.05
157	Harold Baines	.05
158	Willie McGee	.05
159	Bill Doran	.05
160	Steve Balboni	.05
161	Pete Smith	.05
162	Frank Viola	.05
163	Gary Sheffield	.35
164	Bill Landrum	.05
165	Tony Fernandez	.05
166	Mike Heath	.05
167	Jody Reed	.05
168	Wally Joyner	.05
169	Robby Thompson	.05
170	Ken Caminiti	.05
171	Nolan Ryan	1.50
172	Ricky Jordan	.05
173	Lance Blankenship	.05
174	Dwight Gooden	.05
175	Ruben Sierra	.05
176	Carlton Fisk	.50
177	Garry Templeton	.05
178	Mike Devereaux	.05
179	Mookie Wilson	.05
180	Jeff Blauser	.05
181	Scott Bradley	.05
182	Luis Salazar	.05
183	Rafael Ramirez	.05
184	Vince Coleman	.05
185	Doug Drabek	.05
186	Darryl Strawberry	.05
187	Tim Burke	.05
188	Jesse Barfield	.05
189	Barry Larkin	.05
190	Alan Trammell	.05
191	Steve Lake	.05
192	Derek Lilliquist	.05
193	Don Robinson	.05
194	Kevin McReynolds	.05
195	Melido Perez	.05
196	Jose Lind	.05
197	Eric Anthony	.05
198	B.J. Surhoff	.05
199	John Olerud	.05
200	Mike Moore	.05
201	Mark Gubicza	.05
202	Phil Bradley	.05
203	Ozzie Smith	.60
204	Greg Maddux	.60
205	Julio Franco	.05
206	Tom Herr	.05
207	Scott Fletcher	.05
208	Bobby Bonilla	.05
209	Bob Geren	.05
210	Junior Felix	.05
211	Dick Schofield	.05
212	Jim Deshaies	.05
213	Jose Uribe	.05
214	John Kruk	.05
215	Ozzie Guillen	.05
216	Howard Johnson	.05
217	Andy Van Slyke	.05
218	Tim Laudner	.05
219	Manny Lee	.05
220	Checklist	.05
221	Cory Snyder	.05
222	Billy Hatcher	.05
223	Bud Black	.05
224	Will Clark	.05
225	Kevin Tapani	.05
226	Mike Pagliarulo	.05
227	Dave Parker	.05
228	Ben McDonald	.05
229	Carlos Baerga	.05
230	Roger McDowell	.05
231	Delino DeShields	.05
232	Mark Langston	.05
233	Wally Backman	.05
234	Jim Eisenreich	.05
235	Mike Schooler	.05
236	Kevin Bass	.05
237	John Farrell	.05
238	Kal Daniels	.05
239	Tony Phillips	.05
240	Todd Stottlemyre	.05
241	Greg Olson	.05
242	Charlie Hough	.05
243	Mariano Duncan	.05
244	Billy Ripken	.05
245	Joe Carter	.05
246	Tim Belcher	.05
247	Roberto Kelly	.05
248	Candy Maldonado	.05
249	Mike Scott	.05
250	Ken Griffey Jr.	.75
251	Nick Esasky	.05
252	Tom Gordon	.05
253	John Tudor	.05
254	Gary Gaetti	.05
255	Neal Heaton	.05
256	Jerry Browne	.05
257	Jose Rijo	.05
258	Mike Boddicker	.05
259	Brett Butler	.05
260	Andy Benes	.05
261	Kevin Brown	.05
262	Hubie Brooks	.05
263	Randy Milligan	.05
264	John Franco	.05
265	Sandy Alomar	.05
266	Dave Valle	.05
267	Jerome Walton	.05

268	Bob Boone	.05
269	Ken Howell	.05
270	Jose Canseco	.30
271	Joe Magrane	.05
272	Brian DuBois	.05
273	Carlos Quintana	.05
274	Lance Johnson	.05
275	Steve Bedrosian	.05
276	Brook Jacoby	.05
277	Fred Lynn	.05
278	Jeff Ballard	.05
279	Otis Nixon	.05
280	Chili Davis	.05
281	Joe Oliver	.05
282	Brian Holman	.05
283	Juan Samuel	.05
284	Rick Aguilera	.05
285	Jeff Reardon	.05
286	Sammy Sosa	3.00
287	Carmelo Martinez	.05
288	Greg Swindell	.05
289	Erik Hanson	.05
290	Tony Pena	.05
291	Pascual Perez	.05
292	Rickey Henderson	.50
293	Kurt Stillwell	.05
294	Todd Zeile	.05
295	Bobby Thigpen	.05
296	Larry Walker	.05
297	Rob Murphy	.05
298	Mitch Webster	.05
299	Devon White	.05
300	Len Dykstra	.05
301	Keith Hernandez	.05
302	Gene Larkin	.05
303	Jeffrey Leonard	.05
304	Jim Presley	.05
305	Lloyd Moseby	.05
306	John Smoltz	.05
307	Sam Horn	.05
308	Greg Litton	.05
309	Dave Henderson	.05
310	Mark McLemore	.05
311	Gary Pettis	.05
312	Mark Davis	.05
313	Cecil Fielder	.05
314	Jack Armstrong	.05
315	Alvin Davis	.05
316	Doug Jones	.05
317	Eric Yelding	.05
318	Joe Orsulak	.05
319	Chuck Finley	.05
320	Glenn Wilson	.05
321	Harold Reynolds	.05
322	Teddy Higuera	.05
323	Lance Parrish	.05
324	Bruce Hurst	.05
325	Dave West	.05
326	Kirk Gibson	.05
327	Cal Ripken, Jr.	1.50
328	Rick Reuschel	.05
329	Jim Abbott	.05
330	Checklist	.05

George Bush

GEORGE BUSH

As a favor to President George Bush, Topps produced a special run of 100 cards in its 1990 design featuring a photo of the president in his Yale University baseball uniform. At least a few of the cards reportedly were inadvertently included in regular Topps packages and made their way into the hobby.

		NM/M
USA1	George Bush (7/05 Auction)	2,000

Coins

Sixty top stars and promising rookies are featured in this fourth annual coin set. Fronts of the 1-1/2"

diameter coins feature a portrait photo with a symbolic infield. Player name and team appear below. Most coins feature natural aluminum coloring on the rolled edges and on the back. Special coins of major award winners have different colors in the background and edges. Backs feature a coin number, minimal biographical data and a previous season career summary. Coins were sold three per pack which included an offer card for a coin holder and Topps magazine subscription offer.

	NM/M
Factory Set (60):	15.00
Complete Set (60):	7.50
Common Player:	.15
Wax Pack (3):	.75
Wax Box (36):	9.00

1	Robin Yount	.50
2	Bret Saberhagen	.15
3	Gregg Olson	.15
4	Kirby Puckett	.65
5	George Bell	.15
6	Wade Boggs	.65
7	Jerry Browne	.15
8	Ellis Burks	.15
9	Ivan Calderon	.15
10	Tom Candiotti	.15
11	Alvin Davis	.15
12	Chili Davis	.15
13	Chuck Finley	.15
14	Gary Gaetti	.15
15	Tom Gordon	.15
16	Ken Griffey Jr.	.75
17	Rickey Henderson	.50
18	Kent Hrbek	.15
19	Bo Jackson	.20
20	Carlos Martinez	.15
21	Don Mattingly	.75
22	Fred McGriff	.15
23	Paul Molitor	.50
24	Cal Ripken, Jr.	1.00
25	Nolan Ryan	1.00
26	Steve Sax	.15
27	Gary Sheffield	.30
28	Ruben Sierra	.15
29	Dave Stewart	.15
30	Mickey Tettleton	.15
31	Alan Trammell	.15
32	Lou Whitaker	.15
33	Kevin Mitchell	.15
34	Mark Davis	.15
35	Jerome Walton	.15
36	Tony Gwynn	.65
37	Roberto Alomar	.25
38	Tim Belcher	.15
39	Craig Biggio	.15
40	Barry Bonds	1.00
41	Bobby Bonilla	.15
42	Joe Carter	.15
43	Will Clark	.15
44	Eric Davis	.15
45	Glenn Davis	.15
46	Sid Fernandez	.15
47	Pedro Guerrero	.15
48	Von Hayes	.15
49	Tom Herr	.15
50	Howard Johnson	.15
51	Barry Larkin	.15
52	Joe Magrane	.15
53	Dale Murphy	.25
54	Tim Raines	.15
55	Willie Randolph	.15
56	Ryne Sandberg	.65
57	Dwight Smith	.15
58	Lonnie Smith	.15
59	Robby Thompson	.15
60	Tim Wallach	.15

Double Headers

CARLTON FISK

For a second (and final) year, Topps produced an issue of mini cards encased in plastic stands and marketed as Double Headers. Each piece features a 1-5/8" x 2-1/4" reproduction of the player's Topps rookie card, backed by a reproduction of his card from the regular 1990 Topps set. The size of the DH set was increased from 24 in 1989 to 72 for 1990. The novelties were

sold for 50 cents apiece. The unnumbered cards are checklisted here alphabetically.

	NM/M
Complete Set (72):	25.00
Common Player:	.25
Wax Pack (1):	.50
Wax Box (36):	15.00

(1)	Jim Abbott	.25
(2)	Jeff Ballard	.25
(3)	George Bell	.25
(4)	Wade Boggs	1.00
(5)	Barry Bonds	2.50
(6)	Bobby Bonilla	.25
(7)	Ellis Burks	.25
(8)	Jose Canseco	.50
(9)	Joe Carter	.25
(10)	Will Clark	.25
(11)	Roger Clemens	1.25
(12)	Vince Coleman	.25
(13)	Alvin Davis	.25
(14)	Eric Davis	.25
(15)	Glenn Davis	.25
(16)	Mark Davis	.25
(17)	Andre Dawson	.40
(18)	Shawon Dunston	.25
(19)	Dennis Eckersley	.60
(20)	Sid Fernandez	.25
(21)	Tony Fernandez	.25
(22)	Chuck Finley	.25
(23)	Carlton Fisk	.75
(24)	Julio Franco	.25
(25)	Gary Gaetti	.25
(26)	Dwight Gooden	.25
(27)	Mark Grace	.25
(28)	Mike Greenwell	.25
(29)	Ken Griffey Jr.	1.50
(30)	Pedro Guerrero	.25
(31)	Tony Gwynn	1.00
(32)	Von Hayes	.25
(33)	Rickey Henderson	.75
(34)	Orel Hershiser	.25
(35)	Bo Jackson	.35
(36)	Gregg Jefferies	.25
(37)	Howard Johnson	.25
(38)	Ricky Jordan	.25
(39)	Carney Lansford	.25
(40)	Barry Larkin	.25
(41)	Greg Maddux	1.00
(42)	Joe Magrane	.25
(43)	Don Mattingly	1.25
(44)	Fred McGriff	.25
(45)	Mark McGwire	2.00
(46)	Kevin McReynolds	.25
(47)	Kevin Mitchell	.25
(48)	Gregg Olson	.25
(49)	Kirby Puckett	1.00
(50)	Tim Raines	.25
(51)	Harold Reynolds	.25
(52)	Cal Ripken, Jr.	2.50
(53)	Nolan Ryan	2.50
(54)	Bret Saberhagen	.25
(55)	Ryne Sandberg	1.00
(56)	Benito Santiago	.25
(57)	Steve Sax	.25
(58)	Mike Scioscia	.25
(59)	Mike Scott	.25
(60)	Ruben Sierra	.25
(61)	Lonnie Smith	.25
(62)	Ozzie Smith	1.00
(63)	Dave Stewart	.25
(64)	Darryl Strawberry	.25
(65)	Greg Swindell	.25
(66)	Alan Trammell	.25
(67)	Frank Viola	.25
(68)	Tim Wallach	.25
(69)	Jerome Walton	.25
(70)	Lou Whitaker	.25
(71)	Mitch Williams	.25
(72)	Robin Yount	.75

Experimental Mylar Stickers

JOE CARTER

Testing the concept of refractive printing, with stars in the background of these stickers, Topps produced a trial run of Mylar stickers using fronts from its 1990 Traded card set. Fronts of the 2-1/2" x 3-1/2" stickers are printed on metallic foil. Backs are blank.

	NM/M
Complete Set (6):	400.00
Common Player:	60.00

(1)	Joe Carter	60.00
(2)	Shane Mack	60.00
(3)	Alan Mills	60.00
(4)	Alejandro Pena	60.00
(5)	Gerald Perry	60.00
(6)	Dave Winfield	175.00

Gallery of Champions

FRED McGRIFF

The 1990 Topps 1/4-size metal baseball mini-cards were issued only as complete sets in a special display case. As with earlier editions, the 1-1/4" x 1-3/4" ingots do a creditable job of reproducing the players' 1990 Topps cards, right down to the tiny stats on the back. Players in the set represent the winners of major awards and statistical leaders from the previous season. A pewter Nolan Ryan 1/4-size card was issued as a sales incentive for dealers purchasing the Gallery of Champions sets.

	NM/M
Complete Aluminum Set (12):	15.00
Complete Bronze Set (12):	50.00
Complete Silver Set (12):	100.00

(1a)	Mark Davis/Aluminum	1.00
(1b)	Mark Davis/Bronze	2.50
(1s)	Mark Davis/Silver	5.00
(2a)	Jose DeLeon /Aluminum	1.00
(2b)	Jose DeLeon/Bronze	2.50
(2s)	Jose DeLeon/Silver	5.00
(3a)	Tony Gwynn/Aluminum	3.00
(3b)	Tony Gwynn/Bronze	7.50
(3s)	Tony Gwynn/Silver	20.00
(4a)	Fred McGriff/Aluminum	1.00
(4b)	Fred McGriff/Bronze	2.50
(4s)	Fred McGriff/Silver	5.00
(5a)	Kevin Mitchell/Aluminum	1.00
(5b)	Kevin Mitchell/Bronze	2.50
(5s)	Kevin Mitchell/Silver	5.00
(6a)	Gregg Olson/Aluminum	1.00
(6b)	Gregg Olson/Bronze	2.50
(6s)	Gregg Olson/Silver	5.00
(7a)	Kirby Puckett/Aluminum	3.00
(7b)	Kirby Puckett/Bronze	7.50
(7s)	Kirby Puckett/Silver	20.00
(8a)	Jeff Russell/Aluminum	1.00
(8b)	Jeff Russell/Bronze	2.50
(8s)	Jeff Russell/Silver	5.00
(9a)	Nolan Ryan/Aluminum	10.00
(9b)	Nolan Ryan/Bronze	20.00
(9s)	Nolan Ryan/Silver	40.00
(9p)	Nolan Ryan/Pewter	35.00
(10a)	Bret Saberhagen/Aluminum	1.00
(10b)	Bret Saberhagen/Bronze	2.50
(10s)	Bret Saberhagen/Silver	5.00
(11a)	Jerome Walton/Aluminum	1.00
(11b)	Jerome Walton/Bronze	2.50
(11s)	Jerome Walton/Silver	5.00
(12a)	Robin Yount/Aluminum	2.00
(12b)	Robin Yount/Bronze	5.00
(12s)	Robin Yount/Silver	15.00

Golden Spikes Award

ALEX FERNANDEZ

This one-card "set" was given out at the United States Baseball Federation awards luncheon in New York City on Nov. 14, 1990, honoring Alex Fernandez as the outstanding amateur baseball player of the year and winner of the Golden Spikes Award. The rough borders found on many of these cards indi-

cates they were cut from the press sheet by hand. Production was reported as 600 cards.

	NM/M
Alex Fernandez	85.00

Heads Up!

Following up a much rarer test issue of the previous year, the Heads Up! BaseballAll-Stars of 1990 was a 24-piece set which received much wider distribution, but proved unpopular with collectors. On heavy cardboard, die-cut to approximately 5" x 6", these novelties featured only a head-and-cap photo of the player. Backs have the player's name and team, along with an adhesive strip and plastic suction cup which could be used to "hang" the player.

	NM/M
Complete Set (24):	10.00
Common Player:	.50
Wax Pack (1):	.75
Wax Box (24):	10.00

1	Tony Gwynn	2.00
2	Will Clark	.50
3	Dwight Gooden	.50
4	Dennis Eckersley	1.25
5	Ken Griffey Jr.	3.00
6	Craig Biggio	.50
7	Bret Saberhagen	.50
8	Bo Jackson	.75
9	Ryne Sandberg	2.00
10	Gregg Olson	.50
11	John Franco	.50
12	Rafael Palmeiro	1.25
13	Gary Sheffield	1.00
14	Mark McGwire	4.00
15	Kevin Mitchell	.50
16	Jim Abbott	.50
17	Harold Reynolds	.50
18	Jose Canseco	1.00
19	Don Mattingly	2.50
20	Kirby Puckett	2.00
21	Tom Gordon	.50
22	Craig Worthington	.50
23	Dwight Smith	.50
24	Jerome Walton	.50

Magazine

ROYCE

Beginning with its debut issue dated Winter, 1990, Topps Magazine included sportscards in each quarterly issue. Generally printed on perforated panels which could be easily separated from the magazine and the other cards, six to eight cards were included in most issues. Most of the cards were original designs, but some depicted then-current players on Topps designs from previous years. For the duration of their issue, the cards were numbered nonconsecutively with a "TM" prefix.

	NM/M
Complete Set (112):	50.00
Common Player:	.25

1	Dave Staton	.25
2	Dan Peltier	.25
3	Ken Griffey Jr.	2.00
4	Ruben Sierra	.25
5	Bret Saberhagen	.25
6	Jerome Walton	.25
7	Kevin Mitchell	.25
8	Mike Scott	.25
9	Bo Jackson	.30
10	Nolan Ryan	3.00
11	Will Clark	.25
12	Robin Yount	.75
13	Joe Morgan	.75
14	Jim Palmer	.75
15	Ben McDonald	.25
16	John Olerud	.25
17	Don Mattingly	1.50
18	Eric Davis, Barry Larkin, Chris Sabo	.25
19	Jim Abbott	.25
20	Sandy Alomar Jr.	.25
21	Jose Canseco	.50
22	Delino DeShields	.25
23	Wade Boggs	1.00
24	Kirby Puckett	1.00
25	Ryne Sandberg	1.00
26	Roger Clemens	1.25
27	Ken Griffey Jr., Ken Griffey Sr.	1.00
28	Cecil Fielder	.25
29	Steve Avery	.25
30	Rickey Henderson	.75
31	Kevin Maas	.25
32	Len Dykstra	.25
33	Darryl Strawberry	.25
34	Mark McGwire	2.25
35	Matt Williams	.25
36	David Justice	.25
37	Cincinnati Reds	.25
38	Todd Van Poppel	.25
39	Jose Offerman	.25
40	Alex Fernandez	.25
41	Carlton Fisk	.75
42	Barry Bonds	3.00
43	Bobby Bonilla	.25
44	Bob Welch	.25
45	Mo Vaughn	.25
46	Tino Martinez	.25
47	D.J. Dozier	.25
48	Frank Thomas	.75
49	Cal Ripken Jr.	
	('75 Topps Style)	3.00
50	Dave Winfield	
	('75 Topps Style)	.75
51	Dwight Gooden	
	('75 Topps Style)	.25
52	Bo Jackson	
	('75 Topps Style)	.30
53	Kirk Dressendorfer	.25
54	Gary Scott	.25
55	Steve Decker	.25
56	Ray Lankford	.25
57	Ozzie Smith	
	('86 Topps Style)	1.00
58	Joe Carter	
	('86 Topps Style)	.25
59	Dave Henderson	
	('86 Topps Style)	.25
60	Tony Gwynn	
	('86 Topps Style)	1.00
61	Jeff Bagwell	.75
62	Scott Erickson	.25
63	Pat Kelly	.25
64	Orlando Merced	.40
65	Andre Dawson	.40
66	Reggie Sanders	.25
67	Phil Plantier	.25
68	Paul Molitor	.75
69	Terry Pendleton	.25
70	Julio Franco	.25
71	Lee Smith	.25
72	'91 Minnesota Twins	.25
73	Royce Clayton	.25
74	Tom Glavine	.45
75	Roger Salkeld	.25
76	Robin Ventura	.25
77	John Goodman (As Babe Ruth.)	.25
78	Jack Morris	.25
79	Brien Taylor	.25
80	Howard Johnson	.25
81	Barry Larkin	.25
82	Deion Sanders	.30
83	Mike Mussina	.60
84	Juan Gonzalez	.50
85	Roberto Alomar	.50
86	Fred McGriff	.25
87	Doug Drabek	.25
88	George Brett	1.25
89	Otis Nixon	.25
90	Brady Anderson	.25
91	Gary Sheffield	.50
92	Dave Fleming	.25
93	Jeff Reardon	.25
94	Mark McGwire	2.25
95	Larry Walker	.25
96	John Kruk	.25
97	Carlos Baerga	.25
98	Pat Listach	.25
99	'92 Toronto Blue Jays	.25
100	Eric Karros	.25
101	Bret Boone	.25
102	Al Martin	.25
103	Wil Cordero	.25
104	Tim Salmon	.25
105	Danny Tartabull	.25
106	J.T. Snow	.25
107	Mike Piazza	1.50
108	Frank Viola	.25
109	Nolan Ryan (Mets)	2.25
110	Nolan Ryan (Angels)	2.25
111	Nolan Ryan (Astros)	2.25
112	Nolan Ryan (Rangers)	2.25

Mini League Leaders

The last in a five-year string of mini cards, the 1990 league leaders' set offers players who were in the top five in major batting and pitching stats during the 1989 season. Fronts of the 2-1/8" x 3" cards mimic the regular Topps' design for 1990; featuring an action photo with multi-colored borders. Backs offer a round player portrait photo and information about the statistical achievement, all printed in full color. Cards are numbered alphabetically within teams. The 1990 minis are considerably scarcer than the previous years' offerings.

		NM/M
Complete Set (88):		5.00
Common Player:		.05
1	Jeff Ballard	.05
2	Phil Bradley	.05
3	Wade Boggs	.65
4	Roger Clemens	.75
5	Nick Esasky	.05
6	Jody Reed	.05
7	Bert Blyleven	.05
8	Chuck Finley	.05
9	Kirk McCaskill	.05
10	Devon White	.05
11	Ivan Calderon	.05
12	Bobby Thigpen	.05
13	Joe Carter	.05
14	Gary Pettis	.05
15	Tom Gordon	.05
16	Bo Jackson	.10
17	Bret Saberhagen	.05
18	Kevin Seitzer	.05
19	Chris Bosio	.05
20	Paul Molitor	.50
21	Dan Plesac	.05
22	Robin Yount	.50
23	Kirby Puckett	.65
24	Don Mattingly	.75
25	Steve Sax	.05
26	Storm Davis	.05
27	Dennis Eckersley	.40
28	Rickey Henderson	.50
29	Carney Lansford	.05
30	Mark McGwire	1.00
31	Mike Moore	.05
32	Dave Stewart	.05
33	Alvin Davis	.05
34	Harold Reynolds	.05
35	Mike Schooler	.05
36	Cecil Espy	.05
37	Julio Franco	.05
38	Jeff Russell	.05
39	Nolan Ryan	1.50
40	Ruben Sierra	.05
41	George Bell	.05
42	Tony Fernandez	.05
43	Fred McGriff	.05
44	Dave Steib	.05
45	Checklist	.05
46	Lonnie Smith	.05
47	John Smoltz	.05
48	Mike Bielecki	.05
49	Mark Grace	.05
50	Greg Maddux	.65
51	Ryne Sandberg	.65
52	Mitch Williams	.05
53	Eric Davis	.05
54	John Franco	.05
55	Glenn Davis	.05
56	Mike Scott	.05
57	Tim Belcher	.05
58	Orel Hershiser	.05
59	Jay Howell	.05
60	Eddie Murray	.50
61	Tim Burke	.05
62	Mark Langston	.05
63	Tim Raines	.05
64	Tim Wallach	.05
65	David Cone	.05
66	Sid Fernandez	.05
67	Howard Johnson	.05
68	Juan Samuel	.05
69	Von Hayes	.05
70	Barry Bonds	1.50
71	Bobby Bonilla	.05
72	Andy Van Slyke	.05
73	Vince Coleman	.05
74	Jose DeLeon	.05
75	Pedro Guerrero	.05
76	Joe Magrane	.05
77	Roberto Alomar	.20
78	Jack Clark	.05
79	Mark Davis	.05
80	Tony Gwynn	.65
81	Bruce Hurst	.05
82	Eddie Whitson	.05
83	Brett Butler	.05
84	Will Clark	.05
85	Scott Garrelts	.05
86	Kevin Mitchell	.05
87	Rick Reuschel	.05
88	Robby Thompson	.05

Nolan Ryan Bronze

This full-size bronze reproduction of Ryan's 1990 Topps card was given to dealers who made early orders for Topps' 1991 "Tiffany" sets. A 2,500 piece limit was announced.

	NM/M
Nolan Ryan	50.00

Senior League

Topps was among several companies to produce a Senior League set in 1990. The set includes 132 cards and was sold as a boxed set. The card fronts have the Senior Baseball and Topps logo on top and the player's name and team logo on the bottom, with a woodgrain-like border surrounding the front photo. The backs of the card include traditional biographical information, plus career major league statistics, career ML bests and stats from any Senior League experience.

		NM/M
Complete Set (132):		5.00
Common Player:		.05
1	George Foster	.15
2	Dwight Lowry	.05
3	Bob Jones	.05
4	Clete Boyer	.05
5	Rafael Landestoy	.05
6	Bob Shirley	.05
7	Ivan Murrell	.05
8	Jerry White	.05
9	Steve Henderson	.05
10	Marty Castillo	.05
11	Bruce Kison	.05
12	George Hendrick	.05
13	Bernie Carbo	.05
14	Jerry Martin	.05
15	Al Hrabosky	.05
16	Luis Gomez	.05
17	Dick Drago	.05
18	Bobby Ramos	.05
19	Joe Pittman	.05
20	Ike Blessitt	.05
21	Bill Travers	.05
22	Dick Williams	.05
23	Randy Lerch	.05
24	Tom Spencer	.05
25	Graig Nettles	.05
26	Jim Gideon	.05
27	Al Bumbry	.05
28	Tom Murphy	.05
29	Rodney Scott	.05
30	Alan Bannister	.05
31	John D'Acquisto	.05
32	Bert Campaneris	.05
33	Bill Lee	.05
34	Jerry Grote	.05
35	Ken Reitz	.05
36	Al Oliver	.15
37	Tim Stoddard	.05
38	Lenny Randle	.05
39	Rick Manning	.05
40	Bobby Bonds	.15
41	Rick Wise	.05
42	Sal Butera	.05
43	Ed Figueroa	.05
44	Ron Washington	.05
45	Elias Sosa	.05
46	Dan Driessen	.05
47	Wayne Nordhagen	.05
48	Vida Blue	.05
49	Butch Hobson	.05
50	Randy Bass	.05
51	Paul Mirabella	.05
52	Steve Kemp	.05
53	Kim Allen	.05
54	Stan Cliburn	.05
55	Derrel Thomas	.05
56	Pete Falcone	.05
57	Willie Aikens	.05
58	Toby Harrah	.05
59	Bob Tolan	.05
60	Rick Waits	.05
61	Jim Morrison	.05
62	Stan Bahnsen	.05
63	Gene Richards	.05
64	Dave Cash	.05
65	Rollie Fingers	.50
66	Butch Benton	.05
67	Tim Ireland	.05
68	Rick Lysander	.05
69	Cesar Cedeno	.05
70	Jim Willoughby	.05
71	Bill Madlock	.15
72	Lee Lacy	.05
73	Milt Wilcox	.05
74	Ron Pruitt	.05
75	Wayne Krenchicki	.05
76	Earl Weaver	.25
77	Pedro Borbon	.05
78	Jose Cruz	.05
79	Steve Ontiveros	.05
80	Mike Easler	.05
81	Amos Otis	.05
82	Mickey Mahler	.05
83	Orlando Gonzalez	.05
84	Doug Simunic	.05
85	Felix Millan	.05
86	Garth Iorg	.05
87	Pete Broberg	.05
88	Roy Howell	.05
89	Dave LaRoche	.05
90	Jerry Manuel	.05
91	Tony Scott	.05
92	Larvell Blanks	.05
93	Joaquin Andujar	.05
94	Tito Landrum	.05
95	Joe Sambito	.05
96	Pat Dobson	.05
97	Dan Meyer	.05
98	Clint Hurdle	.05
99	Pete LaCock	.05
100	Bob Galasso	.05
101	Dave Kingman	.15
102	Jon Matlack	.05
103	Larry Harlow	.05
104	Rick Peterson	.05
105	Joe Hicks	.05
106	Bill Campbell	.05
107	Tom Paciorek	.05
108	Ray Burris	.05
109	Ken Landreaux	.05
110	Steve McCatty	.05
111	Ron LeFlore	.05
112	Joe Decker	.05
113	Leon Roberts	.05
114	Doug Corbett	.05
115	Mickey Rivers	.05
116	Dock Ellis	.05
117	Ron Jackson	.05
118	Bob Molinaro	.05
119	Fergie Jenkins	.50
120	U.L. Washington	.05
121	Roy Thomas	.05
122	Hal McRae	.15
123	Juan Eichelberger	.05
124	Gary Rajsich	.05
125	Dennis Leonard	.05
126	Walt Williams	.05
127	Rennie Stennett	.05
128	Jim Bibby	.05
129	Dyar Miller	.05
130	Luis Pujols	.05
131	Juan Beniquez	.05
132	Checklist	.05

Stickercards

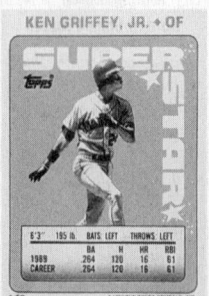

Providing a cardboard backing for its annual series of player stickers, the stickercards are a collectible in themselves. Each 2-1/8" x 3" card is backed by one or two player stickers which could be removed and placed into a special album. The card portion features a player photo set against a solid-color background. A few vitae plus 1989 and career stats are presented in a graduated-color box toward the bottom. The stickercards are sequenced by position within league.

		NM/M
Complete Set (67):		5.00
Common Player:		.05
Wax Pack (5):		.25
Wax Box (48):		10.00
1	Will Clark	.05
2	Glenn Davis	.05
3	Pedro Guerrero	.05
4	Roberto Alomar	.15
5	Gregg Jefferies	.05
6	Ryne Sandberg	.60
7	Bobby Bonilla	.05
8	Howard Johnson	.05
9	Tim Wallach	.05
10	Shawon Dunston	.05
11	Barry Larkin	.05
12	Ozzie Smith	.60
13	Eric Davis	.05
14	Andre Dawson	.25
15	Tony Gwynn	.60
16	Von Hayes	.05
17	Kevin Mitchell	.05
18	Rock Raines	.05
19	Lonnie Smith	.05
20	Darryl Strawberry	.05
21	Jerome Walton	.05
22	Craig Biggio	.05
23	Benito Santiago	.05
24	Mike Scioscia	.05
25	Doc Gooden	.05
26	Rick Reuschel	.05
27	Mike Scott	.05
28	Sid Fernandez	.05
29	Mark Langston	.05
30	Joe Magrane	.05
31	Mark Davis	.05
32	Jay Howell	.05
33	Mitch Williams	.05
34	Don Mattingly	.65
35	Fred McGriff	.05
36	Mark McGwire	.85
37	Julio Franco	.05
38	Steve Sax	.05
39	Lou Whitaker	.05
40	Wade Boggs	.60
41	Gary Gaetti	.05
42	Carney Lansford	.05
43	Tony Fernandez	.05
44	Cal Ripken Jr.	1.00
45	Alan Trammell	.05
46	George Bell	.05
47	Jose Canseco	.35
48	Joe Carter	.05
49	Ken Griffey Jr.	.75
50	Rickey Henderson	.45
51	Bo Jackson	.10
52	Kirby Puckett	.60
53	Ruben Sierra	.05
54	Robin Yount	.45
55	Carlton Fisk	.45
56	Terry Steinbach	.05
57	Mickey Tettleton	.05
58	Nolan Ryan	1.00
59	Bret Saberhagen	.05
60	Dave Stewart	.05
61	Jeff Ballard	.05
62	Chuck Finley	.05
63	Greg Swindell	.05
64	Dennis Eckersley	.40
65	Gregg Olson	.05
66	Jeff Russell	.05
67	Checklist	.05

OPC Stickers

Topps' 1990 stickers were produced in two formats. Some measure 2-1/8" x 3" while there are many pairs of half-size (1-1/2" x 2-1/8") stickers. All stickers are attached to Super Star stickercards from which they can be peeled and affixed in a special yearbook. Stickers have large center photos with a shadowbox effect in the borders, (blues for N.L., reds for A.L.). A tiny black sticker number is in the lower-right corner. There is no player name on the stickers; the albums have a box under each space with player data. The half-size stickers are printed in pairs and are checklisted in that fashion. Values given are for complete sticker(s)/stickercard combinations, but without regard for which sticker is on back. The checklist and values for the O-Pee-Chee version of this set are identical to those for the Topps brand. Packs of five stickers sold for a quarter; the album with Don Mattingly on the cover retailed for 50 cents. Numbers in parentheses in this checklist indicate with which other sticker the named sticker is paired in the smaller format.

		NM/M
Complete Set (328):		7.50
Common Sticker:		.05
Album:		2.00
1	Rick Cerone/321 (Highlight)	.05
2	Kevin Elster/322 (Highlight)	.05
3	Nolan Ryan/323 (Highlight)	.45
4	Vince Coleman/319 (Highlight)	.05
5	Cal Ripken Jr./240 (Highlight)	.45
6	Jeff Reardon/328 (Highlight)	.05
7	Rickey Henderson/320 (Highlight)	.15
8	Wade Boggs/324 (Highlight)	.30
9	Barry Bonds/325 (Highlight)	.45
10	Gregg Olson/236 (Highlight)	.05
11	Tony Fernandez/327 (Highlight)	.05
12	Ryne Sandberg/326 (Highlight)	.30
13	Glenn Davis	.05
14	Danny Darwin/316	.05
15	Bill Doran/298	.05
16	Dave Smith/225	.05
17	Kevin Bass/278	.05
18	Rafael Ramirez/177	.05
19	Mike Scott	.05
20	Ken Caminiti/235	.05
21	Jim Deshaies/272	.05
22	Gerald Young/314	.05
23	Craig Biggio/186	.05
24	Lonnie Smith	.05
25	Dale Murphy/210	.10
26	Tom Glavine	.15
27	Gerald Perry/313	.05
28	Jeff Blauser/269	.05
29	Jeff Treadway/252	.05
30	John Smoltz/299	.05
31	Darrell Evans/295	.05
32	Oddibe McDowell/265	.05
33	Andres Thomas/304	.05
34	Joe Boever/191	.05
35	Pedro Guerrero	.05
36	Ken Dayley/226	.05
37	Milt Thompson/188	.05
38	Jose DeLeon/180	.05
39	Vince Coleman/293	.05
40	Terry Pendleton/225	.05
41	Joe Magrane	.05
42	Ozzie Smith/179	.30
43	Todd Worrell/195	.05
44	Jose Oquendo/238	.05
45	Tom Brunansky/287	.05
46	Ryne Sandberg	.60
47	Andre Dawson/268	.15
48	Mitch Williams	.05
49	Damon Berryhill/204	.05
50	Jerome Walton/274	.05
51	Greg Maddux/315	.30
52	Dwight Smith/248	.05
53	Shawon Dunston/194	.05
55	Mike Bielecki/239	.05
55	Rick Sutcliffe/305	.05
56	Mark Grace/228	.05
57	Eddie Murray	.40
58	Alfredo Griffin/197	.05
59	Fernando Valenzuela/277	.05
60	Kirk Gibson/201	.05
61	Ramon Martinez/190	.05
62	Mike Marshall/309	.05
63	Orel Hershiser	.05
64	Mike Scioscia/271	.05
65	Jay Howell/279	.05
66	Willie Randolph/283	.05
67	Jeff Hamilton/280	.05
68	Denny Martinez	.05
69	Tim Raines/184	.05
70	Mark Langston	.05
71	Dave Martinez/301	.05
72	Tim Burke/258	.05
73	Spike Owen/232	.05
74	Tim Wallach/254	.05
75	Andres Galarraga/208	.05
76	Kevin Gross/234	.05
77	Hubie Brooks/263	.05
78	Bryn Smith/207	.05
79	Kevin Mitchell	.05
80	Craig Lefferts/256	.05
81	Ernest Riles/247	.05
82	Scott Garrelts/185	.05
83	Robby Thompson/251	.05
84	Don Robinson/282	.05
85	Will Clark	.05
86	Steve Bedrosian/183	.05
87	Brett Butler/284	.05
88	Matt Williams/227	.05
89	Rick Reuschel/291	.05
90	Howard Johnson	.05
91	Darryl Strawberry/246	.05
92	Sid Fernandez	.05
93	David Cone/189	.05
94	Kevin McReynolds/311	.05
95	Frank Viola/229	.05
96	Dwight Gooden/206	.05
97	Kevin Elster/267	.05
98	Ron Darling/289	.05
99	Dave Magadan/257	.05
100	Randy Myers/192	.05
101	Tony Gwynn	.60
102	Mark Davis/312	.05
103	Bip Roberts/212	.05
104	Jack Clark/205	.05
105	Chris James/211	.05
106	Mike Pagliarulo/199	.05
107	Ed Whitson	.05
108	Bruce Hurst/245	.05
109	Roberto Alomar/202	.15
110	Benito Santiago/224	.05
111	Eric Show/307	.05
112	Ricky Jordan	.05
113	Steve Jeltz/203	.05
114	Von Hayes	.05
115	Dickie Thon/182	.05
116	Ken Howell/213	.05
117	John Kruk/306	.05
118	Lenny Dykstra/302	.05
119	Jeff Parrett/300	.05
120	Randy Ready/230	.05
121	Roger McDowell/262	.05
122	Tom Herr/250	.05
123	Barry Bonds	.90
124	Andy Van Slyke/219	.05
125	Bob Walk/216	.05
126	R.J. Reynolds/243	.05
127	Gary Redus/249	.05
128	Bill Landrum/276	.05
129	Bobby Bonilla	.05
130	Doug Drabek/218	.05
131	Jose Lind/221	.05
132	John Smiley/241	.05
133	Mike LaValliere/214	.05
134	Eric Davis	.05
135	Tom Browning/270	.05
136	Barry Larkin	.05
137	Jose Rijo/318	.05
138	Todd Benzinger/292	.05
139	Rick Mahler/217	.05
140	Chris Sabo/196	.05
141	Paul O'Neill/175	.05
142	Danny Jackson/273	.05
143	Rolando Roomes/261	.05
144	John Franco/233	.05
145	Ozzie Smith/AS	.30
146	Tony Gwynn/AS	.30
147	Will Clark/AS	.05
148	Kevin Mitchell/AS	.05
149	Eric Davis/AS	.05
150	Howard Johnson/AS	.05
151	Pedro Guerrero/AS	.05
152	Ryne Sandberg/AS	.05
153	Benito Santiago/AS	.05
154	Rick Reuschel/AS	.05
155	Bo Jackson/AS	.05
156	Wade Boggs/AS	.35
157	Kirby Puckett/AS	.30
158	Harold Baines/AS	.05
159	Julio Franco/AS	.05
160	Cal Ripken Jr./AS	.45
161	Ruben Sierra/AS	.05
162	Mark McGwire/AS	.40
163	Terry Steinbach/AS	.05
164	Dave Stewart/AS	.05
165	Bert Blyleven	.05
166	Wally Joyner/285	.05
167	Kirk McCaskill/290	.05
168	Devon White/223	.05
169	Brian Downing/294	.05
170	Lance Parrish/296	.05
171	Chuck Finley	.05
172	Jim Abbott/317	.05
173	Chili Davis/181	.05
174	Johnny Ray/260	.05
175	Bryan Harvey/141	.05
176	Mark McGwire	.75
177	Jose Canseco/18	.15
178	Mike Moore	.05
179	Dave Parker/42	.05
180	Bob Welch/38	.05
181	Rickey Henderson/173	.25
182	Dennis Eckersley/115	.20
183	Carney Lansford/86	.05
184	Dave Henderson/69	.05
185	Dave Stewart/82	.05
186	Terry Steinbach/23	.05
187	Fred McGriff	.05
188	Junior Felix/37	.05
189	Ernie Whitt/93	.05
190	Dave Smith/61	.05
191	Jimmy Key/34	.05
192	George Bell/100	.05
193	Kelly Gruber	.05
194	Tony Fernandez/53	.05
195	John Cerutti/43	.05
196	Tom Henke/140	.05
197	Nelson Liriano/58	.05
198	Robin Yount	.40
199	Paul Molitor/106	.05
200	Dan Plesac	.05
201	Teddy Higuera/60	.05
202	Gary Sheffield/109	.15
203	B.J. Surhoff/113	.05
204	Rob Deer/49	.05

205	Chris Bosio/104	.05
206	Glenn Braggs/96	.05
207	Jim Gantner/78	.05
208	Greg Brock/75	.05
209	Joe Carter	.05
210	Jerry Browne/25	.05
211	Cory Snyder/105	.05
212	Joey Belle/103	.10
213	Bud Black/116	.05
214	Greg Swindell/133	.05
215	Doug Jones	.05
216	Tom Candiotti/125	.05
217	John Farrell/139	.05
218	Pete O'Brien/130	.05
219	Brook Jacoby/124	.05
220	Alvin Davis	.05
221	Harold Reynolds/131	.05
222	Scott Bankhead	.05
223	Jeffrey Leonard/168	.05
224	Jim Presley/110	.05
225	Ken Griffey Jr./40	.40
226	Greg Briley/36	.05
227	Darnell Coles/88	.05
228	Mike Schooler/56	.05
229	Scott Bradley/95	.05
230	Randy Johnson/120	.25
231	Cal Ripken Jr.	.90
232	Jeff Ballard/73	.05
233	Randy Milligan/144	.05
234	Joe Orsulak/76	.05
235	Billy Ripken/20	.05
236	Mark Williamson/10	.05
237	Mickey Tettleton	.05
238	Gregg Olson/44	.05
239	Craig Worthington/54	.05
240	Bob Milacki/5	.05
241	Phil Bradley/132	.05
242	Nolan Ryan	.90
243	Julio Franco/126	.05
244	Ruben Sierra	.05
245	Harold Baines/128	.05
246	Jeff Kunkel/91	.05
247	Pete Incaviglia/81	.05
248	Kevin Brown/52	.05
249	Cecil Espy/127	.05
250	Rafael Palmeiro/122	.20
251	Steve Buechele/83	.05
252	Jeff Russell/29	.05
253	Wade Boggs	.60
254	Mike Greenwell/74	.05
255	Roger Clemens/16	.35
256	Marty Barrett/80	.05
257	Dwight Evans/99	.05
258	Mike Boddicker/72	.05
259	Ellis Burks	.05
260	John Dopson/174	.05
261	Rob Murphy/143	.05
262	Lee Smith/121	.05
263	Nick Esasky/77	.05
264	Bo Jackson	.10
265	George Brett/32	.35
266	Bret Saberhagen	.05
267	Kevin Seitzer/97	.05
268	Tom Gordon/47	.05
269	Kurt Stillwell/28	.05
270	Steve Farr/135	.05
271	Jim Eisenreich/64	.05
272	Mark Gubicza/21	.05
273	Jeff Montgomery/142	.05
274	Danny Tartabull/50	.05
275	Lou Whitaker	.05
276	Jack Morris/128	.05
277	Frank Tanana/59	.05
278	Chet Lemon/17	.05
279	Fred Lynn/65	.05
280	Mike Heath/67	.05
281	Alan Trammell/85	.05
282	Mike Henneman/84	.05
283	Gary Pettis/56	.05
284	Jeff Robinson/87	.05
285	Dave Bergman/166	.05
286	Kirby Puckett	.60
287	Kent Hrbek/45	.05
288	Gary Gaetti	.05
289	Jeff Reardon/98	.05
290	Brian Harper/167	.05
291	Gene Larkin/89	.05
292	Dan Gladden/138	.05
293	Al Newman/39	.05
294	Randy Bush/169	.05
295	Greg Gagne/31	.05
296	Allan Anderson/170	.05
297	Bobby Thigpen	.05
298	Ozzie Guillen/15	.05
299	Ivan Calderon/39	.05
300	Carlos Martinez/119	.05
301	Steve Lyons/71	.05
302	Ron Kittle/118	.05
303	Carlton Fisk	.40
304	Melido Perez/33	.05
305	Dave Gallagher/55	.05
306	Dan Pasqua/117	.05
307	Scott Fletcher/111	.05
308	Don Slaught/137	.65
309	Dave Righetti/62	.05
310	Steve Sax	.05
311	Alvaro Espinoza/94	.05
312	Roberto Kelly/102	.05
313	Mel Hall/27	.05
314	Jesse Barfield/22	.05
315	Chuck Cary/51	.05
316	Bob Geren/14	.05
317	Andy Hawkins/172	.05
318	Don Slaught/137	.05
319	Jim Abbott/4 (Future Star)	.05
320	Greg Briley/7 (Future Star)	.05
321	Bob Geren/1 (Future Star)	.05

322	Tom Gordon/2 (Future Star)	.05
323	Ken Griffey Jr./3 (Future Star)	.30
324	Gregg Jefferies/8 (Future Star)	.10
325	Carlos Martinez/9 (Future Star)	.05
326	Gary Sheffield/12 (Future Star)	.15
327	Jerome Walton/11 (Future Star)	.05
328	Craig Worthington/6 (Future Star)	.05

TV All-Stars

This 66-card boxed set was sold only through a television offer in limited markets. Consequently, production numbers are relatively low and single cards are seldom offered in the hobby market. Most of the game's top stars are included in the issue. Fronts feature a high-gloss surface. On the red-bordered backs there are several lines of biographical data plus each player's "Career Bests" in various statistical categories, set against a pastel background shield. Issue price was $22.90.

		NM/M
Complete Set (66):		45.00
Common Player:		.25
1	Mark McGwire	6.50
2	Julio Franco	.25
3	Ozzie Guillen	.25
4	Carney Lansford	.25
5	Bo Jackson	.75
6	Kirby Puckett	3.50
7	Ruben Sierra	.25
8	Carlton Fisk	3.00
9	Nolan Ryan	9.00
10	Rickey Henderson	3.00
11	Jose Canseco	1.50
12	Mark Davis	.25
13	Dennis Eckersley	2.25
14	Chuck Finley	.25
15	Bret Saberhagen	.25
16	Dave Stewart	.25
17	Don Mattingly	5.00
18	Steve Sax	.25
19	Cal Ripken, Jr.	9.00
20	Wade Boggs	3.50
21	George Bell	.25
22	Mike Greenwell	.25
23	Robin Yount	3.00
24	Mickey Tettleton	.25
25	Roger Clemens	5.00
26	Fred McGriff	.25
27	Jeff Ballard	.25
28	Dwight Evans	.25
29	Paul Molitor	3.00
30	Gregg Olson	.25
31	Dan Plesac	.25
32	Greg Swindell	.25
33	Cito Gaston, Tony LaRussa	.25
34	Will Clark	3.50
35	Roberto Alomar	.75
36	Barry Larkin	.25
37	Ken Caminiti	.25
38	Eric Davis	.25
39	Tony Gwynn	3.50
40	Kevin Mitchell	.25
41	Craig Biggio	.25
42	Mike Scott	.25
43	Joe Carter	.25
44	Jack Clark	.25
45	Glenn Davis	.25
46	Orel Hershiser	.25
47	Jay Howell	.25
48	Bruce Hurst	.25
49	Dave Smith	.25
50	Pedro Guerrero	.25
51	Ryne Sandberg	3.50
52	Ozzie Smith	3.50
53	Howard Johnson	.25
54	Von Hayes	.25
55	Tim Raines	.25
56	Darryl Strawberry	.25
57	Mike LaValliere	.25
58	Dwight Gooden	.25
59	Bobby Bonilla	.25
60	Tim Burke	.25
61	Sid Fernandez	.25

62	Andres Galarraga	.25
63	Mark Grace	.25
64	Joe Magrane	.25
65	Mitch Williams	.25
66	Roger Craig, Don Zimmer	.25

TV Cardinals Team Set

Available only as a boxed set via a limited television offer, this team set includes cards of all players on the opening day roster plus the manager, selected coaches and many of the organization's top prospects. In many cases this is the first card of a player in major league uniform, and in some cases represents the only card which will ever be issued of the player as a major leaguer. Cards feature a high-gloss front surface. Backs have a red border and feature a "ghost image" of the photo on the front as a background to the statistical and biographical data. Because of the relatively limited production and the fact it was sold as a boxed set only, single cards are seldom available.

		NM/M
Complete Set (66):		20.00
Common Player:		.25
1	Whitey Herzog	.25
2	Steve Braun	.25
3	Rich Hacker	.25
4	Dave Ricketts	.25
5	Jim Riggleman	.25
6	Mike Roarke	.25
7	Cris Carpenter	.25
8	John Costello	.25
9	Danny Cox	.25
10	Ken Dayley	.25
11	Jose DeLeon	.25
12	Frank DiPino	.25
13	Ken Hill	.25
14	Howard Hilton	.25
15	Ricky Horton	.25
16	Joe Magrane	.25
17	Greg Mathews	.25
18	Bryn Smith	.25
19	Scott Terry	.25
20	Bob Tewksbury	.25
21	John Tudor	.25
22	Todd Worrell	.25
23	Tom Pagnozzi	.25
24	Todd Zeile	.50
25	Pedro Guerrero	.25
26	Tim Jones	.25
27	Jose Oquendo	.25
28	Terry Pendleton	.25
29	Ozzie Smith	15.00
30	Denny Walling	.25
31	Tom Brunansky	.25
32	Vince Coleman	.50
33	Dave Collins	.25
34	Willie McGee	.50
35	John Morris	.25
36	Milt Thompson	.25
37	Gibson Alba	.25
38	Scott Arnold	.25
39	Rod Brewer	.25
40	Greg Carmona	.25
41	Mark Clark	.25
42	Stan Clarke	.25
43	Paul Coleman	.25
44	Todd Crosby	.25
45	Brad DuVall	.25
46	John Ericks	.25
47	Bien Figueroa	.25
48	Terry Francona	.25
49	Ed Fulton	.25
50	Bernard Gilkey	1.00
51	Ernie Camacho	.25
52	Mike Hinkle	.25
53	Ray Lankford	1.00
54	Julian Martinez	.25
55	Jesus Mendez	.25
56	Mike Milchin	.25
57	Mauricio Nunez	.25
58	Omar Olivares	.25
59	Geronimo Pena	.25
60	Mike Perez	.25
61	Gaylen Pitts	.25
62	Mark Riggins	.25
63	Tim Sherrill	.25
64	Roy Silver	.25
65	Ray Stephens	.25
66	Craig Wilson	.25

TV Cubs Team Set

Sold only in boxed set form via a limited television offer, this 66-card issue includes all players on the team's 1990 opening day roster as well as the manager, selected coaches and some of the organization's top minor league prospects. For the latter group, this sets offers the first - and in many cases the only - card of the player in a major league uniform. The cards have a high-gloss front surface. Card backs feature a "ghost image" of the color photo used on the front as a background to the stats and biographical information. A red border completes the back design. Because the set was sold only in boxed form, and production was relatively low, single cards are seldom seen in the market.

		NM/M
Complete Set (66):		45.00
Common Player:		.35
1	Don Zimmer	.35
2	Joe Altobelli	.35
3	Chuck Cottier	.35
4	Jose Martinez	.35
5	Dick Pole	.35
6	Phil Roof	.35
7	Paul Assenmacher	.35
8	Mike Bielecki	.35
9	Mike Harkey	.35
10	Joe Kraemer	.35
11	Les Lancaster	.35
12	Greg Maddux	20.00
13	Jose Nunez	.35
14	Jeff Pico	.35
15	Rick Sutcliffe	.75
16	Dean Wilkins	.35
17	Mitch Williams	.35
18	Steve Wilson	.35
19	Damon Berryhill	.35
20	Joe Girardi	.35
21	Rick Wrona	.35
22	Shawon Dunston	.50
23	Mark Grace	5.00
24	Domingo Ramos	.35
25	Luis Salazar	.35
26	Ryne Sandberg	20.00
27	Greg Smith	.35
28	Curtis Wilkerson	.35
29	Dave Clark	.35
30	Doug Dascenzo	.35
31	Andre Dawson	7.50
32	Lloyd McClendon	.35
33	Dwight Smith	.35
34	Jerome Walton	.35
35	Marvell Wynne	.35
36	Alex Arias	.35
37	Bob Bafia	.35
38	Brad Bierley	.35
39	Shawn Boskie	.35
40	Danny Clay	.35
41	Rusty Crockett	.35
42	Earl Cunningham	.35
43	Len Damian	.35
44	Darrin Duffy	.35
45	Ty Griffin	.35
46	Brian Guinn	.35
47	Phil Hannon	.35
48	Phil Harrison	.35
49	Jeff Hearron	.35
50	Greg Kallevig	.35
51	Cedric Landrum	.35
52	Bill Long	.35
53	Derrick May	.35
54	Ray Mullino	.35
55	Erik Pappas	.35
56	Steve Parker	.35
57	Dave Pavlas	.35
58	Laddie Renfroe	.35
59	Jeff Small	.35
60	Doug Strange	.35
61	Gary Varsho	.35
62	Hector Villanueva	.35
63	Rick Wilkins	.35
64	Dana Williams	.35
65	Bill Wrona	.35
66	Fernando Zarranz	.35

TV Mets Team Set

CRAIG SHIPLEY

This late-season issue, sold only as a boxed set via a television offer in limited areas, features all of the players on the 1990 opening day roster, plus the manager, selected coaches and many of the organization's top minor league prospects. For many of the prospects, this is the first, if not the only, card on which they appear in major league uniform. A highlight of the back design is a "ghost image" full-color reproduction of the front photo, used as a background to the statistical and biographical information. A red border dominates the remainder of the back design. Because it was sold only as a boxed set, and production was relatively limited, single cards are seldom available.

		NM/M
Complete Set (66):		10.00
Common Player:		.35
1	Dave Johnson	.35
2	Mike Cubbage	.35
3	Doc Edwards	.35
4	Bud Harrelson	.35
5	Greg Pavlick	.35
6	Mel Stottlemyre, Sr.	.35
7	Blaine Beatty	.35
8	David Cone	1.00
9	Ron Darling	.35
10	Sid Fernandez	.35
11	John Franco	.50
12	Dwight Gooden	.50
13	Jeff Innis	.35
14	Julio Machado	.35
15	Jeff Musselman	.35
16	Bob Ojeda	.35
17	Alejandro Pena	.35
18	Frank Viola	.35
19	Wally Whitehurst	.35
20	Barry Lyons	.35
21	Orlando Mercado	.35
22	Mackey Sasser	.35
23	Kevin Elster	.35
24	Gregg Jefferies	.50
25	Howard Johnson	.35
26	Dave Magadan	.35
27	Mike Marshall	.35
28	Tom O'Malley	.35
29	Tim Teufel	.35
30	Mark Carreon	.35
31	Kevin McReynolds	.35
32	Keith Miller	.35
33	Darryl Strawberry	.50
34	Lou Thornton	.35
35	Shawn Barton	.35
36	Tim Bogar	.35
37	Terry Bross	.35
38	Kevin Brown	.35
39	Mike DeButch	.35
40	Alex Diaz	.35
41	Chris Donnels	.35
42	Jeff Gardner	.35
43	Denny Gonzalez	.35
44	Kenny Graves	.35
45	Manny Hernandez	.35
46	Keith Hughes	.35
47	Todd Hundley	.50
48	Chris Jelic	.35
49	Dave Liddell	.35
50	Terry McDaniel	.35
51	Cesar Mejia	.35
52	Scott Nielsen	.35
53	Dale Plummer	.35
54	Darren Reed	.35
55	Gil Roca	.35
56	Jaime Roseboro	.35
57	Roger Samuels	.35
58	Zoilo Sanchez	.35
59	Pete Schourek	.35
60	Craig Shipley	.35
61	Ray Soff	.35
62	Steve Swisher	.35
63	Kelvin Torve	.35
64	Dave Trautwein	.35
65	Julio Valera	.35
66	Alan Zinter	.35

TV Red Sox Team Set

This 66-card set was available only via a television offer in certain limited areas. Production was relatively low and single cards are hard to find. Player selection includes all those on the team's opening day roster in 1990, plus the manager, selected coaches and the team's top minor league prospects. In many cases this represents the first, or even the only, appearance of these prospects on major league baseball cards. Fronts have a high-gloss surface. Card backs, bordered in red, feature a "ghost image" reproduction of the front photo as a background to the statistics and biographical data.

		NM/M
Complete Set (66):		40.00
Common Player:		.35
1	Joe Morgan	.35
2	Dick Berardino	.35
3	Al Bumbry	.35
4	Bill Fischer	.35
5	Richie Hebner	.35
6	Rac Slider	.35
7	Mike Boddicker	.35
8	Roger Clemens	25.00
9	John Dopson	.35
10	Wes Gardner	.35
11	Greg Harris	.35
12	Dana Kiecker	.35
13	Dennis Lamp	.35
14	Rob Murphy	.35
15	Jeff Reardon	.35
16	Mike Rochford	.35
17	Lee Smith	.50
18	Rich Gedman	.35
19	John Marzano	.35
20	Tony Pena	.35
21	Marty Barrett	.35
22	Wade Boggs	15.00
23	Bill Buckner	.50
24	Danny Heep	.35
25	Jody Reed	.35
26	Luis Rivera	.35
27	Billy Jo Robidoux	.35
28	Ellis Burks	.35
29	Dwight Evans	.35
30	Mike Greenwell	.35
31	Randy Kutcher	.35
32	Carlos Quintana	.35
33	Kevin Romine	.35
34	Ed Nottle	.35
35	Mark Meleski	.35
36	Steve Bast	.35
37	Greg Blosser	.35
38	Tom Bolton	.35
39	Scott Cooper	.35
40	Zach Crouch	.35
41	Steve Curry	.35
42	Mike Dalton	.35
43	John Flaherty	.35
44	Angel Gonzalez	.35
45	Eric Hetzel	.35
46	Daryl Irvine	.35
47	Joe Johnson	.35
48	Rick Lancellotti	.35
49	John Leister	.35
50	Derek Livernois	.35
51	Josias Manzanillo	.35
52	Kevin Morton	.35
53	Julius McDougal	.35
54	Tim Naehring	.35
55	Jim Pankovits	.35
56	Mickey Pina	.35
57	Phil Plantier	.35
58	Jerry Reed	.35
59	Larry Shikles	.35
60	Tito Stewart	.35
61	Jeff Stone	.35
62	John Trautwein	.35
63	Gary Tremblay	.35
64	Mo Vaughn	2.50
65	Scott Wade	.35
66	Eric Wedge	.35

TV Yankees Team Set

The first - and in many cases the only - baseball card appearance of top minor league prospects occurs in this special 66-card boxed set which was sold only via a spe-

DON MATTINGLY

SEPTEMBER 1, 1989
MAJOR LEAGUE DEBUT

MIKE BLOWERS

cial television offer in limited markets. The set also includes all players on the team's opening day roster, plus the manager and selected coaches. Card fronts have a high-gloss surface. On back, framed by a red border, the design features a "ghost image" of the color card front photo, used as a background to the statistical and biographical information. Because the cards are sold only as a complete set, single cards are seldom available.

	NM/M
Complete Set (66):	60.00
Common Player:	.35
1 Bucky Dent	.35
2 Mark Connor	.35
3 Billy Connors	.35
4 Mike Ferraro	.35
5 Joe Sparks	.35
6 Champ Summers	.35
7 Greg Cadaret	.35
8 Chuck Cary	.35
9 Lee Guetterman	.35
10 Andy Hawkins	.35
11 Dave LaPoint	.35
12 Tim Leary	.35
13 Lance McCullers	.35
14 Alan Mills	.35
15 Clay Parker	.35
16 Pascual Perez	.35
17 Eric Plunk	.35
18 Dave Righetti	.35
19 Jeff Robinson	.35
20 Rick Cerone	.35
21 Bob Geren	.35
22 Steve Balboni	.35
23 Mike Blowers	.35
24 Alvaro Espinoza	.35
25 Don Mattingly	40.00
26 Steve Sax	.35
27 Wayne Tolleson	.35
28 Randy Velarde	.35
29 Jesse Barfield	.35
30 Mel Hall	.35
31 Roberto Kelly	.35
32 Luis Polonia	.35
33 Deion Sanders	1.00
34 Dave Winfield	15.00
35 Steve Adkins	.35
36 Oscar Azocar	.35
37 Bob Brower	.35
38 Britt Burns	.35
39 Bob Davidson	.35
40 Brian Dorsett	.35
41 Dave Eiland	.35
42 John Fishel	.35
43 Andy Fox	.35
44 John Habyan	.35
45 Cullen Hartzog	.35
46 Sterling Hitchcock	.35
47 Brian Johnson	.35
48 Jimmy Jones	.35
49 Scott Kamieniecki	.35
50 Mark Leiter	.35
51 Jim Leyritz	.35
52 Jason Maas	.35
53 Kevin Maas	.35
54 Hensley Meulens	.35
55 Kevin Mmahat	.35
56 Rich Monteleone	.35
57 Vince Phillips	.35
58 Carlos Rodriguez	.35
59 Dave Sax	.35
60 Willie Smith	.35
61 Van Snider	.35
62 Andy Stankiewicz	.35
63 Wade Taylor	.35
64 Ricky Torres	.35
65 Jim Walewander	.35
66 Bernie Williams	4.00

1989 Major League Debut

This 150-card set chronicles the debut date of all 1989 Major League rookies. Two checklist cards are also included in this boxed set, listing the players in order of debut date, though the cards are numbered alphabetically. The card fronts resemble the 1990 Topps cards in style. A debut banner appears in an upper corner. The flip sides are horizontal and are printed in black on yellow stock, providing an overview of the player's first game. The set is packaged in a special collectors box and was only available through hobby dealers.

	NM/M
Complete Set (150):	10.00
Common Player:	.05
1 Jim Abbott	.05
2 Beau Allred	.05
3 Wilson Alvarez	.05
4 Kent Anderson	.05
5 Eric Anthony	.05
6 Kevin Appier	.05
7 Larry Arndt	.05
8 John Barfield	.05
9 Billy Bates	.05
10 Kevin Batiste	.05
11 Blaine Beatty	.05
12 Stan Belinda	.05
13 Juan Bell	.05
14 Joey Belle	.25
15 Andy Benes	.05
16 Mike Benjamin	.05
17 Geronimo Berroa	.05
18 Mike Blowers	.05
19 Brian Brady	.05
20 Francisco Cabrera	.05
21 George Canale	.05
22 Jose Cano	.05
23 Steve Carter	.05
24 Pat Combs	.05
25 Scott Coolbaugh	.05
26 Steve Cummings	.05
27 Pete Dalena	.05
28 Jeff Datz	.05
29 Bobby Davidson	.05
30 Drew Denson	.05
31 Gary DiSarcina	.05
32 Brian DuBois	.05
33 Mike Dyer	.05
34 Wayne Edwards	.05
35 Junior Felix	.05
36 Mike Fetters	.05
37 Steve Finley	.05
38 Darren Fletcher	.05
39 LaVel Freeman	.05
40 Steve Frey	.05
41 Mark Gardner	.05
42 Joe Girardi	.05
43 Juan Gonzalez	.50
44 Goose Gozzo	.05
45 Tommy Greene	.05
46 Ken Griffey Jr.	3.00
47 Jason Grimsley	.05
48 Marquis Grissom	.05
49 Mark Guthrie	.05
50 Chip Hale	.05
51 John Hardy	.05
52 Gene Harris	.05
53 Mike Hartley	.05
54 Scott Hemond	.05
55 Xavier Hernandez	.05
56 Eric Hetzel	.05
57 Greg Hibbard	.05
58 Mark Higgins	.05
59 Glenallen Hill	.05
60 Chris Hoiles	.05
61 Shawn Holman	.05
62 Dann Howitt	.05
63 Mike Huff	.05
64 Terry Jorgenson	.05
65 Dave Justice	.25
66 Jeff King	.05
67 Matt Kinzer	.05
68 Joe Kraemer	.05
69 Marcus Lawton	.05
70 Derek Lilliquist	.05
71 Scott Little	.05
72 Greg Litton	.05
73 Rick Lueken	.05
74 Julio Machado	.05
75 Tom Magrann	.05
76 Kelly Mann	.05
77 Randy McCament	.05
78 Ben McDonald	.05
79 Chuck McElroy	.05
80 Jeff McKnight	.05
81 Kent Mercker	.05
82 Matt Merullo	.05
83 Hensley Meulens	.05
84 Kevin Mmahat	.05
85 Mike Munoz	.05
86 Dan Murphy	.05
87 Jaime Navarro	.05
88 Randy Nosek	.05
89 John Olerud	.15
90 Steve Olin	.05
91 Joe Oliver	.05
92 Francisco Oliveras	.05
93 Greg Olson	.05
94 John Orton	.05
95 Dean Palmer	.05
96 Ramon Pena	.05
97 Jeff Peterek	.05
98 Marty Pevey	.05
99 Rusty Richards	.05
100 Jeff Richardson	.05
101 Rob Richie	.05
102 Kevin Ritz	.05
103 Rosario Rodriguez	.05
104 Mike Roesler	.05
105 Kenny Rogers	.05
106 Bobby Rose	.05
107 Alex Sanchez	.05
108 Deion Sanders	.25
109 Jeff Schaefer	.05
110 Jeff Schulz	.05
111 Mike Schwabe	.05
112 Dick Scott	.05
113 Scott Scudder	.05
114 Rudy Seanez	.05
115 Joe Skalski	.05
116 Dwight Smith	.05
117 Greg Smith	.05
118 Mike Smith	.05
119 Paul Sorrento	.05
120 Sammy Sosa	3.00
121 Billy Spiers	.05
122 Mike Stanton	.05
123 Phil Stephenson	.05
124 Doug Strange	.05
125 Russ Swan	.05
126 Kevin Tapani	.05
127 Stu Tate	.05
128 Greg Vaughn	.05
129 Robin Ventura	.15
130 Randy Veres	.05
131 Jose Vizcaino	.05
132 Omar Vizquel	.05
133 Larry Walker	.25
134 Jerome Walton	.05
135 Gary Wayne	.05
136 Lenny Webster	.05
137 Mickey Weston	.05
138 Jeff Wetherby	.05
139 John Wetteland	.05
140 Ed Whited	.05
141 Wally Whitehurst	.05
142 Kevin Wickander	.05
143 Dean Wilkins	.05
144 Dana Williams	.05
145 Paul Wilmet	.05
146 Craig Wilson	.05
147 Matt Winters	.05
148 Eric Yelding	.05
149 Clint Zavaras	.05
---- Todd Zeile	.05
---- Checklist (1 of 2)	.05
---- Checklist (2 of 2)	.05

Pre-Production Sample Sheet

To preview its 40th anniversary set, Topps distributed this 7-1/2" x 10-1/2" uncut sheet. Fronts are identical to the issued versions of each player's card while backs are printed in blue with a large anniversary logo, the player's name, a copyright line and "1991 PRE-PRODUCTION / SAMPLE."

	NM/M
Uncut Sheet:	15.00
Complete Set (9):	15.00
Common Player:	1.00
(1) Wade Boggs	3.00
(2) Jose Canseco	2.00
(3) Roger Clemens	6.00
(4) Rickey Henderson	2.50
(5) Bo Jackson	1.50
(6) Kirt Manwaring	1.00
(7) Willie Randolph	1.00
(8) Benny Santiago	1.00
(9) Walt Weiss	1.00

1991 Topps

Topps celebrated its 40th anniversary in 1991 with the biggest promotional campaign in baseball card history. More than 300,000 vintage Topps cards (or certificates redeemable for valuable older cards) produced from 1952 to 1990 were randomly inserted in packs. Also a grand prize winner received a complete set from each year, and others received a single set from 1952-1990. The 1991 Topps card fronts feature the "Topps 40 Years of Baseball" logo in the upper-left corner. Colored borders frame the player photos. All players of the same team have cards with the same frame/border colors. Both action and posed shots appear in full-color on the card fronts. The flip sides are printed horizontally and feature complete statistics. Record Breakers and other special cards were once again included in the set. The cards measure 2-1/2" x 3-1/2". Many cards can be found with variations in the sheet-letter (A-F) designations in the copyright line on back.

	NM/M
Unopened Factory Set, Retail (792):	30.00
Unopened Factory Set, Hobby (792):	25.00
Complete Set (792):	20.00
Common Player:	.05
Wax Pack (15):	.50
Wax Box (36):	12.50
Cello Pack (34):	1.00
Cello Box (24):	15.00
Rack Pack (45):	1.00
Rack Box (24):	15.00
Vending Box (500):	7.50
1 Nolan Ryan	.75
2 George Brett (Record Breaker)	.25
3 Carlton Fisk (Record Breaker)	.20
4 Kevin Maas (Record Breaker)	.05
5 Cal Ripken, Jr. (Record Breaker)	.40
6 Nolan Ryan (Record Breaker)	.40
7 Ryne Sandberg (Record Breaker)	.30
8 Bobby Thigpen (Record Breaker)	.05
9 Darrin Fletcher RC	.05
10 Gregg Olson	.05
11 Roberto Kelly	.05
12 Paul Assenmacher	.05
13 Mariano Duncan	.05
14 Dennis Lamp	.05
15 Von Hayes	.05
16 Mike Heath	.05
17 Jeff Brantley	.05
18 Nelson Liriano	.05
19 Jeff Robinson	.05
20 Pedro Guerrero	.05
21 Joe M. Morgan	.05
22 Storm Davis	.05
23 Jim Gantner	.05
24 Dave Martinez	.05
25 Tim Belcher	.05
26 Luis Sojo	.05
27 Bobby Witt	.05
28 Alvaro Espinoza	.05
29 Bob Walk	.05
30 Gregg Jefferies	.05
31 Colby Ward RC	.05
32 Mike Simms RC	.05
33 Barry Jones	.05
34 Atlee Hammaker	.05
35 Greg Maddux	.50
36 Donnie Hill	.05
37 Tom Bolton	.05
38 Scott Bradley	.05
39 Jim Neidlinger RC	.05
40 Kevin Mitchell	.05
41 Ken Dayley	.05
42a Chris Hoiles RC (White inner photo frame.)	.20
42b Chris Hoiles RC (Gray inner photo frame.)	.10
43 Roger McDowell	.05
44 Mike Felder	.05
45 Chris Sabo	.05
46 Tim Drummond	.05
47 Brook Jacoby	.05
48 Dennis Boyd	.05
49a Pat Borders (40 stolen bases in Kinston 1986)	.20
49b Pat Borders (0 stolen bases in Kinston 1986)	.10
50 Bob Welch	.05
51 Art Howe	.05
52 Francisco Oliveras RC	.05
53 Mike Sharperson	.05
54 Gary Mielke	.05
55 Jeffrey Leonard	.05
56 Jeff Parrett	.05
57 Jack Howell	.05
58 Mel Stottlemyre	.05
59 Eric Yelding	.05
60 Frank Viola	.05
61 Stan Javier	.05
62 Lee Guetterman	.05
63 Milt Thompson	.05
64 Tom Herr	.05
65 Bruce Hurst	.05
66 Terry Kennedy	.05
67 Rick Honeycutt	.05
68 Gary Sheffield	.25
69 Steve Wilson	.05
70 Ellis Burks	.05
71 Jim Acker	.05
72 Junior Ortiz	.05
73 Craig Worthington	.05
74 Shane Andrews RC (#1 Draft Pick)	.10
75 Jack Morris	.05
76 Jerry Browne	.05
77 Drew Hall	.05
78 Geno Petralli	.05
79 Frank Thomas	.35
80a Fernando Valenzuela (No diamond after 104 ER in 1990.)	.25
80b Fernando Valenzuela (Diamond after 104 ER in 1990.)	
81 Cito Gaston	.05
82 Tom Glavine	.20
83 Daryl Boston	.05
84 Bob McClure	.05
85 Jesse Barfield	.05
86 Les Lancaster	.05
87 Tracy Jones	.05
88 Bob Tewksbury	.05
89 Darren Daulton	.05
90 Danny Tartabull	.05
91 Greg Colbrunn RC (Future Star)	.05
92 Danny Jackson	.05
93 Ivan Calderon	.05
94 John Dopson	.05
95 Paul Molitor	.35
96 Trevor Wilson	.05
97a Brady Anderson (3H, 2RBI in Sept. scoreboard)	.25
97b Brady Anderson (14H, 3 RBI in Sept. scoreboard)	.05
98 Sergio Valdez	.05
99 Chris Gwynn	.05
100a Don Mattingly (10 hits 1990)	.50
100b Don Mattingly (101 hits in 1990)	.50
101 Rob Ducey	.05
102 Gene Larkin	.05
103 Tim Costo RC (#1 Draft Pick)	.05
104 Don Robinson	.05
105 Kevin McReynolds	.05
106 Ed Nunez	.05
107 Luis Polonia	.05
108 Matt Young	.05
109 Greg Riddoch	.05
110 Tom Henke	.05
111 Andres Thomas	.05
112 Frank DiPino	.05
113 Carl Everett RC (#1 Draft Pick)	.50
114 Lance Dickson RC (Future Star)	
115 Hubie Brooks	.05
116 Mark Davis	.05
117 Dion James	.05
118 Tom Edens RC	.05
119 Carl Nichols RC	.05
120 Joe Carter	.05
121 Eric King	.05
122 Paul O'Neill	.05
123 Greg Harris	.05
124 Randy Bush	.05
125 Steve Bedrosian	.05
126 Bernard Gilkey RC	.10
127 Joe Price	.05
128 Travis Fryman	.05
129 Mark Eichhorn	.05
130 Ozzie Smith	.50
131a Checklist 1 (Phil Bradley #727.)	.05
131b Checklist 1 (Phil Bradley #717.)	.05
132 Jamie Quirk	.05
133 Greg Briley	.05
134 Kevin Elster	.05
135 Jerome Walton	.05
136 Dave Schmidt	.05
137 Randy Ready	.05
138 Jamie Moyer	.05
139 Jeff Treadway	.05
140 Fred McGriff	.05
141 Nick Leyva	.05
142 Curtis Wilkerson	.05
143 John Smiley	.05
144 Dave Henderson	.05
145 Lou Whitaker	.05
146 Dan Plesac	.05
147 Carlos Baerga	.05
148 Rey Palacios	.05
149 Al Osuna RC	.05
150 Cal Ripken, Jr.	.75
151 Tom Browning	.05
152 Mickey Hatcher	.05
153 Bryan Harvey	.05
154 Jay Buhner	.05
155a Dwight Evans (Diamond after 162 G 1982.)	.10
155b Dwight Evans (No diamond after 162 G 1982.)	
156 Carlos Martinez	.05
157 John Smoltz	.05
158 Jose Uribe	.05
159 Joe Boever	.05
160 Vince Coleman	.05
161 Tim Leary	.05
162 Ozzie Canseco RC	.10
163 Dave Johnson	.05
164 Edgar Diaz	.05
165 Sandy Alomar	.05
166 Harold Baines	.05
167a Randy Tomlin RC ("Harrisburg" 1989-90.)	.10
167b Randy Tomlin RC ("Harrisburg" 1989-90.)	.05
168 John Olerud	.05
169 Luis Aquino	.05
170 Carlton Fisk	.35
171 Tony LaRussa	.05
172 Pete Incaviglia	.05
173 Jason Grimsley	.05
174 Ken Caminiti	.05
175 Jack Armstrong	.05
176 John Orton RC	.05
177 Reggie Harris RC	.05
178 Dave Valle	.05
179 Pete Harnisch	.05
180 Tony Gwynn	.50
181 Duane Ward	.05
182 Junior Noboa	.05
183 Clay Parker	.05
184 Gary Green	.05
185 Joe Magrane	.05
186 Rod Booker	.05
187 Greg Cadaret	.05
188 Damon Berryhill	.05
189 Daryl Irvine RC	.05
190 Matt Williams	.05
191 Willie Blair RC	.05
192 Rob Deer	.05
193 Felix Fermin	.05
194 Xavier Hernandez RC	.05
195 Wally Joyner	.05
196 Jim Vatcher RC	.05
197 Chris Nabholz RC	.05
198 R.J. Reynolds	.05
199 Mike Hartley RC	.05
200 Darryl Strawberry	.05
201 Tom Kelly	.05
202 Jim Leyritz RC	.20
203 Gene Harris	.05
204 Herm Winningham	.05
205 Mike Perez RC	.05
206 Carlos Quintana	.05
207 Gary Wayne	.05
208 Willie Wilson	.05
209 Ken Howell	.05
210 Lance Parrish	.05
211 Brian Barnes RC (Future Star)	
212 Steve Finley	.05
213 Frank Wills	.05
214 Joe Girardi	.05
215 Dave Smith	.05
216 Greg Gagne	.05
217 Chris Bosio	.05
218 Rick Parker RC	.05
219 Jack McDowell	.05
220 Tim Wallach	.05
221 Don Slaught	.05
222 Brian McRae RC	.10
223 Allan Anderson	.05
224 Juan Gonzalez	.20
225 Randy Johnson	.05
226 Alfredo Griffin	.05
227 Steve Avery	.05
228 Rex Hudler	.05
229 Rance Mulliniks	.05
230 Sid Fernandez	.05
231 Doug Rader	.05
232 Jose DeJesus	.05
233 Al Leiter	.05
234 Scott Erickson RC	.10
235 Dave Parker	.05
236a Frank Tanana (No diamond after 269 SO 1975.)	.10
236b Frank Tanana (Diamond after 269 SO 1975.)	
237 Rick Cerone	.05
238 Mike Dunne	.05
239 Darren Lewis RC	.05
240 Mike Scott	.05
241 Dave Clark	.05
242 Mike LaCoss	.05
243 Lance Johnson	.05
244 Mike Jeffcoat	.05
245 Kal Daniels	.05
246 Kevin Wickander	.05
247 Jody Reed	.05
248 Tom Gordon	.05

#	Player	Price
249	Bob Melvin	.05
250	Dennis Eckersley	.30
251	Mark Lemke	.05
252	Mel Rojas RC	.05
253	Garry Templeton	.05
254	Shawn Boskie RC	.05
255	Brian Downing	.05
256	Greg Hibbard	.05
257	Tom O'Malley	.05
258	Chris Hammond RC	.05
259	Hensley Meulens	.05
260	Harold Reynolds	.05
261	Bud Harrelson	.05
262	Tim Jones	.05
263	Checklist 2	.05
264	Dave Hollins RC	.05
265	Mark Gubicza	.05
266	Carmen Castillo	.05
267	Mark Knudson	.05
268	Tom Brookens	.05
269	Joe Hesketh	.05
270a	Mark McGwire (1987 SLG .618)	.75
270b	Mark McGwire (1987 SLG 618)	.75
271	Omar Olivares RC	.05
272	Jeff King	.05
273	Johnny Ray	.05
274	Ken Williams	.05
275	Alan Trammell	.05
276	Bill Swift	.05
277	Scott Coolbaugh	.05
278	Alex Fernandez RC (#1 Draft Pick)	.10
279a	Jose Gonzalez (Photo of Billy Bean, left-handed batter.)	.75
279b	Jose Gonzalez (Correct photo, right-handed batter.)	.05
280	Bret Saberhagen	.05
281	Larry Sheets	.05
282	Don Carman	.05
283	Marquis Grissom	.05
284	Bill Spiers	.05
285	Jim Abbott	.05
286	Ken Oberkfell	.05
287	Mark Grant	.05
288	Derrick May RC	.05
289	Tim Birtsas	.05
290	Steve Sax	.05
291	John Wathan	.05
292	Bud Black	.05
293	Jay Bell	.05
294	Mike Moore	.05
295	Rafael Palmeiro	.30
296	Mark Williamson	.05
297	Manny Lee	.05
298	Omar Vizquel	.05
299	Scott Radinsky RC	.05
300	Kirby Puckett	.50
301	Steve Farr	.05
302	Tim Teufel	.05
303	Mike Boddicker	.05
304	Kevin Reimer RC	.05
305	Mike Scioscia	.05
306a	Lonnie Smith (136 G 1990)	.10
306b	Lonnie Smith (135 G 1990)	.05
307	Andy Benes	.05
308	Tom Pagnozzi	.05
309	Norm Charlton	.05
310	Gary Carter	.35
311	Jeff Pico	.05
312	Charlie Hayes	.05
313	Ron Robinson	.05
314	Gary Pettis	.05
315	Roberto Alomar	.15
316	Gene Nelson	.05
317	Mike Fitzgerald	.05
318	Rick Aguilera	.05
319	Jeff McKnight RC	.05
320	Tony Fernandez	.05
321	Bob Rodgers	.05
322	Terry Shumpert RC	.05
323	Cory Snyder	.05
324a	Ron Kittle ("6 Home Runs" in career summary)	.10
324b	Ron Kittle ("7 Home Runs" in career summary)	.05
325	Brett Butler	.05
326	Ken Patterson	.05
327	Ron Hassey	.05
328	Walt Terrell	.05
329	Dave Justice	.05
330	Dwight Gooden	.05
331	Eric Anthony	.05
332	Kenny Rogers	.05
333	Chipper Jones RC (#1 Draft Pick)	6.00
334	Todd Benzinger	.05
335	Mitch Williams	.05
336	Matt Nokes	.05
337a	Keith Comstock (Mariners logo.)	.05
337b	Keith Comstock (Cubs logo.)	1.50
338	Luis Rivera	.05
339	Larry Walker	.05
340	Ramon Martinez	.05
341	John Moses	.05
342	Mickey Morandini RC	.10
343	Jose Oquendo	.05
344	Jeff Russell	.05
345	Len Dykstra	.05
346	Jesse Orosco	.05
347	Greg Vaughn	.05
348	Todd Stottlemyre	.05
349	Dave Gallagher	.05

#	Player	Price
350	Glenn Davis	.05
351	Joe Torre	.05
352	Frank White	.05
353	Tony Castillo	.05
354	Sid Bream	.05
355	Chili Davis	.05
356	Mike Marshall	.05
357	Jack Savage	.05
358	Mark Parent	.05
359	Chuck Cary	.05
360	Tim Raines	.05
361	Scott Garrelts	.05
362	Hector Villanueva RC	.05
363	Rick Mahler	.05
364	Dan Pasqua	.05
365	Mike Schooler	.05
366a	Checklist 3 (Carl Nichols #19.)	.05
366b	Checklist 3 (Carl Nichols #119.)	.05
367	Dave Walsh RC	.05
368	Felix Jose	.05
369	Steve Searcy	.05
370	Kelly Gruber	.05
371	Jeff Montgomery	.05
372	Spike Owen	.05
373	Darrin Jackson	.05
374	Larry Casian RC	.05
375	Tony Pena	.05
376	Mike Harkey	.05
377	Rene Gonzales	.05
378a	Wilson Alvarez RC (No 1989 Port Charlotte stats.)	.50
378b	Wilson Alvarez RC (1989 Port Charlotte stats)	.20
379	Randy Velarde	.05
380	Willie McGee	.05
381	Jim Leyland	.05
382	Mackey Sasser	.05
383	Pete Smith	.05
384	Gerald Perry	.05
385	Mickey Tettleton	.05
386	Cecil Fielder/AS	.05
387	Julio Franco/AS	.05
388	Kelly Gruber/AS	.05
389	Alan Trammell/AS	.05
390	Jose Canseco/AS	.15
391	Rickey Henderson/AS	.20
392	Ken Griffey Jr./AS	.20
393	Carlton Fisk/AS	.20
394	Bob Welch/AS	.05
395	Chuck Finley/AS	.05
396	Bobby Thigpen/AS	.05
397	Eddie Murray/AS	.20
398	Ryne Sandberg/AS	.30
399	Matt Williams/AS	.05
400	Barry Larkin/AS	.05
401	Barry Bonds/AS	.40
402	Darryl Strawberry/AS	.05
403	Bobby Bonilla/AS	.05
404	Mike Scoscia/AS	.05
405	Doug Drabek/AS	.05
406	Frank Viola/AS	.05
407	John Franco/AS	.05
408	Ernie Riles	.05
409	Mike Stanley	.05
410	Dave Righetti	.05
411	Lance Blankenship	.05
412	Dave Bergman	.05
413	Terry Mulholland	.05
414	Sammy Sosa	.60
415	Rick Sutcliffe	.05
416	Randy Milligan	.05
417	Bill Krueger	.05
418	Nick Esasky	.05
419	Jeff Reed	.05
420	Bobby Thigpen	.05
421	Alex Cole	.05
422	Rick Rueschel	.05
423	Rafael Ramirez	.05
424	Calvin Schiraldi	.05
425	Andy Van Slyke	.05
426	Joe Grahe RC	.05
427	Rick Dempsey	.05
428	John Barfield RC	.05
429	Stump Merrill	.05
430	Gary Gaetti	.05
431	Paul Gibson	.05
432	Delino DeShields	.05
433	Pat Tabler	.05
434	Julio Machado RC	.05
435	Kevin Maas	.05
436	Scott Bankhead	.05
437	Doug Dascenzo	.05
438	Vicente Palacios	.05
439	Dickie Thon	.05
440	George Bell	.05
441	Zane Smith	.05
442	Charlie O'Brien	.05
443	Jeff Innis	.05
444	Glenn Braggs	.05
445	Greg Swindell	.05
446	Craig Grebeck RC	.05
447	John Burkett	.05
448	Craig Lefferts	.05
449	Juan Berenguer	.05
450	Wade Boggs	.50
451	Neal Heaton	.05
452	Bill Schroeder	.05
453	Lenny Harris	.05
454a	Kevin Appier (No 1990 Omaha stats.)	.15
454b	Kevin Appier (1990 Omaha stats)	.05
455	Walt Weiss	.05
456	Charlie Leibrandt	.05
457	Todd Hundley	.05
458	Brian Holman	.05

#	Player	Price
459	Tom Trebelhorn	.05
460	Dave Steib	.05
461a	Robin Ventura (Gray inner photo frame at left.)	.15
461b	Robin Ventura (Red inner photo frame at left.)	.05
462	Steve Frey	.05
463	Dwight Smith	.05
464	Steve Buechele	.05
465	Ken Griffey	.05
466	Charles Nagy RC	.05
467	Dennis Cook	.05
468	Tim Hulett	.05
469	Chet Lemon	.05
470	Howard Johnson	.05
471	Mike Lieberthal RC (#1 Draft Pick)	.50
472	Kirt Manwaring	.05
473	Curt Young	.05
474	Phil Plantier RC	.10
475	Teddy Higuera	.05
476	Glenn Wilson	.05
477	Mike Fetters	.05
478	Kurt Stillwell	.05
479	Bob Patterson	.05
480	Dave Magadan	.05
481	Eddie Whitson	.05
482	Tino Martinez	.05
483	Mike Aldrete	.05
484	Dave LaPoint	.05
485	Terry Pendleton	.05
486	Tommy Greene RC	.05
487	Rafael Belliard	.05
488	Jeff Manto RC	.05
489	Bobby Valentine	.05
490	Kirk Gibson	.05
491	Kurt Miller RC (#1 Draft Pick)	.05
492	Ernie Whitt	.05
493	Jose Rijo	.05
494	Chris James	.05
495	Charlie Hough	.05
496	Marty Barrett	.05
497	Ben McDonald	.05
498	Mark Salas	.05
499	Melido Perez	.05
500	Will Clark	.05
501	Mike Bielecki	.05
502	Carney Lansford	.05
503	Roy Smith	.05
504	Julio Valera RC	.05
505	Chuck Finley	.05
506	Darnell Coles	.05
507	Steve Jeltz	.05
508	Mike York RC	.05
509	Glenallen Hill	.05
510	John Franco	.05
511	Steve Balboni	.05
512	Jose Mesa RC	.05
513	Jerald Clark	.05
514	Mike Stanton	.05
515	Alvin Davis	.05
516	Karl Rhodes RC	.05
517	Joe Oliver	.05
518	Cris Carpenter	.05
519	Sparky Anderson	.10
520	Mark Grace	.05
521	Joe Orsulak	.05
522	Stan Belinda	.05
523	Rodney McCray RC	.05
524	Darrel Akerfelds	.05
525	Willie Randolph	.05
526a	Moises Alou (37 R 1990 Pirates)	.20
526b	Moises Alou (0 R 1990 Pirates)	.15
527a	Checklist 4 (Kevin McReynolds #719)	.05
527b	Checklist 4 (Kevin McReynolds #105)	.05
528	Denny Martinez	.05
529	Mark Newfield RC (#1 Draft Pick)	.05
530	Roger Clemens	.60
531	Dave Rhode RC	.05
532	Kirk McCaskill	.05
533	Oddibe McDowell	.05
534	Mike Jackson	.05
535	Ruben Sierra	.05
536	Mike Witt	.05
537	Jose Lind	.05
538	Bip Roberts	.05
539	Scott Terry	.05
540	George Brett	.60
541	Domingo Ramos	.05
542	Rob Murphy	.05
543	Junior Felix	.05
544	Alejandro Pena	.05
545	Dale Murphy	.15
546	Jeff Ballard	.05
547	Mike Pagliarulo	.05
548	Jaime Navarro	.05
549	John McNamara	.05
550	Eric Davis	.05
551	Bob Kipper	.05
552	Jeff Hamilton	.05
553	Joe Klink RC	.05
554	Brian Harper	.05
555	Turner Ward RC	.05
556	Gary Ward	.05
557	Wally Whitehurst	.05
558	Otis Nixon	.05
559	Adam Peterson	.05
560	Greg Smith RC	.05
561	Tim McIntosh RC (Future Star)	.05
562	Jeff Kunkel	.05
563	Brent Knackert RC	.05

#	Player	Price
564	Dante Bichette	.05
565	Craig Biggio	.05
566	Craig Wilson RC	.05
567	Dwayne Henry	.05
568	Ron Karkovice	.05
569	Curt Schilling	.05
570	Barry Bonds	.75
571	Pat Combs	.05
572	Dave Anderson	.05
573	Rich Rodriguez RC	.05
574	John Marzano	.05
575	Robin Yount	.35
576	Jeff Kaiser RC	.05
577	Bill Doran	.05
578	Dave West	.05
579	Roger Craig	.05
580	Dave Stewart	.05
581	Luis Quinones	.05
582	Marty Clary	.05
583	Tony Phillips	.05
584	Kevin Brown	.05
585	Pete O'Brien	.05
586	Fred Lynn	.05
587	Jose Offerman RC (Future Star)	.05
588a	Mark Whiten (Hand inside left border.)	.05
588b	Mark Whiten (Hand over left border.)	.20
589	Scott Ruskin RC	.05
590	Eddie Murray	.35
591	Ken Hill	.05
592	B.J. Surhoff	.05
593a	Mike Walker RC (No 1990 Canton-Akron stats.)	.15
593b	Mike Walker RC (1990 Canton-Akron stats)	.05
594	Rich Garces RC (Future Star)	.05
595	Bill Landrum	.05
596	Ronnie Walden RC (#1 Draft Pick)	.05
597	Jerry Don Gleaton	.05
598	Sam Horn	.05
599a	Greg Myers (No 1990 Syracuse stats.)	.10
599b	Greg Myers (1990 Syracuse stats)	.05
600	Bo Jackson	.10
601	Bob Ojeda	.05
602	Casey Candaele	.05
603a	Wes Chamberlain RC (Photo of Louie Meadows, no bat.)	.75
603b	Wes Chamberlain RC (Correct photo, holding bat.)	.05
604	Billy Hatcher	.05
605	Jeff Reardon	.05
606	Jim Gott	.05
607	Edgar Martinez	.05
608	Todd Burns	.05
609	Jeff Torborg	.05
610	Andres Galarraga	.05
611	Dave Eiland	.05
612	Steve Lyons	.05
613	Eric Show	.05
614	Luis Salazar	.05
615	Bert Blyleven	.05
616	Todd Zeile	.05
617	Bill Wegman	.05
618	Sil Campusano	.05
619	David Wells	.05
620	Ozzie Guillen	.05
621	Ted Power	.05
622	Jack Daugherty	.05
623	Jeff Blauser	.05
624	Tom Candiotti	.05
625	Terry Steinbach	.05
626	Gerald Young	.05
627	Tim Layana RC	.05
628	Greg Litton	.05
629	Wes Gardner	.05
630	Dave Winfield	.35
631	Mike Morgan	.05
632	Lloyd Moseby	.05
633	Kevin Tapani	.05
634	Henry Cotto	.05
635	Andy Hawkins	.05
636	Geronimo Pena RC	.05
637	Bruce Ruffin	.05
638	Mike Macfarlane	.05
639	Frank Robinson	.05
640	Andre Dawson	.20
641	Mike Henneman	.05
642	Hal Morris	.05
643	Jim Presley	.05
644	Chuck Crim	.05
645	Juan Samuel	.05
646	Andujar Cedeno RC	.05
647	Mark Portugal	.05
648	Lee Stevens RC	.05
649	Bill Sampen RC	.05
650	Jack Clark	.05
651	Alan Mills RC	.05
652	Kevin Romine	.05
653	Anthony Telford RC	.05
654	Paul Sorrento RC	.05
655	Erik Hanson	.05
656a	Checklist 5 (Vincente Palacios #348.)	.05
656b	Checklist 5 (Palacios #433.)	.05
656c	Checklist 5 (Palacios #438.)	.05
657	Mike Kingery	.05
658	Scott Aldred RC	.05
659	Oscar Azocar RC	.05
660	Lee Smith	.05

#	Player	Price
661	Steve Lake	.05
662	Rob Dibble	.05
663	Greg Brock	.05
664	John Farrell	.05
665	Mike LaValliere	.05
666	Danny Darwin	.05
667	Kent Anderson	.05
668	Bill Long	.05
669	Lou Pinella	.05
670	Rickey Henderson	.35
671	Andy McGaffigan	.05
672	Shane Mack	.05
673	Greg Olson RC	.05
674a	Kevin Gross (No diamond after 89 BB 1988.)	.10
674b	Kevin Gross (Diamond after 89 BB 1988.)	.05
675	Tom Brunansky	.05
676	Scott Chiamparino RC	.05
677	Billy Ripken	.05
678	Mark Davidson	.05
679	Bill Bathe RC	.05
680	David Cone	.05
681	Jeff Schaefer RC	.05
682	Ray Lankford RC	.15
683	Derek Lilliquist	.05
684	Milt Cuyler RC	.05
685	Doug Drabek	.05
686	Mike Gallego	.05
687a	John Cerutti (4.46 ERA 1990)	.05
687b	John Cerutti (4.76 ERA 1990)	.05
688	Rosario Rodriguez RC	.05
689	John Kruk	.05
690	Orel Hershiser	.05
691	Mike Blowers	.05
692a	Efrain Valdez RC (No text below stats.)	.15
692b	Efrain Valdez RC (Two lines of text below stats.)	.05
693	Francisco Cabrera	.05
694	Randy Veres	.05
695	Kevin Seitzer	.05
696	Steve Olin	.05
697	Shawn Abner	.05
698	Mark Guthrie	.05
699	Jim Lefebvre	.05
700	Jose Canseco	.25
701	Pascual Perez	.05
702	Tim Naehring RC	.05
703	Juan Agosto	.05
704	Devon White	.05
705	Robby Thompson	.05
706a	Brad Arnsberg (68.2 IP Rangers 1990)	.05
706b	Brad Arnsberg (62.2 IP Rangers 1990)	.05
707	Jim Eisenreich	.05
708	John Mitchell	.05
709	Matt Sinatro	.05
710	Kent Hrbek	.05
711	Jose DeLeon	.05
712	Ricky Jordan	.05
713	Scott Scudder	.05
714	Marvell Wynne	.05
715	Tim Burke	.05
716	Bob Geren	.05
717	Phil Bradley	.05
718	Steve Crawford	.05
719	Keith Miller	.05
720	Cecil Fielder	.05
721	Mark Lee RC	.05
722	Wally Backman	.05
723	Candy Maldonado	.05
724	David Segui RC	.10
725	Ron Gant	.05
726	Phil Stephenson	.05
727	Mookie Wilson	.05
728	Scott Sanderson	.05
729	Don Zimmer	.05
730	Barry Larkin	.05
731	Jeff Gray RC	.05
732	Franklin Stubbs	.05
733	Kelly Downs	.05
734	John Russell	.05
735	Ron Darling	.05
736	Dick Schofield	.05
737	Tim Crews	.05
738	Mel Hall	.05
739	Russ Swan RC	.05
740	Ryne Sandberg	.50
741	Jimmy Key	.05
742	Tommy Gregg	.05
743	Bryn Smith	.05
744	Nelson Santovenia	.05
745	Doug Jones	.05
746	John Shelby	.05
747	Tony Fossas	.05
748	Al Newman	.05
749	Greg Harris	.05
750	Bobby Bonilla	.05
751	Wayne Edwards RC	.05
752	Kevin Bass	.05
753	Paul Marak RC	.05
754	Bill Pecota	.05
755	Mark Langston	.05
756	Jeff Huson	.05
757	Mark Gardner	.05
758	Mike Devereaux	.05
759	Bobby Cox	.05
760	Benny Santiago	.05
761	Larry Andersen	.05
762	Mitch Webster	.05
763	Dana Kiecker RC	.05
764	Mark Carreon	.05
765	Shawon Dunston	.05
766	Jeff Robinson	.05

#	Player	Price
767	Dan Wilson RC (#1 Draft Pick)	.10
768	Donn Pall	.05
769	Tim Sherrill RC	.05
770	Jay Howell	.05
771	Gary Redus	.05
772	Kent Mercker RC	.05
773	Tom Foley	.05
774	Dennis Rasmussen	.05
775	Julio Franco	.05
776	Brent Mayne RC	.05
777	John Candelaria	.05
778	Danny Gladden	.05
779	Carmelo Martinez	.05
780a	Randy Myers (Career losses 15.)	.10
780b	Randy Myers (Career losses 19.)	.05
781	Darryl Hamilton	.05
782	Jim Deshaies	.05
783	Joel Skinner	.05
784	Willie Fraser	.05
785	Scott Fletcher	.05
786	Eric Plunk	.05
787	Checklist 6	.05
788	Bob Milacki	.05
789	Tom Lasorda	.05
790	Ken Griffey Jr.	.60
791	Mike Benjamin RC	.05
792	Mike Greenwell	.05

Tiffany

Topps ended its annual run of special collectors' edition boxed sets in 1991, producing the glossy sets inconsiderably more limited quantity than in previous years. Cards are identical to the regular 1991 Topps set except for the use of white cardboard stock and a high-gloss front finish.

	NM/M
Unopened Set (792):	135.00
Complete Set (792):	85.00
Common Player:	.10

Desert Shield

As a special treat for U.S. armed services personnel serving in the Persian Gulf prior to and during the war with Iraq, Topps produced a special edition featuring a gold-foil overprint honoring the military effort. Enough cards were produced to equal approximately 6,800 sets. While some cards actually reached the troops in the Middle East, many were short-stopped by military supply personnel stateside and sold into the hobby. Many of the cards sent to Saudi Arabia never returned to the U.S., however, making the supply of available cards somewhat scarce. The checklist cards in the set were not overprinted. At least two types of counterfeit overprint have been seen on genuine Topps cards in an attempt to cash in on the scarcity of these war "veterans."

	NM/M
Complete Set (792):	1,200
Common Player:	1.00
Wax Pack:	60.00

Traded

"Team USA" players are featured in the 1991 Topps Traded set. The cards feature the same style as the regular 1991 issue, including the 40th anniversary logo. The set includes 132 cards and showcases rookies and traded players along with "Team USA." The cards are numbered with a "T" designation in alphabetical order. Wax-pack versions have a gray cardboard stock (unlike the box-set's white stock).

Each of the wax-pack cards can be found with one or two asterisks preceding the copyright line on back.

		NM/M
Unopened Retail or Hobby Set		
(132):		12.00
Complete Set (132):		10.00
Common Player:		.05
Wax Pack (7):		.65
Wax Box (36):		15.00
1	Juan Agosto	.05
2	Roberto Alomar	.15
3	Wally Backman	.05
4	Jeff Bagwell RC	3.00
5	Skeeter Barnes RC	.05
6	Steve Bedrosian	.05
7	Derek Bell RC	.05
8	George Bell	.05
9	Rafael Belliard	.05
10	Dante Bichette	.05
11	Bud Black	.05
12	Mike Boddicker	.05
13	Sid Bream	.05
14	Hubie Brooks	.05
15	Brett Butler	.05
16	Ivan Calderon	.05
17	John Candelaria	.05
18	Tom Candiotti	.05
19	Gary Carter	.50
20	Joe Carter	.05
21	Rick Cerone	.05
22	Jack Clark	.05
23	Vince Coleman	.05
24	Scott Coolbaugh	.05
25	Danny Cox	.05
26	Danny Darwin	.05
27	Chili Davis	.05
28	Glenn Davis	.05
29	Steve Decker RC	.05
30	Rob Deer	.05
31	Rich DeLucia RC	.05
32	John Dettmer RC (USA)	.05
33	Brian Downing	.05
34	Darren Dreifort RC (USA)	.25
35	Kirk Dressendorfer	.05
36	Jim Essian	.05
37	Dwight Evans	.05
38	Steve Farr	.05
39	Jeff Fassero RC	.05
40	Junior Felix	.05
41	Tony Fernandez	.05
42	Steve Finley	.05
43	Jim Fregosi	.05
44	Gary Gaetti	.05
45	Jason Giambi RC (USA)	4.00
46	Kirk Gibson	.05
47	Leo Gomez RC	.05
48	Luis Gonzalez RC	1.00
49	Jeff Granger RC (USA)	.10
50	Todd Greene RC (USA)	.15
51	Jeffrey Hammonds RC (USA)	.15
52	Mike Hargrove	.05
53	Pete Harnisch	.05
54	Rick Helling RC (USA)	.10
55	Glenallen Hill	.05
56	Charlie Hough	.05
57	Pete Incaviglia	.05
58	Bo Jackson	.10
59	Danny Jackson	.05
60	Reggie Jefferson RC	.05
61	Charles Johnson RC (USA)	.15
62	Jeff Johnson RC	.05
63	Todd Johnson RC (USA)	.05
64	Barry Jones	.05
65	Chris Jones	.05
66	Scott Kamieniecki	.05
67	Pat Kelly RC	.05
68	Darryl Kile RC	.05
69	Chuck Knoblauch RC	.05
70	Bill Krueger	.05
71	Scott Leius RC	.05
72	Donnie Leshnock RC (USA)	.05
73	Mark Lewis	.05
74	Candy Maldonado	.05
75	Jason McDonald RC (USA)	.05
76	Willie McGee	.05
77	Fred McGriff	.05
78	Billy McMillon RC (USA)	.05
79	Hal McRae	.05
80	Dan Melendez RC (USA)	.05
81	Orlando Merced RC	.05
82	Jack Morris	.05
83	Phil Nevin RC (USA)	.50

84	Otis Nixon	.05
85	Johnny Oates	.05
86	Bob Ojeda	.05
87	Mike Pagliarulo	.05
88	Dean Palmer RC	.05
89	Dave Parker	.05
90	Terry Pendleton	.05
91	Tony Phillips RC (USA)	.10
92	Doug Piatt RC	.05
93	Ron Fox (U.S.A.)	.05
94	Tim Raines	.05
95	Willie Randolph	.05
96	Dave Righetti	.05
97	Ernie Riles	.05
98	Chris Roberts RC (USA)	.05
99	Jeff Robinson (Angels)	.05
100	Jeff Robinson (Orioles)	.05
101	Ivan Rodriguez RC	3.00
102	Steve Rodriguez RC (USA)	.05
103	Tom Runnells	.05
104	Scott Sanderson	.05
105	Bob Scanlan RC	.05
106	Pete Schourek RC	.10
107	Gary Scott RC	.05
108	Paul Shuey RC (USA)	.10
109	Doug Simons RC	.05
110	Dave Smith	.05
111	Cory Snyder	.05
112	Luis Sojo	.05
113	Kennie Steenstra RC (USA)	.05
114	Darryl Strawberry	.05
115	Franklin Stubbs	.05
116	Todd Taylor RC (USA)	.05
117	Wade Taylor RC	.05
118	Garry Templeton	.05
119	Mickey Tettleton	.05
120	Tim Teufel	.05
121	Mike Timlin	.05
122	David Tuttle RC (USA)	.05
123	Mo Vaughn RC	.25
124	Jeff Ware RC (USA)	.05
125	Devon White	.05
126	Mark Whiten	.05
127	Mitch Williams	.05
128	Craig Wilson RC (USA)	.05
129	Willie Wilson	.05
130	Chris Wimmer RC (USA)	.05
131	Ivan Zweig RC (USA)	.05
132	Checklist	.05

Traded Tiffany

The final year of production for Topps "Tiffany" parallel boxed sets saw production levels slashed for the 132-card Traded version. Value of the sets has risen dramatically with the hobby's perception of the set's scarcity and the development of key rookies such as Bagwell, Giambi and I-Rod. Like the regular Traded set, cards are numbered in alphabetical order with a "T" suffix.

	NM/M
Unopened Set (132):	165.00
Complete Set (132):	90.00
Common Player:	.25
Stars and Rookies:	4X

Traded Brooks Robinson Bronze

This 1/4-size metal replica of Robinson's first-ever Topps card was issued to dealers who purchased cases of 1991 Topps Traded sets. Each detail of the 1957 Topps Robinson card is reproduced on the 1-1/4" x 1-3/4" bronze metal mini-card, right down to the stats.

		NM/M
328	Brooks Robinson	15.00

Box Panel Cards

Styled like the standard 1991 Topps cards, this 16-card set honors milestones of the featured players. The cards were found on the bottom of wax pack boxes. The cards are designated in alphabetical order by (A-P) and are not numbered.

	NM/M
Complete Set (16):	6.00

Common Player:		.15
A	Bert Blyleven	.15
B	George Brett	1.25
C	Brett Butler	.15
D	Andre Dawson	.50
E	Dwight Evans	.15
F	Carlton Fisk	.75
G	Alfredo Griffin	.15
H	Rickey Henderson	.75
I	Willie McGee	.15
J	Dale Murphy	.50
K	Eddie Murray	.75
L	Dave Parker	.15
M	Jeff Reardon	.15
N	Nolan Ryan	2.25
O	Juan Samuel	.15
P	Robin Yount	.75

All-Star Glossy Set of 22

Continuing the same basic format used since 1984, these glossy-front rack-pack inserts honor the players, manager and honorary captains of the previous year's All-Star Game. Fronts have a league logo in the lower-left corner, a 1990 All-Star banner above the photo and a Topps 40th anniversary logo superimposed over the photo. Backs have a shield and star design and the legend "1990 All-Star Commemorative Set" above the player's name, position and card number. Backs are printed in red and blue.

		NM/M
Complete Set (22):		3.00
Common Player:		.05
1	Tony LaRussa	.05
2	Mark McGwire	.85
3	Steve Sax	.05
4	Wade Boggs	.50
5	Cal Ripken, Jr.	1.00
6	Rickey Henderson	.40
7	Ken Griffey Jr.	.75
8	Jose Canseco	.30
9	Sandy Alomar, Jr.	.05
10	Bob Welch	.05
11	Al Lopez	.05
12	Roger Craig	.05
13	Will Clark	.50
14	Ryne Sandberg	.50
15	Chris Sabo	.05
16	Ozzie Smith	.50
17	Kevin Mitchell	.05
18	Len Dykstra	.05
19	Andre Dawson	.15
20	Mike Scoscia	.05
21	Jack Armstrong	.05
22	Juan Marichal	.05

Glossy Rookies

Similar in format to previous years' glossy rookies sets, this 33-card issue was available one per pack in 100-card jumbo cello packs. Card fronts have a colored "1990 Rookies" banner above the player photo, with the player's name in red in a yellow bar beneath. The Topps 40th anniversary logo appears in one of the upper corners of the photo. Backs are printed in red and blue and feature a "1990 Rookies Commemorative Set" shield logo. The

player's name, position, team and card number are printed beneath. Cards are numbered alphabetically.

		NM/M
Complete Set (33):		2.00
Common Player:		.10
1	Sandy Alomar, Jr.	.10
2	Kevin Appier	.10
3	Steve Avery	.10
4	Carlos Baerga	.10
5	John Burkett	.10
6	Alex Cole	.10
7	Pat Combs	.10
8	Delino DeShields	.10
9	Travis Fryman	.10
10	Marquis Grissom	.10
11	Mike Harkey	.10
12	Glenallen Hill	.10
13	Jeff Huson	.10
14	Felix Jose	.10
15	Dave Justice	.25
16	Jim Leyritz	.10
17	Kevin Maas	.10
18	Ben McDonald	.10
19	Kent Mercker	.10
20	Hal Morris	.10
21	Chris Nabholz	.10
22	Tim Naehring	.10
23	Jose Offerman	.10
24	John Olerud	.25
25	Scott Radinsky	.10
26	Scott Ruskin	.10
27	Kevin Tapani	.10
28	Frank Thomas	1.50
29	Randy Tomlin	.10
30	Greg Vaughn	.10
31	Robin Ventura	.25
32	Larry Walker	.10
33	Todd Zeile	.10

East Coast National Reprints

Produced in Topps' 40th anniversay year, this four-card set was issued at the 1991 East Coast National card show, the first card show in which Topps had ever participated. A total of 40,000 sets were reportedly issued in the now-standard 2-1/2" x 3-1/2" format. Fronts reproduce first Topps cards of four baseball greats while backs, printed in blue, carry a reprint notice, ad for the card show and Topps copyright.

		NM/M
Complete Set (4):		7.50
Common Card:		1.50
(1)	Mickey Mantle/1952	5.00
(2)	Hank Aaron/1954	3.00
(3)	Frank Robinson/1957	1.50
(4)	Stan Musial/1958	1.50

Gallery of Champions

Topps final issue of metallic mini-cards continued the theme of honoring the previous year's winners of major awards. The 1/4-size (1-1/4" x 1-3/4") ingots were issued in complete boxed sets of aluminum, bronze and silver in special display cases. To promote quantity sales, Topps offered a special pewter version of the Rickey Henderson ingot.

		NM/M
Complete Aluminum Set (12):		22.50
Complete Bronze Set (12):		45.00
Complete Silver Set (12):		180.00
(1a)	Sandy Alomar Jr./ Aluminum	1.00
(1b)	Sandy Alomar Jr./Bronze	2.50
(1s)	Sandy Alomar Jr./Silver	6.00
(2a)	Barry Bonds/Aluminum	10.00
(2b)	Barry Bonds/Bronze	15.00
(2s)	Barry Bonds/Silver	65.00
(3a)	George Brett/Aluminum	7.50
(3b)	George Brett/Bronze	10.00
(3s)	George Brett/Silver	50.00
(4a)	Doug Drabek/Aluminum	1.00
(4b)	Doug Drabek/Bronze	2.50
(4s)	Doug Drabek/Bronze	6.00
(5a)	Cecil Fielder/Aluminum	1.00
(5b)	Cecil Fielder/Bronze	2.50
(5s)	Cecil Fielder/Silver	6.00
(6a)	John Franco/Aluminum	1.00
(6b)	John Franco/Bronze	2.50
(6s)	John Franco/Silver	6.00
(7a)	Rickey Henderson/ Aluminum	3.00
(7b)	Rickey Henderson/ Bronze	6.00
(7s)	Rickey Henderson/ Silver	35.00
(7p)	Rickey Henderson/ Pewter	15.00
(8a)	Dave Justice/Aluminum	1.25
(8b)	Dave Justice/Bronze	3.00
(8s)	Dave Justice/Silver	9.00
(9a)	Willie McGee/Aluminum	1.00
(9b)	Willie McGee/Bronze	2.50
(9s)	Willie McGee/Silver	6.00
(10a)	Ryne Sandberg/ Aluminum	6.00
(10b)	Ryne Sandberg/Bronze	7.50
(10s)	Ryne Sandberg/Silver	40.00
(11a)	Bobby Thigpen/ Aluminum	1.00
(11b)	Bobby Thigpen/Bronze	2.50
(11s)	Bobby Thigpen/Silver	6.00
(12a)	Bob Welch/Aluminum	1.00
(12b)	Bob Welch/Bronze	2.50
(12s)	Bob Welch/Silver	6.00

Golden Spikes Award

Each year the United States Baseball Federation honors the outstanding amateur player with the Golden Spikes Award. This card was handed out at the Nov. 20, 1991 awards banquet honoring Arizona State star Mike Kelly. Production was reported as 600 cards.

	NM/M
Mike Kelly	85.00

Joe Garagiola

Virtually identical to the personal business card which Topps produced for long-time NBC announcer and former major leaguer Joe Garagiola in 1976, this 1991 version makes mention of the Today Show on both front and back. The front is in the format of a 1973 Topps card and has a color portrait. The back resembles the 1976 Topps card, is in black-and-white and provides contact information.

		NM/M
1	Joe Garagiola	8.00

Micro

	NM/M
Complete Set (792):	9.00
Common Player:	.05
Stars/Rookies:	1-1.5X

Babe Ruth

This 11-card set by Topps was released in honor of the NBC movie about Babe Ruth. The cards were released on a limited basis. The card fronts feature full-color photos from the movie, while the flip sides are printed horizontally and describe the front photo. The cards are numbered on the back.

		NM/M
Complete Set (11):		12.50
Common Player:		1.00
1	Sunday Oct. 6, NBC	1.00
2	Stephen Lang as Babe Ruth	1.00
3	Bruce Weitz as Miller Huggins	1.00
4	Lisa Zane as Claire Ruth	1.00
5	Donald Moffat as Jacob Ruppert	1.00
6	Neil McDonough as Lou Gehrig	1.00
7	Pete Rose as Ty Cobb	5.00
8	Baseball Consultant (Rod Carew)	2.50
9	Miller Huggins, Babe Ruth	1.00
10	Ruth In Action	1.00
11	Babe Calls His Shot	1.00

Superstar Stand-Ups

Another of Topps' efforts over the years to market candy containers with a baseball player theme, the 1991 Superstar Stand-Ups were a test issue. Sold in a color-printed paper envelope, Stand-Ups are a hard plastic container filled with candy tablets. In bright see-through colors, the containers measure 2-1/16" x 2-9/16" and are vaguely shaped like a head and shoulders. A paper label attached to the front of the plastic has a player portrait with his team in a banner above and his name in a strip at bottom. Backs have a baseball design on the label with the Topps 40th anniversary logo at top. The player's name, team and position are in color bars at the bottom, with the item number at left. At center are the player's height, weight, birth date, batting and throwing preference and the year and number of his Topps rookie card. Clear (non-colored) plastic containers are also known for each player, though their relative scarcity to the colored pieces is currently undetermined.

	NM/M
Complete Set (36):	45.00
Common Player:	1.00
Wax Pack (1):	1.50
Wax Box (36):	30.00

#	Player	Price
1	Jim Abbott	1.00
2	Sandy Alomar	1.00
3	Wade Boggs	2.50
4	Barry Bonds	5.00
5	Bobby Bonilla	1.00
6	George Brett	3.00
7	Jose Canseco	3.00
8	Will Clark	1.00
9	Roger Clemens	3.00
10	Eric Davis	1.00
11	Andre Dawson	1.50
12	Len Dykstra	1.00
13	Cecil Fielder	1.00
14	Carlton Fisk	2.00
15	Dwight Gooden	1.00
16	Mark Grace	1.00
17	Ken Griffey Jr.	3.50
18	Tony Gwynn	2.50
19	Rickey Henderson	2.00
20	Bo Jackson	1.50
21	Dave Justice	1.00
22	Kevin Maas	1.00
23	Ramon Martinez	1.00
24	Don Mattingly	3.00
25	Ben McDonald	1.00
26	Mark McGwire	4.00
27	Kevin Mitchell	1.00
28	Cal Ripken, Jr.	5.00
29	Nolan Ryan	5.00
30	Ryne Sandberg	2.50
31	Ozzie Smith	2.50
32	Dave Stewart	1.00
33	Darryl Strawberry	1.00
34	Frank Viola	1.00
35	Matt Williams	1.00
36	Robin Yount	2.00

"1953" Topps Archives Promos

This nine-card set was issued to promote Topps' 1953 Archives set. Besides seven of the cards being reprinted from the '53 set, the promo set included two of the "new" 1953-style cards which were included in the Archives issue - cards of Hank Aaron and Eleanor Engle, the first woman to sign a minor league contract in modern times. Card fronts are identical to the issued Archives cards, while the backs are white with red Archives logo and "Pre-production Sample" notation.

	NM/M
Complete Set (9):	75.00
Common Player:	7.50

#	Player	Price
(1)	Hank Aaron	12.00
(2)	Roy Campanella	7.50
(3)	Eleanor Engle	7.50
(4)	Bob Feller	7.50
(5)	Whitey Ford	7.50
(6)	Mickey Mantle	20.00
(7)	Willie Mays	12.00
(8)	Jackie Robinson	10.00
(9)	Satchell Paige	10.00

"1953" Topps Archives

Billed as "The Ultimate 1953 Set," this issue reproduced 273 of the original 274-card 1953 Topps set. (Card #174, Billy Loes, was not reproduced due to lack of permission from the former Dodgers pitcher, though cards with #174 are known with a Loes back and another player on the front.) The Archives issue downsized the cards from their original 2-5/8" x 3-3/4" size to the now-standard 2-1/2" x 3-1/2" format. More than 50 cards of players who were not included in the 1953 Topps set were created as part of the Archives issue. Because Topps chose to use black-and-white photos and colorized backgrounds for most of the "extended" cards, rather than paintings as on the originals, collector interest in the Archives issue was diminished. Only 18,000 cases were reportedly produced.

	NM/M
Complete Set (337):	45.00
Common Player:	.10
Wax Pack (12):	1.50
Wax Box (36):	35.00

#	Player	Price
1	Jackie Robinson	7.50
2	Luke Easter	.10
3	George Crowe	.10
4	Ben Wade	.10
5	Joe Dobson	.10
6	Sam Jones	.10
7	Bob Borkowski	.10
8	Clem Koshorek	.10
9	Joe Collins	.10
10	Smoky Burgess	.10
11	Sal Yvars	.10
12	Howie Judson	.10
13	Conrado Marrero	.10
14	Clem Labine	.10
15	Bobo Newsom	.10
16	Peanuts Lowrey	.10
17	Billy Hitchcock	.10
18	Ted Lepcio	.10
19	Mel Parnell	.10
20	Hank Thompson	.10
21	Billy Johnson	.10
22	Howie Fox	.10
23	Toby Atwell	.10
24	Ferris Fain	.10
25	Ray Boone	.10
26	Dale Mitchell	.10
27	Roy Campanella	1.50
28	Eddie Pellagrini	.10
29	Hal Jeffcoat	.10
30	Willard Nixon	.10
31	Ewell Blackwell	.10
32	Clyde Vollmer	.10
33	Bob Kennedy	.10
34	George Shuba	.10
35	Irv Noren	.10
36	Johnny Groth	.10
37	Eddie Mathews	1.00
38	Jim Hearn	.10
39	Eddie Miksis	.10
40	John Lipon	.10
41	Enos Slaughter	.50
42	Gus Zernial	.10
43	Gil McDougald	.30
44	Ellis Kinder	.10
45	Grady Hatton	.10
46	Johnny Klippstein	.10
47	Bubba Church	.10
48	Bob Del Greco	.10
49	Faye Throneberry	.10
50	Chuck Dressen	.10
51	Frank Campos	.10
52	Ted Gray	.10
53	Sherman Lollar	.10
54	Bob Feller	1.00
55	Maurice McDermott	.10
56	Gerald Staley	.10
57	Carl Scheib	.10
58	George Metkovich	.10
59	Karl Drews	.10
60	Cloyd Boyer	.10
61	Early Wynn	.50
62	Monte Irvin	.50
63	Gus Niarhos	.10
64	Dave Philley	.10
65	Earl Harrist	.10
66	Orestes Minoso	.25
67	Roy Sievers	.10
68	Del Rice	.10
69	Dick Brodowski	.10
70	Ed Yuhas	.10
71	Tony Bartirome	.10
72	Fred Hutchinson	.10
73	Eddie Robinson	.10
74	Joe Rossi	.10
75	Mike Garcia	.10
76	Pee Wee Reese	1.00
77	John Mize	.75
78	Al Schoendienst	.50
79	Johnny Wyrostek	.10
80	Jim Hegan	.10
81	Joe Black	.10
82	Mickey Mantle	12.50
83	Howie Pollet	.10
84	Bob Hooper	.10
85	Bobby Morgan	.10
86	Billy Martin	.35
87	Ed Lopat	.20
88	Willie Jones	.10
89	Chuck Stobbs	.10
90	Hank Edwards	.10
91	Ebba St. Claire	.10
92	Paul Minner	.10
93	Hal Rice	.10
94	William Kennedy	.10
95	Willard Marshall	.10
96	Virgil Trucks	.10
97	Don Kolloway	.10
98	Cal Abrams	.10
99	Dave Madison	.10
100	Bill Miller	.10
101	Ted Wilks	.10
102	Connie Ryan	.10
103	Joe Astroth	.10
104	Yogi Berra	1.50
105	Joe Nuxhall	.10
106	John Antonelli	.10
107	Danny O'Connell	.10
108	Bob Porterfield	.10
109	Alvin Dark	.10
110	Herman Wehmeier	.10
111	Hank Sauer	.10
112	Ned Garver	.10
113	Jerry Priddy	.10
114	Phil Rizzuto	1.00
115	George Spencer	.10
116	Frank Smith	.10
117	Sid Gordon	.10
118	Gus Bell	.10
119	John Sain	.25
120	Davey Williams	.10
121	Walt Dropo	.10
122	Elmer Valo	.10
123	Tommy Byrne	.10
124	Sibby Sisti	.10
125	Dick Williams	.20
126	Bill Connelly	.10
127	Clint Courtney	.10
128	Wilmer Mizell	.10
129	Keith Thomas	.10
130	Turk Lown	.10
131	Harry Byrd	.10
132	Tom Morgan	.10
133	Gil Coan	.10
134	Rube Walker	.10
135	Al Rosen	.25
136	Ken Heintzelman	.10
137	John Rutherford	.10
138	George Kell	.50
139	Sammy White	.10
140	Tommy Glaviano	.10
141	Allie Reynolds	.25
142	Vic Wertz	.10
143	Billy Pierce	.20
144	Bob Schultz	.10
145	Harry Dorish	.10
146	Granville Hamner	.10
147	Warren Spahn	1.00
148	Mickey Grasso	.10
149	Dom DiMaggio	.25
150	Harry Simpson	.10
151	Hoyt Wilhelm	.50
152	Bob Adams	.10
153	Andy Seminick	.10
154	Dick Groat	.20
155	Dutch Leonard	.10
156	Jim Rivera	.10
157	Bob Addis	.10
158	John Logan	.10
159	Wayne Terwilliger	.10
160	Bob Young	.10
161	Vern Bickford	.10
162	Ted Kluszewski	.35
163	Fred Hatfield	.10
164	Frank Shea	.10
165	Billy Hoeft	.10
166	Bill Hunter	.10
167	Art Schult	.10
168	Willard Schmidt	.10
169	Dizzy Trout	.10
170	Bill Werle	.10
171	Bill Glynn	.10
172	Rip Repulski	.10
173	Preston Ward	.10
174	Ron Kline	.10
175	Don Hoak	.10
176	Jim Dyck	.10
177	Jim Waugh	.10
178	Gene Hermanski	.10
179	Virgil Stallcup	.10
180	Al Zarilla	.10
181	Bob Hofman	.10
182	Stu Miller	.10
183	Hal Brown	.10
184	Jim Pendleton	.10
185	Charlie Bishop	.10
186	Jim Fridley	.10
187	Andy Carey	.10
188	Ray Jablonski	.10
189	Dixie Walker	.10
190	Ralph Kiner	.50
191	Wally Westlake	.10
192	Mike Clark	.10
193	Eddie Kazak	.10
194	Ed McGhee	.10
195	Bob Keegan	.10
196	Del Crandall	.10
197	Forrest Main	.10
198	Marion Fricano	.10
199	Gordon Goldsberry	.10
200	Paul La Palme	.10
201	Carl Sawatski	.10
202	Cliff Fannin	.10
203	Dick Bokelmann	.10
205	Vern Benson	.10
206	Ed Bailey	.10
207	Whitey Ford	1.00
208	Jim Wilson	.10
209	Jim Greengrass	.10
210	Bob Cerv	.10
211	J.W. Porter	.10
212	Jack Dittmer	.10
213	Ray Scarborough	.10
214	Bill Bruton	.10
215	Gene Conley	.10
216	Jim Hughes	.10
217	Murray Wall	.10
218	Les Fusselman	.10
219	Pete Runnels	.10
220	Satchell Paige	4.00
221	Bob Milliken	.10
222	Vic Janowicz	.10
223	John O'Brien	.10
224	Lou Sleater	.10
225	Bobby Shantz	.20
226	Ed Erautt	.10
227	Morris Martin	.10
228	Hal Newhouser	.10
229	Rocky Krshnich	.10
230	Johnny Lindell	.10
231	Solly Hemus	.10
232	Dick Kokos	.10
233	Al Aber	.10
234	Ray Murray	.10
235	John Hetki	.10
236	Harry Perkowski	.10
237	Clarence Podbielan	.10
238	Cal Hogue	.10
239	Jim Delsing	.10
240	Freddie Marsh	.10
241	Al Sima	.10
242	Charlie Silvera	.10
243	Carlos Bernier	.10
244	Willie Mays	7.50
245	Bill Norman	.10
246	Roy Face	.10
247	Mike Sandlock	.10
248	Gene Stephens	.10
249	Ed O'Brien	.10
250	Bob Wilson	.10
251	Sid Hudson	.10
252	Henry Foiles	.10
254	Preacher Roe	.10
255	Dixie Howell	.10
256	Les Peden	.10
257	Bob Boyd	.10
258	Jim Gilliam	.35
259	Roy McMillan	.10
260	Sam Calderone	.10
262	Bob Oldis	.10
263	John Podres	.35
264	Gene Woodling	.35
265	Jackie Jensen	.35
266	Bob Cain	.10
269	Duane Pillette	.10
270	Vern Stephens	.10
272	Bill Antonello	.10
273	Harvey Haddix	.25
274	John Riddle	.10
276	Ken Raffensberger	.10
277	Don Lund	.10
278	Willie Miranda	.10
279	Joe Coleman	.10
280	Milt Bolling	.10
281	Jimmie Dykes	.10
282	Ralph Houk	.35
283	Frank Thomas	.10
284	Bob Lemon	.50
285	Joe Adcock	.35
286	Jimmy Piersall	.10
287	Mickey Vernon	.10
288	Robin Roberts	.50
289	Rogers Hornsby	.50
290	Hank Bauer	.10
291	Hoot Evers	.10
292	Whitey Lockman	.10
293	Ralph Branca	.25
294	Wally Post	.10
295	Phil Cavarretta	.10
296	Gil Hodges	.35
297	Roy Smalley	.10
298	Bob Friend	.10
299	Dusty Rhodes	.25
300	Eddie Stanky	.10
301	Harvey Kuenn	.25
302	Marty Marion	.10
303	Sal Maglie	.10
304	Lou Boudreau	.50
305	Carl Furillo	.35
306	Bobo Holloman	.10
307	Steve O'Neill	.10
308	Carl Erskine	.25
309	Leo Durocher	.25
310	Lew Burdette	.10
311	Richie Ashburn	.50
312	Hoyt Wilhelm	.50
313	Bucky Harris	.10
314	Joe Garagiola	.50
315	Johnny Pesky	.10
316	Fred Haney	.10
317	Hank Aaron	7.50
318	Curt Simmons	.10
319	Ted Williams	7.50
320	Don Newcombe	.35
321	Charlie Grimm	.10
322	Paul Richards	.10
323	Wes Westrum	.10
324	Vern Law	.10
325	Casey Stengel	1.00
326	Hall of Fame Inductees (Dizzy Dean, Al Simmons)	1.00
327	Duke Snider	1.00
328	Bill Rigney	.10
329	Al Lopez	.50
330	Bobby Thomson	.35
331	Nellie Fox	.50
332	Eleanor Engle	.10
333	Larry Doby	.50
334	Billy Goodman	.10
335	Checklist 1-140	.10
336	Checklist 141-280	.10
337	Checklist 281-337	.10

1990 Major League Debut

This 171-card set features the players who made their Major League debut in 1990. The cards are styled like the 1991 Topps cards and are numbered in alphabetical order. The card backs are printed horizontally and feature information about the player's debut and statistics. The issue was sold only as a boxed set through hobby channels.

	NM/M
Complete Set (171):	5.00
Common Player:	.05

#	Player	Price
1	Paul Abbott	.05
2	Steve Adkins	.05
3	Scott Aldred	.05
4	Gerald Alexander	.05
5	Moises Alou	.25
6	Steve Avery	.25
7	Oscar Azocar	.05
8	Carlos Baerga	.05
9	Kevin Baez	.05
10	Jeff Baldwin	.05
11	Brian Barnes	.05
12	Kevin Bearse	.05
13	Kevin Belcher	.05
14	Mike Bell	.05
15	Sean Berry	.05
16	Joe Bitker	.05
17	Willie Blair	.05
18	Brian Bohanon	.05
19	Mike Bordick	.05
20	Shawn Boskie	.05
21	Rod Brewer	.05
22	Kevin Brown	.10
23	Dave Burba	.05
24	Jim Campbell	.05
25	Ozzie Canseco	.05
26	Chuck Carr	.05
27	Larry Casian	.05
28	Andujar Cedeno	.05
29	Wes Chamberlain	.05
30	Scott Chiamparino	.05
31	Steve Chitren	.05
32	Pete Coachman	.05
33	Alex Cole	.10
34	Jeff Conine	.10
35	Scott Cooper	.05
36	Milt Cuyler	.05
37	Steve Decker	.05
38	Rich DeLucia	.05
39	Delino DeShields	.50
40	Mark Dewey	.05
41	Carlos Diaz	.05
42	Lance Dickson	.05
43	Narciso Elvira	.05
44	Luis Encarnacion	.05
45	Scott Erickson	.25
46	Paul Faries	.05
47	Howard Farmer	.05
48	Alex Fernandez	.05
49	Travis Fryman	.05
50	Rich Garces	.05
51	Carlos Garcia	.05
52	Mike Gardiner	.05
53	Bernard Gilkey	.05
54	Tom Gilles	.05
55	Jerry Goff	.05
56	Leo Gomez	.05
57	Luis Gonzalez	.75
58	Joe Grahe	.05
59	Craig Grebeck	.05
60	Kip Gross	.05
61	Eric Gunderson	.05
62	Chris Hammond	.05
63	Dave Hansen	.05
64	Reggie Harris	.05
65	Bill Haselman	.05
66	Randy Hennis	.05
67	Carlos Hernandez	.05
68	Howard Hilton	.05
69	Dave Hollins	.05
70	Darren Holmes	.05
71	John Hoover	.05
72	Steve Howard	.05
73	Thomas Howard	.05
74	Todd Hundley	.05
75	Daryl Irvine	.05
76	Chris Jelic	.05
77	Dana Kiecker	.05
78	Brent Knackert	.05
79	Jimmy Kremers	.05
80	Jerry Kutzler	.05
81	Ray Lankford	.05
82	Tim Layana	.05
83	Terry Lee	.05
84	Mark Leiter	.05
85	Scott Leius	.05
86	Mark Leonard	.05
87	Darren Lewis	.05
88	Scott Lewis	.05
89	Jim Leyritz	.05
90	Dave Liddell	.05
91	Luis Lopez	.05
92	Kevin Maas	.05
93	Bob MacDonald	.05
94	Carlos Maldonado	.05
95	Chuck Malone	.05
96	Ramon Manon	.05
97	Jeff Manto	.05
98	Paul Marak	.05
99	Tino Martinez	.25
100	Derrick May	.05
101	Brent Mayne	.05
102	Paul McClellan	.05
103	Rodney McCray	.05
104	Tim McIntosh	.05
105	Brian McRae	.05
106	Jose Melendez	.05
107	Orlando Merced	.05
108	Alan Mills	.05
109	Gino Minutelli	.05
110	Mickey Morandini	.05
111	Pedro Munoz	.05
112	Chris Nabholz	.05
113	Tim Naehring	.05
114	Charles Nagy	.05
115	Jim Neidlinger	.05
116	Rafael Novoa	.05
117	Jose Offerman	.05
118	Omar Olivares	.05
119	Javier Ortiz	.05
120	Al Osuna	.05
121	Rick Parker	.05
122	Dave Pavlas	.05
123	Geronimo Pena	.05
124	Mike Perez	.05
125	Phil Plantier	.05
126	Jim Poole	.05
127	Tom Quinlan	.05
128	Scott Radinsky	.05
129	Darren Reed	.05
130	Karl Rhodes	.05
131	Jeff Richardson	.05
132	Rich Rodriguez	.05
133	Dave Rohde	.05
134	Mel Rojas	.05
135	Vic Rosario	.05
136	Rich Rowland	.05
137	Scott Ruskin	.05
138	Bill Sampen	.05
139	Andres Santana	.05
140	David Segui	.05
141	Jeff Shaw	.05
142	Tim Sherrill	.05
143	Terry Shumpert	.05
144	Mike Simms	.05
145	Daryl Smith	.05
146	Luis Sojo	.05
147	Steve Springer	.05
148	Ray Stephens	.05
149	Lee Stevens	.05
150	Mel Stottlemyre, Jr.	.05
151	Glenn Sutko	.05
152	Anthony Telford	.05
153	Frank Thomas	3.00
154	Randy Tomlin	.05
155	Brian Traxler	.05
156	Efrain Valdez	.05
157	Rafael Valdez	.05
158	Julio Valera	.05
159	Jim Vatcher	.05
160	Hector Villanueva	.05
161	Hector Wagner	.05
162	Dave Walsh	.05
163	Steve Wapnick	.05
164	Colby Ward	.05
165	Turner Ward	.05
166	Terry Wells	.05
167	Mark Whiten	.05
168	Mike York	.05
169	Cliff Young	.05
170	Checklist	.05
171	Checklist	.05

1992 Topps Pre-Production

To preview its 1992 card set for dealers, Topps distributed a nine-card sheet in the basic format of its 1992 issue. The 8" x 10" sheets are often found cut into standard 2-1/2" x 3-1/2" singles. Card numbers on the backs of these promo cards do not correspond to the same cards in the regular set, and the stats for 1991 are not included. The preview cards have an orange oval on back, with the words, "1992 Pre-Production Sample."

ROB DIBBLE

	NM/M
Uncut Sheet:	6.00
Complete Set (9):	6.00
Common Player:	1.00

3	Shawon Dunston	1.00
16	Mike Heath	1.00
18	Todd Frowirth	1.00
20	Bip Roberts	1.00
131	Rob Dibble	1.00
174	Otis Nixon	1.00
273	Dennis Martinez	1.00
325	Brett Butler	1.00
798	Tom Lasorda	1.00

1992 Topps

This 792-card set features white stock much like the 1991 issue. The card fronts feature full-color action and posed photos with a gray inner frame and the player name and position at bottom. Backs feature biographical information, statistics and stadium photos on player cards where space is available. All-Star cards and #1 Draft Pick cards are once again included. Topps brought back four-player rookie cards in 1992. Nine Top Prospect cards of this nature can be found within the set. "Match the Stats" game cards were inserted into packs of 1992 Topps cards. Special bonus cards were given away to winners of this insert game. This was the first Topps regular-issue baseball card set since 1951 which was sold without bubblegum.

	NM/M
Unopened Fact. Set (802):	30.00
Complete Set (792):	20.00
Common Player:	.05
Golds:	4X
Wax Pack (14):	.50
Wax Box (36):	12.50
Cello Pack (34):	1.00
Cello Box (24):	16.00
Vending Box (500):	6.00

1	Nolan Ryan	.75
2	Rickey Henderson (Record Breaker)	.20
3	Jeff Reardon (Record Breaker)	.05
4	Nolan Ryan (Record Breaker)	.40
5	Dave Winfield (Record Breaker)	.20
6	Brien Taylor RC (Draft Pick)	
7	Jim Olander RC	.05
8	Bryan Hickerson RC	.05
9	John Farrell (Draft Pick)	.05
10	Wade Boggs	.45
11	Jack McDowell	.05
12	Luis Gonzalez	.05
13	Mike Scioscia	.05
14	Wes Chamberlain	.05
15	Denny Martinez	.05
16	Jeff Montgomery	.05
17	Randy Milligan	.05
18	Greg Cadaret	.05
19	Jamie Quirk	.05
20	Bip Roberts	.05
21	Buck Rodgers	.05
22	Bill Wegman	.05

23	Chuck Knoblauch	.05
24	Randy Myers	.05
25	Ron Gant	.05
26	Mike Bielecki	.05
27	Juan Gonzalez	.20
28	Mike Schooler	.05
29	Mickey Tettleton	.05
30	John Kruk	.05
31	Bryn Smith	.05
32	Chris Nabholz	.05
33	Carlos Baerga	.05
34	Jeff Juden	.05
35	Dave Righetti	.05
36	Scott Ruffcorn RC (Draft Pick)	.05
37	Luis Polonia	.05
38	Tom Candiotti	.05
39	Greg Olson	.05
40	Cal Ripken, Jr.	.75
41	Craig Lefferts	.05
42	Mike Macfarlane	.05
43	Jose Lind	.05
44	Rick Aguilera	.05
45	Gary Carter	.35
46	Steve Farr	.05
47	Rex Hudler	.05
48	Scott Scudder	.05
49	Damon Berryhill	.05
50	Ken Griffey Jr.	.55
51	Tom Runnells	.05
52	Juan Bell	.05
53	Tommy Gregg	.05
54	David Wells	.05
55	Rafael Palmeiro	.30
56	Charlie O'Brien	.05
57	Donn Pall	.05
58	Top Prospects-Catchers (Brad Ausmus RC, Jim Campanis RC, Dave Nilsson RC, Doug Robbins RC)	.15
59	Mo Vaughn	.05
60	Tony Fernandez	.05
61	Paul O'Neill	.05
62	Gene Nelson	.05
63	Randy Ready	.05
64	Bob Kipper	.05
65	Willie McGee	.05
66	Scott Stahoviak RC (Draft Pick)	.05
67	Luis Salazar	.05
68	Marvin Freeman	.05
69	Kenny Lofton	.05
70	Gary Gaetti	.05
71	Erik Hanson	.05
72	Eddie Zosky RC	.05
73	Brian Barnes	.05
74	Scott Leius	.05
75	Bret Saberhagen	.05
76	Mike Gallego	.05
77	Jack Armstrong	.05
78	Ivan Rodriguez	.35
79	Jesse Orosco	.05
80	Dave Justice	.05
81	Ced Landrum RC	.05
82	Doug Simons RC	.05
83	Tommy Greene	.05
84	Leo Gomez	.05
85	Jose DeLeon	.05
86	Steve Finley	.05
87	Bob MacDonald RC	.05
88	Darrin Jackson	.05
89	Neal Heaton	.05
90	Robin Yount	.35
91	Jeff Reed	.05
92	Lenny Harris	.05
93	Reggie Jefferson	.05
94	Sammy Sosa	.45
95	Scott Bailes	.05
96	Tom McKinnon RC (Draft Pick)	
97	Luis Rivera	.05
98	Mike Harkey	.05
99	Jeff Treadway	.05
100	Jose Canseco	.25
101	Omar Vizquel	.05
102	Scott Kamieniecki RC	.05
103	Ricky Jordan	.05
104	Jeff Ballard	.05
105	Felix Jose	.05
106	Mike Boddicker	.05
107	Dan Pasqua	.05
108	Mike Timlin RC	.10
109	Roger Craig	.05
110	Ryne Sandberg	.45
111	Mark Carreon	.05
112	Oscar Azocar	.05
113	Mike Greenwell	.05
114	Mark Portugal	.05
115	Terry Pendleton	.05
116	Willie Randolph	.05
117	Scott Terry	.05
118	Chili Davis	.05
119	Mark Gardner	.05
120	Alan Trammell	.05
121	Derek Bell	.05
122	Gary Varsho	.05
123	Bob Ojeda	.05
124	Shawn Livsey RC (Draft Pick)	.05
125	Chris Hoiles	.05
126	Top Prospects-1st Baseman (Rico Brogna, John Jaha, Ryan Klesko, Dave Staton)	.05
127	Carlos Quintana	.05
128	Kurt Stillwell	.05
129	Melido Perez	.05
130	Alvin Davis	.05

131	Checklist 1	.05
132	Eric Show	.05
133	Rance Mulliniks	.05
134	Darryl Kile	.05
135	Von Hayes	.05
136	Bill Doran	.05
137	Jeff Robinson	.05
138	Monty Fariss	.05
139	Jeff Innis	.05
140	Mark Grace	.05
141	Jim Leyland	.05
142	Todd Van Poppel	.05
143	Paul Gibson	.05
144	Bill Swift	.05
145	Danny Tartabull	.05
146	Al Newman	.05
147	Cris Carpenter	.05
148	Anthony Young RC	.05
149	Brian Bohanon RC	.05
150	Roger Clemens	.50
151	Jeff Hamilton	.05
152	Charlie Leibrandt	.05
153	Ron Karkovice	.05
154	Hensley Meulens	.05
155	Scott Bankhead	.05
156	Manny Ramirez RC (Draft Pick)	3.00
157	Keith Miller	.05
158	Todd Frowirth	.05
159	Darrin Fletcher	.05
160	Bobby Bonilla	.05
161	Casey Candaele	.05
162	Paul Faries	.05
163	Dana Kiecker	.05
164	Shane Mack	.05
165	Mark Langston	.05
166	Geronimo Pena	.05
167	Andy Allanson	.05
168	Dwight Smith	.05
169	Chuck Crim	.05
170	Alex Cole	.05
171	Bill Plummer	.05
172	Juan Berenguer	.05
173	Brian Downing	.05
174	Steve Frey	.05
175	Orel Hershiser	.05
176	Ramon Garcia RC	.05
177	Danny Gladden	.05
178	Jim Acker	.05
179	Top Prospects-2nd Baseman (Cesar Bernhardt RC, Bobby DeJardin RC, Armando Moreno RC, Andy Stankiewicz RC)	.05
180	Kevin Mitchell	.05
181	Hector Villanueva	.05
182	Jeff Reardon	.05
183	Brent Mayne	.05
184	Jimmy Jones	.05
185	Benny Santiago	.05
186	Cliff Floyd RC (Draft Pick)	.50
187	Ernie Riles	.05
188	Jose Guzman	.05
189	Junior Felix	.05
190	Glenn Davis	.05
191	Charlie Hough	.05
192	Dave Fleming RC	.05
193	Omar Oliveras RC	.05
194	Eric Karros	.05
195	David Cone	.05
196	Frank Castillo RC	.05
197	Glenn Braggs	.05
198	Scott Aldred	.05
199	Jeff Blauser	.05
200	Len Dykstra	.05
201	Buck Showalter	.05
202	Rick Honeycutt	.05
203	Greg Myers	.05
204	Trevor Wilson	.05
205	Jay Howell	.05
206	Luis Sojo	.05
207	Jack Clark	.05
208	Julio Machado	.05
209	Lloyd McClendon	.05
210	Ozzie Guillen	.05
211	Jeremy Hernandez RC	.05
212	Randy Velarde	.05
213	Les Lancaster	.05
214	Andy Mota RC	.05
215	Rich Gossage	.05
216	Brent Gates RC (Draft Pick)	
217	Brian Harper	.05
218	Mike Flanagan	.05
219	Jerry Browne	.05
220	Jose Rijo	.05
221	Skeeter Barnes	.05
222	Jaime Navarro	.05
223	Mel Hall	.05
224	Brett Barberie RC	.05
225	Roberto Alomar	.15
226	Pete Smith	.05
227	Daryl Boston	.05
228	Eddie Whitson	.05
229	Shawn Boskie	.05
230	Dick Schofield	.05
231	Brian Drahman RC	.05
232	John Smiley	.05
233	Mitch Webster	.05
234	Terry Steinbach	.05
235	Jack Morris	.05
236	Bill Pecota	.05
237	Jose Hernandez RC	.05
238	Greg Litton	.05
239	Brian Holman	.05
240	Andres Galarraga	.05
241	Gerald Young	.05
242	Mike Mussina	.30

243	Alvaro Espinoza	.05
244	Darren Daulton	.05
245	John Smoltz	.05
246	Jason Pruitt RC (Draft Pick)	.05
247	Chuck Finley	.05
248	Jim Gantner	.05
249	Tony Fossas	.05
250	Ken Griffey	.05
251	Kevin Elster	.05
252	Dennis Rasmussen	.05
253	Terry Kennedy	.05
254	Ryan Bowen RC	.05
255	Robin Ventura	.05
256	Mike Aldrete	.05
257	Jeff Russell	.05
258	Jim Lindeman	.05
259	Ron Darling	.05
260	Devon White	.05
261	Tom Lasorda	.05
262	Terry Lee RC	.05
263	Bob Patterson	.05
264	Checklist 2	.05
265	Teddy Higuera	.05
266	Roberto Kelly	.05
267	Steve Bedrosian	.05
268	Brady Anderson	.05
269	Ruben Amaro RC	.05
270	Tony Gwynn	.45
271	Tracy Jones	.05
272	Jerry Don Gleaton	.05
273	Craig Grebeck	.05
274	Bob Scanlan RC	.05
275	Todd Zeile	.05
276	Shawn Green RC (Draft Pick)	1.50
277	Scott Chiamparino	.05
278	Darryl Hamilton	.05
279	Jim Clancy	.05
280	Carlos Martinez	.05
281	Kevin Appier	.05
282	John Wehner RC	.05
283	Reggie Sanders	.05
284	Gene Larkin	.05
285	Bob Welch	.05
286	Gilberto Reyes RC	.05
287	Pete Schourek	.05
288	Andujar Cedeno	.05
289	Mike Morgan	.05
290	Bo Jackson	.10
291	Phil Garner	.05
292	Ray Lankford	.05
293	Mike Henneman	.05
294	Dave Valle	.05
295	Alonzo Powell RC	.05
296	Tom Brunansky	.05
297	Kevin Brown	.05
298	Kelly Gruber	.05
299	Charles Nagy	.05
300	Don Mattingly	.50
301	Kirk McCaskill	.05
302	Joey Cora	.05
303	Dan Plesac	.05
304	Joe Oliver	.05
305	Tom Glavine	.25
306	Al Shirley RC (Draft Pick)	.05
307	Bruce Ruffin	.05
308	Craig Shipley RC	.05
309	Dave Martinez	.05
310	Jose Mesa	.05
311	Henry Cotto	.05
312	Mike LaValliere	.05
313	Kevin Tapani	.05
314	Jeff Huson	.05
315	Juan Samuel	.05
316	Curt Schilling	.25
317	Mike Bordick RC	.05
318	Steve Howe	.05
319	Tony Phillips	.05
320	George Bell	.05
321	Lou Pinella	.05
322	Tim Burke	.05
323	Milt Thompson	.05
324	Danny Darwin	.05
325	Joe Orsulak	.05
326	Eric King	.05
327	Jay Buhner	.05
328	Joel Johnston RC	.05
329	Franklin Stubbs	.05
330	Will Clark	.05
331	Steve Lake	.05
332	Chris Jones RC	.05
333	Pat Tabler	.05
334	Kevin Gross	.05
335	Dave Henderson	.05
336	Greg Anthony RC (Draft Pick)	
337	Alejandro Pena	.05
338	Shawn Abner	.05
339	Tom Browning	.05
340	Otis Nixon	.05
341	Bob Geren	.05
342	Tim Spehr RC	.05
343	Jon Vander Wal RC	.20
344	Jack Daugherty	.05
345	Zane Smith	.05
346	Rheal Cormier RC	.05
347	Kent Hrbek	.05
348	Rick Wilkins RC	.10
349	Steve Lyons	.05
350	Gregg Olson	.05
351	Greg Riddoch	.05
352	Ed Nunez	.05
353	Braulio Castillo RC	.05
354	Dave Bergman	.05
355	Warren Newson RC	.05
356	Luis Quinones	.05
357	Mike Witt	.05

358	Ted Wood RC	.05
359	Mike Moore	.05
361	Barry Jones	.05
362	Javier Ortiz RC	.05
363	John Candelaria	.05
364	Glenallen Hill	.05
366	Checklist 3	.05
367	Rafael Belliard	.05
368	Bill Krueger	.05
369	Steve Whitaker RC (Draft Pick)	.05
370	Shawon Dunston	.05
371	Dante Bichette	.05
372	Kip Gross RC	.05
373	Don Robinson	.05
375	Bert Blyleven	.05
377	Chris Donnels RC	.05
378	Bob Zupcic RC	.05
379	Joel Skinner	.05
380	Steve Chitren	.05
380	Sparky Anderson	.10
381	Sid Fernandez	.05
382	Dave Hollins	.05
384	Mark Lee	.05
385	Tim Wallach	.05
386	Will Clark/AS	.05
387	Ryne Sandberg/AS	.20
388	Howard Johnson/AS	.05
389	Barry Larkin/AS	.05
390	Barry Bonds/AS	.40
391	Ron Gant/AS	.05
392	Bobby Bonilla/AS	.05
393	Craig Biggio/AS	.05
394	Denny Martinez/AS	.05
395	Tom Glavine/AS	.05
396	Lee Smith/AS	.05
397	Cecil Fielder/AS	.05
398	Julio Franco/AS	.05
399	Wade Boggs/AS	.20
400	Cal Ripken, Jr./AS	.40
401	Jose Canseco/AS	.15
402	Joe Carter/AS	.05
403	Ruben Sierra/AS	.05
404	Matt Nokes/AS	.05
405	Roger Clemens/AS	.25
406	Jim Abbott/AS	.05
407	Bryan Harvey/AS	.05
408	Bob Milacki	.05
409	Geno Petralli	.05
410	Dave Stewart	.05
411	Mike Jackson	.05
412	Luis Aquino	.05
413	Tim Teufel	.05
414	Jeff Ware (Draft Pick)	.05
415	Jim Deshaies	.05
416	Ellis Burks	.05
417	Allan Anderson	.05
418	Alfredo Griffin	.05
419	Wally Whitehurst	.05
420	Sandy Alomar	.05
421	Juan Agosto	.05
422	Sam Horn	.05
423	Jeff Fassero RC	.05
424	Paul McClellan RC	.05
425	Cecil Fielder	.05
426	Tim Raines	.05
427	Eddie Taubensee RC	.05
428	Dennis Boyd	.05
429	Tony LaRussa	.05
430	Steve Sax	.05
431	Tom Gordon	.05
432	Billy Hatcher	.05
433	Cal Eldred	.05
434	Wally Backman	.05
435	Mark Eichhorn	.05
436	Mookie Wilson	.05
437	Scott Servais RC	.10
438	Mike Maddux	.05
439	Chico Walker RC	.05
440	Doug Drabek	.05
441	Rob Deer	.05
442	Dave West	.05
443	Spike Owen	.05
444	Tyrone Hill RC (Draft Pick)	.05
445	Matt Williams	.05
446	Mark Lewis	.05
447	David Segui	.05
448	Tom Pagnozzi	.05
449	Jeff Johnson RC	.05
450	Mark McGwire	.65
451	Tom Henke	.05
452	Wilson Alvarez	.05
453	Gary Redus	.05
454	Darren Holmes	.05
455	Pete O'Brien	.05
456	Pat Combs	.05
457	Hubie Brooks	.05
458	Frank Tanana	.05
459	Tom Kelly	.05
460	Andre Dawson	.25
461	Doug Jones	.05
462	Rich Rodriguez	.05
463	Mike Simms RC	.05
464	Mike Jeffcoat	.05
465	Barry Larkin	.05
466	Stan Belinda	.05
467	Lonnie Smith	.05
468	Greg Harris	.05
469	Jim Eisenreich	.05
470	Pedro Guerrero	.05
471	Jose DeJesus	.05
472	Rich Rowland RC	.05

473	Top Prospects-3rd Baseman (Frank Bolick RC, Craig Paquette RC, Tom Redington RC, Paul Russo RC)	.05
474	Mike Rossiter RC (Draft Pick)	.05
475	Robby Thompson	.05
476	Randy Bush	.05
477	Greg Hibbard	.05
478	Dale Sveum	.05
479	Chito Martinez RC	.05
480	Scott Sanderson	.05
481	Tino Martinez	.05
482	Jimmy Key	.05
483	Terry Shumpert	.05
484	Mike Hartley	.05
485	Chris Sabo	.05
486	Bob Walk	.05
487	John Cerutti	.05
488	Scott Cooper RC	.05
489	Bobby Cox	.05
490	Julio Franco	.05
491	Jeff Brantley	.05
492	Mike Devereaux	.05
493	Jose Offerman	.05
494	Gary Thurman	.05
495	Carney Lansford	.05
496	Joe Grahe	.05
497	Andy Ashby RC	.10
498	Gerald Perry	.05
499	Dave Otto	.05
500	Vince Coleman	.05
501	Rob Mallicoat RC	.05
502	Greg Briley	.05
503	Pascual Perez	.05
504	Aaron Sele RC (Draft Pick)	.25
505	Bobby Thigpen	.05
506	Todd Benzinger	.05
507	Candy Maldonado	.05
508	Bill Gullickson	.05
509	Doug Dascenzo	.05
510	Frank Viola	.05
511	Kenny Rogers	.05
512	Mike Heath	.05
513	Kevin Bass	.05
514	Kim Batiste RC	.05
515	Delino DeShields	.05
516	Ed Sprague RC	.05
517	Jim Gott	.05
518	Jose Melendez RC	.05
519	Hal McRae	.05
520	Jeff Bagwell	.35
521	Joe Hesketh	.05
522	Milt Cuyler	.05
523	Shawn Hillegas	.05
524	Don Slaught	.05
525	Randy Johnson	.35
526	Doug Piatt RC	.05
527	Checklist 4	.05
528	Steve Foster RC	.05
529	Joe Girardi	.05
530	Jim Abbott	.05
531	Larry Walker	.05
532	Mike Huff	.05
533	Mackey Sasser	.05
534	Benji Gil RC (Draft Pick)	.05
535	Dave Stieb	.05
536	Willie Wilson	.05
537	Mark Leiter RC	.05
538	Jose Uribe	.05
539	Thomas Howard	.05
540	Ben McDonald	.05
541	Jose Tolentino RC	.05
542	Keith Mitchell RC	.05
543	Jerome Walton	.05
544	Cliff Brantley RC	.05
545	Andy Van Slyke	.05
546	Paul Sorrento	.05
547	Herm Winningham	.05
548	Mark Guthrie	.05
549	Joe Torre	.05
550	Darryl Strawberry	.05
551	Top Prospects-Shortstops (Manny Alexander, Alex Arias, Wil Cordero, Chipper Jones)	.25
552	Dave Gallagher	.05
553	Edgar Martinez	.05
554	Donald Harris	.05
555	Frank Thomas	.35
556	Storm Davis	.05
557	Dickie Thon	.05
558	Scott Garrelts	.05
559	Steve Olin	.05
560	Rickey Henderson	.35
561	Jose Vizcaino	.05
562	Wade Taylor RC	.05
563	Pat Borders	.05
564	Jimmy Gonzalez RC (Draft Pick)	
565	Lee Smith	.05
566	Bill Sampen	.05
567	Dean Palmer	.05
568	Bryan Harvey	.05
569	Tony Pena	.05
570	Lou Whitaker	.05
571	Randy Tomlin	.05
572	Greg Vaughn	.05
573	Kelly Downs	.05
574	Steve Avery	.05
575	Kirby Puckett	.45
576	Heathcliff Slocumb RC	.05
577	Kevin Seitzer	.05
578	Lee Guetterman	.05
579	Johnny Oates	.05
580	Greg Maddux	.45
581	Stan Javier	.05

582	Vicente Palacios	.05
583	Mel Rojas	.05
584	Wayne Rosenthal RC	.05
585	Lenny Webster RC	.05
586	Rod Nichols	.05
587	Mickey Morandini	.05
588	Russ Swan	.05
589	Mariano Duncan	.05
590	Howard Johnson	.05
591	Top Prospects-Outfielders (Jacob Brumfield RC, Jeromy Burnitz RC, Alan Cockrell RC, D.J. Dozier RC)	.25
592	Denny Neagle RC	.10
593	Steve Decker	.05
594	Brian Barber RC (Draft Pick)	.05
595	Bruce Hurst	.05
596	Kent Mercker	.05
597	Mike Magnante RC	.05
598	Jody Reed	.05
599	Steve Searcy	.05
600	Paul Molitor	.35
601	Dave Smith	.05
602	Mike Fetters	.05
603	Luis Mercedes RC	.05
604	Chris Gwynn	.05
605	Scott Erickson	.05
606	Brook Jacoby	.05
607	Todd Stottlemyre	.05
608	Scott Bradley	.05
609	Mike Hargrove	.05
610	Eric Davis	.05
611	Brian Hunter RC	.05
612	Pat Kelly	.05
613	Pedro Munoz RC	.05
614	Al Osuna	.05
615	Matt Merullo	.05
616	Larry Andersen	.05
617	Junior Ortiz	.05
618	Top Prospects-Outfielders (Cesar Hernandez RC, Steve Hosey RC, Dan Peltier RC, Jeff McNeely RC)	.10
619	Danny Jackson	.05
620	George Brett	.50
621	Dan Gakeler RC	.05
622	Steve Buechele	.05
623	Bob Tewksbury	.05
624	Shawn Estes RC (Draft Pick)	.25
625	Kevin McReynolds	.05
626	Chris Haney RC	.05
627	Mike Sharperson	.05
628	Mark Williamson	.05
629	Wally Joyner	.05
630	Carlton Fisk	.35
631	Armando Reynoso RC	.05
632	Felix Fermin	.05
633	Mitch Williams	.05
634	Manuel Lee	.05
635	Harold Baines	.05
636	Greg Harris	.05
637	Orlando Merced	.05
638	Chris Bosio	.05
639	Wayne Housie RC	.05
640	Xavier Hernandez	.05
641	David Howard RC	.05
642	Tim Crews	.05
643	Rick Cerone	.05
644	Terry Leach	.05
645	Deion Sanders	.10
646	Craig Wilson	.05
647	Marquis Grissom	.05
648	Scott Fletcher	.05
649	Norm Charlton	.05
650	Jesse Barfield	.05
651	Joe Slusarski RC	.05
652	Bobby Rose	.05
653	Dennis Lamp	.05
654	Allen Watson RC (Draft Pick)	.05
655	Brett Butler	.05
656	Top Prospects-Outfielders (Rudy Pemberton RC, Henry Rodriguez RC, Lee Tinsley RC, Gerald Williams RC)	.10
657	Dave Johnson	.05
658	Checklist 5	.05
659	Brian McRae	.05
660	Fred McGriff	.35
661	Bill Landrum	.05
662	Juan Guzman	.05
663	Greg Gagne	.05
664	Ken Hill	.05
665	Dave Haas RC	.05
666	Tom Foley	.05
667	Roberto Hernandez RC	.10
668	Dwayne Henry	.05
669	Jim Fregosi	.05
670	Harold Reynolds	.05
671	Mark Whiten	.05
672	Eric Plunk	.05
673	Todd Hundley	.05
674	Mo Sanford RC	.05
675	Bobby Witt	.05
676	Top Prospects-Pitchers (Pat Mahomes RC, Sam Militello RC, Roger Salkeld RC, Turk Wendell RC)	.15
677	John Marzano	.05
678	Joe Klink	.05
679	Pete Incaviglia	.05
680	Dale Murphy	.15

681	Rene Gonzales	.05
682	Andy Benes	.05
683	Jim Poole RC	.05
684	Trever Miller RC (Draft Pick)	.10
685	Scott Livingstone RC	.05
686	Rich DeLucia	.05
687	Harvey Pulliam RC	.05
688	Tim Belcher	.05
689	Mark Lemke	.05
690	John Franco	.05
691	Walt Weiss	.05
692	Scott Ruskin	.05
693	Jeff King	.05
694	Mike Gardiner RC	.05
695	Gary Sheffield	.30
696	Joe Boever	.05
697	Mike Felder	.05
698	John Habyan	.05
699	Cito Gaston	.05
700	Ruben Sierra	.05
701	Scott Radinsky	.05
702	Lee Stevens	.05
703	Mark Wohlers RC	.05
704	Curt Young	.05
705	Dwight Evans	.05
706	Rob Murphy	.05
707	Gregg Jefferies	.05
708	Tom Bolton	.05
709	Chris James	.05
710	Kevin Maas	.05
711	Ricky Bones RC	.05
712	Curt Wilkerson	.05
713	Roger McDowell	.05
714	Calvin Reese RC (Draft Pick)	.10
715	Craig Biggio	.05
716	Kirk Dressendorfer RC	.05
717	Ken Dayley	.05
718	B.J. Surhoff	.05
719	Terry Mulholland	.05
720	Kirk Gibson	.05
721	Mike Pagliarulo	.05
722	Walt Terrell	.05
723	Jose Oquendo	.05
724	Kevin Morton RC	.05
725	Dwight Gooden	.05
726	Kirt Manwaring	.05
727	Chuck McElroy	.05
728	Dave Burba RC	.05
729	Art Howe	.05
730	Ramon Martinez	.05
731	Donnie Hill	.05
732	Nelson Santovenia	.05
733	Bob Melvin	.05
734	Scott Hatteberg RC (Draft Pick)	.10
735	Greg Swindell	.05
736	Lance Johnson	.05
737	Kevin Reimer	.05
738	Dennis Eckersley	.35
739	Rob Ducey	.05
740	Ken Caminiti	.05
741	Mark Gubicza	.05
742	Billy Spiers	.05
743	Darren Lewis	.05
744	Chris Hammond	.05
745	Dave Magadan	.05
746	Bernard Gilkey	.05
747	Willie Banks RC	.05
748	Matt Nokes	.05
749	Jerald Clark	.05
750	Travis Fryman	.05
751	Steve Wilson	.05
752	Billy Ripken	.05
753	Paul Assenmacher	.05
754	Charlie Hayes	.05
755	Alex Fernandez	.05
756	Gary Pettis	.05
757	Rob Dibble	.05
758	Tim Naehring	.05
759	Jeff Torborg	.05
760	Ozzie Smith	.45
761	Mike Fitzgerald	.05
762	John Burkett	.05
763	Kyle Abbott	.05
764	Tyler Green RC (Draft Pick)	.05
765	Pete Harnisch	.05
766	Mark Davis	.05
767	Kal Daniels	.05
768	Jim Thome	.35
769	Jack Howell	.05
770	Sid Bream	.05
771	Arthur Rhodes RC	.10
772	Garry Templeton	.05
773	Hal Morris	.05
774	Bud Black	.05
775	Ivan Calderon	.05
776	Doug Henry RC	.05
777	John Olerud	.05
778	Tim Leary	.05
779	Jay Bell	.05
780	Eddie Murray	.35
781	Paul Abbott	.05
782	Phil Plantier	.35
783	Joe Magrane	.05
784	Ken Patterson	.05
785	Albert Belle	.35
786	Royce Clayton	.05
787	Checklist 6	.05
788	Mike Stanton	.05
789	Bobby Valentine	.05
790	Joe Carter	.05
791	Danny Cox	.05
792	Dave Winfield	.35

Gold Promo Sheet

Similar in form and function to the nine-card promo sheet issued for the regular 1992 Topps set, this 8" x 11" sheet previewed the Topps Gold cards for dealers. Fronts are identical to the regular-issue '92 Topps cards. Backs differ in that actual 1991 stats are not printed, and there is a diamond over the stat box which reads, "1992 Pre-Production Sample." Card numbers on the gold preview cards correspond to the regular Topps cards. Single cards in the standard 2-1/2" x 3-1/2" size are frequently offered cut from these sheets.

		NM/M
	Complete Set (Sheet):	8.00
	Complete Set (9):	8.00
	Common Player:	1.00
1	Nolan Ryan	4.00
15	Dennis Martinez	1.00
40	Cal Ripken, Jr.	4.00
261	Tom Lasorda	1.00
370	Shawon Dunston	1.00
512	Mike Heath	1.00
655	Brett Butler	1.00
757	Rob Dibble	1.00

Gold

Topps Gold cards share a checklist and format with the regular-issue 1992 Topps baseball issue except the color bars with the player's name and team printed beneath the photo have been replaced with gold foil. On back the light blue Topps logo printed beneath the stats has been replaced with a gold "ToppsGold" logo. Topps Gold cards were random inserts in all forms of packs. Additionally, factory sets of Gold cards were sold which included an autographed card of Yankees #1 draft pick Brien Taylor, and which had the checklist cards replaced with player cards. Several errors connected with the gold name/team strips are noted; no corrected versions were issued.

		NM/M
	Unopened Fact. Set (793):	75.00
	Complete Set (792):	35.00
	Common Player:	.20
86	Steve Finley (Incorrect name, Mark Davidson, on gold strip.)	.20
131	Terry Mathews	.20
264	Rod Beck	1.00
288	Andujar Cedeno (Incorrect team, Yankees, listed on gold strip.)	.60
366	Tony Perezchica	.20
465	Barry Larkin (Incorrect team, Astros, listed on gold strip.)	2.50
527	Terry McDaniel	.20
532	Mike Huff (Incorrect team, Red Sox, listed on gold strip.)	.20
658	John Ramos	.20
787	Brian Williams	.20
793	Brien Taylor (Autographed edition of 12,000; factory sets only.)	7.50

Gold Winners

A second gold-foil enhanced parallel version of the regular 1992 Topps issue was the Gold Winner cards awarded as prizes in a scratch-off contest found in each pack. Winner cards are identical to the Topps Gold cards except for the addition of a gold-foil "Winner" and star added above the team name. Due to a flaw in the design of the scratch-off game cards, it was easy to win every time and the Winner cards had to be produced in quantities far greater than originally planned, making them rather common. Six checklist cards from the regular issue were replaced with player cards in the Winners edition. Cards were sent to winners in 10-card cello packs.

		NM/M
	Complete Set (792):	30.00
	Common Player:	.10
	Cello Pack (10):	.75
131	Terry Mathews	.15
264	Rod Beck	.25
366	Tony Perezchica	.15
465a	Barry Larkin (Team name incorrect, Astros.)	2.00
465b	Barry Larkin (Team name correct, Reds.)	.75
527	Terry McDaniel	.15
658	John Ramos	.15
787	Brian Williams	.15

Traded

Members of the United States baseball team are featured in this 132-card boxed set released by Topps. The cards are styled after the regular 1992 Topps cards and are numbered alphabetically. Several United States baseball players featured in this set were also featured in the 1991 Topps Traded set.

		NM/M
	Complete Set (132):	50.00
	Common Player:	.05
	Golds:	2-4X
1	Willie Adams RC (USA)	.05
2	Jeff Alkire (USA)	.05
3	Felipe Alou	.05
4	Moises Alou	.10
5	Ruben Amaro	.05
6	Jack Armstrong	.05
7	Scott Bankhead	.05
8	Tim Belcher	.05
9	George Bell	.05
10	Freddie Benavides RC	.05
11	Todd Benzinger	.05
12	Joe Boever	.05
13	Ricky Bones	.05
14	Bobby Bonilla	.05
15	Hubie Brooks	.05
16	Jerry Browne	.05
17	Jim Bullinger	.05
18	Dave Burba	.05
19	Kevin Campbell RC	.05
20	Tom Candiotti	.05
21	Mark Carreon	.05
22	Gary Carter	.75
23	Archi Cianfrocco	.05
24	Phil Clark	.05
25	Chad Curtis RC	.50
26	Eric Davis	.05
27	Tim Davis (USA)	.05
28	Gary DiSarcina	.05
29	Darren Dreifort (USA)	.05
30	Mariano Duncan	.05
31	Mike Fitzgerald	.05
32	John Flaherty RC	.05
33	Darrin Fletcher	.05
34	Scott Fletcher	.05
35	Ron Fraser (USA)	.05
36	Andres Galarraga	.05
37	Dave Gallagher	.05
38	Mike Gallego	.05
39	Nomar Garciaparra RC (USA)	30.00
40	Jason Giambi (USA)	1.00
41	Danny Gladden	.05
42	Rene Gonzales	.05
43	Jeff Granger (USA)	.05
44	Rick Greene (USA)	.05
45	Jeffrey Hammonds (USA)	.05
46	Charlie Hayes	.05
47	Von Hayes	.05
48	Rick Helling (USA)	.05
49	Butch Henry RC	.05
50	Carlos Hernandez RC	.05
51	Ken Hill	.05
52	Butch Hobson	.05
53	Vince Horsman RC	.05
54	Pete Incaviglia	.05
55	Gregg Jefferies	.05
56	Charles Johnson (USA)	.05
57	Doug Jones	.05
58	Brian Jordan RC	2.00
59	Wally Joyner	.05
60	Daron Kirkreit RC (USA)	.20
61	Bill Krueger	.05
62	Gene Lamont	.05
63	Jim Lefebvre	.05
64	Danny Leon RC	.05
65	Pat Listach	.05
66	Kenny Lofton	.05
67	Dave Martinez	.05
68	Derrick May	.05
69	Kirk McCaskill	.05
70	Chad McConnell RC (USA)	.05
71	Kevin McReynolds	.05
72	Rusty Meacham RC	.05
73	Keith Miller	.05
74	Kevin Mitchell	.05
75	Jason Moler RC (USA)	.05
76	Mike Morgan	.05
77	Jack Morris	.05
78	Calvin Murray RC (USA)	.05
79	Eddie Murray	.75
80	Randy Myers	.05
81	Denny Neagle RC	.05
82	Phil Nevin (USA)	.10
83	Dave Nilsson	.05
84	Junior Ortiz	.05
85	Donovan Osborne	.05
86	Bill Pecota	.05
87	Melido Perez	.05
88	Mike Perez RC	.05
89	Hipolito Pena RC	.05
90	Willie Randolph	.05
91	Darren Reed RC	.05
92	Bip Roberts	.05
93	Chris Roberts (USA)	.05
94	Steve Rodriguez (USA)	.05
95	Bruce Ruffin	.05
96	Scott Ruskin	.05
97	Bret Saberhagen	.05
98	Rey Sanchez RC	.05
99	Steve Sax	.05
100	Curt Schilling	.25
101	Dick Schofield	.05
102	Gary Scott	.05
103	Kevin Seitzer	.05
104	Frank Seminara RC	.05
105	Gary Sheffield	.35
106	John Smiley	.05
107	Cory Snyder	.05
108	Paul Sorrento	.05
109	Sammy Sosa	1.50
110	Matt Stairs RC	.25
111	Andy Stankiewicz	.05
112	Kurt Stillwell	.05
113	Rick Sutcliffe	.05
114	Bill Swift	.05
115	Jeff Tackett RC	.05
116	Danny Tartabull	.05
117	Eddie Taubensee RC	.05
118	Dickie Thon	.05
119	Michael Tucker RC (USA)	.25
120	Scooter Tucker RC	.05
121	Marc Valdes (USA)	.05
122	Julio Valera RC	.05
123	Jason Varitek RC (USA)	15.00
124	Ron Villone RC (USA)	.05
125	Frank Viola	.05
126	B.J. Wallace RC (USA)	.05
127	Dan Walters RC	.05
128	Craig Wilson (USA)	.05
129	Chris Wimmer (USA)	.05
130	Dave Winfield	.75
131	Herm Winningham	.05
132	Checklist	.05

Traded Gold

A reported 6,000 sets of 1992 Topps Traded were produced in a gold edition, with gold-foil strips on front bearing the player and team names. The cards are in all other respects identical to the regular boxed Traded issue.

	NM/M
Complete Unopened Set (132):	75.00
Complete Set (132):	65.00
Common Player:	.25
Stars/Rookies:	4X

Golden Spikes Award

At a Nov. 17, 1992 awards ceremony, Phil Nevin was presented with the U.S. Baseball Federation's Golden Spikes Award, emblematic of his selection as the outstanding amateur player in the nation. Topps created and handed out at the affair a reported 600 of these cards.

	NM/M
Phil Nevin	45.00

Kids

In a market which had increasingly become the province of adult collectors, Topps in 1992 offered an issue unashamedly aimed at the youngster. Called "Topps Kids," the 132-card set features bright colors, garish graphics and the game's top stars. Sold at 35 cents per pack (with bubble gum), the issue was even priced for the young collector. Unfortunately, the concept was a flop and was not repeated in subsequent years. Card fronts feature player photos, sometimes only the player's head on a cartoon body, against a background of wild designs or cartoon ballpark action. Player names at bottom were rendered in superhero comic-book style. Backs feature a few 1991 and career stats, and/or a cartoon or two about the player or baseball trivia.

	NM/M
Complete Set (132):	7.50
Common Player:	.05
Wax Pack (7):	.40
Wax Box (36):	6.00
1 Ryne Sandberg	.45
2 Andre Dawson	.25
3 George Bell	.05
4 Mark Grace	.05
5 Shawon Dunston	.05
6 Tim Wallach	.05
7 Ivan Calderon	.05
8 Marquis Grissom	.05
9 Delino DeShields	.05
10 Denny Martinez	.05
11 Dwight Gooden	.05
12 Howard Johnson	.05
13 John Franco	.05
14 Gregg Jefferies	.05
15 Kevin McReynolds	.05
16 David Cone	.05
17 Len Dykstra	.05
18 John Kruk	.05
19 Von Hayes	.05
20 Mitch Williams	.05
21 Barry Bonds	.75
22 Bobby Bonilla	.05
23 Andy Van Slyke	.05
24 Doug Drabek	.05
25 Ozzie Smith	.45
26 Pedro Guerrero	.05
27 Todd Zelle	.05
28 Lee Smith	.05
29 Felix Jose	.05
30 Jose DeLeon	.05
31 David Justice	.05
32 Ron Gant	.05
33 Terry Pendleton	.05
34 Tom Glavine	.25
35 Otis Nixon	.05
36 Steve Avery	.05
37 Barry Larkin	.05
38 Eric Davis	.05
39 Chris Sabo	.05
40 Rob Dibble	.05
41 Paul O'Neill	.05
42 Jose Rijo	.05
43 Craig Biggio	.05
44 Jeff Bagwell	.35
45 Ken Caminiti	.05
46 Steve Finley	.05
47 Darryl Strawberry	.05
48 Ramon Martinez	.05
49 Brett Butler	.05
50 Eddie Murray	.35
51 Kal Daniels	.05
52 Orel Hershiser	.05
53 Tony Gwynn	.45
54 Benny Santiago	.05
55 Fred McGriff	.05
56 Bip Roberts	.05
57 Tony Fernandez	.05
58 Will Clark	.05
59 Kevin Mitchell	.05
60 Matt Williams	.05
61 Willie McGee	.05
62 Dave Righetti	.05
63 Cal Ripken, Jr.	.75
64 Ben McDonald	.05
65 Glenn Davis	.05
66 Gregg Olson	.05
67 Roger Clemens	.50
68 Wade Boggs	.45
69 Mike Greenwell	.05
70 Ellis Burks	.05
71 Sandy Alomar	.05
72 Greg Swindell	.05
73 Albert Belle	.05
74 Mark Whiten	.05
75 Alan Trammell	.05
76 Cecil Fielder	.05
77 Lou Whitaker	.05
78 Travis Fryman	.05
79 Tony Phillips	.05
80 Robin Yount	.35
81 Paul Molitor	.35
82 B.J. Surhoff	.05
83 Greg Vaughn	.05
84 Don Mattingly	.50
85 Steve Sax	.05
86 Kevin Maas	.05
87 Mel Hall	.05
88 Roberto Kelly	.05
89 Joe Carter	.05
90 Roberto Alomar	.15
91 Dave Stieb	.05
92 Kelly Gruber	.05
93 Tom Henke	.05
94 Chuck Finley	.05
95 Wally Joyner	.05
96 Dave Winfield	.35
97 Jim Abbott	.05
98 Mark Langston	.05
99 Frank Thomas	.35
100 Ozzie Guillen	.05
101 Bobby Thigpen	.05
102 Robin Ventura	.05
103 Bo Jackson	.10
104 Tim Raines	.05
105 George Brett	.50
106 Danny Tartabull	.05
107 Bret Saberhagen	.05
108 Brian McRae	.05
109 Kirby Puckett	.45
110 Scott Erickson	.05
111 Kent Hrbek	.05
112 Chuck Knoblauch	.05
113 Chili Davis	.05
114 Rick Aguilera	.05
115 Jose Canseco	.25
116 Dave Henderson	.05
117 Dave Stewart	.05
118 Rickey Henderson	.35
119 Dennis Eckersley	.30
120 Harold Baines	.05
121 Mark McGwire	.60
122 Ken Griffey Jr.	.60
123 Harold Reynolds	.05
124 Erik Hanson	.05
125 Edgar Martinez	.05
126 Randy Johnson	.35
127 Nolan Ryan	.75
128 Ruben Sierra	.05
129 Julio Franco	.05
130 Rafael Palmeiro	.30
131 Juan Gonzalez	.20
132 Checklist	.05

Micro

Topps returned for a second year with a micro parallel of its regular-issue baseball set, in a format about 40% the size of the standard cards. Sold only in complete-set form, the 1" x 1-3/8" cards also included a dozen gold-enhanced star cards. Stars and rookies among the micros are valued at a percentage of the corresponding regular card.

	NM/M
Complete Set (804):	9.00
Common Player:	.05
Stars/Rookies: 50-100 Percent	
1 Nolan Ryan (Record Breaker)	2.00
2 Rickey Henderson (Record Breaker)	.65
10 Wade Boggs	.75
50 Ken Griffey Jr.	1.00
100 Jose Canseco	.60
270 Tony Gwynn	.75
300 Don Mattingly	.90
380 Barry Bonds	2.00
397 Cecil Fielder/AS	.50
403 Ruben Sierra/AS	.50
460 Andre Dawson	.55
725 Dwight Gooden	.50

Triple Header Photo Balls

Picture a slightly oversize ping pong ball painted like a baseball with the heads and facsimile autographs of three different players on it and you've got the idea behind the Triple Headers test issue. Very limited in distribution, the team balls were sold in a small box with a package of candy.

	NM/M
Complete Set (26):	100.00
Common Ball:	3.50
(1) California Angels (Chuck Finley, Dave Winfield, Wally Joyner)	4.00
(2) Houston Astros (Jeff Bagwell, Craig Biggio, Ken Caminiti)	4.50
(3) Oakland Athletics (Dave Henderson, Jose Canseco, Rickey Henderson)	4.50
(4) Toronto Blue Jays (Roberto Alomar, Kelly Gruber, Joe Carter)	4.00
(5) Atlanta Braves (Ron Gant, Tom Glavine, Dave Justice)	4.00
(6) Milwaukee Brewers (Greg Vaughn, Paul Molitor, Robin Yount)	4.50
(7) St. Louis Cardinals (Todd Zeile, Pedro Guerrero, Ozzie Smith)	4.50
(8) Chicago Cubs (Ryne Sandberg, George Bell, Mark Grace)	4.50
(9) Los Angeles Dodgers (Ramon Martinez, Eddie Murray, Darryl Strawberry)	4.50
(10) Montreal Expos (Delino DeShields, Dennis Martinez, Ivan Calderon)	3.50
(11) San Francisco Giants (Will Clark, Kevin Mitchell, Matt Williams)	3.50
(12) Cleveland Indians (Sandy Alomar Jr., Alex Cole, Mark Lewis)	3.50
(13) Seattle Mariners (Ken Griffey Jr., Harold Reynolds, Ken Griffey Sr.)	10.00
(14) New York Mets (Vince Coleman, Dwight Gooden, Howard Johnson)	3.50
(15) Baltimore Orioles (Ben McDonald, Cal Ripken Jr., Gregg Olson)	12.50
(16) San Diego Padres (Benito Santiago, Fred McGriff, Tony Gwynn)	5.00
(17) Philadelphia Phillies (Len Dykstra, John Kruk, Dale Murphy)	3.50
(18) Pittsburgh Pirates (Andy Van Slyke, Barry Bonds, Bobby Bonilla)	12.50
(19) Cincinnati Reds (Chris Sabo, Eric Davis, Barry Larkin)	3.50
(20) Boston Red Sox (Wade Boggs, Mike Greenwell, Roger Clemens)	6.00
(21) Kansas City Royals (George Brett, Danny Tartabull, Bret Saberhagen)	6.00
(22) Texas Rangers (Julio Franco, Nolan Ryan, Juan Gonzalez)	12.50
(23) Minnesota Twins (Scott Erickson, Kirby Puckett, Kent Hrbek)	5.00
(24) Detroit Tigers (Cecil Fielder, Tony Phillips, Alan Trammell)	3.50
(25) Chicago White Sox (Carlton Fisk, Robin Ventura, Frank Thomas)	5.00
(26) New York Yankees (Don Mattingly, Steve Sax, Willie Randolph)	6.00

1991 Major League Debut

This 194-card set highlights the debut date of 1991 Major League rookies. Two checklist cards are also included in this boxed set. The card fronts resemble the 1992 Topps cards. A debut banner appears in the lower-right corner of the card front. The set is packaged in an attractive collector box and the cards are numbered alphabetically. This set was available only through hobby dealers.

	NM/M
Complete Set (194):	12.50
Common Player:	.05
1 Kyle Abbott	.05
2 Dana Allison	.05
3 Rich Amaral	.05
4 Ruben Amaro	.05
5 Andy Ashby	.05
6 Jim Austin	.05
7 Jeff Bagwell	4.00
8 Jeff Banister	.05
9 Willie Banks	.05
10 Bret Barberie	.05
11 Kim Batiste	.05
12 Chris Beasley	.05
13 Rod Beck	.05
14 Derek Bell	.05
15 Esteban Beltre	.05
16 Freddie Benavides	.05
17 Rickey Bones	.05
18 Denis Boucher	.05
19 Ryan Bowen	.05
20 Cliff Brantley	.05
21 John Briscoe	.05
22 Scott Brosius	.05
23 Terry Bross	.05
24 Jarvis Brown	.05
25 Scott Bullett	.05
26 Kevin Campbell	.05
27 Amalio Carreno	.05
28 Matias Carrillo	.05
29 Jeff Carter	.05
30 Vinny Castilla	.05
31 Braulio Castillo	.05
32 Frank Castillo	.05
33 Darrin Chapin	.05
34 Mike Christopher	.05
35 Mark Clark	.05
36 Royce Clayton	.05
37 Stu Cole	.05
38 Gary Cooper	.05
39 Archie Corbin	.05
40 Rheal Cormier	.05
41 Chris Cron	.05
42 Mike Dalton	.05
43 Mark Davis	.05
44 Francisco de la Rosa	.05
45 Chris Donnels	.05
46 Brian Drahman	.05
47 Tom Drees	.05
48 Kirk Dressendorfer	.05
49 Bruce Egloff	.05
50 Cal Eldred	.05
51 Jose Escobar	.05
52 Tony Eusebio	.05
53 Hector Fajardo	.05
54 Monty Farriss	.05
55 Jeff Fassero	.05
56 Dave Fleming	.05
57 Kevin Flora	.05
58 Steve Foster	.05
59 Dan Gakeler	.05
60 Ramon Garcia	.05
61 Chris Gardner	.05
62 Jeff Gardner	.05
63 Chris George	.05
64 Ray Giannelli	.05
65 Tom Goodwin	.05
66 Mark Grater	.05
67 Johnny Guzman	.05
68 Juan Guzman	.05
69 Dave Haas	.05
70 Chris Haney	.05
71 Shawn Hare	.05
72 Donald Harris	.05
73 Doug Henry	.05
74 Pat Hentgen	.05
75 Gil Heredia	.05
76 Jeremy Hernandez	.05
77 Jose Hernandez	.05
78 Roberto Hernandez	.05
79 Bryan Hickerson	.05
80 Milt Hill	.05
81 Vince Horsman	.05
82 Wayne Housie	.05
83 Chris Howard	.05
84 David Howard	.05
85 Mike Humphreys	.05
86 Brian Hunter	.05
87 Jim Hunter	.05
88 Mike Ignasiak	.05
89 Reggie Jefferson	.05
90 Jeff Johnson	.05
91 Joel Johnson	.05
92 Calvin Jones	.05
93 Chris Jones	.05
94 Stacy Jones	.05
95 Jeff Juden	.05
96 Scott Kamieniecki	.05
97 Eric Karros	.05
98 Pat Kelly	.05
99 John Kiely	.05
100 Darryl Kile	.05
101 Wayne Kirby	.05
102 Garland Kiser	.05
103 Chuck Knoblauch	.05
104 Randy Knorr	.05
105 Tom Kramer	.05
106 Ced Landrum	.05
107 Patrick Lennon	.05
108 Jim Lewis	.05
109 Mark Lewis	.05
110 Doug Lindsey	.05
111 Scott Livingstone	.05
112 Kenny Lofton	.10
113 Ever Magallanes	.05
114 Mike Magnante	.05
115 Barry Manuel	.05
116 Josias Manzanillo	.05
117 Chito Martinez	.05
118 Terry Mathews	.05
119 Rob Mauer	.05
120 Tim Mauser	.05
121 Terry McDaniel	.05
122 Rusty Meacham	.05
123 Luis Mercedes	.05
124 Paul Miller	.05
125 Keith Mitchell	.05
126 Bobby Moore	.05
127 Kevin Morton	.05
128 Andy Mota	.05
129 Jose Mota	.05
130 Mike Mussina	2.00
131 Jeff Mutis	.05
132 Denny Neagle	.05
133 Warren Newson	.05
134 Jim Olander	.05
135 Erik Pappas	.05
136 Jorge Pedre	.05
137 Yorkis Perez	.05
138 Mark Petkovsek	.05
139 Doug Piatt	.05
140 Jeff Plympton	.05
141 Harvey Pulliam	.05
142 John Ramos	.05
143 Mike Remlinger	.05
144 Laddie Renfroe	.05
145 Armando Reynoso	.05
146 Arthur Rhodes	.05
147 Pat Rice	.05
148 Nikco Riesgo	.05
149 Carlos Rodriguez	.05
150 Ivan Rodriguez	3.00
151 Wayne Rosenthal	.05
152 Rico Rossy	.05
153 Stan Royer	.05
154 Rey Sanchez	.05
155 Reggie Sanders	.05
156 Mo Sanford	.05
157 Bob Scanlan	.05
158 Pete Schourek	.05
159 Gary Scott	.05
160 Tim Scott	.05
161 Tony Scruggs	.05
162 Scott Servais	.05
163 Doug Simons	.05
164 Heathcliff Slocumb	.05
165 Joe Slusarski	.05
166 Tim Spehr	.05
167 Ed Sprague	.05
168 Jeff Tackett	.05
169 Eddie Taubensee	.05
170 Wade Taylor	.05
171 Jim Thome	2.50
172 Mike Timlin	.05
173 Jose Tolentino	.05
174 John Vander Wal	.05
175 Todd Van Poppel	.05
176 Mo Vaughn	.50
177 Dave Wainhouse	.05
178 Don Wakamatsu	.05
179 Bruce Walton	.05
180 Kevin Ward	.05
181 Dave Weathers	.05
182 Eric Wedge	.05
183 John Wehner	.05
184 Rick Wilkins	.05
185 Bernie Williams	.50
186 Brian Williams	.05
187 Ron Witmeyer	.05
188 Mark Wohlers	.05
189 Ted Wood	.05
190 Anthony Young	.05
191 Eddie Zosky	.05
192 Bob Zupcic	.05
193 Checklist	.05
194 Checklist	.05

Pre-Production

Specially marked 1992 Topps factory sets included this nine-card preview of the coming year's issue. The preview cards are identical to the regular-issue versions except the backs have a gray oval over the stats box with the notation, "1993 Pre-Production Sample."

	NM/M
Complete Set (9):	7.50
Common Player:	.35
1 Robin Yount	.75
2 Barry Bonds	3.00
11 Eric Karros	.50
32 Don Mattingly	1.00
100 Mark McGwire	2.00
150 Frank Thomas	.75
179 Ken Griffey Jr.	1.50
230 Carlton Fisk	.75
250 Chuck Knoblauch	.50

Pre-Production Sheet

Originally produced as an 8" x 11" nine-card sheet, these pre-production sample cards are rarely found as singles. Cards are in the same basic format as the regular-issue 1993 Topps cards. Backs differ in that all cards are numbered "000" with all zeroes for 1992 stats and bogus career highlights. A large gray circle over the stats box reads "1993 Pre-Production Sample For General Look Only."

	NM/M
Uncut Sheet:	6.00
Complete Set (9):	6.00
Common Player:	.50
(1) Roberto Alomar	.60
(2) Bobby Bonilla	.50
(3) Gary Carter	1.00
(4) Andre Dawson	.75
(5) Dave Fleming	.50
(6) Ken Griffey Jr.	3.00
(7) Pete Incaviglia	.50
(8) Spike Owen	.50
(9) Larry Walker	.50

1993 Topps

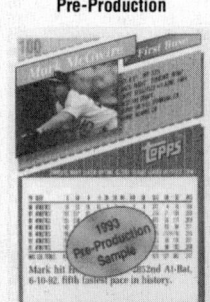

Topps issued in a two-series format in 1993. Series I includes cards #1-396; Series II comprises #397-825. The card fronts feature full-color photos enclosed by a white border. The player's name and team appear at the bottom. The backs feature an additional player photo and biographical information at the top. The bottom box includes statistics and player information. The cards are numbered in red in a yellow flag on the back. The factory set includes the regular 825 cards plus 10 gold parallels, three Black Gold inserts and nine 1994 preview cards.

	NM/M
Unopened Fact. Set (847):	40.00
Complete Set (825):	30.00
Common Player:	.05
Golds:	3X
Series 1 Wax Pack (15):	1.00
Series 1 Wax Box (36):	25.00
Series 2 Wax Pack (15):	.75
Series 2 Wax Box (36):	15.00
Series 1 Jumbo Pack (41):	2.00
Series 1 Jumbo Box (24):	30.00
Series 2 Jumbo Pack (41):	1.50
Series 2 Jumbo Box (24):	20.00
1 Robin Yount	.50
2 Barry Bonds	1.00
3 Ryne Sandberg	.60
4 Roger Clemens	.65
5 Tony Gwynn	.60
6 Jeff Tackett RC	.05
7 Pete Incaviglia	.05
8 Mark Wohlers	.05
9 Kent Hrbek	.05
10 Will Clark	.05
11 Eric Karros	.05
12 Lee Smith	.05
13 Esteban Beltre	.05
14 Greg Briley	.05
15 Marquis Grissom	.05

No.	Player	Price
16	Dan Plesac	.05
17	Dave Hollins	.05
18	Terry Steinbach	.05
19	Ed Nunez	.05
20	Tim Salmon	.05
21	Luis Salazar	.05
22	Jim Eisenreich	.05
23	Todd Stottlemyre	.05
24	Tim Naehring	.05
25	John Franco	.05
26	Skeeter Barnes	.05
27	Carlos Garcia RC	.05
28	Joe Orsulak	.05
29	Dwayne Henry	.05
30	Fred McGriff	.05
31	Derek Lilliquist	.05
32	Don Mattingly	.65
33	B.J. Wallace (1992 Draft Pick)	.05
34	Juan Gonzalez	.25
35	John Smoltz	.05
36	Scott Servais	.05
37	Lenny Webster	.05
38	Chris James	.05
39	Roger McDowell	.05
40	Ozzie Smith	.60
41	Alex Fernandez	.05
42	Spike Owen	.05
43	Ruben Amaro	.05
44	Kevin Seitzer	.05
45	Dave Fleming	.05
46	Eric Fox RC	.05
47	Bob Scanlan	.05
48	Bert Blyleven	.05
49	Brian McRae	.05
50	Roberto Alomar	.20
51	Mo Vaughn	.05
52	Bobby Bonilla	.05
53	Frank Tanana	.05
54	Mike LaValliere	.05
55	Mark McLemore	.05
56	Chad Mottola RC (1992 Draft Pick)	.10
57	Norm Charlton	.05
58	Jose Melendez	.05
59	Carlos Martinez	.05
60	Roberto Kelly	.05
61	Gene Larkin	.05
62	Rafael Belliard	.05
63	Al Osuna	.05
64	Scott Chiamparino	.05
65	Brett Butler	.05
66	John Burkett	.05
67	Felix Jose	.05
68	Omar Vizquel	.05
69	John Vander Wal	.05
70	Roberto Hernandez	.05
71	Ricky Bones	.05
72	Jeff Grotewold RC	.05
73	Mike Moore	.05
74	Steve Buechele	.05
75	Juan Guzman	.05
76	Kevin Appier	.05
77	Junior Felix	.05
78	Greg Harris	.05
79	Dick Schofield	.05
80	Cecil Fielder	.05
81	Lloyd McClendon	.05
82	David Segui	.05
83	Reggie Sanders	.05
84	Kurt Stillwell	.05
85	Sandy Alomar	.05
86	John Habyan	.05
87	Kevin Reimer	.05
88	Mike Stanton	.05
89	Eric Anthony	.05
90	Scott Erickson	.05
91	Craig Colbert	.05
92	Tom Pagnozzi	.05
93	Pedro Astacio RC	.10
94	Lance Johnson	.05
95	Larry Walker	.05
96	Russ Swan	.05
97	Scott Fletcher	.05
98	Derek Jeter RC (1992 Draft Pick)	10.00
99	Mike Williams RC	.05
100	Mark McGwire	.85
101	Jim Bullinger RC	.05
102	Brian Hunter	.05
103	Jody Reed	.05
104	Mike Butcher RC	.05
105	Gregg Jefferies	.05
106	Howard Johnson	.05
107	John Kiely RC	.05
108	Jose Lind	.05
109	Sam Horn	.05
110	Barry Larkin	.05
111	Bruce Hurst	.05
112	Brian Barnes	.05
113	Thomas Howard	.05
114	Mel Hall	.05
115	Robby Thompson	.05
116	Mark Lemke	.05
117	Eddie Taubensee	.05
118	David Hulse	.05
119	Pedro Munoz	.05
120	Ramon Martinez	.05
121	Todd Worrell	.05
122	Joey Cora	.05
123	Moises Alou	.05
124	Franklin Stubbs	.05
125	Pete O'Brien	.05
126	Bob Ayrault RC	.05
127	Carney Lansford	.05
128	Kal Daniels	.05
129	Joe Grahe	.05
130	Jeff Montgomery	.05
131	Dave Winfield	.50
132	Preston Wilson RC (1992 Draft Pick)	.75
133	Steve Wilson	.05
134	Lee Guetterman	.05
135	Mickey Tettleton	.05
136	Jeff King	.05
137	Alan Mills	.05
138	Joe Oliver	.05
139	Gary Gaetti	.05
140	Gary Sheffield	.30
141	Dennis Cook	.05
142	Charlie Hayes	.05
143	Jeff Huson	.05
144	Kent Mercker	.05
145	Eric Young RC	.10
146	Scott Leius	.05
147	Bryan Hickerson	.05
148	Steve Finley	.05
149	Rheal Cormier	.05
150	Frank Thomas	.50
151	Archi Cianfrocco RC	.05
152	Rich DeLucia	.05
153	Greg Vaughn	.05
154	Wes Chamberlain	.05
155	Dennis Eckersley	.40
156	Sammy Sosa	.60
157	Gary DiSarcina	.05
158	Kevin Koslofski RC	.05
159	Doug Linton RC	.05
160	Lou Whitaker	.05
161	Chad McDonnell (1992 Draft Pick)	.05
162	Joe Hesketh	.05
163	Tim Wakefield RC	.10
164	Leo Gomez	.05
165	Jose Rijo	.05
166	Tim Scott RC	.05
167	Steve Olin	.05
168	Kevin Maas	.05
169	Kenny Rogers	.05
170	Dave Justice	.05
171	Doug Jones	.05
172	Jeff Reboulet RC	.05
173	Andres Galarraga	.05
174	Randy Velarde	.05
175	Kirk McCaskill	.05
176	Darren Lewis	.05
177	Lenny Harris	.05
178	Jeff Fassero	.05
179	Ken Griffey Jr.	.75
180	Darren Daulton	.05
181	John Jaha	.05
182	Ron Darling	.05
183	Greg Maddux	.60
184	Damion Easley RC	.10
185	Jack Morris	.05
186	Mike Magnante	.05
187	John Dopson	.05
188	Sid Fernandez	.05
189	Tony Phillips	.05
190	Doug Drabek	.05
191	Sean Lowe RC (1992 Draft Pick)	.05
192	Bob Milacki	.05
193	Steve Foster RC	.05
194	Jerald Clark	.05
195	Pete Harnisch	.05
196	Pat Kelly	.05
197	Jeff Frye	.05
198	Alejandro Pena	.05
199	Junior Ortiz	.05
200	Kirby Puckett	.60
201	Jose Uribe	.05
202	Mike Scioscia	.05
203	Bernard Gilkey	.05
204	Dan Pasqua	.05
205	Gary Carter	.50
206	Henry Cotto	.05
207	Paul Molitor	.50
208	Mike Hartley	.05
209	Jeff Parrett	.05
210	Mark Langston	.05
211	Doug Dascenzo	.05
212	Rick Reed	.05
213	Candy Maldonado	.05
214	Danny Darwin	.05
215	Pat Howell RC	.05
216	Mark Leiter	.05
217	Kevin Mitchell	.05
218	Ben McDonald	.05
219	Bip Roberts	.05
220	Benny Santiago	.05
221	Carlos Baerga	.05
222	Bernie Williams	.05
223	Roger Pavlik RC	.05
224	Sid Bream	.05
225	Matt Williams	.05
226	Willie Banks	.05
227	Jeff Bagwell	.50
228	Tom Goodwin	.05
229	Mike Perez	.05
230	Carlton Fisk	.50
231	John Wetteland	.05
232	Tino Martinez	.05
233	Rick Greene RC (1992 Draft Pick)	.05
234	Tim McIntosh	.05
235	Mitch Williams	.05
236	Kevin Campbell RC	.05
237	Jose Vizcaino	.05
238	Chris Donnels	.05
239	Mike Boddicker	.05
240	John Olerud	.05
241	Mike Gardiner	.05
242	Charlie O'Brien	.05
243	Rob Deer	.05
244	Denny Neagle	.05
245	Chris Sabo	.05
246	Gregg Olson	.05
247	Frank Seminara	.05
248	Scott Scudder	.05
249	Tim Burke	.05
250	Chuck Knoblauch	.05
251	Mike Bielecki	.05
252	Xavier Hernandez	.05
253	Jose Guzman	.05
254	Cory Snyder	.05
255	Orel Hershiser	.05
256	Wil Cordero	.05
257	Luis Alicea	.05
258	Mike Schooler	.05
259	Craig Grebeck	.05
260	Duane Ward	.05
261	Bill Wegman	.05
262	Mickey Morandini	.05
263	Vince Horsman RC	.05
264	Paul Sorrento	.05
265	Andre Dawson	.25
266	Rene Gonzales	.05
267	Keith Miller	.05
268	Derek Bell	.05
269	Todd Steverson RC (1992 Draft Pick)	.05
270	Frank Viola	.05
271	Wally Whitehurst	.05
272	Kurt Knudsen RC	.05
273	Dan Walters RC	.05
274	Rick Sutcliffe	.05
275	Andy Van Slyke	.05
276	Paul O'Neill	.05
277	Mark Whiten	.05
278	Chris Nabholz	.05
279	Todd Burns	.05
280	Tom Glavine	.25
281	Butch Henry RC	.05
282	Shane Mack	.05
283	Mike Jackson	.05
284	Henry Rodriguez	.05
285	Bob Tewksbury	.05
286	Ron Karkovice	.05
287	Mike Gallego	.05
288	Dave Cochrane	.05
289	Jesse Orosco	.05
290	Dave Stewart	.05
291	Tommy Greene	.05
292	Rey Sanchez	.05
293	Rob Ducey	.05
294	Brent Mayne	.05
295	Dave Stieb	.05
296	Luis Rivera	.05
297	Jeff Innis	.05
298	Scott Livingstone	.05
299	Bob Patterson	.05
300	Cal Ripken, Jr.	1.00
301	Cesar Hernandez	.05
302	Randy Myers	.05
303	Brook Jacoby	.05
304	Melido Perez	.05
305	Rafael Palmeiro	.05
306	Damon Berryhill	.05
307	Dan Serafini RC (1992 Draft Pick)	.05
308	Darryl Kile	.05
309	J.T. Bruett RC	.05
310	Dave Righetti	.05
311	Jay Howell	.05
312	Geronimo Pena	.05
313	Greg Hibbard	.05
314	Mark Gardner	.05
315	Edgar Martinez	.05
316	Dave Nilsson	.05
317	Kyle Abbott	.05
318	Willie Wilson	.05
319	Paul Assenmacher	.05
320	Tim Fortugno RC	.05
321	Rusty Meacham	.05
322	Pat Borders	.05
323	Mike Greenwell	.05
324	Willie Randolph	.05
325	Bill Gullickson	.05
326	Gary Varsho	.05
327	Tim Hulett	.05
328	Scott Ruskin	.05
329	Mike Maddux	.05
330	Danny Tartabull	.05
331	Kenny Lofton	.05
332	Geno Petralli	.05
333	Otis Nixon	.05
334	Jason Kendall RC (1992 Draft Pick)	.50
335	Mark Portugal	.05
336	Mike Pagliarulo	.05
337	Kirt Manwaring	.05
338	Bob Ojeda	.05
339	Mark Clark RC	.05
340	John Kruk	.05
341	Mel Rojas	.05
342	Erik Hanson	.05
343	Doug Henry	.05
344	Jack McDowell	.05
345	Harold Baines	.05
346	Chuck McElroy	.05
347	Luis Sojo	.05
348	Andy Stankiewicz	.05
349	Hipolito Pichardo RC	.05
350	Joe Carter	.05
351	Ellis Burks	.05
352	Pete Schourek	.05
353	Buddy Groom RC	.05
354	Jay Bell	.05
355	Brady Anderson	.05
356	Freddie Benavides	.05
357	Phil Stephenson	.05
358	Kevin Wickander	.05
359	Mike Stanley	.05
360	Ivan Rodriguez	.40
361	Scott Bankhead	.05
362	Luis Gonzalez	.05
363	John Smiley	.05
364	Trevor Wilson	.05
365	Tom Candiotti	.05
366	Craig Wilson	.05
367	Steve Sax	.05
368	Delino Deshields	.05
369	Jaime Navarro	.05
370	Dave Valle	.05
371	Mariano Duncan	.05
372	Rod Nichols	.05
373	Mike Morgan	.05
374	Julio Valera	.05
375	Wally Joyner	.05
376	Tom Henke	.05
377	Herm Winningham	.05
378	Orlando Merced	.05
379	Mike Munoz	.05
380	Todd Hundley	.05
381	Mike Flanagan	.05
382	Tim Belcher	.05
383	Jerry Browne	.05
384	Mike Benjamin	.05
385	Jim Leyritz	.05
386	Ray Lankford	.05
387	Devon White	.05
388	Jeremy Hernandez	.05
389	Brian Harper	.05
390	Wade Boggs	.60
391	Derrick May	.05
392	Travis Fryman	.05
393	Ron Gant	.05
394	Checklist 1-132	.05
395	Checklist 133-264	.05
396	Checklist 265-396	.05
397	George Brett	.65
398	Bobby Witt	.05
399	Daryl Boston	.05
400	Bo Jackson	.10
401	Fred McGriff, Frank Thomas/AS	.20
402	Ryne Sandberg, Carlos Baerga/AS	.30
403	Gary Sheffield, Edgar Martinez/AS	.05
404	Barry Larkin, Travis Fryman/AS	.05
405	Andy Van Slyke, Ken Griffey Jr./AS	.40
406	Larry Walker, Kirby Puckett/AS	.20
407	Barry Bonds, Joe Carter/AS	.50
408	Darren Daulton, Brian Harper/AS	.05
409	Greg Maddux, Roger Clemens/AS	.25
410	Tom Glavine, Dave Fleming/AS	.05
411	Lee Smith, Dennis Eckersley/AS	.15
412	Jamie McAndrew	.05
413	Pete Smith	.05
414	Juan Guerrero	.05
415	Todd Frohwirth	.05
416	Randy Tomlin	.05
417	B.J. Surhoff	.05
418	Jim Gott	.05
419	Mark Thompson (1992 Draft Pick)	.05
420	Kevin Tapani	.05
421	Curt Schilling	.25
422	J.T. Snow RC	.40
423	Top Prospects 1B (Ryan Klesko, Ivan Cruz, Bubba Smith, Larry Sutton)	.05
424	John Valentin	.05
425	Joe Girardi	.05
426	Nigel Wilson RC	.05
427	Bob MacDonald	.05
428	Todd Zeile	.05
429	Milt Cuyler	.05
430	Eddie Murray	.50
431	Rich Amaral	.05
432	Pete Young	.05
433	Rockies Future Stars (Roger Bailey, Tom Schmidt)	.05
434	Jack Armstrong	.05
435	Willie McGee	.05
436	Greg Harris	.05
437	Chris Hammond	.05
438	Ritchie Moody RC (1992 Draft Pick)	.05
439	Bryan Harvey	.05
440	Ruben Sierra	.05
441	Marlins Future Stars (Don Lemon, Todd Pridy)	.05
442	Kevin McReynolds	.05
443	Terry Leach	.05
444	David Nied	.05
445	Dale Murphy	.15
446	Luis Mercedes	.05
447	Keith Shepherd RC	.05
448	Ken Caminiti	.05
449	James Austin	.05
450	Darryl Strawberry	.05
451	Top Propsects 2B (Ramon Caraballo, Jon Shave, Brent Gates, Quinton McCracken RC)	.10
452	Bob Wickman	.05
453	Victor Cole	.05
454	John Johnstone RC	.05
455	Chili Davis	.05
456	Scott Taylor	.05
457	Tracy Woodson	.05
458	David Wells	.05
459	Derek Wallace RC (1992 Draft Pick)	.05
460	Randy Johnson	.50
461	Steve Reed RC	.05
462	Felix Fermin	.05
463	Scott Aldred	.05
464	Greg Colbrunn	.05
465	Tony Fernandez	.05
466	Mike Felder	.05
467	Lee Stevens	.05
468	Matt Whiteside	.05
469	Dave Hansen	.05
470	Rob Dibble	.05
471	Dave Gallagher	.05
472	Chris Gwynn	.05
473	Dave Henderson	.05
474	Ozzie Guillen	.05
475	Jeff Reardon	.05
476	Rockies Future Stars (Mark Voisard, Will Scalzitti)	.05
477	Jimmy Jones	.05
478	Greg Cadaret	.05
479	Todd Pratt	.05
480	Pat Listach	.05
481	Ryan Luzinski RC (1992 Draft Pick)	.05
482	Darren Reed	.05
483	Brian Griffiths RC	.05
484	John Wehner	.05
485	Glenn Davis	.05
486	Eric Wedge RC	.05
487	Jesse Hollins	.05
488	Manuel Lee	.05
489	Scott Fredrickson RC	.05
490	Omar Olivares	.05
491	Shawn Hare	.05
492	Tom Lampkin	.05
493	Jeff Nelson	.05
494	Top Prospects 3B (Kevin Young, Adell Davenport, Eduardo Perez, Lou Lucca)	.05
495	Ken Hill	.05
496	Reggie Jefferson	.05
497	Marlins Future Stars (Matt Petersen, Willie Brown)	.05
498	Bud Black	.05
499	Chuck Crim	.05
500	Jose Canseco	.30
501	Major League Managers (Johnny Oates, Bobby Cox)	.05
502	Major League Managers (Butch Hobson, Jim Lefebvre)	.05
503	Major League Managers (Buck Rodgers, Tony Perez)	.05
504	Major League Managers (Gene Lamont, Don Baylor)	.05
505	Major League Managers (Mike Hargrove, Rene Lachemann)	.05
506	Major League Managers (Sparky Anderson, Art Howe)	.10
507	Major League Managers (Hal McRae, Tommy Lasorda)	.05
508	Major League Manager (Phil Garner, Felipe Alou)	.05
509	Major League Managers (Tom Kelly, Jeff Torborg)	.05
510	Major League Managers (Buck Showalter, Jim Fregosi)	.05
511	Major League Managers (Tony LaRussa, Jim Leyland)	.10
512	Major League Managers (Lou Piniella, Joe Torre)	.10
513	Major League Managers (Toby Harrah, Jim Riggleman)	.05
514	Major League Managers (Cito Gaston, Dusty Baker)	.05
515	Greg Swindell	.05
516	Alex Arias	.05
517	Bill Pecota	.05
518	Benji Grigsby RC (1992 Draft Pick)	.05
519	Doug Howard	.05
520	Charlie Hough	.05
521	Kevin Flora	.05
522	Shane Reynolds	.05
523	Doug Bochtler RC	.05
524	Chris Hoiles	.05
525	Scott Sanderson	.05
526	Mike Fetters	.05
527	Mike Fetters	.05
528	Paul Quantrill RC	.05
529	Top Propsects SS (Dave Silvestri, Chipper Jones, Benji Gil, Jeff Patzke)	.25
530	Sterling Hitchcock	.05
531	Joe Millette	.05
532	Tom Brunansky	.05
533	Frank Castillo	.05
534	Randy Knorr	.05
535	Jose Oquendo	.05
536	Dave Haas	.05
537	Rockies Future Stars (Jason Hutchins, Ryan Turner)	.05
538	Jimmy Baron (1992 Draft Pick)	.05
539	Kerry Woodson	.05
540	Ivan Calderon	.05
541	Denis Boucher	.05
542	Royce Clayton	.05
543	Reggie Williams	.05
544	Steve Decker	.05
545	Dean Palmer	.05
546	Hal Morris	.05
547	Ryan Thompson RC	.05
548	Lance Blankenship	.05
549	Hensley Meulens	.05
550	Scott Radinsky	.05
551	Eric Young RC	.10
552	Jeff Blauser	.05
553	Andujar Cedeno	.05
554	Arthur Rhodes	.05
555	Terry Mulholland	.05
556	Darryl Hamilton	.05
557	Pedro Martinez	.50
558	Marlins Future Stars (Ryan Whitman, Mark Skeels)	.05
559	Jamie Arnold RC (1992 Draft Pick)	.05
560	Zane Smith	.05
561	Matt Nokes	.05
562	Bob Zupcic	.05
563	Shawn Boskie	.05
564	Mike Timlin	.05
565	Jerald Clark	.05
566	Rod Brewer	.05
567	Mark Carreon	.05
568	Andy Benes	.05
569	Shawn Barton	.05
570	Tim Wallach	.05
571	Dave Mlicki	.05
572	Trevor Hoffman	.05
573	John Patterson	.05
574	DeShawn Warren (1992 Draft Pick)	.05
575	Monty Fariss	.05
576	Top Prospects OF (Darrell Sherman, Damon Buford, Cliff Floyd, Michael Moore)	.05
577	Tim Costo	.05
578	Dave Magadan	.05
579	Rockies Future Stars (Neil Garret, Jason Bates)	.05
580	Walt Weiss	.05
581	Chris Haney	.05
582	Shawn Abner	.05
583	Marvin Freeman	.05
584	Casey Candaele	.05
585	Ricky Jordan	.05
586	Jeff Tabaka	.05
587	Manny Alexander	.05
588	Mike Trombley	.05
589	Carlos Hernandez	.05
590	Cal Eldred	.05
591	Alex Cole	.05
592	Phil Plantier	.05
593	Brett Merriman	.05
594	Jerry Nielsen	.05
595	Shawon Dunston	.05
596	Jimmy Key	.05
597	Gerald Perry	.05
598	Rico Brogna	.05
599	Marlins Future Stars (Clemente Nunez, Dan Robinson)	.05
600	Bret Saberhagen	.05
601	Craig Shipley	.05
602	Henry Mercedes	.05
603	Jim Thome	.40
604	Rod Beck	.05
605	Chuck Finley	.05
606	J. Owens	.05
607	Dan Smith	.05
608	Bill Doran	.05
609	Lance Parrish	.05
610	Denny Martinez	.05
611	Tom Gordon	.05
612	Byron Mathews (1992 Draft Pick)	.05
613	Joel Adamson	.05
614	Brian Williams	.05
615	Steve Avery	.05
616	Top Prospects OF (Matt Mieske, Tracy Sanders, Midre Cummings, Ryan Freeburg)	.05
617	Craig Lefferts	.05
618	Tony Pena	.05
619	Billy Spiers	.05
620	Todd Benzinger	.05
621	Rockies Future Stars (Mike Kotarski, Greg Boyd)	.05
622	Ben Rivera	.05
623	Al Martin RC	.05
624	Sam Militello	.05
625	Rick Aguilera	.05
626	Danny Gladden	.05
627	Andres Berumen	.05
628	Kelly Gruber	.05
629	Cris Carpenter	.05
630	Mark Grace	.05
631	Jeff Brantley	.05
632	Chris Widger (1992 Draft Pick)	.05

633	Russian Angels (Rodolf Razjigaev, Evgenyi Puchkov, Ilya Bogatyrev)	.10
634	Mo Sanford	.05
635	Albert Belle	.05
636	Tim Teufel	.05
637	Greg Myers	.05
638	Brian Bohanon	.05
639	Mike Bordick	.05
640	Dwight Gooden	.05
641	Marlins Future Stars (Pat Leahy, Gavin Baugh)	.05
642	Milt Hill	.05
643	Luis Aquino	.05
644	Dante Bichette	.05
645	Bobby Thigpen	.05
646	Rich Scheid	.05
647	Brian Sackinsky (1992 Draft Pick)	.05
648	Ryan Hawblitzel	.05
649	Tom Marsh	.05
650	Terry Pendleton	.05
651	Rafael Bournigal **RC**	.05
652	Dave West	.05
653	Steve Hosey	.05
654	Gerald Williams	.05
655	Scott Cooper	.05
656	Gary Scott	.05
657	Mike Harkey	.05
658	Top Prospects OF (Jeromy Burnitz, Melvin Nieves, Rich Becker, Shon Walker)	.05
659	Ed Sprague	.05
660	Alan Trammell	.05
661	Rockies Future Stars (Garvin Alston, Mike Case)	.05
662	Donovan Osborne	.05
663	Jeff Gardner	.05
664	Calvin Jones	.05
665	Darrin Fletcher	.05
666	Glenallen Hill	.05
667	Jim Rosenbohm (1992 Draft Pick)	.05
668	Scott Lewis	.05
669	Kip Vaughn	.05
670	Julio Franco	.05
671	Dave Martinez	.05
672	Kevin Bass	.05
673	Todd Van Poppel	.05
674	Mark Gubicza	.05
675	Tim Raines	.05
676	Rudy Seanez	.05
677	Charlie Leibrandt	.05
678	Randy Milligan	.05
679	Kim Batiste	.05
680	Craig Biggio	.05
681	Darren Holmes	.05
682	John Candelaria	.05
683	Marlins Future Stars (Jerry Stafford, Eddie Christian)	.05
684	Pat Mahomes	.05
685	Bob Walk	.05
686	Russ Springer	.05
687	Tony Sheffield (1992 Draft Picks)	.05
688	Dwight Smith	.05
689	Eddie Zosky	.05
690	Bien Figueroa	.05
691	Jim Tatum	.05
692	Chad Kreuter	.05
693	Rich Rodriguez	.05
694	Shane Turner	.05
695	Kent Bottenfield	.05
696	Jose Mesa	.05
697	Darrell Whitmore **RC**	.05
698	Ted Wood	.05
699	Chad Curtis	.05
700	Nolan Ryan	1.00
701	Top Prospects C (Mike Piazza, Carlos Delgado, Brook Fordyce, Donnie Leshnock)	.85
702	Tim Pugh **RC**	.05
703	Jeff Kent	.05
704	Rockies Future Stars (Jon Goodrich, Danny Figueroa)	.05
705	Bob Welch	.05
706	Sherard Clinkscales (1992 Draft Pick)	.05
707	Donn Pall	.05
708	Greg Olson	.05
709	Jeff Juden	.05
710	Mike Mussina	.30
711	Scott Chiamparino	.05
712	Stan Javier	.05
713	John Doherty	.05
714	Kevin Gross	.05
715	Greg Gagne	.05
716	Steve Cooke	.05
717	Steve Farr	.05
718	Jay Buhner	.05
719	Butch Henry	.05
720	David Cone	.05
721	Rick Wilkins	.05
722	Chuck Carr	.05
723	Kenny Felder **RC** (1992 Draft Pick)	.05
724	Guillermo Velasquez	.05
725	Billy Hatcher	.05
726	Marlins Future Stars (Mike Veneziale, Ken Kendrena)	.05
727	Jonathan Hurst	.05
728	Steve Frey	.05

729	Mark Leonard	.05
730	Charles Nagy	.05
731	Donald Harris	.05
732	Travis Buckley	.05
733	Tom Browning	.05
734	Anthony Young	.05
735	Steve Shifflett	.05
736	Jeff Russell	.05
737	Wilson Alvarez	.05
738	Lance Painter	.05
739	Dave Weathers	.05
740	Len Dykstra	.05
741	Mike Devereaux	.05
742	Top Prospects SP (Rene Arocha, Alan Embree, Tim Crabtree **RC**, Brien Taylor)	.05
743	Dave Landaker (1992 Draft Pick)	.05
744	Chris George	.05
745	Eric Davis	.05
746	Rockies Future Stars (Mark Strittmatter **RC**, LaMarr Rogers)	.05
747	Carl Willis	.05
748	Stan Belinda	.05
749	Scott Kamieniecki	.05
750	Rickey Henderson	.50
751	Eric Hillman	.05
752	Pat Hentgen	.05
753	Jim Corsi	.05
754	Brian Jordan	.05
755	Bill Swift	.05
756	Mike Henneman	.05
757	Harold Reynolds	.05
758	Sean Berry	.05
759	Charlie Hayes	.05
760	Luis Polonia	.05
761	Darrin Jackson	.05
762	Mark Lewis	.05
763	Rob Maurer	.05
764	Willie Greene	.05
765	Vince Coleman	.05
766	Todd Revenig	.05
767	Rich Ireland (1992 Draft Pick)	.05
768	Mike MacFarlane	.05
769	Francisco Cabrera	.05
770	Robin Ventura	.05
771	Kevin Ritz	.05
772	Chito Martinez	.05
773	Cliff Brantley	.05
774	Curtis Leskanic	.05
775	Chris Bosio	.05
776	Jose Offerman	.05
777	Mark Guthrie	.05
778	Don Slaught	.05
779	Rich Monteleone	.05
780	Jim Abbott	.05
781	Jack Clark	.05
782	Marlins Future Stars (Rafael Mendoza, Dan Roman)	.05
783	Heathcliff Slocumb	.05
784	Jeff Branson	.05
785	Kevin Brown	.05
786	Top Prospects RP (Mike Christopher, Ken Ryan, Aaron Taylor, Gus Gandarillas)	.05
787	Mike Matthews (1992 Draft Pick)	.05
788	Mackey Sasser	.05
789	Jeff Conine	.05
790	George Bell	.05
791	Pat Rapp	.05
792	Joe Boever	.05
793	Jim Poole	.05
794	Andy Ashby	.05
795	Deion Sanders	.10
796	Scott Brosius	.05
797	Brad Pennington (Coming Attraction)	.05
798	Greg Blosser (Coming Attraction)	.05
799	Jim Edmonds **RC** (Coming Attraction)	1.00
800	Shawn Jeter (Coming Attraction)	.05
801	Jesse Levis (Coming Attraction)	.05
802	Phil Clark (Coming Attraction)	.05
803	Ed Pierce (Coming Attraction)	.05
804	Jose Valentin **RC** (Coming Attraction)	.05
805	Terry Jorgensen (Coming Attraction)	.05
806	Mark Hutton (Coming Attraction)	.05
807	Troy Neel (Coming Attraction)	.05
808	Bret Boone (Coming Attraction)	.05
809	Chris Colon (Coming Attraction)	.05
810	Domingo Martinez **RC** (Coming Attraction)	.05
811	Javier Lopez (Coming Attraction)	.05
812	Matt Walbeck (Coming Attraction)	.05
813	Dan Wilson (Coming Attraction)	.05
814	Scooter Tucker (Coming Attraction)	.05

815	Billy Ashley **RC** (Coming Attraction)	.05
816	Tim Laker **RC** (Coming Attraction)	.05
817	Bobby Jones (Coming Attraction)	.05
818	Brad Brink (Coming Attraction)	.05
819	William Pennyfeather (Coming Attraction)	.05
820	Stan Royer (Coming Attraction)	.05
821	Doug Brocail (Coming Attraction)	.05
822	Kevin Rogers (Coming Attraction)	.05
823	Checklist 397-528	.05
824	Checklist 541-691	.05
825	Checklist 692-825	.05

Gold

Expanding on the concept begun in 1992, Topps issued a "gold" version of each of its regular 1993 cards as a package insert. One Gold card was found in each wax pack; three per rack-pack and five per jumbo cello pack. Ten Gold cards were included in each factory set. Identical in format to the regular-issue 1993 Topps cards, the Gold version replaces the black or white Topps logo on front with a "ToppsGold" logo in gold-foil. The color bars and angled strips beneath the player photo which carry the player and team ID on regular cards are replaced with a gold-foil version on the insert cards. Backs are identical to the regular cards. The six checklist cards in the regular issue were replaced in the Gold version with cards of players who do not appear in the 1993 Topps set.

	NM/M
Complete Set (825):	40.00
Common Player:	.15
394 Bernardo Brito	.25
395 Jim McNamara	.25
396 Rich Sauveur	.25
823 Keith Brown	.25
824 Russ McGinnis	.25
825 Mike Walker	.25

Black Gold

Randomly inserted in regular 1993 Topps packs, as well as 10 per factory set, Black Gold cards are found in both single-player versions and "Winner" cards. The single-player cards feature an action photo set against a black background and highlighted at top and bottom with gold foil. Backs have another player photo at left, again on a black background. A career summary is printed in a blue box at right. A "Topps Black Gold" logo appears at top-left, and the player's name is printed in gold foil in an art deco device at top-right. The Win-

ner cards picture tiny versions of the Black Gold player cards for which they could be redeemed by mail. Some, perhaps all, of the mail-in cards can also be found on which the miniature card pictures on front do not correspond to the players named on back. In addition, with each mail-in redemption set, a non-redeemable version of the Winner card was also sent.

	NM/M
Complete Set (44):	7.50
Common Player:	.10
Winner A (1-11):	1.00
Winner B (12-22):	1.00
Winner C (23-33):	1.00
Winner D (34-44):	1.00
Winner AB (1-22):	3.00
Winner CD (23-44):	3.00
Winner ABCD (1-44):	5.00
1 Barry Bonds	1.50
2 Will Clark	.10
3 Darren Daulton	.10
4 Andre Dawson	.25
5 Delino DeShields	.10
6 Tom Glavine	.20
7 Marquis Grissom	.10
8 Tony Gwynn	.75
9 Eric Karros	.10
10 Ray Lankford	.10
11 Barry Larkin	.10
12 Greg Maddux	.75
13 Fred McGriff	.10
14 Joe Oliver	.10
15 Terry Pendleton	.10
16 Bip Roberts	.10
17 Ryne Sandberg	.75
18 Gary Sheffield	.40
19 Lee Smith	.10
20 Ozzie Smith	.75
21 Andy Van Slyke	.10
22 Larry Walker	.10
23 Roberto Alomar	.20
24 Brady Anderson	.10
25 Carlos Baerga	.10
26 Joe Carter	.10
27 Roger Clemens	.85
28 Mike Devereaux	.10
29 Dennis Eckersley	.60
30 Cecil Fielder	.10
31 Travis Fryman	.10
32 Juan Gonzalez	.35
33 Ken Griffey Jr.	1.00
34 Brian Harper	.10
35 Pat Listach	.10
36 Kenny Lofton	.10
37 Edgar Martinez	.10
38 Jack McDowell	.10
39 Mark McGwire	1.00
40 Kirby Puckett	.75
41 Mickey Tettleton	.10
42 Frank Thomas	.65
43 Robin Ventura	.10
44 Dave Winfield	.65

Colorado Rockies Inaugural Year

To mark the team's inaugural year in the Major Leagues, Topps produced a special run of 10,000 of its 1993 factory sets in which each card was embossed with a special gold seal incorporating the Rockies logo. Sets sold for $100 at the team's normal souvenir outlets. The factory sets were sealed with a sticker featuring the inaugural year logo.

	NM/M
Complete Set (825):	80.00
Common Player:	.50

Florida Marlins Inaugural Year

To commemorate the team's inaugural year in the Major Leagues, Topps produced a special edition of 6,000 of its 1993 factory sets in which every card was embossed with a special gold seal incorporating the Marlins logo. The sets were sold for $100 at the team's normal

souvenir outlets. Factory sets are sealed with a sticker incorporating the inaugural year logo.

	NM/M
Complete Set (825):	100.00
Common Player:	.50

Traded

The 1993 Topps Traded baseball set features many players in their new uniforms as a result of trades, free agent signings and rookie call-ups. The set also features 35 expansion players from the Colorado Rockies and Florida Marlins, as well as 22 Team USA members exclusive to Topps. The 132-card set is packed in a color deluxe printed box.

	NM/M
Complete Set (132):	20.00
Common Player:	.05
1 Barry Bonds	2.00
2 Rich Renteria	.05
3 Aaron Sele	.05
4 Carlton Loewer **RC** (USA)	.10
5 Erik Pappas	.05
6 Greg McMichael **RC**	.05
7 Freddie Benavides	.05
8 Kirk Gibson	.05
9 Tony Fernandez	.05
10 Jay Gainer **RC**	.05
11 Orestes Destrade	.05
12 A.J. Hinch **RC** (USA)	.40
13 Bobby Munoz	.05
14 Tom Henke	.05
15 Rob Butler	.05
16 Gary Wayne	.05
17 David McCarty	.05
18 Walt Weiss	.05
19 Todd Helton **RC** (USA)	15.00
20 Mark Whiten	.05
21 Ricky Gutierrez	.05
22 Dustin Hermanson **RC** (USA)	.40
23 Sherman Obando **RC**	.05
24 Mike Piazza	2.00
25 Jeff Russell	.05
26 Jason Bere	.05
27 Jack Voight **RC**	.05
28 Chris Bosio	.05
29 Phil Hiatt	.05
30 Matt Beaumont **RC** (USA)	.05
31 Andres Galarraga	.05
32 Greg Swindell	.05
33 Vinny Castilla	.05
34 Pat Clougherty **RC** (USA)	.05
35 Greg Briley	.05
36 Dallas Green, Davey Johnson	.05
37 Tyler Green	.05
38 Craig Paquette	.05
39 Danny Sheaffer	.05
40 Jim Converse	.05
41 Terry Harvey	.05
42 Phil Plantier	.05
43 Doug Saunders **RC**	.05
44 Benny Santiago	.05
45 Dante Powell **RC** (USA)	.10
46 Jeff Parrett	.05
47 Wade Boggs	.85
48 Paul Molitor	.75
49 Turk Wendell	.05
50 David Wells	.05
51 Gary Sheffield	.35

52	Kevin Young	.05
53	Nelson Liriano	.05
54	Greg Maddux	.85
55	Derek Bell	.05
56	Matt Turner **RC**	.05
57	Charlie Nelson **RC** (USA)	.05
58	Mike Hampton	.05
59	Troy O'Leary **RC**	.10
60	Benji Gil	.05
61	Mitch Lyden **RC**	.05
62	J.T. Snow	.05
63	Damon Buford	.05
64	Gene Harris	.05
65	Randy Myers	.05
66	Felix Jose	.05
67	Todd Dunn **RC** (USA)	.05
68	Jimmy Key	.05
69	Pedro Castellano	.05
70	Mark Merila **RC** (USA)	.05
71	Rich Rodriguez	.05
72	Matt Mieske	.05
73	Pete Incaviglia	.05
74	Carl Everett	.05
75	Jim Abbott	.05
76	Luis Aquino	.05
77	Rene Arocha **RC**	.05
78	Jon Shave **RC**	.05
79	Todd Walker **RC** (USA)	1.00
80	Jack Armstrong	.05
81	Jeff Richardson	.05
82	Blas Minor	.05
83	Dave Winfield	.75
84	Paul O'Neill	.05
85	Steve Reich **RC** (USA)	.10
86	Chris Hammond	.05
87	Hilly Hathaway **RC**	.05
88	Fred McGriff	.05
89	Dave Telgheder **RC**	.05
90	Richie Lewis **RC**	.05
91	Brent Gates	.05
92	Andre Dawson	.15
93	Andy Barkett **RC** (USA)	.05
94	Doug Drabek	.05
95	Joe Klink	.05
96	Willie Blair	.05
97	Danny Graves **RC** (USA)	.05
98	Pat Meares	.05
99	Mike Lansing	.05
100	Marcos Armas	.05
101	Darren Grass **RC** (USA)	.05
102	Chris Jones	.05
103	Ken Ryan **RC**	.05
104	Ellis Burks	.05
105	Bobby Kelly	.05
106	Dave Magadan	.05
107	Paul Wilson **RC** (USA)	.25
108	Rob Natal	.05
109	Paul Wagner	.05
110	Jeromy Burnitz	.05
111	Monty Fariss	.05
112	Kevin Mitchell	.05
113	Scott Pose **RC**	.05
114	Dave Stewart	.05
115	Russ Johnson **RC** (USA)	.10
116	Armando Reynoso	.05
117	Geronimo Berroa	.05
118	Woody Williams **RC**	.15
119	Tim Bogar **RC**	.05
120	Bob Scafa **RC** (USA)	.05
121	Henry Cotto	.05
122	Gregg Jefferies	.05
123	Norm Charlton	.05
124	Bret Wagner **RC** (USA)	.05
125	David Cone	.05
126	Daryl Boston	.05
127	Tim Wallach	.05
128	Mike Martin **RC** (USA)	.05
129	John Cummings **RC**	.05
130	Ryan Bowen	.05
131	John Powell **RC** (USA)	.05
132	Checklist	.05

Full Shot Super

Just as rivals Upper Deck and Donruss did, Topps issued a set of 21 oversized cards (3-1/2" x 5") that was available in retail outlets in packages that contained one of the large cards and two packs of regular issue Topps cards from the same year. The Topps Full Shot cards feature many of the top players in the game, and unlike the Upper Deck oversized cards, the Topps cards were not enlarged versions of existing cards but rather photos and a design that appeared only in this format.

	NM/M
Complete Set (21):	65.00
Common Player:	2.00
1 Frank Thomas	4.00
2 Ken Griffey Jr.	8.00
3 Barry Bonds	9.00
4 Juan Gonzalez	2.50
5 Roberto Alomar	2.50
6 Mike Piazza	6.50
7 Tony Gwynn	4.50
8 Jeff Bagwell	3.50
9 Tim Salmon	2.00
10 John Olerud	2.00
11 Cal Ripken, Jr.	9.00
12 David McCarty	2.00
13 Darren Daulton	2.00
14 Carlos Baerga	2.00
15 Roger Clemens	5.00
16 John Kruk	2.00
17 Barry Larkin	2.00
18 Gary Sheffield	2.50
19 Tom Glavine	2.50
20 Andres Galarraga	2.00
21 Fred McGriff	2.00

Golden Spikes Award

Darren Dreifort was the 1993 recipient of the U.S. Baseball Federation's Golden Spikes Award, emblematic of his selection as the outstanding amateur player in the nation. Topps created and handed out at the awards ceremony this special card.

	NM/M
Darren Dreifort	125.00

Magazine Jumbo Rookies

The final four issues of Topps' Magazine in 1993 substituted a 5-1/2" x 8" enlargement of a player's Topps rookie card in place of four of the standard-size inserts found previously. The jumbo rookie cards are identical, front and back, to the original rookie cards but carry a reprint notice on front. In an attempt to increase sales to subscribers and at the newsstands, the stars pictured autographed 100 of their cards to be randomly bound into the magazine and given away in prize drawings.

	NM/M
Complete Set (4):	7.50
Common Player:	1.00
(1) Dennis Eckersley (1976 Topps)	1.00
(2) Dave Winfield (1974 Topps)	1.00
(3) George Brett (1975 Topps)	2.00
(4) Jerry Koosman, Nolan Ryan (1968 Topps)	4.00

Micro

Topps returned for a final year with a micro parallel of its regular-issue baseball set, in a format about 40 percent of the size of the standard cards. Sold only in complete-set form, the 1"x 1-3/8" cards also included a dozen prismatic- foil bordered star cards. Stars and rookies among the micros are valued at a percentage of the corresponding regular card.

	NM/M
Complete Set (837):	11.00
Common Player:	.05
Stars/Rookies:	1-1.5X
1 Robin Yount	.75
20 Tim Salmon	.50
32 Don Mattingly	1.25
50 Roberto Alomar	.60
150 Frank Thomas	.75
155 Dennis Eckersley	.65
179 Ken Griffey Jr.	1.50
200 Kirby Puckett	1.00
397 George Brett	1.25
426 Nigel Wilson	.50
444 David Nied	.50
700 Nolan Ryan	2.00

Preview

Two different versions of this nine-card set exist. A cello-wrapped version, designated (a) in the checklist, was given away to dealers and the hobby press. A second version, designated (b), was included in 1993 Topps factory sets. It is currently unknown which version, if either, will become more valuable due to demand and perceived scarcity. Both versions are similar to the regular-issue '94 Topps cards, except for the sample notation on back.

	NM/M
Complete Set (a)(9):	10.00
Complete Set (b)(9):	10.00
Common Player (a):	.30
Common Player (b):	.30
2a Barry Bonds (Vertical format.)	4.00
2b Barry Bonds (Horizontal)	4.00
6a Jeff Tackett (Full bat label visible.)	.30
6b Jeff Tackett (Partial bat label.)	.30
34a Juan Gonzalez (Green triangle behind "Juan.")	.75
34b Juan Gonzalez (Brown triangle.)	.75
225a Matt Williams (Green triangle behind "Matt.")	.30
225b Matt Williams (Blue triangle.)	.30
294a Carlos Quintana (Team/position yellow.)	.30
294b Carlos Quintana (Team/position black.)	.30
331a Ken Lofton (Team/position white.)	.30
331b Ken Lofton (Team/position black.)	.30
390a Wade Boggs (Team/position yellow.)	2.00
390b Wade Boggs (Team/position black.)	2.00
397a George Brett (Vertical format.)	3.00
397b George Brett (Horizontal)	3.00
700a Nolan Ryan (Vertical format.)	4.00
700b Nolan Ryan (Horizontal)	4.00

1994 Topps

Once again released in two 396-card series, Topps' basic issue for 1994 offers a standard mix of regular player cards, Future Stars, multi-player rookie cards and double-header All-Star cards. On most cards the player photo on front is framed in a home-plate shaped design. The player's name appears in script beneath the photo and a team color-coded strip at bottom carries the team name and position designation. On back is a player photo, a red box at top with biographical details and a marbled panel which carries the stats and a career highlight. Cards are UV coated on each side. Inserts include a gold-foil enhanced parallel card in every pack, plus random Black Gold cards. Factory hobby sets include the 792 base cards plus 10 gold parallels, three Black Gold inserts and three Finest pre-production cards. Factory retails sets have the 792 base cards, 10 Gold, three Black Gold, 10 1995 Topps pre-production cards and three Superstar Sampler cards.

	NM/M
Unopened Retail Set (818):	60.00
Unopened Hobby Set (808):	50.00
Complete Set (792):	35.00
Common Player:	.05
Golds:	2X
Series 1 or 2 Pack (12):	.50
Series 1 or 2 Wax Box (36):	15.00
1 Mike Piazza (All-Star Rookie)	.85
2 Bernie Williams	.05
3 Kevin Rogers	.05
4 Paul Carey (Future Star)	.05
5 Ozzie Guillen	.05
6 Derrick May	.05
7 Jose Mesa	.05
8 Todd Hundley	.05
9 Chris Haney	.05
10 John Olerud	.05
11 Andujar Cedeno	.05
12 John Smiley	.05
13 Phil Plantier	.05
14 Willie Banks	.05
15 Jay Bell	.05
16 Doug Henry	.05
17 Lance Blankenship	.05
18 Greg Harris	.05
19 Scott Livingstone	.05
20 Bryan Harvey	.05
21 Wil Cordero (All-Star Rookie)	.05
22 Roger Pavlik	.05
23 Mark Lemke	.05
24 Jeff Nelson	.05
25 Todd Zeile	.05
26 Billy Hatcher	.05
27 Joe Magrane	.05
28 Tony Longmire (Future Star)	.05
29 Omar Daal	.05
30 Kirt Manwaring	.05
31 Melido Perez	.05
32 Tim Hulett	.05
33 Jeff Schwarz	.05
34 Nolan Ryan	1.00
35 Jose Guzman	.05
36 Felix Fermin	.05
37 Jeff Innis	.05
38 Brent Mayne	.05
39 Huck Flener RC	.05
40 Jeff Bagwell	.50
41 Kevin Wickander	.05
42 Ricky Gutierrez	.05
43 Pat Mahomes	.05
44 Jeff King	.05
45 Cal Eldred	.05
46 Craig Paquette	.05
47 Richie Lewis	.05
48 Tony Phillips	.05
49 Armando Reynoso	.05
50 Moises Alou	.05
51 Manuel Lee	.05
52 Otis Nixon	.05
53 Billy Ashley (Future Star)	.05
54 Mark Whiten	.05
55 Jeff Russell	.05
56 Chad Curtis	.05
57 Kevin Stocker	.05
58 Mike Jackson	.05
59 Matt Nokes	.05
60 Chris Bosio	.05
61 Damon Buford	.05
62 Tim Belcher	.05
63 Glenallen Hill	.05
64 Bill Wertz	.05
65 Eddie Murray	.50
66 Tom Gordon	.05
67 Alex Gonzalez (Future Star)	.05
68 Eddie Taubensee	.05
69 Jacob Brumfield	.05
70 Andy Benes	.05
71 Rich Becker (Future Star)	.05
72 Steve Cooke (All-Star Rookie)	.05
73 Billy Spiers	.05
74 Scott Brosius	.05
75 Alan Trammell	.05
76 Luis Aquino	.05
77 Jerald Clark	.05
78 Mel Rojas	.05
79 OF Prospects (Billy Masse, Stanton Cameron, Tim Clark, Craig McClure)	.05
80 Jose Canseco	.30
81 Greg McMichael (All-Star Rookie)	.05
82 Brian Turang	.05
83 Tom Urban	.05
84 Garret Anderson (Future Star)	.05
85 Tony Pena	.05
86 Ricky Jordan	.05
87 Jim Gott	.05
88 Pat Kelly	.05
89 Bud Black	.05
90 Robin Ventura	.05
91 Rick Sutcliffe	.05
92 Jose Bautista	.05
93 Bob Ojeda	.05
94 Phil Hiatt	.05
95 Tim Pugh	.05
96 Randy Knorr	.05
97 Todd Jones (Future Star)	.05
98 Ryan Thompson	.05
99 Tim Mauser	.05
100 Kirby Puckett	.60
101 Mark Dewey	.05
102 B.J. Surhoff	.05
103 Sterling Hitchcock	.05
104 Alex Arias	.05
105 David Wells	.05
106 Daryl Boston	.05
107 Mike Stanton	.05
108 Gary Redus	.05
109a Delino DeShields (Red "Expos, 2B.")	2.00
109b Delino DeShields (Yellow "Expos, 2B.")	.05
110 Lee Smith	.05
111 Greg Litton	.05
112 Frank Rodriguez (Future Star)	.05
113 Russ Springer	.05
114 Mitch Williams	.05
115 Eric Karros	.05
116 Jeff Brantley	.05
117 Jack Voight	.05
118 Jason Bere	.05
119 Kevin Roberson	.05
120 Jimmy Key	.05
121 Reggie Jefferson	.05
122 Jeromy Burnitz	.05
123 Billy Brewer (Future Star)	.05
124 Willie Canate	.05
125 Greg Swindell	.05
126 Hal Morris	.05
127 Brad Ausmus	.05
128 George Tsamis	.05
129 Denny Neagle	.05
130 Pat Listach	.05
131 Steve Karsay	.05
132 Bret Barberie	.05
133 Mark Leiter	.05
134 Greg Colbrunn	.05
135 David Nied	.05
136 Dean Palmer	.05
137 Steve Avery	.05
138 Bill Haselman	.05
139 Tripp Cromer (Future Star)	.05
140 Frank Viola	.05
141 Rene Gonzales	.05
142 Curt Schilling	.25
143 Tim Wallach	.05
144 Bobby Munoz	.05
145 Brady Anderson	.05
146 Rod Beck	.05
147 Mike LaValliere	.05
148 Greg Hibbard	.05
149 Kenny Lofton	.05
150 Dwight Gooden	.05
151 Greg Gagne	.05
152 Ray McDavid (Future Star)	.05
153 Chris Donnels	.05
154 Dan Wilson	.05
155 Todd Stottlemyre	.05
156 David McCarty	.05
157 Paul Wagner	.05
158 SS Prospects (Orlando Miller, Brandon Wilson, Derek Jeter, Mike Neal)	1.00
159 Mike Fetters	.05
160 Scott Lydy	.05
161 Darrell Whitmore	.05
162 Bob MacDonald	.05
163 Vinny Castilla	.05
164 Denis Boucher	.05
165 Ivan Rodriguez	.40
166 Ron Gant	.05
167 Tim Davis	.05
168 Steve Dixon	.05
169 Scott Fletcher	.05
170 Terry Mulholland	.05
171 Greg Myers	.05
172 Brett Butler	.05
173 Bob Wickman	.05
174 Dave Martinez	.05
175 Fernando Valenzuela	.05
176 Craig Grebeck	.05
177 Shawn Boskie	.05
178 Albie Lopez	.05
179 Butch Huskey (Future Star)	.05
180 George Brett	.65
181 Juan Guzman	.05
182 Eric Anthony	.05
183 Bob Dibble	.05
184 Craig Shipley	.05
185 Kevin Tapani	.05
186 Marcus Moore	.05
187 Graeme Lloyd	.05
188 Mike Bordick	.05
189 Chris Hammond	.05
190 Cecil Fielder	.05
191 Curtis Leskanic	.05
192 Lou Frazier	.05
193 Steve Dreyer	.05
194 Javier Lopez (Future Star)	.05
195 Edgar Martinez	.05
196 Allen Watson	.05
197 John Flaherty	.05
198 Kurt Stillwell	.05
199 Danny Jackson	.05
200 Cal Ripken, Jr.	1.00
201 Mike Bell (Draft Pick)	.05
202 Alan Benes RC (Draft Pick)	.10
203 Matt Farner (Draft Pick)	.05
204 Jeff Granger RC (Draft Pick)	.05
205 Brooks Kieschnick RC (Draft Pick)	.25
206 Jeremy Lee (Draft Pick)	.05
207 Charles Peterson RC (Draft Pick)	.05
208 Andy Rice (Draft Pick)	.05
209 Billy Wagner RC (Draft Pick)	.60
210 Kelly Wunsch (Draft Pick)	.05
211 Tom Candiotti	.05
212 Domingo Jean (Draft Pick)	.05
213 John Burkett	.05
214 George Bell	.05
215 Dan Plesac	.05
216 Manny Ramirez (Future Star)	.60
217 Mike Maddux	.05
218 Kevin McReynolds	.05
219 Pat Borders	.05
220 Doug Drabek	.05
221 Larry Luebbers	.05
222 Trevor Hoffman	.05
223 Pat Meares	.05
224 Danny Miceli (Future Star)	.05
225 Greg Vaughn	.05
226 Scott Hemond	.05
227 Pat Rapp	.05
228 Kirk Gibson	.05
229 Lance Painter	.05
230 Larry Walker	.05
231 Benji Gil (Future Star)	.05
232 Mark Wohlers	.05
233 Rich Amaral	.05
234 Erik Pappas	.05
235 Scott Cooper	.05
236 Mike Butcher	.05
237 OF Prospects (Curtis Pride RC, Shawn Green, Mark Sweeney, Eddie Davis)	.35
238 Kim Batiste	.05
239 Paul Assenmacher	.05
240 Will Clark	.05
241 Jose Offerman	.05
242 Todd Frohwirth	.05
243 Tim Raines	.05
244 Rick Wilkins	.05
245 Bret Saberhagen	.05
246 Thomas Howard	.05
247 Stan Belinda	.05
248 Rickey Henderson	.50
249 Brian Williams	.05
250 Barry Larkin	.05
251 Jose Valentin (Future Star)	.05
252 Lenny Webster	.05
253 Blas Minor	.05
254 Tim Teufel	.05
255 Bobby Witt	.05
256 Walt Weiss	.05
257 Chad Kreuter	.05
258 Roberto Mejia	.05
259 Cliff Floyd (Future Star)	.05
260 Julio Franco	.05
261 Rafael Belliard	.05
262 Marc Newfield	.05
263 Gerald Perry	.05
264 Ken Ryan	.05
265 Chili Davis	.05
266 Dave West	.05
267 Royce Clayton	.05
268 Pedro Martinez	.50
269 Mark Hutton	.05
270 Frank Thomas	.50
271 Brad Pennington	.05
272 Mike Harkey	.05
273 Sandy Alomar	.05
274 Dave Gallagher	.05
275 Wally Joyner	.05
276 Ricky Trlicek	.05
277 Al Osuna	.05
278 Calvin Reese (Future Star)	.05
279 Kevin Higgins	.05
280 Rick Aguilera	.05
281 Orlando Merced	.05
282 Mike Mohler	.05
283 John Jaha	.05
284 Robb Nen	.05
285 Travis Fryman	.05
286 Mark Thompson (Future Star)	.05
287 Mike Lansing (All-Star Rookie)	.05
288 Craig Lefferts	.05
289 Damon Berryhill	.05
290 Randy Johnson	.50
291 Jeff Reed	.05
292 Danny Darwin	.05
293 J.T. Snow (All-Star Rookie)	.05
294 Tyler Green	.05
295 Chris Hoiles	.05
296 Roger McDowell	.05
297 Spike Owen	.05
298 Salomon Torres (Future Star)	.05
299 Wilson Alvarez	.05
300 Ryne Sandberg	.60
301 Derek Lilliquist	.05
302 Howard Johnson	.05
303 Greg Cadaret	.05
304 Pat Hentgen	.05
305 Craig Biggio	.05
306 Scott Service	.05
307 Melvin Nieves	.05
308 Mike Trombley	.05
309 Carlos Garcia (All-Star Rookie)	.05
310 Robin Yount	.50
311 Marcos Armas	.05
312 Rich Rodriguez	.05
313 Justin Thompson (Future Star)	.05
314 Danny Sheaffer	.05
315 Ken Hill	.05
316 P Prospects (Chad Ogea RC, Duff Brumley RC, Terrell Wade RC, Chris Michalak RC)	.10
317 Cris Carpenter	.05
318 Jeff Blauser	.05
319 Ted Power	.05
320 Ozzie Smith	.60
321 John Dopson	.05
322 Chris Turner	.05
323 Pete Incaviglia	.05
324 Alan Mills	.05
325 Jody Reed	.05
326 Rich Monteleone	.05
327 Mark Carreon	.05
328 Donn Pall	.05
329 Matt Walbeck (Future Star)	.05
330 Charles Nagy	.05
331 Jeff McKnight	.05
332 Jose Lind	.05
333 Mike Timlin	.05
334 Doug Jones	.05
335 Kevin Mitchell	.05
336 Luis Lopez	.05
337 Shane Mack	.05
338 Randy Tomlin	.05
339 Matt Mieske	.05
340 Mark McGwire	.85
341 Nigel Wilson (Future Star)	.05
342 Danny Gladden	.05
343 Mo Sanford	.05
344 Sean Berry	.05
345 Kevin Brown	.05
346 Greg Olson	.05
347 Dave Magadan	.05
348 Rene Arocha	.05
349 Carlos Quintana	.05
350 Jim Abbott	.05
351 Gary DiSarcina	.05
352 Ben Rivera	.05
353 Carlos Hernandez	.05
354 Darren Lewis	.05
355 Harold Reynolds	.05
356 Scott Ruffcorn (Future Star)	.05
357 Mark Gubicza	.05
358 Paul Sorrento	.05
359 Anthony Young	.05
360 Mark Grace	.05
361 Rob Butler	.05
362 Kevin Bass	.05
363 Eric Helfand (Future Star)	.05
364 Derek Bell	.05
365 Scott Erickson	.05
366 Al Martin	.05

No.	Player	Price
367	Ricky Bones	.05
368	Jeff Branson	.05
369	3B Prospects (Luis Ortiz, David Bell, Jason Giambi, George Arias RC)	.30
370a	Benny Santiago	.05
370b	Mark McLemore (Originally checklisted as #379.)	.05
371	John Doherty	.05
372	Joe Girardi	.05
373	Tim Scott	.05
374	Marvin Freeman	.05
375	Deion Sanders	.10
376	Roger Salkeld	.05
377	Bernard Gilkey	.05
378	Tony Fossas	.05
380	Darren Daulton	.05
381	Chuck Finley	.05
382	Mitch Webster	.05
383	Gerald Williams	.05
384	Frank Thomas, Fred McGriff/AS	.30
385	Roberto Alomar, Robby Thompson/AS	.05
386	Wade Boggs, Matt Williams/AS	.35
387	Cal Ripken, Jr., Jeff Blauser/AS	.50
388	Ken Griffey Jr., Len Dykstra/AS	.40
389	Juan Gonzalez, Dave Justice/AS	.10
390	Albert Belle, Barry Bonds/AS	.45
391	Mike Stanley, Mike Piazza/AS	.45
392	Jack McDowell, Greg Maddux/AS	.35
393	Jimmy Key, Tom Glavine/AS	.05
394	Jeff Montgomery, Randy Myers/AS	.05
395	Checklist 1	.05
396	Checklist 2	.05
397	Tim Salmon (All-Star Rookie)	.10
398	Todd Benzinger	.05
399	Frank Castillo	.05
400	Ken Griffey Jr.	.75
401	John Kruk	.05
402	Dave Telgheder	.05
403	Gary Gaetti	.05
404	Jim Edmonds	.05
405	Don Slaught	.05
406	Jose Oquendo	.05
407	Bruce Ruffin	.05
408	Phil Clark	.05
409	Joe Klink	.05
410	Lou Whitaker	.05
411	Kevin Seitzer	.05
412	Darrin Fletcher	.05
413	Kenny Rogers	.05
414	Bill Pecota	.05
415	Dave Fleming	.05
416	Luis Alicea	.05
417	Paul Quantrill	.05
418	Damion Easley	.05
419	Wes Chamberlain	.05
420	Harold Baines	.05
421	Scott Radinsky	.05
422	Rey Sanchez	.05
423	Junior Ortiz	.05
424	Jeff Kent	.05
425	Brian McRae	.05
426	Ed Sprague	.05
427	Tom Edens	.05
428	Willie Greene	.05
429	Bryan Hickerson	.05
430	Dave Winfield	.50
431	Pedro Astacio	.05
432	Mike Gallego	.05
433	Dave Burba	.05
434	Bob Walk	.05
435	Darryl Hamilton	.05
436	Vince Horsman	.05
437	Bob Natal	.05
438	Mike Henneman	.05
439	Willie Blair	.05
440	Denny Martinez	.05
441	Dan Peltier	.05
442	Tony Tarasco	.05
443	John Cummings	.05
444	Geronimo Pena	.05
445	Aaron Sele	.05
446	Stan Javier	.05
447	Mike Williams	.05
448	1B Prospects (Greg Pirkl, Roberto Petagine, D.J. Boston, Shawn Wooten)	.05
449	Jim Poole	.05
450	Carlos Baerga	.05
451	Bob Scanlan	.05
452	Lance Johnson	.05
453	Eric Hillman	.05
454	Keith Miller	.05
455	Dave Stewart	.05
456	Pete Harnisch	.05
457	Roberto Kelly	.05
458	Tim Worrell	.05
459	Pedro Munoz	.05
460	Orel Hershiser	.05
461	Randy Velarde	.05
462	Trevor Wilson	.05
463	Jerry Goff	.05
464	Bill Wegman	.05
465	Dennis Eckersley	.40
466	Jeff Conine (All-Star Rookie)	.05
467	Joe Boever	.05
468	Dante Bichette	.05
469	Jeff Shaw	.05
470	Rafael Palmeiro	.40
471	Phil Leftwich RC	.05
472	Jay Buhner	.05
473	Bob Tewksbury	.05
474	Tim Naehring	.05
475	Tom Glavine	.25
476	Dave Hollins	.05
477	Arthur Rhodes	.05
478	Joey Cora	.05
479	Mike Morgan	.05
480	Albert Belle	.25
481	John Franco	.05
482	Hipolito Pichardo	.05
483	Duane Ward	.05
484	Luis Gonzalez	.05
485	Joe Oliver	.05
486	Wally Whitehurst	.05
487	Mike Benjamin	.05
488	Eric Davis	.05
489	Scott Kamieniecki	.05
490	Kent Hrbek	.05
491	John Hope RC	.05
492	Jesse Orosco	.05
493	Troy Neel	.05
494	Ryan Bowen	.05
495	Mickey Tettleton	.05
496	Chris Jones	.05
497	John Wetteland	.05
498	David Hulse	.05
499	Greg Maddux	.60
500	Bo Jackson	.10
501	Donovan Osborne	.05
502	Mike Greenwell	.05
503	Steve Frey	.05
504	Jim Eisenreich	.05
505	Robby Thompson	.05
506	Leo Gomez	.05
507	Dave Staton	.05
508	Wayne Kirby (All-Star Rookie)	.05
509	Tim Bogar	.05
510	David Cone	.05
511	Devon White	.05
512	Xavier Hernandez	.05
513	Tim Costo	.05
514	Gene Harris	.05
515	Jack McDowell	.05
516	Kevin Gross	.05
517	Scott Leius	.05
518	Lloyd McClendon	.05
519	Alex Diaz RC	.05
520	Wade Boggs	.60
521	Bob Welch	.05
522	Henry Cotto	.05
523	Mike Moore	.05
524	Tim Laker	.05
525	Andres Galarraga	.05
526	Jamie Moyer	.05
527	2B Prospects (Norberto Martin, Ruben Santana, Jason Hardtke, Chris Sexton)	.05
528	Sid Bream	.05
529	Erik Hanson	.05
530	Ray Lankford	.05
531	Rob Deer	.05
532	Rod Correia	.05
533	Roger Mason	.05
534	Mike Devereaux	.05
535	Jeff Montgomery	.05
536	Dwight Smith	.05
537	Jeremy Hernandez	.05
538	Ellis Burks	.05
539	Bobby Jones	.05
540	Paul Molitor	.50
541	Jeff Juden	.05
542	Chris Sabo	.05
543	Larry Casian	.05
544	Jeff Gardner	.05
545	Ramon Martinez	.05
546	Paul O'Neill	.05
547	Steve Hosey	.05
548	Dave Nilsson	.05
549	Ron Darling	.05
550	Matt Williams	.05
551	Jack Armstrong	.05
552	Bill Krueger	.05
553	Freddie Benavides	.05
554	Jeff Fassero	.05
555	Chuck Knoblauch	.05
556	Guillermo Velasquez	.05
557	Joel Johnston	.05
558	Tom Lampkin	.05
559	Todd Van Poppel	.05
560	Gary Sheffield	.30
561	Skeeter Barnes	.05
562	Darren Holmes	.05
563	John Vander Wal	.05
564	Mike Ignasiak	.05
565	Fred McGriff	.30
566	Luis Polonia	.05
567	Mike Perez	.05
568	John Valentin	.05
569	Mike Felder	.05
570	Tommy Greene	.05
571	David Segui	.05
572	Roberto Hernandez	.05
573	Steve Wilson	.05
574	Willie McGee	.05
575	Randy Myers	.05
576	Darrin Jackson	.05
577	Eric Plunk	.05
578	Mike MacFarlane	.05
579	Doug Brocail	.05
580	Steve Finley	.05
581	John Roper	.05
582	Danny Cox	.05
583	Chip Hale	.05
584	Scott Bullett	.05
585	Kevin Reimer	.05
586	Brent Gates	.05
587	Matt Turner	.05
588	Rich Rowland	.05
589	Kent Bottenfield	.05
590	Marquis Grissom	.05
591	Doug Strange	.05
592	Jay Howell	.05
593	Omar Vizquel	.05
594	Rheal Cormier	.05
595	Andre Dawson	.25
596	Hilly Hathaway	.05
597	Todd Pratt	.05
598	Mike Mussina	.30
599	Alex Fernandez	.05
600	Don Mattingly	.65
601	Frank Thomas (Measures of Greatness)	.25
602	Ryne Sandberg (Measures of Greatness)	.30
603	Wade Boggs (Measures of Greatness)	.30
604	Cal Ripken, Jr. (Measures of Greatness)	.50
605	Barry Bonds (Measures of Greatness)	.50
606	Ken Griffey Jr. (Measures of Greatness)	.40
607	Kirby Puckett (Measures of Greatness)	.35
608	Darren Daulton (Measures of Greatness)	.05
609	Paul Molitor (Measures of Greatness)	.25
610	Terry Steinbach	.05
611	Todd Worrell	.05
612	Jim Thome	.40
613	Chuck McElroy	.05
614	John Habyan	.05
615	Sid Fernandez	.05
616	OF Prospects (Eddie Zambrano, Glenn Murray, Chad Mottola, Jermaine Allensworth RC)	.05
617	Steve Bedrosian	.05
618	Rob Ducey	.05
619	Tom Browning	.05
620	Tony Gwynn	.60
621	Carl Willis	.05
622	Kevin Young	.05
623	Rafael Novoa	.05
624	Jerry Browne	.05
625	Charlie Hough	.05
626	Chris Gomez	.05
627	Steve Reed	.05
628	Kirk Rueter	.05
629	Matt Whiteside	.05
630	Dave Justice	.05
631	Brad Holman	.05
632	Brian Jordan	.05
633	Scott Bankhead	.05
634	Torey Lovullo	.05
635	Len Dykstra	.05
636	Ben McDonald	.05
637	Steve Howe	.05
638	Jose Vizcaino	.05
639	Bill Swift	.05
640	Darryl Strawberry	.05
641	Steve Farr	.05
642	Tom Kramer	.05
643	Joe Orsulak	.05
644	Tom Henke	.05
645	Joe Carter	.05
646	Ken Caminiti	.05
647	Reggie Sanders	.05
648	Andy Ashby	.05
649	Derek Parks	.05
650	Andy Van Slyke	.05
651	Juan Bell	.05
652	Roger Smithberg	.05
653	Chuck Carr	.05
654	Bill Gullickson	.05
655	Charlie Hayes	.05
656	Chris Nabholz	.05
657	Karl Rhodes	.05
658	Pete Smith	.05
659	Bret Boone	.05
660	Gregg Jefferies	.05
661	Bob Zupcic	.05
662	Steve Sax	.05
663	Mariano Duncan	.05
664	Jeff Tackett	.05
665	Mark Langston	.05
666	Steve Buechele	.05
667	Candy Maldonado	.05
668	Woody Williams	.05
669	Tim Wakefield	.05
670	Danny Tartabull	.05
671	Charlie O'Brien	.05
672	Felix Jose	.05
673	Bobby Ayala	.05
674	Scott Servais	.05
675	Roberto Alomar	.15
676	Pedro Martinez	.05
677	Eddie Guardado	.05
678	Mark Lewis	.05
679	Jaime Navarro	.05
680	Ruben Sierra	.10
681	Rick Renteria	.05
682	Storm Davis	.05
683	Cory Snyder	.05
684	Ron Karkovice	.05
685	Juan Gonzalez	.25
686	C Prospects (Chris Howard, Carlos Delgado, Jason Kendall, Paul Bako)	.40
687	John Smoltz	.05
688	Brian Dorsett	.05
689	Omar Olivares	.05
690	Mo Vaughn	.05
691	Joe Grahe	.05
692	Mickey Morandini	.05
693	Tino Martinez	.05
694	Brian Barnes	.05
695	Mike Stanley	.05
696	Mark Clark	.05
697	Dave Hansen	.05
698	Willie Wilson	.05
699	Pete Schourek	.05
700	Barry Bonds	1.00
701	Kevin Appier	.05
702	Tony Fernandez	.05
703	Darryl Kile	.05
704	Archi Cianfrocco	.05
705	Jose Rijo	.05
706	Brian Harper	.05
707	Zane Smith	.05
708	Dave Henderson	.05
709	Angel Miranda	.05
710	Orestes Destrade	.05
711	Greg Gohr	.05
712	Eric Young	.05
713	P Prospects (Todd Williams, Ron Watson, Kirk Bullinger, Mike Welch)	.05
714	Tim Spehr	.05
715	Hank Aaron (20th Anniversary #715)	.50
716	Nate Minchey	.05
717	Mike Blowers	.05
718	Kent Mercker	.05
719	Tom Pagnozzi	.05
720	Roger Clemens	.65
721	Eduardo Perez	.05
722	Milt Thompson	.05
723	Gregg Olson	.05
724	Kirk McCaskill	.05
725	Sammy Sosa	.60
726	Alvaro Espinoza	.05
727	Henry Rodriguez	.05
728	Jim Leyritz	.05
729	Steve Scarsone	.05
730	Bobby Bonilla	.05
731	Chris Gwynn	.05
732	Al Leiter	.05
733	Bip Roberts	.05
734	Mark Portugal	.05
735	Terry Pendleton	.05
736	Dave Valle	.05
737	Paul Kilgus	.05
738	Greg Harris	.05
739	Jon Ratliff RC (Draft Pick)	.05
740	Kirk Presley RC (Draft Pick)	.05
741	Josue Estrada RC (Draft Pick)	.05
742	Wayne Gomes RC (Draft Pick)	.10
743	Pat Watkins RC (Draft Pick)	.05
744	Jamey Wright RC (Draft Pick)	.05
745	Jay Powell RC (Draft Pick)	.05
746	Ryan McGuire RC (Draft Pick)	.05
747	Marc Barcelo RC (Draft Pick)	.05
748	Sloan Smith RC (Draft Pick)	.05
749	John Wasdin RC (Draft Pick)	.05
750	Marc Valdes (Draft Pick)	.05
751	Dan Ehler RC (Draft Pick)	.05
752	Andre King RC (Draft Pick)	.05
753	Greg Keagle RC (Draft Pick)	.05
754	Jason Myers RC (Draft Pick)	.05
755	Dax Winslett RC (Draft Pick)	.05
756	Casey Whitten RC (Draft Pick)	.05
757	Tony Fuduric RC (Draft Pick)	.05
758	Greg Norton RC (Draft Pick)	.05
759	Jeff D'Amico RC (Draft Pick)	.05
760	Ryan Hancock RC (Draft Pick)	.05
761	David Cooper RC (Draft Pick)	.05
762	Kevin Orie RC (Draft Pick)	.05
763	John O'Donoghue, Mike Oquist (Coming Attractions)	.05
764	Cory Bailey, Scott Hatteberg (Coming Attractions)	.05
765	Mark Holzemer, Paul Swingle (Coming Attractions)	.05
766	James Baldwin, Rod Bolton (Coming Attractions)	.05
767	Jerry DiPoto RC, Julian Tavarez RC (Coming Attractions)	.10
768	Danny Bautista, Sean Bergman (Coming Attractions)	.05
769	Bob Hamelin, Joe Vitiello (Coming Attractions)	.05
770	Mark Kiefer, Troy O'Leary (Coming Attractions)	.05
771	Denny Hocking, Oscar Munoz (Coming Attractions)	.05
772	Russ Davis, Brien Taylor (Coming Attractions)	.05
773	Kurt Abbott, Miguel Jimenez (Coming Attractions)	.05
774	Kevin King, Eric Plantenberg (Coming Attractions)	.05
775	Jon Shave, Desi Wilson (Coming Attractions)	.05
776	Domingo Cedeno, Paul Spoljaric (Coming Attractions)	.05
777	Chipper Jones, Ryan Klesko (Coming Attractions)	.75
778	Steve Trachsel, Turk Wendell (Coming Attractions)	.05
779	Johnny Ruffin, Jerry Spradlin (Coming Attractions)	.05
780	Jason Bates, John Burke (Coming Attractions)	.05
781	Carl Everett, Dave Weathers (Coming Attractions)	.05
782	Gary Mota, James Mouton (Coming Attractions)	.05
783	Raul Mondesi, Ben Van Ryn (Coming Attractions)	.05
784	Gabe White, Rondell White (Coming Attractions)	.05
785	Brook Fordyce, Bill Pulsipher (Coming Attractions)	.05
786	Kevin Foster, Gene Schall (Coming Attractions)	.05
787	Rich Aude, Midre Cummings (Coming Attractions)	.05
788	Brian Barber, Richard Batchelor (Coming Attractions)	.05
789	Brian Johnson RC, Scott Sanders (Coming Attractions)	.05
790	Rikkert Faneyte, J.R. Phillips (Coming Attractions)	.05
791	Checklist 3	.05
792	Checklist 4	.05

Gold

This premium parallel set was issued as inserts in virtually all forms of Topps packaging. Identical in all other ways to the regular Topps cards, the Gold version replaces the white or black Topps logo on front with a gold-foil "Topps Gold" logo, and prints either the player name or card title in gold foil. The four checklist cards from the regular issue are replaced with cards of players not found in the regular Topps set.

	NM/M
Complete Set (792):	50.00
Common Player:	.15

Black Gold

Black Gold inserts returned for 1994 randomly included in all types of Topps packaging. Single cards, as well as cards redeemable by mail for 11, 22 or 44 Black Gold cards, were produced. The basic single-player card features an action photo, the background of which has been almost completely blacked out. At top is the team name in black letters against a gold prismatic foil background. The player name at bottom is in the same gold foil. On back, bordered in white, is a background which fades from black at top to gray at the bottom and is gridded with white lines. At left is another player action photo. The Topps Black Gold logo and player name appear in gold foil; the latter printed on a simulated wooden board "hanging" from the top of the card. A second hanging plank has player stats and rankings from the 1993 season. The multi-card redemption cards come in two versions. The type found in packs has all 11, 22 or 44 of the cards pictured on front in miniature and redemption details printed on back. A second version, returned with the single cards won, has on back a checklist and non-redemption notice. Stated odds of winning Black Gold cards were one in 72 packs for single cards; one in 180 packs for 11-card winners and one in 720 packs (one per foil-pack case) for a 22-card winner.

	NM/M
Complete Set (44):	10.00
Complete Series 1 (22):	6.00
Complete Series 2 (22):	4.00
Common Player:	.10
1 Roberto Alomar	.20
2 Carlos Baerga	.10
3 Albert Belle	.10
4 Joe Carter	.10
5 Cecil Fielder	.10
6 Travis Fryman	.10
7 Juan Gonzalez	.25
8 Ken Griffey Jr.	.75
9 Chris Hoiles	.10
10 Randy Johnson	.45
11 Kenny Lofton	.45
12 Jack McDowell	.10
13 Paul Molitor	.45
14 Jeff Montgomery	.10
15 John Olerud	.10
16 Rafael Palmeiro	.45
17 Kirby Puckett	.60
18 Cal Ripken, Jr.	1.50
19 Tim Salmon	.10
20 Mike Stanley	.10
21 Frank Thomas	.10
22 Robin Ventura	.10
23 Jeff Bagwell	.45
24 Jay Bell	.10
25 Craig Biggio	.10
26 Jeff Blauser	.10
27 Barry Bonds	1.50
28 Darren Daulton	.10
29 Len Dykstra	.10
30 Andres Galarraga	.10
31 Ron Gant	.10
32 Tom Glavine	.10
33 Mark Grace	.10
34 Marquis Grissom	.10
35 Gregg Jefferies	.10
36 Dave Justice	.10
37 John Kruk	.10
38 Greg Maddux	.60
39 Fred McGriff	.60
40 Randy Myers	.10
41 Mike Piazza	1.00
42 Sammy Sosa	.60
43 Robby Thompson	.10
44 Matt Williams	.10
--- Winner A	.50
--- Winner B	.50
--- Winner C	.50
--- Winner D	.50
--- Winner A/B	.60
--- Winner C/D	.60
--- Winner A/B/C/D	.75

Traded

Topps Traded features top prospects and rookies as well as traded veterans. Also included in the boxed set is an eight-card Topps Finest subset of six MVPs and two Rookie of the Year cards. Regular cards have the same design as the previously released '94 Topps set. "Anatomy of a Trade" is a two-card subset that includes Roberto Kelly/Deion Sanders and Pedro Martinez/Delino DeShields on a split, puzzle-like front. There is also a Prospect card, showcasing a top prospect from AAA, AA and A, as well as a top-rated draft pick. In addition, there are 12 Draft Pick cards included in the Traded set. Finally, two cards pay tribute to Ryne Sandberg, one in a Phillies uniform, one with the Cubs.

		NM/M
Complete Set (140):		25.00
Common Player:		.05
1	Paul Wilson (Draft Pick)	.05
2	Bill Taylor	.05
3	Dan Wilson	.05
4	Mark Smith	.05
5	Toby Borland	.05
6	Dave Clark	.05
7	Denny Martinez	.05
8	Dave Gallagher	.05
9	Josias Manzanillo	.05
10	Brian Anderson	.05
11	Damon Berryhill	.05
12	Alex Cole	.05
13	Jacob Shumate (Draft Pick)	.05
14	Oddibe McDowell	.05
15	Willie Banks	.05
16	Jerry Browne	.05
17	Donnie Elliott	.05
18	Ellis Burks	.05
19	Chuck McElroy	.05
20	Luis Polonia	.05
21	Brian Harper	.05
22	Mark Portugal	.05
23	Dave Henderson	.05
24	Mark Acre	.05
25	Julio Franco	.05
26	Darren Hall	.05
27	Eric Anthony	.05
28	Sid Fernandez	.05
29	Rusty Greer **RC**	.25
30	Riccardo Ingram	.05
31	Gabe White	.05
32	Tim Belcher	.05
33	Terrence Long **RC** (Draft Pick)	.50
34	Mark Dalesandro **RC**	.05
35	Mike Kelly	.05
36	Jack Morris	.05
37	Jeff Brantley	.05
38	Larry Barnes **RC** (Draft Pick)	.05
39	Brian Hunter	.05
40	Otis Nixon	.05
41	Bret Wagner (Draft Pick)	.05
42	Anatomy of a Trade (Pedro Martinez, Delino DeShields)	.25
43	Heathcliff Slocumb	.05
44	Ben Grieve **RC** (Draft Pick)	.25
45	John Hudek	.05
46	Shawon Dunston	.05
47	Greg Colbrunn	.05
48	Joey Hamilton	.05
49	Marvin Freeman	.05
50	Terry Mulholland	.05
51	Keith Mitchell	.05
52	Dwight Smith	.05
53	Shawn Boskie	.05
54	Kevin Witt **RC** (Draft Pick)	.05
55	Ron Gant	.05
56	1994 Prospects (Trenidad Hubbard, Jason Schmidt **RC**, Larry Sutton, Stephen Larkin)	3.00
57	Jody Reed	.05
58	Rick Helling	.05
59	John Powell (Draft Pick)	.05
60	Eddie Murray	.60
61	Joe Hall	.05
62	Jorge Fabregas	.05
63	Mike Mordecai	.05
64	Ed Vosberg	.05
65	Rickey Henderson	.60
66	Tim Grieve (Draft Pick)	.05
67	Jon Lieber	.05
68	Chris Howard	.05
69	Matt Walbeck	.05
70	Chan Ho Park	.15
71	Bryan Eversgerd	.05
72	John Dettmer	.05
73	Erik Hanson	.05
74	Mike Thurman (Draft Pick)	.05
75	Bobby Ayala	.05
76	Rafael Palmeiro	.50
77	Bret Boone	.05
78	Paul Shuey (Future Star)	.05
79	Kevin Foster	.05
80	Dave Magadan	.05
81	Bip Roberts	.05
82	Howard Johnson	.05
83	Xavier Hernandez	.05
84	Ross Powell	.05
85	Doug Million **RC** (Draft Pick)	.05
86	Geronimo Berroa	.05
87	Mark Farris **RC** (Draft Pick)	.05
88	Butch Henry	.05
89	Junior Felix	.05
90	Bo Jackson	.25
91	Hector Carrasco	.05
92	Charlie O'Brien	.05
93	Omar Vizquel	.05
94	David Segui	.05
95	Dustin Hermanson (Draft Pick)	.05
96	Gar Finnvold	.05
97	Dave Stevens	.05
98	Corey Pointer (Draft Pick)	.05
99	Felix Fermin	.05
100	Lee Smith	.05
101	Reid Ryan (Draft Pick)	.15
102	Bobby Munoz	.05
103	Anatomy of a Trade (Deion Sanders, Roberto Kelly)	.05
104	Turner Ward	.05
105	William Van Landingham	.05
106	Vince Coleman	.05
107	Stan Javier	.05
108	Darrin Jackson	.05
109	C.J. Nitkowski (Draft Pick)	.05
110	Anthony Young	.05
111	Kurt Miller	.05
112	Paul Konerko **RC** (Draft Pick)	15.00
113	Walt Weiss	.05
114	Daryl Boston	.05
115	Will Clark	.05
116	Matt Smith **RC** (Draft Pick)	.05
117	Mark Leiter	.05
118	Gregg Olson	.05
119	Tony Pena	.05
120	Jose Vizcaino	.05
121	Rick White	.05
122	Rich Rowland	.05
123	Jeff Reboulet	.05
124	Greg Hibbard	.05
125	Chris Sabo	.05
126	Doug Jones	.05
127	Tony Fernandez	.05
128	Carlos Reyes	.05
129	Kevin Brown (Draft Pick)	.05
130	Commemorative (Ryne Sandberg)	1.00
131	Commemorative (Ryne Sandberg)	1.00
132	Checklist 1-132	.05

Traded Finest Inserts

Eight Finest cards were included in the 1994 Topps Traded set. Cards picture the player on a blue and gold background. Either Rookie of the Year or MVP is printed across the bottom opposite the player's name, indicating the player's candidacy for such an award in 1994. Backs offer a portrait photo, stats through the All-Star break and comments on the player's season to that point.

		NM/M
Complete Set (8):		6.00
Common Player:		.25
1	Greg Maddux	1.50
2	Mike Piazza	2.00
3	Matt Williams	.25
4	Raul Mondesi	.25
5	Ken Griffey Jr.	2.00
6	Kenny Lofton	.25
7	Frank Thomas	1.25
8	Manny Ramirez	.25

Bilingual

Produced in a limited edition said to be 5,000 sets, this issue is a close parallel to the regular 1994 Topps baseball card issue. Each card is virtually identical to the regular Topps card except that backs are printed in English and Spanish. The set was test marketed in areas with a high percentage of Hispanic

population and was also sold through Topps' Stadium Club. The bilingual edition was sold only in factory set form. A special feature of the set was the inclusion of 10 "Topps Leyendas/Legends" cards of former Latin stars.

		NM/M
Factory Set (792+10):		225.00
Common Player:		.50
1	Felipe Alou	3.00
2	Ruben Amaro	1.00
3	Luis Aparicio	7.50
4	Rod Carew	7.50
5	Chico Carrasquel	1.50
6	Orlando Cepeda	7.50
7	Juan Marichal	7.50
8	Minnie Minoso	6.00
9	Cookie Rojas	1.00
10	Luis Tiant	2.00

"1954" Archives

Marketed as "The Ultimate 1954 Series," the Archives set was a virtual reproduction of the popular 1954 Topps issue. Of the 250 cards in the original set, 248 were included in the Archives release. Ted Williams, who was on cards #1 and 250 in the '54 set, was contractually prohibited by Upper Deck from appearing in the Archives issue. Eight "1954 Prospect" cards featuring future Hall of Famers and star players were appended to the reproduction cards to create a 256-card Archives issue. Cards were sold in 12-card packs, with one Gold card in each pack. There were 1,954 personally autographed cards of Henry Aaron inserted at random, along with cards that could be redeemed for genuine 1954 Topps cards and complete sets of Gold Archives cards. The Archives cards were produced in the now-standard 2-1/2" x 3-1/2" size, instead of the original 1954 dimensions of 2-5/8" x 3-3/4". That format allowed the Archives cards to have a white border at top which the originals lack. While the card backs identify the Archives issue, they do not specify a 1994 production date anywhere.

		NM/M
Complete Set (256):		90.00
Common Player:		.25
Wax Pack (12):		4.00
Wax Box (24):		65.00
1	Gus Zernial	.25
2	Monte Irvin	.75
3	Hank Sauer	.25
4	Ed Lopat	.40
5	Pete Runnels	.25
6	Ted Kluszewski	.60
7	Bobby Young	.25
8	Harvey Haddix	.25
9	Jackie Robinson	4.50
10	Paul Smith	.25
11	Del Crandall	.25
12	Billy Martin	.60
13		

14	Preacher Roe	.40
15	Al Rosen	.25
16	Vic Janowicz	.25
17	Phil Rizzuto	1.00
18	Walt Dropo	.25
19	Johnny Lipon	.25
20	Warren Spahn	.75
21	Bobby Shantz	.25
22	Jim Greengrass	.25
23	Luke Easter	.25
24	Granny Hamner	.25
25	Harvey Kuenn	.25
26	Ray Jablonski	.25
27	Ferris Fain	.25
28	Paul Minner	.25
29	Jim Hegan	.25
30	Eddie Mathews	.75
31	Johnny Klippstein	.25
32	Duke Snider	1.50
33	Johnny Schmitz	.25
34	Jim Rivera	.25
35	Junior Gilliam	.40
36	Hoyt Wilhelm	.75
37	Whitey Ford	1.25
38	Eddie Stanky	.25
39	Sherman Lollar	.25
40	Mel Parnell	.25
41	Willie Jones	.25
42	Don Mueller	.25
43	Dick Groat	.25
44	Ned Garver	.25
45	Richie Ashburn	.75
46	Ken Raffensberger	.25
47	Ellis Kinder	.25
48	Billy Hunter	.25
49	Ray Murray	.25
50	Yogi Berra	1.50
51	Johnny Lindell	.25
52	Vic Power	.25
53	Jack Dittmer	.25
54	Vern Stephens	.25
55	Phil Cavarretta	.25
56	Willie Miranda	.40
57	Luis Aloma	.25
58	Bob Wilson	.25
59	Gene Conley	.25
60	Frank Baumholtz	.25
61	Bob Cain	.25
62	Eddie Robinson	.40
63	Johnny Pesky	.25
64	Hank Thompson	.25
65	Bob Swift	.25
66	Ted Lepcio	.25
67	Jim Willis	.25
68	Sam Calderone	.25
69	Bud Podbielan	.25
70	Larry Doby	.75
71	Frank Smith	.25
72	Preston Ward	.25
73	Wayne Terwilliger	.25
74	Bill Taylor	.25
75	Fred Haney	.25
76	Bob Scheffing	.25
77	Ray Boone	.25
78	Ted Kazanski	.25
79	Andy Pafko	.25
80	Jackie Jensen	.25
81	Dave Hoskins	.25
82	Milt Bolling	.25
83	Joe Collins	.40
84	Dick Cole	.25
85	Bob Turley	.75
86	Billy Herman	.40
87	Roy Face	.25
88	Matt Batts	.25
89	Howie Pollet	.25
90	Willie Mays	4.50
91	Bob Oldis	.25
92	Wally Westlake	.25
93	Sid Hudson	.25
94	Ernie Banks	4.50
95	Hal Rice	.25
96	Charlie Silvera	.40
97	Jerry Lane	.25
98	Joe Black	.25
99	Bob Hofman	.25
100	Bob Keegan	.25
101	Gene Woodling	.40
102	Gil Hodges	1.25
103	Jim Lemon	.25
104	Mike Sandlock	.25
105	Andy Carey	.40
106	Dick Kokos	.25
107	Duane Pillette	.25
108	Thornton Kipper	.25
109	Bill Bruton	.25
110	Harry Dorish	.25
111	Jim Delsing	.25
112	Bill Renna	.25
113	Bob Boyd	.25
114	Dean Stone	.25
115	"Rip" Repulski	.25
116	Steve Bilko	.25
117	Solly Hemus	.25
118	Carl Scheib	.25
119	Johnny Antonelli	.25
120	Roy McMillan	.25
121	Clem Labine	.40
122	Johnny Logan	.25
123	Bobby Adams	.25
124	Marion Fricano	.25
125	Harry Perkowski	.25
126	Ben Wade	.25
127	Steve O'Neill	.25
128	Hank Aaron	7.50
129	Forrest Jacobs	.25
130	Hank Bauer	.75
131	Reno Bertoia	.25

132	Tom Lasorda	3.00
133	Del Baker	.25
134	Cal Hogue	.25
135	Joe Presko	.25
136	Connie Ryan	.25
137	Wally Moon	.25
138	Bob Borkowski	.25
139	Ed & Johnny O'Brien	.60
140	Tom Wright	.25
141	Joe Jay	.25
142	Tom Poholsky	.25
143	Rollie Hemsley	.25
144	Bill Werle	.25
145	Elmer Valo	.25
146	Don Johnson	.25
147	John Riddle	.25
148	Bob Trice	.25
149	Jim Robertson	.25
150	Dick Kryhoski	.25
151	Alex Grammas	.25
152	Mike Blyzka	.25
153	Rube Walker	.25
154	Mike Fornieles	.25
155	Bob Kennedy	.40
156	Joe Coleman	.25
157	Don Lenhardt	.25
158	Peanuts Lowrey	.25
159	Dave Philley	.25
160	Red Kress	.25
161	John Hetki	.25
162	Herman Wehmeier	.25
163	Frank House	.25
164	Stu Miller	.25
165	Jim Pendleton	.25
166	Johnny Podres	.40
167	Don Lund	.25
168	Morrie Martin	.25
169	Jim Hughes	.25
170	Dusty Rhodes	.25
171	Leo Kiely	.25
172	Hal Brown	.25
173	Jack Harshman	.25
174	Tom Qualters	.25
175	Frank Leja	.40
176	Bob Keely	.25
177	Bob Milliken	.25
178	Bill Glynn	.25
179	Gair Allie	.25
180	Wes Westrum	.25
181	Mel Roach	.25
182	Chuck Harmon	.25
183	Earle Combs	.25
184	Ed Bailey	.25
185	Chuck Stobbs	.25
186	Karl Olson	.25
187	Heinie Manush	.25
188	Dave Jolly	.25
189	Bob Ross	.25
190	Ray Herbert	.25
191	Dick Schofield	.25
192	Cot Deal	.25
193	Johnny Hopp	.25
194	Bill Sarni	.25
195	Bill Consolo	.25
196	Stan Jok	.25
197	Schoolboy Rowe	.25
198	Carl Sawatski	.25
199	Rocky Nelson	.25
200	Larry Jansen	.25
201	Al Kaline	4.50
202	Bob Purkey	.25
203	Harry Brecheen	.25
204	Angel Scull	.25
205	Johnny Sain	.40
206	Ray Crone	.25
207	Tom Oliver	.25
208	Grady Hatton	.25
209	Charlie Thompson	.25
210	Bob Buhl	.25
211	Don Hoak	.40
212	Mickey Micelotta	.25
213	John Fitzpatrick	.25
214	Arnold Portocarrero	.25
215	Ed McGhee	.25
216	Al Sima	.25
217	Paul Schreiber	.25
218	Fred Marsh	.25
219	Charlie Kress	.25
220	Ruben Gomez	.25
221	Dick Brodowski	.25
222	Bill Wilson	.25
223	Joe Haynes	.25
224	Dick Weik	.25
225	Don Liddle	.25
226	Jehosie Heard	.25
227	Buster Mills	.25
228	Gene Hermanski	.25
229	Bob Talbot	.25
230	Bob Kuzava	.40
231	Roy Smalley	.25
232	Lou Limmer	.25
233	Augie Galan	.25
234	Jerry Lynch	.25
235	Vern Law	.25
236	Paul Penson	.25
237	Mike Ryba	.25
238	Al Aber	.25
239	Bill Skowron	.75
240	Sam Mele	.25
241	Bob Miller	.25
242	Curt Roberts	.25
243	Ray Blades	.25
244	Leroy Wheat	.25
245	Roy Sievers	.25
246	Howie Fox	.25
247	Eddie Mayo	.25
248	Al Smith	.25
249	Wilmer Mizell	.25

251	Roberto Clemente	7.50
252	Bob Grim	.40
253	Elston Howard	.75
254	Harmon Killebrew	1.25
255	Camilo Pascual	.25
256	Herb Score	.25
257	Bill Virdon	.25
258	Don Zimmer	.50

"1954" Archives Gold

Issued as a premium insert at the rate of one per foil pack, gold versions of each of the cards in the 1954 Archives set differ from the regular cards only in that the team logo at top and player facsimile autograph on bottom are printed in gold foil. Redemption cards for complete Archives gold sets were also randomly inserted into Archives packs.

		NM/M
Complete Set (256):		150.00
Common Player:		.45
128	Hank Aaron/Auto.	125.00

1995 Topps Pre-Production

The "Baker's Dozen" version of Topps' 1994 factory baseball card set includes a 10-card pre-production sample of the company's 1995 issue. The sample features nine regular-issue cards and one of them in its Spectralite foil-printed version, as used on the Cyberstats insert cards. Cards are virtually identical to the regular '95 Topps except the backs have a "PP" prefix to the card number and "PRE-PRODUCTION SAMPLE" instead of 1994 season stats.

		NM/M
Complete Set (9):		6.00
Complete Set, Cyberstats (9):		20.00
1	Larry Walker	.50
1	Larry Walker (Spectralite)	1.50
2	Mike Piazza	2.50
2	Mike Piazza (Spectralite)	7.50
3	Greg Vaughn	.50
3	Greg Vaughn (Spectralite)	1.50
4	Sandy Alomar Jr.	.50
4	Sandy Alomar Jr. (Spectralite)	1.50
5	Travis Fryman	.50
5	Travis Fryman (Spectralite)	1.50
6	Ken Griffey Jr.	2.50
6	Ken Griffey Jr. (Spectralite)	7.50
7	Mike Devereaux	.50
7	Mike Devereaux (Spectralite)	1.50
8	Roberto Hernandez	.50
8	Roberto Hernandez (Spectralite)	1.50
9	Alex Fernandez	.50
9	Alex Fernandez (Spectralite)	1.50

1995 Topps

Topps 1995 baseball arrived offering Cyberstats, which projected full-season statistics for the strike shortened year, as well as League Leaders and Stadium Club First Day Issue pre-production inserts. Series 1 comprises 396 cards, including subsets of Draft Picks, Star Tracks, a Babe Ruth commemorative card and the Topps All-Stars, featuring two players per card at each position. Regular cards have a ragged white border around the player photo, with his name in gold foil under the picture. Series 2 concluded the Cyberstats inserts and added 264 cards to the regular set. Subsets in Series 2 include a continuation of the Draft Picks as well as two-player On Deck cards and four-player Prospects cards, arranged by position. Besides the 660 base cards, hobby-version factory sets include 10 Stadium Club 1st Day previews and seven Cyberstat Season in Review cards. Two versions of the retail factory sets were made. One has 660 regular cards, 20 Cyberstats parallels and four League Leader inserts. The other has the base set of 660 plus 10 Opening Day cards and seven Cyberstat Season in Review.

		NM/M
Unopened Hobby Set (677):		100.00
Unopened Retail Set (684):		75.00
Unopened Hobby Set (677):		85.00
Complete Set (660):		45.00
Common Player:		.05
Series 1 or 2 Pack (15):		1.25
Series 1 or 2 Wax Box (36):		25.00

#	Player	Price
1	Frank Thomas	.75
2	Mickey Morandini	.05
3a	Babe Ruth (100th Birthday, no gold "Topps" logo)	2.00
3b	Babe Ruth (100th Birthday, gold "Topps" logo)	2.00
4	Scott Cooper	.05
5	David Cone	.05
6	Jacob Shumate (Draft Pick)	.05
7	Trevor Hoffman	.05
8	Shane Mack	.05
9	Delino DeShields	.05
10	Matt Williams	.05
11	Sammy Sosa	1.00
12	Gary DiSarcina	.05
13	Kenny Rogers	.05
14	Jose Vizcaino	.05
15	Lou Whitaker	.05
16	Ron Darling	.05
17	Dave Nilsson	.05
18	Chris Hammond	.05
19	Sid Bream	.05
20	Denny Martinez	.05
21	Orlando Merced	.05
22	John Wetteland	.05
23	Mike Devereaux	.05
24	Rene Arocha	.05
25	Jay Buhner	.05
26	Darren Holmes	.05
27	Hal Morris	.05
28	Brian Buchanan RC (Draft Pick)	.10
29	Keith Miller	.05
30	Paul Molitor	.75
31	Dave West	.05
32	Tony Tarasco	.05
33	Scott Sanders	.05
34	Eddie Zambrano	.05
35	Ricky Bones	.05
36	John Valentin	.05
37	Kevin Tapani	.05
38	Tim Wallach	.05
39	Darren Lewis	.05
40	Travis Fryman	.05
41	Mark Leiter	.05
42	Jose Bautista	.05
43	Pete Smith	.05
44	Bret Barberie	.05
45	Dennis Eckersley	.65
46	Ken Hill	.05
47	Chad Ogea (Star Track)	.05
48	Pete Harnisch	.05
49	James Baldwin (Future Star)	.05
50	Mike Mussina	.45
51	Al Martin	.05
52	Mark Thompson (Star Track)	.05
53	Matt Smith (Draft Pick)	.05
54	Joey Hamilton (All-Star Rookie)	.05
55	Edgar Martinez	.05
56	John Smiley	.05
57	Rey Sanchez	.05
58	Mike Timlin	.05
59	Ricky Bottalico (Star Track)	.05
60	Jim Abbott	.05
61	Mike Kelly	.05
62	Brian Jordan	.05
63	Ken Ryan	.05
64	Matt Mieske	.05
65	Rick Aguilera	.05
66	Ismael Valdes	.05
67	Royce Clayton	.05
68	Junior Felix	.05
69	Harold Reynolds	.05
70	Juan Gonzalez	.35
71	Kelly Stinnett	.05
72	Carlos Reyes	.05
73	Dave Weathers	.05
74	Mel Rojas	.05
75	Doug Drabek	.05
76	Charles Nagy	.05
77	Tim Raines	.05
78	Midre Cummings	.05
79	1B Prospects (Gene Schall, Scott Talanoa RC, Harold Williams RC, Ray Brown RC)	.05
80	Rafael Palmeiro	.65
81	Charlie Hayes	.05
82	Ray Lankford	.05
83	Tim Davis	.05
84	C.J. Nitkowski (Draft Pick)	.05
85	Andy Ashby	.05
86	Gerald Williams	.05
87	Terry Shumpert	.05
88	Heathcliff Slocumb	.05
89	Domingo Cedeno	.05
90	Mark Grace	.05
91	Brad Woodall RC (Star Track)	.10
92	Gar Finnvold	.05
93	Jaime Navarro	.05
94	Carlos Hernandez	.05
95	Mark Langston	.05
96	Chuck Carr	.05
97	Mike Gardiner	.05
98	David McCarty	.05
99	Cris Carpenter	.05
100	Barry Bonds	2.00
101	David Segui	.05
102	Scott Brosius	.05
103	Mariano Duncan	.05
104	Kenny Lofton	.05
105	Ken Caminiti	.05
106	Darrin Jackson	.05
107	Jim Poole	.05
108	Wil Cordero	.05
109	Danny Miceli	.05
110	Walt Weiss	.05
111	Tom Pagnozzi	.05
112	Terrence Long (Draft Pick)	.05
113	Bret Boone	.05
114	Daryl Boston	.05
115	Wally Joyner	.05
116	Rob Butler	.05
117	Rafael Belliard	.05
118	Luis Lopez	.05
119	Tony Fossas	.05
120	Len Dykstra	.05
121	Mike Morgan	.05
122	Denny Hocking	.05
123	Kevin Gross	.05
124	Todd Benzinger	.05
125	John Doherty	.05
126	Eduardo Perez	.05
127	Dan Smith	.05
128	Joe Orsulak	.05
129	Brent Gates	.05
130	Jeff Conine	.05
131	Doug Henry	.05
132	Paul Sorrento	.05
133	Mike Hampton	.05
134	Tim Spehr	.05
135	Julio Franco	.05
136	Mike Dyer	.05
137	Chris Sabo	.05
138	Rheal Cormier	.05
139	Paul Konerko (Draft Pick)	.25
140	Dante Bichette	.05
141	Chuck McElroy	.05
142	Mike Sanders	.05
143	Bob Hamelin (All-Star Rookie)	.05
144	Tommy Greene	.05
145	John Smoltz	.05
146	Ed Sprague	.05
147	Ray McDavid (Star Track)	.05
148	Otis Nixon	.05
149	Turk Wendell	.05
150	Chris James	.05
151	Derek Parks	.05
152	Jose Offerman	.05
153	Tony Clark (Future Star)	.05
154	Chad Curtis	.05
155	Mark Portugal	.05
156	Bill Pulsipher (Future Star)	.05
157	Troy Neel	.05
158	Dave Winfield	.75
159	Bill Wegman	.05
160	Benny Santiago	.05
161	Jose Mesa	.05
162	Luis Gonzalez	.05
163	Alex Fernandez	.05
164	Freddie Benavides	.05
165	Ben McDonald	.05
166	Blas Minor	.05
167	Bret Wagner (Draft Pick)	.05
168	Mac Suzuki (Future Star)	.05
169	Roberto Mejia	.05
170	Wade Boggs	1.00
171	Calvin Reese (Future Star)	.05
172	Hipolito Pichardo	.05
173	Kim Batiste	.05
174	Darren Hall	.05
175	Tom Glavine	.25
176	Phil Plantier	.05
177	Chris Howard	.05
178	Karl Rhodes	.05
179	LaTroy Hawkins (Future Star)	.05
180	Raul Mondesi (All-Star Rookie)	.05
181	Jeff Reed	.05
182	Milt Cuyler	.05
183	Jim Edmonds	.05
184	Hector Fajardo	.05
185	Jeff Kent	.05
186	Wilson Alvarez	.05
187	Geronimo Berroa	.05
188	Billy Spiers	.05
189	Derek Lilliquist	.05
190	Craig Biggio	.05
191	Roberto Hernandez	.05
192	Bob Natal	.05
193	Bobby Ayala	.05
194	Travis Miller RC (Draft Pick)	.10
195	Bob Tewksbury	.05
196	Rondell White	.05
197	Steve Cooke	.05
198	Jeff Branson	.05
199	Derek Jeter (Future Star)	2.00
200	Tim Salmon	.05
201	Steve Frey	.05
202	Kent Mercker	.05
203	Randy Johnson	.75
204	Todd Worrell	.05
205	Mo Vaughn	.05
206	Howard Johnson	.05
207	John Wasdin (Future Star)	.05
208	Eddie Williams	.05
209	Tim Belcher	.05
210	Jeff Montgomery	.05
211	Kirt Manwaring	.05
212	Ben Grieve (Draft Pick)	.05
213	Pat Hentgen	.05
214	Shawon Dunston	.05
215	Mike Greenwell	.05
216	Alex Diaz	.05
217	Pat Mahomes	.05
218	Dave Hanson	.05
219	Kevin Rogers	.05
220	Cecil Fielder	.05
221	Andrew Lorraine (Star Track)	.05
222	Jack Armstrong	.05
223	Todd Hundley	.05
224	Mark Acre	.05
225	Darrell Whitmore	.05
226	Randy Milligan	.05
227	Wayne Kirby	.05
228	Darryl Kile	.05
229	Bob Zupcic	.05
230	Jay Bell	.05
231	Dustin Hermanson (Draft Pick)	.05
232	Harold Baines	.05
233	Alan Benes (Future Star)	.05
234	Felix Fermin	.05
235	Ellis Burks	.05
236	Jeff Brantley	.05
237	OF Prospects (Brian Hunter, Jose Malave, Shane Pullen, Karim Garcia RC)	.40
238	Matt Nokes	.05
239	Ben Rivera	.05
240	Joe Carter	.05
241	Jeff Granger (Star Track)	.05
242	Terry Pendleton	.05
243	Melvin Nieves	.05
244	Frank Rodriguez (Future Star)	.05
245	Darryl Hamilton	.05
246	Brooks Kieschnick (Future Star)	.05
247	Todd Hollandsworth (Future Star)	.05
248	Joe Rosselli (Future Star)	.05
249	Bill Gullickson	.05
250	Chuck Knoblauch	.05
251	Kurt Miller (Star Track)	.05
252	Bobby Jones	.05
253	Lance Blankenship	.05
254	Matt Whiteside	.05
255	Darrin Fletcher	.05
256	Eric Plunk	.05
257	Shane Reynolds	.05
258	Norberto Martin	.05
259	Mike Thurman (Draft Pick)	.05
260	Andy Van Slyke	.05
261	Dwight Smith	.05
262	Allen Watson	.05
263	Dan Wilson	.05
264	Brent Mayne	.05
265	Bip Roberts	.05
266	Sterling Hitchcock	.05
267	Alex Gonzalez (Star Track)	.05
268	Greg Harris	.05
269	Ricky Jordan	.05
270	Johnny Ruffin	.05
271	Mike Stanton	.05
272	Rich Rowland	.05
273	Steve Trachsel	.05
274	Pedro Munoz	.05
275	Ramon Martinez	.05
276	Dave Henderson	.05
277	Chris Gomez (All-Star Rookie)	.05
278	Joe Grahe	.05
279	Rusty Greer	.05
280	John Franco	.05
281	Mike Bordick	.05
282	Jeff D'Amico (Future Star)	.05
283	Dave Magadan	.05
284	Tony Pena	.05
285	Greg Swindell	.05
286	Doug Million (Draft Pick)	.05
287	Gabe White (Star Track)	.05
288	Trey Beamon (Future Star)	.05
289	Arthur Rhodes	.05
290	Juan Guzman	.05
291	Jose Oquendo	.05
292	Willie Blair	.05
293	Eddie Taubensee	.05
294	Steve Howe	.05
295	Greg Maddux	1.00
296	Mike MacFarlane	.05
297	Curt Schilling	.25
298	Phil Clark	.05
299	Woody Williams	.05
300	Jose Canseco	.40
301	Aaron Sele	.05
302	Carl Willis	.05
303	Steve Buechele	.05
304	Dave Burba	.05
305	Orel Hershiser	.05
306	Damion Easley	.05
307	Mike Henneman	.05
308	Josias Manzanillo	.05
309	Kevin Seitzer	.05
310	Ruben Sierra	.05
311	Bryan Harvey	.05
312	Jim Thome	.45
313	Ramon Castro RC (Draft Pick)	.05
314	Lance Johnson	.05
315	Marquis Grissom	.05
316	SP Prospects (Terrell Wade, Juan Acevedo, Matt Arrandale, Eddie Priest RC)	.05
317	Paul Wagner	.05
318	Jamie Moyer	.05
319	Todd Zeile	.05
320	Chris Bosio	.05
321	Steve Reed	.05
322	Erik Hanson	.05
323	Luis Polonia	.05
324	Ryan Klesko	.05
325	Kevin Appier	.05
326	Jim Eisenreich	.05
327	Randy Knorr	.05
328	Craig Shipley	.05
329	Tim Naehring	.05
330	Randy Myers	.05
331	Alex Cole	.05
332	Jim Gott	.05
333	Mike Jackson	.05
334	John Flaherty	.05
335	Chili Davis	.05
336	Benji Gil (Star Track)	.05
337a	Jason Jacome (No Diamond Vision logo on back photo.)	.25
337b	Jason Jacome (Diamond Vision logo on back photo.)	.05
338	Stan Javier	.05
339	Mike Fetters	.05
340	Rick Renteria	.05
341	Kevin Witt (Draft Pick)	.05
342	Scott Servais	.05
343	Craig Grebeck	.05
344	Kirk Rueter	.05
345	Don Slaught	.05
346	Armando Benitez RC (Star Track)	.15
347	Ozzie Smith	1.00
348	Mike Blowers	.05
349	Armando Reynoso	.05
350	Barry Larkin	.05
351	Mike Williams	.05
352	Scott Kamieniecki	.05
353	Gary Gaetti	.05
354	Todd Stottlemyre	.05
355	Fred McGriff	.05
356	Tim Mauser	.05
357	Chris Gwynn	.05
358	Frank Castillo	.05
359	Jeff Reboulet	.05
360	Roger Clemens	1.00
361	Mark Carreon	.05
362	Chad Kreuter	.05
363	Mark Farris (Draft Pick)	.05
364	Bob Welch	.05
365	Dean Palmer	.05
366	Jeromy Burnitz	.05
367	B.J. Surhoff	.05
368	Mike Butcher	.05
369	RP Prospects (Brad Clontz, Steve Phoenix, Scott Gentile, Bucky Buckles)	.05
370	Eddie Murray	.75
371	Orlando Miller (Star Track)	.05
372	Ron Karkovice	.05
373	Richie Lewis	.05
374	Lenny Webster	.05
375	Jeff Tackett	.05
376	Tom Urbani	.05
377	Tino Martinez	.05
378	Mark Dewey	.05
379	Charlie O'Brien	.05
380	Terry Mulholland	.05
381	Thomas Howard	.05
382	Chris Haney	.05
383	Billy Hatcher	.05
384	Jeff Bagwell, Frank Thomas/AS	.45
385	Bret Boone, Carlos Baerga/AS	.05
386	Matt Williams, Wade Boggs/AS	.30
387	Wil Cordero, Cal Ripken Jr./AS	1.00
388	Barry Bonds, Ken Griffey Jr./AS	1.00
389	Tony Gwynn, Albert Belle/AS	.50
390	Dante Bichette, Kirby Puckett/AS	.50
391	Mike Piazza, Mike Stanley/AS	.75
392	Greg Maddux, David Cone/AS	.50
393	Danny Jackson, Jimmy Key/AS	.05
394	John Franco, Lee Smith/AS	.05
395	Checklist 1-198	.05
396	Checklist 199-396	.05
397	Ken Griffey Jr.	1.25
398	Rick Heiserman RC (Draft Pick)	.05
399	Don Mattingly	1.00
400	Henry Rodriguez	.05
401	Lenny Harris	.05
402	Ryan Thompson	.05
403	Darren Oliver	.05
404	Omar Vizquel	.05
405	Jeff Bagwell	.75
406	Doug Webb RC (Draft Pick)	.05
407	Todd Van Poppel	.05
408	Leo Gomez	.05
409	Mark Whiten	.05
410	Pedro Martinez	.05
411	Reggie Sanders	.05
412	Kevin Foster	.05
413	Danny Tartabull	.05
414	Jeff Blauser	.05
415	Mike Magnante	.05
416	Tom Candiotti	.05
417	Rod Beck	.05
418	Jody Reed	.05
419	Vince Coleman	.05
420	Danny Jackson	.05
421	Ryan Nye RC (Draft Pick)	.05
422	Larry Walker	.05
423	Russ Johnson (Draft Pick)	.05
424	Pat Borders	.05
425	Lee Smith	.05
426	Paul O'Neill	.05
427	Devon White	.05
428	Jim Bullinger	.05
429	SP Prospects (Greg Hansell, Brian Sackinsky, Carey Paige, Rob Welch)	.05
430	Steve Avery	.05
431	Tony Gwynn	1.00
432	Pat Meares	.05
433	Bill Swift	.05
434	David Wells	.05
435	John Briscoe	.05
436	Roger Pavlik	.05
437	Jayson Peterson RC (Draft Pick)	.05
438	Roberto Alomar	.15
439	Billy Brewer	.05
440	Gary Sheffield	.40
441	Lou Frazier	.05
442	Terry Steinbach	.05
443	Jay Payton RC (Draft Pick)	.25
444	Jason Bere	.05
445	Denny Neagle	.05
446	Andres Galarraga	.05
447	Hector Carrasco	.05
448	Bill Risley	.05
449	Andy Benes	.05
450	Jim Leyritz	.05
451	Jose Oliva	.05
452	Greg Vaughn	.05
453	Rich Monteleone	.05
454	Tony Eusebio	.05
455	Chuck Finley	.05
456	Kevin Brown	.05
457	Joe Boever	.05
458	Bobby Munoz	.05
459	Bret Saberhagen	.05
460	Kurt Abbott	.05
461	Bobby Witt	.05
462	Cliff Floyd	.05
463	Mark Clark	.05
464	Andujar Cedeno	.05
465	Marvin Freeman	.05
466	Mike Piazza	1.25
467	Willie Greene	.05
468	Pat Kelly	.05
469	Carlos Delgado	.40
470	Willie Banks	.05
471	Matt Walbeck	.05
472	Mark McGwire	1.50
473	McKay Christensen (Draft Pick)	.05
474	Alan Trammell	.05
475	Tom Gordon	.05
476	Greg Colbrunn	.05
477	Darren Daulton	.05
478	Albie Lopez	.05
479	Robin Ventura	.05
480	C Prospects (Eddie Perez RC, Jason Kendall, Einar Diaz RC, Bret Hemphill)	.20
481	Bryan Eversgerd	.05
482	Dave Fleming	.05
483	Scott Livingstone	.05
484	Pete Schourek	.05
485	Bernie Williams	.05
486	Mark Lemke	.05
487	Eric Karros	.05
488	Scott Ruffcorn	.05
489	Billy Ashley	.05
490	Rico Brogna	.05
491	John Burkett	.05
492	Cade Gaspar RC (Draft Pick)	.05
493	Jorge Fabregas	.05
494	Greg Gagne	.05
495	Doug Jones	.05
496	Troy O'Leary	.05
497	Pat Rapp	.05
498	Butch Henry	.05
499	John Olerud	.05
500	John Hudek	.05
501	Jeff King	.05
502	Bobby Bonilla	.05
503	Albert Belle	.05
504	Rick Wilkins	.05
505	John Jaha	.05
506	Nigel Wilson	.05
507	Sid Fernandez	.05
508	Deion Sanders	.05
509	Gil Heredia	.05
510	Scott Elarton RC (Draft Pick)	.10
511	Melido Perez	.05
512	Greg McMichael	.05
513	Rusty Meacham	.05
514	Shawn Green	.35
515	Carlos Garcia	.05
516	Dave Stevens	.05
517	Eric Young	.05
518	Omar Daal	.05
519	Kirk Gibson	.05
520	Spike Owen	.05
521	Jacob Cruz RC (Draft Pick)	.05
522	Sandy Alomar	.05
523	Steve Bedrosian	.05
524	Ricky Gutierrez	.05
525	Dave Veres	.05
526	Gregg Jefferies	.05
527	Jose Valentin	.05
528	Robb Nen	.05
529	Jose Rijo	.05
530	Sean Berry	.05
531	Mike Gallego	.05
532	Roberto Kelly	.05
533	Kevin Stocker	.05
534	Kirby Puckett	1.00
535	Chipper Jones	1.00
536	Russ Davis	.05
537	Jon Lieber	.05
538	Trey Moore RC (Draft Pick)	.05
539	Joe Girardi	.05
540	2B Prospects (Quilvio Veras, Arquimedez Pozo, Miguel Cairo, Jason Camilli)	.05
541	Tony Phillips	.05
542	Brian Anderson	.05
543	Ivan Rodriguez	.65
544	Jeff Cirillo	.05
545	Joey Cora	.05
546	Chris Hoiles	.05
547	Bernard Gilkey	.05
548	Mike Lansing	.05
549	Jimmy Key	.05
550	Mark Wohlers	.05
551	Chris Clemons RC (Draft Pick)	.05
552	Vinny Castilla	.05
553	Mark Guthrie	.05
554	Mike Lieberthal	.05
555	Tommy Davis RC (Draft Pick)	.05
556	Robby Thompson	.05
557	Danny Bautista	.05
558	Will Clark	.05
559	Rickey Henderson	.75
560	Todd Jones	.05
561	Jack McDowell	.05
562	Carlos Rodriguez	.05
563	Mark Eichhorn	.05
564	Jeff Nelson	.05
565	Eric Anthony	.05
566	Randy Velarde	.05
567	Javy Lopez	.05
568	Kevin Mitchell	.05
569	Steve Karsay	.05
570	Brian Meadows RC (Draft Pick)	.10
571	SS Prospects (Rey Ordonez RC, Mike Metcalfe, Ray Holbert, Kevin Orie)	.40

572	John Kruk	.05
573	Scott Leius	.05
574	John Patterson	.05
575	Kevin Brown	.05
576	Mike Moore	.05
577	Manny Ramirez	.75
578	Jose Lind	.05
579	Derrick May	.05
580	Cal Eldred	.05
581	3B Prospects (David Bell, Joel Chelmis, Lino Diaz, Aaron Boone RC)	.15
582	J.T. Snow	.05
583	Luis Sojo	.05
584	Moises Alou	.05
585	Dave Clark	.05
586	Dave Hollins	.05
587	Nomar Garciaparra (Draft Pick)	2.00
588	Cal Ripken Jr.	2.00
589	Pedro Astacio	.05
590	J.R. Phillips	.05
591	Jeff Frye	.05
592	Bo Jackson	.10
593	Steve Ontiveros	.05
594	David Nied	.05
595	Brad Ausmus	.05
596	Carlos Baerga	.05
597	James Mouton	.05
598	Ozzie Guillen	.05
599	OF Prospects (Ozzie Timmons, Curtis Goodwin, Johnny Damon, Jeff Abbott RC)	.25
600	Yorkis Perez	.05
601	Rich Rodriguez	.05
602	Mark McLemore	.05
603	Jeff Fassero	.05
604	John Roper	.05
605	Mark Johnson RC (Draft Pick)	.10
606	Wes Chamberlain	.05
607	Felix Jose	.05
608	Tony Longmire	.05
609	Duane Ward	.05
610	Brett Butler	.05
611	William Van Landingham	.05
612	Mickey Tettleton	.05
613	Brady Anderson	.05
614	Reggie Jefferson	.05
615	Mike Kingery	.05
616	Derek Bell	.05
617	Scott Erickson	.05
618	Bob Wickman	.05
619	Phil Leftwich	.05
620	Dave Justice	.05
621	Paul Wilson (Draft Pick)	.05
622	Pedro Martinez	.75
623	Terry Mathews	.05
624	Brian McRae	.05
625	Bruce Ruffin	.05
626	Steve Finley	.05
627	Ron Gant	.05
628	Rafael Bournigal	.05
629	Darryl Strawberry	.05
630	Luis Alicea	.05
631	Mark Smith, Scott Klingenbeck (On Deck)	.05
632	Cory Bailey, Scott Hatteberg (On Deck)	.05
633	Todd Greene, Troy Percival (On Deck)	.05
634	Rod Bolton, Olmedo Saenz (On Deck)	.05
635	Herb Perry, Steve Kline (On Deck)	.05
636	Sean Bergman, Shannon Penn (On Deck)	.05
637	Joe Vitiello, Joe Randa (On Deck)	.05
638	Jose Mercedes, Duane Singleton (On Deck)	.05
639	Marty Cordova, Marc Barcelo (On Deck)	.10
640	Ruben Rivera, Andy Pettitte (On Deck)	.10
641	Willie Adams, Scott Spiezio (On Deck)	.05
642	Eddie Diaz, Desi Relaford (On Deck)	.05
643	Jon Shave, Terrell Lowery (On Deck)	.05
644	Paul Spoljaric, Angel Martinez (On Deck)	.05
645	Damon Hollins, Tony Graffanino (On Deck)	.05
646	Darron Cox, Doug Glanville (On Deck)	.05
647	Tim Belk, Pat Watkins (On Deck)	.05
648	Rod Pedraza, Phil Schneider (On Deck)	.05
649	Marc Valdes, Vic Darensbourg (On Deck)	.05
650	Rick Huisman, Roberto Petagine (On Deck)	.05
651	Ron Coomer, Roger Cedeno (On Deck)	.05
652	Carlos Perez RC, Shane Andrews (On Deck)	.10
653	Jason Isringhausen, Chris Roberts (On Deck)	.05
654	Kevin Jordan, Wayne Gomes (On Deck)	.05
655	Esteban Loaiza, Steve Pegues (On Deck)	.05
656	John Frascatore, Terry Bradshaw (On Deck)	.05
657	Bryce Florie, Andres Berumen (On Deck)	.05
658	Keith Williams, Dan Carlson (On Deck)	.05
659	Checklist	.05
660	Checklist	.05

Cyberstats

2B/OF — SAN DIEGO PADRES

Inserted into all types of Topps packaging at the rate of about one per 15 cards, this special series attempted to "complete" the statistics from the strike-shortened 1994 baseball season for nearly 400 players. Topps used computer modeling to predict how each player would have ended the season. Fronts of the cards are the same as found in the regular Topps set, except they have been printed on metallic foil. Backs have a black background.

		NM/M
Complete Set (396):		25.00
Common Player:		.10
1	Frank Thomas	.75
2	Mickey Morandini	.10
3	Todd Worrell	.10
4	David Cone	.10
5	Trevor Hoffman	.10
6	Shane Mack	.10
7	Delino DeShields	.10
8	Matt Williams	.10
9	Sammy Sosa	1.00
10	Gary DiSarcina	.10
11	Kenny Rogers	.10
12	Jose Vizcaino	.10
13	Lou Whitaker	.10
14	Ron Darling	.10
15	Dave Nilsson	.10
16	Dennis Martinez	.10
17	Orlando Merced	.10
18	John Wetteland	.10
19	Mike Devereaux	.10
20	Rene Arocha	.10
21	Jay Buhner	.10
22	Hal Morris	.10
23	Paul Molitor	.75
24	Dave West	.10
25	Scott Sanders	.10
26	Eddie Zambrano	.10
27	Ricky Bones	.10
28	John Valentin	.10
29	Kevin Tapani	.10
30	Tim Wallach	.10
31	Darren Lewis	.10
32	Travis Fryman	.10
33	Bret Barberie	.10
34	Dennis Eckersley	.65
35	Ken Hill	.10
36	Pete Harnisch	.10
37	Mike Mussina	.50
38	Dave Winfield	.75
39	Joey Hamilton	.10
40	Edgar Martinez	.10
41	John Smiley	.10
42	Jim Abbott	.10
43	Mike Kelly	.10
44	Brian Jordan	.10
45	Ken Ryan	.10
46	Matt Mieske	.10
47	Rick Aguilera	.10
48	Ismael Valdes	.10
49	Royce Clayton	.10
50	Juan Gonzalez	.35
51	Mel Rojas	.10
52	Doug Drabek	.10
53	Charles Nagy	.10
54	Tim Raines	.10
55	Midre Cummings	.10
56	Rafael Palmeiro	.65
57	Charlie Hayes	.10
58	Ray Lankford	.10
59	Tim Davis	.10
60	Andy Ashby	.10
61	Mark Grace	.10
62	Mark Langston	.10
63	Chuck Carr	.10
64	Barry Bonds	2.00
65	David Segui	.10
66	Mariano Duncan	.10
67	Kenny Lofton	.10
68	Ken Caminiti	.10
69	Darrin Jackson	.10
70	Wil Cordero	.10
71	Walt Weiss	.10
72	Tom Pagnozzi	.10
73	Bret Boone	.10
74	Wally Joyner	.10
75	Luis Lopez	.10
76	Len Dykstra	.10
77	Pedro Munoz	.10
78	Kevin Gross	.10
79	Eduardo Perez	.10
80	Brent Gates	.10
81	Jeff Conine	.10
82	Paul Sorrento	.10
83	Julio Franco	.10
84	Chris Sabo	.10
85	Dante Bichette	.10
86	Mike Stanley	.10
87	Bob Hamelin	.10
88	Tommy Greene	.10
89	Jeff Brantley	.10
90	Ed Sprague	.10
91	Otis Nixon	.10
92	Chad Curtis	.10
93	Chuck McElroy	.10
94	Troy Neel	.10
95	Benito Santiago	.10
96	Jose Mesa	.10
97	Luis Gonzalez	.10
98	Alex Fernandez	.10
99	Ben McDonald	.10
100	Wade Boggs	1.00
101	Tom Glavine	.35
102	Phil Plantier	.10
103	Raul Mondesi	.10
104	Jim Edmonds	.10
105	Jeff Kent	.10
106	Wilson Alvarez	.10
107	Geronimo Berroa	.10
108	Craig Biggio	.10
109	Roberto Hernandez	.10
110	Bobby Ayala	.10
111	Bob Tewksbury	.10
112	Rondell White	.10
113	Steve Cooke	.10
114	Tim Salmon	.10
115	Kent Mercker	.10
116	Randy Johnson	.75
117	Mo Vaughn	.10
118	Eddie Williams	.10
119	Jeff Montgomery	.10
120	Kirt Manwaring	.10
121	Pat Hentgen	.10
122	Shawon Dunston	.10
123	Tim Belcher	.10
124	Cecil Fielder	.10
125	Todd Hundley	.10
126	Mark Acre	.10
127	Darrell Whitmore	.10
128	Darryl Kile	.10
129	Jay Bell	.10
130	Harold Baines	.10
131	Felix Fermin	.10
132	Ellis Burks	.10
133	Joe Carter	.10
134	Terry Pendleton	.10
135	Junior Felix	.10
136	Bill Gullickson	.10
137	Melvin Nieves	.10
138	Chuck Knoblauch	.10
139	Bobby Jones	.10
140	Darrin Fletcher	.10
141	Andy Van Slyke	.10
142	Allen Watson	.10
143	Dan Wilson	.10
144	Bip Roberts	.10
145	Sterling Hitchcock	.10
146	Johnny Ruffin	.10
147	Steve Trachsel	.10
148	Ramon Martinez	.10
149	Dave Henderson	.10
150	Chris Gomez	.10
151	Rusty Greer	.10
152	John Franco	.10
153	Mike Bordick	.10
154	Dave Magadan	.10
155	Greg Swindell	.10
156	Arthur Rhodes	.10
157	Juan Guzman	.10
158	Greg Maddux	1.00
159	Mike Macfarlane	.10
160	Curt Schilling	.35
161	Jose Canseco	.40
162	Aaron Sele	.10
163	Steve Buechele	.10
164	Orel Hershiser	.10
165	Mike Henneman	.10
166	Kevin Seitzer	.10
167	Ruben Sierra	.10
168	Alex Cole	.10
169	Jim Thome	.65
170	Lance Johnson	.10
171	Marquis Grissom	.10
172	Jamie Moyer	.10
173	Todd Zeile	.10
174	Chris Bosio	.10
175	Steve Howe	.10
176	Luis Polonia	.10
177	Ryan Klesko	.10
178	Kevin Appier	.10
179	Tim Naehring	.10
180	Randy Myers	.10
181	Mike Jackson	.10
182	Chili Davis	.10
183	Jason Jacome	.10
184	Stan Javier	.10
185	Scott Servais	.10
186	Kirk Rueter	.10
187	Don Slaught	.10
188	Ozzie Smith	1.00
189	Barry Larkin	.10
190	Gary Gaetti	.10
191	Fred McGriff	.10
192	Roger Clemens	1.00
193	Dean Palmer	.10
194	Jeromy Burnitz	.10
195	Scott Kamieniecki	.10
196	Eddie Murray	.75
197	Ron Karkovice	.10
198	Tino Martinez	.10
199	Ken Griffey Jr.	1.25
200	Don Mattingly	1.00
201	Henry Rodriguez	.10
202	Lenny Harris	.10
203	Ryan Thompson	.10
204	Darren Oliver	.10
205	Omar Vizquel	.10
206	Jeff Bagwell	.75
207	Todd Van Poppel	.10
208	Leo Gomez	.10
209	Mark Whiten	.10
210	Pedro Martinez	.10
211	Reggie Sanders	.10
212	Kevin Foster	.10
213	Danny Tartabull	.10
214	Jeff Blauser	.10
215	Mike Magnante	.10
216	Tom Candiotti	.10
217	Rod Beck	.10
218	Jody Reed	.10
219	Vince Coleman	.10
220	Danny Jackson	.10
221	Larry Walker	.10
222	Pat Borders	.10
223	Lee Smith	.10
224	Paul O'Neill	.10
225	Devon White	.10
226	Jim Bullinger	.10
227	Steve Avery	.10
228	Tony Gwynn	1.00
229	Pat Meares	.10
230	Bill Swift	.10
231	David Wells	.10
232	John Briscoe	.10
233	Roger Pavlik	.10
234	Roberto Alomar	.30
235	Billy Brewer	.10
236	Gary Sheffield	.40
237	Lou Frazier	.10
238	Terry Steinbach	.10
239	Omar Daal	.10
240	Jason Bere	.10
241	Denny Neagle	.10
242	Danny Bautista	.10
243	Hector Carrasco	.10
244	Bill Risley	.10
245	Andy Benes	.10
246	Jim Leyritz	.10
247	Jose Oliva	.10
248	Greg Vaughn	.10
249	Rich Monteleone	.10
250	Tony Eusebio	.10
251	Chuck Finley	.10
252	Joe Boever	.10
253	Bobby Munoz	.10
254	Bret Saberhagen	.10
255	Kurt Abbott	.10
256	Bobby Witt	.10
257	Cliff Floyd	.10
258	Mark Clark	.10
259	Andujar Cedeno	.10
260	Marvin Freeman	.10
261	Mike Piazza	1.25
262	Pat Kelly	.10
263	Carlos Delgado	.45
264	Willie Banks	.10
265	Matt Walbeck	.10
266	Mark McGwire	1.50
267	Alan Trammell	.10
268	Tom Gordon	.10
269	Greg Colbrunn	.10
270	Darren Daulton	.10
271	Albie Lopez	.10
272	Robin Ventura	.10
273	Bryan Eversgerd	.10
274	Dave Fleming	.10
275	Scott Livingstone	.10
276	Pete Schourek	.10
277	Bernie Williams	.10
278	Mark Lemke	.10
279	Eric Karros	.10
280	Billy Ashley	.10
281	Rico Brogna	.10
282	John Burkett	.10
283	Jorge Fabregas	.10
284	Greg Gagne	.10
285	Doug Jones	.10
286	Troy O'Leary	.10
287	Pat Rapp	.10
288	Butch Henry	.10
289	John Olerud	.10
290	John Hudek	.10
291	Jeff King	.10
292	Bobby Bonilla	.10
293	Albert Belle	.10
294	Rick Wilkins	.10
295	John Jaha	.10
296	Sid Fernandez	.10
297	Deion Sanders	.10
298	Gil Heredia	.10
299	Melido Perez	.10
300	Greg McMichael	.10
301	Rusty Meacham	.10
302	Shawn Green	.35
303	Carlos Garcia	.10
304	Dave Stevens	.10
305	Eric Young	.10
306	Kirk Gibson	.10
307	Spike Owen	.10
308	Sandy Alomar	.10
309	Ricky Gutierrez	.10
310	Dave Veres	.10
311	Gregg Jefferies	.10
312	Jose Valentin	.10
313	Robb Nen	.10
314	Jose Rijo	.10
315	Sean Berry	.10
316	Mike Gallego	.10
317	Roberto Kelly	.10
318	Kevin Stocker	.10
319	Kirby Puckett	1.00
320	Jon Lieber	.10
321	Joe Girardi	.10
322	Tony Phillips	.10
323	Brian Anderson	.10
324	Ivan Rodriguez	.65
325	Jeff Cirillo	.10
326	Joey Cora	.10
327	Chris Hoiles	.10
328	Bernard Gilkey	.10
329	Mike Lansing	.10
330	Jimmy Key	.10
331	Vinny Castilla	.10
332	Mark Guthrie	.10
333	Mike Lieberthal	.10
334	Will Clark	.10
335	Rickey Henderson	.75
336	Todd Jones	.10
337	Jack McDowell	.10
338	Carlos Rodriguez	.10
339	Mark Eichhorn	.10
340	Jeff Nelson	.10
341	Eric Anthony	.10
342	Randy Velarde	.10
343	Javier Lopez	.10
344	Kevin Mitchell	.10
345	Steve Bedrosian	.10
346	John Kruk	.10
347	Scott Leius	.10
348	John Patterson	.10
349	Kevin Brown	.10
350	Mike Moore	.10
351	Manny Ramirez	.75
352	Jose Lind	.10
353	Derrick May	.10
354	Cal Eldred	.10
355	J.T. Snow	.10
356	Luis Sojo	.10
357	Moises Alou	.10
358	Dave Clark	.10
359	Dave Hollins	.10
360	Cal Ripken Jr.	2.00
361	Pedro Astacio	.10
362	Tony Longmire	.10
363	Jeff Frye	.10
364	Bo Jackson	.20
365	Steve Ontiveros	.10
366	David Nied	.10
367	Brad Ausmus	.10
368	Carlos Baerga	.10
369	James Mouton	.10
370	Ozzie Guillen	.10
371	Yorkis Perez	.10
372	Rich Rodriguez	.10
373	Mark McLemore	.10
374	Jeff Fassero	.10
375	John Roper	.10
376	Wes Chamberlain	.10
377	Felix Jose	.10
378	Brett Butler	.10
379	William Van Landingham	.10
380	Mickey Tettleton	.10
381	Brady Anderson	.10
382	Reggie Jefferson	.10
383	Mike Kingery	.10
384	Derek Bell	.10
385	Scott Erickson	.10
386	Bob Wickman	.10
387	Phil Leftwich	.10
388	Dave Justice	.10
389	Pedro Martinez	.75
390	Terry Mathews	.10
391	Brian McRae	.10
392	Bruce Ruffin	.10
393	Steve Finley	.10
394	Rafael Bournigal	.10
395	Darryl Strawberry	.10
396	Luis Alicea	.10

This special edition of Cyberstat cards was available only in Topps factory sets. Carrying forward the idea of computerized projections to complete the strike-shortened 1994 season, the Season in Review cards speculate on career milestones and the playoffs that never happened. The Season in Review cards have player action photos printed on a foil background resembling the U.S. flag. Names are in gold foil. Backs have a black background and a recap of the computer simulation.

		NM/M
Complete Set (7):		10.00
Common Player:		1.00
1	Barry Bonds (61 Home Runs)	6.00
2	Jose Canseco (AL West One-Game Playoff)	2.00
3	Juan Gonzalez (AL Divisional Playoffs)	1.50
4	Fred McGriff (NL Divisional Playoffs)	1.00
5	Carlos Baerga (ALCS MVP)	1.00
6	Ryan Klesko (NLCS MVP)	1.00
7	Kenny Lofton (World Series MVP)	1.00

League Leaders

STOLEN BASE LEADER — DEION SANDERS

League Leaders is a 50-card insert set found in one of every six retail packs only of both Series I and II. The set includes the top five players in each league across 10 statistical categories. Cards featured the statistical category running up the right side, with the player's name across the bottom. Photo backgrounds have been darkened and posterized to make the player action stand out. Backs have the player's stat rankings within his division and league, and a bar graph at bottom gives his performance in that statistical category for the previous five seasons.

		NM/M
Complete Set (50):		20.00
Common Player:		.15
1	Albert Belle	.15
2	Kevin Mitchell	.15
3	Wade Boggs	1.50
4	Tony Gwynn	1.50
5	Moises Alou	.15
6	Andres Galarraga	.15
7	Matt Williams	.15
8	Barry Bonds	4.00
9	Frank Thomas	.75
10	Jose Canseco	.50
11	Jeff Bagwell	.75
12	Kirby Puckett	1.50
13	Julio Franco	.15
14	Albert Belle	.15
15	Fred McGriff	.15
16	Kenny Lofton	.15
17	Otis Nixon	.15
18	Brady Anderson	.15
19	Deion Sanders	.15
20	Chuck Carr	.15
21	Pat Hentgen	.15
22	Andy Benes	.15
23	Roger Clemens	1.75
24	Greg Maddux	1.50
25	Pedro Martinez	.75
26	Paul O'Neill	.15
27	Jeff Bagwell	.75
28	Frank Thomas	.75
29	Hal Morris	.15
30	Kenny Lofton	.15
31	Ken Griffey Jr.	2.00
32	Jeff Bagwell	.75
33	Albert Belle	.15
34	Fred McGriff	.15
35	Cecil Fielder	.15
36	Matt Williams	.15
37	Joe Carter	.15
38	Dante Bichette	.15

Cyberstat Season in Review

Juan Gonzalez

39 Frank Thomas .75
40 Mike Piazza 2.00
41 Craig Biggio .15
42 Vince Coleman .15
43 Marquis Grissom .15
44 Chuck Knoblauch .15
45 Darren Lewis .15
46 Randy Johnson .75
47 Jose Rijo .15
48 Chuck Finley .15
49 Bret Saberhagen .15
50 Kevin Appier .15

Total Bases Finest

Printed in Topps Finest technology, including a peel-off plastic protector coating on the front, these cards honor the 1994 statistical leaders in total bases. The cards have a silver waffle-texture background on front as a background to the color action photo. At bottom is a team logo and team-color bar with the player's name. Backs feature a portrait photo and the player's total base stats. These inserts are found in Series II Topps packs at an average rate of one per 36 packs (one box).

	NM/M
Complete Set (15):	12.00
Common Player:	.50
1 Jeff Bagwell	1.25
2 Albert Belle	.50
3 Ken Griffey Jr.	2.00
4 Frank Thomas	1.25
5 Matt Williams	.50
6 Dante Bichette	.50
7 Barry Bonds	2.50
8 Moises Alou	.50
9 Andres Galarraga	.50
10 Kenny Lofton	.50
11 Rafael Palmeiro	1.00
12 Tony Gwynn	1.50
13 Kirby Puckett	1.50
14 Jose Canseco	.75
15 Jeff Conine	.50

Traded and Rookies

Traded players, free agents signed by new teams and all the up-and-coming rookies are the meat of the 1995 Topps Traded and Rookies set, sold for the first time exclusively in foil-pack form. Maintaining the same format used in Series 1 and 2 Topps, the updates also reused the Future Star, Draft Pick and Star Track subsets, along with four-player Prospects cards. New subsets included Rookie of the Year Candidates, All-Stars, On Deck and "At the Break," 10 cards chronicling star players' performances through the first half of the 1995 season. A double-thick, foil-printed version of the "At the Break" cards called "Power Boosters" were the only inserts in the Traded/Rookies set.

	NM/M
Complete Set (165):	30.00
Common Player:	.05
Pack (11):	2.50
Wax Box (36):	60.00
1 Frank Thomas (At The Break)	.50
2 Ken Griffey Jr. (At The Break)	.65
3 Barry Bonds (At The Break)	1.00
4 Albert Belle (At The Break)	.05
5 Cal Ripken Jr. (At The Break)	1.00
6 Mike Piazza (At The Break)	.75
7 Tony Gwynn (At The Break)	.60
8 Jeff Bagwell (At The Break)	.45
9 Mo Vaughn (At The Break)	.05
10 Matt Williams (At The Break)	.05
11 Ray Durham	.05
12 Juan LeBron (Photo Carlos Beltran.) RC (Draft Pick)	5.00
13 Shawn Green (Rookie of the Year Candidate)	.50
14 Kevin Gross	.05
15 Jon Nunnally	.05
16 Brian Maxcy RC	.05
17 Mark Kiefer	.05
18 Carlos Beltran RC (Draft Pick)(Photo actually Juan Beltran.)	15.00
19 Mike Mimbs RC	.05
20 Larry Walker	.05
21 Chad Curtis	.05
22 Jeff Barry	.05
23 Joe Oliver	.05
24 Tomas Perez RC	.05
25 Michael Barrett RC (Draft Pick)	1.50
26 Brian McRae	.05
27 Derek Bell	.05
28 Ray Durham (Rookie of the Year Candidate)	.05
29 Todd Williams	.05
30 Ryan Jaroncyk RC (Draft Pick)	.05
31 Todd Steverson	.05
32 Mike Devereaux	.05
33 Rheal Cormier	.05
34 Benny Santiago	.05
35 Bobby Higginson RC	.50
36 Jack McDowell	.05
37 Mike Macfarlane	.05
38 Tony McKnight RC (Draft Pick)	.05
39 Brian Hunter (Rookie of the Year Candidate)	.05
40 Hideo Nomo (Star Track)	2.00
41 Brett Butler	.05
42 Donovan Osborne	.05
43 Scott Karl	.05
44 Tony Phillips	.05
45 Marty Cordova (Rookie of the Year Candidate)	.20
46 Dave Mlicki	.05
47 Bronson Arroyo RC (Draft Pick)	4.00
48 John Burkett	.05
49 J.D. Smart RC (Draft Pick)	.05
50 Mickey Tettleton	.05
51 Todd Stottlemyre	.05
52 Mike Perez	.05
53 Terry Mulholland	.05
54 Edgardo Alfonzo	.05
55 Zane Smith	.05
56 Jacob Brumfield	.05
57 Andujar Cedeno	.05
58 Jose Parra	.05
59 Manny Alexander	.05
60 Tony Tarasco	.05
61 Orel Hershiser	.05
62 Tim Scott	.05
63 Felix Rodriguez RC	.05
64 Ken Hill	.05
65 Marquis Grissom	.05
66 Lee Smith	.05
67 Jason Bates (Rookie of the Year Candidate)	.05
68 Felipe Lira	.05
69 Alex Hernandez RC (Draft Pick)	.10
70 Tony Fernandez	.05
71 Scott Radinsky	.05
72 Jose Canseco	.50
73 Mark Grudzielanek RC	.50
74 Ben Davis RC (Draft Pick)	.05
75 Jim Abbott	.05
76 Roger Bailey	.05
77 Gregg Jefferies	.05
78 Erik Hanson	.05
79 Brad Radke RC	1.50
80 Jaime Navarro	.05
81 John Wetteland	.05
82 Chad Fonville RC	.10
83 John Mabry	.05
84 Glenallen Hill	.05
85 Ken Caminiti	.05
86 Tom Goodwin	.05
87 Darren Bragg	.05
88 1995 Prospects (Pitchers) (Pat Ahearne RC, Gary Rath RC, Larry Wimberly RC, Robbie Bell RC)	.10
89 Jeff Russell	.05
90 Dave Gallagher	.05
91 Steve Finley	.05
92 Vaughn Eshelman	.05
93 Kevin Jarvis	.05
94 Mark Gubicza	.05
95 Tim Wakefield	.05
96 Bob Tewksbury	.05
97 Sid Roberson RC	.05
98 Tom Henke	.05
99 Michael Tucker (Future Star)	.05
100 Jason Bates	.05
101 Otis Nixon	.05
102 Mark Whiten	.05
103 Dilson Torres	.05
104 Melvin Bunch RC	.05
105 Terry Pendleton	.05
106 Corey Jenkins RC (Draft Pick)	.05
107 On Deck (Glenn Dishman RC, Rob Grable RC)	.05
108 Reggie Taylor RC (Draft Pick)	.05
109 Curtis Goodwin (Rookie of the Year Candidate)	.05
110 David Cone	.05
111 Antonio Osuna	.05
112 Paul Shuey	.05
113 Doug Jones	.05
114 Mark McLemore	.05
115 Kevin Ritz	.05
116 John Kruk	.05
117 Trevor Wilson	.05
118 Jerald Clark	.05
119 Julian Tavarez	.05
120 Tim Pugh	.05
121 Todd Zeile	.05
122 1995 Prospects (Fielders) (Mark Sweeney RC, George Arias, Richie Sexson RC, Brian Schneider RC)	4.00
123 Bobby Witt	.05
124 Hideo Nomo (Rookie of the Year Candidate)	1.00
125 Joey Cora	.05
126 Jim Scharrer RC (Draft Pick)	.05
127 Paul Quantrill	.05
128 Chipper Jones (Rookie of the Year Candidate)	.75
129 Kenny James RC (Draft Pick)	.05
130 On Deck (Lyle Mouton, Mariano Rivera)	.15
131 Tyler Green (Rookie of the Year Candidate)	.05
132 Brad Clontz	.05
133 Jon Nunnally (Rookie of the Year Candidate)	.05
134 Dave Magadan	.05
135 Al Leiter	.05
136 Bret Barberie	.05
137 Bill Swift	.05
138 Scott Cooper	.05
139 Roberto Kelly	.05
140 Charlie Hayes	.05
141 Pete Harnisch	.05
142 Rich Amaral	.05
143 Rudy Seanez	.05
144 Pat Listach	.05
145 Quilvio Veras (Rookie of the Year Candidate)	.05
146 Jose Olmeda RC (Draft Pick)	.05
147 Roberto Petagine	.05
148 Kevin Brown	.05
149 Phil Plantier	.05
150 Carlos Perez RC (Rookie of the Year Candidate)	.05
151 Pat Borders	.05
152 Tyler Green	.05
153 Stan Belinda	.05
154 Dave Stewart	.05
155 Andre Dawson	.05
156 Frank Thomas, Fred McGriff/AS	.30
157 Carlos Baerga, Craig Biggio/AS	.05
158 Wade Boggs, Matt Williams/AS	.35
159 Cal Ripken Jr., Ozzie Smith/AS	.75
160 Ken Griffey Jr., Tony Gwynn/AS	.40
161 Albert Belle, Barry Bonds/AS	.75
162 Kirby Puckett, Len Dykstra/AS	.35
163 Ivan Rodriguez, Mike Piazza/AS	.40
164 Randy Johnson, Hideo Nomo/AS	.25
165 Checklist	.05

Traded and Rookies Power Boosters

Virtually identical to the first 10 cards of the 1995 Topps Traded and Rookies issue, the "At the Break" subset is the only insert found in Traded packs. Cards are printed on double-thick cardboard stock on metallized foil. The chase cards are found at an average rate of one per 36 packs.

	NM/M
Complete Set (10):	20.00
Common Player:	.75

1 Frank Thomas	1.50
2 Ken Griffey Jr.	3.00
3 Barry Bonds	5.00
4 Albert Belle	.75
5 Cal Ripken Jr.	5.00
6 Mike Piazza	3.00
7 Tony Gwynn	2.50
8 Jeff Bagwell	1.50
9 Mo Vaughn	.75
10 Matt Williams	.75

Opening Day

This 10-card set featuring top performers on the belated opening day of the 1995 season was available exclusively in retail factory sets. Card fronts feature color action photos printed on textured foil in a U.S. flag-like design. A large colorful Opening Day logo appears in an upper corner while the player's key stats from that game appear in a foil box at lower-right. Backs have a portrait photo along with complete details and a stats line of the opening day performance.

	NM/M
Complete Set (10):	7.50
Common Player:	.75
1 Kevin Appier	.75
2 Dante Bichette	.75
3 Ken Griffey Jr.	3.50
4 Todd Hundley	.75
5 John Jaha	.75
6 Fred McGriff	.75
7 Raul Mondesi	.75
8 Manny Ramirez	2.50
9 Danny Tartabull	.75
10 Devon White	.75

Archives Brooklyn Dodgers

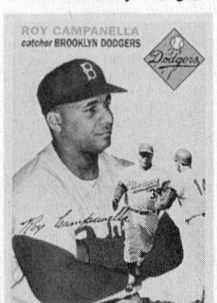

In a departure from its program of complete set reissues, Topps' Archives baseball series for 1995 was a tribute to the 40th anniversary of the Brooklyn Dodgers' 1955 World's Series victory over the archrival Yankees. Besides reprinting all of the Dodgers' cards from the 1952-56 Topps sets and the 1955 Bowman issue, the Archives release included some 30 "cards that never were," done in the styles of the 1952-55 Topps issues.

Those cards are designated with an "N" suffix in parentheses. The old larger format of the vintage cards has been reduced to the standard 2-1/2" x 3-1/2" format for the Archives versions. Cards are UV coated on each side. Each card carries its original or an "extended" card number in the normal location, plus a tiny Archives series card number at the bottom in the fine print. The numbers on cards #97-109 do not coincide with those listed on the checklist card. The only chase cards in the issue are autographed versions of Sandy Koufax's 1956 Archives card. Cards #111-165 are short-printed in relation to cards #1-110.

	NM/M
Complete Set (165):	75.00
Common Player:	.10
Wax Pack (10):	5.00
Wax Box (24):	110.00
1 Andy Pafko (52T)	.25
2 Wayne Terwilliger (52T)	.10
3 Billy Loes (52T)	.25
4 Gil Hodges (52T)	.50
5 Duke Snider (52T)	.75
6 Jim Russell (52T)	.10
7 Chris Van Cuyk (52T)	.10
8 Preacher Roe (52T)	.10
9 Johnny Schmitz (52T)	.10
10 Bud Podbielan (52T)	.10
11 Phil Haugstad (52T)	.10
12 Clyde King (52T)	.10
13 Billy Cox (52T)	.10
14 Rocky Bridges (52T)	.10
15 Carl Erskine (52T)	.10
16 Erv Palica (52T)	.10
17 Ralph Branca (52T)	.10
18 Jackie Robinson (52T)	2.00
19 Roy Campanella (52T)	.75
20 Rube Walker (52T)	.10
21 Johnny Rutherford (52T)	.10
22 Joe Black (52T)	.25
23 George Shuba (52T)	.10
24 Pee Wee Reese (52T)	.75
25 Clem Labine (52T)	.10
26 Bobby Morgan (52T)	.10
27 Cookie Lavagetto (52T)	.10
28 Chuck Dressen (52T)	.10
29 Ben Wade (52T)	.10
30 Rocky Nelson (52T)	.10
31 Billy Herman (52T)	.10
32 Jake Pitler (52T)	.10
33 Dick Williams (52T)	.10
34 Cal Abrams (52N)	.25
35 Carl Furillo (52N)	.25
36 Don Newcombe (52N)	.50
37 Jackie Robinson (53T)	2.00
38 Ben Wade (53T)	.10
39 Clem Labine (53T)	.10
40 Roy Campanella (53T)	.75
41 George Shuba (53T)	.10
42 Chuck Dressen (53T)	.10
43 Pee Wee Reese (53T)	.75
44 Joe Black (53T)	.25
45 Bobby Morgan (53T)	.10
46 Dick Williams (53T)	.10
47 Rube Walker (53T)	.10
48 Johnny Rutherford (53T)	.10
49 Billy Loes (53T)	.15
50 Don Hoak (53T)	.10
51 Jim Hughes (53T)	.10
52 Bob Milliken (53T)	.10
53 Preacher Roe (53T)	.10
54 Dixie Howell (53T)	.10
55 Junior Gilliam (53T)	.25
56 Johnny Podres (53T)	.25
57 Bill Antonello (53T)	.10
58 Ralph Branca (53N)	.25
59 Gil Hodges (53N)	.60
60 Carl Furillo (53N)	.25
61 Carl Erskine (53N)	.25
62 Don Newcombe (53N)	.25
63 Duke Snider (53N)	.75
64 Billy Cox (53N)	.25
65 Russ Meyer (53N)	.10
66 Jackie Robinson (54T)	2.00
67 Preacher Roe (54T)	.10
68 Duke Snider (54T)	.75
69 Junior Gilliam (54T)	.10
70 Billy Herman (54T)	.10
71 Joe Black (54T)	.15
72 Gil Hodges (54T)	.50
73 Clem Labine (54T)	.10
74 Ben Wade (54T)	.10
75 Tommy Lasorda (54T)	1.00
76 Rube Walker (54T)	.10
77 Johnny Podres (54T)	.10
78 Jim Hughes (54T)	.10
79 Bob Milliken (54T)	.10
80 Charlie Thompson (54T)	.10
81 Don Hoak (54T)	.10
82 Roberto Clemente (54N)	1.00
83 Don Zimmer (54N)	.10
84 Roy Campanella (54N)	1.00
85 Billy Cox (54N)	.45
86 Carl Furillo (54N)	.45
87 Carl Furillo (54N)	.45
88 Don Newcombe (54N)	.45
89 Pee Wee Reese (54N)	1.00
90 George Shuba (54N)	.25
91 Junior Gilliam (55T)	.10
92 Billy Herman (55T)	.10
93 Johnny Podres (55T)	.10
94 Don Hoak (55T)	.10
95 Jackie Robinson (55T)	2.00
96 Jim Hughes (55T)	.10
97 Bob Borkowski (55N)	.10
98 Sandy Amoros (55T)	.10
99 Karl Spooner (55T)	.10
100 Don Zimmer (55T)	.10
101 Rube Walker (55T)	.10
102 Bob Milliken (55T)	.10
103 Sandy Koufax (55T)	2.00
104 Joe Black (55T)	.20
105 Clem Labine (55T)	.10
106 Gil Hodges (55T)	.50
107 Ed Roebuck (55T)	.10
108 Bert Hamric (55T)	.10
109 Duke Snider (55T)	.75
110 Walter Alston (55T)	.25
111 Roger Craig (55N)	.75
112 Don Drysdale (55N)	3.00
113 Dixie Howell (55N)	.10
114 Frank Kellert (55N)	.10
115 Tommy Lasorda (55N)	2.50
116 Chuck Templeton (55N)	.50
117 World Series Game 3, Dodgers Stay Alive (Jackie Robinson (55N))	1.00
118 World Series Game 4, Series Knotted (Gil Hodges (55N))	1.00
119 World Series Game 5, Dodgers Lead (Duke Snider (55N))	1.00
120 World Series Game 7, Dodgers Reign (Johnny Podres (55N))	1.00
121 Don Hoak (55B)	.35
122 Roy Campanella (55B)	2.00
123 Pee Wee Reese (55B)	2.00
124 Bob Darnell (55B)	.50
125 Don Zimmer (55B)	.50
126 George Shuba (55B)	.50
127 Johnny Podres (55B)	.50
128 Junior Gilliam (55B)	.65
129 Don Newcombe (55B)	.65
130 Jim Hughes (55B)	.50
131 Gil Hodges (55B)	2.00
132 Carl Furillo (55B)	1.00
133 Carl Erskine (55B)	.50
134 Erv Palica (55B)	.50
135 Russ Meyer (55B)	.50
136 Billy Loes (55B)	.50
137 Walt Moryn (55B)	.50
138 Chico Fernandez (55B)	.50
139 Charley Neal (55B)	.50
140 Ken Lehman (55B)	.50
141 Walter Alston (56T)	1.00
142 Jackie Robinson (56T)	6.00
143 Sandy Amoros (56T)	.50
144 Ed Roebuck (56T)	.50
145 Roger Craig (56T)	.50
146 Sandy Koufax (56T)	5.00
146a Sandy Koufax (56T, autographed)	650.00
147 Karl Spooner (56T)	.50
148 Don Zimmer (56T)	.50
149 Roy Campanella (56T)	3.00
150 Gil Hodges (56T)	4.50
151 Duke Snider (56T)	5.00
152 Team photo (56T)	5.00
153 Johnny Podres (56T)	.50
154 Don Bessent (56T)	.50
155 Carl Furillo (56T)	.50
156 Randy Jackson (56T)	.50
157 Carl Erskine (56T)	.50
158 Don Newcombe (56T)	.65
159 Pee Wee Reese (56T)	2.50
160 Billy Loes (56T)	.65
161 Junior Gilliam (56T)	.65
162 Clem Labine (56T)	.50
163 Charley Neal (56T)	.50
164 Rube Walker (56T)	.50
165 Checklist	.05

1995 Topps DIII

Describing its cards as featuring "infinite depth perspectives" with game-action photos, Topps entered the 3-D card market with its Dimension III product. Utilizing "super thick laminated construction" to provide the illusion of depth, the cards feature borderless action photos on front. Backs are conventionally printed with a color portrait photo and several sets of stats that go beyond the usual to the provide a more in-depth look at the player's performance.

	NM/M
Complete Set (59):	10.00
Common Player:	.15
Retail Pack (3):	.50
Retail Wax Box (24):	9.00
Hobby Pack (5):	.65
Hobby Wax Box (24):	12.50
1 Dave Justice	.15
2 Cal Ripken Jr.	2.50
3 Ruben Sierra	.15
4 Roberto Alomar	.25
5 Dennis Martinez	.15
6 Todd Zeile	.15
7 Albert Belle	.15
8 Chuck Knoblauch	.15
9 Roger Clemens	1.25
10 Cal Eldred	.15
11 Dennis Eckersley	.75
12 Andy Benes	.15
13 Moises Alou	.15
14 Andres Galarraga	.15
15 Jim Thome	.65
16 Tim Salmon	.15
17 Carlos Garcia	.15
18 Scott Leius	.15
19 Jeff Montgomery	.15
20 Brian Anderson	.15
21 Will Clark	.15
22 Bobby Bonilla	.15
23 Mike Stanley	.15
24 Barry Bonds	2.50
25 Jeff Conine	.15
26 Paul O'Neill	.15
27 Mike Piazza	1.50
28 Tom Glavine	.35
29 Jim Edmonds	.15
30 Lou Whitaker	.15
31 Jeff Frye	.15
32 Ivan Rodriguez	.75
33 Bret Boone	.15
34 Mike Greenwell	.15
35 Mark Grace	.15
36 Darren Lewis	.15
37 Don Mattingly	1.25
38 Jose Rijo	.15
39 Robin Ventura	.15
40 Bob Hamelin	.15
41 Tim Wallach	.15
42 Tony Gwynn	1.00
43 Ken Griffey Jr.	1.50
44 Doug Drabek	.15
45 Rafael Palmeiro	.75
46 Dean Palmer	.15
47 Bip Roberts	.15
48 Barry Larkin	.15
49 Dave Nilsson	.15
50 Wil Cordero	.15
51 Travis Fryman	.15
52 Chuck Carr	.15
53 Rey Sanchez	.15
54 Walt Weiss	.15
55 Joe Carter	.15
56 Len Dykstra	.15
57 Orlando Merced	.15
58 Ozzie Smith	1.00
59 Chris Gomez	.15

DIII Zone

A barrage of baseballs in the background, behind a player action photo, are featured on the front of this DIII chase set. Backs have a blazing baseball across the top and a description and stats of the pictured player's hot streaks of the previous season — those times when athletes are said to be "in the zone." The inserts are found on average of one per six packs.

	NM/M
Complete Set (6):	4.00
Common Player:	.50
1 Frank Thomas	1.00
2 Kirby Puckett	1.50
3 Jeff Bagwell	1.00
4 Fred McGriff	.50
5 Raul Mondesi	.50
6 Kenny Lofton	.50

1995 Topps Embossed

DEVON WHITE

Taking the embossed sportscard idea which Action Packed developed years earlier to a new level, Topps Embossed baseball features the tactile image on both sides of the card. Fronts have a lightly textured border while the central player photo is deeply embossed. The player name is embossed in gold-foil letters at bottom. Backs have another embossed player photo and various levels of embossing around the borders and boxes which contain stats and trivia.

	NM/M
Complete Set (140):	7.50
Common Player:	.10
Embossed Golds:	2X
Wax Pack (6+1):	1.50
Wax Box (24):	22.50
1 Kenny Lofton	.75
2 Gary Sheffield	.35
3 Hal Morris	.10
4 Cliff Floyd	.10
5 Pat Hentgen	.10
6 Tony Gwynn	.75
7 Jose Valentin	.10
8 Jason Bere	.10
9 Jeff Kent	.10
10 John Valentin	.10
11 Brian Anderson	.10
12 Deion Sanders	.10
13 Ryan Thompson	.10
14 Ruben Sierra	.10
15 Jay Bell	.10
16 Chuck Carr	.10
17 Brent Gates	.10
18 Bret Boone	.10
19 Paul Molitor	.60
20 Chili Davis	.10
21 Ryan Klesko	.10
22 Will Clark	.10
23 Greg Vaughn	.10
24 Moises Alou	.10
25 Ray Lankford	.10
26 Jose Rijo	.10
27 Bobby Jones	.10
28 Rick Wilkins	.10
29 Cal Eldred	.10
30 Juan Gonzalez	.30
31 Royce Clayton	.10
32 Bryan Harvey	.10
33 Dave Nilsson	.10
34 Chris Hoiles	.10
35 David Nied	.10
36 Javy Lopez	.10
37 Tim Wallach	.10
38 Bobby Bonilla	.10
39 Danny Tartabull	.10
40 Andy Benes	.10
41 Dean Palmer	.10
42 Chris Gomez	.10
43 Kevin Appier	.10
44 Brady Anderson	.10
45 Alex Fernandez	.10
46 Roberto Kelly	.10
47 Dave Hollins	.10
48 Chuck Finley	.10
49 Wade Boggs	.75
50 Travis Fryman	.10
51 Ken Griffey Jr.	1.00
52 John Olerud	.10
53 Delino DeShields	.10
54 Ivan Rodriguez	.50
55 Tommy Greene	.10
56 Tom Pagnozzi	.10
57 Bip Roberts	.10
58 Luis Gonzalez	.10
59 Rey Sanchez	.10
60 Ken Ryan	.10
61 Darren Daulton	.10
62 Rick Aguilera	.10
63 Wally Joyner	.10
64 Mike Greenwell	.10
65 Jay Buhner	.10
66 Craig Biggio	.10
67 Charles Nagy	.10
68 Devon White	.10
69 Randy Johnson	.60
70 Shawon Dunston	.10
71 Kirby Puckett	.75
72 Paul O'Neill	.10
73 Tino Martinez	.10
74 Carlos Garcia	.10

75 Ozzie Smith	.75
76 Cecil Fielder	.10
77 Mike Stanley	.10
78 Lance Johnson	.10
79 Tony Phillips	.10
80 Bobby Munoz	.10
81 Kevin Tapani	.10
82 William Van Landingham	.10
83 Dante Bichette	.10
84 Tom Candiotti	.10
85 Wil Cordero	.10
86 Jeff Conine	.10
87 Joey Hamilton	.10
88 Mark Whiten	.10
89 Jeff Montgomery	.10
90 Andres Galarraga	.10
91 Roberto Alomar	.20
92 Orlando Merced	.10
93 Mike Mussina	.35
94 Pedro Martinez	.60
95 Carlos Baerga	.10
96 Steve Trachsel	.10
97 Lou Whitaker	.10
98 David Cone	.10
99 Chuck Knoblauch	.10
100 Frank Thomas	.60
101 Dave Justice	.10
102 Raul Mondesi	.10
103 Rickey Henderson	.60
104 Doug Drabek	.10
105 Sandy Alomar	.10
106 Roger Clemens	.85
107 Mark McGwire	1.20
108 Tim Salmon	.10
109 Greg Maddux	.75
110 Mike Piazza	1.00
111 Tom Glavine	.30
112 Walt Weiss	.10
113 Cal Ripken Jr.	1.50
114 Eddie Murray	.60
115 Don Mattingly	.85
116 Ozzie Guillen	.10
117 Bob Hamelin	.10
118 Jeff Bagwell	.60
119 Eric Karros	.10
120 Barry Bonds	1.50
121 Mickey Tettleton	.10
122 Mark Langston	.10
123 Robin Ventura	.10
124 Bret Saberhagen	.10
125 Albert Belle	.10
126 Rafael Palmeiro	.50
127 Fred McGriff	.10
128 Jimmy Key	.10
129 Barry Larkin	.10
130 Tim Raines	.10
131 Len Dykstra	.10
132 Todd Zeile	.10
133 Joe Carter	.10
134 Matt Williams	.10
135 Terry Steinbach	.10
136 Manny Ramirez	.60
137 John Wetteland	.10
138 Rod Beck	.10
139 Mo Vaughn	.10
140 Darren Lewis	.10

Embossed Golden Idols

ROYCE CLAYTON

The only insert in the Topps Embossed baseball set was a parallel set of the 140 cards rendered in gold tones on front and inserted at the rate of one per pack. Backs are identical to the regular version.

	NM/M
Complete Set (140):	25.00
Common Player:	.25

Legends of the '60s

Twelve of the true superstars of the 1960s are featured on one of their best Topps card designs in this collection of 6-oz. bronze metal cards. In 2-1/2" x 3-1/2" size, the ingots' fronts reproduce one of the player's 1960s Topps cards. Backs have been modified to present entire career stats. The set was sold in a mail-order subscription plan and included a custom wood box to house the collection.

	NM/M
Complete Set (12):	100.00
Common Player:	7.50

GIANTS

WILLIE MAYS   outfield

(1)	Hank Aaron/1965	10.00
(2)	Roberto Clemente/1965	10.00
(3)	Don Drysdale/1965	7.50
(4)	Bob Gibson/1964	7.50
(5)	Harmon Killebrew/1968	7.50
(6)	Juan Marichal/1966	7.50
(7)	Willie Mays/1964	7.50
(8)	Willie McCovey/1961	7.50
(9)	Brooks Robinson/1969	7.50
(10)	Frank Robinson/1962	7.50
(11)	Billy Williams/1967	7.50
(12)	Carl Yastrzemski/1966	7.50

Own the Game Instant Winner

Randomly packaged at a rate between 1:60 and 1:120, depending on type of packaging, Instant Winner cards were available in 1995 Topps baseball. The grand prize was a $40,000 "Baseball Passport" good for games, flights, hotels, etc., for 60 days during the 1996 season. Other prizes included personalized Topps baseball cards picturing the winner and Topps Spectra Light cards in team sets, league sets or a complete set. Prize cards had to be redeemed by Jan. 31, 1996.

Ted Williams Tunnel Opening Commemorative

TED WILLIAMS

This card was produced as the header for a 13-card set distributed at a luncheon in conjunction with Dec. 15, 1995 opening day ceremonies for the Ted Williams Tunnel, connecting South Boston with the city's airport, running beneath Boston Harbor. Just 3,000 sets were reported produced. This card is in the style of Topps' regular 1996 baseball card set and features gold-foil highlights on front. A career summary is on back. The card was later offered free with a $75 purchase from Topps Stadium Club. (See also 1995 Choice Marketing Ted Williams Tunnel Opening Day Set.)

	NM/M
9 Ted Williams	35.00

"1952" Gold Mickey Mantle

This down-sized (2-1/2" x 3-1/2") version of Topps' first Mickey Mantle card was produced with embossed 22K gold-foil design on front and back and individually serial numbered within an edition of 50,000.

	NM/M
311 Mickey Mantle	10.00

Pre-Production

This set of promo cards was reportedly included in some 1995 Topps factory Hobby sets as an unadvertised insert. Cards are in the format of the forthcoming 1996 issue but do not have 1995 stats or career updates, and are numbered with a "PP" prefix.

	NM/M
Complete Set (9):	25.00
Common Player:	2.00
PP1 Cal Ripken Jr.	10.00
PP2 Thomas Howard	2.00
PP3 Rafael Bournigal	2.00
PP4 Ron Gant	2.00
PP5 Chipper Jones	7.50
PP6 Frank Thomas	6.00
PP7 Barry Bonds	10.00
PP8 Fred McGriff	2.00
PP9 Hideo Nomo	6.00

1996 Topps

MO VAUGHN

At 440 cards, the basic Topps set for 1996 was the smallest regular-issue from the company since it adopted the 2-1/2" x 3-1/2" format in 1957. Honoring the late Mickey Mantle on card No. 7, Topps announced it would hereafter retire that card number. Subsets in the 220-card Series 1 are Star Power, Commemoratives, Draft Picks, Tribute, AAA Stars and Future Stars. Series 2 subsets repeat Star Power and Draft Picks and add Prospects, Now Appearing and Rookie All-Stars. Three different factory sets were available with each including the 440-card base set and various inserts. The "Cereal Box" set, so named because of the

resemblance of its four component boxes to single-serving cereal boxes, has four of the Mantle inserts. The Retail and Hobby sets each include seven randomly packed chase cards, a plastic-cased #7 Mantle card labeled "Last Day Production" and a Mantle Foundation card. In addition the Retail version has one of the 19 Mantle reprints.

	NM/M
Unopened Hobby Set (449):	40.00
Unopened Retail Set (450):	40.00
Unopened Cereal Box	
Set (444):	35.00
Complete Set (440):	25.00
Common Player:	.05
Wax Pack (12):	1.50
Wax Box (36):	35.00
Cello Pack (17):	2.50
Cello Box (24):	40.00
Vending Box (500):	12.50
1 Tony Gwynn (Star Power)	.50
2 Mike Piazza (Star Power)	.75
3 Greg Maddux	
(Star Power)	.50
4 Jeff Bagwell (Star Power)	.40
5 Larry Walker (Star Power)	.05
6 Barry Larkin (Star Power)	.05
7 Mickey Mantle	
(Commemorative)	4.00
8 Tom Glavine (Star Power)	.05
9 Craig Biggio (Star Power)	.05
10 Barry Bonds	
(Star Power)	1.00
11 Heathcliff Slocumb	
(Star Power)	.05
12 Matt Williams	
(Star Power)	.05
13 Todd Helton (Draft Pick)	.75
14 Mark Redman (Draft Pick)	.05
15 Michael Barrett	
(Draft Pick)	.05
16 Ben Davis (Draft Pick)	.05
17 Juan LeBron (Draft Pick)	.05
18 Tony McKnight	
(Draft Pick)	.05
19 Ryan Jaroncyk	
(Draft Pick)	.05
20 Corey Jenkins (Draft Pick)	.05
21 Jim Scharrer (Draft Pick)	.05
22 Mark Bellhorn RC	
(Draft Pick)	.10
23 Jarrod Washburn RC	
(Draft Pick)	.50
24 Geoff Jenkins RC	
(Draft Pick)	1.00
25 Sean Casey RC	
(Draft Pick)	3.00
26 Brett Tomko RC	
(Draft Pick)	.10
27 Tony Fernandez	.05
28 Rich Becker	.05
29 Andujar Cedeno	.05
30 Paul Molitor	.75
31 Brent Gates	.05
32 Glenallen Hill	.05
33 Mike MacFarlane	.05
34 Manny Alexander	.05
35 Todd Zeile	.05
36 Joe Girardi	.05
37 Tony Tarasco	.05
38 Tim Belcher	.05
39 Tom Goodwin	.05
40 Orel Hershiser	.05
41 Tripp Cromer	.05
42 Sean Bergman	.05
43 Troy Percival	.05
44 Kevin Stocker	.05
45 Albert Belle	.05
46 Tony Eusebio	.05
47 Sid Roberson	.05
48 Todd Hollandsworth	.05
49 Mark Wohlers	.05
50 Kirby Puckett	1.00
51 Darren Holmes	.05
52 Ron Karkovice	.05
53 Al Martin	.05
54 Pat Rapp	.05
55 Mark Grace	.05
56 Greg Gagne	.05
57 Stan Javier	.05
58 Scott Sanders	.05
59 J.T. Snow	.05
60 David Justice	.05
61 Royce Clayton	.05
62 Kevin Foster	.05
63 Tim Naehring	.05
64 Orlando Miller	.05
65 Mike Mussina	.35
66 Jim Eisenreich	.05
67 Felix Fermin	.05
68 Bernie Williams	.05
69 Robb Nen	.05
70 Ron Gant	.05
71 Felipe Lira	.05
72 Jacob Brumfield	.05
73 John Mabry	.05
74 Mark Carreon	.05
75 Carlos Baerga	.05
76 Jim Dougherty	.05
77 Ryan Thompson	.05
78 Scott Leius	.05
79 Roger Pavlik	.05
80 Gary Sheffield	.45

#	Player	Price
81	Julian Tavarez	.05
82	Andy Ashby	.05
83	Mark Lemke	.05
84	Omar Vizquel	.05
85	Darren Daulton	.05
86	Mike Lansing	.05
87	Rusty Greer	.05
88	Dave Stevens	.05
89	Jose Offerman	.05
90	Tom Henke	.05
91	Troy O'Leary	.05
92	Michael Tucker	.05
93	Marvin Freeman	.05
94	Alex Diaz	.05
95	John Wetteland	.05
96	Cal Ripken Jr. (Tribute Card)	1.00
97	Mike Mimbs	.05
98	Bobby Higginson	.05
99	Edgardo Alfonzo	.05
100	Frank Thomas	.75
101	Steve Gibralter, Bob Abreu (AAA Stars)	.05
102	Brian Givens, T.J. Mathews (AAA Stars)	.05
103	Chris Pritchett, Trenidad Hubbard (AAA Stars)	.05
104	Eric Owens, Butch Huskey (AAA Stars)	.05
105	Doug Drabek	.05
106	Tomas Perez	.05
107	Mark Leiter	.05
108	Joe Oliver	.05
109	Tony Castillo	.05
110	Checklist	.05
111	Kevin Seitzer	.05
112	Pete Schourek	.05
113	Sean Berry	.05
114	Todd Stottlemyre	.05
115	Joe Carter	.05
116	Jeff King	.05
117	Dan Wilson	.05
118	Kurt Abbott	.05
119	Lyle Mouton	.05
120	Jose Rijo	.05
121	Curtis Goodwin	.05
122	Jose Valentin RC	.05
123	Ellis Burks	.05
124	David Cone	.05
125	Eddie Murray	.75
126	Brian Jordan	.05
127	Darrin Fletcher	.05
128	Curt Schilling	.25
129	Ozzie Guillen	.05
130	Kenny Rogers	.05
131	Tom Pagnozzi	.05
132	Garret Anderson	.05
133	Bobby Jones	.05
134	Chris Gomez	.05
135	Mike Stanley	.05
136	Hideo Nomo	.35
137	Jon Nunnally	.05
138	Tim Wakefield	.05
139	Steve Finley	.05
140	Ivan Rodriguez	.65
141	Quilvio Veras	.05
142	Mike Fetters	.05
143	Mike Greenwell	.05
144	Bill Pulsipher	.05
145	Mark McGwire	1.50
146	Frank Castillo	.05
147	Greg Vaughn	.05
148	Pat Hentgen	.05
149	Walt Weiss	.05
150	Randy Johnson	.75
151	David Segui	.05
152	Benji Gil	.05
153	Tom Candiotti	.05
154	Geronimo Berroa	.05
155	John Franco	.05
156	Jay Bell	.05
157	Mark Gubicza	.05
158	Hal Morris	.05
159	Wilson Alvarez	.05
160	Derek Bell	.05
161	Ricky Bottalico	.05
162	Bret Boone	.05
163	Brad Radke	.05
164	John Valentin	.05
165	Steve Avery	.05
166	Mark McLemore	.05
167	Danny Jackson	.05
168	Tino Martinez	.05
169	Shane Reynolds	.05
170	Terry Pendleton	.05
171	Jim Edmonds	.05
172	Esteban Loaiza	.05
173	Ray Durham	.05
174	Carlos Perez	.05
175	Raul Mondesi	.05
176	Steve Ontiveros	.05
177	Chipper Jones	1.00
178	Otis Nixon	.05
179	John Burkett	.05
180	Gregg Jefferies	.05
181	Denny Martinez	.05
182	Ken Caminiti	.05
183	Doug Jones	.05
184	Brian McRae	.05
185	Don Mattingly	1.00
186	Mel Rojas	.05
187	Marty Cordova	.05
188	Vinny Castilla	.05
189	John Smoltz	.05
190	Travis Fryman	.05
191	Chris Hoiles	.05
192	Chuck Finley	.05
193	Ryan Klesko	.05
194	Alex Fernandez	.05
195	Dante Bichette	.05
196	Eric Karros	.05
197	Roger Clemens	1.00
198	Randy Myers	.05
199	Tony Phillips	.05
200	Cal Ripken Jr.	2.00
201	Rod Beck	.05
202	Chad Curtis	.05
203	Jack McDowell	.05
204	Gary Gaetti	.05
205	Ken Griffey Jr.	1.25
206	Ramon Martinez	.05
207	Jeff Kent	.05
208	Brad Ausmus	.05
209	Devon White	.05
210	Jason Giambi (Future Star)	.45
211	Nomar Garciaparra (Future Star)	1.00
212	Billy Wagner (Future Star)	.05
213	Todd Greene (Future Star)	.05
214	Paul Wilson (Future Star)	.05
215	Johnny Damon (Future Star)	.25
216	Alan Benes (Future Star)	.05
217	Karim Garcia (Future Star)	.10
218	Dustin Hermanson (Future Star)	.05
219	Derek Jeter (Future Star)	2.00
220	Checklist	.05
221	Kirby Puckett (Star Power)	.50
222	Cal Ripken Jr. (Star Power)	1.00
223	Albert Belle (Star Power)	.05
224	Randy Johnson (Star Power)	.40
225	Wade Boggs (Star Power)	.50
226	Carlos Baerga	.05
227	Ivan Rodriguez (Star Power)	.30
228	Mike Mussina (Star Power)	.25
229	Frank Thomas (Star Power)	.40
230	Ken Griffey Jr. (Star Power)	.75
231	Jose Mesa (Star Power)	.05
232	Matt Morris RC (Draft Pick)	1.00
233	Craig Wilson RC (Draft Pick)	.50
234	Alvie Shepherd RC (Draft Pick)	.05
235	Randy Winn RC (Draft Pick)	.05
236	David Yocum RC (Draft Pick)	.05
237	Jason Brester RC (Draft Pick)	.05
238	Shane Monahan RC (Draft Pick)	.05
239	Brian McNichol RC (Draft Pick)	.05
240	Reggie Taylor (Draft Pick)	.05
241	Garrett Long (Draft Pick)	.05
242	Jonathan Johnson RC (Draft Pick)	.05
243	Jeff Liefer RC (Draft Pick)	.05
244	Brian Powell RC (Draft Pick)	.05
245	Brian Buchanan (Draft Pick)	.05
246	Mike Piazza	1.25
247	Edgar Martinez	.05
248	Chuck Knoblauch	.05
249	Andres Galarraga	.05
250	Tony Gwynn	1.00
251	Lee Smith	.05
252	Sammy Sosa	1.00
253	Jim Thome	.45
254	Frank Rodriguez	.05
255	Charlie Hayes	.05
256	Bernard Gilkey	.05
257	John Smiley	.05
258	Brady Anderson	.05
259	Rico Brogna	.05
260	Kirt Manwaring	.05
261	Len Dykstra	.05
262	Tom Glavine	.25
263	Vince Coleman	.05
264	John Olerud	.05
265	Orlando Merced	.05
266	Kent Mercker	.05
267	Terry Steinbach	.05
268	Brian Hunter	.05
269	Jeff Fassero	.05
270	Jay Buhner	.05
271	Jeff Brantley	.05
272	Tim Raines	.05
273	Jimmy Key	.05
274	Mo Vaughn	.25
275	Andre Dawson	.25
276	Jose Mesa	.05
277	Brett Butler	.05
278	Luis Gonzalez	.05
279	Steve Sparks	.05
280	Chili Davis	.05
281	Carl Everett	.05
282	Jeff Cirillo	.05
283	Thomas Howard	.05
284	Paul O'Neill	.05
285	Pat Meares	.05
286	Mickey Tettleton	.05
287	Rey Sanchez	.05
288	Bip Roberts	.05
289	Roberto Alomar	.15
290	Ruben Sierra	.05
291	John Flaherty	.05
292	Bret Saberhagen	.05
293	Barry Larkin	.05
294	Sandy Alomar	.05
295	Ed Sprague	.05
296	Gary DiSarcina	.05
297	Marquis Grissom	.05
298	John Frascatore	.05
299	Will Clark	.05
300	Barry Bonds	2.00
301	Ozzie Smith	1.00
302	Dave Nilsson	.05
303	Pedro Martinez	.75
304	Joey Cora	.05
305	Rick Aguilera	.05
306	Craig Biggio	.05
307	Jose Vizcaino	.05
308	Jeff Montgomery	.05
309	Moises Alou	.05
310	Robin Ventura	.05
311	David Wells	.05
312	Delino DeShields	.05
313	Trevor Hoffman	.05
314	Andy Benes	.05
315	Deion Sanders	.05
316	Jim Bullinger	.05
317	John Jaha	.05
318	Greg Maddux	1.00
319	Tim Salmon	.05
320	Ben McDonald	.05
321	Sandy Martinez RC	.05
322	Dan Miceli	.05
323	Wade Boggs	1.00
324	Ismael Valdes	.05
325	Juan Gonzalez	.35
326	Charles Nagy	.05
327	Ray Lankford	.05
328	Mark Portugal	.05
329	Bobby Bonilla	.05
330	Reggie Sanders	.05
331	Jamie Brewington	.05
332	Aaron Sele	.05
333	Pete Harnisch	.05
334	Cliff Floyd	.05
335	Cal Eldred	.05
336	Jason Bates (Now Appearing)	.05
337	Tony Clark (Now Appearing)	.05
338	Jose Herrera (Now Appearing)	.05
339	Alex Ochoa (Now Appearing)	.05
340	Mark Loretta (Now Appearing)	.05
341	Donne Wall RC (Now Appearing)	.05
342	Jason Kendall (Now Appearing)	.05
343	Shannon Stewart (Now Appearing)	.05
344	Brooks Kieschnick (Now Appearing)	.05
345	Chris Snopek (Now Appearing)	.05
346	Ruben Rivera (Now Appearing)	.05
347	Jeff Suppan (Now Appearing)	.05
348	Phil Nevin (Now Appearing)	.05
349	John Wasdin (Now Appearing)	.05
350	Jay Payton (Now Appearing)	.05
351	Tim Crabtree (Now Appearing)	.05
352	Rick Krivda (Now Appearing)	.05
353	Bob Wolcott (Now Appearing)	.05
354	Jimmy Haynes (Now Appearing)	.05
355	Herb Perry	.05
356	Ryne Sandberg	1.00
357	Harold Baines	.05
358	Chad Ogea	.05
359	Lee Tinsley	.05
360	Matt Williams	.05
361	Randy Velarde	.05
362	Jose Canseco	.40
363	Larry Walker	.05
364	Kevin Appier	.05
365	Darryl Hamilton	.05
366	Jose Lima	.05
367	Javy Lopez	.05
368	Dennis Eckersley	.65
369	Jason Isringhausen	.05
370	Mickey Morandini	.05
371	Scott Cooper	.05
372	Jim Abbott	.05
373	Paul Sorrento	.05
374	Chris Hammond	.05
375	Lance Johnson	.05
376	Kevin Brown	.05
377	Luis Alicea	.05
378	Andy Pettitte	.25
379	Dean Palmer	.05
380	Jeff Bagwell	.75
381	Jaime Navarro	.05
382	Rondell White	.05
383	Erik Hanson	.05
384	Pedro Munoz	.05
385	Heathcliff Slocumb	.05
386	Wally Joyner	.05
387	Bob Tewksbury	.05
388	David Bell	.05
389	Fred McGriff	.05
390	Mike Henneman	.05
391	Robby Thompson	.05
392	Norm Charlton	.05
393	Cecil Fielder	.05
394	Benito Santiago	.05
395	Rafael Palmeiro	.65
396	Ricky Bones	.05
397	Rickey Henderson	.75
398	C.J. Nitkowski	.05
399	Shawon Dunston	.05
400	Manny Ramirez	.75
401	Bill Swift	.05
402	Chad Fonville	.05
403	Joey Hamilton	.05
404	Alex Gonzalez	.05
405	Roberto Hernandez	.05
406	Jeff Blauser	.05
407	LaTroy Hawkins	.05
408	Greg Colbrunn	.05
409	Todd Hundley	.05
410	Glenn Dishman	.05
411	Joe Vitiello	.05
412	Todd Worrell	.05
413	Wil Cordero	.05
414	Ken Hill	.05
415	Carlos Garcia	.05
416	Bryan Rekar	.05
417	Shawn Green (Topps Rookie All-Star)	.40
418	Tyler Green	.05
419	Mike Blowers	.05
420	Kenny Lofton	.05
421	Denny Neagle	.05
422	Jeff Conine	.05
423	Mark Langston	.05
424	Steve Cox, Jesse Ibarra RC, Derrek Lee, Ron Wright RC (Prospects)	.10
425	Jim Bonnici RC, Billy Owens, Richie Sexson, Daryle Ward RC (Prospects)	.10
426	Kevin Jordan, Bobby Morris RC, Desi Relaford, Adam Riggs RC (Prospects)	.10
427	Tim Harkrider, Rey Ordonez, Neifi Perez, Enrique Wilson (Prospects)	.05
428	Bartolo Colon, Doug Million, Rafael Orellano, Ray Ricken RC (Prospects)	.05
429	Jeff D'Amico, Marty Janzen RC, Gary Rath, Clint Sodowsky (Prospects)	.05
430	Matt Drews, Rich Hunter RC, Matt Ruebel RC, Bret Wagner (Prospects)	.05
431	Jaime Bluma, Dave Coggin RC, Steve Montgomery, Brandon Reed (Prospects)	.05
432	Mike Figga, Raul Ibanez RC, Paul Konerko, Julio Mosquera (Prospects)	.25
433	Brian Barber, Marc Kroon, Marc Valdes, Don Wengert (Prospects)	.05
434	George Arias, Chris Haas RC, Scott Rolen, Scott Spiezio (Prospects)	.50
435	Brian Banks RC, Vladimir Guerrero, Andruw Jones, Billy McMillon (Prospects)	.50
436	Roger Cedeno, Derrick Gibson, Ben Grieve, Shane Spencer RC (Prospects)	.50
437	Anton French, Demond Smith, Darond Stovall RC, Keith Williams (Prospects)	.05
438	Michael Coleman RC, Jacob Cruz, Richard Hidalgo, Charles Peterson (Prospects)	.10
439	Trey Beamon, Yamil Benitez, Jermaine Dye, Angel Echevarria (Prospects)	.05
440	Checklist	.05

Head-to-head stats among baseball's top pitchers and hitters are featured in this insert set. The cards were seeded one per pack in the special 50-cent packs sold exclusively at Wal-Mart during the T206 Honus Wagner card giveaway promotion. Fronts have player action poses against a granite background and are highlighted in gold foil. Backs have a portrait photo and stats.

		NM/M
Complete Set (15):		3.50
Common Player:		.06
1	Ken Griffey Jr.	.65
2	Cal Ripken Jr.	1.00
3	Edgar Martinez	.05
4	Kirby Puckett	.45
5	Frank Thomas	.35
6	Barry Bonds	1.00
7	Reggie Sanders	.05
8	Andres Galarraga	.05
9	Tony Gwynn	.45
10	Mike Piazza	.65
11	Randy Johnson	.35
12	Mike Mussina	.25
13	Roger Clemens	.50
14	Tom Glavine	.25
15	Greg Maddux	.45

Mickey Mantle Commemorative Last Day

To mark the last day on which Topps would produce a #7 baseball card, the Mantle card from its 1996 set was issued in this sealed plastic case with a gold-foil logo on back.

		NM/M
7	Mickey Mantle	5.00

Mickey Mantle Reprints

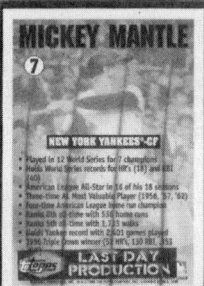

One of Mickey Mantle's regular-issue Bowman or Topps cards from each year 1951-1969 was reproduced in 2-1/2 x 3-1/2 format as a Series 1 insert. Each card carries a gold-foil commemorative seal in one corner of the front. The reprints are found one per six retail packs and, in hobby, once per nine packs. The 1965-69 reprints were somewhat shortprinted (four 1965-69 cards for each five 1951-1964) and are 20 percent scarcer.

		NM/M
Complete Set (19):		90.00
Common Mantle:		5.00
Common SP Mantle (15-19):		8.00
1	1951 Bowman #253	15.00
2	1952 Topps #311	15.00
3	1953 Topps #82	5.00
4	1954 Bowman #65	5.00
5	1955 Bowman #202	5.00
6	1956 Topps #135	5.00
7	1957 Topps #95	5.00
8	1958 Topps #150	5.00
9	1959 Topps #10	5.00
10	1960 Topps #350	5.00
11	1961 Topps #300	5.00
12	1962 Topps #200	5.00
13	1963 Topps #200	5.00
14	1964 Topps #50	5.00
15	1965 Topps #350	8.00
16	1966 Topps #50	8.00
17	1967 Topps #150	8.00
18	1968 Topps #280	6.00
19	1969 Topps #500	8.00

Mickey Mantle Finest Reprints

Nineteen of Mickey Mantle's regular-issue Bowman and Topps cards from 1951-1969 were printed in Finest technology for this Series 2 insert set. Each card's chrome front is protected with a peel-off plastic layer. Average insertion rate for the Mantle Finest reprints is one per 18 packs. The 1965-69 reprints were printed in a ratio of four for every five 1951-64 reprints, making them 20 percent scarcer. Unmarked Refractor versions of each card were inserted at an average rate of 1:144 packs.

		NM/M
Complete Set (19):		90.00
Common Card (1-14):		5.00
Common Shortprint (15-19):		8.00
Refractors:		3X
Inserted 1:144		
1	1951 Bowman #253	15.00
2	1952 Topps #311	15.00
3	1953 Topps #82	6.00
4	1954 Bowman #65	6.00
5	1955 Bowman #202	6.00
6	1956 Topps #135	6.00
7	1957 Topps #95	6.00
8	1958 Topps #150	6.00
9	1959 Topps #10	6.00
10	1960 Topps #350	6.00
11	1961 Topps #300	6.00
12	1962 Topps #200	6.00
13	1963 Topps #200	6.00
14	1964 Topps #50	6.00
15	1965 Topps #350	8.00
16	1966 Topps #50	8.00
17	1967 Topps #150	8.00
18	1968 Topps #280	6.00
19	1969 Topps #500	8.00

Mickey Mantle Case Inserts

Inserted one per case of Series 2 Topps, these special versions of the 19 Mickey Mantle reprint cards come sealed in a soft plastic holder. The plastic sleeve has a gold-foil stamp at bottom-back which reads "FACTORY TOPPS SEAL 1996." Like the other Mantle reprints, the 1965-69 cards are somewhat scarcer due to short-printing.

		NM/M
Complete Set (19):		375.00
Common Mantle:		20.00
Common SP Mantle (15-19):		30.00
1	1951 Bowman #253	60.00
2	1952 Topps #311	60.00
3	1953 Topps #82	30.00
4	1954 Bowman #65	20.00
5	1955 Bowman #202	20.00
6	1956 Topps #135	20.00
7	1957 Topps #95	20.00
8	1958 Topps #150	20.00
9	1959 Topps #10	20.00
10	1960 Topps #350	20.00
11	1961 Topps #300	20.00
12	1962 Topps #200	20.00
13	1963 Topps #200	20.00
14	1964 Topps #50	20.00
15	1965 Topps #350	30.00
16	1966 Topps #50	30.00
17	1967 Topps #150	30.00
18	1968 Topps #280	30.00
19	1969 Topps #500	30.00

Classic Confrontations

Mickey Mantle Redemption

Each of the 19 Mantle reprint cards, minus the commemorative gold-foil stamp on front, was also issued in a sweepstakes set. Seeded one per 108 packs, these cards could be sent in for a chance to win the authentic Mantle card pictured on front. Between one and 10 genuine Mantles were awarded for each of the 19 years. Cards entered in the sweepstakes were not returned when the contest ended Oct. 15, 1996. The sweepstakes cards are a Series 2 exclusive insert.

		NM/M
Complete Set (19):		200.00
Common Mantle:		10.00
Inserted 1:108 Series 2 Retail		
1	1951 Bowman #253	35.00
2	1952 Topps #311	35.00
3	1953 Topps #82	15.00
4	1954 Bowman #65	10.00
5	1955 Bowman #202	10.00
6	1956 Topps #135	10.00
7	1957 Topps #95	10.00
8	1958 Topps #150	10.00
9	1959 Topps #10	10.00
10	1960 Topps #350	10.00
11	1961 Topps #300	10.00
12	1962 Topps #200	10.00
13	1963 Topps #200	10.00
14	1964 Topps #50	10.00
15	1965 Topps #350	10.00
16	1966 Topps #50	10.00
17	1967 Topps #150	10.00
18	1968 Topps #280	10.00
19	1969 Topps #500	10.00

Mickey Mantle Commemorative Card Sheet

In conjunction with its program of reprinting most of the Mick's Topps and Bowman cards of the 1950s-1960s, Topps created this limited edition (numbered to 10,000) framed sheet depicting 20 cards surrounding an enlarged portrait from his famed 1952 Topps card. The sheet is embossed with a gold-foil #7 seal and was sold with a certificate of authenticity from Topps' president. The framed sheet measures about 19-1/2" x 25".

	NM/M
Framed Sheet:	80.00

Mickey Mantle Foundation

This black-and-white card was an insert exclusive to specially marked 1996 Topps factory sets. In standard 2-1/2" x 3-1/2" format, the card offers on its back information about the foundation and its work in health care and organ donation causes.

	NM/M
Mickey Mantle	4.00

Masters of the Game

Appearing at a one per 18 pack rate, these inserts are exclusive to Series 1 hobby packs.

		NM/M
Complete Set (20):		20.00
Common Player:		.35
1	Dennis Eckersley	.75
2	Denny Martinez	.35
3	Eddie Murray	1.00
4	Paul Molitor	1.00
5	Ozzie Smith	1.50
6	Rickey Henderson	1.00
7	Tim Raines	.35
8	Lee Smith	.35
9	Cal Ripken Jr.	4.00
10	Chili Davis	.35
11	Wade Boggs	1.50
12	Tony Gwynn	1.50
13	Don Mattingly	2.00
14	Bret Saberhagen	.35
15	Kirby Puckett	1.50
16	Joe Carter	.35
17	Roger Clemens	2.00
18	Barry Bonds	4.00
19	Greg Maddux	1.50
20	Frank Thomas	1.00

Mystery Finest

Each Mystery Finest insert has an opaque black film over the card front, concealing the identity of the player until removed. The inserts are seeded at the rate of one per 36 packs.

		NM/M
Complete Set (21)		25.00
Common Player:		.50
Refractors:		1.5X
M1	Hideo Nomo	1.00
M2	Greg Maddux	2.00
M3	Randy Johnson	1.50
M4	Chipper Jones	2.00
M5	Marty Cordova	.50
M6	Garret Anderson	.50
M7	Cal Ripken Jr.	4.00
M8	Kirby Puckett	2.00
M9	Tony Gwynn	2.00
M10	Manny Ramirez	1.50
M11	Jim Edmonds	.50
M12	Mike Piazza	2.50
M13	Barry Bonds	4.00
M14	Raul Mondesi	.50
M15	Sammy Sosa	2.00
M16	Ken Griffey Jr.	2.50
M17	Albert Belle	.50
M18	Dante Bichette	.50
M19	Mo Vaughn	.50
M20	Jeff Bagwell	1.50
M21	Frank Thomas	1.50

5-Star Mystery Finest

The 5-Star Mystery Finest inserts have an opaque black film over the card front, like the regular Mystery Finest, but has the words "5-Star" in large letters across the background. They are inserted at the average rate of one per 36 packs.

		NM/M
Complete Set (5):		12.50
Common Player:		2.00
Refractors:		2X
M22	Hideo Nomo	2.00
M23	Cal Ripken Jr.	5.00
M24	Mike Piazza	3.00
M25	Ken Griffey Jr.	3.00
M26	Frank Thomas	2.50

Power Boosters

This insert set is printed in Topps' "Power Matrix" technology, replacing two regular cards when found on the average of once per 36 packs. The Power Boosters reproduce the Star Power and Draft Picks subsets on a double-thick card.

		NM/M
Complete Set (26):		30.00
Common Player:		1.00
1	Tony Gwynn (Star Power)	2.00
2	Mike Piazza (Star Power)	3.00
3	Greg Maddux (Star Power)	2.00
4	Jeff Bagwell (Star Power)	1.50
5	Larry Walker (Star Power)	1.00
6	Barry Larkin (Star Power)	1.00
7	Tom Glavine (Star Power)	1.25
8	Craig Biggio (Star Power)	1.00
9	Barry Bonds (Star Power)	4.00
10	Heathcliff Slocumb (Star Power)	1.00
11	Matt Williams (Star Power)	1.00
12	Todd Helton (Draft Pick)	4.00
13	Mark Redman (Draft Pick)	1.00
14	Michael Barrett (Draft Pick)	1.00
15	Ben Davis (Draft Pick)	1.00
16	Juan LeBron (Draft Pick)	1.00
17	Tony McKnight (Draft Pick)	1.00
18	Ryan Jaroncyk (Draft Pick)	1.00
19	Corey Jenkins (Draft Pick)	1.00
20	Jim Scharrer (Draft Pick)	1.00
21	Mark Bellhorn	1.00
22	Jarrod Washburn (Draft Pick)	1.00
23	Geoff Jenkins (Draft Pick)	1.00
24	Sean Casey (Draft Pick)	2.00
25	Brett Tomko (Draft Pick)	1.00

Profiles-AL

Ten cards from this insert issue can be found in each of Topps Series 1 and 2. Analyzing an up-and-coming star, the cards are found every 12th pack, on average.

		NM/M
Complete Set (20):		8.00
Common Player:		.25
1	Roberto Alomar	.30
2	Carlos Baerga	.25
3	Albert Belle	.25
4	Cecil Fielder	.25
5	Ken Griffey Jr.	1.00
6	Randy Johnson	.60
7	Paul O'Neill	.25
8	Cal Ripken Jr.	1.50
9	Frank Thomas	.60
10	Mo Vaughn	.25
11	Jay Buhner	.25
12	Marty Cordova	.25

13	Jim Edmonds	.25
14	Juan Gonzalez	.35
15	Kenny Lofton	.25
16	Edgar Martinez	.25
17	Don Mattingly	.75
18	Mark McGwire	1.25
19	Rafael Palmeiro	.50
20	Tim Salmon	.25

Profiles-NL

Projected future stars of the National League are featured in this insert set. Ten players each are found in Series 1 and 2 packs at the rate of one per 12, on average.

		NM/M
Complete Set (20):		7.00
Common Player:		.25
1	Jeff Bagwell	.60
2	Derek Bell	.25
3	Barry Bonds	1.50
4	Greg Maddux	.75
5	Fred McGriff	.25
6	Raul Mondesi	.25
7	Mike Piazza	1.00
8	Reggie Sanders	.25
9	Sammy Sosa	.75
10	Larry Walker	.25
11	Dante Bichette	.25
12	Andres Galarraga	.25
13	Ron Gant	.35
14	Tom Glavine	.35
15	Chipper Jones	.75
16	David Justice	.25
17	Barry Larkin	.25
18	Hideo Nomo	.40
19	Gary Sheffield	.40
20	Matt Williams	.25

Road Warriors

These inserts feature top hitters and were only found in Series 2 packs sold at Wal-Mart stores. Cards have an RW prefix to their number. Fronts have action photos and gold foil highlights. Backs feature a portrait photo and hitting stats from the player's favorite out-of-town ballparks.

		NM/M
Complete Set (20):		9.00
Common Player:		.25
1	Derek Bell	.25
2	Albert Belle	.25
3	Craig Biggio	.25
4	Barry Bonds	2.50
5	Jay Buhner	.25
6	Jim Edmonds	.25
7	Gary Gaetti	.25
8	Ron Gant	.25
9	Edgar Martinez	.25
10	Tino Martinez	.25
11	Mark McGwire	1.50
12	Mike Piazza	1.25
13	Manny Ramirez	1.00
14	Tim Salmon	.25
15	Reggie Sanders	.25
16	Frank Thomas	1.00
17	John Valentin	.25
18	Mo Vaughn	.25
19	Robin Ventura	.25
20	Matt Williams	.25

Wrecking Crew

Printed on foilboard stock, cards of 15 players known for their hitting prowess are featured in this insert set. Found only in Series 2 hobby packs, the inserts are a one per 72 packs find, on average. Cards are numbered with a "WC" prefix.

		NM/M
Complete Set (15):		20.00
Common Player:		.50
1	Jeff Bagwell	1.50
2	Albert Belle	.50
3	Barry Bonds	5.00
4	Jose Canseco	.75
5	Joe Carter	.50
6	Cecil Fielder	.50
7	Ron Gant	.50
8	Juan Gonzalez	.75
9	Ken Griffey Jr.	3.00
10	Fred McGriff	.50
11	Mark McGwire	4.00
12	Mike Piazza	3.00
13	Frank Thomas	1.50
14	Mo Vaughn	.50
15	Matt Williams	.50

Team Topps

Some of baseball's most popular players and their teammates are featured on specially marked cards sold in blister packed team sets along with a jumbo "Big Topps" version of the team superstar's card. The team sets were a Wal-Mart exclusive, selling for around $5. Most of the Team Topps cards are identical to the regular-issue versions except for the addition of a gold-foil Team Topps logo on the card front. Several cards in this special issue have had their regular and Star Power backs transposed.

		NM/M
Complete Set (84):		25.00
Common Player:		.10
Orioles Team Set (19):		8.00
Cal Ripken, Jr. Big Topps:		4.00
34	Manny Alexander	.10
65	Mike Mussina (Star Power front, regular back).	.50
96	Cal Ripken Jr. (2,131)	1.25
121	Curtis Goodwin	.10
183	Doug Jones	.10
191	Chris Hoiles	.10
200	Cal Ripken Jr.	2.50
222	Cal Ripken Jr. (Star Power)	1.25
228	Mike Mussina (Regular-card front, Star Power back).	.50
234	Alvie Shepherd (Draft Pick)	.10
258	Brady Anderson	.10
320	Ben McDonald	.10
329	Bobby Bonilla	.10
352	Rick Krivda (Now Appearing)	.10
354	Jimmy Haynes (Now Appearing)	.10
357	Harold Baines	.10
376	Kevin Brown	.10
395	Rafael Palmeiro	.65

Cubs Team Set (16):		5.00
Ryne Sandberg Big Topps:		3.00
35	Todd Zeile	.10
55	Mark Grace	.10
62	Kevin Foster	.10
146	Frank Castillo	.10
184	Brian McRae	.10
198	Randy Myers	.10
239	Brian McNichol (Draft Pick)	.10
252	Sammy Sosa	1.00
278	Luis Gonzalez	.10
287	Rey Sanchez	.10
316	Jim Bullinger	.10
344	Brooks Kieshnick (Now Appearing)	.10
356	Ryne Sandberg	1.00
381	Jaime Navarro	.10
399	Shawon Dunston	.10
White Sox Team Set (15):		5.00
Frank Thomas Big Topps:		2.50
52	Ron Karkovice	.10
100	Frank Thomas	.75
119	Lyle Mouton	.10
129	Ozzie Guillen	.10
159	Wilson Alvarez	.10
173	Ray Durham (All-Star Rookie)	.10
194	Alex Fernandez	.10
229	Frank Thomas (Star Power)	.40
243	Jeff Liefer (Draft Pick)	.10
272	Tim Raines	.10
310	Robin Ventura	.10
345	Chris Snopek (Now Appearing)	.10
375	Lance Johnson	.10
405	Roberto Hernandez	.10
Yankees Team Set (19):		8.00
Derek Jeter Big Topps:		4.00
7	Mickey Mantle	3.00
27	Tony Fernandez	.10
68	Bernie Williams	.10
95	John Wetteland	.10
124	David Cone	.10
135	Mike Stanley	.10
185	Don Mattingly	1.25
203	Jack McDowell	.10
219	Derek Jeter (Future Star)	2.50
225	Wade Boggs (Star Power)	.50
245	Brian Buchanan (Draft Pick)	.10
273	Jimmy Key	.10
284	Paul O'Neill	.10
290	Ruben Sierra	.10
323	Wade Boggs	1.00
346	Ruben Rivera (Now Appearing)	.10
361	Randy Velarde	.10
378	Andy Pettitte	.35
Rangers Team Set (15):		5.00
Juan Gonzalez Big Topps:		2.00
79	Roger Pavlik	.10
87	Rusty Greer	.10
130	Kenny Rogers	.10
140	Ivan Rodriguez	.65
152	Benji Gil	.10
166	Mark McLemore	.10
178	Otis Nixon	.10
227	Ivan Rodriguez (Star Power)	.35
242	Jonathan Johnson (Draft Pick)	.10
286	Mickey Tettleton	.10
299	Will Clark	.10
325	Juan Gonzalez	.35
387	Bob Tewksbury	.10
379	Dean Palmer	.10

American League Champion Cleveland Indians

Sold in a blister pack at Wal-Mart stores, this team set features specially overprinted versions of the Indians' regular '96 Topps cards, along with a super-size "Big Topps" card of Albert Belle. Each card carries a color logo recognizing the Tribe's A.L. Championship season of 1995. Sets sold for around $5.

		NM/M
Complete Set (21):		4.00
Common Player:		.10
Albert Belle Big Topps:		2.00
25	Sean Casey	1.50

40 Orel Hershiser .10
45 Albert Belle .10
75 Carlos Baerga .10
81 Julian Tavarez .10
84 Omar Vizquel .10
125 Eddie Murray .75
181 Denny Martinez .10
223 Albert Belle (Star Power) .10
226 Carlos Baerga (Star Power) .10
231 Jose Mesa (Star Power) .10
253 Jim Thome .65
276 Jose Mesa .10
294 Sandy Alomar .10
326 Charles Nagy .10
355 Herb Perry .10
358 Chad Ogea .10
373 Paul Sorrento .10
400 Manny Ramirez .75
414 Ken Hill .10
420 Kenny Lofton .10

A.L. West Champion Seattle Mariners

These specially marked versions of Topps' regular '96 cards were sold for around $5 in a blister pack with a Ken Griffey, Jr. "Big Topps" card. The team sets were a Wal-Mart exclusive. Each of the Mariners' cards is overprinted with a color A.L. West Champions logo. Cards are otherwise identical to the regular issue.

NM/M
Complete Set (18): 3.50
Common Player: .10
Ken Griffey, Jr. Big Topps: 3.50
38 Tim Belcher .10
67 Felix Fermin .10
94 Alex Diaz .10
117 Dan Wilson .10
150 Randy Johnson .75
168 Tino Martinez .10
205 Ken Griffey Jr. 1.50
224 Randy Johnson (Star Power) .40
230 Ken Griffey Jr. (Star Power) .75
238 Shane Monahan (Draft Pick) .10
247 Edgar Martinez .10
263 Vince Coleman .10
270 Jay Buhner .10
304 Joey Cora .10
314 Andy Benes .10
353 Bob Wolcott (Now Appearing) .10
392 Norm Charlton .10
419 Mike Blowers .10

Dodger Stadium 35th Anniversary L.A. Dodgers

Celebrating 35 seasons of play in Chavez Ravine, this team set of specially marked cards was issued in a blister pack with a jumbo Hideo Nomo "Big Topps" card. Selling for about $5, the team set was a Wal-Mart exclusive. Otherwise identical to the regular '96 Topps cards, these are overprinted with a colorful 35 Seasons logo. The backs of the two Mike Piazza cards in the set were switched. His regular card has the Star Power back (#2) while his Star Power card (#246) has the regular-issue back.

NM/M
Complete Set (16): 5.00
Common Player: .10
Hideo Nomo Big Topps: 2.00
2 Mike Piazza (Star Power back) 2.50
48 Todd Hollandsworth .10
89 Jose Offerman .10
136 Hideo Nomo (All-Star Rookie) 1.00
153 Tom Candiotti .10
175 Raul Mondesi .10
196 Eric Karros .10
206 Ramon Martinez .10
217 Karim Garcia (Future Star) .10
236 David Yocum (Draft Pick) .10
246 Mike Piazza (Star Power front) 2.50
277 Brett Butler .10
312 Delino DeShields .10
324 Ismael Valdes .10
402 Chad Fonville .10
412 Todd Worrell .10

World Champions Atlanta Braves

These specially marked versions of Topps regular 1996 cards feature a color World Champions logo overprinted on the front of each card. They were sold as a team set along with a 3-1/2" x 5" "Big Topps" card at Wal-Mart stores for around $5.

NM/M
Complete Set (17): 4.00
Common Player: .10
Greg Maddux Big Topps: 3.00
3 Greg Maddux (Star Power) .50
8 Tom Glavine (Star Power) .15
12 Jim Scharrer (Draft Pick) .10
49 Mark Wohlers .10
60 David Justice .10
83 Mark Lemke .10
165 Steve Avery .10
177 Chipper Jones (All-Star Rookie) 2.00
189 John Smoltz .10
193 Ryan Klesko .10
262 Tom Glavine .30
266 Kent Mercker .10
297 Marquis Grissom .10
318 Greg Maddux 1.00
367 Javy Lopez .10
389 Fred McGriff .10
406 Jeff Blauser .10

Big Topps

These double-size (3-1/2" x 5") cards are found exclusively in team-set blister packs prepared by Treat Entertainments for sale at Wal-Mart stores. Suggested retail price was just under $5. The Big Topps cards feature the fronts of the players' regular 1996 Topps card set against a marbled green background. Backs are in black-and-white with copyright data and licensors' logos. The unnumbered cards are checklisted here alphabetically.

NM/M
Complete Set (9): 20.00
Common Player: 2.00
(1) Albert Belle 2.00
(2) Juan Gonzalez 2.00
(3) Ken Griffey Jr. 3.50
(4) Derek Jeter 4.00
(5) Greg Maddux 3.00
(6) Hideo Nomo 2.00
(7) Cal Ripken Jr. 4.00
(8) Ryne Sandberg 3.00
(9) Frank Thomas 2.50

1996 Topps Chrome Promo Sheet

This promotional sheet was issued to promote the first annual issue of Topps Chrome baseball cards. The 8" x 5" sheet reproduces three of the card fronts from the forthcoming set in Topps' "Brilliant Chromium" technology. Back of the sheet is conventionally printed and advertises the set and its chase cards.

NM/M
Sheet: 5.00

1996 Topps Chrome

In conjunction with baseball's postseason, Topps introduced the premiere edition of Chrome Baseball. The set has 165 of the elite players from 1996 Topps Series 1 and 2. Card #7 is a Mickey Mantle tribute card. There are two insert sets: Masters of the Game and Wrecking Crew, and scarcer Refractor versions for each.

NM/M
Complete Set (165): 40.00
Common Player: .10
Refractors: 3X
Pack (4): 2.00
Wax Box (24): 30.00
1 Tony Gwynn (Star Power) 1.00
2 Mike Piazza (Star Power) 1.25
3 Greg Maddux (Star Power) 1.00
4 Jeff Bagwell (Star Power) .75
5 Larry Walker (Star Power) .10
6 Barry Larkin (Star Power) .10
7 Mickey Mantle (Commemorative) 9.00
8 Tom Glavine (Star Power) .10
9 Craig Biggio (Star Power) .10
10 Barry Bonds (Star Power) 2.00
11 Heathcliff Slocumb (Star Power) .10
12 Matt Williams (Star Power) .10
13 Todd Helton (Draft Pick) 2.00
14 Paul Molitor 1.50
15 Glenallen Hill .10
16 Troy Percival .10
17 Albert Belle .10
18 Mark Wohlers .10
19 Kirby Puckett 2.00
20 Mark Grace .10
21 J.T. Snow .10
22 David Justice .10
23 Mike Mussina .75
24 Bernie Williams .10
25 Ron Gant .10
26 Carlos Baerga .10
27 Gary Sheffield .65
28 Cal Ripken Jr. (Tribute Card) 2.00
29 Frank Thomas 1.50
30 Kevin Seitzer .10
31 Joe Carter .10
32 Jeff King .10
33 David Cone .10
34 Eddie Murray 1.50
35 Brian Jordan .10
36 Garret Anderson .10
37 Hideo Nomo .75
38 Steve Finley .10
39 Ivan Rodriguez 1.25
40 Quilvio Veras .10
41 Mark McGwire 3.00
42 Greg Vaughn .10
43 Randy Johnson 1.50
44 David Segui .10
45 Derek Bell .10
46 John Valentin .10
47 Steve Avery .10
48 Tino Martinez .10
49 Shane Reynolds .10
50 Jim Edmonds .10
51 Raul Mondesi .10
52 Chipper Jones 2.00
53 Gregg Jefferies .10
54 Ken Caminiti .10
55 Brian McRae .10
56 Don Mattingly 2.25
57 Marty Cordova .10
58 Vinny Castilla .10
59 John Smoltz .10
60 Travis Fryman .10
61 Ryan Klesko .10
62 Alex Fernandez .10
63 Dante Bichette .10
64 Eric Karros .10
65 Roger Clemens 2.25
66 Randy Myers .10
67 Cal Ripken Jr. 4.00
68 Rod Beck .10
69 Jack McDowell .10
70 Ken Griffey Jr. 2.50
71 Ramon Martinez .10
72 Jason Giambi (Future Star) .75
73 Nomar Garciaparra (Future Star) 2.00
74 Billy Wagner (Future Star) .10
75 Todd Greene (Future Star) .10
76 Paul Wilson (Future Star) .10
77 Johnny Damon (Future Star) .35
78 Alan Benes (Future Star) .10
79 Karim Garcia (Future Star) .25
80 Derek Jeter (Future Star) 4.00
81 Kirby Puckett (Star Power) 1.00
82 Cal Ripken Jr. (Star Power) 2.00
83 Albert Belle (Star Power) .10
84 Randy Johnson (Star Power) .40
85 Wade Boggs (Star Power) 1.00
86 Carlos Baerga (Star Power) .10
87 Ivan Rodriguez (Star Power) .35
88 Mike Mussina (Star Power) .30
89 Frank Thomas (Star Power) .75
90 Ken Griffey Jr. (Star Power) 1.25
91 Jose Mesa (Star Power) .10
92 Matt Morris RC (Draft Pick) 1.00
93 Mike Piazza 2.50
94 Edgar Martinez .10
95 Chuck Knoblauch .10
96 Andres Galarraga .10
97 Tony Gwynn 2.00
98 Lee Smith .10
99 Sammy Sosa 2.00
100 Jim Thome 1.25
101 Bernard Gilkey .10
102 Brady Anderson .10
103 Rico Brogna .10
104 Lenny Dykstra .10
105 Tom Glavine .35
106 John Olerud .10
107 Terry Steinbach .10
108 Brian Hunter .10
109 Jay Buhner .10
110 Mo Vaughn .10
111 Jose Mesa .10
112 Brett Butler .10
113 Chili Davis .10
114 Paul O'Neill .10
115 Roberto Alomar .35
116 Barry Larkin .10
117 Marquis Grissom .10
118 Will Clark .10
119 Barry Bonds 4.00
120 Ozzie Smith 2.00
121 Pedro Martinez 1.50
122 Craig Biggio .10
123 Moises Alou .10
124 Robin Ventura .10
125 Greg Maddux 2.00
126 Tim Salmon .10
127 Wade Boggs .10
128 Ismael Valdes .10
129 Juan Gonzalez .75
130 Ray Lankford .10
131 Bobby Bonilla .10
132 Reggie Sanders .10
133 Alex Ochoa (Now Appearing) .10
134 Mark Loretta (Now Appearing) .10
135 Jason Kendall (Now Appearing) .10
136 Brooks Kieschnick (Now Appearing) .10
137 Chris Snopek (Now Appearing) .10
138 Ruben Rivera (Now Appearing) .10
139 Jeff Suppan (Now Appearing) .10
140 John Wasdin (Now Appearing) .10
141 Jay Payton (Now Appearing) .10
142 Rick Krivda (Now Appearing) .10
143 Jimmy Haynes (Now Appearing) .10
144 Ryne Sandberg 2.00
145 Matt Williams .10
146 Jose Canseco .65
147 Larry Walker .10
148 Kevin Appier .10
149 Javy Lopez .10
150 Dennis Eckersley 1.25
151 Jason Isringhausen .10
152 Dean Palmer .10
153 Jeff Bagwell 1.50
154 Rondell White .10
155 Wally Joyner .10
156 Fred McGriff .10
157 Cecil Fielder .10
158 Rafael Palmeiro 1.25
159 Rickey Henderson 1.50
160 Shawon Dunston .10
161 Manny Ramirez 1.50
162 Alex Gonzalez .10
163 Shawn Green .45
164 Kenny Lofton .10
165 Jeff Conine .10

Masters of the Game

These 1996 Topps Chrome inserts were seeded one per every 12 packs. Each of the cards is also reprinted in a Refractor version; these cards are seeded one per every 36 packs.

NM/M
Complete Set (20): 35.00
Common Player: 1.00
Refractors: 1.5X
1 Dennis Eckersley 2.00
2 Denny Martinez 1.00
3 Eddie Murray 2.50
4 Paul Molitor 2.50
5 Ozzie Smith 3.50
6 Rickey Henderson 2.50
7 Tim Raines 1.00
8 Lee Smith 1.00
9 Cal Ripken Jr. 6.00
10 Chili Davis 1.00
11 Wade Boggs 3.50
12 Tony Gwynn 3.50
13 Don Mattingly 4.00
14 Bret Saberhagen 1.00
15 Kirby Puckett 3.50
16 Joe Carter 1.00
17 Roger Clemens 4.00
18 Barry Bonds 6.00
19 Greg Maddux 3.50
20 Frank Thomas 2.50

Wrecking Crew

Wrecking Crew insert cards were inserted one per every 24 packs of 1996 Topps Chrome Baseball. Refractor versions were also made for these cards; they are seeded one per every 72 packs. Cards are numbered with a "WC" prefix.

NM/M
Complete Set (15): 25.00
Common Player: 1.00
Refractors: 1.5X
1 Jeff Bagwell 2.50
2 Albert Belle 1.00
3 Barry Bonds 5.00
4 Jose Canseco 1.50
5 Joe Carter 1.00
6 Cecil Fielder 1.00
7 Ron Gant 1.00
8 Juan Gonzalez 1.25
9 Ken Griffey Jr. 3.50
10 Fred McGriff 1.00
11 Mark McGwire 4.00
12 Mike Piazza 4.00
13 Frank Thomas 2.50
14 Mo Vaughn 1.00
15 Matt Williams 1.00

1996 Topps Gallery

This 180-card set is printed on 24-point stock utilizing metallic inks and a high-definition printing process. Then a high-gloss film is applied to each card, followed by foil stamping. The regular set is broken down into five subsets - The Classics, The Modernists, The Futurists, The Masters and New Editions. Each theme has a different design. Gallery also has four insert sets. Player's Private Issue cards are a parallel set to the main issue; these cards are seeded one per every 12 packs. The backs are sequentially numbered from 0-999, with the first 100 cards sent to the players; the rest are inserted into packs. The backs are UV coated on the photo only, to allow for autographing. The other insert sets are Expressionists, Photo Gallery and a Mickey Mantle Masterpiece card.

NM/M
Complete Set (180): 20.00
Common Player: .10
Private Issue: 8X
Pack (8): 1.50
Wax Box (24): 27.50
1 Tom Glavine .35
2 Carlos Baerga .10
3 Dante Bichette .10
4 Mark Langston .10
5 Ray Lankford .10
6 Moises Alou .10
7 Marquis Grissom .10
8 Ramon Martinez .10
8p Ramon Martinez (Unmarked promo, "Pitcher" spelled out under photo on back.) 2.50
9 Steve Finley .10
10 Todd Hundley .10
11 Brady Anderson .10
12 John Valentin .10
13 Heathcliff Slocumb .10
14 Ruben Sierra .10
15 Jeff Conine .10
16 Jay Buhner .10
16p Jay Buhner (Unmarked promo; height, weight and "Bats" on same line.) 2.50
17 Sammy Sosa 1.00
18 Doug Drabek .10
19 Jose Mesa .10
20 Jeff King .10
21 Mickey Tettleton .10
22 Jeff Montgomery .10
23 Alex Fernandez .10
24 Greg Vaughn .10
25 Chuck Finley .10
26 Terry Steinbach .10
27 Rod Beck .10
28 Jack McDowell .10
29 Mark Wohlers .10
30 Lenny Dykstra .10
31 Bernie Williams .10
32 Travis Fryman .10
33 Jose Canseco .45
34 Ken Caminiti .10
35 Devon White .10
36 Bobby Bonilla .10
37 Paul Sorrento .10
38 Ryne Sandberg 1.00
39 Derek Bell .10
40 Bobby Jones .10

41	J.T. Snow	.10
42	Denny Neagle	.10
43	Tim Wakefield	.10
44	Andres Galarraga	.10
45	David Segui	.10
46	Lee Smith	.10
47	Mel Rojas	.10
48	John Franco	.10
49	Pete Schourek	.10
50	John Wetteland	.10
51	Paul Molitor	.75
52	Ivan Rodriguez	.65
53	Chris Hoiles	.10
54	Mike Greenwell	.10
55	Orel Hershiser	.10
56	Brian McRae	.10
57	Geronimo Berroa	.10
58	Craig Biggio	.10
59	David Justice	.10
59p	David Justice (Unmarked promo; height,weight and "Bats" on same line.)	2.50
60	Lance Johnson	.10
61	Andy Ashby	.10
62	Randy Myers	.10
63	Gregg Jefferies	.10
64	Kevin Appier	.10
65	Rick Aguilera	.10
66	Shane Reynolds	.10
67	John Smoltz	.10
68	Ron Gant	.10
69	Eric Karros	.10
70	Jim Thome	.65
71	Terry Pendleton	.10
72	Kenny Rogers	.10
73	Robin Ventura	.10
74	Dave Nilsson	.10
75	Brian Jordan	.10
76	Glenallen Hill	.10
77	Greg Colbrunn	.10
78	Roberto Alomar	.25
79	Rickey Henderson	.75
80	Carlos Garcia	.10
81	Dean Palmer	.10
82	Mike Stanley	.10
83	Hal Morris	.10
84	Wade Boggs	1.00
85	Chad Curtis	.10
86	Roberto Hernandez	.10
87	John Olerud	.10
88	Frank Castillo	.10
89	Rafael Palmeiro	.65
90	Trevor Hoffman	.10
91	Marty Cordova	.10
92	Hideo Nomo	.35
93	Johnny Damon	.30
94	Bill Pulsipher	.10
95	Garret Anderson	.10
96	Ray Durham	.10
97	Ricky Bottalico	.10
98	Carlos Perez	.10
99	Troy Percival	.10
100	Chipper Jones	1.00
101	Esteban Loaiza	.10
102	John Mabry	.10
103	Jon Nunnally	.10
104	Andy Pettitte	.35
105	Lyle Mouton	.10
106	Jason Isringhausen	.10
107	Brian Hunter	.10
108	Quilvio Veras	.10
109	Jim Edmonds	.10
110	Ryan Klesko	.10
111	Pedro Martinez	.75
112	Joey Hamilton	.10
113	Vinny Castilla	.10
114	Alex Gonzalez	.10
115	Raul Mondesi	.10
116	Rondell White	.10
117	Dan Miceli	.10
118	Tom Goodwin	.10
119	Bret Boone	.10
120	Shawn Green	.35
121	Jeff Cirillo	.10
122	Rico Brogna	.10
123	Chris Gomez	.10
124	Ismael Valdes	.10
125	Javy Lopez	.10
126	Manny Ramirez	.75
127	Paul Wilson	.10
128	Billy Wagner	.10
129	Eric Owens	.10
130	Todd Greene	.10
131	Karim Garcia	.10
132	Jimmy Haynes	.10
133	Michael Tucker	.10
134	John Wasdin	.10
135	Brooks Kieschnick	.10
136	Alex Ochoa	.10
137	Ariel Prieto	.10
138	Tony Clark	.10
139	Mark Loretta	.10
140	Rey Ordonez	.10
141	Chris Snopek	.10
142	Roger Cedeno	.10
143	Derek Jeter	2.00
144	Jeff Suppan	.10
145	Greg Maddux	1.00
146	Ken Griffey Jr.	1.25
147	Tony Gwynn	1.00
148	Darren Daulton	.10
149	Will Clark	.10
150	Mo Vaughn	.10
151	Reggie Sanders	.10
152	Kirby Puckett	1.00
153	Paul O'Neill	.10
154	Tim Salmon	.10
155	Mark McGwire	1.50

156	Barry Bonds	2.00
157	Albert Belle	.10
158	Edgar Martinez	.10
159	Mike Mussina	.35
160	Cecil Fielder	.10
161	Kenny Lofton	.10
162	Randy Johnson	.75
163	Juan Gonzalez	.35
164	Jeff Bagwell	.75
165	Joe Carter	.10
166	Mike Piazza	1.25
167	Eddie Murray	.75
168	Cal Ripken Jr.	2.00
169	Barry Larkin	.10
170	Chuck Knoblauch	.10
171	Chili Davis	.10
172	Fred McGriff	.10
173	Matt Williams	.10
174	Roger Clemens	1.00
175	Frank Thomas	.75
176	Dennis Eckersley	.10
177	Gary Sheffield	.40
178	David Cone	.10
179	Larry Walker	.10
180	Mark Grace	.10

Players Private Issue

The first 999 examples of each of the base cards in the Gallery issue are designated on the front with a gold-foil stamp as "Players Private Issue." The first 100 of those cards were given to the depicted player, the others are randomly packed. Besides the logo on front, the PPI cards are identified on back with an individual serial number.

	NM/M
Complete Set (180):	200.00
Common Player:	1.00
Stars:	8X

Expressionists

These 1996 Topps Gallery inserts feature 20 team leaders printed on triple foil-stamped and texture-embossed cards. Cards are seeded one per every 24 packs.

		NM/M
Complete Set (20):		20.00
Common Player:		.35
1	Mike Piazza	3.00
2	J.T. Snow	.35
3	Ken Griffey Jr.	3.00
4	Kirby Puckett	2.00
5	Carlos Baerga	.35
6	Chipper Jones	2.00
7	Hideo Nomo	.75
8	Mark McGwire	4.00
9	Gary Sheffield	.75
10	Randy Johnson	1.25
11	Ray Lankford	.35
12	Sammy Sosa	2.00
13	Denny Martinez	.35
14	Jose Canseco	.75
15	Tony Gwynn	2.00
16	Edgar Martinez	.35
17	Reggie Sanders	.35
18	Andres Galarraga	.35
19	Albert Belle	.35
20	Barry Larkin	.35

Masterpiece

Masterpiece

Topps continues its tribute to Mickey Mantle with this 1996 Topps Gallery insert card. The card, seeded one per every 48 packs, has three photos of Mantle on the front, with his comprehensive career statistics on the back.

		NM/M
MP1	Mickey Mantle	6.00

Photo Gallery

Photo Gallery is a collection of 15 cards featuring photography of baseball's biggest stars and greatest moments from the last season. The text on the card includes details of the card's front and back photos. The cards are seeded one per every 30 packs. Cards are numbered with a "PG" prefix.

		NM/M
Complete Set (15):		20.00
Common Player:		.75
1	Eddie Murray	2.00
2	Randy Johnson	2.00
3	Cal Ripken Jr.	5.00
4	Bret Boone	.75
5	Frank Thomas	2.00
6	Jeff Conine	.75
7	Johnny Damon	.85
8	Roger Clemens	3.00
9	Albert Belle	.75
10	Ken Griffey Jr.	4.00
11	Kirby Puckett	2.50
12	David Justice	.75
13	Bobby Bonilla	.75
14	Larry Walker, Andres Galarraga, Vinny Castilla, Dante Bichette	1.00
15	Mark Wohlers, Javier Lopez	.75

Derek Jeter Panel

The method of issue for this triple-size (about 7-1/2" x 3-1/2") panel is uncertain. It has been reported that the piece was inserted into some 1995 Topps Hobby factory sets as an unadvertised bonus. The front has an action sequence showing the Yankees shortstop turning a double play. On back is personal data, minor and major league stats, a repeat of the center photo and a few sentences about the budding superstar.

	NM/M
Derek Jeter	7.50

Landmark Medallions

Milestones of the 1995 season are recalled in this set of limited edition (2,000) medallions. Each of the 2-1/2" x 3-1/2" pieces features a Topps Finest technology card bonded to a 1/8" thick, 4-oz. burnished bronze ingot, then clear-coated. Backs have career stats and a description of the milestone minted into

the bronze. The issue was sold only as complete sets through Topps Stadium Club; issue price was $100.

		NM/M
Complete Set (4):		75.00
Common Player:		10.00
1	Greg Maddux (4th straight Cy Young)	20.00
2	Albert Belle (First 50 HR/50 2B season)	10.00
3	Cal Ripken, Jr. (2,131 consecutive games)	35.00
4	Eddie Murray (3,000 hits)	15.00

1996 Topps Laser

Topps' 1996 Laser Baseball was the first set to use laser-cut technology on every card, creating surgically-precise latticework across the entire card. Every card in the 128-card regular issue set features one of four designs laser-cut into 20-point stock. One card from each of the four different designs is found in each four-card pack. Three different laser-cut insert sets were also produced: Bright Spots, Power Cuts and Stadium Stars. Cards 1-8 from each insert set were in Series 1 packs; cards 9-16 were seeded in Series 2 packs. A slightly oversize (1-5/8" x 3-5/8") checklist card in each pack helped protect the delicate die-cut details from damage.

		NM/M
Complete Set (128):		27.50
Common Player:		.10
Series 1 or 2 Pack (4):		1.50
Series 1 or 2 Wax Box (24):		22.50
1	Moises Alou	.10
2	Derek Bell	.10
3	Joe Carter	.10
4	Jeff Conine	.10
5	Darren Daulton	.10
6	Jim Edmonds	.10
7	Ron Gant	.10
8	Juan Gonzalez	.50
9	Brian Jordan	.10
10	Ryan Klesko	.10
11	Paul Molitor	1.00
12	Tony Phillips	.10
13	Manny Ramirez	1.00
14	Sammy Sosa	1.50
15	Devon White	.10
16	Bernie Williams	.10
17	Garret Anderson	.10
18	Jay Bell	.10
19	Craig Biggio	.10
20	Bobby Bonilla	.10
21	Ken Caminiti	.10
22	Shawon Dunston	.10
23	Mark Grace	.10
23p	Mark Grace (Unmarked promo, plain, rather than brushed, gold foil.)	2.00
24	Gregg Jefferies	.10
25	Jeff King	.10
26	Javy Lopez	.10
27	Edgar Martinez	.10
28	Dean Palmer	.10
29	J.T. Snow	.10

30	Mike Stanley	.10
30p	Mike Stanley (Unmarked promo; plain, rather than brushed, gold foil.)	1.00
31	Terry Steinbach	.10
32	Robin Ventura	.10
33	Roberto Alomar	.20
34	Jeff Bagwell	1.00
35	Dante Bichette	.10
36	Wade Boggs	1.50
37	Barry Bonds	3.00
38	Jose Canseco	.50
39	Vinny Castilla	.10
40	Will Clark	.10
41	Marty Cordova	.10
42	Ken Griffey Jr.	2.00
43	Tony Gwynn	1.50
44	Rickey Henderson	1.00
45	Chipper Jones	1.50
46	Mark McGwire	2.50
47	Brian McRae	.10
48	Ryne Sandberg	1.50
49	Andy Ashby	.10
50	Alan Benes	.10
51	Andy Benes	.10
52	Roger Clemens	1.75
53	Doug Drabek	.10
54	Dennis Eckersley	.75
55	Tom Glavine	.35
56	Randy Johnson	1.00
57	Mark Langston	.10
58	Denny Martinez	.10
59	Jack McDowell	.10
60	Hideo Nomo	.50
61	Shane Reynolds	.10
62	John Smoltz	.10
63	Paul Wilson	.10
64	Mark Wohlers	.10
65	Shawn Green	.35
66	Marquis Grissom	.10
67	Dave Hollins	.10
68	Todd Hundley	.10
69	David Justice	.10
70	Eric Karros	.10
71	Ray Lankford	.10
72	Fred McGriff	.10
73	Hal Morris	.10
74	Eddie Murray	1.00
75	Paul O'Neill	.10
76	Rey Ordonez	.10
77	Reggie Sanders	.10
78	Gary Sheffield	.45
79	Jim Thome	.75
80	Rondell White	.10
81	Travis Fryman	.10
82	Derek Jeter	3.00
83	Chuck Knoblauch	.10
84	Barry Larkin	.10
85	Tino Martinez	.10
86	Raul Mondesi	.10
87	John Olerud	.10
88	Rafael Palmeiro	.75
89	Mike Piazza	2.00
90	Cal Ripken Jr.	3.00
91	Ivan Rodriguez	.75
92	Frank Thomas	1.00
93	John Valentin	.10
94	Mo Vaughn	.10
95	Quilvio Veras	.10
96	Matt Williams	.10
97	Brady Anderson	.10
98	Carlos Baerga	.10
99	Albert Belle	.10
100	Jay Buhner	.10
101	Johnny Damon	.35
102	Chili Davis	.10
103	Ray Durham	.10
104	Lenny Dykstra	.10
105	Cecil Fielder	.10
106	Andres Galarraga	.10
107	Brian Hunter	.10
108	Kenny Lofton	.10
109	Kirby Puckett	1.50
110	Tim Salmon	.10
111	Greg Vaughn	.10
112	Larry Walker	.10
113	Rick Aguilera	.10
114	Kevin Appier	.10
115	Kevin Brown	.10
116	David Cone	.10
117	Alex Fernandez	.10
118	Chuck Finley	.10
119	Joey Hamilton	.10
120	Jason Isringhausen	.10
121	Greg Maddux	1.50
122	Pedro Martinez	1.00
123	Jose Mesa	.10
124	Jeff Montgomery	.10
125	Mike Mussina	.50
126	Randy Myers	.10
127	Kenny Rogers	.10
128	Ismael Valdes	.10
	Series 1 Checklist	.05
	Series 2 Checklist	.05

Bright Spots

Top young stars are featured on these insert cards, which use etched silver and gold diffraction foil. The cards are seeded one per 20 packs. Numbers 1-8 are in Series 1 packs; cards 9-16 are in Series 2 packs.

		NM/M
Complete Set (16):		17.50
Common Player:		.50

1	Brian Hunter	.50
2	Derek Jeter	4.50
3	Jason Kendall	.50
4	Brooks Kieschnick	.50
5	Rey Ordonez	.50
6	Jason Schmidt	.50
7	Chris Snopek	.50
8	Bob Wolcott	.50
9	Alan Benes	.50
10	Marty Cordova	.50
11	Jimmy Haynes	.50
12	Todd Hollandsworth	.50
13	Derek Jeter	4.50
14	Chipper Jones	3.00
15	Hideo Nomo	1.00
16	Paul Wilson	.50

Power Cuts

This insert set spotlights 16 of the game's top power hitters on etched foil and gold diffraction foil cards. These cards were seeded one per 40 packs; numbers 1-8 were in Series 1 packs; cards 9-16 were in Series 2 packs.

		NM/M
Complete Set (16):		20.00
Common Player:		.75
1	Albert Belle	.75
2	Jay Buhner	.75
3	Fred McGriff	.75
4	Mike Piazza	3.00
5	Tim Salmon	.75
6	Frank Thomas	2.00
7	Mo Vaughn	.75
8	Matt Williams	.75
9	Jeff Bagwell	2.00
10	Barry Bonds	5.00
11	Jose Canseco	1.00
12	Cecil Fielder	.75
13	Juan Gonzalez	2.00
14	Ken Griffey Jr.	3.00
15	Sammy Sosa	2.50
16	Larry Walker	.75

Stadium Stars

These 1996 Topps Laser cards are the most difficult to find; they are seeded one per every 60 packs. The 16 cards feature a laser-sculpted cover that folds back to reveal striated silver and gold etched diffraction foil on each card front. Cards 1-8 were in Series I packs; numbers 9-16 were in Series II inserts.

		NM/M
Complete Set (16):		45.00
Common Player:		1.50
1	Carlos Baerga	1.50
2	Barry Bonds	10.00
3	Andres Galarraga	1.50
4	Ken Griffey Jr.	7.50
5	Barry Larkin	1.50
6	Raul Mondesi	1.50
7	Kirby Puckett	5.00
8	Cal Ripken Jr.	10.00

No.	Player	Price
9	Will Clark	1.50
10	Roger Clemens	6.00
11	Tony Gwynn	5.00
12	Randy Johnson	4.00
13	Kenny Lofton	1.50
14	Edgar Martinez	1.50
15	Ryne Sandberg	5.00
16	Frank Thomas	4.00

League Leaders Finest Bronze

Specially designed Topps Finest cards are bedded to a slab of bronze and clear-coated in this set honoring major award winners from the 1995 season. A "League Leaders" logo at top has the player's award inscribed. Backs of the 2-3/4" x 3-3/4" ingots are silk-screened with season and career stats. The issue was sold only in complete sets (2,000 limit) through Topps Stadium Club for $80.

		NM/M
Complete Set (6):		75.00
Common Player:		10.00
(1)	Mo Vaughn (A.L. MVP)	10.00
(2)	Barry Larkin (N.L. MVP)	10.00
(3)	Randy Johnson (A.L. CY)	15.00
(4)	Greg Maddux (N.L. CY)	30.00
(5)	Marty Cordova (A.L. ROY)	10.00
(6)	Hideo Nomo (N.L. ROY)	15.00

Legends of the '50s

A dozen of the greatest players of the 1950s ever to grace a Topps card are featured in this set of bronze replicas. Each player's card is reproduced in a 4-oz. bronze version in 2-1/2" x 3-1/2" format. The card fronts are faithfully reproduced on each ingot, while the backs have been modified to present the player's lifetime stats. The ingots were sold through Topps' Stadium Club for about $45 apiece through a monthly subscription plan. The complete set was housed in a special wooden display case. The ingots are checklisted here alphabetically, with the year of Topps card reproduced noted parenthetically.

		NM/M
Complete Set (12):		275.00
Common Player:		20.00
(1)	Ernie Banks/1954	20.00
(2)	Yogi Berra/1952	20.00
(3)	Roy Campanella/1952	20.00
(4)	Whitey Ford/1953	20.00
(5)	Mickey Mantle/1952	35.00
(6)	Eddie Mathews/1952	20.00
(7)	Willie Mays/1953	25.00
(8)	Stan Musial/1959	20.00
(9)	Jackie Robinson/1952	20.00
(10)	Duke Snider/1955	20.00
(11)	Warren Spahn/1952	20.00
(12)	Ted Williams/1954 (#250)	20.00

"1952" Gold Willie Mays

This reproduction of Topps' 1952 card #261 is embossed and covered in 22-karat gold foil. Each full-size replica card is serially numbered within an edition of 50,000.

		NM/M
261	Willie Mays	12.00

"1954" Ted Williams Gold

This reproduction of Topps' 1954 card #1, Ted Williams, is embossed and covered in 22-karat gold foil. Each full-size replica card is serially numbered within an edition of 50,000.

		NM/M
1	Ted Williams	12.00

"1959" Stan Musial Gold

Topps' first regular-issue card of Stan Musial was reproduced in a full-size (2-1/2" x 3-1/2") 22-karat gold foil edition sold through Topps' Stadium Club. Each of the gold replicas bears a unique serial number. Issue price of the card was about $30.

		NM/M
150	Stan Musial	10.00

1997 Topps

Topps' 1997 set includes the first-ever player cards of the expansion Diamondbacks and Devil Rays; 16 Mickey Mantle reprints; a special Jackie Robinson tribute card; 27 Willie Mays Topps and Bowman reprints; randomly-inserted Willie Mays autographed reprint cards; and Inter-League Finest and Finest Refractors cards. The base set has 275 cards in Series 1 and 220 cards in Series 2. Each card front has a glossy coating on the photo and a spot matte finish on the border, with gold-foil graphics. Card backs have informative text, complete player stats and biographies, and a second photo. Mantle reprints, seeded one per 12 packs, feature the 16 remaining Mantle cards which were not reprinted in 1996, stamped with a gold foil logo, and numbered from #21 to #36. Willie Mays has 27 of his cards reprinted and seeded one per eight packs. Each card also has a gold foil stamp. As a special hobby-exclusive bonus, 1,000 Mays reprints were autographed and randomly inserted in packs. Five other insert sets were made: All-Stars, Inter-League Finest and Inter-League Finest Refractors, Sweet Strokes and Hobby Masters. Two factory sets, comprising the 495 base cards and either seven or eight random inserts were produced and currently enjoy a significant premium over hand-collated sets.

	NM/M
Unopened Fact. Set (504):	110.00
Unopened Fact. Set (503):	145.00
Complete Set (495):	65.00
Common Player:	.05
Ser. 1 or 2 Pack (11):	1.00
Ser. 1 or 2 Wax Box (36):	20.00
Ser. 1 or 2 Vending Box (500):	12.00

No.	Player	Price
1	Barry Bonds	2.00
2	Tom Pagnozzi	.05
3	Terrell Wade	.05
4	Jose Valentin	.05
5	Mark Clark	.05
6	Brady Anderson	.05
7	Wade Boggs	1.00
8	Scott Stahoviak	.05
9	Andres Galarraga	.05
10	Steve Avery	.05
11	Rusty Greer	.05
12	Derek Jeter	2.00
13	Ricky Bottalico	.05
14	Andy Ashby	.05
15	Paul Shuey	.05
16	F.P. Santangelo	.05
17	Royce Clayton	.05
18	Mike Mohler	.05
20	Mike Piazza	1.50
21	Jaime Navarro	.05
22	Billy Wagner	.05
23	Mike Timlin	.05
24	Garret Anderson	.05
25	Ben McDonald	.05
26	Mel Rojas	.05
27	John Burkett	.05
28	Jeff King	.05
29	Reggie Jefferson	.05
30	Kevin Appier	.05
31	Felipe Lira	.05
32	Kevin Tapani	.05
33	Mark Portugal	.05
34	Carlos Garcia	.05
35	Joey Cora	.05
36	David Segui	.05
37	Mark Grace	.05
38	Erik Hanson	.05
39	Jeff D'Amico	.05
40	Jay Buhner	.05
41	B.J. Surhoff	.05
42	Jackie Robinson	1.50
43	Roger Pavlik	.05
44	Hal Morris	.05
45	Mariano Duncan	.05
46	Harold Baines	.05
47	Jorge Fabregas	.05
48	Jose Herrera	.05
49	Jeff Cirillo	.05
50	Tom Glavine	.05
51	Pedro Astacio	.05
52	Mark Gardner	.05
53	Arthur Rhodes	.05
54	Troy O'Leary	.05
55	Bip Roberts	.05
56	Mike Lieberthal	.05
57	Shane Andrews	.05
58	Scott Karl	.05
59	Gary DiSarcina	.05
60	Andy Pettitte	.25
61a	Kevin Elster	.05
61b	Mike Fetters (Should be #84.)	
62	Mark McGwire	1.75
63	Dan Wilson	.05
64	Mickey Morandini	.05
65	Chuck Knoblauch	.05
66	Tim Wakefield	.05
67	Raul Mondesi	.05
68	Todd Jones	.05
69	Albert Belle	.05
70	Trevor Hoffman	.05
71	Eric Young	.05
72	Robert Perez	.05
73	Butch Huskey	.05
74	Brian McRae	.05
75	Jim Edmonds	.05
76	Mike Henneman	.05
77	Frank Rodriguez	.05
78	Danny Tartabull	.05
79	Robby Nen	.05
80	Reggie Sanders	.05
81	Ron Karkovice	.05
82	Benny Santiago	.05
83	Mike Lansing	.05
85	Craig Biggio	.05
86	Mike Bordick	.05
87	Ray Lankford	.05
88	Charles Nagy	.05
89	Paul Wilson	.05
90	John Wetteland	.05
91	Tom Candiotti	.05
92	Carlos Delgado	.45
93	Derek Bell	.05
94	Mark Lemke	.05
95	Edgar Martinez	.05
96	Rickey Henderson	.75
97	Greg Myers	.05
98	Jim Leyritz	.05
99	Mark Johnson	.05
100	Dwight Gooden (Season Highlights)	.05
101	Al Leiter (Season Highlights)	.05
102a	John Mabry (Season Highlights)(Last line on back ends "... Mabry.")	.05
102b	John Mabry (Season Highlights) (Last line on back ends "...walked.")	.05
103	Alex Ochoa (Season Highlights)	.05
104	Mike Piazza (Season Highlights)	.75
105	Jim Thome	.65
106	Ricky Otero	.05
107	Jamey Wright	.05
108	Frank Thomas	.75
109	Jody Reed	.05
110	Orel Hershiser	.05
111	Terry Steinbach	.05
112	Mark Loretta	.05
113	Turk Wendell	.05
114	Marvin Benard	.05
115	Kevin Brown	.05
116	Robert Person	.05
117	Joey Hamilton	.05
118	Francisco Cordova	.05
119	John Smiley	.05
120	Travis Fryman	.05
121	Jimmy Key	.05
122	Tom Goodwin	.05
123	Mike Greenwell	.05
124	Juan Gonzalez	.35
125	Pete Harnisch	.05
126	Roger Cedeno	.05
127	Ron Gant	.05
128	Mark Langston	.05
129	Tim Crabtree	.05
130	Greg Maddux	1.00
131	William Van Landingham	.05
132	Wally Joyner	.05
133	Randy Myers	.05
134	John Valentin	.05
135	Bret Boone	.05
136	Bruce Ruffin	.05
137	Chris Snopek	.05
138	Paul Molitor	.75
139	Mark McLemore	.05
140	Rafael Palmeiro	.65
141	Herb Perry	.05
142	Luis Gonzalez	.05
143	Doug Drabek	.05
144	Ken Ryan	.05
145	Todd Hundley	.05
146	Ellis Burks	.05
147	Ozzie Guillen	.05
148	Rich Becker	.05
149	Sterling Hitchcock	.05
150	Bernie Williams	.05
151	Mike Stanley	.05
152	Roberto Alomar	.25
153	Jose Mesa	.05
154	Steve Trachsel	.05
155	Alex Gonzalez	.05
156	Troy Percival	.05
157	John Smoltz	.05
158	Pedro Martinez	.75
159	Jeff Conine	.05
160	Bernard Gilkey	.05
161	Jim Eisenreich	.05
162	Mickey Tettleton	.05
163	Justin Thompson	.05
164	Jose Offerman	.05
165	Tony Phillips	.05
166	Ismael Valdes	.05
167	Ryne Sandberg	1.00
168	Matt Mieske	.05
169	Geronimo Berroa	.05
170	Otis Nixon	.05
171	John Mabry	.05
172	Shawon Dunston	.05
173	Omar Vizquel	.05
174	Chris Holles	.05
175	Doc Gooden	.05
176	Wilson Alvarez	.05
177	Todd Hollandsworth	.05
178	Roger Salkeld	.05
179	Rey Sanchez	.05
180	Rey Ordonez	.05
181	Denny Martinez	.05
182	Ramon Martinez	.05
183	Dave Nilsson	.05
184	Marquis Grissom	.05
185	Randy Velarde	.05
186	Ron Coomer	.05
187	Tino Martinez	.05
188	Jeff Brantley	.05
189	Steve Finley	.05
190	Andy Benes	.05
191	Terry Adams	.05
192	Mike Blowers	.05
193	Russ Davis	.05
194	Darryl Hamilton	.05
195	Jason Kendall	.25
196	Johnny Damon	.05
197	Dave Martinez	.05
198	Mike Macfarlane	.05
199	Norm Charlton	.05
200	Doug Million, Damian Moss, Bobby Rodgers (Prospect)	.05
201	Geoff Jenkins, Raul Ibanez, Mike Cameron (Prospect)	.05
202	Sean Casey, Jim Bonnici, Dmitri Young (Prospect)	.15
203	Jed Hansen, Homer Bush, Felipe Crespo (Prospect)	.05
204	Kevin Orie, Gabe Alvarez, Aaron Boone (Prospect)	.05
205	Ben Davis, Kevin Brown, Bobby Estalella (Prospect)	.05
206	Billy McMillon, Bubba Trammell RC, Dante Powell (Prospect)	.05
207	Jarrod Washburn, Marc Wilkins RC, Glendon Rusch (Prospect)	.05
208	Brian Hunter	.05
209	Jason Giambi	.45
210	Henry Rodriguez	.05
211	Edgar Renteria	.05
212	Edgardo Alfonzo	.05
213	Fernando Vina	.05
214	Shawn Green	.40
215	Ray Durham	.05
216	Joe Randa	.05
217	Armando Reynoso	.05
218	Eric Davis	.05
219	Bob Tewksbury	.05
220	Jacob Cruz	.05
221	Glenallen Hill	.05
222	Gary Gaetti	.05
223	Donne Wall	.05
224	Brad Clontz	.05
225	Marty Janzen	.05
226	Todd Worrell	.05
227	John Franco	.05
228	David Wells	.05
229	Gregg Jefferies	.05
230	Tim Naehring	.05
231	Thomas Howard	.05
232	Roberto Hernandez	.05
233	Kevin Ritz	.05
234	Julian Tavarez	.05
235	Ken Hill	.05
236	Greg Gagne	.05
237	Bobby Chouinard	.05
238	Joe Carter	.05
239	Jermaine Dye	.05
240	Antonio Osuna	.05
241	Julio Franco	.05
242	Mike Grace	.05
243	Aaron Sele	.05
244	David Justice	.05
245	Sandy Alomar	.05
246	Jose Canseco	.45
247	Paul O'Neill	.05
248	Sean Berry	.05
249	Nick Bierbrodt RC, Kevin Sweeney RC (Diamond Backs)	.05
250	Larry Rodriguez RC, Vladimir Nunez RC (Diamond Backs)	.10
251	Ron Hartman, David Hayman (Diamond Backs)	.05
252	Alex Sanchez, Matt Quatraro (Devil Rays)	.05
253	Ronni Seberino, Pablo Ortega RC (Devil Rays)	.05
254	Rex Hudler	.05
255	Orlando Miller	.05
256	Mariano Rivera	.10
257	Brad Radke	.05
258	Bobby Higginson	.05
259	Jay Bell	.05
260	Mark Grudzielanek	.05
261	Lance Johnson	.05
262	Ken Caminiti	.05
263	J.T. Snow	.05
264	Gary Sheffield	.45
265	Darrin Fletcher	.05
266	Eric Owens	.05
267	Luis Castillo	.05
268	Scott Rolen	.65
269	Todd Noel RC, John Oliver (Draft Pick)	.05
270	Robert Stratton RC, Corey Lee RC (Draft Pick)	.05
271	Gil Meche RC, Matt Halloran RC (Draft Pick)	.50
272	Eric Milton RC, Dermal Brown (Draft Pick)	.25
273	Josh Garrett RC, Chris Reitsma RC (Draft Pick)	.10
274	A.J. Zapp RC, Jason Marquis RC (Draft Pick)	.50
275	Checklist	.05
276a	Checklist	.05
276b	Chipper Jones (Should be #277.)	1.00
278	Orlando Merced	.05
279	Ariel Prieto	.05
280	Al Leiter	.05
281	Pat Meares	.05
282	Darryl Strawberry	.05
283	Jamie Moyer	.05
284	Scott Servais	.05
285	Delino DeShields	.05
286	Danny Graves	.05
287	Gerald Williams	.05
288	Todd Greene	.05
289	Rico Brogna	.05
290	Derrick Gibson	.05
291	Joe Girardi	.05
292	Darren Lewis	.05
293	Nomar Garciaparra	1.00
294	Greg Colbrunn	.05
295	Jeff Bagwell	.75
296	Brent Gates	.05
297	Jose Vizcaino	.05
298	Alex Ochoa	.05
299	Sid Fernandez	.05
300	Ken Griffey Jr.	1.50
301	Chris Gomez	.05
302	Wendell Magee	.05
303	Darren Oliver	.05
304	Mel Nieves	.05
305	Sammy Sosa	1.00
306	George Arias	.05
307	Jack McDowell	.05
308	Stan Javier	.05
309	Kimera Bartee	.05
310	James Baldwin	.05
311	Rocky Coppinger	.05
312	Keith Lockhart	.05
313	C.J. Nitkowski	.05
314	Allen Watson	.05
315	Darryl Kile	.05
316	Amaury Telemaco	.05
317	Jason Isringhausen	.05
318	Manny Ramirez	.75
319	Terry Pendleton	.05
320	Tim Salmon	.05
321	Eric Karros	.05
322	Mark Whiten	.05
323	Rick Krivda	.05
324	Brett Butler	.05
325	Randy Johnson	.75
326	Eddie Taubensee	.05
327	Mark Leiter	.05
328	Kevin Gross	.05
329	Ernie Young	.05
330	Pat Hentgen	.05
331	Rondell White	.05
332	Bobby Witt	.05
333	Eddie Murray	.75
334	Tim Raines	.05
335	Jeff Fassero	.05
336	Chuck Finley	.05
337	Willie Adams	.05
338	Chan Ho Park	.05
339	Jay Powell	.05
340	Ivan Rodriguez	.05
341	Jermaine Allensworth	.05
342	Jay Payton	.05
343	T.J. Mathews	.05
344	Tony Batista	.05
345	Ed Sprague	.05
346	Jeff Kent	.05
347	Scott Erickson	.05
348	Jeff Suppan	.05
349	Pete Schourek	.05
350	Kenny Lofton	.05
351	Alan Benes	.05
352	Fred McGriff	.05
353	Charlie O'Brien	.05
354	Darren Bragg	.05
355	Alex Fernandez	.05
356	Al Martin	.05
357	Bob Wells	.05
358	Chad Mottola	.05
359	Devon White	.05
360	David Cone	.05
361	Bobby Jones	.05
362	Scott Sanders	.05
363	Karim Garcia	.15
364	Kirt Manwaring	.05
365	Chili Davis	.05
366	Mike Hampton	.05
367	Chad Ogea	.05
368	Curt Schilling	.25
369	Phil Nevin	.05
370	Roger Clemens	1.25
371	Willie Greene	.05
372	Kenny Rogers	.05
373	Jose Rijo	.05
374	Bobby Bonilla	.05
375	Mike Mussina	.35
376	Curtis Pride	.05
377	Todd Walker	.05
378	Jason Bere	.05
379	Heathcliff Slocumb	.05
380	Dante Bichette	.05
381	Carlos Baerga	.05
382	Livan Hernandez	.05
383	Jason Schmidt	.05
384	Kevin Stocker	.05
385	Matt Williams	.05
386	Bartolo Colon	.05
387	Will Clark	.05
388	Dennis Eckersley	.65
389	Brooks Kieschnick	.05
390	Ryan Klesko	.05
391	Mark Carreon	.05
392	Tim Worrell	.05
393	Dean Palmer	.05
394	Wil Cordero	.05
395	Javy Lopez	.05
396	Rich Aurilia	.05
397	Greg Vaughn	.05
398	Vinny Castilla	.05
399	Jeff Montgomery	.05
400	Cal Ripken Jr.	2.00
401	Walt Weiss	.05
402	Brad Ausmus	.05
403	Ruben Rivera	.05
404	Mark Wohlers	.05
405	Rick Aguilera	.05
406	Tony Clark	.05
407	Lyle Mouton	.05
408	Bill Pulsipher	.05
409	Jose Rosado	.05
410	Tony Gwynn	1.00
411	Cecil Fielder	.05
412	John Flaherty	.05
413	Lenny Dykstra	.05
414	Ugueth Urbina	.05
415	Brian Jordan	.05
416	Bob Abreu	.05
417	Craig Paquette	.05
418	Sandy Martinez	.05
419	Jeff Blauser	.05
420	Barry Larkin	.05
421	Kevin Seitzer	.05
422	Tim Belcher	.05
423	Paul Sorrento	.05
424	Cal Eldred	.05
425	Robin Ventura	.05
426	John Olerud	.05
427	Bob Wolcott	.05
428	Matt Lawton	.05
429	Rod Beck	.05
430	Shane Reynolds	.05
431	Mike James	.05
432	Steve Wojciechowski	.05
433	Vladimir Guerrero	.75
434	Dustin Hermanson	.05
435	Marty Cordova	.05
436	Marc Newfield	.05
437	Todd Stottlemyre	.05
438	Jeffrey Hammonds	.05
439	Dave Stevens	.05
440	Hideo Nomo	.35
441	Mark Thompson	.05
442	Mark Lewis	.05
443	Quinton McCracken	.05
444	Cliff Floyd	.05
445	Denny Neagle	.05
446	John Jaha	.05
447	Mike Sweeney	.05
448	John Wasdin	.05
449	Chad Curtis	.05
450	Mo Vaughn	.05
451	Donovan Osborne	.05
452	Ruben Sierra	.05
453	Michael Tucker	.05
454	Kurt Abbott	.05
455	Andruw Jones	.75
456	Shannon Stewart	.05
457	Scott Brosius	.05
458	Juan Guzman	.05
459	Ron Villone	.05
460	Moises Alou	.05
461	Larry Walker	.05
462	Eddie Murray (Season Highlights)	.40

463	Paul Molitor (Season Highlights)	.40
464	Hideo Nomo (Season Highlights)	.20
465	Barry Bonds (Season Highlights)	1.00
466	Todd Hundley (Season Highlights)	.05
467	Rheal Cormier	.05
468	Jason Conti RC	.05
469	Rod Barajas RC	.05
470	Jared Sandberg, Cedric Bowers RC	.05
471	Paul Wilders, Chie Gunner RC	.05
472	Mike Decelle, Marcus McCain RC	.05
473	Todd Zeile	.05
474	Neifi Perez	.05
475	Jeromy Burnitz	.05
476	Trey Beamon	.05
477	John Patterson, Braden Looper RC (Draft Picks)	.15
478	Danny Peoples RC, Jake Westbrook RC (Draft Picks)	.25
479	Eric Chavez RC, Adam Eaton (Draft Picks)	.25
480	Joe Lawrence RC, Pete Tucci (Draft Picks)	.05
481	Kris Benson, Billy Koch RC (Draft Picks)	.25
482	John Nicholson, Andy Prater (Draft Picks)	.05
483	Mark Kotsay RC, Mark Johnson (Draft Picks)	.25
484	Armando Benitez	.05
485	Mike Matheny	.05
486	Jeff Reed	.05
487	Mark Bellhorn, Russ Johnson, Enrique Wilson (Prospects)	.05
488	Ben Grieve, Richard Hidalgo, Scott Morgan RC (Prospects)	.05
489	Paul Konerko, Derrek Lee, Ron Wright (Prospects)	.50
490	Wes Helms, Bill Mueller RC, Brad Seitzer (Prospects)	.50
491	Jeff Abbott, Shane Monahan, Edgard Velazquez (Prospects)	.05
492	Jimmy Anderson RC, Ron Blazier, Gerald Witasick Jr. (Prospects)	.05
493	Darin Blood, Heath Murray, Carl Pavano (Prospects)	.05
494	Mark Redman, Mike Villano RC, Nelson Figueroa (Prospects)	.05
495	Checklist	.05
496	Checklist	.05

All-Stars

Topps' 1997 All-Stars insert cards, printed on a dazzling rainbow foilboard, feature the top players from each position. There are 22 cards, 11 from each league, which showcase the top three players from each position as voted by Topps' sports department. On the front of each card is a photo of a "first team" all-star player; the back has a different photo of that player, who appears alongside the "second team" and "third team" selections. These cards are seeded one per every 18 1997 Topps Series I packs. Cards are numbered with an "AS" prefix.

		NM/M
Complete Set (22):		12.00
Common Player:		.25
1	Ivan Rodriguez	.75
2	Todd Hundley	.25
3	Frank Thomas	1.00
4	Andres Galarraga	.25
5	Chuck Knoblauch	.25
6	Eric Young	.25
7	Jim Thome	.75

8	Chipper Jones	1.50
9	Cal Ripken Jr.	3.00
10	Barry Larkin	.25
11	Albert Belle	.25
12	Barry Bonds	3.00
13	Ken Griffey Jr.	2.00
14	Ellis Burks	.25
15	Juan Gonzalez	.60
16	Gary Sheffield	.50
17	Andy Pettitte	.35
18	Tom Glavine	.35
19	Pat Hentgen	.25
20	John Smoltz	.25
21	Roberto Hernandez	.25
22	Mark Wohlers	.25

Awesome Impact

This flashy insert exclusive to Series 2 retail packaging features young players who have quickly made their mark in the big leagues. Fronts have player action photos against a background of silver prismatic geometric shapes. Backs are horizontal with a player portrait photo, recent stats and a few words about the player's current and projected impact. Stated odds of finding this insert are one per 18 packs. Cards are numbered with an "AI" prefix.

		NM/M
Complete Set (20):		20.00
Common Player:		.40
1	Jaime Bluma	.40
2	Tony Clark	.40
3	Jermaine Dye	.40
4	Nomar Garciaparra	4.50
5	Vladimir Guerrero	3.00
6	Todd Hollandsworth	.40
7	Derek Jeter	6.00
8	Andruw Jones	3.00
9	Chipper Jones	4.50
10	Jason Kendall	.40
11	Brooks Kieschnick	.40
12	Alex Ochoa	.40
13	Rey Ordonez	.40
14	Neifi Perez	.40
15	Edgar Renteria	.40
16	Mariano Rivera	.50
17	Ruben Rivera	.40
18	Scott Rolen	2.25
19	Billy Wagner	.40
20	Todd Walker	.40

Inter-League Match Ups

The double-sided Inter-League Finest and Inter-League Finest Refractors (seeded one in 36 and one in 216 Topps Series 1 packs respectively) feature top individual matchups from inter-league rivalries. One player from each major league team is represented, for a total of 28 players on 14 different cards. Each card is covered with a Finest clear protector. Cards are numbered with an "ILM" prefix.

		NM/M
Complete Set (14):		16.00
Common Card:		.50
	Refractors:	1.5X
1	Mark McGwire, Barry Bonds	3.00

2	Tim Salmon, Mike Piazza	2.00
3	Ken Griffey Jr., Dante Bichette	2.00
4	Juan Gonzalez, Tony Gwynn	1.50
5	Frank Thomas, Sammy Sosa	1.50
6	Albert Belle, Barry Larkin	.50
7	Johnny Damon, Brian Jordan	.75
8	Paul Molitor, Jeff King	1.00
9	John Jaha, Jeff Bagwell	1.00
10	Bernie Williams, Todd Hundley	.50
11	Joe Carter, Henry Rodriguez	.50
12	Cal Ripken Jr., Gregg Jefferies	3.00
13	Mo Vaughn, Chipper Jones	1.50
14	Travis Fryman, Gary Sheffield	.75

Derek Jeter Autograph

An authentically autographed card honoring Derek Jeter as Rookie of the Year was a random insert found on average of one per 576 packs of Topps Series 2.

	NM/M
Derek Jeter	130.00

Hobby Masters

These 20 cards lead the way as dealers' top selections. The cards, printed on 28-point diffraction foilboard, replace two regular cards in every 36th pack of 1997 Topps Series 1 product. Cards are numbered with a "HM" prefix.

		NM/M
Complete Set (20):		30.00
Common Player:		.75
1	Ken Griffey Jr.	3.00
2	Cal Ripken Jr.	4.50
3	Greg Maddux	2.25
4	Albert Belle	.75
5	Tony Gwynn	2.25
6	Jeff Bagwell	1.50
7	Randy Johnson	1.50
8	Raul Mondesi	.75
9	Juan Gonzalez	1.00
10	Kenny Lofton	.75
11	Frank Thomas	1.50
12	Mike Piazza	3.00
13	Chipper Jones	2.25
14	Brady Anderson	.75
15	Ken Caminiti	.75
16	Barry Bonds	4.50
17	Mo Vaughn	.75
18	Derek Jeter	4.50
19	Sammy Sosa	2.25
20	Andres Galarraga	.75

Mickey Mantle Reprints

All 16 remaining Mickey Mantle cards that were not reprinted in 1996 Topps Baseball are found in this insert, seeded every 12 packs of Series I Topps. The set starts off with No. 21 and runs through No. 36 since the '96 reprints were numbered 1-20.

AMERICAN LEAGUE ALL-STAR

MICKEY MANTLE

OUTFIELD

		NM/M
Complete Set (16):		60.00
Common Card:		5.00
Inserted 1:12 Series 1		
21	1953 Bowman #44	5.00
22	1953 Bowman #59	5.00
23	1957 Topps #407	5.00
24	1958 Topps #418	5.00
25	1958 Topps #487	5.00
26	1959 Topps #461	5.00
27	1959 Topps #564	5.00
28	1960 Topps #160	5.00
29	1960 Topps #563	5.00
30	1961 Topps #406	5.00
31	1961 Topps #475	5.00
32	1961 Topps #578	5.00
33	1962 Topps #18	5.00
34	1962 Topps #318	5.00
35	1962 Topps #471	5.00
36	1964 Topps #331	5.00

Mickey Mantle Finest

The Mickey Mantle reprint inserts found in Series 1 were re-issued in Series 2 in Finest technology, found on average of every 24 packs. Refractor versions of each Finest reprint were inserted at a 1:216 rate.

		NM/M
Complete Set (16):		70.00
Common Card:		5.00
Inserted 1:24 Series 2		
	Refractor:	4X
Inserted 1:216		
21	1953 Bowman #44	5.00
22	1953 Bowman #59	7.50
23	1957 Topps #407	5.00
24	1958 Topps #418	5.00
25	1958 Topps #487	5.00
26	1959 Topps #461	5.00
27	1959 Topps #564	5.00
28	1960 Topps #160	5.00
29	1960 Topps #563	5.00
30	1961 Topps #406	5.00
31	1961 Topps #475	5.00
32	1961 Topps #578	5.00
33	1962 Topps #18	5.00
34	1962 Topps #318	5.00
35	1962 Topps #471	5.00
36	1964 Topps #331	5.00

Mickey Mantle Case Inserts

WORLD SERIES BATTING FOES
MICKEY MANTLE - HANK AARON

Inserted one per case of Series 1 Topps, these reprints of 16 Mickey Mantle special cards of the 1950s-1960s come sealed in a soft

plastic holder. The plastic sleeve has a gold-foil stamp at bottom-back which reads "FACTORY TOPPS SEAL 1997."

		NM/M
Complete Set (16):		160.00
Common Card:		12.50
21	1953 Bowman #44	12.50
22	1953 Bowman #59	18.00
23	1957 Topps #407	12.50
24	1958 Topps #418	12.50
25	1958 Topps #487	12.50
26	1959 Topps #461	12.50
27	1959 Topps #564	12.50
28	1960 Topps #160	12.50
29	1960 Topps #563	12.50
30	1961 Topps #406	12.50
31	1961 Topps #475	12.50
32	1961 Topps #578	12.50
33	1962 Topps #18	12.50
34	1962 Topps #318	12.50
35	1962 Topps #471	12.50
36	1964 Topps #331	12.50

Willie Mays Reprints

GIANTS

WILLIE MAYS outfield

There are 27 different Willie Mays cards reprinted in Series 1 and seeded every eight packs. The inserts form a collection of Topps and Bowman cards from throughout Mays' career and each is highlighted by a special commemorative gold foil stamp. Many of the Mays reprints can also be found in an autographed edition, bearing a special "Certified Autograph Issue" gold-foil logo.

		NM/M
Complete Set (27):		50.00
Common Card:		3.00
Autographed Card:		120.00
1	1951 Bowman #305	6.00
2	1952 Topps #261	4.00
3	1953 Topps #244	3.00
4	1954 Bowman #89	3.00
5	1954 Topps #90	3.00
6	1955 Bowman #184	3.00
7	1955 Topps #194	3.00
8	1956 Topps #130	3.00
9	1957 Topps #10	3.00
10	1958 Topps #5	3.00
11	1959 Topps #50	3.00
12	1960 Topps #200	3.00
13	1960 Topps #564	3.00
14	1961 Topps #150	3.00
15	1961 Topps #579	3.00
16	1962 Topps #300	3.00
17	1963 Topps #300	3.00
18	1964 Topps #150	3.00
19	1965 Topps #250	3.00
20	1966 Topps #1	3.00
21	1967 Topps #200	3.00
22	1968 Topps #50	3.00
23	1969 Topps #190	3.00
24	1970 Topps #600	3.00
25	1971 Topps #600	3.00
26	1972 Topps #49	3.00
27	1973 Topps #305	3.00

Willie Mays Reprint Autographs

According to Topps, only 19 of the 27 different Willie Mays cards reprinted in Series 1 exist in authentically autographed form, bearing a special "Certified Autograph Issue" gold-foil logo.

		NM/M
Common Card:		120.00
1	1951 Bowman #305	150.00
2	1952 Topps #261	120.00
3	1953 Topps #244	120.00
6	1955 Bowman #184	120.00
7	1955 Topps #194	120.00
9	1957 Topps #10	120.00
10	1958 Topps #5	120.00
12	1960 Topps #200	120.00
13	1960 Topps #564	120.00
14	1961 Topps #150	120.00
15	1961 Topps #579	120.00
17	1963 Topps #300	120.00
18	1964 Topps #150	120.00
19	1965 Topps #250	120.00
20	1966 Topps #1	120.00
23	1969 Topps #190	120.00
24	1970 Topps #600	120.00
26	1972 Topps #49	120.00
27	1973 Topps #305	120.00

Willie Mays Finest

Series 2 offered collectors a chance to find Finest technology versions of each of the 27 commemorative reprint Topps and Bowman cards from throughout Mays' career. The Finest reprints are found one in every 30 packs, on average, with Refractor versions seeded 1:180.

		NM/M
Complete Set (27):		60.00
Common Card:		3.00
	Refractor:	3X
Inserted 1:180		
1	1951 Bowman #305	6.00
2	1952 Topps #261	4.00
3	1953 Topps #244	3.00
4	1954 Bowman #89	3.00
5	1954 Topps #90	3.00
6	1955 Bowman #184	3.00
7	1955 Topps #194	3.00
8	1956 Topps #130	3.00
9	1957 Topps #10	3.00
10	1958 Topps #5	3.00
11	1959 Topps #50	3.00
12	1960 Topps #200	3.00
13	1960 Topps #564	3.00
14	1961 Topps #150	3.00
15	1961 Topps #579	3.00
16	1962 Topps #300	3.00
17	1963 Topps #300	3.00
18	1964 Topps #150	3.00
19	1965 Topps #250	3.00
20	1966 Topps #1	3.00
21	1967 Topps #200	3.00
22	1968 Topps #50	3.00
23	1969 Topps #190	3.00
24	1970 Topps #600	3.00
25	1971 Topps #600	3.00
26	1972 Topps #49	3.00
27	1973 Topps #305	3.00

Willie Mays Commemorative Super

WILLIE MAYS

This oversize (4-1/4" x 5-3/4") version of card #2 (1952 Topps) in the Willie Mays Commemorative Reprint series was available exclusively in a special retail packaging of 10 1997 Topps Series 1 foil packs. Like the regular-size reprints, it has a gold-foil commemorative stamp on front.

		NM/M
2	Willie Mays (1952 Topps)	5.00

Season's Best

Season's Best features 25 players on prismatic illusion foilboard, and can be found every six packs. The set has the top five players from five statistical categories: home runs, RBIs, batting average, steals, and wins. Season's Best were found in

NUMBER CRUNCHERS — FRANK THOMAS

packs of Topps Series II, and later reprinted on chromium stock as part of Topps Chrome.

		NM/M
Complete Set (25):		12.00
Common Player:		.25
1	Tony Gwynn	1.50
2	Frank Thomas	1.25
3	Ellis Burks	.25
4	Paul Molitor	1.25
5	Chuck Knoblauch	.25
6	Mark McGwire	3.00
7	Brady Anderson	.25
8	Ken Griffey Jr.	2.00
9	Albert Belle	.25
10	Andres Galarraga	.25
11	Andres Galarraga	.25
12	Albert Belle	.25
13	Juan Gonzalez	.75
14	Mo Vaughn	.25
15	Rafael Palmeiro	1.00
16	John Smoltz	.25
17	Andy Pettitte	.50
18	Pat Hentgen	.25
19	Mike Mussina	.50
20	Andy Benes	.25
21	Kenny Lofton	.25
22	Tom Goodwin	.25
23	Otis Nixon	.25
24	Eric Young	.25
25	Lance Johnson	.25

Series 2 Supers

CHIPPER JONES

At 3-3/4" x 5-1/4", these premium cards are nearly identical to the regular-issue versions except for size. Also, whereas the regular cards have a front format which combines a high-gloss central area with a matte finish near the borders, the supers have just one finish on the front which is a semi-gloss. The supers also have different card numbers on back. One of the supers was included in each boxed lot of 15 Series II foil packs sold at large retail outlets with a price tag of about $15.

		NM/M
Complete Set (3):		10.00
1	Chipper Jones	3.00
2	Ken Griffey Jr.	4.00
3	Cal Ripken Jr.	5.00

Sweet Strokes

These retail-exclusive Sweet Strokes insert cards consist of 15 Power Matrix foil cards of the top hitters in the game. These players have the swings to produce game winning-hits. The cards were seed-

ed one per every 12 1997 Topps Series I retail packs. Cards are numbered with a "SS" prefix.

		NM/M
Complete Set (15):		15.00
Common Player:		.35
1	Roberto Alomar	.50
2	Jeff Bagwell	1.25
3	Albert Belle	.35
4	Barry Bonds	3.00
5	Mark Grace	.35
6	Ken Griffey Jr.	2.00
7	Tony Gwynn	1.50
8	Chipper Jones	1.50
9	Edgar Martinez	.35
10	Mark McGwire	2.50
11	Rafael Palmeiro	1.00
12	Mike Piazza	2.00
13	Gary Sheffield	.75
14	Frank Thomas	1.25
15	Mo Vaughn	.35

Team Timber

TEAM TIMBER

Team Timber was a 16-card insert that was exclusive to retail packs and inserted one per 36. The set displays the game's top sluggers on laminated litho wood cards. Cards are numbered with a "TT" prefix.

		NM/M
Complete Set (16):		24.00
Common Player:		.50
1	Ken Griffey Jr.	3.00
2	Ken Caminiti	.50
3	Bernie Williams	.50
4	Jeff Bagwell	1.50
5	Frank Thomas	1.50
6	Andres Galarraga	.50
7	Barry Bonds	5.00
8	Rafael Palmeiro	1.25
9	Brady Anderson	.50
10	Juan Gonzalez	.75
11	Mo Vaughn	.50
12	Mark McGwire	4.00
13	Gary Sheffield	.90
14	Albert Belle	.50
15	Chipper Jones	2.50
16	Mike Piazza	3.00

1997 Topps Chrome

JOSE VALENTIN

Chrome Baseball reprinted the top 165 cards from Topps Series I and II baseball on a chromium, metallized stock. Chrome was sold in four-card packs and included three insert sets: Diamond Duos, which was created exclusively for this product, Season's Best and Topps All-Stars, which were both reprinted from Topps products. Refractor versions of each card were found every 12 packs.

		NM/M
Complete Set (165):		35.00
Common Player:		.10
Refractors:		2X
Pack (4):		1.50
Wax Box (24):		25.00
1	Barry Bonds	3.00
2	Jose Valentin	.10
3	Brady Anderson	.10
4	Wade Boggs	1.50
5	Andres Galarraga	.10
6	Rusty Greer	.10
7	Derek Jeter	3.00
8	Ricky Bottalico	.10
9	Mike Piazza	2.00
10	Garret Anderson	.10
11	Jeff King	.10
12	Kevin Appier	.10
13	Mark Grace	.10
14	Jeff D'Amico	.10
15	Jay Buhner	.10
16	Hal Morris	.10
17	Harold Baines	.10
18	Jeff Cirillo	.10
19	Tom Glavine	.35
20	Andy Pettitte	.35
21	Mark McGwire	2.50
22	Chuck Knoblauch	.10
23	Raul Mondesi	.10
24	Albert Belle	.10
25	Trevor Hoffman	.10
26	Eric Young	.10
27	Brian McRae	.10
28	Jim Edmonds	.10
29	Robb Nen	.10
30	Reggie Sanders	.10
31	Mike Lansing	.10
32	Craig Biggio	.10
33	Ray Lankford	.10
34	Charles Nagy	.10
35	Paul Wilson	.10
36	John Wetteland	.10
37	Derek Bell	.10
38	Edgar Martinez	.10
39	Rickey Henderson	1.00
40	Jim Thome	.75
41	Frank Thomas	1.00
42	Jackie Robinson (Tribute)	2.00
43	Terry Steinbach	.10
44	Kevin Brown	.10
45	Joey Hamilton	.10
46	Travis Fryman	.10
47	Juan Gonzalez	.50
48	Ron Gant	.10
49	Greg Maddux	1.50
50	Wally Joyner	.10
51	John Valentin	.10
52	Bret Boone	.10
53	Paul Molitor	1.00
54	Rafael Palmeiro	.75
55	Todd Hundley	.10
56	Ellis Burks	.10
57	Bernie Williams	.10
58	Roberto Alomar	.25
59	Jose Mesa	.10
60	Troy Percival	.10
61	John Smoltz	.10
62	Jeff Conine	.10
63	Bernard Gilkey	.10
64	Mickey Tettleton	.10
65	Justin Thompson	.10
66	Tony Phillips	.10
67	Ryne Sandberg	1.50
68	Geronimo Berroa	.10
69	Todd Hollandsworth	.10
70	Rey Ordonez	.10
71	Marquis Grissom	.10
72	Tino Martinez	.10
73	Steve Finley	.10
74	Andy Benes	.10
75	Jason Kendall	.10
76	Johnny Damon	.35
77	Jason Giambi	.10
78	Henry Rodriguez	.10
79	Edgar Renteria	.10
80	Ray Durham	.10
81	Gregg Jefferies	.10
82	Roberto Hernandez	.10
83	Joe Carter	.10
84	Jermaine Dye	.10
85	Julio Franco	.10
86	David Justice	.10
87	Jose Canseco	.50
88	Paul O'Neill	.10
89	Mariano Rivera	.15
90	Bobby Higginson	.10
91	Mark Grudzielanek	.10
92	Lance Johnson	.10
93	Ken Caminiti	.10
94	Gary Sheffield	.50
95	Luis Castillo	.10
96	Scott Rolen	.75
97	Chipper Jones	1.50
98	Darryl Strawberry	.10
99	Nomar Garciaparra	1.50
100	Jeff Bagwell	1.00
101	Ken Griffey Jr.	2.00
102	Sammy Sosa	1.50
103	Jack McDowell	.10
104	James Baldwin	.10
105	Rocky Coppinger	.10
106	Manny Ramirez	1.00
107	Tim Salmon	.10
108	Eric Karros	.10
109	Brett Butler	.10
110	Randy Johnson	1.00
111	Pat Hentgen	.10
112	Rondell White	.10
113	Eddie Murray	1.00
114	Ivan Rodriguez	.75
115	Jermaine Allensworth	.10
116	Ed Sprague	.10
117	Kenny Lofton	.10
118	Alan Benes	.10
119	Fred McGriff	.10
120	Alex Fernandez	.10
121	Al Martin	.10
122	Devon White	.10
123	David Cone	.10
124	Karim Garcia	.25
125	Chili Davis	.10
126	Roger Clemens	1.75
127	Bobby Bonilla	.10
128	Mike Mussina	.50
129	Todd Walker	.10
130	Dante Bichette	.10
131	Carlos Baerga	.10
132	Matt Williams	.10
133	Will Clark	.10
134	Dennis Eckersley	.75
135	Ryan Klesko	.10
136	Dean Palmer	.10
137	Javy Lopez	.10
138	Greg Vaughn	.10
139	Vinny Castilla	.10
140	Cal Ripken Jr.	3.00
141	Ruben Rivera	.10
142	Mark Wohlers	.10
143	Tony Clark	.10
144	Jose Rosado	.10
145	Tony Gwynn	1.50
146	Cecil Fielder	.10
147	Brian Jordan	.10
148	Bob Abreu	.10
149	Barry Larkin	.10
150	Robin Ventura	.10
151	John Olerud	.10
152	Rod Beck	.10
153	Vladimir Guerrero	1.00
154	Marty Cordova	.10
155	Todd Stottlemyre	.10
156	Hideo Nomo	.50
157	Denny Neagle	.10
158	John Jaha	.10
159	Mo Vaughn	.10
160	Andruw Jones	1.00
161	Moises Alou	.10
162	Larry Walker	.10
163	Eddie Murray (Season Highlights)	.75
164	Paul Molitor (Season Highlights)	.75
165	Checklist	.10

All-Stars

Topps Chrome All-Stars display the same 22 cards found in Topps Series I, however these are reprinted on a Chrome stock. Regular versions are seeded every 24 packs, while Refractor versions arrive every 72 packs. Cards are numbered with an "AS" prefix.

		NM/M
Complete Set (22):		25.00
Common Player:		.75
Refractors:		1.5X
1	Ivan Rodriguez	1.50
2	Todd Hundley	.75
3	Frank Thomas	2.00
4	Andres Galarraga	.75
5	Chuck Knoblauch	.75
6	Eric Young	.75
7	Jim Thome	1.50
8	Chipper Jones	3.00
9	Cal Ripken Jr.	6.00
10	Barry Larkin	.75
11	Albert Belle	.75
12	Barry Bonds	6.00
13	Ken Griffey Jr.	4.00
14	Ellis Burks	.75
15	Juan Gonzalez	1.00
16	Gary Sheffield	1.25
17	Andy Pettitte	1.00
18	Tom Glavine	1.00
19	Pat Hentgen	.75
20	John Smoltz	.75
21	Roberto Hernandez	.75
22	Mark Wohlers	.75

Diamond Duos

Diamond Duos is the only one of the three insert sets in Chrome Baseball that was developed exclusively for this product. The set has 10 cards featuring two superstar teammates on double-sided chromium cards. Diamond Duos are found every 36 packs, while Refractor versions are found every 108 packs. Cards are numbered with a "DD" prefix.

DIAMOND DUOS

		NM/M
Complete Set (10):		17.50
Common Player:		.50
Refractors:		1.5X
1	Chipper Jones, Andruw Jones	2.00
2	Derek Jeter, Bernie Williams	4.00
3	Ken Griffey Jr., Jay Buhner	2.50
4	Kenny Lofton, Manny Ramirez	1.50
5	Jeff Bagwell, Craig Biggio	1.50
6	Juan Gonzalez, Ivan Rodriguez	1.25
7	Cal Ripken Jr., Brady Anderson	4.00
8	Mike Piazza, Hideo Nomo	2.50
9	Andres Galarraga, Dante Bichette	.50
10	Frank Thomas, Albert Belle	1.50

Season's Best

Season's Best includes the 25 players found in Topps Series II, but in a chromium version. The top five players from five statistical categories, including Leading Looters, Bleacher Reachers and Kings of Swing. Regular versions are seeded every 18 packs, with Refractors every 54 packs.

		NM/M
Complete Set (25):		17.50
Common Player:		.50
Refractors:		1.5X
1	Tony Gwynn	2.00
2	Frank Thomas	1.50
3	Ellis Burks	.50
4	Paul Molitor	1.50
5	Chuck Knoblauch	.50
6	Mark McGwire	4.00
7	Brady Anderson	.50
8	Ken Griffey Jr.	3.00
9	Albert Belle	.50
10	Andres Galarraga	.50
11	Andres Galarraga	.50
12	Albert Belle	.50
13	Juan Gonzalez	.75
14	Mo Vaughn	.50
15	Rafael Palmeiro	1.25
16	John Smoltz	.50
17	Andy Pettitte	.75
18	Pat Hentgen	.50
19	Mike Mussina	.75
20	Andy Benes	.50
21	Kenny Lofton	.50
22	Tom Goodwin	.50
23	Otis Nixon	.50
24	Eric Young	.50
25	Lance Johnson	.50

Jumbos

MIKE PIAZZA

These large-format (3-3/4" x 5-1/4") Topps Chrome cards were produced for sale in special retail packaging offering one jumbo card and five packs of Topps Chrome for about $15. The jumbos are identical in design to the regular-issue Chrome cards of the same players. Because they were

offered in a windowed retail package, it was easy for collectors to pick the card they wanted.

		NM/M
Complete Set (6):		10.00
Common Player:		.75
9	Mike Piazza	2.00
94	Gary Sheffield	.75
97	Chipper Jones	1.50
101	Ken Griffey Jr.	2.00
102	Sammy Sosa	1.50
140	Cal Ripken Jr.	3.00

1997 Topps Gallery Pre-Production

In its second year Topps Gallery was produced in a greatly improved combination of card stock, graphic highlights and inserts. To reintroduce the hobby to the issue, Topps distributed these promotional samples to dealers and the press. Except for the "PP" prefix to the card number on front, the samples are virtually identical to the issued versions.

		NM/M
Complete Set (4):		25.00
Common Player:		3.00
1	Andruw Jones	5.00
2	Derek Jeter	9.00
3	Mike Piazza	10.00
4	Craig Biggio	3.00

1997 Topps Gallery

ANDRUW JONES

The second year of Gallery features 180 cards printed on extra-thick 24-point stock. Card fronts feature a player photo surrounded by an embossed foil "frame" to give each card the look of a piece of artwork. Backs contain career stats and biographical information on each player. Inserts include Peter Max Serigraphs, Signature Series Serigraphs, Player's Private Issue (parallel set), Photo Gallery and Gallery of Heroes. Cards were sold exclusively in hobby shops in eight-card packs for $4 each.

		NM/M
Complete Set (180):		20.00
Common Player:		.10
Pack (8):		1.50
Wax Box (24):		25.00
1	Paul Molitor	.75
2	Devon White	.10
3	Andres Galarraga	.10
4	Cal Ripken Jr.	3.00
5	Tony Gwynn	1.50
6	Mike Stanley	.10
7	Orel Hershiser	.10
8	Jose Canseco	.50
9	Chili Davis	.10
10	Harold Baines	.10
11	Rickey Henderson	.75
12	Darryl Strawberry	.10
13	Todd Worrell	.10
14	Cecil Fielder	.10
15	Gary Gaetti	.10
16	Bobby Bonilla	.10
17	Will Clark	.10
18	Kevin Brown	.10
19	Tom Glavine	.35
20	Wade Boggs	1.50
21	Edgar Martinez	.10
22	Lance Johnson	.10
23	Gregg Jefferies	.10
24	Bip Roberts	.10
25	Tony Phillips	.10
26	Greg Maddux	1.50
27	Mickey Tettleton	.10
28	Terry Steinbach	.10
29	Ryne Sandberg	1.50
30	Wally Joyner	.10
31	Joe Carter	.10
32	Ellis Burks	.10
33	Fred McGriff	.10
34	Barry Larkin	.10
35	John Franco	.10
36	Rafael Palmeiro	.65

37	Mark McGwire	2.50
38	Ken Caminiti	.10
39	David Cone	.10
40	Julio Franco	.10
41	Roger Clemens	1.75
42	Barry Bonds	3.00
43	Dennis Eckersley	.65
44	Eddie Murray	.75
45	Paul O'Neill	.10
46	Craig Biggio	.10
47	Roberto Alomar	.20
48	Mark Grace	.10
49	Matt Williams	.10
50	Jay Buhner	.10
51	John Smoltz	.10
52	Randy Johnson	.75
53	Ramon Martinez	.10
54	Curt Schilling	.35
55	Gary Sheffield	.50
56	Jack McDowell	.10
57	Brady Anderson	.10
58	Dante Bichette	.10
59	Ron Gant	.10
60	Alex Fernandez	.10
61	Moises Alou	.10
62	Travis Fryman	.10
63	Dean Palmer	.10
64	Todd Hundley	.10
65	Jeff Brantley	.10
66	Bernard Gilkey	.10
67	Geronimo Berroa	.10
68	John Wetteland	.10
69	Robin Ventura	.10
70	Ray Lankford	.10
71	Kevin Appier	.10
72	Larry Walker	.10
73	Juan Gonzalez	.40
74	Jeff King	.10
75	Greg Vaughn	.10
76	Steve Finley	.10
77	Brian McRae	.10
78	Paul Sorrento	.10
79	Ken Griffey Jr.	2.00
80	Omar Vizquel	.10
81	Jose Mesa	.10
82	Albert Belle	.10
83	Glenallen Hill	.10
84	Sammy Sosa	1.50
85	Andy Benes	.10
86	David Justice	.10
87	Marquis Grissom	.10
88	John Olerud	.10
89	Tino Martinez	.10
90	Frank Thomas	.75
91	Raul Mondesi	.10
92	Steve Trachsel	.10
93	Jim Edmonds	.10
94	Rusty Greer	.10
95	Joey Hamilton	.10
96	Ismael Valdes	.10
97	Dave Nilsson	.10
98	John Jaha	.10
99	Alex Gonzalez	.10
100	Javy Lopez	.10
101	Ryan Klesko	.10
102	Tim Salmon	.10
103	Bernie Williams	.10
104	Roberto Hernandez	.10
105	Chuck Knoblauch	.10
106	Mike Lansing	.10
107	Vinny Castilla	.10
108	Reggie Sanders	.10
109	Mo Vaughn	.10
110	Rondell White	.10
111	Ivan Rodriguez	.65
112	Mike Mussina	.40
113	Carlos Baerga	.10
114	Jeff Conine	.10
115	Jim Thome	.65
116	Manny Ramirez	.75
117	Kenny Lofton	.10
118	Wilson Alvarez	.10
119	Eric Karros	.10
120	Robb Nen	.10
121	Mark Wohlers	.10
122	Ed Sprague	.10
123	Pat Hentgen	.10
124	Juan Guzman	.10
125	Derek Bell	.10
126	Jeff Bagwell	.75
127	Eric Young	.10
128	John Valentin	.10
129	Al Martin (Photo actually Javy Lopez.)	.10
130	Trevor Hoffman	.10
131	Henry Rodriguez	.10
132	Pedro Martinez	.75
133	Mike Piazza	2.00
134	Brian Jordan	.10
135	Jose Valentin	.10
136	Jeff Cirillo	.10
137	Chipper Jones	1.50
138	Ricky Bottalico	.10
139	Hideo Nomo	.40
140	Troy Percival	.10
141	Rey Ordonez	.10
142	Edgar Renteria	.10
143	Luis Castillo	.10
144	Vladimir Guerrero	.75
145	Jeff D'Amico	.10
146	Andruw Jones	.75
147	Darin Erstad	.25
148	Bob Abreu	.10
149	Carlos Delgado	.45
150	Jamey Wright	.10
151	Nomar Garciaparra	1.50
152	Jason Kendall	.10
153	Jermaine Allensworth	.10
154	Scott Rolen	.65
155	Rocky Coppinger	.10
156	Paul Wilson	.10
157	Garret Anderson	.10
158	Mariano Rivera	.15
159	Ruben Rivera	.10
160	Andy Pettitte	.35
161	Derek Jeter	3.00
162	Neifi Perez	.10
163	Ray Durham	.10
164	James Baldwin	.10
165	Marty Cordova	.10
166	Tony Clark	.10
167	Michael Tucker	.10
168	Mike Sweeney	.10
169	Johnny Damon	.25
170	Jermaine Dye	.10
171	Alex Ochoa	.10
172	Jason Isringhausen	.10
173	Mark Grudzielanek	.10
174	Jose Rosado	.10
175	Todd Hollandsworth	.10
176	Alan Benes	.10
177	Jason Giambi	.45
178	Billy Wagner	.10
179	Justin Thompson	.10
180	Todd Walker	.10

Players Private Issue

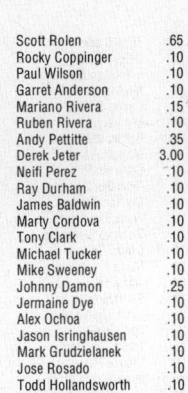

A parallel version of the Gallery issue called Players Private Issue was produced as a 1:12 pack insert. The PPI cards differ from the regular version in the use of a "PPI-" prefix to the card number on front and the application of a small silver PPI seal in a lower corner. On back, the line "One of 250 Issued" has been added.

	NM/M
Common Player:	1.00
Stars:	5X

Gallery of Heroes

This 10-card die-cut insert features a design resembling stained glass. Cards were inserted 1:36 packs. Cards are numbered with a "GH" prefix.

		NM/M
Complete Set (10):		30.00
Common Player:		1.50
1	Derek Jeter	6.00
2	Chipper Jones	3.00
3	Frank Thomas	2.50
4	Ken Griffey Jr.	4.00
5	Cal Ripken Jr.	6.00
6	Mark McGwire	5.00
7	Mike Piazza	4.00
8	Jeff Bagwell	2.50
9	Tony Gwynn	3.00
10	Mo Vaughn	1.50

Peter Max

Noted artist Peter Max has painted renditions of 10 superstar players and offered his commentary about those players on the backs. Cards were inserted 1:24 packs. In addition, Max-autographed cards signed and numbered from an edition of 40 are inserted 1:1,200 packs.

		NM/M
Complete Set (10):		60.00
Common Player:		3.00
Peter Max Autographed:		100.00
1	Derek Jeter	10.00
2	Albert Belle	3.00
3	Ken Caminiti	3.00
4	Chipper Jones	6.00
5	Ken Griffey Jr.	7.50
6	Frank Thomas	5.00
7	Cal Ripken Jr.	10.00
8	Mark McGwire	9.00
9	Barry Bonds	10.00
10	Mike Piazza	7.50

Photo Gallery

This 21-card set features full-bleed, high-gloss action photos of some of the game's top stars. Cards were inserted 1:24 packs. They are numbered with a "PG" prefix.

		NM/M
Complete Set (16):		15.00
Common Player:		.50
1	World Series	.50
2	Paul Molitor	1.00
3	Eddie Murray	1.00
4	Ken Griffey Jr.	2.50
5	Chipper Jones	1.50
6	Derek Jeter	3.50
7	Frank Thomas	1.00
8	Mark McGwire	3.00
9	Kenny Lofton	.50
10	Gary Sheffield	.65
11	Mike Piazza	2.50
12	Vinny Castilla	.50
13	Andres Galarraga	.50
14	Andy Pettitte	.50
15	Robin Ventura	.50
16	Barry Larkin	.50

Screenplays

Twenty of the game's top stars were featured in this multi-part collectible. The packaging is a 5-1/8" diameter lithographed steel can. The can was shrink-wrapped at the factory with a round checklist disc covering the color player photo on top of the can. The top has a woodgrain border around the photo and a gold facsimile autograph. The back of the topper disc has a career summary of the player. Inside the tin is a 2-1/2" x 3-1/2" plastic motion card with several seconds of game action shown as the angle of view changes. The card is covered by a peel-off protective layer on front and back. Foam pieces in the package allow both the can and card to be displayed upright. Issue price was about $10 per can. The unnumbered cans are checklisted here alphabetically. Values shown are for can/card combinations.

	NM/M
Complete Set (20):	25.00
Common Player:	1.00

Pack (1):		2.50
Wax Box (21):		30.00
(1)	Jeff Bagwell	2.00
(2)	Albert Belle	1.00
(3)	Barry Bonds	5.00
(4)	Andres Galarraga	1.00
(5)	Nomar Garciaparra	2.50
(6)	Juan Gonzalez	1.25
(7)	Ken Griffey Jr.	3.00
(8)	Tony Gwynn	2.50
(9)	Derek Jeter	5.00
(10)	Randy Johnson	2.00
(11)	Andruw Jones	2.00
(12)	Chipper Jones	2.50
(13)	Kenny Lofton	1.00
(14)	Mark McGwire	4.00
(15)	Paul Molitor	2.00
(16)	Hideo Nomo	1.25
(17)	Cal Ripken Jr.	5.00
(18)	Sammy Sosa	2.50
(19)	Frank Thomas	2.00
(20)	Jim Thome	1.50

Screenplays Inserts

		NM/M
Complete Set (6):		35.00
Common Player:		2.00
1	Larry Walker	2.00
2	Cal Ripken Jr.	12.50
3	Chipper Jones	6.00
4	Frank Thomas	5.00
5	Mike Piazza	7.50
6	Ken Griffey Jr.	7.50

1997 Topps Stars Promos

These promo cards introduced Topps' new line of premium cards. They are in the same basic format as the regular issue, but are marked "PRE-PRODUCTION / SAMPLE" in the stats box on back.

		NM/M
Complete Set (3):		5.00
Common Player:		1.00
PP1	Larry Walker	1.00
PP2	Roger Clemens	3.00
PP3	Frank Thomas	2.00

1997 Topps Stars

The premiere version of this product was sold only to hobby shops that were members of the Topps Home Team Advantage program. Each of the 125 regular cards in the set is printed on 20-point stock. Card fronts feature spot UV coating with a textured star pattern running down one side of the card. Inserts include the parallel Always Mint set, as well as '97 All-Stars, Future All-Stars, All-Star memories, and Autographed Rookie Reprints. Cards were sold in seven-card packs for $3 each.

		NM/M
Complete Set (125):		30.00
Common Player:		.10
Always Mint Stars, RC's:		8X
Pack (7):		3.00
Wax Box (24):		65.00
1	Larry Walker	.10
2	Tino Martinez	.10
3	Cal Ripken Jr.	3.00
4	Ken Griffey Jr.	2.00
5	Chipper Jones	1.50
6	David Justice	.10
7	Mike Piazza	2.00
8	Jeff Bagwell	1.00
9	Ron Gant	.10
10	Sammy Sosa	2.00
11	Tony Gwynn	1.50
12	Carlos Baerga	.10
13	Frank Thomas	1.00
14	Moises Alou	.10
15	Barry Larkin	.10
16	Ivan Rodriguez	.75
17	Greg Maddux	1.50
18	Jim Edmonds	.10
19	Jose Canseco	.50
20	Rafael Palmeiro	.75
21	Paul Molitor	1.00
22	Kevin Appier	.10
23	Raul Mondesi	.10
24	Lance Johnson	.10
25	Edgar Martinez	.10
26	Andres Galarraga	.10
27	Mo Vaughn	.10
28	Ken Caminiti	.10
29	Cecil Fielder	.10
30	Harold Baines	.10
31	Roberto Alomar	.25
32	Shawn Estes	.10
33	Tom Glavine	.35
34	Dennis Eckersley	.75
35	Manny Ramirez	1.00
36	John Olerud	.50
37	Juan Gonzalez	.50
38	Chuck Knoblauch	.10
39	Albert Belle	.10
40	Vinny Castilla	.10
41	John Smoltz	.10
42	Barry Bonds	3.00
43	Randy Johnson	1.00
44	Brady Anderson	.10
45	Jeff Blauser	.10
46	Craig Biggio	.10
47	Jeff Conine	.10
48	Marquis Grissom	.10
49	Mark Grace	.10
50	Roger Clemens	1.75
51	Mark McGwire	2.50
52	Fred McGriff	.10
53	Gary Sheffield	.50
54	Bobby Jones	.10
55	Eric Young	.10
56	Robin Ventura	.10
57	Wade Boggs	1.50
58	Joe Carter	.10
59	Ryne Sandberg	1.50
60	Matt Williams	.10
61	Todd Hundley	.10
62	Dante Bichette	.10
63	Chili Davis	.10
64	Kenny Lofton	.10
65	Jay Buhner	.10
66	Will Clark	.10
67	Travis Fryman	.10
68	Pat Hentgen	.10
69	Ellis Burks	.10
70	Mike Mussina	.40
71	Hideo Nomo	.50
72	Sandy Alomar	.10
73	Bobby Bonilla	.10
74	Rickey Henderson	1.00
75	David Cone	.10
76	Terry Steinbach	.10
77	Pedro Martinez	1.00
78	Jim Thome	.75
79	Rod Beck	.10
80	Randy Myers	.10
81	Charles Nagy	.10
82	Mark Wohlers	.10
83	Paul O'Neill	.10
84	Curt Schilling	.35
85	Joey Cora	.10
86	John Franco	.10
87	Kevin Brown	.10
88	Benito Santiago	.10
89	Ray Lankford	.10
90	Bernie Williams	.10
91	Jason Dickson	.10
92	Jeff Cirillo	.10
93	Nomar Garciaparra	2.00
94	Mariano Rivera	.15
95	Javy Lopez	.10
96	Tony Womack RC	.25
97	Jose Rosado	.10
98	Denny Neagle	.10
99	Darryl Kile	.10
100	Justin Thompson	.10
101	Juan Encarnacion	.10
102	Brad Fullmer	.10
103	Kris Benson RC	.75
104	Todd Helton	1.00
105	Paul Konerko	.10
106	Travis Lee RC	.10
107	Todd Greene	.10
108	Mark Kotsay RC	.50
109	Carl Pavano	.10
110	Kerry Wood RC	4.00
111	Jason Romano RC	.10
112	Geoff Goetz RC	.10
113	Scott Hodges RC	.10
114	Aaron Akin RC	.10
115	Vernon Wells RC	6.00
116	Chris Stowe RC	.10
117	Brett Caradonna RC	.10
118	Adam Kennedy RC	1.00
119	Jayson Werth RC	.10
120	Glenn Davis RC	.10
121	Troy Cameron RC	.10
122	J.J. Davis RC	.10
123	Jason Dellaero RC	.10
124	Jason Standridge RC	.10
125	Lance Berkman RC	2.00

Always Mint

This set parallels the regular Topps Stars issue and was inserted at the announced rate of one card per 12 packs. Identical in design to the regular version, the Always Mint cards have metallic foil background on the player portion of the front photos. Backs of the Always Mint parallels have a shiny metallic silver background.

	NM/M
Complete Set (125):	250.00
Common Player:	.50
Stars/Rookies:	8X

All-Star Memories

This 10-card insert features stars who have had memorable performances in previous All-Star Games. Cards feature a laser-cut cascade of stars on a foilboard stock. Backs have another photo and a description of the All-Star memory. The cards were inserted 1:24 packs. Cards are numbered with an "ASM" prefix.

		NM/M
Complete Set (10):		20.00
Common Player:		1.00
1	Cal Ripken Jr.	6.00
2	Jeff Conine	1.00
3	Mike Piazza	4.00
4	Randy Johnson	2.00
5	Ken Griffey Jr.	4.00
6	Fred McGriff	1.00
7	Moises Alou	1.00
8	Hideo Nomo	1.25
9	Larry Walker	1.00
10	Sandy Alomar	1.00

Future All-Stars

This 15-card set showcases the top candidates to make their All-Star Game debut in 1998. Cards feature a prismatic rainbow foil background and were inserted 1:12 packs. Cards are numbered with a "FAS" prefix.

	NM/M
Complete Set (15):	17.50
Common Player:	.75
1 Derek Jeter	4.00
2 Andruw Jones	2.50
3 Vladimir Guerrero	3.00
4 Scott Rolen	2.50
5 Jose Guillen	.75
6 Jose Cruz, Jr.	.75
7 Darin Erstad	2.50
8 Tony Clark	.75
9 Scott Spiezio	.75
10 Kevin Orie	.75
11 Calvin Reese	.75
12 Billy Wagner	.75
13 Matt Morris	.75
14 Jeremi Gonzalez	.75
15 Hideki Irabu	.75

Rookie Reprints

Fifteen Topps rookie cards of Hall of Famers were reprinted as a one-per-six-packs insert. Regardless of original size, all reprints are 2-1/2" x 3-1/2" with a reprint notice on back.

	NM/M
Complete Set (15):	25.00
Common Player:	2.00
(1) Luis Aparicio	2.00
(2) Richie Ashburn	2.00
(3) Jim Bunning	2.00
(4) Bob Feller	2.00
(5) Rollie Fingers	2.00
(6) Monte Irvin	2.00
(7) Al Kaline	3.00
(8) Ralph Kiner	2.00
(9) Eddie Mathews	3.00
(10) Hal Newhouser	2.00
(11) Gaylord Perry	2.00
(12) Robin Roberts	2.00
(13) Brooks Robinson	3.00
(14) Enos Slaughter	2.00
(15) Earl Weaver	2.00

Autographed Rookie Reprints

Fourteen different Hall of Famers autographed reprinted versions of their Topps rookie cards as a one-per-30-pack insert. Each card features a special certified stamp. Richie Ashburn was to have been card #2, but he died before he could autograph them.

	NM/M
Common Player:	15.00
(1) Luis Aparicio	20.00
(3) Jim Bunning	30.00
(4) Bob Feller	35.00
(5) Rollie Fingers	15.00
(6) Monte Irvin	15.00
(7) Al Kaline	30.00
(8) Ralph Kiner	25.00
(9) Eddie Mathews	75.00
(10) Hal Newhouser	40.00
(11) Gaylord Perry	15.00
(12) Robin Roberts	30.00
(13) Brooks Robinson	40.00
(14) Enos Slaughter	30.00
(15) Earl Weaver	20.00

1997 All-Stars

This 20-card insert honors participants of the 1997 All-Star Game in Cleveland. Cards were inserted 1:24 packs. Fronts are printed on prismatic foil with hundreds of stars in the background. On back is another player photo and his All-Star Game 1997 and career stats. Cards are numbered with an "AS" prefix.

	NM/M
Complete Set (20):	60.00
Common Player:	1.50
1 Greg Maddux	6.00
2 Randy Johnson	4.50
3 Tino Martinez	1.50
4 Jeff Bagwell	4.50
5 Ivan Rodriguez	3.50
6 Mike Piazza	7.50
7 Cal Ripken Jr.	12.00
8 Ken Caminiti	1.50
9 Tony Gwynn	6.00
10 Edgar Martinez	1.50
11 Craig Biggio	1.50
12 Roberto Alomar	2.00
13 Larry Walker	1.50
14 Brady Anderson	1.50
15 Barry Bonds	12.00
16 Ken Griffey Jr.	7.50
17 Ray Lankford	1.50
18 Paul O'Neill	1.50
19 Jeff Blauser	1.50
20 Sandy Alomar	1.50

Dodger Rookie of the Year Collection

Available only through Topps Stadium Club and at Dodger Stadium, this set of special cards honors the five consecutive (1992-96) N.L. Rookies of the Year - all L.A. Dodgers - as well as the first-ever Rookie of the Year, Jackie Robinson. The cards feature reproductions of the players' rookie cards printed on front in metallic foil and with an N.L. Rookie of the Year logo and year banner. Backs are virtually identical to the regular-issue cards, but include a reprint line in the fine print. Raul Mondesi's card is a different version of the '94 Topps Coming Attractions subset card which he shared with Ben Van Ryn. Production was reported at 4,000 sets.

	NM/M
Complete Set (6):	35.00
Common Player:	3.00
1 Jackie Robinson (1952 Topps)	20.00
2 Mike Piazza (1992 Bowman)	10.00
3 Eric Karros (1993 Topps)	3.00
4 Raul Mondesi (1994 Topps)	3.00
5 Hideo Nomo (1995 Topps Traded)	7.50
6 Todd Hollandsworth (1996 Topps)	3.00

"Pro Shooters" Photo Marbles

This limited distribution test issue was another attempt to market marbles with baseball player photos. The hard plastic 1" diameter marbles have a black composite band around the circumference. On one side is a player portrait, on the other is a team logo at center with the player name in a strip below and a number "... of 60" in a strip above. The Topps name does not appear. They were sold two per pack.

	NM/M
Complete Set (60):	1,000
Common Player:	10.00
1 Roberto Alomar	15.00
2 Brady Anderson	10.00
3 Carlos Baerga	10.00
4 Jeff Bagwell	30.00
5 Albert Belle	10.00
6 Dante Bichette	10.00
7 Craig Biggio	10.00
8 Wade Boggs	40.00
9 Barry Bonds	60.00
10 Jay Buhner	10.00
11 Ken Caminiti	10.00
12 Jose Canseco	15.00
13 Roger Clemens	42.50
14 David Cone	10.00
15 Cecil Fielder	10.00
16 Travis Fryman	10.00
17 Andres Galarraga	10.00
18 Ron Gant	10.00
19 Bernard Gilkey	10.00
20 Tom Glavine	12.50
21 Juan Gonzalez	30.00
22 Mark Grace	10.00
23 Ken Griffey Jr.	45.00
24 Tony Gwynn	40.00
25 Todd Hundley	10.00
26 John Jaha	10.00
27 Derek Jeter	60.00
28 Lance Johnson	10.00
29 Randy Johnson	30.00
30 Andruw Jones	30.00
31 Chipper Jones	40.00
32 Brian Jordan	10.00
33 Jason Kendall	10.00
34 Chuck Knoblauch	10.00
35 Ray Lankford	10.00
36 Barry Larkin	10.00
37 Kenny Lofton	10.00
38 Greg Maddux	40.00
39 Edgar Martinez	10.00
40 Fred McGriff	10.00
41 Mark McGwire	50.00
42 Paul Molitor	30.00
43 Raul Mondesi	10.00
44 Eddie Murray	30.00
45 Mike Mussina	15.00
46 Hideo Nomo	15.00
47 Rafael Palmeiro	25.00
48 Andy Pettitte	15.00
49 Mike Piazza	45.00
50 Cal Ripken Jr.	60.00
51 Ivan Rodriguez	25.00
52 Tim Salmon	10.00
53 Ryne Sandberg	40.00
54 Gary Sheffield	15.00
55 John Smoltz	10.00
56 Sammy Sosa	40.00
57 Frank Thomas	30.00
58 Mo Vaughn	10.00
59 Bernie Williams	10.00
60 Matt Williams	10.00
1 of 2 Checklist Card 1-30	30.00
2 of 2 Checklist Card 31-60	30.00

22k Gold

These 22-karat gold-foil cards were created for direct sale by Topps. They reproduce, front and back, Griffey's and Ripken's regular-issue 1997 Topps cards, and feature a 1997-style card of Irabu, who did not appear on a regular Topps card that year. The 2-1/2" x 3-1/2" cards are individually serial numbered and were sold in a protective display holder. Initially priced at $30 apiece, they were discounted in a later offer to $19.95.

	NM/M
Complete Set (3):	60.00
Common Player:	20.00
300 Ken Griffey Jr.	15.00
400 Cal Ripken Jr.	20.00
---- Hideki Irabu	15.00

1998 Topps Pre-Production

To give potential customers a feel for its 1998 baseball cards, Topps issued this series of pre-production samples. Cards are identical in format to the issued versions except they are numbered with a "PP" prefix and the 1997 stats line reads "PRE-PRODUCTION SAMPLE."

	NM/M
Complete Set (6):	4.00
Common Player:	.25
PP1 Carlos Baerga	.25
PP2 Jeff Bagwell	.75
PP3 Marquis Grissom	.25
PP4 Derek Jeter	1.50
PP5 Randy Johnson	.75
PP6 Mike Piazza	1.00

1998 Topps

Topps issued two series in 1998, a total of 503 base cards; 282 in Series 1 and 221 in Series 2. Cards feature a gold border instead of the traditional white of past years. The product features Roberto Clemente inserts and a tribute card No. 21 in the base set. Series 1 subsets Series Highlights, Expansion Team Prospects, Interleague Highlights, Season Highlights, Prospects and Draft Picks. Subsets in Series II included: Expansion Teams, InterLeague Preview, Season Highlights, Prospects and Draft Picks. Every card in the set is paralleled in a Minted in Cooperstown insert that was stamped on-site at the Baseball Hall of Fame in Cooperstown. Inserts in Series 1 include: Roberto Clemente Reprints, Clemente Finest, Clemente Tribute, Memorabilia Madness, Etch a Sketch, Mystery Finest, Flashback and Baby Boomers. Inserts in Series 2 included: Clemente Reprints, Clemente Finest, 1998 Rookie Class, Mystery Finest, Milestones, Focal Points, and Clout 9. A factory set includes the 503 base cards, eight randomly selected inserts and one Clemente card sealed in a gold-foil stamped soft plastic case.

	NM/M
Unopened Fact. Set (511):	85.00
Complete Set (503):	40.00
Common Player:	.05
Minted:	6X
Inserted 1:8	
Series 1 or 2 Pack (11):	1.00
Series 1 or 2 Wax Box (36):	25.00
1 Tony Gwynn	1.00
2 Larry Walker	.05
3 Billy Wagner	.05
4 Denny Neagle	.05
5 Vladimir Guerrero	.75
6 Kevin Brown	.05
7 Mariano Rivera	.10

9 Tony Clark	.05
10 Deion Sanders	.05
11 Francisco Cordova	.05
12 Matt Williams	.05
13 Carlos Baerga	.05
14 Mo Vaughn	.05
15 Bobby Witt	.05
16 Matt Stairs	.05
17 Chan Ho Park	.05
18 Mike Bordick	.05
19 Michael Tucker	.05
20 Frank Thomas	.75
21 Roberto Clemente	1.50
22 Dmitri Young	.05
23 Steve Trachsel	.05
24 Jeff Kent	.05
25 Scott Rolen	.50
26 John Thomson	.05
27 Joe Vitiello	.05
28 Eddie Guardado	.05
29 Charlie Hayes	.05
30 Juan Gonzalez	.40
31 Garret Anderson	.05
32 John Jaha	.05
33 Omar Vizquel	.05
34 Brian Hunter	.05
35 Jeff Bagwell	.75
36 Mark Lemke	.05
37 Doug Glanville	.05
38 Dan Wilson	.05
39 Steve Cooke	.05
40 Chili Davis	.05
41 Mike Cameron	.05
42 F.P. Santangelo	.05
43 Brad Ausmus	.05
44 Gary DiSarcina	.05
45 Pat Hentgen	.05
46 Wilton Guerrero	.05
47 Devon White	.05
48 Danny Patterson	.05
49 Pat Meares	.05
50 Rafael Palmeiro	.65
51 Mark Gardner	.05
52 Jeff Blauser	.05
53 Dave Hollins	.05
54 Carlos Garcia	.05
55 Ben McDonald	.05
56 John Mabry	.05
57 Trevor Hoffman	.05
58 Tony Fernandez	.05
59 Rich Loiselle	.05
60 Mark Leiter	.05
61 Pat Kelly	.05
62 John Flaherty	.05
63 Roger Bailey	.05
64 Tom Gordon	.05
65 Ryan Klesko	.05
66 Darryl Hamilton	.05
67 Jim Eisenreich	.05
68 Butch Huskey	.05
69 Mark Grudzielanek	.05
70 Marquis Grissom	.05
71 Mark McLemore	.05
72 Gary Gaetti	.05
73 Greg Gagne	.05
74 Lyle Mouton	.05
75 Jim Edmonds	.05
76 Shawn Green	.25
77 Greg Vaughn	.05
78 Terry Adams	.05
79 Kevin Polcovich RC	.05
80 Troy O'Leary	.05
81 Jeff Shaw	.05
82 Rich Becker	.05
83 David Wells	.05
84 Steve Karsay	.05
85 Charles Nagy	.05
86 B.J. Surhoff	.05
87 Jamey Wright	.05
88 James Baldwin	.05
89 Edgardo Alfonzo	.05
90 Jay Buhner	.05
91 Brady Anderson	.05
92 Scott Servais	.05
93 Edgar Renteria	.05
94 Mike Lieberthal	.05
95 Rick Aguilera	.05
96 Walt Weiss	.05
97 Deivi Cruz	.05
98 Kurt Abbott	.05
99 Henry Rodriguez	.05
100 Mike Piazza	1.25
101 Bill Taylor	.05
102 Todd Zeile	.05
103 Rey Ordonez	.05
104 Willie Greene	.05
105 Tony Womack	.05
106 Mike Sweeney	.05
107 Jeffrey Hammonds	.05
108 Kevin Orie	.05
109 Alex Gonzalez	.05
110 Jose Canseco	.50
111 Paul Sorrento	.05
112 Joey Hamilton	.05
113 Brad Radke	.05
114 Steve Avery	.05
115 Esteban Loaiza	.05
116 Stan Javier	.05
117 Chris Gomez	.05
118 Royce Clayton	.05
119 Orlando Merced	.05
120 Kevin Appier	.05
121 Mel Nieves	.05
122 Joe Girardi	.05
123 Rico Brogna	.05
124 Kent Mercker	.05
125 Manny Ramirez	.75
126 Jeromy Burnitz	.05

127 Kevin Foster	.05
128 Matt Morris	.05
129 Jason Dickson	.05
130 Tom Glavine	.05
131 Wally Joyner	.05
132 Rick Reed	.05
133 Todd Jones	.05
134 Dave Martinez	.05
135 Sandy Alomar	.05
136 Mike Lansing	.05
137 Sean Berry	.05
138 Doug Jones	.05
139 Todd Stottlemyre	.05
140 Jay Bell	.05
141 Jaime Navarro	.05
142 Chris Hoiles	.05
143 Joey Cora	.05
144 Scott Spiezio	.05
145 Joe Carter	.05
146 Jose Guillen	.05
147 Damion Easley	.05
148 Lee Stevens	.05
149 Alex Fernandez	.05
150 Randy Johnson	.75
151 J.T. Snow	.05
152 Chuck Finley	.05
153 Bernard Gilkey	.05
154 David Segui	.05
155 Dante Bichette	.05
156 Kevin Stocker	.05
157 Carl Everett	.05
158 Jose Valentin	.05
159 Pokey Reese	.05
160 Derek Jeter	2.00
161 Roger Pavlik	.05
162 Mark Wohlers	.05
163 Ricky Bottalico	.05
164 Ozzie Guillen	.05
165 Mike Mussina	.50
166 Gary Sheffield	.05
167 Hideo Nomo	.40
168 Mark Grace	.05
169 Aaron Sele	.05
170 Darryl Kile	.05
171 Shawn Estes	.05
172 Vinny Castilla	.05
173 Ron Coomer	.05
174 Jose Rosado	.05
175 Kenny Lofton	.05
176 Jason Giambi	.50
177 Hal Morris	.05
178 Darren Bragg	.05
179 Orel Hershiser	.05
180 Ray Lankford	.05
181 Hideki Irabu	.05
182 Kevin Young	.05
183 Javy Lopez	.05
184 Jeff Montgomery	.05
185 Mike Holtz	.05
186 George Williams	.05
187 Cal Eldred	.05
188 Tom Candiotti	.05
189 Glenallen Hill	.05
190 Brian Giles	.05
191 Dave Mlicki	.05
192 Garrett Stephenson	.05
193 Jeff Frye	.05
194 Joe Oliver	.05
195 Bob Hamelin	.05
196 Luis Sojo	.05
197 LaTroy Hawkins	.05
198 Kevin Elster	.05
199 Jeff Reed	.05
200 Dennis Eckersley	.65
201 Bill Mueller	.05
202 Russ Davis	.05
203 Armando Benitez	.05
204 Quilvio Veras	.05
205 Tim Naehring	.05
206 Quinton McCracken	.05
207 Raul Casanova	.05
208 Matt Lawton	.05
209 Luis Alicea	.05
210 Luis Gonzalez	.05
211 Allen Watson	.05
212 Gerald Williams	.05
213 David Bell	.05
214 Todd Hollandsworth	.05
215 Wade Boggs	1.00
216 Jose Mesa	.05
217 Jamie Moyer	.05
218 Darren Daulton	.05
219 Mickey Morandini	.05
220 Rusty Greer	.05
221 Jim Bullinger	.05
222 Jose Offerman	.05
223 Matt Karchner	.05
224 Woody Williams	.05
225 Mark Loretta	.05
226 Mike Hampton	.05
227 Willie Adams	.05
228 Scott Hatteberg	.05
229 Rich Amaral	.05
230 Terry Steinbach	.05
231 Glendon Rusch	.05
232 Bret Boone	.05
233 Robert Person	.05
234 Jose Hernandez	.05
235 Doug Drabek	.05
236 Jason McDonald	.05
237 Chris Widger	.05
238 Tom Martin RC	.05
239 Dave Burba	.05
240 Pete Rose II	.05
241 Bobby Ayala	.05
242 Tim Wakefield	.05
243 Dennis Springer	.05
244 Tim Belcher	.05

#	Player	Price
245	Jon Garland, Geoff Goetz (Draft Pick)	.05
246	Glenn Davis, Lance Berkman (Draft Pick)	.05
247	Vernon Wells, Aaron Akin (Draft Pick)	.10
248	Adam Kennedy, Jason Romano (Draft Pick)	.10
249	Jason Dellaero, Troy Cameron (Draft Pick)	.05
250	Alex Sanchez, Jared Sandberg RC (Expansion Team Prospects)	.10
251	Pablo Ortega, Jim Manias (Expansion Team Prospects)	.05
252	Jason Conti, Mike Stoner RC (Expansion Team Prospects)	.10
253	John Patterson, Larry Rodriguez (Expansion Team Prospects)	.05
254	Adrian Beltre, Ryan Minor RC, Aaron Boone (Prospect)	.15
255	Ben Grieve, Brian Buchanan, Dermal Brown (Prospect)	.05
256	Carl Pavano, Kerry Wood, Gil Meche (Prospect)	.15
257	David Ortiz, Daryle Ward, Richie Sexson (Prospect)	.50
258	Randy Winn, Juan Encarnacion, Andrew Vessel (Prospect)	.10
259	Kris Benson, Travis Smith, Courtney Duncan (Prospect)	.05
260	Chad Hermansen, Brent Butler, Warren Morris RC (Prospect)	.05
261	Ben Davis, Elieser Marrero, Ramon Hernandez (Prospect)	.05
262	Eric Chavez, Russell Branyan, Russ Johnson (Prospect)	.20
263	Todd Dunwoody, John Barnes, Ryan Jackson RC (Prospect)	.10
264	Matt Clement, Roy Halladay, Brian Fuentes RC (Prospect)	.05
265	Randy Johnson (Season Highlight)	.15
266	Kevin Brown (Season Highlight)	.05
267	Ricardo Rincon, Francisco Cordova (Season Highlight)	.05
268	Nomar Garciaparra (Season Highlight)	.50
269	Tino Martinez (Season Highlight)	.05
270	Chuck Knoblauch (Interleague)	.05
271	Pedro Martinez (Interleague)	.40
272	Denny Neagle (Interleague)	.05
273	Juan Gonzalez (Interleague)	.20
274	Andres Galarraga (Interleague)	.05
275	Checklist	.05
276	Checklist	.05
277	Moises Alou (World Series)	.05
278	Sandy Alomar (World Series)	.05
279	Gary Sheffield (World Series)	.05
280	Matt Williams (World Series)	.05
281	Livan Hernandez (World Series)	.05
282	Chad Ogea (World Series)	.05
283	Marlins Win (World Series)	.05
284	Tino Martinez	.05
285	Roberto Alomar	.20
286	Jeff King	.05
287	Brian Jordan	.05
288	Darin Erstad	.15
289	Ken Caminiti	.05
290	Jim Thome	.60
291	Paul Molitor	.75
292	Ivan Rodriguez	.65
293	Bernie Williams	.05
294	Todd Hundley	.05
295	Andres Galarraga	.05
296	Greg Maddux	1.00
297	Edgar Martinez	.05
298	Ron Gant	.05
299	Derek Bell	.05
300	Roger Clemens	1.00
301	Rondell White	.05
302	Barry Larkin	.05
303	Robin Ventura	.05
304	Jason Kendall	.05
305	Chipper Jones	1.00
306	John Franco	.05
307	Sammy Sosa	1.00
308	Troy Percival	.05
309	Chuck Knoblauch	.05
310	Ellis Burks	.05
311	Al Martin	.05

#	Player	Price
312	Tim Salmon	.05
313	Moises Alou	.05
314	Lance Johnson	.05
315	Justin Thompson	.05
316	Will Clark	.05
317	Barry Bonds	2.00
318	Craig Biggio	.05
319	John Smoltz	.05
320	Cal Ripken Jr.	2.00
321	Ken Griffey Jr.	1.25
322	Paul O'Neill	.05
323	Todd Helton	.65
324	John Olerud	.05
325	Mark McGwire	1.50
326	Jose Cruz Jr.	.05
327	Jeff Cirillo	.05
328	Dean Palmer	.05
329	John Wetteland	.05
330	Steve Finley	.05
331	Albert Belle	.05
332	Curt Schilling	.25
333	Raul Mondesi	.05
334	Andruw Jones	.75
335	Nomar Garciaparra	1.00
336	David Justice	.05
337	Andy Pettitte	.25
338	Pedro Martinez	.75
339	Travis Miller	.05
340	Chris Stynes	.05
341	Gregg Jefferies	.05
342	Jeff Fassero	.05
343	Craig Counsell	.05
344	Wilson Alvarez	.05
345	Bip Roberts	.05
346	Kelvim Escobar	.05
347	Mark Bellhorn	.05
348	Cory Lidle RC	.05
349	Fred McGriff	.05
350	Chuck Carr	.05
351	Bob Abreu	.05
352	Juan Guzman	.05
353	Fernando Vina	.05
354	Andy Benes	.05
355	Dave Nilsson	.05
356	Bobby Bonilla	.05
357	Ismael Valdes	.05
358	Carlos Perez	.05
359	Kirk Rueter	.05
360	Bartolo Colon	.05
361	Mel Rojas	.05
362	Johnny Damon	.25
363	Geronimo Berroa	.05
364	Reggie Sanders	.05
365	Jermaine Allensworth	.05
366	Orlando Cabrera	.05
367	Jorge Fabregas	.05
368	Scott Stahoviak	.05
369	Ken Cloude	.05
370	Donovan Osborne	.05
371	Roger Cedeno	.05
372	Neifi Perez	.05
373	Chris Holt	.05
374	Cecil Fielder	.05
375	Marty Cordova	.05
376	Tom Goodwin	.05
377	Jeff Suppan	.05
378	Jeff Brantley	.05
379	Mark Langston	.05
380	Shane Reynolds	.05
381	Mike Fetters	.05
382	Todd Greene	.05
383	Ray Durham	.05
384	Carlos Delgado	.30
385	Jeff D'Amico	.05
386	Brian McRae	.05
387	Alan Benes	.05
388	Heathcliff Slocumb	.05
389	Eric Young	.05
390	Travis Fryman	.05
391	David Cone	.05
392	Otis Nixon	.05
393	Jeremi Gonzalez	.05
394	Jeff Juden	.05
395	Jose Vizcaino	.05
396	Ugueth Urbina	.05
397	Ramon Martinez	.05
398	Robb Nen	.05
399	Harold Baines	.05
400	Delino DeShields	.05
401	John Burkett	.05
402	Sterling Hitchcock	.05
403	Mark Clark	.05
404	Terrell Wade	.05
405	Scott Brosius	.05
406	Chad Curtis	.05
407	Brian Johnson	.05
408	Roberto Kelly	.05
409	Dave Dellucci RC	.15
410	Michael Tucker	.05
411	Mark Kotsay	.05
412	Mark Lewis	.05
413	Ryan McGuire	.05
414	Shawon Dunston	.05
415	Brad Rigby	.05
416	Scott Erickson	.05
417	Bobby Jones	.05
418	Darren Oliver	.05
419	John Smiley	.05
420	T.J. Mathews	.05
421	Dustin Hermanson	.05
422	Mike Timlin	.05
423	Willie Blair	.05
424	Manny Alexander	.05
425	Bob Tewksbury	.05
426	Pete Schourek	.05
427	Reggie Jefferson	.05
428	Ed Sprague	.05
429	Jeff Conine	.05

#	Player	Price
430	Roberto Hernandez	.05
431	Tom Pagnozzi	.05
432	Jaret Wright	.05
433	Livan Hernandez	.05
434	Andy Ashby	.05
435	Todd Dunn	.05
436	Bobby Higginson	.05
437	Rod Beck	.05
438	Jim Leyritz	.05
439	Matt Williams	.05
440	Brett Tomko	.05
441	Joe Randa	.05
442	Chris Carpenter	.05
443	Dennis Reyes	.05
444	Al Leiter	.05
445	Jason Schmidt	.05
446	Ken Hill	.05
447	Shannon Stewart	.05
448	Enrique Wilson	.05
449	Fernando Tatis	.05
450	Jimmy Key	.05
451	Darrin Fletcher	.05
452	John Valentin	.05
453	Kevin Tapani	.05
454	Eric Karros	.05
455	Jay Bell	.05
456	Walt Weiss	.05
457	Devon White	.05
458	Carl Pavano	.05
459	Mike Lansing	.05
460	John Flaherty	.05
461	Richard Hidalgo	.05
462	Quinton McCracken	.05
463	Karim Garcia	.15
464	Miguel Cairo	.05
465	Edwin Diaz	.05
466	Bobby Smith	.05
467	Yamil Benitez	.05
468	Rich Butler RC	.05
469	Ben Ford RC	.05
470	Bubba Trammell	.05
471	Brent Brede	.05
472	Brooks Kieschnick	.05
473	Carlos Castillo	.05
474	Brad Radke (Season Highlight)	.05
475	Roger Clemens (Season Highlight)	.50
476	Curt Schilling (Season Highlight)	.05
477	John Olerud (Season Highlight)	.05
478	Mark McGwire (Season Highlight)	.75
479	Mike Piazza, Ken Griffey Jr. (Interleague)	.75
480	Jeff Bagwell, Frank Thomas (Interleague)	.50
481	Chipper Jones, Nomar Garciaparra (Interleague)	.75
482	Larry Walker, Juan Gonzalez (Interleague)	.30
483	Gary Sheffield, Tino Martinez (Interleague)	.05
484	Derrick Gibson, Michael Coleman, Norm Hutchins (Prospect)	.05
485	Braden Looper, Cliff Politte, Brian Rose (Prospect)	.05
486	Eric Milton, Jason Marquis, Corey Lee (Prospect)	.05
487	A.J. Hinch, Mark Osborne, Robert Fick RC (Prospect)	.10
488	Aramis Ramirez, Alex Gonzalez, Sean Casey (Prospect)	.15
489	Donnie Bridges RC, Tim Drew RC (Draft Pick)	.10
490	Ntema Ndungidi RC, Darnell McDonald RC (Draft Pick)	.10
491	Ryan Anderson RC, Mark Mangum (Draft Pick)	.25
492	J.J. Davis, Troy Glaus RC (Draft Pick)	2.00
493	Jayson Werth, Dan Reichert RC (Draft Pick)	.10
494	John Curtice RC, Mike Cuddyer RC (Draft Pick)	.25
495	Jack Cust RC, Jason Standridge (Draft Pick)	1.00
496	Brian Anderson (Expansion Team Prospect)	.05
497	Tony Saunders (Expansion Team Prospect)	.05
498	Vladimir Nunez, Jhensy Sandoval RC (Expansion Team Prospect)	.10
499	Brad Penny, Nick Bierbrodt (Expansion Team Prospect)	.05
500	Dustin Carr RC, Luis Cruz RC (Expansion Team Prospect)	.05
501	Marcus McCain RC, Cedrick Bowers RC (Expansion Team Prospect)	.10
502	Checklist	.05
503	Checklist	.05
504	Alex Rodriguez	1.50

Minted in Cooperstown

As part of an effort to promote interest in the various major sports' halls of fame, Topps produced this parallel version of its Series 1 baseball set. A special embossing machine was set up at the National Baseball Hall of Fame in Cooperstown to apply a bronze-foil "MINTED IN COOPERSTOWN" logo to cards. Twenty-card sheets of the logoed cards were sold on the premises and single cards were inserted into foil packs.

	NM/M
Common Card:	.50
Stars/Rookies:	6X

Arizona Diamondbacks Inaugural Season

To mark the team's inaugural year in the Major Leagues, Topps produced a special run of 5,000 factory sets in which each card was embossed with a special gold seal incorporating the D-Backs logo. Sets were sold only at the team's normal souvenir outlets.

	NM/M
Complete Set (503):	80.00
Common Player:	.50
Stars/Rookies:	6X

Tampa Bay Devil Rays Inaugural Season

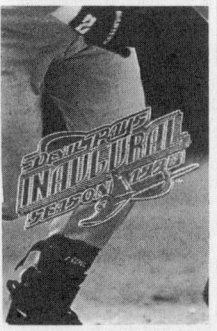

To mark the team's inaugural year in the Major Leagues, Topps produced a special run of 5,000 factory sets in which each card was embossed with a special gold seal incorporating the D-Rays logo. Sets were sold only at the team's normal souvenir outlets.

	NM/M
Complete Set (503):	100.00
Common Player:	.50
Stars/Rookies:	6X

Baby Boomers

This 15-card retail exclusive insert was seeded one per 36 packs of Series 1. It featured some of the top young players in the game and was numbered with a "BB" prefix.

	NM/M
Complete Set (15):	15.00
Common Player:	.75
Inserted 1:36 Retail	

#		Price
1	Derek Jeter	6.00
2	Scott Rolen	1.00

#		Price
3	Nomar Garciaparra	3.50
4	Jose Cruz Jr.	.75
5	Darin Erstad	.85
6	Todd Helton	1.50
7	Tony Clark	.75
8	Jose Guillen	.75
9	Andruw Jones	1.00
10	Vladimir Guerrero	1.50
11	Mark Kotsay	.75
12	Todd Greene	.75
13	Andy Pettitte	.85
14	Justin Thompson	.75
15	Alan Benes	.75

Roberto Clemente Reprints

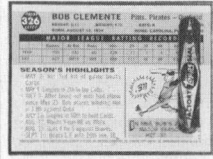

Nineteen different Topps Clemente cards were reprinted with a gold foil stamp and included 1998 Topps. Odd numbers were included in Series I, while even numbers were inserted into Series II, both at a rate of one per 18 packs. The insert was created to honor the memory of the 25th anniversary of Clemente's death.

	NM/M
Complete Set (19):	50.00
Common Card:	2.50
Inserted 1:18	
1	1955	4.00
2	1956	2.50
3	1957	2.50
4	1958	2.50
5	1959	2.50
6	1960	2.50
7	1961	2.50
8	1962	2.50
9	1963	2.50
10	1964	2.50
11	1965	2.50
12	1966	2.50
13	1967	2.50
14	1968	2.50
15	1969	2.50
16	1970	2.50
17	1971	2.50
18	1972	2.50
19	1973	2.50

Roberto Clemente Finest

Clemente Finest inserts were included in both Series I and II at a rate of one per 72 packs. There were a total of 19 different, with odd numbers in Series I and even numbers in Series II. The insert helped honor the memory of the 25th anniversary of his death.

	NM/M
Complete Set (19):	60.00
Common Card:	4.00
Inserted 1:72	
Refractors:	2X
Inserted 1:288	
1	1955	6.00
2	1956	4.00
3	1957	4.00
4	1958	4.00
5	1959	4.00
6	1960	4.00
7	1961	4.00
8	1962	4.00
9	1963	4.00
10	1964	4.00
11	1965	4.00
12	1966	4.00
13	1967	4.00
14	1968	4.00
15	1969	4.00
16	1970	4.00
17	1971	4.00
18	1972	4.00
19	1973	4.00

Roberto Clemente "Tin" Reprints

Each of the 19 basic Clemente reprint cards can also be found in a factory-sealed, gold-foil stamped soft plastic case. These were inserted in special retail-only tin boxes and one per factory set of 1998 Topps.

	NM/M
Complete Set (19):	60.00
Common Card:	4.00
1	1955	8.00
2	1956	4.00
3	1957	4.00
4	1958	4.00
5	1959	4.00
6	1960	4.00
7	1961	4.00
8	1962	4.00
9	1963	4.00
10	1964	4.00
11	1965	4.00
12	1966	4.00
13	1967	4.00
14	1968	4.00
15	1969	4.00
16	1970	4.00
17	1971	4.00
18	1972	4.00
19	1973	4.00

Roberto Clemente Commemorative Tins

This series of commemorative tin card "packs" reproduces in an enlarged (about 3" x 4-5/8" x 3/4") format the front and back of four of Roberto Clemente's Topps cards. Each tin, originally retailing for about $5, contains a plastic-sealed Clemente reprint card.

	NM/M
Complete Set (4):	10.00
Roberto Clemente/1955	3.50
Roberto Clemente/1956	2.50
Roberto Clemente/1965	2.50
Roberto Clemente/1971	2.50

Roberto Clemente Tribute

Five Clemente Tribute cards were produced for Series I and inserted in one per 12 packs. The set features some classic photos of Clemente and honor his memory in the 25th anniversary of his death. Clemente Tribute cards are numbered with a "RC" prefix.

	NM/M
Complete Set (5):	3.00
Common Clemente:	.75
Inserted 1:12	
1-5 Roberto Clemente	.75

Clout 9

Clout 9 captured nine players known for their statistical supremacy. Cards were numbered with a "C" prefix and inserted one per 72 packs of Series 2.

		NM/M
Complete Set (9):		17.50
Common Player:		1.00
Inserted 1:72		
1	Edgar Martinez	1.00
2	Mike Piazza	5.00
3	Frank Thomas	2.00
4	Craig Biggio	1.00
5	Vinny Castilla	1.00
6	Jeff Blauser	1.00
7	Barry Bonds	7.50
8	Ken Griffey Jr.	5.00
9	Larry Walker	1.00

Etch-A-Sketch

Etch-a-Sketch featured nine different players depicted by nationally acclaimed artist George Vlosich III. Known as "The Etch-a-Sketch Kid," Vlosich created each one of these Series I inserts, which were inserted at a rate of one per 36 packs. Cards are numbered with an "ES" prefix.

		NM/M
Complete Set (9):		20.00
Common Player:		1.00
Inserted 1:36		
1	Albert Belle	1.00
2	Barry Bonds	6.00
3	Ken Griffey Jr.	4.00
4	Greg Maddux	3.00
5	Hideo Nomo	1.50
6	Mike Piazza	4.00
7	Cal Ripken Jr.	6.00
8	Frank Thomas	2.00
9	Mo Vaughn	1.00

Flashback

This double-sided insert offers "then and now" photos of 10 top major leaguers. One side pic-

---

tures the player circa 1998, while the other side shows him at the beginning of his major league career. Flashback inserts were seeded one per 72 packs and numbered with a "FB" prefix.

		NM/M
Complete Set (10):		22.50
Common Player:		1.00
Inserted 1:72		
1	Barry Bonds	7.50
2	Ken Griffey Jr.	5.00
3	Paul Molitor	2.00
4	Randy Johnson	2.00
5	Cal Ripken Jr.	7.50
6	Tony Gwynn	3.00
7	Kenny Lofton	1.00
8	Gary Sheffield	1.50
9	Deion Sanders	1.00
10	Brady Anderson	1.00

Focal Point

This hobby exclusive insert focuses on the skills that have made the players great. Focal Point inserts were available in Series 2 packs, seeded one per 36, and are numbered with a "FP" prefix.

		NM/M
Complete Set (15):		25.00
Common Player:		.75
Inserted 1:36		
1	Juan Gonzalez	.85
2	Nomar Garciaparra	2.50
3	Jose Cruz Jr.	.75
4	Cal Ripken Jr.	5.00
5	Ken Griffey Jr.	3.50
6	Ivan Rodriguez	1.00
7	Larry Walker	.75
8	Barry Bonds	5.00
9	Roger Clemens	3.00
10	Frank Thomas	1.50
11	Chuck Knoblauch	.75
12	Mike Piazza	3.50
13	Greg Maddux	2.50
14	Vladimir Guerrero	1.50
15	Andruw Jones	1.50

Hallbound

Hall Bound features players who were considered locks to be inducted into the Hall of Fame when their career was over. This insert was exclusive to Series 1 hobby packs and seeded one per 36. Cards are numbered with a "HB" prefix.

		NM/M
Complete Set (15):		45.00
Common Player:		1.50
1	Paul Molitor	2.50
2	Tony Gwynn	3.50
3	Wade Boggs	3.50
4	Roger Clemens	4.00
5	Dennis Eckersley	2.00
6	Cal Ripken Jr.	7.50
7	Greg Maddux	3.50
8	Rickey Henderson	2.50
9	Ken Griffey Jr.	5.00
10	Frank Thomas	3.00
11	Mark McGwire	6.00
12	Barry Bonds	7.50
13	Mike Piazza	5.00
14	Juan Gonzalez	1.50
15	Randy Johnson	2.50

Inter-League Mystery Finest

Five of the 1997 season's most intriguing inter-league matchups are showcased with four cards each in Inter-League Mystery Finest. Regular versions of this Series 1 insert are seeded one per 36 packs, while Refractor versions are seeded one per 144 packs. Cards are numbered with an "ILM" prefix.

		NM/M
Complete Set (20):		35.00
Common Player:		.75
Inserted 1:36		
Refractors:		1.5X
Inserted 1:144		
1	Chipper Jones	3.00
2	Cal Ripken Jr.	6.50
3	Greg Maddux	3.00
4	Rafael Palmeiro	1.50
5	Todd Hundley	.75
6	Derek Jeter	6.50
7	John Olerud	.75
8	Tino Martinez	.75
9	Larry Walker	.75
10	Ken Griffey Jr.	4.00
11	Andres Galarraga	.75
12	Randy Johnson	2.00
13	Mike Piazza	4.00
14	Jim Edmonds	.75
15	Eric Karros	.75
16	Tim Salmon	.75
17	Sammy Sosa	3.00
18	Frank Thomas	2.00
19	Mark Grace	.75
20	Albert Belle	.75

Milestones

Milestones features 10 records from 1998 that could be broken during the 1998 season and the players who have the best shot at breaking them. This retail exclusive insert is seeded one per 36 packs and is numbered with a "MS" prefix.

		NM/M
Complete Set (10):		17.50
Common Player:		.75
Inserted 1:12		
MS1	Barry Bonds	5.00
MS2	Roger Clemens	2.50
MS3	Dennis Eckersley	1.00
MS4	Juan Gonzalez	.75
MS5	Ken Griffey Jr.	3.00
MS6	Tony Gwynn	2.00
MS7	Greg Maddux	2.00
MS8	Mark McGwire	4.00
MS9	Cal Ripken Jr.	5.00
MS10	Frank Thomas	1.25

Mystery Finest

This 20-card insert set features top players on bordered and borderless designs, with Refractor

---

versions of each. Exclusive to Series 2 packs, bordered cards are seeded 1:36 packs, borderless are seeded 1:72 packs, bordered Refractors are 1:108 and borderless Refractors are seeded 1:288 packs. Mystery Finest inserts are numbered with a "M" prefix.

		NM/M
Complete Set (20):		25.00
Common Player:		.50
Inserted 1:36		
Bordered 1:72:		1.5X
Bordered Refractors 1:108:		1.5X
Borderless Refractors 1:288:		2X
1	Nomar Garciaparra	1.50
2	Chipper Jones	1.50
3	Scott Rolen	.75
4	Albert Belle	.50
5	Mo Vaughn	.50
6	Jose Cruz Jr.	.50
7	Mark McGwire	3.00
8	Derek Jeter	3.50
9	Tony Gwynn	1.00
10	Frank Thomas	1.00
11	Tino Martinez	.50
12	Greg Maddux	1.50
13	Juan Gonzalez	.75
14	Larry Walker	.50
15	Mike Piazza	2.50
16	Cal Ripken Jr.	3.50
17	Jeff Bagwell	1.00
18	Andruw Jones	1.00
19	Barry Bonds	3.50
20	Ken Griffey Jr.	2.50

Rookie Class

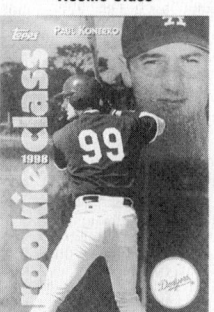

Rookie Class features 10 young stars from 1998 and was exclusive to Series II packs. The cards were inserted one per 12 packs and numbered with a "R" prefix.

		NM/M
Complete Set (10):		4.00
Common Player:		.25
Inserted 1:12		
1	Travis Lee	1.00
2	Richard Hidalgo	.25
3	Todd Helton	2.00
4	Paul Konerko	.75
5	Mark Kotsay	.25
6	Derrek Lee	1.50
7	Eli Marrero	.25
8	Fernando Tatis	.25
9	Juan Encarnacion	.25
10	Ben Grieve	.25

1998 Topps Chrome

All 502 1998 Topps cards were reprinted in chromium versions for Topps Chrome. Chrome was released in two series; Series 1 containing 282 cards and Series 2 including 220 cards. Four-card packs had a suggested retail price of $3. Card fronts include a Topps Chrome logo. The issue offers a sampling of the inserts from Topps, along with Refractor versions of every card and insert. Series 1 inserts included: Flashbacks, Baby

---

Boomers and Hallbound. Series 2 inserts included: Milestones, '98 Rookie Class and Clout 9.

		NM/M
Complete Set (502):		100.00
Common Player:		.10
Refractors:		5X
Inserted 1:12		
Foil Pack (4):		1.50
Foil Box (24):		25.00
1	Tony Gwynn	2.00
2	Larry Walker	.10
3	Billy Wagner	.10
4	Denny Neagle	.10
5	Vladimir Guerrero	1.50
6	Kevin Brown	.10
8	Mariano Rivera	.10
9	Tony Clark	.10
10	Deion Sanders	.10
11	Francisco Cordova	.10
12	Matt Williams	.10
13	Carlos Baerga	.10
14	Mo Vaughn	.10
15	Bobby Witt	.10
16	Matt Stairs	.10
17	Chan Ho Park	.10
18	Mike Bordick	.10
19	Michael Tucker	.10
20	Frank Thomas	1.50
21	Roberto Clemente (Tribute)	2.50
22	Dmitri Young	.10
23	Steve Trachsel	.10
24	Jeff Kent	.10
25	Scott Rolen	.75
26	John Thomson	.10
27	Joe Vitiello	.10
28	Eddie Guardado	.10
29	Charlie Hayes	.10
30	Juan Gonzalez	.75
31	Garret Anderson	.10
32	John Jaha	.10
33	Omar Vizquel	.10
34	Brian Hunter	.10
35	Jeff Bagwell	1.50
36	Mark Lemke	.10
37	Doug Glanville	.10
38	Dan Wilson	.10
39	Steve Cooke	.10
40	Chili Davis	.10
41	Mike Cameron	.10
42	F.P. Santangelo	.10
43	Brad Ausmus	.10
44	Gary DiSarcina	.10
45	Pat Hentgen	.10
46	Wilton Guerrero	.10
47	Devon White	.10
48	Danny Patterson	.10
49	Pat Meares	.10
50	Rafael Palmeiro	1.00
51	Mark Gardner	.10
52	Jeff Blauser	.10
53	Dave Hollins	.10
54	Carlos Garcia	.10
55	Ben McDonald	.10
56	John Mabry	.10
57	Trevor Hoffman	.10
58	Tony Fernandez	.10
59	Rich Loiselle	.10
60	Mark Leiter	.10
61	Pat Kelly	.10
62	John Flaherty	.10
63	Roger Bailey	.10
64	Tom Gordon	.10
65	Ryan Klesko	.10
66	Darryl Hamilton	.10
67	Jim Eisenreich	.10
68	Butch Huskey	.10
69	Mark Grudzielanek	.10
70	Marquis Grissom	.10
71	Mark McLemore	.10
72	Gary Gaetti	.10
73	Greg Gagne	.10
74	Lyle Mouton	.10
75	Jim Edmonds	.10
76	Shawn Green	.35
77	Terry Vaughn	.10
78	Terry Adams	.10
79	Kevin Polcovich RC	.10
80	Troy O'Leary	.10
81	Jeff Shaw	.10
82	Rich Becker	.10
83	David Wells	.10
84	Steve Karsay	.10
85	Charles Nagy	.10
86	B.J. Surhoff	.10
87	Jamey Wright	.10
88	James Baldwin	.10
89	Edgardo Alfonzo	.10
90	Jay Buhner	.10
91	Brady Anderson	.10
92	Scott Servais	.10
93	Edgar Renteria	.10
94	Mike Lieberthal	.10
95	Rick Aguilera	.10
96	Walt Weiss	.10
97	Deivi Cruz	.10
98	Kurt Abbott	.10
99	Henry Rodriguez	.10
100	Mike Piazza	2.25
101	Bill Taylor	.10
102	Todd Zeile	.10
103	Rey Ordonez	.10
104	Willie Greene	.10
105	Tony Womack	.10
106	Mike Sweeney	.10
107	Jeffrey Hammonds	.10

		NM/M
108	Kevin Orie	.10
109	Alex Gonzalez	.10
110	Jose Canseco	.60
111	Paul Sorrento	.10
112	Joey Hamilton	.10
113	Brad Radke	.10
114	Steve Avery	.10
115	Esteban Loaiza	.10
116	Stan Javier	.10
117	Chris Gomez	.10
118	Royce Clayton	.10
119	Orlando Merced	.10
120	Kevin Appier	.10
121	Mel Nieves	.10
122	Joe Girardi	.10
123	Rico Brogna	.10
124	Kent Mercker	.10
125	Manny Ramirez	1.50
126	Jeromy Burnitz	.10
127	Kevin Foster	.10
128	Matt Morris	.10
129	Jason Dickson	.10
130	Tom Glavine	.35
131	Wally Joyner	.10
132	Rick Reed	.10
133	Todd Jones	.10
134	Dave Martinez	.10
135	Sandy Alomar	.10
136	Mike Lansing	.10
137	Sean Berry	.10
138	Doug Jones	.10
139	Todd Stottlemyre	.10
140	Jay Bell	.10
141	Jaime Navarro	.10
142	Chris Hoiles	.10
143	Joey Cora	.10
144	Scott Spiezio	.10
145	Joe Carter	.10
146	Jose Guillen	.10
147	Damion Easley	.10
148	Lee Stevens	.10
149	Alex Fernandez	.10
150	Randy Johnson	1.50
151	J.T. Snow	.10
152	Chuck Finley	.10
153	Bernard Gilkey	.10
155	David Segui	.10
155	Dante Bichette	.10
156	Kevin Stocker	.10
157	Carl Everett	.10
158	Jose Valentin	.10
159	Pokey Reese	.10
160	Derek Jeter	3.00
161	Roger Pavlik	.10
162	Mark Wohlers	.10
163	Ricky Bottalico	.10
164	Ozzie Guillen	.10
165	Mike Mussina	.60
166	Gary Sheffield	.50
167	Hideo Nomo	.75
168	Mark Grace	.10
169	Aaron Sele	.10
170	Darryl Kile	.10
171	Shawn Estes	.10
172	Vinny Castilla	.10
173	Ron Coomer	.10
174	Jose Rosado	.10
175	Kenny Lofton	.10
176	Jason Giambi	.65
177	Hal Morris	.10
178	Darren Bragg	.10
179	Orel Hershiser	.10
180	Ray Lankford	.10
181	Hideki Irabu	.10
182	Kevin Young	.10
183	Javy Lopez	.10
184	Jeff Montgomery	.10
185	Mike Holtz	.10
186	George Williams	.10
187	Cal Eldred	.10
188	Tom Candiotti	.10
189	Glenallen Hill	.10
190	Brian Giles	.10
191	Dave Mlicki	.10
192	Garrett Stephenson	.10
193	Jeff Frye	.10
194	Joe Oliver	.10
195	Bob Hamelin	.10
196	Luis Sojo	.10
197	LaTroy Hawkins	.10
198	Kevin Elster	.10
199	Jeff Reed	.10
200	Dennis Eckersley	1.00
201	Bill Mueller	.10
202	Russ Davis	.10
203	Armando Benitez	.10
204	Quilvio Veras	.10
205	Tim Naehring	.10
206	Quinton McCracken	.10
207	Raul Casanova	.10
208	Matt Lawton	.10
209	Luis Alicea	.10
210	Luis Gonzalez	.10
211	Allen Watson	.10
212	Gerald Williams	.10
213	David Bell	.10
214	Todd Hollandsworth	.10
215	Wade Boggs	2.00
216	Jose Mesa	.10
217	Jamie Moyer	.10
218	Darren Daulton	.10
219	Mickey Morandini	.10
220	Rusty Greer	.10
221	Jim Bullinger	.10
222	Jose Offerman	.10
223	Matt Karchner	.10
224	Woody Williams	.10
225	Mark Loretta	.10

#	Player	Price
226	Mike Hampton	.10
227	Willie Adams	.10
228	Scott Hatteberg	.10
229	Rich Amaral	.10
230	Terry Steinbach	.10
231	Glendon Rusch	.10
232	Bret Boone	.10
233	Robert Person	.10
234	Jose Hernandez	.10
235	Doug Drabek	.10
236	Jason McDonald	.10
237	Chris Widger	.10
238	Tom Martin RC	.10
239	Dave Burba	.10
240	Pete Rose	.10
241	Bobby Ayala	.10
242	Tim Wakefield	.10
243	Dennis Springer	.10
244	Tim Belcher	.10
245	Jon Garland, Geoff Goetz (Draft Pick)	.10
246	Glenn Davis, Lance Berkman (Draft Pick)	.25
247	Vernon Wells, Aaron Akin (Draft Pick)	.15
248	Adam Kennedy, Jason Romano (Draft Pick)	.25
249	Jason Dellaero, Troy Cameron (Draft Pick)	.10
250	Alex Sanchez, Jared Sandberg RC (Expansion)	.25
251	Pablo Ortega, James Manias RC (Expansion)	.10
252	Jason Conti, Mike Stoner RC (Expansion)	.10
253	John Patterson, Larry Rodriguez (Expansion)	.10
254	Adrian Beltre, Ryan Minor RC, Aaron Boone (Prospect)	.25
255	Ben Grieve, Brian Buchanan, Dermal Brown (Prospect)	.10
256	Carl Pavano, Kerry Wood, Gil Meche (Prospect)	.75
257	David Ortiz, Daryle Ward, Richie Sexson (Prospect)	.65
258	Randy Winn, Juan Encarnacion, Andrew Vessel (Prospect)	.15
259	Kris Benson, Travis Smith, Courtney Duncan (Prospect)	.15
260	Chad Hermansen, Brent Butler, Warren Morris RC (Prospect)	.15
261	Ben Davis, Elieser Marrero, Ramon Hernandez (Prospect)	.10
262	Eric Chavez, Russell Branyan, Russ Johnson (Prospect)	.25
263	Todd Dunwoody, John Barnes, Ryan Jackson RC (Prospect)	.15
264	Matt Clement, Roy Halladay, Brian Fuentes (Prospect)	.20
265	Randy Johnson (Season Highlight)	.50
266	Kevin Brown (Season Highlight)	.10
267	Francisco Cordova, Ricardo Rincon (Season Highlight)	.10
268	Nomar Garciaparra (Season Highlight)	.75
269	Tino Martinez (Season Highlight)	.10
270	Chuck Knoblauch (Inter-League)	.10
271	Pedro Martinez (Inter-League)	.40
272	Denny Neagle (Inter-League)	.10
273	Juan Gonzalez (Inter-League)	.20
274	Andres Galarraga (Inter-League)	.10
275	Checklist	.10
276	Checklist	.10
277	Moises Alou (World Series)	.10
278	Sandy Alomar (World Series)	.10
279	Gary Sheffield (World Series)	.10
280	Matt Williams (World Series)	.10
281	Livan Hernandez (World Series)	.10
282	Chad Ogea (World Series)	.10
283	Marlins Win (World Series)	.10
284	Tino Martinez	.35
285	Roberto Alomar	.35
286	Jeff King	.10
287	Brian Jordan	.10
288	Darin Erstad	.30
289	Ken Caminiti	.10
290	Jim Thome	.90
291	Paul Molitor	1.50
292	Ivan Rodriguez	1.00
293	Bernie Williams	.10
294	Todd Hundley	.10
295	Andres Galarraga	.10
296	Greg Maddux	2.00
297	Edgar Martinez	.10
298	Ron Gant	.10
299	Derek Bell	.10
300	Roger Clemens	2.00
301	Rondell White	.10
302	Barry Larkin	.10
303	Robin Ventura	.10
304	Jason Kendall	.10
305	Chipper Jones	2.00
306	John Franco	.10
307	Sammy Sosa	2.00
308	Troy Percival	.10
309	Chuck Knoblauch	.10
310	Ellis Burks	.10
311	Al Martin	.10
312	Tim Salmon	.10
313	Moises Alou	.10
314	Lance Johnson	.10
315	Justin Thompson	.10
316	Will Clark	.10
317	Barry Bonds	3.00
318	Craig Biggio	.10
319	John Smoltz	.10
320	Cal Ripken Jr.	3.00
321	Ken Griffey Jr.	2.25
322	Paul O'Neill	.10
323	Todd Helton	1.50
324	John Olerud	.10
325	Mark McGwire	2.50
326	Jose Cruz Jr.	.10
327	Jeff Cirillo	.10
328	Dean Palmer	.10
329	John Wetteland	.10
330	Steve Finley	.10
331	Albert Belle	.10
332	Curt Schilling	.35
333	Raul Mondesi	.10
334	Andruw Jones	1.50
335	Nomar Garciaparra	2.00
336	David Justice	.10
337	Andy Pettitte	.30
338	Pedro Martinez	1.50
339	Travis Miller	.10
340	Chris Stynes	.10
341	Gregg Jefferies	.10
342	Jeff Fassero	.10
343	Craig Counsell	.10
344	Wilson Alvarez	.10
345	Bip Roberts	.10
346	Kelvim Escobar	.10
347	Mark Bellhorn	.10
348	Cory Lidle	.10
349	Fred McGriff	.10
350	Chuck Carr	.10
351	Bob Abreu	.10
352	Juan Guzman	.10
353	Fernando Vina	.10
354	Andy Benes	.10
355	Dave Nilsson	.10
356	Bobby Bonilla	.10
357	Ismael Valdes	.10
358	Carlos Perez	.10
359	Kirk Rueter	.10
360	Bartolo Colon	.10
361	Mel Rojas	.10
362	Johnny Damon	.35
363	Geronimo Berroa	.10
364	Reggie Sanders	.10
365	Jermaine Allensworth	.10
366	Orlando Cabrera	.10
367	Jorge Fabregas	.10
368	Scott Stahoviak	.10
369	Ken Cloude	.10
370	Donovan Osborne	.10
371	Roger Cedeno	.10
372	Neifi Perez	.10
373	Chris Holt	.10
374	Cecil Fielder	.10
375	Marty Cordova	.10
376	Tom Goodwin	.10
377	Jeff Suppan	.10
378	Jeff Brantley	.10
379	Mark Langston	.10
380	Shane Reynolds	.10
381	Mike Fetters	.10
382	Todd Greene	.10
383	Ray Durham	.10
384	Carlos Delgado	.35
385	Jeff D'Amico	.10
386	Brian McRae	.10
387	Alan Benes	.10
388	Heathcliff Slocumb	.10
389	Eric Young	.10
390	Travis Fryman	.10
391	David Cone	.10
392	Otis Nixon	.10
393	Jeremi Gonzalez	.10
394	Jeff Juden	.10
395	Jose Vizcaino	.10
396	Ugueth Urbina	.10
397	Ramon Martinez	.10
398	Robb Nen	.10
399	Harold Baines	.10
400	Delino DeShields	.10
401	John Burkett	.10
402	Sterling Hitchcock	.10
403	Mark Clark	.10
404	Terrell Wade	.10
405	Scott Brosius	.10
406	Chad Curtis	.10
407	Brian Johnson	.10
408	Roberto Kelly	.10
409	Dave Dellucci RC	.25
410	Michael Tucker	.10
411	Mark Kotsay	.10
412	Mark Lewis	.10
413	Ryan McGuire	.10
414	Shawon Dunston	.10
415	Brad Rigby	.10
416	Scott Erickson	.10
417	Bobby Jones	.10
418	Darren Oliver	.10
419	John Smiley	.10
420	T.J. Mathews	.10
421	Dustin Hermanson	.10
422	Mike Timlin	.10
423	Willie Blair	.10
424	Manny Alexander	.10
425	Bob Tewksbury	.10
426	Pete Schourek	.10
427	Reggie Jefferson	.10
428	Ed Sprague	.10
429	Jeff Conine	.10
430	Roberto Hernandez	.10
431	Tom Pagnozzi	.10
432	Jaret Wright	.10
433	Livan Hernandez	.10
434	Andy Ashby	.10
435	Todd Dunn	.10
436	Bobby Higginson	.10
437	Rod Beck	.10
438	Jim Leyritz	.10
439	Matt Williams	.10
440	Brett Tomko	.10
441	Joe Randa	.10
442	Chris Carpenter	.10
443	Dennis Reyes	.10
444	Al Leiter	.10
445	Jason Schmidt	.10
446	Ken Hill	.10
447	Shannon Stewart	.10
448	Enrique Wilson	.10
449	Fernando Tatis	.10
450	Jimmy Key	.10
451	Darrin Fletcher	.10
452	John Valentin	.10
453	Kevin Tapani	.10
454	Eric Karros	.10
455	Jay Bell	.10
456	Walt Weiss	.10
457	Devon White	.10
458	Carl Pavano	.10
459	Mike Lansing	.10
460	John Flaherty	.10
461	Richard Hidalgo	.10
462	Quinton McCracken	.10
463	Karim Garcia	.20
464	Miguel Cairo	.10
465	Edwin Diaz	.10
466	Bobby Smith	.10
467	Yamil Benitez	.10
468	Rich Butler RC	.10
469	Ben Ford RC	.10
470	Bubba Trammell	.10
471	Brent Brede	.10
472	Brooks Kieschnick	.10
473	Carlos Castillo	.10
474	Brad Radke (Season Highlight)	.10
475	Roger Clemens (Season Highlight)	1.00
476	Curt Schilling (Season Highlight)	.15
477	John Olerud (Season Highlight)	.10
478	Mark McGwire (Season Highlight)	1.25
479	Mike Piazza, Ken Griffey Jr. (Interleague)	1.25
480	Jeff Bagwell, Frank Thomas (Interleague)	1.00
481	Chipper Jones, Nomar Garciaparra (Interleague)	1.00
482	Larry Walker, Juan Gonzalez (Interleague)	.20
483	Gary Sheffield, Tino Martinez (Interleague)	.10
484	Derrick Gibson, Michael Coleman, Norm Hutchins (Prospect)	.10
485	Braden Looper, Cliff Politte, Brian Rose (Prospect)	.15
486	Eric Milton, Jason Marquis, Corey Lee (Prospect)	.25
487	A.J. Hinch, Mark Osborne, Robert Fick RC (Prospect)	.25
488	Aramis Ramirez, Alex Gonzalez, Sean Casey (Prospect)	.25
489	Donnie Bridges RC, Tim Drew RC (Draft Pick)	.20
490	Ntema Ndungidi RC, Darnell McDonald RC (Draft Pick)	.10
491	Ryan Anderson RC, Mark Mangum (Draft Pick)	.50
492	J.J. Davis, Troy Glaus RC (Draft Pick)	3.00
493	Jayson Werth, Dan Reichert (Draft Pick)	.10
494	John Curtice RC, Mike Cuddyer RC (Draft Pick)	.50
495	Jack Cust RC, Jason Standridge (Draft Pick)	4.00
496	Brian Anderson (Expansion Team Prospect)	.10
497	Tony Saunders (Expansion Team Prospect)	.10
498	Vladimir Nunez, Jhensy Sandoval RC (Expansion Team Prospect)	.10
499	Brad Penny, Nick Bierbrodt (Expansion Team Prospect)	.10
500	Dustin Carr RC, Luis Cruz RC (Expansion Team Prospect)	.10
501	Marcus McCain RC, Cedrick Bowers RC (Expansion Team Prospect)	.10
502	Checklist	.10
503	Checklist	.10
504	Alex Rodriguez	2.50

Refractors

Each card in the regular Topps Series 1 and Series 2 Chrome issue could also be found in a refractor version seeded approximately one per 12 packs. Refractor versions are so designated above the card number on back.

	NM/M
Common Player:	.50
Stars/Rookies:	5X

Baby Boomers

This 15-card insert featured players with less than three years of experience. Cards were inserted one per 24 packs, with Refractor versions found every 72 packs of Series I. Cards were numbered with a "BB" prefix.

	NM/M
Complete Set (15):	16.00
Common Player:	.75
Inserted 1:24	
Refractors:	1.5X
Inserted 1:72	
1 Derek Jeter	6.00
2 Scott Rolen	.90
3 Nomar Garciaparra	3.50
4 Jose Cruz Jr.	.75
5 Darin Erstad	.90
6 Todd Helton	1.50
7 Tony Clark	.75
8 Jose Guillen	.75
9 Andruw Jones	1.50
10 Vladimir Guerrero	1.50
11 Mark Kotsay	.75
12 Todd Greene	.75
13 Andy Pettitte	.90
14 Justin Thompson	.75
15 Alan Benes	.75

Clout 9

This nine-card insert included players for their statistical supremacy. Clout 9 cards were found in Series II packs at a rate of one per 24 packs, with Refractor versions every 72 packs. Cards are numbered with a "C" prefix.

	NM/M
Complete Set (9):	15.00
Common Player:	.75
Inserted 1:24	
Refractors:	1.5X
Inserted 1:72	
1 Edgar Martinez	.75
2 Mike Piazza	3.50
3 Frank Thomas	1.50
4 Craig Biggio	.75
5 Vinny Castilla	.75
6 Jeff Blauser	.75
7 Barry Bonds	6.00
8 Ken Griffey Jr.	3.50
9 Larry Walker	.75

Flashback

This 10-card double-sided insert features top players as they looked in 1998 on one side, and how they looked when they first appeared in the majors on the other side. Flashback inserts were seeded one per 24 packs of Series I, with Refractors every 72 packs. This insert was numbered with a "FB" prefix.

	NM/M
Complete Set (10):	16.00
Common Player:	.75
Inserted 1:24	
Refractors:	1.5X
Inserted 1:72	
1 Barry Bonds	6.00
2 Ken Griffey Jr.	3.50
3 Paul Molitor	1.50
4 Randy Johnson	1.50
5 Cal Ripken Jr.	6.00
6 Tony Gwynn	2.50
7 Kenny Lofton	1.50
8 Gary Sheffield	.85
9 Deion Sanders	.75
10 Brady Anderson	.75

Hallbound

Hallbound highlighted 15 players destined for the Hall of Fame on die-cut cards. Inserted at a rate of one per 24 packs of Series I, with Refractors every 72 packs, these were numbered with a "HB" prefix.

	NM/M
Complete Set (15):	35.00
Common Player:	1.50
Inserted 1:24	
Refractors:	1.5X
Inserted 1:72	
1 Paul Molitor	2.00
2 Tony Gwynn	2.50
3 Wade Boggs	2.50
4 Roger Clemens	3.00
5 Dennis Eckersley	1.50
6 Cal Ripken Jr.	6.00
7 Greg Maddux	2.50
8 Rickey Henderson	1.50
9 Ken Griffey Jr.	3.50
10 Frank Thomas	2.00
11 Mark McGwire	4.00
12 Barry Bonds	6.00
13 Mike Piazza	3.50
14 Juan Gonzalez	1.50
15 Randy Johnson	2.00

Milestones

Ten superstars who were within reach of major records for the 1998 season are featured in Milestones. This Series II insert was seeded one per 24 packs, with Refractor versions seeded one per 72 packs. Milestones were numbered with a "MS" prefix.

	NM/M
Complete Set (10):	25.00
Common Player:	1.00
Inserted 1:24	
Refractors:	1.5X
Inserted 1:72	
1 Barry Bonds	6.00
2 Roger Clemens	3.00
3 Dennis Eckersley	1.00
4 Juan Gonzalez	1.00
5 Ken Griffey Jr.	3.50
6 Tony Gwynn	2.50
7 Greg Maddux	2.50
8 Mark McGwire	4.50
9 Cal Ripken Jr.	6.00
10 Frank Thomas	1.50

Rookie Class

This insert featured 10 players with less than one year of major league experience. Inserted in Series II packs at a rate of one per 12 packs, with Refractors every 24 packs, '98 Rookie Class inserts were numbered with a "R" prefix.

	NM/M
Complete Set (10):	10.00
Common Player:	.75
Inserted 1:12	
Refractors:	1.5X
Inserted 1:24	
1 Travis Lee	1.00
2 Richard Hidalgo	.75
3 Todd Helton	4.50
4 Paul Konerko	1.50
5 Mark Kotsay	.75
6 Derek Lee	3.00
7 Eli Marrero	.75
8 Fernando Tatis	.75
9 Juan Encarnacion	.75
10 Ben Grieve	1.00

Super Chrome

This 36-card oversized set featured some of the top players from Chrome on 4-1/8" x 5-3/4" cards. The product sold in three-card packs and featured the same photography as Topps and Topps Chrome before it, but added a Super Chrome logo. Refractor versions of each card were also available, inserted one per 12 packs.

	NM/M
Complete Set (36):	20.00
Common Player:	.25
Refractors:	1.5X
Inserted 1:12	
Pack (3):	2.50
Wax Box (12):	25.00
1 Tony Gwynn	1.00
2 Larry Walker	.25
3 Vladimir Guerrero	.75
4 Mo Vaughn	.25
5 Frank Thomas	.75
6 Barry Larkin	.25
7 Scott Rolen	.65
8 Juan Gonzalez	.75
9 Jeff Bagwell	.75
10 Ryan Klesko	.25
11 Mike Piazza	1.50
12 Randy Johnson	.75
13 Derek Jeter	3.00
14 Gary Sheffield	.50
15 Hideo Nomo	.50
16 Tino Martinez	.25
17 Ivan Rodriguez	.65
18 Bernie Williams	.25
19 Greg Maddux	1.00
20 Roger Clemens	1.25
21 Roberto Clemente	2.00
22 Chipper Jones	1.00
23 Sammy Sosa	.75
24 Tony Clark	.25
25 Barry Bonds	3.00
26 Craig Biggio	.25
27 Cal Ripken Jr.	3.00
28 Ken Griffey Jr.	.65
29 Todd Helton	.65
30 Mark McGwire	2.00
31 Jose Cruz	.25
32 Albert Belle	.25
33 Andruw Jones	.75
34 Nomar Garciaparra	1.00
35 Andy Pettitte	.45
36 Alex Rodriguez	1.50

1998 Topps Gallery Pre-Production Samples

To introduce its premium Gallery line for 1998, Topps issued this set of pre-production samples showcasing several of the different technologies to be found in the issue. The samples are virtually identical to the issued versions except for the use of a "PP" prefix to the card number.

		NM/M
Complete Set (5):		7.50
Common Player:		1.50
PP1	Andruw Jones (Portraits)	1.50
PP2	Juan Gonzalez (Permanent Collection)	1.00
PP3	Barry Bonds (Expressionists)	3.00
PP4	Derek Jeter (Exhibitions)	3.00
PP5	Nomar Garciaparra (Impressions)	2.00

1998 Topps Gallery

Gallery returned in 1998 with a 150-card set broken up into five different subsets - Exhibitions, Impressions, Expressionists, Portraits and Permanent Collection. The set was paralleled twice - first in a Player's Private Issue set and, second in Gallery Proofs. Gallery cards were made to look like works of art instead of simply a photo of the player on cardboard, and were sold in six-card packs. Inserts in this single-series product include: Photo Gallery, Gallery of Heroes and Awards Gallery.

		NM/M
Complete Set (150):		15.00
Common Player:		.10
Pack (6):		1.50
Wax Box (24):		25.00
1	Andruw Jones	1.00
2	Fred McGriff	.10
3	Wade Boggs	1.50
4	Pedro Martinez	1.00
5	Matt Williams	.10
6	Wilson Alvarez	.10
7	Henry Rodriguez	.10
9	Jay Bell	.10
9	Marquis Grissom	.10
10	Darryl Kile	.10
11	Chuck Knoblauch	.10
12	Kenny Lofton	.10
13	Quinton McCracken	.10
14	Andres Galarraga	.10
15	Brian Jordan	.10
16	Mike Lansing	.10
17	Travis Fryman	.10
18	Tony Saunders	.10
19	Moises Alou	.10
20	Travis Lee	.10
21	Garret Anderson	.10
22	Ken Caminiti	.10
23	Pedro Astacio	.10
24	Ellis Burks	.10
25	Albert Belle	.10
26	Alan Benes	.10
27	Jay Buhner	.10
28	Derek Bell	.10
29	Jeromy Burnitz	.10

30	Kevin Appier	.10
31	Jeff Cirillo	.10
32	Bernard Gilkey	.10
33	David Cone	.10
34	Jason Dickson	.10
35	Jose Cruz Jr.	.10
36	Marty Cordova	.10
37	Ray Durham	.10
38	Jaret Wright	.10
39	Billy Wagner	.10
40	Roger Clemens	1.75
41	Juan Gonzalez	.50
42	Jeremi Gonzalez	.10
43	Mark Grudzielanek	.10
44	Tom Glavine	.35
45	Barry Larkin	.10
46	Lance Johnson	.10
47	Bobby Higginson	.10
48	Mike Mussina	.50
49	Al Martin	.10
50	Mark McGwire	2.50
51	Todd Hundley	.10
52	Ray Lankford	.10
53	Jason Kendall	.10
54	Javy Lopez	.10
55	Ben Grieve	.10
56	Randy Johnson	1.00
57	Jeff King	.10
58	Mark Grace	.10
59	Rusty Greer	.10
60	Greg Maddux	1.50
61	Jeff Kent	.10
62	Rey Ordonez	.10
63	Hideo Nomo	.50
64	Charles Nagy	.10
65	Rondell White	.10
66	Todd Helton	.75
67	Jim Thome	.75
68	Denny Neagle	.10
69	Ivan Rodriguez	.75
70	Vladimir Guerrero	1.00
71	Jorge Posada	.10
72	J.T. Snow Jr.	.10
73	Reggie Sanders	.10
74	Scott Rolen	.75
75	Robin Ventura	.10
76	Mariano Rivera	.15
77	Cal Ripken Jr.	3.00
78	Justin Thompson	.10
79	Mike Piazza	2.00
80	Kevin Brown	.10
81	Sandy Alomar	.10
82	Craig Biggio	.10
83	Vinny Castilla	.10
84	Eric Young	.10
85	Bernie Williams	.10
86	Brady Anderson	.10
87	Bobby Bonilla	.10
88	Tony Clark	.10
89	Dan Wilson	.10
90	John Wetteland	.10
91	Barry Bonds	3.00
92	Chan Ho Park	.10
93	Carlos Delgado	.35
94	David Justice	.10
95	Chipper Jones	1.50
96	Shawn Estes	.10
97	Jason Giambi	.60
98	Ron Gant	.10
99	John Olerud	.10
100	Frank Thomas	1.00
101	Jose Guillen	.10
102	Brad Radke	.10
103	Troy Percival	.10
104	John Smoltz	.10
105	Edgardo Alfonzo	.10
106	Dante Bichette	.10
107	Larry Walker	.10
108	John Valentin	.10
109	Roberto Alomar	.30
110	Mike Cameron	.10
111	Eric Davis	.10
112	Johnny Damon	.35
113	Darin Erstad	.30
114	Omar Vizquel	.10
115	Derek Jeter	3.00
116	Tony Womack	.10
117	Edgar Renteria	.10
118	Raul Mondesi	.10
119	Tony Gwynn	1.50
120	Ken Griffey Jr.	2.00
121	Jim Edmonds	.10
122	Brian Hunter	.10
123	Neifi Perez	.10
124	Dean Palmer	.10
125	Alex Rodriguez	2.50
126	Tim Salmon	.10
127	Curt Schilling	.35
128	Kevin Orie	.10
129	Andy Pettitte	.30
130	Gary Sheffield	.50
131	Jose Rosado	.10
132	Manny Ramirez	1.00
133	Rafael Palmeiro	.75
134	Sammy Sosa	1.50
135	Jeff Bagwell	1.00
136	Delino DeShields	.10
137	Ryan Klesko	.10
138	Mo Vaughn	.10
139	Steve Finley	.10
140	Nomar Garciaparra	1.50
141	Paul Molitor	1.00
142	Pat Hentgen	.10
143	Eric Karros	.10
144	Bobby Jones	.10
145	Tino Martinez	.10
146	Matt Morris	.10
147	Livan Hernandez	.10

148	Edgar Martinez	.10
149	Paul O'Neill	.10
150	Checklist	.10

Player's Private Issue

Player's Private Issue inserts parallel the 150-card base set with a distinct design and embossing. The average insertion rate is one per 12 packs.

	NM/M
Common Player:	1.00
Stars/Rookies:	4X
Production 250 Sets	

Player's Private Issue Auction Cards

These special auction points cards were seeded one per pack of Gallery. Fronts are identical to the much scarcer PPI cards. Backs, however, differ greatly. Where regular PPI cards have a player photo, serial number, etc., these auction points cards have details of the procedure by which points could be accumulated and used to bid for original photos and printing plates. The redemption period ended Oct. 16, 1998.

	NM/M
Complete Set (150):	60.00
Common Player:	.25
Stars/Rookies:	1.5X

Gallery Proofs

This hobby-only parallel set included all 150 cards in the base set. Gallery Proofs were sequentially numbered to 125 sets.

	NM/M
Common Player:	1.50
Stars/Rookies:	4X
Production 125 Sets	

Awards Gallery

Awards Gallery featured 10 players who earned the highest honors in the game on a horizontal design. Fronts featured a shot of the player and the award he won on silver foilboard. These were inserted every 24 packs and numbered with an "AG" prefix.

		NM/M
Complete Set (10):		18.00
Common Player:		1.00
Inserted 1:24		
1	Ken Griffey Jr.	4.00
2	Larry Walker	1.00
3	Roger Clemens	2.50
4	Pedro Martinez	1.50
5	Nomar Garciaparra	1.00
6	Scott Rolen	1.00
7	Frank Thomas	2.00
8	Tony Gwynn	2.00
9	Mark McGwire	5.00
10	Livan Hernandez	1.00

Gallery of Heroes

Gallery of Heroes is a 15-card insert printed on colored, die-cut plastic that resembles a stained glass window. Cards were inserted one per 24 packs and numbered with a "GH" prefix. More is less in the case in the jumbo (3-1/4" x 4-1/2") version of the cards which were inserted one per hobby box. Cards are numbered with a "GH" prefix.

		NM/M
Complete Set (15):		80.00
Common Player:		1.25
Inserted 1:24		
Jumbo Version (1:24): 75 Percent		
1	Ken Griffey Jr.	8.00
2	Derek Jeter	15.00
3	Barry Bonds	15.00
4	Alex Rodriguez	12.00
5	Frank Thomas	4.00
6	Nomar Garciaparra	6.00
7	Mark McGwire	12.00
8	Mike Piazza	8.00
9	Cal Ripken Jr.	15.00
10	Jose Cruz Jr.	1.25
11	Jeff Bagwell	4.00
12	Chipper Jones	6.00
13	Juan Gonzalez	2.00
14	Hideo Nomo	2.00
15	Greg Maddux	6.00

Photo Gallery

This 10-card insert captured unique shots of players on a silver foilboard design. Photo Gallery inserts were seeded one per 24 packs and numbered with a "PG" prefix.

		NM/M
Complete Set (10):		25.00
Common Player:		1.00
Inserted 1:24		
1	Alex Rodriguez	3.00
2	Frank Thomas	2.00
3	Derek Jeter	4.00
4	Cal Ripken Jr.	4.00
5	Ken Griffey Jr.	2.50
6	Mike Piazza	2.50
7	Nomar Garciaparra	2.25
8	Tim Salmon	1.00
9	Jeff Bagwell	2.00
10	Barry Bonds	4.00

Printing Plates

The aluminum press plates used to print the Gallery cards were issued as random pack inserts. Each card's front and back can be found in four different color variations. Because of the unique nature of each plate, assignment of catalog values is not feasible.

	NM/M
Common Player, Front:	50.00
Common Player, Back:	35.00

Gold Label Class 1 (Fielding, Follow-Thru)

Topps debuted its Gold Label brand with 100 cards printed on 30-point "spectral-reflective stock" with gold foil stamping and two shots of the player on each card front. Cards arrived in Gold Label, Black Label and Red Label versions, each with varying levels of scarcity. The rarity of the cards was determined by the photo and foil stamping on the cards. In the foreground of each card front, the photograph is the same, but in the background one of three shots is featured. Class 1, fielding, are considered base cards; Class 2: running (inserted 1:4 packs) and Class 3, hitting (inserted 1:8 packs) are seeded levels. For pitching the cards are: Class 1, set position (base); Class 2, throwing (inserted 1:4 packs) and Class 3, follow-through (inserted 1:8 packs). Black Label cards are scarcer, while Red Label cards are scarcer yet. In addition, 1 of 1 cards exist for each Class and version. Class 1 cards have matte gold-foil graphic highlights on front. Black Label Class 1 cards were inserted one per eight packs. Red Label Class 1 cards are a 1:99 insert and are serially numbered to 100.

		NM/M
Complete Set (100):		12.00
Gold Label Common Player:		.10
Black Label Common Player:		.35
Black Label Stars/RC's:		4X
Red Label Common Player:		1.50
Red Label Stars/RC's:		12X
Pack (5):		2.00
Wax Box (24):		40.00
1	Kevin Brown	.10
2	Greg Maddux	1.25
3	Albert Belle	.10
4	Andres Galarraga	.10
5	Craig Biggio	.10
6	Matt Williams	.10
7	Derek Jeter	3.00
8	Randy Johnson	1.00
9	Jay Bell	.10
10	Jim Thome	.75
11	Roberto Alomar	.30
12	Tom Glavine	.35
13	Reggie Sanders	.10
14	Tony Gwynn	1.25
15	Mark McGwire	2.00
16	Jeromy Burnitz	.10
17	Andruw Jones	1.00
18	Jay Buhner	.10
19	Robin Ventura	.10
20	Jeff Bagwell	1.00
21	Roger Clemens	1.25
22	Masato Yoshii RC	.25
23	Travis Fryman	.10
24	Rafael Palmeiro	.75
25	Alex Rodriguez	2.00
26	Sandy Alomar	.10
27	Chipper Jones	1.25
28	Rusty Greer	.10
29	Cal Ripken Jr.	3.00
30	Tony Clark	.10
31	Derek Bell	.10
32	Fred McGriff	.10
33	Paul O'Neill	.10
34	Moises Alou	.10
35	Henry Rodriguez	.10
36	Steve Finley	.10
37	Marquis Grissom	.10
38	Jason Giambi	.60
39	Javy Lopez	.10
40	Damion Easley	.10
41	Mariano Rivera	.15
42	Mo Vaughn	.10
43	Mike Mussina	.40
44	Jason Kendall	.10

45	Pedro Martinez	1.00
46	Frank Thomas	1.00
47	Jim Edmonds	.10
48	Hideki Irabu	.10
49	Eric Karros	.10
50	Juan Gonzalez	.50
51	Ellis Burks	.10
52	Dean Palmer	.10
53	Scott Rolen	.60
54	Raul Mondesi	.10
55	Quinton McCraken	.10
56	John Olerud	.10
57	Ken Caminiti	.10
58	Brian Jordan	.10
59	Wade Boggs	1.25
60	Mike Piazza	1.50
61	Darin Erstad	.30
62	Curt Schilling	.35
63	David Justice	.10
64	Kenny Lofton	.10
65	Barry Bonds	3.00
66	Ray Lankford	.10
67	Brian Hunter	.10
68	Chuck Knoblauch	.10
69	Vinny Castilla	.10
70	Vladimir Guerrero	1.00
71	Tim Salmon	.10
72	Larry Walker	.10
73	Paul Molitor	1.00
74	Barry Larkin	.10
75	Edgar Martinez	.10
76	Bernie Williams	.10
77	Dante Bichette	.10
78	Nomar Garciaparra	1.25
79	Ben Grieve	.10
80	Ivan Rodriguez	.75
81	Todd Helton	.75
82	Ryan Klesko	.10
83	Sammy Sosa	1.25
84	Travis Lee	.10
85	Jose Cruz	.10
86	Mark Kotsay	.10
87	Richard Hidalgo	.10
88	Rondell White	.10
89	Greg Vaughn	.10
90	Gary Sheffield	.50
91	Paul Konerko	.25
92	Mark Grace	.10
93	Kevin Millwood RC	.10
94	Manny Ramirez	1.00
95	Tino Martinez	.10
96	Brad Fullmer	.10
97	Todd Walker	.10
98	Carlos Delgado	.45
99	Kerry Wood	.60
100	Ken Griffey Jr.	1.50

Gold Label Class 2 (Running, Set Position)

Class 2 Gold Label and parallels feature background photos on front of position players running and pitchers in the set position. Class 2 cards have sparkling silver-foil graphic highlights on front and were inserted one per two packs. Black Label Class 2 cards were inserted one per 16 packs. Red Label Class 2 cards are a 1:198 insert and are serially numbered to 50.

	NM/M
Complete Set (100)	50.00
Gold Label Common Player:	.35
Gold Label Stars/RC's:	2X
Black Label Common Player:	1.00
Black Label Stars/RC's:	4X
Red Label Common Player:	4.00
Red Label Stars/RC's:	25X

Gold Label Class 3 (Hitting, Throwing)

Class 3 Gold Label and parallels feature background photos on front of position players hitting and pitchers throwing. Class 3 cards have sparkling gold-foil graphic highlights on front and were inserted one per four packs. Black Label Class 3 cards were inserted one per 32 packs. Red Label Class 2 cards are a 1:396 insert and are serially numbered to 25.

	NM/M
Complete Set (100):	120.00
Common Player:	.75
Gold Label Stars/RC's:	2.5X
Black Label Common Player:	2.00
Black Label Stars/RC's:	6X
Red Label Common Player:	6.00
Red Label Stars/RC's:	35X

Gold Label 1 of 1

Each of the Classes and color versions of Topps Gold Label cards was paralleled in a 1 of 1 insert which was to be found on average of one per 1,085 packs. Each player, thus, can be found on nine different 1 of 1 cards in the issue.

Gold Label Home Run Race

Home Run Race of '98 was a four-card insert set. Each of the current players' cards features a background shot of Roger Maris, while the fourth card features two shots of Maris. Gold, Black and Red Label versions are identified by the different foil-stamp logos. Gold cards were inserted 1:12 packs, Black Label cards were inserted 1:48 packs and Red Label cards were sequentially numbered to 61 and inserted 1:4,055 packs. The Home Run Race inserts are exclusive to Topps Home Team Advantage boxes.

	NM/M
Complete Set (4):	7.50
Common Player:	2.00
Black Label:	2X
Red Label:	4X
HR1 Roger Maris	3.00
HR2 Mark McGwire	3.00
HR3 Ken Griffey Jr.	2.50
HR4 Sammy Sosa	2.00

Opening Day

Topps Opening Day was a retail exclusive product comprising 165 cards, with 110 from Series 1 and 55 from Series 2. The cards from Series 2 were available in this product prior to the regular-issue cards being re-

leased. Opening Day cards feature a silver border vs. the gold border in the regular set, and include a silver-foil Opening Day stamp.

	NM/M
Complete Set (165):	10.00
Common Player:	.05
Wax Pack (7):	.65
Wax Box (22):	10.00
1 Tony Gwynn	.65
2 Larry Walker	.05
3 Billy Wagner	.05
4 Denny Neagle	.05
5 Vladimir Guerrero	.50
6 Kevin Brown	.05
7 Mariano Rivera	.15
8 Tony Clark	.05
9 Deion Sanders	.05
10 Matt Williams	.05
11 Carlos Baerga	.05
12 Mo Vaughn	.05
13 Chan Ho Park	.05
14 Frank Thomas	.50
15 John Jaha	.05
16 Steve Trachsel	.05
17 Jeff Kent	.05
18 Scott Rolen	.40
19 Juan Gonzalez	.25
20 Garret Anderson	.05
21 Roberto Clemente	1.00
22 Omar Vizquel	.05
23 Brian Hunter	.05
24 Jeff Bagwell	.50
25 Chili Davis	.05
26 Mike Cameron	.05
27 Pat Hentgen	.05
28 Wilton Guerrero	.05
29 Devon White	.05
30 Rafael Palmeiro	.40
31 Jeff Blauser	.05
32 Dave Nilsson	.05
33 Trevor Hoffman	.05
34 Ryan Klesko	.05
35 Butch Huskey	.05
36 Mark Grudzielanek	.05
37 Marquis Grissom	.05
38 Jim Edmonds	.05
39 Greg Vaughn	.05
40 David Wells	.05
41 Charles Nagy	.05
42 B.J. Surhoff	.05
43 Edgardo Alfonzo	.05
44 Jay Buhner	.05
45 Brady Anderson	.05
46 Edgar Renteria	.05
47 Rick Aguilera	.05
48 Henry Rodriguez	.05
49 Mike Piazza	.75
50 Todd Zeile	.05
51 Rey Ordonez	.05
52 Tony Womack	.05
53 Mike Sweeney	.05
54 Jeffrey Hammonds	.05
55 Kevin Orie	.05
56 Alex Gonzalez	.05
57 Jose Canseco	.35
58 Joey Hamilton	.05
59 Brad Radke	.05
60 Kevin Appier	.05
61 Manny Ramirez	.50
62 Jeromy Burnitz	.05
63 Matt Morris	.05
64 Jason Dickson	.05
65 Tom Glavine	.25
66 Wally Joyner	.05
67 Todd Jones	.05
68 Sandy Alomar	.05
69 Mike Lansing	.05
70 Todd Stottlemyre	.05
71 Jay Bell	.05
72 Joey Cora	.05
73 Scott Spiezio	.05
74 Joe Carter	.05
75 Jose Guillen	.05
76 Damion Easley	.05
77 Alex Fernandez	.05
78 Randy Johnson	.50
79 J.T. Snow	.05
80 Bernard Gilkey	.05
81 David Segui	.05
82 Dante Bichette	.05
83 Derek Jeter	1.50
84 Mark Wohlers	.05
85 Ricky Bottalico	.05
86 Mike Mussina	.35
87 Gary Sheffield	.35

88 Hideo Nomo	.25
89 Mark Grace	.05
90 Darryl Kile	.05
91 Shawn Estes	.05
92 Vinny Castilla	.05
93 Jose Rosado	.05
94 Kenny Lofton	.05
95 Jason Giambi	.35
96 Ray Lankford	.05
97 Hideki Irabu	.05
98 Javy Lopez	.05
99 Jeff Montgomery	.05
100 Dennis Eckersley	.40
101 Armando Benitez	.05
102 Tim Naehring	.05
103 Luis Gonzalez	.05
104 Todd Hollandsworth	.05
105 Wade Boggs	.65
106 Mickey Morandini	.05
107 Rusty Greer	.05
108 Terry Steinbach	.05
109 Pete Rose II	.05
110 Checklist	.05
111 Tino Martinez	.05
112 Roberto Alomar	.20
113 Jeff King	.05
114 Brian Jordan	.05
115 Darin Erstad	.25
116 Ken Caminiti	.05
117 Jim Thome	.60
118 Paul Molitor	.50
119 Ivan Rodriguez	.40
120 Bernie Williams	.05
121 Todd Hundley	.05
122 Andres Galarraga	.05
123 Greg Maddux	.65
124 Edgar Martinez	.05
125 Ron Gant	.05
126 Derek Bell	.05
127 Roger Clemens	.70
128 Rondell White	.05
129 Barry Larkin	.05
130 Robin Ventura	.05
131 Jason Kendall	.05
132 Chipper Jones	.75
133 John Franco	.05
134 Sammy Sosa	.65
135 Chuck Knoblauch	.05
136 Ellis Burks	.05
137 Al Martin	.05
138 Tim Salmon	.05
139 Moises Alou	.05
140 Lance Johnson	.05
141 Justin Thompson	.05
142 Will Clark	.05
143 Barry Bonds	1.50
144 Craig Biggio	.05
145 John Smoltz	.05
146 Cal Ripken Jr.	1.50
147 Ken Griffey Jr.	.75
148 Paul O'Neill	.05
149 Todd Helton	.40
150 John Olerud	.05
151 Mark McGwire	1.00
152 Jose Cruz Jr.	.05
153 Jeff Cirillo	.05
154 Dean Palmer	.05
155 John Wetteland	.05
156 Eric Karros	.05
157 Steve Finley	.05
158 Albert Belle	.05
159 Curt Schilling	.25
160 Raul Mondesi	.05
161 Andruw Jones	.50
162 Nomar Garciaparra	.65
163 David Justice	.05
164 Andy Pettitte	.20
165 Pedro Martinez	.50

SportzCubz Prototypes

This rare "Product Prototype" (says so right on the back) was designed to allow collectors to get creative in making their own 3-D structures featuring their favorite ballplayers. About 3" square, the plastic pieces have slots and tabs which would allow them to be connected in a variety of ways. Fronts have action photos on a large team logo. Backs have a portrait photo, personal data, recent stats, a career highlight or two and essential licensing data. The product was never rolled out for public consumption and it is unknown to what extent the prototypes were produced or have found their way into collectors' hands. Therefore, no pricing is provided.

Complete Set (25):

1998 Topps Stars Pre-Production

These promotional cards introduced the new Stars brand from Topps to dealers and the hobby press. The cards are virtually identical to the regularly-issued version except for the numbering on back, which has a "PP" prefix and serial numbers "000/000."

	NM/M
Complete Set (6):	5.00
Common Player:	.50
PP1 Mike Piazza	3.00
PP2 Darin Erstad	.60
PP3 Vinny Castilla	.50
PP4 Craig Biggio	.50
PP5 Ivan Rodriguez	.75
PP6 Pedro Martinez	1.00

1998 Topps Stars

Topps Stars adopted an all-sequential numbering format in 1998 with a 150-card set. Every card was available in a bronze (numbered to 9,799), red (9,799), silver (4,399), gold (2,299) and gold rainbow format (99) with different color foil to distinguish the groups. Players were each judged in five categories: arm strength, hit for average, power, defense and speed. Inserts in the product include: Galaxy, Luminaries, Supernovas, Rookie Reprints and Rookie Reprint Autographs. All regular-issue cards and inserts were individually numbered except the Rookie Reprints.

	NM/M
Complete Set, Red or Bronze (150):	24.00
Common Player, Red or Bronze:	.10
Production 9,799 sets each.	
Pack (6):	1.25
Wax Box (24):	25.00
1 Greg Maddux	1.50
2 Darryl Kile	.10
3 Rod Beck	.10
4 Ellis Burks	.10
5 Gary Sheffield	.40
6 David Ortiz	.10
7 Marquis Grissom	.10
8 Tony Womack	.10
9 Mike Mussina	.60
10 Bernie Williams	.10
11 Andy Benes	.10
12 Rusty Greer	.10
13 Carlos Delgado	.35
14 Jim Edmonds	.10
15 Raul Mondesi	.10
16 Andres Galarraga	.10
17 Wade Boggs	1.50
18 Paul O'Neill	.10
19 Edgar Renteria	.10
20 Tony Clark	.10
21 Vladimir Guerrero	1.00
22 Moises Alou	.10
23 Bernard Gilkey	.10
24 Lance Johnson	.10
25 Ben Grieve	.10
26 Sandy Alomar	.10
27 Ray Durham	.10
28 Shawn Estes	.10
29 David Segui	.10
30 Javy Lopez	.10
31 Steve Finley	.10
32 Rey Ordonez	.10
33 Derek Jeter	3.00
34 Henry Rodriguez	.10
35 Mo Vaughn	.10
36 Richard Hidalgo	.10
37 Omar Vizquel	.10
38 Johnny Damon	.35
39 Brian Hunter	.10
40 Matt Williams	.10
41 Chuck Finley	.10
42 Jeromy Burnitz	.10
43 Livan Hernandez	.10
44 Delino DeShields	.10
45 Charles Nagy	.10

46 Scott Rolen	.75
47 Neifi Perez	.10
48 John Wetteland	.10
49 Eric Milton	.10
50 Mike Piazza	2.00
51 Cal Ripken Jr.	3.00
52 Mariano Rivera	.25
53 Butch Huskey	.10
54 Quinton McCracken	.10
55 Jose Cruz Jr.	.10
56 Brian Jordan	.10
57 Hideo Nomo	.50
58 Masato Yoshii	.10
59 Cliff Floyd	.10
60 Jose Guillen	.10
61 Jeff Shaw	.10
62 Edgar Martinez	.10
63 Rondell White	.10
64 Hal Morris	.10
65 Barry Larkin	.10
66 Eric Young	.10
67 Ray Lankford	.10
68 Derek Bell	.10
69 Charles Johnson	.10
70 Robin Ventura	.10
71 Chuck Knoblauch	.10
72 Kevin Brown	.10
73 Jose Valentin	.10
74 Jay Buhner	.10
75 Tony Gwynn	1.50
76 Andy Pettitte	.30
77 Edgardo Alfonzo	.10
78 Kerry Wood	.40
79 Darin Erstad	.30
80 Paul Konerko	.15
81 Jason Kendall	.10
82 Tino Martinez	.10
83 Brad Radke	.10
84 Jeff King	.10
85 Travis Lee	.10
86 Jeff Kent	.10
87 Trevor Hoffman	.10
88 David Cone	.10
89 Jose Canseco	.40
90 Juan Gonzalez	.50
91 Todd Hundley	.10
92 John Valentin	.10
93 Sammy Sosa	1.50
94 Jason Giambi	.40
95 Chipper Jones	1.50
96 Jeff Blauser	.10
97 Brad Fullmer	.10
98 Derrek Lee	.60
99 Denny Neagle	.10
100 Ken Griffey Jr.	2.00
101 David Justice	.10
102 Tim Salmon	.10
103 J.T. Snow	.10
104 Fred McGriff	.10
105 Brady Anderson	.10
106 Larry Walker	.10
107 Jeff Cirillo	.10
108 Andruw Jones	1.00
109 Manny Ramirez	1.00
110 Justin Thompson	.10
111 Vinny Castilla	.10
112 Chan Ho Park	.10
113 Mark Grudzielanek	.10
114 Mark Grace	.10
115 Ken Caminiti	.10
116 Ryan Klesko	.10
117 Rafael Palmeiro	.75
118 Pat Hentgen	.10
119 Eric Karros	.10
120 Randy Johnson	1.00
121 Roberto Alomar	.25
122 John Olerud	.10
123 Paul Molitor	1.00
124 Dean Palmer	.10
125 Nomar Garciaparra	1.50
126 Curt Schilling	.30
127 Jay Bell	.10
128 Craig Biggio	.10
129 Marty Cordova	.10
130 Ivan Rodriguez	.75
131 Todd Helton	.75
132 Jim Thome	.65
133 Albert Belle	.10
134 Mike Lansing	.10
135 Mark McGwire	2.50
136 Roger Clemens	1.75
137 Tom Glavine	.30
138 Ron Gant	.10
139 Alex Rodriguez	2.50
140 Jeff Bagwell	1.00
141 John Smoltz	.10
142 Kenny Lofton	.10
143 Dante Bichette	.10
144 Pedro Martinez	1.00
145 Barry Bonds	3.00
146 Travis Fryman	.10
147 Bobby Jones	.10
148 Bobby Higginson	.10
149 Reggie Sanders	.10
150 Frank Thomas	1.00
Checklist	.05

Silver

	NM/M
Common Silver:	.50
Silver Stars:	1.5X
Production 4,399 Sets	

Gold

	NM/M
Common Gold:	1.00
Gold Stars:	2X
Production 2,299 Sets	

Gold Rainbow

Each card in Topps Stars was available in a Gold Rainbow version. This was the most limited of the five parallels and was numbered to 99. Cards featured gold prismatic foil on the front and were seeded every 46 packs.

	NM/M
Common Gold Rainbow:	4.00
Gold Rainbow Stars:	8X
Production 99 Sets	

Galaxy

Galaxy featured 10 players who possess all five skills featured in Topps Stars Baseball. Four versions were available and sequentially numbered, including: Bronze (numbered to 100, inserted 1:682 packs), Silver (numbered to 75, inserted 1:910), Gold (numbered to 50, inserted 1:1,364) and Gold Rainbow (numbered to 5, inserted 1:13,643).

	NM/M
Complete Set (10):	150.00
Common Player:	7.50
Production 100 Sets	
Silvers:	1.5X
Production 75 Sets	
Golds:	2X
Production 50 Sets	
Gold Rainbows: Values Undetermined	
Production Five Sets	
G1 Barry Bonds	40.00
G2 Jeff Bagwell	15.00
G3 Nomar Garciaparra	20.00
G4 Chipper Jones	20.00
G5 Ken Griffey Jr.	25.00
G6 Sammy Sosa	20.00
G7 Larry Walker	7.50
G8 Alex Rodriguez	35.00
G9 Craig Biggio	7.50
G10 Raul Mondesi	7.50

Luminaries

Luminaries feature three top players in each "tool" group. The 15-card insert has four parallel sequentially numbered versions inserted as follows: bronze (numbered to 100, inserted 1:455), silver (numbered to 75, inserted 1:606), gold (numbered to 50, inserted 1:910) and gold rainbow (numbered to 5, inserted 1:9,095).

		NM/M
Complete Set (15):		140.00
Common Player:		4.00
Production 100 Sets		
Silver (75 Sets):		1.5X
Gold (50 Sets):		1.5X
Gold Rainbow (Five Sets):		
Values Undetermined		
L1	Ken Griffey Jr.	15.00
L2	Mark McGwire	20.00
L3	Juan Gonzalez	5.00
L4	Tony Gwynn	12.50
L5	Frank Thomas	10.00
L6	Mike Piazza	15.00
L7	Chuck Knoblauch	4.00
L8	Kenny Lofton	4.00
L9	Barry Bonds	25.00
L10	Matt Williams	4.00
L11	Raul Mondesi	4.00
L12	Ivan Rodriguez	7.50
L13	Alex Rodriguez	20.00
L14	Nomar Garciaparra	12.50
L15	Ken Caminiti	4.00

Supernovas

Supernovas was a 10-card insert in Topps Stars who included rookies and prospects who either have all five tools focused on in the product, or excel dramatically in one of the five. Four sequentially numbered levels were available, with insert rates as follows: bronze (numbered to 100, inserted 1:682), silver (numbered to 75, inserted 1:910), gold (numbered to 50, inserted 1:1,364) and gold rainbow (numbered to 5, inserted 1:13,643).

		NM/M
Complete Set (10):		35.00
Common Player:		2.00
Production 100 Sets		
Silver:		1.5X
Production 75 Sets		
Gold:		1.5X
Production 50 Sets		
Gold Rainbow: Values Undetermined		
Production Five Sets		
S1	Ben Grieve	2.00
S2	Travis Lee	2.00
S3	Todd Helton	10.00
S4	Adrian Beltre	4.00
S5	Derrek Lee	6.00
S6	David Ortiz	6.00
S7	Brad Fullmer	2.00
S8	Mark Kotsay	2.00
S9	Paul Konerko	4.00
S10	Kerry Wood	6.00

Rookie Reprints

Topps reprinted the rookie cards of five Hall of Famers in Rookie Reprints. The cards are inserted one per 24 packs and have UV coating.

		NM/M
Complete Set (5):		7.00
Common Player:		1.50
1968	Johnny Bench	1.50
1953	Whitey Ford	1.50
1965	Joe Morgan	1.50
1973	Mike Schmidt	2.50
1960	Carl Yastrzemski	2.00

Rookie Reprints Autographs

Autographed versions of all five Rookie Reprint inserts were available and seeded one per 273 packs. Each card arrive with a Topps "Certified Autograph Issue" stamp to ensure its authenticity.

		NM/M
Complete Set (5):		175.00
Common Player:		25.00
1968	Johnny Bench	75.00
1953	Whitey Ford	50.00
1965	Joe Morgan	25.00
1973	Mike Schmidt	90.00
1960	Carl Yastrzemski	90.00

1998 Topps Stars 'N Steel

Stars 'N Steel was a 44-card set printed on four-colored textured film laminate bonded to a sheet of 25-gauge metal. Regular cards featured a silver colored border while gold versions were also available and seeded one per 12 packs. Stars 'N Steel was available only to Home Team Advantage members and was packaged in three-card packs that arrived in a sturdy, tri-fold stand-up display unit. A second parallel version was also available featuring gold holographic technology and was seeded one per 40 packs.

		NM/M
Complete Set (44):		40.00
Common Player:		.25
Golds:		2X
Holographics:		7X
Pack (3):		3.50
Wax Box (12):		30.00
1	Roberto Alomar	.50
2	Jeff Bagwell	1.25
3	Albert Belle	.25
4	Dante Bichette	.25
5	Barry Bonds	4.00
6	Jay Buhner	.25
7	Ken Caminiti	.25
8	Vinny Castilla	.25
9	Roger Clemens	2.25
10	Jose Cruz Jr.	.25
11	Andres Galarraga	.25
12	Nomar Garciaparra	2.00
13	Juan Gonzalez	.65
14	Mark Grace	.25
15	Ken Griffey Jr.	2.50
16	Tony Gwynn	2.00
17	Todd Hundley	.25
18	Derek Jeter	4.00
19	Randy Johnson	1.25
20	Andruw Jones	1.25
21	Chipper Jones	2.00
22	David Justice	.25
23	Ray Larkin	.25
24	Barry Larkin	.25
25	Kenny Lofton	.25
26	Greg Maddux	2.00
27	Edgar Martinez	.25
28	Tino Martinez	.25
29	Mark McGwire	3.00
30	Paul Molitor	1.25
31	Rafael Palmeiro	1.00
32	Mike Piazza	2.50
33	Manny Ramirez	1.25
34	Cal Ripken Jr.	4.00
35	Ivan Rodriguez	1.00
36	Scott Rolen	.75
37	Tim Salmon	.25
38	Gary Sheffield	.50
39	Sammy Sosa	2.00
40	Frank Thomas	1.25
41	Jim Thome	1.00
42	Mo Vaughn	.25
43	Larry Walker	.25
44	Bernie Williams	.25

1998 Topps TEK Pre-Production

Each of three players' Tek cards can also be found in two versions marked diagonally across the card number on back "Pre-production." The gold-foil version is much scarcer than the silver.

		NM/M
Complete Set, Silver (3):		10.00
Complete Set, Gold (3):		45.00
23	Mark McGwire/Silver	6.00
23	Mark McGwire/Gold	30.00
45	Roger Clemens/Silver	5.00
45	Roger Clemens/Gold	20.00
?	Raul Mondesi/Silver	.50
?	Raul Mondesi/Gold	2.50

1998 Topps TEK

A myriad of collecting methods was created with this innovative product which features 90 different players each printed on an acetate stock with 90 different background patterns. A parallel series utilizing Diffraction technology was inserted at the rate of one per six packs. Each of the 8,100 different cards was created in the same quantity, so there is no differentiation in value among patterns.

		NM/M
Complete Set (90):		75.00
Common Player:		.25
Pack (4):		4.00
Wax Box (20):		80.00
1	Ben Grieve	.25
2	Kerry Wood	1.50
3	Barry Bonds	8.00
4	John Olerud	.25
5	Ivan Rodriguez	2.00
6	Frank Thomas	2.50
7	Bernie Williams	.25
8	Dante Bichette	.25
9	Alex Rodriguez	6.00
10	Tom Glavine	.50
11	Eric Karros	.25
12	Craig Biggio	.25
13	Mark McGwire	6.00
14	Derek Jeter	8.00
15	Nomar Garciaparra	4.00
16	Brady Anderson	.25
17	Vladimir Guerrero	2.50
18	David Justice	.25
19	Chipper Jones	4.00
20	Jim Edmonds	.25
21	Roger Clemens	4.50
22	Mark Kotsay	.25
23	Tony Gwynn	4.00
24	Todd Walker	.25
25	Tino Martinez	.25
26	Andruw Jones	2.50
27	Sandy Alomar	.25
28	Sammy Sosa	4.00
29	Gary Sheffield	1.50
30	Ken Griffey Jr.	5.00
31	Aramis Ramirez	.25
32	Curt Schilling	.50
33	Robin Ventura	.25
34	Larry Walker	.25
35	Darin Erstad	1.25
36	Todd Dunwoody	.25
37	Paul O'Neill	.25
38	Vinny Castilla	.25
39	Randy Johnson	2.50
40	Rafael Palmeiro	2.00
41	Pedro Martinez	2.50
42	Derek Bell	.25
43	Carlos Delgado	.50
44	Matt Williams	.25
45	Kenny Lofton	.25
46	Edgar Renteria	.25
47	Albert Belle	.25
48	Jeromy Burnitz	.25
49	Adrian Beltre	.40
50	Greg Maddux	4.00
51	Cal Ripken Jr.	8.00
52	Jason Kendall	.25
53	Ellis Burks	.25
54	Paul Molitor	2.50
55	Moises Alou	.25
56	Raul Mondesi	.25
57	Barry Larkin	.25
58	Tony Clark	.25
59	Travis Lee	.25
60	Juan Gonzalez	1.25
61	Troy Glaus **RC**	3.00
62	Jose Cruz Jr.	.25
63	Paul Konerko	.40
64	Edgar Martinez	.25
65	Javy Lopez	.25
66	Manny Ramirez	2.50
67	Roberto Alomar	.75
68	Ken Caminiti	.25
69	Todd Helton	1.50
70	Chuck Knoblauch	.25
71	Kevin Brown	.25
72	Tim Salmon	.25
73	Orlando Hernandez **RC**	1.00
74	Jeff Bagwell	2.50
75	Brian Jordan	.25
76	Derrek Lee	1.50
77	Brad Fullmer	.25
78	Mark Grace	.25
79	Jeff King	.25
80	Mike Mussina	1.50
81	Jay Buhner	.25
82	Quinton McCracken	.25
83	A.J. Hinch	.25
84	Richard Hidalgo	.25
85	Andres Galarraga	.25
86	Mike Piazza	5.00
87	Mo Vaughn	.25
88	Scott Rolen	1.50
89	Jim Thome	2.00
90	Ray Lankford	.25

Diffraction

Not only can each of the 90 cards in Topps TEK be found in 90 different background patterns, but each can be found in a parallel edition printed with diffraction foil. The parallels are inserted on an average of one per six packs. Like the regular issue TEKs, all patterns were produced equally and there is no value differentiation among them.

	NM/M
Complete Set (90):	400.00
Common Player:	4.00
Stars/RC's:	4X

1999 Topps Pre-Production

To give potential customers a feel for its 1999 baseball cards, Topps issued this series of pre-production samples. Cards are identical in format to the issued versions except they are numbered with a "PP" prefix and the 1998 stats line reads "PRE-PRODUCTION SAMPLE."

		NM/M
Complete Set (6):		7.00

		NM/M
Common Player:		.50
PP1	Roger Clemens	2.00
PP2	Sammy Sosa	2.00
PP3	Derek Jeter	2.50
PP4	Walt Weiss	.50
PP5	Darin Erstad	.75
PP6	Jason Kendall	.50

1999 Topps

Released in two series, the 462-card set includes two home run record subsets, featuring McGwire and Sosa. McGwire's subset card #220 has 70 different versions, commemorating each of his home runs, including where it was hit, the pitcher, date and estimated distance. Sosa's subset card #461 has 66 different versions. Other subsets include World Series Highlights, Prospects, Draft Picks and Season Highlights. Each pack contains 11 cards with an SRP of $1.29. MVPs are the only parallel. They feature a special Topps MVP logo; 100 cards of each player exist. If the player on the card was named a weekly Topps MVP, collectors won a special set of redemption cards.

		NM/M
Unop. Hobby Set (462):		40.00
Unop. Retail Set (463):		50.00
Complete Set (462):		35.00
Common Player:		.05
MVP Stars/Rookies:		20X
Ser. 1 or 2 Hobby Pack (11):		1.25
Ser. 1 or 2 Hobby Box (36):		40.00
Ser. 1 or 2 Retail Pack (8):		1.00
Ser. 1 or 2 Retail Box (22):		20.00
Ser. 1 or 2 Jumbo Pack (40):		3.50
Ser. 1 or 2 Jumbo Box (12):		30.00
1	Roger Clemens	1.00
2	Andres Galarraga	.05
3	Scott Brosius	.05
4	John Flaherty	.05
5	Jim Leyritz	.05
6	Ray Durham	.05
7	Joe Vizcaino	.05
8	Will Clark	.05
9	David Wells	.05
10	Jose Guillen	.05
11	Scott Hatteberg	.05
12	Edgardo Alfonzo	.05
13	Mike Bordick	.05
14	Manny Ramirez	.75
15	Greg Maddux	1.00
16	David Segui	.05
17	Darryl Strawberry	.05
18	Brad Radke	.05
19	Kerry Wood	.40
20	Matt Anderson	.05
21	Derek Lee	.60
22	Mickey Morandini	.05
23	Paul Konerko	.15
24	Travis Lee	.15
25	Ken Hill	.05
26	Kenny Rogers	.05
27	Paul Sorrento	.05
28	Quilvio Veras	.05
29	Todd Walker	.05
30	Ryan Jackson	.05
31	John Olerud	.05
32	Doug Glanville	.05
33	Nolan Ryan	2.00
34	Ray Lankford	.05
36	Mark Loretta	.05
37	Jason Dickson	.05
38	Sean Bergman	.05
39	Quinton McCracken	.05
40	Bartolo Colon	.05
41	Brady Anderson	.05
42	Chris Stynes	.05
43	Jorge Posada	.05
44	Justin Thompson	.05
45	Johnny Damon	.30
46	Armando Benitez	.05
47	Brant Brown	.05
48	Charlie Hayes	.05
49	Darren Dreifort	.05
50	Juan Gonzalez	.40
51	Chuck Knoblauch	.05
52	Todd Helton (Rookie All-Star)	.75
53	Rick Reed	.05
54	Chris Gomez	.05
55	Gary Sheffield	.45
56	Rod Beck	.05
57	Rey Sanchez	.05
58	Garret Anderson	.05
59	Jimmy Haynes	.05
60	Steve Woodard	.05
61	Rondell White	.05
62	Vladimir Guerrero	.75
63	Eric Karros	.05
64	Russ Davis	.05
65	Mo Vaughn	.05
66	Sammy Sosa	1.00
67	Troy Percival	.05
68	Kenny Lofton	.05
69	Bill Taylor	.05
70	Mark McGwire	1.50
71	Roger Cedeno	.05
72	Javy Lopez	.05
73	Damion Easley	.05
74	Andy Pettitte	.25
75	Tony Gwynn	1.00
76	Ricardo Rincon	.05
77	F.P. Santangelo	.05
78	Jay Bell	.05
79	Scott Servais	.05
80	Jose Canseco	.40
81	Roberto Hernandez	.05
82	Todd Dunwoody	.05
83	John Wetteland	.05
84	Mike Caruso (Rookie All-Star)	.05
85	Derek Jeter	2.00
86	Aaron Sele	.05
87	Jose Lima	.05
88	Ryan Christenson	.05
89	Jeff Cirillo	.05
90	Jose Hernandez	.05
91	Mark Kotsay (Rookie All-Star)	.05
92	Darren Bragg	.05
93	Albert Belle	.05
94	Matt Lawton	.05
95	Pedro Martinez	.75
96	Greg Vaughn	.05
97	Neifi Perez	.05
98	Gerald Williams	.05
99	Derek Bell	.05
100	Ken Griffey Jr.	1.25
101	David Cone	.05
102	Brian Johnson	.05
103	Dean Palmer	.05
104	Javier Valentin	.05
105	Trevor Hoffman	.05
106	Butch Huskey	.05
107	Dave Martinez	.05
108	Billy Wagner	.05
109	Shawn Green	.30
110	Ben Grieve (Rookie All-Star)	.05
111	Tom Goodwin	.05
112	Jaret Wright	.05
113	Aramis Ramirez	.05
114	Dmitri Young	.05
115	Hideki Irabu	.05
116	Roberto Kelly	.05
117	Jeff Fassero	.05
118	Mark Clark	.05
119	Jason McDonald	.05
120	Matt Williams	.05
121	Dave Burba	.05
122	Bret Saberhagen	.05
123	Deivi Cruz	.05
124	Chad Curtis	.05
125	Scott Rolen	.65
126	Lee Stevens	.05
127	J.T. Snow Jr.	.05
128	Rusty Greer	.05
129	Brian Meadows	.05
130	Jim Edmonds	.05
131	Ron Gant	.05
132	A.J. Hinch (Rookie All-Star)	.05
133	Shannon Stewart	.05
134	Brad Fullmer	.05
135	Cal Eldred	.05
136	Matt Walbeck	.05
137	Carl Everett	.05
138	Walt Weiss	.05
139	Fred McGriff	.25
140	Darin Erstad	.25
141	Dave Nilsson	.05
142	Eric Young	.05
143	Dan Wilson	.05
144	Jeff Reed	.05
145	Brett Tomko	.05
146	Terry Steinbach	.05
147	Seth Greisinger	.05
148	Pat Meares	.05

149	Livan Hernandez	.05
150	Jeff Bagwell	.75
151	Bob Wickman	.05
152	Omar Vizquel	.05
153	Eric Davis	.05
154	Larry Sutton	.05
155	Magglio Ordonez (Rookie All-Star)	.40
156	Eric Milton	.05
157	Darren Lewis	.05
158	Rick Aguilera	.05
159	Mike Lieberthal	.05
160	Robb Nen	.05
161	Brian Giles	.05
162	Jeff Brantley	.05
163	Gary DiSarcina	.05
164	John Valentin	.05
165	David Dellucci	.05
166	Chan Ho Park	.05
167	Masato Yoshii	.05
168	Jason Schmidt	.05
169	LaTroy Hawkins	.05
170	Bret Boone	.05
171	Jerry DiPoto	.05
172	Mariano Rivera	.10
173	Mike Cameron	.05
174	Scott Erickson	.05
175	Charles Johnson	.05
176	Bobby Jones	.05
177	Francisco Cordova	.05
178	Todd Jones	.05
179	Jeff Montgomery	.05
180	Mike Mussina	.40
181	Bob Abreu	.05
182	Ismael Valdes	.05
183	Andy Fox	.05
184	Woody Williams	.05
185	Denny Neagle	.05
186	Jose Valentin	.05
187	Darrin Fletcher	.05
188	Gabe Alvarez	.05
189	Eddie Taubensee	.05
190	Edgar Martinez	.05
191	Jason Kendall	.05
192	Darryl Kile	.05
193	Jeff King	.05
194	Rey Ordonez	.05
195	Andruw Jones	.75
196	Tony Fernandez	.05
197	Jamey Wright	.05
198	B.J. Surhoff	.05
199	Vinny Castilla	.05
200	David Wells (Season Highlight)	.05
201	Mark McGwire (Season Highlight)	.75
202	Sammy Sosa (Season Highlight)	.50
203	Roger Clemens (Season Highlight)	.50
204	Kerry Wood (Season Highlight)	.15
205	Lance Berkman, Mike Frank, Gabe Kapler (Prospects)	.15
206	Alex Escobar RC, Ricky Ledee, Mike Stoner (Prospects)	.25
207	Peter Bergeron RC, Jeremy Giambi, George Lombard (Prospects)	.30
208	Michael Barrett, Ben Davis, Robert Fick (Prospects)	.05
209	Pat Cline, Ramon Hernandez, Jayson Werth (Prospects)	.05
210	Bruce Chen, Chris Enochs, Ryan Anderson (Prospects)	.05
211	Mike Lincoln, Octavio Dotel, Brad Penny (Prospects)	.05
212	Chuck Abbott, Brent Butler, Danny Klassen (Prospects)	.05
213	Chris Jones, Jeff Urban RC (Draft Pick)	.05
214	Arturo McDowell RC, Tony Torcato RC (Draft Pick)	.25
215	Josh McKinley RC, Jason Tyner RC (Draft Pick)	.25
216	Matt Burch RC, Seth Etherton RC (Draft Pick)	.25
217	Mamon Tucker RC, Rick Elder RC (Draft Pick)	.10
218	J.M. Gold RC, Ryan Mills RC (Draft Pick)	.10
219	Adam Brown RC, Choo Freeman RC (Draft Pick)	.25
220	Home Run Record #1 (M. McGwire)	20.00
220	HR Record #2-60 (M. McGwire)	6.00
220	HR Record #61-62 (M. McGwire)	10.00
220	HR Record #63-69 (M. McGwire)	15.00
220	HR Record #70 (Mark McGwire)	40.00
221	Larry Walker (League Leader)	.05
222	Bernie Williams (League Leader)	.05
223	Mark McGwire (League Leader)	.75

224	Ken Griffey Jr. (League Leader)	.65
225	Sammy Sosa (League Leader)	.50
226	Juan Gonzalez (League Leader)	.20
227	Dante Bichette (League Leader)	.05
228	Alex Rodriguez (League Leader)	.75
229	Sammy Sosa (League Leader)	.50
230	Derek Jeter (League Leader)	1.00
231	Greg Maddux (League Leader)	.50
232	Roger Clemens (League Leader)	.50
233	Ricky Ledee (World Series)	.05
234	Chuck Knoblauch (World Series)	.05
235	Bernie Williams (World Series)	.05
236	Tino Martinez (World Series)	.05
237	Orlando Hernandez (World Series)	.05
238	Scott Brosius (World Series)	.05
239	Andy Pettitte (World Series)	.05
240	Mariano Rivera (World Series)	.05
241	Checklist	.05
242	Checklist	.05
243	Tom Glavine	.25
244	Andy Benes	.05
245	Sandy Alomar	.05
246	Wilton Guerrero	.05
247	Alex Gonzalez	.05
248	Roberto Alomar	.30
249	Ruben Rivera	.05
250	Eric Chavez	.15
251	Ellis Burks	.05
252	Richie Sexson	.05
253	Steve Finley	.05
254	Dwight Gooden	.05
255	Dustin Hermanson	.05
256	Kirk Rueter	.05
257	Steve Trachsel	.05
258	Gregg Jefferies	.05
259	Matt Stairs	.05
260	Shane Reynolds	.05
261	Gregg Olson	.05
262	Kevin Tapani	.05
263	Matt Morris	.05
264	Carl Pavano	.05
265	Nomar Garciaparra	1.00
266	Kevin Young	.05
267	Rick Helling	.05
268	Mark Leiter	.05
269	Brian McRae	.05
270	Cal Ripken Jr.	2.00
271	Jeff Abbott	.05
272	Tony Batista	.05
273	Bill Simas	.05
274	Brian Hunter	.05
275	John Franco	.05
276	Devon White	.05
277	Rickey Henderson	.75
278	Chuck Finley	.05
279	Mike Blowers	.05
280	Mark Grace	.05
281	Randy Winn	.05
282	Bobby Bonilla	.05
283	David Justice	.05
284	Shane Monahan	.05
285	Kevin Brown	.05
286	Todd Zeile	.05
287	Al Martin	.05
288	Troy O'Leary	.05
289	Darryl Hamilton	.05
290	Tino Martinez	.05
291	David Ortiz	.45
292	Tony Clark	.05
293	Ryan Minor	.05
294	Reggie Sanders	.05
295	Wally Joyner	.05
296	Cliff Floyd	.05
297	Shawn Estes	.05
298	Pat Hentgen	.05
299	Scott Elarton	.05
300	Alex Rodriguez	1.50
301	Ozzie Guillen	.05
302	Manny Martinez	.05
303	Ryan McGuire	.05
304	Brad Ausmus	.05
305	Alex Gonzalez	.05
306	Brian Jordan	.05
307	John Jaha	.05
308	Mark Grudzielanek	.05
309	Juan Guzman	.05
310	Tony Womack	.05
311	Dennis Reyes	.05
312	Marty Cordova	.05
313	Ramiro Mendoza	.05
314	Robin Ventura	.05
315	Rafael Palmeiro	.60
316	Ramon Martinez	.05
317	John Mabry	.05
318	Dave Hollins	.05
319	Tom Candiotti	.05
320	Al Leiter	.05
321	Rico Brogna	.05
322	Jimmy Key	.05
323	Bernard Gilkey	.05
324	Jason Giambi	.45

325	Craig Biggio	.05
326	Troy Glaus	.65
327	Delino DeShields	.05
328	Fernando Vina	.05
329	John Smoltz	.05
330	Jeff Kent	.05
331	Roy Halladay	.05
332	Andy Ashby	.05
333	Tim Wakefield	.05
334	Tim Belcher	.05
335	Bernie Williams	.05
336	Desi Relaford	.05
337	John Burkett	.05
338	Mike Hampton	.05
339	Royce Clayton	.05
340	Mike Piazza	1.25
341	Jeremi Gonzalez	.05
342	Mike Lansing	.05
343	Jamie Moyer	.05
344	Ron Coomer	.05
345	Barry Larkin	.05
346	Fernando Tatis	.05
347	Chili Davis	.05
348	Bobby Higginson	.05
349	Hal Morris	.05
350	Larry Walker	.05
351	Carlos Guillen	.05
352	Miguel Tejada	.05
353	Travis Fryman	.05
354	Jarrod Washburn	.05
355	Chipper Jones	1.00
356	Todd Stottlemyre	.05
357	Henry Rodriguez	.05
358	Eli Marrero	.05
359	Alan Benes	.05
360	Tim Salmon	.05
361	Luis Gonzalez	.05
362	Scott Spiezio	.05
363	Chris Carpenter	.05
364	Bobby Howry	.05
365	Raul Mondesi	.05
366	Ugueth Urbina	.05
367	Tom Evans	.05
368	Kerry Ligtenberg RC	.15
369	Adrian Beltre	.15
370	Ryan Klesko	.05
371	Wilson Alvarez	.05
372	John Thomson	.05
373	Tony Saunders	.05
374	Mike Stanley	.05
375	Ken Caminiti	.05
376	Jay Buhner	.05
377	Bill Mueller	.05
378	Jeff Blauser	.05
379	Edgar Renteria	.05
380	Jim Thome	.60
381	Joey Hamilton	.05
382	Calvin Pickering	.05
383	Marquis Grissom	.05
384	Omar Daal	.05
385	Curt Schilling	.25
386	Jose Cruz Jr.	.05
387	Chris Widger	.05
388	Pete Harnisch	.05
389	Charles Nagy	.05
390	Tom Gordon	.05
391	Bobby Smith	.05
392	Derrick Gibson	.05
393	Jeff Conine	.05
394	Carlos Perez	.05
395	Barry Bonds	2.00
396	Mark McLemore	.05
397	Juan Encarnacion	.05
398	Wade Boggs	1.00
399	Ivan Rodriguez	.65
400	Moises Alou	.05
401	Jeromy Burnitz	.05
402	Sean Casey	.10
403	Jose Offerman	.05
404	Joe Fontenot	.05
405	Kevin Millwood	.05
406	Lance Johnson	.05
407	Richard Hidalgo	.05
408	Mike Jackson	.05
409	Brian Anderson	.05
410	Jeff Shaw	.05
411	Preston Wilson	.05
412	Todd Hundley	.05
413	Jim Parque	.05
414	Justin Baughman	.05
415	Dante Bichette	.05
416	Paul O'Neill	.05
417	Miguel Cairo	.05
418	Randy Johnson	.75
419	Jesus Sanchez	.05
420	Carlos Delgado	.30
421	Ricky Ledee	.05
422	Orlando Hernandez	.05
423	Frank Thomas	.75
424	Pokey Reese	.05
425	Carlos Lee, Mike Lowell, Kit Pellow (Prospect)	.25
426	Michael Cuddyer, Mark DeRosa, Jerry Hairston Jr. (Prospect)	.05
427	Marlon Anderson, Ron Belliard, Orlando Cabrera (Prospect)	.10
428	Micah Bowie RC, Phil Norton RC, Randy Wolf (Prospect)	.05
429	Jack Cressend, Jason Rakers, John Rocker (Prospect)	.05
430	Ruben Mateo, Scott Morgan, Mike Zywica RC (Prospect)	.10

431	Jason LaRue, Matt LeCroy RC, Mitch Meluskey (Prospect)	.10
432	Gabe Kapler, Armando Rios, Fernando Seguignol (Prospect)	.05
433	Adam Kennedy, Mickey Lopez RC, Jackie Rexrode (Prospect)	.10
434	Jose Fernandez RC, Jeff Liefer, Chris Truby (Prospect)	.10
435	Corey Koskie, Doug Mientkiewicz, Damon Minor (Prospect)	.10
436	Roosevelt Brown RC, Dernell Stenson, Vernon Wells (Prospect)	.10
437	A.J. Burnett RC, John Nicholson, Billy Koch (Prospect)	.25
438	Matt Belisle RC, Matt Roney RC (Draft Pick)	.10
439	Austin Kearns RC, Chris George RC (Draft Pick)	2.50
440	Nate Bump RC, Nate Cornejo RC (Draft Pick)	.40
441	Brad Lidge RC, Mike Nannini RC (Draft Pick)	.25
442	Matt Holiday RC, Jeff Winchester RC (Draft Pick)	.25
443	Adam Everett RC, Chip Ambres RC (Draft Pick)	.25
444	Pat Burrell RC, Eric Valent RC (Draft Pick)	1.50
445	Roger Clemens (Strikeout Kings)	.50
446	Kerry Wood (Strikeout Kings)	.15
447	Curt Schilling (Strikeout Kings)	.05
448	Randy Johnson (Strikeout Kings)	.40
449	Pedro Martinez (Strikeout Kings)	.40
450	Jeff Bagwell, Andres Galarraga, Mark McGwire (All-Topps)	.50
451	John Olerud, Jim Thome, Tino Martinez (All-Topps)	.30
452	Alex Rodriguez, Nomar Garciaparra, Derek Jeter (All-Topps)	.60
453	Vinny Castilla, Chipper Jones, Scott Rolen (All-Topps)	.40
454	Sammy Sosa, Ken Griffey Jr., Juan Gonzalez (All-Topps)	.60
455	Barry Bonds, Manny Ramirez, Larry Walker (All-Topps)	.60
456	Frank Thomas, Tim Salmon, David Justice (All-Topps)	.25
457	Travis Lee, Todd Helton, Ben Grieve (All-Topps)	.30
458	Vladimir Guerrero, Greg Vaughn, Bernie Williams (All-Topps)	.25
459	Mike Piazza, Ivan Rodriguez, Jason Kendall (All-Topps)	.50
460	Roger Clemens, Kerry Wood, Greg Maddux (All-Topps)	.45
461	Home Run Parade #1 (Sammy Sosa)	10.00
461	HR Parade #2-60 (Sammy Sosa)	4.00
461	HR Parade #61-62 (Sammy Sosa)	10.00
461	HR Parade #63-65 (Sammy Sosa)	6.00
461	HR Parade #66 (Sammy Sosa)	20.00
462	Checklist	.05
463	Checklist	.05

MVP Promotion

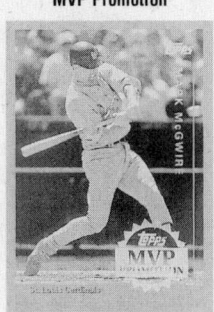

Each of the 198 regular-issue players' cards in Series 1 and cards #243-444 in Series 2 were issued in a parallel version of 100 each for use in an MVP of the Week sweepstakes. Overprinted with a large gold-foil seal on front, the MVP cards have contest rules on back. The MVP cards were inserted at ratios of between 1:142 (HTA) and 1:515 (Hobby) packs. Cards of players who won MVP of the Week during the 1999 season could be redeemed for a special set of MVP cards prior to the Dec. 31, 1999 deadline. Winning players' cards are checklisted here according to their regular-issue card number. Because they were not returned when redeemed, they are in shorter supply than non-winning cards, though market value is not significantly affected.

	NM/M
Common Player:	3.00
Stars/Rookies:	20X

MVP Redemption

Person redeeming winning MVP contest cards prior to Dec. 31, 1999, received this set of 25 cards corresponding to the weekly winners. Cards have an MVP prefix.

		NM/M
Complete Set (25):		30.00
Common Player:		.50
1	Raul Mondesi	.50
2	Tim Salmon	.50
3	Fernando Tatis	.50
4	Larry Walker	.50
5	Fred McGriff	.50
6	Nomar Garciaparra	3.00
7	Rafael Palmeiro	1.50
8	Randy Johnson	2.00
9	Mike Lieberthal	.50
10	B.J. Surhoff	.50
11	Todd Helton	2.00
12	Tino Martinez	.50
13	Scott Rolen	1.50
14	Mike Piazza	4.00
15	David Cone	.50
16	Tony Clark	.50
17	Roberto Alomar	.60
18	Miguel Tejada	.75
19	Alex Rodriguez	5.00
20	J.T. Snow	.50
21	Ray Lankford	.50
22	Mo Vaughn	.50
23	Paul O'Neill	.50
24	Chipper Jones	3.00
25	Mark McGwire	5.00

All-Matrix

This 30-card set features holo-foil card fronts and features the top stars in the game. Each card is numbered with a "AM" prefix on card backs and are seeded 1:18 packs.

		NM/M
Complete Set (30):		45.00
Common Player:		.75
Inserted 1:18		
AM1	Mark McGwire	6.00
AM2	Sammy Sosa	3.50
AM3	Ken Griffey Jr.	4.50
AM4	Greg Vaughn	.75
AM5	Albert Belle	.75
AM6	Vinny Castilla	.75
AM7	Jose Canseco	1.25
AM8	Juan Gonzalez	1.25
AM9	Manny Ramirez	2.50
AM10	Andres Galarraga	.75
AM11	Rafael Palmeiro	2.00
AM12	Alex Rodriguez	6.00
AM13	Mo Vaughn	.75
AM14	Eric Chavez	1.25
AM15	Gabe Kapler	.75
AM16	Calvin Pickering	.75
AM17	Ruben Mateo	.75
AM18	Roy Halladay	.75
AM19	Jeremy Giambi	.75
AM20	Alex Gonzalez	.75
AM21	Ron Belliard	.75
AM22	Marlon Anderson	.75
AM23	Carlos Lee	.75
AM24	Kerry Wood	1.25
AM25	Roger Clemens	3.50
AM26	Curt Schilling	.75
AM27	Kevin Brown	.75
AM28	Randy Johnson	2.50
AM29	Pedro Martinez	2.50
AM30	Orlando Hernandez	.75

All-Topps Mystery Finest

This 33-card set features a black opaque covering that collectors peel off to reveal the player. Each card is numbered with a "M" prefix and inserted 1:36 packs. A parallel Refractor version is also randomly seeded and inserted 1:144 packs.

		NM/M
Complete Set (33):		100.00
Common Player:		1.00
Inserted 1:36		
Refractors:		1.5X
Inserted 1:144		
M1	Jeff Bagwell	4.25
M2	Andres Galarraga	1.00
M3	Mark McGwire	9.00
M4	John Olerud	1.00
M5	Jim Thome	2.50
M6	Tino Martinez	1.00
M7	Alex Rodriguez	9.00
M8	Nomar Garciaparra	9.00
M9	Derek Jeter	12.50
M10	Vinny Castilla	1.00
M11	Chipper Jones	5.00
M12	Scott Rolen	3.00
M13	Sammy Sosa	9.00
M14	Ken Griffey Jr.	7.50
M15	Juan Gonzalez	2.00
M16	Barry Bonds	12.50
M17	Manny Ramirez	4.50
M18	Larry Walker	1.00
M19	Frank Thomas	4.50
M20	Tim Salmon	1.00
M21	David Justice	1.00
M22	Travis Lee	1.50
M23	Todd Helton	4.50
M24	Ben Grieve	1.00
M25	Vladimir Guerrero	4.50
M26	Greg Vaughn	1.00
M27	Bernie Williams	1.00
M28	Mike Piazza	7.50
M29	Ivan Rodriguez	3.50
M30	Jason Kendall	1.00
M31	Roger Clemens	6.00
M32	Kerry Wood	2.00
M33	Greg Maddux	5.00

Autographs

Autographs were inserted exclusively in hobby packs in both Topps series 1 and 2. Each series had eight cards with each one carrying the Topps Certified Autograph Issue stamp. Series 1 Autographs were seeded 1:532 packs while Series 2 were found 1:501 packs.

		NM/M
Common Player:		8.00
Series 1 Inserted 1:532 H		
Series 2 Inserted 1:501 H		
A1	Roger Clemens	100.00
A2	Chipper Jones	50.00
A3	Scott Rolen	25.00
A4	Alex Rodriguez	100.00
A5	Andres Galarraga	8.00
A6	Rondell White	8.00
A7	Ben Grieve	8.00
A8	Troy Glaus	20.00
A9	Moises Alou	15.00

A10	Barry Bonds	180.00
A11	Vladimir Guerrero	35.00
A12	Andruw Jones	10.00
A13	Darin Erstad	12.00
A14	Shawn Green	16.00
A15	Eric Chavez	15.00
A16	Pat Burrell	30.00

Hall of Fame

Found exclusively in hobby packs, Hall of Fame Collection is a 10-card set featured on cards that silhouette their images against their respective Hall of Fame plaques. These were seeded 1:12 packs.

		NM/M
Complete Set (10):		8.00
Common Player:		.50
Inserted 1:12 H		
HOF1	Mike Schmidt	1.50
HOF2	Brooks Robinson	.75
HOF3	Stan Musial	1.50
HOF4	Willie McCovey	.50
HOF5	Eddie Mathews	.75
HOF6	Reggie Jackson	1.50
HOF7	Ernie Banks	1.00
HOF8	Whitey Ford	.75
HOF9	Bob Feller	.50
HOF10	Yogi Berra	1.00

Lords of the Diamond

Inserted in every 18 packs this 15-card set features the top players in the game including Barry Bonds and Ken Griffey Jr. Card fronts include a holographic look with die-cutting across the top of the card on a silver background.

		NM/M
Complete Set (15):		13.00
Common Player:		.25
Inserted 1:18		
LD1	Ken Griffey Jr.	1.25
LD2	Chipper Jones	1.00
LD3	Sammy Sosa	1.00
LD4	Frank Thomas	.75
LD5	Mark McGwire	1.50
LD6	Jeff Bagwell	.75
LD7	Alex Rodriguez	1.50
LD8	Juan Gonzalez	.40
LD9	Barry Bonds	2.00
LD10	Nomar Garciaparra	1.00
LD11	Darin Erstad	.35
LD12	Tony Gwynn	1.00
LD13	Andres Galarraga	.25
LD14	Mike Piazza	1.25
LD15	Greg Maddux	1.00

New Breed

The next generation of stars are featured in this 15-card set that showcases the young talent on a silver foil card. These are seeded 1:18 packs.

		NM/M
Complete Set (15):		9.00
Common Player:		.25
Inserted 1:18		
NB1	Darin Erstad	.50
NB2	Brad Fullmer	.25
NB3	Kerry Wood	.50
NB4	Nomar Garciaparra	1.50
NB5	Travis Lee	.35
NB6	Scott Rolen	.75

NB7	Todd Helton	.75
NB8	Vladimir Guerrero	1.00
NB9	Derek Jeter	3.00
NB10	Alex Rodriguez	2.00
NB11	Ben Grieve	.25
NB12	Andruw Jones	1.00
NB13	Paul Konerko	.40
NB14	Aramis Ramirez	.25
NB15	Adrian Beltre	.35

Picture Perfect

This 10-card set features a full bleed photo of baseball's biggest stars, including Derek Jeter and Ken Griffey Jr. These are found one per eight packs.

		NM/M
Complete Set (10):		5.00
Common Player:		.25
Inserted 1:8		
P1	Ken Griffey Jr.	.75
P2	Kerry Wood	.30
P3	Pedro Martinez	.45
P4	Mark McGwire	.90
P5	Greg Maddux	.60
P6	Sammy Sosa	.60
P7	Greg Vaughn	.25
P8	Juan Gonzalez	.30
P9	Jeff Bagwell	.45
P10	Derek Jeter	1.50

Power Brokers

This 20-card set features baseball's biggest superstars including McGwire, Sosa and Chipper Jones. The cards are die-cut at the top and printed on Finest technology. Power Brokers are inserted in every 36 packs. A Refractor parallel version also exists, which are seeded 1:144 packs.

		NM/M
Complete Set (20):		20.00
Common Player:		.25
Inserted 1:36		
Refractors:		1.5X
Inserted 1:144		
PB1	Mark McGwire	3.00
PB2	Andres Galarraga	.25
PB3	Ken Griffey Jr.	2.00
PB4	Sammy Sosa	1.50
PB5	Juan Gonzalez	1.00
PB6	Alex Rodriguez	3.00
PB7	Frank Thomas	1.00
PB8	Jeff Bagwell	1.00

PB9	Vinny Castilla	.25
PB10	Mike Piazza	2.00
PB11	Greg Vaughn	.25
PB12	Barry Bonds	4.00
PB13	Mo Vaughn	.25
PB14	Jim Thome	.65
PB15	Larry Walker	.25
PB16	Chipper Jones	1.50
PB17	Nomar Garciaparra	1.50
PB18	Manny Ramirez	1.00
PB19	Roger Clemens	1.75
PB20	Kerry Wood	.65

Record Numbers

This 10-card set highlights achievements from the game's current stars, including Nomar Garciaparra's 30 game hitting streak, the longest by a rookie in major league history. These inserts are randomly seeded 1:8 packs, each card is numbered on the back with a "RN" prefix.

		NM/M
Complete Set (10):		8.00
Common Player:		.50
Inserted 1:8		
RN1	Mark McGwire	1.50
RN2	Mike Piazza	1.00
RN3	Curt Schilling	.75
RN4	Ken Griffey Jr.	1.50
RN5	Sammy Sosa	.75
RN6	Nomar Garciaparra	.75
RN7	Kerry Wood	.50
RN8	Roger Clemens	1.50
RN9	Cal Ripken Jr.	2.00
RN10	Mark McGwire	1.50

Record Numbers Gold

This is a parallel of the Record Numbers insert set, each card features the appropriate sequential numbering based on the featured players' highlighted record. Each card is numbered with a "RN" prefix on the back.

		NM/M
Common Player:		8.00
RN1	Mark McGwire/70	40.00
RN2	Mike Piazza/362	15.00
RN3	Curt Schilling/319	8.00
RN4	Ken Griffey Jr./350	20.00
RN5	Sammy Sosa/20	20.00
RN6	Nomar Garciaparra/30	20.00
RN7	Kerry Wood/20	20.00
RN8	Roger Clemens/20	40.00
RN9	Cal Ripken Jr./2,632	15.00
RN10	Mark McGwire/162	20.00

Nolan Ryan Reprints

Topps reprinted all 27 of Nolan Ryan's basic Topps cards, with 14 odd numbers appearing in Series 1 and the remaining 13 even cards inserted into Series 2 packs. Each card is stamped with a gold Topps commemorative stamp on the front for identification. Reprints were seeded in every 18 packs. Ryan also autographed a number of the reprints for both series. Series 1 Ryan autographs are seeded 1:4,260, with Series 2 autographs

found 1:5,007 packs. Ryan autographs were inserted exclusively in hobby packs.

		NM/M
Complete Set (27):		40.00
Common Ryan:		3.00
Inserted 1:18		
Nolan Ryan Autograph:		150.00
1	Nolan Ryan/1968	7.50
2	Nolan Ryan/1969	4.50
3	Nolan Ryan/1970	3.00
4	Nolan Ryan/1971	3.00
5	Nolan Ryan/1972	3.00
6	Nolan Ryan/1973	3.00
7	Nolan Ryan/1974	3.00
8	Nolan Ryan/1975	3.00
9	Nolan Ryan/1976	3.00
10	Nolan Ryan/1977	3.00
11	Nolan Ryan/1978	3.00
12	Nolan Ryan/1979	3.00
13	Nolan Ryan/1980	3.00
14	Nolan Ryan/1981	3.00
15	Nolan Ryan/1982	3.00
16	Nolan Ryan/1983	3.00
17	Nolan Ryan/1984	3.00
18	Nolan Ryan/1985	3.00
19	Nolan Ryan/1986	3.00
20	Nolan Ryan/1987	3.00
21	Nolan Ryan/1988	3.00
22	Nolan Ryan/1989	3.00
23	Nolan Ryan/1990	3.00
24	Nolan Ryan/1991	3.00
25	Nolan Ryan/1992	3.00
26	Nolan Ryan/1993	3.00
27	Nolan Ryan/1994	3.00

Nolan Ryan Reprint Autographs

Topps reprinted all 27 of Nolan Ryan's basic Topps cards, with 14 odd numbers appearing in Series 1 and the remaining 13 even cards inserted into Series 2 packs. Each card is stamped with a gold Topps commemorative stamp on the front for identification. Ryan-autographed reprints, found exclusively in hobby packs, are seeded 1:4,260 in Series 1, with Series 2 autographs found 1:5,007 packs.

		NM/M
Common Card:		150.00
1	Nolan Ryan/1968	200.00
2	Nolan Ryan/1969	150.00
3	Nolan Ryan/1970	150.00
4	Nolan Ryan/1971	150.00
5	Nolan Ryan/1972	150.00
6	Nolan Ryan/1973	150.00
7	Nolan Ryan/1974	150.00
8	Nolan Ryan/1975	150.00
9	Nolan Ryan/1976	150.00
10	Nolan Ryan/1977	150.00
11	Nolan Ryan/1978	150.00
12	Nolan Ryan/1979	150.00
13	Nolan Ryan/1980	150.00
14	Nolan Ryan/1981	150.00
15	Nolan Ryan/1982	150.00
16	Nolan Ryan/1983	150.00
17	Nolan Ryan/1984	150.00
18	Nolan Ryan/1985	150.00
19	Nolan Ryan/1986	150.00
20	Nolan Ryan/1987	150.00
21	Nolan Ryan/1988	150.00
22	Nolan Ryan/1989	150.00
23	Nolan Ryan/1990	150.00
24	Nolan Ryan/1991	150.00
25	Nolan Ryan/1992	150.00
26	Nolan Ryan/1993	150.00
27	Nolan Ryan/1994	150.00

Nolan Ryan Finest Reprints

This 27-card set reprinted all 27 of Ryan's basic Topps cards. Odd numbers were distributed in Series 1 packs, with even numbers distributed in Series 2 packs. These are seeded 1:72 packs in both series 1 and 2 packs. A Refractor parallel version is inserted 1:288 packs.

		NM/M
Complete Set (27):		125.00
Common Card:		5.00
Inserted 1:72		
Refractors:		2X
Inserted 1:288		
1	1968	12.50
2	1969	7.50
3	1970	5.00
4	1971	5.00
5	1972	5.00
6	1973	5.00
7	1974	5.00
8	1975	5.00
9	1976	5.00
10	1977	5.00
11	1978	5.00
12	1979	5.00
13	1980	5.00
14	1981	5.00
15	1982	5.00
16	1983	5.00
17	1984	5.00
18	1985	5.00
19	1986	5.00
20	1987	5.00
21	1988	5.00
22	1989	5.00
23	1990	5.00
24	1991	5.00
25	1992	5.00
26	1992	5.00
27	1992	5.00

Traded and Rookies

Identical in design to the base 1999 Topps cards the 121- card set includes players involved in pre and mid-season transactions as well as top prospects and 1999 Draft Picks. Released in a boxed set, each set includes one autographed card from the 75 rookie/draft pick cards in the set.

		NM/M
Unopened Set (122):		40.00
Complete Set, No Autograph (121):		15.00
Common Player:		.10
1	Seth Etherton	.10
2	Mark Harriger RC	.10
3	Matt Wise RC	.25
4	Carlos Hernandez RC	.15
5	Julio Lugo RC	.25
6	Mike Nannini	.10
7	Justin Bowles RC	.10
8	Mark Mulder RC	.75
9	Roberto Vaz RC	.10
10	Felipe Lopez RC	.75
11	Matt Belisle	.10
12	Micah Bowie	.10
13	Ruben Quevedo RC	.10
14	Jose Garcia RC	.10
15	David Kelton RC	.25
16	Phillip Norton	.10

17	Corey Patterson RC	.75
18	Ron Walker RC	.10
19	Paul Hoover RC	.10
20	Ryan Rupe RC	.15
21	J.D. Closser RC	.10
22	Rob Ryan RC	.10
23	Steve Colyer RC	.10
24	Bubba Crosby RC	.50
25	Luke Prokopec RC	.10
26	Matt Blank RC	.10
27	Josh McKinley RC	.10
28	Nate Bump	.10
29	Giuseppe Chiaramonte RC	.10
30	Arturo McDowell RC	.10
31	Tony Torcato	.10
32	Dave Roberts	.10
33	C.C. Sabathia RC	2.00
34	Sean Spencer RC	.10
35	Chip Ambres	.10
36	A.J. Burnett RC	.15
37	Mo Bruce RC	.10
38	Jason Tyner	.10
39	Mamon Tucker	.10
40	Sean Burroughs RC	.25
41	Kevin Eberwein RC	.10
42	Junior Herndon RC	.10
43	Bryan Wolff RC	.10
44	Pat Burrell	.50
45	Eric Valent	.10
46	Carlos Pena RC	1.00
47	Mike Zywica	.10
48	Adam Everett	.10
49	Juan Pena	.50
50	Adam Dunn RC	3.00
51	Austin Kearns	.75
52	Jacobo Sequea RC	.10
53	Choo Freeman	.10
54	Jeff Winchester	.10
55	Matt Burch	.10
56	Chris George	.10
57	Scott Mullen RC	.10
58	Kit Pellow	.10
59	Mark Quinn RC	.15
60	Nate Cornejo	.10
61	Ryan Mills RC	.25
62	Kevin Beirne RC	.10
63	Kip Wells RC	.50
64	Juan Rivera RC	.25
65	Alfonso Soriano RC	4.00
66	Josh Hamilton RC	8.00
67	Josh Girdley RC	.10
68	Kyle Snyder RC	.15
69	Mike Paradis RC	.10
70	Jason Jennings RC	.25
71	David Walling RC	.10
72	Omar Ortiz RC	.10
73	Jay Gehrke RC	.10
74	Casey Burns RC	.10
75	Carl Crawford RC	2.00
76	Reggie Sanders	.10
77	Will Clark	.10
78	David Wells	.10
79	Paul Konerko	.20
80	Armando Benitez	.10
81	Brant Brown	.10
82	Mo Vaughn	.10
83	Jose Canseco	.25
84	Albert Belle	.10
85	Dean Palmer	.10
86	Greg Vaughn	.10
87	Mark Clark	.10
88	Pat Meares	.10
89	Eric Davis	.10
90	Brian Giles	.10
91	Jeff Brantley	.10
92	Bret Boone	.10
93	Ron Gant	.10
94	Mike Cameron	.10
95	Charles Johnson	.10
96	Denny Neagle	.10
97	Brian Hunter	.10
98	Jose Hernandez	.10
99	Rick Aguilera	.10
100	Tony Batista	.10
101	Roger Cedeno	.10
102	Creighton Gubanich	.10
103	Tim Belcher	.10
104	Bruce Aven	.10
105	Brian Daubach RC	.25
106	Ed Sprague	.10
107	Michael Tucker	.10
108	Homer Bush	.10
109	Armando Reynoso	.10
110	Brook Fordyce	.10
111	Matt Mantei	.10
112	Jose Guillen	.10
113	Kenny Rogers	.10
114	Livan Hernandez	.10
115	Butch Huskey	.10
116	David Segui	.10
117	Darryl Hamilton	.10
118	Jim Leyritz	.10
119	Randy Velarde	.10
120	Bill Taylor	.10
121	Kevin Appier	.10

Traded and Rookies Autographs

These autographs have identical photos and design from the Traded and Rookies set. Seeded one per boxed set, each card has a "Topps Certified Autograph Issue" stamp ensuring its authenticity. Cards of the first 75 rookies/draft picks included in the 121-card boxed set can be found in this autographed version.

		NM/M
	Common Player:	3.00
	Inserted 1:Set	
1	Seth Etherton	3.00
2	Mark Harriger	3.00
3	Matt Wise	5.00
4	Carlos Hernandez	5.00
5	Julio Lugo	20.00
6	Mike Nannini	3.00
7	Justin Bowles	3.00
8	Mark Mulder	15.00
9	Roberto Vaz	3.00
10	Felipe Lopez	15.00
11	Matt Belisle	3.00
12	Micah Bowie	3.00
13	Ruben Quevedo	5.00
14	Jose Garcia	5.00
15	David Kelton	5.00
16	Phillip Norton	5.00
17	Corey Patterson	15.00
18	Ron Walker	3.00
19	Paul Hoover	3.00
20	Ryan Rupe	4.00
21	J.D. Closser	5.00
22	Rob Ryan	5.00
23	Steve Colyer	5.00
24	Bubba Crosby	10.00
25	Luke Prokopec	3.00
26	Matt Blank	3.00
27	Josh McKinley	5.00
28	Nate Bump	5.00
29	Giuseppe Chiaramonte	3.00
30	Arturo McDowell	3.00
31	Tony Torcato	5.00
32	Dave Roberts	10.00
33	C.C. Sabathia	100.00
34	Sean Spencer	3.00
35	Chip Ambres	3.00
36	A.J. Burnett	25.00
37	Mo Bruce	3.00
38	Jason Tyner	3.00
39	Mamon Tucker	3.00
40	Sean Burroughs	3.00
41	Kevin Eberwein	3.00
42	Junior Herndon	3.00
43	Bryan Wolff	3.00
44	Pat Burrell	35.00
45	Eric Valent	5.00
46	Carlos Pena	30.00
47	Mike Zywica	3.00
48	Adam Everett	10.00
49	Juan Pena	5.00
50	Adam Dunn	80.00
51	Austin Kearns	15.00
52	Jacobo Sequea	3.00
53	Choo Freeman	5.00
54	Jeff Winchester	3.00
55	Matt Burch	3.00
56	Chris George	4.00
57	Scott Mullen	3.00
58	Kit Pellow	3.00
59	Mark Quinn	3.00
60	Nate Cornejo	5.00
61	Ryan Mills	3.00
62	Kevin Beirne	4.00
63	Kip Wells	5.00
64	Juan Rivera	8.00
65	Alfonso Soriano	125.00
66	Josh Hamilton	200.00
67	Josh Girdley	5.00
68	Kyle Snyder	5.00
69	Mike Paradis	5.00
70	Jason Jennings	10.00
71	David Walling	3.00
72	Omar Ortiz	3.00
73	Jay Gehrke	5.00
74	Casey Burns	3.00
75	Carl Crawford	50.00

Supers

These oversize (3-1/2" x 5") versions of Topps cards were issued one per box in hobby and Home Team Advantage boxes. Eight cards were issued in each of Series 1 and 2. Other than their size and the card numbers on back, the supers are identical to the regular versions.

	NM/M
Complete Set (16):	17.50
Common Player:	.50

1	Roger Clemens	1.25
2	Greg Maddux	1.25
3	Kerry Wood	.75
4	Juan Gonzalez	.75
5	Sammy Sosa	1.25
6	Mark McGwire	2.50
7	Ken Griffey Jr.	2.00
8	Ben Grieve	.50
1	Nomar Garciaparra	1.25
2	Cal Ripken Jr.	3.00
3	Alex Rodriguez	2.00
4	Mike Piazza	1.50
5	Larry Walker	.50
6	Chipper Jones	1.25
7	Barry Bonds	3.00
8	Frank Thomas	1.00

Action Flats

"Dynamic action poses . . . painstakingly capturing one of their signature plays" are featured in this issue of plastic player figures. The figures are about 3" tall by 2-1/2" wide and stand on a plastic base. In the manner of early 20th Century tin soldiers, there is little depth to the figures. Each handpainted figure is sold in a plastic-windowed box which includes a special foil-stamped version of the player's 1999 Topps card inside. Each figure was also produced in a short-printed "away" jersey version, with 10 of the players seeded at the rate of one per 12 figures, Sosa at a 1:24 rate and McGwire at a 1:36 rate. Suggested retail price at issue was $2.99. Values shown are for un-opened packages.

		NM/M
Complete Set, "Home" (12):		6.00
Complete Set, "Away" (12):		12.00
Common Player, "Home":		.50
Common Player, "Away":		.75
1	Chipper Jones	.50
2	Greg Maddux	.50
3	Mark McGwire	1.00
4	Sammy Sosa	.50
5	Kerry Wood	.50
6	Barry Bonds	1.50
7	Alex Rodriguez	1.00
8	Ken Griffey Jr.	.75
9	Cal Ripken Jr.	1.50
10	Juan Gonzalez	.50
11	Nomar Garciaparra	.50
12	Derek Jeter	1.50
1	Chipper Jones	.75
2	Greg Maddux	.75
3	Mark McGwire	1.50
4	Sammy Sosa	.75
5	Kerry Wood	.75
6	Barry Bonds	2.00
7	Alex Rodriguez	1.50
8	Ken Griffey Jr.	1.00
9	Cal Ripken Jr.	2.00
10	Juan Gonzalez	.50
11	Nomar Garciaparra	.75
12	Derek Jeter	1.50

1999 Topps Chrome

The 462-card base set is a chromium parallel version of Topps baseball. Included are the Mark McGwire #220 and Sammy Sosa #461 home

run subset cards, which commemorate each of their home runs. Each pack contains four cards with a S.R.P. of $3.00 per pack.

	NM/M
Complete Set (461):	75.00
Common Player:	.15
Refractors:	4X
Inserted 1:12	
Ser. 1 or 2 Pack (4):	1.50
Ser. 1 or 2 Box (24):	30.00

1	Roger Clemens	1.75
2	Andres Galarraga	.15
3	Scott Brosius	.15
4	John Flaherty	.15
5	Jim Leyritz	.15
6	Ray Durham	.15
7	Joe Vizcaino	.15
8	Will Clark	.15
9	David Wells	.15
10	Jose Guillen	.15
11	Scott Hatteberg	.15
12	Edgardo Alfonzo	.15
13	Mike Bordick	.15
14	Manny Ramirez	1.00
15	Greg Maddux	1.50
16	David Segui	.15
17	Darryl Strawberry	.15
18	Brad Radke	.15
19	Kerry Wood	.40
20	Matt Anderson	.15
21	Derek Lee	.60
22	Mickey Morandini	.15
23	Paul Konerko	.30
24	Travis Lee	.15
25	Ken Hill	.15
26	Kenny Rogers	.15
27	Paul Sorrento	.15
28	Quilvio Veras	.15
29	Todd Walker	.15
30	Ryan Jackson	.15
31	John Olerud	.15
32	Doug Glanville	.15
33	Nolan Ryan	3.00
34	Ray Lankford	.15
35	Mark Loretta	.15
36	Jason Dickson	.15
37	Sean Bergman	.15
38	Quinton McCracken	.15
39	Bartolo Colon	.15
40	Brady Anderson	.15
41	Chris Stynes	.15
42	Jorge Posada	.15
43	Justin Thompson	.15
44	Johnny Damon	.40
45	Armando Benitez	.15
46	Brant Brown	.15
47	Charlie Hayes	.15
48	Darren Dreifort	.15
49	Juan Gonzalez	.50
50	Chuck Knoblauch	.15
51	Todd Helton (Rookie All-Star)	1.00
52	Rick Reed	.15
53	Chris Gomez	.15
54	Gary Sheffield	.50
55	Rod Beck	.15
56	Rey Sanchez	.15
57	Garret Anderson	.15
58	Jimmy Haynes	.15
59	Steve Woodard	.15
60	Rondell White	.15
61	Vladimir Guerrero	1.00
62	Eric Karros	.15
63	Russ Davis	.15
64	Mo Vaughn	.15
65	Sammy Sosa	1.50
66	Troy Percival	.15
67	Kenny Lofton	.15
68	Bill Taylor	.15
69	Mark McGwire	2.50
70	Roger Cedeno	.15
71	Javy Lopez	.15
72	Damion Easley	.15
73	Andy Pettitte	.35
74	Tony Gwynn	1.50
75	Ricardo Rincon	.15
76	F.P. Santangelo	.15
77	Jay Bell	.15
78	Scott Servais	.15
79	Jose Canseco	.50
80	Roberto Hernandez	.15
81	Todd Dunwoody	.15
82	John Wetteland	.15
83	Mike Caruso (Rookie All-Star)	.15
84	Derek Jeter	3.00
85	Aaron Sele	.15
86	Jose Lima	.15
87	Ryan Christenson	.15
88	Jeff Cirillo	.15
89	Jose Hernandez	.15
90	Mark Kotsay (Rookie All-Star)	.15
91	Darren Bragg	.15
92	Albert Belle	.15
93	Matt Lawton	.15
94	Pedro Martinez	1.00
95	Greg Vaughn	.15
96	Neifi Perez	.15
97	Gerald Williams	.15
98	Derek Bell	.15
99	Ken Griffey Jr.	2.00
100	David Cone	.15
101	Brian Johnson	.15
102	George Lombard (Prospects)	.15
103	Dean Palmer	.15

104	Javier Valentin	.15
105	Trevor Hoffman	.15
106	Butch Huskey	.15
107	Dave Martinez	.15
108	Billy Wagner	.15
109	Shawn Green	.35
110	Ben Grieve (Rookie All-Star)	.15
111	Tom Goodwin	.15
112	Jaret Wright	.15
113	Aramis Ramirez	.15
114	Dmitri Young	.15
115	Hideki Irabu	.15
116	Roberto Kelly	.15
117	Jeff Fassero	.15
118	Mark Clark	.15
119	Jason McDonald	.15
120	Matt Williams	.15
121	Dave Burba	.15
122	Bret Saberhagen	.15
123	Deivi Cruz	.15
124	Chad Curtis	.15
125	Scott Rolen	.75
126	Lee Stevens	.15
127	J.T. Snow Jr.	.15
128	Rusty Greer	.15
129	Brian Meadows	.15
130	Jim Edmonds	.15
131	Ron Gant	.15
132	A.J. Hinch (Rookie All-Star)	.15
133	Shannon Stewart	.15
134	Brad Fullmer	.15
135	Cal Eldred	.15
136	Matt Walbeck	.15
137	Carl Everett	.15
138	Walt Weiss	.15
139	Fred McGriff	.15
140	Darin Erstad	.40
141	Dave Nilsson	.15
142	Eric Young	.15
143	Dan Wilson	.15
144	Jeff Reed	.15
145	Brett Tomko	.15
146	Terry Steinbach	.15
147	Seth Greisinger	.15
148	Pat Meares	.15
149	Livan Hernandez	.15
150	Jeff Bagwell	1.00
151	Bob Wickman	.15
152	Omar Vizquel	.15
153	Eric Davis	.15
154	Larry Sutton	.15
155	Magglio Ordonez (Rookie All-Star)	.45
156	Eric Milton	.15
157	Darren Lewis	.15
158	Rick Aguilera	.15
159	Mike Lieberthal	.15
160	Robb Nen	.15
161	Brian Giles	.15
162	Jeff Brantley	.15
163	Gary DiSarcina	.15
164	John Valentin	.15
165	David Dellucci	.15
166	Chan Ho Park	.15
167	Masato Yoshii	.15
168	Jason Schmidt	.15
169	LaTroy Hawkins	.15
170	Bret Boone	.15
171	Jerry DiPoto	.15
172	Mariano Rivera	.25
173	Mike Cameron	.15
174	Scott Erickson	.15
175	Charles Johnson	.15
176	Bobby Jones	.15
177	Francisco Cordova	.15
178	Todd Jones	.15
179	Jeff Montgomery	.15
180	Mike Mussina	.50
181	Bob Abreu	.15
182	Ismael Valdes	.15
183	Andy Fox	.15
184	Woody Williams	.15
185	Denny Neagle	.15
186	Jose Valentin	.15
187	Darrin Fletcher	.15
188	Gabe Alvarez	.15
189	Eddie Taubensee	.15
190	Edgar Martinez	.15
191	Jason Kendall	.15
192	Darryl Kile	.15
193	Jeff King	.15
194	Rey Ordonez	.15
195	Andruw Jones	1.00
196	Tony Fernandez	.15
197	Jamey Wright	.15
198	B.J. Surhoff	.15
199	Vinny Castilla	.15
200	David Wells (Season Highlight)	.15
201	Mark McGwire (Season Highlight)	1.25
202	Sammy Sosa (Season Highlight)	.75
203	Roger Clemens (Season Highlight)	.85
204	Kerry Wood (Season Highlight)	.20
205	Lance Berkman, Mike Frank, Gabe Kapler (Prospects)	.15
206	Alex Escobar RC, Ricky Ledee, Mike Stoner (Prospects)	.50
207	Peter Bergeron RC, Jeremy Giambi, George Lombard (Prospects)	.15

208	Michael Barrett, Ben Davis, Robert Fick (Prospects)	.15
209	Pat Cline, Ramon Hernandez, Jayson Werth (Prospects)	.20
210	Bruce Chen, Chris Enochs, Ryan Anderson (Prospects)	.15
211	Mike Lincoln, Octavio Dotel, Brad Penny (Prospects)	.15
212	Chuck Abbott, Brent Butler, Danny Klassen (Prospects)	.15
213	Chris Jones, Jeff Urban RC (Draft Pick)	.15
214	Arturo McDowell RC, Tony Torcato RC (Draft Pick)	.25
215	Josh McKinley RC, Jason Tyner RC (Draft Pick)	.30
216	Matt Burch RC, Seth Etherton RC (Draft Pick)	.15
217	Mamon Tucker RC, Rick Elder RC (Draft Pick)	.20
218	J.M. Gold RC, Ryan Mills RC (Draft Pick)	.15
219	Adam Brown RC, Choo Freeman RC (Draft Pick)	.20
220	Mark McGwire HR #1 (Record Breaker)	15.00
220	Mark McGwire HR #2-60	10.00
220	McGwire HR #61-62	15.00
220	McGwire HR #63-69	12.50
220	McGwire HR #70	40.00
221	Larry Walker (League Leader)	.15
222	Bernie Williams (League Leader)	.15
223	Mark McGwire (League Leader)	1.25
224	Ken Griffey Jr. (League Leader)	1.00
225	Sammy Sosa (League Leader)	.75
226	Juan Gonzalez (League Leader)	.35
227	Dante Bichette (League Leader)	.15
228	Alex Rodriguez (League Leader)	1.25
229	Sammy Sosa (League Leader)	.75
230	Derek Jeter (League Leader)	1.50
231	Greg Maddux (League Leader)	.75
232	Roger Clemens (League Leader)	.75
233	Ricky Ledee (World Series)	.15
234	Chuck Knoblauch (World Series)	.15
235	Bernie Williams (World Series)	.15
236	Tino Martinez (World Series)	.15
237	Orlando Hernandez (World Series)	.15
238	Scott Brosius (World Series)	.15
239	Andy Pettitte (World Series)	.15
240	Mariano Rivera (World Series)	.15
241	Checklist	.15
242	Checklist	.15
243	Tom Glavine	.35
244	Andy Benes	.15
245	Sandy Alomar	.15
246	Wilton Guerrero	.15
247	Alex Gonzalez	.15
248	Roberto Alomar	.30
249	Ruben Rivera	.15
250	Eric Chavez	.15
251	Ellis Burks	.15
252	Richie Sexson	.15
253	Steve Finley	.15
254	Dwight Gooden	.15
255	Dustin Hermanson	.15
256	Kirk Rueter	.15
257	Steve Trachsel	.15
258	Gregg Jefferies	.15
259	Matt Stairs	.15
260	Shane Reynolds	.15
261	Gregg Olson	.15
262	Kevin Tapani	.15
263	Matt Morris	.15
264	Carl Pavano	.15
265	Nomar Garciaparra	1.50
266	Kevin Young	.15
267	Rick Helling	.15
268	Matt Franco	.15
269	Brian McRae	.15
270	Cal Ripken Jr.	3.00
271	Jeff Abbott	.15
272	Tony Batista	.15
273	Bill Simas	.15
274	Brian Hunter	.15
275	John Franco	.15
276	Devon White	.15
277	Rickey Henderson	1.00
278	Chuck Finley	.15
279	Mike Blowers	.15
280	Mark Grace	.15
281	Randy Winn	.15

282	Bobby Bonilla	.15
283	David Justice	.15
284	Shane Monahan	.15
285	Kevin Brown	.15
286	Todd Zeile	.15
287	Al Martin	.15
288	Troy O'Leary	.15
289	Darryl Hamilton	.15
290	Tino Martinez	.15
291	David Ortiz	.50
292	Tony Clark	.15
293	Ryan Minor	.15
294	Reggie Sanders	.15
295	Wally Joyner	.15
296	Cliff Floyd	.15
297	Shawn Estes	.15
298	Pat Hentgen	.15
299	Scott Elarton	.15
300	Alex Rodriguez	2.50
301	Ozzie Guillen	.15
302	Hideo Martinez	.15
303	Ryan McGuire	.15
304	Brad Ausmus	.15
305	Alex Gonzalez	.15
306	Brian Jordan	.15
307	John Jaha	.15
308	Mark Grudzielanek	.15
309	Juan Guzman	.15
310	Tony Womack	.15
311	Dennis Reyes	.15
312	Marty Cordova	.15
313	Ramiro Mendoza	.15
314	Robin Ventura	.15
315	Rafael Palmeiro	.65
316	Ramon Martinez	.15
317	Pedro Astacio	.15
318	Dave Hollins	.15
319	Tom Candiotti	.15
320	Al Leiter	.15
321	Rico Brogna	.15
322	Reggie Jefferson	.15
323	Bernard Gilkey	.15
324	Jason Giambi	.40
325	Craig Biggio	.15
326	Troy Glaus	.75
327	Delino DeShields	.15
328	Fernando Vina	.15
329	John Smoltz	.15
330	Jeff Kent	.15
331	Roy Halladay	.15
332	Andy Ashby	.15
333	Tim Wakefield	.15
334	Roger Clemens	1.75
335	Bernie Williams	.15
336	Desi Relaford	.15
337	John Burkett	.15
338	Mike Hampton	.15
339	Royce Clayton	.15
340	Mike Piazza	2.00
341	Jeremi Gonzalez	.15
342	Mike Lansing	.15
343	Jamie Moyer	.15
344	Ron Coomer	.15
345	Barry Larkin	.15
346	Fernando Tatis	.15
347	Chili Davis	.15
348	Bobby Higginson	.15
349	Hal Morris	.15
350	Larry Walker	.15
351	Carlos Guillen	.15
352	Miguel Tejada	.30
353	Travis Fryman	.15
354	Jarrod Washburn	.15
355	Chipper Jones	1.50
356	Todd Stottlemyre	.15
357	Henry Rodriguez	.15
358	Eli Marrero	.15
359	Alan Benes	.15
360	Tim Salmon	.15
361	Luis Gonzalez	.15
362	Scott Spiezio	.15
363	Chris Carpenter	.15
364	Bobby Howry	.15
365	Raul Mondesi	.15
366	Ugueth Urbina	.15
367	Tom Evans	.15
368	Kerry Ligtenberg RC	.15
369	Adrian Beltre	.35
370	Ryan Klesko	.15
371	Wilson Alvarez	.15
372	John Thomson	.15
373	Tony Saunders	.15
374	Mike Stanley	.15
375	Ken Caminiti	.15
376	Jay Buhner	.15
377	Bill Mueller	.15
378	Jeff Blauser	.15
379	Edgar Renteria	.15
380	Jim Thome	.60
381	Joey Hamilton	.15
382	Calvin Pickering	.15
383	Marquis Grissom	.15
384	Omar Daal	.15
385	Curt Schilling	.35
386	Jose Cruz Jr.	.15
387	Chris Widger	.15
388	Pete Harnisch	.15
389	Charles Nagy	.15
390	Tom Gordon	.15
391	Bobby Smith	.15
392	Derrick Gibson	.15
393	Jeff Conine	.15
394	Carlos Perez	.15
395	Barry Bonds	3.00
396	Mark McLemore	.15
397	Juan Encarnacion	.15
398	Wade Boggs	1.50
399	Ivan Rodriguez	.75

400	Moises Alou	.15
401	Jeromy Burnitz	.15
402	Sean Casey	.25
403	Jose Offerman	.15
404	Joe Fontenot	.15
405	Kevin Millwood	.15
406	Lance Johnson	.15
407	Richard Hidalgo	.15
408	Mike Jackson	.15
409	Brian Anderson	.15
410	Jeff Shaw	.15
411	Preston Wilson	.15
412	Todd Hundley	.15
413	Jim Parque	.15
414	Justin Baughman	.15
415	Dante Bichette	.15
416	Paul O'Neill	.15
417	Miguel Cairo	.15
418	Randy Johnson	1.00
419	Jesus Sanchez	.15
420	Carlos Delgado	.35
421	Ricky Ledee	.15
422	Orlando Hernandez	.15
423	Frank Thomas	1.00
424	Pokey Reese	.15
425	Carlos Lee, Mike Lowell, Kit Pellow RC (Prospect)	.40
426	Michael Cuddyer, Mark DeRosa, Jerry Hairston Jr. RC (Prospect)	.60
427	Marlon Anderson, Ron Belliard, Orlando Cabrera (Prospect)	.45
428	Micah Bowie RC, Phil Norton RC, Randy Wolf (Prospect)	.35
429	Jack Cressend, Jason Rakers, John Rocker (Prospect)	.25
430	Ruben Mateo, Scott Morgan, Mike Zywica RC (Prospect)	.25
431	Jason LaRue, Matt LeCroy RC, Mitch Meluskey RC (Prospect)	.25
432	Gabe Kapler, Armando Rios RC, Fernando Seguignol (Prospect)	.25
433	Adam Kennedy, Mickey Lopez RC, Jackie Rexrode (Prospect)	.25
434	Jose Fernandez RC, Jeff Liefer, Chris Truby (Prospect)	.25
435	Corey Koskie, Doug Mientkiewicz RC, Damon Minor (Prospect)	.60
436	Roosevelt Brown RC, Dernell Stenson, Vernon Wells (Prospect)	.25
437	A.J. Burnett RC, John Nicholson, Billy Koch (Prospect)	.75
438	Matt Belisle RC, Matt Roney RC (Draft Pick)	.30
439	Austin Kearns RC, Chris George RC (Draft Pick)	3.00
440	Nate Bump RC, Nate Cornejo RC (Draft Pick)	.40
441	Brad Lidge RC, Mike Nannini RC (Draft Pick)	.60
442	Matt Holliday RC, Jeff Winchester RC (Draft Pick)	8.00
443	Adam Everett RC, Chip Ambres RC (Draft Pick)	.30
444	Pat Burrell RC, Eric Valent RC (Draft Pick)	3.00
445	Roger Clemens (Strikeout Kings)	.85
446	Kerry Wood (Strikeout Kings)	.20
447	Curt Schilling (Strikeout Kings)	.15
448	Randy Johnson (Strikeout Kings)	.50
449	Pedro Martinez (Strikeout Kings)	.50
450	Jeff Bagwell, Andres Galarraga, Mark McGwire (All-Topps)	1.25
451	John Olerud, Jim Thome, Tino Martinez (All-Topps)	.40
452	Alex Rodriguez, Nomar Garciaparra, Derek Jeter (All-Topps)	1.50
453	Vinny Castilla, Chipper Jones, Scott Rolen (All-Topps)	.75
454	Sammy Sosa, Ken Griffey Jr., Juan Gonzalez (All-Topps)	1.00
455	Barry Bonds, Manny Ramirez, Larry Walker (All-Topps)	1.50
456	Frank Thomas, Tim Salmon, Ivan Rodriguez (All-Topps)	.60
457	Travis Lee, Todd Helton, Ben Grieve (All-Topps)	.50
458	Vladimir Guerrero, Greg Vaughn, Bernie Williams (All-Topps)	.50

459	Mike Piazza, Ivan Rodriguez, Jason Kendall (All-Topps)	1.00
460	Roger Clemens, Kerry Wood, Greg Maddux (All-Topps)	1.00
461	Sammy Sosa #1 (Home Run Parade)	10.00
461	Sammy Sosa HR #2-60	6.00
461	S. Sosa HR #61-62	10.00
461	S. Sosa HR #63-65	7.50
461	S. Sosa HR #66	20.00
---	Checklist 1-100	.15
---	Checklist - inserts	.15

All-Etch

Inserted in Series 2 packs, All-Etch has three different styles of inserts. '99 Rookie Rush features rookies who have the best shot of winning '99 Rookie of the Year. Club 40 features 13 players who hit 40 homers or more in 1998, and Club K features seven pitchers known for their strikeout abilities. Each is inserted 1:6 packs, while Refractor versions are seeded 1:24 packs.

		NM/M
Complete Set (30):		15.00
Common Player:		.35
Inserted 1:6		
Refractors:		1.5X
Inserted 1:24		
1	Mark McGwire	3.00
2	Sammy Sosa	1.50
3	Ken Griffey Jr.	2.00
4	Greg Vaughn	.25
5	Albert Belle	.25
6	Vinny Castilla	.25
7	Jose Canseco	.50
8	Juan Gonzalez	.50
9	Manny Ramirez	1.00
10	Andres Galarraga	.25
11	Rafael Palmeiro	.75
12	Alex Rodriguez	3.00
13	Mo Vaughn	.25
14	Eric Chavez	.40
15	Gabe Kapler	.25
16	Calvin Pickering	.25
17	Ruben Mateo	.25
18	Roy Halladay	.40
19	Jeremy Giambi	.25
20	Alex Gonzalez	.25
21	Ron Belliard	.25
22	Marlon Anderson	.25
23	Carlos Lee	.25
24	Kerry Wood	.50
25	Roger Clemens	1.50
26	Curt Schilling	.50
27	Kevin Brown	.25
28	Randy Johnson	1.00
29	Pedro Martinez	1.00
30	Orlando Hernandez	.25

Early Road to the Hall

This insert set spotlights players with less than 10 years in the Majors but who are gunning towards their respective spots in Cooperstown. The cards feature chromium technology, with an insert rate of 1:12 packs. A Refractor parallel edition, numbered to 100 each, was a 1:944 hobby-only insert.

	NM/M
Complete Set (10):	12.00
Common Player:	.50
Inserted 1:12	
Refractors (#'d to 100):	6X
ER1	Nomar Garciaparra	1.50
ER2	Derek Jeter	3.00
ER3	Alex Rodriguez	2.50
ER4	Juan Gonzalez	.50
ER5	Ken Griffey Jr.	2.00
ER6	Chipper Jones	1.50
ER7	Vladimir Guerrero	1.00
ER8	Jeff Bagwell	1.00
ER9	Ivan Rodriguez	.75
ER10	Frank Thomas	1.00

Fortune 15

Fortune 15 showcases the baseball's best players and hot rookies. They are inserted in Series 2 packs at a rate of 1:12. A Refractor version is found exclusively in hobby packs at a rate of 1:627 packs. Refractors are sequentially numbered to 100.

		NM/M
Complete Set (15):		17.50
Common Player:		.50
Inserted 1:12		
Refractors (#'d to 100):		4X
1	Alex Rodriguez	2.25
2	Nomar Garciaparra	1.25
3	Derek Jeter	3.00
4	Troy Glaus	.75
5	Ken Griffey Jr.	1.50
6	Vladimir Guerrero	1.00
7	Kerry Wood	.65
8	Eric Chavez	.65
9	Greg Maddux	1.25
10	Mike Piazza	1.50
11	Sammy Sosa	1.25
12	Mark McGwire	2.25
13	Ben Grieve	.50
14	Chipper Jones	1.25
15	Manny Ramirez	1.00

Home Run Heroes

These cards were part of an unannounced multi-manufacturer (Fleer, Upper Deck, Topps, Pacific) insert program exclusive to Wal-Mart. Each company produced cards of Mark McGwire and Sammy Sosa, along with two other premier sluggers. Each company's cards share a "Power Elite" logo at top and "Home Run Heroes" logo vertically at right.

		NM/M
Complete Set (4):		5.00
Common Player:		1.00
9	Mark McGwire	2.00
10	Sammy Sosa	1.50
11	Alex Rodriguez	1.00
12	Vladimir Guerrero	1.00

Lords of the Diamond

Parallel to the Topps version, this insert set features die-cutting across the card top and is seeded 1:8 in Series 1 packs. Refractor versions can be found 1:24 packs.

randomly in Series 2 packs at a rate of 1:36 packs. Refractor parallel versions are seeded 1:144 packs.

		NM/M
Complete Set (10):		20.00
Common Player:		.50
Inserted 1:36		
Refractors:		1.5X
Inserted 1:144		
1	Mark McGwire	3.00
2	Craig Biggio	.50
3	Barry Bonds	4.00
4	Ken Griffey Jr.	2.50
5	Sammy Sosa	2.00
6	Alex Rodriguez	3.00
7	Kerry Wood	1.00
8	Roger Clemens	2.00
9	Cal Ripken Jr.	4.00
10	Mark McGwire	3.00

Traded and Rookies

Actually issued in 2000, this parallel of the Topps Traded set utilizing Chromium technology was issued in complete set form.

		NM/M
Complete Set (121):		40.00
Common Player:		.15
1	Seth Etherton	.15
2	Mark Harriger RC	.25
3	Matt Wise RC	.50
4	Carlos Hernandez RC	.25
5	Julio Lugo RC	1.00
6	Mike Nannini	.15
7	Justin Bowles RC	.15
8	Mark Mulder RC	1.00
9	Roberto Vaz RC	.15
10	Felipe Lopez RC	1.50
11	Matt Belisle	.15
12	Micah Bowie	.15
13	Ruben Quevedo RC	.25
14	Jose Garcia RC	.15
15	David Kelton RC	.50
16	Phillip Norton	.15
17	Corey Patterson RC	1.00
18	Ron Walker RC	.25
19	Paul Hoover RC	.15
20	Ryan Rupe RC	.25
21	J.D. Closser RC	.15
22	Rob Ryan RC	.15
23	Steve Colyer RC	.15
24	Bubba Crosby RC	.50
25	Luke Prokopec RC	.15
26	Matt Blank RC	.15
27	Josh McKinley RC	.15
28	Nate Bump	.15
29	Giuseppe Chiaramonte RC	.15
30	Arturo McDowell RC	.15
31	Tony Torcato	.15
32	Dave Roberts	.15
33	C.C. Sabathia RC	6.00
34	Sean Spencer RC	.15
35	Chip Ambres	.15
36	A.J. Burnett	.50
37	Mo Bruce RC	.15
38	Jason Tyner	.15
39	Mamon Tucker	.15
40	Sean Burroughs RC	.50
41	Kevin Eberwein RC	.15
42	Junior Herndon RC	.25
43	Bryan Wolff RC	.15
44	Pat Burrell	1.00
45	Eric Valent	.15
46	Carlos Pena RC	3.00
47	Mike Zywica	.15
48	Adam Everett	.15
49	Juan Pena RC	.15
50	Adam Dunn RC	10.00
51	Austin Kearns	1.00
52	Jacobo Sequea RC	.15
53	Choo Freeman	.50
54	Jeff Winchester	.15
55	Matt Burch	.15
56	Chris George	.25
57	Scott Mullen RC	.15
58	Kit Pellow	.15
59	Mark Quinn RC	.50
60	Nate Cornejo	.15
61	Ryan Mills RC	.15
62	Kevin Beirne RC	.15
63	Kip Wells RC	.50
64	Juan Rivera RC	1.00
65	Alfonso Soriano RC	10.00
66	Josh Hamilton RC	18.00
67	Josh Girdley RC	.15
68	Kyle Snyder RC	.25

New Breed

A parallel version utilizing chromium technology, this insert set features the top young stars in the game and is seeded 1:24 packs. A Refractor version also exists, found 1:72 packs.

		NM/M
Complete Set (15):		30.00
Common Player:		.50
Inserted 1:24		
Refractors:		1.5X
Inserted 1:72		
NB1	Darin Erstad	.75
NB2	Brad Fullmer	.50
NB3	Kerry Wood	.75
NB4	Nomar Garciaparra	5.00
NB5	Travis Lee	.65
NB6	Scott Rolen	2.00
NB7	Todd Helton	3.00
NB8	Vladimir Guerrero	3.00
NB9	Derek Jeter	7.50
NB10	Alex Rodriguez	6.00
NB11	Ben Grieve	.50
NB12	Andruw Jones	3.00
NB13	Paul Konerko	.75
NB14	Aramis Ramirez	.50
NB15	Adrian Beltre	.75

Record Numbers

This insert set salutes nine record-setters who have earned a mark of distinction, including Cal Ripken Jr. for his record setting consecutive game streak. Inserted

69	Mike Paradis RC	.25
70	Jason Jennings RC	.25
71	David Walling RC	.25
72	Omar Ortiz RC	.15
73	Jay Gehrke RC	.15
74	Casey Burns RC	.15
75	Carl Crawford RC	8.00
76	Reggie Sanders	.15
77	Will Clark	.15
78	David Wells	.15
79	Paul Konerko	.25
80	Armando Benitez	.15
81	Brant Brown	.15
82	Mo Vaughn	.15
83	Jose Canseco	.50
84	Albert Belle	.15
85	Dean Palmer	.15
86	Greg Vaughn	.15
87	Mark Clark	.15
88	Pat Meares	.15
89	Eric Davis	.15
90	Brian Giles	.15
91	Jeff Brantley	.15
92	Bret Boone	.15
93	Ron Gant	.15
94	Mike Cameron	.15
95	Charles Johnson	.15
96	Denny Neagle	.15
97	Brian Hunter	.15
98	Jose Hernandez	.15
99	Rick Aguilera	.15
100	Tony Batista	.15
101	Roger Cedeno	.15
102	Creighton Gubanich	.15
103	Tim Belcher	.15
104	Bruce Aven	.15
105	Brian Daubach RC	.50
106	Ed Sprague	.15
107	Michael Tucker	.15
108	Homer Bush	.15
109	Armando Reynoso	.15
110	Brook Fordyce	.15
111	Matt Mantei	.15
112	Jose Guillen	.15
113	Kenny Rogers	.15
114	Livan Hernandez	.15
115	Butch Huskey	.15
116	David Segui	.15
117	Darryl Hamilton	.15
118	Jim Leyritz	.15
119	Randy Velarde	.15
120	Bill Taylor	.15
121	Kevin Appier	.15

Super Chrome

Using identical photos from Topps Chrome Baseball, Topps supersized 36 players to 4-1/8" x 5-3/4" card size. The cards are done on standard chromium technology. Each pack contains three oversized cards and sells for S.R.P. of $4.99. There also is a Refractor parallel set, which are seeded 1:12 packs.

		NM/M
Complete Set (36):		45.00
Common Player:		.50
Refractors:		2X
Inserted 1:12		
Pack (3):		4.50
Wax Box (12):		48.00
1	Roger Clemens	2.25
2	Andres Galarraga	.50
3	Manny Ramirez	1.50
4	Greg Maddux	2.00
5	Kerry Wood	.75
6	Travis Lee	.75
7	Nolan Ryan	4.50
8	Juan Gonzalez	.75
9	Vladimir Guerrero	1.50
10	Sammy Sosa	2.00
11	Mark McGwire	3.00
12	Javy Lopez	.50
13	Tony Gwynn	2.00
14	Derek Jeter	4.50
15	Albert Belle	.50
16	Pedro Martinez	1.50
17	Greg Vaughn	.50
18	Ken Griffey Jr.	2.50
19	Ben Grieve	.50
20	Vinny Castilla	.50
21	Moises Alou	.50
22	Barry Bonds	4.50
23	Nomar Garciaparra	2.00
24	Chipper Jones	2.00
25	Mike Piazza	2.50

26	Alex Rodriguez	3.00
27	Ivan Rodriguez	1.25
28	Frank Thomas	1.50
29	Larry Walker	.50
30	Troy Glaus	1.00
31	David Wells (Season Highlight)	.50
32	Roger Clemens (Season Highlight)	1.00
33	Kerry Wood (Season Highlight)	.50
34	Mark McGwire (Home Run Record)	3.00
35	Sammy Sosa (Home Run Parade)	2.00
36	World Series	.50

1999 Topps Gallery Pre-Production

Topps debuted its 1999 Gallery set with this trio of sample cards. Format is virtually identical to issued cards except for the use of a "PP" prefix to the card numbers on back.

		NM/M
Complete Set (3):		5.00
Common Player:		2.00
PP1	Scott Rolen	2.00
PP2	Andres Galarraga (Masters)	2.00
PP3	Brad Fullmer (Artisans)	2.00

1999 Topps Gallery

This 150-card base set features a white textured border surrounding the player image with the player's name, team name and Topps Gallery logo stamped in gold foil. The first 100 cards in the set portray veteran players while the final 50 cards are short-printed in three subsets: Masters, Artisans and Apprentices. Card backs have a monthly batting or pitching record from the '98 season, a player photo and vital information.

		NM/M
Complete Set (150):		60.00
Common Player (1-100):		.10
Common Player (101-150):		.25
Player's Private Issue:		5X
PPI SP's:		3X
Production 250 Sets		
Pack (6):		3.00
Wax Box (24):		45.00
1	Mark McGwire	1.50
2	Jim Thome	.35
3	Bernie Williams	.10
4	Larry Walker	.10
5	Juan Gonzalez	.30
6	Ken Griffey Jr.	1.00
7	Raul Mondesi	.10
8	Sammy Sosa	.75
9	Greg Maddux	.75
10	Jeff Bagwell	.60
11	Vladimir Guerrero	.60
12	Scott Rolen	.50
13	Nomar Garciaparra	.75
14	Mike Piazza	1.00
15	Travis Lee	.15
16	Carlos Delgado	.35
17	Darin Erstad	.25
18	David Justice	.10

19	Cal Ripken Jr.	2.00
20	Derek Jeter	2.00
21	Tony Clark	.10
22	Barry Larkin	.10
23	Greg Vaughn	.10
24	Jeff Kent	.10
25	Wade Boggs	.75
26	Andres Galarraga	.10
27	Ken Caminiti	.10
28	Jason Kendall	.10
29	Todd Helton	.60
30	Chuck Knoblauch	.10
31	Roger Clemens	.85
32	Jeromy Burnitz	.10
33	Javy Lopez	.10
34	Roberto Alomar	.25
35	Eric Karros	.10
36	Ben Grieve	.10
37	Eric Davis	.10
38	Rondell White	.10
39	Dmitri Young	.10
40	Ivan Rodriguez	.50
41	Paul O'Neill	.10
42	Jeff Cirillo	.10
43	Kerry Wood	.30
44	Albert Belle	.10
45	Frank Thomas	.60
46	Manny Ramirez	.60
47	Tom Glavine	.25
48	Mo Vaughn	.10
49	Jose Cruz Jr.	.10
50	Sandy Alomar	.10
51	Edgar Martinez	.10
52	John Olerud	.10
53	Todd Walker	.10
54	Tim Salmon	.10
55	Derek Bell	.10
56	Matt Williams	.10
57	Alex Rodriguez	1.50
58	Rusty Greer	.10
59	Vinny Castilla	.10
60	Jason Giambi	.30
61	Mark Grace	.10
62	Jose Canseco	.40
63	Gary Sheffield	.40
64	Brad Fullmer	.10
65	Trevor Hoffman	.10
66	Mark Kotsay	.10
67	Mike Mussina	.25
68	Johnny Damon	.30
69	Tino Martinez	.10
70	Curt Schilling	.25
71	Jay Buhner	.10
72	Kenny Lofton	.10
73	Randy Johnson	.60
74	Kevin Brown	.10
75	Brian Jordan	.10
76	Craig Biggio	.10
77	Barry Bonds	2.00
78	Tony Gwynn	.75
79	Jim Edmonds	.10
80	Shawn Green	.35
81	Todd Hundley	.10
82	Cliff Floyd	.10
83	Jose Guillen	.10
84	Dante Bichette	.10
85	Moises Alou	.10
86	Chipper Jones	.75
87	Ray Lankford	.10
88	Fred McGriff	.10
89	Rod Beck	.10
90	Dean Palmer	.10
91	Pedro Martinez	.60
92	Andruw Jones	.60
93	Robin Ventura	.10
94	Ugueth Urbina	.10
95	Orlando Hernandez	.10
96	Sean Casey	.15
97	Denny Neagle	.10
98	Troy Glaus	.60
99	John Smoltz	.10
100	Al Leiter	.10
101	Ken Griffey Jr.	1.50
102	Frank Thomas	.75
103	Mark McGwire	2.00
104	Sammy Sosa	1.00
105	Chipper Jones	1.00
106	Alex Rodriguez	2.00
107	Nomar Garciaparra	1.00
108	Juan Gonzalez	.40
109	Derek Jeter	3.00
110	Mike Piazza	1.50
111	Barry Bonds	3.00
112	Tony Gwynn	1.00
113	Cal Ripken Jr.	3.00
114	Greg Maddux	1.00
115	Roger Clemens	1.25
116	Brad Fullmer	.25
117	Kerry Wood	.50
118	Ben Grieve	.25
119	Todd Helton	.65
120	Kevin Millwood	.25
121	Sean Casey	.35
122	Vladimir Guerrero	.75
123	Travis Lee	.75
124	Troy Glaus	.65
125	Bartolo Colon	.25
126	Andruw Jones	.75
127	Scott Rolen	.60
128	Alfonso Soriano **RC**	4.00
129	Nick Johnson **RC**	1.00
130	Matt Belisle **RC**	.25
131	Jorge Toca **RC**	.25
132	Masao Kida **RC**	.25
133	Carlos Pena **RC**	1.50
134	Adrian Beltre	.40
135	Eric Chavez	.40
136	Carlos Beltran	.65

137	Alex Gonzalez	.25
138	Ryan Anderson	.25
139	Ruben Mateo	.25
140	Bruce Chen	.25
141	Pat Burrell **RC**	3.00
142	Michael Barrett	.25
143	Carlos Lee	.25
144	Mark Mulder **RC**	1.00
145	Choo Freeman **RC**	.50
146	Gabe Kapler	.25
147	Juan Encarnacion	.25
148	Jeremy Giambi	.25
149	Jason Tyner **RC**	.35
150	George Lombard	.25
	Checklist Folder 1 (1:3 Packs)	.10
	Checklist Folder 2 (1:3)	.10
	Checklist Folder 3 (1:3)	.10
	Checklist Folder 4 (1:12)	.25
	Checklist Folder 5 (1:240)	1.50
	Checklist Folder 6 (1:640)	3.00

Player's Private Issue

This parallel to the 150 regular cards in 1999 Gallery is limited to 250 serially numbered cards of each. Stated odds of insertion were one per 17 packs.

	NM/M
Common Player:	1.00
Stars:	5X
SP's:	3X
Production 250 Sets	

Autograph Cards

Three of baseball's top young third basemen are featured in this autographed set. The insertion odds are 1:209.

		NM/M
Common Player:		10.00
Inserted 1:209		
GA1	Troy Glaus	15.00
GA2	Adrian Beltre	10.00
GA3	Eric Chavez	10.00

Awards Gallery

This 10-card set features players who have earned the highest honors in baseball. Each insert commemorates the player's award by stamping his achievement on the bottom of the card front. Card

fronts have silver borders surrounding the player's image. These are seeded 1:12 and card numbers have a "AG" prefix.

		NM/M
Complete Set (10):		12.50
Common Player:		.50
Inserted 1:12		
AG1	Kerry Wood	.75
AG2	Ben Grieve	.50
AG3	Roger Clemens	2.50
AG4	Tom Glavine	.75
AG5	Juan Gonzalez	.75
AG6	Sammy Sosa	3.00
AG7	Ken Griffey Jr.	3.00
AG8	Mark McGwire	3.00
AG9	Bernie Williams	.50
AG10	Larry Walker	.50

Exhibitions

This 20-card set is done on textured 24-point stock and features baseball's top stars. Exhibitions are seeded 1:48 packs.

		NM/M
Complete Set (20):		75.00
Common Player:		2.00
Inserted 1:48		
E1	Sammy Sosa	4.50
E2	Mark McGwire	7.50
E3	Greg Maddux	4.50
E4	Roger Clemens	5.00
E5	Ben Grieve	2.00
E6	Kerry Wood	2.25
E7	Ken Griffey Jr.	6.00
E8	Tony Gwynn	4.50
E9	Cal Ripken Jr.	10.00
E10	Frank Thomas	4.00
E11	Jeff Bagwell	4.00
E12	Derek Jeter	10.00
E13	Alex Rodriguez	7.50
E14	Nomar Garciaparra	4.50
E15	Manny Ramirez	4.00
E16	Vladimir Guerrero	4.00
E17	Darin Erstad	2.25
E18	Scott Rolen	3.00
E19	Mike Piazza	6.00
E20	Andres Galarraga	2.00

Gallery of Heroes

This 10-card set is done on card stock that simulates medieval stained glass. Gallery of Heroes are found 1:24 packs.

		NM/M
Complete Set (10):		30.00
Common Player:		.75
Inserted 1:24		
GH1	Mark McGwire	6.00
GH2	Sammy Sosa	3.50
GH3	Ken Griffey Jr.	4.50
GH4	Mike Piazza	4.50
GH5	Derek Jeter	7.50
GH6	Nomar Garciaparra	4.50
GH7	Kerry Wood	1.50
GH8	Ben Grieve	.75
GH9	Chipper Jones	3.50
GH10	Alex Rodriguez	6.00

Heritage

Nineteen contemporary legends and Hall-of-Famer Hank Aaron are artistically depicted using the 1953 Topps design as a template. For a chance to bid on the

original art used in the development of this insert set, collectors were able to enter the Topps Gallery Auction. Collectors could accumulate auction points found in Topps Gallery packs. Heritages are seeded 1:12 packs. A parallel called Heritage Proofs are also randomly inserted 1:48 packs and have a chrome styrene finish.

		NM/M
Complete Set (20):		100.00
Common Player:		2.50
Inserted 1:12		
Heritage Proofs:		1.5X
Inserted 1:48		
TH1	Hank Aaron	10.00
TH2	Ben Grieve	2.50
TH3	Nomar Garciaparra	7.50
TH4	Roger Clemens	8.50
TH5	Travis Lee	2.50
TH6	Tony Gwynn	7.50
TH7	Alex Rodriguez	12.50
TH8	Ken Griffey Jr.	10.00
TH9	Derek Jeter	15.00
TH10	Sammy Sosa	7.50
TH11	Scott Rolen	2.50
TH12	Chipper Jones	7.50
TH13	Cal Ripken Jr.	15.00
TH14	Kerry Wood	3.00
TH15	Barry Bonds	15.00
TH16	Juan Gonzalez	3.00
TH17	Mike Piazza	10.00
TH18	Greg Maddux	7.50
TH19	Frank Thomas	6.00
TH20	Mark McGwire	12.50

Heritage Proofs

Heritage Proofs are a parallel to the 1953-style inserts. Printed on chrome styrene, the proofs have a silver metallic background on front and the notation on bottom-back, "1953 TOPPS HERITAGE PROOF." The proof versions are found on average of one per 48 packs.

		NM/M
Complete Set (20):		175.00
Common Player:		3.00
TH1	Hank Aaron	15.00
TH2	Ben Grieve	3.00
TH3	Nomar Garciaparra	10.00
TH4	Roger Clemens	11.50
TH5	Travis Lee	3.00
TH6	Tony Gwynn	10.00
TH7	Alex Rodriguez	15.00
TH8	Ken Griffey Jr.	12.50
TH9	Derek Jeter	20.00
TH10	Sammy Sosa	12.50
TH11	Scott Rolen	5.00
TH12	Chipper Jones	10.00
TH13	Cal Ripken Jr.	20.00
TH14	Kerry Wood	4.00
TH15	Barry Bonds	20.00
TH16	Juan Gonzalez	7.50
TH17	Mike Piazza	12.50
TH18	Greg Maddux	10.00
TH19	Frank Thomas	7.50
TH20	Mark McGwire	15.00

Heritage Lithographs

Eight of the paintings used to create the Heritage inserts for 1999 Topps Gallery were reproduced as enlarged limited-edition offset lithographs. The paintings of Bill Purdom and James Fiorentino were reproduced in an 18" x 25" serially-numbered, artist-signed edition of 600 pieces each. The lithos were offered through Bill Goff Inc / Good Sports at $60 each unframed.

		NM/M
Complete Set (8):		480.00
Single Player:		60.00
(1)	Roger Clemens	60.00
(2)	Nomar Garciaparra	60.00
(3)	Ken Griffey Jr.	60.00
(4)	Derek Jeter	60.00
(5)	Mark McGwire	60.00
(6)	Mike Piazza	60.00
(7)	Cal Ripken Jr.	60.00
(8)	Sammy Sosa	60.00

Heritage Super Promos

Actually issued as a Topps handout at the 2000 National Sports Collectors Convention Corporate Block Party, this set depicts eight of the 1953 Topps-style cards which had been created for the Gallery Heritage insert series in 1999. The super-size (3-3/4" x 5-1/8") promos are printed on thin, glossy stock. Fronts have card-style artwork by Bill Goff or Bill Purdom. Backs are in black-and-white with player information and advertising by the artists, along with MLB and MLBPA licensor logos. The unnumbered cards are checklisted here alphabetically.

		NM/M
Complete Set (8):		40.00
Common Player:		4.00
(1)	Roger Clemens	4.50
(2)	Nomar Garciaparra	4.00
(3)	Ken Griffey Jr.	5.00
(4)	Derek Jeter	7.50
(5)	Mark McGwire	6.00
(6)	Mike Piazza	5.00
(7)	Cal Ripken Jr.	7.50
(8)	Sammy Sosa	4.00

Press Plates

The aluminum press plates used to print the Gallery cards were inserted at a rate of one per 985 packs. Each card's front and back can be found in four different color variations. Because of the unique nature of each plate, assignment of catalog values is not feasible.

	NM/M
Common Player:	25.00

1999 Topps Gold Label Pre-Production

This trio of pre-production samples previews Topps' 1999 version of its high-end Gold Label brand. Cards are nearly identical in format to the issued version except for the "PP" prefix to card numbers on back.

		NM/M
Complete Set (3):		3.00
Common Player:		1.00
PP1	Tom Glavine	1.00
PP2	Tino Martinez	1.00
PP3	Jim Thome	2.00

1999 Topps Gold Label Class 1

Pedro Martinez

This set consists of 100 cards on 35-point spectral-reflective rainbow stock with gold foil stamping. All cards are available in three versions each with the same foreground photo, but with different background photos that vary by category: Class 1 (fielding), Class 2 (running, 1:2), Class 3 (hitting, 1:4). In addition each variation has a different version of the player's team logo in the background. Variations for pitchers are Class 1, set position; Class 2, wind-up, and Class 3, throwing. Black Label parallels were inserted at the rate of between 1:8 and 1:12, depending on packaging. Red Label parallels, serially numbered to 100 each were inserted at rates from 1:118 to 1:148. A One to One parallel version also exists and is limited to one numbered card for each variation and color (Gold, Black and Red), for a total of 900 cards inserted about one per 1,500 packs.

		NM/M
Complete Set (100):		30.00
Common Gold Label:		.10
Common Black Label:		.10
Black Label Stars:		3X
Common Red Label:		2.00
Red Label Stars:		12X
Pack (5):		3.00
Wax Box (24):		50.00
1	Mike Piazza	2.00
2	Andres Galarraga	.10
3	Mark Grace	.10
4	Tony Clark	.10
5	Jim Thome	.60
6	Tony Gwynn	1.50
7	Kelly Dransfeldt RC	.15
8	Eric Chavez	.25
9	Brian Jordan	.10
10	Todd Hundley	.10
11	Rondell White	.10
12	Dmitri Young	.10
13	Jeff Kent	.10
14	Derek Bell	.10
15	Todd Helton	.75
16	Chipper Jones	1.50
17	Albert Belle	.40
18	Barry Larkin	.40
19	Dante Bichette	.10

20	Gary Sheffield	.50
21	Cliff Floyd	.10
22	Derek Jeter	3.00
23	Jason Giambi	.50
24	Ray Lankford	.10
25	Alex Rodriguez	2.50
26	Ruben Mateo	.10
27	Wade Boggs	1.50
28	Carlos Delgado	.45
29	Tim Salmon	.10
30	Alfonso Soriano RC	5.00
31	Javy Lopez	.10
32	Jason Kendall	.10
33	Nick Johnson RC	1.00
34	A.J. Burnett RC	1.00
35	Troy Glaus	.75
36	Pat Burrell RC	3.00
37	Jeff Cirillo	.10
38	David Justice	.10
39	Ivan Rodriguez	.75
40	Bernie Williams	.10
41	Jay Buhner	.10
42	Mo Vaughn	.10
43	Randy Johnson	1.00
44	Pedro Martinez	1.00
45	Larry Walker	.10
46	Todd Walker	.10
47	Roberto Alomar	.25
48	Kevin Brown	.10
49	Mike Mussina	.40
50	Tom Glavine	.25
51	Curt Schilling	.25
52	Ken Caminiti	.10
53	Brad Fullmer	.10
54	Bobby Seay RC	.10
55	Orlando Hernandez	.10
56	Sean Casey	.10
57	Al Leiter	.10
58	Sandy Alomar	.10
59	Mark Kotsay	.10
60	Matt Williams	.10
61	Raul Mondesi	.10
62	Joe Crede RC	5.00
63	Jim Edmonds	.10
64	Jose Cruz Jr.	.10
65	Juan Gonzalez	.50
66	Sammy Sosa	1.50
67	Cal Ripken Jr.	3.00
68	Vinny Castilla	.10
69	Craig Biggio	.10
70	Mark McGwire	2.50
71	Greg Vaughn	.10
72	Greg Maddux	1.50
73	Paul O'Neill	.10
74	Scott Rolen	.65
75	Ben Grieve	.10
76	Vladimir Guerrero	1.00
77	John Olerud	.10
78	Eric Karros	.10
79	Jeromy Burnitz	.10
80	Jeff Bagwell	1.00
81	Kenny Lofton	.10
82	Manny Ramirez	1.00
83	Andruw Jones	1.00
84	Travis Lee	.15
85	Darin Erstad	.25
86	Nomar Garciaparra	1.50
87	Frank Thomas	1.00
88	Moises Alou	.10
89	Tino Martinez	.10
90	Carlos Pena RC	1.50
91	Shawn Green	.40
92	Rusty Greer	.10
93	Matt Belisle RC	.25
94	Adrian Beltre	.25
95	Roger Clemens	1.75
96	John Smoltz	.10
97	Mark Mulder RC	1.00
98	Kerry Wood	.50
99	Barry Bonds	3.00
100	Ken Griffey Jr.	2.00
	Checklist folder	.05

Class 2

Joe Crede

Background photos for Class 2 Gold Label and color parallels show position players running and pitchers in their windup. Class 2 Gold Label cards are inserted at the rate of one in two Home Team Advantage packs, and one in four retail packs. Black Label versions are inserted 1:16 HTA and 1:24 R. Red Labels, numbered to 50 each, are found in HTA at a 1:237 rate, and in retail at 1:296.

	NM/M
Complete Set (100):	75.00
Common Gold Label:	.25
Gold Label Stars:	1.5X
Common Black Label:	2.00
Black Label Stars:	4X
Common Red Label:	6.00
Red Label Stars:	15X

Class 3

Pat Burrell

Background photos for Class 3 Gold Label and color parallels show position players hitting and pitchers pitching. Class 3 Gold Label cards are inserted at the rate of one in four Home Team Advantage packs, and one in eight retail packs. Black Label versions are inserted 1:32 HTA and 1:48 R. Red Labels, numbered to 25 each, are found in HTA at a 1:473 rate, and in retail at 1:591.

	NM/M
Complete Set (100):	125.00
Common Gold Label:	.50
Gold Label Stars: 2	
Common Black Label:	3.00
Black Label Stars:	6X
Common Red Label:	12.00
Red Label Stars:	35X

One to One

Nomar Garciaparra

Depending on type of packaging, these rare parallels are found at the rate of only one per approximately 1,200-1,600 packs. Each of the three Classes in Gold, Red and Black versions can be found as a One to One insert, for a total of nine "unique" cards for each player in the base set and three in the Race to Aaron insert series. Backs of the One to One cards are printed in silver foil with a "1/1" foil serial number.

	NM/M
Common Player, Base Set:	50.00
Common Player, Race to Aaron:	150.00

Race to Aaron

This 10-card set features the best current players who are chasing Hank Aaron's career home run

and career RBI records. Each player is pictured in the foreground with Aaron silhouetted in the background on the card front. These are seeded 1:12 packs. Two parallel versions also exist: Black and Red. Blacks have black foil stamping and are seeded 1:48 packs. Reds have red foil stamping and are limited to 44 sequentially numbered sets.

		NM/M
Complete Set (10):		20.00
Common Player:		1.00
Blacks:		2X
Reds:		12X
1	Mark McGwire	4.50
2	Ken Griffey Jr.	3.00
3	Alex Rodriguez	4.50
4	Vladimir Guerrero	1.50
5	Albert Belle	1.00
6	Nomar Garciaparra	2.50
7	Ken Griffey Jr.	3.00
8	Alex Rodriguez	4.50
9	Juan Gonzalez	1.00
10	Barry Bonds	7.50

Name Mismatches

Because of faulty alignment when the gold-foil logo and player name were applied to card fronts, some Gold Label cards are found with the wrong name on front. Because each of these error cards is rare or possibly unique, and the demand is dependent on the combination of photo and name, it is not possible to assign values.

1999 Topps Opening Day

This retail exclusive product is comprised of 165 cards. Base cards have a silver border, and the Opening Day logo stamped with silver foil. Packs are pre-priced at $.99, each pack has seven cards. Hank Aaron autographs are randomly seeded and are stamped with the Topps "Certified Autograph Issue" stamp. The insertion rate for the autograph is 1:29,642 packs.

		NM/M
Complete Set (165):		20.00
Common Player:		.10
Hank Aaron Autograph:		150.00
Pack (7):		1.50
Wax Box (24):		20.00
1	Hank Aaron	3.00
2a	Roger Clemens	1.25
2b	Andres Galarraga (Should be #3.)	.10
4	Scott Brosius	.10
5	Ray Durham	.10
6	Will Clark	.10
7	David Wells	.10
8	Jose Guillen	.10
9	Edgardo Alfonzo	.10
10	Manny Ramirez	.75
11	Greg Maddux	1.00
12	David Segui	.10
13	Darryl Strawberry	.10
14	Brad Radke	.10
15	Kerry Wood	.35
16	Paul Konerko	.30

17	Travis Lee	.25
18	Kenny Rogers	.10
19	Todd Walker	.10
20	John Olerud	.10
21	Nolan Ryan	2.00
22	Ray Lankford	.10
23	Bartolo Colon	.10
24	Brady Anderson	.10
25	Jorge Posada	.10
26	Justin Thompson	.10
27	Juan Gonzalez	.40
28	Chuck Knoblauch	.10
29	Todd Helton	.65
30	Gary Sheffield	.40
31	Rod Beck	.10
32	Garret Anderson	.10
33	Rondell White	.10
34	Vladimir Guerrero	.75
35	Eric Karros	.10
36	Mo Vaughn	.10
37	Sammy Sosa	1.00
38	Kenny Lofton	.10
39	Mark McGwire	2.00
40	Javy Lopez	.10
41	Damion Easley	.10
42	Andy Pettitte	.30
43	Tony Gwynn	1.00
44	Jay Bell	.10
45	Jose Canseco	.45
46	John Wetteland	.10
47	Mike Caruso	.10
48	Derek Jeter	3.00
49	Aaron Sele	.10
50	Jeff Cirillo	.10
51	Mark Kotsay	.10
52	Albert Belle	.10
53	Matt Lawton	.10
54	Pedro Martinez	.75
55	Greg Vaughn	.10
56	Neifi Perez	.10
57	Derek Bell	.10
58	Ken Griffey Jr.	1.50
59	David Cone	.10
60	Dean Palmer	.10
61	Trevor Hoffman	.10
62	Billy Wagner	.10
63	Shawn Green	.25
64	Ben Grieve	.10
65	Tom Goodwin	.10
66	Jaret Wright	.10
67	Dmitri Young	.10
68	Hideki Irabu	.10
69	Jeff Fassero	.10
70	Matt Williams	.10
71	Bret Saberhagen	.10
72	Chad Curtis	.10
73	Scott Rolen	.60
74	J.T. Snow Jr.	.10
75	Rusty Greer	.10
76	Jim Edmonds	.10
77	Ron Gant	.10
78	A.J. Hinch	.10
79	Shannon Stewart	.10
80	Brad Fullmer	.10
81	Walt Weiss	.10
82	Fred McGriff	.10
83	Darin Erstad	.25
84	Eric Young	.10
85	Livan Hernandez	.10
86	Jeff Bagwell	.75
87	Omar Vizquel	.10
88	Eric Davis	.10
89	Magglio Ordonez	.25
90	John Valentin	.10
91	Dave Dellucci	.10
92	Chan Ho Park	.10
93	Masato Yoshii	.10
94	Bret Boone	.10
95	Mariano Rivera	.20
96	Bobby Jones	.10
97	Francisco Cordova	.10
98	Mike Mussina	.40
99	Denny Neagle	.10
100	Edgar Martinez	.10
101	Jason Kendall	.10
102	Jeff King	.10
103	Rey Ordonez	.10
104	Andruw Jones	.75
105	Vinny Castilla	.10
106	Troy Glaus	.65
107	Tom Glavine	.40
108	Moises Alou	.10
109	Carlos Delgado	.40
110	Raul Mondesi	.10
111	Shane Reynolds	.10
112	Jason Giambi	.60
113	Jose Cruz Jr.	.10
114	Craig Biggio	.10
115	Tim Salmon	.10
116	Chipper Jones	1.00
117	Andy Benes	.10
118	John Smoltz	.10
119	Jeromy Burnitz	.10
120	Randy Johnson	.75
121	Mark Grace	.10
122	Henry Rodriguez	.10
123	Ryan Klesko	.10
124	Kevin Millwood	.10
125	Sean Casey	.20
126	Brian Jordan	.10
127	Kevin Brown	.10
128	Orlando Hernandez	.10
129	Barry Bonds	3.00
130	David Justice	.10
131	Carlos Perez	.10
132	Andy Ashby	.10
133	Paul O'Neill	.10
134	Curt Schilling	.40

135	Alex Rodriguez	2.00
136	Cliff Floyd	.10
137	Rafael Palmeiro	.60
138	Nomar Garciaparra	1.00
139	Mike Piazza	1.50
140	Roberto Alomar	.30
141	Todd Hundley	.10
142	Jeff Kent	.10
143	Barry Larkin	.10
144	Cal Ripken Jr.	3.00
145	Jay Buhner	.10
146	Kevin Young	.10
147	Ivan Rodriguez	.65
148	Al Leiter	.10
149	Sandy Alomar	.10
150	Bernie Williams	.10
151	Ellis Burks	.10
152	Wally Joyner	.10
153	Bobby Higginson	.10
154	Tony Clark	.10
155	Larry Walker	.10
156	Frank Thomas	.75
157	Tino Martinez	.10
158	Jim Thome	.60
159	Dante Bichette	.10
160	David Wells (Season Highlights)	.10
161	Roger Clemens (Season Highlights)	.50
162	Kerry Wood (Season Highlights)	.15
163	Mark McGwire (HR Record #70)	4.00
164	Sammy Sosa (HR Record #66)	1.50
165	Checklist	.10

1999 Topps Stars Pre-Production

Five-card cello packs of pre-production samples were distributed to introduce Topps' new concept for its Stars brand. The samples follow the format of the issued versions except for the use of a "PP" prefix to the card number on back.

		NM/M
Complete Set (5):		5.00
Common Player:		.75
PP1	Paul O'Neill (Base card.)	.75
PP2	Vinny Castilla (One-star.)	.75
PP3	Darin Erstad (Two-star.)	1.00
PP4	Kerry Wood (Three-star.)	1.50
PP5	Chipper Jones (Four-star.)	3.00

1999 Topps Stars

Topps Stars consists of 180 cards on 20-point stock with foil stamping and metallic inks. The set is comprised of 150 base cards and 30 subset cards: Luminaries and Supernovas. Packs contain six cards; three base cards, two One-Star cards and one Two-Star card on the average.

		NM/M
Complete Set (180):		20.00
Common Player:		.05
Pack (6):		1.50
Wax Box (24):		25.00
1	Ken Griffey Jr.	
2	Chipper Jones	.50
3	Mike Piazza	.75
4	Nomar Garciaparra	.50

5	Derek Jeter	1.50
6	Frank Thomas	.40
7	Ben Grieve	.05
8	Mark McGwire	1.00
9	Sammy Sosa	.50
10	Alex Rodriguez	1.00
11	Troy Glaus	.35
12	Eric Chavez	.25
13	Kerry Wood	.30
14	Barry Bonds	1.50
15	Vladimir Guerrero	.40
16	Albert Belle	.05
17	Juan Gonzalez	.20
18	Roger Clemens	.60
19	Ruben Mateo	.05
20	Cal Ripken Jr.	1.50
21	Darin Erstad	.25
22	Jeff Bagwell	.40
23	Roy Halladay	.10
24	Todd Helton	.35
25	Michael Barrett	.05
26	Manny Ramirez	.40
27	Fernando Seguignol	.05
28	Pat Burrell RC	2.00
29	Andruw Jones	.40
30	Randy Johnson	.40
31	Jose Canseco	.30
32	Brad Fullmer	.05
33	Alex Escobar RC	.10
34	Alfonso Soriano RC	3.00
35	Larry Walker	.05
36	Matt Clement	.05
37	Mo Vaughn	.05
38	Bruce Chen	.05
39	Travis Lee	.20
40	Adrian Beltre	.10
41	Alex Gonzalez	.05
42	Jason Tyner RC	.10
43	George Lombard	.05
44	Scott Rolen	.25
45	Mark Mulder RC	.50
46	Gabe Kapler	.05
47	Choo Freeman RC	.10
48	Tony Gwynn	.50
49	A.J. Burnett RC	.25
50	Matt Belisle RC	.10
51	Greg Maddux	.50
52	John Smoltz	.05
53	Mark Grace	.05
54	Wade Boggs	.50
55	Bernie Williams	.05
56	Pedro Martinez	.40
57	Barry Larkin	.05
58	Orlando Hernandez	.05
59	Jason Kendall	.05
60	Mark Kotsay	.05
61	Jim Thome	.35
62	Gary Sheffield	.30
63	Preston Wilson	.05
64	Rafael Palmeiro	.35
65	David Wells	.05
66	Shawn Green	.30
67	Tom Glavine	.25
68	Jeromy Burnitz	.05
69	Kevin Brown	.05
70	Rondell White	.05
71	Roberto Alomar	.25
72	Cliff Floyd	.05
73	Craig Biggio	.05
74	Greg Vaughn	.05
75	Ivan Rodriguez	.35
76	Vinny Castilla	.05
77	Todd Walker	.05
78	Paul Konerko	.15
79	Andy Brown RC	.05
80	Todd Hundley	.05
81	Dmitri Young	.05
82	Tony Clark	.05
83	Nick Johnson RC	.50
84	Mike Caruso	.05
85	David Ortiz	.35
86	Matt Williams	.05
87	Raul Mondesi	.05
88	Kenny Lofton	.05
89	Miguel Tejada	.10
90	Dante Bichette	.05
91	Jorge Posada	.05
92	Carlos Beltran	.25
93	Carlos Delgado	.30
94	Javy Lopez	.05
95	Aramis Ramirez	.05
96	Neifi Perez	.05
97	Marlon Anderson	.05
98	David Cone	.05
99	Moises Alou	.05
100	John Olerud	.05
101	Tim Salmon	.05
102	Jason Giambi	.30
103	Sandy Alomar	.05
104	Curt Schilling	.25
105	Andres Galarraga	.05
106	Rusty Greer	.05
107	Bobby Seay RC	.05
108	Eric Young	.05
109	Brian Jordan	.05
110	Eric Davis	.05
111	Will Clark	.05
112	Andy Ashby	.05
113	Edgardo Alfonzo	.05
114	Paul O'Neill	.05
115	Denny Neagle	.05
116	Eric Karros	.05
117	Ken Caminiti	.05
118	Garret Anderson	.05
119	Todd Stottlemyre	.05
120	David Justice	.05
121	Francisco Cordova	.05
122	Robin Ventura	.05

123	Mike Mussina	.25
124	Hideki Irabu	.05
125	Justin Thompson	.05
126	Mariano Rivera	.15
127	Delino DeShields	.05
128	Steve Finley	.05
129	Jose Cruz Jr.	.05
130	Ray Lankford	.05
131	Jim Edmonds	.05
132	Charles Johnson	.05
133	Al Leiter	.05
134	Jose Offerman	.05
135	Eric Milton	.05
136	Dean Palmer	.05
137	Johnny Damon	.25
138	Andy Pettitte	.20
139	Ray Durham	.05
140	Ugueth Urbina	.05
141	Marquis Grissom	.05
142	Ryan Klesko	.05
143	Brady Anderson	.05
144	Bobby Higginson	.05
145	Chuck Knoblauch	.05
146	Rickey Henderson	.40
147	Kevin Millwood	.05
148	Fred McGriff	.05
149	Damion Easley	.05
150	Tino Martinez	.05
151	Greg Maddux (Luminaries)	.30
152	Scott Rolen (Luminaries)	.20
153	Pat Burrell (Luminaries)	.75
154	Roger Clemens (Luminaries)	.35
155	Albert Belle (Luminaries)	.05
156	Troy Glaus (Luminaries)	.25
157	Cal Ripken Jr. (Luminaries)	.75
158	Alfonso Soriano (Luminaries)	.75
159	Manny Ramirez (Luminaries)	.25
160	Eric Chavez (Luminaries)	.10
161	Kerry Wood (Luminaries)	.20
162	Tony Gwynn (Luminaries)	.30
163	Barry Bonds (Luminaries)	.75
164	Ruben Mateo (Luminaries)	.05
165	Todd Helton (Luminaries)	.05
166	Darin Erstad (Luminaries)	.05
167	Jeff Bagwell (Luminaries)	.25
168	Juan Gonzalez (Luminaries)	.15
169	Mo Vaughn (Luminaries)	.05
170	Vladimir Guerrero (Luminaries)	.25
171	Nomar Garciaparra (Supernovas)	.35
172	Derek Jeter (Supernovas)	.75
173	Alex Rodriguez (Supernovas)	.50
174	Ben Grieve (Supernovas)	.05
175	Mike Piazza (Supernovas)	.40
176	Chipper Jones (Supernovas)	.50
177	Frank Thomas (Supernovas)	.25
178	Ken Griffey Jr. (Supernovas)	.40
179	Sammy Sosa (Supernovas)	.35
180	Mark McGwire (Supernovas)	.50
	Checklist 1 (1-45)	.05
	Checklist 2 (46-136)	.05
	Checklist 3 (137-150, inserts)	.05

Foil

MIGUEL TEJADA

Metallic foil in the background and a serial number on back from within a specific edition identifies this parallel. Stated odds of insertion were one in 15 packs for parallels of the 180 base cards, numbered to 299 each. One-Star foil parallels are numbered to 249 and inserted 1:33. The Two-Star Foils are numbered to 199 each and found on average of one per 82 packs. With insertion odds of 1:410, the Three-Star Foil parallels are numbered within an edition of 99. At the top of the scarcity scale,

the Foil Four-Star parallels are sequentially numbered to 49 and are a one per 650-pack find.

	NM/M
Complete Base Set (180):	90.00
Common Foil Player:	.15
Foil Stars:	3X

One-Star

★ ALEX RODRIGUEZ

One-Star inserts include card numbers 1-100 from the base set and have silver foil stamping with one star on the bottom left portion of the card front. These are seeded two per pack. A foil One-Star parallel also is randomly seeded and sequentially numbered to 249 sets. These are a 1:33 pack insert.

		NM/M
Complete Set (100):		25.00
Common Player:		.10
Foils (249 Each):		2X
1	Ken Griffey Jr.	1.25
2	Chipper Jones	1.00
3	Mike Piazza	1.25
4	Nomar Garciaparra	1.00
5	Derek Jeter	2.00
6	Frank Thomas	.75
7	Ben Grieve	.10
8	Mark McGwire	1.50
9	Sammy Sosa	1.00
10	Alex Rodriguez	1.50
11	Troy Glaus	.65
12	Eric Chavez	.25
13	Kerry Wood	.35
14	Barry Bonds	2.00
15	Vladimir Guerrero	.75
16	Albert Belle	.10
17	Juan Gonzalez	.40
18	Roger Clemens	1.00
19	Ruben Mateo	.10
20	Cal Ripken Jr.	2.00
21	Darin Erstad	.30
22	Jeff Bagwell	.75
23	Roy Halladay	.10
24	Todd Helton	.65
25	Michael Barrett	.10
26	Manny Ramirez	.75
27	Fernando Seguignol	.10
28	Pat Burrell	1.00
29	Andruw Jones	.75
30	Randy Johnson	.75
31	Jose Canseco	.40
32	Brad Fullmer	.10
33	Alex Escobar	.10
34	Alfonso Soriano	2.00
35	Larry Walker	.10
36	Matt Clement	.25
37	Mo Vaughn	.10
38	Bruce Chen	.10
39	Travis Lee	.15
40	Adrian Beltre	.20
41	Alex Gonzalez	.10
42	Jason Tyner	.10
43	George Lombard	.10
44	Scott Rolen	.50
45	Mark Mulder	.50
46	Gabe Kapler	.10
47	Choo Freeman	.10
48	Tony Gwynn	1.00
49	A.J. Burnett	.15
50	Matt Belisle	.10
51	Greg Maddux	1.00
52	John Smoltz	.10
53	Mark Grace	.10
54	Wade Boggs	1.00
55	Bernie Williams	.10
56	Pedro Martinez	.75
57	Barry Larkin	.10
58	Orlando Hernandez	.10
59	Jason Kendall	.10
60	Mark Kotsay	.10
61	Jim Thome	.45
62	Gary Sheffield	.40
63	Preston Wilson	.10
64	Rafael Palmeiro	.60
65	David Wells	.10
66	Shawn Green	.30
67	Tom Glavine	.30
68	Jeromy Burnitz	.10
69	Kevin Brown	.10
70	Rondell White	.10
71	Roberto Alomar	.25
72	Cliff Floyd	.10
73	Craig Biggio	.10
74	Greg Vaughn	.10
75	Ivan Rodriguez	.60
76	Vinny Castilla	.10
77	Todd Walker	.10
78	Paul Konerko	.20
79	Andy Brown	.10
80	Todd Hundley	.10
81	Dmitri Young	.10
82	Tony Clark	.10
83	Nick Johnson	.50
84	Mike Caruso	.10
85	David Ortiz	.40
86	Matt Williams	.10
87	Raul Mondesi	.10
88	Kenny Lofton	.10
89	Miguel Tejada	.20
90	Dante Bichette	.10
91	Jorge Posada	.10
92	Carlos Beltran	.25
93	Carlos Delgado	.20
94	Javy Lopez	.10
95	Aramis Ramirez	.10
96	Neifi Perez	.10
97	Marlon Anderson	.10
98	David Cone	.10
99	Moises Alou	.10
100	John Olerud	.10

Two-Star

Two-Stars are inserted one per pack and feature light gold metallic inks and foil stamping. Two-Stars include card numbers 1-50 from the base set. A Two-Star foil parallel is also randomly seeded and limited to 199 sequentially numbered sets.

		NM/M
Complete Set (50):		50.00
Common Player:		.25
Foils:		3X
1	Ken Griffey Jr.	2.00
2	Chipper Jones	1.50
3	Mike Piazza	2.00
4	Nomar Garciaparra	1.50
5	Derek Jeter	3.00
6	Frank Thomas	1.00
7	Ben Grieve	.25
8	Mark McGwire	2.50
9	Sammy Sosa	1.50
10	Alex Rodriguez	2.50
11	Troy Glaus	.75
12	Eric Chavez	.30
13	Kerry Wood	.40
14	Barry Bonds	3.00
15	Vladimir Guerrero	1.00
16	Albert Belle	.25
17	Juan Gonzalez	.50
18	Roger Clemens	1.75
19	Ruben Mateo	.25
20	Cal Ripken Jr.	3.00
21	Darin Erstad	.75
22	Jeff Bagwell	1.00
23	Roy Halladay	.40
24	Todd Helton	.75
25	Michael Barrett	.25
26	Manny Ramirez	1.00
27	Fernando Seguignol	.25
28	Pat Burrell	1.50
29	Andruw Jones	1.00
30	Randy Johnson	1.00
31	Jose Canseco	.50
32	Brad Fullmer	.25
33	Alex Escobar	.25
34	Alfonso Soriano	1.50
35	Larry Walker	.25
36	Matt Clement	.30
37	Mo Vaughn	.25
38	Bruce Chen	.25
39	Travis Lee	.30
40	Adrian Beltre	.30
41	Alex Gonzalez	.25
42	Jason Tyner	.25
43	George Lombard	.25
44	Scott Rolen	.65
45	Mark Mulder	.45
46	Gabe Kapler	.25
47	Choo Freeman	.25
48	Tony Gwynn	1.50
49	A.J. Burnett	.30
50	Matt Belisle	.25

Three-Star

Three-Star inserts are a partial parallel from the base set including cards 1-20. Inserted 1:5 packs, these cards feature refractive silver foil

stamping along with gold metallic inks. A Three-Star parallel also is randomly inserted featuring gold stamping and limited to 99 serial numbered sets, inserted one per 410 packs.

		NM/M
Complete Set (20):		30.00
Common Player:		.50
Foils:		4X
1	Ken Griffey Jr.	2.50
2	Chipper Jones	2.00
3	Mike Piazza	2.50
4	Nomar Garciaparra	2.00
5	Derek Jeter	4.00
6	Frank Thomas	1.50
7	Ben Grieve	.30
8	Mark McGwire	3.00
9	Sammy Sosa	2.00
10	Alex Rodriguez	3.00
11	Troy Glaus	1.25
12	Eric Chavez	.60
13	Kerry Wood	.75
14	Barry Bonds	4.00
15	Vladimir Guerrero	1.50
16	Albert Belle	.50
17	Juan Gonzalez	.75
18	Roger Clemens	2.25
19	Ruben Mateo	.50
20	Cal Ripken Jr.	4.00

Four-Star

Four-Star inserts include cards numbered 1-10 from the base set and are seeded 1:12 packs. The cards feature dark metallic inks and refractive foil stamping on front. A Four-Star parallel is also randomly seeded and has gold metallic inks. Sequentially numbered to 49, it is inserted at the rate of one per 650 packs.

		NM/M
Complete Set (10):		30.00
Common Player:		1.00
Foils:		2X
1	Ken Griffey Jr.	4.00
2	Chipper Jones	3.00
3	Mike Piazza	4.00
4	Nomar Garciaparra	3.00
5	Derek Jeter	6.00
6	Frank Thomas	2.50
7	Ben Grieve	1.00
8	Mark McGwire	5.00
9	Sammy Sosa	3.00
10	Alex Rodriguez	5.00

Bright Futures

BRIGHT FUTURES

This 10-card set features top prospects with a brilliant future ahead of them. Each card features foil stamping and is sequentially numbered to 1,999. Cards have a "BF" prefix to the number. A metallized foil parallel version is also randomly seeded (1:2,702) and limited to 30 numbered sets.

		NM/M
Complete Set (10):		20.00
Common Player:		1.50
Production 1,999 Sets		
Foil (30 Each):		8X
1	Troy Glaus	3.00
2	Eric Chavez	2.00
3	Adrian Beltre	2.00

4	Michael Barrett	1.50
5	Fernando Seguignol	1.50
6	Alex Gonzalez	1.50
7	Matt Clement	1.50
8	Pat Burrell	6.00
9	Ruben Mateo	1.50
10	Alfonso Soriano	6.00

Galaxy

Galaxy

MARK McGWIRE

This 10-card set highlights the top players in baseball with foil stamping and limited to 1,999 numbered sets, inserted at the rate of one per 41 packs. Each card is numbered on the back with a "G" prefix. A Galaxy foil parallel version is randomly seeded (1:2,702) and sequentially numbered to 30 sets.

		NM/M
Complete Set (10):		25.00
Common Player:		1.00
Production 1,999 Sets		
Foil (30 Each):		8X
1	Mark McGwire	5.00
2	Roger Clemens	3.00
3	Nomar Garciaparra	4.00
4	Alex Rodriguez	5.00
5	Kerry Wood	1.50
6	Ben Grieve	1.00
7	Derek Jeter	6.00
8	Vladimir Guerrero	2.50
9	Ken Griffey Jr.	4.00
10	Sammy Sosa	3.00

Rookie Reprints

bob gibson

ST. LOUIS CARDINALS
PITCHER

Topps reprinted five Hall of Famers' rookie cards. The rookie reprints are inserted 1:65 packs and limited to 2,500 numbered sets.

		NM/M
Complete Set (5):		10.00
Common Player:		2.00
Production 2,500 Sets		
1	Frank Robinson	2.00
2	Ernie Banks	3.00
3	Yogi Berra	3.00
4	Bob Gibson	3.00
5	Tom Seaver	3.00

Rookie Reprints Autographs

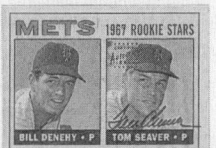

METS 1967 ROOKIE STARS
BILL DENEHY · P
TOM SEAVER · P

These foil stamped inserts feature the "Topps Certified Autograph Issue" stamp and are inserted 1:406 packs. The Ernie Banks autograph is inserted 1:812 packs.

		NM/M
Complete Set (5):		150.00
Common Player:		20.00
Inserted 1:406		
Banks Inserted 1:812		
1	Frank Robinson	25.00
2	Ernie Banks	70.00
3	Yogi Berra	35.00
4	Bob Gibson	20.00
5	Tom Seaver	65.00

1999 Topps Stars 'N Steel

Using Serilusion technology, each borderless card features a four-colored textured film laminate bonded to a sheet of strong 25-gauge metal. Each pack contains three cards, packaged in a stand-up tri-fold display unit, at an S.R.P. of $9.99. There are two parallels to the 44-card set, Gold and Domed Holographics. Golds are seeded 1:12 packs, Holographics are found every 24 packs.

	NM/M
Complete Set (44):	65.00
Common Player:	.50
Gold:	4X
Inserted 1:12	
Holographic Dome:	6X
Inserted 1:24	
Pack (3):	4.00
Wax Box (12):	40.00
1 Kerry Wood	1.00
2 Ben Grieve	.50
3 Chipper Jones	3.00
4 Alex Rodriguez	5.00
5 Mo Vaughn	.50
6 Bernie Williams	.50
7 Juan Gonzalez	1.00
8 Vinny Castilla	.50
9 Tony Gwynn	3.00
10 Manny Ramirez	2.00
11 Raul Mondesi	.50
12 Roger Clemens	3.50
13 Darin Erstad	.75
14 Barry Bonds	4.00
15 Cal Ripken Jr.	6.00
16 Barry Larkin	.50
17 Scott Rolen	1.00
18 Albert Belle	.50
19 Craig Biggio	.50
20 Tony Clark	.50
21 Mark McGwire	5.00
22 Andres Galarraga	.50
23 Kenny Lofton	.50
24 Pedro Martinez	2.00
25 Paul O'Neill	.50
26 Ken Griffey Jr.	4.00
27 Travis Lee	.75
28 Tim Salmon	.50
29 Frank Thomas	2.00
30 Larry Walker	.50
31 Moises Alou	.50
32 Vladimir Guerrero	2.00
33 Ivan Rodriguez	1.50
34 Derek Jeter	6.00
35 Greg Vaughn	.50
36 Gary Sheffield	1.00
37 Carlos Delgado	1.00
38 Greg Maddux	3.00
39 Sammy Sosa	3.00
40 Mike Piazza	4.00
41 Nomar Garciaparra	3.00
42 Dante Bichette	.50
43 Jeff Bagwell	2.00
44 Jim Thome	1.50

'N Steel Gold Domed Holographics

This parallel edition was inserted at a rate of one per box. Cards are basically the same as the regular-issue, except for the use of holographic foil highlights on front and the presence of a thick plastic dome which covers the front.

	NM/M
Complete Set (44):	600.00
Common Player:	6.00
Stars:	8X

1999 Topps TEK Pre-Production

The second edition of Topps TEK was introduced with this trio of star cards. The preview cards are virtually identical in format to the issued version, except for the use of "PP" prefixes to card numbers on back.

	NM/M
Complete Set (3):	5.00
Common Player:	1.00
PP1A Derek Jeter	4.00
PP2A Moises Alou	1.00
PP3A Tony Clark	1.00

1999 Topps TEK

Topps TEK baseball contains 45 players, with all cards printed on a transparent, 27-point stock. Each player is featured in two different versions (A & B), which are noted on the card back. The versions are differentiated by type of player uniform (home is version A and away uniforms are version B). Each version also has 30 different baseball-focused background patterns; as a result every player in the 45-card set has 60 total cards. There also is a Gold parallel set that has a gold design and all versions are paralleled. Each gold card is numbered to 10, with an insertion rate of 1:15 packs.

	NM/M
Complete Set (45):	30.00
Common Player:	.25
Common Gold	
(10 Each Variation):	2.00
Gold Stars:	10X
Pack (4):	3.00
Wax Box (20):	45.00
1 Ben Grieve	.25
2 Andres Galarraga	.25
3 Travis Lee	.35
4 Larry Walker	.25
5 Ken Griffey Jr.	2.50
6 Sammy Sosa	1.50
7 Mark McGwire	3.00
8 Roberto Alomar	.40
9 Wade Boggs	2.00
10 Troy Glaus	.75
11 Craig Biggio	.25
12 Kerry Wood	.50
13 Vladimir Guerrero	1.00
14 Albert Belle	.25
15 Mike Piazza	2.50
16 Chipper Jones	2.00
17 Randy Johnson	1.00
18 Adrian Beltre	.45
19 Barry Bonds	4.00
20 Jim Thome	.65
21 Greg Vaughn	.25
22 Scott Rolen	.65
23 Ivan Rodriguez	.75
24 Derek Jeter	4.00
25 Cal Ripken Jr.	4.00
26 Mark Grace	.25
27 Bernie Williams	.25
28 Darin Erstad	.75
29 Eric Chavez	.35
30 Tom Glavine	.50
31 Jeff Bagwell	1.00
32 Manny Ramirez	1.00
33 Tino Martinez	.25
34 Todd Helton	.75
35 Jason Kendall	.25
36 Pat Burrell RC	2.50
37 Tony Gwynn	2.00
38 Nomar Garciaparra	2.00
39 Frank Thomas	1.00
40 Orlando Hernandez	.25
41 Juan Gonzalez	.50
42 Alex Rodriguez	3.00
43 Greg Maddux	2.00
44 Mo Vaughn	.25
45 Roger Clemens	2.25
Version A Checklist Folder (Orange)	.05
Version B Checklist Folder (Green)	.05

Gold

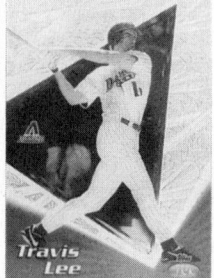

Each of the two player versions on each of the 30 background patterns was paralleled in a gold insert version. Cards share the same front and back designs and photos but feature gold graphics. Each card is serially numbered within an edition of just 10. Insertion rate is one per 15 packs.

	NM/M
Common Gold:	2.00
Gold Stars:	10X

Fantastek Phenoms

This 10-card set highlights top young prospects on a transparent plastic stock with silver and blue highlighting. These are inserted 1:18 packs.

	NM/M
Complete Set (10):	15.00
Common Player:	.75
Inserted 1:18	
F1 Eric Chavez	1.50
F2 Troy Glaus	4.00
F3 Pat Burrell	4.00
F4 Alex Gonzalez	.75
F5 Carlos Lee	1.00
F6 Ruben Mateo	.75
F7 Carlos Beltran	2.00
F8 Adrian Beltre	1.50
F9 Bruce Chen	.75
F10 Ryan Anderson	.75

Teknicians

This 10-card set focuses on baseball's top stars on a clear, plastic stock utilizing metallic blue, silver and red inks. These are inserted 1:18 packs.

	NM/M
Complete Set (10):	24.00
Common Player:	1.00
Inserted 1:18	
T1 Ken Griffey Jr.	3.00
T2 Mark McGwire	4.00
T3 Kerry Wood	1.00
T4 Ben Grieve	1.00
T5 Sammy Sosa	2.50
T6 Derek Jeter	6.00
T7 Alex Rodriguez	4.00
T8 Roger Clemens	2.50
T9 Nomar Garciaparra	2.50
T10 Vladimir Guerrero	1.50

2000 Topps Pre-Production

Though carrying a "PP" prefix as previous years' pre-production samples, this three-card issue was not distributed until July-August at the National and SportsFest conventions. The three-card cello packs contain cards which differ from the regular issued versions only in their numbers and the fact that they have white borders, rather than the pewter borders found on regular-issue cards.

	NM/M
Complete Set (3):	5.00
Common Player:	2.00
PP1 Brady Anderson	2.00
PP2 Jason Kendall	2.00
PP3 Ryan Klesko	2.00

2000 Topps

Released in two series the card fronts have a silver border with the Topps logo, player name and position stamped with gold foil. Card backs have complete year-by-year statistics along with a small photo in the upper right portion and the player's vital information. Subsets within the first series 239-card set include Draft Picks, Prospects, Magic Moments, Season Highlights and 20th Century's Best. The Topps MVP promotion is a parallel of 200 of the base cards, excluding subsets, with a special Topps MVP logo. 100 cards of each player was produced and if the featured player is named MVP for a week, collectors win a prize.

	NM/M
Complete Set (478):	50.00
Complete Series I Set (239):	25.00
Complete Series II Set (239):	25.00
Common Player:	.10
MVP Stars:	20-40X
Yng Stars & RC's:	10-20X
Production 100 Sets	
5 Versions for 236-240, 475-479	
Pack (11):	1.00
Wax Box (36):	30.00
1 Mark McGwire	1.00
2 Tony Gwynn	.75
3 Wade Boggs	.75
4 Cal Ripken Jr.	1.50
5 Matt Williams	.10
6 Jay Buhner	.10
7 Jeff Conine	.10
8 Todd Greene	.10
9 Mike Lieberthal	.10
10 Steve Avery	.10
11 Bret Saberhagen	.10
12 Magglio Ordonez	.20
13	
14 Brad Radke	.10
15 Derek Jeter	1.50
16 Javy Lopez	.10
17 Russ David	.10
18 Armando Benitez	.10
19 B.J. Surhoff	.10
20 Darryl Kile	.10
21 Mark Lewis	.10
22 Mike Williams	.10
23 Mark McLemore	.10
24 Sterling Hitchcock	.10
25 Darin Erstad	.20
26 Ricky Gutierrez	.10
27 John Jaha	.10
28 Homer Bush	.10
29 Darrin Fletcher	.10
30 Mark Grace	.10
31 Fred McGriff	.10
32 Omar Daal	.10
33 Eric Karros	.10
34 Orlando Cabrera	.15
35 J.T. Snow Jr.	.10
36 Luis Castillo	.10
37 Rey Ordonez	.10
38 Bob Abreu	.20
39 Warren Morris	.10
40 Juan Gonzalez	.20
41 Mike Lansing	.10
42 Chili Davis	.10
43 Dean Palmer	.10
44 Hank Aaron	1.00
45 Jeff Bagwell	.60
46 Jose Valentin	.10
47 Shannon Stewart	.10
48 Kent Bottenfield	.10
49 Jeff Shaw	.10
50 Sammy Sosa	.75
51 Randy Johnson	.60
52 Benny Agbayani	.10
53 Dante Bichette	.10
54 Pete Harnisch	.10
55 Frank Thomas	.60
56 Jorge Posada	.10
57 Todd Walker	.10
58 Juan Encarnacion	.15
59 Mike Sweeney	.10
60 Pedro Martinez	.60
61 Lee Stevens	.10
62 Brian Giles	.10
63 Chad Ogea	.10
64 Ivan Rodriguez	.50
65 Roger Cedeno	.10
66 David Justice	.10
67 Steve Trachsel	.10
68 Eli Marrero	.10
69 Dave Nilsson	.10
70 Ken Caminiti	.10
71 Tim Raines	.10
72 Brian Jordan	.10
73 Jeff Blauser	.10
74 Bernard Gilkey	.10
75 John Flaherty	.10
76 Brent Mayne	.10
77 Jose Vidro	.10
78 Jeff Fassero	.10
79 Bruce Aven	.10
80 John Olerud	.10
81 Pokey Reese	.10
82 Woody Williams	.10
83 Ed Sprague	.10
84 Joe Girardi	.10
85 Barry Larkin	.10
86 Mike Caruso	.10
87 Bobby Higginson	.10
88 Roberto Kelly	.10
89 Edgar Martinez	.10
90 Mark Kotsay	.10
91 Paul Sorrento	.10
92 Eric Young	.10
93 Carlos Delgado	.40
94 Troy Glaus	.50
95 Ben Grieve	.10
96 Jose Lima	.10
97 Garret Anderson	.10
98 Luis Gonzalez	.10
99 Carl Pavano	.10
100 Alex Rodriguez	1.25
101 Preston Wilson	.10
102 Ron Gant	.10
103 Harold Baines	.10
104 Rickey Henderson	.60
105 Gary Sheffield	.40
106 Mickey Morandini	.10
107 Jim Edmonds	.10
108 Kris Benson	.10
109 Adrian Beltre	.20
110 Alex Fernandez	.10
111 Dan Wilson	.10
112 Mark Clark	.10
113 Greg Vaughn	.10
114 Neifi Perez	.10
115 Paul O'Neill	.10
116 Jermaine Dye	.10
117 Todd Jones	.10
118 Terry Steinbach	.10
119 Greg Norton	.10
120 Curt Schilling	.25
121 Todd Zeile	.10
122 Edgardo Alfonzo	.10
123 Ryan Jackson	.10
124 Stan Javier	.10
125 John Smoltz	.10
126 Bob Wickman	.10
127 Richard Hidalgo	.10
128 Chuck Finley	.10
129 Billy Wagner	.10
130 Todd Hundley	.10
131 Dwight Gooden	.10
132 Russ Ortiz	.10
133 Mike Lowell	.10
134 Reggie Sanders	.10
135 John Valentin	.10
136 Brad Ausmus	.10
137 Chad Kreuter	.10
138 David Cone	.10
139 Brook Fordyce	.10
140 Roberto Alomar	.25
141 Charles Nagy	.10
142 Brian Hunter	.10
143 Mike Mussina	.30
144 Robin Ventura	.10
145 Kevin Brown	.10
146 Pat Hentgen	.10
147 Ryan Klesko	.10
148 Derek Bell	.10
149 Andy Sheets	.10
150 Larry Walker	.10
151 Scott Williamson	.10
152 Jose Offerman	.10
153 Doug Mientkiewicz	.10
154 John Snyder RC	.10
155 Sandy Alomar	.10
156 Joe Nathan	.10
157 Lance Johnson	.10
158 Odalis Perez	.10
159 Hideo Nomo	.25
160 Steve Finley	.10
161 Dave Martinez	.10
162 Matt Walbeck	.10
163 Bill Spiers	.10
164 Fernando Tatis	.10
165 Kenny Lofton	.10
166 Paul Byrd	.10
167 Aaron Sele	.10
168 Eddie Taubensee	.10
169 Reggie Jefferson	.10
170 Roger Clemens	.85
171 Francisco Cordova	.10
172 Mike Bordick	.10
173 Wally Joyner	.10
174 Marvin Benard	.10
175 Jason Kendall	.10
176 Mike Stanley	.10
177 Chad Allen	.10
178 Carlos Beltran	.25
179 Deivi Cruz	.10
180 Chipper Jones	.75
181 Vladimir Guerrero	.60
182 Dave Burba	.10
183 Tom Goodwin	.10
184 Brian Daubach	.10
185 Jay Bell	.10
186 Roy Halladay	.25
187 Miguel Tejada	.25
188 Armando Rios	.10
189 Fernando Vina	.10
190 Eric Davis	.10
191 Henry Rodriguez	.10
192 Joe McEwing	.10
193 Jeff Kent	.10
194 Mike Jackson	.10
195 Mike Morgan	.10
196 Jeff Montgomery	.10
197 Jeff Zimmerman	.10
198 Tony Fernandez	.10
199 Jason Giambi	.40
200 Jose Canseco	.40
201 Alex Gonzalez	.10
202 Jack Cust, Mike Colangelo, Dee Brown	.10
203 Felipe Lopez, Alfonso Soriano, Pablo Ozuna	.75
204 Erubiel Durazo, Pat Burrell, Nick Johnson	.25
205 John Sneed RC, Kip Wells, Matt Blank	.10
206 Josh Kalinowski RC, Michael Tejera RC, Chris Mears	.10
207 Roosevelt Brown, Corey Patterson, Lance Berkman	.25
208 Kit Pellow, Kevin Barker, Russ Branyan	.10
209 B.J. Garbe RC, Larry Bigbie RC	1.00
210 Eric Munson, Bobby Bradley RC	.25
211 Josh Girdley, Kyle Snyder	.10
212 Chance Caple RC, Jason Jennings	.25
213 Ryan Christiansen RC, Brett Myers RC	1.50
214 Jason Stumm RC, Rob Purvis RC	.25
215 David Walling, Mike Paradis	.10
216 Omar Ortiz, Jay Gehrke	.10
217 David Cone (Season Highlights)	.10
218 Jose Jimenez (Season Highlights)	.10
219 Chris Singleton (Season Highlights)	.10
220 Fernando Tatis (Season Highlights)	.10
221 Todd Helton (Season Highlights)	.20
222 Kevin Millwood (Post-Season Highlights)	.15
223 Todd Pratt (Post-Season Highlights)	.10
224 Orlando Hernandez (Post-Season Highlights)	.20
225 (Post-Season Highlights)	.10

226	(Post-Season Highlights)	.10
227	Bernie Williams	
	(Post-Season Highlights)	.25
228	Mariano Rivera	
	(Post-Season Highlights)	.20
229	Tony Gwynn	
	(20th Century's Best)	.50
230	Wade Boggs	
	(20th Century's Best)	.25
231	Tim Raines	
	(20th Century's Best)	.10
232	Mark McGwire	
	(20th Century's Best)	2.00
233	Rickey Henderson	
	(20th Century's Best)	.25
234	Rickey Henderson	
	(20th Century's Best)	.25
235	Roger Clemens	
	(20th Century's Best)	1.50
236	Mark McGwire	
	(Magic Moments)	2.00
237	Hank Aaron	
	(Magic Moments)	2.00
238	Cal Ripken Jr.	
	(Magic Moments)	3.00
239	Wade Boggs	
	(Magic Moments)	.75
240	Tony Gwynn	
	(Magic Moments)	1.00
	Series 1 checklist (1-201)	.05
	Series 1 checklist	
	(202-240, inserts)	.05
241	Tom Glavine	.25
242	David Wells	.10
243	Kevin Appier	.10
244	Troy Percival	.10
245	Ray Lankford	.10
246	Marquis Grissom	.10
247	Randy Winn	.10
248	Miguel Batista	.10
249	Darren Dreifort	.10
250	Barry Bonds	1.50
251	Harold Baines	.10
252	Cliff Floyd	.10
253	Freddy Garcia	.10
254	Kenny Rogers	.10
255	Ben Davis	.10
256	Charles Johnson	.10
257	John Burkett	.10
258	Desi Relaford	.10
259	Al Martin	.10
260	Andy Pettitte	.20
261	Carlos Lee	.10
262	Matt Lawton	.10
263	Andy Fox	.10
264	Chan Ho Park	.10
265	Billy Koch	.10
266	Dave Roberts	.10
267	Carl Everett	.10
268	Orel Hershiser	.10
269	Trot Nixon	.10
270	Rusty Greer	.10
271	Will Clark	.10
272	Quilvio Veras	.10
273	Rico Brogna	.10
274	Devon White	.10
275	Tim Hudson	.25
276	Mike Hampton	.10
277	Miguel Cairo	.10
278	Darren Oliver	.10
279	Jeff Cirillo	.10
280	Al Leiter	.10
281	Brant Brown	.10
282	Carlos Febles	.10
283	Pedro Astacio	.10
284	Juan Guzman	.10
285	Orlando Hernandez	.20
286	Paul Konerko	.15
287	Tony Clark	.10
288	Aaron Boone	.10
289	Ismael Valdes	.10
290	Moises Alou	.10
291	Kevin Tapani	.10
292	John Franco	.10
293	Todd Zeile	.10
294	Jason Schmidt	.15
295	Johnny Damon	.25
296	Scott Brosius	.10
297	Travis Fryman	.10
298	Jose Vizcaino	.10
299	Eric Chavez	.20
300	Mike Piazza	1.00
301	Matt Clement	.10
302	Cristian Guzman	.10
303	Darryl Strawberry	.10
304	Jeff Abbott	.10
305	Brett Tomko	.10
306	Mike Lansing	.10
307	Eric Owens	.10
308	Livan Hernandez	.10
309	Rondell White	.10
310	Todd Stottlemyre	.10
311	Chris Carpenter	.10
312	Ken Hill	.10
313	Mark Loretta	.10
314	John Rocker	.10
315	Richie Sexson	.25
316	Ruben Mateo	.10
317	Joe Randa	.10
318	Mike Sirotka	.10
319	Jose Rosado	.10
320	Matt Mantei	.10
321	Kevin Millwood	.10
322	Gary DiSarcina	.10
323	Dustin Hermanson	.10
324	Mike Stanton	.10
325	Kirk Rueter	.10
326	Damian Miller	.10

327	Doug Glanville	.10
328	Scott Rolen	.50
329	Ray Durham	.10
330	Butch Huskey	.10
331	Mariano Rivera	.20
332	Darren Lewis	.10
333	Ramiro Mendoza	.10
334	Mark Grudzielanek	.10
335	Mike Cameron	.10
336	Kelvim Escobar	.10
337	Bret Boone	.10
338	Mo Vaughn	.10
339	Craig Biggio	.10
340	Michael Barrett	.10
341	Marlon Anderson	.10
342	Bobby Jones	.10
343	John Halama	.10
344	Todd Ritchie	.10
345	Chuck Knoblauch	.10
346	Rick Reed	.10
347	Kelly Stinnett	.10
348	Tim Salmon	.10
349	A.J. Hinch	.10
350	Jose Cruz Jr.	.10
351	Roberto Hernandez	.10
352	Edgar Renteria	.10
353	Jose Hernandez	.10
354	Brad Fullmer	.10
355	Trevor Hoffman	.10
356	Troy O'Leary	.10
357	Justin Thompson	.10
358	Kevin Young	.10
359	Hideki Irabu	.10
360	Jim Thome	.50
361	Todd Dunwoody	.10
362	Octavio Dotel	.10
363	Omar Vizquel	.10
364	Raul Mondesi	.10
365	Shane Reynolds	.10
366	Bartolo Colon	.10
367	Chris Widger	.10
368	Gabe Kapler	.10
369	Bill Simas	.10
370	Tino Martinez	.10
371	John Thomson	.10
372	Delino DeShields	.10
373	Carlos Perez	.10
374	Eddie Perez	.10
375	Jeromy Burnitz	.10
376	Jimmy Haynes	.10
377	Travis Lee	.10
378	Darryl Hamilton	.10
379	Jamie Moyer	.10
380	Alex Gonzalez	.10
381	John Wetteland	.10
382	Vinny Castilla	.10
383	Jeff Suppan	.10
384	Chad Curtis	.10
385	Robb Nen	.10
386	Wilson Alvarez	.10
387	Andres Galarraga	.10
388	Mike Remlinger	.10
389	Geoff Jenkins	.10
390	Matt Stairs	.10
391	Bill Mueller	.10
392	Mike Lowell	.10
393	Andy Ashby	.10
394	Ruben Rivera	.10
395	Todd Helton	.50
396	Bernie Williams	.10
397	Royce Clayton	.10
398	Manny Ramirez	.60
399	Kerry Wood	.25
400	Ken Griffey Jr.	.75
401	Enrique Wilson	.10
402	Joey Hamilton	.10
403	Shawn Estes	.10
404	Ugueth Urbina	.10
405	Albert Belle	.10
406	Rick Helling	.10
407	Steve Parris	.10
408	Eric Milton	.10
409	Dave Mlicki	.10
410	Shawn Green	.25
411	Jaret Wright	.10
412	Tony Womack	.10
413	Vernon Wells	.15
414	Ron Belliard	.10
415	Ellis Burks	.10
416	Scott Erickson	.10
417	Rafael Palmeiro	.35
418	Damion Easley	.10
419	Jamey Wright	.10
420	Corey Koskie	.10
421	Bobby Howry	.10
422	Ricky Ledee	.10
423	Dmitri Young	.10
424	Sidney Ponson	.10
425	Greg Maddux	.75
426	Jose Guillen	.10
427	Jon Lieber	.10
428	Andy Benes	.10
429	Randy Velarde	.10
430	Sean Casey	.20
431	Torii Hunter	.20
432	Ryan Rupe	.10
433	David Segui	.10
434	Rich Aurilia	.10
435	Nomar Garciaparra	.75
436	Denny Neagle	.10
437	Ron Coomer	.10
438	Chris Singleton	.10
439	Tony Batista	.10
440	Andruw Jones	.60
441	Adam Piatt, Aubrey Huff, Sean Burroughs (Prospects)	.20

442	Rafael Furcal, Jason Dallero, Travis Dawkins (Prospects)	.20
443	Wilton Veras, Joe Crede, Mike Lamb **RC** (Prospects)	.10
444	Julio Zuleta **RC**, Dernell Stenson, Jorge Toca (Prospects)	.20
445	Tim Raines Jr., Gary Mathews Jr., Garry Maddox Jr. **RC** (Prospects)	.20
446	Matt Riley, Mark Mulder, C.C. Sabathia (Prospects)	.25
447	Scott Downs **RC**, Chris George, Matt Belisle (Prospects)	.10
448	Doug Mirabelli, Ben Petrick, Jayson Werth (Prospects)	.10
449	Josh Hamilton, Corey Myers **RC** (Draft Picks)	.50
450	Ben Christensen **RC**, Brett Myers (Draft Picks)	.20
451	Barry Zito **RC**, Ben Sheets **RC** (Draft Picks)	2.00
452	Ty Howington **RC**, Kurt Ainsworth **RC** (Draft Picks)	.25
453	Rick Asadoorian **RC**, Vince Faison **RC** (Draft Picks)	.10
454	Keith Reed **RC**, Jeff Heaverlo **RC** (Draft Picks)	.20
455	Mike MacDougal **RC**, Jay Gehrke (Draft Picks)	.25
456	Mark McGwire (Season Highlights)	.75
457	Cal Ripken Jr. (Season Highlights)	1.00
458	Wade Boggs (Season Highlights)	.25
459	Tony Gwynn (Season Highlights)	.50
460	Jesse Orosco (Season Highlights)	.10
461	Nomar Garciaparra, Larry Walker (League Leaders)	.50
462	Mark McGwire, Ken Griffey Jr. (League Leaders)	.50
463	Mark McGwire, Manny Ramirez (League Leaders)	.50
464	Randy Johnson, Pedro Martinez (League Leaders)	.25
465	Randy Johnson, Pedro Martinez (League Leaders)	.25
466	Luis Gonzalez, Derek Jeter (League Leaders)	.50
467	Manny Ramirez, Larry Walker (League Leaders)	.25
468	Tony Gwynn (20th Century's Best)	.75
469	Mark McGwire (20th Century's Best)	2.00
470	Frank Thomas (20th Century's Best)	.50
471	Harold Baines (20th Century's Best)	.10
472	Roger Clemens (20th Century's Best)	.75
473	John Franco (20th Century's Best)	.10
474	John Franco (20th Century's Best)	.10
475	Ken Griffey Jr. (Magic Moments)	1.50
476	Barry Bonds (Magic Moments)	2.00
477	Sammy Sosa (Magic Moments)	1.25
478	Derek Jeter (Magic Moments)	2.50
479	Alex Rodriguez (Magic Moments)	2.00

Hank Aaron Reprints

This 23-card set reprints all of Aaron's 23-regular issued Topps cards and are seeded 1:18 packs.

Hank Aaron Chrome Reprints

This 23-card set reprints Aaron's regular issued Topps cards utilizing Chromium technology. Each card has a commemorative logo and are seeded 1:72 packs. A Refractor parallel version is also randomly inserted 1:288 packs and have Refractor printed underneath the number on the card back.

	NM/M
Complete Set (23):	90.00
Common Aaron:	5.00
Inserted 1:72	
Refractors:	3X
Inserted 1:288	
1 Hank Aaron/1954	10.00
2 Hank Aaron/1955	5.00
3 Hank Aaron/1956	5.00
4 Hank Aaron/1957	5.00
5 Hank Aaron/1958	5.00
6 Hank Aaron/1959	5.00
7 Hank Aaron/1960	5.00
8 Hank Aaron/1961	5.00
9 Hank Aaron/1962	5.00
10 Hank Aaron/1963	5.00
11 Hank Aaron/1964	5.00
12 Hank Aaron/1965	5.00
13 Hank Aaron/1966	5.00
14 Hank Aaron/1967	5.00
15 Hank Aaron/1968	5.00
16 Hank Aaron/1969	5.00
17 Hank Aaron/1970	5.00
18 Hank Aaron/1971	5.00
19 Hank Aaron/1972	5.00
20 Hank Aaron/1973	5.00
21 Hank Aaron/1974	5.00
22 Hank Aaron/1975	5.00
23 Hank Aaron/1976	5.00

All-Star Rookie Team

	NM/M
Complete Set (10):	10.00
Common Player:	.25
Inserted 1:36	

	NM/M
Complete Set (23):	60.00
Common Aaron:	3.00
Inserted 1:18	
Autographed:	300.00
"Limited Edition" 4,000 Sets:	1X
1 Hank Aaron/1954	8.00
2 Hank Aaron/1955	3.00
3 Hank Aaron/1956	3.00
4 Hank Aaron/1957	3.00
5 Hank Aaron/1958	3.00
6 Hank Aaron/1959	3.00
7 Hank Aaron/1960	3.00
8 Hank Aaron/1961	3.00
9 Hank Aaron/1962	3.00
10 Hank Aaron/1963	3.00
11 Hank Aaron/1964	3.00
12 Hank Aaron/1965	3.00
13 Hank Aaron/1966	3.00
14 Hank Aaron/1967	3.00
15 Hank Aaron/1968	3.00
16 Hank Aaron/1969	3.00
17 Hank Aaron/1970	3.00
18 Hank Aaron/1971	3.00
19 Hank Aaron/1972	3.00
20 Hank Aaron/1973	3.00
21 Hank Aaron/1974	3.00
22 Hank Aaron/1975	3.00
23 Hank Aaron/1976	3.00

Autographs

Inserted exclusively in Series 1 and 2 hobby packs, each card features the "Topps Certified Autograph Issue" stamp and is autographed on the card front.

	NM/M
Common Player:	8.00
Group A 1:7,589	
Group B 1:4,553	
Group C 1:518	
Group D 1:911	
Group E 1:1,138	
1 Alex Rodriguez (A)	100.00
2 Tony Gwynn (A)	50.00
3 Vinny Castilla (B)	15.00
4 Sean Casey (B)	15.00
5 Shawn Green (C)	25.00
6 Rey Ordonez (C)	8.00
7 Matt Lawton (C)	15.00
8 Tony Womack (C)	8.00
9 Gabe Kapler (D)	10.00
10 Pat Burrell (D)	20.00
11 Preston Wilson (D)	15.00
12 Troy Glaus (D)	30.00

13	Carlos Beltran (D)	40.00
14	Josh Girdley (E)	8.00
15	B.J. Garbe (E)	8.00
16	Derek Jeter (A)	125.00
17	Cal Ripken Jr. (A)	150.00
18	Ivan Rodriguez (B)	40.00
19	Rafael Palmeiro (B)	40.00
20	Vladimir Guerrero (E)	45.00
21	Raul Mondesi (C)	15.00
22	Scott Rolen (C)	40.00
23	Billy Wagner (C)	10.00
24	Fernando Tatis (C)	8.00
25	Ruben Mateo (D)	8.00
26	Carlos Febles (D)	8.00
27	Mike Sweeney (E)	10.00
28	Alex Gonzalez (D)	10.00
29	Miguel Tejada (D)	40.00
30	Josh Hamilton (E)	50.00

All-Topps Team

This insert set spotlights 10 National League (Series 1) and 10 A.L. (Series 2) players who are deemed the best at their respective position. On front, a Hall of Fame style plaque design features gold-foil highlights. Backs offer stat comparisons to contemporary players and Hall of Fame greats at their position. These were seeded 1:12 packs. Cards are numbered with an "AT" prefix.

	NM/M
Complete Set (20):	15.00
Common Player:	.25
Inserted 1:12	
"Limited Edition" 4,000 Sets:	1X
1 Greg Maddux	1.50
2 Mike Piazza	1.50
3 Mark McGwire	2.50
4 Craig Biggio	.40
5 Chipper Jones	1.50
6 Barry Larkin	.40
7 Barry Bonds	2.50
8 Andruw Jones	.75
9 Sammy Sosa	1.50
10 Larry Walker	.40
11 Pedro Martinez	1.00
12 Ivan Rodriguez	.50
13 Rafael Palmeiro	.50
14 Roberto Alomar	.50
15 Cal Ripken Jr.	3.00
16 Derek Jeter	3.00
17 Albert Belle	.25
18 Ken Griffey Jr.	1.50
19 Manny Ramirez	.75
20 Jose Canseco	.50

Century Best

	NM/M
Common Player:	2.00
Ser. 1 1:869 H	
Ser. 2 1:362	
CB1 Tony Gwynn/339	8.00
CB2 Wade Boggs/578	4.00
CB3 Lance Johnson/117	2.00
CB4 Mark McGwire/522	20.00
CB5 Rickey Henderson/1,334	4.00
CB6 Rickey Henderson/2,103	4.00
CB7 Roger Clemens/247	12.00
CB8 Tony Gwynn/3,067	6.00
CB9 Mark McGwire/587	20.00
CB10 Frank Thomas/440	6.00
CB11 Harold Baines/1,583	2.00
CB12 Roger Clemens/3,316	8.00
CB13 John Franco/264	2.00
CB14 John Franco/416	2.00

Combos

	NM/M
Complete Set (10):	15.00
Common Card:	1.00
Inserted 1:18	
"Limited Edition" 4,000 Sets:	1X
1 Roberto Alomar, Manny Ramirez, Kenny Lofton, Jim Thome	1.00
2 Tom Glavine, Greg Maddux, John Smoltz	1.50
3 Derek Jeter, Bernie Williams, Tino Martinez	3.00
4 Ivan Rodriguez, Mike Piazza	1.50
5 Nomar Garciaparra, Alex Rodriguez, Derek Jeter	3.00
6 Sammy Sosa, Mark McGwire	3.00
7 Pedro Martinez, Randy Johnson	1.00
8 Barry Bonds, Ken Griffey Jr.	2.50
9 Chipper Jones, Ivan Rodriguez	1.50
10 Cal Ripken Jr., Tony Gwynn, Wade Boggs	

Hands of Gold

This seven-card insert set highlights players who have won at least five gold gloves. Each card is foil stamped and die-cut and is seeded 1:18 packs.

	NM/M
Complete Set (7):	5.00

Hands of Gold

Common Player:		.25
Inserted 1:18		
"Limited Edition" 4,000 Sets:		1X
1	Barry Bonds	2.50
2	Ivan Rodriguez	.75
3	Ken Griffey Jr.	1.50
4	Roberto Alomar	.75
5	Tony Gwynn	1.00
6	Omar Vizquel	.25
7	Greg Maddux	1.50

Mark McGwire 1985 Rookie Reprint

This insert pays tribute to baseball's reigning single season home run record holder by reprinting his '85 Topps Rookie card. Card fronts have a commemorative gold stamp and is seeded 1:36 packs.

	NM/M
Complete Set (1):	6.00
Mark McGwire	6.00

Own the Game

		NM/M
Complete Set (30):		15.00
Common Player:		.15
Inserted 1:12		
"Limited Edition" 4,000 Sets:		1X
1	Derek Jeter	2.00
2	B.J. Surhoff	.15
3	Luis Gonzalez	.25
4	Manny Ramirez	.50
5	Rafael Palmeiro	.40
6	Mark McGwire	1.50
7	Mark McGwire	1.50
8	Sammy Sosa	1.00
9	Ken Griffey Jr.	1.00
10	Larry Walker	.25
11	Nomar Garciaparra	1.50
12	Derek Jeter	2.00
13	Larry Walker	.25
14	Mark McGwire	1.50
15	Manny Ramirez	.50
16	Pedro Martinez	.75
17	Randy Johnson	.25
18	Kevin Millwood	.25
19	Pedro Martinez	.75
20	Randy Johnson	.75
21	Kevin Brown	.25
22	Chipper Jones	1.00
23	Ivan Rodriguez	.50
24	Mariano Rivera	.25
25	Scott Williamson	.15
26	Carlos Beltran	.25
27	Randy Johnson	.75
28	Pedro Martinez	.75
29	Sammy Sosa	1.00
30	Manny Ramirez	.50

Perennial All-Stars

This 10-card set highlights 10 superstars who have consistently achieved All-Star recognition. Card fronts feature a silver holographic foil throughout, while card backs have the featured player's career All-Star statistics. These were seeded 1:18 packs. Cards are numbered with a "PA" prefix.

		NM/M
Complete Set (10):		10.00
Common Player:		.50
Inserted 1:18		
"Limited Edition" 4,000 Sets:		1X
1	Ken Griffey Jr.	1.00
2	Derek Jeter	2.00
3	Sammy Sosa	1.00
4	Cal Ripken Jr.	2.00
5	Mike Piazza	1.00
6	Nomar Garciaparra	1.50
7	Jeff Bagwell	.50
8	Barry Bonds	1.50
9	Alex Rodriguez	1.50
10	Mark McGwire	1.50

Power Players

This 20-card set highlights the top power hitters in the game and are printed on a holographic silver foil front. They are numbered with a "P" prefix and are seeded 1:8 packs.

		NM/M
Complete Set (20):		10.00
Common Player:		.25
Inserted 1:8		
"Limited Edition" 4,000 Sets:		1X
1	Juan Gonzalez	.50
2	Ken Griffey Jr.	1.00
3	Mark McGwire	1.50
4	Nomar Garciaparra	1.50
5	Barry Bonds	1.50
6	Mo Vaughn	.25
7	Larry Walker	.25
8	Alex Rodriguez	1.50
9	Jose Canseco	.25
10	Jeff Bagwell	.50
11	Manny Ramirez	.50
12	Albert Belle	.25
13	Frank Thomas	.50
14	Mike Piazza	1.00
15	Chipper Jones	1.00
16	Sammy Sosa	1.00
17	Vladimir Guerrero	.50
18	Scott Rolen	.50
19	Raul Mondesi	.25
20	Derek Jeter	2.00

Stadium Relics

Inserted exclusively in Home-Team Advantage packs, this five-card set features historical baseball stadiums and the autograph of the players who made them sacred. Besides the player autograph, the cards also have a piece of base from the featured stadium embedded into each card. These were seeded 1:165 HTA packs and are numbered with a "SR" prefix.

		NM/M
Common Player:		40.00
Inserted 1:165 HTA		
1	Don Mattingly	150.00
2	Carl Yastrzemski	100.00
3	Ernie Banks	75.00
4	Johnny Bench	75.00
5	Willie Mays	150.00
6	Mike Schmidt	100.00
7	Lou Brock	50.00
8	Al Kaline	75.00
9	Paul Molitor	60.00
10	Eddie Matthews	75.00

2000 Topps Traded and Rookies

		NM/M
Complete Set (135):		25.00
Common Player:		.10
Unopened Set (136):		50.00
1	Mike MacDougal	.20
2	Andy Tracy RC	.20
3	Brandon Phillips RC	1.00
4	Brandon Inge RC	.75
5	Robbie Morrison RC	.25
6	Josh Pressley RC	.20
7	Todd Moser RC	.25
8	Rob Purvis RC	.25
9	Chance Caple RC	.75
10	Ben Sheets RC	.75
11	Russ Jacobson RC	.10
12	Brian Cole RC	.10
13	Brad Baker RC	.25
14	Alex Cintron RC	.40
15	Lyle Overbay RC	.75
16	Mike Edwards RC	.20
17	Sean McGowan RC	.25
18	Jose Molina RC	.20
19	Marcos Castillo RC	.20
20	Josue Espada RC	.20
21	Alex Gordon RC	.10
22	Rob Pugmire RC	.10
23	Jason Stumm RC	.25
24	Ty Howington RC	.40
25	Brett Myers RC	.50
26	Maicer Izturis RC	.10
27	John McDonald RC	.10
28	Wilfredo Rodriguez RC	.25
29	Carlos Zambrano RC	3.00
30	Alejandro Diaz RC	.20
31	Geraldo Guzman RC	.20
32	J.R. House RC	.50
33	Elvin Nina RC	.50
34	Juan Pierre RC	.50
35	Ben Johnson RC	.50
36	Jeff Bailey RC	.20
37	Miguel Olivo RC	.20
38	Francisco Rodriguez RC	2.00
39	Tony Pena Jr. RC	.25
40	Miguel Cabrera RC	10.00
41	Asdrubal Oropeza RC	.10
42	Junior Zamora RC	.10
43	Jovanny Cedeno RC	.25
44	John Sneed RC	.10
45	Josh Kalinowski RC	.10
46	Mike Young RC	3.00
47	Rico Washington RC	.10
48	Chad Durbin RC	.40
49	Junior Brignac RC	.25
50	Carlos Hernandez RC	.40
51	Cesar Izturis RC	.50
52	Oscar Salazar RC	.25
53	Pat Strange RC	.25
54	Rick Asadoorian RC	.15
55	Keith Reed RC	.25
56	Leo Estrella RC	.10
57	Wascar Serrano RC	.10
58	Richard Gomez RC	.25
59	Ramon Santiago RC	.25
60	Jovanny Sosa RC	.25
61	Aaron Rowand RC	.25
62	Junior Guerrero RC	.25
63	Luis Terrero RC	.25
64	Brian Sanches RC	.10
65	Scott Sobkowiak RC	.25
66	Gary Majewski RC	.25
67	Barry Zito RC	.75
68	Ryan Christianson RC	.40
69	Cristian Guerrero RC	.40
70	Tomas de la Rosa RC	.10
71	Andrew Beinbrink RC	.10
72	Ryan Knox RC	.10
73	Alex Graman RC	.10
74	Juan Guzman RC	.10
75	Ruben Salazar RC	.40
76	Luis Matos RC	.40
77	Tony Mota RC	.10
78	Doug Davis RC	.50
79	Ben Christensen RC	.25
80	Mike Lamb RC	.10
81	Adrian Gonzalez RC (Draft Picks)	2.00
82	Mike Stodolka RC (Draft Picks)	.25
83	Adam Johnson RC (Draft Picks)	.25
84	Matt Wheatland RC (Draft Picks)	.25
85	Corey Smith RC (Draft Picks)	.50
86	Rocco Baldelli RC (Draft Picks)	1.00
87	Keith Bucktrot RC (Draft Picks)	.25
88	Adam Wainwright RC (Draft Picks)	1.50
89	Scott Thorman RC (Draft Picks)	.50
90	Tripper Johnson RC (Draft Picks)	.50
91	Jim Edmonds	.25
92	Masato Yoshii	.10
93	Adam Kennedy	.10
94	Darryl Kile	.10
95	Mark McLemore	.10
96	Ricky Gutierrez	.10
97	Juan Gonzalez	.40
98	Melvin Mora	.10
99	Dante Bichette	.10
100	Lee Stevens	.10
101	Roger Cedeno	.10
102	John Olerud	.25
103	Eric Young	.10
104	Mickey Morandini	.10
105	Travis Lee	.10
106	Greg Vaughn	.10
107	Todd Zeile	.10
108	Chuck Finley	.10
109	Ismael Valdes	.10
110	Ron Henika	.10
111	Pat Hentgen	.10
112	Ryan Klesko	.10
113	Derek Bell	.10
114	Hideo Nomo	.40
115	Aaron Sele	.10
116	Fernando Vina	.10
117	Wally Joyner	.10
118	Brian Hunter	.10
119	Joe Girardi	.10
120	Omar Daal	.10
121	Brook Fordyce	.10
122	Jose Valentin	.10
123	Curt Schilling	.40
124	B.J. Surhoff	.10
125	Henry Rodriguez	.10
126	Mike Bordick	.10
127	David Justice	.25
128	Charles Johnson	.10
129	Will Clark	.25
130	Dwight Gooden	.10
131	David Segui	.10
132	Denny Neagle	.10
133	Andy Ashby	.10
134	Bruce Chen	.10
135	Jason Bere	.10

Supers

Each box of Topps foil packs includes one upwrapped box-topper card in an oversize (3-1/2" x 5") format. Except for its size, the super version differs from the same players' issued cards only in the numbering on back which designates each card "x of 8."

		NM/M
Complete Set (16):		35.00
Common Player:		1.00
Inserted 1:box		
1	Mark McGwire	5.00
2	Hank Aaron	5.00
3	Derek Jeter	3.00
4	Sammy Sosa	3.00
5	Alex Rodriguez	3.00
6	Chipper Jones	4.00
7	Cal Ripken Jr.	4.00
8	Pedro Martinez	2.00
1	Barry Bonds	1.50
2	Orlando Hernandez	1.00
3	Mike Piazza	3.00
4	Manny Ramirez	1.50
5	Ken Griffey Jr.	4.00
6	Rafael Palmeiro	1.00
7	Greg Maddux	2.50
8	Nomar Garciaparra	3.00

21st Century Topps

Printed on a silver holographic foil front, this 10-card set highlights young players who are poised to thrive into the next millennium. These are seeded 1:18 packs and are numbered on the card backs with a "C" prefix.

		NM/M
Complete Set (10):		5.00
Common Player:		.25
Inserted 1:18		
"Limited Edition" 4,000 Sets:		1X
1	Ben Grieve	.25
2	Alex Gonzalez	.25
3	Derek Jeter	2.00
4	Sean Casey	.25
5	Nomar Garciaparra	1.50
6	Alex Rodriguez	1.50
7	Scott Rolen	.50
8	Andruw Jones	.50
9	Vladimir Guerrero	.50
10	Todd Helton	.50

Autographs

		NM/M
Common Player:		4.00
Inserted 1:Set		
1	Mike MacDougal	4.00
2	Andy Tracy	8.00
3	Brandon Phillips	50.00
4	Brandon Inge	15.00
5	Robbie Morrison	4.00
6	Josh Pressley	4.00
7	Todd Moser	4.00
8	Rob Purvis	4.00
9	Chance Caple	4.00
10	Ben Sheets	40.00
11	Russ Jacobson	4.00
12	Brian Cole	4.00
13	Brad Baker	4.00
14	Alex Cintron	4.00
15	Lyle Overbay	20.00
16	Mike Edwards	4.00
17	Sean McGowan	4.00
18	Jose Molina	4.00
19	Marcos Castillo	4.00
20	Josue Espada	4.00
21	Alex Gordon	4.00
22	Rob Pugmire	4.00
23	Jason Stumm	4.00
24	Ty Howington	4.00
25	Brett Myers	20.00
26	Maicer Izturis	8.00
27	John McDonald	4.00
28	Wilfredo Rodriguez	4.00
29	Carlos Zambrano	150.00
30	Alejandro Diaz	4.00
31	Geraldo Guzman	4.00
32	J.R. House	8.00
33	Elvin Nina	4.00
34	Juan Pierre	25.00
35	Ben Johnson	10.00
36	Jeff Bailey	4.00
37	Miguel Olivo	10.00
38	Francisco Rodriguez	50.00
39	Tony Pena Jr.	4.00
40	Miguel Cabrera	450.00
41	Asdrubal Oropeza	4.00
42	Junior Zamora	4.00
43	Jovanny Cedeno	4.00
44	John Sneed	4.00
45	Josh Kalinowski	8.00
46	Mike Young	100.00
47	Rico Washington	4.00
48	Chad Durbin	4.00
49	Junior Brignac	4.00
50	Carlos Hernandez	8.00
51	Cesar Izturis	10.00
52	Oscar Salazar	4.00
53	Pat Strange	4.00
54	Rick Asadoorian	4.00
55	Keith Reed	4.00
56	Leo Estrella	4.00
57	Wascar Serrano	4.00
58	Richard Gomez	4.00
59	Ramon Santiago	4.00
60	Jovanny Sosa	4.00
61	Aaron Rowand	35.00
62	Junior Guerrero	4.00
63	Luis Terrero	10.00
64	Brian Sanches	4.00
65	Scott Sobkowiak	4.00
66	Gary Majewski	4.00
67	Barry Zito	30.00
68	Ryan Christianson	8.00
69	Cristian Guerrero	4.00
70	Tomas de la Rosa	4.00
71	Andrew Beinbrink	4.00
72	Ryan Knox	4.00
73	Alex Graman	4.00
74	Juan Guzman	4.00
75	Ruben Salazar	4.00
76	Luis Matos	8.00
77	Tony Mota	4.00
78	Doug Davis	10.00
79	Ben Christensen	4.00
80	Mike Lamb	10.00

2000 Topps Opening Day

Essentially identical in design to 2000 Topps regular cards, Opening Day has a silver border with "2000 Opening Day" stamped in silver foil on the card front. The checklist is made up of cards from Series 1 and 2 from Topps base set with identical photos. The rookie reprint card of Hank Aaron was intended to carry card #110, but it does not appear, only the original '54 Topps card #128.

		NM/M
Complete Set (165):		30.00
Common Player:		.15
Pack (8):		1.00
Wax Box (36):		25.00
1	Mark McGwire	2.00
2	Tony Gwynn	1.00
3	Wade Boggs	.40
4	Cal Ripken Jr.	2.50
5	Matt Williams	.20
6	Jay Buhner	.15
7	Mike Lieberthal	.15
8	Magglio Ordonez	.25
9	Derek Jeter	2.00
10	Javy Lopez	.25
11	Armando Benitez	.15
12	Darin Erstad	.25
13	Mark Grace	.25
14	Eric Karros	.15
15	J.T. Snow Jr.	.15
16	Luis Castillo	.15
17	Rey Ordonez	.15
18	Bob Abreu	.15
19	Warren Morris	.15
20	Juan Gonzalez	.25
21	Dean Palmer	.15
22	Hank Aaron	2.00
23	Jeff Bagwell	.75
24	Sammy Sosa	1.50
25	Randy Johnson	.75
26	Dante Bichette	.15
27	Frank Thomas	.75
28	Pedro Martinez	.75

No.	Player	Price
29	Brian Giles	.20
30	Ivan Rodriguez	.50
31	Roger Cedeno	.15
32	David Justice	.25
33	Ken Caminiti	.15
34	Brian Jordan	.15
35	John Olerud	.25
36	Pokey Reese	.15
37	Barry Larkin	.25
38	Edgar Martinez	.15
39	Carlos Delgado	.50
40	Troy Glaus	.40
41	Ben Grieve	.15
42	Jose Lima	.15
43	Luis Gonzalez	.15
44	Alex Rodriguez	2.00
45	Preston Wilson	.20
46	Rickey Henderson	.40
47	Gary Sheffield	.25
48	Jim Edmonds	.25
49	Greg Vaughn	.15
50	Neifi Perez	.15
51	Paul O'Neill	.25
52	Jermaine Dye	.15
53	Curt Schilling	.25
54	Edgardo Alfonzo	.15
55	John Smoltz	.20
56	Chuck Finley	.15
57	Billy Wagner	.15
58	David Cone	.25
59	Roberto Alomar	.50
60	Charles Nagy	.15
61	Mike Mussina	.50
62	Robin Ventura	.25
63	Kevin Brown	.15
64	Pat Hentgen	.15
65	Ryan Klesko	.15
66	Derek Bell	.15
67	Larry Walker	.25
68	Scott Williamson	.15
69	Jose Offerman	.15
70	Doug Mientkiewicz	.15
71	John Snyder	.15
72	Sandy Alomar	.15
73	Joe Nathan	.15
74	Steve Finley	.15
75	Dave Martinez	.15
76	Fernando Tatis	.15
77	Kenny Lofton	.20
78	Paul Byrd	.15
79	Aaron Sele	.15
80	Roger Clemens	1.50
81	Francisco Cordova	.15
82	Wally Joyner	.15
83	Jason Kendall	.25
84	Carlos Beltran	.15
85	Chipper Jones	1.50
86	Vladimir Guerrero	.75
87	Tom Goodwin	.15
88	Brian Daubach	.15
89	Jay Bell	.15
90	Roy Halladay	.25
91	Miguel Tejada	.40
92	Eric Davis	.15
93	Henry Rodriguez	.15
94	Joe McEwing	.15
95	Jeff Kent	.25
96	Jeff Zimmerman	.15
97	Tony Fernandez	.15
98	Jason Giambi	.75
99	Jose Canseco	.40
100	Alex Gonzalez	.15
101	Erubiel Durazo, Pat Burrell, Nick Johnson (Prospects)	.40
102	Corey Patterson, Roosevelt Brown, Lance Berkman (Prospects)	.25
103	Eric Munson, Bobby Bradley **RC** (Draft Picks)	.25
104	Josh Hamilton, Corey Myers **RC** (Draft Picks)	.25
105	Mark McGwire (Magic Moments)	2.00
106	Hank Aaron (Magic Moments)	2.00
107	Cal Ripken Jr. (Magic Moments)	2.50
108	Wade Boggs (Magic Moments)	.40
109	Tony Gwynn (Magic Moments)	1.00
(110)	Hank Aaron (Rookie Reprint)	2.00
111	Tom Glavine	.40
112	Mo Vaughn	.20
113	Tino Martinez	.25
114	Craig Biggio	.25
115	Tim Hudson	.25
116	John Wetteland	.15
117	Ellis Burks	.15
118	David Wells	.15
119	Rico Brogna	.15
120	Greg Maddux	1.50
121	Jeromy Burnitz	.15
122	Raul Mondesi	.25
123	Rondell White	.25
124	Barry Bonds	2.00
125	Orlando Hernandez	.15
126	Bartolo Colon	.15
127	Tim Salmon	.25
128	Kevin Young	.15
129	Troy O'Leary	.15
130	Jim Thome	.50
131	Ray Durham	.15
132	Tony Clark	.15
133	Mariano Rivera	.25
134	Omar Vizquel	.15
135	Ken Griffey Jr.	1.50
136	Shawn Green	.40
137	Cliff Floyd	.15
138	Al Leiter	.15
139	Mike Hampton	.15
140	Mike Piazza	1.50
141	Andy Pettitte	.25
142	Albert Belle	.20
143	Scott Rolen	.75
144	Rusty Greer	.15
145	Kevin Millwood	.25
146	Ivan Rodriguez	.75
147	Nomar Garciaparra	1.50
148	Denny Neagle	.15
149	Manny Ramirez	.75
150	Vinny Castilla	.15
151	Andruw Jones	.50
152	Johnny Damon	.15
153	Eric Milton	.15
154	Todd Helton	.50
155	Rafael Palmeiro	.50
156	Damion Easley	.15
157	Carlos Febles	.15
158	Paul Konerko	.25
159	Bernie Williams	.50
160	Ken Griffey Jr. (Magic Moments)	1.50
161	Barry Bonds (Magic Moments)	2.00
162	Sammy Sosa (Magic Moments)	2.00
163	Derek Jeter (Magic Moments)	2.00
164	Alex Rodriguez (Magic Moments)	2.00
165	Checklist (Magic Moments)	.15

Autographs

		NM/M
	Common Player:	25.00
1	Edgardo Alfonzo	25.00
2	Wade Boggs	60.00
3	Robin Ventura	25.00
4	Josh Hamilton	50.00
5	Vernon Wells	30.00

2000 Topps Chrome

The base set consists of 478 cards utilizing Topps Chromium technology and features the same photos and basic design as the 2000 Topps base set. Subsets include Prospects, Draft Picks, 20th Century's Best, Magic Moments and Post Season Highlights. A parallel Refractor version is also available 1:12 packs.

		NM/M
	Complete Set (478):	100.00
	Complete Series I Set (239):	50.00
	Complete Series II Set (239):	50.00
	Common Player:	.25
	Pack (4):	1.50
	Wax Box (24):	30.00
1	Mark McGwire	3.00
2	Tony Gwynn	1.50
3	Wade Boggs	.75
4	Cal Ripken Jr.	4.00
5	Matt Williams	.40
6	Jay Buhner	.40
7	Jeff Conine	.25
8	Todd Greene	.25
9	Todd Greene	
10	Mike Lieberthal	.25
11	Steve Avery	.25
12	Bret Saberhagen	.25
13	Magglio Ordonez	.50
14	Brad Radke	.25
15	Derek Jeter	4.00
16	Javy Lopez	.50
17	Russ David	.25
18	Armando Benitez	.25
19	B.J. Surhoff	.25
20	Darryl Kile	.25
21	Mark Lewis	.25
22	Mike Williams	.25
23	Mark McLemore	.25
24	Sterling Hitchcock	.25
25	Darin Erstad	.50
26	Ricky Gutierrez	.25
27	John Jaha	.25
28	Homer Bush	.25
29	Darrin Fletcher	.25
30	Mark Grace	.75
31	Fred McGriff	.50
32	Omar Daal	.25
33	Eric Karros	.40
34	Orlando Cabrera	.40
35	J.T. Snow Jr.	.25
36	Luis Castillo	.25
37	Rey Ordonez	.25
38	Bob Abreu	.40
39	Warren Morris	.25
40	Juan Gonzalez	1.00
41	Mike Lansing	.25
42	Chili Davis	.25
43	Dean Palmer	.25
44	Hank Aaron	3.00
45	Jeff Bagwell	1.00
46	Jose Valentin	.25
47	Shannon Stewart	.25
48	Kent Bottenfield	.25
49	Jeff Shaw	.25
50	Sammy Sosa	2.00
51	Randy Johnson	1.50
52	Benny Agbayani	.25
53	Dante Bichette	.25
54	Pete Harnisch	.25
55	Frank Thomas	1.00
56	Jorge Posada	.75
57	Todd Walker	.25
58	Juan Encarnacion	.40
59	Mike Sweeney	.25
60	Pedro Martinez	1.50
61	Lee Stevens	.25
62	Brian Giles	.50
63	Chad Ogea	.25
64	Ivan Rodriguez	1.00
65	Roger Clemens	.50
66	David Justice	.50
67	Steve Trachsel	.25
68	Eli Marrero	.25
69	Dave Nilsson	.25
70	Ken Caminiti	.25
71	Tim Raines	.25
72	Brian Jordan	.25
73	Jeff Blauser	.25
74	Bernard Gilkey	.25
75	John Flaherty	.25
76	Brent Mayne	.25
77	Jose Vidro	.25
78	Jeff Fassero	.25
79	Bruce Aven	.25
80	John Olerud	.50
81	Juan Guzman	.25
82	Woody Williams	.25
83	Ed Sprague	.25
84	Joe Girardi	.25
85	Barry Larkin	.50
86	Mike Caruso	.25
87	Bobby Higginson	.25
88	Roberto Kelly	.25
89	Edgar Martinez	.40
90	Mark Kotsay	.25
91	Paul Sorrento	.25
92	Eric Young	.25
93	Carlos Delgado	1.00
94	Troy Glaus	1.00
95	Ben Grieve	.25
96	Jose Lima	.25
97	Garret Anderson	.50
98	Luis Gonzalez	.50
99	Carl Pavano	.25
100	Alex Rodriguez	3.00
101	Preston Wilson	.40
102	Ron Gant	.25
103	Harold Baines	.25
104	Rickey Henderson	.50
105	Gary Sheffield	.75
106	Mickey Morandini	.25
107	Jim Edmonds	.25
108	Kris Benson	.25
109	Adrian Beltre	.25
110	Alex Fernandez	.25
111	Dan Wilson	.25
112	Mark Clark	.25
113	Greg Vaughn	.25
114	Neifi Perez	.25
115	Paul O'Neill	.50
116	Jermaine Dye	.25
117	Todd Jones	.25
118	Terry Steinbach	.25
119	Greg Norton	.25
120	Curt Schilling	.75
121	Todd Zeile	.25
122	Edgardo Alfonzo	.25
123	Ryan McGuire	.25
124	Stan Javier	.25
125	John Smoltz	.40
126	Bob Wickman	.25
127	Richard Hidalgo	.25
128	Chuck Finley	.25
129	Billy Wagner	.25
130	Todd Hundley	.25
131	Dwight Gooden	.40
132	Russ Ortiz	.25
133	Mike Lowell	.25
134	Reggie Sanders	.25
135	John Valentin	.25
136	Brad Ausmus	.25
137	Chad Kreuter	.25
138	David Cone	.40
139	Brook Fordyce	.25
140	Roberto Alomar	.75
141	Charles Nagy	.25
142	Brian Hunter	.25
143	Mike Mussina	.75
144	Robin Ventura	.25
145	Kevin Brown	.40
146	Pat Hentgen	.25
147	Ryan Klesko	.40
148	Derek Bell	.25
149	Andy Sheets	.25
150	Larry Walker	.50
151	Scott Williamson	.25
152	Jose Offerman	.25
153	Doug Mientkiewicz	.25
154	John Snyder **RC**	.40
155	Sandy Alomar	.25
156	Joe Nathan	.25
157	Lance Johnson	.25
158	Odalis Perez	.25
159	Hideo Nomo	.75
160	Steve Finley	.25
161	Dave Martinez	.25
162	Matt Walbeck	.25
163	Bill Spiers	.25
164	Fernando Tatis	.25
165	Kenny Lofton	.40
166	Paul Byrd	.25
167	Aaron Sele	.25
168	Eddie Taubensee	.25
169	Reggie Jefferson	.25
170	Roger Clemens	2.50
171	Francisco Cordova	.25
172	Mike Bordick	.25
173	Wally Joyner	.25
174	Marvin Benard	.25
175	Jason Kendall	.40
176	Mike Stanley	.25
177	Chad Allen	.25
178	Carlos Beltran	.50
179	Deivi Cruz	.25
180	Chipper Jones	2.00
181	Vladimir Guerrero	1.50
182	Dave Burba	.25
183	Tom Goodwin	.25
184	Brian Daubach	.25
185	Jay Bell	.25
186	Roy Halladay	.25
187	Miguel Tejada	.50
188	Armando Rios	.25
189	Fernando Vina	.25
190	Eric Davis	.40
191	Henry Rodriguez	.25
192	Joe McEwing	.25
193	Jeff Kent	.50
194	Mike Jackson	.25
195	Mike Morgan	.25
196	Jeff Montgomery	.25
197	Jeff Zimmerman	.25
198	Tony Fernandez	.25
199	Jason Giambi	1.00
200	Jose Canseco	.75
201	Alex Gonzalez	.25
202	Jack Cust, Mike Colangelo, Dee Brown	.50
203	Felipe Lopez, Alfonso Soriano, Pablo Ozuna	3.00
204	Erubiel Durazo, Pat Burrell, Nick Johnson	.75
205	John Sneed **RC**, Kip Wells, Matt Blank	.50
206	Josh Kalinowski **RC**, Michael Tejera **RC**, Chris Mears	.50
207	Roosevelt Brown, Corey Patterson, Lance Berkman	.50
208	Kit Pellow, Kevin Barker, Russ Branyan	.40
209	B.J. Garbe **RC**, Larry Bigbie **RC**	3.00
210	Eric Munson, Bobby Bradley **RC**	.75
211	Josh Girdley, Kyle Snyder	.50
212	Chance Caple **RC**, Jason Jennings	.50
213	Ryan Christiansen **RC**, Brett Myers **RC**	6.00
214	Jason Stumm **RC**, Rob Purvis **RC**	.75
215	David Walling, Mike Paradis	.40
216	Omar Ortiz, Jay Gehrke	.25
217	David Cone (Season Highlights)	.40
218	Jose Jimenez (Season Highlights)	.25
219	Chris Singleton (Season Highlights)	.25
220	Fernando Tatis (Season Highlights)	.25
221	Todd Helton (Season Highlights)	1.00
222	Kevin Millwood (Post-Season Highlights)	.50
223	Todd Pratt (Post-Season Highlights)	.25
224	Orlando Hernandez (Post-Season Highlights)	.25
225	Post-Season Highlights	.25
226	Post-Season Highlights	.25
227	Bernie Williams (Post-Season Highlights)	.75
228	Mariano Rivera (Post-Season Highlights)	.50
229	Tony Gwynn (20th Century's Best)	1.50
230	Wade Boggs (20th Century's Best)	.50
231	Tim Raines (20th Century's Best)	.25
232	Mark McGwire (20th Century's Best)	3.00
233	Rickey Henderson (20th Century's Best)	.75
234	Rickey Henderson (20th Century's Best)	.75
235	Roger Clemens (20th Century's Best)	2.00
236	Mark McGwire (Magic Moments)	5.00
237	Hank Aaron (Magic Moments)	5.00
238	Cal Ripken Jr. (Magic Moments)	6.00
239	Wade Boggs (Magic Moments)	1.00
240	Tony Gwynn (Magic Moments)	3.00
	Series 1 checklist (1-201)	.05
	Series 1 checklist (202-240, inserts)	.05
241	Tom Glavine	.50
242	David Wells	.25
243	Kevin Appier	.25
244	Troy Percival	.25
245	Ray Lankford	.25
246	Marquis Grissom	.25
247	Randy Winn	.25
248	Miguel Batista	.25
249	Darren Dreifort	.25
250	Barry Bonds	3.00
251	Harold Baines	.25
252	Cliff Floyd	.25
253	Freddy Garcia	.40
254	Kenny Rogers	.25
255	Ben Davis	.25
256	Charles Johnson	.25
257	John Burkett	.25
258	Desi Relaford	.25
259	Al Martin	.25
260	Andy Pettitte	.50
261	Carlos Lee	.25
262	Matt Lawton	.25
263	Andy Fox	.25
264	Chan Ho Park	.25
265	Billy Koch	.25
266	Dave Roberts	.25
267	Carl Everett	.25
268	Orel Hershiser	.25
269	Trot Nixon	.25
270	Rusty Greer	.25
271	Will Clark	.75
272	Quilvio Veras	.25
273	Rico Brogna	.25
274	Devon White	.25
275	Tim Hudson	.50
276	Mike Hampton	.25
277	Miguel Cairo	.25
278	Darren Oliver	.25
279	Jeff Cirillo	.25
280	Al Leiter	.25
281	Brant Brown	.25
282	Carlos Febles	.25
283	Pedro Astacio	.25
284	Juan Guzman	.25
285	Orlando Hernandez	.25
286	Paul Konerko	.25
287	Tony Clark	.25
288	Aaron Boone	.50
289	Ismael Valdes	.25
290	Moises Alou	.50
291	Kevin Tapani	.25
292	John Franco	.25
293	Todd Zeile	.25
294	Jason Schmidt	.25
295	Johnny Damon	.40
296	Scott Brosius	.25
297	Travis Fryman	.40
298	Jose Vizcaino	.25
299	Eric Chavez	.50
300	Mike Piazza	2.00
301	Matt Stairs	.25
302	Cristian Guzman	.25
303	Darryl Strawberry	.40
304	Jeff Abbott	.25
305	Brett Tomko	.25
306	Mike Lansing	.25
307	Eric Owens	.25
308	Livan Hernandez	.25
309	Rondell White	.25
310	Todd Stottlemyre	.25
311	Chris Carpenter	.25
312	Ken Hill	.25
313	Mark Loretta	.25
314	John Rocker	.25
315	Richie Sexson	.25
316	Ruben Mateo	.25
317	Ramon Martinez	.25
318	Mike Sirotka	.25
319	Jose Rosado	.25
320	Matt Mantei	.25
321	Kevin Millwood	.50
322	Gary DiSarcina	.25
323	Dustin Hermanson	.25
324	Mike Stanton	.25
325	Kirk Rueter	.25
326	Damian Miller	.25
327	Doug Glanville	.25
328	Scott Rolen	1.00
329	Ray Durham	.25
330	Butch Huskey	.25
331	Mariano Rivera	.50
332	Darren Lewis	.25
333	Ramiro Mendoza	.25
334	Mark Grudzielanek	.25
335	Mike Cameron	.25
336	Kelvim Escobar	.25
337	Bret Boone	.40
338	Mo Vaughn	.40
339	Craig Biggio	.40
340	Michael Barrett	.25
341	Marlon Anderson	.25
342	Bobby Jones	.25
343	John Halama	.25
344	Todd Ritchie	.25
345	Chuck Knoblauch	.25
346	Rick Reed	.25
347	Kelly Stinnett	.25
348	Tim Salmon	.50
349	A.J. Hinch	.25
350	Jose Cruz Jr.	.25
351	Roberto Hernandez	.25
352	Edgar Renteria	.25
353	Jose Hernandez	.25
354	Brad Fullmer	.25
355	Trevor Hoffman	.25
356	Troy O'Leary	.25
357	Justin Thompson	.25
358	Kevin Young	.25
359	Hideki Irabu	.25
360	Jim Thome	1.00
361	Todd Dunwoody	.25
362	Octavio Dotel	.25
363	Omar Vizquel	.40
364	Raul Mondesi	.40
365	Shane Reynolds	.25
366	Bartolo Colon	.25
367	Chris Widger	.25
368	Gabe Kapler	.25
369	Bill Simas	.25
370	Tino Martinez	.50
371	John Thomson	.25
372	Delino DeShields	.25
373	Carlos Perez	.25
374	Eddie Perez	.25
375	Jeromy Burnitz	.25
376	Jimmy Haynes	.25
377	Travis Lee	.25
378	Darryl Hamilton	.25
379	Jamie Moyer	.25
380	Alex Gonzalez	.25
381	John Wetteland	.25
382	Vinny Castilla	.40
383	Jeff Suppan	.25
384	Chad Curtis	.25
385	Robb Nen	.25
386	Wilson Alvarez	.25
387	Andres Galarraga	.50
388	Mike Remlinger	.25
389	Geoff Jenkins	.40
390	Matt Stairs	.25
391	Bill Mueller	.25
392	Mike Lowell	.25
393	Andy Ashby	.25
394	Ruben Rivera	.25
395	Todd Helton	1.00
396	Bernie Williams	.75
397	Royce Clayton	.25
398	Manny Ramirez	1.00
399	Kerry Wood	.75
400	Ken Griffey Jr.	2.00
401	Enrique Wilson	.25
402	Joey Hamilton	.25
403	Shawn Estes	.25
404	Ugueth Urbina	.25
405	Albert Belle	.30
406	Rick Helling	.25
407	Steve Parris	.25
408	Eric Milton	.25
409	Dave Mlicki	.25
410	Shawn Green	.50
411	Jaret Wright	.25
412	Tony Womack	.25
413	Vernon Wells	.50
414	Ron Belliard	.25
415	Ellis Burks	.25
416	Scott Erickson	.25
417	Rafael Palmeiro	.75
418	Damion Easley	.25
419	Jamey Wright	.25
420	Corey Koskie	.25
421	Bobby Howry	.25
422	Ricky Ledee	.25
423	Dmitri Young	.25
424	Sidney Ponson	.25
425	Greg Maddux	2.00
426	Jose Guillen	.25
427	Jon Lieber	.25
428	Andy Benes	.25
429	Randy Velarde	.25
430	Sean Casey	.25
431	Torii Hunter	.50
432	Ryan Rupe	.25
433	David Segui	.25
434	Rich Aurilia	.25
435	Nomar Garciaparra	3.00
436	Denny Neagle	.25
437	Ron Coomer	.25
438	Chris Singleton	.25
439	Tony Batista	.25
440	Andruw Jones	1.00

441	Adam Piatt, Aubrey Huff, Sean Burroughs (Prospects)	.50
442	Rafael Furcal, Jason Dallero, Travis Dawkins (Prospects)	.50
443	Wilton Veras, Joe Crede, Mike Lamb RC (Prospects)	.25
444	Julio Zuleta RC, Dernell Stenson, Jorge Toca (Prospects)	.25
445	Tim Raines Jr., Gary Mathews Jr., Garry Maddox Jr. RC (Prospects)	.50
446	Matt Riley, Mark Mulder, C.C. Sabathia (Prospects)	.25
447	Scott Downs RC, Chris George, Matt Belisle (Prospects)	.50
448	Doug Mirabelli, Ben Petrick, Jayson Werth (Prospects)	.25
449	Josh Hamilton, Corey Myers RC (Draft Picks)	.75
450	Ben Christensen RC, Brett Myers (Draft Picks)	.50
451	Barry Zito RC, Ben Sheets RC (Draft Picks)	10.00
452	Ty Howington RC, Kurt Ainsworth RC (Draft Picks)	2.00
453	Rick Asadoorian RC, Vince Faison RC (Draft Picks)	.50
454	Keith Reed RC, Jeff Heaverlo RC (Draft Picks)	.50
455	Mike MacDougal RC, Jay Gehrke (Draft Picks)	1.50
456	Mark McGwire (Season Highlights)	3.00
457	Cal Ripken Jr. (Season Highlights)	4.00
458	Wade Boggs (Season Highlights)	.75
459	Tony Gwynn (Season Highlights)	1.50
460	Jesse Orosco (Season Highlights)	.25
461	Nomar Garciaparra, Larry Walker (League Leaders)	1.50
462	Mark McGwire, Ken Griffey Jr. (League Leaders)	1.50
463	Mark McGwire, Manny Ramirez (League Leaders)	1.50
464	Randy Johnson, Pedro Martinez (League Leaders)	1.00
465	Randy Johnson, Pedro Martinez (League Leaders)	1.00
466	Luis Gonzalez, Derek Jeter (League Leaders)	2.00
467	Manny Ramirez, Larry Walker (League Leaders)	.75
468	Tony Gwynn (20th Century's Best)	1.50
469	Mark McGwire (20th Century's Best)	3.00
470	Frank Thomas (20th Century's Best)	.75
471	Harold Baines (20th Century's Best)	.25
472	Roger Clemens (20th Century's Best)	1.50
473	John Franco (20th Century's Best)	
474	John Franco (20th Century's Best)	
475	Ken Griffey Jr. (Magic Moments)	3.00
476	Barry Bonds (Magic Moments)	5.00
477	Sammy Sosa (Magic Moments)	4.00
478	Derek Jeter (Magic Moments)	6.00
479	Alex Rodriguez (Magic Moments)	5.00

Refractors

A parallel to the base set, Refractors have a reflective sheen to them when held up to light. They are seeded 1:12 packs and have "Refractor" written underneath the card number on the back.

Stars:	3-5X
Young Stars/RC's:	1-2X
Inserted 1:12	

All-Star Rookie Team

This 10-card set highlights players who lived up to the high expectations placed on them during their rookie season. These are seeded 1:16 packs and are numbered with an "RT" prefix on the card back. A Refractor parallel is also randomly inserted, seeded 1:80 packs. "Refractor" is printed under the card number on the back.

		NM/M
Complete Set (10):		10.00
Common Player:		.50
Inserted 1:16		
Refractors:		2-3X
Inserted 1:80		
1	Mark McGwire	3.00
2	Chuck Knoblauch	.50
3	Chipper Jones	2.00
4	Cal Ripken Jr.	4.00
5	Manny Ramirez	1.00
6	Jose Canseco	.75
7	Ken Griffey Jr.	3.00
8	Mike Piazza	2.00
9	Dwight Gooden	.50
10	Billy Wagner	.50

All-Topps Team

These feature top National League players and picks a top player for each position. They have a brown border utilizing Topps Chromium technology. Card backs have a small photo along with statistical comparisons made to current and former greats for their respective position. Backs are numbered with an "AT" prefix and are seeded 1:32 packs. A Refractor parallel is inserted 1:160 packs.

		NM/M
Complete Set (20):		40.00
Complete Series I Set (10):		20.00
Complete Series II Set (10):		20.00
Common Player:		.50
Inserted 1:32		
Refractors:		2-3X
Inserted 1:160		
1	Greg Maddux	3.00
2	Mike Piazza	3.00
3	Mark McGwire	5.00
4	Craig Biggio	1.00
5	Chipper Jones	3.00
6	Barry Larkin	1.00
7	Barry Bonds	5.00
8	Andruw Jones	1.50
9	Sammy Sosa	3.00
10	Larry Walker	1.00
11	Pedro Martinez	2.00
12	Ivan Rodriguez	1.00
13	Rafael Palmeiro	1.00
14	Roberto Alomar	

15	Cal Ripken Jr.	6.00
16	Derek Jeter	6.00
17	Albert Belle	.50
18	Ken Griffey Jr.	3.00
19	Manny Ramirez	1.50
20	Jose Canseco	.50

Allegiance

Allegiance features 20 stars who have spent their entire career with one team. They are seeded 1:16 and are numbered with a "TA" prefix. There is also a hobby-exclusive Refractor parallel version, sequentially numbered to 100 and inserted 1:424 packs.

		NM/M
Complete Set (20):		30.00
Common Player:		.75
Inserted 1:16		
Refractors:		5X
Inserted 1:424		
1	Derek Jeter	6.00
2	Ivan Rodriguez	1.00
3	Alex Rodriguez	5.00
4	Cal Ripken Jr.	6.00
5	Mark Grace	1.00
6	Tony Gwynn	2.00
7	Juan Gonzalez	1.50
8	Frank Thomas	1.50
9	Manny Ramirez	1.50
10	Barry Larkin	.75
11	Bernie Williams	1.50
12	Raul Mondesi	.75
13	Vladimir Guerrero	1.50
14	Craig Biggio	.75
15	Nomar Garciaparra	4.00
16	Andruw Jones	1.50
17	Jim Thome	1.50
18	Scott Rolen	1.50
19	Chipper Jones	3.00
20	Ken Griffey Jr.	3.00

Combos

Ten player combinations linked by a common element are featured in this set. Combos are found 1:16 packs and are numbered with a "TC" prefix on the card back. A Refractor parallel is randomly seeded 1:80 packs and have "Refractor" printed under the card number on the back.

		NM/M
Complete Set (10):		20.00
Common Player:		1.00
Inserted 1:16		
Refractors:		2-3X
Inserted 1:80		
1	Manny Ramirez, Kenny Lofton, Jim Thome, Roberto Alomar	1.50
2	Tom Glavine, Greg Maddux, John Smoltz	2.00
3	Derek Jeter, Bernie Williams, Tino Martinez	4.00
4	Ivan Rodriguez, Mike Piazza	2.00
5	Nomar Garciaparra, Alex Rodriguez, Derek Jeter	4.00
6	Sammy Sosa, Mark McGwire	4.00
7	Pedro Martinez, Randy Johnson	1.50

8	Barry Bonds, Ken Griffey Jr.	3.00
9	Chipper Jones, Ivan Rodriguez	2.00
10	Cal Ripken Jr., Tony Gwynn, Wade Boggs	4.00

Kings

This 10-card set spotlights hitters who have averaged 30 or more homeruns per season for their career. Kings are seeded 1:32 packs and are numbered with an "CK" prefix on the card back. A Refractor parallel is also randomly inserted and are serially numbered to the featured player's career homerun total.

		NM/M
Complete Set (10):		25.00
Common Player:		1.50
Inserted 1:32		
1	Mark McGwire	5.00
2	Sammy Sosa	3.00
3	Ken Griffey Jr.	3.00
4	Mike Piazza	3.00
5	Alex Rodriguez	5.00
6	Manny Ramirez	1.50
7	Barry Bonds	6.00
8	Nomar Garciaparra	4.00
9	Chipper Jones	3.00
10	Vladimir Guerrero	1.50

Mark McGwire 1985 Rookie Reprint

This insert is a chromium re-printed version of McGwire's 1985 Topps rookie card. Each card features a commemorative gold-foil stamp. The insertion rate is 1:32 packs. A hobby-exclusive Refractor version is also inserted, limited to 70 sequentially numbered sets and seeded 1:12,116 packs.

		NM/M
Complete Set (1):		5.00
Inserted 1:32		
Refractor:		50.00
Production 70 cards.		
	Mark McGwire	5.00

Millennium Stars

This 10-card set features stars who had less than three years major league experience in 2000.

Millennium Stars are seeded 1:32 packs and are numbered with an "NMS" prefix. A Refractor parallel is randomly inserted in 1:160 packs and has "Refractor" printed under the card number on the back.

		NM/M
Complete Set (10):		10.00
Common Player:		.50
Inserted 1:32		
Refractors:		2-3X
Inserted 1:160		
1	Nomar Garciaparra	4.00
2	Vladimir Guerrero	1.50
3	Sean Casey	.75
4	Richie Sexson	1.00
5	Todd Helton	1.50
6	Carlos Beltran	.75
7	Kevin Millwood	.75
8	Ruben Mateo	.50
9	Pat Burrell	1.00
10	Alfonso Soriano	2.00

Own the Game

This 30-card set spotlights statistical stars and 1999 Major League Baseball award winners. These were seeded 1:11 packs and are numbered with an "OTG" prefix on the card back. A Refractor parallel is randomly inserted 1:55 packs and has "Refractor" written under the card number on the back.

		NM/M
Complete Set (30):		30.00
Common Player:		.25
Inserted 1:12		
Refractors:		2-3X
Inserted 1:55		
1	Derek Jeter	4.00
2	B.J. Surhoff	.25
3	Luis Gonzalez	.50
4	Manny Ramirez	1.00
5	Rafael Palmeiro	1.00
6	Mark McGwire	3.00
7	Mark McGwire	3.00
8	Sammy Sosa	2.00
9	Ken Griffey Jr.	2.00
10	Larry Walker	.50
11	Nomar Garciaparra	3.00
12	Derek Jeter	4.00
13	Larry Walker	.50
14	Mark McGwire	3.00
15	Manny Ramirez	1.00
16	Pedro Martinez	1.50
17	Randy Johnson	1.00
18	Kevin Millwood	1.50
19	Pedro Martinez	1.50
20	Randy Johnson	1.50
21	Kevin Brown	.50
22	Chipper Jones	2.00
23	Ivan Rodriguez	1.50
24	Mariano Rivera	.50
25	Scott Williamson	.25
26	Carlos Beltran	.50
27	Randy Johnson	1.50
28	Pedro Martinez	1.50
29	Sammy Sosa	2.00
30	Manny Ramirez	1.00

Power Players

Twenty of the leading power hitters are featured on a colorful design. They are seeded 1:8 packs and are numbered with a "P" prefix. A Refractor parallel is also randomly seeded 1:40 packs.

		NM/M
Complete Set (20):		25.00
Common Player:		.25
Inserted 1:8		
Refractors:		2-3X
Inserted 1:40		
1	Juan Gonzalez	1.00
2	Ken Griffey Jr.	2.00
3	Mark McGwire	3.00
4	Nomar Garciaparra	3.00
5	Barry Bonds	3.00
6	Mo Vaughn	.40
7	Larry Walker	.50
8	Alex Rodriguez	3.00
9	Jose Canseco	.75
10	Jeff Bagwell	1.00

11	Manny Ramirez	1.00
12	Albert Belle	.25
13	Frank Thomas	1.00
14	Mike Piazza	2.00
15	Chipper Jones	2.00
16	Sammy Sosa	2.00
17	Vladimir Guerrero	1.00
18	Scott Rolen	1.00
19	Raul Mondesi	.40
20	Derek Jeter	4.00

21st Century Topps

This 10-card set focuses on the top young stars in baseball heading into the next century. These were seeded 1:16 packs and are numbered with a "C" prefix on the card back. A Refractor parallel version is also seeded 1:80 packs.

		NM/M
Complete Set (10):		10.00
Common Player:		.25
Inserted 1:16		
Refractors:		2-3X
Inserted 1:80		
1	Ben Grieve	.25
2	Alex Gonzalez	.25
3	Derek Jeter	4.00
4	Sean Casey	.50
5	Nomar Garciaparra	3.00
6	Alex Rodriguez	3.00
7	Scott Rolen	1.00
8	Andruw Jones	1.00
9	Vladimir Guerrero	1.00
10	Todd Helton	1.00

Traded and Rookies

		NM/M
Complete Set (135):		60.00
Common Player:		.25
1	Mike MacDougal RC	.50
2	Andy Tracy RC	.50
3	Brandon Phillips RC	3.00
4	Brandon Inge RC	1.50
5	Robbie Morrison RC	.50
6	Josh Pressley RC	.50
7	Todd Moser RC	.50
8	Rob Purvis RC	.50
9	Chance Caple RC	.50
10	Ben Sheets	2.00
11	Russ Jacobson RC	.50
12	Brian Cole RC	.50
13	Brad Baker RC	.50
14	Alex Cintron RC	.50
15	Lyle Overbay RC	1.50
16	Mike Edwards RC	.50
17	Sean McGowan RC	.50
18	Jose Molina RC	.50
19	Marcos Castillo RC	.50
20	Josue Espada RC	.50
21	Alex Gordon RC	.50
22	Rob Pugmire RC	.50
23	Jason Stumm RC	.50
24	Ty Howington RC	.50
25	Brett Myers	.50
26	Maicer Izturis RC	.50
27	John McDonald RC	.50
28	Wilfredo Rodriguez RC	.50
29	Carlos Zambrano RC	6.00
30	Alejandro Diaz RC	.50
31	Geraldo Guzman RC	.50
32	J.R. House RC	.50
33	Elvin Nina RC	.50
34	Juan Pierre RC	2.00
35	Ben Johnson RC	.50
36	Jeff Bailey RC	.50
37	Miguel Olivo RC	.50

38 Francisco Rodriguez **RC** 4.00
39 Tony Pena Jr. **RC** .50
40 Miguel Cabrera **RC** 30.00
41 Asdrubal Oropeza **RC** .50
42 Junior Zamora **RC** .50
43 Jovanny Cedeno **RC** .50
44 John Sneed **RC** .50
45 Josh Kalinowski **RC** .50
46 Mike Young **RC** 6.00
47 Rico Washington **RC** .50
48 Chad Durbin **RC** .50
49 Junior Brignac **RC** .50
50 Carlos Hernandez **RC** .50
51 Cesar Izturis **RC** .50
52 Oscar Salazar **RC** .50
53 Pat Strange **RC** .50
54 Rick Asadoorian **RC** .50
55 Keith Reed **RC** .50
56 Leo Estrella **RC** .50
57 Wascar Serrano **RC** .50
58 Richard Gomez **RC** .50
59 Ramon Santiago **RC** .50
60 Jovanny Sosa **RC** .50
61 Aaron Rowand **RC** 3.00
62 Junior Guerrero **RC** .50
63 Luis Terrero **RC** .50
64 Brian Sanches **RC** .50
65 Scott Sobkowiak **RC** .50
66 Gary Majewski **RC** .50
67 Barry Zito **RC** 2.00
68 Ryan Christianson **RC** .50
69 Cristian Guerrero **RC** .50
70 Tomas de la Rosa **RC** .50
71 Andrew Beinbrink **RC** .50
72 Ryan Knox **RC** .50
73 Alex Graman **RC** .50
74 Juan Guzman **RC** .50
75 Ruben Salazar **RC** .50
76 Luis Matos **RC** .50
77 Tony Mota **RC** .50
78 Doug Davis **RC** .50
79 Ben Christensen **RC** .50
80 Mike Lamb **RC** .50
81 Adrian Gonzalez **RC**
   (Draft Picks) 5.00
82 Mike Stodolka **RC**
   (Draft Picks) .50
83 Adam Johnson **RC**
   (Draft Picks) .50
84 Matt Wheatland **RC**
   (Draft Picks) .50
85 Corey Smith **RC**
   (Draft Picks) .50
86 Rocco Baldelli **RC**
   (Draft Picks) 4.00
87 Keith Bucktrot **RC**
   (Draft Picks) .50
88 Adam Wainwright **RC**
   (Draft Picks) 5.00
89 Scott Thorman **RC**
   (Draft Picks) 1.00
90 Tripper Johnson **RC**
   (Draft Picks) .50
91 Jim Edmonds .50
92 Masato Yoshii .25
93 Adam Kennedy .25
94 Darryl Kile .25
95 Mark McLemore .25
96 Ricky Gutierrez .25
97 Juan Gonzalez .50
98 Melvin Mora .25
99 Dante Bichette .25
100 Lee Stevens .25
101 Roger Cedeno .25
102 John Olerud .40
103 Eric Young .25
104 Mickey Morandini .25
105 Travis Lee .25
106 Greg Vaughn .25
107 Todd Zeile .25
108 Chuck Finley .25
109 Ismael Valdes .25
110 Ron Henika .25
111 Pat Hentgen .25
112 Ryan Klesko .40
113 Derek Bell .25
114 Hideo Nomo 1.00
115 Aaron Sele .25
116 Fernando Vina .25
117 Wally Joyner .25
118 Brian Hunter .25
119 Joe Girardi .25
120 Omar Daal .25
121 Brook Fordyce .25
122 Jose Valentin .25
123 Curt Schilling .50
124 B.J. Surhoff .25
125 Henry Rodriguez .25
126 Mike Bordick .25
127 David Justice .25
128 Charles Johnson .25
129 Will Clark .50
130 Dwight Gooden .25
131 David Segui .25
132 Denny Neagle .25
133 Andy Ashby .25
134 Bruce Chen .25
135 Jason Bere .25

FanFest Honus Wagner T206 Reprint

In conjunction with the forthcoming sale of the finest-known T206 Honus Wagner card in July 2000, Topps produced this reprint as a promotional device for the seller (Robert Edwards Auction) and prin-

cipal venue (eBay). The card was distributed at the All-Star FanFest in Atlanta. Front of the 1-1/2" x 2-5/8" card reproduces the 1909 Wagner card. The black-and-white back details the history of the card and makes note of the upcoming sale.

	NM/M
Honus Wagner	5.00

2000 Topps Gallery

The base set consists of 150 cards. Cards 101-150 are broken down into two subsets Masters of the Game (20 cards) and Students of the Game (30 cards). The subset cards are found one per pack. Card fronts have a tan textured border around the player photo with the player name, team and Gallery logo stamped in gold foil. Card backs have a small photo, brief career note and the featured player's '99 statistics. Gallery was a hobby exclusive product. Five-card packs carried a $3 SRP.

	NM/M
Complete Set (150):	40.00
Common Player:	.15
Common (101-150):	.50
Inserted 1:1	
Pack (6):	2.00
Wax Box (24):	40.00
1 Nomar Garciaparra	1.50
2 Kevin Millwood	.25
3 Jay Bell	.15
4 Rusty Greer	.15
5 Bernie Williams	.50
6 Barry Larkin	.25
7 Carlos Beltran	.25
8 Damion Easley	.15
9 Maggio Ordonez	.25
10 Matt Williams	.20
11 Shannon Stewart	.15
12 Ray Lankford	.15
13 Vinny Castilla	.20
14 Miguel Tejada	.25
15 Craig Biggio	.25
16 Chipper Jones	1.00
17 Albert Belle	.20
18 Doug Glanville	.15
19 Brian Giles	.25
20 Shawn Green	.25
21 J.T. Snow Jr.	.15
22 Luis Gonzalez	.25
23 Carlos Delgado	.50
24 J.D. Drew	.50
25 Ivan Rodriguez	.50
26 Tino Martinez	.25
27 Erubiel Durazo	.20
28 Scott Rolen	.50
29 Gary Sheffield	.40
30 Manny Ramirez	.50
31 Luis Castillo	.15
32 Fernando Tatis	.15
33 Darin Erstad	.25
34 Tim Hudson	.25
35 Sammy Sosa	1.00
36 Jason Kendall	.25

37 Todd Walker	.15
38 Orlando Hernandez	.25
39 Pokey Reese	.15
40 Mike Piazza	1.00
41 B.J. Surhoff	.15
42 Tony Gwynn	.75
43 Kevin Brown	.25
44 Preston Wilson	.15
45 Kenny Lofton	.25
46 Rondell White	.20
47 Frank Thomas	.50
48 Neifi Perez	.15
49 Edgardo Alfonzo	.15
50 Ken Griffey Jr.	1.00
51 Barry Bonds	1.50
52 Brian Jordan	.15
53 Raul Mondesi	.25
54 Troy Glaus	.50
55 Curt Schilling	.40
56 Mike Mussina	.50
57 Brian Daubach	.15
58 Roger Clemens	1.00
59 Carlos Febles	.15
60 Todd Helton	.50
61 Mark Grace	.40
62 Randy Johnson	.75
63 Jeff Bagwell	.50
64 Tom Glavine	.25
65 Adrian Beltre	.20
66 Rafael Palmeiro	.50
67 Paul O'Neill	.25
68 Robin Ventura	.25
69 Ray Durham	.15
70 Mark McGwire	1.50
71 Greg Vaughn	.15
72 Javy Lopez	.25
73 Jeromy Burnitz	.15
74 Mike Lieberthal	.15
75 Cal Ripken Jr.	2.00
76 Juan Gonzalez	.50
77 Sean Casey	.25
78 Jermaine Dye	.25
79 John Olerud	.25
80 Jose Canseco	.40
81 Eric Karros	.15
82 Roberto Alomar	.40
83 Ben Grieve	.15
84 Greg Maddux	1.00
85 Pedro Martinez	.75
86 Tony Clark	.15
87 Richie Sexson	.25
88 Cliff Floyd	.15
89 Eric Chavez	.25
90 Andruw Jones	.50
91 Vladimir Guerrero	.50
92 Alex Gonzalez	.15
93 Jim Thome	.50
94 Bob Abreu	.25
95 Derek Jeter	2.00
96 Larry Walker	.25
97 John Smoltz	.25
98 Mo Vaughn	.20
99 Jason Giambi	.50
100 Alex Rodriguez	1.50
101 Mark McGwire (Masters of the Game)	2.50
102 Sammy Sosa (Masters of the Game)	1.50
103 Alex Rodriguez (Masters of the Game)	2.50
104 Derek Jeter (Masters of the Game)	3.00
105 Greg Maddux (Masters of the Game)	1.50
106 Jeff Bagwell (Masters of the Game)	.75
107 Nomar Garciaparra (Masters of the Game)	2.00
108 Mike Piazza (Masters of the Game)	1.50
109 Pedro Martinez (Masters of the Game)	1.00
110 Chipper Jones (Masters of the Game)	1.50
111 Randy Johnson (Masters of the Game)	1.00
112 Barry Bonds (Masters of the Game)	2.50
113 Ken Griffey Jr. (Masters of the Game)	1.50
114 Manny Ramirez (Masters of the Game)	.75
115 Ivan Rodriguez (Masters of the Game)	.75
116 Juan Gonzalez (Masters of the Game)	.75
117 Vladimir Guerrero (Masters of the Game)	.75
118 Tony Gwynn (Masters of the Game)	1.00
119 Larry Walker (Masters of the Game)	.50
120 Cal Ripken Jr. (Masters of the Game)	3.00
121 Josh Hamilton (Students of the Game)	.50
122 Corey Patterson (Students of the Game)	.50
123 Pat Burrell (Students of the Game)	.50
124 Nick Johnson (Students of the Game)	.50
125 Adam Piatt (Students of the Game)	.50
126 Rick Ankiel (Students of the Game)	.50
127 A.J. Burnett (Students of the Game)	.50

128 Ben Petrick (Students of the Game)	.50
129 Rafael Furcal (Students of the Game)	.75
130 Alfonso Soriano (Students of the Game)	2.00
131 Dee Brown (Students of the Game)	.50
132 Ruben Mateo (Students of the Game)	.50
133 Pablo Ozuna (Students of the Game)	.50
134 Sean Burroughs (Students of the Game)	.75
135 Mark Mulder (Students of the Game)	.75
136 Jason Jennings (Students of the Game)	.50
137 Eric Munson (Students of the Game)	.50
138 Vernon Wells (Students of the Game)	.75
139 Brett Myers **RC** (Students of the Game)	3.00
140 Ben Christensen **RC** (Students of the Game)	.50
141 Bobby Bradley **RC** (Students of the Game)	.50
142 Ruben Salazar **RC** (Students of the Game)	.50
143 Ryan Christianson **RC** (Students of the Game)	.50
144 Corey Myers **RC** (Students of the Game)	.50
145 Aaron Rowand **RC** (Students of the Game)	1.00
146 Julio Zuleta **RC** (Students of the Game)	.50
147 Kurt Ainsworth **RC** (Students of the Game)	1.00
148 Scott Downs **RC** (Students of the Game)	.50
149 Larry Bigbie **RC** (Students of the Game)	1.50
150 Chance Caple **RC** (Students of the Game)	.50

Players Private Issue

A parallel to the 150-card base set, Players Private Issue differ from the base cards with silver foil stamping on the card front and "Players Private Issue" stamped in silver foil across the card bottom. Card backs are serial numbered in an edition of 250 sets.

Stars (1-100):	4-8X
SPs (101-150):	2-4X
Production 250 Sets	

Autographs

This five-card set features top prospects. Each card is stamped with the Topps Certified Autograph Issue logo and the Topps Authentication sticker. Autographs are seeded 1:153 packs.

	NM/M
Common Player:	5.00
Inserted 1:153	
RA Rick Ankiel	15.00
RM Ruben Mateo	5.00
CP Corey Patterson	15.00
BP Ben Petrick	5.00
VW Vernon Wells	20.00

Gallery Exhibits

This 30-card set traces the history of art from medieval to contemporary. Card fronts have gold foil stamping and the card backs are numbered with a "GE" prefix and are found 1:18 packs.

	NM/M
Complete Set (30):	50.00
Common Player:	.50
Inserted 1:18	
1 Mark McGwire	5.00
2 Jeff Bagwell	1.50
3 Mike Piazza	3.00
4 Alex Rodriguez	4.00
5 Nomar Garciaparra	4.00
6 Ivan Rodriguez	1.50
7 Chipper Jones	3.00
8 Cal Ripken Jr.	6.00
9 Tony Gwynn	2.00
10 Jose Canseco	1.00
11 Albert Belle	.50
12 Greg Maddux	3.00
13 Barry Bonds	5.00
14 Ken Griffey Jr.	3.00
15 Juan Gonzalez	1.50
16 Rickey Henderson	1.00
17 Craig Biggio	.75
18 Vladimir Guerrero	1.50
19 Rey Ordonez	.50
20 Roberto Alomar	1.00
21 Derek Jeter	6.00
22 Manny Ramirez	1.50
23 Shawn Green	1.00
24 Sammy Sosa	3.00
25 Larry Walker	1.00
26 Pedro Martinez	2.00
27 Randy Johnson	2.00
28 Pat Burrell	1.00
29 Josh Hamilton	1.50
30 Corey Patterson	1.00

Gallery of Heroes

This 10-card set is printed on an acetate stock that simulates stained glass. Gallery of Heroes are found on the average of 1:24 packs and are numbered with a "GH" prefix on the card back.

	NM/M
Complete Set (10):	20.00
Common Player:	1.00
Inserted 1:24	
1 Alex Rodriguez	3.00
2 Chipper Jones	2.00
3 Pedro Martinez	1.50
4 Sammy Sosa	2.00
5 Mark McGwire	3.00
6 Nomar Garciaparra	3.00
7 Vladimir Guerrero	1.00
8 Ken Griffey Jr.	2.00
9 Mike Piazza	2.00
10 Derek Jeter	4.00

Press Plates

The aluminum press plates used to print the Gallery cards were inserted at a rate of one per 1,200 packs. Each card's front and back can be found in four different color variations. Because of the unique nature of each plate, assignment of catalog values in not feasible.

	NM/M
Common Player:	50.00

Proof Positive

This 10-card set features both positive and negative photography. Done on a horizontal format the inserts pair a current star with a top prospect at the same position. Printed on a clear polycarbonate stock they were inserted 1:48 packs and are numbered with a "P" prefix.

	NM/M
Complete Set (10):	40.00
Common Player:	3.00
Inserted 1:48	
1 Ken Griffey Jr., Ruben Mateo	4.00
2 Derek Jeter, Alfonso Soriano	6.00
3 Mark McGwire, Pat Burrell	6.00
4 Pedro Martinez, A.J. Burnett	3.00
5 Alex Rodriguez, Rafael Furcal	6.00
6 Sammy Sosa, Corey Patterson	4.00
7 Randy Johnson, Rick Ankiel	3.00
8 Chipper Jones, Adam Piatt	4.00
9 Nomar Garciaparra, Pablo Ozuna	6.00
10 Mike Piazza, Eric Munson	4.00

Topps Heritage

Twenty current players are artistically depicted using the 1954 Topps card design as a template. They are seeded 1:12 packs and are numbered on the card back with a "TGH" prefix. As an added bonus the original artwork used in the development of the set is available through the Topps Gallery Auction. Auction points cards are found in every pack of Gallery.

	NM/M
Complete Set (20):	100.00
Common Player:	2.00
Inserted 1:12	
Proofs:	1-2X
Inserted 1:27	
1 Mark McGwire	12.00
2 Sammy Sosa	8.00
3 Greg Maddux	8.00
4 Mike Piazza	8.00
5 Ivan Rodriguez	4.00
6 Manny Ramirez	4.00
7 Jeff Bagwell	4.00
8 Sean Casey	4.00

9	Orlando Hernandez	2.00
10	Randy Johnson	5.00
11	Pedro Martinez	5.00
12	Vladimir Guerrero	4.00
13	Shawn Green	2.50
14	Ken Griffey Jr.	8.00
15	Alex Rodriguez	12.00
16	Nomar Garciaparra	10.00
17	Derek Jeter	15.00
18	Tony Gwynn	5.00
19	Chipper Jones	8.00
20	Cal Ripken Jr.	15.00

Lithos

Eight cards from the Topps Gallery set were issued in the form of limited edition lithographs by Bill Goff Inc. Measuring 18" x 25", the lithographs were each produced in an edition of 600, with 60 artist's proofs. Issue price on the lithos was $80 for single-player pieces and $100 for the multi-player prints.

		NM/M
Complete Set (8):		675.00
Common Player:		80.00
(1)	Shawn Green (1954 Topps Style)	80.00
(2)	Ken Griffey Jr. (1954 Topps Style)	80.00
(3)	Chipper Jones (1954 Topps Style)	80.00
(4)	Pedro Martinez (1954 Topps Style)	80.00
(5)	Alex Rodriguez (1954 Topps Style)	80.00
(6)	Ivan Rodriguez (1954 Topps Style)	80.00
(7)	Three of a Kind (Nomar Garciaparra, Alex Rodriguez, Derek Jeter)	100.00
(8)	Torre's Terrors (Paul O'Neill, Derek Jeter, Bernie Williams, Tino Martinez)	100.00

2000 Topps Gold Label Pre-Production

A Derek Jeter card in each of the three classes of Gold Label was produced as a promo and distributed in three-card cello packs.

		NM/M
Complete Set (3):		7.50
Common Card:		3.00
PP1	Derek Jeter/Btg	3.00
PP2	Derek Jeter/Fldg	3.00
PP3	Derek Jeter/Running	3.00

2000 Topps Gold Label Class 1

Larry Walker

Each base card in the 100-card set has three different classes, each noted on the card back below the featured player's team logo. Each base card is also printed on 35-point rainbow styrene stock with gold foil stamping. Besides the notation on the card back, Class 1's can also be identified by the action in the background photo. Hitters are hitting and pitchers are at the start of their wind-up. A Gold die-cut parallel is also randomly seeded and are serially numbered to 100.

		NM/M
Complete Set (100):		25.00
Common Player:		.25
Gold Parallel:		4-8X
Production 100 Sets		
Pack (3):		2.00
Wax Box (24):		30.00
1	Sammy Sosa	1.50
2	Greg Maddux	1.50
3	Dee Brown	.25
4	Rondell White	.40
5	Fernando Tatis	.25
6	Troy Glaus	.75
7	Nick Johnson	.40
8	Albert Belle	.30
9	Scott Rolen	.75
10	Rafael Palmeiro	.50

11	Tony Gwynn	1.00
12	Kevin Brown	.40
13	Roberto Alomar	.50
14	John Olerud	.40
15	Rick Ankiel	.25
16	Chipper Jones	1.50
17	Craig Biggio	.40
18	Mark Mulder	.40
19	Carlos Delgado	.75
20	Alex Gonzalez	.25
21	Gabe Kapler	.25
22	Derek Jeter	3.00
23	Carlos Beltran	.40
24	Todd Helton	.75
25	Mark McGwire	2.50
26	Ben Grieve	.25
27	Rafael Furcal	.40
28	Vernon Wells	.40
29	Greg Vaughn	.25
30	Vladimir Guerrero	.75
31	Mike Piazza	1.50
32	Roger Clemens	2.00
33	Barry Larkin	.40
34	Pedro Martinez	1.00
35	Matt Williams	.30
36	Mo Vaughn	.40
37	Tim Hudson	.40
38	Andruw Jones	.75
39	Vinny Castilla	.25
40	Frank Thomas	.75
41	Pokey Reese	.25
42	Corey Patterson	.40
43	Jeromy Burnitz	.40
44	Preston Wilson	.40
45	Juan Gonzalez	.75
46	Brian Giles	.40
47	Todd Walker	.25
48	Magglio Ordonez	.40
49	Alfonso Soriano	1.00
50	Ken Griffey Jr.	1.50
51	Michael Barrett	.25
52	Shawn Green	.40
53	Erubiel Durazo	.40
54	Adam Piatt	.25
55	Pat Burrell	.50
56	Mike Mussina	.50
57	Bernie Williams	.75
58	Sean Casey	.40
59	Randy Johnson	1.00
60	Jeff Bagwell	.75
61	Eric Chavez	.40
62	Josh Hamilton	.50
63	A.J. Burnett	.25
64	Jim Thome	.40
65	Raul Mondesi	.40
66	Jason Kendall	.25
67	Mike Lieberthal	.25
68	Robin Ventura	.40
69	Ivan Rodriguez	.40
70	Larry Walker	.40
71	Eric Munson	.25
72	Brian Jordan	.25
73	Edgardo Alfonzo	.25
74	Curt Schilling	.50
75	Nomar Garciaparra	2.00
76	Mark Grace	.50
77	Shannon Stewart	.25
78	J.D. Drew	.40
79	Jack Cust	.25
80	Cal Ripken Jr.	3.00
81	Bob Abreu	.40
82	Ruben Mateo	.25
83	Orlando Hernandez	.25
84	Kris Benson	.25
85	Barry Bonds	2.50
86	Manny Ramirez	.75
87	Jose Canseco	.50
88	Sean Burroughs	.25
89	Kevin Millwood	.40
90	Alex Rodriguez	2.50
91	Brett Myers **RC**	3.00
92	Rick Asadoorian **RC**	.40
93	Ben Christensen **RC**	.40
94	Bobby Bradley **RC**	.50
95	Corey Myers **RC**	.50
96	Brad Baisley **RC**	.50
97	Aaron McNeal **RC**	.50
98	Aaron Rowand **RC**	.75
99	Scott Downs **RC**	.40
100	Michael Tejera **RC**	.50

Class 2

Kevin Brown

Each base card in the 100-card set has three different classes, each noted on the card back below the featured player's team logo. Each base card is also printed on 35-point rainbow styrene stock with gold foil stamping. Besides the notation on the card back, Class 2's can also be identified by the action in the background photo. Hitters are fielding and pitchers are in a throwing motion. A Gold die-cut parallel is also randomly seeded and are serially numbered to 100.

Same prices as Class 1.

Gold Parallel:	4-8X

Class 3

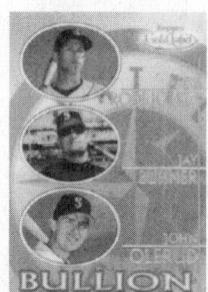

Ivan Rodriguez

Each base card in the 100-card set has three different classes, each noted on the card back below the featured player's team logo. Each base card is also printed on 35-point rainbow styrene stock with gold foil stamping. Besides the notation on the card back, Class 3's can also be identified by the action in the background photo. Hitters are running and pitchers are in their follow through. A Gold die-cut parallel is also randomly seeded and are serially numbered to 100.

Same prices as Class 1.

Gold Parallel:	4-8X
Production 100 Sets	

Bullion

BULLION

This 10-card set features three teammates superimposed over their team logo on a gold holo-foiled front with gold foil stamping. They are seeded 1:53 packs and are numbered on the card back with a "B" prefix.

		NM/M
Complete Set (10):		125.00
Common Player:		4.00
Inserted 1:53		
1	Jim Thome, Manny Ramirez, Roberto Alomar	6.00
2	Derek Jeter, Orlando Hernandez, Bernie Williams	15.00
3	Chipper Jones, Andruw Jones, Greg Maddux	12.00
4	Alex Rodriguez, Jay Buhner, John Olerud	
5	Nomar Garciaparra, Pedro Martinez, Brian Daubach	15.00
6	Mark McGwire, J.D. Drew, Rick Ankiel	
7	Sammy Sosa, Mark Grace, Kerry Wood	20.00
8	Ken Griffey Jr., Sean Casey, Barry Larkin	20.00
9	Mike Piazza, Edgardo Alfonzo, Robin Ventura	15.00
10	Randy Johnson, Matt Williams, Erubiel Durazo	6.00

35-point rainbow styrene stock with gold foil stamping. Besides the notation on the card back, Class 2's can also be identified by the action in the background photo. Hitters are fielding and pitchers are in a throwing motion. A Gold die-cut parallel is also randomly seeded and are serially numbered to 100.

Same prices as Class 1.

Gold Parallel:	4-8X

End of the Rainbow

End of the Rainbow

This 15-card set highlights some of baseball's top prospects on a silver holo foiled card front with gold foil stamping. Card backs are numbered with an "ER" prefix and are seeded 1:11 packs.

		NM/M
Complete Set (15):		8.00
Common Player:		.50
Inserted 1:11		
1	Pat Burrell	1.50
2	Corey Patterson	1.00
3	Josh Hamilton	1.50
4	Eric Munson	.50
5	Sean Burroughs	.75
6	Jack Cust	.50
7	Rafael Furcal	.75
8	Ruben Salazar	.50
9	Brett Myers	1.00
10	Wes Anderson	.50
11	Nick Johnson	1.00
12	Scott Downs	.50
13	Choo Freeman	.50
14	Brad Baisley	.50
15	A.J. Burnett	.75

Prospector's Dream

Prospector's Dream — Shawn Green

These inserts feature 10 players whose success was projected early in their careers. Card fronts feature gold holo foil with the player name, Gold Label logo and insert name stamped in gold foil. Card backs are numbered with a "PD" prefix. They are inserted 1:26 packs.

		NM/M
Complete Set (10):		15.00
Common Player:		.50
Inserted 1:26		
1	Mark McGwire	3.00
2	Alex Rodriguez	3.00
3	Nomar Garciaparra	3.00
4	Pat Burrell	.75
5	Todd Helton	1.00
6	Derek Jeter	4.00
7	Adam Piatt	.50
8	Chipper Jones	2.00
9	Shawn Green	.75
10	Josh Hamilton	1.50

The Treasury

THE TREASURY — MARK MULDER

This 25-card set spotlights 15 veterans and 10 prospects on a silver holo foiled front with gold foil stamp-

ing. They have an insertion ratio of 1:21 packs and are numbered on the card back with an "T" prefix.

		NM/M
Complete Set (25):		40.00
Common Player:		.50
Inserted 1:21		
1	Ken Griffey Jr.	3.00
2	Derek Jeter	6.00
3	Chipper Jones	3.00
4	Manny Ramirez	1.50
5	Nomar Garciaparra	4.00
6	Sammy Sosa	3.00
7	Cal Ripken Jr.	6.00
8	Alex Rodriguez	5.00
9	Mike Piazza	3.00
10	Pedro Martinez	2.00
11	Vladimir Guerrero	1.50
12	Jeff Bagwell	1.50
13	Shawn Green	1.00
14	Greg Maddux	3.00
15	Mark McGwire	5.00
16	Josh Hamilton	1.50
17	Corey Patterson	1.00
18	Dee Brown	.50
19	Rafael Furcal	.75
20	Pat Burrell	1.00
21	Alfonso Soriano	3.00
22	Adam Piatt	.50
23	A.J. Burnett	.75
24	Mark Mulder	.75
25	Ruben Mateo	.50

Name Mismatches

Because of faulty alignment when the gold-foil logo and player name were applied to card fronts, some Gold Label cards are found with the wrong name on front. Because each of these error cards is rare or possibly unique, and the demand is dependent on the combination of photo and name, it is not possible to assign values.

2000 Topps HD

TONY GWYNN — PADRES

This super-premium product consists of 100 regular base cards comprised of 88 veterans and 12 rookies. The base cards feature hyper-color technology and printed on a very thick 50-pt. card stock. Card backs have a small photo, career highlight and complete year-by-year statistics. A Platinum parallel to the base set is also randomly seeded and are sequentially numbered to 99 sets.

		NM/M
Complete Set (100):		30.00
Common Player:		.25
Platinums:		4-8X
Production 99 Sets		
Pack (4):		1.50
Wax Box (20):		30.00
1	Derek Jeter	3.00
2	Andruw Jones	.75
3	Ben Grieve	.25
4	Carlos Beltran	.40
5	Randy Johnson	1.00
6	Javy Lopez	.40
7	Gary Sheffield	.50
8	John Olerud	.40
9	Vinny Castilla	.25
10	Barry Larkin	.40
11	Tony Clark	.25
12	Roberto Alomar	.50
13	Brian Jordan	.25
14	Wade Boggs	.50
15	Carlos Febles	.25
16	Alfonso Soriano	1.50
17	A.J. Burnett	.25
18	Matt Williams	.25
19	Alex Gonzalez	.25
20	Larry Walker	.40
21	Jeff Bagwell	.75
22	Al Leiter	.25
23	Ken Griffey Jr.	1.50
24	Ruben Mateo	.25
25	Mark Grace	.50
26	Carlos Delgado	.75
27	Vladimir Guerrero	.75
28	Kenny Lofton	.40

29	Rusty Greer	.25
30	Pedro Martinez	1.00
31	Todd Helton	.75
32	Ray Lankford	.25
33	Jose Canseco	.50
34	Raul Mondesi	.40
35	Mo Vaughn	.40
36	Eric Chavez	.40
37	Manny Ramirez	.75
38	Jason Kendall	.40
39	Mike Mussina	.50
40	Dante Bichette	.25
41	Troy Glaus	.75
42	Rickey Henderson	.50
43	Pablo Ozuna	.25
44	Michael Barrett	.25
45	Tony Gwynn	1.00
46	John Smoltz	.50
47	Rafael Palmeiro	.50
48	Curt Schilling	.50
49	Todd Walker	.25
50	Greg Vaughn	.25
51	Orlando Hernandez	.25
52	Jim Thome	.75
53	Pat Burrell	.40
54	Tim Salmon	.40
55	Tom Glavine	.50
56	Travis Lee	.25
57	Gabe Kapler	.25
58	Greg Maddux	1.50
59	Scott Rolen	.75
60	Cal Ripken Jr.	3.00
61	Preston Wilson	.40
62	Ivan Rodriguez	.50
63	Johnny Damon	.40
64	Bernie Williams	.50
65	Barry Bonds	2.50
66	Sammy Sosa	1.50
67	Robin Ventura	.40
68	Tony Fernandez	.25
69	Jay Bell	.25
70	Mark McGwire	2.50
71	Jeromy Burnitz	.25
72	Chipper Jones	1.50
73	Josh Hamilton	.50
74	Darin Erstad	.40
75	Alex Rodriguez	2.50
76	Sean Casey	.40
77	Tino Martinez	.40
78	Juan Gonzalez	.75
79	Cliff Floyd	.25
80	Craig Biggio	.40
81	Shawn Green	.50
82	Adrian Beltre	.25
83	Mike Piazza	1.50
84	Nomar Garciaparra	2.00
85	Kevin Brown	.40
86	Roger Clemens	2.00
87	Frank Thomas	.75
88	Albert Belle	.25
89	Erubiel Durazo	.25
90	David Walling	.25
91	John Sneed **RC**	.50
92	Larry Bigbie **RC**	1.50
93	B.J. Garbe **RC**	.50
94	Bobby Bradley **RC**	.75
95	Ryan Christiansen **RC**	.50
96	Jay Gerhke **RC**	.50
97	Jason Stumm **RC**	.50
98	Brett Myers **RC**	4.00
99	Chance Caple **RC**	.50
100	Corey Myers **RC**	.75

Autographs

This two-card set features Cal Ripken Jr. and Derek Jeter. Card fronts include the Topps "Certified Autograph Issue" logo stamp as well as the Topps 3M authentication sticker to verify its authenticity. The insert rate for Jeter is 1:859 and Ripken Jr. 1:4,386.

	NM/M
Jeter 1:859	
Ripken 1:4,386	
1 Derek Jeter	150.00
2 Cal Ripken Jr.	250.00

Ballpark Figures

This 10-card set features a baseball field designed die-cut. These are seeded 1:11 packs and are numbered with a "BF" prefix on the card back.

BALLPARK FIGURES

JUAN GONZALEZ

		NM/M
Complete Set (10):		15.00
Common Player:		.50
Inserted 1:11		
1	Mark McGwire	3.00
2	Ken Griffey Jr.	2.00
3	Nomar Garciaparra	3.00
4	Derek Jeter	4.00
5	Sammy Sosa	2.00
6	Mike Piazza	2.00
7	Juan Gonzalez	1.00
8	Larry Walker	.75
9	Ben Grieve	.50
10	Barry Bonds	3.00

Clearly Refined

CLEARLY REFINED

ADAM PIATT

This 10-card set focuses on baseball's top young stars heading into the 2000 season. They are printed on high definition card stock and are seeded 1:20 packs. These are numbered with a "CR" prefix on the card back.

		NM/M
Complete Set (10):		8.00
Common Player:		.50
Inserted 1:20		
1	Alfonso Soriano	3.00
2	Ruben Mateo	1.00
3	Josh Hamilton	1.00
4	Chad Hermansen	.50
5	Ryan Anderson	.50
6	Nick Johnson	1.00
7	Octavio Dotel	.50
8	Peter Bergeron	.50
9	Adam Piatt	.50
10	Pat Burrell	2.00

Image

This 10-card insert set highlights those batters with the best eyes at the plate. These were seeded 1:44 packs and are numbered with a "HD" prefix on the card back.

		NM/M
Complete Set (10):		30.00
Common Player:		1.00
Inserted 1:44		
1	Sammy Sosa	3.00
2	Mark McGwire	5.00
3	Derek Jeter	6.00
4	Albert Belle	1.00
5	Vladimir Guerrero	1.50
6	Ken Griffey Jr.	3.00
7	Mike Piazza	3.00
8	Alex Rodriguez	5.00
9	Barry Bonds	5.00
10	Nomar Garciaparra	4.00

On The Cutting Edge

This 10-card insert set is die-cut down the right hand side of the card highlighting the five-tool stars top five baseball attributes. These are inserted 1:22 packs and are numbered with a "CE" prefix on the card back.

		NM/M
Complete Set (10):		15.00
Common Player:		.50
Inserted 1:22		
1	Andruw Jones	1.00
2	Nomar Garciaparra	3.00
3	Barry Bonds	3.00

On The Cutting Edge

Jeff Bagwell

4	Larry Walker	.50
5	Vladimir Guerrero	1.00
6	Jeff Bagwell	1.00
7	Derek Jeter	4.00
8	Sammy Sosa	2.00
9	Alex Rodriguez	3.00
10	Ken Griffey Jr.	2.00

Opening Day 2K

Ivan Rodriguez
Texas Rangers

As part of a multi-manufacturer promotion, Topps issued eight cards of an "Opening Day 2K" set. Packages containing some of the 32 cards in the issue were distributed by MLB teams early in the season. The cards were also available exclusively as inserts in Topps Opening Day packs sold at KMart stores early in the season. The Topps OD2K cards have gold-foil graphic highlights on front. Backs have portrait photos, stats and are numbered with an "OD" prefix.

		NM/M
Complete Set (8):		6.00
Common Player:		.50
1	Mark McGwire	2.00
2	Barry Bonds	.75
3	Ivan Rodriguez	.75
4	Sean Casey	.65
5	Derek Jeter	1.00
6	Vladimir Guerrero	1.00
7	Preston Wilson	.65
8	Ben Grieve	.50

2000 Topps Stars

GREG MADDUX

The base set consists of 200 cards, including a 50-card Spotlights subset (151-200). Card fronts have a shadow image of the featured player in the background of the player photo. The Topps Stars logo, player name, team logo and position are stamped in silver foil.

		NM/M
Complete Set (200):		35.00
Common Player:		.10
Pack (6):		2.00
Box (24):		40.00
1	Vladimir Guerrero	.75
2	Eric Karros	.10
3	Omar Vizquel	.20
4	Ken Griffey Jr.	1.50
5	Preston Wilson	.20
6	Albert Belle	.20

7	Ryan Klesko	.10
8	Bob Abreu	.20
9	Warren Morris	.10
10	Rafael Palmeiro	.40
11	Nomar Garciaparra	2.00
12	Dante Bichette	.10
13	Jeff Cirillo	.10
14	Carlos Beltran	.10
15	Tony Clark	.10
16	Ray Durham	.10
17	Mark McGwire	2.00
18	Jim Thome	.50
19	Todd Walker	.10
20	Richie Sexson	.40
21	Adrian Beltre	.10
22	Jay Bell	.10
23	Craig Biggio	.25
24	Ben Grieve	.15
25	Greg Maddux	1.50
26	Fernando Tatis	.10
27	Jeromy Burnitz	.10
28	Vinny Castilla	.10
29	Mark Grace	.25
30	Derek Jeter	2.00
31	Larry Walker	.25
32	Ivan Rodriguez	.50
33	Curt Schilling	.40
34	Mike Lamb RC	.25
35	Kevin Brown	.20
36	Andruw Jones	.40
37	Chris Mears RC	.25
38	Bartolo Colon	.10
39	Edgardo Alfonzo	.15
40	Brady Anderson	.20
41	Andres Galarraga	.25
42	Scott Rolen	.50
43	Manny Ramirez	.75
44	Carlos Delgado	.50
45	David Cone	.10
46	Carl Everett	.10
47	Chipper Jones	1.50
48	Barry Bonds	2.00
49	Dean Palmer	.10
50	Frank Thomas	.75
51	Paul O'Neill	.25
52	Mo Vaughn	.20
53	Todd Helton	.75
54	Jason Giambi	1.00
55	Brian Jordan	.10
56	Luis Gonzalez	.25
57	Alex Rodriguez	2.00
58	J.D. Drew	.10
59	Javy Lopez	.20
60	Tony Gwynn	1.00
61	Jason Kendall	.20
62	Pedro Martinez	.75
63	Matt Williams	.20
64	Gary Sheffield	.40
65	Roberto Alomar	.50
66	Lyle Overbay RC	1.00
67	Jeff Bagwell	.75
68	Tim Hudson	.40
69	Sammy Sosa	1.50
70	Keith Reed RC	.10
71	Robin Ventura	.20
72	Cal Ripken Jr.	2.50
73	Alex Gonzalez	.10
74	Aaron McNeal RC	.10
75	Mike Lieberthal	.10
76	Brian Giles	.25
77	Kevin Millwood	.10
78	Troy O'Leary	.10
79	Raul Mondesi	.20
80	John Olerud	.20
81	David Justice	.25
82	Erubiel Durazo	.10
83	Shawn Green	.40
84	Tino Martinez	.20
85	Greg Vaughn	.15
86	Tom Glavine	.25
87	Jose Canseco	.40
88	Kenny Lofton	.25
89	Brian Daubach	.10
90	Mike Piazza	1.50
91	Randy Johnson	.75
92	Pokey Reese	.10
93	Troy Glaus	.50
94	Kerry Wood	.25
95	Sean Casey	.20
96	Magglio Ordonez	.40
97	Bernie Williams	.50
98	Juan Gonzalez	.75
99	Barry Larkin	.25
100	Orlando Hernandez	.20
101	Roger Clemens	1.50
102	Bob Gibson (Retired Stars)	.40
103	Gary Carter (Retired Stars)	.10
104	Willie Stargell (Retired Stars)	.10
105	Joe Morgan (Retired Stars)	.10
106	Brooks Robinson (Retired Stars)	.50
107	Ozzie Smith (Retired Stars)	.50
108	Carl Yastrzemski (Retired Stars)	.25
109	Al Kaline (Retired Stars)	.40
110	Frank Robinson (Retired Stars)	.50
111	Lance Berkman (Shining Prospects)	.10
112	Adam Piatt (Shining Prospects)	.20
113	Vernon Wells (Shining Prospects)	.25

114	Rafael Furcal (Shining Prospects)	.25
115	Rick Ankiel (Shining Prospects)	.25
116	Corey Patterson (Shining Prospects)	.25
117	Josh Hamilton (Shining Prospects)	.50
118	Jack Cust (Shining Prospects)	.20
119	Josh Girdley (Shining Prospects)	.10
120	Pablo Ozuna (Shining Prospects)	.10
121	Sean Burroughs (Shining Prospects)	.25
122	Pat Burrell (Shining Prospects)	.25
123	Chad Hermansen (Shining Prospects)	.10
124	Ruben Mateo (Shining Prospects)	.10
125	Ben Petrick (Shining Prospects)	.10
126	Dee Brown (Shining Prospects)	.10
127	Eric Munson (Shining Prospects)	.10
128	Ruben Salazar (Shining Prospects)	.10
129	Kip Wells (Shining Prospects)	.10
130	Alfonso Soriano (Shining Prospects)	1.00
131	Mark Mulder (Shining Prospects)	.25
132	Roosevelt Brown (Shining Prospects)	.10
133	Nick Johnson (Shining Prospects)	.40
134	Kyle Snyder (Shining Prospects)	.10
135	David Walling (Shining Prospects)	.10
136	Geraldo Guzman RC	.25
137	John Sneed RC	.25
138	Ben Christensen RC	.40
139	Corey Myers RC	.25
140	Jose Ortiz RC	3.00
141	Ryan Christianson RC	.25
142	Brett Myers RC	3.00
143	Bobby Bradley RC	.25
144	Rick Asadoorian RC	.25
145	Julio Zuleta RC	.40
146	Ty Howington RC	.40
147	Josh Kalinowski RC	.40
148	B.J. Garbe RC	.50
149	Scott Downs RC	.25
150	Dan Wright RC	.25
151	Jeff Bagwell (Veterans)	.40
152	Vladimir Guerrero (Veterans)	.50
153	Mike Piazza (Veterans)	1.00
154	Juan Gonzalez (Veterans)	.40
155	Ivan Rodriguez (Veterans)	.40
156	Manny Ramirez (Veterans)	.40
157	Sammy Sosa (Veterans)	1.00
158	Chipper Jones (Veterans)	.75
159	Shawn Green (Veterans)	.25
160	Ken Griffey Jr. (Veterans)	.75
161	Cal Ripken Jr. (Veterans)	1.25
162	Nomar Garciaparra (Veterans)	1.00
163	Derek Jeter (Veterans)	1.00
164	Barry Bonds (Veterans)	1.00
165	Greg Maddux (Veterans)	.75
166	Mark McGwire (Veterans)	1.00
167	Roberto Alomar (Veterans)	.25
168	Alex Rodriguez (Veterans)	1.25
169	Randy Johnson (Veterans)	.40
170	Tony Gwynn (Veterans)	.50
171	Pedro Martinez (Veterans)	.40
172	Bob Gibson (Retired Stars)	.25
173	Gary Carter (Retired Stars)	.10
174	Willie Stargell (Retired Stars)	.25
175	Joe Morgan (Retired Stars)	.25
176	Brooks Robinson (Retired Stars)	.25
177	Ozzie Smith (Retired Stars)	.50
178	Carl Yastrzemski (Retired Stars)	.20
179	Al Kaline (Retired Stars)	.25
180	Frank Robinson (Retired Stars)	.40
181	Adam Piatt (Prospects)	.20
182	Alfonso Soriano (Prospects)	.75
183	Corey Patterson (Prospects)	.25
184	Vernon Wells (Prospects)	.40
185	Pat Burrell (Prospects)	.20
186	Mark Mulder (Prospects)	.10
187	Eric Munson (Prospects)	.10
188	Rafael Furcal (Prospects)	.15
189	Rick Ankiel (Prospects)	.25
190	Ruben Mateo (Prospects)	.10
191	Sean Burroughs (Prospects)	.20
192	Josh Hamilton (Prospects)	.75
193	Brett Myers	1.00
194	Ben Christensen	.25

195	Ty Howington	.25
196	Rick Asadoorian	.20
197	Josh Kalinowski	.20
198	Corey Myers	.25
199	Ryan Christianson	.25
200	John Sneed	.25

Blue

A parallel to the 200-card base set the player shadow has blue tint and the Topps Stars logo, player name, team logo and position are stamped in blue foil. Cards 1-150 are serially numbered on the card back to 299 and cards 151-200 are serially numbered to 99.

Stars (1-150):	3-5X
Production 299 Sets	
Stars (151-180):	4-8X
Rookies (181-200):	2-4X
Production 99 Sets	

All-Star Authority

Manny Ramirez

This 14-card set features a gold and silver holo foiled front with gold etching. Card backs are numbered with an "AS" prefix. They are found on the the average of 1:13 packs.

		NM/M
Complete Set (14):		25.00
Common Player:		1.00
Inserted 1:13		
1	Mark McGwire	3.00
2	Sammy Sosa	2.00
3	Ken Griffey Jr.	2.00
4	Cal Ripken Jr.	4.00
5	Tony Gwynn	1.50
6	Barry Bonds	4.00
7	Mike Piazza	2.00
8	Pedro Martinez	1.50
9	Chipper Jones	2.00
10	Manny Ramirez	2.00
11	Alex Rodriguez	3.00
12	Derek Jeter	4.00
13	Nomar Garciaparra	3.00
14	Roberto Alomar	1.00

Autographs

A combination of retired and current players make up this 13-card set. The set is broken down into two levels: A and B. Level A autographs are seeded 1:382 packs and Level B autographs are found in 1:1,636 packs. Each card features the Topps "Certified Autograph Issue" stamp and the Topps "Genuine Issue" sticker on the card back. Card backs are numbered with the featured player's initials.

		NM/M
Common Player:		10.00
Group A 1:382		
Group B 1:1,636		
RA	Rick Ankiel/A	15.00
GC	Gary Carter/A	15.00
RF	Rafael Furcal/A	15.00
BG	Bob Gibson/A	25.00
DJ	Derek Jeter/A	90.00
AK	Al Kaline/A	50.00
KM	Kevin Millwood/A	15.00
JM	Joe Morgan/B	40.00
BR	Brooks Robinson/B	40.00

FR	Frank Robinson/B	20.00
OS	Ozzie Smith/B	35.00
WS	Willie Stargell/B	50.00
CY	Carl Yastrzemski/B	65.00

Game Gear Bats

A piece of the featured player's game-used bat is embedded into the card front and are seeded 1:175 packs.

		NM/M
Common Player:		10.00
Group A 1:2,289		
Group B 1:1,153		
Group C 1:409		
1	Rafael Furcal/C	10.00
2	Sean Burroughs/B	10.00
3	Corey Patterson/B	10.00
4	Chipper Jones/B	40.00
5	Vernon Wells/C	15.00
6	Alfonso Soriano/B	25.00
7	Eric Munson/C	10.00
8	Ben Petrick/B	10.00
9	Dee Brown/A	10.00
10	Lance Berkman/C	15.00

Game Gear Jersey

A piece of the featured player's game-used jersey is embedded into the card front and are seeded 1:382 packs.

		NM/M
Common Player:		10.00
Inserted 1:382		
1	Kevin Millwood	10.00
2	Brad Penny	10.00
3	J.D. Drew	15.00

Progression

Each of the nine cards features three players on a horizontal format, progressing from past, present and future stars at each of the nine positions. They were seeded 1:13 packs and are numbered on the back with a "P" prefix.

		NM/M
Complete Set (9):		15.00
Common Player:		1.00
Inserted 1:13		
1	Bob Gibson, Pedro Martinez, Rick Ankiel	1.50
2	Gary Carter, Mike Piazza, Ben Petrick	2.00
3	Willie Stargell, Mark McGwire, Pat Burrell	3.00
4	Joe Morgan, Roberto Alomar, Ruben Salazar	1.00
5	Brooks Robinson, Chipper Jones, Sean Burroughs	2.00
6	Ozzie Smith, Derek Jeter, Rafael Furcal	3.00
7	Carl Yastrzemski, Barry Bonds, Josh Hamilton	4.00
8	Al Kaline, Ken Griffey Jr., Ruben Mateo	2.00
9	Frank Robinson, Manny Ramirez, Corey Patterson	1.50

Walk of Fame

This 15-card set spotlights the top stars on a silver and gold holo foiled card front. Card backs feature comparative commentary with the all-time best at their respective positions and are numbered with an "WF" prefix. They are seeded 1:8 packs.

Subway Series Parade Promos

	NM/M
Complete Set (15):	15.00
Common Player:	.75
Inserted 1:8	
1 Cal Ripken Jr.	3.00
2 Ken Griffey Jr.	1.50
3 Mark McGwire	2.00
4 Sammy Sosa	1.50
5 Alex Rodriguez	2.00
6 Derek Jeter	2.50
7 Nomar Garciaparra	2.00
8 Chipper Jones	1.50
9 Manny Ramirez	1.50
10 Mike Piazza	1.50
11 Vladimir Guerrero	1.00
12 Barry Bonds	3.00
13 Tony Gwynn	1.00
14 Roberto Alomar	.75
15 Pedro Martinez	1.00

Subway Series Parade Promos

During the October 30 World Series victory parade in New York, Topps randomly distributed a pair of special cards promoting its forthcoming Subway Series boxed set. Besides regular versions of each card, a foil version was also produced in a hand-numbered edition of 1,000 each, with 500 given to Topps employees. Cards have group photos of the team's celebrating on front, with the title in a black band on top, along with a team logo and the subway station number. Backs are in blue and orange on white and have a team logo printed beneath a short post-season summary. At bottom are ads for Topps' Subway Series commemorative set and information on a sweepstakes for 2001 Yankees or Mets tickets.

	NM/M
N.L. Champs	3.00
N.L. Champs (Foil)	6.00
Yankees Win Subway Series	5.00
Yankees Win Subway Series (Foil)	10.00

Subway Series Parade Promos - Mets Win

To cover themselves in the event the Mets had won the 2000 Subway Series against the Yankees, Topps printed up a "Mets Win" card for distribution as a promo for its Subway Series set. When the Yankees won, the Mets Win card was not released. Early in 2002, a quantity (50) of these cards surfaced, reportedly having been given to a Topps employee in 2000. The Mets Win cards are nearly identical to the issued Yankees version, with an on-field celebration group hug on front and information about

the Series on back, along with information about the Subway Series card set and other Topps products.

	NM/M
Mets Win Subway Series	90.00

Subway Series

Rick Reed P
2000 New York City Subway Series

	NM/M
Complete Fact. Set (101):	70.00
Complete Set (100):	20.00
Common Player:	.20
1 Mike Piazza	3.00
2 Jay Payton	.20
3 Edgardo Alfonzo	.40
4 Todd Pratt	.20
5 Todd Zeile	.20
6 Mike Bordick	.20
7 Robin Ventura	.40
8 Benny Agbayani	.20
9 Timo Perez	.50
10 Kurt Abbott	.20
11 Matt Franco	.20
12 Bubba Trammell	.20
13 Darryl Hamilton	.20
14 Lenny Harris	.20
15 Joe McEwing	.20
16 Mike Hampton	.40
17 Al Leiter	.40
18 Rick Reed	.20
19 Bobby Jones	.20
20 Glendon Rusch	.20
21 Armando Benitez	.20
22 John Franco	.20
23 Rick White	.20
24 Dennis Cook	.20
25 Turk Wendell	.20
26 Bobby Valentine	.20
27 Derek Jeter	4.00
28 Chuck Knoblauch	.40
29 Tino Martinez	.30
30 Jorge Posada	.40
31 Luis Sojo	.20
32 Scott Brosius	.20
33 Chris Turner	.20
34 Bernie Williams	.75
35 David Justice	.75
36 Paul O'Neill	.40
37 Glenallen Hill	.20
38 Jose Vizcaino	.20
39 Luis Polonia	.20
40 Clay Bellinger	.20
41 Orlando Hernandez	.40
42 Roger Clemens	1.50
43 Andy Pettitte	.50
44 Denny Neagle	.20
45 Dwight Gooden	.30
46 David Cone	.20
47 Mariano Rivera	.50
48 Jeff Nelson	.20
49 Mike Stanton	.20
50 Jason Grimsley	.20
51 Jose Canseco	.75
52 Joe Torre	.50
53 Edgardo Alfonzo	.40
54 Darryl Hamilton	.20
55 John Franco	.20
56 Benny Agbayani	.20
57 Bobby Jones	.20
58 New York Mets	.20
59 Bobby Valentine	.20
60 Mike Piazza	3.00
61 Armando Benitez	.20
62 Mike Piazza	3.00
63 Mike Piazza	3.00
64 Todd Zeile	.20
65 Timo Perez	.50
66 Timo Perez	.50
67 Mike Hampton	.40
68 Andy Pettitte	.50
69 Tino Martinez	.30
70 Joe Torre	.50
71 New York Yankees	.40
72 Orlando Hernandez	.40
73 Bernie Williams	.75
74 Andy Pettitte	.50
75 Mariano Rivera	.50
76 New York Yankees	.40
77 Roger Clemens	1.50
78 Derek Jeter	4.00
79 David Justice	.75
80 Mariano Rivera	.50
81 Tino Martinez	.30
82 New York Yankees	.40
83 Jorge Posada	.40
84 Chuck Knoblauch	.40
85 Jose Vizcaino	.20
86 Roger Clemens	1.50
87 Mike Piazza	3.00
88 Clay Bellinger	.20
89 Robin Ventura	.40
90 Benny Agbayani	.20
91 Orlando Hernandez	.40
92 Derek Jeter	4.00
93 Mike Piazza	3.00
94 Mariano Rivera	.50
95 Derek Jeter	3.00
96 Luis Sojo	.20
97 New York Yankees	.40
98 Mike Hampton	.40
99 David Justice	.75
100 Derek Jeter	4.00

Series Fan Fare

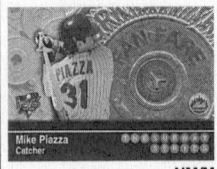

Mike Piazza
Catcher

	NM/M
Common Player:	25.00
Inserted 1:Set	
1 Timo Perez	35.00
2 Edgardo Alfonzo	40.00
3 Mike Piazza	120.00
4 Robin Ventura	35.00
5 Todd Zeile	25.00
6 Benny Agbayani	25.00
7 Jay Payton	25.00
8 Mike Bordick	25.00
9 Matt Franco	25.00
10 Mike Hampton	40.00
11 Al Leiter	40.00
12 Rick Reed	25.00
13 Bobby Jones	25.00
14 Glendon Rusch	25.00
15 Darryl Hamilton	25.00
16 Turk Wendell	25.00
17 John Franco	25.00
18 Armando Benitez	25.00
19 Chuck Knoblauch	35.00
20 Derek Jeter	200.00
21 David Justice	40.00
22 Bernie Williams	50.00
23 Jorge Posada	40.00
24 Paul O'Neill	50.00
25 Tino Martinez	35.00
26 Luis Sojo	25.00
27 Scott Brosius	25.00
28 Jose Canseco	50.00
29 Orlando Hernandez	35.00
30 Roger Clemens	100.00
31 Andy Pettitte	40.00
32 Denny Neagle	25.00
33 David Cone	25.00
34 Jeff Nelson	25.00
35 Mike Stanton	25.00
36 Mariano Rivera	60.00

2000 Topps TEK

Forty-five players make up this set including 5 rookies (41-45). Each card is printed on a transparent, polycarbonate stock, with patterns 1-15 featuring silver foil metalization. All 45 players are featured on 20 different player focused background patterns. Card backs have two numbers, the first is the player's card number within the set and the second is the pattern number. Patterns 16-20 have color variations and have an insertion rate of 1:10 packs. Each pack contains 4 TEK cards with an SRP of $5.

	NM/M
Complete Set (45):	25.00
Common Player:	.40
Common Rookie (41-45):	.75
2,000 serial numbered rookies.	
Pack (4):	2.00
Box (30):	30.00
1 Mike Piazza	1.50
2 Chipper Jones	1.50
3 Juan Gonzalez	.75
4 Ivan Rodriguez	.50

5 Cal Ripken Jr.	3.00
6 A.J. Burnett	.40
7 Jim Thome	.75
8 Mo Vaughn	.40
9 Andruw Jones	.75
10 Mark McGwire	2.00
11 Jose Canseco	.50
12 Shawn Green	.50
13 Barry Bonds	3.00
14 Bernie Williams	.50
15 Manny Ramirez	.75
16 Greg Maddux	1.50
17 Carlos Beltran	.40
18 Pedro Martinez	1.00
19 Jeff Bagwell	.75
20 Sammy Sosa	2.00
21 J.D. Drew	.40
22 Randy Johnson	1.00
23 Larry Walker	.40
24 Frank Thomas	.75
25 Orlando Hernandez	.40
26 Scott Rolen	.75
27 Tony Gwynn	1.00
28 Rick Ankiel	.50
29 Roberto Alomar	.75
30 Ken Griffey Jr.	1.50
31 Vladimir Guerrero	1.00
32 Derek Jeter	3.00
33 Nomar Garciaparra	2.00
34 Alex Rodriguez	2.50
35 Sean Casey	.40
36 Adam Piatt (Prospects)	.40
37 Corey Patterson (Prospects)	.40
38 Josh Hamilton (Prospects)	.50
39 Pat Burrell (Prospects)	.50
40 Eric Munson (Prospects)	.40
41 Ruben Salazar RC (Rookies)	.75
42 John Sneed RC (Rookies)	.75
43 Josh Girdley RC (Rookies)	.75
44 Brett Myers RC (Rookies)	4.00
45 Rick Asadoorian RC (Rookies)	.75

Color

Color variations make up patterns 16-20 of the base set and instead of metallic silver foil they have a different color background. They are seeded on the average of 1:10 packs.

	NM/M
Patterns 16-20:	1-2X
Inserted 1:10	

Gold

This parallel to the base set has a rounded top corner and rounded bottom corner with a gold background. Each pattern is serially numbered on the card back in an edition of 10 sets.

Stars:	8-15X
Rookies:	4-8X
Production 10 Sets	

ArchiTEKs

Printed on a clear, polycarbonate card stock the TEK logo, and player name is stamped in gold foil. Card backs are numbered with an "A" prefix. They are found on the average of 1:5 packs.

ArchiTEKs

	NM/M
Complete Set (18):	20.00
Common Player:	.50
Inserted 1:5	
1 Nomar Garciaparra	2.00
2 Derek Jeter	3.00
3 Chipper Jones	1.50
4 Vladimir Guerrero	1.00
5 Mark McGwire	2.50
6 Ken Griffey Jr.	1.50
7 Mike Piazza	1.50
8 Jeff Bagwell	1.00
9 Larry Walker	.50
10 Manny Ramirez	1.00
11 Alex Rodriguez	2.00
12 Sammy Sosa	2.00
13 Shawn Green	.50
14 Juan Gonzalez	.75
15 Barry Bonds	2.00
16 Pedro Martinez	1.00
17 Cal Ripken Jr.	3.00
18 Ivan Rodriguez	.75

DramaTEK Performers

Printed on a clear, polycarbonate stock, the insert name and TEK logo are stamped in blue foil. Card backs are numbered with a "DP" prefix and are seeded 1:10 packs.

	NM/M
Complete Set (9):	15.00
Common Player:	1.50
Inserted 1:10	
1 Mark McGwire	3.00
2 Sammy Sosa	2.50
3 Ken Griffey Jr.	2.00
4 Nomar Garciaparra	3.00
5 Chipper Jones	2.00
6 Mike Piazza	2.00
7 Alex Rodriguez	3.00
8 Derek Jeter	3.00
9 Vladimir Guerrero	1.50

TEKtonics

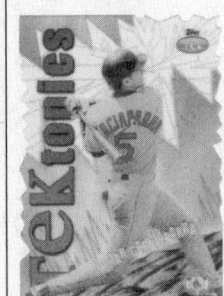

This nine-card set features baseball's top hitters on a die-cut design on a clear, polycarbonate stock. Card backs are numbered with a "TT" prefix and are inserted 1:30 packs.

	NM/M
Complete Set (9):	35.00
Common Player:	4.00
Inserted 1:30	
1 Derek Jeter	6.00
2 Mark McGwire	6.00

3 Ken Griffey Jr.	4.00
4 Mike Piazza	4.00
5 Alex Rodriguez	6.00
6 Chipper Jones	4.00
7 Nomar Garciaparra	6.00
8 Sammy Sosa	5.00
9 Cal Ripken Jr.	8.00

1984 Toronto Blue Jays Fire Safety

TONY FERNANDEZ
1
infielder

This 35-card set was issued in conjuction with the Toronto Sun newspaper and various Ontario area fire departments. The cards feature full-color action photos on the fronts, along with the player name, number and position. Rather than the customary wide white border on front, the Blue Jays fire safety set features bright blue borders. The card backs include brief player biographies and a fire safety tip. The 2-1/2" x 3-1/2" cards were distributed five at a time at two-week intervals during the summer of 1984.

	NM/M
Complete Set (35):	6.00
Common Player:	.25
1 Tony Fernandez	.30
3 Jimy Williams	.25
4 Alfredo Griffin	.25
5 Rance Mulliniks	.25
6 Bobby Cox	.50
7 Damaso Garcia	.25
8 John Sullivan	.25
9 Rick Leach	.25
10 Dave Collins	.25
11 George Bell	.40
12 Ernie Whitt	.25
13 Buck Martinez	.25
15 Lloyd Moseby	.25
16 Garth Iorg	.25
17 Kelly Gruber	.25
18 Jim Clancy	.25
23 Mitch Webster	.25
24 Willie Aikens	.25
25 Roy Lee Jackson	.25
26 Willie Upshaw	.25
27 Jimmy Key	.50
29 Jesse Barfield	.25
31 Jim Acker	.25
33 Doyle Alexander	.25
34 Stan Clarke	.25
35 Bryan Clark	.25
37 Dave Stieb	.40
38 Jim Gott	.25
41 Al Widmar	.25
42 Billy Smith	.25
43 Cito Gaston	.25
44 Cliff Johnson	.25
48 Luis Leal	.25
53 Dennis Lamp	.25
--- Team Logo/Checklist	.25

1985 Toronto Blue Jays Fire Safety

JESSE BARFIELD
29
outfielder

The Toronto Blue Jays issued a 35-card fire safety set for the second year in a row in 1985. Cards feature players, coaches, manager, checklist and team picture. The full-color photos are on the card fronts with a blue border. The backs feature player stats and a safety tip. The cards measure 2-1/2" x 3-1/2" and were distributed throughout the Province of Ontario, Canada.

		NM/M
Complete Set (36):		5.00
Common Player:		.25
1	Tony Fernandez	.30
3	Jimy Williams	.25
4	Manny Lee	.25
5	Rance Mulliniks	.25
6	Bobby Cox	.40
7	Damaso Garcia	.25
8	John Sullivan	.25
11	George Bell	.30
12	Ernie Whitt	.25
13	Buck Martinez	.25
15	Lloyd Moseby	.25
16	Garth Iorg	.25
17	Kelly Gruber	.25
18	Jim Clancy	.25
22	Jimmy Key	.35
23	Mitch Webster	.25
24	Willie Aikens	.25
25	Len Matuszek	.25
26	Willie Upshaw	.25
28	Lou Thornton	.25
29	Jesse Barfield	.25
30	Ron Musselman	.25
31	Jim Acker	.25
33	Doyle Alexander	.25
36	Bill Caudill	.25
37	Dave Stieb	.30
41	Al Widmar	.25
42	Billy Smith	.25
43	Cito Gaston	.25
44	Jeff Burroughs	.25
46	Gary Lavelle	.25
48	Luis Leal	.25
50	Tom Henke	.30
53	Dennis Lamp	.25
---	Team Logo/Checklist	.25
---	Team Photo/Schedule	.25

1986 Toronto Blue Jays Fire Safety

LLOYD MOSEBY
15
outfielder

This was the third consecutive year the Toronto Blue Jays issued a fire safety set of 36 baseball cards. The cards were given out at many fire stations in Ontario, Canada. The cards are printed in full color and include players and other personnel. The set was co-sponsored by the local fire departments, Bubble Yum and the Toronto Star. The cards measure 2-1/2" x 3-1/2".

		NM/M
Complete Set (36):		6.00
Common Player:		.25
1	Tony Fernandez	.30
3	Jimy Williams	.25
5	Rance Mulliniks	.25
7	Damaso Garcia	.25
8	John Sullivan	.25
9	Rick Leach	.25
11	George Bell	.30
12	Ernie Whitt	.25
13	Buck Martinez	.25
15	Lloyd Moseby	.25
16	Garth Iorg	.25
17	Kelly Gruber	.25
18	Jim Clancy	.25
22	Jimmy Key	.30
23	Cecil Fielder	2.00
24	John McLaren	.25
25	Steve Davis	.25
26	Willie Upshaw	.25
29	Jesse Barfield	.25
31	Jim Acker	.25
33	Doyle Alexander	.25
36	Bill Caudill	.25
37	Dave Stieb	.30
38	Mark Eichhorn	.25
39	Don Gordon	.25
41	Al Widmar	.25
42	Billy Smith	.25
43	Cito Gaston	.25
44	Cliff Johnson	.25
46	Gary Lavelle	.25
49	Tom Filer	.25
50	Tom Henke	.25
53	Dennis Lamp	.25
54	Jeff Hearron	.25
---	Team Photo	.25
---	10th Anniversary Logo Card	.25

1987 Toronto Blue Jays Fire Safety

JESSE BARFIELD
29
outfielder

For the fourth consecutive year, the Toronto Blue Jays issued a fire safety set of 36 cards. As in 1986, the set was sponsored by the local fire departments and governing agencies, Bubble Yum and the Toronto Star. The card fronts feature a full-color photo surrounded by a white border. The backs carry a fire safety tip and logos of all sponsors, plus player personal data and statistics. Produced on thin stock, cards in the set are the standard 2-1/2" x 3-1/2" size.

		NM/M
Complete Set (36):		6.00
Common Player:		.25
1	Tony Fernandez	.30
3	Jimy Williams	.25
5	Rance Mulliniks	.25
8	John Sullivan	.25
9	Rick Leach	.25
10	Mike Sharperson	.25
11	George Bell	.30
12	Ernie Whitt	.25
15	Lloyd Moseby	.25
16	Garth Iorg	.25
17	Kelly Gruber	.25
18	Jim Clancy	.25
19	Fred McGriff	2.00
22	Jimmy Key	.30
23	Cecil Fielder	.50
24	John McLaren	.25
26	Willie Upshaw	.25
29	Jesse Barfield	.25
31	Duane Ward	.25
33	Joe Johnson	.25
35	Jeff Musselman	.25
37	Dave Stieb	.30
38	Mark Eichhorn	.25
40	Rob Ducey	.25
41	Al Widmar	.25
42	Billy Smith	.25
43	Cito Gaston	.25
45	Jose Nunez	.25
47	Gary Lavelle	.25
47	Matt Stark	.25
48	Craig McMurtry	.25
50	Tom Henke	.25
54	Jeff Hearron	.25
55	John Cerutti	.25
---	Logo/Won-Loss Record	.25
---	Team Photo/Checklist	.25

1988 Toronto Blue Jays Fire Safety

PAT BORDERS
catcher

This 36-card set features action photos on 3-1/2" x 5" cards with white borders. Card numbers (player's uniform #) appear lower-left; team logo lower-right; player's name and position are printed bottom center. Card backs are blue on white and include personal and career info, 1987 and career stats, sponsor logos and a fire safety tip. The set includes 34 player cards, a team photo checklist card and a team logo card with a year-by-year won/loss record. The set was

sponsored by the Ontario Fire Chief Association, Ontario's Solicitor General, The Toronto Star and Bubble Yum and was distributed free as part of a community service project. At least some of the cards have been seen in a blank-back version, apparently used to answer fans autograph requests.

		NM/M
Complete Set (36):		5.00
Common Player:		.25
1	Tony Fernandez	.30
2	Nelson Liriano	.25
3	Jimy Williams	.25
4	Manny Lee	.25
5	Rance Mulliniks	.25
6	Silvestre Campusano	.25
7	John McLaren	.25
8	John Sullivan	.25
9	Rick Leach	.25
10	Pat Borders	.30
11	George Bell	.25
12	Ernie Whitt	.25
13	Jeff Musselman	.25
15	Lloyd Moseby	.25
17	Todd Stottlemyre	.75
17	Kelly Gruber	.25
18	Jim Clancy	.25
19	Fred McGriff	.75
21	Juan Beniquez	.25
22	Jimmy Key	.25
23	Cecil Fielder	.30
29	Jesse Barfield	.25
31	Duane Ward	.25
36	David Wells	1.00
37	Dave Stieb	.30
38	Mark Eichhorn	.25
40	Rob Ducey	.25
41	Al Widmar	.25
42	Billy Smith	.25
43	Cito Gaston	.25
46	Mike Flanagan	.25
50	Tom Henke	.25
55	John Cerutti	.25
57	Winston Llenas	.25
---	Team Photo	.25
---	Team Logo	.25

1989 Toronto Blue Jays Fire Safety

37 DAVE STIEB
Pitcher

The 1989 Blue Jays safety set consists of 36 standard-size cards co-sponsored by the Ontario Association of Fire Chiefs, Oh Henry! candy bars and A&P supermarkets. Card fronts feature color photos with the player's uniform number in large type in the upper left corner. His name and position are to the right above the photo. The Blue Jays "On the Move" logo is centered at the bottom. The backs of the cards include fire safety messages.

		NM/M
Complete Set (36):		6.00
Common Player:		.25
1	Tony Fernandez	.30
2	Nelson Liriano	.25
3	Jimy Williams	.25
4	Manny Lee	.25
5	Rance Mulliniks	.25
6	Silvestre Campusano	.25
7	John McLaren	.25
8	John Sullivan	.25
9	Bob Brenly	.25
10	Pat Borders	.25
11	George Bell	.30
12	Ernie Whitt	.25
13	Jeff Musselman	.25
15	Lloyd Moseby	.25
16	Greg Myers	.25
17	Kelly Gruber	.25
18	Tom Lawless	.25
19	Fred McGriff	.25
22	Jimmy Key	.30
25	Mike Squires	.25
28	Sal Butera	.25
29	Jesse Barfield	.25
30	Todd Stottlemyre	.25
31	Duane Ward	.25
36	David Wells	.50
37	Dave Stieb	.30

40	Rob Ducey	.25
41	Al Widman	.25
43	Cito Gaston	.25
44	Frank Wills	.25
45	Jose Nunez	.25
46	Mike Flanagan	.25
50	Tom Henke	.25
55	John Cerutti	.25
---	Team Photo	.25
---	Team Logo	.25

1990 Toronto Blue Jays Fire Safety

FRED McGRIFF
Infielder

This 35-card set was co-sponsored by the Ontario Association of Fire Chiefs, The Ministry of the Solicitor General, A & P/Dominion, Oh Henry, and the Toronto Blue Jays. The card fronts feature full-color photos on white stock and display a special Blue Jays fan club logo in the upper left corner. The flip sides feature biographical information, statistics, and a fire fact. The cards are checklisted here by uniform number.

		NM/M
Complete Set (35):		6.00
Common Player:		.25
1	Tony Fernandez	.30
2	Nelson Liriano	.25
3	Mookie Wilson	.25
4	Manny Lee	.25
5	Rance Mulliniks	.25
7	John McLaren	.25
8	John Sullivan	.25
9	John Olerud	2.00
10	Pat Borders	.25
11	George Bell	.30
15	Gene Tenace	.25
19	Tom Lawless	.25
19	Fred McGriff	.50
21	Greg Myers	.25
22	Jimmy Key	.30
23	Alex Sanchez	.25
24	Glenallen Hill	.25
25	Mike Squires	.25
26	Ozzie Virgil	.25
27	Willie Blair	.25
28	Al Leiter	.30
30	Todd Stottlemyre	.25
31	Duane Ward	.25
34	Jim Acker	.25
36	David Wells	.50
37	Dave Stieb	.30
39	Paul Kilgus	.25
42	Galen Cisco	.25
43	Cito Gaston	.25
44	Frank Wills	.25
49	Junior Felix	.25
50	Tom Henke	.25
55	John Cerutti	.25
---	Skydome/Checklist	.25
---	Logo/Schedule	.25

1991 Toronto Blue Jays Fire Safety

29
JOE CARTER
Outfielder

The Blue Jays played host to the 1991 All-Star Game and the team's annual fire safety set prominently featured that honor. A header-card with the Jays All-Star logo was included in the set and each card carried the logo in full color on

the front. The 2-1/2" x 3-1/2" cards have a color action photo at top which bleeds off the top and sides. Beneath the photo is a white border with the player's name, position and uniform number. Backs are printed in black-and-white and have a few biographical notes, 1990 and career stats, a Fire Fact safety message and logos of the cards' sponsors.

		NM/M
Complete Set (36):		6.00
Common Player:		.25
3	Mookie Wilson	.25
4	Manuel Lee	.25
5	Rance Mulliniks	.25
6	Mike Squires	.25
8	Rich Hacker	.25
8	John Sullivan	.25
9	John Olerud	.50
10	Pat Borders	.25
12	Roberto Alomar	3.00
14	Kenny Williams	.25
15	Pat Tabler	.25
17	Kelly Gruber	.25
18	Gene Tenace	.25
20	Rob Ducey	.25
21	Greg Myers	.25
22	Jimmy Key	.30
23	Mark Whiten	.25
24	Glenallen Hill	.25
28	Devon White	.35
28	Al Leiter	.30
29	Joe Carter	.50
30	Todd Stottlemyre	.25
31	Duane Ward	.25
34	Jim Acker	.25
35	Denis Boucher	.25
36	David Wells	.25
37	Dave Stieb	.30
42	Galen Cisco	.25
43	Cito Gaston	.25
44	Frank Wills	.25
46	Ken Dayley	.25
50	Tom Henke	.25
56	Hector Torres	.25
88	Rene Gonzales	.25
---	BJ Birdy (Mascot)	.25
---	All-Star Season Header/Checklist Card	.25

1992 Toronto Blue Jays Fire Safety

10 PAT BORDERS
CATCHER

Hidden amid the myriad sponsors' logos on the backs of these cards is a fire safety message. The 2-1/2" x 3-1/2" cards are printed on thin cardboard and feature color player photos on front, along with a red, white and blue "Toronto Blue Jays Fanatic" logo. Fronts also carry uniform numbers, by which the set is checklisted here. Backs are printed in black-and-white with a few biographical details, 1991 and career stats.

		NM/M
Complete Set (36):		8.00
Common Player:		.25
1	Eddie Zosky	.25
2	Manuel Lee	.25
3	Bob Bailor	.25
4	Alfredo Griffin	.25
5	Rance Mulliniks	.25
7	Rich Hacker	.25
8	John Sullivan	.25
9	John Olerud	.50
10	Pat Borders	.25
12	Roberto Alomar	1.00
14	Derek Bell	.25
15	Pat Tabler	.25
17	Kelly Gruber	.25
18	Gene Tenace	.25
20	Rob Ducey	.25
21	Greg Myers	.25
22	Jimmy Key	.35
23	Candy Maldonado	.25
24	Turner Ward	.25
28	Devon White	.35
29	Joe Carter	.35
30	Todd Stottlemyre	.30
31	Duane Ward	.25

32	Dave Winfield	1.50
36	David Wells	.45
37	Dave Steib	.30
39	Larry Hisle	.25
40	Mike Timlin	.25
42	Galen Cisco	.25
43	Cito Gaston	.25
45	Bob MacDonald	.25
46	Ken Dayley	.25
47	Jack Morris	.25
50	Tom Henke	.25
66	Juan Guzman	.25
---	Checklist	.25

1993 Toronto Blue Jays Fire Safety

Todd Stottlemyre

The Blue Jays produced a fire safety set for the 10th year in a row in 1993. In the first year of offering the item as a boxed set, the cards feature a full-bleed color photo on the front, with the player's name printed in white over a blue stripe across the top of the card. The Blue Jay's 1992 World Champions logo appears in the upper left corner. Cards are checklisted here by uniform number.

		NM/M
Complete Set (36):		6.00
Common Player:		.25
1	Eddie Zosky	.25
2	Luis Sojo	.25
3	Bob Bailor	.25
4	Alfredo Griffin	.25
5	Domingo Martinez	.25
7	Rich Hacker	.25
8	John Sullivan	.25
9	John Olerud	.40
10	Pat Borders	.25
11	Darnell Coles	.25
12	Roberto Alomar	.75
14	Darrin Jackson	.25
16	Tom Quinlin	.25
18	Gene Tenace	.25
19	Paul Molitor	1.50
22	Dick Schofield	.25
24	Turner Ward	.25
27	Devon White	.30
27	Randy Knorr	.25
28	Al Leiter	.30
29	Joe Carter	.30
30	Todd Stottlemyre	.30
31	Duane Ward	.25
33	Ed Sprague	.25
34	Dave Stewart	.25
39	Larry Hisle	.25
40	Mike Timlin	.25
41	Pat Hentgen	.25
42	Galen Cisco	.25
43	Cito Gaston	.25
46	Ken Davley	.25
47	Jack Morris	.25
48	Mark Eichhorn	.25
50	Danny Cox	.25
66	Juan Guzman	.25
---	World's Champion Trophy/Checklist	.25

2002 Toronto Blue Jays Team Issue

JOE LAWRENCE
INFIELDER

This boxed set was a stadium giveaway. It features current players, coaches and a handful of "alumni." Backs have Major League stats, biographical data and either 2001 highlights or a short biography.

	NM/M
Complete Set (34):	10.00
Common Player:	.35
2 Dave Berg	.35
5 Chris Woodward	.35
6 Joe Lawrence	.35
7 Felipe Lopez	.35
9 Darrin Fletcher	.35
10 Vernon Wells	.50
11 Eric Hinske	.50
14 Carlos Tosca	.35
15 Tom Wilson	.35
19 Cliff Politte	.35
20 Ken Huckaby	.35
21 Esteban Loaiza	.35
23 Jose Cruz Jr.	.35
24 Shannon Stewart	.45
25a Carlos Delgado	.50
25b Devon White	.35
26 Cris Carpenter	.35
29 Scott Eyre	.35
32 Roy Halladay	.45
35 Corey Thurman	.35
39 Steve Parris	.35
40 Scott Cassidy	.35
41 Pete Walker	.35
43 Cito Gaston	.35
44 Luke Prokopec	.35
45 Kelvim Escobar	.35
47a Jack Morris	.35
47b Gil Patterson	.35
49 Felix Heredia	.35
51 Tom Henke	.35
52 Bruce Walton	.35
53 John Gibbons	.35
55 Brian Butterfield	.35
56 Mike Barnett	.35

1987 Toys "R" Us

Marked as a collectors' edition set and titled "Baseball Rookies," the 1987 Toys "R" Us issue was produced by Topps for the toy store chain. The set is comprised of 33 glossy-coated cards, each measuring 2-1/2" x 3-1/2". The card fronts are very colorful, employing nine different colors including deep black borders. The backs, printed in blue and orange, contain career highlights and composite minor and major league statistics. The set was distributed in a specially designed box and sold for $1.99 in retail outlets.

	NM/M
Complete Set (33):	15.00
Common Player:	.10
1 Andy Allanson	.10
2 Paul Assenmacher	.10
3 Scott Bailes	.10
4 Barry Bonds	12.50
5 Jose Canseco	.50
6 John Cerutti	.10
7 Will Clark	.10
8 Kal Daniels	.10
9 Jim Deshaies	.10
10 Mark Eichhorn	.10
11 Ed Hearn	.10
12 Pete Incaviglia	.10
13 Bo Jackson	.50
14 Wally Joyner	.10
15 Charlie Kerfeld	.10
16 Eric King	.10
17 John Kruk	.10
18 Barry Larkin	.10
19 Mike LaValliere	.10
20 Greg Mathews	.10
21 Kevin Mitchell	.10
22 Dan Plesac	.10
23 Bruce Ruffin	.10
24 Ruben Sierra	.10
25 Cory Snyder	.10
26 Kurt Stillwell	.10
27 Dale Sveum	.10
28 Danny Tartabull	.10
29 Andres Thomas	.10
30 Robby Thompson	.10
31 Jim Traber	.10
32 Mitch Williams	.10
33 Todd Worrell	.10

1988 Toys "R" Us Rookies

This 33-card boxed edition was produced by Topps for exclusive distribution at Toys "R" Us stores. The glossy standard-size cards spotlight rookies in both close-ups and action photos on a bright blue background inlaid with yellow. The Toys "R" Us logo frames the top left corner, above a curving white banner that reads "Topps 1988 Collectors' Edition Rookies." A black Topps logo hugs the upper right-hand edge of the photo. The player name, red-lettered on a tube of yellow, frames the bottom. Card backs are horizontal, blue and pink on a bright pink background and include the player name, personal information and career highlights and stats.

	NM/M
Complete Set (33):	3.00
Common Player:	.10
1 Todd Benzinger	.10
2 Bob Brower	.10
3 Jerry Browne	.10
4 DeWayne Buice	.10
5 Ellis Burks	.10
6 Ken Caminiti	.10
7 Casey Candaele	.10
8 Dave Cone	.10
9 Kelly Downs	.10
10 Mike Dunne	.10
11 Ken Gerhart	.10
12 Mike Greenwell	.10
13 Mike Henneman	.10
14 Sam Horn	.10
15 Joe Magrane	.10
16 Fred Manrique	.10
17 John Marzano	.10
18 Fred McGriff	.10
19 Mark McGwire	2.50
20 Jeff Musselman	.10
21 Randy Myers	.10
22 Matt Nokes	.10
23 Al Pedrique	.10
24 Luis Polonia	.10
25 Billy Ripken	.10
26 Benny Santiago	.10
27 Kevin Seitzer	.10
28 John Smiley	.10
29 Mike Stanley	.10
30 Terry Steinbach	.10
31 B.J. Surhoff	.10
32 Bobby Thigpen	.10
33 Devon White	.10

1989 Toys "R" Us Rookies

This glossy set of 33 top rookies was produced by Topps for the Toys "R" Us chain and was sold in a special box. Each player's name and position appear below the full-color photo, while the Toys "R" Us logo and "Topps 1989 Collector's Edition" appear along the top. Major and minor league stats are on the back. The set is numbered alphabetically.

	NM/M
Complete Set (33):	3.00

1990 Toys "R" Us Rookies

Common Player:	.10
1 Roberto Alomar	.50
2 Brady Anderson	.10
3 Tim Belcher	.10
4 Damon Berryhill	.10
5 Jay Buhner	.10
6 Sherman Corbett	.10
7 Kevin Elster	.10
8 Cecil Espy	.10
9 Dave Gallagher	.10
10 Ron Gant	.10
11 Paul Gibson	.10
12 Mark Grace	.50
13 Bryan Harvey	.10
14 Darrin Jackson	.10
15 Gregg Jefferies	.10
16 Ron Jones	.10
17 Ricky Jordan	.10
18 Roberto Kelly	.10
19 Al Leiter	.10
20 Jack McDowell	.10
21 Melido Perez	.10
22 Jeff Pico	.10
23 Jody Reed	.10
24 Chris Sabo	.10
25 Nelson Santovenia	.10
26 Mackey Sasser	.10
27 Mike Schooler	.10
28 Gary Sheffield	1.50
29 Pete Smith	.10
30 Pete Stanicek	.10
31 Jeff Treadway	.10
32 Walt Weiss	.10
33 Dave West	.10

1990 Toys "R" Us Rookies

This 33-card set marks the fourth straight year that Topps has produced a set to be sold exclusively at Toys "R" Us stores. The card fronts contain full-color photos of 1989 rookies. The flip sides are horizontal and provide both minor and major league totals. The complete set is packaged in a special box which features a checklist on the back.

	NM/M
Complete Set (33):	3.00
Common Player:	.10
1 Jim Abbott	.10
2 Eric Anthony	.10
3 Joey Belle	.50
4 Andy Benes	.10
5 Greg Briley	.10
6 Kevin Brown	.10
7 Mark Carreon	.10
8 Mike Devereaux	.10
9 Junior Felix	.10
10 Mark Gardner	.10
11 Bob Geren	.10
12 Tom Gordon	.10
13 Ken Griffey Jr.	2.50
14 Pete Harnisch	.10
15 Ken Hill	.10
16 Gregg Jefferies	.10
17 Derek Lilliquist	.10
18 Carlos Martinez	.10
19 Ramon Martinez	.10
20 Bob Milacki	.10
21 Gregg Olson	.10
22 Kenny Rogers	.10
23 Alex Sanchez	.10
24 Gary Sheffield	.50
25 Dwight Smith	.10
26 Billy Spiers	.10
27 Greg Vaughn	.10
28 Robin Ventura	.10
29 Jerome Walton	.10
30 Dave West	.10
31 John Wetteland	.10
32 Craig Worthington	.10
33 Todd Zeile	.10

1991 Toys "R" Us Rookies

Produced by Topps, this 33-card set features baseball's top young players. The cards are styled much like past Toys "R" Us issues featuring glossy photos. The backs are printed horizontally and include player information and statistics. This set is the fifth of its kind produced by Topps for Toys "R" Us.

	NM/M
Complete Set (33):	3.00

	NM/M
Complete Set (33):	3.00
Common Player:	.10
1 Sandy Alomar, Jr.	.10
2 Kevin Appier	.10
3 Steve Avery	.10
4 Carlos Baerga	.10
5 Alex Cole	.10
6 Pat Combs	.10
7 Delino DeShields	.10
8 Travis Fryman	.10
9 Marquis Grissom	.10
10 Mike Harkey	.10
11 Glenallen Hill	.10
12 Jeff Huson	.10
13 Felix Jose	.10
14 Dave Justice	.50
15 Dana Kiecker	.10
16 Kevin Maas	.10
17 Ben McDonald	.10
18 Brian McRae	.10
19 Kent Mercker	.10
20 Hal Morris	.10
21 Chris Nabholz	.10
22 Tim Naehring	.10
23 Jose Offerman	.10
24 John Olerud	.25
25 Scott Radinsky	.10
26 Bill Sampen	.10
27 Frank Thomas	1.50
28 Randy Tomlin	.10
29 Greg Vaughn	.10
30 Robin Ventura	.10
31 Larry Walker	.50
32 Wally Whitehurst	.10
33 Todd Zeile	.10

1993 Toys "R" Us Topps Stadium Club

Featuring subsets labeled "Young Stars," "Future Stars," and "Rookie Stars," this 100-card set was sold in a plastic replica of a Toys "R" Us store, packaged with a dozen "Master Photos." Similar to regular 1993 Topps Stadium Club cards, the Toys "R" Us version features full-bleed photos on front, highlighted with goil-foil and a color Toys "R" Us logo in one of the upper corners. Backs have a background of a cloud-filled blue sky and green grass. A small player photo is at upper-right. Back information offers a few personal details, 1992 and career stats and a few career highlights. At bottom are the logos of all involved parties. The cards are UV-coated front and back. Each card is designated on the front as "Rookie Star," "Young Star" or "Future Star" in gold foil.

	NM/M
Unopened Set (100+12):	10.00
Complete Set (100):	6.00
Common Player:	.05
1 Ken Griffey Jr.	1.50
2 Chad Curtis	.05
3 Mike Bordick	.05
4 Ryan Klesko	.05
5 Pat Listach	.05
6 Jim Bullinger	.05
7 Tim Laker	.05
8 Mike Devereaux	.05
9 Kevin Young	.05
10 John Valentin	.05
11 Pat Mahomes	.05
12 Todd Hundley	.05
13 Roberto Alomar	.25
14 David Justice	.05
15 Mike Perez	.05
16 Royce Clayton	.05
17 Ryan Thompson	.05
18 Dave Hollins	.05
19 Brien Taylor	.05
20 Melvin Nieves	.05
21 Rheal Cormier	.05
22 Mike Piazza	1.50
23 Larry Walker	.05
24 Tim Wakefield	.05
25 Tim Costo	.05
26 Pedro Munoz	.05
27 Reggie Sanders	.05
28 Arthur Rhodes	.05
29 Scott Cooper	.05
30 Marquis Grissom	.05
31 Dave Nilsson	.05
32 John Patterson	.05
33 Ivan Rodriguez	.50
34 Andy Stankiewicz	.05
35 Bret Boone	.05
36 Gerald Williams	.05
37 Mike Mussina	.45
38 Henry Rodriguez	.05
39 Chuck Knoblauch	.05
40 Bob Wickman	.05
41 Donovan Osborne	.05
42 Mike Timlin	.05
43 Damion Easley	.05
44 Pedro Astacio	.05
45 David Segui	.05
46 Willie Greene	.05
47 Mike Trombley	.05
48 Bernie Williams	.05
49 Eric Anthony	.05
50 Tim Naehring	.05
51 Carlos Baerga	.05
52 Brady Anderson	.05
53 Mo Vaughn	.05
54 Willie Banks	.05
55 Mark Wohlers	.05
56 Jeff Bagwell	.75
57 Frank Seminara	.05
58 Robin Ventura	.05
59 Alan Embree	.05
60 Rey Sanchez	.05
61 Delino DeShields	.05
62 Todd Van Poppel	.05
63 Eric Karros	.05
64 Gary Sheffield	.35
65 Dan Wilson	.05
66 Frank Thomas	.75
67 Tim Salmon	.05
68 Dan Smith	.05
69 Kenny Lofton	.05
70 Carlos Garcia	.05
71 Scott Livingstone	.05
72 Sam Militello	.05
73 Juan Guzman	.05
74 Greg Colbrunn	.05
75 David Hulse	.05
76 Rusty Meacham	.05
77 Dave Fleming	.05
78 Rene Arocha	.05
79 Derrick May	.05
80 Cal Eldred	.05
81 Bernard Gilkey	.05
82 Deion Sanders	.05
83 Reggie Jefferson	.05
84 Jeff Kent	.05
85 Juan Gonzalez	.35
86 Bill Ashley	.05
87 Travis Fryman	.05
88 Roberto Hernandez	.05
89 Hipolito Pichardo	.05
90 Wil Cordero	.05
91 John Jaha	.05
92 Javy Lopez	.05
93 Derek Bell	.05
94 Jeff Juden	.05
95 Steve Avery	.05
96 Moises Alou	.05
97 Brian Jordan	.05
98 Brian Williams	.05
99 Bob Zupcic	.05
100 Ray Lankford	.05

Master Photos

Each boxed set of Toys "R" Us Stadium Club cards comes with a set of 12 Master Photos. Similar to the regular 1993 S.C. Master Photos, they feature at center a larger 2-3/4" x 3-3/4", uncropped version of the photo used on the Toys "R" Us card. A gold holographic box on the photo delineates the dimensions of the regular card, while another separates the photo from the 5" by 7" white background. Topps, Toys "R" Us, and Master Photo logos appear at the top of the card. Blank white backs have a few logos and copyrights printed in black.

	NM/M
Complete Set (12):	4.00
Common Player:	.25
(1) Willie Greene	.25
(2) Frank Thomas	1.00
(3) Chuck Knoblauch	.25
(4) Marquis Grissom	.25
(5) Scott Livingstone	.25
(6) Ken Griffey Jr.	2.00
(7) Carlos Baerga	.25
(8) Ivan Rodriguez	.75
(9) Moises Alou	.25
(10) Sam Militello	.25
(11) Eric Anthony	.25
(12) Gary Sheffield	.50

Ty Cobb

This special gold-foil bordered card was available exclusively at TRU stores as part of a package of 65 plastic sheets sold by Megacards. The card is in the design of the contemporary Conlon Collection issue from Megacards and features on its front the classic photo of Cobb sliding into base. On the back, Conlon describes how he came to take the photo.

	NM/M
Ty Cobb	4.00

1992 Triple Play Previews

To introduce its base-brand Triple Play set in 1992, Donruss issued these preview cards. The format and photos on the previews are exactly like the issued versions; backs, however, differ in the numbering "X of 8" and the appearance of the word "PREVIEW" between the MLBPA and MLB logos at bottom.

	NM/M
Complete Set (8):	25.00
Common Player:	1.00
1 Ken Griffey Jr.	9.00
2 Darryl Strawberry	1.00
3 Andy Van Slyke (Little Hotshots)	1.00
4 Don Mattingly	7.50
5 Awesome Action (Gary Carter, Steve Finley)	1.00
6 Frank Thomas	5.00
7 Kirby Puckett	6.00
8 Fun at the Ballpark	1.00

1992 Triple Play

This set was released only in wax pack form. Cards feature red borders. Boyhood photos, mascots and ballparks are among the featured cards. This set was designed to give collectors an alternative product to the high-end card sets. The cards are standard size.

NM/M
Complete Set (264): 6.00
Common Player: .05
Wax Pack (12): .40
Wax Box (36): 7.50
1 SkyDome .05
2 Tom Foley .05
3 Scott Erickson .05
4 Matt Williams .05
5 Dave Valle .05
6 Andy Van Slyke (Little Hotshot) .05
7 Tom Glavine .25
8 Kevin Appier .05
9 Pedro Guerrero .05
10 Terry Steinbach .05
11 Terry Mulholland .05
12 Mike Boddicker .05
13 Gregg Olson .05
14 Tim Burke .05
15 Candy Maldonado .05
16 Orlando Merced .05
17 Robin Ventura .05
18 Eric Anthony .05
19 Greg Maddux .60
20 Erik Hanson .05
21 Bob Ojeda .05
22 Nolan Ryan 1.00
23 Dave Righetti .05
24 Reggie Jefferson .05
25 Jody Reed .05
26 Awesome Action (Steve Finley, Gary Carter) .10
27 Chili Davis .05
28 Hector Villanueva .05
29 Cecil Fielder .05
30 Hal Morris .05
31 Barry Larkin .05
32 Bobby Thigpen .05
33 Andy Benes .05
34 Harold Baines .05
35 David Cone .05
36 Mark Langston .05
37 Bryan Harvey .05
38 John Kruk .05
39 Scott Sanderson .05
40 Lonnie Smith .05
41 Awesome Action (Rex Hudler) .05
42 George Bell .05
43 Steve Finley .05
44 Mickey Tettleton .05
45 Robby Thompson .05
46 Pat Kelly .05
47 Marquis Grissom .05
48 Tony Pena .05
49 Alex Cole .05
50 Steve Buechele .05
51 Ivan Rodriguez .45
52 John Smiley .05
53 Gary Sheffield .25
54 Greg Olson .05
55 Ramon Martinez .05
56 B.J. Surhoff .05
57 Bruce Hurst .05
58 Todd Stottlemyre .05
59 Brett Butler .05
60 Glenn Davis .05
61 Awesome Action (Glenn Braggs, Kirt Manwaring) .05
62 Lee Smith .05
63 Rickey Henderson .45
64 Fun at the Ballpark (David Cone, Jeff Innis, John Franco) .05
65 Rick Aguilera .05
66 Kevin Elster .05
67 Dwight Evans .05
68 Andujar Cedeno .05
69 Brian McRae .05
70 Benito Santiago .05
71 Randy Johnson .45
72 Roberto Kelly .05
73 Awesome Action (Juan Samuel) .05
74 Alex Fernandez .05
75 Felix Jose .05
76 Brian Harper .05
77 Scott Sanderson (Little Hotshot) .05
78 Ken Caminiti .05
79 Mo Vaughn .05
80 Roger McDowell .05
81 Robin Yount .45
82 Dave Magadan .05
83 Julio Franco .05
84 Roberto Alomar .25
85 Steve Avery .05
86 Travis Fryman .05
87 Fred McGriff .05
88 Dave Stewart .05
89 Larry Walker .05
90 Chris Sabo .05
91 Chuck Finley .05
92 Dennis Martinez .05
93 Jeff Johnson .05
94 Len Dykstra .05
95 Mark Whiten .05
96 Wade Taylor .05
97 Lance Dickson .05
98 Kevin Tapani .05
99 Awesome Action (Luis Polonia, Tony Phillips) .05
100 Milt Cuyler .05
101 Willie McGee .05
102 Awesome Action (Tony Fernandez, Ryne Sandberg) .15
103 Albert Belle .05
104 Todd Hundley .05
105 Ben McDonald .05
106 Doug Drabek .05
107 Tim Raines .05
108 Joe Carter .05
109 Reggie Sanders .05
110 John Olerud .05
111 Darren Lewis .05
112 Juan Gonzalez .25
113 Awesome Action (Andre Dawson) .05
114 Mark Grace .05
115 George Brett .65
116 Barry Bonds 1.00
117 Lou Whitaker .05
118 Jose Oquendo .05
119 Lee Stevens .05
120 Phil Plantier .05
121 Awesome Action (Devon White, Matt Merullo) .05
122 Greg Vaughn .05
123 Royce Clayton .05
124 Bob Welch .05
125 Juan Samuel .05
126 Ron Gant .05
127 Edgar Martinez .05
128 Andy Ashby .05
129 Jack McDowell .05
130 Awesome Action (Dave Henderson, Jerry Browne) .05
131 Leo Gomez .05
132 Checklist 1-88 .05
133 Phillie Phanatic .05
134 Bret Barbarie .05
135 Kent Hrbek .05
136 Hall of Fame .05
137 Omar Vizquel .05
138 The Famous Chicken .05
139 Terry Pendleton .05
140 Jim Eisenreich .05
141 Todd Zeile .05
142 Todd Van Poppel .05
143 Darren Daulton .05
144 Mike Macfarlane .05
145 Luis Mercedes .05
146 Trevor Wilson .05
147 Dave Steib .05
148 Andy Van Slyke .05
149 Carlton Fisk .45
150 Craig Biggio .05
151 Joe Girardi .05
152 Ken Griffey Jr. .65
153 Jose Offerman .05
154 Bobby Witt .05
155 Will Clark .05
156 Steve Olin .05
157 Greg Harris .05
158 Dale Murphy (Little Hotshot) .05
159 Don Mattingly .65
160 Shawon Dunston .05
161 Bill Gullickson .05
162 Paul O'Neill .05
163 Norm Charlton .05
164 Bo Jackson .10
165 Tony Fernandez .05
166 Dave Henderson .05
167 Dwight Gooden .05
168 Junior Felix .05
169 Lance Parrish .05
170 Pat Combs .05
171 Chuck Knoblauch .05
172 John Smoltz .05
173 Wrigley Field .05
174 Andre Dawson .25
175 Pete Harnisch .05
176 Alan Trammell .05
177 Kirk Dressendorfer .05
178 Matt Nokes .05
179 Wil Cordero .05
180 Scott Cooper .05
181 Glenallen Hill .05
182 John Franco .05
183 Rafael Palmeiro .40
184 Jay Bell .05
185 Bill Wegman .05
186 Deion Sanders .05
187 Darryl Strawberry .05
188 Jaime Navarro .05
189 Darren Jackson .05
190 Eddie Zosky .05
191 Mike Scioscia .05
192 Chito Martinez .05
193 Awesome Action (Pat Kelly, Ron Tingley) .05
194 Ray Lankford .05
195 Dennis Eckersley .35
196 Awesome Action (Ivan Calderon, Mike Maddux) .05
197 Shane Mack .05
198 Checklist 89-176 .05
199 Cal Ripken, Jr. 1.00
200 Jeff Bagwell .45
201 David Howard .05
202 Kirby Puckett .60
203 Harold Reynolds .05
204 Jim Abbott .05
205 Mark Lewis .05
206 Frank Thomas .45
207 Rex Hudler .05
208 Vince Coleman .05
209 Delino DeShields .05
210 Luis Gonzalez .05
211 Wade Boggs .60
212 Orel Hershiser .05
213 Cal Eldred .05
214 Jose Canseco .25
215 Jose Guzman .05
216 Roger Clemens .65
217 Dave Justice .05
218 Tony Phillips .05
219 Tony Gwynn .60
220 Mitch Williams .05
221 Bill Sampen .05
222 Billy Hatcher .05
223 Gary Gaetti .05
224 Tim Wallach .05
225 Kevin Maas .05
226 Kevin Brown .05
227 Sandy Alomar .05
228 John Habyan .05
229 Ryne Sandberg .60
230 Greg Gagne .05
231 Autographs (Mark McGwire) .40
232 Mike LaValliere .05
233 Mark Gubicza .05
234 Lance Parrish (Little Hotshot) .05
235 Carlos Baerga .05
236 Howard Johnson .05
237 Mike Mussina .25
238 Ruben Sierra .05
239 Lance Johnson .05
240 Devon White .05
241 Dan Wilson .05
242 Kelly Gruber .05
243 Brett Butler (Little Hotshot) .05
244 Ozzie Smith .60
245 Chuck McElroy .05
246 Shawn Boskie .05
247 Mark Davis .05
248 Bill Landrum .05
249 Frank Tanana .05
250 Darryl Hamilton .05
251 Gary DiSarcina .05
252 Mike Greenwell .05
253 Cal Ripken, Jr. (Little Hotshot) .35
254 Paul Molitor .45
255 Tim Teufel .05
256 Chris Hoiles .05
257 Rob Dibble .05
258 Sid Bream .05
259 Chito Martinez .05
260 Dale Murphy .15
261 Greg Hibbard .05
262 Mark McGwire .75
263 Oriole Park .05
264 Checklist 177-264 .05

Gallery of Stars

DANNY TARTABULL

Two levels of scarcity are represented in this insert issue. Cards #1-6 (all cards have a GS prefix to the card number) feature in their new uniforms players who changed teams for 1993. Those inserts were found in the standard Triple Play foil packs and are somewhat more common than cards #7-12, which were found only in jumbo packs and which feature a better selection of established stars and rookies. All of the inserts feature the artwork of Dick Perez, with player portraits set against a colorful background. Silver-foil accents highlight the front design. Backs are red with a white "tombstone" containing a career summary.

NM/M
Complete Set (12): 4.00
Common Player: .15
1 Bobby Bonilla .15
2 Wally Joyner .15
3 Jack Morris .15
4 Steve Sax .15
5 Danny Tartabull .15
6 Frank Viola .15
7 Jeff Bagwell .60
8 Ken Griffey Jr. 1.00
9 David Justice .15
10 Ryan Klesko .15
11 Cal Ripken, Jr. 1.50
12 Frank Thomas .75

1993 Triple Play Promos

This set was given to dealers to preview the 1993 Donruss Triple Play issue. Cards are virtually identical to the regular-issue cards except for a large promotional sample notation printed on back.

NM/M
Complete Set (12): 100.00
Common Player: 5.00
1 Ken Griffey Jr. 25.00
2 Roberto Alomar 6.00
3 Cal Ripken, Jr. 40.00
4 Eric Karros 5.00
5 Cecil Fielder 5.00
6 Gary Sheffield 7.50
7 Darren Daulton 5.00
8 Andy Van Slyke 5.00
9 Dennis Eckersley 10.00
10 Ryne Sandberg 25.00
11 Mark Grace (Little Hotshots) 5.00
12 Awesome Action #1 (Luis Polonia, David Segui) 5.00

1993 Triple Play

MARK LEMKE 2B

For the second year, Leaf-Donruss used the "Triple Play" brand name for its base-level card set aimed at the younger collector. The 264-card set was available in several types of retail packaging and included a number of special subsets, such as childhood photos (labeled LH - Little Hotshots - in the checklist) and insert sets. Checklist card #264 incorrectly shows card #129, Joe Robbie Stadium, as #259. There is a second card, "Equipment," which also bears #129. An "Action Baseball" scratch-off game card was included in each foil pack.

NM/M
Complete Set (264): 10.00
Common Player: .05
Wax Pack (12): .60
Wax Box (36): 15.00
1 Ken Griffey Jr. .50
2 Roberto Alomar .10
3 Cal Ripken, Jr. .75
4 Eric Karros .05
5 Cecil Fielder .05
6 Gary Sheffield .15
7 Darren Daulton .05
8 Andy Van Slyke .05
9 Dennis Eckersley .20
10 Ryne Sandberg .35
11 Mark Grace (Little Hotshots) .05
12 Awesome Action #1 (Luis Polonia, David Segui) .05
13 Mike Mussina .15
14 Vince Coleman .05
15 Rafael Belliard .05
16 Ivan Rodriguez .20
17 Eddie Taubensee .05
18 Cal Eldred .05
19 Rick Wilkins .05
20 Edgar Martinez .05
21 Brian McRae .05
22 Darren Holmes .05
23 Mark Whiten .05
24 Todd Zeile .05
25 Scott Cooper .05
26 Frank Thomas .25
27 Wil Cordero .05
28 Juan Guzman .05
29 Pedro Astacio .05
30 Steve Avery .05
31 Barry Larkin .05
32 President Clinton 2.00
33 Scott Erickson .05
34 Mike Devereaux .05
35 Tino Martinez .05
36 Brent Mayne .05
37 Tim Salmon .05
38 Dave Hollins .05
39 Royce Clayton .05
40 Shawon Dunston .05
41 Eddie Murray .25
42 Larry Walker .05
43 Jeff Bagwell .25
44 Milt Cuyler .05
45 Mike Bordick .05
46 Mike Greenwell .05
47 Steve Sax .05
48 Chuck Knoblauch .05
49 Charles Nagy .05
50 Tim Wakefield .05
51 Tony Gwynn .35
52 Rob Dibble .05
53 Mickey Morandini .05
54 Steve Hosey .05
55 Mike Piazza .50
56 Bill Wegman .05
57 Kevin Maas .05
58 Gary DiSarcina .05
59 Travis Fryman .05
60 Ruben Sierra .05
61 Awesome Action #2 (Ken Caminiti) .05
62 Brian Jordan .05
63 Scott Chiamparino .05
64 Awesome Action #3 (Mike Bordick, George Brett) .05
65 Carlos Garcia .05
66 Checklist 1-66 .05
67 John Smoltz .05
68 Awesome Action #4 (Mark McGwire, Brian Harper) .20
69 Kurt Stillwell .05
70 Chad Curtis .05
71 Rafael Palmeiro .20
72 Kevin Young .05
73 Glenn Davis .05
74 Dennis Martinez .05
75 Sam Militello .05
76 Mike Morgan .05
77 Frank Thomas (Little Hotshots) .20
78 Staying Fit (Bip Roberts, Mike Devereaux) .05
79 Steve Buechele .05
80 Carlos Baerga .05
81 Robby Thompson .05
82 Kirk McCaskill .05
83 Lee Smith .05
84 Gary Scott .05
85 Tony Pena .05
86 Howard Johnson .05
87 Mark McGwire .60
88 Bip Roberts .05
89 Devon White .05
90 John Franco .05
91 Tom Browning .05
92 Mickey Tettleton .05
93 Jeff Conine .05
94 Albert Belle .05
95 Fred McGriff .05
96 Nolan Ryan .75
97 Paul Molitor (Little Hotshots) .10
98 Juan Bell .05
99 Dave Fleming .05
100 Craig Biggio .05
101a Andy Stankiewicz (White name on front.) .05
101b Andy Stankiewicz (Red name on front.) .25
102 Delino DeShields .05
103 Damion Easley .05
104 Kevin McReynolds .05
105 David Nied .05
106 Rick Sutcliffe .05
107 Will Clark .05
108 Tim Raines .05
109 Eric Anthony .05
110 Mike LaValliere .05
111 Dean Palmer .05
112 Eric Davis .05
113 Damon Berryhill .05
114 Felix Jose .05
115 Ozzie Guillen .05
116 Pat Listach .05
117 Tom Glavine .15
118 Roger Clemens .40
119 Dave Henderson .05
120 Don Mattingly .40
121 Orel Hershiser .05
122 Ozzie Smith .35
123 Bret Saberhagen .05
124 Mitch Williams .05
125 Jerald Clark .05
127 Mile High Stadium .05
128 Kent Hrbek .05
129a Equipment (Curt Schilling, Mark Whiten) .05
129b Joe Robbie Stadium .05
130 Gregg Jefferies .05
131 John Orton .05
132 Checklist 67-132 .05
133 Bret Boone .05
134 Pat Borders .05
135 Gregg Olson .05
136 Brett Butler .05
137 Rob Deer .05
138 Darrin Jackson .05
139 John Kruk .05
140 Jay Bell .05
141 Bobby Witt .05
142 New Cubs (Dan Plesac, Randy Myers, Jose Guzman) .05
143 Wade Boggs (Little Hotshots) .15
144 Awesome Action #5 (Kenny Lofton) .05
145 Ben McDonald .05
146 Dwight Gooden .05
147 Terry Pendleton .05
148 Julio Franco .05
149 Ken Caminiti .05
150 Greg Vaughn .05
151 Sammy Sosa .05
152 David Valle .05
153 Wally Joyner .05
154 Dante Bichette .05
155 Mark Lewis .05
156 Bob Tewksbury .05
157 Billy Hatcher .05
158 Jack McDowell .05
159 Marquis Grissom .05
160 Jack Morris .05
161 Ramon Martinez .05
162 Deion Sanders .05
163 Tim Belcher .05
164 Mascots .05
165 Scott Leius .05
166 Brady Anderson .05
167 Randy Johnson .25
168 Mark Gubicza .05
169 Chuck Finley .05
170 Terry Mulholland .05
171 Matt Williams .05
172 Dwight Smith .05
173 Bobby Bonilla .05
174 Ken Hill .05
175 Doug Jones .05
176 Tony Phillips .05
177 Terry Steinbach .05
178 Frank Viola .05
179 Robin Ventura .05
180 Shane Mack .05
181 Kenny Lofton .05
182 Jeff King .05
183 Tim Teufel .05
184 Chris Sabo .05
185 Lenny Dykstra .05
186 Trevor Wilson .05
187 Darryl Strawberry .05
188 Robin Yount .25
189 Bob Wickman .05
190 Luis Polonia .05
191 Alan Trammell .05
192 Bob Welch .05
193 Awesome Action #6 .05
194 Tom Pagnozzi .05
195 Bret Barberie .05
196 Awesome Action #7 (Mike Scioscia) .05
197 Randy Tomlin .05
198 Checklist 133-198 .05
199 Ron Gant .05
200 Awesome Action #8 (Roberto Alomar) .05
201 Andy Benes .05
202 Pepper .05
203 Steve Finley .05
204 Steve Olin .05
205 Chris Hoiles .05
206 John Wetteland .05
207 Danny Tartabull .05
208 Bernard Gilkey .05
209 Tom Glavine (Little Hotshots) .05
210 Benito Santiago .05
211 Mark Grace .05
212 Glenallen Hill .05
213 Jeff Brantley .05
214 George Brett .40
215 Mark Lemke .05
216 Ron Karkovice .05
217 Tom Brunansky .05
218 Todd Hundley .05
219 Rickey Henderson .05
220 Joe Oliver .05
221 Juan Gonzalez .15
222 John Olerud .05
223 Hal Morris .05
224 Lou Whitaker .05
225 Bryan Harvey .05
226 Mike Gallego .05
227 Willie McGee .05
228 Jose Oquendo .05
229 Darren Daulton (Little Hotshots) .05
230 Curt Schilling .10
231 Jay Buhner .05
232 New Astros (Doug Drabek, Greg Swindell) .05
233 Jaime Navarro .05

234	Kevin Appier	.05
235	Mark Langston	.05
236	Jeff Montgomery	.05
237	Joe Girardi	.05
238	Ed Sprague	.05
239	Dan Walters	.05
240	Kevin Tapani	.05
241	Pete Harnisch	.05
242	Al Martin	.05
243	Jose Canseco	.15
244	Moises Alou	.05
245	Mark McGwire (Little Hotshots)	.25
246	Luis Rivera	.05
247	George Bell	.05
248	B.J. Surhoff	.05
249	Dave Justice	.05
250	Brian Harper	.05
251	Sandy Alomar, Jr.	.05
252	Kevin Brown	.05
253	New Dodgers (Tim Wallach, Jody Reed, Todd Worrell)	.05
254	Ray Lankford	.05
255	Derek Bell	.05
256	Joe Grahe	.05
257	Charlie Hayes	.05
258	New Yankees (Wade Boggs, Jim Abbott)	.25
259	Joe Robbie Stadium	.05
260	Kirby Puckett	.35
261	Fun at the Ballpark (Jay Bell, Vince Coleman)	.05
262	Bill Swift	.05
263	Fun at the Ballpark (Roger McDowell)	.05
264	Checklist 199-264	.05

Action Baseball

These game folders were inserted in each 1993 Triple Play foil pack. Because collation of the folders was very bad, few collectors bothered to save them. Measuring 2-1/2" x 5", fronts have an action photo of an unnamed player. Printed over the bottom of the photo are two full-color team logos, with a white "Versus" between. Inside the folder is a baseball diamond diagram, a three-inning scoreboard, rules for playing the game and 32 scratch-off squares for playing. Backs have a number designating the folder as "of 30."

		NM/M
Complete Set (30):		3.00
Common Player:		.10
1	Andy Van Slyke	.10
2	Bobby Bonilla	.10
3	Ozzie Smith	.30
4	Ryne Sandberg	.30
5	Darren Daulton	.10
6	Larry Walker	.10
7	Eric Karros	.10
8	Barry Larkin	.10
9	Deion Sanders	.10
10	Gary Sheffield	.20
11	Will Clark	.10
12	Jeff Bagwell	.25
13	Roberto Alomar	.15
14	Roger Clemens	.35
15	Cecil Fielder	.10
16	Robin Yount	.25
17	Cal Ripken, Jr.	.50
18	Carlos Baerga	.10
19	Don Mattingly	.35
20	Kirby Puckett	.30
21	Frank Thomas	.25
22	Juan Gonzalez	.15
23	Mark McGwire	.45
24	Ken Griffey Jr.	.40
25	Wally Joyner	.10
26	Chad Curtis	.10
27	Batting glove	.10
28	Juan Guzman	.10
29	Dave Justice	.10
30	Joe Carter	.10

Gallery

The Gallery of Stars cards were found as random inserts in Triple Play jumbo packs. The cards feature Dick Perez painted representations of the players.

		NM/M
Complete Set (10):		7.00
Common Player:		.50
1	Barry Bonds	3.00
2	Andre Dawson	.65
3	Wade Boggs	1.50
4	Greg Maddux	1.50
5	Dave Winfield	1.00
6	Paul Molitor	1.00
7	Jim Abbott	.50
8	J.T. Snow	.50
9	Benito Santiago	.50
10	David Nied	.50

League Leaders

These "double-headed" cards feature one player on each side. The six cards were random inserts in Triple Play retail packs.

		NM/M
Complete Set (6):		7.00
Common Player:		.50
1	Barry Bonds, Dennis Eckersley	3.50
2	Greg Maddux, Dennis Eckersley	2.00
3	Eric Karros, Pat Listach	.75
4	Fred McGriff, Juan Gonzalez	.75
5	Darren Daulton, Cecil Fielder	.50
6	Gary Sheffield, Edgar Martinez	.50

Nicknames

Popular nicknames of 10 of the game's top stars are featured in silver foil on this insert set found in Triple Play foil packs.

		NM/M
Complete Set (10):		10.00
Common Player:		.75
1	Frank Thomas (Big Hurt)	1.25
2	Roger Clemens (Rocket)	2.00
3	Ryne Sandberg (Ryno)	1.50
4	Will Clark (Thrill)	.75
5	Ken Griffey Jr. (Junior)	3.00
6	Dwight Gooden (Doc)	.75
7	Nolan Ryan (Express)	4.00
8	Deion Sanders (Prime Time)	.75
9	Ozzie Smith (Wizard)	1.50
10	Fred McGriff (Crime Dog)	.75

1994 Triple Play Promos

This set was given to dealers to preview the 1994 Donruss Triple Play issue. Cards are virtually identical to the regular-issue cards except for a large black "Promotional Sample" printed diagonally in black on both front and back. Cards are numbered as "X of 10" on the promos.

		NM/M
Complete Set (10):		9.00
Common Player:		.50
1	Juan Gonzalez	.60
2	Frank Thomas	.85
3	Barry Bonds	3.00
4	Ken Griffey Jr.	1.50
5	Paul Molitor	.75
6	Mike Piazza	1.50
7	Tim Salmon	.50
8	Lenny Dykstra	.50
9	Don Mattingly	1.25
10	Greg Maddux	1.00

1994 Triple Play

Triple Play cards returned for a third year in 1994, this time with a borderless design. According to company officials, production was less than 1994 Donruss Series I baseball, which was roughly 17,500 20-box cases. In the regular-issue 300-card set, 10 players from each team were featured, along with a 17-card Rookie Review subset and several insert sets.

		NM/M
Complete Set (300):		7.50
Common Player:		.05
Wax Pack (12):		.50
Wax Box (36):		12.00
1	Mike Bordick	.05
2	Dennis Eckersley	.35
3	Brent Gates	.05
4	Rickey Henderson	.40
5	Mark McGwire	.65
6	Troy Neel	.05
7	Craig Paquette	.05
8	Ruben Sierra	.05
9	Terry Steinbach	.05
10	Bobby Witt	.05
11	Chad Curtis	.05
12	Chili Davis	.05
13	Gary DiSarcina	.05
14	Damion Easley	.05
15	Chuck Finley	.05
16	Joe Grahe	.05
17	Mark Langston	.05
18	Eduardo Perez	.05
19	Tim Salmon	.05
20	J.T. Snow	.05
21	Jeff Bagwell	.40
22	Craig Biggio	.05
23	Ken Caminiti	.05
24	Andujar Cedeno	.05
25	Doug Drabek	.05
26	Steve Finley	.05
27	Luis Gonzalez	.05
28	Pete Harnisch	.05
29	Darryl Kile	.05
30	Mitch Williams	.05
31	Roberto Alomar	.20
32	Joe Carter	.05
33	Juan Guzman	.05
34	Pat Hentgen	.05
35	Paul Molitor	.40
36	John Olerud	.05
37	Ed Sprague	.05
38	Dave Stewart	.05
39	Duane Ward	.05
40	Devon White	.05
41	Steve Avery	.05
42	Jeff Blauser	.05
43	Ron Gant	.05
44	Tom Glavine	.20
45	Dave Justice	.05
46	Greg Maddux	.45
47	Fred McGriff	.05
48	Terry Pendleton	.05
49	Deion Sanders	.05
50	John Smoltz	.05
51	Ricky Bones	.05
52	Cal Eldred	.05
53	Darryl Hamilton	.05
54	John Jaha	.05
55	Pat Listach	.05
56	Jaime Navarro	.05
57	Dave Nilsson	.05
58	B.J. Surhoff	.05
59	Greg Vaughn	.05
60	Robin Yount	.40
61	Bernard Gilkey	.05
62	Gregg Jefferies	.05
63	Brian Jordan	.05
64	Ray Lankford	.05
65	Tom Pagnozzi	.05
66	Ozzie Smith	.45
67	Bob Tewksbury	.05
68	Allen Watson	.05
69	Mark Whiten	.05
70	Todd Zeile	.05
71	Steve Buechele	.05
72	Mark Grace	.05
73	Jose Guzman	.05
74	Derrick May	.05
75	Mike Morgan	.05
76	Randy Myers	.05
77	Ryne Sandberg	.45
78	Sammy Sosa	.50
79	Jose Vizcaino	.05
80	Rick Wilkins	.05
81	Pedro Astacio	.05
82	Brett Butler	.05
83	Delino DeShields	.05
84	Orel Hershiser	.05
85	Eric Karros	.05
86	Ramon Martinez	.05
87	Jose Offerman	.05
88	Mike Piazza	.50
89	Darryl Strawberry	.05
90	Tim Wallach	.05
91	Moises Alou	.05
92	Wil Cordero	.05
93	Jeff Fassero	.05
94	Darrin Fletcher	.05
95	Marquis Grissom	.05
96	Ken Hill	.05
97	Mike Lansing	.05
98	Kirk Rueter	.05
99	Larry Walker	.05
100	John Wetteland	.05
101	Rod Beck	.05
102	Barry Bonds	.75
103	John Burkett	.05
104	Royce Clayton	.05
105	Darren Lewis	.05
106	Kirt Manwaring	.05
107	Willie McGee	.05
108	Bill Swift	.05
109	Robby Thompson	.05
110	Matt Williams	.20
111	Sandy Alomar Jr.	.05
112	Carlos Baerga	.05
113	Albert Belle	.05
114	Wayne Kirby	.05
115	Kenny Lofton	.05
116	Jose Mesa	.05
117	Eddie Murray	.40
118	Charles Nagy	.05
119	Paul Sorrento	.05
120	Jim Thome	.35
121	Rich Amaral	.05
122	Eric Anthony	.05
123	Mike Blowers	.05
124	Chris Bosio	.05
125	Jay Buhner	.05
126	Dave Fleming	.05
127	Ken Griffey Jr.	.50
128	Randy Johnson	.40
129	Edgar Martinez	.05
130	Tino Martinez	.05
131	Bret Barberie	.05
132	Ryan Bowen	.05
133	Chuck Carr	.05
134	Jeff Conine	.05
135	Orestes Destrade	.05
136	Chris Hammond	.05
137	Bryan Harvey	.05
138	Dave Magadan	.05
139	Benito Santiago	.05
140	Gary Sheffield	.30
141	Bobby Bonilla	.05
142	Jeromy Burnitz	.05
143	Dwight Gooden	.05
144	Todd Hundley	.05
145	Bobby Jones	.05
146	Jeff Kent	.05
147	Joe Orsulak	.05
148	Bret Saberhagen	.05
149	Pete Schourek	.05
150	Ryan Thompson	.05
151	Brady Anderson	.05
152	Harold Baines	.05
153	Mike Devereaux	.05
154	Chris Hoiles	.05
155	Ben McDonald	.05
156	Mark McLemore	.05
157	Mike Mussina	.25
158	Rafael Palmeiro	.40
159	Cal Ripken, Jr.	.75
160	Chris Sabo	.05
161	Brad Ausmus	.05
162	Derek Bell	.05
163	Andy Benes	.05
164	Doug Brocail	.05
165	Archi Cianfrocco	.05
166	Ricky Gutierrez	.05
167	Tony Gwynn	.45
168	Gene Harris	.05
169	Pedro Martinez	.40
170	Phil Plantier	.05
171	Darren Daulton	.05
172	Mariano Duncan	.05
173	Len Dykstra	.05
174	Tommy Greene	.05
175	Dave Hollins	.05
176	Danny Jackson	.05
177	John Kruk	.05
178	Terry Mulholland	.05
179	Curt Schilling	.20
180	Kevin Stocker	.05
181	Jay Bell	.05
182	Steve Cooke	.05
183	Carlos Garcia	.05
184	Joel Johnston	.05
185	Jeff King	.05
186	Al Martin	.05
187	Orlando Merced	.05
188	Don Slaught	.05
189	Andy Van Slyke	.05
190	Kevin Young	.05
191	Kevin Brown	.05
192	Jose Canseco	.25
193	Will Clark	.05
194	Juan Gonzalez	.20
195	Tom Henke	.05
196	David Hulse	.05
197	Dean Palmer	.05
198	Roger Pavlik	.05
199	Ivan Rodriguez	.35
200	Kenny Rogers	.05
201	Roger Clemens	.45
202	Scott Cooper	.05
203	Andre Dawson	.20
204	Mike Greenwell	.05
205	Billy Hatcher	.05
206	Jeff Russell	.05
207	Aaron Sele	.05
208	John Valentin	.05
209	Mo Vaughn	.05
210	Frank Viola	.05
211	Rob Dibble	.05
212	Willie Greene	.05
213	Roberto Kelly	.05
214	Barry Larkin	.05
215	Kevin Mitchell	.05
216	Hal Morris	.05
217	Joe Oliver	.05
218	Jose Rijo	.05
219	Reggie Sanders	.05
220	John Smiley	.05
221	Dante Bichette	.05
222	Ellis Burks	.05
223	Andres Galarraga	.05
224	Joe Girardi	.05
225	Charlie Hayes	.05
226	Darren Holmes	.05
227	Howard Johnson	.05
228	Roberto Mejia	.05
229	David Nied	.05
230	Armando Reynoso	.05
231	Kevin Appier	.05
232	David Cone	.05
233	Greg Gagne	.05
234	Tom Gordon	.05
235	Felix Jose	.05
236	Wally Joyner	.05
237	Jose Lind	.05
238	Brian McRae	.05
239	Mike MacFarlane	.05
240	Jeff Montgomery	.05
241	Eric Davis	.05
242	John Doherty	.05
243	Cecil Fielder	.05
244	Travis Fryman	.05
245	Bill Gullickson	.05
246	Mike Henneman	.05
247	Tony Phillips	.05
248	Mickey Tettleton	.05
249	Alan Trammell	.05
250	Lou Whitaker	.05
251	Rick Aguilera	.05
252	Scott Erickson	.05
253	Kent Hrbek	.05
254	Chuck Knoblauch	.05
255	Shane Mack	.05
256	Dave McCarty	.05
257	Pat Meares	.05
258	Kirby Puckett	.45
259	Kevin Tapani	.05
260	Dave Winfield	.40
261	Wilson Alvarez	.05
262	Jason Bere	.05
263	Alex Fernandez	.05
264	Ozzie Guillen	.05
265	Roberto Hernandez	.05
266	Lance Johnson	.05
267	Jack McDowell	.05
268	Tim Raines	.05
269	Frank Thomas	.40
270	Robin Ventura	.05
271	Jim Abbott	.05
272	Wade Boggs	.45
273	Mike Gallego	.05
274	Pat Kelly	.05
275	Jimmy Key	.05
276	Don Mattingly	.50
277	Paul O'Neill	.05
278	Mike Stanley	.05
279	Danny Tartabull	.05
280	Bernie Williams	.05
281	Chipper Jones	.50
282	Ryan Klesko	.05
283	Javier Lopez	.05
284	Jeffrey Hammonds	.05
285	Jeff McNeely	.05
286	Manny Ramirez	.40
287	Billy Ashley	.05
288	Raul Mondesi	.05
289	Cliff Floyd	.05
290	Rondell White	.05
291	Steve Karsay	.05
292	Midre Cummings	.05
293	Salomon Torres	.05
294	J.R. Phillips	.05
295	Marc Newfield	.05
296	Carlos Delgado	.30
297	Butch Huskey	.05
298	Checklist (Frank Thomas)	.05
299	Checklist (Barry Bonds)	.05
300	Checklist (Juan Gonzalez)	.05

Bomb Squad

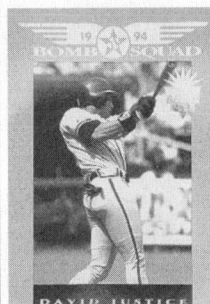

Ten of the top major league home run hitters are included in this insert set. Fronts feature sepia-toned player photos within a wide brown frame. Gold foil enhances the typography. Backs have a white background with representations of vintage airplanes. A bar chart at left gives the player's home run totals by year. A small color portrait photo is at upper-right. Below are a few words about his homer history.

		NM/M
Complete Set (10):		5.00
Common Player:		.25
1	Frank Thomas	1.00
2	Cecil Fielder	.25
3	Juan Gonzalez	.45
4	Barry Bonds	2.50
5	Dave Justice	.25
6	Fred McGriff	.25
7	Ron Gant	.25
8	Ken Griffey Jr.	1.50
9	Albert Belle	.25
10	Matt Williams	.25

Medalists

Statistical performance over the 1992-93 seasons was used to rank the players appearing in the Medalists insert set. Horizontal format cards have photos of the first, second and third place winners in appropriate boxes of gold, silver and bronze foil. "Medalists," the "medals" and "Triple Play 94" are embossed on the front. Backs have color action photos of each player along with team logos and a few stats.

		NM/M
Complete Set (15):		10.00
Common Player:		.50
1	A.L. Catchers (Chris Hoiles, Mickey Tettleton, Brian Harper)	.50

2	N.L. Catchers (Darren Daulton, Rick Wilkins, Kirt Manwaring)	.50
3	A.L. First Basemen (Frank Thomas, Rafael Palmeiro, John Olerud)	1.00
4	N.L. First Basemen (Mark Grace, Fred McGriff, Jeff Bagwell)	1.00
5	A.L. Second Basemen (Roberto Alomar, Carlos Baerga, Lou Whitaker)	.50
6	N.L. Second Basemen (Ryne Sandberg, Craig Biggio, Robby Thompson)	1.25
7	A.L. Shortstops (Tony Fernandez, Cal Ripken, Alan Trammell)	2.00
8	N.L. Shortstops (Barry Larkin, Jay Bell, Jeff Blauser)	.50
9	A.L. Third Basemen (Robin Ventura, Travis Fryman, Wade Boggs)	1.25
10	N.L. Third Basemen (Terry Pendleton, Dave Hollins, Gary Sheffield)	.50
11	A.L. Outfielders (Ken Griffey Jr., Kirby Puckett, Albert Belle)	1.50
12	N.L. Outfielders (Barry Bonds, Andy Van Slyke, Len Dykstra)	2.00
13	A.L. Starters (Jack McDowell, Kevin Brown, Randy Johnson)	.60
14	N.L. Starters (Greg Maddux, Jose Rijo, Billy Swift)	1.25
15	Designated Hitters (Paul Molitor, Dave Winfield, Harold Baines)	.60

Nicknames

Eight of baseball's most colorful team nicknames are featured in this insert set. Fronts feature a background photo representative of the nickname, with a player photo is superimposed over that. Backs have another player photo and a history of the team's nickname.

		NM/M
	Complete Set (8):	10.00
	Common Player:	.75
1	Cecil Fielder	.75
2	Ryne Sandberg	1.50
3	Gary Sheffield	.90
4	Joe Carter	.75
5	John Olerud	.75
6	Cal Ripken, Jr.	3.00
7	Mark McGwire	2.50
8	Gregg Jefferies	.75

1990 Tropicana Team Mets

In 1990, Tropicana orange juice took over as sponsor of the junior Mets fan club. One of the membership perks was a nine-card

---

sheet. Action photos were surrounded by team-color stripes of blue and orange and a white outer border. Backs have Team Mets and Tropicana logos, 1989 highlights and stats, career numbers and personal data. Individual cards measure 2-1/2" x 3-1/2", though they are not often sold other than as an original 7-1/2" x 10-1/2" sheet. Cards are checklisted here on the basis of uniform numbers found on the cards' fronts.

		NM/M
	Complete Set (9):	4.00
	Common Player:	.50
9	Gregg Jefferies	.50
16	Dwight Gooden	.50
18	Darryl Strawberry	.50
20	Howard Johnson	.50
21	Kevin Elster	.50
25	Keith Miller	.50
29	Frank Viola	.50
44	David Cone	.50
50	Sid Fernandez	.50

1991 Tropicana Team Mets

This nine-card sheet was a perk for members of the junior Mets fan club - Team Mets. Sponsored by Tropicana fruit juices for the second straight year, the 2-1/2" x 3-1/2" individual cards on the 7-1/2" x 10-1/2" sheet feature color action photos of the players, surrounded by team-color blue and orange stripes and an outer white border. Backs have 1990 highlights and stats, career stats and biographical details, along with the Team Mets and Tropicana logos. Cards are checklisted here according to the uniform numbers found on the front.

		NM/M
	Complete Set (9):	4.00
	Common Player:	.50
2	Mackey Sasser	.50
9	Gregg Jefferies	.50
10	Dave Magadan	.50
16	Dwight Gooden	.50
20	Howard Johnson	.50
22	Kevin McReynolds	.50
29	Frank Viola	.50
31	John Franco	.50
44	David Cone	.50

1983 True Value White Sox

Issued by the White Sox and True Value hardware stores, these 2-5/8" x 4-1/8" cards are among the scarcer early 1980s regional sets. The issue was originally scheduled as part of a promotion in which cards were given out at special Tuesday night games. The idea was sound, but rainouts forced the cancellation of some games so those scheduled cards were never given

---

out. They were, however, smuggled out to hobby channels making it possible, although not easy, to assemble complete sets. The cards feature a large color photo with a wide white border. A team logo is at lower-left while the player's name, position and uniform number are in the lower-right. Backs feature a True Value ad along with statistics. The three cards which were never given out through the normal channels are considered scarcer than the others. They are Marc Hill, Harold Baines and Salome Barojas.

		NM/M
	Complete Set (23):	12.00
	Common Player:	.25
1	Scott Fletcher	.25
2	Harold Baines	3.50
5	Vance Law	.25
7	Marc Hill	2.00
10	Tony LaRussa	.40
11	Rudy Law	.25
17	Tony Bernazard	.25
19	Greg Luzinski	.25
24	Floyd Bannister	.25
25	Mike Squires	.25
30	Salome Barojas	2.00
31	LaMarr Hoyt	.25
34	Richard Dotson	.25
36	Jerry Koosman	.25
40	Britt Burns	.25
41	Dick Tidrow	.25
42	Ron Kittle	.25
44	Tom Paciorek	.25
45	Kevin Hickey	.25
53	Dennis Lamp	.25
67	Jim Kern	.25
72	Carlton Fisk	1.50

1984 True Value White Sox

CARLTON FISK
Catcher 72

True Value hardware stores and the White Sox gave the Tuesday night baseball card promotion at Comiskey Park another try in 1984. The cards measure 2-5/8" x 4-1/8". In addition to the players, there are cards for manager Tony LaRussa, the coaching staff, and former Sox greats Luis Aparicio and Minnie Minoso. Card design is very similar to the 1983 cards. As the cards were given out two at a time, it was very difficult to acquire a complete set. Additionally, as numbers available vary because of attendance, some cards are scarcer than others.

		NM/M
	Complete Set (30):	25.00
	Common Player:	.50
1	Scott Fletcher	.50
3	Harold Baines	1.00
5	Vance Law	.50
7	Marc Hill	.50
8	Dave Stegman	.50
10	Tony LaRussa	1.00
11	Rudy Law	.50
16	Julio Cruz	.50
17	Jerry Hairston Sr.	.50
19	Greg Luzinski	.50
20	Jerry Dybzinski	.50
24	Floyd Bannister	.50
25	Mike Squires	.50
27	Ron Reed	.50
29	Greg Walker	.50
30	Salome Barojas	.50
31	LaMarr Hoyt	.50
32	Tim Hulett	.50
34	Richard Dotson	.50
40	Britt Burns	.50
41	Tom Seaver	5.00
42	Ron Kittle	.50
44	Tom Paciorek	.50
50	Juan Agosto	.50
59	Tom Brennan	.50

72	Carlton Fisk	3.00
---	Minnie Minoso	3.00
---	Luis Aparicio	3.00
---	Nancy Faust (organist)	.50
---	The Coaching Staff (Ed Brinkman, Dave Duncan, Art Kusnyer, Tony LaRussa, Jim Leyland, Dave Nelson, Joe Nossek)	.50

1986 True Value

A 30-card set of 2-1/2" x 3-1/2" cards was available in three-card folders at True Value hardware stores with a purchase of $5 or more. Fronts feature a portrait flanked by stars with balls and bats at the bottom. The player's ID and a Major League Players Association logo are at bottom. Team insignia have been removed from the uniforms. Backs feature some personal information and brief 1985 statistics. Along with the player cards, the folders contained a sweepstakes card offering trips to postseason games and other prizes.

		NM/M
	Complete Panel Set (10):	6.00
	Complete Singles Set (30):	5.00
	Common Player:	.05
Panel (1)		.50
1	Pedro Guerrero	.05
2	Steve Garvey	.10
3	Eddie Murray	.25
Panel (2)		1.25
4	Pete Rose	.60
5	Don Mattingly	.50
6	Fernando Valenzuela	.05
Panel (3)		.50
7	Jim Rice	.15
8	Kirk Gibson	.05
9	Ozzie Smith	.35
Panel (4)		.75
10	Dale Murphy	.15
11	Robin Yount	.25
12	Tom Seaver	.25
Panel (5)		.75
13	Reggie Jackson	.35
14	Ryne Sandberg	.35
15	Bruce Sutter	.25
Panel (6)		.75
16	Gary Carter	.25
17	George Brett	.50
18	Rick Sutcliffe	.05
Panel (7)		.25
19	Dave Steib	.05
20	Buddy Bell	.05
21	Alvin Davis	.05
Panel (8)		1.00
22	Cal Ripken Jr.	.75
23	Bill Madlock	.05
24	Kent Hrbek	.05
Panel (9)		1.00
25	Lou Whitaker	.05
26	Nolan Ryan	.75
27	Dwayne Murphy	.05
Panel (10)		1.00
28	Mike Schmidt	.50
29	Andre Dawson	.15
30	Wade Boggs	.35

U

1991 Ultra

GEORGE BELL
CUBS OUTFIELD

This 400-card set was originally going to be called the Elite set, but Fleer chose to use the Ultra label. The card fronts feature gray borders surrounding full-color action photos. The backs feature

---

three player photos and statistics. Hot Prospects and Great Performers are among the special cards featured within the set.

		NM/M
	Complete Set (400):	12.00
	Common Player:	.05
	Wax Pack (14):	.50
	Wax Box (36):	9.00
1	Steve Avery	.05
2	Jeff Blauser	.05
3	Francisco Cabrera	.05
4	Ron Gant	.05
5	Tom Glavine	.25
6	Tommy Gregg	.05
7	Dave Justice	.05
8	Oddibe McDowell	.05
9	Greg Olson	.05
10	Terry Pendleton	.05
11	Lonnie Smith	.05
12	John Smoltz	.05
13	Jeff Treadway	.05
14	Glenn Davis	.05
15	Mike Devereaux	.05
16	Leo Gomez	.05
17	Chris Hoiles	.05
18	Dave Johnson	.05
19	Ben McDonald	.05
20	Randy Milligan	.05
21	Gregg Olson	.05
22	Joe Orsulak	.05
23	Bill Ripken	.05
24	Cal Ripken, Jr.	1.50
25	David Segui	.05
26	Craig Worthington	.05
27	Wade Boggs	.60
28	Tom Bolton	.05
29	Tom Brunansky	.05
30	Ellis Burks	.05
31	Roger Clemens	.65
32	Mike Greenwell	.05
33	Greg Harris	.05
34	Daryl Irvine	.05
35	Mike Marshall	.05
36	Tim Naehring	.05
37	Tony Pena	.05
38	Phil Plantier **RC**	.05
39	Carlos Quintana	.05
40	Jeff Reardon	.05
41	Jody Reed	.05
42	Luis Rivera	.05
43	Jim Abbott	.05
44	Chuck Finley	.05
45	Bryan Harvey	.05
46	Donnie Hill	.05
47	Jack Howell	.05
48	Wally Joyner	.05
49	Mark Langston	.05
50	Kirk McCaskill	.05
51	Lance Parrish	.05
52	Dick Schofield	.05
53	Lee Stevens	.05
54	Dave Winfield	.50
55	George Bell	.05
56	Damon Berryhill	.05
57	Mike Bielecki	.05
58	Andre Dawson	.25
59	Shawon Dunston	.05
60	Joe Girardi	.05
61	Mark Grace	.05
62	Mike Harkey	.05
63	Les Lancaster	.05
64	Greg Maddux	.60
65	Derrick May	.05
66	Ryne Sandberg	.60
67	Luis Salazar	.05
68	Dwight Smith	.05
69	Hector Villanueva	.05
70	Jerome Walton	.05
71	Mitch Williams	.05
72	Carlton Fisk	.50
73	Scott Fletcher	.05
74	Ozzie Guillen	.05
75	Greg Hibbard	.05
76	Lance Johnson	.05
77	Steve Lyons	.05
78	Jack McDowell	.05
79	Dan Pasqua	.05
80	Melido Perez	.05
81	Tim Raines	.05
82	Sammy Sosa	.60
83	Cory Snyder	.05
84	Bobby Thigpen	.05
85	Frank Thomas	.05
86	Robin Ventura	.05
87	Todd Benzinger	.05
88	Glenn Braggs	.05
89	Tom Browning	.05
90	Norm Charlton	.05
91	Eric Davis	.05
92	Rob Dibble	.05
93	Bill Doran	.05
94	Mariano Duncan	.05
95	Billy Hatcher	.05
96	Barry Larkin	.05
97	Randy Myers	.05
98	Hal Morris	.05
99	Joe Oliver	.05
100	Paul O'Neill	.05
101a	Jeff Reed	.05
101b	Beau Allred (Should be #104.)	.05
102	Jose Rijo	.05
103a	Chris Sabo	.05
103b	Carlos Baerga (Should be #106.)	.05

105	Sandy Alomar, Jr.	.05
107	Albert Belle	.05
108	Jerry Browne	.05
109	Tom Candiotti	.05
110	Alex Cole	.05
111a	John Farrell	.05
111b	Chris James (Should be #114.)	.05
112	Felix Fermin	.05
113	Brook Jacoby	.05
115	Doug Jones	.05
116a	Steve Olin	.05
116b	Mitch Webster (Should be #119.)	.05
117	Greg Swindell	.05
118	Turner Ward	.05
120	Dave Bergman	.05
121	Cecil Fielder	.05
122	Travis Fryman	.05
123	Mike Henneman	.05
124	Lloyd Moseby	.05
125	Dan Petry	.05
126	Tony Phillips	.05
127	Mark Salas	.05
128	Frank Tanana	.05
129	Alan Trammell	.05
130	Lou Whitaker	.05
131	Eric Anthony	.05
132	Craig Biggio	.05
133	Ken Caminiti	.05
134	Casey Candaele	.05
135	Andujar Cedeno	.05
136	Mark Davidson	.05
137	Jim Deshaies	.05
138	Mark Portugal	.05
139	Rafael Ramirez	.05
140	Mike Scott	.05
141	Eric Yelding	.05
142	Gerald Young	.05
143	Kevin Appier	.05
144	George Brett	.65
145	Jeff Conine **RC**	.40
146	Jim Eisenreich	.05
147	Tom Gordon	.05
148	Mark Gubicza	.05
149	Bo Jackson	.10
150	Brent Mayne	.05
151	Mike Macfarlane	.05
152	Brian McRae **RC**	.10
153	Jeff Montgomery	.05
154	Bret Saberhagen	.05
155	Kevin Seitzer	.05
156	Terry Shumpert	.05
157	Kurt Stillwell	.05
158	Danny Tartabull	.05
159	Tim Belcher	.05
160	Kal Daniels	.05
161	Alfredo Griffin	.05
162	Lenny Harris	.05
163	Jay Howell	.05
164	Ramon Martinez	.05
165	Mike Morgan	.05
166	Eddie Murray	.50
167	Jose Offerman	.05
168	Juan Samuel	.05
169	Mike Scioscia	.05
170	Mike Sharperson	.05
171	Darryl Strawberry	.05
172	Greg Brock	.05
173	Chuck Crim	.05
174	Jim Gantner	.05
175	Ted Higuera	.05
176	Mark Knudson	.05
177	Tim McIntosh	.05
178	Paul Molitor	.50
179	Dan Plesac	.05
180	Gary Sheffield	.35
181	Bill Spiers	.05
182	B.J. Surhoff	.05
183	Greg Vaughn	.05
184	Robin Yount	.50
185	Rick Aguilera	.05
186	Greg Gagne	.05
187	Dan Gladden	.05
188	Brian Harper	.05
189	Kent Hrbek	.05
190	Gene Larkin	.05
191	Shane Mack	.05
192	Pedro Munoz	.05
193	Al Newman	.05
194	Junior Ortiz	.05
195	Kirby Puckett	.60
196	Kevin Tapani	.05
197	Dennis "Oil Can" Boyd	.05
198	Tim Burke	.05
199	Ivan Calderon	.05
200	Delino DeShields	.05
201	Mike Fitzgerald	.05
202	Steve Frey	.05
203	Andres Galarraga	.05
204	Marquis Grissom	.05
205	Dave Martinez	.05
206	Dennis Martinez	.05
207	Junior Noboa	.05
208	Spike Owen	.05
209	Scott Ruskin	.05
210	Tim Wallach	.05
211	Daryl Boston	.05
212	Vince Coleman	.05
213	David Cone	.05
214	Ron Darling	.05
215	Kevin Elster	.05
216	Sid Fernandez	.05
217	John Franco	.05
218	Dwight Gooden	.05
219	Tom Herr	.05
220	Todd Hundley	.05
221	Gregg Jefferies	.05

#	Player	Price
222	Howard Johnson	.05
223	Dave Magadan	.05
224	Kevin McReynolds	.05
225	Keith Miller	.05
226	Mackey Sasser	.05
227	Frank Viola	.05
228	Jesse Barfield	.05
229	Greg Cadaret	.05
230	Alvaro Espinoza	.05
231	Bob Geren	.05
232	Lee Guetterman	.05
233	Mel Hall	.05
234	Andy Hawkins	.05
235	Roberto Kelly	.05
236	Tim Leary	.05
237	Jim Leyritz	.05
238	Kevin Maas	.05
239	Don Mattingly	.65
240	Hensley Meulens	.05
241	Eric Plunk	.05
242	Steve Sax	.05
243	Todd Burns	.05
244	Jose Canseco	.35
245	Dennis Eckersley	.40
246	Mike Gallego	.05
247	Dave Henderson	.05
248	Rickey Henderson	.50
249	Rick Honeycutt	.05
250	Carney Lansford	.05
251	Mark McGwire	1.00
252	Mike Moore	.05
253	Terry Steinbach	.05
254	Dave Stewart	.05
255	Walt Weiss	.05
256	Bob Welch	.05
257	Curt Young	.05
258	Wes Chamberlain	.05
259	Pat Combs	.05
260	Darren Daulton	.05
261	Jose DeJesus	.05
262	Len Dykstra	.05
263	Charlie Hayes	.05
264	Von Hayes	.05
265	Ken Howell	.05
266	John Kruk	.05
267	Roger McDowell	.05
268	Mickey Morandini	.05
269	Terry Mulholland	.05
270	Dale Murphy	.15
271	Randy Ready	.05
272	Dickie Thon	.05
273	Stan Belinda	.05
274	Jay Bell	.05
275	Barry Bonds	1.50
276	Bobby Bonilla	.05
277	Doug Drabek	.05
278	Carlos Garcia RC	.05
279	Neal Heaton	.05
280	Jeff King	.05
281	Bill Landrum	.05
282	Mike LaValliere	.05
283	Jose Lind	.05
284	Orlando Merced RC	.10
285	Gary Redus	.05
286	Don Slaught	.05
287	Andy Van Slyke	.05
288	Jose DeLeon	.05
289	Pedro Guerrero	.05
290	Ray Lankford	.05
291	Joe Magrane	.05
292	Jose Oquendo	.05
293	Tom Pagnozzi	.05
294	Bryn Smith	.05
295	Lee Smith	.05
296	Ozzie Smith	.60
297	Milt Thompson	.05
298	Craig Wilson RC	.05
299	Todd Zeile	.05
300	Shawn Abner	.05
301	Andy Benes	.05
302	Paul Faries	.05
303	Tony Gwynn	.60
304	Greg Harris	.05
305	Thomas Howard	.05
306	Bruce Hurst	.05
307	Craig Lefferts	.05
308	Fred McGriff	.05
309	Dennis Rasmussen	.05
310	Bip Roberts	.05
311	Benito Santiago	.05
312	Garry Templeton	.05
313	Ed Whitson	.05
314	Dave Anderson	.05
315	Kevin Bass	.05
316	Jeff Brantley	.05
317	John Burkett	.05
318	Will Clark	.05
319	Steve Decker	.05
320	Scott Garrelts	.05
321	Terry Kennedy	.05
322	Mark Leonard	.05
323	Darren Lewis	.05
324	Greg Litton	.05
325	Willie McGee	.05
326	Kevin Mitchell	.05
327	Don Robinson	.05
328	Andres Santana	.05
329	Robby Thompson	.05
330	Jose Uribe	.05
331	Matt Williams	.05
332	Scott Bradley	.05
333	Henry Cotto	.05
334	Alvin Davis	.05
335	Ken Griffey Sr.	.05
336	Ken Griffey Jr.	.75
337	Erik Hanson	.05
338	Brian Holman	.05
339	Randy Johnson	.50
340	Edgar Martinez	.05
341	Tino Martinez	.05
342	Pete O'Brien	.05
343	Harold Reynolds	.05
344	David Valle	.05
345	Omar Vizquel	.05
346	Brad Arnsberg	.05
347	Kevin Brown	.05
348	Julio Franco	.05
349	Jeff Huson	.05
350	Rafael Palmeiro	.40
351	Geno Petralli	.05
352	Gary Pettis	.05
353	Kenny Rogers	.05
354	Jeff Russell	.05
355	Nolan Ryan	1.50
356	Ruben Sierra	.05
357	Bobby Witt	.05
358	Roberto Alomar	.15
359	Pat Borders	.05
360	Joe Carter	.05
361	Kelly Gruber	.05
362	Tom Henke	.05
363	Glenallen Hill	.05
364	Jimmy Key	.05
365	Manny Lee	.05
366	Rance Mulliniks	.05
367	John Olerud	.05
368	Dave Stieb	.05
369	Duane Ward	.05
370	David Wells	.05
371	Mark Whiten	.05
372	Mookie Wilson	.05
373	Willie Banks	.05
374	Steve Carter	.05
375	Scott Chiamparino	.05
376	Steve Chitren	.05
377	Darrin Fletcher	.05
378	Rich Garces	.05
379	Reggie Jefferson	.05
380	Eric Karros RC	.50
381	Pat Kelly	.05
382	Chuck Knoblauch	.05
383	Denny Neagle	.05
384	Dan Opperman	.05
385	John Ramos	.05
386	Henry Rodriguez RC	.05
387	Mo Vaughn	.05
388	Gerald Williams	.05
389	Mike York	.05
390	Eddie Zosky	.05
391	Barry Bonds (Great Performer)	.75
392	Cecil Fielder (Great Performer)	.05
393	Rickey Henderson (Great Performer)	.25
394	Dave Justice (Great Performer)	.05
395	Nolan Ryan (Great Performer)	.75
396	Bobby Thigpen (Great Performer)	.05
397	Checklist	.05
398	Checklist	.05
399	Checklist	.05
400	Checklist	.05

Gold

BO JACKSON
KANSAS CITY ROYALS • OUTFIELD

A pair of action photos flanking and below a portrait in a home plate frame at top-center are featured on these cards. Background is a graduated gold coloring. The Fleer Ultra Team logo is in the upper-left corner. Backs have narrative career information. The Puckett and Sandberg cards feature incorrect historical information on the backs.

		NM/M
	Complete Set (10):	5.00
	Common Player:	.15
1	Barry Bonds	2.50
2	Will Clark	.15
3	Doug Drabek	.15
4	Ken Griffey Jr.	1.50
5	Rickey Henderson	.75
6	Bo Jackson	.25
7	Ramon Martinez	.15
8	Kirby Puckett	1.00
9	Chris Sabo	.15
10	Ryne Sandberg	1.00

Update

RICK WILKINS CUBS CATCHER

This 120-card set was produced as a supplement to the premier Fleer Ultra set. Cards feature the same style as the regular Fleer Ultra cards. The cards were sold only as complete sets in full color, shrinkwrapped boxes.

		NM/M
	Complete Set (120):	15.00
	Common Player:	.05
1	Dwight Evans	.05
2	Chito Martinez	.05
3	Bob Melvin	.05
4	Mike Mussina RC	3.00
5	Jack Clark	.05
6	Dana Kiecker	.05
7	Steve Lyons	.05
8	Gary Gaetti	.05
9	Dave Gallagher	.05
10	Dave Parker	.05
11	Luis Polonia	.05
12	Luis Sojo	.05
13	Wilson Alvarez	.05
14	Alex Fernandez	.05
15	Craig Grebeck	.05
16	Ron Karkovice	.05
17	Warren Newson	.05
18	Scott Radinsky	.05
19	Glenallen Hill	.05
20	Charles Nagy	.05
21	Mark Whiten	.05
22	Milt Cuyler	.05
23	Paul Gibson	.05
24	Mickey Tettleton	.05
25	Todd Benzinger	.05
26	Storm Davis	.05
27	Kirk Gibson	.05
28	Bill Pecota	.05
29	Gary Thurman	.05
30	Darryl Hamilton	.05
31	Jaime Navarro	.05
32	Willie Randolph	.05
33	Bill Wegman	.05
34	Randy Bush	.05
35	Chili Davis	.05
36	Scott Erickson	.05
37	Chuck Knoblauch	.05
38	Scott Leius	.05
39	Jack Morris	.05
40	John Habyan	.05
41	Pat Kelly	.05
42	Matt Nokes	.05
43	Scott Sanderson	.05
44	Bernie Williams	.05
45	Harold Baines	.05
46	Brook Jacoby	.05
47	Ernest Riles	.05
48	Willie Wilson	.05
49	Jay Buhner	.05
50	Rich DeLucia	.05
51	Mike Jackson	.05
52	Bill Krueger	.05
53	Bill Swift	.05
54	Brian Downing	.05
55	Juan Gonzalez	.75
56	Dean Palmer	.05
57	Kevin Reimer	.05
58	Ivan Rodriguez RC	6.00
59	Tom Candiotti	.05
60	Juan Guzman	.05
61	Bob MacDonald	.05
62	Greg Myers	.05
63	Ed Sprague	.05
64	Devon White	.05
65	Rafael Belliard	.05
66	Juan Berenguer	.05
67	Brian Hunter	.05
68	Kent Mercker	.05
69	Otis Nixon	.05
70	Danny Jackson	.05
71	Chuck McElroy	.05
72	Gary Scott	.05
73	Heathcliff Slocumb	.05
74	Chico Walker	.05
75	Rick Wilkins	.05
76	Chris Hammond	.05
77	Luis Quinones	.05
78	Herm Winningham	.05
79	Jeff Bagwell RC	6.00
80	Jim Corsi	.05
81	Steve Finley	.05
82	Luis Gonzalez RC	1.00
83	Pete Harnisch	.05
84	Darryl Kile	.05
85	Brett Butler	.05
86	Gary Carter	1.00
87	Tim Crews	.05
88	Orel Hershiser	.05
89	Bob Ojeda	.05
90	Bret Barberie	.05
91	Barry Jones	.05
92	Gilberto Reyes	.05
93	Larry Walker	.05
94	Hubie Brooks	.05
95	Tim Burke	.05
96	Rick Cerone	.05
97	Jeff Innis	.05
98	Wally Backman	.05
99	Tommy Greene	.05
100	Ricky Jordan	.05
101	Mitch Williams	.05
102	John Smiley	.05
103	Randy Tomlin	.05
104	Gary Varsho	.05
105	Cris Carpenter	.05
106	Ken Hill	.05
107	Felix Jose	.05
108	Omar Oliveras RC	.05
109	Gerald Perry	.05
110	Jerald Clark	.05
111	Tony Fernandez	.05
112	Darrin Jackson	.05
113	Mike Maddux	.05
114	Tim Teufel	.05
115	Bud Black	.05
116	Kelly Downs	.05
117	Mike Felder	.05
118	Willie McGee	.05
119	Trevor Wilson	.05
120	Checklist	.05

1992 Ultra Pre-Production Samples

ROGER CLEMENS

These cards were produced and distributed to hobby dealers to give them a preview of Ultra's second-year offering. Cards are virtually identical to the issued versions except for a white oval on back which has a "1992 / PRE-PRODUCTION / SAMPLE" notice printed in black. Each card (except the Gwynn) can also be found in a version with no card number on back; they are worth a small premium over the numbered promos. Two strips were issued, each with a different Gwynn card.

		NM/M
	Uncut Strip:	25.00
	Complete Set (6):	25.00
	Common Player:	1.00
118	Todd Van Poppel	1.00
180	Rey Sanchez	1.00
271	Ozzie Smith	7.50
288	Royce Clayton	1.00
6/25	Roger Clemens (Award Winners)	10.00
2/10	Tony Gwynn (Commemorative Series)	7.50
7/10	Tony Gwynn (Commemorative Series)	7.50

1992 Ultra

JOE CARTER TORONTO BLUE JAYS • OUTFIELD

Fleer released its second annual Ultra set in 1992. Card fronts feature full-color action photos with a marble accent at the card bottom. The flip sides are horizontal with two additional player photos. Many insert sets were randomly included in foil packs as premiums. These included rookie, All-Star and award winners, among others. A two-card Tony Gwynn send-away set was also available through an offer from Fleer. For $1 and 10 Ultra wrappers, collectors could receive the Gwynn cards. The set is numbered by team; cards #1-300 comprise Series I, cards #301-600 are Series II.

		NM/M
	Complete Set (600):	12.00
	Common Player:	.05
	Ser. 1 or 2 Pack (14):	.60
	Ser. 1 or 2 Box (36):	12.50
	Tony Gwynn Auto.	60.00
1	Glenn Davis	.05
2	Mike Devereaux	.05
3	Dwight Evans	.05
4	Leo Gomez	.05
5	Chris Hoiles	.05
6	Sam Horn	.05
7	Chito Martinez	.05
8	Randy Milligan	.05
9	Mike Mussina	.30
10	Billy Ripken	.05
11	Cal Ripken, Jr.	1.00
12	Tom Brunansky	.05
13	Ellis Burks	.05
14	Jack Clark	.05
15	Roger Clemens	.60
16	Mike Greenwell	.05
17	Joe Hesketh	.05
18	Tony Pena	.05
19	Carlos Quintana	.05
20	Jeff Reardon	.05
21	Jody Reed	.05
22	Luis Rivera	.05
23	Mo Vaughn	.05
24	Gary DiSarcina	.05
25	Chuck Finley	.05
26	Gary Gaetti	.05
27	Bryan Harvey	.05
28	Lance Parrish	.05
29	Luis Polonia	.05
30	Dick Schofield	.05
31	Luis Sojo	.05
32	Wilson Alvarez	.05
33	Carlton Fisk	.40
34	Craig Grebeck	.05
35	Ozzie Guillen	.05
36	Greg Hibbard	.05
37	Charlie Hough	.05
38	Lance Johnson	.05
39	Ron Karkovice	.05
40	Jack McDowell	.05
41	Donn Pall	.05
42	Melido Perez	.05
43	Tim Raines	.05
44	Frank Thomas	.40
45	Sandy Alomar, Jr.	.05
46	Carlos Baerga	.05
47	Albert Belle	.05
48	Jerry Browne	.05
49	Felix Fermin	.05
50	Reggie Jefferson	.05
51	Mark Lewis	.05
52	Carlos Martinez	.05
53	Steve Olin	.05
54	Jim Thome	.35
55	Mark Whiten	.05
56	Dave Bergman	.05
57	Milt Cuyler	.05
58	Rob Deer	.05
59	Cecil Fielder	.05
60	Travis Fryman	.05
61	Scott Livingstone	.05
62	Tony Phillips	.05
63	Mickey Tettleton	.05
64	Alan Trammell	.05
65	Lou Whitaker	.05
66	Kevin Appier	.05
67	Mike Boddicker	.05
68	George Brett	.60
69	Jim Eisenreich	.05
70	Mark Gubicza	.05
71	David Howard	.05
72	Joel Johnston	.05
73	Mike Macfarlane	.05
74	Brent Mayne	.05
75	Brian McRae	.05
76	Jeff Montgomery	.05
77	Terry Shumpert	.05
78	Don August	.05
79	Dante Bichette	.05
80	Ted Higuera	.05
81	Paul Molitor	.40
82	Jamie Navarro	.05
83	Gary Sheffield	.30
84	Bill Spiers	.05
85	B.J. Surhoff	.05
86	Greg Vaughn	.05
87	Robin Yount	.40
88	Rick Aguilera	.05
89	Chili Davis	.05
90	Scott Erickson	.05
91	Brian Harper	.05
92	Kent Hrbek	.05
93	Chuck Knoblauch	.05
94	Scott Leius	.05
95	Shane Mack	.05
96	Mike Pagliarulo	.05
97	Kirby Puckett	.50
98	Kevin Tapani	.05
99	Jesse Barfield	.05
100	Alvaro Espinoza	.05
101	Mel Hall	.05
102	Pat Kelly	.05
103	Roberto Kelly	.05
104	Kevin Maas	.05
105	Don Mattingly	.60
106	Hensley Meulens	.05
107	Matt Nokes	.05
108	Steve Sax	.05
109	Harold Baines	.05
110	Jose Canseco	.30
111	Ron Darling	.05
112	Mike Gallego	.05
113	Dave Henderson	.05
114	Rickey Henderson	.75
115	Mark McGwire	.75
116	Terry Steinbach	.05
117	Dave Stewart	.05
118	Todd Van Poppel	.05
119	Bob Welch	.05
120	Greg Briley	.05
121	Jay Buhner	.05
122	Rich DeLucia	.05
123	Ken Griffey Jr.	.65
124	Erik Hanson	.05
125	Randy Johnson	.40
126	Edgar Martinez	.05
127	Tino Martinez	.05
128	Pete O'Brien	.05
129	Harold Reynolds	.05
130	Dave Valle	.05
131	Julio Franco	.05
132	Juan Gonzalez	.20
133	Jeff Huson	.05
134	Mike Jeffcoat	.05
135	Terry Mathews	.05
136	Rafael Palmeiro	.35
137	Dean Palmer	.05
138	Geno Petralli	.05
139	Ivan Rodriguez	.35
140	Jeff Russell	.05
141	Nolan Ryan	1.00
142	Ruben Sierra	.05
143	Roberto Alomar	.15
144	Pat Borders	.05
145	Joe Carter	.05
146	Kelly Gruber	.05
147	Jimmy Key	.05
148	Manny Lee	.05
149	Rance Mulliniks	.05
150	Greg Myers	.05
151	John Olerud	.05
152	Dave Stieb	.05
153	Todd Stottlemyre	.05
154	Duane Ward	.05
155	Devon White	.05
156	Eddie Zosky	.05
157	Steve Avery	.05
158	Rafael Belliard	.05
159	Jeff Blauser	.05
160	Sid Bream	.05
161	Ron Gant	.05
162	Tom Glavine	.25
163	Brian Hunter	.05
164	Dave Justice	.05
165	Mark Lemke	.05
166	Greg Olson	.05
167	Terry Pendleton	.05
168	Lonnie Smith	.05
169	John Smoltz	.05
170	Mike Stanton	.05
171	Jeff Treadway	.05
172	Paul Assenmacher	.05
173	George Bell	.05
174	Shawon Dunston	.05
175	Mark Grace	.05
176	Danny Jackson	.05
177	Les Lancaster	.05
178	Greg Maddux	.50
179	Luis Salazar	.05
180	Rey Sanchez	.05
181	Ryne Sandberg	.50
182	Jose Vizcaino	.05
183	Chico Walker	.05
184	Jerome Walton	.05
185	Glenn Braggs	.05
186	Tom Browning	.05
187	Rob Dibble	.05
188	Bill Doran	.05
189	Chris Hammond	.05
190	Billy Hatcher	.05
191	Barry Larkin	.05
192	Hal Morris	.05
193	Joe Oliver	.05
194	Paul O'Neill	.05
195	Jeff Reed	.05
196	Jose Rijo	.05
197	Chris Sabo	.05
198	Jeff Bagwell	.40
199	Craig Biggio	.05
200	Ken Caminiti	.05
201	Andujar Cedeno	.05
202	Steve Finley	.05
203	Luis Gonzalez	.05
204	Pete Harnisch	.05
205	Xavier Hernandez	.05
206	Darryl Kile	.05
207	Al Osuna	.05
208	Curt Schilling	.25
209	Brett Butler	.05
210	Kal Daniels	.05
211	Lenny Harris	.05
212	Stan Javier	.05
213	Ramon Martinez	.05

No.	Player	Price
214	Roger McDowell	.05
215	Jose Offerman	.05
216	Juan Samuel	.05
217	Mike Scioscia	.05
218	Mike Sharperson	.05
219	Darryl Strawberry	.05
220	Delino DeShields	.05
221	Tom Foley	.05
222	Steve Frey	.05
223	Dennis Martinez	.05
224	Spike Owen	.05
225	Gilberto Reyes	.05
226	Tim Wallach	.05
227	Daryl Boston	.05
228	Tim Burke	.05
229	Vince Coleman	.05
230	David Cone	.05
231	Kevin Elster	.05
232	Dwight Gooden	.05
233	Todd Hundley	.05
234	Jeff Innis	.05
235	Howard Johnson	.05
236	Dave Magadan	.05
237	Mackey Sasser	.05
238	Anthony Young	.05
239	Wes Chamberlain	.05
240	Darren Daulton	.05
241	Len Dykstra	.05
242	Tommy Greene	.05
243	Charlie Hayes	.05
244	Dave Hollins	.05
245	Ricky Jordan	.05
246	John Kruk	.05
247	Mickey Morandini	.05
248	Terry Mulholland	.05
249	Dale Murphy	.25
250	Jay Bell	.05
251	Barry Bonds	1.00
252	Steve Buechele	.05
253	Doug Drabek	.05
254	Mike LaValliere	.05
255	Jose Lind	.05
256	Lloyd McClendon	.05
257	Orlando Merced	.05
258	Don Slaught	.05
259	John Smiley	.05
260	Zane Smith	.05
261	Randy Tomlin	.05
262	Andy Van Slyke	.05
263	Pedro Guerrero	.05
264	Felix Jose	.05
265	Ray Lankford	.05
266	Omar Olivares	.05
267	Jose Oquendo	.05
268	Tom Pagnozzi	.05
269	Bryn Smith	.05
270	Lee Smith	.05
271	Ozzie Smith	.50
272	Milt Thompson	.05
273	Todd Zeile	.05
274	Andy Benes	.05
275	Jerald Clark	.05
276	Tony Fernandez	.05
277	Tony Gwynn	.50
278	Greg Harris	.05
279	Thomas Howard	.05
280	Bruce Hurst	.05
281	Mike Maddux	.05
282	Fred McGriff	.05
283	Benito Santiago	.05
284	Kevin Bass	.05
285	Jeff Brantley	.05
286	John Burkett	.05
287	Will Clark	.05
288	Royce Clayton	.05
289	Steve Decker	.05
290	Kelly Downs	.05
291	Mike Felder	.05
292	Darren Lewis	.05
293	Kirt Manwaring	.05
294	Willie McGee	.05
295	Robby Thompson	.05
296	Matt Williams	.05
297	Trevor Wilson	.05
298	Checklist 1-108 (Sandy Alomar, Jr.)	
299	Checklist 109-208 (Rey Sanchez)	.05
300	Checklist 209-300 (Nolan Ryan)	.25
301	Brady Anderson	.05
302	Todd Frohwirth	.05
303	Ben McDonald	.05
304	Mark McLemore	.05
305	Jose Mesa	.05
306	Bob Milacki	.05
307	Gregg Olson	.05
308	David Segui	.05
309	Rick Sutcliffe	.05
310	Jeff Tackett	.05
311	Wade Boggs	.50
312	Scott Cooper	.05
313	John Flaherty	.05
314	Wayne Housie	.05
315	Peter Hoy	.05
316	John Marzano	.05
317	Tim Naehring	.05
318	Phil Plantier	.05
319	Frank Viola	.05
320	Matt Young	.05
321	Jim Abbott	.05
322	Hubie Brooks	.05
323	Chad Curtis RC	.25
324	Alvin Davis	.05
325	Junior Felix	.05
326	Von Hayes	.05
327	Mark Langston	.05
328	Scott Lewis	.05
329	Don Robinson	.05
330	Bobby Rose	.05
331	Lee Stevens	.05
332	George Bell	.05
333	Esteban Beltre	.05
334	Joey Cora	.05
335	Alex Fernandez	.05
336	Roberto Hernandez	.05
337	Mike Huff	.05
338	Kirk McCaskill	.05
339	Dan Pasqua	.05
340	Scott Radinsky	.05
341	Steve Sax	.05
342	Bobby Thigpen	.05
343	Robin Ventura	.05
344	Jack Armstrong	.05
345	Alex Cole	.05
346	Dennis Cook	.05
347	Glenallen Hill	.05
348	Thomas Howard	.05
349	Brook Jacoby	.05
350	Kenny Lofton	.05
351	Charles Nagy	.05
352	Rod Nichols	.05
353	Junior Ortiz	.05
354	Dave Otto	.05
355	Tony Perezchica	.05
356	Scott Scudder	.05
357	Paul Sorrento	.05
358	Skeeter Barnes	.05
359	Mark Carreon	.05
360	John Doherty	.05
361	Dan Gladden	.05
362	Bill Gullickson	.05
363	Shawn Hare	.05
364	Mike Henneman	.05
365	Chad Kreuter	.05
366	Mark Leiter	.05
367	Mike Munoz	.05
368	Kevin Ritz	.05
369	Mark Davis	.05
370	Tom Gordon	.05
371	Chris Gwynn	.05
372	Gregg Jefferies	.05
373	Wally Joyner	.05
374	Kevin McReynolds	.05
375	Keith Miller	.05
376	Rico Rossy	.05
377	Curtis Wilkerson	.05
378	Ricky Bones	.05
379	Chris Bosio	.05
380	Cal Eldred	.05
381	Scott Fletcher	.05
382	Jim Gantner	.05
383	Darryl Hamilton	.05
384	Doug Henry	.05
385	Pat Listach RC	.05
386	Tim McIntosh	.05
387	Edwin Nunez	.05
388	Dan Plesac	.05
389	Kevin Seitzer	.05
390	Franklin Stubbs	.05
391	William Suero	.05
392	Bill Wegman	.05
393	Willie Banks	.05
394	Jarvis Brown	.05
395	Greg Gagne	.05
396	Mark Guthrie	.05
397	Bill Krueger	.05
398	Pat Mahomes RC	.05
399	Pedro Munoz	.05
400	John Smiley	.05
401	Gary Wayne	.05
402	Lenny Webster	.05
403	Carl Willis	.05
404	Greg Cadaret	.05
405	Steve Farr	.05
406	Mike Gallego	.05
407	Charlie Hayes	.05
408	Steve Howe	.05
409	Dion James	.05
410	Jeff Johnson	.05
411	Tim Leary	.05
412	Jim Leyritz	.05
413	Melido Perez	.05
414	Scott Sanderson	.05
415	Andy Stankiewicz	.05
416	Mike Stanley	.05
417	Danny Tartabull	.05
418	Lance Blankenship	.05
419	Mike Bordick	.05
420	Scott Brosius RC	.05
421	Dennis Eckersley	.35
422	Scott Hemond	.05
423	Carney Lansford	.05
424	Henry Mercedes	.05
425	Mike Moore	.05
426	Gene Nelson	.05
427	Randy Ready	.05
428	Bruce Walton	.05
429	Willie Wilson	.05
430	Rich Amaral	.05
431	Dave Cochrane	.05
432	Henry Cotto	.05
433	Calvin Jones	.05
434	Kevin Mitchell	.05
435	Clay Parker	.05
436	Omar Vizquel	.05
437	Floyd Bannister	.05
438	Kevin Brown	.05
439	John Cangelosi	.05
440	Brian Downing	.05
441	Monty Fariss	.05
442	Jose Guzman	.05
443	Donald Harris	.05
444	Kevin Reimer	.05
445	Kenny Rogers	.05
446	Wayne Rosenthal	.05
447	Dickie Thon	.05
448	Derek Bell	.05
449	Juan Guzman	.05
450	Tom Henke	.05
451	Candy Maldonado	.05
452	Jack Morris	.05
453	David Wells	.05
454	Dave Winfield	.40
455	Juan Berenguer	.05
456	Damon Berryhill	.05
457	Mike Bielecki	.05
458	Marvin Freeman	.05
459	Charlie Leibrandt	.05
460	Kent Mercker	.05
461	Otis Nixon	.05
462	Alejandro Pena	.05
463	Ben Rivera	.05
464	Deion Sanders	.10
465	Mark Wohlers	.05
466	Shawn Boskie	.05
467	Frank Castillo	.05
468	Andre Dawson	.25
469	Joe Girardi	.05
470	Chuck McElroy	.05
471	Mike Morgan	.05
472	Ken Patterson	.05
473	Bob Scanlan	.05
474	Gary Scott	.05
475	Dave Smith	.05
476	Sammy Sosa	.50
477	Hector Villanueva	.05
478	Scott Bankhead	.05
479	Tim Belcher	.05
480	Freddie Benavides	.05
481	Jacob Brumfield	.05
482	Norm Charlton	.05
483	Dwayne Henry	.05
484	Dave Martinez	.05
485	Bip Roberts	.05
486	Reggie Sanders	.05
487	Greg Swindell	.05
488	Ryan Bowen	.05
489	Casey Candaele	.05
490	Juan Guerrero	.05
491	Pete Incaviglia	.05
492	Jeff Juden	.05
493	Rob Murphy	.05
494	Mark Portugal	.05
495	Rafael Ramirez	.05
496	Scott Servais	.05
497	Ed Taubensee	.05
498	Brian Williams	.05
499	Todd Benzinger	.05
500	John Candelaria	.05
501	Tom Candiotti	.05
502	Tim Crews	.05
503	Eric Davis	.05
504	Jim Gott	.05
505	Dave Hansen	.05
506	Carlos Hernandez	.05
507	Orel Hershiser	.05
508	Eric Karros	.05
509	Bob Ojeda	.05
510	Steve Wilson	.05
511	Moises Alou	.05
512	Bret Barberie	.05
513	Ivan Calderon	.05
514	Gary Carter	.40
515	Archi Cianfrocco	.05
516	Jeff Fassero	.05
517	Darrin Fletcher	.05
518	Marquis Grissom	.05
519	Chris Haney	.05
520	Ken Hill	.05
521	Chris Nabholz	.05
522	Bill Sampen	.05
523	John VanderWal	.05
524	David Wainhouse	.05
525	Larry Walker	.05
526	John Wetteland	.05
527	Bobby Bonilla	.05
528	Sid Fernandez	.05
529	John Franco	.05
530	Dave Gallagher	.05
531	Paul Gibson	.05
532	Eddie Murray	.40
533	Junior Noboa	.05
534	Charlie O'Brien	.05
535	Bill Pecota	.05
536	Willie Randolph	.05
537	Bret Saberhagen	.05
538	Dick Schofield	.05
539	Pete Schourek	.05
540	Ruben Amaro	.05
541	Andy Ashby	.05
542	Kim Batiste	.05
543	Cliff Brantley	.05
544	Mariano Duncan	.05
545	Jeff Grotewold	.05
546	Barry Jones	.05
547	Julio Peguero	.05
548	Curt Schilling	.25
549	Mitch Williams	.05
550	Stan Belinda	.05
551	Scott Bullett	.05
552	Cecil Espy	.05
553	Jeff King	.05
554	Roger Mason	.05
555	Paul Miller	.05
556	Denny Neagle	.05
557	Vicente Palacios	.05
558	Bob Patterson	.05
559	Tom Prince	.05
560	Gary Redus	.05
561	Gary Varsho	.05
562	Juan Agosto	.05
563	Cris Carpenter	.05
564	Mark Clark RC	.05
565	Jose DeLeon	.05
566	Rich Gedman	.05
567	Bernard Gilkey	.05
568	Rex Hudler	.05
569	Tim Jones	.05
570	Donovan Osborne	.05
571	Mike Perez	.05
572	Gerald Perry	.05
573	Bob Tewksbury	.05
574	Todd Worrell	.05
575	Dave Eiland	.05
576	Jeremy Hernandez	.05
577	Craig Lefferts	.05
578	Jose Melendez	.05
579	Randy Myers	.05
580	Gary Pettis	.05
581	Rich Rodriguez	.05
582	Gary Sheffield	.30
583	Craig Shipley	.05
584	Kurt Stillwell	.05
585	Tim Teufel	.05
586	Rod Beck RC	.05
587	Dave Burba	.05
588	Craig Colbert	.05
589	Bryan Hickerson	.05
590	Mike Jackson	.05
591	Mark Leonard	.05
592	Jim McNamara	.05
593	John Patterson	.05
594	Dave Righetti	.05
595	Cory Snyder	.05
596	Bill Swift	.05
597	Ted Wood	.05
598	Checklist 301-403 (Scott Sanderson)	.05
599	Checklist 404-498 (Junior Ortiz)	.05
600	Checklist 499-600 (Mike Morgan)	.05

Award Winners

The 25 cards in this insert issue were randomly packaged with Series 1 Ultra. One of the Cal Ripken cards (#21) can be found with a photo made from a reversed negative, as well as with the proper orientation. Neither version carries a premium.

		NM/M
Complete Set (26):		10.00
Common Player:		.20
1	Jack Morris	.20
2	Chuck Knoblauch	.20
3	Jeff Bagwell	.20
4	Terry Pendleton	.20
5	Cal Ripken, Jr.	2.00
6	Roger Clemens	1.25
7	Tom Glavine	.35
8	Tom Pagnozzi	.20
9	Ozzie Smith	1.00
10	Andy Van Slyke	1.00
11	Barry Bonds	2.00
12	Tony Gwynn	1.00
13	Matt Williams	.20
14	Will Clark	1.00
15	Robin Ventura	.20
16	Mark Langston	.20
17	Devon White	.20
18	Don Mattingly	1.25
19	Roberto Alomar	.40
21a	Cal Ripken, Jr. (Reversed negative.)	2.00
21b	Cal Ripken, Jr. (Correct)	2.00
22	Ken Griffey Jr.	1.50
23	Kirby Puckett	1.00
24	Greg Maddux	1.00
25	Ryne Sandberg	1.00

All-Rookies

The 10 promising rookies in this set could be found on special cards inserted in Ultra Series 2 foil packs.

		NM/M
Complete Set (10):		2.00
Common Player:		.25
1	Eric Karros	.35
2	Andy Stankiewicz	.25
3	Gary DiSarcina	.25
4	Archi Cianfrocco	.25
5	Jim McNamara	.25
6	Chad Curtis	.25
7	Kenny Lofton	.35
8	Reggie Sanders	.25
9	Pat Mahomes	.25
10	Donovan Osborne	.25

All-Stars

An All-Star team from each league, with two pitchers, could be assembled by collecting these inserts from Ultra Series 2 foil packs.

		NM/M
Complete Set (20):		7.50
Common Player:		.15
1	Mark McGwire	1.25
2	Roberto Alomar	.30
3	Cal Ripken, Jr.	1.50
4	Wade Boggs	.75
5	Mickey Tettleton	.15
6	Ken Griffey Jr.	1.00
7	Roberto Kelly	.15
8	Kirby Puckett	.75
9	Frank Thomas	.65
10	Jack McDowell	.15
11	Will Clark	.15
12	Ryne Sandberg	.75
13	Barry Larkin	.15
14	Gary Sheffield	.35
15	Tom Pagnozzi	.15
16	Barry Bonds	1.50
17	Deion Sanders	.15
18	Darryl Strawberry	.15
19	David Cone	.15
20	Tom Glavine	.30

Tony Gwynn

This 12-card subset of Ultra's spokesman features 10 cards which were available as inserts in Series I foil packs, plus two cards labeled "Special No. 1" and "Special No. 2" which could only be obtained in a send-away offer. Some 2,000 of these cards carry a "certified" Gwynn autograph. Not part of the issue, but similar in format were a pair of extra Tony Gwynn cards. One pictures him with Fleer CEO Paul Mullan, the other shows him with the poster child for Casa de Amparo, a children's shelter in San Diego County.

		NM/M
Complete Set (12):		9.00
Common Card:		.75
Certified Autograph Card:		60.00
1	Tony Gwynn/Fldg	.75
2	Tony Gwynn/Btg	.75
3	Tony Gwynn/Fldg	.75
4	Tony Gwynn/Btg	.75
5	Tony Gwynn/Base-Running	.75
6	Tony Gwynn/Awards	.75
7	Tony Gwynn/Btg	.75
8	Tony Gwynn/Bunting	.75
9	Tony Gwynn (Running)	.75
10	Tony Gwynn/Btg	.75
1	Tony Gwynn/Btg	2.00
2	Tony Gwynn/Fldg	2.00
---	Tony Gwynn, Paul Mullan	3.00
---	Tony Gwynn (Casa de Amparo)	7.50

1993 Ultra

The first series of 300 cards retains Fleer's successful features from 1992, including additional gold foil stamping, UV coating, and team color-coded marbled bars on the fronts. The backs feature a stylized ballpark background, which creates a 3-D effect, stats and portrait and an action photo. Dennis Eckersley is featured in a limited-edition "Career Highlights" set and personally autographed more than 2,000 of his cards, to be randomly inserted into both series' packs. A 10-card Home Run Kings subset and 25-card Ultra Awards Winners subset were also randomly inserted in packs. Ultra Rookies cards are included in both series. Ultra's second series has three limited-edition subsets: Ultra All-Stars, Ultra All-Rookie Team, and Strikeout Kings, plus cards featuring Colorado Rockies and Florida Marlins players.

		NM/M
Complete Set (650):		15.00
Common Player:		.05
Series 1 or 2 Pack (14):		.75
Series 1 or 2 Wax Box (36):		15.00
1	Steve Avery	.05
2	Rafael Belliard	.05
3	Damon Berryhill	.05
4	Sid Bream	.05
5	Ron Gant	.05
6	Tom Glavine	.05
7	Ryan Klesko	.05
8	Mark Lemke	.05
9	Javier Lopez	.05
10	Greg Olson	.05
11	Terry Pendleton	.05
12	Deion Sanders	.05
13	Mike Stanton	.05
14	Paul Assenmacher	.05
15	Steve Buechele	.05
16	Frank Castillo	.05
17	Shawon Dunston	.05
18	Mark Grace	.05
19	Derrick May	.05
20	Chuck McElroy	.05
21	Mike Morgan	.05
22	Bob Scanlan	.05
23	Dwight Smith	.05
24	Sammy Sosa	.60
25	Rick Wilkins	.05
26	Tim Belcher	.05
27	Jeff Branson	.05
28	Bill Doran	.05
29	Chris Hammond	.05
30	Barry Larkin	.05
31	Hal Morris	.05
32	Joe Oliver	.05
33	Jose Rijo	.05
34	Bip Roberts	.05
35	Chris Sabo	.05
36	Reggie Sanders	.05
37	Craig Biggio	.05
38	Ken Caminiti	.05
39	Steve Finley	.05
40	Luis Gonzalez	.05
41	Juan Guerrero	.05
42	Pete Harnisch	.05
43	Xavier Hernandez	.05
44	Doug Jones	.05
45	Al Osuna	.05
46	Eddie Taubensee	.05
47	Scooter Tucker	.05
48	Brian Williams	.05
49	Pedro Astacio	.05

No.	Player	Price	No.	Player	Price	No.	Player	Price	No.	Player	Price	No.	Player	Price	No.	Player	Price
50	Rafael Bournigal	.05	168	Luis Polonia	.05	280	Jeff Huson	.05	398	Tom Goodwin	.05	516	Jeff Russell	.05	634	Gary Redus	.05
51	Brett Butler	.05	169	Julio Valera	.05	281	Rafael Palmeiro	.40	399	Kevin Gross	.05	517	Ken Ryan RC	.05	635	Bill Ripken	.05
52	Tom Candiotti	.05	170	Wilson Alvarez	.05	282	Dean Palmer	.05	400	Carlos Hernandez	.05	518	Chili Davis	.05	636	Nolan Ryan	1.50
53	Eric Davis	.05	171	George Bell	.05	283	Roger Pavlik	.05	401	Ramon Martinez	.05	519	Jim Edmonds RC	1.50	637	Dan Smith	.05
54	Lenny Harris	.05	172	Joey Cora	.05	284	Ivan Rodriguez	.40	402	Raul Mondesi	.05	520	Gary Gaetti	.05	638	Matt Whiteside RC	.05
55	Orel Hershiser	.05	173	Alex Fernandez	.05	285	Kenny Rogers	.05	403	Jody Reed	.05	521	Torey Lovullo	.05	639	Roberto Alomar	.25
56	Eric Karros	.05	174	Lance Johnson	.05	286	Derek Bell	.05	404	Mike Sharperson	.05	522	Tony Percival RC	.05	640	Juan Guzman	.05
57	Pedro Martinez	.50	175	Ron Karkovice	.05	287	Pat Borders	.05	405	Cory Snyder	.05	523	Tim Salmon	.05	641	Pat Hentgen	.05
58	Roger McDowell	.05	176	Jack McDowell	.05	288	Joe Carter	.05	406	Darryl Strawberry	.05	524	Scott Sanderson	.05	642	Darrin Jackson	.05
59	Jose Offerman	.05	177	Scott Radinsky	.05	289	Bob MacDonald	.05	407	Rick Trlicek RC	.05	525	J.T. Snow RC	.75	643	Randy Knorr	.05
60	Mike Piazza	.75	178	Tim Raines	.05	290	Jack Morris	.05	408	Tim Wallach	.05	526	Jerome Walton	.05	644	Domingo Martinez RC	.05
61	Moises Alou	.05	179	Steve Sax	.05	291	John Olerud	.05	409	Todd Worrell	.05	527	Jason Bere	.05	645	Paul Molitor	.50
62	Kent Bottenfield	.05	180	Bobby Thigpen	.05	292	Ed Sprague	.05	410	Tavo Alvarez	.05	528	Rod Bolton RC	.05	646	Dick Schofield	.05
63	Archi Cianfrocco	.05	181	Frank Thomas	.50	293	Todd Stottlemyre	.05	411	Sean Berry RC	.05	529	Ellis Burks	.05	647	Dave Stewart	.05
64	Greg Colbrunn	.05	182	Sandy Alomar Jr.	.05	294	Mike Timlin	.05	412	Frank Bolick RC	.05	530	Carlton Fisk	.50	648	Checklist (Rey Sanchez)	.05
65	Wil Cordero	.05	183	Carlos Baerga	.05	295	Duane Ward	.05	413	Cliff Floyd	.05	531	Craig Grebeck	.05	649	Checklist (Jeremy Hernandez)	.05
66	Delino DeShields	.05	184	Felix Fermin	.05	296	David Wells	.05	414	Mike Gardiner	.05	532	Ozzie Guillen	.05	650	Checklist (Junior Ortiz)	.05
67	Darrin Fletcher	.05	185	Thomas Howard	.05	297	Devon White	.05	415	Marquis Grissom	.05	533	Roberto Hernandez	.05			
68	Ken Hill	.05	186	Mark Lewis	.05	298	Checklist (Ray Lankford)	.05	416	Tim Laker RC	.05	534	Bo Jackson	.10			
69	Chris Nabholz	.05	187	Derek Lilliquist	.05	299	Checklist (Bobby Witt)	.05	417	Mike Lansing RC	.10	535	Kirk McCaskill	.05			
70	Mel Rojas	.05	188	Carlos Martinez	.05	300	Checklist (Mike Piazza)	.40	418	Dennis Martinez	.05	536	Dave Stieb	.05			
71	Larry Walker	.05	189	Charles Nagy	.05	301	Steve Bedrosian	.05	419	John Vander Wal	.05	537	Robin Ventura	.05			
72	Sid Fernandez	.05	190	Scott Scudder	.05	302	Jeff Blauser	.05	420	John Wetteland	.05	538	Albert Belle	.05			
73	John Franco	.05	191	Paul Sorrento	.05	303	Francisco Cabrera	.05	421	Rondell White	.05	539	Mike Bielecki	.05			
74	Dave Gallagher	.05	192	Jim Thome	.40	304	Marvin Freeman	.05	422	Bobby Bonilla	.05	540	Glenallen Hill	.05			
75	Todd Hundley	.05	193	Mark Whiten	.05	305	Brian Hunter	.05	423	Jeromy Burnitz	.05	541	Reggie Jefferson	.05			
76	Howard Johnson	.05	194	Milt Cuyler	.05	306	Dave Justice	.05	424	Vince Burnitz RC	.05	542	Kenny Lofton	.05			
77	Jeff Kent	.05	195	Rob Deer	.05	307	Greg Maddux	.60	425	Mike Draper RC	.05	543	Jeff Mutis RC	.05			
78	Eddie Murray	.50	196	John Doherty	.05	308	Greg McMichael RC	.05	426	Tony Fernandez	.05	544	Junior Ortiz	.05			
79	Bret Saberhagen	.05	197	Travis Fryman	.05	309	Kent Mercker	.05	427	Dwight Gooden	.05	545	Manny Ramirez	.50			
80	Chico Walker	.05	198	Dan Gladden	.05	310	Otis Nixon	.05	428	Jeff Innis	.05	546	Jeff Treadway	.05			
81	Anthony Young	.05	199	Mike Henneman	.05	311	Pete Smith	.05	429	Bobby Jones RC	.05	547	Kevin Wickander	.05			
82	Kyle Abbott	.05	200	John Kiely	.05	312	John Smoltz	.05	430	Mike Maddux	.05	548	Cecil Fielder	.05			
83	Ruben Amaro Jr.	.05	201	Chad Kreuter	.05	313	Jose Guzman	.05	431	Charlie O'Brien	.05	549	Kirk Gibson	.05			
84	Juan Bell	.05	202	Scott Livingstone	.05	314	Mike Harkey	.05	432	Joe Orsulak	.05	550	Greg Gohr RC	.05			
85	Wes Chamberlain	.05	203	Tony Phillips	.05	315	Greg Hibbard	.05	433	Pete Schourek	.05	551	David Haas	.05			
86	Darren Daulton	.05	204	Alan Trammell	.05	316	Candy Maldonado	.05	434	Frank Tanana	.05	552	Bill Krueger	.05			
87	Mariano Duncan	.05	205	Mike Boddicker	.05	317	Randy Myers	.05	435	Ryan Thompson RC	.05	553	Mike Moore	.05			
88	Dave Hollins	.05	206	George Brett	.65	318	Dan Plesac	.05	436	Kim Batiste	.05	554	Mickey Tettleton	.05			
89	Ricky Jordan	.05	207	Tom Gordon	.05	319	Rey Sanchez	.05	437	Mark Davis	.05	555	Lou Whitaker	.05			
90	John Kruk	.05	208	Mark Gubicza	.05	320	Ryne Sandberg	.60	438	Jose DeLeon	.05	556	Kevin Appier	.05			
91	Mickey Morandini	.05	209	Gregg Jefferies	.05	321	Tommy Shields RC	.05	439	Len Dykstra	.05	557	Billy Brewer RC	.05			
92	Terry Mulholland	.05	210	Wally Joyner	.05	322	Jose Vizcaino	.05	440	Jim Eisenreich	.05	558	David Cone	.05			
93	Ben Rivera	.05	211	Kevin Koslofski	.05	323	Matt Walbeck RC	.05	441	Tommy Greene	.05	559	Greg Gagne	.05			
94	Mike Williams	.05	212	Brent Mayne	.05	324	Willie Wilson	.05	442	Pete Incaviglia	.05	560	Mark Gardner	.05			
95	Stan Belinda	.05	213	Brian McRae	.05	325	Tom Browning	.05	443	Danny Jackson	.05	561	Phil Hiatt	.05			
96	Jay Bell	.05	214	Kevin McReynolds	.05	326	Tim Costo	.05	444	Todd Pratt RC	.05	562	Felix Jose	.05			
97	Jeff King	.05	215	Rusty Meacham	.05	327	Rob Dibble	.05	445	Curt Schilling	.20	563	Jose Lind	.05			
98	Mike LaValliere	.05	216	Steve Shifflett	.05	328	Steve Foster	.05	446	Milt Thompson	.05	564	Mike Macfarlane	.05			
99	Lloyd McClendon	.05	217	James Austin	.05	329	Roberto Kelly	.05	447	David West	.05	565	Keith Miller	.05			
100	Orlando Merced	.05	218	Cal Eldred	.05	330	Randy Milligan	.05	448	Mitch Williams	.05	566	Jeff Montgomery	.05			
101	Zane Smith	.05	219	Darryl Hamilton	.05	331	Kevin Mitchell	.05	449	Steve Cooke	.05	567	Hipolito Pechardo	.05			
102	Randy Tomlin	.05	220	Doug Henry	.05	332	Tim Pugh RC	.05	450	Carlos Garcia	.05	568	Ricky Bones	.05			
103	Andy Van Slyke	.05	221	John Jaha	.05	333	Jeff Reardon	.05	451	Al Martin	.05	569	Tom Brunansky	.05			
104	Tim Wakefield	.05	222	Dave Nilsson	.05	334	John Roper RC	.05	452	Blas Minor RC	.05	570	Joe Kmak RC	.05			
105	John Wehner	.05	223	Jesse Orosco	.05	335	Juan Samuel	.05	453	Dennis Moeller	.05	571	Pat Listach	.05			
106	Bernard Gilkey	.05	224	B.J. Surhoff	.05	336	John Smiley	.05	454	Denny Neagle	.05	572	Graeme Lloyd RC	.05			
107	Brian Jordan	.05	225	Greg Vaughn	.05	337	San Wilson	.05	455	Don Slaught	.05	573	Carlos Maldonado RC	.05			
108	Ray Lankford	.05	226	Bill Wegman	.05	338	Scott Aldred	.05	456	Lonnie Smith	.05	574	Josias Manzanillo RC	.05			
109	Donovan Osborne	.05	227	Robin Yount	.50	339	Andy Ashby	.05	457	Paul Wagner	.05	575	Matt Mieske	.05			
110	Tom Pagnozzi	.05	228	Rick Aguilera	.05	340	Freddie Benavides	.05	458	Bob Walk	.05	576	Kevin Reimer	.05			
111	Mike Perez	.05	229	J.T. Bruett	.05	341	Dante Bichette	.05	459	Kevin Young	.05	577	Bill Spiers	.05			
112	Lee Smith	.05	230	Scott Erickson	.05	342	Willie Blair	.05	460	Rene Arocha RC	.05	578	Dickie Thon	.05			
113	Ozzie Smith	.60	231	Kent Hrbek	.05	343	Daryl Boston	.05	461	Brian Barber	.05	579	Willie Banks	.05			
114	Bob Tewksbury	.05	232	Terry Jorgensen	.05	344	Vinny Castilla	.05	462	Rheal Cormier	.05	580	Jim Deshaies	.05			
115	Todd Zeile	.05	233	Scott Leius	.05	345	Jerald Clark	.05	463	Gregg Jefferies	.05	581	Mark Guthrie	.05			
116	Andy Benes	.05	234	Pat Mahomes	.05	346	Alex Cole	.05	464	Joe Magrane	.05	582	Brian Harper	.05			
117	Greg Harris	.05	235	Pedro Munoz	.05	347	Andres Galarraga	.05	465	Omar Olivares	.05	583	Chuck Knoblauch	.05			
118	Darrin Jackson	.05	236	Kirby Puckett	.60	348	Joe Girardi	.05	466	Geronimo Pena	.05	584	Gene Larkin	.05			
119	Fred McGriff	.05	237	Kevin Tapani	.05	349	Ryan Hawblitzel RC	.05	467	Allen Watson	.05	585	Shane Mack	.05			
120	Rich Rodriguez	.05	238	Lenny Webster	.05	350	Charlie Hayes	.05	468	Mark Whiten	.05	586	David McCarty	.05			
121	Frank Seminara	.05	239	Carl Willis	.05	351	Butch Henry	.05	469	Derek Bell	.05	587	Mike Pagliarulo	.05			
122	Gary Sheffield	.35	240	Mike Gallego	.05	352	Darren Holmes	.05	470	Phil Clark	.05	588	Mike Trombley	.05			
123	Craig Shipley	.05	241	John Habyan	.05	353	Dale Murphy	.20	471	Pat Gomez RC	.05	589	Dave Winfield	.50			
124	Kurt Stillwell	.05	242	Pat Kelly	.05	354	David Nied	.05	472	Tony Gwynn	.60	590	Jim Abbott	.05			
125	Dan Walters	.05	243	Kevin Maas	.05	355	Jeff Parrett	.05	473	Jeremy Hernandez	.05	591	Wade Boggs	.60			
126	Rod Beck	.05	244	Don Mattingly	.65	356	Steve Reed RC	.05	474	Bruce Hurst	.05	592	Russ Davis RC	.05			
127	Mike Benjamin	.05	245	Hensley Meulens	.05	357	Bruce Ruffin	.05	475	Phil Plantier	.05	593	Steve Farr	.05			
128	Jeff Brantley	.05	246	Sam Militello	.05	358	Danny Sheaffer RC	.05	476	Scott Sanders RC	.05	594	Steve Howe	.05			
129	John Burkett	.05	247	Matt Nokes	.05	359	Bryn Smith	.05	477	Tim Scott RC	.05	595	Mike Humphreys RC	.05			
130	Will Clark	.05	248	Melido Perez	.05	360	Jim Tatum RC	.05	478	Darrell Sherman RC	.05	596	Jimmy Key	.05			
131	Royce Clayton	.05	249	Andy Stankiewicz	.05	361	Eric Young	.05	479	Guillermo Velasquez	.05	597	Jim Leyritz	.05			
132	Steve Hosey	.05	250	Randy Velarde	.05	362	Gerald Young	.05	480	Tim Worrell RC	.05	598	Bobby Munoz RC	.05			
133	Mike Jackson	.05	251	Bob Wickman	.05	363	Luis Aquino	.05	481	Todd Benzinger	.05	599	Paul O'Neill	.05			
134	Darren Lewis	.05	252	Bernie Williams	.05	364	Alex Arias RC	.05	482	Bud Black	.05	600	Spike Owen	.05			
135	Kirt Manwaring	.05	253	Lance Blankenship	.05	365	Jack Armstrong	.05	483	Barry Bonds	1.50	601	Mike Stanley	.05			
136	Bill Swift	.05	254	Mike Bordick	.05	366	Bret Barberie	.05	484	Dave Burba	.05	602	Danny Tartabull	.05			
137	Robby Thompson	.05	255	Jerry Browne	.05	367	Ryan Bowen	.05	485	Bryan Hickerson	.05	603	Scott Brosius	.05			
138	Brady Anderson	.05	256	Ron Darling	.05	368	Greg Briley	.05	486	Dave Martinez	.05	604	Storm Davis	.05			
139	Glenn Davis	.05	257a	Dennis Eckersley	.40	369	Cris Carpenter	.05	487	Willie McGee	.05	605	Eric Fox	.05			
140	Leo Gomez	.05	257b	Dennis Eckersley (Wt. 195; no "MLBPA" on back - unmarked sample card.)	1.50	370	Chuck Carr	.05	488	Jeff Reed	.05	606	Goose Gossage	.05			
141	Chris Martinez	.05	257c	Dennis Eckersley (Wt, 195; no "Printed in USA" on back - unmarked sample card.)	1.50	371	Jeff Conine RC	.25	489	Kevin Rogers	.05	607	Scott Hammond	.05			
142	Ben McDonald	.05	258	Rickey Henderson	.50	372	Steve Decker	.05	490	Matt Williams	.05	608	Dave Henderson	.05			
143	Alan Mills	.05	259	Vince Horsman	.05	373	Orestes Destrade	.05	491	Trevor Wilson	.05	609	Mark McGwire	1.00			
144	Mike Mussina	.30	260	Troy Neel	.05	374	Monty Fariss	.05	492	Harold Baines	.05	610	Mike Mohler RC	.05			
145	Gregg Olson	.05	261	Jeff Parrett	.05	375	Junior Felix	.05	493	Mike Devereaux	.05	611	Edwin Nunez	.05			
146	David Segui	.05	262	Terry Steinbach	.05	376	Chris Hammond	.05	494	Todd Frohwirth	.05	612	Kevin Seitzer	.05			
147	Jeff Tackett	.05	263	Bob Welch	.05	377	Bryan Harvey	.05	495	Chris Hoiles	.05	613	Ruben Sierra	.05			
148	Jack Clark	.05	264	Bobby Witt	.05	378	Trevor Hoffman RC	.25	496	Luis Mercedes	.05	614	Chris Bosio	.05			
149	Scott Cooper	.05	265	Rich Amaral	.05	379	Charlie Hough	.05	497	Sherman Obando RC	.05	615	Norm Charlton	.05			
150	Danny Darwin	.05	266	Bret Boone	.05	380	Joe Klink	.05	498	Brad Pennington RC	.05	616	Jim Converse RC	.05			
151	John Dopson	.05	267	Jay Buhner	.05	381	Richie Lewis RC	.05	499	Harold Reynolds	.05	617	John Cummings RC	.05			
152	Mike Greenwell	.05	268	Dave Fleming	.05	382	Dave Magadan	.05	500	Arthur Rhodes	.05	618	Mike Felder	.05			
153	Tim Naehring	.05	269	Randy Johnson	.50	383	Bob McClure	.05	501	Cal Ripken, Jr.	1.50	619	Ken Griffey Jr.	.75			
154	Tony Pena	.05	270	Edgar Martinez	.05	384	Scott Pose RC	.05	502	Rick Sutcliffe	.05	620	Mike Hampton	.05			
155	Paul Quantrill	.05	271	Mike Schooler	.05	385	Rich Renteria RC	.05	503	Fernando Valenzuela	.05	621	Erik Hanson	.05			
156	Mo Vaughn	.05	272	Russ Swan	.05	386	Benito Santiago	.05	504	Mark Williamson	.05	622	Bill Haselman	.05			
157	Frank Viola	.05	273	Dave Valle	.05	387	Walt Weiss	.05	505	Scott Bankhead	.05	623	Tino Martinez	.05			
158	Bob Zupcic	.05	274	Omar Vizquel	.05	388	Nigel Wilson	.05	506	Greg Blosser	.05	624	Lee Tinsley	.05			
159	Chad Curtis	.05	275	Kerry Woodson	.05	389	Eric Anthony	.05	507	Ivan Calderon	.05	625	Fernando Vina RC	.05			
160	Gary DiSarcina	.05	276	Kevin Brown	.05	390	Jeff Bagwell	.65	508	Roger Clemens	.65	626	David Wainhouse RC	.05			
161	Damion Easley	.05	277	Julio Franco	.05	391	Andujar Cedeno	.05	509	Andre Clemens	.05	627	Jose Canseco	.30			
162	Chuck Finley	.05	278	Jeff Frye	.05	392	Doug Drabek	.05	510	Scott Fletcher	.05	628	Benji Gil	.05			
163	Tim Fortugno	.05	279	Juan Gonzalez	.25	393	Darryl Kile	.05	511	Greg Harris	.05	629	Tom Henke	.05			
164	Rene Gonzales	.05				394	Mark Portugal	.05	512	Billy Hatcher	.05	630	David Hulse RC	.05			
165	Joe Grahe	.05				395	Karl Rhodes	.05	513	Bob Melvin	.05	631	Manuel Lee	.05			
166	Mark Langston	.05				396	Scott Servais	.05	514	Carlos Quintana	.05	632	Craig Lefferts	.05			
167	John Orton	.05				397	Greg Swindell	.05	515	Luis Rivera	.05	633	Robb Nen RC	.05			

All-Rookies

These insert cards are foil stamped on both sides and were randomly inserted into Series 2 packs. The cards have black fronts, with six different colors of type. The player's uniform number and position are located in the upper-right corner. The player's name and Ultra logo are gold-foil stamped. Backs have a black background with a player photo and career summary.

		NM/M
Complete Set (10):		4.00
Common Player:		.25
1	Rene Arocha	.25
2	Jeff Conine	.25
3	Phil Hiatt	.25
4	Mike Lansing	.25
5	Al Martin	.25
6	David Nied	.25
7	Mike Piazza	3.00
8	Tim Salmon	.50
9	J.T. Snow	.45
10	Kevin Young	.25

All-Stars

This 20-card set features 10 of the top players from each league. Cards were randomly inserted into Series II packs and are foil stamped on both sides.

		NM/M
Complete Set (20):		17.50
Common Player:		.25
1	Darren Daulton	.25
2	Will Clark	.35
3	Ryne Sandberg	1.50
4	Barry Larkin	.25
5	Gary Sheffield	.40
6	Barry Bonds	3.00
7	Ray Lankford	.25
8	Larry Walker	.25
9	Greg Maddux	1.50
10	Lee Smith	.25
11	Ivan Rodriguez	.75
12	Mark McGwire	2.50
13	Carlos Baerga	.25
14	Cal Ripken, Jr.	3.00
15	Edgar Martinez	.25
16	Juan Gonzalez	1.00
17	Ken Griffey Jr.	2.00
18	Kirby Puckett	1.50
19	Frank Thomas	1.25
20	Mike Mussina	.65

Award Winners

This insert set features 18 Top Glove players (nine from each league), two rookies of the year, three MVPs (both leagues and World Series), both Cy Young Award winners and one Player of the Year. All cards are UV coated and foil stamped on both sides and were found in Series I packs. Two formats are seen. Cards #1-18 are horizontal with player portrait and action photos on a marbled black background. Gold-foil graphics identify the player. Cards #19-25 are verticial with a black background that has "Fleer Ultra Award Winners" splashed around in trendy colors. The Ultra logo, player's name and his award are spelled out in gold foil. Horizontally arranged backs share many of their respective front elements, and have a summary of the season's performance which led to the award. There is a close-up player photo, as well.

		NM/M
Complete Set (25):		12.00
Common Player:		.25
1	Greg Maddux	.75
2	Tom Pagnozzi	.25
3	Mark Grace	.25
4	Jose Lind	.25
5	Terry Pendleton	.25
6	Ozzie Smith	.75
7	Barry Bonds	2.00
8	Andy Van Slyke	.25
9	Larry Walker	.25
10	Mark Langston	.25
11	Ivan Rodriguez	.60
12	Don Mattingly	.75
13	Roberto Alomar	.35
14	Robin Ventura	.25
15	Cal Ripken, Jr.	2.00
16	Ken Griffey Jr.	1.00
17	Kirby Puckett	.75
18	Devon White	.25
19	Pat Listach	.25
20	Eric Karros	.25
21	Pat Borders	.25
22	Greg Maddux	.75
23	Dennis Eckersley	.60
24	Barry Bonds	2.00
25	Gary Sheffield	.45

1993 Ultra Career Highlights Promo Sheet

To introduce its "Career Highlights" insert cards in Fleer and Fleer Ultra, the company distributed this promo sheet picturing one card each from the Tom Glavine and Dennis Eckersley sets, overprinted with a gray "PROMOTIONAL SAMPLE" across front and back. A third panel on the sheet provides details of the mail-in offer through which additional cards from the sets could be ordered. The sheet measures 7-1/2"x3-1/2".

	NM/M
Three-Panel Strip:	2.50

Dennis Eckersley Career Highlights

This limited-edition subset chronicles Dennis Eckersley's illustrious career. Cards, which are UV coated and silver foil-stamped on both sides, were randomly inserted into both series' packs. Eckersley autographed more than 2,000 of the cards, which were also randomly inserted into packs. By sending in 10 Fleer Ultra wrappers plus $1, collectors could receive two additional Eckersley cards which were not available in regular packs. Card fronts have a

---

color action photo, the background of which has been colorized into shades of purple. A black marble strip at bottom has the city name and years he was with the team in silver foil. A large black marble box in one corner has the "Dennis Eckersley Career Highlights" logo in silver foil. On back, a purple box is dropped out of a color photo, and silver-foil typography describes some phrase of Eck's career.

		NM/M
Complete Set (12):		6.00
Common Card:		.50
Autographed Card:		35.00
1	"Perfection" (A's 1987-92)	.50
2	"The Kid" (Indians 1975-77)	.50
3	"The Warrior" (Indians 1975-77)	.50
4	"Beantown Blazer" (Red Sox 1978-84)	.50
5	"Eckspeak" (Red Sox 1978-84)	.50
6	"Down to Earth" (Red Sox 1978-84)	.50
7	"Wrigley Bound" (Cubs 1984-86)	.50
8	"No Relief" (A's 1987-92)	.50
9	"In Control" (A's 1987-92)	.50
10	"Simply the Best" (A's 1987-92)	.50
11	"Reign of Perfection" (A's 1987-92)	.50
12	"Leaving His Mark" (A's 1987-92)	.50

1993 Ultra Commemorative

Photos of Fleer's CEO and the company's spokesman, 1992 Cy Young/MVP winner Dennis Eckersley are superimposed on a background of Oakland-Alameda County Stadium on this promo card. The back gives details of the forthcoming 1993 Fleer Ultra issue.

	NM/M
Dennis Eckersley, Paul Mullan	5.00

Home Run Kings

This insert set features top home run kings. Cards, which are UV coated and have gold foil stamping on both sides, were inserts in Series I packs.

		NM/M
Complete Set (10):		8.00
Common Player:		.50
1	Juan Gonzalez	.65
2	Mark McGwire	2.50
3	Cecil Fielder	.50
4	Fred McGriff	.50
5	Albert Belle	.50
6	Barry Bonds	2.50
7	Joe Carter	.50

8	Gary Sheffield	.65
9	Darren Daulton	.50
10	Dave Hollins	.50

Performers

An Ultra Performers set of Fleer Ultra baseball cards was offered directly to collectors in 1993. The set, available only by mail, was limited to 150,000 sets. The cards featured gold-foil stamping and UV coating on each side and a six-photo design, including five on the front of the card. Each card was identified on the back by set serial number jet-printed in black in a strip at bottom.

		NM/M
Complete Set (10):		5.00
Common Player:		.25
1	Barry Bonds	2.50
2	Juan Gonzalez	.30
3	Ken Griffey Jr.	1.00
4	Eric Karros	.25
5	Pat Listach	.25
6	Greg Maddux	.75
7	David Nied	.25
8	Gary Sheffield	.40
9	J.T. Snow	.25
10	Frank Thomas	.65

Strikeout Kings

Five of baseball's top strikeout pitchers are featured in this second-series Ultra insert set. Cards are UV coated and foil stamped on both sides. Each card front has a picture of a pitcher winding up to throw. A baseball is in the background, with the pitcher in the forefront.

		NM/M
Complete Set (5):		7.50
Common Player:		.25
1	Roger Clemens	2.50
2	Juan Guzman	.25
3	Randy Johnson	1.25
4	Nolan Ryan	5.00
5	John Smoltz	.50

1994 Ultra

Issued in two series of 300 cards each, Ultra for 1994 represented a new highwater mark in production values for a mid-priced brand. Each side of the basic cards is UV coated and gold-foil embossed. Fronts feature full-bleed action photos. At bottom the player name, team, position and Fleer Ultra logo appear in gold foil above a gold-foil strip. Some rookie cards are specially designated with a large gold "ROOKIE" above the Ultra logo. Backs feature a basic background that is team color coordinated. Three more player action photos are featured on the back, along with a team logo and a modicum of stats and personal data. There is a gold stripe along the left edge and the player's name and card number appear in gold in the lower-left corner. The set features seven types of insert cards, packaged one per pack.

		NM/M
Complete Set (600):		15.00
Common Player:		.50
Series 1 or 2 Pack (14):		.50
Series 1 or 2 Wax Box (36):		15.00
1	Jeffrey Hammonds	.05
2	Chris Hoiles	.05
3	Ben McDonald	.05
4	Mark McLemore	.05
5	Alan Mills	.05
6	Jamie Moyer	.05
7	Brad Pennington	.05
8	Jim Poole	.05
9	Cal Ripken, Jr.	1.50
10	Jack Voigt	.05
11	Roger Clemens	.65
12	Danny Darwin	.05
13	Andre Dawson	.25
14	Scott Fletcher	.05
15	Greg Harris	.05
16	Billy Hatcher	.05
17	Jeff Russell	.05
18	Aaron Sele	.05
19	Mo Vaughn	.30
20	Mike Butcher	.05
21	Rod Correia	.05
22	Steve Frey	.05
23	Phil Leftwich RC	.05
24	Torey Lovullo	.05
25	Ken Patterson	.05
26	Eduardo Perez	.05
27	Tim Salmon	.25
28	J.T. Snow	.05
29	Chris Turner	.05
30	Wilson Alvarez	.05
31	Jason Bere	.05
32	Joey Cora	.05
33	Alex Fernandez	.05
34	Roberto Hernandez	.05
35	Lance Johnson	.05
36	Ron Karkovice	.05
37	Kirk McCaskill	.05
38	Jeff Schwarz	.05
39	Frank Thomas	.50
40	Sandy Alomar Jr.	.05
41	Albert Belle	.25
42	Felix Fermin	.05
43	Wayne Kirby	.05
44	Tom Kramer	.05
45	Kenny Lofton	.25
46	Jose Mesa	.05
47	Eric Plunk	.05
48	Paul Sorrento	.05
49	Jim Thome	.35
50	Bill Wertz	.05
51	John Doherty	.05
52	Cecil Fielder	.25
53	Travis Fryman	.25
54	Chris Gomez	.05
55	Mike Henneman	.05
56	Chad Kreuter	.05
57	Bob MacDonald	.05
58	Mike Moore	.05
59	Tony Phillips	.05
60	Lou Whitaker	.05
61	Kevin Appier	.05
62	Greg Gagne	.05
63	Chris Gwynn	.05

64	Bob Hamelin	.05
65	Chris Haney	.05
66	Phil Hiatt	.05
67	Felix Jose	.05
68	Jose Lind	.05
69	Mike Macfarlane	.05
70	Jeff Montgomery	.05
71	Hipolito Pichardo	.05
72	Juan Bell	.05
73	Cal Eldred	.05
74	Darryl Hamilton	.05
75	Doug Henry	.05
76	Mike Ignasiak	.05
77	John Jaha	.05
78	Graeme Lloyd	.05
79	Angel Miranda	.05
80	Dave Nilsson	.05
81	Troy O'Leary	.05
82	Kevin Reimer	.05
83	Willie Banks	.05
84	Larry Casian	.05
85	Scott Erickson	.05
86	Eddie Guardado	.05
87	Kent Hrbek	.05
88	Terry Jorgensen	.05
89	Chuck Knoblauch	.05
90	Pat Meares	.05
91	Mike Trombley	.05
92	Dave Winfield	.50
93	Wade Boggs	.60
94	Scott Kamieniecki	.05
95	Pat Kelly	.05
96	Jimmy Key	.05
97	Jim Leyritz	.05
98	Bobby Munoz	.05
99	Paul O'Neill	.05
100	Melido Perez	.05
101	Mike Stanley	.05
102	Danny Tartabull	.05
103	Bernie Williams	.05
104	Kurt Abbott RC	.05
105	Mike Bordick	.05
106	Ron Darling	.05
107	Brent Gates	.05
108	Miguel Jimenez	.05
109	Steve Karsay	.05
110	Scott Lydy	.05
111	Mark McGwire	1.00
112	Troy Neel	.05
113	Craig Paquette	.05
114	Bob Welch	.05
115	Bobby Witt	.05
116	Rich Amaral	.05
117	Mike Blowers	.05
118	Jay Buhner	.05
119	Dave Fleming	.05
120	Ken Griffey Jr.	.75
121	Tino Martinez	.05
122	Marc Newfield	.05
123	Ted Power	.05
124	Mackey Sasser	.05
125	Omar Vizquel	.05
126	Kevin Brown	.05
127	Juan Gonzalez	.25
128	Tom Henke	.05
129	David Hulse	.05
130	Dean Palmer	.05
131	Roger Pavlik	.05
132	Ivan Rodriguez	.40
133	Kenny Rogers	.05
134	Doug Strange	.05
135	Pat Borders	.05
136	Joe Carter	.05
137	Darnell Coles	.05
138	Pat Hentgen	.05
139	Al Leiter	.05
140	Paul Molitor	.50
141	John Olerud	.05
142	Ed Sprague	.05
143	Dave Stewart	.05
144	Mike Timlin	.05
145	Duane Ward	.05
146	Devon White	.05
147	Steve Avery	.05
148	Steve Bedrosian	.05
149	Damon Berryhill	.05
150	Jeff Blauser	.05
151	Tom Glavine	.20
152	Chipper Jones	.05
153	Mark Lemke	.05
154	Fred McGriff	.25
155	Greg McMichael	.05
156	Deion Sanders	.25
157	John Smoltz	.05
158	Mark Wohlers	.05
159	Jose Bautista	.05
160	Steve Buechele	.05
161	Mike Harkey	.05
162	Greg Hibbard	.05
163	Chuck McElroy	.05
164	Mike Morgan	.05
165	Kevin Roberson	.05
166	Ryne Sandberg	.60
167	Jose Vizcaino	.05
168	Rick Wilkins	.05
169	Willie Wilson	.05
170	Willie Greene	.05
171	Roberto Kelly	.05
172	Larry Luebbers	.05
173	Kevin Mitchell	.05
174	Joe Oliver	.05
175	John Roper	.05
176	Johnny Ruffin	.05
177	Reggie Sanders	.05
178	John Smiley	.05
179	Jerry Spradlin	.05
180	Freddie Benavides	.05
181	Dante Bichette	.05

182	Willie Blair	.05
183	Kent Bottenfield	.05
184	Jerald Clark	.05
185	Joe Girardi	.05
186	Roberto Mejia	.05
187	Steve Reed	.05
188	Armando Reynoso	.05
189	Bruce Ruffin	.05
190	Eric Young	.05
191	Luis Aquino	.05
192	Bret Barberie	.05
193	Ryan Bowen	.05
194	Chuck Carr	.05
195	Orestes Destrade	.05
196	Richie Lewis	.05
197	Dave Magadan	.05
198	Bob Natal	.05
199	Gary Sheffield	.30
200	Matt Turner	.05
201	Darrell Whitmore	.05
202	Eric Anthony	.05
203	Jeff Bagwell	.50
204	Andujar Cedeno	.05
205	Luis Gonzalez	.05
206	Xavier Hernandez	.05
207	Doug Jones	.05
208	Darryl Kile	.05
209	Scott Servais	.05
210	Greg Swindell	.05
211	Brian Williams	.05
212	Pedro Astacio	.05
213	Brett Butler	.05
214	Omar Daal	.05
215	Jim Gott	.05
216	Raul Mondesi	.05
217	Jose Offerman	.05
218	Mike Piazza	.75
219	Cory Snyder	.05
220	Tim Wallach	.05
221	Todd Worrell	.05
222	Moises Alou	.05
223	Sean Berry	.05
224	Wil Cordero	.05
225	Jeff Fassero	.05
226	Darrin Fletcher	.05
227	Cliff Floyd	.05
228	Marquis Grissom	.05
229	Ken Hill	.05
230	Mike Lansing	.05
231	Kirk Rueter	.05
232	John Wetteland	.05
233	Rondell White	.05
234	Tim Bogar	.05
235	Jeromy Burnitz	.05
236	Dwight Gooden	.05
237	Todd Hundley	.05
238	Jeff Kent	.05
239	Josias Manzanillo	.05
240	Joe Orsulak	.05
241	Ryan Thompson	.05
242	Kim Batiste	.05
243	Darren Daulton	.05
243a	Darren Daulton (Promotional Sample)	1.00
244	Tommy Greene	.05
245	Dave Hollins	.05
246	Pete Incaviglia	.05
247	Danny Jackson	.05
248	Ricky Jordan	.05
249	John Kruk	.05
249a	John Kruk (Promotional Sample)	1.00
250	Mickey Morandini	.05
251	Terry Mulholland	.05
252	Ben Rivera	.05
253	Kevin Stocker	.05
254	Jay Bell	.05
255	Steve Cooke	.05
256	Jeff King	.05
257	Al Martin	.05
258	Danny Miceli	.05
259	Blas Minor	.05
260	Don Slaught	.05
261	Paul Wagner	.05
262	Tim Wakefield	.05
263	Kevin Young	.05
264	Rene Arocha	.05
265	Richard Batchelor RC	.05
266	Gregg Jefferies	.05
267	Brian Jordan	.05
268	Jose Oquendo	.05
269	Donovan Osborne	.05
270	Erik Pappas	.05
271	Mike Perez	.05
272	Bob Tewksbury	.05
273	Mark Whiten	.05
274	Todd Zeile	.05
275	Andy Ashby	.05
276	Brad Ausmus	.05
277	Phil Clark	.05
278	Jeff Gardner	.05
279	Ricky Gutierrez	.05
280	Tony Gwynn	.60
281	Tim Mauser	.05
282	Scott Sanders	.05
283	Frank Seminara	.05
284	Wally Whitehurst	.05
285	Rod Beck	.05
286	Barry Bonds	1.50
287	Dave Burba	.05
288	Mark Carreon	.05
289	Royce Clayton	.05
290	Mike Jackson	.05
291	Darren Lewis	.05
292	Kirt Manwaring	.05
293	Dave Martinez	.05
294	Billy Swift	.05
295	Salomon Torres	.05

296	Matt Williams	.05	410	Carlos Reyes **RC**	.05
297	Checklist 1-103		411	Ruben Sierra	.05
	(Joe Orsulak)	.05	412	Terry Steinbach	.05
298	Checklist 104-201		413	Bill Taylor	.05
	(Pete Incaviglia)	.05	414	Todd Van Poppel	.05
299	Checklist 202-300		415	Eric Anthony	.05
	(Todd Hundley)	.05	416	Bobby Ayala	.05
300	Checklist - Inserts		417	Chris Bosio	.05
	(John Doherty)	.05	418	Tim Davis	.05
301	Brady Anderson	.05	419	Randy Johnson	.50
302	Harold Baines	.05	420	Kevin King	.05
303	Damon Buford	.05	421	Anthony Manahan **RC**	.05
304	Mike Devereaux	.05	422	Edgar Martinez	.05
305	Sid Fernandez	.05	423	Keith Mitchell	.05
306	Rick Krivda	.05	424	Roger Salkeld	.05
307	Mike Mussina	.30	425	Mac Suzuki **RC**	.05
308	Rafael Palmeiro	.40	426	Dan Wilson	.05
309	Arthur Rhodes	.05	427	Duff Brumley **RC**	.05
310	Chris Sabo	.05	428	Jose Canseco	.30
311	Lee Smith	.05	429	Will Clark	.05
312	Gregg Zaun **RC**	.05	430	Steve Dreyer	.05
313	Scott Cooper	.05	431	Rick Helling	.05
314	Mike Greenwell	.05	432	Chris James	.05
315	Tim Naehring	.05	433	Matt Whiteside	.05
316	Otis Nixon	.05	434	Roberto Alomar	.20
317	Paul Quantrill	.05	435	Scott Brow	.05
318	John Valentin	.05	436	Domingo Cedeno **RC**	.05
319	Dave Valle	.05	437	Carlos Delgado	.35
320	Frank Viola	.05	438	Juan Guzman	.05
321	Brian Anderson **RC**	.10	439	Paul Spoljaric	.05
322	Garret Anderson	.05	440	Todd Stottlemyre	.05
323	Chad Curtis	.05	441	Woody Williams	.05
324	Chili Davis	.05	442	Dave Justice	.05
325	Gary DiSarcina	.05	443	Mike Kelly	.05
326	Damion Easley	.05	444	Ryan Klesko	.05
327	Jim Edmonds	.05	445	Javier Lopez	.05
328	Chuck Finley	.05	446	Greg Maddux	.60
329	Joe Grahe	.05	447	Kent Mercker	.05
330	Bo Jackson	.10	448	Charlie O'Brien	.05
331	Mark Langston	.05	449	Terry Pendleton	.05
332	Harold Reynolds	.05	450	Mike Stanton	.05
333	James Baldwin	.05	451	Tony Tarasco	.05
334	Ray Durham **RC**	.50	452	Terrell Wade **RC**	.05
335	Julio Franco	.05	453	Willie Banks	.05
336	Craig Grebeck	.05	454	Shawon Dunston	.05
337	Ozzie Guillen	.05	455	Mark Grace	.05
338	Joe Hall	.05	456	Jose Guzman	.05
339	Darrin Jackson	.05	457	Jose Hernandez	.05
340	Jack McDowell	.05	458	Glenallen Hill	.05
341	Tim Raines	.05	459	Blaise Ilsley	.05
342	Robin Ventura	.05	460	Brooks Kieschnick **RC**	.05
343	Carlos Baerga	.05	461	Derrick May	.05
344	Derek Lilliquist	.05	462	Randy Myers	.05
345	Dennis Martinez	.05	463	Karl Rhodes	.05
346	Jack Morris	.05	464	Sammy Sosa	.60
347	Eddie Murray	.50	465	Steve Trachsel **RC**	.10
348	Chris Nabholz	.05	466	Anthony Young	.05
349	Charles Nagy	.05	467	Eddie Zambrano **RC**	.05
350	Chad Ogea	.05	468	Bret Boone	.05
351	Manny Ramirez	.50	469	Tom Browning	.05
352	Omar Vizquel	.05	470	Hector Carrasco **RC**	.05
353	Tim Belcher	.05	471	Rob Dibble	.05
354	Eric Davis	.05	472	Erik Hanson	.05
355	Kirk Gibson	.05	473	Thomas Howard	.05
356	Rick Greene	.05	474	Barry Larkin	.05
357	Mickey Tettleton	.05	475	Hal Morris	.05
358	Alan Trammell	.05	476	Jose Rijo	.05
359	David Wells	.05	477	John Burke	.05
360	Stan Belinda	.05	478	Ellis Burks	.05
361	Vince Coleman	.05	479	Marvin Freeman	.05
362	David Cone	.05	480	Andres Galarraga	.05
363	Gary Gaetti	.05	481	Greg Harris	.05
364	Tom Gordon	.05	482	Charlie Hayes	.05
365	Dave Henderson	.05	483	Darren Holmes	.05
366	Wally Joyner	.05	484	Howard Johnson	.05
367	Brent Mayne	.05	485	Marcus Moore **RC**	.05
368	Brian McRae	.05	486	David Nied	.05
369	Michael Tucker	.05	487	Mark Thompson	.05
370	Ricky Bones	.05	488	Walt Weiss	.05
371	Brian Harper	.05	489	Kurt Abbott	.05
372	Tyrone Hill	.05	490	Matias Carrillo	.05
373	Mark Kiefer	.05	491	Jeff Conine	.05
374	Pat Listach	.05	492	Chris Hammond	.05
375	Mike Matheny **RC**	.10	493	Bryan Harvey	.05
376	Jose Mercedes **RC**	.05	494	Charlie Hough	.05
377	Jody Reed	.05	495	Yorkis Perez **RC**	.05
378	Kevin Seitzer	.05	496	Pat Rapp	.05
379	B.J. Surhoff	.05	497	Benito Santiago	.05
380	Greg Vaughn	.05	498	David Weathers	.05
381	Turner Ward	.05	499	Craig Biggio	.05
382	Wes Weger **RC**	.05	500	Ken Caminiti	.05
383	Bill Wegman	.05	501	Doug Drabek	.05
384	Rick Aguilera	.05	502	Tony Eusebio **RC**	.10
385	Rich Becker	.05	503	Steve Finley	.05
386	Alex Cole	.05	504	Pete Harnisch	.05
387	Steve Dunn	.05	505	Brian Hunter	.05
388	Keith Garagozzo **RC**	.05	506	Domingo Jean	.05
389	LaTroy Hawkins **RC**	.05	507	Todd Jones	.05
390	Shane Mack	.05	508	Orlando Miller	.05
391	David McCarty	.05	509	James Mouton	.05
392	Pedro Munoz	.05	510	Roberto Petagine	.05
393	Derek Parks **RC**	.05	511	Shane Reynolds	.05
394	Kirby Puckett	.60	512	Mitch Williams	.05
395	Kevin Tapani	.05	513	Billy Ashley	.05
396	Matt Walbeck	.05	514	Tom Candiotti	.05
397	Jim Abbott	.05	515	Delino DeShields	.05
398	Mike Gallego	.05	516	Kevin Gross	.05
399	Xavier Hernandez	.05	517	Orel Hershiser	.05
400	Don Mattingly	.65	518	Eric Karros	.05
401	Terry Mulholland	.05	519	Ramon Martinez	.05
402	Matt Nokes	.05	520	Chan Ho Park **RC**	.75
403	Luis Polonia	.05	521	Henry Rodriguez	.05
404	Bob Wickman	.05	522	Joey Eischen	.05
405	Mark Acre	.05	523	Rod Henderson	.05
406	Fausto Cruz **RC**	.05	524	Pedro Martinez	.50
407	Dennis Eckersley	.45	525	Mel Rojas	.05
408	Rickey Henderson	.50	526	Larry Walker	.05
409	Stan Javier	.05	527	Gabe White **RC**	.10

528	Bobby Bonilla	.05
529	Jonathan Hurst	.05
530	Bobby Jones	.05
531	Kevin McReynolds	.05
532	Bill Pulsipher	.05
533	Bret Saberhagen	.05
534	David Segui	.05
535	Pete Smith	.05
536	Kelly Stinnett **RC**	.05
537	Dave Telgheder	.05
538	Quilvio Veras **RC**	.05
539	Jose Vizcaino	.05
540	Pete Walker	.05
541	Ricky Bottalico	.05
542	Wes Chamberlain	.05
543	Mariano Duncan	.05
544	Len Dykstra	.05
545	Jim Eisenreich	.05
546	Phil Geisler **RC**	.05
547	Wayne Gomes **RC**	.10
548	Doug Jones	.05
549	Jeff Juden	.05
550	Mike Lieberthal	.05
551	Tony Longmire **RC**	.05
552	Tom Marsh	.05
553	Bobby Munoz	.05
554	Curt Schilling	.15
555	Carlos Garcia	.05
556	Ravelo Manzanillo **RC**	.05
557	Orlando Merced	.05
558	Will Pennyfeather **RC**	.05
559	Zane Smith	.05
560	Andy Van Slyke	.05
561	Rick White	.05
562	Luis Alicea	.05
563	Brian Barber **RC**	.05
564	Clint Davis **RC**	.05
565	Bernard Gilkey	.05
566	Ray Lankford	.05
567	Tom Pagnozzi	.05
568	Ozzie Smith	.60
569	Rick Sutcliffe	.05
570	Allen Watson	.05
571	Dmitri Young	.05
572	Derek Bell	.05
573	Andy Benes	.05
574	Archi Cianfrocco	.05
575	Joey Hamilton	.05
576	Gene Harris	.05
577	Trevor Hoffman	.05
578	Tim Hyers **RC**	.05
579	Brian Johnson **RC**	.05
580	Keith Lockhart **RC**	.05
581	Pedro Martinez	.05
582	Ray McDavid	.05
583	Phil Plantier	.05
584	Bip Roberts	.05
585	Dave Staton	.05
586	Todd Benzinger	.05
587	John Burkett	.05
588	Bryan Hickerson	.05
589	Willie McGee	.05
590	John Patterson	.05
591	Mark Portugal	.05
592	Kevin Rogers	.05
593	Joe Rosselli **RC**	.05
594	Steve Soderstrom **RC**	.05
595	Robby Thompson	.05
596	125th Anniversary card	.05
597	Checklist	.05
598	Checklist	.05
599	Checklist	.05
600	Checklist	.05

1994 Ultra All-Rookie Team Supers

This super-size (3-1/2" x 5-1/2") version of the Fleer Ultra II insert set featuring top rookies was included one per case of hobby packaging. Cards are identical to the smaller version. Both sides are gold-foil enhanced and UV-coated.

		NM/M
Complete Set (10):		5.00
Common Player:		.50
1	Kurt Abbott	.50
2	Carlos Delgado	3.00
3	Cliff Floyd	.50
4	Jeffrey Hammonds	.50
5	Ryan Klesko	.50
6	Javier Lopez	.50
7	Raul Mondesi	.50
8	James Mouton	.50
9	Chan Ho Park	.75
10	Dave Staton	.50

All-Stars

Fleer's opinion of the top 20 players in 1994 are featured in this most common of the Series II Ultra insert sets. Silver-foil highlights enhance the chase cards, found, according to stated odds, once per three packs, on average. National Leaguers have purple backgrounds front and back, American Leaguers have red.

		NM/M
Complete Set (20):		5.00
Common Player:		.15
1	Chris Hoiles	.15
2	Frank Thomas	.35
3	Roberto Alomar	.20
4	Cal Ripken, Jr.	1.00
5	Robin Ventura	.15
6	Albert Belle	.15
7	Juan Gonzalez	.20
8	Ken Griffey Jr.	.50
9	John Olerud	.15
10	Jack McDowell	.15
11	Mike Piazza	.50
12	Fred McGriff	.15
13	Ryne Sandberg	.40
14	Jay Bell	.15
15	Matt Williams	.15
16	Barry Bonds	1.00
17	Len Dykstra	.15
18	Dave Justice	.15
19	Tom Glavine	.20
20	Greg Maddux	.40

All-Rookie Team

A stylized sunrise landscape is the background for this insert set featuring top rookies and inserted into Ultra Series II packs at the rate of about one per 10. Backs repeat the motif with an action photo. Both sides are gold-foil enhanced and UV-coated.

		NM/M
Complete Set (10):		4.00
Common Player:		.35
1	Kurt Abbott	.35
2	Carlos Delgado	3.00
3	Cliff Floyd	.35
4	Jeffrey Hammonds	.35
5	Ryan Klesko	.35
6	Javier Lopez	.35
7	Raul Mondesi	.35
8	James Mouton	.35
9	Chan Ho Park	.50
10	Dave Staton	.35

Award Winners

The most common of the Fleer Ultra insert sets for 1994 is the 25-card "Award Winners." Horizontal format cards feature front and back background with a gold-embossed look. A player action photo appears on the front. A gold-foil seal on the front has a symbolic player representation flanked by the pictured player's name and award. A gold Fleer Ultra logo is at top. Backs have a player portrait photo and a write-up about the award. The name of the award and the player's name appear in gold foil at the top. Stated odds of finding an Award Winners card were one in three packs.

		NM/M
Complete Set (25):		5.00
Common Player:		.10
1	Ivan Rodriguez	.25
2	Don Mattingly	.45
3	Roberto Alomar	.20
4	Robin Ventura	.10
5	Omar Vizquel	.10
6	Ken Griffey Jr.	.50
7	Kenny Lofton	.10
8	Devon White	.10
9	Mark Langston	.10
10	Kirt Manwaring	.10
11	Mark Grace	.10
12	Robby Thompson	.10
13	Matt Williams	.10
14	Jay Bell	.10
15	Barry Bonds	.60
16	Marquis Grissom	.10
17	Larry Walker	.10
18	Greg Maddux	.40
19	Frank Thomas	.35
20	Barry Bonds	.60
21	Paul Molitor	.35
22	Jack McDowell	.10
23	Greg Maddux	.40
24	Tim Salmon	.10
25	Mike Piazza	.50

Career Achievement Awards

The outstanding careers of five of baseball's top veteran stars are recognized in this chase set, inserted on average once every 21 packs of Ultra Series II. The gold-highlighted horizontal fronts combine a current color photo with a background single-tint photo from the player's earlier days. Backs flip-flop the photo use, with the current photo in the background and the earlier photo in full color in the foreground. The gold Ultra Career Achievement Award seal is repeated on back, as well.

		NM/M
Complete Set (5):		4.00
Common Player:		.50
1	Joe Carter	.50
2	Paul Molitor	.75
3	Cal Ripken, Jr.	2.00
4	Ryne Sandberg	1.00
5	Dave Winfield	.75

Firemen

Ten of the major leagues' leading relief pitchers are featured in this Ultra insert set. Cards have an action photo of the player superimposed over a background photo of a fire truck. A shield at top, in gold foil, has a smoke-eater's helmet, stylized flames and proclaims the player an "Ultra Fireman." Backs are horizontal in format and feature the pumper's control panel in the background photo. A color player portrait photo appears on one side, with a description of his relief role and successes in a whitened box. Fireman cards are found, on average, once per 11 packs, according to stated odds.

		NM/M
Complete Set (10):		2.00
Common Player:		.25
1	Jeff Montgomery	.25
2	Duane Ward	.25
3	Tom Henke	.25
4	Roberto Hernandez	.25
5	Dennis Eckersley	1.25
6	Randy Myers	.25
7	Rod Beck	.25
8	Bryan Harvey	.25
9	John Wetteland	.25
10	Mitch Williams	.25

Hitting Machines

A heavy metal background of gears and iron-letter logo is featured in this insert set honoring the game's top hitters. The cards turn up about once in every five packs of Ultra Series II. Both front and back are highlighted in silver foil.

		NM/M
Complete Set (10):		4.00
Common Player:		.15
1	Roberto Alomar	.25
2	Carlos Baerga	.15
3	Barry Bonds	2.00
4	Andres Galarraga	.15
5	Juan Gonzalez	.25
6	Tony Gwynn	.50
7	Paul Molitor	.40
8	John Olerud	.15
9	Mike Piazza	.75
10	Frank Thomas	.40

Home Run Kings

One of two high-end insert sets in '94 Ultra is the 12-card "Home Run Kings" found exclusively in 14-card foil packs, on an average of once per 36-pack box. Featuring the technology Fleer calls "etched metallization," the cards have a black background with a red and blue foil representation of a batter. An action photo of a player taking a mighty cut or starting his home-run trot is featured. A large gold-foil "Home Run King" crown-and-shield device are in an upper corner, while the Ultra logo and player name are in gold foil at bottom. Backs have a white background with the red and blue batter symbol. The player's name appears in gold foil at the top, along with a portrait photo and a summary of his home run prowess.

		NM/M
Complete Set (12):		15.00
Common Player:		.75
1	Juan Gonzalez	1.00
2	Ken Griffey Jr.	2.50
3	Frank Thomas	2.00
4	Albert Belle	.75
5	Rafael Palmeiro	1.50
6	Joe Carter	.75
7	Barry Bonds	4.00
8	Dave Justice	.75
9	Matt Williams	.75
10	Fred McGriff	.75
11	Ron Gant	.75
12	Mike Piazza	2.50

League Leaders

Arguably the least attractive of the '94 Ultra inserts are the "League Leaders." Fronts feature a full-bleed action photo on which the bottom has been re-colored to a team hue giving the effect of teal, purple and magenta miasmas rising from the turf. An Ultra logo appears in gold foil in an upper corner, with the player's name in gold foil at about the dividing line between the natural color and colorized portions of the photo. A large "League Leader" appears in the bottom half of the photo, with the category led printed in the lower-left. Backs repeat the team color at top, fading to white at the bottom. In gold foil are "League Leader" and the category. A portrait photo appears at bottom. Several paragraphs detail the league leading performance of the previous season.

		NM/M
Complete Set (10):		3.00
Common Player:		.25
1	John Olerud	.25
2	Rafael Palmeiro	1.00
3	Kenny Lofton	.25
4	Jack McDowell	.25
5	Randy Johnson	1.50
6	Andres Galarraga	.25
7	Len Dykstra	.25
8	Chuck Carr	.25
9	Tom Glavine	.35
10	Jose Rijo	.25

On-Base Leaders

One of the lesser-known, but most valuable, stats - on-base percentage - is featured in this subset found exclusively in 17-card packs, at the rate of about one per 37 packs. The fronts feature color photos against a stat-filled printed-foil background.

		NM/M
Complete Set (12):		25.00
Common Player:		1.50
1	Roberto Alomar	2.00
2	Barry Bonds	6.50
3	Len Dykstra	1.50
4	Andres Galarraga	1.50
5	Mark Grace	1.50
6	Ken Griffey Jr.	5.00
7	Gregg Jefferies	1.50
8	Orlando Merced	1.50
9	Paul Molitor	3.50
10	John Olerud	1.50
11	Tony Phillips	1.50
12	Frank Thomas	3.50

Phillies Finest

As a tribute to two of Fleer's home-team heroes, the Philadelphia-based card company created an Ultra insert set featuring 12 cards each of "Phillies Finest," John Kruk and Darren Daulton. Twenty of the cards were issued as

Series 1 and 2 inserts, about one in every eight packs, while four were available only by a mail-in offer. Fronts feature action photos with large block letters popping out of the background. The Ultra logo and player name appear in gold foil. Backs have portrait photos and career summaries, with the player's name and card number in gold foil. Daulton and Kruk each autographed 1,000 of the inserts. Stated odds of finding the autographed cards were one in 11,000 packs. Values listed are per card.

		NM/M
Complete Set (24):		4.00
Common Player:		.25
Autographed Daulton:		45.00
Autographed Kruk:		30.00
1-5	Darren Daulton	.25
6-10	John Kruk	.25
11-15	Darren Daulton	.25
16-20	John Kruk	.25
9a	John Kruk(PROMOTIONAL SAMPLE)	1.50
1M, 3M	Darren Daulton	.75
2M, 4M	John Kruk	.75

RBI Kings

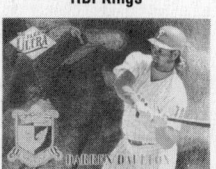

Exclusive to the 19-card jumbo packs of Fleer Ultra are a series of 12 "RBI Kings" insert cards, found, according to stated odds, one per 36 packs. The horizontal-format card front uses Fleer's "etched metallized" technology to produce a sepia-toned background action photo, in front of which is a color player photo. An Ultra logo appears in gold foil in an upper corner while a fancy shield-and-scroll "RBI King" logo and the player's name are in gold at the bottom. Backs repeat the basic front motif and include a color player portrait photo, his name in gold foil and a paragraph justifying his selection as an RBI King.

		NM/M
Complete Set (12):		16.00
Common Player:		1.00
1	Albert Belle	1.00
2	Frank Thomas	2.50
3	Joe Carter	1.00
4	Juan Gonzalez	1.25
5	Cecil Fielder	1.00
6	Carlos Baerga	1.00
7	Barry Bonds	5.00
8	David Justice	1.00
9	Ron Gant	1.00
10	Mike Piazza	3.50
11	Matt Williams	1.00
12	Darren Daulton	1.00

Rising Stars

An outer space background printed on metallic foil sets this chase set apart from most of the rest of the Ultra Series II inserts. The silver-foil enhanced cards of projected superstars of tomorrow are found on average once every 37 packs.

		NM/M
Complete Set (12):		15.00
Common Player:		1.00
1	Carlos Baerga	1.00
2	Jeff Bagwell	5.00

3	Albert Belle	1.00
4	Cliff Floyd	1.00
5	Travis Fryman	1.00
6	Marquis Grissom	1.00
7	Kenny Lofton	1.00
8	John Olerud	1.00
9	Mike Piazza	7.50
10	Kirk Rueter	1.00
11	Tim Salmon	1.00
12	Aaron Sele	1.00

Second Year Standouts

Approximately once every 11 packs, the Ultra insert find is a "Second Year Standout" card. Ten of the game's sophomore stars are featured. Fronts feature a pair of action photos against a team-color background. Gold-foil highlights are the Ultra logo, the player's name and a "Second Year Standout" shield. The shield and player name are repeated in gold foil on the back, as is the team color background. There is a player portrait photo at bottom and a summary of the player's 1993 season.

		NM/M
Complete Set (10):		5.00
Common Player:		.25
1	Jason Bere	.25
2	Brent Gates	.25
3	Jeffrey Hammonds	.25
4	Tim Salmon	.50
5	Aaron Sele	.25
6	Chuck Carr	.25
7	Jeff Conine	.25
8	Greg McMichael	.25
9	Mike Piazza	4.00
10	Kevin Stocker	.25

Strikeout Kings

A gold-foil "Strikeout Kings" crown-and-shield logo is featured on the front of this chase set. Cards are found on average once per seven packs. Each of the cards features the K-king in sequential action photos. Backs have a larger action photo with a large version of the Strikeout King shield in the background.

	NM/M
Complete Set (5):	2.00
Common Player:	.25

1	Randy Johnson	.75
2	Mark Langston	.25
3	Greg Maddux	1.00
4	Jose Rijo	.25
5	John Smoltz	.25

1995 Ultra

A clean design enhanced with three different colors of metallic foil graphics is featured on the basic cards of 1995 Fleer Ultra. Two series of 250 cards each were issued with cards arranged alphabetically within team, also sequenced alphabetically. Fronts have a gold-foil Ultra logo in an upper corner, with the player's name and team logo in a team-color coded foil at bottom. There are no other graphic elements on the borderless photos. Backs have a large photo rendered in a single color, again team-coded. A postage-stamp sized color photo in one corner is flanked by a few vital stats in silver foil. Career and '94 stats are printed at bottom, enhanced by the foil color from the front. Cards were issued in 12-card retail and hobby packs at $1.99 and jumbo pre-priced ($2.69) magazine packs. Each pack contains one of the several insert series from the appropriate series.

	NM/M
Complete Set (450):	10.00
Common Player:	.05
Gold Medallion:	2X
Series 1 or 2 Pack (12):	.50
Series 1 or 2 Wax Box (36):	12.50

1	Brady Anderson	.05
2	Sid Fernandez	.05
3	Jeffrey Hammonds	.05
4	Chris Hoiles	.05
5	Ben McDonald	.05
6	Mike Mussina	.35
7	Rafael Palmeiro	.65
8	Jack Voigt	.05
9	Wes Chamberlain	.05
10	Roger Clemens	1.00
11	Chris Howard	.05
12	Tim Naehring	.05
13	Otis Nixon	.05
14	Rich Rowland	.05
15	Ken Ryan	.05
16	John Valentin	.05
17	Mo Vaughn	.75
18	Brian Anderson	.05
19	Chili Davis	.05
20	Damion Easley	.05
21	Jim Edmonds	.05
22	Mark Langston	.05
23	Tim Salmon	.25
24	J.T. Snow	.05
25	Chris Turner	.05
26	Wilson Alvarez	.05
27	Joey Cora	.05
28	Alex Fernandez	.05
29	Roberto Hernandez	.05
30	Lance Johnson	.05
31	Ron Karkovice	.05
32	Kirk McCaskill	.05
33	Tim Raines	.05
34	Frank Thomas	.75
35	Sandy Alomar	.05
36	Albert Belle	.05
37	Mark Clark	.05
38	Kenny Lofton	.75
39	Eddie Murray	.05
40	Eric Plunk	.05
41	Manny Ramirez	.75
42	Jim Thome	.60
43	Omar Vizquel	.05
44	Danny Bautista	.05
45	Junior Felix	.05
46	Cecil Fielder	.05
47	Chris Gomez	.05
48	Chad Kreuter	.05
49	Mike Moore	.05
50	Tony Phillips	.05
51	Alan Trammell	.05
52	David Wells	.05
53	Kevin Appier	.05
54	Billy Brewer	.05
55	David Cone	.05
56	Greg Gagne	.05
57	Bob Hamelin	.05
58	Jose Lind	.05
59	Brent Mayne	.05
60	Brian McRae	.05
61	Terry Shumpert	.05
62	Ricky Bones	.05
63	Mike Fetters	.05
64	Darryl Hamilton	.05
65	John Jaha	.05
66	Graeme Lloyd	.05
67	Matt Mieske	.05
68	Kevin Seitzer	.05
69	Jose Valentin	.05
70	Turner Ward	.05
71	Rick Aguilera	.05
72	Rich Becker	.05
73	Alex Cole	.05
74	Scott Leius	.05
75	Pat Meares	.05
76	Kirby Puckett	1.00
77	Dave Stevens	.05
78	Kevin Tapani	.05
79	Matt Walbeck	.05
80	Wade Boggs	1.00
81	Scott Kamieniecki	.05
82	Pat Kelly	.05
83	Jimmy Key	.05
84	Paul O'Neill	.05
85	Luis Polonia	.05
86	Mike Stanley	.05
87	Danny Tartabull	.05
88	Bob Wickman	.05
89	Mark Acre	.05
90	Geronimo Berroa	.05
91	Mike Bordick	.05
92	Ron Darling	.05
93	Stan Javier	.05
94	Mark McGwire	1.50
95	Troy Neel	.05
96	Ruben Sierra	.05
97	Terry Steinbach	.05
98	Eric Anthony	.05
99	Chris Bosio	.05
100	Dave Fleming	.05
101	Ken Griffey Jr.	1.25
102	Reggie Jefferson	.05
103	Randy Johnson	.75
104	Edgar Martinez	.05
105	Bill Risley	.05
106	Dan Wilson	.05
107	Cris Carpenter	.05
108	Will Clark	.05
109	Juan Gonzalez	.40
110	Rusty Greer	.05
111	David Hulse	.05
112	Roger Pavlik	.05
113	Ivan Rodriguez	.75
114	Doug Strange	.05
115	Matt Whiteside	.05
116	Roberto Alomar	.20
117	Brad Cornett	.05
118	Carlos Delgado	.45
119	Alex Gonzalez	.05
120	Darren Hall	.05
121	Pat Hentgen	.05
122	Paul Molitor	.75
123	Ed Sprague	.05
124	Devon White	.05
125	Tom Glavine	.25
126	Dave Justice	.05
127	Roberto Kelly	.05
128	Mark Lemke	.05
129	Greg Maddux	1.00
130	Charles Johnson	.05
131	Kent Mercker	.05
132	Charlie O'Brien	.05
133	John Smoltz	.05
134	Willie Banks	.05
135	Steve Buechele	.05
136	Kevin Foster	.05
137	Glenallen Hill	.05
138	Ray Sanchez	.05
139	Sammy Sosa	1.00
140	Steve Trachsel	.05
141	Rick Wilkins	.05
142	Jeff Brantley	.05
143	Hector Carrasco	.05
144	Kevin Jarvis	.05
145	Barry Larkin	.05
146	Chuck McElroy	.05
147	Jose Rijo	.05
148	Johnny Ruffin	.05
149	Deion Sanders	.05
150	Eddie Taubensee	.05
151	Dante Bichette	.05
152	Ellis Burks	.05
153	Joe Girardi	.05
154	Charlie Hayes	.05
155	Mike Kingery	.05
156	Kevin Ritz	.05
157	Bruce Ruffin	.05
158	Eric Young	.05
159	Kurt Abbott	.05
160	Chuck Carr	.05
161	Chris Hammond	.05
162	Bryan Harvey	.05
163	Terry Mathews	.05
164	Yorkis Perez	.05
165	Pat Rapp	.05
166	Gary Sheffield	.40
167	Dave Weathers	.05
168	Jeff Bagwell	.75
169	Ken Caminiti	.05
170	Doug Drabek	.05
171	Steve Finley	.05
172	Steve Finley	.05
173	John Hudek	.05
174	Todd Jones	.05
175	James Mouton	.05
176	Shane Reynolds	.05
177	Scott Servais	.05
178	Tom Candiotti	.05
179	Omar Daal	.05
180	Darren Dreifort	.05
181	Eric Karros	.05
182	Ramon Martinez	.05
183	Raul Mondesi	.05
184	Henry Rodriguez	.05
185	Todd Worrell	.05
186	Moises Alou	.05
187	Sean Berry	.05
188	Wil Cordero	.05
189	Jeff Fassero	.05
190	Darrin Fletcher	.05
191	Butch Henry	.05
192	Ken Hill	.05
193	Mel Rojas	.05
194	John Wetteland	.05
195	Bobby Bonilla	.05
196	Rico Brogna	.05
197	Bobby Jones	.05
198	Jeff Kent	.05
199	Josias Manzanillo	.05
200	Kelly Stinnett	.05
201	Ryan Thompson	.05
202	Jose Vizcaino	.05
203	Lenny Dykstra	.05
204	Jim Eisenreich	.05
205	Dave Hollins	.05
206	Mike Lieberthal	.05
207	Mickey Morandini	.05
208	Bobby Munoz	.05
209	Curt Schilling	.20
210	Heathcliff Slocumb	.05
211	David West	.05
212	Dave Clark	.05
213	Steve Cooke	.05
214	Midre Cummings	.05
215	Carlos Garcia	.05
216	Jeff King	.05
217	Jon Lieber	.05
218	Orlando Merced	.05
219	Don Slaught	.05
220	Rick White	.05
221	Rene Arocha	.05
222	Bernard Gilkey	.05
223	Brian Jordan	.05
224	Tom Pagnozzi	.05
225	Vicente Palacios	.05
226	Geronimo Pena	.05
227	Ozzie Smith	1.00
228	Allen Watson	.05
229	Mark Whiten	.05
230	Brad Ausmus	.05
231	Derek Bell	.05
232	Andy Benes	.05
233	Tony Gwynn	1.00
234	Joey Hamilton	.05
235	Luis Lopez	.05
236	Pedro A. Martinez	.05
237	Scott Sanders	.05
238	Eddie Williams	.05
239	Rod Beck	.05
240	Dave Burba	.05
241	Darren Lewis	.05
242	Kirt Manwaring	.05
243	Mark Portugal	.05
244	Darryl Strawberry	.05
245	Robby Thompson	.05
246	William Van Landingham	.05
247	Matt Williams	.05
248	Checklist	.05
249	Checklist	.05
250	Checklist	.05
251	Harold Baines	.05
252	Bret Barberie	.05
253	Armando Benitez	.05
254	Mike Devereaux	.05
255	Leo Gomez	.05
256	Jamie Moyer	.05
257	Arthur Rhodes	.05
258	Cal Ripken Jr.	2.00
259	Luis Alicea	.05
260	Jose Canseco	.45
261	Scott Cooper	.05
262	Andre Dawson	.25
263	Mike Greenwell	.05
264	Aaron Sele	.05
265	Garret Anderson	.05
266	Chad Curtis	.05
267	Gary DiSarcina	.05
268	Chuck Finley	.05
269	Rex Hudler	.05
270	Andrew Lorraine	.05
271	Spike Owen	.05
272	Lee Smith	.05
273	Jason Bere	.05
274	Ozzie Guillen	.05
275	Norberto Martin	.05
276	Scott Ruffcorn	.05
277	Robin Ventura	.05
278	Carlos Baerga	.05
279	Jason Grimsley	.05
280	Dennis Martinez	.05
281	Charles Nagy	.05
282	Paul Sorrento	.05
283	Dave Winfield	.75
284	John Doherty	.05
285	Travis Fryman	.05
286	Kirk Gibson	.05
287	Lou Whitaker	.05
288	Gary Gaetti	.05
289	Tom Gordon	.05
290	Mark Gubicza	.05

291	Wally Joyner	.05
292	Mike Macfarlane	.05
293	Jeff Montgomery	.05
294	Jeff Cirillo	.05
295	Cal Eldred	.05
296	Pat Listach	.05
297	Jose Mercedes	.05
298	Dave Nilsson	.05
299	Duane Singleton	.05
300	Greg Vaughn	.05
301	Scott Erickson	.05
302	Denny Hocking	.05
303	Chuck Knoblauch	.05
304	Pat Mahomes	.05
305	Pedro Munoz	.05
306	Erik Schullstrom	.05
307	Jim Abbott	.05
308	Tony Fernandez	.05
309	Sterling Hitchcock	.05
310	Jim Leyritz	.05
311	Don Mattingly	1.00
312	Jack McDowell	.05
313	Melido Perez	.05
314	Bernie Williams	.05
315	Scott Brosius	.05
316	Dennis Eckersley	.65
317	Brent Gates	.05
318	Rickey Henderson	.75
319	Steve Karsay	.05
320	Steve Ontiveros	.05
321	Bill Taylor	.05
322	Todd Van Poppel	.05
323	Bob Welch	.05
324	Bobby Ayala	.05
325	Mike Blowers	.05
326	Jay Buhner	.05
327	Felix Fermin	.05
328	Tino Martinez	.05
329	Marc Newfield	.05
330	Greg Pirkl	.05
331	Alex Rodriguez	1.50
332	Kevin Brown	.05
333	John Burkett	.05
334	Jeff Frye	.05
335	Kevin Gross	.05
336	Dean Palmer	.05
337	Joe Carter	.05
338	Shawn Green	.35
339	Juan Guzman	.05
340	Mike Huff	.05
341	Al Leiter	.05
342	John Olerud	.05
343	Dave Stewart	.05
344	Todd Stottlemyre	.05
345	Steve Avery	.05
346	Jeff Blauser	.05
347	Chipper Jones	1.00
348	Mike Kelly	.05
349	Ryan Klesko	.05
350	Javier Lopez	.05
351	Fred McGriff	.05
352	Jose Oliva	.05
353	Terry Pendleton	.05
354	Mike Stanton	.05
355	Tony Tarasco	.05
356	Mark Wohlers	.05
357	Jim Bullinger	.05
358	Shawon Dunston	.05
359	Mark Grace	.05
360	Derrick May	.05
361	Randy Myers	.05
362	Karl Rhodes	.05
363	Bret Boone	.05
364	Brian Dorsett	.05
365	Ron Gant	.05
366	Brian R. Hunter	.05
367	Hal Morris	.05
368	Jack Morris	.05
369	John Roper	.05
370	Reggie Sanders	.05
371	Pete Schourek	.05
372	John Smiley	.05
373	Marvin Freeman	.05
374	Andres Galarraga	.05
375	Mike Munoz	.05
376	David Nied	.05
377	Walt Weiss	.05
378	Greg Colbrunn	.05
379	Jeff Conine	.05
380	Charles Johnson	.05
381	Kurt Miller	.05
382	Robb Nen	.05
383	Benito Santiago	.05
384	Craig Biggio	.05
385	Tony Eusebio	.05
386	Luis Gonzalez	.05
387	Brian L. Hunter	.05
388	Darryl Kile	.05
389	Orlando Miller	.05
390	Phil Plantier	.05
391	Greg Swindell	.05
392	Billy Ashley	.05
393	Pedro Astacio	.05
394	Brett Butler	.05
395	Delino DeShields	.05
396	Orel Hershiser	.05
397	Garey Ingram	.05
398	Chan Ho Park	.05
399	Mike Piazza	1.25
400	Ismael Valdes	.05
401	Tim Wallach	.05
402	Cliff Floyd	.05
403	Marquis Grissom	.05
404	Mike Lansing	.05
405	Pedro Martinez	.75
406	Kirk Rueter	.05
407	Tim Scott	.05
408	Jeff Shaw	.05

409	Larry Walker	.05
410	Rondell White	.05
411	John Franco	.05
412	Todd Hundley	.05
413	Jason Jacome	.05
414	Joe Orsulak	.05
415	Bret Saberhagen	.05
416	David Segui	.05
417	Darren Daulton	.05
418	Mariano Duncan	.05
419	Tommy Greene	.05
420	Gregg Jefferies	.05
421	John Kruk	.05
422	Kevin Stocker	.05
423	Jay Bell	.05
424	Al Martin	.05
425	Denny Neagle	.05
426	Zane Smith	.05
427	Andy Van Slyke	.05
428	Paul Wagner	.05
429	Tom Henke	.05
430	Danny Jackson	.05
431	Ray Lankford	.05
432	John Mabry	.05
433	Bob Tewksbury	.05
434	Todd Zeile	.05
435	Andy Ashby	.05
436	Andujar Cedeno	.05
437	Donnie Elliott	.05
438	Bryce Florie	.05
439	Trevor Hoffman	.05
440	Melvin Nieves	.05
441	Bip Roberts	.05
442	Barry Bonds	2.00
443	Royce Clayton	.05
444	Mike Jackson	.05
445	John Patterson	.05
446	J.R. Phillips	.05
447	Bill Swift	.05
448	Checklist	.05
449	Checklist	.05
450	Checklist	.05

1995 Ultra Gold Medallion

Less than 10 percent of the production run of Fleer Ultra (regular and insert sets) was produced in a special parallel Gold Medallion edition. On these special cards an embossed round gold seal replaces the Fleer Ultra logo in the upper corner. One Gold Medallion card was inserted into each Ultra foil pack.

	NM/M
Complete Set (450):	60.00
Common Player:	.25
Stars/Rookies:	2X

All-Rookies

Enlarged pieces of the central color action photo, set on a white background, make up the front design on these inserts. The player's name, card title and Ultra logo are printed in silver foil. Horizontal backs have another color photo, which is also repeated in single-color fashion. A career summary is printed over the larger photo. The All-Rookie inserts are found only in 12-card packs, at the rate of about one per four packs.

	NM/M
Complete Set (10):	2.25

Common Player:		.15
Gold Medallion:		2X
1	Cliff Floyd	.15
2	Chris Gomez	.15
3	Rusty Greer	.15
4	Bob Hamelin	.15
5	Joey Hamilton	.15
6	John Hudek	.15
7	Ryan Klesko	.15
8	Raul Mondesi	.15
9	Manny Ramirez	2.00
10	Steve Trachsel	.15

All-Stars

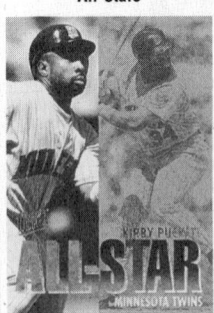

Twenty of the top players in the majors were chosen as Ultra All-Stars in this Series II chase set. Fronts have a color player photo at left. At right is a second photo, printed in only one color. A large "ALL-STAR" is at bottom, with the player's name above and team below in silver foil. An Ultra logo is at left. Backs have another color photo, with a '94 season summary printed in a black panel at right. These cards were found one per five packs, on average.

	NM/M
Complete Set (20):	7.50

Common Player:		.15
Gold Medallion:		2X
1	Moises Alou	.15
2	Albert Belle	.15
3	Craig Biggio	.15
4	Wade Boggs	.60
5	Barry Bonds	1.50
6	David Cone	.15
7	Ken Griffey Jr.	.75
8	Tony Gwynn	.60
9	Chuck Knoblauch	.15
10	Barry Larkin	.15
11	Kenny Lofton	.15
12	Greg Maddux	.60
13	Fred McGriff	.15
14	Paul O'Neill	.15
15	Mike Piazza	.75
16	Kirby Puckett	.75
17	Cal Ripken Jr.	1.50
18	Ivan Rodriguez	.45
19	Frank Thomas	.50
20	Matt Williams	.15

Award Winners

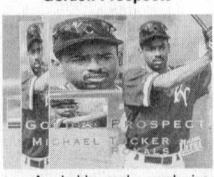

Various official and unofficial award winners from the 1994 season are featured in this Series I insert set. Horizontal cards have a color player photo on the right side, with a single-color, vertically compressed action photo at left. The player's award is printed in a white strip at top, while his name and team logo, along with the Ultra logo, are at bottom. All front typography is in gold foil. Backs repeat the compressed photo at left, combined with another color photo at right. A season summary is printed over the photo at left. The Award Winners inserts were common to all types of packaging, found at the rate of about one per four packs.

	NM/M
Complete Set (25):	6.00

Common Player:		.10
Gold Medallion:		2X
1	Ivan Rodriguez	.30
2	Don Mattingly	.65
3	Roberto Alomar	.20
4	Wade Boggs	.60
5	Omar Vizquel	.10
6	Ken Griffey Jr.	.75
7	Kenny Lofton	.10
8	Devon White	.10
9	Mark Langston	.10
10	Tom Pagnozzi	.10
11	Jeff Bagwell	.45
12	Craig Biggio	.10
13	Matt Williams	.10
14	Barry Larkin	.10
15	Barry Bonds	1.00
16	Marquis Grissom	.10
17	Darren Lewis	.10
18	Greg Maddux	.60
19	Frank Thomas	.45
20	Jeff Bagwell	.45
21	David Cone	.10
22	Greg Maddux	.60
23	Bob Hamelin	.10
24	Raul Mondesi	.10
25	Moises Alou	.10

Golden Prospects

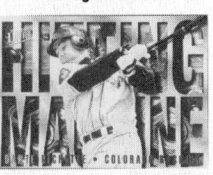

A hobby-pack exclusive, found at the rate of one per eight packs on average in Series I. Fronts feature a player photo at right, with three horizontally and vertically compressed versions of the same photo at right. The photo's background has been rendered in a single color. All typography - Ultra logo, card title, name and team - is in gold foil. Backs are also horizontal and have a color player photo and career summary.

	NM/M
Complete Set (10):	5.00

Common Player:		.10
Gold Medallion:		2X
1	James Baldwin	.10
2	Alan Benes	.10
3	Armando Benitez	.10
4	Ray Durham	.10
5	LaTroy Hawkins	.10
6	Brian Hunter	.10
7	Derek Jeter	3.00
8	Charles Johnson	.10
9	Alex Rodriguez	2.00
10	Michael Tucker	.10

1995 Ultra Gold Medallion Rookies Mail-in

This set of 20 was available only by mailing in 10 Fleer Ultra wrappers plus $5.95. A reported 100,000 sets were produced. The cards are in the same format as the regular-issue Fleer Ultra. Each card has a team logo, player name and "ROOKIE" notation in gold foil at bottom, and the round Gold Medallion seal in an upper-corner of the borderless game-action photo front. Backs have two more action photos, a large one in one-color and a small one in full-color. Much of the typography on back is rendered in gold foil. Card numbers have an M prefix.

	NM/M
Complete Set (20):	3.00

Common Player:		.10
M-1	Manny Alexander	.10
M-2	Edgardo Alfonzo	.10
M-3	Jason Bates	.10
M-4	Andrés Berumen	.10
M-5	Darren Bragg	.10
M-6	Jamie Brewington	.10
M-7	Jason Christiansen	.10
M-8	Brad Clontz	.10
M-9	Marty Cordova	.10
M-10	Johnny Damon	1.50
M-11	Vaughn Eshelman	.10
M-12	Chad Fonville	.10
M-13	Curtis Goodwin	.10
M-14	Tyler Green	.10
M-15	Bob Higginson	.10
M-16	Jason Isringhausen	.10
M-17	Hideo Nomo	1.50
M-18	Jon Nunnally	.10
M-19	Carlos Perez	.10
M-20	Julian Tavarez	.10

Hitting Machines

Various mechanical devices and dynamics make up the letters of "HITTING MACHINE" behind the color player action photo in this insert set. Both of those elements, along with the gold-foil player name, team and Ultra logo are in UV-coated contrast to the matte-finish gray background. Backs are also horizontal in format and feature a portrait photo at right, against a gray-streaked background. A career summary is printed at right. The Hitting Machines series is found only in Series II Ultra retail packs, at the rate of one card per eight packs, on average.

	NM/M
Complete Set (10):	6.00

Common Player:		.40
Gold Medallion:		2X
1	Jeff Bagwell	.65
2	Albert Belle	.25
3	Dante Bichette	.25
4	Barry Bonds	2.50
5	Jose Canseco	.50
6	Ken Griffey Jr.	1.00
7	Tony Gwynn	.75
8	Fred McGriff	.25
9	Mike Piazza	1.00
10	Frank Thomas	.65

Home Run Kings

Retail packaging of Fleer Ultra Series I was the hiding place for this sluggers' chase set. An average of one out of eight packs yielded a Home Run King insert. Fronts have a photo of the player's home run cut, while large letters "H," "R" and "K" are stacked vertically down one side. All front typography is in gold foil. Backs have another batting photo and a couple of sentences of recent career slugging prowess.

	NM/M
Complete Set (10):	7.50

Common Player:		.25
Gold Medallion:		2X
1	Ken Griffey Jr.	2.00
2	Frank Thomas	.75
3	Albert Belle	.25
4	Jose Canseco	.50
5	Cecil Fielder	.25
6	Matt Williams	.25
7	Jeff Bagwell	.75
8	Barry Bonds	3.00
9	Fred McGriff	.25
10	Andres Galarraga	.25

League Leaders

Top performers in major statistical categories are featured in this Series I insert. Cards were seeded in all types of Ultra packaging at the rate of about one card per three packs. Cards have a horizontal orientation with a color player action photo printed over a black logo of the appropriate league. American Leaguers' cards have a light brown overall background color, National Leaguers have dark green. The player's name, team and Ultra logos, and box with his league-leading category are printed in silver foil. The background from the front is carried over to the back, where a color portrait photo is at left, and a '94 season summary printed at right.

	NM/M
Complete Set (10):	2.50

Common Player:		.15
Gold Medallion:		2X
1	Paul O'Neill	.15
2	Kenny Lofton	.15
3	Jimmy Key	.15
4	Randy Johnson	.50
5	Lee Smith	.15
6	Tony Gwynn	.75
7	Craig Biggio	.15
8	Greg Maddux	.50
9	Andy Benes	.15
10	John Franco	.15

On-Base Leaders

Numerous smaller versions in several sizes of the central action photo against a graduated color background from the front design of this Series II insert set. The player name, card title and Ultra logo are printed in gold foil down one side. Backs have a horizontal player photo with a large team logo at top, a smaller version at bottom and a 1994 season summary. One out of eight (on average) pre-priced packs yielded an On-Base Leaders insert.

	NM/M
Complete Set (10):	15.00

Common Player:		1.00
Gold Medallion:		2X
1	Jeff Bagwell	2.00
2	Albert Belle	1.00
3	Craig Biggio	1.00
4	Wade Boggs	2.50
5	Barry Bonds	6.00
6	Will Clark	1.00
7	Tony Gwynn	2.50
8	Dave Justice	1.00
9	Paul O'Neill	1.00
10	Frank Thomas	2.00

Power Plus

The scarcest of the Series I Ultra inserts are the Power Plus cards, printed on 100% etched foil and inserted at the rate of less than one per box. Fronts have a player action photo overprinted on a background of "POWER PLUS" logos in various metallic colors. A team logo and player name are at bottom in gold foil, as is the Ultra logo at top. Backs are conventionally printed and have a player photo on one side and season summary on the other.

		NM/M
Complete Set (6):		7.50
Common Player:		.50
Gold Medallion:		2X
1	Albert Belle	.50
2	Ken Griffey Jr.	2.00
3	Frank Thomas	1.00
4	Jeff Bagwell	1.00
5	Barry Bonds	4.00
6	Matt Williams	.50

RBI Kings

A bright aura surrounds the central player action photo on these cards, separating the player image from an indistinct colored background. At center is a large gold-foil "RBI KING" with the player's name above and team below. Backs have a similar design with a white box at bottom covering the player's RBI abilities. This set is found only in Series I jumbo packs, at an average rate of one per eight packs.

		NM/M
Complete Set (10):		12.00
Common Player:		.50
Gold Medallion:		2X
1	Kirby Puckett	3.00
2	Joe Carter	.50
3	Albert Belle	.50
4	Frank Thomas	2.00
5	Julio Franco	.50
6	Jeff Bagwell	2.00
7	Matt Williams	.50
8	Dante Bichette	.50
9	Fred McGriff	.50
10	Mike Piazza	4.00

Rising Stars

The top of the line among Series II chase cards is this set printed on 100% etched foil and seeded at the rate of less than one per box, on average. Horizontal-format cards have two player photos on a background of multi-colored rays. The Ultra logo, card title, player name and team are printed in gold foil. Backs repeat the colored rays, have another player photo and a career summary.

		NM/M
Complete Set (9):		7.00
Common Player:		.50
Gold Medallion:		2X
1	Moises Alou	1.50
2	Jeff Bagwell	1.50
3	Albert Belle	.65
4	Juan Gonzalez	1.50
5	Chuck Knoblauch	.50
6	Kenny Lofton	.50
7	Raul Mondesi	.50
8	Mike Piazza	2.50
9	Frank Thomas	1.50

Second Year Standouts

Fifteen of the game's sophomore stars are featured in this Series I insert set. Horizontal-format cards have player action photos front and back set against a background of orange and yellow rays. Besides the player name, card title and Ultra logo in gold-foil, the front features a pair of leafed branches flanking a team logo, all in embossed gold-foil. Backs have a career summary. The series was seeded at the average rate of one per six packs.

		NM/M
Complete Set (15):		3.50
Common Player:		.15
Gold Medallion:		2X
1	Cliff Floyd	.15
2	Chris Gomez	.15
3	Rusty Greer	.15
4	Darren Hall	.15
5	Bob Hamelin	.15
6	Joey Hamilton	.15
7	Jeffrey Hammonds	.15
8	John Hudek	.15
9	Ryan Klesko	.15
10	Raul Mondesi	.15
11	Manny Ramirez	3.00
12	Bill Risley	.15
13	Steve Trachsel	.15
14	William Van Landingham	.15
15	Rondell White	.15

Strikeout Kings

A purple background with several types of concentric and overlapping circular designs in white are the background of this Series II chase set. An action color photo of the K-King is at center, while down one side are stacked photos of the grips used for various pitches. The player name, card title and Ultra logo are in silver foil. Backs have a portrait photo and career summary with purple circles behind and a black background. Stated odds of finding a Strikeout King card are one in five packs, on average.

		NM/M
Complete Set (6):		3.00
Common Player:		.10
Gold Medallion:		2X
1	Andy Benes	.10
2	Roger Clemens	1.50
3	Randy Johnson	.75
4	Greg Maddux	1.00
5	Pedro Martinez	.75
6	Jose Rijo	.10

1996 Ultra Promotional Samples

A six-page glossy folder which was die-cut to hold three sample cards introduced Fleer's Ultra line for 1996. The fronts of all three cards are similar in format to the issued versions, but only the back of the basic-card sample rep-

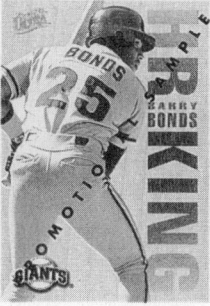

licates the issued version. Backs of the chase card samples contained product information.

		NM/M
Complete Set (8):		7.50
Common Player:		1.00
(1)	Ken Griffey Jr. (Basic Card)	1.50
(2)	Matt Williams (Basic Card)	1.00
(3)	Barry Bonds (HR King)	2.50
(4)	Frank Thomas (HR King)	1.25
(5)	Roberto Alomar (Prime Leather)	1.00
(6)	Cal Ripken Jr. (Prime Leather)	2.50
2	Tony Gwynn (Season Crown)	1.50
4	Kenny Lofton (Season Crown)	1.00

1996 Ultra

A 40% thicker cardboard stock and silver-foil highlights are featured in this year's edition. Fronts are very basic with a borderless action photo and silver-foil graphics. Backs feature a three-photo montage along with 1995 and career stats. The set was released in two 300-card series; each card is also reprinted as part of a limited-edition Gold Medallion parallel set. One Gold Medallion card is found in every pack. Each series has eight insert sets. Series 1 inserts are RBI Kings, Home Run Kings, Fresh Foundations, Diamond Producers, Power Plus, Season Crowns, Golden Prospects and Prime Leather. Series 2 inserts are Call to the Hall, Golden Prospects, Hitting Machines, On-Base Leaders, RESPECT, Rawhide, Rising Stars and Thunderclap. Checklist cards were also randomly inserted into packs from both series.

		NM/M
Complete Set (600):		22.50
Common Player:		.05
Gold Medallions:		2X
Series 1 or 2 Pack (12):		1.25
Series 1 or 2 Wax Box (24):		20.00
1	Manny Alexander	.05
2	Brady Anderson	.05
3	Bobby Bonilla	.05
4	Scott Erickson	.05
5	Curtis Goodwin	.05
6	Chris Hoiles	.05
7	Doug Jones	.05
8	Jeff Manto	.05
9	Mike Mussina	.35
10	Rafael Palmeiro	.35
11	Cal Ripken Jr.	1.50
12	Rick Aguilera	.05
13	Luis Alicea	.05
14	Stan Belinda	.05
15	Jose Canseco	.40
16	Roger Clemens	.85
17	Mike Greenwell	.05
18	Mike Macfarlane	.05
19	Tim Naehring	.05
20	Troy O'Leary	.05
21	John Valentin	.05
22	Mo Vaughn	.05
23	Tim Wakefield	.05
24	Brian Anderson	.05
25	Garret Anderson	.05
26	Chili Davis	.05
27	Gary DiSarcina	.05
28	Jim Edmonds	.05
29	Jorge Fabregas	.05
30	Chuck Finley	.05
31	Mark Langston	.05
32	Troy Percival	.05
33	Tim Salmon	.05
34	Lee Smith	.05
35	Wilson Alvarez	.05
36	Ray Durham	.05
37	Alex Fernandez	.05
38	Ozzie Guillen	.05
39	Roberto Hernandez	.05
40	Lance Johnson	.05
41	Ron Karkovice	.05
42	Lyle Mouton	.05
43	Tim Raines	.05
44	Frank Thomas	.60
45	Carlos Baerga	.05
46	Albert Belle	.60
47	Orel Hershiser	.05
48	Kenny Lofton	.05
49	Dennis Martinez	.05
50	Jose Mesa	.05
51	Eddie Murray	.60
52	Chad Ogea	.05
53	Manny Ramirez	.60
54	Jim Thome	.50
55	Omar Vizquel	.05
56	Dave Winfield	.60
57	Chad Curtis	.05
58	Cecil Fielder	.05
59	John Flaherty	.05
60	Travis Fryman	.05
61	Chris Gomez	.05
62	Bob Higginson	.05
63	Felipe Lira	.05
64	Brian Maxcy	.05
65	Alan Trammell	.05
66	Lou Whitaker	.05
67	Kevin Appier	.05
68	Gary Gaetti	.05
69	Tom Goodwin	.05
70	Tom Gordon	.05
71	Jason Jacome	.05
72	Wally Joyner	.05
73	Brent Mayne	.05
74	Jeff Montgomery	.05
75	Jon Nunnally	.05
76	Joe Vitiello	.05
77	Ricky Bones	.05
78	Jeff Cirillo	.05
79	Mike Fetters	.05
80	Darryl Hamilton	.05
81	David Hulse	.05
82	Dave Nilsson	.05
83	Kevin Seitzer	.05
84	Steve Sparks	.05
85	B.J. Surhoff	.05
86	Jose Valentin	.05
87	Greg Vaughn	.05
88	Marty Cordova	.05
89	Chuck Knoblauch	.05
90	Pat Meares	.05
91	Pedro Munoz	.05
92	Kirby Puckett	.75
93	Brad Radke	.05
94	Scott Stahoviak	.05
95	Dave Stevens	.05
96	Mike Trombley	.05
97	Matt Walbeck	.05
98	Wade Boggs	.75
99	Russ Davis	.05
100	Jim Leyritz	.05
101	Don Mattingly	.85
102	Jack McDowell	.05
103	Paul O'Neill	.05
104	Andy Pettitte	.30
105	Mariano Rivera	.15
106	Ruben Sierra	.05
107	Darryl Strawberry	.05
108	John Wetteland	.05
109	Bernie Williams	.05
110	Geronimo Berroa	.05
111	Scott Brosius	.05
112	Dennis Eckersley	.50
113	Brent Gates	.05
114	Rickey Henderson	.60
115	Mark McGwire	1.25
116	Ariel Prieto	.05
117	Terry Steinbach	.05
118	Todd Stottlemyre	.05
119	Todd Van Poppel	.05
120	Steve Wojciechowski	.05
121	Rich Amaral	.05
122	Bobby Ayala	.05
123	Mike Blowers	.05
124	Chris Bosio	.05
125	Joey Cora	.05
126	Ken Griffey Jr.	1.00
127	Randy Johnson	.60
128	Edgar Martinez	.05
129	Tino Martinez	.05
130	Alex Rodriguez	1.25
131	Dan Wilson	.05
132	Will Clark	.05
133	Jeff Frye	.05
134	Benji Gil	.05
135	Juan Gonzalez	.30
136	Rusty Greer	.05
137	Mark McLemore	.05
138	Roger Pavlik	.05
139	Ivan Rodriguez	.50
140	Kenny Rogers	.05
141	Mickey Tettleton	.05
142	Roberto Alomar	.20
143	Joe Carter	.05
144	Tony Castillo	.05
145	Alex Gonzalez	.05
146	Shawn Green	.35
147	Pat Hentgen	.05
148	Sandy Martinez RC	.05
149	Paul Molitor	.60
150	John Olerud	.05
151	Ed Sprague	.05
152	Jeff Blauser	.05
153	Brad Clontz	.05
154	Tom Glavine	.30
155	Marquis Grissom	.05
156	Chipper Jones	.75
157	David Justice	.05
158	Ryan Klesko	.05
159	Javier Lopez	.05
160	Greg Maddux	.75
161	John Smoltz	.05
162	Mark Wohlers	.05
163	Jim Bullinger	.05
164	Frank Castillo	.05
165	Shawon Dunston	.05
166	Kevin Foster	.05
167	Luis Gonzalez	.05
168	Mark Grace	.05
169	Rey Sanchez	.05
170	Scott Servais	.05
171	Sammy Sosa	.75
172	Ozzie Timmons	.05
173	Steve Trachsel	.05
174	Bret Boone	.05
175	Jeff Branson	.05
176	Jeff Brantley	.05
177	Dave Burba	.05
178	Ron Gant	.05
179	Barry Larkin	.05
180	Darren Lewis	.05
181	Mark Portugal	.05
182	Reggie Sanders	.05
183	Pete Schourek	.05
184	John Smiley	.05
185	Jason Bates	.05
186	Dante Bichette	.05
187	Ellis Burks	.05
188	Vinny Castilla	.05
189	Andres Galarraga	.05
190	Darren Holmes	.05
191	Armando Reynoso	.05
192	Kevin Ritz	.05
193	Bill Swift	.05
194	Larry Walker	.05
195	Kurt Abbott	.05
196	John Burkett	.05
197	Greg Colbrunn	.05
198	Jeff Conine	.05
199	Andre Dawson	.25
200	Chris Hammond	.05
201	Charles Johnson	.05
202	Robb Nen	.05
203	Terry Pendleton	.05
204	Quilvio Veras	.05
205	Jeff Bagwell	.60
206	Derek Bell	.05
207	Doug Drabek	.05
208	Tony Eusebio	.05
209	Mike Hampton	.05
210	Brian Hunter	.05
211	Todd Jones	.05
212	Orlando Miller	.05
213	James Mouton	.05
214	Shane Reynolds	.05
215	Dave Veres	.05
216	Billy Ashley	.05
217	Brett Butler	.05
218	Chad Fonville	.05
219	Todd Hollandsworth	.05
220	Eric Karros	.05
221	Ramon Martinez	.05
222	Raul Mondesi	.05
223	Hideo Nomo	.30
224	Mike Piazza	1.00
225	Kevin Tapani	.05
226	Ismael Valdes	.05
227	Todd Worrell	.05
228	Moises Alou	.05
229	Wil Cordero	.05
230	Jeff Fassero	.05
231	Darrin Fletcher	.05
232	Mike Lansing	.05
233	Pedro Martinez	.60
234	Carlos Perez	.05
235	Mel Rojas	.05
236	David Segui	.05
237	Tony Tarasco	.05
238	Rondell White	.05
239	Edgardo Alfonzo	.05
240	Rico Brogna	.05
241	Carl Everett	.05
242	Todd Hundley	.05
243	Butch Huskey	.05
244	Jason Isringhausen	.05
245	Bobby Jones	.05
246	Jeff Kent	.05
247	Bill Pulsipher	.05
248	Jose Vizcaino	.05
249	Ricky Bottalico	.05
250	Darren Daulton	.05
251	Jim Eisenreich	.05
252	Tyler Green	.05
253	Charlie Hayes	.05
254	Gregg Jefferies	.05
255	Tony Longmire	.05
256	Michael Mimbs	.05
257	Mickey Morandini	.05
258	Paul Quantrill	.05
259	Heathcliff Slocumb	.05
260	Jay Bell	.05
261	Jacob Brumfield	.05
262	Angelo Encarnacion RC	.05
263	John Ericks	.05
264	Mark Johnson	.05
265	Esteban Loaiza RC	.05
266	Al Martin	.05
267	Orlando Merced	.05
268	Dan Miceli	.05
269	Denny Neagle	.05
270	Brian Barber	.05
271	Scott Cooper	.05
272	Tripp Cromer	.05
273	Bernard Gilkey	.05
274	Tom Henke	.05
275	Brian Jordan	.05
276	John Mabry	.05
277	Tom Pagnozzi	.05
278	Mark Petkovsek RC	.05
279	Ozzie Smith	.75
280	Andy Ashby	.05
281	Brad Ausmus	.05
282	Ken Caminiti	.05
283	Glenn Dishman	.05
284	Tony Gwynn	.75
285	Joey Hamilton	.05
286	Trevor Hoffman	.05
287	Phil Plantier	.05
288	Jody Reed	.05
289	Eddie Williams	.05
290	Barry Bonds	1.50
291	Jamie Brewington	.05
292	Mark Carreon	.05
293	Royce Clayton	.05
294	Glenallen Hill	.05
295	Mark Leiter	.05
296	Kirt Manwaring	.05
297	J.R. Phillips	.05
298	Deion Sanders	.05
299	William Van Landingham	.05
300	Matt Williams	.05
301	Roberto Alomar	.20
302	Armando Benitez	.05
303	Mike Devereaux	.05
304	Jeffrey Hammonds	.05
305	Jimmy Haynes	.05
306	Scott McClain RC	.05
307	Kent Mercker	.05
308	Randy Myers	.05
309	B.J. Surhoff	.05
310	Tony Tarasco	.05
311	David Wells	.05
312	Wil Cordero	.05
313	Alex Delgado	.05
314	Tom Gordon	.05
315	Dwayne Hosey	.05
316	Jose Malave	.05
317	Kevin Mitchell	.05
318	Jamie Moyer	.05
319	Aaron Sele	.05
320	Heathcliff Slocumb	.05
321	Mike Stanley	.05
322	Jeff Suppan	.05
323	Jim Abbott	.05
324	George Arias	.05
325	Todd Greene	.05
326	Bryan Harvey	.05
327	J.T. Snow	.05
328	Randy Velarde	.05
329	Tim Wallach	.05
330	Harold Baines	.05
331	Jason Bere	.05
332	Darren Lewis	.05
333	Norberto Martin	.05
334	Tony Phillips	.05
335	Bill Simas	.05
336	Chris Snopek	.05
337	Kevin Tapani	.05
338	Danny Tartabull	.05
339	Robin Ventura	.05
340	Sandy Alomar	.05
341	Julio Franco	.05
342	Jack McDowell	.05
343	Charles Nagy	.05
344	Julian Tavarez	.05
345	Kimera Bartee	.05
346	Greg Keagle	.05
347	Mark Lewis	.05
348	Jose Lima	.05
349	Melvin Nieves	.05
350	Mark Parent	.05
351	Eddie Williams	.05
352	Johnny Damon	.30
353	Sal Fasano	.05
354	Mark Gubicza	.05
355	Bob Hamelin	.05
356	Chris Haney	.05
357	Keith Lockhart	.05
358	Mike Macfarlane	.05
359	Jose Offerman	.05
360	Bip Roberts	.05
361	Michael Tucker	.05
362	Chuck Carr	.05
363	Bobby Hughes	.05
364	John Jaha	.05
365	Mark Loretta	.05
366	Mike Matheny	.05
367	Ben McDonald	.05
368	Matt Mieske	.05
369	Angel Miranda	.05
370	Fernando Vina	.05
371	Rick Aguilera	.05
372	Rich Becker	.05
373	LaTroy Hawkins	.05

374	Dave Hollins	.05
375	Roberto Kelly	.05
376	Matt Lawton **RC**	.05
377	Paul Molitor	.60
378	Dan Naulty **RC**	.05
379	Rich Robertson	.05
380	Frank Rodriguez	.05
381	David Cone	.05
382	Mariano Duncan	.05
383	Andy Fox **RC**	.05
384	Joe Girardi	.05
385	Dwight Gooden	.05
386	Derek Jeter	1.50
387	Pat Kelly	.05
388	Jimmy Key	.05
389	Matt Luke **RC**	.05
390	Tino Martinez	.05
391	Jeff Nelson	.05
392	Melido Perez	.05
393	Tim Raines	.05
394	Ruben Rivera	.05
395	Kenny Rogers	.05
396	Tony Batista **RC**	.25
397	Allen Battle	.05
398	Mike Bordick	.05
399	Steve Cox	.05
400	Jason Giambi	.40
401	Doug Johns	.05
402	Pedro Munoz	.05
403	Phil Plantier	.05
404	Scott Spiezio	.05
405	George Williams	.05
406	Ernie Young	.05
407	Darren Bragg	.05
408	Jay Buhner	.05
409	Norm Charlton	.05
410	Russ Davis	.05
411	Sterling Hitchcock	.05
412	Edwin Hurtado	.05
413	Raul Ibanez **RC**	2.00
414	Mike Jackson	.05
415	Luis Sojo	.05
416	Paul Sorrento	.05
417	Bob Wolcott	.05
418	Damon Buford	.05
419	Kevin Gross	.05
420	Darryl Hamilton	.05
421	Mike Henneman	.05
422	Ken Hill	.05
423	Dean Palmer	.05
424	Bobby Witt	.05
425	Tilson Brito	.05
426	Giovanni Carrara	.05
427	Domingo Cedeno	.05
428	Felipe Crespo	.05
429	Carlos Delgado	.40
430	Juan Guzman	.05
431	Erik Hanson	.05
432	Marty Janzen **RC**	.05
433	Otis Nixon	.05
434	Robert Perez	.05
435	Paul Quantrill	.05
436	Bill Risley	.05
437	Steve Avery	.05
438	Jermaine Dye	.05
439	Mark Lemke	.05
440	Marty Malloy **RC**	.05
441	Fred McGriff	.05
442	Greg McMichael	.05
443	Wonderful Monds	.05
444	Eddie Perez	.05
445	Jason Schmidt	.05
446	Terrell Wade	.05
447	Terry Adams	.05
448	Scott Bullett	.05
449	Robin Jennings **RC**	.05
450	Doug Jones	.05
451	Brooks Kieschnick	.05
452	Dave Magadan	.05
453	Jason Maxwell **RC**	.05
454	Brian McRae	.05
455	Rodney Myers	.05
456	Jaime Navarro	.05
457	Ryne Sandberg	.75
458	Vince Coleman	.05
459	Eric Davis	.05
460	Steve Gibralter	.05
461	Thomas Howard	.05
462	Mike Kelly	.05
463	Hal Morris	.05
464	Eric Owens	.05
465	Jose Rijo	.05
466	Chris Sabo	.05
467	Eddie Taubensee	.05
468	Trenidad Hubbard	.05
469	Curt Leskanic	.05
470	Quinton McCracken	.05
471	Jayhawk Owens	.05
472	Steve Reed	.05
473	Bryan Rekar	.05
474	Bruce Ruffin	.05
475	Bret Saberhagen	.05
476	Walt Weiss	.05
477	Eric Young	.05
478	Kevin Brown	.05
479	Al Leiter	.05
480	Pat Rapp	.05
481	Gary Sheffield	.35
482	Devon White	.05
483	Bob Abreu	.05
484	Sean Berry	.05
485	Craig Biggio	.05
486	Jim Dougherty	.05
487	Richard Hidalgo	.05
488	Darryl Kile	.05
489	Derrick May	.05
490	Greg Swindell	.05
491	Rick Wilkins	.05

492	Mike Blowers	.05
493	Tom Candiotti	.05
494	Roger Cedeno	.05
495	Delino DeShields	.05
496	Greg Gagne	.05
497	Karim Garcia	.10
498	Wilton Guerrero **RC**	.05
499	Chan Ho Park	.05
500	Israel Alcantara	.05
501	Shane Andrews	.05
502	Yamil Benitez	.05
503	Cliff Floyd	.05
504	Mark Grudzielanek	.05
505	Ryan McGuire	.05
506	Sherman Obando	.05
507	Jose Paniagua	.05
508	Henry Rodriguez	.05
509	Kirk Rueter	.05
510	Juan Acevedo	.05
511	John Franco	.05
512	Bernard Gilkey	.05
513	Lance Johnson	.05
514	Rey Ordonez	.05
515	Robert Person	.05
516	Paul Wilson	.05
517	Toby Borland	.05
518	David Doster **RC**	.05
519	Lenny Dykstra	.05
520	Sid Fernandez	.05
521	Mike Grace **RC**	.05
522	Rich Hunter **RC**	.05
523	Benito Santiago	.05
524	Gene Schall	.05
525	Curt Schilling	.15
526	Kevin Sefcik **RC**	.05
527	Lee Tinsley	.05
528	David West	.05
529	Mark Whiten	.05
530	Todd Zeile	.05
531	Carlos Garcia	.05
532	Charlie Hayes	.05
533	Jason Kendall	.05
534	Jeff King	.05
535	Mike Kingery	.05
536	Nelson Liriano	.05
537	Dan Plesac	.05
538	Paul Wagner	.05
539	Luis Alicea	.05
540	David Bell	.05
541	Alan Benes	.05
542	Andy Benes	.05
543	Mike Busby **RC**	.05
544	Royce Clayton	.05
545	Dennis Eckersley	.05
546	Gary Gaetti	.05
547	Ron Gant	.05
548	Aaron Holbert	.05
549	Ray Lankford	.05
550	T.J. Mathews	.05
551	Willie McGee	.05
552	Miguel Mejia **RC**	.05
553	Todd Stottlemyre	.05
554	Sean Bergman	.05
555	Willie Blair	.05
556	Andujar Cedeno	.05
557	Steve Finley	.05
558	Rickey Henderson	.60
559	Wally Joyner	.05
560	Scott Livingstone	.05
561	Marc Newfield	.05
562	Bob Tewksbury	.05
563	Fernando Valenzuela	.05
564	Rod Beck	.05
565	Doug Creek	.05
566	Shawon Dunston	.05
567	Osvaldo Fernandez **RC**	.20
568	Stan Javier	.05
569	Marcus Jensen	.05
570	Steve Scarsone	.05
571	Robby Thompson	.05
572	Allen Watson	.05
573	Roberto Alomar (Ultra Stars)	.10
574	Jeff Bagwell (Ultra Stars)	.30
575	Albert Belle (Ultra Stars)	.05
576	Wade Boggs (Ultra Stars)	.40
577	Barry Bonds (Ultra Stars)	.75
578	Juan Gonzalez (Ultra Stars)	.15
579	Ken Griffey Jr. (Ultra Stars)	.50
580	Tony Gwynn (Ultra Stars)	.40
581	Randy Johnson (Ultra Stars)	.30
582	Chipper Jones (Ultra Stars)	.40
583	Barry Larkin (Ultra Stars)	.05
584	Kenny Lofton (Ultra Stars)	.05
585	Greg Maddux (Ultra Stars)	.40
586	Raul Mondesi (Ultra Stars)	.05
587	Mike Piazza (Ultra Stars)	.50
588	Cal Ripken Jr. (Ultra Stars)	.75
589	Tim Salmon (Ultra Stars)	.05
590	Frank Thomas (Ultra Stars)	.35
591	Mo Vaughn (Ultra Stars)	.05
592	Matt Williams (Ultra Stars)	.05
593	Marty Cordova (Raw Power)	.05
594	Jim Edmonds (Raw Power)	.05
595	Cliff Floyd (Raw Power)	.05
596	Chipper Jones (Raw Power)	.40
597	Ryan Klesko (Raw Power)	.05
598	Raul Mondesi (Raw Power)	.05

599	Manny Ramirez (Raw Power)	.30
600	Ruben Rivera (Raw Power)	.05

1996 Ultra Gold Medallion

Limited to less than 10 percent of the regular edition's production, the Gold Medallion parallel set replaces the front photo's background with gold foil featuring a large embossed Fleer Ultra Gold Medallion seal at center. One Gold Medallion card is found in each foil pack.

	NM/M
Complete Set (600):	75.00
Common Player:	.25

Call to the Hall

Ten probable future Hall of Famers are featured on these cards, which use classic style original illustrations of the players. The cards were seeded one per every 24 Series 2 packs.

		NM/M
Complete Set (10):		10.00
Common Player:		1.00
Gold Medallion Edition:		2X
1	Barry Bonds	3.00
2	Ken Griffey Jr.	2.00
3	Tony Gwynn	1.25
4	Rickey Henderson	1.00
5	Greg Maddux	1.25
6	Eddie Murray	1.00
7	Cal Ripken Jr.	3.00
8	Ryne Sandberg	1.25
9	Ozzie Smith	1.25
10	Frank Thomas	1.00

Checklists

Fleer Ultra featured 10 checklist cards that were inserted every four packs. These cards featured a superstar player on the front and, throughout the set, a full checklist of all cards in the 1996 Ultra set on the back.

		NM/M
Complete Set (20):		9.00
Common Player:		.15
1	Jeff Bagwell	.50

2	Barry Bonds	1.00
3	Juan Gonzalez	.25
4	Ken Griffey Jr.	.65
5	Chipper Jones	.60
6	Mike Piazza	.65
7	Manny Ramirez	.50
8	Cal Ripken Jr.	1.00
9	Frank Thomas	.50
10	Matt Williams	.15
1	Albert Belle	.15
2	Cecil Fielder	.15
3	Ken Griffey Jr.	.65
4	Tony Gwynn	.60
5	Derek Jeter	1.00
6	Jason Kendall	.15
7	Ryan Klesko	.15
8	Greg Maddux	.60
9	Cal Ripken Jr.	1.00
10	Frank Thomas	.50

1996 Ultra Diamond Dust

This card commemorates Cal Ripken's history-making 1995 record of playing in 2,131 consecutive regular-season games. Horizontal in format, the front has a color action photo of Ripken on a simulated leather background. Back has a photo of Ripken on the night he set the new record. Sandwiched between front and back is a dime-sized plastic capsule of dirt certified, according to the facsimile autograph of the team's head groundskeeper, to have been used on the infield at Oriole Park in Camden Yards during the 1995 season. Two versions of the card were made. A hand-numbered version limited to 2,131 was offered direct to dealers for $39.99. An unnumbered version was available to collectors as a wrapper redemption for $24.99.

	NM/M
Cal Ripken Jr. (Numbered)	40.00
Cal Ripken Jr. (Unnumbered)	20.00

Diamond Producers

A horizontal layout and two versions of the same photo printed on holographic foil are featured in this insert set. Stated odds of finding a Diamond Producers card are one per every 20 Series I packs.

		NM/M
Complete Set (12):		15.00
Common Player:		.50
Gold Medallions:		2X
1	Albert Belle	.50
2	Barry Bonds	3.00
3	Ken Griffey Jr.	2.00
4	Tony Gwynn	1.50
5	Greg Maddux	1.50
6	Hideo Nomo	.75
7	Mike Piazza	2.00
8	Kirby Puckett	1.50
9	Cal Ripken Jr.	3.00
10	Frank Thomas	1.25
11	Mo Vaughn	.50
12	Matt Williams	.50

Fresh Foundations

Rising stars who can carry their teams' fortunes into the next century are featured in this foil-printed insert set, found on average of one card per every three Series I foil packs.

		NM/M
Complete Set (10):		2.00
Common Player:		.15
Gold Medallions:		2X
1	Garret Anderson	.15
2	Marty Cordova	.15
3	Jim Edmonds	.15
4	Brian Hunter	.15
5	Chipper Jones	.50

6	Ryan Klesko	.15
7	Raul Mondesi	.15
8	Hideo Nomo	.25
9	Manny Ramirez	.40
10	Rondell White	.15

Golden Prospects, Series 1

A hobby-pack-only insert, these horizontal format cards have rainbow foil ballpark backgrounds and feature 1996's rookie crop. They are found on average of one per every five Series I packs.

		NM/M
Complete Set (10):		7.00
Common Player:		.25
Gold Medallions:		2X
1	Yamil Benitez	.25
2	Alberto Castillo	.25
3	Roger Cedeno	.25
4	Johnny Damon	1.00
5	Micah Franklin	.25
6	Jason Giambi	1.00
7	Jose Herrera	.25
8	Derek Jeter	5.00
9	Kevin Jordan	.25
10	Ruben Rivera	.25

Golden Prospects, Series 2

The Golden Prospects insert series continued with 15 more young stars found exclusively in Series 2 hobby packs, though in much lower numbers than the Series 1 inserts.

		NM/M
Complete Set (15):		10.00
Common Player:		1.00
Gold Medallions:		2X
1	Bob Abreu	1.50
2	Israel Alcantara	1.00
3	Tony Batista	1.00
4	Mike Cameron	1.00
5	Steve Cox	1.00
6	Jermaine Dye	1.00
7	Wilton Guerrero	1.00
8	Richard Hidalgo	1.00
9	Raul Ibanez	1.00
10	Marty Janzen	1.00
11	Robin Jennings	1.00
12	Jason Maxwell	1.00
13	Scott McClain	1.00
14	Wonderful Monds	1.00
15	Chris Singleton	1.00

Hitting Machines

These die-cut 1996 Fleer Ultra Series II insert cards showcase the heaviest hitters on cards featuring a machine-gear design. The cards were seeded one per every 288 Series II packs.

	NM/M
Complete Set (10):	35.00

	NM/M
Common Player:	2.00
Gold Medallion:	2X
1	Albert Belle	2.00
2	Barry Bonds	12.00
3	Juan Gonzalez	2.50
4	Ken Griffey Jr.	6.00
5	Edgar Martinez	2.00
6	Rafael Palmeiro	3.00
7	Mike Piazza	6.00
8	Tim Salmon	2.00
9	Frank Thomas	4.00
10	Matt Williams	2.00

1996 Ultra Home Run Kings Exchange Cards

Printed on cardboard, these super-scarce inserts are found at the rate of only one per 75 packs. Because of quality control problems, the cards were initially released as exchange cards, with instructions on back for a mail-in redemption offer for the actual wooden card. The redemption period expired Dec. 1, 1996.

		NM/M
Complete Set (12):		20.00
Common Player:		.75
1	Albert Belle	.75
2	Dante Bichette	.75
3	Barry Bonds	5.00
4	Jose Canseco	1.50
5	Juan Gonzalez	1.25
6	Ken Griffey Jr.	3.00
7	Mark McGwire	4.00
8	Manny Ramirez	2.50
9	Tim Salmon	.75
10	Frank Thomas	2.50
11	Mo Vaughn	.75
12	Matt Williams	.75

Home Run Kings

Printed on a thin wood veneer, these super-scarce inserts are seeded one per every 75 Series 1 packs. Because of quality control problems, the cards were initially released as exchange cards, with instructions on back for a mail-in redemption offer for the actual wooden card.

		NM/M
Complete Set (12):		50.00
Common Player:		2.50
Gold Medallions:		2X
1	Albert Belle	2.50
2	Dante Bichette	2.50
3	Barry Bonds	12.50
4	Jose Canseco	5.00
5	Juan Gonzalez	3.00
6	Ken Griffey Jr.	9.00
7	Mark McGwire	10.00
8	Manny Ramirez	6.50
9	Tim Salmon	2.50
10	Frank Thomas	6.50

11	Mo Vaughn	2.50
12	Matt Williams	2.50

On-Base Leaders

These 1996 Fleer Ultra Series II inserts feature 10 of the game's top on-base leaders. The cards were seeded one per every four packs.

		NM/M
Complete Set (10):		4.50
Common Player:		.25
Gold Medallion:		2X
1	Wade Boggs	.75
2	Barry Bonds	2.00
3	Tony Gwynn	.75
4	Rickey Henderson	.60
5	Chuck Knoblauch	.25
6	Edgar Martinez	.25
7	Mike Piazza	1.00
8	Tim Salmon	.25
9	Frank Thomas	.60
10	Jim Thome	.50

Power Plus

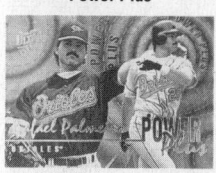

Etched-foil backgrounds, multiple player photos and a horizontal format are featured in this chase set. Stated odds of finding one of the dozen Power Plus cards are one per every 10 Series I packs.

		NM/M
Complete Set (12):		10.00
Common Player:		.40
Gold Medallions:		2X
1	Jeff Bagwell	1.25
2	Barry Bonds	3.00
3	Ken Griffey Jr.	2.00
4	Raul Mondesi	.40
5	Rafael Palmeiro	1.00
6	Mike Piazza	2.00
7	Manny Ramirez	1.25
8	Tim Salmon	.40
9	Reggie Sanders	.40
10	Frank Thomas	1.25
11	Larry Walker	.40
12	Matt Williams	.40

Prime Leather

An embossed leather-feel background is featured on these cards of top fielders, seeded one per every eight Series I packs, on average.

		NM/M
Complete Set (18):		17.50
Common Player:		.50
Gold Medallions:		2X
1	Ivan Rodriguez	1.50
2	Will Clark	.50
3	Roberto Alomar	.65
4	Cal Ripken Jr.	4.00
5	Wade Boggs	2.00
6	Ken Griffey Jr.	2.50
7	Kenny Lofton	.50
8	Kirby Puckett	2.00
9	Tim Salmon	.65
10	Mike Piazza	2.50
11	Mark Grace	.50
12	Craig Biggio	.50
13	Barry Larkin	.50
14	Matt Williams	.50
15	Barry Bonds	4.00
16	Tony Gwynn	2.00

17	Brian McRae	.50
18	Raul Mondesi	.50

Rawhide

Ten top fielders are featured on these 1996 Fleer Ultra Series II inserts. The cards were seeded one per every eight packs.

		NM/M
Complete Set (10):		10.00
Common Player:		.45
Gold Medallion:		2X
1	Roberto Alomar	.65
2	Barry Bonds	3.00
3	Mark Grace	.45
4	Ken Griffey Jr.	1.50
5	Kenny Lofton	.45
6	Greg Maddux	1.00
7	Raul Mondesi	.45
8	Mike Piazza	1.50
9	Cal Ripken Jr.	3.00
10	Matt Williams	.45

RBI Kings

Retail packs are the exclusive provenance of this 10-card set of top RBI men. Stated odds of finding an RBI King card are one per every five Series I packs.

		NM/M
Complete Set (10):		4.00
Common Player:		.10
Gold Medallions:		2X
1	Derek Bell	.10
2	Albert Belle	.10
3	Dante Bichette	.10
4	Barry Bonds	2.00
5	Jim Edmonds	.15
6	Manny Ramirez	1.00
7	Reggie Sanders	.10
8	Sammy Sosa	1.50
9	Frank Thomas	1.00
10	Mo Vaughn	.10

R-E-S-P-E-C-T

These cards feature 10 players held in high esteem by their major league peers. The cards were seeded one per every 18 1996 Ultra Series II packs.

		NM/M
Complete Set (10):		20.00
Common Player:		.50
Gold Medallion:		2X
1	Joe Carter	.50
2	Ken Griffey Jr.	3.00
3	Tony Gwynn	2.50
4	Greg Maddux	2.50
5	Eddie Murray	2.00
6	Kirby Puckett	2.50
7	Cal Ripken Jr.	5.00
8	Ryne Sandberg	2.50
9	Frank Thomas	2.00
10	Mo Vaughn	.50

Rising Stars

Ten of baseball's best young players are spotlighted on these 1996 Fleer Ultra Series II inserts. Cards were seeded one per every four packs.

		NM/M
Complete Set (10):		4.00
Common Player:		.20
Gold Medallion:		2X
1	Garret Anderson	.20
2	Marty Cordova	.20
3	Jim Edmonds	.35
4	Cliff Floyd	.20
5	Brian Hunter	.20
6	Chipper Jones	2.00
7	Ryan Klesko	.20
8	Hideo Nomo	.65
9	Manny Ramirez	1.25
10	Rondell White	.20

Season Crowns

Large coats-of-arms printed on "Ultra Crystal" clear plastic are the background for player action photos in this insert set. Odds of one per every 10 Series II packs were stated.

		NM/M
Complete Set (10):		12.50
Common Player:		.75
Gold Medallions:		2X
1	Barry Bonds	4.00
2	Tony Gwynn	2.00
3	Randy Johnson	1.25
4	Kenny Lofton	.75
5	Greg Maddux	2.00
6	Edgar Martinez	.75
7	Hideo Nomo	1.00
8	Cal Ripken Jr.	4.00
9	Frank Thomas	1.25
10	Tim Wakefield	.75

Thunderclap

The active career home run leaders are featured in this retail-exclusive Ultra insert set. Seeded only one per 72 packs, the Thunderclap cards have action photos on front with simulated lightning in the background and other graphic highlights rendered in holographic foil. Backs have a large portrait photo and career summary. Each of these scarce retail inserts can also be found in an even more elusive Gold Medallion version.

		NM/M
Complete Set (20):		45.00
Common Player:		1.00
Gold Medallion:		2X
1	Albert Belle	1.00
2	Barry Bonds	7.50
3	Bobby Bonilla	1.00
4	Jose Canseco	1.50
5	Joe Carter	1.00
6	Will Clark	1.00
7	Andre Dawson	1.50
8	Cecil Fielder	1.00
9	Andres Galarraga	1.00
10	Juan Gonzalez	1.50
11	Ken Griffey Jr.	5.00
12	Fred McGriff	1.00
13	Mark McGwire	6.00
14	Eddie Murray	2.50
15	Rafael Palmeiro	2.00
16	Kirby Puckett	4.00
17	Cal Ripken Jr.	7.50
18	Ryne Sandberg	4.00
19	Frank Thomas	2.50
20	Matt Williams	1.00

1997 Ultra Promo Strip

To introduce the concept of its new non-parallel parallel set, Fleer issued this three-card promo strip picturing regular (left), Gold Medallion (center) and Platinum Medallion (right) Cal Ripken, Jr., cards. Fronts have a "PROMOTIONAL SAMPLE," overprint in foil to match the cards' graphic highlights (silver, gold and prismatic). Backs, which have stats only through the 1995 season, have the same overprint in red.

	NM/M
Three-Card Strip:	10.00

1997 Ultra

Ultra was issued in a 300-card Series 1 and 252-card Series 2, each with two parallel sets, Gold and Platinum, which feature "G" and "P" prefixes on the card number, respectively. Cards were issued in 10-card packs. Player names and the Ultra logo are in silver holographic foil. Backs contains complete year-by-year statistics, plus two photos of the player. This also marked the first time that the Gold and Platinum parallel sets displayed a different photo than the base cards. Inserts in Ultra included: Rookie Reflections, Double Trouble, Checklists, Season Crowns, RBI Kings, Power Plus, Fielder's Choice, Diamond Producers, HR Kings, and Baseball Rules.

		NM/M
Complete Set (553):		80.00
Common Player:		.05
Gold Medallion:		3X
Platinum Medallion:		25X
Series 1 Wax Pack (10):		1.25
Series 1 Wax Box (24):		20.00
Series 2 Wax Pack (10):		5.00
Series 2 Wax Box (24):		90.00
1	Roberto Alomar	.25
2	Brady Anderson	.05
3	Rocky Coppinger	.05
4	Jeffrey Hammonds	.05
5	Chris Hoiles	.05
6	Eddie Murray	.75
7	Mike Mussina	.45
8	Jimmy Myers	.05
9	Randy Myers	.05
10	Arthur Rhodes	.05
11	Cal Ripken Jr.	2.50
12	Jose Canseco	.50
13	Roger Clemens	1.25
14	Tom Gordon	.05
15	Jose Malave	.05
16	Tim Naehring	.05
17	Troy O'Leary	.05
18	Bill Selby	.05
19	Heathcliff Slocumb	.05
20	Mike Stanley	.05
21	Mo Vaughn	.05
22	Garret Anderson	.05
23	George Arias	.05
24	Chili Davis	.05
25	Jim Edmonds	.05
26	Darin Erstad	.25
27	Chuck Finley	.05
28	Todd Greene	.05
29	Troy Percival	.05
30	Tim Salmon	.05
31	Jeff Schmidt	.05
32	Randy Velarde	.05
33	Shad Williams	.05
34	Wilson Alvarez	.05
35	Harold Baines	.05
36	James Baldwin	.05
37	Mike Cameron	.05
38	Ray Durham	.05
39	Ozzie Guillen	.05
40	Roberto Hernandez	.05
41	Darren Lewis	.05
42	Jose Munoz	.05
43	Tony Phillips	.05
44	Frank Thomas	.75
45	Sandy Alomar Jr.	.05
46	Albert Belle	.05
47	Mark Carreon	.05
48	Julio Franco	.05
49	Orel Hershiser	.05
50	Kenny Lofton	.05
51	Jack McDowell	.05
52	Jose Mesa	.05
53	Charles Nagy	.05
54	Manny Ramirez	.75
55	Julian Tavarez	.05
56	Omar Vizquel	.05
57	Raul Casanova	.05
58	Tony Clark	.05
59	Travis Fryman	.05
60	Bob Higginson	.05
61	Melvin Nieves	.05
62	Curtis Pride	.05
63	Justin Thompson	.05
64	Alan Trammell	.05
65	Kevin Appier	.05
66	Johnny Damon	.35
67	Keith Lockhart	.05
68	Jeff Montgomery	.05
69	Jose Offerman	.05
70	Bip Roberts	.05
71	Jose Rosado	.05
72	Chris Stynes	.05
73	Mike Sweeney	.05
74	Jeff Cirillo	.05
75	Jeff D'Amico	.05
76	John Jaha	.05
77	Scott Karl	.05
78	Mike Matheny	.05
79	Ben McDonald	.05
80	Matt Mieske	.05
81	Marc Newfield	.05
82	Dave Nilsson	.05
83	Jose Valentin	.05
84	Fernando Vina	.05
85	Rick Aguilera	.05
86	Marty Cordova	.05
87	Chuck Knoblauch	.05
88	Matt Lawton	.05
89	Pat Meares	.05
90	Paul Molitor	.75
91	Greg Myers	.05
92	Dan Naulty	.05
93	Kirby Puckett	1.00
94	Frank Rodriguez	.05
95	Wade Boggs	1.00
96	Cecil Fielder	.05
97	Joe Girardi	.05
98	Dwight Gooden	.05
99	Derek Jeter	2.50
100	Tino Martinez	.05
101	Ramiro Mendoza RC	.05
102	Andy Pettitte	.20
103	Mariano Rivera	.15
104	Ruben Rivera	.05
105	Kenny Rogers	.05
106	Darryl Strawberry	.05
107	Bernie Williams	.05
108	Tony Batista	.05
109	Geronimo Berroa	.05
110	Bobby Chouinard	.05
111	Brent Gates	.05
112	Jason Giambi	.60
113	Damon Mashore RC	.05
114	Mark McGwire	2.00
115	Scott Spiezio	.05
116	John Wasdin	.05
117	Steve Wojciechowski	.05
118	Ernie Young	.05
119	Norm Charlton	.05
120	Joey Cora	.05
121	Ken Griffey Jr.	1.50
122	Sterling Hitchcock	.05
123	Raul Ibanez	.05
124	Randy Johnson	.75
125	Edgar Martinez	.05
126	Alex Rodriguez	2.00
127	Matt Wagner	.05
128	Bob Wells	.05
129	Dan Wilson	.05
130	Will Clark	.05
131	Kevin Elster	.05
132	Juan Gonzalez	.40
133	Rusty Greer	.05
134	Darryl Hamilton	.05
135	Mike Henneman	.05
136	Ken Hill	.05
137	Mark McLemore	.05
138	Dean Palmer	.05
139	Roger Pavlik	.05
140	Ivan Rodriguez	.65
141	Joe Carter	.05
142	Carlos Delgado	.50
143	Alex Gonzalez	.05
144	Juan Guzman	.05
145	Pat Hentgen	.05
146	Marty Janzen	.05
147	Otis Nixon	.05
148	Charlie O'Brien	.05
149	John Olerud	.05
150	Robert Perez	.05
151	Jermaine Dye	.05
152	Tom Glavine	.30
153	Andruw Jones	.75
154	Chipper Jones	1.00
155	Ryan Klesko	.05
156	Javier Lopez	.05
157	Greg Maddux	1.00
158	Fred McGriff	.05
159	Wonderful Monds	.05
160	John Smoltz	.05
161	Terrell Wade	.05
162	Mark Wohlers	.05
163	Brant Brown	.05
164	Mark Grace	.05
165	Tyler Houston	.05
166	Robin Jennings	.05
167	Jason Maxwell	.05
168	Ryne Sandberg	1.00
169	Sammy Sosa	1.00
170	Amaury Telemaco	.05
171	Steve Trachsel	.05
172	Pedro Valdes RC	.05
173	Tim Belk	.05
174	Bret Boone	.05
175	Jeff Brantley	.05
176	Eric Davis	.05
177	Barry Larkin	.05
178	Chad Mottola	.05
179	Mark Portugal	.05
180	Reggie Sanders	.05
181	John Smiley	.05
182	Eddie Taubensee	.05
183	Dante Bichette	.05
184	Ellis Burks	.05
185	Andres Galarraga	.05
186	Curt Leskanic	.05
187	Quinton McCracken	.05
188	Jeff Reed	.05
189	Kevin Ritz	.05
190	Walt Weiss	.05
191	Jamey Wright	.05
192	Eric Young	.05
193	Kevin Brown	.05
194	Luis Castillo	.05
195	Jeff Conine	.05
196	Andre Dawson	.25
197	Charles Johnson	.05
198	Al Leiter	.05
199	Ralph Milliard	.05
200	Robb Nen	.05
201	Edgar Renteria	.05
202	Gary Sheffield	.40
203	Bob Abreu	.10
204	Jeff Bagwell	.75
205	Derek Bell	.05
206	Sean Berry	.05
207	Richard Hidalgo	.05
208	Todd Jones	.05
209	Darryl Kile	.05
210	Orlando Miller	.05
211	Shane Reynolds	.05
212	Billy Wagner	.05
213	Donne Wall	.05
214	Roger Cedeno	.05
215	Greg Gagne	.05
216	Karim Garcia	.10
217	Wilton Guerrero	.05
218	Todd Hollandsworth	.05
219	Ramon Martinez	.05
220	Raul Mondesi	.40
221	Hideo Nomo	.40
222	Chan Ho Park	.05
223	Mike Piazza	1.50
224	Ismael Valdes	.05
225	Moises Alou	.05
226	Derek Aucoin	.05
227	Yamil Benitez	.05
228	Jeff Fassero	.05
229	Darrin Fletcher	.05
230	Mark Grudzielanek	.05
231	Barry Manuel	.05
232	Pedro Martinez	.75
233	Henry Rodriguez	.05

No.	Player		No.	Player		No.	Player	
234	Ugueth Urbina	.05	352	Mark Whiten	.05	470	Dmitri Young	.05
235	Rondell White	.05	353	Ricky Bottalico	.05	471	Shannon Stewart	.05
236	Carlos Baerga	.05	354	Brian Giles **RC**	.75	472	Rick Helling	.05
237	John Franco	.05	355	Eric Karros	.05	473	Bill Haselman	.05
238	Bernard Gilkey	.05	356	Jimmy Key	.05	474	Albie Lopez	.05
239	Todd Hundley	.05	357	Carlos Perez	.05	475	Glendon Rusch	.05
240	Butch Huskey	.05	358	Alex Fernandez	.05	476	Derrick May	.05
241	Jason Isringhausen	.05	359	J.T. Snow	.05	477	Chad Ogea	.05
242	Lance Johnson	.05	360	Bobby Bonilla	.05	478	Kirk Reuter	.05
243	Bobby Jones	.05	361	Scott Brosius	.05	479	Chris Hammond	.05
244	Alex Ochoa	.05	362	Greg Swindell	.05	480	Russ Johnson	.05
245	Rey Ordonez	.05	363	Jose Vizcaino	.05	481	James Mouton	.05
246	Paul Wilson	.05	364	Matt Williams	.25	482	Mike Macfarlane	.05
247	Ron Blazier	.05	365	Darren Daulton	.05	483	Scott Ruffcorn	.05
248	David Doster	.05	366	Shane Andrews	.05	484	Jeff Frye	.05
249	Jim Eisenreich	.05	367	Jim Eisenreich	.05	485	Richie Sexson	.05
250	Mike Grace	.05	368	Ariel Prieto	.05	486	Emil Brown **RC**	.05
251	Mike Lieberthal	.05	369	Bob Tewksbury	.05	487	Desi Wilson	.05
252	Wendell Magee	.05	370	Mike Bordick	.05	488	Brent Gates	.05
253	Mickey Morandini	.05	371	Rheal Cormier	.05	489	Tony Graffanino	.05
254	Ricky Otero	.05	372	Cliff Floyd	.05	490	Dan Miceli	.05
255	Scott Rolen	.60	373	David Justice	.05	491	Orlando Cabrera **RC**	.65
256	Curt Schilling	.20	374	John Wetteland	.05	492	Tony Womack **RC**	.20
257	Todd Zeile	.05	375	Mike Blowers	.05	493	Jerome Walton	.05
258	Jermaine Allensworth	.05	376	Jose Canseco	.50	494	Mark Thompson	.05
259	Trey Beamon	.05	377	Roger Clemens	1.25	495	Jose Guillen	.05
260	Carlos Garcia	.05	378	Kevin Mitchell	.05	496	Willie Blair	.05
261	Mark Johnson	.05	379	Todd Zeile	.05	497	T.J. Staton **RC**	.05
262	Jason Kendall	.05	380	Jim Thome	.60	498	Scott Kamieniecki	.05
263	Jeff King	.05	381	Turk Wendell	.05	499	Vince Coleman	.05
264	Al Martin	.05	382	Rico Brogna	.05	500	Jeff Abbott	.05
265	Denny Neagle	.05	383	Eric Davis	.05	501	Chris Widger	.05
266	Matt Ruebel	.05	384	Mike Lansing	.05	502	Kevin Tapani	.05
267	Marc Wilkins **RC**	.05	385	Devon White	.05	503	Carlos Castillo **RC**	.05
268	Alan Benes	.05	386	Marquis Grissom	.05	504	Luis Gonzalez	.05
269	Dennis Eckersley	.65	387	Todd Worrell	.05	505	Tim Belcher	.05
270	Ron Gant	.05	388	Jeff Kent	.05	506	Armando Reynoso	.05
271	Aaron Holbert	.05	389	Mickey Tettleton	.05	507	Jamie Moyer	.05
272	Brian Jordan	.05	390	Steve Avery	.05	508	Randall Simon **RC**	.05
273	Ray Lankford	.05	391	David Cone	.05	509	Vladimir Guerrero	.75
274	John Mabry	.05	392	Scott Cooper	.05	510	Wady Almonte **RC**	.05
275	T.J. Mathews	.05	393	Lee Stevens	.05	511	Dustin Hermanson	.05
276	Ozzie Smith	1.00	394	Kevin Elster	.05	512	Deivi Cruz **RC**	.25
277	Todd Stottlemyre	.05	395	Tom Goodwin	.05	513	Luis Alicea	.05
278	Mark Sweeney	.05	396	Shawn Green	.25	514	Felix Heredia **RC**	.15
279	Andy Ashby	.05	397	Pete Harnisch	.05	515	Don Slaught	.05
280	Steve Finley	.05	398	Eddie Murray	.75	516	Shigetosi Hasegawa	.05
281	John Flaherty	.05	399	Joe Randa	.05	517	Matt Walbeck	.05
282	Chris Gomez	.05	400	Scott Sanders	.05	518	David Arias **RC** (Last name actually Ortiz.)	40.00
283	Tony Gwynn	1.00	401	John Valentin	.05	519	Brady Raggio **RC**	.05
284	Joey Hamilton	.05	402	Todd Jones	.05	520	Rudy Pemberton	.05
285	Rickey Henderson	.75	403	Terry Adams	.05	521	Wayne Kirby	.05
286	Trevor Hoffman	.05	404	Brian Hunter	.05	522	Calvin Maduro	.05
287	Jason Thompson	.05	405	Pat Listach	.05	523	Mark Lewis	.05
288	Fernando Valenzuela	.05	406	Kenny Lofton	.25	524	Mike Jackson	.05
289	Greg Vaughn	.05	407	Hal Morris	.05	525	Sid Fernandez	.05
290	Barry Bonds	2.50	408	Ed Sprague	.05	526	Mike Bielecki	.05
291	Jay Canizaro	.05	409	Rich Becker	.05	527	Bubba Trammell **RC**	.05
292	Jacob Cruz	.05	410	Edgardo Alfonzo	.05	528	Brent Brede **RC**	.05
293	Shawon Dunston	.05	411	Albert Belle	.25	529	Matt Morris	.05
294	Shawn Estes	.05	412	Jeff King	.05	530	Joe Borowski	.05
295	Mark Gardner	.05	413	Kirt Manwaring	.05	531	Orlando Miller	.05
296	Marcus Jensen	.05	414	Jason Schmidt	.05	532	Jim Bullinger	.05
297	Bill Mueller **RC**	.35	415	Allen Watson	.05	533	Robert Person	.05
298	Chris Singleton	.05	416	Lee Tinsley	.05	534	Doug Glanville	.05
299	Allen Watson	.05	417	Brett Butler	.05	535	Terry Pendleton	.05
300	Matt Williams	.05	418	Carlos Garcia	.05	536	Jorge Posada	.05
301	Rod Beck	.05	419	Mark Lemke	.05	537	Marc Sagmoen **RC**	.05
302	Jay Bell	.05	420	Jaime Navarro	.05	538	Fernando Tatis **RC**	.20
303	Shawon Dunston	.05	421	David Segui	.05	539	Aaron Sele	.05
304	Reggie Jefferson	.05	422	Ruben Sierra	.05	540	Brian Banks	.05
305	Darren Oliver	.05	423	B.J. Surhoff	.05	541	Derrek Lee	.50
306	Benito Santiago	.05	424	Julian Tavarez	.05	542	John Wasdin	.05
307	Gerald Williams	.05	425	Billy Taylor	.05	543	Justin Towle **RC**	.05
308	Damon Buford	.05	426	Ken Caminiti	.05	544	Pat Cline	.05
309	Jeromy Burnitz	.05	427	Chuck Carr	.05	545	Dave Magadan	.05
310	Sterling Hitchcock	.05	428	Benji Gil	.05	546	Jeff Blauser	.05
311	Dave Hollins	.05	429	Terry Mulholland	.05	547	Phil Nevin	.05
312	Mel Rojas	.05	430	Mike Stanton	.05	548	Todd Walker	.05
313	Robin Ventura	.05	431	Wil Cordero	.05	549	Elieser Marrero	.05
314	David Wells	.05	432	Chili Davis	.05	550	Bartolo Colon	.05
315	Cal Eldred	.05	433	Mariano Duncan	.05	551	Jose Cruz Jr. **RC**	.50
316	Gary Gaetti	.05	434	Orlando Merced	.05	552	Todd Dunwoody	.05
317	John Hudek	.05	435	Kent Mercker	.05	553	Hideki Irabu **RC**	.25
318	Brian Johnson	.05	436	John Olerud	.05			
319	Denny Neagle	.05	437	Quilvio Veras	.05			
320	Larry Walker	.05	438	Mike Fetters	.05			
321	Russ Davis	.05	439	Glenallen Hill	.05			
322	Delino DeShields	.05	440	Bill Swift	.05			
323	Charlie Hayes	.05	441	Tim Wakefield	.05			
324	Jermaine Dye	.05	442	Pedro Astacio	.05			
325	John Ericks	.05	443	Vinny Castilla	.05			
326	Jeff Fassero	.05	444	Doug Drabek	.05			
327	Nomar Garciaparra	1.00	445	Alan Embree	.05			
328	Willie Greene	.05	446	Lee Smith	.05			
329	Greg McMichael	.05	447	Darryl Hamilton	.05			
330	Damion Easley	.05	448	Brian McRae	.05			
331	Ricky Bones	.05	449	Mike Timlin	.05			
332	John Burkett	.05	450	Bob Wickman	.05			
333	Royce Clayton	.05	451	Jason Dickson	.05			
334	Greg Colbrunn	.05	452	Chad Curtis	.05			
335	Tony Eusebio	.05	453	Mark Leiter	.05			
336	Gregg Jefferies	.05	454	Damon Berryhill	.05			
337	Wally Joyner	.05	455	Kevin Orie	.05			
338	Jim Leyritz	.05	456	Dave Burba	.05			
339	Paul O'Neill	.05	457	Chris Holt	.05			
340	Bruce Ruffin	.05	458	Ricky Ledee **RC**	.10			
341	Michael Tucker	.05	459	Mike Devereaux	.05			
342	Andy Benes	.05	460	Pokey Reese	.05			
343	Craig Biggio	.05	461	Tim Raines	.05			
344	Rex Hudler	.05	462	Ryan Jones	.05			
345	Brad Radke	.05	463	Shane Mack	.05			
346	Deion Sanders	.05	464	Darren Dreifort	.05			
347	Moises Alou	.05	465	Mark Parent	.05			
348	Brad Ausmus	.05	466	Mark Portugal	.05			
349	Armando Benitez	.05	467	Dante Powell	.05			
350	Mark Gubicza	.05	468	Craig Grebeck	.05			
351	Terry Steinbach	.05	469	Ron Villone	.05			

1997 Ultra Gold Medallion Edition

A new concept in parallel editions was debuted by Ultra in Series I. While sharing the card numbers with regular-issue Ultra cards, the Gold Medallion Edition features a "G" prefix to the card number and gold-foil highlights on front. Unlike past parallels, how-

ever, the '97 Ultra Gold Medallion and Platinum Medallion inserts share a photograph which is entirely different from the regular Ultra base cards. Gold Medallion Edition cards are identified as such in the lower-right corner and were inserted at a rate of one per pack.

	NM/M
Complete Set (553):	100.00
Common Player:	.25
Stars/Rookies:	3X

1997 Ultra Platinum Medallion Edition

A new concept in parallel editions was debuted by Ultra in Series I. While sharing the card numbers with regular-issue Ultra cards, the Platinum Medallion Edition features a "P" prefix to the card number and holographic-foil highlights on front. Unlike past parallels, however, the '97 Ultra Gold Medallion and Platinum Medallion inserts share a photograph which is entirely different from the regular Ultra base cards are identified as such in the lower-right corner and were inserted at a rate of one per 100 packs.

	NM/M
Common Player:	2.00
Stars/Rookies:	25X

Baseball Rules!

Baseball Rules was a 10-card insert that was found only in retail packs at a rate of one per 36 packs. The cards are die-cut with a player in front of a mound of baseballs with embossed seams on the front, while each card back explains a baseball term or rule.

		NM/M
Complete Set (10):		45.00
Common Player:		.50
1	Barry Bonds	10.00
2	Ken Griffey Jr.	6.00
3	Derek Jeter	10.00
4	Chipper Jones	5.00
5	Greg Maddux	5.00
6	Mark McGwire	7.50
7	Troy Percival	.50
8	Mike Piazza	6.00
9	Cal Ripken Jr.	10.00
10	Frank Thomas	4.00

Checklists

There are 10 Checklist cards in each series of Ultra baseball covering all regular-issue cards and inserts. The front of the card features a superstar, while the back contains a portion of the set checklist. The cards have the player's name and "CHECKLIST" in bold, all caps across the bottom in silver foil.

		NM/M
Complete Set (20):		5.00
Common Player:		.05
1	Dante Bichette	.05
2	Barry Bonds	.75
3	Ken Griffey Jr.	.35
4	Greg Maddux	.25
5	Mark McGwire	.50
6	Mike Piazza	.35
7	Cal Ripken Jr.	.75
8	John Smoltz	.05
9	Sammy Sosa	.25
10	Frank Thomas	.20
1	Andruw Jones	.20
2	Ken Griffey Jr.	.35
3	Frank Thomas	.20
4	Alex Rodriguez	.60
5	Cal Ripken Jr.	.75
6	Mike Piazza	.35
7	Greg Maddux	.25
8	Chipper Jones	.25
9	Derek Jeter	.75
10	Juan Gonzalez	.10

Diamond Producers

Printed on textured, uniform-like material, this 12-card insert contains some of the most consistent producers in baseball. Horizontal backs are conventionally printed with another color player photo on a pin-striped background and a few words about him. This was the most difficult insert Ultra foil-pack insert, with a ratio of one per 288.

		NM/M
Complete Set (12):		110.00
Common Player:		2.50
1	Jeff Bagwell	7.00
2	Barry Bonds	20.00
3	Ken Griffey Jr.	12.50
4	Chipper Jones	10.00
5	Kenny Lofton	2.50
6	Greg Maddux	10.00
7	Mark McGwire	15.00
8	Mike Piazza	12.50
9	Cal Ripken Jr.	20.00
10	Alex Rodriguez	15.00
11	Frank Thomas	7.50
12	Matt Williams	2.50

Double Trouble

Double Trouble is a 20-card, team color coded set pairing two stars from the same team on a horizontal front. These inserts were found every four packs.

		NM/M
Complete Set (20):		10.00
Common Player:		.15
1	Roberto Alomar, Cal Ripken Jr.	1.50
2	Mo Vaughn, Jose Canseco	.40
3	Jim Edmonds, Tim Salmon	.15
4	Harold Baines, Frank Thomas	.50
5	Albert Belle, Kenny Lofton	.15
6	Chuck Knoblauch, Marty Cordova	.15
7	Andy Pettitte, Derek Jeter	1.50
8	Jason Giambi, Mark McGwire	1.00
9	Ken Griffey Jr., Alex Rodriguez	1.00
10	Juan Gonzalez, Will Clark	.30
11	Greg Maddux, Chipper Jones	.75
12	Mark Grace, Sammy Sosa	.60
13	Dante Bichette, Andres Galarraga	.15
14	Jeff Bagwell, Derek Bell	.50
15	Hideo Nomo, Mike Piazza	.75
16	Henry Rodriguez, Moises Alou	.15
17	Rey Ordonez, Alex Ochoa	.15
18	Ray Lankford, Ron Gant	.15
19	Tony Gwynn, Rickey Henderson	.60
20	Barry Bonds, Matt Williams	1.50

Fame Game

This eight-card hobby-exclusive insert showcases players who have displayed Hall of Fame potential. The player photo on front and Fame Game logo are embossed and highlighted in gold and silver foil. Backs have a color portrait photo and a few words about the player. Cards were inserted 1:8 packs.

		NM/M
Complete Set (18):		20.00
Common Player:		.35
1	Ken Griffey Jr.	1.75
2	Frank Thomas	1.00
3	Alex Rodriguez	2.00
4	Cal Ripken Jr.	3.00
5	Mike Piazza	1.75
6	Greg Maddux	1.25
7	Derek Jeter	3.00
8	Jeff Bagwell	1.00
9	Juan Gonzalez	.50
10	Albert Belle	.35
11	Tony Gwynn	1.25
12	Mark McGwire	2.00
13	Andy Pettitte	.45
14	Kenny Lofton	.35
15	Roberto Alomar	.40
16	Ryne Sandberg	1.25
17	Barry Bonds	3.00
18	Eddie Murray	1.00

Fielder's Choice

Fielder's Choice highlights 18 of the top defensive players in baseball. Fronts of the horizontal cards have a leather look and feel and are highlighted in gold foil. Backs are conventionally printed with another player photo and some words about his fielding ability. Fielder's Choice inserts were found every 144 packs.

		NM/M
Complete Set (18):		80.00
Common Player:		1.00
1	Roberto Alomar	1.50
2	Jeff Bagwell	6.00
3	Wade Boggs	7.50
4	Barry Bonds	15.00
5	Mark Grace	1.00
6	Ken Griffey Jr.	10.00
7	Marquis Grissom	1.00
8	Charles Johnson	1.00

9	Chuck Knoblauch	1.00
10	Barry Larkin	1.00
11	Kenny Lofton	1.00
12	Greg Maddux	7.50
13	Raul Mondesi	1.00
14	Rey Ordonez	1.00
15	Cal Ripken Jr.	15.00
16	Alex Rodriguez	12.50
17	Ivan Rodriguez	5.00
18	Matt Williams	1.00

Golden Prospects

This 10-card set was exclusive to hobby shop packs and highlighted the top young players in baseball. Action photos on front and portraits on back are set on a sepia background. Cards were inserted 1:4 packs.

		NM/M
Complete Set (10):		3.00
Common Player:		.25
1	Andruw Jones	1.00
2	Vladimir Guerrero	1.50
3	Todd Walker	.25
4	Karim Garcia	.25
5	Kevin Orie	.25
6	Brian Giles	.25
7	Jason Dickson	.25
8	Jose Guillen	.25
9	Ruben Rivera	.25
10	Derrek Lee	1.00

Hitting Machines

This 36-card insert was only found in hobby packs and showcases the game's top hitters. Cards were inserted at a ratio of 1:36 packs.

		NM/M
Complete Set (18):		60.00
Common Player:		1.00
1	Andruw Jones	3.00
2	Ken Griffey Jr.	5.00
3	Frank Thomas	3.00
4	Alex Rodriguez	6.50
5	Cal Ripken Jr.	9.00
6	Mike Piazza	5.00
7	Derek Jeter	9.00
8	Albert Belle	1.00
9	Tony Gwynn	4.00
10	Jeff Bagwell	3.00
11	Mark McGwire	6.50
12	Kenny Lofton	1.00
13	Manny Ramirez	3.00
14	Roberto Alomar	1.25
15	Ryne Sandberg	4.00
16	Eddie Murray	3.00
17	Sammy Sosa	4.00
18	Ken Caminiti	1.00

HR Kings

HR Kings are printed on clear plastic with transparent refractive holofoil crowns and other objects in the plastic. Backs contain a white silhouette of the player with career summary and logos within the figure. Stated odds of finding an HR King card were one per 36 packs.

		NM/M
Complete Set (12):		30.00
Common Player:		1.00
1	Albert Belle	

2	Barry Bonds	7.50
3	Juan Gonzalez	1.50
4	Ken Griffey Jr.	4.50
5	Todd Hundley	1.00
6	Ryan Klesko	1.00
7	Mark McGwire	6.00
8	Mike Piazza	4.50
9	Sammy Sosa	3.50
10	Frank Thomas	2.50
11	Mo Vaughn	1.00
12	Matt Williams	1.00

Leather Shop

Baseball's best fielders are honored in this 12-card hobby-exclusive insert. Cards were inserted at a ratio of 1:6 packs and feature an embossed grain-like finish on the fronts.

		NM/M
Complete Set (12):		9.00
Common Player:		.25
1	Ken Griffey Jr.	1.25
2	Alex Rodriguez	1.50
3	Cal Ripken Jr.	2.00
4	Derek Jeter	2.00
5	Juan Gonzalez	.45
6	Tony Gwynn	1.00
7	Jeff Bagwell	.75
8	Roberto Alomar	.40
9	Ryne Sandberg	1.00
10	Ken Caminiti	.25
11	Kenny Lofton	.25
12	John Smoltz	.25

Power Plus Series 1

Series 1 Power Plus is a 12-card insert utilizing silver rainbow holofoil in the background, with the featured player in the foreground. Backs have another action photo and the player's credentials. The insert captures power hitters that also excel in other areas of the game. Power Plus inserts can be found every 24 packs.

		NM/M
Complete Set (12):		15.00
Common Player:		.50
1	Jeff Bagwell	.75
2	Barry Bonds	3.00
3	Juan Gonzalez	.60
4	Ken Griffey Jr.	1.50
5	Chipper Jones	1.00
6	Mark McGwire	2.00

7	Mike Piazza	1.50
8	Cal Ripken Jr.	3.00
9	Alex Rodriguez	2.00
10	Sammy Sosa	1.00
11	Frank Thomas	.75
12	Matt Williams	.50

Power Plus Series 2

Similar in design to the Power Plus insert in Series I, this 12-card insert salutes the game's top sluggers and was found only in hobby packs. Cards were inserted at a ratio of 1:8 packs. Front design features gold holographic foil graphics. Backs have another photo and a description of the player's skills.

		NM/M
Complete Set (12):		6.50
Common Player:		.25
1	Ken Griffey Jr.	.75
2	Frank Thomas	.50
3	Alex Rodriguez	1.00
4	Cal Ripken Jr.	1.50
5	Mike Piazza	.75
6	Chipper Jones	.75
7	Albert Belle	.25
8	Juan Gonzalez	.35
9	Jeff Bagwell	.50
10	Mark McGwire	1.00
11	Mo Vaughn	.25
12	Barry Bonds	1.50

RBI Kings

Ten different players are featured in RBI Kings, which contain a metallic paisley background, with an English shield of armor and latin words in the background. RBI Kings were inserted every 18 packs of Series I.

		NM/M
Complete Set (10):		12.50
Common Player:		.75
1	Jeff Bagwell	1.50
2	Albert Belle	.75
3	Dante Bichette	.75
4	Barry Bonds	4.00
5	Jay Buhner	.75
6	Juan Gonzalez	1.00
7	Ken Griffey Jr.	2.50
8	Sammy Sosa	2.00
9	Frank Thomas	1.50
10	Mo Vaughn	.75

Rookie Reflections

Rookie Reflections features 10 of the 1996 season's top first-year stars. Cards are inserted every four packs. Front features an action photo on a black-and-silver starburst pattern. Horizontal backs have another photo and a career summary of the prospect.

		NM/M
Complete Set (10):		3.50
Common Player:		.25
1	James Baldwin	.25
2	Jermaine Dye	.25
3	Darin Erstad	.40
4	Todd Hollandsworth	.25
5	Derek Jeter	3.00

6	Jason Kendall	.25
7	Alex Ochoa	.25
8	Rey Ordonez	.25
9	Edgar Renteria	.25
10	Scott Rolen	.50

Season Crowns

Season Crowns were found at a rate of one per eight packs of Ultra I Baseball. This etched, silver-foil insert contained 12 statistical leaders and award winners from the 1996 season.

		NM/M
Complete Set (12):		10.00
Common Player:		.50
1	Albert Belle	.50
2	Dante Bichette	.50
3	Barry Bonds	3.00
4	Kenny Lofton	.50
5	Edgar Martinez	.50
6	Mark McGwire	2.00
7	Andy Pettitte	.50
8	Mike Piazza	1.50
9	Alex Rodriguez	2.00
10	John Smoltz	.50
11	Sammy Sosa	1.25
12	Frank Thomas	1.00

Starring Role

Another hobby-exclusive insert, these 12 cards salute baseball's clutch performers and were found 1:288 packs.

		NM/M
Complete Set (12):		175.00
Common Player:		7.50
1	Andruw Jones	12.00
2	Ken Griffey Jr.	20.00
3	Frank Thomas	12.00
4	Alex Rodriguez	25.00
5	Cal Ripken Jr.	30.00
6	Mike Piazza	20.00
7	Greg Maddux	15.00
8	Chipper Jones	15.00
9	Derek Jeter	30.00
10	Juan Gonzalez	9.00
11	Albert Belle	7.50
12	Tony Gwynn	15.00

Thunderclap

This 10-card hobby-exclusive insert showcases hitters who strike fear in opposing pitchers. Cards were inserted 1:18 packs.

Fronts are highlighted by streaks of gold prismatic foil lightning in a stormy sky. Backs have another player photo and a few words about him.

		NM/M
Complete Set (10):		20.00
Common Player:		.75
1	Barry Bonds	5.00
2	Mo Vaughn	.75
3	Mark McGwire	4.00
4	Jeff Bagwell	1.50
5	Juan Gonzalez	1.00
6	Alex Rodriguez	4.00
7	Chipper Jones	2.50
8	Ken Griffey Jr.	3.00
9	Mike Piazza	3.00
10	Frank Thomas	2.00

Top 30

This 30-card insert was found only in retail store packs and salutes the 30 most collectible players in the game. Cards were inserted one per pack. A Top 30 Gold Medallion parallel set, die-cut around the top, was also produced and inserted 1:18 packs.

		NM/M
Complete Set (30):		12.00
Common Player:		.20
Gold Medallions:		6X
1	Andruw Jones	.75
2	Ken Griffey Jr.	1.25
3	Frank Thomas	.75
4	Alex Rodriguez	1.50
5	Cal Ripken Jr.	2.00
6	Mike Piazza	1.25
7	Greg Maddux	1.00
8	Chipper Jones	1.00
9	Derek Jeter	2.00
10	Juan Gonzalez	.40
11	Albert Belle	.20
12	Tony Gwynn	1.00
13	Jeff Bagwell	.75
14	Mark McGwire	1.50
15	Andy Pettitte	.30
16	Mo Vaughn	.20
17	Kenny Lofton	.20
18	Manny Ramirez	.75
19	Roberto Alomar	.40
20	Ryne Sandberg	1.00
21	Hideo Nomo	.40
22	Barry Bonds	2.00
23	Eddie Murray	.75
24	Ken Caminiti	.20
25	John Smoltz	.20
26	Pat Hentgen	.20
27	Todd Hollandsworth	.20
28	Matt Williams	.20
29	Bernie Williams	.20
30	Brady Anderson	.20

1997 Ultra FanFest Larry Doby

In the same basic style as its regular-issue Ultra baseball series of 1997, Fleer issued a special Larry Doby card in conjunction with the All-Star FanFest in Cleveland, recognizing Doby's 50th anniversary of breaking the American League color barrier. The card has a black-and-white batting

pose of Doby on front with his name, team and Fleer Ultra logo in red-shaded silver holographic foil. A color All-Star Game logo also appears on front. Backs have a red duotone photo of Doby fielding, his career stats and a few words about his career.

	NM/M
Larry Doby	4.00

1998 Ultra

Ultra was released in two series with a total of 501 cards; 250 in Series 1 and 251 in Series 2. Ten-card packs carried an SRP of $2.59. There were three parallel sets: Gold Medallion, Platinum Medallion and Masterpieces. Series 1 has 210 regular cards, 25 Prospects (seeded 1:4 packs), 10 Season's Crowns (1:12) and five Checklists (1:8). Series 2 has 202 regular cards, 25 Pizzazz (1:4), 20 New Horizons and three checklists. Series 2 also added a Mike Piazza N.Y. Mets card as #501, inserted every 20 packs. Inserts in Series 1 include: Big Shots, Double Trouble, Kid Gloves, Back to the Future, Artistic Talents, Fall Classics, Power Plus, Prime Leather, Diamond Producers, Diamond Ink and Million Dollar Moments. Series 2 included: Notables, Rocket to Stardom, Millennium Men, Win Now, Ticket Studs, Diamond Immortals, Diamond Ink, Top 30 and 750 sequentially numbered Alex Rodriguez autographed promo cards.

		NM/M
Complete Set (501):		75.00
Common Player:		.05
Alex Rodriguez		
Autograph (750):		50.00
Pack (10):		1.25
Wax Box (24):		20.00
1	Ken Griffey Jr.	1.25
2	Matt Morris	.05
3	Roger Clemens	1.00
4	Matt Williams	.05
5	Roberto Hernandez	.05
6	Rondell White	.05
7	Tim Salmon	.05
8	Brad Radke	.05
9	Brett Butler	.05
10	Carl Everett	.05
11	Chili Davis	.05
12	Chuck Finley	.05
13	Darryl Kile	.05
14	Deivi Cruz	.05
15	Gary Gaetti	.05
16	Matt Stairs	.05
17	Pat Meares	.05
18	Will Cunnane	.05
19	Steve Woodard RC	.15
20	Andy Ashby	.05
21	Bobby Higginson	.05
22	Brian Jordan	.05
23	Craig Biggio	.05

#	Player	$		#	Player	$		#	Player	$		#	Player	$		#	Player	$
24	Jim Edmonds	.05		142	Bobby Bonilla	.05		244	Andrew Vessel (Prospect)	.25		362	Craig Counsell	.05		467	Wade Boggs (New Horizons)	1.00
25	Ryan McGuire	.05		143	Cal Ripken Jr.	2.00		245	Chris Carpenter (Prospect)	.25		363	Jose Offerman	.05		468	Fred McGriff (New Horizons)	.05
26	Scott Hatteberg	.05		144	Chad Fox RC	.05		246	Checklist (Ken Griffey Jr.)	.65		364	Tony Fernandez	.05		469	Paul Sorrento (New Horizons)	.05
27	Willie Greene	.05		145	Dante Bichette	.05		247	Checklist (Andruw Jones)	.50		365	Jason McDonald	.05		470	Kevin Stocker (New Horizons)	.05
28	Albert Belle	.05		146	Dennis Eckersley	.65		248	Checklist (Alex Rodriguez)	.75		366	Sterling Hitchcock	.05		471	Bubba Trammell (New Horizons)	.05
29	Ellis Burks	.05		147	Mariano Rivera	.15		249	Checklist (Frank Thomas)	.60		367	Donovan Osborne	.05		472	Quinton McCracken (New Horizons)	.05
30	Hideo Nomo	.40		148	Mo Vaughn	.05		250	Checklist (Cal Ripken Jr.)	1.00		368	Troy Percival	.05		473	Checklist (Ken Griffey Jr.)	.65
31	Jeff Bagwell	.75		149	Reggie Sanders	.05		251	Carlos Perez	.05		369	Henry Rodriguez	.05		474	Checklist (Cal Ripken Jr.)	1.00
32	Kevin Brown	.05		150	Derek Jeter	2.00		252	Larry Sutton	.05		370	Dmitri Young	.05		475	Checklist (Frank Thomas)	.60
33	Nomar Garciaparra	1.00		151	Rusty Greer	.05		253	Brad Rigby	.05		371	Jay Powell	.05		476	Ken Griffey Jr. (Pizzazz)	1.75
34	Pedro Martinez	.75		152	Brady Anderson	.05		254	Wally Joyner	.05		372	Jeff Conine	.05		477	Cal Ripken Jr. (Pizzazz)	3.00
35	Raul Mondesi	.05		153	Brett Tomko	.05		255	Todd Stottlemyre	.05		373	Orlando Cabrera	.10		478	Frank Thomas (Pizzazz)	2.00
36	Ricky Bottalico	.05		154	Jaime Navarro	.05		256	Nerio Rodriguez	.05		374	Butch Huskey	.05		479	Alex Rodriguez (Pizzazz)	2.00
37	Shawn Estes	.05		155	Kevin Orie	.05		257	Jeff Frye	.05		375	Mike Lowell RC	1.00		480	Nomar Garciaparra (Pizzazz)	1.50
38	Shawon Dunston	.05		156	Roberto Alomar	.20		258	Pedro Astacio	.05		376	Kevin Young	.05		481	Derek Jeter (Pizzazz)	3.00
39	Terry Steinbach	.05		157	Edgar Martinez	.05		259	Cal Eldred	.05		377	Jamie Moyer	.05		482	Andruw Jones (Pizzazz)	1.00
40	Tom Glavine	.25		158	John Olerud	.05		260	Chili Davis	.05		378	Jeff D'Amico	.05		483	Chipper Jones (Pizzazz)	1.50
41	Todd Dunwoody	.05		159	John Smoltz	.05		261	Freddy Garcia	.05		379	Scott Erickson	.05		484	Greg Maddux (Pizzazz)	1.50
42	Deion Sanders	.05		160	Ryne Sandberg	1.00		262	Bobby Witt	.05		380	Magglio Ordonez RC	2.50		485	Mike Piazza (Pizzazz)	1.75
43	Gary Sheffield	.45		161	Billy Taylor	.05		263	Michael Coleman	.05		381	Melvin Nieves	.05		486	Juan Gonzalez (Pizzazz)	.60
44	Mike Lansing	.05		162	Chris Holt	.05		264	Mike Caruso	.05		382	Ramon Martinez	.05		487	Jose Cruz (Pizzazz)	.60
45	Mike Lieberthal	.05		163	Damion Easley	.05		265	Mike Lansing	.05		383	A.J. Hinch	.05		488	Jaret Wright (Pizzazz)	.60
46	Paul Sorrento	.05		164	Darin Erstad	.25		266	Dennis Reyes	.05		384	Jeff Brantley	.05		489	Hideo Nomo (Pizzazz)	.60
47	Paul O'Neill	.05		165	Joe Carter	.05		267	F.P. Santangelo	.05		385	Kevin Elster	.05		490	Scott Rolen (Pizzazz)	.65
48	Tom Goodwin	.05		166	Kelvim Escobar	.05		268	Darryl Hamilton	.05		386	Allen Watson	.05		491	Tony Gwynn (Pizzazz)	1.50
49	Andruw Jones	.75		167	Ken Caminiti	.05		269	Mike Fetters	.05		387	Moises Alou	.05		492	Roger Clemens (Pizzazz)	1.60
50	Barry Bonds	2.00		168	Pokey Reese	.05		270	Charlie Hayes	.05		388	Jeff Blauser	.05		493	Darin Erstad (Pizzazz)	.50
51	Bernie Williams	.05		169	Ray Lankford	.05		271	Royce Clayton	.05		389	Pete Harnisch	.05		494	Mark McGwire (Pizzazz)	2.00
52	Jeremi Gonzalez	.05		170	Livan Hernandez	.05		272	Doug Drabek	.05		390	Shane Andrews	.05		495	Jeff Bagwell (Pizzazz)	1.00
53	Mike Piazza	1.25		171	Steve Kline	.05		273	James Baldwin	.05		391	Rico Brogna	.05		496	Mo Vaughn (Pizzazz)	.50
54	Russ Davis	.05		172	Tom Gordon	.05		274	Brian Hunter	.05		392	Stan Javier	.05		497	Albert Belle (Pizzazz)	.50
55	Vinny Castilla	.05		173	Travis Fryman	.05		275	Chan Ho Park	.05		393	David Howard	.05		498	Kenny Lofton (Pizzazz)	.50
56	Rod Beck	.05		174	Al Martin	.05		276	John Franco	.05		394	Darryl Strawberry	.05		499	Ben Grieve (Pizzazz)	.50
57	Andres Galarraga	.05		175	Andy Pettitte	.25		277	David Wells	.05		395	Kent Mercker	.05		500	Barry Bonds (Pizzazz)	2.50
58	Ben McDonald	.05		176	Jeff Kent	.05		278	Eli Marrero	.05		396	Juan Encarnacion	.05		501	Mike Piazza (Mets)	1.50
59	Billy Wagner	.05		177	Jimmy Key	.05		279	Kerry Wood	.40		397	Sandy Alomar	.05				
60	Charles Johnson	.05		178	Mark Grudzielanek	.05		280	Donnie Sadler	.05		398	Al Leiter	.05				
61	Fred McGriff	.05		179	Tony Saunders	.05		281	Scott Winchester RC	.05		399	Tony Graffanino	.05				
62	Dean Palmer	.05		180	Barry Larkin	.05		282	Hal Morris	.05		400	Terry Adams	.05				
63	Frank Thomas	.75		181	Bubba Trammell	.05		283	Brad Fullmer	.05		401	Bruce Aven	.05				
64	Ismael Valdes	.05		182	Carlos Delgado	.50		284	Bernard Gilkey	.05		402	Derrick Gibson	.05				
65	Mark Bellhorn	.05		183	Carlos Baerga	.05		285	Ramiro Mendoza	.05		403	Jose Cabrera	.05				
66	Jeff King	.05		184	Derek Bell	.05		286	Kevin Brown	.05		404	Rich Becker	.05				
67	John Wetteland	.05		185	Henry Rodriguez	.05		287	David Segui	.05		405	David Ortiz	.50				
68	Mark Grace	.05		186	Jason Dickson	.05		288	Willie McGee	.05		406	Brian McRae	.05				
69	Mark Kotsay	.05		187	Ron Gant	.05		289	Darren Oliver	.05		407	Bobby Estalella	.05				
70	Scott Rolen	.60		188	Tony Womack	.05		290	Antonio Alfonseca	.05		408	Bill Mueller	.05				
71	Todd Hundley	.05		189	Justin Thompson	.05		291	Eric Davis	.05		409	Dennis Eckersley	.65				
72	Todd Worrell	.05		190	Fernando Tatis	.05		292	Mickey Morandini	.05		410	Sandy Martinez	.05				
73	Wilson Alvarez	.05		191	Mark Wohlers	.05		293	Frank Catalanotto RC	.20		411	Jose Vizcaino	.05				
74	Bobby Jones	.05		192	Takashi Kashiwada	.05		294	Derrek Lee	.50		412	Jermaine Allensworth	.05				
75	Jose Canseco	.50		193	Garret Anderson	.05		295	Todd Zeile	.05		413	Miguel Tejada	.20				
76	Kevin Appier	.05		194	Jose Cruz, Jr.	.05		296	Chuck Knoblauch	.05		414	Turner Ward	.05				
77	Neifi Perez	.05		195	Ricardo Rincon	.05		297	Wilson Delgado	.05		415	Glenallen Hill	.05				
78	Paul Molitor	.75		196	Tim Naehring	.05		298	Raul Ibanez	.05		416	Lee Stevens	.05				
79	Quilvio Veras	.05		197	Moises Alou	.05		299	Orel Hershiser	.05		417	Cecil Fielder	.05				
80	Randy Johnson	.75		198	Eric Karros	.05		300	Ozzie Guillen	.05		418	Ruben Sierra	.05				
81	Glendon Rusch	.05		199	John Jaha	.05		301	Aaron Sele	.05		419	Jon Nunnally	.05				
82	Curt Schilling	.15		200	Marty Cordova	.05		302	Joe Carter	.05		420	Rod Myers	.05				
83	Alex Rodriguez	1.50		201	Travis Lee	.10		303	Darryl Kile	.05		421	Dustin Hermanson	.05				
84	Rey Ordonez	.05		202	Mark Davis	.05		304	Shane Reynolds	.05		422	James Mouton	.05				
85	Jeff Juden	.05		203	Vladimir Nunez	.05		305	Todd Dunn	.05		423	Dan Wilson	.05				
86	Mike Cameron	.05		204	Stanton Cameron	.05		306	Bob Abreu	.10		424	Roberto Kelly	.05				
87	Ryan Klesko	.05		205	Mike Stoner RC	.05		307	Doug Strange	.05		425	Antonio Osuna	.05				
88	Trevor Hoffman	.05		206	Rolando Arrojo RC	.40		308	Jose Canseco	.50		426	Jacob Cruz	.05				
89	Chuck Knoblauch	.05		207	Rick White	.05		309	Lance Johnson	.05		427	Brent Mayne	.05				
90	Larry Walker	.05		208	Luis Polonia	.05		310	Harold Baines	.05		428	Matt Karchner	.05				
91	Mark McLemore	.05		209	Greg Blosser	.05		311	Todd Pratt	.05		429	Damian Jackson	.05				
92	B.J. Surhoff	.05		210	Cesar Devarez	.05		312	Greg Colbrunn	.05		430	Roger Cedeno	.05				
93	Darren Daulton	.05		211	Jeff Bagwell (Season Crown)	1.00		313	Masato Yoshii RC	.25		431	Rickey Henderson	.75				
94	Ray Durham	.05		212	Barry Bonds (Season Crown)	3.00		314	Felix Heredia	.05		432	Joe Randa	.05				
95	Sammy Sosa	1.00		213	Roger Clemens (Season Crown)	1.75		315	Dennis Martinez	.05		433	Greg Vaughn	.05				
96	Eric Young	.05		214	Nomar Garciaparra (Season Crown)	1.50		316	Geronimo Berroa	.05		434	Andres Galarraga	.05				
97	Gerald Williams	.05		215	Ken Griffey Jr. (Season Crown)	2.00		317	Darren Lewis	.05		435	Rod Beck	.05				
98	Javy Lopez	.05		216	Tony Gwynn (Season Crown)	1.50		318	Billy Ripken	.05		436	Curtis Goodwin	.05				
99	John Smiley	.05		217	Randy Johnson (Season Crown)	1.00		319	Enrique Wilson	.05		437	Brad Ausmus	.05				
100	Juan Gonzalez	.40		218	Mark McGwire (Season Crown)	3.00		320	Alex Ochoa	.05		438	Bob Hamelin	.05				
101	Shawn Green	.30		219	Scott Rolen (Season Crown)	.75		321	Doug Glanville	.05		439	Todd Walker	.05				
102	Charles Nagy	.05		220	Frank Thomas (Season Crown)	1.25		322	Mike Stanley	.05		440	Scott Brosius	.05				
103	David Justice	.05		221	Matt Perisho (Prospect)	.25		323	Gerald Williams	.05		441	Lenny Dykstra	.25				
104	Joey Hamilton	.05		222	Wes Helms (Prospect)	.25		324	Pedro Martinez	.75		442	Abraham Nunez	.05				
105	Pat Hentgen	.05		223	David Dellucci RC (Prospect)	.25		325	Jaret Wright	.05		443	Brian Johnson	.05				
106	Raul Casanova	.05		224	Todd Helton (Prospect)	1.00		326	Terry Pendleton	.05		444	Randy Myers	.05				
107	Tony Phillips	.05		225	Brian Rose (Prospect)	.25		327	LaTroy Hawkins	.05		445	Bret Boone	.15				
108	Tony Gwynn	1.00		226	Aaron Boone (Prospect)	.25		328	Emil Brown	.05		446	Oscar Henriquez	.05				
109	Will Clark	.05		227	Keith Foulke (Prospect)	.25		329	Walt Weiss	.05		447	Mike Sweeney	.05				
110	Jason Giambi	.50		228	Homer Bush (Prospect)	.25		330	Omar Vizquel	.05		448	Kenny Rogers	.05				
111	Jay Bell	.05		229	Shannon Stewart (Prospect)	.25		331	Carl Everett	.05		449	Mark Langston	.05				
112	Johnny Damon	.30		230	Richard Hidalgo (Prospect)	.25		332	Fernando Vina	.05		450	Luis Gonzalez	.05				
113	Alan Benes	.05		231	Russ Johnson (Prospect)	.25		333	Mike Blowers	.05		451	John Burkett	.05				
114	Jeff Suppan	.05		232	Henry Blanco RC (Prospect)	.25		334	Dwight Gooden	.05		452	Bip Roberts	.05				
115	Kevin Polcovich RC	.05		233	Paul Konerko (Prospect)	.35		335	Mark Lewis	.05		453	Travis Lee (New Horizons)	.15				
116	Shigetosi Hasegawa	.05		234	Antone Williamson (Prospect)	.25		336	Jim Leyritz	.05		454	Felix Rodriguez (New Horizons)	.05				
117	Steve Finley	.05		235	Shane Bowers (Prospect) (Prospect)	.25		337	Kenny Lofton	.05		455	Andy Benes (New Horizons)	.05				
118	Tony Clark	.05		236	Jose Vidro (Prospect)	.25		338	John Halama RC	.05		456	Willie Blair (New Horizons)	.05				
119	David Cone	.05		237	Derek Wallace (Prospect)	.25		339	Jose Valentin	.05		457	Brian Anderson (New Horizons)	.05				
120	Jose Guillen	.05		238	Ricky Ledee (Prospect)	.25		340	Desi Relaford	.05		458	Jay Bell (New Horizons)	.05				
121	Kevin Millwood RC	1.00		239	Ben Grieve (Prospect)	.25		341	Dante Powell	.05		459	Matt Williams (New Horizons)	.05				
122	Greg Maddux	1.00		240	Lou Collier (Prospect)	.25		342	Ed Sprague	.05		460	Devon White (New Horizons)	.05				
123	Dave Nilsson	.05		241	Derrek Lee (Prospect)	.65		343	Reggie Jefferson	.05		461	Karim Garcia (New Horizons)	.10				
124	Hideki Irabu	.05		242	Ruben Rivera (Prospect)	.25		344	Mike Hampton	.05		462	Jorge Fabregas (New Horizons)	.05				
125	Jason Kendall	.05		243	Jorge Velandia (Prospect)	.25		345	Marquis Grissom	.05		463	Wilson Alvarez (New Horizons)	.05				
126	Jim Thome	.60						346	Heathcliff Slocumb	.05		464	Roberto Hernandez (New Horizons)	.05				
127	Delino DeShields	.05						347	Francisco Cordova	.05		465	Tony Saunders (New Horizons)	.05				
128	Edgar Renteria	.05						348	Ken Cloude	.05		466	Rolando Arrojo RC (New Horizons)	.35				
129	Edgardo Alfonzo	.05						349	Benito Santiago	.05								
130	J.T. Snow	.05						350	Denny Neagle	.05								
131	Jeff Abbott	.05						351	Sean Casey	.15								
132	Jeffrey Hammonds	.05						352	Robb Nen	.05								
133	Rich Loiselle	.05						353	Orlando Merced	.05								
134	Vladimir Guerrero	.75						354	Adrian Brown	.05								
135	Jay Buhner	.05						355	Gregg Jefferies	.05								
136	Jeff Cirillo	.05						356	Otis Nixon	.05								
137	Jeromy Burnitz	.05						357	Michael Tucker	.05								
138	Mickey Morandini	.05						358	Eric Milton	.05								
139	Tino Martinez	.05						359	Travis Fryman	.05								
140	Jeff Shaw	.05						360	Gary DiSarcina	.05								
141	Rafael Palmeiro	.65						361	Mario Valdez	.05								

prismatic foil. Backs are in color with the serial number printed in silver foil at bottom. Series 2 checklist cards #473-475 were not printed in Platinum, and the short-prints from the regular issue are not short-printed in this parallel edition.

	NM/M
Common Player:	5.00
Stars/RC's:	25X
Checklists:	25X
Season Crowns:	8X
Prospects:	8X
Pizzazz:	8X

Masterpiece

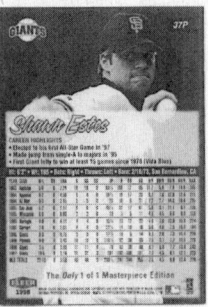

This top of the line parallel to '98 Ultra consists of a 1 of 1 version of each regular card.

	NM/M
Common Player:	50.00

1998 Ultra Gold Medallion

This parallel to the Ultra set is found seeded on a one per pack ratio. Cards are similar to the regular-issue Ultra except for a gold presentation of the embossed player name on front and a shower of gold specks in the photo background. Backs have a "G" suffix to the card number and a "GOLD MEDALLION EDITION" notation at bottom. The short-printed subset cards from the regular Ultra edition are not short-printed in Gold Medallion.

	NM/M
Common Player:	.25
Stars/RC's:	2X
Checklists:	2X
Season Crowns:	1X
Prospects:	1X
Pizzazz:	1X

1998 Ultra Platinum Medallion

Insertion odds on this super-scarce insert set are not given but each card is produced and serially numbered in an edition of only 100 (Series 1) and 98 (Series 2). Fronts are similar to regular Ultra cards except the photo is black-and-white and the name is rendered in silver

Artistic Talents

This 18-card insert featured top players in the game on a canvas-like surface with the insert name in silver holographic letters across the top. The backs are done in black and white and numbered with an "AT" suffix.

		NM/M
Complete Set (18):		12.00
Common Player:		.40
Inserted 1:8		
1	Ken Griffey Jr.	1.00
2	Andruw Jones	.60
3	Alex Rodriguez	1.25
4	Frank Thomas	.60
5	Cal Ripken Jr.	1.50
6	Derek Jeter	1.50
7	Chipper Jones	.75
8	Greg Maddux	.75
9	Mike Piazza	1.00
10	Albert Belle	.40
11	Darin Erstad	.50
12	Juan Gonzalez	.50
13	Jeff Bagwell	.60
14	Tony Gwynn	.75
15	Mark McGwire	1.25
16	Scott Rolen	.50
17	Barry Bonds	1.50
18	Kenny Lofton	.40

Back to the Future

This 15-card insert was printed in a horizontal format with a baseball field background. Cards were numbered with a "BF" suffix.

		NM/M
Complete Set (15):		4.00
Common Player:		.10
Inserted 1:6		
1	Andruw Jones	.50

2	Alex Rodriguez	1.00
3	Derek Jeter	1.50
4	Darin Erstad	.25
5	Mike Cameron	.10
6	Scott Rolen	.35
7	Nomar Garciaparra	.75
8	Hideki Irabu	.10
9	Jose Cruz, Jr.	.10
10	Vladimir Guerrero	.50
11	Mark Kotsay	.10
12	Tony Womack	.10
13	Jason Dickson	.10
14	Jose Guillen	.10
15	Tony Clark	.10

Big Shots

CHIPPER JONES

Big Shots is a 15-card insert displaying some of the top home run hitters in baseball. A generic stadium is pictured across the bottom with the insert name running up the left side. Cards are numbered with a "BS" suffix and inserted one per four Series 1 packs.

		NM/M
Complete Set (15):		4.00
Common Player:		.10
Inserted 1:4		
1	Ken Griffey Jr.	.75
2	Frank Thomas	.35
3	Chipper Jones	.50
4	Albert Belle	.10
5	Juan Gonzalez	.25
6	Jeff Bagwell	.35
7	Mark McGwire	1.00
8	Barry Bonds	1.50
9	Manny Ramirez	.35
10	Mo Vaughn	.10
11	Matt Williams	.10
12	Jim Thome	.30
13	Tino Martinez	.10
14	Mike Piazza	.75
15	Tony Clark	.10

Diamond Immortals

This Series 2 insert showcases 15 top players on an intricate silver holographic foil design. Cards are numbered with a "DI" suffix.

		NM/M
Complete Set (15):		330.00
Common Player:		7.50
Inserted 1:288		
1	Ken Griffey Jr.	30.00
2	Frank Thomas	12.50
3	Alex Rodriguez	40.00
4	Cal Ripken Jr.	50.00
5	Mike Piazza	30.00
6	Mark McGwire	40.00
7	Greg Maddux	20.00
8	Andruw Jones	12.50
9	Chipper Jones	20.00
10	Derek Jeter	50.00
11	Tony Gwynn	20.00
12	Juan Gonzalez	9.00
13	Jose Cruz	7.50
14	Roger Clemens	25.00
15	Barry Bonds	50.00

Diamond Producers

This 15-card insert captures players on a prismatic silver design, with a wood backdrop and a black felt frame around the border.

Cards were seeded one per 288 Series 1 packs and numbered with a "DP" suffix.

		NM/M
Complete Set (15):		180.00
Common Player:		7.50
Inserted 1:288		
1	Ken Griffey Jr.	30.00
2	Andruw Jones	12.50
3	Alex Rodriguez	40.00
4	Frank Thomas	12.50
5	Cal Ripken Jr.	50.00
6	Derek Jeter	50.00
7	Chipper Jones	20.00
8	Greg Maddux	20.00
9	Mike Piazza	30.00
10	Juan Gonzalez	9.00
11	Jeff Bagwell	12.50
12	Tony Gwynn	20.00
13	Mark McGwire	40.00
14	Barry Bonds	50.00
15	Jose Cruz, Jr.	7.50

Double Trouble

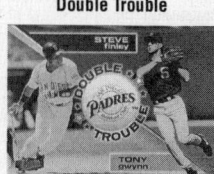

Double Trouble includes 20 cards and pairs teammates on a horizontal format with the team's logo and the insert name featured in a silver holographic circle in the middle. These are numbered with a "DT" suffix and exclusive to Series 1 packs.

		NM/M
Complete Set (20):		12.00
Common Player:		.15
Inserted 1:4		
1	Ken Griffey Jr., Alex Rodriguez	1.25
2	Vladimir Guerrero, Pedro Martinez	.60
3	Andruw Jones, Kenny Lofton	.60
4	Chipper Jones, Greg Maddux	.75
5	Derek Jeter, Tino Martinez	1.50
6	Frank Thomas, Albert Belle	.60
7	Cal Ripken Jr., Roberto Alomar	1.50
8	Mike Piazza, Hideo Nomo	1.00
9	Darin Erstad, Jason Dickson	.15
10	Juan Gonzalez, Ivan Rodriguez	.25
11	Jeff Bagwell, Darryl Kile	.60
12	Tony Gwynn, Steve Finley	.65
13	Mark McGwire, Ray Lankford	1.00
14	Barry Bonds, Jeff Kent	1.50
15	Andy Pettitte, Bernie Williams	.25
16	Mo Vaughn, Nomar Garciaparra	.65
17	Matt Williams, Jim Thome	.15
18	Hideki Irabu, Mariano Rivera	.25
19	Roger Clemens, Jose Cruz, Jr.	.75
20	Manny Ramirez, David Justice	.60

Fall Classics

This Series 1 insert pictures 15 stars on a green holographic background. They are numbered with a "FC" suffix.

		NM/M
Complete Set (15):		35.00
Common Player:		1.00
Inserted 1:18		
1	Ken Griffey Jr.	3.00
2	Andruw Jones	1.50
3	Alex Rodriguez	4.00

4	Frank Thomas	1.50
5	Cal Ripken Jr.	5.00
6	Derek Jeter	5.00
7	Chipper Jones	2.00
8	Greg Maddux	2.00
9	Mike Piazza	4.00
10	Albert Belle	1.00
11	Juan Gonzalez	1.00
12	Jeff Bagwell	1.50
13	Tony Gwynn	2.00
14	Mark McGwire	3.00
15	Barry Bonds	5.00

Kid Gloves

Kid Gloves features top fielders on an embossed glove background. Exclusive to Series 1 packs, they are numbered with a "KG" suffix.

		NM/M
Complete Set (12):		9.00
Common Player:		.25
Inserted 1:8		
1	Andruw Jones	.75
2	Alex Rodriguez	2.00
3	Derek Jeter	3.00
4	Chipper Jones	1.00
5	Darin Erstad	.35
6	Todd Walker	.25
7	Scott Rolen	.65
8	Nomar Garciaparra	1.00
9	Jose Cruz, Jr.	.25
10	Charles Johnson	.25
11	Rey Ordonez	.25
12	Vladimir Guerrero	.75

Millennium Men

Millenium Men is a hobby-only insert exclusive to Series 2 packs. The tri-fold cards feature an embossed wax seal design and can be unfolded to reveal another shot of the player, team logo and statistics. They are numbered with a "MM" suffix.

		NM/M
Complete Set (15):		30.00
Common Player:		.75
Inserted 1:35		
1	Jose Cruz	.75
2	Ken Griffey Jr.	3.50
3	Cal Ripken Jr.	6.00
4	Derek Jeter	6.00
5	Andruw Jones	2.00
6	Alex Rodriguez	4.50
7	Chipper Jones	2.50
8	Scott Rolen	1.00

9	Nomar Garciaparra	2.50
10	Frank Thomas	2.00
11	Mike Piazza	3.50
12	Greg Maddux	2.50
13	Juan Gonzalez	1.00
14	Ben Grieve	.75
15	Jaret Wright	.75

Notables

This insert pictures a player on a holographic background with either an American League or National League logo in the background. Notables were seeded in Series 2 packs and numbered with a "N" suffix.

		NM/M
Complete Set (20):		13.50
Common Player:		.20
Inserted 1:4		
1	Frank Thomas	.50
2	Ken Griffey Jr.	1.25
3	Edgar Renteria	.20
4	Albert Belle	.20
5	Juan Gonzalez	.30
6	Jeff Bagwell	.50
7	Mark McGwire	1.50
8	Barry Bonds	2.25
9	Scott Rolen	.40
10	Mo Vaughn	.20
11	Andruw Jones	.50
12	Chipper Jones	.75
13	Tino Martinez	.20
14	Mike Piazza	1.25
15	Tony Clark	.20
16	Jose Cruz	.20
17	Nomar Garciaparra	.75
18	Cal Ripken Jr.	2.25
19	Alex Rodriguez	1.50
20	Derek Jeter	2.25

Power Plus

This insert is exclusive to Series 1 packs. Cards picture the player on an embossed blue background featuring plus signs. These are numbered with a "PP" suffix.

		NM/M
Complete Set (10):		16.00
Common Player:		1.00
Inserted 1:36		
1	Ken Griffey Jr.	4.00
2	Andruw Jones	2.00
3	Alex Rodriguez	3.00
4	Frank Thomas	2.00
5	Mike Piazza	3.00
6	Albert Belle	1.00
7	Juan Gonzalez	1.25
8	Jeff Bagwell	2.00
9	Barry Bonds	5.00
10	Jose Cruz	1.00

Prime Leather

This insert features top fielders on a leather-like card stock, with a large baseball in the background. Cards are seeded in Series 1 packs and numbered with a "PL" suffix.

		NM/M
Complete Set (18):		135.00
Common Player:		2.00
Inserted 1:144		
1	Ken Griffey Jr.	12.50
2	Andruw Jones	7.50
3	Alex Rodriguez	15.00

PRIME LEATHER

4	Frank Thomas	7.50
5	Cal Ripken Jr.	20.00
6	Derek Jeter	20.00
7	Chipper Jones	10.00
8	Greg Maddux	10.00
9	Mike Piazza	12.50
10	Albert Belle	2.00
11	Darin Erstad	3.00
12	Juan Gonzalez	3.00
13	Jeff Bagwell	7.50
14	Tony Gwynn	10.00
15	Roberto Alomar	2.50
16	Barry Bonds	20.00
17	Kenny Lofton	2.00
18	Jose Cruz, Jr.	2.00

Rocket to Stardom

This insert set is exclusive to Series 2 packs. Cards are in black-and-white and are die-cut, embossed and numbered with an "RS" suffix.

		NM/M
Complete Set (15):		15.00
Common Player:		.75
Inserted 1:20		
1	Ben Grieve	.75
2	Magglio Ordonez	4.00
3	Travis Lee	1.00
4	Carl Pavano	.75
5	Brian Rose	.75
6	Brad Fullmer	.75
7	Michael Coleman	.75
8	Juan Encarnacion	.75
9	Karim Garcia	1.00
10	Todd Helton	7.50
11	Richard Hildalgo	.75
12	Paul Konerko	1.50
13	Rod Myers	.75
14	Jaret Wright	.75
15	Miguel Tejada	1.50

Ticket Studs

Fifteen players are featured on fold-out ticket-like cards in Ticket Studs. The cards arrive folded across the middle and open to reveal a full-length shot of the player with prismatic team color stripes over a white background that has section, seat and row numbers. Cards were inserted in Series 2 packs and are numbered with a "TS" suffix.

		NM/M
Complete Set (15):		150.00
Common Player:		2.50
Inserted 1:144		
1	Travis Lee	3.00
2	Tony Gwynn	12.00
3	Scott Rolen	6.00
4	Nomar Garciaparra	12.00
5	Mike Piazza	15.00
6	Mark McGwire	17.50
7	Ken Griffey Jr.	15.00
8	Juan Gonzalez	5.00
9	Jose Cruz	2.50
10	Frank Thomas	9.00
11	Derek Jeter	20.00

TICKET STUDS

12	Chipper Jones	12.00
13	Cal Ripken Jr.	20.00
14	Andruw Jones	9.00
15	Alex Rodriguez	17.50

Top 30

Top 30 is a retail-only insert found only in Series 2.

		NM/M
Complete Set (30):		20.00
Common Player:		.15
Inserted 1:1 R		
1	Barry Bonds	2.00
2	Ivan Rodriguez	.65
3	Kenny Lofton	.15
4	Albert Belle	.15
5	Mo Vaughn	.15
6	Jeff Bagwell	.75
7	Mark McGwire	1.50
8	Darin Erstad	.35
9	Roger Clemens	1.00
10	Tony Gwynn	1.00
11	Scott Rolen	.45
12	Hideo Nomo	.35
13	Juan Gonzalez	.35
14	Mike Piazza	1.25
15	Greg Maddux	1.00
16	Chipper Jones	1.00
17	Andruw Jones	.75
18	Derek Jeter	2.00
19	Nomar Garciaparra	1.00
20	Alex Rodriguez	1.50
21	Frank Thomas	.75
22	Cal Ripken Jr.	2.00
23	Ken Griffey Jr.	1.25
24	Jose Cruz Jr.	.15
25	Jaret Wright	.15
26	Travis Lee	.30
27	Wade Boggs	1.00
28	Chuck Knoblauch	.15
29	Joe Carter	.15
30	Ben Grieve	.15

Win Now

This Series 2 insert has top players printed on plastic card stock, with a color shot of the player on the left side and a close-up shot on the right with black lines through it. Cards are numbered with a "WN" suffix.

	NM/M
Complete Set (20):	100.00
Common Player:	2.50
Inserted 1:72	
1 Alex Rodriguez	10.00
2 Andruw Jones	4.00
3 Cal Ripken Jr.	12.50
4 Chipper Jones	5.00
5 Darin Erstad	3.00
6 Derek Jeter	12.50
7 Frank Thomas	4.00
8 Greg Maddux	5.00
9 Hideo Nomo	3.00
10 Jeff Bagwell	4.00
11 Jose Cruz	2.50
12 Juan Gonzalez	3.00
13 Ken Griffey Jr.	7.50
14 Mark McGwire	10.00
15 Mike Piazza	7.50
16 Mo Vaughn	2.50
17 Nomar Garciaparra	5.00
18 Roger Clemens	6.00
19 Scott Rolen	3.00
20 Tony Gwynn	5.00

1999 Ultra Sample Sheet

This six-card sheet was issued to introduce potential customers to '99 Ultra's base cards. The sheet measures 7-1/2" x 7". Cards are virtually identical to the issued version, except for the diagonal black-and-white "PROMOTIONAL SAMPLE" overprint on front and back.

	NM/M
Complete Sheet:	5.00

1999 Ultra

Base cards feature the full career stats by year in 15 categories and career highlights. There are short-printed subsets including Season Crowns (216-225) found 1:8 packs and Prospects (226-250) found 1:4 packs. Card fronts feature full bleed photography, and metallic foil stamping. There are three parallel versions Gold Medallion seeded 1 per pack with Prospects 1:40 and Season Crowns 1:80. Platinum Medallions are numbered to 99 with Prospects numbered to 65 and Season Crowns numbered to 50 sets. One of One Masterpiece parallels also exist. Packs consist of 10 cards with a S.R.P. of $2.69.

	NM/M
Complete Set (250):	35.00
Common Player:	.05
Common Season Crown:	.25
Inserted 1:8	
Common Prospect:	.25
Inserted 1:4	
Gold Medallion (1-215):	2X
Inserted 1:1	
Gold Medall. Prospect:	4X
Inserted 1:40	
Gold Medall. Season Crown:	3X

Inserted 1:80	
Platinums (1-215):	25X
Production 99 Sets	
Platinum Prospects:	6X
Production 65 Sets	
Platinum Season Crowns:	20X
Production 50 Sets	
Pack (10):	1.50
Wax Box (24):	25.00
1 Greg Maddux	1.00
2 Greg Vaughn	.05
3 John Wetteland	.05
4 Tino Martinez	.05
5 Todd Walker	.05
6 Troy O'Leary	.05
7 Barry Larkin	.05
8 Mike Lansing	.05
9 Delino DeShields	.05
10 Brett Tomko	.05
11 Carlos Perez	.05
12 Mark Langston	.05
13 Jamie Moyer	.05
14 Jose Guillen	.05
15 Bartolo Colon	.05
16 Brady Anderson	.05
17 Walt Weiss	.05
18 Shane Reynolds	.05
19 David Segui	.05
20 Vladimir Guerrero	.75
21 Freddy Garcia	.05
22 Carl Everett	.05
23 Jose Cruz Jr.	.05
24 David Ortiz	.40
25 Andruw Jones	.75
26 Darren Lewis	.05
27 Ray Lankford	.05
28 Wally Joyner	.05
29 Charles Johnson	.05
30 Derek Jeter	2.00
31 Sean Casey	.10
32 Bobby Bonilla	.05
33 Todd Zeile	.05
34 Todd Helton	.65
35 David Wells	.05
36 Darin Erstad	.30
37 Ivan Rodriguez	.65
38 Antonio Osuna	.05
39 Mickey Morandini	.05
40 Rusty Greer	.05
41 Rod Beck	.05
42 Larry Sutton	.05
43 Edgar Renteria	.05
44 Otis Nixon	.05
45 Eli Marrero	.05
46 Reggie Jefferson	.05
47 Trevor Hoffman	.05
48 Andres Galarraga	.05
49 Scott Brosius	.05
50 Vinny Castilla	.05
51 Bret Boone	.05
52 Masato Yoshii	.05
53 Matt Williams	.05
54 Robin Ventura	.05
55 Jay Powell	.05
56 Dean Palmer	.05
57 Eric Milton	.05
58 Willie McGee	.05
59 Tony Gwynn	1.00
60 Tom Gordon	.05
61 Dante Bichette	.05
62 Jaret Wright	.05
63 Devon White	.05
64 Frank Thomas	.75
65 Mike Piazza	1.25
66 Jose Offerman	.05
67 Pat Meares	.05
68 Brian Meadows	.05
69 Nomar Garciaparra	1.00
70 Mark McGwire	1.50
71 Tony Graffanino	.05
72 Ken Griffey Jr.	1.25
73 Ken Caminiti	.05
74 Todd Jones	.05
75 A.J. Hinch	.05
76 Marquis Grissom	.05
77 Jay Buhner	.05
78 Albert Belle	.05
79 Brian Anderson	.05
80 Quinton McCracken	.05
81 Omar Vizquel	.05
82 Todd Stottlemyre	.05
83 Cal Ripken Jr.	2.00
84 Magglio Ordonez	.30
85 John Olerud	.05
86 Hal Morris	.05
87 Derrek Lee	.40
88 Doug Glanville	.05
89 Marty Cordova	.05
90 Kevin Brown	.05
91 Kevin Young	.05
92 Rico Brogna	.05
93 Wilson Alvarez	.05
94 Bob Wickman	.05
95 Jim Thome	.50
96 Mike Mussina	.35
97 Al Leiter	.05
98 Travis Lee	.10
99 Jeff King	.05
100 Kerry Wood	.40
101 Cliff Floyd	.05
102 Jose Valentin	.05
103 Manny Ramirez	.75
104 Butch Huskey	.05
105 Scott Erickson	.05
106 Ray Durham	.05
107 Johnny Damon	.05
108 Craig Counsell	.05
109 Rolando Arrojo	.05

110 Bob Abreu	.05
111 Tony Womack	.05
112 Mike Stanley	.05
113 Kenny Lofton	.05
114 Eric Davis	.05
115 Jeff Conine	.05
116 Carlos Baerga	.05
117 Rondell White	.05
118 Billy Wagner	.05
119 Ed Sprague	.05
120 Jason Schmidt	.05
121 Edgar Martinez	.05
122 Travis Fryman	.05
123 Armando Benitez	.05
124 Matt Stairs	.05
125 Roberto Hernandez	.05
126 Jay Bell	.05
127 Justin Thompson	.05
128 John Jaha	.05
129 Mike Caruso	.05
130 Miguel Tejada	.20
131 Geoff Jenkins	.05
132 Wade Boggs	1.00
133 Andy Benes	.05
134 Aaron Sele	.05
135 Bret Saberhagen	.05
136 Mariano Rivera	.15
137 Neifi Perez	.05
138 Paul Konerko	.15
139 Barry Bonds	2.00
140 Garret Anderson	.05
141 Bernie Williams	.05
142 Gary Sheffield	.40
143 Rafael Palmeiro	.65
144 Orel Hershiser	.05
145 Craig Biggio	.05
146 Dmitri Young	.05
147 Damion Easley	.05
148 Henry Rodriguez	.05
149 Brad Radke	.05
150 Pedro Martinez	.75
151 Mike Lieberthal	.05
152 Jim Leyritz	.05
153 Chuck Knoblauch	.05
154 Darryl Kile	.05
155 Brian Jordan	.05
156 Chipper Jones	1.00
157 Pete Harnisch	.05
158 Moises Alou	.05
159 Ismael Valdes	.05
160 Stan Javier	.05
161 Mark Grace	.05
162 Jason Giambi	.40
163 Chuck Finley	.05
164 Juan Encarnacion	.05
165 Chan Ho Park	.05
166 Randy Johnson	.75
167 J.T. Snow	.05
168 Tim Salmon	.05
169 Brian Hunter	.05
170 Rickey Henderson	.75
171 Cal Eldred	.05
172 Curt Schilling	.25
173 Alex Rodriguez	1.50
174 Dustin Hermanson	.05
175 Mike Hampton	.05
176 Shawn Green	.30
177 Roberto Alomar	.20
178 Sandy Alomar Jr.	.05
179 Larry Walker	.05
180 Mo Vaughn	.05
181 Raul Mondesi	.05
182 Hideki Irabu	.05
183 Jim Edmonds	.05
184 Shawn Estes	.05
185 Tony Clark	.05
186 Dan Wilson	.05
187 Michael Tucker	.05
188 Jeff Shaw	.05
189 Mark Grudzielanek	.05
190 Roger Clemens	1.00
191 Juan Gonzalez	.40
192 Sammy Sosa	1.00
193 Troy Percival	.05
194 Robb Nen	.05
195 Bill Mueller	.05
196 Ben Grieve	.05
197 Luis Gonzalez	.05
198 Will Clark	.05
199 Jeff Cirillo	.05
200 Scott Rolen	.50
201 Reggie Sanders	.05
202 Fred McGriff	.05
203 Denny Neagle	.05
204 Brad Fullmer	.05
205 Royce Clayton	.05
206 Jose Canseco	.50
207 Jeff Bagwell	.75
208 Hideo Nomo	.40
209 Karim Garcia	.15
210 Kenny Rogers	.05
211 Checklist (Kerry Wood)	1.00
212 Checklist (Alex Rodriguez)	.75
213 Checklist (Cal Ripken Jr.)	1.00
214 Checklist (Frank Thomas)	.50
215 Checklist (Ken Griffey Jr.)	.65
216 Alex Rodriguez (Season Crowns)	1.00
217 Greg Maddux (Season Crowns)	.50
218 Juan Gonzalez (Season Crowns)	.20
219 Ken Griffey Jr. (Season Crowns)	.75
220 Kerry Wood (Season Crowns)	.25
221 Mark McGwire (Season Crowns)	1.00

222 Mike Piazza (Season Crowns)	.75
223 Rickey Henderson (Season Crowns)	.40
224 Sammy Sosa (Season Crowns)	.50
225 Travis Lee (Season Crowns)	.25
226 Gabe Alvarez (Prospects)	.25
227 Matt Anderson (Prospects)	.25
228 Adrian Beltre (Prospects)	.35
229 Orlando Cabrera (Prospects)	.35
230 Orlando Hernandez (Prospects)	.25
231 Aramis Ramirez (Prospects)	.25
232 Troy Glaus (Prospects)	1.00
233 Gabe Kapler (Prospects)	.25
234 Jeremy Giambi (Prospects)	.25
235 Derrick Gibson (Prospects)	.25
236 Carlton Loewer (Prospects)	.25
237 Mike Frank (Prospects)	.25
238 Carlos Guillen (Prospects)	.25
239 Alex Gonzalez (Prospects)	.25
240 Enrique Wilson (Prospects)	.25
241 J.D. Drew (Prospects)	.75
242 Bruce Chen (Prospects)	.25
243 Ryan Minor (Prospects)	.25
244 Preston Wilson (Prospects)	.35
245 Josh Booty (Prospects)	.25
246 Luis Ordaz (Prospects)	.25
247 George Lombard (Prospects)	.25
248 Matt Clement (Prospects)	.25
249 Eric Chavez (Prospects)	.35
250 Corey Koskie (Prospects)	.30

Gold Medallion

The basic cards (#1-215) in this parallel set are found one per pack, while the short-printed versions are seen one per 40 packs (Prospects) or one per 80 packs (Season Crowns). Sharing the photos and format of the regular-issue cards, these inserts have a gold-foil background on front. On back, "GOLD MEDALLION EDITION" is printed in gold foil.

	NM/M
Common Player (1-215):	.25
Stars/RC's:	2X
Season Crowns (216-225):	4X
Prospects (226-250):	3X

Platinum Medallion

The basic cards (#1-215) in this parallel set are found in an individually serial numbered edition of 99. The short-printed cards were released in editions of 65 (Prospects) and 50 (Season Crowns). Sharing the photos and format of the regular-issue cards, these inserts have a silver-foil background on front. On back,

"PLATINUM MEDALLION" is printed in silver foil along with the serial number.

	NM/M
Common Player (1-215):	5.00
Stars/RC's:	25X
Season Crowns (216-225):	20X
Prospects (226-250):	6X

Masterpiece

This top of the line parallel to '99 Ultra consists of a 1 of 1 version of each regular card.

	NM/M
Common Player:	50.00

Book On

This set features insider scouting reports on the game's best players, utilizing embossing and gold foil stamping.

	NM/M
Complete Set (20):	13.50
Common Player:	.25
Inserted 1:6	
1 Kerry Wood	.35
2 Ken Griffey Jr.	1.00
3 Frank Thomas	.65
4 Albert Belle	.25
5 Juan Gonzalez	.35
6 Jeff Bagwell	.65
7 Mark McGwire	1.25
8 Barry Bonds	1.50
9 Andruw Jones	.65
10 Mo Vaughn	.25
11 Scott Rolen	.40
12 Travis Lee	.25
13 Tony Gwynn	.75
14 Greg Maddux	.75
15 Mike Piazza	1.00
16 Chipper Jones	.75
17 Nomar Garciaparra	.75
18 Cal Ripken Jr.	1.50
19 Derek Jeter	1.50
20 Alex Rodriguez	1.25

Damage Inc.

This insert set has a buisness card design, for players who mean business.

	NM/M
Complete Set (15):	50.00
Common Player:	1.00
Inserted 1:72	
1 Alex Rodriguez	5.00
2 Greg Maddux	3.50
3 Cal Ripken Jr.	7.50
4 Chipper Jones	4.00
5 Derek Jeter	7.50
6 Frank Thomas	2.50
7 Juan Gonzalez	1.50
8 Ken Griffey Jr.	4.00
9 Kerry Wood	1.25
10 Mark McGwire	5.00
11 Mike Piazza	4.00
12 Nomar Garciaparra	3.50
13 Scott Rolen	1.50
14 Tony Gwynn	3.50
15 Travis Lee	1.00

Diamond Producers

This die-cut set uses full-foil plastic with custom embossing.

	NM/M
Complete Set (10):	140.00
Common Player:	6.00
Inserted 1:288	
1 Ken Griffey Jr.	17.50
2 Frank Thomas	12.00
3 Alex Rodriguez	20.00
4 Cal Ripken Jr.	25.00
5 Mike Piazza	17.50
6 Mark McGwire	20.00

KEN GRIFFEY, JR.

7 Greg Maddux	15.00
8 Kerry Wood	6.00
9 Chipper Jones	15.00
10 Derek Jeter	25.00

RBI Kings

	NM/M
Complete Set (30):	12.00
Common Player:	.15
Inserted 1:1 R	
1 Rafael Palmeiro	.40
2 Mo Vaughn	.15
3 Ivan Rodriguez	.40
4 Barry Bonds	1.25
5 Albert Belle	.15
6 Jeff Bagwell	.45
7 Mark McGwire	1.00
8 Darin Erstad	.25
9 Manny Ramirez	.45
10 Chipper Jones	.75
11 Jim Thome	.40
12 Scott Rolen	.35
13 Tony Gwynn	.60
14 Juan Gonzalez	.25
15 Mike Piazza	.75
16 Sammy Sosa	.60
17 Andruw Jones	.45
18 Derek Jeter	1.25
19 Nomar Garciaparra	.60
20 Alex Rodriguez	1.00
21 Frank Thomas	.45
22 Cal Ripken Jr.	1.25
23 Ken Griffey Jr.	.75
24 Travis Lee	.25
25 Paul O'Neill	.15
26 Greg Vaughn	.15
27 Andres Galarraga	.15
28 Tino Martinez	.15
29 Jose Canseco	.30
30 Ben Grieve	.15

Thunderclap

This set highlights the top hitters in the game. Card fronts feature a lightning bolt in the background.

	NM/M
Complete Set (15):	35.00
Common Player:	.75
Inserted 1:36	
1 Alex Rodriguez	4.00
2 Andruw Jones	1.50
3 Cal Ripken Jr.	6.00
4 Chipper Jones	2.50

5	Darin Erstad	.75
6	Derek Jeter	6.00
7	Frank Thomas	1.50
8	Jeff Bagwell	1.50
9	Juan Gonzalez	.75
10	Ken Griffey Jr.	3.00
11	Mark McGwire	4.00
12	Mike Piazza	3.00
13	Travis Lee	.75
14	Nomar Garciaparra	2.50
15	Scott Rolen	1.00

World Premiere

This set highlights rookies who made debuts in 1998.

		NM/M
Complete Set (15):		8.00
Common Player:		.50
Inserted 1:18		
1	Gabe Alvarez	.50
2	Kerry Wood	1.50
3	Orlando Hernandez	.60
4	Mike Caruso	.50
5	Matt Anderson	.50
6	Randall Simon	.50
7	Adrian Beltre	.65
8	Scott Elarton	.50
9	Karim Garcia	.60
10	Mike Frank	.50
11	Richard Hidalgo	.50
12	Paul Konerko	.60
13	Travis Lee	.65
14	J.D. Drew	1.50
15	Miguel Tejada	.75

2000 Ultra Sample

Product spokesman Alex Rodriguez is featured on the promo card for 2000 Ultra. Virtually identical in format to the issued version, the card has a "PROMOTIONAL SAMPLE" overprint diagonally on front and back.

		NM/M
1	Alex Rodriguez	2.00

2000 Ultra

The 300-card base set features a borderless design with silver holographic foil stamping on the card front. Card backs have an action image along with complete year-by-year statistics. The base set includes a 50-card short-printed Prospects (1:4) subset. A Masterpiece one-of-one parallel was produced.

		NM/M
Complete Set (300):		35.00
Common Player:		.10
Common Player (251-300):		.50
Inserted 1:4		
Pack (10):		2.00
Wax Box (24):		35.00
1	Alex Rodriguez	1.50
2	Shawn Green	.25
3	Magglio Ordonez	.25
4	Tony Gwynn	.75
5	Joe McEwing	.10
6	Jose Rosado	.10
7	Sammy Sosa	1.00
8	Gary Sheffield	.25
9	Mickey Morandini	.10
10	Mo Vaughn	.15
11	Todd Hollandsworth	.10
12	Tom Gordon	.10
13	Charles Johnson	.10
14	Derek Bell	.10
15	Kevin Young	.10
16	Jay Buhner	.15
17	J.T. Snow	.10
18	Jay Bell	.10
19	John Rocker	.10
20	Ivan Rodriguez	.40
21	Pokey Reese	.10
22	Paul O'Neill	.20
23	Ronnie Belliard	.10
24	Ryan Rupe	.10
25	Travis Fryman	.20
26	Trot Nixon	.10
27	Wally Joyner	.10
28	Andy Pettitte	.25
29	Dan Wilson	.10
30	Orlando Hernandez	.20
31	Dmitri Young	.10
32	Edgar Renteria	.10
33	Eric Karros	.20
34	Fernando Seguignol	.10
35	Jason Kendall	.20
36	Jeff Shaw	.10
37	Matt Lawton	.10
38	Robin Ventura	.20
39	Scott Williamson	.10
40	Ben Grieve	.10
41	Billy Wagner	.10
42	Javy Lopez	.20
43	Joe Randa	.10
44	Neifi Perez	.10
45	David Justice	.20
46	Ray Durham	.10
47	Dustin Hermanson	.10
48	Andres Galarraga	.20
49	Brad Fullmer	.10
50	Nomar Garciaparra	1.50
51	David Cone	.15
52	David Nilsson	.10
53	David Wells	.10
54	Miguel Tejada	.25
55	Ismael Valdes	.10
56	Jose Lima	.10
57	Juan Encarnacion	.10
58	Fred McGriff	.20
59	Kenny Rogers	.10
60	Vladimir Guerrero	.75
61	Benito Santiago	.10
62	Chris Singleton	.10
63	Carlos Lee	.10
64	Sean Casey	.20
65	Tom Goodwin	.10
66	Todd Hundley	.10
67	Ellis Burks	.10
68	Tim Hudson	.25
69	Matt Stairs	.10
70	Chipper Jones	1.00
71	Craig Biggio	.20
72	Brian Rose	.10
73	Carlos Delgado	.40
74	Eddie Taubensee	.10
75	John Smoltz	.20
76	Ken Caminiti	.15
77	Rafael Palmeiro	.40
78	Sidney Ponson	.10
79	Todd Helton	.50
80	Juan Gonzalez	.50
81	Bruce Aven	.10
82	Desi Relaford	.10
83	Johnny Damon	.20
84	Albert Belle	.15
85	Mark McGwire	1.50
86	Rico Brogna	.10
87	Tom Glavine	.25
88	Harold Baines	.10
89	Chad Allen	.10
90	Barry Bonds	2.00
91	Mark Grace	.25
92	Paul Byrd	.10
93	Roberto Alomar	.40
94	Roberto Hernandez	.10
95	Steve Finley	.10
96	Bret Boone	.20
97	Charles Nagy	.10
98	Eric Chavez	.20
99	Jamie Moyer	.10
100	Ken Griffey Jr.	1.00
101	J.D. Drew	.20
102	Todd Stottlemyre	.10
103	Tony Fernandez	.10
104	Jeromy Burnitz	.10
105	Jeremi Giambi	.10
106	Livan Hernandez	.10
107	Marlon Anderson	.10
108	Troy Glaus	.50
109	Troy O'Leary	.10
110	Scott Rolen	.50
111	Bernard Gilkey	.10
112	Brady Anderson	.15
113	Chuck Knoblauch	.10
114	Jeff Weaver	.10
115	B.J. Surhoff	.10
116	Alex Gonzalez	.10
117	Vinny Castilla	.10
118	Tim Salmon	.20
119	Brian Jordan	.10
120	Corey Koskie	.10
121	Dean Palmer	.10
122	Gabe Kapler	.15
123	Jim Edmonds	.25
124	John Jaha	.10
125	Mark Grudzielanek	.10
126	Mike Bordick	.10
127	Mike Lieberthal	.10
128	Pete Harnisch	.10
129	Russ Ortiz	.10
130	Kevin Brown	.20
131	Troy Percival	.10
132	Alex Gonzalez	.10
133	Bartolo Colon	.10
134	John Valentin	.10
135	Jose Hernandez	.10
136	Marquis Grissom	.10
137	Wade Boggs	.25
138	Dante Bichette	.10
139	Bobby Higginson	.10
140	Frank Thomas	.50
141	Geoff Jenkins	.10
142	Jason Giambi	.50
143	Jeff Cirillo	.10
144	Sandy Alomar Jr.	.10
145	Luis Gonzalez	.20
146	Preston Wilson	.10
147	Carlos Beltran	.20
148	Greg Vaughn	.10
149	Carlos Febles	.10
150	Jose Canseco	.40
151	Kris Benson	.10
152	Chuck Finley	.10
153	Michael Barrett	.10
154	Rey Ordonez	.10
155	Adrian Beltre	.10
156	Andruw Jones	.50
157	Barry Larkin	.20
158	Brian Giles	.10
159	Carl Everett	.10
160	Manny Ramirez	.50
161	Darryl Kile	.10
162	Edgar Martinez	.15
163	Jeff Kent	.20
164	Matt Williams	.20
165	Mike Piazza	1.00
166	Pedro J. Martinez	.75
167	Ray Lankford	.10
168	Roger Cedeno	.10
169	Ron Coomer	.10
170	Cal Ripken Jr.	2.00
171	Jose Offerman	.10
172	Kenny Lofton	.10
173	Kent Bottenfield	.10
174	Kevin Millwood	.10
175	Omar Daal	.10
176	Orlando Cabrera	.10
177	Pat Hentgen	.10
178	Tino Martinez	.20
179	Tony Clark	.10
180	Roger Clemens	1.25
181	Brad Radke	.10
182	Darin Erstad	.20
183	Jose Jimenez	.10
184	Jim Thome	.50
185	John Wetteland	.10
186	Justin Thompson	.10
187	John Hamala	.10
188	Lee Stevens	.10
189	Miguel Cairo	.10
190	Mike Mussina	.25
191	Raul Mondesi	.15
192	Armando Rios	.10
193	Trevor Hoffman	.10
194	Tony Batista	.10
195	Will Clark	.40
196	Brad Ausmus	.10
197	Chili Davis	.10
198	Cliff Floyd	.10
199	Curt Schilling	.25
200	Derek Jeter	2.00
201	Henry Rodriguez	.10
202	Jose Cruz Jr.	.10
203	Omar Vizquel	.20
204	Randy Johnson	.75
205	Reggie Sanders	.10
206	Al Leiter	.10
207	Damion Easley	.10
208	David Bell	.10
209	Fernando Tatis	.10
210	Kerry Wood	.25
211	Kevin Appier	.10
212	Mariano Rivera	.20
213	Mike Caruso	.10
214	Moises Alou	.10
215	Randy Winn	.10
216	Roy Halladay	.20
217	Shannon Stewart	.10
218	Todd Walker	.10
219	Jim Parque	.10
220	Travis Lee	.10
221	Andy Ashby	.10
222	Ed Sprague	.10
223	Larry Walker	.20
224	Rick Helling	.10
225	Rusty Greer	.10
226	Todd Zeile	.10
227	Freddy Garcia	.15
228	Hideo Nomo	.40
229	Marty Cordova	.10
230	Greg Maddux	1.00
231	Rondell White	.20
232	Paul Konerko	.15
233	Warren Morris	.10
234	Bernie Williams	.40
235	Bobby Abreu	.10
236	John Olerud	.25
237	Doug Glanville	.10
238	Eric Young	.10
239	Robb Nen	.10
240	Jeff Bagwell	.50
241	Sterling Hitchcock	.10
242	Todd Greene	.10
243	Bill Mueller	.10
244	Rickey Henderson	.20
245	Chan Ho Park	.10
246	Jason Schmidt	.10
247	Jeff Zimmerman	.10
248	Jermaine Dye	.10
249	Randall Simon	.10
250	Richie Sexson	.40
251	Micah Bowie	.50
252	Joe Nathan	.50
253	Chris Woodward	.50
254	Lance Berkman	.75
255	Ruben Mateo	.50
256	Russell Branyan	.50
257	Randy Wolf	.75
258	A.J. Burnett	.75
259	Mark Quinn	.50
260	Buddy Carlyle	.50
261	Ben Davis	.50
262	Yamid Haad	.50
263	Mike Colangelo	.50
264	Rick Ankiel	.75
265	Jacque Jones	.75
266	Kelly Dransfeldt	.50
267	Matt Riley	.50
268	Adam Kennedy	.50
269	Octavio Dotel	.50
270	Francisco Cordero	.50
271	Wilton Veras	.50
272	Calvin Pickering	.50
273	Alex Sanchez	.50
274	Tony Armas Jr.	.50
275	Pat Burrell	1.00
276	Chad Meyers	.50
277	Ben Petrick	.50
278	Ramon Hernandez	.50
279	Ed Yarnall	.50
280	Erubiel Durazo	.50
281	Vernon Wells	1.00
282	Gary Matthews	.50
283	Kip Wells	.50
284	Peter Bergeron	.50
285	Travis Dawkins	.50
286	Jorge Toca	.50
287	Cole Liniak	.50
288	Chad Hermansen	.50
289	Eric Gagne	.50
290	Chad Hutchinson	.50
291	Eric Munson	.50
292	Wiki Gonzalez	.50
293	Alfonso Soriano	1.50
294	Trent Durrington	.50
295	Ben Molina	.50
296	Aaron Myette	.50
297	Willi Mo Pena	.75
298	Kevin Barker	.50
299	Geoff Blum	.50
300	Josh Beckett	.75

Gold Medallion

A parallel to the 300-card base set these have gold foil stamping over a metallic gold background. Cards 1-250 are seeded one per pack, Prospects 251-300 are seeded 1:24 packs. Card backs are numbered with a "G" suffix.

Stars:	2X
Inserted 1:1	
Prospects (251-300):	2-4X
Inserted 1:24	

Platinum Medallion

Platinum Medallion are a parallel to the 300-card base set and are die-cut like the Gold Medallion parallel inserts. Card fronts are stamped with silver foil over a me-tallic silver background. Card backs are serially numbered with cards 1-250 limited to 50 sets and Prospects limited to 25 numbered sets. Card backs are numbered with a "P" suffix.

Stars:	15-30X
Production 50 Sets	
Prospects (251-300):	4-8X
Production 25 Sets	

Masterpiece Edition

Masterpiece Edition is a 1 of 1 parallel to the 300-card base set and are "tombstone" die-cut like the Gold and Platinum Medallion inserts. Card fronts are stamped with purple foil over a metallic purple background. Card backs are overprinted with "The only 1 of 1 Masterpiece."

Club 3000

This three-card set is die-cut around the number 3,000 and commemorates 3,000 hit club members Wade Boggs, Tony Gwynn and Carl Yastrzemski. These were seeded 1:24 packs.

	NM/M
Common Player:	3.00
Inserted 1:24	
Wade Boggs	2.00
Tony Gwynn	3.00
Carl Yastrzemski	3.00

Club 3000 Memorabilia

Each featured player has a total of four different memorabilia based inserts: hat, jersey, bat/jersey and bat/hat/jersey.

	NM/M
Wade Boggs/Bat/250	20.00
Wade Boggs/Hat/100	40.00
Wade Boggs/Jsy/440	20.00
Wade Boggs/Bat, Hat, Jsy/25	40.00
Wade Boggs/Bat/100	150.00
Tony Gwynn/Bat/260	40.00
Tony Gwynn/Hat/115	60.00
Tony Gwynn/Jsy/450	25.00
Tony Gwynn/Bat, Jsy/100	65.00
Tony Gwynn/Bat, Hat, Jsy/25	375.00
Carl Yastrzemski/Bat/250	40.00
Carl Yastrzemski/Hat/100	60.00
Carl Yastrzemski/Jsy/440	25.00
Carl Yastrzemski/Bat, Jsy/100	75.00
Carl Yastrzemski/Bat, Hat, Jsy/25	300.00

Crunch Time

This 15-card insert set is printed on suede stock with gold foil stamping. These were seeded 1:72 packs and numbered with a "CT" suffix on the card back.

		NM/M
Complete Set (15):		50.00
Common Player:		2.00
Inserted 1:72		
1	Nomar Garciaparra	8.00
2	Ken Griffey Jr.	5.00
3	Mark McGwire	8.00
4	Alex Rodriguez	8.00
5	Derek Jeter	8.00
6	Sammy Sosa	6.00
7	Mike Piazza	5.00
8	Cal Ripken Jr.	10.00
9	Frank Thomas	3.00
10	Juan Gonzalez	3.00
11	J.D. Drew	2.00
12	Greg Maddux	3.00
13	Tony Gwynn	3.00
14	Vladimir Guerrero	3.00
15	Ben Grieve	2.00

Diamond Mine

These were printed on a silver foil card front with Diamond Mine stamped in the background of the player image. These were inserted 1:6 packs and numbered with a "DM" suffix on the card back.

		NM/M
Complete Set (15):		20.00
Common Player:		1.00
Inserted 1:6		
1	Greg Maddux	1.50
2	Mark McGwire	2.00
3	Ken Griffey Jr.	1.50
4	Cal Ripken Jr.	3.00
5	Nomar Garciaparra	2.50
6	Mike Piazza	2.00
7	Alex Rodriguez	2.50
8	Frank Thomas	2.00
9	Juan Gonzalez	1.00
10	Derek Jeter	2.50
11	Tony Gwynn	1.00
12	Chipper Jones	1.50
13	Sammy Sosa	1.00
14	Roger Clemens	1.50
15	Vladimir Guerrero	1.00

Feel the Game

These memorabilia based inserts have a piece of game worn jersey or batting glove embedded into the card front.

	NM/M
Common Player:	5.00
Roberto Alomar	10.00
J.D. Drew	5.00
Tony Gwynn/SP	40.00
Randy Johnson	20.00
Greg Maddux	20.00
Edgar Martinez	10.00
Pedro Martinez	20.00
Kevin Millwood	10.00
Cal Ripken Jr.	40.00

	NM/M
Alex Rodriguez	25.00
Scott Rolen	10.00
Curt Schilling	10.00
Chipper Jones	20.00
Frank Thomas/SP	40.00
Robin Ventura	5.00

Fresh Ink

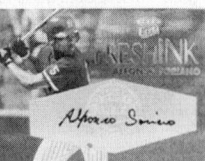

These autographed cards have the words "Fresh Ink" printed continually in the background image of the player. The signature is in a designated blank box intended for the autograph. Production numbers vary from player to player and are listed in parentheses after the player name.

	NM/M
Common Player:	5.00
1 Bobby Abreu/400	10.00
2 Chad Allen/1,000	5.00
3 Marlon Anderson/1,000	5.00
4 Glen Barker/1,000	5.00
5 Michael Barrett/1,000	5.00
6 Carlos Beltran/1,000	15.00
7 Adrian Beltre/1,000	8.00
8 Wade Boggs/250	40.00
9 Barry Bonds/250	150.00
10 Peter Bergeron/1,000	5.00
11 Pat Burrell/500	20.00
12 Roger Cedeno/500	5.00
13 Eric Chavez/750	10.00
14 Bruce Chen/600	5.00
15 Johnny Damon/750	8.00
16 Ben Davis/1,000	5.00
17 Carlos Delgado/300	10.00
18 Einar Diaz/1,000	6.00
19 Octavio Dotel/1,000	6.00
20 J.D. Drew/600	8.00
21 Scott Elarton/1,000	5.00
22 Freddy Garcia/500	8.00
23 Jeremy Giambi/1,000	5.00
24 Troy Glaus/500	20.00
25 Shawn Green/350	30.00
26 Tony Gwynn/250	50.00
27 Richard Hidalgo/500	8.00
28 Bobby Higginson/1,000	6.00
29 Tim Hudson/1,000	10.00
30 Norm Hutchins/1,000	5.00
31 Derek Jeter/95	200.00
32 Randy Johnson/150	50.00
33 Gabe Kapler/750	8.00
34 Jason Kendall/400	8.00
35 Paul Konerko/500	8.00
36 Matt Lawton/1,000	6.00
37 Carlos Lee/1,000	8.00
38 Jose Macias/1,000	5.00
39 Greg Maddux/250	65.00
40 Ruben Mateo/250	8.00
41 Kevin Millwood/500	10.00
42 Warren Morris/1,000	5.00
43 Eric Munson/1,000	6.00
44 Heath Murray/1,000	5.00
45 Joe Nathan/1,000	5.00
46 Magglio Ordonez/350	10.00
47 Angel Pena/1,000	5.00
48 Cal Ripken Jr./350	125.00
49 Alex Rodriguez/350	80.00
50 Scott Rolen/250	35.00
51 Ryan Rupe/1,000	5.00
52 Curt Schilling/375	25.00
53 Randall Simon/1,000	5.00
54 Alfonso Soriano/1,000	60.00
55 Shannon Stewart/300	5.00
56 Miguel Tejada/1,000	25.00
57 Frank Thomas/150	60.00
58 Jeff Weaver/1,000	6.00
59 Randy Wolf/1,000	8.00
60 Ed Yarnall/1,000	5.00
61 Kevin Young/1,000	5.00
62 Tony Gwynn, Wade Boggs, Nolan Ryan/100	450.00
63 Rick Ankiel/500	10.00

Swing King

Printed on a clear, plastic stock this 10-card set features the top hitters in the game. Card fronts also utilize silver foil stamping. These were seeded 1:24 packs and are numbered on the card back with a "SK" suffix.

	NM/M
Complete Set (10):	20.00
Common Player:	1.00
Inserted 1:24	
1 Cal Ripken Jr.	4.00
2 Nomar Garciaparra	3.00
3 Frank Thomas	1.00
4 Tony Gwynn	1.50
5 Ken Griffey Jr.	3.00
6 Chipper Jones	2.00
7 Mark McGwire	3.00
8 Sammy Sosa	2.50
9 Derek Jeter	3.00
10 Alex Rodriguez	3.00

Ultra Talented

Available exclusively in hobby packs these were printed on a holo-foil background with gold foil stamping. Each card is serially numbered to 100 and are numbered on the card back with a "UT" suffix.

	NM/M
Common Player:	5.00
Production 100 Sets	
1 Sammy Sosa	15.00
2 Derek Jeter	20.00
3 Alex Rodriguez	20.00
4 Mike Piazza	15.00
5 Ken Griffey Jr.	20.00
6 Nomar Garciaparra	20.00
7 Mark McGwire	20.00
8 Cal Ripken Jr.	25.00
9 Frank Thomas	8.00
10 J.D. Drew	5.00

World Premiere

This insert set highlights ten young potential stars on a die-cut, silver foil etched design. These were inserted 1:12 packs and are numbered with a "WP" suffix on the card back.

	NM/M
Complete Set (10):	5.00
Common Player:	.50
Inserted 1:12	
1 Ruben Mateo	.50
2 Lance Berkman	1.00
3 Octavio Dotel	.50
4 Ben Davis	.50
5 Warren Morris	.50
6 Carlos Beltran	.75
7 Rick Ankiel	.50
8 Adam Kennedy	.50
9 Tim Hudson	1.00
10 Jorge Toca	.50

1989 Upper Deck Promos

WALLY JOYNER

In 1988 Upper Deck produced a two-card test set to be distributed as samples for the 1989 set; 18,000 of each card were produced. The cards were distributed to dealers at the 1988 National Sports Collectors Convention. Two other variations of the promo cards exist. Both variations involve differences in where the hologram was placed. Fewer than 5,000 of one of the hologram variations exist, while less than 1,000 of the third variation exist. Joyner and Buice were selected for the promo cards because of a reported investment interest in Upper Deck; they were later required to sell their interest in the card company due to their active-player status.

	NM/M
Complete Set A (2):	5.00
Complete Set B (2):	9.00
Complete Set C (2):	15.00
1a DeWayne Buice (1/2" x 3/16" hologram at bottom)	2.00
1b DeWayne Buice (Hologram extends to bottom edge.)	3.00
1c DeWayne Buice (Hologram at top.)	5.00
700a Wally Joyner (1/2" x 3/16" hologram at bottom)	2.50
700b Wally Joyner (Hologram extends to bottom edge.)	6.00
700c Wally Joyner (Hologram at top.)	10.00

1989 Upper Deck Show Samples

Tommy John

At the Nov. 26-27, 1988 Anaheim card show, Upper Deck distributed samples of its forthcoming premiere set. While card fronts are nearly identical to the same players' issued versions (except they lack the position indicator at top-right), the backs are blank, also lacking the hologram. All cards in this sample distribution are from the range of card numbers between 206-250, in five contiguous groups of five, with gaps of five between them. The samples are listed here in alphabetical order. Uncut sheets of the samples were reported to be widely available at the show.

	NM/M
Complete Set (25):	90.00
Common Player:	3.00
Uncut Sheet (25):	100.00
Mike Aldrete	3.00
Andy Allanson	3.00
Scott Bailes	3.00
Phil Bradley	3.00
Scott Bradley	3.00
Jay Buhner	3.00
Brett Butler	3.00
John Candelaria	3.00
Bruce Fields	3.00
Von Hayes	3.00
Rickey Henderson	15.00
Steve Jeltz	3.00
Tommy John	4.50
Ron Kittle	3.00
Bob Melvin	3.00
Lance Parrish	3.00
Willie Randolph	4.50
Harold Reynolds	3.00
Rafael Santana	3.00
Rod Scurry	3.00
Chris Speier	3.00
Greg Swindell	3.00
Kent Tekulve	3.00
Matt Williams	3.00
Paul Zuvella	3.00

1989 Upper Deck

Dale Murphy

This premiere "Collector's Choice" issue from Upper Deck contains 700 cards (2-1/2" x 3-1/2") with full-color photos on both sides. The first 26 cards feature Star Rookies. The set also includes 26 special portrait cards with team checklist backs and seven numbered checklist cards. Major 1988 award winners (Cy Young, Rookie of Year, MVP) are honored on 10 cards in the set, in addition to their individual player cards. There are also special cards for the Most Valuable Players in both League Championship series and the World Series. The card fronts feature player photos framed by a white border. A vertical brown and green artist's rendition of the runner's lane that leads from home plate to first base is found along the right margin. Backs carry full-color action poses that fill the card back, except for a compact (yet complete) stats chart. A high-number series, cards 701-800, featuring rookies and traded players, was released in mid-season in foil packs mixed within the complete set, in boxed complete sets and in high number set boxes.

	NM/M
Unopened Fact. Set (800):	80.00
Complete Set (800):	45.00
Complete Low Set (700):	40.00
Complete High Set (100):	5.00
Common Player:	.05
Low Foil Pack (15):	4.00
Low Foil Box (36):	100.00
High Foil Pack (15):	2.00
High Foil Box (36):	60.00
1 Ken Griffey Jr. RC	40.00
2 Luis Medina RC	.05
3 Tony Chance RC	.05
4 Dave Otto RC	.05
5 Sandy Alomar, Jr. RC	1.00
6 Rolando Roomes RC	.05
7 David West RC	.05
8 Cris Carpenter RC	.25
9 Gregg Jefferies	.25
10 Doug Dascenzo RC	.05
11 Ron Jones RC	.05
12 Luis de los Santos RC	.05
13a Gary Sheffield RC ("SS" upside-down)	8.00
13b Gary Sheffield RC ("SS" correct)	8.00
14 Mike Harkey RC	.05
15 Lance Blankenship RC	.05
16 William Brennan RC	.05
17 John Smoltz RC	.45
18 Ramon Martinez RC	.25
19 Mark Lemke RC	.05
20 Juan Bell RC	.05
21 Rey Palacios RC	.05
22 Felix Jose RC	.05
23 Van Snider RC	.05
24 Dante Bichette RC	.75
25 Randy Johnson RC	10.00
26 Carlos Quintana RC	.05
27 Star Rookie Checklist 1-26	.05
28 Mike Schooler RC	.05
29 Randy St. Claire	.05
30 Jerald Clark RC	.05
31 Kevin Gross	.05
32 Dan Firova RC	.05
33 Jeff Calhoun	.05
34 Tommy Hinzo	.05
35 Ricky Jordan RC	.05
36 Bret Saberhagen	.05
37 Mike Smithson	.05
38 Dave Dravecky	.05
39 Ed Romero	.05
40 Jeff Musselman	.05
41 Ed Hearn	.05
42 Rance Mulliniks	.05
43 Jim Eisenreich	.05
44 Sil Campusano RC	.05
45 Mike Krukow	.05
46 Paul Gibson RC	.05
47 Mike LaCoss	.05
48 Larry Herndon	.05
49 Scott Garrelts	.05
50 Dwayne Henry	.05
51 Jim Acker	.05
52 Steve Sax	.05
53 Pete O'Brien	.05
54 Paul Runge	.05
55 Rick Rhoden	.05
56 John Dopson RC	.05
57 Casey Candaele	.05
58 Dave Righetti	.05
59 Joe Hesketh	.05
60 Frank DiPino	.05
61 Tim Laudner	.05
62 Jamie Moyer	.05
63 Fred Toliver	.05
64 Mitch Webster	.05
65 John Tudor	.05
66 John Cangelosi	.05
67 Mike Devereaux	.05
68 Brian Fisher	.05
69 Mike Marshall	.05
70 Zane Smith	.05
72a Brian Holton (Ball not visible on card front, photo actually Shawn Hillegas.)	.75
72b Brian Holton (Ball visible, correct photo.)	.05
73 Jose Guzman	.05
74 Rick Mahler	.05
75 John Shelby	.05
76 Jim Deshaies	.05
77 Bobby Meacham	.05
78 Bryn Smith	.05
79 Joaquin Andujar	.05
80 Richard Dotson	.05
81 Charlie Lea	.05
82 Calvin Schiraldi	.05
83 Les Straker	.05
84 Les Lancaster	.05
85 Allan Anderson	.05
86 Junior Ortiz	.05
87 Jesse Orosco	.05
88 Felix Fermin	.05
89 Dave Anderson	.05
90 Rafael Belliard	.05
91 Franklin Stubbs	.05
92 Cecil Espy	.05
93 Albert Hall	.05
94 Tim Leary	.05
95 Mitch Williams	.05
96 Tracy Jones	.05
97 Danny Darwin	.05
98 Gary Ward	.05
99 Neal Heaton	.05
100 Jim Pankovits	.05
101 Bill Doran	.05
102 Tim Wallach	.20
103 Joe Magrane	.05
104 Ozzie Virgil	.05
105 Alvin Davis	.05
106 Tom Brookens	.05
107 Shawon Dunston	.05
108 Tracy Woodson	.05
109 Nelson Liriano	.05
110 Devon White	.05
111 Steve Balboni	.05
112 Buddy Bell	.05
113 German Jimenez RC	.05
114 Ken Dayley	.05
115 Andres Galarraga	.05
116 Mike Scioscia	.05
117 Gary Pettis	.05
118 Ernie Whitt	.05
119 Bob Boone	.05
120 Ryne Sandberg	1.50
121 Bruce Benedict	.05
122 Hubie Brooks	.05
123 Mike Moore	.05
124 Wallace Johnson	.05
125 Bob Horner	.05
126 Chili Davis	.05
127 Manny Trillo	.05
128 Chet Lemon	.05
129 John Cerutti	.05
130 Orel Hershiser	.05
131 Terry Pendleton	.05
132 Jeff Blauser	.05
133 Mike Fitzgerald	.05
134 Henry Cotto	.05
135 Gerald Young	.05
136 Luis Salazar	.05
137 Alejandro Pena	.05
138 Jack Howell	.05
139 Tony Fernandez	.05
140 Mark Grace	.05
141 Ken Caminiti	.05
142 Mike Jackson	.05
143 Larry McWilliams	.05
144 Andres Thomas	.05
145 Nolan Ryan	2.00
146 Mike Davis	.05
147 DeWayne Buice	.05
148 Jody Davis	.05
149 Jesse Barfield	.05
150 Matt Nokes	.05
151 Jerry Reuss	.05
152 Rick Cerone	.05
153 Storm Davis	.05
154 Marvell Wynne	.05
155 Will Clark	.05
156 Luis Aguayo	.05
157 Willie Upshaw	.05
158 Randy Bush	.05
159 Ron Darling	.05
160 Kal Daniels	.05
161 Spike Owen	.05
162 Luis Polonia	.05
163 Kevin Mitchell	.05
164 Dave Gallagher RC	.05
165 Benito Santiago	.05
166 Greg Gagne	.05
167 Ken Phelps	.05
168 Sid Fernandez	.05
169 Bo Diaz	.05
170 Cory Snyder	.05
171 Eric Show	.05
172 Robby Thompson	.05
173 Marty Barrett	.05
174 Dave Henderson	.05
175 Ozzie Guillen	.05
176 Barry Lyons	.05
177 Kelvin Torve RC	.05
178 Don Slaught	.05
179 Steve Lombardozzi	.05
180 Chris Sabo RC	.05
181 Jose Uribe	.05
182 Shane Mack	.05
183 Ron Karkovice	.05
184 Todd Benzinger	.05
185 Dave Stewart	.05
186 Julio Franco	.05
187 Ron Robinson	.05
188 Wally Backman	.05
189 Randy Velarde	.05
190 Joe Carter	.05
191 Bob Welch	.05
192 Kelly Paris	.05
193 Chris Brown	.05
194 Rick Reuschel	.05
195 Roger Clemens	1.60
196 Dave Concepcion	.05
197 Al Newman	.05
198 Brook Jacoby	.05
199 Mookie Wilson	.05
200 Don Mattingly	1.60
201 Dick Schofield	.05
202 Mark Gubicza	.05
203 Gary Gaetti	.05
204 Dan Pasqua	.05
205 Andre Dawson	.35
206 Chris Speier	.05
207 Kent Tekulve	.05
208 Rod Scurry	.05
209 Scott Bailes	.05
210 Rickey Henderson	1.00
211 Harold Baines	.05
212 Tony Armas	.05
213 Kent Hrbek	.05
214 Darrin Jackson	.05
215 George Brett	1.60
216 Rafael Santana	.05
217 Andy Allanson	.05
218 Brett Butler	.05
219 Steve Jeltz	.05
220 Jay Buhner	.05
221 Bo Jackson	.15
222 Angel Salazar	.05
223 Kirk McCaskill	.05
224 Steve Lyons	.05
225 Bert Blyleven	.05
226 Scott Bradley	.05
227 Bob Melvin	.05
228 Ron Kittle	.05
229 Phil Bradley	.05
230 Tommy John	.05
231 Greg Walker	.05
232 Juan Berenguer	.05
233 Pat Tabler	.05
234 Terry Clark RC	.05
235 Rafael Palmeiro	.75
236 Paul Zuvella	.05
237 Willie Randolph	.05
238 Bruce Fields	.05
239 Mike Aldrete	.05
240 Lance Parrish	.05
241 Greg Maddux	1.50
242 John Moses	.05
243 Melido Perez	.05
244 Willie Wilson	.05
245 Mark McLemore	.05
246 Von Hayes	.05
247 Matt Williams	.05
248 John Candelaria	.05
249 Harold Reynolds	.05
250 Greg Swindell	.05

No.	Player	Price
251	Juan Agosto	.05
252	Mike Felder	.05
253	Vince Coleman	.05
254	Larry Sheets	.05
255	George Bell	.05
256	Terry Steinbach	.05
257	Jack Armstrong RC	.05
258	Dickie Thon	.05
259	Ray Knight	.05
260	Darryl Strawberry	.05
261	Doug Sisk	.05
262	Alex Trevino	.05
263	Jeff Leonard	.05
264	Tom Henke	.05
265	Ozzie Smith	1.50
266	Dave Bergman	.05
267	Tony Phillips	.05
268	Mark Davis	.05
269	Kevin Elster	.05
270	Barry Larkin	.05
271	Manny Lee	.05
272	Tom Brunansky	.05
273	Craig Biggio	.05
274	Jim Gantner	.05
275	Eddie Murray	1.00
276	Jeff Reed	.05
277	Tim Teufel	.05
278	Rick Honeycutt	.05
279	Guillermo Hernandez	.05
280	John Kruk	.05
281	Luis Alicea RC	.15
282	Jim Clancy	.05
283	Billy Ripken	.05
284	Craig Reynolds	.05
285	Robin Yount	1.00
286	Jimmy Jones	.05
287	Ron Oester	.05
288	Terry Leach	.05
289	Dennis Eckersley	.75
290	Alan Trammell	.05
291	Jimmy Key	.05
292	Chris Bosio	.05
293	Jose DeLeon	.04
294	Jim Traber	.05
295	Mike Scott	.05
296	Roger McDowell	.05
297	Garry Templeton	.05
298	Doyle Alexander	.05
299	Nick Esasky	.05
300	Mark McGwire	1.75
301	Darryl Hamilton RC	.05
302	Dave Smith	.05
303	Rick Sutcliffe	.05
304	Dave Stapleton	.05
305	Alan Ashby	.05
306	Pedro Guerrero	.05
307	Ron Guidry	.05
308	Steve Farr	.05
309	Curt Ford	.05
310	Claudell Washington	.05
311	Tom Prince	.05
312	Chad Kreuter RC	.15
313	Ken Oberkfell	.05
314	Jerry Browne	.05
315	R.J. Reynolds	.05
316	Scott Bankhead	.05
317	Milt Thompson	.05
318	Mario Diaz	.05
319	Bruce Ruffin	.05
320	Dave Valle	.05
321a	Gary Varsho RC (Batting righty on card back, photo actually Mike Bielecki.)	.05
321b	Gary Varsho RC (Batting lefty on card back, correct photo.)	.05
322	Paul Mirabella	.05
323	Chuck Jackson	.05
324	Drew Hall	.05
325	Don August	.05
326	Israel Sanchez RC	.05
327	Denny Walling	.05
328	Joel Skinner	.05
329	Danny Tartabull	.05
330	Tony Pena	.05
331	Jim Sundberg	.05
332	Jeff Robinson	.05
333	Odibbe McDowell	.05
334	Jose Lind	.05
335	Paul Kilgus	.05
336	Juan Samuel	.05
337	Mike Campbell	.05
338	Mike Maddux	.05
339	Darnell Coles	.05
340	Bob Dernier	.05
341	Rafael Ramirez	.05
342	Scott Sanderson	.05
343	B.J. Surhoff	.05
344	Billy Hatcher	.05
345	Pat Perry	.05
346	Jack Clark	.05
347	Gary Thurman	.05
348	Timmy Jones RC	.05
349	Dave Winfield	1.00
350	Frank White	.05
351	Dave Collins	.05
352	Jack Morris	.05
353	Eric Plunk	.05
354	Leon Durham	.05
355	Ivan DeJesus	.05
356	Brian Holman RC	.05
357a	Dale Murphy (Reversed negative.)	25.00
357b	Dale Murphy (Corrected)	.25
358	Mark Portugal	.05
359	Andy McGaffigan	.05
360	Tom Glavine	.25
361	Keith Moreland	.05
362	Todd Stottlemyre	.05
363	Dave Leiper	.05
364	Cecil Fielder	.05
365	Carmelo Martinez	.05
366	Dwight Evans	.05
367	Kevin McReynolds	.05
368	Rich Gedman	.05
369	Len Dykstra	.05
370	Jody Reed	.05
371	Jose Canseco	.60
372	Rob Murphy	.05
373	Mike Henneman	.05
374	Walt Weiss	.05
375	Rob Dibble RC	.05
376	Kirby Puckett	1.50
377	Denny Martinez	.05
378	Ron Gant	.05
379	Brian Harper	.05
380	Nelson Santovenia RC	.05
381	Lloyd Moseby	.05
382	Lance McCullers	.05
383	Dave Stieb	.05
384	Tony Gwynn	1.50
385	Mike Flanagan	.05
386	Bob Ojeda	.05
387	Bruce Hurst	.05
388	Dave Magadan	.05
389	Wade Boggs	1.50
390	Gary Carter	1.00
391	Frank Tanana	.05
392	Curt Young	.05
393	Jeff Treadway	.05
394	Darrell Evans	.05
395	Glenn Hubbard	.05
396	Chuck Cary	.05
397	Frank Viola	.05
398	Jeff Parrett	.05
399	Terry Blocker RC	.05
400	Dan Gladden	.05
401	Louie Meadows RC	.05
402	Tim Raines	.05
403	Joey Meyer	.05
404	Larry Andersen	.05
405	Rex Hudler	.05
406	Mike Schmidt	1.60
407	John Franco	.05
408	Brady Anderson	.05
409	Don Carman	.05
410	Eric Davis	.05
411	Bob Stanley	.05
412	Pete Smith	.05
413	Jim Rice	.25
414	Bruce Sutter	.75
415	Dennis "Oil Can" Boyd	.05
416	Ruben Sierra	.05
417	Mike LaValliere	.05
418	Steve Buechele	.05
419	Gary Redus	.05
420	Scott Fletcher	.05
421	Dale Sveum	.05
422	Bob Knepper	.05
423	Luis Rivera	.05
424	Ted Higuera	.05
425	Kevin Bass	.05
426	Ken Gerhart	.05
427	Shane Rawley	.05
428	Paul O'Neill	.05
429	Joe Orsulak	.05
430	Jackie Gutierrez	.05
431	Gerald Perry	.05
432	Mike Greenwell	.05
433	Jerry Royster	.05
434	Ellis Burks	.05
435	Ed Olwine	.05
436	Dave Rucker	.05
437	Charlie Hough	.05
438	Bob Walk	.05
439	Bob Brower	.05
440	Barry Bonds	2.00
441	Tom Foley	.05
442	Rob Deer	.05
443	Glenn Davis	.05
444	Dave Martinez	.05
445	Bill Wegman	.05
446	Lloyd McClendon	.05
447	Dave Schmidt	.05
448	Darren Daulton	.05
449	Frank Williams	.05
450	Don Aase	.05
451	Lou Whitaker	.05
452	Goose Gossage	.05
453	Ed Whitson	.05
454	Jim Walewander	.05
455	Damon Berryhill	.05
456	Tim Burke	.05
457	Barry Jones	.05
458	Joel Youngblood	.05
459	Floyd Youmans	.05
460	Mark Salas	.05
461	Jeff Russell	.05
462	Darrell Miller	.05
463	Jeff Kunkel	.05
464	Sherman Corbett RC	.05
465	Curtis Wilkerson	.05
466	Bud Black	.05
467	Cal Ripken, Jr.	2.00
468	John Farrell	.05
469	Terry Kennedy	.05
470	Tom Candiotti	.05
471	Roberto Alomar	.20
472	Jeff Robinson	.05
473	Vance Law	.05
474	Randy Ready	.05
475	Walt Terrell	.05
476	Kelly Downs	.05
477	Johnny Paredes RC	.05
478	Shawn Hillegas	.05
479	Bob Brenly	.05
480	Otis Nixon	.05
481	Johnny Ray	.05
482	Geno Petralli	.05
483	Stu Cliburn	.05
484	Pete Incaviglia	.05
485	Brian Downing	.05
486	Jeff Stone	.05
487	Carmen Castillo	.05
488	Tom Niedenfuer	.05
489	Jay Bell	.05
490	Rick Schu	.05
491	Jeff Pico RC	.05
492	Mark Parent RC	.05
493	Eric King	.05
494	Al Nipper	.05
495	Andy Hawkins	.05
496	Daryl Boston	.05
497	Ernie Riles	.05
498	Pascual Perez	.05
499	Bill Long	.05
500	Kirt Manwaring	.05
501	Chuck Crim	.05
502	Candy Maldonado	.05
503	Dennis Lamp	.05
504	Glenn Braggs	.05
505	Joe Price	.05
506	Ken Williams	.05
507	Bill Pecota	.05
508	Rey Quinones	.05
509	Jeff Bittiger RC	.05
510	Kevin Seitzer	.05
511	Steve Bedrosian	.05
512	Todd Worrell	.05
513	Chris James	.05
514	Jose Oquendo	.05
515	David Palmer	.05
516	John Smiley	.05
517	Dave Clark	.05
518	Mike Dunne	.05
519	Ron Washington	.05
520	Bob Kipper	.05
521	Lee Smith	.05
522	Juan Castillo	.05
523	Don Robinson	.05
524	Kevin Romine	.05
525	Paul Molitor	1.00
526	Mark Langston	.05
527	Donnie Hill	.05
528	Larry Owen	.05
529	Jerry Reed	.05
530	Jack McDowell	.05
531	Greg Mathews	.05
532	John Russell	.05
533	Dan Quisenberry	.05
534	Greg Gross	.05
535	Danny Cox	.05
536	Terry Francona	.05
537	Andy Van Slyke	.05
538	Mel Hall	.05
539	Jim Gott	.05
540	Doug Jones	.05
541	Criag Lefferts	.05
542	Mike Boddicker	.05
543	Greg Brock	.05
544	Atlee Hammaker	.05
545	Tom Bolton	.05
546	Mike Macfarlane RC	.25
547	Rich Renteria RC	.05
548	John Davis	.05
549	Floyd Bannister	.05
550	Mickey Brantley	.05
551	Duane Ward	.05
552	Dan Petry	.05
553	Mickey Tettleton	.05
554	Rick Leach	.05
555	Mike Witt	.05
556	Sid Bream	.05
557	Bobby Witt	.05
558	Tommy Herr	.05
559	Randy Milligan	.05
560	Jose Cecena RC	.05
561	Mackey Sasser	.05
562	Carney Lansford	.05
563	Rick Aguilera	.05
564	Ron Hassey	.05
565	Dwight Gooden	.05
566	Paul Assenmacher	.05
567	Neil Allen	.05
568	Jim Morrison	.05
569	Mike Pagliarulo	.05
570	Ted Simmons	.05
571	Mark Thurmond	.05
572	Fred McGriff	.05
573	Wally Joyner	.05
574	Jose Bautista RC	.05
575	Kelly Gruber	.05
576	Cecilio Guante	.05
577	Mark Davidson	.05
578	Bobby Bonilla	.05
579	Mike Stanley	.05
580	Gene Larkin	.05
581	Stan Javier	.05
582	Howard Johnson	.05
583a	Mike Gallego (Photo on card back reversed.)	.75
583b	Mike Gallego (Correct photo.)	.05
584	David Cone	.05
585	Doug Jennings RC	.05
586	Charlie Hudson	.05
587	Dion James	.05
588	Al Leiter	.05
589	Charlie Puleo	.05
590	Roberto Kelly	.05
591	Thad Bosley	.05
592	Pete Stanicek	.05
593	Pat Borders RC	.25
594	Bryan Harvey RC	.05
595	Jeff Ballard	.05
596	Jeff Reardon	.05
597	Doug Drabek	.05
598	Edwin Correa	.05
599	Keith Atherton	.05
600	Dave LaPoint	.05
601	Don Baylor	.05
602	Tom Pagnozzi	.05
603	Tim Flannery	.05
604	Gene Walter	.05
605	Dave Parker	.05
606	Mike Diaz	.05
607	Chris Gwynn	.05
608	Odell Jones	.05
609	Carlton Fisk	1.00
610	Jay Howell	.05
611	Tim Crews	.05
612	Keith Hernandez	.05
613	Willie Fraser	.05
614	Jim Eppard	.05
615	Jeff Hamilton	.05
616	Kurt Stillwell	.05
617	Tom Browning	.05
618	Jeff Montgomery	.10
619	Jose Rijo	.05
620	Jamie Quirk	.05
621	Willie McGee	.05
622	Mark Grant	.05
623	Bill Swift	.05
624	Orlando Mercado	.05
625	John Costello RC	.05
626	Jose Gonzalez	.05
627a	Bill Schroeder (Putting on shin guards on card back, photo actually Ronn Reynolds.)	.75
627b	Bill Schroeder (Arms crossed on card back, correct photo.)	.05
628a	Fred Manrique (Throwing on card back, photo actually Ozzie Guillen.)	.75
628b	Fred Manrique (Batting on card back, correct photo.)	.05
629	Ricky Horton	.05
630	Dan Plesac	.05
631	Alfredo Griffin	.05
632	Chuck Finley	.05
633	Kirk Gibson	.05
634	Randy Myers	.05
635	Greg Minton	.05
636	Herm Winningham	.05
637	Charlie Leibrandt	.05
638	Tim Birtsas	.05
639	Bill Buckner	.05
640	Danny Jackson	.05
641	Greg Booker	.05
642	Jim Presley	.05
643	Gene Nelson	.05
644	Rod Booker	.05
645	Dennis Rasmussen	.05
646	Juan Nieves	.05
647	Bobby Thigpen	.05
648	Tim Belcher	.05
649	Mike Young	.05
650	Ivan Calderon	.05
651	Oswaldo Peraza RC	.05
652a	Pat Sheridan (No position on front.)	8.00
652b	Pat Sheridan (Position on front.)	.05
653	Mike Morgan	.05
654	Mike Heath	.05
655	Jay Tibbs	.05
656	Fernando Valenzuela	.05
657	Lee Mazzilli	.05
658	Frank Viola	.05
659	Jose Canseco	.60
660	Walt Weiss	.05
661	Orel Hershiser	.05
662	Kirk Gibson	.05
663	Chris Sabo	.05
664	Dennis Eckersley	.75
665	Orel Hershiser	.05
666	Kirk Gibson	.05
667	Orel Hershiser	.05
668	Wally Joyner (TC)	.05
669	Nolan Ryan (TC)	1.00
670	Jose Canseco (TC)	.30
671	Fred McGriff (TC)	.05
672	Dale Murphy (TC)	.20
673	Paul Molitor (TC)	.50
674	Ozzie Smith (TC)	.75
675	Ryne Sandberg (TC)	.40
676	Kirk Gibson (TC)	.05
677	Andres Galarraga (TC)	.05
678	Will Clark (TC)	.05
679	Cory Snyder (TC)	.05
680	Alvin Davis (TC)	.05
681	Darryl Strawberry (TC)	.05
682	Cal Ripken, Jr. (TC)	1.00
683	Tony Gwynn (TC)	.40
684	Mike Schmidt (TC)	.85
685	Andy Van Slyke (TC)	.05
686	Ruben Sierra (TC)	.05
687	Wade Boggs (TC)	.40
688	Eric Davis (TC)	.05
689	George Brett (TC)	.85
690	Alan Trammell (TC)	.05
691	Frank Viola (TC)	.05
692	Harold Baines (TC)	.05
693	Don Mattingly (TC)	.85
694	Checklist 1-100	.05
695	Checklist 101-200	.05
696	Checklist 201-300	.05
697	Checklist 301-400	.05
698	Checklist 401-500	.05
699	Checklist 501-600	.05
700	Checklist 601-700	.05
701	Checklist 701-800	.05
702	Jessie Barfield	.05
703	Walt Terrell	.05
704	Dickie Thon	.05
705	Al Leiter	.05
706	Dave LaPoint	.05
707	Charlie Hayes RC	.05
708	Andy Hawkins	.05
709	Mickey Hatcher	.05
710	Lance McCullers	.05
711	Ron Kittle	.05
712	Bert Blyleven	.05
713	Rick Dempsey	.05
714	Ken Williams	.05
715	Steve Rosenberg RC	.05
716	Joe Skalski RC	.05
717	Spike Owen	.05
718	Todd Burns	.05
719	Kevin Gross	.05
720	Tommy Herr	.05
721	Rob Ducey	.05
722	Gary Green RC	.05
723	Gregg Olson RC	.10
724	Greg Harris RC	.05
725	Craig Worthington RC	.05
726	Tom Howard RC	.05
727	Dale Mohorcic	.05
728	Rich Yett	.05
729	Mel Hall	.05
730	Floyd Youmans	.05
731	Lonnie Smith	.05
732	Wally Backman	.05
733	Trevor Wilson	.05
734	Jose Alvarez	.05
735	Bob Milacki RC	.05
736	Tom Gordon RC	.50
737	Wally Whitehurst RC	.05
738	Mike Aldrete	.05
739	Keith Miller	.05
740	Randy Milligan	.05
741	Jeff Parrett	.05
742	Steve Finley RC	.75
743	Junior Felix RC	.05
744	Pete Harnisch RC	.25
745	Bill Spiers RC	.05
746	Hensley Meulens RC	.05
747	Juan Bell	.05
748	Steve Sax	.05
749	Phil Bradley	.05
750	Rey Quinones	.05
751	Tommy Gregg RC	.05
752	Kevin Brown RC	.25
753	Derek Lilliquist RC	.05
754	Todd Zeile RC	.75
755	Jim Abbott	.05
756	Ozzie Canseco RC	.05
757	Nick Esasky	.05
758	Mike Moore	.05
759	Rob Murphy	.05
760	Rick Mahler	.05
761	Fred Lynn	.05
762	Kevin Blankenship RC	.05
763	Eddie Murray	1.00
764	Steve Searcy RC	.05
765	Jerome Walton RC	.05
766	Erik Hanson RC	.05
767	Bob Boone	.05
768	Edgar Martinez RC	.05
769	Jose DeJesus RC	.05
770	Greg Briley RC	.05
771	Steve Peters RC	.05
772	Rafael Palmeiro	.75
773	Jack Clark	.05
774	Nolan Ryan	2.00
775	Lance Parrish	.05
776	Joe Girardi RC	.30
777	Willie Randolph	.05
778	Mitch Williams	.05
779	Dennis Cook RC	.05
780	Dwight Smith RC	.05
781	Lenny Harris RC	.10
782	Torey Lovullo RC	.05
783	Norm Charlton RC	.15
784	Chris Brown	.05
785	Todd Benzinger	.05
786	Shane Rawley	.05
787	Omar Vizquel RC	2.00
788	LaVel Freeman RC	.05
789	Jeffrey Leonard	.05
790	Eddie Williams RC	.05
791	Jamie Moyer	.05
792	Bruce Hurst	.05
793	Julio Franco	.05
794	Claudell Washington	.05
795	Jody Davis	.05
796	Odibbe McDowell	.05
797	Paul Kilgus	.05
798	Tracy Jones	.05
799	Steve Wilson RC	.05
800	Pete O'Brien	.05

Tom Gordon

outs. The cards are similar in design to the 1989 issue. The high-number series (701-800) was released as a boxed set, in factory sets and in foil packs at mid-season. Cards #101-199 can be found either with or without the copyright line on back; no premium attaches to either.

	NM/M
Unopened Factory Set (800):	20.00
Complete Set (800):	15.00
Complete Low Set (700):	12.00
Complete High Set (100):	5.00
Common Player:	.05
Low or High Foil Pack (15):	.50
Low or High Foil Box (36):	12.00

No.	Player	Price
1	Star Rookie Checklist	.05
2	Randy Nosek RC	.05
3	Tom Drees RC	.05
4	Curt Young	.05
5	Angels checklist (Devon White)	.05
6	Luis Salazar	.05
7	Phillies checklist (Von Hayes)	.05
8	Jose Bautista	.05
9	Marquis Grissom RC	.50
10	Dodgers checklist (Orel Hershiser)	.05
11	Rick Aguilera	.05
12	Padres checklist (Benito Santiago)	.05
13	Deion Sanders	.10
14	Marvell Wynne	.05
15	David West	.05
16	Pirates checklist (Bobby Bonilla)	.05
17	Sammy Sosa RC	5.00
18	Yankees checklist (Steve Sax)	.05
19	Jack Howell	.05
20	Mike Schmidt Retires (Mike Schmidt)	.75
21	Robin Ventura	.05
22	Brian Meyer RC	.05
23	Blaine Beatty RC	.05
24	Mariners checklist (Ken Griffey Jr.)	.50
25	Greg Vaughn	.05
26	Xavier Hernandez RC	.05
27	Jason Grimsley RC	.05
28	Eric Anthony RC	.05
29	Expos checklist (Tim Raines)	.05
30	David Wells	.05
31	Hal Morris RC	.05
32	Royals checklist (Bo Jackson)	.10
33	Kelly Mann RC	.05
34	Nolan Ryan 5000 Strikeouts (Nolan Ryan)	1.00
35	Scott Service RC	.05
36	Athletics checklist (Mark McGwire)	.50
37	Tino Martinez	.05
38	Chili Davis	.05
39	Scott Sanderson	.05
40	Giants checklist (Kevin Mitchell)	.05
41	Tigers checklist (Lou Whitaker)	.05
42	Scott Coolbaugh RC	.05
43	Jose Cano RC	.05
44	Jose Vizcaino RC	.10
45	Bob Hamelin RC	.05
46	Jose Offerman RC	.15
47	Kevin Blankenship	.05
48	Twins checklist (Kirby Puckett)	.40
49	Tommy Greene RC	.05
50	N.L. Top Vote Getter (Will Clark)	.05
51	Rob Nelson RC	.05
52	Chris Hammond RC	.15
53	Indians checklist (Joe Carter)	.05
54a	Ben McDonald RC (Orioles Logo)	1.00
54b	Ben McDonald RC (Star Rookie logo)	.25
55	Andy Benes	.05
56	John Olerud RC	1.00
57	Red Sox checklist (Roger Clemens)	.45
58	Tony Armas	

1990 Upper Deck

Following the success of its first issue, Upper Deck released another 800-card set in 1990. The cards feature full-color photos on both sides in the standard 2-1/2" x 3-1/2" format. The artwork of Vernon Wells Sr. is featured on the front of all team checklist cards. The 1990 set also introduces two new Wells illustrations - a tribute to Mike Schmidt upon his retirement and one commemorating Nolan Ryan's 5,000 career strike-

#	Player	Price
59	George Canale RC	.05
60a	Orioles checklist (Mickey Tettleton) (#683 Jamie Weston)	1.00
60b	Orioles checklist (Mickey Tettleton) (#683 Mickey Weston)	
61	Mike Stanton RC	.05
62	Mets checklist (Dwight Gooden)	
63	Kent Mercker RC	.10
64	Francisco Cabrera RC	
65	Steve Avery RC	
66	Jose Canseco	.35
67	Matt Merullo RC	.05
68	Cardinals checklist (Vince Coleman)	.05
69	Ron Karkovice	.05
70	Kevin Maas RC	.05
71	Dennis Cook	.05
72	Juan Gonzalez RC	2.00
73	Cubs checklist (Andre Dawson)	.10
74	Dean Palmer RC	.25
75	A.L. Top Vote Getter (Bo Jackson)	.10
76	Rob Richie RC	.05
77	Bobby Rose RC	.05
78	Brian DuBois RC	.05
79	White Sox checklist (Ozzie Guillen)	.05
80	Gene Nelson	.05
81	Bob McClure	.05
82	Rangers checklist (Julio Franco)	.05
83	Greg Minton	.05
84	Braves checklist (John Smoltz)	.05
85	Willie Fraser	.05
86	Neal Heaton	.05
87	Kevin Tapani RC	.05
88	Astros Checklist (Mike Scott)	.05
89a	Jim Gott (Incorrect photo.)	1.00
89b	Jim Gott (Correct photo.)	.05
90	Lance Johnson	.05
91	Brewers checklist (Robin Yount)	.35
92	Jeff Parrett	.05
93	Julio Machado RC	.05
94	Ron Jones	.05
95	Blue Jays checklist (George Bell)	.05
96	Jerry Reuss	.05
97	Brian Fisher	.05
98	Kevin Ritz RC	.05
99	Reds Checklist (Barry Larkin)	.05
100	Checklist 1-100	.05
101	Gerald Perry	.05
102	Kevin Appier	.05
103	Julio Franco	.05
104	Craig Biggio	.05
105	Bo Jackson	.10
106	Junior Felix RC	.05
107	Mike Harkey RC	.05
108	Fred McGriff	.05
109	Rick Sutcliffe	.05
110	Pete O'Brien	.05
111	Kelly Gruber	.05
112	Pat Borders	.05
113	Dwight Evans	.05
114	Dwight Gooden	.05
115	Kevin Batiste RC	.05
116	Eric Davis	.05
117	Kevin Mitchell	.05
118	Ron Oester	.05
119	Brett Butler	.05
120	Danny Jackson	.05
121	Tommy Gregg	.05
122	Ken Caminiti	.05
123	Kevin Brown	.05
124	George Brett	.85
125	Mike Scott	.05
126	Cory Snyder	.05
127	George Bell	.05
128	Mark Grace	.05
129	Devon White	.05
130	Tony Fernandez	.05
131	Don Aase	.05
132	Rance Mulliniks	.05
133	Marty Barrett	.05
134	Nelson Liriano	.05
135	Mark Carreon RC	.05
136	Candy Maldonado	.05
137	Tim Birtsas	.05
138	Tom Brookens	.05
139	John Franco	.05
140	Mike LaCoss	.05
141	Jeff Treadway	.05
142	Pat Tabler	.05
143	Darrell Evans	.05
144	Rafael Ramirez	.05
145	Oddibe McDowell	.05
146	Brian Downing	.05
147	Curtis Wilkerson	.05
148	Ernie Whitt	.05
149	Bill Schroeder	.05
150	Domingo Ramos	.05
151	Rick Honeycutt	.05
152	Don Slaught	.05
153	Mitch Webster	.05
154	Tony Phillips	.05
155	Paul Kilgus	.05
156	Ken Griffey Jr.	1.50
157	Gary Sheffield	.35
158	Wally Backman	.05
159	B.J. Surhoff	.05
160	Louie Meadows	.05
161	Paul O'Neill	.05
162	Jeff McKnight RC	.05
163	Alvaro Espinoza RC	.05
164	Scott Scudder RC	.05
165	Jeff Reed	.05
166	Gregg Jefferies	.05
167	Barry Larkin	.05
168	Gary Carter	.60
169	Robby Thompson	.05
170	Rolando Roomes	.05
171	Mark McGwire	1.50
172	Steve Sax	.05
173	Mark Williamson	.05
174	Mitch Williams	.05
175	Brian Holton	.05
176	Rob Deer	.05
177	Tim Raines	.05
178	Mike Felder	.05
179	Harold Reynolds	.05
180	Terry Francona	.05
181	Chris Sabo	.05
182	Darryl Strawberry	.05
183	Willie Randolph	.05
184	Billy Ripken	.05
185	Mackey Sasser	.05
186	Todd Benzinger	.05
187	Kevin Elster	.05
188	Jose Uribe	.05
189	Tom Browning	.05
190	Keith Miller	.05
191	Don Mattingly	.85
192	Dave Parker	.05
193	Roberto Kelly	.05
194	Phil Bradley	.05
195	Ron Hassey	.05
196	Gerald Young	.05
197	Hubie Brooks	.05
198	Bill Doran	.05
199	Al Newman	.05
200	Checklist 101-200	.05
201	Terry Puhl	.05
202	Frank DiPino	.05
203	Jim Clancy	.05
204	Bob Ojeda	.05
205	Alex Trevino	.05
206	Dave Henderson	.05
207	Henry Cotto	.05
208	Rafael Belliard	.05
209	Stan Javier	.05
210	Jerry Reed	.05
211	Doug Dascenzo	.05
212	Andres Thomas	.05
213	Greg Maddux	.75
214	Mike Schooler	.05
215	Lonnie Smith	.05
216	Jose Rijo	.05
217	Greg Gagne	.05
218	Jim Gantner	.05
219	Allan Anderson	.05
220	Rick Mahler	.05
221	Jim Deshaies	.05
222	Keith Hernandez	.05
223	Vince Coleman	.05
224	David Cone	.05
225	Ozzie Smith	.75
226	Matt Nokes	.05
227	Barry Bonds	2.00
228	Felix Jose	.05
229	Dennis Powell	.05
230	Mike Gallego	.05
231	Shawon Dunston	.05
232	Ron Gant	.05
233	Omar Vizquel	.05
234	Derek Lilliquist	.05
235	Erik Hanson	.05
236	Kirby Puckett	.75
237	Bill Spiers	.05
238	Dan Gladden	.05
239	Bryan Clutterbuck RC	.05
240	John Moses	.05
241	Ron Darling	.05
242	Joe Magrane	.05
243	Dave Magadan	.05
244	Pedro Guerrero	.05
245	Glenn Davis	.05
246	Terry Steinbach	.05
247	Fred Lynn	.05
248	Gary Redus	.05
249	Kenny Williams	.05
250	Sid Bream	.05
251	Bob Welch	.05
252	Bill Buckner	.05
253	Carney Lansford	.05
254	Paul Molitor	.60
255	Jose DeJesus	.05
256	Orel Hershiser	.05
257	Tom Brunansky	.05
258	Mike Davis	.05
259	Jeff Ballard	.05
260	Scott Terry	.05
261	Sid Fernandez	.05
262	Mike Marshall	.05
263	Howard Johnson	.05
264	Kirk Gibson	.05
265	Kevin McReynolds	.05
266	Cal Ripken, Jr.	2.00
267	Ozzie Guillen	.05
268	Jim Traber	.05
269	Bobby Thigpen	.05
270	Joe Orsulak	.05
271	Bob Boone	.05
272	Dave Stewart	.05
273	Tim Wallach	.05
274	Luis Aquino	.05
275	Mike Moore	.05
276	Tony Pena	.05
277	Eddie Murray	.60
278	Milt Thompson	.05
279	Alejandro Pena	.05
280	Ken Dayley	.05
281	Carmen Castillo	.05
282	Tom Henke	.05
283	Mickey Hatcher	.05
284	Roy Smith	.05
285	Manny Lee	.05
286	Dan Pasqua	.05
287	Larry Sheets	.05
288	Garry Templeton	.05
289	Eddie Williams	.05
290	Brady Anderson	.05
291	Spike Owen	.05
292	Storm Davis	.05
293	Chris Bosio	.05
294	Jim Eisenreich	.05
295	Don August	.05
296	Jeff Hamilton	.05
297	Mickey Tettleton	.05
298	Mike Scioscia	.05
299	Kevin Hickey RC	.05
300	Checklist 201-300	.05
301	Shawn Abner	.05
302	Kevin Bass	.05
303	Bip Roberts RC	.05
304	Joe Girardi	.05
305	Danny Darwin	.05
306	Mike Heath	.05
307	Mike Macfarlane	.05
308	Ed Whitson	.05
309	Tracy Jones	.05
310	Scott Fletcher	.05
311	Darnell Coles	.05
312	Mike Brumley	.05
313	Bill Swift	.05
314	Charlie Hough	.05
315	Jim Presley	.05
316	Luis Polonia	.05
317	Mike Morgan	.05
318	Lee Guetterman	.05
319	Jose Oquendo	.05
320	Wayne Tolleson	.05
321	Jody Reed	.05
322	Damon Berryhill	.05
323	Roger Clemens	.85
324	Ryne Sandberg	.75
325	Benito Santiago	.05
326	Bret Saberhagen	.05
327	Lou Whitaker	.05
328	Dave Gallagher	.05
329	Mike Pagliarulo	.05
330	Doyle Alexander	.05
331	Jeffrey Leonard	.05
332	Torey Lovullo	.05
333	Pete Incaviglia	.05
334	Rickey Henderson	.60
335	Rafael Palmeiro	.50
336	Ken Hill RC	.05
337	Dave Winfield	.60
338	Alfredo Griffin	.05
339	Andy Hawkins	.05
340	Ted Power	.05
341	Steve Wilson	.05
342	Jack Clark	.05
343	Ellis Burks	.05
344	Tony Gwynn	.75
345	Jerome Walton	.05
346	Roberto Alomar	.20
347	Carlos Martinez RC	.05
348	Chet Lemon	.05
349	Willie Wilson	.05
350	Greg Walker	.05
351	Tom Bolton	.05
352	German Gonzalez RC	.05
353	Harold Baines	.05
354	Mike Greenwell	.05
355	Ruben Sierra	.05
356	Andres Galarraga	.05
357	Andre Dawson	.25
358	Jeff Brantley RC	.05
359	Mike Bielecki	.05
360	Ken Oberkfell	.05
361	Kurt Stillwell	.05
362	Brian Holman	.05
363	Kevin Seitzer	.05
364	Alvin Davis	.05
365	Tom Gordon	.05
366	Bobby Bonilla	.05
367	Carlton Fisk	.60
368	Steve Carter RC	.05
369	Joel Skinner	.05
370	John Cangelosi	.05
371	Cecil Espy	.05
372	Gary Wayne RC	.05
373	Jim Rice	.20
374	Mike Dyer RC	.05
375	Joe Carter	.05
376	Dwight Smith	.05
377	John Wetteland RC	.15
378	Ernie Riles	.05
379	Otis Nixon	.05
380	Vance Law	.05
381	Dave Bergman	.05
382	Frank White	.05
383	Scott Bradley	.05
384	Israel Sanchez	.05
385	Gary Pettis	.05
386	Donn Pall RC	.05
387	Ken Smiley	.05
388	Tom Candiotti	.05
389	Junior Ortiz	.05
390	Steve Lyons	.05
391	Brian Harper	.05
392	Fred Manrique	.05
393	Lee Smith	.05
394	Jeff Kunkel	.05
395	Claudell Washington	.05
396	John Tudor	.05
397	Terry Kennedy	.05
398	Lloyd McClendon	.05
399	Craig Lefferts	.05
400	Checklist 301-400	.05
401	Keith Moreland	.05
402	Rich Gedman	.05
403	Jeff Robinson	.05
404	Randy Ready	.05
405	Rick Cerone	.05
406	Jeff Blauser	.05
407	Larry Andersen	.05
408	Joe Boever	.05
409	Felix Fermin	.05
410	Glenn Wilson	.05
411	Rex Hudler	.05
412	Mark Grant	.05
413	Dennis Martinez	.05
414	Darrin Jackson	.05
415	Mike Aldrete	.05
416	Roger McDowell	.05
417	Jeff Reardon	.05
418	Darren Daulton	.05
419	Tim Laudner	.05
420	Don Carman	.05
421	Lloyd Moseby	.05
422	Doug Drabek	.05
423	Lenny Harris	.05
424	Jose Lind	.05
425	Dave Johnson RC	.05
426	Jerry Browne	.05
427	Eric Yelding RC	.05
428	Brad Komminsk	.05
429	Jody Davis	.05
430	Mariano Duncan RC	.05
431	Mark Davis	.05
432	Nelson Santovenia	.05
433	Bruce Hurst	.05
434	Jeff Huson RC	.05
435	Chris James	.05
436	Mark Guthrie RC	.05
437	Charlie Hayes RC	.05
438	Shane Rawley	.05
439	Dickie Thon	.05
440	Juan Berenguer	.05
441	Kevin Romine	.05
442	Bill Landrum	.05
443	Todd Frohwirth	.05
444	Craig Worthington	.05
445	Fernando Valenzuela	.05
446	Albert Belle	.05
447	Ed Whited RC	.05
448	Dave Smith	.05
449	Dave Clark	.05
450	Juan Agosto	.05
451	Dave Valle	.05
452	Kent Hrbek	.05
453	Von Hayes	.05
454	Gary Gaetti	.05
455	Greg Briley	.05
456	Glenn Braggs	.05
457	Kirt Manwaring	.05
458	Mel Hall	.05
459	Brook Jacoby	.05
460	Pat Sheridan	.05
461	Rob Murphy	.05
462	Jimmy Key	.05
463	Nick Esasky	.05
464	Rob Ducey	.05
465	Carlos Quintana	.05
466	Larry Walker RC	1.00
467	Todd Worrell	.05
468	Kevin Gross	.05
469	Terry Pendleton	.05
470	Dave Martinez	.05
471	Gene Larkin	.05
472	Len Dykstra	.05
473	Barry Lyons	.05
474	Terry Mulholland RC	.05
475	Chip Hale RC	.05
476	Jesse Barfield	.05
477	Dan Plesac	.05
478a	Scott Garrelts (Photo actually Bill Bathe.)	1.00
478b	Scott Garrelts (Correct photo.)	.05
479	Dave Righetti	.05
480	Gus Polidor RC	.05
481	Mookie Wilson	.05
482	Luis Rivera	.05
483	Mike Flanagan	.05
484	Dennis "Oil Can" Boyd	.05
485	John Cerutti	.05
486	John Costello	.05
487	Pascual Perez	.05
488	Tommy Herr	.05
489	Tom Foley	.05
490	Curt Ford	.05
491	Steve Lake	.05
492	Tim Teufel	.05
493	Randy Bush	.05
494	Mike Jackson	.05
495	Steve Jeltz	.05
496	Paul Gibson	.05
497	Steve Balboni	.05
498	Bud Black	.05
499	Dale Sveum	.05
500	Checklist 401-500	.05
501	Timmy Jones	.05
502	Mark Portugal	.05
503	Ivan Calderon	.05
504	Rick Rhoden	.05
505	Willie McGee	.05
506	Kirk McCaskill	.05
507	Dave LaPoint	.05
508	Jay Howell	.05
509	Johnny Ray	.05
510	Dave Anderson	.05
511	Chuck Crim	.05
512	Joe Hesketh	.05
513	Dennis Eckersley	.40
514	Greg Brock	.05
515	Tim Burke	.05
516	Frank Tanana	.05
517	Jay Bell	.05
518	Guillermo Hernandez	.05
519	Randy Kramer RC	.05
520	Charles Hudson	.05
521	Jim Corsi RC	.05
522	Steve Rosenberg	.05
523	Cris Carpenter	.05
524	Matt Winters RC	.05
525	Melido Perez	.05
526	Chris Gwynn RC	.05
527	Bert Blyleven	.05
528	Chuck Cary RC	.05
529	Daryl Boston	.05
530	Dale Mohorcic	.05
531	Geronimo Berroa RC	.05
532	Edgar Martinez	.05
533	Dale Murphy	.20
534	Jay Buhner	.05
535	John Smoltz	.05
536	Andy Van Slyke	.05
537	Mike Henneman RC	.05
538	Miguel Garcia RC	.05
539	Frank Williams RC	.05
540	R.J. Reynolds	.05
541	Shawn Hillegas RC	.05
542	Walt Weiss	.05
543	Greg Hibbard RC	.05
544	Nolan Ryan	2.00
545	Todd Zeile	.05
546	Hensley Meulens	.05
547	Tim Belcher RC	.05
548	Mike Witt	.05
549	Greg Cadaret RC	.05
550	Franklin Stubbs	.05
551	Tony Castillo RC	.05
552	Jeff Robinson	.05
553	Steve Olin RC	.05
554	Alan Trammell	.05
555	Wade Boggs	.75
556	Will Clark	.05
557	Jeff King	.05
558	Mike Fitzgerald	.05
559	Ken Howell RC	.05
560	Bob Kipper	.05
561	Scott Bankhead	.05
562a	Jeff Innis RC (Photo actually David West.)	1.00
562b	Jeff Innis RC (Correct photo.)	.05
563	Randy Johnson	.60
564	Wally Whitehurst RC	.05
565	Gene Harris RC	.05
566	Norm Charlton RC	.05
567	Robin Yount	.60
568	Joe Oliver RC	.05
569	Mark Parent	.05
570	John Farrell RC	.05
571	Tom Glavine	.20
572	Rod Nichols RC	.05
573	Jack Morris	.05
574	Greg Swindell RC	.05
575	Steve Searcy RC	.05
576	Ricky Jordan RC	.05
577	Matt Williams	.05
578	Mike LaValliere RC	.05
579	Bryn Smith	.05
580	Bruce Ruffin RC	.05
581	Randy Myers	.05
582	Rick Wrona RC	.05
583	Juan Samuel	.05
584	Les Lancaster RC	.05
585	Jeff Musselman	.05
586	Rob Dibble RC	.05
587	Eric Show	.05
588	Jesse Orosco	.05
589	Herm Winningham	.05
590	Andy Allanson	.05
591	Dion James	.05
592	Carmelo Martinez	.05
593	Luis Quinones RC	.05
594	Dennis Rasmussen RC	.05
595	Rich Yett	.05
596	Bob Walk RC	.05
597a	Andy McGaffigan (Player #48, photo actually Rich Thompson.)	.75
597b	Andy McGaffigan (Player #27, correct photo.)	.05
598	Billy Hatcher RC	.05
599	Bob Knepper	.05
600	Checklist 501-600	.05
601	Joey Cora RC	.05
602	Steve Finley RC	.20
603	Kal Daniels	.05
604	Gregg Olson	.05
605	Dave Steib	.05
606	Kenny Rogers RC	.05
607	Zane Smith	.05
608	Bob Geren RC	.05
609	Chad Kreuter	.05
610	Mike Smithson RC	.05
611	Jeff Wetherby RC	.05
612	Gary Mielke RC	.05
613	Pete Smith	.05
614	Jack Daugherty RC	.05
615	Lance McCullers	.05
616	Don Robinson RC	.05
617	Jose Guzman	.05
618	Steve Bedrosian RC	.05
619	Jamie Moyer	.05
620	Atlee Hammaker	.05
621	Rick Luecken RC	.05
622	Greg W. Harris RC	.05
623	Pete Harnisch	.05
624	Jerald Clark RC	.05
625	Jack McDowell	.05
626	Frank Viola	.05
627	Ted Higuera	.05
628	Marty Pevey RC	.05
629	Bill Wegman	.05
630	Eric Plunk RC	.05
631	Drew Hall	.05
632	Doug Jones RC	.05
633	Geno Petralli	.05
634	Jose Alvarez RC	.05
635	Bob Milacki	.05
636	Bobby Witt RC	.05
637	Trevor Wilson	.05
638	Jeff Russell RC	.05
639	Mike Krukow	.05
640	Rick Leach RC	.05
641	Dave Schmidt	.05
642	Terry Leach RC	.05
643	Calvin Schiraldi	.05
644	Bob Melvin RC	.05
645	Jim Abbott	.05
646	Jaime Navarro RC	.05
647	Mark Langston	.05
648	Juan Nieves RC	.05
649	Damaso Garcia	.05
650	Charlie O'Brien RC	.05
651	Eric King	.05
652	Mike Boddicker	.05
653	Duane Ward	.05
654	Bob Stanley	.05
655	Sandy Alomar, Jr.	.05
656	Danny Tartabull	.05
657	Randy McCament RC	.05
658	Charlie Leibrandt	.05
659	Dan Quisenberry	.05
660	Paul Assenmacher RC	.05
661	Walt Terrell	.05
662	Tim Leary	.05
663	Randy Milligan	.05
664	Bo Diaz RC	.05
665	Mark Lemke	.05
666	Jose Gonzalez	.05
667	Chuck Finley	.05
668	John Kruk	.05
669	Dick Schofield	.05
670	Tim Crews	.05
671	John Dopson	.05
672	John Orton RC	.05
673	Eric Hetzel RC	.05
674	Lance Parrish	.05
675	Ramon Martinez	.05
676	Mark Gubicza	.05
677	Greg Litton	.05
678	Greg Mathews	.05
679	Dave Dravecky	.05
680	Steve Farr RC	.05
681	Mike Devereaux	.05
682	Ken Griffey Sr.	.05
683a	Jamie Weston RC (First name incorrect.)	1.00
683b	Mickey Weston RC (Corrected)	.05
684	Jack Armstrong	.05
685	Steve Buechele	.05
686	Bryan Harvey	.05
687	Lance Blankenship	.05
688	Dante Bichette	.05
689	Todd Burns RC	.05
690	Dan Petry	.05
691	Kent Anderson RC	.05
692	Todd Stottlemyre	.05
693	Wally Joyner	.05
694	Mike Rochford RC	.05
695	Floyd Bannister	.05
696	Rick Reuschel	.05
697	Jose DeLeon RC	.05
698	Jeff Montgomery	.05
699	Kelly Downs	.05
700a	Checklist 601-700 (#683 Jamie Weston)	.05
700b	Checklist 601-700 (# 683 Mickey Weston)	.05
701	Jim Gott	.05
702	"Rookie Threats" (Delino DeShields, Larry Walker, Marquis Grissom)	.25
703	Alejandro Pena	.05
704	Willie Randolph	.05
705	Tim Leary	.05
706	Chuck McElroy RC	.05
707	Gerald Perry RC	.05
708	Tom Brunansky	.05
709	John Franco	.05
710	Mark Davis	.05
711	Dave Justice RC	1.50
712	Storm Davis	.05
713	Scott Ruskin RC	.05
714	Glenn Braggs	.05
715	Kevin Bearse RC	.05
716	Jose Nunez RC	.05
717	Tim Layana RC	.05
718	Greg Myers RC	.05
719	Pete O'Brien	.05
720	John Candelaria	.05
721	Craig Grebeck	.05
722	Shawn Boskie RC	.05
723	Jim Leyritz RC	.10
724	Bill Sampen RC	.05
725	Scott Radinsky RC	.05
726	Todd Hundley RC	.25
727	Scott Hemond RC	.05
728	Lenny Webster RC	.05
729	Jeff Reardon	.05

730	Mitch Webster	.05
731	Brian Bohanon **RC**	.05
732	Rick Parker **RC**	.05
733	Terry Shumpert **RC**	.05
734a	Nolan Ryan (300-win stripe on front)	1.50
734b	Nolan Ryan (No stripe.)	4.00
735	John Burkett	.05
736	Derrick May **RC**	.05
737	Carlos Baerga **RC**	.05
738	Greg Smith **RC**	.05
739	Joe Kraemer **RC**	.05
740	Scott Sanderson **RC**	.05
741	Hector Villanueva **RC**	.05
742	Mike Fetters **RC**	.05
743	Mark Gardner **RC**	.05
744	Mark Nokes **RC**	.05
745	Dave Winfield	.60
746	Delino DeShields **RC**	.15
747	Dann Howitt **RC**	.05
748	Tony Pena	.05
749	Dennis "Oil Can" Boyd	.05
750	Mike Benjamin **RC**	.05
751	Alex Cole **RC**	.05
752	Eric Gunderson **RC**	.05
753	Howard Farmer **RC**	.05
754	Joe Carter	.05
755	Ray Lankford **RC**	.25
756	Sandy Alomar, Jr.	.05
757	Alex Sanchez **RC**	.05
758	Nick Esasky	.05
759	Stan Belinda **RC**	.05
760	Jim Presley **RC**	.05
761	Gary DiSarcina **RC**	.05
762	Wayne Edwards **RC**	.05
763	Pat Combs **RC**	.05
764	Mickey Pina **RC**	.05
765	Wilson Alvarez **RC**	.25
766	Dave Parker	.05
767	Mike Blowers **RC**	.05
768	Tony Phillips	.05
769	Pascual Perez	.05
770	Gary Pettis	.05
771	Fred Lynn	.05
772	Mel Rojas **RC**	.10
773	David Segui **RC**	.25
774	Gary Carter	.60
775	Rafael Valdez **RC**	.05
776	Glenallen Hill **RC**	.05
777	Keith Hernandez	.05
778	Billy Hatcher	.05
779	Marty Clary **RC**	.05
780	Candy Maldonado **RC**	.05
781	Mike Marshall	.05
782	Billy Jo Robidoux **RC**	.05
783	Mark Langston	.05
784	Paul Sorrento **RC**	.05
785	Dave Hollins **RC**	.05
786	Cecil Fielder	.05
787	Matt Young	.05
788	Jeff Huson	.05
789	Lloyd Moseby	.05
790	Ron Kittle	.05
791	Hubie Brooks	.05
792	Craig Lefferts	.05
793	Kevin Bass	.05
794	Bryn Smith **RC**	.05
795	Juan Samuel	.05
796	Sam Horn	.05
797	Randy Myers	.05
798	Chris James **RC**	.05
799	Bill Gullickson	.05
800	Checklist 701-800	.05

Baseball Heroes Reggie Jackson

This Baseball Heroes set is devoted to Reggie Jackson. The cards, numbered 1-9, are the first in a continuing series of cards issued in subsequent years. An unnumbered cover card that says "Baseball Heroes" was also issued. The Jackson cards were randomly inserted in high number foil packs only. Jackson also autographed 2,500 numbered cards, which were randomly included in high number packs.

		NM/M
Complete Set (10):		5.00
Common Player:		.50
Autographed Card:		100.00
1	1969 Emerging Superstar (Reggie Jackson)	.50

2	1973 An MVP Year (Reggie Jackson)	.50
3	1977 "Mr. October" (Reggie Jackson)	.50
4	1978 Jackson vs. Welch (Reggie Jackson)	.50
5	1982 Under the Halo (Reggie Jackson)	.50
6	1984 500! (Reggie Jackson)	.50
7	1986 Moving Up the List (Reggie Jackson)	.50
8	1987 A Great Career Ends (Reggie Jackson)	.50
9	Heroes Checklist 1-9 (Reggie Jackson)	.50
----	Header Card	.50

1990 Upper Deck Black-Box Variations

It appears that card #702 in 1990 UD was originally intended to be Mike Witt, but that it was replaced by a "Rookie Threats" card picturing three Expos. At least a few examples of the Witt card, factory cancelled with a large black ink box on back, have made their way into the market, along with a #800 checklist card naming Witt as #702.

		NM/M
702	Mike Witt	450.00
800	Checklist 701-800	250.00

1991 Upper Deck

More than 110 rookies are included among the first 700 cards in the 1991 Upper Deck set. A 100-card high-number series was released in late summer. Cards feature top quality white stock and color photos on front and back. A nine-card "Baseball Heroes" bonus set honoring Nolan Ryan, is among the many insert specials in the '91 UD set. Others include a card of Chicago Bulls superstar Michael Jordan. Along with the Ryan bonus cards, 2,500 cards personally autographed and numbered by Ryan were randomly inserted. Upper Deck cards are packaged in tamper-proof foil packs. Each pack contains 15 cards and a 3-1/2" x 2-1/2" 3-D team logo hologram sticker.

	NM/M
Unopened Factory Set (800):	20.00
Complete Set (800):	10.00
Complete Low Series (700):	9.00
Complete High Series (100):	1.00
Common Player:	.05
Low or High Wax Pack (15):	.60
Low or High Wax Box (36):	13.50

1	Star Rookie Checklist	.05
2	Phil Plantier **RC**	.05
3	D.J. Dozier **RC**	.05
4	Dave Hansen **RC**	.05
5	Mo Vaughn **RC**	.10
6	Leo Gomez **RC**	.05
7	Scott Aldred **RC**	.05
8	Scott Chiamparino **RC**	.05

9	Lance Dickson **RC**	.05
10	Sean Berry **RC**	.05
11	Bernie Williams **RC**	.25
12	Brian Barnes **RC**	.05
13	Narciso Elvira **RC**	.05
14	Mike Gardiner **RC**	.05
15	Greg Colbrunn **RC**	.05
16	Bernard Gilkey **RC**	.05
17	Mark Lewis **RC**	.05
18	Mickey Morandini **RC**	.05
19	Charles Nagy **RC**	.05
20	Geronimo Pena **RC**	.05
21	Henry Rodriguez **RC**	.05
22	Scott Cooper **RC**	.05
23	Andujar Cedeno **RC**	.05
24	Eric Karros **RC**	.25
25	Steve Decker **RC**	.05
26	Kevin Belcher **RC**	.05
27	Jeff Conine **RC**	.25
28	Oakland Athletics Checklist (Dave Stewart)	.05
29	Chicago White Sox Checklist (Carlton Fisk)	.20
30	Texas Rangers Checklist (Rafael Palmeiro)	.20
31	California Angels Checklist (Chuck Finley)	.05
32	Seattle Mariners Checklist (Harold Reynolds)	.05
33	Kansas City Royals Checklist (Bret Saberhagen)	.05
34	Minnesota Twins Checklist (Gary Gaetti)	.05
35	Scott Leius	.05
36	Neal Heaton	.05
37	Terry Lee **RC**	.05
38	Gary Redus	.05
39	Barry Jones	.05
40	Chuck Knoblauch **RC**	.05
41	Larry Andersen	.05
42	Darryl Hamilton	.05
43	Boston Red Sox Checklist (Mike Greenwell)	.05
44	Toronto Blue Jays Checklist (Kelly Gruber)	.05
45	Detroit Tigers Checklist (Jack Morris)	.05
46	Cleveland Indians Checklist (Sandy Alomar Jr.)	.05
47	Baltimore Orioles Checklist (Gregg Olson)	.05
48	Milwaukee Brewers Checklist (Dave Parker)	.05
49	New York Yankees Checklist (Roberto Kelly)	.05
50	Top Prospect '91 checklist	.05
51	Kyle Abbott **RC** (Top Prospect)	.10
52	Jeff Juden **RC** (Top Prospect)	.05
53	Todd Van Poppel **RC** (Top Prospect)	.10
54	Steve Karsay **RC** (Top Prospect)	.10
55	Chipper Jones **RC** (Top Prospect)	6.00
56	Chris Johnson **RC** (Top Prospect)	.05
57	John Ericks **RC** (Top Prospect)	.05
58	Gary Scott **RC** (Top Prospect)	.05
59	Kiki Jones **RC** (Top Prospect)	.05
60	Wil Cordero **RC** (Top Prospect)	.05
61	Royce Clayton **RC** (Top Prospect)	.05
62	Tim Costo **RC** (Top Prospect)	.05
63	Roger Salkeld **RC** (Top Prospect)	.05
64	Brook Fordyce **RC** (Top Prospect)	.05
65	Mike Mussina **RC** (Top Prospect)	1.00
66	Dave Staton **RC** (Top Prospect)	.05
67	Mike Lieberthal **RC** (Top Prospect)	.50
68	Kurt Miller **RC** (Top Prospect)	.05
69	Dan Peltier **RC** (Top Prospect)	.05
70	Greg Blosser **RC** (Top Prospect)	.05
71	Reggie Sanders **RC** (Top Prospect)	.25
72	Brent Mayne **RC** (Top Prospect)	.05
73	Rico Brogna **RC** (Top Prospect)	.05
74	Willie Banks **RC** (Top Prospect)	.05
75	Len Brutcher **RC** (Top Prospect)	.05
76	Pat Kelly **RC** (Top Prospect)	.05
77	Cincinnati Reds Checklist (Chris Sabo)	.05
78	Los Angeles Dodgers Checklist (Ramon Martinez)	.05
79	San Francisco Giants Checklist (Matt Williams)	.05
80	San Diego Padres Checklist (Roberto Alomar)	.05

81	Houston Astros checklist (Glenn Davis)	.05
82	Atlanta Braves checklist (Ron Gant)	.05
83	"Fielder's Feat" (Cecil Fielder)	.05
84	Orlando Merced **RC**	.10
85	Domingo Ramos	.05
86	Tom Bolton	.05
87	Andres Santana **RC**	.05
88	John Dopson **RC**	.05
89	Kenny Williams	.05
90	Marty Barrett	.05
91	Tom Pagnozzi	.05
92	Carmelo Martinez	.05
93	"Save Master" (Bobby Thigpen)	.05
94	Pittsburgh Pirates Checklist (Barry Bonds)	.50
95	New York Mets Checklist (Gregg Jefferies)	.05
96	Montreal Expos Checklist (Tim Wallach)	.05
97	Philadelphia Phillies Checklist (Lenny Dykstra)	.05
98	St. Louis Cardinals Checklist (Pedro Guerrero)	.05
99	Chicago Cubs Checklist (Mark Grace)	.05
100	Checklist 1-100	.05
101	Kevin Elster	.05
102	Tom Brookens	.05
103	Mackey Sasser	.05
104	Felix Fermin **RC**	.05
105	Kevin McReynolds	.05
106	Dave Steib	.05
107	Jeffrey Leonard	.05
108	Dave Henderson	.05
109	Sid Bream	.05
110	Henry Cotto	.05
111	Shawon Dunston	.05
112	Mariano Duncan **RC**	.05
113	Joe Girardi	.05
114	Billy Hatcher	.05
115	Greg Maddux	.50
116	Jerry Browne **RC**	.05
117	Juan Samuel	.05
118	Steve Olin	.05
119	Alfredo Griffin	.05
120	Mitch Webster **RC**	.05
121	Joel Skinner	.05
122	Frank Viola	.05
123	Cory Snyder	.05
124	Howard Johnson	.05
125	Carlos Baerga	.05
126	Tony Fernandez	.05
127	Dave Stewart	.05
128	Jay Buhner	.05
129	Mike LaValliere	.05
130	Scott Bradley	.05
131	Tony Phillips	.05
132	Ryne Sandberg	.50
133	Paul O'Neill	.05
134	Mark Grace	.05
135	Chris Sabo	.05
136	Ramon Martinez	.05
137	Brook Jacoby	.05
138	Candy Maldonado	.05
139	Mike Scioscia	.05
140	Chris James **RC**	.05
141	Craig Worthington	.05
142	Manny Lee	.05
143	Tim Raines	.05
144	Sandy Alomar, Jr.	.05
145	John Olerud	.05
146	Ozzie Canseco **RC**	.05
147	Pat Borders	.05
148	Harold Reynolds	.05
149	Tom Henke	.05
150	R.J. Reynolds	.05
151	Mike Gallego	.05
152	Bobby Bonilla	.05
153	Terry Steinbach	.05
154	Barry Bonds	1.00
155	Jose Canseco	.30
156	Gregg Jefferies	.05
157	Matt Williams	.05
158	Craig Biggio	.05
159	Daryl Boston	.05
160	Ricky Jordan	.05
161	Stan Belinda	.05
162	Ozzie Smith	.50
163	Tom Brunansky	.05
164	Todd Zeile	.05
165	Mike Greenwell	.05
166	Kal Daniels	.05
167	Kent Hrbek	.05
168	Franklin Stubbs	.05
169	Dick Schofield	.05
170	Junior Ortiz	.05
171	Hector Villanueva **RC**	.05
172	Dennis Eckersley	.35
173	Mitch Williams	.05
174	Mark McGwire	.75
175	Fernando Valenzuela	.05
176	Gary Carter	.40
177	Dave Magadan	.05
178	Robby Thompson	.05
179	Bob Ojeda	.05
180	Ken Caminiti	.05
181	Don Slaught	.05
182	Luis Rivera	.05
183	Jay Bell	.05
184	Jody Reed	.05
185	Wally Backman	.05
186	Dave Martinez	.05
187	Luis Polonia	.05
188	Shane Mack	.05

189	Spike Owen	.05
190	Scott Bailes	.05
191	John Russell	.05
192	Walt Weiss	.05
193	Jose Oquendo	.05
194	Carney Lansford	.05
195	Jeff Huson	.05
196	Keith Miller	.05
197	Eric Yelding	.05
198	Ron Darling	.05
199	John Kruk	.05
200	Checklist 101-200	.05
201	John Shelby	.05
202	Bob Geren	.05
203	Lance McCullers	.05
204	Alvaro Espinoza	.05
205	Mark Salas	.05
206	Mike Pagliarulo	.05
207	Jose Uribe	.05
208	Jim Deshaies **RC**	.05
209	Ron Karkovice	.05
210	Rafael Ramirez	.05
211	Donnie Hill	.05
212	Brian Harper **RC**	.05
213	Jack Howell	.05
214	Wes Gardner	.05
215	Tim Burke	.05
216	Doug Jones **RC**	.05
217	Hubie Brooks	.05
218	Tom Candiotti	.05
219	Gerald Perry	.05
220	Jose DeLeon **RC**	.05
221	Wally Whitehurst	.05
222	Alan Mills **RC**	.05
223	Alan Trammell	.05
224	Dwight Gooden	.05
225	Travis Fryman	.05
226	Joe Carter	.05
227	Julio Franco	.05
228	Craig Lefferts	.05
229	Gary Pettis	.05
230	Dennis Rasmussen	.05
231a	Brian Downing (No position on front.)	2.00
231b	Brian Downing (DH on front)	.05
232	Carlos Quintana **RC**	.05
233	Gary Gaetti	.05
234	Mark Langston	.05
235	Tim Wallach	.05
236	Greg Swindell	.05
237	Eddie Murray	.40
238	Jeff Manto **RC**	.05
239	Lenny Harris	.05
240	Jesse Orosco	.05
241	Scott Lusader	.05
242	Sid Fernandez	.05
243	Jim Leyritz	.05
244	Cecil Fielder	.05
245	Darryl Strawberry	.05
246	Frank Thomas **RC**	.50
247	Kevin Mitchell	.05
248	Lance Johnson **RC**	.05
249	Rick Rueschel	.05
250	Mark Portugal	.05
251	Derek Lilliquist	.05
252	Brian Holman **RC**	.05
253	Rafael Valdez	.05
254	B.J. Surhoff	.05
255	Tony Gwynn	.50
256	Andy Van Slyke	.05
257	Todd Stottlemyre	.05
258	Jose Lind	.05
259	Greg Myers	.05
260	Jeff Ballard **RC**	.05
261	Bobby Thigpen	.05
262	Jimmy Kremers **RC**	.05
263	Robin Ventura	.05
264	John Smoltz	.05
265	Sammy Sosa	.50
266	Gary Sheffield	.30
267	Len Dykstra	.05
268	Bill Spiers	.05
269	Charlie Hayes	.05
270	Brett Butler	.05
271	Bip Roberts	.05
272	Rob Deer	.05
273	Fred Lynn	.05
274	Dave Parker	.05
275	Andy Benes	.05
276	Glenallen Hill **RC**	.05
277	Steve Howard **RC**	.05
278	Doug Drabek	.05
279	Joe Oliver	.05
280	Todd Benzinger	.05
281	Eric King	.05
282	Jim Presley	.05
283	Ken Patterson **RC**	.05
284	Jack Daugherty **RC**	.05
285	Ivan Calderon	.05
286	Edgar Diaz **RC**	.05
287	Kevin Bass	.05
288	Don Carman **RC**	.05
289	Greg Brock	.05
290	John Franco	.05
291	Joey Cora	.05
292	Bill Wegman	.05
293	Eric Show	.05
294	Scott Bankhead	.05
295	Garry Templeton	.05
296	Mickey Tettleton	.05
297	Luis Sojo	.05
298	Jose Rijo	.05
299	Dave Johnson	.05
300	Checklist 201-300	.05
301	Mark Grant	.05
302	Pete Harnisch	.05
303	Greg Olson	.05

304	Anthony Telford **RC**	.05
305	Lonnie Smith	.05
306	Chris Hoiles	.05
307	Bryn Smith	.05
308	Mike Devereaux	.05
309a	Milt Thompson ("86" in stats obscured by "bull's eye")	.50
309b	Milt Thompson ("86" visible)	.05
310	Bob Melvin	.05
311a	Luis Salazar (Circled dot over "i" in Luis on back.)	2.00
311b	Luis Salazar (Corrected)	.05
312	Ed Whitson **RC**	.05
313	Charlie Hough	.05
314	Dave Clark	.05
315	Eric Gunderson **RC**	.05
316	Dan Petry	.05
317	Dante Bichette	.05
318	Mike Heath	.05
319	Damon Berryhill	.05
320	Walt Terrell	.05
321	Scott Fletcher	.05
322	Dan Plesac	.05
323	Jack McDowell	.05
324	Paul Molitor	.40
325	Ozzie Guillen	.05
326	Gregg Olson	.05
327	Pedro Guerrero	.05
328	Bob Milacki **RC**	.05
329	John Tudor	.05
330	Steve Finley	.05
331	Jack Clark	.05
332	Jerome Walton	.05
333	Andy Hawkins	.05
334	Derrick May	.05
335	Roberto Alomar	.20
336	Jack Morris	.05
337	Dave Winfield	.40
338	Steve Searcy	.05
339	Chili Davis	.05
340	Larry Sheets	.05
341	Ted Higuera	.05
342	David Segui **RC**	.10
343	Greg Cadaret	.05
344	Robin Yount	.40
345	Nolan Ryan	1.00
346	Ray Lankford	.05
347	Cal Ripken, Jr.	1.00
348	Lee Smith	.05
349	Brady Anderson	.05
350	Frank DiPino	.05
351	Hal Morris	.05
352	Deion Sanders	.10
353	Barry Larkin	.05
354	Don Mattingly	.60
355	Eric Davis	.05
356	Jose Offerman	.05
357	Mel Rojas	.05
358	Rudy Seanez **RC**	.05
359	Dennis "Oil Can" Boyd	.05
360	Nelson Liriano	.05
361	Ron Gant	.05
362	Howard Farmer **RC**	.05
363	Dave Justice	.05
364	Delino DeShields	.05
365	Steve Avery	.05
366	David Cone	.05
367	Lou Whitaker	.05
368	Von Hayes	.05
369	Frank Tanana	.05
370	Tim Teufel	.05
371	Randy Myers	.05
372	Roberto Kelly	.05
373	Jack Armstrong	.05
374	Kelly Gruber	.05
375	Kevin Maas	.05
376	Randy Johnson	.40
377	David West	.05
378	Brent Knackert **RC**	.05
379	Rick Honeycutt	.05
380	Kevin Gross	.05
381	Tom Foley	.05
382	Jeff Blauser	.05
383	Scott Ruskin **RC**	.05
384	Andres Thomas **RC**	.05
385	Dennis Martinez	.05
386	Mike Henneman	.05
387	Felix Jose	.05
388	Alejandro Pena	.05
389	Chet Lemon	.05
390	Craig Wilson **RC**	.05
391	Chuck Crim	.05
392	Mel Hall	.05
393	Mark Knudson	.05
394	Norm Charlton	.05
395	Mike Felder	.05
396	Tim Layana **RC**	.05
397	Steve Frey **RC**	.05
398	Bill Doran	.05
399	Dion James	.05
400	Checklist 301-400	.05
401	Ron Hassey	.05
402	Don Robinson	.05
403	Gene Nelson	.05
404	Terry Kennedy	.05
405	Todd Burns	.05
406	Roger McDowell	.05
407	Bob Kipper	.05
408	Darren Daulton	.05
409	Chuck Cary	.05
410	Bruce Ruffin	.05
411	Juan Berenguer	.05
412	Gary Ward	.05
413	Al Newman	.05
414	Danny Jackson	.05
415	Greg Gagne	.05

416	Tom Herr	.05
417	Jeff Parrett	.05
418	Jeff Reardon	.05
419	Mark Lemke	.05
420	Charlie O'Brien RC	.05
421	Willie Randolph	.05
422	Steve Bedrosian	.05
423	Mike Moore	.05
424	Jeff Brantley RC	.05
425	Bob Welch	.05
426	Terry Mulholland	.05
427	Willie Blair RC	.05
428	Darrin Fletcher RC	.05
429	Mike Witt	.05
430	Joe Boever	.05
431	Tom Gordon	.05
432	Pedro Munoz RC	.05
433	Kevin Seitzer	.05
434	Kevin Tapani	.05
435	Bret Saberhagen	.05
436	Ellis Burks	.05
437	Chuck Finley	.05
438	Mike Boddicker	.05
439	Francisco Cabrera	.05
440	Todd Hundley	.05
441	Kelly Downs	.05
442	Dann Howitt RC	.05
443	Scott Garrelts	.05
444	Rickey Henderson	.40
445	Will Clark	.05
446	Ben McDonald	.05
447	Dale Murphy	.20
448	Dave Righetti	.05
449	Dickie Thon	.05
450	Ted Power	.05
451	Scott Coolbaugh	.05
452	Dwight Smith	.05
453	Pete Incaviglia	.05
454	Andre Dawson	.25
455	Ruben Sierra	.05
456	Andres Galarraga	.05
457	Alvin Davis	.05
458	Tony Castillo	.05
459	Pete O'Brien	.05
460	Charlie Leibrandt	.05
461	Vince Coleman	.05
462	Steve Sax	.05
463	Omar Oliveras RC	.05
464	Oscar Azocar RC	.05
465	Joe Magrane RC	.05
466	Karl Rhodes RC	.05
467	Benito Santiago	.05
468	Joe Klink RC	.05
469	Sil Campusano RC	.05
470	Mark Parent	.05
471	Shawn Boskie RC	.05
472	Kevin Brown	.05
473	Rick Sutcliffe	.05
474	Rafael Palmeiro	.35
475	Mike Harkey	.05
476	Jaime Navarro	.05
477	Marquis Grissom	.05
478	Marty Clary	.05
479	Greg Briley RC	.05
480	Tom Glavine	.25
481	Lee Guetterman	.05
482	Rex Hudler	.05
483	Dave LaPoint RC	.05
484	Terry Pendleton	.05
485	Jesse Barfield	.05
486	Jose DeJesus	.05
487	Paul Abbott RC	.05
488	Ken Howell	.05
489	Greg W. Harris	.05
490	Roy Smith	.05
491	Paul Assenmacher	.05
492	Geno Petralli	.05
493	Steve Wilson	.05
494	Kevin Reimer RC	.05
495	Bill Long	.05
496	Mike Jackson RC	.05
497	Oddibe McDowell	.05
498	Bill Swift	.05
499	Jeff Treadway	.05
500	Checklist 401-500	.05
501	Gene Larkin	.05
502	Bob Boone	.05
503	Allan Anderson	.05
504	Luis Aquino RC	.05
505	Mark Guthrie	.05
506	Joe Orsulak	.05
507	Dana Kiecker RC	.05
508	Dave Gallagher RC	.05
509	Greg A. Harris	.05
510	Mark Williamson	.05
511	Casey Candaele	.05
512	Mookie Wilson	.05
513	Dave Smith	.05
514	Chuck Carr RC	.05
515	Glenn Wilson	.05
516	Mike Fitzgerald RC	.05
517	Devon White	.05
518	Dave Hollins	.05
519	Mark Eichhorn	.05
520	Otis Nixon	.05
521	Terry Shumpert RC	.05
522	Scott Erickson RC	.15
523	Danny Tartabull	.05
524	Orel Hershiser	.05
525	George Brett	.60
526	Greg Vaughn	.05
527	Tim Naehring RC	.05
528	Curt Schilling RC	.25
529	Chris Bosio	.05
530	Sam Horn	.05
531	Mike Scott	.05
532	George Bell	.05
533	Eric Anthony	.05
534	Julio Valera RC	.05
535	Glenn Davis	.05
536	Larry Walker	.05
537	Pat Combs	.05
538	Chris Nabholz RC	.05
539	Kirk McCaskill	.05
540	Randy Ready	.05
541	Mark Gubicza	.05
542	Rick Aguilera	.05
543	Brian McRae RC	.05
544	Kirby Puckett	.50
545	Bo Jackson	.10
546	Wade Boggs	.50
547	Tim McIntosh RC	.05
548	Randy Milligan RC	.05
549	Dwight Evans	.05
550	Billy Ripken	.05
551	Erik Hanson	.05
552	Lance Parrish	.05
553	Tino Martinez	.05
554	Jim Abbott	.05
555	Ken Griffey Jr.	.65
556	Milt Cuyler RC	.05
557	Mark Leonard RC	.05
558	Jay Howell	.05
559	Lloyd Moseby	.05
560	Chris Gwynn	.05
561	Mark Whiten RC	.05
562	Harold Baines	.05
563	Junior Felix	.05
564	Darren Lewis	.05
565	Fred McGriff	.05
566	Kevin Appier	.05
567	Luis Gonzalez RC	1.00
568	Frank White	.05
569	Juan Agosto	.05
570	Mike Macfarlane	.05
571	Bert Blyleven	.05
572	Ken Griffey Sr.	.05
573	Lee Stevens RC	.05
574	Edgar Martinez	.05
575	Wally Joyner	.05
576	Tim Belcher	.05
577	John Burkett	.05
578	Mike Morgan	.05
579	Paul Gibson	.05
580	Jose Vizcaino RC	.05
581	Duane Ward	.05
582	Scott Sanderson	.05
583	David Wells	.05
584	Willie McGee	.05
585	John Cerutti	.05
586	Danny Darwin	.05
587	Kurt Stillwell	.05
588	Rich Gedman	.05
589	Mark Davis	.05
590	Bill Gullickson	.05
591	Matt Young	.05
592	Bryan Harvey RC	.05
593	Omar Vizquel	.05
594	Scott Lewis RC	.05
595	Dave Valle	.05
596	Tim Crews RC	.05
597	Mike Bielecki	.05
598	Mike Sharperson	.05
599	Dave Bergman	.05
600	Checklist 501-600	.05
601	Steve Lyons	.05
602	Bruce Hurst	.05
603	Donn Pall	.05
604	Jim Vatcher RC	.05
605	Dan Pasqua	.05
606	Kenny Rogers	.05
607	Jeff Schulz RC	.05
608	Brad Arnsberg RC	.05
609	Willie Wilson	.05
610	Jamie Moyer	.05
611	Ron Oester	.05
612	Dennis Cook RC	.05
613	Rick Mahler	.05
614	Bill Landrum	.05
615	Scott Scudder	.05
616	Tom Edens RC	.05
617	"1917 Revisited" (Chicago White Sox team photo.)	.05
618	Jim Gantner	.05
619	Darrel Akerfelds RC	.05
620	Ron Robinson	.05
621	Scott Radinsky	.05
622	Pete Smith	.05
623	Melido Perez	.05
624	Jerald Clark RC	.05
625	Carlos Martinez	.05
626	Wes Chamberlain RC	.05
627	Bobby Witt	.05
628	Ken Dayley RC	.05
629	John Barfield RC	.05
630	Bob Tewksbury	.05
631	Glenn Braggs	.05
632	Jim Neidlinger RC	.05
633	Tom Browning	.05
634	Kirk Gibson	.05
635	Rob Dibble	.05
636	"Stolen Base Leaders" (Lou Brock, Rickey Henderson)	.15
637	Jeff Montgomery	.05
638	Mike Schooler	.05
639	Storm Davis	.05
640	Rich Rodriguez RC	.05
641	Phil Bradley	.05
642	Kent Mercker	.05
643	Carlton Fisk	.40
644	Mike Bell	.05
645	Alex Fernandez RC	.05
646	Juan Gonzalez	.30
647	Ken Hill	.05
648	Jeff Russell	.05
649	Chuck Malone RC	.05
650	Steve Buechele	.05
651	Mike Benjamin	.05
652	Tony Pena	.05
653	Trevor Wilson	.05
654	Alex Cole	.05
655	Roger Clemens	.60
656	"The Bashing Years" (Mark McGwire)	.50
657	Joe Grahe RC	.05
658	Jim Eisenreich	.05
659	Dan Gladden	.05
660	Steve Farr RC	.05
661	Bill Sampen RC	.05
662	Dave Rohde RC	.05
663	Mark Gardner	.05
664	Mike Simms RC	.05
665	Moises Alou	.05
666	Mickey Hatcher	.05
667	Jimmy Key	.05
668	John Wetteland	.05
669	John Smiley	.05
670	Jim Acker	.05
671	Pascual Perez	.05
672	Reggie Harris RC	.05
673	Matt Nokes	.05
674	Rafael Novoa RC	.05
675	Hensley Meulens	.05
676	Jeff M. Robinson RC	.05
677	"Ground Breaking" (New Comiskey Park)	.15
678	Johnny Ray	.05
679	Greg Hibbard	.05
680	Paul Sorrento	.05
681	Mike Marshall	.05
682	Jim Clancy	.05
683	Rob Murphy	.05
684	Dave Schmidt RC	.05
685	Jeff Gray RC	.05
686	Mike Hartley RC	.05
687	Jeff King	.05
688	Stan Javier RC	.05
689	Bob Walk	.05
690	Jim Gott	.05
691	Mike LaCoss	.05
692	John Farrell	.05
693	Tim Leary	.05
694	Mike Walker RC	.05
695	Eric Plunk	.05
696	Mike Fetters	.05
697	Wayne Edwards	.05
698	Tim Drummond RC	.05
699	Willie Fraser	.05
700	Checklist 601-700	.05
701	Mike Heath	.05
702	"Rookie Threats" (Luis Gonzalez, Karl Rhodes, Jeff Bagwell)	.45
703	Jose Mesa	.05
704	Dave Smith RC	.05
705	Danny Darwin	.05
706	Rafael Belliard	.05
707	Rob Murphy	.05
708	Terry Pendleton	.05
709	Mike Pagliarulo	.05
710	Sid Bream	.05
711	Junior Felix	.05
712	Dante Bichette	.05
713	Kevin Gross	.05
714	Luis Sojo	.05
715	Bob Ojeda	.05
716	Julio Machado RC	.05
717	Steve Farr	.05
718	Franklin Stubbs	.05
719	Mike Boddicker	.05
720	Willie Randolph	.05
721	Willie McGee	.05
722	Chili Davis	.05
723	Danny Jackson	.05
724	Cory Snyder	.05
725	"MVP Lineup" (Andre Dawson, George Bell, Ryne Sandberg)	.20
726	Rob Deer	.05
727	Rich DeLucia RC	.05
728	Mike Perez RC	.05
729	Mickey Tettleton	.05
730	Mike Blowers	.05
731	Gary Gaetti	.05
732	Brett Butler	.05
733	Dave Parker	.05
734	Eddie Zosky RC	.05
735	Jack Clark	.05
736	Jack Morris	.05
737	Kirk Gibson	.05
738	Steve Bedrosian	.05
739	Candy Maldonado	.05
740	Matt Young	.05
741	Rich Garces RC	.05
742	George Bell	.05
743	Deion Sanders	.10
744	Bo Jackson	.10
745	Luis Mercedes RC	.05
746	Reggie Jefferson RC	.05
747	Pete Incaviglia	.05
748	Chris Hammond	.05
749	Mike Stanton	.05
750	Scott Sanderson	.05
751	Paul Faries RC	.05
752	Al Osuna RC	.05
753	Steve Chitren RC	.05
754	Tony Fernandez	.05
755	Jeff Bagwell RC	1.50
756	Kirk Dressendorfer RC	.05
757	Glenn Davis	.05
758	Gary Carter	.40
759	Zane Smith	.05
760	Vance Law	.05
761	Denis Boucher RC	.05
762	Turner Ward RC	.05
763	Roberto Alomar	.20
764	Albert Belle	.05
765	Joe Carter	.05
766	Pete Schourek RC	.05
767	Heathcliff Slocumb RC	.05
768	Vince Coleman	.05
769	Mitch Williams	.05
770	Brian Downing	.05
771	Dana Allison RC	.05
772	Pete Harnisch	.05
773	Tim Raines	.05
774	Darryl Kile RC	.05
775	Fred McGriff	.05
776	Dwight Evans	.05
777	Joe Slusarski	.05
778	Dave Righetti	.05
779	Jeff Hamilton	.05
780	Ernest Riles	.05
781	Ken Dayley	.05
782	Eric King	.05
783	Devon White	.05
784	Beau Allred RC	.05
785	Mike Timlin RC	.05
786	Ivan Calderon	.05
787	Hubie Brooks	.05
788	Juan Agosto RC	.05
789	Barry Jones	.05
790	Wally Backman	.05
791	Jim Presley	.05
792	Charlie Hough	.05
793	Larry Andersen	.05
794	Steve Finley	.05
795	Shawn Abner	.05
796	Jeff M. Robinson	.05
797	Joe Bitker RC	.05
798	Eric Show	.05
799	Bud Black	.05
800	Checklist 701-800	.05
SP1	Michael Jordan	3.00
SP2	"A Day to Remember" (Rickey Henderson, Nolan Ryan)	1.00
HH1	Hank Aaron (Hologram)	.05

Baseball Heroes Hank Aaron

This set devoted to Hank Aaron is numbered 19-27 and includes an unnumbered "Baseball Heroes" cover card. The cards are found in foil and jumbo packs of Upper Deck high-number cards.

		NM/M
Complete Set (10):		4.00
Common Aaron:		.50
Autographed Card:		180.00
Aaron Header:		1.00
19	1954 Rookie Year	.50
20	1957 MVP	.50
21	1966 Move to Atlanta	.50
22	1970 3,000	.50
23	1974 715	.50
24	1975 Return to Milwaukee	.50
25	1976 755	.50
26	1982 Hall of Fame	.50
27	Checklist - Heroes 19-27	.50

Baseball Heroes Nolan Ryan

This set devoted to Nolan Ryan is numbered 10-18 and includes an unnumbered "Baseball Heroes" cover card. The cards are found in low-number foil and jumbo boxes.

One out of every hundred of the autographed cards was specially inscribed "Strike Out King."

		NM/M
Complete Set (10):		3.00
Common Player:		.50
Ryan Header Card:		1.00
Autographed Card:		200.00
"Strike Out King" Auto.:		575.00
10	1968 Victory #1	.50
11	1973 A Career Year	.50
12	1975 Double Milestone	.50
13	1979 Back Home	.50
14	1981 All-Time Leader	.50
15	1989 5,000	.50
16	1990 The Sixth	.50
17	1990 ... and Still Counting	.50
18	Checklist - Heroes 10-18	.50

1991 Upper Deck Heroes of Baseball

This four-card set features three members of Baseball's Hall of Fame: Harmon Killebrew, Gaylord Perry and Ferguson Jenkins. Each has a card for himself, plus there's a card which features all three players. The cards were found in specially-marked low number foil packs. The cards are numbered H1-H4. Upper Deck also produced 3,000 autographed and numbered cards for each player.

		NM/M
Complete Set (4):		7.00
Common Card:		2.00
1	Harmon Killebrew	2.00
1a	Harmon Killebrew/Auto.	10.00
2	Gaylord Perry	2.00
2a	Gaylord Perry/Auto.	10.00
3	Ferguson Jenkins	2.00
3a	Ferguson Jenkins/Auto.	10.00
4	Gaylord Perry, Ferguson Jenkins, Harmon Killebrew	2.00

Silver Sluggers

Each year the "Silver Slugger" award is presented to the player at each position with the highest batting average in each league. Upper Deck produced special cards in honor of the 1990 season award winners. The cards were randomly inserted in jumbo packs of Upper Deck cards. The cards feature a "SS" designation along with the card number. The cards are designed like the regular issue Upper Deck cards from 1991, but feature a Silver Slugger bat along the left border of the card.

		NM/M
Complete Set (18):		5.00
Common Player:		.15
1	Julio Franco	.15
2	Alan Trammell	.15
3	Rickey Henderson	.75
4	Jose Canseco	.50
5	Barry Bonds	2.00
6	Eddie Murray	.75
7	Kelly Gruber	.15
8	Ryne Sandberg	1.00
9	Darryl Strawberry	.15
10	Ellis Burks	.15
11	Lance Parrish	.15
12	Cecil Fielder	.15
13	Matt Williams	.15
14	Dave Parker	.15
15	Bobby Bonilla	.15
16	Don Robinson	.15
17	Benito Santiago	.15
18	Barry Larkin	.15

Final Edition

Oil Can Boyd

Upper Deck surprised the hobby with the late-season release of this 100-card boxed set. The cards are numbered with an "F" designation. A special "Minor League Diamond Skills" subset (cards #1-21) features several top prospects. An All-Star subset (cards #79-99) is also included in this set. The cards are styled like the regular 1991 Upper Deck issue. Special team hologram cards are included with the set.

		NM/M
Complete Set (100):		9.00
Common Player:		.05
1	Ryan Klesko, Reggie Sanders (Minor League Diamond Skills Checklist)	.10
2	Pedro Martinez RC	5.00
3	Lance Dickson RC	.05
4	Royce Clayton	.05
5	Scott Bryant RC	.05
6	Dan Wilson RC	.05
7	Dmitri Young RC	.50
8	Ryan Klesko RC	.50
9	Tom Goodwin RC	.05
10	Rondell White RC	.25
11	Reggie Sanders	.05
12	Todd Van Poppel	.05
13	Arthur Rhodes RC	.05
14	Eddie Zosky	.05
15	Gerald Williams RC	.05
16	Robert Eenhoorn RC	.05
17	Jim Thome RC	3.00
18	Marc Newfield RC	.05
19	Kerwin Moore RC	.05
20	Jeff McNeely RC	.05
21	Frankie Rodriguez RC	.05
22	Andy Mota RC	.05
23	Chris Haney RC	.05
24	Kenny Lofton RC	.25
25	Dave Nilsson RC	.05
26	Derek Bell	.05
27	Frank Castillo RC	.05
28	Candy Maldonado	.05
29	Chuck McElroy	.05
30	Chito Martinez RC	.05
31	Steve Howe RC	.05
32	Freddie Benavides RC	.05
33	Scott Kamieniecki	.05
34	Denny Neagle RC	.05
35	Mike Humphreys RC	.05
36	Mike Remlinger RC	.05
37	Scott Coolbaugh	.05
38	Darren Lewis	.05
39	Thomas Howard RC	.05
40	John Candelaria	.05
41	Todd Benzinger	.05
42	Wilson Alvarez	.05
43	Patrick Lennon RC	.05
44	Rusty Meacham RC	.05
45	Ryan Bowen RC	.05
46	Rick Wilkins RC	.10
47	Ed Sprague RC	.05
48	Bob Scanlan RC	.05
49	Tom Candiotti	.05
50	Dennis Martinez (Perfecto)	.05
51	Dennis "Oil Can" Boyd	.05
52	Glenallen Hill	.05
53	Scott Livingstone RC	.05
54	Brian Hunter RC	.05
55	Ivan Rodriguez RC	1.50
56	Keith Mitchell RC	.05
57	Roger McDowell	.05
58	Otis Nixon	.05
59	Juan Bell RC	.05
60	Bill Krueger	.05
61	Chris Donnels RC	.05
62	Tommy Greene	.05
63	Doug Simons RC	.05
64	Andy Ashby RC	.15
65	Anthony Young RC	.05
66	Kevin Morton RC	.05
67	Bret Barberie RC	.05
68	Scott Servais RC	.05
69	Ron Darling	.05
70	Vicente Palacios	.05
71	Tim Burke RC	.05
72	Gerald Alexander RC	.05
73	Reggie Jefferson	.05

74 Dean Palmer .05
75 Mark Whiten .05
76 Randy Tomlin **RC** .05
77 Mark Wohlers **RC** .05
78 Brook Jacoby .05
79 Ken Griffey Jr., Ryne Sandberg (All-Star Checklist) .25
80 Jack Morris/AS .05
81 Sandy Alomar, Jr./AS .05
82 Cecil Fielder/AS .05
83 Roberto Alomar/AS .10
84 Wade Boggs/AS .25
85 Cal Ripken, Jr./AS .60
86 Rickey Henderson/AS .15
87 Ken Griffey Jr./AS .60
88 Dave Henderson/AS .05
89 Danny Tartabull/AS .05
90 Tom Glavine/AS .10
91 Benito Santiago/AS .05
92 Will Clark/AS .05
93 Ryne Sandberg/AS .50
94 Chris Sabo/AS .05
95 Ozzie Smith/AS .50
96 Ivan Calderon/AS .05
97 Tony Gwynn/AS .25
98 Andre Dawson/AS .05
99 Bobby Bonilla/AS .05
100 Checklist .05

1991 Upper Deck Comic Ball 2 Promos

Among the most sought-after promo cards in the promo-card mania that marked the 1991 National Sports Collectors Convention in Anaheim, Calif., was this set of Upper Deck preview cards for its Comic Ball 2 set. One card was given out each day of the National, from July 4-7, with the giveaway date noted in a banner at top. Fronts picture Reggie Jackson and Nolan Ryan with various Looney Tunes cartoon characters. Backs have information on the upcoming Comic Ball 2 issue against a cartoon puzzle background.

NM/M
Complete Set (4): 6.00
Common Player: 1.00
7/4/91 Nolan Ryan (w/Bugs Bunny, Daffy Duck) 2.50
7/5/91 Reggie Jackson (w/Taz) 1.00
7/6/91 Nolan Ryan (w/Speedy Gonzalez) 2.50
7/7/91 Reggie Jackson (w/Sylvester, Elmer Fudd) 1.00

1991 Upper Deck Comic Ball 2

Despite featuring two popular superstars on dozens of the cards, this 198-piece issue has found little favor with collectors. Most cards are arranged in 18-card sequences which tell a baseball-related cartoon tale starring Bugs Bunny, Daffy Duck, Wile E. Coyote and the rest of the Looney Tune characters. Actual-photo "guest appearances" by Nolan Ryan and Reggie Jackson highlight these presentations. There are also "Seventh Inning Stretch" cards featuring the ballplayers in scenes with the cartoon figures. When arranged in nine-pocket plastic sheets, card backs form a cartoon picture puzzle. Cards are typical Upper Deck quality with semi-gloss front and back surfaces and a circular hologram on the backs in the standard 2-1/2" x 3-1/2" format. Nine hologram stickers featuring Ryan and Jackson along with the cartoon characters were produced as random pack inserts. Because the cards are licensed by Major League Baseball, the players and cartoon critters are depicted in Major League uniforms.

NM/M
Complete Set (198): 5.00
Common Card, Cartoon: .05
Common Card, Ryan/Jackson: .10
Hologram Sticker: 2.00
Wax Pack: .50
Wax Box (36): 7.50

1991 Upper Deck Comic Ball 2 Holograms

Nine silver-foil hologram stickers combine photos of Reggie Jackson and/or Nolan Ryan with various Warner Brothers cartoon stars and were issued as random pack inserts in Comic Ball 2. The 2-1/2" x 3-1/2" round-cornered stickers are blank-backed and unnumbered.

NM/M
Complete Set (9): 17.50
Common Player: 3.00
(1) Reggie Jackson (w/Daffy) 3.00
(2) Reggie Jackson (w/Speedy) 3.00
(3) Reggie Jackson (w/Sylvester) 3.00
(4) Reggie Jackson (w/Taz) 3.00
(5) Reggie Jackson, Nolan Ryan (w/Roadrunner & Wile) 3.00
(6) Nolan Ryan (w/Bugs) 3.00
(7) Nolan Ryan (w/Sylvester) 3.00
(8) Nolan Ryan (w/?) 3.00
(9) Nolan Ryan (w/?) 3.00

1992 Upper Deck

Upper Deck introduced a new look in 1992. The baseline style was no longer used. The cards feature full-color action photos on white stock, with the player's name and the Upper Deck logo along the top border. The team name is in the photo's bottom-right corner. Once again a 100-card high number series was released in late summer. Ted Williams autographed 2,500 Baseball Heroes cards which were randomly inserted into packs. Subsets featured in the 1992 issue include Star Rookies and Top Prospects. Cards originating from factory sets have gold-foil holograms on back, rather than silver.

NM/M
Unopened Fact. Set (800): 20.00
Complete Set (800): 15.00
Common Player: .05
Low or High Pack (15): .50
Low or High Box (36): 12.50

Jumbo Pack (27): 1.00
Jumbo Box (20): 16.00
Bench/Morgan Auto. 75.00
Ted Williams Auto. 425.00
1 Star Rookie Checklist (Ryan Klesko, Jim Thome) .25
2 Royce Clayton/SR .05
3 Brian Jordan/SR .30
4 Dave Fleming/SR **RC** .05
5 Jim Thome/SR) .40
6 Jeff Juden/SR .05
7 Roberto Hernandez/SR **RC** .15
8 Kyle Abbott/SR **RC** .05
9 Chris George/SR **RC** .05
10 Rob Maurer/SR **RC** .05
11 Donald Harris/SR **RC** .05
12 Ted Wood/SR **RC** .05
13 Patrick Lennon/SR **RC** .05
14 Willie Banks/SR .05
15 Roger Salkeld/SR **RC** .05
16 Wil Cordero/SR .05
17 Arthur Rhodes/SR **RC** .05
18 Pedro Martinez/SR .40
19 Andy Ashby/SR **RC** .10
20 Tom Goodwin/SR .05
21 Braulio Castillo/SR .05
22 Todd Van Poppel/SR .05
23 Brian Williams/SR **RC** .05
24 Ryan Klesko/SR .05
25 Kenny Lofton/SR .05
26 Derek Bell/SR .05
27 Reggie Sanders/SR .05
28 Dave Winfield (Winfield's 400th) .25
29 Atlanta Braves Checklist (Dave Justice) .05
30 Cincinnati Reds Checklist (Rob Dibble) .05
31 Houston Astros Checklist (Craig Biggio **RC**) .05
32 Los Angeles Dodgers Checklist (Eddie Murray) .20
33 San Diego Padres Checklist (Fred McGriff) .05
34 San Francisco Giants Checklist (Willie McGee) .05
35 Chicago Cubs Checklist (Shawon Dunston) .05
36 Montreal Expos Checklist (Delino DeShields) .05
37 New York Mets Checklist (Howard Johnson) .05
38 Philadelphia Phillies Checklist (John Kruk) .05
39 Pittsburgh Pirates Checklist (Doug Drabek) .05
40 St. Louis Cardinals Checklist (Todd Zeile) .05
41 Steve Avery (Playoff Perfection) .05
42 Jeremy Hernandez **RC** .05
43 Doug Henry **RC** .05
44 Chris Donnels **RC** .05
45 Mo Sanford **RC** .05
46 Scott Kamieniecki **RC** .10
47 Mark Lemke .05
48 Steve Farr .05
49 Francisco Oliveras .05
50 Ced Landrum **RC** .05
51 Top Prospect Checklist (Rondell White, Marc Newfield) .05
52 Eduardo Perez **RC** (Top Prospect) .10
53 Tom Nevers **RC** (Top Prospect) .05
54 David Zancanaro **RC** (Top Prospect) .05
55 Shawn Green **RC** (Top Prospect) 1.50
56 Mark Wohlers **RC** (Top Prospect) .05
57 Dave Nilsson (Top Prospect) .05
58 Dmitri Young **RC** (Top Prospect) .05
59 Ryan Hawblitzel **RC** (Top Prospect) .05
60 Raul Mondesi **RC** (Top Prospect) .05
61 Rondell White **RC** (Top Prospect) .05
62 Steve Hosey **RC** (Top Prospect) .05
63 Manny Ramirez **RC** (Top Prospect) 2.00
64 Marc Newfield **RC** (Top Prospect) .05
65 Jeromy Burnitz **RC** (Top Prospect) .05
66 Mark Smith **RC** (Top Prospect) .05
67 Joey Hamilton **RC** (Top Prospect) .10
68 Tyler Green **RC** (Top Prospect) .05
69 John Farrell **RC** (Top Prospect) .05
70 Kurt Miller **RC** (Top Prospect) .05
71 Jeff Plympton **RC** (Top Prospect) .05
72 Dan Wilson **RC** (Top Prospect) .05
73 Joe Vitiello **RC** (Top Prospect) .05
74 Rico Brogna (Top Prospect) .05
75 David McCarty **RC** (Top Prospect) .05
76 Bob Wickman **RC** (Top Prospect) .05
77 Carlos Rodriguez **RC** (Top Prospect) .05
78 Jim Abbott (Stay in School) .05
79 Bloodlines (Pedro Martinez, Ramon Martinez) .05
80 Bloodlines (Kevin Mitchell, Keith Mitchell) .05
81 Bloodlines (Sandy Jr. & Roberto Alomar, Sandy Jr. & Roberto Alomar) .10
82 Bloodlines (Cal Jr. & Billy Ripken, Cal Jr. & Billy Ripken) .40
83 Bloodlines (Tony & Chris Gwynn, Tony & Chris Gwynn) .20
84 Bloodlines (Dwight Gooden, Gary Sheffield) .15
85 Bloodlines (Ken, Sr.; Ken, Jr.; & Craig Griffey, Ken, Sr.; Ken, Jr.; & Craig Griffey, Ken, Sr.; Ken, Jr.; & Craig Griffey) .30
86 California Angels Checklist (Jim Abbott) .05
87 Chicago White Sox Checklist (Frank Thomas) .25
88 Kansas City Royals Checklist (Danny Tartabull) .05
89 Minnesota Twins Checklist (Scott Erickson) .05
90 Oakland Athletics Checklist (Rickey Henderson) .25
91 Seattle Mariners Checklist (Edgar Martinez) .05
92 Texas Rangers Checklist (Nolan Ryan) .50
93 Baltimore Orioles Checklist (Ben McDonald) .05
94 Boston Red Sox Checklist (Ellis Burks) .05
95 Cleveland Indians Checklist (Greg Swindell) .05
96 Detroit Tigers Checklist (Cecil Fielder) .05
97 Milwaukee Brewers Checklist (Greg Vaughn) .05
98 New York Yankees Checklist (Kevin Maas) .05
99 Toronto Blue Jays Checklist (Dave Stieb) .05
100 Checklist 1-100 .05
101 Joe Oliver .05
102 Hector Villanueva .05
103 Ed Whitson .05
104 Danny Jackson .05
105 Chris Hammond .05
106 Ricky Jordan .05
107 Kevin Bass .05
108 Darrin Fletcher .05
109 Junior Ortiz .05
110 Tom Bolton .05
111 Jeff King .05
112 Dave Magadan .05
113 Mike LaValliere .05
114 Hubie Brooks .05
115 Jay Bell .05
116 David Wells .05
117 Jim Leyritz .05
118 Manuel Lee .05
119 Alvaro Espinoza .05
120 B.J. Surhoff .05
121 Hal Morris .05
122 Shawon Dunston .05
123 Chris Sabo .05
124 Andre Dawson .25
125 Eric Davis .05
126 Chili Davis .05
127 Dale Murphy .15
128 Kirk McCaskill .05
129 Terry Mulholland .05
130 Rick Aguilera .05
131 Vince Coleman .05
132 Andy Van Slyke .05
133 Gregg Jefferies .05
134 Barry Bonds 1.00
135 Dwight Gooden .05
136 Dave Stieb .05
137 Albert Belle .05
138 Teddy Higuera .05
139 Jesse Barfield .05
140 Pat Borders .05
141 Bip Roberts .05
142 Rob Dibble .05
143 Mark Grace .05
144 Barry Larkin .05
145 Ryne Sandberg .50
146 Scott Erickson .05
147 Luis Polonia .05
148 John Burkett .05
149 Luis Sojo .05
150 Dickie Thon .05
151 Walt Weiss .05
152 Mike Scioscia .05
153 Mark McGwire .75
154 Matt Williams .05
155 Rickey Henderson .25
156 Sandy Alomar, Jr. .05
157 Brian McRae .05
158 Harold Baines .05
159 Kevin Appier .05
160 Felix Fermin .05
161 Leo Gomez .05
162 Craig Biggio .05
163 Ben McDonald .05
164 Randy Johnson .40
165 Cal Ripken, Jr. 1.00
166 Frank Thomas .40
167 Delino DeShields .05
168 Greg Gagne .05
169 Ron Karkovice .05
170 Charlie Leibrandt .05
171 Dave Righetti .05
172 Dave Henderson .05
173 Steve Decker .05
174 Darryl Strawberry .05
175 Will Clark .05
176 Ruben Sierra .05
177 Ozzie Smith .50
178 Charles Nagy .05
179 Gary Pettis .05
180 Kirk Gibson .05
181 Randy Milligan .05
182 Dave Valle .05
183 Chris Hoiles .05
184 Tony Phillips .05
185 Brady Anderson .05
186 Scott Fletcher .05
187 Gene Larkin .05
188 Lance Johnson .05
189 Greg Olson .05
190 Melido Perez .05
191 Lenny Harris .05
192 Terry Kennedy .05
193 Mike Gallego .05
194 Willie McGee .05
195 Juan Samuel .05
196 Jeff Huson .05
197 Alex Cole .05
198 Ron Robinson .05
199 Joel Skinner .05
200 Checklist 101-200 .05
201 Kevin Reimer .05
202 Stan Belinda .05
203 Pat Tabler .05
204 Jose Guzman .05
205 Jose Lind .05
206 Spike Owen .05
207 Joe Orsulak .05
208 Charlie Hayes .05
209 Mike Devereaux .05
210 Mike Fitzgerald .05
211 Willie Randolph .05
212 Rod Nichols .05
213 Mike Boddicker .05
214 Bill Spiers .05
215 Steve Olin .05
216 David Howard **RC** .05
217 Gary Varsho .05
218 Mike Harkey .05
219 Luis Aquino .05
220 Chuck McElroy **RC** .05
221 Doug Drabek .05
222 Dave Winfield .05
223 Rafael Palmeiro .35
224 Joe Carter .05
225 Bobby Bonilla .05
226 Ivan Calderon .05
227 Gregg Olson .05
228 Tim Wallach .05
229 Terry Pendleton .05
230 Gilberto Reyes **RC** .05
231 Carlos Baerga .05
232 Greg Vaughn .05
233 Bret Saberhagen .05
234 Gary Sheffield .30
235 Mark Lewis .05
236 George Bell .05
237 Danny Tartabull .05
238 Willie Wilson .05
239 Doug Dascenzo .05
240 Bill Pecota .05
241 Julio Franco .05
242 Ed Sprague .05
243 Juan Gonzalez .20
244 Chuck Finley .05
245 Ivan Rodriguez .35
246 Len Dykstra .05
247 Deion Sanders .10
248 Dwight Evans .05
249 Larry Walker .05
250 Billy Ripken .05
251 Mickey Tettleton .05
252 Tony Pena .05
253 Benito Santiago .05
254 Kirby Puckett .50
255 Cecil Fielder .05
256 Howard Johnson .05
257 Andujar Cedeno .05
258 Jose Rijo .05
259 Al Osuna .05
260 Todd Hundley .05
261 Orel Hershiser .05
262 Ray Lankford .05
263 Robin Ventura .05
264 Felix Jose .05
265 Eddie Murray .40
266 Kevin Mitchell .05
267 Gary Carter .40
268 Mike Benjamin .05
269 Dick Schofield .05
270 Jose Uribe .05
271 Pete Incaviglia .05
272 Tony Fernandez .05
273 Alan Trammell .05
274 Tony Gwynn .50
275 Mike Greenwell .05
276 Jeff Bagwell .40
277 Frank Viola .05
278 Randy Myers .05
279 Ken Caminiti .05
280 Bill Doran .05
281 Dan Pasqua .05
282 Alfredo Griffin .05
283 Jose Oquendo .05
284 Kal Daniels .05
285 Bobby Thigpen .05
286 Robby Thompson .05
287 Mark Eichhorn .05
288 Mike Felder .05
289 Dave Gallagher .05
290 Dave Anderson .05
291 Mel Hall .05
292 Jerald Clark .05
293 Al Newman .05
294 Rob Deer .05
295 Matt Nokes .05
296 Jack Armstrong .05
297 Jim Deshaies .05
298 Jeff Innis .05
299 Jeff Reed .05
300 Checklist 201-300 .05
301 Lonnie Smith .05
302 Jimmy Key .05
303 Junior Felix .05
304 Mike Heath .05
305 Mark Langston .05
306 Greg W. Harris .05
307 Brett Butler .05
308 Luis Rivera **RC** .05
309 Bruce Ruffin .05
310 Paul Faries .05
311 Terry Leach .05
312 Scott Brosius **RC** .10
313 Scott Leius .05
314 Harold Reynolds .05
315 Jack Morris .05
316 David Segui .05
317 Bill Gullickson .05
318 Todd Frohwirth .05
319 Mark Leiter **RC** .05
320 Jeff M. Robinson .05
321 Gary Gaetti .05
322 John Smoltz .05
323 Andy Benes .05
324 Kelly Gruber .05
325 Jim Abbott .05
326 John Kruk .05
327 Kevin Seitzer .05
328 Darrin Jackson .05
329 Kurt Stillwell **RC** .05
330 Mike Maddux .05
331 Dennis Eckersley .35
332 Dan Gladden .05
333 Jose Canseco .30
334 Kent Hrbek .05
335 Ken Griffey Sr. .05
336 Greg Swindell .05
337 Trevor Wilson **RC** .05
338 Sam Horn .05
339 Mike Henneman .05
340 Jerry Browne .05
341 Glenn Braggs .05
342 Tom Glavine .20
343 Wally Joyner .05
344 Fred McGriff .05
345 Ron Gant .05
346 Ramon Martinez .05
347 Wes Chamberlain .05
348 Terry Shumpert .05
349 Tim Teufel .05
350 Wally Backman .05
351 Joe Girardi .05
352 Devon White .05
353 Greg Maddux .50
354 Ryan Bowen **RC** .05
355 Roberto Alomar .20
356 Don Mattingly .60
357 Pedro Guerrero .05
358 Steve Sax .05
359 Joey Cora .05
360 Jim Gantner .05
361 Brian Barnes **RC** .05
362 Kevin McReynolds .05
363 Bret Barberie **RC** .05
364 David Cone .05
365 Dennis Martinez .05
366 Brian Hunter **RC** .05
367 Edgar Martinez .05
368 Steve Finley .05
369 Greg Briley .05
370 Jeff Blauser .05
371 Todd Stottlemyre .05
372 Luis Gonzalez .05
373 Rick Wilkins .05
374 Darryl Kile **RC** .05
375 John Olerud .05
376 Lee Smith .05
377 Kevin Maas .05
378 Dante Bichette .05
379 Tom Pagnozzi .05
380 Mike Flanagan .05
381 Charlie O'Brien .05
382 Dave Martinez .05
383 Keith Miller .05
384 Scott Ruskin .05
385 Kevin Elster .05
386 Alvin Davis .05
387 Casey Candaele .05
388 Pete O'Brien .05
389 Jeff Treadway **RC** .05
390 Scott Bradley .05
391 Mookie Wilson .05
392 Jimmy Jones .05
393 Candy Maldonado .05
394 Eric Yelding .05

#	Player	Price
395	Tom Henke	.05
396	Franklin Stubbs	.05
397	Milt Thompson	.05
398	Mark Carreon	.05
399	Randy Velarde	.05
400	Checklist 301-400	.05
401	Omar Vizquel	.05
402	Joe Boever	.05
403	Bill Krueger	.05
404	Jody Reed	.05
405	Mike Schooler RC	.05
406	Jason Grimsley	.05
407	Greg Myers	.05
408	Randy Ready	.05
409	Mike Timlin RC	.15
410	Mitch Williams	.05
411	Garry Templeton	.05
412	Greg Cadaret	.05
413	Donnie Hill	.05
414	Wally Whitehurst	.05
415	Scott Sanderson	.05
416	Thomas Howard	.05
417	Neal Heaton	.05
418	Charlie Hough	.05
419	Jack Howell	.05
420	Greg Hibbard	.05
421	Carlos Quintana	.05
422	Kim Batiste RC	.05
423	Paul Molitor	.40
424	Ken Griffey Jr.	.65
425	Phil Plantier	.05
426	Denny Neagle	.05
427	Von Hayes	.05
428	Shane Mack	.05
429	Darren Daulton	.05
430	Dwayne Henry	.05
431	Lance Parrish	.05
432	Mike Humphreys RC	.05
433	Tim Burke	.05
434	Bryan Harvey	.05
435	Pat Kelly	.05
436	Ozzie Guillen	.05
437	Bruce Hurst	.05
438	Sammy Sosa	.50
439	Dennis Rasmussen	.05
440	Ken Patterson	.05
441	Jay Buhner	.05
442	Pat Combs	.05
443	Wade Boggs	.50
444	George Brett	.60
445	Mo Vaughn	.05
446	Chuck Knoblauch	.05
447	Tom Candiotti	.05
448	Mark Portugal	.05
449	Mickey Morandini	.05
450	Duane Ward	.05
451	Otis Nixon	.05
452	Bob Welch	.05
453	Rusty Meacham	.05
454	Keith Mitchell	.05
455	Marquis Grissom	.05
456	Robin Yount	.40
457	Harvey Pulliam RC	.05
458	Jose DeLeon RC	.05
459	Mark Gubicza	.05
460	Darryl Hamilton	.05
461	Tom Browning	.05
462	Monty Fariss	.05
463	Jerome Walton	.05
464	Paul O'Neill	.05
465	Dean Palmer	.05
466	Travis Fryman	.05
467	John Smiley	.05
468	Lloyd Moseby	.05
469	John Wehner RC	.05
470	Skeeter Barnes RC	.05
471	Steve Chitren	.05
472	Kent Mercker	.05
473	Terry Steinbach	.05
474	Andres Galarraga	.05
475	Steve Avery	.05
476	Tom Gordon	.05
477	Cal Eldred	.05
478	Omar Olivares RC	.05
479	Julio Machado	.05
480	Bob Milacki	.05
481	Les Lancaster	.05
482	John Candelaria	.05
483	Brian Downing	.05
484	Roger McDowell	.05
485	Scott Scudder	.05
486	Zane Smith	.05
487	John Cerutti	.05
488	Steve Buechele	.05
489	Paul Gibson	.05
490	Curtis Wilkerson	.05
491	Marvin Freeman	.05
492	Tom Foley	.05
493	Juan Berenguer	.05
494	Ernest Riles	.05
495	Sid Bream	.05
496	Chuck Crim	.05
497	Mike Macfarlane	.05
498	Dale Sveum	.05
499	Storm Davis	.05
500	Checklist 401-500	.05
501	Jeff Reardon	.05
502	Shawn Abner	.05
503	Tony Fossas	.05
504	Cory Snyder	.05
505	Matt Young	.05
506	Allan Anderson RC	.05
507	Mark Lee	.05
508	Gene Nelson	.05
509	Mike Pagliarulo	.05
510	Rafael Belliard	.05
511	Jay Howell	.05
512	Bob Tewksbury	.05
513	Mike Morgan	.05
514	John Franco	.05
515	Kevin Gross	.05
516	Lou Whitaker	.05
517	Orlando Merced	.05
518	Todd Benzinger	.05
519	Gary Redus	.05
520	Walt Terrell	.05
521	Jack Clark	.05
522	Dave Parker	.05
523	Tim Naehring	.05
524	Mark Whiten	.05
525	Ellis Burks	.05
526	Frank Castillo RC	.05
527	Brian Harper	.05
528	Brook Jacoby	.05
529	Rick Sutcliffe	.05
530	Joe Klink	.05
531	Terry Bross	.05
532	Jose Offerman	.05
533	Todd Zeile	.05
534	Eric Karros	.05
535	Anthony Young RC	.05
536	Milt Cuyler	.05
537	Randy Tomlin	.05
538	Scott Livingstone RC	.05
539	Jim Eisenreich	.05
540	Don Slaught	.05
541	Scott Cooper	.05
542	Joe Grahe RC	.05
543	Tom Brunansky	.05
544	Eddie Zosky	.05
545	Roger Clemens	.60
546	Dave Justice	.05
547	Dave Stewart	.05
548	David West	.05
549	Dave Smith	.05
550	Dan Plesac	.05
551	Alex Fernandez	.05
552	Bernard Gilkey	.05
553	Jack McDowell	.05
554	Tino Martinez	.05
555	Bo Jackson	.10
556	Bernie Williams	.05
557	Mark Gardner	.05
558	Glenallen Hill	.05
559	Dennis "Oil Can" Boyd	.05
560	Chris James	.05
561	Scott Servais RC	.05
562	Rey Sanchez RC	.05
563	Paul McClellan RC	.05
564	Andy Mota RC	.05
565	Darren Lewis	.05
566	Jose Melendez RC	.05
567	Tommy Greene	.05
568	Rich Rodriguez	.05
569	Heathcliff Slocumb RC	.05
570	Joe Hesketh RC	.05
571	Carlton Fisk	.40
572	Erik Hanson	.05
573	Wilson Alvarez	.05
574	Rheal Cormier RC	.05
575	Tim Raines	.05
576	Bobby Witt	.05
577	Roberto Kelly	.05
578	Kevin Brown	.05
579	Chris Nabholz	.05
580	Jesse Orosco	.05
581	Jeff Brantley	.05
582	Rafael Ramirez	.05
583	Kelly Downs	.05
584	Mike Simms	.05
585	Mike Remlinger RC	.05
586	Dave Hollins	.05
587	Larry Andersen	.05
588	Mike Gardiner	.05
589	Craig Lefferts	.05
590	Paul Assenmacher RC	.05
591	Bryn Smith	.05
592	Donn Pall	.05
593	Mike Jackson	.05
594	Scott Radinsky	.05
595	Brian Holman	.05
596	Geronimo Pena	.05
597	Mike Jeffcoat	.05
598	Carlos Martinez RC	.05
599	Geno Petralli	.05
600	Checklist 501-600	.05
601	Jerry Don Gleaton	.05
602	Adam Peterson RC	.05
603	Craig Grebeck	.05
604	Mark Guthrie	.05
605	Frank Tanana	.05
606	Hensley Meulens RC	.05
607	Mark Davis	.05
608	Eric Plunk	.05
609	Mark Williamson	.05
610	Lee Guetterman RC	.05
611	Bobby Rose	.05
612	Bill Wegman	.05
613	Mike Hartley	.05
614	Chris Beasley RC	.05
615	Chris Bosio	.05
616	Henry Cotto	.05
617	Chico Walker RC	.05
618	Russ Swan RC	.05
619	Bob Walk	.05
620	Billy Swift	.05
621	Warren Newson RC	.05
622	Steve Bedrosian RC	.05
623	Ricky Bones RC	.05
624	Kevin Tapani	.05
625	Juan Guzman RC	.05
626	Jeff Johnson RC	.05
627	Jeff Montgomery	.05
628	Ken Hill	.05
629	Gary Thurman	.05
630	Steve Howe RC	.05
631	Jose DeJesus	.05
632	Bert Blyleven	.05
633	Jaime Navarro	.05
634	Lee Stevens RC	.05
635	Pete Harnisch	.05
636	Bill Landrum	.05
637	Rich DeLucia	.05
638	Luis Salazar RC	.05
639	Rob Murphy	.05
640	A.L. Diamond Skills Checklist (Rickey Henderson, Jose Canseco)	.05
641	Roger Clemens (Diamond Skills)	.40
642	Jim Abbott (Diamond Skills)	.05
643	Travis Fryman (Diamond Skills)	.05
644	Jesse Barfield (Diamond Skills)	.05
645	Cal Ripken, Jr. (Diamond Skills)	.50
646	Wade Boggs (Diamond Skills)	.35
647	Cecil Fielder (Diamond Skills)	.05
648	Rickey Henderson (Diamond Skills)	.20
649	Jose Canseco (Diamond Skills)	.15
650	Ken Griffey Jr. (Diamond Skills)	.45
651	Kenny Rogers	.05
652	Luis Mercedes RC	.05
653	Mike Stanton	.05
654	Glenn Davis	.05
655	Nolan Ryan	1.00
656	Reggie Jefferson	.05
657	Javier Ortiz RC	.05
658	Greg A. Harris	.05
659	Mariano Duncan	.05
660	Jeff Shaw	.05
661	Mike Moore	.05
662	Chris Haney RC	.05
663	Joe Slusarski RC	.05
664	Wayne Housie RC	.05
665	Carlos Garcia	.05
666	Bob Ojeda	.05
667	Bryan Hickerson RC	.05
668	Tim Belcher	.05
669	Ron Darling	.05
670	Rex Hudler RC	.05
671	Sid Fernandez	.05
672	Chito Martinez RC	.05
673	Pete Schourek RC	.05
674	Armando Renoso RC	.05
675	Mike Mussina	.30
676	Kevin Morton RC	.05
677	Norm Charlton	.05
678	Danny Darwin	.05
679	Eric King	.05
680	Ted Power	.05
681	Barry Jones	.05
682	Carney Lansford	.05
683	Mel Rojas	.05
684	Rick Honeycutt	.05
685	Jeff Fassero RC	.05
686	Cris Carpenter RC	.05
687	Tim Crews	.05
688	Scott Terry	.05
689	Chris Gwynn	.05
690	Gerald Perry	.05
691	John Barfield	.05
692	Bob Melvin	.05
693	Juan Agosto	.05
694	Alejandro Pena RC	.05
695	Jeff Russell	.05
696	Carmelo Martinez	.05
697	Bud Black	.05
698	Dave Otto RC	.05
699	Billy Hatcher	.05
700	Checklist 601-700	.05
701	Clemente Nunez RC	.05
702	"Rookie Threats" (Donovan Osborne, Brian Jordan, Mark Clark)	.05
703	Mike Morgan	.05
704	Keith Miller	.05
705	Kurt Stillwell	.05
706	Damon Berryhill	.05
707	Von Hayes	.05
708	Rick Sutcliffe	.05
709	Hubie Brooks	.05
710	Ryan Turner RC	.05
711	N.L. Diamond Skills Checklist (Barry Bonds, Andy Van Slyke)	.30
712	Jose Rijo (Diamond Skills)	.05
713	Tom Glavine (Diamond Skills)	.05
714	Shawon Dunston (Diamond Skills)	.05
715	Andy Van Slyke (Diamond Skills)	.05
716	Ozzie Smith (Diamond Skills)	.35
717	Tony Gwynn (Diamond Skills)	.35
718	Will Clark (Diamond Skills)	.35
719	Marquis Grissom (Diamond Skills)	.05
720	Howard Johnson (Diamond Skills)	.05
721	Barry Bonds (Diamond Skills)	.50
722	Kirk McCaskill	.05
723	Sammy Sosa	.50
724	George Bell	.05
725	Gregg Jefferies	.05
726	Gary DiSarcina RC	.05
727	Mike Bordick	.05
728	Eddie Murray (400 Home Run Club)	.20
729	Rene Gonzales	.05
730	Mike Bielecki	.05
731	Calvin Jones RC	.05
732	Jack Morris	.05
733	Frank Viola	.05
734	Dave Winfield	.40
735	Kevin Mitchell	.05
736	Billy Swift	.05
737	Dan Gladden	.05
738	Mike Jackson	.05
739	Mark Carreon	.05
740	Kirt Manwaring	.05
741	Randy Myers	.05
742	Kevin McReynolds	.05
743	Steve Sax	.05
744	Wally Joyner	.05
745	Gary Sheffield	.25
746	Danny Tartabull	.05
747	Julio Valera	.05
748	Denny Neagle	.05
749	Lance Blankenship	.05
750	Mike Gallego	.05
751	Bret Saberhagen	.05
752	Ruben Amaro RC	.05
753	Eddie Murray	.40
754	Kyle Abbott RC	.05
755	Bobby Bonilla	.05
756	Eric Davis	.05
757	Eddie Taubensee RC	.05
758	Andres Galarraga	.05
759	Pete Incaviglia	.05
760	Tom Candiotti	.05
761	Tim Belcher	.05
762	Ricky Bones	.05
763	Bip Roberts	.05
764	Pedro Munoz	.05
765	Greg Swindell	.05
766	Kenny Lofton	.05
767	Gary Carter	.40
768	Charlie Hayes	.05
769	Dickie Thon	.05
770	Diamond Debuts Checklist (Donovan Osborne)	.05
771	Bret Boone (Diamond Debuts)	.10
772	Archi Cianfrocco RC (Diamond Debuts)	.05
773	Mark Clark RC (Diamond Debuts)	.20
774	Chad Curtis RC (Diamond Debuts)	.05
775	Pat Listach RC (Diamond Debuts)	.05
776	Pat Mahomes RC (Diamond Debuts)	.05
777	Donovan Osborne RC (Diamond Debuts)	.05
778	John Patterson RC (Diamond Debuts)	.05
779	Andy Stankiewicz RC (Diamond Debuts)	.05
780	Turk Wendell RC (Diamond Debuts)	.10
781	Bill Krueger	.05
782	Rickey Henderson (Grand Theft)	.20
783	Kevin Seitzer	.05
784	Dave Martinez	.05
785	John Smiley	.05
786	Matt Stairs	.05
787	Scott Scudder	.05
788	John Wetteland	.05
789	Jack Armstrong	.05
790	Ken Hill	.05
791	Dick Schofield	.05
792	Mariano Duncan	.05
793	Bill Pecota	.05
794	Mike Kelly RC	.05
795	Willie Randolph	.05
796	Butch Henry RC	.05
797	Carlos Hernandez RC	.05
798	Doug Jones	.05
799	Melido Perez	.05
800	Checklist	.05
SP3	"Prime Time's Two" (Deion Sanders)	.25
SP4	"Mr. Baseball" (Tom Selleck, Frank Thomas)	2.00
HH2	Ted Williams (Hologram)	2.00

Baseball Heroes Bench/Morgan

This set is devoted to two of the vital cogs in Cincinnati's Big Red Machine: Hall of Famers Johnny Bench and Joe Morgan. Cards, numbered 37-45, were included in high number packs. An unnumbered cover card was also produced. Both players autographed 2,500 of card #45, the painting of the Reds duo by sports artist Vernon Wells.

		NM/M
Complete Set (10):		4.00
Common Card:		.50
Autographed Card:		65.00
---	Header Card	.75
37	1968 Rookie of the Year (Johnny Bench)	.75
38	1968-77 Ten Straight Gold Gloves (Johnny Bench)	.75
39	1970 & 1972 MVP (Johnny Bench)	.75
40	1965 Rookie Year (Joe Morgan)	.50
41	1975-76 Back-to-Back MVP (Joe Morgan)	.50
42	1980-83 The Golden Years (Joe Morgan)	.50
43	1972-79 Big Red Machine (Johnny Bench, Joe Morgan)	.60
44	1989 & 1990 Hall of Fame (Johnny Bench, Joe Morgan)	.60
45	Checklist - Heroes 37-45 (Johnny Bench, Joe Morgan)	.60

Bench-Morgan Box Bottoms

The eight Heroes of Baseball high-number cards featuring Johnny Bench and/or Joe Morgan were also issued in a box-bottom version measuring about 5" x 7". The blank-back box bottoms are listed here according to the corresponding number of the regular-size cards.

		NM/M
Complete Set (8):		7.00
Common Card:		1.00
(37)	1968 Rookie of the Year (Johnny Bench)	1.00
(38)	1968-77 Ten Straight Gold Gloves (Johnny Bench)	1.00
(39)	1970 & 1972 MVP (Johnny Bench)	1.00
(40)	1965 Rookie Year (Joe Morgan)	1.00
(41)	1975-76 Back-to-Back MVP (Joe Morgan)	1.00
(42)	1980-83 The Golden Years (Joe Morgan)	1.00
(43)	1972-79 Big Red Machine (Johnny Bench, Joe Morgan)	1.00
(44)	1989 & 1990 Hall of Fame (Johnny Bench, Joe Morgan)	1.00

Baseball Heroes Ted Williams

This Baseball Heroes set devoted to Ted Williams continues where previous efforts left off by numbering it from 28-36. An unnumbered "Baseball Heroes" cover card is also included. Cards were found in low-number foil and jumbo packs. Williams also autographed 2,500 cards, which were numbered and randomly inserted in low-number packs.

		NM/M
Complete Set (10):		3.00
Common Player:		.50
Autographed Card:		425.00
---	Header Card	.75
28	1939 Rookie Year (Ted Williams)	.50
29	1941 .406! (Ted Williams)	.50
30	1942 Triple Crown Year (Ted Williams)	.50
31	1946 & 1949 MVP (Ted Williams)	.50
32	1947 Second Triple Crown (Ted Williams)	.50
33	1950s Player of the Decade (Ted Williams)	.50
34	1960 500 Home Run Club (Ted Williams)	.50
35	1966 Hall of Fame (Ted Williams)	.50
36	Checklist - Heroes 28-36 (Ted Williams)	.50

Ted Williams Box Bottoms

Foil-pack boxes of low-number 1992 Upper Deck baseball featured on their bottom an oversize reproduction of the front of one of the Ted Williams "Baseball Heroes" insert cards. Eight different box-bottom cards were produced, measuring 5" x 7" and printed on a mottled orange background. The box-bottom cards are blank-backed and unnumbered. They are checklisted here according to the card numbers of the regular-size version.

		NM/M
Complete Set (8):		6.00
Common Player:		1.00
(28)	1939 - Rookie Year (Ted Williams)	1.00
(29)	1941 - .406 (Ted Williams)	1.00
(30)	1942 - Triple Crown Year (Ted Williams)	1.00
(31)	1946, 1949 - MVP (Ted Williams)	1.00
(32)	1947 - Second Triple Crown (Ted Williams)	1.00
(33)	1950s - Player of the Decade (Ted Williams)	1.00
(34)	1960 - 500 Hokme Run Club (Ted Williams)	1.00
(35)	1966 - Hall of Fame (Ted Williams)	1.00

College POY Holograms

This three-card hologram set features the College Player of the Year winners from 1989-91. Cards were randomly inserted in high number foil packs and have a CP prefix for numbering.

		NM/M
Complete Set (3):		.75
Common Player:		.25
1	David McCarty	.25
2	Mike Kelly	.25
3	Ben McDonald	.25

Hall of Fame Heroes

This set features three top players from the 1970s: Vida Blue, Lou Brock and Rollie Fingers. The cards continue from last year's set by using numbers H5-H8. The three players are each on one card; the fourth card features all three. They were found in low-number foil packs and specially-marked jumbo packs. Both types of packs could also contain autographed cards; each player signed 3,000 cards.

		NM/M
Complete Set (4):		2.50
Common Player:		.50
5	Vida Blue	.50
5a	Vida Blue/Auto.	20.00
6	Lou Brock	1.00
6a	Lou Brock/Auto.	35.00
7	Rollie Fingers	.50
7a	Rollie Fingers/Auto.	30.00
8	Vida Blue, Lou Brock, Rollie Fingers	1.00

Heroes Highlights

Special packaging of 1992 Upper Deck high numbers produced for sales to dealers at its Heroes of Baseball show series included these cards of former players as inserts. Cards have a Heroes Highlights banner including the player's name and the date of his career highlight beneath the photo. In a tombstone frame on back, the highlight is chronicled. Cards are numbered alphabetically by player name, with the card number carrying an HI prefix.

		NM/M
Complete Set (10):		4.00
Common Player:		.45
1	Bobby Bonds	.45
2	Lou Brock	.45
3	Rollie Fingers	.45
4	Bob Gibson	.45
5	Reggie Jackson	.75
6	Gaylord Perry	.45
7	Robin Roberts	.45
8	Brooks Robinson	.45
9	Billy Williams	.45
10	Ted Williams	2.00

Home Run Heroes

This 26-card set features a top home run hitter from each major league team. The cards, numbered HR1-HR26, were found in low-number jumbo packs, one per pack.

		NM/M
Complete Set (26):		5.00
Common Player:		.15
1	Jose Canseco	.45
2	Cecil Fielder	.15
3	Howard Johnson	.15
4	Cal Ripken, Jr.	1.50
5	Matt Williams	.15
6	Joe Carter	.15
7	Ron Gant	.15
8	Frank Thomas	.75
9	Andre Dawson	.40
10	Fred McGriff	.15
11	Danny Tartabull	.15
12	Chili Davis	.15
13	Albert Belle	.15
14	Jack Clark	.15
15	Paul O'Neill	.15

16	Darryl Strawberry	.15
17	Dave Winfield	.75
18	Jay Buhner	.15
19	Juan Gonzalez	.25
20	Greg Vaughn	.15
21	Barry Bonds	1.50
22	Matt Nokes	.15
23	John Kruk	.15
24	Ivan Calderon	.15
25	Jeff Bagwell	.75
26	Todd Zeile	.15

Scouting Report

These cards were randomly inserted in Upper Deck high-number jumbo packs. The set is numbered SR1-SR25 and features 25 top prospects, including 1992 Rookies of the Year Pat Listach and Eric Karros. "Scouting Report" is written down the side on the front in silver lettering. The back features a clipboard which shows a photo, a player profile and a major league scouting report.

		NM/M
Complete Set (25):		2.00
Common Player:		.25
1	Andy Ashby	.25
2	Willie Banks	.25
3	Kim Batiste	.25
4	Derek Bell	.25
5	Archi Cianfrocco	.25
6	Royce Clayton	.25
7	Gary DiSarcina	.25
8	Dave Fleming	.25
9	Butch Henry	.25
10	Todd Hundley	.25
11	Brian Jordan	.25
12	Eric Karros	.25
13	Pat Listach	.25
14	Scott Livingstone	.25
15	Kenny Lofton	.25
16	Pat Mahomes	.25
17	Denny Neagle	.25
18	Dave Nilsson	.25
19	Donovan Osborne	.25
20	Reggie Sanders	.25
21	Andy Stankiewicz	.25
22	Jim Thome	1.50
23	Julio Valera	.25
24	Mark Wohlers	.25
25	Anthony Young	.25

Ted Williams' Best Hitters/Future

Twenty of the best hitters in baseball according to legend Ted Williams are featured in this special insert set from Upper Deck. The cards are styled much like the 1992 FanFest cards and showcase each chosen player. Each card is numbered with a "T" designation.

		NM/M
Complete Set (20):		3.00
Common Player:		.12
1	Wade Boggs	.50
2	Barry Bonds	1.00
3	Jose Canseco	.25
4	Will Clark	.10
5	Cecil Fielder	.10
6	Tony Gwynn	.50
7	Rickey Henderson	.40

8	Fred McGriff	.10
9	Kirby Puckett	.50
10	Ruben Sierra	.20
11	Roberto Alomar	.20
12	Jeff Bagwell	.40
13	Albert Belle	.10
14	Juan Gonzalez	.20
15	Ken Griffey Jr.	.75
16	Chris Hoiles	.10
17	Dave Justice	.10
18	Phil Plantier	.10
19	Frank Thomas	.40
20	Robin Ventura	.10

FanFest

This 54-card boxed set was made available through special offers at the 1992 National Sports Collectors Convention and at the 1992 All-Star FanFest in San Diego. Card fronts feature a glossy UV finish, silver-foil stamping and the All-Star FanFest logo. The card backs include a player profile. Both "Future Heroes" and past and present "All-Star Heroes" are featured. The complete set was packaged in an attractive blue box with white pinstripes.

		NM/M
Complete Set (54):		6.00
Common Player:		.10
1	Steve Avery	.10
2	Ivan Rodriguez	.60
3	Jeff Bagwell	.75
4	Delino DeShields	.10
5	Royce Clayton	.10
6	Robin Ventura	.10
7	Phil Plantier	.10
8	Ray Lankford	.10
9	Juan Gonzalez	.40
10	Frank Thomas	.75
11	Roberto Alomar	.30
12	Sandy Alomar, Jr.	.10
13	Wade Boggs	1.25
14	Barry Bonds	2.50
15	Bobby Bonilla	.10
16	George Brett	1.50
17	Jose Canseco	.60
18	Will Clark	.10
19	Roger Clemens	1.50
20	Eric Davis	.10
21	Rob Dibble	.10
22	Cecil Fielder	.10
23	Dwight Gooden	.10
24	Ken Griffey Jr.	2.00
25	Tony Gwynn	1.25
26	Bryan Harvey	.10
27	Rickey Henderson	.75
28	Howard Johnson	.10
29	Wally Joyner	.10
30	Barry Larkin	.10
31	Don Mattingly	1.50
32	Mark McGwire	2.25
33	Dale Murphy	.30
34	Rafael Palmeiro	.60
35	Kirby Puckett	1.25
36	Cal Ripken, Jr.	2.50
37	Nolan Ryan	2.50
38	Chris Sabo	.10
39	Ryne Sandberg	1.25
40	Benito Santiago	.10
41	Ruben Sierra	.10
42	Ozzie Smith	1.25
43	Darryl Strawberry	.10
44	Robin Yount	.75
45	Rollie Fingers	.20
46	Reggie Jackson	1.25
47	Billy Williams	.20
48	Lou Brock	.20
49	Gaylord Perry	.20
50	Ted Williams	2.00
51	Brooks Robinson	.50
52	Bob Gibson	.20
53	Bobby Bonds	.20
54	Robin Roberts	.20

FanFest Gold

One out of every 60 sets of Upper Deck FanFest All-Stars was produced with gold-foil printing highlights rather than silver. The sets were randomly inserted into cases.

	NM/M
Complete Set (54):	30.00
Common Player:	.25

FanFest Ted Williams Super

This large-format (8-1/2" x 11") card is essentially an enlargement of Ted Williams' card issued with the FanFest All-Star Heroes boxed set by UD. The Williams super cards were distributed at the FanFest event and are serially numbered on back within an edition of 2,500.

	NM/M
Ted Williams	25.00

MVP Holograms

State of the art holography is presented in this 54-card plastic-cased set featuring a top pitcher and a top position player from each major league team, plus 1991 MVPs Terry Pendleton and Cal Ripken, Jr. The hologram on the front of each card feature a close-up and a field-action photo of the player; his name and position are in a strip at bottom. Full-color backs have a player photo on the right and career summary on the left. A custom album for the set was available via a mail offer for $10. Each set includes a numbered certificate of authenticity, verifying its position within a total issue of 216,000 sets.

		NM/M
Complete Set (54):		6.00
Common Player:		.10
1	A.L. Checklist (Cal Ripken, Jr.)	.40
2	N.L. Checkklist (Terry Pendleton)	.10
3	Jim Abbott	.10
4	Roberto Alomar	.25
5	Kevin Appier	.10
6	Steve Avery	.10
7	Jeff Bagwell	.40
8	Albert Belle	.10
9	Andy Benes	.10
10	Wade Boggs	.50
11	Barry Bonds	1.00
12	George Brett	.60
13	Ivan Calderon	.10
14	Jose Canseco	.30
15	Will Clark	.10
16	Roger Clemens	.60
17	David Cone	.10
18	Doug Drabek	.10
19	Dennis Eckersley	.35
20	Scott Erickson	.10
21	Cecil Fielder	.10
22	Ken Griffey Jr.	.75
23	Bill Gullickson	.10
24	Juan Guzman	.10
25	Pete Harnisch	.10
26	Howard Johnson	.10
27	Randy Johnson	.40
28	John Kruk	.10
29	Barry Larkin	.10
30	Greg Maddux	.50
31	Dennis Martinez	.10
32	Ramon Martinez	.10
33	Don Mattingly	.60
34	Jack McDowell	.10
35	Fred McGriff	.10
36	Paul Molitor	.40
37	Charles Nagy	.10
38	Gregg Olson	.10
39	Terry Pendleton	.10
40	Luis Polonia	.10

41	Kirby Puckett	.50
42	Dave Righetti	.10
43	Jose Rijo	.10
44	Cal Ripken, Jr.	1.00
45	Nolan Ryan	1.00
46	Ryne Sandberg	.50
47	Scott Sanderson	.10
48	Ruben Sierra	.10
49	Lee Smith	.10
50	Ozzie Smith	.50
51	Darryl Strawberry	.10
52	Frank Thomas	.40
53	Bill Wegman	.10
54	Mitch Williams	.10

Comic Ball 3

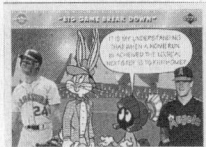

The third series of Comic Ball cards was issued in 1992 and was the second to combine photos of real ballplayers with Looney Tune cartoon characters in several cartoon strip-style series. Players featured in the set with Bugs, Taz and the gang were Jim Abbott and the Ken Griffeys, Sr. and Jr. Each of the 198 regular cards features a puzzle-piece back. A special album to house the set was sold separately. A series of holograms which also combined the players and cartoon figures was issued as pack inserts.

		NM/M
Complete Set (198):		6.00
Common Card:		.05
Hologram:		1.00

Holograms

These blank-back holograms which combine player pictures with those of cartoon characters were issued as inserts in Comic Ball 3 foil packs.

		NM/M
Common Hologram:		.50
(1)	Jim Abbott (w/Tweety)	1.00
(2)	Jim Abbott (w/Taz)	1.00
(3)	Ken Griffey Jr. (w/Bugs)	2.00
(4)	Ken Griffey Jr. (w/Wile E. Coyote)	2.00
(5)	Chuck Jones (Artist) (w/Bugs)	.50

1993 Upper Deck

Upper Deck introduced its 1993 set in a two-series format to adjust to expansion. Cards 1-420 make up the first series. Special subsets in Series 1 include rookies, teammates and community heroes. Fronts feature color player photos surrounded by a white border. Backs feature vertical photos, a change from the past, and more complete statistics than Upper Deck had in the past. The hologram appears in the lower-left corner on the card back. One out of 20 factory sets featured cards with gold, rather than silver, holograms.

		NM/M
Unopened Fact. Set (840):		30.00
Complete Set (840):		25.00
Common Player:		.05
Gold Hologram:		4X
Series 1 or 2 Pack (15):		.75
Series 1 or 2 Wax Box (36):		17.50
Jumbo Pack, USA (27):		1.50
Jumbo Box, USA (20):		17.50
Jumbo Pack, Canada (23):		2.00
Jumbo Box, Canada (20):		20.00

1	Tim Salmon (Checklist)	.05
2	Mike Piazza/SR	1.25
3	Rene Arocha/SR RC	.05
4	Willie Greene/SR RC	.05
5	Manny Alexander/SR RC	.05
6	Dan Wilson/SR	.05
7	Dan Smith/SR RC	.05
8	Kevin Rogers/SR RC	.05
9	Nigel Wilson/SR RC	.05
10	Joe Vitko/SR RC	.05
11	Tim Costo/SR RC	.05
12	Alan Embree/SR	.05
13	Jim Tatum/SR RC	.05
14	Cris Colon/SR RC	.05
15	Steve Hosey/SR RC	.05
16	Sterling Hitchcock/SR RC	.15
17	Dave Mlicki/SR RC	.05
18	Jessie Hollins/SR RC	.05
19	Bobby J. Jones/SR RC	.05
21	Kurt Miller/SR RC	.05
22	Melvin Nieves/SR RC	.05
23	Billy Ashley/SR RC	.05
22	J.T. Snow/SR RC/SR	.50
24	Chipper Jones/SR	1.00
25	Tim Salmon/SR	.25
26	Tim Pugh/SR RC	.05
27	David Nied/SR	.05
28	Mike Trombley/SR RC	.05
29	Javier Lopez/SR)	.05
30	Community Heroes Checklist (Jim Abbott)	.05
31	Jim Abbott (Community Heroes)	.05
32	Dale Murphy (Community Heroes)	.10
33	Tony Pena (Community Heroes)	.05
34	Kirby Puckett (Community Heroes)	.40
35	Harold Reynolds (Community Heroes)	.05
36	Cal Ripken, Jr. (Community Heroes)	.65
37	Nolan Ryan (Community Heroes)	.65
38	Ryne Sandberg (Community Heroes)	.35
39	Dave Stewart (Community Heroes)	.05
40	Dave Winfield (Community Heroes)	.25
41	Teammates Checklist (Joe Carter, Mark McGwire)	.50
42	Blockbuster Trade (Joe Carter, Roberto Alomar)	.05
43	Brew Crew (Pat Listach, Robin Yount, Paul Molitor)	.15
44	Iron and Steal (Brady Anderson, Cal Ripken, Jr.)	.45
45	Youthful Tribe (Albert Belle, Sandy Alomar Jr., Jim Thome, Carlos Baerga, Kenny Lofton)	.25
46	Motown Mashers (Cecil Fielder, Mickey Tettleton)	.05
47	Yankee Pride (Roberto Kelly, Don Mattingly)	.45
48	Boston Cy Sox (Frank Viola, Roger Clemens)	.30
49	Bash Brothers (Ruben Sierra, Mark McGwire)	.50
50	Twin Titles (Kent Hrbek, Kirby Puckett)	.35
51	Southside Sluggers (Robin Ventura, Frank Thomas)	.35
52	Latin Stars (Jose Canseco, Ivan Rodriguez, Rafael Palmeiro, Juan Gonzalez)	.35
53	Lethal Lefties (Mark Langston, Jim Abbott, Chuck Finley)	.05
54	Royal Family (Gregg Jefferies, George Brett, Wally Joyner)	.35
55	Pacific Sox Exchange (Kevin Mitchell, Jay Buhner, Ken Griffey Jr.)	.40
56	George Brett	.85
57	Scott Cooper	.05
58	Mike Maddux	.05
59	Rusty Meacham RC	.05
60	Wil Cordero	.05
61	Tim Teufel	.05
62	Jeff Montgomery	.05
63	Scott Livingstone RC	.05
64	Doug Dascenzo	.05
65	Bret Boone	.05
66	Tim Wakefield RC	.10
67	Curt Schilling	.05
68	Frank Tanana	.05
69	Len Dykstra	.05
70	Derek Lilliquist	.05
71	Anthony Young RC	.05
72	Hipolito Pichardo RC	.05
73	Rod Beck RC	.05
74	Kent Hrbek	.05
75	Tom Glavine	.20
76	Kevin Brown	.05
77	Chuck Finley	.05
78	Bob Walk	.05
79	Rheal Cormier	.05
80	Rick Sutcliffe	.05

No.	Player	Price
81	Harold Baines	.05
82	Lee Smith	.05
83	Geno Petralli	.05
84	Jose Oquendo	.05
85	Mark Gubicza	.05
86	Mickey Tettleton	.05
87	Bobby Witt	.05
88	Mark Lewis	.05
89	Kevin Appier	.05
90	Mike Stanton	.05
91	Rafael Belliard	.05
92	Kenny Rogers	.05
93	Randy Velarde	.05
94	Luis Sojo	.05
95	Mark Leiter	.05
96	Jody Reed	.05
97	Pete Harnisch	.05
98	Tom Candiotti	.05
99	Mark Portugal	.05
100	Dave Valle	.05
101	Shawon Dunston	.05
102	B.J. Surhoff	.05
103	Jay Bell	.05
104	Sid Bream	.05
105	Checklist 1-105 (Frank Thomas)	.35
106	Mike Morgan	.05
107	Bill Doran	.05
108	Lance Blankenship	.05
109	Mark Lemke	.05
110	Brian Harper	.05
111	Brady Anderson	.05
112	Bip Roberts	.05
113	Mitch Williams	.05
114	Craig Biggio	.05
115	Eddie Murray	.65
116	Matt Nokes	.05
117	Lance Parrish	.05
118	Bill Swift	.05
119	Jeff Innis	.05
120	Mike LaValliere	.05
121	Hal Morris	.05
122	Walt Weiss	.05
123	Ivan Rodriguez	.60
124	Andy Van Slyke	.05
125	Roberto Alomar	.20
126	Robby Thompson	.05
127	Sammy Sosa	.75
128	Mark Langston	.05
129	Jerry Browne	.05
130	Chuck McElroy	.05
131	Frank Viola	.05
132	Leo Gomez	.05
133	Ramon Martinez	.05
134	Don Mattingly	.85
135	Roger Clemens	.85
136	Rickey Henderson	.65
137	Darren Daulton	.05
138	Ken Hill	.05
139	Ozzie Guillen	.05
140	Jerald Clark	.05
141	Dave Fleming	.05
142	Delino DeShields	.05
143	Matt Williams	.05
144	Larry Walker	.05
145	Ruben Sierra	.05
146	Ozzie Smith	.75
147	Chris Sabo	.05
148	Carlos Hernandez RC	.05
149	Pat Borders	.05
150	Orlando Merced	.05
151	Royce Clayton	.05
152	Kurt Stillwell	.05
153	Dave Hollins	.05
154	Mike Greenwell	.05
155	Nolan Ryan	1.50
156	Felix Jose	.05
157	Junior Felix	.05
158	Derek Bell	.05
159	Steve Buechele	.05
160	John Burkett	.05
161	Pat Howell RC	.05
162	Milt Cuyler	.05
163	Terry Pendleton	.05
164	Jack Morris	.05
165	Tony Gwynn	.75
166	Deion Sanders	.10
167	Mike Devereaux	.05
168	Ron Darling	.05
169	Orel Hershiser	.05
170	Mike Jackson	.05
171	Doug Jones	.05
172	Dan Walters RC	.05
173	Darren Lewis	.05
174	Carlos Baerga	.05
175	Ryne Sandberg	.75
176	Gregg Jefferies	.05
177	John Jaha	.05
178	Luis Polonia	.05
179	Kirt Manwaring	.05
180	Mike Magnante	.05
181	Billy Ripken	.05
182	Mike Moore	.05
183	Eric Anthony	.05
184	Lenny Harris	.05
185	Tony Pena	.05
186	Mike Felder	.05
187	Greg Olson	.05
188	Rene Gonzales	.05
189	Mike Bordick	.05
190	Mel Rojas	.05
191	Todd Frohwirth	.05
192	Darryl Hamilton	.05
193	Mike Fetters	.05
194	Omar Olivares RC	.05
195	Tony Phillips	.05
196	Paul Sorrento	.05
197	Trevor Wilson	.05
198	Kevin Gross	.05
199	Ron Karkovice	.05
200	Brook Jacoby	.05
201	Mariano Duncan	.05
202	Dennis Cook	.05
203	Daryl Boston	.05
204	Mike Perez	.05
205	Manuel Lee	.05
206	Steve Olin	.05
207	Charlie Hough	.05
208	Scott Scudder	.05
209	Charlie O'Brien	.05
210	Checklist 106-210 (Barry Bonds)	.60
211	Jose Vizcaino	.05
212	Scott Leius	.05
213	Kevin Mitchell	.05
214	Brian Barnes	.05
215	Pat Kelly	.05
216	Chris Hammond	.05
217	Rob Deer	.05
218	Cory Snyder	.05
219	Gary Carter	.65
220	Danny Darwin	.05
221	Tom Gordon	.05
222	Gary Sheffield	.40
223	Joe Carter	.05
224	Jay Buhner	.05
225	Jose Offerman	.05
226	Jose Rijo	.05
227	Mark Whiten	.05
228	Randy Milligan	.05
229	Bud Black	.05
230	Gary DiSarcina	.05
231	Steve Finley	.05
232	Dennis Martinez	.05
233	Mike Mussina	.30
234	Joe Oliver	.05
235	Chad Curtis	.05
236	Shane Mack	.05
237	Jaime Navarro	.05
238	Brian McRae	.05
239	Chili Davis	.05
240	Jeff King	.05
241	Dean Palmer	.05
242	Danny Tartabull	.05
243	Charles Nagy	.05
244	Ray Lankford	.05
245	Barry Larkin	.05
246	Steve Avery	.05
247	John Kruk	.05
248	Derrick May	.05
249	Stan Javier	.05
250	Roger McDowell	.05
251	Dan Gladden	.05
252	Wally Joyner	.05
253	Pat Listach	.05
254	Chuck Knoblauch	.05
255	Sandy Alomar Jr.	.05
256	Jeff Bagwell	.65
257	Andy Stankiewicz	.05
258	Darrin Jackson	.05
259	Brett Butler	.05
260	Joe Orsulak	.05
261	Andy Benes	.05
262	Kenny Lofton	.05
263	Robin Ventura	.05
264	Ron Gant	.05
265	Ellis Burks	.05
266	Juan Guzman	.05
267	Wes Chamberlain	.05
268	John Smiley	.05
269	Franklin Stubbs	.05
270	Tom Browning	.05
271	Dennis Eckersley	.60
272	Carlton Fisk	.65
273	Lou Whitaker	.05
274	Phil Plantier	.05
275	Bobby Bonilla	.05
276	Ben McDonald	.05
277	Bob Zupcic	.05
278	Terry Steinbach	.05
279	Terry Mulholland	.05
280	Lance Johnson	.05
281	Willie McGee	.05
282	Bret Saberhagen	.05
283	Randy Myers	.05
284	Randy Tomlin	.05
285	Mickey Morandini	.05
286	Brian Williams	.05
287	Tino Martinez	.05
288	Jose Melendez	.05
289	Jeff Huson	.05
290	Joe Grahe	.05
291	Mel Hall	.05
292	Otis Nixon	.05
293	Todd Hundley	.05
294	Casey Candaele	.05
295	Kevin Seitzer	.05
296	Eddie Taubensee	.05
297	Moises Alou	.05
298	Scott Radinsky	.05
299	Thomas Howard	.05
300	Kyle Abbott	.05
301	Omar Vizquel	.05
302	Keith Miller	.05
303	Rick Aguilera	.05
304	Bruce Hurst	.05
305	Ken Caminiti	.05
306	Mike Pagliarulo	.05
307	Frank Seminara	.05
308	Andre Dawson	.30
309	Jose Lind	.05
310	Joe Boever	.05
311	Jeff Parrett RC	.05
312	Alan Mills	.05
313	Kevin Tapani	.05
314	Darryl Kile	.05
315	Checklist 211-315 (Will Clark)	.05
316	Mike Sharperson	.05
317	John Orton	.05
318	Bob Tewksbury	.40
319	Xavier Hernandez	.05
320	Paul Assenmacher	.05
321	John Franco	.05
322	Mike Timlin	.05
323	Jose Guzman	.05
324	Pedro Martinez	.65
325	Bill Spiers	.05
326	Melido Perez	.05
327	Mike Macfarlane	.05
328	Ricky Bones	.05
329	Scott Bankhead	.05
330	Rich Rodriguez	.05
331	Geronimo Pena	.05
332	Bernie Williams	.05
333	Paul Molitor	.65
334	Roger Mason	.05
335	David Cone	.05
336	Randy Johnson	.65
337	Pat Mahomes	.05
338	Erik Hanson	.05
339	Duane Ward	.05
340	Al Martin	.05
341	Pedro Munoz	.05
342	Greg Colbrunn	.05
343	Julio Valera	.05
344	John Olerud	.05
345	George Bell	.05
346	Devon White	.05
347	Donovan Osborne	.05
348	Mark Gardner	.05
349	Zane Smith	.05
350	Wilson Alvarez	.05
351	Kevin Koslofski RC	.05
352	Roberto Hernandez	.05
353	Glenn Davis	.05
354	Reggie Sanders	.05
355	Ken Griffey Jr.	1.00
355a	Ken Griffey Jr. (Promo, 1992-dated hologram on back.)	3.00
355b	Ken Griffey Jr. (8-1/2" x 11" limited edition of 1,000)	15.00
356	Marquis Grissom	.05
357	Jack McDowell	.05
358	Jimmy Key	.05
359	Stan Belinda	.05
360	Gerald Williams	.05
361	Sid Fernandez	.05
362	Alex Fernandez	.05
363	John Smoltz	.05
364	Travis Fryman	.05
365	Jose Canseco	.50
366	Dave Justice	.05
367	Pedro Astacio RC	.10
368	Tim Belcher	.05
369	Steve Sax	.05
370	Gary Gaetti	.05
371	Jeff Frye	.05
372	Bob Wickman	.05
373	Ryan Thompson RC	.05
374	David Hulse RC	.05
375	Cal Eldred	.05
376	Ryan Klesko	.05
377	Damion Easley RC	.10
378	John Kiely RC	.05
379	Jim Bullinger RC	.05
380	Brian Bohanon	.05
381	Rod Brewer	.05
382	Fernando Ramsey RC	.05
383	Sam Militello	.05
384	Arthur Rhodes	.05
385	Eric Karros	.05
386	Rico Brogna	.05
387	John Valentin RC	.10
388	Kerry Woodson RC	.05
389	Ben Rivera RC	.05
390	Matt Whiteside RC	.05
391	Henry Rodriguez	.05
392	John Wetteland	.05
393	Kent Mercker	.05
394	Bernard Gilkey	.05
395	Doug Henry	.05
396	Mo Vaughn	.05
397	Scott Erickson	.05
398	Bill Gullickson	.05
399	Mark Guthrie	.05
400	Dave Martinez	.05
401	Jeff Kent RC	.05
402	Chris Hoiles	.05
403	Mike Henneman	.05
404	Chris Nabholz	.05
405	Tom Pagnozzi	.05
406	Kelly Gruber	.05
407	Bob Welch	.05
408	Frank Castillo	.05
409	John Dopson	.05
410	Steve Farr	.05
411	Henry Cotto	.05
412	Bob Patterson	.05
413	Todd Stottlemyre	.05
414	Greg A. Harris	.05
415	Denny Neagle	.05
416	Bill Wegman	.05
417	Willie Wilson	.05
418	Terry Leach	.05
419	Willie Randolph	.05
420	Checklist 316-420 (Mark McGwire)	.65
421	Calvin Murray (Top Prospects Checklist)	.05
422	Pete Janicki RC (Top Prospect)	.05
423	Todd Jones RC (Top Prospect)	.05
424	Mike Neill (Top Prospect)	.05
425	Carlos Delgado (Top Prospect)	.40
426	Jose Oliva (Top Prospect)	.05
427	Tyrone Hill (Top Prospect)	.05
428	Dmitri Young (Top Prospect)	.05
429	Derek Wallace RC (Top Prospect)	.05
430	Michael Moore RC (Top Prospect)	.05
431	Cliff Floyd (Top Prospect)	.05
432	Calvin Murray (Top Prospect)	.05
433	Manny Ramirez (Top Prospect)	.75
434	Marc Newfield (Top Prospect)	.05
435	Charles Johnson (Top Prospect)	.05
436	Butch Huskey (Top Prospect)	.05
437	Brad Pennington (Top Prospect)	.05
438	Ray McDavid RC (Top Prospect)	.05
439	Chad McConnell (Top Prospect)	.05
440	Midre Cummings RC (Top Prospect)	.05
441	Benji Gil (Top Prospect)	.05
442	Frank Rodriguez (Top Prospect)	.05
443	Chad Mottola RC (Top Prospect)	.05
444	John Burke RC (Top Prospect)	.05
445	Michael Tucker (Top Prospect)	.05
446	Rick Greene (Top Prospect)	.05
447	Rich Becker (Top Prospect)	.05
448	Mike Robertson (Top Prospect)	.05
449	Derek Jeter RC (Top Prospect)	10.00
450	Checklist 451-470 Inside the Numbers (David McCarty, Ivan Rodriguez)	.05
451	Jim Abbott (Inside the Numbers)	.05
452	Jeff Bagwell (Inside the Numbers)	.40
453	Jason Bere (Inside the Numbers)	.05
454	Delino DeShields (Inside the Numbers)	.05
455	Travis Fryman (Inside the Numbers)	.05
456	Alex Gonzalez (Inside the Numbers)	.05
457	Phil Hiatt (Inside the Numbers)	.05
458	Dave Hollins (Inside the Numbers)	.05
459	Chipper Jones (Inside the Numbers)	.75
460	Dave Justice (Inside the Numbers)	.05
461	Ray Lankford (Inside the Numbers)	.05
462	David McCarty (Inside the Numbers)	.05
463	Mike Mussina (Inside the Numbers)	.15
464	Jose Offerman (Inside the Numbers)	.05
465	Dean Palmer (Inside the Numbers)	.05
466	Geronimo Pena (Inside the Numbers)	.05
467	Eduardo Perez (Inside the Numbers)	.05
468	Ivan Rodriguez (Inside the Numbers)	.25
469	Reggie Sanders (Inside the Numbers)	.05
470	Bernie Williams (Inside the Numbers)	.05
471	Checklist 472-485 Team Stars (Matt Williams, Will Clark, Barry Bonds)	.45
472	Strike Force (John Smoltz, Steve Avery, Greg Maddux, Tom Glavine)	.10
473	Red October (Jose Rijo, Rob Dibble, Roberto Kelly, Reggie Sanders, Barry Larkin)	.10
474	Four Corners (Gary Sheffield, Phil Plantier, Tony Gwynn, Fred McGriff)	.20
475	Shooting Stars (Doug Drabek, Craig Biggio, Jeff Bagwell)	.15
476	Giant Sticks (Will Clark, Barry Bonds, Matt Williams)	.40
477	Boyhood Friends (Darryl Strawberry, Eric Davis)	.05
478	Rock Solid (Dante Bichette, David Nied, Andres Galarraga)	.05
479	Inaugural Catch (Dave Magadan, Orestes Destrade, Bret Barbarie, Jeff Conine)	.05
480	Steel City Champions (Tim Wakefield, Andy Van Slyke, Jay Bell)	.05
481	"Les Grandes Etoiles" (Marquis Grissom, Delino DeShields, Dennis Martinez, Larry Walker)	.05
482	Runnin' Redbirds (Geronimo Pena, Ray Lankford, Ozzie Smith, Bernard Gilkey)	.10
483	Ivy Leaguers (Ryne Sandberg, Mark Grace, Randy Myers)	.15
484	Big Apple Power Switch (Eddie Murray, Bobby Bonilla, Howard Johnson)	.10
485	Hammers & Nails (John Kruk, Dave Hollins, Darren Daulton, Len Dykstra)	.05
486	Barry Bonds (Award Winners)	.60
487	Dennis Eckersley (Award Winners)	.30
488	Greg Maddux (Award Winners)	.40
489	Dennis Eckersley (Award Winners)	.30
490	Eric Karros (Award Winners)	.05
491	Pat Listach (Award Winners)	.05
492	Gary Sheffield (Award Winners)	.10
493	Mark McGwire (Award Winners)	.75
494	Gary Sheffield (Award Winners)	.10
495	Edgar Martinez (Award Winners)	.05
496	Fred McGriff (Award Winners)	.05
497	Juan Gonzalez (Award Winners)	.20
498	Darren Daulton (Award Winners)	.05
499	Cecil Fielder (Award Winners)	.05
500	Checklist 501-510 Diamond Debuts (Brent Gates)	.05
501	Tavo Alvarez (Diamond Debuts)	.05
502	Rod Bolton (Diamond Debuts)	.05
503	John Cummings RC (Diamond Debuts)	.05
504	Brent Gates (Diamond Debuts)	.05
505	Tyler Green (Diamond Debuts)	.05
506	Jose Martinez RC (Diamond Debuts)	.05
507	Troy Percival (Diamond Debuts)	.05
508	Kevin Stocker (Diamond Debuts)	.05
509	Matt Walbeck RC (Diamond Debuts)	.10
510	Rondell White (Diamond Debuts)	.05
511	Billy Ripken	.05
512	Mike Moore	.05
513	Jose Lind	.05
514	Chito Martinez	.05
515	Jose Guzman	.05
516	Kim Batiste	.05
517	Jeff Tackett	.05
518	Charlie Hough	.05
519	Marvin Freeman	.05
520	Carlos Martinez	.05
521	Eric Young	.05
522	Pete Incaviglia	.05
523	Scott Fletcher	.05
524	Orestes Destrade	.05
525	Checklist 421-525 (Ken Griffey Jr.)	.40
526	Ellis Burks	.05
527	Juan Samuel	.05
528	Dave Magadan	.05
529	Jeff Parrett	.05
530	Bill Krueger	.05
531	Frank Bolick	.05
532	Alan Trammell	.05
533	Walt Weiss	.05
534	David Cone	.05
535	Greg Maddux	.75
536	Kevin Young	.05
537	Dave Hansen	.05
538	Alex Cole	.05
539	Greg Hibbard	.05
540	Gene Larkin	.05
541	Jeff Reardon	.05
542	Felix Jose	.05
543	Jimmy Key	.05
544	Reggie Jefferson	.05
545	Gregg Jefferies	.05
546	Dave Stewart	.05
547	Tim Wallach	.05
548	Spike Owen	.05
549	Tommy Greene	.05
550	Fernando Valenzuela	.05
551	Rich Amaral	.05
552	Bret Barberie	.05
553	Edgar Martinez	.05
554	Jim Abbott	.05
555	Frank Thomas	.65
556	Wade Boggs	.75
557	Tom Henke	.05
558	Matt Thompson	.05
559	Lloyd McClendon	.05
560	Vinny Castilla	.05
561	Ricky Jordan	.05
562	Andujar Cedeno	.05
563	Greg Vaughn	.05
564	Cecil Fielder	.05
565	Kirby Puckett	.75
566	Mark McGwire	1.25
567	Barry Bonds	1.50
568	Jody Reed	.05
569	Todd Zeile	.05
570	Mark Carreon	.05
571	Joe Girardi	.05
572	Luis Gonzalez	.05
573	Mark Grace	.60
574	Rafael Palmeiro	.05
575	Darryl Strawberry	.05
576	Will Clark	.05
577	Fred McGriff	.05
578	Kevin Reimer	.05
579	Dave Righetti	.05
580	Juan Bell	.05
581	Jeff Brantley	.05
582	Brian Hunter	.05
583	Tim Naehring	.05
584	Glenallen Hill	.05
585	Cal Ripken, Jr.	1.50
586	Albert Belle	.65
587	Robin Yount	.05
588	Chris Bosio	.05
589	Pete Smith	.05
590	Chuck Carr	.05
591	Jeff Blauser	.05
592	Kevin McReynolds	.05
593	Andres Galarraga	.05
594	Kevin Maas	.05
595	Eric Davis	.05
596	Brian Jordan	.05
597	Tim Raines	.05
598	Rick Wilkins	.05
599	Steve Cooke	.05
600	Mike Gallego	.05
601	Mike Munoz	.05
602	Luis Rivera	.05
603	Junior Ortiz	.05
604	Brent Mayne	.05
605	Luis Alicea	.05
606	Damon Berryhill	.05
607	Dave Henderson	.05
608	Kirk McCaskill	.05
609	Jeff Fassero	.05
610	Mike Harkey	.05
611	Francisco Cabrera	.05
612	Rey Sanchez	.05
613	Scott Servais	.05
614	Darrin Fletcher	.05
615	Felix Fermin	.05
616	Kevin Seitzer	.05
617	Bob Scanlan	.05
618	Billy Hatcher	.05
619	John Vander Wal	.05
620	Joe Hesketh	.05
621	Hector Villanueva	.05
622	Randy Milligan	.05
623	Tony Tarasco RC	.05
624	Russ Swan	.05
625	Willie Wilson	.05
626	Frank Tanana	.05
627	Pete O'Brien	.05
628	Lenny Webster	.05
629	Mark Clark	.05
630	Checklist 526-630 (Roger Clemens)	.40
631	Alex Arias	.05
632	Chris Gwynn	.05
633	Tom Bolton	.05
634	Greg Briley	.05
635	Kent Bottenfield	.05
636	Kelly Downs	.05
637	Manuel Lee	.05
638	Al Leiter	.05
639	Jeff Gardner	.05
640	Mike Gardiner	.05
641	Mark Gardner	.05
642	Jeff Branson	.05
643	Paul Wagner	.05
644	Sean Berry	.05
645	Phil Hiatt	.05
646	Kevin Mitchell	.05
647	Charlie Hayes	.05
648	Jim Deshaies	.05
649	Dan Pasqua	.05
650	Mike Maddux	.05
651	Domingo Martinez RC	.05
652	Greg McMichael RC	.05
653	Eric Wedge RC	.05
654	Mark Whiten	.05
655	Bobby Kelly	.05
656	Julio Franco	.05
657	Gene Harris	.05
658	Pete Schourek	.05
659	Mike Bielecki	.05
660	Ricky Gutierrez	.05
661	Chris Hammond	.05
662	Tim Scott	.05
663	Norm Charlton	.05
664	Doug Drabek	.05
665	Dwight Gooden	.05
666	Jim Gott	.05
667	Randy Myers	.05
668	Darren Holmes	.05
669	Tim Spehr	.05
670	Bruce Ruffin	.05

671 Bobby Thigpen .05
672 Tony Fernandez .05
673 Darrin Jackson .05
674 Gregg Olson .05
675 Rob Dibble .05
676 Howard Johnson .05
677 Mike Lansing RC .15
678 Charlie Leibrandt .05
679 Kevin Bass .05
680 Hubie Brooks .05
681 Scott Brosius .05
682 Randy Knorr .05
683 Dante Bichette .05
684 Bryan Harvey .05
685 Greg Gohr .05
686 Willie Banks .05
687 Robb Nen .05
688 Mike Scioscia .05
689 John Farrell .05
690 John Candelaria .05
691 Damon Buford .05
692 Todd Worrell .05
693 Pat Hentgen .05
694 John Smiley .05
695 Greg Swindell .05
696 Derek Bell .05
697 Terry Jorgensen .05
698 Jimmy Jones .05
699 David Wells .05
700 Dave Martinez .05
701 Steve Bedrosian .05
702 Jeff Russell .05
703 Joe Magrane .05
704 Matt Mieske .05
705 Paul Molitor .65
706 Dale Murphy .15
707 Steve Howe .05
708 Greg Gagne .05
709 Dave Eiland .05
710 David West .05
711 Luis Aquino .05
712 Joe Orsulak .05
713 Eric Plunk .05
714 Mike Felder .05
715 Joe Klink .05
716 Lonnie Smith .05
717 Monty Fariss .05
718 Craig Lefferts .05
719 John Habyan .05
720 Willie Blair .05
721 Darnell Coles .05
722 Mark Williamson .05
723 Bryn Smith .05
724 Greg W. Harris .05
725 Graeme Lloyd RC .05
726 Cris Carpenter .05
727 Chico Walker .05
728 Tracy Woodson .05
729 Jose Uribe .05
730 Stan Javier .05
731 Jay Howell .05
732 Freddie Benavides .05
733 Jeff Reboulet .05
734 Scott Sanderson .05
735 Checklist 631-735 (Ryne Sandberg) .20
736 Archi Cianfrocco .05
737 Daryl Boston .05
738 Craig Grebeck .05
739 Doug Dascenzo .05
740 Gerald Young .05
741 Candy Maldonado .05
742 Joey Cora .05
743 Don Slaught .05
744 Steve Decker .05
745 Blas Minor .05
746 Storm Davis .05
747 Carlos Quintana .05
748 Vince Coleman .05
749 Todd Burns .05
750 Steve Frey .05
751 Ivan Calderon .05
752 Steve Reed RC .05
753 Danny Jackson .05
754 Jeff Conine .05
755 Juan Gonzalez .35
756 Mike Kelly .05
757 John Doherty .05
758 Jack Armstrong .05
759 John Wehner .05
760 Scott Bankhead .05
761 Jim Tatum .05
762 Scott Pose RC .05
763 Andy Ashby .05
764 Ed Sprague .05
765 Harold Baines .05
766 Kirk Gibson .05
767 Troy Neel .05
768 Dick Schofield .05
769 Dickie Thon .05
770 Butch Henry .05
771 Junior Felix .05
772 Ken Ryan RC .05
773 Trevor Hoffman .05
774 Phil Plantier .05
775 Bo Jackson .10
776 Benito Santiago .05
777 Andre Dawson .25
778 Bryan Hickerson .05
779 Dennis Moeller .05
780 Ryan Bowen .05
781 Eric Fox .05
782 Joe Kmak .05
783 Mike Hampton .05
784 Darrell Sherman RC .05
785 J.T. Snow .05
786 Dave Winfield .65
787 Jim Austin .05

788 Craig Shipley .05
789 Greg Myers .05
790 Todd Benzinger .05
791 Cory Snyder .05
792 David Segui .05
793 Armando Reynoso .05
794 Chili Davis .05
795 Dave Nilsson .05
796 Paul O'Neill .05
797 Jerald Clark .05
798 Jose Mesa .05
799 Brian Holman .05
800 Jim Eisenreich .05
801 Mark McLemore .05
802 Luis Sojo .05
803 Harold Reynolds .05
804 Dan Plesac .05
805 Dave Stieb .05
806 Tom Brunansky .05
807 Kelly Gruber .05
808 Bob Ojeda .05
809 Dave Burba .05
810 Joe Boever .05
811 Jeremy Hernandez .05
812 Angels Checklist (Tim Salmon) .05
813 Astros Checklist (Jeff Bagwell) .35
814 Athletics Checklist (Mark McGwire) .75
815 Blue Jays Checklist (Roberto Alomar) .10
816 Braves Checklist (Steve Avery) .05
817 Brewers Checklist (Pat Listach) .05
818 Cardinals Checklist (Gregg Jefferies) .05
819 Cubs Checklist (Sammy Sosa) .40
820 Dodgers Checklist (Darryl Strawberry) .05
821 Expos Checklist (Dennis Martinez) .05
822 Giants Checklist (Robby Thompson) .05
823 Indians Checklist (Albert Belle) .05
824 Mariners Checklist (Randy Johnson) .30
825 Marlins Checklist (Nigel Wilson) .05
826 Mets Checklist (Bobby Bonilla) .05
827 Orioles Checklist (Glenn Davis) .05
828 Padres Checklist (Gary Sheffield) .10
829 Phillies Checklist (Darren Daulton) .05
830 Pirates Checklist (Jay Bell) .05
831 Rangers Checklist (Juan Gonzalez) .20
832 Red Sox Checklist (Andre Dawson) .10
833 Reds Checklist (Hal Morris) .05
834 Rockies Checklist (David Nied) .05
835 Royals Checklist (Felix Jose) .05
836 Tigers Checklist (Travis Fryman) .05
837 Twins Checklist (Shane Mack) .05
838 White Sox Checklist (Robin Ventura) .05
839 Yankees Checklist (Danny Tartabull) .05
840 Checklist 736-840 (Roberto Alomar) .10
SP5 3,000 Hits (Robin Yount, George Brett) .50
SP6 Nolan Ryan 1.50

Gold Holograms

Unlike 1992, when gold holograms were found on the back of every card originating in a factory set, in 1993 the use of gold holograms was limited to just one factory set per 20-set case, creating a scarce parallel version.

NM/M
Complete Fact. Set (840): 200.00
Common Player: .50

Baseball Heroes Reggie Jackson Supers

Upper Deck issued a large version of its 1990 Heroes Reggie Jackson cards that was available in retail outlets. Just as in the case of the regular issue Jackson insert cards, there are 10 cards (nine numbered and one unnumbered header card). The cards are 3-1/2" x 5" and identical to the smaller Heroes cards in every other respect. Each of the individual cards carries a sequential number out of a limit of 10,000. The cards were sold one to a package that also included two packs of 1993 Upper Deck cards for about $5.

NM/M
Complete Set (10): 25.00
Common Card: 3.00
1 1969 Emerging Superstar (Reggie Jackson) 3.00
2 1973 An MVP Year (Reggie Jackson) 3.00
3 1977 "Mr. October" (Reggie Jackson) 3.00
4 1978 Jackson vs. Welch (Reggie Jackson) 3.00
5 1982 Under the Halo (Reggie Jackson) 3.00
6 1984 500! (Reggie Jackson) 3.00
7 1986 Moving Up the List (Reggie Jackson) 3.00
8 1987 A Great Career Ends (Reggie Jackson) 3.00
9 Heroes Checklist (Reggie Jackson) 3.00
--- Header Card 3.00

Baseball Heroes Willie Mays

This 10-card insert set includes eight individually-titled cards, an illustrated checklist and one header card. The set is a continuation of Upper Deck's previous Heroes efforts, honoring greats such as Hank Aaron, Nolan Ryan and Reggie Jackson, and is numbered 46-54. Cards were randomly inserted into Series 1 foil packs.

NM/M
Complete Set (10): 4.00
Common Card: .50
Header Card: 1.00
46 1951 Rookie-of-the-Year .50
47 1954 The Catch .50
48 1956-57 30-30 Club .50
49 1961 Four-Homer Game .50
50 1965 Most Valuable Player .50
51 1969 600-Home Run Club .50
52 1972 New York Homecoming .50
53 1979 Hall of Fame .50
54 Checklist - Heroes 46-54 .50

Clutch Performers

Reggie Jackson has selected the players who perform the best under pressure for this 20-card insert set. Cards were available only in Series II retail packs and use the prefix "R" for numbering. Fronts have a black bottom panel with "Clutch Performers" printed in dark gray. Jackson's facsimile autograph is overprinted in gold foil. On back, under a second player photo, is Jackson's picture and his

assessment of the player. There are a few lines of stats to support the player's selection to this exclusive company.

NM/M
Complete Set (20): 8.00
Common Player: .25
1 Roberto Alomar .30
2 Wade Boggs 1.00
3 Barry Bonds 2.50
4 Jose Canseco .40
5 Joe Carter .25
6 Will Clark .25
7 Roger Clemens 1.25
8 Dennis Eckersley .60
9 Cecil Fielder .25
10 Juan Gonzalez .60
11 Ken Griffey Jr. 2.00
12 Rickey Henderson .75
13 Barry Larkin .25
14 Don Mattingly 1.25
15 Fred McGriff .25
16 Terry Pendleton .25
17 Kirby Puckett 1.00
18 Ryne Sandberg 1.00
19 John Smoltz .25
20 Frank Thomas .75

Future Heroes

This insert set includes eight player cards, a checklist and an unnumbered header card. The cards are numbered 55-63 as a continuation of previous Heroes sets, but this one features more than one player; previous sets featured only one player. Card fronts have a Future Heroes logo and a facsimile autograph. The player's name is revealed using a peeled-back paper effect. Cards were randomly inserted in Series II foil packs.

NM/M
Complete Set (10): 5.00
Common Player: .50
Header Card: .25
55 Roberto Alomar .50
56 Barry Bonds 2.50
57 Roger Clemens 1.00
58 Juan Gonzalez .50
59 Ken Griffey Jr. 1.50
60 Mark McGwire 2.00
61 Kirby Puckett .85
62 Frank Thomas .75
63 Checklist .05

Highlights

These 20 insert cards commemorate highlights from the 1992 season. Cards, which were randomly inserted in Series II packs, have a '92 Season Highlights logo on the bottom, with the player's name inside a banner trailing from the logo. The date of the significant event is under the player's name. Card backs have the logo at the top and are numbered with an "HI" prefix. A headline describes what highlight occurred, while the text describes the event.

NM/M
Complete Set (20): 20.00
Common Player: .25
1 Roberto Alomar .50
2 Steve Avery .25
3 Harold Baines .25
4 Damon Berryhill .25
5 Barry Bonds 7.50
6 Bret Boone .25
7 George Brett 4.00
8 Francisco Cabrera .25
9 Ken Griffey Jr. 5.00
10 Rickey Henderson 2.00
11 Kenny Lofton .25
12 Mickey Morandini .25
13 Eddie Murray 2.00
14 David Nied .25
15 Jeff Reardon .25
16 Bip Roberts .25
17 Nolan Ryan 7.50
18 Ed Sprague .25
19 Dave Winfield 2.00
20 Robin Yount 2.00

Home Run Heroes

Albert Belle

This 28-card insert set features the top home run hitters from each team for 1992. Cards, inserted in Series I jumbo packs, are numbered with an "HR" prefix. The card fronts have "Home Run Heroes" printed vertically at the left edge and an embossed bat with the player's name and Upper Deck trademark at bottom. Backs have a purple or pink posterized photo and a few words about the player.

NM/M
Complete Set (28): 7.50
Common Player: .15
1 Juan Gonzalez
2 Mark McGwire 2.25
3 Cecil Fielder .15
4 Fred McGriff .15
5 Albert Belle .15
6 Barry Bonds 2.50
7 Joe Carter .15
8 Darren Daulton .15
9 Ken Griffey Jr. 2.00
10 Dave Hollins .15
11 Ryne Sandberg 1.00
12 George Bell .15
13 Danny Tartabull .15
14 Mike Devereaux .15
15 Greg Vaughn .15
16 Larry Walker .15
17 Dave Justice .15
18 Terry Pendleton .15
19 Eric Karros .15
20 Ray Lankford .15
21 Matt Williams .15
22 Eric Anthony .15
23 Bobby Bonilla .15
24 Kirby Puckett 1.00
25 Mike Macfarlane .15
26 Tom Brunansky .15
27 Paul O'Neill .15
28 Gary Gaetti .15

Looss Collection

Sports photographer Walter Iooss Jr. has captured 26 current players in this insert set featuring their candid portraits. Cards have full-bleed photos and gold foil

stamping. Backs have biographical sketches and are numbered using a WI prefix. They are available in Series I retail packs.

NM/M
Complete Set (27): 10.00
Common Player: .25
Header Card: .25
1 Tim Salmon .25
2 Jeff Bagwell .75
3 Mark McGwire 1.50
4 Roberto Alomar .35
5 Steve Avery .25
6 Paul Molitor .75
7 Ozzie Smith 1.00
8 Mark Grace .25
9 Eric Karros .25
10 Delino DeShields .25
11 Will Clark .25
12 Albert Belle .35
13 Ken Griffey Jr. 1.50
14 Howard Johnson .25
15 Cal Ripken, Jr. 2.00
16 Fred McGriff .25
17 Darren Daulton .25
18 Andy Van Slyke .25
19 Nolan Ryan 2.00
20 Wade Boggs 1.00
21 Barry Larkin .25
22 George Brett 1.25
23 Cecil Fielder .25
24 Kirby Puckett 1.00
25 Frank Thomas .75
26 Don Mattingly 1.25

Looss Collection Supers

Upper Deck issued a series of 27 individually numbered oversized cards identical to the Iooss Collection inserts from the regular 1993 Upper Deck set. The cards are 3-1/2" x 5" and each is numbered on back to a limit of 10,000. The cards were available in retail outlets such as WalMart, packaged in blister packs with two foil packs of 1993 Upper Deck cards for around $5. Authentically autographed and numbered (on card fronts) of some players' cards were sold by Upper Deck Authenticated.

NM/M
Complete Set (27): 20.00
Common Player: .50
Header Card: .25
1 Tim Salmon .50
2 Jeff Bagwell 1.00
3 Mark McGwire 2.00
4 Roberto Alomar .75
5 Steve Avery .50
6 Paul Molitor 1.00
7 Ozzie Smith 1.25
8 Mark Grace .50
9 Eric Karros .50
10 Delino DeShields .50
11 Will Clark .50
12 Albert Belle .50
13 Ken Griffey Jr. 2.00
14 Howard Johnson .50
15 Cal Ripken, Jr. 2.50
16 Fred McGriff .50
17 Darren Daulton .50
18 Andy Van Slyke .50
19 Nolan Ryan 2.50
20 Wade Boggs 1.25
21 Barry Larkin .50
22 George Brett 1.50
23 Cecil Fielder .50
24 Kirby Puckett 1.25
25 Frank Thomas 1.00
26 Don Mattingly 1.50

On Deck

These UV-coated cards feature 25 of the game's top players. Each card has a full-bleed photo on the front and questions and answers on the back. Available only in Series II jumbo packs, the cards have a D prefix for numbering.

NM/M
Complete Set (25): 10.00

Common Player:		.15
1	Jim Abbott	.15
2	Roberto Alomar	.25
3	Carlos Baerga	.15
4	Albert Belle	.15
5	Wade Boggs	1.00
6	George Brett	1.25
7	Jose Canseco	.45
8	Will Clark	.15
9	Roger Clemens	1.25
10	Dennis Eckersley	.65
11	Cecil Fielder	.15
12	Juan Gonzalez	.40
13	Ken Griffey Jr.	1.50
14	Tony Gwynn	1.00
15	Bo Jackson	.20
16	Chipper Jones	1.00
17	Eric Karros	.15
18	Mark McGwire	2.00
19	Kirby Puckett	1.00
20	Nolan Ryan	2.50
21	Tim Salmon	.15
22	Ryne Sandberg	1.00
23	Darryl Strawberry	.15
24	Frank Thomas	.75
25	Andy Van Slyke	.15

Supers

A series of six 1993 Upper Deck cards and one from 1991 was re-issued in an 8-1/2" x 11" format, though the manner of distribution is unclear. The cards are virtually identical in design to the regularly issued versions, except for the size, the lack of a hologram on back, and a 1993 dated seal with an individual serial number. The Ryan card was issued in an edition of 5,000, the Karros and Finley cards were issued in an edition of 2,500; the others were limited to 1,000 each.

		NM/M
Complete Set (7):		24.00
Common Card:		3.00
6	Kirby Puckett (Triple Crown Contender)	4.50
10	Barry Bonds/SP	3.00
24	Eric Karros/1991	3.00
75	Tom Glavine/1993	3.00
77	Chuck Finley	3.00
155	Nolan Ryan	7.50
199	Roger Clemens/SP	5.00

Then And Now

This 18-card lithogram set features both Hall of Famers and current players. The cards feature a combination of four-color player photos and a holographic background. They were random inserts in both Series I and Series II packs. Numbering includes the prefix TN. A limited edition of 2,500 supersize

---

5" by 7" Mickey Mantle Then And Now cards was created for sale through Upper Deck Authenticated.

		NM/M
Complete Set (18):		30.00
Common Player:		.75
1	Wade Boggs	2.00
2	George Brett	2.50
3	Rickey Henderson	1.25
4	Cal Ripken, Jr.	4.00
5	Nolan Ryan	4.00
6	Ryne Sandberg	2.00
7	Ozzie Smith	2.00
8	Darryl Strawberry	.75
9	Dave Winfield	1.25
10	Dennis Eckersley	1.00
11	Tony Gwynn	2.00
12	Howard Johnson	.75
13	Don Mattingly	2.50
14	Eddie Murray	1.25
15	Robin Yount	1.25
16	Reggie Jackson	2.00
17	Mickey Mantle	6.00
17a	Mickey Mantle (5" x 7")	13.50
18	Willie Mays	3.00

1993 Upper Deck 5th Anniversary Supers

Gary Sheffield

This set of oversized (3-1/2" x 5") cards is simply an enlarged version of the Upper Deck 5th Anniversary subset that was inserted with the company's 1993 cards. There are 15 cards in the set, which are reprinted versions of some of the most popular cards in the last five years from Upper Deck. Each of the cards carries a number on the back out of an edition of 10,000. The cards were sold individually in blister packs at retail outlets along with two packs of 1993 Upper Deck.

		NM/M
Complete Set (15):		17.50
Common Player:		1.00
1	Ken Griffey Jr.	2.50
2	Gary Sheffield	1.25
3	Roberto Alomar	1.25
4	Jim Abbott	1.00
5	Nolan Ryan	3.00
6	Juan Gonzalez	1.25
7	David Justice	1.00
8	Carlos Baerga	1.00
9	Reggie Jackson	2.00
10	Eric Karros	1.00
11	Chipper Jones	2.00
12	Ivan Rodriguez	1.50
13	Pat Listach	1.00
14	Frank Thomas	1.75
15	Tim Salmon	1.00

1993 Upper Deck Heroes of Baseball Previews

This four-card preview set was produced in conjunction with the All-Star FanFest in Baltimore to re-introduce the concept of T202-style "triplefolder" baseball cards. The preview set came in a specially decorated box. The 5-1/4" x 2-1/4" cards feature Ted Williams, Mickey Mantle and Reggie Jackson in various combinations of photos and artwork on each card. Backs are printed in red and gold and include an infield-shaped hologram. Written summaries of the players and their careers are featured. Cards have an "HOB" prefix to their number. A special offering of uncut 27" x 20" sheets containing eight complete sets of the preview cards was sold by UD Authenticated in a numbered edition of 2,000.

		NM/M
Complete Set (4):		5.00
Common Card:		1.00
Uncut UDA Sheet:		20.00
1	Triple Threat (Mickey Mantle, Ted Williams)	2.00
2	Changing of the Guard (Mickey Mantle, Reggie Jackson)	1.50
3	Night and Day (Reggie Jackson, Ted Williams)	1.00
4	Hall-of-Fame Trio (Reggie Jackson, Mickey Mantle, Ted Williams)	1.50

Triple Crown Contenders

FRED McGRIFF

These insert cards were available in 1993 Upper Deck Series I foil packs sold by hobby dealers. The set features 10 players who are candidates to win baseball's Triple Crown. Card fronts have a crown and the player's name at the bottom. Backs put that material at the top and explain why the player might lead the league in home runs, batting average and runs batted in.

		NM/M
Complete Set (10):		6.00
Common Player:		.25
1	Barry Bonds	1.50
2	Jose Canseco	.45
3	Will Clark	.25
4	Ken Griffey Jr.	1.25
5	Fred McGriff	.25
6	Kirby Puckett	.75
7	Cal Ripken, Jr.	1.50
8	Gary Sheffield	.35
9	Frank Thomas	.60
10	Larry Walker	.25

5th Anniversary

Chipper Jones

This 15-card insert set replicates 15 of Upper Deck's most popular cards from its first five years. Foil stamping and a fifth-anniversary logo appear on the cards, which are otherwise reproductions of the originals. The prefix A appears before each card number. The cards were available in Series II hobby packs only.

		NM/M
Complete Set (15):		7.00
Common Player:		.25
1	Ken Griffey Jr.	1.50
2	Gary Sheffield	.35
3	Roberto Alomar	.35
4	Jim Abbott	.35
5	Nolan Ryan	2.00
6	Juan Gonzalez	.35
7	Dave Justice	.25

1993UD All-Time Heroes

This 1993 set pays homage to one of the classiest, turn-of-the-century card sets, the T202 Hassan Triple Folders. The All-Time Heroes cards are 2-1/4" x 5-1/4" and feature two side panels and a larger middle panel, which features an action shot of the player. A portrait of the player and the Baseball Assistance Team (BAT) logo flank the action photo. Card backs have a biography and career summary. A Classic Combinations subset of 35 cards features artwork or photographs of two or more great players together, plus individual photos on the side panels. Production was limited to 5,140 numbered cases of 12-card foil packs. Ten T202 reprints were also produced and were randomly inserted in the foil packs.

		NM/M
Complete Set (165):		35.00
Common Player:		.10
Wax Pack (12):		2.00
Wax Box (24):		30.00
1	Hank Aaron	2.00
2	Tommie Agee	.10
3	Bob Allison	.10
4	Matty Alou	.10
5	Sal Bando	.10
6	Hank Bauer	.15
7	Don Baylor	.10
8	Glenn Beckert	.10
9	Yogi Berra	.50
10	Buddy Biancalana	.10
11	Jack Billingham	.10
12	Joe Black	.10
13	Paul Blair	.10
14	Steve Blass	.10
15	Ray Boone	.10
16	Lou Boudreau	.15
17	Ken Brett	.10
18	Nellie Briles	.10
19	Bobby Brown	.10
20	Bill Buckner	.10
21	Don Buford	.10
22	Al Bumbry	.10
23	Lew Burdette	.10
24	Jeff Burroughs	.10
25	Johnny Callison	.10
26	Bert Campaneris	.10
27	Rico Carty	.10
28	Dave Cash	.10
29	Cesar Cedeno	.10
30	Frank Chance	.25
31	Joe Charboneau	.15
32	Ty Cobb	2.00
33	Jerry Coleman	.10
34	Cecil Cooper	.10
35	Frankie Crosetti	.10
36	Alvin Dark	.10
37	Tommy Davis	.10
38	Dizzy Dean	.25
39	Doug DeCinces	.10
40	Bucky Dent	.10
41	Larry Dierker	.10
42	Larry Doby	.20
43	Moe Drabowsky	.10
44	Dave Dravecky	.10
45	Del Ennis	.10
46	Carl Erskine	.10
47	Johnny Evers	.25
48	Elroy Face	.10
49	Rick Ferrell	.10
50	Mark Fidrych	.15
51	Curt Flood	.10
52	Whitey Ford	.50
53	George Foster	.10
54	Jimmie Foxx	.25
55	Jim Fregosi	.10
56	Phil Garner	.10
57	Ralph Garr	.10
58	Lou Gehrig	2.00
59	Bobby Grich	.10
60	Jerry Grote	.10
61	Harvey Haddix	.10
62	Toby Harrah	.10
63	Bud Harrelson	.10
64	Jim Hegan	.10
65	Gil Hodges	.25
66	Ken Holtzman	.10
67	Bob Horner	.10
68	Rogers Hornsby	.25
69	Carl Hubbell	.25
70	Ron Hunt	.10
71	Monte Irvin	.10
72a	Reggie Jackson (Regular issue, black printing on back.)	.50
72b	Reggie Jackson (Dealer promo, red printing on back.)	6.00
73	Larry Jansen	.10

74	Ferguson Jenkins	.10
75	Tommy John	.10
76	Cliff Johnson	.10
77	Davey Johnson	.10
78	Walter Johnson	.45
79	George Kell	.10
80	Don Kessinger	.10
81	Vern Law	.10
82	Dennis Leonard	.10
83	Johnny Logan	.10
84	Mickey Lolich	.10
85	Jim Lonborg	.10
86	Bill Madlock	.10
87	Mickey Mantle	4.00
88	Billy Martin	.25
89	Christy Mathewson	.45
90	Lee May	.10
91	Willie Mays	2.00
92	Bill Mazeroski	.25
93	Gil McDougald	.15
94	Sam McDowell	.10
95	Minnie Minoso	.15
96	Johnny Mize	.25
97	Rick Monday	.10
98	Wally Moon	.10
99	Manny Mota	.10
100	Bobby Murcer	.10
101	Ron Necciai	.10
102	Al Oliver	.10
103	Mel Ott	.15
104	Mel Parnell	.10
105	Jimmy Piersall	.10
106	Johnny Podres	.15
107	Bobby Richardson	.15
108	Robin Roberts	.15
109	Al Rosen	.10
110	Babe Ruth	3.00
111	Joe Sambito	.10
112	Manny Sanguillen	.10
113	Ron Santo	.10
114	Bill Skowron	.15
115	Enos Slaughter	.15
116	Warren Spahn	.20
117	Tris Speaker	.20
118	Frank Thomas	.15
119	Bobby Thomson	.10
120	Andre Thornton	.10
121	Marv Throneberry	.10
122	Luis Tiant	.10
123	Joe Tinker	.25
124	Honus Wagner	.50
125	Bill White	.10
126	Ted Williams	1.00
127	Earl Wilson	.10
128	Joe Wood	.10
129	Cy Young	.40
130	Richie Zisk	.10
131	Babe Ruth, Lou Gehrig	2.00
132	Ted Williams, Rogers Hornsby	1.00
133	Lou Gehrig, Babe Ruth	2.00
134	Babe Ruth, Mickey Mantle	3.00
135	Mickey Mantle, Reggie Jackson	1.00
136	Mel Ott, Carl Hubbell	.15
137	Mickey Mantle, Willie Mays	2.00
138	Cy Young, Walter Johnson	.25
139	Honus Wagner, Rogers Hornsby	.25
140	Mickey Mantle, Whitey Ford	2.00
141	Mickey Mantle, Billy Martin	2.00
142	Cy Young, Walter Johnson	.25
143	Christy Mathewson, Walter Johnson	.25
144	Warren Spahn, Christy Mathewson	.15
145	Honus Wagner, Ty Cobb	.50
146	Babe Ruth, Ty Cobb	1.00
147	Joe Tinker, Johnny Evers	.15
148	Johnny Evers, Frank Chance	.15
149	Hank Aaron, Babe Ruth	1.00
150	Willie Mays, Hank Aaron	1.00
151	Babe Ruth, Willie Mays	1.00
152	Babe Ruth, Whitey Ford	1.00
153	Larry Doby, Minnie Minoso	.25
154	Joe Black, Monte Irvin	.15
155	Joe Wood, Christy Mathewson	.15
156	Christy Mathewson, Cy Young	.25
157	Cy Young, Joe Wood	.15
158	Cy Young, Whitey Ford	.20
159	Cy Young, Ferguson Jenkins	.15
160	Ty Cobb, Rogers Hornsby	.45
161	Tris Speaker, Ted Williams	1.00
162	Rogers Hornsby, Ted Williams	1.00
163	Willie Mays, Monte Irvin	.50
164	Willie Mays, Bobby Thomson	.50
165	Reggie Jackson, Mickey Mantle	2.00

All-Time Heroes T202 Reprints

A series of 10 reprints of the classic 1912 Hassan "Triplefolders" baseball cards on which the All-Time Heroes set was patterned

---

was included as random inserts in the Upper Deck Old-Timers set. The reprints measure 5-1/4" x 2-1/4" (same as the originals). The Hassan cigarette ads on the backs of the originals have been replaced on the reprints by an Upper Deck holo-gram and the logos of the card company, B.A.T., Major League Baseball and the Cooperstown Collection. The Hassan cards are known as T202, their designation in the "American Card Catalog." The reprints are unnumbered and are checklisted here alphabetically in order of the player appearing on the left end of each card.

		NM/M
Complete Set (10):		10.00
Common Player:		.50
(1)	Art Devlin, Christy Mathewson	1.00
(2)	Hugh Jennings, Ty Cobb	2.00
(3)	John Kling, Cy Young	1.00
(4)	Jack Knight, Walter Johnson	.75
(5)	John McGraw, Hugh Jennings	.50
(6)	George Moriarty, Ty Cobb	2.00
(7)	Charley O'Leary, Ty Cobb	2.00
(8)	Charley O'Leary, Ty Cobb	2.00
(9)	Joe Tinker, Frank Chance	1.00
(10)	Joe Wood, Tris Speaker	.50

1993 Upper Deck Diamond Gallery

Utilizing something the company calls lithogram technology, Upper Deck produced a 36-card set that combines four-color photography and a holographic image. The set features one star from each of the 28 teams, along with a subset spotlighting top rookies from 1993 and cards saluting Nolan Ryan, Rickey Henderson and Ozzie Smith. The set comes in a specially-designed box, with a numbered checklist card. The set was limited to a total of 123,600.

		NM/M
Complete Set (36):		6.00
Common Player:		.10
1	Tim Salmon	.15
2	Jeff Bagwell	.30
3	Mark McGwire	.75
4	Roberto Alomar	.25
5	Terry Pendleton	.10
6	Robin Yount	.30
7	Ray Lankford	.10
8	Ryne Sandberg	.40
9	Darryl Strawberry	.10
10	Marquis Grissom	.10
11	Barry Bonds	1.00
12	Carlos Baerga	.10
13	Ken Griffey Jr.	.65
14	Benito Santiago	.10
15	Dwight Gooden	.10
16	Cal Ripken, Jr.	1.00
17	Tony Gwynn	.40
18	Dave Hollins	.10
19	Andy Van Slyke	.10
20	Juan Gonzalez	.25
21	Roger Clemens	.50
22	Barry Larkin	.10
23	Dave Nied	.10
24	George Brett	.50
25	Travis Fryman	.10
26	Kirby Puckett	.40
27	Frank Thomas	.30
28	Don Mattingly	.50
29	Rickey Henderson	.30
30	Nolan Ryan	.40
31	Ozzie Smith	.20
32	Wil Cordero	.10
33	Phil Hiatt	.10
34	Mike Piazza	.65
35	J.T. Snow	.10
36	Kevin Young	.10

1993 Upper Deck Fun Packs

Aimed at the younger audience, this product features 150 "regular" player cards and 75 specialty cards in a variety of subsets, plus two different types of insert cards. Basic player cards feature a photo (generally in action) on a background of purple, green and red, highlighted by yellow and orange stripes. On back is a white panel on red, yellow and orange blended stripes. In the panel are a cartoon, a trivia question and answer, brief biographical details, stats, and career summary. The basic player cards are arranged within the set alphabetically by team. The teams are also arranged alphabetically by nickname. Leading off each team's roster is a "Glow Stars" sticker, featuring a player photo against a parti-colored background. The area around the photo is die-cut to allow the picture to be separated from the background and stuck to a wall, where the white and green outlines glow in the dark. Cards #1-9 are designated "Stars of Tomorrow." Both front and back have a background of a star-studded purple sky. Cards #10-21 are "Hot Shots" - heat-sensitive cards. When touched the black textured ink surrounding the player photo turns clear, revealing a colored pattern beneath. The Hot Shot cards were available only via mail-in redemption. Cards #22-27 are "Kid Stars" and feature a childhood photo. Cards #28-37 are checklisted as "Upper Deck Heroes," though that designation does not appear on the cards. The subset is done in comic-book art style. Cards #216-220 are double-size (2-1/2"x7") "Fold-outs." The five checklist cards which conclude the set have player photos on front.

		NM/M
Complete Set (225):		15.00
Common Player:		.05
Wax Pack (6):		.50
Wax Box (36):		15.00
1	Wil Cordero (Stars of Tomorrow)	.05
2	Brent Gates (Stars of Tomorrow)	.05
3	Benji Gil (Stars of Tomorrow)	.05
4	Phil Hiatt (Stars of Tomorrow)	.05
5	David McCarty (Stars of Tomorrow)	.05
6	Mike Piazza (Stars of Tomorrow)	1.50
7	Tim Salmon (Stars of Tomorrow)	.05
8	J.T. Snow RC (Stars of Tomorrow)	.50
9	Kevin Young (Stars of Tomorrow)	.15
10	Roberto Alomar (Hot Shots)	.25
11	Barry Bonds (Hot Shots)	1.50
12	Jose Canseco (Hot Shots)	.35
13	Will Clark (Hot Shots)	.25
14	Roger Clemens (Hot Shots)	.75
15	Juan Gonzalez (Hot Shots)	.25
16	Ken Griffey Jr. (Hot Shots)	1.00
17	Mark McGwire (Hot Shots)	1.25
18	Nolan Ryan (Hot Shots)	1.50
19	Ryne Sandberg (Hot Shots)	.65
20	Gary Sheffield (Hot Shots)	.30
21	Frank Thomas (Hot Shots)	.60
22	Roberto Alomar (Kid Stars)	.10
23	Roger Clemens (Kid Stars)	.45
24	Ken Griffey Jr. (Kid Stars)	.50
25	Gary Sheffield (Kid Stars)	.15
26	Nolan Ryan (Kid Stars)	.75
27	Frank Thomas (Kid Stars)	.40
28	Reggie Jackson (Heroes)	.45
29	Roger Clemens (Heroes)	.45
30	Ken Griffey Jr. (Heroes)	.50
31	Bo Jackson (Heroes)	.10
32	Cal Ripken, Jr. (Heroes)	.75
33	Nolan Ryan (Heroes)	.75
34	Deion Sanders (Heroes)	.10
35	Ozzie Smith (Heroes)	.40
36	Frank Thomas (Heroes)	.35
37	Tim Salmon (Glow Stars)	.05
38	Chili Davis	.05
39	Chuck Finley	.05
40	Mark Langston	.05
41	Luis Polonia	.05
42	Jeff Bagwell (Glow Stars)	.30
43	Jeff Bagwell	.50
44	Craig Biggio	.05
45	Ken Caminiti	.05
46	Doug Drabek	.05
47	Steve Finley	.05
48	Mark McGwire (Glow Stars)	.65
49	Dennis Eckersley	.45
50	Rickey Henderson	.50
51	Mark McGwire	1.25
52	Ruben Sierra	.05
53	Terry Steinbach	.05
54	Roberto Alomar (Glow Stars)	.10
55	Roberto Alomar	.20
56	Joe Carter	.05
57	Juan Guzman	.05
58	Paul Molitor	.50
59	Jack Morris	.05
60	John Olerud	.05
61	Tom Glavine (Glow Stars)	.10
62	Steve Avery	.05
63	Tom Glavine	.20
64	Dave Justice	.05
65	Greg Maddux	.65
66	Terry Pendleton	.05
67	Deion Sanders	.10
68	John Smoltz	.05
69	Robin Yount (Glow Stars)	.30
70	Cal Eldred	.05
71	Pat Listach	.05
72	Greg Vaughn	.05
73	Robin Yount	.50
74	Ozzie Smith (Glow Stars)	.45
75	Gregg Jefferies	.05
76	Ray Lankford	.05
77	Lee Smith	.05
78	Ozzie Smith	.65
79	Bob Tewksbury	.05
80	Ryne Sandberg (Glow Stars)	.35
81	Mark Grace	.05
82	Mike Morgan	.05
83	Randy Myers	.05
84	Ryne Sandberg	.65
85	Sammy Sosa	.65
86	Eric Karros (Glow Stars)	.05
87	Brett Butler	.05
88	Orel Hershiser	.05
89	Eric Karros	.05
90	Ramon Martinez	.05
91	Jose Offerman	.05
92	Darryl Strawberry	.05
93	Marquis Grissom (Glow Stars)	.05
94	Delino DeShields	.05
95	Marquis Grissom	.05
96	Ken Hill	.05
97	Dennis Martinez	.05
98	Larry Walker	.05
99	Barry Bonds (Glow Stars)	.65
100	Barry Bonds	1.50
101	Will Clark	.05
102	Bill Swift	.05
103	Robby Thompson	.05
104	Matt Williams	.05
105	Carlos Baerga (Glow Stars)	.05
106	Sandy Alomar, Jr.	.05
107	Carlos Baerga	.05
108	Albert Belle	.05
109	Kenny Lofton	.05
110	Charles Nagy	.05
111	Ken Griffey Jr. (Glow Stars)	.50
112	Jay Buhner	.05
113	Dave Fleming	.05
114	Ken Griffey Jr.	1.00
115	Randy Johnson	.50
116	Edgar Martinez	.05
117	Benito Santiago (Glow Stars)	.05
118	Bret Barberie	.05
119	Jeff Conine	.05
120	Brian Harvey	.05
121	Benito Santiago	.05
122	Walt Weiss	.05
123	Dwight Gooden (Glow Stars)	.05
124	Bobby Bonilla	.05
125	Tony Fernandez	.05
126	Dwight Gooden	.05
127	Howard Johnson	.05
128	Eddie Murray	.50
129	Bret Saberhagen	.05
130	Cal Ripken, Jr. (Glow Stars)	.75
131	Brady Anderson	.05
132	Mike Devereaux	.05
133	Ben McDonald	.05
134	Mike Mussina	.30
135	Cal Ripken, Jr.	1.50
136	Fred McGriff (Glow Stars)	.05
137	Andy Benes	.05
138	Tony Gwynn	.65
139	Fred McGriff	.05
140	Phil Plantier	.05
141	Gary Sheffield	.25
142	Darren Daulton (Glow Stars)	.05
143	Darren Daulton	.05
144	Len Dykstra	.05
145	Dave Hollins	.05
146	John Kruk	.05
147	Mitch Williams	.05
148	Andy Van Slyke (Glow Stars)	.05
149	Jay Bell	.05
150	Zane Smith	.05
151	Andy Van Slyke	.05
152	Tim Wakefield	.05
153	Juan Gonzalez (Glow Stars)	.15
154	Kevin Brown	.05
155	Jose Canseco	.35
156	Juan Gonzalez	.25
157	Rafael Palmeiro	.40
158	Dean Palmer	.05
159	Ivan Rodriguez	.45
160	Nolan Ryan	1.50
161	Roger Clemens (Glow Stars)	.50
162	Roger Clemens	.75
163	Andre Dawson	.25
164	Mike Greenwell	.05
165	Tony Pena	.05
166	Frank Viola	.05
167	Barry Larkin (Glow Stars)	.05
168	Rob Dibble	.05
169	Roberto Kelly	.05
170	Barry Larkin	.05
171	Kevin Mitchell	.05
172	Bip Roberts	.05
173	Andres Galarraga (Glow Stars)	.05
174	Dante Bichette	.05
175	Jerald Clark	.05
176	Andres Galarraga	.05
177	Charlie Hayes	.05
178	David Nied	.05
179	David Cone (Glow Stars)	.05
180	Kevin Appier	.05
181	George Brett	.75
182	David Cone	.05
183	Felix Jose	.05
184	Wally Joyner	.05
185	Cecil Fielder (Glow Stars)	.05
186	Cecil Fielder	.05
187	Travis Fryman	.05
188	Tony Phillips	.05
189	Mickey Tettleton	.05
190	Lou Whitaker	.05
191	Kirby Puckett (Glow Stars)	.35
192	Scott Erickson	.05
193	Chuck Knoblauch	.05
194	Shane Mack	.05
195	Kirby Puckett	.65
196	Dave Winfield	.50
197	Frank Thomas (Glow Stars)	.40
198	George Bell	.05
199	Bo Jackson	.10
200	Jack McDowell	.05
201	Tim Raines	.05
202	Frank Thomas	.50
203	Robin Ventura	.05
204	Jim Abbott (Glow Stars)	.05
205	Jim Abbott	.05
206	Wade Boggs	.65
207	Jimmy Key	.05
208	Don Mattingly	.75
209	Danny Tartabull	.05
210	Brett Butler (All-Star Advice)	.05
211	Tony Gwynn (All-Star Advice)	.35
212	Rickey Henderson (All-Star Advice)	.25
213	Ramon Martinez (All-Star Advice)	.05
214	Nolan Ryan (All-Star Advice)	.75
215	Ozzie Smith (All-Star Advice)	.35
216	Marquis Grissom (Fold-Out)	.05
217	Dean Palmer (Fold-Out)	.05
218	Cal Ripken, Jr. (Fold-Out)	.75
219	Deion Sanders (Fold-Out)	.05
220	Darryl Strawberry (Fold-Out)	.05
221	David McCarty (Checklist)	.05
222	Barry Bonds (Checklist)	.05
223	Juan Gonzalez (Checklist)	.15
224	Ken Griffey Jr. (Checklist)	.50
225	Frank Thomas (Checklist)	.05
	Trade Upper Deck ("Hot Shots" redemption card.)	.05

Fun Packs Mascot Madness

Upper Deck's high-tech lithogram process of combining color photos and holograms was used to create the five-card "Mascot Madness" inserts which were randomly found in Fun Packs. Backs have a description of the mascot and explain his role with the team.

		NM/M
Complete Set (5):		2.50
Common Card:		.50
1	Phillie Phanatic	.50
2	Pirate Parrot	.50
3	Fredbird	.50
4	BJ Birdy	.50
5	Youppi (Mascot)	.50

Fun Packs All-Star Scratch-Off

Randomly inserted into Fun Packs was a series of nine "All-Star Scratch-Off" game cards. Fronts and backs have a star-studded blue background. Inside the folded, double-size (2-1/2" x 7") cards are American and National League line-ups which can be used to play a baseball game, the rules of which are explained on the card backs. On front are photos of two of the players in the line-up, matched by position from each league. The inserts are numbered with an "AS" prefix.

		NM/M
Complete Set (9):		5.00
Common Player:		.25
1	Fred McGriff, Frank Thomas	.45
2	Darren Daulton, Ivan Rodriguez	.35
3	Mark McGwire, Will Clark	1.25
4	Ryne Sandberg, Roberto Alomar	.50
5	Robin Ventura, Terry Pendleton	.25
6	Cal Ripken Jr., Ozzie Smith	1.50
7	Barry Bonds, Juan Gonzalez	1.50
8	Marquis Grissom, Ken Griffey Jr.	1.00
9	Tony Gwynn, Kirby Puckett	.50

1994 Upper Deck

Upper Deck's 1994 offering was a typical presentation, combining high-quality regular-issue cards with innovative subsets and high-tech chase cards. Series 1, besides the standard player cards, features subsets including Star Rookies with metallic borders, "Fantasy Team" stars, Home Field Advantage cards showcasing National League stadiums, and, stars under the age of 25 in a subset titled, "The Future is Now." Regular-issue cards feature a color photo on front and a second, black-and-white version of the same photo at left in a vertically stretched format. The player's name, team and Upper Deck logo appear on front in copper foil. Backs have a color photo, stats and an infield-shaped hologram. Series 2 offered in addition to regular cards, subsets of American League Home Field Advantage cards, a group of "Classic Alumni" minor league players, a selection of "Diamond Debuts" cards and a group of "Top Prospects." Series 1 retail packaging contained a special Mickey Mantle/Ken Griffey, Jr. card that could be found bearing either one or both of the players' autographs in an edition of 1,000 each. Series 2 retail packs offered a chance to find an autographed version of Alex Rodriguez' Classic Alumni card.

	NM/M
Complete Set (550):	30.00
Complete Series 1 (280):	25.00
Complete Series 2 (270):	5.00
Common Player:	.05
Series 1 Hobby Pack (12):	2.50
Series 1 Hobby Box (36):	65.00
Series 1 Retail Pack (12):	2.00
Series 1 Retail Box (36):	40.00
Series 2 Hobby Pack (12):	.75
Series 2 Hobby Box (36):	20.00
Series 2 Retail Pack (12):	1.25
Series 2 Retail Box (36):	25.00

1	Brian Anderson/SR RC	.15
2	Shane Andrews/SR	.05
3	James Baldwin/SR	.05
4	Rich Becker/SR	.05
5	Greg Blosser/SR	.05
6	Ricky Bottalico/SR RC	.05
7	Midre Cummings/SR	.05
8	Carlos Delgado/SR	.50
9	Steve Dreyer/SR RC	.05
10	Joey Eischen/SR RC	.05
11	Carl Everett/SR	.05
12	Cliff Floyd/SR	.05
13	Alex Gonzalez/SR	.05
14	Jeff Granger/SR	.05
15	Shawn Green/SR	.35
16	Brian Hunter/SR	.05
17	Butch Huskey/SR	.05
18	Mark Hutton/SR	.05
19	Michael Jordan/SR RC	5.00
20	Steve Karsay/SR	.05
21	Jeff McNeely/SR	.05
22	Marc Newfield/SR	.05
23	Manny Ramirez/SR	.60
24	Alex Rodriguez/SR RC	20.00
25	Scott Ruffcorn/SR	.05
27	Salomon Torres/SR	.05
28	Steve Trachsel/SR	.05
29	Chris Turner/SR RC	.05
30	Gabe White/SR	.05
31	Randy Johnson (Fantasy Team)	.40
32	John Wetteland (Fantasy Team)	.05
33	Mike Piazza (Fantasy Team)	.65
34	Rafael Palmeiro (Fantasy Team)	.35
35	Roberto Alomar (Fantasy Team)	.10
36	Matt Williams (Fantasy Team)	.05
37	Travis Fryman (Fantasy Team)	.05
38	Barry Bonds (Fantasy Team)	1.00
39	Marquis Grissom (Fantasy Team)	.05
40	Albert Belle (Fantasy Team)	.05
41	Steve Avery (Future/Now)	.05
42	Jason Bere (Future/Now)	.05
43	Alex Fernandez (Future/Now)	.05
44	Mike Mussina (Future/Now)	.15
45	Aaron Sele (Future/Now)	.05
46	Rod Beck (Future/Now)	.05
47	Mike Piazza (Future/Now)	.65
48	John Olerud (Future/Now)	.05
49	Carlos Baerga (Future/Now)	.05
50	Gary Sheffield (Future/Now)	.20
51	Travis Fryman (Future/Now)	.05
52	Juan Gonzalez (Future/Now)	.20
53	Ken Griffey Jr. (Future/Now)	.65
54	Tim Salmon (Future/Now)	.05
55	Frank Thomas (Future/Now)	.45
56	Tony Phillips	.05
57	Julio Franco	.05
58	Kevin Mitchell	.05
59	Raul Mondesi	.75
60	Rickey Henderson	.05
61	Jay Buhner	.05
62	Bill Swift	.05
63	Brady Anderson	.05
64	Ryan Klesko	.05
65	Darren Daulton	.05
66	Damion Easley	.05
67	Mark McGwire	1.50
68	John Roper	.05
69	Dave Telgheder	.05
70	Dave Nied	.05
71	Mo Vaughn	.05
72	Tyler Green	.05
73	Dave Magadan	.05
74	Chili Davis	.05
75	Archi Cianfrocco	.05
76	Joe Girardi	.05
77	Chris Hoiles	.05
78	Ryan Bowen	.05
79	Greg Gagne	.05
80	Aaron Sele	.05
81	Dave Winfield	.75
82	Chad Curtis	.05
83	Andy Van Slyke	.05
84	Kevin Stocker	.05
85	Deion Sanders	.05
86	Bernie Williams	.05
87	John Smoltz	.05
88	Ruben Santana RC	.05
89	Dave Stewart	.05
90	Don Mattingly	1.00
91	Joe Carter	.05
92	Ryne Sandberg	.90
93	Chris Gomez	.05
94	Tino Martinez	.05
95	Terry Pendleton	.05
96	Andre Dawson	.25
97	Wil Cordero	.05
98	Kent Hrbek	.05
99	John Olerud	.05
100	Kirt Manwaring	.05
101	Tim Bogar	.05
102	Mike Mussina	.30
103	Nigel Wilson	.05
104	Ricky Gutierrez	.05
105	Roberto Mejia	.05
106	Tom Pagnozzi	.05
107	Mike Macfarlane	.05
108	Jose Bautista	.05
109	Luis Ortiz	.05
110	Brent Gates	.05
111	Tim Salmon	.05
112	Wade Boggs	.90
113	Tripp Cromer RC	.05
114	Denny Hocking	.05
115	Carlos Baerga	.05
116	J.R. Phillips RC	.05
117	Bo Jackson	.10
118	Lance Johnson	.05
119	Bobby Jones	.05
120	Bobby Witt	.05
121	Ron Karkovice	.05
122	Jose Vizcaino	.05
123	Danny Darwin	.05
124	Eduardo Perez	.05
125	Brian Looney	.05
126	Pat Hentgen	.05
127	Frank Viola	.05
128	Darren Holmes	.05
129	Wally Whitehurst	.05
130	Matt Walbeck	.05
131	Albert Belle	.05
132	Steve Cooke	.05
133	Kevin Appier	.05
134	Joe Oliver	.05
135	Benji Gil	.05
136	Steve Buechele	.05
137	Devon White	.05
138	Sterling Hitchcock	.05
139	Phil Leftwich RC	.05
140	Jose Canseco	.45
141	Rick Aguilera	.05
142	Rod Beck	.05
143	Jose Rijo	.05
144	Tom Glavine	.25
145	Phil Plantier	.05
146	Jason Bere	.05
147	Jamie Moyer	.05
148	Wes Chamberlain	.05
149	Glenallen Hill	.05
150	Mark Whiten	.05
151	Bret Barberie	.05
152	Chuck Knoblauch	.05
153	Trevor Hoffman	.05
154	Rick Wilkins	.05
155	Juan Gonzalez	.40
156	Ozzie Guillen	.05
157	Jim Eisenreich	.05
158	Pedro Astacio	.05
159	Joe Magrane	.05
160	Ryan Thompson	.05
161	Jose Lind	.05
162	Jeff Conine	.05
163	Todd Benzinger	.05
164	Roger Salkeld	.05
165	Gary DiSarcina	.05
166	Kevin Gross	.05

#	Player	Price
167	Charlie Hayes	.05
168	Tim Costo	.05
169	Wally Joyner	.05
170	Johnny Ruffin	.05
171	Kirk Rueter RC	.10
172	Len Dykstra	.05
173	Ken Hill	.05
174	Mike Bordick	.05
175	Billy Hall	.05
176	Rob Butler	.05
177	Jay Bell	.05
178	Jeff Kent	.05
179	David Wells	.05
180	Dean Palmer	.05
181	Mariano Duncan	.05
182	Orlando Merced	.05
183	Brett Butler	.05
184	Milt Thompson	.05
185	Chipper Jones	1.00
186	Paul O'Neill	.05
187	Mike Greenwell	.05
188	Harold Baines	.05
189	Todd Stottlemyre	.05
190	Jeromy Burnitz	.05
191	Rene Arocha	.05
192	Jeff Fassero	.05
193	Robby Thompson	.05
194	Greg W. Harris	.05
195	Todd Van Poppel	.05
196	Jose Guzman	.05
197	Shane Mack	.05
198	Carlos Garcia	.05
199	Kevin Roberson	.05
200	David McCarty	.05
201	Alan Trammell	.05
202	Chuck Carr	.05
203	Tommy Greene	.05
204	Wilson Alvarez	.05
205	Dwight Gooden	.05
206	Tony Tarasco	.05
207	Darren Lewis	.05
208	Eric Karros	.05
209	Chris Hammond	.05
210	Jeffrey Hammonds	.05
211	Rich Amaral	.05
212	Danny Tartabull	.05
213	Jeff Russell	.05
214	Dave Staton	.05
215	Kenny Lofton	.05
216	Manuel Lee	.05
217	Brian Koelling	.05
218	Scott Lydy	.05
219	Tony Gwynn	.90
220	Cecil Fielder	.05
221	Royce Clayton	.05
222	Reggie Sanders	.05
223	Brian Jordan	.05
224	Ken Griffey Jr.	1.25
224a	Ken Griffey Jr. (Promo Card)	3.00
225	Fred McGriff	.05
226	Felix Jose	.05
227	Brad Pennington	.05
228	Chris Bosio	.05
229	Mike Stanley	.05
230	Willie Greene	.05
231	Alex Fernandez	.05
232	Brad Ausmus	.05
233	Darrell Whitmore	.05
234	Marcus Moore	.05
235	Allen Watson	.05
236	Jose Offerman	.05
237	Rondell White	.05
238	Jeff King	.05
239	Luis Alicea	.05
240	Dan Wilson	.05
241	Ed Sprague	.05
242	Todd Hundley	.05
243	Al Martin	.05
244	Mike Lansing	.05
245	Ivan Rodriguez	.65
246	Dave Fleming	.05
247	John Doherty	.05
248	Mark McLemore	.05
249	Bob Hamelin	.05
250	Curtis Pride RC	.05
251	Zane Smith	.05
252	Eric Young	.05
253	Brian McRae	.05
254	Tim Raines	.05
255	Javier Lopez	.05
256	Melvin Nieves	.05
257	Randy Myers	.05
258	Willie McGee	.05
259	Jimmy Key	.05
260	Tom Candiotti	.05
261	Eric Davis	.05
262	Craig Paquette	.05
263	Robin Ventura	.05
264	Pat Kelly	.05
265	Gregg Jefferies	.05
266	Cory Snyder	.05
267	Dave Justice	.05
	(Home Field Advantage)	.05
268	Sammy Sosa	.05
	(Home Field Advantage)	.45
269	Barry Larkin	.05
	(Home Field Advantage)	.05
270	Andres Galarraga	.05
	(Home Field Advantage)	.05
271	Gary Sheffield	.05
	(Home Field Advantage)	.20
272	Jeff Bagwell	.05
	(Home Field Advantage)	.40
273	Mike Piazza	.05
	(Home Field Advantage)	.65
274	Larry Walker	.05
	(Home Field Advantage)	.05

#	Player	Price
275	Bobby Bonilla	.05
	(Home Field Advantage)	.05
276	John Kruk	.05
	(Home Field Advantage)	.05
277	Jay Bell	.05
	(Home Field Advantage)	.05
278	Ozzie Smith	.05
	(Home Field Advantage)	.45
279	Tony Gwynn	.05
	(Home Field Advantage)	.45
280	Barry Bonds	.05
	(Home Field Advantage)	1.00
281	Cal Ripken, Jr.	.05
	(Home Field Advantage)	1.00
282	Mo Vaughn	.05
	(Home Field Advantage)	.05
283	Tim Salmon	.05
	(Home Field Advantage)	.05
284	Frank Thomas	.05
	(Home Field Advantage)	.40
285	Albert Belle	.05
	(Home Field Advantage)	.05
286	Cecil Fielder	.05
	(Home Field Advantage)	.05
287	Wally Joyner	.05
288	Greg Vaughn	.05
	(Home Field Advantage)	.05
289	Kirby Puckett	.05
	(Home Field Advantage)	.45
290	Don Mattingly	.05
	(Home Field Advantage)	.50
291	Terry Steinbach	.05
	(Home Field Advantage)	.05
292	Ken Griffey Jr.	.05
	(Home Field Advantage)	.90
293	Juan Gonzalez	.05
	(Home Field Advantage)	.20
294	Paul Molitor	.05
	(Home Field Advantage)	.40
295	Tavo Alvarez (Classic Alumni)	.05
296	Matt Brunson (Classic Alumni)	.05
297	Shawn Green (Classic Alumni)	.20
298	Alex Rodriguez (Classic Alumni)	2.00
299	Shannon Stewart (Classic Alumni)	.05
300	Frank Thomas	.75
301	Mickey Tettleton	.05
302	Pedro Munoz	.05
303	Jose Valentin	.05
304	Orestes Destrade	.05
305	Pat Listach	.05
306	Scott Brosius	.05
307	Kurt Miller RC	.05
308	Rob Dibble	.05
309	Mike Blowers	.05
310	Jim Abbott	.05
311	Mike Jackson	.05
312	Craig Biggio	.05
313	Kurt Abbott RC	.05
314	Chuck Finley	.05
315	Andres Galarraga	.05
316	Mike Moore	.05
317	Doug Strange	.05
318	Pedro J. Martinez	.75
319	Kevin McReynolds	.05
320	Greg Maddux	.90
321	Mike Henneman	.05
322	Scott Leius	.05
323	John Franco	.05
324	Jeff Blauser	.05
325	Kirby Puckett	.90
326	Darryl Hamilton	.05
327	John Smiley	.05
328	Derrick May	.05
329	Jose Vizcaino	.05
330	Randy Johnson	.75
331	Jack Morris	.05
332	Graeme Lloyd	.05
333	Dave Valle	.05
334	Greg Myers	.05
335	John Wetteland	.05
336	Jim Gott	.05
337	Tim Naehring	.05
338	Mike Kelly	.05
339	Jeff Montgomery	.05
340	Rafael Palmeiro	.65
341	Eddie Murray	.75
342	Xavier Hernandez	.05
343	Bobby Munoz	.05
344	Bobby Bonilla	.05
345	Travis Fryman	.05
346	Steve Finley	.05
347	Chris Sabo	.05
348	Armando Reynoso	.05
349	Ramon Martinez	.05
350	Will Clark	.05
351	Moises Alou	.05
352	Jim Thome	.50
353	Bob Tewksbury	.05
354	Andujar Cedeno	.05
355	Orel Hershiser	.05
356	Mike Devereaux	.05
357	Mike Perez	.05
358	Dennis Martinez	.05
359	Dave Nilsson	.05
360	Ozzie Smith	.90
361	Eric Anthony	.05
362	Scott Sanders	.05
363	Paul Sorrento	.05
364	Tim Belcher	.05
365	Dennis Eckersley	.60
366	Mel Rojas	.05
367	Tom Henke	.05

#	Player	Price
368	Randy Tomlin	.05
369	B.J. Surhoff	.05
370	Larry Walker	.05
371	Joey Cora	.05
372	Mike Harkey	.05
373	John Valentin	.05
374	Doug Jones	.05
375	Dave Justice	.05
376	Vince Coleman	.05
377	David Hulse	.05
378	Kevin Seitzer	.05
379	Pete Harnisch	.05
380	Ruben Sierra	.05
381	Mark Lewis	.05
382	Bip Roberts	.05
383	Paul Wagner	.05
384	Stan Javier	.05
385	Barry Larkin	.05
386	Mark Portugal	.05
387	Roberto Kelly	.05
388	Andy Benes	.05
389	Felix Fermin	.05
390	Marquis Grissom	.05
391	Troy Neel	.05
392	Chad Kreuter	.05
393	Gregg Olson	.05
394	Charles Nagy	.05
395	Jack McDowell	.05
396	Luis Gonzalez	.05
397	Benito Santiago	.05
398	Chris James	.05
399	Terry Mulholland	.05
400	Barry Bonds	2.00
401	Joe Grahe	.05
402	Duane Ward	.05
403	John Burkett	.05
404	Scott Servais	.05
405	Bryan Harvey	.05
406	Bernard Gilkey	.05
407	Greg McMichael	.05
408	Tim Wallach	.05
409	Ken Caminiti	.05
410	John Kruk	.05
411	Darrin Jackson	.05
412	Mike Gallego	.05
413	David Cone	.05
414	Lou Whitaker	.05
415	Sandy Alomar Jr.	.05
416	Bill Wegman	.05
417	Pat Borders	.05
418	Roger Pavlik	.05
419	Pete Smith	.05
420	Steve Avery	.05
421	David Segui	.05
422	Rheal Cormier	.05
423	Harold Reynolds	.05
424	Edgar Martinez	.05
425	Cal Ripken, Jr.	2.00
426	Jaime Navarro	.05
427	Sean Berry	.05
428	Bret Saberhagen	.05
429	Bob Welch	.05
430	Juan Guzman	.05
431	Cal Eldred	.05
432	Dave Hollins	.05
433	Sid Fernandez	.05
434	Willie Banks	.05
435	Darryl Kile	.05
436	Henry Rodriguez	.05
437	Tony Fernandez	.05
438	Walt Weiss	.05
439	Kevin Tapani	.05
440	Mark Grace	.05
441	Brian Harper	.05
442	Kent Mercker	.05
443	Anthony Young	.05
444	Todd Zeile	.05
445	Greg Vaughn	.05
446	Ray Lankford	.05
447	David Weathers	.05
448	Bret Boone	.05
449	Charlie Hough	.05
450	Roger Clemens	1.00
451	Mike Morgan	.05
452	Doug Drabek	.05
453	Danny Jackson	.05
454	Dante Bichette	.05
455	Roberto Alomar	.20
456	Ben McDonald	.05
457	Kenny Rogers	.05
458	Bill Gullickson	.05
459	Darrin Fletcher	.05
460	Curt Schilling	.20
461	Billy Hatcher	.05
462	Howard Johnson	.05
463	Mickey Morandini	.05
464	Frank Castillo	.05
465	Delino DeShields	.05
466	Gary Gaetti	.05
467	Steve Farr	.05
468	Roberto Hernandez	.05
469	Jack Armstrong	.05
470	Paul Molitor	.75
471	Melido Perez	.05
472	Greg Hibbard	.05
473	Jody Reed	.05
474	Tom Gordon	.05
475	Gary Sheffield	.35
476	John Jaha	.05
477	Shawon Dunston	.05
478	Reggie Jefferson	.05
479	Don Slaught	.05
480	Jeff Bagwell	.75
481	Tim Pugh	.05
482	Kevin Young	.05
483	Ellis Burks	.05
484	Greg Swindell	.05
485	Mark Langston	.05

#	Player	Price
486	Omar Vizquel	.05
487	Kevin Brown	.05
488	Terry Steinbach	.05
489	Mark Lemke	.05
490	Matt Williams	.05
491	Pete Incaviglia	.05
492	Karl Rhodes	.05
493	Shawn Green	.30
494	Hal Morris	.05
495	Derek Bell	.05
496	Luis Polonia	.05
497	Otis Nixon	.05
498	Ron Darling	.05
499	Mitch Williams	.05
500	Mike Piazza	1.25
501	Pat Meares	.05
502	Scott Cooper	.05
503	Scott Erickson	.05
504	Jeff Juden	.05
505	Lee Smith	.05
506	Bobby Ayala	.05
507	Dave Henderson	.05
508	Erik Hanson	.05
509	Bob Wickman	.05
510	Sammy Sosa	.90
511	Hector Carrasco (Diamond Debuts)	.05
512	Tim Davis (Diamond Debuts)	.05
513	Joey Hamilton (Diamond Debuts)	.05
514	Robert Eenhoorn (Diamond Debuts)	.05
515	Jorge Fabregas (Diamond Debuts)	.05
516	Tim Hyers (Diamond Debuts)	.05
517	John Hudek (Diamond Debuts)	.05
518	James Mouton RC (Diamond Debuts)	.05
519	Herbert Perry (Diamond Debuts)	.05
520	Chan Ho Park RC (Diamond Debuts)	.75
521	Bill VanLandingham (Diamond Debuts)	.05
522	Paul Shuey (Diamond Debuts)	.05
523	Ryan Hancock RC (Top Prospects)	.05
524	Billy Wagner RC (Top Prospects)	.25
525	Jason Giambi (Top Prospects)	.50
526	Jose Silva RC (Top Prospects)	.05
527	Terrell Wade RC (Top Prospects)	.05
528	Todd Dunn (Top Prospects)	.05
529	Alan Benes RC (Top Prospects)	.05
530	Brooks Kieschnick RC (Top Prospects)	.05
531	Todd Hollandsworth (Top Prospects)	.05
532	Brad Fullmer RC (Top Prospects)	.15
533	Steve Soderstrom RC (Top Prospects)	.05
534	Daron Kirkreit (Top Prospects)	.05
535	Arquimedez Pozo RC (Top Prospects)	.05
536	Charles Johnson (Top Prospects)	.05
537	Preston Wilson (Top Prospects)	.10
538	Alex Ochoa (Top Prospects)	.05
539	Derrek Lee RC (Top Prospects)	3.00
540	Wayne Gomes RC (Top Prospects)	.05
541	Jermaine Allensworth RC (Top Prospects)	.05
542	Mike Bell RC (Top Prospects)	.05
543	Trot Nixon RC (Top Prospects)	1.25
544	Pokey Reese (Top Prospects)	.05
545	Neifi Perez RC (Top Prospects)	.30
546	Johnny Damon (Top Prospects)	.05
547	Matt Brunson (Top Prospects)	.05
548	LaTroy Hawkins RC (Top Prospects)	.05
549	Eddie Pearson RC (Top Prospects)	.05
550	Derek Jeter (Top Prospects)	2.00

Electric Diamond

Each of the regular-issue and subset cards from 1994 Upper Deck was also produced in a limited edition premium insert "Electric Diamond" version. Where the regular cards have the Upper Deck logo, player and team name in copper foil, the Electric Diamond version has those elements in a silver pris-

matic foil, along with an "Electric Diamond" identification line next to the UD logo. Backs are identical to the regular cards. (Forty-five of the first series cards can be found with player names on back in either silver or copper.) Electric Diamond cards are found, on average, about every other pack.

	NM/M
Complete Set (550):	75.00
Common Player:	.25
Stars:	1.5X

Baseball Heroes Mickey Mantle

Mickey Mantle Baseball Hero is a 10-card set that chronicles his career. The cards, which include an unnumbered header card, were randomly inserted into both hobby and retail packs of Series II Upper Deck Baseball. This set starts with his rookie season in 1951 and concludes with his induction into The Hall of Fame. It is numbered 64-72 and was the eighth in the continuing "Baseball Heroes" series, which began in 1990.

		NM/M
Complete Set (10):		25.00
Common Player:		3.00
64	1951 - The Early Years (Mickey Mantle)	3.00
65	1953 - Tape Measure Home Runs (Mickey Mantle)	3.00
66	1956 - Triple Crown Season (Mickey Mantle)	3.00
67	1957 - 2nd Consecutive MVP (Mickey Mantle)	3.00
68	1961 - Chases The Babe (Mickey Mantle)	3.00
69	1964 - Series Home Run Record (Mickey Mantle)	3.00
70	1967 - 500th Home Run (Mickey Mantle)	3.00
71	1974: Hall of Fame (Mickey Mantle)	3.00
72	Mickey Mantle/Portrait	3.00
----	Header Card (Mickey Mantle)	5.00

Diamond Collection

The premium chase cards in 1994 Upper Deck are a series of Diamond Collection cards issued in regional subsets. Ten cards are found unique to each of three geographic areas of distribution. Western region cards carry a "W" prefix to the card number, Central cards have a "C" prefix and Eastern cards

have an "E" prefix. The region is also indicated in silver-foil printing on the front of the card, with a large "W," "C" or "E" in a compass design. The player's name and team are presented in a foil strip at bottom. A "Diamond Collection" logo is shown in embossed-look typography in the background. Diamond Collection cards are inserted only in hobby packs.

	NM/M
Complete Set (30):	40.00
Common Player:	.50
Complete Central (10):	20.00
1 Michael Jordan	10.00
2 Jeff Bagwell	2.00
3 Barry Larkin	1.00
4 Kirby Puckett	4.00
5 Manny Ramirez	3.00
6 Ryne Sandberg	3.00
7 Ozzie Smith	3.00
8 Frank Thomas	3.00
9 Andy Van Slyke	.50
10 Robin Yount	3.00
Complete East (10):	12.00
1 Roberto Alomar	1.00
2 Roger Clemens	4.00
3 Len Dykstra	.50
4 Cecil Fielder	.50
5 Cliff Floyd	.50
6 Dwight Gooden	.50
7 Dave Justice	.50
8 Don Mattingly	3.00
9 Cal Ripken, Jr.	6.00
10 Gary Sheffield	.50
Complete West (10):	15.00
1 Barry Bonds	5.00
2 Andres Galarraga	.50
3 Juan Gonzalez	1.00
4 Ken Griffey Jr.	4.00
5 Tony Gwynn	2.50
6 Rickey Henderson	1.50
7 Bo Jackson	1.00
8 Mark McGwire	3.00
9 Mike Piazza	3.00
10 Tim Salmon	.50

Jumbo Checklists

Each hobby foil box of 1994 Upper Deck contains one jumbo checklist card. Each of the 5" x 7" cards features Ken Griffey, Jr. There is a large color action photo along with a hologram of the player on front, highlighted by copper-foil printing. Backs have one of four checklists and are numbered with a "CL" prefix.

	NM/M
Complete Set (4):	4.00
Common Card:	1.00
1 Numerical Checklist (Ken Griffey Jr.)	1.00
2 Alphabetical Checklist (Ken Griffey Jr.)	1.00
3 Team Checklist (Ken Griffey Jr.)	1.00
4 Insert Checklist (Ken Griffey Jr.)	1.00

Mickey Mantle's Long Shots

Retail packaging was the exclusive venue for this insert set of contemporary high-ball sluggers. Horizontal fronts feature game-action photos with holographic foil rendering of the background. In one of the lower corners appears the logo "1994 Mickey Mantle's Long Shots." Backs have a color player photo at top, with a photo of Mantle beneath and a statement by him about the featured player. Previous season and career stats are included. Cards are numbered with an "MM" prefix. Besides the 20 current player cards there is a

Mickey Mantle card and two trade cards which could be redeemed for complete insert card sets.

	NM/M
Complete Set (21):	20.00
Common Player:	.50
Electric Diamonds:	1X

(1)	Mickey Mantle Trade Card (Silver): (Redeemable for 21-card Mantle Long Shots set.)	4.00
(2)	Mickey Mantle Trade Card (Blue): (Redeemable for Electric Diamond version Mantle Long Shots set.)	4.00
1	Jeff Bagwell	1.50
2	Albert Belle	.50
3	Barry Bonds	4.00
4	Jose Canseco	.75
5	Joe Carter	.50
6	Carlos Delgado	.75
7	Cecil Fielder	.50
8	Cliff Floyd	.50
9	Juan Gonzalez	.75
10	Ken Griffey Jr.	2.50
11	David Justice	.50
12	Fred McGriff	.50
13	Mark McGwire	3.00
14	Dean Palmer	.50
15	Mike Piazza	2.50
16	Manny Ramirez	1.50
17	Tim Salmon	.50
18	Frank Thomas	1.50
19	Mo Vaughn	.50
20	Matt Williams	.50
21	Header (Mickey Mantle)	4.00

Mantle-Griffey Autographed Inserts

First series retail packs of '94 UD were the exclusive venue for a special card featuring spokesmen Ken Griffey Jr. and Mickey Mantle. The front has a painting of the two stars. On back are career highlights and a comparison of the players' first five seasons. A large numbered elliptical hologram on back authenticates the autographs. One thousand cards were issued with either or both signatures.

		NM/M
KG1	Ken Griffey Jr., Mickey Mantle (Griffey Autograph)	250.00
MM1	Ken Griffey Jr., Mickey Mantle (Mantle Autograph)	650.00
GM1	Ken Griffey Jr., Mickey Mantle (Both Autographs)	1,150

Next Generation

Next Generation linked 18 top stars with all-time greats, using the HoloView printing technology. Next Generation Electric Diamond Trade Cards could be redeemed for a complete set of Electic Diamond versions of the Next Generation set. The insert cards were a retail-only find at a rate of one per 20 packs, while the Electric Diamond Trade card was inserted one per case.

	NM/M
Complete Set (18):	100.00
Common Player:	1.50
Electic Diamond	
Complete Set (18):	
Electic Diamond Singles (1.5X)	
1	Roberto Alomar	2.50
2	Carlos Delgado	4.00
3	Cliff Floyd	1.50
4	Alex Gonzalez	1.50

5	Juan Gonzalez	3.00
6	Ken Griffey Jr.	10.00
7	Jeffrey Hammonds	1.50
8	Michael Jordan	30.00
9	Dave Justice	1.50
10	Ryan Klesko	1.50
11	Javier Lopez	1.50
12	Raul Mondesi	1.50
13	Mike Piazza	10.00
14	Kirby Puckett	7.50
15	Manny Ramirez	6.50
16	Alex Rodriguez	30.00
17	Tim Salmon	1.50
18	Gary Sheffield	4.00
	ED Trade Card (Ken Griffey Jr.)	30.00

Alex Rodriguez Autograph

Available exclusively in Series 2 retail packaging was this special version of A-Rod's Classic Alumni card. The card is authentically signed in blue Sharpie and carries on its back an authentication hologram.

		NM/M
A298	Alex Rodriguez/Auto. (Classic Alumni)	500.00

SP Insert

Fifteen SP Preview cards were inserted into Series II packs of Upper Deck baseball. The cards were inserted with regional distribution and gave collectors a chance to see what the SP super-premium cards would look like. There were five cards available in the East, Central and West and were inserted at a rate of about one per 36 packs. Most of the preview inserts have different front and back photos than the regularly issued SPs, along with other differences in typography and graphics elements.

	NM/M
Complete Set (15):	60.00
Common Player:	.50
EASTERN REGION	
1	Roberto Alomar	1.00
2	Cliff Floyd	.50
3	Javier Lopez	.50
4	Don Mattingly	6.00
5	Cal Ripken, Jr.	10.00
CENTRAL REGION	
1	Jeff Bagwell	3.00
2	Michael Jordan	10.00
3	Kirby Puckett	6.00
4	Manny Ramirez	3.00
5	Frank Thomas	4.00
WESTERN REGION	
1	Barry Bonds	10.00
2	Juan Gonzalez	1.50
3	Ken Griffey Jr.	5.00
4	Mike Piazza	5.00
5	Tim Salmon	.50

Ken Griffey Jr. 5th Anniversary Jumbo

The origins of this card are unknown. Besides producing 15-card sets of top players in a black-bordered 5th Anniversary insert set in regular and 3-1/2" x 5-1/2" formats, UD issued an 8-1/2" x 11" 5th Anniversary card of Griffey. In virtually all respects except size, the jumbo card is identical to the others. It is, however, numbered on back from within an edition of 5,000.

	NM/M
Ken Griffey Jr.	20.00

All-Stars

Produced in commemoration of the 1994 All-Star Game, this boxed set features photography by Walter Iooss, Jr. on most cards, shown to its best advantage on a large 3-1/2" x 5" format. The front of each card has a foil seal of the Pittsburgh All-Star Game logo. On most sets, the seal is in green foil; every 40th set has the seals in gold. The left side of the card backs features a smaller version of the front photo and a few sentences about the player. Some cards feature a second, larger photo of the player on back, but most have a photo and write-up of a teammate. The last six cards in the set honor the 125th anniversary of professional baseball. An album to house the set was made available for $10 via a mail-in offer card in the set.

	NM/M
Complete Set (48):	9.00
Common Player:	.15
Gold:	4X
1	Ken Griffey Jr.	1.00
2	Ruben Sierra, Todd Van Poppel	.15
3	Bryan Harvey, Gary Sheffield	.35
4	Gregg Jefferies, Brian Jordan	.15
5	Ryne Sandberg	.75
6	Matt Williams, John Burkett	.15
7	Darren Daulton, John Kruk	.15
8	Don Mattingly, Wade Boggs	.75
9	Pat Listach, Greg Vaughn	.15
10	Tim Salmon, Eduardo Perez	.25
11	Fred McGriff, Tom Glavine	.25
12	Mo Vaughn, Andre Dawson	.35
13	Brian McRae, Kevin Appier	.15
14	Kirby Puckett, Kent Hrbek	.75
15	Cal Ripken, Jr.	2.00
16	Roberto Alomar, Paul Molitor	.65
17	Tony Gwynn, Phil Plantier	.75
18	Greg Maddux, Steve Avery	.75
19	Mike Mussina, Chris Hoiles	.50
20	Randy Johnson	.65
21	Roger Clemens, Aaron Sele	.75
22	Will Clark, Dean Palmer	.15
23	Cecil Fielder, Travis Fryman	.15
24	John Olerud, Joe Carter	.15
25	Juan Gonzalez	.65
26	Jose Rijo, Barry Larkin	.15
27	Andy Van Slyke, Jeff King	.15
28	Larry Walker, Marquis Grissom	.15
29	Kenny Lofton, Albert Belle	.25
30	Mark Grace, Sammy Sosa	1.00
31	Mike Piazza	1.00
32	Ramon Martinez, Orel Hershiser	.15
33	Dave Justice, Terry Pendleton	.15
34	Ivan Rodriguez, Jose Canseco	.15
35	Barry Bonds	2.00
36	Jeff Bagwell, Craig Biggio	.65
37	Jay Bell, Orlando Merced	.15
38	Jeff Kent, Dwight Gooden	.15
39	Andres Galarraga, Charlie Hayes	.15
40	Frank Thomas	.70
41	Bobby Bonilla	.15
42	Jack McDowell, Tim Raines	.15
43	1869 Red Stockings	.15
44	Ty Cobb	.50
45	Babe Ruth	1.50
46	Mickey Mantle	2.50
47	Reggie Jackson	.50

48	Ken Griffey Jr.	1.00
48a	Ken Griffey Jr. (Promo Card)	1.00

1994 UD All-Time Heroes

The All-Time Heroes set provided collectors with both Ted Williams cards from Topps 1954 reprint set, from which they were absent due to a contractual obligation between Ted Williams and the Upper Deck Co. An agreement between Topps and Upper Deck allowed both Williams' cards to be offered in the All-Time Heroes set. There is also a 1954 Mickey Mantle inserted that has no number, but bears the same design as original 1954 Topps cards. The basic All-Time Heroes of Baseball set contains 225 cards. The cards were patterned after cards from the early 60's, with black borders across the top and bottom. Black-and-white photographs give the 2-1/2" x 3-1/2" cards a nostalgic appearance. All-Time Heroes also has autographed cards of Mantle, Brett, Jackson and Seaver, along with a Next in Line insert set and a parallel, bronze-foil 125th anniversary set. Cards #1-18 comprise an Off the Wire subset. Cards #101-125 are a Major League 125th Anniversary subset. Cards #151-177 are a Diamond Legends subset. Cards #208-224 are a subset titled Heroes of Baseball.

	NM/M
Complete Set (225):	20.00
Common Player:	.10
Wax Box:	65.00
1	Ted Williams (OTW)	.75
2	Johnny Vander Meer (OTW)	.10
3	Lou Brock (OTW)	.10
4	Lou Gehrig (OTW)	.75
5	Hank Aaron (OTW)	.50
6	Tommie Agee (OTW)	.10
7	Mickey Mantle (OTW)	1.50
8	Bill Mazeroski (OTW)	.30
9	Reggie Jackson, Bud Harrelson (OTW)	.20
10	Willie Mays, Mickey Mantle (OTW)	1.25
11	Roy Campanella (OTW)	.20
12	Harvey Haddix (OTW)	.10
13	Jimmy Piersall (OTW)	.10
14	Enos Slaughter (OTW)	.10
15	Nolan Ryan (OTW)	.75
16	Bobby Thomson (OTW)	.10
17	Willie Mays (OTW)	.50
18	Bucky Dent (OTW)	.10
19	Joe Garagiola	.20
20	George Brett	.75
21	Cecil Cooper	.10
22	Ray Boone	.10
23	King Kelly	.10
24	Willie Mays	.50
25	Napoleon Lajoie	.10
26	Gil McDougald	.10
27	Nelson Briles	.10
28	Bucky Dent	.10
29	Manny Sanguillen	.10
30	Ty Cobb	.50
31	Jim Grant	.10
32	Del Ennis	.10
33	Ron Hunt	.10
34	Nolan Ryan	1.50
35	Christy Mathewson	.75
36	Robin Roberts	.10
37	Frank Crosetti	.10
38	Johnny Vander Meer	.10
39	Virgil Trucks	.10
40	Lou Gehrig	1.50
41	Luke Appling	.10
42	Rico Petrocelli	.10
43	Harry Walker	.10
44	Reggie Jackson	.65
44a	Reggie Jackson (Promo card.)	4.00
45	Mel Ott	.10
46	Phil Cavaretta	.10

47	Larry Doby	.10
48	Johnny Mize	.10
49	Ralph Kiner	.10
50	Ted Williams	1.50
51	Bobby Thomson	.10
52	Joe Black	.10
53	Monte Irvin	.10
54	Bill Virdon	.10
55	Honus Wagner	1.00
56	Herb Score	.10
57	Jerry Coleman	.10
58	Jimmie Foxx	.30
59	Elroy Face	.10
60	Babe Ruth	2.00
61	Jimmy Piersall	.10
62	Ed Charles	.10
63	Johnny Podres	.10
64	Charlie Neal	.10
65	Bill White	.10
66	Bill Skowron	.10
67	Al Rosen	.10
68	Eddie Lopat	.10
69	Bud Harrelson	.10
70	Steve Carlton	.10
71	Vida Blue	.10
72	Don Newcombe	.10
73	Al Bumbry	.10
74	Bill Madlock	.10
(75)	Checklist 1-75 (Hank Aaron)	.50
76	Bill Mazeroski	.50
77	Ron Cey	.10
78	Tommy John	.10
79	Lou Brock	.10
80	Walter Johnson	.75
81	Harvey Haddix	.10
82	Al Oliver	.10
83	Johnny Logan	.10
84	Dave Dravecky	.10
85	Tony Oliva	.10
86	Dave Kingman	.10
87	Luis Tiant	.10
88	Sal Bando	.10
89	Cesar Cedeno	.10
90	Warren Spahn	.10
91	Mickey Lolich	.10
92	Lew Burdette	.10
93	Hank Bauer	.10
94	Marv Throneberry	.10
95	Willie Stargell	.10
96	George Kell	.10
97	Fergie Jenkins	.10
98	Al Kaline	.10
99	Billy Martin	.10
100	Mickey Mantle	3.00
101	1869 - Red Stockings (125th)	.20
102	1892 (King Kelly (125th))	.10
103	1901 (Nap Lajoie (125th))	.10
104	1905 (Christy Mathewson (125th))	.40
105	1910 (Cy Young (125th))	.40
106	1915 (Ty Cobb (125th))	.75
(107)	Checklist 136-180 (Reggie Jackson)	.40
108	1924 (Rogers Hornsby (125th))	.10
109	1926 (Walter Johnson (125th))	.40
110	1927 (Babe Ruth (125th))	1.00
111	1930 (Hack Wilson (125th))	.10
112	1939 (Lou Gehrig (125th))	.75
113	1941 (Ted Williams (125th))	.75
113a	1941 (Ted Williams (125th)(Autographed edition of 2,500.))	250.00
114	1949 (Joe Berra (125th))	.30
115	1951 (Bobby Thomson (125th))	.10
116	1953 (Mickey Mantle (125th))	1.50
117	1954 (Willie Mays (125th))	.50
118	1960 (Bill Mazeroski (125th))	.30
119	1967 (Bob Gibson (125th))	.10
120	1969 Miracle Mets (125th)	.50
121	1974 (Hank Aaron (125th))	.50
122	1977 (Reggie Jackson (125th))	.40
123	1980 (George Brett (125th))	.20
124	1982 (Steve Carlton (125th))	.10
125	1991 (Nolan Ryan (125th))	.75
126	Frank Thomas	.10
127	Sam McDowell	.10
128	Jim Lonberg	.10
129	Bert Campaneris	.10
130	Bob Gibson	.10
131	Bobby Richardson	.10
132	Bobby Grich	.10
133	Billy Pierce	.10
(135)	Checklist 181-225 (Honus Wagner)	.50
136	Orlando Cepeda	.10
137	Rennie Stennett	.10
138	Gene Alley	.10
139	Manny Mota	.10
140	Rogers Hornsby	.10
141	Joe Charboneau	.20

142	Rick Farrell	.10
143	Toby Harrah	.10
144	Hank Aaron	1.00
145	Yogi Berra	.50
146	Whitey Ford	.50
147	Roy Campanella	.10
148	Graig Nettles	.10
149	Bobby Brown	.10
150	Checklist 76-150 (Willie Mays)	.50
151	Cy Young (DL)	.40
152	Walter Johnson (DL)	.40
153	Christy Mathewson (DL)	.40
154	Warren Spahn (DL)	.10
155	Steve Carlton (DL)	.10
156	Bob Gibson (DL)	.10
157	Whitey Ford (DL)	.30
158	Yogi Berra (DL)	.30
159	Roy Campanella (DL)	.10
160	Lou Gehrig (DL)	.75
161	Johnny Mize (DL)	.10
162	Rogers Hornsby (DL)	.10
163	Honus Wagner (DL)	.50
164	Hank Aaron (DL)	.50
165	Babe Ruth (DL)	1.00
166	Willie Mays (DL)	.50
167	Reggie Jackson (DL)	.40
168	Mickey Mantle (DL)	1.50
169	Jimmie Foxx (DL)	.10
170	Ted Williams (DL)	.75
171	Mel Ott (DL)	.10
172	Willie Stargell (DL)	.10
173	Al Kaline (DL)	.10
174	Ty Cobb (DL)	.75
175	Napoleon Lajoie (DL)	.10
176	Lou Brock (DL)	.10
177	Tom Seaver (DL)	.10
178	Mark Fidrych	.20
179	Don Baylor	.10
180	Tom Seaver	.10
181	Jerry Grote	.10
182	George Foster	.10
183	Buddy Bell	.10
184	Ralph Garr	.10
185	Steve Garvey	.10
186	Joe Torre	.10
187	Carl Erskine	.10
188	Tommy Davis	.10
189	Bill Buckner	.10
190	Hack Wilson	.10
191	Steve Bass	.10
192	Ken Brett	.10
193	Lee May	.10
194	Bob Horner	.10
195	Boog Powell	.10
196	Darrell Evans	.10
197	Paul Blair	.10
198	Johnny Callison	.10
199	Jimmie Reese	.10
200	Cy Young	.75
201	Ron Santo	.10
202	Rico Carty	.10
203	Ron Necciai	.10
204	Lou Boudreau	.10
205	Minnie Minoso	.10
206	Eddie Yost	.10
207	Tommie Agee	.10
208	Dave Kingman (Heroes)	.10
209	Tony Oliva (Heroes)	.10
210	Reggie Jackson (Heroes)	.40
211	Paul Blair (Heroes)	.10
212	Fergie Jenkins (Heroes)	.10
213	Steve Garvey (Heroes)	.10
214	Bert Campaneris (Heroes)	.10
215	Orlando Cepeda (Heroes)	.10
216	Bill Madlock (Heroes)	.10
217	Rennie Stennett (Heroes)	.10
218	Frank Thomas (Heroes)	.10
219	Bob Gibson (Heroes)	.10
220	Lou Brock (Heroes)	.10
221	Rico Carty (Heroes)	.10
222	Mickey Mantle (Heroes)	1.50
223	Robin Roberts (Heroes)	.10
224	Manny Sanguillen (Heroes)	.10
225	Checklist 151-225 (Mickey Mantle)	1.50

1994 Upper Deck All-Time Heroes 125th Anniversary

This parallel set was issued at the rate of one card per pack of Upper Deck All-Time Heroes cards. They are identical to the regular-issue version except for the presence on front of bronze-foil stamping which reads, "Major League Baseball / 125th Anniversary."

	NM/M
Complete Set (225):	40.00
Common Player:	.25
Stars:	2X
15	Nolan Ryan (OTW)
	(Overprint at left.)	1.00
15	Nolan Ryan (OTW)
	(Overprint at right.)	1.00

All-Time Heroes Autographs

Four players' autographed cards were randomly inserted into packs of All-Time Heroes at a reported rate of about 1:385. Seaver, Jackson and Mantle signed 1,000 each, Brett signed 2,000.

	NM/M
Complete Set (4):	650.00
Common Player:	45.00
(1)	Mickey Mantle	550.00
(2)	Reggie Jackson	40.00
(3)	George Brett	60.00
(4)	Tom Seaver	25.00

All-Time Heroes Next In Line

The Next in Line insert set includes 20 top minor leaguers. These cards were randomly inserted into every 39 packs with only 2,500 of each card produced.

		NM/M
Complete Set (20):		40.00
Common Player:		1.00
1	Mike Bell	1.00
2	Alan Benes	1.00
3	D.J. Boston	1.00
4	Johnny Damon	5.00
5	Brad Fullmer	1.00
6	LaTroy Hawkins	1.00
7	Derek Jeter	25.00
8	Daron Kirkreit	1.00
9	Trot Nixon	3.00
10	Alex Ochoa	1.00
11	Kirk Presley	1.00
12	Jose Silva	1.00
13	Terrell Wade	1.00
14	Billy Wagner	1.50
15	Glenn Williams	1.00
16	Preston Wilson	1.50
17	Wayne Gomes	1.00
18	Ben Grieve	1.00
19	Dustin Hermanson	1.00
20	Paul Wilson	1.00

All-Time Heroes 1954 Topps Archives

Two cards that were not included in the Topps 1954 Archives Set and one that wasn't even in the original 1954 set were randomly inserted into All-Time Heroes foil packs. Both Ted Williams cards, numbers 1 and 250, were left out of the Archives set because of contractual obligations of Williams with Upper Deck. In addition, a Mickey Mantle card with the original 1954 design was randomly inserted. Mantle was signed exclu-

sively with Bowman in 1954 and 1955, and therefore, was not in either Topps set.

		NM/M
Complete Set (3):		150.00
1	Ted Williams	50.00
250	Ted Williams	50.00
259	Mickey Mantle	75.00

American Epic

Baseball, The American Epic traces the history of the game, highlighting players, personalities, events and stadiums that have contributed to the national pastime. The set was patterned after a 1994 18-hour TV documentary. This boxed set contains 80 cards. It explains the roots of the game and showcases some of baseball's great players and events. Each set contains a randomly inserted card of either Michael Jordan, Babe Ruth or Mickey Mantle. Cards from the regular set are in black-and-white, with the player name and the featured year running down the left side in white print. Card backs contain half color, depending on what "inning" the card is from, and half white. The color side tells a story, the white side gives statistics and highlights.

		NM/M
Complete Set (81):		12.50
Common Player:		.15
1	1880s - Our Game	.15
2	1845 -	
	Alexander Cartwright	.15
3	1857 - Henry Chadwick	.15
4	1866 - The Fair Sex	.15
5	1869 - Harry Wright	.15
6	1876 - Albert Goodwill	
	Spalding	.15
7	1883 - Cap Anson	.15
8	1884 - Moses Fleetwood	
	Walker	.25
9	1886 - King Kelly	.15
10	1890 - John Montgomery	
	Ward	.15
11	1909 - Ty Cobb	.75
12	1904 - John McGraw	.15
13	1904 - Rube Waddell	.15
14	1905 - Christy Mathewson	.25
15	1907 - Walter Johnson	.25
16	1908 - Alta Weiss	.15
17	1908 - Fred Merkle	.15
18	1908 - Take Me Out To	
	The Ball Game	.15
19	1909 - John Henry Lloyd	.15
20	1909 - Honus Wagner	.40
21	1915 - Woodrow Wilson	.15
22	1910 - Napoleon Lajoie	.15
23	1911 - Addie Joss	.15
24	1912 - Joe Wood	.15
25	1912 - Royal Rooters	.15
26	1912 - Ebbets Field	.15
27	1914 - Johnny Evers	.15
28	1918 - World War II	.15
29	1919 - Joe Jackson	.75
30	1927 - Babe Ruth	1.50
31	1920 - Rube Foster	.15
32	1920 - Ray Chapman	.15
33	1921 - Kenesaw M. Landis	.15

34	1923 - Yankee Stadium	.15
35	1924 - Rogers Hornsby	.15
36	1923 - Warren G. Harding	.15
37	1925 - Lou Gehrig	.75
38	1926 - Grover C.	
	Alexander	.15
39	1929 - House of David	.15
40	1933 - Satchel Paige	.40
41	1931 - Lefty Grove	.15
42	1932 - Jimmie Foxx	.15
43	1932 - Connie Mack	.15
44	1937 - Josh Gibson	.15
45	1934 - Dizzy Dean	.15
46	1934 - Carl Hubbell	.15
47	1937 - Franklin D.	
	Roosevelt	.15
48	1938 - Bob Feller	.15
49	1939 - Cool Papa Bell	.15
50	1947 - Jackie Robinson	.75
51	1941 - Ted Williams	.75
52	1941 - Sym-Phony Band	.15
53	1944 - Annabel Lee	.15
54	1945 - Hank Greenberg	.15
55	1947 - Branch Rickey	.15
56	1948 - Harry S. Truman	.15
57	1953 - Casey Stengel	.15
58	1951 - Bobby Thomson	.15
59	1952 - Dwight D.	
	Eisenhower	.15
60	1952 - Mario Cuomo	.15
61	1952 - Buck O'Neil	.15
62	1955 - Yogi Berra	.15
63	1956 - Mickey Mantle	2.00
64	1956 - Don Larsen	.15
65	1961 - John F. Kennedy	.15
66	1960 - Bill Mazeroski	.15
67	1961 - Roger Maris	.25
68	1966 - Frank Robinson	.15
69	1969 - Bob Gibson	.15
70	1970 - Tom Seaver	.15
71	1969 - Curt Flood	.15
72	1972 - Roberto Clemente	.75
73	1975 - Luis Tiant	.15
74	1975 - Marvin Miller	.15
75	1977 - Reggie Jackson	.25
76	1979 - Willie Stargell	.15
77	1985 - Pete Rose	.75
78	1994 - Bill Clinton	.15
79	1991 - Nolan Ryan	.75
80	1993 - George Brett	.75
---	Checklist	.08

American Epic Inserts

In addition to the regular 80-card set, each boxed set contains one special insert card, depending on where it was purchased. At retail locations, an additional Babe Ruth card was included. Michael Jordan was included in sets purchased through direct mail outlets. Mickey Mantle was featured in sets purchased from QVC (sets purchased from Upper Deck Authenticated included an autographed card of Mantle). The inserts are numbered BC1- BC3.

		NM/M
Complete Set (3):		6.00
Common Player:		2.00
1	Mickey Mantle	2.00
2	Michael Jordan	2.00
3	Babe Ruth	2.00

American Epic Little Debbie Mail-in

Fifteen of the cards from Upper Deck's "An American Epic" card set were chosen for use in a mail-in promotion with Little Debbie snack cakes. These cards are identical to the Epic versions except for the card numbers, which

include an "LD" prefix. The back of card LD1 is a checklist for the set and includes a Little Debbie logo. Sets sold for about $4, with proofs of purchase.

		NM/M
Complete Set (15):		4.50
Common Player:		.25
1	Our Game/Checklist	.05
2	Alexander Cartwright	.25
3	King Kelly	.25
4	John McGraw	.25
5	Christy Mathewson	.40
6	Walter Johnson	.40
7	Ted Williams	.75
8	Annabel Lee	.25
9	Jackie Robinson	.50
10	Bobby Thomson	.25
11	Buck O'Neil	.25
12	Mickey Mantle	1.50
13	Bob Gibson	.25
14	Curt Flood	.25
15	Reggie Jackson	.40

1994 Upper Deck Fun Packs

In its second year this product aimed at the young collector again offered a basic set of some 160 players, surrounded by several special subsets. The first nine cards feature Stars of Tomorrow. There is a group of 18 Stand Out cards on which the background can be folded to create a player figure. Profiles cards feature playing tips from six young stars. A group of nine Headline Stars cards features two players on each which fold back to reveal a holographic photo. What's the Call cards offer game problems and cartoon caricatures of nine players. There are nine Fold Outs cards which open to reveal action photos. The subsets concluded with seven heat-activated Fun Cards on which the background temporarily appears when body heat is applied. Each five-card foil pack also includes a scratch-off game card; one for each major league team and one All-Star team for each league.

		NM/M
Complete Set (240):		35.00
Common Player:		.05
Wax Box:		15.00
1	Manny Ramirez	
	(Stars of Tomorrow)	.75
2	Cliff Floyd	
	(Stars of Tomorrow)	.05
3	Rondell White	
	(Stars of Tomorrow)	.05
4	Carlos Delgado	
	(Stars of Tomorrow)	.50
5	Chipper Jones	
	(Stars of Tomorrow)	1.25
6	Javier Lopez	
	(Stars of Tomorrow)	.15
7	Ryan Klesko	
	(Stars of Tomorrow)	.05
8	Steve Karsay	
	(Stars of Tomorrow)	.05
9	Rich Becker	
	(Stars of Tomorrow)	.05
10	Gary Sheffield	.35
11	Jeffrey Hammonds	.05
12	Roberto Alomar	.20
13	Brent Gates	.05
14	Andres Galarraga	.05
15	Tim Salmon	.05
16	Dwight Gooden	.05
17	Mark Grace	.05
18	Andy Van Slyke	.05
19	Juan Gonzalez	.40
20	Mickey Tettleton	.05
21	Roger Clemens	1.25
22	Will Clark	.05
23	Dave Justice	.15
24	Ken Griffey Jr.	1.50
24a	Ken Griffey Jr.	
	(Promo Card)	1.50
25	Barry Bonds	2.50

26	Bill Swift	.05
27	Fred McGriff	.05
28	Randy Myers	.05
29	Joe Carter	.05
30	Nigel Wilson	.05
31	Mike Piazza	1.50
32	Dave Winfield	.75
33	Steve Avery	.05
34	Kirby Puckett	.90
35	Frank Thomas	.05
36	Aaron Sele	.05
37	Ricky Gutierrez	.05
38	Curt Schilling	.25
39	Mike Greenwell	.05
40	Andy Benes	.05
41	Kevin Brown	.05
42	Mo Vaughn	.05
43	Dennis Eckersley	.60
44	Ken Hill	.05
45	Cecil Fielder	.05
46	Bobby Jones	.05
47	Tom Glavine	.25
48	Wally Joyner	.05
49	Ellis Burks	.05
50	Jason Bere	.05
51	Randy Johnson	.75
52	Darryl Kile	.05
53	Jeff Montgomery	.05
54	Alex Fernandez	.05
55	Kevin Appier	.05
56	Brian McRae	.05
57	John Wetteland	.05
58	Bob Tewksbury	.05
59	Todd Van Poppel	.05
60	Ryne Sandberg	.90
61	Bret Barberie	.05
62	Phil Plantier	.05
63	Chris Hoiles	.05
64	Tony Phillips	.05
65	Salomon Torres	.05
66	Juan Guzman	.05
67	Paul O'Neill	.05
68	Dante Bichette	.05
69	Len Dykstra	.05
70	Ivan Rodriguez	.65
71	Dean Palmer	.05
72a	Brett Butler	.05
72b	Phil Hiatt	
	(Checklisted as #172.)	.05
73	Rick Aguilera	.05
74	Robby Thompson	.05
75	Jim Abbott	.05
76	Al Martin	.05
77	Roberto Hernandez	.05
78	Jay Buhner	.05
79	Devon White	.05
80	Travis Fryman	.05
81	Jeromy Burnitz	.05
82	John Burkett	.05
83	Orlando Merced	.05
84	Jose Rijo	.05
85	Eddie Murray	.75
86	Howard Johnson	.05
87	Chuck Carr	.05
88	Pedro J. Martinez	.75
89	Charlie Hayes	.05
90	Matt Williams	.05
91	Steve Finley	.05
92	Pat Listach	.05
93	Sandy Alomar, Jr.	.05
94	Delino DeShields	.05
95	Rod Beck	.05
97	Todd Zeile	
	(Checklisted as #96.)	.05
98a	Darryl Hamilton	.05
98b	Duane Ward	
	(Checklisted as #97.)	.05
99	John Olerud	.05
100	Andre Dawson	.25
101	Ozzie Smith	.90
102	Rick Wilkins	.05
103	Alan Trammell	.05
104	Jeff Blauser	.05
105	Bret Boone	.05
106	J.T. Snow	.05
107	Kenny Lofton	.05
108	Cal Ripken, Jr.	2.50
109	Carlos Baerga	.05
110	Bip Roberts	.05
111	Barry Larkin	.05
112	Mark Langston	.05
113	Ozzie Guillen	.05
114	Chad Curtis	.05
115	Dave Hollins	.05
116	Reggie Sanders	.05
117	Jeff Conine	.05
118	Mark Whiten	.05
119	Tony Gwynn	.90
120	John Kruk	.05
121	Eduardo Perez	.05
122	Walt Weiss	.05
123	Don Mattingly	1.00
124	Rickey Henderson	.75
125	Mark McGwire	2.00
126	Wade Boggs	.90
127	Bobby Bonilla	.05
128	Jeff King	.05
129	Jack McDowell	.05
130	Albert Belle	.05
131	Greg Maddux	.90
132	Dennis Martinez	.05
133	Jose Canseco	.40
134	Bryan Harvey	.05
135	Dave Fleming	.05
136	Larry Walker	.05
137	Ken Caminiti	.05
138	Doug Drabek	.05
139	Ron Gant	.05

140	Darren Daulton	.05
141	Ruben Sierra	.05
142	Kirk Rueter	.05
143	Raul Mondesi	.05
144	Greg Vaughn	.05
145	Danny Tartabull	.05
146	Eric Karros	.05
147	Chuck Knoblauch	.05
148	Mike Mussina	.30
149	Brady Anderson	.05
150	Paul Molitor	.75
151	Bo Jackson	.10
152	Jeff Bagwell	.75
153	Gregg Jefferies	.05
154	Rafael Palmeiro	.65
155	Orel Hershiser	.05
156	Derek Bell	.05
157	Jeff Kent	.05
158	Craig Biggio	.05
159	Marquis Grissom	.05
160	Matt Mieske	.05
161	Jay Bell	.05
162	Sammy Sosa	.90
163	Robin Ventura	.05
164	Deion Sanders	.05
165	Jimmy Key	.05
166	Cal Eldred	.05
167	David McCarty	.05
168	Carlos Garcia	.05
169	Willie Greene	.05
170	Michael Jordan RC	2.50
171	Roberto Mejia	.05
173	Marc Newfield	.05
174	Kevin Stocker	.05
175	Randy Johnson	
	(Standouts)	.40
176	Ivan Rodriguez	
	(Standouts)	.30
177	Frank Thomas (Standouts)	.45
178	Roberto Alomar	
	(Standouts)	.10
179	Travis Fryman (Standouts)	.05
180	Cal Ripken, Jr.	
	(Standouts)	1.25
181	Juan Gonzalez (Standouts)	.30
182	Ken Griffey Jr. (Standouts)	.75
183	Albert Belle (Standouts)	.05
184	Greg Maddux (Standouts)	.50
185	Mike Piazza (Standouts)	.75
186	Fred McGriff (Standouts)	.05
187	Robby Thompson	
	(Standouts)	.05
188	Matt Williams (Standouts)	.05
189	Jeff Blauser (Standouts)	.05
190	Barry Bonds (Standouts)	1.25
191	Len Dykstra (Standouts)	.05
192	Dave Justice (Standouts)	.05
193	Ken Griffey Jr. (Profiles)	.75
194	Barry Bonds (Profiles)	1.25
195	Frank Thomas (Profiles)	.45
196	Juan Gonzalez (Profiles)	.30
197	Randy Johnson (Profiles)	.40
198	Chuck Carr (Profiles)	.05
199	Barry Bonds, Juan Gonzalez	
	(Headline Stars)	1.00
200	Ken Griffey Jr., Don Mattingly	
	(Headline Stars)	.75
201	Roberto Alomar,	
	Carlos Baerga	
	(Headline Stars)	.10
202	Dave Winfield, Robin Yount	
	(Headline Stars)	.40
203	Mike Piazza, Tim Salmon	
	(Headline Stars)	.75
204	Albert Belle, Frank Thomas	
	(Headline Stars)	.45
205	Cliff Floyd, Rondell White	
	(Headline Stars)	.05
206	Kirby Puckett, Tony Gwynn	
	(Headline Stars)	.50
207	Roger Clemens, Greg Maddux	
	(Headline Stars)	.50
208	Mike Piazza	
	(What's The Call)	.75
209	Jose Canseco	
	(What's The Call)	.20
210	Frank Thomas	
	(What's The Call)	.45
211	Roberto Alomar	
	(What's The Call)	.10
212	Barry Bonds	
	(What's The Call)	1.25
213	Rickey Henderson	
	(What's The Call)	.40
214	John Kruk	
	(What's The Call)	.05
215	Juan Gonzalez	
	(What's The Call)	.40
216	Ken Griffey Jr.	
	(What's The Call)	.75
217	Roberto Alomar (Foldouts)	.10
218	Craig Biggio (Foldouts)	.05
219	Cal Ripken, Jr. (Foldouts)	1.25
220	Mike Piazza (Foldouts)	.05
221	Brent Gates (Foldouts)	.05
222	Walt Weiss (Foldouts)	.05
223	Bobby Bonilla (Foldouts)	.05
224	Ken Griffey Jr. (Foldouts)	.05
225	Barry Bonds (Foldouts)	1.25
226	Barry Bonds (Fun Cards)	1.25
227	Joe Carter (Fun Cards)	.05
228	Mike Greenwell	
	(Fun Cards)	.05
229	Ken Griffey Jr. (Fun Cards)	.75
230	John Kruk (Fun Cards)	.05
231	Mike Piazza (Fun Cards)	.75
232	Kirby Puckett (Fun Cards)	.50
233	John Smoltz (Fun Cards)	.05

234 Rick Wilkins (Fun Cards) .05
235 Checklist 1-40 (Ken Griffey Jr.) .65
236 Checklist 41-80 (Frank Thomas) .45
237 Checklist 81-120 (Barry Bonds) 1.00
238 Checklist 121-160 (Mike Piazza) .65
239 Checklist 161-200 (Tim Salmon) .05
240 Checklist 201-240 (Juan Gonzalez) .35

Scratch-off Game Cards:
(1) National League .05
(2) Atlanta Braves .05
(3) Chicago Cubs .05
(4) Cincinnati Reds .05
(5) Colorado Rockies .05
(6) Florida Marlins .05
(7) Houston Astros .05
(8) Los Angeles Dodgers .05
(9) Montreal Expos .05
(10) New York Mets .05
(11) Philadelphia Phillies .05
(12) Pittsburgh Pirates .05
(13) St. Louis Cardinals .05
(14) San Diego Padres .05
(15) San Francisco Giants .05

GM "Baseball" Previews

This nine-card set is closely related to the 80-card issue subsequently released in conjunction with the public television series "Baseball" by Ken Burns. This preview issue, carrying the logo of General Motors (principal sponsor of the TV series), was issued in cello and foil packs and was available, generally with a test drive, at GM automobile dealerships. Card backs have some biographical and statistical highlights and a career summary.

NM/M
Complete Set (9): 6.00
Common Player: .50
1 Hank Aaron 1.25
2 Roberto Clemente 1.50
3 Ty Cobb .50
4 Hank Greenberg .50
5 Mickey Mantle 3.00
6 Satchel Paige .50
7 Jackie Robinson .75
8 Babe Ruth 2.00
9 Ted Williams 1.00

GTS Mickey Mantle Phone Cards

Upper Deck and Global Telecommunication Solutions combined to produce this set of phone cards paralleling the Mantle Heroes insert cards found in the regular UD issue. The phone cards were sold in two series of five cards each for $59.95 per series. Fronts of the 2-1/8" x 3-3/8" plastic cards feature black-and-white or color photos of Mantle, along with mention of a career highlight.

Backs are printed in black and have instructions for use of the card. A card picturing the 1869 Cincinnati Red Stockings was included as a random insert in the first series of Mantle phone card sets.

NM/M
Complete Set (10): 20.00
Common Card: 3.00
(1) Mickey Mantle/Portrait 3.00
(2) Mickey Mantle (1951: The Early Years) 3.00
(3) Mickey Mantle (1953: Tape Measure Home Runs) 3.00
(4) Mickey Mantle (1956: Triple Crown Season) 3.00
(5) Mickey Mantle (1957: Second Consecutive MVP) 3.00
(6) Mickey Mantle (1961: Chasing the Babe) 3.00
(7) Mickey Mantle (1964: Series Home Run Record) 3.00
(8) Mickey Mantle (1967: 500th Home Run) 3.00
(9) Mickey Mantle (1974: Hall of Fame) 3.00
(10) Mickey Mantle/Portrait 3.00
(11) 1869 Cincinnati Red Stockings 10.00

1995 Upper Deck

Issued in two series of 225 base cards each, with loads of subsets and inserts, the 1995 Upper Deck set was a strong collector favorite from the outset. Basic cards feature a borderless front photo with the player's name and UD logo in bronze foil. Backs have another large color photo, recent stats and career totals and appropriate logos, along with the infield-shaped hologram. Subsets in each series include Star Rookies and Top Prospects, each with special designs highlighting the game's young stars. Series I has a "'90s Midpoint Analysis" subset studying the decade's superstars, and Series II has another hot rookies' subset, Diamond Debuts. The set closes with a five-card "Final Tribute" subset summarizing the careers of five recently retired superstars. Retail and hobby versions were sold with each featuring some unique insert cards. Basic packaging of each type was the 12-card foil pack at $1.99, though several other configurations were also released.

NM/M
Complete Set (450): 20.00
Common Player: .05
Electric Diamond: 2X
Electric Diamond Golds: 8X
Series 1 or 2 Pack (12): .85
Series 1 or 2 Wax Box (36): 20.00
1 Ruben Rivera (Top Prospect) .05
2 Bill Pulsipher (Top Prospect) .05
3 Ben Grieve (Top Prospect) .05
4 Curtis Goodwin (Top Prospect) .05
5 Damon Hollins (Top Prospect) .05
6 Todd Greene (Top Prospect) .05
7 Glenn Williams (Top Prospect) .05
8 Bret Wagner (Top Prospect) .05
9 Karim Garcia RC (Top Prospect) .50
10 Nomar Garciaparra (Top Prospect) 1.00
11 Raul Casanova RC (Top Prospect) .10
12 Matt Smith (Top Prospect) .05
13 Paul Wilson (Top Prospect) .05
14 Jason Isringhausen (Top Prospect) .05
15 Reid Ryan (Top Prospect) .05
16 Lee Smith .05
17 Chili Davis .05
18 Brian Anderson .05
19 Gary DiSarcina .05
20 Bo Jackson .10
21 Chuck Finley .05
22 Darryl Kile .05
23 Shane Reynolds .05
24 Tony Eusebio .05
25 Craig Biggio .05
26 Doug Drabek .05
27 Brian L. Hunter .05
28 James Mouton .05
29 Geronimo Berroa .05
30 Rickey Henderson .75
31 Steve Karsay .05
32 Steve Ontiveros .05
33 Ernie Young .05
34 Dennis Eckersley .65
35 Mark McGwire 1.50
36 Dave Stewart .05
37 Pat Hentgen .05
38 Carlos Delgado .45
39 Joe Carter .05
40 Roberto Alomar .20
41 John Olerud .05
42 Devon White .05
43 Roberto Kelly .05
44 Jeff Blauser .05
45 Fred McGriff .05
46 Tom Glavine .25
47 Mike Kelly .05
48 Javy Lopez .05
49 Greg Maddux 1.00
50 Matt Mieske .05
51 Troy O'Leary .05
52 Jeff Cirillo .05
53 Cal Eldred .05
54 Pat Listach .05
55 Jose Valentin .05
56 John Mabry .05
57 Bob Tewksbury .05
58 Brian Jordan .05
59 Gregg Jefferies .05
60 Ozzie Smith 1.00
61 Geronimo Pena .05
62 Mark Whiten .05
63 Rey Sanchez .05
64 Willie Banks .05
65 Mark Grace .05
66 Randy Myers .05
67 Steve Trachsel .05
68 Derrick May .05
69 Brett Butler .05
70 Eric Karros .05
71 Tim Wallach .05
72 Delino DeShields .05
73 Darren Dreifort .05
74 Orel Hershiser .05
75 Billy Ashley .05
76 Sean Berry .05
77 Ken Hill .05
78 John Wetteland .05
79 Moises Alou .05
80 Cliff Floyd .05
81 Marquis Grissom .05
82 Larry Walker .05
83 Rondell White .05
84 William VanLandingham .05
85 Matt Williams .05
86 Rod Beck .05
87 Darren Lewis .05
88 Robby Thompson .05
89 Darryl Strawberry .05
90 Kenny Lofton .05
91 Charles Nagy .05
92 Sandy Alomar Jr. .05
93 Mark Clark .05
94 Dennis Martinez .05
95 Dave Winfield .75
96 Jim Thome .60
97 Manny Ramirez .75
98 Goose Gossage .05
99 Tino Martinez .05
100 Ken Griffey Jr. 1.25
100a Ken Griffey Jr./OPS 2.00
101 Greg Maddux (Analysis: '90s Midpoint) .50
102 Randy Johnson (Analysis: '90s Midpoint) .40
103 Barry Bonds (Analysis: '90s Midpoint) 1.00
104 Juan Gonzalez (Analysis: '90s Midpoint) .20
105 Frank Thomas (Analysis: '90s Midpoint) .40
106 Matt Williams (Analysis: '90s Midpoint) .05
107 Paul Molitor (Analysis: '90s Midpoint) .40
108 Fred McGriff (Analysis: '90s Midpoint) .05
109 Carlos Baerga (Analysis: '90s Midpoint) .05
110 Ken Griffey Jr. (Analysis: '90s Midpoint) .65
111 Reggie Jefferson .05
112 Randy Johnson .75
113 Marc Newfield .05
114 Robb Nen .05
115 Jeff Conine .05
116 Kurt Abbott .05
117 Charlie Hough .05
118 Dave Weathers .05
119 Juan Castillo .05
120 Bret Saberhagen .05
121 Rico Brogna .05
122 John Franco .05
123 Todd Hundley .05
124 Jason Jacome .05
125 Bobby Jones .05
126 Bret Barberie .05
127 Ben McDonald .05
128 Harold Baines .05
129 Jeffrey Hammonds .05
130 Mike Mussina .30
131 Chris Hoiles .05
132 Brady Anderson .05
133 Eddie Williams .05
134 Andy Benes .05
135 Tony Gwynn 1.00
136 Bip Roberts .05
137 Joey Hamilton .05
138 Luis Lopez .05
139 Ray McDavid .05
140 Lenny Dykstra .05
141 Mariano Duncan .05
142 Fernando Valenzuela .05
143 Bobby Munoz .05
144 Kevin Stocker .05
145 John Kruk .05
146 Jon Lieber .05
147 Zane Smith .05
148 Steve Cooke .05
149 Andy Van Slyke .05
150 Jay Bell .05
151 Carlos Garcia .05
152 John Dettmer .05
153 Darren Oliver .05
154 Dean Palmer .05
155 Otis Nixon .05
156 Rusty Greer .05
157 Rick Helling .05
158 Jose Canseco .40
159 Roger Clemens 1.00
160 Andre Dawson .25
161 Mo Vaughn .05
162 Aaron Sele .05
163 John Valentin .05
164 Brian Hunter .05
165 Bret Boone .05
166 Hector Carrasco .05
167 Pete Schourek .05
168 Willie Greene .05
169 Kevin Mitchell .05
170 Deion Sanders .05
171 John Roper .05
172 Charlie Hayes .05
173 David Nied .05
174 Ellis Burks .05
175 Dante Bichette .05
176 Marvin Freeman .05
177 Eric Young .05
178 David Cone .05
179 Greg Gagne .05
180 Bob Hamelin .05
181 Wally Joyner .05
182 Jeff Montgomery .05
183 Jose Lind .05
184 Chris Gomez .05
185 Travis Fryman .05
186 Kirk Gibson .05
187 Mike Moore .05
188 Lou Whitaker .05
189 Sean Bergman .05
190 Shane Mack .05
191 Rick Aguilera .05
192 Denny Hocking .05
193 Chuck Knoblauch .05
194 Kevin Tapani .05
195 Kent Hrbek .05
196 Ozzie Guillen .05
197 Wilson Alvarez .05
198 Tim Raines .05
199 Scott Ruffcorn .05
200 Michael Jordan 2.00
201 Robin Ventura .05
202 Jason Bere .05
203 Darrin Jackson .05
204 Russ Davis .05
205 Jimmy Key .05
206 Jack McDowell .05
207 Jim Abbott .05
208 Paul O'Neill .05
209 Bernie Williams .05
210 Don Mattingly 1.00
211 Orlando Miller/SR .05
212 Alex Gonzalez/SR .05
213 Terrell Wade/SR .05
214 Jose Oliva/SR .05
215 Alex Rodriguez/SR 1.50
216 Garret Anderson/SR .05
217 Alan Benes/SR .05
218 Armando Benitez/SR .05
219 Dustin Hermanson/SR .05
220 Charles Johnson/SR .05
221 Julian Tavarez/SR .05
222 Jason Giambi/SR .50
223 LaTroy Hawkins/SR .05
224 Todd Hollandsworth/SR .05
225 Derek Jeter/SR 2.00
226 Hideo Nomo/SR RC 2.00
227 Tony Clark/SR .05
228 Roger Cedeno/SR .05
229 Scott Stahoviak/SR .05
230 Michael Tucker/SR .05
231 Joe Rosselli/SR .05
232 Antonio Osuna/SR .05
233 Bobby Higginson/SR RC .25
234 Mark Grudzielanek/SR RC .25
235 Ray Durham/SR .05
236 Frank Rodriguez/SR .05
237 Quilvio Veras/SR .05
238 Darren Bragg/SR .05
239 Ugueth Urbina/SR .05
240 Jason Bates/SR .05
241 David Bell (Diamond Debuts) .05
242 Ron Villone (Diamond Debuts) .05
243 Joe Randa (Diamond Debuts) .05
244 Carlos Perez RC (Diamond Debuts) .05
245 Brad Clontz (Diamond Debuts) .05
246 Steve Rodriguez (Diamond Debuts) .05
247 Joe Vitiello (Diamond Debuts) .05
248 Ozzie Timmons (Diamond Debuts) .05
249 Rudy Pemberton (Diamond Debuts) .05
250 Marty Cordova (Diamond Debuts) .05
251 Tony Graffanino (Top Prospect) .05
252 Mark Johnson RC (Top Prospect) .05
253 Tomas Perez RC (Top Prospect) .05
254 Jimmy Hurst (Top Prospect) .05
255 Edgardo Alfonzo (Top Prospect) .05
256 Jose Malave (Top Prospect) .05
257 Brad Radke RC (Top Prospect) .30
258 Jon Nunnally (Top Prospect) .05
259 Dilson Torres (Top Prospect) .05
260 Esteban Loaiza (Top Prospect) .05
261 Freddy Garcia RC (Top Prospect) .05
262 Don Wengert (Top Prospect) .05
263 Robert Person RC (Top Prospect) .05
264 Tim Unroe RC (Top Prospect) .05
265 Juan Acevedo (Top Prospect) .05
266 Eduardo Perez .05
267 Tony Phillips .05
268 Jim Edmonds .05
269 Jorge Fabregas .05
270 Tim Salmon .05
271 Mark Langston .05
272 J.T. Snow .05
273 Phil Plantier .05
274 Derek Bell .05
275 Jeff Bagwell .75
276 Luis Gonzalez .05
277 John Hudek .05
278 Todd Stottlemyre .05
279 Mark Acre .05
280 Ruben Sierra .05
281 Mike Bordick .05
282 Ron Darling .05
283 Brent Gates .05
284 Todd Van Poppel .05
285 Paul Molitor .75
286 Ed Sprague .05
287 Juan Guzman .05
288 David Cone .05
289 Shawn Green .30
290 Marquis Grissom .05
291 Kent Mercker .05
292 Steve Avery .05
293 Chipper Jones 1.00
294 John Smoltz .05
295 Dave Justice .05
296 Ryan Klesko .05
297 Joe Oliver .05
298 Ricky Bones .05
299 John Jaha .05
300 Greg Vaughn .05
301 Dave Nilsson .05
302 Kevin Seitzer .05
303 Bernard Gilkey .05
304 Allen Battle .05
305 Ray Lankford .05
306 Tom Pagnozzi .05
307 Allen Watson .05
308 Danny Jackson .05
309 Ken Hill .05
310 Todd Zeile .05
311 Kevin Roberson .05
312 Steve Buechele .05
313 Rick Wilkins .05
314 Kevin Foster .05
315 Sammy Sosa 1.00
316 Howard Johnson .05
317 Greg Hansell .05
318 Pedro Astacio .05
319 Rafael Bournigal .05
320 Mike Piazza 1.25
321 Ramon Martinez .05
322 Raul Mondesi .05
323 Ismael Valdes .05
324 Wil Cordero .05
325 Tony Tarasco .05
326 Roberto Kelly .05
327 Jeff Fassero .05
328 Mike Lansing .05
329 Pedro J. Martinez .75
330 Kirk Rueter .05
331 Glenallen Hill .05
332 Kirt Manwaring .05
333 Royce Clayton .05
334 J.R. Phillips .05
335 Barry Bonds 2.00
336 Mark Portugal .05
337 Terry Mulholland .05
338 Omar Vizquel .05
339 Carlos Baerga .05
340 Albert Belle .75
341 Eddie Murray .75
342 Wayne Kirby .05
343 Chad Ogea .05
344 Tim Davis .05
345 Jay Buhner .05
346 Bobby Ayala .05
347 Mike Blowers .05
348 Dave Fleming .05
349 Edgar Martinez .05
350 Andre Dawson .30
351 Darrell Whitmore .05
352 Chuck Carr .05
353 John Burkett .05
354 Chris Hammond .05
355 Gary Sheffield .40
356 Pat Rapp .05
357 Greg Colbrunn .05
358 David Segui .05
359 Jeff Kent .05
360 Bobby Bonilla .05
361 Pete Harnisch .05
362 Ryan Thompson .05
363 Jose Vizcaino .05
364 Brett Butler .05
365 Cal Ripken Jr. 2.00
366 Rafael Palmeiro .65
367 Leo Gomez .05
368 Andy Van Slyke .05
369 Arthur Rhodes .05
370 Ken Caminiti .05
371 Steve Finley .05
372 Melvin Nieves .05
373 Andujar Cedeno .05
374 Trevor Hoffman .05
375 Fernando Valenzuela .05
376 Ricky Bottalico .05
377 Dave Hollins .05
378 Charlie Hayes .05
379 Tommy Greene .05
380 Darren Daulton .05
381 Curt Schilling .25
382 Midre Cummings .05
383 Al Martin .05
384 Jeff King .05
385 Orlando Merced .05
386 Denny Neagle .05
387 Don Slaught .05
388 Dave Clark .05
389 Kevin Gross .05
390 Will Clark .05
391 Ivan Rodriguez .65
392 Benji Gil .05
393 Jeff Frye .05
394 Kenny Rogers .05
395 Juan Gonzalez .40
396 Mike Macfarlane .05
397 Lee Tinsley .05
398 Tim Naehring .05
399 Tim Vanegmond .05
400 Mike Greenwell .05
401 Ken Ryan .05
402 John Smiley .05
403 Tim Pugh .05
404 Reggie Sanders .05
405 Barry Larkin .05
406 Hal Morris .05
407 Jose Rijo .05
408 Lance Painter .05
409 Joe Girardi .05
410 Andres Galarraga .05
411 Mike Kingery .05
412 Roberto Mejia .05
413 Walt Weiss .05
414 Bill Swift .05
415 Larry Walker .05
416 Billy Brewer .05
417 Pat Borders .05
418 Tom Gordon .05
419 Kevin Appier .05
420 Gary Gaetti .05
421 Greg Gohr .05
422 Felipe Lira .05
423 John Doherty .05
424 Chad Curtis .05
425 Cecil Fielder .05
426 Alan Trammell .05
427 David McCarty .05
428 Scott Erickson .05
429 Pat Mahomes .05
430 Kirby Puckett 1.00
431 Dave Stevens .05
432 Pedro Munoz .05
433 Chris Sabo .05
434 Alex Fernandez .05
435 Frank Thomas .75
436 Roberto Hernandez .05
437 Lance Johnson .05
438 Jim Abbott .05
439 John Wetteland .05
440 Melido Perez .05
441 Tony Fernandez .05
442 Pat Kelly .05
443 Mike Stanley .05
444 Danny Tartabull .05
445 Wade Boggs 1.00

446	Robin Yount (Final Tribute)	.75
447	Ryne Sandberg (Final Tribute)	1.00
448	Nolan Ryan (Final Tribute)	2.00
449	George Brett (Final Tribute)	1.00
450	Mike Schmidt (Final Tribute)	1.00

Electric Diamond

Included as an insert at the rate of one per retail foil pack and two per jumbo pack, this set parallels the regular issue. The only differences are that the Electric Diamond cards utilize silver-foil highlights on front, compared to the copper foil on the regular cards. The Electric Diamond cards also include a home-plate shaped logo printed in silver foil in one of the upper corners.

	NM/M
Complete Set (1-450):	60.00
Common Player:	.25
Stars/Rookies:	2X

Electric Diamond Gold

A parallel set of a parallel set, the Electric Diamond Gold cards were found at an average rate of one per 36 retail packs. They differ from the standard ED inserts in that the home plate-shaped Electric Diamond logo in the upper corner and the player's name at bottom are printed in gold foil, rather than the silver of the ED cards or the copper of the regular-issue UD cards.

	NM/M
Complete Set (450):	650.00
Common Player:	2.00
Stars/Rookies:	8X

Update Trade Cards

Inserted into Series 2 at the rate of about one per 11 packs was this five-card series of trade cards. Each card could be mailed in with $2 to receive nine cards from a special UD Update set picturing traded or free agent players in the uniforms of their new teams. The front of each trade card pictures one of the traded players in his old uniform against a red and blue background. Backs have instructions for redeeming the trade cards. The mail-in offer expired Feb. 1, 1996. Cards are numbered with a "TC" prefix.

	NM/M
Complete Set (5):	6.00
Common Player:	1.00
1 Orel Hershiser	1.00
2 Terry Pendleton	1.00
3 Benito Santiago	1.00
4 Kevin Brown	1.00
5 Gregg Jefferies	1.00

Update

These cards depicting traded and free agent players in the uniforms of their new 1995 teams were available only by redeeming trade cards found in Series 2 packs. Each trade-in card was good for one nine-card segment of the Update series when sent with $2 prior to the Feb. 1, 1996 deadline. Update cards share the same format as the regular 1995 Upper Deck set.

	NM/M
Complete Set (45):	7.50
Common Player:	.25
451 Jim Abbott	.25
452 Danny Tartabull	.25
453 Ariel Prieto	.25
454 Scott Cooper	.25
455 Tom Henke	.25
456 Todd Zeile	.25
457 Brian McRae	.25
458 Luis Gonzalez	.25
459 Jaime Navarro	.25
460 Todd Worrell	.25
461 Roberto Kelly	.25
462 Chad Fonville	.25
463 Shane Andrews	.25
464 David Segui	.25
465 Deion Sanders	.50
466 Orel Hershiser	.25
467 Ken Hill	.25
468 Andy Benes	.25
469 Terry Pendleton	.25
470 Bobby Bonilla	.25
471 Scott Erickson	.25
472 Kevin Brown	.25
473 Glenn Dishman	.25
474 Phil Plantier	.25
475 Gregg Jefferies	.25
476 Tyler Green	.25
477 Heathcliff Slocumb	.25
478 Mark Whiten	.25
479 Mickey Tettleton	.25
480 Tim Wakefield	.25
481 Vaughn Eshelman	.25
482 Rick Aguilera	.25
483 Erik Hanson	.25
484 Willie McGee	.25
485 Troy O'Leary	.25
486 Benito Santiago	.25
487 Darren Lewis	.25
488 Dave Burba	.25
489 Ron Gant	.25
490 Bret Saberhagen	.25
491 Vinny Castilla	.25
492 Frank Rodriguez	.25
493 Andy Pettitte	5.00
494 Ruben Sierra	.25
495 Alex Cone	.25

Autograph Trade Cards

On the average of once every 72 packs (two boxes) of Series II hobby, a trade card good for an autographed player card could be found as an insert. The cards feature the player name, but no picture, on front, while the reverse has instructions for redeeming the card for a $5 fee. The autograph trade cards expired on Nov. 1, 1995.

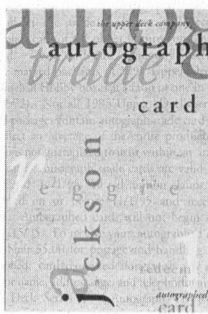

	NM/M
Complete Set (5):	15.00
Common Player:	2.00
(1) Roger Clemens	4.00
(2) Reggie Jackson	3.00
(3) Willie Mays	6.00
(4) Raul Mondesi	2.00
(5) Frank Robinson	3.00

Autograph Redemption Cards

These cards were sent to collectors who redeemed Autograph Trade cards found in Series II Upper Deck baseball. A certificate of authenticity with a holographic serial number matching that on the card back was issued with each card.

	NM/M
Complete Set (5):	220.00
Common Player:	15.00
AC1 Reggie Jackson	20.00
AC2 Willie Mays	100.00
AC3 Frank Robinson	30.00
AC4 Roger Clemens	125.00
AC5 Raul Mondesi	10.00

Autographed Jumbos

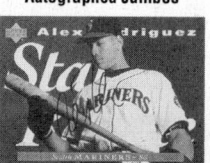

By sending in quantities of foil wrappers from Upper Deck baseball cards, collectors could receive a jumbo 5" x 7" blow-up of a player's card. The offer was limited to 8,000 Roger Clemens cards (Series I) and 6,000 Alex Rodriguez cards (Series II). Each card bears a serial number hologram on back and comes with a matching Upper Deck Authenticated authenticity guarantee card.

	NM/M
Complete Set (2):	100.00
(1) Roger Clemens	50.00
(2) Alex Rodriguez	75.00

Award Winners Predictors (Hobby)

Candidates for 1995 MVP and Rookie of the Year in each league are featured in the interactive insert series called Predictors. Twenty potential award winners were released in each of Series 1 and 2 at the rate of one per 30 packs on average. Cards feature on front a player photo inside a diamond cutout on a rich looking black and marbled background. In gold foil are his name and team at top, and "PREDICTOR" and the category at bottom. Backs feature game rules and details for redeem-

ing the card if the pictured player wins the specified award. Winners could trade in the card for a foil-enhanced set of Predictor cards. The trade-in offer expired at the end of 1995. Cards are numbered with a "H" prefix.

	NM/M
Complete Set (40):	50.00
Common Player:	.50
Winner Exchange Cards:	2X
1 Albert Belle	.50
2 Juan Gonzalez	1.50
3 Ken Griffey Jr.	3.00
4 Kirby Puckett	2.50
5 Frank Thomas	2.00
6 Jeff Bagwell	2.00
7 Barry Bonds	5.00
8 Mike Piazza	3.00
9 Matt Williams	.50
10 1995 MVP Long Shot (Winner)	.50
11 Armando Benitez	.50
12 Alex Gonzalez	.50
13 Shawn Green	1.50
14 Derek Jeter	5.00
15 Alex Rodriguez	4.00
16 Alan Benes	.50
17 Brian L. Hunter	.50
18 Charles Johnson	.50
19 Jose Oliva	.50
20 1995 ROY Long Shot	.50
21 Cal Ripken Jr.	5.00
22 Don Mattingly	2.75
23 Roberto Alomar	.75
24 Kenny Lofton	.50
25 Will Clark	.50
26 Mark McGwire	4.00
27 Greg Maddux	2.50
28 Fred McGriff	.50
29 Andres Galarraga	.50
30 Jose Canseco	1.50
31 Ray Durham	.50
32 Mark Grudzielanek	.50
33 Scott Ruffcorn	.50
34 Michael Tucker	.50
35 Garret Anderson	.50
36 Darren Bragg	.50
37 Quilvio Veras	.50
38 Hideo Nomo (Winner)	4.00
39 Chipper Jones	2.50
40 Marty Cordova (Winner)	1.50

Baseball Heroes Babe Ruth

In the 100th anniversary year of his birth, Babe Ruth was the featured star in Upper Deck continuing its "Heroes" insert set. Ten cards, including an unnumbered header, were issued in Series 2 packs. The cards featured colorized photos printed on metallic foil on the front. Backs have stats and/or biographical data. On average, one Babe Ruth Heroes card is found per 34 packs.

	NM/M
Complete Set (10):	45.00
Common Card:	6.00
73 1914-18 Pitching Career (Babe Ruth)	6.00
74 1919 - Move to Outfield (Babe Ruth)	6.00

75	1920 - Renaissance Man (Babe Ruth)	6.00
76	1923 - House That Ruth Built (Babe Ruth)	6.00
77	1927 - 60-Homer Season (Babe Ruth)	6.00
78	1928 - Three-homer Game (Babe Ruth)	6.00
79	1932 - The Called Shot (Babe Ruth)	6.00
80	1930-35 - Milestones (Babe Ruth)	6.00
81	1935 - The Last Hurrah (Babe Ruth)	6.00
---	Header Card	7.50

Checklists

Upscale checklists for the 1995 UD set were part of the insert card program, seeded about one per 17 packs, on average. Horizontally formatted fronts are printed on metallic foil and include a career highlight of the pictured player. Backs have the checklist data. Five checklists were issued in each of Series I and Series II.

	NM/M
Complete Set (10):	3.00
Common Player:	.25
1 Checklist 1-75 (Montreal Expos)	.25
2 Checklist 76-150 (Fred McGriff)	.25
3 Checklist 151-225 (John Valentin (Unassisted triple play.))	.25
4 Special Edition Checklist (Greg Maddux)	.75
5 Special Edition Checklist 69-135 (Kenny Rogers (Perfect Game))	.25
1 Checklist 226-300 (Cecil Fielder)	.25
2 Checklist 301-375 (Tony Gwynn)	.75
3 Checklist 376-450 (Greg Maddux)	.75
4 Special Edition Checklist 136-203 (Randy Johnson)	.50
5 Special Edition Checklist 204-270 (Mike Schmidt)	.75

League Leaders Predictors (Retail)

Candidates for the Triple Crown categories of league leaders in hits, home runs and RBIs are featured in this retail-only insert set, found at the average rate of one per 30 packs in both Series 1 and 2. If the player pictured on the card front won the category specified on his card, it could be redeemed for a special foil-enhanced version of the subset prior to the Dec. 31, 1995 deadline. Cards are numbered with a "R" prefix.

	NM/M
Complete Set (60):	65.00
Common Player:	.50
Winner Exchange Cards:	2X
1 Albert Belle (Winner)	1.50
2 Jose Canseco	1.50
3 Juan Gonzalez	1.00
4 Ken Griffey Jr.	3.00
5 Frank Thomas	2.00
6 Jeff Bagwell	2.00
7 Barry Bonds	5.00
8 Fred McGriff	.50
9 Matt Williams	.50
10 1995 Home Run Long Shot (Winner)	.50

11	Albert Belle (Winner)	1.50
12	Joe Carter	.50
13	Cecil Fielder	.50
14	Kirby Puckett	2.50
15	Frank Thomas	2.00
16	Jeff Bagwell	2.00
17	Barry Bonds	5.00
18	Mike Piazza	3.00
19	Matt Williams	.50
20	1995 RBI Long Shot (Winner)	.50
21	Wade Boggs	2.50
22	Kenny Lofton	.50
23	Paul Molitor	2.00
24	Paul O'Neill	.50
25	Frank Thomas	2.00
26	Jeff Bagwell	.50
27	Tony Gwynn (Winner)	5.00
28	Gregg Jefferies	.50
29	Hal Morris	.50
30	1995 Batting Long Shot (Winner)	.50
31	Joe Carter	.50
32	Cecil Fielder	.50
33	Rafael Palmeiro	1.50
34	Larry Walker	.50
35	Manny Ramirez	2.00
36	Tim Salmon	.50
37	Mike Piazza	3.00
38	Andres Galarraga	.50
39	Dave Justice	.50
40	Gary Sheffield	1.50
41	Juan Gonzalez	1.00
42	Jose Canseco	.50
43	Will Clark	.50
44	Rafael Palmeiro	1.50
45	Ken Griffey Jr.	3.00
46	Ruben Sierra	.50
47	Larry Walker	.50
48	Fred McGriff	.50
49	Dante Bichette (Winner)	.50
50	Darren Daulton	.50
51	Will Clark	.50
52	Ken Griffey Jr.	3.00
53	Don Mattingly	2.75
54	John Olerud	.50
55	Kirby Puckett	2.50
56	Raul Mondesi	.50
57	Moises Alou	.50
58	Bret Boone	.50
59	Albert Belle	.50
60	Mike Piazza	3.00

Steal of a Deal

A horizontal format with an action photo printed over a green foil background and a large bronze seal indicating how the player was acquired are featured in this 15-card insert set. The front has a terra-cotta border, which is carried over to the back. A large green box on back details the transaction and describes why it can be categorized as a "steal" for the player's new team. These top-of-the-line chase cards were seeded in both hobby and retail packs of Series I at the average rate of one per 34 packs. Cards are numbered with a "SD" prefix.

	NM/M
Complete Set (15):	25.00
Common Player:	1.00
1 Mike Piazza	6.00
2 Fred McGriff	1.00
3 Kenny Lofton	1.00
4 Jose Oliva	1.00
5 Jeff Bagwell	3.00
6 Roberto Alomar, Joe Carter	1.00
7 Steve Karsay	1.00
8 Ozzie Smith	4.00
9 Dennis Eckersley	2.00
10 Jose Canseco	1.50
11 Carlos Baerga	1.00
12 Cecil Fielder	1.00
13 Don Mattingly	5.00
14 Bret Boone	1.00
15 Michael Jordan	10.00

Special Edition

Printed on metallic foil on front, and inserted into hobby packs only at the rate of one per pack, this insert set is found in both Series 1 (#1-135) and Series 2 (#136-270). Each card top has the name of the issue and the issuer, while stacked black and silver bars at bottom have the player name, team and position. Backs are conventionally printed and have another color photo, career data and 1994 and lifetime stats.

	NM/M
Complete Set (270):	60.00
Common Player:	.10
Gold:	3X

1	Cliff Floyd	.10
2	Wil Cordero	.10
3	Pedro Martinez	1.50
4	Larry Walker	.10
5	Derek Jeter	4.00
6	Mike Stanley	.10
7	Melido Perez	.10
8	Jim Leyritz	.10
9	Danny Tartabull	.10
10	Wade Boggs	2.00
11	Ryan Klesko	.10
12	Steve Avery	.10
13	Damon Hollins	.10
14	Chipper Jones	2.00
15	Dave Justice	.10
16	Glenn Williams	.10
17	Jose Oliva	.10
18	Terrell Wade	.10
19	Alex Fernandez	.10
20	Frank Thomas	1.50
21	Ozzie Guillen	.10
22	Roberto Hernandez	.10
23	Albie Lopez	.10
24	Eddie Murray	1.50
25	Albert Belle	.10
26	Omar Vizquel	.10
27	Carlos Baerga	.10
28	Jose Rijo	.10
29	Hal Morris	.10
30	Reggie Sanders	.10
31	Jack Morris	.10
32	Raul Mondesi	.10
33	Karim Garcia	.15
34	Todd Hollandsworth	.10
35	Mike Piazza	2.50
36	Chan Ho Park	.10
37	Ramon Martinez	.10
38	Kenny Rogers	.10
39	Will Clark	.10
40	Juan Gonzalez	.75
41	Ivan Rodriguez	1.25
42	Orlando Miller	.10
43	John Hudek	.10
44	Luis Gonzalez	.10
45	Jeff Bagwell	1.50
46	Cal Ripken Jr.	4.00
47	Mike Oquist	.10
48	Armando Benitez	.10
49	Ben McDonald	.10
50	Rafael Palmeiro	1.25
51	Curtis Goodwin	.10
52	Vince Coleman	.10
53	Tom Gordon	.10
54	Mike Macfarlane	.10
55	Brian McRae	.10
56	Matt Smith	.10
57	David Segui	.10
58	Paul Wilson	.10
59	Bill Pulsipher	.10
60	Bobby Bonilla	.10
61	Jeff Kent	.10
62	Ryan Thompson	.10
63	Jason Isringhausen	.10
64	Ed Sprague	.10
65	Paul Molitor	1.50
66	Juan Guzman	.10
67	Alex Gonzalez	.10
68	Shawn Green	.50
69	Mark Portugal	.10
70	Barry Bonds	4.00
71	Robby Thompson	.10
72	Royce Clayton	.10
73	Ricky Bottalico	.10
74	Doug Jones	.10
75	Darren Daulton	.10
76	Gregg Jefferies	.10
77	Scott Cooper	.10
78	Nomar Garciaparra	2.00
79	Ken Ryan	.10
80	Mike Greenwell	.10
81	LaTroy Hawkins	.10
82	Rich Becker	.10
83	Scott Erickson	.10
84	Pedro Munoz	.10
85	Kirby Puckett	2.00
86	Orlando Merced	.10
87	Jeff King	.10
88	Midre Cummings	.10
89	Bernard Gilkey	.10

90	Ray Lankford	.10
91	Todd Zeile	.10
92	Alan Benes	.10
93	Bret Wagner	.10
94	Rene Arocha	.10
95	Cecil Fielder	.10
96	Alan Trammell	.10
97	Tony Phillips	.10
98	Junior Felix	.10
99	Brian Harper	.10
100	Greg Vaughn	.10
101	Ricky Bones	.10
102	Walt Weiss	.10
103	Lance Painter	.10
104	Roberto Mejia	.10
105	Andres Galarraga	.10
106	Todd Van Poppel	.10
107	Ben Grieve	.10
108	Brent Gates	.10
109	Jason Giambi	1.00
110	Ruben Sierra	.10
111	Terry Steinbach	.10
112	Chris Hammond	.10
113	Charles Johnson	.10
114	Jesus Tavarez	.10
115	Gary Sheffield	.40
116	Chuck Carr	.10
117	Bobby Ayala	.10
118	Randy Johnson	1.50
119	Edgar Martinez	.10
120	Alex Rodriguez	3.00
121	Kevin Foster	.10
122	Kevin Roberson	.10
123	Sammy Sosa	2.00
124	Steve Trachsel	.10
125	Eduardo Perez	.10
126	Tim Salmon	.10
127	Todd Greene	.10
128	Jorge Fabregas	.10
129	Mark Langston	.10
130	Mitch Williams	.10
131	Raul Casanova	.10
132	Mel Nieves	.10
133	Andy Benes	.10
134	Dustin Hermanson	.10
135	Trevor Hoffman	.10
136	Mark Grudzielanek	.10
137	Ugueth Urbina	.10
138	Moises Alou	.10
139	Roberto Kelly	.10
140	Rondell White	.10
141	Paul O'Neill	.10
142	Jimmy Key	.10
143	Jack McDowell	.10
144	Ruben Rivera	.10
145	Don Mattingly	2.25
146	John Wetteland	.10
147	Tom Glavine	.25
148	Marquis Grissom	.10
149	Javy Lopez	.10
150	Fred McGriff	.10
151	Greg Maddux	2.00
152	Chris Sabo	.10
153	Ray Durham	.10
154	Robin Ventura	.10
155	Jim Abbott	.10
156	Jimmy Hurst	.10
157	Tim Raines	.10
158	Dennis Martinez	.10
159	Kenny Lofton	.10
160	Dave Winfield	1.50
161	Manny Ramirez	1.50
162	Jim Thome	1.00
163	Barry Larkin	.10
164	Bret Boone	.10
165	Deion Sanders	.10
166	Ron Gant	.10
167	Benito Santiago	.10
168	Hideo Nomo	.75
169	Billy Ashley	.10
170	Roger Cedeno	.10
171	Ismael Valdes	.10
172	Eric Karros	.10
173	Rusty Greer	.10
174	Rick Helling	.10
175	Nolan Ryan	4.00
176	Dean Palmer	.10
177	Phil Plantier	.10
178	Darryl Kile	.10
179	Derek Bell	.10
180	Doug Drabek	.10
181	Craig Biggio	.10
182	Kevin Brown	.10
183	Harold Baines	.10
184	Jeffrey Hammonds	.10
185	Chris Hoiles	.10
186	Mike Mussina	.50
187	Bob Hamelin	.10
188	Jeff Montgomery	.10
189	Michael Tucker	.10
190	George Brett	2.25
191	Edgardo Alfonzo	.10
192	Brett Butler	.10
193	Bobby Jones	.10
194	Todd Hundley	.10
195	Bret Saberhagen	.10
196	Pat Hentgen	.10
197	Roberto Alomar	.30
198	David Cone	.10
199	Carlos Delgado	1.00
200	Joe Carter	.10
201	William Van Landingham	.10
202	Rod Beck	.10
203	J.R. Phillips	.10
204	Darren Lewis	.10
205	Matt Williams	.10
206	Lenny Dykstra	.10
207	Dave Hollins	.10

208	Mike Schmidt	2.25
209	Charlie Hayes	.10
210	Mo Vaughn	.10
211	Jose Malave	.10
212	Roger Clemens	2.25
213	Jose Canseco	.75
214	Mark Whiten	.10
215	Marty Cordova	.10
216	Rick Aguilera	.10
217	Kevin Tapani	.10
218	Chuck Knoblauch	.10
219	Al Martin	.10
220	Jay Bell	.10
221	Carlos Garcia	.10
222	Freddy Garcia	.10
223	Jon Lieber	.10
224	Danny Jackson	.10
225	Ozzie Smith	2.00
226	Brian Jordan	.10
227	Ken Hill	.10
228	Scott Cooper	.10
229	Chad Curtis	.10
230	Lou Whitaker	.10
231	Kirk Gibson	.10
232	Travis Fryman	.10
233	Jose Valentin	.10
234	Dave Nilsson	.10
235	Cal Eldred	.10
236	Matt Mieske	.10
237	Bill Swift	.10
238	Marvin Freeman	.10
239	Jason Bates	.10
240	Larry Walker	.10
241	David Nied	.10
242	Dante Bichette	.10
243	Dennis Eckersley	1.25
244	Todd Stottlemyre	.10
245	Rickey Henderson	1.50
246	Geronimo Berroa	.10
247	Mark McGwire	3.00
248	Quilvio Veras	.10
249	Terry Pendleton	.10
250	Andre Dawson	.30
251	Jeff Conine	.10
252	Kurt Abbott	.10
253	Jay Buhner	.10
254	Darren Bragg	.10
255	Ken Griffey Jr.	2.50
256	Tino Martinez	.10
257	Mark Grace	.10
258	Ryne Sandberg	2.00
259	Randy Myers	.10
260	Howard Johnson	.10
261	Lee Smith	.10
262	J.T. Snow	.10
263	Chili Davis	.10
264	Chuck Finley	.10
265	Eddie Williams	.10
266	Joey Hamilton	.10
267	Ken Caminiti	.10
268	Andujar Cedeno	.10
269	Steve Finley	.10
270	Tony Gwynn	2.00

Special Edition Gold

An insert set within an insert set, gold-foil enhanced versions of the Special Edition cards were seeded into hobby packs at the rate of about one per box. The substitution of gold ink for silver is also carried over onto the background of the card back.

	NM/M
Complete Set (270):	350.00
Common Player:	1.50
Stars/Rookies:	3X

Cal Ripken Commemorative Jumbo

To commemorate Cal Ripken's 2,131st consecutive game, UD issued this 5" x 3" die-cut card. Five thousand of the cards were issued with silver foil highlights;

2,131 with gold trim. Each card is serially numbered in the lower-right corner on back.

	NM/M
Cal Ripken Jr. (Silver edition of 5,000.)	10.00
Cal Ripken Jr. (Gold edition of 2,131.)	13.50

Sports Drink Reggie Jackson

UD partnered with Energy Foods to produce "Upper Deck Authentic Sports Drink." Each $2.99 six pack contained a cello-wrapped Reggie Jackson card. The cards are 2-1/2" x 3-1/2" and have a color photo on front on which the team logos have been removed. Backs has a subdued photo of a player swinging a bat with a stadium scene in the background. A few career highlights are presented along with the sports drink logo and UD hologram. Each card could also be found in a version with a gold-foil facsimile autograph on front.

	NM/M
Complete Set (3):	5.00
Common Card:	2.00
Gold:	1-1.5X
1/3	Reggie Jackson (Swinging bat.)	2.00
2/3	Reggie Jackson/Portrait	2.00
3/3	Reggie Jackson (Batting follow-thru.)	2.00

Eagle Snacks Ballpark Legends

Nine Hall of Famers comprise this set which was produced by UD for the Eagle snack food company. Sets were available via mail-in redemption for proofs of purchase and $1. Fronts have sepia photos on which uniform logos have been removed. The Eagle Ballpark Legends is at upper-left, the UD logo is at lower-left, followed by the player name. Backs of the 2-1/2" x 3-1/2" cards have career summary and personal data. Autographed cards of Harmon Killebrew were random inserts.

	NM/M
Complete Set (9):	3.00
Common Player:	.25
1	Nolan Ryan	1.00
2	Reggie Jackson	.50
3	Tom Seaver	.50
4	Harmon Killebrew	.25
4a	Harmon Killebrew (Autographed)	20.00
5	Ted Williams	.75
6	Whitey Ford	.50
7	Al Kaline	.50
8	Willie Stargell	.50
9	Bob Gibson	.25

GTS Phone Cards

In conjunction with Global Telecommunications Service, Upper Deck issued a series of 15 phone cards described as being the first licensed by Major League Baseball and the Player's Association. Measuring about 2-1/8" x 3-3/8" with round corners, the cards were printed on heavy plastic and utilized the basic format and photos from the players' 1994 Upper Deck baseball cards. Issue price, with phone time, was $12 each. Cards are numbered with a "MLB" prefix.

	NM/M
Complete Set (15):	21.00
Common Player:	1.00
01	Tony Gwynn	2.00
02	Fred McGriff	1.00
03	Frank Thomas	1.50
04	Ken Griffey Jr.	2.50
05	Cecil Fielder	1.00
06	Barry Bonds	3.00
07	Don Mattingly	2.25
08	Dave Justice	1.00
09	Roger Clemens	2.25
10	Cal Ripken Jr.	3.00
11	Roberto Alomar	1.25
12	Gary Sheffield	1.25
13	Jeff Bagwell	1.50
14	Kirby Puckett	2.00
15	Ozzie Smith	2.00

Metallic Impressions Michael Jordan

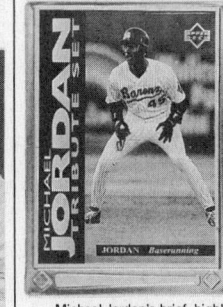

Michael Jordan's brief, highly publicized baseball career is chronicled in this metallic card set produced for UD by Metallic Impressions and sold in a special lithographed tin box. Each of the 2-5/8" x 3-9/16" cards has a gold-tone rolled edge. Fronts feature photos of Jordan in action. Backs have another photo and a career summary in a horizontal format. Cards are numbered with a "JT" prefix.

	NM/M
Complete Boxed Set (5):	7.50
Common Card:	1.50
1	Starting Out (Michael Jordan)	1.50
2	West to Arizona (Michael Jordan)	1.50
3	Hitting (Michael Jordan)	1.50
4	Baserunning (Michael Jordan)	1.50
5	Fielding (Michael Jordan)	1.50

Metallic Impressions Mickey Mantle

Sharing the card-front images with the UD phone cards of 1994, these metal cards trace the career of Mickey Mantle. Sold in an embossed metal box, the cards measure 2-5/8" x 3-9/16" and have rolled gold-tone metal borders.

Fronts have black-and-white or color photos of Mantle. Backs have a career summary in a red box against a background of pin-striped flannel, along with a small color photo of Mantle. The issue was reportedly limited to 19,950 sets.

	NM/M
Complete Boxed Set (10):	17.50
Common Player:	3.00
1	The Commerce Comet (Mickey Mantle)	3.00
2	1951 - The Early Years (Mickey Mantle)	3.00
3	1953 - Tape-Measure Home Runs (Mickey Mantle)	3.00
4	1956 - Triple Crown Season (Mickey Mantle)	3.00
5	1957 - Second Consecutive MVP (Mickey Mantle)	3.00
6	1961 - Chasing the Babe (Mickey Mantle)	3.00
7	1964 - Series Home Run Record (Mickey Mantle)	3.00
8	1967 - 500th Home Run (Mickey Mantle)	3.00
9	1974 - Hall of Famer (Mickey Mantle)	3.00
10	Checklist (Mickey Mantle)	3.00

1996 Upper Deck Promo

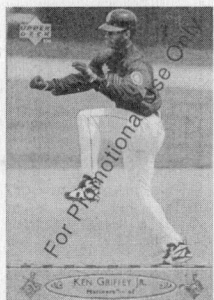

To debut its 1996 issue, Upper Deck issued this sample card. It is identical in format to the regular-issue card, except that it is numbered 100 and overprinted diagonally on each side, "For Promotional Use Only."

	NM/M
100	Ken Griffey Jr.	2.00

1996 Upper Deck

Upper Deck Series 1 consists of 240 base cards. There are 187 regular player cards plus subsets of Star Rookies, Young at Heart, Beat the Odds, Milestones, Postseason, checklists, and expansion logos. The issue was marketed in 10-card foil packs in hobby and retail versions Series 1 insert sets are Blue Chip Prospects, Future Shock and Power Driven. Cal Ripken Jr. Collection cards are inserted in both series, as are Retail Predictor (home runs, batting average and RBIs) and Hobby Predictor (Player of the Month, Pitcher of the Month and rookie hits leaders) cards. Series 2 has 240 cards, including subsets for Star Rookies, Diamond Debuts, Strange But True, Managerial Salutes and Best of a Generation. Insert sets include Hot Commodities, Hideo Nomo Highlights, Run Producers and the Lovero Collection. Factory sets comprising both regular series and the Update series were issued in two serially numbered versions, a regular boxed set in an edition of 15,000 and a wooden boxed set numbered to 500.

	NM/M
Unopened Wood Box Set (510):	40.00
Unopened Fact. Set (510):	35.00
Complete Set (480):	20.00
Common Player:	.05
Wax Pack (10):	.75
Wax Box (32):	17.50
1 Cal Ripken Jr. (Milestones)	1.00
2 Eddie Murray (Milestones)	.40
3 Mark Wohlers	.05
4 Dave Justice	.05
5 Chipper Jones	1.00
6 Javier Lopez	.05
7 Mark Lemke	.05
8 Marquis Grissom	.05
9 Tom Glavine	.25
10 Greg Maddux	1.00
11 Manny Alexander	.05
12 Curtis Goodwin	.05
13 Scott Erickson	.05
14 Chris Hoiles	.05
15 Rafael Palmeiro	.65
16 Rick Krivda	.05
17 Jeff Manto	.05
18 Mo Vaughn	.05
19 Tim Wakefield	.05
20 Roger Clemens	1.00
21 Tim Naehring	.05
22 Troy O'Leary	.05
23 Mike Greenwell	.05
24 Stan Belinda	.05
25 John Valentin	.05
26 J.T. Snow	.05
27 Gary DiSarcina	.05
28 Mark Langston	.05
29 Brian Anderson	.05
30 Jim Edmonds	.05
31 Garret Anderson	.05
32 Orlando Palmeiro	.05
33 Brian McRae	.05
34 Kevin Foster	.05
35 Sammy Sosa	1.00
36 Todd Zeile	.05
37 Jim Bullinger	.05
38 Luis Gonzalez	.05
39 Lyle Mouton	.05
40 Ray Durham	.05
41 Ozzie Guillen	.05
42 Alex Fernandez	.05
43 Brian Keyser	.05
44 Robin Ventura	.05
45 Reggie Sanders	.05
46 Pete Schourek	.05
47 John Smiley	.05
48 Jeff Brantley	.05
49 Thomas Howard	.05
50 Bret Boone	.05
51 Kevin Jarvis	.05
52 Jeff Branson	.05
53 Carlos Baerga	.05
54 Jim Thome	.50
55 Manny Ramirez	.75
56 Omar Vizquel	.05
57 Jose Mesa	.05
58 Julian Tavarez	.05
59 Orel Hershiser	.05
60 Larry Walker	.05
61 Bret Saberhagen	.05
62 Vinny Castilla	.05
63 Eric Young	.05
64 Bryan Rekar	.05
65 Andres Galarraga	.05
66 Steve Reed	.05
67 Chad Curtis	.05
68 Bobby Higginson	.05
69 Phil Nevin	.05
70 Cecil Fielder	.05
71 Felipe Lira	.05
72 Chris Gomez	.05
73 Charles Johnson	.05
74 Quilvio Veras	.05
75 Jeff Conine	.05
76 John Burkett	.05
77 Greg Colbrunn	.05
78 Terry Pendleton	.05
79 Shane Reynolds	.05
80 Jeff Bagwell	.75
81 Orlando Miller	.05
82 Mike Hampton	.05
83 James Mouton	.05
84 Brian L. Hunter	.05
85 Derek Bell	.05

86 Kevin Appier	.05
87 Joe Vitiello	.05
88 Wally Joyner	.05
89 Michael Tucker	.05
90 Johnny Damon	.20
91 Jon Nunnally	.05
92 Jason Jacome	.05
93 Chad Fonville	.05
94 Chan Ho Park	.05
95 Hideo Nomo	.40
96 Ismael Valdes	.05
97 Greg Gagne	.05
98 Diamondbacks-Devil Rays (Expansion Card)	.10
99 Raul Mondesi	.05
100 Dave Winfield (Young at Heart)	.75
101 Dennis Eckersley (Young at Heart)	.35
102 Andre Dawson (Young at Heart)	.15
103 Dennis Martinez (Young at Heart)	.05
104 Lance Parrish (Young at Heart)	.05
105 Eddie Murray (Young at Heart)	.40
106 Alan Trammell (Young at Heart)	.40
107 Lou Whitaker (Young at Heart)	.05
108 Ozzie Smith (Young at Heart)	.50
109 Paul Molitor (Young at Heart)	.40
110 Rickey Henderson (Young at Heart)	.40
111 Tim Raines (Young at Heart)	.18
112 Harold Baines (Young at Heart)	.05
113 Lee Smith (Young at Heart)	.05
114 Fernando Valenzuela (Young at Heart)	.05
115 Cal Ripken Jr. (Young at Heart)	1.00
116 Tony Gwynn (Young at Heart)	.50
117 Wade Boggs (Young at Heart)	.50
118 Todd Hollandsworth	.05
119 Dave Nilsson	.05
120 Jose Valentin RC	.05
121 Steve Sparks	.05
122 Chuck Carr	.05
123 John Jaha	.05
124 Scott Karl	.05
125 Chuck Knoblauch	.05
126 Brad Radke	.05
127 Pat Meares	.05
128 Ron Coomer	.05
129 Pedro Munoz	.05
130 Kirby Puckett	1.00
131 David Segui	.05
132 Mark Grudzielanek	.05
133 Mike Lansing	.05
134 Sean Berry	.05
135 Rondell White	.05
136 Pedro Martinez	.75
137 Carl Everett	.05
138 Dave Mlicki	.05
139 Bill Pulsipher	.05
140 Jason Isringhausen	.05
141 Rico Brogna	.05
142 Edgardo Alfonzo	.05
143 Jeff Kent	.05
144 Andy Pettitte	.25
145 Mike Piazza (Beat the Odds)	.65
146 Cliff Floyd (Beat the Odds)	.05
147 Jason Isringhausen (Beat the Odds)	.05
148 Tim Wakefield (Beat the Odds)	.05
149 Chipper Jones (Beat the Odds)	.50
150 Hideo Nomo (Beat the Odds)	.20
151 Mark McGwire (Beat the Odds)	.75
152 Ron Gant (Beat the Odds)	.05
153 Gary Gaetti (Beat the Odds)	.05
154 Don Mattingly	1.00
155 Paul O'Neill	.05
156 Derek Jeter	2.00
157 Joe Girardi	.05
158 Ruben Sierra	.05
159 Jorge Posada	.05
160 Geronimo Berroa	.05
161 Steve Ontiveros	.05
162 George Williams	.05
163 Doug Johns	.05
164 Ariel Prieto	.05
165 Scott Brosius	.05
166 Mike Bordick	.05
167 Tyler Green	.05
168 Mickey Morandini	.05
169 Darren Daulton	.05
170 Gregg Jefferies	.05
171 Jim Eisenreich	.05
172 Heathcliff Slocumb	.05
173 Kevin Stocker	.05
174 Esteban Loaiza	.05
175 Jeff King	.05
176 Mark Johnson	.05
177 Denny Neagle	.05

178 Orlando Merced	.05
179 Carlos Garcia	.05
180 Brian Jordan	.05
181 Mike Morgan	.05
182 Mark Petkovsek	.05
183 Bernard Gilkey	.05
184 John Mabry	.05
185 Tom Henke	.05
186 Glenn Dishman	.05
187 Andy Ashby	.05
188 Bip Roberts	.05
189 Melvin Nieves	.05
190 Ken Caminiti	.05
191 Brad Ausmus	.05
192 Deion Sanders	.05
193 Jamie Brewington	.05
194 Glenallen Hill	.05
195 Barry Bonds	2.00
196 William Van Landingham	.05
197 Mark Carreon	.05
198 Royce Clayton	.05
199 Joey Cora	.05
200 Ken Griffey Jr.	1.25
201 Jay Buhner	.05
202 Alex Rodriguez	1.50
203 Norm Charlton	.05
204 Andy Benes	.05
205 Edgar Martinez	.05
206 Juan Gonzalez	.40
207 Will Clark	.05
208 Kevin Gross	.05
209 Roger Pavlik	.05
210 Ivan Rodriguez	.65
211 Rusty Greer	.05
212 Angel Martinez	.05
213 Tomas Perez	.05
214 Alex Gonzalez	.05
215 Joe Carter	.05
216 Shawn Green	.30
217 Edwin Hurtado	.05
218 Edgar Martinez, Tony Pena (Post Season Checklist)	.05
219 Chipper Jones, Barry Larkin (Post Season Checklist)	.25
220 Orel Hershiser (Post Season Checklist)	.05
221 Mike Devereaux (Post Season Checklist)	.05
222 Tom Glavine (Post Season Checklist)	.05
223 Karim Garcia/SR	.10
224 Arquimedez Pozo/SR	.05
225 Billy Wagner/SR	.05
226 John Wasdin/SR	.05
227 Jeff Suppan/SR	.05
228 Steve Gibralter/SR	.05
229 Jimmy Haynes/SR	.05
230 Ruben Rivera/SR	.05
231 Chris Snopek/SR	.05
232 Alex Ochoa/SR	.05
233 Shannon Stewart/SR	.05
234 Quinton McCracken/SR	.05
235 Trey Beamon/SR	.05
236 Billy McMillon/SR	.05
237 Steve Cox/SR	.05
238 George Arias/SR	.05
239 Yamil Benitez/SR	.05
240 Todd Greene/SR	.05
241 Jason Kendall/SR	.05
242 Brooks Kieschnick/SR	.05
243 Osvaldo Fernandez/SR RC	.15
244 Livan Hernandez/SR RC	.35
245 Rey Ordonez/SR	.05
246 Mike Grace/SR RC	.05
247 Jay Canizaro/SR	.05
248 Bob Wolcott/SR	.05
249 Jermaine Dye/SR	.05
250 Jason Schmidt/SR	.05
251 Mike Sweeney/SR RC	1.00
252 Marcus Jensen/SR	.05
253 Mendy Lopez/SR	.05
254 Wilton Guerrero/SR RC	.10
255 Paul Wilson/SR	.05
256 Edgar Renteria/SR	.05
257 Richard Hidalgo/SR	.05
258 Bob Abreu/SR	.10
259 Robert Smith RC (Diamond Debuts)	.05
260 Sal Fasano (Diamond Debuts)	.05
261 Enrique Wilson (Diamond Debuts)	.05
262 Rich Hunter RC (Diamond Debuts)	.05
263 Sergio Nunez (Diamond Debuts)	.05
264 Dan Serafini (Diamond Debuts)	.05
265 David Doster RC (Diamond Debuts)	.05
266 Ryan McGuire (Diamond Debuts)	.05
267 Scott Spiezio (Diamond Debuts)	.05
268 Rafael Orellano (Diamond Debuts)	.05
269 Steve Avery	.05
270 Fred McGriff	.05
271 John Smoltz	.05
272 Ryan Klesko	.05
273 Jeff Blauser	.05
274 Brad Clontz	.05
275 Roberto Alomar	.20
276 B.J. Surhoff	.05
277 Jeffrey Hammonds	.05
278 Brady Anderson	.05
279 Bobby Bonilla	.05
280 Cal Ripken Jr.	2.00

281 Mike Mussina	.30
282 Wil Cordero	.05
283 Mike Stanley	.05
284 Aaron Sele	.05
285 Jose Canseco	.40
286 Tom Gordon	.05
287 Heathcliff Slocumb	.05
288 Lee Smith	.05
289 Troy Percival	.05
290 Tim Salmon	.05
291 Chuck Finley	.05
292 Jim Abbott	.05
293 Chili Davis	.05
294 Steve Trachsel	.05
295 Mark Grace	.05
296 Rey Sanchez	.05
297 Scott Servais	.05
298 Jaime Navarro	.05
299 Frank Castillo	.05
300 Frank Thomas	.75
301 Jason Bere	.05
302 Danny Tartabull	.05
303 Darren Lewis	.05
304 Roberto Hernandez	.05
305 Tony Phillips	.05
306 Wilson Alvarez	.05
307 Jose Rijo	.05
308 Hal Morris	.05
309 Mark Portugal	.05
310 Barry Larkin	.05
311 Dave Burba	.05
312 Eddie Taubensee	.05
313 Sandy Alomar Jr.	.05
314 Dennis Martinez	.05
315 Albert Belle	.15
316 Eddie Murray	.75
317 Charles Nagy	.05
318 Chad Ogea	.05
319 Kenny Lofton	.05
320 Dante Bichette	.05
321 Armando Reynoso	.05
322 Walt Weiss	.05
323 Ellis Burks	.05
324 Kevin Ritz	.05
325 Bill Swift	.05
326 Jason Bates	.05
327 Tony Clark	.05
328 Travis Fryman	.05
329 Mark Parent	.05
330 Alan Trammell	.05
331 C.J. Nitkowski	.05
332 Jose Lima	.05
333 Phil Plantier	.05
334 Kurt Abbott	.05
335 Andre Dawson	.25
336 Chris Hammond	.05
337 Robb Nen	.05
338 Pat Rapp	.05
339 Al Leiter	.05
340 Gary Sheffield	.35
341 Todd Jones	.05
342 Doug Drabek	.05
343 Greg Swindell	.05
344 Tony Eusebio	.05
345 Craig Biggio	.05
346 Darryl Kile	.05
347 Mike Macfarlane	.05
348 Jeff Montgomery	.05
349 Chris Haney	.05
350 Bip Roberts	.05
351 Tom Goodwin	.05
352 Mark Gubicza	.05
353 Joe Randa	.05
354 Ramon Martinez	.05
355 Eric Karros	.05
356 Delino DeShields	.05
357 Brett Butler	.05
358 Todd Worrell	.05
359 Mike Blowers	.05
360 Mike Piazza	1.25
361 Ben McDonald	.05
362 Ricky Bones	.05
363 Greg Vaughn	.05
364 Matt Mieske	.05
365 Kevin Seitzer	.05
366 Jeff Cirillo	.05
367 LaTroy Hawkins	.05
368 Frank Rodriguez	.05
369 Rick Aguilera	.05
370 Roberto Alomar (Best of a Generation)	.15
371 Albert Belle (Best of a Generation)	.05
372 Wade Boggs (Best of a Generation)	.50
373 Barry Bonds (Best of a Generation)	1.00
374 Roger Clemens (Best of a Generation)	.65
375 Dennis Eckersley (Best of a Generation)	.35
376 Ken Griffey Jr. (Best of a Generation)	.65
377 Tony Gwynn (Best of a Generation)	.50
378 Rickey Henderson (Best of a Generation)	.40
379 Greg Maddux (Best of a Generation)	.50
380 Fred McGriff (Best of a Generation)	.05
381 Paul Molitor (Best of a Generation)	.40
382 Eddie Murray (Best of a Generation)	.40
383 Mike Piazza (Best of a Generation)	.65

384 Kirby Puckett (Best of a Generation)	.50
385 Cal Ripken Jr. (Best of a Generation)	1.00
386 Ozzie Smith (Best of a Generation)	.50
387 Frank Thomas (Best of a Generation)	.45
388 Matt Walbeck	.05
389 Dave Stevens	.05
390 Marty Cordova	.05
391 Darrin Fletcher	.05
392 Cliff Floyd	.05
393 Mel Rojas	.05
394 Shane Andrews	.05
395 Moises Alou	.05
396 Carlos Perez	.05
397 Jeff Fassero	.05
398 Bobby Jones	.05
399 Todd Hundley	.05
400 John Franco	.05
401 Jose Vizcaino	.05
402 Bernard Gilkey	.05
403 Pete Harnisch	.05
404 Pat Kelly	.05
405 David Cone	.05
406 Bernie Williams	.05
407 John Wetteland	.05
408 Scott Kamieniecki	.05
409 Tim Raines	.05
410 Wade Boggs	1.00
411 Terry Steinbach	.05
412 Jason Giambi	.40
413 Todd Van Poppel	.05
414 Pedro Munoz	.05
415 Eddie Murray-1990 (Strange But True)	.40
416 Dennis Eckersley-1990 (Strange But True)	.35
417 Bip Roberts-1992 (Strange But True)	.05
418 Glenallen Hill-1992 (Strange But True)	.05
419 John Hudek-1994 (Strange But True)	.05
420 Derek Bell-1995 (Strange But True)	.05
421 Larry Walker-1995 (Strange But True)	.05
422 Greg Maddux-1995 (Strange But True)	.50
423 Ken Caminiti-1995 (Strange But True)	.05
424 Brent Gates	.05
425 Mark McGwire	1.50
426 Mark Whiten	.05
427 Sid Fernandez	.05
428 Ricky Bottalico	.05
429 Mike Mimbs	.05
430 Lenny Dykstra	.05
431 Todd Zeile	.05
432 Benito Santiago	.05
433 Danny Miceli	.05
434 Al Martin	.05
435 Jay Bell	.05
436 Charlie Hayes	.05
437 Mike Kingery	.05
438 Paul Wagner	.05
439 Tom Pagnozzi	.05
440 Ozzie Smith	1.00
441 Ray Lankford	.05
442 Dennis Eckersley	.65
443 Ron Gant	.05
444 Alan Benes	.05
445 Rickey Henderson	.75
446 Jody Reed	.05
447 Trevor Hoffman	.05
448 Andujar Cedeno	.05
449 Steve Finley	.05
450 Tony Gwynn	1.00
451 Joey Hamilton	.05
452 Mark Leiter	.05
453 Rod Beck	.05
454 Kirt Manwaring	.05
455 Matt Williams	.05
456 Robby Thompson	.05
457 Shawon Dunston	.05
458 Russ Davis	.05
459 Paul Sorrento	.05
460 Randy Johnson	.75
461 Chris Bosio	.05
462 Luis Sojo	.05
463 Sterling Hitchcock	.05
464 Benji Gil	.05
465 Mickey Tettleton	.05
466 Mark McLemore	.05
467 Darryl Hamilton	.05
468 Ken Hill	.05
469 Dean Palmer	.05
470 Carlos Delgado	.40
471 Ed Sprague	.05
472 Otis Nixon	.05
473 Pat Hentgen	.05
474 Juan Guzman	.05
475 John Olerud	.05
476 Checklist (Buck Showalter)	.05
477 Checklist (Bobby Cox)	.05
478 Checklist (Tommy Lasorda)	.05
479 Checklist (Jim Leyland)	.05
480 Checklist (Sparky Anderson)	.05

1996 Upper Deck Update

Available only via a mail-in wrapper redemption or in factory sets, this update set offers cards of players who changed teams after the base card set was issued, as well as a few rookies and others. Cards share the earlier issue's format and are numbered with a "U" suffix.

	NM/M
Complete Set (30):	8.00
Common Player:	.25
481 Randy Myers	.25
482 Kent Mercker	.25
483 David Wells	.35
484 Kevin Mitchell	.25
485 Randy Velarde	.25
486 Ryne Sandberg	4.00
487 Doug Jones	.25
488 Terry Adams	.25
489 Kevin Tapani	.25
490 Harold Baines	.25
491 Eric Davis	.25
492 Julio Franco	.25
493 Jack McDowell	.25
494 Devon White	.25
495 Kevin Brown	.35
496 Rick Wilkins	.25
497 Sean Berry	.25
498 Keith Lockhart	.25
499 Mark Loretta	.25
500 Paul Molitor	2.50
501 Roberto Kelly	.25
502 Lance Johnson	.25
503 Tino Martinez	.25
504 Kenny Rogers	.25
505 Todd Stottlemyre	.25
506 Gary Gaetti	.25
507 Royce Clayton	.25
508 Andy Benes	.25
509 Wally Joyner	.25
510 Erik Hanson	.25

A Cut Above

No Pricing

Blue Chip Prospects

Twenty top young stars who could make a major impact in the major leagues in upcoming seasons are featured in this insert set. Each card is highlighted with blue-foil printing and double die-cut technology, which includes a zig-zag pattern around the top and a die-cut around both bottom corners. The cards are found one per 20 packs in Series 1 foil packs. Cards are numbered with a "BC" prefix.

	NM/M
Complete Set (20):	50.00
Common Player:	1.00
1 Hideo Nomo	4.00
2 Johnny Damon	3.50
3 Jason Isringhausen	1.00
4 Bill Pulsipher	1.00
5 Marty Cordova	1.00
6 Michael Tucker	1.00
7 John Wasdin	1.00
8 Karim Garcia	1.50
9 Ruben Rivera	1.00
10 Chipper Jones	10.00
11 Billy Wagner	1.00
12 Brooks Kieschnick	1.00

13	Alex Ochoa	1.00
14	Roger Cedeno	1.00
15	Alex Rodriguez	15.00
16	Jason Schmidt	1.00
17	Derek Jeter	20.00
18	Brian L. Hunter	1.00
19	Garret Anderson	1.00
20	Manny Ramirez	7.50

Diamond Destiny

This late-season release is found exclusively in retail foil packs labeled "Upper Deck Tech." They are inserted at a rate of one per pack, sold with eight regular 1996 Upper Deck cards at a suggested retail of around $3. The cards have three versions of the same action photo; in color and black-and-white on front, and in black-and-white on back. A large team logo also appears on front and back. In the upper half of the card is a 1-3/16" diameter round color transparency portrait of the player. The basic version of this chase set had bronze foil highlights. Parallel silver and gold versions are found on average of one per 35 and one per 143 packs, respectively. Cards are numbered with a "DD" prefix.

		NM/M
Complete Set (Bronze):		35.00
Common Player (Bronze):		.30
Silver:		6X
Gold:		12X
1	Chipper Jones	1.50
2	Fred McGriff	.30
3	Ryan Klesko	.30
4	John Smoltz	.30
5	Greg Maddux	1.50
6	Cal Ripken Jr.	3.00
7	Roberto Alomar	.45
8	Eddie Murray	1.25
9	Brady Anderson	.30
10	Mo Vaughn	.30
11	Roger Clemens	1.75
12	Darin Erstad	.60
13	Sammy Sosa	1.50
14	Frank Thomas	1.25
15	Barry Larkin	.30
16	Albert Belle	.30
17	Manny Ramirez	1.25
18	Kenny Lofton	.30
19	Dante Bichette	.30
20	Gary Sheffield	.75
21	Jeff Bagwell	1.25
22	Hideo Nomo	.65
23	Mike Piazza	2.00
24	Kirby Puckett	1.50
25	Paul Molitor	1.25
26	Chuck Knoblauch	.30
27	Wade Boggs	1.50
28	Derek Jeter	3.00
29	Rey Ordonez	.30
30	Mark McGwire	2.50
31	Ozzie Smith	1.50
32	Tony Gwynn	1.50
33	Barry Bonds	3.00
34	Matt Williams	.30
35	Ken Griffey Jr.	2.00
36	Jay Buhner	.30
37	Randy Johnson	1.25
38	Alex Rodriguez	2.00
39	Juan Gonzalez	.65
40	Joe Carter	.30

Future Stock

Future Stock inserts are found on average of one per six packs of Series 1, highlighting 20 top young stars on a die-cut design. Each card has a blue border, vertical photo and silver-foil stamping on the front. Cards are numbered with a "FS" prefix.

		NM/M
Complete Set (20):		4.00
Common Player:		.25
1	George Arias	.25
2	Brian Barnes	.25

3	Trey Beamon	.25
4	Yamil Benitez	.25
5	Jamie Brewington	.25
6	Tony Clark	.25
7	Steve Cox	.25
8	Carlos Delgado	.75
9	Chad Fonville	.25
10	Steve Gibralter	.25
11	Curtis Goodwin	.25
12	Todd Greene	.25
13	Jimmy Haynes	.25
14	Quinton McCracken	.25
15	Billy McMillon	.25
16	Chan Ho Park	.25
17	Arquimedez Pozo	.25
18	Chris Snopek	.25
19	Shannon Stewart	.25
20	Jeff Suppan	.25

Gameface

This insert was exclusive to $1.50 Wal-Mart retail packs. Fronts have an action photo vignetted in white with a gold-foil Gameface logo. Backs have another photo and a few sentences about the player. One Gameface card was found in each pack.

		NM/M
Complete Set (10):		6.00
Common Player:		.15
1	Ken Griffey Jr.	1.00
2	Frank Thomas	.65
3	Barry Bonds	1.50
4	Albert Belle	.15
5	Cal Ripken Jr.	1.50
6	Mike Piazza	1.00
7	Chipper Jones	.75
8	Matt Williams	.15
9	Hideo Nomo	.40
10	Greg Maddux	.75

Hobby Predictor

These inserts depict 60 top players as possible winners in the categories of Player of the Month, Pitcher of the Month and Rookie Hits Leader. If the pictured player won that category any month of the season the card was redeemable for a 10-card set with a different look, action photos and printed on silver-foil stock. Hobby Predictor inserts are found on average once per dozen packs in both series. Winning cards are indicated by (W).

		NM/M
Complete Set (60):		35.00
Common Player:		.40
H1	Albert Belle	.40
H2	Kenny Lofton	.40
H3	Rafael Palmeiro	.65
H4	Ken Griffey Jr.	2.00
H5	Tim Salmon	.40
H6	Cal Ripken Jr.	3.00
H7	Mark McGwire (W)	4.50
H8	Frank Thomas (W)	1.25
H9	Mo Vaughn (W)	.60
H10	Player of the Month Long Shot (W)	.40
H11	Roger Clemens	1.75
H12	David Cone	.40
H13	Jose Mesa	.40
H14	Randy Johnson	.75
H15	Steve Finley	.40
H16	Mike Mussina	.50
H17	Kevin Appier	.40
H18	Kenny Rogers	.40
H19	Lee Smith	.40
H20	Pitcher of the Month Long Shot (W)	.40
H21	George Arias	.40
H22	Jose Herrera	.40
H23	Tony Clark	.40
H24	Todd Greene	.40
H25	Derek Jeter (W)	6.00
H26	Arquimedez Pozo	.40
H27	Matt Lawton	.40
H28	Shannon Stewart	.40
H29	Chris Snopek	.40
H30	Rookie Hits Long Shot	.40
H31	Jeff Bagwell (W)	1.25
H32	Dante Bichette	.40
H33	Barry Bonds (W)	6.00
H34	Tony Gwynn	1.50
H35	Chipper Jones	1.50
H36	Eric Karros	.40
H37	Barry Larkin	.40
H38	Mike Piazza	2.00
H39	Matt Williams	.40
H40	Player of the Month Long Shot (W)	.40
H41	Osvaldo Fernandez	.40
H42	Tom Glavine	.60
H43	Jason Isringhausen	.40
H44	Greg Maddux	1.50
H45	Pedro Martinez	.75
H46	Hideo Nomo	.60
H47	Pete Schourek	.40
H48	Paul Wilson	.40
H49	Mark Wohlers	.40
H50	Pitcher of the Month Long Shot	.40
H51	Bob Abreu	.40
H52	Trey Beamon	.40
H53	Yamil Benitez	.40
H54	Roger Cedeno (W)	.60
H55	Todd Hollandsworth (W)	.40
H56	Marvin Benard	.40
H57	Jason Kendall	.40
H58	Brooks Kieschnick	.40
H59	Rey Ordonez (W)	.60
H60	Rookie Hits Long Shot (W)	.40

Hobby Predictor Redemption

Persons who redeemed winning cards from UD's interactive Predictor insert series received a 10-card set of the top players in various statistical categories. The redemption cards are similar in format to the Predictor cards, but have fronts printed on silver-foil. In place of the contest rules found on the backs of Predictor cards, the redemption cards have a career summary.

		NM/M
Complete Set (60):		45.00
Common Player:		.50
H1	Albert Belle	.50
H2	Kenny Lofton	.50
H3	Rafael Palmeiro	.75
H4	Ken Griffey Jr.	2.50
H5	Tim Salmon	.50
H6	Cal Ripken Jr.	4.00
H7	Mark McGwire	3.00
H8	Frank Thomas	1.00
H9	Mo Vaughn	.50
H10	Player of the Month Long Shot	.50
H11	Roger Clemens	2.25
H12	David Cone	.50
H13	Jose Mesa	.50
H14	Randy Johnson	1.00
H15	Steve Finley	.50
H16	Mike Mussina	.65
H17	Kevin Appier	.50
H18	Kenny Rogers	.50
H19	Lee Smith	.50
H20	Pitcher of the Month Long Shot	.50
H21	George Arias	.50
H22	Jose Herrera	.50
H23	Tony Clark	.50
H24	Todd Greene	.50
H25	Derek Jeter	4.00
H26	Arquimedez Pozo	.50
H27	Matt Lawton	.50
H28	Shannon Stewart	.50
H29	Chris Snopek	.50
H30	Rookie Hits Long Shot	.50
H31	Jeff Bagwell	1.00
H32	Dante Bichette	.50
H33	Barry Bonds	4.00
H34	Tony Gwynn	2.00
H35	Chipper Jones	2.00
H36	Eric Karros	.50
H37	Barry Larkin	.50
H38	Mike Piazza	2.50
H39	Matt Williams	.50
H40	Player of the Month Long Shot	.50
H41	Osvaldo Fernandez	.50
H42	Tom Glavine	.65
H43	Jason Isringhausen	.50
H44	Greg Maddux	2.00
H45	Pedro Martinez	1.00
H46	Hideo Nomo	.65
H47	Pete Schourek	.50
H48	Paul Wilson	.50
H49	Mark Wohlers	.50
H50	Pitcher of the Month Long Shot	.50
H51	Bob Abreu	.50
H52	Trey Beamon	.50
H53	Yamil Benitez	.50
H54	Roger Cedeno	.50
H55	Todd Hollandsworth	.50
H56	Marvin Benard	.50
H57	Jason Kendall	.50
H58	Brooks Kieschnick	.50
H59	Rey Ordonez	.50
H60	Rookie Hits Long Shot	.50

Hot Commodities

These 20 die-cut cards were seeded one per every 37 1996 Upper Deck Series 2 packs. Cards are numbered with a "HC" prefix.

		NM/M
Complete Set (20):		30.00
Common Player:		.75
1	Ken Griffey Jr.	3.00
2	Hideo Nomo	1.50
3	Roberto Alomar	1.50
4	Paul Wilson	.75
5	Albert Belle	.75
6	Manny Ramirez	2.25
7	Kirby Puckett	2.50
8	Johnny Damon	2.00
9	Randy Johnson	2.25
10	Greg Maddux	2.50
11	Chipper Jones	2.50
12	Barry Bonds	5.00
13	Mo Vaughn	.75
14	Mike Piazza	3.00
15	Cal Ripken Jr.	5.00
16	Tim Salmon	.75
17	Sammy Sosa	2.50
18	Kenny Lofton	.75
19	Tony Gwynn	2.50
20	Frank Thomas	2.25

Lovero Collection

Every sixth pack of 1996 Upper Deck Series II has a V.J. Lovero insert card. This 20-card set features unique shots from Lovero, one of the most well-known photographers in the country. Some of the cards feature Randy Johnson wearing a cone-

head, Frank Thomas blowing a bubble while throwing the ball, and Jay Buhner and his child both chewing on a bat. Cards are numbered with a "VJ" prefix.

		NM/M
Complete Set (20):		17.50
Common Player:		.25
1	Rod Carew	1.00
2	Hideo Nomo	.50
3	Derek Jeter	3.00
4	Barry Bonds	3.00
5	Greg Maddux	1.50
6	Mark McGwire (W/Will Clark.)	2.50
7	Jose Canseco	.50
8	Ken Caminiti	.50
9	Raul Mondesi	.50
10	Ken Griffey Jr.	2.50
11	Jay Buhner	.25
12	Randy Johnson	1.00
13	Roger Clemens	2.00
14	Brady Anderson	.25
15	Frank Thomas	1.00
16	Angels Outfielders	.25
17	Mike Piazza	2.00
18	Dante Bichette	.25
19	Tony Gwynn	1.50
20	Jim Abbott	.25

Nomo Highlights

The 1995 rookie season of Los Angeles Dodgers' pitcher Hideo Nomo is recapped in this five-card 1996 Upper Deck insert set. The cards were seeded one per every 23 Series 2 packs. A 5" x 7" version of each card was also issued as a retail box insert. Values are the same as for small cards.

		NM/M
Complete Set (5):		3.00
Common Card:		.75
1-5	Hideo Nomo	.75

Power Driven

Twenty of the game's top power hitters are analyzed in depth by baseball writer Peter Gammons on these Series 1 insert cards. Found once per 36 packs, on average, the cards are printed on an embossed light F/X design. Cards are numbered with a "PD" prefix.

		NM/M
Complete Set (20):		24.00
Common Player:		.30
1	Albert Belle	.30
2	Barry Bonds	5.00
3	Jay Buhner	.30
4	Jose Canseco	.75
5	Cecil Fielder	.30
6	Juan Gonzalez	.75
7	Ken Griffey Jr.	3.00
8	Eric Karros	.30
9	Fred McGriff	.30
10	Mark McGwire	4.00
11	Rafael Palmeiro	1.25
12	Mike Piazza	3.00
13	Manny Ramirez	1.50
14	Tim Salmon	.30
15	Reggie Sanders	.30
16	Sammy Sosa	2.50
17	Frank Thomas	1.50
18	Mo Vaughn	.30
19	Larry Walker	.30
20	Matt Williams	.30

Retail Predictor

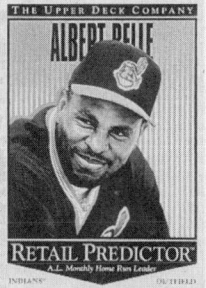

Retail Predictor inserts feature 60 possible winners in the categories of monthly leader in home runs, batting average and RBIs. If the pictured player led a category in any month, his card was redeemable for a 10-card set featuring action photos on silver foil. Retail Predictors are found on average once per 12 packs in each series. Winning cards are indicated by (W).

		NM/M
Complete Set (60):		40.00
Common Player:		.40
R1	Albert Belle (W)	.60
R2	Jay Buhner (W)	.60
R3	Juan Gonzalez	.50
R4	Ken Griffey Jr.	2.00
R5	Mark McGwire (W)	4.00
R6	Rafael Palmeiro	.65
R7	Tim Salmon	.40
R8	Frank Thomas	1.00
R9	Mo Vaughn (W)	.60
R10	Home Run Long Shot (W)	.40
R11	Albert Belle (W)	.60
R12	Jay Buhner	.40
R13	Jim Edmonds	.40
R14	Cecil Fielder	.40
R15	Ken Griffey Jr.	2.00
R16	Edgar Martinez	.40
R17	Manny Ramirez	.75
R18	Frank Thomas	1.00
R19	Mo Vaughn (W)	.60
R20	RBI Long Shot (W)	.40
R21	Roberto Alomar (W)	1.00
R22	Carlos Baerga	.40
R23	Wade Boggs	1.50
R24	Ken Griffey Jr.	2.00
R25	Chuck Knoblauch	.40
R26	Kenny Lofton	.40
R27	Edgar Martinez	.40
R28	Tim Salmon	.40
R29	Frank Thomas	2.00
R30	Batting Average Long Shot (W)	.40
R31	Dante Bichette	.40
R32	Barry Bonds (W)	4.50
R33	Ron Gant	.40
R34	Chipper Jones	1.50
R35	Fred McGriff	.40
R36	Mike Piazza	2.00
R37	Sammy Sosa	1.50
R38	Larry Walker	.40
R39	Matt Williams	.40
R40	Home Run Long Shot	.40
R41	Jeff Bagwell (W)	1.25
R42	Dante Bichette	.40
R43	Barry Bonds (W)	4.50
R44	Jeff Conine	.40
R45	Andres Galarraga	.40
R46	Mike Piazza	2.00
R47	Reggie Sanders	.40
R48	Sammy Sosa	1.50
R49	Matt Williams	.40
R50	RBI Long Shot	.75
R51	Jeff Bagwell	.75
R52	Derek Bell	.40
R53	Dante Bichette	.40
R54	Craig Biggio	.40
R55	Barry Bonds	2.50
R56	Bret Boone	.40
R57	Tony Gwynn	1.50
R58	Barry Larkin	.40
R59	Mike Piazza	3.50
R60	AVG Long Shot	.40

Retail Predictor Redemption

Persons who redeemed winning cards from UD's interactive Predictor insert series received a 10-card set of the top players in various statistical categories. The redemption cards are similar in format to the Predictor cards, but have fronts printed on silver-foil. In place of the contest rules found on the backs of Predictor cards, the redemption cards have a career summary.

		NM/M
Complete Set (60):		25.00
Common Player:		.25
R1	Albert Belle	.25
R2	Jay Buhner	.25
R3	Juan Gonzalez	.35
R4	Ken Griffey Jr.	1.00
R5	Mark McGwire	1.50
R6	Rafael Palmeiro	.50
R7	Tim Salmon	.25
R8	Frank Thomas	.60
R9	Mo Vaughn	.25
R10	Home Run Long Shot	.25
R11	Albert Belle	.25
R12	Jay Buhner	.25
R13	Jim Edmonds	.25
R14	Cecil Fielder	.25
R15	Ken Griffey Jr.	1.00
R16	Edgar Martinez	.25
R17	Manny Ramirez	.60
R18	Frank Thomas	.60
R19	Mo Vaughn	.25
R20	RBI Long Shot	.25
R21	Roberto Alomar	.35
R22	Carlos Baerga	.25
R23	Wade Boggs	.75
R24	Ken Griffey Jr.	1.00
R25	Chuck Knoblauch	.25
R26	Kenny Lofton	.25
R27	Edgar Martinez	.25
R28	Tim Salmon	.25
R29	Frank Thomas	.60
R30	Batting Average Long Shot	.25
R31	Dante Bichette	.25
R32	Barry Bonds	2.00
R33	Ron Gant	.25
R34	Chipper Jones	.75
R35	Fred McGriff	.25
R36	Mike Piazza	1.00
R37	Sammy Sosa	.75
R38	Larry Walker	.25
R39	Matt Williams	.25
R40	Home Run Long Shot	.25
R41	Jeff Bagwell	.60
R42	Dante Bichette	.25
R43	Barry Bonds	2.00
R44	Jeff Conine	.25
R45	Andres Galarraga	.25
R46	Mike Piazza	1.00
R47	Reggie Sanders	.25
R48	Sammy Sosa	.75
R49	Matt Williams	.25
R50	RBI Long Shot	.25
R51	Jeff Bagwell	.60
R52	Derek Bell	.25
R53	Dante Bichette	.25
R54	Craig Biggio	.25
R55	Barry Bonds	2.00
R56	Bret Boone	.25
R57	Tony Gwynn	.75
R58	Barry Larkin	.25
R59	Mike Piazza	1.00
R60	AVG Long Shot	.25

Cal Ripken Collection

Part of a cross-brand insert set, four cards are included as Series I inserts at the rate of one per 24 packs. Five cards are also included in Series II, one per every 23 packs. They chronicle Cal Ripken's career and highlights.

		NM/M
Complete Set (8):		12.50
Common Card:		2.00
Header:		2.00
5	Cal Ripken Jr.	2.00
6	Cal Ripken Jr.	2.00
7	Cal Ripken Jr.	2.00
8	Cal Ripken Jr.	2.00
13	Cal Ripken Jr.	2.00

14	Cal Ripken Jr.	2.00
15	Cal Ripken Jr.	2.00
16	Cal Ripken Jr.	2.00
17	Cal Ripken Jr.	2.00

Cal Ripken Collection Supers

The career of Cal Ripken Jr. to the point of his 2,131st consecutive major league game is chronicled in this boxed set of 3-1/2" x 5" cards. The tale is told in reverse order, with card #1 marking the record and #22 detailing Ripken's first major league experience. Fronts have photos of Ripken in various stages of his career and feature a gold-foil facsimile autograph. Backs have a green and black background with a portrait of Ripken at top. At center are a few sentences about his career and a season's stats.

		NM/M
Complete Set (22):		10.00
Common Player:		.75
1	Cal Ripken Jr.	.75
2	Cal Ripken Jr. (w/Barry Bonds)	1.00
3-21	Cal Ripken Jr.	.75
22	Cal Ripken Jr. (w/Eddie Murray)	.75

Run Producers

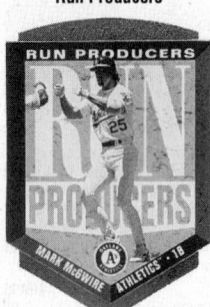

These double die-cut, embossed and color foil-stamped cards feature 20 of the game's top RBI men. The cards were seeded one per every 71 packs of 1996 Upper Deck Series II. Cards are numbered with a "RP" prefix.

		NM/M
Complete Set (20):		50.00
Common Player:		1.00
1	Albert Belle	1.00
2	Dante Bichette	1.00
3	Barry Bonds	10.00
4	Jay Buhner	1.00
5	Jose Canseco	2.00
6	Juan Gonzalez	1.50
7	Ken Griffey Jr.	6.00
8	Tony Gwynn	5.00
9	Kenny Lofton	1.00
10	Edgar Martinez	1.00
11	Fred McGriff	1.00
12	Mark McGwire	7.50
13	Rafael Palmeiro	2.50
14	Mike Piazza	6.00
15	Manny Ramirez	3.00
16	Tim Salmon	1.00
17	Sammy Sosa	5.00
18	Frank Thomas	3.00
19	Mo Vaughn	1.00
20	Matt Williams	1.00

All-Star Supers

The starting line-ups of the 1996 All-Star Game are featured in super-size (3-1/2" x 5") versions of their 1996 Upper Deck cards in this special boxed set sold at Wal-Mart late in the year for around $18. Other than a large silver-foil All-Star Game logo in the lower-left corner of each photo, these cards are identical to the regular-issue versions, right down to the silver- and bronze-foil highlights on front and the card numbers on back.

		NM/M
Complete Set (18):		7.50
Common Player:		.25
80	Jeff Bagwell	.75
195	Barry Bonds	2.00
200	Ken Griffey Jr.	1.25
271	John Smoltz	.25
275	Roberto Alomar	.45
280	Cal Ripken Jr.	2.00
300	Frank Thomas	.75
310	Barry Larkin	.25
313	Sandy Alomar Jr.	.25
315	Albert Belle	.25
317	Charles Nagy	.25
319	Kenny Lofton	.25
320	Dante Bichette	.25
345	Craig Biggio	.25
360	Mike Piazza	1.25
410	Wade Boggs	1.00
450	Tony Gwynn	1.00
455	Matt Williams	.25

Ken Griffey Jr. All-Star

Junior's seventh All-Star team selection was marked with the issue of this special jumbo (3-1/2" x 5") card. The front has an action photo with the 1996 All-Star Game logo and is highlighted in silver foil, including a reproduction of his autograph. The top is die-cut. On back is a portrait photo with Griffey's All-Star history overprinted, and a serial number from within an edition of 2,500. The card was an exclusive to a TV shopping network.

	NM/M
Ken Griffey Jr.	12.00

Ken Griffey Jr. 22kt Gold

This standard-size card has a gold-foil facsimile autograph on front and is serially numbered on back from within an edition of 5,000. A certificate of authenticity accompanied the card when sold new.

National Heroes

	NM/M
Ken Griffey Jr.	7.50

Two baseball stars are included in this series of collector issues believed to have been a TV shop-at-home exclusive. Measuring 3-1/2" x 5", the cards are die-cut into a torn ticket shape. Fronts have color action photos on a gold-foil background. Two versions of each card were issued, an edition of 5,000 unsigned cards and an autographed edition serially numbered on front to a limit of 250.

		NM/M
Complete Set (2):		20.00
Complete Set,		
	Autographed (2):	190.00
(1)	Ken Griffey Jr.	7.50
(1a)	Ken Griffey Jr./Auto.	90.00
(2)	Cal Ripken Jr.	10.00
(2a)	Cal Ripken Jr./Auto.	100.00

Hideo Nomo R.O.Y.

The Japanese pitcher's 1995 Rookie of the Year season was commemorated with this large-format (3-1/2" x 5"), die-cut card sold only via TV shopping programs. The card has an action photo of Nomo on front and is highlighted in gold foil, including a replica of his autograph. On back is an action photo, major league career summary and stats and a serial number from within an edition of 5,000 pieces.

	NM/M
Hideo Nomo	15.00

Meet the Stars

These 7" x 5" cards were issued in conjunction with UD's "Meet the Stars" promotion.

		NM/M
Complete Set (2):		12.00
(1)	Dynamic Debut/1989 (Ken Griffey Jr.)	5.00
(2)	Magic Memories/1995 (Ken Griffey Jr.)	5.00

Statistics Leaders Supers

National League and American League winners of important statistical categories, along with major award winners for the 1996 season are featured in this boxed set of large-format (3-1/2" x 5") cards. Besides the size, these cards differ from the regular-issue 1996 UD cards of the same players only in the addition of a silver-foil award shield on front and the card number on back. Players with multiple awards have identical cards. The set was sold only at retail outlets with a suggested price of about $20.

		NM/M
Complete Set (23):		4.00
Common Player:		.15
1	Alex Rodriguez (AL Batting)	1.50
2	Tony Gwynn (NL Batting)	.60
3	Mark McGwire (AL HR)	1.50
4	Andres Galarraga (NL HR)	.15
5	Albert Belle (AL RBI)	.15
6	Andres Galarraga (NL RBI)	.15
7	Kenny Lofton (AL Steals)	.15
8	Eric Young (NL Steals)	.15
9	Andy Pettitte (AL Wins)	.25
10	John Smoltz (NL Wins)	.15
11	Roger Clemens (AL Ks)	.75
12	John Smoltz (NL Ks)	.15
13	Juan Guzman (AL ERA)	.15
14	Kevin Brown (NL ERA)	.15
15	John Wetteland (AL Saves)	.15
16	Jeff Brantley (NL Saves)	.15
17	Todd Worrell (NL Saves)	.15
18	Derek Jeter (AL ROY)	2.00
19	Todd Hollandsworth (NL ROY)	.15
20	Juan Gonzalez (AL MVP)	.30
21	Ken Caminiti (NL MVP)	.15
22	Pat Hentgen (AL CY)	.15
23	John Smoltz (NL CY)	.15

1997 Upper Deck

The 520-card set was issued in two series in 12-card packs. Base card fronts feature a game-action shot with the player's name near the bottom edge above a bronze-gold, wood-grain stripe. A team logo is in the lower-left corner in silver foil. Each card front has the date of the game pictured with a brief description. Backs contain more detailed game highlight descriptions and statistics, along with a small action shot in the upper-left quadrant. Series 1 subsets are: Jackie Robinson Tribute (1-9), Strike Force (65-72), Defensive Gems (136-153), Global Impact (181-207), Season Highlights Checklist (214-222) and Star Rookies (223-240). A 30-card update to Series 1 was released early in the season featuring 1996 post-season highlights and star rookies. Those card faces have red or purple borders and are numbered 241 to 270. Second series subsets include Star Rookie (271-288), Season Highlights (316-324), Capture the Flag (370-387), the short-printed (about one per seven packs) Griffey Hot List (415-424), and Diamond Debuts (469-483). A second update set of 30 was released near the end of the 1997 season, numbered 521-550 and featuring traded players and rookies. Both of the update sets were available only via a mail-in redemption offer.

	NM/M
Complete Set (550):	75.00
Complete Series 1 Set (240):	35.00
Complete Update Set (241-270):	5.00
Complete Series 2 Set (271-520):	35.00
Complete Update Set (521-550):	7.50
Common Player:	.05
Series 1 or 2 Pack (12):	1.50
Series 1 or 2 Wax Box (28):	25.00
1-9	Jackie Robinson	.50
10	Chipper Jones	1.00
11	Marquis Grissom	.05
12	Jermaine Dye	.05
13	Mark Lemke	.05
14	Terrell Wade	.05
15	Fred McGriff	.05
16	Tom Glavine	.20
17	Mark Wohlers	.05
18	Randy Myers	.05
19	Roberto Alomar	.25
20	Cal Ripken Jr.	2.00
21	Rafael Palmeiro	.65
22	Mike Mussina	.30
23	Brady Anderson	.05
24	Jose Canseco	.50
25	Mo Vaughn	.05
26	Roger Clemens	1.00
27	Tim Naehring	.05
28	Jeff Suppan	.05
29	Troy Percival	.05
30	Sammy Sosa	1.00
31	Amaury Telemaco	.05
32	Rey Sanchez	.05
33	Scott Servais	.05
34	Steve Trachsel	.05
35	Mark Grace	.05
36	Wilson Alvarez	.05
37	Harold Baines	.05
38	Tony Phillips	.05
39	James Baldwin	.05
40	Frank Thomas (Wrong (Ken Griffey Jr.'s) vital data.)	.85
41	Lyle Mouton	.05
42	Chris Snopek	.05
43	Hal Morris	.05
44	Eric Davis	.05
45	Barry Larkin	.05
46	Reggie Sanders	.05
47	Pete Schourek	.05
48	Lee Smith	.05
49	Charles Nagy	.05
50	Albert Belle	.05
51	Julio Franco	.05
52	Kenny Lofton	.05
53	Orel Hershiser	.05
54	Omar Vizquel	.05
55	Eric Young	.05
56	Curtis Leskanic	.05
57	Quinton McCracken	.05
58	Kevin Ritz	.05
59	Walt Weiss	.05
60	Dante Bichette	.05
61	Marc Lewis	.05
62	Tony Clark	.05
63	Travis Fryman	.05
64	John Smoltz (Strike Force)	.05
65	Greg Maddux (Strike Force)	.50
66	Tom Glavine (Strike Force)	.10
67	Mike Mussina (Strike Force)	.15
68	Andy Pettitte (Strike Force)	.15
69	Mariano Rivera (Strike Force)	.10
70	Hideo Nomo (Strike Force)	.20
71	Kevin Brown (Strike Force)	.05
72	Randy Johnson (Strike Force)	.40
73	Felipe Lira	.05
74	Kimera Bartee	.05
75	Alan Trammell	.05
76	Kevin Brown	.05
77	Edgar Renteria	.05
78	Al Leiter	.05
79	Charles Johnson	.05
80	Andre Dawson	.05
81	Billy Wagner	.05
82	Donne Wall	.05
83	Jeff Bagwell	.75
84	Keith Lockhart	.05
85	Jeff Montgomery	.05
86	Tom Goodwin	.05
87	Tim Belcher	.05
88	Mike Macfarlane	.05
89	Joe Randa	.05
90	Brett Butler	.05
91	Todd Worrell	.05
92	Todd Hollandsworth	.05
93	Ismael Valdes	.05
94	Hideo Nomo	.40
95	Mike Piazza	1.25
96	Jeff Cirillo	.05
97	Ricky Bones	.05
98	Fernando Vina	.05
99	Ben McDonald	.05

No.	Player	Price
100	John Jaha	.05
101	Mark Loretta	.05
102	Paul Molitor	.75
103	Rick Aguilera	.05
104	Marty Cordova	.05
105	Kirby Puckett	1.00
106	Dan Naulty	.05
107	Frank Rodriguez	.05
108	Shane Andrews	.05
109	Henry Rodriguez	.05
110	Mark Grudzielanek	.05
111	Pedro Martinez	.75
112	Ugueth Urbina	.05
113	David Segui	.05
114	Rey Ordonez	.05
115	Bernard Gilkey	.05
116	Butch Huskey	.05
117	Paul Wilson	.05
118	Alex Ochoa	.05
119	John Franco	.05
120	Dwight Gooden	.05
121	Ruben Rivera	.05
122	Andy Pettitte	.20
123	Tino Martinez	.05
124	Bernie Williams	.05
125	Wade Boggs	1.00
126	Paul O'Neill	.05
127	Scott Brosius	.05
128	Ernie Young	.05
129	Doug Johns	.05
130	Geronimo Berroa	.05
131	Jason Giambi	.50
132	John Wasdin	.05
133	Jim Eisenreich	.05
134	Ricky Otero	.05
135	Ricky Bottalico	.05
136	Mark Langston (Defensive Gems)	.05
137	Greg Maddux (Defensive Gems)	.50
138	Ivan Rodriguez (Defensive Gems)	.35
139	Charles Johnson (Defensive Gems)	.05
140	J.T. Snow (Defensive Gems)	.05
141	Mark Grace (Defensive Gems)	.05
142	Roberto Alomar (Defensive Gems)	.15
143	Craig Biggio (Defensive Gems)	.05
144	Ken Caminiti (Defensive Gems)	.05
145	Matt Williams (Defensive Gems)	.05
146	Omar Vizquel (Defensive Gems)	.05
147	Cal Ripken Jr. (Defensive Gems)	1.00
148	Ozzie Smith (Defensive Gems)	.40
149	Rey Ordonez (Defensive Gems)	.05
150	Ken Griffey Jr. (Defensive Gems)	.65
151	Devon White (Defensive Gems)	.05
152	Barry Bonds (Defensive Gems)	1.00
153	Kenny Lofton (Defensive Gems)	.05
154	Mickey Morandini	.05
155	Gregg Jefferies	.05
156	Curt Schilling	.20
157	Jason Kendall	.05
158	Francisco Cordova	.05
159	Dennis Eckersley	.65
160	Ron Gant	.05
161	Ozzie Smith	1.00
162	Brian Jordan	.05
163	John Mabry	.05
164	Andy Ashby	.05
165	Steve Finley	.05
166	Fernando Valenzuela	.05
167	Archi Cianfrocco	.05
168	Wally Joyner	.05
169	Greg Vaughn	.05
170	Barry Bonds	2.00
171	William Van Landingham	.05
172	Marvin Benard	.05
173	Rich Aurilia	.05
174	Jay Canizaro	.05
175	Ken Griffey Jr.	1.25
176	Bob Wells	.05
177	Jay Buhner	.05
178	Sterling Hitchcock	.05
179	Edgar Martinez	.05
180	Rusty Greer	.05
181	Dave Nilsson (Global Impact)	.05
182	Larry Walker (Global Impact)	.05
183	Edgar Renteria (Global Impact)	.05
184	Rey Ordonez (Global Impact)	.05
185	Rafael Palmeiro (Global Impact)	.35
186	Osvaldo Fernandez (Global Impact)	.05
187	Raul Mondesi (Global Impact)	.05
188	Manny Ramirez (Global Impact)	.40
189	Sammy Sosa (Global Impact)	.50

No.	Player	Price
190	Robert Eenhoorn (Global Impact)	.05
191	Devon White (Global Impact)	.05
192	Hideo Nomo (Global Impact)	.20
193	Mac Suzuki (Global Impact)	.05
194	Chan Ho Park (Global Impact)	.05
195	Fernando Valenzuela (Global Impact)	.05
196	Andruw Jones (Global Impact)	.40
197	Vinny Castilla (Global Impact)	.05
198	Dennis Martinez (Global Impact)	.05
199	Ruben Rivera (Global Impact)	.05
200	Juan Gonzalez (Global Impact)	.20
201	Roberto Alomar (Global Impact)	.30
202	Edgar Martinez (Global Impact)	.05
203	Ivan Rodriguez (Global Impact)	.35
204	Carlos Delgado (Global Impact)	.20
205	Andres Galarraga (Global Impact)	.05
206	Ozzie Guillen (Global Impact)	.05
207	Midre Cummings (Global Impact)	.05
208	Roger Pavlik	.05
209	Darren Oliver	.05
210	Dean Palmer	.05
211	Ivan Rodriguez	.65
212	Otis Nixon	.05
213	Pat Hentgen	.05
214	Ozzie Smith, Andre Dawson, Kirby Puckett CL (Season Highlights)	.10
215	Barry Bonds, Gary Sheffield, Brady Anderson (Checklist/Season Highlights)	.25
216	Ken Caminiti (Checklist/Season Highlights)	.05
217	John Smoltz (Checklist/Season Highlights)	.05
218	Eric Young (Checklist/Season Highlights)	.10
219	Juan Gonzalez (Checklist/Season Highlights)	.10
220	Eddie Murray (Checklist/Season Highlights)	.15
221	Tommy Lasorda (Checklist/Season Highlights)	.05
222	Paul Molitor (Checklist/Season Highlights)	.15
223	Luis Castillo	.05
224	Justin Thompson	.05
225	Rocky Coppinger	.05
226	Jermaine Allensworth	.05
227	Jeff D'Amico	.05
228	Jamey Wright	.05
229	Scott Rolen	.60
230	Darin Erstad	.25
231	Marty Janzen	.05
232	Jacob Cruz	.05
233	Raul Ibanez	.25
234	Nomar Garciaparra	1.00
235	Todd Walker	.05
236	Brian Giles RC	.75
237	Matt Beech	.05
238	Mike Cameron	.05
239	Jose Paniagua	.05
240	Andruw Jones	.75
241	Brant Brown/SR	.25
242	Robin Jennings/SR	.25
243	Willie Adams/SR	.25
244	Ken Caminiti/SR	.25
245	Brian Jordan (Division Series)	.25
246	Chipper Jones (Division Series)	2.50
247	Juan Gonzalez (Division Series)	1.00
248	Bernie Williams (Division Series)	.05
249	Roberto Alomar (Division Series)	.30
250	Bernie Williams (Post-Season)	.05
251	David Wells (Post-Season)	.25
252	Cecil Fielder (Post-Season)	.05
253	Darryl Strawberry (Post-Season)	.05
254	Andy Pettitte (Post-Season)	.05
255	Javier Lopez (Post-Season)	.05
256	Gary Gaetti (Post-Season)	.25
257	Ron Gant (Post-Season)	.25
258	Brian Jordan (Post-Season)	.25
259	John Smoltz (Post-Season)	.25

No.	Player	Price
260	Greg Maddux (Post-Season)	2.50
261	Tom Glavine (Post-Season)	.45
262	Chipper Jones (World Series)	2.50
263	Greg Maddux (World Series)	2.50
264	David Cone (World Series)	.25
265	Jim Leyritz (World Series)	.25
266	Andy Pettitte (World Series)	.40
267	John Wetteland (World Series)	.05
268	Dario Veras/SR RC	.25
269	Neifi Perez/SR	.25
270	Bill Mueller/SR	.25
271	Vladimir Guerrero/SR	.75
272	Dmitri Young/SR	.05
273	Nerio Rodriguez/SR RC	.05
274	Kevin Orie/SR	.05
275	Felipe Crespo/SR	.05
276	Danny Graves/SR	.05
277	Roderick Myers/SR	.05
278	Felix Heredia/SR RC	.25
279	Ralph Milliard/SR	.05
280	Greg Norton/SR	.05
281	Derek Wallace/SR	.05
282	Trot Nixon/SR	.10
283	Bobby Chouinard/SR	.05
284	Jay Witasick/SR	.05
285	Travis Miller/SR	.05
286	Brian Bevil/SR	.05
287	Bobby Estalella/SR	.05
288	Steve Soderstrom/SR	.05
289	Mark Langston	.05
290	Tim Salmon	.05
291	Jim Edmonds	.05
292	Garret Anderson	.05
293	George Arias	.05
294	Gary DiSarcina	.05
295	Chuck Finley	.05
296	Todd Greene	.05
297	Randy Velarde	.05
298	David Justice	.05
299	Ryan Klesko	.05
300	John Smoltz	.05
301	Javier Lopez	.05
302	Greg Maddux	1.00
303	Denny Neagle	.05
304	B.J. Surhoff	.05
305	Chris Hoiles	.05
306	Eric Davis	.05
307	Scott Erickson	.05
308	Mike Bordick	.05
309	John Valentin	.05
310	Heathcliff Slocumb	.05
311	Tom Gordon	.05
312	Mike Stanley	.05
313	Reggie Jefferson	.05
314	Darren Bragg	.05
315	Troy O'Leary	.05
316	John Mabry (Season Highlight)	.05
317	Mark Whiten (Season Highlight)	.05
318	Edgar Martinez (Season Highlight)	.05
319	Alex Rodriguez (Season Highlight)	.75
320	Mark McGwire (Season Highlight)	.75
321	Hideo Nomo (Season Highlight)	.20
322	Todd Hundley (Season Highlight)	.05
323	Barry Bonds (Season Highlight)	1.00
324	Andruw Jones (Season Highlight)	.40
325	Ryne Sandberg	1.00
326	Brian McRae	.05
327	Frank Castillo	.05
328	Shawon Dunston	.05
329	Ray Durham	.05
330	Robin Ventura	.05
331	Ozzie Guillen	.05
332	Roberto Hernandez	.05
333	Albert Belle	.25
334	Dave Martinez	.05
335	Willie Greene	.05
336	Jeff Brantley	.05
337	Kevin Jarvis	.05
338	John Smiley	.05
339	Eddie Taubensee	.05
340	Bret Boone	.05
341	Kevin Seitzer	.05
342	Jack McDowell	.05
343	Sandy Alomar Jr.	.05
344	Chad Curtis	.05
345	Manny Ramirez	.75
346	Chad Ogea	.05
347	Jim Thome	.05
348	Mark Thompson	.05
349	Ellis Burks	.05
350	Andres Galarraga	.05
351	Vinny Castilla	.05
352	Kirt Manwaring	.05
353	Larry Walker	.05
354	Omar Olivares	.05
355	Bobby Higginson	.05
356	Melvin Nieves	.05
357	Brian Johnson	.05
358	Devon White	.05
359	Jeff Conine	.05
360	Gary Sheffield	.35
361	Robb Nen	.05
362	Mike Hampton	.05

No.	Player	Price
363	Bob Abreu	.10
364	Luis Gonzalez	.05
365	Derek Bell	.05
366	Sean Berry	.05
367	Craig Biggio	.05
368	Darryl Kile	.05
369	Shane Reynolds	.05
370	Jeff Bagwell (Capture the Flag)	.40
371	Ron Gant (Capture the Flag)	.05
372	Andy Benes (Capture the Flag)	.05
373	Gary Gaetti (Capture the Flag)	.05
374a	Ramon Martinez (Capture the Flag)(Gold back.)	.05
374b	Ramon Martinez (Capture the Flag)(White back.)	.05
375	Raul Mondesi (Capture the Flag)	.05
376a	Steve Finley (Capture the Flag)(Gold back.)	.05
376b	Steve Finley (Capture the Flag)(White back.)	.05
377	Ken Caminiti (Capture the Flag)	.05
378	Tony Gwynn (Capture the Flag)	.40
379	Dario Veras (Capture the Flag)	.05
380	Andy Pettitte (Capture the Flag)	.10
381	Ruben Rivera (Capture the Flag)	.05
382	David Cone (Capture the Flag)	.05
383	Roberto Alomar (Capture the Flag)	.20
384	Edgar Martinez (Capture the Flag)	.05
385	Ken Griffey Jr. (Capture the Flag)	.65
386	Mark McGwire (Capture the Flag)	.75
387	Rusty Greer (Capture the Flag)	.05
388	Jose Rosado	.05
389	Kevin Appier	.05
390	Johnny Damon	.25
391	Jose Offerman	.05
392	Michael Tucker	.05
393	Craig Paquette	.05
394	Bip Roberts	.05
395	Ramon Martinez	.05
396	Greg Gagne	.05
397	Chan Ho Park	.05
398	Karim Garcia	.10
399	Wilton Guerrero	.05
400	Eric Karros	.05
401	Raul Mondesi	.05
402	Matt Mieske	.05
403	Mike Fetters	.05
404	Dave Nilsson	.05
405	Jose Valentin	.05
406	Scott Karl	.05
407	Marc Newfield	.05
408	Cal Eldred	.05
409	Rich Becker	.05
410	Terry Steinbach	.05
411	Chuck Knoblauch	.05
412	Pat Meares	.05
413	Brad Radke	.05
415a	Kirby Puckett (Should be #414.)	1.00
415b	Andruw Jones (Griffey Hot List)	1.50
416	Chipper Jones (Griffey Hot List)	2.00
417	Mo Vaughn (Griffey Hot List)	.50
418	Frank Thomas (Griffey Hot List)	1.50
419	Albert Belle (Griffey Hot List)	.50
420	Mark McGwire (Griffey Hot List)	3.00
421	Derek Jeter (Griffey Hot List)	4.50
422	Alex Rodriguez (Griffey Hot List)	3.00
423	Juan Gonzalez (Griffey Hot List)	.75
424	Ken Griffey Jr. (Griffey Hot List)	2.50
425	Rondell White	.05
426	Darrin Fletcher	.05
427	Cliff Floyd	.05
428	Mike Lansing	.05
429	F.P. Santangelo	.05
430	Todd Hundley	.05
431	Mark Clark	.05
432	Pete Harnisch	.05
433	Jason Isringhausen	.05
434	Bobby Jones	.05
435	Lance Johnson	.05
436	Carlos Baerga	.05
437	Mariano Duncan	.05
438	David Cone	.05
439	Mariano Rivera	.15
440	Derek Jeter	2.00
441	Joe Girardi	.05
442	Charlie Hayes	.05
443	Tim Raines	.05
444	Darryl Strawberry	.05
445	Cecil Fielder	.05
446	Ariel Prieto	.05
447	Tony Batista	.05

No.	Player	Price
448	Brent Gates	.05
449	Scott Spiezio	.05
450	Mark McGwire	1.50
451	Don Wengert	.05
452	Mike Lieberthal	.05
453	Lenny Dykstra	.05
454	Rex Hudler	.05
455	Darren Daulton	.05
456	Kevin Stocker	.05
457	Trey Beamon	.05
458	Midre Cummings	.05
459	Mark Johnson	.05
460	Al Martin	.05
461	Kevin Elster	.05
462	Jon Lieber	.05
463	Jason Schmidt	.05
464	Paul Wagner	.05
465	Andy Benes	.05
466	Alan Benes	.05
467	Royce Clayton	.05
468	Gary Gaetti	.05
469	Curt Lyons (Diamond Debuts)	.05
470	Eugene Kingsale (Diamond Debuts)	.05
471	Damian Jackson (Diamond Debuts)	.05
472	Wendell Magee (Diamond Dubuts)	.05
473	Kevin L. Brown (Diamond Debuts)	.05
474	Raul Casanova (Diamond Debuts)	.05
475	Ramiro Mendoza RC (Diamond Debuts)	.25
476	Todd Dunn (Diamond Debuts)	.05
477	Chad Mottola (Diamond Debuts)	.05
478	Andy Larkin (Diamond Debuts)	.05
479	Jaime Bluma (Diamond Debuts)	.05
480	Mac Suzuki (Diamond Debuts)	.05
481	Brian Banks (Diamond Debuts)	.05
482	Desi Wilson (Diamond Debuts)	.05
483	Einar Diaz (Diamond Debuts)	.05
484	Tom Pagnozzi	.05
485	Ray Lankford	.05
486	Todd Stottlemyre	.05
487	Donovan Osborne	.05
488	Trevor Hoffman	.05
489	Chris Gomez	.05
490	Ken Caminiti	.05
491	John Flaherty	.05
492	Tony Gwynn	1.00
493	Joey Hamilton	.05
494	Rickey Henderson	.75
495	Glenallen Hill	.05
496	Rod Beck	.05
497	Osvaldo Fernandez	.05
498	Rick Wilkins	.05
499	Joey Cora	.05
500	Alex Rodriguez	1.50
501	Randy Johnson	.75
502	Paul Sorrento	.05
503	Dan Wilson	.05
504	Jamie Moyer	.05
505	Will Clark	.05
506	Mickey Tettleton	.05
507	John Burkett	.05
508	Ken Hill	.05
509	Mark McLemore	.05
510	Juan Gonzalez	.40
511	Bobby Witt	.05
512	Carlos Delgado	.40
513	Alex Gonzalez	.05
514	Shawn Green	.05
515	Joe Carter	.05
516	Juan Guzman	.05
517	Charlie O'Brien	.05
518	Ed Sprague	.05
519	Mike Timlin	.05
520	Roger Clemens	1.00
521	Eddie Murray	2.00
522	Jason Dickson	.25
523	Jim Leyritz	.25
524	Michael Tucker	.25
525	Kenny Lofton	.25
526	Jimmy Key	.25
527	Mel Rojas	.25
528	Deion Sanders	.25
529	Bartolo Colon	.25
530	Matt Williams	.25
531	Marquis Grissom	.25
532	David Justice	.25
533	Bubba Trammell RC	.35
534	Moises Alou	.25
535	Bobby Bonilla	.25
536	Alex Fernandez	.25
537	Jay Bell	.25
538	Chili Davis	.25
539	Jeff King	.25
540	Todd Zeile	.25
541	John Olerud	.25
542	Jose Guillen	.25
543	Derrek Lee	1.00
544	Dante Powell	.25
545	J.T. Snow	.25
546	Jeff Kent	.25
547	Jose Cruz Jr. RC	.75
548	John Wetteland	.25
549	Orlando Merced	.25
550	Hideki Irabu RC	.50

Amazing Greats

The 20-card, regular-sized insert set was included every 138 packs of 1997 Upper Deck baseball. The cards include real wood with two player shots imaged on the card front. The team logo appears in the upper right corner of the horizontal card. The cards are numbered with the "AG" prefix.

		NM/M
Complete Set (20):		140.00
Common Player:		2.50
1	Ken Griffey Jr.	12.50
2	Roberto Alomar	3.00
3	Alex Rodriguez	15.00
4	Paul Molitor	7.50
5	Chipper Jones	10.00
6	Tony Gwynn	10.00
7	Kenny Lofton	2.50
8	Albert Belle	2.50
9	Matt Williams	2.50
10	Frank Thomas	7.50
11	Greg Maddux	10.00
12	Sammy Sosa	10.00
13	Kirby Puckett	10.00
14	Jeff Bagwell	7.50
15	Cal Ripken Jr.	20.00
16	Manny Ramirez	7.50
17	Barry Bonds	20.00
18	Mo Vaughn	2.50
19	Eddie Murray	7.50
20	Mike Piazza	12.50

Blue Chip Prospects

This 20-card insert was found in packs of Series II and features a die-cut design. Cards appear to have a photo slide attached to them featuring a portrait shot of the promising youngster depicted on the card. A total of 500 of each card were produced. Cards are numbered with a "BC" prefix.

		NM/M
Common Player:		6.00
Production 500 Sets		
1	Andruw Jones	25.00
2	Derek Jeter	60.00
3	Scott Rolen	15.00
4	Manny Ramirez	25.00
5	Todd Walker	6.00
6	Rocky Coppinger	6.00
7	Nomar Garciaparra	30.00
8	Darin Erstad	7.50
9	Jermaine Dye	6.00
10	Vladimir Guerrero	25.00
11	Edgar Renteria	6.00
12	Bob Abreu	7.50
13	Karim Garcia	6.00
14	Jeff D'Amico	6.00
15	Chipper Jones	30.00
16	Todd Hollandsworth	6.00
17	Andy Pettitte	9.00
18	Ruben Rivera	6.00
19	Jason Kendall	6.00
20	Alex Rodriguez	40.00

Game Jersey

The three-card, regular-sized set was inserted every 800 packs of Upper Deck Series I. The cards contained a square of the player's game-used jersey, and carried a "GJ" card number prefix.

		NM/M
Complete Set (3):		160.00
Common Player:		15.00
GJ1	Ken Griffey Jr.	150.00
GJ2	Tony Gwynn	25.00
GJ3	Rey Ordonez	15.00

Hot Commodities

This 20-card insert from Series II features a flame pattern behind the image of the player depicted on the front of the card. Odds of finding a card were 1:13 packs. Cards are numbered with a "HC" prefix.

		NM/M
Complete Set (20):		20.00
Common Player:		.30
1	Alex Rodriguez	2.00
2	Andruw Jones	1.00
3	Derek Jeter	2.50
4	Frank Thomas	1.00
5	Ken Griffey Jr.	1.50
6	Chipper Jones	1.25
7	Juan Gonzalez	.50
8	Cal Ripken Jr.	2.50
9	John Smoltz	.30
10	Mark McGwire	2.00
11	Barry Bonds	2.50
12	Albert Belle	.30
13	Mike Piazza	1.50
14	Manny Ramirez	1.00
15	Mo Vaughn	.30
16	Tony Gwynn	1.25
17	Vladimir Guerrero	1.00
18	Hideo Nomo	.50
19	Greg Maddux	1.25
20	Kirby Puckett	1.25

Long Distance Connection

This 20-card insert from Series II features the top home run hitters in the game. Odds of finding a card were 1:35 packs. Cards are numbered with a "LD" prefix.

		NM/M
Complete Set (20):		32.50
Common Player:		.60
1	Mark McGwire	4.00
2	Brady Anderson	.60
3	Ken Griffey Jr.	3.00
4	Albert Belle	.60
5	Juan Gonzalez	1.25
6	Andres Galarraga	.60
7	Jay Buhner	.60
8	Mo Vaughn	.60
9	Barry Bonds	5.00
10	Gary Sheffield	1.25
11	Todd Hundley	.60
12	Frank Thomas	2.00
13	Sammy Sosa	2.50
14	Rafael Palmeiro	1.75
15	Alex Rodriguez	4.00
16	Mike Piazza	3.00
17	Ken Caminiti	.60
18	Chipper Jones	2.50
19	Manny Ramirez	2.00
20	Andruw Jones	2.00

Memorable Moments

This issue was a one per pack insert in special Series 1 and 2 Collector's Choice six-card retail packs. In standard 2-1/2" x 3-1/2", the cards are die-cut at top and bottom in a wave pattern. Fronts, highlighted in matte bronze foil, have action photos and a career highlight. Backs have another photo and a more complete explanation of the Memorable Moment.

		NM/M
Complete Set (20):		20.00
Common Player:		.50
1	Andruw Jones	.75
2	Chipper Jones	1.00
3	Cal Ripken Jr.	2.50
4	Frank Thomas	.75
5	Manny Ramirez	.75
6	Mike Piazza	1.50
7	Mark McGwire	2.00
8	Barry Bonds	2.50
9	Ken Griffey Jr.	1.50
10	Alex Rodriguez	2.00
1	Ken Griffey Jr.	1.50
2	Albert Belle	.50
3	Derek Jeter	2.50
4	Greg Maddux	1.00
5	Tony Gwynn	1.00
6	Ryne Sandberg	1.00
7	Juan Gonzalez	.60
8	Roger Clemens	1.25
9	Jose Cruz Jr.	.50
10	Mo Vaughn	.50

Power Package

The 20-card, regular-sized, die-cut set was inserted every 23 packs of 1997 Upper Deck baseball. The player's name is printed in gold foil along the top border of the card face, which also features Light F/X. The die-cut cards have a silver-foil border and team-color frame with a "Power Package" logo in gold foil centered on the bottom border. The card backs have a short highlight in a brown box bordered by team colors and are numbered with the "PP" prefix.

		NM/M
Complete Set (20):		30.00
Common Player:		1.00
1	Ken Griffey Jr.	3.50
2	Joe Carter	1.00
3	Rafael Palmeiro	1.75
4	Jay Buhner	1.00
5	Sammy Sosa	1.00
6	Fred McGriff	1.00
7	Jeff Bagwell	2.00
8	Albert Belle	1.00
9	Matt Williams	1.00
10	Mark McGwire	4.00
11	Gary Sheffield	1.25
12	Tim Salmon	1.00
13	Ryan Klesko	1.00
14	Manny Ramirez	2.00
15	Mike Piazza	3.50
16	Barry Bonds	5.00
17	Mo Vaughn	1.00
18	Jose Canseco	1.25

19	Juan Gonzalez	1.25
20	Frank Thomas	2.00

Power Package Jumbos

Unlike the regular Power Package inserts found in Series 1 packs, these jumbo versions are not die-cut. The 5" x 7" jumbos are found one per retail foil box of Series 1. Cards are numbered with a "PP" prefix.

		NM/M
Complete Set (20):		30.00
Common Player:		1.00
1	Ken Griffey Jr.	3.50
2	Joe Carter	1.00
3	Rafael Palmeiro	1.75
4	Jay Buhner	1.00
5	Sammy Sosa	3.00
6	Fred McGriff	1.00
7	Jeff Bagwell	2.00
8	Albert Belle	1.00
9	Matt Williams	1.00
10	Mark McGwire	4.00
11	Gary Sheffield	1.25
12	Tim Salmon	1.00
13	Ryan Klesko	1.00
14	Manny Ramirez	2.00
15	Mike Piazza	3.50
16	Barry Bonds	5.00
17	Mo Vaughn	1.25
18	Jose Canseco	1.25
19	Juan Gonzalez	1.25
20	Frank Thomas	2.00

Predictor

A new concept in interactive cards was UD's Series II Predictor inserts. Each player's card has four scratch-off baseball bats at the top-right. Under each bat is printed a specific accomplishment - hit for cycle, CG shutout, etc. - If the player attained that goal during the '97 season, and if the collector had scratched off the correct bat among the four, the Predictor card could be redeemed (with $2) for a premium TV cel card of the player. Thus if the player made one of his goals, the collector had a 25 percent chance of choosing the right bat. Two goals gave a 50 percent chance, etc. The Predictor cards have color action photos of the players at the left end of the horizontal format. The background at left and bottom is a red scorecard motif. Behind the bats is a black-and-white stadium scene. Backs repeat the red scorecard design with contest rules printed in white. A (W) in the checklist here indicates the player won one or more of his goals, making his card eligible for redemption. The redemption period ended Nov. 22, 1997. Values shown are for unscratched cards.

		NM/M
Complete Set (30):		15.00
Common Player:		.10
Values for unscratched cards.		
1	Andruw Jones	.40
2	Chipper Jones	.50
3	Greg Maddux (W)	1.00
4	Fred McGriff (W)	.25
5	John Smoltz (W)	.25
6	Brady Anderson (W)	.25
7	Cal Ripken Jr. (W)	2.00
8	Mo Vaughn (W)	.25
9	Sammy Sosa	.50

10	Albert Belle (W)	.25
11	Frank Thomas	.40
12	Kenny Lofton (W)	.25
13	Jim Thome	.30
14	Dante Bichette (W)	.25
15	Andres Galarraga	.10
16	Gary Sheffield	.25
17	Hideo Nomo (W)	.40
18	Mike Piazza (W)	1.25
19	Derek Jeter (W)	2.00
20	Bernie Williams	.10
21	Mark McGwire (W)	1.50
22	Ken Caminiti (W)	.25
23	Tony Gwynn (W)	1.00
24	Barry Bonds (W)	2.00
25	Jay Buhner (W)	.25
26	Ken Griffey Jr. (W)	1.25
27	Alex Rodriguez (W)	1.50
28	Juan Gonzalez (W)	.40
29	Dean Palmer (W)	.25
30	Roger Clemens (W)	1.00

Predictor Prize Cards

Persons who redeemed winning Predictor scratch-off cards prior to the Nov. 22, 1997 deadline received a premium version of that player's card. A $2 per card handling fee was charged. The Predictor prize cards are in a format similar to the scratch-off cards, with a red background on front and back depicting the motif of a baseball score card. The prize cards are printed on plastic in 3-1/2" x 2-1/2" format. Fronts have a player portrait photo at left. At right is a large semi-circular mirrored window with an action photo visible when held to the light. Backs have a few stats, copyright data, logos, etc., with a reverse image in the window. Card fronts were covered with a sheet of peel-off protection plastic. The prize cards are numbered on back with a "P" prefix.

		NM/M
Complete Set (22):		35.00
Common Player:		.60
3	Greg Maddux	2.50
4	Fred McGriff	.60
5	John Smoltz	.60
6	Brady Anderson	.60
7	Cal Ripken Jr.	5.00
8	Mo Vaughn	.60
11	Frank Thomas	1.75
12	Kenny Lofton	.60
14	Dante Bichette	.60
17	Hideo Nomo	1.00
18	Mike Piazza	3.00
19	Derek Jeter	5.00
21	Mark McGwire	4.00
22	Ken Caminiti	.60
23	Tony Gwynn	2.50
24	Barry Bonds	5.00
25	Jay Buhner	.60
26	Ken Griffey Jr.	3.00
27	Alex Rodriguez	4.00
28	Juan Gonzalez	1.00
29	Dean Palmer	.60
30	Roger Clemens	2.75

Rock Solid Foundation

The 20-card, regular-sized set was inserted every seven packs of 1997 Upper Deck baseball. The card fronts feature rainbow foil with the player's name in silver foil along the top border. The team logo appears in gold foil in the lower right corner with "Rock Solid Foundation" also printed in gold foil over

a marbled background. The card backs have the same marbled background with a close-up shot on the upper half. A short text is also included and the cards are numbered with the "RS" prefix.

		NM/M
Complete Set (20):		7.50
Common Player:		.15
1	Alex Rodriguez	1.50
2	Rey Ordonez	.15
3	Derek Jeter	2.00
4	Darin Erstad	.35
5	Chipper Jones	1.25
6	Johnny Damon	.35
7	Ryan Klesko	.15
8	Charles Johnson	.15
9	Andy Pettitte	.30
10	Manny Ramirez	.75
11	Ivan Rodriguez	.65
12	Jason Kendall	.15
13	Rondell White	.15
14	Alex Ochoa	.15
15	Javy Lopez	.15
16	Pedro Martinez	.75
17	Carlos Delgado	.15
18	Paul Wilson	.15
19	Alan Benes	.15
20	Raul Mondesi	.15

Run Producers

A 24-card insert found in Series II, Run Producers salutes the top offensive players in the game. Cards were inserted 1:69 packs. Die-cut into a shield shape, the cards have an action photo in a home-plate shaped center section and several colors of foil highlights. Backs have recent stats and career highlights. Cards are numbered with a "RP" prefix.

		NM/M
Complete Set (24):		45.00
Common Player:		.50
1	Ken Griffey Jr.	5.00
2	Barry Bonds	7.50
3	Albert Belle	.50
4	Mark McGwire	6.00
5	Frank Thomas	3.00
6	Juan Gonzalez	1.50
7	Brady Anderson	.50
8	Andres Galarraga	.50
9	Rafael Palmeiro	2.50
10	Alex Rodriguez	6.00
11	Jay Buhner	.50
12	Gary Sheffield	1.50
13	Sammy Sosa	4.00
14	Dante Bichette	.50
15	Mike Piazza	5.00
16	Manny Ramirez	.50
17	Kenny Lofton	.50
18	Mo Vaughn	.50
19	Tim Salmon	.50
20	Chipper Jones	.50
21	Jim Thome	2.00
22	Ken Caminiti	.50
23	Jeff Bagwell	3.00
24	Paul Molitor	3.00

Star Attractions

These die-cut cards were inserted one per pack of retail "Memorabila Madness" Collector's Choice (#11-20) and Upper Deck

(#1-10) cards. Fronts have action photos, backs have portrait photos. A gold version of the inserts was exclusive to retail packaging.

		NM/M
Complete Set (20):		30.00
Common Player:		.30
Gold:		1.5X
1	Ken Griffey Jr.	3.00
2	Barry Bonds	5.00
3	Jeff Bagwell	2.50
4	Nomar Garciaparra	2.50
5	Tony Gwynn	2.50
6	Roger Clemens	2.75
7	Chipper Jones	2.50
8	Tino Martinez	.30
9	Albert Belle	.30
10	Kenny Lofton	.30
11	Alex Rodriguez	4.00
12	Mark McGwire	4.00
13	Cal Ripken Jr.	5.00
14	Larry Walker	.30
15	Mike Piazza	3.00
16	Frank Thomas	2.00
17	Juan Gonzalez	.65
18	Greg Maddux	2.50
19	Jose Cruz Jr.	.30
20	Mo Vaughn	.30

Ticket to Stardom

The 20-card, regular-sized, die-cut set was inserted every 34 packs of 1997 Upper Deck baseball. Card fronts have a gold-foil border on three sides with a portrait and action photo. Half of the player's league emblem appears on either the left or right border of the horizontal cards, as two cards can be placed together to form a "ticket." The card backs feature an in-depth text with the same headshot as the card front and are numbered with the "TS" prefix.

		NM/M
Complete Set (20):		35.00
Common Player:		.75
1	Chipper Jones	5.00
2	Jermaine Dye	.75
3	Rey Ordonez	.75
4	Alex Ochoa	.75
5	Derek Jeter	7.50
6	Ruben Rivera	.75
7	Billy Wagner	.75
8	Jason Kendall	.75
9	Darin Erstad	1.00
10	Alex Rodriguez	6.00
11	Bob Abreu	.75
12	Richard Hidalgo	.75
13	Karim Garcia	1.00
14	Andruw Jones	4.00
15	Carlos Delgado	1.50
16	Rocky Coppinger	.75
17	Jeff D'Amico	.75
18	Johnny Damon	2.00
19	John Wasdin	.75
20	Manny Ramirez	4.00

Ticket to Stardom Retail

Double-size "full ticket" versions of Upper Deck's Series 1 Ticket to Stardom inserts were produced as an incentive for collectors to buy a boxed three-pack of Collector's Choice cards in a special retail-only packaging. Unlike the insert Ticket cards which feature only one player and measure 3-1/2" x 2-1/2", the retail version measures 5" x 2-1/2" and features two players. The basic format of the retail cards follows the inserts, with gold-foil background, a vignetted player portrait at one end with an action photo toward center and a league logo at center. Arrangement of graphics on the retail ticket prevent unscrupulous persons from cutting them in half and passing them off as the more valuable insert cards. Backs repeat the player portrait photo and present a career summary. Cards are numbered in the upper-left

corner. Seven players were dropped from the original Ticket checklist and replaced in the retail issue with new faces. Cards are numbered with a "TS" prefix.

		NM/M
Complete Set (10):		24.00
Common Player:		1.50
1	Chipper Jones, Andruw Jones	4.00
2	Rey Ordonez, Kevin Orie	1.50
3	Derek Jeter, Nomar Garciaparra	6.00
4	Billy Wagner, Jason Kendall	1.50
5	Darin Erstad, Alex Rodriguez	5.00
6	Bob Abreu, Jose Guillen	1.50
7	Wilton Guerrero, Vladimir Guerrero	3.00
8	Carlos Delgado, Rocky Coppinger	2.00
9	Jason Dickson, Johnny Damon	2.00
10	Bartolo Colon, Manny Ramirez	3.00

Ken Griffey Jr. Highlight Reel

Using its trademarked Diamond Vision technology to provide action scenes on these 5" x 3-1/2" plastic cards. Each card has two scenes which go into action as the angle of vision is changed. Cards were sold in retail outlets in plastic blister packs at a suggested $9.99 price.

		NM/M
Complete Set (5):		12.50
Common Card:		3.00
1	Record Setter (Ken Griffey Jr.)	3.00
2	Long Distance Connection (Ken Griffey Jr.)	3.00
3	Home Run Derby (Ken Griffey Jr.)	3.00
4	Swing for the Ages (Ken Griffey Jr.)	3.00
5	Postseason Power (Ken Griffey Jr.)	3.00

Tony Gwynn Commemorative

Tony Gwynn's record-tying eighth batting title in 1997 is commemorated on this 3-1/2" x 4-7/8" card marketed by UD Authenticated. The card has a batting pose on front with a die-cut background of bats citing the year and average of each of his batting titles. The back has three color photos and is numbered within an edition of 2,500.

	NM/M
Tony Gwynn	7.50

Home Team Heroes

These large-format cards were issued both as a 12-card boxed set (original price about $20) and as a blister-pack insert to enhance the sales of special Collector's Choice team sets at Wal-Mart. Each $4.99 pack contains a 14-card team set and a Home Team Heroes card of one of 12 teams, plus a random assortment of Collector's Choice cards. The Heroes cards are 5" x 3-1/2" with a die-cut pattern at top. Fronts are rendered in team colors with two player action photos superimposed on a background of the players' home ballpark. The ballpark scene is executed in etched silver foil and there are silver-foil graphics around the card front. Backs are conventionally printed with small photos and a few sentences about each player.

		NM/M
Complete Set (12):		10.00
Common Player:		.50
1	Alex Rodriguez, Ken Griffey Jr.	2.00
2	Bernie Williams, Derek Jeter	2.50
3	Bernard Gilkey, Randy Hundley	.50
4	Hideo Nomo, Mike Piazza	1.50
5	Andruw Jones, Chipper Jones	1.00
6	John Smoltz, Greg Maddux	1.00
7	Mike Mussina, Cal Ripken Jr.	2.50
8	Andres Galarraga, Dante Bichette	.50
9	Juan Gonzalez, Ivan Rodriguez	.65
10	Albert Belle, Frank Thomas	.75
11	Jim Thome, Manny Ramirez	.75
12	Ken Caminiti, Tony Gwynn	1.00

Jackie Robinson Jumbos

The nine Jackie Robinson commemorative cards which lead off the '97 Upper Deck set were also issued in a large-format (3-1/2" x 5") version as a complete boxed set. The jumbos are printed in sepia tones on gold-foil backgrounds and, like the standard-size cards, are highlighted with silver-foil graphics on front. Backs are also identical to the regular cards. Complete sets only were sold in a gold-foil stamped box with the 50th anniversary logo.

		NM/M
Complete Set (10):		13.50
Common Player:		2.00
1	The Beginnings (Jackie Robinson)	2.00
2	Breaking the Barrier (Jackie Robinson)	2.00
3	The MVP Season (Jackie Robinson)	2.00
4	The '51 Season (Jackie Robinson)	2.00
5	The '52 and '53 Seasons (Jackie Robinson)	2.00
6	The '54 Season (Jackie Robinson)	2.00
7	The '55 Season (Jackie Robinson)	2.00
8	The '56 Season (Jackie Robinson)	2.00
9	The Hall of Fame (Jackie Robinson)	2.00
--	Checklist	.10

Jackie Robinson Tribute

This retail exclusive card commemorates the 50th anniversary of Robinson's major league debut. The 5" x 3-1/2" card has a tombstone contour top edge and a sepia photo on front of Robinson at bat. Also on front are 50th anniversary and UD logos and a large gold-foil facsimile autograph. Back has a photo of Robinson sliding into home plate, his career stats and a serial number from within an edition of 5,000.

	NM/M
Jackie Robinson	3.50

1997 Upper Deck UD3

Released in April, this 60-card set is broken down into three different 20-card subsets, each utilizing a different print technology. There are 20 PROmotion cards (Light F/X cards featuring a special foil stock), 20 Future Impact cards (Cel-Chrome cards that feature a 3-D image on transparent chromium), and 20 Homerun Heroes (Electric Wood cards printed on an embossed wood/paper stock). Cards were sold in three-card packs (with one subset card per pack) for $3.99 each. Inserts include Superb Signatures, Generation Next and Marquee Attraction.

		NM/M
Complete Set (60):		30.00
Common Player:		.15
Pack (3):		1.50
Wax Box (24):		30.00
1	Mark McGwire	2.50
2	Brady Anderson	.15
3	Ken Griffey Jr.	2.00
4	Albert Belle	.15
5	Andres Galarraga	.15
6	Juan Gonzalez	.40
7	Jay Buhner	.15
8	Mo Vaughn	.15
9	Barry Bonds	3.00
10	Gary Sheffield	.40
11	Todd Hundley	.15
12	Ellis Burks	.15
13	Ken Caminiti	.15
14	Vinny Castilla	.15
15	Sammy Sosa	1.50
16	Frank Thomas	.75
17	Rafael Palmeiro	.65
18	Mike Piazza	2.00
19	Matt Williams	.15
20	Eddie Murray	.75
21	Roger Clemens	1.75
22	Tim Salmon	.15
23	Robin Ventura	.15
24	Ron Gant	.15
25	Cal Ripken Jr.	3.00
26	Bernie Williams	.15
27	Hideo Nomo	.40
28	Ivan Rodriguez	.65
29	John Smoltz	.15
30	Paul Molitor	.75
31	Greg Maddux	1.50
32	Raul Mondesi	.15
33	Roberto Alomar	.25
34	Barry Larkin	.15
35	Tony Gwynn	1.50
36	Jim Thome	.60
37	Kenny Lofton	.15
38	Jeff Bagwell	.75
39	Ozzie Smith	1.50
40	Kirby Puckett	1.50
41	Andruw Jones	.75
42	Vladimir Guerrero	.75
43	Edgar Renteria	.15
44	Luis Castillo	.15
45	Darin Erstad	.30
46	Nomar Garciaparra	1.50
47	Todd Greene	.15
48	Jason Kendall	.15
49	Rey Ordonez	.15
50	Alex Rodriguez	2.50
51	Manny Ramirez	.75
52	Todd Walker	.15
53	Ruben Rivera	.15
54	Andy Pettitte	.30
55	Derek Jeter	3.00
56	Todd Hollandsworth	.15
57	Rocky Coppinger	.15
58	Scott Rolen	.60
59	Jermaine Dye	.15
60	Chipper Jones	1.50

Generation Next

A 20-card insert saluting the game's up-and-coming stars with two different photos of the player on each card front. Odds of finding these cards were 1:11 packs. Cards are numbered with a "GN" prefix.

		NM/M
Complete Set (20):		35.00
Common Player:		1.00
1	Alex Rodriguez	5.00
2	Vladimir Guerrero	2.50
3	Luis Castillo	1.00
4	Rey Ordonez	1.00
5	Andruw Jones	2.50
6	Darin Erstad	1.25
7	Edgar Renteria	1.00
8	Jason Kendall	1.00
9	Jermaine Dye	1.00
10	Chipper Jones	3.00
11	Rocky Coppinger	1.00
12	Andy Pettitte	1.25
13	Todd Greene	1.00
14	Todd Hollandsworth	1.00
15	Derek Jeter	6.00
16	Ruben Rivera	1.00
17	Todd Walker	1.00
18	Nomar Garciaparra	3.00
19	Scott Rolen	2.00
20	Manny Ramirez	2.50

Marquee Attraction

The game's top names are featured in this insert set, inserted 1:144 packs. Cards featured a peel-off protector that would expose a holographic image on the card fronts. Cards are numbered with a "MA" prefix.

		NM/M
Complete Set (10):		40.00
Common Player:		1.25
1	Ken Griffey Jr.	6.00
2	Mark McGwire	7.50
3	Juan Gonzalez	1.75
4	Barry Bonds	9.00
5	Frank Thomas	2.50
6	Albert Belle	1.25
7	Mike Piazza	6.00
8	Cal Ripken Jr.	9.00
9	Mo Vaughn	1.25
10	Alex Rodriguez	7.50

Superb Signatures

Autographed cards of Ken Griffey Jr., Ken Caminiti, Vladimir Guerrero, and Derek Jeter were inserted 1:1,500 packs.

		NM/M
Complete Set (4):		450.00
Common Autograph:		15.00
1	Ken Caminiti	45.00
2	Ken Griffey Jr.	150.00
3	Vladimir Guerrero	50.00
4	Derek Jeter	225.00

Pepsi Mariners Insert

Though unmarked as such, this set was sponsored by Pepsi with single cards inserted into 12-packs of soda in the Northwest. Format of the cards is similar to UD's regular 1996 issue, with borderless color photos on front and back. At bottom-front is a Mariners-blue foil area with the player identification. Backs differ from the regular '96 UD cards in the use of a "M" prefix to the card number.

		NM/M
Complete Set (19):		12.00
Common Player:		.25
1	Joey Cora	.25
2	Ken Griffey Jr.	5.00
3	Jay Buhner	.50
4	Alex Rodriguez	6.00
5	Norm Charlton	.25
6	Edgar Martinez	.50
7	Paul Sorrento	.25
8	Randy Johnson	2.00
9	Rich Amaral	.25
10	Russ Davis	.25
11	Bob Wolcott	.25
12	Jamie Moyer	.25
13	Bob Wells	.25
14	Makoto Suzuki	.25
15	Dan Wilson	.25
16	Tim Davis	.25
17	Bobby Ayala	.25
18	Salomon Torres	.25
19	Raul Ibanez	.25

1997 Upper Deck/Pepsi Mariners SGA

This team set, sponsored by Pepsi, was a stadium give-away to the first 20,000 fans attending the July 12 game at the Kingdome. Format of the cards is similar to UD's regular 1996 issue, with borderless color photos on front and back. At bottom-front is a Mariners-blue foil area with the player identification. Backs differ from the regular '96 UD cards in the use of a "P" prefix to the card number and the inclusion of a Pepsi logo at lower-left.

		NM/M
Complete Set (21):		12.00
Common Player:		.25
1	Joey Cora	.25
2	Ken Griffey Jr.	5.00
3	Jay Buhner	.50
4	Alex Rodriguez	6.00
5	Norm Charlton	.25
6	Edgar Martinez	.50
7	Paul Sorrento	.25
8	Randy Johnson	2.00
9	Rich Amaral	.25
10	Russ Davis	.25
11	Greg McCarthy	.25
12	Jamie Moyer	.25
13	Jeff Fassero	.25
14	Scott Sanders	.25
15	Dan Wilson	.25
16	Mike Blowers	.25
17	Bobby Ayala	.25
18	Brent Gates	.25
19	John Marzano	.25
20	Lou Piniella	.25
---	Pepsi Header Card/Coupon	.05

Shimano

Two ballplayers are included with four professional fishermen in this set produced by Upper Deck as a premium with the purchase of Shimano fishing reels. Fronts have pictures of the fishermen displaying their trophy. Backs have a portrait photo, baseball and fishing stats and data.

		NM/M
5	Jay Buhner	3.00
6	Tony Gwynn	30.00

1998 Upper Deck

Upper Deck Baseball was released in three series. Series 1 consists of 270 base cards, with five subsets. Inserts included A Piece of the Action, Amazing Greats, National Pride, Ken Griffey Jr.'s Home Run Chronicles and 10th Anniversary Preview. The 270-card Series 2 also has five subsets. Inserts include Prime Nine, Ken Griffey Jr.'s Home Run Chronicles, Tape Measure Titans, Blue Chip Prospects, Clearly Dominant and A Piece of the Action. The third series, Upper Deck Rookie Edition, has a 210-card base set. Cards #601-630, the Eminent Prestige subset, are short-printed, about one per four packs. Mike Piazza's card in Series 3 can be found depicting him either as a Marlin or a Met. Insert sets were Ken Griffey Jr. Game Jersey, Game Jersey Rookie Cards, Unparalleled, Destination Stardom, All-Star Credentials and Retrospectives.

		NM/M
Complete Set (750):		100.00
Complete Series 1 Set (270):		25.00
Complete Series 2 Set (270):		25.00
Complete Series 3 Set (210):		75.00
Common Emminent Prestige (601-630):		.25
Common Player:		.05
Series 1 or 2 Pack (12):		1.50
Series 3 Pack (10):		1.50
Series 1 or 2 Wax Box (24):		35.00
Series 3 Wax Box (24):		35.00
1	Tino Martinez (History in the Making)	.05
2	Jimmy Key (History in the Making)	.05
3	Jay Buhner (History in the Making)	.05
4	Mark Gardner (History in the Making)	.05
5	Greg Maddux (History in the Making)	.25
6	Pedro Martinez (History in the Making)	.20
7	Hideo Nomo, Shigetosi Hasegawa (History in the Making)	.25
8	Sammy Sosa (History in the Making)	.35
9	Mark McGwire (Griffey Hot List)	.50
10	Ken Griffey Jr. (Griffey Hot List)	.45
11	Larry Walker (Griffey Hot List)	.05
12	Tino Martinez (Griffey Hot List)	.05
13	Mike Piazza (Griffey Hot List)	.40
14	Jose Cruz, Jr. (Griffey Hot List)	.05
15	Tony Gwynn (Griffey Hot List)	.25

No.	Player	Price
16	Greg Maddux (Griffey Hot List)	.25
17	Roger Clemens (Griffey Hot List)	.35
18	Alex Rodriguez (Griffey Hot List)	.50
19	Shigetosi Hasegawa	.05
20	Eddie Murray	.50
21	Jason Dickson	.05
22	Darin Erstad	.25
23	Chuck Finley	.05
24	Dave Hollins	.05
25	Garret Anderson	.05
26	Michael Tucker	.05
27	Kenny Lofton	.05
28	Javier Lopez	.05
29	Fred McGriff	.05
30	Greg Maddux	.65
31	Jeff Blauser	.05
32	John Smoltz	.05
33	Mark Wohlers	.05
34	Scott Erickson	.05
35	Jimmy Key	.05
36	Harold Baines	.05
37	Randy Myers	.05
38	B.J. Surhoff	.05
39	Eric Davis	.05
40	Rafael Palmeiro	.35
41	Jeffrey Hammonds	.05
42	Mo Vaughn	.05
43	Tom Gordon	.05
44	Tim Naehring	.05
45	Darren Bragg	.05
46	Aaron Sele	.05
47	Troy O'Leary	.05
48	John Valentin	.05
49	Doug Glanville	.05
50	Ryne Sandberg	.65
51	Steve Trachsel	.05
52	Mark Grace	.05
53	Kevin Foster	.05
54	Kevin Tapani	.05
55	Kevin Orie	.05
56	Lyle Mouton	.05
57	Ray Durham	.05
58	Jaime Navarro	.05
59	Mike Cameron	.05
60	Albert Belle	.05
61	Doug Drabek	.05
62	Chris Snopek	.05
63	Eddie Taubensee	.05
64	Terry Pendleton	.05
65	Barry Larkin	.05
66	Willie Greene	.05
67	Deion Sanders	.05
68	Pokey Reese	.05
69	Jeff Shaw	.05
70	Jim Thome	.15
71	Orel Hershiser	.05
72	Omar Vizquel	.05
73	Brian Giles	.05
74	David Justice	.05
75	Bartolo Colon	.05
76	Sandy Alomar Jr.	.05
77	Neifi Perez	.05
78	Eric Young	.05
79	Vinny Castilla	.05
80	Dante Bichette	.05
81	Quinton McCracken	.05
82	Jamey Wright	.05
83	John Thomson	.05
84	Damion Easley	.05
85	Justin Thompson	.05
86	Willie Blair	.05
87	Raul Casanova	.05
88	Bobby Higginson	.05
89	Bubba Trammell	.05
90	Tony Clark	.05
91	Livan Hernandez	.05
92	Charles Johnson	.05
93	Edgar Renteria	.05
94	Alex Fernandez	.05
95	Gary Sheffield	.30
96	Moises Alou	.05
97	Tony Saunders	.05
98	Robb Nen	.05
99	Darryl Kile	.05
100	Craig Biggio	.05
101	Chris Holt	.05
102	Bob Abreu	.10
103	Luis Gonzalez	.05
104	Billy Wagner	.05
105	Brad Ausmus	.05
106	Chili Davis	.05
107	Tim Belcher	.05
108	Dean Palmer	.05
109	Jeff King	.05
110	Jose Rosado	.05
111	Mike Macfarlane	.05
112	Jay Bell	.05
113	Todd Worrell	.05
114	Chan Ho Park	.05
115	Raul Mondesi	.05
116	Brett Butler	.05
117	Greg Gagne	.05
118	Hideo Nomo	.05
119	Todd Zeile	.05
120	Eric Karros	.05
121	Cal Eldred	.05
122	Jeff D'Amico	.05
123	Antone Williamson	.05
124	Doug Jones	.05
125	Dave Nilsson	.05
126	Gerald Williams	.05
127	Fernando Vina	.05
128	Ron Coomer	.05
129	Matt Lawton	.05
130	Paul Molitor	.50
131	Todd Walker	.05
132	Rick Aguilera	.05
133	Brad Radke	.05
134	Bob Tewksbury	.05
135	Vladimir Guerrero	.50
136	Tony Gwynn (Define The Game)	.25
137	Roger Clemens (Define The Game)	.35
138	Dennis Eckersley (Define The Game)	.15
139	Brady Anderson (Define The Game)	.05
140	Ken Griffey Jr. (Define The Game)	.40
141	Derek Jeter (Define The Game)	.75
142	Ken Caminiti (Define The Game)	.05
143	Frank Thomas (Define The Game)	.20
144	Barry Bonds (Define The Game)	.75
145	Cal Ripken Jr. (Define The Game)	.75
146	Alex Rodriguez (Define The Game)	.50
147	Greg Maddux (Define The Game)	.25
148	Kenny Lofton (Define The Game)	.05
149	Mike Piazza (Define The Game)	.40
150	Mark McGwire (Define The Game)	.50
151	Andruw Jones (Define The Game)	.20
152	Rusty Greer (Define The Game)	.05
153	F.P. Santangelo (Define The Game)	.05
154	Mike Lansing	.05
155	Lee Smith	.05
156	Carlos Perez	.05
157	Pedro Martinez	.50
158	Ryan McGuire	.05
159	F.P. Santangelo	.05
160	Rondell White	.05
161	Takashi Kashiwada RC	.05
162	Butch Huskey	.05
163	Edgardo Alfonzo	.05
164	John Franco	.05
165	Todd Hundley	.05
166	Rey Ordonez	.05
167	Armando Reynoso	.05
168	John Olerud	.05
169	Bernie Williams	.05
170	Andy Pettitte	.15
171	Wade Boggs	.05
172	Paul O'Neill	.05
173	Cecil Fielder	.05
174	Charlie Hayes	.05
175	David Cone	.05
176	Hideki Irabu	.05
177	Mark Bellhorn	.05
178	Steve Karsay	.05
179	Damon Mashore	.05
180	Jason McDonald	.05
181	Scott Spiezio	.05
182	Ariel Prieto	.05
183	Jason Giambi	.30
184	Wendell Magee	.05
185	Rico Brogna	.05
186	Garrett Stephenson	.05
187	Wayne Gomes	.05
188	Ricky Bottalico	.05
189	Mickey Morandini	.05
190	Mike Lieberthal	.05
191	Kevin Polcovich RC	.05
192	Francisco Cordova	.05
193	Kevin Young	.05
194	Jon Lieber	.05
195	Kevin Elster	.05
196	Tony Womack	.05
197	Lou Collier	.05
198	Mike Defelice RC	.05
199	Gary Gaetti	.05
200	Dennis Eckersley	.40
201	Alan Benes	.05
202	Willie McGee	.05
203	Ron Gant	.05
204	Fernando Valenzuela	.05
205	Mark McGwire	1.00
206	Archi Cianfrocco	.05
207	Andy Ashby	.05
208	Steve Finley	.05
209	Quilvio Veras	.05
210	Ken Caminiti	.05
211	Rickey Henderson	.50
212	Joey Hamilton	.05
213	Derrek Lee	.30
214	Bill Mueller	.05
215	Shawn Estes	.05
216	J.T. Snow	.05
217	Mark Gardner	.05
218	Terry Mulholland	.05
219	Dante Powell	.05
220	Jeff Kent	.05
221	Jamie Moyer	.05
222	Joey Cora	.05
223	Jeff Fassero	.05
224	Dennis Martinez	.05
225	Ken Griffey Jr.	.75
226	Edgar Martinez	.05
227	Russ Davis	.05
228	Dan Wilson	.05
229	Will Clark	.05
230	Ivan Rodriguez	.40
231	Benji Gil	.05
232	Lee Stevens	.05
233	Mickey Tettleton	.05
234	Julio Santana	.05
235	Rusty Greer	.05
236	Bobby Witt	.05
237	Ed Sprague	.05
238	Pat Hentgen	.05
239	Kevin Escobar	.05
240	Joe Carter	.05
241	Carlos Delgado	.05
242	Shannon Stewart	.05
243	Benito Santiago	.05
244	Tino Martinez (Season Highlights)	.05
245	Ken Griffey Jr. (Season Highlights)	.40
246	Kevin Brown (Season Highlights)	.05
247	Ryne Sandberg (Season Highlights)	.35
248	Mo Vaughn (Season Highlights)	.20
249	Darryl Hamilton (Season Highlights)	.05
250	Randy Johnson (Season Highlights)	.20
251	Steve Finley (Season Highlights)	.05
252	Bobby Higginson (Season Highlights)	.05
253	Brett Tomko/SR	.05
254	Mark Kotsay/SR	.05
255	Jose Guillen/SR	.05
256	Elieser Marrero/SR	.05
257	Dennis Reyes/SR	.05
258	Richie Sexson/SR	.05
259	Pat Cline/SR	.05
260	Todd Helton/SR	.50
261	Juan Melo/SR	.05
262	Matt Morris/SR	.05
263	Jeremi Gonzalez/SR	.05
264	Jeff Abbott/SR	.05
265	Aaron Boone/SR	.05
266	Todd Dunwoody/SR	.05
267	Jaret Wright/SR	.05
268	Derrick Gibson/SR	.05
269	Mario Valdez/SR	.05
270	Fernando Tatis/SR	.05
271	Craig Counsell/SR	.05
272	Brad Rigby/SR	.05
273	Danny Clyburn/SR	.05
274	Brian Rose/SR	.05
275	Miguel Tejada/SR	.15
276	Jason Varitek/SR	.05
277	David Dellucci/SR RC	.15
278	Michael Coleman/SR	.05
279	Adam Riggs/SR	.05
280	Ben Grieve/SR	.05
281	Brad Fullmer/SR	.05
282	Ken Cloude/SR	.05
283	Tom Evans/SR	.05
284	Kevin Millwood/SR RC	.05
285	Paul Konerko/SR	.15
286	Juan Encarnacion/SR	.05
287	Chris Carpenter/SR	.05
288	Tom Fordham/SR	.05
289	Gary DiSarcina	.05
290	Tim Salmon	.05
291	Troy Percival	.05
292	Todd Greene	.05
293	Ken Hill	.05
294	Dennis Springer	.05
295	Jim Edmonds	.05
296	Allen Watson	.05
297	Brian Anderson	.05
298	Keith Lockhart	.05
299	Tom Glavine	.20
300	Chipper Jones	.75
301	Randall Simon	.05
302	Mark Lemke	.05
303	Ryan Klesko	.05
304	Denny Neagle	.05
305	Andruw Jones	.50
306	Mike Mussina	.30
307	Brady Anderson	.05
308	Chris Hoiles	.05
309	Mike Bordick	.05
310	Cal Ripken Jr.	1.50
311	Geronimo Berroa	.05
312	Armando Benitez	.05
313	Roberto Alomar	.25
314	Tim Wakefield	.05
315	Reggie Jefferson	.05
316	Jeff Frye	.05
317	Scott Hatteberg	.05
318	Steve Avery	.05
319	Robinson Checo	.05
320	Nomar Garciaparra	.65
321	Lance Johnson	.05
322	Tyler Houston	.05
323	Mark Clark	.05
324	Terry Adams	.05
325	Sammy Sosa	.65
326	Scott Servais	.05
327	Manny Alexander	.05
328	Norberto Martin	.05
329	Scott Eyre RC	.05
330	Frank Thomas	.50
331	Robin Ventura	.05
332	Matt Karchner	.05
333	Keith Foulke	.05
334	James Baldwin	.05
335	Chris Stynes	.05
336	Bret Boone	.05
337	Jon Nunnally	.05
338	Dave Burba	.05
339	Eduardo Perez	.05
340	Reggie Sanders	.05
341	Mike Remlinger	.05
342	Pat Watkins	.05
343	Chad Ogea	.05
344	John Smiley	.05
345	Kenny Lofton	.05
346	Jose Mesa	.05
347	Charles Nagy	.05
348	Bruce Aven	.05
349	Enrique Wilson	.05
350	Manny Ramirez	.50
351	Jerry DiPoto	.05
352	Ellis Burks	.05
353	Kirt Manwaring	.05
354	Vinny Castilla	.05
355	Larry Walker	.05
356	Kevin Ritz	.05
357	Pedro Astacio	.05
358	Scott Sanders	.05
359	Deivi Cruz	.05
360	Brian L. Hunter	.05
361	Pedro Martinez (History in the Making)	.20
362	Tom Glavine (History in the Making)	.05
363	Willie McGee (History in the Making)	.05
364	J.T. Snow (History in the Making)	.05
365	Rusty Greer (History in the Making)	.05
366	Mike Grace (History in the Making)	.05
367	Tony Clark (History in the Making)	.05
368	Ben Grieve (History in the Making)	.05
369	Gary Sheffield (History in the Making)	.10
370	Joe Oliver	.05
371	Todd Jones	.05
372	Frank Catalanotto RC	.10
373	Brian Moehler	.05
374	Cliff Floyd	.05
375	Bobby Bonilla	.05
376	Al Leiter	.05
377	Josh Booty	.05
378	Darren Daulton	.05
379	Jay Powell	.05
380	Felix Heredia	.05
381	Jim Eisenreich	.05
382	Richard Hidalgo	.05
383	Mike Hampton	.05
384	Shane Reynolds	.05
385	Jeff Bagwell	.50
386	Derek Bell	.05
387	Ricky Gutierrez	.05
388	Bill Spiers	.05
389	Jose Offerman	.05
390	Johnny Damon	.25
391	Jermaine Dye	.05
392	Jeff Montgomery	.05
393	Glendon Rusch	.05
394	Mike Sweeney	.05
395	Kevin Appier	.05
396	Joe Vitiello	.05
397	Ramon Martinez	.05
398	Darren Dreifort	.05
399	Wilton Guerrero	.05
400	Mike Piazza	.75
401	Eddie Murray	.50
402	Ismael Valdes	.05
403	Todd Hollandsworth	.05
404	Mark Loretta	.05
405	Jeromy Burnitz	.05
406	Jeff Cirillo	.05
407	Scott Karl	.05
408	Mike Matheny	.05
409	Jose Valentin	.05
410	John Jaha	.05
411	Terry Steinbach	.05
412	Torii Hunter	.05
413	Pat Meares	.05
414	Marty Cordova	.05
415	Jaret Wright (Postseason Headliners)	.05
416	Mike Mussina (Postseason Headliners)	.10
417	John Smoltz (Postseason Headliners)	.05
418	Devon White (Postseason Headliners)	.05
419	Denny Neagle (Postseason Headliners)	.05
420	Livan Hernandez (Postseason Headliners)	.05
421	Kevin Brown (Postseason Headliners)	.05
422	Marquis Grissom (Postseason Headliners)	.05
423	Mike Mussina (Postseason Headliners)	.10
424	Eric Davis (Postseason Headliners)	.05
425	Tony Fernandez (Postseason Headliners)	.05
426	Moises Alou (Postseason Headliners)	.05
427	Sandy Alomar Jr. (Postseason Headliners)	.05
428	Gary Sheffield (Postseason Headliners)	.10
429	Jaret Wright (Postseason Headliners)	.05
430	Livan Hernandez (Postseason Headliners)	.05
431	Chad Ogea (Postseason Headliners)	.05
432	Edgar Renteria (Postseason Headliners)	.05
433	LaTroy Hawkins	.05
434	Rich Robertson	.05
435	Chuck Knoblauch	.05
436	Jose Vidro	.05
437	Dustin Hermanson	.05
438	Jim Bullinger	.05
439	Orlando Cabrera/SR	.10
440	Vladimir Guerrero	.50
441	Ugueth Urbina	.05
442	Brian McRae	.05
443	Matt Franco	.05
444	Bobby Jones	.05
445	Bernard Gilkey	.05
446	Dave Mlicki	.05
447	Brian Bohanon	.05
448	Mel Rojas	.05
449	Tim Raines	.05
450	Derek Jeter	1.50
451	Roger Clemens (Upper Echelon)	.35
452	Nomar Garciaparra (Upper Echelon)	.35
453	Mike Piazza (Upper Echelon)	.40
454	Mark McGwire (Upper Echelon)	.50
455	Ken Griffey Jr. (Upper Echelon)	.40
456	Larry Walker (Upper Echelon)	.05
457	Alex Rodriguez (Upper Echelon)	.50
458	Tony Gwynn (Upper Echelon)	.25
459	Frank Thomas (Upper Echelon)	.20
460	Tino Martinez	.05
461	Chad Curtis	.05
462	Ramiro Mendoza	.05
463	Joe Girardi	.05
464	David Wells	.05
465	Mariano Rivera	.15
466	Willie Adams	.05
467	George Williams	.05
468	Dave Telgheder	.05
469	Dave Magadan	.05
470	Matt Stairs	.05
471	Billy Taylor	.05
472	Jimmy Haynes	.05
473	Gregg Jefferies	.05
474	Midre Cummings	.05
475	Curt Schilling	.15
476	Mike Grace	.05
477	Mark Leiter	.05
478	Matt Beech	.05
479	Scott Rolen	.35
480	Jason Kendall	.05
481	Esteban Loaiza	.05
482	Jermaine Allensworth	.05
483	Mark Smith	.05
484	Jason Schmidt	.05
485	Jose Guillen	.05
486	Al Martin	.05
487	Delino DeShields	.05
488	Todd Stottlemyre	.05
489	Brian Jordan	.05
490	Ray Lankford	.05
491	Matt Morris	.05
492	Royce Clayton	.05
493	John Mabry	.05
494	Wally Joyner	.05
495	Trevor Hoffman	.05
496	Chris Gomez	.05
497	Sterling Hitchcock	.05
498	Pete Smith	.05
499	Greg Vaughn	.05
500	Tony Gwynn	.65
501	Will Cunnane	.05
502	Darryl Hamilton	.05
503	Brian Johnson	.05
504	Kirk Rueter	.05
505	Barry Bonds	1.50
506	Osvaldo Fernandez	.05
507	Stan Javier	.05
508	Julian Tavarez	.05
509	Rich Aurilia	.05
510	Alex Rodriguez	1.00
511	David Segui	.05
512	Rich Amaral	.05
513	Raul Ibanez	.25
514	Jay Buhner	.05
515	Randy Johnson	.50
516	Heathcliff Slocumb	.05
517	Tony Saunders	.05
518	Kevin Elster	.05
519	John Burkett	.05
520	Juan Gonzalez	.25
521	John Wetteland	.05
522	Domingo Cedeno	.05
523	Darren Oliver	.05
524	Roger Pavlik	.05
525	Jose Cruz Jr.	.05
526	Woody Williams	.05
527	Alex Gonzalez	.05
528	Robert Person	.05
529	Juan Guzman	.05
530	Roger Clemens	.70
531	Shawn Green	.20
532	Cordova, Ricon, Smith (Season Highlights)	.05
533	Nomar Garciaparra (Season Highlights)	.35
534	Roger Clemens (Season Highlights)	.35
535	Mark McGwire (Season Highlights)	.50
536	Larry Walker (Season Highlights)	.05
537	Mike Piazza (Season Highlights)	.40
538	Curt Schilling (Season Highlights)	.05
539	Tony Gwynn (Season Highlights)	.25
540	Ken Griffey Jr. (Season Highlights)	.40
541	Carl Pavano/SR	.05
542	Shane Monahan/SR	.05
543	Gabe Kapler/SR RC	.25
544	Eric Milton/SR	.05
545	Gary Matthews Jr./SR RC	.05
546	Mike Kinkade/SR	.05
547	Ryan Christenson/SR RC	.10
548	Corey Koskie/SR RC	.25
549	Norm Hutchins/SR	.05
550	Russell Branyan/SR	.05
551	Masato Yoshii/SR RC	.25
552	Jesus Sanchez/SR RC	.05
553	Anthony Sanders/SR	.05
554	Edwin Diaz/SR	.05
555	Gabe Alvarez/SR	.05
556	Carlos Lee/SR RC	.25
557	Mike Darr/SR	.05
558	Kerry Wood/SR	.20
559	Carlos Guillen/SR	.05
560	Sean Casey/SR	.15
561	Manny Aybar/SR	.05
562	Octavio Dotel/SR	.05
563	Jarrod Washburn/SR	.05
564	Mark L. Johnson/SR	.05
565	Ramon Hernandez/SR	.05
566	Rich Butler/SR	.05
567	Mike Caruso/SR	.05
568	Cliff Politte/SR	.05
569	Scott Elarton/SR	.05
570	Magglio Ordonez/SR RC	1.50
571	Adam Butler/SR RC	.05
572	Marlon Anderson/SR	.05
573	Julio Ramirez/SR RC	.05
574	Darron Ingram/SR RC	.05
575	Bruce Chen/SR	.05
576	Steve Woodard/SR RC	.05
577	Hiram Bocachica/SR	.05
578	Kevin Witt/SR	.05
579	Javier Vazquez/SR	.10
580	Alex Gonzalez/SR	.05
581	Brian Powell/SR	.05
582	Wes Helms/SR	.05
583	Ron Wright/SR	.05
584	Rafael Medina/SR	.05
585	Daryle Ward/SR	.05
586	Geoff Jenkins/SR	.05
587	Preston Wilson/SR	.10
588	Jim Chamblee/SR RC	.05
589	Mike Lowell/SR RC	2.00
590	A.J. Hinch/SR	.05
591	Francisco Cordero/SR RC	.10
592	Rolando Arrojo/SR RC	.25
593	Braden Looper/SR	.05
594	Sidney Ponson/SR	.05
595	Matt Clement/SR	.05
596	Carlton Loewer/SR	.05
597	Brian Meadows/SR	.05
598	Danny Klassen/SR	.05
599	Larry Sutton/SR	.15
600	Travis Lee/SR	.15
601	Randy Johnson (Eminent Prestige)	1.50
602	Greg Maddux (Eminent Prestige)	2.00
603	Roger Clemens (Eminent Prestige)	2.25
604	Jaret Wright (Eminent Prestige)	.25
605	Mike Piazza (Eminent Prestige)	2.50
606	Tino Martinez (Eminent Prestige)	.25
607	Frank Thomas (Eminent Prestige)	1.50
608	Mo Vaughn (Eminent Prestige)	.25
609	Todd Helton (Eminent Prestige)	1.00
610	Mark McGwire (Eminent Prestige)	3.00
611	Jeff Bagwell (Eminent Prestige)	1.50
612	Travis Lee (Eminent Prestige)	.40
613	Scott Rolen (Eminent Prestige)	1.00
614	Cal Ripken Jr. (Eminent Prestige)	4.00
615	Chipper Jones (Eminent Prestige)	2.00
616	Nomar Garciaparra (Eminent Prestige)	2.00
617	Alex Rodriguez (Eminent Prestige)	3.00
618	Derek Jeter (Eminent Prestige)	4.00
619	Tony Gwynn (Eminent Prestige)	2.00
620	Ken Griffey Jr. (Eminent Prestige)	2.50
621	Kenny Lofton (Eminent Prestige)	.25
622	Juan Gonzalez (Eminent Prestige)	.75
623	Jose Cruz Jr. (Eminent Prestige)	.25
624	Larry Walker (Eminent Prestige)	.25

#	Player	Price
625	Barry Bonds (Eminent Prestige)	4.00
626	Ben Grieve (Eminent Prestige)	.25
627	Andruw Jones (Eminent Prestige)	1.50
628	Vladimir Guerrero (Eminent Prestige)	1.50
629	Paul Konerko (Eminent Prestige)	.50
630	Paul Molitor (Eminent Prestige)	1.50
631	Cecil Fielder	.05
632	Jack McDowell	.05
633	Mike James	.05
634	Brian Anderson	.05
635	Jay Bell	.05
636	Devon White	.05
637	Andy Stankiewicz	.05
638	Tony Batista	.05
639	Omar Daal	.05
640	Matt Williams	.05
641	Brent Brede	.05
642	Jorge Fabregas	.05
643	Karim Garcia	.10
644	Felix Rodriguez	.05
645	Andy Benes	.05
646	Willie Blair	.05
647	Jeff Suppan	.05
648	Yamil Benitez	.05
649	Walt Weiss	.05
650	Andres Galarraga	.05
651	Doug Drabek	.05
652	Ozzie Guillen	.05
653	Joe Carter	.05
654	Dennis Eckersley	.40
655	Pedro Martinez	.50
656	Jim Leyritz	.05
657	Henry Rodriguez	.05
658	Rod Beck	.05
659	Mickey Morandini	.05
660	Jeff Blauser	.05
661	Ruben Sierra	.05
662	Mike Sirotka	.05
663	Pete Harnisch	.05
664	Damian Jackson	.05
665	Dmitri Young	.05
666	Steve Cooke	.05
667	Geronimo Berroa	.05
668	Shawon Dunston	.05
669	Mike Jackson	.05
670	Travis Fryman	.05
671	Dwight Gooden	.05
672	Paul Assenmacher	.05
673	Eric Plunk	.05
674	Mike Lansing	.05
675	Darryl Kile	.05
676	Luis Gonzalez	.05
677	Frank Castillo	.05
678	Joe Randa	.05
679	Bip Roberts	.05
680	Derrek Lee	.30
681a	Mike Piazza (Marlins)	2.00
681b	Mike Piazza (Mets)	1.00
682	Sean Berry	.05
683	Ramon Garcia	.05
684	Carl Everett	.05
685	Moises Alou	.05
686	Hal Morris	.05
687	Jeff Conine	.05
688	Gary Sheffield	.25
689	Jose Vizcaino	.05
690	Charles Johnson	.05
691	Bobby Bonilla	.05
692	Marquis Grissom	.05
693	Alex Ochoa	.05
694	Mike Morgan	.05
695	Orlando Merced	.05
696	David Ortiz	.30
697	Brent Gates	.05
698	Otis Nixon	.05
699	Trey Moore	.05
700	Derrick May	.05
701	Rich Becker	.05
702	Al Leiter	.05
703	Chili Davis	.05
704	Scott Brosius	.05
705	Chuck Knoblauch	.05
706	Kenny Rogers	.05
707	Mike Blowers	.05
708	Mike Fetters	.05
709	Tom Candiotti	.05
710	Rickey Henderson	.50
711	Bob Abreu	.05
712	Mark Lewis	.05
713	Doug Glanville	.05
714	Desi Relaford	.05
715	Kent Mercker	.05
716	J. Kevin Brown	.05
717	James Mouton	.05
718	Mark Langston	.05
719	Greg Myers	.05
720	Orel Hershiser	.05
721	Charlie Hayes	.05
722	Robb Nen	.05
723	Glenallen Hill	.05
724	Tony Saunders	.05
725	Wade Boggs	.65
726	Kevin Stocker	.05
727	Wilson Alvarez	.05
728	Albie Lopez	.05
729	Dave Martinez	.05
730	Fred McGriff	.05
731	Quinton McCracken	.05
732	Bryan Rekar	.05
733	Paul Sorrento	.05
734	Roberto Hernandez	.05
735	Bubba Trammell	.05
736	Miguel Cairo	.05
737	John Flaherty	.05
738	Terrell Wade	.05
739	Roberto Kelly	.05
740	Mark Mclemore (McLemore)	.05
741	Danny Patterson	.05
742	Aaron Sele	.05
743	Tony Fernandez	.05
744	Randy Myers	.05
745	Jose Canseco	.30
746	Darrin Fletcher	.05
747	Mike Stanley	.05
748	Marquis Grissom (Season Highlights)	.05
749	Fred McGriff (Season Highlights)	.05
750	Travis Lee (Season Highlights)	.05

Amazing Greats

The 30-card Amazing Greats insert is printed on acetate. The cards are labeled "One of 2,000." A die-cut parallel was sequentially numbered to 250. Amazing Greats was an insert in Upper Deck Series One packs. Cards carry an "AG" prefix.

		NM/M
	Complete Set (30):	75.00
	Common Player:	.60
	Die-Cuts (250):	8X
1	Ken Griffey Jr.	5.00
2	Derek Jeter	7.50
3	Alex Rodriguez	6.00
4	Paul Molitor	3.00
5	Jeff Bagwell	3.00
6	Larry Walker	.60
7	Kenny Lofton	.60
8	Cal Ripken Jr.	7.50
9	Juan Gonzalez	1.50
10	Chipper Jones	4.00
11	Greg Maddux	4.00
12	Roberto Alomar	1.25
13	Mike Piazza	5.00
14	Andres Galarraga	.60
15	Barry Bonds	7.50
16	Andy Pettitte	1.25
17	Nomar Garciaparra	4.00
18	Hideki Irabu	.60
19	Tony Gwynn	4.00
20	Frank Thomas	3.00
21	Roger Clemens	4.50
22	Sammy Sosa	5.00
23	Jose Cruz, Jr.	.60
24	Manny Ramirez	3.00
25	Mark McGwire	6.00
26	Randy Johnson	3.00
27	Mo Vaughn	.60
28	Gary Sheffield	1.50
29	Andruw Jones	3.00
30	Albert Belle	.60

A Piece of the Action

A Piece of the Action was inserted in Series 1, 2 and 3 packs. Series 1 featured 10 cards: five with a piece of game-used jersey and five with a piece of game-used bat. Series 2 offered a piece of game-used bat and jersey on four cards. Series 3 inserts featured a piece of jersey only. The cards were inserted one per 2,500 packs in Series 1 and 2; the insertion rate in Series 3 was not revealed.

		NM/M
	Complete Set (14):	250.00
	Common Player:	5.00
	Inserted 1:2,500	
(1)	Jay Buhner/Bat	20.00
(2)	Tony Gwynn/Bat	25.00
(3)	Tony Gwynn/Jsy	25.00
(4)	Todd Hollandsworth/Bat	5.00
(5)	Todd Hollandsworth/Jsy	5.00
(6)	Greg Maddux/Jsy	40.00
(7)	Alex Rodriguez/Bat	40.00
(8)	Alex Rodriguez/Jsy	40.00
(9)	Gary Sheffield/Bat	15.00
(10)	Gary Sheffield/Jsy	15.00
RA	Roberto Alomar	35.00
JB	Jay Buhner	10.00
AJ	Andruw Jones	20.00
GS	Gary Sheffield	15.00

Blue Chip Prospects

Inserted in Series 2 packs, these inserts are printed on die-cut acetate. They are sequentially numbered to 2,000. They carry a "BC" prefix.

		NM/M
	Complete Set (30):	75.00
	Common Player:	2.00
1	Nomar Garciaparra	8.00
2	Scott Rolen	5.00
3	Jason Dickson	2.00
4	Darin Erstad	3.00
5	Brad Fullmer	2.00
6	Jaret Wright	2.00
7	Justin Thompson	2.00
8	Matt Morris	2.00
9	Fernando Tatis	2.00
10	Alex Rodriguez	12.00
11	Todd Helton	6.50
12	Andy Pettitte	2.50
13	Jose Cruz Jr.	2.00
14	Mark Kotsay	2.00
15	Derek Jeter	15.00
16	Paul Konerko	3.00
17	Todd Dunwoody	2.00
18	Vladimir Guerrero	6.00
19	Miguel Tejada	5.00
20	Chipper Jones	8.00
21	Kevin Orie	2.00
22	Juan Encarnacion	2.00
23	Brian Rose	2.00
24	Andruw Jones	6.00
25	Livan Hernandez	2.00
26	Brian Giles	2.00
27	Brett Tomko	2.00
28	Jose Guillen	2.00
29	Aaron Boone	2.00
30	Ben Grieve	2.00

Clearly Dominant

Clearly Dominant was an insert in Series 2. Printed on Light F/X plastic stock, the 30-card set is sequentially numbered to 250. They carry a "CD" prefix.

		NM/M
	Complete Set (30):	300.00
	Common Player:	3.00
	Production 250 Sets	
1	Mark McGwire	25.00
2	Derek Jeter	30.00
3	Alex Rodriguez	25.00
4	Paul Molitor	12.00
5	Jeff Bagwell	12.00
6	Ivan Rodriguez	10.00
7	Kenny Lofton	3.00
8	Cal Ripken Jr.	30.00
9	Albert Belle	3.00
10	Chipper Jones	15.00
11	Gary Sheffield	5.00
12	Roberto Alomar	4.00
13	Mo Vaughn	3.00
14	Andres Galarraga	3.00
15	Nomar Garciaparra	15.00
16	Randy Johnson	12.00
17	Mike Mussina	3.00
18	Greg Maddux	15.00
19	Tony Gwynn	15.00
20	Frank Thomas	12.00
21	Roger Clemens	17.50
22	Dennis Eckersley	10.00
23	Juan Gonzalez	6.00
24	Tino Martinez	3.00
25	Andruw Jones	12.00
26	Larry Walker	3.00
27	Ken Caminiti	3.00
28	Mike Piazza	20.00
29	Barry Bonds	30.00
30	Ken Griffey Jr.	20.00

Ken Griffey Jr.'s HR Chronicles

Griffey's Home Run Chronicles was inserted in both Series 1 and 2 packs. Series 1 had cards spotlighting one of Junior's first 30 home runs of the 1997 season. Series 2 had 26 cards highlighting the rest of his 1997 home run output. In both series, the cards were inserted one per nine packs. Cards are numbered "XX of 56" and printed on silver-metallic foil on front.

	NM/M
Complete Set (56):	45.00
Common Card:	1.00
Inserted 1:9	

National Pride

National Pride is a 42-card insert printed on die-cut rainbow foil. The set honors the nationality of the player with their country's flag in the background. The cards were inserted one per 24 packs. Cards are numbered with a "NP" prefix.

		NM/M
	Complete Set (42):	65.00
	Common Player:	.75
1	Dave Nilsson	.75
2	Larry Walker	.75
3	Edgar Renteria	.75
4	Jose Canseco	1.25
5	Rey Ordonez	.75
6	Rafael Palmeiro	2.50
7	Livan Hernandez	.75
8	Andruw Jones	3.00
9	Manny Ramirez	3.00
10	Sammy Sosa	4.00
11	Raul Mondesi	.75
12	Moises Alou	.75
13	Pedro Martinez	3.00
14	Vladimir Guerrero	3.00
15	Chili Davis	.75
16	Hideo Nomo	1.50
17	Hideki Irabu	.75
18	Shigetosi Hasegawa	.75
19	Takashi Kashiwada	.75
20	Chan Ho Park	.75
21	Fernando Valenzuela	1.50
22	Vinny Castilla	.75
23	Armando Reynoso	.75
24	Karim Garcia	1.00
25	Marvin Benard	.75
26	Mariano Rivera	1.00
27	Juan Gonzalez	1.50
28	Roberto Alomar	1.00
29	Ivan Rodriguez	2.50
30	Carlos Delgado	1.00
31	Bernie Williams	3.00
32	Edgar Martinez	.75
33	Frank Thomas	3.00
34	Barry Bonds	7.50
35	Mike Piazza	5.00
36	Chipper Jones	4.00
37	Cal Ripken Jr.	7.50
38	Alex Rodriguez	6.00
39	Ken Griffey Jr.	5.00
40	Andres Galarraga	.75
41	Omar Vizquel	.75
42	Ozzie Guillen	.75

Tape Measure Titans

Tape Measure Titans is a 30-card insert seeded 1:23 in Series 2. The set honors the game's top home run hitters. A parallel gold version was also created with each card serially numbered to 2,667 on front.

		NM/M
	Complete Set (30):	45.00
	Common Player:	.40
	Inserted 1:23	
	Gold:	1.5X
1	Mark McGwire	5.00

Prime Nine

Nine of the most popular players are featured in this insert set. The cards are printed on silver-foil stock and inserted 1:5 in Series 2 packs.

		NM/M
	Complete Set (60):	50.00
	Common Griffey:	1.00
	Common Piazza:	1.25
	Common Thomas:	.60
	Common McGwire:	1.25
	Common Ripken:	1.75
	Common Gonzalez:	.50
	Common Gwynn:	.70
	Common Bonds:	1.75
	Common Maddux:	.70
	Inserted 1:5	
PN1	Ken Griffey Jr./1989-1992	1.00
PN2	Ken Griffey Jr./1993	1.00
PN3	Ken Griffey Jr./1994	1.00
PN4	Ken Griffey Jr./1995	1.00
PN5	Ken Griffey Jr./1996	1.00
PN6	Ken Griffey Jr./1997	1.00
PN7	Ken Griffey Jr./1997	1.00
PN8	Mike Piazza/1991	1.00
PN9	Mike Piazza/1992	1.00
PN10	Mike Piazza/1993	1.00
PN11	Mike Piazza/1994	1.00
PN12	Mike Piazza/1995	1.00
PN13	Mike Piazza/1996	1.00
PN14	Mike Piazza/1997	1.00
PN15	Frank Thomas/1991	.60
PN16	Frank Thomas/1992	.60
PN17	Frank Thomas/1993	.60
PN18	Frank Thomas/1994	.60
PN19	Frank Thomas/1995	.60
PN20	Frank Thomas/1996	.60
PN21	Frank Thomas/1997	.60
PN22	Mark McGwire/1987	1.25
PN23	Mark McGwire/1988-1990	1.25
PN24	Mark McGwire/1992	1.25
PN25	Mark McGwire/1995-1996	1.25
PN26	Mark McGwire/1997	1.25
PN27	Mark McGwire/1997	1.25
PN28	Mark McGwire/1997	1.25
PN29	Cal Ripken Jr./1982	1.75
PN30	Cal Ripken Jr./1983	1.75
PN31	Cal Ripken Jr./1989	1.75
PN32	Cal Ripken Jr./1991	1.75
PN33	Cal Ripken Jr./1995	1.75
PN34	Cal Ripken Jr./1996	1.75
PN35	Cal Ripken Jr./1997	1.75
PN36	Juan Gonzalez/1992	.50
PN37	Juan Gonzalez/1993	.50
PN38	Juan Gonzalez/1994	.50
PN39	Juan Gonzalez/1995	.50
PN40	Juan Gonzalez/1996	.50
PN41	Juan Gonzalez/1996	.50
PN42	Juan Gonzalez/1997	.50
PN43	Tony Gwynn/1984	.75
PN44	Tony Gwynn/1987-1989	.75
PN45	Tony Gwynn/1990-1993	.75
PN46	Tony Gwynn/1994	.75
PN47	Tony Gwynn/1996	.75
PN48	Tony Gwynn/1997	.75
PN49	Tony Gwynn/1997	.75
PN50	Barry Bonds/1986-1992	1.75
PN51	Barry Bonds/1990-1993	1.75
PN52	Barry Bonds/1993	1.75
PN53	Barry Bonds/1994	1.75
PN54	Barry Bonds/1996	1.75
PN55	Barry Bonds/1997	1.75
PN56	Greg Maddux/1992	.75
PN57	Greg Maddux/1993-1994	.75
PN58	Greg Maddux/1995	.75
PN59	Greg Maddux/1996	.75
PN60	Greg Maddux/1997	.75
2	Andres Galarraga	.40
3	Jeff Bagwell	2.00
4	Larry Walker	.40
5	Frank Thomas	2.50
6	Rafael Palmeiro	1.50
7	Nomar Garciaparra	4.00
8	Mo Vaughn	.40
9	Albert Belle	.60
10	Ken Griffey Jr.	5.00
11	Manny Ramirez	2.00
12	Jim Thome	.40
13	Tony Clark	.40
14	Juan Gonzalez	2.00
15	Mike Piazza	4.00
16	Jose Canseco	1.00
17	Jay Buhner	.40
18	Alex Rodriguez	5.00
19	Jose Cruz Jr.	.40
20	Tino Martinez	.40
21	Carlos Delgado	.75
22	Andruw Jones	2.00
23	Chipper Jones	3.00
24	Fred McGriff	.40
25	Matt Williams	.40
26	Sammy Sosa	4.00
27	Vinny Castilla	.60
28	Tim Salmon	.60
29	Ken Caminiti	.40
30	Barry Bonds	6.00

10th Anniversary Preview

10th Anniversary Preview is a 60-card set. The foil cards have the same design as the 1989 Upper Deck base cards. The set was inserted one per five packs. Retail versions have the words "PREVIEW EDITION" stamped vertically in gold foil at left. While scarcer than the hobby version, they do not command a premium.

		NM/M
	Complete Set (60):	45.00
	Common Player:	.30
1	Greg Maddux	2.00
2	Mike Mussina	.50
3	Roger Clemens	2.25
4	Hideo Nomo	.75
5	David Cone	.30
6	Tom Glavine	.45
7	Andy Pettitte	.60
8	Jimmy Key	.30
9	Randy Johnson	1.50
10	Dennis Eckersley	1.00
11	Lee Smith	.30
12	John Franco	.30
13	Randy Myers	.30
14	Mike Piazza	2.50
15	Ivan Rodriguez	1.25
16	Todd Hundley	.30
17	Sandy Alomar Jr.	.30
18	Frank Thomas	1.50
19	Rafael Palmeiro	1.25
20	Mark McGwire	3.00
21	Mo Vaughn	.30
22	Fred McGriff	.30
23	Andres Galarraga	.30
24	Mark Grace	.30
25	Jeff Bagwell	1.50
26	Roberto Alomar	.45
27	Chuck Knoblauch	.30
28	Ryne Sandberg	2.00
29	Eric Young	.30
30	Craig Biggio	.30
31	Carlos Baerga	.30
32	Robin Ventura	.30

33	Matt Williams	.30
34	Wade Boggs	2.00
35	Dean Palmer	.30
36	Chipper Jones	2.00
37	Vinny Castilla	.30
38	Ken Caminiti	.30
39	Omar Vizquel	.30
40	Cal Ripken Jr.	3.50
41	Derek Jeter	3.50
42	Alex Rodriguez	3.00
43	Barry Larkin	.30
44	Mark Grudzielanek	.30
45	Albert Belle	.30
46	Manny Ramirez	1.50
47	Jose Canseco	.75
48	Ken Griffey Jr.	2.50
49	Juan Gonzalez	.75
50	Kenny Lofton	.30
51	Sammy Sosa	2.00
52	Larry Walker	.30
53	Gary Sheffield	.60
54	Rickey Henderson	1.50
55	Tony Gwynn	1.50
56	Barry Bonds	3.50
57	Paul Molitor	1.50
58	Edgar Martinez	.30
59	Chili Davis	.30
60	Eddie Murray	1.50

Jumbos

For $3 and 10 foil-pack wrappers, collectors could receive this set of large-format (3-1/2" x 5") cards in a mail-in redemption. The cards are identical to the standard-size versions.

		NM/M
Complete Set (15):		6.00
Common Player:		.25
27	Kenny Lofton	.25
30	Greg Maddux	.75
40	Rafael Palmeiro	.50
50	Ryne Sandberg	.75
60	Albert Belle	.25
65	Barry Larkin	.25
67	Deion Sanders	.25
95	Gary Sheffield	.40
130	Paul Molitor	.60
135	Vladimir Guerrero	.60
176	Hideki Irabu	.25
205	Mark McGwire	2.00
211	Rickey Henderson	.60
225	Ken Griffey Jr.	1.50
230	Ivan Rodriguez	.50

5x7 Inserts

Each box of specially marked Series 2 retail packs contains one of these oversize (5" x 7") versions of UD cards. Besides being four times the size of the regular cards, the jumbo versions do not have the metallic-foil highlights on front nor the hologram on back.

		NM/M
Complete Set (10):		30.00
Common Player:		1.00
310	Cal Ripken Jr.	6.00
320	Nomar Garciaparra	3.00
330	Frank Thomas	2.50
355	Larry Walker	1.00
385	Jeff Bagwell	2.50
400	Mike Piazza	4.00
450	Derek Jeter	6.00
500	Tony Gwynn	3.00
510	Alex Rodriguez	5.00
530	Roger Clemens	3.50

Richie Ashburn Tribute

As part of the company's participation at SportsFest in May 1998, the company issued a tribute card for Phillies Hall of Famer and broadcasting great Richie Ash-

burn. The card front features a color action photo, part of which is repeated on the back along with Ashburn's career stats and highlights.

		NM/M
1	Richie Ashburn	4.00

Ken Griffey Most Memorable Home Runs

This retail-exclusive boxed set features 11 large-format (3-1/2" x 5") cards depicting Junior's key home runs. The cards have brushed gold-foil graphic highlights on front and a large photo with details of the memorable home run on back. Each card in the set also exists in an autographed and numbered edition of 10 which were randomly inserted. The set was originally sold with a 4" x 6" lucite card holder for about $12.

		NM/M
Complete Set (11):		7.50
Common Card:		1.00
Autographed Card:		225.00
1	Ken Griffey Jr. (First ML HR)	1.00
2	Ken Griffey Jr. (Father-son HRs)	1.00
3	Ken Griffey Jr. (1992 All-Star HR)	1.00
4	Ken Griffey Jr. (HR in eight straight)	1.00
5	Ken Griffey Jr. (32 HR in June 1994)	1.00
6	Ken Griffey Jr. (Game-winning HR)	1.00
7	Ken Griffey Jr. (5th Divison Series HR)	1.00
8	Ken Griffey Jr. (April record)	1.00
9	Ken Griffey Jr. (50th HR in 1997)	1.00
10	Ken Griffey Jr. (56th in 1997)	1.00
11	Ken Griffey Jr. (300th)	1.00

Mark McGwire's Chase for 62

This boxed set chronicles the Cardinal slugger's quest for the single-season home run record. Sold only as a boxed set of 30 cards in standard 2-1/2" x 3-1/2" format, plus a 3-1/2" x 5" card picturing home runs No. 61 and 62, these sets were offered only on a television home shopping show (individually serial numbered red box) and in selected retail stores (unnumbered yellow box). The cards in each version are identical. Issue price was about $20. Card fronts have color poses or action photos at right; at left is a monochrome portrait photo in red. Backs repeat the large front photo, also in red monochrome, and have a few words about a McGwire homer or other highlight. Each card has a silver-foil UD logo on front and a diamond-shaped hologram on back.

		NM/M
Complete Boxed Set:		7.50
Common Card:		.50
1-30	Mark McGwire	.50
---	Mark McGwire (3-1/2" x 5" HR #61/62)	3.00

Mark McGwire - Sept. 8, 1998

This is one of many special issues from Upper Deck commemorating McGwire's record-breaking 1998 season. Most such cards were produced for retail-only sales, or for home shopping television shows. This blank-back, round-cornered card is 5" x 3" and has flicker-action scenes of Big Mac's home run swing and his salute to the crowd following his historic blast.

	NM/M
Mark McGwire	6.00

Mark McGwire 70/62 Home Runs

This 3-1/2" x 5" die-cut card was one of many special issues from UD commemorating McGwire's record-breaking season in 1998. This card is highlighted on front with red foil and has a photo of the player with details of his 70th HR. On back in similar format is another photo and details of his 62nd home run, along with a serial number from within the edition of 17,000.

	NM/M
Mark McGwire	4.00

PowerDeck Audio Card

A late-1990s reinvention of the "talking" baseball card, this was the first application of UD's "PowerDeck" technology to the trading card field. Specially marked hobby boxes of '98 UD baseball could contain one of three Ken Griffey, Jr., audio cards. The cards are standard 2-1/2" x 3-1/2" and were made to be inserted into a "dummy" plastic disc which could then be played in any audio CD, offering comments from Griffey, trivia, and career highlights. Insertion rate of each of the Griffey cards varies and is detailed in the listings.

		NM/M
Complete Set (3):		45.00
Common Card:		2.00
(1)	Ken Griffey Jr. (Gray jersey, 1:46 packs.)	3.00
(2)	Ken Griffey Jr. (Blue jersey, 1:500 packs.)	12.00
(3)	Ken Griffey Jr. (White jersey, 1:2,400 packs.)	35.00

Rookie Edition Preview

		NM/M
Complete Set (10):		5.00
Common Player:		.50
1	Nomar Garciaparra	2.00
2	Scott Rolen	1.00
3	Mark Kotsay	.50
4	Todd Helton	1.50
5	Paul Konerko	.60
6	Juan Encarnacion	.50
7	Brad Fullmer	.50
8	Miguel Tejada	.65
9	Richard Hidalgo	.50
10	Ben Grieve	.50

Rookie Edition A Piece of the Action

A Piece of the Action consists of five Game Jersey cards. Three rookie Game Jersey cards were sequentially numbered to 200, while a Ken Griffey Jr. Game Jersey card was numbered to 300. Griffey also signed and hand-numbered 24 Game Jersey cards.

		NM/M
Common Card:		15.00
KG	Ken Griffey Jr./300	100.00
KGS	Ken Griffey Jr./Auto./24	300.00
BG	Ben Grieve/200	15.00
JC	Jose Cruz Jr./200	15.00
TL	Travis Lee/200	15.00

Rookie Edition All-Star Credentials

All-Star Credentials is a 30-card insert seeded 1:9. It features the game's top players.

		NM/M
Complete Set (30):		25.00
Common Player:		.25
Inserted 1:9		
AS1	Ken Griffey Jr.	1.50
AS2	Travis Lee	.40
AS3	Ben Grieve	.25
AS4	Jose Cruz Jr.	.25
AS5	Andruw Jones	.75
AS6	Craig Biggio	.25
AS7	Hideo Nomo	.40
AS8	Cal Ripken Jr.	2.50
AS9	Jaret Wright	.25
AS10	Alex Rodriguez	2.50
AS11	Derek Jeter	2.50
AS12	Scott Rolen	.60
AS13	Jeff Bagwell	.75
AS14	Manny Ramirez	.75
AS15	Alex Rodriguez	2.00
AS16	Chipper Jones	1.00
AS17	Larry Walker	.25
AS18	Barry Bonds	2.50
AS19	Tony Gwynn	1.00
AS20	Mike Piazza	1.50
AS21	Roger Clemens	1.25
AS22	Greg Maddux	1.00
AS23	Jim Thome	.60
AS24	Tino Martinez	.25
AS25	Nomar Garciaparra	1.00
AS26	Juan Gonzalez	.40
AS27	Kenny Lofton	.25
AS28	Randy Johnson	.75
AS29	Todd Helton	.65
AS30	Frank Thomas	.75

Rookie Edition Destination Stardom

This 60-card insert features top young players. Fronts are printed on a foil background. The insertion rate was one card per five packs. Cards have a "DS" prefix to the card number.

		NM/M
Complete Set (60):		40.00
Common Player:		.50
Inserted 1:5		
1	Travis Lee	.75
2	Nomar Garciaparra	3.50
3	Alex Gonzalez	.50
4	Richard Hidalgo	.50
5	Jaret Wright	.50
6	Mike Kinkade	.50
7	Matt Morris	.50
8	Gary Mathews Jr.	.50
9	Brett Tomko	.50
10	Todd Helton	2.00
11	Scott Elarton	.50
12	Scott Rolen	1.50
13	Jose Cruz Jr.	.50
14	Jarrod Washburn	.50
15	Sean Casey	.50
16	Magglio Ordonez	2.00
17	Gabe Alvarez	.50
18	Todd Dunwoody	.50
19	Kevin Witt	.50
20	Ben Grieve	.50
21	Daryle Ward	.50
22	Matt Clement	.50
23	Carlton Loewer	.50
24	Javier Vazquez	.50
25	Paul Konerko	.75
26	Preston Wilson	.60
27	Wes Helms	.50
28	Derek Jeter	5.00
29	Corey Koskie	.50
30	Russell Branyan	.50
31	Vladimir Guerrero	2.50
32	Ryan Christenson	.50
33	Carlos Lee	.60
34	David Dellucci	.50
35	Bruce Chen	.50
36	Ricky Ledee	.50
37	Ron Wright	.50
38	Derek Lee	1.50
39	Miguel Tejada	.75
40	Brad Fullmer	.50
41	Rich Butler	.50
42	Chris Carpenter	.50
43	Alex Rodriguez	4.00
44	Darron Ingram	.50
45	Kerry Wood	1.50
46	Jason Varitek	.50
47	Ramon Hernandez	.50
48	Aaron Boone	.50
49	Juan Encarnacion	.50
50	A.J. Hinch	.50
51	Mike Lowell	1.00
52	Fernando Tatis	.50
53	Jose Guillen	.50
54	Mike Caruso	.50
55	Carl Pavano	.50
56	Chris Clemons	.50
57	Mark L. Johnson	.50
58	Ken Cloude	.50
59	Rolando Arrojo	.50
60	Mark Kotsay	.50

Rookie Edition Eminent Prestige 5x7

This 4X super-size (5" x 7") version is a partial parallel of the Rookie Edition Eminent Prestige subset. It was available only in specially marked retail packaging.

		NM/M
Complete Set (10):		25.00
Common Player:		2.00
605	Mike Piazza	3.50
607	Frank Thomas	2.50
610	Mark McGwire	4.00
611	Jeff Bagwell	2.50
612	Travis Lee	2.00
614	Cal Ripken Jr.	3.50
616	Nomar Garciaparra	3.00
617	Alex Rodriguez	4.00
619	Tony Gwynn	3.00
620	Ken Griffey Jr.	3.50

Rookie Edition Retrospectives

Retrospectives is a 30-card insert seeded 1:24. The cards offer a look back at the careers of baseball's top stars.

		NM/M
Complete Set (30):		55.00
Common Player:		.50
Inserted 1:24		
1	Dennis Eckersley	2.50
2	Rickey Henderson	3.00
3	Harold Baines	.50
4	Cal Ripken Jr.	7.50
5	Tony Gwynn	4.00
6	Wade Boggs	4.00
7	Orel Hershiser	.50
8	Joe Carter	.50
9	Roger Clemens	4.50
10	Barry Bonds	7.50
11	Mark McGwire	6.00
12	Greg Maddux	4.00
13	Fred McGriff	.50
14	Rafael Palmeiro	3.00
15	Craig Biggio	.50
16	Brady Anderson	.50
17	Randy Johnson	3.00
18	Gary Sheffield	1.00
19	Albert Belle	.50
20	Ken Griffey Jr.	5.00
21	Juan Gonzalez	1.50
22	Larry Walker	.50
23	Tino Martinez	.50
24	Frank Thomas	5.00
25	Jeff Bagwell	3.00
26	Kenny Lofton	.50
27	Mo Vaughn	.50
28	Mike Piazza	5.00
29	Alex Rodriguez	6.00
30	Chipper Jones	4.00

Rookie Edition Unparalleled

Unparalleled is a 20-card, hobby-only insert. The set consists of holo-pattern foil-stamped cards. They were inserted one per 72 packs.

		NM/M
Complete Set (20):		75.00
Common Player:		1.00
Inserted 1:72		
1	Ken Griffey Jr.	6.00
2	Travis Lee	1.50

3	Ben Grieve	1.00	
4	Jose Cruz Jr.	1.00	
5	Nomar Garciaparra	5.00	
6	Hideo Nomo	1.75	
7	Kenny Lofton	1.00	
8	Cal Ripken Jr.	10.00	
9	Roger Clemens	5.50	
10	Mike Piazza	6.00	
11	Jeff Bagwell	3.50	
12	Chipper Jones	5.00	
13	Greg Maddux	5.00	
14	Randy Johnson	3.50	
15	Alex Rodriguez	7.50	
16	Barry Bonds	10.00	
17	Frank Thomas	3.50	
18	Juan Gonzalez	1.75	
19	Tony Gwynn	5.00	
20	Mark McGwire	7.50	

1998 Upper Deck Special F/X

Special F/X is a retail-only product. The 150-card set consists of 125 regular cards, the 15-card Star Rookies subset and a 10-card subset called Ken Griffey Jr.'s Hot List. The base cards are printed on 20-point stock. The only insert is Power Zone which has four levels: Level One, Level Two - Octoberbest, Level Three - Power Driven and Level Four - Superstar Xcitement.

		NM/M
Complete Set (150):		30.00
Common Player:		.05
1	Ken Griffey Jr.	
	(Griffey Hot List)	1.00
2	Mark McGwire	
	(Griffey Hot List)	1.25
3	Alex Rodriguez	
	(Griffey Hot List)	2.50
4	Larry Walker	
	(Griffey Hot List)	.05
5	Tino Martinez	
	(Griffey Hot List)	.05
6	Mike Piazza	
	(Griffey Hot List)	2.50
7	Jose Cruz Jr.	
	(Griffey Hot List)	.05
8	Greg Maddux	
	(Griffey Hot List)	.75
9	Tony Gwynn	
	(Griffey Hot List)	.75
10	Roger Clemens	
	(Griffey Hot List)	1.75
11	Jason Dickson	.05
12	Darin Erstad	.25
13	Chuck Finley	.05
14	Dave Hollins	.05
15	Garret Anderson	.05
16	Michael Tucker	.05
17	Javier Lopez	.05
18	John Smoltz	.05
19	Mark Wohlers	.05
20	Greg Maddux	1.50
21	Scott Erickson	.05
22	Jimmy Key	.05
23	B.J. Surhoff	.05
24	Eric Davis	.05
25	Rafael Palmeiro	.75
26	Tim Naehring	.05
27	Darren Bragg	.05
28	Troy O'Leary	.05
29	John Valentin	.05
30	Mo Vaughn	.75
31	Mark Grace	.05
32	Kevin Foster	.05
33	Kevin Tapani	.05
34	Kevin Orie	.05
35	Albert Belle	.05
36	Ray Durham	.05
37	Jaime Navarro	.05
38	Mike Cameron	.05
39	Eddie Taubensee	.05
40	Barry Larkin	.05
41	Willie Greene	.05
42	Jeff Shaw	.05
43	Omar Vizquel	.05
44	Brian Giles	.05
45	Jim Thome	.60
46	David Justice	.05
47	Sandy Alomar Jr.	.05
48	Neifi Perez	.05
49	Dante Bichette	.05
50	Vinny Castilla	.05

51	John Thomson	.05	
52	Damion Easley	.05	
53	Justin Thompson	.05	
54	Bobby Higginson	.05	
55	Tony Clark	.05	
56	Charles Johnson	.05	
57	Edgar Renteria	.05	
58	Alex Fernandez	.05	
59	Gary Sheffield	.50	
60	Livan Hernandez	.05	
61	Craig Biggio	.05	
62	Chris Holt	.05	
63	Billy Wagner	.05	
64	Brad Ausmus	.05	
65	Dean Palmer	.05	
66	Tim Belcher	.05	
67	Jeff King	.05	
68	Jose Rosado	.05	
69	Chan Ho Park	.05	
70	Raul Mondesi	.05	
71	Hideo Nomo	.50	
72	Todd Zeile	.05	
73	Eric Karros	.05	
74	Cal Eldred	.05	
75	Jeff D'Amico	.05	
76	Doug Jones	.05	
77	Dave Nilsson	.05	
78	Todd Walker	.05	
79	Rick Aguilera	.05	
80	Paul Molitor	1.00	
81	Brad Radke	.05	
82	Vladimir Guerrero	1.00	
83	Carlos Perez	.05	
84	F.P. Santangelo	.05	
85	Rondell White	.05	
86	Butch Huskey	.05	
87	Edgardo Alfonzo	.05	
88	John Franco	.05	
89	John Olerud	.05	
90	Todd Hundley	.05	
91	Bernie Williams	.05	
92	Andy Pettitte	.30	
93	Paul O'Neill	.05	
94	David Cone	.05	
95	Jason Giambi	.50	
96	Damon Mashore	.05	
97	Scott Spiezio	.05	
98	Ariel Prieto	.05	
99	Rico Brogna	.05	
100	Mike Lieberthal	.05	
101	Garrett Stephenson	.05	
102	Ricky Bottalico	.05	
103	Kevin Polcovich	.05	
104	Jon Lieber	.05	
105	Kevin Young	.05	
106	Tony Womack	.05	
107	Gary Gaetti	.05	
108	Alan Benes	.05	
109	Willie McGee	.05	
110	Mark McGwire	2.50	
111	Ron Gant	.05	
112	Andy Ashby	.05	
113	Steve Finley	.05	
114	Quilvio Veras	.05	
115	Ken Caminiti	.05	
116	Joey Hamilton	.05	
117	Bill Mueller	.05	
118	Mark Gardner	.05	
119	Shawn Estes	.05	
120	J.T. Snow	.05	
121	Dante Powell	.05	
122	Jeff Kent	.05	
123	Jamie Moyer	.05	
124	Joey Cora	.05	
125	Ken Griffey Jr.	2.00	
126	Jeff Fassero	.05	
127	Edgar Martinez	.05	
128	Will Clark	.05	
129	Lee Stevens	.05	
130	Ivan Rodriguez	.75	
131	Rusty Greer	.05	
132	Ed Sprague	.05	
133	Pat Hentgen	.05	
134	Shannon Stewart	.05	
135	Carlos Delgado	.40	
136	Brett Tomko/SR	.05	
137	Jose Guillen/SR	.05	
138	Elieser Marrero/SR	.05	
139	Dennis Reyes/SR	.05	
140	Mark Kotsay/SR	.05	
141	Richie Sexson/SR	.05	
142	Todd Helton/SR	.75	
143	Jeremi Gonzalez/SR	.05	
144	Jeff Abbott/SR	.05	
145	Matt Morris/SR	.05	
146	Aaron Boone/SR	.05	
147	Todd Dunwoody/SR	.05	
148	Mario Valdez/SR	.05	
149	Fernando Tatis/SR	.05	
150	Jaret Wright/SR	.05	

OctoberBest

OctoberBest is Level Two of the Power Zone insert. This 20-card insert is die-cut and printed on silver foil. Inserted one per 34 packs, the set features the post-season exploits of 20 players from Power Zone Level One.

		NM/M
Complete Set (15):		40.00
Common Player:		1.00
Inserted 1:34		
PZ1	Frank Thomas	3.00
PZ2	Juan Gonzalez	1.50
PZ3	Mike Piazza	5.00

PZ4	Mark McGwire	6.00
PZ5	Jeff Bagwell	3.00
PZ6	Barry Bonds	7.50
PZ7	Ken Griffey Jr.	5.00
PZ8	John Smoltz	1.00
PZ9	Andruw Jones	3.00
PZ10	Greg Maddux	4.00
PZ11	Sandy Alomar Jr.	1.00
PZ12	Roberto Alomar	1.25
PZ13	Chipper Jones	4.00
PZ14	Kenny Lofton	1.00
PZ15	Tom Glavine	1.25

Power Driven

Power Driven is Level Three of the Power Zone insert. Inserted 1:69, the set features the top 10 power hitters from Power Zone Level Two. The cards feature gold Light F/X technology.

		NM/M
Complete Set (10):		40.00
Common Player:		1.50
Inserted 1:69		
PZ1	Frank Thomas	4.50
PZ2	Juan Gonzalez	2.50
PZ3	Mike Piazza	6.00
PZ4	Larry Walker	1.50
PZ5	Mark McGwire	7.50
PZ6	Jeff Bagwell	4.50
PZ7	Mo Vaughn	1.50
PZ8	Barry Bonds	10.00
PZ9	Tino Martinez	1.50
PZ10	Ken Griffey Jr.	6.00

Power Zone

Power Zone Level One is seeded one per seven packs. The cards are printed using silver Light F/X technology.

		NM/M
Complete Set (20):		40.00
Common Player:		.50
Inserted 1:7		
PZ1	Jose Cruz Jr.	.50
PZ2	Frank Thomas	2.50
PZ3	Juan Gonzalez	1.25
PZ4	Mike Piazza	4.50
PZ5	Mark McGwire	4.50
PZ6	Barry Bonds	6.00
PZ7	Greg Maddux	3.00
PZ8	Alex Rodriguez	4.50
PZ9	Nomar Garciaparra	3.00
PZ10	Ken Griffey Jr.	3.50
PZ11	John Smoltz	.50
PZ12	Andruw Jones	2.50

PZ13	Sandy Alomar Jr.	.50
PZ14	Roberto Alomar	1.00
PZ15	Chipper Jones	3.00
PZ16	Kenny Lofton	.50
PZ17	Larry Walker	.50
PZ18	Jeff Bagwell	2.50
PZ19	Mo Vaughn	.50
PZ20	Tom Glavine	1.00

Superstar Xcitement

Printed on Light F/X gold foil, this 10-card set features the same players as the Power Driven insert. This set is Power Zone Level Four and is sequentially numbered to 250.

		NM/M
Complete Set (10):		275.00
Common Player:		10.00
Production 250 Sets		
PZ1	Jose Cruz Jr.	10.00
PZ2	Frank Thomas	25.00
PZ3	Juan Gonzalez	10.00
PZ4	Mike Piazza	40.00
PZ5	Mark McGwire	45.00
PZ6	Barry Bonds	50.00
PZ7	Greg Maddux	35.00
PZ8	Alex Rodriguez	45.00
PZ9	Nomar Garciaparra	35.00
PZ10	Ken Griffey Jr.	40.00

1998 Upper Deck UD 3

The 270-card base set of UD 3 is actually three levels of the same 90 players. Light FX cards comprise #1-90. The first 30 cards are Future Impact players. Cards #31-60 are Power Corps and cards #61-90 are The Establishment. Cards #91-180 repeat the three subsets in Embossed technology while the final 90 cards repeat the basic sequence in Rainbow technology. Because each subset at each level is seeded at a different rate, few collectors bother to try to understand the relative scarcities and the issue is largely ignored. The insertion ratio for each tier is shown in the checklist. UD 3 was offered in three-card packs at an SRP of $3.99.

	NM/M
Complete Set (270):	200.00
Common Future Impact (1-30):	.50
Inserted 1:12	
Die-Cuts (2,000 Sets):	1X
Common Power Corps (31-60):	.25
Inserted 1:1	
Die-Cuts (2,000 Sets):	3X
Common Establishment (61-90):	.25
Inserted 1:6	
Die-Cuts (2,000 Sets):	2X
Common Future Impact Embossed (91-120):	.25
Inserted 1:4	
Die-Cuts (1,000 Sets):	3X
Common Power Corps Embossed (121-150):	.25
Inserted 1:1	
Die-Cuts (1,000 Sets):	6X
Common Establishment Embossed (151-180):	.25
Inserted 1:1	
Die-Cuts (1,000 Sets):	12X
Common Future Impact Rainbow (181-210):	.25
Inserted 1:1	
Die-Cuts (1,000 Sets):	15X
Common Power Corps Rainbow (211-240):	.50
Inserted 1:12	
Die-Cuts (100 Sets):	8X

	Common Establishment Rainbow	
	(241-270):	.75
	Inserted 1:24	
	Die-Cuts (100 Sets):	5X
	Pack (3):	1.00
	Wax Box (24):	20.00
1	Travis Lee	.50
2	A.J. Hinch	.50
3	Mike Caruso	.25
4	Miguel Tejada	.75
5	Brad Fullmer	.50
6	Eric Milton	.50
7	Mark Kotsay	.25
8	Darin Erstad	.75
9	Magglio Ordonez	1.00
10	Ben Grieve	.50
11	Brett Tomko	.50
12	Mike Kinkade **RC**	.75
13	Rolando Arrojo	.50
14	Todd Helton	1.00
15	Scott Rolen	1.00
16	Bruce Chen	.50
17	Daryle Ward	.50
18	Jaret Wright	.50
19	Sean Casey	.65
20	Paul Konerko	.65
21	Kerry Wood	1.00
22	Russell Branyan	.50
23	Gabe Alvarez	.50
24	Juan Encarnacion	.50
25	Andruw Jones	1.50
26	Vladimir Guerrero	1.50
27	Eli Marrero	.50
28	Matt Clement	.50
29	Gary Matthews Jr.	.50
30	Derrek Lee	1.50
31	Ken Caminiti	.25
32	Gary Sheffield	.50
33	Jay Buhner	.25
34	Ryan Klesko	.25
35	Nomar Garciaparra	.75
36	Vinny Castilla	.25
37	Tony Clark	.25
38	Sammy Sosa	.75
39	Tino Martinez	.25
40	Mike Piazza	1.00
41	Manny Ramirez	.65
42	Larry Walker	.25
43	Jose Cruz Jr.	.25
44	Matt Williams	.25
45	Frank Thomas	.65
46	Jim Edmonds	.25
47	Raul Mondesi	.25
48	Alex Rodriguez	1.50
49	Albert Belle	.25
50	Mark McGwire	1.50
51	Tim Salmon	.25
52	Andres Galarraga	.25
53	Jeff Bagwell	.65
54	Jim Thome	.50
55	Barry Bonds	2.50
56	Carlos Delgado	.40
57	Mo Vaughn	.25
58	Chipper Jones	.75
59	Juan Gonzalez	.40
60	Ken Griffey Jr.	1.00
61	David Cone	.25
62	Hideo Nomo	.75
63	Edgar Martinez	.25
64	Fred McGriff	.25
65	Cal Ripken Jr.	4.00
66	Todd Hundley	.25
67	Barry Larkin	.25
68	Dennis Eckersley	1.00
69	Randy Johnson	1.50
70	Paul Molitor	1.50
71	Eric Karros	.25
72	Rafael Palmeiro	1.00
73	Chuck Knoblauch	.25
74	Ivan Rodriguez	1.25
75	Greg Maddux	2.00
76	Dante Bichette	.25
77	Brady Anderson	.25
78	Craig Biggio	.25
79	Derek Jeter	4.00
80	Roger Clemens	2.25
81	Roberto Alomar	.40
82	Wade Boggs	2.00
83	Charles Johnson	.25
84	Mark Grace	.25
85	Kenny Lofton	.25
86	Mike Mussina	1.00
87	Pedro Martinez	1.50
88	Curt Schilling	.50
89	Bernie Williams	.25
90	Tony Gwynn	2.00
91	Travis Lee	.40
92	A.J. Hinch	.25
93	Mike Caruso	.25
94	Miguel Tejada	.40
95	Brad Fullmer	.25
96	Eric Milton	.25
97	Mark Kotsay	.25
98	Darin Erstad	1.00
99	Magglio Ordonez	1.00
100	Ben Grieve	.25
101	Brett Tomko	.25
102	Mike Kinkade **RC**	.40
103	Rolando Arrojo	.25
104	Todd Helton	1.00
105	Scott Rolen	1.00
106	Bruce Chen	.25
107	Daryle Ward	.25
108	Jaret Wright	.25
109	Sean Casey	.25
110	Paul Konerko	.40
111	Kerry Wood	1.00
112	Russell Branyan	.25

113	Gabe Alvarez	.25
114	Juan Encarnacion	.25
115	Andruw Jones	1.50
116	Vladimir Guerrero	1.50
117	Eli Marrero	.25
118	Matt Clement	.25
119	Gary Matthews Jr.	.25
120	Derrek Lee	1.00
121	Ken Caminiti	.25
122	Gary Sheffield	.50
123	Jay Buhner	.25
124	Ryan Klesko	.25
125	Nomar Garciaparra	1.50
126	Vinny Castilla	.25
127	Tony Clark	.25
128	Sammy Sosa	1.50
129	Tino Martinez	.25
130	Mike Piazza	2.00
131	Manny Ramirez	1.00
132	Larry Walker	.25
133	Jose Cruz Jr.	.25
134	Matt Williams	.25
135	Frank Thomas	1.00
136	Jim Edmonds	.25
137	Raul Mondesi	.25
138	Alex Rodriguez	3.00
139	Albert Belle	.25
140	Mark McGwire	3.00
141	Tim Salmon	.25
142	Andres Galarraga	.25
143	Jeff Bagwell	1.00
144	Jim Thome	.75
145	Barry Bonds	5.00
146	Carlos Delgado	.50
147	Mo Vaughn	.25
148	Chipper Jones	1.50
149	Juan Gonzalez	.50
150	Ken Griffey Jr.	2.00
151	David Cone	.25
152	Hideo Nomo	.40
153	Edgar Martinez	.25
154	Fred McGriff	.25
155	Cal Ripken Jr.	2.00
156	Todd Hundley	.25
157	Barry Larkin	.25
158	Dennis Eckersley	.65
159	Randy Johnson	.75
160	Paul Molitor	.75
161	Eric Karros	.25
162	Rafael Palmeiro	.65
163	Chuck Knoblauch	.25
164	Ivan Rodriguez	.65
165	Greg Maddux	1.00
166	Dante Bichette	.25
167	Brady Anderson	.25
168	Craig Biggio	.25
169	Derek Jeter	2.00
170	Roger Clemens	1.25
171	Roberto Alomar	.30
172	Wade Boggs	1.00
173	Charles Johnson	.25
174	Mark Grace	.25
175	Kenny Lofton	.25
176	Mike Mussina	.40
177	Pedro Martinez	.75
178	Curt Schilling	.40
179	Bernie Williams	.25
180	Tony Gwynn	1.00
181	Travis Lee	.40
182	A.J. Hinch	.25
183	Mike Caruso	.25
184	Miguel Tejada	.40
185	Brad Fullmer	.25
186	Eric Milton	.25
187	Mark Kotsay	.25
188	Darin Erstad	.50
189	Magglio Ordonez	1.25
190	Ben Grieve	.25
191	Brett Tomko	.25
192	Mike Kinkade **RC**	.40
193	Rolando Arrojo	.25
194	Todd Helton	.65
195	Scott Rolen	.60
196	Bruce Chen	.25
197	Daryle Ward	.25
198	Jaret Wright	.25
199	Sean Casey	.40
200	Paul Konerko	.25
201	Kerry Wood	.60
202	Russell Branyan	.25
203	Gabe Alvarez	.25
204	Juan Encarnacion	.25
205	Andruw Jones	1.50
206	Vladimir Guerrero	1.50
207	Eli Marrero	.25
208	Matt Clement	.25
209	Gary Matthews Jr.	.25
210	Derrek Lee	1.00
211	Ken Caminiti	.50
212	Gary Sheffield	.50
213	Jay Buhner	.50
214	Ryan Klesko	.50
215	Nomar Garciaparra	3.00
216	Vinny Castilla	.50
217	Tony Clark	.50
218	Sammy Sosa	.50
219	Tino Martinez	.50
220	Mike Piazza	4.00
221	Manny Ramirez	2.00
222	Larry Walker	.50
223	Jose Cruz Jr.	.50
224	Matt Williams	.50
225	Frank Thomas	2.00
226	Jim Edmonds	.50
227	Raul Mondesi	.50
228	Alex Rodriguez	6.00
229	Albert Belle	.50
230	Mark McGwire	6.00

231	Tim Salmon	.50
232	Andres Galarraga	.50
233	Jeff Bagwell	2.00
234	Jim Thome	1.50
235	Barry Bonds	9.00
236	Carlos Delgado	.75
267	Mo Vaughn	.50
238	Chipper Jones	3.00
239	Juan Gonzalez	1.00
240	Ken Griffey Jr.	4.00
241	David Cone	.75
242	Hideo Nomo	1.50
243	Edgar Martinez	.75
244	Fred McGriff	.75
245	Cal Ripken Jr.	12.00
246	Todd Hundley	.75
247	Barry Larkin	.75
248	Dennis Eckersley	3.00
249	Randy Johnson	4.50
250	Paul Molitor	4.50
251	Eric Karros	.75
252	Rafael Palmeiro	3.50
253	Chuck Knoblauch	.75
254	Ivan Rodriguez	4.00
255	Greg Maddux	6.00
256	Dante Bichette	.75
257	Brady Anderson	.75
258	Craig Biggio	.75
259	Derek Jeter	12.00
260	Roger Clemens	6.50
261	Roberto Alomar	1.25
262	Wade Boggs	6.00
263	Charles Johnson	.75
264	Mark Grace	.75
265	Kenny Lofton	.75
266	Mike Mussina	1.25
267	Pedro Martinez	4.50
268	Curt Schilling	1.50
269	Bernie Williams	.75
270	Tony Gwynn	6.00

Die-Cut

Die-cut versions of all 270 cards in UD 3 were available in three sequentially numbered tiers. Light FX were numbered to 2,000 sets; Embossed cards were numbered to 1,000 and Rainbow cards were numbered to 100.

Light FX Die-Cuts (2,000 Each)
Future Impact (1-30): .75X
Power Corps (31-60): 3X
Establishment (61-90): 2X
Embossed Die-Cuts (1,000 Each)
Future Impact (91-120): 1X
Power Corps (121-150): 3X
Establishment (151-180): 6X
Rainbow Die-Cuts (100 Each)
Future Impact (181-210): 20X
Power Corps (211-240): 4X
Establishment (241-270): 12X

Power Corps Jumbos

Ten of the Power Corps cards from UD 3 were selected to be reproduced in jumbo 4X (5" x 7") format as box-toppers for special retail packaging of UD 3.

		NM/M
Complete Set (10):		60.00
Common Player:		2.50
35	Ken Griffey Jr.	7.50
38	Sammy Sosa	6.00
40	Mike Piazza	7.50
45	Frank Thomas	5.00
48	Alex Rodriguez	10.00
50	Mark McGwire	12.50
55	Barry Bonds	12.50
58	Chipper Jones	6.00
59	Juan Gonzalez	2.50
60	Ken Griffey Jr.	7.50

1998 UD Retro

The 129-card set is comprised of 99 regular player cards and 30 Futurama subset cards. Card fronts have a white border encasing the player photo. Retro is packaged in a lunchbox featuring one of six players. Each lunchbox contains 24 six-card packs.

	NM/M
Complete Set (129):	15.00

Common Player:		.05
Pack (6):		2.25
Lunchbox (24):		40.00
1	Jim Edmonds	.05
2	Darin Erstad	.25
3	Tim Salmon	.05
4	Jay Bell	.05
5	Matt Williams	.05
6	Andres Galarraga	.05
7	Andruw Jones	.60
8	Chipper Jones	.75
9	Greg Maddux	.75
10	Rafael Palmeiro	.50
11	Cal Ripken Jr.	2.00
12	Brooks Robinson	.15
13	Nomar Garciaparra	.75
14	Pedro Martinez	.60
15	Mo Vaughn	.05
16	Ernie Banks	.50
17	Mark Grace	.05
18	Gary Matthews	.05
19	Sammy Sosa	.75
20	Albert Belle	.05
21	Carlton Fisk	.15
22	Frank Thomas	.60
23	Ken Griffey Sr.	.05
24	Paul Konerko	.15
25	Barry Larkin	.05
26	Sean Casey	.10
27	Tony Perez	.05
28	Bob Feller	.15
29	Kenny Lofton	.05
30	Manny Ramirez	.60
31	Jim Thome	.45
32	Omar Vizquel	.05
33	Dante Bichette	.05
34	Larry Walker	.05
35	Tony Clark	.05
36	Damion Easley	.05
37	Cliff Floyd	.05
38	Livan Hernandez	.05
39	Jeff Bagwell	.60
40	Craig Biggio	.05
41	Al Kaline	.15
42	Johnny Damon	.20
43	Dean Palmer	.05
44	Charles Johnson	.05
45	Eric Karros	.05
46	Gaylord Perry	.05
47	Raul Mondesi	.05
48	Gary Sheffield	.30
49	Eddie Mathews	.15
50	Warren Spahn	.15
51	Jeromy Burnitz	.05
52	Jeff Cirillo	.05
53	Marquis Grissom	.05
54	Paul Molitor	.60
55	Kirby Puckett	.75
56	Brad Radke	.05
57	Todd Walker	.05
58	Vladimir Guerrero	.60
59	Brad Fullmer	.05
60	Rondell White	.05
61	Bobby Jones	.05
62	Hideo Nomo	.30
63	Mike Piazza	1.00
64	Tom Seaver	.15
65	Frank J. Thomas	.05
66	Yogi Berra	.50
67	Derek Jeter	2.00
68	Tino Martinez	.05
69	Paul O'Neill	.05
70	Andy Pettitte	.20
71	Rollie Fingers	.05
72	Rickey Henderson	.60
73	Matt Stairs	.05
74	Scott Rolen	.50
75	Curt Schilling	.25
76	Jose Guillen	.05
77	Jason Kendall	.05
78	Lou Brock	.10
79	Bob Gibson	.10
80	Ray Lankford	.05
81	Mark McGwire	1.50
83	Kevin Brown	.05
85	Ken Caminiti	.05
86	Tony Gwynn	.75
87	Greg Vaughn	.05
88	Barry Bonds	2.00
89	Willie Stargell	.10
89	Willie McCovey	.10
90	Ken Griffey Jr.	1.00
91	Randy Johnson	.60
92	Alex Rodriguez	1.50
93	Quinton McCracken	.05
94	Fred McGriff	.05
95	Juan Gonzalez	.30
96	Ivan Rodriguez	.50

97	Nolan Ryan	1.50
98	Jose Canseco	.45
99	Roger Clemens	.90
100	Jose Cruz Jr.	.05
101	Justin Baughman RC	.05
102	David Dellucci RC (Futurama)	.15
103	Travis Lee (Futurama)	.15
104	Troy Glaus RC (Futurama)	1.00
105	Kerry Wood (Futurama)	.40
106	Mike Caruso (Futurama)	.05
107	Jim Parque RC (Futurama)	.10
108	Brett Tomko (Futurama)	.05
109	Russell Branyan (Futurama)	.05
110	Jaret Wright (Futurama)	.05
111	Todd Helton (Futurama)	.60
112	Gabe Alvarez (Futurama)	.05
113	Matt Anderson RC (Futurama)	.10
114	Alex Gonzalez (Futurama)	.05
115	Mark Kotsay (Futurama)	.10
116	Derrek Lee (Futurama)	.50
117	Richard Hidalgo (Futurama)	.05
118	Adrian Beltre (Futurama)	.10
119	Geoff Jenkins (Futurama)	.05
120	Eric Milton (Futurama)	.05
121	Brad Fullmer (Futurama)	.05
122	Vladimir Guerrero (Futurama)	.60
123	Carl Pavano (Futurama)	.05
124	Orlando Hernandez RC (Futurama)	.25
125	Ben Grieve (Futurama)	.05
126	A.J. Hinch (Futurama)	.05
127	Matt Clement (Futurama)	.05
128	Gary Matthews Jr. RC (Futurama)	.05
129	Aramis Ramirez (Futurama)	.05
130	Rolando Arrojo (Futurama)	.05

Big Boppers

The game's heavy hitters are the focus of this insert set. Cards have a color action photo on a sepia background. Each card is individually serial numbered in red foil in the upper-right, within an edition of 500. Backs repeat part of the front photo, in sepia only, and have recent stats and hitting highlights. Cards are numbered with a "B" prefix.

		NM/M
Complete Set (30):		80.00
Common Player:		1.00
Production 500 Sets		
B1	Darin Erstad	1.50
B2	Rafael Palmeiro	3.00
B3	Cal Ripken Jr.	10.00
B4	Nomar Garciaparra	5.00
B5	Mo Vaughn	1.00
B6	Frank Thomas	4.00
B7	Albert Belle	1.00
B8	Jim Thome	2.50
B9	Manny Ramirez	4.00
B10	Tony Clark	1.00
B11	Tino Martinez	1.00
B12	Ben Grieve	.05
B13	Ken Griffey Jr.	6.00
B14	Alex Rodriguez	7.50
B15	Jay Buhner	1.00
B16	Juan Gonzalez	2.00
B17	Jose Cruz Jr.	.05
B18	Jose Canseco	2.50
B19	Travis Lee	1.50
B20	Chipper Jones	5.00
B21	Andres Galarraga	4.00
B22	Andruw Jones	4.00
B23	Sammy Sosa	5.00
B24	Vinny Castilla	1.00
B25	Larry Walker	1.00
B26	Jeff Bagwell	4.00
B27	Gary Sheffield	2.00
B28	Mike Piazza	6.00
B29	Mark McGwire	7.50
B30	Barry Bonds	10.00

Groovy Kind of Glove

This 30-card set showcases baseball's top defensive players on a psychedelic, wavy and colorful background. They were inserted 1:7 packs.

		NM/M
Complete Set (30):		50.00
Common Player:		.60
Inserted 1:7		
G1	Roberto Alomar	1.00
G2	Cal Ripken Jr.	7.50
G3	Nomar Garciaparra	3.50
G4	Frank Thomas	2.25
G5	Robin Ventura	.60
G6	Omar Vizquel	.60
G7	Kenny Lofton	.60
G8	Ben Grieve	.60
G9	Alex Rodriguez	6.00
G10	Ken Griffey Jr.	5.00
G11	Ivan Rodriguez	1.50
G12	Travis Lee	.75
G13	Matt Williams	.60
G14	Greg Maddux	3.50
G15	Andres Galarraga	.60
G16	Andruw Jones	2.25
G17	Kerry Wood	1.25
G18	Mark Grace	.60
G19	Craig Biggio	.60
G20	Charles Johnson	.60
G21	Raul Mondesi	.60
G22	Mike Piazza	5.00
G23	Rey Ordonez	.60
G24	Derek Jeter	7.50
G25	Scott Rolen	1.25
G26	Mark McGwire	6.00
G27	Ken Caminiti	.60
G28	Tony Gwynn	3.50
G29	J.T. Snow	.60
G30	Barry Bonds	7.50

Legendary Cut

This insert features an actual Babe Ruth cut signature and is limited to a total of three cards.

		NM/M
LC	Babe Ruth (Three issued; 1/04 auction.)	9,500

New Frontier

This set spotlights 30 of baseball's top young prospects and is limited to 1,000 sequentially numbered sets.

		NM/M
Complete Set (30):		45.00
Common Player:		1.00
Production 1,000 Sets		
NF1	Justin Baughman	1.00
NF2	David Dellucci	1.00
NF3	Travis Lee	1.50
NF4	Troy Glaus	6.00
NF5	Mike Caruso	1.00
NF6	Jim Parque	1.00
NF7	Kerry Wood	2.00
NF8	Brett Tomko	1.00
NF9	Russell Branyan	1.00
NF10	Jaret Wright	1.00
NF11	Todd Helton	5.00
NF12	Gabe Alvarez	1.00
NF13	Matt Anderson	1.00
NF14	Alex Gonzalez	1.00
NF15	Mark Kotsay	1.00
NF16	Derrek Lee	3.00
NF17	Richard Hidalgo	1.00
NF18	Adrian Beltre	2.00
NF19	Geoff Jenkins	1.00
NF20	Eric Milton	1.00
NF21	Brad Fullmer	1.00
NF22	Vladimir Guerrero	6.00
NF23	Carl Pavano	1.00
NF24	Orlando Hernandez	1.25
NF25	Ben Grieve	1.00
NF26	A.J. Hinch	1.00
NF27	Matt Clement	1.00
NF28	Gary Matthews	1.00
NF29	Aramis Ramirez	1.00
NF30	Rolando Arrojo	1.00

Quantum Leap

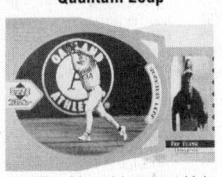

This 30-card insert set highlights the technological advancements of Upper Deck products on a horizontal format. A total of 50 serially numbered sets were produced.

		NM/M
Common Player:		15.00
Production 50 Sets		
Q1	Darin Erstad	20.00
Q2	Cal Ripken Jr.	100.00
Q3	Nomar Garciaparra	50.00
Q4	Frank Thomas	40.00
Q5	Kenny Lofton	15.00
Q6	Ben Grieve	15.00
Q7	Ken Griffey Jr.	60.00
Q8	Alex Rodriguez	75.00
Q9	Juan Gonzalez	20.00
Q10	Jose Cruz Jr.	15.00
Q11	Roger Clemens	55.00
Q12	Travis Lee	15.00
Q13	Chipper Jones	50.00
Q14	Greg Maddux	50.00
Q15	Kerry Wood	20.00
Q16	Jeff Bagwell	40.00
Q17	Mike Piazza	60.00
Q18	Scott Rolen	30.00
Q19	Mark McGwire	75.00
Q20	Tony Gwynn	50.00
Q21	Larry Walker	15.00
Q22	Derek Jeter	100.00
Q23	Sammy Sosa	50.00
Q24	Barry Bonds	100.00
Q25	Mo Vaughn	15.00
Q26	Roberto Alomar	20.00
Q27	Todd Helton	30.00
Q28	Ivan Rodriguez	30.00
Q29	Vladimir Guerrero	40.00
Q30	Albert Belle	15.00

Sign of the Times

This retro-style autographed 31-card set features both retired legends and current players. They were inserted 1:36 packs.

		NM/M
Common Autograph:		7.50
Inserted 1:36		
EB	Ernie Banks/300	40.00
YB	Yogi Berra/150	60.00
RB	Russell Branyan/750	8.00
LB	Lou Brock/300	25.00
JC	Jose Cruz Jr./300	8.00
RF	Rollie Fingers/600	10.00
BF	Bob Feller/300	20.00
CF	Carlton Fisk/600	30.00
BGi	Bob Gibson/300	30.00
BGr	Ben Grieve/300	5.00
KGj	Ken Griffey Jr./100	185.00
KGs	Ken Griffey Sr./600	15.00
TG	Tony Gwynn/200	35.00
AK	Al Kaline/600	30.00
PK	Paul Konerko/750	15.00
TLe	Travis Lee/300	8.00
EM	Eddie Mathews/600	60.00
GMj	Gary Matthews Jr./750	8.00
GMs	Gary Matthews/600	8.00
WM	Willie McCovey/600	30.00
TP	Tony Perez/600	10.00
GP	Gaylord Perry/1,000	10.00
KP	Kirby Puckett/450	80.00
BR	Brooks Robinson/300	30.00
SR	Scott Rolen/300	20.00
NR	Nolan Ryan/500	100.00
TS	Tom Seaver/300	30.00
WS	Warren Spahn/600	40.00
WiS	Willie Stargell/600	50.00
FT	Frank Thomas/600	15.00
KW	Kerry Wood/200	25.00

Time Capsule

Another retro-styled card that featured current stars who were destined to earn a place in baseball history. They were inserted 1:2 packs.

		NM/M
Complete Set (50):		35.00
Common Player:		.25
Inserted 1:2		
TC1	Mike Mussina	.50
TC2	Rafael Palmeiro	.65
TC3	Cal Ripken Jr.	3.00
TC4	Nomar Garciaparra	1.50
TC5	Pedro Martinez	.25
TC6	Mo Vaughn	.25
TC7	Albert Belle	.25
TC8	Frank Thomas	1.00
TC9	David Justice	.25
TC10	Kenny Lofton	.25
TC11	Manny Ramirez	1.00
TC12	Jim Thome	.60
TC13	Derek Jeter	3.00
TC14	Tino Martinez	.25
TC15	Ben Grieve	.25
TC16	Rickey Henderson	1.00
TC17	Ken Griffey Jr.	2.00
TC18	Randy Johnson	1.00
TC19	Alex Rodriguez	2.50
TC20	Wade Boggs	1.50
TC21	Fred McGriff	.25
TC22	Juan Gonzalez	.50
TC23	Ivan Rodriguez	.75
TC24	Nolan Ryan	2.50
TC25	Jose Canseco	.50
TC26	Roger Clemens	1.75
TC27	Jose Cruz Jr.	.25
TC28	Travis Lee	.40
TC29	Matt Williams	.25
TC30	Andres Galarraga	.25
TC31	Andruw Jones	1.00
TC32	Chipper Jones	1.50
TC33	Greg Maddux	1.50
TC34	Kerry Wood	.50
TC35	Barry Larkin	.25
TC36	Dante Bichette	.25
TC37	Larry Walker	.25
TC38	Livan Hernandez	.25
TC39	Jeff Bagwell	1.00
TC40	Craig Biggio	.25
TC41	Charles Johnson	.25
TC42	Gary Sheffield	.50
TC43	Marquis Grissom	.25
TC44	Mike Piazza	2.00
TC45	Scott Rolen	.65
TC46	Curt Schilling	.40
TC47	Mark McGwire	2.50
TC48	Ken Caminiti	.25
TC49	Tony Gwynn	1.50
TC50	Barry Bonds	3.00

Lunchbox

Lunchboxes were the form of packaging for UD Retro. Six different players are featured with each lunchbox containing 24 six-card packs, with a SRP of $4.99.

		NM/M
Complete Set (6):		40.00
Common Lunchbox:		4.00
	Nomar Garciaparra	6.00
	Ken Griffey Jr.	7.50
	Chipper Jones	6.00
	Travis Lee	4.00
	Mark McGwire	10.00
	Cal Ripken Jr.	12.00

1999 Upper Deck

Released in two series, base card fronts feature a textured silver border along the left and right sides. The player name and Upper Deck logo also are stamped in silver foil. Backs have a small photo, with stats and career highlights. Randomly seeded in packs are 100 Ken Griffey Jr. rookie cards that were bought back by Upper Deck from the hobby and autographed. Upper

Deck also re-inserted one pack of '89 Upper Deck inside every hobby box. Ten-card hobby packs carry a S.R.P. of $2.99. Cards #256-265 were never produced.

	NM/M
Complete Set (525):	45.00
Complete Series 1 (255):	25.00
Complete Series 2 (270):	20.00
Common Player:	.05
Exclusive Stars/RC's:	15X
Production 100 each	
Pack (10):	1.50
Wax Box (24):	35.00

#	Player	Price
1	Troy Glaus/SR	.60
2	Adrian Beltre/SR	.25
3	Matt Anderson/SR	.05
4	Eric Chavez/SR	.15
5	Jin Cho/SR	.05
6	Robert Smith/SR RC	.05
7	George Lombard/SR	.05
8	Mike Kinkade/SR	.05
9	Seth Greisinger/SR	.05
10	J.D. Drew/SR	.50
11	Aramis Ramirez/SR	.05
12	Carlos Guillen/SR	.05
13	Justin Baughman/SR	.05
14	Jim Parque/SR	.05
15	Ryan Jackson/SR	.05
16	Ramon Martinez/SR	.05
17	Orlando Hernandez/SR	.05
18	Jeremy Giambi/SR	.05
19	Gary DiSarcina	.05
20	Darin Erstad	.25
21	Troy Glaus	.50
22	Chuck Finley	.05
23	Dave Hollins	.05
24	Troy Percival	.05
25	Tim Salmon	.05
26	Brian Anderson	.05
27	Jay Bell	.05
28	Andy Benes	.05
29	Brent Brede	.05
30	David Dellucci	.05
31	Karim Garcia	.10
32	Travis Lee	.20
33	Andres Galarraga	.05
34	Ryan Klesko	.05
35	Keith Lockhart	.05
36	Kevin Millwood	.05
37	Denny Neagle	.05
38	John Smoltz	.05
39	Michael Tucker	.05
40	Walt Weiss	.05
41	Dennis Martinez	.05
42	Javy Lopez	.05
43	Brady Anderson	.05
44	Harold Baines	.05
45	Mike Bordick	.05
46	Roberto Alomar	.20
47	Scott Erickson	.05
48	Mike Mussina	.30
49	Cal Ripken Jr.	2.00
50	Darren Bragg	.05
51	Dennis Eckersley	.50
52	Nomar Garciaparra	.05
53	Scott Hatteberg	.05
54	Troy O'Leary	.05
55	Bret Saberhagen	.05
56	John Valentin	.05
57	Rod Beck	.05
58	Jeff Blauser	.05
59	Brant Brown	.05
60	Mark Clark	.05
61	Mark Grace	.05
62	Kevin Tapani	.05
63	Henry Rodriguez	.05
64	Mike Cameron	.05
65	Mike Caruso	.05
66	Ray Durham	.05
67	Jaime Navarro	.05
68	Magglio Ordonez	.30
69	Mike Sirotka	.05
70	Sean Casey	.15
71	Barry Larkin	.05
72	Jon Nunnally	.05
73	Paul Konerko	.15
74	Chris Stynes	.05
75	Brett Tomko	.05
76	Dmitri Young	.05
77	Sandy Alomar	.05
78	Bartolo Colon	.05
79	Travis Fryman	.05
80	Brian Giles	.05
81	David Justice	.05
82	Omar Vizquel	.05

#	Player	Price
83	Jaret Wright	.05
84	Jim Thome	.40
85	Charles Nagy	.05
86	Pedro Astacio	.05
87	Todd Helton	.50
88	Darryl Kile	.05
89	Mike Lansing	.05
90	Neifi Perez	.05
91	John Thomson	.05
92	Larry Walker	.05
93	Tony Clark	.05
94	Deivi Cruz	.05
95	Damion Easley	.05
96	Brian L. Hunter	.05
97	Todd Jones	.05
98	Brian Moehler	.05
99	Gabe Alvarez	.05
100	Craig Counsell	.05
101	Cliff Floyd	.05
102	Livan Hernandez	.05
103	Andy Larkin	.05
104	Derrek Lee	.35
105	Brian Meadows	.05
106	Moises Alou	.05
107	Sean Berry	.05
108	Craig Biggio	.05
109	Ricky Gutierrez	.05
110	Mike Hampton	.05
111	Jose Lima	.05
112	Billy Wagner	.05
113	Hal Morris	.05
114	Johnny Damon	.30
115	Jeff King	.05
116	Jeff Montgomery	.05
117	Glendon Rusch	.05
118	Larry Sutton	.05
119	Bobby Bonilla	.05
120	Jim Eisenreich	.05
121	Eric Karros	.05
122	Matt Luke	.05
123	Ramon Martinez	.05
124	Gary Sheffield	.40
125	Eric Young	.05
126	Charles Johnson	.05
127	Jeff Cirillo	.05
128	Marquis Grissom	.05
129	Jeromy Burnitz	.05
130	Bob Wickman	.05
131	Scott Karl	.05
132	Mark Loretta	.05
133	Fernando Vina	.05
134	Matt Lawton	.05
135	Pat Meares	.05
136	Eric Milton	.05
137	Paul Molitor	.60
138	David Ortiz	.35
139	Todd Walker	.05
140	Shane Andrews	.05
141	Brad Fullmer	.05
142	Vladimir Guerrero	.60
143	Dustin Hermanson	.05
144	Ryan McGuire	.05
145	Ugueth Urbina	.05
146	John Franco	.05
147	Butch Huskey	.05
148	Bobby Jones	.05
149	John Olerud	.05
150	Rey Ordonez	.05
151	Mike Piazza	1.25
152	Hideo Nomo	.30
153	Masato Yoshii	.05
154	Derek Jeter	2.00
155	Chuck Knoblauch	.05
156	Paul O'Neill	.05
157	Andy Pettitte	.20
158	Mariano Rivera	.15
159	Darryl Strawberry	.05
160	David Wells	.05
161	Jorge Posada	.05
162	Ramiro Mendoza	.05
163	Miguel Tejada	.15
164	Ryan Christenson	.05
165	Rickey Henderson	.60
166	A.J. Hinch	.05
167	Ben Grieve	.05
168	Kenny Rogers	.05
169	Matt Stairs	.05
170	Bob Abreu	.05
171	Rico Brogna	.05
172	Doug Glanville	.05
173	Mike Grace	.05
174	Desi Relaford	.05
175	Scott Rolen	.40
176	Jose Guillen	.05
177	Francisco Cordova	.05
178	Al Martin	.05
179	Jason Schmidt	.05
180	Turner Ward	.05
181	Kevin Young	.05
182	Mark McGwire	1.50
183	Delino DeShields	.05
184	Eli Marrero	.05
185	Tom Lampkin	.05
186	Ray Lankford	.05
187	Willie McGee	.05
188	Matt Morris	.05
189	Andy Ashby	.05
190	Kevin Brown	.05
191	Ken Caminiti	.05
192	Trevor Hoffman	.05
193	Wally Joyner	.05
194	Greg Vaughn	.05
195	Danny Darwin	.05
196	Shawn Estes	.05
197	Orel Hershiser	.05
198	Jeff Kent	.05
199	Bill Mueller	.05
200	Robb Nen	.05

#	Player	Price
201	J.T. Snow	.05
202	Ken Cloude	.05
203	Russ Davis	.05
204	Jeff Fassero	.05
205	Ken Griffey Jr.	1.00
206	Shane Monahan	.05
207	David Segui	.05
208	Dan Wilson	.05
209	Wilson Alvarez	.05
210	Wade Boggs	.75
211	Miguel Cairo	.05
212	Bubba Trammell	.05
213	Quinton McCracken	.05
214	Paul Sorrento	.05
215	Kevin Stocker	.05
216	Will Clark	.05
217	Rusty Greer	.05
218	Rick Helling	.05
219	Mike McLemore	.05
220	Ivan Rodriguez	.50
221	John Wetteland	.05
222	Jose Canseco	.40
223	Roger Clemens	.85
224	Carlos Delgado	.25
225	Darrin Fletcher	.05
226	Alex Gonzalez	.05
227	Jose Cruz Jr.	.05
228	Shannon Stewart	.05
229	Rolando Arrojo (Foreign Focus)	.05
230	Livan Hernandez (Foreign Focus)	.05
231	Orlando Hernandez (Foreign Focus)	.05
232	Raul Mondesi (Foreign Focus)	.05
233	Moises Alou (Foreign Focus)	.05
234	Pedro Martinez (Foreign Focus)	.30
235	Sammy Sosa (Foreign Focus)	.50
236	Vladimir Guerrero (Foreign Focus)	.40
237	Bartolo Colon (Foreign Focus)	.05
238	Miguel Tejada (Foreign Focus)	.05
239	Ismael Valdes (Foreign Focus)	.05
240	Mariano Rivera (Foreign Focus)	.05
241	Jose Cruz Jr. (Foreign Focus)	.05
242	Juan Gonzalez (Foreign Focus)	.20
243	Ivan Rodriguez (Foreign Focus)	.15
244	Sandy Alomar (Foreign Focus)	.05
245	Roberto Alomar (Foreign Focus)	.10
246	Magglio Ordonez (Foreign Focus)	.05
247	Kerry Wood (Highlights Checklist)	.10
248	Mark McGwire (Highlights Checklist)	.75
249	David Wells (Highlights Checklist)	.05
250	Rolando Arrojo (Highlights Checklist)	.05
251	Ken Griffey Jr. (Highlights Checklist)	.65
252	Trevor Hoffman (Highlights Checklist)	.05
253	Travis Lee (Highlights Checklist)	.05
254	Roberto Alomar (Highlights Checklist)	.10
255	Sammy Sosa (Highlights Checklist)	.05
266	Pat Burrell/SR RC	2.00
267	Shea Hillenbrand/SR RC	.65
268	Robert Fick/SR	.05
269	Roy Halladay/SR	.05
270	Ruben Mateo/SR	.05
271	Bruce Chen/SR	.05
272	Angel Pena/SR	.05
273	Michael Barrett/SR	.05
274	Kevin Witt/SR	.05
275	Damon Minor/SR	.05
276	Ryan Minor/SR	.05
277	A.J. Pierzynski/SR	.05
278	A.J. Burnett/SR RC	.50
279	Dermal Brown/SR	.05
280	Joe Lawrence/SR	.05
281	Derrick Gibson/SR	.05
282	Carlos Febles/SR	.05
283	Chris Haas/SR	.05
284	Cesar King/SR	.05
285	Calvin Pickering/SR	.05
286	Mitch Meluskey/SR	.05
287	Carlos Beltran/SR	.50
288	Ron Belliard/SR	.05
289	Jerry Hairston Jr./SR	.05
290	Fernando Seguignol/SR	.05
291	Kris Benson/SR	.05
292	Chad Hutchinson/SR RC	.05
293	Jarrod Washburn	.05
294	Jason Dickson	.05
295	Mo Vaughn	.05
296	Garrett Anderson	.05
297	Jim Edmonds	.05
298	Ken Hill	.05
299	Shigetosi Hasegawa	.05
300	Todd Stottlemyre	.05
301	Randy Johnson	.60

#	Player	Price
302	Omar Daal	.05
303	Steve Finley	.05
304	Matt Williams	.05
305	Danny Klassen	.05
306	Tony Batista	.05
307	Brian Jordan	.05
308	Greg Maddux	.75
309	Chipper Jones	.75
310	Bret Boone	.05
311	Ozzie Guillen	.05
312	John Rocker	.05
313	Tom Glavine	.25
314	Andruw Jones	.60
315	Albert Belle	.05
316	Charles Johnson	.05
317	Will Clark	.05
318	B.J. Surhoff	.05
319	Delino DeShields	.05
320	Heathcliff Slocumb	.05
321	Sidney Ponson	.05
322	Juan Guzman	.05
323	Reggie Jefferson	.05
324	Mark Portugal	.05
325	Tim Wakefield	.05
326	Jason Varitek	.05
327	Jose Offerman	.05
328	Pedro Martinez	.60
329	Trot Nixon	.05
330	Kerry Wood	.05
331	Sammy Sosa	.75
332	Glenallen Hill	.05
333	Gary Gaetti	.05
334	Mickey Morandini	.05
335	Benito Santiago	.05
336	Jeff Blauser	.05
337	Frank Thomas	.65
338	Paul Konerko	.15
339	James Navarro	.05
340	Carlos Lee	.05
341	Brian Simmons	.05
342	Mark Johnson	.05
343	Jeff Abbot	.05
344	Steve Avery	.05
345	Mike Cameron	.05
346	Michael Tucker	.05
347	Greg Vaughn	.05
348	Hal Morris	.05
349	Pete Harnisch	.05
350	Denny Neagle	.05
351	Manny Ramirez	.60
352	Roberto Alomar	.20
353	Dwight Gooden	.05
354	Kenny Lofton	.05
355	Mike Jackson	.05
356	Charles Nagy	.05
357	Enrique Wilson	.05
358	Russ Branyan	.05
359	Richie Sexson	.05
360	Vinny Castilla	.05
361	Dante Bichette	.05
362	Kirt Manwaring	.05
363	Darryl Hamilton	.05
364	Jamey Wright	.05
365	Curt Leskanic	.05
366	Jeff Reed	.05
367	Bobby Higginson	.05
368	Justin Thompson	.05
369	Brad Ausmus	.05
370	Dean Palmer	.05
371	Gabe Kapler	.05
372	Juan Encarnacion	.05
373	Karim Garcia	.10
374	Alex Gonzalez	.05
375	Braden Looper	.05
376	Preston Wilson	.05
377	Todd Dunwoody	.05
378	Alex Fernandez	.05
379	Mark Kotsay	.05
380	Mark Mantei	.05
381	Ken Caminiti	.05
382	Scott Elarton	.05
383	Jeff Bagwell	.60
384	Derek Bell	.05
385	Ricky Gutierrez	.05
386	Richard Hildago	.05
387	Shane Reynolds	.05
388	Carl Everett	.05
389	Scott Service	.05
390	Jeff Suppan	.05
391	Joe Randa	.05
392	Kevin Appier	.05
393	Shane Halter	.05
394	Chad Kreuter	.05
395	Mike Sweeney	.05
396	Kevin Brown	.05
397	Devon White	.05
398	Todd Hollandsworth	.05
399	Todd Hundley	.05
400	Chan Ho Park	.05
401	Mark Grudzielanek	.05
402	Raul Mondesi	.05
403	Ismael Valdes	.05
404	Rafael Roque	.05
405	Sean Berry	.05
406	Kevin Barker	.05
407	Dave Nilsson	.05
408	Geoff Jenkins	.05
409	Jim Abbott	.05
410	Bobby Hughes	.05
411	Corey Koskie	.05
412	Rick Aguilera	.05
413	LaTroy Hawkins	.05
414	Ron Coomer	.05
415	Denny Hocking	.05
416	Marty Cordova	.05
417	Terry Steinbach	.05
418	Rondell White	.05
419	Wilton Guerrero	.05

#	Player	Price
420	Shane Andrews	.05
421	Orlando Cabrera	.05
422	Carl Pavano	.05
423	Jeff Vasquez	.05
424	Chris Widger	.05
425	Robin Ventura	.05
426	Rickey Henderson	.60
427	Al Leiter	.05
428	Bobby Jones	.05
429	Brian McRae	.05
430	Roger Cedeno	.05
431	Bobby Bonilla	.05
432	Edgardo Alfonzo	.05
433	Bernie Williams	.05
434	Ricky Ledee	.05
435	Chili Davis	.05
436	Tino Martinez	.05
437	Scott Brosius	.05
438	David Cone	.05
439	Joe Girardi	.05
440	Roger Clemens	.85
441	Chad Curtis	.05
442	Hideki Irabu	.05
443	Jason Giambi	.40
444	Scott Spezio	.05
445	Tony Phillips	.05
446	Ramon Hernandez	.05
447	Mike Macfarlane	.05
448	Tom Candiotti	.05
449	Billy Taylor	.05
450	Bobby Estella	.05
451	Curt Schilling	.25
452	Carlton Loewer	.05
453	Marlon Anderson	.05
454	Kevin Jordan	.05
455	Ron Gant	.05
456	Chad Ogea	.05
457	Abraham Nunez	.05
458	Jason Kendall	.05
459	Pat Meares	.05
460	Brant Brown	.05
461	Brian Giles	.05
462	Chad Hermansen	.05
463	Freddy Garcia	.05
464	Edgar Renteria	.05
465	Fernando Tatis	.05
466	Eric Davis	.05
467	Darren Bragg	.05
468	Donovan Osborne	.05
469	Manny Aybar	.05
470	Jose Jimenez	.05
471	Kent Mercker	.05
472	Reggie Sanders	.05
473	Ruben Rivera	.05
474	Tony Gwynn	.75
475	Jim Leyritz	.05
476	Chris Gomez	.05
477	Matt Clement	.05
478	Carlos Hernandez	.05
479	Sterling Hitchcock	.05
480	Ellis Burks	.05
481	Barry Bonds	2.00
482	Marvin Bernard	.05
483	Kirk Rueter	.05
484	F.P. Santangelo	.05
485	Stan Javier	.05
486	Jeff Kent	.05
487	Alex Rodriguez	1.50
488	Tom Lampkin	.05
489	Jose Mesa	.05
490	Jay Buhner	.05
491	Edgar Martinez	.05
492	Butch Huskey	.05
493	John Mabry	.05
494	Jamie Moyer	.05
495	Roberto Hernandez	.05
496	Tony Saunders	.05
497	Fred McGriff	.05
498	Dave Martinez	.05
499	Jose Canseco	.40
500	Rolando Arrojo	.05
501	Esteban Yan	.05
502	Juan Gonzalez	.30
503	Rafael Palmeiro	.50
504	Aaron Sele	.05
505	Royce Clayton	.05
506	Todd Zeile	.05
507	Tom Goodwin	.05
508	Lee Stevens	.05
509	Esteban Loaiza	.05
510	Joey Hamilton	.05
511	Homer Bush	.05
512	Willie Greene	.05
513	Shawn Green	.25
514	David Wells	.05
515	Kelvim Escobar	.05
516	Tony Fernandez	.05
517	Pat Hentgen	.05
518	Mark McGwire (Arms Race)	.75
519	Ken Griffey Jr. (Arms Race)	.65
520	Sammy Sosa (Arms Race)	.50
521	Juan Gonzalez (Arms Race)	.50
522	J.D. Drew (Arms Race)	.10
523	Chipper Jones (Arms Race)	.50
524	Alex Rodriguez (Arms Race)	.75
525	Mike Piazza (Arms Race)	.65
526	Nomar Garciaparra (Arms Race)	.50
527	Season Highlights Checklist (Mark McGwire)	.75
528	Season Highlights Checklist (Sammy Sosa)	.50

#		Price
529	Season Highlights Checklist (Scott Brosius)	.05
530	Season Highlights Checklist (Cal Ripken Jr.)	1.00
531	Season Highlights Checklist (Barry Bonds)	1.00
532	Season Highlights Checklist (Roger Clemens)	.40
533	Season Highlights Checklist (Ken Griffey Jr.)	.65
534	Season Highlights Checklist (Alex Rodriguez)	.75
535	Season Highlights Checklist (Curt Schilling)	.05

Exclusives

Randomly inserted into hobby packs, this parallel issue is individually serial numbered on back from within an edition of 100 of each card. Besides the serial number, the inserts are readily apparent by the use of copper metallic foil graphic highlights on front. Series 1 Exclusive cards have the serial number on back in gold foil; Series 2 Exclusives have the number ink-jetted in black. A green-foil parallel of the parallel was issued in quantities of just one card each for Series 1, and 10 cards each for Series 2.

	NM/M
Common Player:	3.00
Stars/Rookies:	15X
Greens (1-255): Values Undetermined	
Greens (266-535):	100X

Crowning Glory

These double-sided cards feature players who reached milestones during the '98 season. There are three cards in the set, with four different versions of each card. The regular version is seeded 1:23 packs. Doubles are numbered to 1,000, Triples numbered to 25 and Home Runs are limited to one each.

	NM/M
Complete Set (3):	22.50
Common Player:	6.00
Inserted 1:23	
Doubles (1,000 Sets):	2X
Triples (25 Sets):	8X
Home Runs (1 Set):	Values Undetermined

CG1	Roger Clemens, Kerry Wood	6.00
CG2	Mark McGwire, Barry Bonds	12.00
CG3	Ken Griffey Jr., Mark McGwire	7.50

Forte

This 30-card set features the top players in the game, highlighted by blue holofoil treatment. Numbers on card backs have an "F" prefix and are seeded 1:23 packs. There are also die-cut parallels to Forte: Double, Triple and Home Run. Doubles are sequen-

MP	Mike Piazza HR1	20.00
MR	Manny Ramirez H2	10.00
AR	Alex Rodriguez HR1	25.00
IR	Ivan Rodriguez H1	7.50
NRa	Nolan Ryan/Astros H2	25.00
NRas	Nolan Ryan H2/	
	Auto./34	450.00
NRb	Nolan Ryan/	
	Rangers HR2	25.00
SS	Sammy Sosa H2	20.00
BT	Bubba Trammell H2	6.00
FT	Frank Thomas HR2	15.00
KW	Kerry Wood HR1	15.00
KWs	Kerry Wood/	
	Auto./34 HR1	150.00

Grand Slam Record Breakers

tially numbered to 2,000 sets, Triples are limited to 100 numbered sets and Home Runs are limited to 10 numbered sets.

		NM/M
Complete Set (30):		50.00
Common Player:		.50
Inserted 1:23		
Doubles (2,000 Sets):		3X
Triples (100):		15X
Quadruples (10):		40X
1	Darin Erstad	1.00
2	Troy Glaus	1.50
3	Mo Vaughn	.50
4	Greg Maddux	2.50
5	Andres Galarraga	.50
6	Chipper Jones	2.50
7	Cal Ripken Jr.	5.00
8	Albert Belle	.50
9	Nomar Garciaparra	2.50
10	Sammy Sosa	2.50
11	Kerry Wood	1.00
12	Frank Thomas	2.00
13	Jim Thome	1.50
14	Jeff Bagwell	2.00
15	Vladimir Guerrero	2.00
16	Mike Piazza	3.00
17	Derek Jeter	5.00
18	Ben Grieve	.50
19	Eric Chavez	.50
20	Scott Rolen	1.50
21	Mark McGwire	4.00
22	J.D. Drew	1.00
23	Tony Gwynn	2.50
24	Barry Bonds	5.00
25	Alex Rodriguez	4.00
26	Ken Griffey Jr.	3.00
27	Ivan Rodriguez	1.50
28	Juan Gonzalez	1.00
29	Roger Clemens	2.75
30	Andruw Jones	2.00

Game Jersey

A piece of game-worn jersey is framed by a baseball diamond schematic. A round portrait photo appears at top-right, along with the player's uniform number. A small action photo is at bottom center. Backs have another round portrait photo and a statement of authenticity. Game Jersey cards bearing an H1 or H2 designation were hobby-only inserts at a rate of one per 288 packs in the appropriate series. Cards with an HR1 or HR2 notation were found in both hobby and retail packs at a rate of 1:2,500. Autographed versions of some cards were produced, with the edition number noted.

		NM/M
Common Player:		6.00
AB	Adrian Beltre H1	10.00
EC	Eric Chavez H2	6.00
JD	J.D. Drew H2	10.00
JDs	J.D. Drew/Auto./8 H2	150.00
DE	Darin Erstad H1	10.00
BF	Brad Fullmer H2	4.50
JG	Juan Gonzalez HR1	15.00
BG	Ben Grieve H1	6.00
KG	Ken Griffey Jr. H1	20.00
KGs	Ken Griffey Jr./	
	Auto./24 H1	150.00
JR	Ken Griffey Jr. HR2	20.00
JRs	Ken Griffey Jr./	
	Auto./24 HR2	150.00
TGw	Tony Gwynn H2	15.00
TH	Todd Helton H2	15.00
CJ	Charles Johnson HR1	6.00
CJ	Chipper Jones H2	15.00
TL	Travis Lee H1	6.00
GM	Greg Maddux HR2	15.00

company's cards share a "Power Elite" logo at top and "Home Run Heroes" logo vertically at right.

		NM/M
Complete Set (4):		5.00
Common Player:		1.00
5	Mark McGwire	2.00
6	Sammy Sosa	1.25
7	Ken Griffey Jr.	1.50
8	Frank Thomas	1.00

Immaculate Perception

These gold-foil accented cards were inserts in a limited distribution retail packaging.

		NM/M
Complete Set (10):		7.50
Common Player:		.50
G1	Mark McGwire	1.50
G2	Sammy Sosa	1.50
G3	Ken Griffey Jr.	1.50
G4	Roger Clemens	1.00
G5	Kerry Wood	.75
G6	Cal Ripken Jr.	2.00
G7	Barry Bonds	2.00
G8	David Wells	.50
G9	Sammy Sosa	1.50
G10	Mark McGwire	1.50

Homerun Heroes

These gold-foil enhanced cards were inserted one per specially marked five-card foil pack, plus one as a topper in each tin can of this retail exclusive product. The first six players on the checklist were featured on the cans in which the cards were sold.

		NM/M
Complete Set (10):		10.00
Common Player:		.50
Complete Set Cans (6):		10.00
Common Player Can:		
H1	Ken Griffey Jr.	1.25
H2	Mark McGwire	2.00
H3	Sammy Sosa	1.00
H4	Troy Glaus	.75
H5	Mike Piazza	2.00
H6	Chipper Jones	1.00
H7	Vladimir Guerrero	.75
H8	Frank Thomas	.75
H9	Juan Gonzalez	.50
H10	Alex Rodriguez	2.00
1	Ken Griffey Jr.	2.50
2	Mark McGwire	2.50
3	Sammy Sosa	2.00
4	Troy Glaus	1.50
5	Mike Piazza	2.50
6	Chipper Jones	2.00

Home Run Heroes

These cards were part of an unannounced multi-manufacturer (Fleer, Upper Deck, Topps, Pacific) insert program which was exclusive to Wal-Mart. Each company produced cards of Mark McGwire and Sammy Sosa, along with two other premier sluggers. Each

		NM/M
Complete Set (10):		10.00
Common Player:		.50
S1	Ken Griffey Jr.	1.50
S2	Mark McGwire	1.50
S3	Sammy Sosa	1.00
S4	Cal Ripken Jr.	2.00
S5	Nomar Garciaparra	1.00
S6	Alex Rodriguez	1.50
S7	Kerry Wood	.50
S8	Juan Gonzalez	.50
S9	Derek Jeter	2.00
S10	Greg Maddux	1.00

Piece of History 500 Club Babe Ruth

Limited to a reported 50 pieces and inserted into Series 2 Upper Deck packs, this card differs from the Piece of History Ruth bat cards on the photos used and the 500 Club notation.

		NM/M
BR	Babe Ruth/50	4,000

Babe Ruth Piece of History Bat

Limited to approximately 400, this card has an imbedded chip of a bat from an actual game-used Louisville Slugger swung by the Bambino himself. A "signed" version of this card also exists, which incorporates a cut signature of Ruth along with a piece of his game-used bat; only three exist.

		NM/M
PH	Babe Ruth/Bat	900.00
PHLC	Babe Ruth/Legendary	
	Cut Auto.	25,000

Textbook Excellence

This 30-card set features the game's most fundamentally sound performers. Card fronts have a photo of the featured player on a silver-foil stamped grid background. Vertically at left is player identification on a brown background. These are seeded 1:23 packs. Three hobby-only parallels were also issued: Double, Triple and Home Run. Doubles are numbered to 2,000 sets, Triples are limited to 100 numbered sets and Home Runs are limited to 10 numbered sets. Cards are numbered with a "T" prefix.

		NM/M
Complete Set (30):		12.50
Common Player:		.25
Inserted 1:4		
Doubles (2,000 Sets):		1.5X
Triples (100):		5X
Quadruples (10):		40X
T1	Mo Vaughn	.25
T2	Greg Maddux	.75
T3	Chipper Jones	.75
T4	Andruw Jones	.60
T5	Cal Ripken Jr.	2.00
T6	Albert Belle	.25
T7	Roberto Alomar	.30
T8	Nomar Garciaparra	.75
T9	Kerry Wood	.30
T10	Sammy Sosa	.75
T11	Greg Vaughn	.25
T12	Jeff Bagwell	.25
T13	Kevin Brown	.25
T14	Vladimir Guerrero	.60
T15	Mike Piazza	1.00
T16	Bernie Williams	.25
T17	Derek Jeter	2.00
T18	Ben Grieve	.25
T19	Eric Chavez	.25
T29	Scott Rolen	.50
T21	Mark McGwire	1.50
T22	David Wells	.25
T23	J.D. Drew	.50
T24	Tony Gwynn	.75
T25	Barry Bonds	2.00
T26	Alex Rodriguez	1.50
T27	Ken Griffey Jr.	1.00
T28	Juan Gonzalez	.30
T29	Ivan Rodriguez	.50
T30	Roger Clemens	.85

View to a Thrill

This 30-card set focuses on baseball's best overall athletes. There are two photos of the featured player on the card front, highlighted by silver foil and some embossing. These are inserted 1:7 packs. Numbered parallel sets were produced of: Doubles (2,000), Triples (100) and Quadruples (10).

		NM/M
Complete Set (30):		25.00
Common Player:		.35
Inserted 1:7		
Doubles (2,000 Sets):		1.5X
Triples (100):		4X
Quadruples (10):		30X
V1	Mo Vaughn	.35
V2	Darin Erstad	.40
V3	Travis Lee	.40
V4	Chipper Jones	1.50
V5	Greg Maddux	1.50
V6	Gabe Kapler	.35
V7	Cal Ripken Jr.	3.00
V8	Nomar Garciaparra	1.50
V9	Kerry Wood	.40
V10	Frank Thomas	1.00
V11	Manny Ramirez	1.00
V12	Larry Walker	.35
V13	Tony Clark	.35
V14	Jeff Bagwell	1.00
V15	Craig Biggio	.35
V16	Vladimir Guerrero	1.00
V17	Mike Piazza	2.00
V18	Bernie Williams	.35
V19	Derek Jeter	3.00
V20	Ben Grieve	.35
V21	Eric Chavez	.35
V22	Scott Rolen	.65
V23	Mark McGwire	2.50
V24	Tony Gwynn	1.50
V25	Barry Bonds	3.00
V26	Ken Griffey Jr.	2.00
V27	Alex Rodriguez	2.50
V28	J.D. Drew	.65
V29	Juan Gonzalez	.50
V30	Roger Clemens	1.75

Wonder Years

These inserts look like a throwback to the groovin' '70s, with brightly striped green and pink borders. "Wonder Years" is across the top of the front in yellow. Backs have the player's three best seasons' stats along with a mention of a milestone. The cards are numbered with a WY prefix and are seeded 1:7 packs. There are three parallel ver-

sions: Doubles numbered to 1,000, Triples numbered to 25 and Home Runs that are limited to one.

		NM/M
Complete Set (30):		30.00
Common Player:		.50
Inserted 1:7		
Doubles (2,000):		2.5X
Triples (50):		10X
Home Runs (1): Values Undetermined		
WY1	Kerry Wood	.75
WY2	Travis Lee	.65
WY3	Jeff Bagwell	1.50
WY4	Barry Bonds	4.00
WY5	Roger Clemens	2.25
WY6	Jose Cruz Jr.	.50
WY7	Andres Galarraga	.50
WY8	Nomar Garciaparra	2.00
WY9	Juan Gonzalez	.75
WY10	Ken Griffey Jr.	2.50
WY11	Tony Gwynn	2.00
WY12	Derek Jeter	4.00
WY13	Randy Johnson	1.50
WY14	Andruw Jones	1.50
WY15	Chipper Jones	2.00
WY16	Kenny Lofton	.50
WY17	Greg Maddux	2.00
WY18	Tino Martinez	.50
WY19	Mark McGwire	3.00
WY20	Paul Molitor	1.50
WY21	Mike Piazza	2.50
WY22	Manny Ramirez	1.50
WY23	Cal Ripken Jr.	4.00
WY24	Alex Rodriguez	3.00
WY25	Sammy Sosa	2.00
WY26	Frank Thomas	1.50
WY27	Mo Vaughn	.50
WY28	Larry Walker	.50
WY29	Scott Rolen	1.00
WY30	Ben Grieve	.50

10th Anniversary Team

This 30-card set commemorates Upper Deck's 10th Anniversary, as collectors selected their favorite players for this set. Regular versions are seeded 1:4 packs, Doubles numbered to 4,000, Triples numbered to 100 and Home Runs which are limited to one set.

		NM/M
Complete Set (30):		20.00
Common Player:		.15
Inserted 1:4		
Doubles (4,000 Sets):		2X
Triples (100):		6X
Home Runs (1): Values Undetermined		
X1	Mike Piazza	1.50
X2	Mark McGwire	2.00
X3	Roberto Alomar	.30
X4	Chipper Jones	1.00
X5	Cal Ripken Jr.	3.00
X6	Ken Griffey Jr.	1.50
X7	Barry Bonds	3.00
X8	Tony Gwynn	1.00
X9	Nolan Ryan	3.00
X10	Randy Johnson	.75
X11	Dennis Eckersley	.65
X12	Ivan Rodriguez	.65
X13	Frank Thomas	.75
X14	Craig Biggio	.15
X15	Wade Boggs	.75
X16	Alex Rodriguez	2.00
X17	Albert Belle	.15
X18	Juan Gonzalez	.40
X19	Rickey Henderson	.25
X20	Greg Maddux	1.00
X21	Tom Glavine	.35
X22	Randy Myers	.15
X23	Sandy Alomar	.15
X24	Jeff Bagwell	.25
X25	Derek Jeter	3.00
X26	Matt Williams	.15
X27	Kenny Lofton	.15
X28	Sammy Sosa	1.00
X29	Larry Walker	.15
X30	Roger Clemens	1.25

Ken Griffey Jr. Supers

These large-format (5" x 7") reproductions of each of Junior's regular-issue UD cards from 1989-98 were issued as a Wal-Mart exclusive in Series 1 UD

Opening Season Superstars

These gold-foil enhanced cards were inserted one per specially marked five-card foil pack, in limited retail-exclusive distribution.

baseball. Autographed versions of the super-sized Griffey cards were also found in the boxes. The supers were also distributed at the July 1999 National Sports Collectors Convention as a wrapper-redemption premium at the card company's booth. Other than the lack of a hologram on back, the cards are identical 4X blowups of the issued cards.

	NM/M
Complete Set (10):	15.00
Common Card:	2.00
Autographed Card:	75.00
1 Ken Griffey Jr./1989	5.00
156 Ken Griffey Jr./1990	2.00
555 Ken Griffey Jr./1991	2.00
424 Ken Griffey Jr./1992	2.00
355 Ken Griffey Jr./1993	2.00
224 Ken Griffey Jr./1994	2.00
100 Ken Griffey Jr./1995	2.00
200 Ken Griffey Jr./1996	2.00
175 Ken Griffey Jr./1997	2.00
225 Ken Griffey Jr./1998	2.00

Ken Griffey Jr. 1989 Buyback Autograph

One hundred authentically autographed 1989 Ken Griffey Jr. Upper Deck rookie cards were seeded into Series 1 packs. UD bought the cards on the open market, had them autographed by Griffey and added a diamond-shaped authentication hologram on back

	NM/M
Ken Griffey Jr./100	1,250

1999 Upper Deck Black Diamond

This 120-card base set features metallic foil fronts, while card backs have the featured player's vital information along with a close-up photo. The Diamond Debut subset (91-120) are short-printed and seeded 1:4 packs.

	NM/M
Complete Set (120):	30.00
Common Player:	.10

		NM/M
Common Diamond Debut (91-120):		.25
Inserted 1:4		
Double Diamonds (3,000 Each):		3X
Double Diamond Debuts (2,500):		2X
Triple Diamonds (1,500):		6X
Triple Diamond Debuts (1,000):		3X
Pack (6):		2.00
Wax Box (30):		40.00
1	Darin Erstad	.10
2	Tim Salmon	.10
3	Jim Edmonds	.10
4	Matt Williams	.10
5	David Dellucci	.10
6	Jay Bell	.10
7	Andres Galarraga	.10
8	Chipper Jones	1.00
9	Greg Maddux	1.00
10	Andruw Jones	.75
11	Cal Ripken Jr.	2.50
12	Rafael Palmeiro	.65
13	Brady Anderson	.10
14	Mike Mussina	.40
15	Nomar Garciaparra	1.00
16	Mo Vaughn	.10
17	Pedro Martinez	.75
18	Sammy Sosa	1.00
19	Henry Rodriguez	.10
20	Frank Thomas	.75
21	Magglio Ordonez	.40
22	Albert Belle	.10
23	Paul Konerko	.20
24	Sean Casey	.10
25	Jim Thome	.60
26	Kenny Lofton	.10
27	Sandy Alomar Jr.	.10
28	Jaret Wright	.10
29	Larry Walker	.10
30	Todd Helton	.65
31	Vinny Castilla	.10
32	Tony Clark	.10
33	Damion Easley	.10
34	Mark Kotsay	.10
35	Derrek Lee	.50
36	Moises Alou	.10
37	Jeff Bagwell	.10
38	Craig Biggio	.10
39	Randy Johnson	.75
40	Dean Palmer	.10
41	Johnny Damon	.35
42	Chan Ho Park	.10
43	Raul Mondesi	.10
44	Gary Sheffield	.40
45	Jeromy Burnitz	.10
46	Marquis Grissom	.10
47	Jeff Cirillo	.10
48	Paul Molitor	.75
49	Todd Walker	.10
50	Vladimir Guerrero	.75
51	Brad Fullmer	.10
52	Mike Piazza	1.50
53	Hideo Nomo	.40
54	Carlos Baerga	.10
55	John Olerud	.10
56	Derek Jeter	2.50
57	Hideki Irabu	.10
58	Tino Martinez	.10
59	Bernie Williams	.10
60	Miguel Tejada	.25
61	Ben Grieve	.10
62	Jason Giambi	.55
63	Scott Rolen	.60
64	Doug Glanville	.10
65	Desi Relaford	.10
66	Tony Womack	.10
67	Jason Kendall	.10
68	Jose Guillen	.10
69	Tony Gwynn	1.00
70	Ken Caminiti	.10
71	Greg Vaughn	.10
72	Kevin Brown	.10
73	Barry Bonds	2.50
74	J.T. Snow	.10
75	Jeff Kent	.10
76	Ken Griffey Jr.	1.50
77	Alex Rodriguez	2.00
78	Edgar Martinez	.10
79	Jay Buhner	.10
80	Mark McGwire	2.00
81	Delino DeShields	.10
82	Brian Jordan	.10
83	Quinton McCracken	.10
84	Fred McGriff	.10
85	Juan Gonzalez	.40
86	Ivan Rodriguez	.65
87	Will Clark	.10
88	Roger Clemens	1.25
89	Jose Cruz Jr.	.10
90	Babe Ruth	2.00
91	Troy Glaus (Diamond Debut)	1.00
92	Jarrod Washburn (Diamond Debut)	.25
93	Travis Lee (Diamond Debut)	.75
94	Bruce Chen (Diamond Debut)	.25
95	Mike Caruso (Diamond Debut)	.25
96	Jim Parque (Diamond Debut)	.25
97	Kerry Wood (Diamond Debut)	.50
98	Jeremy Giambi (Diamond Debut)	.25
99	Matt Anderson (Diamond Debut)	.10

100	Seth Greisinger (Diamond Debut)	.25
101	Gabe Alvarez (Diamond Debut)	.25
102	Rafael Medina (Diamond Debut)	.25
103	Daryle Ward (Diamond Debut)	.25
104	Alex Cora (Diamond Debut)	.25
105	Adrian Beltre (Diamond Debut)	.50
106	Geoff Jenkins (Diamond Debut)	.25
107	Eric Milton (Diamond Debut)	.25
108	Carl Pavano (Diamond Debut)	.25
109	Eric Chavez (Diamond Debut)	.50
110	Orlando Hernandez (Diamond Debut)	.25
111	A.J. Hinch (Diamond Debut)	.25
112	Carlton Loewer (Diamond Debut)	.25
113	Aramis Ramirez (Diamond Debut)	.25
114	Cliff Politte (Diamond Debut)	.25
115	Matt Clement (Diamond Debut)	.25
116	Alex Gonzalez (Diamond Debut)	.25
117	J.D. Drew (Diamond Debut)	.75
118	Shane Monahan (Diamond Debut)	.25
119	Rolando Arrojo (Diamond Debut)	.25
120	George Lombard (Diamond Debut)	.25

Double Diamond

Double Diamonds are the most common parallels to the Black Diamond base set. Cards feature a red metallic-foil background or highlights. Regular-player cards (#1-90) are serially numbered on back from within an edition of 3,000 each. Diamond Debut cards (#91-120) are individually numbered within an edition of 2,500 each.

	NM/M
Complete Set (120):	200.00
Common Player (1-90):	.25
Common Diamond Debut (91-120):	1.00
Stars (1-90):	3X
Diamond Debuts (91-120):	2X

Triple Diamond

Triple Diamonds are the mid-level of scarcity among the parallel inserts to the Black Diamond base cards. They feature yellow metallic-foil backgrounds (1-90) and highlights (91-120). Regular-player cards are serially numbered on back from within an edition of

1,500 each. Diamond Debut cards are individually numbered within an edition of 1,000 each.

	NM/M
Common Player (1-90):	1.00
Common Diamond Debut (91-120):	1.50
Stars (1-90):	6X
Diamond Debuts (91-120):	3X

Quadruple Diamond

Quadruple Diamonds are the scarcest of the parallel inserts to the Black Diamond base cards. The regular player cards (#1-90) feature a green metallic-foil background and are serially numbered on back from within an edition of 150 each. Diamond Debut cards (#91-120) also feature green foil highlights on front and are individually numbered within an edition of 100 each. Quad Diamond cards of Sosa, Griffey and McGwire were limited to the number of home runs each hit the previous season.

	NM/M
Common Player (1-90):	4.00
Production 150 each.	
Common Diamond Debut (91-120):	6.00
Production 100 each.	
Stars (1-90):	25X
Diamond Debuts (91-120):	8X
18 Sammy Sosa/66	50.00
76 Ken Griffey Jr./56	60.00
80 Mark McGwire/70	75.00

A Piece of History

This six-card set features green metallic foil fronts with a diamond-shaped piece of game-used bat from the featured player embedded on the card front. No insertion ratio was released.

	NM/M
Common Player:	5.00
JG Juan Gonzalez	7.50
TG Tony Gwynn	10.00
BW Bernie Williams	5.00
MM Mark McGwire	200.00
MV Mo Vaughn	5.00
SS Sammy Sosa	25.00

Diamond Dominance

This 30-card set features full-bleed metallic foil fronts and includes the top stars of the game along with Babe Ruth. Each card is numbered with a "D" prefix and is limited to 1,500 sequentially numbered sets.

	NM/M
Complete Set (30):	65.00
Common Player:	.50
Production 1,500 Sets	
D01 Kerry Wood	1.00
D02 Derek Jeter	6.00
D03 Alex Rodriguez	5.00
D04 Frank Thomas	2.00
D05 Jeff Bagwell	2.00
D06 Mo Vaughn	.50
D07 Ivan Rodriguez	1.50
D08 Cal Ripken Jr.	6.00
D09 Rolando Arrojo	.50
D10 Chipper Jones	3.00
D11 Kenny Lofton	.50
D12 Paul Konerko	.75
D13 Mike Piazza	4.00
D14 Ben Grieve	.50
D15 Nomar Garciaparra	3.00
D16 Travis Lee	.65
D17 Scott Rolen	1.00
D18 Juan Gonzalez	1.00
D19 Tony Gwynn	3.00
D20 Tony Clark	.50
D21 Roger Clemens	3.50
D22 Sammy Sosa	3.00
D23 Larry Walker	.50
D24 Ken Griffey Jr.	4.00
D25 Mark McGwire	5.00
D26 Barry Bonds	6.00
D27 Vladimir Guerrero	2.00
D28 Tino Martinez	.50
D29 Greg Maddux	3.00
D30 Babe Ruth	5.00

Mystery Numbers

The player's card number determines scarcity in this hobby-only insert set. The basic set has an action photo set against a silver-foil background of repeated numerals. Backs have a portrait photo and significant stat numbers from the 1998 season. Each base Mystery Numbers card is individually numbered within an edition of 100 cards times the card number within the 30-card set (i.e., card #24 has an edition of 2,400 for a total of 46,500 cards. An emerald version of the Mystery Numbers cards has a total issue of 465 cards, with cards issued to a limit of the player's card number multiplied by 1.

	NM/M
Complete Set (30):	100.00
Common Player:	.75
M1 Babe Ruth/100	25.00
M2 Ken Griffey Jr./200	12.50
M3 Kerry Wood/300	4.00
M4 Mark McGwire/400	12.50
M5 Alex Rodriguez/500	12.50
M6 Chipper Jones/600	6.00
M7 Nomar Garciaparra/700	6.00
M8 Derek Jeter/800	10.00
M9 Mike Piazza/900	6.00
M10 Roger Clemens/1,000	4.50
M11 Greg Maddux/1,100	4.00
M12 Scott Rolen/1,200	1.25
M13 Cal Ripken Jr./1,300	7.50
M14 Ben Grieve/1,400	.75
M15 Troy Glaus/1,500	3.00
M16 Sammy Sosa/1,600	4.50
M17 Darin Erstad/1,700	1.25
M18 Juan Gonzalez/1,800	1.25
M19 Pedro Martinez/1,900	1.50
M20 Larry Walker/2,000	.75
M21 Vladimir Guerrero/2,100	1.50
M22 Jeff Bagwell/2,200	1.50
M23 Jaret Wright/2,300	.75
M24 Travis Lee/2,400	.75
M25 Barry Bonds/2,500	4.50
M26 Orlando Hernandez/2,600	.75
M27 Frank Thomas/2,700	1.50
M28 Tony Gwynn/2,800	2.00

M29 Andres Galarraga/2,900	.75
M30 Craig Biggio/3,000	.75

Piece of History 500 Club

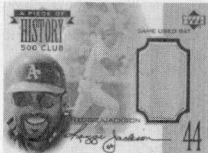

A veneer of lumber from one of Mr. October's war clubs is included in this special insert card. A facsimile autograph is also featured on front. A premium version with an authentic autograph serially numbered from within an edition of 44 (his uniform number) was also issued. Backs have a congratulatory authentication message from Upper Deck CEO Richard McWilliam.

	NM/M
Reggie Jackson	165.00
Reggie Jackson/Auto.	500.00

1999 Upper Deck Century Legends

The first 47 cards in the 131-card set are taken from The Sporting News' list of Baseball's 100 Greatest Players. Each card bears a Sporting News photo of the featured player and his ranking in silver and copper foil. The next 50 cards tout Upper Deck's rankings of the Top 50 contemporary players. Rounding out the base set are two subsets: 21st Century Phenoms and Century Memories. Because of contractual problems, cards #11, 25, 26 and 126 were never issued. A die-cut parallel version of each card, serially numbered to 100 each, was produced as the "Century Collection."

	NM/M
Complete Set (131):	20.00
Common Player:	.10
Century Collection:	20X
Production 100 Sets	
Pack (5):	3.00
Wax Box (24):	60.00
1 Babe Ruth (Top 50)	2.00
1 Babe Ruth (SAMPLE overprint on back.)	2.00
2 Willie Mays (Top 50)	1.00
3 Ty Cobb (Top 50)	1.00
4 Walter Johnson (Top 50)	.40
5 Hank Aaron (Top 50)	1.00
6 Lou Gehrig (Top 50)	1.50
7 Christy Mathewson (Top 50)	.40
8 Ted Williams (Top 50)	1.25
9 Rogers Hornsby (Top 50)	.25
10 Stan Musial (Top 50)	.65
12 Grover Alexander (Top 50)	.25
13 Honus Wagner (Top 50)	.40
14 Cy Young (Top 50)	.40
15 Jimmie Foxx (Top 50)	.25
16 Johnny Bench (Top 50)	.40
17 Mickey Mantle (Top 50)	2.00
18 Josh Gibson (Top 50)	.40
19 Satchel Paige (Top 50)	.50
20 Roberto Clemente (Top 50)	1.50
21 Warren Spahn (Top 50)	.20
22 Frank Robinson (Top 50)	.20
23 Lefty Grove (Top 50)	.20
24 Eddie Collins (Top 50)	.25
27 Tris Speaker (Top 50)	.25
28 Mike Schmidt (Top 50)	.50
29 Napoleon LaJoie (Top 50)	.20
30 Steve Carlton (Top 50)	.25
31 Bob Gibson (Top 50)	.25
32 Tom Seaver (Top 50)	.25
33 George Sisler (Top 50)	.10

34 Barry Bonds (Top 50) 1.50
35 Joe Jackson (Top 50) 1.25
36 Bob Feller (Top 50) .25
37 Hank Greenberg (Top 50) .25
38 Ernie Banks (Top 50) .40
39 Greg Maddux (Top 50) .75
40 Yogi Berra (Top 50) .40
41 Nolan Ryan (Top 50) 2.00
42 Mel Ott (Top 50) .25
43 Al Simmons (Top 50) .10
44 Jackie Robinson (Top 50) 1.25
45 Carl Hubbell (Top 50) .25
46 Charley Gehringer (Top 50) .10
47 Buck Leonard (Top 50) .10
48 Reggie Jackson (Top 50) .40
49 Tony Gwynn (Top 50) .75
50 Roy Campanella (Top 50) .40
51 Ken Griffey Jr. (Contemporaries) 1.00
52 Barry Bonds (Contemporaries) 1.50
53 Roger Clemens (Contemporaries) .85
54 Tony Gwynn (Contemporaries) .75
55 Cal Ripken Jr. (Contemporaries) 1.50
56 Greg Maddux (Contemporaries) .75
57 Frank Thomas (Contemporaries) .65
58 Mark McGwire (Contemporaries) 1.25
59 Mike Piazza (Contemporaries) 1.00
60 Wade Boggs (Contemporaries) .75
61 Alex Rodriguez (Contemporaries) 1.25
62 Juan Gonzalez (Contemporaries) .30
63 Mo Vaughn (Contemporaries) .10
64 Albert Belle (Contemporaries) .10
65 Sammy Sosa (Contemporaries) .75
66 Nomar Garciaparra (Contemporaries) .75
67 Derek Jeter (Contemporaries) 1.50
68 Kevin Brown (Contemporaries) .10
69 Jose Canseco (Contemporaries) .35
70 Randy Johnson (Contemporaries) .60
71 Tom Glavine (Contemporaries) .25
72 Barry Larkin (Contemporaries) .10
73 Curt Schilling (Contemporaries) .25
74 Moises Alou (Contemporaries) .10
75 Fred McGriff (Contemporaries) .10
76 Pedro Martinez (Contemporaries) .65
77 Andres Galarraga (Contemporaries) .10
78 Will Clark (Contemporaries) .10
79 Larry Walker (Contemporaries) .10
80 Ivan Rodriguez (Contemporaries) .50
81 Chipper Jones (Contemporaries) .75
82 Jeff Bagwell (Contemporaries) .60
83 Craig Biggio (Contemporaries) .10
84 Kerry Wood (Contemporaries) .35
85 Roberto Alomar (Contemporaries) .20
86 Vinny Castilla (Contemporaries) .10
87 Kenny Lofton (Contemporaries) .10
88 Rafael Palmeiro (Contemporaries) .50
89 Manny Ramirez (Contemporaries) .60
90 David Wells (Contemporaries) .10
91 Mark Grace (Contemporaries) .10
92 Bernie Williams (Contemporaries) .10
93 David Cone (Contemporaries) .10
94 John Olerud (Contemporaries) .10
95 John Smoltz (Contemporaries) .10
96 Tino Martinez (Contemporaries) .10
97 Raul Mondesi (Contemporaries) .10
98 Gary Sheffield (Contemporaries) .35
99 Orel Hershiser (Contemporaries) .10

100 Rickey Henderson (Contemporaries) .65
101 J.D. Drew (21st Century Phenoms) .50
102 Troy Glaus (21st Century Phenoms) .50
103 Nomar Garciaparra (21st Century Phenoms) .75
104 Scott Rolen (21st Century Phenoms) .45
105 Ryan Minor (21st Century Phenoms) .10
106 Travis Lee (21st Century Phenoms) .20
107 Roy Halladay (21st Century Phenoms) .10
108 Carlos Beltran (21st Century Phenoms) .50
109 Alex Rodriguez (21st Century Phenoms) 1.25
110 Eric Chavez (21st Century Phenoms) .20
111 Vladimir Guerrero (21st Century Phenoms) .60
112 Ben Grieve (21st Century Phenoms) .15
113 Kerry Wood (21st Century Phenoms) .30
114 Alex Gonzalez (21st Century Phenoms) .10
115 Darin Erstad (21st Century Phenoms) .30
116 Derek Jeter (21st Century Phenoms) 1.50
117 Jaret Wright (21st Century Phenoms) .10
118 Jose Cruz Jr. (21st Century Phenoms) .10
119 Chipper Jones (21st Century Phenoms) .75
120 Gabe Kapler (21st Century Phenoms) .10
121 Satchel Paige (Century Memories) .50
122 Willie Mays (Century Memories) 1.00
123 Roberto Clemente (Century Memories) 1.50
124 Lou Gehrig (Century Memories) 1.50
125 Mark McGwire (Century Memories) 1.25
127 Bob Gibson (Century Memories) .25
128 Johnny Vander Meer (Century Memories) .10
129 Walter Johnson (Century Memories) .25
130 Ty Cobb (Century Memories) .75
131 Don Larsen (Century Memories) .20
132 Jackie Robinson (Century Memories) 1.00
133 Tom Seaver (Century Memories) .25
134 Johnny Bench (Century Memories) .35
135 Frank Robinson (Century Memories) .25

All-Century Team

This 10-card set highlights Upper Deck's all-time all-star team. These were seeded 1:23 packs.

		NM/M
Complete Set (10):		30.00
Common Player:		2.50
Inserted 1:23		
1	Babe Ruth	7.50
2	Ty Cobb	3.50
3	Willie Mays	3.50
4	Lou Gehrig	6.00
5	Jackie Robinson	5.00
6	Mike Schmidt	2.50
7	Ernie Banks	2.50
8	Johnny Bench	2.50
9	Cy Young	2.50
10	Lineup Sheet	.25

Century Artifacts

A total of nine cards were inserted, redeemable for memorabilia from some of the top players of the century. Due to the limited nature of these one-of-one inserts and the fact that most or all were redeemed, no pricing is assigned. Each cut signature was framed with the player's Century Legends card.

Century MVPs

This collection selects 100 cards from Upper Deck's '99 MVP brand and adds a rainbow-foil shift to each card. These are limited to only one numbered set.

One Set Produced
Values Undetermined

Epic Milestones

This nine-card set showcases nine of the most impressive milestones established in major league history. Each card is numbered with an "EM" prefix and are seeded 1:12 packs. Because of a contractual dispute, card #1 was never issued.

		NM/M
Complete Set (9):		5.00
Common Player:		.25
Inserted 1:12		
2	Jackie Robinson	.75
3	Nolan Ryan	1.00
4	Mark McGwire	.75
5	Roger Clemens	.60
6	Sammy Sosa	.50
7	Cal Ripken Jr.	1.00
8	Rickey Henderson	.25
9	Hank Aaron	.75
10	Barry Bonds	1.00

Epic Signatures

This 30-card set features autographs from retired and current stars on a horizonal format. A player portrait appears over a ballpark background on front. The portrait is repeated on back with a statement of authenticity. Cards are numbered with player initials. These autographed cards are seeded 1:24 packs. Exchange cards of Fisk, Bench, Berra and McCovey were originally inserted into packs and had to be mailed in for the autographed card. They are valued about 10 percent of the corresponding signed card.

		NM/M
Common Player:		10.00
Inserted 1:24		
EB	Ernie Banks	65.00
JB	Johnny Bench	40.00
YB	Yogi Berra	50.00
BB	Barry Bonds	180.00
SC	Steve Carlton	20.00
BD	Bucky Dent	10.00
BF	Bob Feller	15.00
CF	Carlton Fisk	25.00
BG	Bob Gibson	25.00
JG	Juan Gonzalez	20.00
Jr.	Ken Griffey Jr.	100.00
Sr.	Ken Griffey Sr.	10.00
VG	Vladimir Guerrero	30.00
TG	Tony Gwynn	40.00
RJ	Reggie Jackson	40.00
HK	Harmon Killebrew	30.00
DL	Don Larsen	15.00
GM	Greg Maddux	100.00
EMa	Eddie Mathews	80.00
BM	Bill Mazeroski	30.00
WMc	Willie McCovey	20.00
SM	Stan Musial	80.00
FR	Frank Robinson	30.00
AR	Alex Rodriguez	150.00
NR	Nolan Ryan	150.00
MS	Mike Schmidt	50.00
TS	Tom Seaver	40.00
WS	Warren Spahn	60.00
FT	Frank Thomas	50.00
BT	Bobby Thomson	10.00

Century Epic Signatures

This 32-card autographed set features signatures from retired and current stars. The cards have a horizontal format and have gold foil stamping. Each card is hand numbered to 100.

		NM/M
Common Player:		20.00
Production 100 Sets		
EB	Ernie Banks	85.00
JB	Johnny Bench	90.00
YB	Yogi Berra	75.00
BB	Barry Bonds	240.00
SC	Steve Carlton	50.00
BD	Bucky Dent	20.00
BF	Bob Feller	50.00
CF	Carlton Fisk	40.00
BG	Bob Gibson	60.00
JG	Juan Gonzalez	60.00
Jr.	Ken Griffey Jr.	165.00
Sr.	Ken Griffey Sr.	20.00
VG	Vladimir Guerrero	70.00
TG	Tony Gwynn	90.00
RJ	Reggie Jackson	60.00
HK	Harmon Killebrew	75.00
DL	Don Larsen	30.00
GM	Greg Maddux	150.00
EMa	Eddie Mathews	90.00
WM	Willie Mays	300.00
BM	Bill Mazeroski	25.00
WMc	Willie McCovey	50.00
SM	Stan Musial	100.00
FR	Frank Robinson	50.00
AR	Alex Rodriguez	200.00
NR	Nolan Ryan	200.00
MS	Mike Schmidt	125.00
TS	Tom Seaver	75.00
WS	Warren Spahn	80.00
FT	Frank Thomas	80.00
BT	Bobby Thomson	20.00
TW	Ted Williams	750.00

Jerseys of the Century

This nine-card set features a swatch of game-worn jersey from the featured current and retired player.

		NM/M
Common Player:		12.50
Inserted 1:418		
GB	George Brett	25.00
RC	Roger Clemens	25.00
TG	Tony Gwynn	20.00
GM	Greg Maddux	20.00
EM	Eddie Murray	15.00
NR	Nolan Ryan	90.00
MS	Mike Schmidt	25.00
OZ	Ozzie Smith	20.00
DW	Dave Winfield	15.00

Legendary Cuts

A total of nine of these one-fo-one inserts exist. These are actual "cut" signatures from some of baseball's all-time greats.

Values Undetermined
CY Cy Young (11/00 Auction) 1,850

Memorable Shots

This 10-card insert set focuses on the most memorable home runs launched during this century. The player's image is framed in an embossed foil, frame-like design. These are seeded 1:12 packs, each card back is numbered with an "HR" prefix.

		NM/M
Complete Set (10):		15.00
Common Player:		.50
Inserted 1:12		
1	Babe Ruth	5.00
2	Bobby Thomson	1.00
3	Kirk Gibson	.50

4	Carlton Fisk	.50
5	Bill Mazeroski	1.00
6	Bucky Dent	.50
7	Mark McGwire	2.00
8	Mickey Mantle	5.00
9	Joe Carter	.50
10	Mark McGwire	2.00

500 Club Piece History

This Jimmie Foxx insert has a piece of of a game-used Louisville Slugger once swung by Foxx, embedded into the card front. An estimated 350 cards of this one exist.

		NM/M
JF	Jimmie Foxx	125.00

1999 Upper Deck Challengers for 70

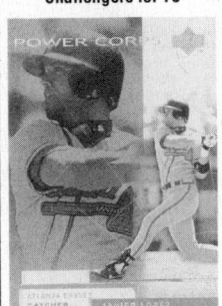

Celebrating Mark McGwire's record-setting season of 1998, and featuring those who would chase his single-season home run crown in 1999, Upper Deck issued this specialty product. The base set of 90 cards is fractured into subsets of Power Elite (#1-10), Power Corps (#11-40), Rookie Power (#41-45), and Home Run Highlights (#46-90). Several styles of inserts and numbered parallels were included in the 5-card foil packs. A parallel set with each card serially numbered to 600 was also issued, titled "Challengers Edition".

		NM/M
Complete Set (90):		15.00
Common Player:		.05
Challenger's Edition (600 Sets):		5X
Pack (5):		2.00
Wax Box (20):		25.00
1	Mark McGwire (Power Elite)	1.50
2	Sammy Sosa (Power Elite)	1.00
3	Ken Griffey Jr. (Power Elite)	1.25
4	Alex Rodriguez (Power Elite)	1.50
5	Albert Belle (Power Elite)	.05
6	Mo Vaughn (Power Elite)	.05
7	Mike Piazza (Power Elite)	1.25
8	Frank Thomas (Power Elite)	.75
9	Juan Gonzalez (Power Elite)	.35
10	Barry Bonds (Power Elite)	2.00
11	Rafael Palmeiro (Power Corps)	.60
12	Jose Canseco (Power Corps)	.50

13 Nomar Garciaparra (Power Corps) 1.00
14 Carlos Delgado (Power Corps) .20
15 Brian Jordan (Power Corps) .05
16 Vladimir Guerrero (Power Corps) .65
17 Vinny Castilla (Power Corps) .05
18 Chipper Jones (Power Corps) 1.00
19 Jeff Bagwell (Power Corps) .65
20 Moises Alou (Power Corps) .05
21 Tony Clark (Power Corps) .05
22 Jim Thome (Power Corps) .50
23 Tino Martinez (Power Corps) .05
24 Greg Vaughn (Power Corps) .05
25 Javy Lopez (Power Corps) .05
26 Jeromy Burnitz (Power Corps) .05
27 Cal Ripken Jr. (Power Corps) 2.00
28 Manny Ramirez (Power Corps) .65
29 Darin Erstad (Power Corps) .25
30 Ken Caminiti (Power Corps) .05
31 Edgar Martinez (Power Corps) .05
32 Ivan Rodriguez (Power Corps) .60
33 Larry Walker (Power Corps) .05
34 Todd Helton (Power Corps) .60
35 Andruw Jones (Power Corps) .65
36 Ray Lankford (Power Corps) .05
37 Travis Lee (Power Corps) .10
38 Raul Mondesi (Power Corps) .05
39 Scott Rolen (Power Corps) .50
40 Ben Grieve (Power Corps) .05
41 J.D. Drew (Rookie Power) .50
42 Troy Glaus (Rookie Power) .60
43 Eric Chavez (Rookie Power) .10
44 Gabe Kapler (Rookie Power) .05
45 Michael Barrett (Rookie Power) .05
46 Mark McGwire (HR Highlights) .75
47 Jose Canseco (HR Highlights) .25
48 Greg Vaughn (HR Highlights) .05
49 Albert Belle (HR Highlights) .05
50 Mark McGwire (HR Highlights) .75
51 Vinny Castilla (HR Highlights) .05
52 Vladimir Guerrero (HR Highlights) .35
53 Andres Galarraga (HR Highlights) .05
54 Rafael Palmeiro (HR Highlights) .30
55 Juan Gonzalez (HR Highlights) .20
56 Ken Griffey Jr. (HR Highlights) .60
57 Barry Bonds (HR Highlights) 1.00
58 Mo Vaughn (HR Highlights) .05
59 Nomar Garciaparra (HR Highlights) .50
60 Tino Martinez (HR Highlights) .05
61 Mark McGwire (HR Highlights) .75
62 Mark McGwire (HR Highlights) .75
63 Mark McGwire (HR Highlights) .75
64 Mark McGwire (HR Highlights) .75
65 Mark McGwire (HR Highlights) .75
66 Sammy Sosa (HR Highlights) .50
67 Mark McGwire (HR Highlights) .75
68 Mark McGwire (HR Highlights) .75
69 Mark McGwire (HR Highlights) .75
70 Mark McGwire (HR Highlights) .75
71 Mark McGwire (HR Highlights) .75
72 Scott Brosius (HR Highlights) .05
73 Tony Gwynn (HR Highlights) .40
74 Chipper Jones (HR Highlights) .50

75	Jeff Bagwell	
	(HR Highlights)	.35
76	Moises Alou	
	(HR Highlights)	.05
77	Manny Ramirez	
	(HR Highlights)	.35
78	Carlos Delgado	
	(HR Highlights)	.05
79	Kerry Wood	
	(HR Highlights)	.20
80	Ken Griffey Jr.	
	(HR Highlights)	.60
81	Cal Ripken Jr.	
	(HR Highlights)	1.00
82	Alex Rodriguez	
	(HR Highlights)	.75
83	Barry Bonds	
	(HR Highlights)	1.00
84	Ken Griffey Jr.	
	(HR Highlights)	.60
85	Travis Lee (HR Highlights)	.15
86	George Lombard	
	(HR Highlights)	.05
87	Michael Barrett	
	(HR Highlights)	.05
88	Jeremy Giambi	
	(HR Highlights)	.05
89	Troy Glaus	
	(HR Highlights)	.30
90	J.D. Drew (HR Highlights)	.25

Challengers Insert

Found one per pack, this insert series identifies 30 top contenders for the 1999 home run crown. Action photos on front are highlighted by red graphics and silver-foil. Backs repeat a detail of the front photo and present a capsule of the player's 1998 season. Cards have a "C" prefix to the number. A parallel edition, utilizing refractive foil details on front, is serially numbered within an edition of 70 each.

		NM/M
Complete Set (30):		9.00
Common Player:		.15
Parallel Edition (70 Sets):		15X
1	Mark McGwire	1.00
2	Sammy Sosa	.65
3	Ken Griffey Jr.	.75
4	Alex Rodriguez	1.00
5	Albert Belle	.45
6	Mo Vaughn	.15
7	Mike Piazza	.75
8	Frank Thomas	.50
9	Juan Gonzalez	.45
10	Barry Bonds	1.50
11	Rafael Palmeiro	.35
12	Nomar Garciaparra	.65
13	Vladimir Guerrero	.45
14	Vinny Castilla	.15
15	Chipper Jones	.75
16	Jeff Bagwell	.45
17	Moises Alou	.15
18	Tony Clark	.15
19	Jim Thome	.35
20	Tino Martinez	.15
21	Greg Vaughn	.15
22	Manny Ramirez	.45
23	Darin Erstad	.25
24	Ken Caminiti	.15
25	Ivan Rodriguez	.35
26	Andruw Jones	.45
27	Travis Lee	.25
28	Scott Rolen	.35
29	Ben Grieve	.15
30	J.D. Drew	.35

Longball Legends

Top home-run threats are featured in this insert series. The action photos on front are repeated in a diffused version on back, where they are joined by a second photo and a bargraph of the player's home run production in recent seasons. Cards have an "L" prefix to the number. Stated odds of picking a Longball Legends card are one per 39 packs.

		NM/M
Complete Set (30):		20.00

Common Player:		.50
1	Ken Griffey Jr.	1.50
2	Mark McGwire	2.00
3	Sammy Sosa	1.00
4	Cal Ripken Jr.	2.50
5	Barry Bonds	2.50
6	Larry Walker	.50
7	Fred McGriff	.50
8	Alex Rodriguez	2.00
9	Frank Thomas	.75
10	Juan Gonzalez	.60
11	Jeff Bagwell	.75
12	Mo Vaughn	.50
13	Albert Belle	.50
14	Mike Piazza	1.50
15	Vladimir Guerrero	.75
16	Chipper Jones	1.00
17	Ken Caminiti	.50
18	Rafael Palmeiro	.65
19	Nomar Garciaparra	1.00
20	Jim Thome	.60
21	Edgar Martinez	.50
22	Ivan Rodriguez	.65
23	Andres Galarraga	.50
24	Scott Rolen	.60
25	Darin Erstad	.65
26	Moises Alou	.50
27	J.D. Drew	.65
28	Andruw Jones	.75
29	Manny Ramirez	.75
30	Tino Martinez	.50

Mark on History

The details of Mark McGwire's successful assault on the single-season home run record are captured in this 25-card insert set, found on average of one per five packs. Cards have action photos set against a split red-and-black background and are highlighted in red metallic foil. Backs have details of the home run featured on front, a quote from McGwire and another photo. Cards have an "M" prefix to the number. A parallel edition numbered to 70 was also issued.

		NM/M
Complete Set (25):		25.00
Common McGwire:		1.50
Parallel:		8X
01-25 Mark McGwire		1.50

Piece of History 500

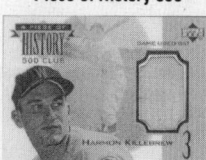

A piece of game-used bat from 500-HR club member Harmon Killebrew is featured on these inserts. Only 350 cards were issued, along with three (his uniform number) authentically autographed versions. Backs have an action photo and a congratulatory authentication message from UD CEO Richard McWilliam.

	NM/M
Harmon Killebrew	120.00
Harmon Killebrew/	
Auto.	450.00

Swinging/Fences

Fifteen top sluggers are included in this insert set. The players' power swing is captured on a muted textured-look background. Back has a color portrait photo and an "S" prefix to the card number. Stated insertion rate is one per 19 packs.

		NM/M
Complete Set (15):		15.00
Common Player:		.50
1	Ken Griffey Jr.	1.50
2	Mark McGwire	2.00
3	Sammy Sosa	1.25
4	Alex Rodriguez	2.00
5	Nomar Garciaparra	1.25
6	J.D. Drew	.75
7	Vladimir Guerrero	1.00
8	Ben Grieve	.50
9	Chipper Jones	1.25
10	Gabe Kapler	.50
11	Travis Lee	.60
12	Todd Helton	.75
13	Juan Gonzalez	.60
14	Mike Piazza	1.50
15	Mo Vaughn	.50

Autographed Swinging

A total of 2,700 autographed versions of Swinging for the Fences inserts were featured in the Challengers for 70 issue. Only six of the 15 players' cards were included in this premium version.

		NM/M
Complete Set (6):		200.00
Common Player:		5.00
JR	Ken Griffey Jr.	95.00
VG	Vladimir Guerrero	25.00
TH	Todd Helton	15.00
GK	Gabe Kapler	5.00
TL	Travis Lee	7.50
AR	Alex Rodriguez	90.00

1999 Upper Deck UD Choice Previews

A month prior to the release of its new UD Choice brand baseball series, Upper Deck issued this 55-card Preview version. Sold in five-card cello packs for about 75 cents only at retail outlets, the cards are identical to the issued versions of the same players except for the appearance at top front of a gold foil-stamped "PREVIEW."

		NM/M
Complete Set (55):		16.00
Common Player:		.10
46	Tim Salmon	.10
48	Chuck Finley	.10
50	Matt Williams	.10
52	Travis Lee	.20
54	Andres Galarraga	.10
56	Greg Maddux	.75
58	Cal Ripken Jr.	1.50
60	Rafael Palmeiro	.50
62	Nomar Garciaparra	.75
64	Pedro Martinez	.60
66	Kerry Wood	.35
67	Sammy Sosa	.75
70	Albert Belle	.10
72	Frank Thomas	.60
74	Pete Harnisch	.10
76	Manny Ramirez	.60
78	Travis Fryman	.10
80	Kenny Lofton	.10
82	Larry Walker	.10
84	Gabe Alvarez	.10
86	Damion Easley	.10
88	Mark Kotsay	.10
90	Jeff Bagwell	.60
93	Craig Biggio	.10
94	Larry Sutton	.10
96	Johnny Damon	.30
98	Gary Sheffield	.35
100	Mark Grudzielanek	.10
102	Jeff Cirillo	.10
104	Mark Loretta	.10
106	David Ortiz	.40
108	Brad Fullmer	.10
110	Vladimir Guerrero	.60
112	Brian McRae	.10
114	Rey Ordonez	.10
118	Derek Jeter	1.50
118	Paul O'Neill	.10
120	A.J. Hinch	.10
122	Miguel Tejada	.15
124	Scott Rolen	.45
128	Bobby Abreu	.10
128	Jason Kendall	.10
130	Mark McGwire	1.25
132	Eli Marrero	.10
136	Kevin Brown	.10
137	Tony Gwynn	.75
138	Bill Mueller	.10
140	Barry Bonds	1.50
142	Ken Griffey Jr.	1.00
143	Alex Rodriguez	1.25
146	Rolando Arrojo	.10
148	Quinton McCracken	.10
150	Will Clark	.10
152	Juan Gonzalez	.30
154	Carlos Delgado	.25

1999 Upper Deck UD Choice

The 155-card base set consists of 110 regular player cards and two subsets, 27 Star Rookies and 18 Cover Glory subset cards. Card fronts have a white border, with the Upper Deck UD Choice logo on the bottom right of the front. Card backs have complete year-by-year stats along with some vital information. Each pack contains 12 cards. A parallel version also exists, called Prime Choice Reserve and are numbered to 100.

	NM/M
Complete Set (155):	7.50
Common Player:	.03
Prime Choice Reserve Stars:	10X
Production 100 Sets	
Pack (12):	.50
Wax Box (36):	10.00
1	Gabe Kapler	
	(Rookie Class)	.05
2	Jin Ho Cho (Rookie Class)	.05
3	Matt Anderson	
	(Rookie Class)	.05
4	Ricky Ledee	
	(Rookie Class)	.05
5	Bruce Chen (Rookie Class)	.05
6	Alex Gonzalez	
	(Rookie Class)	.05
7	Ryan Minor	
	(Rookie Class)	.05
8	Michael Barrett	
	(Rookie Class)	.05
9	Carlos Beltran	
	(Rookie Class)	.50
10	Ramon Martinez	
	(Rookie Class)	.05
11	Dermal Brown	
	(Rookie Class)	.05
12	Robert Fick (Rookie Class)	.05
13	Preston Wilson	
	(Rookie Class)	.05
14	Orlando Hernandez	
	(Rookie Class)	.05
15	Troy Glaus (Rookie Class)	.65
16	Calvin Pickering	
	(Rookie Class)	.05
17	Corey Koskie	
	(Rookie Class)	.05
18	Fernando Seguignol	
	(Rookie Class)	.05
19	Carlos Guillen	
	(Rookie Class)	.05
20	Kevin Witt (Rookie Class)	.05
21	Mike Kinkade	
	(Rookie Class)	.05
22	Eric Chavez	
	(Rookie Class)	.15
23	Mike Lowell	
	(Rookie Class)	.10
24	Adrian Beltre	
	(Rookie Class)	.10
25	George Lombard	
	(Rookie Class)	.05
26	Jeremy Giambi	
	(Rookie Class)	.05
27	J.D. Drew (Rookie Class)	.40
28	Mark McGwire	
	(Cover Glory)	.60
29	Kerry Wood (Cover Glory)	.15
30	David Wells (Cover Glory)	.05
31	Juan Gonzalez	
	(Cover Glory)	.15
32	Randy Johnson	
	(Cover Glory)	.35
33	Derek Jeter (Cover Glory)	.75
34	Tony Gwynn (Cover Glory)	.45
35	Greg Maddux	
	(Cover Glory)	.45
36	Cal Ripken Jr.	
	(Cover Glory)	.75
37	Ken Griffey Jr.	
	(Cover Glory)	.50
38	Bartolo Colon	
	(Cover Glory)	.05
39	Troy Glaus (Cover Glory)	.30
40	Ben Grieve (Cover Glory)	.05
41	Roger Clemens	
	(Cover Glory)	.50
42	Chipper Jones	
	(Cover Glory)	.50
43	Scott Rolen (Cover Glory)	.25
44	Nomar Garciaparra	
	(Cover Glory)	.45
45	Sammy Sosa	
	(Cover Glory)	.45
46	Tim Salmon	.05
47	Darin Erstad	.25
48	Chuck Finley	.05
49	Garrett Anderson	.05
50	Matt Williams	.05
51	Jay Bell	.05
52	Travis Lee	.10
53	Andruw Jones	.65
54	Andres Galarraga	.05
55	Chipper Jones	.75
56	Greg Maddux	.75
57	Javy Lopez	.05
58	Cal Ripken Jr.	1.50
59	Brady Anderson	.05
60	Rafael Palmeiro	.50
61	B.J. Surhoff	.05
62	Nomar Garciaparra	.75
63	Troy O'Leary	.05
64	Pedro Martinez	.65
65	Jason Varitek	.05
66	Kerry Wood	.35
67	Sammy Sosa	.75
68	Mark Grace	.05
69	Mickey Morandini	.05
70	Albert Belle	.05
71	Mike Caruso	.05
72	Frank Thomas	.65
73	Sean Casey	.10
74	Pete Harnisch	.05
75	Dmitri Young	.05
76	Manny Ramirez	.65
77	Omar Vizquel	.05
78	Travis Fryman	.05
79	Jim Thome	.40
80	Kenny Lofton	.05
81	Todd Helton	.50
82	Larry Walker	.05
83	Vinny Castilla	.05
84	Gabe Alvarez	.05
85	Tony Clark	.05
86	Damion Easley	.05
87	Livan Hernandez	.05
88	Mark Kotsay	.05
89	Cliff Floyd	.05
90	Jeff Bagwell	.65
91	Moises Alou	.05
92	Randy Johnson	.65
93	Craig Biggio	.05
94	Larry Sutton	.05
95	Dean Palmer	.05
96	Johnny Damon	.20
97	Charles Johnson	.05
98	Gary Sheffield	.25
99	Raul Mondesi	.05
100	Mark Grudzielanek	.05
101	Jeromy Burnitz	.05
102	Jeff Cirillo	.05
103	Jose Valentin	.05
104	Mark Loretta	.05
105	Todd Walker	.05
106	David Ortiz	.35
107	Brad Radke	.05
108	Brad Fullmer	.05
109	Rondell White	.05
110	Vladimir Guerrero	.65
111	Mike Piazza	1.00
112	Brian McRae	.05
113	John Olerud	.05
114	Rey Ordonez	.05
115	Derek Jeter	1.50
116	Bernie Williams	.05
117	David Wells	.05
118	Paul O'Neill	.05
119	Tino Martinez	.05
120	A.J. Hinch	.05
121	Jason Giambi	.30
122	Miguel Tejada	.10
123	Ben Grieve	.05
124	Scott Rolen	.50
125	Desi Relaford	.05
126	Bobby Abreu	.10
127	Jose Guillen	.05
128	Jason Kendall	.05
129	Aramis Ramirez	.05
130	Mark McGwire	1.25
131	Ray Lankford	.05
132	Eli Marrero	.05
133	Wally Joyner	.05
134	Greg Vaughn	.05
135	Trevor Hoffman	.05
136	Kevin Brown	.05
137	Tony Gwynn	.75
138	Bill Mueller	.05
139	Ellis Burks	.05
140	Barry Bonds	1.50
141	Robb Nen	.05
142	Ken Griffey Jr.	1.00
143	Alex Rodriguez	1.25
144	Jay Buhner	.05
145	Edgar Martinez	.05
146	Rolando Arrojo	.05
147	Robert Smith	.05
148	Quinton McCracken	.05
149	Ivan Rodriguez	.50
150	Will Clark	.05
151	Mark McLemore	.05
152	Juan Gonzalez	.35
153	Jose Cruz Jr.	.05
154	Carlos Delgado	.25
155	Roger Clemens	.85

Prime Choice Reserve

Each card in the UD Choice set is also found in a parallel version with the words "Prime Choice Reserve" repeated in the background of the photo in refractive foil. On back, the parallels are individually serial numbered within an edition of 100 each.

	NM/M
Common Player:	2.50
Stars:	10X

All-Star Game '99

These super-size (3-1/2" x 5") versions of 1999 UD Choice cards were issued as a boxed set exclusively for retail outlet sales. The cards are in a format identical to the regular-issue UD Choice except for a large All-Star Game logo in one of the upper corners. Fronts have game-action photos; backs have a small portrait, major league stats and career highlights. The set was sold in a green-foil enhanced box with a special card commemorating the 1999 game July 13 in Boston.

		NM/M
Complete Set (21):		12.50
Common Player:		.35
1	Kenny Lofton	.35
2	Pedro Martinez	.75
3	Nomar Garciaparra	1.00
4	Ken Griffey Jr.	1.25
5	Derek Jeter	2.00
6	Manny Ramirez	.75
7	Ivan Rodriguez	.65
8	Bernie Williams	.35
9	Cal Ripken Jr.	2.00
10	Jim Thome	.60
11	Mike Piazza	1.25
12	Jeff Bagwell	.75
13	Craig Biggio	.35
14	Mark McGwire	1.50
15	Matt Williams	.35
16	Chipper Jones	1.00
17	Tony Gwynn	1.00
18	Sammy Sosa	1.00
19	Raul Mondesi	.35
20	Larry Walker	.35
---	Header Card	.05

Mini Bobbing Head

Inserted 1:5 packs, some of the game's best players can be assembled into a miniature bobbing head figure by following the instructions on the card backs.

		NM/M
Complete Set (30):		15.00
Common Player:		.25
Inserted 1:5		
B1	Randy Johnson	.50
B2	Troy Glaus	.50
B3	Chipper Jones	.75
B4	Cal Ripken Jr.	1.50
B5	Nomar Garciaparra	.65
B6	Pedro Martinez	.50
B7	Kerry Wood	.35
B8	Sammy Sosa	.65
B9	Frank Thomas	.50
B10	Paul Konerko	.35
B11	Omar Vizquel	.25
B12	Kenny Lofton	.25
B13	Gabe Kapler	.25
B14	Adrian Beltre	.35
B15	Orlando Hernandez	.25
B16	Derek Jeter	1.50
B17	Mike Piazza	.75
B18	Tino Martinez	.25
B19	Ben Grieve	.25
B20	Rickey Henderson	.50
B21	Scott Rolen	.40
B22	Aramis Ramirez	.25
B23	Greg Vaughn	.25
B24	Tony Gwynn	.65
B25	Barry Bonds	1.50
B26	Alex Rodriguez	1.00
B27	Ken Griffey Jr.	.75
B28	Mark McGwire	1.00
B29	J.D. Drew	.45
B30	Juan Gonzalez	.30

Piece of History 500 Club

A piece from an Eddie Murray game-used bat was incorporated into each of these cards, which are limited to 350.

		NM/M
EM	Eddie Murray/350	150.00

StarQuest

This four-tiered 30-card set features four different colors for each of the levels. Singles are seeded one per pack and have blue foil etching, Doubles (1:8) have green foil etching, Triples (1:23) have red foil etching and Home Runs are limited to 100 numbered sets with gold foil etching.

		NM/M
Complete Set (30):		7.50
Common Player:		.10
Inserted 1:1		
Green (1:8):		1.5X
Red (1:23):		3X
Gold (100 Sets): 50X		
SQ1	Ken Griffey Jr.	.60
SQ2	Sammy Sosa	.50
SQ3	Alex Rodriguez	.75
SQ4	Derek Jeter	1.00
SQ5	Troy Glaus	.35
SQ6	Mike Piazza	.60
SQ7	Barry Bonds	1.00
SQ8	Tony Gwynn	.50
SQ9	Juan Gonzalez	.20
SQ10	Chipper Jones	.50
SQ11	Greg Maddux	.50
SQ12	Randy Johnson	.40
SQ13	Roger Clemens	.55
SQ14	Ben Grieve	.10
SQ15	Nomar Garciaparra	.50
SQ16	Travis Lee	.15
SQ17	Frank Thomas	.40
SQ18	Vladimir Guerrero	.40
SQ19	Scott Rolen	.30
SQ20	Ivan Rodriguez	.35
SQ21	Cal Ripken Jr.	1.00
SQ22	Mark McGwire	.75
SQ23	Jeff Bagwell	.40
SQ24	Tony Clark	.10
SQ25	Kerry Wood	.25
SQ26	Kenny Lofton	.10
SQ27	Adrian Beltre	.15
SQ28	Larry Walker	.10
SQ29	Curt Schilling	.25
SQ30	Jim Thome	.40

Yard Work

This 30-card set showcases the top power hitters in the game. The right side of the card is covered in bronze foil and stamped with Yard Work. They are numbered with a Y-prefix and seeded 1:13 packs.

		NM/M
Complete Set (30):		20.00
Common Player:		.35
Inserted 1:13		
Y1	Andres Galarraga	.35
Y2	Chipper Jones	1.50
Y3	Rafael Palmeiro	.75
Y4	Nomar Garciaparra	1.50
Y5	Sammy Sosa	1.50
Y6	Frank Thomas	1.00
Y7	J.D. Drew	.75
Y8	Albert Belle	.35
Y9	Jim Thome	.60
Y10	Manny Ramirez	1.00
Y11	Larry Walker	.35
Y12	Vinny Castilla	.35
Y13	Tony Clark	.35
Y14	Jeff Bagwell	1.00
Y15	Moises Alou	.35
Y16	Dean Palmer	.35
Y17	Gary Sheffield	.50
Y18	Vladimir Guerrero	1.00
Y19	Mike Piazza	1.75
Y20	Tino Martinez	.35
Y21	Ben Grieve	.35
Y22	Greg Vaughn	.35
Y23	Ken Caminiti	.35
Y24	Barry Bonds	3.00
Y25	Ken Griffey Jr.	1.75
Y26	Alex Rodriguez	2.25
Y27	Mark McGwire	2.25
Y28	Juan Gonzalez	.50
Y29	Jose Canseco	.50
Y30	Jose Cruz Jr.	.35

1999 Upper Deck Encore

Encore is a 180-card partial parallel of Upper Deck Series 1, utilizing a special holo-foil treatment on each card. The Encore set consists of 90 base cards and three short-printed subsets: 45 Star Rookies (1:4), 30 Homer Odyssey (1:6) and 15 Stroke of Genius (1:8).

		NM/M
Complete Set (180):		75.00
Common Player (1-90):		.05
Common Player (91-135):		.25
Inserted 1:4		
Common Player (136-165):		.35
Inserted 1:6		
Common Player (166-180):		.50
Inserted 1:8		
Gold (1-90):		10X
Gold (91-135):		1.5X
Gold (136-165):		3X
Gold (166-180):		4X
Production 125 Sets		
Pack (6):		1.50
Wax Box (24):		25.00
1	Darin Erstad	.25
2	Mo Vaughn	.05
3	Travis Lee	.15
4	Randy Johnson	.60
5	Matt Williams	.05
6	John Smoltz	.05
7	Greg Maddux	.75
8	Chipper Jones	.75
9	Tom Glavine	.25
10	Andruw Jones	.60
11	Cal Ripken Jr.	1.50
12	Mike Mussina	.30
13	Albert Belle	.05
14	Nomar Garciaparra	.75
15	Jose Offerman	.05
16	Pedro Martinez	.60
17	Trot Nixon	.10
18	Kerry Wood	.40
19	Sammy Sosa	.75
20	Frank Thomas	.60
21	Paul Konerko	.15
22	Sean Casey	.15
23	Barry Larkin	.05
24	Greg Vaughn	.05
25	Travis Fryman	.05
26	Jaret Wright	.05
27	Jim Thome	.45
28	Manny Ramirez	.60
29	Roberto Alomar	.20
30	Kenny Lofton	.05
31	Todd Helton	.60
32	Larry Walker	.05
33	Vinny Castilla	.05
34	Dante Bichette	.05
35	Tony Clark	.05
36	Dean Palmer	.05
37	Gabe Kapler	.05
38	Juan Encarnacion	.05
39	Alex Gonzalez	.05
40	Preston Wilson	.05
41	Mark Kotsay	.05
42	Moises Alou	.05
43	Craig Biggio	.05
44	Ken Caminiti	.05
45	Jeff Bagwell	.60
46	Johnny Damon	.30
47	Gary Sheffield	.05
48	Kevin Brown	.05
49	Raul Mondesi	.05
50	Jeff Cirillo	.05
51	Jeromy Burnitz	.05
52	Todd Walker	.05
53	Corey Koskie	.05
54	Brad Fullmer	.05
55	Vladimir Guerrero	.60
56	Mike Piazza	1.25
57	Robin Ventura	.05
58	Rickey Henderson	.60
59	Derek Jeter	1.50
60	Paul O'Neill	.05
61	Bernie Williams	.05
62	Tino Martinez	.05
63	Roger Clemens	.85
64	Ben Grieve	.05
65	Jason Giambi	.35
66	Bob Abreu	.10
67	Scott Rolen	.40
68	Curt Schilling	.25
69	Marlon Anderson	.05
70	Kevin Young	.05
71	Jason Kendall	.05
72	Brian Giles	.05
73	Mark McGwire	1.25
74	Fernando Tatis	.05
75	Eric Davis	.05
76	Trevor Hoffman	.05
77	Tony Gwynn	.75
78	Matt Clement	.05
79	Robb Nen	.05
80	Barry Bonds	1.50
81	Ken Griffey Jr.	1.00
82	Alex Rodriguez	1.25
83	Wade Boggs	.75
84	Fred McGriff	.05
85	Jose Canseco	.30
86	Ivan Rodriguez	.50
87	Juan Gonzalez	.30
88	Rafael Palmeiro	.50
89	Carlos Delgado	.25
90	David Wells	.05
91	Troy Glaus/SR	1.00
92	Adrian Beltre/SR	.50
93	Matt Anderson/SR	.25
94	Eric Chavez/SR	.40
95	Jeff Weaver/SR RC	.25
96	Warren Morris/SR	.25
97	George Lombard/SR	.25
98	Mike Kinkade/SR	.25
99	Kyle Farnsworth/SR RC	.25
100	J.D. Drew/SR	.50
101	Joe McEwing/SR RC	.50
102	Carlos Guillen/SR	.25
103	Kelly Dransfeldt/SR RC	.25
104	Eric Munson/SR	.50
105	Armando Rios/SR	.25
106	Ramon Martinez/SR	.25
107	Orlando Hernandez/SR	.45
108	Jeremy Giambi/SR	.25
109	Pat Burrell/SR RC	2.50
110	Shea Hillenbrand/SR RC	.50
111	Billy Koch/SR	.25
112	Roy Halladay/SR	.35
113	Ruben Mateo/SR	.25
114	Bruce Chen/SR	.25
115	Angel Pena/SR	.25
116	Michael Barrett/SR	.25
117	Kevin Witt/SR	.25
118	Damon Minor/SR	.25
119	Ryan Minor/SR	.25
120	A.J. Pierzynski/SR	.25
121	A.J. Burnett/SR RC	.50
122	Christian Guzman/SR	.25
123	Joe Lawrence/SR	.25
124	Derrick Gibson/SR	.25
125	Carlos Febles/SR	.25
126	Chris Haas/SR	.25
127	Cesar King/SR	.25
128	Calvin Pickering/SR	.25
129	Mitch Meluskey/SR	.25
130	Carlos Beltran/SR	1.00
131	Ron Belliard/SR	.25
132	Jerry Hairston Jr./SR	.25
133	Fernando Seguignol/SR	.25
134	Kris Benson/SR	.25
135	Chad Hutchinson/SR RC	.25
136	Ken Griffey Jr. (Homer Odyssey)	1.50
137	Mark McGwire (Homer Odyssey)	2.00
138	Sammy Sosa (Homer Odyssey)	1.25
139	Albert Belle (Homer Odyssey)	.35
140	Mo Vaughn (Homer Odyssey)	.35
141	Alex Rodriguez (Homer Odyssey)	2.00
142	Manny Ramirez (Homer Odyssey)	.75
143	J.D. Drew (Homer Odyssey)	.50
144	Juan Gonzalez (Homer Odyssey)	.45
145	Vladimir Guerrero (Homer Odyssey)	.75
146	Fernando Tatis (Homer Odyssey)	.35
147	Mike Piazza (Homer Odyssey)	2.00
148	Barry Bonds (Homer Odyssey)	2.50
149	Ivan Rodriguez (Homer Odyssey)	.60
150	Jeff Bagwell (Homer Odyssey)	.75
151	Raul Mondesi (Homer Odyssey)	.35
152	Nomar Garciaparra (Homer Odyssey)	1.25
153	Jose Canseco (Homer Odyssey)	.50
154	Greg Vaughn (Homer Odyssey)	.35
155	Scott Rolen (Homer Odyssey)	.50
156	Vinny Castilla (Homer Odyssey)	.35
157	Troy Glaus (Homer Odyssey)	.65
158	Craig Biggio (Homer Odyssey)	.35
159	Tino Martinez (Homer Odyssey)	.35
160	Jim Thome (Homer Odyssey)	.60
161	Frank Thomas (Homer Odyssey)	1.00
162	Tony Clark (Homer Odyssey)	.35
163	Ben Grieve (Homer Odyssey)	.35
164	Matt Williams (Homer Odyssey)	.35
165	Derek Jeter (Homer Odyssey)	2.50
166	Ken Griffey Jr. (Strokes of Genius)	2.00
167	Tony Gwynn (Strokes of Genius)	1.50
168	Mike Piazza (Strokes of Genius)	2.00
169	Mark McGwire (Strokes of Genius)	2.50
170	Sammy Sosa (Strokes of Genius)	1.50
171	Juan Gonzalez (Strokes of Genius)	.60
172	Mo Vaughn (Strokes of Genius)	.50
173	Derek Jeter (Strokes of Genius)	3.00
174	Bernie Williams (Strokes of Genius)	.50
175	Ivan Rodriguez (Strokes of Genius)	.75
176	Barry Bonds (Strokes of Genius)	3.00
177	Scott Rolen (Strokes of Genius)	.75
178	Larry Walker (Strokes of Genius)	.50
179	Chipper Jones (Strokes of Genius)	1.50
180	Alex Rodriguez (Strokes of Genius)	2.50

FX Gold

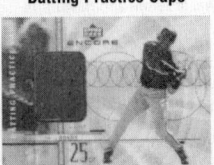

This is a 180-card parallel to the base set featuring gold holo-foil treatment and limited to 125 sequentially numbered sets.

		NM/M
Common Player:		1.00
Gold (1-90):		10X
Gold (91-135):		1.5X
Gold (136-165):		3X
Gold (166-180):		4X

Batting Practice Caps

This 15-card set features actual swatch pieces of the highlighted players' batting practice cap embedded into each card. These are seeded 1:750 packs.

		NM/M
Complete Set (15):		85.00
Common Player:		4.00
Inserted 1:750		
CB	Carlos Beltran	8.00
BB	Barry Bonds	30.00
VC	Vinny Castilla	4.00
EC	Eric Chavez	6.00
TC	Tony Clark	4.00
JD	J.D. Drew	6.00
VG	Vladimir Guerrero	8.00
TG	Tony Gwynn	15.00
TH	Todd Helton	8.00
GK	Gabe Kapler	4.00
JK	Jason Kendall	4.00
DP	Dean Palmer	4.00
BH	Frank Thomas	8.00
GV	Greg Vaughn	4.00
TW	Todd Walker	4.00

Driving Forces

This 15-card set is highlighted by holo-foil treatment on the card fronts on a thick card stock. Baseball's top performers are featured in this set and are seeded 1:23 packs. A Gold parallel exists and is limited to 10 sets.

		NM/M
Complete Set (15):		30.00
Common Player:		1.00
Inserted 1:23		
Gold (10 Sets):		30X
D1	Ken Griffey Jr.	3.00
D2	Mark McGwire	4.00
D3	Sammy Sosa	2.50
D4	Albert Belle	1.00
D5	Alex Rodriguez	4.00
D6	Mo Vaughn	1.00
D7	Juan Gonzalez	1.00
D8	Jeff Bagwell	2.00
D9	Mike Piazza	3.00
D10	Frank Thomas	2.00
D11	Barry Bonds	5.00
D12	Vladimir Guerrero	2.00
D13	Chipper Jones	2.50
D14	Tony Gwynn	2.50
D15	J.D. Drew	1.50

McGwired!

This 10-card set salutes baseball's reigning single season home run king. These are seeded 1:23 packs. A gold parallel also is randomly seeded and is limited to 500 sequentially numbered sets. A small photo of the pitcher McGwire hit the historic home run off of is pictured as well.

		NM/M
Complete Set (10):		12.50
Common Card:		1.50
Inserted 1:23		
Parallel:		2X
Production 500 Sets		
1	Mark McGwire, Carl Pavano	1.50
2	Mark McGwire, Michael Morgan	1.50
3	Mark McGwire, Steve Trachsel	1.50
4	Mark McGwire	2.50
5	Mark McGwire	2.50
6	Mark McGwire, Scott Elarton	1.50
7	Mark McGwire, Jim Parque	1.50
8	Mark McGwire	2.50
9	Mark McGwire, Rafael Roque	1.50
10	Mark McGwire, Jaret Wright	1.50

Pure Excitement

This 30-card set features Light F/X technology and includes the top players in baseball. These are seeded 1:7 packs.

		NM/M
Complete Set (30):		35.00
Common Player:		.50
Inserted 1:7		
1	Mo Vaughn	.50
2	Darin Erstad	.75
3	Travis Lee	.65
4	Chipper Jones	1.50
5	Greg Maddux	1.50
6	Gabe Kapler	.50
7	Cal Ripken Jr.	4.00
8	Nomar Garciaparra	1.50
9	Kerry Wood	.75
10	Frank Thomas	1.00
11	Manny Ramirez	1.00
12	Larry Walker	.50
13	Tony Clark	.50
14	Jeff Bagwell	1.00
15	Craig Biggio	.50
16	Vladimir Guerrero	1.00
17	Mike Piazza	2.00
18	Bernie Williams	.60
19	Derek Jeter	4.00
20	Ben Grieve	.60
21	Eric Chavez	.60
22	Scott Rolen	.75
23	Mark McGwire	3.00
24	Tony Gwynn	1.50
25	Barry Bonds	4.00
26	Ken Griffey Jr.	2.00
27	Alex Rodriguez	3.00
28	J.D. Drew	.75
29	Juan Gonzalez	.60
30	Roger Clemens	1.75

Rookie Encore

This 10-card set highlights the top rookie prospects in 1999, including J.D. Drew and Gabe Kapler. These are seeded 1:23 packs. A parallel version is also randomly seeded and limited to 500 sequentially numbered sets.

		NM/M
Complete Set (10):		17.50
Common Player:		1.00
Inserted 1:23		
FX Gold:		2X
Production 500 Sets		
1	J.D. Drew	2.00
2	Eric Chavez	1.00
3	Gabe Kapler	1.00
4	Bruce Chen	1.00
5	Carlos Beltran	3.00
6	Troy Glaus	5.00
7	Roy Halladay	1.00
8	Adrian Beltre	2.00
9	Michael Barrett	1.00
10	Pat Burrell	5.00

UD Authentics

This six-card autographed set features signatures of Griffey Jr. and Nomar Garciaparra. These are seeded 1:288 packs.

		NM/M
Complete Set (6):		130.00
Common Player:		5.00
Inserted 1:288		

		NM/M
MB	Michael Barrett	4.00
PB	Pat Burrell	10.00
JD	J.D. Drew	12.00
NG	Nomar Garciaparra	70.00
TG	Troy Glaus	12.00
JR	Ken Griffey Jr.	90.00

Upper Realm

This 15-card set focuses on the top stars of the game. Card fronts utilize holo-foil treatment, with the initials UR lightly foiled. Card backs are numbered with a "U" prefix and are seeded 1:11 packs.

		NM/M
Complete Set (15):		13.00
Common Player:		.30
Inserted 1:11		
1	Ken Griffey Jr.	1.25
2	Mark McGwire	1.50
3	Sammy Sosa	.75
4	Tony Gwynn	.75
5	Alex Rodriguez	1.50
6	Juan Gonzalez	.40
7	J.D. Drew	.50
8	Roger Clemens	.85
9	Greg Maddux	.75
10	Randy Johnson	.60
11	Mo Vaughn	.30
12	Derek Jeter	2.00
13	Vladimir Guerrero	.60
14	Cal Ripken Jr.	2.00
15	Nomar Garciaparra	.75

2K Countdown

This set recognizes the countdown to the next century with a salute to baseball's next century of superstars including Derek Jeter and Alex Rodriguez. These are done on a horizontal format and inserted 1:11 packs.

		NM/M
Complete Set (10):		16.00
Common Player:		.75
Inserted 1:11		
1	Ken Griffey Jr.	2.00
2	Derek Jeter	3.00
3	Mike Piazza	2.00
4	J.D. Drew	.75
5	Vladimir Guerrero	1.00
6	Chipper Jones	1.50
7	Alex Rodriguez	2.50
8	Nomar Garciaparra	1.50
9	Mark McGwire	2.50
10	Sammy Sosa	1.50

Ken Griffey Jr. Santa Hat Card

A swatch of red velvet, ostensibly from "a special holiday-worn Santa hat," is featured on this card given to customers and associates of UD. The standard-size card is

highlighted in gold-foil front and back and features pictures of the spokesman in a Santa hat on each side, as well.

		NM/M
HH-1	Ken Griffey Jr.	40.00

1999 Upper Deck HoloGrFX Sample

Numbered 60, rather than 56 as in the regular-issue version, this card, which also bears a white "SAMPLE" notation on back, was issued to preview the new UD brand.

		NM/M
60	Ken Griffey Jr.	2.50

1999 Upper Deck HoloGrFX

HoloGrFX was distributed exclusively to retail and the base set is comprised of 60 base cards, each utilizing holographic technology. A parallel gold-enhanced AUsome version is found about once every eight packs.

		NM/M
Complete Set (60):		12.00
Common Player:		.10
AUsome:		1.5X
Inserted 1:8		
Pack (3):		1.00
Wax Box (36):		20.00
1	Mo Vaughn	.10
2	Troy Glaus	.60
3	Tim Salmon	.10
4	Randy Johnson	.65
5	Travis Lee	.25
6	Chipper Jones	.75
7	Greg Maddux	.75
8	Andruw Jones	.65
9	Tom Glavine	.25
10	Cal Ripken Jr.	1.50
11	Albert Belle	.10
12	Nomar Garciaparra	.75
13	Pedro J. Martinez	.65
14	Sammy Sosa	.75
15	Frank Thomas	.65
16	Greg Vaughn	.10
17	Kenny Lofton	.10
18	Jim Thome	.50
19	Manny Ramirez	.65
20	Todd Helton	.60
21	Larry Walker	.10
22	Tony Clark	.10
23	Juan Encarnacion	.10
24	Mark Kotsay	.10
25	Jeff Bagwell	.65
26	Craig Biggio	.10
27	Ken Caminiti	.10
28	Carlos Beltran	.50
29	Jeremy Giambi	.10
30	Raul Mondesi	.10
31	Kevin Brown	.10
32	Jeromy Burnitz	.10

33	Corey Koskie	.10
34	Todd Walker	.10
35	Vladimir Guerrero	.65
36	Mike Piazza	1.00
37	Robin Ventura	.10
38	Derek Jeter	1.50
39	Roger Clemens	.85
40	Bernie Williams	.10
41	Orlando Hernandez	.10
42	Ben Grieve	.10
43	Eric Chavez	.15
44	Scott Rolen	.45
45	Pat Burrell RC	1.50
46	Warren Morris	.10
47	Jason Kendall	.10
48	Mark McGwire	1.25
49	J.D. Drew	.50
50	Tony Gwynn	.75
51	Trevor Hoffman	.10
52	Barry Bonds	1.50
53	Ken Griffey Jr.	1.00
54	Alex Rodriguez	1.25
55	Jose Canseco	.35
56	Juan Gonzalez	.30
57	Ivan Rodriguez	.60
58	Rafael Palmeiro	.60
59	David Wells	.10
60	Carlos Delgado	.25

Future Fame

This six-card set focuses on players who are destined for Hall of Fame greatness. Card fronts feature a horizontal format on a die-cut design. These are seeded 1:34 packs. A parallel Gold (AU) version is also randomly seeded in every 1:432 packs.

		NM/M
Complete Set (6):		15.00
Common Player:		2.50
Inserted 1:34		
Gold:		2X
Inserted 1:210		
1	Tony Gwynn	2.50
2	Cal Ripken Jr.	5.00
3	Mark McGwire	4.00
4	Ken Griffey Jr.	3.50
5	Greg Maddux	2.50
6	Roger Clemens	3.00

Launchers

This 15-card set highlights the top home run hitters on holographic patterned foil fronts, including McGwire and Sosa. These are seeded 1:3 packs. A Gold (AU) parallel version is also seeded 1:105 packs.

		NM/M
Complete Set (15):		20.00
Common Player:		.50
Inserted 1:3		
Gold:		2X
Inserted 1:105		
1	Mark McGwire	3.00
2	Ken Griffey Jr.	2.50
3	Sammy Sosa	2.00
4	J.D. Drew	.75
5	Mo Vaughn	.50
6	Juan Gonzalez	.50
7	Mike Piazza	2.50
8	Alex Rodriguez	3.00
9	Chipper Jones	2.00
10	Nomar Garciaparra	2.00
11	Vladimir Guerrero	1.00
12	Albert Belle	.50
13	Barry Bonds	4.00
14	Frank Thomas	1.00
15	Jeff Bagwell	1.00

StarView

This nine-card set highlights the top players in the game on a rainbow foil, full bleed design. These are seeded 1:17 packs. A Gold parallel version is also randomly seeded 1:210 packs.

		NM/M
Complete Set (9):		25.00
Common Player:		2.50
Inserted 1:17		
Gold:		2X
Inserted 1:210		
1	Mark McGwire	5.00
2	Ken Griffey Jr.	4.00
3	Sammy Sosa	2.50
4	Nomar Garciaparra	2.50
5	Roger Clemens	3.00
6	Greg Maddux	2.50
7	Mike Piazza	3.00
8	Alex Rodriguez	5.00
9	Chipper Jones	2.50

UD Authentics

This autographed set is done on a horizontal format, with the player signature across the front of a shadow image of the featured player in the background.

		NM/M
Common Player:		4.00
Inserted 1:431		
CB	Carlos Beltran	25.00
BC	Bruce Chen	4.00
JD	J.D. Drew	12.00
AG	Alex Gonzalez	4.00
JR	Ken Griffey Jr.	80.00
CJ	Chipper Jones	50.00
GK	Gabe Kapler	6.00
MK	Mike Kinkade	4.00
CK	Corey Koskie	7.50
GL	George Lombard	4.00
RM	Ryan Minor	4.00
SM	Shane Monahan	4.00

500 Club Piece of History

This two card collection features game-used bat chips from bats swung by Willie McCovey and Eddie Mathews embedded into each card. 350 cards of each player exist. Each player also autographed these inserts to their respective jersey numbers: McCovey (44) and Mathews (41).

		NM/M
Eddie Mathews/350		150.00
Eddie Mathews/		
Auto./41		550.00
Willie McCovey 350		120.00
Willie McCovey/		
Auto./44		650.00

Hitter.Net Ted Williams

To promote Ted Williams; web site, UD issued this card to persons attending the 1999 All-Star Game July 13 at Fenway Park in Boston. Enclosed in a cellophane wrapper, the 2-1/2" x 3-1/2" card has a sepia photo of a young Williams superimposed on an

aerial view of the ballpark. There is a facsimile autograph on front as well as the hitter.net logo. On back are various advertisements for the service, along with a photo of an autographed baseball.

		NM/M
9	Ted Williams	7.50

1999 UD Ionix

Ionix is a 90-card set that includes a 30-card "Techno" short-printed subset (1:4 packs). Four-card packs sold for $4.99. The first 60 cards of the set are included in a parallel set in which the photo from the back of the regular card was put on the front of a rainbow-foil Reciprocal card. These cards are sequentially numbered to 750. The Techno subset cards were also paralleled on a Reciprocal version sequentially numbered to 100. Due to an error, all Techno card numbers bear the "R" prefix intended for the Reciprocals; actual Reciprocal cards also bear a dot-matrix serial number on front.

		NM/M
Complete Set (90):		45.00
Common Player (1-60):		.25
Common Techno (61-90):		.50
Inserted 1:4		
Reciprocals (1-60):		3X
Production 750 Sets		
Techno Reciprocals (61-90):		1.5X
Production 100 Sets		
Pack (4):		2.00
Wax Box (20):		25.00
1	Troy Glaus	.60
2	Darin Erstad	.50
3	Travis Lee	.35
4	Matt Williams	.25
5	Chipper Jones	.75
6	Greg Maddux	.75
7	Andruw Jones	.65
8	Andres Galarraga	.25
9	Tom Glavine	.35
10	Cal Ripken Jr.	2.00
11	Ryan Minor	.25
12	Nomar Garciaparra	1.00
13	Mo Vaughn	.25
14	Pedro Martinez	.65
15	Sammy Sosa	.75
16	Kerry Wood	.50
17	Albert Belle	.25
18	Frank Thomas	.25
19	Sean Casey	.25
20	Kenny Lofton	.25
21	Manny Ramirez	.65
22	Jim Thome	.60
23	Bartolo Colon	.25
24	Jaret Wright	.25
25	Larry Walker	.25
26	Tony Clark	.25
27	Gabe Kapler	.25
28	Edgar Renteria	.25
29	Randy Johnson	.65
30	Craig Biggio	.25
31	Jeff Bagwell	.65
32	Moises Alou	.25
33	Johnny Damon	.50
34	Adrian Beltre	.35

35	Jeromy Burnitz	.25
36	Todd Walker	.25
37	Corey Koskie	.25
38	Vladimir Guerrero	.65
39	Mike Piazza	1.00
40	Hideo Nomo	.35
41	Derek Jeter	2.00
42	Tino Martinez	.25
43	Orlando Hernandez	.25
44	Ben Grieve	.25
45	Rickey Henderson	.65
46	Scott Rolen	.60
47	Curt Schilling	.25
48	Aramis Ramirez	.25
49	Tony Gwynn	.75
50	Kevin Brown	.25
51	Barry Bonds	2.00
52	Ken Griffey Jr.	1.00
53	Alex Rodriguez	1.50
54	Mark McGwire	1.50
55	J.D. Drew	.60
56	Rolando Arrojo	.25
57	Ivan Rodriguez	.35
58	Juan Gonzalez	.35
59	Roger Clemens	.85
60	Jose Cruz Jr.	.25
61	Travis Lee (Techno)	.65
62	Andres Galarraga (Techno)	.50
63	Andruw Jones (Techno)	1.50
64	Chipper Jones (Techno)	2.00
65	Greg Maddux (Techno)	2.00
66	Cal Ripken Jr. (Techno)	4.00
67	Nomar Garciaparra (Techno)	2.00
68	Mo Vaughn (Techno)	.50
69	Sammy Sosa (Techno)	2.00
70	Frank Thomas (Techno)	1.50
71	Kerry Wood (Techno)	.75
72	Kenny Lofton (Techno)	.50
73	Manny Ramirez (Techno)	1.50
74	Larry Walker (Techno)	.50
75	Jeff Bagwell (Techno)	1.50
76	Randy Johnson (Techno)	1.50
77	Paul Molitor (Techno)	1.50
78	Derek Jeter (Techno)	4.00
79	Tino Martinez (Techno)	.50
80	Mike Piazza (Techno)	2.50
81	Ben Grieve (Techno)	.50
82	Scott Rolen (Techno)	.75
83	Mark McGwire (Techno)	3.00
84	Tony Gwynn (Techno)	2.00
85	Barry Bonds (Techno)	4.00
86	Ken Griffey Jr. (Techno)	3.00
87	Alex Rodriguez (Techno)	3.00
88	Juan Gonzalez (Techno)	.75
89	Roger Clemens (Techno)	2.25
90	J.D. Drew (Techno)	1.00
100	Ken Griffey Jr. (SAMPLE)	2.50

Reciprocal

Reciprocal is a parallel of the Ionix base set in which the front and back photos have been switched. Card numbers carry an "R" prefix. The first 60 Reciprocal parallels were produced in an edition of 750 each; the Techno subset Reciprocals (#61-90) are an edition of just 100 each.

Stars (1-60):		3X
Stars (61-90):		1.5X

Cyber

This insert set consisted of 25-cards of baseball's superstars and red-hot rookies. One card was inserted every 53 packs.

		NM/M
Complete Set (25):		125.00
Common Player:		2.00
C01	Ken Griffey Jr.	8.00
C02	Cal Ripken Jr.	12.50
C03	Frank Thomas	5.00
C04	Greg Maddux	6.50
C05	Mike Piazza	8.00
C06	Alex Rodriguez	10.00
C07	Chipper Jones	8.00
C08	Derek Jeter	12.50
C09	Mark McGwire	10.00
C10	Juan Gonzalez	2.50
C11	Kerry Wood	2.50
C12	Tony Gwynn	6.50
C13	Scott Rolen	4.00
C14	Nomar Garciaparra	6.50
C15	Roger Clemens	7.00
C16	Sammy Sosa	6.50
C17	Travis Lee	2.00
C18	Ben Grieve	2.00
C19	Jeff Bagwell	5.00
C20	Ivan Rodriguez	4.00
C21	Barry Bonds	12.50
C22	J.D. Drew	4.00
C23	Kenny Lofton	4.00
C24	Andruw Jones	5.00
C25	Vladimir Guerrero	5.00

HoloGrFX

This insert set consisted of 10-cards, and featured only the best players in the game. The cards in this set were holographically enhanced. These cards were rare with one card inserted every 1,500 packs.

		NM/M
Complete Set (10):		800.00
Common Player:		50.00
Inserted 1:1,500		
HG01	Ken Griffey Jr.	100.00
HG02	Cal Ripken Jr.	150.00
HG03	Frank Thomas	75.00
HG04	Greg Maddux	90.00
HG05	Mike Piazza	100.00
HG06	Alex Rodriguez	125.00
HG07	Chipper Jones	90.00
HG08	Derek Jeter	150.00
HG09	Mark McGwire	125.00
HG10	Juan Gonzalez	50.00

Hyper

This insert set featured the top players in baseball, and consisted of 20-cards. Hyper cards were inserted one per nine packs.

		NM/M
Complete Set (20):		37.00
Common Player:		.75
Inserted 1:9		
H01	Ken Griffey Jr.	3.00
H02	Cal Ripken Jr.	4.50
H03	Frank Thomas	1.50
H04	Greg Maddux	2.25
H05	Mike Piazza	3.00
H06	Alex Rodriguez	3.75
H07	Chipper Jones	2.50
H08	Derek Jeter	4.50
H09	Mark McGwire	3.75
H10	Juan Gonzalez	.75
H11	Kerry Wood	1.00

H12	Tony Gwynn	2.25
H13	Scott Rolen	1.00
H14	Nomar Garciaparra	2.25
H15	Roger Clemens	2.75
H16	Sammy Sosa	2.25
H17	Travis Lee	1.00
H18	Ben Grieve	.75
H19	Jeff Bagwell	1.50
H20	J.D. Drew	1.00

Nitro

Baseball's ten most collectible players are featured in this 10-card insert set. Each card features Ionix technology with rainbow foil and a unique color pattern. Nitro cards were inserted one per 18 packs.

		NM/M
Complete Set (10):		18.00
Common Player:		1.00
Inserted 1:18		
N01	Ken Griffey Jr.	2.50
N02	Cal Ripken Jr.	4.00
N03	Frank Thomas	1.50
N04	Greg Maddux	2.00
N05	Mike Piazza	2.50
N06	Alex Rodriguez	3.00
N07	Chipper Jones	2.00
N08	Derek Jeter	4.00
N09	Mark McGwire	3.00
N10	J.D. Drew	1.00

Warp Zone

This 15-card insert set contained a special holographic foil enhancement. Warp Zone cards were inserted one per 216 packs.

		NM/M
Complete Set (15):		195.00
Common Player:		6.00
Inserted 1:216		
WZ1	Ken Griffey Jr.	20.00
WZ2	Cal Ripken Jr.	30.00
WZ3	Frank Thomas	10.00
WZ4	Greg Maddux	15.00
WZ5	Mike Piazza	20.00
WZ6	Alex Rodriguez	25.00
WZ7	Chipper Jones	15.00
WZ8	Derek Jeter	30.00
WZ9	Mark McGwire	25.00
WZ10	Juan Gonzalez	10.00
WZ11	Kerry Wood	10.00
WZ12	Tony Gwynn	15.00
WZ13	Scott Rolen	6.00
WZ14	Nomar Garciaparra	15.00
WZ15	J.D. Drew	6.00

500 Club Piece of History

These cards feature an actual piece of game-used bat from one of Hall-of-Famer Frank Robinson's Louisville Sluggers. Approximately 350 were made. Robinson also autographed 20 of his Piece of History inserts.

		NM/M
FR	Frank Robinson/350	165.00
FRA	Frank Robinson/	
	Auto. 20	650.00

Mark McGwire Tribute Lunchbox

One of many special issues produced by Upper Deck in celebration of McGwire's short-lived season home run record, this 30-card set was sold in a metal lunchbox. Each 2-1/2" x 3-1/2" card has a large action photo on front and a small round portrait, along with the card title. The back has the same photos, with the large photo in a ghosted image as a background for the description of the highight presented on the card.

		NM/M
Complete Boxed Set (30):		10.00
Common Card:		.50
1-30	Mark McGwire	.50

Mark McGwire 70 HR - A New Record

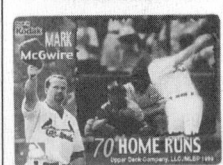

This is one of many special issues from Upper Deck commemorating McGwire's record-breaking 1998 season. Most such cards were produced for retail-only sales, or for home shopping television shows. This blank-back, round-cornered card is 3-1/2" x 2-1/2" and has a flicker-action scene of Big Mac's home run swing.

	NM/M
Mark McGwire	4.00

Mark McGwire 500 Home Run Card Set

This TV-exclusive product depicts milestone home runs leading up to Big Mac's 500th career clout on Aug. 5, 1999. Sold in a shrink-wrapped decorative box, the basic design of the 2-1/2" x 3-1/2" card has a central photo, usually an action shot, with a black pinstriped border at left and a red striped border at right. The word "MILE-STONES" appears at the top of the picture. In a gray tab at left is a date or year, while his name is in a matching black tab at right. A silver-foil UD logo is at bottom. Backs have a grainy red monochromatic background photo on which are overprinted the details of the pictured blast, along with appropriate logos. Some cards have a silver-foil home run number printed on front. A special card pictures his 1st and 500th career homers. Issue price was about $30.

		NM/M
Complete Boxed Set (30):		7.00
Common Card:		.35
1-30	Mark McGwire	.35

1999 Upper Deck MVP Samples

		NM/M
S3	Ken Griffey Jr.	2.00
S3	Ken Griffey Jr. (Silver signature.)	2.00

1999 Upper Deck MVP

Card fronts of the 220-card set feature silver foil stamping and a white border. Backs feature year-by-year statistics, a small photo of the featured player and a brief career note. MVP was distributed in 36-pack boxes, with a SRP of $1.59 for 10-card packs.

		NM/M
Complete Set (220):		10.00
Common Player:		.05
Silver Script:		1X
Inserted 1:2		
Gold Script:		10X
Production 100 Sets		
Super Script:		30X
Production 25 Sets		
Pack (10):		1.00
Wax Box (36):		20.00
1	Mo Vaughn	.05
2	Tim Belcher	.05
3	Jack McDowell	.05
4	Troy Glaus	.60
5	Darin Erstad	.40
6	Tim Salmon	.15
7	Jim Edmonds	.05
8	Randy Johnson	.60
9	Steve Finley	.05
10	Travis Lee	.15
11	Matt Williams	.05
12	Todd Stottlemyre	.05
13	Jay Bell	.05
14	David Dellucci	.05
15	Chipper Jones	.75
16	Andruw Jones	.60
17	Greg Maddux	.75
18	Tom Glavine	.25
19	Javy Lopez	.05
20	Brian Jordan	.05
21	George Lombard	.05
22	John Smoltz	.05
23	Cal Ripken Jr.	1.50
24	Charles Johnson	.05
25	Albert Belle	.15
26	Brady Anderson	.05
27	Mike Mussina	.35
28	Calvin Pickering	.05
29	Ryan Minor	.05
30	Jerry Hairston Jr.	.05
31	Nomar Garciaparra	1.00
32	Pedro Martinez	.60
33	Jason Varitek	.05
34	Troy O'Leary	.05
35	Donnie Sadler	.05
36	Mark Portugal	.05
37	John Valentin	.05
38	Kerry Wood	.35
39	Sammy Sosa	1.00
40	Mark Grace	.10
41	Henry Rodriguez	.05
42	Rod Beck	.05
43	Benito Santiago	.05
44	Kevin Tapani	.05

45	Frank Thomas	.60
46	Mike Caruso	.05
47	Magglio Ordonez	.40
48	Paul Konerko	.05
49	Ray Durham	.05
50	Jim Parque	.05
51	Carlos Lee	.05
52	Denny Neagle	.05
53	Pete Harnisch	.05
54	Michael Tucker	.05
55	Sean Casey	.15
56	Eddie Taubensee	.05
57	Barry Larkin	.05
58	Pokey Reese	.05
59	Sandy Alomar	.05
60	Roberto Alomar	.25
61	Bartolo Colon	.05
62	Kenny Lofton	.05
63	Omar Vizquel	.05
64	Travis Fryman	.05
65	Jim Thome	.05
66	Manny Ramirez	.60
67	Jaret Wright	.05
68	Darryl Kile	.05
69	Kirt Manwaring	.05
70	Vinny Castilla	.05
71	Todd Helton	.60
72	Dante Bichette	.05
73	Larry Walker	.05
74	Derrick Gibson	.05
75	Gabe Kapler	.05
76	Dean Palmer	.05
77	Matt Anderson	.05
78	Bobby Higginson	.05
79	Damion Easley	.05
80	Tony Clark	.05
81	Juan Encarnacion	.05
82	Livan Hernandez	.05
83	Alex Gonzalez	.05
84	Preston Wilson	.05
85	Derrek Lee	.05
86	Mark Kotsay	.05
87	Todd Dunwoody	.05
88	Cliff Floyd	.05
89	Ken Caminiti	.05
90	Jeff Bagwell	.60
91	Moises Alou	.05
92	Craig Biggio	.05
93	Billy Wagner	.05
94	Richard Hidalgo	.05
95	Derek Bell	.05
96	Hipolito Pichardo	.05
97	Jeff King	.05
98	Carlos Beltran	.40
99	Jeremy Giambi	.05
100	Larry Sutton	.05
101	Johnny Damon	.20
102	Dee Brown	.05
103	Kevin Brown	.10
104	Chan Ho Park	.05
105	Raul Mondesi	.05
106	Eric Karros	.05
107	Adrian Beltre	.15
108	Devon White	.05
109	Gary Sheffield	.35
110	Sean Berry	.05
111	Alex Ochoa	.05
112	Marquis Grissom	.05
113	Fernando Vina	.05
114	Jeff Cirillo	.05
115	Geoff Jenkins	.05
116	Jeromy Burnitz	.05
117	Brad Radke	.05
118	Eric Milton	.05
119	A.J. Pierzynski	.05
120	Todd Walker	.05
121	David Ortiz	.05
122	Corey Koskie	.05
123	Vladimir Guerrero	.60
124	Rondell White	.05
125	Brad Fullmer	.05
126	Ugueth Urbina	.05
127	Dustin Hermanson	.05
128	Michael Barrett	.05
129	Fernando Seguignol	.05
130	Mike Piazza	1.00
131	Rickey Henderson	.60
132	Rey Ordonez	.05
133	John Olerud	.05
134	Robin Ventura	.05
135	Hideo Nomo	.60
136	Mike Kinkade	.05
137	Al Leiter	.05
138	Brian McRae	.05
139	Derek Jeter	1.50
140	Bernie Williams	.15
141	Paul O'Neill	.15
142	Scott Brosius	.05
143	Tino Martinez	.15
144	Roger Clemens	.85
145	Orlando Hernandez	.10
146	Mariano Rivera	.10
147	Ricky Ledee	.05
148	A.J. Hinch	.05
149	Ben Grieve	.10
150	Eric Chavez	.15
151	Miguel Tejada	.15
152	Matt Stairs	.05
153	Ryan Christenson	.05
154	Jason Giambi	.35
155	Curt Schilling	.05
156	Scott Rolen	.45
157	Pat Burrell RC	1.50
158	Doug Glanville	.05
159	Bobby Abreu	.05
160	Rico Brogna	.05
161	Ron Gant	.05
162	Jason Kendall	.05

163	Aramis Ramirez	.05
164	Jose Guillen	.05
165	Emil Brown	.05
166	Pat Meares	.05
167	Kevin Young	.05
168	Brian Giles	.05
169	Mark McGwire	1.25
170	J.D. Drew	.40
171	Edgar Renteria	.05
172	Fernando Tatis	.05
173	Matt Morris	.05
174	Eli Marrero	.05
175	Ray Lankford	.05
176	Tony Gwynn	.75
177	Sterling Hitchcock	.05
178	Ruben Rivera	.05
179	Wally Joyner	.05
180	Trevor Hoffman	.05
181	Jim Leyritz	.05
182	Carlos Hernandez	.05
183	Barry Bonds	1.50
184	Ellis Burks	.05
185	F.P. Santangelo	.05
186	J.T. Snow	.05
187	Ramon Martinez	.05
188	Jeff Kent	.05
189	Robb Nen	.05
190	Ken Griffey Jr.	1.00
191	Alex Rodriguez	1.25
192	Shane Monahan	.05
193	Carlos Guillen	.05
194	Edgar Martinez	.05
195	David Segui	.05
196	Jose Mesa	.05
197	Jose Canseco	.35
198	Rolando Arrojo	.05
199	Wade Boggs	.75
200	Fred McGriff	.05
201	Quinton McCracken	.05
202	Bobby Smith	.05
203	Bubba Trammell	.05
204	Juan Gonzalez	.60
205	Ivan Rodriguez	.45
206	Rafael Palmeiro	.45
207	Royce Clayton	.05
208	Rick Helling	.05
209	Todd Zeile	.05
210	Rusty Greer	.05
211	David Wells	.05
212	Roy Halladay	.05
213	Carlos Delgado	.25
214	Darrin Fletcher	.05
215	Shawn Green	.15
216	Kevin Witt	.05
217	Jose Cruz Jr.	.05
218	Checklist (Ken Griffey Jr.)	.45
219	Checklist (Sammy Sosa)	.45
220	Checklist (Mark McGwire)	.50

Scripts/Super Scripts

Three different parallels of the 220 base cards in MVP are inserted bearing a metallic-foil facsimile autograph on front. Silver Script cards are found about every other pack. Gold Script cards are hobby-only and serially numbered to 100 apiece. Also hobby-only are Super Script versions on which the autograph is in holographic foil and the cards are numbered on the back to 25 apiece.

Silver Script:	1X
Gold Script:	10X
Super Script:	30X

All-Star Game

In conjunction with FanFest held in Boston prior to the All-Star Game, UD issued a set of specially marked versions of its MVP issue. It was reported that 15,000 three-card packs were distributed at the show, with some cards reportedly short-printed. The cards have a format virtually identical to the regular-issue MVP cards, except for the presence on front of a bright silver-foil All-Star logo and an AS prefix to the card number on back.

	NM/M
Complete Set (30):	12.50
Common Player:	.25

Dynamics

1	Mo Vaughn	.25
2	Randy Johnson	.60
3	Chipper Jones	.75
4	Greg Maddux	.75
5	Cal Ripken Jr.	2.00
6	Albert Belle	.35
7	Nomar Garciaparra	1.00
8	Pedro Martinez	.60
9	Sammy Sosa	1.00
10	Frank Thomas	.60
11	Sean Casey	.35
12	Roberto Alomar	.30
13	Manny Ramirez	.60
14	Larry Walker	.25
15	Jeff Bagwell	.60
16	Craig Biggio	.25
17	Raul Mondesi	.25
18	Vladimir Guerrero	.60
19	Mike Piazza	1.00
20	Derek Jeter	2.00
21	Roger Clemens	.85
22	Scott Rolen	.40
23	Mark McGwire	1.50
24	Tony Gwynn	.75
25	Barry Bonds	2.00
26	Ken Griffey Jr.	1.00
27	Alex Rodriguez	1.50
28	Jose Canseco	.40
29	Juan Gonzalez	.60
30	Ivan Rodriguez	.50

This 15-card set features holofoil treatment on the card fronts with silver foil stamping. Card backs are numbered with a "D" prefix and are inserted 1:28 packs.

		NM/M
Complete Set (15):		17.50
Common Player:		.60
Inserted 1:28		
1	Ken Griffey Jr.	2.00
2	Alex Rodriguez	2.50
3	Nomar Garciaparra	2.00
4	Mike Piazza	2.00
5	Mark McGwire	2.25
6	Sammy Sosa	2.00
7	Chipper Jones	1.50
8	Mo Vaughn	.60
9	Tony Gwynn	1.50
10	Vladimir Guerrero	1.25
11	Derek Jeter	3.00
12	Jeff Bagwell	1.25
13	Cal Ripken Jr.	3.00
14	Juan Gonzalez	1.25
15	J.D. Drew	.90

Game-Used Souvenirs

This set has a piece of game-used bat from the featured player embedded into each card. These are found exclusively in hobby packs at a rate of 1:144 packs.

	NM/M
Complete Set (9):	75.00

Common Player:		5.00
Inserted 1:144		
JB	Jeff Bagwell	8.00
BB	Barry Bonds	20.00
JD	J.D. Drew	8.00
KGj	Ken Griffey Jr.	15.00
CJ	Chipper Jones	10.00
MP	Mike Piazza	15.00
CR	Cal Ripken Jr.	20.00
SR	Scott Rolen	8.00
MV	Mo Vaughn	5.00

Signed Game-Used Souvenirs

Ken Griffey Jr. and Chipper Jones both signed their Game Used Souvenir inserts to their jersey number, Griffey (24) and Jones (10). These were seeded exclusively in hobby packs.

		NM/M
KGj	Ken Griffey Jr.	300.00
CJ	Chipper Jones	200.00

Power Surge

This 15-card set features baseball's top home run hitters, utilizing rainbow-foil technology. Card backs are numbered with a "P" prefix and are seeded 1:9 packs.

		NM/M
Complete Set (15):		12.50
Common Player:		.50
Inserted 1:9		
1	Mark McGwire	1.50
2	Sammy Sosa	1.25
3	Ken Griffey Jr.	1.25
4	Alex Rodriguez	1.50
5	Juan Gonzalez	.75
6	Nomar Garciaparra	1.25
7	Vladimir Guerrero	.75
8	Chipper Jones	1.00
9	Albert Belle	.50
10	Frank Thomas	.75
11	Mike Piazza	1.25
12	Jeff Bagwell	.75
13	Manny Ramirez	.75
14	Mo Vaughn	.50
15	Barry Bonds	2.00

ProSign

This 30-card autographed set is randomly seeded exclusively in retail packs at a rate of 1:216 packs. Card backs are numbered with the featured player's initials.

		NM/M
Common Autograph:		5.00
Inserted 1:216 R		
MA	Matt Anderson	5.00
CB	Carlos Beltran	15.00
RB	Russ Branyan	5.00
EC	Eric Chavez	10.00
BC	Bruce Chen	5.00
BF	Brad Fuller	5.00
NG	Nomar Garciaparra	80.00
JG	Jeremy Giambi	5.00
DG	Derrick Gibson	5.00
CG	Chris Gomez	5.00
AG	Alex Gonzalez	5.00
BG	Ben Grieve	5.00
JR.	Ken Griffey Jr.	80.00
RH	Richard Hidalgo	5.00
SH	Shea Hillenbrand	10.00
CJ	Chipper Jones/SP	50.00

GK	Gabe Kapler	6.00
SK	Scott Karl	5.00
CK	Corey Koskie	7.50
RL	Ricky Ledee	5.00
ML	Mike Lincoln	5.00
GL	George Lombard	5.00
MLo	Mike Lowell	7.50
RM	Ryan Minor	5.00
SM	Shane Monahan	5.00
AN	Abraham Nunez	5.00
JP	Jim Parque	5.00
CP	Calvin Pickering	5.00
JRa	Jason Rakers	5.00
RR	Ruben Rivera	5.00
IR	Ivan Rodriguez/SP	50.00
KW	Kevin Witt	5.00

Scout's Choice

Utilizing Light F/X technology, this 15-card set highlights the top young prospects in the game. Card backs are numbered with an "SC" prefix and are seeded 1:9 packs.

		NM/M
Complete Set (15):		5.00
Common Player:		.25
Inserted 1:9		
1	J.D. Drew	.65
2	Ben Grieve	.35
3	Troy Glaus	1.50
4	Gabe Kapler	.25
5	Carlos Beltran	.45
6	Aramis Ramirez	.25
7	Pat Burrell	1.00
8	Kerry Wood	.65
9	Ryan Minor	.25
10	Todd Helton	1.00
11	Eric Chavez	.25
12	Russ Branyon	.25
13	Travis Lee	.35
14	Ruben Mateo	.35
15	Roy Halladay	.35

Super Tools

This 15-card insert set focuses on baseball's top stars and utilizes holo foil technology on the card fronts. Card backs are numbered with a "T" prefix and are seeded 1:14 packs.

		NM/M
Complete Set (15):		25.00
Common Player:		.50
Inserted 1:14		
1	Ken Griffey Jr.	2.50
2	Alex Rodriguez	3.00
3	Sammy Sosa	2.00
4	Derek Jeter	4.00
5	Vladimir Guerrero	1.50
6	Ben Grieve	.50
7	Mike Piazza	2.50
8	Kenny Lofton	.50
9	Barry Bonds	4.00
10	Darin Erstad	1.00
11	Nomar Garciaparra	2.00
12	Cal Ripken Jr.	4.00
13	J.D. Drew	1.00
14	Larry Walker	.50
15	Chipper Jones	2.00

Swing Time

This 12-card set focuses on top hitters in the game and points out three aspects why the featured player is such a successful hitter. Printed on a full foiled front these are seeded 1:6 packs. Cards are numbered with an "S" prefix.

		NM/M
Complete Set (12):		5.00
Common Player:		.35
Inserted 1:6		
1	Ken Griffey Jr.	.75

2	Mark McGwire	1.00
3	Sammy Sosa	.60
4	Tony Gwynn	.60
5	Alex Rodriguez	1.00
6	Nomar Garciaparra	.60
7	Barry Bonds	1.50
8	Frank Thomas	.45
9	Chipper Jones	.60
10	Ivan Rodriguez	.35
11	Mike Piazza	.75
12	Derek Jeter	1.50

500 Club Piece of History

This insert has a piece of game-used bat once swung by Mike Schmidt embedded into each card. A total of 350 of this insert was produced. Schmidt also signed 20 of the inserts.

	NM/M
Mike Schmidt/350	160.00
Mike Schmidt/Auto./20	1,250

1999 Upper Deck Ovation

Cards 1-60 in the base set have the look and feel of an actual baseball. A player photo is in the foreground with a partial image of a baseball in the background on the card front. Cards 61-90 make up two subsets: World Premiere (61-80) is a 20-card collection consisting of 20 rookie prospects and Superstar Spotlight (81-90) is a 10-card lineup of baseball's biggest stars. Both subsets are short-printed, World Premiere are seeded 1:3.5 packs and Superstar Spotlight 1:6 packs. Five-card packs carry a S.R.P. of $3.99 per pack.

	NM/M
Complete Set (90):	20.00
Common Player:	.05
Common World Premiere:	.15
Inserted 1:3.5	
Common Superstar Spotlight:	.60
Inserted 1:6	
Pack (5):	2.00
Box (20):	30.00

1	Ken Griffey Jr.	1.50
2	Rondell White	.05
3	Tony Clark	.05
4	Barry Bonds	2.50
5	Larry Walker	.05
6	Greg Vaughn	.05
7	Mark Grace	.05
8	John Olerud	.05
9	Matt Williams	.05
10	Craig Biggio	.05
11	Quinton McCracken	.05
12	Kerry Wood	.35
13	Derek Jeter	2.50
14	Frank Thomas	.75
15	Tino Martinez	.05

16	Albert Belle	.05
17	Ben Grieve	.05
18	Cal Ripken Jr.	2.50
19	Johnny Damon	.30
20	Jose Cruz Jr.	.05
21	Barry Larkin	.05
22	Jason Giambi	.45
23	Sean Casey	.10
24	Scott Rolen	.60
25	Jim Thome	.45
26	Curt Schilling	.25
27	Moises Alou	.05
28	Alex Rodriguez	2.00
29	Mark Kotsay	.05
30	Darin Erstad	.25
31	Mike Mussina	.30
32	Todd Walker	.05
33	Nomar Garciaparra	1.00
34	Vladimir Guerrero	.75
35	Jeff Bagwell	.75
36	Mark McGwire	2.00
37	Travis Lee	.15
38	Dean Palmer	.05
39	Fred McGriff	.05
40	Sammy Sosa	1.00
41	Mike Piazza	1.50
42	Andres Galarraga	.05
43	Pedro Martinez	.75
44	Juan Gonzalez	.40
45	Greg Maddux	1.00
46	Jeromy Burnitz	.05
47	Roger Clemens	1.25
48	Vinny Castilla	.05
49	Kevin Brown	.05
50	Mo Vaughn	.05
51	Raul Mondesi	.05
52	Randy Johnson	.75
53	Ray Lankford	.05
54	Jaret Wright	.05
55	Tony Gwynn	1.00
56	Chipper Jones	1.00
57	Gary Sheffield	.40
58	Ivan Rodriguez	.65
59	Kenny Lofton	.05
60	Jason Kendall	.05
61	J.D. Drew (World Premiere)	.75
62	Gabe Kapler (World Premiere)	.15
63	Adrian Beltre (World Premiere)	.40
64	Carlos Beltran (World Premiere)	.50
65	Eric Chavez (World Premiere)	.35
66	Mike Lowell (World Premiere)	.25
67	Troy Glaus (World Premiere)	1.00
68	George Lombard (World Premiere)	.15
69	Alex Gonzalez (World Premiere)	.15
70	Mike Kinkade (World Premiere)	.15
71	Jeremy Giambi (World Premiere)	.15
72	Bruce Chen (World Premiere)	.15
73	Preston Wilson (World Premiere)	.25
74	Kevin Witt (World Premiere)	.15
75	Carlos Guillen (World Premiere)	.15
76	Ryan Minor (World Premiere)	.15
77	Corey Koskie (World Premiere)	.15
78	Robert Fick (World Premiere)	.15
79	Michael Barrett (World Premiere)	.15
80	Calvin Pickering (World Premiere)	.15
81	Ken Griffey Jr. (Superstar Spotlight)	1.00
82	Mark McGwire (Superstar Spotlight)	1.50
83	Cal Ripken Jr. (Superstar Spotlight)	2.00
84	Derek Jeter (Superstar Spotlight)	2.00
85	Chipper Jones (Superstar Spotlight)	.75
86	Nomar Garciaparra (Garciaparra) (Superstar Spotlight)	.75
87	Sammy Sosa (Superstar Spotlight)	.75
88	Juan Gonzalez (Superstar Spotlight)	.30
89	Mike Piazza (Superstar Spotlight)	1.00
90	Alex Rodriguez (Superstar Spotlight)	1.50

Standing Ovation

Stars (1-60):	3X
World Premiere (61-80):	1.5X

World Premiere

Superstar Spotlight (81-90): 2X
Production 500 Sets

Curtain Calls

This 20-card set focuses on the most memorable accomplishments posted during the '98 season. Card fronts have two images of the player, one on the right half and a smaller image on the bottom left. Copper foil stamping is used to enhance the card front. These are numbered with a "R" prefix and are seeded 1:8 packs.

		NM/M
Complete Set (20):		20.00
Common Player:		.25
Inserted 1:8		
R1	Mark McGwire	2.00
R2	Sammy Sosa	1.00
R3	Ken Griffey Jr.	1.50
R4	Alex Rodriguez	2.00
R5	Roger Clemens	1.25
R6	Cal Ripken Jr.	2.50
R7	Barry Bonds	2.50
R8	Kerry Wood	.40
R9	Nomar Garciaparra	1.00
R10	Derek Jeter	2.50
R11	Juan Gonzalez	.50
R12	Greg Maddux	1.00
R13	Pedro Martinez	1.00
R14	David Wells	.25
R15	Moises Alou	.25
R16	Tony Gwynn	1.00
R17	Albert Belle	.25
R18	Mike Piazza	1.50
R19	Ivan Rodriguez	.65
R20	Randy Johnson	.75

Major Production

This 20-card set utilizes thermography technology to simulate the look and feel of home plate and highlights some of the game's most productive players. These are inserted 1:45 packs and are numbered with an "S" prefix.

		NM/M
Complete Set (20):		45.00
Common Player:		.75
Inserted 1:45		
S1	Mike Piazza	4.00
S2	Mark McGwire	5.00
S3	Chipper Jones	3.00
S4	Cal Ripken Jr.	6.00

S5	Ken Griffey Jr.	4.00
S6	Barry Bonds	6.00
S7	Tony Gwynn	3.00
S8	Randy Johnson	2.50
S9	Ivan Rodriguez	2.00
S10	Frank Thomas	2.50
S11	Alex Rodriguez	5.00
S12	Albert Belle	.75
S13	Juan Gonzalez	1.25
S14	Greg Maddux	3.00
S15	Jeff Bagwell	2.50
S16	Derek Jeter	6.00
S17	Matt Williams	.75
S18	Kenny Lofton	.75
S19	Sammy Sosa	3.00
S20	Roger Clemens	3.50

Piece of History

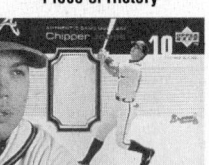

This 16-card set has actual pieces of game-used bat, from the featured player, imbedded into the card. These are inserted 1:247 packs. Ben Grieve autographed 25 versions of his Piece of History insert cards. Although there is no regular Piece of History Kerry Wood card, Upper Deck inserted 25 autographed Piece of History game-used baseball cards. These have a piece of one of Wood's game-hurled baseballs from the 1998 season.

		NM/M
Common Player:		5.00
Inserted 1:247		
BB	Barry Bonds	25.00
CJ	Chipper Jones	15.00
BW	Bernie Williams	5.00
KGj	Ken Griffey Jr.	20.00
NG	Nomar Garciaparra	15.00
JG	Juan Gonzalez	15.00
DJ	Derek Jeter	25.00
SS	Sammy Sosa	15.00
TG	Tony Gwynn	15.00
AR	Alex Rodriguez	20.00
CR	Cal Ripken Jr.	25.00
BG	Ben Grieve	5.00
VG	Vladimir Guerrero	10.00
MP	Mike Piazza	20.00
BGAU	Ben Grieve/Auto./25	30.00
KWAU	Kerry Wood/Auto./25	50.00

ReMarkable

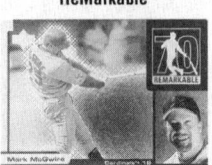

This three-tiered 15-card insert showcases Mark McGwire's historic '98 season. Cards #1-5 are Bronze and inserted 1:9 packs; cards #6-10 are Silver and inserted 1:25 packs; and cards #11-15 are Gold and inserted 1:99 packs.

		NM/M
Complete Set (15):		20.00
Common #1-5:		1.50
Inserted 1:9		
Common #6-10:		2.25
Inserted 1:25		
Common # 11-15:		3.00
Inserted 1:99		
MM1-5	Mark McGwire	1.50
MM6-10	Mark McGwire	3.00
MM11-15	Mark McGwire	5.00

500 Club Piece of History

Each of these cards actually has a piece of game-used Louisville Slugger, once swung by Mickey Mantle, embedded. Approximately 350 cards exist. There is also one card with a cut signature of Mantle and a piece of his game-used bat on it.

		NM/M
MIC-P	Mickey Mantle/350	600.00
	Mickey Mantle/Bat Auto.	8,000

1999 Upper Deck PowerDeck

This 25-card set is comprised of 25 digital PowerDeck interactive trading cards, complete with video and audio content. There is also a parallel "paper" version of the base set called Auxiliary Power. Each digital card includes 32 megabytes of information and is compatible with almost any internet ready computer. One PowerDeck digital card comes in every three-card pack.

		NM/M
Complete Set (25):		20.00
Common Player:		.50
Pack (3):		1.50
Wax Box (24):		20.00
1	Ken Griffey Jr.	2.00
2	Mark McGwire	2.50
3	Cal Ripken Jr.	3.00
4	Sammy Sosa	1.50
5	Derek Jeter	3.00
6	Mike Piazza	2.00
7	Nomar Garciaparra	1.50
8	Greg Maddux	1.50
9	Tony Gwynn	1.50
10	Roger Clemens	1.75
11	Scott Rolen	1.00
12	Alex Rodriguez	2.50
13	Manny Ramirez	1.25
14	Chipper Jones	1.50
15	Juan Gonzalez	.65
16	Ivan Rodriguez	1.00
17	Frank Thomas	1.25
18	Mo Vaughn	.50
19	Barry Bonds	3.00
20	Vladimir Guerrero	1.25
21	Jose Canseco	.65
22	Jeff Bagwell	1.25
23	Pedro Martinez	1.25
24	Gabe Kapler	.50
25	J.D. Drew	.75
---	Checklist	.10

Auxiliary Power

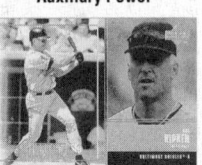

A "paper" parallel version of the 25-card digital set. These have a horizontal format with silver-foil graphics. Backs repeat the front portrait photo along with the player's past five years of statistics and a brief career highlight. Card numbers are prefixed with "AUX-."

		NM/M
Complete Set (25):		6.00
Common Player:		.10
1	Ken Griffey Jr.	.50
2	Mark McGwire	.60
3	Cal Ripken Jr.	.75
4	Sammy Sosa	.40
5	Derek Jeter	.75
6	Mike Piazza	.50
7	Nomar Garciaparra	.40
8	Greg Maddux	.40
9	Tony Gwynn	.40
10	Roger Clemens	.45
11	Scott Rolen	.25
12	Alex Rodriguez	.60
13	Manny Ramirez	.30
14	Chipper Jones	.40
15	Juan Gonzalez	.15
16	Ivan Rodriguez	.30
17	Frank Thomas	.30
18	Mo Vaughn	.10
19	Barry Bonds	.75
20	Vladimir Guerrero	.30
21	Jose Canseco	.20
22	Jeff Bagwell	.30
23	Pedro Martinez	.30
24	Gabe Kapler	.10
25	J.D. Drew	.25

Most Valuable Performances

This seven-card digital insert set consists of capturing true MVP performances from some of baseball's greatest players. These were seeded 1:287 packs.

		NM/M
Complete Set (7):		75.00
Common Player:		6.00
Inserted 1:287		
1	Sammy Sosa	10.00
2	Barry Bonds	20.00
3	Cal Ripken Jr.	20.00
4	Juan Gonzalez	6.00
5	Ken Griffey Jr.	12.50
6	Roger Clemens	10.00
7	Mark McGwire, Sammy Sosa	12.50

MVP Auxiliary

A "paper" parallel version of the digital set, these also were inserted 1:287 packs. They have a horizontal format using silver holofoil and also have different photos from the digital version.

		NM/M
Complete Set (7):		60.00
Common Player:		4.00
Inserted 1:287		
1	Sammy Sosa	7.50
2	Barry Bonds	15.00
3	Cal Ripken Jr.	15.00
4	Juan Gonzalez	4.00
5	Ken Griffey Jr.	10.00
6	Roger Clemens	7.50
7	Mark McGwire, Sammy Sosa	12.50

Powerful Moments

This six-card digital interactive set has game-action footage pinpointing specific milestones in each of the featured players' careers. These were inserted 1:7 packs.

		NM/M
Complete Set (6):		10.00
Common Player:		1.00
Inserted 1:7		
1	Mark McGwire	2.00
2	Sammy Sosa	1.00
3	Cal Ripken Jr.	3.00
4	Ken Griffey Jr.	1.50
5	Derek Jeter	3.00
6	Alex Rodriguez	2.00

Powerful Moments Auxiliary

This "paper" parallel version of the digital set is also inserted 1:7 packs on a horizontal format. Different photos were used from the digital set.

		NM/M
Complete Set (6):		10.00
Common Player:		1.00
Inserted 1:7		
Gold (One each.): Value Undetermined		
1	Mark McGwire	2.00
2	Sammy Sosa	1.00
3	Cal Ripken Jr.	3.00
4	Ken Griffey Jr.	1.50
5	Derek Jeter	3.00
6	Alex Rodriguez	2.00

Time Capsule

Six MLB Rookies of the Year are honored in this digital set with the digital content going back to the rookie seasons of the featured players. These were seeded 1:23 packs.

		NM/M
Complete Set (6):		12.50
Common Player:		1.00
Inserted 1:23		
1	Ken Griffey Jr.	2.50
2	Mike Piazza	2.50
3	Mark McGwire	3.00
4	Derek Jeter	4.00
5	Jose Canseco	1.00
6	Nomar Garciaparra	2.00

Time Capsule-Auxiliary Power

This "paper" parallel set of the digital version utilizes a similar design as the digital insert and uses different photos as well. Horizontal fronts have a thin vertical monochromatic portrait at left. At right is an action photos set on a metallized background. Backs repeat the front portrait and have a screen simulation along with stats and data. These were inserted 1:23 packs.

		NM/M
Complete Set (6):		15.00
Common Player:		1.00
Inserted 1:23		
Gold (One of each.): Values Undetermined		
1	Ken Griffey Jr.	2.50
2	Mike Piazza	2.50
3	Mark McGwire	3.00
4	Derek Jeter	4.00
5	Jose Canseco	1.00
6	Nomar Garciaparra	2.00

A Season to Remember

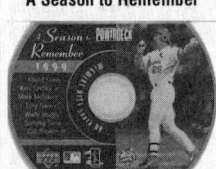

This special box-topper CD insert presents audio-visual highlights of the 1999 season, featuring players like David Cone, Ken Griffey, Jr., Mark McGwire, Tony Gwynn, Wade Boggs, Sammy Sosa and Cal Ripken, Jr. McGwire is pictured on this CD hitting his 500th home run.

		NM/M
	Mark McGwire	3.00

Athletes of the Century

Babe Ruth was baseball's representative in a four-sport set of CD "cards" produced by Upper Deck.

		NM/M
	Babe Ruth	1.00

World Series Power Deck

This CD-ROM card titled "Season to Remember" was distributed at Yankee Stadium during

Game 4 of the 1999 World Series and features highlights of the Yankees championship season.

		NM/M
	Season to Remember (1999 Yankees)	12.00

1999 UD Retro

The 110-card base set is comprised of 88 current stars and 22 retired greats. Card fronts have a tan, speckled border while card backs have a year-by-year compilation of the player's stats along with a career note. Retro is packaged in lunchboxes, 24 packs to a box with an S.R.P. of $4.99 per six-card pack.

		NM/M
Complete Set (110):		15.00
Common Player:		.05
Gold:		12X
Production 250 Sets		
Platinum 1/1: Values Undetermined		
Wax Pack (6):		2.50
Lunchbox (24):		45.00
1	Mo Vaughn	.05
2	Troy Glaus	.65
3	Tim Salmon	.05
4	Randy Johnson	.75
5	Travis Lee	.15
6	Matt Williams	.05
7	Greg Maddux	.85
8	Chipper Jones	1.00
9	Andruw Jones	.75
10	Tom Glavine	.05
11	Javy Lopez	.05
12	Albert Belle	.05
13	Cal Ripken Jr.	2.00
14	Brady Anderson	.05
15	Nomar Garciaparra	.85
16	Pedro J. Martinez	.75
17	Sammy Sosa	.85
18	Mark Grace	.05
19	Frank Thomas	.75
20	Ray Durham	.05
21	Sean Casey	.10
22	Greg Vaughn	.05
23	Barry Larkin	.05
24	Manny Ramirez	.75
25	Jim Thome	.50
26	Jaret Wright	.05
27	Kenny Lofton	.05
28	Larry Walker	.05
29	Todd Helton	.65
30	Vinny Castilla	.05
31	Tony Clark	.05
32	Juan Encarnacion	.05
33	Dean Palmer	.05
34	Mark Kotsay	.05
35	Alex Gonzalez	.05
36	Shane Reynolds	.05
37	Ken Caminiti	.05
38	Jeff Bagwell	.75
39	Craig Biggio	.05
40	Carlos Febles	.05
41	Carlos Beltran	.35
42	Jeremy Giambi	.05
43	Raul Mondesi	.05
44	Adrian Beltre	.10
45	Kevin Brown	.05
46	Jeromy Burnitz	.05
47	Jeff Cirillo	.05
48	Corey Koskie	.05
49	Todd Walker	.05
50	Vladimir Guerrero	.75
51	Michael Barrett	.05
52	Mike Piazza	1.00
53	Robin Ventura	.05
54	Edgardo Alfonzo	.05
55	Derek Jeter	2.00
56	Roger Clemens	.90
57	Tino Martinez	.05
58	Orlando Hernandez	.05
59	Chuck Knoblauch	.05
60	Bernie Williams	.05
61	Eric Chavez	.10
62	Ben Grieve	.05
63	Jason Giambi	.40
64	Scott Rolen	.60
65	Curt Schilling	.25
66	Bobby Abreu	.05
67	Jason Kendall	.05
68	Kevin Young	.05
69	Mark McGwire	1.50

70	J.D. Drew	.60
71	Eric Davis	.05
72	Tony Gwynn	.85
73	Trevor Hoffman	.05
74	Barry Bonds	2.00
75	Robb Nen	.05
76	Ken Griffey Jr.	1.00
77	Alex Rodriguez	1.50
78	Jay Buhner	.05
79	Carlos Guillen	.05
80	Jose Canseco	.40
81	Bobby Smith	.05
82	Juan Gonzalez	.40
83	Ivan Rodriguez	.65
84	Rafael Palmeiro	.65
85	Rick Helling	.05
86	Jose Cruz Jr.	.05
87	David Wells	.05
88	Carlos Delgado	.20
89	Nolan Ryan	1.50
90	George Brett	.90
91	Robin Yount	.50
92	Paul Molitor	.50
93	Dave Winfield	.50
94	Steve Garvey	.25
95	Ozzie Smith	.85
96	Ted Williams	1.50
97	Don Mattingly	.90
98	Mickey Mantle	2.50
99	Harmon Killebrew	.25
100	Rollie Fingers	.10
101	Kirk Gibson	.05
102	Bucky Dent	.05
103	Willie Mays	1.00
104	Babe Ruth	1.50
105	Gary Carter	.50
106	Reggie Jackson	.85
107	Frank Robinson	.25
108	Ernie Banks	.50
109	Eddie Murray	.50
110	Mike Schmidt	.90

Gold/Platinum

This is a 110-card parallel to the base set. Cards have a gold-tone front and are sequentially numbered to 250 sets. A one-of-one Platinum parallel to the base set also is randomly seeded.

NM/M
Common Gold: 1.00
Gold Stars: 15X
Platinum 1/1: Values Undetermined

Distant Replay

This 15-card set recounts the most memorable plays from the 1998 season. Card fronts have a black-and-white photo of the player and along the bottom of the photo a date of the memorable play and brief description are given. These are seeded 1:8 packs. A parallel version, Level 2, is also randomly seeded, limited to 100 sequentially numbered sets.

NM/M
Complete Set (15): 30.00
Common Player: 1.00
Inserted 1:8
Level 2: 6X
Production 100 Sets
1 Ken Griffey Jr. 2.50
2 Mark McGwire 3.00
3 Cal Ripken Jr. 4.00

4	Greg Maddux	2.00
5	Nomar Garciaparra	2.00
6	Roger Clemens	2.25
7	Alex Rodriguez	3.00
8	Frank Thomas	1.50
9	Mike Piazza	2.50
10	Chipper Jones	2.00
11	Juan Gonzalez	1.00
12	Tony Gwynn	2.00
13	Barry Bonds	4.00
14	Ivan Rodriguez	1.00
15	Derek Jeter	4.00

INKredible

INKredible is an autographed insert set that consists of both current players and retired stars. Card fronts have a small photo in the upper left portion of the featured player and a large signing area. These are seeded 1:23 packs.

NM/M
Common Player: 4.00
Inserted 1:23
CBe Carlos Beltran 30.00
GB George Brett/SP 80.00
PB Pat Burrell 10.00
SC Sean Casey 10.00
TC Tony Clark 4.00
BD Bucky Dent 8.00
DE Darin Erstad 15.00
RF Rollie Fingers 8.00
SG Steve Garvey 10.00
KG Kirk Gibson 10.00
RG Rusty Greer 4.00
JR Ken Griffey Jr. 80.00
TG Tony Gwynn 30.00
CJ Chipper Jones 40.00
GK Gabe Kapler 5.00
HK Harmon Killebrew 30.00
FL Fred Lynn 10.00
DM Don Mattingly 50.00
PM Paul Molitor 20.00
EM Eddie Murray/SP 50.00
PO Paul O'Neill 15.00
AP Angel Pena 4.00
MR Manny Ramirez 30.00
IR Ivan Rodriguez 25.00
NR Nolan Ryan 150.00
OZ Ozzie Smith 30.00
DWe David Wells 15.00
BW Bernie Williams 40.00
DW Dave Winfield 20.00
RY Robin Yount 35.00

INKredible Level 2

A parallel to INKredible autographed inserts, these are hand-numbered to the featured player's jersey number.

NM/M
Common Player: 10.00
Limited to player's jersey #.
CBe Carlos Beltran/36 60.00
PB Pat Burrell/76 50.00
SC Sean Casey/21 40.00
TC Tony Clark/17 20.00
BD Bucky Dent/20 25.00
DE Darin Erstad/17 50.00
RF Rollie Fingers/34 25.00
KG Kirk Gibson/23 50.00
RG Rusty Greer/29 20.00
JR Ken Griffey Jr./24 200.00
TG Tony Gwynn/19 150.00
GK Gabe Kapler/23 40.00
FL Fred Lynn/19 30.00
DM Don Mattingly/23 200.00
EM Eddie Murray/33 80.00
PO Paul O'Neill/21 50.00
AP Angel Pena/36 10.00
MR Manny Ramirez/24 80.00
NR Nolan Ryan/34 400.00
DWe David Wells/33 25.00
BW Bernie Williams/51 60.00
DW Dave Winfield/31 60.00
RY Robin Yount/19 90.00

Old/New School

This 30-card insert set captures 15 Old School players and 15 New School players. Each card is sequentially numbered to 1,000. A parallel version is also randomly

white is, "throwback attack." There is a white border. Backs have a ghosted image of the front photo and career highlights. Cards are numbered with a "T" prefix and are seeded 1:5 packs. A parallel version is also randomly seeded and limited to 500 numbered sets.

NM/M
Complete Set (15): 20.00
Common Player: .50
Inserted 1:5
Level 2: 3X
Production 500 Sets
1 Ken Griffey Jr. 2.00
2 Mark McGwire 2.50
3 Sammy Sosa 1.25
4 Roger Clemens 1.50
5 J.D. Drew .75
6 Alex Rodriguez 2.50
7 Greg Maddux 1.25
8 Mike Piazza 2.00
9 Juan Gonzalez .50
10 Mo Vaughn .50
11 Cal Ripken Jr. 3.00
12 Frank Thomas 1.00
13 Nomar Garciaparra 1.25
14 Vladimir Guerrero 1.25
15 Tony Gwynn 1.25

Piece of History 500 Club

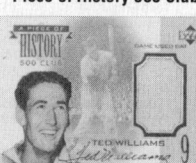

Each one of these inserts features a piece of game-used bat swung by Ted Williams embedded into each card. A total of 350 of these were issued. Williams also autographed nine of the 500 Club Piece of History cards.

NM/M
TW Ted Williams/350 250.00

Throwback Attack

These inserts have a "Retro" look, borrowing heavily from 1959 Topps. Highlighting top players, the set features card fronts with a circular player photo on a bright orange background. At top in

seeded and is limited to 50 sequentially numbered sets. Old School cards are basically black-and-white with color graphic highlights on front and back. New School cards have multiple computer-enhanced color photos and silver-foil highlights.

NM/M
Complete Set (30): 35.00
Common Player: .40
Production 1,000 Sets
Level 2: 5X
Production 50 Sets
1 Ken Griffey Jr. 2.50
2 Alex Rodriguez 3.00
3 Frank Thomas 1.50
4 Cal Ripken Jr. 4.00
5 Chipper Jones 2.00
6 Craig Biggio .40
7 Greg Maddux 2.00
8 Jeff Bagwell 1.50
9 Juan Gonzalez .75
10 Mark McGwire 3.00
11 Mike Piazza 2.50
12 Mo Vaughn .40
13 Roger Clemens 2.25
14 Sammy Sosa 2.00
15 Tony Gwynn 2.00
16 Gabe Kapler .40
17 J.D. Drew 1.00
18 Pat Burrell 1.00
19 Roy Halladay .40
20 Jeff Weaver .40
21 Troy Glaus 1.00
22 Vladimir Guerrero 1.50
23 Michael Barrett .40
24 Carlos Beltran .40
25 Scott Rolen 1.00
26 Nomar Garciaparra 2.00
27 Warren Morris .40
28 Alex Gonzalez .40
29 Kyle Farnsworth .40
30 Derek Jeter 4.00

Lunchbox

Lunchboxes were the packaging for UD Retro. Each lunchbox contains 24 six-card packs and features 16 different current or retired baseball legends including Babe Ruth.

NM/M
Complete Set (17): 140.00
Common Lunchbox: 7.50
One dual-player per case.
Roger Clemens 7.50
Ken Griffey Jr. 7.50
Mickey Mantle 10.00
Mark McGwire 10.00
Mike Piazza 7.50
Alex Rodriguez 7.50
Babe Ruth 10.00
Sammy Sosa 7.50
Ted Williams 10.00
Ken Griffey Jr., Mark McGwire 12.50
Ken Griffey Jr., Babe Ruth 12.50
Ken Griffey Jr., Ted Williams 12.50
Mickey Mantle, Babe Ruth 15.00
Mark McGwire, Mickey Mantle 15.00
Mark McGwire, Babe Ruth 15.00
Mark McGwire, Ted Williams 15.00

1999 Upper Deck Ultimate Victory

The 180-card base set includes two 30-card short-printed (1:4) subsets: McGwire Magic (151-180) and 1999 Rookie (121-150). The base cards have a silver foil border with the featured players' last five seasons of statistics along with a brief career highlight. There are two parallels randomly inserted: Victory Collection and Ultimate Collection. Victory Collection is seeded 1:12 packs with

a holographic, prismatic look. Ultimate Collection has a gold holographic, prismatic look and are serially numbered "xxx/100" on the card front.

NM/M
Complete Set (180): 125.00
Common Player: .10
Common 99 Rookie (121-150): .50
Common McGwire Magic (151-180): 1.00
Victory (1-120): 3.5X
Victory SP (121-180): 2X
Inserted 1:12
Ultimate (1-120): 12X
Ultimate SP (121-180): 5X
Production 100 Sets
Pack (5): 4.50
Wax Box (24): 75.00
1 Troy Glaus .65
2 Tim Salmon .10
3 Mo Vaughn .10
4 Garret Anderson .10
5 Darin Erstad .30
6 Randy Johnson .75
7 Matt Williams .10
8 Travis Lee .25
9 Jay Bell .10
10 Steve Finley .10
11 Luis Gonzalez .10
12 Greg Maddux 1.00
13 Chipper Jones 1.00
14 Javy Lopez .10
15 Tom Glavine .35
16 John Smoltz .10
17 Cal Ripken Jr. 3.00
18 Charles Johnson .10
19 Albert Belle .10
20 Mike Mussina .40
21 Pedro Martinez .75
22 Nomar Garciaparra 1.00
23 Jose Offerman .10
24 Sammy Sosa 1.00
25 Mark Grace .10
26 Kerry Wood .35
27 Frank Thomas .75
28 Ray Durham .10
29 Paul Konerko .20
30 Pete Harnisch .10
31 Greg Vaughn .10
32 Sean Casey .20
33 Manny Ramirez .75
34 Jim Thome .65
35 Sandy Alomar .10
36 Roberto Alomar .30
37 Travis Fryman .10
38 Kenny Lofton .10
39 Omar Vizquel .10
40 Larry Walker .10
41 Todd Helton .65
42 Vinny Castilla .10
43 Tony Clark .10
44 Juan Encarnacion .10
45 Dean Palmer .10
46 Damion Easley .10
47 Mark Kotsay .10
48 Cliff Floyd .10
49 Jeff Bagwell .75
50 Ken Caminiti .10
51 Craig Biggio .10
52 Moises Alou .10
53 Johnny Damon .35
54 Larry Sutton .10
55 Kevin Brown .10
56 Adrian Beltre .25
57 Raul Mondesi .10
58 Gary Sheffield .50
59 Jeromy Burnitz .10
60 Sean Berry .10
61 Jeff Cirillo .10
62 Brad Radke .10
63 Todd Walker .10
64 Matt Lawton .10
65 Vladimir Guerrero .75
66 Rondell White .10
67 Dustin Hermanson .10
68 Mike Piazza 2.00
69 Rickey Henderson .75
70 Robin Ventura .10
71 John Olerud .10
72 Derek Jeter 3.00
73 Roger Clemens 1.25
74 Orlando Hernandez .10
75 Paul O'Neill .10
76 Bernie Williams .10
77 Chuck Knoblauch .10
78 Tino Martinez .10
79 Jason Giambi .50
80 Ben Grieve .10
81 Matt Stairs .10
82 Scott Rolen .60
83 Ron Gant .10
84 Bobby Abreu .10
85 Curt Schilling .35
86 Brian Giles .10
87 Jason Kendall .10
88 Kevin Young .10
89 Mark McGwire 2.00
90 Fernando Tatis .10
91 Ray Lankford .10
92 Eric Davis .10
93 Tony Gwynn 1.00
94 Reggie Sanders .10
95 Wally Joyner .10
96 Trevor Hoffman .10
97 Robb Nen .10

98 Barry Bonds 3.00
99 Jeff Kent .10
100 J.T. Snow .10
101 Ellis Burks .10
102 Ken Griffey Jr. 1.50
103 Alex Rodriguez 2.00
104 Jay Buhner .10
105 Edgar Martinez .10
106 David Bell .10
107 Bobby Smith .10
108 Wade Boggs 1.00
109 Fred McGriff .10
110 Rolando Arrojo .10
111 Jose Canseco .50
112 Ivan Rodriguez .65
113 Juan Gonzalez .40
114 Rafael Palmeiro .65
115 Rusty Greer .10
116 Todd Zeile .10
117 Jose Cruz Jr. .10
118 Carlos Delgado .35
119 Shawn Green .30
120 David Wells .10
121 Eric Munson RC (99 Rookie) 2.50
122 Lance Berkman (99 Rookie) 2.00
123 Ed Yarnall (99 Rookie) .50
124 Jacque Jones (99 Rookie) 1.00
125 Kyle Farnsworth (99 Rookie) 1.00
126 Ryan Rupe (99 Rookie) .50
127 Jeff Weaver RC (99 Rookie) 2.00
128 Gabe Kapler (99 Rookie) .50
129 Alex Gonzalez (99 Rookie) .50
130 Randy Wolf (99 Rookie) .50
131 Ben Davis (99 Rookie) .50
132 Carlos Beltran (99 Rookie) 2.00
133 Jim Morris (99 Rookie) 2.00
134 Jeff Zimmerman (99 Rookie) .50
135 Bruce Aven (99 Rookie) .50
136 Alfonso Soriano RC (99 Rookie) 50.00
137 Tim Hudson RC (99 Rookie) 10.00
138 Josh Beckett RC (99 Rookie) 50.00
139 Michael Barrett (99 Rookie) .50
140 Eric Chavez (99 Rookie)
141 Pat Burrell RC (99 Rookie) 10.00
142 Kris Benson (99 Rookie) 1.00
143 J.D. Drew (99 Rookie) 2.00
144 Matt Clement (99 Rookie) 1.00
145 Rick Ankiel RC (99 Rookie) 25.00
146 Vernon Wells (99 Rookie) 1.00
147 Ruben Mateo (99 Rookie) .50
148 Roy Halladay (99 Rookie) 1.00
149 Joe McEwing (99 Rookie) .50
150 Freddy Garcia RC (99 Rookie) 8.00
151 Mark McGwire (McGwire Magic) 1.00
152 Mark McGwire (McGwire Magic) 1.00
153 Mark McGwire (McGwire Magic) 1.00
154 Mark McGwire (McGwire Magic) 1.00
155 Mark McGwire (McGwire Magic) 1.00
156 Mark McGwire (McGwire Magic) 1.00
157 Mark McGwire (McGwire Magic) 1.00
158 Mark McGwire (McGwire Magic) 1.00
159 Mark McGwire (McGwire Magic) 1.00
160 Mark McGwire (McGwire Magic) 1.00
161 Mark McGwire (McGwire Magic) 1.00
162 Mark McGwire (McGwire Magic) 1.00
163 Mark McGwire (McGwire Magic) 1.00
164 Mark McGwire (McGwire Magic) 1.00
165 Mark McGwire (McGwire Magic) 1.00
166 Mark McGwire (McGwire Magic) 1.00
167 Mark McGwire (McGwire Magic) 1.00
168 Mark McGwire (McGwire Magic) 1.00
169 Mark McGwire (McGwire Magic) 1.00
170 Mark McGwire (McGwire Magic) 1.00
171 Mark McGwire (McGwire Magic) 1.00
172 Mark McGwire (McGwire Magic) 1.00
173 Mark McGwire (McGwire Magic) 1.00
174 Mark McGwire (McGwire Magic) 1.00

175	Mark McGwire (McGwire Magic)	1.00
176	Mark McGwire (McGwire Magic)	1.00
177	Mark McGwire (McGwire Magic)	1.00
178	Mark McGwire (McGwire Magic)	1.00
179	Mark McGwire (McGwire Magic)	1.00
180	Mark McGwire (McGwire Magic)	1.00

Victory Collection

This parallel of the base set features a prismatic foil design on front. The cards are found on average of one per 12 packs. A 1-of-1 edition also exists, but is not priced here due to rarity and demand variability.

	NM/M
Common Player (1-120, 151-180):	1.00
Common Player (121-150):	5.00
Stars (1-120):	3.5X
Stars (121-150):	2X

Ultimate Collection

This parallel insert set is individually serial numbered on front from within an edition of 100 cards each. Card fronts have silver holographic prismatic foil background and a silver-foil serial number. Backs are identical to the regular-issue cards.

	NM/M
Common Player (1-120, 151-180):	2.00
Common Player (121-150):	12.00
Stars (1-120):	12X
Stars (121-150):	5X

Bleacher Reachers

This 11-card set focuses on the hitters who were vying for the 1999 home run title. They have a horizontal format with a holographic foil card front. Card backs have a small photo along with three-year statistical totals. They are numbered with a "BR" prefix and were inserted 1:23 packs.

		NM/M
Complete Set (11):		20.00
Common Player:		.75
Inserted 1:23		
1	Ken Griffey Jr.	2.50
2	Mark McGwire	3.00
3	Sammy Sosa	1.50
4	Barry Bonds	4.00
5	Nomar Garciaparra	2.00
6	Juan Gonzalez	.75
7	Jose Canseco	.75
8	Manny Ramirez	1.50
9	Mike Piazza	2.50
10	Jeff Bagwell	1.50
11	Alex Rodriguez	3.00

Fame-Used Memorabilia

This four-card set has a piece of game-used bat embedded into each card, from either George Brett, Robin Yount, Nolan Ryan or Orlando Cepeda. Approximately 350 bat cards of each player were produced.

		NM/M
Complete Set (4):		50.00
Common Player:		7.50
Production 350 Cards		
GB	George Brett	20.00
OC	Orlando Cepeda	7.50
NR	Nolan Ryan	25.00
RY	Robin Yount	10.00

Fame-Used Combo

This insert has a piece of game-used bat from each of the 1999 Hall of Fame inductees and is limited to 99 sequentially numbered singles.

		NM/M
Edition of 99:		
HOF	Nolan Ryan, George Brett, Robin Yount, Orlando Cepeda	250.00

Frozen Ropes

This 10-card set spotlights baseball's top hitters and are seeded 1:23 packs.

		NM/M
Complete Set (10):		15.00
Common Player:		.50
Inserted 1:23		
1	Ken Griffey Jr.	2.00
2	Mark McGwire	2.50
3	Sammy Sosa	1.50
4	Derek Jeter	3.00
5	Tony Gwynn	1.50
6	Nomar Garciaparra	1.50
7	Alex Rodriguez	2.00
8	Mike Piazza	2.00
9	Mo Vaughn	.50
10	Craig Biggio	.50

STATure

This 15-card set highlights players with outstanding statistical achievements. The featured stat for the player runs down the right side of the card. Fronts are printed on metallic foil with a textured pattern behind the player photo. Conventionally printed backs repeat the front design numbered with an "S" prefix. These were seeded 1:6 packs.

		NM/M
Complete Set (15):		9.00
Common Player:		.30
Inserted 1:6		
1	Ken Griffey Jr.	.75
2	Mark McGwire	1.00
3	Sammy Sosa	.65
4	Nomar Garciaparra	.65
5	Roger Clemens	.65
6	Greg Maddux	.65
7	Alex Rodriguez	1.00
8	Derek Jeter	1.50
9	Juan Gonzalez	.30
10	Manny Ramirez	.50
11	Mike Piazza	.75
12	Tony Gwynn	.65
13	Chipper Jones	.75
14	Pedro Martinez	.50
15	Frank Thomas	.50

Tribute 1999

This four-card set is devoted to 1999's Hall of Fame inductees. Card fronts have a horizontal format over a holographic foil design. Card backs have the featured players' year-by-year statistics and are numbered with a "T" prefix.

		NM/M
Complete Set (4):		5.00
Common Player:		1.00
Inserted 1:11		
1	Nolan Ryan	2.00
2	Robin Yount	1.50
3	George Brett	1.50
4	Orlando Cepeda	1.00

Ultimate Competitors

This 12-card set has a close-up photo, along with two miniature action photos in the foreground, all printed on silver foil. Backs repeat the front photos and have a few words about the player's competitive desire. These were seeded 1:23 packs and are numbered with a "U" prefix on the card back.

		NM/M
Complete Set (12):		20.00
Common Player:		.60
Inserted 1:23		
1	Ken Griffey Jr.	3.00
2	Roger Clemens	2.50
3	Scott Rolen	1.00
4	Greg Maddux	2.00
5	Mark McGwire	4.00
6	Derek Jeter	5.00
7	Randy Johnson	1.50
8	Cal Ripken Jr.	5.00
9	Craig Biggio	.50
10	Kevin Brown	.50
11	Chipper Jones	2.00
12	Vladimir Guerrero	1.50

Ultimate Hit Men

This insert set spotlights the eight candidates who competed for the 1999 batting titles. Inserted on the average of 1:23 packs they were numbered with an "H" prefix on the card back.

		NM/M
Complete Set (8):		15.00
Common Player:		1.00
Inserted 1:23		
1	Tony Gwynn	2.00
2	Cal Ripken Jr.	4.00
3	Wade Boggs	2.00
4	Larry Walker	1.00
5	Alex Rodriguez	3.00
6	Derek Jeter	4.00
7	Ivan Rodriguez	1.25
8	Ken Griffey Jr.	2.50

1999 Upper Deck Victory

This 470-card base set is printed on 20-point stock and has a white border with UV coating. The set consists of a number of subsets including, 30-card Mark McGwire Magic, 30 team checklist cards, 50 '99 rookies, 15 Power Trip, 20 Rookie Flashback, 15 Big Play Makers and 10 History in the Making. Twelve-card packs had an SRP of $.99.

		NM/M
Complete Set (470):		30.00
Common Player:		.05
Pack (12):		.75
Wax Box (36):		20.00
1	Anaheim Angels (Team Checklist)	.05
2	Mark Harriger RC (99 Rookie)	.10
3	Mo Vaughn (Power Trip)	.05
4	Darin Erstad (Big Play Makers)	.10
5	Troy Glaus	.45
6	Tim Salmon	.05
7	Mo Vaughn	.05
8	Darin Erstad	.25
9	Garret Anderson	.05
10	Todd Greene	.05
11	Troy Percival	.05
12	Chuck Finley	.05
13	Jason Dickson	.05
14	Jim Edmonds	.05
15	Arizona Diamondbacks (Team Checklist)	.05
16	Randy Johnson	.50
17	Matt Williams	.05
18	Travis Lee	.15
19	Jay Bell	.05
20	Tony Womack	.05
21	Steve Finley	.05
22	Bernard Gilkey	.05
23	Tony Batista	.05
24	Todd Stottlemyre	.05
25	Omar Daal	.05
26	Atlanta Braves (Team Checklist)	.05
27	Bruce Chen (99 Rookie)	.05
28	George Lombard (99 Rookie)	.05
29	Chipper Jones (Power Trip)	.40
30	Chipper Jones (Big Play Makers)	.40
31	Greg Maddux	.65
32	Chipper Jones	.75
33	Javy Lopez	.05
34	Tom Glavine	.25
35	John Smoltz	.05
36	Andruw Jones	.50
37	Brian Jordan	.05
38	Walt Weiss	.05
39	Bret Boone	.05
40	Andres Galarraga	.05
41	Baltimore Orioles (Team Checklist)	.05
42	Ryan Minor (99 Rookie)	.05
43	Jerry Hairston Jr. (99 Rookie)	.05
44	Calvin Pickering (99 Rookie)	.05
45	Cal Ripken Jr. (History in the Making)	.75
46	Cal Ripken Jr.	1.50
47	Charles Johnson	.05
48	Albert Belle	.05
49	Delino DeShields	.05
50	Mike Mussina	.30
51	Scott Erickson	.05
52	Brady Anderson	.05
53	B.J. Surhoff	.05
54	Harold Baines	.05
55	Will Clark	.05
56	Boston Red Sox (Team Checklist)	.05
57	Shea Hillenbrand RC (99 Rookie)	.50
58	Trot Nixon (99 Rookie)	.10
59	Jin Ho Cho (99 Rookie)	.05
60	Nomar Garciaparra (Power Trip)	.35
61	Nomar Garciaparra (Big Play Makers)	.35
62	Pedro Martinez	.50
63	Nomar Garciaparra	.65
64	Jose Offerman	.05
65	Jason Varitek	.05
66	Darren Lewis	.05
67	Troy O'Leary	.05
68	Donnie Sadler	.05
69	John Valentin	.05
70	Tim Wakefield	.05
71	Bret Saberhagen	.05
72	Chicago Cubs (Team Checklist)	.05
73	Kyle Farnsworth RC (99 Rookie)	.10
74	Sammy Sosa (Power Trip)	.35
75	Sammy Sosa (Big Play Makers)	.35
76	Sammy Sosa (History in the Making)	.35
77	Kerry Wood (History in the Making)	.10
78	Sammy Sosa	.65
79	Mark Grace	.05
80	Kerry Wood	.25
81	Kevin Tapani	.05
82	Benito Santiago	.05
83	Gary Gaetti	.05
84	Mickey Morandini	.05
85	Glenallen Hill	.05
86	Henry Rodriguez	.05
87	Rod Beck	.05
88	Chicago White Sox (Team Checklist)	.05
89	Carlos Lee (99 Rookie)	.10
90	Mark Johnson (99 Rookie)	.05
91	Frank Thomas (Power Trip)	.50
92	Frank Thomas	.50
93	Jim Parque	.05
94	Mike Sirotka	.05
95	Mike Caruso	.05
96	Ray Durham	.05
97	Magglio Ordonez	.25
98	Paul Konerko	.15
99	Bob Howry	.05
100	Brian Simmons	.05
101	Jaime Navarro	.05
102	Cincinnati Reds (Team Checklist)	.05
103	Denny Neagle	.05
104	Pete Harnisch	.05
105	Greg Vaughn	.05
106	Brett Tomko	.05
107	Mike Cameron	.05
108	Sean Casey	.10
109	Aaron Boone	.05
110	Michael Tucker	.05
111	Dmitri Young	.05
112	Barry Larkin	.05
113	Cleveland Indians (Team Checklist)	.05
114	Russ Branyan (99 Rookie)	.05
115	Jim Thome (Power Trip)	.20
116	Manny Ramirez (Power Trip)	.05
117	Manny Ramirez	.50
118	Jim Thome	.40
119	David Justice	.05
120	Sandy Alomar	.05
121	Roberto Alomar	.20
122	Jaret Wright	.05
123	Bartolo Colon	.05
124	Travis Fryman	.05
125	Kenny Lofton	.05
126	Omar Vizquel	.05
127	Colorado Rockies (Team Checklist)	.05
128	Derrick Gibson (99 Rookie)	.05
129	Larry Walker (Big Play Makers)	.05
130	Larry Walker	.05
131	Dante Bichette	.05
132	Todd Helton	.45
133	Neifi Perez	.05
134	Vinny Castilla	.05
135	Darryl Kile	.05
136	Pedro Astacio	.05
137	Darryl Hamilton	.05
138	Mike Lansing	.05
139	Kirt Manwaring	.05
140	Detroit Tigers (Team Checklist)	.05
141	Jeff Weaver RC (99 Rookie)	.50
142	Gabe Kapler (99 Rookie)	.05
143	Tony Clark (Power Trip)	.05
144	Tony Clark	.05
145	Juan Encarnacion	.05
146	Dean Palmer	.05
147	Damion Easley	.05
148	Bobby Higginson	.05
149	Karim Garcia	.05
150	Justin Thompson	.05
151	Matt Anderson	.05
152	Willie Blair	.05
153	Brian Hunter	.05
154	Florida Marlins (Team Checklist)	.05
155	Alex Gonzalez (99 Rookie)	.05
156	Mark Kotsay	.05
157	Livan Hernandez	.05
158	Cliff Floyd	.05
159	Todd Dunwoody	.05
160	Alex Fernandez	.05
161	Mark Mantei	.05
162	Derrek Lee	.40
163	Kevin Orie	.05
164	Craig Counsell	.05
165	Rafael Medina	.05
166	Houston Astros (Team Checklist)	.05
167	Daryle Ward (99 Rookie)	.05
168	Mitch Meluskey (99 Rookie)	.05
169	Jeff Bagwell (Power Trip)	.25
170	Jeff Bagwell	.50
171	Ken Caminiti	.05
172	Craig Biggio	.05
173	Derek Bell	.05
174	Moises Alou	.05
175	Billy Wagner	.05
176	Shane Reynolds	.05
177	Carl Everett	.05
178	Scott Elarton	.05
179	Richard Hidalgo	.05
180	Kansas City Royals (Team Checklist)	.05
181	Carlos Beltran (99 Rookie)	.60
182	Carlos Febles (99 Rookie)	.05
183	Jeremy Giambi (99 Rookie)	.05
184	Johnny Damon	.30
185	Joe Randa	.05
186	Jeff King	.05
187	Hipolito Pichardo	.05
188	Kevin Appier	.05
189	Chad Kreuter	.05
190	Rey Sanchez	.05
191	Larry Sutton	.05
192	Jeff Montgomery	.05
193	Jermaine Dye	.05
194	Los Angeles Dodgers (Team Checklist)	.05
195	Adam Riggs (99 Rookie)	.05
196	Angel Pena (99 Rookie)	.05
197	Todd Hundley	.05
198	Kevin Brown	.05
199	Ismael Valdes	.05
200	Chan Ho Park	.05
201	Adrian Beltre	.15
202	Mark Grudzielanek	.05
203	Raul Mondesi	.35
204	Gary Sheffield	.05
205	Eric Karros	.05
206	Devon White	.05
207	Milwaukee Brewers (Team Checklist)	.05
208	Ron Belliard (99 Rookie)	.05
209	Rafael Roque (99 Rookie)	.05
210	Jeromy Burnitz	.05
211	Fernando Vina	.05
212	Scott Karl	.05
213	Jim Abbott	.05
214	Sean Berry	.05
215	Marquis Grissom	.05
216	Geoff Jenkins	.05
217	Jeff Cirillo	.05
218	Dave Nilsson	.05
219	Jose Valentin	.05
220	Minnesota Twins (Team Checklist)	.05
221	Corey Koskie (99 Rookie)	.05
222	Christian Guzman (99 Rookie)	.05
223	A.J. Pierzynski (99 Rookie)	.05
224	David Ortiz	.05
225	Brad Radke	.05
226	Todd Walker	.05
227	Matt Lawton	.05
228	Rick Aguilera	.05
229	Eric Milton	.05
230	Marty Cordova	.05
231	Torii Hunter	.05
232	Ron Coomer	.05
233	LaTroy Hawkins	.05
234	Montreal Expos (Team Checklist)	.05
235	Fernando Seguignol (99 Rookie)	.05
236	Michael Barrett (99 Rookie)	.05
237	Vladimir Guerrero (Big Play Makers)	.25
238	Vladimir Guerrero	.50
239	Brad Fullmer	.05
240	Rondell White	.05
241	Ugueth Urbina	.05
242	Dustin Hermanson	.05
243	Orlando Cabrera	.05
244	Wilton Guerrero	.05
245	Carl Pavano	.05
246	Javier Vasquez	.05
247	Chris Widger	.05
248	New York Mets (Team Checklist)	.05
249	Mike Kinkade (99 Rookie)	.05
250	Octavio Dotel (99 Rookie)	.05
251	Mike Piazza (Power Trip)	.40
252	Mike Piazza	.75

No.	Player	Price
253	Rickey Henderson	.50
254	Edgardo Alfonzo	.05
255	Robin Ventura	.05
256	Al Leiter	.05
257	Brian McRae	.05
258	Rey Ordonez	.05
259	Bobby Bonilla	.05
260	Orel Hershiser	.05
261	John Olerud	.05
262	New York Yankees (Team Checklist)	
263	Ricky Ledee (99 Rookie)	.05
264	Bernie Williams (Big Play Makers)	.05
265	Derek Jeter (Big Play Makers)	.75
266	Scott Brosius (History in the Making)	.05
267	Derek Jeter	1.50
268	Roger Clemens	.65
269	Orlando Hernandez	.05
270	Scott Brosius	.05
271	Paul O'Neill	.05
272	Bernie Williams	.05
273	Chuck Knoblauch	.05
274	Tino Martinez	.05
275	Mariano Rivera	.10
276	Jorge Posada	.05
277	Oakland Athletics (Team Checklist)	.05
278	Eric Chavez (99 Rookie)	.15
279	Ben Grieve (History in the Making)	.05
280	Jason Giambi	.30
281	John Jaha	.05
282	Miguel Tejada	.15
283	Ben Grieve	.05
284	Matt Stairs	.05
285	Ryan Christenson	.05
286	A.J. Hinch	.05
287	Kenny Rogers	.05
288	Tom Candiotti	.05
289	Scott Spezio	.05
290	Philadelphia Phillies (Team Checklist)	.05
291	Pat Burrell RC (99 Rookie)	1.50
292	Marlon Anderson (99 Rookie)	.05
293	Scott Rolen (Big Play Makers)	.20
294	Scott Rolen	.40
295	Doug Glanville	.05
296	Rico Brogna	.05
297	Ron Gant	.05
298	Bobby Abreu	.05
299	Desi Relaford	.05
300	Curt Schilling	.25
301	Chad Ogea	.05
302	Kevin Jordan	.05
303	Carlton Loewer	.05
304	Pittsburgh Pirates (Team Checklist)	.05
305	Kris Benson (99 Rookie)	.05
306	Brian Giles	.05
307	Jason Kendall	.05
308	Jose Guillen	.05
309	Pat Meares	.05
310	Brant Brown	.05
311	Kevin Young	.05
312	Ed Sprague	.05
313	Francisco Cordova	.05
314	Aramis Ramirez	.05
315	Freddy Garcia	.05
316	Saint Louis Cardinals (Team Checklist)	.05
317	J.D. Drew (99 Rookie)	.40
318	Chad Hutchinson RC (99 Rookie)	.05
319	Mark McGwire (Power Trip)	.50
320	J.D. Drew (Power Trip)	.20
321	Mark McGwire (Big Play Makers)	.50
322	Mark McGwire (History in the Making)	.50
323	Mark McGwire	1.00
324	Fernando Tatis	.05
325	Edgar Renteria	.05
326	Ray Lankford	.05
327	Willie McGee	.05
328	Ricky Bottalico	.05
329	Eli Marrero	.05
330	Matt Morris	.05
331	Eric Davis	.05
332	Darren Bragg	.05
333	Padres (Team Checklist)	.05
334	Matt Clement (99 Rookie)	.05
335	Ben Davis (99 Rookie)	.05
336	Gary Matthews Jr. (99 Rookie)	.05
337	Tony Gwynn (Big Play Makers)	.35
338	Tony Gwynn (History in the Making)	.35
339	Tony Gwynn	.65
340	Reggie Sanders	.05
341	Ruben Rivera	.05
342	Wally Joyner	.05
343	Sterling Hitchcock	.05
344	Carlos Hernandez	.05
345	Andy Ashby	.05
346	Trevor Hoffman	.05
347	Chris Gomez	.05
348	Jim Leyritz	.05
349	San Francisco Giants (Team Checklist)	.05
350	Armando Rios (99 Rookie)	.05
351	Barry Bonds (Power Trip)	.75
352	Barry Bonds (Big Play Makers)	.75
353	Barry Bonds (History in the Making)	.75
354	Robb Nen	.05
355	Bill Mueller	.05
356	Barry Bonds	1.50
357	Jeff Kent	.05
358	J.T. Snow	.05
359	Ellis Burks	.05
360	F.P. Santangelo	.05
361	Marvin Benard	.05
362	Stan Javier	.05
363	Shawn Estes	.05
364	Seattle Mariners (Team Checklist)	.05
365	Carlos Guillen (99 Rookie)	.05
366	Ken Griffey Jr. (Power Trip)	.40
367	Alex Rodriguez (Power Trip)	.50
368	Ken Griffey Jr. (Big Play Makers)	.40
369	Alex Rodriguez (Big Play Makers)	.50
370	Ken Griffey Jr. (History in the Making)	.40
371	Alex Rodriguez (History in the Making)	.50
372	Ken Griffey Jr.	.75
373	Alex Rodriguez	1.00
374	Jay Buhner	.05
375	Edgar Martinez	.05
376	Jeff Fassero	.05
377	David Bell	.05
378	David Segui	.05
379	Russ Davis	.05
380	Dan Wilson	.05
381	Jamie Moyer	.05
382	Tampa Bay Devil Rays (Team Checklist)	.05
383	Roberto Hernandez	.05
384	Bobby Smith	.05
385	Wade Boggs	.65
386	Fred McGriff	.05
387	Rolando Arrojo	.05
388	Jose Canseco	.35
389	Wilson Alvarez	.05
390	Kevin Stocker	.05
391	Miguel Cairo	.05
392	Quinton McCracken	.05
393	Texas Rangers (Team Checklist)	.05
394	Ruben Mateo (99 Rookie)	.05
395	Cesar King (99 Rookie)	.05
396	Juan Gonzalez (Power Trip)	.15
397	Juan Gonzalez (Big Play Makers)	.15
398	Ivan Rodriguez	.40
399	Juan Gonzalez	.25
400	Rafael Palmeiro	.40
401	Rick Helling	.05
402	Aaron Sele	.05
403	John Wetteland	.05
404	Rusty Greer	.05
405	Todd Zeile	.05
406	Royce Clayton	.05
407	Tom Goodwin	.05
408	Toronto Blue Jays (Team Checklist)	.05
409	Kevin Witt (99 Rookie)	.05
410	Roy Halladay (99 Rookie)	.05
411	Jose Cruz Jr.	.05
412	Carlos Delgado	.30
413	Willie Greene	.05
414	Shawn Green	.25
415	Homer Bush	.05
416	Shannon Stewart	.05
417	David Wells	.05
418	Kelvim Escobar	.05
419	Joey Hamilton	.05
420	Alex Gonzalez	.05
421	Mark McGwire (McGwire Magic)	
422	Mark McGwire (McGwire Magic)	.20
423	Mark McGwire (McGwire Magic)	.20
424	Mark McGwire (McGwire Magic)	.20
425	Mark McGwire (McGwire Magic)	.20
426	Mark McGwire (McGwire Magic)	.20
427	Mark McGwire (McGwire Magic)	.20
428	Mark McGwire (McGwire Magic)	.20
429	Mark McGwire (McGwire Magic)	.20
430	Mark McGwire (McGwire Magic)	.20
431	Mark McGwire (McGwire Magic)	.20
432	Mark McGwire (McGwire Magic)	.20
433	Mark McGwire (McGwire Magic)	.20
434	Mark McGwire (McGwire Magic)	.20
435	Mark McGwire (McGwire Magic)	.20
436	Mark McGwire (McGwire Magic)	.20
437	Mark McGwire (McGwire Magic)	.20
438	Mark McGwire (McGwire Magic)	.20
439	Mark McGwire (McGwire Magic)	.20
440	Mark McGwire (McGwire Magic)	.20
441	Mark McGwire (McGwire Magic)	.20
442	Mark McGwire (McGwire Magic)	.20
443	Mark McGwire (McGwire Magic)	.20
444	Mark McGwire (McGwire Magic)	.20
445	Mark McGwire (McGwire Magic)	.20
446	Mark McGwire (McGwire Magic)	.20
447	Mark McGwire (McGwire Magic)	.20
448	Mark McGwire (McGwire Magic)	.20
449	Mark McGwire (McGwire Magic)	.20
450	Mark McGwire (McGwire Magic)	.20
451	Chipper Jones '93 (Rookie Flashback)	.40
452	Cal Ripken Jr. '81 (Rookie Flashback)	.75
453	Roger Clemens '84 (Rookie Flashback)	.40
454	Wade Boggs '82 (Rookie Flashback)	.35
455	Greg Maddux '86 (Rookie Flashback)	.35
456	Frank Thomas '90 (Rookie Flashback)	.30
457	Jeff Bagwell '91 (Rookie Flashback)	.25
458	Mike Piazza '92 (Rookie Flashback)	.45
459	Randy Johnson '88 (Rookie Flashback)	.25
460	Mo Vaughn '91 (Rookie Flashback)	.05
461	Mark McGwire '86 (Rookie Flashback)	.50
462	Rickey Henderson '79 (Rookie Flashback)	.25
463	Barry Bonds '86 (Rookie Flashback)	.75
464	Tony Gwynn '82 (Rookie Flashback)	.35
465	Ken Griffey Jr. '89 (Rookie Flashback)	.45
466	Alex Rodriquez '94 (Rookie Flashback)	.50
467	Sammy Sosa '89 (Rookie Flashback)	.35
468	Juan Gonzalez '89 (Rookie Flashback)	.15
469	Kevin Brown '86 (Rookie Flashback)	.05
470	Fred McGriff '86 (Rookie Flashback)	.05

2000 Upper Deck

Released in two 270-card series, the base cards feature full-bleed fronts with gold foil etching and stamping. Card backs have complete year-by-year statistics.

	NM/M
Complete Set (540):	40.00
Complete Series I (270):	20.00
Complete Series II (270):	20.00
Common Player:	.15
Silver Stars:	5-10X
Rookies:	2-4X
Hobby Pack (10):	3.00
Hobby Box (24):	55.00

No.	Player	Price
1	Rick Ankiel/SR	.25
2	Vernon Wells/SR	.50
3	Ryan Anderson/SR	.15
4	Ed Yarnall/SR	.15
5	Brian McNichol/SR	.15
6	Ben Petrick/SR	.15
7	Kip Wells/SR	.15
8	Eric Munson/SR	.20
9	Matt Riley/SR	.15
10	Peter Bergeron/SR	.15
11	Eric Gagne/SR	.25
12	Ramon Ortiz/SR	.15
13	Josh Beckett/SR	.50
14	Alfonso Soriano/SR	1.50
15	Jorge Toca/SR	.15
16	Buddy Carlyle/SR	.15
17	Chad Hermansen/SR	.15
18	Matt Perisho/SR	.15
19	Tomokazu Ohka/SR RC	.75
20	Jacque Jones/SR	.15
21	Josh Paul/SR	.15
22	Dermal Brown/SR	.15
23	Adam Kennedy/SR	.15
24	Chad Harville/SR	.15
25	Calvin Murray/SR	.15
26	Chad Meyers/SR	.15
27	Brian Cooper/SR	.15
28	Troy Glaus	.50
29	Ben Molina	.15
30	Troy Percival	.15
31	Ken Hill	.15
32	Chuck Finley	.15
33	Todd Greene	.15
34	Tim Salmon	.25
35	Gary DiSarcina	.15
36	Luis Gonzalez	.25
37	Tony Womack	.15
38	Omar Daal	.15
39	Randy Johnson	.50
40	Erubiel Durazo	.20
41	Jay Bell	.15
42	Steve Finley	.15
43	Travis Lee	.15
44	Greg Maddux	1.00
45	Bret Boone	.25
46	Brian Jordan	.15
47	Kevin Millwood	.25
48	Odalis Perez	.15
49	Javy Lopez	.25
50	John Smoltz	.25
51	Bruce Chen	.15
52	Albert Belle	.15
53	Jerry Hairston Jr.	.15
54	Will Clark	.40
55	Sidney Ponson	.15
56	Charles Johnson	.15
57	Cal Ripken Jr.	2.00
58	Ryan Minor	.15
59	Mike Mussina	.40
60	Tom Gordon	.15
61	Jose Offerman	.15
62	Trot Nixon	.15
63	Pedro Martinez	.75
64	John Valentin	.15
65	Jason Varitek	.15
66	Juan Pena	.15
67	Troy O'Leary	.15
68	Sammy Sosa	1.25
69	Henry Rodriguez	.15
70	Kyle Farnsworth	.15
71	Glenallen Hill	.15
72	Lance Johnson	.15
73	Mickey Morandini	.15
74	Jon Lieber	.15
75	Kevin Tapani	.15
76	Carlos Lee	.15
77	Ray Durham	.15
78	Jim Parque	.15
79	Bob Howry	.15
80	Magglio Ordonez	.25
81	Paul Konerko	.20
82	Mike Caruso	.15
83	Chris Singleton	.15
84	Sean Casey	.20
85	Barry Larkin	.25
86	Pokey Reese	.15
87	Eddie Taubensee	.15
88	Scott Williamson	.15
89	Jason LaRue	.15
90	Aaron Boone	.20
91	Jeffrey Hammonds	.15
92	Omar Vizquel	.20
93	Manny Ramirez	.50
94	Kenny Lofton	.20
95	Jaret Wright	.15
96	Einar Diaz	.15
97	Charles Nagy	.15
98	David Justice	.25
99	Richie Sexson	.25
100	Steve Karsay	.15
101	Todd Helton	.50
102	Dante Bichette	.15
103	Larry Walker	.25
104	Pedro Astacio	.15
105	Neifi Perez	.15
106	Brian Bohanon	.15
107	Edgard Clemente	.15
108	Dave Veres	.15
109	Gabe Kapler	.15
110	Juan Encarnacion	.15
111	Jeff Weaver	.15
112	Damion Easley	.15
113	Justin Thompson	.15
114	Brad Ausmus	.15
115	Frank Catalanotto	.15
116	Todd Jones	.15
117	Preston Wilson	.25
118	Cliff Floyd	.15
119	Mike Lowell	.15
120	Jorge Fabregas	.15
121	Alex Gonzalez	.15
122	Braden Looper	.15
123	Bruce Aven	.15
124	Richard Hidalgo	.15
125	Mitch Meluskey	.15
126	Jeff Bagwell	.50
127	Jose Lima	.15
128	Derek Bell	.15
129	Billy Wagner	.15
130	Shane Reynolds	.15
131	Moises Alou	.15
132	Carlos Beltran	.25
133	Carlos Febles	.15
134	Jermaine Dye	.15
135	Jeremy Giambi	.15
136	Joe Randa	.15
137	Jose Rosado	.15
138	Chad Kreuter	.15
139	Jose Vizcaino	.15
140	Adrian Beltre	.25
141	Kevin Brown	.25
142	Ismael Valdes	.15
143	Angel Pena	.15
144	Chan Ho Park	.15
145	Mark Grudzielanek	.15
146	Jeff Shaw	.15
147	Geoff Jenkins	.20
148	Jeromy Burnitz	.15
149	Hideo Nomo	.15
150	Ron Belliard	.15
151	Sean Berry	.15
152	Mark Loretta	.15
153	Steve Woodard	.15
154	Joe Mays	.15
155	Eric Milton	.15
156	Corey Koskie	.15
157	Ron Coomer	.15
158	Brad Radke	.15
159	Terry Steinbach	.15
160	Christian Guzman	.15
161	Vladimir Guerrero	.50
162	Wilton Guerrero	.15
163	Michael Barrett	.15
164	Chris Widger	.15
165	Fernando Seguignol	.15
166	Ugueth Urbina	.15
167	Dustin Hermanson	.15
168	Kenny Rogers	.15
169	Edgardo Alfonzo	.15
170	Orel Hershiser	.15
171	Robin Ventura	.20
172	Octavio Dotel	.15
173	Rickey Henderson	.25
174	Roger Cedeno	.15
175	John Olerud	.25
176	Derek Jeter	2.00
177	Tino Martinez	.20
178	Orlando Hernandez	.20
179	Chuck Knoblauch	.15
180	Bernie Williams	.40
181	Chili Davis	.15
182	David Cone	.20
183	Ricky Ledee	.15
184	Paul O'Neill	.25
185	Jason Giambi	.50
186	Eric Chavez	.25
187	Matt Stairs	.15
188	Miguel Tejada	.25
189	Olmedo Saenz	.15
190	Tim Hudson	.40
191	John Jaha	.15
192	Randy Velarde	.15
193	Rico Brogna	.15
194	Mike Lieberthal	.20
195	Marlon Anderson	.15
196	Bobby Abreu	.25
197	Ron Gant	.15
198	Randy Wolf	.15
199	Desi Relaford	.15
200	Doug Glanville	.15
201	Warren Morris	.15
202	Kris Benson	.15
203	Kevin Young	.15
204	Brian Giles	.15
205	Jason Schmidt	.15
206	Ed Sprague	.15
207	Francisco Cordova	.15
208	Mark McGwire	2.00
209	Jose Jimenez	.15
210	Fernando Tatis	.15
211	Kent Bottenfield	.15
212	Eli Marrero	.15
213	Edgar Renteria	.15
214	Joe McEwing	.15
215	J.D. Drew	.20
216	Tony Gwynn	.75
217	Gary Matthews Jr.	.15
218	Eric Owens	.15
219	Damian Jackson	.15
220	Reggie Sanders	.15
221	Trevor Hoffman	.15
222	Ben Davis	.15
223	Shawn Estes	.15
224	F.P. Santangelo	.15
225	Livan Hernandez	.15
226	Ellis Burks	.15
227	J.T. Snow	.15
228	Jeff Kent	.25
229	Robb Nen	.15
230	Marvin Benard	.15
231	Ken Griffey Jr.	1.00
232	John Halama	.15
233	Gil Meche	.15
234	David Bell	.15
235	Brian L. Hunter	.15
236	Jay Buhner	.25
237	Edgar Martinez	.25
238	Jose Mesa	.15
239	Wilson Alvarez	.15
240	Wade Boggs	.40
241	Fred McGriff	.25
242	Jose Canseco	.40
243	Kevin Stocker	.15
244	Bubba Trammell	.15
245	John Flaherty	.15
246	Roberto Hernandez	.15
247	Ivan Rodriguez	.40
248	Rusty Greer	.15
249	Rafael Palmeiro	.40
250	Jeff Zimmerman	.15
251	Royce Clayton	.15
252	Todd Zeile	.15
253	John Wetteland	.15
254	Ruben Mateo	.15
255	Kelvim Escobar	.15
256	David Wells	.15
257	Shawn Green	.40
258	Homer Bush	.15
259	Shannon Stewart	.15
260	Carlos Delgado	.50
261	Roy Halladay	.25
262	Fernando Tatis CL	.15
263	Jose Jimenez CL	.15
264	Tony Gwynn CL	.40
265	Wade Boggs CL	.25
266	Cal Ripken Jr. CL	1.00
267	David Cone CL	.15
268	Mark McGwire CL	.75
269	Pedro Martinez CL	.40
270	Nomar Garciaparra CL	.75
271	Nick Johnson/SR	.40
272	Mark Quinn/SR	.15
273	Roosevelt Brown/SR	.15
274	Adam Everett/SR	.15
275	Jason Marquis/SR	.15
276	Kazuhio Sasaki/SR RC	1.50
277	Aaron Myette/SR	.15
278	Danys Baez/SR RC	.50
279	Travis Dawkins/SR	.15
280	Mark Mulder/SR	.25
281	Chris Haas/SR	.15
282	Milton Bradley/SR	.25
283	Brad Penny/SR	.15
284	Rafael Furcal/SR	.25
285	Luis Matos/SR RC	1.00
286	Victor Santos/SR	.15
287	Rico Washington/SR RC	.15
288	Rob Bell/SR	.15
289	Joe Crede/SR	.15
290	Pablo Ozuna/SR	.15
291	Wascar Serrano/SR RC	.15
292	Sang-Hoon Lee/SR RC	.25
293	Chris Wakeland/SR	.15
294	Luis Rivera/SR	.15
295	Mike Lamb/SR RC	.20
296	Wily Pena/SR	.15
297	Mike Meyers/SR RC	.15
298	Mo Vaughn	.15
299	Darin Erstad	.25
300	Garret Anderson	.15
301	Tim Belcher	.15
302	Scott Spiezio	.15
303	Kent Bottenfield	.15
304	Orlando Palmeiro	.15
305	Jason Dickson	.15
306	Matt Williams	.20
307	Brian Anderson	.15
308	Hanley Frias	.15
309	Todd Stottlemyre	.15
310	Matt Mantei	.15
311	David Dellucci	.15
312	Armando Reynoso	.15
313	Bernard Gilkey	.15
314	Chipper Jones	1.00
315	Tom Glavine	.25
316	Quilvio Veras	.50
317	Andruw Jones	.50
318	Bobby Bonilla	.15
319	Reggie Sanders	.15
320	Andres Galarraga	.20
321	George Lombard	.15
322	John Rocker	.15
323	Wally Joyner	.15
324	B.J. Surhoff	.15
325	Scott Erickson	.15
326	Delino DeShields	.15
327	Jeff Conine	.15
328	Mike Timlin	.15
329	Brady Anderson	.15
330	Mike Bordick	.15
331	Harold Baines	.15
332	Nomar Garciaparra	1.50
333	Bret Saberhagen	.15
334	Ramon Martinez	.15
335	Donnie Sadler	.15
336	Wilton Veras	.15
337	Mike Stanley	.15
338	Brian Rose	.15
339	Carl Everett	.15
340	Tim Wakefield	.15
341	Mark Grace	.15
342	Kerry Wood	.30
343	Eric Young	.15
344	Jose Nieves	.15
345	Ismael Valdes	.15
346	Joe Girardi	.15
347	Damon Buford	.15
348	Ricky Gutierrez	.15
349	Frank Thomas	.50
350	Brian Simmons	.15
351	James Baldwin	.15
352	Brook Fordyce	.15
353	Jose Valentin	.15
354	Mike Sirotka	.15
355	Greg Norton	.15
356	Dante Bichette	.15
357	Deion Sanders	.25
358	Ken Griffey Jr.	1.00
359	Denny Neagle	.15
360	Dmitri Young	.15
361	Pete Harnisch	.15
362	Michael Tucker	.15
363	Roberto Alomar	.40
364	Dave Roberts	.15
365	Jim Thome	.15
366	Bartolo Colon	.15
367	Travis Fryman	.20
368	Chuck Finley	.15
369	Russell Branyan	.15

370	Alex Ramirez	.15
371	Jeff Cirillo	.15
372	Jeffrey Hammonds	.15
373	Scott Karl	.15
374	Brent Mayne	.15
375	Tom Goodwin	.15
376	Jose Jimenez	.15
377	Rolando Arrojo	.15
378	Terry Shumpert	.15
379	Juan Gonzalez	.50
380	Bobby Higginson	.15
381	Tony Clark	.15
382	Dave Mlicki	.15
383	Deivi Cruz	.15
384	Brian Moehler	.15
385	Dean Palmer	.15
386	Luis Castillo	.15
387	Mike Redmond	.15
388	Alex Fernandez	.15
389	Brant Brown	.15
390	Dave Berg	.15
391	A.J. Burnett	.15
392	Mark Kotsay	.15
393	Craig Biggio	.20
394	Daryle Ward	.15
395	Lance Berkman	.25
396	Roger Cedeno	.15
397	Scott Elarton	.15
398	Octavio Dotel	.15
399	Ken Caminiti	.15
400	Johnny Damon	.25
401	Mike Sweeney	.15
402	Jeff Suppan	.15
403	Rey Sanchez	.15
404	Blake Stein	.15
405	Ricky Bottalico	.15
406	Jay Witasick	.15
407	Shawn Green	.40
408	Orel Hershiser	.15
409	Gary Sheffield	.40
410	Todd Hollandsworth	.15
411	Terry Adams	.15
412	Todd Hundley	.15
413	Eric Karros	.15
414	F.P. Santangelo	.15
415	Alex Cora	.15
416	Marquis Grissom	.15
417	Henry Blanco	.15
418	Jose Hernandez	.15
419	Kyle Peterson	.15
420	John Snyder **RC**	.15
421	Bob Wickman	.15
422	Jamey Wright	.15
423	Chad Allen	.15
424	Todd Walker	.15
425	J.C. Romero **RC**	.15
426	Butch Huskey	.15
427	Jacque Jones	.15
428	Matt Lawton	.15
429	Rondell White	.25
430	Jose Vidro	.15
431	Hideki Irabu	.15
432	Javier Vazquez	.15
433	Lee Stevens	.15
434	Mike Thurman	.15
435	Geoff Blum	.15
436	Mike Hampton	.15
437	Mike Piazza	1.00
438	Al Leiter	.15
439	Derek Bell	.15
440	Armando Benitez	.15
441	Rey Ordonez	.15
442	Todd Zeile	.15
443	Roger Clemens	1.25
444	Ramiro Mendoza	.15
445	Andy Pettitte	.25
446	Scott Brosius	.15
447	Mariano Rivera	.25
448	Jim Leyritz	.15
449	Jorge Posada	.25
450	Omar Olivares	.15
451	Ben Grieve	.15
452	A.J. Hinch	.15
453	Gil Heredia	.15
454	Kevin Appier	.15
455	Ryan Christenson	.15
456	Ramon Hernandez	.15
457	Scott Rolen	.50
458	Alex Arias	.15
459	Andy Ashby	.15
460		.15
461	Robert Person	.15
462	Paul Byrd	.15
463	Curt Schilling	.25
464	Mike Jackson	.15
465	Jason Kendall	.25
466	Pat Meares	.15
467	Bruce Aven	.15
468	Todd Ritchie	.15
469	Wil Cordero	.15
470	Aramis Ramirez	.15
471	Andy Benes	.15
472	Ray Lankford	.15
473	Fernando Vina	.15
474a	Jim Edmonds	.25
474b	Kevin Jordan (Should be #460.)	.15
475	Craig Paquette	.15
476	Pat Hentgen	.15
477	Darryl Kile	.15
478	Sterling Hitchcock	.15
479	Ruben Rivera	.15
480	Ryan Klesko	.15
481	Phil Nevin	.15
482	Woody Williams	.15
483	Carlos Hernandez	.15
484	Brian Meadows	.15
485	Bret Boone	.25

486	Barry Bonds	1.50
487	Russ Ortiz	.15
488	Bobby Estalella	.15
489	Rich Aurilia	.15
490	Bill Mueller	.15
491	Joe Nathan	.15
492	Russ Davis	.15
493	John Olerud	.25
494	Alex Rodriguez	1.50
495	Fred Garcia	.15
496	Carlos Guillen	.15
497	Aaron Sele	.15
498	Brett Tomko	.15
499	Jamie Moyer	.15
500	Mike Cameron	.15
501	Vinny Castilla	.15
502	Gerald Williams	.15
503	Mike DiFelice	.15
504	Ryan Rupe	.15
505	Greg Vaughn	.15
506	Miguel Cairo	.15
507	Juan Guzman **RC**	.15
508	Jose Guillen	.15
509	Gabe Kapler	.15
510	Rick Helling	.15
511	David Segui	.15
512	Doug Davis	.15
513	Justin Thompson	.15
514	Chad Curtis	.15
515	Tony Batista	.15
516	Billy Koch	.15
517	Raul Mondesi	.20
518	Joey Hamilton	.15
519	Darrin Fletcher	.15
520	Brad Fullmer	.15
521	Jose Cruz Jr.	.15
522	Kevin Witt	.15
523	Mark McGwire (All-UD Team)	1.00
524	Roberto Alomar (All-UD Team)	.25
525	Chipper Jones (All-UD Team)	.50
526	Derek Jeter (All-UD Team)	1.00
527	Ken Griffey Jr. (All-UD Team)	.50
528	Sammy Sosa (All-UD Team)	.75
529	Manny Ramirez (All-UD Team)	.40
530	Ivan Rodriguez (All-UD Team)	.25
531	Pedro J. Martinez (All-UD Team)	.40
532	Mariano Rivera (Season Highlights Checklist)	.15
533	Sammy Sosa (Season Highlights Checklist)	.75
534	Cal Ripken Jr. (Season Highlights Checklist)	1.00
535	Vladimir Guerrero (Season Highlights Checklist)	.40
536	Tony Gwynn (Season Highlights Checklist)	.25
537	Mark McGwire (Season Highlights Checklist)	1.00
538	Bernie Williams (Season Highlights Checklist)	.25
539	Pedro J. Martinez (Season Highlights Checklist)	.40
540	Ken Griffey Jr. (Season Highlights Checklist)	.50

Inserted 1:23

1	Roger Clemens	3.00
2	Cal Ripken Jr.	5.00
3	Ken Griffey Jr.	3.00
4	Mike Piazza	3.00
5	Tony Gwynn	2.00
6	Sammy Sosa	2.50
7	Jose Canseco	1.00
8	Larry Walker	.75
9	Barry Bonds	4.00
10	Greg Maddux	2.50
11	Derek Jeter	5.00
12	Mark McGwire	4.00
13	Randy Johnson	2.00
14	Frank Thomas	1.50
15	Jeff Bagwell	1.50

e-Card

Randomly inserted in series 2 packs, each e-card has an ID number stamped on the card front that can be entered on Upper Deck's website. Collectors then find out if that card "evolves" into a signature card, jersey card or a signed jersey card. They are seeded 1:9 packs and are numbered with an "E" prefix on the card back.

	NM/M
Complete Set (6):	10.00
Common Player:	1.00

Inserted 1:12

1	Ken Griffey Jr.	2.00
2	Alex Rodriguez	3.00
3	Cal Ripken Jr.	3.00
4	Jeff Bagwell	1.00
5	Barry Bonds	3.00
6	Manny Ramirez	1.00

Exclusives

Labeled "UD Exclusives," these parallel sets were issued in two versions, silvers numbered to 100 each, and golds which were 1-of-1. Except for the appropriately colored foil highlights on front and dot-matrix serial number, the Exclusives are identical to the regular-issue cards. They were inserted exclusively into hobby packs. Because of their rarity and variable demand, the unique gold cards are not priced.

	NM/M
Common Silver Exclusive:	1.00
Silver Stars/Rookies:	8X

Cooperstown Calling

This insert set features players deemed by Upper Deck as future Hall of Famers. Card fronts feature silver holo-foil with gold foil stamping. Card backs are numbered with a "CC" prefix and are seeded 1:23 packs.

	NM/M
Complete Set (15):	25.00
Common Player:	.75

2	Alex Rodriguez	150.00
3	Cal Ripken Jr.	200.00
4	Jeff Bagwell	60.00
5	Barry Bonds	150.00
6	Manny Ramirez	60.00

eVolve Signature

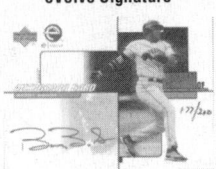

	NM/M
Common Player:	40.00
Production 200 Sets	

1	Ken Griffey Jr.	85.00
2	Alex Rodriguez	85.00
3	Cal Ripken Jr.	150.00
4	Jeff Bagwell	40.00
5	Barry Bonds	120.00
6	Manny Ramirez	40.00

Faces of the Game

Randomly inserted in Series 1 at a rate of 1:11 packs, card fronts feature a close-up photo of the featured player with bronze foil etching and stamping. Backs are numbered with an "F" prefix. Two parallel versions are available, Silvers are serially numbered to 100 and golds limited to one set.

	NM/M
Complete Set (20):	30.00
Common Player:	.75
Inserted 1:11	
Silver:	4-8X
Production 100 Sets	

1	Ken Griffey Jr.	2.50
2	Mark McGwire	3.00
3	Sammy Sosa	2.00
4	Alex Rodriguez	3.00
5	Manny Ramirez	1.00
6	Derek Jeter	4.00
7	Jeff Bagwell	1.00
8	Roger Clemens	2.00
9	Scott Rolen	.75
10	Tony Gwynn	1.50
11	Nomar Garciaparra	2.50
12	Randy Johnson	1.50
13	Greg Maddux	2.00
14	Mike Piazza	2.50
15	Frank Thomas	1.00
16	Cal Ripken Jr.	4.00
17	Ivan Rodriguez	.75
18	Mo Vaughn	.75
19	Chipper Jones	2.00
20	Sean Casey	.75

Five-Tool Talents

Randomly inserted in series 2 at a rate of 1:11 packs, this 15-card set spotlights players who have "five tools." Card fronts have silver holo-foil throughout with silver foil stamping. Card backs are numbered with an "FT" prefix.

	NM/M
Complete Set (15):	15.00

Common Player:	.50
Inserted 1:11	

1	Vladimir Guerrero	1.50
2	Barry Bonds	3.00
3	Jason Kendall	.50
4	Derek Jeter	4.00
5	Ken Griffey Jr.	2.50
6	Andruw Jones	.75
7	Bernie Williams	.75
8	Jose Canseco	.75
9	Scott Rolen	.75
10	Shawn Green	.50
11	Nomar Garciaparra	2.50
12	Jeff Bagwell	1.00
13	Larry Walker	.75
14	Chipper Jones	2.00
15	Alex Rodriguez	3.00

Game Balls

These inserts feature a piece of game-used baseball embedded into the card from the featured player. Card backs are numbered with the featured player's initials and are found on the average of 1:287 series 2 packs.

		NM/M
Common Player:		10.00
JB	Jeff Bagwell	10.00
RC	Roger Clemens	30.00
KG	Ken Griffey Jr.	25.00
VG	Vladimir Guerrero	15.00
TG	Tony Gwynn	25.00
DJ	Derek Jeter	40.00
CJ	Chipper Jones	20.00
GM	Greg Maddux	20.00
MM	Mark McGwire	50.00
AR	Alex Rodriguez	30.00
BW	Bernie Williams	10.00

Game Jersey

These have a piece of game-used jersey from the featured player embedded into the card. This regular version is found both in hobby and retail packs at a rate of 1:2,500 packs.

		NM/M
Common Player:		10.00
Inserted 1:2,500		
JC	Jose Canseco	15.00
JG	Juan Gonzalez	15.00
VG	Vladimir Guerrero	20.00
TH	Todd Helton	15.00
CJ	Chipper Jones	25.00
GK	Gabe Kapler	10.00
GM	Greg Maddux	35.00
MR	Manny Ramirez	20.00
CR	Cal Ripken Jr.	60.00
GV	Greg Vaughn	10.00

Game Jersey Series 2

These jersey inserts are found in both hobby and retail packs and are seeded 1:287 packs.

		NM/M
Common Player:		10.00
AR	Alex Rodriguez	30.00
TG	Tony Gwynn	20.00
FT	Frank Thomas	15.00
MW	Matt Williams	10.00
JT	Jim Thome	15.00
MV	Mo Vaughn	10.00
TGl	Tom Glavine	15.00
BG	Ben Grieve	10.00
TrG	Troy Glaus	15.00
RJ	Randy Johnson	20.00
KM	Kevin Millwood	10.00
KG	Ken Griffey Jr.	25.00
AB	Albert Belle	10.00
DC	David Cone	10.00
MH	Mike Hampton	10.00
EC	Eric Chavez	10.00

Common Player:	.50
Inserted 1:11	
1	Vladimir Guerrero	1.50
2	Barry Bonds	3.00
3	Jason Kendall	.50
4	Derek Jeter	4.00
5	Ken Griffey Jr.	2.50
6	Andruw Jones	.75
7	Bernie Williams	.75
8	Jose Canseco	.75
9	Scott Rolen	.75
10	Shawn Green	.50
11	Nomar Garciaparra	2.50
12	Jeff Bagwell	1.00
13	Larry Walker	.75
14	Chipper Jones	2.00
15	Alex Rodriguez	3.00

EM	Edgar Martinez	15.00
PW	Preston Wilson	10.00
RV	Robin Ventura	10.00

Game Jersey Hobby

These game-used memorabilia inserts were found exclusively in series 1 packs at a rate of 1:288.

		NM/M
Common Player:		10.00
Inserted 1:288		
JB	Jeff Bagwell	15.00
TG	Troy Glaus	15.00
CY	Tom Glavine	10.00
Jr.	Ken Griffey Jr.	25.00
DJ	Derek Jeter	40.00
PM	Pedro J. Martinez	20.00
MP	Mike Piazza	30.00
AR	Alex Rodriguez	30.00
FT	Frank Thomas	15.00
LW	Larry Walker	10.00

Game Jersey Auto. Hobby Series 2

Found exclusively in series 2 packs these autographed game-used memorabilia inserts are found only in hobby packs at a rate of 1:287.

		NM/M
Common Player:		30.00
H-KG	Ken Griffey Jr.	100.00
H-CR	Cal Ripken Jr.	150.00
H-DJ	Derek Jeter	150.00
H-IR	Ivan Rodriguez	40.00
H-AR	Alex Rodriguez	100.00
H-MR	Manny Ramirez	50.00
H-JC	Jose Canseco	30.00
H-BB	Barry Bonds	180.00
H-SR	Scott Rolen	40.00
H-PO	Paul O'Neill	40.00
H-JK	Jason Kendall	30.00
H-VG	Vladimir Guerrero	50.00
H-JB	Jeff Bagwell	40.00

Game Jersey Patch

Inserted in Series 1 packs at a rate of 1:10,000, these memorabilia inserts have a piece of game-used uniform patch embedded. A 1-of-1 patch of each player was also issued, but cannot be priced due to rarity.

		NM/M
Common Player:		40.00
Inserted 1:10,000		
JB	Jeff Bagwell	60.00
JC	Jose Canseco	60.00
TG	Troy Glaus	50.00
CY	Tom Glavine	60.00
Jr.	Ken Griffey Jr.	100.00
VG	Vladimir Guerrero	100.00
TH	Todd Helton	60.00
DJ	Derek Jeter	150.00
CJ	Chipper Jones	75.00
GK	Gabe Kapler	40.00
GM	Greg Maddux	100.00
PM	Pedro J. Martinez	100.00
MP	Mike Piazza	100.00
MR	Manny Ramirez	80.00
CR	Cal Ripken Jr.	200.00
AR	Alex Rodriguez	125.00
FT	Frank Thomas	80.00
GV	Greg Vaughn	50.00
LW	Larry Walker	50.00

Game Jersey Patch Series 2

Inserted in Series 2 packs, these memorabilia inserts have a game-used uniform patch embedded and are seeded 1:7,500 packs. A limited one-of-one patch insert

eVolve Jersey

	NM/M
Common Player:	15.00
Production 300 Sets	

1	Ken Griffey Jr.	30.00
2	Alex Rodriguez	40.00
3	Cal Ripken Jr.	50.00
4	Jeff Bagwell	15.00
5	Barry Bonds	40.00
6	Manny Ramirez	20.00

eVolve Signed Jersey

	NM/M
Common Player:	80.00
Production 50 Sets	
1	Ken Griffey Jr.	150.00

for each player is also randomly seeded and are not priced due to their limited nature.

		NM/M
JB	Jeff Bagwell	75.00
BB	Barry Bonds	200.00
JC	Jose Canseco	75.00
TGl	Troy Glaus	75.00
KG	Ken Griffey Jr.	125.00
VG	Vladimir Guerrero	100.00
TG	Tony Gwynn	100.00
DJ	Derek Jeter	150.00
RJ	Randy Johnson	100.00
AJ	Andruw Jones	80.00
CJ	Chipper Jones	100.00
GM	Greg Maddux	100.00
PM	Pedro Martinez	100.00
MR	Manny Ramirez	100.00
CR	Cal Ripken Jr.	200.00
SR	Scott Rolen	75.00
AR	Alex Rodriguez	150.00
IR	Ivan Rodriguez	90.00
FT	Frank Thomas	100.00
MV	Mo Vaughn	50.00
MW	Matt Williams	50.00

Hit Brigade

Fifteen of the game's top hitters are featured on a full foiled front with bronze foil stamping. Card backs are numbered with an "H" prefix and are found in series 1 packs at a rate of 1:8. Two parallels are randomly inserted: Silvers are serial numbered to 100 and Golds are limited to one set.

		NM/M
Complete Set (15):		15.00
Common Player:		.50
Inserted 1:8		
Silver:		5-10X
Production 100 Sets		
1	Ken Griffey Jr.	2.00
2	Tony Gwynn	1.00
3	Alex Rodriguez	2.50
4	Derek Jeter	3.00
5	Mike Piazza	2.00
6	Sammy Sosa	1.50
7	Juan Gonzalez	.75
8	Scott Rolen	.50
9	Nomar Garciaparra	2.00
10	Barry Bonds	2.50
11	Craig Biggio	.75
12	Chipper Jones	1.50
13	Frank Thomas	.75
14	Larry Walker	.75
15	Mark McGwire	2.50

Hot Properties

This set spotlights rookies and prospects who have a bright future. Card fronts have a horizontal format on a holo-foiled stock with silver foil stamping. Card backs are numbered with an "HP" prefix and are found in series 2 packs at a rate of 1:11.

		NM/M
Complete Set (15):		10.00
Common Player:		.50
Inserted 1:11		

1	Carlos Beltran	1.00
2	Rick Ankiel	.50
3	Sean Casey	1.00
4	Preston Wilson	1.00
5	Vernon Wells	1.00
6	Pat Burrell	1.50
7	Eric Chavez	1.00
8	J.D. Drew	1.00
9	Alfonso Soriano	2.00
10	Gabe Kapler	.50
11	Rafael Furcal	1.00
12	Ruben Mateo	.50
13	Corey Koskie	.75
14	Kip Wells	.50
15	Ramon Ortiz	.75

The People's Choice

This 15-card set is printed on a full holo-foiled front with gold foil stamping. Card backs are numbered with a "PC" prefix and are seeded 1:23 packs.

		NM/M
Complete Set (15):		20.00
Common Player:		.75
Inserted 1:23		
1	Mark McGwire	3.00
2	Nomar Garciaparra	3.00
3	Derek Jeter	3.00
4	Shawn Green	.75
5	Manny Ramirez	1.00
6	Pedro Martinez	1.50
7	Ivan Rodriguez	.75
8	Alex Rodriguez	3.00
9	Juan Gonzalez	1.00
10	Ken Griffey Jr.	2.00
11	Sammy Sosa	2.50
12	Jeff Bagwell	1.00
13	Chipper Jones	1.50
14	Cal Ripken Jr.	4.00
15	Mike Piazza	2.00

Pennant Driven

This 10-card horizontal set has a holo-foiled card front with silver foil stamping. Card backs are numbered with a "PD" prefix and are seeded 1:4 packs.

		NM/M
Complete Set (10):		8.00
Common Player:		.50
Inserted 1:4		
1	Derek Jeter	2.00
2	Roberto Alomar	.50
3	Chipper Jones	1.50
4	Jeff Bagwell	.75
5	Roger Clemens	1.00
6	Nomar Garciaparra	1.50
7	Manny Ramirez	.75
8	Mike Piazza	1.50
9	Ivan Rodriguez	.50
10	Randy Johnson	.75

Piece of History-500 Club

This card features a piece of a game-used Louisville Slugger once swung by Aaron. Approximately 350 cards were produced. Also randomly inserted are 44 autographed versions.

		NM/M
755HR Hank Aaron		300.00
HAAU Hank Aaron/Auto./44		1,200

Power Deck

Collectors need access to a CD-ROM in order to enjoy these interactive cards. Found exclusively in hobby packs cards 1-8 are seeded 1:23 packs and cards 9-11 are found 1:287 packs.

		NM/M
Complete Set (11):		60.00
Common Player:		2.50
Inserted 1:23		
1	Ken Griffey Jr.	5.00
2	Cal Ripken Jr.	7.50
3	Mark McGwire	6.00
4	Tony Gwynn	3.50
5	Roger Clemens	3.50
6	Alex Rodriguez	6.00
7	Sammy Sosa	3.50
8	Derek Jeter	7.50
9	Ken Griffey Jr.	25.00
10	Mark McGwire	30.00
11	Reggie Jackson	15.00

Power MARK

		NM/M
Complete Set (10):		25.00
Common McGwire:		3.00
Inserted 1:23		
Silver:		5-10X
Production 100 Sets		
1-10	Mark McGwire	3.00

Power Rally

This 15-card set highlights the top hitters and are numbered with an "P" prefix on the card back. They are found 1:11 packs. Two parallel version are also seeded: Coppers are limited to 100 serial numbered sets and Golds are limited to one set.

		NM/M
Complete Set (15):		20.00
Common Player:		.75
Inserted 1:11		
Silver:		4-8X
Production 100 Sets		
1	Ken Griffey Jr.	2.50
2	Mark McGwire	3.00
3	Sammy Sosa	2.00
4	Jose Canseco	.75
5	Juan Gonzalez	1.00
6	Bernie Williams	.75
7	Jeff Bagwell	1.00
8	Chipper Jones	2.00
9	Vladimir Guerrero	1.50
10	Mo Vaughn	.75
11	Derek Jeter	4.00
12	Mike Piazza	2.50
13	Barry Bonds	3.00
14	Alex Rodriguez	3.00
15	Nomar Garciaparra	2.50

Prime Performers

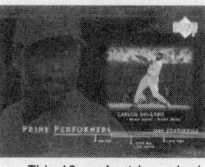

This 10-card set has a horizontal format on a full holo foiled front, with silver foil etching and stamping. Card backs are numbered with a "PP" prefix and found 1:8 packs.

		NM/M
Complete Set (10):		10.00
Common Player:		.50
Inserted 1:8		
1	Manny Ramirez	.75
2	Pedro Martinez	1.00
3	Carlos Delgado	.50
4	Ken Griffey Jr.	2.00
5	Derek Jeter	3.00
6	Chipper Jones	1.50
7	Sean Casey	.50
8	Shawn Green	.50
9	Sammy Sosa	1.50
10	Alex Rodriguez	2.50

STATitude

This 30-card set spotlights the most statistically dominant players on a horizontal format with silver foil stamping. Card backs are numbered with an "S" prefix and are inserted 1:4. Two parallel versions are randomly inserted: Coppers are limited to 100 serial numbered sets and Golds are limited to one set.

		NM/M
Complete Set (30):		25.00
Common Player:		.40
Inserted 1:4		
Silver:		5-10X
Production 100 Sets		
1	Mo Vaughn	.40
2	Matt Williams	.40
3	Travis Lee	.40
4	Chipper Jones	1.50
5	Greg Maddux	1.50
6	Gabe Kapler	.40
7	Cal Ripken Jr.	3.00
8	Nomar Garciaparra	2.00
9	Sammy Sosa	1.50
10	Frank Thomas	.75
11	Manny Ramirez	.75
12	Larry Walker	.50
13	Ivan Rodriguez	.50
14	Jeff Bagwell	.75
15	Craig Biggio	.50
16	Vladimir Guerrero	1.00
17	Mike Piazza	2.00
18	Bernie Williams	.50
19	Derek Jeter	3.00
20	Jose Canseco	.50
21	Eric Chavez	.50
22	Scott Rolen	.50
23	Mark McGwire	2.50
24	Tony Gwynn	1.00
25	Barry Bonds	2.50
26	Ken Griffey Jr.	2.00
27	Alex Rodriguez	2.50
28	J.D. Drew	.50
29	Juan Gonzalez	.50
30	Roger Clemens	1.50

2K Plus

This 12-card set showcases the talents of baseball's next millennium. They are numbered with an "2K" prefix on the card back and are seeded 1:23 packs. Two parallel versions are also randomly inserted: Coppers are limited to 100 serial numbered sets and Golds are limited on one set produced.

		NM/M
Complete Set (12):		15.00
Common Player:		.50
Inserted 1:23		
Silver:		5-10X
Production 100 Sets		
1	Ken Griffey Jr.	2.00
2	J.D. Drew	.50
3	Derek Jeter	3.00
4	Nomar Garciaparra	3.00
5	Pat Burrell	.75
6	Ruben Mateo	.50
7	Carlos Beltran	.50
8	Vladimir Guerrero	1.00
9	Scott Rolen	1.00
10	Chipper Jones	2.00
11	Alex Rodriguez	3.00
12	Magglio Ordonez	.75

3,000 Hit Club Series 1

Game-used memorabilia from Orioles teammates Ripken and Murray were inserted in the cross-brand 3,000 Hit Club inserts in Series 1 UD.

		NM/M
CR-B	Cal Ripken Jr./Bat/350	25.00
CR-J	Cal Ripken Jr./Jsy/350	25.00
CR-JB	Cal Ripken Jr./Jsy/Bat/100	150.00
EM-B	Eddie Murray/Bat/350	10.00
EM-J	Eddie Murray/Jsy/350	8.00
EM-JB	Eddie Murray/Jsy/Bat/100	60.00

3,000 Hit Club Series 2

This cross-brand series spotlights Hank Aaron. The series includes a Jersey card (350 produced), Bat card (350 produced), Jersey/Bat combo (100 produced) and Autographed Jersey/Bat combo (44 produced).

		NM/M
HA-B	Hank Aaron/Bat/350	75.00
HA-JB	Hank Aaron/Bat/Jsy/100	150.00
HA-J	Hank Aaron/Jsy/350	75.00
HA-JBS	Hank Aaron/Auto. Bat/Jsy/44	1,000

2000 Upper Deck Black Diamond

The base set consists of 120-cards, including a 30 card Diamond Debut (91-120) subset that are seeded 1:4 packs. Card fronts are full foiled with silver etching.

Card backs have the player's past five years of statistics, a brief career note and small photo.

		NM/M
Complete Set (120):		25.00
Common Player:		.15
Common Diamond Debut:		.50
Pack (6):		1.50
Wax Box (24):		30.00
1	Darin Erstad	.25
2	Tim Salmon	.25
3	Mo Vaughn	.20
4	Matt Williams	.25
5	Travis Lee	.15
6	Randy Johnson	.75
7	Tom Glavine	.40
8	Chipper Jones	1.50
9	Greg Maddux	1.50
10	Andruw Jones	.50
11	Brian Jordan	.15
12	Cal Ripken Jr.	2.50
13	Albert Belle	.20
14	Mike Mussina	.50
15	Nomar Garciaparra	2.00
16	Troy O'Leary	.15
17	Pedro J. Martinez	1.00
18	Sammy Sosa	1.50
19	Henry Rodriguez	.15
20	Frank Thomas	.75
21	Magglio Ordonez	.40
22	Greg Vaughn	.15
23	Barry Larkin	.25
24	Sean Casey	.25
25	Jim Thome	.75
26	Kenny Lofton	.25
27	Roberto Alomar	.50
28	Manny Ramirez	.75
29	Larry Walker	.25
30	Todd Helton	.75
31	Gabe Kapler	.15
32	Tony Clark	.15
33	Dean Palmer	.15
34	Cliff Floyd	.15
35	Alex Gonzalez	.15
36	Moises Alou	.15
37	Jeff Bagwell	.75
38	Craig Biggio	.25
39	Richard Hidalgo	.15
40	Carlos Beltran	.25
41	Johnny Damon	.25
42	Adrian Beltre	.25
43	Gary Sheffield	.40
44	Kevin Brown	.25
45	Jeromy Burnitz	.15
46	Jeff Cirillo	.15
47	Joe Mays	.15
48	Todd Walker	.15
49	Vladimir Guerrero	.75
50	Michael Barrett	.15
51	Rickey Henderson	.40
52	Mike Piazza	1.50
53	Robin Ventura	.25
54	John Olerud	.25
55	Edgardo Alfonzo	.15
56	Derek Jeter	2.00
57	Orlando Hernandez	.15
58	Tino Martinez	.25
59	Bernie Williams	.50
60	Roger Clemens	1.50
61	Eric Chavez	.25
62	Ben Grieve	.15
63	Jason Giambi	1.00
64	Scott Rolen	.50
65	Bobby Abreu	.25
66	Curt Schilling	.40
67	Mike Lieberthal	.15
68	Warren Morris	.15
69	Brian Giles	.25
70	Eric Owens	.15
71	Tony Gwynn	1.00
72	Reggie Sanders	.15
73	Barry Bonds	2.00
74	J.T. Snow	.15
75	Jeff Kent	.25
76	Ken Griffey Jr.	1.50
77	Alex Rodriguez	2.00
78	Edgar Martinez	.25
79	Jay Buhner	.15
80	Mark McGwire	2.00
81	J.D. Drew	.25
82	Eric Davis	.15
83	Fernando Tatis	.15
84	Wade Boggs	.50
85	Fred McGriff	.25
86	Juan Gonzalez	.75
87	Ivan Rodriguez	.50
88	Rafael Palmeiro	.50
89	Shawn Green	.40
90	Carlos Delgado	.60
91	Pat Burrell (Diamond Debut)	1.00
92	Eric Munson (Diamond Debut)	.50
93	Jorge Toca (Diamond Debut)	.50
94	Rick Ankiel (Diamond Debut)	.50
95	Tony Armas Jr. (Diamond Debut)	.75
96	Byung-Hyun Kim (Diamond Debut)	.75
97	Alfonso Soriano (Diamond Debut)	3.00
98	Mark Quinn (Diamond Debut)	.50
99	Ryan Rupe (Diamond Debut)	.50

100	Adam Kennedy (Diamond Debut)	.50
101	Jeff Weaver (Diamond Debut)	.75
102	Ramon Ortiz (Diamond Debut)	.75
103	Eugene Kingsale (Diamond Debut)	.50
104	Josh Beckett (Diamond Debut)	1.00
105	Eric Gagne (Diamond Debut)	1.00
106	Peter Bergeron (Diamond Debut)	.50
107	Erubiel Durazo (Diamond Debut)	.75
108	Chad Meyers (Diamond Debut)	.50
109	Kip Wells (Diamond Debut)	.50
110	Chad Harville (Diamond Debut)	.50
111	Matt Riley (Diamond Debut)	.50
112	Ben Petrick (Diamond Debut)	.50
113	Ed Yarnall (Diamond Debut)	.50
114	Calvin Murray (Diamond Debut)	.50
115	Vernon Wells (Diamond Debut)	1.00
116	A.J. Burnett (Diamond Debut)	.75
117	Jacque Jones (Diamond Debut)	.75
118	Francisco Cordero (Diamond Debut)	.50
119	Tomokazu Ohka RC (Diamond Debut)	1.50
120	Julio Ramirez (Diamond Debut)	.50

Reciprocal Cut

A parallel to the 120-card base set, the die-cut design can be used to differentiate them from base cards. Card backs are also numbered with an "R" prefix. Cards 1-90 are found 1:7 packs and Diamond Debuts (91-120) are seeded 1:12 packs.

Stars (1-90):	2-5X
Diamond Debuts	1-1.5X
1-90 inserted 1:7	
Diamond Debuts inserted 1:12	

Final Cut

A parallel to the 120-card base set the die-cut design can be used to distinguish them from base cards, the card backs are also numbered with an "F" prefix. Each card is serial numbered within an edition of 100 sets.

Stars (1-90):	5-10X
Diamond Debuts:	2-4X
Production 100 Sets	

A Piece of History Single

These memorabilia inserts have a piece of game-used bat embedded into the card front and are seeded 1:179 packs.

		NM/M
Common Player:		8.00
Inserted 1:179		
AB	Albert Belle	8.00
BB	Barry Bonds	40.00
JC	Jose Canseco	10.00
DE	Darin Erstad	8.00
JR	Ken Griffey Jr.	25.00
VG	Vladimir Guerrero	15.00
TG	Tony Gwynn	20.00
TH	Todd Helton	10.00
DJ	Derek Jeter	40.00
AJ	Andruw Jones	10.00
CJ	Chipper Jones	20.00
TL	Travis Lee	8.00
RM	Raul Mondesi	8.00
MP	Mike Piazza	25.00
CAL	Cal Ripken Jr.	50.00
AR	Alex Rodriguez	25.00
IR	Ivan Rodriguez	10.00
SR	Scott Rolen	10.00
MV	Mo Vaughn	8.00

A Piece of History Double

These memorabilia inserts have two pieces of game-used bat embedded into the card front and are a parallel to the single set. They are inserted 1:1,079 packs.

		NM/M
Common Player:		10.00
Inserted 1:1079		
AB	Albert Belle	10.00
BB	Barry Bonds	75.00
JC	Jose Canseco	20.00
DE	Darin Erstad	15.00
JR	Ken Griffey Jr.	50.00
VG	Vladimir Guerrero	30.00
TG	Tony Gwynn	40.00
TH	Todd Helton	15.00
DJ	Derek Jeter	75.00
AJ	Andruw Jones	15.00
CJ	Chipper Jones	40.00
TL	Travis Lee	10.00
RM	Raul Mondesi	10.00
MP	Mike Piazza	50.00
CAL	Cal Ripken Jr.	80.00
AR	Alex Rodriguez	50.00
IR	Ivan Rodriguez	15.00
SR	Scott Rolen	15.00
MV	Mo Vaughn	10.00

Barrage

This 10-card set features a prismatic background with silver foil stamping. Card backs are numbered with a "B" prefix and are seeded 1:29 packs.

		NM/M
Complete Set (10):		15.00
Common Player:		1.00
Inserted 1:29		
1	Mark McGwire	3.00
2	Ken Griffey Jr.	2.00
3	Sammy Sosa	2.50
4	Jeff Bagwell	1.00
5	Juan Gonzalez	1.00
6	Alex Rodriguez	3.00
7	Manny Ramirez	1.00
8	Ivan Rodriguez	1.00
9	Chipper Jones	2.00
10	Mike Piazza	2.00

Constant Threat

A 10-card set spotlighting the top hitters in the game. Card backs are numbered with a "T" prefix and are seeded 1:29 packs.

		NM/M
Complete Set (10):		20.00
Common Player:		1.00
Inserted 1:29		
1	Ken Griffey Jr.	2.00
2	Vladimir Guerrero	1.00
3	Alex Rodriguez	3.00
4	Sammy Sosa	2.50
5	Juan Gonzalez	1.00
6	Derek Jeter	3.00
7	Nomar Garciaparra	3.00
8	Barry Bonds	4.00
9	Chipper Jones	2.00
10	Mike Piazza	2.00

Diamonation

This 10-card set has a holo-foil background with gold foil etching and stamping. Card backs are numbered with a "D" prefix and have an insertion ratio of 1:4 packs.

		NM/M
Complete Set (10):		6.00
Common Player:		.50
Inserted 1:4		
1	Ken Griffey Jr.	1.00
2	Randy Johnson	1.00
3	Mark McGwire	1.50
4	Manny Ramirez	.75
5	Scott Rolen	.75
6	Bernie Williams	.75
7	Roger Clemens	1.50
8	Mo Vaughn	.50
9	Frank Thomas	.75
10	Sean Casey	.50

Diamond Gallery

This 10-card set spotlights the featured player in a baseball diamond frame with a prismatic background. Gold foil etching and stamping is also used throughout. Card backs are numbered with a "G" prefix and are seeded 1:14 packs.

		NM/M
Complete Set (10):		20.00
Common Player:		1.50
Inserted 1:14		
1	Derek Jeter	3.00
2	Alex Rodriguez	3.00
3	Nomar Garciaparra	3.00
4	Cal Ripken Jr.	4.00
5	Sammy Sosa	2.50
6	Tony Gwynn	1.50
7	Mark McGwire	3.00
8	Roger Clemens	2.50
9	Greg Maddux	2.00
10	Pedro Martinez	1.50

DiamondMight

DiamondMight's have a horizontal format, utilizing holo-foil and gold foil stamping. Card backs are numbered with an "M" prefix and are seeded 1:14 packs.

		NM/M
Complete Set (10):		15.00
Common Player:		1.00
Inserted 1:14		
1	Ken Griffey Jr.	2.00
2	Mark McGwire	3.00
3	Sammy Sosa	2.50
4	Manny Ramirez	1.00
5	Jeff Bagwell	1.00
6	Frank Thomas	1.00
7	Mike Piazza	2.00
8	Juan Gonzalez	1.00
9	Barry Bonds	4.00
10	Alex Rodriguez	3.00

Diamonds in the Rough

This 10-card set has a horizontal format utilizing holo-foil and gold foil stamping. Card backs are numbered with an "R" prefix and seeded 1:9 packs.

		NM/M
Complete Set (10):		8.00
Common Player:		.75
Inserted 1:9		
1	Pat Burrell	2.00
2	Eric Munson	.75
3	Alfonso Soriano	3.00
4	Ruben Mateo	.75
5	A.J. Burnett	1.00
6	Ben Davis	.75
7	Lance Berkman	1.50
8	Ed Yarnall	.75
9	Rick Ankiel	1.00
10	Ryan Bradley	.75

500 Club Piece of History

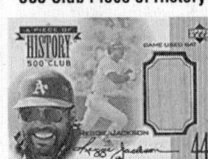

These Reggie Jackson inserts are part of a cross brand insert series paying tribute to baseball's 500 home run club members. These have a piece of Jackson's game-used bat embedded. An autographed version signed to his jersey number (44) are also randomly inserted.

	NM/M
Reggie Jackson	165.00
Reggie Jackson Auto./44	500.00

2000 UD Rookie Edition

		NM/M
Complete Set (154):		200.00
Common Player:		.15
Common Rookie Gem (91-120):		4.00
Production 1,000		
Rookie Jersey Gems (121-136):		
Inserted 1:24		
USA Authentics (137-154):		
Inserted 1:96		
Golds (1-90):		2-4X
Gold Gems (91-120):		1X
Gold Jerseys (121-136):		1-2X
Pack (6):		2.00
Box (24):		40.00
1	Troy Glaus	.75

2	Mo Vaughn	.40
3	Darin Erstad	.40
4	Jason Giambi	.40
5	Tim Hudson	.25
6	Ben Grieve	.25
7	Eric Chavez	.25
8	Tony Batista	.15
9	Carlos Delgado	.60
10	David Wells	.15
11	Greg Vaughn	.15
12	Fred McGriff	.25
13	Manny Ramirez	.75
14	Roberto Alomar	.60
15	Jim Thome	.40
16	Alex Rodriguez	2.50
17	Edgar Martinez	.15
18	John Olerud	.20
19	Albert Belle	.40
20	Mike Mussina	.40
21	Cal Ripken Jr.	2.50
22	Ivan Rodriguez	.75
23	Rafael Palmeiro	.15
24	Pedro J. Martinez	.75
25	Nomar Garciaparra	2.00
26	Carl Everett	.15
27	Jermaine Dye	.15
28	Mike Sweeney	.15
29	Juan Gonzalez	.75
30	Bobby Higginson	.15
31	Dean Palmer	.15
32	Jacque Jones	.15
33	Eric Milton	.15
34	Matt Lawton	.15
35	Magglio Ordonez	.25
36	Paul Konerko	.15
37	Frank Thomas	1.00
38	Ray Durham	.15
39	Roger Clemens	1.00
40	Derek Jeter	2.50
41	Bernie Williams	.50
42	Jose Canseco	.25
43	Craig Biggio	.25
44	Richard Hidalgo	.15
45	Jeff Bagwell	.75
46	Greg Maddux	1.50
47	Chipper Jones	1.50
48	Rafael Furcal	.40
49	Andruw Jones	.50
50	Geoff Jenkins	.15
51	Jeromy Burnitz	.15
52	Mark McGwire	3.00
53	Rick Ankiel	.50
54	Jim Edmonds	.50
55	Kerry Wood	.25
56	Sammy Sosa	2.00
57	Matt Williams	.25
58	Randy Johnson	.75
59	Steve Finley	.15
60	Curt Schilling	.15
61	Kevin Brown	.15
62	Gary Sheffield	.30
63	Shawn Green	.30
64	Jose Vidro	.15
65	Vladimir Guerrero	1.00
66	Jeff Kent	.15
67	Barry Bonds	1.00
68	Ryan Dempster	.15
69	Cliff Floyd	.15
70	Preston Wilson	.15
71	Mike Piazza	2.00
72	Al Leiter	.15
73	Edgardo Alfonzo	.25
74	Derek Bell	.15
75	Ryan Klesko	.15
76	Tony Gwynn	1.00
77	Bobby Abreu	.15
78	Pat Burrell	.50
79	Scott Rolen	.50
80	Mike Lieberthal	.15
81	Jason Kendall	.15
82	Brian Giles	.25
83	Ken Griffey Jr.	2.00
84	Pokey Reese	.15
85	Dmitri Young	.15
86	Sean Casey	.15
87	Jeff Cirillo	.15
88	Todd Helton	.75
89	Jeffrey Hammonds	.15
90	Larry Walker	.30
91	Barry Zito RC	15.00
92	Keith Ginter RC	6.00
93	Dane Sardinha RC	4.00
94	Kenny Kelly RC	4.00
95	Ryan Kohlmeier RC	4.00
96	Leo Estrella RC	4.00
97	Danys Baez RC	4.00
98	Paul Rigdon RC	4.00
99	Mike Lamb RC	4.00
100	Aaron McNeal RC	4.00
101	Juan Pierre RC	6.00
102	Rico Washington RC	4.00
103	Luis Matos RC	8.00
104	Adam Bernero RC	4.00
105	Wascar Serrano RC	4.00
106	Chris Richard RC	4.00
107	Justin Miller RC	4.00
108	Julio Zuleta RC	4.00
109	Alex Cabrera RC	4.00
110	Gene Stechschulte RC	4.00
111	Tony Mota RC	4.00
112	Tomokazu Ohka RC	4.00
113	Geraldo Guzman RC	4.00
114	Scott Downs RC	4.00
115	Timoniel Perez RC	4.00
116	Chad Durbin RC	4.00
117	Sun-Woo Kim RC	4.00
118	Tomas de la Rosa RC	4.00
119	Javier Cardona RC	4.00

120	Kazuhiro Sasaki RC	6.00
121	Brad Cresse RC (Rookie Jersey Gems)	5.00
122	Matt Wheatland RC (Rookie Jersey Gems)	5.00
123	Joe Torres RC (Rookie Jersey Gems)	5.00
124	Dave Krynzel RC (Rookie Jersey Gems)	5.00
125	Ben Diggins RC (Rookie Jersey Gems)	8.00
126	Sean Burnett RC (Rookie Jersey Gems)	5.00
127	David Espinosa RC (Rookie Jersey Gems)	5.00
128	Scott Heard RC (Rookie Jersey Gems)	5.00
129	Daylan Holt RC (Rookie Jersey Gems)	5.00
130	Koyie Hill RC (Rookie Jersey Gems)	5.00
131	Mark Buehrle RC (Rookie Jersey Gems)	15.00
132	Xavier Nady RC (Rookie Jersey Gems)	8.00
133	Mike Tonis RC (Rookie Jersey Gems)	5.00
134	Matt Ginter RC (Rookie Jersey Gems)	5.00
135	Lorenzo Barcelo RC (Rookie Jersey Gems)	5.00
136	Cory Vance RC (Rookie Jersey Gems)	5.00
137	Sean Burroughs (USA Authentics)	8.00
138	Todd Williams (USA Authentics)	5.00
139	Brad Wilkerson RC (USA Authentics)	5.00
140	Ben Sheets RC (USA Authentics)	20.00
141	Kurt Ainsworth RC (USA Authentics)	8.00
142	Anthony Sanders (USA Authentics)	5.00
143	Ryan Franklin (USA Authentics)	5.00
144	Shane Heams RC (USA Authentics)	5.00
145	Roy Oswalt RC (USA Authentics)	20.00
146	Jon Rauch RC (USA Authentics)	5.00
147	Brent Abernathy RC (USA Authentics)	5.00
148	Ernie Young (USA Authentics)	5.00
149	Chris George RC (USA Authentics)	5.00
150	Gookie Dawkins (USA Authentics)	5.00
151	Adam Everett (USA Authentics)	5.00
152	John Cotton RC (USA Authentics)	5.00
153	Pat Borders (USA Authentics)	5.00
154	Doug Mientkiewicz (USA Authentics)	5.00

Rookie Edition Authentics

		NM/M
Jeter Authentic Pinstripes		
APJ	Derek Jeter/Jsy/1,000	35.00
APB	Derek Jeter/Bat/1,000	35.00
APC	Derek Jeter/Cap/200	70.00
APG	Derek Jeter/Glv/200	80.00

Combos

	NM/M
Random game-used inserts. 25 produced of each combo bat. 100 produced of combo jersey.	
JDM	Derek Jeter, Joe DiMaggio, Mickey Mantle/Bat	925.00
JWO	Derek Jeter, Bernie Williams, Paul O'Neill/Jsy	150.00

Rookie Editon Diamonation

		NM/M
Complete Set (9):		10.00
Common Player:		.50
Inserted 1:12		
1	Pedro J. Martinez	1.00
2	Derek Jeter	2.50
3	Jason Giambi	1.00
4	Todd Helton	.75
5	Nomar Garciaparra	2.50
6	Randy Johnson	

7	Jeff Bagwell	.75
8	Cal Ripken Jr.	3.00
9	Ivan Rodriguez	.50

Gallery

		NM/M
Complete Set (6):		10.00
Common Player:		1.00
Inserted 1:20		
1	Sammy Sosa	2.00
2	Barry Bonds	3.00
3	Vladimir Guerrero	1.00
4	Cal Ripken Jr.	3.00
5	Mike Piazza	1.50
6	Mark McGwire	2.00

Might

		NM/M
Complete Set (9):		10.00
Common Player:		.50
Inserted 1:12		
1	Mark McGwire	2.50
2	Mike Piazza	1.50
3	Frank Thomas	.75
4	Ken Griffey Jr.	1.50
5	Sammy Sosa	2.00
6	Alex Rodriguez	2.50
7	Carlos Delgado	.50
8	Vladimir Guerrero	1.00
9	Barry Bonds	3.00

Skills

		NM/M
Complete Set (6):		8.00
Common Player:		.75
Inserted 1:20		
1	Alex Rodriguez	2.50
2	Chipper Jones	1.50
3	Ken Griffey Jr.	1.00
4	Pedro J. Martinez	1.00
5	Ivan Rodriguez	.75
6	Derek Jeter	2.50

Brooklyn Dodgers Master Collection

Following on the success of its Yankees Master Collection, UD produced a more limited edition set featuring the Brooklyn Dodgers. Only 250 numbered boxed sets were produced. Each set includes 15 base cards, 11 Legends of Flatbush memorabilia/autograph cards and a mystery pack containing a premium memorabilia/autograph card. The set concentrates on Dodgers of the 1950s, along with Zach Wheat. The set was issued in a laser-engraved wooden box.

	NM/M
Complete Unopened Set:	1,250
Complete Opened Set:	800.00

Brooklyn Dodgers Master Collection Base Set

Portrait and action photos are combined on a horizontal format for the base cards in the Dodgers Masters Collection. Cards are numbered on back with a "BD" prefix.

		NM/M
Complete Set (15):		230.00
Common Player:		10.00
1	Jackie Robinson	50.00
2	Duke Snider	25.00
3	Pee Wee Reese	25.00
4	Gil Hodges	25.00
5	Carl Furillo	15.00
6	Don Newcombe	10.00
7	Sandy Koufax	50.00
8	Roy Campanella	25.00
9	Jim Gilliam	10.00
10	Don Drysdale	20.00
11	Sandy Amoros	10.00
12	Joe Black	10.00
13	Carl Erskine	10.00
14	Johnny Podres	10.00
15	Zack Wheat	10.00

Brooklyn Dodgers Master Collection Legends

The "Legends of Flatbush" are remembered in this series of memorabilia cards inserted into each Dodgers Master Collection. Each card's number has a "LOF" prefix.

		NM/M
Complete Set (11):		800.00
Common Player:		20.00
1	Gil Hodges/Bat	35.00
2	Jackie Robinson/Bat	100.00
3	Pee Wee Reese/Bat	30.00
4	Jim Gilliam/Bat	20.00
5	Roy Campanella/Bat	20.00
6	Zack Wheat/Bat	20.00
7	Carl Furillo/Bat	20.00
8	Don Newcombe/Bat/Auto.	40.00
9	Duke Snider/Bat/Auto.	80.00
10	Don Drysdale/Jsy	40.00
11	Sandy Koufax/Jsy/Auto.	650.00

Brooklyn Dodgers Master Collection Mystery Pack

Each of the Master Collection sets included a sealed mystery pack containing a premium autograph/memorabilia card. Numbers produced are indicated where known.

	NM/M
Values Undetermined	

JR-BC	Jackie Robinson/Bat/Cut Sig/5	3,500
PW-BC	Pee Wee Reese/Bat/Cut Sig/8	325.00

2000 Upper Deck Gold Reserve

Gold Reserve is primarily a retail product that has virtually the same design as regular 2000 Upper Deck base cards. The set consists of 300-cards each with the Upper Deck logo and the featured player's last name stamped in gold foil. Above the player name "Gold Reserve" is stamped in gold foil. The Fantastic Finds subset (268-297) are serial stamped within an edition of 2,500 for each of the subset cards.

		NM/M
Complete Set (300):		75.00
Common Player:		.15
Common 268-297:		3.00
Production 2,500 Sets		
Pack (10):		2.00
Box (24):		40.00
1	Mo Vaughn	.20
2	Darin Erstad	.25
3	Garret Anderson	.25
4	Troy Glaus	.50
5	Troy Percival	.15
6	Kent Bottenfield	.15
7	Orlando Palmeiro	.15
8	Tim Salmon	.25
9	Jason Giambi	.75
10	Eric Chavez	.25
11	Matt Stairs	.15
12	Miguel Tejada	.40
13	Tim Hudson	.25
14	John Jaha	.15
15	Ben Grieve	.15
16	Kevin Appier	.15
17	David Wells	.15
18	Jose Cruz Jr.	.15
19	Homer Bush	.15
20	Shannon Stewart	.15
21	Carlos Delgado	.50
22	Roy Halladay	.25
23	Tony Batista	.15
24	Raul Mondesi	.25
25	Fred McGriff	.25
26	Jose Canseco	.40
27	Roberto Hernandez	.15
28	Vinny Castilla	.15
29	Gerald Williams	.15
30	Ryan Rupe	.15
31	Greg Vaughn	.15
32	Miguel Cairo	.15
33	Roberto Alomar	.40
34	Jim Thome	.50
35	Bartolo Colon	.15
36	Omar Vizquel	.25
37	Manny Ramirez	.50
38	Chuck Finley	.15
39	Travis Fryman	.25
40	Kenny Lofton	.25
41	Richie Sexson	.40
42	Charles Nagy	.15
43	John Halama	.15
44	David Bell	.15
45	Jay Buhner	.15
46	Edgar Martinez	.25
47	Alex Rodriguez	1.50
48	Fred Garcia	.15
49	Aaron Sele	.15
50	Jamie Moyer	.15
51	Mike Cameron	.15
52	Albert Belle	.20
53	Jerry Hairston Jr.	.15
54	Sidney Ponson	.15
55	Cal Ripken Jr.	2.00
56	Mike Mussina	.40
57	B.J. Surhoff	.15
58	Brady Anderson	.15
59	Mike Bordick	.15
60	Ivan Rodriguez	.40
61	Rusty Greer	.15
62	Rafael Palmeiro	.40
63	John Wetteland	.15
64	Ruben Mateo	.15
65	Gabe Kapler	.15
66	David Segui	.15
67	Justin Thompson	.15
68	Rick Helling	.15

69	Jose Offerman	.15
70	Trot Nixon	.15
71	Pedro Martinez	.75
72	Jason Varitek	.15
73	Troy O'Leary	.15
74	Nomar Garciaparra	1.50
75	Carl Everett	.15
76	Wilton Veras	.15
77	Tim Wakefield	.15
78	Ramon Martinez	.15
79	Johnny Damon	.25
80	Mike Sweeney	.15
81	Rey Sanchez	.15
82	Carlos Beltran	.25
83	Carlos Febles	.15
84	Jermaine Dye	.15
85	Joe Randa	.15
86	Jose Rosado	.15
87	Jeff Suppan	.15
88	Juan Encarnacion	.15
89	Damion Easley	.15
90	Brad Ausmus	.15
91	Todd Jones	.15
92	Juan Gonzalez	.50
93	Bobby Higginson	.15
94	Tony Clark	.15
95	Brian Moehler	.15
96	Dean Palmer	.15
97	Joe Mays	.15
98	Eric Milton	.15
99	Corey Koskie	.15
100	Ron Coomer	.15
101	Brad Radke	.15
102	Todd Walker	.15
103	Butch Huskey	.15
104	Jacque Jones	.15
105	Frank Thomas	.50
106	Mike Sirotka	.15
107	Carlos Lee	.15
108	Ray Durham	.15
109	Bob Howry	.15
110	Magglio Ordonez	.25
111	Paul Konerko	.15
112	Chris Singleton	.15
113	James Baldwin	.15
114	Derek Jeter	2.00
115	Tino Martinez	.25
116	Orlando Hernandez	.25
117	Chuck Knoblauch	.15
118	Bernie Williams	.25
119	David Cone	.15
120	Paul O'Neill	.25
121	Roger Clemens	1.25
122	Mariano Rivera	.25
123	Ricky Ledee	.15
124	Richard Hidalgo	.25
125	Jeff Bagwell	.50
126	Jose Lima	.15
127	Billy Wagner	.15
128	Shane Reynolds	.15
129	Moises Alou	.25
130	Craig Biggio	.25
131	Roger Cedeno	.15
132	Octavio Dotel	.15
133	Greg Maddux	1.00
134	Brian Jordan	.15
135	Kevin Millwood	.25
136	Javy Lopez	.25
137	Bruce Chen	.15
138	Chipper Jones	1.00
139	Tom Glavine	.40
140	Andruw Jones	.40
141	Andres Galarraga	.25
142	Reggie Sanders	.15
143	Geoff Jenkins	.25
144	Jeromy Burnitz	.15
145	Ron Belliard	.15
146	Mark Loretta	.15
147	Steve Woodard	.15
148	Marquis Grissom	.15
149	Bob Wickman	.15
150	Mark McGwire	1.50
151	Fernando Tatis	.15
152	Edgar Renteria	.15
153	J.D. Drew	.25
154	Ray Lankford	.15
155	Fernando Vina	.15
156	Pat Hentgen	.15
157	Jim Edmonds	.25
158	Mark Grace	.25
159	Kerry Wood	.40
160	Eric Young	.15
161	Ismael Valdes	.15
162	Sammy Sosa	1.25
163	Henry Rodriguez	.15
164	Kyle Farnsworth	.15
165	Glenallen Hill	.15
166	Jon Lieber	.15
167	Luis Gonzalez	.25
168	Tony Womack	.15
169	Omar Daal	.15
170	Randy Johnson	.75
171	Erubiel Durazo	.15
172	Jay Bell	.15
173	Steve Finley	.15
174	Travis Lee	.15
175	Matt Williams	.25
176	Matt Mantei	.15
177	Adrian Beltre	.25
178	Kevin Brown	.25
179	Chan Ho Park	.15
180	Mark Grudzielanek	.15
181	Jeff Shaw	.15
182	Shawn Green	.25
183	Gary Sheffield	.40
184	Todd Hundley	.15
185	Eric Karros	.25
186	Kevin Elster	.15

187	Vladimir Guerrero	.75
188	Michael Barrett	.15
189	Chris Widger	.15
190	Ugueth Urbina	.15
191	Dustin Hermanson	.15
192	Rondell White	.15
193	Jose Vidro	.15
194	Hideki Irabu	.15
195	Lee Stevens	.15
196	Livan Hernandez	.15
197	Ellis Burks	.15
198	J.T. Snow	.15
199	Jeff Kent	.25
201	Robb Nen	.15
202	Marvin Benard	.15
202	Barry Bonds	1.50
203	Russ Ortiz	.15
204	Rich Aurilia	.15
205	Joe Nathan	.15
206	Preston Wilson	.25
207	Cliff Floyd	.15
208	Mike Lowell	.15
209	Ryan Dempster	.15
210	Luis Castillo	.15
211	Alex Fernandez	.15
212	Mark Kotsay	.15
213	Brant Brown	.15
214	Edgardo Alfonzo	.15
215	Robin Ventura	.25
216	Rickey Henderson	.25
217	Mike Hampton	.15
218	Mike Piazza	1.00
219	Al Leiter	.15
220	Derek Bell	.15
221	Armando Benitez	.15
222	Rey Ordonez	.15
223	Todd Zeile	.15
224	Tony Gwynn	.75
225	Eric Owens	.15
226	Damian Jackson	.15
227	Trevor Hoffman	.15
228	Ben Davis	.15
229	Sterling Hitchcock	.15
230	Ruben Rivera	.15
231	Ryan Klesko	.25
232	Phil Nevin	.15
233	Mike Lieberthal	.15
234	Bobby Abreu	.25
235	Doug Glanville	.15
236	Rico Brogna	.15
237	Scott Rolen	.50
238	Andy Ashby	.15
239	Robert Person	.15
240	Curt Schilling	.25
241	Mike Jackson	.15
242	Warren Morris	.15
243	Kris Benson	.15
244	Kevin Young	.15
245	Brian Giles	.25
246	Jason Schmidt	.15
247	Jason Kendall	.25
248	Todd Ritchie	.15
249	Wil Cordero	.15
250	Aramis Ramirez	.15
251	Sean Casey	.25
252	Barry Larkin	.25
253	Pokey Reese	.15
254	Scott Williamson	.15
255	Aaron Boone	.25
256	Dante Bichette	.15
257	Ken Griffey Jr.	1.00
258	Denny Neagle	.15
259	Dmitri Young	.15
260	Todd Helton	.50
261	Larry Walker	.25
262	Pedro Astacio	.15
263	Neifi Perez	.15
264	Jeff Cirillo	.15
265	Jeffrey Hammonds	.15
266	Tom Goodwin	.15
267	Rolando Arrojo	.15
268	Rick Ankiel (Fantastic Finds)	3.00
269	Pat Burrell (Fantastic Finds)	4.00
270	Eric Munson (Fantastic Finds)	3.00
271	Rafael Furcal (Fantastic Finds)	5.00
272	Brad Penny (Fantastic Finds)	3.00
273	Adam Kennedy (Fantastic Finds)	3.00
274	Mike Lamb **RC** (Fantastic Finds)	3.00
275	Matt Riley (Fantastic Finds)	3.00
276	Eric Gagne (Fantastic Finds)	5.00
277	Kazuhiro Sasaki **RC** (Fantastic Finds)	3.00
278	Julio Lugo (Fantastic Finds)	3.00
279	Kip Wells (Fantastic Finds)	3.00
280	Danys Baez **RC** (Fantastic Finds)	3.00
281	Josh Beckett (Fantastic Finds)	4.00
282	Alfonso Soriano (Fantastic Finds)	4.00
283	Vernon Wells (Fantastic Finds)	3.00
284	Nick Johnson (Fantastic Finds)	3.00
285	Ramon Ortiz (Fantastic Finds)	3.00

286	Peter Bergeron (Fantastic Finds)	3.00
287	Wascar Serrano **RC** (Fantastic Finds)	3.00
288	Josh Paul (Fantastic Finds)	3.00
289	Mark Quinn (Fantastic Finds)	3.00
290	Jason Marquis (Fantastic Finds)	3.00
291	Rob Bell (Fantastic Finds)	3.00
292	Pablo Ozuna (Fantastic Finds)	3.00
293	Milton Bradley (Fantastic Finds)	3.00
294	Roosevelt Brown (Fantastic Finds)	3.00
295	Terrence Long (Fantastic Finds)	3.00
296	Chad Durbin **RC** (Fantastic Finds)	3.00
297	Matt LeCroy (Fantastic Finds)	3.00
298	Ken Griffey Jr. (Checklist)	.50
299	Mark McGwire (Checklist)	.75
300	Derek Jeter (Checklist)	1.00

Game-Used Ball

		NM/M
Common Player:		10.00
Inserted 1:480		
JB	Jeff Bagwell	25.00
BB	Barry Bonds	70.00
SC	Sean Casey	10.00
RC	Roger Clemens	35.00
NG	Nomar Garciaparra	40.00
SG	Shawn Green	10.00
KG	Ken Griffey Jr.	30.00
TG	Tony Gwynn	25.00
DJ	Derek Jeter	60.00
AJ	Andruw Jones	15.00
CJ	Chipper Jones	30.00
GM	Greg Maddux	30.00
MM	Mark McGwire	60.00
MP	Mike Piazza	30.00
MR	Manny Ramirez	15.00
IR	Ivan Rodriguez	15.00
SR	Scott Rolen	10.00
GS	Gary Sheffield	10.00
SS	Sammy Sosa	30.00
BW	Bernie Williams	10.00

Setting the Standard

This 15-card set spotlights the top hitters and are inserted 1:11 packs. Card fronts feature gold foil stamping and card backs are numbered with an "S" prefix.

		NM/M
Complete Set (15):		25.00
Common Player:		.50
Inserted 1:11		
1	Tony Gwynn	1.50
2	Manny Ramirez	1.00
3	Derek Jeter	3.00
4	Cal Ripken Jr.	4.00
5	Mo Vaughn	.50
6	Jose Canseco	.75
7	Barry Bonds	4.00
8	Nomar Garciaparra	3.00
9	Juan Gonzalez	1.00
10	Mark McGwire	3.00
11	Alex Rodriguez	3.00
12	Jeff Bagwell	1.00
13	Ken Griffey Jr.	2.00
14	Frank Thomas	1.00
15	Sammy Sosa	2.50

Solid Gold Gallery

This 12-card set features close-up shots of the featured player accentuated by gold foil

		NM/M
10	Chipper Jones	2.00
11	Carlos Delgado	1.00
12	Alex Rodriguez	3.00
13	Randy Johnson	1.50
14	Tony Gwynn	1.50
15	Shawn Green	.75

3,000 Hit Club

This on-going cross brand insert series features Al Kaline. Each card features a piece of Kaline's game-used bat, he also signed six cards.

		NM/M
AK-B	Al Kaline/Bat/400	20.00

2000 Upper Deck Hitter's Club

The 90-card base set includes only hitters and features past and current stars. The base set consists of 50 regular cards, 25 Why 3K?, and 15 Hitting the Show subset cards. Card backs of the 50 regular cards have complete year-by-year statistics.

		NM/M
Complete Set (90):		20.00
Common Player:		.15
Pack (5):		1.50
Wax Box (24):		25.00
1	Mo Vaughn	.20
2	Troy Glaus	.40
3	Jeff Bagwell	.50
4	Craig Biggio	.25
5	Jason Giambi	.75
6	Eric Chavez	.25
7	Carlos Delgado	.50
8	Chipper Jones	1.00
9	Andruw Jones	.50
10	Andres Galarraga	.20
11	Jeromy Burnitz	.15
12	Mark McGwire	1.50
13	Mark Grace	.25
14	Sammy Sosa	1.25
15	Jose Canseco	.40
16	Vinny Castilla	.15
17	Matt Williams	.25
18	Gary Sheffield	.25
19	Shawn Green	.25
20	Vladimir Guerrero	.50
21	Barry Bonds	1.50
22	Manny Ramirez	.50
23	Roberto Alomar	.40
24	Jim Thome	.50
25	Ken Griffey Jr.	1.00
26	Alex Rodriguez	1.50
27	Edgar Martinez	.15
28	Preston Wilson	.25
29	Mike Piazza	1.00
30	Robin Ventura	.25
31	Albert Belle	.20
32	Cal Ripken Jr.	2.00
33	Tony Gwynn	.75
34	Scott Rolen	.50
35	Bob Abreu	.25
36	Brian Giles	.25
37	Ivan Rodriguez	.40
38	Rafael Palmeiro	.40
39	Nomar Garciaparra	1.50
40	Sean Casey	.20
41	Larry Walker	.25
42	Todd Helton	.25
43	Carlos Beltran	.25
44	Dean Palmer	.15
45	Juan Gonzalez	.50
46	Corey Koskie	.15
47	Frank Thomas	.50
48	Magglio Ordonez	.25
49	Derek Jeter	2.00
50	Bernie Williams	.40
51	Paul Waner (Why 3k?)	.25
52	Honus Wagner (Why 3k?)	.50
53	Tris Speaker (Why 3k?)	.25
54	Nap Lajoie (Why 3k?)	.25
55	Eddie Collins (Why 3k?)	.25
56	Roberto Clemente (Why 3k?)	1.00
57	Ty Cobb (Why 3k?)	1.50
58	Cap Anson (Why 3k?)	.50
59	Robin Yount (Why 3k?)	.50
60	Carl Yastrzemski (Why 3k?)	.50
61	Dave Winfield (Why 3k?)	.25
62	Stan Musial (Why 3k?)	1.00

UD Authentics

		NM/M
Inserted 1:480		
CB	Carlos Beltran	40.00
JC	Jose Canseco	35.00
SG	Shawn Green	20.00
TG	Tony Gwynn	30.00
CJ	Chipper Jones	60.00
MR	Manny Ramirez	25.00
CR	Cal Ripken Jr.	100.00
AR	Alex Rodriguez	80.00
IR	Ivan Rodriguez	20.00

UD Authentics Gold

Values Undetermined

24-Karat Gems

This 15-card set features gold foil stamping on the front and are numbered on the back with a "K" prefix. They are found on the average of 1:7 packs.

		NM/M
Complete Set (15):		12.00
Common Player:		.50
Inserted 1:7		
1	Pedro Martinez	1.50
2	Scott Rolen	1.00
3	Jason Giambi	1.50
4	Jeromy Burnitz	.50
5	Rafael Palmeiro	1.00
6	Rick Ankiel	.50
7	Carlos Beltran	.75
8	Derek Jeter	3.00
9	Jason Kendall	.50

		NM/M
63	Eddie Murray (Why 3k?)	.40
64	Paul Molitor (Why 3k?)	.50
65	Willie Mays (Why 3k?)	1.50
66	Al Kaline (Why 3k?)	.50
67	Tony Gwynn (Why 3k?)	.75
68	Rod Carew (Why 3k?)	.40
69	Lou Brock (Why 3k?)	.25
70	George Brett (Why 3k?)	1.00
71	Wade Boggs (Why 3k?)	.25
72	Hank Aaron (Why 3k?)	1.50
73	Jorge Luis Toca (Hitting the Show)	.15
74	J.D. Drew (Hitting the Show)	.15
75	Pat Burrell (Hitting the Show)	.25
76	Vernon Wells (Hitting the Show)	.25
77	Julio Ramirez (Hitting the Show)	.15
78	Gabe Kapler (Hitting the Show)	.15
79	Erubiel Durazo (Hitting the Show)	.15
80	Lance Berkman (Hitting the Show)	.25
81	Peter Bergeron (Hitting the Show)	.15
82	Alfonso Soriano (Hitting the Show)	.75
83	Jacque Jones (Hitting the Show)	.15
84	Ben Petrick (Hitting the Show)	.15
85	Jerry Hairston Jr. (Hitting the Show)	.15
86	Kevin Witt (Hitting the Show)	.15
87	Dermal Brown (Hitting the Show)	.15
88	Chad Hermansen (Hitting the Show)	.15
89	Ruben Mateo (Hitting the Show)	.15
90	Checklist (Ken Griffey Jr.)	.50

Accolades

These inserts have a full foiled front with gold foil stamping. Card backs are numbered with an "A" prefix and are seeded 1:11 packs.

		NM/M
Complete Set (10):		12.00
Common Player:		.75
Inserted 1:11		
1	Robin Yount	1.00
2	Tony Gwynn	1.00
3	Sammy Sosa	2.00
4	Mike Piazza	1.50
5	Cal Ripken Jr.	3.00
6	Mark McGwire	2.50
7	Barry Bonds	2.50
8	Wade Boggs	.75
9	Ken Griffey Jr.	1.50
10	Willie Mays	2.00

Autographs

Former and current players are featured in this signature set, which are seeded 1:215 packs. Card backs are numbered with the featured player's initials.

		NM/M
Common Player:		15.00
Inserted 1:215		
HA	Hank Aaron #44	275.00

		NM/M
WB	Wade Boggs #12	30.00
GB	George Brett #5	80.00
Lou	Lou Brock #20	15.00
Rod	Rod Carew #29	15.00
TG	Tony Gwynn #19	40.00
Al	Al Kaline #6	30.00
WM	Willie Mays #24	150.00
PM	Paul Molitor #4	30.00
EM	Eddie Murray #33	30.00
Man	Stan Musial #6	75.00
Cal	Cal Ripken Jr. #8	150.00
DW	Dave Winfield #31	20.00
Yaz	Carl Yastrzemski #7	60.00
RY	Robin Yount #19	40.00

Epic Performances

This 10-card set (#EP2 was not issued) showcases some of baseball's top performances on a fully foiled card front with gold-foil stamping. Card backs are numbered with an "EP" prefix.

		NM/M
Complete Set (10):		12.00
Common Player:		1.00
Inserted 1:3		
2	Mark McGwire	2.50
3	Sammy Sosa	2.00
4	Ken Griffey Jr.	1.50
5	Carl Yastrzemski	1.00
6	Tony Gwynn	1.00
7	Nomar Garciaparra	2.50
8	Cal Ripken Jr.	3.00
9	George Brett	1.50
10	Hank Aaron	2.00
11	Wade Boggs	1.00

Eternals

These inserts were printed on a fully foiled front with "Eternals" printed a number of times in the background. The player name and Upper Deck logo are stamped in gold foil at bottom. Card backs are numbered with an "E" prefix.

		NM/M
Complete Set (10):		20.00
Common Player:		1.00
Inserted 1:23		
1	Cal Ripken Jr.	4.00
2	Mark McGwire	3.00
3	Ken Griffey Jr.	2.00
4	Nomar Garciaparra	3.00
5	Tony Gwynn	1.50
6	Derek Jeter	3.00
7	Jose Canseco	1.00
8	Mike Piazza	2.00
9	Alex Rodriguez	3.00
10	Barry Bonds	4.00

Generations of Excellence

This 10-card insert set features two players who are linked either by team or position. Gold-foil stamping is used throughout. Card backs are numbered with a "GE" prefix.

		NM/M
Complete Set (10):		15.00
Common Player:		1.00
Inserted 1:6		
1	Cal Ripken Jr., Eddie Murray	3.00

		NM/M
2	Vladimir Guerrero, Roberto Clemente	2.00
3	George Brett, Robin Yount	2.00
4	Barry Bonds, Willie Mays	3.00
5	Chipper Jones, Hank Aaron	2.00
6	Mark McGwire, Sammy Sosa	2.00
7	Tony Gwynn, Wade Boggs	1.00
8	Rickey Henderson, Lou Brock	1.00
9	Derek Jeter, Nomar Garciaparra	3.00
10	Alex Rodriguez, Ken Griffey Jr.	2.50

On Target

This 10-card set is printed on a full foiled front with silver foil stamping. Card backs are numbered with an "OT" prefix and are seeded 1:23 packs.

		NM/M
Complete Set (10):		12.00
Common Player:		.50
Inserted 1:23		
1	Nomar Garciaparra	3.00
2	Sean Casey	.50
3	Alex Rodriguez	3.00
4	Troy Glaus	1.00
5	Ivan Rodriguez	1.00
6	Chipper Jones	2.00
7	Manny Ramirez	1.00
8	Derek Jeter	3.00
9	Vladimir Guerrero	1.00
10	Scott Rolen	1.00

The Hitters' Club

These inserts are seeded 1:95 packs and are numbered on the back with an "HC" prefix.

		NM/M
Complete Set (10):		60.00
Common Player:		3.00
1	Rod Carew	5.00
2	Alex Rodriguez	15.00
3	Willie Mays	10.00
4	George Brett	10.00
5	Tony Gwynn	8.00
6	Stan Musial	8.00
7	Frank Thomas	5.00
8	Wade Boggs	3.00
9	Larry Walker	3.00
10	Nomar Garciaparra	15.00

3,000 Hit Club

Upper Deck's cross brand series pays tribute to players who have reached 3,000 hits. Hitter's Club features Wade Boggs and Tony Gwynn inserts with Bat, Bat and Cap and Autographed versions randomly inserted.

stamping. Card backs are numbered with a "G" prefix, these were seeded 1:13 packs.

		NM/M
Complete Set (12):		20.00
Common Player:		1.00
Inserted 1:13		
1	Ken Griffey Jr.	2.00
2	Alex Rodriguez	3.00
3	Mike Piazza	2.00
4	Sammy Sosa	2.50
5	Derek Jeter	3.00
6	Jeff Bagwell	1.00
7	Mark McGwire	3.00
8	Cal Ripken Jr.	4.00
9	Pedro Martinez	1.50
10	Chipper Jones	2.00
11	Ivan Rodriguez	1.00
12	Vladimir Guerrero	1.00

2000 Upper Deck HoloGrFX

The base set consists of 90-cards on a horizontal format. The cards have a holo-foil front utilizing HoloGrFX technology.

		NM/M
Complete Set (90):		20.00
Common Player:		.15
Pack (4):		1.50
Wax Box (32):		25.00
1	Mo Vaughn	.20
2	Troy Glaus	.50
3	Daryle Ward	.15
4	Jeff Bagwell	.50
5	Craig Biggio	.25
6	Jose Lima	.15
7	Jason Giambi	.75
8	Eric Chavez	.25
9	Tim Hudson	.25
10	Raul Mondesi	.25
11	Carlos Delgado	.50
12	David Wells	.15
13	Chipper Jones	1.00
14	Greg Maddux	1.00
15	Andruw Jones	.50
16	Brian Jordan	.15
17	Jeromy Burnitz	.15
18	Ron Belliard	.15
19	Mark McGwire	1.50
20	Fernando Tatis	.15
21	J.D. Drew	.25
22	Sammy Sosa	1.00
23	Mark Grace	.40
24	Greg Vaughn	.15
25	Jose Canseco	.40
26	Vinny Castilla	.15
27	Fred McGriff	.25
28	Matt Williams	.25
29	Randy Johnson	.75
30	Erubiel Durazo	.15
31	Shawn Green	.25
32	Gary Sheffield	.25
33	Kevin Brown	.15
34	Vladimir Guerrero	.50
35	Michael Barrett	.15
36	Russ Ortiz	.15
37	Barry Bonds	1.50
38	Jeff Kent	.25
39	Kenny Lofton	.25
40	Manny Ramirez	.50
41	Roberto Alomar	.40
42	Richie Sexson	.25
43	Edgar Martinez	.25
44	Alex Rodriguez	1.50
45	Fred Garcia	.15
46	Preston Wilson	.15
47	Alex Gonzalez	.15
48	Mike Hampton	.15
49	Mike Piazza	1.00
50	Robin Ventura	.25
51	Edgardo Alfonzo	.15
52	Albert Belle	.15
53	Cal Ripken Jr.	2.00
54	B.J. Surhoff	.15
55	Tony Gwynn	.75
56	Trevor Hoffman	.15
57	Mike Lieberthal	.15
58	Scott Rolen	.25
59	Bob Abreu	.25
60	Curt Schilling	.40
61	Jason Kendall	.25
62	Brian Giles	.25
63	Kris Benson	.15
64	Rafael Palmeiro	.40
65	Ivan Rodriguez	.40
66	Gabe Kapler	.40
67	Nomar Garciaparra	1.50
68	Pedro Martinez	.75
69	Troy O'Leary	.15
70	Barry Larkin	.25
71	Dante Bichette	.15
72	Sean Casey	.20
73	Ken Griffey Jr.	1.00
74	Jeff Cirillo	.15
75	Todd Helton	.50
76	Larry Walker	.25
77	Carlos Beltran	.25
78	Jermaine Dye	.15
79	Juan Gonzalez	.50
80	Juan Encarnacion	.15
81	Dean Palmer	.15
82	Corey Koskie	.15
83	Eric Milton	.15
84	Frank Thomas	

		NM/M
Common Player:		25.00
WB	Wade Boggs/Bat/350	25.00
WB	Wade Boggs/Bat & Cap/50	65.00
TG	Tony Gwynn/Bat/350	25.00
TG	Tony Gwynn/Bat & Cap/50	100.00
TG	Tony Gwynn AU/19	550.00
GB	Tony Gwynn, Wade Boggs/Bat/99	85.00

85 Magglio Ordonez .25
86 Carlos Lee .15
87 Derek Jeter 2.00
88 Tino Martinez .25
89 Bernie Williams .50
90 Roger Clemens 1.50

A Piece of the Series

This inserts have a piece of game-used base from a 1999 World Series game embedded. These were inserted at a rate of 1:215 packs.

		NM/M
Common Player:		5.00
Inserted 1:215		
1	Derek Jeter	40.00
2	Chipper Jones	20.00
3	Roger Clemens	30.00
4	Greg Maddux	30.00
5	Bernie Williams	10.00
6	Andruw Jones	10.00
7	Tino Martinez	8.00
8	Brian Jordan	5.00
9	Mariano Rivera	8.00
11	Paul O'Neill	8.00
12	Tom Glavine	10.00

A Piece of Series Autograph

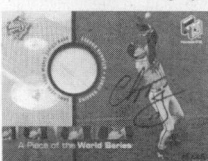

This is an autographed parallel of the Piece of Series insert set that is limited to 25 sets.

		NM/M
Common Player:		40.00
Production 25 Sets		
PSA1	Derek Jeter	300.00
PSA2	Chipper Jones	125.00
PSA3	Roger Clemens	220.00
PSA4	Greg Maddux	220.00
PSA6	Andruw Jones	85.00
PSA7	Tino Martinez	65.00
PSA8	Brian Jordan	40.00
PSA11	Paul O'Neill	75.00
PSA12	Tom Glavine	100.00

Bomb Squad

This set highlights top home run hitters in a horizontal format with complete holo-foiled fronts. Card backs are numbered with a "BS" prefix.

		NM/M
Complete Set (6):		15.00
Common Player:		2.00
Inserted 1:34		
1	Ken Griffey Jr.	2.00
2	Mark McGwire	3.00
3	Chipper Jones	2.00
4	Alex Rodriguez	3.00
5	Sammy Sosa	2.50
6	Barry Bonds	4.00

Future Fame

This six-card set has a horizontal format that is completely holo-foiled with silver foil stamping. Card backs are numbered with an "FF" prefix and seeded 1:34 packs.

		NM/M
Complete Set (6):		10.00
Common Player:		2.00
Inserted 1:34		

1 Cal Ripken Jr. 4.00
2 Mark McGwire 3.00
3 Greg Maddux 2.00
4 Tony Gwynn 1.50
5 Ken Griffey Jr. 2.00
6 Roger Clemens 2.50

Longball Legacy

This 15-card set spotlights the top home run hitters on a horizontal format and completely holo-foiled. Card backs are numbered with an "LL" prefix and seeded 1:6 packs.

		NM/M
Complete Set (15):		15.00
Common Player:		.50
Inserted 1:6		
1	Mike Piazza	2.00
2	Ivan Rodriguez	.75
3	Jeff Bagwell	1.00
4	Alex Rodriguez	3.00
5	Jose Canseco	.75
6	Mark McGwire	3.00
7	Scott Rolen	.75
8	Carlos Delgado	.75
9	Mo Vaughn	.50
10	Manny Ramirez	1.00
11	Matt Williams	.50
12	Sammy Sosa	2.50
13	Ken Griffey Jr.	2.00
14	Nomar Garciaparra	3.00
15	Larry Walker	.50

Stars of the System

This 10-card set features some of baseball's top prospects on a horizontal format. The fronts are completely holo-foiled with silver foil stamping. Card backs are numbered with an "SS" prefix and seeded 1:8 packs.

		NM/M
Complete Set (10):		8.00
Common Player:		.75
Inserted 1:8		
1	Rick Ankiel	.75
2	Alfonso Soriano	2.00
3	Vernon Wells	1.00
4	Ben Petrick	.75
5	Francisco Cordero	.75
6	Matt Riley	.75
7	A.J. Burnett	1.00
8	Pat Burrell	1.50
9	Ed Yarnall	.75
10	Dermal Brown	.75

StarView

This eight-card set features top stars on a horizontal format. Card backs are numbered with an "SV" prefix and inserted 1:11 packs.

		NM/M
Complete Set (8):		15.00
Common Player:		2.00
Inserted 1:11		
1	Ken Griffey Jr.	3.00
2	Nomar Garciaparra	3.00
3	Chipper Jones	2.00
4	Mark McGwire	3.00
5	Sammy Sosa	2.50
6	Derek Jeter	4.00
7	Mike Piazza	3.00
8	Alex Rodriguez	3.00

3,000 Hit Club

Upper Deck pays tribute to members of the 3,000 Hit Club with this cross-brand insert series. Robin Yount and George Brett are featured on a game-used bat card (350 produced), game-used jersey card (350

YOUNT

produced), a bat combo of both players (99 produced) and an autographed combo (10 produced).

		NM/M
Common Card:		20.00
RY	Robin Yount/Bat/350	20.00
RYJ	Robin Yount/Jsy/350	20.00
GB	George Brett/Bat/350	35.00
GBJ	George Brett/Jsy/350	35.00
BY	George Brett, Robin Yount/Bat/99	120.00
BYJ	George Brett, Robin Yount/Jsy/99	120.00

2000 UD Ionix

The base set consists of 90 cards, including a 30-card Futuristics subset that were seeded 1:4 packs. A Reciprocal parallel to the base set are also randomly inserted. The cards can distinguished by a holo-foiled front and the number on the back has an "R" prefix. Reciprocals 1-60 are found 1:4 packs, while Futuristics Reciprocals are found on the average of 1:11 packs.

		NM/M
Complete Set (90):		50.00
Common Player:		.15
Common Futuristic:		.15
Inserted 1:4		
Reciprocal (1-60):		1.5-2X
Reciprocal (61-90):		1-1.5X
Inserted 1:4		
Future Recip. 1:11		
Pack (4):		2.00
Wax Box (24):		35.00
1	Mo Vaughn	.20
2	Troy Glaus	.75
3	Jeff Bagwell	.75
4	Craig Biggio	.40
5	Jose Lima	.15
6	Jason Giambi	1.00
7	Tim Hudson	.40
8	Shawn Green	.50
9	Carlos Delgado	.75
10	Chipper Jones	1.50
11	Andruw Jones	.75
12	Greg Maddux	1.50
13	Jeromy Burnitz	.15
14	Mark McGwire	2.00
15	J.D. Drew	.25
16	Sammy Sosa	2.00
17	Jose Canseco	.50
18	Fred McGriff	.40
19	Randy Johnson	.75
20	Matt Williams	.25
21	Kevin Brown	.40
22	Gary Sheffield	.40
23	Vladimir Guerrero	.75
24	Barry Bonds	2.50
25	Jim Thome	.75
26	Manny Ramirez	.75
27	Roberto Alomar	.50
28	Kenny Lofton	.25
29	Ken Griffey Jr.	1.50
30	Alex Rodriguez	2.50
31	Alex Gonzalez	.15
32	Preston Wilson	.15
33	Mike Piazza	1.50
34	Robin Ventura	.25
35	Cal Ripken Jr.	2.50
36	Albert Belle	.20
37	Tony Gwynn	1.00
38	Scott Rolen	.75
39	Curt Schilling	.50
40	Brian Giles	.25
41	Juan Gonzalez	.75
42	Ivan Rodriguez	.75
43	Rafael Palmeiro	.60
44	Pedro J. Martinez	1.00
45	Nomar Garciaparra	2.00
46	Sean Casey	.25
47	Aaron Boone	.25
48	Barry Larkin	.40
49	Larry Walker	.25
50	Vinny Castilla	.20
51	Carlos Beltran	.25
52	Gabe Kapler	.15
53	Dean Palmer	.15
54	Eric Milton	.15
55	Corey Koskie	.15
56	Frank Thomas	.75
57	Magglio Ordonez	.40
58	Roger Clemens	2.00
59	Bernie Williams	.75
60	Derek Jeter	2.50
61	Josh Beckett (Futuristics)	1.50
62	Eric Munson (Futuristics)	1.00
63	Rick Ankiel (Futuristics)	1.00
64	Matt Riley (Futuristics)	1.00
65	Robert Ramsay (Futuristics)	1.00
66	Vernon Wells (Futuristics)	2.00
67	Eric Gagne (Futuristics)	1.50
68	Robert Fick (Futuristics)	1.00
69	Mark Quinn (Futuristics)	1.00
70	Kip Wells (Futuristics)	1.00
71	Peter Bergeron (Futuristics)	1.00
72	Ed Yarnall (Futuristics)	1.00
73	Jorge Luis Toca (Futuristics)	1.00
74	Alfonso Soriano (Futuristics)	4.00
75	Calvin Murray (Futuristics)	1.00
76	Ramon Ortiz (Futuristics)	1.50
77	Chad Meyers (Futuristics)	1.00
78	Jason LaRue (Futuristics)	1.00
79	Pat Burrell (Futuristics)	2.00
80	Chad Hermansen (Futuristics)	1.00
81	Lance Berkman (Futuristics)	1.50
82	Erubiel Durazo (Futuristics)	1.50
83	Juan Pena (Futuristics)	1.00
84	Adam Kennedy (Futuristics)	1.00
85	Ben Petrick (Futuristics)	1.00
86	Kevin Barker (Futuristics)	1.00
87	Bruce Chen (Futuristics)	1.00
88	Jerry Hairston Jr. (Futuristics)	1.00
89	A.J. Burnett (Futuristics)	1.00
90	Gary Matthews Jr. (Futuristics)	1.00

Atomic

This 15-card insert set has a horizontal format on a holo-foil front. Card backs are numbered with an "A" prefix and are found 1:8 packs.

		NM/M
Complete Set (15):		25.00
Common Player:		1.00
Inserted 1:8		
1	Pedro J. Martinez	1.50
2	Mark McGwire	3.00
3	Ken Griffey Jr.	2.00
4	Jeff Bagwell	1.00
5	Greg Maddux	2.00
6	Derek Jeter	3.00
7	Cal Ripken Jr.	4.00
8	Manny Ramirez	1.00
9	Randy Johnson	1.50
10	Nomar Garciaparra	3.00
11	Tony Gwynn	1.50
12	Bernie Williams	1.00
13	Mike Piazza	2.00
14	Roger Clemens	3.00
15	Alex Rodriguez	3.00

Awesome Powers

The title of this insert set is a takeoff from the Austin Powers movie that was popular at the time of this release. The cards have a holo-foil front with a "groovin" '70s backdrop. Card backs are numbered with an "AP" prefix.

		NM/M
Complete Set (15):		50.00
Common Player:		1.00
Inserted 1:23		
1	Ken Griffey Jr.	4.00
2	Mike Piazza	4.00
3	Carlos Delgado	2.00
4	Mark McGwire	6.00
5	Chipper Jones	4.00
6	Scott Rolen	2.00
7	Cal Ripken Jr.	8.00
8	Alex Rodriguez	6.00
9	Larry Walker	1.00
10	Sammy Sosa	5.00
11	Barry Bonds	6.00
12	Nomar Garciaparra	6.00
13	Jose Canseco	1.50
14	Manny Ramirez	2.00
15	Jeff Bagwell	2.00

BIOrhythm

This 15-card set has a holo-foil front and are seeded 1:11 packs. Card backs have a brief career note and are numbered with a "B" prefix.

		NM/M
Complete Set (15):		25.00
Common Player:		.50
Inserted 1:11		
1	Randy Johnson	1.50
2	Derek Jeter	3.00
3	Sammy Sosa	2.50
4	Jose Lima	.50
5	Chipper Jones	2.00
6	Barry Bonds	4.00
7	Ken Griffey Jr.	2.00
8	Nomar Garciaparra	3.00
9	Frank Thomas	1.00
10	Pedro Martinez	1.50
11	Larry Walker	.50
12	Greg Maddux	2.00
13	Alex Rodriguez	3.00
14	Mark McGwire	3.00
15	Cal Ripken Jr.	4.00

Pyrotechnics

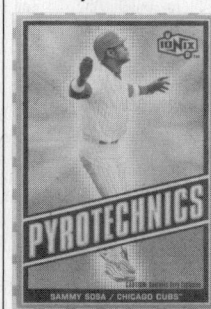

This 15-card set has a holo-foiled front with an insertion ratio of 1:72 packs. Card backs are numbered with a "P" prefix.

		NM/M
Complete Set (15):		125.00
Common Player:		5.00
Inserted 1:72		
1	Roger Clemens	12.00
2	Chipper Jones	10.00
3	Alex Rodriguez	15.00
4	Jeff Bagwell	5.00
5	Mark McGwire	15.00
6	Pedro Martinez	6.00
7	Manny Ramirez	5.00
8	Cal Ripken Jr.	20.00
9	Mike Piazza	10.00
10	Derek Jeter	15.00
11	Ken Griffey Jr.	10.00
12	Frank Thomas	5.00
13	Sammy Sosa	12.00
14	Nomar Garciaparra	15.00
15	Greg Maddux	10.00

Shockwave

Baseball's top hitters are spotlighted on a holo-foil front. They are found on the average of 1:4 packs and are numbered on the card back with an "S" prefix.

		NM/M
Complete Set (15):		15.00
Common Player:		.50
Inserted 1:4		
1	Mark McGwire	2.00
2	Sammy Sosa	2.00
3	Manny Ramirez	1.00
4	Ken Griffey Jr.	1.50
5	Vladimir Guerrero	.75
6	Barry Bonds	2.50
7	Albert Belle	.50
8	Ivan Rodriguez	.75
9	Chipper Jones	1.50
10	Mo Vaughn	.50
11	Jose Canseco	.75
12	Jeff Bagwell	1.00
13	Matt Williams	.50
14	Alex Rodriguez	2.50
15	Carlos Delgado	.75

UD Authentics

These autographed inserts have a horizontal format and are found on the average of 1:144 packs.

		NM/M
Common Player:		10.00
Inserted 1:144		
CBE	Carlos Beltran	30.00
AB	Adrian Beltre	15.00
PB	Pat Burrell	15.00
JC	Jose Canseco	25.00
SC	Sean Casey	15.00
BD	Ben Davis	10.00
SG	Shawn Green	20.00
JR	Ken Griffey Jr.	100.00
VG	Vladimir Guerrero	30.00
DJ	Derek Jeter	100.00
GK	Gabe Kapler	10.00
RM	Ruben Mateo	10.00
RB	Joe McEwing	10.00
MR	Manny Ramirez	35.00
SR	Scott Rolen	30.00
MW	Matt Williams	15.00

Warp Zone

This 15-card set has a holo-foiled front with an insertion ratio of 1:288 packs. Card backs are numbered with a "WZ" prefix.

		NM/M
Complete Set (15):		250.00
Common Player:		8.00
Inserted 1:288		
1	Cal Ripken Jr.	30.00
2	Barry Bonds	30.00

3	Ken Griffey Jr.	20.00
4	Nomar Garciaparra	25.00
5	Chipper Jones	20.00
6	Ivan Rodriguez	8.00
7	Greg Maddux	20.00
8	Derek Jeter	25.00
9	Mike Piazza	20.00
10	Sammy Sosa	20.00
11	Roger Clemens	10.00
12	Alex Rodriguez	25.00
13	Vladimir Guerrero	10.00
14	Pedro Martinez	10.00
15	Mark McGwire	25.00

3,000 Hit Club

Upper Deck's cross-brand insert series paying tribute to baseball's 3,000 Hit Club members spotlights Roberto Clemente in UD Ionix. Three versions were randomly inserted: A game-used bat card, bat/cut signature card and a cut signature card.

| | | NM/M |
| RC1 | Roberto Clemente/ Bat/350 | 125.00 |

2000 Upper Deck Legends

The 135-card base set consists of 90 regular player cards, 30 20th Century Legends (1:5) and 15 Generation Y2K (1:9). The base cards have a full foiled front with silver foil stamping. Card backs have complete year-by-year statistics.

		NM/M
Complete Set (135):		80.00
Common Player:		.15
Common Y2K:		.75
Inserted 1:9		
Common 20th Century Legend		1.00
Inserted 1:5		
Pack (7):		5.00
Box (24):		90.00
1	Darin Erstad	.25
2	Troy Glaus	.75
3	Mo Vaughn	.20
4	Craig Biggio	.25
5	Jeff Bagwell	.75
6	Reggie Jackson	1.00
7	Tim Hudson	.25
8	Jason Giambi	1.00
9	Hank Aaron	2.00
10	Greg Maddux	1.50
11	Chipper Jones	1.50
12	Andres Galarraga	.25
13	Robin Yount	.50
14	Jeromy Burnitz	.15
15	Paul Molitor	.50
16	David Wells	.15
17	Carlos Delgado	.75
18	Ernie Banks	.75
19	Sammy Sosa	2.00
20	Kerry Wood	.40
21	Stan Musial	.75
22	Bob Gibson	.50
23	Mark McGwire	2.00
24	Fernando Tatis	.15
25	Randy Johnson	1.00
26	Matt Williams	.40
27	Jackie Robinson	2.00
28	Sandy Koufax	1.50
29	Shawn Green	.40
30	Kevin Brown	.25
31	Gary Sheffield	.40
32	Greg Vaughn	.15
33	Jose Canseco	.50
34	Gary Carter	.15
35	Vladimir Guerrero	.75
36	Willie Mays	2.00
37	Barry Bonds	2.00
38	Jeff Kent	.25
39	Bob Feller	.40
40	Roberto Alomar	.50

41	Jim Thome	.75
42	Manny Ramirez	.75
43	Alex Rodriguez	2.00
44	Preston Wilson	.15
45	Tom Seaver	.75
46	Robin Ventura	.15
47	Mike Piazza	1.50
48	Mike Hampton	.15
49	Brooks Robinson	.75
50	Frank Robinson	.75
51	Cal Ripken Jr.	2.50
52	Albert Belle	.20
53	Eddie Murray	.40
54	Tony Gwynn	1.00
55	Roberto Clemente	1.50
56	Willie Stargell	.25
57	Brian Giles	.25
58	Jason Kendall	.25
59	Mike Schmidt	1.00
60	Bob Abreu	.25
61	Scott Rolen	.50
62	Curt Schilling	.40
63	Johnny Bench	1.00
64	Sean Casey	.15
65	Barry Larkin	.25
66	Ken Griffey Jr.	1.50
67	George Brett	1.50
68	Carlos Beltran	.15
69	Nolan Ryan	3.00
70	Ivan Rodriguez	.75
71	Rafael Palmeiro	.40
72	Larry Walker	.25
73	Todd Helton	.75
74	Jeff Cirillo	.15
75	Carl Everett	.15
76	Nomar Garciaparra	2.00
77	Pedro Martinez	1.00
78	Harmon Killebrew	.50
79	Corey Koskie	.15
80	Ty Cobb	2.00
81	Dean Palmer	.15
82	Juan Gonzalez	.75
83	Carlton Fisk	.15
84	Frank Thomas	.75
85	Magglio Ordonez	.25
86	Lou Gehrig	2.00
87	Babe Ruth	3.00
88	Derek Jeter	2.50
89	Roger Clemens	1.50
90	Bernie Williams	.50
91	Rick Ankiel (Generation Y2K)	.75
92	Kip Wells (Generation Y2K)	.75
93	Pat Burrell (Generation Y2K)	1.50
94	Mark Quinn (Generation Y2K)	.75
95	Ruben Mateo (Generation Y2K)	.75
96	Adam Kennedy (Generation Y2K)	.75
97	Brad Penny (Generation Y2K)	.75
98	Kazuhiro Sasaki RC (Generation Y2K)	2.00
99	Peter Bergeron (Generation Y2K)	.75
100	Rafael Furcal (Generation Y2K)	1.00
101	Eric Munson (Generation Y2K)	.75
102	Nick Johnson (Generation Y2K)	1.00
103	Rob Bell (Generation Y2K)	.75
104	Vernon Wells (Generation Y2K)	1.00
105	Ben Petrick (Generation Y2K)	.75
106	Babe Ruth (20th Century Legends)	8.00
107	Mark McGwire (20th Century Legends)	6.00
108	Nolan Ryan (20th Century Legends)	8.00
109	Hank Aaron (20th Century Legends)	5.00
110	Barry Bonds (20th Century Legends)	6.00
111	Nomar Garciaparra (20th Century Legends)	5.00
112	Roger Clemens (20th Century Legends)	2.50
113	Johnny Bench (20th Century Legends)	2.50
114	Alex Rodriguez (20th Century Legends)	6.00
115	Cal Ripken Jr. (20th Century Legends)	8.00
116	Willie Mays (20th Century Legends)	6.00
117	Mike Piazza (20th Century Legends)	4.00
118	Reggie Jackson (20th Century Legends)	2.00
119	Tony Gwynn (20th Century Legends)	3.00
120	Cy Young (20th Century Legends)	2.00
121	George Brett (20th Century Legends)	4.00
122	Greg Maddux (20th Century Legends)	4.00
123	Yogi Berra (20th Century Legends)	2.00
124	Sammy Sosa (20th Century Legends)	5.00

125	Randy Johnson (20th Century Legends)	2.50
126	Bob Gibson (20th Century Legends)	2.00
127	Lou Gehrig (20th Century Legends)	6.00
128	Ken Griffey Jr. (20th Century Legends)	4.00
129	Derek Jeter (20th Century Legends)	6.00
130	Mike Schmidt (20th Century Legends)	3.00
131	Pedro Martinez (20th Century Legends)	2.50
132	Jackie Robinson (20th Century Legends)	5.00
133	Jose Canseco (20th Century Legends)	1.00
134	Ty Cobb (20th Century Legends)	5.00
135	Stan Musial (20th Century Legends)	3.00

Gold

Gold graphic enhancements are featured on this parallel edition. On back, a dot-matrix printed "1/1" attests to the status of these cards as unique specimens. Because only one of each card was produced, attaching values can be problematic. Values shown here represent specimens offered at auction shortly after the cards were issued.

		NM/M
Common Player:		75.00
10	Greg Maddux	340.00
13	Robin Yount	450.00
15	Paul Molitor	450.00
31	Gary Sheffield	175.00
36	Willie Mays	1,175
53	Eddie Murray	1,000
82	Juan Gonzalez	230.00
87	Babe Ruth	2,025
89	Roger Clemens	250.00
107	Mark McGwire (20th Century Legends)	1,580
119	Tony Gwynn (20th Century Legends)	190.00
126	Bob Gibson (20th Century Legends)	275.00
130	Mike Schmidt (20th Century Legends)	900.00

Commemorative Collection

A metallized photo background on front distinguishes these 1-of-100 inserts from their base-card parallels. Backs have an ink-jetted serial number from within each card's edition of 100.

Stars (1-90):	4-8X
Y2K:	1-2X
20th Century Legends:	2-3X
Production 100 Sets	

Defining Moments

A 10-card set highlights the featured player's greatest baseball moment with a date stamped in gold foil on the front and a description of the moment

on the back. Card backs are numbered with a "DM" prefix and seeded 1:12 packs.

		NM/M
Complete Set (10):		20.00
Common Player:		1.00
Inserted 1:12		
1	Reggie Jackson	1.50
2	Hank Aaron	3.00
3	Babe Ruth	4.00
4	Cal Ripken Jr.	4.00
5	Carlton Fisk	1.00
6	Ken Griffey Jr.	2.00
7	Nolan Ryan	4.00
8	Roger Clemens	2.50
9	Willie Mays	3.00
10	Mark McGwire	3.00

Eternal Glory

This six-card set has a full holo-foiled front with gold foil stamping. Card backs are numbered with an "EG" prefix and are inserted 1:24 packs.

		NM/M
Complete Set (7):		15.00
Common Player:		2.00
Inserted 1:24		
1	Nolan Ryan	4.00
2	Ken Griffey Jr.	2.00
5	Sammy Sosa	2.50
4	Derek Jeter	4.00
6	Willie Mays	3.00
7	Roger Clemens	3.00

Legendary Jerseys

This game-used memorabilia insert set has a swatch of game-used jersey embedded and were inserted 1:48 packs.

		NM/M
Common Player:		8.00
Inserted 1:48		
HA	Hank Aaron	40.00
JB	Jeff Bagwell	10.00
JB	Johnny Bench	20.00
WB	Wade Boggs	10.00
BaB	Barry Bonds	40.00
BoB	Bobby Bonds	8.00
GB	George Brett	30.00
LB	Lou Brock	8.00
JC	Jose Canseco	10.00
RC	Roger Clemens	30.00
DC	Dave Concepcion	8.00
DD	Don Drysdale	25.00
RF	Rollie Fingers	8.00
LG	Lou Gehrig/Pants	250.00
BG	Bob Gibson/Pants	20.00
KG	Ken Griffey Jr.	35.00
TG	Tony Gwynn	20.00
RJ	Reggie Jackson	10.00
DJ	Derek Jeter	40.00
RaJ	Randy Johnson	20.00
CJ	Chipper Jones	20.00
SK	Sandy Koufax	250.00
SK	Sandy Koufax/Auto./32	1,200
GM	Greg Maddux	30.00
MM	Mickey Mantle	150.00
RM	Roger Maris/Pants	60.00
EM	Eddie Mathews	30.00
WM	Willie Mays/SP/29	675.00
BM	Bill Mazeroski	8.00
WMc	Willie McCovey	10.00
TM	Thurman Munson	30.00
DM	Dale Murphy	10.00
SM	Stan Musial/SP/28	650.00
JP	Jim Palmer	8.00
GP	Gaylord Perry	8.00
MR	Manny Ramirez	10.00
CR	Cal Ripken Jr.	40.00
BR	Brooks Robinson	20.00
FR	Frank Robinson	10.00
AR	Alex Rodriguez	35.00
NR	Nolan Ryan	40.00

MS	Mike Schmidt	25.00
TS	Tom Seaver	20.00
OS	Ozzie Smith	20.00
WS	Willie Stargell	8.00
FT	Frank Thomas	10.00
JT	Joe Torre	8.00
EW	Earl Weaver	8.00
MW	Matt Williams	8.00
MW	Maury Wills	8.00
DW	Dave Winfield	10.00

Legendary Signatures

These autographed inserts are signed in blue Sharpie on the bottom panel. A Gold parallel version is also randomly seeded which has gold-foil stamping and is individually numbered to 50.

		NM/M
Common Player:		8.00
Inserted 1:23		
Golds:		1-2X
Production 50 Sets		
HA	Hank Aaron/SP/94	300.00
JB	Johnny Bench	30.00
BB	Bobby Bonds	8.00
LB	Lou Brock	8.00
GB	George Brett	60.00
JC	Jose Canseco	20.00
GC	Gary Carter	10.00
SC	Sean Casey	8.00
RC	Roger Clemens	80.00
DC	Dave Concepcion	8.00
AD	Andre Dawson	10.00
KG	Ken Griffey Jr.	85.00
VG	Vladimir Guerrero	30.00
TG	Tony Gwynn	40.00
RJ	Reggie Jackson	20.00
DJ	Derek Jeter SP/61	60.00
RaJ	Randy Johnson	50.00
CJ	Chipper Jones	50.00
HK	Harmon Killebrew	25.00
FL	Fred Lynn	8.00
DM	Dale Murphy	15.00
SM	Stan Musial	50.00
PN	Phil Niekro	8.00
JP	Jim Palmer	10.00
MP	Mike Piazza	120.00
MR	Manny Ramirez/SP/141	60.00
CR	Cal Ripken Jr.	120.00
AR	Alex Rodriguez	85.00
IR	Ivan Rodriguez	25.00
NR	Nolan Ryan	85.00
MS	Mike Schmidt	50.00
TS	Tom Seaver	30.00
OS	Ozzie Smith	40.00
WS	Willie Stargell	60.00
FT	Frank Thomas	30.00
AT	Alan Trammell	10.00
BW	Matt Williams	8.00

Ones for the Ages

This seven-card set has a holo-foiled front with gold foil etching and stamping. The player image is in a classic picture framed design. Card backs are numbered with an "O" prefix and seeded 1:24 packs.

		NM/M
Complete Set (7):		15.00
Inserted 1:24		
01	Ty Cobb	2.50
02	Cal Ripken Jr.	4.00
03	Babe Ruth	4.00
04	Jackie Robinson	2.50

05	Mark McGwire	3.00
06	Alex Rodriguez	3.00
07	Mike Piazza	4.00

Reflections in Time

This 10-card horizontal insert set features two players, past and present, linked by significant events or statistics. Card fronts are completely holo-foiled with gold foil stamping. Card backs are numbered with an "R" prefix and inserted 1:12 packs.

		NM/M
Complete Set (10):		25.00
Common Player:		2.00
Inserted 1:12		
1	Ken Griffey Jr., Hank Aaron	3.00
2	Sammy Sosa, Roberto Clemente	3.00
3	Roger Clemens, Nolan Ryan	4.00
4	Ivan Rodriguez, Johnny Bench	2.00
5	Alex Rodriguez, Ernie Banks	3.00
6	Tony Gwynn, Stan Musial	2.00
7	Barry Bonds, Willie Mays	4.00
8	Cal Ripken Jr., Lou Gehrig	4.00
9	Chipper Jones, Mike Schmidt	2.50
10	Mark McGwire, Babe Ruth	4.00

UD Millennium Team

This nine-card set has a complete holo-foiled front with silver foil stamping. The set is Upper Deck's selections for the all-time 20th century team and are inserted 1:4 packs. Card backs are numbered with an "UD" prefix.

		NM/M
Complete Set (10):		15.00
Common Player:		1.50
Inserted 1:4		
1	Mark McGwire	2.00
2	Jackie Robinson	2.00
3	Mike Schmidt	1.50
4	Cal Ripken Jr.	3.00
5	Babe Ruth	3.00
6	Willie Mays	4.00
8	Johnny Bench	1.50
9	Nolan Ryan	3.00
10	Ken Griffey Jr.	1.50

3,000 Hit Club

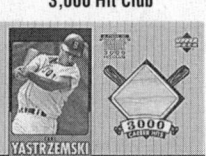

Upper Deck's continuing series pays tribute to Carl Yastrzemski and Paul Molitor. The series includes 350 Bat cards, 350 Jersey cards, 100 Bat/Jersey combo cards and eight autographed Bat/Jersey combo cards from Yastrzemski and 350 Bat cards from Molitor.

		NM/M
CY	Carl Yastrzemski/ Bat/350	30.00
CY	Carl Yastrzemski/ Jsy/350	30.00
CY	Carl Yastrzemski/ Bat/Jsy/100	80.00

2000 Upper Deck MVP

The base set consists of 220 cards with a white bordered design and bronze foil stamping. Card backs have a maximum of 10 year-by-year statistics.

	NM/M
Complete Set (220):	20.00
Common Player:	.10
Pack (10):	1.25
Wax Box (28):	25.00
1	Garret Anderson	.25
2	Mo Vaughn	.15
3	Tim Salmon	.20
4	Ramon Ortiz	.10
5	Darin Erstad	.20
6	Troy Glaus	.50
7	Troy Percival	.10
8	Jeff Bagwell	.50
9	Ken Caminiti	.10
10	Daryle Ward	.10
11	Craig Biggio	.25
12	Jose Lima	.10
13	Moises Alou	.20
14	Octavio Dotel	.10
15	Ben Grieve	.20
16	Jason Giambi	.50
17	Tim Hudson	.20
18	Eric Chavez	.20
19	Matt Stairs	.10
20	Miguel Tejada	.25
21	John Jaha	.10
22	Chipper Jones	1.00
23	Kevin Millwood	.20
24	Brian Jordan	.10
25	Andruw Jones	.25
26	Andres Galarraga	.20
27	Greg Maddux	1.00
28	Reggie Sanders	.10
29	Javy Lopez	.10
30	Jeromy Burnitz	.10
31	Kevin Barker	.10
32	Jose Hernandez	.10
33	Ron Belliard	.10
34	Henry Blanco	.10
35	Marquis Grissom	.10
36	Geoff Jenkins	.20
37	Carlos Delgado	.50
38	Raul Mondesi	.20
39	Roy Halladay	.20
40	Tony Batista	.10
41	David Wells	.10
42	Shannon Stewart	.10
43	Vernon Wells	.20
44	Sammy Sosa	1.00
45	Ismael Valdes	.10
46	Joe Girardi	.10
47	Mark Grace	.20
48	Henry Rodriguez	.10
49	Kerry Wood	.25
50	Eric Young	.10
51	Mark McGwire	2.00
52	Daryle Kile	.10
53	Fernando Vina	.10
54	Ray Lankford	.10
55	J.D. Drew	.20
56	Fernando Tatis	.10
57	Rick Ankiel	.10
58	Matt Williams	.20
59	Erubiel Durazo	.15
60	Tony Womack	.10
61	Jay Bell	.10
62	Randy Johnson	.75
63	Steve Finley	.10
64	Matt Mantei	.10
65	Luis Gonzalez	.20
66	Gary Sheffield	.25
67	Eric Gagne	.10
68	Adrian Beltre	.20
69	Mark Grudzielanek	.10
70	Kevin Brown	.20
71	Chan Ho Park	.10
72	Shawn Green	.40
73	Vinny Castilla	.15
74	Fred McGriff	.20
75	Wilson Alvarez	.10
76	Greg Vaughn	.10
77	Gerald Williams	.10
78	Ryan Rupe	.10
79	Jose Canseco	.25
80	Vladimir Guerrero	.50
81	Dustin Hermanson	.10
82	Michael Barrett	.10
83	Rondell White	.20
84	Tony Armas Jr.	.10
85	Wilton Guerrero	.10

86	Jose Vidro	.10
87	Barry Bonds	1.50
88	Russ Ortiz	.10
89	Ellis Burks	.10
90	Jeff Kent	.20
91	Russ Davis	.10
92	J.T. Snow	.10
93	Roberto Alomar	.40
94	Manny Ramirez	.50
95	Chuck Finley	.10
96	Kenny Lofton	.20
97	Jim Thome	.50
98	Bartolo Colon	.10
99	Omar Vizquel	.20
100	Richie Sexson	.25
101	Mike Cameron	.10
102	Brett Tomko	.10
103	Edgar Martinez	.20
104	Alex Rodriguez	1.50
105	John Olerud	.20
106	Fred Garcia	.10
107	Kazuhiro Sasaki RC	1.00
108	Preston Wilson	.20
109	Luis Castillo	.10
110	A.J. Burnett	.10
111	Mike Lowell	.10
112	Cliff Floyd	.10
113	Brad Penny	.10
114	Alex Gonzalez	.10
115	Mike Piazza	1.00
116	Derek Bell	.10
117	Edgardo Alfonzo	.10
118	Rickey Henderson	.20
119	Todd Zeile	.10
120	Mike Hampton	.10
121	Al Leiter	.20
122	Robin Ventura	.20
123	Cal Ripken Jr.	1.50
124	Mike Mussina	.40
125	B.J. Surhoff	.10
126	Jerry Hairston Jr.	.10
127	Brady Anderson	.10
128	Albert Belle	.10
129	Sidney Ponson	.10
130	Tony Gwynn	.75
131	Ryan Klesko	.10
132	Sterling Hitchcock	.10
133	Eric Owens	.10
134	Trevor Hoffman	.10
135	Al Martin	.10
136	Bret Boone	.25
137	Brian Giles	.25
138	Chad Hermansen	.10
139	Kevin Young	.10
140	Kris Benson	.10
141	Warren Morris	.10
142	Jason Kendall	.20
143	Wil Cordero	.10
144	Scott Rolen	.50
145	Curt Schilling	.40
146	Doug Glanville	.10
147	Mike Lieberthal	.10
148	Mike Jackson	.10
149	Rico Brogna	.10
150	Andy Ashby	.10
151	Sean Casey	.20
152	Sean Casey	.20
153	Pete Harnisch	.10
154	Dante Bichette	.10
155	Pokey Reese	.10
156	Aaron Boone	.20
157	Ken Griffey Jr.	1.00
158	Barry Larkin	.25
159	Scott Williamson	.10
160	Carlos Beltran	.20
161	Jermaine Dye	.10
162	Jose Rosado	.10
163	Joe Randa	.10
164	Johnny Damon	.10
165	Mike Sweeney	.10
166	Mark Quinn	.10
167	Ivan Rodriguez	.40
168	Rusty Greer	.10
169	Ruben Mateo	.10
170	Doug Davis	.10
171	Gabe Kapler	.10
172	Justin Thompson	.10
173	Rafael Palmeiro	.40
174	Larry Walker	.20
175	Neifi Perez	.10
176	Rolando Arrojo	.10
177	Jeffrey Hammonds	.10
178	Todd Helton	.50
179	Pedro Astacio	.10
180	Jeff Cirillo	.10
181	Pedro Martinez	.75
182	Carl Everett	.10
183	Troy O'Leary	.10
184	Nomar Garciaparra	1.25
185	Jose Offerman	.10
186	Bret Saberhagen	.10
187	Trot Nixon	.10
188	Jason Varitek	.10
189	Todd Walker	.10
190	Eric Milton	.10
191	Chad Allen	.10
192	Jacque Jones	.10
193	Brad Radke	.10
194	Corey Koskie	.10
195	Joe Mays	.10
196	Juan Gonzalez	.20
197	Jeff Weaver	.10
198	Juan Encarnacion	.10
199	Deivi Cruz	.10
200	Damion Easley	.10
201	Tony Clark	.20
202	Dean Palmer	.10
203	Frank Thomas	.50

204	Carlos Lee	.10
205	Mike Sirotka	.10
206	Kip Wells	.10
207	Magglio Ordonez	.20
208	Paul Konerko	.20
209	Chris Singleton	.10
210	Derek Jeter	1.50
211	Tino Martinez	.25
212	Mariano Rivera	.20
213	Roger Clemens	.75
214	Nick Johnson	.25
215	Paul O'Neill	.20
216	Bernie Williams	.40
217	David Cone	.10
218	Checklist (Ken Griffey Jr.)	.50
219	Checklist (Sammy Sosa)	.50
220	Checklist (Mark McGwire)	.75

Silver

A parallel to the 220-card base set. These 1:2 pack inserts can be distinguished from the base cards by the silver foil stamping and a silver foiled facsimile signature of the featured player on the card bottom.

Stars:	1-2X
Inserted 1:2	

Gold

A parallel to the base set, these can be distinguished from base cards with gold script stamping. Each card is also serial numbered on the card front within an edition of 50 sets.

Stars:	10-20X
Production 50 Sets	

Super

A parallel to the 220-card base set, these inserts can be distinguished from the base cards by the holo-foil stamping used on the Upper Deck logo and the featured player's facsimile signature on the card bottom. The card fronts are also serial numbered within an edition of 25 sets.

Stars:	15-30X
Production 25 Sets	

2000 Upper Deck MVP All-Star Game

	NM/M
Complete Set (30):	25.00
Common Player:	.25
AS1	Mo Vaughn	.25
AS2	Jeff Bagwell	.75
AS3	Jason Giambi	.75
AS4	Chipper Jones	1.50
AS5	Greg Maddux	1.00
AS6	Tony Batista	.25
AS7	Sammy Sosa	2.00
AS8	Mark McGwire	2.50
AS9	Randy Johnson	.75
AS10	Shawn Green	.50
AS11	Greg Vaughn	.25
AS12	Vladimir Guerrero	.75
AS13	Barry Bonds	2.50
AS14	Manny Ramirez	.75
AS15	Alex Rodriguez	2.50
AS16	Preston Wilson	.25
AS17	Mike Piazza	1.50
AS18	Cal Ripken Jr.	3.00
AS19	Tony Gwynn	1.00
AS20	Scott Rolen	.75
AS21	Ken Griffey Jr.	1.50
AS22	Carlos Beltran	.25
AS23	Ivan Rodriguez	.60
AS24	Larry Walker	.25
AS25	Nomar Garciaparra	2.00
AS26	Pedro Martinez	.75
AS27	Juan Gonzalez	.75
AS28	Frank Thomas	.75
AS29	Derek Jeter	2.50
AS30	Bernie Williams	.50

Drawing Power

This seven-card set has a holo-foil front with silver foil stamping. Card backs are numbered with a "DP" prefix.

	NM/M
Complete Set (7):	12.00
Common Player:	1.00
Inserted 1:28	
1	Mark McGwire	3.00
2	Ken Griffey Jr.	2.00
3	Mike Piazza	2.00
4	Chipper Jones	2.00
5	Nomar Garciaparra	3.00
6	Sammy Sosa	2.50
7	Jose Canseco	1.00

Game-Used Souvenirs

These memorabilia inserts feature a game-used piece of glove embedded and are found exclusively in hobby packs at a rate of 1:130 packs.

	NM/M
Common Glove:	8.00
Inserted 1:130	
RA	Roberto Alomar	15.00
JB	Jeff Bagwell	20.00
AB	Albert Belle	8.00
BB	Barry Bonds	65.00
JC	Jose Canseco	15.00
WC	Will Clark	20.00
AF	Alex Fernandez	8.00
JG	Jason Giambi	15.00
TGI	Troy Glaus	15.00
AG	Alex Gonzalez	8.00
BG	Ben Grieve	8.00
KG	Ken Griffey Jr.	40.00
VG	Vladimir Guerrero	15.00
TG	Tony Gwynn	30.00
AJ	Andruw Jones	15.00
CJ	Chipper Jones	30.00
KL	Kenny Lofton	8.00
RM	Raul Mondesi	8.00
PO	Paul O'Neill	10.00
RP	Rafael Palmeiro	8.00
MR	Manny Ramirez	15.00
CR	Cal Ripken Jr.	65.00
AR	Alex Rodriguez	40.00
IR	Ivan Rodriguez	15.00
NR	Nolan Ryan	65.00
TS	Tim Salmon	8.00
LW	Larry Walker	8.00
BW	Bernie Williams	8.00
MW	Matt Williams	8.00

Game-Used Souvenirs - Bats

These memorabilia inserts have a piece of game-used bat embedded and are seeded exclusively in hobby packs at a rate of 1:130 packs.

	NM/M
Common Bat:	8.00

	NM/M
Inserted 1:130	
BB	Barry Bonds	40.00
JC	Jose Canseco	15.00
KG	Ken Griffey Jr.	20.00
VG	Vladimir Guerrero	10.00
TG	Tony Gwynn	15.00
CJ	Chipper Jones	15.00
MR	Manny Ramirez	10.00
AR	Alex Rodriguez	20.00
IR	Ivan Rodriguez	10.00
BW	Bernie Williams	10.00

Game Used Souvenirs - Bats Auto.

Production 25 Sets
Values Undetermined

Prolifics

This seven-card set features a full holo-foiled front with silver foil stamping and are seeded 1:28 packs. Card backs are numbered with a "P" prefix.

	NM/M
Complete Set (7):	10.00
Common Player:	.50
Inserted 1:28	
1	Manny Ramirez	1.00
2	Vladimir Guerrero	1.00
3	Derek Jeter	3.00
4	Pedro Martinez	1.50
5	Shawn Green	.50
6	Alex Rodriguez	3.00
7	Cal Ripken Jr.	4.00

ProSign

These autographed inserts are found exclusively in retail packs at a rate of 1:216.

	NM/M
Common Player:	5.00
Inserted 1:216 R	
RA	Rick Ankiel	10.00
MB	Michael Barrett	5.00
RB	Rob Bell	5.00
CB	Carlos Beltran	20.00
LB	Lance Berkman	25.00
RB	Rico Brogna	5.00
SC	Sean Casey	8.00
DD	Doug Davis	5.00
ED	Erubiel Durazo	8.00
RF	Robert Fick	5.00
NG	Nomar Garciaparra	65.00
AG	Alex Gonzalez	8.00
KG	Ken Griffey Jr.	60.00
TG	Tony Gwynn	50.00
TH	Tim Hudson	15.00
DJ	Derek Jeter	80.00
CJ	Chipper Jones	50.00
MM	Mike Meyers	5.00
EM	Eric Milton	5.00
JM	Jim Morris	5.00
WM	Warren Morris	5.00
TN	Trot Nixon	5.00
BP	Ben Petrick	5.00
AP	Adam Piatt	5.00
MP	Mike Piazza	60.00
MQ	Mark Quinn	5.00
MR	Manny Ramirez	25.00
RR	Rob Ramsay	5.00
MRe	Mike Redmond	5.00
MRi	Mariano Rivera	5.00
AR	Alex Rodriguez	65.00
MS	Mike Sweeney	8.00
BT	Bubba Trammell	5.00

JV	Jose Vidro	8.00
DW	Daryle Ward	5.00
KW	Kip Wells	8.00
SW	Scott Williamson	5.00
PW	Preston Wilson	8.00
KW	Kevin Witt	5.00
TW	Tony Womack	8.00
EY	Ed Yarnall	5.00
JZ	Jeff Zimmerman	5.00

Pure Grit

These 1:6 pack inserts have a full holo-foiled front with silver foil stamping. Card backs are numbered with a "G" prefix.

	NM/M
Complete Set (10):	10.00
Common Player:	.50
Inserted 1:6	
1	Derek Jeter	2.00
2	Kevin Brown	.50
3	Craig Biggio	.50
4	Ivan Rodriguez	.75
5	Scott Rolen	.75
6	Carlos Beltran	.50
7	Ken Griffey Jr.	1.50
8	Cal Ripken Jr.	2.50
9	Nomar Garciaparra	2.00
10	Randy Johnson	1.00

Scout's Choice

This ten-card set spotlights some of the best prospects in 2000. The inserts have a full holo-foiled front with silver foil stamping. Card backs are numbered with an "SC" prefix and are seeded 1:14 packs.

	NM/M
Complete Set (10):	8.00
Common Player:	.50
Inserted 1:14	
1	Rick Ankiel	.50
2	Vernon Wells	1.00
3	Pat Burrell	1.50
4	Travis Dawkins	.50
5	Eric Munson	.50
6	Nick Johnson	1.00
7	Dermal Brown	.50
8	Alfonso Soriano	2.00
9	Ben Petrick	.50
10	Adam Everett	.50

Second Season Standouts

This 10-card set has a full holo-foiled card front with silver foil stamping. Card backs are numbered with an "SS" prefix and inserted 1:6 packs.

		NM/M
Complete Set (10):		6.00
Common Player:		.25
Inserted 1:6		
1	Pedro Martinez	1.00
2	Mariano Rivera	.40
3	Orlando Hernandez	.25
4	Ken Caminiti	.25
5	Bernie Williams	.50
6	Jim Thome	.75
7	Nomar Garciaparra	2.00
8	Edgardo Alfonzo	.25
9	Derek Jeter	2.50
10	Kevin Millwood	.40

3,000 Hit Club

Upper Deck used this cross-brand insert series to salute the players who accomplished 3,000 hits in their career. Stan Musial is featured and offers a game-used memorabilia bat, jersey, jersey/bat combo and combo autograph versions.

		NM/M
Common Player:		
SM	Stan Musial/Jsy/350	30.00
SM	Stan Musial/Bat/350	30.00
SM	Stan Musial/ Jsy/Bat/100	80.00

2000 UD N.Y. Yankees Master Collection

The most popular franchise in sports history was the subject of this Master Collection limited to 500 numbered sets. Issued in a serially-numbered mahogany box with pewter team-logo inlay, each set contains 25 cards honoring the Yankees' World Championships between 1923-1999. There is also a "Team of the Century" card set with 10 game-used bat cards and a special Gehrig commemorative. Each set also includes a Mystery Pack containing one of 14 autographed memorabilia cards. Retail price at time of issue was around $6,000. Because unopened sets may contain one of the better "Mystery Pack" cards, they maintain a significant premium.

	NM/M
Complete Boxed Set, Unopened:	3,250
Complete Boxed Set, Opened:	1,650
N.Y. Yankees Master Collection Wood Box	100.00

Mystery Cards

Each Master Collection set contains one foil-pack Mystery Card ranging from autographed player memorabilia-cards to cut signatures. The Gehrig, Mantle,

Martin, Munson and Ruth cards are each uniquely numbered on back with the player's initials or initials plus "C" (for cut signature) as a prefix. The Berra, Ford, Jackson and Jeter cards are not "numbered," but are identified by player initials and type of memorabilia. The number issued of each card is shown in parentheses. Some cards remain unpriced due to rarity.

		NM/M
Unopened Mystery Pack:		600.00
BM	Billy Martin/Bat-Cut/2 (8/05 Auction)	615.00
BR	Babe Ruth/Bat-Cut/3	9,500
BR-C	Babe Ruth/Cut/3	7,500
DJ-B	Derek Jeter/ Bat-Auto./100	450.00
DJ-J	Derek Jeter/ Jsy-Auto./100	500.00
LG-C	Lou Gehrig/Cut/3	3,000
MM	Mickey Mantle/ Bat-Cut/7	4,000
RJ-B	Reggie Jackson/ Bat-Auto./100	400.00
WF-J	Whitey Ford/ Bat-Auto./100	450.00
YB-B	Yogi Berra/ Bat-Auto./80	450.00

Team of the Century

An 11-player "Team of the Century" card set within the Yankees Master Collection features game-used bat cards from 10 of the players and a special Lou Gehrig commemorative card (Upper Deck could not get a Gehrig gamer to cut up for the cards). Each card carries an individual serial number from an edition of 500 each.

		NM/M
Complete Set (11):		1,575
Common Player:		35.00
ATY1	Babe Ruth	400.00
ATY2	Mickey Mantle	550.00
ATY3	Reggie Jackson	135.00
ATY4	Don Mattingly	135.00
ATY5	Billy Martin	90.00
ATY6	Graig Nettles	55.00
ATY7	Derek Jeter	110.00
ATY8	Yogi Berra	135.00
ATY9	Thurman Munson	145.00
ATY10	Whitey Ford	110.00
ATY11	Lou Gehrig	35.00

Series Champions

Each of the Yankees' 25 World Series Championships between 1923-1999 is marked with one of these "base" cards in the Master Collection. Fronts of the 2-1/2" x 3-1/2" cards have black-and-white or color poses or action photos highlighted with holographic foil. Backs have a portrait photo, a World Series summary and the player's career and Series stats. Each card is serially numbered within an edition of 500.

		NM/M
Complete Set (25):		480.00
Common Player:		12.50
NYY1	Babe Ruth/1923	50.00
NYY2	Lou Gehrig/1927	35.00
NYY3	Tony Lazzeri/1928	12.50
NYY4	Babe Ruth/1932	50.00
NYY5	Lou Gehrig/1936	35.00
NYY6	Lefty Gomez/1937	25.00
NYY7	Bill Dickey/1938	25.00
NYY8	Bill Dickey/1939	25.00
NYY9	Tommy Henrich/1941	17.50
NYY10	Spud Chandler/1943	12.50
NYY11	Tommy Henrich/1947	17.50
NYY12	Phil Rizzuto/1949	25.00
NYY13	Whitey Ford/1950	25.00
NYY14	Yogi Berra/1951	30.00
NYY15	Casey Stengel/1952	17.50
NYY16	Billy Martin/1953	17.50
NYY17	Don Larsen/1956	22.00
NYY18	Elston Howard/1958	12.50
NYY19	Roger Maris/1961	30.00
NYY20	Mickey Mantle/1962	50.00
NYY21	Reggie Jackson/1977	30.00
NYY22	Bucky Dent/1978	15.00
NYY23	Derek Jeter/1996	25.00
NYY24	Derek Jeter/1998	25.00
NYY25	Derek Jeter/1999	25.00

2000 Upper Deck Opening Day 2K

As part of a multi-manufacturer promotion, UD issued eight cards of an "Opening Day 2K" set. Packages containing some of the 32 cards in the issue were distributed by MLB teams early in the season. The cards were also available exclusively as inserts in Upper Deck Victory and Hitters Club packs sold at K-Mart stores early in the season. The Upper Deck OD2K cards have gold-foil graphic highlights on front. Backs have a monochromatic version of the front photo and are numbered with an "OD" prefix.

		NM/M
Complete Set (8):		6.00
Common Player:		.50
17	Ken Griffey Jr.	1.50
18	Sammy Sosa	1.00
19	Pedro Martinez	.75
20	Manny Ramirez	.65
21	Shawn Green	.65
22	Carlos Beltran	.40
23	Juan Gonzalez	.50
24	Jeromy Burnitz	.50

2000 Upper Deck Ovation

The base set consists of 90-cards, including a 20-card World Premiere subset and 10-card Superstar Spotlight subset. World Premiere's are found 1:3 packs and Superstar Spotlight's 1:6 packs. Card fronts are embossed, intended to resemble the feel of a baseball and also has silver foil stamping.

		NM/M
Complete Set (90):		65.00
Common Player:		.25
Common World Prem. (61-80):		1.00

Inserted 1:3		
Common Super. Spot (81-90):		1.50
Inserted 1:6		
Pack (5):		2.00
Wax Box (20):		30.00
1	Mo Vaughn	.25
2	Troy Glaus	.75
3	Jeff Bagwell	.75
4	Craig Biggio	.40
5	Mike Hampton	.25
6	Jason Giambi	.75
7	Tim Hudson	.40
8	Chipper Jones	1.50
9	Greg Maddux	1.50
10	Kevin Millwood	.25
11	Brian Jordan	.25
12	Jeromy Burnitz	.25
13	David Wells	.25
14	Carlos Delgado	.75
15	Sammy Sosa	2.50
16	Mark McGwire	3.00
17	Matt Williams	.25
18	Randy Johnson	.75
19	Erubiel Durazo	.40
20	Kevin Brown	.40
21	Shawn Green	.75
22	Gary Sheffield	.50
23	Jose Canseco	.50
24	Vladimir Guerrero	1.00
25	Barry Bonds	3.00
26	Manny Ramirez	.75
27	Roberto Alomar	.75
28	Richie Sexson	.40
29	Jim Thome	.75
30	Alex Rodriguez	2.50
31	Ken Griffey Jr.	1.50
32	Preston Wilson	.25
33	Mike Piazza	1.50
34	Al Leiter	.25
35	Robin Ventura	.25
36	Cal Ripken Jr.	3.00
37	Albert Belle	.25
38	Tony Gwynn	1.00
39	Brian Giles	.40
40	Jason Kendall	.40
41	Scott Rolen	.75
42	Bob Abreu	.40
43	Ken Griffey Jr.	1.50
44	Sean Casey	.25
45	Carlos Beltran	.40
46	Gabe Kapler	.25
47	Ivan Rodriguez	.75
48	Rafael Palmeiro	.50
49	Larry Walker	.40
50	Nomar Garciaparra	2.00
51	Pedro J. Martinez	1.00
52	Eric Milton	.25
53	Juan Gonzalez	.75
54	Tony Clark	.25
55	Frank Thomas	.75
56	Magglio Ordonez	.40
57	Roger Clemens	1.50
58	Derek Jeter	2.50
59	Bernie Williams	.50
60	Orlando Hernandez	.40
61	Rick Ankiel (World Premiere)	1.00
62	Josh Beckett (World Premiere)	1.50
63	Vernon Wells (World Premiere)	1.50
64	Alfonso Soriano (World Premiere)	3.00
65	Pat Burrell (World Premiere)	2.00
66	Eric Munson (World Premiere)	1.00
67	Chad Hutchinson (World Premiere)	1.00
68	Eric Gagne (World Premiere)	1.00
69	Peter Bergeron (World Premiere)	1.00
70	Ryan Anderson (Supposed to have been withdrawn, all known cards have embossed UD racing mark.)	300.00
71	A.J. Burnett (World Premiere)	1.00
72	Jorge Luis Toca (World Premiere)	1.00
73	Matt Riley (World Premiere)	1.00
74	Chad Hermansen (World Premiere)	1.00
75	Doug Davis (World Premiere)	1.00
76	Jim Morris (World Premiere)	1.00
77	Ben Petrick (World Premiere)	1.00
78	Mark Quinn (World Premiere)	1.00
79	Ed Yarnall (World Premiere)	1.00
80	Ramon Ortiz (World Premiere)	1.00
81	Ken Griffey Jr. (Superstar Spotlight)	3.00
82	Mark McGwire (Superstar Spotlight)	5.00
83	Derek Jeter (Superstar Spotlight)	5.00
84	Jeff Bagwell (Superstar Spotlight)	1.50
85	Nomar Garciaparra (Superstar Spotlight)	5.00
86	Sammy Sosa (Superstar Spotlight)	4.00
87	Mike Piazza (Superstar Spotlight)	3.00
88	Alex Rodriguez (Superstar Spotlight)	5.00
89	Cal Ripken Jr. (Superstar Spotlight)	6.00
90	Pedro Martinez (Superstar Spotlight)	2.00

Standing Ovation

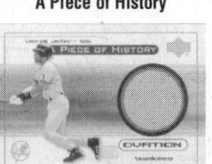

A parallel to the 120-card base set, these are identical to the base cards besides the holographic silver stamping on the card front and the backs serially numbered to 50.

Stars (1-60):	8-15X
World Prem. (61-80):	2-3X
Super. Spot. (81-90):	3-5X
Production 50 Sets	

A Piece of History

These memorabilia inserts feature a piece of game-used bat embedded and are limited to 400 sets produced.

		NM/M
Common Player:		5.00
Production 400 Sets		
JB	Jeff Bagwell	10.00
CB	Carlos Beltran	10.00
SC	Sean Casey	5.00
KG	Ken Griffey Jr.	25.00
DJ	Derek Jeter	35.00
TG	Tony Gwynn	15.00
AJ	Andruw Jones	10.00
CJ	Chipper Jones	20.00
RP	Rafael Palmeiro	10.00
MP	Mike Piazza	20.00
MR	Manny Ramirez	10.00
CR	Cal Ripken Jr.	35.00
AR	Alex Rodriguez	25.00
SR	Scott Rolen	15.00
SS	Sammy Sosa	25.00
FT	Frank Thomas	10.00

A Piece of History - Signed

Values Undetermined

Center Stage

Ten of baseball's top performers are highlighted on a card that features gold foil stamping and etching. Card backs are numbered with an "CS" prefix and are seeded 1:9 packs. Two parallels to this insert set are randomly inserted: Golds are found 1:39 packs and Rainbows are seeded 1:99 packs.

		NM/M
Complete Set (10):		20.00
Common Player:		1.00
Inserted 1:9		

Gold:		2X
Inserted 1:39		
Rainbow:		3-4X
Inserted 1:99		
1	Jeff Bagwell	1.00
2	Ken Griffey Jr.	2.00
3	Nomar Garciaparra	3.00
4	Mike Piazza	2.00
5	Mark McGwire	3.00
6	Alex Rodriguez	3.00
7	Cal Ripken Jr.	4.00
8	Derek Jeter	3.00
9	Chipper Jones	2.00
10	Sammy Sosa	2.50

Curtain Calls

This 20-card set features gold foil stamping and highlights some memorable playoff moments. Card backs are numbered with a "CC" prefix.

		NM/M
Complete Set (20):		15.00
Common Player:		.50
Inserted 1:3		
1	David Cone	.50
2	Mark McGwire	2.00
3	Sammy Sosa	2.00
4	Eric Milton	.50
5	Bernie Williams	.75
6	Tony Gwynn	1.00
7	Nomar Garciaparra	2.00
8	Manny Ramirez	1.00
9	Wade Boggs	.50
10	Randy Johnson	1.00
11	Cal Ripken Jr.	3.00
12	Pedro J. Martinez	1.00
13	Alex Rodriguez	2.00
14	Fernando Tatis	.50
15	Vladimir Guerrero	.50
16	Robin Ventura	.50
17	Larry Walker	.50
18	Carlos Beltran	.50
19	Jose Canseco	.75
20	Ken Griffey Jr.	1.50

Diamond Futures

This 10-card set highlights some of baseball's top prospects on a full foiled front with silver foil stamping. Card backs are numbered with a "DM" prefix.

		NM/M
Complete Set (10):		8.00
Common Player:		.50
Inserted 1:6		
1	J.D. Drew	.75
2	Alfonso Soriano	2.50
3	Preston Wilson	.75
4	Erubiel Durazo	.75
5	Rick Ankiel	.50
6	Octavio Dotel	.50
7	A.J. Burnett	.75
8	Carlos Beltran	.75
9	Vernon Wells	1.00
10	Troy Glaus	2.00

Lead Performers

Upper Deck chose 10 players for this set who are thought of as leaders on and off the field. Card fronts have silver foil stamping and card backs are numbered with an "LP" prefix.

Upper Deck's cross brand insert series pays tribute to members of the elite 3,000 Hit Club. Ovation features Willie Mays in the series, which has four versions: Bat card, 300 produced; Jersey card, 350 produced; Bat/Jersey combo, 50 produced; and Bat/Jersey autograph, 24 produced.

		NM/M
1	Willie Mays/Jsy/350	40.00
2	Willie Mays/Bat/300	40.00
3	Willie Mays/Jsy/Bat/50	180.00
4	Willie Mays/ Jsy/Bat/Auto./24	675.00

2000 Upper Deck PowerDeck

		NM/M
Complete Set (12):		50.00
Common Card:		3.00
Pack (1):		4.00
Box:		40.00
1	Sammy Sosa	6.00
2	Ken Griffey Jr.	6.00
3	Mark McGwire	8.00
4	Derek Jeter	6.00
5	Alex Rodriguez	8.00
6	Nomar Garciaparra	6.00
7	Mike Piazza	6.00
8	Cal Ripken Jr.	8.00
9	Ivan Rodriguez	3.00
10	Chipper Jones	5.00
11	Pedro Martinez	3.00
12	Manny Ramirez	3.00

Magical Moments

		NM/M
Inserted 1:10 H		
KG	Ken Griffey Jr.	6.00
CR	Cal Ripken Jr.	10.00

Magical Moments Autograph

		NM/M
Each signed 50 cards.		
KG	Ken Griffey Jr.	180.00
CR	Cal Ripken Jr.	275.00

Power Trio

		NM/M
Complete Set (3):		15.00
Common Player:		5.00
Inserted 1:7		
PT1	Derek Jeter	6.00
PT2	Ken Griffey Jr.	5.00
PT3	Mark McGwire	6.00

2000 Upper Deck Pros and Prospects

This 20-card set is printed on a full foiled card front enhanced by silver foil stamping and etching. Card backs are numbered with an "ST" prefix.

		NM/M
Complete Set (20):		20.00
Common Player:		.50
Inserted 1:19		
1	Ivan Rodriguez	1.00
2	Brian Giles	.50
3	Bernie Williams	1.00
4	Greg Maddux	2.00
5	Frank Thomas	1.00
6	Sean Casey	.50
7	Mo Vaughn	.50
8	Carlos Delgado	1.00
9	Tony Gwynn	1.50
10	Pedro Martinez	1.50
11	Scott Rolen	1.00
12	Mark McGwire	3.00
13	Manny Ramirez	1.00
14	Rafael Palmeiro	.75
15	Jose Canseco	.75
16	Randy Johnson	1.50
17	Gary Sheffield	.75
18	Larry Walker	.75
19	Barry Bonds	4.00
20	Roger Clemens	3.00

3,000 Hit Club

The 132-card base set consists of 90 regular player cards, a 30-card Prospective Superstars subset and a 12-card Pro-Fame subset. Prospective Superstars are serially numbered to 1,350 and Pro-Fame are serially numbered to 1,000. Card fronts have a white-bordered design with silver foil stamping. Both subsets are serially numbered on the card front.

	NM/M
Complete Set (132):	300.00
Common Player (1-90):	.15
Common (91-120):	5.00
Production 1,350 Sets	
Common (121-132):	4.00
Production 1,000 Sets	
Pack (5):	2.50
Box (24):	40.00
1	Darin Erstad	.40

2	Troy Glaus	.75
3	Mo Vaughn	.20
4	Jason Giambi	.75
5	Tim Hudson	.25
6	Ben Grieve	.15
7	Eric Chavez	.25
8	Shannon Stewart	.15
9	Raul Mondesi	.25
10	Carlos Delgado	.75
11	Jose Canseco	.40
12	Fred McGriff	.25
13	Greg Vaughn	.15
14	Manny Ramirez	.75
15	Roberto Alomar	.50
16	Jim Thome	.75
17	Alex Rodriguez	2.50
18	Fred Garcia	.15
19	John Olerud	.25
20	Cal Ripken Jr.	2.50
21	Albert Belle	.20
22	Mike Mussina	.40
23	Ivan Rodriguez	.50
24	Rafael Palmeiro	.50
25	Ruben Mateo	.15
26	Gabe Kapler	.15
27	Pedro Martinez	1.00
28	Nomar Garciaparra	2.00
29	Carl Everett	.15
30	Carlos Beltran	.25
31	Jermaine Dye	.15
32	Johnny Damon	.25
33	Juan Gonzalez	.75
34	Juan Encarnacion	.15
35	Dean Palmer	.15
36	Jacque Jones	.15
37	Matt Lawton	.15
38	Frank Thomas	.75
39	Paul Konerko	.15
40	Magglio Ordonez	.25
41	Derek Jeter	2.00
42	Bernie Williams	.50
43	Mariano Rivera	.25
44	Roger Clemens	1.50
45	Jeff Bagwell	.75
46	Craig Biggio	.25
47	Richard Hidalgo	.25
48	Chipper Jones	1.50
49	Andres Galarraga	.25
50	Andruw Jones	.50
51	Greg Maddux	1.50
52	Jeromy Burnitz	.15
53	Geoff Jenkins	.25
54	Mark McGwire	2.00
55	Jim Edmonds	.25
56	Fernando Tatis	.15
57	J.D. Drew	.15
58	Sammy Sosa	2.00
59	Kerry Wood	.50
60	Randy Johnson	.75
61	Matt Williams	.25
62	Erubiel Durazo	.15
63	Shawn Green	.25
64	Kevin Brown	.25
65	Gary Sheffield	.25
66	Adrian Beltre	.25
67	Vladimir Guerrero	.75
68	Jose Vidro	.15
69	Barry Bonds	2.00
70	Jeff Kent	.25
71	Preston Wilson	.15
72	Ryan Dempster	.15
73	Mike Lowell	.15
74	Mike Piazza	1.50
75	Robin Ventura	.25
76	Edgardo Alfonzo	.15
77	Derek Bell	.15
78	Tony Gwynn	1.00
79	Matt Clement	.15
80	Scott Rolen	.75
81	Bobby Abreu	.25
82	Curt Schilling	.40
83	Brian Giles	.25
84	Jason Kendall	.25
85	Kris Benson	.15
86	Ken Griffey Jr.	1.50
87	Sean Casey	.25
88	Pokey Reese	.15
89	Larry Walker	.25
90	Todd Helton	.75
91	Rick Ankiel (Prospective Superstars)	5.00
92	Milton Bradley (Prospective Superstars)	5.00
93	Vernon Wells (Prospective Superstars)	6.00
94	Rafael Furcal (Prospective Superstars)	6.00
95	Kazuhiro Sasaki RC (Prospective Superstars)	8.00
96	Joe Torres RC (Prospective Superstars)	5.00
97	Adam Kennedy (Prospective Superstars)	5.00
98	Adam Piatt (Prospective Superstars)	5.00
99	Matt Wheatland RC (Prospective Superstars)	5.00
100	Alex Cabrera RC (Prospective Superstars)	5.00
101	Barry Zito RC (Prospective Superstars)	25.00
102	Mike Lamb RC (Prospective Superstars)	5.00
103	Scott Heard RC (Prospective Superstars)	5.00
104	Danys Baez RC (Prospective Superstars)	8.00

105	Matt Riley (Prospective Superstars)	5.00
106	Mark Mulder (Prospective Superstars)	6.00
107	Wilfredo Rodriguez RC (Prospective Superstars)	5.00
108	Luis Matos RC (Prospective Superstars)	10.00
109	Alfonso Soriano (Prospective Superstars)	8.00
110	Pat Burrell (Prospective Superstars)	6.00
111	Mike Tonis RC (Prospective Superstars)	5.00
112	Aaron McNeal RC (Prospective Superstars)	5.00
113	Dave Krynzel RC (Prospective Superstars)	8.00
114	Josh Beckett (Prospective Superstars)	5.00
115	Sean Burnett RC (Prospective Superstars)	5.00
116	Eric Munson (Prospective Superstars)	5.00
117	Scott Downs RC (Prospective Superstars)	5.00
118	Brian Tollberg RC (Prospective Superstars)	5.00
119	Nick Johnson (Prospective Superstars)	5.00
120	Leo Estrella RC (Prospective Superstars)	5.00
121	Ken Griffey Jr. (Pro Fame)	8.00
122	Frank Thomas (Pro Fame)	4.00
123	Cal Ripken Jr. (Pro Fame)	15.00
124	Ivan Rodriguez (Pro Fame)	4.00
125	Derek Jeter (Pro Fame)	12.00
126	Mark McGwire (Pro Fame)	12.00
127	Pedro Martinez (Pro Fame)	5.00
128	Chipper Jones (Pro Fame)	8.00
129	Sammy Sosa (Pro Fame)	10.00
130	Alex Rodriguez (Pro Fame)	10.00
131	Vladimir Guerrero (Pro Fame)	4.00
132	Jeff Bagwell (Pro Fame)	4.00

Future Forces

This 10-card set highlights top prospects on a card front featuring gold foil stamping and etching. Card backs are numbered with an "F" prefix.

		NM/M
Complete Set (10):		5.00
Common Player:		.50
Inserted 1:6		
1	Pat Burrell	2.00
2	Brad Penny	.50
3	Rick Ankiel	.50
4	Adam Kennedy	.50
5	Eric Munson	.50
6	Rafael Furcal	.75
7	Mark Mulder	.75
8	Vernon Wells	.75
9	Matt Riley	.50
10	Nick Johnson	.75

ProMotion

Complete Set (10):	20.00
Common Player:	1.00
Inserted 1:19	
1	Mark McGwire	3.00
2	Derek Jeter	3.00
3	Vladimir Guerrero	1.00
4	Mike Piazza	2.00
5	Cal Ripken Jr.	4.00
6	Sammy Sosa	2.50
7	Jeff Bagwell	1.00
8	Nomar Garciaparra	3.00
9	Chipper Jones	2.00
10	Ken Griffey Jr.	2.00

Super Signatures

This two-card insert set features Ken Griffey Jr. and Mike Piazza. Spotlighting the autographs of Griffey and Piazza, Super Signatures is issued in three versions: Silver, numbered to 100; Gold, numbered to 50; and Rainbow, numbered to 10.

		NM/M
Common Card:		
KG	Ken Griffey/Gold/50	180.00
KG	Ken Griffey/Silver/100	100.00
MP	Mike Piazza/Gold/50	180.00
MP	Mike Piazza/Silver/100	150.00

Superstar Theatre

Rare Breed

Baseball's top performers are spotlighted in this 12-card set on a full foiled silver front with gold foil stamping. Card backs are numbered with an "R" prefix and are inserted 1:12 packs.

		NM/M
Complete Set (12):		15.00
Common Player:		.50
Inserted 1:12		
1	Mark McGwire	3.00
2	Frank Thomas	1.00
3	Mike Piazza	2.00
4	Barry Bonds	4.00
5	Manny Ramirez	1.00
6	Ken Griffey Jr.	2.00
7	Nomar Garciaparra	3.00
8	Randy Johnson	1.50
9	Vladimir Guerrero	1.00
10	Jeff Bagwell	1.00
11	Rick Ankiel	.50
12	Alex Rodriguez	3.00

Signed Game-Worn Jerseys

Each of these Game Jersey cards has a piece of jersey swatch and autograph from the featured player. A Level 2 "Gold" version is limited to the player's corresponding uniform number.

		NM/M
Common Player:		25.00
Inserted 1:96		
BB	Barry Bonds	200.00
JC	Jose Canseco	40.00
JD	J.D. Drew	25.00
TG	Tom Glavine	40.00
LG	Luis Gonzalez	25.00
KG	Ken Griffey Jr.	100.00
TG	Tony Gwynn	50.00
DJ	Derek Jeter/SP	350.00
RJ	Randy Johnson	80.00
CJ	Chipper Jones	50.00
KL	Kenny Lofton	25.00
CR	Cal Ripken Jr.	140.00
AR	Alex Rodriguez	120.00
IR	Ivan Rodriguez	40.00
SR	Scott Rolen	50.00
GS	Gary Sheffield	40.00
FT	Frank Thomas	40.00
MV	Mo Vaughn	25.00
RV	Robin Ventura	25.00
MW	Matt Williams	25.00
PW	Preston Wilson	25.00

The Best in the Bigs

This 10-card set spotlights some of baseball's best all-around talents using gold foil stamping. Card backs are numbered with a "P" prefix and are seeded 1:6 packs.

		NM/M
Complete Set (10):		15.00
Common Player:		.75
Inserted 1:6		
1	Derek Jeter	3.00
2	Mike Piazza	1.50
3	Mark McGwire	2.50
4	Ivan Rodriguez	.75
5	Kerry Wood	.75
6	Nomar Garciaparra	2.00
7	Sammy Sosa	2.00
8	Alex Rodriguez	2.50
9	Ken Griffey Jr.	1.50
10	Vladimir Guerrero	1.00

Rare Breed

This 10-card set spotlights baseball's best performers on a white bordered design with gold foil stamping. Card backs are numbered with a "B" prefix.

		NM/M
Complete Set (10):		15.00
Common Player:		1.00
Inserted 1:12		
1	Sammy Sosa	2.50
2	Tony Gwynn	1.50
3	Pedro Martinez	1.50
4	Mark McGwire	3.00
5	Chipper Jones	2.00
6	Derek Jeter	3.00
7	Ken Griffey Jr.	2.00
8	Cal Ripken Jr.	4.00
9	Greg Maddux	2.00
10	Ivan Rodriguez	1.00

3,000 Hit Club

Upper Deck's continuing series features Lou Brock and Rod Carew. The series features 350 numbered bat cards, 350 numbered jersey cards and 100 numbered bat/jersey combos. Each player also signed the bat/jersey combos to their jersey number, as Brock signed 20 and Carew 29.

		NM/M
Lou Brock/Bat/350		20.00
Lou Brock/Jsy/350		20.00
Lou Brock/Bat/Jsy/100		40.00
Rod Carew/Bat/350		20.00
Rod Carew/Jsy/350		20.00
Rod Carew/Bat/Jsy/100		40.00

2000 Upper Deck Rookie Update

		NM/M
Common Player:		.25
Common Rookie:		5.00
Pack (4):		4.50
Box (15):		50.00
SP Authentic Update		
(136-164) Production 1,700		
136	Barry Zito RC (Future Watch)	25.00
137	Aaron McNeal RC (Future Watch)	5.00
138	Teofilo Perez (Future Watch)	5.00
139	Sun-Woo Kim RC (Future Watch)	5.00
140	Xavier Nady RC (Future Watch)	15.00
141	Matt Wheatland RC (Future Watch)	5.00
142	Brent Abernathy RC (Future Watch)	5.00
143	Cory Vance RC (Future Watch)	5.00
144	Scott Heard RC (Future Watch)	5.00
145	Mike Meyers RC (Future Watch)	5.00
146	Ben Diggins RC (Future Watch)	5.00
147	Luis Matos RC (Future Watch)	5.00
148	Ben Sheets RC (Future Watch)	15.00

149	Kurt Ainsworth RC	
	(Future Watch)	5.00
150	Dave Krynzel RC	
	(Future Watch)	5.00
151	Alex Cabrera RC	
	(Future Watch)	5.00
152	Mike Tonis RC	
	(Future Watch)	5.00
153	Dane Sardinha RC	
	(Future Watch)	5.00
154	Keith Ginter RC	
	(Future Watch)	5.00
155	David Espinosa RC	
	(Future Watch)	5.00
156	Joe Torres RC	
	(Future Watch)	5.00
157	Daylan Holt RC	
	(Future Watch)	5.00
158	Koyie Hill RC	
	(Future Watch)	5.00
159	Brad Wilkerson RC	
	(Future Watch)	8.00
160	Juan Pierre RC	
	(Future Watch)	10.00
161	Matt Ginter RC	
	(Future Watch)	5.00
162	Dane Artman RC	
	(Future Watch)	5.00
163	Jon Rauch RC	
	(Future Watch)	5.00
164	Sean Burnett RC	
	(Future Watch)	5.00
166	Darin Erstad	.50
167	Ben Grieve	.25
168	David Wells	.25
169	Fred McGriff	.40
170	Bob Wickman	.25
171	Al Martin	.25
172	Melvin Mora	.25
173	Ricky Ledee	.25
174	Dante Bichette	.25
175	Mike Sweeney	.25
176	Bobby Higginson	.25
177	Matt Lawton	.25
178	Charles Johnson	.25
179	David Justice	.50
180	Richard Hidalgo	.40
181	B.J. Surhoff	.25
182	Richie Sexson	.50
183	Jim Edmonds	.50
184	Rondell White	.25
185	Curt Schilling	.50
186	Tom Goodwin	.25
187	Jose Vidro	.25
188	Ellis Burks	.25
189	Henry Rodriguez	.25
190	Mike Bordick	.25
191	Eric Owens	.25
192	Travis Lee	.25
193	Kevin Young	.25
194	Aaron Boone	.40
195	Todd Hollandsworth	.25

SPx Update
(121-135, 182-196) 1,600
(136-151) Production 1,500

	Common Autograph	10.00
121	Brad Wilkerson RC	15.00
122	Roy Oswalt RC	100.00
123	Wascar Serrano RC	5.00
124	Sean Burnett RC	10.00
125	Alex Cabrera RC	5.00
126	Timoniel Perez RC	5.00
127	Juan Pierre RC	15.00
128	Daylan Holt RC	5.00
129	Tomokazu Ohka RC	5.00
130	Kazuhiro Sasaki RC	10.00
131	Kurt Ainsworth RC	5.00
132	Brent Abernathy RC	5.00
133	Danys Baez RC	5.00
134	Brad Cresse RC	5.00
135	Ryan Franklin	5.00
136	Mike Lamb RC	10.00
137	David Espinosa RC	5.00
138	Matt Wheatland RC	5.00
139	Xavier Nady RC	50.00
140	Scott Heard RC	5.00
141	Pascual Coco RC	5.00
142	Justin Miller RC	5.00
143	Dave Krynzel RC	10.00
144	Dane Sardinha RC	5.00
145	Ben Sheets RC	40.00
146	Leo Estrella RC	10.00
147	Ben Diggins RC	10.00
148	Barry Zito RC	40.00
149	Joe Torres RC	10.00
150	Mike Meyers RC	10.00
151	Kris Wilson RC	10.00
152	Darin Erstad	.50
153	Richard Hidalgo	.40
154	Eric Chavez	.50
155	B.J. Surhoff	.25
156	Richie Sexson	.75
157	Raul Mondesi	.50
158	Rondell White	.50
159	Jim Edmonds	.75
160	Curt Schilling	.75
161	Tom Goodwin	.25
162	Fred McGriff	.50
163	Jose Vidro	.25
164	Ellis Burks	.25
165	David Segui	.25
166	Aaron Sele	.25
167	Henry Rodriguez	.25
168	Mike Bordick	.25
169	Mike Mussina	1.00
170	Ryan Klesko	.25
171	Kevin Young	.25
172	Travis Lee	.25

173	Aaron Boone	.50
174	Jermaine Dye	.25
175	Ricky Ledee	.25
176	Jeffrey Hammonds	.25
177	Carl Everett	.25
178	Matt Lawton	.25
179	Bobby Higginson	.25
180	Charles Johnson	.25
181	David Justice	.75
182	Joey Nation RC	4.00
183	Rico Washington RC	4.00
184	Luis Matos RC	10.00
185	Chris Wakeland RC	4.00
186	Sun-Woo Kim RC	4.00
187	Keith Ginter RC	5.00
188	Geraldo Guzman RC	4.00
189	Jay Spurgeon RC	4.00
190	Jace Brewer RC	4.00
191	Juan Guzman RC	4.00
192	Ross Gload RC	4.00
193	Paxton Crawford RC	4.00
194	Ryan Kohlmeier RC	4.00
195	Julio Zuleta RC	4.00
196	Matt Ginter RC	4.00

UD Pros & Prospects Update
(133-162) Production 1,600

133	Dane Artman RC	5.00
134	Juan Pierre RC	8.00
135	Jace Brewer RC	5.00
136	Sun-Woo Kim RC	6.00
137	Jon Rauch RC	6.00
138	Juan Guzman RC	5.00
139	Daylan Holt RC	5.00
140	Rico Washington RC	5.00
141	Ben Diggins RC	8.00
142	Mike Meyers RC	5.00
143	Chris Wakeland RC	5.00
144	Cory Vance RC	5.00
145	Keith Ginter RC	8.00
146	Koyie Hill RC	8.00
147	Julio Zuleta RC	5.00
148	Geraldo Guzman RC	5.00
149	Jay Spurgeon RC	5.00
150	Ross Gload RC	5.00
151	Ben Sheets RC	15.00
152	Josh Kalinowski RC	6.00
153	Kurt Ainsworth RC	5.00
154	Paxton Crawford RC	5.00
155	Xavier Nady RC	8.00
156	Brad Wilkerson RC	10.00
157	Kris Wilson RC	5.00
158	Paul Rigdon RC	5.00
159	Ryan Kohlmeier RC	5.00
160	Dane Sardinha RC	5.00
161	Javier Cardona RC	5.00
162	Brad Cresse RC	5.00
163	Ron Gant	.25
164	Mark Mulder	.50
165	David Wells	.25
166	Jason Tyner	.25
167	David Segui	.25
168	Al Martin	.25
169	Melvin Mora	.25
170	Ricky Ledee	.25
171	Rolando Arrojo	.25
172	Mike Sweeney	.25
173	Bobby Higginson	.25
174	Eric Milton	.25
175	Charles Johnson	.25
176	David Justice	.50
177	Moises Alou	.25
178	Andy Ashby	.25
179	Richie Sexson	.75
180	Will Clark	.75
181	Rondell White	.40
182	Curt Schilling	.75
183	Tom Goodwin	.25
184	Lee Stevens	.25
185	Ellis Burks	.25
186	Henry Rodriguez	.25
187	Mike Bordick	.25
188	Ryan Klesko	.50
189	Travis Lee	.25
190	Kevin Young	.25
191	Barry Larkin	.75
192	Jeff Cirillo	.25

Winning Materials

		NM/M
	Common Card:	10.00
	Inserted 1:15	
NG-PM	Nomar Garciaparra,	
	Pedro Martinez	40.00
DJ-AR	Derek Jeter,	
	Alex Rodriguez	40.00
DJ-NG	Derek Jeter,	
	Nomar Garciaparra	40.00
MM-KG	Mark McGwire,	
	Ken Griffey Jr.	40.00
MM-SS	Mark McGwire,	
	Sammy Sosa	40.00
MM-RA	Mark McGwire,	
	Rick Ankiel	30.00
KG-SS	Ken Griffey Jr.,	
	Sammy Sosa	25.00
RC-PM	Roger Clemens,	
	Pedro Martinez	30.00
CR-TG	Cal Ripken Jr.,	
	Tony Gwynn	40.00
JC-BB	Jose Canseco,	
	Barry Bonds	30.00
FT-MO	Frank Thomas,	
	Magglio Ordonez	10.00
JB-CB	Jeff Bagwell,	
	Craig Biggio	10.00
MP-RV	Mike Piazza,	
	Robin Ventura	25.00
IR-RP	Ivan Rodriguez,	
	Rafael Palmeiro	10.00
J-G-R	Derek Jeter,	
	Nomar Garciaparra,	
	Alex Rodriguez	75.00
G-S-R	Ken Griffey Jr.,	
	Sammy Sosa,	
	Alex Rodriguez	40.00

Winning Materials Gold

		NM/M
	Common Player:	5.00
JC	John Cotton	5.00
BS	Ben Sheets	15.00
SB	Sean Burroughs	8.00
MN	Mike Neill	5.00
DM	Doug Mientkiewicz	8.00
EY	Ernie Young	5.00
GD	Travis Dawkins,	
	Mike Kinkade	5.00
BS	Sean Burroughs,	
	Ben Sheets	15.00
AE	Brent Abernathy,	
	Adam Everett	5.00
EY	Brad Wilkerson,	
	Ernie Young	8.00

2000 Upper Deck Ultimate Victory

		NM/M
	Complete Set (120):	200.00
	Common Player:	.15
	Common Ultimate Rookie	
	(91-120):	4.00
	Varying Production Levels	
	Pack (5):	1.50
	Box (24):	25.00
1	Mo Vaughn	.20
2	Darin Erstad	.40
3	Troy Glaus	.75
4	Adam Kennedy	.15
5	Jason Giambi	.75
6	Ben Grieve	.15
7	Terrence Long	.15
8	Tim Hudson	.25
9	David Wells	.15
10	Carlos Delgado	.75
11	Shannon Stewart	.15
12	Greg Vaughn	.15
13	Gerald Williams	.15
14	Manny Ramirez	.75
15	Roberto Alomar	.60
16	Jim Thome	.75
17	Edgar Martinez	.25
18	Alex Rodriguez	2.50
19	Matt Riley	.15
20	Cal Ripken Jr.	2.50
21	Mike Mussina	.50
22	Albert Belle	.20
23	Ivan Rodriguez	.50
24	Rafael Palmeiro	.50
25	Nomar Garciaparra	2.00
26	Pedro Martinez	1.00
27	Carl Everett	.15
28	Tomokazu Ohka RC	.40
29	Jermaine Dye	.15
30	Johnny Damon	.25
31	Dean Palmer	.15
32	Juan Gonzalez	.75
33	Eric Milton	.15
34	Matt Lawton	.15
35	Frank Thomas	.75
36	Paul Konerko	.15
37	Magglio Ordonez	.25
38	Jon Garland	.15
39	Derek Jeter	2.50
40	Roger Clemens	1.50
41	Bernie Williams	.50
42	Nick Johnson	.15
43	Julio Lugo	.15
44	Jeff Bagwell	.75
45	Richard Hidalgo	.15
46	Chipper Jones	1.50
47	Greg Maddux	1.50
48	Andruw Jones	.50
49	Andres Galarraga	.25
50	Rafael Furcal	.50
51	Jeromy Burnitz	.15
52	Geoff Jenkins	.25
53	Mark McGwire	2.00
54	Jim Edmonds	.25
55	Rick Ankiel	.25
56	Sammy Sosa	2.00
57	Julio Zuleta RC	.25
58	Kerry Wood	.40
59	Randy Johnson	.75
60	Matt Williams	.25
61	Steve Finley	.25
62	Gary Sheffield	.40
63	Kevin Brown	.25
64	Shawn Green	.25
65	Milton Bradley	.15
66	Vladimir Guerrero	.75
67	Jose Vidro	.15
68	Barry Bonds	2.00
69	Jeff Kent	.25
70	Preston Wilson	.15
71	Mike Lowell	.15
72	Mike Piazza	2.00
73	Robin Ventura	.25
74	Edgardo Alfonzo	.15
75	Jay Payton	.15
76	Tony Gwynn	1.00
77	Adam Eaton	.15
78	Phil Nevin	.15
79	Scott Rolen	.75
80	Bob Abreu	.25
81	Pat Burrell	.50
82	Brian Giles	.25
83	Jason Kendall	.15
84	Kris Benson	.15
85	Gookie Dawkins	.15
86	Ken Griffey Jr.	1.50
87	Barry Larkin	.40
88	Larry Walker	.25
89	Todd Helton	.75
90	Ben Petrick	.15
91	Alex Cabrera 3,500 RC	
	(Ultimate Rookie 2000)	4.00
92	Matt Wheatland 1,000 RC	
	(Ultimate Rookie 2000)	4.00
93	Joe Torres 1,000 RC	
	(Ultimate Rookie 2000)	4.00
94	Xavier Nady 1,000 RC	
	(Ultimate Rookie 2000)	12.00
95	Kenny Kelly 3,500 RC	
	(Ultimate Rookie 2000)	4.00
96	Matt Ginter 3,500 RC	
	(Ultimate Rookie 2000)	4.00
97	Ben Diggins 1,000 RC	
	(Ultimate Rookie 2000)	8.00
98	Danys Baez 3,500 RC	
	(Ultimate Rookie 2000)	6.00
99	Daylan Holt 2,500 RC	
	(Ultimate Rookie 2000)	4.00
100	Kazuhiro Sasaki 3,500 RC	
	(Ultimate Rookie 2000)	5.00
101	Dane Artman 2,500 RC	
	(Ultimate Rookie 2000)	4.00
102	Mike Tonis 1,000 RC	
	(Ultimate Rookie 2000)	4.00
103	Timoniel Perez 2,500 RC	
	(Ultimate Rookie 2000)	4.00
104	Barry Zito 2,500 RC (Ultimate	
	Rookie 2000)	20.00
105	Koyie Hill 2,500 RC (Ultimate	
	Rookie 2000)	4.00
106	Brad Wilkerson 2,500 RC	
	(Ultimate Rookie 2000)	8.00
107	Juan Pierre 3,500 RC	
	(Ultimate Rookie 2000)	8.00
108	Aaron McNeal 3,500 RC	
	(Ultimate Rookie 2000)	4.00
109	Jay Spurgeon 3,500 RC	
	(Ultimate Rookie 2000)	4.00
110	Sean Burnett 1,000 RC	
	(Ultimate Rookie 2000)	8.00
111	Luis Matos 3,500 RC	
	(Ultimate Rookie 2000)	8.00
112	Dave Krynzel 1,000 RC	
	(Ultimate Rookie 2000)	6.00
113	Scott Heard 1,000 RC	
	(Ultimate Rookie 2000)	4.00
114	Ben Sheets 2,500 RC	
	(Ultimate Rookie 2000)	15.00
115	Dane Sardinha 1,000 RC	
	(Ultimate Rookie 2000)	4.00
116	David Espinosa 1,000 RC	
	(Ultimate Rookie 2000)	4.00
117	Leo Estrella 3,500 RC	
	(Ultimate Rookie 2000)	4.00
118	Kurt Ainsworth 2,500 RC	
	(Ultimate Rookie 2000)	4.00
119	Jon Rauch 2,500 RC	
	(Ultimate Rookie 2000)	4.00
120	Ryan Franklin 2,500 (Ultimate	
	Rookie 2000)	4.00

Collection

Parallel 25 Stars:	20-40X
Rookies (91-120):	2-4X
Production 25 Sets	
Parallel 100 Stars:	4-8X
Rookies (91-120):	1-2X
Production 100 Sets	
Parallel 250 Stars:	2-4X
Rookies (91-120):	1-2X
Production 250 Sets	

Diamond Dignitaries

		NM/M
	Complete Set (10):	20.00
	Common Player:	1.00
	Inserted 1:23	
1	Ken Griffey Jr.	2.00
2	Nomar Garciaparra	3.00
3	Chipper Jones	2.00
4	Ivan Rodriguez	1.00
5	Mark McGwire	3.00
6	Cal Ripken Jr.	4.00
7	Vladimir Guerrero	1.00
8	Alex Rodriguez	3.00
9	Sammy Sosa	2.50
10	Derek Jeter	3.00

HOF Game Jersey

		NM/M
	Common Card:	8.00
SA	Sparky Anderson	8.00
CF	Carlton Fisk	10.00
TP	Tony Perez	8.00

HOF Game Jersey Combo

		NM/M
UV-C	Sparky Anderson, Carlton Fisk,	
	Tony Perez	40.00

Lasting Impressions

		NM/M
	Complete Set (10):	15.00
	Common Player:	1.00
	Inserted 1:11	
1	Barry Bonds	3.00
2	Mike Piazza	2.00
3	Manny Ramirez	1.00
4	Pedro J. Martinez	1.50
5	Mark McGwire	2.00
6	Ken Griffey Jr.	2.00
7	Ivan Rodriguez	1.00
8	Jeff Bagwell	1.00
9	Randy Johnson	1.50
10	Alex Rodriguez	3.00

Starstruck

		NM/M
	Complete Set (10):	20.00
	Common Player:	1.00
	Inserted 1:11	
1	Alex Rodriguez	3.00
2	Frank Thomas	1.00
3	Derek Jeter	3.00
4	Mark McGwire	3.00
5	Nomar Garciaparra	3.00
6	Chipper Jones	2.00
7	Cal Ripken Jr.	4.00
8	Sammy Sosa	2.00
9	Vladimir Guerrero	1.00
10	Ken Griffey Jr.	2.00

Victory

Victory offers no inserts just your standard 440-card base set that features a white bordered design, with two player images on the card front. The base set includes three subsets: Rookie 2000 (331-370); Big Play Makers (371-390) and JUNIOR Circuit (391-440).

		NM/M
	Complete Set (440):	20.00
	Complete Factory Set (466):	25.00

	Common Player:	.10
	Common Griffey (391-440):	.50
	Common USA (441-466):	.40
	Pack (12):	1.00
	Wax Box (36):	25.00
1	Mo Vaughn	.15
2	Garret Anderson	.20
3	Tim Salmon	.20
4	Troy Percival	.10
5	Orlando Palmeiro	.10
6	Darin Erstad	.20
7	Ramon Ortiz	.10
8	Ben Molina	.10
9	Troy Glaus	.40
10	Jim Edmonds	.20
11	Mo Vaughn, Troy Percival	.15
12	Craig Biggio	.25
13	Roger Cedeno	.10
14	Shane Reynolds	.10
15	Jeff Bagwell	.50
16	Octavio Dotel	.10
17	Moises Alou	.20
18	Jose Lima	.10
19	Ken Caminiti	.15
20	Richard Hidalgo	.10
21	Billy Wagner	.10
22	Lance Berkman	.20
23	Jeff Bagwell, Jose Lima	.25
24	Jason Giambi	.50
25	Randy Velarde	.10
26	Miguel Tejada	.25
27	Matt Stairs	.10
28	A.J. Hinch	.10
29	Olmedo Saenz	.10
30	Ben Grieve	.10
31	Ryan Christenson	.10
32	Eric Chavez	.20
33	Tim Hudson	.20
34	John Jaha	.10
35	Jason Giambi, Matt Stairs	.25
36	Raul Mondesi	.20
37	Tony Batista	.10
38	David Wells	.10
39	Homer Bush	.10
40	Carlos Delgado	.40
41	Billy Koch	.10
42	Darrin Fletcher	.10
43	Tony Fernandez	.10
44	Shannon Stewart	.10
45	Roy Halladay	.20
46	Chris Carpenter	.10
47	Carlos Delgado,	
	David Wells	.20
48	Chipper Jones	1.00
49	Greg Maddux	1.00
50	Andruw Jones	.40
51	Andres Galarraga	.20
52	Tom Glavine	.20
53	Brian Jordan	.10
54	John Smoltz	.15
55	John Rocker	.10
56	Javy Lopez	.15
57	Eddie Perez	.10
58	Kevin Millwood	.10
59	Chipper Jones,	
	Greg Maddux	.50
60	Jeromy Burnitz	.10
61	Steve Woodard	.10
62	Ron Belliard	.10
63	Geoff Jenkins	.20
64	Bob Wickman	.10
65	Marquis Grissom	.10
66	Henry Blanco	.10
67	Mark Loretta	.10
68	Alex Ochoa	.10
69	Marquis Grissom,	
	Jeromy Burnitz	.10
70	Mark McGwire	1.50
71	Edgar Renteria	.10
72	Dave Veres	.10
73	Eli Marrero	.10
74	Fernando Tatis	.10
75	J.D. Drew	.20
76	Ray Lankford	.10
77	Daryle Kile	.10
78	Kent Bottenfield	.10
79	Joe McEwing	.10
80	Mark McGwire,	
	Ray Lankford	.75
81	Sammy Sosa	1.25
82	Jose Nieves	.10
83	Jon Lieber	.10
84	Henry Rodriguez	.10
85	Mark Grace	.20
86	Eric Young	.10
87	Kerry Wood	.20
88	Ismael Valdes	.10
89	Glenallen Hill	.10

#	Player	Price
90	Sammy Sosa, Mark Grace	.60
91	Greg Vaughn	.10
92	Fred McGriff	.20
93	Ryan Rupe	.10
94	Bubba Trammell	.10
95	Miguel Cairo	.10
96	Roberto Hernandez	.10
97	Jose Canseco	.40
98	Wilson Alvarez	.10
99	John Flaherty	.10
100	Vinny Castilla	.15
101	Jose Canseco, Roberto Hernandez	.25
102	Randy Johnson	.50
103	Matt Williams	.15
104	Matt Mantei	.10
105	Steve Finley	.10
106	Luis Gonzalez	.20
107	Travis Lee	.10
108	Omar Daal	.10
109	Jay Bell	.10
110	Erubiel Durazo	.10
111	Tony Womack	.10
112	Todd Stottlemyre	.10
113	Randy Johnson, Matt Williams	.25
114	Gary Sheffield	.25
115	Adrian Beltre	.10
116	Kevin Brown	.20
117	Todd Hundley	.10
118	Eric Karros	.10
119	Shawn Green	.40
120	Chan Ho Park	.10
121	Mark Grudzielanek	.10
122	Todd Hollandsworth	.10
123	Jeff Shaw	.10
124	Darren Dreifort	.10
125	Gary Sheffield, Kevin Brown	.15
126	Vladimir Guerrero	.50
127	Michael Barrett	.10
128	Dustin Hermanson	.10
129	Jose Vidro	.10
130	Chris Widger	.10
131	Mike Thurman	.10
132	Wilton Guerrero	.10
133	Brad Fullmer	.10
134	Rondell White	.10
135	Ugueth Urbina	.10
136	Vladimir Guerrero, Rondell White	.40
137	Barry Bonds	1.50
138	Russ Ortiz	.10
139	J.T. Snow	.10
140	Joe Nathan	.10
141	Rich Aurilia	.10
142	Jeff Kent	.20
143	Armando Rios	.10
144	Ellis Burks	.10
145	Robb Nen	.10
146	Marvin Benard	.10
147	Barry Bonds, Russ Ortiz	.75
148	Manny Ramirez	.50
149	Bartolo Colon	.10
150	Kenny Lofton	.20
151	Sandy Alomar Jr.	.10
152	Travis Fryman	.15
153	Omar Vizquel	.15
154	Roberto Alomar	.40
155	Richie Sexson	.25
156	David Justice	.20
157	Jim Thome	.50
158	Manny Ramirez, Roberto Alomar	.25
159	Ken Griffey Jr.	1.00
160	Edgar Martinez	.15
161	Fred Garcia	.10
162	Alex Rodriguez	1.50
163	John Halama	.10
164	Russ Davis	.10
165	David Bell	.10
166	Gil Meche	.10
167	Jamie Moyer	.10
168	John Olerud	.20
169	Ken Griffey Jr., Fred Garcia	.50
170	Preston Wilson	.20
171	Antonio Alfonseca	.10
172	A.J. Burnett	.10
173	Luis Castillo	.10
174	Mike Lowell	.10
175	Alex Fernandez	.10
176	Mike Redmond	.10
177	Alex Gonzalez	.10
178	Vladimir Nunez	.10
179	Mark Kotsay	.10
180	Preston Wilson, Luis Castillo	.10
181	Mike Piazza	1.00
182	Darryl Hamilton	.10
183	Al Leiter	.20
184	Robin Ventura	.20
185	Rickey Henderson	.20
186	Rey Ordonez	.10
187	Edgardo Alfonzo	.10
188	Derek Bell	.10
189	Mike Hampton	.10
190	Armando Benitez	.10
191	Mike Piazza, Rickey Henderson	.75
192	Cal Ripken Jr.	1.50
193	B.J. Surhoff	.10
194	Mike Mussina	.20
195	Albert Belle	.15
196	Jerry Hairston Jr.	.10
197	Will Clark	.20
198	Sidney Ponson	.10
199	Brady Anderson	.10
200	Scott Erickson	.10
201	Ryan Minor	.10
202	Cal Ripken Jr., Albert Belle	.75
203	Tony Gwynn	.75
204	Bret Boone	.20
205	Ryan Klesko	.10
206	Ben Davis	.10
207	Matt Clement	.10
208	Eric Owens	.10
209	Trevor Hoffman	.10
210	Sterling Hitchcock	.10
211	Phil Nevin	.10
212	Tony Gwynn, Trevor Hoffman	.40
213	Scott Rolen	.50
214	Bob Abreu	.10
215	Curt Schilling	.25
216	Rico Brogna	.10
217	Robert Person	.10
218	Doug Glanville	.10
219	Mike Lieberthal	.10
220	Andy Ashby	.10
221	Randy Wolf	.10
222	Bob Abreu, Curt Schilling	.20
223	Brian Giles	.20
224	Jason Kendall	.20
225	Kris Benson	.10
226	Warren Morris	.10
227	Kevin Young	.10
228	Al Martin	.10
229	Wil Cordero	.10
230	Bruce Aven	.10
231	Todd Ritchie	.10
232	Jason Kendall, Brian Giles	.10
233	Ivan Rodriguez	.50
234	Rusty Greer	.10
235	Ruben Mateo	.10
236	Justin Thompson	.10
237	Rafael Palmeiro	.25
238	Chad Curtis	.10
239	Royce Clayton	.10
240	Gabe Kapler	.10
241	Jeff Zimmerman	.10
242	John Wetteland	.10
243	Ivan Rodriguez, Rafael Palmeiro	.25
244	Nomar Garciaparra	1.25
245	Pedro Martinez	.75
246	Jose Offerman	.10
247	Jason Varitek	.10
248	Troy O'Leary	.10
249	John Valentin	.10
250	Trot Nixon	.10
251	Carl Everett	.10
252	Wilton Veras	.10
253	Bret Saberhagen	.10
254	Nomar Garciaparra, Pedro J. Martinez	.60
255	Sean Casey	.10
256	Barry Larkin	.25
257	Pokey Reese	.10
258	Pete Harnisch	.10
259	Aaron Boone	.10
260	Dante Bichette	.10
261	Scott Williamson	.10
262	Steve Parris	.10
263	Dmitri Young	.10
264	Mike Cameron	.10
265	Sean Casey, Scott Williamson	.10
266	Larry Walker	.25
267	Rolando Arrojo	.10
268	Pedro Astacio	.10
269	Todd Helton	.50
270	Jeff Cirillo	.10
271	Neifi Perez	.10
272	Brian Bohanon	.10
273	Jeffrey Hammonds	.10
274	Tom Goodwin	.10
275	Larry Walker, Todd Helton	.25
276	Carlos Beltran	.15
277	Jermaine Dye	.10
278	Mike Sweeney	.10
279	Joe Randa	.10
280	Jose Rosado	.10
281	Carlos Febles	.10
282	Jeff Suppan	.10
283	Johnny Damon	.20
284	Jeremy Giambi	.10
285	Mike Sweeney, Carlos Beltran	.10
286	Tony Clark	.10
287	Damion Easley	.10
288	Jeff Weaver	.10
289	Dean Palmer	.10
290	Juan Gonzalez	.50
291	Juan Encarnacion	.10
292	Todd Jones	.10
293	Karim Garcia	.10
294	Deivi Cruz	.10
295	Dean Palmer, Juan Encarnacion	.10
296	Corey Koskie	.10
297	Brad Radke	.10
298	Doug Mientkiewicz	.10
299	Ron Coomer	.10
300	Joe Mays	.10
301	Eric Milton	.10
302	Jacque Jones	.10
303	Chad Allen	.10
304	Cristian Guzman	.10
305	Jason Ryan	.10
306	Todd Walker	.10
307	Corey Koskie, Eric Milton	.10
308	Frank Thomas	.50
309	Paul Konerko	.10
310	Mike Sirotka	.10
311	Jim Parque	.10
312	Magglio Ordonez	.25
313	Bob Howry	.10
314	Carlos Lee	.10
315	Ray Durham	.10
316	Chris Singleton	.10
317	Brook Fordyce	.10
318	Frank Thomas, Magglio Ordonez	.25
319	Derek Jeter	1.50
320	Roger Clemens	1.00
321	Paul O'Neill	.20
322	Bernie Williams	.40
323	Mariano Rivera	.20
324	Tino Martinez	.20
325	David Cone	.20
326	Chuck Knoblauch	.20
327	Darryl Strawberry	.20
328	Orlando Hernandez	.10
329	Ricky Ledee	.10
330	Derek Jeter, Bernie Williams	.75
331	Pat Burrell (Rookie 2000)	.50
332	Alfonso Soriano (Rookie 2000)	.75
333	Josh Beckett (Rookie 2000)	.25
334	Matt Riley (Rookie 2000)	.15
335	Brian Cooper (Rookie 2000)	.10
336	Eric Munson (Rookie 2000)	.20
337	Vernon Wells (Rookie 2000)	.25
338	Juan Pena (Rookie 2000)	.10
339	Mark DeRosa (Rookie 2000)	.10
340	Kip Wells (Rookie 2000)	.10
341	Roosevelt Brown (Rookie 2000)	.10
342	Jason LaRue (Rookie 2000)	.10
343	Ben Petrick (Rookie 2000)	.10
344	Mark Quinn (Rookie 2000)	.10
345	Julio Ramirez (Rookie 2000)	.10
346	Rod Barajas (Rookie 2000)	.10
347	Robert Fick (Rookie 2000)	.10
348	David Newhan (Rookie 2000)	.10
349	Eric Gagne (Rookie 2000)	.15
350	Jorge Toca (Rookie 2000)	.10
351	Mitch Meluskey (Rookie 2000)	.10
352	Ed Yarnall (Rookie 2000)	.10
353	Chad Hermansen (Rookie 2000)	.10
354	Peter Bergeron (Rookie 2000)	.10
355	Dermal Brown (Rookie 2000)	.10
356	Adam Kennedy (Rookie 2000)	.10
357	Kevin Barker (Rookie 2000)	.10
358	Francisco Cordero (Rookie 2000)	.10
359	Travis Dawkins (Rookie 2000)	.10
360	Jeff Williams (Rookie 2000)	.10
361	Chad Hutchinson (Rookie 2000)	.10
362	D'Angelo Jimenez (Rookie 2000)	.10
363	Derrick Gibson (Rookie 2000)	.10
364	Calvin Murray (Rookie 2000)	.10
365	Doug Davis (Rookie 2000)	.10
366	Rob Ramsay (Rookie 2000)	.10
367	Mark Redman (Rookie 2000)	.10
368	Rick Ankiel (Rookie 2000)	.10
369	Domingo Guzman (Rookie 2000)	.10
370	Eugene Kingsale (Rookie 2000)	.10
371	Nomar Garciaparra (Big Play Makers)	.75
372	Ken Griffey Jr. (Big Play Makers)	.50
373	Randy Johnson (Big Play Makers)	.25
374	Jeff Bagwell (Big Play Makers)	.25
375	Ivan Rodriguez (Big Play Makers)	.25
376	Derek Jeter (Big Play Makers)	.75
377	Carlos Beltran (Big Play Makers)	.10
378	Vladimir Guerrero (Big Play Makers)	.40
379	Sammy Sosa (Big Play Makers)	.60
380	Barry Bonds (Big Play Makers)	.75
381	Pedro Martinez (Big Play Makers)	.40
382	Chipper Jones (Big Play Makers)	.50
383	Mo Vaughn (Big Play Makers)	.10
384	Mike Piazza (Big Play Makers)	.50
385	Alex Rodriguez (Big Play Makers)	.75
386	Manny Ramirez (Big Play Makers)	.25
387	Mark McGwire (Big Play Makers)	.75
388	Tony Gwynn (Big Play Makers)	.40
389	Sean Casey (Big Play Makers)	.10
390	Cal Ripken Jr. (Big Play Makers)	.75
391-440	Ken Griffey Jr.	.40
441	Tommy Lasorda	.50
442	Sean Burroughs	.75
443	Rick Krivda	.40
444	Ben Sheets RC	1.50
445	Pat Borders	.40
446	Brent Abernathy RC	.75
447	Tim Young	.40
448	Adam Everett	.50
449	Anthony Sanders	.40
450	Ernie Young	.40
451	Brad Wilkerson RC	1.50
452	Kurt Ainsworth	1.00
453	Ryan Franklin	.40
454	Todd Williams	.40
455	Jon Rauch RC	.50
456	Roy Oswalt RC	5.00
457	Shane Heams	.50
458	Chris George	.50
459	Bobby Seay	.40
460	Mike Kinkade	.40
461	Marcus Jensen	.40
462	Travis Dawkins	.50
463	Doug Mientkiewicz	.40
464	John Cotton	.40
465	Mike Neill	.40
466	Team Photo USA	2.50

2000 Upper Deck Yankees Legends Sample

This promo card was issued to preview the Yankees Legends set. With silver-foil graphics on front, it is identical in design to the base cards in the regularly issued version. Back has a "SAMPLE" overprint across the stats.

		NM/M
NY7	Mickey Mantle	5.00

2000 Upper Deck Yankees Legends

		NM/M
Complete Set (90):		20.00
Common Player:		.15
Pack (5):		6.00
Box (24):		100.00
1	Babe Ruth	2.00
2	Mickey Mantle	2.00
3	Lou Gehrig	2.00
4	Joe DiMaggio	2.00
5	Yogi Berra	.75
6	Don Mattingly	1.00
7	Reggie Jackson	.75
8	Dave Winfield	.40
9	Bill Skowron	.15
10	Willie Randolph	.15
11	Phil Rizzuto	.15
12	Tony Kubek	.15
13	Thurman Munson	1.00
14	Roger Maris	1.00
15	Billy Martin	.40
16	Elston Howard	.15
17	Graig Nettles	.15
18	Whitey Ford	.50
19	Earl Combes	.15
20	Tony Lazzeri	.15
21	Bob Meusel	.15
22	Joe Gordon	.15
23	Jerry Coleman	.15
24	Joe Torre	.50
25	Bucky Dent	.15
26	Don Larsen	.40
27	Bobby Richardson	.15
28	Ron Guidry	.15
29	Bobby Murcer	.15
30	Tommy Henrich	.15
31	Hank Bauer	.15
32	Joe Pepitone	.15
33	Clete Boyer	.15
34	Chris Chambliss	.15
35	Tommy John	.15
36	Goose Gossage	.15
37	Red Ruffing	.15
38	Charlie Keller	.15
39	Billy Gardner	.15
40	Hector Lopez	.15
41	Cliff Johnson	.15
42	Oscar Gamble	.15
43	Allie Reynolds	.15
44	Mickey Rivers	.15
45	Bill Dickey	.40
46	Dave Righetti	.15
47	Mel Stottlemyre	.15
48	Waite Hoyt	.15
49	Lefty Gomez	.15
50	Wade Boggs	.50
51	Billy Martin (Magic Numbers)	.25
52	Babe Ruth (Magic Numbers)	1.00
53	Lou Gehrig (Magic Numbers)	1.00
54	Joe DiMaggio (Magic Numbers)	1.00
55	Mickey Mantle (Magic Numbers)	1.00
56	Yogi Berra (Magic Numbers)	.40
57	Bill Dickey (Magic Numbers)	.25
58	Roger Maris (Magic Numbers)	.50
59	Phil Rizzuto (Magic Numbers)	.25
60	Thurman Munson (Magic Numbers)	.50
61	Whitey Ford (Magic Numbers)	.25
62	Don Mattingly (Magic Numbers)	.50
63	Elston Howard (Magic Numbers)	.15
64	Casey Stengel (Magic Numbers)	.15
65	Reggie Jackson (Magic Numbers)	.50
66	Babe Ruth/1923 (The Championship Years)	1.00
67	Lou Gehrig/1927 (The Championship Years)	1.00
68	Tony Lazzeri/1928 (The Championship Years)	.15
69	Babe Ruth/1932 (The Championship Years)	1.00
70	Lou Gehrig/1936 (The Championship Years)	1.00
71	Lefty Gomez/1937 (The Championship Years)	.15
72	Bill Dickey/1938 (The Championship Years)	.25
73	Tommy Henrich/1939 (The Championship Years)	.15
74	Joe DiMaggio/1941 (The Championship Years)	1.00
75	Spud Chandler/1943 (The Championship Years)	.15
76	Tommy Henrich/1947 (The Championship Years)	.15
77	Phil Rizzuto/1949 (The Championship Years)	.15
78	Whitey Ford/1950 (The Championship Years)	.15
79	Yogi Berra/1951 (The Championship Years)	.40
80	Casey Stengel/1952 (The Championship Years)	.15
81	Billy Martin/1953 (The Championship Years)	.25
82	Don Larsen/1956 (The Championship Years)	.25
83	Elston Howard/1958 (The Championship Years)	.15
84	Roger Maris/1961 (The Championship Years)	.50
85	Mickey Mantle/1962 (The Championship Years)	1.00
86	Reggie Jackson/1977 (The Championship Years)	.50
87	Bucky Dent/1978 (The Championship Years)	.15
88	Wade Boggs/1996 (The Championship Years)	.25
89	Joe Torre/1998 (The Championship Years)	.25
90	Joe Torre/1999 (The Championship Years)	.25

DiMaggio Memorabilia

		NM/M
YLB-JD	Joe DiMaggio/Bat	125.00

		NM/M
YLG-JD	Joe DiMaggio/Gold Bat/56	200.00
YLC-JD	Joe DiMaggio/Bat, Cut Sig./5	650.00

Legendary Lumber

		NM/M
Common Player:		5.00
Inserted 1:23		
HB	Hank Bauer	8.00
YB	Yogi Berra	20.00
PB	Paul Blair	5.00
CB	Clete Boyer	5.00
CC	Chris Chambliss	8.00
BD	Bucky Dent	8.00
JD	Joe DiMaggio	140.00
OG	Oscar Gamble	5.00
BG	Billy Gardner	5.00
TH	Tommy Henrich	5.00
RH	Ralph Houk	8.00
EH	Elston Howard	8.00
RJ	Reggie Jackson	20.00
TJ	Tommy John	8.00
CJ	Cliff Johnson	5.00
CK	Charlie Keller	5.00
TK	Tony Kubek	8.00
HL	Hector Lopez	5.00
MM	Mickey Mantle	165.00
RM	Roger Maris	70.00
DM	Don Mattingly	45.00
TM	Thurman Munson	35.00
BM	Bobby Murcer	8.00
GN	Graig Nettles	10.00
JP	Joe Pepitone	6.00
WR	Willie Randolph	6.00
MR	Mickey Rivers	5.00
BR	Babe Ruth	185.00
MS	Moose Skowron	6.00
DW	Dave Winfield	15.00

Leg. Lumber/Sign. Cut

		NM/M
MM-LC	Mickey Mantle/7	4,000

Legendary Pinstripes

		NM/M
Common Player:		20.00
Inserted 1:144		
BD	Bucky Dent	20.00
WF	Whitey Ford	50.00
LG	Lou Gehrig	300.00
GG	Goose Gossage	20.00
RG	Ron Guidry	20.00
TH	Tommy Henrich	20.00
EH	Elston Howard	20.00
RJ	Reggie Jackson	40.00
HL	Hector Lopez	20.00
MM	Mickey Mantle	250.00
RM	Roger Maris	75.00
BM	Billy Martin	40.00
DM	Don Mattingly	60.00
TM	Thurman Munson	75.00
JP	Joe Pepitone	20.00
AR	Allie Reynolds	20.00
BR	Bobby Richardson	20.00
PR	Phil Rizzuto	40.00
DW	Dave Winfield	40.00

Auto. Legend. Pinstripe

		NM/M
Common Player:		30.00
BD	Bucky Dent	30.00
WF	Whitey Ford	60.00
GG	Goose Gossage	30.00
RG	Ron Guidry	35.00
TH	Tommy Henrich	30.00
GM	Gil MacDougald	30.00
DM	Don Mattingly	150.00
JP	Joe Pepitone	30.00
PR	Phil Rizzuto	60.00
DW	Dave Winfield	35.00

Monument Park

		NM/M
Complete Set (6):		20.00
Common Player:		1.50
Inserted 1:23		3.00
1	Lou Gehrig	6.00
2	Babe Ruth	6.00
3	Mickey Mantle	6.00
4	Joe DiMaggio	6.00
5	Thurman Munson	3.00
6	Elston Howard	1.50

Murderer's Row

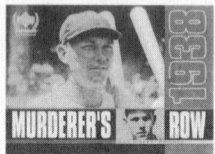

		NM/M
Complete Set (10):		17.50
Common Player:		1.50
Inserted 1:11		
1	Tony Lazzeri	1.50
2	Babe Ruth	6.00
3	Bob Meusel	1.50
4	Lou Gehrig	6.00
5	Joe Dugan	1.50
6	Bill Dickey	1.50
7	Waite Hoyt	1.50
8	Red Ruffing	1.50
9	Earl Combes	1.50
10	Lefty Gomez	1.50

Pride of the Pinstripes

		NM/M
Complete Set (6):		17.50
Common Player:		2.50
Inserted 1:23		
1	Babe Ruth	6.00
2	Mickey Mantle	6.00
3	Joe DiMaggio	5.00
4	Lou Gehrig	5.00
5	Reggie Jackson	2.50
6	Yogi Berra	2.50

The Golden Years

		NM/M
Complete Set (10):		20.00

Common Player:		1.50
Inserted 1:11		
1	Joe DiMaggio	6.00
2	Phil Rizzuto	2.50
3	Yogi Berra	3.00
4	Billy Martin	2.50
5	Whitey Ford	2.50
6	Roger Maris	5.00
7	Mickey Mantle	7.50
8	Elston Howard	1.50
9	Tommy Henrich	1.50
10	Joe Gordon	1.50

The New Dynasty

		NM/M
Complete Set (10):		15.00
Common Player:		1.50
Inserted 1:11		
1	Reggie Jackson	3.50
2	Graig Nettles	1.50
3	Don Mattingly	6.50
4	Goose Gossage	1.50
5	Dave Winfield	3.00
6	Chris Chambliss	1.50
7	Thurman Munson	4.00
8	Willie Randolph	1.50
9	Ron Guidry	2.50
10	Bucky Dent	2.50

22kt Gold Ken Griffey Jr. Rookie Card

A 22-karat gold embossed card replicating in all important details the 1989 Upper Deck Ken Griffey Jr. rookie card was issued by UD. The card was accompanied by a commemorative collectors' sheet describing the original rookie card and the gold version. The gold card was offered to members of UD's Collectors Club for $24.

		NM/M
1	Ken Griffey Jr.	24.00

1993 USA Rice

To promote rice consumption and raise money for the pictured athletes' favorite charities, the USA Rice Council issued this multi-sport card set and made it available by mail for a $2 donation. All players are pictured in civilian clothes with either a blue or red border around. Backs of most cards have rice recipes and indicate the charity to which the athlete is donating their portion of the proceeds. Cards are standard 2-1/2" x 3-1/2".

		NM/M
Complete Set (10):		10.00
Common Card:		.50
1	Steve Sax (Cooking)	1.00

2	Troy Aikman (Football)	3.00
3	Roger Clemens	7.50
4	Zina Garrison (Tennis)	.50
5	Warren Moon (Football)	2.00
6	Summer Sanders (Swimming)	.50
7	Steve Sax (Lifting weights.)	1.00
8	Brian Shimer (Bobsledder)	.50
9	Food Guide Pyramid	.25
10	Healthy Eating Tips	.25

1999 U.S. Cellular Milwaukee Brewers

The four Milwaukee Brewers who have had their uniform numbers retired by the team, plus Jackie Robinson, whose #42 was retired by MLB edict, are honored on this foldout promotion given to fans October 2 at County Stadium. Five 4" x 6" cards make up the panel, which is perforated between the cards for ease of separation. Cards have player action photos on front (color except for Robinson) on a muted blue-green stadium photo background. At lower-right is a gold-foil seal with the player's name and number. At top is a sponsor logo and part of the legend "COMMEMORATING GREATNESS" which runs contiguously across the panel. Backs have a black-and-white photo, career data and highlights.

		NM/M
Complete Set, Panel:		12.00
Complete Set, Singles (5):		8.00
Common Player:		1.00
4	Paul Molitor	4.00
19	Robin Yount	4.00
34	Rollie Fingers	1.00
42	Jackie Robinson	3.00
44	Hank Aaron	5.00

1993 U.S. Department of Transportation Safety Set

This six-card set (issued in three-card panels) was sponsored by the U.S. Department of Transportation and distributed at the Little League World Series. Standard size cards have red and blue borders on front, along with the Little League logo. Backs are printed in red and blue and include a highway safety message and sponsors/licensors logos.

		NM/M
Complete Set (6):		11.00
Common Player:		1.50
	Panel 1	4.00
1	Orel Hershiser	.50
2	Don Mattingly	3.00
3	Mike Mussina	1.00
	Panel 2	6.00
(4)	Mike Piazza	2.50
(5)	Cal Ripken Jr.	4.00
(6)	Mo Vaughn	.50

1987 U.S. Forestry Service Smokey Bear's Team

The U.S. Forestry Service and Major League Baseball united in an effort to promote National Smokey the Bear Day. Two perforated sheets of baseball cards, one each for the American and National Leagues, were produced. The sheet of American Leaguers measures 18" x 24" and contains 16 full-color cards. The National League sheet measures 20" x 18" and contains 15 cards. Each individual card is 4" x 6" and contains a fire prevention tip on the back. An average number of 25,000 sets was sent to all teams.

		NM/M
Complete Set (31):		12.00
Complete A.L. Sheet:		7.00
Complete N.L. Sheet:		7.00
Common Player:		.25
1A	Jose Canseco	.75
1N	Steve Sax	.25
2A	Dennis "Oil Can" Boyd	.25
2Na	Dale Murphy (Shirttail out.)	5.00
2Nb	Dale Murphy (Shirttail in.)	.90
3A	John Candelaria	.25
3Na	Jody Davis (Standing)	3.00
3Nb	Jody Davis (Kneeling)	.25
4A	Harold Baines	.25
4N	Bill Gullickson	.25
5A	Joe Carter	.25
5N	Mike Scott	.25
6A	Jack Morris	.25
6N	Roger McDowell	.25
7A	Buddy Biancalana	.25
7N	Steve Bedrosian	.25
8A	Kirby Puckett	3.00
8N	Johnny Ray	.25
9A	Mike Pagliarulo	.25
9N	Ozzie Smith	3.00
10A	Larry Sheets	.25
10N	Steve Garvey	.50
11A	Mike Moore	.25
11N	Smokey Bear Logo Card	.05
12A	Charlie Hough	.25
12N	Mike Krukow	.25
13A	Smokey Bear Logo Card	.05
13N	Smokey Bear	.05
14A	Tom Henke	.25
14N	Mike Fitzgerald	.25
15A	Jim Gantner	.25
15N	National League Logo Card	.05
16A	American League Logo Card	.05

1990 U.S. Playing Card All-Stars

Sold as a boxed set, these cards are the standard 2-1/2" x 3-1/2" format but feature rounded corners. Each card features a color player photo with the upper-left and lower-right corners inset to provide for playing card designations. A team logo appears in the lower-left corner. On American

League players' cards (Clubs and Spades) the player's name and position appear in white in a blue box beneath the photo. On National Leaguers' cards (Hearts and Diamonds) the box is red and the printing black. Card backs are identical, with blue borders and a multi-colored "1990 Baseball Major League All-Stars" logo on a pinstriped white center panel. A premium version with the cards' edges silvered was also issued. These cards have a small diagonal "nip" at each rounded corner.

		NM/M
Complete Set (56):		5.00
Common Player:		.05
HEARTS		
J	Bobby Bonilla	.05
Q	Kevin Mitchell	.05
K	Darryl Strawberry	.05
A	Ramon Martinez	.05
2	Mike Scioscia	.05
3	Jeff Brantley	.05
4	Ryne Sandberg	.75
5	Chris Sabo	.05
6	Ozzie Smith	.75
7	John Franco	.05
8	Matt Williams	.05
9	Andre Dawson	.25
10	Benito Santiago	.05
CLUBS		
J	Wade Boggs	.75
Q	George Bell	.05
K	Rickey Henderson	.50
A	Bob Welch	.05
2	Lance Parrish	.05
3	Bret Saberhagen	.05
4	Gregg Olson	.05
5	Brook Jacoby	.05
6	Ozzie Guillen	.05
7	Ellis Burks	.05
8	Dennis Eckersley	.40
9	Bobby Thigpen	.05
10	Dave Stieb	.05
DIAMONDS		
J	Tony Gwynn	.75
Q	Will Clark	.05
K	Barry Bonds	1.50
A	Frank Viola	.05
2	Greg Olson	.05
3	Dennis Martinez	.05
4	Roberto Alomar	.20
5	Tim Wallach	.05
6	Barry Larkin	.05
7	Neal Heaton	.05
8	Dave Smith	.05
9	Lenny Dykstra	.05
10	Shawon Dunston	.05
SPADES		
J	Ken Griffey Jr.	1.00
Q	Dave Parker	.05
K	Cecil Fielder	.05
A	Roger Clemens	.85
2	Sandy Alomar	.05
3	Randy Johnson	.50
4	Steve Sax	.05
5	Kelly Gruber	.05
6	Chuck Finley	.05
7	Doug Jones	.05
8	Kirby Puckett	.75
9	Cal Ripken, Jr.	1.50
10	Alan Trammell	.05
WILD CARDS/JOKERS		
---	Jack Armstrong (Joker)	.05
---	Julio Franco (Joker)	.05
---	Rob Dibble, Randy Myers (Wild Card)	.05
---	Mark McGwire, Jose Canseco (Wild Card)	1.00

1991 U.S. Playing Card All-Stars

In standard 2-1/2" x 3-1/2" format, though with rounded corners, this 56-card set was produced by the country's leading maker of playing cards and sold as a boxed set. Fronts have a color player photo with the top-left and bottom-right corners inset to include playing card designations. A team logo

appears in the upper-right corner. On American Leaguers' cards (Hearts and Diamonds), the player's name and position appear in white in a green stripe beneath the photo. National League players (Clubs and Spades) have a yellow stripe with black printing. Backs are red-bordered with a colorful "1991 Baseball Major League All-Stars" logo on a pinstriped white center panel. A silver-edged premium version was also issued. These cards have a diagonal "nip" at each rounded corner. A Canadian version, with the imprint of International Playing Card, also exists.

		NM/M
Complete Set (56):		4.00
Common Player:		.05
HEARTS		
J	Rickey Henderson	.50
Q	Roberto Alomar	.20
K	Dave Henderson	.05
A	Jack Morris	.05
2	Ozzie Guillen	.05
3	Jack McDowell	.05
4	Joe Carter	.05
5	Mark Langston	.05
6	Julio Franco	.05
7	Rick Aguilera	.05
8	Paul Molitor	.50
9	Ruben Sierra	.05
10	Roger Clemens	.85
CLUBS		
J	Andre Dawson	.25
Q	Chris Sabo	.05
K	Ivan Calderon	.05
A	Tony Gwynn	.75
2	Paul O'Neill	.05
3	John Smiley	.05
4	Howard Johnson	.05
5	Mike Morgan	.05
6	Barry Larkin	.05
7	Frank Viola	.05
8	Juan Samuel	.05
9	Craig Biggio	.05
10	Lee Smith	.05
DIAMONDS		
J	Sandy Alomar	.05
Q	Cecil Fielder	.05
K	Cal Ripken, Jr.	1.50
A	Ken Griffey Jr.	1.00
2	Carlton Fisk	.50
3	Scott Sanderson	.05
4	Kirby Puckett	.75
5	Jeff Reardon	.05
6	Rafael Palmeiro	.40
7	Bryan Harvey	.05
8	Jimmy Key	.05
9	Harold Baines	.05
10	Dennis Eckersley	.40
SPADES		
J	Benito Santiago	.05
Q	Ryne Sandberg	.75
K	Ozzie Smith	.75
A	Tom Glavine	.10
2	Eddie Murray	.60
3	Pete Harnisch	.05
4	John Kruk	.05
5	Tom Browning	.05
6	George Bell	.05
7	Dennis Martinez	.05
8	Brett Butler	.05
9	Terry Pendleton	.05
10	Rob Dibble	.05
WILD CARDS/JOKERS		
---	Bobby Bonilla (Joker)	.05
---	Danny Tartabull	.05
---	Wade Boggs (Wild Card)	.75
---	Will Clark (Wild Card)	.05

1992 U.S. Playing Card Aces

This 56-card boxed set features 13 top players in each of four major statistical categories, ranked by performance. Hearts feature RBI leaders, Clubs depict home run hitters, batting average leaders are featured on Diamonds and Spades have pitchers with lowest ERAs. Card fronts feature full-bleed color photos, with the playing card suit and rank overprinted in opposing corners. A team logo is in the lower-left, along with a black box containing the player's name and position in gold. Backs have a red, white and gold "Major League Baseball 1992 Aces" against a black background. The 2-1/2" x 3-1/2" cards have rounded corners.

		NM/M
Complete Set (56):		4.00
Common Player:		.05

HEARTS

J	Will Clark	.05
Q	Howard Johnson	.05
K	Jose Canseco	.35
A	Cecil Fielder	.05
2	Juan Gonzalez	.25
3	Andre Dawson	.25
4	Ron Gant	.05
5	Fred McGriff	.05
6	Joe Carter	.05
7	Frank Thomas	.50
8	Cal Ripken (Ripken)	1.50
9	Ruben Sierra	.05
10	Barry Bonds	1.50

CLUBS

J	Cal Ripken (Ripken)	1.50
Q	Howard Johnson	.05
K	Cecil Fielder	.05
A	Jose Canseco	.40
2	Chili Davis	.05
3	Mickey Tettleton	.05
4	Danny Tartabull	.05
5	Fred McGriff	.05
6	Andre Dawson	.25
7	Frank Thomas	.75
8	Ron Gant	.05
9	Cal Ripken (Ripken)	1.50
10	Matt Williams	.05

DIAMONDS

J	Ken Griffey Jr.	1.00
Q	Willie Randolph	.05
K	Wade Boggs	.75
A	Julio Franco	.05
2	Danny Tartabull	.05
3	Tony Gwynn	.75
4	Frank Thomas	.60
5	Hal Morris	.05
6	Kirby Puckett	.75
7	Terry Pendleton	.05
8	Rafael Palmeiro	.50
9	Cal Ripkin (Ripken)	1.50
10	Paul Molitor	.60

SPADES

J	Tim Belcher	.05
Q	Tom Glavine	.15
K	Jose Rijo	.05
A	Dennis Martinez	.05
2	Mike Moore	.05
3	Nolan Ryan	1.50
4	Jim Abbott	.05
5	Bill Wegman	.05
6	Mike Morgan	.05
7	Jose DeLeon	.05
8	Pete Harnisch	.05
9	Tom Candiotti	.05
10	Roger Clemens	.85

JOKERS

---	Roger Clemens (Joker)	.85
---	Tom Glavine (Joker)	.15
---	Home Run Rummy Game Instructions	.05
---	Header Card	.05

All-Stars

Players from the 1992 All-Star Game are featured in this set of 56 playing cards. In playing card format of 2-1/2" x 3-1/2" with rounded corners, the cards have a photo on front with a team logo in the upper-right corner. Traditional playing card suits and values are in the upper-left and lower-right corners. Player names are in a yellow (American League) or red (National League) box beneath the photo. Backs have a large product logo on a white background with a dark blue-green border. Appropriate licensor and manufacturer logos appear at bottom. The set was sold in a box featuring miniature representations of some of the cards.

		NM/M
Complete Set (56):		5.00
Common Player:		.05

AC	Roberto Alomar	.20
2C	Joe Carter	.05
3C	Juan Guzman	.05
4C	Charles Nagy	.05
5C	Robin Ventura	.05
6C	Chuck Knoblauch	.05
7C	Ruben Sierra	.05
8C	Paul Molitor	.60
9C	Carlos Baerga	.05
10C	Edgar Martinez	.05
JC	Sandy Alomar Jr.	.05
QC	Mark McGwire	1.25
KC	Wade Boggs	.75
AS	Ken Griffey Jr.	1.00
2S	Ivan Rodriguez	.50
3S	Roberto Kelly	.05
4S	Brady Anderson	.05
5S	Travis Fryman	.05
6S	Jeff Montgomery	.05
7S	Jack McDowell	.05
8S	Rick Aguilera	.05
9S	Kevin Brown	.05
10S	Roger Clemens	.85
JS	Jose Canseco	.35
QS	Cal Ripken Jr.	1.50
KS	Kirby Puckett	.75
AH	Andy Van Slyke	.05
2H	Greg Maddux	.75
3H	Larry Walker	.05
4H	Tom Pagnozzi	.05
5H	David Cone	.05
6H	Tony Fernandez	.05
7H	Will Clark	.05
8H	Gary Sheffield	.30
9H	Mike Sharperson	.05
10H	John Kruk	.05
JH	Ryne Sandberg	.75
QH	Ozzie Smith	.75
KH	Fred McGriff	.05
AD	Tony Gwynn	.75
2D	Bob Tewksbury	.05
3D	Ron Gant	.05
4D	Doug Jones	.05
5D	Craig Biggio	.05
6D	Bip Roberts	.05
7D	Norm Charlton	.05
8D	John Smoltz	.05
9D	Lee Smith	.05
10D	Tom Glavine	.25
JD	Benito Santiago	.05
QD	Terry Pendleton	.05
KD	Barry Bonds	1.50
WILD	Dennis Eckersley	.50
JOKER	Mike Mussina, Mark Langston	.15
JOKER	Darren Daulton, Dennis Martinez	.05
---	Advertising Card	.05

Team Sets

Besides two All-Star sets, the U.S. Playing Card Co. in 1992 issued playing card team sets for five teams. All were issued as 56-card boxed sets in a similar format. Cards are 2-1/2" x 3-1/2" with rounded corners. Fronts feature player photos with insets at the upper-left and lower-right corners displaying card suit designations and rankings. The player's name and position appear in a colored strip beneath the photo. Backs feature a large color team logo set on a gray background with either dark blue or red pinstriping and heavy vertical side bars. A silver-edged World Series premium version of the Braves and Twins sets were also issued; on these cards each rounded corner has a diagonal "nip."

Atlanta Braves

		NM/M
Complete Set (56):		5.00
Common Player:		.10

HEARTS

J	Dave Justice	.10
Q	Juan Berenguer	.10
K	Ron Gant	.10
A	Otis Nixon	.10
2	Deion Sanders	.20
3	Mike Stanton	.10
4	Sid Bream	.10
5	Armando Reynoso	.10
6	Brian Hunter	.10
7	Kent Mercker	.10
8	Lonnie Smith	.10
9	Jeff Treadway	.10
10	Tom Glavine	.35

CLUBS

J	Pete Smith	.10
Q	Jeff Blauser	.10
K	Charlie Leibrandt	.10
A	Terry Pendleton	.10
2	Mark Lemke	.10
3	Armando Reynoso	.10
4	Kent Mercker	.10
5	Marvin Freeman	.10
6	Rico Rossy	.10
7	Dave Justice	.10
8	Juan Berenguer	.10
9	Ron Gant	.10
10	Otis Nixon	.10

DIAMONDS

J	Brian Hunter	.10
Q	Rafael Belliard	.10
K	Greg Olson	.10
A	Steve Avery	.10
2	Marvin Freeman	.10
3	Pete Smith	.10
4	Mike Heath	.10
5	Jeff Blauser	.10
6	Jim Clancy	.10
7	Rico Rossy	.10
8	John Smoltz	.10
9	Charlie Leibrandt	.10
10	Terry Pendleton	.10

SPADES

J	John Smoltz	.10
Q	Lonnie Smith	.10
K	Jeff Treadway	.10
A	Tom Glavine	.35
2	Jim Clancy	.10
3	Deion Sanders	.20
4	Mark Lemke	.10
5	Mike Heath	.10
6	Mike Stanton	.10
7	Sid Bream	.10
8	Rafael Belliard	.10
9	Greg Olson	.10
10	Steve Avery	.10

JOKERS

---	N.L. Logo (Joker)	.05
---	N.L. Logo (Joker)	.05
---	'92 Braves Home Schedule	.05
---	Atlanta Braves History	.05

World Series - Braves

		NM/M
Complete Set (56):		5.00
Common Player:		.05

AC	Charlie Leibrandt	.10
2C	Vinny Castilla	.10
3C	Alejandro Pena	.10
4C	Mark Lemke	.10
5C	Marvin Freeman	.10
6C	Dave Justice	.10
7C	Mike Stanton	.10
8C	Terry Pendleton	.10
9C	Jeff Treadway	.10
10C	Brian Hunter	.10
JC	Steve Avery	.10
QC	Jeff Blauser	.10
KC	Ron Gant	.10
AS	Terry Pendleton	.10
2S	Ryan Klesko	.10
3S	Jeff Treadway	.10
4S	Pete Smith	.10
5S	Ron Gant	.10
6S	Sid Bream	.10
7S	Deion Sanders	.15
8S	Tom Glavine	.35
9S	Kent Mercker	.10
10S	Lonnie Smith	.10
JS	Damon Berryhill	.10
QS	Marvin Freeman	.10
KS	John Smoltz	.10
AH	Dave Justice	.10
2H	Kent Mercker	.10
3H	Lonnie Smith	.10
4H	Greg Olson	.10
5H	Jeff Reardon	.10
6H	Steve Avery	.10
7H	Otis Nixon	.10
8H	Juan Berenguer	.10
9H	Greg Olson	.10
10H	Mike Bielecki	.10
JH	Mike Stanton	.10
QH	Deion Sanders	.15
KH	Pete Smith	.10
AD	Otis Nixon	.10
2D	Juan Berenguer	.10
3D	Francisco Cabrera	.10
4D	Damon Berryhill	.10
5D	Brian Hunter	.10
6D	Charlie Leibrandt	.10
7D	Jeff Blauser	.10
8D	John Smoltz	.10
9D	Alejandro Pena	.10
10D	Mark Lemke	.10
JD	Jeff Reardon	.10
QD	Sid Bream	.10
KD	Tom Glavine	.35
WILD	Mike Bielecki	.10
WILD	David Nied	.10
WILD	Mark Wohlers	.10
JOKER	Checklist	.05

Boston Red Sox

		NM/M
Complete Set (56):		5.00
Common Player:		.10

HEARTS

J	Jack Clark	.10
Q	Jeff Gray	.10
K	Greg Harris	.10
A	Roger Clemens	1.00
2	Matt Young	.10
3	John Marzano	.10
4	Dennis Lamp	.10
5	Danny Darwin	.10
6	Jeff Reardon	.10
7	Phil Plantier	.10
8	Tony Fossas	.10
9	Carlos Quintana	.10
10	Wade Boggs	.75

CLUBS

J	Luis Rivera	.10
Q	John Marzano	.10
K	Jody Reed	.10
A	Mike Greenwell	.10
2	Danny Darwin	.10
3	Dan Petry	.10
4	Dana Kiecker	.10
5	Greg Harris	.10
6	Tony Pena	.10
7	Dan Petry	.10
8	Jeff Gray	.10
9	Jack Clark	.10
10	Roger Clemens	1.00

DIAMONDS

J	Tom Brunansky	.10
Q	Mo Vaughn	.25
K	Ellis Burks	.10
A	Joe Hesketh	.10
2	Steve Lyons	.10
3	Dana Kiecker	.10
4	Tony Fossas	.10
5	Matt Young	.10
6	Luis Rivera	.10
7	Tom Bolton	.10
8	Kevin Morton	.10
9	Jody Reed	.10
10	Mike Greenwell	.10

SPADES

J	Tony Pena	.10
Q	Phil Plantier	.10
K	Carlos Quintana	.10
A	Wade Boggs	.75
2	Tom Bolton	.10
3	Mo Vaughn	.25
4	Kevin Morton	.10
5	Steve Lyons	.10
6	Tom Brunansky	.10
7	Dennis Lamp	.10
8	Joe Hesketh	.10
9	Ellis Burks	.10
10	Jeff Reardon	.10

JOKERS

---	A.L. Logo (Joker)	.10
---	A.L. Logo (Joker) (Joker)	.10
---	'92 Red Sox Home Schedule	.10
---	Boston Red Sox Team History	.10

Chicago Cubs

		NM/M
Complete Set (56):		5.00
Common Player:		.10

HEARTS

J	Jerome Walton	.10
Q	Chico Walker	.10
K	Chuck McElroy	.10
A	Andre Dawson	.30
2	Dwight Smith	.10
3	Rick Wilkins	.10
4	Doug Dascenzo	.10
5	Bob Scanlan	.10
6	Chico Walker	.10
7	Paul Assenmacher	.10
8	Mark Grace	.25
9	Ryne Sandberg	1.00
10	Danny Jackson	.10

CLUBS

J	Hector Villanueva	.10
Q	Doug Dascenzo	.10
K	Shawon Dunston	.10
A	George Bell	.10
2	Greg Scott	.10
3	Jose Vizcaino	.10
4	Heathcliff Slocumb	.10
5	Danny Jackson	.10
6	Shawn Boskie	.10
7	Luis Salazar	.10
8	Chuck McElroy	.10
9	Andre Dawson	.30
10	Dave Smith	.10

DIAMONDS

J	Frank Castillo	.10
Q	Les Lancaster	.10
K	Paul Assenmacher	.10
A	Greg Maddux	1.00
2	Shawn Boskie	.10
3	Ced Landrum	.10
4	Gary Scott	.10
5	Ced Landrum	.10
6	Jose Vizcaino	.10
7	Mike Harkey	.10
8	Jerome Walton	.10
9	George Bell	.10
10	Frank Castillo	.10

SPADES

J	Bob Scanlan	.10
Q	Luis Salazar	.10
K	Mark Grace	.25
A	Ryne Sandberg	1.00
2	Frank Castillo	.10
3	Mike Harkey	.10
4	Dave Smith	.10
5	Les Lancaster	.10
6	Hector Villanueva	.10
7	Shawon Dunston	.10
8	Heathcliff Slocumb	.10
9	Greg Maddux	1.00
10	Dwight Smith	.10

JOKERS

---	N.L. logo (Joker)	.10
---	N.L. logo (Joker)	.10
---	'92 Cubs Home Schedule	.10
---	Chicago Cubs Team History	.10

Detroit Tigers

		NM/M
Complete Set (56):		5.00
Common Player:		.10

HEARTS

J	Lloyd Moseby	.10
Q	Walt Terrell	.10
K	Mickey Tettleton	.10
A	Cecil Fielder	.10
2	Andy Allanson	.10
3	Dave Bergman	.10
4	Steve Searcy	.10
5	Dan Gakeler	.10
6	Jerry Don Gleaton	.10
7	Paul Gibson	.10
8	Alan Trammell	.25
9	Frank Tanana	.10
10	John Cerutti	.10

CLUBS

J	Rob Deer	.10
Q	Skeeter Barnes	.10
K	Pete Incaviglia	.10
A	Tony Phillips	.10
2	Dan Gakeler	.10
3	Walt Terrell	.10
4	David Haas	.10
5	Pete Incaviglia	.10
6	Travis Fryman	.10
7	Scott Aldred	.10
8	Skeeter Barnes	.10
9	Mickey Tettleton	.10
10	Cecil Fielder	.10

DIAMONDS

J	Milt Cuyler	.10
Q	Travis Fryman	.10
K	Lou Whitaker	.10
A	Bill Gullickson	.10
2	John Cerutti	.10
3	Steve Searcy	.10
4	David Haas	.10
5	Lloyd Moseby	.10
6	Scott Livingstone	.10
7	John Shelby	.10
8	Mike Henneman	.10
9	Dave Bergman	.10
10	Tony Phillips	.10

SPADES

J	Alan Trammell	.25
Q	Jerry Don Gleaton	.10
K	Mike Henneman	.10
A	Frank Tanana	.10
2	Scott Aldred	.10
3	Scott Livingstone	.10
4	John Shelby	.10
5	Rob Deer	.10
6	Milt Cuyler	.10
7	Andy Allanson	.10
8	Paul Gibson	.10
9	Lou Whitaker	.10
10	Bill Gullickson	.10

JOKERS

---	A.L. Logo (Joker)	.10
---	A.L. Logo (Joker)	.10
---	'92 Tigers Home Schedule	.10
---	Detroit Tigers Team History	.10

Minnesota Twins

		NM/M
Complete Set (56):		5.00
Common Player:		.10

HEARTS

J	Scott Leius	.10
Q	Rick Aguilera	.10
K	Jack Morris	.10
A	Kirby Puckett	.75
2	Junior Ortiz	.10
3	Paul Abbott	.10
4	Steve Bedrosian	.10
5	Pedro Munoz	.10
6	Mike Pagliarulo	.10
7	Greg Gagne	.10
8	Chuck Knoblauch	.10
9	Kevin Tapani	.10
10	Scott Erickson	.10

CLUBS

J	Carl Willis	.10
Q	Dan Gladden	.10
K	Kent Hrbek	.10
A	Shane Mack	.10
2	Allan Anderson	.10
3	Al Newman	.10
4	Junior Ortiz	.10
5	Mike Pagliarulo	.10
6	Terry Leach	.10
7	Scott Leius	.10
8	Rick Aguilera	.10
9	Jack Morris	.10
10	Kirby Puckett	.75

DIAMONDS

J	Gene Larkin	.10
Q	Randy Bush	.10
K	Chili Davis	.10
A	Brian Harper	.10
2	Al Newman	.10
3	Allan Anderson	.10
4	David West	.10
5	Terry Leach	.10
6	Mark Guthrie	.10
7	Carl Willis	.10
8	Dan Gladden	.10
9	Kent Hrbek	.10
10	Shane Mack	.10

SPADES

J	Greg Gagne	.10
Q	Chuck Knoblauch	.10
K	Kevin Tapani	.10
A	Scott Erickson	.10
2	Paul Abbott	.10
3	David West	.10
4	Steve Bedrosian	.10
5	Mark Guthrie	.10
6	Pedro Munoz	.10
7	Gene Larkin	.10
8	Randy Bush	.10
9	Chili Davis	.10
10	Brian Harper	.10

JOKERS

---	A.L. Logo (Joker)	.10
---	A.L. Logo (Joker)	.10
---	'92 Twins Home Schedule	.10
---	Minnesota Twins Team History	.10

1993 U.S. Playing Card Aces

Major league superstars with the top 1992 statistical performance in four major categories are featured in this set of playing cards. Spades feature the 13 lowest ERAs; Hearts depict the baker's dozen stolen base leaders; the 13 players with highest home run totals and batting average are featured on clubs and diamonds, respectively. The 2-1/2" x 3-1/2" cards have rounded corners and traditional trading card suits and values in the upper-left and lower-right corners. Borderless color player photos are featured on front, with color team logos at lower-left. Player names and positions are printed in a black box at bottom. Backs have a red background with a large product logo and smaller licensor and manufacturer logos at bottom. The box in which the cards were sold is enhanced with gold foil and features miniature representations of some of the cards.

		NM/M
Complete Set (56):		4.00
Common Player:		.05
AC	Juan Gonzalez	.15
2C	Dave Hollins	.05
3C	Darren Daulton	.05
4C	Ken Griffey Jr.	.75
5C	Rob Deer	.05
6C	Mickey Tettleton	.05
7C	Gary Sheffield	.25
8C	Joe Carter	.05
9C	Albert Belle	.05
10C	Barry Bonds	1.50
JC	Fred McGriff	.05
QC	Cecil Fielder	.05
KC	Mark McGwire	1.00
AS	Bill Swift	.05
2S	Tom Glavine	.35
3S	Sid Fernandez	.05
4S	Greg Swindell	.05
5S	Juan Guzman	.05
6S	Jose Rijo	.05
7S	Mike Morgan	.05
8S	Mike Mussina	.35
9S	Dennis Martinez	.05
10S	Kevin Appier	.05
JS	Roger Clemens	.65
QS	Curt Schilling	.35
KS	Greg Maddux	.60
AH	Marquis Grissom	.05
2H	Chad Curtis	.05
3H	Ozzie Smith	.60
4H	Bip Roberts	.05
5H	Steve Finley	.05
6H	Tim Raines	.05
7H	Delino DeShields	.05
8H	Rickey Henderson	.50
9H	Roberto Alomar	.10
10H	Luis Polonia	.05
JH	Brady Anderson	.05
QH	Pat Listach	.05
KH	Kenny Lofton	.05
AD	Edgar Martinez	.05
2D	Roberto Alomar	.10
3D	Terry Pendleton	.05
4D	Carlos Baerga	.05
5D	Shane Mack	.05
6D	Tony Gwynn	.60
7D	Paul Molitor	.50
8D	Frank Thomas	.50
9D	Bip Roberts	.05
10D	John Kruk	.05
JD	Andy Van Slyke	.05
QD	Kirby Puckett	.60
KD	Gary Sheffield	.05
WILD	Cal Ripken Jr.	1.50
JOKER	National League Logo	.05
JOKER	American League Logo	.05
---	Advertising Card	.05

1992 Rookies

Top rookies of the 1992 season are featured in full-color on the fronts of these playing cards. Player name and position are printed in white in a green stripe beneath the photo. A team logo is in the upper-right corner. Backs are printed in dark green with gold pinstripes and a large gold, red and purple logo.

		NM/M
Complete Boxed Set (56):		4.00
Common Player:		.10
AC	Kenny Lofton	.10
2C	Eric Fox	.10
3C	Mark Wohlers	.10
4C	John Patterson	.10
5C	Eric Young	.10
6C	Arthur Rhodes	.10
7C	Jeff Frye	.10
8C	Scott Servais	.10
9C	Ruben Amaro Jr.	.10
10C	Reggie Sanders	.10
JC	Alan Mills	.10
QC	Bob Zupcic	.10
KC	Cal Eldred	.10
AS	Eric Karros	.10
2S	Butch Henry	.10
3S	Wil Cordero	.10
4S	Pedro Astacio	.10
5S	Derek Bell	.10
6S	David Nied	.10
7S	Jeff Kent	.35
8S	David Haas	.10
9S	Ed Taubensee	.10
10S	Royce Clayton	.10
JS	Moises Alou	.10
QS	Rusty Meacham	.10
KS	Chad Curtis	.10
AH	Pat Listach	.10
2H	Pat Mahomes	.10
3H	Greg Colbrunn	.10
4H	Dan Walters	.10
5H	John Vander Wal	.10
6H	Jeff Branson	.10
7H	Monty Fariss	.10
8H	Rey Sanchez	.10
9H	Robert Wickman	.10
10H	Derrick May	.10
JH	Donovan Osborne	.10
QH	Scott Livingstone	.10
KH	Gary DiSarcina	.10
AD	Dave Fleming	.10
2D	Reggie Jefferson	.10
3D	Anthony Young	.10
4D	Kevin Koslofski	.10
5D	Brian Williams	.10
6D	Brian Jordan	.10
7D	John Doherty	.10
8D	Lenny Webster	.10
9D	Roberto Hernandez	.10
10D	Frank Seminara	.10
JD	Scott Cooper	.10
QD	Andy Stankiewicz	.10
KD	Tim Wakefield	.10
JOKER	Eric Karros (N.L. ROY)	.10
JOKER	Pat Listach (A.L. ROY)	.10
---	Rookie Qualification Rules	.10
---	Checklist	.10

Team Sets

For a second year the leading U.S. manufacturer of playing cards produced several team sets depicting ballplayers. Each was sold as a 56-card set in standard 2-1/2" x 3-1/2" round-corner playing card format in a colorful flip-top box. Backs of each team set carry a team logo. Fronts have portrait or action photo and playing card suits and values. Most players are represented twice in each team set in different photos.

Cincinnati Reds

		NM/M
Complete Set (56):		4.00
Common Player:		.10
AC	Tim Belcher	.10
2C	Jacob Brumfield	.10
3C	Rob Dibble	.10
4C	Jose Rijo	.10
5C	Dan Wilson	.10
6C	Cecil Espy	.10
7C	Tom Browning	.10
8C	Steve Foster	.10
9C	Jacob Brumfield	.10
10C	Jeff Branson	.10
JC	Greg Cadaret	.10
QC	Hal Morris	.10
KC	Joe Oliver	.10
AS	Bip Roberts	.10
2S	Cesar Hernandez	.10
3S	Chris Hammond	.10
4S	Scott Ruskin	.10
5S	John Smiley	.10
6S	Roberto Kelly	.10
7S	Barry Larkin	.25
8S	Gary Varsho	.10
9S	Hal Morris	.10
10S	Dwayne Henry	.10
JS	Tommy Gregg	.10
QS	Kevin Mitchell	.10
KS	Rob Dibble	.10
AH	Barry Larkin	.25
2H	Willie Greene	.10
3H	Steve Foster	.10
4H	Greg Cadaret	.10
5H	Chris Sabo	.10
6H	Joe Oliver	.10
7H	Milton Hill	.10
8H	Tim Belcher	.10
9H	Scott Ruskin	.10
10H	Cecil Espy	.10
JH	Roberto Kelly	.10
QH	Tom Browning	.10
KH	Reggie Sanders	.10
AD	Jose Rijo	.10
2D	Dwayne Henry	.10
3D	Jeff Branson	.10
4D	Milton Hill	.10
5D	Tim Costo	.10
6D	Bip Roberts	.10
7D	Kevin Mitchell	.10
8D	Tim Pugh	.10
9D	Reggie Sanders	.10
10D	Chris Hammond	.10
JD	Gary Varsho	.10
QD	John Smiley	.10
KD	Chris Sabo	.10
WILD	Tony Perez	.50
JOKER	Riverfront Stadium	.10
---	Reds Schedule	.10
---	Checklist	.10

Colorado Rockies

		NM/M
Complete Set (56):		4.00
Common Player:		.10
AC	Jim Tatum	.10
2C	Charlie Hayes	.10
3C	Dale Murphy	.50
4C	Scott Aldred	.10
5C	Braulio Castillo	.10
6C	Danny Sheaffer	.10
7C	Jerald Clark	.10
8C	Willie Blair	.10
9C	Daryl Boston	.10
10C	Andy Ashby	.10
JC	Butch Henry	.10
QC	Alex Cole	.10
KC	Vinny Castilla	.10
AS	David Nied	.10
2S	Andres Galarraga	.10
3S	Gary Wayne	.10
4S	Freddie Benavides	.10
5S	Butch Henry	.10
6S	Gerald Young	.10
7S	Jeff Parrett	.10
8S	Braulio Castillo	.10
9S	Darren Holmes	.10
10S	Dale Murphy	.50
JS	Eric Young	.10
QS	Bruce Ruffin	.10
KS	Joe Girardi	.10
AH	Charlie Hayes	.10
2H	Jim Tatum	.10
3H	Andy Ashby	.10
4H	Vinny Castilla	.10
5H	Steve Reed	.10
6H	Daryl Boston	.10
7H	Alex Cole	.10
8H	Bryn Smith	.10
9H	Danny Sheaffer	.10
10H	Willie Blair	.10
JH	Dante Bichette	.10
QH	Jerald Clark	.10
DH	Scott Aldred	.10
AD	Andres Galarraga	.10
2D	David Nied	.10
3D	Dante Bichette	.10
4D	Joe Girardi	.10
5D	Bryn Smith	.10
6D	Darren Holmes	.10
7D	Bruce Ruffin	.10
8D	Eric Young	.10
9D	Gerald Young	.10
10D	Gary Wayne	.10
JD	Steve Reed	.10
QD	Jeff Parrett	.10
KD	Freddie Benavides	.10

Florida Marlins

		NM/M
Complete Set (56):		4.00
Common Player:		.10
AC	Walt Weiss	.10
2C	Dave Magadan	.10
3C	Chris Carpenter	.10
4C	Dave Magadan	.10
5C	Bob McClure	.10
6C	Junior Felix	.10
7C	Walt Weiss	.10
8C	Steve Decker	.10
9C	Jeff Conine	.15
10C	Bryan Harvey	.10
JC	Orestes Destrade	.10
QC	Chris Hammond	.10
KC	Monty Fariss	.10
AS	Alex Arias	.10
2S	Benito Santiago	.10
3S	Ryan Bowen	.10
4S	Steve Decker	.10
5S	Jeff Conine	.15
6S	Bret Barberie	.10
7S	Orestes Destrade	.10
8S	Greg Briley	.10
9S	Charlie Hough	.10
10S	Bob Natal	.10
JS	Jack Armstrong	.10
QS	Junior Felix	.10
KS	Richie Lewis	.10
AH	Benito Santiago	.10
2H	Walt Weiss	.10
3H	Monty Fariss	.10
4H	Chris Hammond	.10
5H	Joe Klink	.10
6H	Chuck Carr	.10
7H	Alex Arias	.10
8H	Charlie Hough	.10
9H	Junior Felix	.10
10H	Jim Corsi	.10
JH	Jeff Conine	.15
QH	Trevor Hoffman	.10
KH	Rich Renteria	.10
AD	Dave Magadan	.10
2D	Jack Armstrong	.10
3D	Bryan Harvey	.10
4D	Richie Lewis	.10
5D	Scott Pose	.10
6D	Rich Renteria	.10
7D	Trevor Hoffman	.10
8D	Jim Corsi	.10
9D	Ryan Bowen	.10
10D	Orestes Destrade	.10
JD	Bret Barberie	.10
QD	Chuck Carr	.10
KD	Chris Carpenter	.10
JOKER	N.L. Logo	.10
JOKER	N.L. Logo	.10
---	Opening Day Roster	.10
---	Marlins Schedule	.10

1994 U.S. Playing Card Aces

ANDRES GALARRAGA FIRST BASE

Statistical leaders from the 1993 season are featured in this deck of playing cards. Pitchers with the lowest ERAs are shown on the spades; stolen base leaders are featured on the hearts; home run hitters are depicted on the clubs, and diamonds host the batting average leaders. Cards are 2-1/2" x 3-1/2" with rounded corners. Fronts have full-bleed photos with the suit and value of the playing card in the upper-left and lower-right corners. The player's name, position and team logo are at lower-left. Backs are printed in dark blue with vertical silver stripes at each side and a red, white and blue "Baseball Aces" logo at top. Licensing logos appear at the bottom. Besides the 52 player cards in the boxed set, there is a checklist card, A.L. and N.L. logo cards and a U.S. Playing Card Co. advertising card.

		NM/M
Complete Set (56):		6.00
Common Player:		.10
AC	Barry Bonds	1.50
2C	Phil Plantier	.10
3C	Bobby Bonilla	.10
4C	Mike Piazza	1.00
5C	Ron Gant	.10
6C	Rafael Palmeiro	.50
7C	Fred McGriff	.10
8C	Matt Williams	.10
9C	Albert Belle	.10
10C	Dave Justice	.10
JC	Frank Thomas	.60
QC	Ken Griffey Jr.	1.00
KC	Juan Gonzalez	.30
AS	Greg Maddux	.75
2S	Tom Candiotti	.10
3S	Jimmy Key	.10
4S	Jack McDowell	.10
5S	John Burkett	.10
6S	Tom Glavine	.25
7S	Pete Harnisch	.10
8S	Wilson Alvarez	.10
9S	Steve Avery	.10
10S	Bill Swift	.10
JS	Mark Portugal	.10
QS	Kevin Appier	.10
KS	Jose Rijo	.10
AH	Kenny Lofton	.10
2H	Brett Butler	.10
3H	Eric Young	.10
4H	Delino DeShields	.10
5H	Darren Lewis	.10
6H	Gregg Jefferies	.10
7H	Otis Nixon	.10
8H	Chad Curtis	.10
9H	Rickey Henderson	.60
10H	Marquis Grissom	.10
JH	Luis Polonia	.10
QH	Roberto Alomar	.20
KH	Chuck Carr	.10
AD	Andres Galarraga	.10
2D	John Kruk	.10
3D	Frank Thomas	.60
4D	Mike Piazza	1.00
5D	Jeff Bagwell	.60
6D	Carlos Baerga	.10
7D	Mark Grace	.10
8D	Kenny Lofton	.10
9D	Roberto Alomar	.20
10D	Paul Molitor	.60
JD	Barry Bonds	1.50
QD	Gregg Jefferies	.10
KD	John Olerud	.10
Joker	National League Logo	.05
Joker	American League Logo	.05
---	Checklist	.05
---	Advertising Card	.05

Atlanta Braves

MIKE KELLY ♦ OF

The most popular Braves are pictured on up to three of the cards in this deck. In 2-1/2" x 3-1/2" round-cornered format, the large color photos on the card fronts have their upper-left and lower-right corners clipped to display traditional playing card suits and values. The player name and position are printed in black in a gold strip below the photo. Backs have the Braves logo on a dark blue background with red stripes on the left and right edges. Brand and licensor logos are at bottom. The cards were sold in a colorful box.

		NM/M
Complete Set (56):		4.00
Common Player:		.10
AC	Ron Gant	.10
2C	Chipper Jones	1.00
3C	Terry Pendleton	.10
4C	Mark Wohlers	.10
5C	Pedro Borbon	.10
6C	Steve Avery	.10
7C	Deion Sanders	.10
8C	Dave Justice	.10
9C	Dave Gallagher	.10
10C	Rafael Belliard	.10
JC	Greg McMichael	.10
QC	John Smoltz	.10
KC	Fred McGriff	.10
AS	Jeff Blauser	.10
2S	Mike Stanton	.10
3S	Ryan Klesko	.10
4S	Mike Potts	.10
5S	Charlie O'Brien	.10
6S	Steve Bedrosian	.10
7S	Javier Lopez	.10
8S	Greg Maddux	.75
9S	Deion Sanders	.15
10S	Ramon Caraballo	.10
JS	Kent Mercker	.10
QS	Mark Wohlers	.10
KS	Tom Glavine	.25
AH	Dave Justice	.10
2H	Mark Lemke	.10
3H	Javier Lopez	.10
4H	Rafael Belliard	.10
5H	Bill Pecota	.10
6H	Tom Glavine	.25
7H	Milt Hill	.10
8H	Jeff Blauser	.10
9H	Ryan Klesko	.10
10H	Terry Pendleton	.10
JH	Mike Stanton	.10
QH	Steve Avery	.10
KH	Deion Sanders	.15
AD	Greg Maddux	.75
2D	Ron Gant	.10
3D	Kent Mercker	.10
4D	Greg McMichael	.10
5D	Tony Tarasco	.10
6D	John Smoltz	.10
7D	Fred McGriff	.10
8D	Ron Gant	.10
9D	Mike Kelly	.10
10D	Steve Bedrosian	.10
JD	Bill Pecota	.10
QD	Mark Lemke	.10
KD	Terry Pendleton	.10
Joker	Atlanta Braves Logo	.10
Joker	National League Logo	.10
---	Checklist	.10
---	'94 Braves Home Schedule	.10

Baltimore Orioles

The 1994 Baltimore Orioles are featured in this deck of playing cards. Color photos of the players have clipped corners to display traditional playing card suits and values in the upper-left and lower-right corners. Beneath the photo is an orange strip with the player's name and position in white. Backs have a large Orioles logo on a pin-striped background. Company and licensor logos are at the bottom. Cards measure 2-1/2" x 3-1/2" with rounded corners. The set was sold in a colorful cardboard box.

		NM/M
Complete Set (56):		4.00
Common Player:		.10
AC	Chris Hoiles	.10
2C	Mike Cook	.10
3C	Paul Carey	.10
4C	Jeff Tackett	.10
5C	Arthur Rhodes	.10
6C	Damon Buford	.10
7C	David Segui	.10
8C	Ben McDonald	.10
9C	Cal Ripken Jr.	1.00
10C	Brad Pennington	.10
JC	Jack Voigt	.10
QC	Jeffrey Hammonds	.10
KC	Rafael Palmeiro	.60
AS	Mark McLemore	.10
2S	Manny Alexander	.10
3S	Kevin McGehee	.10
4S	Jim Poole	.10
5S	Leo Gomez	.10
6S	Tim Hulett	.10
7S	Mike Devereaux	.10
8S	Brady Anderson	.10
9S	Mike Mussina	.40
10S	Sherman Obando	.10
JS	Alan Mills	.10
QS	Jamie Moyer	.10
KS	Harold Baines	.10
AH	Cal Ripken Jr.	1.00
2H	Harold Baines	.10
3H	John O'Donoghue	.10
4H	Sid Fernandez	.10
5H	Alan Mills	.10
6H	Jamie Moyer	.10
7H	Harold Baines	.10
8H	Mark McLemore	.10
9H	Jeff Tackett	.10
10H	Arthur Rhodes	.10
JH	Damon Buford	.10
QH	David Segui	.10
KH	Ben McDonald	.10
AD	Mike Mussina	.40
2D	Mike Oquist	.10
3D	Brad Pennington	.10
4D	Jeffrey Hammonds	.10
5D	Jack Voigt	.10
6D	Chris Sabo	.10
7D	Rafael Palmeiro	.60
8D	Chris Hoiles	.10
9D	Jim Poole	.10
10D	Leo Gomez	.10
JD	Tim Hulett	.10
QD	Mike Devereaux	.10
KD	Brady Anderson	.10
Joker	Baltimore Orioles Logo	.10
Joker	American League Logo	.10
---	Checklist	.10
---	'94 Orioles Home Schedule	.10

Philadelphia Phillies

JOHN KRUK • 1B

Veterans and rookies on the roster of the '94 Phils are featured in this deck of playing cards; the most popular players appear on up to three cards each. In standard 2-1/2" x 3-1/2" round-cornered format, the large color photos have their top-left and bottom-right corners clipped to display traditional playing card suits and values. The player's name and position are printed in black on a red strip beneath the photo. Backs have a large Phillies logo on a gray pinstriped background. Company and licensor logos are at bottom. The cards were sold in a decorative box.

		NM/M
Complete Set (56):		4.00
Common Player:		.10
AC	Pete Incaviglia	.10
2C	Lenny Dykstra	.10
3C	Milt Thompson	.10
4C	Mickey Morandini	.10
5C	Kevin Stocker	.10
6C	Terry Mulholland	.10
7C	Curt Schilling	.35
8C	Darren Daulton	.10
9C	Terry Mulholland	.10
10C	Roger Mason	.10
JC	Mariano Duncan	.10
QC	Ben Rivera	.10
KC	John Kruk	.10
AS	Dave Hollins	.10
2S	Danny Jackson	.10
3S	Todd Pratt	.10
4S	David West	.10
5S	Lenny Dykstra	.10
6S	Wes Chamberlain	.10
7S	Tommy Greene	.10
8S	Tony Longmire	.10
9S	Brad Brink	.10
10S	Ricky Jordan	.10
JS	Kim Batiste	.10
QS	Tyler Green	.10
KS	Jim Eisenreich	.10
AH	Lenny Dykstra	.10
2H	Tony Longmire	.10
3H	Kim Batiste	.10
4H	Pete Incaviglia	.10
5H	Ben Rivera	.10
6H	Ricky Jordan	.10
7H	Dave Hollins	.10
8H	Kevin Foster	.10
9H	Kevin Stocker	.10
10H	Mike Williams	.10
JH	Milt Thompson	.10
QH	Curt Schilling	.10
KH	Darren Daulton	.10
AD	Terry Mulholland	.10
2D	Brad Brink	.10
3D	Roger Mason	.10
4D	Mariano Duncan	.10
5D	Danny Jackson	.10
6D	Jim Eisenreich	.10
7D	John Kruk	.10
8D	David West	.10
9D	Todd Pratt	.10
10D	Wes Chamberlain	.10
JD	Jim Eisenreich	.10
QD	Mickey Morandini	.10
KD	Tommy Greene	.10
Joker	Phillies Logo	.10
Joker	National League Logo	.10
---	Checklist	.10
---	'94 Phillies Home Schedule	.10

S.F. Giants

Veterans and rookies on the roster of the '94 Giants are featured in this deck of playing cards; the most popular players appear on up to three cards each. In standard 2-1/2" x 3-1/2" round-cornered format, the large color photos have their top-left and bottom-right corners clipped to display traditional playing card suits and values. The player's name and position are printed in white on an orange strip beneath the photo.

ROYCE CLAYTON • SS

Backs have a large Giants logo on a gray pinstriped background. Company and licensor logos are at bottom. The cards were sold in a decorative box.

		NM/M
Complete Set (56):		4.00
Common Player:		.10
AC	Matt Williams	.10
2C	John Patterson	.10
3C	Steve Hosey	.10
4C	Jeff Reed	.10
5C	Mike Jackson	.10
6C	Kirt Manwaring	.10
7C	Royce Clayton	.10
8C	Robby Thompson	.10
9C	Luis Mercedes	.10
10C	Mike Benjamin	.10
JC	Mark Carreon	.10
QC	Dave Burba	.10
KC	John Burkett	.10
AS	Barry Bonds	1.00
2S	Salomon Torres	.10
3S	Kevin Rogers	.10
4S	Todd Benzinger	.10
5S	Dave Martinez	.10
6S	Darren Lewis	.10
7S	Willie McGee	.10
8S	Bill Swift	.10
9S	Paul Faries	.10
10S	Trevor Wilson	.10
JS	Steve Scarsone	.10
QS	Bryan Hickerson	.10
KS	Rod Beck	.10
AH	Robby Thompson	.10
2H	Paul Faries	.10
3H	Trevor Wilson	.10
4H	Steve Scarsone	.10
5H	Bryan Hickerson	.10
6H	Rod Beck	.10
7H	Barry Bonds	1.00
8H	John Patterson	.10
9H	J.R. Phillips	.10
10H	Jeff Reed	.10
JH	Mike Jackson	.10
QH	Kirt Manwaring	.10
KH	Royce Clayton	.10
AD	Bill Swift	.10
2D	Luis Mercedes	.10
3D	Mike Benjamin	.10
4D	Mark Carreon	.10
5D	Dave Burba	.10
6D	John Burkett	.10
7D	Matt Williams	.10
8D	Salomon Torres	.10
9D	Kevin Rogers	.10
10D	Todd Benzinger	.10
JD	Dave Martinez	.10
QD	Darren Lewis	.10
KD	Willie McGee	.10
JOKER	Giants Home Schedule	.10
JOKER	Checklist	.10
---	N.L. Logo	.10
---	Giants Logo	.10

1993 Rookies

CHUCK CARR • CF

The top rookies from the 1993 season are featured on this deck of playing cards; several players appear on more than one card in the deck. Fronts have color player photos at center, with traditional playing card suits and values in the upper-left and lower-right borders. A team logo is at upper-right. The player's name

and position appear in white in a purple strip at lower-left. Backs are purple with a large product logo at top-center and licensor/licensee logos at bottom. Cards measure 2-1/2" x 3-1/2" with rounded corners and were sold in a specially decorated cardboard box.

		NM/M
Complete Set (56):		4.00
Common Player:		.10
AC	Mike Piazza	1.00
2C	Vinny Castilla	.10
3C	Wil Cordero	.10
4C	Ryan Thompson	.10
5C	Craig Paquette	.10
6C	Carlos Garcia	.10
7C	Jeff Conine	.10
8C	Bret Boone	.10
9C	Jeromy Burnitz	.10
10C	J.T. Snow	.10
JC	Al Martin	.10
QC	Troy Neel	.10
KC	Tim Salmon	.10
AS	Greg McMichael	.10
2S	Paul Quantrill	.10
3S	Steve Reed	.10
4S	Trevor Hoffman	.10
5S	Tim Pugh	.10
6S	Angel Miranda	.10
7S	Steve Cooke	.10
8S	Aaron Sele	.10
9S	Kirk Rueter	.10
10S	Rene Arocha	.10
JS	Pedro Martinez	.75
QS	Armando Reynoso	.10
KS	Jason Bere	.10
AH	Kevin Stocker	.10
2H	Alex Arias	.10
3H	Carlos Garcia	.10
4H	Erik Pappas	.10
5H	Al Martin	.10
6H	Tim Salmon	.10
7H	Mike Lansing	.10
8H	Rich Amaral	.10
9H	Brent Gates	.10
10H	David Hulse	.10
JH	Troy Neel	.10
QH	Jeff Conine	.10
KH	Mike Piazza	1.00
AD	Chuck Carr	.10
2D	Jeff McNeeley	.10
3D	Joe Kmak	.10
4D	Phil Hiatt	.10
5D	Brent Gates	.10
6D	Wil Cordero	.10
7D	Al Martin	.10
8D	Wayne Kirby	.10
9D	Lou Frazier	.10
10D	Carlos Garcia	.10
JD	Rich Amaral	.10
QD	Mike Lansing	.10
KD	David Hulse	.10
Joker	Tim Salmon (Rookie of the Year)	.10
Joker	Mike Piazza (Rookie of the Year)	.75
--	Checklist	.10
--	Rookie Qualification Rules	.10

1995 U.S. Playing Card Aces

WADE BOGGS THIRD BASE

Baseball's 1994 statistical leaders in home runs (clubs), ERA (spades), stolen bases (hearts) and batting average (diamonds) are featured in this deck of playing cards. Measuring a standard 2-1/2" x 3-1/2" with rounded corners, cards have borderless action photos on front with traditional playing card suits and denominations in the upper-left and lower-right corners. The player's color team logo, name and position appear in the lower-left corner. Backs are silver with black side stripes and a red-and-black Aces logo at center. Sets were sold in a colorful cardboard box.

		NM/M
Complete Set (56):		5.00
Common Player:		.10
AC	"Wee" Willie Keeler	.10
2C	Bob Feller	.10
3C	Luke Appling	.10
4C	Jerome "Dizzy" Dean	.15
5C	Johnny Bench	.25
6C	Lou Brock	.10
7C	Joe Cronin	.10
8C	Mickey Cochrane	.10
9C	Rod Carew	.10
10C	Bill Dickey	.10
JC	Josh Gibson	.10
QC	Lou Gehrig	.75
KC	Jackie Robinson	.75
AS	Babe Ruth	1.00

AC	Matt Williams	.10
2C	Joe Carter	.10
3C	Dante Bichette	.10
4C	Cecil Fielder	.10
5C	Kevin Mitchell	.10
6C	Andres Galarraga	.10
7C	Jose Canseco	.35
8C	Fred McGriff	.10
9C	Albert Belle	.10
10C	Barry Bonds	1.00
JC	Frank Thomas	.50
QC	Jeff Bagwell	.50
KC	Ken Griffey Jr.	.75
AS	Greg Maddux	.60
2S	Steve Trachsel	.10
3S	Randy Johnson	.50
4S	Bobby Jones	.10
5S	Jose Rijo	.10
6S	Mike Mussina	.30
7S	Shane Reynolds	.10
8S	Jeff Fassero	.10
9S	David Cone	.10
10S	Roger Clemens	.65
JS	Doug Drabek	.10
QS	Bret Saberhagen	.10
KS	Steve Ontiveros	.10
AH	Kenny Lofton	.10
2H	Brian McRae	.10
3H	Alex Cole	.10
4H	Barry Bonds	1.00
5H	Darren Lewis	.10
6H	Brady Anderson	.10
7H	Chuck Carr	.10
8H	Chuck Knoblauch	.10
9H	Marquis Grissom	.10
10H	Deion Sanders	.15
JH	Craig Biggio	.10
QH	Otis Nixon	.10
KH	Vince Coleman	.10
AD	Tony Gwynn	.60
2D	Gregg Jefferies	.10
3D	Kevin Mitchell	.10
4D	Will Clark	.10
5D	Hal Morris	.10
6D	Moises Alou	.10
7D	Paul Molitor	.50
8D	Wade Boggs	.60
9D	Kenny Lofton	.10
10D	Frank Thomas	.50
JD	Albert Belle	.10
QD	Paul O'Neill	.10
KD	Jeff Bagwell	.50
Joker	American League logo	.05
Joker	National League logo	.05
---	Checklist	.05
---	MicroMini Team card order form	.05

2000 U.S. Playing Card All Century Baseball Team

Robert Feller

Fifty-two members of baseball's All Century team are featured on this deck of playing cards. On round-cornered playing card stock in 2-1/2" x 3-1/2" format, cards have black-and-white photos vignetted on front with the player name at bottom. In opposite corners are a color baseball with the card's value at center and the suit printed in red or black below. Backs are predominantly blue with gold borders and pinstriping. The cards were issued with four All Century team logos in a cardboard box within an embossed lithographed steel case.

		NM/M
Complete Boxed Set (56):		6.00
Common Player:		.10

2S	Leroy "Satchel" Paige	.40
3S	Willie McCovey	.10
4S	Joe Morgan	.10
5S	Mel Ott	.10
6S	Jim Palmer	.10
7S	Frank Robinson	.10
8S	Mike Schmidt	.40
9S	George Sisler	.10
10S	Al Simmons	.10
JS	Denton "Cy" Young	.10
QS	Ozzie Smith	.25
KS	Tris Speaker	.10
AH	Bob Gibson	.10
2H	Whitey Ford	.10
3H	Christy Mathewson	.15
4H	Ralph Kiner	.10
5H	Juan Marichal	.10
6H	Bob "Lefty" Grove	.10
7H	Carl Hubbell	.10
8H	Al Kaline	.15
9H	Rogers Hornsby	.10
10H	Harmon Killebrew	.10
JH	Walter Johnson	.10
QH	Jimmie Foxx	.10
KH	Carlton Fisk	.10
AD	Eddie Collins	.10
2D	Robin Roberts	.10
3D	Honus Wagner	.20
4D	Warren Spahn	.10
5D	Mickey Mantle	1.50
6D	Brooks Robinson	.10
7D	Hank Aaron	.75
8D	Rollie Fingers	.10
9D	Dennis Eckersley	.10
10D	Ty Cobb	.75
JD	Joe Medwick	.10
QD	Ernie Banks	.15
KD	Grover Cleveland Alexander	.10

1989 U.S. Postal Service Legends

Roberto Clemente
USA 20c

In 1989 the U.S. Postal Service offered to collectors a Legends set for $7.95. The set consists of a heavily illustrated 24-page "Baseball Scrapbook and Stamp Album," a set of the four U.S. postage stamps which had been issued to that time honoring individual players, and a set of cards matching the stamps. The 2-1/2" x 3-1/2" cards have color reproductions of the stamps on front, bordered in white with red and blue striping. Backs are in red, black and orange and feature player data and major league stats.

		NM/M
Complete Set, Album, Stamps,	Cards:	24.00
Card Set (4):		15.00
3	Babe Ruth	4.00
4	Lou Gehrig	3.00
21	Roberto Clemente	5.00
42	Jackie Robinson	3.00

2000 U.S. Postal Service Legends of Baseball Stamps

Legends of Baseball

Twenty of the players nominated to baseball's All-Century team are featured on this souvenir sheet of 33-cent stamps issued by the USPS during ceremonies in Atlanta prior to the 2000 All-Star Game. The players chosen to appear were all Hall of Famers and, as per post office rules, had been deceased at least 10 years

prior to the stamps' issue. Many of the pastel paintings by Joseph Saffold are familiar to card collectors because the illustrations are based on earlier photos which have been seen on vintage cards. A total of 225 million of the self-adhesive 1-1/4" x 1-9/16" stamps was produced, with the 7-1/8" x 7-13/16" souvenir panel originally retailing at face value - $6.60. It was reported that 11,250,000 sheets were printed.

		NM/M
Complete Sheet:		8.00
Common Player:		.35
(1)	Roberto Clemente	.60
(2)	Ty Cobb	.45
(3)	Mickey Cochrane	.35
(4)	Eddie Collins	.35
(5)	Dizzy Dean	.35
(6)	Jimmie Foxx	.35
(7)	Lou Gehrig	.50
(8)	Josh Gibson	.35
(9)	Lefty Grove	.35
(10)	Rogers Hornsby	.35
(11)	Walter Johnson	.35
(12)	Christy Mathewson	.35
(13)	Satchel Paige	.45
(14)	Jackie Robinson	.60
(15)	Babe Ruth	.60
(16)	George Sisler	.35
(17)	Tris Speaker	.35
(18)	Pie Traynor	.35
(19)	Honus Wagner	.35
(20)	Cy Young	.35

2000 USPS Legends of Baseball Post Cards

USA 33
NEW YORK
CHRISTY MATHEWSON

In conjunction with the issue of a souvenir sheet of 33-cent stamps, the USPS also issued a boxed set of "Legends of Baseball" post cards. The 5" x 7" cards have a large reproduction of each stamp on front against a beige background. Postcard-style backs have color logos of the USPS and MLB's All-Century Team, along with address lines and a stamp box. At upper-left is a summary of the player's career. The cards were issued in a colorful folder with an All-Century Team hologram. The boxed sets sold for $5.95. Production was reported as 62,500 sets.

		NM/M
Complete Boxed Set (20):		9.00
Common Player:		.75
(1)	Roberto Clemente	1.50
(2)	Ty Cobb	1.25
(3)	Mickey Cochrane	.75
(4)	Eddie Collins	.75
(5)	Dizzy Dean	.75
(6)	Jimmie Foxx	.75
(7)	Lou Gehrig	1.25
(8)	Josh Gibson	.75
(9)	Lefty Grove	.75
(10)	Rogers Hornsby	.75
(11)	Walter Johnson	.75
(12)	Christy Mathewson	.75
(13)	Satchel Paige	1.25
(14)	Jackie Robinson	1.50
(15)	Babe Ruth	1.50
(16)	George Sisler	.75
(17)	Tris Speaker	.75
(18)	Pie Traynor	.75
(19)	Honus Wagner	.75
(20)	Cy Young	.75

2000 USPS Legends of Baseball Postal Card Booklet

In conjunction with the issue of a souvenir sheet of 33-cent stamps, the USPS also issued a bound booklet of "Legends of Baseball" postal cards. By definition, postal cards have the "stamp" preprinted. The 4-1/4" x 6-1/16" cards have borderless color artwork on front, pastel paintings which reproduce the stamps' artwork. On the divided back a 20-cent "stamp" version of the player picture is printed at top-right. There is a short biography at top-left. The cards were perforated with an 11/16" stub attaching it to the bound book. With a $4 face value, the booklets were originally sold for $8.95 at the post office. Production was reported as 105,000 sets.

		NM/M
Complete Booklet (20):		12.50
Common Player:		.75
(1)	Roberto Clemente	1.50
(2)	Ty Cobb	1.25
(3)	Mickey Cochrane	.75
(4)	Eddie Collins	.75
(5)	Dizzy Dean	.75
(6)	Jimmie Foxx	.75
(7)	Lou Gehrig	1.25
(8)	Josh Gibson	.75
(9)	Lefty Grove	.75
(10)	Rogers Hornsby	.75
(11)	Walter Johnson	.75
(12)	Christy Mathewson	.75
(13)	Satchel Paige	1.25
(14)	Jackie Robinson	1.50
(15)	Babe Ruth	1.50
(16)	George Sisler	.75
(17)	Tris Speaker	.75
(18)	Pie Traynor	.75
(19)	Honus Wagner	.75
(20)	Cy Young	.75

V

2000 Verizon Tampa Bay Devil Rays

This team set was a stadium giveaway at a promotional date. Fronts of the 2-1/2" x 3-1/2" cards have game-action photos on which a silver dollar-size portion remains in natural color while the balance of the picture is a purple duo-tone. Backs are in gray with a purple box for complete pro stats, capped by a dime-size color player portrait. The set is listed here according to uniform numbers which appear on back.

		NM/M
Complete Set (28):		7.50
Common Player:		.25
1	Miguel Cairo	.25
2	Randy Winn	.25
4	Gerald Williams	.25
6	John Flaherty	.25
8	Mike DiFelice	.25
9	Vinny Castilla	.25
10	Russ Johnson	.25
11	Larry Rothschild	.25
15	Ozzie Guillen	.25
16	Felix Martinez	.25
21	Bubba Trammell	.25
23	Greg Vaughn	.25
28	Steve Cox	.25
29	Fred McGriff	.50
30	Jose Guillen	.25
32	Albie Lopez	.25
33	Jose Canseco	2.50
35	Bryan Rekar	.25
39	Roberto Hernandez	.25
40	Wilson Alvarez	.25
41	Esteban Yan	.25
46	Steve Trachsel	.25
57	Rick White	.25
57	Juan Guzman	.25
---	Coaches (Orlando Gomez, Billy Hatcher, Bill Russell, Jose Cardenal, Bill Fischer, Leon Roberts)	.25
00	Raymond (Mascot)	.25
---	Wade Boggs (Literacy Champion)	3.50
---	A's for the Rays	.10

1989 Very Fine Pirates

BILL LANDRUM 43

This 30-card set Pirates set was sponsored by Veryfine fruit juices and issued in the form of two uncut, perforated panels, each containing 15 standard-size cards. A third panel featured color action photographs. The panels were distributed in a promotion to fans attending the April 23 game at Three Rivers Stadium. The cards display the Pirates' traditional black and gold color scheme. The backs include player data and complete stats.

		NM/M
Complete Three-Panel Set:		15.00
Complete Singles Set (30):		13.50
Common Player:		.25
0	Junior Ortiz	.25
2	Gary Redus	.25
3	Jay Bell	.25
5	Sid Bream	.25
6	Rafael Belliard	.25
10	Jim Leyland	.25
11	Glenn Wilson	.25
12	Mike La Valliere	.25
13	Jose Lind	.25
14	Ken Oberkfell	.25
15	Doug Drabek	.25
16	Bob Kipper	.25
17	Bob Walk	.25
18	Andy Van Slyke	.25
23	R.J. Reynolds	.25
24	Barry Bonds	12.00
25	Bobby Bonilla	.25
26	Neal Heaton	.25
30	Benny Distefano	.25
35	Jim Gott	.25
41	Mike Dunne	.25
43	Bill Landrum	.25
44	John Cangelosi	.25
49	Jeff Robinson	.25
52	Dorn Taylor	.25
54	Brian Fisher	.25
57	John Smiley	.25
31/37	Ray Miller, Tommy Sandt	.25
32/36	Bruce Kimm, Gene Lamont	.25
39/45	Milt May, Rich Donnelly	.25
---	Rich Donnelly (39-45)	.25

2002 Viagra Rafael Palmeiro

RAFAEL PALMEIRO

Spokesman Rafael Palmeiro is featured on five of the nine cards in this set issued to promote the drug Viagra. (Models are pictured on the other four cards.) Sets were issued in a cello-wrapped pack with a detailed information sheet on the drug. Evidently distributed to medical professionals, the exact manner and range of the cards' distribution is unknown. In standard 2-1/2" x 3-1/2" format, cards are printed on rather thin stock which is UV coated on each side. Except for one card which has a Palmeiro portrait photo on back along with personal data and stats, the backs have information on the drug.

	NM/M
Complete Set (9):	4.50
Common Card:	.05

(1)	Rafael Palmeiro (Game-action photo.)	1.25
(2)	Rafael Palmeiro (Bat at ready pose.)	1.25
(3)	Rafael Palmeiro (Batting follow-through.)	1.25
(4)	Rafael Palmeiro (Jersey close-up.)	1.25
(5)	Rafael Palmeiro/Portrait	1.25
(6)	Communication	.05
(7)	Diabetes	.05
(8)	Hyperlipidemia	.05
(9)	Hypertension	.05

1991 Vine Line Chicago Cubs

VINE LINE

23   Ryne Sandberg   IF

This set was produced in conjunction with the official fan magazine of the Chicago Cubs, "Vine Line." Issued in nine-card panels for insertion into issues of the magazine, the panels were apparently also offered as a complete set via a mail-in offer. Cards measure the standard 2-1/2" x 3-1/2" and will be perforated on two, three or four sides, depending on their placement on the panel. Fronts are bordered in black with white typography that has the player name, position and uniform number. The player photo is in color with the background in stippled black-and-white. Backs have a black-and-white player portrait, biographical data, career highlights, 1990 and career stats and a brown and green background. The cards are listed here by uniform number.

		NM/M
Complete Singles Set (36):		6.00
Complete Panel Set (4):		7.50
Common Card:		.25
3	Jose Martinez	.25
4	Don Zimmer	.25
5	Chuck Cottier	.25
6	Joe Altobelli	.25
7	Joe Girardi	.25
8	Andre Dawson	.45
9	Damon Berryhill	.25
10	Luis Salazar	.25
11	George Bell	.25
16	Shawon Dunston	.25
16	Jose Vizcaino	.25
17	Mark Grace	.50
18	Dwight Smith	.25
19	Hector Villanueva	.25
20	Jerome Walton	.25
22	Mike Harkey	.25
23	Ryne Sandberg	2.00
24	Chico Walker	.25
25	Gary Scott	.25
29	Doug Dascenzo	.25
31	Greg Maddux	2.00
32	Danny Jackson	.25
34	Dick Pole	.25
35	Chuck McElroy	.25
36	Mike Bielecki	.25
37	Erik Pappas	.25
42	Rick Sutcliffe	.25
42	Dave Smith	.25
44	Steve Wilson	.25
45	Paul Assenmacher	.25
47	Shawn Boskie	.25
48	Phil Roof	.25
50	Les Lancaster	.25
53	Heathcliff Slocumb	.25
31	Fergie Jenkins (Hall of Fame)	.50
---	Most Valuable Players (Ryne Sandberg, Andre Dawson, George Bell)	.40

1994 Vine Line Chicago Cubs Postcards

Chicago Cubs Vine Line, the team's official monthly paper, produced this set of promotional postcards. The 4" x 5-1/2" cards have black-and-white or color pictures with maroon borders. Backs

are in color with a description of the front photo. The unnumbered cards are checklisted here in chronological order.

		NM/M
Complete Set (10):		10.00
Common Card:		1.00
(1)	Wrigley Field 1914-1994/ 1935	1.00
(2)	Wrigley Field 1914-1994/ 1988	1.00
(3)	Harry Caray 50 Seasons (7th inning stretch)	1.00
(4)	Harry Caray 50 Seasons (1989 w/Stan Musial)	1.00
(5)	1969 (Team composite.)	2.50
(6)	1969 (Ken Holtzman No-hitter.))	1.50
(7)	1984 (Clinching NL East)	1.00
(8)	1969 (Final game celebration)	1.00
(9)	1989 (Boys of Zimmer)	1.00
(10)	1989 (Clinching NL East)	1.00

1998 Virginia Lottery Baseball Legends Cards

BASEBALL LEGENDS

PHIL NIEKRO HALL OF FAME: 1997

This set of cards was one of several consolation prizes available in the commonwealth's scratch-off lottery game featuring Hall of Famers who had played in Virginia. The 2-1/2" x 3-1/2" cards have larger versions of the player photos found on the tickets. Borders are in red, white, blue, and black. Black-and-white backs have career highlights and stats. Cards can be found in either signed or autographed versions.

	NM/M
Complete Set (4):	4.00
Autographed Set (4):	25.00
Common Player:	1.00
Common Autograph:	8.00
(1)	Yogi Berra	2.00
(1)	Yogi Berra/Auto.	15.00
(2)	Willie McCovey	1.00
(2)	Willie McCovey/Auto.	10.00
(3)	Phil Niekro	1.00
(3)	Phil Niekro/Auto.	8.00
(4)	Duke Snider	1.50
(4)	Duke Snider/Auto.	12.00

W

1986 Wallich Enterprises Padres Sports Cards

This set of artwork postcards was designed to be the first in a series which never materialized. The cards feature color artwork on front with a wide border and player name beneath.

		NM/M
Complete Set (15):		35.00
Common Player:		3.00
(1)	Kurt Bevacqua	3.00
(2)	Dave Dravecky	4.00

1998 Washington Senators 1969 Reunion

SENATORS

Frank Howard   OF/1st BASE

In conjunction with a card-show reunion of the '69 Nats, this set of cards was issued in uncut sheet form at the reunion breakfast. Featuring original artwork portraits atop cartoon bodies in the style of 1938 Goudey Heads-Up cards, the 2-1/2" x 2-7/8" cards have a reunion logo in an upper-corner. Backs have a team logo, player personal data, 1969 and career stats, and a quote about the player by Washington sports talk radio personality Phil Wood. Cards are listed here alphabetically.

		NM/M
Complete Set, Uncut Sheet:		15.00
Complete Set, Singles (28):		12.00
Common Player:		.25
(1)	Bernie Allen	.25
(2)	Hank Allen	.25
(3)	Frank Bertaina	.25
(4)	Dick Billings	.25
(5)	Dick Bosman	.25
(6)	Ed Brinkman	.25
(7)	Joe Camacho	.25
(8)	Casey Cox	.25
(9)	Tim Cullen	.25
(10)	Mike Epstein	.40
(11)	Jim French	.25
(12)	Jim Hannan	.25
(13)	Dennis Higgins	.25
(14)	Johnny Holliday (Announcer)	.25
(15)	Frank Howard	.50
(16)	Sid Hudson	.25
(17)	Bob Humphreys	.25
(18)	Frank Kreutzer	.25
(19)	Lee Maye	.25
(20)	Ken McMullen	.25
(21)	Ron Menchine (Announcer)	.25
(22)	Ed Stroud	.25
(23)	Wayne Terwilliger	.25
(24)	Del Unser	.25
(25)	Fred Valentine	.25
(26)	Shelby Whitfield (Announcer)	.25
(27)	Ted Williams	6.00
(28)	Checklist	.25

1988 Weis Winners Super Stars Discs

1985 Wendy's Tigers

This set contains 22 cards measuring 2-1/2" x 3-1/2", which carry both Wendy's Hamburgers and Coca-Cola logos and were produced by Topps. The cards feature a color photo with the player's identification underneath the picture. Backs are identical to 1985 Topps cards except they have different card numbers and are done in a red and black color scheme.

		NM/M
		(first header)

(3)	Tim Flannery, Jerry Royster	
(4)	Steve Garvey	6.00
(5)	Rich Gossage	4.00
(6)	Tony Gwynn	9.00
(7)	Andy Hawkins	3.00
(8)	LaMarr Hoyt	3.00
(9)	Terry Kennedy	3.00
(10)	Carmelo Martinez	3.00
(11)	Kevin McReynolds	4.00
(12)	Graig Nettles	4.00
(13)	Eric Show	3.00
(14)	Garry Templeton	4.00
(15)	Player composite	3.00

(Note: Tim Flannery, Jerry Royster row shows 3.00)

1994 Wendy's Roberto Clemente Hologram

DETROIT TIGERS
DAN PETRY

Cards were distributed three to a pack along with a "Header" checklist in a cellophane package at selected Wendy's outlets in Michigan only.

		NM/M
Complete Set (22):		5.00
Common Player:		.25
1	Sparky Anderson	.50
2	Doug Bair	.25
3	Juan Berenguer	.25
4	Dave Bergman	.25
5	Tom Brookens	.25
6	Marty Castillo	.25
7	Darrell Evans	.40
8	Barbaro Garbey	.25
9	Kirk Gibson	.65
10	Johnny Grubb	.25
11	Willie Hernandez	.25
12	Larry Herndon	.25
13	Rusty Kuntz	.25
14	Chet Lemon	.25
15	Aurelio Lopez	.25
16	Jack Morris	.35
17	Lance Parrish	.65
18	Dan Petry	.25
19	Bill Scherrer	.25
20	Alan Trammell	1.00
21	Lou Whitaker	.50
22	Milt Wilcox	.25

1994 Wendy's Roberto Clemente Hologram

This single-card set was issued by the restaurant chain in a stated edition of 90,000. The front has a black-bordered hologram picturing Clemente at bat, with the number 3,000 in a box at upper-right. The back has a couple of color photos of the Pirates' star along with biographical data and a career summary.

		NM/M
(1)	Roberto Clemente	6.00

1993 Whataburger Nolan Ryan

Issued in two-card cello packs at Whataburger restaurants, this set honors the career of Nolan Ryan. Cards have action photos set against colorized backgrounds and overlayed with ribbed plastic to create a 3-D effect. A card title is printed in white in the lower-left corner, with the logo of Triad (the card's maker) in the lower-right. In the upper-left corner is a red "Nolan Ryan's Recollections" logo. Backs have color logos of the hamburger chain, Triad, Coca-Cola and Major League Baseball, along with a quote from Ryan about the career highlight and a facsimile autograph. The cards are unnumbered.

		NM/M
Complete Set (10):		6.00
Common Card:		1.00
(1)	Nolan Ryan (1st No-hitter)	1.00
(2)	Nolan Ryan (2nd No-hitter)	1.00
(3)	Nolan Ryan (3rd No-hitter)	1.00
(4)	Nolan Ryan (4th No-hitter)	1.00
(5)	Nolan Ryan (5th No-hitter)	1.00
(6)	Nolan Ryan (6th No-hitter)	1.00
(7)	Nolan Ryan (7th No-hitter)	1.00
(8)	Nolan Ryan (5,000th Strikeout)	1.00
(9)	Nolan Ryan (300th Win)	1.00
(10)	Nolan Ryan (On horse.)	1.00

1982 Wheaties Indians

These 2-13/16" x 4-1/8" cards were given out ten at a time during three special promotional games; later the complete set was placed on sale at the Indians' gift shop. The cards represented the first time in 30 years that Wheaties had been associated with a baseball card set. Fronts feature color photos surrounded by a wide white border with the player's name and position below the picture. The Indians logo is in the lower-left corner while the Wheaties logo is in the lower-right. Card backs have a Wheaties ad.

		NM/M
Complete Set (30):		7.50
Common Player:		.25
(1)	Chris Bando	.25
(2)	Alan Bannister	.25
(3)	Len Barker	.25
(4)	Bert Blyleven	.75
(5)	Tom Brennan	.25
(6)	Joe Charboneau	1.00
(7)	Rodney Craig	.25
(8)	John Denny	.25
(9)	Miguel Dilone	.25
(10)	Jerry Dybzinski	.25
(11)	Mike Fischlin	.25
(12)	Dave Garcia	.25
(13)	Johnny Goryl	.25
(14)	Mike Hargrove	.50
(15)	Toby Harrah	.50
(16)	Ron Hassey	.25
(17)	Von Hayes	.25
(18)	Dennis Lewallyn	.25
(19)	Rick Manning	.25
(20)	Bake McBride	.25
(21)	Tommy McCraw	.25
(22)	Jack Perconte	.25
(23)	Mel Queen	.25
(24)	Dennis Sommers	.25
(25)	Lary Sorensen	.25
(26)	Dan Spillner	.25
(27)	Rick Sutcliffe	.75
(28)	Andre Thornton	.50
(29)	Rick Waits	.25
(30)	Eddie Whitson	.25

1983 Wheaties Indians

A 32-card set marked the second year of Wheaties involvement with the Indians. Distribution of the 2-13/16" x 4-1/8" cards changed slightly in that the entire set was given away on the day of the special promotional game. As happened in 1982, the set was then placed on sale at the team's gift shop. The set includes 27 players, four coaches and the manager. The format of the cards remained basically the same

on the front although the backs of player cards were changed to include complete major and minor league statistics.

		NM/M
Complete Set (32):		5.00
Common Player:		.25
(1)	Bud Anderson	.25
(2)	Jay Baller	.25
(3)	Chris Bando	.25
(4)	Alan Bannister	.25
(5)	Len Barker	.25
(6)	Bert Blyleven	.50
(7)	Wil Culmer	.25
(8)	Miguel Dilone	.25
(9)	Juan Eichelberger	.25
(10)	Jim Essian	.25
(11)	Mike Ferraro	.25
(12)	Mike Fischlin	.25
(13)	Julio Franco	.35
(14)	Ed Glynn	.25
(15)	Johnny Goryl	.25
(16)	Mike Hargrove	.35
(17)	Toby Harrah	.35
(18)	Ron Hassey	.25
(19)	Neal Heaton	.25
(20)	Rick Manning	.25
(21)	Bake McBride	.25
(22)	Don McMahon	.25
(23)	Ed Napoleon	.25
(24)	Broderick Perkins	.25
(25)	Dennis Sommers	.25
(26)	Lary Sorensen	.25
(27)	Dan Spillner	.25
(28)	Rick Sutcliffe	.35
(29)	Andre Thornton	.35
(30)	Manny Trillo	.25
(31)	George Vukovich	.25
(32)	Rick Waits	.25

1984 Wheaties Indians

The 2-13/16" x 4-1/8" cards again were given out at Municipal Stadium as part of a promotion involving Wheaties and the Indians on July 22. The set was down from 32 cards in 1983 to 29. There are 26 players as well as cards for the manager, coaches and team mascot. Design of the cards is virtually identical to prior years. The 1984 set is numbered by uniform number. A total of 15,000 sets were printed and any left over from the promotion were placed on sale in the team's gift shop.

		NM/M
Complete Set (29):		9.00
Common Player:		.50
2	Brett Butler	.75
4	Tony Bernazard	.50
8	Carmelo Castillo	.50
10	Pat Tabler	.50
13	Ernie Camacho	.50
14	Julio Franco	.75
15	Broderick Perkins	.50
16	Jerry Willard	.50
18	Pat Corrales	.50
21	Mike Hargrove	.75
22	Mike Fischlin	.50
23	Chris Bando	.50
24	George Vukovich	.50
26	Brook Jacoby	.50
27	Steve Farr	.50
28	Bert Blyleven	1.00
29	Andre Thornton	.75
30	Joe Carter	1.50
31	Steve Comer	.50
33	Roy Smith	.50
34	Mel Hall	.50
36	Jamie Easterly	.50
37	Don Schulze	.50
38	Luis Aponte	.50
44	Neal Heaton	.50
46	Mike Jeffcoat	.50
54	Tom Waddell	.50
---	Coaching Staff (Bobby Bonds, John Goryl, Don McMahon, Ed Napoleon, Dennis Sommers)	.50
---	Tom-E-Hawk (Mascot)	.50

1997 Wheaties All-Stars

Forty-five years after it last printed baseball cards on its cereal boxes, Wheaties issued a cross-brand set of 30 cards in 1997. Top players are generally grouped by positions in groups of six on the box backs. Boxes also feature three player photos on front and an ad for obtaining a player photoball. The three series of cards found on 18 oz. boxes of Wheaties carry a Topps logo in upper-right corner. The top of the cards' fronts have action photos. A blue box below the photo has the player name and career highlights in white. A green, blue or orange border surrounds the card, which is separated from the rest of the box back by a black dotted line. Backs, printed inside the box, have limited personal data and full major league stats. Perfectly cut cards from these boxes measure about 2-1/2" x 3-13/16". Somewhat smaller at 2-1/16" x 3-3/8", though identical in format, are the cards found on the backs of Honey Frosted Wheaties and Crispy Wheaties 'n Raisins. Cards on the former carry a Pinnacle logo; the latter are marked Upper Deck. Both have orange borders surrounding the cards.

		NM/M
Complete Set, Boxes (5):		12.00
Complete Set, Singles (30):		15.00
Common Player:		.25
	All-Star Players Complete Box:	3.50
(1)	Ken Griffey Jr.	.75
(2)	Greg Maddux	.65
(3)	Paul Molitor	.50
(4)	Cal Ripken Jr.	1.50
(5)	Frank Thomas	.50
(6)	Mo Vaughn	.25
	All-Star Players Complete Box:	3.00
(7)	Barry Bonds	1.50
(8)	Ken Caminiti	.25
(9)	Ken Griffey Jr.	.75
(10)	Chipper Jones	.65
(11)	Chuck Knoblauch	.25
(12)	Alex Rodriguez	1.00
	All-Star Infielders Complete Box:	2.50
(13)	Jeff Bagwell	.50
(14)	Mark McGwire	1.00
(15)	Mike Piazza	.75
(16)	Cal Ripken Jr.	1.50
(17)	Ryne Sandberg	.65
(18)	Frank Thomas	.50
	All-Star Outfielders Complete Box:	2.50
(19)	Barry Bonds	1.50
(20)	Ellis Burks	.25
(21)	Juan Gonzalez	.35
(22)	Ken Griffey Jr.	.75
(23)	Tony Gwynn	.65
(24)	Bernie Williams	.25
	All-Star Pitchers Complete Box:	2.00
(25)	Andy Benes	.25
(26)	David Cone	.25
(27)	Greg Maddux	.65
(28)	Mike Mussina	.35
(29)	Hideo Nomo	.35
(30)	John Smoltz	.50

1995 Wienerschnitzel L.A. Dodgers POGs

The Dodger Stadium hot dog concessionaire sponsored this promotion which was given away to youngsters attending a May 13 Dodgers game. The issue consists of 14 POGs die cut from an 8-1/2" x 10-3/4" cardboard sheet. The POGs picture the team's winners of the Rookie of the Year Award from Jackie Robinson in 1947 through Raul Mondesi in 1994. The individual POGs measure 1-5/8" in diameter. Fronts have a sepia or color player portrait at center, with a blue border of lighter blue stars. Backs are printed in red and blue on white and have a bit of player information plus the logos of the team, sponsor and World POG Federation.

		NM/M
Complete Set, Panel:		8.00
Complete Set, Singles (14):		7.00
Common Player:		.25
1	Jackie Robinson	3.00
2	Don Newcombe	.50
3	Joe Black	.50
4	Jim Gilliam	.35
5	Frank Howard	.35
6	Jim Lefebvre	.25
7	Ted Sizemore	.25
8	Rick Sutcliffe	.25
9	Steve Howe	.25
10	Fernando Valenzuela	.35
11	Steve Sax	.25
12	Eric Karros	.25
13	Mike Piazza	2.00
14	Raul Mondesi	.25

1993 Ted Williams Co. Promos

Though they are unmarked as sample cards, the promos issued for the debut Ted Williams Card Co. set are easily distinguished from the regularly issued versions. The #1 Williams card has different front photos and his name in green, rather than orange, and the Paige and Gonzalez cards have text backs in the promo version, rather than checklists.

		NM/M
Complete Set (3):		10.00
Common Player:		2.00
1	Ted Williams	5.00
115	Satchel Paige	3.00
160	Juan Gonzalez	2.00

1993 Ted Williams Card Company

Without a license from the players' union, the premiere issue of the Ted Williams Card Company relied on innovative subsets to create interest in its "old-timers" set. The first 96 cards in the set comprise the base set. Those cards feature a black-and-white or color action photo set against a background of a second ghost-image photo. The player's name is at bottom with the card company logo conspicuous at top. Backs have some biographical detail, a career summary, the player's five best seasons' and career stats. Subsets numbered contiguously with the base set include a 19-card Negro Leagues series highlighted with green-foil; five cards featuring the All-American Girls Professional Baseball League; a 10-card "Ted's Greatest Hitters" series; 10 "Barrier Breakers" cards featuring Negro Leagues veterans who later played in the majors; a 10-card "Goin' North" subset featuring major league stars of the 1940s-1970s in minor league photos, and, a pair of five-card "Dawning of a Legacy" series featuring Juan Gonzalez and Jeff Bagwell. There were also several insert card series which are listed separately. The cards were packaged with a pair of die-cut player or team logo POGs.

		NM/M
Complete Set (160):		12.00
Common Player:		.05
Wax Pack (12):		.75
Wax Box (36):		20.00
1	Ted Williams	3.00
2	Rick Ferrell	.05
3	Jim Lonborg	.05
4	Mel Parnell	.05
5	Jim Piersall	.05
6	Luis Tiant	.05
7	Carl Yastrzemski	.50
8	Ralph Branca	.05
9	Roy Campanella	.50
10	Ron Cey	.05
11	Tommy Davis	.05
12	Don Drysdale	.35
13	Carl Erskine	.10
14	Steve Garvey	.10
15	Don Newcombe	.10
16	Duke Snider	.50
17	Maury Wills	.05
18	Jim Fregosi	.05
19	Bobby Grich	.05
20	Bill Buckner	.05
21	Billy Herman	.05
22	Ferguson Jenkins	.10
23	Ron Santo	.05
24	Billy Williams	.10
25	Luis Aparicio	.10
26	Luke Appling	.10
27	Minnie Minoso	.15
28	Johnny Bench	.50
29	George Foster	.05
30	Joe Morgan	.15
31	Buddy Bell	.05
32	Lou Boudreau	.10
33	Rocky Colavito	.05
34	Jim "Mudcat" Grant	.05
35	Tris Speaker	.10
36	Ray Boone	.05
37	Darrell Evans	.05
38	Al Kaline	.35
39	George Kell	.10
40	Mickey Lolich	.05
41	Cesar Cedeno	.05
42	Sal Bando	.05
43	Vida Blue	.05
44	Bert Campaneris	.05
45	Ken Holtzman	.05
46	Lew Burdette	.05
47	Bob Horner	.05
48	Warren Spahn	.10
49	Cecil Cooper	.05
50	Tony Oliva	.10
51	Bobby Bonds	.05
52	Alvin Dark	.05
53	Dave Dravecky	.05
54	Monte Irvin	.05
55	Willie Mays	1.00
56	Bud Harrelson	.05
57	Dave Kingman	.05
58	Yogi Berra	.50
59	Don Baylor	.05
60	Jim Bouton	.05
61	Bobby Brown	.05
62	Whitey Ford	.40
63	Lou Gehrig	1.50
64	Charlie Keller	.05
65	Eddie Lopat	.05
66	Johnny Mize	.10
67	Bobby Murcer	.05
68	Graig Nettles	.05
69	Bobby Shantz	.05
70	Richie Ashburn	.10
71	Larry Bowa	.05
72	Steve Carlton	.40
73	Robin Roberts	.10
74	Matty Alou	.05
75	Harvey Haddix	.05
76	Ralph Kiner	.10
77	Bill Madlock	.05
78	Bill Mazeroski	.35
79	Al Oliver	.05
80	Manny Sanguillen	.05
81	Willie Stargell	.10
82	Al Brumbry	.05
83	Davey Johnson	.05
84	Boog Powell	.10
85	Earl Weaver	.10
86	Lou Brock	.10
87	Orlando Cepeda	.10
88	Curt Flood	.05
89	Joe Garagiola	.35
90	Bob Gibson	.10
91	Rogers Hornsby	.20
92	Enos Slaughter	.10
93	Joe Torre	.10
94	Gaylord Perry	.10
95	Checklist 1-49	.05
96	Checklist 50-96	.05
97	Cool Papa Bell	.10
98	Garnett Blair	.05
99	Gene Benson	.05
100	Lyman Bostock, Sr.	.05
101	Marlin Carter	.05
102	Oscar Charleston	.10
103	Ray Dandridge	.10
104	Mahlon Duckett	.05
105	Josh Gibson	.20
106	Cowan Hyde	.05
107	"Judy" Johnson	.10
108	Buck Leonard	.10
109	Pop Lloyd	.10
110	Lester Lockett	.05
111	Max Manning	.05
112	Satchel Paige	.50
113	Armando Vazquez	.05
114	Smokey Joe Williams	.05
115	Negro Leagues Checklist (Satchel Paige)	.05
116	Alice Hohlmayer	.05
117	Dotty Kamenshek	.05
118	Pepper Davis	.05
119	Marge Wenzell	.05
120	AAGPBA Checklist	.05
121	The Babe (Babe Ruth)	1.50
122	The Iron Horse (Lou Gehrig)	.75
123	Double X (Jimmie Foxx)	.20
124	Rajah (Rogers Hornsby)	.10
125	The Georgia Peach (Ty Cobb)	.75
126	The Say Hey Kid (Willie Mays)	.50
127	Ralph (Ralph Kiner)	.10
128	The Grey Eagle (Tris Speaker)	.10
129	The Big Cat (Johnny Mize)	.10
130	Ted's Greatest Hitters Checklist	.05
131	Satchel Paige	.25
132	Joe Black	.10
133	Roy Campanella	.25
134	Larry Doby	.10
135	Jim Gilliam	.10
136	Monte Irvin	.10
137	Sam Jethroe	.05
138	Willie Mays	.50
139	Don Newcombe	.10
140	Barrier Breakers Checklist	.05
141	Roy Campanella	.25
142	Bob Gibson	.10
143	Boog Powell	.10
144	Willie Mays	.50
145	Johnny Mize	.10
146	Monte Irvin	.10
147	Earl Weaver	.10
148	Ted Williams	1.50
149	Jim Gilliam	.05
150	Goin' North Checklist	.05
151	Juan Gonzalez (Footsteps to Greatness)	.25
151a	Juan Gonzalez/Auto. (Edition of 43.)	60.00
152	Juan Gonzalez (Sign 'em Up)	.25
152a	Juan Gonzalez/Auto. (Edition of 43.)	60.00
153	Juan Gonzalez (The Road to Success)	.25
153a	Juan Gonzalez/Auto. (Edition of 43.)	60.00
154	Juan Gonzalez (Looking Ahead)	.25
154a	Juan Gonzalez/Auto. (Edition of 43.)	60.00
155	"Dawning of a Legacy" Checklist	.05
156	Jeff Bagwell (Born with Red Sox Blood)	.50
157	Jeff Bagwell (Movin' Up, Then Out)	.50
158	Jeff Bagwell (Year 1)	.50
159	Jeff Bagwell (Year 2)	.50
160	"Dawning of a Legacy" Checklist (Juan Gonzalez)	.05

Etched in Stone

This 10-card insert set documents the career of Roberto Clemente, using sepia-toned and color photographs on the card front, highlighted by a gold-foil embossed "Tribute '93" logo in the lower-left corner and an "Etched in Stone" logo at upper-right. Backs have a detailed biography. Cards are numbered ES1 through ES10.

		NM/M
Complete Set (10):		12.00
Common Player:		2.00
1	Youth (Roberto Clemente)	2.00

		NM/M
2	Sign Up (Roberto Clemente)	2.00
3	Try-Out (Roberto Clemente)	2.00
4	Playing Mad (Roberto Clemente)	2.00
5	Minor Leagues (Roberto Clemente)	2.00
6	1955-1959 (Roberto Clemente)	2.00
7	1960 (Roberto Clemente)	2.00
8	1963 (Roberto Clemente)	2.00
9	1970 (Roberto Clemente)	2.00
10	Etched in Stone Checklist	2.00

Locklear Collection

The paintings of former major leaguer Gene Locklear are featured in this 10-card insert set. The central image of the player is set against a background of multiple player images in orange, red and purple tones. The player's name is in dark blue on the left edge and a "Gene Locklear Collection" logo is in lower-right. On back is a commentary on the player, a card number with an "LC" suffix and, at bottom center, a serial number. The cards of Ted Williams can be found in an autographed insert version numbered on back from within an edition of 406.

		NM/M
Complete Set (10):		12.00
Common Player:		.75
Ted Williams Autographed:		500.00
1	Yogi Berra	1.00
2	Lou Brock	.75
3	Willie Mays	2.00
4	Johnny Mize	.75
5	Satchel Paige	1.50
6	Babe Ruth	3.00
7	Enos Slaughter	.75
8	Carl Yastrzemski	1.00
9	Ted Williams	2.50
10	Locklear Collection Checklist	.10

Memories

Four historical World Series of the 1950s-1970s are featured in five-card runs within the "Memories" insert set. Fronts have black-and-white or color player photos.

In the lower-left corner is a vintage press camera with "Memories" and the year emanating from the flashbulb. The Ted Williams Card Co. logo is at upper-right. The player's name is in white at bottom-center. Cards are numbered with an "M" prefix on back and feature a headline announcing the team's World Series victory and a summary of the featured player's performance in that Fall Classic.

		NM/M
Complete Set (20):		45.00
Common Player:		1.00

1955 BROOKLYN DODGERS

1	Roy Campanella	3.50
2	Jim Gilliam	2.00
3	Gil Hodges	3.50
4	Duke Snider	3.50
5	1955 Dodgers Checklist	.60

1963 L.A. DODGERS

6	Don Drysdale	3.50
7	Tommy Davis	2.25
8	Johnny Podres	2.25
9	Maury Wills	3.50
10	1963 Dodgers Checklist	.60

1971 PITTSBURGH PIRATES

11	Roberto Clemente	9.00
12	Al Oliver	1.00
13	Manny Sanguillen	1.00
14	Willie Stargell	2.00
15	1971 Pirates Checklist	.60

1975 CINCINNATI REDS

16	Johnny Bench	4.50
17	George Foster	1.25
18	Joe Morgan	3.00
19	Tony Perez	2.00
20	1975 Red Checklist	.60

POGs

These 26 cards featuring two die-cut POGs on each were issued as inserts in 1993 Ted Williams packs. Fronts of the extra-thick cardboard cards have a black background with the logos of the card company and the Cooperstown Collection. Two 1-5/8" diameter POGs appear on each card, picturing either players or team logos. Backs are blank. The unnumbered POG cards are listed here alphabetically, with player POGs listed first.

		NM/M
Complete Set (26):		4.00
Common Player:		.25
(1)	Yogi Berra, Roy Campanella	1.00
(2)	Brooklyn Dodgers (Roy Campanella)	.50
(3)	Tommy Davis, George Foster	.25
(4)	Lou Gehrig, Ted Williams	2.00
(5)	New York Yankees (Lou Gehrig)	1.50
(6)	Ted Williams, #9 patch	.25
(7)	1993 World Series patch	.25
(8)	Baltimore Elite Giants	.25
(9)	New York Mets	.25
(10)	New York Cuban Stars	.25
(11)	Minnesota Twins	.25
(12)	St. Louis Browns	.25
(13)	Detroit Tigers	.25
(14)	Kansas City Royals	.25
(15)	Detroit Stars	.25
(16)	Kansas City Athletics	.25
(17)	Florida Marlins	.25
(18)	New York Black Yankees	.25
(19)	New York Yankees	.25
(20)	New York Harlem Stars	.25
(21)	Philadelphia Stars	.25
(22)	New York Giants	.25
(23)	San Diego Padres	.25
(24)	Negro Leagues Classic Teams	.25
(25)	#21 (Clemente) patch	.25
(26)	St. Louis Cardinals	.25

Brooks Robinson

This 10-card insert set, numbered BR1 through BR10, traces the baseball career of Hall of Fame Orioles third baseman Brooks Robinson. Card fronts feature sepia-toned or color photos highlighted by the player's name in gold foil down the left side and a "Brooks Robinson Collection" diamond logo at lower-right. Backs include a career summary or batting or fielding stats. Autographed versions were a random retail packaging insert.

		NM/M
Complete Set (10):		7.50
Common Player:		1.00
Autographed:		20.00
1BR	Salad Days (Brooks Robinson)	1.00
2BR	Career Batting Stats (Brooks Robinson)	1.00
3BR	'66 World Series (Brooks Robinson)	1.00
4BR	Career Fielding Stats (Brooks Robinson)	1.00
5BR	'70 Series #2 (Brooks Robinson)	1.00
6BR	'70 Series #1 (Brooks Robinson)	1.00
7BR	Comin' Up (Brooks Robinson)	1.00
8BR	All Star Games (Brooks Robinson)	1.00
9BR	1964 (Brooks Robinson)	1.00
10BR	Brooks Robinson Collection Checklist	1.00

1994 Ted Williams Card Company

Lack of a players' association license again limited the company to using two major leaguers in its second annual card set, but it spiced up its 1994 edition with hot prospects in the minor leagues, more high-tech production values and innovative subsets and chase cards. The base set for 1994 includes 162 cards. The first 92 feature retired or deceased players. Those cards feature a color or colorized photo set against a background of a second ghost-image photo or the actual photo background. Vertically at right is a stone image on which the player's name is printed in extremely difficult to read gold letters. The edge of the stone and the card company logo are embossed. Backs have biographical and career details, and stats for the player's five top seasons. Subsets numbered consecutively with the base cards include a seven-card "Women of Baseball" series; 18 Negro Leaguers, 18 current minor leaguers in a series titled "The Campaign;" 10 "Goin' North"

cards of former superstars as minor leaguers; nine "Swingin' for the Fences" cards of home run hitters, and, a nine-card "Dawning of a Legacy" series featuring Cliff Floyd and Tim Salmon. The several insert card series are listed separately. Autographed cards of Leon Day were random pack inserts.

		NM/M
Complete Set (162):		15.00
Common Player:		.10
Wax Pack (12):		1.00
Wax Box (36):		30.00
Jumbo Pack(20):		2.00
Jumbo Box (24):		35.00
1	Ted Williams	4.00
P1	Ted Williams (Promo card.)	2.50
2	Bernie Carbo	.10
3	Bobby Doerr	.10
4	Fred Lynn	.10
5	Johnny Pesky	.10
6	Rico Petrocelli	.10
7	Cy Young	.25
8	Paul Blair	.10
9	Andy Etchebarren	.10
10	Brooks Robinson	.20
11	Gil Hodges	.20
12	Tommy John	.15
13	Rick Monday	.10
14	Dean Chance	.10
15	Doug DeCinces	.10
16	Gabby Hartnett	.10
17	Don Kessinger	.10
18	Bruce Sutter	.20
19	Eddie Collins	.10
20	Nellie Fox	.10
21	Carlos May	.10
22	Ted Kluszewski	.25
23	Vada Pinson	.10
24	Johnny Vander Meer	.10
25	Bob Feller	.25
26	Mike Garcia	.10
27	Sam McDowell	.10
28	Al Rosen	.10
29	Norm Cash	.15
30	Ty Cobb	1.50
31	Mark Fidrych	.20
32	Hank Greenberg	.25
33	Denny McLain	.10
34	Virgil Trucks	.10
35	Enos Cabell	.10
36	Mike Scott	.10
37	Bob Watson	.10
38	Amos Otis	.10
39	Frank White	.10
40	Joe Adcock	.10
41	Rico Carty	.10
42	Ralph Garr	.10
43	Eddie Mathews	.20
44	Ben Oglivie	.10
45	Gorman Thomas	.10
46	Earl Battey	.10
47	Rod Carew	.20
48	Jim Kaat	.10
49	Harmon Killebrew	.20
50	Gary Carter	.25
51	Steve Rogers	.10
52	Rusty Staub	.10
53	Sal Maglie	.10
54	Juan Marichal	.20
55	Mel Ott	.20
56	Bobby Thomson	.10
57	Tommie Agee	.10
58	Tug McGraw	.10
59	Elston Howard	.15
60	Sparky Lyle	.10
61	Billy Martin	.15
62	Thurman Munson	.25
63	Bobby Richardson	.15
64	Bill Skowron	.15
65	Mickey Cochrane	.10
66	Rollie Fingers	.10
67	Lefty Grove	.10
68	Catfish Hunter	.10
69	Connie Mack	.10
70	Al Simmons	.10
71	Dick Allen	.15
72	Bob Boone	.10
73	Del Ennis	.10
74	Chuck Klein	.10
75	Mike Schmidt	.50
76	Dock Ellis	.10
77	Elroy Face	.10
78	Phil Garner	.10
79	Bill Mazeroski	.10
80	Pie Traynor	.10
81	Honus Wagner	.25
82	Dizzy Dean	.25
83	Red Schoendienst	.10
84	Randy Jones	.10
85	Nate Colbert	.10
86	Jeff Burroughs	.10
87	Jim Sundberg	.10
88	Frank Howard	.10
89	Walter Johnson	.20
90	Eddie Yost	.10
91	Checklist 1-46	.10
92	Checklist 47-92	.10
93	Faye Dancer	.10
94	Snookie Doyle	.10
95	Maddy English	.10
96	Nickie Fox	.10
97	Sophie Kurys	.10
98	Alma Ziegler	.10
99	Women of Baseball Checklist	.10
100	Newton Allen	.10
101	Willard Brown	.10
102	Larry Brown	.10
103	Leon Day	.10
103a	Leon Day/Auto.	20.00
104	John Donaldson	.10
105	Rube Foster	.10
106	Bud Fowler	.10
107	Vic Harris	.10
108	Webster McDonald	.10
109	John "Buck" O'Neil	.10
110	Ted "Double Duty" Radcliffe	.10
111	Wilber "Bullet" Rogan	.10
112	Toni Stone	.10
113	Jim Taylor	.10
114	Moses "Fleetwood" Walker	.15
115	George Wilson	.10
116	Judson Wilson	.10
117	Negro Leagues Checklist	.10
118	Howard Battle	.10
119	John Burke	.10
120	Brian Dubose	.10
121	Alex Gonzalez	.15
122	Jose Herrera	.10
123	Jason Giambi	1.00
124	Derek Jeter	4.50
125	Charles Johnson	.25
126	Daron Kirkreit	.10
127	Jason Moler	.10
128	Vince Moore	.10
129	Chad Mottola	.10
130	Jose Silva	.10
131	Makato Suzuki (Makoto)	.10
132	Brien Taylor	.10
133	Michael Tucker	.10
134	Billy Wagner	.25
135	The Campaign Checklist	.10
136	Gary Carter	.10
137	Tony Conigliaro	.10
138	Sparky Lyle	.10
139	Roger Maris	.45
140	Vada Pinson	.10
141	Mike Schmidt	.50
142	Frank White	.10
143	Ted Williams	2.50
144	Goin' North Checklist	.10
145	Joe Adcock	.10
146	Rocky Colavito	.25
147	Lou Gehrig	2.00
148	Gil Hodges	.25
149	Bob Horner	.10
150	Willie Mays	1.50
151	Mike Schmidt	.50
152	Pat Seery	.10
153	Swingin' for the Fences Checklist	.10
154	Cliff Floyd (The Honors Begin)	.15
155	Cliff Floyd (The Top Polecat)	.15
156	Cliff Floyd (Minor League Team of the Year)	.15
157	Cliff Floyd (Major League Debut)	.15
158	Tim Salmon (Award Winner)	.15
159	Tim Salmon (Early Professional Career)	.15
160	Tim Salmon (An MVP Season)	.15
161	Tim Salmon (Rookie of the Year)	.15
162	Dawning of a Legacy Checklist	.10

Etched in Stone

A metallized effect highlights the front design of this insert series commemorating the career of Roger Maris. Color (or colorized) photos appear to have been revealed by chiseling away a rock face which forms much of the front border. Backs have career write-ups overprinted on a design which forms a large "Etched in Stone" design when the cards are laid together in order. Cards have an "ES" prefix to the card number. Cards can be found with either brown or red "rock" borders. The red version is valued at double the brown.

		NM/M
Complete Set (9):		7.50
Common Player:		1.00
1	Roger Maris (Scouting Report)	1.00
2	Roger Maris (Traded)	1.00
3	Roger Maris (Career Year)	1.00
4	Roger Maris/1961	1.00
5	Roger Maris (Silent Accomplishments)	1.00
6	Roger Maris (Team Player)	1.00
7	Roger Maris (Reborn)	1.00
8	Roger Maris (Hero's Welcome)	1.00
9	Checklist (Roger Maris)	.20

Dan Gardiner

Sports artist Dan Gardiner was commissioned to produce a series of nine insert cards depicting hot minor league prospects for this insert set. Players are depicted in posed portraits on front and in action paintings on the back. Cards carry a "DG" prefix to the card number and each card is serially numbered in the upper-left corner.

		NM/M
Complete Set (9):		6.00
Common Player:		.25
1	Michael Jordan	2.50
2	Michael Tucker	.25
3	Derek Jeter	3.50
4	Charles Johnson	.25
5	Howard Battle	.25
6	Quilvio Vergas (Veras)	.25
7	Brian Hunter	.25
8	Brien Taylor	.25
9	Checklist	.05

Locklear Collection

Paintings of eight Hall of Famers plus a checklist are featured in this insert set. The art is the work of former major leaguer Gene Locklear. The cards are numbered with an "LC" suffix.

		NM/M
Complete Set (9):		7.50
Common Player:		1.00
11	Ty Cobb	2.00
12	Bob Feller	1.00
13	Lou Gehrig	2.00
14	Josh Gibson	1.00
15	Walter Johnson	1.00
16	Casey Stengel	1.00
17	Honus Wagner	1.00
18	Cy Young	1.00
19	Checklist	.05

LP Cards

Two premium insert cards in the 1994 Ted Williams Co. set carry an "LP" card number prefix. One depicts basketball superstar Larry Bird playing baseball during his college days at Indiana State University. The other card depicts

Ted Williams speaking at the opening of the Ted Williams Museum. Fronts use a metallized technology. Backs describe the action. A few genuinely autographed Bird cards are known, featuring an embossed seal of authenticity.

	NM/M
Complete Set (2):	8.00
1 Larry Bird	5.00
1a Larry Bird/Auto.	200.00
2 Ted Williams	5.00

Memories

Continuing the card numbers from the 1993 Memories insert set, the 1994 version features highlights of the 1954, 1961, 1968 and 1975 World Series. Card fronts feature metallized images in a snapshot format. The year is noted in large pink numbers at lower-left. Backs describe each player's participation in that particular World Series and are numbered with an "M" prefix.

	NM/M
Complete Set (20):	11.00
Common Player:	.50
21 Monte Irvin	.50
22 Sal Maglie	.50
23 Dusty Rhodes	.50
24 Hank Thompson	.50
25 Yogi Berra	1.25
26 Elston Howard	.75
27 Roger Maris	1.50
28 Bobby Richardson	.75
29 Norm Cash	.75
30 Al Kaline	1.00
31 Mickey Lolich	.50
32 Denny McLain	.50
33 Bernie Carbo	.50
34 Fred Lynn	.50
35 Rico Petrocelli	.50
36 Luis Tiant	.50
37 Checklist	.05

Mike Schmidt Collection

This nine-card insert set honors the career of Hall of Fame Phillies third baseman Mike Schmidt. Fronts feature full-bleed metallized color photos. Backs have a

Phillies flag design with a career biography. Cards are numbered with an "MS" prefix.

	NM/M
Complete Set (9):	7.50
Common Player:	1.00
1 Mike Schmidt (Mike)	1.00
2 Mike Schmidt (The White House)	1.00
3 Mike Schmidt (Soaping Up)	1.00
4 Mike Schmidt (The Promised Land)	1.00
5 Mike Schmidt (Who's Who)	1.00
6 Mike Schmidt (The Call)	1.00
7 Mike Schmidt (Leading the Way)	1.00
8 Mike Schmidt (Award Winner)	1.00
9 Checklist	.35

The 500 Club

Major leaguers with 500 or more career home runs are featured in this nine-card insert set. Fronts have full-bleed metallized photos, some in color and some which have been colorized. A logo picturing a hanging "The 500 Club" sign appears at lower-left, with the player's name in gold. Backs have a basic design that looks for all the world like a toilet seat, in which the player's home run prowess is recalled. Cards are numbered with a "5C" prefix. Two versions of each card exist, one has brown graphic highlights on front, one has red. The red highlighted cards are worth about 25 percent more than the brown.

	NM/M
Complete Set (9):	7.50
Common Player:	.75
1 Hank Aaron	1.50
2 Reggie Jackson	1.25
3 Harmon Killebrew	.75
4 Mickey Mantle	2.25
5 Jimmie Foxx	.75
6 Babe Ruth	2.00
7 Mike Schmidt	1.25
8 Ted Williams	1.50
9 Checklist	.05

Trade for Babe

This nine-card set was available to persons who found a randomly packaged "Trade for Babe" redemption card in packs of Ted Williams Co. cards. A $4.50 postage/handling fee was necessary for redemption and a reported 9,999 trade sets were available. Card fronts feature colorized photos of Ruth while backs have text concerning the front theme. Cards are numbered with a "TB" prefix.

	NM/M
Complete Set (9):	15.00
Common Player:	2.00

----	Babe Ruth (Redemption card, expired Nov. 30, 1994.)	2.00
1	Babe Ruth (George Herman Ruth)	2.00
2	Babe Ruth (King of the Hill)	2.00
3	Babe Ruth (On to New York)	2.00
4	Babe Ruth (Called Shot?)	2.00
5	Babe Ruth (The Bambino and the Iron Horse)	2.00
6	Babe Ruth (Larger Than Life)	2.00
7	Babe Ruth (Always a Yankee)	2.00
8	Babe Ruth (The Babe)	2.00
9	Babe Ruth (Checklist)	2.00

1990 Windwalker Discs

The origins of this disc set, even its name, are not recorded. The set is comprised on nine dual-headed 3-7/8" discs. Each disc features two players from the 1990 American League All-Star team. No similar issue is known for the National League. Each side has a color action photo and a facsimile autograph. The unnumbered discs are checklisted here alphabetically.

		NM/M
Complete Set (9):		15.00
Common Disc:		.70
(1)	Sandy Alomar Jr., Dave Parker	.75
(2)	George Bell, Julio Franco	.75
(3)	Wade Boggs, Kirby Puckett	3.00
(4)	Jose Canseco, Rickey Henderson	2.50
(5)	Roger Clemens, Bob Welch	3.50
(6)	Cecil Fielder, Bret Saberhagen	.75
(7)	Chuck Finley, Kelly Gruber	.75
(8)	Ken Griffey Jr., Steve Sax	4.00
(9)	Ozzie Guillen, Cal Ripken Jr.	5.00

1991 Wiz Mets

This 450-card issue was one of several sponsored by the East Coast WIZ home entertainment stores in the early 1990s. Virtually every player in Mets history is included in the set. Each of three series of 15-card perforated sheets was co-sponsored by a large electronics manufacturer: AT&T, Fisher or Maxell. Sheets measure 10" x 9", with individual cards measuring 2" x 3". Card fronts have a black-and-white photo at center with the player's name at left and position at right. A color Mets logo is above and a WIZ logo below. Blue corner decorations complete the front design. Backs are printed in black-and-white, have Mets and sponsors' logos, years the player appeared with the Mets and his Mets career stats. Single cards from this set are seldom available.

	NM/M
Complete Set (450):	45.00
Common Player:	.10

1	Don Aase	.10
2	Tommie Agee	.30
3	Rick Aguilera	.20
4	Jack Aker	.10
5	Neil Allen	.10
6	Bill Almon	.10
7	Sandy Alomar	.10
8	Jesus Alou	.10
9	George Altman	.10
10	Luis Alvarado	.10
11	Craig Anderson	.10
12	Rick Anderson	.10
13	Bob Apodaca	.10
14	Gerry Arrigo	.10
15	Richie Ashburn	6.00
16	Tucker Ashford	.10
17	Bob Aspromonte	.10
18	Benny Ayala	.10
19	Wally Backman	.10
20	Kevin Baez	.10
21	Bob Bailor	.10
22	Rick Baldwin	.10
23	Billy Baldwin	.10
24	Lute Barnes	.10
25	Ed Bauta	.10
26	Billy Beane	.10
27	Larry Bearnarth	.10
28	Blaine Beatty	.10
29	Jim Beauchamp	.10
30	Gus Bell	.30
31	Dennis Bennett	.10
32	Butch Benton	.10
33	Juan Berenguer	.10
34	Bruce Berenyi	.10
35	Dwight Bernard	.10
36	Yogi Berra	6.00
37	Jim Bethke	.10
38	Mike Bishop	.10
39	Terry Blocker	.10
40	Bruce Bochy	.10
41	Bruce Boisclair	.10
42	Dan Boitano	.10
43	Mark Bomback	.10
44	Don Bosch	.10
45	Daryl Boston	.10
46	Ken Boswell	.10
47	Ed Bouchee	.10
48	Larry Bowa	.20
49	Ken Boyer	.50
50	Mark Bradley	.10
51	Eddie Bressoud	.10
52	Hubie Brooks	.30
53	Kevin Brown	.10
54	Leon Brown	.10
55	Mike Bruhert	.10
56	Jerry Buchek	.10
57	Larry Burright	.10
58	Ray Burris	.10
59	John Candelaria	.10
60	Chris Cannizzaro	.10
61	Buzz Capra	.10
62	Jose Cardenal	.10
63	Don Cardwell	.10
64	Duke Carmel	.10
65	Chuck Carr	.10
66	Mark Carreon	.10
67	Gary Carter	4.00
68	Elio Chacon	.10
69	Dean Chance	.10
70	Kelvin Chapman	.10
71	Ed Charles	.40
72	Rich Chiles	.10
73	Harry Chiti	.10
74	John Christensen	.10
75	Joe Christopher	.10
76	Galen Cisco	.10
77	Donn Clendenon	.40
78	Gene Clines	.10
79	Choo Choo Coleman	.40
80	Kevin Collins	.10
81	David Cone	.75
82	Bill Connors	.10
83	Cliff Cook	.10
84	Tim Corcoran	.10
85	Mardie Cornejo	.10
86	Billy Cowan	.10
87	Roger Craig	.10
88	Jerry Cram	.10
89	Mike Cubbage	.10
90	Ron Darling	.20
91	Ray Daviault	.10
92	Tommie Davis	.10
93	John DeMerit	.10
94	Bill Denehy	.10
95	Jack DiLauro	.10
96	Carlos Diaz	.10
97	Mario Diaz	.10
98	Steve Dillon	.10
99	Sammy Drake	.10
100	Jim Dwyer	.10
101	Duffy Dyer	.10
102	Len Dykstra	.50
103	Tom Edens	.10
104	Dave Eilers	.10
105	Larry Elliot	.10
106	Dock Ellis	.10
107	Kevin Elster	.20
108	Nino Espinosa	.10
109	Chuck Estrada	.10
110	Francisco Estrada	.10
111	Pete Falcone	.10
112	Sid Fernandez	.20
113	Chico Fernandez	.10
114	Sergio Ferrer	.10
115	Jack Fisher	.10
116	Mike Fitzgerald	.10
117	Shaun Fitzmaurice	.10
118	Gil Flores	.10

119	Doug Flynn	.10
120	Tim Foli	.10
121	Rich Folkers	.10
122	Larry Foss	.10
123	George Foster	.30
124	Leo Foster	.10
125	Joe Foy	.10
126	John Franco	.30
127	Jim Fregosi	.20
128	Bob Friend	.10
129	Danny Frisella	.10
130	Brent Gaff	.10
131	Bob Gallagher	.10
132	Ron Gardenhire	.10
133	Rob Gardner	.10
134	Wes Gardner	.10
135	Wayne Garrett	.10
136	Rod Gaspar	.10
137	Gary Gentry	.10
138	Jim Gibbons	.10
139	Bob Gibson	.10
140	Brian Giles	.10
141	Joe Ginsberg	.10
142	Ed Glynn	.10
143	Jesse Gonder	.30
144	Dwight Gooden	1.00
145	Greg Goossen	.10
146	Tom Gorman	.10
147	Jim Gosger	.10
148	Bill Graham	.10
149	Wayne Graham	.10
150	Dallas Green	.30
151	Pumpsie Green	.10
152	Tom Grieve	.10
153	Jerry Grote	.20
154	Joe Grzenda	.10
155	Don Hahn	.10
156	Tom Hall	.10
157	Jack Hamilton	.10
158	Ike Hampton	.10
159	Tim Harkness	.10
160	Bud Harrelson	.40
161	Greg Harris	.10
162	Greg Harts	.10
163	Andy Hassler	.10
164	Tom Hausman	.10
165	Ed Hearn	.10
166	Richie Hebner	.30
167	Danny Heep	.10
168	Jack Heidemann	.10
169	Bob Heise	.10
170	Ken Henderson	.10
171	Steve Henderson	.10
172	Bob Hendley	.10
173	Phil Hennigan	.10
174	Bill Hepler	.10
175	Ron Herbel	.10
176	Manny Hernandez	.10
177	Keith Hernandez	.50
178	Tommy Herr	.10
179	Rick Herrscher	.10
180	Jim Hickman	.10
181	Joe Hicks	.10
182	Chuck Hiller	.10
183	Dave Hillman	.10
184	Jerry Hinsley	.10
185	Gil Hodges	2.00
186	Ron Hodges	.10
187	Scott Holman	.10
188	Jay Hook	.10
189	Mike Howard	.10
190	Jesse Hudson	.10
191	Keith Hughes	.10
192	Todd Hundley	.30
193	Ron Hunt	.10
194	Willard Hunter	.10
195	Clint Hurdle	.10
196	Jeff Innis	.10
197	Al Jackson	.10
198	Roy Lee Jackson	.10
199	Gregg Jefferies	1.00
200	Stan Jefferson	.10
201	Chris Jelic	.10
202	Bob Johnson	.10
203	Howard Johnson	.75
204	Bob W. Johnson	.10
205	Randy Jones	.10
206	Sherman Jones	.10
207	Cleon Jones	.30
208	Ross Jones	.10
209	Mike Jorgensen	.10
210	Rod Kanehl	.10
211	Dave Kingman	.50
212	Bobby Klaus	.10
213	Jay Kleven	.10
214	Lou Klimchock	.10
215	Ray Knight	.30
216	Kevin Kobel	.10
217	Gary Kolb	.10
218	Cal Koonce	.10
219	Jerry Koosman	.30
220	Ed Kranepool	.30
221	Gary Kroll	.10
222	Clem Labine	.30
223	Jack Lamabe	.10
224	Hobie Landrith	.10
225	Frank Lary	.10
226	Bill Latham	.10
227	Terry Leach	.10
228	Tim Leary	.10
229	John Lewis	.10
230	David Liddell	.10
231	Phil Linz	.10
232	Ron Locke	.10
233	Skip Lockwood	.10
234	Mickey Lolich	.30
235	Phil Lombardi	.10
236	Al Luplow	.10

237	Ed Lynch	.10
238	Barry Lyons	.10
239	Ken MacKenzie	.10
240	Julio Machado	.10
241	Elliot Maddox	.10
243	Dave Magadan	.10
244	Phil Mankowski	.10
245	Felix Mantilla	.10
246	Mike Marshall	.10
247	Dave Marshall	.10
248	Jim Marshall	.10
249	Mike A. Marshall	.10
250	J.C. Martin	.10
251	Jerry Martin	.10
252	Teddy Martinez	.10
253	Jon Matlack	.20
254	Jerry May	.10
255	Willie Mays	15.00
256	Lee Mazzilli	.20
257	Jim McAndrew	.10
258	Bob McClure	.10
259	Roger McDowell	.30
260	Tug McGraw	.40
261	Jeff McKnight	.10
262	Roy McMillan	.10
263	Kevin McReynolds	.30
264	George Medich	.20
265	Orlando Mercado	.10
266	Butch Metzger	.10
267	Felix Millan	.10
268	Bob G. Miller	.10
269	Bob L. Miller	.10
270	Dyar Miller	.10
271	Larry Miller	.10
272	Keith Miller	.10
273	Randy Milligan	.10
274	John Milner	.10
275	John Mitchell	.10
276	Kevin Mitchell	.30
277	Wilmer Mizell	.10
278	Herb Moford	.10
279	Willie Montanez	.10
280	Joe Moock	.10
281	Tommy Moore	.10
282	Bob Moorhead	.10
283	Jerry Morales	.10
284	Al Moran	.10
285	Jose Moreno	.10
286	Bill Murphy	.10
287	Dale Murray	.10
288	Dennis Musgraves	.10
289	Jeff Musselman	.10
290	Randy Myers	.30
291	Bob Myrick	.10
292	Danny Napoleon	.10
293	Charlie Neal	.10
294	Randy Niemann	.10
295	Joe Nolan	.10
296	Dan Norman	.10
297	Ed Nunez	.10
298	Charlie O'Brien	.10
299	Tom O'Malley	.10
300	Bob Ojeda	.30
301	Jose Oquendo	.10
302	Jesse Orosco	.10
303	Junior Ortiz	.10
304	Brian Ostrosser	.10
305	Amos Otis	.30
306	Rick Ownbey	.10
307	John Pacella	.10
308	Tom Paciorek	.10
309	Harry Parker	.10
310	Tom Parsons	.10
311	Al Pedrique	.10
312	Brock Pemberton	.10
313	Alejandro Pena	.10
314	Bobby Pfeil	.10
315	Mike Phillips	.10
316	Jim Piersall	.30
317	Joe Pignatano	.10
318	Grover Powell	.10
319	Rich Puig	.10
320	Charlie Puleo	.10
321	Gary Rajsich	.10
322	Mario Ramirez	.10
323	Lenny Randle	.10
324	Bob Rauch	.10
325	Jeff Reardon	.30
326	Darren Reed	.10
327	Hal Reniff	.10
328	Ronn Reynolds	.10
329	Tom Reynolds	.10
330	Dennis Ribant	.10
331	Gordie Richardson	.10
332	Dave Roberts	.10
333	Les Rohr	.10
334	Luis Rosado	.10
335	Don Rose	.10
336	Don Rowe	.10
337	Dick Rusteck	.10
338	Nolan Ryan	15.00
339	Ray Sadecki	.10
340	Joe Sambito	.10
341	Amado Samuel	.10
342	Juan Samuel	.10
343	Ken Sanders	.10
344	Rafael Santana	.10
345	Mackey Sasser	.10
346	Mac Scarce	.10
347	Jim Schaffer	.10
348	Dan Schatzeder	.10
349	Calvin Schiraldi	.10
350	Al Schmelz	.10
351	Dave Schneck	.10
352	Ted Schreiber	.10
353	Don Schulze	.10
354	Mike Scott	.30
355	Ray Searage	.10

356 Tom Seaver 10.00
357 Dick Selma .10
358 Art Shamsky .30
359 Bob Shaw .10
360 Don Shaw .10
361 Norm Sherry .10
362 Craig Shipley .10
363 Bart Shirley .10
364 Bill Short .10
365 Paul Siebert .10
366 Ken Singleton .30
367 Doug Sisk .10
368 Bobby Gene Smith .10
369 Charley Smith .10
370 Dick Smith .10
371 Duke Snider 10.00
372 Warren Spahn 4.00
373 Larry Stahl .10
374 Roy Staiger .10
375 Tracy Stallard .10
376 Leroy Stanton .10
377 Rusty Staub 1.00
378 John Stearns .10
379 John Stephenson .10
380 Randy Sterling .10
381 George Stone .10
382 Darryl Strawberry 1.00
383 John Strohmayer .10
384 Brent Strom .10
385 Dick Stuart .10
386 Tom Sturdivant .10
387 Bill Sudakis .10
388 John Sullivan .10
389 Darrell Sutherland .10
390 Ron Swoboda .30
391 Craig Swan .10
392 Rick Sweet .10
393 Pat Tabler .10
394 Kevin Tapani .10
395 Randy Tate .10
396 Frank Taveras .10
397 Chuck Taylor .10
398 Ron Taylor .10
399 Bob Taylor .10
400 Sammy Taylor .10
401 Walt Terrell .10
402 Ralph Terry .10
403 Tim Teufel .30
404 George Theodore .10
405 Frank Thomas .20
406 Lou Thornton .10
407 Marv Throneberry .50
408 Dick Tidrow .10
409 Rusty Tillman .10
410 Jackson Todd .10
411 Joe Torre 1.50
412 Mike Torrez .10
413 Kelvin Torve .10
414 Alex Trevino .10
415 Wayne Twitchell .10
416 Del Unser .10
417 Mike Vail .10
418 Bobby Valentine .40
419 Ellis Valentine .10
420 Julio Valera .10
421 Tom Veryzer .10
422 Frank Viola .30
423 Bill Wakefield .10
424 Gene Walter .10
425 Claudell Washington .10
426 Hank Webb .10
427 Al Weis .10
428 Dave West .10
429 Wally Whitehurst .10
430 Carl Willey .10
431 Nick Willhite .10
432 Charlie Williams .10
433 Mookie Wilson .60
434 Herm Winningham .10
435 Gene Woodling .30
436 Billy Wynne .10
437 Joel Youngblood .10
438 Pat Zachry .10
439 Don Zimmer .30
(440) Checklist 1-40 .10
(441) Checklist 41-80 .10
(442) Checklist 81-120 .10
(443) Checklist 121-160 .10
(444) Checklist 161-200 .10
(445) Checklist 201-240 .10
(446) Checklist 241-280 .10
(447) Checklist 281-320 .10
(448) Checklist 321-360 .10
(449) Checklist 361-400 .10
(450) Checklist 401-439 .10

1991 Wiz Yankees of the '50's

Yankees players from the 1950s dynasty are featured in this set distributed in several series at various promotional games. The cards were produced in a perforated sheet format, the 2" x 3" individual cards can be separated with ease. Fronts feature blue-and-white duo-tone photos with the familiar Yankee Stadium facade in blue at top and the player name in black below. Backs are printed in blue on white. The series name is printed beneath the top name bar, along with a line indicating the player's years with the Yankees and a few career stats. At bottom of all cards are Wiz Home Enter-

tainment Centers and AT&T logos, along with a Yankees Classics logo. The unnumbered cards are checklisted here alphabetically.

NM/M
Complete Set, Panels (9): 20.00
Complete Set, Singles (125): 20.00
Common Player: .25
(1) Loren Babe .25
(2) Hank Bauer .40
(3) Zeke Bella .25
(4) Lou Berberet .25
(5) Yogi Berra 2.00
(6) Ewell Blackwell .35
(7) Johnny Blanchard .25
(8) Gary Blaylock .25
(9) Don Bollweg .25
(10) Clete Boyer .35
(11) Ralph Branca .25
(12) Fritzie Brickell .25
(13) Jim Brideweser .25
(14) Jim Bronstad .50
(15) Bobby Brown .35
(16) Lew Burdette .35
(17) Harry Byrd .25
(18) Tommy Byrne .25
(19) Andy Carey .25
(20) Tommy Carroll .25
(21) Bob Cerv .35
(22) Al Cicotte .25
(23) Jim Coates .25
(24) Jerry Coleman .25
(25) Rip Coleman .25
(26) Joe Collins .25
(27) Clint Courtney .25
(28) Bobby Del Greco .25
(29) Jim Delsing .25
(30) Murry Dickson .25
(31) Joe DiMaggio 6.00
(32) Art Ditmar .25
(33) Sonny Dixon .25
(34) Ryne Duren .35
(35) Tom Ferrick .25
(36) Whitey Ford 2.00
(37) Mark Freeman .25
(38) Tom Gorman .25
(39) Ted Gray .25
(40) Eli Grba .25
(41) Bob Grim .25
(42) Woodie Held .25
(43) Tommy Henrich .35
(44) Johnny Hopp .25
(45) Ralph Houk .35
(46) Elston Howard .50
(47) Ken Hunt .25
(48) Billy Hunter .25
(49) Johnny James .25
(50) Jackie Jensen .45
(51) Billy Johnson .25
(52) Darrell Johnson .25
(53) Charlie Keller .35
(54) Jim Konstanty .25
(55) Steve Kraly .25
(56) Jack Kramer .25
(57) Tony Kubek .25
(58) Johnny Kucks .25
(59) Bob Kuzava .25
(60) Don Larsen 1.00
(61) Frank Leja .25
(62) Johnny Lindell .25
(63) Ed Lopat .40
(64) Hector Lopez .25
(65) Jerry Lumpe .25
(66) Duke Maas .25
(67) Dave Madison .25
(68) Sal Maglie .35
(69) Mickey Mantle 12.00
(70) Cliff Mapes .25
(71) Billy Martin 1.50
(72) Mickey McDermott .25
(73) Jim McDonald .25
(74) Gil McDougald .45
(75) Bill Miller .25
(76) Willie Miranda .25
(77) Johnny Mize .50
(78) Zack Monroe .25
(79) Tom Morgan .25
(80) Bob Muncrief .25
(81) Ernie Nevel .50
(82) Irv Noren .25
(83) Joe Ostrowski .25
(84) Stubby Overmire .25
(85) Joe Page .25
(86) Duane Pillette .25
(87) Jim Pisoni .25
(88) Bob Porterfield .25
(89) Vic Raschi .50
(90) Bill Renna .25
(91) Allie Reynolds .50
(92) Bobby Richardson .75
(93) Phil Rizzuto 2.00
(94) Eddie Robinson .25
(95) Johnny Sain .50
(96) Fred Sanford .25
(97) Ray Scarborough .25
(98) Harry Schaeffer .25
(99) Art Schallock (Schallock) .50
(100) Johnny Schmitz .25
(101) Art Schults .50
(102) Kal Segrist .25
(103) Bobby Shantz .50
(104) Spec Shea .25
(105) Norm Siebern .25
(106) Charlie Silvera .25
(107) Harry Simpson .35
(108) Lou Skizas .25

(109) Bill Skowron .75
(110) Enos Slaughter 1.00
(111) Gerry Staley .25
(112) Snuffy Stirnweiss .25
(113) Marlin Stuart .25
(114) Tom Sturdivant .25
(115) Bill Terry .25
(116) Dick Tettelbach .50
(117) Marv Throneberry .35
(118) Gus Triandos .35
(119) Virgil Trucks .35
(120) Bob Turley .50
(121) Frank Verdi .25
(122) Dick Wakefield .25
(123) Bob Wiesler .25
(124) Archie Wilson .25
(125) George Wilson .25

1992 Wiz Yankees Classics

TUCKER ASHFORD

More than 600 different Yankees players from the turn of the century through the 1980s are featured in this set. Produced and distributed in five series at various promotional games, the cards share a common design and theme. Originally in a 10" x 9" perforated sheet format, the 2" x 3" individual cards can be separated with ease. Fronts feature blue-and-white duo-tone photos with the familiar Yankee Stadium facade in blue at top and the player name in black below. Backs are printed in blue on white. The series name is printed beneath the top name bar, along with a line indicating the player's years with the Yankees and a few career stats. At bottom of all cards are the Yankees Classics and Wiz Home Entertainment Centers logos, along with the logo of the co-sponsor. The Yankees of the '60s and All-Star series were co-sponsored by American Express; the '70s series by Fisher; the '80s by Minolta and the Hall of Famers by Aiwa. The unnumbered cards are checklisted here alphabetically within series.

NM/M
Complete Set (638): 95.00
Common Player: .20
Complete Series, Yankees of the '60s: 25.00
(1) Jack Aker .20
(2) Ruben Amaro .20
(3) Luis Arroyo .20
(4) Stan Bahnsen .20
(5) Steve Barber .20
(6) Ray Barker .20
(7) Rich Beck .20
(8) Yogi Berra 2.00
(9) Johnny Blanchard .50
(10) Gil Blanco .20
(11) Ron Blomberg .20
(12) Len Boehmer .20
(13) Jim Bouton .50
(14) Clete Boyer .50
(15) Jim Brenneman .20
(16) Marshall Bridges .20
(17) Harry Bright .20
(18) Hal Brown .20
(19) Billy Bryan .20
(20) Bill Burbach .20
(21) Andy Carey .20
(22) Duke Carmel .20
(23) Bob Cerv .20
(24) Horace Clarke .20
(25) Tex Clevenger .20
(26) Lu Clinton .20
(27) Jim Coates .20
(28) Rocky Colavito 1.50
(29) Billy Cowan .20
(30) Bobby Cox .50
(31) Jack Cullen .20
(32) John Cumberland .20
(33) Bud Daley .20
(34) Joe DeMaestri .20
(35) Art Ditmar .20
(36) Al Downing .30

(37) Ryne Duren .30
(38) Doc Edwards .20
(39) John Ellis .20
(40) Frank Fernandez .20
(41) Mike Ferraro .20
(42) Whitey Ford 2.00
(43) Bob Friend .20
(44) John Gabler .20
(45) Billy Gardner .20
(46) Jake Gibbs .20
(47) Jesse Gonder .20
(48) Pedro Gonzalez .20
(49) Eli Grba .20
(50) Kent Hadley .20
(51) Bob Hale .20
(52) Jimmie Hall .20
(53) Steve Hamilton .20
(54) Mike Hegan .30
(55) Bill Henry .20
(56) Elston Howard .90
(57) Dick Howser .50
(58) Ken Hunt .20
(59) Johnny James .20
(60) Elvio Jiminez .20
(61) Deron Johnson .30
(62) Ken Johnson .20
(63) Mike Jurewicz .50
(64) Mike Kekich .20
(65) John Kennedy .20
(66) Jerry Kenney .20
(67) Fred Kipp .20
(68) Ron Klimkowski .20
(69) Andy Kosco .20
(70) Tony Kubek .75
(71) Bill Kunkel .20
(72) Phil Linz .20
(73) Dale Long .20
(74) Art Lopez .20
(75) Hector Lopez .20
(76) Jim Lyttle .20
(77) Duke Maas .20
(78) Mickey Mantle 10.00
(79) Roger Maris 4.00
(80) Lindy McDaniel .20
(81) Danny McDevitt .20
(82) Dave McDonald .20
(83) Gil McDougald .50
(84) Tom Metcalf .20
(85) Bob Meyer .20
(86) Gene Michael .30
(87) Pete Mikkelsen .20
(88) John Miller .20
(89) Bill Monbouquette .20
(90) Archie Moore .20
(91) Ross Moschitto .20
(92) Thurman Munson 2.00
(93) Bobby Murcer .75
(94) Don Nottebart .20
(95) Nate Oliver .20
(96) Joe Pepitone .50
(97) Cecil Perkins .20
(98) Fritz Peterson .20
(99) Jim Pisoni .20
(100) Pedro Ramos .20
(101) Jack Reed .20
(102) Hal Reniff .20
(103) Roger Repoz .20
(104) Bobby Richardson .90
(105) Dale Roberts .50
(106) Bill Robinson .20
(107) Ellie Rodriguez .20
(108) Charlie Sands .20
(109) Bob Schmidt .20
(110) Dick Schofield .30
(111) Billy Shantz .20
(112) Bobby Shantz .30
(113) Rollie Sheldon .20
(114) Tom Shopay .20
(115) Bill Short .20
(116) Dick Simpson .20
(117) Bill Skowron .50
(118) Charley Smith .20
(119) Tony Solaita .20
(120) Bill Stafford .20
(121) Mel Stottlemyre .30
(122) Hal Stowe .20
(123) Fred Talbot .20
(124) Frank Tepedino .20
(125) Ralph Terry .20
(126) Lee Thomas .20
(127) Bobby Tiefenauer .20
(128) Bob Tillman .20
(129) Thad Tillotson .20
(130) Earl Torgeson .20
(131) Tom Tresh .50
(132) Bob Turley .40
(133) Elmer Valo .20
(134) Joe Verbanic .20
(135) Steve Whitaker .20
(136) Roy White .40
(137) Stan Williams .20
(138) Dooley Womack .20
(139) Ron Woods .20
(140) John Wyatt .20

Complete Series, Yankees of the '70s: 16.00
(1) Jack Aker .20
(2) Doyle Alexander .20
(3) Bernie Allen .20
(4) Sandy Alomar .20
(5) Felipe Alou .25
(6) Matty Alou .20
(7) Dell Alston .20
(8) Rick Anderson .20
(9) Stan Bahnsen .20
(10) Frank Baker .20
(11) Jim Beattie .20
(12) Fred Beene .20

(13) Juan Beniquez .20
(14) Dave Bergman .20
(15) Juan Bernhardt .20
(16) Rick Bladt .20
(17) Paul Blair .20
(18) Wade Blasingame .20
(19) Steve Blateric .20
(21) Ron Blomberg .20
(22) Len Boehmer .20
(23) Bobby Bonds .30
(24) Ken Brett .20
(25) Ed Brinkman .20
(26) Bobby Brown .20
(27) Bill Burbach .20
(28) Ray Burris .20
(29) Tom Buskey .20
(30) Johnny Callison .20
(31) Danny Cater .20
(32) Chris Chambliss .30
(33) Horace Clarke .20
(34) Ken Clay .20
(35) Al Closter .20
(36) Rich Coggins .20
(37) Loyd Colson .20
(38) Casey Cox .20
(39) John Cumberland .20
(40) Ron Davis .20
(41) Jim Deidel .20
(42) Rick Dempsey .30
(43) Bucky Dent .40
(44) Kerry Dineen .20
(45) Pat Dobson .20
(46) Brian Doyle .20
(47) Rawly Eastwick .20
(48) Dock Ellis .20
(49) John Ellis .20
(50) Ed Figueroa .20
(51) Oscar Gamble .20
(52) Damaso Garcia .20
(53) Rob Gardner .20
(54) Jake Gibbs .20
(55) Fernando Gonzalez .20
(56) Rich Gossage .40
(57) Larry Gowell .20
(58) Wayne Granger .20
(59) Mike Griffin .20
(60) Ron Guidry .75
(61) Brad Gulden .20
(62) Don Gullett .20
(63) Larry Gura .20
(64) Roger Hambright .20
(65) Steve Hamilton .20
(66) Ron Hansen .20
(67) Jim Hardin .20
(68) Fran Healy .20
(69) Mike Heath .20
(70) Mike Hegan .30
(71) Elrod Hendricks .20
(72) Ed Herrmann .20
(73) Rich Hinton .20
(74) Ken Holtzman .20
(75) Don Hood .20
(76) Catfish Hunter 1.00
(77) Grant Jackson .20
(78) Reggie Jackson 2.00
(79) Tommy John .90
(80) Alex Johnson .20
(81) Cliff Johnson .20
(82) Jay Johnstone .30
(83) Darryl Jones .20
(84) Gary Jones .20
(85) Jim Kaat .40
(86) Bob Kammeyer .20
(87) Mike Kekich .20
(88) Jerry Kenney .20
(89) Dave Kingman .50
(90) Ron Klimkowski .20
(91) Steve Kline .20
(92) Mickey Klutts .20
(93) Hal Lanier .20
(94) Eddie Leon .20
(95) Terry Ley .20
(96) Paul Lindblad .20
(97) Gene Locklear .20
(98) Sparky Lyle .40
(99) Jim Lyttle .20
(100) Elliott Maddox .20
(101) Jim Magnuson .20
(102) Tippy Martinez .20
(103) Jim Mason .20
(104) Carlos May .20
(105) Rudy May .20
(106) Larry McCall .20
(107) Mike McCormick .20
(108) Lindy McDaniel .20
(109) Sam McDowell .30
(110) Rich McKinney .20
(111) George Medich .20
(112) Andy Messersmith .30
(113) Gene Michael .20
(114) Paul Mirabella .20
(115) Bobby Mitchell .20
(116) Gerry Moses .20
(117) Thurman Munson 2.00
(118) Bobby Murcer .75
(119) Larry Murray .20
(120) Jerry Narron .20
(121) Graig Nettles .40
(122) Bob Oliver .20
(123) Dave Pagan .20
(124) Gil Patterson .20
(125) Marty Perez .20
(126) Fritz Peterson .20
(127) Lou Piniella .50
(128) Dave Rajsich .20
(129) Domingo Ramos .20

(131) Lenny Randle .20
(132) Willie Randolph .50
(133) Dave Righetti .20
(134) Mickey Rivers .30
(135) Bruce Robinson .20
(136) Jim Roland .20
(137) Celerino Sanchez .20
(138) Rick Sawyer .20
(139) George Scott .30
(140) Duke Sims .20
(141) Roger Slagle .20
(142) Jim Spencer .20
(143) Charlie Spikes .20
(144) Roy Staiger .20
(145) Fred Stanley .30
(146) Bill Sudakis .20
(147) Ron Swoboda .20
(148) Frank Tepedino .20
(149) Stan Thomas .20
(150) Gary Thomasson .20
(151) Luis Tiant .40
(152) Dick Tidrow .20
(153) Rusty Torres .20
(154) Mike Torrez .20
(155) Cesar Tovar .20
(156) Cecil Upshaw .20
(157) Otto Velez .20
(158) Joe Verbanic .20
(159) Mike Wallace .20
(160) Danny Walton .20
(161) Pete Ward .20
(162) Gary Waslewski .20
(163) Dennis Werth .20
(164) Roy White .30
(165) Terry Whitfield .20
(166) Walt Williams .20
(167) Ron Woods .20
(168) Dick Woodson .20
(169) Ken Wright .20
(170) Jimmy Wynn .20
(171) Jim York .20
(172) George Zeber .20

Complete Series, Yankees of the '80s: 17.50
(1) Luis Aguayo .20
(2) Doyle Alexander .20
(3) Neil Allen .20
(4) Mike Armstrong .20
(5) Brad Arnsberg .20
(6) Tucker Ashford .20
(7) Steve Balboni .20
(8) Jesse Barfield .20
(9) Don Baylor .40
(10) Dale Berra .20
(11) Doug Bird .20
(12) Paul Blair .20
(13) Mike Blowers .20
(14) Juan Bonilla .20
(15) Rich Bordi .20
(16) Scott Bradley .20
(17) Marshall Brant .20
(18) Tom Brookens .20
(19) Bob Brower .20
(20) Bobby Brown .20
(21) Curt Brown .20
(22) Jay Buhner .50
(23) Marty Bystrom .20
(24) Greg Cadaret .20
(25) Bert Campaneris .30
(26) John Candelaria .30
(27) Chuck Cary .20
(28) Bill Castro .20
(29) Rick Cerone .20
(30) Chris Chambliss .30
(31) Clay Christiansen .20
(32) Jack Clark .20
(33) Pat Clements .20
(34) Dave Collins .25
(35) Don Cooper .20
(36) Henry Cotto .20
(37) Joe Cowley .20
(38) Jose Cruz .20
(39) Bobby Davidson .20
(40) Ron Davis .20
(41) Brian Dayett .20
(42) Ivan DeJesus .20
(43) Bucky Dent .50
(44) Jim Deshaies .20
(45) Orestes Destrade .20
(46) Brian Dorsett .20
(47) Rich Dotson .20
(48) Brian Doyle .20
(49) Doug Drabek .30
(50) Mike Easler .20
(51) Dave Eiland .20
(52) Roger Erickson .20
(53) Juan Espino .20
(54) Alvaro Espinoza .20
(55) Barry Evans .20
(56) Ed Figueroa .20
(57) Pete Filson .20
(58) Mike Fischlin .20
(59) Brian Fisher .20
(60) Tim Foli .20
(61) Ray Fontenot .20
(62) Barry Foote .20
(63) George Frazier .20
(64) Bill Fulton .20
(65) Oscar Gamble .20
(66) Bob Geren .20
(67) Rich Gossage .40
(68) Mike Griffin .20
(69) Ken Griffey .30
(70) Cecilio Guante .20
(71) Lee Guetterman .20
(72) Ron Guidry .50
(73) Brad Gulden .20
(74) Don Gullett .20

(75)	Bill Gullickson	.20
(76)	Mel Hall	.20
(77)	Toby Harrah	.25
(78)	Ron Hassey	.20
(79)	Andy Hawkins	.20
(80)	Rickey Henderson	1.50
(81)	Leo Hernandez	.20
(82)	Butch Hobson	.20
(83)	Al Holland	.20
(84)	Roger Holt	.20
(85)	Jay Howell	.25
(86)	Rex Hudler	.20
(87)	Charles Hudson	.20
(88)	Keith Hughes	.20
(89)	Reggie Jackson	2.00
(90)	Stan Javier	.20
(91)	Stan Jefferson	.20
(92)	Tommy John	.50
(93)	Jimmy Jones	.20
(94)	Ruppert Jones	.20
(95)	Jim Kaat	.30
(96)	Curt Kaufman	.20
(97)	Roberto Kelly	.30
(98)	Steve Kemp	.25
(99)	Matt Keough	.20
(100)	Ron Kittle	.20
(101)	Steve Kiefer	.20
(102)	Dave LaPoint	.20
(103)	Marcus Lawton	.20
(104)	Joe Lefebvre	.20
(105)	Al Leiter	.20
(106)	Jim Lewis	.20
(107)	Bryan Little	.20
(108)	Tim Lollar	.20
(109)	Phil Lombardi	.20
(110)	Vic Mata	.20
(111)	Don Mattingly	4.00
(112)	Rudy May	.20
(113)	John Mayberry	.20
(114)	Lee Mazzilli	.25
(115)	Lance McCullers	.20
(116)	Andy McGaffigan	.20
(117)	Lynn McGlothen	.20
(118)	Bobby Meacham	.20
(119)	Hensley Muelens	.30
(120)	Larry Milbourne	.20
(121)	Kevin Mmahat	.20
(122)	Dale Mohorcic	.20
(123)	John Montefusco	.20
(124)	Omar Moreno	.20
(125)	Mike Morgan	.20
(126)	Jeff Moronko	.20
(127)	Hal Morris	.25
(128)	Jerry Mumphrey	.20
(129)	Bobby Murcer	.35
(130)	Dale Murray	.20
(131)	Gene Nelson	.20
(132)	Joe Niekro	.30
(133)	Phil Niekro	.90
(134)	Scott Nielsen	.20
(135)	Otis Nixon	.20
(136)	Johnny Oates	.20
(137)	Mike O'Berry	.20
(138)	Rowland Office	.20
(139)	John Pacella	.20
(140)	Mike Pagliarulo	.30
(141)	Clay Parker	.20
(142)	Dan Pasqua	.20
(143)	Mike Patterson	.20
(144)	Hipolito Pena	.20
(145)	Gaylord Perry	.50
(146)	Ken Phelps	.20
(147)	Lou Piniella	.40
(148)	Eric Plunk	.20
(149)	Luis Polonia	.30
(150)	Alfonso Pulido	.20
(151)	Jamie Quirk	.20
(152)	Bobby Ramos	.20
(153)	Willie Randolph	.40
(154)	Dennis Rasmussen	.20
(155)	Shane Rawley	.20
(156)	Rick Reuschel	.20
(157)	Dave Revering	.20
(158)	Rick Rhoden	.20
(159)	Dave Righetti	.30
(160)	Jose Rijo	.20
(161)	Andre Robertson	.20
(162)	Bruce Robinson	.20
(163)	Aurelio Rodriguez	.20
(164)	Edwin Rodriguez	.20
(165)	Gary Roenicke	.20
(166)	Jerry Royster	.20
(167)	Lenn Sakata	.20
(168)	Mark Salas	.20
(169)	Billy Sample	.20
(170)	Deion Sanders	1.00
(171)	Rafael Santana	.20
(172)	Steve Sax	.30
(173)	Don Schulze	.20
(174)	Rodney Scott	.20
(175)	Rod Scurry	.20
(176)	Dennis Sherrill	.20
(177)	Steve Shields	.20
(178)	Bob Shirley	.20
(179)	Joel Skinner	.20
(180)	Don Slaught	.30
(181)	Roy Smalley	.20
(182)	Keith Smith	.20
(183)	Eric Soderholm	.20
(184)	Jim Spencer	.20
(185)	Fred Stanley	.20
(186)	Dave Stegman	.20
(187)	Tim Stoddard	.20
(188)	Walt Terrell	.20
(189)	Bob Tewksbury	.20
(190)	Luis Tiant	.40
(191)	Wayne Tolleson	.20
(192)	Steve Trout	.20

(193)	Tom Underwood	.20
(194)	Randy Velarde	.30
(195)	Gary Ward	.20
(196)	Claudell Washington	.30
(197)	Bob Watson	.20
(198)	Dave Wehrmeister	.20
(199)	Dennis Werth	.20
(200)	Stefan Wever	.20
(201)	Ed Whitson	.20
(202)	Ted Wilborn	.20
(203)	Dave Winfield	1.00
(204)	Butch Wynegar	.20
(205)	Paul Zuvella	.20

Complete Series, Yankees
All-Stars 17.50

(1)	Luis Arroyo	.20
(2)	Hank Bauer	.35
(3)	Yogi Berra	2.00
(4)	Bobby Bonds	.30
(5)	Ernie Bonham	.20
(6)	Hank Borowy	.20
(7)	Jim Bouton	.30
(8)	Tommy Byrne	.20
(9)	Chris Chambliss	.20
(10)	Spud Chandler	.20
(11)	Ben Chapman	.20
(12)	Jim Coates	.20
(13)	Jerry Coleman	.20
(14)	Frank Crosetti	.20
(15)	Ron Davis	.20
(16)	Bucky Dent	.30
(17)	Bill Dickey	.50
(18)	Joe DiMaggio	6.00
(19)	Al Downing	.20
(20)	Ryne Duren	.20
(21)	Whitey Ford	2.00
(22)	Lou Gehrig	6.00
(23)	Lefty Gomez	.40
(24)	Joe Gordon	.30
(25)	Rich Gossage	.30
(26)	Bob Grim	.20
(27)	Ron Guidry	.30
(28)	Rollie Hemsley	.20
(29)	Rickey Henderson	1.50
(30)	Tommy Henrich	.20
(31)	Elston Howard	.35
(32)	Catfish Hunter	.30
(33)	Reggie Jackson	2.00
(34)	Tommy John	.30
(35)	Billy Johnson	.20
(36)	Charlie Keller	.20
(37)	Tony Kubek	.35
(38)	Johnny Kucks	.20
(39)	Tony Lazzeri	.30
(40)	Johnny Lindell	.20
(41)	Ed Lopat	.30
(42)	Sparky Lyle	.20
(43)	Mickey Mantle	10.00
(44)	Roger Maris	4.00
(45)	Billy Martin	.75
(46)	Don Mattingly	4.00
(47)	Gil McDougald	.30
(48)	George McQuinn	.20
(49)	Johnny Mize	.40
(50)	Thurman Munson	2.00
(51)	Bobby Murcer	.30
(52)	Johnny Murphy	.20
(53)	Graig Nettles	.20
(54)	Phil Niekro	.80
(55)	Irv Noren	.20
(56)	Joe Page	.20
(57)	Monte Pearson	.20
(58)	Joe Pepitone	.30
(59)	Fritz Peterson	.20
(60)	Willie Randolph	.30
(61)	Vic Raschi	.30
(62)	Allie Reynolds	.30
(63)	Bobby Richardson	.35
(64)	Dave Righetti	.20
(65)	Mickey Rivers	.20
(66)	Phil Rizzuto	2.00
(67)	Aaron Robinson	.20
(68)	Red Rolfe	.20
(69)	Buddy Rosar	.20
(70)	Red Ruffing	.20
(71)	Marius Russo	.20
(72)	Babe Ruth	7.50
(73)	Johnny Sain	.40
(74)	Scott Sanderson	.20
(75)	Steve Sax	.20
(76)	George Selkirk	.20
(77)	Bobby Shantz	.20
(78)	Spec Shea	.20
(79)	Snuffy Stirnweiss	.20
(80)	Mel Stottlemyre	.20
(81)	Ralph Terry	.20
(82)	Tom Tresh	.20
(83)	Bob Turley	.20
(84)	Roy White	.30
(85)	Dave Winfield	1.00

Complete Series, Yankees
Hall of Famers 15.00

(1)	Home Run Baker	.50
(2)	Ed Barrow	.20
(3)	Yogi Berra	2.00
(4)	Frank Chance	.50
(5)	Jack Chesbro	.20
(6)	Earle Combs	.20
(7)	Stan Coveleski	.20
(8)	Bill Dickey	.50
(9)	Joe DiMaggio	6.00
(10)	Whitey Ford	2.00
(11)	Lou Gehrig	6.00
(12)	Lefty Gomez	.50
(13)	Clark C. Griffith	.20
(14)	Burleigh Grimes	.20
(15)	Bucky Harris	.20

(16)	Waite Hoyt	.20
(17)	Miller Huggins	.20
(18)	Catfish Hunter	.30
(19)	Willie Keeler	.20
(20)	Tony Lazzeri	.20
(21)	Larry MacPhail	.20
(22)	Mickey Mantle	10.00
(23)	Joe McCarthy	.20
(24)	Johnny Mize	.35
(25)	Herb Pennock	.20
(26)	Gaylord Perry	.20
(27)	Branch Rickey	.20
(28)	Red Ruffing	.20
(29)	Babe Ruth	7.50
(30)	Joe Sewell	.20
(31)	Enos Slaughter	.30
(32)	Casey Stengel	.30
(33)	Dazzy Vance	.20
(34)	Paul Waner	.20
(35)	George M. Weiss	.20

1990 Wonder Stars

The cards were found in specially marked loaves of Wonder Bread, in a special plastic pocket to protect them from product stains (and vice versa). Uncut sheets could also be obtained for $3 and proofs of purchase. Produced by Mike Schechter Associates, the photos at the center of the cards have team logos airbrushed away for lack of a license from MLB; the cards are licensed by the players' union. A red border surrounds the photo on front. Backs are printed in red and blue on white and have up to five years' worth of stats, a few lines of career highlights and a facsimile autograph.

		NM/M
Complete Set (20):		9.00
Common Player:		.25
Uncut Sheet:		12.50
1	Bo Jackson	.30
2	Roger Clemens	1.00
3	Jim Abbott	.25
4	Orel Hershiser	.25
5	Ozzie Smith	.75
6	Don Mattingly	1.00
7	Kevin Mitchell	.25
8	Jerome Walton	.25
9	Kirby Puckett	.75
10	Darryl Strawberry	.25
11	Robin Yount	.60
12	Tony Gwynn	.75
13	Alan Trammell	.25
14	Jose Canseco	.50
15	Greg Swindell	.25
16	Nolan Ryan	2.00
17	Howard Johnson	.25
18	Ken Griffey Jr.	2.00
19	Will Clark	.25
20	Ryne Sandberg	.60

1985 Woolworth

This 44-card boxed set was produced by Topps for the Woolworth's chain stores, though "Woolworth's" does not appear anywhere on the individual cards. Featuring a combination of black-and-white and color photos of baseball record holders from all eras, the set is in the standard 2-1/2" x 3-1/2" format. Backs, printed in blue and orange, give career details and personal data. Because it combined old-timers with current players, the set did not achieve a great deal of collector popularity. The set was reissued in 1987 in a different box at the Boardwalk and Baseball theme park in Florida.

		NM/M
Complete Set (44):		7.50
Common Player:		.10
1	Hank Aaron	.60
2	Grover Alexander	.15
3	Ernie Banks	.30
4	Yogi Berra	.30
5	Lou Brock	.10
6	Steve Carlton	.25
7	Jack Chesbro	.10
8	Ty Cobb	.60
9	Sam Crawford	.10
10	Rollie Fingers	.10
11	Whitey Ford	.30
12	Johnny Frederick	.10
13	Frankie Frisch	.10
14	Lou Gehrig	.75
15	Jim Gentile	.10
16	Dwight Gooden	.10
17	Rickey Henderson	.40
18	Rogers Hornsby	.10
19	Frank Howard	.10
20	Cliff Johnson	.10
21	Walter Johnson	.25
22	Hub Leonard	.10
23	Mickey Mantle	2.00
24	Roger Maris	.50
25	Christy Mathewson	.25
26	Willie Mays	.60
27	Stan Musial	.50
28	Dan Quisenberry	.10
29	Frank Robinson	.25
30	Pete Rose	1.00
31	Babe Ruth	1.50
32	Nolan Ryan	1.50
33	George Sisler	.10
34	Tris Speaker	.10
35	Ed Walsh	.10
36	Lloyd Waner	.10
37	Earl Webb	.10
38	Ted Williams	.75
39	Maury Wills	.10
40	Hack Wilson	.10
41	Owen Wilson	.10
42	Willie Wilson	.10
43	Rudy York	.10
44	Cy Young	.25

1986 Woolworth

Labeled "Topps' Collector Series" in a red band at the top of the front, this set marked the second year of Topps' production of a special boxed set for the Woolworth chain of stores, though Woolworth's name does not appear anywhere on the card. The 2-1/2"x3-1/2" cards feature a color photo with its lower-right corner rolled up to reveal the words "Super Star" on a bright yellow border. The player's name appears in the lower-left corner.

		NM/M
Complete Set (33):		6.00
Common Player:		.10
1	Tony Armas	.10
2	Don Baylor	.10
3	Wade Boggs	.75
4	George Brett	1.00
5	Bill Buckner	.10
6	Rod Carew	.75
7	Gary Carter	.75
8	Cecil Cooper	.10
9	Darrell Evans	.10
10	Dwight Evans	.10
11	George Foster	.10
12	Bobby Grich	.10
13	Tony Gwynn	.75
14	Keith Hernandez	.10
15	Reggie Jackson	.75
16	Dave Kingman	.10
17	Carney Lansford	.10
18	Fred Lynn	.10
19	Bill Madlock	.10
20	Don Mattingly	1.50
21	Willie McGee	.10
22	Hal McRae	.10
23	Dale Murphy	.35
24	Eddie Murray	.20
25	Ben Oglivie	.10
26	Al Oliver	.10
27	Dave Parker	.10
28	Jim Rice	.35
29	Pete Rose	1.50
30	Mike Schmidt	1.00
31	Gorman Thomas	.10
32	Willie Wilson	.10
33	Dave Winfield	.75

1987 Woolworth

The "Baseball Highlights" boxed set of 33 cards was prepared by Topps for distribution at stores in the Woolworth's chain, although the retailer's name does not appear on the cards. Each card measures 2-1/2" x 3-1/2" in size and features a memorable baseball event that occurred during the 1986 season. The glossy set sold for $1.99.

		NM/M
Complete Set (33):		2.00
Common Player:		.05
1	Steve Carlton	.20
2	Cecil Cooper	.05
3	Rickey Henderson	.20
4	Reggie Jackson	.35
5	Jim Rice	.15
6	Don Sutton	.15
7	Roger Clemens	.40
8	Mike Schmidt	.40
9	Jesse Barfield	.05
10	Wade Boggs	.35
11	Tim Raines	.05
12	Jose Canseco	.25
13	Todd Worrell	.05
14	Dave Righetti	.05
15	Don Mattingly	.40
16	Tony Gwynn	.25
17	Marty Barrett	.05
18	Mike Scott	.05
19	World Series Game #1 (Bruce Hurst)	.05
20	World Series Game #1 (Calvin Schiraldi)	.05
21	World Series Game #2 (Dwight Evans)	.05
22	World Series Game #2 (Dave Henderson)	.05
23	World Series Game #3 (Len Dykstra)	.05
24	World Series Game #3 (Bob Ojeda)	.05
25	World Series Game #4 (Gary Carter)	.05
26	World Series Game #4 (Ron Darling)	.05
27	Jim Rice	.15
28	Bruce Hurst	.05
29	World Series Game #6 (Darryl Strawberry)	.05
30	World Series Game #6 (Ray Knight)	.05
31	World Series Game #6 (Keith Hernandez)	.05
32	World Series Game #7 (Mets Celebrate)	.05
33	Ray Knight	.05

1988 Woolworth

This 33-card boxed set was produced by Topps for exclusive distribution at Woolworth stores. The set includes 18 individual player cards and 15 World Series game-action photo cards. World Series cards include two for each game of the Series, plus a card of 1987 Series MVP Frank Viola. A white-lettered caption beneath the photo consists of either the player's name or a World Series game notation. Card backs are red, white and blue and contain a brief description of the photo on the front.

		NM/M
Complete Set (33):		2.00
Common Player:		.05
1	Don Baylor	.05
2	Vince Coleman	.05
3	Darrell Evans	.05
4	Don Mattingly	.60
5	Eddie Murray	.35
6	Nolan Ryan	.75
7	Mike Schmidt	.60
8	Andre Dawson	.20
9	George Bell	.05
10	Steve Bedrosian	.05
11	Roger Clemens	.60
12	Tony Gwynn	.50
13	Wade Boggs	.50
14	Benny Santiago	.05
15	Mark McGwire	.65
16	Dave Righetti	.05
17	Jeffrey Leonard	.05
18	Gary Gaetti	.05
19	World Series Game #1 (Frank Viola)	.05
20	World Series Game #1 (Dan Gladden)	.05
21	World Series Game #2 (Bert Blyleven)	.05
22	World Series Game #2 (Gary Gaetti)	.05
23	World Series Game #3 (John Tudor)	.05
24	World Series Game #3 (Todd Worrell)	.05
25	World Series Game #4 (Tom Lawless)	.05
26	World Series Game #5 (Willie McGee)	.05
27	World Series Game #5 (Danny Cox)	.05
28	World Series Game #5 (Curt Ford)	.05
29	World Series Game #6 (Don Baylor)	.05
30	World Series Game #6 (Kent Hrbek)	.05
31	World Series Game #7 (Kirby Puckett)	.35
32	World Series Game #7 (Greg Gagne)	.05
33	World Series MVP (Frank Viola)	.05

1989 Woolworth

This 33-card set was produced by Topps for the Woolworth store chain and was sold in a special box with a checklist on the back. The glossy-coated cards commemorate the most memorable moments in baseball from the 1988 season. The backs include a description of the various highlights.

		NM/M
Complete Set (33):		4.00
Common Player:		.05
1	Jose Canseco	.30
2	Kirk Gibson	.05
3	Frank Viola	.05
4	Orel Hershiser	.05
5	Walt Weiss	.05
6	Chris Sabo	.05
7	George Bell	.05
8	Wade Boggs	.65
9	Tom Browning	.05
10	Gary Carter	.50
11	Andre Dawson	.20
12	John Franco	.05
13	Randy Johnson	.50

14	Doug Jones	.05
15	Kevin McReynolds	.05
16	Gene Nelson	.05
17	Jeff Reardon	.05
18	Pat Tabler	.05
19	Tim Belcher	.05
20	Dennis Eckersley	.35
21	Orel Hershiser	.05
22	Gregg Jefferies	.05
23	Jose Canseco	.30
24	Kirk Gibson	.05
25	Orel Hershiser	.05
26	Mike Marshall	.05
27	Mark McGwire	1.00
28	Rick Honeycutt	.05
29	Tim Belcher	.05
30	Jay Howell	.05
31	Mickey Hatcher	.05
32	Mike Davis	.05
33	Orel Hershiser	.05

1990 Woolworth

This 33-card boxed set recalls baseball highlights of 1989. The cards are styled like past Woolworth sets, with game-action or posed photos framed in green. Backs are in blue, white and black with a headline and explanation of the commemoration. The set features award winners and regular and post-season highlights.

		NM/M
Complete Set (33):		2.50
Common Player:		.05
1	Robin Yount	.30
2	Kevin Mitchell	.05
3	Bret Saberhagen	.05
4	Mark Davis	.05
5	Gregg Olson	.05
6	Jerome Walton	.05
7	Bert Blyleven	.05
8	Wade Boggs	.45
9	George Brett	.50
10	Vince Coleman	.05
11	Andre Dawson	.20
12	Dwight Evans	.05
13	Carlton Fisk	.30
14	Rickey Henderson	.30
15	Dale Murphy	.15
16	Eddie Murray	.30
17	Jeff Reardon	.05
18	Rick Reuschel	.05
19	Cal Ripken, Jr.	.75
20	Nolan Ryan	.75
21	Ryne Sandberg	.45
22	Robin Yount	.30
23	Rickey Henderson	.30
24	Will Clark	.05
25	Dave Stewart	.05
26	Walt Weiss	.05
27	Mike Moore	.05
28	Terry Steinbach	.05
29	Dave Henderson	.05
30	Matt Williams	.05
31	Rickey Henderson	.30
32	Kevin Mitchell	.05
33	Dave Stewart	.05

1991 Woolworth

This 33-card boxed set was produced by Topps for distribution at Woolworth stores. Yellow borders are featured on the fronts of the glossy cards. The backs feature baseball highlights from the

---

previous season. Award winners, regular season and World Series highlights are showcased.

		NM/M
Complete Set (33):		3.00
Common Player:		.05
1	Barry Bonds	.75
2	Rickey Henderson	.45
3	Doug Drabek	.05
4	Bob Welch	.05
5	Dave Justice	.10
6	Sandy Alomar, Jr.	.05
7	Bert Blyleven	.05
8	George Brett	.60
9	Andre Dawson	.25
10	Dwight Evans	.05
11	Alex Fernandez	.05
12	Carlton Fisk	.45
13	Kevin Maas	.05
14	Dale Murphy	.20
15	Eddie Murray	.45
16	Dave Parker	.05
17	Jeff Reardon	.05
18	Cal Ripken, Jr.	.75
19	Nolan Ryan	.75
20	Ryne Sandberg	.50
21	Bobby Thigpen	.05
22	Robin Yount	.45
23	Nasty Boys (Rob Dibble, Randy Myers)	.05
24	Dave Stewart	.05
25	Eric Davis	.05
26	Rickey Henderson	.45
27	Billy Hatcher	.05
28	Joe Oliver	.05
29	Chris Sabo	.05
30	Barry Larkin	.05
31	Jose Rijo	.05
32	Reds Celebrate	.05
33	Jose Rijo (World Series MVP)	.05

1986-88 World Wide Sports Conlon Collection

Marketed as complete series through World Wide Sports, five sets of black-and-white cards featuring the game's great players of the 1905-1935 era were made utilizing the photos of Charles Martin Conlon. The 2-1/2" x 3-1/2" cards carry the copyright of "The Sporting News," owner of the Conlon photos. The 60 cards of Series one each feature a Babe Ruth logo in the lower-left corner, the only graphic on the borderless card front. Series two has no front logo. Series 3-5 have a sliding Ty Cobb logo. Backs feature a line of career stats, a few bits of biographical data and a paragraph of highlights written by TSN historian Paul Mac-Farlane. The first two series were produced in an edition of 12,000 sets each; production of the other series was not announced. Cards in Series 3-5 are not numbered and are checklisted here alphabetically. Series designations are in small print at back-bottom.

		NM/M
Complete Set (211):		100.00
Common Player:		.25
Series 1 - 1986:		**18.00**
1	Lou Gehrig	1.50
2	Ty Cobb	1.00
3	Grover C. Alexander	.35
4	Walter Johnson	.50
5	Bill Klem	.25
6	Ty Cobb	1.00
7	Gordon S. Cochrane	.25
8	Paul Waner	.25
9	Joe Cronin	.25
10	Jay Hannah Dean	.25
11	Leo Durocher	.25
12	Jimmie Foxx	.25
13	Babe Ruth	2.00
14	Mike Gonzalez, Frank Frisch, Clyde Wares	.25
15	Carl Hubbell	.25
16	Miller Huggins	.25

17	Lou Gehrig	1.50
18	Connie Mack	.25
19	Heinie Manush	.25
20	Babe Ruth	2.00
21	Al Simmons	.25
22	Pepper Martin	.25
23	Christy Mathewson	.50
24	Ty Cobb	1.00
25	Stanley Harris	.25
26	Waite Hoyt	.25
27	Rube Marquard	.25
28	Joe McCarthy	.25
29	John McGraw	.25
30	Tris Speaker	.25
31	Bill Terry	.25
32	Christy Mathewson	.50
33	Casey Stengel	.25
34	Robert W. Meusel	.25
35	George Edward Waddell	.25
36	Mel Ott	.25
37	Roger Peckinpaugh	.25
38	Pie Traynor	.25
39	Chief Bender	.25
40	John W. Coombs	.25
41	Ty Cobb	1.00
42	Harry Heilmann	.25
43	Charlie Gehringer	.25
44	Rogers Hornsby	.25
45	Vernon Gomez	.25
46	Christy Mathewson	.50
47	Robert M. Grove	.25
48	Babe Ruth	2.00
49	Fred Merkle	.25
50	Babe Ruth	2.00
51	Herb Pennock	.25
52	Lou Gehrig	1.50
53	Fred Clarke	.25
54	Babe Ruth	2.00
55	John P. Wagner	.50
56	Hack Wilson	.25
57	Lou Gehrig	1.50
58	Lloyd Waner	.25
59	Charles Martin Conlon	.25
60	Charles & Margie Conlon	.25
---	Header Card	.25
Series 2 - 1987:		**15.00**
1	Lou Gehrig	1.50
2	Vernon Gomez	.25
3	Christy Mathewson	.50
4	Grover Alexander	.25
5	Ty Cobb	1.00
6	Walter Johnson	.50
7	Charles (Babe) Adams	.25
8	Nick Altrock	.25
9	Al Schacht	.25
10	Hugh Critz	.25
11	Henry Cullop	.25
12	Jake Daubert	.25
13	Bill Donovan	.25
14	Chick Hafey	.25
15	Bill Hallahan	.25
16	Fred Haney	.25
17	Charles Hartnett	.25
18	Walter Henline	.25
19	Ed Rommel	.25
20	Ralph "Babe" Pinelli	.25
21	Bob Meusel	.25
22	Emil Meusel	.25
23	Smead Jolley	.25
24	Ike Boone	.25
25	Earl Webb	.25
26	Charles Comiskey	.25
27	Edward Collins	.25
28	Geroge (Buck) Weaver	.50
29	Eddie Cicotte	.50
30	Sam Crawford	.25
31	Chuck Dressen	.25
32	Arthur Fletcher	.25
33	Hugh Duffy	.25
34	Ira Flagstead	.25
35	Harry Hooper	.25
36	George E. Lewis	.25
37	James Dykes	.25
38	Leon Goslin	.25
39	Henry Gowdy	.25
40	Charles Grimm	.25
41	Mark Koenig	.25
42	James Hogan	.25
43	William Jacobson	.25
44	Fielder Jones	.25
45	George Kelly	.25
46	Adolfo Luque	.40
47	Walter Maranville	.25
48	Carl Mays	.25
49	Eddie Plank	.25
50	Hubert Pruett	.25
51	John (Picus) Quinn	.25
52	Charles (Flint) Rhem	.25
53	Amos Rusie	.25
54	Edd Roush	.25
55	Ray Schalk	.25
56	Ernie Shore	.25
57	Joe Wood	.25
58	George Sisler	.25
59	James Thorpe	3.00
60	Earl Whitehill	.25
Series 3 - 1988:		**35.00**
(1)	Ace Adams	1.00
(2)	Grover C. Alexander	2.00
(3)	Eldon Auker	1.00
(4)	Jack Barry	1.00
(5)	Wally Berger	1.00
(6)	Ben Chapman	1.00
(7)	Mickey Cochrane	1.00
(8)	Frank Crosetti	1.00
(9)	Paul Dean	1.00
(10)	Leo Durocher	1.00
(11)	Wes Ferrell	1.00

---

(12)	Hank Gowdy	1.00
(13)	Andy High	1.00
(14)	Rogers Hornsby	2.00
(15)	Carl Hubbell	1.00
(16)	Joe Judge	1.00
(17)	Tony Lazzeri	1.00
(18)	Pepper Martin	1.00
(19)	Lee Meadows	1.00
(20)	Jimmy Murphy	1.00
(21)	Steve O'Neill	1.00
(22)	Ed Plank	1.00
(23)	John P. Quinn	1.00
(24)	Charlie Root	1.00
(25)	Babe Ruth	6.00
(26)	Fred Snodgrass	1.00
(27)	Tris Speaker	2.00
(28)	Bill Terry	1.00
(29)	Jeff Tesreau	1.00
(30)	George Torporcer	1.00
Series 4 - 1988:		**30.00**
(1)	Dale Alexander	1.00
(2)	Morris "Red" Badgro	1.00
(3)	Dick Bartell	1.00
(4)	Max Bishop	1.00
(5)	Hal Chase	1.50
(6)	Ty Cobb	2.00
(7)	Nick Cullop	1.00
(8)	Dizzy Dean	2.50
(9)	Chuck Dressen	1.00
(10)	Jimmy Dykes	1.00
(11)	Art Fletcher	1.00
(12)	Charlie Grimm	1.00
(13)	Lefty Grove	1.00
(14)	Baby Doll Jacobson	1.00
(15)	Bill Klem	1.00
(16)	Mark Koenig	1.00
(17)	Duffy Lewis	1.00
(18)	Carl Mays	1.00
(19)	Fred Merkle	1.00
(20)	Greasy Neale	1.50
(21)	Mel Ott	1.00
(22)	"Babe" Pinelli	1.00
(23)	Flint Rhem	1.00
(24)	Slim Sallee	1.00
(25)	Al Simmons	1.00
(26)	George Sisler	1.00
(27)	Riggs Stephenson	1.00
(28)	Jim Thorpe	4.00
(29)	Bill Wambsganss	1.00
(30)	Cy Young	2.50
Series 5 - 1988:		**30.00**
(1)	Nick Altrock	1.00
(2)	Del Baker	1.00
(3)	Moe Berg	4.50
(4)	Zeke Bonura	1.00
(5)	Eddie Collins	1.00
(6)	Hugh Critz	1.00
(7)	George Dauss	1.00
(8)	Joe Dugan	1.00
(9)	Howard Ehmke	1.00
(10)	Jimmie Foxx	2.50
(11)	Frank Frisch	1.00
(12)	Lou Gehrig	6.00
(13)	Charlie Gehringer	1.00
(14)	Kid Gleason	1.00
(15)	Lefty Gomez	1.00
(16)	Babe Herman	1.00
(17)	Bill James	1.00
(18)	Joe Kuhel	1.00
(19)	Dolf Luque	1.50
(20)	John McGraw	1.00
(21)	Stuffy McInnis	1.00
(22)	Bob Meusel	1.00
(23)	Lefty O'Doul	1.00
(24)	Hub Pruett	1.00
(25)	Paul Richards	1.00
(26)	Bob Shawkey	1.00
(27)	Gabby Street	1.00
(28)	Johnny Tobin	1.00
(29)	Rube Waddell	1.00
(30)	Billy Werber	1.00

1988 World Wide Sports 1933 All-Stars

The photos of Charles M. Conlon in The Sporting News' archive are the basis for this collectors' issue depicting the players of the original All-Star Game of 1933. Fronts have sepia photo of the players on a 2-1/2" x 3-1/2" format. The only graphics added to the front are in the upper-right corner designating the league which the player represented. Backs have 1933 and career stats, along with a career sum-

---

mary. The unnumbered cards are checklisted here in alphabetical order within league.

		NM/M
Complete Set (48):		12.00
Common Player:		.25
American League		**6.00**
(1)	Luke Appling	.25
(2)	Earl Averill	.25
(3)	Tommy Bridges	.25
(4)	Ben Chapman	.25
(5)	Mickey Cochrane	.25
(6)	Joe Cronin	.25
(7)	Alvin Crowder	.25
(8)	Bill Dickey	.35
(9)	Jimmie Foxx	.45
(10)	Lou Gehrig	1.00
(11)	Charlie Gehringer	.35
(12)	Lefty Gomez	.25
(13)	Lefty Grove	.25
(14)	Mel Harder	.25
(15)	Pinky Higgins	.25
(16)	Urban Hodapp	.25
(17)	Roy Johnson	.25
(18)	Joe Kuhel	.25
(19)	Tony Lazzeri	.25
(20)	Heinie Manush	.25
(21)	Babe Ruth	1.50
(22)	Al Simmons	.25
(23)	Evar Swanson	.25
(24)	Earl Whitehill	.25
National League		**6.00**
(1)	Wally Berger	.25
(2)	Guy Bush	.25
(3)	Ripper Collins	.25
(4)	Spud Davis	.25
(5)	Dizzy Dean	.45
(6)	Johnny Frederick	.25
(7)	Larry French	.25
(8)	Frank Frisch	.25
(9)	Chick Fullis	.25
(10)	Chick Hafey	.25
(11)	Carl Hubbell	.25
(12)	Chuck Klein	.25
(13)	Freddie Lindstrom	.25
(14)	Pepper Martin	.25
(15)	Ducky Medwick	.25
(16)	Tony Piet	.25
(17)	Wes Schulmerich	.25
(18)	Hal Schumacher	.25
(19)	Riggs Stephenson	.25
(20)	Bill Terry	.25
(21)	Paul Traynor	.25
(22)	Arky Vaughan	.25
(23)	Paul Waner	.25
(24)	Lon Warneke	.25

1988 World Wide Sports 1933 Negro All Stars

The photos of Charles M. Conlon in The Sporting News' archive are the basis for this collectors' issue depicting "1933 Negro All Stars. Fronts have borderless sepia photos of the players on a 2-1/2" x 3-1/2" format. The only graphics added to the front are in the upper-right corner designating the All-Star status. Backs have a few personal data along with a career summary. The unnumbered cards are checklisted here in alphabetical order.

		NM/M
Complete Set (12):		7.50
Common Player:		1.00
(1)	Cool Papa Bell	1.00
(2)	Oscar Charleston	1.00
(3)	Martin Dihigo	1.00
(4)	Andrew "Rube" Foster	1.00
(5)	Josh Gibson	2.00
(6)	Judy Johnson	1.00
(7)	Buck Leonard	1.00
(8)	Pop Lloyd	1.00
(9)	Dave Malarcher	1.00
(10)	Satchel Paige	2.50
(11)	Willie Wells	1.00
(12)	Joe Williams	1.00

1989 W/R Associates Mark Grace

This collectors' issue traces the career of Mark Grace on a nine-card panel which includes eight standard 2-1/2" x 3-1/2" cards and a 5" x 7" card on a sheet with overall dimensions of 10-5/8" x 14". Because the issue was licensed only by the player, and not Major League Baseball, all Cubs uniform logos have been removed from the photos. Cards are numbered on front and back with a year identifying the photo. Backs are printed in red, white and blue and include biographical data and career summary. The large-format card offers complete major and minor league stats on back. The cards on the sheet are not perforated and individual cards are rarely encountered. Sheets were offered in either autographed or unautographed form with production limited to 15,000 sheets.

		NM/M
Complete Sheet:		7.50
Complete Sheet, Autographed:		25.00
Complete Set, Cut (9):		7.50
Common Card:		.50
73	Mark Grace (Boyhood photo.)	.50
83	Mark Grace (San Diego State)	.50
86	Mark Grace (Minor League)	.50
87	Mark Grace (Throwing)	.50
88a	Mark Grace/Fldg	.50
88b	Mark Grace (Wedding)	.50
89a	Mark Grace, Mark Grace/Btg	.50
89b	Mark Grace, Mark Grace/Btg	.50
----	Mark Grace (5" x 7" Portrait, Autographed)	25.00
----	Mark Grace (5" x 7" Portrait, Unsigned)	4.00

1985 WTBS Atlanta Braves

This set of large-format (8-1/4" x 10-3/4") cards was issued by the Braves' TV broadcaster, WTBS. The sets were given to potential sponsors as part of a "kit" inviting them to Florida to attend a spring training game. It was reported that only 600 sets were printed and 150 of them were destroyed. Fronts feature player portraits on brightly colored backgrounds. There is a facsimile autograph and a large star-boxed "AMERICA'S TEAM." Backs are in red and black and have some vital data and stats for the 1982-84 seasons. Cards are numbered according to uniform number.

		NM/M
Complete Set (4):		50.00
Common Player:		7.50
3	Dale Murphy	35.00
7	Brad Komminsk	7.50

15	Claudell Washington	7.50
42	Bruce Sutter	15.00

1991 WWOR N.Y. Mets

This set of 5-1/2" x 7-1/2" cards was issued by WWOR-TV in New York City, which carried the Mets telecasts in 1991. The cards were evidently intended for use as a sales promotion, as the backs detail Neilsen ratings for the games. Fronts have game action photos with green borders in a design not unlike 1991 Donruss.

		NM/M
	Complete Set (12):	15.00
	Common Player:	2.00
(1)	Darryl Boston	2.00
(2)	Vince Coleman	2.00
(3)	David Cone	2.00
(4)	Kevin Elster	2.00
(5)	Sid Fernandez	2.00
(6)	John Franco	2.00
(7)	Dwight Gooden	2.00
(8)	Jeff Innis	2.00
(9)	Howard Johnson	2.00
(10)	Dave Magadan	2.00
(11)	Mackey Sasser	2.00
(12)	Wally Whitehurst	2.00

Y

1993 Yoo-Hoo

The Yoo-Hoo beverage company, which had a promotional affiliation with Yogi Berra as far back as the 1950's, made Berra the #1 card in a 1993 set of 20 baseball legends that was released in two series. All of the players included in the set are retired, and all but five are Hall of Famers (at this printing). The unnumbered cards feature a yellow border with a color photo on the front; the backs have the player's statistics and biographical information.

		NM/M
	Complete Set (20):	7.00
	Common Player:	.25
Series 1		
(1)	Yogi Berra	.50
(2)	Joe Morgan	.35
(3)	Duke Snider	.50
(4)	Steve Garvey	.30
(5)	Jim Rice	.35
(6)	Bob Feller	.35
(7)	Pete Rose	1.00
(8)	Rod Carew	.35
(9)	Gaylord Perry	.35
(10)	Graig Nettles	.25
Series 2		
(1)	Johnny Bench	.40
(2)	Lou Brock	.35
(3)	Stan Musial	1.00
(4)	Willie McCovey	.35
(5)	Whitey Ford	.50
(6)	Phil Rizzuto	.50
(7)	Tom Seaver	.50
(8)	Willie Stargell	.35
(9)	Brooks Robinson	.35
(10)	Al Kaline	.45

1994 Yoo-Hoo

Issued in conjunction with Rawling's, sponsor of the Gold Glove Award, this set features past winners. Cards have color photos on which team logos have been airbrushed away. Borders are bright yellow. Backs have career stats and highlights. A limited number of Yaz autographed cards were randomly inserted into the packs in which the cards were distributed.

		NM/M
	Complete Set (20):	6.00
	Common Player:	.25
	Yastrzemski Autograph:	30.00
1	Luis Aparicio	.25
2	Bobby Bonds	.25
3	Bob Boone	.25
4	Steve Carlton	.35
5	Roberto Clemente	2.00
6	Bob Gibson	.25
7	Keith Hernandez	.25
8	Jim Kaat	.25
9	Roger Maris	.60
10	Don Mattingly	1.00
11	Thurman Munson	.60
12	Phil Rizzuto	.50
13	Brooks Robinson	.40
14	Ryne Sandberg	.75
15	Mike Schmidt	1.00
16	Carl Yastrzemski	.60
17	Fact Card	.05
18	Fact Card	.05
19	Fact Card	.05
20	Fact Card	.05

Z

1982 Zellers Expos

Issued by Zellers department stores in Canada, this 60-card set was produced in the form of 20 three-card panels. The cards feature a round photo of the player on a yellow background. A red "Zellers" is above the photo and on either side of it are the words "Baseball Pro Tips" in English on the left and in French on the right. The player's name and the title of the playing tip are under the photo. Backs have the playing tip in both languages. Single cards measure 2-1/2" x 3-1/2" while the whole panel is 7-1/2" x 3-1/2". Although a number of stars are depicted, this set is not terribly popular as collectors do not generally like the playing tips idea. Total panels are worth more than separated cards.

		NM/M
	Complete Set (20):	6.00
	Common Player:	.25
1	Gary Carter (Catching Position)	1.50
2	Steve Rogers (Pitching Stance)	.25
3	Tim Raines (Sliding)	.50
4	Andre Dawson (Batting Stance)	.60
5	Terry Francona (Contact Hitting)	.25
6	Gary Carter (Fielding Pop Fouls)	1.50
7	Warren Cromartie (Fielding at First Base)	.25
8	Chris Speier (Fielding at Shortstop)	.25
9	Billy DeMars (Signals)	.25
10	Andre Dawson (Batting Stroke)	.60
11	Terry Francona (Outfield Throws)	.25
12	Woodie Fryman (Holding the Runner-Left Handed)	.25
13	Gary Carter (Fielding Low Balls)	1.50
14	Andre Dawson (Playing Centerfield)	.60
15	Bill Gullickson (The Slurve)	.25
16	Gary Carter (Catching Stance)	1.50
17	Scott Sanderson (Fielding as a Pitcher)	.25
18	Warren Cromartie (Handling Bad Throws)	.25
19	Gary Carter (Hitting Stride)	1.50
20	Ray Burris (Holding the Runner-Right Handed)	.25

1995 Zenith Samples

As Pinnacle extended its top-of-the-line brand name into baseball, this nine-card cello-wrapped samples set was sent to dealers to familiarize them with the product. Using the same state of the art all-foil metalized printing on extra heavy 24-point cardboard stock, the samples are virtually identical to the issued version, except for a white "SAMPLE" printed diagonally across front and back.

		NM/M
	Complete Set (9):	10.00
	Common Player:	.75
12	Cal Ripken Jr.	3.00
20	Dante Bichette	.75
51	Jim Thome	1.00
70	Mark Grace	1.00
97	Ryan Klesko	.75
111	Chipper Jones (Rookie)	1.00
113	Curtis Goodwin (Rookie)	.75
7	Hideo Nomo (Rookie Roll Call)	2.00
---	Header Card	.05

1995 Zenith

At the top of the pyramid of Pinnacle's baseball card lines for 1995 was Zenith, a super-premium brand utilizing all-foil metalized printing technology on double-thick 24-point cardboard stock to emphasize the quality look and feel. Six-card packs carried a retail price of $3.99. Two styles comprise the 150-card base set. The 110 veteran player cards are curiously arranged in alphabetical order according to the player's first names (with the exception of card #48, a special Japanese-language card of Hideo Nomo). These cards have a color player action photo on a black and gold background - which is a view of a pyramid from its pinnacle. One the horizontal back, a portrait photo of the player in a partly-cloudy blue sky overlooks a playing field which offers his hit location preferences versus righty and lefty pitching. A scoreboard has his 1994 and career stats. The Pinnacle anti-counterfeiting optical-variable bar is in the lower-right corner. The rookie cards which comprise the final 40 cards in the set have a color photo at center with a gold-tone version of the same picture in the back-ground. A large gold "ROOKIE" is vertically at right. Backs are similar to those on the veterans' cards except they have a scouting report in place of the hit-location chart.

		NM/M
	Complete Set (150):	15.00
	Common Player:	.10
	Pack (6):	1.50
	Wax Box (24):	17.50
1	Albert Belle	.10
2	Alex Fernandez	.10
3	Andy Benes	.10
4	Barry Larkin	.10
5	Barry Bonds	2.50
6	Ben McDonald	.10
7	Bernard Gilkey	.10
8	Billy Ashley	.10
9	Bobby Bonilla	.10
10	Bret Saberhagen	.10
11	Brian Jordan	.10
12	Cal Ripken Jr.	2.50
13	Carlos Baerga	.10
14	Carlos Delgado	.35
15	Cecil Fielder	.10
16	Chili Davis	.10
17	Chuck Knoblauch	.10
18	Craig Biggio	.10
19	Danny Tartabull	.10
20	Dante Bichette	.10
21	Darren Daulton	.10
22	Dave Justice	.10
23	Dave Winfield	.75
24	David Cone	.10
25	Dean Palmer	.10
26	Deion Sanders	.20
27	Dennis Eckersley	.65
28	Derek Bell	.10
29	Don Mattingly	1.50
30	Edgar Martinez	.10
31	Eric Karros	.10
32	Erik Hanson	.10
33	Frank Thomas	.75
34	Fred McGriff	.10
35	Gary Sheffield	.45
36	Gary Gaetti	.10
37	Greg Maddux	1.25
38	Gregg Jefferies	.10
39	Ivan Rodriguez	.65
40	Kenny Rogers	.10
41	J.T. Snow	.10
42	Hal Morris	.10
43	Eddie Murray (3,000 hit)	.50
44	Javier Lopez	.10
45	Jay Bell	.10
46	Jeff Conine	.10
47	Jeff Bagwell	.75
48	Hideo Nomo RC	2.00
49	Jeff Kent	.10
50	Jeff King	.10
51	Jim Thome	.65
52	Jimmy Key	.10
53	Joe Carter	.10
54	John Valentin	.10
55	John Olerud	.10
56	Jose Canseco	.45
57	Jose Rijo	.10
58	Jose Offerman	.10
59	Juan Gonzalez	.45
60	Ken Caminiti	.10
61	Ken Griffey Jr.	1.75
62	Kenny Lofton	.10
63	Kevin Appier	.10
64	Kevin Seitzer	.10
65	Kirby Puckett	1.25
66	Kirk Gibson	.10
67	Larry Walker	.10
68	Lenny Dykstra	.10
69	Manny Ramirez	.75
70	Mark Grace	.10
71	Mark McGwire	2.00
72	Marquis Grissom	.10
73	Jim Edmonds	.10
74	Matt Williams	.45
75	Mike Mussina	.10
76	Mike Piazza	1.75
77	Mo Vaughn	.10
78	Moises Alou	.10
79	Ozzie Smith	1.25
80	Paul O'Neill	.10
81	Paul Molitor	.75
82	Rafael Palmeiro	.65
83	Randy Johnson	.10
84	Raul Mondesi	.10
85	Ray Lankford	.10
86	Reggie Sanders	.10
87	Rickey Henderson	.75
88	Rico Brogna	.10
89	Roberto Alomar	.25
90	Robin Ventura	.10
91	Roger Clemens	1.50
92	Ron Gant	.10
93	Rondell White	.10
94	Royce Clayton	.10
95	Ruben Sierra	.10
96	Rusty Greer	.10
97	Ryan Klesko	.10
98	Sammy Sosa	1.25
99	Shawon Dunston	.10
100	Steve Ontiveros	.10
101	Tim Naehring	.10
102	Tim Salmon	.10
103	Tino Martinez	.10
104	Tony Gwynn	1.25
105	Travis Fryman	.10
106	Vinny Castilla	.10
107	Wade Boggs	1.25
108	Wally Joyner	.10
109	Wil Cordero	.10
110	Will Clark	.10
111	Chipper Jones	1.25
112	C.J. Nitkowski	.10
113	Curtis Goodwin	.10
114	Tim Unroe	.10
115	Vaughn Eshelman	.10
116	Marty Cordova	.10
117	Dustin Hermanson	.10
118	Rich Becker	.10
119	Ray Durham	.10
120	Shane Andrews	.10
121	Scott Ruffcorn	.10
122	Mark Grudzielanek RC	.25
123	James Baldwin	.10
124	Carlos Perez RC	.10
125	Julian Tavarez	.10
126	Joe Vitiello	.10
127	Jason Bates	.10
128	Edgardo Alfonzo	.10
129	Juan Acevedo	.10
130	Bill Pulsipher	.10
131	Bob Higginson RC	.25
132	Russ Davis	.10
133	Charles Johnson	.10
134	Derek Jeter	2.50
135	Phil Nevin	.10
136	LaTroy Hawkins	.10
137	Brian Hunter	.10
138	Roberto Petagine	.10
139	Jim Pittsley	.10
140	Garret Anderson	.10
141	Ugueth Urbina	.10
142	Antonio Osuna	.10
143	Michael Tucker	.10
144	Benji Gil	.10
145	Jon Nunnally	.10
146	Alex Rodriguez	2.00
147	Todd Hollandsworth	.10
148	Alex Gonzalez	.10
149	Hideo Nomo RC	2.00
150	Shawn Green	.30
---	Numeric Checklist	.10
---	Chase Program Checklist	.10

All-Star Salute

The most common of the Zenith inserts is a series of 18 All-Star Salute cards. Fronts have action photos printed on foil. Backs have the 1995 All-Star Game logo and a large photo of the player taken at the game, with a few words about his All-Star history. The Salute cards are seeded at the rate of one per six packs, on average.

		NM/M
	Complete Set (18):	16.00
	Common Player:	.50
1	Cal Ripken Jr.	3.00
2	Frank Thomas	1.00
3	Mike Piazza	2.00
4	Kirby Puckett	1.50
5	Manny Ramirez	1.00
6	Tony Gwynn	1.50
7	Hideo Nomo	.75
8	Matt Williams	1.00
9	Randy Johnson	1.00
10	Raul Mondesi	.50
11	Albert Belle	.50
12	Ivan Rodriguez	1.00
13	Barry Bonds	3.00
14	Carlos Baerga	.50
15	Ken Griffey Jr.	2.00
16	Jeff Conine	.50
17	Frank Thomas	1.00
18	Cal Ripken Jr., Barry Bonds	2.00

Rookie Roll Call

Dufex foil printing technology on both front and back is featured on this insert set. Fronts have a large and a small player photo on a green background dominated by a large star. Backs have another photo on a green and gold background. A prestigious black and gold box at left in the horizontally formatted design has a few good words about the pros-pect. Stated odds of finding a Rookie Roll Call card are one per 24 packs, on average.

		NM/M
	Complete Set (18):	17.50
	Common Player:	.60
1	Alex Rodriguez	6.00
2	Derek Jeter	7.50
3	Chipper Jones	5.00
4	Shawn Green	1.50
5	Todd Hollandsworth	.60
6	Bill Pulsipher	.60
7	Hideo Nomo	1.50
8	Ray Durham	.60
9	Curtis Goodwin	.60
10	Brian Hunter	.60
11	Julian Tavarez	.60
12	Marty Cordova	.60
13	Michael Tucker	.60
14	Edgardo Alfonzo	.60
15	LaTroy Hawkins	.60
16	Carlos Perez	.60
17	Charles Johnson	.60
18	Benji Gil	.60

Z-Team

The scarcest of the Zenith insert cards are those of 18 "living legends" profiled in the Z-Team series. Found at an average rate of only one per 72 packs, the cards are printed in technology Pinnacle calls 3-D Dufex.

		NM/M
	Complete Set (18):	85.00
	Common Player:	2.00
1	Cal Ripken Jr.	15.00
2	Ken Griffey Jr.	10.00
3	Frank Thomas	6.00
4	Matt Williams	2.00
5	Mike Piazza	10.00
6	Barry Bonds	15.00
7	Raul Mondesi	2.00
8	Greg Maddux	7.50
9	Jeff Bagwell	6.00
10	Manny Ramirez	6.00
11	Larry Walker	2.00
12	Tony Gwynn	7.50
13	Will Clark	2.00
14	Albert Belle	2.00
15	Kenny Lofton	2.00
16	Rafael Palmeiro	4.50
17	Don Mattingly	9.00
18	Carlos Baerga	2.00

1996 Zenith

Pinnacle's 1996 Zenith set has 150 cards in the regular set, including 30 Rookies, 20 Honor roll and two checklist cards. Each card in the set has a parallel Artist's Proof version (seeded one per every 35 packs). Insert sets include Z Team, Mozaics and two versions of Diamond Club. Normal Dufex versions of Diamond Club appear one every 24 packs; parallel versions, which have an actual diamond chip incorporated into the card design, were seeded one per every 350 packs.

	NM/M
Complete Set (150):	15.00
Common Player:	.10
Common Artist's Proofs:	2.00
Star Artist's Proofs:	12X
Pack (6):	1.50
Wax Box (24):	25.00
1 Ken Griffey Jr.	2.00
2 Ozzie Smith	1.50
3 Greg Maddux	1.50
4 Rondell White	.10
5 Mark McGwire	2.50
6 Jim Thome	.75
7 Ivan Rodriguez	.75
8 Marc Newfield	.10
9 Travis Fryman	.10
10 Fred McGriff	.10
11 Shawn Green	.25
12 Mike Piazza	2.00
13 Dante Bichette	.10
14 Tino Martinez	.10
15 Sterling Hitchcock	.10
16 Ryne Sandberg	1.50
17 Rico Brogna	.10
18 Roberto Alomar	.25
19 Barry Larkin	.10
20 Bernie Williams	.10
21 Gary Sheffield	.50
22 Frank Thomas	1.00
23 Gregg Jefferies	.10
24 Jeff Bagwell	1.00
25 Marty Cordova	.10
26 Jim Edmonds	.10
27 Jay Bell	.10
28 Ben McDonald	.10
29 Barry Bonds	3.00
30 Mo Vaughn	.10
31 Johnny Damon	.35
32 Dean Palmer	.10
33 Ismael Valdes	.10
34 Manny Ramirez	1.00
35 Edgar Martinez	.10
36 Cecil Fielder	.10
37 Ryan Klesko	.10
38 Ray Lankford	.10
39 Tim Salmon	.10
40 Joe Carter	.10
41 Jason Isringhausen	.10
42 Rickey Henderson	1.00
43 Lenny Dykstra	.10
44 Andre Dawson	.25
45 Paul O'Neill	.10
46 Ray Durham	.10
47 Raul Mondesi	.10
48 Jay Buhner	.10
49 Eddie Murray	1.00
50 Henry Rodriguez	.10
51 Hal Morris	.10
52 Mike Mussina	.50
53 Wally Joyner	.10
54 Will Clark	.10
55 Chipper Jones	1.50
56 Brian Jordan	.10
57 Larry Walker	.10
58 Wade Boggs	1.50
59 Melvin Nieves	.10
60 Charles Johnson	.10
61 Juan Gonzalez	.50
62 Carlos Delgado	.35
63 Reggie Sanders	.10
64 Brian Hunter	.10
65 Edgardo Alfonzo	.10
66 Kenny Lofton	1.00
67 Paul Molitor	1.00
68 Mike Bordick	.10
69 Garret Anderson	.10
70 Orlando Merced	.10
71 Craig Biggio	.10
72 Chuck Knoblauch	.50
73 Mark Grace	.10
74 Jack McDowell	.10
75 Randy Johnson	1.00
76 Cal Ripken Jr.	3.00
77 Matt Williams	.10
78 Benji Gil	.10
79 Moises Alou	.10
80 Robin Ventura	.10
81 Greg Vaughn	.10
82 Carlos Baerga	.10
83 Roger Clemens	1.75
84 Hideo Nomo	.50
85 Pedro Martinez	.50
86 John Valentin	.10
87 Andres Galarraga	.10
88 Andy Pettitte	.30
89 Derek Bell	.10
90 Kirby Puckett	1.50
91 Tony Gwynn	1.50
92 Brady Anderson	.10
93 Derek Jeter	3.00
94 Michael Tucker	.10
95 Albert Belle	.10
96 David Cone	.10
97 J.T. Snow	.10
98 Tom Glavine	.35
99 Alex Rodriguez	2.50
100 Sammy Sosa	1.50
101 Karim Garcia	.15
102 Alan Benes	.10

103 Chad Mottola	.10
104 Robin Jennings RC	.10
105 Bob Abreu	.10
106 Tony Clark	.10
107 George Arias	.10
108 Jermaine Dye	.10
109 Jeff Suppan	.10
110 Ralph Milliard RC	.10
111 Ruben Rivera	.10
112 Billy Wagner	.10
113 Jason Kendall	.10
114 Mike Grace RC	.10
115 Edgar Renteria	.10
116 Jason Schmidt	.10
117 Paul Wilson	.10
118 Rey Ordonez	.10
119 Rocky Coppinger RC	.10
120 Wilton Guerrero RC	.10
121 Brooks Kieschnick	.10
122 Raul Casanova	.10
123 Alex Ochoa	.10
124 Chan Ho Park	.10
125 John Wasdin	.10
126 Eric Owens	.10
127 Justin Thompson	.10
128 Chris Snopek	.10
129 Terrell Wade	.10
130 Darin Erstad RC	1.50
131 Albert Belle (Honor Roll)	.10
132 Cal Ripken Jr. (Honor Roll)	1.50
133 Frank Thomas (Honor Roll)	.60
134 Greg Maddux (Honor Roll)	.75
135 Ken Griffey Jr. (Honor Roll)	1.00
136 Mo Vaughn (Honor Roll)	.10
137 Chipper Jones (Honor Roll)	.75
138 Mike Piazza (Honor Roll)	1.00
139 Ryan Klesko (Honor Roll)	.10
140 Hideo Nomo (Honor Roll)	.20
141 Roberto Alomar (Honor Roll)	.10
142 Manny Ramirez (Honor Roll)	.60
143 Gary Sheffield (Honor Roll)	.10
144 Barry Bonds (Honor Roll)	1.50
145 Matt Williams (Honor Roll)	.10
146 Jim Edmonds (Honor Roll)	.10
147 Derek Jeter (Honor Roll)	1.50
148 Sammy Sosa (Honor Roll)	.75
149 Kirby Puckett (Honor Roll)	.75
150 Tony Gwynn (Honor Roll)	.75

1996 Zenith Artist's Proofs

Each card in the '96 Zenith base set can also be found in a specially marked Artist's Proof version. The AP cards were found on average of once per 35 packs.

	NM/M
Common Player:	2.00
Stars:	12X

Diamond Club

Mike Piazza

Twenty different players are featured on these two 1996 Pinnacle Zenith insert cards. Normal Dufex versions are inserted one per every 24 packs. Parallel versions of these cards, containing an

actual diamond chip incorporated into the design, were seeded one per every 350 packs.

	NM/M
Complete Set (20):	17.50
Common Player:	.45
Diamond Versions:	12X
1 Albert Belle	.45
2 Mo Vaughn	.45
3 Ken Griffey Jr.	1.50
4 Mike Piazza	1.50
5 Cal Ripken Jr.	2.50
6 Jermaine Dye	.45
7 Jeff Bagwell	1.00
8 Frank Thomas	1.00
9 Alex Rodriguez	2.00
10 Ryan Klesko	.45
11 Roberto Alomar	.60
12 Sammy Sosa	1.25
13 Matt Williams	.45
14 Gary Sheffield	.75
15 Ruben Rivera	.45
16 Darin Erstad	.60
17 Randy Johnson	1.00
18 Greg Maddux	1.25
19 Karim Garcia	.60
20 Chipper Jones	1.25

Mozaics

Each of these 1996 Pinnacle Zenith cards contains multiple player images for the team represented on the card. The cards were inserted one per every 10 packs.

	NM/M
Complete Set (25):	30.00
Common Card:	.45
1 Greg Maddux, Chipper Jones, Ryan Klesko	3.00
2 Juan Gonzalez, Will Clark, Ivan Rodriguez	1.00
3 Frank Thomas, Robin Ventura, Ray Durham	1.00
4 Matt Williams, Barry Bonds, Osvaldo Fernandez	5.00
5 Ken Griffey Jr., Randy Johnson, Alex Rodriguez	4.00
6 Sammy Sosa, Ryne Sandberg, Mark Grace	4.00
7 Jim Edmonds, Tim Salmon, Garret Anderson	.45
8 Cal Ripken Jr., Roberto Alomar, Mike Mussina	5.00
9 Mo Vaughn, Roger Clemens, John Valentin	3.50
10 Barry Larkin, Reggie Sanders, Hal Morris	.45
11 Ray Lankford, Brian Jordan, Ozzie Smith	1.50
12 Dante Bichette, Larry Walker, Andres Galarraga	.45
13 Mike Piazza, Hideo Nomo, Raul Mondesi	4.00
14 Ben McDonald, Greg Vaughn, Kevin Seitzer	.45
15 Joe Carter, Carlos Delgado, Alex Gonzalez	.60
16 Gary Sheffield, Charles Johnson, Jeff Conine	.45
17 Rondell White, Moises Alou, Henry Rodriguez	.45
18 Albert Belle, Manny Ramirez, Carlos Baerga	1.00
19 Kirby Puckett, Paul Molitor, Chuck Knoblauch	1.50
20 Tony Gwynn, Rickey Henderson, Wally Joyner	2.00
21 Mark McGwire, Mike Bordick, Scott Brosius	4.00
22 Paul O'Neill, Bernie Williams, Wade Boggs	1.50
23 Jay Bell, Orlando Merced, Jason Kendall	.45
24 Rico Brogna, Paul Wilson, Jason Isringhausen	.45
25 Jeff Bagwell, Craig Biggio, Derek Bell	1.00

1996 Zenith Z-Team Samples

CHIPPER JONES

Each of the first nine microetched plastic-printed Z-Team insert cards can also be found in an edition which is overprinted "SAMPLE" on the front. These cards were distributed to hobby dealers.

	NM/M
Complete Set (9):	35.00
Common Player:	3.00
1 Ken Griffey Jr.	4.50
2 Albert Belle	3.00
3 Cal Ripken Jr.	7.50
4 Frank Thomas	3.50
5 Greg Maddux	4.00
6 Mo Vaughn	3.00
7 Chipper Jones	4.00
8 Mike Piazza	4.50
9 Ryan Klesko	4.00

Z-Team

GARY SHEFFIELD

Pinnacle's 1996 Zenith baseball continues the Z-Team insert concept with a new clear plastic treatment that is micro-etched for a see-through design that allows light to shine through etched highlights and a green baseball field background. The 18 cards were seeded one per every 72 packs.

	NM/M
Complete Set (18):	100.00
Common Player:	3.00
1 Ken Griffey Jr.	12.50
2 Albert Belle	3.00
3 Cal Ripken Jr.	20.00
4 Frank Thomas	7.50
5 Greg Maddux	10.00
6 Mo Vaughn	3.00
7 Chipper Jones	10.00
8 Mike Piazza	12.50
9 Ryan Klesko	3.00
10 Hideo Nomo	4.50
11 Roberto Alomar	3.00
12 Manny Ramirez	6.00
13 Gary Sheffield	3.50
14 Barry Bonds	20.00
15 Matt Williams	3.00
16 Jim Edmonds	3.00
17 Kirby Puckett	10.00
18 Sammy Sosa	10.00

1997 Zenith Samples

SAMPLE

The extent of the sample-marked version of the standard-size '97 Zenith cards is unknown.

	NM/M
Common Player:	1.50
S1 Ken Griffey Jr.	5.00
S6 Kenny Lofton	1.50

1997 Zenith

This set combines standard size trading cards with cards in an 8" x 10" format. The standard size set consists of 60 cards. Card fronts feature full-bleed photos and the word "Zenith," but no reference to the player's name or team is found on the fronts. Backs have another player photo, a hit location chart and 1996/career stats. There are four inserts in the set, all of which are printed in the larger size format - 8" x 10", 8" x 10" Dufex, 8" x 10" V-2, and Z-Team. Each sale unit contained one pack of five standard-size cards and two larger size cards for a suggested retail price of $9.99.

	NM/M
Complete Set (50):	15.00
Common Player:	.10
Pack (Five Cards, Two 8 x 10)	2.00
Wax Box (12):	25.00
1 Frank Thomas	.75
2 Tony Gwynn	1.00
3 Jeff Bagwell	.75
4 Paul Molitor	.75
5 Roberto Alomar	.20
6 Mike Piazza	1.25
7 Albert Belle	.10
8 Greg Maddux	1.00
9 Barry Larkin	.10
10 Tony Clark	.10
11 Larry Walker	.10
12 Chipper Jones	1.00
13 Juan Gonzalez	.40
14 Barry Bonds	2.00
15 Ivan Rodriguez	.65
16 Sammy Sosa	1.00
17 Derek Jeter	2.00
18 Hideo Nomo	.40
19 Roger Clemens	1.00
20 Ken Griffey Jr.	1.25
21 Andy Pettitte	.25
22 Alex Rodriguez	1.50
23 Tino Martinez	.10
24 Bernie Williams	.10
25 Ken Caminiti	.10
26 John Smoltz	.10
27 Javier Lopez	.10
28 Mark McGwire	1.50
29 Gary Sheffield	.50
30 David Justice	.10
31 Randy Johnson	.75
32 Chuck Knoblauch	.10
33 Mike Mussina	.40
34 Deion Sanders	.20
35 Cal Ripken Jr.	2.00
36 Darin Erstad	.30
37 Kenny Lofton	.10
38 Jay Buhner	.10
39 Brady Anderson	.10
40 Edgar Martinez	.10
41 Mo Vaughn	.10
42 Ryne Sandberg	1.00
43 Andruw Jones	.75
44 Nomar Garciaparra	1.00
45 Hideki Irabu RC	.25
46 Wilton Guerrero	.10
47 Jose Cruz Jr. RC	.45
48 Vladimir Guerrero	.75
49 Scott Rolen	.65
50 Jose Guillen	.10

V-2

This eight-card die-cut insert utilizes motion technology as well as foil printing to create a very high-tech 8" x 10" card. Cards were inserted 1:47 packs.

	NM/M
Complete Set (8):	45.00
Common Player:	5.00

DEREK JETER

1 Ken Griffey Jr.	7.50
2 Andruw Jones	5.00
3 Frank Thomas	5.00
4 Mike Piazza	7.50
5 Alex Rodriguez	10.00
6 Cal Ripken Jr.	12.00
7 Derek Jeter	12.00
8 Vladimir Guerrero	5.00

Z-Team

This nine-card 8" x 10" insert is printed on a mirror gold mylar foil stock with each card sequentially numbered to 1,000.

	NM/M
Complete Set (9):	60.00
Common Player:	3.00
1 Ken Griffey Jr.	9.00
2 Larry Walker	3.00
3 Frank Thomas	6.00
4 Alex Rodriguez	10.00
5 Mike Piazza	9.00
6 Cal Ripken Jr.	12.50
7 Derek Jeter	12.50
8 Andruw Jones	6.00
9 Roger Clemens	7.50

8x10 and 8x10 Dufex

This 24-card insert takes select cards from the standard set and blows them up to an 8" x 10" format. Cards were inserted one per pack. A Dufex version of each 8" x 10" insert card was also available at a rate of one per pack (except in packs which contained either a Z-Team or V-2 card).

	NM/M
Complete Set (24):	20.00
Common Player:	.50
Dufex versions:	1X
Samples:	1X
1 Frank Thomas	1.00
2 Tony Gwynn	1.50
3 Jeff Bagwell	1.00
4 Ken Griffey Jr.	2.00
5 Mike Piazza	2.00
6 Greg Maddux	1.50
7 Ken Caminiti	.50
8 Albert Belle	.50
9 Ivan Rodriguez	.75
10 Sammy Sosa	1.50
11 Mark McGwire	2.50
12 Roger Clemens	1.75
13 Alex Rodriguez	2.50
14 Chipper Jones	1.50
15 Juan Gonzalez	.60
16 Barry Bonds	3.00
17 Derek Jeter	3.00
18 Hideo Nomo	.60
19 Cal Ripken Jr.	3.00
20 Hideki Irabu	.50
21 Andruw Jones	1.50
22 Nomar Garciaparra	1.50
23 Vladimir Guerrero	1.00
24 Scott Rolen	.75

1998 Zenith Samples

To introduce its "Dare to Tear" concept, Zenith's promo cards for 1998 included a specially-marked standard-size (2-1/2" x 3-1/2") sample card within a 5" x 7" card. All cards are marked "SAMPLE" on back, but are otherwise identical to the issued versions.

		NM/M
Complete Set, Large (9):		17.50
Common Player, Large:		1.00
Complete Set, Small (6):		12.00
Common Player, Small:		1.00
Z1	Nomar Garciaparra	1.50
Z3	Greg Maddux	2.00
Z4	Frank Thomas	1.50
Z9	Andruw Jones	1.50
Z15	Derek Jeter	4.00
Z21	Mike Piazza	2.50
Z22	Tony Gwynn	2.00
Z35	Ivan Rodriguez	1.50
Z40	Ken Griffey Jr.	2.50
2	Ken Griffey Jr.	2.50
12	Greg Maddux	2.00
14	Mike Piazza	2.50
17	Derek Jeter	4.00
18	Nomar Garciaparra	2.00
19	Ivan Rodriguez	1.00

1998 Zenith

CHARLES Johnson

Zenith was part of Pinnacle's "Dare to Tear" program. Sold in three-card packs, the set consists of 5" x 7" cards, each with a standard-size card packaged inside. Collectors had to decide whether to keep the large cards or tear them open to get the smaller card inside. Eighty 5" x 7" cards and 100 regular cards comprise the set. The regular, or Z2, cards were paralleled twice - Z-Silver (1:7) and Z-Gold (numbered to 100). The large cards also had two parallels - Impulse (1:7) and Gold Impulse (numbered to 100).

		NM/M
Complete Set (100):		25.00
Common Player:		.10
Silvers:		2X
Inserted 1:7		
Pack (3):		2.50
Wax Box (18):		35.00
1	Larry Walker	.10
2	Ken Griffey Jr.	1.75
3	Cal Ripken Jr.	2.50
4	Sammy Sosa	1.50
5	Andruw Jones	1.00
6	Frank Thomas	1.00
7	Tony Gwynn	1.50
8	Rafael Palmeiro	.75
9	Tim Salmon	.10
10	Randy Johnson	1.00
11	Juan Gonzalez	1.00
12	Greg Maddux	1.50
13	Vladimir Guerrero	1.00
14	Mike Piazza	1.75
15	Andres Galarraga	.10
16	Alex Rodriguez	2.00
17	Derek Jeter	2.50
18	Nomar Garciaparra	1.50
19	Ivan Rodriguez	.75
20	Chipper Jones	1.50
21	Barry Larkin	.10
22	Mo Vaughn	.10
23	Albert Belle	.10
24	Scott Rolen	.65
25	Sandy Alomar Jr.	.10
26	Roberto Alomar	.30
27	Andy Pettitte	.30
28	Chuck Knoblauch	.10
29	Jeff Bagwell	1.00
30	Mike Mussina	.30
31	Fred McGriff	.10
32	Roger Clemens	.75
33	Rusty Greer	.10
34	Edgar Martinez	.10
35	Paul Molitor	1.00
36	Mark Grace	.10
37	Darin Erstad	.30
38	Kenny Lofton	.10
39	Tom Glavine	.35
40	Javier Lopez	.10
41	Will Clark	.10
42	Tino Martinez	.10
43	Raul Mondesi	.10
44	Brady Anderson	.10
45	Chan Ho Park	.10
46	Jason Giambi	.75
47	Manny Ramirez	1.00
48	Jay Buhner	.10
49	Dante Bichette	.10
50	Jose Cruz Jr.	.10
51	Charles Johnson	.10
52	Bernard Gilkey	.10
53	Johnny Damon	.35
54	David Justice	.10
55	Justin Thompson	.10
56	Bobby Higginson	.10
57	Todd Hundley	.10
58	Gary Sheffield	.50
59	Barry Bonds	2.50
60	Mark McGwire	2.00
61	John Smoltz	.10
62	Tony Clark	.10
63	Brian Jordan	.10
64	Jason Kendall	.10
65	Mariano Rivera	.20
66	Pedro Martinez	1.00
67	Jim Thome	.75
68	Neifi Perez	.10
69	Kevin Brown	.10
70	Hideo Nomo	.50
71	Craig Biggio	.10
72	Bernie Williams	.10
73	Jose Guillen	.10
74	Ken Caminiti	.10
75	Livan Hernandez	.10
76	Ray Lankford	.10
77	Jim Edmonds	.10
78	Matt Williams	.10
79	Mark Kotsay	.10
80	Moises Alou	.10
81	Antone Williamson	.10
82	Jaret Wright	.10
83	Jacob Cruz	.10
84	Abraham Nunez	.10
85	Raul Ibanez	.10
86	Miguel Tejada	.10
87	Derek Lee	.50
88	Juan Encarnacion	.10
89	Todd Helton	.75
90	Travis Lee	.10
91	Ben Grieve	.10
92	Ryan McGuire	.10
93	Richard Hidalgo	.10
94	Paul Konerko	.15
95	Shannon Stewart	.10
96	Homer Bush	.10
97	Lou Collier	.10
98	Jeff Abbott	.10
99	Brett Tomko	.10
100	Fernando Tatis	.10

Z-Silver

This parallel set reprinted all 100 standard sized cards in Zenith on silver foilboard, with a "Z-Silver" logo across the bottom center. Z-Silvers were inserted one per seven packs.

	NM/M
Common Player:	1.00
Stars/RC's:	2X
Inserted 1:7	

Z-Gold

	NM/M
Common Player:	3.00
Stars/Rookies	12X
Production 100 Sets	

Epix

Epix is a cross-brand insert. The set honors Plays, Games, Seasons and Moments in the careers of top baseball players. Epix consisted of 24 cards in Zenith, inserted 1:11. The cards have orange, purple and emerald versions.

		NM/M
Complete Set (24):		95.00
Common (Orange) Card:		1.50
Purples:		1X
Emeralds:		2X
1	Ken Griffey Jr./S	7.50
2	Juan Gonzalez/S	2.50
3	Jeff Bagwell/S	4.50
4	Ivan Rodriguez/S	4.00
5	Nomar Garciaparra/S	6.00
6	Ryne Sandberg/S	6.00
7	Frank Thomas/M	4.50
8	Derek Jeter/M	12.00
9	Tony Gwynn/M	6.00
10	Albert Belle/M	1.50
11	Scott Rolen/M	3.50
12	Barry Larkin/M	1.50
13	Alex Rodriguez/P	9.00
14	Cal Ripken Jr./P	12.00
15	Chipper Jones/P	6.00
16	Roger Clemens/P	6.50
17	Mo Vaughn/P	1.50
18	Mark McGwire/P	9.00
19	Mike Piazza/G	7.50
20	Andruw Jones/G	4.50
21	Greg Maddux/G	6.00
22	Barry Bonds/G	12.00
23	Paul Molitor/G	4.50
24	Eddie Murray/G	4.50

Raising the Bar

Andruw Jones RAISING the BAR

Raising the Bar is a 15-card insert seeded 1:25. The set features players who have set high standards for other players to follow.

		NM/M
Complete Set (15):		25.00
Common Player:		1.25
Inserted 1:25		
1	Ken Griffey Jr.	3.00
2	Frank Thomas	1.50
3	Alex Rodriguez	3.50
4	Tony Gwynn	2.50
5	Mike Piazza	3.00
6	Ivan Rodriguez	1.25
7	Cal Ripken Jr.	4.50
8	Greg Maddux	2.50
9	Hideo Nomo	1.25
10	Mark McGwire	3.50
11	Juan Gonzalez	1.25
12	Andruw Jones	1.50
13	Jeff Bagwell	1.50
14	Chipper Jones	2.50
15	Nomar Garciaparra	2.50

Rookie Thrills

Rookie Thrills is a 15-card insert seeded 1:25. The set features many of the top rookies of 1998 in action photos printed on a silver-foil background. Backs have a few words about the player's career to that point.

		NM/M
Complete Set (15):		20.00
Common Player:		1.50
Inserted 1:25		
1	Travis Lee	1.50
2	Juan Encarnacion	1.50
3	Derrek Lee	1.50
4	Raul Ibanez	1.50
5	Ryan McGuire	1.50
6	Todd Helton	3.00
7	Jacob Cruz	1.50
8	Abraham Nunez	1.50
9	Paul Konerko	2.00
10	Ben Grieve	1.50
11	Jeff Abbott	1.50
12	Richard Hidalgo	1.50
13	Jaret Wright	1.50
14	Lou Collier	1.50
15	Miguel Tejada	2.00

Z-Team

The Z Team insert was created in 5" x 7" and standard-size versions, each inserted at a 1:35 pack rate. The nine Rookie Z Team cards were seeded 1:58 and gold versions of both were found 1:175.

		NM/M
Complete Set (18):		35.00
Common Player:		1.25
Golds:		2X
Inserted 1:175		
1	Frank Thomas	2.50
2	Ken Griffey Jr.	3.50
3	Mike Piazza	3.50
4	Cal Ripken Jr.	6.00
5	Alex Rodriguez	5.00
6	Greg Maddux	3.00
7	Derek Jeter	6.00
8	Chipper Jones	3.00
9	Roger Clemens	3.25
10	Ben Grieve	1.25
11	Derek Lee	1.75
12	Jose Cruz Jr.	1.25
13	Nomar Garciaparra	3.00
14	Travis Lee	1.50
15	Todd Helton	2.00
16	Paul Konerko	1.75
17	Miguel Tejada	1.25
18	Scott Rolen	2.00

Z-Team 5x7

The 5" x 7" Z-Team insert is a nine-card set seeded one per 35 packs.

		NM/M
Complete Set (9):		40.00
Common Player:		3.00
Inserted 1:35		
1	Frank Thomas	3.00
2	Ken Griffey Jr.	5.00
3	Mike Piazza	5.00
4	Cal Ripken Jr.	7.50
5	Alex Rodriguez	6.00
6	Greg Maddux	4.00
7	Derek Jeter	7.50
8	Chipper Jones	4.00
9	Roger Clemens	4.50

5x7

VLADIMIR Guerrero

The 80 Zenith 5" x 7" cards all contained a regular-size card. Collectors could tear open the 5" x 7" to get at the smaller card inside.

		NM/M
The set has two parallels: 5" x 7" Impulse (1:7) and 5" x 7" Gold Impulse (1:43).		
		NM/M
Complete Set (80):		30.00
Common Player:		.25
Impulse Silvers:		1.5X
Inserted 1:7		
1	Nomar Garciaparra	2.00
2	Andres Galarraga	.25
3	Greg Maddux	2.00
4	Frank Thomas	1.00
5	Mark McGwire	3.00
6	Rafael Palmeiro	.75
7	John Smoltz	.25
8	Jeff Bagwell	1.00
9	Andruw Jones	1.00
10	Rusty Greer	.25
11	Paul Molitor	1.00
12	Bernie Williams	.25
13	Kenny Lofton	.25
14	Alex Rodriguez	3.00
15	Derek Jeter	4.00
15s	Derek Jeter ("SAMPLE" overprint on back.)	
16	Scott Rolen	.65
17	Albert Belle	.25
18	Mo Vaughn	.25
19	Chipper Jones	2.00
20	Chuck Knoblauch	.25
21	Mike Piazza	3.00
22	Tony Gwynn	2.00
22s	Tony Gwynn ("SAMPLE" overprint on back.)	
23	Juan Gonzalez	.50
24	Andy Pettitte	.35
25	Tim Salmon	.25
26	Brady Anderson	.25
27	Mike Mussina	.40
28	Edgar Martinez	.25
29	Jose Guillen	.25
30	Hideo Nomo	.50
31	Jim Thome	.65
32	Mark Grace	.25
33	Darin Erstad	.50
34	Bobby Higginson	.25
35	Ivan Rodriguez	.75
36	Todd Hundley	.25
37	Sandy Alomar Jr.	.25
38	Gary Sheffield	.40
39	David Justice	.25
40	Ken Griffey Jr.	2.50
40s	Ken Griffey Jr. ("SAMPLE" overprint on back.)	2.50
41	Vladimir Guerrero	1.00
42	Larry Walker	.25
43	Barry Bonds	4.00
44	Randy Johnson	1.00
45	Roger Clemens	2.25
46	Raul Mondesi	.25
47	Tino Martinez	.25
48	Jason Giambi	.50
49	Matt Williams	.25
50	Cal Ripken Jr.	4.00
51	Barry Larkin	.25
52	Jim Edmonds	.25
53	Ken Caminiti	.25
54	Sammy Sosa	2.00
55	Tony Clark	.25
56	Manny Ramirez	1.00
57	Bernard Gilkey	.25
58	Jose Cruz Jr.	.25
59	Brian Jordan	.25
60	Kevin Brown	.25
61	Craig Biggio	.25
62	Javier Lopez	.25
63	Jay Buhner	.25
64	Roberto Alomar	.40
65	Justin Thompson	.25
66	Todd Helton	.75
67	Travis Lee	.25
68	Paul Konerko	.35
69	Jaret Wright	.25
70	Ben Grieve	.25
71	Juan Encarnacion	.25
72	Ryan McGuire	.25
73	Derrek Lee	.60
74	Abraham Nunez	.25
75	Richard Hidalgo	.25
76	Miguel Tejada	.25
77	Jacob Cruz	.25
78	Homer Bush	.25
79	Jeff Abbott	.25
80	Lou Collier	.25
	Checklist	.10

5x7 Impulse Silver

MARK McGwire

These silver parallels reprinted each of the 80 cards in the 5" x 7" set and carried that logo on the front and were inserted one per seven packs. Since these cards contained other cards inside them, they are condition sensitive and only worth full price if left in mint condition and not cut open.

	NM/M
Common Player:	2.00
Stars/RC's:	1.5X
Inserted 1:7	

1998 Zenith 5x7 Impulse Gold

RICHARD Hidalgo

These gold parallels reprint each of the 80 cards in the 5" x 7" set. Cards carry a Gold Impulse logo on front and are serially numbered from within an edition of 100 each on back. Silver or Gold Impulse parallels were inserted one per seven packs. Since these cards contained other cards inside them, they are condition sensitive and only worth full price if left in mint condition and not cut open.

	NM/M
Common Player:	5.00
Stars/RC's:	20X
Inserted 1:7	

1992 Ziploc

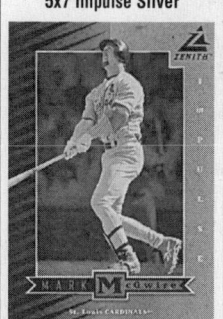

HANK AARON

Dow Brands produced an 11-card set of All-Stars in 1992 that featured mostly Hall of Famers, with the exception only of Nellie Fox. The cards were included in specially-marked Ziploc packages, and also could be purchased by mail.

		NM/M
Complete Set (11):		4.00
Common Player:		.45
1	Warren Spahn	.50
2	Bob Gibson	.50
3	Rollie Fingers	.50
4	Carl Yastrzemski	1.00
5	Brooks Robinson	.50
6	Pee Wee Reese	.75
7	Willie McCovey	.50
8	Willie Mays	2.00
9	Nellie Fox	.50
10	Yogi Berra	.75
11	Hank Aaron	2.00

MINOR LEAGUE (1867-1969)

Prior to 1970 virtually all minor league baseball cards were issued as single cards rather than the complete sets. Like contemporary major league cards they were usually intended as premiums given away with the purchase of goos and services.

The listings which follow offer individual card prices in three grades of preservation to allow accurate valuations of superstar and other special interest cards, along with cards that were short-printed or otherwise are scarce.

A

1959 APCO Meat Packing Co. San Antonio Missions

The extent of this issue, as well as its distribution are not known. The 3-1/2" x 4-1/2" black-and-white cards may have been packaged with meat products and/or given away at the ballpark. The team was Class AA affiliate of the Chicago Cubs.

		NM	EX	VG
Common Player:		50.00	25.00	15.00
(1)	Russell Gragg	50.00	25.00	15.00
(2)	Mike Lutz	50.00	25.00	15.00
	(In Corpus Christi uniform.)			

1960 Armour Meats Denver Bears

Ten cards from this Class AA farm team of the Detroit Tigers have been checklisted, with others possibly to be discovered. The black-and-white blank-backed cards measure 2-1/2" x 3-1/4" and were issued with a coupon attached to the right side. The unnumbered cards are checklisted here alphabetically.

		NM	EX	VG
Complete Set (10):		650.00	325.00	195.00
Common Player:		75.00	37.00	22.00
(1)	George Alusik	75.00	37.00	22.00
(2)	Tony Bartirome	75.00	37.00	22.00
(3)	Edward J. Donnelly	75.00	37.00	22.00
(4)	James R. McDaniel	75.00	37.00	22.00
(5)	Charlie Metro	75.00	37.00	22.00
(6)	Harry Perkowski	75.00	37.00	22.00
(7)	Vernon E. Rapp	75.00	37.00	22.00
(8)	James Stump	75.00	37.00	22.00
(9)	Ozzie Virgil	75.00	37.00	22.00
(10)	Robert Walz	75.00	37.00	22.00

1940 Associated Stations San Francisco Seals

This album and sticker set was created as a premium by a Northern California gas company. Individual stickers were given away each week at participating service stations. The blank-backed, 1-3/4" x 2-5/8" stickers have the player's name in a black strip at the bottom. Pages in the accompanying 3-1/2" x 6" album have space for an autograph and a few career highlights for each player. The checklist is presented in page order of the album.

		NM	EX	VG
Complete Set (26):		500.00	250.00	125.00
Common Player:		20.00	10.00	6.00
Album:		100.00	50.00	30.00
(1)	"Lefty" O'Doul	40.00	20.00	12.00

(2)	Sam Gibson	20.00	10.00	6.00
(3)	Brooks Holder	20.00	10.00	6.00
(4)	Ted Norbert	20.00	10.00	6.00
(5)	Win Ballou	20.00	10.00	6.00
(6)	Al Wright	20.00	10.00	6.00
(7)	Al Epperly	20.00	10.00	6.00
(8)	Orville Jorgens	20.00	10.00	6.00
(9)	Larry Powell	20.00	10.00	6.00
(10)	Joe Sprinz	20.00	10.00	6.00
(11)	Harvey Storey	20.00	10.00	6.00
(12)	Jack Burns	20.00	10.00	6.00
(13)	Bob Price	20.00	10.00	6.00
(14)	Larry Guay	20.00	10.00	6.00
(15)	Frank Dasso	20.00	10.00	6.00
(16)	Eddie Stutz	20.00	10.00	6.00
(17)	John Barrett	20.00	10.00	6.00
(18)	Eddie Botelho	20.00	10.00	6.00
(19)	Ferris Fain	30.00	15.00	9.00
(20)	Larry Woodall	20.00	10.00	6.00
(21)	Ted Jennings	20.00	10.00	6.00
(22)	Jack Warner	20.00	10.00	6.00
(23)	Wil Leonard	20.00	10.00	6.00
(24)	Gene Kiley	20.00	10.00	6.00
(25)	Bob Jensen	20.00	10.00	6.00
(26)	Wilfrid Le Febvre	20.00	10.00	6.00

1952 Atlanta Crackers Souvenir Pictures Album

Rather than a set of individual baseball cards, the Class AA Southern Association farm club of the Boston Braves issued this souvenir picture album depicting players (including future major leaguers like Chuck Tanner, Art Fowler and Carl Wiley), staff and media. About 8-1/8" x 7-1/2", the album has embossed metallic light blue covers and dark blue graphics. Inside are eight black-and-white pages with three card-like images per page. The pictures are in about the same size and format as Globe Printing's contemporary minor league baseball card team sets.

	NM	EX	VG
Complete Souvenir Book:	400.00	200.00	120.00
1952 Atlanta Crackers	.00	.00	.00

1910 A.W.H./A.W.A. Caramels Virginia League (E222)

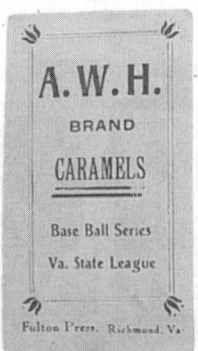

This rare set of cards picturing players from the Virginia League was issued by the A.W.H. (or A.W.A.) Caramel Co. in 1910. The cards measure 1-1/2" x 2-3/4" and feature player portraits in either red, black, brown or blue duotones. Examples of 12 different cards have been found. The front of the card displays the player's last name and team below his photo. The back states "A.W.H. (or A.W.A.) Brand Caramels" in large letters with "Base Ball Series/Va. State League" below. At least four variations in back typography and borders are known.

		NM	EX	VG
Complete Set (12):		100,000	40,000	25,000
Common Player:		9,000	3,600	2,250
(1)	Tom Guiheen	9,000	3,600	2,250
(2)	Hooker	9,000	3,600	2,250
(3)	Ison	9,000	3,600	2,250
(4)	Lipe	9,000	3,600	2,250
(5)	McCauley	9,000	3,600	2,250
(6)	Otey	9,000	3,600	2,250
(7)	Revelle	9,000	3,600	2,250
(8)	Ryan	9,000	3,600	2,250
(9)	Shaughessy	9,000	3,600	2,250
(10)	Sieber	9,000	3,600	2,250
(11)	Smith	9,000	3,600	2,250
(12)	Titman	9,000	3,600	2,250

B

1910 Baltimore News Orioles

The Eastern League Baltimore Orioles are featured in this set of schedule cards issued by a local newspaper. Cards measure 2-3/4" x 3-1/2" and feature player photographs on front, with a wide border. Player name, position, team and league are printed at the bottom of the photo. Backs have both the "Home" and "Abroad" schedule for the team, along with ads at top and bottom for the newspaper. All printing on front is in red-and-white; backs are in black-and-white. The checklist here is likely incomplete.

		NM	EX	VG
Common Player:		1,200	600.00	350.00
(1)	Byers	1,200	600.00	350.00
(2)	Jim Egan	1,200	600.00	350.00
(3)	Maisel	1,200	600.00	350.00
(4)	Malloy	1,200	600.00	350.00
(5)	Jimmy Murray	1,200	600.00	350.00

1914 Baltimore News Orioles

The International League Baltimore Orioles are one of two teams featured (along with the city's Federal League team) in this set of newspaper promotional cards. The 2-5/8" x 3-5/8" cards are monochrome printed in either blue or red with wide borders on front framing full-length action poses on which the background has been erased in favor of artificial shadows. Player name, position and league are printed on front. Backs have a "HOME" and "ABROAD" schedule with an ad for the paper at top and a line at bottom which reads, "This Card is Given to," with space for a signature. At least one card, a Babe Ruth, has been seen with "Compliments Baltimore International League" replacing the newspaper ad at top. Only the minor league Orioles players are listed here, the Terrapins cards are listed in the major league section of this catalog. This checklist is almost certainly incomplete.

		NM	EX	VG
Common Player:		3,000	1,500	900.00
(1)	Neal Ball	3,000	1,500	900.00
(2)	Ensign Cottrell	3,000	1,500	900.00
(3)	Birdie Cree	3,000	1,500	900.00
(4)	Bert Daniels	3,000	1,500	900.00
(5)	Davidson	3,000	1,500	900.00
(6)	Jack Dunn	4,500	2,250	1,350
(7)	Gleichmann	3,000	1,500	900.00
(8)	Allen Russell (Allan)	3,000	1,500	900.00

(10) Babe Ruth ((Blue PSA 4 (VG-EX) card sold in 5/05 auction for $244,000. Red PSA 1 (Poor- Fair) sold in 4/06 auction for $150,800. Ungraded VG sold in 5/07 auction for $517,000.) Red VG sold 5/08 auction for 440,000. Red VG sold in 5/08 auction for $440,000.)

(11)	Ernie Shore	3,000	1,500 900.00
(12)	George Twombley (Twombly)	3,000	1,500 900.00
(13)	Orioles Team w/Ruth (slabbed authentic, sold in 5/08 auction for 52,875) (Slabbed authentic sold in 5/08 auction for $52,875.)		

1952 Baltimore Orioles Team Issue

ROY WEATHERLY

While most of the company's issues were for minor league teams in the lower classifications, Globe Printing of San Jose, Calif., also produced a set for the International League Baltimore Orioles. Similar to the company's other issues, the black-and-white cards measure about 2-1/4" x 3-3/8". Reliable reports indicate that individual cards were given away with ice cream purchases at the ballpark. The checklist here is obviously incomplete. In 1952 the O's were the top farm club of the Philadelphia Phillies.

		NM	EX	VG
Common Player:		75.00	37.50	22.50
(1)	Al Cihocki	75.00	37.50	22.50
(2)	Blix Donnelly	75.00	37.50	22.50
(3)	Bob Greenwood	75.00	37.50	22.50
(4)	Don Heffner	75.00	37.50	22.50
(5)	Russ Kerns	75.00	37.50	22.50
(6)	Howie Moss	75.00	37.50	22.50
(7)	Dee Phillips	75.00	37.50	22.50
(8)	Jerry Scala	75.00	37.50	22.50
(9)	Danny Schell	75.00	37.50	22.50
(10)	Paul Stuffel	75.00	37.50	22.50
(11)	Roy Weatherly	75.00	37.50	22.50

1923 Baltimore Shirt Co. Kansas City Blues

LENA BLACKBURNE

Kansas City's Pennant Winning BLUES 1923

Compliments Baltimore Shirt 4 Stores KANSAS CITY, MO.

This unusual souvenir of the American Association Champion K.C. Blues is in the form of a 48" x 3-5/8" accordian-fold packet. Individual 1-7/8" x 3-1/4" black-and-white photos of the players are glued onto the black backing paper. Because the photos are rather easily removed, they may be encountered as singles. The players are checklisted here as they originally appeared, from left to right, on the foldout. There is no advertising on the individual pictures, just on the outer covers.

		NM	EX	VG
Complete Foldout:		1,000	500.00	300.00
Complete Set, Singles:		750.00	375.00	225.00
Common Player:		50.00	25.00	15.00
(1)	Wilbur Good	50.00	25.00	15.00
(2)	Bill Skiff	50.00	25.00	15.00
(3)	Lew McCarty	50.00	25.00	15.00
(4)	Dudley Branom	50.00	25.00	15.00
(5)	Lena Blackburne	55.00	27.50	16.50
(6)	Walter Hammond	50.00	25.00	15.00
(7)	Glen Wright (Glenn)	60.00	30.00	18.00
(8)	Geo. Armstrong	50.00	25.00	15.00
(9)	Beals Becker	50.00	25.00	15.00
(10)	"Dutch" Zwilling	50.00	25.00	15.00
(11)	Pete Scott	50.00	25.00	15.00
(12)	"Bunny" Brief	50.00	25.00	15.00
(13)	Jimmie Zinn	50.00	25.00	15.00
(14)	Ferd Schupp	50.00	25.00	15.00
(15)	Roy Wilkinson	50.00	25.00	15.00
(16)	Ray Caldwell	50.00	25.00	15.00

(17)	Joe Dawson	50.00	25.00	15.00
(18)	John Saladna	50.00	25.00	15.00
(19)	Herb Thormahlen	50.00	25.00	15.00
(20)	"Nick" Carter	50.00	25.00	15.00
(21)	George Muehlebach (President)	50.00	25.00	15.00

1909 Bastian Gum Pin

It is unknown whether other members of the championship 1909 Rochester Bronchos of the Eastern League were honored on these black-and-white pinback celluloid buttons or only their manager. The pin measures about 1-1/4" in diameter and as originally issued had a paper insert in back crediting it to Bastian Bros. Gum.

	NM	EX	VG
John H. Ganzel	150.00	75.00	45.00

1961 Bee Hive Starch Toronto Maple Leafs

DAVE POPE, outfielder · 1961

This 24-card set features players of the Toronto Maple Leafs, an independent team in the International League which featured future Hall of Fame Manager Sparky Anderson as its second baseman. The black-and-white cards are printed on thin, blank-backed stock and measure approximately 2-1/2" x 3-1/4". As the cards are not numbered, the checklist below is presented alphabetically.

		NM	EX	VG
Complete Set (24):		2,400	1,200	725.00
Common Player:		90.00	45.00	25.00
(1)	George Anderson	450.00	225.00	135.00
(2)	Fritzie Brickell	90.00	45.00	25.00
(3)	Ellis Burton	90.00	45.00	25.00
(4)	Bob Chakales	90.00	45.00	25.00
(5)	Rip Coleman	90.00	45.00	25.00
(6)	Steve Demeter	90.00	45.00	25.00
(7)	Joe Hannah	90.00	45.00	25.00
(8)	Earl Hersh	90.00	45.00	25.00
(9)	Lou Jackson	90.00	45.00	25.00
(10)	Ken Johnson	90.00	45.00	25.00
(11)	Lou Johnson	90.00	45.00	25.00
(12)	John Lipon	90.00	45.00	25.00
(13)	Carl Mathias	90.00	45.00	25.00
(14)	Bill Moran	90.00	45.00	25.00
(15)	Ron Negray	90.00	45.00	25.00
(16)	Herb Plews	90.00	45.00	25.00
(17)	Dave Pope	90.00	45.00	25.00
(18)	Steve Ridzik	90.00	45.00	25.00
(19)	Raul Sanchez	90.00	45.00	25.00
(20)	Pat Scantlebury	90.00	45.00	25.00
(21)	Bill Smith	90.00	45.00	25.00
(22)	Bob Smith	90.00	45.00	25.00
(23)	Chuck Tanner	125.00	65.00	35.00
(24)	Tim Thompson	90.00	45.00	25.00

1911 Big Eater Sacramento Solons

This very rare set was issued circa 1911 and includes only members of the Pacific Coast League Sacramento Solons. The black-and-white cards measure 2-1/8" x 4" and feature action photos. The lower part of the card contains a three-line caption that includes the player's last name, team designation (abbreviated to "Sac'to"), and the promotional line: "He Eats 'Big Eater'." Although the exact origin is undetermined, it is believed that "Big Eaters" were a candy novelty.

BYRAM SACTO HE EATS "BIG EATER"

		NM	EX	VG
Complete Set (20):		50,000	20,000	12,000
Common Player:		2,750	1,100	700.00
(1)	Frank Arellanes	2,750	1,100	700.00
(2)	Spider Baum	2,750	1,100	700.00
(3)	Herb Byram	2,750	1,100	700.00
(4)	Babe Danzig	2,750	1,100	700.00
(5)	Jack Fitzgerald	2,750	1,100	700.00
(6)	George Gaddy	2,750	1,100	700.00
(7)	Al Heister	2,750	1,100	700.00
(8)	Ben Hunt	2,750	1,100	700.00
(9)	Butch Kerns	2,750	1,100	700.00
(10)	Mickey LaLonge	2,750	1,100	700.00
(11)	Dutch Lerchen	2,750	1,100	700.00
(12)	Jimmy Lewis	2,750	1,100	700.00
(13)	Chris Mahoney	2,750	1,100	700.00
(14)	Dick Nebinger	2,750	1,100	700.00
(15)	Patsy O'Rourke	2,750	1,100	700.00
(16)	Jimmy Shinn	2,750	1,100	700.00
(17)	Chester Thomas	2,750	1,100	700.00
(18)	Fuller Thompson	2,750	1,100	700.00
(19)	Frank Thornton	2,750	1,100	700.00
(20)	Deacon Van Buren	2,750	1,100	700.00

1950 Big League Stars (V362)

Chuck Connors
MONTREAL ROYALS
Infielder
Born at Brooklyn, N.Y., on April 10, 1921. Bats left. Throws left. 6'5". 210 lbs. Hit .319, 20 homers and batted in 108 runs with Royals in 1949.

Champ intérieur
Né à Brooklyn, N.Y., le 10 avril 1921. Frappe de la gauche, lance de la gauche. 6'5", 210 livres. Frappe .319, 20 coups de circuit et participa à 108 buts avec les Royaux en 1949.

BIG LEAGUE STARS — No. 2

International League players are featured in this 48-card set. Measuring 3-1/4" x 2-5/8", the blank-backed cards are printed in blue-on-white with English and French stats and biographical data.

		NM	EX	VG
Complete Set (48):		4,500	2,750	1,200
Common Player:		90.00	40.00	25.00
1	Rocky Bridges	100.00	50.00	30.00
2	Chuck Connors	650.00	325.00	200.00
3	Jake Wade	90.00	40.00	25.00
4	Al Cihocki	90.00	40.00	25.00
5	John Simmons	90.00	40.00	25.00
6	Frank Trechock	90.00	40.00	25.00
7	Steve Lembo	90.00	40.00	25.00
8	Johnny Welaj	90.00	40.00	25.00
9	Seymour Block	90.00	40.00	25.00
10	Pat McGlothlin	90.00	40.00	25.00
11	Bryan Stephens	90.00	40.00	25.00
12	Clarence Podbielan	90.00	40.00	25.00
13	Clem Hausmann	90.00	40.00	25.00
14	Turk Lown	90.00	40.00	25.00
15	Joe Payne	90.00	40.00	25.00
16	Coacker Triplett (Coaker)	90.00	40.00	25.00
17	Nick Strincevich	90.00	40.00	25.00
18	Charlie Thompson	90.00	40.00	25.00
19	Erick Silverman	90.00	40.00	25.00
20	George Schmees	90.00	40.00	25.00
21	George Binks	90.00	40.00	25.00
22	Gino Cimoli	100.00	50.00	30.00
23	Marty Tabacheck	90.00	40.00	25.00
24	Al Gionfriddo	100.00	50.00	30.00
25	Ronnie Lee	90.00	40.00	25.00
26	Clyde King	90.00	40.00	25.00
27	Harry Heslet	90.00	40.00	25.00
28	Jerry Scala	90.00	40.00	25.00
29	Boris Woyt	90.00	40.00	25.00
30	Jack Collum	90.00	40.00	25.00
31	Chet Laabs	90.00	40.00	25.00
32	Carden Gillwater	90.00	40.00	25.00
33	Irving Medlinger	90.00	40.00	25.00
34	Toby Atwell	90.00	40.00	25.00
35	Charlie Marshall	90.00	40.00	25.00
36	Johnny Mayo	90.00	40.00	25.00
37	Gene Markland	90.00	40.00	25.00
38	Russ Kerns	90.00	40.00	25.00

		NM	EX	VG
39	Jim Prendergast	90.00	40.00	25.00
40	Lou Welaj	90.00	40.00	25.00
41	Clyde Kluttz	90.00	40.00	25.00
42	Bill Glynn	90.00	40.00	25.00
43	Don Richmond	90.00	40.00	25.00
44	Hank Biasatti	90.00	40.00	25.00
45	Tom Lasorda	600.00	300.00	180.00
46	Al Roberge	90.00	40.00	25.00
47	George Byam	90.00	40.00	25.00
48	Dutch Mele	90.00	40.00	25.00

1910 Bishop & Co. P.C.L. Teams (E221)

A very rare issue, this series of team pictures of clubs in the Pacific Coast League was distributed by Bishop & Co. of Los Angeles in 1910. The team photos were printed on a thin, news-print-type paper that measures an elongated 10" x 2-3/4". Although there were six teams in the PCL at the time, only five clubs have been found - the sixth team, Sacramento, was apparently never issued. The cards indicate that they were issued with five-cent packages of Bishop's Milk Chocolate and that the photos were taken by the Los Angeles Examiner. The black-and-white team photos are found with red, blue, yellow, purple, or green background.

		NM	EX	VG
Complete Set (5):		32,000	13,000	8,000
Common Team:		6,000	2,700	1,700
(1)	Los Angeles	6,000	2,700	1,700
(2)	Oakland	6,000	2,700	1,700
(3)	Portland	6,000	2,700	1,700
(4)	San Francisco	6,000	2,700	1,700
(5)	Vernon	6,000	2,700	1,700

1910 Bishop & Co. P.C.L. (E99)

Hap. Hogan, c. Vernon

The first of two obscure sets produced by the Los Angeles candy maker Bishop & Co., this 30-card set was issued in 1910 and depicts players from the Pacific Coast League, showing five players from each of the six teams. The cards measure approximately 1-1/2" x 2-3/4" and feature black-and-white player photos with colored backgrounds (green, blue, purple, yellow, or rarely, black). The player's last name, position and team appear along the bottom. The backs of the cards contain the complete checklist in groups of five, according to team, with each name indented slightly more than the name above. Cards in the 1910 set do not contain the name "Bishop & Company, California" along the bottom on the back.

		NM	EX	VG
Complete Set (30):		50,000	21,000	13,000
Common Player:		1,750	700.00	435.00
(1)	Bodie	2,000	800.00	500.00
(2)	N. Brashear	1,750	700.00	435.00
(3)	Briggs	1,750	700.00	435.00
(4)	Byones (Byrnes)	1,750	700.00	435.00
(5)	Cameron	1,750	700.00	435.00
(6)	Casey	1,750	700.00	435.00
(7)	Cutshaw	1,750	700.00	435.00
(8)	Delmas	1,750	700.00	435.00
(9)	Dillon	1,750	700.00	435.00
(10)	Hasty	1,750	700.00	435.00
(11)	Hitt	1,750	700.00	435.00
(12)	Hap. Hogan	1,750	700.00	435.00
(13)	Hunt	1,750	700.00	435.00
(14)	Krapp	1,750	700.00	435.00
(15)	John Lindsay	1,750	700.00	435.00
(16)	Maggert	1,750	700.00	435.00
(17)	McArdle	1,750	700.00	435.00
(18)	McCredie (McCreedie)	1,750	700.00	435.00
(19)	Melchior	1,750	700.00	435.00
(20)	Mohler	1,750	700.00	435.00
(21)	Nagle	1,750	700.00	435.00
(22)	Nelson	1,750	700.00	435.00
(23)	Nourse	1,750	700.00	435.00
(24)	Olsen	1,750	700.00	435.00
(25)	Raymer	1,750	700.00	435.00
(26)	Smith	1,750	700.00	435.00
(27)	Tennent (Tennant)	1,750	700.00	435.00
(28)	Thorsen	1,750	700.00	435.00
(29)	Van Buren	1,750	700.00	435.00
(30)	Wolverton	1,750	700.00	435.00

1911 Bishop & Co. P.C.L. Type I (E100)

P. O'Rourke, 2b Sacramento

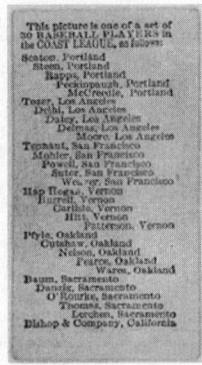

This set was issued by the confectioner Bishop & Co. of Los Angeles, which had produced a similar set a year earlier. Both sets showcased star players from the Pacific Coast League. The cards measure approximately 1-1/2" x 2-3/4" and feature black-and-white photos with a background of green, blue, yellow, purple or red. The backs contain the complete checklist of the set, listing the players in groups of five by team, with one line indented slightly more than the previous one. In addition to the checklist, the 1911 set can be differentiated from the previous year because the line "Bishop & Company, California" appears along the bottom.

		NM	EX	VG
Complete Set (30):		55,000	22,000	13,500
Common Player:		1,700	675.00	425.00
(1)	Spider Baum	1,700	675.00	425.00
(2)	Burrell	1,700	675.00	425.00
(3)	Carlisle	1,700	675.00	425.00
(4)	Cutshaw	1,700	675.00	425.00
(5)	Pete Daley	1,700	675.00	425.00
(6)	Danzig	1,700	675.00	425.00
(7)	Delhi	1,700	675.00	425.00
(8)	Delmas	1,700	675.00	425.00
(9)	Hitt	1,700	675.00	425.00
(10)	Hap Hogan (Actually Walter Bray.)	1,700	675.00	425.00
(11)	Lerchen	1,700	675.00	425.00
(12)	McCreddie (McCreedie)	1,700	675.00	425.00
(13)	Mohler	1,700	675.00	425.00
(14)	Moore	1,700	675.00	425.00
(15)	Slim Nelson	1,700	675.00	425.00
(16)	P. O'Rourke	1,700	675.00	425.00
(17)	Patterson	1,700	675.00	425.00
(18)	Bunny Pearce	1,700	675.00	425.00
(19)	Peckinpaugh	1,700	675.00	425.00
(20)	Monte Pfyle (Pfyl)	1,700	675.00	425.00
(21)	Powell	1,700	675.00	425.00
(22)	Rapps	1,700	675.00	425.00
(23)	Seaton	1,700	675.00	425.00
(24)	Steen	1,700	675.00	425.00
(25)	Suter	1,700	675.00	425.00
(26)	Tennant	1,700	675.00	425.00
(27)	Thomas	1,700	675.00	425.00
(28)	Tozer	1,700	675.00	425.00
(29)	Clyde Wares	1,700	675.00	425.00
(30)	Weaver	6,500	2,600	1,625

1911 Bishop & Co. P.C.L. Type II (E100)

Sutor, p., Frisco.

Currently little over half of the checklist of Bishop & Co. (E100) has been found in a second version. These cards have thus far been seen only with green and orange backgrounds, are blank-backed, have larger, reversed negatives, cropping of the photos and have caption differences.

		NM	EX	VG
Common Player:		1,850	750.00	450.00
(1)	Burrell	1,850	750.00	450.00
(2)	Danzig	1,850	750.00	450.00
(3)	Delhi	1,850	750.00	450.00
(4)	Hitt	1,850	750.00	450.00
(5)	Lerchen	1,850	750.00	450.00
(6)	McCreddie (McCreedie)	1,850	750.00	450.00
(7)	Slim Nelson	1,850	750.00	450.00
(8)	P. O'Rourke	1,850	750.00	450.00
(9)	Patterson	1,850	750.00	450.00
(10)	Bunny Pearce	1,850	750.00	450.00
(11)	Monte Pfyle	1,850	750.00	450.00
(12)	Rapps	1,850	750.00	450.00
(13)	Seaton	1,850	750.00	450.00
(14)	Steen	1,850	750.00	450.00
(15)	Suter	1,850	750.00	450.00
(16)	Tennant	1,850	750.00	450.00
(17)	Weaver	6,500	2,600	1,625

1954 Blossom Dairy Charleston Senators

JOE TORPEY

The Class AAA farm team of the Chicago White Sox is featured in this team set sponsored by a Charleston, W. Va., dairy. The 2-1/4" x 3-3/16" black-and-white cards are either a late issue by Globe Printing (which issued many minor league sets from 1951-52) or were patterned after the Globe issues, right down to the issue of an album to house the cards. A white box is superimposed over the posed action photos and contains the player and sponsor identification. Cards are blank-backed.

		NM	EX	VG
Complete Set (22):		2,200	1,100	650.00
Common Player:		100.00	50.00	30.00
Album:		150.00	75.00	45.00
(1)	Al Baro	100.00	50.00	30.00
(2)	Joe Becker	100.00	50.00	30.00
(3)	Joe Carroll	100.00	50.00	30.00
(4)	Gerald "Red" Fahr	100.00	50.00	30.00
(5)	Dick Fowler	100.00	50.00	30.00
(6)	Alex Garbowski	100.00	50.00	30.00
(7)	Gordon Goldsberry	100.00	50.00	30.00
(8)	Ross Grimsley	100.00	50.00	30.00
(9)	Sam Hairston	125.00	65.00	35.00
(10)	Phil Haugstad	100.00	50.00	30.00
(11)	Tom Hurd	100.00	50.00	30.00
(12)	Bill Killinger	100.00	50.00	30.00
(13)	John Kropf	100.00	50.00	30.00
(14)	Bob Masser	100.00	50.00	30.00
(15)	Danny Menendez	100.00	50.00	30.00
(16)	Bill Paolisso	100.00	50.00	30.00
(17)	Bill Pope	100.00	50.00	30.00
(18)	Lou Sleater	100.00	50.00	30.00
(19)	Dick Strahs	100.00	50.00	30.00
(20)	Joe Torpey	100.00	50.00	30.00
(21)	Bill Voiselle	100.00	50.00	30.00
(22)	Al Ware	100.00	50.00	30.00

1958 Bond Bread Buffalo Bisons

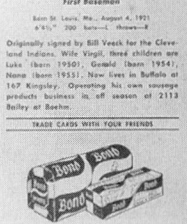

Nine members of the International League affiliate of the Kansas City Athletics are featured in this set. The 2-1/2" x 3-1/2" cards are printed on very thin cardboard. Fronts have a black-and-white player photo, the player's name and position, and an ad for a TV Western. Card backs are printed in red and blue and include a few biographical details and a career summary, along with an illustrated ad.

		NM	EX	VG
Complete Set (9):		350.00	175.00	100.00
Common Player:		40.00	20.00	12.00
(1)	Al Aber	40.00	20.00	12.00
(2)	Joe Caffie	40.00	20.00	12.00
(3)	Phil Cavaretta	40.00	20.00	12.00
(4)	Rip Coleman	40.00	20.00	12.00
(5)	Luke Easter	60.00	30.00	18.00
(6)	Ken Johnson	40.00	20.00	12.00
(7)	Lou Ortiz	40.00	20.00	12.00
(8)	Jack Phillips	40.00	20.00	12.00
(9)	Jim Small	40.00	20.00	12.00

1949 Bowman Pacific Coast League

One of the scarcest issues of the postwar period, the 1949 Bowman PCL set was issued only on the West Coast. Like the 1949 Bowman regular issue, the cards contain black-and-white photos overprinted with various pastel colors. Thirty-six cards, which measure 2-1/16" x 2-1/2", make up the set. It is believed

Top right table (continuation of 1911 Type I (E100)):

		NM	EX	VG
(12)	Rapps	1,850	750.00	450.00
(13)	Seaton	1,850	750.00	450.00
(14)	Steen	1,850	750.00	450.00
(15)	Suter	1,850	750.00	450.00
(16)	Tennant	1,850	750.00	450.00
(17)	Weaver	6,500	2,600	1,625

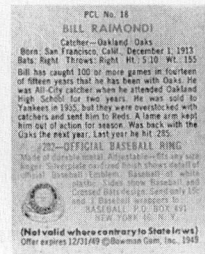

that the cards may have been issued only in sheets and not sold in gum packs. Consequently, many cards are found which display evidence of having been cut with a scissors.

		NM	EX	VG
Complete Set (36):		15,000	7,500	4,500
Common Player:		500.00	240.00	145.00
1	Lee Anthony	500.00	240.00	145.00
2	George Metkovich	500.00	240.00	145.00
3	Ralph Hodgin	500.00	240.00	145.00
4	George Woods	500.00	240.00	145.00
5	Xavier Rescigno	500.00	240.00	145.00
6	Mickey Grasso	500.00	240.00	145.00
7	Johnny Rucker	500.00	240.00	145.00
8	Jack Brewer	500.00	240.00	145.00
9	Dom D'Allessandro	500.00	240.00	145.00
10	Charlie Gassaway	500.00	240.00	145.00
11	Tony Freitas	500.00	240.00	145.00
12	Gordon Maltzberger	500.00	240.00	145.00
13	John Jensen	500.00	240.00	145.00
14	Joyner White	500.00	240.00	145.00
15	Harvey Storey	500.00	240.00	145.00
16	Dick Lajeski	500.00	240.00	145.00
17	Albie Glossop	500.00	240.00	145.00
18	Bill Raimondi	500.00	240.00	145.00
19	Ken Holcombe	500.00	240.00	145.00
20	Don Ross	500.00	240.00	145.00
21	Pete Coscarart	500.00	240.00	145.00
22	Tony York	500.00	240.00	145.00
23	Jake Mooty	500.00	240.00	145.00
24	Charles Adams	500.00	240.00	145.00
25	Les Scarsella	500.00	240.00	145.00
26	Joe Marty	500.00	240.00	145.00
27	Frank Kelleher	500.00	240.00	145.00
28	Lee Handley	500.00	240.00	145.00
29	Herman Besse	500.00	240.00	145.00
30	John Lazor	500.00	240.00	145.00
31	Eddie Malone	500.00	240.00	145.00
32	Maurice Van Robays	500.00	240.00	145.00
33	Jim Tabor	500.00	240.00	145.00
34	Gene Handley	500.00	240.00	145.00
35	Tom Seats	500.00	240.00	145.00
36	Ora Burnett	500.00	240.00	145.00

1933 Buffalo Bisons Jigsaw Puzzles

Produced as a stadium promotional giveaway, this set consists of 19 player puzzles and one for Hall of Fame Manager Ray Schalk. Each of the 11" x 14", 200-piece, black-and-white puzzles was produced in an edition of 10,000. Puzzles carried a red serial number, and certain numbers could be redeemed for tickets and other prizes. The known puzzles are checklisted below in alphabetical order.

		NM	EX	VG
Complete Set (15):		5,000	2,500	1,500
Common Player:		335.00	165.00	100.00
(1)	Joe Bartulis	335.00	165.00	100.00
(2)	Joe Bloomer	335.00	165.00	100.00
(3)	Ollie Carnegie	335.00	165.00	100.00
(4)	Clyde "Buck" Crouse	335.00	165.00	100.00
(5)	Harry Danning	335.00	165.00	100.00
(6)	Gilbert English	335.00	165.00	100.00
(7)	Fred Fussell	335.00	165.00	100.00
(8)	Bob Gould	335.00	165.00	100.00
(9)	Len Koenecke	335.00	165.00	100.00
(10)	Ray Lucas	335.00	165.00	100.00
(11)	Clarence Mueller	335.00	165.00	100.00
(12)	Ray Schalk	500.00	250.00	150.00
(13)	Jack Smith	335.00	165.00	100.00
(14)	Roy Tarr	335.00	165.00	100.00
(15)	Johnny Wilson	335.00	165.00	100.00

1934 Buffalo Bisons Team Issue

Apparently a team issue, these 4" x 7-1/16" black-and-white blank-backed cards feature posed action photos with white borders and a facsimile autograph. The player's full

---

name and position are printed in the bottom border, along with a career summary. This checklist is probably incomplete though the exact scope of the issue is unknown.

		NM	EX	VG
Common Player:		200.00	100.00	60.00
(1)	Kenneth L. Ash	200.00	100.00	60.00
(2)	Harold "Ace" Elliott	200.00	100.00	60.00
(3)	Gregory T. Mulleavy	200.00	100.00	60.00
(4)	Irving M. Plummer	200.00	100.00	60.00

1940 Buffalo Bisons Team Issue

Many former and future big leaguers are included in this set of black-and-white, 2" x 3" cards. Fronts picture the players in poses at old Offerman Stadium. The player's name and position are printed in the white border at bottom. Backs have a career summary and highlights. The unnumbered cards are checklisted here alphabetically.

		NM	EX	VG
Complete Set (24):		4,500	2,250	1,350
Common Player:		200.00	100.00	60.00
(1)	Ollie Carnegie	200.00	100.00	60.00
(2)	Dan Carnevale	200.00	100.00	60.00
(3)	Earl Cook	200.00	100.00	60.00
(4)	Les Fleming	200.00	100.00	60.00
(5)	Floyd Giebel	200.00	100.00	60.00
(6)	Jimmy Hutch	200.00	100.00	60.00
(7)	Fred Hutchinson	200.00	100.00	60.00
(8)	Art Jacobs	200.00	100.00	60.00
(9)	John Kroner	200.00	100.00	60.00
(10)	Sal Maglie	300.00	150.00	90.00
(11)	Joe Martin	200.00	100.00	60.00
(12)	Clyde McCullough	200.00	100.00	60.00
(13)	Greg Mulleavy	200.00	100.00	60.00
(14)	Pat Mullin	200.00	100.00	60.00
(15)	Hank Nowak	200.00	100.00	60.00
(16)	Steve O'Neil	200.00	100.00	60.00
(17)	Jimmy Outlaw	200.00	100.00	60.00
(18)	Joe Rogalski	200.00	100.00	60.00
(19)	Les Scarsella	200.00	100.00	60.00
(20)	Mayo Smith	200.00	100.00	60.00
(21)	Floyd Stromme	200.00	100.00	60.00
(22)	Jim Trexler	200.00	100.00	60.00
(23)	Hal White	200.00	100.00	60.00
(24)	Frank Zubik	200.00	100.00	60.00

1947 Buffalo Bisons Team Issue

Despite some anomalies among the players checklisted thus far, this appears to have been a 1947 team-issued set of 8" a 10" black-and-white player photographs. Fronts include player identification in the form of a facsimile autograph. Backs are blank.

		NM	EX	VG
Common Player:		30.00	15.00	9.00
(1)	Johnny Bero	30.00	15.00	9.00
(2)	Hank Biasatti	30.00	15.00	9.00
(3)	Eddie Boland	30.00	15.00	9.00
(4)	Ray Coleman	30.00	15.00	9.00
(5)	Zeb "Red" Eaton	30.00	15.00	9.00
(6)	Lonny Frey	30.00	15.00	9.00
(7)	Freddie Hancock	30.00	15.00	9.00
(8)	Gabby Hartnett	65.00	32.00	19.50
(9)	Clem Hausman	30.00	15.00	9.00
(10)	Manuel Hidalgo	30.00	15.00	9.00
(11)	Chet Laabs	30.00	15.00	9.00
(12)	Johnny McHale	30.00	15.00	9.00
(13)	Edward Mierkowicz	30.00	15.00	9.00
(14)	Eddie Mordarski	30.00	15.00	9.00
(15)	Hank Perry	30.00	15.00	9.00
(16)	Billy Pierce, Ted Gray	45.00	22.00	13.50
(17)	Bill Radulovich	30.00	15.00	9.00
(18)	Earl Rapp, Clint Conatser, Anse Moore, Coaker Triplett	30.00	15.00	9.00
(19)	Vic Wertz	40.00	20.00	12.00

1950 Bush & Hancock/Oak Hall Roanoke Red Sox

These blank-back, black-and-white cards have a portrait photo on front surrounded by a white border. Beneath the photo is a credit line and space for an autograph. Cards exist in 3-1/2" x 5" size with sponsor's credit reading "Compliments of Bush & Hancock," and in 4" x 6" format with sponsor's credit reading, "Compliments of Oak Hall." It is not known whether the checklist presented here is complete. Roanoke was a Class B Piedmont League farm club.

		NM	EX	VG
Common Player:		50.00	25.00	15.00
(1)	Tom Casey	50.00	25.00	15.00
(2)	George Contratto	50.00	25.00	15.00
(3)	Ike Delock	65.00	32.50	20.00
(4)	Red Marion	50.00	25.00	15.00
(5)	Rod Morgan	50.00	25.00	15.00
(6)	Julio Ondani	50.00	25.00	15.00
(7)	Joe Reedy	50.00	25.00	15.00
(8)	Johnny Sehrt	50.00	25.00	15.00
(9)	Sammy White	65.00	32.50	20.00
(10)	Bob Wilson	50.00	25.00	15.00

C

1943 Centennial Flour Seattle Rainiers

The 25 cards in this 4" x 5" black-and-white set feature players of the Pacific Coast League Seattle Rainiers. Identical in format to the set issued in 1944, the '43s can be identified by the lines of type at the bottom of the card back reading, "Compliments of/CENTENNIAL FLOURING MILLS."

		NM	EX	VG
Complete Set (25):		1,100	550.00	325.00
Common Player:		60.00	30.00	18.00
(1)	John Babich	60.00	30.00	18.00
(2)	Nick Bonarigo (Buonarigo)	60.00	30.00	18.00
(3)	Eddie Carnett	60.00	30.00	18.00
(4)	Lloyd Christopher	60.00	30.00	18.00
(5)	Joe Demoran	60.00	30.00	18.00
(6)	Joe Dobbins	60.00	30.00	18.00
(7)	Glenn Elliott	60.00	30.00	18.00
(8)	Carl Fischer	60.00	30.00	18.00
(9)	Leonard Gabrielson	60.00	30.00	18.00
(10)	Stanley Gray	60.00	30.00	18.00
(11)	Dick Gyselman	60.00	30.00	18.00
(12)	Jim Jewell	60.00	30.00	18.00
(13)	Syl Johnson	60.00	30.00	18.00
(14)	Pete Jonas	60.00	30.00	18.00
(15)	Bill Kats	60.00	30.00	18.00
(16)	Lynn King	60.00	30.00	18.00
(17)	Bill Lawrence	60.00	30.00	18.00
(18)	Clarence Marshall	60.00	30.00	18.00
(19)	Bill Matheson	60.00	30.00	18.00
(20)	Ford Mullen	60.00	30.00	18.00
(21)	Bill Skiff	60.00	30.00	18.00
(22)	Byron Speece	60.00	30.00	18.00
(23)	Hal Sueme	60.00	30.00	18.00
(24)	Hal Turpin	60.00	30.00	18.00
(25)	John Yelovic	60.00	30.00	18.00

1944 Centennial Flour Seattle Rainiers

Identical in format to the previous year's issue, the 25 black-and-white 4" x 5" cards issued in 1944 can be differentiated from the 1943 set by the two lines of type at the bottom of each card's back. In the 1944 set, it reads, "Compliments of/CENTENNIAL HOTCAKE AND WAFFLE FLOUR."

	NM	EX	VG
Complete Set (25):	1,350	675.00	400.00

Common Player:			
(1)	John Babich	60.00	30.00	18.00
(2)	Paul Carpenter	60.00	30.00	18.00
(3)	Lloyd Christopher	60.00	30.00	18.00
(4)	Joe Demoran	60.00	30.00	18.00
(5)	Joe Dobbins	60.00	30.00	18.00
(6)	Glenn Elliott	60.00	30.00	18.00
(7)	Carl Fischer	60.00	30.00	18.00
(8)	Bob Garbould (Gorbould)	60.00	30.00	18.00
(9)	Stanley Gray	60.00	30.00	18.00
(10)	Dick Gyselman	60.00	30.00	18.00
(11)	Gene Holt	60.00	30.00	18.00
(12)	Roy Johnson	60.00	30.00	18.00
(13)	Syl Johnson	60.00	30.00	18.00
(14)	Al Libke	60.00	30.00	18.00
(15)	Bill Lyman	60.00	30.00	18.00
(16)	Bill Matheson	60.00	30.00	18.00
(17)	Jack McClure	60.00	30.00	18.00
(18)	Jimmy Ripple	60.00	30.00	18.00
(19)	Bill Skiff	60.00	30.00	18.00
(20)	Byron Speece	60.00	30.00	18.00
(21)	Hal Sueme	60.00	30.00	18.00
(22)	Frank Tincup	60.00	30.00	18.00
(23)	Jack Treece	60.00	30.00	18.00
(24)	Hal Turpin	60.00	30.00	18.00
(25)	Sicks Stadium	65.00	32.50	20.00

1945 Centennial Flour Seattle Rainiers

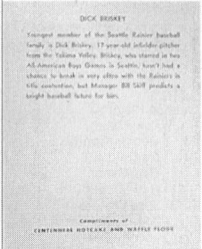

The 27 blue-and-white cards in the third consecutive issue for this Pacific Coast League team are distinguished from the two previous issues by the borderless photo on the front and the fact that the name and team are printed in a black bar at the bottom. The set can be distinguished from the 1947 issue by virtue of the fact that the player biography on back is not surrounded by a frame. The cards measure slightly narrower but longer than the 1943-44 issues, at 3-7/8" x 5-1/8".

		NM	EX	VG
Complete Set (27):		1,500	750.00	450.00
Common Player:		60.00	30.00	18.00
(1)	Charley Aleno	60.00	30.00	18.00
(2)	Dick Briskey	60.00	30.00	18.00
(3)	John Carpenter	60.00	30.00	18.00
(4)	Joe Demoran	60.00	30.00	18.00
(5)	Joe Dobbins	60.00	30.00	18.00
(6)	Glenn Elliott	60.00	30.00	18.00
(7)	Bob Finley	60.00	30.00	18.00
(8)	Carl Fischer	60.00	30.00	18.00
(9)	Keith Frazier	60.00	30.00	18.00
(10)	Johnny Gill	60.00	30.00	18.00
(11)	Bob Gorbould	60.00	30.00	18.00
(12)	Chet Johnson	60.00	30.00	18.00
(13)	Syl Johnson	60.00	30.00	18.00
(14)	Bill Kats	60.00	30.00	18.00
(15)	Billy Lyman	60.00	30.00	18.00
(16)	Bill Matheson	60.00	30.00	18.00
(17)	George McDonald	60.00	30.00	18.00
(18)	Ted Norbert	60.00	30.00	18.00
(19)	Alex Palica	60.00	30.00	18.00
(20)	Joe Passero	60.00	30.00	18.00
(21)	Hal Patchett	60.00	30.00	18.00
(22)	Bill Skiff	60.00	30.00	18.00
(23)	Byron Speece	60.00	30.00	18.00
(24)	Hal Sueme	60.00	30.00	18.00
(25)	Eddie Taylor	60.00	30.00	18.00
(26)	Hal Turpin	60.00	30.00	18.00
(27)	Jack Whipple	60.00	30.00	18.00

1947 Centennial Flour Seattle Rainiers

After a lapse of one year, Centennial Flour returned to issue a final black-and-white 32-card set for 1947. Identical in size (3-7/8" x 5-1/8") and front format to the 1945 issue, the '47s can be identified by the white framed box on back containing the player's biography.

	NM	EX	VG
Complete Set (32):	1,100	550.00	325.00
Common Player:	50.00	25.00	15.00

(1)	Dick Barrett	50.00	25.00	15.00
(2)	Joe Buzas	50.00	25.00	15.00
(3)	Paul Carpenter	50.00	25.00	15.00
(4)	Rex Cecil	50.00	25.00	15.00
(5)	Tony Criscola	50.00	25.00	15.00
(6)	Walter Dubiel	50.00	25.00	15.00
(7)	Doug Ford	50.00	25.00	15.00
(8)	Rollie Hemsley	50.00	25.00	15.00
(9)	Jim Hill	50.00	25.00	15.00
(10)	Jim Hopper	50.00	25.00	15.00
(11)	Sigmund Jakucki	50.00	25.00	15.00
(12)	Bob Johnson	60.00	30.00	18.00
(13)	Pete Jonas	50.00	25.00	15.00
(14)	Joe Kaney	50.00	25.00	15.00
(15)	Hillis Layne	50.00	25.00	15.00
(16)	Lou Novikoff	50.00	25.00	15.00
(17)	Johnny O'Neil	50.00	25.00	15.00
(18)	John Orphal	50.00	25.00	15.00
(19)	Ike Pearson	50.00	25.00	15.00
(20)	Bill Posedel	50.00	25.00	15.00
(21)	Don Pulford	50.00	25.00	15.00
(22)	Tom Reis	50.00	25.00	15.00
(23)	Charley Ripple	50.00	25.00	15.00
(24)	Mickey Rocco	50.00	25.00	15.00
(25)	Johnny Rucker	50.00	25.00	15.00
(26)	Earl Sheely	50.00	25.00	15.00
(27)	Bob Stagg	50.00	25.00	15.00
(28)	Hal Sueme	50.00	25.00	15.00
(29)	Eddie Taylor	50.00	25.00	15.00
(30)	Ed Vanni	50.00	25.00	15.00
(31)	JoJo White	50.00	25.00	15.00
(32)	Tony York	50.00	25.00	15.00

1957-58 Chattanooga Lookouts Team Issue

Based on the known and certainly incomplete checklist seen thus far, this issue of 8" x 10" black-and-white, blank-back player photos can only be generally attributed to year of issue. With a credit line to Moss Photo Service of New York City, the pictures feature action poses of the players taken in historic Engel Stadium. Facsimile autographs are pre-printed on the front. During the late 1950s the Lookouts were the top farm club of the Washington Senators.

		NM	EX	VG
Common Player:		30.00	15.00	9.00
(1)	Bobby Brown	30.00	15.00	9.00
(2)	Hal Griggs	30.00	15.00	9.00
(2)	Harmon Killebrew	200.00	100.00	60.00
(3)	Jesse Levan	30.00	15.00	9.00
(3)	Ernie Oravetz	30.00	15.00	9.00
(4)	Stan Roseboro	30.00	15.00	9.00
(5)	Bunky Stewart	30.00	15.00	9.00

1967 Chevron/Uniroyal Vancouver Mounties

These 2" x 3" black-and-white cards were distributed by local gas stations and picture members of the top farm club of the Kansas City A's. Backs are printed in red and black on white.

		NM	EX	VG
Complete Set (27):		4,500	2,250	1,300
Common Player:		200.00	100.00	60.00
(1)	Sal Bando	350.00	175.00	105.00
(2)	Frank Bastrire (Trainer)	200.00	100.00	60.00
(3)	Ossie Chavarria	200.00	100.00	60.00
(4)	Jim Dickson	200.00	100.00	60.00
(5)	John Donaldson	200.00	100.00	60.00
(6)	Jim Driscoll	200.00	100.00	60.00
(7)	Bob Duliba	200.00	100.00	60.00
(8)	Bill Edgerton	200.00	100.00	60.00
(9)	Larry Elliot	200.00	100.00	60.00
(10)	Ernie Foli	200.00	100.00	60.00
(11)	Joe Gaines	200.00	100.00	60.00
(12)	Vern Handrann	200.00	100.00	60.00
(13)	Jim Hughes	200.00	100.00	60.00
(14)	Woody Huyke	200.00	100.00	60.00

(15)	Rene Lachemann	225.00	110.00	67.00
(16)	Bob Meyer	200.00	100.00	60.00
(17)	Wayne Norton	200.00	100.00	60.00
(18)	Gerry Reimer	200.00	100.00	60.00
(19)	Roberto Rodriguez	200.00	100.00	60.00
(20)	Ken Sanders	200.00	100.00	60.00
(21)	Randy Schwartz	200.00	100.00	60.00
(22)	Diego Segui	275.00	135.00	82.00
(23)	Paul Seitz	200.00	100.00	60.00
(24)	Ron Tompkins	200.00	100.00	60.00
(25)	Mickey Vernon	350.00	175.00	105.00
(26)	Jim Ward	200.00	100.00	60.00
(27)	Don Yingling	200.00	100.00	60.00

1909 Clement Bros. Bread (D380-1)

This set features only players of the Rochester team in the Eastern League. According to the bakery ad on back, the cards were distributed one per loaf of bread. The 1-1/2" x 2-3/4" cards feature a player photo on front in an oval frame against a white background. The player's last name, position and "Rochester" are printed beneath.

		NM	EX	VG
Complete Set (8):		25,000	12,500	7,500
Common Player:		5,000	2,500	1,500
(1)	Anderson	5,000	2,500	1,500
(2)	Heinie Batch	5,000	2,500	1,500
(3)	Butler	5,000	2,500	1,500
(4)	Ed Holly	5,000	2,500	1,500
(5)	Holmes	5,000	2,500	1,500
(6)	McConnell	5,000	2,500	1,500
(7)	Osborn	5,000	2,500	1,500
(8)	Partee	5,000	2,500	1,500

1910 Clement Bros. Bread (D380)

For the second of two annual issues, the bakery added an unknown number of major league players' cards to those of six of the hometeam Rochester club of the Eastern League. While the backs remained identical to the previous issue, featuring advertising for the bakery's bread and pies, the fronts adopted the standard format of the era, black-and-white player photos surrounded by a white border, with the player's last name, position and city printed at bottom. Size remained 1-1/2" x 2-3/4".

		NM	EX	VG
Common Player:		5,750	2,850	1,700
(1)	Whitey Alperman	5,750	2,850	1,700
(2)	Bailey	5,750	2,850	1,700
(3)	Walter Blair	5,750	2,850	1,700
(4)	Ty Cobb	40,000	25,000	15,000
(5)	Eddie Collins	15,000	10,000	6,000
(6)	Roy Hartzell	5,750	2,850	1,700
(7)	Harry Howell	5,750	2,850	1,700
(8)	Addie Joss	15,000	10,000	6,000
(9)	Ditus Lagoe	5,750	2,850	1,700
(10)	McConnell	5,750	2,850	1,700
(11)	George Mullin	5,750	2,850	1,700
(12)	Wilfred Osborn	5,750	2,850	1,700
(13)	Harry Patee	5,750	2,850	1,700
(14)	Don Carlos Ragan	5,750	2,850	1,700
(15)	Oscar Stanage	5,750	2,850	1,700
(16)	George Stone	5,750	2,850	1,700
(17)	Ed Summers	5,750	2,850	1,700
(18)	Joe Tinker	15,000	10,000	6,000

		NM	EX	VG
(19)	Bert Tooley	5,750	2,850	1,700
(20)	Heinie Zimmerman	5,750	2,850	1,700

1953 Coca-Cola Galveston White Caps

This set may have been an issue of the Globe Printing Co., which produced many lower-minors team sets in the years preceding, or it may just share the format. The 2-1/4" x 3-3/8" cards have borderless black-and-white photos on front and blank backs. In a white box near the bottom of the picture is the player name and "Compliments of / Coca-Cola Bottling Co." Galveston was champion of the 1953 Class B Gulf Coast League and not affiliated with any major league team.

		NM	EX	VG
Complete Set (16):		1,000	500.00	300.00
Common Player:		75.00	37.50	22.00
(1)	Ed Bohnslav	75.00	37.50	22.00
(2)	Mike Conovan	75.00	37.50	22.00
(3)	Pop Faucett	75.00	37.50	22.00
(4)	Bobby Flis	75.00	37.50	22.00
(5)	Stan Goletz	75.00	37.50	22.00
(6)	Jerry Kleinsmith	75.00	37.50	22.00
(7)	Charlie Lehrmann	75.00	37.50	22.00
(8)	Jim Logan	75.00	37.50	22.00
(9)	Bob Miller	75.00	37.50	22.00
(10)	Tom Moore	75.00	37.50	22.00
(11)	Bob Pugatch	75.00	37.50	22.00
(12)	Bob Ramsey	75.00	37.50	22.00
(13)	Hank Robinson	75.00	37.50	22.00
(14)	Charlie Schmidt	75.00	37.50	22.00
(15)	Barnie White	75.00	37.50	22.00
(16)	Hank Yzquierdo (Izquierdo)	75.00	37.50	22.00

1952 Colorado Springs Sky Sox Team Issue

From the Class A Western League runners-up, this is one of many minor league sets issued in the early 1950s by the Globe Printing Co., of San Jose, Calif. The '52 Sky Sox were a farm team of the Chicago White Sox. Players included former Negro Leaguers and future major leaguers Connie Johnson and Sam Hairston, plus bonus-baby bust Gus Keriazakos. Cards are about 2-1/4" x 3-1/4", printed in black-and-white with blank backs. An album with die-cut pages to allow the corners of the cards to be slipped in was also available. Cards were likely given away one or two at a time at home games.

		NM	EX	VG
Complete Set (19):		1,200	600.00	360.00
Common Player:		60.00	30.00	18.00
Album:		100.00	50.00	30.00
(1)	Jerry Crosby	60.00	30.00	18.00
(2)	Vic Fucci	60.00	30.00	18.00
(3)	Don Gutteridge	60.00	30.00	18.00
(4)	Sam Hairston	90.00	45.00	27.00
(5)	Al Jacinto	60.00	30.00	18.00
(6)	Connie Johnson	75.00	37.50	22.00
(7)	Bob Kellogg	60.00	30.00	18.00
(8)	Gus Keriazakos	60.00	30.00	18.00
(9)	Ken Landenberger	60.00	30.00	18.00
(10)	George Noga	60.00	30.00	18.00
(11)	Floyd Penfold	60.00	30.00	18.00
(12)	Bill Pope	60.00	30.00	18.00
(13)	J.W. Porter	60.00	30.00	18.00
(14)	Bill (Red) Rose	60.00	30.00	18.00
(15)	Don Rudolph	60.00	30.00	18.00
(16)	Andy Skurski	60.00	30.00	18.00
(17)	Dick Strahs	60.00	30.00	18.00
(18)	Bill Wells	60.00	30.00	18.00
(19)	Dick Welteroth	60.00	30.00	18.00

1952 Columbus Cardinals Team Issue

This set of cards was a product of the Globe Printing Co. of San Jose, Calif. The cards were given away at Golden Park during the 1952 season. The cards measure 2-1/8" x 3-3/8" and have black-and-white photos of players with the player's name in a white box in the bottom-left corner of the photograph. The backs are blank. The cards are unnumbered and listed in alphabetical order, although this checklist may not be complete. The team was a Class A South Atlantic League affiliate of the St. Louis Cardinals.

		NM	EX	VG
Complete Set (17):		1,000	500.00	300.00
Common Player:		60.00	30.00	18.00
(1)	Chief Bender	60.00	30.00	18.00
(2)	Bob Betancourt	60.00	30.00	18.00
(3)	Tom Burgess	60.00	30.00	18.00
(4)	Jack Byers	60.00	30.00	18.00
(5)	Mike Curnan	60.00	30.00	18.00
(6)	Gil Daley	60.00	30.00	18.00
(7)	Bill Harris	60.00	30.00	18.00
(8)	Ev Joyner	60.00	30.00	18.00
(9)	Bob Kerce	60.00	30.00	18.00
(10)	Ted Lewandowski	60.00	30.00	18.00
(11)	John Mackey	60.00	30.00	18.00
(12)	Bill Paolisso	60.00	30.00	18.00
(13)	Dennis Reeder	60.00	30.00	18.00
(14)	Whit Ulrich	60.00	30.00	18.00
(15)	Norman Shope	60.00	30.00	18.00
(16)	Don Swartz	60.00	30.00	18.00
(17)	Len Wile	60.00	30.00	18.00

1955 Columbus Jets Photos

A top farm club of the Kansas City A's in 1955 the Columbus (Ohio) Jets issued these black-and-white glossy photocards. In 3-5/8" x 5-5/8" format, the cards have a facsimile autograph on front. It is possible that the checklist presented here in alphabetical order of the unnumbered cards may be incomplete.

		NM	EX	VG
Complete Set (21):		900.00	450.00	275.00
Common Player:		45.00	22.50	13.50
(1)	Hal Bevan	45.00	22.50	13.50
(2)	Paul Burris	45.00	22.50	13.50
(3)	Ted Del Guercio	45.00	22.50	13.50
(4)	Carl Duser	45.00	22.50	13.50
(5)	Charlie Haag	45.00	22.50	13.50
(6)	Forrest "Spook" Jacobs	60.00	30.00	18.00
(7)	Dick Kryhoski	45.00	22.50	13.50
(8)	Mike Kume	45.00	22.50	13.50
(9)	Al Lakeman	45.00	22.50	13.50
(10)	Jackie Mayo	45.00	22.50	13.50
(11)	Jim Miller	45.00	22.50	13.50
(12)	Al Pinkston	50.00	25.00	15.00
(13)	Al Romberger	45.00	22.50	13.50
(14)	Bill Stewart	45.00	22.50	13.50
(15)	Russ Sullivan	45.00	22.50	13.50
(16)	"Jake" Thies	45.00	22.50	13.50
(17)	Bob Trice	45.00	22.50	13.50
(18)	Ozzie VanBrabant	45.00	22.50	13.50
(19)	Frank Verdi	45.00	22.50	13.50
(20)	Leroy Wheat	45.00	22.50	13.50
(21)	Spider Wilhelm	45.00	22.50	13.50

1957 Columbus Jets Postcards

In 1957, the Columbus (Ohio) Jets began a long association as a top farm team of the Pittsburgh Pirates. That year, the team issued this set of postcards. The black-and-white

glossy cards measure 3-9/16" x 5-1/2" and have the player name and position overprinted in black block letters near the bottom of the photo. Backs have postcard indicia and a notice of printing by the Howard Photo Service of New York City. The unnumbered cards are presented here alphabetically but it is unknown whether this checklist is complete at 20.

		NM	EX	VG
Complete Set (20):		900.00	450.00	275.00
Common Player:		45.00	22.50	13.50
(1)	Dick Barone	45.00	22.50	13.50
(2)	Ron Blackburn	45.00	22.50	13.50
(3)	Jackie Brown	45.00	22.50	13.50
(4)	Ed Burtschy	45.00	22.50	13.50
(5)	Whammy Douglas	50.00	25.00	15.00
(6)	Howie Goss	45.00	22.50	13.50
(7)	Al Grunwald	45.00	22.50	13.50
(8)	Gail Henley	45.00	22.50	13.50
(9)	Don Kildoo	45.00	22.50	13.50
(10)	Danny Kravitz	45.00	22.50	13.50
(11)	Bob Kuzava	45.00	22.50	13.50
(12)	Johnny Lipon	45.00	22.50	13.50
(13)	Cholly Naranjo	45.00	22.50	13.50
(14)	Eddie O'Brien	60.00	30.00	18.00
(15)	Frank Oceak	45.00	22.50	13.50
(16)	Harding Peterson	60.00	30.00	18.00
(17)	John Powers	45.00	22.50	13.50
(18)	James Rice	45.00	22.50	13.50
(19)	Russ Sullivan	45.00	22.50	13.50
(20)	Ken Toothman	45.00	22.50	13.50

1958 Columbus Jets Photos

In format similar to the postcard issue of the previous year, and sharing some of the same pictures, this set of photocards is smaller, at 4" x 5", and is blank-backed. It is unknown whether the alphabetical checklist of the unnumbered cards presented here is complete.

		NM	EX	VG
Complete Set (17):		650.00	325.00	200.00
Common Player:		40.00	20.00	12.00
(1)	Gair Allie	40.00	20.00	12.00
(2)	Luis Arroyo	40.00	20.00	12.00
(3)	Tony Bartirome	45.00	22.50	13.50
(4)	Jim Baumer	40.00	20.00	12.00
(5)	Bill Causion	40.00	20.00	12.00
(6)	Whammy Douglas	40.00	20.00	12.00
(7)	Joe Gibbon	40.00	20.00	12.00
(8)	Howie Goss	40.00	20.00	12.00
(9)	Spook Jacobs	50.00	25.00	15.00
(10)	Clyde King	40.00	20.00	12.00
(11)	Cholly Naranjo	40.00	20.00	12.00
(12)	George O'Donnell	40.00	20.00	12.00
(13)	Laurin Pepper	40.00	20.00	12.00
(14)	Dick Rand	40.00	20.00	12.00
(15)	Leo Rodriguez	40.00	20.00	12.00
(16)	Don Rowe	40.00	20.00	12.00
(17)	Art Swanson	40.00	20.00	12.00

1910 Contentnea First Series (T209)

The 1910 Contentnea minor league set actually consists of two distinctively different series, both featuring players from the Virginia League, Carolina Association and Eastern Carolina League. The cards were distributed in packages of Contentnea cigarettes. The first series, featuring color photographs, consists of just 16 cards, each measuring 1-9/16" x 2-11/16". The front of the card has the player's last name and team printed at the bottom, while the back identifies the card as "First Series" and carries an advertisement for Contentnea cigarettes. Many first series cards are also found with rubber-stamped "Factory

No. 12, 4th Dist. N.C." on back. The second series, belived to have been issued later in 1910, is a massive 221-card set consisting of black-and- white player photos. The cards in this series are slightly larger, measuring 1-5/8" x 2-3/4". They carry the words "Photo Series" on the back, along with the cigarette advertisement. Only a handful of the players in the Contentnea set ever advanced to the major leagues and the set contains no major stars. Subsequently, it generally holds interest only to collectors who specialize in the old southern minor leagues.

	NM	EX	VG
Complete Set (16):	12,500	6,250	3,725
Common Player:	1,000	600.00	300.00
(1) Armstrong	1,000	600.00	300.00
(2) Booles	1,000	600.00	300.00
(3) Bourquise (Bourquoise)	1,000	600.00	300.00
(4) Cooper	1,000	600.00	300.00
(5) Cowell	1,000	600.00	300.00
(6) Crockett	1,000	600.00	300.00
(7) Fullenwider	1,000	600.00	300.00
(8) Gilmore	1,000	600.00	300.00
(9) Hoffman	1,000	600.00	300.00
(10) Lane	1,000	600.00	300.00
(11) Martin	1,000	600.00	300.00
(12) McGeehan	1,000	600.00	300.00
(13) Pope	1,200	800.00	400.00
(14) Sisson	1,000	600.00	300.00
(15) Stubbe	1,000	600.00	300.00
(16) Walsh	1,000	600.00	300.00

1910 Contentnea Photo Series (T209)

WOOLUMS, LYNCHBURG

PHOTO SERIES OF Virginia Carolina Association Eastern Carolina Leagues. PACKED WITH CONTENTNEA CIGARETTES Factory No. 12, 4th Dist., N.C.

	NM	EX	VG
Common Player:	550.00	275.00	150.00
(1) Abercrombie	550.00	275.00	150.00
(2) Andrada	550.00	275.00	150.00
(3) Armstrong	550.00	275.00	150.00
(4) Averett	550.00	275.00	150.00
(5) Baker	550.00	275.00	150.00
(6) Banner (Bonner)	550.00	275.00	150.00
(7) Bausewein (Bansewein)	550.00	275.00	150.00
(8) Beatty	550.00	275.00	150.00
(9) Bentley	550.00	275.00	150.00
(10) Beusse	550.00	275.00	150.00
(11) Biel	550.00	275.00	150.00
(12) Bigbie (Raleigh)	550.00	275.00	150.00
(13) Bigbie (Richmond)	550.00	275.00	150.00
(14) Blackstone	550.00	275.00	150.00
(15) Bonner	550.00	275.00	150.00
(16) Bourquin	550.00	275.00	150.00
(17) Bowen	550.00	275.00	150.00
(18) Boyle	550.00	275.00	150.00
(19) Brandon	550.00	275.00	150.00
(20) Brazelle (Brazell)	550.00	275.00	150.00
(21) Brent	550.00	275.00	150.00
(22) Brown	550.00	275.00	150.00
(23) Busch	550.00	275.00	150.00
(24) Bussey	550.00	275.00	150.00
(25) Byrd	550.00	275.00	150.00
(26) Cafalu (Cefalu)	550.00	275.00	150.00
(27) Callahan	550.00	275.00	150.00
(28) Chandler	550.00	275.00	150.00
(29) Clapp	550.00	275.00	150.00
(30) Clark (Clarke)	550.00	275.00	150.00
(31) Clemens	550.00	275.00	150.00
(32) Clunk	550.00	275.00	150.00
(33) Cooper	550.00	275.00	150.00
(34) Corbett	550.00	275.00	150.00
(35) Cote	550.00	275.00	150.00
(36) Coutts	550.00	275.00	150.00
(37) Cowan (Cowen)	550.00	275.00	150.00
(38) Cowells (Cowell)	550.00	275.00	150.00
(39) Creagan (Cregan)	550.00	275.00	150.00
(40) Crockett	550.00	275.00	150.00
(41) Lave Cross	550.00	275.00	150.00
(42) Dailey	550.00	275.00	150.00
(43) C. Derrck (Derrick)	550.00	275.00	150.00
(44) F. Derrick	550.00	275.00	150.00
(45) Doak (Greensboro)	550.00	275.00	150.00
(46) Doak (Wilmington)	550.00	275.00	150.00
(47) Dobard	550.00	275.00	150.00
(48) Dobson	550.00	275.00	150.00
(49) Doyle	550.00	275.00	150.00
(50) Drumm	550.00	275.00	150.00
(51) Duvie	550.00	275.00	150.00
(52) Ebinger	550.00	275.00	150.00
(53) Eldridge	550.00	275.00	150.00
(54) Evans	550.00	275.00	150.00
(55) Fairbanks	550.00	275.00	150.00
(56) Farmer	550.00	275.00	150.00
(57) Ferrell	550.00	275.00	150.00
(58) Fisher	550.00	275.00	150.00
(59) Flowers	550.00	275.00	150.00
(60) Fogarty	550.00	275.00	150.00
(61) Foltz	550.00	275.00	150.00
(62) Foreman	550.00	275.00	150.00
(63) Forque	550.00	275.00	150.00
(64) Francis	550.00	275.00	150.00
(65) Fulton	550.00	275.00	150.00
(66) Galvin	550.00	275.00	150.00
(67) Gardin	550.00	275.00	150.00
(68) Garman	550.00	275.00	150.00
(69) Gastmeyer	550.00	275.00	150.00
(70) Gaston	550.00	275.00	150.00
(71) Gates	550.00	275.00	150.00
(72) Gehring	550.00	275.00	150.00
(73) Gillespie	550.00	275.00	150.00
(74) Gorham	550.00	275.00	150.00
(75) Griffin (Danville)	550.00	275.00	150.00
(76) Griffin (Lynchburg)	550.00	275.00	150.00
(77) Guiheen	550.00	275.00	150.00
(78) Gunderson	550.00	275.00	150.00
(79) Hale	550.00	275.00	150.00
(80) Halland (Holland)	550.00	275.00	150.00
(81) Hamilton	550.00	275.00	150.00
(82) Hammersley	550.00	275.00	150.00
(83) Handiboe	550.00	275.00	150.00
(84) Hannifen (Hannifan)	550.00	275.00	150.00
(85) Hargrave	550.00	275.00	150.00
(86) Harrington	550.00	275.00	150.00
(87) Harris	550.00	275.00	150.00
(88) Hart	550.00	275.00	150.00
(89) Hartley	550.00	275.00	150.00
(90) Hawkins	550.00	275.00	150.00
(91) Hearne (Hearn)	550.00	275.00	150.00
(92) Hicks	550.00	275.00	150.00
(93) Hobbs	550.00	275.00	150.00
(94) Hoffman	550.00	275.00	150.00
(95) Hooker	550.00	275.00	150.00
(96) Howard	550.00	275.00	150.00
(97) Howedel (Howedell)	550.00	275.00	150.00
(98) Hudson	550.00	275.00	150.00
(99) Humphrey	550.00	275.00	150.00
(100) Hyames	600.00	300.00	175.00
(101) Irvine	550.00	275.00	150.00
(102) Irving	550.00	275.00	150.00
(103) Jackson (Greensboro)	550.00	275.00	150.00
(104) Jackson (Spartanburg)	550.00	275.00	150.00
(105) Jenkins (Greenville)	550.00	275.00	150.00
(106) Jenkins (Roanoke)	550.00	275.00	150.00
(107) Jobson	550.00	275.00	150.00
(108) Johnson	550.00	275.00	150.00
(109) Keating	550.00	275.00	150.00
(110) Kelley	550.00	275.00	150.00
(111) Kelly (Anderson)	550.00	275.00	150.00
(112) Kelly (Goldsboro)	550.00	275.00	150.00
(113) "King" Kelly	550.00	275.00	150.00
(114) King	550.00	275.00	150.00
(115) Kite	550.00	275.00	150.00
(116) Kunkle	550.00	275.00	150.00
(117) Landgraff	550.00	275.00	150.00
(118) Lane	550.00	275.00	150.00
(119) Lathrop	550.00	275.00	150.00
(120) Lavoia	550.00	275.00	150.00
(121) Levy	550.00	275.00	150.00
(122) Lloyd	550.00	275.00	150.00
(123) Loval	550.00	275.00	150.00
(124) Lucia	550.00	275.00	150.00
(125) Luyster	550.00	275.00	150.00
(126) MacConachie	550.00	275.00	150.00
(127) Malcolm	550.00	275.00	150.00
(128) Martin	550.00	275.00	150.00
(129) Mayberry	550.00	275.00	150.00
(130) A. McCarthy	550.00	275.00	150.00
(131) J. McCarthy	550.00	275.00	150.00
(132) McCormick	550.00	275.00	150.00
(133) McFarland	550.00	275.00	150.00
(134) McFarlin	550.00	275.00	150.00
(135) C. McGeehan	550.00	275.00	150.00
(136) Dan McGeehan	550.00	275.00	150.00
(137) McHugh	550.00	275.00	150.00
(138) McKeavitt (McKevitt)	550.00	275.00	150.00
(139) Merchant	550.00	275.00	150.00
(140) Midkiff	550.00	275.00	150.00
(141) Miller	550.00	275.00	150.00
(142) Missitt	550.00	275.00	150.00
(143) Morgan	550.00	275.00	150.00
(144) Morrissey (Morrisey)	550.00	275.00	150.00
(145) Mullany (Mullaney)	550.00	275.00	150.00
(146) Mullinix	550.00	275.00	150.00
(147) Mundell	600.00	300.00	175.00
(148) Munsen (Munson)	550.00	275.00	150.00
(149) Murdock (Murdoch)	550.00	275.00	150.00
(150) Newton	550.00	275.00	150.00
(151) Noojin	550.00	275.00	150.00
(152) Novak	550.00	275.00	150.00
(153) Ochs	550.00	275.00	150.00
(154) Painter	550.00	275.00	150.00
(155) Peloguin	550.00	275.00	150.00
(156) Phealean (Phelan)	550.00	275.00	150.00
(157) Phoenix	550.00	275.00	150.00
(158) Powell	550.00	275.00	150.00
(159) Presley (Pressley), Pritchard	800.00	400.00	200.00
(160) Priest	550.00	275.00	150.00
(161) Prim	550.00	275.00	150.00
(162) Pritchard	550.00	275.00	150.00
(163) Rawe (Rowe)	550.00	275.00	150.00
(164) Redfern (Redfearn)	550.00	275.00	150.00
(165) Reggy	550.00	275.00	150.00
(166) Richardson	550.00	275.00	150.00
(167) Rickard	550.00	275.00	150.00
(168) Rickert	550.00	275.00	150.00
(169) Ridgeway (Ridgway)	550.00	275.00	150.00
(170) Roth	550.00	275.00	150.00
(171) Salve	550.00	275.00	150.00
(172) Schmidt	550.00	275.00	150.00
(173) Schrader	550.00	275.00	150.00
(174) Schumaker	550.00	275.00	150.00
(175) Sexton	550.00	275.00	150.00
(176) Shanghnessy (Shaughnessy)	550.00	275.00	150.00
(177) Sharp	550.00	275.00	150.00
(178) Shaw	550.00	275.00	150.00
(179) Simmons	550.00	275.00	150.00
(180) A. Smith	550.00	275.00	150.00
(181) D. Smith	550.00	275.00	150.00
(182) Smith (Portsmouth)	550.00	275.00	150.00
(183) Spratt	550.00	275.00	150.00
(184) Springs	550.00	275.00	150.00
(185) Stewart	550.00	275.00	150.00
(186) Stoehr	550.00	275.00	150.00
(187) Stouch	550.00	275.00	150.00
(188) Sullivan	550.00	275.00	150.00
(189) Swindell	550.00	275.00	150.00
(190) Taxis	550.00	275.00	150.00
(191) Templin	600.00	300.00	175.00
(192) Thompson	550.00	275.00	150.00
(193) B.E. Thompson	2,500	1,250	750.00
(Dressed as Uncle Sam.)			
(194) Tiedeman	550.00	275.00	150.00
(195) Titman	550.00	275.00	150.00
(196) Toner	550.00	275.00	150.00
(197) Turner	550.00	275.00	150.00
(198) Tydeman	550.00	275.00	150.00
(199) Vail	550.00	275.00	150.00
(200) Verbout	550.00	275.00	150.00
(201) Vickery	550.00	275.00	150.00
(202) Walker (Norfolk)	550.00	275.00	150.00
(203) Walker (Spartanburg)	550.00	275.00	150.00
(204) Wallace	550.00	275.00	150.00
(205) Walsh	550.00	275.00	150.00
(206) Walters	550.00	275.00	150.00
(207) Waters	550.00	275.00	150.00
(208) Waymack	550.00	275.00	150.00
(209) Webb	550.00	275.00	150.00
(210) Wehrell	550.00	275.00	150.00
(211) Weldon	550.00	275.00	150.00
(212) Welsher	550.00	275.00	150.00
(213) Westlake	550.00	275.00	150.00
(214) Williams	550.00	275.00	150.00
(215) Willis	550.00	275.00	150.00
(216) Wingo	550.00	275.00	150.00
(217) Wolf	600.00	300.00	150.00
(218) Wood	550.00	275.00	150.00
(219) Woolums	550.00	275.00	150.00
(220) Workman	550.00	275.00	150.00
(221) Wright	600.00	300.00	150.00
(222) Wynne	550.00	275.00	150.00

1924 Crescent Ice Cream Hanbury

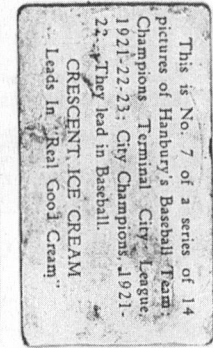

7—Art Morse Short Stop

This is No. 7 of a series of 14 pictures of Hanbury's Baseball Team. Champions of Hanbury's Terminal City League. 1921-22-23; City Champions 1921-22. They lead in Baseball. CRESCENT ICE CREAM Leads In "Real Good Cream."

Rather than a professional minor league team, this Canadian set features members of an amateur or semi-pro team sponsored by the Hanbury Sawmill in the Vancouver, B.C., Terminal Amateur League. The 2-1/4" x 1-5/8" black-and-white cards have a player portrait photo in an oval on front, with identification and card number below. On back is an identically worded summation of the team's recent seasons' championships, the card number, and an ad for the sponsor.

	NM	EX	VG
Complete Set (14):	4,000	1,350	800.00
Common Player:	300.00	150.00	90.00
1 Jack Lester (Mascot)	300.00	150.00	90.00
2 Frank Coyle	300.00	150.00	90.00
3 Fred Inch	300.00	150.00	90.00
4 Robt. Mills	300.00	150.00	90.00
5 John Daniels (Capt.)	300.00	150.00	90.00
6 Doug. May	300.00	150.00	90.00
7 Art Morse	300.00	150.00	90.00
8 Chas. Stevenson	300.00	150.00	90.00
9 Tom Raftery	300.00	150.00	90.00
10 Frank Williams	300.00	150.00	90.00
11 Unknown	300.00	150.00	90.00
12 Don Stewart	300.00	150.00	90.00
13 Roy Goodall	300.00	150.00	90.00
14 Cecil Kimberley	300.00	150.00	90.00

1940 Crowley's Milk Binghamton Triplets

Members of the Binghamton, N.Y., Eastern League team are known in this set of 3" x 5" cards. Some have been seen with stamped postcard backs. Blue-and-white player photos are framed by a red rendition of a ballpark scene on the front of the unnumbered cards. Each card has a facsimile autograph ostensibly written by the pictured player. It is unknown whether the checklist below is complete. Several of the players later appeared with the N.Y. Yankees and other teams.

		NM	EX	VG
Complete Set (18):		6,000	3,000	1,800
Common Player:		400.00	200.00	120.00
(1)	Jimmy Adlam	400.00	200.00	120.00
(2)	Russ Bergman	400.00	200.00	120.00
(3)	Bruno Betzel	400.00	200.00	120.00
(4)	Bill Bevens	400.00	200.00	120.00
(5)	Johnny Bianco	400.00	200.00	120.00
(6)	Fred Collins	400.00	200.00	120.00
(7)	Vince DeBiassi	400.00	200.00	120.00
(8)	Jack Graham	400.00	200.00	120.00
(9)	Randy Gumpert	400.00	200.00	120.00
(10)	Al Gurske	400.00	200.00	120.00
(11)	Mike Milosevich	400.00	200.00	120.00
(12)	Billie O'Donnell (Trainer)	200.00	100.00	60.00
(13)	Earl Reid	400.00	200.00	120.00
(14)	Aaron Robinson	400.00	200.00	120.00
(15)	Frankie Silvanic	400.00	200.00	120.00
(16)	Pete Suder	400.00	200.00	120.00
(17)	Ray Volps	400.00	200.00	120.00
(18)	Herb White	400.00	200.00	120.00

D

1952 Dallas Eagles Team Issue

A Class AA Texas League farm team of the Cleveland Indians, the Eagles were one of the higher minor league teams chronicled by Globe Printing in its series of 2-1/4" x 3-3/8" blank-back, black-and-white cards sets of the early 1950s. The checklist here is not complete.

		NM	EX	VG
Common Player:		60.00	30.00	18.00
(1)	Dick Aylward	60.00	30.00	18.00
(2)	Jodie Beeler	60.00	30.00	18.00
(3)	Bob Bundy	60.00	30.00	18.00
(4)	Hal Erickson	60.00	30.00	18.00
(5)	Dave Hoskins	60.00	30.00	18.00
(6)	Edward Knoblauch	60.00	30.00	18.00
(7)	Joe Kotrany	60.00	30.00	18.00
(8)	Joe Macko	60.00	30.00	18.00
(9)	Peter Mazar	60.00	30.00	18.00
(10)	Harry Sullivan	60.00	30.00	18.00
(11)	Edward Varhely	60.00	30.00	18.00

1959 Darigold Farms Spokane Indians

The unnumbered cards in this set were glued to milk cartons by a folded tab at the top of each card. The basic card measures 2-1/2" x 2-3/8", with a 2-1/2" x 2-1/8" tab. Black-and-white player photos are set against colored backgrounds of yellow (1-8), red (9-16) and blue (17-22). Player biographical details and stats are printed in black on the back. Values shown are for cards without the superfluous tabs.

		NM	EX	VG
Complete Set (22):		4,500	2,250	1,350
Common Player:		200.00	100.00	60.00
(1)	Facundo Barragan	200.00	100.00	60.00
(2)	Steve Bilko	225.00	110.00	65.00
(3)	Bobby Bragan	225.00	110.00	65.00
(4)	Chuck Churn	200.00	100.00	60.00
(5)	Tom Davis	450.00	225.00	135.00
(6)	Dom Domenichelli	200.00	100.00	60.00
(7)	Bob Giallombardo	200.00	100.00	60.00
(8)	Connie Grob	200.00	100.00	60.00
(9)	Fred Hatfield	200.00	100.00	60.00
(10)	Bob Lillis	225.00	110.00	65.00
(11)	Lloyd Merritt	200.00	100.00	60.00
(12)	Larry Miller	200.00	100.00	60.00
(13)	Chris Nicolosi	200.00	100.00	60.00
(14)	Allen Norris	200.00	100.00	60.00
(15)	Phil Ortega	200.00	100.00	60.00
(16)	Phillips Paine	200.00	100.00	60.00
(17)	Bill Parsons	200.00	100.00	60.00

(18)	Hisel Patrick	200.00	100.00	60.00
(19)	Tony Roig	200.00	100.00	60.00
(20)	Tom Saffell	200.00	100.00	60.00
(21)	Norm Sherry	250.00	125.00	75.00
(22)	Ben Wade	200.00	100.00	60.00

1960 Darigold Farms Spokane Indians

 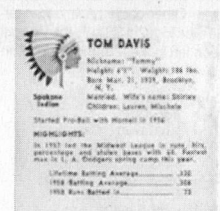

For its second annual baseball card set, the dairy added two cards and numbered the issue on the back. Card fronts were black-and-white photos against colored backgrounds of yellow (1-8), green (9-16) and red (17-24). A facsimile autograph appears on the front as well. The basic card measures 2-3/8" x 2-11/16", with a folded 2-3/8" x 2-1/16" tab at the top, by which the card was glued to a milk carton. Backs are black-and-white. Values shown are for cards without the superfluous tab.

		NM	EX	VG
Complete Set (24):		4,500	2,250	1,350
Common Player:		145.00	75.00	40.00
1	Chris Nicolosi	145.00	75.00	40.00
2	Jim Pagliaroni	145.00	75.00	40.00
3	Roy Smalley	145.00	75.00	40.00
4	Bill Bethel	145.00	75.00	40.00
5	Joe Liscio	145.00	75.00	40.00
6	Curt Roberts	145.00	75.00	40.00
7	Ed Palmquist	145.00	75.00	40.00
8	Willie Davis	300.00	150.00	90.00
9	Bob Giallombardo	145.00	75.00	40.00
10	Pedro Gomez	145.00	75.00	40.00
11	Mel Nelson	145.00	75.00	40.00
12	Charley Smith	145.00	75.00	40.00
13	Clarence Churn	145.00	75.00	40.00
14	Ramon Conde	145.00	75.00	40.00
15	George O'Donnell	145.00	75.00	40.00
16	Tony Roig	145.00	75.00	40.00
17	Frank Howard	450.00	225.00	135.00
18	Billy Harris	145.00	75.00	40.00
19	Mike Brumley	145.00	75.00	40.00
20	Earl Robinson	145.00	75.00	40.00
21	Ron Fairly	400.00	200.00	120.00
22	Joe Frazier	145.00	75.00	40.00
23	Allen Norris	145.00	75.00	40.00
24	Ford Young	145.00	75.00	40.00

E

1928 Pacific Coast League Exhibits

This regional series of 32 cards pictures players from the six California teams in the Pacific Coast League. Like the 1928 major league Exhibits, the PCL cards have a blue tint and are not numbered. They are blank-backed and measure 3-3/8" x 5-3/8". The set includes several misspellings. Cards are occasionally found with a corner clipped, the card corner to be used as a coupon with redemption value.

		NM	EX	VG
Complete Set (32):		17,500	8,750	5,250
Common Player:		500.00	250.00	150.00
1	Buzz Arlett	800.00	400.00	240.00
2	Earl Averill	1,750	875.00	525.00
3	Carl Berger (Walter)	800.00	400.00	240.00
4	"Ping" Bodie	700.00	350.00	210.00
5	Carl Dittmar	500.00	250.00	150.00
6	Jack Fenton	500.00	250.00	150.00
7	Neal "Mickey" Finn (Cornelius)	500.00	250.00	150.00
8	Ray French	500.00	250.00	150.00
9	Tony Governor	500.00	250.00	150.00
10	"Truck" Hannah	500.00	250.00	150.00
11	Mickey Heath	500.00	250.00	150.00
12	Wally Hood	500.00	250.00	150.00
13	"Fuzzy" Hufft	500.00	250.00	150.00
14	Snead Jolly (Smead Jolley)	600.00	300.00	180.00

15	Bobby "Ducky" Jones	500.00	250.00	150.00
16	Rudy Kallio	500.00	250.00	150.00
17	Ray Keating	500.00	250.00	150.00
18	Johnny Kerr	500.00	250.00	150.00
19	Harry Krause	500.00	250.00	150.00
20	Lynford H. Larry (Lary)	500.00	250.00	150.00
21	Dudley Lee	500.00	250.00	150.00
22	Walter "Duster" Mails	500.00	250.00	150.00
23	Jimmy Reese	650.00	325.00	200.00
24	"Dusty" Rhodes	500.00	250.00	150.00
25	Hal Rhyne	500.00	250.00	150.00
26	Hank Severied (Severeid)	500.00	250.00	150.00
27	Earl Sheely	500.00	250.00	150.00
28	Frank Shellenback	500.00	250.00	150.00
29	Gordon Slade	500.00	250.00	150.00
30	Hollis Thurston	500.00	250.00	150.00
31	"Babe" Twombly	500.00	250.00	150.00
32	Earl "Tex" Weathersby	500.00	250.00	150.00

1953 Montreal Royals Exhibits

Twenty-four Montreal Royals, including many future Brooklyn and L.A. Dodgers and Hall of Fame managers Walt Alston and Tommy Lasorda, were included in a 64-card Canadian issue by Exhibit Supply Co., of Chicago. The cards are slightly smaller, at 3-1/4" x 5-1/4", than standard Exhibits and printed - blank-backed - on gray stock. Numbered on front, cards of the Montreal players can be found in either blue or reddish-brown tint. Only the Royals players from the issue are checklisted here.

		NM	EX	VG
Complete Set (24):		450.00	225.00	135.00
Common Player:		15.00	7.50	4.50
33	Don Hoak	25.00	12.50	7.50
34	Bob Alexander	15.00	7.50	4.50
35	John Simmons	15.00	7.50	4.50
36	Steve Lembo	15.00	7.50	4.50
37	Norm Larker	20.00	10.00	6.00
38	Bob Ludwick	15.00	7.50	4.50
39	Walt Moryn	20.00	10.00	6.00
40	Charlie Thompson	15.00	7.50	4.50
41	Ed Roebuck	20.00	10.00	6.00
42	Russell Rose	15.00	7.50	4.50
43	Edmundo (Sandy) Amoros	25.00	12.50	7.50
44	Bob Milliken	15.00	7.50	4.50
45	Art Fabbro	15.00	7.50	4.50
46	Spook Jacobs	15.00	7.50	4.50
47	Carmen Mauro	15.00	7.50	4.50
48	Walter Fiala	15.00	7.50	4.50
49	Rocky Nelson	15.00	7.50	4.50
50	Tom La Sorda (Lasorda)	60.00	30.00	18.00
51	Ronnie Lee	15.00	7.50	4.50
52	Hampton Coleman	15.00	7.50	4.50
53	Frank Marchio	15.00	7.50	4.50
54	William Sampson	15.00	7.50	4.50
55	Gil Mills	15.00	7.50	4.50
56	Al Ronning	15.00	7.50	4.50
61	Walt Alston	40.00	20.00	12.00

F

1953 Fargo-Moorhead Twins Team Issue

This set of team-issued cards includes the first of future home-run king Roger Maris (spelled Maras in the traditional family manner). The cards are about 3-1/4" x 5-5/16" with a white border surrounding a black-and-white posed photo. Player identification is in three lines of white type at lower-left. Backs are blank, except some cards which bear a rubber-stamped promotional message from the "Red River Scenes" newspaper. The unnumbered cards are checklisted here in alphabetical order. Three of the players are known in two or more poses.

		NM	EX	VG
Complete Set (21):		3,500	1,750	1,000
Common Player:		60.00	30.00	18.00
(1)	Zeke Bonura	60.00	30.00	18.00
(2)	Bob Borovicka	60.00	30.00	18.00
(3)	Ken Braeseke	60.00	30.00	18.00
(4)	Joe Camacho	60.00	30.00	18.00
(5)	Galen Fiss	60.00	30.00	18.00
(6)	Frank Gravino (Batting follow-through.)	60.00	30.00	18.00
(7)	Frank Gravino (Hands on hips.)	60.00	30.00	18.00
(8)	Frank Gravino (Hands on knees.)	60.00	30.00	18.00
(9)	Santo Luberto (Fielding)	60.00	30.00	18.00
(10)	Roger Maras (Fielding)	1,250	625.00	375.00
(11)	Roger Maras (Batting)	1,250	625.00	375.00
(12)	Jerry Mehlish (Mehlisch)	60.00	30.00	18.00
(13)	Bob Melton	60.00	30.00	18.00
(14)	Ray Mendoza (Stretching at 1B, ball in glove.)	60.00	30.00	18.00
(15)	Ray Mendoza (Stretching at 1B, no ball.)	60.00	30.00	18.00
(16)	John Morse	60.00	30.00	18.00
(17)	Don Nance	60.00	30.00	18.00
(18)	Ray Seif	60.00	30.00	18.00
(19)	Will Sirois	60.00	30.00	18.00
(20)	Dick Wegner	60.00	30.00	18.00
(21)	Don Wolf	60.00	30.00	18.00

1966 Foremost Milk St. Petersburg Cardinals

This 20-card black-and-white set includes players and the manager, Sparky Anderson, of the Florida State League farm club of the St. Louis Cardinals. The unnumbered, blank-backed cards measure 3-1/2" x 5-1/2".

		NM	EX	VG
Complete Set (20):		50.00	25.00	15.00
Common Player:		2.50	1.25	.75
(1)	George "Sparky" Anderson	17.50	8.75	5.25
(2)	Dave Bakenhaster	2.50	1.25	.75
(3)	Leonard Boyer	4.00	2.00	1.25
(4)	Ron Braddock	2.50	1.25	.75
(5)	Thomas "Chip" Coulter	2.50	1.25	.75
(6)	Ernest "Sweet Pea" Davis	2.50	1.25	.75
(7)	Phil Knuckles	2.50	1.25	.75
(8)	Doug Lukens	2.50	1.25	.75
(9)	Terry Milani	2.50	1.25	.75
(10)	Tim Morgan	2.50	1.25	.75
(11)	Harry Parker	2.50	1.25	.75
(12)	Jerry Robertson	2.50	1.25	.75
(13)	Francisco Rodriguez	2.50	1.25	.75
(14)	John "Sonny" Ruberto	2.50	1.25	.75
(15)	Charlie Stewart	2.50	1.25	.75
(16)	Gary L. Stone	2.50	1.25	.75
(17)	Charles "Tim" Thompson	2.50	1.25	.75
(18)	Jose Villar	2.50	1.25	.75
(19)	Archie L. Wade	2.50	1.25	.75
(20)	Jim Williamson	2.50	1.25	.75

1921 Frederick Foto Service

This issue comprises a mix of Pacific Coast League and Major League players. Because Frederick Foto was located in Sacramento, a preponderance of the minor leaguers are Sacra-

mento Senators. The method of the cards' distribution is unknkown. The cards are black-and-white glossy photographs glued to a cardboard backing. The photos are bordered in white with top and bottom borders considerably wider than those on the sides. About 1-3/16" x 2-5/8", the cards have blank backs. On front is the player's last name and city, printed in a hand-lettered style. Most cards have a "Freredick / Foto." credit in the same style. Other cards have a banner-and-circle "Foto / Frederick / Service logo." It is likely this checklist is not complete. Gaps have been left in the assigned numbering for future additions.

		NM	EX	VG
Common Player:		300.00	150.00	90.00
(1)	Alexander	300.00	150.00	90.00
(2)	Ike Caveny (Caveney)	300.00	150.00	90.00
(3)	Pete Compton	300.00	150.00	90.00
(4)	Les Cook (Batting)	300.00	150.00	90.00
(5)	Les Cook (Fielding)	300.00	150.00	90.00
(7)	Carroll Canfield	300.00	150.00	90.00
(8)	Brick Eldred	300.00	150.00	90.00
(9)	Rowdy Elliott	300.00	150.00	90.00
(11)	Tony Faeth	300.00	150.00	90.00
(12)	Paul Fittery	300.00	150.00	90.00
(14)	Griffith	300.00	150.00	90.00
(15)	Charlie Hollocher	300.00	150.00	90.00
(17)	Willie Kamm	300.00	150.00	90.00
(18)	Manny Kopp	300.00	150.00	90.00
(19)	Earl Kuntz (Kunz)	300.00	150.00	90.00
(21)	Duster Mails (Arms at sides.)	300.00	150.00	90.00
(22)	Duster Mails (Hands at chest.)	300.00	150.00	90.00
(23)	Duster Mails (Follow-through.)	300.00	150.00	90.00
(24)	Duster Mails (Wind-up.)	300.00	150.00	90.00
(26)	Patsy McGaffigan	300.00	150.00	90.00
(27)	Roxie Middleton	300.00	150.00	90.00
(28)	Hack Miller	350.00	175.00	105.00
(31)	Dick Niehaus	300.00	150.00	90.00
(32)	Billy Orr (Batting)	300.00	150.00	90.00
(32)	Billy Orr (Hands on knees.)	300.00	150.00	90.00
(33)	Dode Paskert	300.00	150.00	90.00
(34)	Ken Penner (Right foot off ground.)	300.00	150.00	90.00
(35)	Ken Penner (Right foot on ground.)	300.00	150.00	90.00
(36)	Charlie Pick	300.00	150.00	90.00
(37)	Babe Pinelli	400.00	200.00	120.00
(39)	Bill Prough	300.00	150.00	90.00
(41)	Addison Read	300.00	150.00	90.00
(43)	Bill Rodgers	300.00	150.00	90.00
(44)	Pete Rose	300.00	150.00	90.00
(45)	Babe Ruth	20,000	10,000	6,000
(46)	Buddy Ryan (Holding bat, 3/4 length.)	300.00	150.00	90.00
(47)	Buddy Ryan (Holding bat, full-length.)	300.00	150.00	90.00
(48)	Buddy Ryan (Swinging bat.)	300.00	150.00	90.00
(50)	Bobby Schang	300.00	150.00	90.00
(52)	Les Sheehan	300.00	150.00	90.00
(60)	Kettle Wirts (Chicago)	300.00	150.00	90.00
(61)	Kettle Wirts (Dallas)	300.00	150.00	90.00
(62)	Archie Yelle	300.00	150.00	90.00
	Unidentified player, arms folded.	300.00	150.00	90.00
	Unidentified player, batting follow-through.	300.00	150.00	90.00

1951 Fresno Cardinals Team Issue

These 2-1/4" x 3-3/8" black-and-white, unnumbered, blank-backed cards were one of many minor league team sets issued by Globe Printing of San Jose, Calif., in the early 1950s. Cards were usually given away at the ballpark on a one-per-week or one-per-homestand basis, accounting for the rarity of surviving sets. The team was a California League (Class C) affiliate of the St. Louis Cardinals.

		NM	EX	VG
Complete Set (17):		1,000	500.00	300.00
Common Player:		60.00	30.00	18.00
(1)	Hal Atkinson	60.00	30.00	18.00
(2)	Larry Barton	60.00	30.00	18.00
(3)	Charlie Brooks	60.00	30.00	18.00
(4)	Bill Burton	60.00	30.00	18.00
(5)	Ray Herrera	60.00	30.00	18.00
(6)	Earl Jones	60.00	30.00	18.00
(7)	Jim King	60.00	30.00	18.00
(8)	Whitey Lageman	60.00	30.00	18.00
(9)	Wally Lamers	60.00	30.00	18.00
(10)	John McNamara	75.00	37.00	22.00
(11)	Gerry Mertz	60.00	30.00	18.00
(12)	Frank Olasin	60.00	30.00	18.00
(13)	Howie Phillips	60.00	30.00	18.00
(14)	Jack Ramsey	60.00	30.00	18.00
(15)	Tony Stathos	60.00	30.00	18.00
(16)	Whit Ulrich	60.00	30.00	18.00
(17)	Pete Younie	60.00	30.00	18.00

1952 Frostade

(See 1952 Parkhurst.)

1954 Fruiterie Saint Louis Tommy Lasorda

The date of issue attributed is only a best guess. It is also unknown how many other Montreal Royals players may be found in this issue. Printed in black-and-white on fairly thick 5-1/2" x 7" cardboard, this card features a portrait photo of the Royals' pitcher and future Hall of Fame manager along with a facsimile autograph on the borderless front. Rubber-stamped at top of the otherwise blank back is: "Fruiterie / Saint Louis De Franos / 515 RUE ROY PL. 1729," presumably identification of a Montreal business which distributed the card.

	NM	EX	VG
Tommy Lasorda	100.00	50.00	30.00

G

1911 Gilmartin Printing Co. S.F. Seals

These extremely scarce cards were issued as a premium by the Gilmartin Printing Co. of San Francisco and feature only members of the city's PCL Seals team. The 5" x 7" cards have full-length posed portraits of the players at center, printed in a blue-green tone and surrounded by a wide white border. The player's name, position team and year are scripted in the lower-left corner of the photo. Backs are blank. This checklist is known to be incomplete. Some cards have the sponsor's imprint below the photo.

		NM	EX	VG
Common Player:		3,000	1,500	900.00
(1)	Claude Berry	3,000	1,500	900.00
(2)	Frank Browning	3,000	1,500	900.00
(6)	Willard Meikle	3,000	1,500	900.00
(7)	Frank Miller	3,000	1,500	900.00
(9)	Harry Sutor	3,000	1,500	900.00
(10)	Tom Tennant	3,000	1,500	900.00
(12)	Geo. Weaver	9,000	4,500	2,700

1956-57 Gil's Drive-Ins Seattle Rainiers

(See 1956-57 Seattle Popcorn for checklist and values.)

1951-1954 Globe Printing

The team-issue card sets and souvenir picture albums listed in previous editions under the heading of Globe Printing are now found alphabetically by team name as per this list:

	NM	EX	VG
1951 Fresno Cardinals	.00	.00	.00
1951 San Jose Red Sox	.00	.00	.00
1952 Atlanta Crackers	.00	.00	.00
1952 Baltimore Orioles	.00	.00	.00
1952 Colorado Springs Sky Sox	.00	.00	.00
1952 Columbus Cardinals	.00	.00	.00
1952 Dallas Eagles	.00	.00	.00
1952 Ft. Worth Cats	.00	.00	.00
1952 Great Falls Electrics	.00	.00	.00
1952 Jamestown Falcons	.00	.00	.00
1952 Miami Beach Flamingos	.00	.00	.00
1952 Ogden Reds	.00	.00	.00
1952 Oshkosh Giants	.00	.00	.00
1952 San Diego Padres	.00	.00	.00
1952 Shawnee Hawks	.00	.00	.00
1952-1953 Sioux City Soos	.00	.00	.00
1952 Syracuse Chiefs	.00	.00	.00
1952 Ventura Braves	.00	.00	.00
1954 Sioux City Soos	.00	.00	.00

1943 Golden Quality Ice Cream Wilkes-Barre Barons

This rare war-time minor league issue depicts the Hall of Fame manager, Tony Lazzeri, and players on the Class A Eastern League Barons. The 4" x 5" black-and-white cards have facsimile player autographs. Printed in the bottom border at left are the team and year; at right is "Compliments of Golden Quality Ice Cream Co."

		NM	EX	VG
Complete Set (6):		600.00	300.00	180.00
Common Player:		75.00	37.50	22.50
(1)	Alex Damalitron	75.00	37.50	22.50
(2)	Tony Lazzeri (Bat on shoulder.)	175.00	90.00	55.00
(3)	Tony Lazzeri (Hands on knees.)	175.00	90.00	55.00
(4)	Jim McDonnell	75.00	37.50	22.50
(5)	Joe Pennington	75.00	37.50	22.50
(6)	Ned Tryon	75.00	37.50	22.50

1957 Golden State Dairy S.F. Seals Stickers

There are 23 stickers known in this set, featuring the last minor league team in San Francisco. Virtually every player who appeared in more than 10 games for the Seals that season is included in the set. The stickers measure approximately 2" x 2-1/2", are printed in black-and-white, and blank-backed. A 3-1/2" x 6" album to house the stickers was also issued, with biographical data and space for an autograph on each player's page. The stickers are checklisted here alphabetically, as the stickers are unnumbered.

		NM	EX	VG
Complete Set (23):		550.00	275.00	165.00
Common Player:		25.00	12.50	7.50
Album:		150.00	75.00	45.00
(1)	William "Bill" Abernathie	25.00	12.50	7.50
(2)	Kenneth "Chip" Aspromonte	25.00	12.50	7.50
(3)	Harry "Fritz" Dorish	25.00	12.50	7.50
(4)	Joe "Flash" Gordon	25.00	12.50	7.50
(5)	Grady Hatton Jr.	25.00	12.50	7.50
(6)	Thomas "Tommy" Hurd	25.00	12.50	7.50
(7)	Frank Kellert	25.00	12.50	7.50
(8)	Richard "Marty" Keough	25.00	12.50	7.50
(9)	Leo "Black Cat" Kiely	25.00	12.50	7.50
(10)	Harry William Malmberg	25.00	12.50	7.50
(11)	John McCall	25.00	12.50	7.50
(12)	Albert "Albie" Pearson	40.00	20.00	12.00
(13)	Jack Phillips	25.00	12.50	7.50
(14)	William "Bill" Renna	25.00	12.50	7.50
(15)	Edward "Ed" Sadowski	25.00	12.50	7.50
(16)	Robert W. Smith	25.00	12.50	7.50
(17)	Jack Spring	25.00	12.50	7.50
(18)	Joseph H. Tanner	25.00	12.50	7.50
(19)	Salvador "Sal" Taormina	25.00	12.50	7.50
(20)	Maynard "Bert" Thiel	25.00	12.50	7.50
(21)	Anthony "Nini" Tornay	25.00	12.50	7.50
(22)	Thomas "Tommy" Umphlett	25.00	12.50	7.50
(23)	Glenn "Cap" Wright	25.00	12.50	7.50

1943 Grand Studio Milwaukee Brewers

It's unknown how these blank-backed, black-and-white, 3-1/2" x 5-1/2" pictures were distributed. The only identification is "PHOTO BY GRAND STUDIO" in the lower-right corner. It's likely the pictures were sold as a set at Borchert Field.

		NM	EX	VG
Complete Set (22):		1,000	500.00	300.00
Common Player:		60.00	30.00	20.00
(1)	Joe Berry	60.00	30.00	20.00
(2)	Bob Bowman	60.00	30.00	20.00
(3)	Earl Caldwell	60.00	30.00	20.00
(4)	Grey Clarke	60.00	30.00	20.00
(5)	Merv Conner	60.00	30.00	20.00
(6)	Paul Erickson	60.00	30.00	20.00
(7)	Charlie Grimm	80.00	40.00	25.00
(8)	Hank Helf	60.00	30.00	20.00
(9)	Don Johnson	60.00	30.00	20.00
(10)	Wes Livengood	60.00	30.00	20.00
(11)	Hershell Martin	60.00	30.00	20.00
(12)	Tommy Nelson	60.00	30.00	20.00
(13)	Ted Norbert	60.00	30.00	20.00
(14)	Bill Norman	60.00	30.00	20.00
(15)	Henry Oana	125.00	65.00	40.00
(16)	Jimmy Pruett	60.00	30.00	20.00
(17)	Bill Sahlin	60.00	30.00	20.00
(18)	Frank Secroy	60.00	30.00	20.00
(19)	Red Smith	60.00	30.00	20.00
(20)	Charles Sproull	60.00	30.00	20.00
(21)	Hugh Todd	60.00	30.00	20.00
(22)	Tony York	60.00	30.00	20.00

1944 Grand Studio Milwaukee Brewers

Future Hall of Fame manager Casey Stengel is featured in the second of three annual team-issued photocard sets. The 3-1/2" x 5-1/2" cards have black-and-white portrait photos with facsimile autographs, bordered in white. Backs are blank.

		NM	EX	VG
Complete Set (26):		900.00	450.00	275.00
Common Player:		50.00	25.00	15.00
(1)	Julio Acosta	50.00	25.00	15.00
(2)	Heinz Becker	50.00	25.00	15.00
(3)	George Binks	50.00	25.00	15.00
(4)	Bob Bowman	50.00	25.00	15.00
(5)	Earl Caldwell	50.00	25.00	15.00
(6)	Dick Culler	50.00	25.00	15.00
(7)	Roy Easterwood	50.00	25.00	15.00
(8)	Jack Farmer	50.00	25.00	15.00
(9)	Charles Gassaway	50.00	25.00	15.00
(10)	Dick Hearn	50.00	25.00	15.00
(11)	Don Hendrickson	50.00	25.00	15.00
(12)	Ed Levy	50.00	25.00	15.00
(13)	Hershel Martin	50.00	25.00	15.00
(14)	Bill Nagel	50.00	25.00	15.00
(15)	Tommy Nelson	50.00	25.00	15.00
(16)	Bill Norman	50.00	25.00	15.00
(17)	Hal Peck	50.00	25.00	15.00
(18)	Jimmy Pruett	50.00	25.00	15.00
(19)	Ken Raddant	50.00	25.00	15.00
(20)	Owen Scheetz	50.00	25.00	15.00
(21)	Eddie Scheive	50.00	25.00	15.00
(22)	Frank Secory	50.00	25.00	15.00
(23)	Red Smith	50.00	25.00	15.00
(24)	Floyd Speer	50.00	25.00	15.00
(25)	Charlie Sproull	50.00	25.00	15.00
(26)	Casey Stengel	300.00	150.00	90.00

1945 Grand Studio Milwaukee Brewers

The format remained unchanged for the last of three annual team-issued photocard sets. The 3-1/2" x 5-1/2" cards have black-and-white portrait photos with facsimile autographs, bordered in white. Backs are blank.

		NM	EX	VG
Complete Set (16):		625.00	300.00	175.00
Common Player:		50.00	25.00	15.00
(1)	Julio Acosta	50.00	25.00	15.00
(2)	Arky Biggs	50.00	25.00	15.00
(3)	Bill Burgo	50.00	25.00	15.00
(4)	Nick Cullop	50.00	25.00	15.00
(5)	Wendell "Peaches" Davis	50.00	25.00	15.00
(6)	Otto Denning	50.00	25.00	15.00
(7)	Lew Flick	50.00	25.00	15.00
(8)	Don Hendrickson	50.00	25.00	15.00
(9)	Ed Kobersky	50.00	25.00	15.00
(10)	Carl Lindquist	50.00	25.00	15.00
(11)	Jack McGillen	50.00	25.00	15.00
(12)	Gene Nance	50.00	25.00	15.00
(13)	Bill Norman	50.00	25.00	15.00
(14)	Joe Rullo	50.00	25.00	15.00
(15)	Owen Scheetz	50.00	25.00	15.00
(16)	Floyd Speer	50.00	25.00	15.00

1952 Great Falls Electrics Team Issue

Formatted like the other known minor league issues from Globe Printing of San Jose, Calif., in the early 1950s, this set chronicles the 1952 version of the Class C (Pioneer League) Great Falls (Montana) Electrics, a farm club of the Brooklyn Dodgers. The blank-backed cards are black-and-white and measure about 2-1/4" x 3-3/8". An album was issued with the cards.

		NM	EX	VG
Complete Set (16):		800.00	400.00	240.00
Common Player:		60.00	30.00	18.00
(1)	Don Bricker	60.00	30.00	18.00
(2)	Larry Hampshire	60.00	30.00	18.00
(3)	Ernie Jordan	60.00	30.00	18.00
(4)	Lou Landini	60.00	30.00	18.00
(5)	Joe Oliffe	60.00	30.00	18.00
(6)	Len Payne	60.00	30.00	18.00
(7)	Lou Rochelli	60.00	30.00	18.00
(8)	Earl Silverthorn	60.00	30.00	18.00
(9)	Eddie Serrano	60.00	30.00	18.00
(10)	Rick Small	60.00	30.00	18.00
(11)	Dick Smith	60.00	30.00	18.00
(12)	Hal Snyder	60.00	30.00	18.00
(13)	Armando Suarez	60.00	30.00	18.00
(14)	Emy Unzicker	60.00	30.00	18.00
(15)				
Album:		100.00	50.00	30.00

1888 Gypsy Queen California League

Until further specimens are reported, the attributed date of issue is speculative between about 1887-89. Undiscovered until 1998 was the fact that Gypsy Queen, a cigarette manufactured by Goodwin & Co. (Old Judge, etc.) had issued minor league cards, presumably of the relatively new California League. Like some contemporary issues, the card is a stiff piece of cardboard with a sepia-toned player photo glued to it. Size is about 1-1/2" x 2-1/2". As of November 2001, only one card was known from this issue. In Fair to Good condition it was sold at auction for $80,273, then a record price for any 19th Century card.

(1)   Jas McDonald

H

1949 Hage's Dairy

Hage's Dairy of California began a three-year run of regional baseball cards featuring Pacific Coast League players in 1949. The cards were distributed inside popcorn boxes at the concession stand in Lane Field Park, home of the P.C.L. San Diego Padres. The 1949 set, like the following two years, was printed on thin stock measuring on average 2-5/8" x 3-1/8". The checklist includes several different poses for some of the players. Cards were continually being added or withdrawn to reflect roster changes on the minor league clubs. The Hage's sets were dominated by San Diego players, but also included representatives from the seven other P.C.L. teams. The 1949 cards can be found in four different tints: sepia, green, blue, and black-and-white. The unnumbered cards have blank backs or advertising messages on back. The player's name and team appear inside a box on the front of the card, and the 1949 cards can be dated by the large (quarter-inch) type used for the team names, which are sometimes referred to by city and other times by nickname.

		NM	EX	VG
Complete Set (107):		40,000	20,000	10,000
Common Player:		400.00	200.00	100.00
(1)	"Buster" Adams	400.00	200.00	100.00
(2)	"Red" Adams	400.00	200.00	100.00
(3)	Lee Anthony	400.00	200.00	100.00
(4)	Rinaldo Ardizoia	400.00	200.00	100.00
(5)	Del Baker	400.00	200.00	100.00
(6)	Ed Basinski	400.00	200.00	100.00
(7)	Jim Baxes	400.00	200.00	100.00
(8)	H. Becker	400.00	200.00	100.00
(9)	Herman Besse	400.00	200.00	100.00
(10)	Tom Bridges	400.00	200.00	100.00
(11)	Gene Brocker	400.00	200.00	100.00
(12)	Ralph Buxton	400.00	200.00	100.00
(13)	Mickey Burnett	400.00	200.00	100.00
(14)	Dain Clay (Pose)	400.00	200.00	100.00
(15)	Dain Clay (Batting)	400.00	200.00	100.00
(16)	Dain Corriden, Jim Reese	475.00	235.00	120.00
(17)	Pete Coscarart	400.00	200.00	100.00
(18)	Dom Dallessandro	400.00	200.00	100.00
(19)	Con Dempsey	400.00	200.00	100.00
(20)	Vince DiBiasi	400.00	200.00	100.00

(21)	Luke Easter (Batting stance.)	600.00	300.00	150.00
(22)	Luke Easter (Batting follow through.)	600.00	300.00	150.00
(23)	Ed Fernandez	400.00	200.00	100.00
(24)	Les Fleming	400.00	200.00	100.00
(25)	Jess Flores	400.00	200.00	100.00
(26)	Cecil Garriott	400.00	200.00	100.00
(27)	Charles Gassaway	400.00	200.00	100.00
(28)	Johnny Gorsica	400.00	200.00	100.00
(29)	Mickey Grasso	400.00	200.00	100.00
(30)	Will Hafey (Pitching)	400.00	200.00	100.00
(31)	Will Hafey (Pose)	400.00	200.00	100.00
(32)	"Jeep" Handley	400.00	200.00	100.00
(33)	"Bucky" Harris (Pose)	600.00	300.00	150.00
(34)	"Bucky" Harris (Shouting)	600.00	300.00	150.00
(35)	Roy Helser	400.00	200.00	100.00
(36)	Lloyd Hittle	400.00	200.00	100.00
(37)	Ralph Hodgin	400.00	200.00	100.00
(38)	Leroy Jarvis	400.00	200.00	100.00
(39)	John Jensen	400.00	200.00	100.00
(40)	Al Jurisich	400.00	200.00	100.00
(41)	Herb Karpel	600.00	300.00	150.00
(42)	Frank Kelleher	400.00	200.00	100.00
(43)	Bill Kelly	400.00	200.00	100.00
(44)	Bob Kelly	400.00	200.00	100.00
(45)	Frank Kerr	400.00	200.00	100.00
(46)	Thomas Kipp	400.00	200.00	100.00
(47)	Al Lien	400.00	200.00	100.00
(48)	Lyman Linde (Pose)	400.00	200.00	100.00
(49)	Lyman Linde (Pitching)	400.00	200.00	100.00
(50)	Dennis Luby	400.00	200.00	100.00
(51)	"Red" Lynn	400.00	200.00	100.00
(52)	Pat Malone	400.00	200.00	100.00
(53)	Billy Martin	1,250	625.00	375.00
(54)	Joe Marty	400.00	200.00	100.00
(55)	Cliff Melton	400.00	200.00	100.00
(56)	Steve Mesner	400.00	200.00	100.00
(57)	Leon Mohr	400.00	200.00	100.00
(58)	"Butch" Moran	400.00	200.00	100.00
(59)	Glen Moulder	400.00	200.00	100.00
(60)	Steve Nagy	400.00	200.00	100.00
(61)	Roy Nicely	400.00	200.00	100.00
(62)	Walt Nothe	400.00	200.00	100.00
(63)	John O'Neill	400.00	200.00	100.00
(64)	"Pluto" Oliver	400.00	200.00	100.00
(65)	Al Olsen (Pose)	400.00	200.00	100.00
(66)	Al Olsen (Throwing)	400.00	200.00	100.00
(67)	John Ostrowski	400.00	200.00	100.00
(68)	Roy Partee	400.00	200.00	100.00
(69)	Bill Raimondi	400.00	200.00	100.00
(70)	Bill Ramsey	400.00	200.00	100.00
(71)	Len Ratto	400.00	200.00	100.00
(72)	Xavier Rescigno	400.00	200.00	100.00
(73)	John Ritchey (Batting)	400.00	200.00	100.00
(74)	John Ritchey (Catching)	400.00	200.00	100.00
(75)	Mickey Rocco	400.00	200.00	100.00
(76)	John Rucker	400.00	200.00	100.00
(77)	Clarence Russell	400.00	200.00	100.00
(78)	Jack Salverson	400.00	200.00	100.00
(79)	Charlie Schanz	400.00	200.00	125.00
(80)	Bill Schuster	400.00	200.00	100.00
(81)	Tom Seats	400.00	200.00	100.00
(82)	Neil Sheridan	400.00	200.00	100.00
(83)	Vince Shupe	400.00	200.00	100.00
(84)	Joe Sprinz	400.00	200.00	100.00
(85)	Chuck Stevens	400.00	200.00	100.00
(86)	Harvey Storey	400.00	200.00	100.00
(87)	Jim Tabor (Sacramento)	400.00	200.00	100.00
(88)	Jim Tabor (Seattle)	400.00	200.00	100.00
(89)	"Junior" Thompson	400.00	200.00	100.00
(90)	Arky Vaughn	625.00	310.00	175.00
(91)	Jackie Warner	400.00	200.00	100.00
(92)	Jim Warner	400.00	200.00	100.00
(93)	Dick Wenner	400.00	200.00	100.00
(94)	Max West (Pose)	400.00	200.00	100.00
(95)	Max West (Batting swing.)	400.00	200.00	100.00
(96)	Max West (Batting follow through.)	400.00	200.00	100.00
(97)	Hank Weyse	400.00	200.00	100.00
(98)	"Fuzzy" White	400.00	200.00	100.00
(99)	Jo Jo White	400.00	200.00	100.00
(100)	Artie Wilson	400.00	200.00	100.00
(101)	Bill Wilson	400.00	200.00	100.00
(102)	Bobbie Wilson (Pose)	400.00	200.00	100.00
(103)	Bobbie Wilson (Fielding)	400.00	200.00	100.00
(104)	"Pinky" Woods	400.00	200.00	100.00
(105)	Tony York	400.00	200.00	100.00
(106)	Del Young	400.00	200.00	100.00
(107)	Frank Zak	400.00	200.00	100.00

1950 Hage's Dairy

The 1950 P.C.L. set from Hage's Dairy was similar in design and size (about 2-5/8" x 3-1/8") to the previous year and was again distributed in popcorn boxes at San Diego's Lane Field. The 1950 cards are in black-and-white with a back containing an advertisement for Hage's Milk, Ice Cream or Ice Cream Bars. The advertising backs also contain the player's name and either brief 1949 statistics or career highlights at bottom. Many players were issued in more than one pose.

Again, Padres dominate the unnumbered set with lesser representation from the other P.C.L. clubs. For the 1950 edition all team names are referred to by city (no nicknames) and the typeface is smaller. Gaps have been left in the assigned numbering to accommodate future additions to the checklist.

		NM	EX	VG
Complete Set (128):		45,000	22,500	13,500
Common Player:		375.00	185.00	110.00
(1)	"Buster" Adams (Kneeling)	375.00	185.00	110.00
(2a)	"Buster" Adams (Batting follow-through, with inscription.)	375.00	185.00	110.00
(2b)	"Buster" Adams (Batting follow-through, no inscription.)	375.00	185.00	110.00
(2c)	"Buster" Adams (Batting follow-through, body to left.)	375.00	185.00	110.00
(3a)	"Buster" Adams (Batting stance, caption box touching waist.)	375.00	185.00	110.00
(3b)	"Buster" Adams (Batting stance, caption box not touching waist.)	375.00	185.00	110.00
(4)	"Red" Adams	375.00	185.00	110.00
(5)	Dewey Adkins (Photo actually Albie Glossop.)	375.00	185.00	110.00
(6)	Rinaldo Ardizoia	375.00	185.00	110.00
(7)	Jose Bache	375.00	185.00	110.00
(8a)	Del Baker, Jim Reese (Bat visible at lower right.)	375.00	185.00	110.00
(8b)	Del Baker, Jim Reese (No bat visible.)	375.00	185.00	110.00
(9)	George Bamberger	375.00	185.00	110.00
(10)	Richard Barrett	375.00	185.00	110.00
(11)	Frank Baumholtz	375.00	185.00	110.00
(12)	Henry Behrman	375.00	185.00	110.00
(13)	Bill Bevens	375.00	185.00	110.00
(14)	Ernie Bickhaus	375.00	185.00	110.00
(15)	Bill Burgher (Pose)	375.00	185.00	110.00
(16)	Bill Burgher (Catching)	375.00	185.00	110.00
(17)	Mark Christman	375.00	185.00	110.00
(18)	Clint Conatser	375.00	185.00	110.00
(19)	Herb Conyers (Fielding)	375.00	185.00	110.00
(20)	Herb Conyers (Batting)	375.00	185.00	110.00
(21)	Jim Davis	375.00	185.00	110.00
(22)	Ted Del Guercio	375.00	185.00	110.00
(23)	Vince DiBiasi	375.00	185.00	110.00
(24)	Jess Dobernic	375.00	185.00	110.00
(25)	"Red" Embree (Pose)	375.00	185.00	110.00
(26)	"Red" Embree (Pitching)	375.00	185.00	110.00
(27)	Elbie Fletcher	375.00	185.00	110.00
(28)	Guy Fletcher	375.00	185.00	110.00
(30)	Tony Freitas	375.00	185.00	110.00
(31)	Denny Galehouse	375.00	185.00	110.00
(32)	Jack Graham (Pose, looking to left.)	375.00	185.00	110.00
(33)	Jack Graham (Pose, looking straight ahead.)	375.00	185.00	110.00
(34)	Jack Graham (Batting swing.)	375.00	185.00	110.00
(35)	Jack Graham (Batting stance.)	375.00	185.00	110.00
(36)	Orval Grove	375.00	185.00	110.00
(37)	Lee Handley	375.00	185.00	110.00
(38)	Ralph Hodgin	375.00	185.00	110.00
(39)	Don Johnson	375.00	185.00	110.00
(40)	Al Jurisich (Pose)	375.00	185.00	110.00
(41)	Al Jurisich (Pitching wind-up.)	375.00	185.00	110.00
(42)	Al Jurisich (Pitching follow-through.)	375.00	185.00	110.00
(43)	Bill Kelly	375.00	185.00	110.00
(44)	Frank Kerr	375.00	185.00	110.00
(45)	Tom Kipp (Pose)	375.00	185.00	110.00
(46)	Tom Kipp (Pitching)	375.00	185.00	110.00
(47)	Mel Knezovich	375.00	185.00	110.00
(48)	Red Kress	375.00	185.00	110.00
(49)	Dario Lodigiani	375.00	185.00	110.00
(50)	Dennis Luby (Pose)	375.00	185.00	110.00
(51)	Dennis Luby (Fielding)	375.00	185.00	110.00
(52)	Al Lyons	375.00	185.00	110.00
(53)	Clarence Maddern	375.00	185.00	110.00
(54)	Joe Marty	375.00	185.00	110.00
(55)	Bob McCall	375.00	185.00	110.00
(56)	Cal McIrvin	375.00	185.00	110.00
(57)	Orestes Minoso (Batting follow-through.)	850.00	425.00	250.00
(58)	Orestes Minoso (Bunting)	850.00	425.00	250.00
(59)	Leon Mohr	375.00	185.00	110.00
(60)	Dee Moore (Batting)	375.00	185.00	110.00
(61)	Dee Moore (Catching)	375.00	185.00	110.00
(62)	Jim Moran	375.00	185.00	110.00
(63)	Glen Moulder	375.00	185.00	110.00
(64)	Milt Neilsen (Pose)	375.00	185.00	110.00
(65)	Milt Neilsen (Batting)	375.00	185.00	110.00
(66)	Milt Neilsen (Throwing)	375.00	185.00	110.00
(67)	Rube Novotney	375.00	185.00	110.00
(68)	Al Olsen	375.00	185.00	110.00
(69)	Manny Perez	375.00	185.00	110.00
(70)	Bill Raemondi (Raimondi)	375.00	185.00	110.00
(71)	Len Ratto	375.00	185.00	110.00
(72)	Mickey Rocco	375.00	185.00	110.00
(73)	Marv Rotblatt	375.00	185.00	110.00
(74)	Lynwood Rowe (Pose)	400.00	200.00	120.00
(75)	Lynwood Rowe (Pitching)	400.00	200.00	120.00
(76)	Clarence Russell	375.00	185.00	110.00
(77)	Hal Saltzman (Pitching follow-through.)	375.00	185.00	110.00
(78)	Hal Saltzman (Pitching wind-up.)	375.00	185.00	110.00
(79)	Hal Saltzman (Pitching, leg in air.)	375.00	185.00	110.00
(81)	Mike Sandlock	375.00	185.00	110.00
(82)	Bob Savage (Pose)	375.00	185.00	110.00
(83)	Bob Savage (Pitching)	375.00	185.00	110.00
(84)	Charlie Schanz	375.00	185.00	110.00
(85)	Bill Schuster	375.00	185.00	110.00
(86)	Neill Sheridan	375.00	185.00	110.00
(87)	Harry Simpson (Batting swing)	525.00	260.00	150.00
(88)	Harry Simpson (Batting stance.)	525.00	260.00	150.00
(89)	Harry Simpson (Batting stance, close up.)	525.00	260.00	150.00
(90)	Harry Simpson (Batting follow-through.)	525.00	260.00	150.00

		NM	EX	VG
(91)	Elmer Singleton	375.00	185.00	110.00
(92)	Al Smith (Pose)	375.00	185.00	110.00
(93)	Al Smith (Batting stance.)	375.00	185.00	110.00
(94)	Al Smith (Fielding)	375.00	185.00	110.00
(95)	Alphonse Smith (Glove above knee.)	375.00	185.00	110.00
(96)	Alphonse Smith (Glove below knee.)	375.00	185.00	110.00
(97)	Steve Souchock	375.00	185.00	110.00
(98)	Jim Steiner	375.00	185.00	110.00
(99)	Harvey Storey (Batting stance.)	375.00	185.00	110.00
(100)	Harvey Storey (Swinging bat.)	375.00	185.00	110.00
(101)	Harvey Storey (Throwing)	375.00	185.00	110.00
(102)	Harvey Storey (Fielding, ball in glove.)	375.00	185.00	110.00
(103)	Max Surkont	375.00	185.00	110.00
(104)	Jim Tabor	375.00	185.00	110.00
(105)	Forrest Thompson	375.00	185.00	110.00
(106)	Mike Tresh (Pose)	375.00	185.00	110.00
(107)	Mike Tresh (Catching)	375.00	185.00	110.00
(108)	Ben Wade	375.00	185.00	110.00
(109)	Kenny Washington	375.00	185.00	110.00
(110)	Bill Waters (Pose)	375.00	185.00	110.00
(111)	Bill Waters (Pitching)	375.00	185.00	110.00
(112)	Roy Welmaker (Pose)	375.00	185.00	110.00
(113)	Roy Welmaker (Pitching)	375.00	185.00	110.00
(114)	Max West (Pose)	375.00	185.00	110.00
(115)	Max West (Batting stance.)	375.00	185.00	110.00
(116)	Max West (Kneeling)	375.00	185.00	110.00
(117)	Max West (Batting follow-through.)	375.00	185.00	110.00
(118)	Al White	375.00	185.00	110.00
(119)	"Whitey" Wietelmann (Pose)	375.00	185.00	110.00
(120)	"Whitey" Wietelmann (Bunting)	375.00	185.00	110.00
(121)	"Whitey" Wietelmann (Batting stance.)	375.00	185.00	110.00
(122)	"Whitey" Wietelmann (Throwing)	375.00	185.00	110.00
(123)	Bobbie Wilson	375.00	185.00	110.00
(124)	Bobby Wilson	375.00	185.00	110.00
(125)	Roy Zimmerman	375.00	185.00	110.00
(126)	George Zuverink	375.00	185.00	110.00

1951 Hage's Dairy

The final year of the Hage's P.C.L. issues saw the set reduced to 53 different unnumbered cards, all but 12 of them Padres. Among them are seven cards of Cleveland Indians players, which were issued during an exhibition series with the major league club, and six cards picturing members of the Hollywood Stars. No other P.C.L. teams are represented. The cards maintained the same size and style of the previous two years but were printed in more color tints, including blue, green, burgundy, gold, gray and sepia (but not black-and-white). The 1951 cards have blank backs and were again distributed in popcorn boxes at the San Diego stadium. The 1951 cards are the most common of the three sets issued by Hage's Dairy. The Indians and Stars players were issued in lesser quantities than the Padres, however, and command a higher value.

		NM	EX	VG
Complete Set (54):		18,000	9,000	5,500
Common Player:		300.00	150.00	90.00
(1)	"Buster" Adams	300.00	150.00	90.00
(2)	Del Baker	300.00	150.00	90.00
(3)	Ray Boone	850.00	425.00	250.00
(4)	Russ Christopher	300.00	150.00	90.00
(5)	Allie Clark	850.00	425.00	250.00
(6)	Herb Conyers	300.00	150.00	90.00
(7)	Luke Easter	450.00	225.00	135.00
(8)	"Red" Embree (Pitching, foot in air.)	300.00	150.00	90.00
(9)	"Red" Embree (Pitching, hands up.)	300.00	150.00	90.00
(10)	Jess Flores	850.00	425.00	250.00
(11)	Murray Franklin	300.00	150.00	90.00
(12)	Jack Graham (Portrait)	300.00	150.00	90.00
(13)	Jack Graham (Batting)	300.00	150.00	90.00
(14)	Gene Handley	300.00	150.00	90.00
(15)	Charles Harris	300.00	150.00	90.00
(16)	Sam Jones (Pitching, hands back.)	300.00	150.00	90.00
(17)	Sam Jones (Pitching, hands up.)	300.00	150.00	90.00
(18)	Sam Jones (Pitching, leg in air.)	300.00	150.00	90.00
(19)	Al Jurisich	300.00	150.00	90.00
(20)	Frank Kerr (Batting)	300.00	150.00	90.00
(21)	Frank Kerr (Catching)	300.00	150.00	90.00
(22)	Dick Kinaman	300.00	150.00	90.00
(23)	Clarence Maddern (Batting)	300.00	150.00	90.00
(24)	Clarence Maddern (Fielding)	300.00	150.00	90.00
(25)	Harry Malmberg (Bunting)	300.00	150.00	90.00
(26)	Harry Malmberg (Batting follow-through.)	300.00	150.00	90.00
(27)	Harry Malmberg (Fielding)	300.00	150.00	90.00
(28)	Gordon Maltzberger	300.00	150.00	90.00
(29)	Al Olsen (Cleveland)	850.00	425.00	250.00

		NM	EX	VG
(30)	Al Olsen (San Diego)	300.00	150.00	90.00
(31)	Jimmy Reese (Clapping)	350.00	175.00	100.00
(32)	Jimmy Reese (Hands on knees.)	350.00	175.00	100.00
(33)	Al Rosen	900.00	450.00	270.00
(34)	Joe Rowell	300.00	150.00	90.00
(35)	Mike Sandlock	300.00	150.00	90.00
(36)	George Schmees	300.00	150.00	90.00
(37)	Harry Simpson	300.00	150.00	90.00
(38)	Charlie Sipple	300.00	150.00	90.00
(39)	Harvey Storey (Batting follow-through.)	300.00	150.00	90.00
(40)	Harvey Storey (Batting stance.)	300.00	150.00	90.00
(41)	Harvey Storey (Fielding)	300.00	150.00	90.00
(42)	Jack Tobin	300.00	150.00	90.00
(43)	Frank Tornay	300.00	150.00	90.00
(44)	Thurman Tucker	300.00	150.00	90.00
(45)	Ben Wade	300.00	150.00	90.00
(46)	Roy Welmaker	300.00	150.00	90.00
(47)	Leroy Wheat	300.00	150.00	90.00
(48)	Don White	300.00	150.00	90.00
(49)	"Whitey" Wietelman (Batting)	300.00	150.00	90.00
(50)	"Whitey" Wietelman (Fielding)	300.00	150.00	90.00
(51)	Bobby Wilson (Batting)	300.00	150.00	90.00
(52)	Bobby Wilson (Fielding)	300.00	150.00	90.00
(53)	Tony York	300.00	150.00	90.00
(54)	George Zuverink	850.00	425.00	250.00

1886 Hancock's Syracuse Stars

Currently representing the earliest known minor league baseball cards is this issue by a Syracuse department store's menswear department. The 1-5/8" x 3-3/16" cards feature sepia photos glued to a stiff black cardboard backing with a gilt edge. The photos show the players in suits, presumably from the sponsor's racks. Backs have the player name and position printed at top. At center is an ad for Hancock's. At bottom is a credit line to "Goodwin" as photographer. Each card is currently known in only a single example. It is possible other players of the International League Stars may yet be discovered.

Values Undetermined				
(1)	Richard D. Buckley	.00	.00	.00
(2)	Douglas Crothers (SGC-graded Ex., 2005 auction, $18,304.)	.00	.00	.00
(3)	Philip H. Tomney	.00	.00	.00

1960 Henry House Wieners Seattle Rainiers

Eighteen different cards are known in this hot dog set; most players played major league prior to their appearance with the Pacific Coast League Seattle Rainiers in 1960. Printed in red, the 4-1/2" x 3-3/4" cards are skip-numbered by player uniform number.

		NM	EX	VG
Complete Set (18):		5,500	2,750	1,600
Common Player:		300.00	150.00	90.00
2	Harry Malmberg	300.00	150.00	90.00
3	Francisco Obregon	300.00	150.00	90.00
4	Johnny O'Brien	375.00	185.00	110.00
5	Gordon Coleman	300.00	150.00	90.00
6	Bill Hain	300.00	150.00	90.00
8	Dick Sisler	300.00	150.00	90.00
9	Jerry Zimmerman	300.00	150.00	90.00
10	Hal Bevan	300.00	150.00	90.00

		NM	EX	VG
14	Rudy Regaldo	300.00	150.00	90.00
15	Paul Pettit	300.00	150.00	90.00
20	Buddy Gilbert	300.00	150.00	90.00
21	Erv Palica	300.00	150.00	90.00
22	Joe Taylor	300.00	150.00	90.00
25	Bill Kennedy	300.00	150.00	90.00
26	Dave Stenhouse	300.00	150.00	90.00
28	Ray Ripplemeyer	300.00	150.00	90.00
30	Charlie Beamon	300.00	150.00	90.00
33	Don Rudolph	300.00	150.00	90.00

1888 S.F. Hess California League (N321)

One of several tobacco card sets produced by S.F. Hess & Co. of Rochester, this rare 40-card issue features players from the California League. The cards measure 2-7/8" x 1-1/2" and feature color drawings of players. The player's name and team are printed along the top margin of the card, while the words "S.F. Hess and Co.'s/Creole Cigarettes" appear at the bottom. "California League" is also printed in large capital letters above the player drawing, while the 1888 copyright date appears below. There are 35 players (including one umpire) in the set, and five players are pictured on two cards each, resulting in 40 different cards. One example each of 30 of the cards have been discovered printed on thin paper stock, though the exact nature of that version is undetermined; currently values are about equal to the regular-issue version.

		NM	EX	VG
Common Player:		5,400	3,000	2,250
(1)	Bennett	5,400	3,000	2,250
(2)	Borchers	5,400	3,000	2,250
(3)	Buckley	5,400	3,000	2,250
(4)	Burke (Batting)	5,400	3,000	2,250
(5)	Burke (Ready to pitch.)	5,400	3,000	2,250
(6)	Burnett	5,400	3,000	2,250
(7)	Carroll	5,400	3,000	2,250
(8)	Donohue	5,400	3,000	2,250
(9)	Donovan	5,400	3,000	2,250
(10)	Finn	5,400	3,000	2,250
(11)	Gagus	5,400	3,000	2,250
(12)	Hanley	5,400	3,000	2,250
(13)	Hardie (C., wearing mask.)	5,400	3,000	2,250
(14)	Hardie (C.F., with bat.)	5,400	3,000	2,250
(15)	Hayes	5,400	3,000	2,250
(16)	Lawton	5,400	3,000	2,250
(17)	Levy	5,400	3,000	2,250
(18)	Long	5,400	3,000	2,250
(19)	McCord	5,400	3,000	2,250
(20)	Meegan	5,400	3,000	2,250
(21)	Moore	5,400	3,000	2,250
(22)	Mullee	5,400	3,000	2,250
(23)	Newhert	5,400	3,000	2,250
(24)	Noonan	5,400	3,000	2,250
(25)	O'Day	5,400	3,000	2,250
(26)	Perrier	5,400	3,000	2,250
(27)	Powers (1st B., catching)	5,400	3,000	2,250
(28)	Powers (1st B. & Capt., with bat)	5,400	3,000	2,250
(29)	Ryan	5,400	3,000	2,250
(30)	Selna	5,400	3,000	2,250
(31)	Shea	5,400	3,000	2,250
(32)	J. Sheridan (Umpire)	5,400	3,000	2,250
(33)	"Big" Smith	5,400	3,000	2,250
(34)	H. Smith	5,400	3,000	2,250
(35)	J. Smith	5,400	3,000	2,250
(36)	Smett	5,400	3,000	2,250
(37)	Stockwell (Throwing)	5,400	3,000	2,250
(38)	Stockwell (With bat.)	5,400	3,000	2,250
(39)	Sweeney	5,400	3,000	2,250
(40)	Whitehead	5,400	3,000	2,250

1888 S.F. Hess California League (N338-1)

This tobacco card set picturing players from the California League is one of the rarest of all 19th Century issues. Issued in the late 1880s by S.F. Hess & Co. of Rochester, these 2-7/8" x 1-1/2" cards are so rare that only several examples are known to exist. Some of the photos in the N338-1 set are identical to the drawings in the N321 set, issued by S.F. Hess in 1888. The N338-1 cards are found with the words "California League" printed in an arc either above or below the player photo. The player's name appears below the photo. At the bottom of the card the words "S.F. Hess & Co.'s Creole Cigarettes" are printed in a rolling style.

		NM	EX	VG
Common Player:		18,000	9,000	5,250
(1)	Borsher	18,000	9,000	5,250
(2)	Buckley	18,000	9,000	5,250
(3)	Carroll	18,000	9,000	5,250
(4)	Ebright	18,000	9,000	5,250
(5)	Gagur (Gagus)	18,000	9,000	5,250
(6)	Incell	18,000	9,000	5,250
(7)	Lawton	18,000	9,000	5,250
(8)	Levy (Throwing)	18,000	9,000	5,250
(9)	Levy (With bat.)	18,000	9,000	5,250
(10)	McDonald	18,000	9,000	5,250
(11)	McGinty	20,250	10,125	6,075
(12)	Meegan	18,000	9,000	5,250
(13)	Newhert	18,000	9,000	5,250
(14)	Noonan	18,000	9,000	5,250
(15)	Perrier	18,000	9,000	5,250
(16)	Perrier, H. Smith	18,000	9,000	5,250
(17)	Ryan	18,000	9,000	5,250
(18)	J. Smith, N. Smith	18,000	9,000	5,250
(19)	Sweeney	18,000	9,000	5,250

1888 S.F. Hess Newsboys League (N333)

Although not picturing professional baseball players, these cards issued by S.F. Hess and Co. have a baseball theme. Cards measure 1-1/2" x 2-7/8" and feature pictures of "newsies" from papers in eight different cities (Rochester, Cleveland, Philadelphia, Boston, Albany, Detroit, New York and Syracuse). The boys are pictured in a photographs wearing baseball uniforms, often bearing the name of their newspaper. The boy's name, position and newspaper are printed below, while the words "Newsboys League" appears in capital letters at the top of the card. No identification is provided for the four Philadelphia newsboys, so a photo description is provided in the checklist that follows. Gaps have been left in the assigned numbering for future additions.

		NM	EX	VG
Common Player:		2,400	1,200	725.00
(1)	R.J. Bell	2,400	1,200	725.00
(2)	Bibby (Boston Globe)	2,400	1,200	725.00
(3)	Binden	2,400	1,200	725.00
(4)	Bowen	2,400	1,200	725.00
(5)	Boyle	2,400	1,200	725.00
(6)	Britcher	2,400	1,200	725.00
(7)	Caine	2,400	1,200	725.00
(8)	I. Cohen	2,400	1,200	725.00
(9)	R. Cohen	2,400	1,200	725.00
(10)	Collins (Boston Globe)	2,400	1,200	725.00
(11)	Cross	2,400	1,200	725.00
(12)	F. Cuddy	2,400	1,200	725.00
(13)	E. Daisey	2,400	1,200	725.00
(14)	Davis	2,400	1,200	725.00
(15)	B. Dinsmore	2,400	1,200	725.00
(16)	Donovan	2,400	1,200	725.00
(17)	A. Downer	2,400	1,200	725.00
(18)	Fanelly	2,400	1,200	725.00
(19)	J. Flood	2,400	1,200	725.00
(21)	C. Gallagher	2,400	1,200	725.00
(22)	M.H. Gallagher	2,400	1,200	725.00
(23)	D. Galligher	2,400	1,200	725.00
(24)	J. Galligher	2,400	1,200	725.00
(25)	Haskins	2,400	1,200	725.00
(26)	Herze	2,400	1,200	725.00

(27)	Holmes (Press & Knickerbocker)	2,400	1,200	725.00
(28)	F. Horan	2,400	1,200	725.00
(29)	Hosler	2,400	1,200	725.00
(30)	Hyde	2,400	1,200	725.00
(31)	Keilty	2,400	1,200	725.00
(32)	C. Kellogg	2,400	1,200	725.00
(33)	Mahoney (Rochester Post-Express)	2,400	1,200	725.00
(34)	Mayer	2,400	1,200	725.00
(35)	McCourt (Boston Globe)	2,400	1,200	725.00
(36)	I. McDonald	2,400	1,200	725.00
(37)	McDowell (Rochester)	2,400	1,200	725.00
(38)	McGrady	2,400	1,200	725.00
(39)	O'Brien	2,400	1,200	725.00
(41)	E.C. Murphy	2,400	1,200	725.00
(42)	Sabin	2,400	1,200	725.00
(43)	Shedd	2,400	1,200	725.00
(44)	R. Sheehan	2,400	1,200	725.00
(45)	Smith	2,400	1,200	725.00
(46)	Talbot	2,400	1,200	725.00
(47)	Walsh	2,400	1,200	725.00
(48)	Whitman	2,400	1,200	725.00
(49)	Yeomans	2,400	1,200	725.00
(50)	Cleveland Newsboy (In cap, facing right.)	2,400	1,200	725.00
(51)	Philadelphia Newsboy (Hair parted on right side.)	2,400	1,200	725.00
(52)	Philadelphia Newsboy (Hair parted on left side.)	2,400	1,200	725.00
(53)	Philadelphia Newsboy (No part in hair.)	2,400	1,200	725.00
(54)	Philadelphia Newsboy (Head shaved.)	2,400	1,200	725.00

1949 Hollywood Stars Team Issue

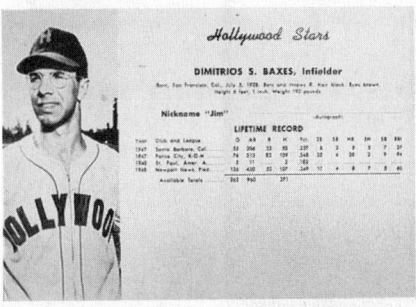

A team issue probably related to similar 1948-49 cards produced by Pacific Coast League cross-town rivals the L.A. Angels, these cards were likely produced by the publisher of the teams' yearbooks and sold at stadium souvenir stands. The cards are blank-backed, printed in black-and-white on thin semi-gloss cardboard, measuring 7-1/16" x 4-7/8". Portrait or posed action photos appear at left with complete major and minor league stats at right. A space for an autograph appears beneath the player's biographical data. The unnumbered cards are checklisted here in alphabetical order.

		NM	EX	VG
Complete Set (24):		500.00	250.00	150.00
Common Player:		25.00	12.50	7.50
(1)	Jim Baxes	25.00	12.50	7.50
(2)	George Fallon	25.00	12.50	7.50
(3)	John Fitzpatrick	25.00	12.50	7.50
(4)	George Genovese	25.00	12.50	7.50
(5)	Herb Gorman	75.00	37.50	22.50
(6)	Gene Handley	25.00	12.50	7.50
(7)	Fred Haney	25.00	12.50	7.50
(8)	Jim Hughes	25.00	12.50	7.50
(9)	Frank Kelleher	25.00	12.50	7.50
(10)	Gordy Maltzberger	25.00	12.50	7.50
(11)	Glen Moulder	25.00	12.50	7.50
(12)	Irv Noren	25.00	12.50	7.50
(13)	Ed Oliver	25.00	12.50	7.50
(14)	Karl Olsen	25.00	12.50	7.50
(15)	John O'Neil	25.00	12.50	7.50
(16)	Jack Paepke	25.00	12.50	7.50
(17)	Willard Ramsdell	25.00	12.50	7.50
(18)	Jack Salveson	25.00	12.50	7.50
(19)	Mike Sandlock	25.00	12.50	7.50
(20)	Art Shallock	25.00	12.50	7.50
(21)	Andy Skurski	25.00	12.50	7.50
(22)	Chuck Stevens	25.00	12.50	7.50
(23)	Al Unser	25.00	12.50	7.50
(24)	George Woods	25.00	12.50	7.50

1950 Hollywood Stars Team Issue

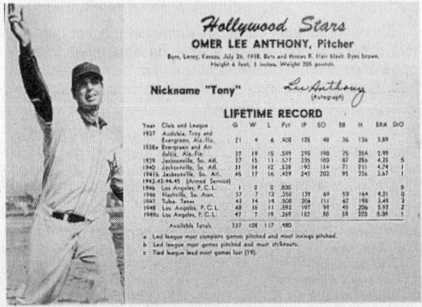

Virtually identical in format to the previous year's issue, the 1950 set differs principally in the inclusion of a facsimile autograph on front. In 1950, the Hollywood Stars were the PCL affiliate of the Brooklyn Dodgers. Both sets were listed in "The American Card Catalog" as W720.

		NM	EX	VG
Complete Set (32):		850.00	425.00	250.00
Common Player:		25.00	12.50	7.50
(1)	Lee Anthony	25.00	12.50	7.50
(2)	Bill Antonello	25.00	12.50	7.50
(3)	Dick Barrett	25.00	12.50	7.50
(4)	Jim Baxes	25.00	12.50	7.50
(5)	Clint Conatser	25.00	12.50	7.50
(6)	Cliff Dapper	25.00	12.50	7.50
(7)	George Fallon	25.00	12.50	7.50
(8)	John Fitzpatrick	25.00	12.50	7.50
(9)	Murray Franklin	25.00	12.50	7.50
(10)	Herb Gorman	75.00	37.50	22.50
(11)	Gene Handley	25.00	12.50	7.50
(12)	Fred Haney	25.00	12.50	7.50
(13)	Clarence Hicks	25.00	12.50	7.50
(14)	Herb Karpel	200.00	100.00	60.00
(15)	Frank Kelleher	25.00	12.50	7.50
(16)	Ken Lehman	25.00	12.50	7.50
(17)	Johnny Lindell	25.00	12.50	7.50
(18)	Gordy Maltzberger	25.00	12.50	7.50
(19)	Dan Menendez	25.00	12.50	7.50
(20)	Pershing Mondroff	25.00	12.50	7.50
(21)	Glen Moulder	25.00	12.50	7.50
(22)	John O'Neil	25.00	12.50	7.50
(23)	Jack Paepke	25.00	12.50	7.50
(24)	Jean Roy	25.00	12.50	7.50
(25)	Jack Salveson	25.00	12.50	7.50
(26)	Mike Sandlock	25.00	12.50	7.50
(27)	Ed Saver	25.00	12.50	7.50
(28)	George Schmees	25.00	12.50	7.50
(29)	Art Shallock	25.00	12.50	7.50
(30)	Chuck Stevens	25.00	12.50	7.50
(31)	Ben Wade	25.00	12.50	7.50
(32)	George Woods	25.00	12.50	7.50

1957 Hollywood Stars Team Issue

Presumably issued by the team, which had a working relationship with the Pittsburgh Pirates, this 23-card set features black-and-white blank-backed photos in a 4-1/8" x 6-3/16" format. Each picture has a facsimile autograph printed in black across the front. The unnumbered cards are checklisted here alphabetically.

		NM	EX	VG
Complete Set (23):		900.00	450.00	275.00
Common Player:		40.00	20.00	12.00
(1)	Jim Baumer	40.00	20.00	12.00
(2)	Carlos Bernier	40.00	20.00	12.00
(3)	Bill Causion	40.00	20.00	12.00
(4)	Chuck Churn	40.00	20.00	12.00
(5)	Bennie Daniels	40.00	20.00	12.00
(6)	Joe Duhem	40.00	20.00	12.00
(7)	John Fitzpatrick	40.00	20.00	12.00
(8)	Bob Garber	40.00	20.00	12.00
(9)	Bill Hall	40.00	20.00	12.00
(10)	Forrest "Spook" Jacobs	50.00	25.00	15.00
(11)	Clyde King	40.00	20.00	12.00
(12)	Nick Koback	40.00	20.00	12.00
(13)	Pete Naton	40.00	20.00	12.00
(14)	George O'Donnell	40.00	20.00	12.00
(15)	Paul Pettit	40.00	20.00	12.00
(16)	Curt Raydon	40.00	20.00	12.00
(17)	Leo Rodriguez	40.00	20.00	12.00
(18)	Don Rowe	40.00	20.00	12.00
(19)	Dick Smith	40.00	20.00	12.00
(20)	R.C. Stevens	40.00	20.00	12.00
(21)	Ben Wade	40.00	20.00	12.00
(22)	Fred Waters	40.00	20.00	12.00
(23)	George Witt	40.00	20.00	12.00

1912 Home Run Kisses (E136)

This 90-card set of Pacific Coast League players was produced in 1912 by the San Francisco candy company of Collins-McCarthy. Each card measures about 2-1/4" x 4-3/16" and features sepia-toned player photos surrounded by an ornate frame. The front of the card has the words "Home Run Kisses" above the player's name. Most cards found are blank-backed, but others exist with a back that advises "Save Home Run Kisses Pictures for Valuable Premiums" along with other details of the Collins-McCarthy promotion. A third type of back exists with an advertising logo for "BARDELL / SEPIA/ SAN FRANCISCO." Redeemed cards were punch-cancelled, often with a heart-shaped hole.

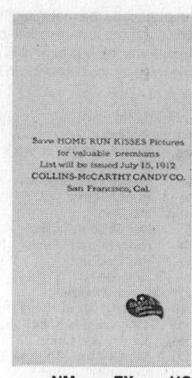

		NM	EX	VG
	Complete Set (90):	70,000	28,000	16,000
	Common Player:	750.00	300.00	185.00
(1)	Ables	750.00	300.00	185.00
(2)	Agnew	750.00	300.00	185.00
(3)	Altman	750.00	300.00	185.00
(4)	Frank Arrelanes (Arellanes)	750.00	300.00	185.00
(5)	Auer	750.00	300.00	185.00
(6)	Bancroft	3,500	1,400	875.00
(7)	Bayless	750.00	300.00	185.00
(8)	Berry	750.00	300.00	185.00
(9)	Boles	750.00	300.00	185.00
(10)	Brashear	750.00	300.00	185.00
(11)	Brooks (Los Angeles)	750.00	300.00	185.00
(12)	Brooks (Oakland)	750.00	300.00	185.00
(13)	Brown	750.00	300.00	185.00
(14)	Burrell	750.00	300.00	185.00
(15)	Butler	750.00	300.00	185.00
(16)	Carlisle	750.00	300.00	185.00
(17)	Carson	750.00	300.00	185.00
(18)	Castleton	750.00	300.00	185.00
(19)	Chadbourne	750.00	300.00	185.00
(20)	Check	750.00	300.00	185.00
(21)	Core	750.00	300.00	185.00
(22)	Corhan	750.00	300.00	185.00
(23)	Coy	750.00	300.00	185.00
(24)	Daley	750.00	300.00	185.00
(25)	Dillon	750.00	300.00	185.00
(26)	Doane	750.00	300.00	185.00
(27)	Driscoll	750.00	300.00	185.00
(28)	Fisher	750.00	300.00	185.00
(29)	Flater	750.00	300.00	185.00
(30)	Gaddy	750.00	300.00	185.00
(31)	Gregg	750.00	300.00	185.00
(32)	Gregory	750.00	300.00	185.00
(33)	Harkness	750.00	300.00	185.00
(34)	Heitmuller	750.00	300.00	185.00
(35)	Henley	750.00	300.00	185.00
(36)	Hiester	750.00	300.00	185.00
(37)	Hoffman	750.00	300.00	185.00
(38)	Hogan	750.00	300.00	185.00
(39)	Hosp	750.00	300.00	185.00
(40)	Howley	750.00	300.00	185.00
(41)	Ireland	750.00	300.00	185.00
(42)	Johnson	750.00	300.00	185.00
(43)	Kane	750.00	300.00	185.00
(44)	Klawitter	750.00	300.00	185.00
(45)	Kreitz	750.00	300.00	185.00
(46)	Krueger	750.00	300.00	185.00
(47)	Leard	750.00	300.00	185.00
(48)	Leverenz	750.00	300.00	185.00
(49)	Lewis	750.00	300.00	185.00
(50)	Bill Lindsay	750.00	300.00	185.00
(51)	Litschi	750.00	300.00	185.00
(52)	Lober	750.00	300.00	185.00
(53)	Malarkey	750.00	300.00	185.00
(54)	Martinoni	750.00	300.00	185.00
(55)	McArdle	750.00	300.00	185.00
(56)	McCorry	750.00	300.00	185.00
(57)	McDowell	750.00	300.00	185.00
(58)	McIver	750.00	300.00	185.00
(59)	Metzger	750.00	300.00	185.00
(60)	Miller	750.00	300.00	185.00
(61)	Mundorf	750.00	300.00	185.00
(62)	Nagle	750.00	300.00	185.00
(63)	Noyes	750.00	300.00	185.00
(64)	Olmstead	750.00	300.00	185.00
(65)	O'Rourke	750.00	300.00	185.00
(66)	Page	750.00	300.00	185.00
(67)	Parkins	750.00	300.00	185.00
(68)	Patterson (Oakland)	750.00	300.00	185.00
(69)	Patterson (Vernon)	750.00	300.00	185.00
(70)	Pernoll	750.00	300.00	185.00
(71)	Powell	750.00	300.00	185.00
(72)	Price	750.00	300.00	185.00
(73)	Raftery	750.00	300.00	185.00
(74)	Raleigh	750.00	300.00	185.00
(75)	Rogers	750.00	300.00	185.00
(76)	Schmidt	750.00	300.00	185.00
(77)	Schwenk	750.00	300.00	185.00
(78)	Sheehan	750.00	300.00	185.00
(79)	Shinn	750.00	300.00	185.00
(80)	Slagle	750.00	300.00	185.00
(81)	Smith	750.00	300.00	185.00
(82)	Stone	750.00	300.00	185.00
(83)	Swain	750.00	300.00	185.00
(84)	Taylor	750.00	300.00	185.00
(85)	Tiedeman	750.00	300.00	185.00
(86)	Toner	750.00	300.00	185.00
(87)	Tozer	750.00	300.00	185.00
(88)	Van Buren	750.00	300.00	185.00
(89)	Williams	750.00	300.00	185.00
(90)	Zacher	750.00	300.00	185.00

1940 Hughes Frozen Confections Sacramento Solons

These borderless 2" x 3" black-and-white cards of the Sacramento Solons can be found in two versions, either blank-backed or with the 1940 Solons Pacific Coast League schedule printed on back. Fronts featured action poses with a facsimile autograph.

		NM	EX	VG
	Complete Set (20):	7,500	3,750	2,250
	Common Player:	400.00	200.00	125.00
(1)	Mel Almada	400.00	200.00	125.00
(2)	Frank Asbell	400.00	200.00	125.00
(3)	Larry Barton	400.00	200.00	125.00
(4)	Robert Blattner	400.00	200.00	125.00
(5)	Bennie Borgmann	400.00	200.00	125.00
(6)	Tony Freitas	400.00	200.00	125.00
(7)	Art Garibaldi	400.00	200.00	125.00
(8)	Jim Grilk	400.00	200.00	125.00
(9)	Gene Handley	400.00	200.00	125.00
(10)	Oscar Judd	400.00	200.00	125.00
(11)	Lynn King	400.00	200.00	125.00
(12)	Norbert Kleinke	400.00	200.00	125.00
(13)	Max Marshall	400.00	200.00	125.00
(14)	William McLaughlin	400.00	200.00	125.00
(15)	Bruce Ogrodowski	400.00	200.00	125.00
(16)	Franich Riel	400.00	200.00	125.00
(17)	Bill Schmidt	400.00	200.00	125.00
(18)	Melvin Wasley	400.00	200.00	125.00
(19)	Chet Wieczorek	400.00	200.00	125.00
(20)	Deb Williams	400.00	200.00	125.00

1957 Hygrade Meats Seattle Rainiers

While the front of the cards mentions a complete set of 22 cards, only a dozen have been checklisted to date. The round-cornered cards measure 4-1/2" x 3-3/4" and are printed in red on white. Backs are blank. The cards feature only players of the Pacific Coast League Seattle Rainiers. The cards are unnumbered.

		NM	EX	VG
	Common Player:	400.00	200.00	120.00
(1)	Dick Aylward	400.00	200.00	120.00
(2)	Bob Balcena	400.00	200.00	120.00
(3)	Jim Dyck	400.00	200.00	120.00
(4)	Marion Fricano	400.00	200.00	120.00
(5)	Bill Glynn	400.00	200.00	120.00
(6)	Larry Jansen	400.00	200.00	120.00
(7)	Bill Kennedy	400.00	200.00	120.00
(8)	Jack Lohrke	400.00	200.00	120.00
(9)	Frank O'Doul	800.00	400.00	240.00
(10)	Ray Orteig	400.00	200.00	120.00
(11)	Joe Taylor	400.00	200.00	120.00
(12)	Morrie (Maury) Wills	800.00	400.00	240.00

I

1912 Imperial Tobacco (C46)

This minor league set, issued in 1912 by the Imperial Tobacco Co., is the only tobacco baseball set issued in Canada. Designated as C46 in the American Card Catalog, each sepia-toned card measures 1-1/2" x 2-5/8" and features a distinctive card design that pictures the player inside an oval surrounded by a simulated woodgrain background featuring a

bat, ball and glove in the borders. The player's last name appears in capital letters in a panel beneath the oval. (An exception is the card of James Murray, whose caption includes both first and last names.) The backs include the player's name and team at the top, followed by a brief biography. The 90 subjects in the set are members of the eight teams in the Eastern League (Rochester, Toronto, Buffalo, Newark, Providence, Baltimore, Montreal and Jersey City), even though the card backs refer to it as the International League. The set contains many players with major league experience, including Hall of Famers Joe Kelley and Joe "Iron Man" McGinnity.

		NM	EX	VG
	Complete Set (90):	13,000	6,500	4,000
	Common Player:	150.00	75.00	40.00
1	William O'Hara	180.00	90.00	55.00
2	James McGinley	160.00	80.00	50.00
3	"Frenchy" LeClaire	150.00	75.00	40.00
4	John White	150.00	75.00	40.00
5	James Murray	150.00	75.00	40.00
6	Joe Ward	150.00	75.00	40.00
7	Whitey Alperman	150.00	75.00	40.00
8	"Natty" Nattress	150.00	75.00	40.00
9	Fred Sline	150.00	75.00	40.00
10	Royal Rock	150.00	75.00	40.00
11	Ray Demmitt	150.00	75.00	40.00
12	"Butcher Boy" Schmidt	150.00	75.00	40.00
13	Samuel Frock	150.00	75.00	40.00
14	Fred Burchell	150.00	75.00	40.00
15	Jack Kelley	150.00	75.00	40.00
16	Frank Barberich	150.00	75.00	40.00
17	Frank Corridon	150.00	75.00	40.00
18	"Doc" Adkins	150.00	75.00	40.00
19	Jack Dunn	150.00	75.00	40.00
20	James Walsh	150.00	75.00	40.00
21	Charles Hanford	150.00	75.00	40.00
22	Dick Rudolph	150.00	75.00	40.00
23	Curt Elston	150.00	75.00	40.00
24	Phil Silton (Sitton)	150.00	75.00	40.00
25	Charlie French	150.00	75.00	40.00
26	John Ganzel	150.00	75.00	40.00
27	Joe Kelley	750.00	375.00	230.00
28	Benny Meyers	150.00	75.00	40.00
29	George Schirm	150.00	75.00	40.00
30	William Purtell	150.00	75.00	40.00
31	Bayard Sharpe	150.00	75.00	40.00
32	Tony Smith	150.00	75.00	40.00
33	John Lush	150.00	75.00	40.00
34	William Collins	150.00	75.00	40.00
35	Art Phelan	150.00	75.00	40.00
36	Edward Phelps	150.00	75.00	40.00
37	"Rube" Vickers	150.00	75.00	40.00
38	Cy Seymour	150.00	75.00	40.00
39	"Shadow" Carroll	150.00	75.00	40.00
40	Jake Gettman	150.00	75.00	40.00
41	Luther Taylor	300.00	150.00	95.00
42	Walter Justis	150.00	75.00	40.00
43	Robert Fisher	150.00	75.00	40.00
44	Fred Parent	150.00	75.00	40.00
45	James Dygert	150.00	75.00	40.00
46	Johnnie Butler	150.00	75.00	40.00
47	Fred Mitchell	150.00	75.00	40.00
48	Heinie Batch	150.00	75.00	40.00
49	Michael Corcoran	150.00	75.00	40.00
50	Edward Doescher	150.00	75.00	40.00
51	George Wheeler	150.00	75.00	40.00
52	Elijah Jones	150.00	75.00	40.00
53	Fred Truesdale	150.00	75.00	40.00
54	Fred Beebe	150.00	75.00	40.00
55	Louis Brockett	150.00	75.00	40.00
56	Robt. Wells	150.00	75.00	40.00
57	"Lew" McAllister	150.00	75.00	40.00
58	Ralph Stroud	150.00	75.00	40.00
59	James Manser	150.00	75.00	40.00
60	Jim Holmes	150.00	75.00	40.00
61	Rube Dessau	150.00	75.00	40.00
62	Fred Jacklitsch	150.00	75.00	40.00
63	Stanley Graham	150.00	75.00	40.00
64	Noah Henline	150.00	75.00	40.00
65	"Chick" Gandil	775.00	385.00	240.00
66	Tom Hughes	150.00	75.00	40.00
67	Joseph Delehanty	150.00	75.00	40.00
68	Geo. Pierce	150.00	75.00	40.00
69	Bob Gaunt (Gantt)	150.00	75.00	40.00
70	Edward Fitzpatrick	150.00	75.00	40.00
71	Wyatt Lee	150.00	75.00	40.00
72	John Kissinger	150.00	75.00	40.00
73	William Malarkey	150.00	75.00	40.00
74	William Byers	150.00	75.00	40.00
75	George Simmons	150.00	75.00	40.00
76	Daniel Moeller	150.00	75.00	40.00
77	Joseph McGinnity	750.00	375.00	230.00

		NM	EX	VG
78	Alex Hardy	150.00	75.00	40.00
79	Bob Holmes	150.00	75.00	40.00
80	William Baxter	150.00	75.00	40.00
81	Edward Spencer	150.00	75.00	40.00
82	Bradley Kocher	150.00	75.00	40.00
83	Robert Shaw	150.00	75.00	40.00
84	Joseph Yeager	150.00	75.00	40.00
85	Anthony Carlo	150.00	75.00	40.00
86	William Abstein	150.00	75.00	40.00
87	Tim Jordan	150.00	75.00	40.00
88	Dick Breen	150.00	75.00	40.00
89	Tom McCarty	150.00	75.00	46.00
90	Ed Curtis	160.00	80.00	50.00

1923 Indianapolis Indians Foldout

Twenty-one players and staff are featured in this black-and-white accordian-fold souvenir. Each of the cards measures about 2" x 3".

	NM	EX	VG
Complete Foldout:	650.00	325.00	195.00
(Checklist not available.)			

1950 Indianapolis Indians Team Issue

Action poses are featured in this set of team-issue 8" x 10" black-and-white glossy photos. Players are identified by a facsimile autograph on front. It is unknown whether the checklist is complete. The Indians were the Class AAA American Association affiliate of the Pittsburgh Pirates in 1950.

		NM	EX	VG
Common Player:		30.00	15.00	9.00
(1)	Monty Basgall	30.00	15.00	9.00
(2)	Ted Beard	30.00	15.00	9.00
(3)	Gus Bell	40.00	20.00	12.00
(4)	Eddie Bockman	30.00	15.00	9.00
(5)	Dale Coogan	30.00	15.00	9.00
(6)	"Del" Dallessandro	30.00	15.00	9.00
(7)	Nanny Fernandez	30.00	15.00	9.00
(8)	Eddy Fitz Gerald	30.00	15.00	9.00
(9)	Al Grunwald	30.00	15.00	9.00
(10)	Frank Kalin	30.00	15.00	9.00
(11)	Paul LaPalme	30.00	15.00	9.00
(12)	Royce Lint	30.00	15.00	9.00
(13)	Al Lopez	45.00	22.00	13.50
(14)	Forrest Main	30.00	15.00	9.00
(15)	Danny O'Connell	30.00	15.00	9.00
(16)	Frank Papish	30.00	15.00	9.00
(17)	Eddie Stevens	30.00	15.00	9.00
(18)	Leo Wells	30.00	15.00	9.00

J

1952 Jamestown Falcons Team Issue

CHARLEY LAU

This Class D farm club of the Detroit Tigers won the 1952 Pony (Pennsylvania-Ontario-New York) League playoffs. Like other issues of Globe Printing, the roughly 2-1/4" x 3-3/8" cards are black-and-white with blank backs and the player name in a white strip at bottom-front. A light green album slotted to hold the cards is known for this issue.

		NM	EX	VG
Complete Set (18):		800.00	400.00	240.00
Common Player:		60.00	30.00	18.00
Album:		100.00	50.00	30.00
(1)	Dick Barr	60.00	30.00	18.00
(2)	Jerry Davie	60.00	30.00	18.00
(3)	John Fickinger	60.00	30.00	18.00
(4)	Paul Franks	60.00	30.00	18.00
(5)	Red Gookin	60.00	30.00	18.00
(6)	Bill Harbour	60.00	30.00	18.00
(7)	Dick Hatfield	60.00	30.00	18.00
(8)	Charley Lau	90.00	45.00	30.00
(9)	Dick Lisiecki	60.00	30.00	18.00
(10)	Tony Lupien	60.00	30.00	18.00
(11)	Joe Melago	60.00	30.00	18.00
(12)	Claude Mitschele	60.00	30.00	18.00
(13)	Bob Neebling	60.00	30.00	18.00
(14)	Fran Oneto	60.00	30.00	18.00
(15)	George Risley	60.00	30.00	18.00
(16)	Bob Szabo	60.00	30.00	18.00
(17)	Ken Walters	60.00	30.00	18.00
(18)	Gabby Witucki	60.00	30.00	18.00

1909 Walter Johnson "Weiser Wonder" Postcards

This issue-date(s) on these postcards are conjectural. Two distinct styles are known using versions of the same full-length portrait of Johnson in a studio standing on an ornate rug in front of a curtain depicting drapes, urn, etc. Johnson is wearing the uniform of the Weiser (Idaho) semi-pro team for whom he pitched prior to beginning his Hall of Fame career with the Washington Senators in 1907. The earlier of the cards utilizes the undivided-back postcard format which was current only until 1908. It is printed in sepia tones and identifies Johnson as the "Weiser Wonder" in a line of white type at the bottom. A later version, on a post-1908 divided-back postcard, is printed in bluetone. The card identifies him in a white strip at bottom. It is likely one or both of these cards continued to be produced or at least available after Johnson became a major league star. Both cards are in standard 3-1/2" x 5-1/2" format.

	NM	EX	VG
Walter Johnson (Bluetone)	2,500	1,250	750.00
Walter Johnson (Sepia)	2,500	1,250	750.00

1967 Jones Dairy Buffalo Bison All-Stars

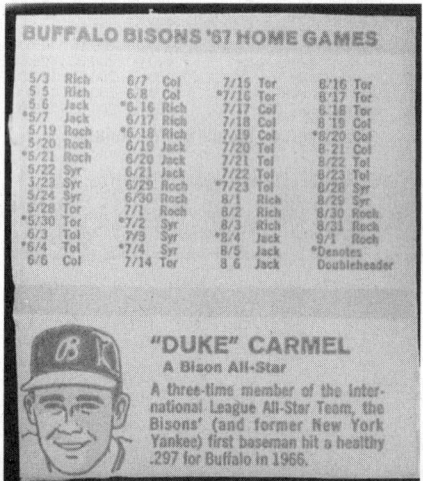

Apparently printed as part of a milk carton, only a single player is known for this issue. Printed in red and yellow, the piece includes a 1967 team home schedule, a player drawing and career highlights in a 2-3/4" x 3-1/8" format. Other players may yet surface.

		NM	EX	VG
(1)	"Duke" Carmel	80.00	40.00	25.00

K

1962 Kahn's Wieners Atlanta Crackers

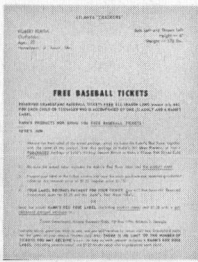

Compliments of Kahn's
"THE WIENER THE WORLD AWAITED"

Kahn's made a single foray into the minor league market in 1962 with a separate 24-card set of Atlanta Crackers. The cards feature the same basic format, 3-1/4" x 4", borderless black-and-white photos with a Kahn's ad message in a white panel below

the picture, as the major league issue. The backs are slightly different, having a free ticket offer in place of the player stats. Atlanta was the top farm club of the St. Louis Cardinals in 1962. The most famous alumnus in the set is Tim McCarver.

		NM	EX	VG
Complete Set (24):		850.00	425.00	250.00
Common Player:		35.00	17.50	10.00
(1)	James (Jimmy) Edward Beauchamp	35.00	17.50	10.00
(2)	Gerald Peter Buchek	35.00	17.50	10.00
(3)	Robert Burda	35.00	17.50	10.00
(4)	Hal Deitz	35.00	17.50	10.00
(5)	Robert John Duliba	35.00	17.50	10.00
(6)	Harry Michael Fanok	35.00	17.50	10.00
(7)	Phil Gagliano	35.00	17.50	10.00
(8)	John Glenn	35.00	17.50	10.00
(9)	Leroy Gregory	35.00	17.50	10.00
(10)	Richard (Dick) Henry Hughes	35.00	17.50	10.00
(11)	John Charles Kucks, Jr.	35.00	17.50	10.00
(12)	Johnny Joe Lewis	35.00	17.50	10.00
(13)	James (Mac - Timmie) Timothy McCarver	75.00	37.50	22.00
(14)	Robert F. Milliken	35.00	17.50	10.00
(15)	Joe Morgan	35.00	17.50	10.00
(16)	Ronald Charles Plaza	35.00	17.50	10.00
(17)	Bob Sadowski	35.00	17.50	10.00
(18)	Jim Saul	35.00	17.50	10.00
(19)	Willard Schmidt	35.00	17.50	10.00
(20)	Joe Schultz	35.00	17.50	10.00
(21)	Thomas Michael (Mike) Shannon	50.00	25.00	15.00
(22)	Paul Louis Toth	35.00	17.50	10.00
(23)	Andrew Lou Vickery	35.00	17.50	10.00
(24)	Fred Dwight Whitfield	35.00	17.50	10.00

1939 Kimball Automobile Trois-Rivieres Photocards

This set of 18 postcards and an accompanying envelope features the player of the Trois-Rivieres (Three Rivers) club of the Quebec Provincial League. Until 1940, the six-team QPL was not a part of organized baseball's minor league system. Several of the players were either former or future minor leaguers within OB. Paul "Pepper" Martin in the set is not the Pepper Martin of the contemporary, Gas House Gang St. Louis Cardinals. The black-and-white cards are about postcard-size and blank-backed, printed on sturdy card stock.

		NM	EX	VG
Complete Set (18):		1,350	675.00	400.00
Common Player:		90.00	45.00	25.00
(1)	George Andrews	90.00	45.00	25.00
(2)	Norm Bell	90.00	45.00	25.00
(3)	Henry Block	90.00	45.00	25.00
(4)	Addie Copple	90.00	45.00	25.00
(5)	Phil Corrigan	90.00	45.00	25.00
(6)	Joe Dickinson	90.00	45.00	25.00
(7)	Bill Hoffner	90.00	45.00	25.00
(8)	Jack Leroy	90.00	45.00	25.00
(9)	Leo Maloney	90.00	45.00	25.00
(10)	Martin	90.00	45.00	25.00
(11)	McGurk	90.00	45.00	25.00
(12)	Connie O'Leary	90.00	45.00	25.00
(13)	James Pickens	90.00	45.00	25.00
(14)	Dutch Prather	90.00	45.00	25.00
(15)	Jamie Skelton	90.00	45.00	25.00
(16)	Byron Speece	90.00	45.00	25.00
(17)	Gene Sullivan	90.00	45.00	25.00
(18)	Grover Wearshing	90.00	45.00	25.00

1952 Knowles Service Stations Stockton Ports

FIBBER HIRAYAMA

Contemporary, and sharing a format with the many Globe minor league issues of the early '50s, this set of Stockton Ports (Class C California League) cards carries the advertising of Knowles Service Stations. The blank-backed, black-and-white cards measure 2-1/4" x 3-1/2" and are unnumbered. Among the players is a Japanese national whose card is in strong demand.

		NM	EX	VG
Complete Set (11):		1,000	500.00	300.00
Common Player:		90.00	45.00	25.00
Album:		150.00	75.00	45.00
(1)	Wayne Clary	90.00	45.00	25.00
(2)	Harry Clements	90.00	45.00	25.00
(3)	John Crocco	90.00	45.00	25.00
(4)	Tony Freitas	90.00	45.00	25.00
(5)	Fibber Hirayama	250.00	125.00	75.00
(6)	Dave Mann	90.00	45.00	25.00
(7)	Larry Mann	90.00	45.00	25.00

		NM	EX	VG
(8)	Hank Moreno	90.00	45.00	25.00
(9)	Frank Romero	90.00	45.00	25.00
(10)	Chuck Thomas	90.00	45.00	25.00
(11)	Bud Watkins	90.00	45.00	25.00

1922-23 Kolb's Mothers' Bread Pins (PB4)

Over a two-year period, Kolb's bakery sponsored a series of pins featuring members of the Reading (Pa.) Aces of the International League. The pins are 7/8" in diameter with black-and-white portraits on a white background. The player name (last name only, usually) and position are indicated beneath the photo. Above the photo, in red, is the sponsor's identification. The pins issued in 1922 have "MOTHERS'" in all capital letters; the 1923 pins have "Mothers'" in upper and lower case.

		NM	EX	VG
	Complete Set (32):	675.00	350.00	200.00
	Common Player:	50.00	25.00	15.00
(1)	Spencer Abbott	50.00	25.00	15.00
(2)	Charlie Babington	50.00	25.00	15.00
(3)	Bill Barrett	50.00	25.00	15.00
(4)	R. Bates	50.00	25.00	15.00
(5)	Chief Bender	75.00	37.50	22.50
(6)	Myrl Brown	50.00	25.00	15.00
(7)	Fred Carts	50.00	25.00	15.00
(8)	Nig Clarke	50.00	25.00	15.00
(9)	Tom Connelly	50.00	25.00	15.00
(10)	Gus Getz	50.00	25.00	15.00
(11)	Frank Gilhooley	50.00	25.00	15.00
(12)	Ray Gordonier	50.00	25.00	15.00
(13)	Hinkey Haines	60.00	30.00	18.00
(14)	Francis Karpp	50.00	25.00	15.00
(15)	Joseph Kelley	50.00	25.00	15.00
(16)	Andrew Kotch	50.00	25.00	15.00
(17)	William Lightner	50.00	25.00	15.00
(18)	Byrd Lynn	50.00	25.00	15.00
(19)	Al Mamaux	50.00	25.00	15.00
(20)	Martin	50.00	25.00	15.00
(21)	Ralph Miller	50.00	25.00	15.00
(22)	Otto Pahlman	50.00	25.00	15.00
(23)	Sam Post	50.00	25.00	15.00
(24)	Al Schacht	62.00	31.00	18.50
(25)	John Scott	50.00	25.00	15.00
(26)	Walt Smallwood	50.00	25.00	15.00
(27)	Ross Swartz	50.00	25.00	15.00
(28)	Fred Thomas	50.00	25.00	15.00
(29)	Myles Thomas	50.00	25.00	15.00
(30)	Walt Tragesser	50.00	25.00	15.00
(31)	Washburn	50.00	25.00	15.00
(32)	Walter Wolfe	50.00	25.00	15.00

L

1952 La Patrie Album Sportif

Ballplayers from Montreal of the International League and several of the teams from the Class C Provincial (Quebec) League were featured in a series of colorized photos printed in the Sunday rotogravure section of the "La Patrie" newspaper. The photos are approximately 11" x 15-3/8" with red left and bottom trim and a vertical blue stripe at far left. Player information is printed in black and is in French. A number of the players went on to stardom with the Brooklyn and/or Los Angeles Dodgers.

		NM	EX	VG
	Complete Set (18):	650.00	325.00	175.00
	Common Player:	25.00	12.50	7.50
(1)	Bob Alexander	25.00	12.50	7.50

		NM	EX	VG
(2)	Hampton Coleman	25.00	12.50	7.50
(3)	Walter Fiala	25.00	12.50	7.50
(4)	Jim Gilliams (Gilliam)	45.00	22.50	13.50
(5)	Tom Hackett	25.00	12.50	7.50
(6)	Don Hoak	35.00	17.50	10.00
(7)	Herbie Lash	25.00	12.50	7.50
(8)	Tommy Lasorda	150.00	75.00	45.00
(9)	Mal Mallette	25.00	12.50	7.50
(10)	Georges Maranda (Aug. 17)	25.00	12.50	7.50
(11)	Carmen Mauro	25.00	12.50	7.50
(12)	Solly Mohn	25.00	12.50	7.50
(13)	Jacques Monette	25.00	12.50	7.50
(14)	Johnny Podres	75.00	37.50	22.50
(15)	Ed Roebuck	25.00	12.50	7.50
(16)	Charlie Thompson	25.00	12.50	7.50
(17)	Don Thompson	25.00	12.50	7.50
(18)	John Wingo	25.00	12.50	7.50

1928-1932 La Presse Baseball Rotos

Players from Montreal's team in the International League (and occasionally other major and minor league teams' stars) were featured in a series of photos between 1928-32 in the Saturday rotogravure section of Montreal's "La Presse" newspaper. The format remained fairly consistent over the years. Large hand-tinted player photos were featured on the approximately 11" x 17-3/4" pages, with writeup in French below. On back was whatever features and ads happened to appear on the following page. The known baseball player list is presented here in chronological order. Other athletes were also featured in the issue, but are not listed here. Gaps have been left in the numbering to better accommodate future additions to this list.

		NM	EX	VG
	Common Player:	60.00	30.00	20.00
	1928	.00	.00	.00
(2)	Aldrick Gaudette (May 19)	60.00	30.00	20.00
(4)	Robert Shawkey (June 2)	80.00	40.00	24.00
(5)	Lachine team photo, portraits of starting nine (June 9)	60.00	30.00	20.00
(6)	Roy Buckalew, Frank Dunagan, Chester Fowler, Thomas Gulley, Peter Radwan, Richard Smith (June 16)	60.00	30.00	20.00
(7)	Seymour Edward Bailey (June 23)	60.00	30.00	20.00
(8)	Wilson F. Fewster (June 30)	60.00	30.00	20.00
(10)	Tom Daly (July 14)	60.00	30.00	20.00
(14)	Red Holt (Aug. 11)	60.00	30.00	20.00
(17)	George Herman Ruth (Oct. 13)	750.00	375.00	225.00
(20)	Johnny Prud'homme (Nov. 3)	60.00	30.00	20.00
	1929	.00	.00	.00
(2)	Walter Paul Gautreau (April 13)	60.00	30.00	20.00
(4)	Herb Thormahlen (April 27)	60.00	30.00	20.00
(9)	Elon Hogsett (July 13)	60.00	30.00	20.00
(12)	Robert M. "Lefty" Grove (Oct. 19)	200.00	100.00	60.00
(15)	Philadelphia A's Stars (Mickey Cochrane, Jimmie Foxx, Connie Mack, Al Simmons, Rube Walberg, Bing Miller) (Nov. 16)	90.00	45.00	27.00
	1930	.00	.00	.00
(3)	Martin Griffin, John Pomorski, Arthur Smith, Herb Thormahlen (May 31)	60.00	30.00	20.00
(4)	James Calleran, Edward Conley, Lee Head, Jimmy Ripple (June 7)	60.00	30.00	20.00
(7)	Del Bissonette (June 28)	60.00	30.00	20.00
(9)	Joe Hauser (July 12)	75.00	37.00	22.00
(14)	Gowell Sylvester Claset (Sept. 13)	60.00	30.00	20.00
(17)	Hack Wilson (Oct. 11)	200.00	100.00	60.00
	1931	.00	.00	.00
(2)	Chuck Klein (May 30)	175.00	87.00	52.00
(3)	Jocko Conlan (June 6)	100.00	50.00	30.00
(5)	Lee Head (June 20)	60.00	30.00	20.00
(9)	Jimmy Ripple (July 4)	60.00	30.00	20.00
(9)	Sol Mishkin (July 18)	60.00	30.00	20.00
(11)	Walter Brown (Aug. 15)	60.00	30.00	20.00
(15)	Johnny Allen, Frank Barnes, Guy Cantrell, Ken Strong (Nov. 14)	60.00	30.00	20.00
(16)	John Pepper Martin (Nov. 21)	80.00	40.00	24.00
	1932	.00	.00	.00
(2)	Johnny Grabowski (May 28)	60.00	30.00	20.00
(3)	Charles Sullivan (June 4)	60.00	30.00	20.00
(5)	Walter "Doc" Gautreau (June 18)	60.00	30.00	20.00
(6)	John Clancy (June 25)	60.00	30.00	20.00
(7)	Buck Walters (July 2)	75.00	37.00	22.00
(8)	Bill McAfee (July 9)	60.00	30.00	20.00
(9)	George Puccinelli (July 16)	60.00	30.00	20.00
(11)	Buck Crouse (Aug. 6)	60.00	30.00	20.00

		NM	EX	VG
(12)	Ollie Carnegie (Aug. 13)	60.00	30.00	20.00
(13)	Leo Mangum (Aug. 20)	60.00	30.00	20.00
(17)	Roy Parmelee (Nov. 19)	60.00	30.00	20.00
	(Dates of issue not confirmed.)			
	Dan Howley	60.00	30.00	20.00

1952 Laval Dairy Provincial League

This scarce Canadian minor league issue includes only players from the Class C Provincial League, centered in Quebec. The black-and-white cards are blank-backed and measure 1-3/4" x 2-1/2". The player name, position, date and place of birth and card number is in French. Teams represented in the set are Quebec (Braves), St. Jean (Pirates), Three Rivers (Independent), Drummondville (Senators), Granby (Phillies) and Ste. Hyacinthe (Philadelphia A's).

		NM	EX	VG
	Complete Set (114):	4,000	2,000	1,200
	Common Player:	35.00	17.50	10.00
1	Georges McQuinn	35.00	17.50	10.00
2	Cliff Statham	35.00	17.50	10.00
3	Frank Wilson	35.00	17.50	10.00
4	Frank Neri	35.00	17.50	10.00
5	Georges Maranda	35.00	17.50	10.00
6	Richard "Dick" Cordeiro	35.00	17.50	10.00
7	Roger McCardell	35.00	17.50	10.00
8	Joseph Janiak	35.00	17.50	10.00
9	Herbert Shankman	35.00	17.50	10.00
10	Joe Subbiondo	35.00	17.50	10.00
11	Jack Brenner	35.00	17.50	10.00
12	Donald Buchanan	35.00	17.50	10.00
13	Robert Smith	35.00	17.50	10.00
14	Raymond Lague	35.00	17.50	10.00
15	Mike Fandozzi	35.00	17.50	10.00
16	Dick Moler	35.00	17.50	10.00
17	Edward Bazydio	35.00	17.50	10.00
18	Danny Mazurek	35.00	17.50	10.00
19	Edwin Charles	35.00	17.50	10.00
20	Jack Nullaney	35.00	17.50	10.00
21	Bob Bolan	35.00	17.50	10.00
22	Bob Long	35.00	17.50	10.00
23	Cleo Lewright	35.00	17.50	10.00
24	Herb Taylor	35.00	17.50	10.00
25	Frankie Gaeta	35.00	17.50	10.00
26	Bill Truitt	35.00	17.50	10.00
27	Jean Prats	35.00	17.50	10.00
28	Tex Taylor	35.00	17.50	10.00
29	Ron Delbianco	35.00	17.50	10.00
30	Joe DiLorenzo	35.00	17.50	10.00
31	Johnny Paszek	35.00	17.50	10.00
32	Ken Suess	35.00	17.50	10.00
33	Harry Sims	35.00	17.50	10.00
34	William Jackson	35.00	17.50	10.00
35	Jerry Mayers	35.00	17.50	10.00
36	Gordon Maltzberger	35.00	17.50	10.00
37	Gerry Cabana	35.00	17.50	10.00
38	Gary Rutkey	35.00	17.50	10.00
39	Ken Hatcher	35.00	17.50	10.00
40	Vincent Cosenza	35.00	17.50	10.00
41	Edward Yaeger	35.00	17.50	10.00
42	Jimmy Orr	35.00	17.50	10.00
43	Johnny Di Matino	35.00	17.50	10.00
44	Lenny Wisneski	35.00	17.50	10.00
45	Pete Caniglia	35.00	17.50	10.00
46	Guy Coleman	35.00	17.50	10.00
47	Herb Fleischer	35.00	17.50	10.00
48	Charles Yahrling	35.00	17.50	10.00
49	Roger Bedard	35.00	17.50	10.00
50	Al Barillari	35.00	17.50	10.00
51	Hugh Mulcahy	50.00	25.00	15.00
52	Vincent Canepa	35.00	17.50	10.00
53	Bob Loranger	35.00	17.50	10.00
54	Georges Carpentier	35.00	17.50	10.00
55	Bill Hamilton	35.00	17.50	10.00
56	Hector Lopez	65.00	32.00	19.50
57	Joel Taylor	35.00	17.50	10.00
58	Alonzo Brathwaite	100.00	50.00	30.00
59	Carl McQuillen	35.00	17.50	10.00
60	Robert Trice	35.00	17.50	10.00
61	John Dworak	35.00	17.50	10.00
62	Al Pinkston	50.00	25.00	15.00
63	William Shannon	35.00	17.50	10.00
64	Stanley Wotychowisz	35.00	17.50	10.00
65	Roger Herbert	35.00	17.50	10.00
66	Troy Spencer	35.00	17.50	10.00
67	Johnny Rohan	35.00	17.50	10.00
68	John Sosh	35.00	17.50	10.00
69	Ramon Mason	35.00	17.50	10.00
70	Tom Smith	35.00	17.50	10.00
71	Douglas McBean	35.00	17.50	10.00
72	Bill Babik	35.00	17.50	10.00
73	Dante Cozzi	35.00	17.50	10.00
74	Melville Doxtater	35.00	17.50	10.00

75	William Gilray	35.00	17.50	10.00
76	Armando Diaz	35.00	17.50	10.00
77	Ackroyd Smith	35.00	17.50	10.00
78	Germain Pizarro	35.00	17.50	10.00
79	Jim Heap	35.00	17.50	10.00
80	Herbert Crompton	35.00	17.50	10.00
81	Howard Bodell	35.00	17.50	10.00
82	Andre Schreiser	35.00	17.50	10.00
83	John Wingo	35.00	17.50	10.00
84	Salvatore Arduini	35.00	17.50	10.00
85	Fred Pallito	35.00	17.50	10.00
86	Aaron Osofsky	35.00	17.50	10.00
87	Jack DiGrace	35.00	17.50	10.00
88	Alphonso Chico Girard (Gerrard)	35.00	17.50	10.00
89	Manuel Trabous	35.00	17.50	10.00
90	Tom Barnes	35.00	17.50	10.00
91	Humberto Robinson	35.00	17.50	10.00
92	Jack Bukowatz	35.00	17.50	10.00
93	Marco Mainini	35.00	17.50	10.00
94	Claude St. Vincent	35.00	17.50	10.00
95	Fernand Brosseau	35.00	17.50	10.00
96	John Malangone	35.00	17.50	10.00
97	Pierre Nantel	35.00	17.50	10.00
98	Donald Stevens	35.00	17.50	10.00
99	Jim Prappas	35.00	17.50	10.00
100	Richard Fitzgerald	35.00	17.50	10.00
101	Yves Aubin	35.00	17.50	10.00
102	Frank Novosel	35.00	17.50	10.00
103	Tony Campos	35.00	17.50	10.00
104	Gelso Oviedo .	35.00	17.50	10.00
105	Guly Becker	35.00	17.50	10.00
106	Aurelio Ala	35.00	17.50	10.00
107	Orlando Andux	35.00	17.50	10.00
108	Tom Hackett	35.00	17.50	10.00
109	Guillame Vargas	35.00	17.50	10.00
110	Fransisco Salfran	35.00	17.50	10.00
111	Jean-Marc Blais	35.00	17.50	10.00
112	Vince Pizzitola	35.00	17.50	10.00
113	John Olsen	35.00	17.50	10.00
114	Jacques Monette	35.00	17.50	10.00

1948 Los Angeles Angels Team Issue

A team-issued set sold in a paper envelope for $1 at the ballpark, these cards were produced by the same firm which published the team's yearbook, Pacific Coast Sports Publishing Co., of Los Angeles. The blank-backed cards measure 6-3/4" x 4-3/4" and are printed in black-and-white on thin cardboard with a semi-gloss front surface. Cards feature a facsimile player autograph on front, along with a posed action or portrait photo and complete major and minor league stats. The cards are listed in the American Card Catalog, along with the subsequent year's issue, as W725. Many of the players on this Pacific Coast League team were former or future Chicago Cubs. The unnumbered cards are checklisted here alphabetically.

		NM	EX	VG
Complete Set (26):		650.00	325.00	200.00
Common Player:		30.00	15.00	9.00
(1)	Cliff Aberson	30.00	15.00	9.00
(2)	Red Adams	30.00	15.00	9.00
(3)	John Adkins	30.00	15.00	9.00
(4)	Lee Anthony	30.00	15.00	9.00
(5)	Russ Bauers	30.00	15.00	9.00
(6)	Ora Burnett	30.00	15.00	9.00
(7)	Donald Carlsen	30.00	15.00	9.00
(8)	Dom Dallessandro	30.00	15.00	9.00
(9)	Cecil Garriott	30.00	15.00	9.00
(10)	Paul Gillespie	30.00	15.00	9.00
(11)	Al Glossop	30.00	15.00	9.00
(12)	Tom Hafey	30.00	15.00	9.00
(13)	Don Johnson	30.00	15.00	9.00
(14)	Bill Kelly	30.00	15.00	9.00
(15)	Hal Kleine	30.00	15.00	9.00
(16)	Walt Lanfranconi	30.00	15.00	9.00
(17)	Ed Lukon	30.00	15.00	9.00
(18)	Red Lynn	30.00	15.00	9.00
(19)	Eddie Malone	30.00	15.00	9.00
(20)	Len Merullo	30.00	15.00	9.00
(21)	Ralph Novotney	30.00	15.00	9.00
(22)	John Ostrowski	30.00	15.00	9.00
(23)	John Sanford	30.00	15.00	9.00
(24)	Ed Sauer	30.00	15.00	9.00
(25)	Bill Schuster	30.00	15.00	9.00
(26)	John Warner	30.00	15.00	9.00

1949 Los Angeles Angels Team Issue

Little changed in the second year of this team issue. Cards remained at 6-3/4" x 4-3/4" in format, printed black-and-white on semi-gloss cardboard with a blank back. Many of the players (and even some of the photos) were repeated from the previous year. The unnumbered cards are checklisted here in alphabetical order.

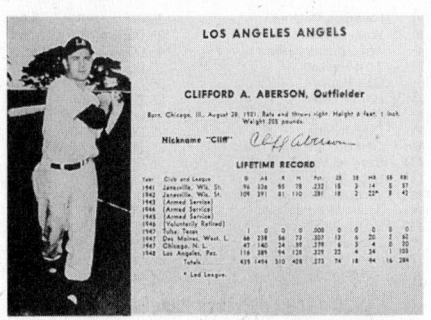

		NM	EX	VG
Complete Set (39):		1,000	500.00	300.00
Common Player:		30.00	15.00	9.00
(1)	Cliff Aberson	30.00	15.00	9.00
(2)	Donald Alfano	30.00	15.00	9.00
(3)	Quentin Altizer	30.00	15.00	9.00
(4)	Lee Anthony	30.00	15.00	9.00
(5)	Nels Burbrink	30.00	15.00	9.00
(6)	Smoky Burgess	75.00	37.50	22.00
(7)	Don Carlsen	30.00	15.00	9.00
(8)	Joe Damato	30.00	15.00	9.00
(9)	Bill Emmerich	30.00	15.00	9.00
(10)	Ken Gables	30.00	15.00	9.00
(11)	Cecil Garriott	30.00	15.00	9.00
(12)	Al Glossop	30.00	15.00	9.00
(13)	Gordon Goldsberry	30.00	15.00	9.00
(14)	Frank Gustine	30.00	15.00	9.00
(15)	Lee Handley	30.00	15.00	9.00
(16)	Alan Ihde	30.00	15.00	9.00
(17)	Bob Kelley (Announcer)	30.00	15.00	9.00
(18)	Bill Kelly	30.00	15.00	9.00
(19)	Bob Kelly	30.00	15.00	9.00
(20)	Walt Lanfranconi	30.00	15.00	9.00
(21)	Red Lynn	30.00	15.00	9.00
(22)	Clarence Maddern	30.00	15.00	9.00
(23)	Eddie Malone	30.00	15.00	9.00
(24)	Carmen Mauro	30.00	15.00	9.00
(25)	Booker McDaniels	75.00	37.50	22.00
(26)	Cal McLish	50.00	25.00	15.00
(27)	Butch Moran	30.00	15.00	9.00
(28)	Ralph Novotney	30.00	15.00	9.00
(29)	John Ostrowski	30.00	15.00	9.00
(30)	Bobby Rhawn	30.00	15.00	9.00
(31)	Bill Schuster	30.00	15.00	9.00
(32)	Pat Seerey	30.00	15.00	9.00
(33)	Bryan Stephens	30.00	15.00	9.00
(34)	Bob Sturgeon	30.00	15.00	9.00
(35)	Wayne Terwilliger	45.00	22.00	13.50
(36)	Gordon Van Dyke	30.00	15.00	9.00
(37)	John Warner	30.00	15.00	9.00
(38)	Don Watkins	30.00	15.00	9.00
(39)	Trainers, Bat Boys	30.00	15.00	9.00
	(Dickie Evans, Joe Liscio, Dave Flores, Billy Lund)			

1930-31 Lucke Badge & Button Baltimore Orioles Pins

These 7/8" diameter celluloid pinback buttons were produced by the Baltimore novelty firm of Lucke Badge & Button Co. Issued to honor fan favorites on their "Day," the buttons have black-and-white portrait photos at center, surrounded by a white rim. At top is the player name, at bottom is the team name and year. A paper label inside the back of the button identifies the maker and includes a union label.

	NM	EX	VG
Joe Hauser (1930)	300.00	150.00	90.00
Don Heffner (1931)	200.00	100.00	60.00

M

1910 Mascot Gum Pins

Only players from the Eastern League champion Rochester Bronchos are known on these 7/8" diameter pinback buttons. Fronts have a black-and-white player photo on a blue background with the player's last name at left and "ROCHESTER" at right. A paper insert on the reverse advertises "Ball Player's Buttons Free With Mascot Gum." This checklist may not be complete.

		NM	EX	VG
Common Player:		250.00	125.00	80.00
(1)	Anderson	250.00	125.00	80.00
(2)	Heinie Batch	250.00	125.00	80.00
(3)	Blair	250.00	125.00	80.00
(4)	Holmes	250.00	125.00	80.00
(5)	Lafitte	250.00	125.00	80.00
(6)	Manning	250.00	125.00	80.00
(7)	McConnell	250.00	125.00	80.00
(8)	Moeller	250.00	125.00	80.00
(9)	Moran	250.00	125.00	80.00
(10)	Osborn	250.00	125.00	80.00
(11)	Don Carlos Ragan	250.00	125.00	80.00
(12)	Savidge	250.00	125.00	80.00
(13)	Simmons	250.00	125.00	80.00
(14)	Spencer	250.00	125.00	80.00
(15)	Tooley	250.00	125.00	80.00

1952 May Co. Chuck Stevens Premium

The date given is speculative, about midway through the player's term with the Hollywood Stars of the Pacific Coast League. The 4-1/2" x 6" blank-backed black-and-white card features a portrait of what the caption at bottom calls the "popular first baseman." The caption also calls the piece a "MAY CO. 'Back To School' Party Souvenir Photo." The cards are often found bearing the player's autograph, presumably obtained at the event.

	NM	EX	VG
Chuck Stevens	75.00	40.00	25.00

1960s-70s J.D. McCarthy Postcards

For details of J.D. McCarthy's prolific body of black-and-white player postcards, see the introductory material in the vintage major league section.

Common Player: $1-3
SPOKANE INDIANS
(1) Roy Hartsfield

TOLEDO MUD HENS
(1) Loren Babe
(2) Stan Bahnsen
(3) Bill Bethea
(4) Joe Cherry
(5) Horace Clark
(6) Wayne Comer
(7) Jack Cullen (2)
(8) Jack Curtis (2)
(9) Gil Downs
(10) Joe Faraci
(11) Frank Fernandez
(12) Mike Ferraro
(13) Mickey Harrington
(14) Mike Hegan
(15) Jim Horsford (2)
(16) Dick Hughes
(17) Elvio Jiminez (2)
(18) Robert Lasko
(19) Artie Lopez
(20) Roy Majtyka
(21) Tom Martz
(22) Ed Merritt (2)
(23) Archie Moore (2)
(24) Al Moran
(25) Bobby Murcer
(26) Tony Przybycien
(27) Bill Roman
(28) Bob Schmidt (2)
(29) Tom Shafer
(30) Billy Shantz
(31) Shantz-Senger-Babe
(32) Bob Tiefenauer
(33) Paul Toth (2)
(34) Andrew Vickery
(35) Jerry Walker
(36) Don Wallace
(37) Dooley Womack

1954 MD Super Service Sacramento Solons

HANK SCHENZ
M D Super Service
56th and T Streets

This issue features only players of the Pacific Coast League Sacramento Solons. The unnumbered cards are printed in black-and-white and carry an ad for a local gas station. The borderless, blank-backed cards measure 2-1/8" x 3-3/8".

	NM	EX	VG
Complete Set (6):	850.00	425.00	250.00
Common Player:	150.00	75.00	45.00
(1) Joe Brovia	150.00	75.00	45.00
(2) Al Cicotte	150.00	75.00	45.00
(3) Nippy Jones	150.00	75.00	45.00
(4) Richie Meyers	150.00	75.00	45.00
(5) Hank Schenz	150.00	75.00	45.00
(6) Bud Sheeley	150.00	75.00	45.00

1952 Miami Beach Flamingos Team Issue

GEORGE HANDY

These 2-1/4" x 3-3/8" black-and-white, unnumbered, blank-backed cards were one of many minor league team sets issued by Globe Printing of San Jose, Calif., in the early 1950s. Cards were usually given away at the ballpark on a one-per-week or one-per-homestand basis, accounting for the rarity of surviving sets. An embossed album slotted to accommodate the cards was also issued. The Flamingos were an unaffiliated team in the Class B Florida International League.

	NM	EX	VG
Complete Set (25):	1,000	500.00	300.00
Common Player:	60.00	30.00	18.00
Album:	100.00	50.00	30.00
(1) Billy Barrett	60.00	30.00	18.00
(2) Art Bosch	60.00	30.00	18.00
(3) Jack Caro	60.00	30.00	18.00
(4) Chuck Ehlman	60.00	30.00	18.00
(5) Oscar Garmendia	60.00	30.00	18.00
(6) George Handy	60.00	30.00	18.00
(7) Clark Henry	60.00	30.00	18.00
(8) Dario Jiminez	60.00	30.00	18.00
(9) Jesse Levan	60.00	30.00	18.00
(10) Bobby Lyons	60.00	30.00	18.00
(11) Pepper Martin	125.00	62.00	37.00
(12) Dick McMillin	60.00	30.00	18.00
(13) Pete Morant	60.00	30.00	18.00
(14) Chico Morilla	60.00	30.00	18.00
(15) Ken Munroe	60.00	30.00	18.00
(16) Walt Nothe	60.00	30.00	18.00
(17) Marshall O'Coine	60.00	30.00	18.00
(18) Whitey Platt	60.00	30.00	18.00
(19) Johnny Podgajny	60.00	30.00	18.00
(20) Knobby Rosa	60.00	30.00	18.00
(21) Harry Raulerson	60.00	30.00	18.00
(22) Mort Smith	60.00	30.00	18.00
(23) Tommy Venn	60.00	30.00	18.00
(24) George Wehmeyer	60.00	30.00	18.00
(25) Ray Williams	60.00	30.00	18.00

1963 Milwaukee Sausage Seattle Rainiers

Inserted into meat packages by a Seattle sausage company, the 11 cards known in this set are all Seattle Rainiers players, several of whom had big league experience. Cards measure approximately 4-1/4"-square and are printed in blue, red and yellow. The unnumbered cards are checklisted in alphabetical order.

	NM	EX	VG
Complete Set (11):	6,000	3,000	1,800
Common Player:	600.00	300.00	180.00
(1) Dave Hall	600.00	300.00	180.00
(2) Bill Harrell	600.00	300.00	180.00
(3) Pete Jernigan	600.00	300.00	180.00
(4) Bill McLeod	600.00	300.00	180.00
(5) Mel Parnell	650.00	325.00	200.00
(6) Elmer Singleton	600.00	300.00	180.00
(7) Archie Skeen	600.00	300.00	180.00
(8) Paul Smith	600.00	300.00	180.00
(9) Pete Smith	600.00	300.00	180.00
(10) Bill Spanswick	600.00	300.00	180.00
(11) George Spencer	600.00	300.00	180.00

1909 Minneapolis Tribune/St. Paul Pioneer Press Mirrors

From the few players known, it is apparent these mirrors were issued in 1909 by two of the Twin Cities' daily newspapers. Each mirror is 2-1/8" diameter with a celluloid back. At center is a black-and-white player photo. All typography is in b/w, as well. A pair of concentric circles around the photo contain the player's name and a short description of his prowess. Olmstead's reads, "Unhittable in the Pinches"; Carisch's reads, "Nails 'em to the Cross Every Time." The outer circle contains an ad for the newspaper. This checklist is probably incomplete.

	NM	EX	VG
Common Player:	200.00	100.00	60.00
(1) Fred Carisch	200.00	100.00	60.00
(2) Michael Kelly	200.00	100.00	60.00
(3) Fred Olmstead	200.00	100.00	60.00

1911 Mono Cigarettes (T217)

As was common with many tobacco issues of the period, the T217 set - distributed on the West Coast by Mono Cigarettes - feature both baseball players and "Leading Actresses." The 23 baseball players in the Mono set are all from the Pacific Coast League. Two of the players (Delhi and Hughie Smith) are shown in two poses, resulting in a total of 25 different cards. The players are pictured in black-and-white photos on a card that measures approximately 1-1/2" x 2-5/8", the standard size of a tobacco card. The player's name and team appear at the bottom, while the back of the card carries

an advertisement for Mono Cigarettes. The Mono set, which can be dated to the 1909-1911 period, is among the rarest of all tobacco cards.

	NM	EX	VG
Complete Set (25):	100,000	50,000	30,000
Common Player:	4,250	2,000	1,100
(1) Aiken	4,250	2,000	1,100
(2) Curtis Bernard	4,250	2,000	1,100
(3) L. Burrell	4,250	2,000	1,100
(4) Chadbourn	4,250	2,000	1,100
(5) R. Couchman	4,250	2,000	1,100
(6) Elmer Criger	4,250	2,000	1,100
(7) Pete Daley	4,250	2,000	1,100
(8) W. Delhi (Glove at chest level.)	4,250	2,000	1,100
(9) W. Delhi (Glove at shoulder level.)	4,250	2,000	1,100
(10) Bert Delmas	4,250	2,000	1,100
(11) Ivan Howard	4,250	2,000	1,100
(12) Kitty Knight	4,250	2,000	1,100
(13) Gene Knapp (Krapp)	4,250	2,000	1,100
(14) Metzger	4,250	2,000	1,100
(15) Carl Mitze	4,250	2,000	1,100
(16) J. O'Rourke	4,250	2,000	1,100
(17) R. Peckinpaugh	4,250	2,000	1,100
(18) Walter Schmidt	4,250	2,000	1,100
(19) Hughie Smith (Batting)	4,250	2,000	1,100
(20) Hughie Smith (Fielding)	4,250	2,000	1,100
(21) Wm. Stein	4,250	2,000	1,100
(22) Elmer Thorsen	4,250	2,000	1,100
(23) Oscar Vitt	4,250	2,000	1,100
(24) Clyde Wares	4,250	2,000	1,100
(25) Geo. Wheeler	4,250	2,000	1,100

1961 Jeffrey W. Morey Postcards

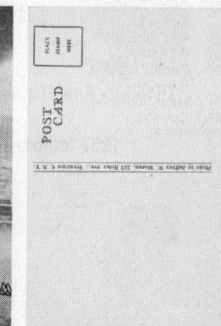

This set of 3-1/2" x 5-1/2", black-and-white postcards was produced to accomodate fan mail requests by two players each from the Columbus Clippers and Syracuse Chiefs. Fronts have a facsimile autograph. Divided-postcard backs have a credit line to the photographer and standard postcard markings.

	NM	EX	VG
Complete Set (4):	125.00	65.00	37.50
Common Player:	35.00	17.50	10.50
(1) Larry Elliot	35.00	17.50	10.50
(2) Don Rowe	35.00	17.50	10.50
(3) Ted Sadowski	35.00	17.50	10.50
(4) Ron Stillwell	35.00	17.50	10.50

1947 Morley Studios Team Cards

Besides issuing individual player cards of the Tacoma team, Morley Studios also issued postcard-size pictures of the teams in the Class B Western International League of 1947. The 3-1/2" x 5-1/2" cards are blank-backed and carry a "Morley Studios / 1947" imprint on front.

	NM	EX	VG
Complete Set (8):	600.00	300.00	180.00
Common Player:	75.00	37.50	22.50
(1) Bremerton Bluejackets	75.00	37.50	22.50
(2) Salem Senators	75.00	37.50	22.50
(3) Spokane Indians	75.00	37.50	22.50
(4) Tacoma Tigers	75.00	37.50	22.50
(5) Vancouver Capilanos	75.00	37.50	22.50
(6) Victoria Athletics	75.00	37.50	22.50
(7) Yakima Stars	75.00	37.50	22.50
(8) Wenatchee Chiefs	75.00	37.50	22.50

1947 Morley Studios Tacoma Tigers

This set of Tacoma Tigers (Western International League) features borderless black-and-white posed action photos with a facsimile autograph on front. A "Morley Sports Photos" or "Morley Studios" credit line appears at the bottom. Backs of the first seven cards are blank, while the others feature player biographies credited to "Jordan's (bread sponsor) Broadcaster" Clay Huntington and a Series A through F designation (though some cards lack the letter code). The unnumbered cards measure 2-1/2" x 3-1/2".

		NM	EX	VG
	Complete Set (28):	3,500	1,750	1,000
	Common Player:	125.00	65.00	40.00
	Blank-Backed	.00	.00	.00
(1)	Hank Bartolomei	125.00	65.00	40.00
(2)	Rod Belcher (Broadcaster)	125.00	65.00	40.00
(3)	Tip Berg (Trainer)	125.00	65.00	40.00
(4)	Gene Clough	125.00	65.00	40.00
(5)	Clay Huntington (Broadcaster)	125.00	65.00	40.00
(6)	Donald Mooney (Bat boy.)	125.00	65.00	40.00
(7)	Buck Tinsley	125.00	65.00	40.00
	Series A	.00	.00	.00
(8)	Richard A. Greco	125.00	65.00	40.00
(9)	Cy Greenlaw	125.00	65.00	40.00
(10)	Bob Joratz	125.00	65.00	40.00
(11)	Earl Kuper	125.00	65.00	40.00
	Series B	.00	.00	.00
(12)	Neil Clifford	125.00	65.00	40.00
(13)	Red Harvel	125.00	65.00	40.00
(14)	Julian Morgan	125.00	65.00	40.00
(15)	Pete Tedeschi	125.00	65.00	40.00
	Series C	.00	.00	.00
(16)	Stanley Gilson	125.00	65.00	40.00
(17)	Harry Nygard	125.00	65.00	40.00
(18)	Cleve Ramsey	125.00	65.00	40.00
(19)	Pete Sabutis	125.00	65.00	40.00
	Series D	.00	.00	.00
(20)	Mitch Chetkovich	125.00	65.00	40.00
(21)	Leroy Paton	125.00	65.00	40.00
(22)	Carl Shaply	125.00	65.00	40.00
(23)	Glenn Stetter	125.00	65.00	40.00
	Series E	.00	.00	.00
(24)	Bob Hedington	125.00	65.00	40.00
(25)	Ed Keehan	125.00	65.00	40.00
(26)	Gordon Walden	125.00	65.00	40.00
	Series F	.00	.00	.00
(27)	Maury Donovan	125.00	65.00	40.00
(28)	Guy Miller	125.00	65.00	40.00

1952 Mother's Cookies

This is one of the most popular regional minor league sets ever issued. Cards of Pacific Coast League players were included in packages of cookies. Distribution was limited to the West Coast. The 64 cards feature full color photos on a colored background, with player name and team. The cards measure 2-13/16" x 3-1/2", though the cards' rounded corners cause some variation in listed size. Card backs feature a very brief player statistic, card numbers and an offer for purchasing postage stamps. Five cards (11, 16, 29, 37 and 43) are considered scarce, while card #4 (Chuck Connors) is the most popular.

		NM	EX	VG
	Complete Set (64):	4,500	2,100	1,250
	Common Player:	60.00	30.00	20.00
1a	Johnny Lindell (Regular back.)	80.00	40.00	25.00
1b	Johnny Lindell ('52 Hollywood schedule on back)	80.00	40.00	25.00
2	Jim Davis	60.00	30.00	20.00
3	Al Gettle (Gettel)	60.00	30.00	20.00
4	Chuck Connors	600.00	300.00	200.00
5	Joe Grace	60.00	30.00	20.00
6	Eddie Basinski	60.00	30.00	20.00
7a	Gene Handley (Regular back.)	60.00	30.00	20.00
7b	Gene Handley (Schedule back.)	60.00	30.00	20.00
8	Walt Judnich	60.00	30.00	20.00
9	Jim Marshall	60.00	30.00	20.00
10	Max West	60.00	30.00	20.00
11	Bill MacCawley	120.00	60.00	35.00
12	Moreno Peiretti	60.00	30.00	20.00
13a	Fred Haney (Regular back.)	75.00	37.50	22.50
13b	Fred Haney ('52 Hollywood schedule on back)	75.00	37.50	22.50
14	Earl Johnson	60.00	30.00	20.00
15	Dave Dahle	60.00	30.00	20.00
16	Bob Talbot	120.00	60.00	35.00
17	Smokey Singleton	60.00	30.00	20.00
18	Frank Austin	60.00	30.00	20.00
19	Joe Gordon	90.00	45.00	27.50
20	Joe Marty	60.00	30.00	20.00
21	Bob Gillespie	60.00	30.00	20.00
22	Red Embree	60.00	30.00	20.00
23a	Lefty Olsen (Brown belt.)	60.00	30.00	20.00
23b	Lefty Olsen (Black belt.)	90.00	45.00	27.50
24a	Whitey Wietelmann (Large photo, much of bat missing.)	60.00	30.00	20.00
24b	Whitey Wietelmann (Small photo, more bat shows.)	60.00	30.00	20.00
25	Frank O'Doul	100.00	50.00	30.00
26	Memo Luna	60.00	30.00	20.00
27	John Davis	60.00	30.00	20.00
28	Dick Faber	60.00	30.00	20.00
29	Buddy Peterson	225.00	110.00	67.00
30	Hank Schenz	60.00	30.00	20.00
31	Tookie Gilbert	60.00	30.00	20.00
32	Mel Ott	200.00	100.00	60.00
33	Sam Chapman	60.00	30.00	20.00
34a	John Ragni (Outfielder)	60.00	30.00	20.00
34b	John Ragni (Pitcher)	100.00	50.00	30.00
35	Dick Cole	60.00	30.00	20.00
36	Tom Saffell	60.00	30.00	20.00
37	Roy Welmaker	120.00	60.00	35.00
38	Lou Stringer	60.00	30.00	20.00
39a	Chuck Stevens (Team on back Hollywood.)	60.00	30.00	20.00
39b	Chuck Stevens (Team on back Seattle.)	60.00	30.00	20.00
39c	Chuck Stevens (No team on back.)	60.00	30.00	20.00
40	Artie Wilson	90.00	45.00	20.00
41	Charlie Schanz	60.00	30.00	20.00
42	Al Lyons	60.00	30.00	20.00
43	Joe Erautt	300.00	150.00	90.00
44	Clarence Maddern	60.00	30.00	20.00
45	Gene Baker	60.00	30.00	20.00
46	Tom Heath	60.00	30.00	20.00
47	Al Lien	60.00	30.00	20.00
48	Bill Reeder	60.00	30.00	20.00
49	Bob Thurman	60.00	30.00	20.00
50	Ray Orteig	60.00	30.00	20.00
51	Joe Brovia	60.00	30.00	20.00
52	Jim Russell	60.00	30.00	20.00
53	Fred Sanford	60.00	30.00	20.00
54	Jim Gladd	60.00	30.00	20.00
55	Clay Hopper	60.00	30.00	20.00
56	Bill Glynn	60.00	30.00	20.00
57	Mike McCormick	60.00	30.00	20.00
58	Richie Myers	60.00	30.00	20.00
59	Vinnie Smith	60.00	30.00	20.00
60a	Stan Hack (Brown belt.)	80.00	40.00	25.00
60b	Stan Hack (Black belt.)	80.00	40.00	25.00
61	Bob Spicer	60.00	30.00	20.00
62	Jack Hollis	60.00	30.00	20.00
63	Ed Chandler	60.00	30.00	20.00
64	Bill Moisan	85.00	45.00	25.00

1953 Mother's Cookies

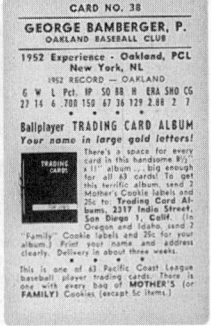

The 1953 Mother's Cookies cards are again 2-3/16" x 3-1/2", with rounded corners. There are 63 players from Pacific Coast League teams included. The full-color fronts have facsimile autographs rather than printed player names, and card backs offer a trading card album. Cards are generally more plentiful than in the 1952 set, with 11 of the cards apparently double printed.

		NM	EX	VG
	Complete Set (63):	1,725	850.00	525.00
	Common Player:	30.00	15.00	9.00
	Album:	125.00	65.00	40.00
1	Lee Winter	35.00	17.50	10.00
2	Joe Ostrowski	30.00	15.00	9.00
3	Will Ramsdell	30.00	15.00	9.00
4	Bobby Bragan	40.00	20.00	12.00
5	Fletcher Robbe	30.00	15.00	9.00
6	Aaron Robinson	30.00	15.00	9.00
7	Augie Galan	30.00	15.00	9.00
8	Buddy Peterson	30.00	15.00	9.00
9	Frank Lefty O'Doul	65.00	32.50	20.00
10	Walt Pocekay	30.00	15.00	9.00
11	Nini Tornay	30.00	15.00	9.00
12	Jim Moran	30.00	15.00	9.00
13	George Schmees	30.00	15.00	9.00
14	Al Widmar	30.00	15.00	9.00
15	Ritchie Myers	30.00	15.00	9.00
16	Bill Howerton	30.00	15.00	9.00
17	Chuck Stevens	30.00	15.00	9.00
18	Joe Brovia	30.00	15.00	9.00
19	Max West	30.00	15.00	9.00
20	Eddie Malone	30.00	15.00	9.00
21	Gene Handley	30.00	15.00	9.00
22	William D. McCawley	30.00	15.00	9.00
23	Bill Sweeney	30.00	15.00	9.00
24	Tom Alston	30.00	15.00	9.00
25	George Vico	30.00	15.00	9.00
26	Hank Arft	30.00	15.00	9.00
27	Al Benton	30.00	15.00	9.00
28	"Pete" Milne	30.00	15.00	9.00
29	Jim Gladd	30.00	15.00	9.00
30	Earl Rapp	35.00	17.50	10.00
31	Ray Orteig	30.00	15.00	9.00
32	Eddie Basinski	30.00	15.00	9.00
33	Reno Cheso	30.00	15.00	9.00
34	Clarence Maddern	30.00	15.00	9.00
35	Marino Pieretti	30.00	15.00	9.00
36	Bill Raimondi	30.00	15.00	9.00
37	Frank Kelleher	30.00	15.00	9.00
38	George Bamberger	35.00	17.50	10.00
39	Dick Smith	30.00	15.00	9.00
40	Charley Schanz	30.00	15.00	9.00
41	John Van Cuyk	30.00	15.00	9.00
42	Lloyd Hittle	30.00	15.00	9.00
43	Tommy Heath	30.00	15.00	9.00
44	Frank Kalin	30.00	15.00	9.00
45	Jack Tobin	30.00	15.00	9.00
46	Jim Davis	30.00	15.00	9.00
47	Claude Christie	30.00	15.00	9.00
48	Elvin Tappe	30.00	15.00	9.00
49	Stan Hack	60.00	30.00	18.00
50	Fred Richards	30.00	15.00	9.00
51	Clay Hopper	30.00	15.00	9.00
52	Roy Welmaker	30.00	15.00	9.00
53	Red Adams	30.00	15.00	9.00
54	Piper Davis	60.00	30.00	18.00
55	Spider Jorgensen	30.00	15.00	9.00
56	Lee Walls	30.00	15.00	9.00
57	Jack Phillips	30.00	15.00	9.00
58	Red Lynn	30.00	15.00	9.00
59	Eddie Beckman	30.00	15.00	9.00
60	Gene Desautels	30.00	15.00	9.00
61	Bob Dillinger	30.00	15.00	9.00
62	Al Federoff	55.00	27.50	16.50
63	Bill Boemler	30.00	15.00	9.00

1920 Mrs. Sherlock's Bread Pins

Members of the Toledo Mud Hens of the American Association are featured on this set of pins sponsored by Mrs. Sherlock's Bread. The 7/8" celluloid pins have a player portrait in black-and-white at center, with his name and position indicated below. At top, in either red or black type is, "Mrs. Sherlock's Home Made Bread." Backs credit manufacture to Bastian Bros. of Rochester, N.Y., "Mfr's of ribbon metal and celluloid novelties." The unnumbered pins are checklisted here alphabetically.

		NM	EX	VG
	Complete Set (19):	850.00	425.00	250.00
	Common Player:	60.00	30.00	18.00
(1)	Brady	60.00	30.00	18.00
(2)	Roger Bresnahan	90.00	45.00	27.00
(3)	Jean Dubuc	60.00	30.00	18.00
(4)	Dyer	60.00	30.00	18.00
(5)	Fox	60.00	30.00	18.00
(6)	Ham Hyatt	60.00	30.00	18.00
(7)	Jones	60.00	30.00	18.00
(8)	Joe Kelly	60.00	30.00	18.00
(9)	M. Kelly	60.00	30.00	18.00
(10)	Art Kores	60.00	30.00	18.00
(11)	McColl	60.00	30.00	18.00
(12)	Norm McNeill (McNeil)	60.00	30.00	18.00
(13)	Middleton	60.00	30.00	18.00
(14)	Murphy	60.00	30.00	18.00
(15)	Nelson	60.00	30.00	18.00
(16)	Dutch Stryker	60.00	30.00	18.00
(17)	Thompson	60.00	30.00	18.00
(18)	Al Wickland	60.00	30.00	18.00
(19)	Joe Wilhoit	60.00	30.00	18.00

1922 Mrs. Sherlock's Bread Pins (PB5)

Members of the Toledo Mud Hens of the American Association are featured on this set of pins sponsored by Mrs. Sherlock's Bread. The 5/8" celluloid pins have a player portrait in brown or green at center, with his name and position indicated below. At top, in either brown or green type, is "Eat Mrs. Sherlock's Bread." The pins are numbered at lower-left.

		NM	EX	VG
	Complete Set (21):	900.00	450.00	275.00
	Common Player:	60.00	30.00	18.00
1	Roger Bresnahan	90.00	45.00	27.00
2	Brad Kocher	60.00	30.00	18.00
3	Hill	60.00	30.00	18.00
4	Huber	60.00	30.00	18.00
5	Doc Ayers	60.00	30.00	18.00
6	Parks	60.00	30.00	18.00
7	Giard	60.00	30.00	18.00
8	Grimes	60.00	30.00	18.00
9	McCullough	60.00	30.00	18.00
10	Shoup	60.00	30.00	18.00
11	Al Wickland	60.00	30.00	18.00
12	Baker	60.00	30.00	18.00
13	Schauffle	60.00	30.00	18.00
14	Wright	60.00	30.00	18.00
15	Lamar	60.00	30.00	18.00
16	Sallee	60.00	30.00	18.00
17	Fred Luderus	60.00	30.00	18.00
18	Walgomat	60.00	30.00	18.00
19	Ed Konetchy	60.00	30.00	18.00
20	O'Neill	60.00	30.00	18.00
21	Hugh Bedient	60.00	30.00	18.00

1933 Mrs. Sherlock's Bread Pins

Members of the Toledo Mud Hens of the American Association are featured on this set of pins sponsored by Mrs. Sherlock's Bread. The 7/8" celluloid pins have a player portrait in black-and-white at center, with his name and position indicated below. At top, in red type, is "Mrs. Sherlock's Home Made Bread" in two lines. The unnumbered pins are checklisted here alphabetically.

		NM	EX	VG
Complete Set (18):		800.00	400.00	240.00
Common Player:		50.00	25.00	15.00
(1)	LeRoy Bachman	50.00	25.00	15.00
(2)	George Detore	50.00	25.00	15.00
(3)	Frank Doljack	50.00	25.00	15.00
(4)	Milt Galatzer	50.00	25.00	15.00
(5)	Walter Henline	50.00	25.00	15.00
(6)	Roxie Lawson	50.00	25.00	15.00
(7)	Thornton Lee	50.00	25.00	15.00
(8)	Ed Montague	50.00	25.00	15.00
(9)	Steve O'Neill	50.00	25.00	15.00
(10)	Monte Pearson	50.00	25.00	15.00
(11)	Bob Reis	50.00	25.00	15.00
(12)	Scott	50.00	25.00	15.00
(13)	Bill Sweeney	50.00	25.00	15.00
(14)	Hal Trosky	50.00	25.00	15.00
(15)	Pete Turgeon	50.00	25.00	15.00
(16)	Forrest Twogood	50.00	25.00	15.00
(17)	Max West	50.00	25.00	15.00
(18)	Ralph Winegarner	50.00	25.00	15.00

1956 Mutual Savings Dick Stuart

Possibly issued in conjunction with an autograph appearance at the bank, Dick Stuart is pictured on this black-and-white postcard-sized photocard as an outfielder for the Western League Lincoln Chiefs in 1956, the season in which he hit 66 home runs.

	NM	EX	VG
Dick Stuart	100.00	50.00	30.00

N

1960 National Bank of Washington Tacoma Giants

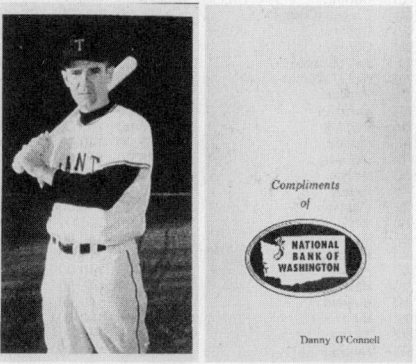

These 3" x 5" unnumbered cards have color photos on front and are usually found with black-and-white backs with the bank's advertising. Uncut sheets of the cards were sold at Cheney Stadium in Tacoma either blank-backed or with a message from the Tacoma Athletic Commission. Only members of the Pacific Coast League Tacoma Giants are included in the set. The set contains the first card issued of Hall of Fame pitcher Juan Marichal. Unfortunately, fellow Hall of Famer Willie McCovey, who played in 17 games for Tacoma in 1960, is not included in the set.

		NM	EX	VG
Complete Set (21):		1,000	500.00	300.00
Common Player:		30.00	15.00	9.00
(1)	Matty Alou	75.00	37.00	22.00
(2)	Ossie Alvarez	30.00	15.00	9.00
(3)	Don Choate	30.00	15.00	9.00
(4)	Red Davis	30.00	15.00	9.00
(5)	Bob Farley	30.00	15.00	9.00
(6)	Eddie Fisher	30.00	15.00	9.00
(7)	Tom Haller	30.00	15.00	9.00
(8)	Sherman Jones	30.00	15.00	9.00
(9)	Juan Marichal	400.00	200.00	120.00
(10)	Ray Monzant	30.00	15.00	9.00
(11)	Danny O'Connell	30.00	15.00	9.00
(12)	Jose Pagan	30.00	15.00	9.00
(13)	Bob Perry	30.00	15.00	9.00
(14)	Dick Phillips	30.00	15.00	9.00
(15)	Bobby Prescott	30.00	15.00	9.00
(16)	Marshall Renfroe	30.00	15.00	9.00
(17)	Frank Reveira	30.00	15.00	9.00
(18)	Dusty Rhodes	35.00	17.50	10.00
(19)	Sal Taormina	30.00	15.00	9.00
(20)	Verle Tiefenthaler	30.00	15.00	9.00
(21)	Dom Zanni	30.00	15.00	9.00

1961 National Bank of Washington Tacoma Giants

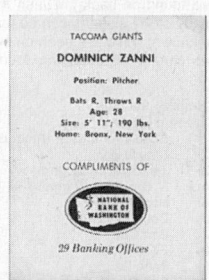

These 3" x 4" cards feature borderless sepia photos on the front. Backs have a sponsor's ad and a few player stats printed in dark blue. The unnumbered cards are checklisted here in alphabetical order.

		NM	EX	VG
Complete Set (21):		800.00	400.00	240.00
Common Player:		30.00	15.00	10.00
(1)	Rafael Alomar	40.00	20.00	12.00
(2)	Ernie Bowman	30.00	15.00	10.00
(3)	Bud Byerly	30.00	15.00	10.00
(4)	Ray Daviault	30.00	15.00	10.00
(5)	Red Davis	30.00	15.00	10.00
(6)	Bob Farley	30.00	15.00	10.00
(7)	Gil Garrido	30.00	15.00	10.00
(8)	John Goetz	30.00	15.00	10.00
(9)	Bill Hain	30.00	15.00	10.00
(10)	Ronald Herbel	30.00	15.00	10.00
(11)	Lynn Lovenguth	30.00	15.00	10.00
(12)	Georges H. Maranda	30.00	15.00	10.00
(13)	Manuel Mota	100.00	50.00	30.00
(14)	John Orsino	30.00	15.00	10.00
(15)	Bob Perry	30.00	15.00	10.00
(16)	Gaylord Perry	175.00	90.00	55.00
(17)	Dick Phillips	30.00	15.00	10.00
(18)	Frank Reveira	30.00	15.00	10.00
(19)	Dusty Rhodes	40.00	20.00	12.00
(20)	Verle Tiefenthaler	30.00	15.00	10.00
(21)	Dom Zanni	30.00	15.00	10.00

1907 Newark Evening World Supplements

The Newark Sailors of the Class A Eastern League are featured in this set of supplements from a local newspaper. The 7-1/2" x 10-15/16" pieces are printed in either sepia or black-and-white. An ornate border surrounds a player pose on a plain

background. In a box beneath is player identification. Backs are blank. The unnumbered supplements are checklisted here in alphabetical order, though the list may not yet be complete.

		NM	EX	VG
Common Player:		400.00	200.00	120.00
(1)	William Carrick	400.00	200.00	120.00
(2)	James Cockman	400.00	200.00	120.00
(3)	Clyde Engle	400.00	200.00	120.00
(4)	James Jones	400.00	200.00	120.00
(5)	Paul Krichell	400.00	200.00	120.00
(6)	Henry LaBelle	400.00	200.00	120.00
(7)	William Mahling	400.00	200.00	120.00
(8)	Chas. McCafferty	400.00	200.00	120.00
(9)	Thomas McCarthy	400.00	200.00	120.00
(10)	James Mullen (Mullin)	400.00	200.00	120.00
(11)	Al Pardee	400.00	200.00	120.00
(12)	Bayard Sharpe	400.00	200.00	120.00
(13)	John E. Shea	400.00	200.00	120.00
(14)	Oscar Stanage	400.00	200.00	120.00
(15)	Elmer Zacher	400.00	200.00	120.00

O

1950 Oak Hall Roanoke Red Sox

(See 1950 Bush & Hancock Roanoke Red Sox.)

1913 Oakland Oaks Team Issue

Stylistically similar to contemporary Zeenuts cards, little is known about this series. The blank-back, approximately 2" x 3-5/8" cards have full-length sepiatone player poses on a sepiatone background. The player's last name and city are printed in all caps in two lines at bottom. It is unknown whether the cards on the list comprise a complete set. Their manner of distribution is likewise unknown, they may have been a strip card issue or a candy insert.

		NM	EX	VG
Common Player:		2,400	1,200	700.00
(1)	Ody Abbott	2,400	1,200	700.00
(2)	Harry Ables	2,400	1,200	700.00
(3)	Jesse Becker	2,400	1,200	700.00
(4)	W.W. Cook	2,400	1,200	700.00
(5)	Bert Coy	2,400	1,200	700.00
(6)	Rube Gardner	2,400	1,200	700.00
(7)	Howard Gregory	2,400	1,200	700.00
(8)	Gus Hetling	2,400	1,200	700.00
(9)	Jack Killilay	2,400	1,200	700.00
(10)	Bill Leard	2,400	1,200	700.00
(11)	John Malarkey	2,400	1,200	700.00
(12)	Carl Mitze	2,400	1,200	700.00
(13)	John Ness	2,400	1,200	700.00
(14)	Henry Olmstead	2,400	1,200	700.00
(15)	Cy Parkin	2,400	1,200	700.00
(16)	W.J. Pearce	2,400	1,200	700.00
(17)	Heine Pernoll	2,400	1,200	700.00
(18)	Ashley Pope	2,400	1,200	700.00
(19)	George Schirm	2,400	1,200	700.00
(20)	Elmer Zacher	2,400	1,200	700.00

1909 Obak (T212)

Produced annually from 1909 to 1911, the Obak cards were actually three separate and distinct sets, but they were all grouped together under a single T212 designation in the American Card Catalog. The Obak sets are closely related in style to the more popular T206 "White Border" set issued over the same three-year period, and, in fact, were produced by the California branch of the same American Tobacco Co. conglomerate. The Obaks are the standard tobacco card size, about 1-1/2" x 2-5/8", and feature a colored lithograph, along with the player's name and team, on the front of the card. The year of issue can easily be determined by examing the back. The 1909 issue has blue printing with the name "Obak" appearing in an "Old English" type style. For 1910 the type face was changed to straight block letters; and in 1911 the backs were printed in red and include a brief biography and player statistics. The 1909 edition featured only teams from the Pacific Coast League. Cards can be found with backs that have or do not have a border around the text, though neither version appears to be scarcer than the other. Many 1909 Obaks with the "no-frame" back design show evidence of having been cut by hand from sheets, rather than machine-cut.

		NM	EX	VG
Complete Set (76):		45,000	27,500	11,000
Common Player:		550.00	275.00	125.00
(1)	Baum	550.00	275.00	125.00
(2)	Beall	550.00	275.00	125.00
(3)	Bernard	550.00	275.00	125.00
(4)	Berry	550.00	275.00	125.00
(5)	Bodie	550.00	275.00	125.00
(6)	Boyce	550.00	275.00	125.00
(7)	Brackenridge	550.00	275.00	125.00
(8)	N. Brashear	550.00	275.00	125.00
(9)	Breen	550.00	275.00	125.00
(10)	Brown	550.00	275.00	125.00
(11)	D. Brown	550.00	275.00	125.00
(12)	Browning	550.00	275.00	125.00
(13)	Byrnes	550.00	275.00	125.00
(14)	Cameron	550.00	275.00	125.00
(15)	Carroll	550.00	275.00	125.00
(16)	Carson	550.00	275.00	125.00
(17)	Christian	550.00	275.00	125.00
(18)	Coy	550.00	275.00	125.00
(19)	Delmas	550.00	275.00	125.00
(20)	Dillon	550.00	275.00	125.00
(21)	Eagan	550.00	275.00	125.00
(22)	Easterly (Eastley)	550.00	275.00	125.00
(23)	Ehman	550.00	275.00	125.00
(24)	Fisher	550.00	275.00	125.00
(25)	Fitzgerald	550.00	275.00	125.00
(26)	Flannagan	550.00	275.00	125.00
(27)	Gandil	4,000	2,000	1,500
(28)	Garrett	550.00	275.00	125.00
(29)	Graham	550.00	275.00	125.00
(30)	Graney	550.00	275.00	125.00
(31)	Griffin	550.00	275.00	125.00
(32)	Guyn	550.00	275.00	125.00
(33)	Haley	550.00	275.00	125.00
(34)	Harkins	550.00	275.00	125.00
(35)	Henley	550.00	275.00	125.00
(36)	Hitt	550.00	275.00	125.00
(37)	Hogan	550.00	275.00	125.00
(38)	W. Hogan	550.00	275.00	125.00
(39)	Howard	550.00	275.00	125.00
(40)	Howse	550.00	275.00	125.00
(41)	Jansing	550.00	275.00	125.00
(42)	LaLonge	550.00	275.00	125.00
(43)	C. Lewis	550.00	275.00	125.00
(44)	D. Lewis	550.00	275.00	125.00
(45)	J. Lewis	550.00	275.00	125.00
(46)	Martinke	550.00	275.00	125.00
(47)	McArdle	550.00	275.00	125.00
(48)	McCredie	550.00	275.00	125.00
(49)	McKune	550.00	275.00	125.00
(50)	Melchior	550.00	275.00	125.00
(51)	Mohler	550.00	275.00	125.00
(52)	Mott	550.00	275.00	125.00
(53)	Mundorff	550.00	275.00	125.00
(54)	Murphy	550.00	275.00	125.00
(55)	Nagle	550.00	275.00	125.00
(56)	Nelson	550.00	275.00	125.00
(57)	Olson	550.00	275.00	125.00
(58)	Ornsdorff	550.00	275.00	125.00
(59)	Ort	550.00	275.00	125.00
(60)	Ragan	550.00	275.00	125.00
(61)	Raymer	550.00	275.00	125.00
(62)	Reidy	550.00	275.00	125.00
(63)	Ryan	550.00	275.00	125.00
(64)	Shinn	550.00	275.00	125.00
(65)	Smith	550.00	275.00	125.00
(66)	Speas	550.00	275.00	125.00
(67)	Stoval (Stovall)	550.00	275.00	125.00
(68)	Tennant	550.00	275.00	125.00
(69)	Whalen	550.00	275.00	125.00
(70)	Wheeler	45,000	275.00	125.00
(71)	Wiggs	550.00	275.00	125.00
(72)	Willett	550.00	275.00	125.00
(73)	J. Williams	550.00	275.00	125.00
(74)	R. Williams	550.00	275.00	125.00
(75)	Willis	550.00	275.00	125.00
(76)	Zeider	550.00	275.00	125.00

1910 Obak 150 Subjects (T212)

The most common, yet most complex, of the three annual T212 baseball card issues from Obak Cigarettes is the 1910 edition. Besides players from the six Pacific Coast League teams, cards were also issued for the four-team Northwestern League. This change caused the addition of a league abbreviation, along with the player's last name and city on front. Backs are again printed in blue, but utilize a less ornate typography than the 1909 cards. The 1910 Obak set is formatted similar to the more popular T206 "White Border" set issued at the same time "back East," and, in fact, was produced by the

California branch of the same American Tobacco Company conglomerate. Obaks are the standard tobacco-card size, about 1-1/2" x 2-5/8", featuring a color lithograph on front. The 1910 issue comprises two major types, one which mentions "150 SUBJECTS," on back, the other specifying "175 SUB-JECTS." Forty player cards, all from the PCL, are known to exist in both 150- and 175-subject versions, the former being much scarcer. Many of the 150-subject cards can be found with significant picture variations, such as missing team names on jerseys, plain versus striped caps, different background colors or different picture cropping. Unique to the 1910 Obaks is a selection of 35 different advertising slogans which are found on back between the boxed text elements. How many of the slogans can be found on each player's cards is unknown; some are seen on only a handful of different players' cards while others are found on dozens.

		NM	EX	VG
Complete Set (40):		25,000	13,000	5,500
Common Player:		600.00	320.00	125.00
(1)	Charlie Armbuster (Ambruster)	600.00	320.00	125.00
(2)	Claude Berry	600.00	320.00	125.00
(3)	John Brackenridge	600.00	320.00	125.00
(4)	N. Brashear (Norman)	600.00	320.00	125.00
(5)	Hap Briggs	600.00	320.00	125.00
(6)	Don Cameron	600.00	320.00	125.00
(7)	Bert Coy	600.00	320.00	125.00
(8)	Elmer Criger	600.00	320.00	125.00
(9)	Babe Danzig	600.00	320.00	125.00
(10)	Cap Dillon	600.00	320.00	125.00
(11)	Bill Fisher	600.00	320.00	125.00
(12)	Ed Griffin	600.00	320.00	125.00
(13)	Cack Henley	600.00	320.00	125.00
(14)	Al Hiester	600.00	320.00	125.00
(15)	Happy Hogan	600.00	320.00	125.00
(16)	Ivan Howard	600.00	320.00	125.00
(17)	Gene Krapp	600.00	320.00	125.00
(18)	Mickey LaLonge	600.00	320.00	125.00
(19)	George Manush	600.00	320.00	125.00
(20)	Roy McArdle	600.00	320.00	125.00
(21)	Walt McCredie	600.00	320.00	125.00
(22)	Henry Melchoir	600.00	320.00	125.00
(23)	Kid Mohler	600.00	320.00	125.00
(24)	Walter Moser	600.00	320.00	125.00
(25)	Howard Mundorf	600.00	320.00	125.00
(26)	Howard Murphy	600.00	320.00	125.00
(27)	George Ort	600.00	320.00	125.00
(28)	Hank Perry	600.00	320.00	125.00
(29)	Bill Rapps	600.00	320.00	125.00
(30)	H. Smith (Hugh)	600.00	320.00	125.00
(31)	J. Smith (Jud)	600.00	320.00	125.00
(32)	Bill Steen	600.00	320.00	125.00
(33)	Harry Stewart	600.00	320.00	125.00
(34)	Pinky Swander	600.00	320.00	125.00
(35)	Lefty Tonnesen (Tonneson)	600.00	320.00	125.00
(36)	Jimmy Whalen	600.00	320.00	125.00
(37)	Roy Willett	600.00	320.00	125.00
(38)	Jimmy Williams	600.00	320.00	125.00
(39)	Ralph Willis	600.00	320.00	125.00
(40)	Harry Wolverton	600.00	320.00	125.00

1910 Obak 175 Subjects (T212)

The most common, yet most complex, of the three annual T212 baseball card issues from Obak Cigarettes is the 1910 edition. Besides players from the six Pacific Coast League teams, cards were also issued for the four-team Northwestern

League. This change caused the addition of a league abbreviation, along with the player's last name and city on front. Backs are again printed in blue, but utilize a less ornate typography than the 1909 cards. The 1910 Obak set is formatted similar to the more popular T206 "White Border" set issued at the same time "back East," and, in fact, was produced by the California branch of the same American Tobacco Co. conglomerate. Obaks are the standard tobacco-card size, about 1-1/2" x 2-5/8", featuring a color lithograph on front. The 1910 issue comprises two major types, one which mentions "150 SUBJECTS," on back, the other specifying "175 SUBJECTS." Forty player cards, all from the PCL, are known to exist in both 150- and 175-subject versions, the former being much scarcer. Many of the 150-subject cards can be found with significant picture variations, such as missing team names on jerseys, plain versus striped caps, different background colors or different picture cropping. Unique to the 1910 Obaks is a selection of 35 different advertising slogans which are found on back between the boxed text elements. How many of the slogans can be found on each player's cards is unknown; some are seen on only a handful of different players' cards while others are found on dozens.

		NM	EX	VG
Complete Set (175):		38,000	20,000	9,000
Common Player:		275.00	140.00	65.00
(1)	Agnew	275.00	140.00	65.00
(2)	Akin	275.00	140.00	65.00
(3)	Ames	275.00	140.00	65.00
(4)	Annis	275.00	140.00	65.00
(5)	Armbuster (Armbruster)	275.00	140.00	65.00
(6)	Baker	275.00	140.00	65.00
(7)	Bassey	275.00	140.00	65.00
(8)	Baum	275.00	140.00	65.00
	Beall (Now believed not to exist.)	275.00	140.00	65.00
(9)	Bennett	275.00	140.00	65.00
(10)	Bernard	275.00	140.00	65.00
(11)	Berry	275.00	140.00	65.00
(12)	Blankenship	275.00	140.00	65.00
(13)	Boardman	275.00	140.00	65.00
(14)	Bodie	275.00	140.00	65.00
(15)	Bonner	275.00	140.00	65.00
(16)	Brackenridge	275.00	140.00	65.00
(17)	N. Brashear	275.00	140.00	65.00
(18)	R. Brashear	275.00	140.00	65.00
(19)	Breen	275.00	140.00	65.00
(20)	Briggs	275.00	140.00	65.00
(21)	Brinker	275.00	140.00	65.00
(22)	Briswalter	275.00	140.00	65.00
(23)	Brooks	275.00	140.00	65.00
(24)	Brown (Sacramento)	275.00	140.00	65.00
(25)	Brown (Vernon)	275.00	140.00	65.00
(26)	D. Brown	275.00	140.00	65.00
(27)	Browning	275.00	140.00	65.00
(28)	Burrell	275.00	140.00	65.00
(29)	Byrd	275.00	140.00	65.00
(30)	Byrnes	275.00	140.00	65.00
(31)	Cameron	275.00	140.00	65.00
(32)	Capron	275.00	140.00	65.00
(33)	Carlisle	275.00	140.00	65.00
(34)	Carroll	275.00	140.00	65.00
(35)	Cartwright	275.00	140.00	65.00
(36)	Casey	275.00	140.00	65.00
(37)	Caslleton (Castleton)	400.00	200.00	100.00
(38)	Chenault	275.00	140.00	65.00
(39)	Christian	275.00	140.00	65.00
(40)	Coleman	275.00	140.00	65.00
(41)	Cooney	275.00	140.00	65.00
(42)	Coy	275.00	140.00	65.00
(43)	Criger	275.00	140.00	65.00
(44)	Custer	275.00	140.00	65.00
(45)	Cutshaw	275.00	140.00	65.00
(46)	Daley	275.00	140.00	65.00
(47)	Danzig	275.00	140.00	65.00
(48)	Daringer	275.00	140.00	65.00
(49)	Davis	275.00	140.00	65.00
(50)	Delhi	275.00	140.00	65.00
(51)	Delmas	275.00	140.00	65.00
(52)	Dillon	275.00	140.00	65.00
(53)	Dretchko	275.00	140.00	65.00
(54)	Eastley	275.00	140.00	65.00
(55)	Erickson	275.00	140.00	65.00
(56)	Flannagan	275.00	140.00	65.00
(57)	Fisher (Portland)	275.00	140.00	65.00
(58)	Fisher (Vernon)	275.00	140.00	65.00
(59)	Fitzgerald	275.00	140.00	65.00
(60)	Flood	275.00	140.00	65.00
(61)	Fournier	275.00	140.00	65.00
(62)	Frisk	275.00	140.00	65.00
(63)	Gaddy	275.00	140.00	65.00
(64)	Gardner	275.00	140.00	65.00
(65)	Garrett	275.00	140.00	65.00
(66)	Greggs (Gregg)	275.00	140.00	65.00
(67)	Griffin	275.00	140.00	65.00
(68)	Gurney	275.00	140.00	65.00
(69)	Hall (Seattle)	275.00	140.00	65.00
(70)	Hall (Tacoma)	275.00	140.00	65.00
(71)	Harkins	275.00	140.00	65.00
(72)	Hartman	275.00	140.00	65.00
(73)	Hendrix	275.00	140.00	65.00
(74)	Henley	275.00	140.00	65.00
(75)	Hensling	275.00	140.00	65.00
(76)	Hetling	275.00	140.00	65.00
(77)	Hickey	275.00	140.00	65.00
(78)	Hiester	275.00	140.00	65.00
(79)	Hitt	275.00	140.00	65.00
(80)	Hogan (Oakland)	275.00	140.00	65.00
(81)	Hogan (Vernon)	275.00	140.00	65.00
(82)	Hollis	275.00	140.00	65.00
(83)	Holm	275.00	140.00	65.00
(84)	Howard	275.00	140.00	65.00
(85)	Hunt	275.00	140.00	65.00
(86)	James	275.00	140.00	65.00
(87)	Jansing	275.00	140.00	65.00

		NM	EX	VG
(88)	Jensen	275.00	140.00	65.00
(89)	Johnston	275.00	140.00	65.00
(90)	Keener	275.00	140.00	65.00
(91)	Killilay	275.00	140.00	65.00
(92)	Kippert	275.00	140.00	65.00
(93)	Klein	275.00	140.00	65.00
(94)	Krapp	275.00	140.00	65.00
(95)	Kusel	275.00	140.00	65.00
(96)	LaLonge	275.00	140.00	65.00
(97)	Lewis	275.00	140.00	65.00
(98)	J. Lewis	275.00	140.00	65.00
(99)	John Lindsay	275.00	140.00	65.00
(100)	Lively	275.00	140.00	65.00
(101)	Lynch	275.00	140.00	65.00
(102)	Manush	275.00	140.00	65.00
(103)	Martinke	275.00	140.00	65.00
(104)	McArdle	275.00	140.00	65.00
(105)	McCredie	275.00	140.00	65.00
(106)	Melchior	275.00	140.00	65.00
(107)	Miller (San Francisco)	275.00	140.00	65.00
(108)	Miller (Seattle)	275.00	140.00	65.00
(109)	Mitze	275.00	140.00	65.00
(110)	Mohler	275.00	140.00	65.00
(111)	Moser	275.00	140.00	65.00
(112)	Mott	275.00	140.00	65.00
(113)	Mundorff (Mundorf)	275.00	140.00	65.00
(114)	Murphy	275.00	140.00	65.00
(115)	Nagle	275.00	140.00	65.00
(116)	Nelson	275.00	140.00	65.00
(117)	Netzel	275.00	140.00	65.00
(118)	Nourse	275.00	140.00	65.00
(119)	Nordyke	275.00	140.00	65.00
(120)	Olson	275.00	140.00	65.00
(121)	Orendorff (Orsnsdorff)	275.00	140.00	65.00
(122)	Ort	275.00	140.00	65.00
(123)	Ostdiek	275.00	140.00	65.00
(124)	Pennington	275.00	140.00	65.00
(125)	Perrine	275.00	140.00	65.00
(126)	Perry	275.00	140.00	65.00
(127)	Persons	275.00	140.00	65.00
(128)	Rapps	275.00	140.00	65.00
(129)	Raymer	275.00	140.00	65.00
(130)	Raymond	275.00	140.00	65.00
(131)	Rockenfield	275.00	140.00	65.00
(132)	Roth	275.00	140.00	65.00
(133)	D. Ryan	275.00	140.00	65.00
(134)	J. Ryan	275.00	140.00	65.00
(135)	Scharnweber	275.00	140.00	65.00
(136)	Schmutz	275.00	140.00	65.00
(137)	Seaton (Portland)	275.00	140.00	65.00
(138)	Seaton (Seattle)	275.00	140.00	65.00
(139)	Shafer	275.00	140.00	65.00
(140)	Shaw	275.00	140.00	65.00
(141)	Shea	275.00	140.00	65.00
(142)	Shinn	275.00	140.00	65.00
(143)	Smith	275.00	140.00	65.00
(144)	H. Smith	275.00	140.00	65.00
(145)	J. Smith	275.00	140.00	65.00
(146)	Speas	275.00	140.00	65.00
(147)	Spiesman	275.00	140.00	65.00
(148)	Starkell	275.00	140.00	65.00
(149)	Steen	275.00	140.00	65.00
(150)	Stevens	275.00	140.00	65.00
(151)	Stewart	275.00	140.00	65.00
(152)	Stovell (Stovall)	275.00	140.00	65.00
(153)	Streib	275.00	140.00	65.00
(154)	Sugden	275.00	140.00	65.00
(155)	Sutor	275.00	140.00	65.00
(156)	Swain	275.00	140.00	65.00
(157)	Swander	275.00	140.00	65.00
(158)	Tennant	275.00	140.00	65.00
(159)	Thomas	275.00	140.00	65.00
(160)	Thompson	275.00	140.00	65.00
(161)	Thorsen	275.00	140.00	65.00
(162)	Tonnesen (Tonneson)	275.00	140.00	65.00
(163)	Tozer	275.00	140.00	65.00
(164)	Van Buren	275.00	140.00	65.00
(165)	Vitt	275.00	140.00	65.00
(166)	Wares	275.00	140.00	65.00
(167)	Waring	275.00	140.00	65.00
(168)	Warren	275.00	140.00	65.00
(169)	Weed	275.00	140.00	65.00
(170)	Whalen	275.00	140.00	65.00
(171)	Willett	275.00	140.00	65.00
(172)	Williams	275.00	140.00	65.00
(173)	Willis	275.00	140.00	65.00
(174)	Wolverton	275.00	140.00	65.00
(175)	Zackert	275.00	140.00	65.00

1911 Obak (T212)

WEAVER, the hardest hitting utility player in the League, has played sensational ball in both infield and outfield. Has a wonderful throwing arm and is one of the most natural ball players in the game today. Can play any position on the infield, covers lots of ground, is very fast and shows up like a star.

1910... AB. 291 B.H. 84 P.C. 289

OBAK

SPEAKS QUALITY

IN ANY COMPANY

FACTORY N9 171 1ST DIST CAL.

WEAVER, SAN FRANCISCO, P. C. L.

The last of the three annual T212 baseball card issues from Obak Cigarettes is the 1911 edition, again featuring play-

---

ers from the six Pacific Coast League teams and the four-team Northwestern League. Often using the same chromolithographic picture on front as the 1910 cards, the 1911s are easily distinguished by the use of red, rather than blue, printing on back. Also new to the 1911s was the addition of a sentence or two about the player and, on most cards, recent years' statistics, an innovation also seen on the contemporary T205 cards "back East." In fact the Obaks were produced by the California branch of the same American Tobacco Company conglomerate. Obaks are the standard tobacco card size, about 1-1/2" x 2-5/8".

		NM	EX	VG
Complete Set (175):		55,000	28,000	11,000
Common Player:		320.00	160.00	75.00
(1)	Abbott	320.00	160.00	75.00
(2)	Ables	320.00	160.00	75.00
(3)	Adams	320.00	160.00	75.00
(4)	Agnew	320.00	160.00	75.00
(5)	Akin	320.00	160.00	75.00
(6)	Annis	320.00	160.00	75.00
(7)	Arrelanes (Arellanes)	320.00	160.00	75.00
(8)	Barry	320.00	160.00	75.00
(9)	Bassey	320.00	160.00	75.00
(10)	Baum	320.00	160.00	75.00
(11)	Bennett	320.00	160.00	75.00
(12)	Bernard	320.00	160.00	75.00
(13)	Berry	320.00	160.00	75.00
(14)	Bloomfield	320.00	160.00	75.00
(15)	Bonner	320.00	160.00	75.00
(16)	Brackenridge	320.00	160.00	75.00
(17)	Brashear	320.00	160.00	75.00
(18)	R. Brashear	320.00	160.00	75.00
(19)	Brinker	320.00	160.00	75.00
(20)	Brown	320.00	160.00	75.00
(21)	Browning	320.00	160.00	75.00
(22)	Bues	320.00	160.00	75.00
(23)	Burrell	320.00	160.00	75.00
(24)	Burns	320.00	160.00	75.00
(25)	Butler	320.00	160.00	75.00
(26)	Byram	320.00	160.00	75.00
(27)	Carlisle	320.00	160.00	75.00
(28)	Carson	320.00	160.00	75.00
(29)	Cartwright	320.00	160.00	75.00
(30)	Casey	320.00	160.00	75.00
(31)	Castleton	400.00	200.00	125.00
(32)	Chadbourne	320.00	160.00	75.00
(33)	Christian	320.00	160.00	75.00
(34)	Coleman	320.00	160.00	75.00
(35)	Cooney	320.00	160.00	75.00
(36)	Coy	320.00	160.00	75.00
(37)	Criger	320.00	160.00	75.00
(38)	Crukshank	320.00	160.00	75.00
(39)	Cutshaw	320.00	160.00	75.00
(40)	Daley	320.00	160.00	75.00
(41)	Danzig	320.00	160.00	75.00
(42)	Dashwood	320.00	160.00	75.00
(43)	Davis	320.00	160.00	75.00
(44)	Delhi	320.00	160.00	75.00
(45)	Delmas	320.00	160.00	75.00
(46)	Dillon	320.00	160.00	75.00
(47)	Engel	320.00	160.00	75.00
(48)	Erickson	320.00	160.00	75.00
(49)	Fitzgerald	320.00	160.00	75.00
(50)	Flater	320.00	160.00	75.00
(51)	Frisk	320.00	160.00	75.00
(52)	Fullerton	320.00	160.00	75.00
(53)	Garrett	320.00	160.00	75.00
(54)	Goodman	320.00	160.00	75.00
(55)	Gordon	320.00	160.00	75.00
(56)	Grindle	320.00	160.00	75.00
(57)	Hall	320.00	160.00	75.00
(58)	Harris	320.00	160.00	75.00
(59)	Hasty	320.00	160.00	75.00
(60)	Henderson	320.00	160.00	75.00
(61)	Henley	320.00	160.00	75.00
(62)	Hetling	320.00	160.00	75.00
(63)	Hiester	320.00	160.00	75.00
(64)	Higgins	320.00	160.00	75.00
(65)	Hitt	320.00	160.00	75.00
(66)	Hoffman	320.00	160.00	75.00
(67)	Hogan	320.00	160.00	75.00
(68)	Holm	320.00	160.00	75.00
(69)	Householder	320.00	160.00	75.00
(70)	Hosp	320.00	160.00	75.00
(71)	Howard	320.00	160.00	75.00
(72)	Hunt	320.00	160.00	75.00
(73)	James	320.00	160.00	75.00
(74)	Jensen	320.00	160.00	75.00
(75)	Kading	320.00	160.00	75.00
(76)	Kane	320.00	160.00	75.00
(77)	Kippert	320.00	160.00	75.00
(78)	Knight	320.00	160.00	75.00
(79)	Koestner	320.00	160.00	75.00
(80)	Krueger	320.00	160.00	75.00
(81)	Kuhn	320.00	160.00	75.00
(82)	LaLonge	320.00	160.00	75.00
(83)	Lamline	320.00	160.00	75.00
(84)	Leard	320.00	160.00	75.00
(85)	Lerchen	320.00	160.00	75.00
(86)	Lewis	320.00	160.00	75.00
(87)	Madden	320.00	160.00	75.00
(88)	Maggert	320.00	160.00	75.00
(89)	Mahoney	320.00	160.00	75.00
(90)	McArdle	320.00	160.00	75.00
(91)	McCredie	320.00	160.00	75.00
(92)	McDonnell	320.00	160.00	75.00
(93)	Meikle	320.00	160.00	75.00
(94)	Melchior	320.00	160.00	75.00
(95)	Mensor	650.00	310.00	210.00
(96)	Metzger	320.00	160.00	75.00
(97)	Miller (Oakland)	320.00	160.00	75.00
(98)	Miller (San Francisco)	320.00	160.00	75.00
(99)	Ten Million	3,000	1,500	750.00
(100)	Mitze	320.00	160.00	75.00
(101)	Mohler	320.00	160.00	75.00
(102)	Moore	320.00	160.00	75.00
(103)	Morse	320.00	160.00	75.00
(104)	Moskiman	320.00	160.00	75.00
(105)	Mundorff	320.00	160.00	75.00
(106)	Murray	320.00	160.00	75.00
(107)	Netzel	320.00	160.00	75.00
(108)	Nordyke	320.00	160.00	75.00
(109)	Nourse	320.00	160.00	75.00
(110)	O'Rourke	320.00	160.00	75.00
(111)	Ostdiek	320.00	160.00	75.00
(112)	Patterson	320.00	160.00	75.00
(113)	Pearce	320.00	160.00	75.00
(114)	Peckinpaugh	320.00	160.00	75.00
(115)	Pernoll	320.00	160.00	75.00
(116)	Pfyl	320.00	160.00	75.00
(117)	Powell	320.00	160.00	75.00
(118)	Raleigh	320.00	160.00	75.00
(119)	Rapps	320.00	160.00	75.00
(120)	Raymer	320.00	160.00	75.00
(121)	Raymond	320.00	160.00	75.00
(122)	Reddick	320.00	160.00	75.00
(123)	Roche	320.00	160.00	75.00
(124)	Rockenfield	320.00	160.00	75.00
(125)	Rogers	320.00	160.00	75.00
(126)	Ross	320.00	160.00	75.00
(127)	Ryan	320.00	160.00	75.00
(128)	J. Ryan	320.00	160.00	75.00
(129)	Scharnweber	320.00	160.00	75.00
(130)	Schmidt	320.00	160.00	75.00
(131)	Schmutz	320.00	160.00	75.00
(132)	Seaton (Portland)	320.00	160.00	75.00
(133)	Seaton (Seattle)	320.00	160.00	75.00
(134)	Shaw	320.00	160.00	75.00
(135)	Shea	320.00	160.00	75.00
(136)	Sheehan (Portland)	320.00	160.00	75.00
(137)	Sheehan (Vernon)	320.00	160.00	75.00
(138)	Shinn	320.00	160.00	75.00
(139)	Skeels	320.00	160.00	75.00
(140)	H. Smith	320.00	160.00	75.00
(141)	Speas	320.00	160.00	75.00
(142)	Spencer	320.00	160.00	75.00
(143)	Spiesman	320.00	160.00	75.00
(144)	Starkel	320.00	160.00	75.00
(145)	Steen	320.00	160.00	75.00
(146)	Stewart	320.00	160.00	75.00
(147)	Stinson	320.00	160.00	75.00
(148)	Stovall	320.00	160.00	75.00
(149)	Strand	320.00	160.00	75.00
(150)	Sutor	320.00	160.00	75.00
(151)	Swain	320.00	160.00	75.00
(152)	Tennant	320.00	160.00	75.00
(153)	Thomas (Sacramento)	320.00	160.00	75.00
(154)	Thomas (Victoria)	320.00	160.00	75.00
(155)	Thompson	320.00	160.00	75.00
(156)	Thornton	320.00	160.00	75.00
(157)	Thorsen	320.00	160.00	75.00
(158)	Tiedeman	320.00	160.00	75.00
(159)	Tozer	320.00	160.00	75.00
(160)	Van Buren	320.00	160.00	75.00
(161)	Vitt	320.00	160.00	75.00
(162)	Ward	320.00	160.00	75.00
(163)	Wares	320.00	160.00	75.00
(164)	Warren	320.00	160.00	75.00
(165)	Weaver	7,000	3,500	1,750
(166)	Weed	320.00	160.00	75.00
(167)	Wheeler	320.00	160.00	75.00
(168)	Wiggs	320.00	160.00	75.00
(169)	Willett	320.00	160.00	75.00
(170)	Williams	320.00	160.00	75.00
(171)	Wolverton	320.00	160.00	75.00
(172)	Zacher	320.00	160.00	75.00
(173)	Zackert	320.00	160.00	75.00
(174)	Zamlock	320.00	160.00	75.00
(175)	Zimmerman	320.00	160.00	75.00

1911 Obak Cabinets (T4)

Among the scarcest of all the 20th Century tobacco issues, the T4 Obak Premiums are cabinet-sized cards distributed in conjunction with the better-known Obak T212 card set of players from the Northwestern and Pacific Coast Leagues. The Obak Premiums measure about 5" x 7" and are printed on a cardboard-like paper. The cards featured a black-and-white player photo inside a 3-1/2" x 5" oval. There is no printing on the front of the card to identify the player or indicate the manufacturer. The backs are blank. In most cases the photos used for the premiums are identical to the T212 pictures, except for some cropping differences. Under the Obak mail-in promotion, 50 coupons from cigarette packages were required to obtain just one premium card, which explains their extreme scarcity today. All 175 players pictured in the T212 set were theoretically available as premium cards, but to date many remain undiscovered. Only those cards that have been confirmed to survive are listed with a value here. Most of the Obak premiums that exist in original condition contain a number, written in pencil on the back of the card, that corresponds to the checklist printed on the coupon. A large group of the cabinets, most of which had been cut down to just the oval portrait, was offered in a September 2002 auction.

		NM	EX	VG
	Common Player:	6,750	3,500	2,200
	LOS ANGELES			
1	H. Smith	5,750	2,875	1,725
2	Tozer	5,750	2,875	1,725
3	Howard	5,750	2,875	1,725
4	Daley	5,750	2,875	1,725
5	Bernard			
6	Dillon	5,750	2,875	1,725
7	Delmas			
8	Delhi	5,750	2,875	1,725
9	Criger			
10	Thorsen	5,750	2,875	1,725
11	Agnew			
12	Akin			
13	Metzger			
14	Abbott			
15	Wheeler	5,750	2,875	1,725
16	Moore			
17	Grindle			
	OAKLAND			
18	Wolverton			
19	Mitze	5,750	2,875	1,725
20	Wares			
21	Cutshaw	5,750	2,875	1,725
22	Christian	5,750	2,875	1,725
23	Wiggs			
24	Maggert	5,750	2,875	1,725
25	Pfyl			
26	Pearce			
27	Hetling			
28	Hoffman			
29	Pernoll			
30	Coy			
31	Tiedeman	5,750	2,875	1,725
32	Knight	.00	.00	.00
33	Flater	5,750	2,875	1,725
34	Zacher	5,750	2,875	1,725
35	Ables	5,750	2,875	1,725
36	Miller			
	PORTLAND (PCL)			
37	Ryan	5,750	2,875	1,725
38	Rapps	5,750	2,875	1,725
39	McCredie			
40	Seaton			
41	Steen			
42	Chadbourne	5,750	2,875	1,725
43	Krueger			
44	Sheehan			
45	Roger Peckinpaugh	5,750	2,875	1,725
46	Bill Rodgers	5,750	2,875	1,725
47	Murray			
48	Fullerton			
49	Kuhn	5,750	2,875	1,725
50	Koestner			
51	Henderson			
52	Barry			
	SACRAMENTO			
53	LaLonge			
54	Heister			
55	Hunt			
56	Van Buren			
57	Fitzgerald	5,750	2,875	1,725
58	Danzig	5,750	2,875	1,725
59	Baum	5,750	2,875	1,725
60	Shinn	5,750	2,875	1,725
61	Nourse			
62	O'Rourke			
63	Lerchen			
64	Thornton			
65	Thomas	5,750	2,875	1,725
66	Thompson			
67	Byram			
68	Frank Arrelanes (Arellanes)			
69	Mahoney			
	SAN FRANCISCO			
70	McArdle			
71	Melchior	5,750	2,875	1,725
72	Vitt	5,750	2,875	1,725
73	Henley			
74	Berry	5,750	2,875	1,725
75	Miller	5,750	2,875	1,725
76	Tennant	5,750	2,875	1,725
77	Mohler	5,750	2,875	1,725
78	Shaw			
79	Sutor	5,750	2,875	1,725
80	Browning	5,750	2,875	1,725
81	Ryan	5,750	2,875	1,725
82	Powell	5,750	2,875	1,725
83	Schmidt	5,750	2,875	1,725
84	Meikle	5,750	2,875	1,725
85	Madden	5,750	2,875	1,725
86	Buck Weaver (VG-EX example auctioned in 2005 for $26,435.)			
87	Moskiman	5,750	2,875	1,725
88	Zamlock	5,750	2,875	1,725
	VERNON			
89	Brown			
90	Hogan			
91	Brashear			
92	Carlisle	5,750	2,875	1,725
93	Burrell	5,750	2,875	1,725
94	Brackenridge	5,750	2,875	1,725
95	Hitt			
96	Willett	5,750	2,875	1,725
97	Stewart	5,750	2,875	1,725
98	Carson	5,750	2,875	1,725
99	Raleigh	5,750	2,875	1,725
100	Ham Patterson	5,750	2,875	1,725

		NM	EX	VG
101	Hosp			
102	Sheehan			
103	Castleton			
104	Ross			
105	Stinson	5,750	2,875	1,725
106	McDonnell	5,750	2,875	1,725
107	Kane	5,750	2,875	1,725
	PORTLAND (NWL)			
108	Harris			
109	Garrett			
110	Stovall			
111	Mundorff	5,750	2,875	1,725
112	Lamline			
113	Bloomfield			
114	Williams			
115	Mensor			
116	Casey			
117	Speas			
	SPOKANE			
118	Netzel			
119	Strand			
120	Hasty			
121	Zimmerman			
122	Cooney			
123	Frisk			
124	Nordyke			
125	Kippert			
126	Bonner			
127	Ostdiek			
128	Cartwright			
129	Holm			
	TACOMA			
130	Higgins			
131	Warren			
132	Morse			
133	Burns			
134	Gordon			
135	Bassey			
136	Rockenfield			
137	Coleman			
138	Schmutz			
139	Hall			
140	Annis	5,750	2,875	1,725
	VANCOUVER			
141	Engel			
142	Brashear			
143	Adams			
144	Spiesman			
145	Brinker			
146	Bennett			
147	James			
148	Lewis			
149	Scharnweber			
150	Swain			
151	Jensen			
152	Erickson			
	VICTORIA			
153	Roche			
154	Davis			
155	Goodman			
156	Ward			
157	Reddick			
158	Householder	5,750	2,875	1,725
159	Dashwood	5,750	2,875	1,725
160	Starkel			
161	Thomas			
162	Ten Million			
163	Raymer			
	SEATTLE			
164	Bues			
165	Crukshank			
166	Kading			
167	Spencer	5,750	2,875	1,725
168	Leard			
169	Seaton			
170	Shea			
171	Butler			
172	Skeels			
173	Weed			
174	Raymond	5,750	2,875	1,725
175	Zackert			

1911 Obak Coupon

About 3" x 3", this coupon was found in each box of Obak cigarettes. Printed in green on white, the coupon has a list of the cabinet cards which could be obtained by redeeming 50 of the coupons.

	NM	EX	VG
Obak Coupon	100.00	50.00	30.00

1908 Offerman Buffalo Bisons Postcards

Virtually identical in format to the Major League player postcards issued by American League Publishing Co., Cleveland, these cards carry the imprint of F.J. Offerman and depict Bufalo Bisons players of the Eastern League. The 3-1/2" x 4-1/2" black-and-white cards have a large posed action photo on a white background with a vignetted oval portrait at top. Player information and stats are printed below. The back has typical postcard markings. It is unknown whether this checklist is complete.

		NM	EX	VG
	Common Player:	600.00	300.00	180.00
(1)	James Archer	600.00	300.00	180.00
(2)	Larry Hesterfer	600.00	300.00	180.00
(3)	William H. Keister	600.00	300.00	180.00
(4)	Charles Kisinger	600.00	300.00	180.00
(5)	Lewis Knapp	600.00	300.00	180.00
(6)	George McConnell	600.00	300.00	180.00
(7)	William J. Milligan	600.00	300.00	180.00
(8)	William Nattress	600.00	300.00	180.00
(9)	John B. Ryan	600.00	300.00	180.00
(10)	George Schirm	600.00	300.00	180.00
(11)	George Smith	600.00	300.00	180.00
(12)	John White	600.00	300.00	180.00
(13)	Merton Whitney	600.00	300.00	180.00

1952 Ogden Reds Team Issue

These 2-1/4" x 3-3/8" black-and-white, unnumbered, blank-backed cards were one of many minor league team sets issued by Globe Printing of San Jose, Calif., in the early 1950s. Cards were usually given away at the ballpark on a one-per-week or one-per-homestand basis, accounting for the rarity of surviving sets. The O-Reds were a Class C Pioneer League farm club of the Cincinnati Reds.

		NM	EX	VG
	Complete Set (18):	800.00	400.00	240.00
	Common Player:	60.00	30.00	18.00
	Album:	100.00	50.00	30.00
(1)	Ralph Birkofer	60.00	30.00	18.00
(2)	William A. Bowman	60.00	30.00	18.00
(3)	David Bristol	60.00	30.00	18.00
(4)	Vincent E. Capece	60.00	30.00	18.00
(5)	Gerald Davis	60.00	30.00	18.00
(6)	Ralph Dollinger	60.00	30.00	18.00
(7)	Robert E. Dumbaugh	60.00	30.00	18.00
(8)	Raymond Estes	60.00	30.00	18.00
(9)	Robert J. Flowers	60.00	30.00	18.00
(10)	Nunzio Izzo	60.00	30.00	18.00
(11)	Howard E. Leister	60.00	30.00	18.00
(12)	Steve Mesner	60.00	30.00	18.00
(13)	Dee C. Moore	60.00	30.00	18.00
(14)	Augie Navarro (Announcer)	60.00	30.00	18.00
(15)	John Omerza	60.00	30.00	18.00
(16)	James W. St. Claire	60.00	30.00	18.00
(17)	Grady N. Watts	60.00	30.00	18.00
(18)	Carl M. Wells	60.00	30.00	18.00

1955 Old Homestead Franks Des Moines Bruins

A very rare minor league issue, this set features players of the Class A Western League farm team of the Chicago Cubs. Many of the players were future major leaguers. Cards measure about 2-1/2" x 3-3/4" and have black-and-white portrait photos of the players with a facsimile autograph across the jersey. A black strip at the bottom of the card has the player and team name, and the position. Backs have an ad for the issuing hot dog company.

		NM	EX	VG
	Complete Set (21):	5,000	2,500	1,500
	Common Player:	250.00	125.00	75.00
(1)	Bob Andersoon	250.00	125.00	75.00
(2)	Ray Bellino	250.00	125.00	75.00
(3)	Don Biebel	250.00	125.00	75.00
(4)	Bobby Cooke	250.00	125.00	75.00
(5)	Dave Cunningham	250.00	125.00	75.00
(6)	Bert Flammini	250.00	125.00	75.00
(7)	Gene Fodge	250.00	125.00	75.00
(8)	Eddie Haas	250.00	125.00	75.00
(9)	Paul Hoffmeister	250.00	125.00	75.00
(10)	Pepper Martin	350.00	175.00	100.00
(11)	Jim McDaniel	250.00	125.00	75.00

		NM	EX	VG
(12)	Bob McKee	250.00	125.00	75.00
(13)	Paul Menking	250.00	125.00	75.00
(14)	Vern Morgan	250.00	125.00	75.00
(15)	Joe Pearson	250.00	125.00	75.00
(16)	John Pramesa	250.00	125.00	75.00
(17)	Joe Stanka	250.00	125.00	75.00
(18)	Jim Stoddard	250.00	125.00	75.00
(19)	Bob Thorpe	250.00	125.00	75.00
(20)	Burdy Thurlby	250.00	125.00	75.00
(21)	Don Watkins	250.00	125.00	75.00

1959 O'Keefe Ale Montreal Royals

TOM LASORDA
Lanceur gaucher — L. H. Pitcher

This set of large (3" x 4") player stamps was issued in conjunction with an album as a promotion by O'Keefe Ale in Quebec. The pictures are black-and-white with player identification in the bottom border. Backs are blank and the edges are perforated. Many former Brooklyn Dodgers are included in the issue. The unnumbered stamps are listed here in alphabetical order.

		NM	EX	VG
Complete Set (24):		900.00	450.00	275.00
Common Player:		30.00	15.00	9.00
Album:		200.00	100.00	60.00
(1)	Edmundo Amoros	45.00	22.50	13.50
(2)	Bob Aspromonte	35.00	17.50	10.00
(3)	Batters Records	12.50	6.25	3.75
(4)	Babe Birrer	30.00	15.00	9.00
(5)	Clay Bryant	30.00	15.00	9.00
(6)	Mike Brumley	30.00	15.00	9.00
(7)	Yvon Dunn (Trainer)	20.00	10.00	6.00
(8)	Bill George	30.00	15.00	9.00
(9)	Mike Goliat	30.00	15.00	9.00
(10)	John Gray	30.00	15.00	9.00
(11)	Billy Harris	30.00	15.00	9.00
(12)	Jim Koranda	30.00	15.00	9.00
(13)	Paul LaPalme	30.00	15.00	9.00
(14)	Tom Lasorda	200.00	100.00	60.00
(15)	Bob Lennon	30.00	15.00	9.00
(16)	Clyde Parris	30.00	15.00	9.00
(17)	Pitchers Records	12.50	6.25	3.75
(18)	Ed Rakow	30.00	15.00	9.00
(19)	Curt Roberts	30.00	15.00	9.00
(20)	Freddy Rodriguez	30.00	15.00	9.00
(21)	Harry Schwegman	30.00	15.00	9.00
(22)	Angel Scull	30.00	15.00	9.00
(23)	Dick Teed	30.00	15.00	9.00
(24)	Rene Valdes (Valdez)	30.00	15.00	9.00

1910 Old Mill Cigarettes Series 1 (S. Atlantic League)

SHIELDS, AUGUSTA

Because of their distinctive red borders, this 1910 minor league tobacco issue is often called the Red Border set by collectors. It's ACC designation is T210. A massive set, it consists of some 640 cards, each measuring 1-1/2" x 2-5/8". Fronts feature a glossy black-and-white photo, while the backs carry an ad for Old Mill Cigarettes. Each of the eight series is devoted to a different minor league. Series 1 features players from the South Atlantic League; Series 2 pictures players from the Virginia League; Series 3 is devoted to the Texas League; Series 4 features players from the Virginia Valley League; Series 5 pictures players from the Carolina Associations; Series 6 spotlights the Blue Grass League; Series 7 is devoted to the Eastern Carolina League; and Series 8 show players from the Southern Association. The various series are identified by a number along the top on the back of the cards. Collectors generally agree that Series 8 cards, which are often found irregularly sized due to

hand-cutting from original sheets, are the scarcest of the series. The relative scarcity of the various series is reflected in the prices listed. Collectors should be aware that some Series 3 cards (Texas League) can be found with orange, rather than red, borders - apparently because not enough red ink was used during part of the print run.

		NM	EX	VG
Common Player:		325.00	140.00	80.00
(1)	Bagwell	325.00	140.00	80.00
(2)	Balenti	360.00	160.00	95.00
(3)	Becker	325.00	140.00	80.00
(4)	Bensen	325.00	140.00	80.00
(5)	Benton	360.00	160.00	95.00
(6)	Bierkortte	325.00	140.00	80.00
(7)	Bierman	325.00	140.00	80.00
(8)	Breitenstein	325.00	140.00	80.00
(9)	Bremmerhof	325.00	140.00	80.00
(10)	Carter	325.00	140.00	80.00
(11)	Cavender	325.00	140.00	80.00
(12)	Collins	325.00	140.00	80.00
(13)	DeFraites	325.00	140.00	80.00
(14)	Dudley	325.00	140.00	80.00
(15)	Dwyer	325.00	140.00	80.00
(16)	Edwards	325.00	140.00	80.00
(17)	Enbanks	360.00	160.00	95.00
(18)	Eubank	325.00	140.00	80.00
(19)	Fox	325.00	140.00	80.00
(20)	Hannifan	325.00	140.00	80.00
(21)	Hartley	325.00	140.00	80.00
(22)	Hauser	325.00	140.00	80.00
(23)	Hille	325.00	140.00	80.00
(24)	Howard	325.00	140.00	80.00
(25)	Hoyt	325.00	140.00	80.00
(26)	Huber	325.00	140.00	80.00
(27)	Ison	325.00	140.00	80.00
(28)	Jones	325.00	140.00	80.00
(29)	Kalkhoff	325.00	140.00	80.00
(30)	Krebs	325.00	140.00	80.00
(31)	Lawrence	325.00	140.00	80.00
(32)	Lee (Jacksonville)	325.00	140.00	80.00
(33)	Lee (Macon)	325.00	140.00	80.00
(34)	Lewis (Columbia)	325.00	140.00	80.00
(35)	Lewis (Columbus)	325.00	140.00	80.00
(36)	Lipe (Batting)	325.00	140.00	80.00
(37)	Lipe (Portrait)	325.00	140.00	80.00
(38)	Long	325.00	140.00	80.00
(39)	Magoon	325.00	140.00	80.00
(40)	Manion	325.00	140.00	80.00
(41)	Marshall	325.00	140.00	80.00
(42)	Martin	325.00	140.00	80.00
(43)	Martina	325.00	140.00	80.00
(44)	Massing	325.00	140.00	80.00
(45)	McLeod	325.00	140.00	80.00
(46)	McMahon	325.00	140.00	80.00
(47)	Morse	325.00	140.00	80.00
(48)	Mullane	325.00	140.00	80.00
(49)	Mulldowney	325.00	140.00	80.00
(50)	Murch	325.00	140.00	80.00
(51)	Norcum	325.00	140.00	80.00
(52)	Pelkey	325.00	140.00	80.00
(53)	Petit	325.00	140.00	80.00
(54)	Pierce	325.00	140.00	80.00
(55)	Pope	325.00	140.00	80.00
(56)	Radebaugh	360.00	160.00	95.00
(57)	Raynolds	325.00	140.00	80.00
(58)	Reagan	325.00	140.00	80.00
(59)	Redfern (Redfearn)	325.00	140.00	80.00
(60)	Reynolds	325.00	140.00	80.00
(61)	Schulz	360.00	160.00	95.00
(62)	Schulze	325.00	140.00	80.00
(63)	Schwietzka	325.00	140.00	80.00
(64)	Shields	360.00	160.00	95.00
(65)	Sisson	325.00	140.00	80.00
(66)	Smith	500.00	200.00	125.00
(67)	Sweeney	325.00	140.00	80.00
(68)	Taffee	325.00	140.00	80.00
(69)	Toren	325.00	140.00	80.00
(70)	Viola	325.00	140.00	80.00
(71)	Wagner	325.00	140.00	80.00
(72)	Wahl	325.00	140.00	80.00
(73)	Weems	325.00	140.00	80.00
(74)	Wells	325.00	140.00	80.00
(75)	Wohlleben	325.00	140.00	80.00

1910 Old Mill Cigarettes Series 2 (Virginia League)

		NM	EX	VG
Common Player:		275.00	135.00	80.00
(1)	Andrada	275.00	135.00	80.00
(2)	Archer	275.00	135.00	80.00
(3)	Baker	275.00	135.00	80.00
(4)	Beham	280.00	140.00	85.00
(5)	Bonner	275.00	135.00	80.00
(6)	Bowen	275.00	135.00	80.00
(7)	Brandon	275.00	135.00	80.00
(8)	Breivogel	275.00	135.00	80.00
(9)	Brooks	275.00	135.00	80.00
(10)	Brown	275.00	135.00	80.00
(11)	Busch	275.00	135.00	80.00
(12)	Bussey	275.00	135.00	80.00
(13)	Cefalu	275.00	135.00	80.00
(14)	Chandler	275.00	135.00	80.00
(15)	Clarke	280.00	140.00	85.00
(16)	Clunk	275.00	135.00	80.00
(17)	Cote	280.00	140.00	85.00
(18)	Cowan	275.00	135.00	80.00
(19)	Decker	275.00	135.00	80.00
(20)	Doyle	275.00	135.00	80.00
(21)	Eddowes	275.00	135.00	80.00
(22)	Fisher	275.00	135.00	80.00
(23)	Fox	275.00	135.00	80.00
(24)	Foxen	275.00	135.00	80.00
(25)	Gaston	275.00	135.00	80.00
(26)	Gehring	275.00	135.00	80.00
(27)	Griffin (Danville)	275.00	135.00	80.00
(28)	Griffin (Lynchburg)	275.00	135.00	80.00
(29)	Hale	275.00	135.00	80.00
(30)	Hamilton	275.00	135.00	80.00
(31)	Hanks	275.00	135.00	80.00
(32)	Hannafin	275.00	135.00	80.00
(33)	Hoffman	280.00	140.00	85.00
(34)	Holland	275.00	135.00	80.00
(35)	Hooker	275.00	135.00	80.00
(36)	Irving	275.00	135.00	80.00
(37)	Jackson (Lynchburg)	280.00	140.00	85.00
(38)	Jackson (Norfolk)	275.00	135.00	80.00
(39)	Jackson (Portsmouth)	275.00	135.00	80.00
(40)	Jackson (Richmond)	275.00	135.00	80.00
(41)	Jenkins	275.00	135.00	80.00
(42)	Keifel	275.00	135.00	80.00
(43)	Kirkpatrick	280.00	140.00	85.00
(44)	Kunkel	275.00	135.00	80.00
(45)	Landgraff	275.00	135.00	80.00
(46)	Larkins	275.00	135.00	80.00
(47)	Laughlin	275.00	135.00	80.00
(48)	Lawlor	275.00	135.00	80.00
(49)	Levy	275.00	135.00	80.00
(50)	Lloyd	275.00	135.00	80.00
(51)	Loos	280.00	140.00	85.00
(52)	Lovell	275.00	135.00	80.00
(53)	Lucia	275.00	135.00	80.00
(54)	MacConachie	275.00	135.00	80.00
(55)	Mayberry	275.00	135.00	80.00
(56)	McFarland	280.00	140.00	85.00
(57)	Messitt	280.00	140.00	85.00
(58)	Michel	275.00	135.00	80.00
(59)	Mullaney	275.00	135.00	80.00
(60)	Munson	275.00	135.00	80.00
(61)	Neuton	275.00	135.00	80.00
(62)	Nimmo	275.00	135.00	80.00
(63)	Norris	275.00	135.00	80.00
(64)	Peterson	275.00	135.00	80.00
(65)	Powell	275.00	135.00	80.00
(66)	Pressly (Pressley)	275.00	135.00	80.00
(67)	Pritchard	275.00	135.00	80.00
(68)	Revelle	275.00	135.00	80.00
(69)	Rowe	275.00	135.00	80.00
(70)	Schmidt	280.00	140.00	85.00
(71)	Schrader	275.00	135.00	80.00
(72)	Sharp	275.00	135.00	80.00
(73)	Shaw	275.00	135.00	80.00
(74)	Smith (Lynchburg, batting.)	275.00	135.00	80.00
(75)	Smith (Lynchburg, catching.)	275.00	135.00	80.00
(76)	Smith (Portsmouth)	280.00	140.00	85.00
(77)	Spicer	275.00	135.00	80.00
(78)	Titman	275.00	135.00	80.00
(79)	Toner	275.00	135.00	80.00
(80)	Tydeman	275.00	135.00	80.00
(81)	Vail	290.00	145.00	90.00
(82)	Verbout	275.00	135.00	80.00
(83)	Walker	275.00	135.00	80.00
(84)	Wallace	275.00	135.00	80.00
(85)	Waymack	275.00	135.00	80.00
(86)	Woolums	275.00	135.00	80.00
(87)	Zimmerman	275.00	135.00	80.00

1910 Old Mill Cigarettes Series 3 (Texas League)

SERIES No 3 — OLD MILL CIGARETTES — BASE BALL SUBJECTS — LARGE ASSORTMENT

		NM	EX	VG
Common Player:		275.00	125.00	80.00
(1)	Alexander	275.00	125.00	80.00
(2)	Ash	275.00	125.00	80.00
(3)	Bandy	275.00	125.00	80.00
(4)	Barenkemp	275.00	125.00	80.00
(5)	Belew	275.00	125.00	80.00
(6)	Bell	275.00	125.00	80.00
(7)	Bennett	275.00	125.00	80.00
(8)	Berlck	275.00	125.00	80.00
(9)	Billiard	275.00	125.00	80.00
(10)	Blanding	275.00	125.00	80.00
(11)	Blue	275.00	125.00	80.00
(12)	Burch	275.00	125.00	80.00
(13)	Burk	275.00	125.00	80.00
(14)	Carlin	275.00	125.00	80.00
(15)	Conaway	275.00	125.00	80.00
(16)	Corkhill	275.00	125.00	80.00
(17)	Cowan	275.00	125.00	80.00
(18)	Coyle	275.00	125.00	80.00
(19)	Crable	275.00	125.00	80.00
(20)	Curry	275.00	125.00	80.00
(21)	Dale	275.00	125.00	80.00
(22)	Davis	275.00	125.00	80.00
(23)	Deardorff	275.00	125.00	80.00
(24)	Donnelley	275.00	125.00	80.00
(25)	Doyle	275.00	125.00	80.00
(26)	Druke	275.00	125.00	80.00
(27)	Dugey	275.00	125.00	80.00
(28)	Ens	275.00	125.00	80.00

#	Player	NM	EX	VG
(29)	Evans	275.00	125.00	80.00
(30)	Fillman	275.00	125.00	80.00
(31)	Firestine	275.00	125.00	80.00
(32)	Francis	275.00	125.00	80.00
(33)	Galloway	275.00	125.00	80.00
(34)	Gardner	275.00	125.00	80.00
(35)	Gear	275.00	125.00	80.00
(36)	Glawe	275.00	125.00	80.00
(37)	Gordon	275.00	125.00	80.00
(38)	Gowdy	275.00	125.00	80.00
(39)	Harbison	275.00	125.00	80.00
(40)	Harper	275.00	125.00	80.00
(41)	Hicks	275.00	125.00	80.00
(42)	Hill	275.00	125.00	80.00
(43)	Hinninger	275.00	125.00	80.00
(44)	Hirsch	275.00	125.00	80.00
(45)	Hise	275.00	125.00	80.00
(46)	Hooks	275.00	125.00	80.00
(47)	Hornsby	275.00	125.00	80.00
(48)	Howell	275.00	125.00	80.00
(49)	Johnston	275.00	125.00	80.00
(50)	Jolley	275.00	125.00	80.00
(51)	Jones	275.00	125.00	80.00
(52)	Kaphan	275.00	125.00	80.00
(53)	Kipp	275.00	125.00	80.00
(54)	Leidy	275.00	125.00	80.00
(55)	Malloy	275.00	125.00	80.00
(56)	Maloney	275.00	125.00	80.00
(57)	Meagher	275.00	125.00	80.00
(58)	Merritt	275.00	125.00	80.00
(59)	McKay	275.00	125.00	80.00
(60)	Mills	275.00	125.00	80.00
(61)	Morris	275.00	125.00	80.00
(62)	Mullen	275.00	125.00	80.00
(63)	Munsell	275.00	125.00	80.00
(64)	Nagel	275.00	125.00	80.00
(65)	Northen	275.00	125.00	80.00
(66)	Ogle	275.00	125.00	80.00
(67)	Onslow	290.00	140.00	85.00
(68)	Pendleton	275.00	125.00	80.00
(69)	Powell	275.00	125.00	80.00
(70)	Riley	275.00	125.00	80.00
(71)	Robertson	275.00	125.00	80.00
(72)	Rose	275.00	125.00	80.00
(73)	Salazor	275.00	125.00	80.00
(74)	Shindel	275.00	125.00	80.00
(75)	Shontz	275.00	125.00	80.00
(76)	Slaven	275.00	125.00	80.00
(77)	Smith (Bat over shoulder.)	275.00	125.00	80.00
(78)	Smith (Bat at hip level.)	275.00	125.00	80.00
(79)	Spangler	275.00	125.00	80.00
(80)	Stadeli	275.00	125.00	80.00
(81)	Stinson	275.00	125.00	80.00
(82)	Storch	275.00	125.00	80.00
(83)	Stringer	275.00	125.00	80.00
(84)	Tesreau	300.00	150.00	90.00
(85)	Thebo	290.00	140.00	85.00
(86)	Tullas	275.00	125.00	80.00
(87)	Walsh	275.00	125.00	80.00
(88)	Watson	275.00	125.00	80.00
(89)	Weber	275.00	125.00	80.00
(90)	Weeks	275.00	125.00	80.00
(91)	Wertherford	275.00	125.00	80.00
(92)	Wickenhofer	275.00	125.00	80.00
(93)	Williams	275.00	125.00	80.00
(94)	Woodburn	275.00	125.00	80.00
(95)	Yantz	275.00	125.00	80.00

1910 Old Mill Cigarettes Series 4 (Va. Valley Leag.)

#	Player	NM	EX	VG
	Common Player:	400.00	175.00	100.00
(1)	Aylor	400.00	175.00	100.00
(2)	Benney	400.00	175.00	100.00
(3)	Best	400.00	175.00	100.00
(4)	Bonno	400.00	175.00	100.00
(5)	Brown	400.00	175.00	100.00
(6)	Brumfield	400.00	175.00	100.00
(7)	Campbell	400.00	175.00	100.00
(8)	Canepa	400.00	175.00	100.00
(9)	Carney	400.00	175.00	100.00
(10)	Carter	400.00	175.00	100.00
(11)	Cochrane	400.00	175.00	100.00
(12)	Coller	400.00	175.00	100.00
(13)	Connolly	400.00	175.00	100.00
(14)	Davis	400.00	175.00	100.00
(15)	Connell	400.00	175.00	100.00
(16)	Doshmer	400.00	175.00	100.00
(17)	Dougherty	400.00	175.00	100.00
(18)	Erlewein	400.00	175.00	100.00
(19)	Farrell	400.00	175.00	100.00
(20)	Geary	400.00	175.00	100.00
(21)	Halterman	400.00	175.00	100.00
(22)	Headly	400.00	175.00	100.00
(23)	Hollis	400.00	175.00	100.00
(24)	Hunter	400.00	175.00	100.00
(25)	Johnson	400.00	175.00	100.00
(26)	Kane	400.00	175.00	100.00
(27)	Kuehn	400.00	175.00	100.00
(28)	Leonard	400.00	175.00	100.00
(29)	Lux	400.00	175.00	100.00
(30)	McClain	400.00	175.00	100.00
(31)	Mollenkamp	410.00	180.00	105.00
(32)	Moore	400.00	175.00	100.00
(33)	Moye	400.00	175.00	100.00
(34)	O'Connor	400.00	175.00	100.00
(35)	Orcutt	400.00	175.00	100.00
(36)	Pick	410.00	180.00	105.00
(37)	Pickels	400.00	175.00	100.00
(38)	Schafer	400.00	175.00	100.00
(39)	Seaman	400.00	175.00	100.00
(40)	Spicer	400.00	175.00	100.00
(41)	Stanley	400.00	175.00	100.00
(42)	Stockum	400.00	175.00	100.00
(43)	Titlow	400.00	175.00	100.00
(44)	Waldron	400.00	175.00	100.00
(45)	Wills	400.00	175.00	100.00
(46)	Witter	400.00	175.00	100.00
(47)	Womach	400.00	175.00	100.00
(48)	Young	400.00	175.00	100.00
(49)	Zurlage	400.00	175.00	100.00

1910 Old Mill Cigarettes Series 5 (Carolina Assn.)

#	Player	NM	EX	VG
	Common Player:	400.00	175.00	100.00
(1)	Abercrombie	400.00	175.00	100.00
(2)	Averett	400.00	175.00	100.00
(3)	Bansewein	400.00	175.00	100.00
(4)	Bentley	400.00	175.00	100.00
(5)	C.G. Beusse	400.00	175.00	100.00
(6)	Fred Beusse	400.00	175.00	100.00
(7)	Bigbie	400.00	175.00	100.00
(8)	Bivens	400.00	175.00	100.00
(9)	Blackstone	400.00	175.00	100.00
(10)	Brannon	400.00	175.00	100.00
(11)	Brazell	400.00	175.00	100.00
(12)	Brent	400.00	175.00	100.00
(13)	Bullock	400.00	175.00	100.00
(14)	Cashion	425.00	190.00	120.00
(15)	Corbett (3/4 length view)	400.00	175.00	100.00
(16)	Corbett (Full length view.)	400.00	175.00	100.00
(17)	Coutts	400.00	175.00	100.00
(18)	Lave Cross	425.00	190.00	120.00
(19)	Crouch	400.00	175.00	100.00
(20)	C.L. Derrick	410.00	180.00	110.00
(21)	F.B. Derrick	400.00	175.00	100.00
(22)	Dobard	400.00	175.00	100.00
(23)	Drumm	400.00	175.00	100.00
(24)	Duvie	400.00	175.00	100.00
(25)	Ehrhardt	400.00	175.00	100.00
(26)	Eldridge	400.00	175.00	100.00
(27)	Fairbanks	400.00	175.00	100.00
(28)	Farmer	400.00	175.00	100.00
(29)	Ferrell	400.00	175.00	100.00
(30)	Finn	400.00	175.00	100.00
(31)	Flowers	400.00	175.00	100.00
(32)	Fogarty	400.00	175.00	100.00
(33)	Francisco	400.00	175.00	100.00
(34)	Gardin	400.00	175.00	100.00
(35)	Gilmore	400.00	175.00	100.00
(36)	Gorham	400.00	175.00	100.00
(37)	Gorman	400.00	175.00	100.00
(38)	Guss	400.00	175.00	100.00
(39)	Hammersley	400.00	175.00	100.00
(40)	Hargrave	400.00	175.00	100.00
(41)	Harrington	400.00	175.00	100.00
(42)	Harris	400.00	175.00	100.00
(43)	Hartley	400.00	175.00	100.00
(44)	Hayes	400.00	175.00	100.00
(45)	Hicks	400.00	175.00	100.00
(46)	Humphrey	410.00	180.00	110.00
(47)	Jackson	400.00	175.00	100.00
(48)	James	400.00	175.00	100.00
(49)	Jenkins	400.00	175.00	100.00
(50)	Johnston	400.00	175.00	100.00
(51)	Kelly	400.00	175.00	100.00
(52)	Laval	400.00	175.00	100.00
(53)	Lothrop	400.00	175.00	100.00
(54)	MacConachie	400.00	175.00	100.00
(55)	Mangum	400.00	175.00	100.00
(56)	A. McCarthy	400.00	175.00	100.00
(57)	J. McCarthy	400.00	175.00	100.00
(58)	McEnroe	400.00	175.00	100.00
(59)	McFarlin	400.00	175.00	100.00
(60)	McHugh	400.00	175.00	100.00
(61)	McKevitt	400.00	175.00	100.00
(62)	Midkiff	400.00	175.00	100.00
(63)	Moore	400.00	175.00	100.00
(64)	Noojin	400.00	175.00	100.00
(65)	Ochs	400.00	175.00	100.00
(66)	Painter	400.00	175.00	100.00
(67)	Redfern (Redfearn)	400.00	175.00	100.00
(68)	Reis	400.00	175.00	100.00
(69)	Rickard	400.00	175.00	100.00
(70)	Roth (Batting)	400.00	175.00	100.00
(71)	Roth (Fielding)	400.00	175.00	100.00
(72)	Smith	400.00	175.00	100.00
(73)	Springs	400.00	175.00	100.00
(74)	Stouch	400.00	175.00	100.00
(75)	Taxis	400.00	175.00	100.00
(76)	Templin	400.00	175.00	100.00
(77)	Thrasher	400.00	175.00	100.00
(78)	Trammell	400.00	175.00	100.00
(79)	Walker	400.00	175.00	100.00
(80)	Walters	400.00	175.00	100.00
(81)	Wehrell	400.00	175.00	100.00
(82)	Weldon	400.00	175.00	100.00
(83)	Williams	400.00	175.00	100.00
(84)	Wingo	400.00	175.00	100.00
(85)	Workman	400.00	175.00	100.00
(86)	Wynne	400.00	175.00	100.00
(87)	Wysong	400.00	175.00	100.00

1910 Old Mill Cigarettes Series 6 (Blue Grass Leag.)

#	Player	NM	EX	VG
	Common Player:	600.00	250.00	150.00
(1)	Angermeier (Fielding)	800.00	400.00	200.00
(2)	Angermeier (Portrait)	800.00	400.00	200.00
(3)	Atwell	600.00	250.00	150.00
(4)	Badger	600.00	250.00	150.00
(5)	Barnett	600.00	250.00	150.00
(6)	Barney	600.00	250.00	150.00
(7)	Beard	600.00	250.00	150.00
(8)	Bohannon	600.00	250.00	150.00
(9)	Callahan	650.00	275.00	160.00
(10)	Chapman	600.00	250.00	150.00
(11)	Chase	600.00	250.00	150.00
(12)	Coleman	600.00	250.00	150.00
(13)	Cornell (Frankfort)	600.00	250.00	150.00
(14)	Cornell (Winchester)	600.00	250.00	150.00
(15)	Creager	600.00	250.00	150.00
(16)	Dailey	600.00	250.00	150.00
(17)	Edington	650.00	275.00	160.00
(18)	Elgin	600.00	250.00	150.00
(19)	Ellis	600.00	250.00	150.00
(20)	Everden	600.00	250.00	150.00
(21)	Gisler	600.00	250.00	150.00
(22)	Goodman	600.00	250.00	150.00
(23)	Goostree (Hands behind back.)	600.00	250.00	150.00
(24)	Goostree (Leaning on bat.)	800.00	400.00	200.00
(25)	Haines	600.00	250.00	150.00
(26)	Harold	600.00	250.00	150.00
(27)	Heveron	600.00	250.00	150.00
(28)	Hicks	600.00	250.00	150.00
(29)	Hoffmann	600.00	250.00	150.00
(30)	Horn	600.00	250.00	150.00
(31)	Kaiser	650.00	275.00	160.00
(32)	Keifel	600.00	250.00	150.00
(33)	Kimbrough	600.00	250.00	150.00
(34)	Kircher (Shelbyville)	600.00	250.00	150.00
(35)	Kircher (Winchester)	600.00	250.00	150.00
(36)	Kuhlman (3/4 length)	600.00	250.00	150.00
(37)	Kuhlmann (Portrait)	600.00	250.00	150.00
(38)	L'Heureux	600.00	250.00	150.00
(39)	McIlvain	600.00	250.00	150.00
(40)	McKernan	600.00	250.00	150.00
(41)	Meyers	600.00	250.00	150.00
(42)	Moloney	650.00	275.00	160.00
(43)	Mullin	600.00	250.00	150.00
(44)	Olson	600.00	250.00	150.00
(45)	Oyler	600.00	250.00	150.00
(46)	Reed	600.00	250.00	150.00
(47)	Ross	600.00	250.00	150.00
(48)	Scheneberg (Fielding)	650.00	275.00	160.00
(49)	Scheneberg (Portrait)	650.00	275.00	160.00
(50)	Schultz	600.00	250.00	150.00
(51)	Scott	600.00	250.00	150.00
(52)	Sinex	600.00	250.00	150.00
(53)	Stengel	.00	40,000	20,000
(54)	Thoss	600.00	250.00	150.00
(55)	Tilford	600.00	250.00	150.00
(56)	Toney	650.00	275.00	160.00
(57)	Van Landingham (Valladingham) (Lexington)	600.00	250.00	150.00
(58)	Van Landingham (Valladingham) (Shelbyville)	600.00	250.00	150.00
(59)	Viox	650.00	275.00	160.00
(60)	Walden	600.00	250.00	150.00
(61)	Whitaker	600.00	250.00	150.00
(62)	Wills	600.00	250.00	150.00
(63)	Womble	600.00	250.00	150.00
(64)	Wright	600.00	250.00	150.00
(65)	Yaeger	650.00	275.00	160.00
(66)	Yancey	600.00	250.00	150.00

1910 Old Mill Cigarettes Series 7 (E. Carolina League)

#	Player	NM	EX	VG
	Common Player:	450.00	200.00	125.00
(1)	Armstrong	450.00	200.00	125.00
(2)	Beatty	450.00	200.00	125.00
(3)	Biel	450.00	200.00	125.00
(4)	Bonner	450.00	200.00	125.00
(5)	Brandt	450.00	200.00	125.00
(6)	Brown	450.00	200.00	125.00
(7)	Cantwell	450.00	200.00	125.00
(8)	Carrol	450.00	200.00	125.00
(9)	Cooney	450.00	200.00	125.00
(10)	Cooper	450.00	200.00	125.00
(11)	Cowell	450.00	200.00	125.00
(12)	Creager (Cregan)	450.00	200.00	125.00
(13)	Crockett	475.00	220.00	135.00
(14)	Dailey	450.00	200.00	125.00
(15)	Dobbs	450.00	200.00	125.00
(16)	Dussault	450.00	200.00	125.00
(17)	Dwyer	450.00	200.00	125.00
(18)	Evans	450.00	200.00	125.00
(19)	Forgue	450.00	200.00	125.00
(20)	Fulton	450.00	200.00	125.00
(21)	Galvin	450.00	200.00	125.00
(22)	Gastmeyer (Batting)	600.00	300.00	150.00
(23)	Gastmeyer (Fielding)	600.00	300.00	150.00
(24)	Gates	450.00	200.00	125.00
(25)	Gillespie	450.00	200.00	125.00
(26)	Griffin	450.00	200.00	125.00
(27)	Gunderson	450.00	200.00	125.00
(28)	Ham	450.00	200.00	125.00
(29)	Handibe (Handiboe)	475.00	220.00	135.00
(30)	Hart	450.00	200.00	125.00
(31)	Hartley	450.00	200.00	125.00
(32)	Hobbs	450.00	200.00	125.00
(33)	Hyames	450.00	200.00	125.00
(34)	Irving	450.00	200.00	125.00
(35)	Kaiser	450.00	200.00	125.00
(36)	Kelley	450.00	200.00	125.00
(37)	Kelly	450.00	200.00	125.00
(38)	Kelly (Mascot, Goldsboro.)	1,000	600.00	350.00
(39)	Luyster	450.00	200.00	125.00
(40)	MacDonald	450.00	200.00	125.00
(41)	Malcolm	450.00	200.00	125.00

		NM	EX	VG
(42)	J. Erskine Mayer	475.00	220.00	135.00
(43)	McCormac (McCormick)	450.00	200.00	125.00
(44)	McGeeham (McGeehan)	475.00	220.00	135.00
(45)	Merchant	450.00	200.00	125.00
(46)	Mills	450.00	200.00	125.00
(47)	Morgan	475.00	220.00	135.00
(48)	Morris	450.00	200.00	125.00
(49)	Munson	450.00	200.00	125.00
(50)	Newman	450.00	200.00	125.00
(51)	Noval (Novak)	450.00	200.00	125.00
(52)	O'Halloran	450.00	200.00	125.00
(53)	Phelan	450.00	200.00	125.00
(54)	Prim	450.00	200.00	125.00
(55)	Reeves	450.00	200.00	125.00
(56)	Richardson	450.00	200.00	125.00
(57)	Schumaker	450.00	200.00	125.00
(58)	Sharp	450.00	200.00	125.00
(59)	Sherrill	450.00	200.00	125.00
(60)	Simmons	450.00	200.00	125.00
(61)	Steinbach	450.00	200.00	125.00
(62)	Stoehr	450.00	200.00	125.00
(63)	Taylor	450.00	200.00	125.00
(64)	Webb	450.00	200.00	125.00
(65)	Whelan	450.00	200.00	125.00
(66)	Wolf	450.00	200.00	125.00
(67)	Wright	450.00	200.00	125.00

1910 Old Mill Cigarettes Series 8 (Southern Assn.)

		NM	EX	VG
Common Player:		700.00	325.00	200.00
(1)	Allen (Memphis)	700.00	325.00	200.00
(2)	Allen (Mobile)	750.00	350.00	210.00
(3)	Anderson	700.00	325.00	200.00
(4)	Babb	750.00	350.00	210.00
(5)	Bartley	750.00	350.00	210.00
(6)	Bauer	700.00	325.00	200.00
(7)	Bay	800.00	400.00	225.00
(8)	Bayliss	700.00	325.00	200.00
(9)	Berger	750.00	350.00	210.00
(10)	Bernhard	700.00	325.00	200.00
(11)	Bitroff	700.00	325.00	200.00
(12)	Breitenstein	800.00	400.00	225.00
(13)	Bronkie	750.00	350.00	210.00
(14)	Brooks	700.00	325.00	200.00
(15)	Burnett	750.00	350.00	210.00
(16)	Cafalu	700.00	325.00	200.00
(17)	Carson	700.00	325.00	200.00
(18)	Case	750.00	350.00	210.00
(19)	Chappelle	750.00	350.00	210.00
(20)	Cohen	700.00	325.00	200.00
(21)	Collins	700.00	325.00	200.00
(22)	Crandall	700.00	325.00	200.00
(23)	Cross	700.00	325.00	200.00
(24)	Jud. Daly	750.00	350.00	210.00
(25)	Davis	700.00	325.00	200.00
(26)	Demaree	750.00	350.00	210.00
(27)	DeMontreville	700.00	325.00	200.00
(28)	E. DeMontreville	750.00	350.00	210.00
(29)	Dick	700.00	325.00	200.00
(30)	Dobbs	750.00	350.00	210.00
(31)	Dudley	700.00	325.00	200.00
(32)	Dunn	750.00	350.00	210.00
(33)	Elliot	750.00	350.00	210.00
(34)	Emery	700.00	325.00	200.00
(35)	Erloff	700.00	325.00	200.00
(36)	Farrell	700.00	325.00	200.00
(37)	Fisher	750.00	350.00	210.00
(38)	Fleharty	700.00	325.00	200.00
(39)	Flood	750.00	350.00	210.00
(40)	Foster	750.00	350.00	210.00
(41)	Fritz	800.00	400.00	225.00
(42)	Greminger	750.00	350.00	210.00
(43)	Gribbon	700.00	325.00	200.00
(44)	Griffin	700.00	325.00	200.00
(45)	Gygli	700.00	325.00	200.00
(46)	Hanks	700.00	325.00	200.00
(47)	Hart	800.00	400.00	225.00
(48)	Hess	750.00	350.00	210.00
(49)	Hickman	750.00	350.00	210.00
(50)	Hohnhorst	750.00	350.00	210.00
(51)	Huelsman	750.00	350.00	210.00
(52)	Jackson			150,000
(53)	Jordan	800.00	400.00	225.00
(54)	Kane	700.00	325.00	200.00
(55)	Kelly	700.00	325.00	200.00
(56)	Kerwin	750.00	350.00	210.00
(57)	Keupper	750.00	350.00	210.00
(58)	LaFitte	700.00	325.00	200.00

		NM	EX	VG
(59)	Larsen	700.00	325.00	200.00
(60)	Bill Lindsay	750.00	350.00	210.00
(61)	Lynch	700.00	325.00	200.00
(62)	Manuel	750.00	350.00	210.00
(63)	Manush	700.00	325.00	200.00
(64)	Marcan	700.00	325.00	200.00
(65)	Maxwell	750.00	350.00	210.00
(66)	McBride	700.00	325.00	200.00
(67)	McCreery	750.00	350.00	210.00
(68)	McGilvray	750.00	350.00	210.00
(69)	McLaurin	750.00	350.00	210.00
(70)	McTigue	750.00	350.00	210.00
(71)	Miller (Chattanooga)	750.00	350.00	210.00
(72)	Miller (Montgomery)	700.00	325.00	200.00
(73)	Molesworth	750.00	350.00	210.00
(74)	Moran	750.00	350.00	210.00
(75)	Newton	700.00	325.00	200.00
(76)	Nolley	700.00	325.00	200.00
(77)	Osteen	750.00	350.00	210.00
(78)	Ower	700.00	325.00	200.00
(79)	Paige	750.00	350.00	210.00
(80)	Patterson	750.00	350.00	210.00
(81)	Pepe	700.00	325.00	200.00
(82)	Perdue	800.00	400.00	225.00
(83)	Peters	750.00	350.00	210.00
(84)	Phillips	700.00	325.00	200.00
(85)	Pratt	750.00	350.00	210.00
(86)	Rementer	750.00	350.00	210.00
(87)	Rhodes	700.00	325.00	200.00
(88)	Rhoton	700.00	325.00	200.00
(89)	Robertson	700.00	325.00	200.00
(90)	Rogers	700.00	325.00	200.00
(91)	Rohe	750.00	350.00	210.00
(92)	Seabough (Seabaugh)	700.00	325.00	200.00
(93)	Seitz	700.00	325.00	200.00
(94)	Schlitzer	750.00	350.00	210.00
(95)	Schopp	700.00	325.00	200.00
(96)	Siegle	750.00	350.00	210.00
(97)	Smith (Montgomery)	700.00	325.00	200.00
(98)	Sid. Smith (Atlanta)	800.00	400.00	225.00
(99)	Steele	700.00	325.00	200.00
(100)	Swacina	750.00	350.00	210.00
(101)	Sweeney	750.00	350.00	210.00
(102)	Thomas (Fielding)	750.00	350.00	210.00
(103)	Thomas (Portrait)	750.00	350.00	210.00
(104)	Vinson	700.00	325.00	200.00
(105)	Wagner (Birmingham)	700.00	325.00	200.00
(106)	Wagner (Mobile)	700.00	325.00	200.00
(107)	Walker	700.00	325.00	200.00
(108)	Wanner	750.00	350.00	210.00
(109)	Welf	750.00	350.00	210.00
(110)	Whiteman	750.00	350.00	210.00
(111)	Whitney	700.00	325.00	200.00
(112)	Wilder	700.00	325.00	200.00
(113)	Wiseman	700.00	325.00	200.00
(114)	Yerkes	800.00	400.00	225.00

1910 Old Mill Cabinets (H801-7)

 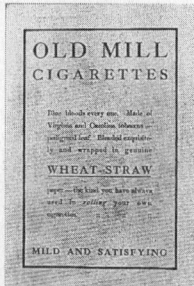

Similar in size and style to the more popular T3 Turkey Red cabinet cards of the same period, the Old Mill cabinets are much scarcer and picture fewer players. Issued in 1910 as a premium by Old Mill Cigarettes, these minor league cards measure approximately 5-3/8" x 7-5/8". Unlike the Turkey Reds, which feature full-color lithographs, the Old Mill cabinet cards picture the players in black-and-white photos surrounded by a wide tan border. The player's last name is printed in black in the lower-left corner, while his team designation appears in the lower-right. Backs carry an advertisement for Old Mill. There are currently 34 known subjects in the set. The Old Mill cabinet cards carry the ACC designation H801-7. Gaps have been left in the numbering to accomodate future additions to this checklist.

		NM	EX	VG
Common Player:		7,500	3,750	2,250
(1)	Armstrong	7,500	3,750	2,250
(2)	Bentley	7,500	3,750	2,250
(3)	Bonner	7,500	3,750	2,250
(4)	Bowen	7,500	3,750	2,250
(5)	Brazille (Brazell)	7,500	3,750	2,250
(6)	Bush (Busch)	7,500	3,750	2,250
(7)	Bussey	7,500	3,750	2,250
(8)	Cross	7,500	3,750	2,250
(9)	Derrick	7,500	3,750	2,250
(10)	Doane	7,500	3,750	2,250
(11)	Doyle	7,500	3,750	2,250
(12)	Fox	7,500	3,750	2,250
(13)	Galvin	7,500	3,750	2,250
(14)	Griffin	7,500	3,750	2,250
(15)	Hearn	7,500	3,750	2,250
(16)	Hobbs	7,500	3,750	2,250
(17)	Hooker	7,500	3,750	2,250
(18)	Kirkpatrick	7,500	3,750	2,250
(19)	Laughlin	7,500	3,750	2,250
(20)	Luyster	.00	.00	.00
(21)	McKevitt	7,500	3,750	2,250

		NM	EX	VG
(22)	Munson	7,500	3,750	2,250
(23)	Noojn (Noojin)	7,500	3,750	2,250
(24)	O'Halloran	7,500	3,750	2,250
(25)	Pressly	7,500	3,750	2,250
(26)	Revelle	7,500	3,750	2,250
(27)	Richardson	7,500	3,750	2,250
(28)	Rickard	7,500	3,750	2,250
(29)	Simmons	7,500	3,750	2,250
(30)	A. Smith	7,500	3,750	2,250
(31)	Spratt	7,500	3,750	2,250
(32)	Titman	7,500	3,750	2,250
(33)	Walters	7,500	3,750	2,250
(34)	Wallace	7,500	3,750	2,250
(35)	Weherell (Wehrell)	7,500	3,750	2,250
(36)	Ivey Wingo	7,500	3,750	2,250
(37)	Woolums	7,500	3,750	2,250

1949 Omaha Cardinals Player Picture Book

JIM BARKLEY, Outfield

While not baseball cards, this team booklet served the same purpose - providing fans with pictures of the local Western League (Class A) affiliate of the St. Louis Cardinals. It's also possible that individual player pages of the book have made their way into card collections over the years. The booklet is 5" x 3-1/4" in size, with 20 pages of photos and semi-gloss front and back covers, stapled together at the spine. The front has printed in red: "OMAHA CARDINALS / BASEBALL TEAM / 1949." Each inside page has back-to-back black-and-white photos with identification beneath. The pairings are checklisted here in the order in which they appear in the booklet.

		NM	EX	VG
Complete Booklet:		350.00	175.00	100.00
(1-2)	Ced Durst, Russ Kerns			
(3-4)	Nick Adzick, Bob Rausch			
(5-6)	Ed Nietopski, Fran Haus			
(7-8)	Fritz Marolewski, Bernie Creger			
(9-10)	Vaughn Hazen, Sid Langston			
(11-12)	Bob Reash, Jim Barkley			
(13-14)	Marty Garlock, Hank Williams			
(15-16)	Lou Ciola, Joe Presko			
(17-18)	Dave Thomas, Bob Mahoney			
(19-20)	Stadium Photo (Dick Bokelmann)			

1956 Omaha Cardinals Picture-Pak

Evidently a concession stand souvenir, this "Picture-Pak" is a comb-bound set of 3-1/2" x 4-3/8" black-and-white player portraits. Each picture is printed on semi-gloss cardboard with a white facsimile autograph.

		NM	EX	VG
Complete Book:		300.00	150.00	90.00
(1)	Tom Alston			
(2)	Alberto Baro			
(3)	Nels Burbrink			
(4)	Tom Cheney			
(5)	Ray Coleman			
(6)	Jim Command			
(7)	Chuck Harmon			
(8)	Walt Jamison (?)			
(9)	Stan Jok			
(10)	Gordon Jones			
(11)	Johnny Keane			
(12)	Marty Kutyna			
(13)	Ed Mayer			
(14)	Herb Moford			
(15)	Mo Mozzali			
(16)	Jim Pearce			
(17)	Charlie Peete			
(18)	Danny Schell			
(19)	Dick Schofield			
(20)	Barney Schultz			
(21)	Wally Shannon			
(22)	Glen Stabelfeld			

1957 Omaha Cardinals Picture-Pak

These 3-3/8" x 4-3/8" black-and-white, blank-back photos were sold in a team picture pack. Fronts have a facsimile autograph. The unnumbered cards are checklisted here in alphabetical order.

		NM	EX	VG
Complete Set (25):		800.00	400.00	240.00
Common Player:		35.00	17.50	10.00
(1)	Frank Barnes	35.00	17.50	10.00
(2)	Bill Bergesch	35.00	17.50	10.00
(3)	Dick Brown	35.00	17.50	10.00
(4)	Tom Cheney	35.00	17.50	10.00
(5)	Nels Chittum	35.00	17.50	10.00
(6)	Jim Command	35.00	17.50	10.00
(7)	Chuck Diering	35.00	17.50	10.00
(8)	Sherry Dixon	35.00	17.50	10.00
(9)	Bob Dumbaugh	35.00	17.50	10.00
(10)	Glen Gorbous	35.00	17.50	10.00
(11)	Johnny Keane	35.00	17.50	10.00
(12)	Jim King	35.00	17.50	10.00
(13)	Paul Kippels	35.00	17.50	10.00
(14)	Don Lassetter	35.00	17.50	10.00
(15)	Don Liddle	35.00	17.50	10.00
(16)	Lou Limmer	35.00	17.50	10.00
(17)	Boyd Linker	35.00	17.50	10.00
(18)	Bob Mabe	35.00	17.50	10.00
(19)	Herb Moford	35.00	17.50	10.00
(20)	Rance Pless	35.00	17.50	10.00
(21)	Kelton Russell	35.00	17.50	10.00
(22)	Barney Schultz	35.00	17.50	10.00
(23)	Milt Smith	35.00	17.50	10.00
(24)	Glen Stabelfeld	35.00	17.50	10.00
(25)	Header Card	35.00	17.50	10.00

1958 Omaha Cardinals Picture-Pak

This rare late-1950s minor league issue contains the first card of Hall of Fame pitcher Bob Gibson. Probably sold as a complete set in format similar to major league picture packs of the era, there are 23 player cards and a header card. Cards measure 3-3/8" x 4-3/8", have a black-and-white player picture and facsimile autograph. They are blank-backed. The checklist of the unnumbered cards is printed here in alphabetical order.

		NM	EX	VG
Complete Set (24):		1,500	750.00	450.00
Common Player:		40.00	20.00	12.00
(1)	Tony Alomar	60.00	30.00	18.00
(2)	Dave Benedict	40.00	20.00	12.00
(3)	Bill Bergesch	40.00	20.00	12.00
(4)	Bob Blaylock	40.00	20.00	12.00
(5)	Prentice "Pidge" Browne	40.00	20.00	12.00
(6)	Chris Cannizzaro	40.00	20.00	12.00
(7)	Nels Chittum	40.00	20.00	12.00
(8)	Don Choate	40.00	20.00	12.00
(9)	Phil Clark	40.00	20.00	12.00
(10)	Jim Frey	75.00	37.50	22.50
(11)	Bob Gibson	500.00	250.00	150.00
(12)	Ev Joyner	40.00	20.00	12.00
(13)	Johnny Keane	40.00	20.00	12.00
(14)	Paul Kippels	40.00	20.00	12.00
(15)	Boyd Linker	40.00	20.00	12.00
(16)	Bob Mabe	40.00	20.00	12.00
(17)	Bernard Mateosky	40.00	20.00	12.00
(18)	Ronnie Plaza	40.00	20.00	12.00
(19)	Bill Queen	40.00	20.00	12.00
(20)	Bill Smith	40.00	20.00	12.00
(21)	Bobby G. Smith	40.00	20.00	12.00
(22)	Lee Tate	40.00	20.00	12.00
(23)	Benny Valenzuela	40.00	20.00	12.00
(24)	Header card	40.00	20.00	12.00

1962 Omaha Dodgers

This unnumbered black-and-white set measures 3-3/8" x 4-1/4" and is blank-backed. It was produced by photographer/collector Mel Bailey in an edition of 1,000 sets, sold for 50 cents by mail and at the stadium concession stand. Cards bear a facsimile autograph.

		NM	EX	VG
Complete Set (22):		175.00	90.00	50.00
Common Player:		12.50	6.25	3.75
(1)	Joe Altobelli	12.50	6.25	3.75
(2)	Jim Barbieri	12.50	6.25	3.75
(3)	Scott Breeden	12.50	6.25	3.75
(4)	Mike Brumley	12.50	6.25	3.75
(5)	Jose Cesar	12.50	6.25	3.75
(6)	Bill Hunter	12.50	6.25	3.75
(7)	Don LeJohn	12.50	6.25	3.75
(8)	Jack Lutz	12.50	6.25	3.75
(9)	Ken McMullen	12.50	6.25	3.75
(10)	Danny Ozark	12.50	6.25	3.75
(11)	Curt Roberts	12.50	6.25	3.75
(12)	Ernie Rodriguez	12.50	6.25	3.75
(13)	Dick Scarbrough	12.50	6.25	3.75
(14)	Bart Shirley	12.50	6.25	3.75
(15)	Dick Smith	12.50	6.25	3.75
(16)	Jack Smith	12.50	6.25	3.75
(17)	Nate Smith	12.50	6.25	3.75
(18)	Gene Snyder	12.50	6.25	3.75
(19)	Burbon Wheeler	12.50	6.25	3.75
(20)	Nick Wilhite (Willhite)	12.50	6.25	3.75
(21)	Jim Williams	12.50	6.25	3.75
(22)	Larry Williams	12.50	6.25	3.75

1952 Oshkosh Giants Team Issue

GORDON WINDHORN

These 2-1/4" x 3-3/8" black-and-white, unnumbered, blank-backed cards were one of many minor league team sets issued by Globe Printing of San Jose, Calif., in the early 1950s. Cards were usually given away at the ballpark on a one-per-week or one-per-homestand basis, accounting for the rarity of surviving sets. The O-Giants were the Wisconsin State League affiliate of the N.Y. Giants. For a Class D team, a surprising number of the Oshkosh players graduated to the major leagues.

		NM	EX	VG
Complete Set (19):		1,000	500.00	300.00
Common Player:		60.00	30.00	18.00
Album:		100.00	50.00	30.00
(1)	Dan Banaszak	60.00	30.00	18.00
(2)	Paul Bentley	60.00	30.00	18.00
(3)	Joe Berke	60.00	30.00	18.00
(4)	Joe DeBellis	60.00	30.00	18.00
(5)	Ron Edwards	60.00	30.00	18.00
(6)	Dave Garcia	60.00	30.00	18.00
(7)	Weldon Grimesley	60.00	30.00	18.00
(8)	Cam Lewis	60.00	30.00	18.00
(9)	Paul McAuley	60.00	30.00	18.00
(10)	Don Mills	60.00	30.00	18.00
(11)	Ed Opich	60.00	30.00	18.00
(12)	John Practico	60.00	30.00	18.00
(13)	Rob R. Schmidt	60.00	30.00	18.00
(14)	Rob W. Schmidt	60.00	30.00	18.00
(15)	Frank Szekula	60.00	30.00	18.00
(16)	Victor Vick	60.00	30.00	18.00
(17)	Donald Wall	60.00	30.00	18.00
(18)	Ken Whitehead	60.00	30.00	18.00
(19)	Gordon Windhorn	60.00	30.00	18.00

P

1911 Pacific Coast Biscuit (D310)

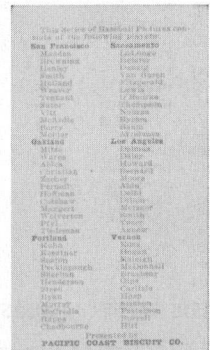

A dozen players each from six Pacific Coast League teams are represented in this set. Cards are about 2-1/2" x 4-1/4" with either black-and-white or sepia pictures on front. Backs have a checklist arranged by team.

		NM	EX	VG
Complete Set (72):		45,000	27,500	13,500
Common Player:		575.00	300.00	175.00
(1)	Ables	575.00	300.00	175.00
(2)	Agnew	575.00	300.00	175.00
(3)	Akin	575.00	300.00	175.00
(4)	Frank Arrelanes (Arellanes)	575.00	300.00	175.00
(5)	Baum	575.00	300.00	175.00
(6)	Bernard	575.00	300.00	175.00
(7)	Berry	575.00	300.00	175.00
(8)	Brashear	575.00	300.00	175.00
(9)	Browning	575.00	300.00	175.00
(10)	Burrell	575.00	300.00	175.00
(11)	Byram	575.00	300.00	175.00
(12)	Carlisle	575.00	300.00	175.00
(13)	Chadbourne	575.00	300.00	175.00
(14)	Christian	575.00	300.00	175.00
(15)	Cutshaw	575.00	300.00	175.00
(16)	Daley	575.00	300.00	175.00
(17)	Danzig	575.00	300.00	175.00
(18)	Delhi	575.00	300.00	175.00
(19)	Delmas	575.00	300.00	175.00
(20)	Dillon	575.00	300.00	175.00
(21)	Fitzgerald	575.00	300.00	175.00
(22)	Gipe	575.00	300.00	175.00
(23)	Heister	575.00	300.00	175.00
(24)	Henderson	575.00	300.00	175.00
(25)	Henley	575.00	300.00	175.00
(26)	Hitt	575.00	300.00	175.00
(27)	Hoffman	575.00	300.00	175.00
(28)	Hogan	575.00	300.00	175.00
(29)	Holland	575.00	300.00	175.00
(30)	Hosp	575.00	300.00	175.00
(31)	Howard	575.00	300.00	175.00
(32)	Kostner	575.00	300.00	175.00
(33)	Kuhn	575.00	300.00	175.00
(34)	LaLonge	575.00	300.00	175.00
(35)	Lewis	575.00	300.00	175.00
(36)	Maddern	575.00	300.00	175.00
(37)	Maggert	575.00	300.00	175.00
(38)	McArdle	575.00	300.00	175.00
(39)	McCredie	575.00	300.00	175.00
(40)	McDonnell	575.00	300.00	175.00
(41)	Metzger	575.00	300.00	175.00
(42)	Mitze	575.00	300.00	175.00
(43)	Mohler	575.00	300.00	175.00
(44)	Moore	575.00	300.00	175.00
(45)	Murray	575.00	300.00	175.00
(46)	Nourse	575.00	300.00	175.00
(47)	O'Rourke	575.00	300.00	175.00
(48)	Patterson	575.00	300.00	175.00
(49)	Peckinpaugh	600.00	300.00	180.00
(50)	Pernoll	575.00	300.00	175.00
(51)	Pfyl	575.00	300.00	175.00
(52)	Raleigh	575.00	300.00	175.00
(53)	Rapps	575.00	300.00	175.00
(54)	Ross	575.00	300.00	175.00
(55)	Ryan	575.00	300.00	175.00
(56)	Seaton	575.00	300.00	175.00
(57)	Sheehan	575.00	300.00	175.00
(58)	A. Smith	575.00	300.00	175.00
(59)	H. Smith	575.00	300.00	175.00
(60)	Steen	575.00	300.00	175.00
(61)	Stinson	575.00	300.00	175.00
(62)	Sutor	575.00	300.00	175.00
(63)	Tennant	575.00	300.00	175.00
(64)	Thompson	575.00	300.00	175.00
(65)	Tiedeman	575.00	300.00	175.00
(66)	Tozer	575.00	300.00	175.00
(67)	Van Buren	575.00	300.00	175.00
(68)	Witt	575.00	300.00	175.00
(69)	Wares	575.00	300.00	175.00
(70)	Weaver	6,000	3,000	1,800
(71)	Wolverton	575.00	300.00	175.00
(72)	Zacher	575.00	300.00	175.00

1911 Pacific Coast Biscuit (D311)

A dozen players each from six Pacific Coast League teams are represented in this set. Cards are about 1-1/2" x 2-5/8" with pastel colored pictures on front. Backs have a checklist arranged by team.

	NM	EX	VG
Complete Set (72):	40,000	20,000	12,000
Common Player:	575.00	300.00	175.00
(1) Agnew	575.00	300.00	175.00
(2) Akin	575.00	300.00	175.00
(3) Frank Arrelanes (Arellanes)	575.00	300.00	175.00
(4) Baum	575.00	300.00	175.00
(5) Bernard	575.00	300.00	175.00
(6) Berry	575.00	300.00	175.00
(7) Brashear	575.00	300.00	175.00
(8) Brown	575.00	300.00	175.00
(9) Browning	575.00	300.00	175.00
(10) Burrell	575.00	300.00	175.00
(11) Byram	575.00	300.00	175.00
(12) Castleton	575.00	300.00	175.00
(13) Chadbourne	575.00	300.00	175.00
(14) Christian	575.00	300.00	175.00
(15) Cutshaw	575.00	300.00	175.00
(16) Daley	575.00	300.00	175.00
(17) Danzig	575.00	300.00	175.00
(18) Delhi	575.00	300.00	175.00
(19) Delmas	575.00	300.00	175.00
(20) Dillon	575.00	300.00	175.00
(21) Fitzgerald	575.00	300.00	175.00
(22) Gipe	575.00	300.00	175.00
(23) Gregory	575.00	300.00	175.00
(24) Harkness	575.00	300.00	175.00
(25) Heister	575.00	300.00	175.00
(26) Henderson	575.00	300.00	175.00
(27) Hoffman	575.00	300.00	175.00
(28) Hogan	575.00	300.00	175.00
(29) Holland	575.00	300.00	175.00
(30) Hosp	575.00	300.00	175.00
(31) Howard	575.00	300.00	175.00
(32) Kuhn	575.00	300.00	175.00
(33) LaLonge	575.00	300.00	175.00
(34) Lewis	575.00	300.00	175.00
(35) Maggert	575.00	300.00	175.00
(36) McArdle	575.00	300.00	175.00
(37) McCredie	575.00	300.00	175.00
(38) McDonnell	575.00	300.00	175.00
(39) Meikle	575.00	300.00	175.00
(40) Melchior	575.00	300.00	175.00
(41) Metzger	575.00	300.00	175.00
(42) Mitze	575.00	300.00	175.00
(43) Mohler	575.00	300.00	175.00
(44) Moore	575.00	300.00	175.00
(45) Murray	575.00	300.00	175.00
(46) Nourse	575.00	300.00	175.00
(47) O'Rourke	575.00	300.00	175.00
(48) Patterson	575.00	300.00	175.00
(49) Pearce	575.00	300.00	175.00
(50) Peckinpaugh	600.00	300.00	180.00
(51) Pernoll	575.00	300.00	175.00
(52) Pfyl	575.00	300.00	175.00
(53) Raleigh	575.00	300.00	175.00
(54) Rapps	575.00	300.00	175.00
(55) Ryan	575.00	300.00	175.00
(56) Schmidt	575.00	300.00	175.00
(57) Seaton	575.00	300.00	175.00
(58) Sheehan	575.00	300.00	175.00
(59) A. Smith	575.00	300.00	175.00
(60) H. Smith	575.00	300.00	175.00
(61) Stamfield	575.00	300.00	175.00
(62) Steen	575.00	300.00	175.00
(63) Stinson	575.00	300.00	175.00
(64) Sutor	575.00	300.00	175.00
(65) Tennant	575.00	300.00	175.00
(66) Thompson	575.00	300.00	175.00
(67) Tiedeman	575.00	300.00	175.00
(68) Tozer	575.00	300.00	175.00
(69) Van Buren	575.00	300.00	175.00
(70) Vitt	575.00	300.00	175.00
(71) Wares	575.00	300.00	175.00
(72) Wolverton	575.00	300.00	175.00

1943-47 Parade Sportive

Over a period of years in the mid-1940s, Montreal sports radio personality Paul Stuart's Parade Sportive program issued a series of baseball player pictures of Montreal Royals and, occasionally, other International League stars. The pictures were issued in 5" x 9-1/2" and 7" x 10" black-and-white, blank-back format. Each picture carries the name of the radio station on which Stuart's program was broadcast, along with an ad at the bottom for one of his sponsors. The unnumbered pictures are listed here alphabetically; it is unknown whether this list constitutes the complete issue.

	NM	EX	VG
Common Player:	30.00	15.00	9.00
(1) Jack Banta	30.00	15.00	9.00

		NM	EX	VG
(2)	Stan Briard	30.00	15.00	9.00
(3)	Les Burge	30.00	15.00	9.00
(4)	Paul Calvert	30.00	15.00	9.00
(5)	Al Campanis	45.00	22.50	13.50
(6)	Red Durrett	30.00	15.00	9.00
(7)	Herman Franks	30.00	15.00	9.00
(8)	John Gabbard	30.00	15.00	9.00
(9)	Roland Gladu	30.00	15.00	9.00
(10)	Ray Hathaway	30.00	15.00	9.00
(11)	Clay Hopper	30.00	15.00	9.00
(12)	John Jorgensen	30.00	15.00	9.00
(13)	Paul "Pepper" Martin	30.00	15.00	9.00
(14)	Steve Nagy	30.00	15.00	9.00
(15)	Roy Portlow (Partlow)	40.00	20.00	12.00
(16)	Marv Rackley	30.00	15.00	9.00
(17)	Jackie Robinson	300.00	150.00	90.00
(18)	Jean-Pierre Roy	30.00	15.00	9.00
(19)	1944 Montreal Royals Team Photo	50.00	25.00	15.00
(20)	1945 Montreal Royals Team Photo (CLUB MONTREAL (ROYAUX) 1945)	60.00	30.00	18.00
(21)	1945 Montreal Royals Team Photo (Les "Royaux" 1945)	60.00	30.00	18.00
(22)	1946 Montreal Royals Team Photo	200.00	100.00	60.00
(23)	Stan Briard, Roland Gladu, Jean-Pierre Roy	30.00	15.00	9.00
(24)	Checklist (Paul Stuart)	30.00	15.00	9.00

1952 Parkhurst

Produced by a Canadian competitor to Kool-Aid, this 100-card set features players from three International League teams, the Toronto Maple Leafs, Montreal Royals and Ottawa Athletics, along with cards featuring baseball playing tips and quizzes. Measuring 2" x 2-1/2", the cards feature black-and-white player photos on front. Backs are printed in red and have a few biographical details, 1951 stats and an ad for Frostade.

	NM	EX	VG
Complete Set (100):	2,400	1,200	725.00
Common Player (1-25, 49-100):	25.00	12.50	7.50
Common Card (26-48):	10.00	5.00	3.00
1 Joe Becker	80.00	35.00	9.00
2 Aaron Silverman	75.00	37.50	22.50
3 Bobby Rhawn	25.00	12.50	7.50
4 Russ Bauers	25.00	12.50	7.50
5 Bill Jennings	25.00	12.50	7.50
6 Grover Bowers	25.00	12.50	7.50
7 Vic Lombardi	25.00	12.50	7.50
8 Billy DeMars	25.00	12.50	7.50
9 Frank Colman	25.00	12.50	7.50
10 Charley Grant	25.00	12.50	7.50
11 Irving Medlinger	25.00	12.50	7.50
12 Burke McLaughlin	25.00	12.50	7.50
13 Lew Morton	25.00	12.50	7.50
14 Red Barrett	25.00	12.50	7.50
15 Leon Foulk	25.00	12.50	7.50
16 Neil Sheridan	25.00	12.50	7.50
17 Ferrell Anderson	25.00	12.50	7.50
18 Roy Shore	25.00	12.50	7.50
19 Duke Markell	75.00	37.50	22.50
20 Bobby Balcena	25.00	12.50	7.50
21 Wilmer Fields	25.00	12.50	7.50
22 Charlie White	25.00	12.50	7.50
23 Red Fahr	25.00	12.50	7.50
24 Jose Bracho	25.00	12.50	7.50
25 Ed Stevens	25.00	12.50	7.50
26 Maple Leaf Stadium	25.00	12.50	7.50
27 Throwing Home	15.00	7.50	4.50
28 Regulation Baseball Diamond	15.00	7.50	4.50
29 Gripping the Bat	15.00	7.50	4.50
30 Hiding the Pitch	15.00	7.50	4.50
31 Catcher's Stance	15.00	7.50	4.50
32 Quiz: "How long does..."	15.00	7.50	4.50
33 Finger and Arm Exercises	15.00	7.50	4.50
34 First Baseman	15.00	7.50	4.50
35 Pitcher's Stance	15.00	7.50	4.50
36 Swinging Bats	15.00	7.50	4.50
37 Quiz: "Can a player advance..."	15.00	7.50	4.50
38 Watch the Ball	15.00	7.50	4.50
39 Quiz: "Can a team..."	15.00	7.50	4.50
40 Quiz: "Can a player put ..."	15.00	7.50	4.50
41 How to Bunt	15.00	7.50	4.50
42 Wrist Snap	15.00	7.50	4.50
43 Pitching Practice	15.00	7.50	4.50
44 Stealing Bases	15.00	7.50	4.50
45 Pitching 1	15.00	7.50	4.50
46 Pitching 2	15.00	7.50	4.50
47 Signals	15.00	7.50	4.50
48 Regulation baseballs	15.00	7.50	4.50
49 Al Ronning	25.00	12.50	7.50
50 Bill Lane	25.00	12.50	7.50
51 Will Sampson	25.00	12.50	7.50
52 Charlie Thompson	25.00	12.50	7.50
53 Ezra McGlothin	25.00	12.50	7.50
54 Spook Jacobs	30.00	15.00	9.00
55 Art Fabbro	25.00	12.50	7.50
56 Jim Hughes	25.00	12.50	7.50
57 Don Hoak	30.00	15.00	9.00

		NM	EX	VG
58	Tommy Lasorda	100.00	50.00	30.00
59	Gil Mills	25.00	12.50	7.50
60	Malcolm Mallette	25.00	12.50	7.50
61	Rocky Nelson	25.00	12.50	7.50
62	John Simmons	25.00	12.50	7.50
63	Bob Alexander	25.00	12.50	7.50
64	Dan Bankhead	35.00	17.50	10.00
65	Solomon Coleman	25.00	12.50	7.50
66	Walt Alston	100.00	50.00	30.00
67	Walt Fiala	25.00	12.50	7.50
68	Jim Gilliam	40.00	20.00	12.00
69	Jim Pendleton	25.00	12.50	7.50
70	Gino Cimoli	30.00	15.00	9.00
71	Carmen Mauro	25.00	12.50	7.50
72	Walt Moryn	25.00	12.50	7.50
73	Jim Romano	25.00	12.50	7.50
74	Joe Lutz	25.00	12.50	7.50
75	Ed Roebuck	25.00	12.50	7.50
76	Johnny Podres	40.00	20.00	12.00
77	Walter Novik	25.00	12.50	7.50
78	Lefty Gohl	25.00	12.50	7.50
79	Tom Kirk	25.00	12.50	7.50
80	Bob Betz	25.00	12.50	7.50
81	Bill Hockenbury	25.00	12.50	7.50
82	Al Rubeling	25.00	12.50	7.50
83	Julius Watlington	25.00	12.50	7.50
84	Frank Fanovich	25.00	12.50	7.50
85	Hank Foiles	25.00	12.50	7.50
86	Lou Limmer	25.00	12.50	7.50
87	Ed Hrabcsak	25.00	12.50	7.50
88	Bob Gardner	25.00	12.50	7.50
89	John Metkovich	25.00	12.50	7.50
90	Jean-Pierre Roy	25.00	12.50	7.50
91	Frank Skaff	25.00	12.50	7.50
92	Harry Desert	25.00	12.50	7.50
93	Stan Jok	25.00	12.50	7.50
94	Russ Swingle	25.00	12.50	7.50
95	Bob Wellman	25.00	12.50	7.50
96	John Conway	25.00	12.50	7.50
97	George Maskovich	25.00	12.50	7.50
98	Charlie Bishop	25.00	12.50	7.50
99	Joe Murray	25.00	12.50	7.50
100	Mike Kume	25.00	12.50	7.50

1935 Pebble Beach Clothiers

This series of black-and-white postcards includes only members of the three Bay area Pacific Coast League teams - the Oakland Oaks, Mission Reds and San Francisco Seals. The 3-1/2" x 5-3/8" cards have player identification at left in the bottom white border. The logotype of the clothier which sponsored the issue is at lower-right. The cards - each authentically autographed - were distributed by an area radio station. Backs have typical postcard indicia. This checklist may not be complete.

		NM	EX	VG
Common Player:		750.00	375.00	225.00
(1)	Leroy Anton	750.00	375.00	225.00
(2)	Joe DiMaggio	7,500	3,750	2,250
(3)	Wee Ludolph	750.00	375.00	225.00
(4)	Walter "The Great" Mails	750.00	375.00	225.00
(5)	Lefty O'Doul	3,650	1,825	1,100
(6)	Gabby Street	1,200	600.00	360.00
(7)	Oscar Vitt	900.00	450.00	270.00

1962 Pepsi-Cola Tulsa Oilers

The Texas League farm club of the St. Louis Cardinals is featured in this issue of sepia-colored 2-1/2" x 3-1/2" cards issued regionally by Pepsi. The unnumbered cards are checklisted here alphabetically.

	NM	EX	VG
Complete Set (24):	275.00	135.00	80.00

Common Player:		12.00	6.00	3.50
(1)	Bob Blaylock	12.00	6.00	3.50
(2)	Bud Bloomfield	12.00	6.00	3.50
(3)	Dick Hughes	12.00	6.00	3.50
(4)	Gary Kolb	12.00	6.00	3.50
(5)	Chris Krug	12.00	6.00	3.50
(6)	Hank Kuhlmann	12.00	6.00	3.50
(7)	Whitey Kurowski	12.00	6.00	3.50
(8)	Johnny Joe Lewis	12.00	6.00	3.50
(9)	Elmer Lindsey	12.00	6.00	3.50
(10)	Jeoff Long	12.00	6.00	3.50
(11)	Pepper Martin	15.00	7.50	4.50
(12)	Jerry Marx	12.00	6.00	3.50
(13)	Weldon Maudin	12.00	6.00	3.50
(14)	Dal Maxvill	15.00	7.50	4.50
(15)	Bill McNamee	12.00	6.00	3.50
(16)	Joe Patterson	12.00	6.00	3.50
(17)	Gordon Richardson	12.00	6.00	3.50
(18)	Daryl Robertson	12.00	6.00	3.50
(19)	Tom Schwaner	12.00	6.00	3.50
(20)	Joe Shipley	12.00	6.00	3.50
(21)	Jon Smith	12.00	6.00	3.50
(22)	Clint Stark	12.00	6.00	3.50
(23)	Terry Tucker	12.00	6.00	3.50
(24)	Bill Wakefield	12.00	6.00	3.50

1963 Pepsi-Cola Tulsa Oilers

These 2-1/2" x 3-1/2", unnumbered, cards were issued in two-card panels with a holed top panel to hang on bottles. Each player's name could also be found under the cork liner of the bottle caps and when all 24 cards and caps were collected, a $24 prize could be collected. It must be assumed that some player caps were short-printed.

		NM	EX	VG
Complete Set, Singles (24):		75.00	37.50	22.50
Complete Set, Panels (12):		90.00	45.00	27.50
Common Player:		4.00	2.00	1.25
(1)	Dennis Aust	4.00	2.00	1.25
(2)	Jimmy Beauchamp	4.00	2.00	1.25
(3)	"Bud" Bloomfield	4.00	2.00	1.25
(4)	Felix de Leon	4.00	2.00	1.25
(5)	Don Dennis	4.00	2.00	1.25
(6)	Lamar Drummonds	4.00	2.00	1.25
(7)	Tom Hilgendorf	4.00	2.00	1.25
(8)	Gary Kolb	4.00	2.00	1.25
(9)	Chris Krug	4.00	2.00	1.25
(10)	"Bee" Lindsey	4.00	2.00	1.25
(11)	Roy Majtyka	4.00	2.00	1.25
(12)	Pepper Martin	7.50	3.75	2.25
(13)	Jerry Marx	4.00	2.00	1.25
(14)	"Hunkey" Mauldin	4.00	2.00	1.25
(15)	Joe Patterson	4.00	2.00	1.25
(16)	Grover Resinger	4.00	2.00	1.25
(17)	Gordon Richardson	4.00	2.00	1.25
(18)	Jon Smith	4.00	2.00	1.25
(19)	Chuck Taylor	4.00	2.00	1.25
(20)	Terry Tucker (Batboy)	4.00	2.00	1.25
(21)	Lou Vickery	4.00	2.00	1.25
(22)	Bill Wakefield	4.00	2.00	1.25
(23)	Harry Watts	4.00	2.00	1.25
(24)	Jerry Wild	4.00	2.00	1.25

1964 Pepsi-Cola Tulsa Oiler Autograph Cards

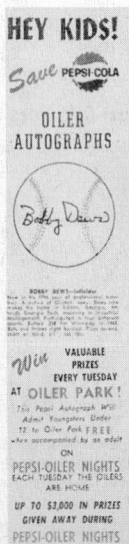

These unusual baseball cards - they don't have pictures! - were one of several 1960s issues by Pepsi in conjunction with the Tulsa Oilers. Apparently carton stuffers (they measure 2-3/16" x 9"), the cards provided free children's admission on special Pepsi-Oiler nights. The cards are printed in red, white and blue and have short player biographies under the baseball containing the facsimile autograph. The unnumbered cards are listed here in alphabetical order.

		NM	EX	VG
Complete Set (8):		30.00	15.00	9.00
Common Player:		5.00	2.50	1.50
(1)	Bob Blaylock	5.00	2.50	1.50
(2)	Nelson Briles	5.00	2.50	1.50
(3)	Bobby Dews	5.00	2.50	1.50
(4)	Roy Majtyka	5.00	2.50	1.50
(5)	Otto Meischner	5.00	2.50	1.50
(6)	Rogers Robinson	5.00	2.50	1.50
(7)	Jerry Wild	5.00	2.50	1.50
(8)	Lou Vickery	5.00	2.50	1.50

1966 Pepsi-Cola Tulsa Oilers

These 2-1/2" x 3-1/2" unnumbered cards were issued in two-card panels. Four cards were double-printed, each appearing on two different panels. Each player's name could also be found under the cork liner of the bottle caps and when all 24 cards and caps were collected, a $24 prize could be collected. It must be assumed that some player cards or caps were short-printed.

		NM	EX	VG
Complete Set (24):		175.00	90.00	55.00
Complete Panel Set (16):		225.00	115.00	70.00
Common Player:		10.00	5.00	3.00
Common Panel:		15.00	7.50	4.50
(1)	Florian Ackley	10.00	5.00	3.00
(2)	Dennis Aust	10.00	5.00	3.00
(3)	Elio Chacon (DP)	10.00	5.00	3.00
(4)	James Cosman	10.00	5.00	3.00
(5)	Mack Creager	10.00	5.00	3.00
(6)	Robert Dews (DP)	10.00	5.00	3.00
(7)	Harold Gilson	10.00	5.00	3.00
(8)	Larry Jaster	10.00	5.00	3.00
(9)	Alex Johnson	10.00	5.00	3.00
(10)	George Kernek (DP)	10.00	5.00	3.00
(11)	Jose Laboy	10.00	5.00	3.00
(12)	Richard LeMay	10.00	5.00	3.00
(13)	Charles Metro	10.00	5.00	3.00
(14)	David Pavlesic	10.00	5.00	3.00
(15)	Robert Pfeil	10.00	5.00	3.00
(16)	Ronald Piche	10.00	5.00	3.00
(17)	Robert Radovich	10.00	5.00	3.00
(18)	David Ricketts (DP)	10.00	5.00	3.00
(19)	Theodore Savage	10.00	5.00	3.00
(20)	George Schultz	10.00	5.00	3.00
(21)	Edward Spiezio	10.00	5.00	3.00
(22)	Clint Stark	10.00	5.00	3.00
(23)	Robert Tolan	10.00	5.00	3.00
(24)	Walter Williams	10.00	5.00	3.00

1956 Portland Beaver All-Star Pins

Stars of the Pacific Coast League Portland Beavers, all former and/or future major leaguers, are featured on these 1" black-and-white celluloid pins.

		NM	EX	VG
Complete Set (8):		1,300	650.00	375.00
Common Player:		175.00	90.00	55.00
(1)	Jim Baxes	175.00	90.00	55.00
(2)	Bob Borkowski	175.00	90.00	55.00
(3)	Sam Calderone	175.00	90.00	55.00
(4)	Jack Littrell	175.00	90.00	55.00
(5)	Luis Marquez	175.00	90.00	55.00
(6)	Ed Mickelson	175.00	90.00	55.00
(7)	Tom Saffell	175.00	90.00	55.00
(8)	Rene Valdez	175.00	90.00	55.00

R

1958 Ralph's Thriftway Seattle Rainiers

(See 1958 Seattle Popcorn for checklist and values.)

1968 Red Barn Memphis Blues

A regional issue from a Memphis chain of fast-food restaurants, these 2-1/2" x 3-3/4" cards feature members of the New York Mets' Class AA farm team. Cards have a blue-tinted player photo within an orange barn design. Player information is printed below. Backs are blank. The cards are checklisted here by uniform number.

		NM	EX	VG
Complete Set (8):		600.00	300.00	180.00
Common Player:		75.00	37.50	22.50
3	Mike "Spider" Jorgensen	75.00	37.50	22.50
6	Joe Moock	75.00	37.50	22.50
9	Rod Gaspar	75.00	37.50	22.50
16	Barry "Chief" Raziano	75.00	37.50	22.50
17	Curtis "Bubba" Brown	75.00	37.50	22.50
18	Roger Stevens	75.00	37.50	22.50
19	Ron Paul	75.00	37.50	22.50
24	Steve "Teddy" Christopher	75.00	37.50	22.50

1910 Red Sun (T211)

The 1910 minor league tobacco set issued by Red Sun Cigarettes features 75 players from the Southern Association. The Red Sun issue is similar in size and style to the massive 640-card Old Mill set (T210) issued the same year. Cards in both sets measure 1-1/2" x 2-5/8" and feature glossy black-and-white player photos. Unlike the Old Mill set, however, the Red Sun cards have a green border surrounding the photograph and a bright red and white advertisement for Red Sun cigarettes on the back. A line at the bottom promotes the cards as "First Series 1 to 75," implying that additional sets would follow, but apparently none ever did. Each of the 75 subjects in the Red Sun set was also pictured in Series Eight of the Old Mill set. Because of the "Glossy" nature of the photographs, cards in both the Old Mill and Red Sun sets are susceptible to cracking, making condition and proper grading of these cards especially important to collectors.

		NM	EX	VG
Complete Set (75):		65,000	35,000	20,000
Common Player:		1,300	500.00	300.00
(1)	Allen	1,300	500.00	300.00
(2)	Anderson	1,300	500.00	300.00
(3)	Babb	1,300	500.00	300.00
(4)	Bartley	1,300	500.00	300.00
(5)	Bay	1,300	500.00	300.00
(6)	Bayliss	1,300	500.00	300.00
(7)	Berger	1,300	500.00	300.00
(8)	Bernard	1,300	500.00	300.00
(9)	Bitroff	1,300	500.00	300.00
(10)	Breitenstein	1,300	500.00	300.00
(11)	Bronkie	1,300	500.00	300.00
(12)	Brooks	1,300	500.00	300.00
(13)	Cafalu	1,300	500.00	300.00
(14)	Case	1,300	500.00	300.00
(15)	Chappelle	1,300	500.00	300.00
(16)	Cohen	1,300	500.00	300.00
(17)	Cross	1,300	500.00	300.00
(18)	Jud. Daly	1,300	500.00	300.00
(19)	Davis	1,300	500.00	300.00
(20)	DeMontreville	1,300	500.00	300.00
(21)	E. DeMontreville	1,300	500.00	300.00
(22)	Dick	1,300	500.00	300.00
(23)	Dunn	1,300	500.00	300.00
(24)	Erloff	1,300	500.00	300.00
(25)	Fisher	1,300	500.00	300.00
(26)	Flood	1,300	500.00	300.00
(27)	Foster	1,300	500.00	300.00
(28)	Fritz	1,300	500.00	300.00
(29)	Greminger	1,300	500.00	300.00
(30)	Gribbon	1,300	500.00	300.00
(31)	Griffin	1,300	500.00	300.00
(32)	Gygli	1,300	500.00	300.00
(33)	Hanks	1,300	500.00	300.00
(34)	Hart	1,300	500.00	300.00
(35)	Hess	1,300	500.00	300.00
(36)	Hickman	1,300	500.00	300.00
(37)	Hohnhorst	1,300	500.00	300.00
(38)	Huelsman	1,300	500.00	300.00
(39)	Jordan	1,300	500.00	300.00

(40)	Kane	1,300	500.00	300.00
(41)	Kelly	1,300	500.00	300.00
(42)	Kerwin	1,300	500.00	300.00
(43)	Keupper	1,300	500.00	300.00
(44)	LaFitte	1,300	500.00	300.00
(45)	Bill Lindsay	1,300	500.00	300.00
(46)	Lynch	1,300	500.00	300.00
(47)	Manush	1,300	500.00	300.00
(48)	McCreery	1,300	500.00	300.00
(49)	Miller	1,300	500.00	300.00
(50)	Molesworth	1,300	500.00	300.00
(51)	Moran	1,300	500.00	300.00
(52)	Nolley	1,300	500.00	300.00
(53)	Paige	1,300	500.00	300.00
(54)	Pepe	1,300	500.00	300.00
(55)	Perdue	1,300	500.00	300.00
(56)	Pratt	1,300	500.00	300.00
(57)	Rhoton	1,300	500.00	300.00
(58)	Robertson	1,300	500.00	300.00
(59)	Rogers	1,300	500.00	300.00
(60)	Rohe	1,300	500.00	300.00
(61)	Seabaugh	1,300	500.00	300.00
(62)	Seitz	1,300	500.00	300.00
(63)	Siegle	1,300	500.00	300.00
(64)	Smith	1,300	500.00	300.00
(65)	Sid. Smith	1,300	500.00	300.00
(66)	Steele	1,300	500.00	300.00
(67)	Swacina	1,300	500.00	300.00
(68)	Sweeney	1,300	500.00	300.00
(69)	Thomas	1,300	500.00	300.00
(70)	Vinson	1,300	500.00	300.00
(71)	Wagner	1,300	500.00	300.00
(72)	Walker	1,300	500.00	300.00
(73)	Welf	1,300	500.00	300.00
(74)	Wilder	1,300	500.00	300.00
(75)	Wiseman	1,300	500.00	300.00

1945 Remar Bread Oakland Oaks

This 4-7/8" x 3-5/8" card features on front a black-and-white team photo, borderless at the top and sides. In the white strip at bottom, the players are identified. The back is printed in black with red highlights and presents the season stats for batting average and pitchers' won-lost percentage. At right is a picture of a loaf of the sponsor's bread. At present, only two examples of this card are known to exist.

	NM	EX	VG
Oakland Oaks Team Photo	2,500	1,250	750.00

1946 Remar Bread Oakland Oaks

CHARLES (Casey) STENGEL
Oaks Manager 10

Remar Baking Co. issued several baseball card sets in the northern California area from 1946-1950, all picturing members of the Oakland Oaks of the Pacific Coast League. The 1946 set consists of 23 cards (five unnumbered, 18 numbered). Measuring 2" x 3", the cards were printed on heavy paper and feature black and white photos with the player's name, team and position at the bottom. The backs contain a brief write-up plus an ad for Remar Bread printed in red. The cards were distributed one per week. The first five cards were unnumbered. The rest of the set is numbered on the front, but begins with number "5," rather than "6."

		NM	EX	VG
Complete Set (23):		600.00	300.00	180.00
Common Player:		25.00	12.50	7.50
5	Hershell Martin (Herschel)	25.00	12.50	7.50
6	Bill Hart	25.00	12.50	7.50
7	Charlie Gassaway	25.00	12.50	7.50
8	Wally Westlake	25.00	12.50	7.50
9	Mickey Burnett	25.00	12.50	7.50
10	Charles (Casey) Stengel	110.00	55.00	35.00
11	Charlie Metro	25.00	12.50	7.50
12	Tom Hafey	25.00	12.50	7.50
13	Tony Sabol	25.00	12.50	7.50
14	Ed Kearse	25.00	12.50	7.50

15	Bud Foster (Announcer)	25.00	12.50	7.50
16	Johnny Price	25.00	12.50	7.50
17	Gene Bearden	25.00	12.50	7.50
18	Floyd Speer	25.00	12.50	7.50
19	Bryan Stephens	25.00	12.50	7.50
20	Rinaldo (Rugger) Ardizoia	25.00	12.50	7.50
21	Ralph Buxton	25.00	12.50	7.50
22	Ambrose (Bo) Palica	25.00	12.50	7.50
----	Brooks Holder	25.00	12.50	7.50
----	Henry (Cotton) Pippen	25.00	12.50	7.50
----	Billy Raimondi	90.00	45.00	27.50
----	Les Scarsella	25.00	12.50	7.50
----	Glen (Gabby) Stewart	25.00	12.50	7.50

1947 Remar Bread Oakland Oaks

BILLY RAIMONDI
Oaks Catcher

BILLY RAIMONDI, 33, has been with the Oaks for 16 years. Managed Acorns part of '45. Believes it's bad luck to cross bats or walk between umpire and catcher. Learned baseball on San Francisco sandlots. Boyhood idol: Baby Ruth; present-day favorite: Joe Di Maggio. Hobby is photography.

"Let's Be Friends"

REMAR BAKING CO.

Remar's second set consisted of 25 numbered cards, again measuring 2" x 3". The cards are nearly identical to the previous year's set, except the loaf of bread on the back is printed in blue, rather than red.

		NM	EX	VG
Complete Set (25):		600.00	300.00	180.00
Common Player:		25.00	12.50	7.50
1	Billy Raimondi	25.00	12.50	7.50
2	Les Scarsella	25.00	12.50	7.50
3	Brooks Holder	25.00	12.50	7.50
4	Charlie Gassaway	25.00	12.50	7.50
5	Mickey Burnett	25.00	12.50	7.50
6	Ralph Buxton	25.00	12.50	7.50
7	Ed Kearse	25.00	12.50	7.50
8	Charles (Casey) Stengel	75.00	37.50	22.50
9	Bud Foster (Announcer)	25.00	12.50	7.50
10	Ambrose (Bo) Palica	25.00	12.50	7.50
11	Tom Hafey	25.00	12.50	7.50
12	Hershel Martin (Herschel)	25.00	12.50	7.50
13	Henry (Cotton) Pippen	25.00	12.50	7.50
14	Floyd Speer	25.00	12.50	7.50
15	Tony Sabol	25.00	12.50	7.50
16	Will Hafey	25.00	12.50	7.50
17	Ray Hamrick	25.00	12.50	7.50
18	Maurice Van Robays	25.00	12.50	7.50
19	Dario Lodigiani	25.00	12.50	7.50
20	Mel (Dizz) Duezabou	25.00	12.50	7.50
21	Damon Hayes	25.00	12.50	7.50
22	Gene Lillard	25.00	12.50	7.50
23	Aldon Wilkie	25.00	12.50	7.50
24	Dewey Soriano	25.00	12.50	7.50
25	Glen Crawford	25.00	12.50	7.50

1948 Remar/Sunbeam Bread Oakland Oaks

1948 Oakland OAKS

Let's Be Friends... REACH FOR SUNBEAM BREAD

One of the great minor league rarities, only two examples of this 3-1/4" x 5-1/2" black-and-white team photo card are known.

	NM	EX	VG
1948 Oakland Oaks Team Photo	2,500	1,250	750.00

1949 Remar Bread Oakland Oaks

BILLY MARTIN
Oaks Infielder

Vital Statistics on Billy Martin

REMAR BAKING CO.

The 1949 Remar Bread issue was increased to 32 cards, again measuring 2" x 3". Unlike the two earlier sets, photos in the 1949 Remar set are surrounded by a thin, white border and are unnumbered. The player's name, team and position appear below the black and white photo. The backs are printed in blue and include the player's 1948 statistics and the distinctive loaf of bread.

		NM	EX	VG
Complete Set (32):		700.00	350.00	210.00
Common Player:		20.00	10.00	6.00
(1)	Ralph Buxton	20.00	10.00	6.00
(2)	Milo Candini	20.00	10.00	6.00
(3)	Rex Cecil	20.00	10.00	6.00
(4)	Loyd Christopher (Lloyd)	20.00	10.00	6.00
(5)	Charles Dressen	20.00	10.00	6.00
(6)	Mel Duezabou	20.00	10.00	6.00
(7)	Bud Foster (Sportscaster)	20.00	10.00	6.00
(8)	Charlie Gassaway	20.00	10.00	6.00
(9)	Ray Hamrick	20.00	10.00	6.00
(10)	Jack Jensen	25.00	12.50	7.50
(11)	Earl Jones	20.00	10.00	6.00
(12)	George Kelly	60.00	30.00	18.00
(13)	Frank Kerr	20.00	10.00	6.00
(14)	Richard Kryhoski	20.00	10.00	6.00
(15)	Harry Lavagetto	20.00	10.00	6.00
(16)	Dario Lodigiani	20.00	10.00	6.00
(17)	Billy Martin	75.00	37.50	22.50
(18)	George Metkovich	20.00	10.00	6.00
(19)	Frank Nelson	20.00	10.00	6.00
(20)	Don Padgett	20.00	10.00	6.00
(21)	Alonzo Perry	40.00	20.00	12.00
(22)	Bill Raimondi	20.00	10.00	6.00
(23)	Earl Rapp	20.00	10.00	6.00
(24)	Eddie Samcoff	20.00	10.00	6.00
(25)	Les Scarsella	20.00	10.00	6.00
(26)	Forest Thompson (Forrest)	20.00	10.00	6.00
(27)	Earl Toolson	20.00	10.00	6.00
(28)	Lou Tost	20.00	10.00	6.00
(29)	Maurice Van Robays	20.00	10.00	6.00
(30)	Jim Wallace	20.00	10.00	6.00
(31)	Arthur Lee Wilson	40.00	20.00	12.00
(32)	Parnell Woods	20.00	10.00	6.00

1950 Remar Bread Oakland Oaks

RAFAEL (RAY) NOBLE
Oaks Catcher

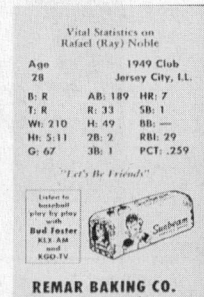

Vital Statistics on Rafael (Ray) Noble

REMAR BAKING CO.

The most common of the Remar Bread issues, the 1950 set contains 27 unnumbered cards, again measuring 2" x 3" and featuring members of the Oakland Oaks. The cards are nearly identical to the previous year's set but can be differentiated by the 1949 statistics on the back.

		NM	EX	VG
Complete Set (27):		500.00	250.00	150.00
Common Player:		20.00	10.00	6.00
(1)	George Bamberger	20.00	10.00	6.00
(2)	Hank Behrman	20.00	10.00	6.00
(3)	Loyd Christopher (Lloyd)	20.00	10.00	6.00
(4)	Chuck Dressen	20.00	10.00	6.00
(5)	Mel Duezabou	20.00	10.00	6.00
(6)	Augie Galan	20.00	10.00	6.00
(7)	Charlie Gassaway	20.00	10.00	6.00
(8)	Allen Gettel	20.00	10.00	6.00
(9)	Ernie W. Groth	20.00	10.00	6.00
(10)	Ray Hamrick	20.00	10.00	6.00
(11)	Earl Harrist	20.00	10.00	6.00
(12)	Billy Herman	60.00	30.00	18.00
(13)	Bob Hofman	20.00	10.00	6.00
(14)	George Kelly	60.00	30.00	18.00
(15)	Harry Lavagetto	20.00	10.00	6.00
(16)	Eddie Malone	20.00	10.00	6.00
(17)	George Metkovich	20.00	10.00	6.00
(18)	Frank Nelson	20.00	10.00	6.00
(19)	Rafael (Ray) Noble	20.00	10.00	6.00
(20)	Don Padgett	20.00	10.00	6.00
(21)	Earl Rapp	20.00	10.00	6.00
(22)	Clyde Shoun	20.00	10.00	6.00
(23)	Forrest Thompson	20.00	10.00	6.00
(24)	Louis Tost	20.00	10.00	6.00
(25)	Dick Wakefield	20.00	10.00	6.00
(26)	Artie Wilson	40.00	20.00	12.00
(27)	Roy Zimmerman	20.00	10.00	6.00

1958 Richmond Virginians Team Issue

This set of black-and-white cards features members of the N.Y. Yankees' top farm club in posed action photos with a stadium background. Issued on a pair of 8-1/2" x 10" sheets, single cards measure about 2-1/8" x 3", including the white borders around the picture. The player name is in a white strip within the photo. Backs have only the player name and a two-line credit at bottom to Galeski Photo Finishing.

	NM	EX	VG
Complete Set (21):	1,200	600.00	360.00
Common Player:	60.00	30.00	18.00

(1)	Billy Bethel	60.00	30.00	18.00
(2)	Cletis Boyer	90.00	45.00	27.50
(3)	Wade Browning	60.00	30.00	18.00
(4)	Bob Chakales	60.00	30.00	18.00
(5)	Jim Coates	60.00	30.00	18.00
(6)	Jim Command	60.00	30.00	18.00
(7)	Bobby Deakin	60.00	30.00	18.00
(8)	Bob Del Greco	60.00	30.00	18.00
(9)	John Jaciuk	60.00	30.00	18.00
(10)	John James	60.00	30.00	18.00
(11)	Deron Johnson	75.00	37.50	22.50
(12)	Len Johnston	60.00	30.00	18.00
(13)	Bob Kline	60.00	30.00	18.00
(14)	Ed Lopat	80.00	40.00	24.00
(15)	Bob Oldis	60.00	30.00	18.00
(16)	Wilson Parsons	60.00	30.00	18.00
(17)	Rance Pless	60.00	30.00	18.00
(18)	Jim Post	60.00	30.00	18.00
(19)	Danny Schell	60.00	30.00	18.00
(20)	Gerry Thomas	60.00	30.00	18.00
(21)	Bob Weisler	60.00	30.00	18.00

1959 Richmond Virginians

Photos of half a dozen local favorites of the International League Richmond Virginians were featured on ticket stubs during the 1959 season. The black-and-white player portions of the stub measure 2" x 3" and are blank-backed. The unnumbered cards are listed here alphabetically. Richmond was a farm club of the N.Y. Yankees.

		NM	EX	VG
Complete Set (6):		1,200	625.00	375.00
Common Player:		90.00	45.00	25.00
(1)	Clete Boyer	300.00	150.00	90.00
(2)	Jim Coates	200.00	100.00	60.00
(3)	Eli Grba	200.00	100.00	60.00
(4)	John James	200.00	100.00	60.00
(5)	Dick Sanders	200.00	100.00	60.00
(6)	Bill Short	200.00	100.00	60.00

1960 Richmond Virginians

Jerry Thomas
MADISON HEIGHTS, VA.

In 1960, the Richmond Virginians of the International League continued the practice of using player photos on their game tickets. Black-and-white with a blank-back, the player portions of the tickets can be found in two sizes. Unnumbered cards are checklisted here alphabetically. The Richmond team was a farm club of the N.Y. Yankees.

		NM	EX	VG
Complete Set (6):		1,750	875.00	525.00
Common Player:		300.00	150.00	90.00
SMALL SIZE (2" x 2-3/4")		.00	.00	.00
(1)	Bob Martyn	300.00	150.00	90.00
(2)	Jack Reed	300.00	150.00	90.00
LARGE SIZE (2-3/8" x 2-7/8")		.00	.00	.00
(1)	Tony Asaro	300.00	150.00	90.00
(2)	Bill Shantz	300.00	150.00	90.00
(3)	Jerry Thomas	300.00	150.00	90.00
(4)	Bob Weisler	300.00	150.00	90.00

1966 Royal Crown Cola Columbus Yankees

This set of 20 cards was distributed in eight packs of Royal Crown Cola, then based in Columbus, Ga. They were part of a strip measuring 2-1/4" wide. The first 3" of the 9-1/2" strip has a black-and-white photo of the player with his name, position and other biographical data, along with an RC logo in blue and red. The bottom of the strip has a promotion sponsored by the ball club and RC, offering a case of cola for turning in a complete set in an album provided for the cards. Those who turned in the cards were also eligible to win baseball equipment or picnic coolers in a giveaway at a July 31 game that year. Most cards have the advertisement removed. Strips that include the advertisement should be valued at 1.5X of values shown. The cards are unnumbered and listed in alphabetical order.

		NM	EX	VG
Complete Set (20):		800.00	400.00	240.00
Common Player:		40.00	20.00	12.00
Album:		800.00	400.00	240.00
(1)	Gil Blanco	40.00	20.00	12.00
(2)	Ronnie Boyer	50.00	25.00	15.00
(3)	Jim Brenneman	40.00	20.00	12.00
(4)	Butch Cretara	40.00	20.00	12.00
(5)	Bill Henry	40.00	20.00	12.00
(6)	Joe Jeran	40.00	20.00	12.00
(7)	Jerry Kenney	40.00	20.00	12.00
(8)	Ronnie Kirk	40.00	20.00	12.00
(9)	Tom Kowalski	40.00	20.00	12.00
(10)	Jim Marrujo	40.00	20.00	12.00
(11)	Dave McDonald	40.00	20.00	12.00
(12)	Ed Merritt	40.00	20.00	12.00
(13)	Jim Palma	40.00	20.00	12.00
(14)	Cecil Perkins	40.00	20.00	12.00
(15)	Jack Reed	40.00	20.00	12.00
(16)	Ellie Rodriguez	60.00	30.00	18.00
(17)	John Schroeppel	40.00	20.00	12.00
(18)	Dave Truelock	40.00	20.00	12.00
(19)	Steve Whitaker	40.00	20.00	12.00
(20)	Earl Willoughby	40.00	20.00	12.00

S

1952 San Diego Padres Team Issue

LONNIE SUMMERS

The Padres were one of the highest classification minor league teams for which Globe Printing produced baseball cards in the early 1950s. Like other sets from the San Jose, Calif., printer, the 2-1/8" x 3-3/8" cards are black-and-white, blank-backed and feature the player's name on a white strip on front. Because the Padres are quite often found as a team set, it's likely they were not distributed a card at a time as seems to have been the case with other sets. In 1952, the team was in the Open Classification Pacific Coast League.

		NM	EX	VG
Complete Set (18):		1,000	500.00	300.00
Common Player:		60.00	30.00	18.00
(1)	Al Benton	60.00	30.00	18.00
(2)	Dain Clay	60.00	30.00	18.00
(3)	John Davis	125.00	62.00	37.00
(4)	Dick Faber	60.00	30.00	18.00
(5)	Ben Flowers	60.00	30.00	18.00
(6)	Murray Franklin	60.00	30.00	18.00
(7)	Herb Gorman	90.00	45.00	27.50
(8)	Jack Graham	60.00	30.00	18.00
(9)	Memo Luna	60.00	30.00	18.00
(10)	Lefty O'Doul (Seated, light background.)	125.00	62.00	37.00
(11)	Lefty O'Doul (Standing, dark background.)	125.00	62.00	37.00
(12)	Al Olsen	60.00	30.00	18.00
(13)	Jimmie Reese	100.00	50.00	30.00
(14)	Al Richter	60.00	30.00	18.00
(15)	Jack Salveson	60.00	30.00	18.00
(16)	Lou Stringer	60.00	30.00	18.00
(17)	Lonnie Summers	60.00	30.00	18.00
(18)	Jack Tobin	60.00	30.00	18.00

1950 San Francisco Seals Popcorn

These 3-1/4" x 4-1/2" black-and-white cards were issued with the purchase of caramel corn at Sicks Stadium.

		NM	EX	VG
Complete Set (13):		700.00	350.00	210.00
Common Player:		60.00	30.00	17.50
(1)	Dick Briskey	60.00	30.00	17.50
(2)	Ralph Buxton	60.00	30.00	17.50
(3)	Harry Feldman	60.00	30.00	17.50
(4)	Chet Johnson	60.00	30.00	17.50
(5)	Al Lien	60.00	30.00	17.50
(6)	Dario Lodigiani	60.00	30.00	17.50
(7)	Cliff Melton	60.00	30.00	17.50
(8)	Roy Nicely	60.00	30.00	17.50
(9)	Roy Partee	60.00	30.00	17.50
(10)	Manny Perez	60.00	30.00	17.50
(11)	Neill Sheridan	60.00	30.00	17.50
(12)	Elmer Singleton	60.00	30.00	17.50
(13)	Jack Tobin	60.00	30.00	17.50

1953 San Francisco Seals Team Issue

This set of 25 cards was sold at Seals Stadium and by mail for 25 cents. Fronts of the 4" x 5" black-and-white cards contain a player photo with facsimile autograph. The player's name, team and position are printed in the white bottom border. Backs of the unnumbered cards are blank. Melton is a rare short-print which has been reprinted.

		NM	EX	VG
Complete Set (25):		600.00	300.00	180.00
Common Player:		30.00	15.00	9.00
(1)	Bill Boemler	30.00	15.00	9.00
(2)	Bill Bradford	30.00	15.00	9.00
(3)	Reno Cheso	30.00	15.00	9.00
(4)	Harlond Clift	30.00	15.00	9.00
(5)	Walt Clough	30.00	15.00	9.00
(6)	Cliff Coggin	30.00	15.00	9.00
(7)	Tommy Heath	30.00	15.00	9.00
(8)	Leo Hughes (Trainer)	30.00	15.00	9.00
(9)	Frank Kalin	30.00	15.00	9.00
(10)	Al Lien	30.00	15.00	9.00
(11)	Al Lyons	30.00	15.00	9.00
(12)	John McCall	30.00	15.00	9.00
(13)	Bill McCawley	30.00	15.00	9.00
(14)	Dave Melton (SP)	200.00	100.00	60.00
(15)	Jim Moran	30.00	15.00	9.00
(16)	Bob Muncrief	30.00	15.00	9.00
(17)	Leo Righetti	30.00	15.00	9.00
(18)	Ted Shandor	30.00	15.00	9.00
(19)	Elmer Singleton	30.00	15.00	9.00
(20)	Lou Stringer	30.00	15.00	9.00
(21)	Sal Taormina	30.00	15.00	9.00
(22)	Will Tiesiera	30.00	15.00	9.00
(23)	Nini Tornay	30.00	15.00	9.00
(24)	George Vico	30.00	15.00	9.00
(25)	Jerry Zuvela	30.00	15.00	9.00

1951 San Jose Red Sox Team Issue

MARVIN OWEN

These 2-1/4" x 3-3/8" black-and-white, unnumbered, blank-backed cards were one of many minor league team sets issued by Globe Printing of San Jose, Calif., in the early 1950s. Cards were usually given away at the ballpark on a one-per-week or one-per-homestand basis, accounting for the rarity of surviving sets. The team was a Class C farm club for the Boston Red Sox in the California League. An album exists for the set, but curiously, it is dated 1952.

		NM	EX	VG
Complete Set (18):		1,000	500.00	300.00
Common Player:		60.00	30.00	18.00
(1)	Ken Aspromonte	75.00	37.00	22.00
(2)	Joe Buck	60.00	30.00	18.00
(3)	Harold Buckwalter	60.00	30.00	18.00
(4)	Al Curtis	60.00	30.00	18.00
(5)	Marvin Eyre	60.00	30.00	18.00
(6)	Jack Heinen	60.00	30.00	18.00
(7)	John Kinney	60.00	30.00	18.00
(8)	Walt Lucas	60.00	30.00	18.00
(9)	Syl McNinch	60.00	30.00	18.00
(10)	Stan McWilliams	60.00	30.00	18.00

(11)	Marvin Owen	60.00	30.00	18.00
(12)	Dick Piedrotti	60.00	30.00	18.00
(13)	Al Schroll	60.00	30.00	18.00
(14)	Ed Sobczak	60.00	30.00	18.00
(15)	Joe Stephenson	60.00	30.00	18.00
(16)	George Storti	60.00	30.00	18.00
(17)	Allan Van Alstyne	60.00	30.00	18.00
(18)	Floyd Warr	60.00	30.00	18.00

1963 Scheible Press Rochester Red Wings

Stephen Thomas Bilko — First Baseman
Born—Nanticoke, Pa., Nov. 13, 1928.
Bats — Right   Weight — 242
Throws — Right   Height — 6' 1"

Steve began his baseball career with Salisbury in the East Shore League in 1946. No stranger to Rochester fans, Steve played here briefly in 1948, and followed with good years in '49, '50, '51 and '52. His biggest years with the bat came in 1956 and 1957 with Los Angeles of the Pacific Coast League with 55 and 56 basemurns. His lifetime total of home runs is 287. Steve's last two years were played with the Los Angeles Angels of the American League.

Apparently sold as a stadium concession stand item in a paper and cellophane envelope, the full-color 3-13/16" x 5-7/8" cards are found printed on either a heavy paper stock or thin cardboard stock, each with identical black-and-white back. Two blank-backed cards in slightly larger (4" x 5-7/8") format are checklisted here, although their relationship to the other photos is unknown. The '63 Red Wings were the International League affiliate of the Baltimore Orioles.

		NM	EX	VG
Complete Set (11):		250.00	125.00	75.00
Common Player:		20.00	10.00	6.00
(1)	Joe Altobelli	25.00	12.50	7.50
(2)	Steve Bilko	25.00	12.50	7.50
(3)	Sam E. Bowens	20.00	10.00	6.00
(4)	Don Brummer	20.00	10.00	6.00
(5)	Nelson Chittum (Cardboard only.)	20.00	10.00	6.00
(6a)	Luke Easter (Small format.)	40.00	20.00	12.00
(6b)	Luke Easter (Large format.)	75.00	40.00	25.00
(7)	Darrell Johnson, Chris Krug (Paper only.)	25.00	12.50	7.50
(8)	Ron Kabbes (Large format.)	20.00	10.00	6.00
(9)	Fred Valentine	20.00	10.00	6.00
(10)	Ozzie Virgil	20.00	10.00	6.00
(11)	Ray Youngdahl	20.00	10.00	6.00

1954-1968 Seattle Rainiers/Angels Popcorn

One of the longest-running minor league baseball card promotions was the 1954-68 Seattle popcorn cards. The principal sponsor was Centennial Mills, which had issued cards in the 1940s. Similar in format throughout their period of issue, the cards are 2" x 3" in size, black-and-white, usually featuring portrait photos on the front with the player's name or name and position below. In some years the cards were printed on semi-glossy stock. Some years' card backs are blank, in other years, backs feature ads for various local businesses; in a few years, cards could be found with both blank and printed backs. Many photo and spelling variations are known throughout the series; most are noted in the appropriate checklists. The unnumbered cards are checklisted alphabetically. It is possible a few stragglers will be added to these checklists in the future. In most years a group of 20 cards was released early in the year, supplemented later in the season as roster changes dictated. The cards were given away with the purchase of a box of popcorn sold at Seattle's Sicks stadium. During the card-issuing era, Seattle was an independent team in the Pacific Coast League in 1954-55. From 1956-60 they were a top farm team in the Reds system. They were a Red Sox affiliate from 1961-64, before tying up with the California Angels in 1965.

(Consult checklists for attribution of blank-back cards.)

1954 Seattle Rainiers Popcorn

BOB HALL
Pitcher

(Blank-back. Most players photographed in dark cap with light "S.")

		NM	EX	VG
Complete Set (26):		2,500	1,250	750.00
Common Player:		110.00	55.00	35.00
(1)	Gene Bearden	110.00	55.00	35.00
(2)	Al Brightman	110.00	55.00	35.00
(3)	Jack Burkowatz	110.00	55.00	35.00
(4)	Tommy Byrne (Photo reversed, backwards "S" on cap.)	110.00	55.00	35.00
(5)	Joe Erautt	110.00	55.00	35.00
(6)	Bill Evans	110.00	55.00	35.00
(7)	Van Fletcher	110.00	55.00	35.00
(8)	Bob Hall	110.00	55.00	35.00
(9)	Pete Hernandez	110.00	55.00	35.00
(10)	Lloyd Jenney	110.00	55.00	35.00
(11)	Joe Joshua	110.00	55.00	35.00
(12)	Vern Kindsfather	110.00	55.00	35.00
(13)	Tom Lovrich	110.00	55.00	35.00
(14)	Clarence Maddern	110.00	55.00	35.00
(15)	Don Mallott	110.00	55.00	35.00
(16)	Loren Meyers	110.00	55.00	35.00
(17)	Steve Nagy	110.00	55.00	35.00
(18)	Ray Orteig	110.00	55.00	35.00
(19)	Gerry Priddy	110.00	55.00	35.00
(20)	George Schmees	110.00	55.00	35.00
(21)	Bill Schuster	110.00	55.00	35.00
(22)	Leo Thomas	110.00	55.00	35.00
(23)	Jack Tobin	110.00	55.00	35.00
(24)	Al Widmer	110.00	55.00	35.00
(25)	Artie Wilson	175.00	85.00	50.00
(26)	Al Zarilla	110.00	55.00	35.00

1955 Seattle Rainiers Popcorn

(Blank-back. All players wearing light caps with "R" logo.)

		NM	EX	VG
Complete Set (22):		2,000	1,000	600.00
Common Player:		110.00	55.00	35.00
(1)	Bob Balcena	110.00	55.00	35.00
(2)	Monty Basgall	110.00	55.00	35.00
(3)	Ewell Blackwell	135.00	65.00	40.00
(4)	Bill Brenner	110.00	55.00	35.00
(5)	Jack Burkowatz	110.00	55.00	35.00
(6)	Van Fletcher	110.00	55.00	35.00
(7)	Joe Ginsberg	110.00	55.00	35.00
(8)	Jehosie Heard	110.00	55.00	35.00
(9)	Fred Hutchinson	110.00	55.00	35.00
(10)	Larry Jansen	110.00	55.00	35.00
(11)	Bob Kelly	110.00	55.00	35.00
(12)	Bill Kennedy	110.00	55.00	35.00
(13)	Lou Kretlow	110.00	55.00	35.00
(14)	Rocco Krsnich	110.00	55.00	35.00
(15)	Carmen Mauro	110.00	55.00	35.00
(16)	John Oldham	110.00	55.00	35.00
(17)	George Schmees	110.00	55.00	35.00
(18)	Elmer Singleton	110.00	55.00	35.00
(19)	Alan Strange	110.00	55.00	35.00
(20)	Gene Verble	110.00	55.00	35.00
(21)	Marv Williams	110.00	55.00	35.00
(22)	Harvey Zernia	110.00	55.00	35.00

1956 Seattle Rainiers Popcorn

JOE TAYLOR
Outfielder

(Blank-back or Gil's Drive-Ins (two locations) ad on back. Players wearing light cap with white "R.")

		NM	EX	VG
Complete Set (27):		2,500	1,250	750.00
Common Player:		110.00	55.00	35.00
(1)	Fred Baczewski	110.00	55.00	35.00
(2)	Bob Balcena	110.00	55.00	35.00
(3)	Bill Brenner	110.00	55.00	35.00
(4)	Sherry Dixon	110.00	55.00	35.00
(5)	Don Fracchia	110.00	55.00	35.00
(6)	Bill Glynn	110.00	55.00	35.00
(7)	Larry Jansen	110.00	55.00	35.00
(8)	Howie Judson	110.00	55.00	35.00
(9)	Bill Kennedy	110.00	55.00	35.00
(10)	Jack Lohrke	110.00	55.00	35.00
(11)	Vic Lombardi	110.00	55.00	35.00
(12)	Carmen Mauro	110.00	55.00	35.00
(13)	Ray Orteig	110.00	55.00	35.00
(14)	Bud Podbielan	110.00	55.00	35.00
(15)	Leo Righetti	110.00	55.00	35.00
(16)	Jim Robertson	110.00	55.00	35.00
(17)	Art Shallock (Schallock)	110.00	55.00	35.00
(18)	Art Schult	110.00	55.00	35.00
(19)	Luke Sewell	135.00	65.00	40.00
(20)	Elmer Singleton	110.00	55.00	35.00
(21a)	Milt Smith (Action)	110.00	55.00	35.00
(21b)	Milt Smith (Portrait)	110.00	55.00	35.00
(22)	Vern Stephens	110.00	55.00	35.00
(23)	Alan Strange	110.00	55.00	35.00
(24)	Joe Taylor	110.00	55.00	35.00
(25)	Artie Wilson	175.00	85.00	50.00
(26)	Harvey Zernia	110.00	55.00	35.00

1957 Seattle Rainiers Popcorn

JIM DYCK
Infielder

By presenting any nine different pictures to either of GIL'S DRIVE-INS you will receive FREE an 8" x 10" player picture of your choice and you still keep your nine small pictures.

Three locations to serve you

GIL'S DRIVE-IN
4406 Rainier Avenue
1 mile south of Sicks' Stadium

3500 Avalon Way
35th S.W. and Avalon Way
West Seattle

Burien
1st South and South 152nd

(Blank-back or Gil's Drive-Ins (three locations) ad on back. Players wearing lighter caps with white "R." No base on letter "T" on outfielders or pitchers cards.)

		NM	EX	VG
Complete Set (24):		2,000	1,000	600.00
Common Player:		100.00	50.00	30.00
(1)	Dick Aylward	100.00	50.00	30.00
(2)	Bob Balcena	100.00	50.00	30.00
(3)	Eddie Basinki	100.00	50.00	30.00
(4)	Hal Bevan	100.00	50.00	30.00
(5)	Joe Black	125.00	65.00	35.00
(6)	Juan Delis	100.00	50.00	30.00
(7)	Jim Dyck	100.00	50.00	30.00
(8)	Marion Fricano	100.00	50.00	30.00
(9)	Bill Glynn	100.00	50.00	30.00
(10)	Larry Jansen	100.00	50.00	30.00
(11)	Howie Judson	100.00	50.00	30.00
(12)	Bill Kennedy	100.00	50.00	30.00
(13)	Jack Lohrke	100.00	50.00	30.00
(14)	Carmen Mauro	100.00	50.00	30.00
(15)	George Munger	100.00	50.00	30.00
(16)	Lefty O'Doul	150.00	75.00	45.00
(17)	Ray Orteig	100.00	50.00	30.00
(18)	Duane Pillette	100.00	50.00	30.00
(19)	Bud Podbielan	100.00	50.00	30.00
(20)	Charley Rabe	100.00	50.00	30.00
(21)	Leo Righetti	100.00	50.00	30.00
(22)	Joe Taylor	100.00	50.00	30.00
(23)	Edo Vanni	100.00	50.00	30.00
(24)	Morrie Wills (Maury)	250.00	125.00	75.00

1958 Seattle Rainiers Popcorn

(All cards have Ralph's Thriftway Market ad on back.)

		NM	EX	VG
Complete Set (19):		1,250	625.00	375.00
Common Player:		75.00	35.00	20.00
(1)	Bob Balcena	75.00	35.00	20.00
(2)	Ed Basinki	75.00	35.00	20.00
(3)	Hal Bevan	75.00	35.00	20.00
(4)	Jack Bloomfield	75.00	35.00	20.00
(5)	Juan Delis	75.00	35.00	20.00
(6)	Dutch Dotterer	75.00	35.00	20.00
(7)	Jim Dyck	75.00	35.00	20.00
(8)	Al Federoff	90.00	45.00	27.50
(9)	Art Fowler	75.00	35.00	20.00
(10)	Bill Kennedy	75.00	35.00	20.00
(11)	Marty Kutyna	75.00	35.00	20.00
(12)	Ray Orteig	75.00	35.00	20.00
(13)	Duane Pillette	75.00	35.00	20.00
(14)	Vada Pinson	225.00	110.00	70.00
(15)	Connie Ryan	75.00	35.00	20.00
(16)	Phil Shartzer	75.00	35.00	20.00
(17)	Max Surkont	75.00	35.00	20.00
(18)	Gale Wade	75.00	35.00	20.00
(19)	Ted Wieand	75.00	35.00	20.00

1959 Seattle Rainiers Popcorn

DON RUDOLPH
Pitcher

(Blank-back. First printing cards have players in lighter cap with white "R." Second printing cards have darker caps with shadow around "R.")

		NM	EX	VG
Complete Set (37):		2,500	1,250	750.00
Common Player:		75.00	35.00	20.00
(1)	Bobby Adams	75.00	35.00	20.00
(2)	Frank Amaya	75.00	35.00	20.00
(3)	Hal Bevan	75.00	35.00	20.00
(4)	Jack Bloomfield	75.00	35.00	20.00
(5)	Clarence Churn	75.00	35.00	20.00

(6)	Jack Dittmer	75.00	35.00	20.00
(7)	Jim Dyck	75.00	35.00	20.00
(8)	Dee Fondy	75.00	35.00	20.00
(9)	Mark Freeman	75.00	35.00	20.00
(10)	Dick Hanlon	75.00	35.00	20.00
(11)	Carroll Hardy	75.00	35.00	20.00
(12)	Bobby Henrich	75.00	35.00	20.00
(13)	Jay Hook	75.00	35.00	20.00
(14)	Fred Hutchinson	75.00	35.00	20.00
(15)	Jake Jenkins	75.00	35.00	20.00
(16)	Eddie Kazak	75.00	35.00	20.00
(17)	Bill Kennedy	75.00	35.00	20.00
(18)	Harry Lowrey	75.00	35.00	20.00
(19a)	Harry Malmbeg (Malmberg)	75.00	35.00	20.00
(19b)	Harry Malmbeg	75.00	35.00	20.00
(20)	Bob Mape (Mabe)	75.00	35.00	20.00
(21)	Darrell Martin	75.00	35.00	20.00
(22)	John McCall	75.00	35.00	20.00
(23)	Claude Osteen	75.00	35.00	20.00
(24)	Paul Pettit	75.00	35.00	20.00
(25)	Charley Rabe	75.00	35.00	20.00
(26)	Rudy Regalado	75.00	35.00	20.00
(27)	Eric Rodin	75.00	35.00	20.00
(28)	Don Rudolph	75.00	35.00	20.00
(29)	Lou Skizas	75.00	35.00	20.00
(30)	Dave Stenhouse	75.00	35.00	20.00
(31)	Alan Strange	75.00	35.00	20.00
(32)	Max Surkont	75.00	35.00	20.00
(33)	Ted Tappe	75.00	35.00	20.00
(34)	Elmer Valo	75.00	35.00	20.00
(35)	Gale Wade	75.00	35.00	20.00
(36)	Bill Wight	75.00	35.00	20.00
(37)	Ed Winceniak	75.00	35.00	20.00

1960 Seattle Rainiers Popcorn

JOHNNY O'BRIEN
Infielder

(Blank-back. All players posed against outfield fence wearing dark caps with shadowed "R.")

		NM	EX	VG
Complete Set (18):		1,200	600.00	350.00
Common Player:		75.00	35.00	20.00
(1)	Charlie Beamon	75.00	35.00	20.00
(2)	Hal Bevan	75.00	35.00	20.00
(3)	Whammy Douglas	75.00	35.00	20.00
(4)	Buddy Gilbert	75.00	35.00	20.00
(5)	Hal Jeffcoat	75.00	35.00	20.00
(6)	Leigh Lawrence	75.00	35.00	20.00
(7)	Darrell Martin	75.00	35.00	20.00
(8)	Francisco Obregon	75.00	35.00	20.00
(9)	Johnny O'Brien	90.00	45.00	27.50
(10)	Paul Pettitt	75.00	35.00	20.00
(11)	Ray Rippelmeyer (Ripplemeyer)	75.00	35.00	20.00
(12)	Don Rudolph	75.00	35.00	20.00
(13)	Willard Schmidt	75.00	35.00	20.00
(14)	Dick Sisler	75.00	35.00	20.00
(15)	Lou Skizas	75.00	35.00	20.00
(16)	Joe Taylor	75.00	35.00	20.00
(17)	Bob Thurman	75.00	35.00	20.00
(18)	Gerald Zimmerman	75.00	35.00	20.00

1961 Seattle Rainiers Popcorn

JOHN TILLMAN
Infielder

(Blank-back. New uniforms: dark cap with stylized "S," "Rainiers" on chest. Many players have both portrait and action poses. Tough to distinguish from 1962 set; names on '61s are more compact, bold than on '62 which has taller, lighter names.)

		NM	EX	VG
Complete Set (29):		2,000	1,000	600.00
Common Player:		75.00	35.00	20.00
(1)	Galen Cisco	75.00	35.00	20.00
(2)	Marlan Coughtry (Batting)	75.00	35.00	20.00
(3)	Marlin Coughtry (Portrait)	75.00	35.00	20.00
(4)	Pete Cronin	75.00	35.00	20.00
(5)	Arnold Earley	75.00	35.00	20.00
(6)	Bob Heffner (Pitching)	75.00	35.00	20.00
(7)	Bob Heffner (Portrait)	75.00	35.00	20.00
(8)	Curt Jensen (Action)	75.00	35.00	20.00
(9)	Curt Jensen (Portrait)	75.00	35.00	20.00
(10)	Harry Malmberg (Coach)	75.00	35.00	20.00
(11)	Harry Malmberg (Player-coach.)	75.00	35.00	20.00
(12)	Dave Mann	75.00	35.00	20.00
(13)	Darrell Martin	75.00	35.00	20.00
(14)	Erv Palica (Pitching)	75.00	35.00	20.00
(15)	Ervin Palica (Portrait)	75.00	35.00	20.00
(16)	Johnny Pesky (Action)	90.00	45.00	27.50
(17)	Johnny Pesky (Portrait)	90.00	45.00	27.50
(18)	Dick Radatz	100.00	50.00	30.00
(19)	Ted Schreiber (Batting)	75.00	35.00	20.00
(20)	Ted Shreiber (Portrait)	75.00	35.00	20.00
(21)	Paul Smith (Action)	75.00	35.00	20.00
(22)	Paul Smith (Portrait)	75.00	35.00	20.00
(23)	John Tillman (Infielder)	75.00	35.00	20.00
(24)	Bob Tillman (Catcher)	75.00	35.00	20.00
(25)	Bo Toft	75.00	35.00	20.00
(26)	Tom Umphlett (Action)	75.00	35.00	20.00
(27)	Tom Umphlett (Portrait)	75.00	35.00	20.00
(28)	Earl Wilson	75.00	35.00	20.00
(29)	Ken Wolfe	75.00	35.00	20.00

1962 Seattle Rainiers Popcorn

BILLY HARRELL

(Blank-back. Nearly identical to '61s except for player name. On 1961 cards, name is compact and bold; on '62s the name is taller, lighter. Some photos repeated from 1961.)

		NM	EX	VG
Complete Set (19):		1,250	625.00	375.00
Common Player:		75.00	35.00	20.00
(1)	Dave Hall	75.00	35.00	20.00
(2)	Billy Harrell	75.00	35.00	20.00
(3)	Curt Jensen (Jenson)	75.00	35.00	20.00
(4)	Stew MacDonald	75.00	35.00	20.00
(5)	Bill MacLeod	75.00	35.00	20.00
(6)	Dave Mann (Action)	75.00	35.00	20.00
(7)	Dave Mann (Portrait)	75.00	35.00	20.00
(8)	Dave Morehead	75.00	35.00	20.00
(9)	John Pesky	90.00	45.00	27.50
(10)	Ted Schreiber (Second baseman.)	75.00	35.00	20.00
(11)	Ted Schreiber (Infielder)	75.00	35.00	20.00
(12)	Elmer Singleton	75.00	35.00	20.00
(13)	Archie Skeen	75.00	35.00	20.00
(14)	Pete Smith	75.00	35.00	20.00
(15)	George Spencer	75.00	35.00	20.00
(16)	Bo Toft (1961 photo)	75.00	35.00	20.00
(17)	Bo Toft (New photo.)	75.00	35.00	20.00
(18)	Tom Umphlett	75.00	35.00	20.00
(19)	Ken Wolfe	75.00	35.00	20.00

1963 Seattle Rainiers Popcorn

(Blank-back. No positions stated on cards except for manager and coach. Impossible to differentiate 1963 issue from 1964 except by player selection.)

		NM	EX	VG
Complete Set (15):		800.00	400.00	240.00
Common Player:		60.00	30.00	17.50
(1)	Don Gile	60.00	30.00	17.50
(2)	Dave Hall	60.00	30.00	17.50
(3)	Billy Harrell	60.00	30.00	17.50
(4)	Pete Jernigan	60.00	30.00	17.50
(5)	Stan Johnson	60.00	30.00	17.50
(6)	Dalton Jones	60.00	30.00	17.50
(7)	Mel Parnell	60.00	30.00	17.50
(8)	Joe Pedrazzini	60.00	30.00	17.50
(9)	Elmer Singleton	60.00	30.00	17.50
(10)	Archie Skeen	60.00	30.00	17.50
(11)	Rac Slider	60.00	30.00	17.50
(12)	Pete Smith	60.00	30.00	17.50
(13)	Bill Spanswick	60.00	30.00	17.50
(14)	George Spencer	60.00	30.00	17.50
(15)	Wilbur Wood	90.00	45.00	27.50

1964 Seattle Rainiers Popcorn

(Blank-back. Impossible to differentiate between 1963 and 1964 issues except by player selection.)

EARL AVERILL

		NM	EX	VG
Complete Set (18):		1,000	500.00	300.00
Common Player:		60.00	30.00	17.50
(1)	Earl Averill	60.00	30.00	17.50
(2)	Billy Gardner	60.00	30.00	17.50
(3)	Russ Gibson	60.00	30.00	17.50
(4)	Guido Grilli	60.00	30.00	17.50
(5)	Bob Guindon	60.00	30.00	17.50
(6)	Billy Harrell	60.00	30.00	17.50
(7)	Fred Holmes	60.00	30.00	17.50
(8)	Stan Johnson	60.00	30.00	17.50
(9)	Hal Kolstad	60.00	30.00	17.50
(10)	Felix Maldonado	60.00	30.00	17.50
(11)	Gary Modrell	60.00	30.00	17.50
(12)	Merlin Nippert	60.00	30.00	17.50
(13)	Rico Petrocelli	100.00	50.00	30.00
(14)	Jay Ritchie	60.00	30.00	17.50
(15)	Barry Shetrone	60.00	30.00	17.50
(16)	Pete Smith	60.00	30.00	17.50
(17)	Bill Tuttle	60.00	30.00	17.50
(18)	Edo Vanni	60.00	30.00	17.50

1965 Seattle Angels Popcorn

(Back has cartoon angel batting. Several cards, issued prior to the season, have blank-backs.)

		NM	EX	VG
Complete Set (22):		600.00	300.00	180.00
Common Player:		30.00	15.00	9.00
(1)	Earl Averill	30.00	15.00	9.00
(2)	Tom Burgmeier	30.00	15.00	9.00
(3)	Bob Guindon	30.00	15.00	9.00
(4)	Jack Hernandez	30.00	15.00	9.00
(5)	Fred Holmes	30.00	15.00	9.00
(6)	Ed Kirkpatrick	30.00	15.00	9.00
(7)	Hal Kolstad	30.00	15.00	9.00
(8)	Joe Koppe	30.00	15.00	9.00
(9)	Les Kuhnz	30.00	15.00	9.00
(10)	Bob Lemon	60.00	30.00	17.50
(11)	Bobby Locke	30.00	15.00	9.00
(12)	Jim McGlothlin	30.00	15.00	9.00
(13a)	Bob Radovich (Blank-back.)	30.00	15.00	9.00
(13b)	Bob Radovich (Ad-back.)	30.00	15.00	9.00
(14)	Merritt Ranew	30.00	15.00	9.00
(15)	Jimmie Reese (Blank-back.)	45.00	22.50	13.50
(16a)	Rick Reichardt (Blank-back.)	30.00	15.00	9.00
(16b)	Rick Reichardt (Ad-back.)	30.00	15.00	9.00
(17)	Tom Satriano	30.00	15.00	9.00
(18)	Dick Simpson	30.00	15.00	9.00
(19)	Jack Spring (Blank-back.)	30.00	15.00	9.00
(20)	Ed Sukla	30.00	15.00	9.00
(21)	Jackie Warner	30.00	15.00	9.00
(22)	Stan Williams	30.00	15.00	9.00

1966 Seattle Angels Popcorn

JIM CAMPANIS

SEATTLE ANGELS GAMES BROADCAST ON KVI RADIO 570

Presented by
CHEVRON DEALERS
STANDARD STATIONS
WESTERN AIRLINES
HOUSEHOLD FINANCE CORP.
WHEATIES, BREAKFAST OF CHAMPIONS

(Cartoon angel pitching on back, first "Presented by" advertiser at bottom is Chevron Dealers.)

		NM	EX	VG
Complete Set (29):		900.00	450.00	275.00
Common Player:		30.00	15.00	9.00
(1)	Del Bates	30.00	15.00	9.00
(2)	Tom Burgmeier	30.00	15.00	9.00
(3)	Jim Campanis	40.00	20.00	12.00
(4)	Jim Coates	30.00	15.00	9.00
(5)	Tony Cortopassi	30.00	15.00	9.00
(6)	Chuck Estrada	30.00	15.00	9.00
(7)	Ray Hernandez	30.00	15.00	9.00
(8)	Jay Johnstone	50.00	25.00	15.00
(9)	Bill Kelso	30.00	15.00	9.00
(10)	Vic LaRose	30.00	15.00	9.00
(11)	Bobby Locke	30.00	15.00	9.00
(12)	Rudy May	30.00	15.00	9.00

		NM	EX	VG
(13)	Andy Messersmith	50.00	25.00	15.00
(14)	Bubba Morton	30.00	15.00	9.00
(15)	Cotton Nash	30.00	15.00	9.00
(16)	John Olerud	50.00	25.00	15.00
(17)	Marty Pattin	30.00	15.00	9.00
(18)	Merritt Ranew	30.00	15.00	9.00
(19)	Minnie Rojas	30.00	15.00	9.00
(20)	George Rubio	30.00	15.00	9.00
(21)	Al Spangler	30.00	15.00	9.00
(22)	Ed Sukla	30.00	15.00	9.00
(23)	Felix Torres	30.00	15.00	9.00
(24)	Hector Torres	30.00	15.00	9.00
(25)	Ken Turner	30.00	15.00	9.00
(26)	Chuck Vinson	30.00	15.00	9.00
(27)	Don Wallace	30.00	15.00	9.00
(28)	Jack D. Warner	30.00	15.00	9.00
(29)	Mike White	30.00	15.00	9.00

1967 Seattle Angels Popcorn

(Cartoon angel pitching on back, first "Presented by" advertiser is Western Airlines.)

		NM	EX	VG
Complete Set (19):		500.00	250.00	150.00
Common Player:		30.00	15.00	9.00
(1)	George Banks	30.00	15.00	9.00
(2)	Tom Burgmeier	30.00	15.00	9.00
(3)	Jim Coates	30.00	15.00	9.00
(4)	Chuck Cottier	30.00	15.00	9.00
(5)	Tony Curry	30.00	15.00	9.00
(6)	Vern Geishert	30.00	15.00	9.00
(7)	Jesse Hickman	30.00	15.00	9.00
(8)	Bill Kelso	30.00	15.00	9.00
(9)	Ed Kirkpatrick	30.00	15.00	9.00
(10)	Chris Krug	30.00	15.00	9.00
(11)	Bobby Locke	30.00	15.00	9.00
(12)	Bill Murphy	30.00	15.00	9.00
(13)	Marty Pattin	30.00	15.00	9.00
(14)	Merritt Ranew	30.00	15.00	9.00
(15)	Bob Sadowski	30.00	15.00	9.00
(16)	Ed Sukla	30.00	15.00	9.00
(17)	Hector Torres	30.00	15.00	9.00
(18)	Chuck Vinson	30.00	15.00	9.00
(19)	Don Wallace	30.00	15.00	9.00

1968 Seattle Angels Popcorn

JARVIS TATUM

(Blank-back.)

		NM	EX	VG
Complete Set (18):		500.00	250.00	150.00
Common Player:		30.00	15.00	9.00
(1)	Ethan Blackaby	30.00	15.00	9.00
(2)	Jim Coates	30.00	15.00	9.00
(3)	Tom Egan	30.00	15.00	9.00
(4)	Larry Elliott (Elliot)	30.00	15.00	9.00
(5)	Jim Engelhardt	30.00	15.00	9.00
(6)	Gus Gil	30.00	15.00	9.00
(7)	Bill Harrelson	30.00	15.00	9.00
(8)	Steve Hovley	30.00	15.00	9.00
(9)	Jim Mahoney	30.00	15.00	9.00
(10)	Mickey McGuire	30.00	15.00	9.00
(11)	Joe Overton	30.00	15.00	9.00
(12)	Marty Pattin	30.00	15.00	9.00
(13)	Larry Sherry	30.00	15.00	9.00
(14)	Marv Staehle	30.00	15.00	9.00
(15)	Ed Sukla	30.00	15.00	9.00
(16)	Jarvis Tatum	30.00	15.00	9.00
(17)	Hawk Taylor	30.00	15.00	9.00
(18)	Chuck Vinson	30.00	15.00	9.00

1952 Shawnee Hawks Team Issue

LOYD McPHERSON

Formatted like the other known minor league issues from Globe Printing of San Jose, Calif., this set chronicles the 1952 version of the Class D (Sooner State League) Shawnee (Okla.) Hawks. The blank-backed cards are black-and-white and measure about 2-1/4" x 3-3/8". The checklist here is incomplete, the set probably having been originally issued with about 18 cards.

		NM	EX	VG
Common Player:		60.00	30.00	18.00
(1)	Russell Bland (Blanco)	60.00	30.00	18.00
(2)	Perry Haddock	60.00	30.00	18.00
(3)	Jim Kenaga	60.00	30.00	18.00
(4)	Hal Long	60.00	30.00	18.00
(5)	Loyd McPherson	60.00	30.00	18.00
(6)	Rolando Olmo	60.00	30.00	18.00
(7)	Dave Rolette	60.00	30.00	18.00
(8)	Hank Salazar	60.00	30.00	18.00

1960 Shopsy's Frankfurters Toronto Maple Leafs

SHOPSY'S PLAYER PHOTO

ARCHIE WILSON - 1960

Only the Toronto Maple Leafs of the International League - including many former and future major leaguers - are included in this set. The cards are about 2-1/4" x 3-1/4", blank-back and printed in black-and-white. The unnumbered cards are checklisted here alphabetically.

		NM	EX	VG
Complete Set (23):		2,000	1,000	600.00
Common Player:		90.00	45.00	30.00
Album:		100.00	50.00	30.00
(1)	George Anderson (Sparky)	150.00	75.00	45.00
(2)	Bob Chakales	90.00	45.00	30.00
(3)	Al Cicotte	90.00	45.00	30.00
(4)	Rip Coleman	90.00	45.00	30.00
(5)	Steve Demeter	90.00	45.00	30.00
(6)	Don Dillard	90.00	45.00	30.00
(7)	Frank Funk	90.00	45.00	30.00
(8)	Russ Heman	90.00	45.00	30.00
(9)	Earl Hersh	90.00	45.00	30.00
(10)	Allen Jones	90.00	45.00	30.00
(11)	Jim King	90.00	45.00	30.00
(12)	Jack Kubiszyn	90.00	45.00	30.00
(13)	Mel McGaha	90.00	45.00	30.00
(14)	Bill Moran	90.00	45.00	30.00
(15)	Ron Negray	90.00	45.00	30.00
(16)	Herb Plews	90.00	45.00	30.00
(17)	Steve Ridzik	90.00	45.00	30.00
(18)	Pat Scantlebury	90.00	45.00	30.00
(19)	Bill Smith (Trainer)	90.00	45.00	30.00
(20)	Bob Smith	90.00	45.00	30.00
(21)	Tim Thompson	90.00	45.00	30.00
(22)	Jack Waters	90.00	45.00	30.00
(23)	Archie Wilson	90.00	45.00	30.00

1947 Signal Gasoline Pacific Coast League

Five of the eight PCL teams participated in this baseball card promotion, giving away cards of hometeam players. Because of vagaries of local distribution, some teams, notably Sacramento and Seattle, are scarcer than others, and there are specific player rarities among other teams. The black-and-white cards are 5-9/16" x 3-1/2" and feature on the front a drawing of the player and several personal or career highlights in cartoon form. The artwork was done by former N.Y. Giants pitcher Al Demaree. On the backs are player biographical details, an ad for Signal Gas and an ad for the co-sponsoring radio station in each locale. Cards are unnumbered.

	NM	EX	VG
Complete Set (89):	6,000	3,000	1,800
(Team sets listed below.)			

1947 Signal Gasoline Hollywood Stars

		NM	EX	VG
Complete Set (20):		1,200	600.00	350.00
Common Player:		50.00	25.00	15.00
(1)	Ed Albosta	50.00	25.00	15.00
(2)	Carl Cox	50.00	25.00	15.00
(3)	Frank Dasso	50.00	25.00	15.00
(4)	Tod Davis	50.00	25.00	15.00
(5)	Jim Delsing	50.00	25.00	15.00
(6)	Jimmy Dykes	50.00	25.00	15.00
(7)	Paul Gregory	50.00	25.00	15.00
(8)	Fred Haney	50.00	25.00	15.00
(9)	Frank Kelleher	50.00	25.00	15.00
(10)	Joe Krakauskas	50.00	25.00	15.00
(11)	Al Libke	50.00	25.00	15.00
(12)	Tony Lupien	50.00	25.00	15.00
(13)	Xaiver Rescigno	50.00	25.00	15.00
(14)	Jack Sherman	50.00	25.00	15.00
(15)	Andy Skurski	50.00	25.00	15.00
(16)	Glen (Glenn) Stewart	50.00	25.00	15.00
(17)	Al Unser	50.00	25.00	15.00
(18)	Fred Vaughn	50.00	25.00	15.00
(19)	Woody Williams	250.00	125.00	75.00
(20)	Dutch (Gus) Zernial	75.00	37.00	22.00

1947 Signal Gasoline Los Angeles Angels

		NM	EX	VG
Complete Set (18):		700.00	350.00	210.00
Common Player:		40.00	20.00	12.00
(1)	Red Adams	40.00	20.00	12.00
(2)	Larry Barton	40.00	20.00	12.00
(3)	Cliff Chambers	40.00	20.00	12.00
(4)	Lloyd Christopher	40.00	20.00	12.00
(5)	Cece Garriott	40.00	20.00	12.00
(6)	Al Glossop	40.00	20.00	12.00
(7)	Bill Kelly	40.00	20.00	12.00
(8)	Red Lynn	40.00	20.00	12.00
(9)	Eddie Malone	40.00	20.00	12.00
(10)	Dutch McCall	40.00	20.00	12.00
(11)	Don Osborne	40.00	20.00	12.00
(12)	John Ostrowski	40.00	20.00	12.00
(13)	Reggie Otero	40.00	20.00	12.00
(14)	Ray Prim	40.00	20.00	12.00
(15)	Ed Sauer	40.00	20.00	12.00
(16)	Bill Schuster	40.00	20.00	12.00
(17)	Tuck Stainback	40.00	20.00	12.00
(18)	Lou Stringer	40.00	20.00	12.00

1947 Signal Gasoline Oakland Oaks

		NM	EX	VG
Complete Set (19):		800.00	400.00	240.00
Common Player:		40.00	20.00	12.00
(1)	Vic Buccola	40.00	20.00	12.00
(2)	Mickey Burnett	40.00	20.00	12.00
(3)	Ralph Buxton	40.00	20.00	12.00
(4)	Vince DiMaggio	95.00	47.00	28.00
(5)	Dizz Duezabou	40.00	20.00	12.00
(6)	Bud Foster	40.00	20.00	12.00
(7)	Sherriff Gassaway	40.00	20.00	12.00
(8)	Tom Hafey	40.00	20.00	12.00
(9)	Brooks Holder	40.00	20.00	12.00
(10)	Gene Lillard	40.00	20.00	12.00
(11)	Dario Lodigiani	40.00	20.00	12.00
(12)	Hershel Martin	40.00	20.00	12.00
(13)	Cotton Pippen	40.00	20.00	12.00
(14)	Billy Raimondi	40.00	20.00	12.00
(15)	Tony Sabol	40.00	20.00	12.00
(16)	Les Scarsella	40.00	20.00	12.00
(17)	Floyd Speer	40.00	20.00	12.00
(18)	Casey Stengel	100.00	50.00	30.00
(19)	Maurice Van Robays	40.00	20.00	12.00

1947 Signal Gasoline Sacramento Solons

		NM	EX	VG
Complete Set (16):		2,000	1,000	600.00
Common Player:		60.00	30.00	18.00
(1)	Bud Beasley	60.00	30.00	18.00
(2)	Frank Dasso	60.00	30.00	18.00
(3)	Ed Fitzgerald (Fitz Gerald)	60.00	30.00	18.00
(4)	Guy Fletcher	60.00	30.00	18.00
(5)	Tony Freitas	60.00	30.00	18.00
(6)	Red Mann	60.00	30.00	18.00
(7)	Joe Marty	60.00	30.00	18.00
(8)	Steve Mesner	60.00	30.00	18.00
(9)	Bill Ramsey	60.00	30.00	18.00
(10)	Charley Ripple	250.00	125.00	75.00
(11)	John Rizzo	250.00	125.00	75.00
(12)	Al Smith	250.00	125.00	75.00
(13)	Ronnie Smith	250.00	125.00	75.00
(14)	Tommy Thompson	250.00	125.00	75.00
(15)	Jim Warner	115.00	55.00	35.00
(16)	Ed Zipay	115.00	55.00	35.00

1947 Signal Gasoline Seattle Rainiers

TONY YORK STAR SEATTLE INFIELDER

	NM	EX	VG
Complete Set (16):	1,750	875.00	525.00

		NM	EX	VG
	Common Player:	75.00	37.00	22.00
(1)	Kewpie Barrett	100.00	50.00	30.00
(2)	Herman Besse	100.00	50.00	30.00
(3)	Guy Fletcher	100.00	50.00	30.00
(4)	Jack Jakucki	100.00	50.00	30.00
(5)	Bob Johnson	100.00	50.00	30.00
(6)	Pete Jonas	275.00	135.00	82.00
(7)	Hillis Layne	100.00	50.00	30.00
(8)	Red Mann	100.00	50.00	30.00
(9)	Lou Novikoff	100.00	50.00	30.00
(10)	John O'Neill	100.00	50.00	30.00
(11)	Bill Ramsey	100.00	50.00	30.00
(12)	Mickey Rocco	100.00	50.00	30.00
(13)	George Scharein	100.00	50.00	30.00
(14)	Hal Sueme	100.00	50.00	30.00
(15)	Jo Jo White	100.00	50.00	30.00
(16)	Tony York	100.00	50.00	30.00

1948 Signal Gasoline Oakland Oaks

Issued by Signal Oil in the Oakland area in 1948, this 24-card set features members of the Oakland Oaks of the Pacific Coast League. The unnumbered cards, measuring 2-3/8" x 3-1/2", were given away at gas stations. The front consists of a color photo, while the backs (printed in either blue or black) contain a brief player write-up along with a Signal Oil ad and logo.

		NM	EX	VG
	Complete Set (24):	900.00	450.00	275.00
	Common Player:	40.00	20.00	12.00
(1)	John C. Babich	40.00	20.00	12.00
(2)	Ralph Buxton	40.00	20.00	12.00
(3)	Loyd E. Christopher (Lloyd)	40.00	20.00	12.00
(4)	Merrill Russell Combs	40.00	20.00	12.00
(5)	Melvin E. Deuzabou	40.00	20.00	12.00
(6)	Nicholas ("Nick") Etten	40.00	20.00	12.00
(7)	Bud Foster (Announcer)	40.00	20.00	12.00
(8)	Charles Gassaway	40.00	20.00	12.00
(9)	Will Hafey	40.00	20.00	12.00
(10)	Ray Hamrick	40.00	20.00	12.00
(11)	Brooks Richard Holder	40.00	20.00	12.00
(12)	Earl Jones	40.00	20.00	12.00
(13)	Harry "Cookie" Lavagetto	40.00	20.00	12.00
(14)	Robert E. Lillard	40.00	20.00	12.00
(15)	Dario Lodigiani	40.00	20.00	12.00
(16)	Ernie Lombardi	75.00	37.50	22.50
(17a)	Alfred Manuel Martin (Born 1921.)	65.00	32.50	20.00
(17b)	Alfred Manuel Martin (Born 1928.)	75.00	37.50	22.50
(18)	George Michael Metkovich	40.00	20.00	12.00
(19)	William L. Raimondi	40.00	20.00	12.00
(20)	Les George Scarsella	40.00	20.00	12.00
(21)	Floyd Vernie Speer	40.00	20.00	12.00
(22)	Charles "Casey" Stengel	115.00	57.00	34.00
(23)	Maurice Van Robays	40.00	20.00	12.00
(24)	Aldon Jay Wilkie	40.00	20.00	12.00

1951 Sioux City Soos Postcards

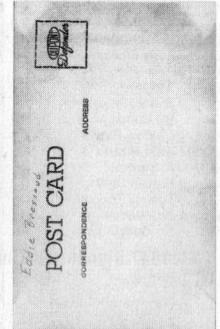

These black-and-white team-issued postcards feature on their fronts posed full-length photos of members of the Class A Western League farm team of the New York Giants. In standard 3-1/2" x 5-1/2" size, the cards have a wide border at bottom which has the team name, the year and a logo featuring an ear of corn. Backs have typical postcard indicia. Players are not identified anywhere on the cards. It is presumed this checklist is incomplete.

		NM	EX	VG
	Common Player:	60.00	30.00	18.00
(1)	Ray Berns	60.00	30.00	18.00
(2)	Ed Bressoud	60.00	30.00	18.00
(3)	Mario Picone	60.00	30.00	18.00
(4)	Bob Reid	60.00	30.00	18.00

1952-1953 Sioux City Soos Team Issue

JIM SINGLETON

From the Class A Western League, this is one of many minor league team sets issued in the early 1950s by Globe Printing of San Jose, Calif. The early 1950s Soos were a farm team of the New York Giants. Cards are about 2-1/4" x 3-3/8", printed in black-and-white with blank backs. It appears as if the Soos were the only team to have issued cards in both 1952 and 1953, since some cards are known with players unique to each season as well as cards of players who were with Sioux City in both 1952 and 1953.

		NM	EX	VG
	Complete Set (29):	1,500	750.00	450.00
	Common Player:	60.00	30.00	18.00
	Album:	100.00	50.00	30.00
	1952			
(1)	Ray Berns	60.00	30.00	18.00
(2)	Eddie Bressoud	60.00	30.00	18.00
(3)	Irv Burton	60.00	30.00	18.00
(4)	Bob Easterbrook	60.00	30.00	18.00
(5)	George Erath	60.00	30.00	18.00
(6)	Don Fracchia	60.00	30.00	18.00
(7)	Dick Hamlin	60.00	30.00	18.00
(8)	Gail Harris	60.00	30.00	18.00
(9)	Chico Ibanez	60.00	30.00	18.00
(10)	Bob Lee	60.00	30.00	18.00
(11)	Bill McMillan	60.00	30.00	18.00
(12)	Dick Messner	60.00	30.00	18.00
(13)	Roy Pardue	60.00	30.00	18.00
(14)	Mario Picone	60.00	30.00	18.00
(15)	Jim Singleton	60.00	30.00	18.00
(16)	John Uber	60.00	30.00	18.00
(17)	Ernie Yelen	60.00	30.00	18.00
	1952/1953			
(18)	Bob Giddings	60.00	30.00	18.00
(19)	Ray Johnson	60.00	30.00	18.00
(20)	Denny Landry (Bat boy.)	60.00	30.00	18.00
(21)	Vince LaSala	60.00	30.00	18.00
(22)	Ray Mueller	60.00	30.00	18.00
	1953			
(23)	Dick Getter	60.00	30.00	18.00
(24)	Dick Hamlin	60.00	30.00	18.00
(25)	Jake Jenkins	60.00	30.00	18.00
(26)	Jim Jones	60.00	30.00	18.00
(27)	Bob Myers	60.00	30.00	18.00
(28)	Clyde Stevens	60.00	30.00	18.00
(29)	Joe Stupak	60.00	30.00	18.00

1954 Sioux City Soos Souvenir Pictures Album

Rather than a set of individual baseball cards, the Class A Western League farm club of the New York Giants issued this souvenir picture album depicting players (including future major league star and N.L. president Bill White), staff and media. About 8-1/8" x 7-1/2", the album has embossed metallic gold covers and orange graphics. Inside are eight black-and-white pages with three card-like images per page. The pictures are in about the same size and format as Globe Printing's contemporary minor league baseball card team sets.

	NM	EX	VG
Complete Souvenir Book:	300.00	150.00	90.00
1954 Sioux City Soos			

1947 Smith's Oakland Oaks

CHARLES (Casey) STENGEL
Oaks Manager 1

Peppery CASEY STENGEL is a baseball veteran of 36 seasons. Stengel, a speedy, hard-hitting outfielder, performed with Brooklyn, New York Giants, Boston Braves, He has managed Dodgers, Braves and Milwaukee. Cagey Casey is noted for his ability to develop young players.

This regional set of Oakland Oaks (Pacific Coast League) cards was issued in 1947 by Smith's Clothing stores and is numbered in the lower right corner. The card fronts include a black and white photo with the player's name, team and posi-

tion below. The backs carry a brief player write-up and an advertisement for Smith's Clothing. The cards measure 2" x 3". The Max Marshall card was apparently short-printed and is much scarcer than the rest of the set.

		NM	EX	VG
	Complete Set (25):	800.00	400.00	240.00
	Common Player:	25.00	12.50	7.50
1	Charles (Casey) Stengel	125.00	65.00	35.00
2	Billy Raimondi	25.00	12.50	7.50
3	Les Scarsella	25.00	12.50	7.50
4	Brooks Holder	25.00	12.50	7.50
5	Ray Hamrick	25.00	12.50	7.50
6	Gene Lillard	25.00	12.50	7.50
7	Maurice Van Robays	25.00	12.50	7.50
8	Charlie (Sheriff) Gassaway	25.00	12.50	7.50
9	Henry (Cotton) Pippen	25.00	12.50	7.50
10	James Arnold	25.00	12.50	7.50
11	Ralph (Buck) Buxton	25.00	12.50	7.50
12	Ambrose (Bo) Palica	25.00	12.50	7.50
13	Tony Sabol	25.00	12.50	7.50
14	Ed Kearse	25.00	12.50	7.50
15	Bill Hart	25.00	12.50	7.50
16	Donald (Snuffy) Smith	25.00	12.50	7.50
17	Oral (Mickey) Burnett	25.00	12.50	7.50
18	Tom Hafey	25.00	12.50	7.50
19	Will Hafey	25.00	12.50	7.50
20	Paul Gillespie	25.00	12.50	7.50
21	Damon Hayes	25.00	12.50	7.50
22	Max Marshall	350.00	175.00	100.00
23	Mel (Dizz) Duezabou	25.00	12.50	7.50
24	Mel Reeves	25.00	12.50	7.50
25	Joe Faria	25.00	12.50	7.50

1948 Smith's Oakland Oaks

BILLY MARTIN
Oaks Third Baseman 17

Newcomer BILLY MARTIN, 19, comes to the Oaks from Phoenix where he led the league last year with his .393 batting average, 174 R.B.I., 230 base hits and 48 2-base hits. Lives in Berkeley where he was born.

The 1948 Smith's Clothing issue was another 25-card regional set featuring members of the Oakland Oaks of the Pacific Coast League. Almost identical to the 1947 Smith's issue, the black and white cards again measure 2" x 3" but were printed on heavier, glossy stock. The player's name, team and position appear below the photo with the card number in the lower right corner. The back has a brief player write-up and an ad for Smith's clothing.

		NM	EX	VG
	Complete Set (25):	700.00	350.00	210.00
	Common Player:	25.00	12.50	7.50
1	Billy Raimondi	25.00	12.50	7.50
2	Brooks Holder	25.00	12.50	7.50
3	Will Hafey	25.00	12.50	7.50
4	Nick Etten	25.00	12.50	7.50
5	Lloyd Christopher	25.00	12.50	7.50
6	Les Scarsella	25.00	12.50	7.50
7	Ray Hamrick	25.00	12.50	7.50
8	Gene Lillard	25.00	12.50	7.50
9	Maurice Van Robays	25.00	12.50	7.50
10	Charlie Gassaway	25.00	12.50	7.50
11	Ralph (Buck) Buxton	25.00	12.50	7.50
12	Tom Hafey	25.00	12.50	7.50
13	Damon Hayes	25.00	12.50	7.50
14	Mel (Dizz) Duezabou	25.00	12.50	7.50
15	Dario Lodigiani	25.00	12.50	7.50
16	Vic Buccola	25.00	12.50	7.50
17	Billy Martin	90.00	45.00	27.00
18	Floyd Speer	25.00	12.50	7.50
19	Eddie Samcoff	25.00	12.50	7.50
20	Charles (Casey) Stengel	90.00	45.00	27.00
21	Lloyd Hittle	25.00	12.50	7.50
22	Johnny Babich	25.00	12.50	7.50
23	Merrill Combs	25.00	12.50	7.50
24	Eddie Murphy	25.00	12.50	7.50
25	Bob Klinger	25.00	12.50	7.50

1948 Sommer & Kaufmann San Francisco Seals

WILFRED "BILL" LEONARD
Seals Catcher 20

WILFRED "BILL" LEONARD, catcher, has to his credit, hitting a home run with all bases loaded when his club was 4 runs behind. With the Seals in 1939 and 1940. Salt Lake Pennant Winning Pioneer League in 1946. Became a Seals catcher in 1947.

One of the more common of the many Pacific Coast League issues of the late 1940s, this emission from the San Francisco boys' clothier features 30 black-and-white 2" x 3" cards. Fronts have a player photo, name, position and card number. Backs have a few biographical details and stats, along with an ad. The 1948 issue can be differentiated from the 1949 issue by the words "BOYS SHOP" above the company logo on back.

		NM	EX	VG
	Complete Set (30):	1,500	750.00	450.00
	Common Player:	60.00	30.00	18.50
1	Lefty O'Doul	100.00	50.00	30.00
2	Jack Brewer	60.00	30.00	18.50
3	Con Dempsey	60.00	30.00	18.50
4	Tommy Fine	60.00	30.00	18.50
5	Kenneth Gables	60.00	30.00	18.50
6	Robert Joyce	60.00	30.00	18.50
7	Al Lien	60.00	30.00	18.50
8	Cliff Melton	60.00	30.00	18.50
9	Frank Shofner	60.00	30.00	18.50
10	Don Trower	60.00	30.00	18.50
11	Joe Brovia	60.00	30.00	18.50
12	Dino Paul Restelli	60.00	30.00	18.50
13	Gene Woodling	75.00	37.00	22.00
14	Ben Guintini	60.00	30.00	18.50
15	Felix Mackiewicz	60.00	30.00	18.50
16	John Patrick Tobin	60.00	30.00	18.50
17	Manuel Perez	60.00	30.00	18.50
18	Bill Werle	60.00	30.00	18.50
19	Homer Howell	60.00	30.00	18.50
20	Wilfred Leonard	60.00	30.00	18.50
21	Bruce Ogrodowski	60.00	30.00	18.50
22	Dick Lajeskie	60.00	30.00	18.50
23	Hugh Luby	60.00	30.00	18.50
24	Roy Nicely	60.00	30.00	18.50
25	Ray Orteig	60.00	30.00	18.50
26	Michael Rocco	60.00	30.00	18.50
27	Del Young	60.00	30.00	18.50
28	Joe Sprinz	60.00	30.00	18.50
29	Doc Hughes	60.00	30.00	18.50
30	Batboys (Don Rode, Albert Boro, Charlie Barnes)	60.00	30.00	18.50

1949 Sommer & Kaufmann San Francisco Seals

JACK NICHOLAS BACCIOCCO, outfielder, Born, San Francisco, Feb. 10, 1925. Height 6', weight 185. Throws and bats right. Italian-Swedish descent. With Salt Lake and Reno in 1947. With Salt Lake in 1948. Hit .277.

Sommer & Kaufmann

838 MARKET ST., 2600 OCEAN AVE.
SAN FRANCISCO
25 FOURTH AVE., SAN MATEO
Famous for Boys' "Hot Rod" Shoes

JACK NICHOLAS BACCIOCCO
Seals Outfielder 19

Twenty-eight black-and-white cards numbered 1-29 (#24 unknown) make up the second and final card issue of the "Frisco area clothier." Measuring 2" x 3", the cards are nearly identical to the '48 issue. The '49s can be identified by the mention of "Hot Rod" shoes on the back. Fronts feature a borderless player photo with a panel at the bottom giving name, position and card number. Backs have the ad for the boy's shop and a brief biographical player sketch.

		NM	EX	VG
	Complete Set (29):	2,000	1,000	600.00
	Common Player:	75.00	37.00	22.00
1	Lefty O'Doul	100.00	50.00	30.00
2	Jack Brewer	75.00	37.00	22.00
3	Kenneth Gables	75.00	37.00	22.00
4	Con Dempsey	75.00	37.00	22.00
5	Al Lien	75.00	37.00	22.00
6	Cliff Melton	75.00	37.00	22.00
7	Steve Nagy	75.00	37.00	22.00
8	Manny Perez	75.00	37.00	22.00
9	Roy Jarvis	75.00	37.00	22.00
10	Roy Partee	75.00	37.00	22.00
11	Reno Cheso	75.00	37.00	22.00
12	Dick Lajeskie	75.00	37.00	22.00
13	Roy Nicely	75.00	37.00	22.00
14	Mickey Rocco	75.00	37.00	22.00
15	Frank Shofner	75.00	37.00	22.00
16	Richard Holder	75.00	37.00	22.00
17	Dino Restelli	75.00	37.00	22.00
18	Floyd J. "Arky" Vaughan	150.00	75.00	45.00
19	Jackie Baccioccu	75.00	37.00	22.00
20	Bob Drilling	75.00	37.00	22.00
21	Del Young	75.00	37.00	22.00
22	Joe Sprinz	75.00	37.00	22.00
23	Doc Hughes	75.00	37.00	22.00
24	Unknown			
25	Bert Singleton	75.00	37.00	22.00
26	John Brocker	75.00	37.00	22.00
27	Jack Tobin	75.00	37.00	22.00
28	Walt Judnich	75.00	37.00	22.00
29	Hal Feldman	75.00	37.00	22.00

1909 Spargo Hartford Senators Postcards

Members on the Connecticut League (Class B) champion Hartford Senators are pictured on these black-and-white postcards. Player portraits are featured in an oval on front with identication below. A photo credit to "Oliver" is provided. The typically formatted back has a credit line for the publisher, A.W. Spargo. It is likely other members of the team exist on cards yet to be reported.

C. P. ARBOGAST.

		NM	EX	VG
	Common Player:	700.00	350.00	200.00
(1)	C.P. Arbogast	700.00	350.00	200.00
(2)	Tom J. Connery	700.00	350.00	200.00
(3)	Ray L. Fisher	700.00	350.00	200.00
(4)	C.A. Wadleigh	700.00	350.00	200.00

1867 Sterey Photographers Troy Haymakers

Pre-dating the use of baseball cards as promotional premiums for other products, this issue comprises cartes de visites of members of the Troy Haymakers, one of the powerhouse "amateur" teams in the days prior to the 1871 formation of the National Association, the first professional baseball league. The approximately 2-1/2" x 4" cards have black-and-white player portrait photos glued to a heavy cardboard backing which on its reverse carries in blue the advertising of E.S. Sterey & Co., Photographers, of Lansingburgh, N.Y. The players are not identified on the cards except for the names and, sometimes, positions pencilled on back. While many CDVs of individual players of the era, along with team poses and composites, are known, this issue is important because it represents one of the first efforts to create a "team set." It is likely cards of other Troy players were issued and may surface someday.

		NM	EX	VG
	Common Player:	3,000	1,500	900.00
(1)	Abrams	3,000	1,500	900.00
(2)	Bill Craver	4,000	2,000	1,200
(3)	Steve King	4,500	2,250	1,350
(4)	Bub McAtee	4,500	2,250	1,350
(5)	Peter McKeon	3,000	1,500	900.00
(6)	McQuide	3,000	1,500	900.00

1933 St. Paul Daily News

(See 1933 Worch Cigar American Association.)

1946 Sunbeam Bread Sacramento Solons

STEVE "LITTLE GOLIATH" MESNER, 28, born Los Angeles, Calif.; second season with Solons. Greatest baseball thrill: hitting three home runs in one game. Played in majors with Chicago White Sox, St. Louis Cards, Cincinnati Reds. Hobby: collecting all articles pertaining to baseball.

Listen to Baseball Play by Play With "Tony" Koester KFBK

STEVE MESNER
1946 Solons Third Baseman
Photo by Joe Benetti

Sunbeam BREAD
The BREAD That Broadcasts BASEBALL

The 21 unnumbered cards in this Pacific Coast League team set are printed with black-and-white fronts containing a borderless player photo with a panel beneath containing name, position and a photo credit. Backs are printed in blue, red and yellow and contain a brief career summary and an ad for the bread brand. Each card can be found with two versions of the ad on back. One has a smaller loaf of bread and the

word "Sunbeam" in blue, the other has a larger picture and "Sunbeam" in red. The cards measure approximately 2" x 3". Players are checklisted here in alphabetical order.

		NM	EX	VG
	Complete Set (21):	900.00	450.00	240.00
	Common Player:	75.00	35.00	20.00
(1)	Bud Beasley	75.00	35.00	20.00
(2)	Jack Calvey	75.00	35.00	20.00
(3)	Gene Corbett	75.00	35.00	20.00
(4)	Bill Conroy	75.00	35.00	20.00
(5)	Guy Fletcher	75.00	35.00	20.00
(6)	Tony Freitas	75.00	35.00	20.00
(7)	Ted Greenhalgh	75.00	35.00	20.00
(8)	Al Jarlett	75.00	35.00	20.00
(9)	Jesse Landrum	75.00	35.00	20.00
(10)	Gene Lillard	75.00	35.00	20.00
(11)	Garth Mann	75.00	35.00	20.00
(12)	Lilo Marcucci	75.00	35.00	20.00
(13)	Joe Marty (SP)	225.00	110.00	65.00
(14)	Steve Mesner	75.00	35.00	20.00
(15)	Herm Pillette	75.00	35.00	20.00
(16)	Earl Sheely	75.00	35.00	20.00
(17)	Al Smith	75.00	35.00	20.00
(18)	Gerald Staley	75.00	35.00	20.00
(19)	Averett Thompson	75.00	35.00	20.00
(20)	Jo Jo White	75.00	35.00	20.00
(21)	Bud Zipay	75.00	35.00	20.00

1947 Sunbeam Bread Sacramento Solons

THE BREAD THAT BROADCASTS BASEBALL

Photo by Joe Benetti
TOMMY THOMPSON
1947 Solons Outfielder

Similar in format to the 1946 issue, the 26 cards in the '47 set again featured black-and-white player photos on front, with a panel beneath giving player name, position and photo credit. Backs of the 2" x 3" cards had a color depiction of a loaf of the sponsoring company's bread. The unnumbered cards are alphabetically checklisted here.

		NM	EX	VG
	Complete Set (26):	1,250	625.00	375.00
	Common Player:	50.00	25.00	15.00
(1)	Gene Babbit	50.00	25.00	15.00
(2)	Bob Barthelson	50.00	25.00	15.00
(3)	Bud Beasley	50.00	25.00	15.00
(4)	Chuck Cronin	50.00	25.00	15.00
(5)	Eddie Fernandes	50.00	25.00	15.00
(6)	Ed Fitz Gerald	50.00	25.00	15.00
(7)	Guy Fletcher	50.00	25.00	15.00
(8)	Tony Freitas	50.00	25.00	15.00
(9)	Garth Mann	50.00	25.00	15.00
(10)	Joe Marty	50.00	25.00	15.00
(11)	Lou McCollum	50.00	25.00	15.00
(12)	Steve Mesner	50.00	25.00	15.00
(13)	Frank Nelson	50.00	25.00	15.00
(14)	Tommy Nelson	50.00	25.00	15.00
(15)	Joe Orengo	50.00	25.00	15.00
(16)	Hugh Orphan	50.00	25.00	15.00
(17)	Nick Pesut	50.00	25.00	15.00
(18)	Bill Ramsey	50.00	25.00	15.00
(19)	Johnny Rizzo	50.00	25.00	15.00
(20)	Mike Schemer	250.00	125.00	75.00
(21)	Al Smith	50.00	25.00	15.00
(22)	Tommy Thompson	50.00	25.00	15.00
(23)	Jim Warner	50.00	25.00	15.00
(24)	Mel Wasley	50.00	25.00	15.00
(25)	Leo Wells	50.00	25.00	15.00
(26)	Eddie Zipay	50.00	25.00	15.00

1949 Sunbeam/Pureta Sacramento Solons

FRANKIE DASSO

They bring you Baseball

Always made in HELT!
Meat Prepared Meats and PURETA Sausages
BREAD
Sunbeam

Let's be Friends!

Mrs Lillie Rodgers
1754 Helena Ave
North Sacramento Calif

Players of the Pacific Coast League's Sacramento Solons were featured in this postcard-size (3-1/4" x 5-1/2") set. Fronts featured black-and-white player photos and the logo of the team's radio broadcaster. Backs feature ads for Sunbeam Bread and Pureta meats.

		NM	EX	VG
Complete Set (12):		2,000	1,000	600.00
Common Player:		250.00	125.00	80.00
(1)	Del Baker	250.00	125.00	80.00
(2)	Frankie Dasso	250.00	125.00	80.00
(3)	Walt Dropo	325.00	160.00	100.00
(4)	Bob Gillespie	250.00	125.00	80.00
(5)	Joe Grace	250.00	125.00	80.00
(6)	Ralph Hodgin	250.00	125.00	80.00
(7)	Freddie Marsh	250.00	125.00	80.00
(8)	Joe Marty	250.00	125.00	80.00
(9)	Len Ratto	250.00	125.00	80.00
(10)	Jim Tabor	250.00	125.00	80.00
(11)	Al White	250.00	125.00	80.00
(12)	Bill Wilson	250.00	125.00	80.00

1949 Sunbeam Bread Stockton Ports

These 2" x 3" unnumbered cards can be found printed in either black-and-white or blue tinted. The Ports were the Class C California League farm club of the Chicago White Sox.

		NM	EX	VG
Complete Set (12):		3,000	1,500	900.00
Common Player:		275.00	135.00	85.00
(1)	Nino Bongiovanni	275.00	135.00	85.00
(2)	Lou Bronzan	275.00	135.00	85.00
(3)	Jimmie Brown	275.00	135.00	85.00
(4)	Rocco Cardinale	275.00	135.00	85.00
(5)	Harry Clements	275.00	135.00	85.00
(6)	Norm Grabar	275.00	135.00	85.00
(7)	Bud Guldborg	275.00	135.00	85.00
(8)	Carl Hoberg	275.00	135.00	85.00
(9)	Eddie Murphy	275.00	135.00	85.00
(10)	Sandy Sandel	275.00	135.00	85.00
(11)	Dick Stone	275.00	135.00	85.00
(12)	Matt Zidich	275.00	135.00	85.00

1950 Sunbeam Bread Stockton Ports

These 2" x 3" unnumbered cards are printed in black-and-white. The Ports were an unaffiliated team in the Class C California League.

		NM	EX	VG
Complete Set (13):		1,800	900.00	550.00
Common Player:		150.00	75.00	45.00
(1)	Richard L. Adams	150.00	75.00	45.00
(2)	James Edward Brown	150.00	75.00	45.00
(3)	Harry Clements	150.00	75.00	45.00
(4)	John Burton Goldborg	150.00	75.00	45.00
(5)	Gerald Lee Haines	150.00	75.00	45.00
(6)	Alfred Michael Heist	150.00	75.00	45.00
(7)	Don Masterson	150.00	75.00	45.00
(8)	Lauren Hugh Monroe	150.00	75.00	45.00
(9)	Frank E. Murray	150.00	75.00	45.00
(10)	Lauren Keith Simon Jr.	150.00	75.00	45.00
(11)	George Anthony Stanich	150.00	75.00	45.00
(12)	Robert Louis Stevens	150.00	75.00	45.00
(13)	Harold Lee Zurcher	150.00	75.00	45.00

1962 Supertest Toronto Maple Leafs

The extent of the checklist for this issue is unknown. It is assumed the cards were given away with gasoline purchases. Printed on thick, porous paper in a 5-1/2" x 8-1/2" format, the cards have a black-and-white photo, facsimile autograph and sponsor's logo on front. Backs are blank.

		NM	EX	VG
Common Player:		60.00	30.00	18.00
(1)	Chuck Dressen	75.00	37.50	22.50
(2)	Russ Heman	60.00	30.00	18.00

1952 Syracuse Chiefs Team Issue

Like the other contemporary issues of Globe Printing, the cards of the '52 Chiefs (International League, unaffiliated) share a blank-back, black-and-white format. Player names are in black in a white strip on front. Cards measure about 2-1/4" x 3-3/8". The checklist here is incomplete.

		NM	EX	VG
Common Player:		60.00	30.00	18.00
(1)	Bruno Betzel	60.00	30.00	18.00
(2)	Johnny Blatnick	60.00	30.00	18.00
(3)	Charles Eisenmann	60.00	30.00	18.00
(4)	Myron Hayworth	60.00	30.00	18.00
(5)	John Welaj	60.00	30.00	18.00

T

1966 Toledo Mud Hens Team Issue

(3-1/4" x 5-1/2") (Unnumbered)

		NM	EX	VG
Complete Set (25):		1,000	500.00	300.00
Common Player:		40.00	20.00	12.00
(1)	Loren Babe	40.00	20.00	12.00
(2)	Stan Bahnsen	40.00	20.00	12.00
(3)	Bill Bethea	40.00	20.00	12.00
(4)	Wayne Comer	40.00	20.00	12.00
(5)	Jack Cullen	40.00	20.00	12.00
(6)	Jack Curtis	40.00	20.00	12.00
(7)	Gil Downs	40.00	20.00	12.00
(8)	Joe Faroci	40.00	20.00	12.00
(9)	Frank Fernandez	40.00	20.00	12.00
(10)	Mike Ferraro	40.00	20.00	12.00
(11)	Doc Foley	40.00	20.00	12.00
(12)	Mike Hegan	40.00	20.00	12.00
(13)	Jim Horsford	40.00	20.00	12.00
(14)	Dick Hughes	40.00	20.00	12.00
(15)	Elvio Jiminez	40.00	20.00	12.00
(16)	Bob Lasko	40.00	20.00	12.00
(17)	Jim Merritt	40.00	20.00	12.00
(18)	Archie Moore	40.00	20.00	12.00
(19)	Bobby Murcer	90.00	45.00	27.00
(20)	Tony Preybycian	40.00	20.00	12.00
(21)	Bob Schmidt	40.00	20.00	12.00
(22)	Charlie Senger, Loren Babe, Bill Shantz	40.00	20.00	12.00
(23)	Bill Shantz	40.00	20.00	12.00
(24)	Paul Toth	40.00	20.00	12.00
(25)	Jerry Walker	40.00	20.00	12.00

1964 True Ade / WGR Buffalo Bisons

Members of the International League Buffalo Bisons, Class AAA farm club of the N.Y. Mets are featured in this set of contest cards. Persons who assembled a complete nine-player set could redeem the cards for ballgame tickets. The cards were found in cartons of Tru Ade beverage. The blank-back cards are printed in red and about 1-1/4" x 6-1/2" overall. At bottom is a player photo with his name and position above, and team below, separated by a dotted line from the upper portion of the card which has contest details and logos of the sponsoring beverage company and WGR radio. The player portion of the card measures about 1-1/4" x 1-1/4". It is evident that at least nine players were issued in the set, possibly with some short-printed; this checklist is, therefore, incomplete. The unnumbered cards are listed here in alphabetical order.

		NM	EX	VG
Common Player:		150.00	75.00	45.00
(1)	Ed Bauta	150.00	75.00	45.00
(2)	Choo Choo Coleman	200.00	100.00	60.00
(3)	Pumpsie Green	300.00	150.00	90.00
(4)	Cleon Jones	200.00	100.00	60.00

1960 Tulsa Oilers Team Issue

This team issue by the St. Louis Cardinals' farm club consists of a dozen black-and-white player photos. Players are identifed by a facsimile autograph on front. Backs of the approximately 4-1/8" x 5" photos are blank.

		NM	EX	VG
Complete Set (18):		350.00	175.00	100.00
Common Player:		20.00	10.00	6.00
(1)	Jim Beauchamp	15.00	7.50	4.50
(2)	Bob Blaylock	20.00	10.00	6.00
(3)	Artie Burnett	20.00	10.00	6.00
(4)	Bill Carpenter	20.00	10.00	6.00
(5)	Julio Gotay	20.00	10.00	6.00
(6)	Jim Hickman	20.00	10.00	6.00
(7)	Ray Katt	20.00	10.00	6.00
(8)	Harry Keister	20.00	10.00	6.00
(9)	Fred Koenig	20.00	10.00	6.00
(10)	Gordon Richardson	20.00	10.00	6.00
(11)	Rich Rogers	20.00	10.00	6.00
(12)	Lynn Rube	20.00	10.00	6.00
(13)	Jim Schaffer	20.00	10.00	6.00
(14)	Clint Stark	20.00	10.00	6.00
(15)	Ted Thiem	20.00	10.00	6.00
(16)	Dixie Walker	20.00	10.00	6.00
(17)	Harry Watts	20.00	10.00	6.00
(18)	Fred Whitfield	20.00	10.00	6.00

U

1888 Uhlman St. Paul Cabinets

While this cabinet-card issue utilizes the same format (about 4-1/4" x 6-1/2") and the same Goodwin & Co. copyright photos found on contemporary Old Judge cards, they are, according to advertising on the bottom, the product of Uhlman (presumably a studio) in St. Joseph, Mo. All cards known to date depict members of the St. Paul Apostles of the newly formed Western Association.

		NM	EX	VG
Common Player:		900.00	525.00	275.00
(1)	Cal Broughton	900.00	525.00	275.00
(2)	George Treadway	900.00	525.00	275.00
(3)	A.M. Tuckerman	900.00	525.00	275.00

1958 Union Oil Sacramento Solons

Ten members of the independent Pacific Coast League team were included in a black-and-white card set distributed at Union 76 gas stations in that locale. Fronts feature borderless player photos with a wide white strip at the bottom on which is printed the player, team name and the position. Backs have brief stats, a "76 Sports Club" pennant and information about a specific game for which the card can be exchanged for admission by a child. Cards measure approximately 2-1/2" x 3-1/4".

	NM	EX	VG
Complete Set (10):	500.00	250.00	150.00
Common Player:	50.00	25.00	15.00
(1) Marshall Bridges	65.00	32.00	19.50
(2) Dick Cole	50.00	25.00	15.00
(3) Jim Greengrass	50.00	25.00	15.00
(4) Al Heist	50.00	25.00	15.00
(5) Nippy Jones	50.00	25.00	15.00
(6) Carlos Paula	50.00	25.00	15.00
(7) Kal Segrist	50.00	25.00	15.00
(8) Sibbi Sisti	50.00	25.00	15.00
(9) Joe Stanka	80.00	40.00	24.00
(10) Bud Watkins	50.00	25.00	15.00

1960 Union Oil Seattle Rainiers

Given away at Union 76 gas stations in the Seattle area, this set of nine full-color cards measure approximately 3-1/8" x 4". Backs have brief biographical data, a career summary and a large Union 76 logo. The cards are skip-numbered.

	NM	EX	VG
Complete Set (9):	200.00	100.00	60.00
Common Player:	12.00	6.00	3.50
4 Francisco Obregon	20.00	10.00	6.00
6 Drew Gilbert	12.00	6.00	3.50
7 Bill Hain	12.00	6.00	3.50
10 Ray Rippelmeyer	100.00	50.00	30.00
13 Joe Taylor	12.00	6.00	3.50
15 Lou Skizas	12.00	6.00	3.50
17 Don Rudolph	12.00	6.00	3.50
19 Gordy Coleman	15.00	7.50	4.50
22 Hal Beven	12.00	6.00	3.50

1961 Union Oil Pacific Coast League

The last of three Union Oil PCL issues, the 67 cards in this set feature sepia-toned borderless photos on front in a 3" to 3-1/8" x 4" format. Backs are printed in blue and feature biographical data, a career summary, and ads by the issuing oil company and participating radio station co-sponsors. Six of the eight teams in the '61 PCL are featured, with Salt Lake City and Vancouver not participating in the promotion. Presumably because of smaller print runs, the cards distributed in Hawaii and Spokane bring a premium price. Hall of Fame pitcher Gaylord Perry is featured on his first baseball card in this set. Only the Tacoma cards are numbered and they are skip-numbered.

(Team sets listed below.)

1961 Union Oil Hawaii Islanders

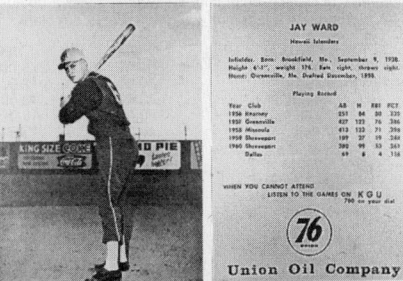

	NM	EX	VG
Complete Set (10):	375.00	185.00	110.00
Common Player:	40.00	20.00	12.00
(1) Ray Jablonski	40.00	20.00	12.00
(2) Jim McManus	40.00	20.00	12.00
(3) George Prescott	75.00	37.50	22.50
(4) Diego Segui	45.00	22.50	13.50
(5) Rachel Slider	40.00	20.00	12.00
(6) Jim Small	40.00	20.00	12.00
(7) Milt Smith	40.00	20.00	12.00
(8) Dave Thies	40.00	20.00	12.00
(9) Jay Ward	40.00	20.00	12.00
(10) Bill Werle	40.00	20.00	12.00

1961 Union Oil Portland Beavers

	NM	EX	VG
Complete Set (13):	150.00	75.00	45.00
Common Player:	12.00	6.00	3.50
(1) Ed Bauta	12.00	6.00	3.50
(2) Vern Benson	12.00	6.00	3.50
(3) Jerry Buchek	12.00	6.00	3.50
(4) Bob Burda	12.00	6.00	3.50
(5) Duke Carmel	12.00	6.00	3.50
(6) Don Choate	12.00	6.00	3.50
(7) Phil Gagliano	12.00	6.00	3.50
(8) Jim Hickman	12.00	6.00	3.50
(9) Ray Katt	12.00	6.00	3.50
(10) Mel Nelson	12.00	6.00	3.50
(11) Jim Shaffer	12.00	6.00	3.50
(12) Mike Shannon	17.50	8.75	5.25
(13) Clint Stark	12.00	6.00	3.50

1961 Union Oil San Diego Padres

	NM	EX	VG
Complete Set (12):	175.00	90.00	45.00
Common Player:	12.00	6.00	3.50
(1) Dick Barone	12.00	6.00	3.50
(2) Jim Bolger	12.00	6.00	3.50
(3) Kent Hadley	12.00	6.00	3.50
(4) Mike Hershberger	15.00	7.50	4.50
(5) Stan Johnson	12.00	6.00	3.50
(6) Dick Lines	12.00	6.00	3.50
(7) Jim Napier	12.00	6.00	3.50
(8) Tony Roig	12.00	6.00	3.50
(9) Herb Score	40.00	20.00	12.00
(10) Harry Simpson	20.00	10.00	6.00
(11) Joe Taylor	12.00	6.00	3.50
(12) Ben Wade	12.00	6.00	3.50

1961 Union Oil Seattle Rainiers

	NM	EX	VG
Complete Set (11):	100.00	50.00	30.00
Common Player:	10.00	5.00	3.00
(1) Galen Cisco	10.00	5.00	3.00
(2) Lou Clinton	10.00	5.00	3.00
(3) Marlan Coughtry	10.00	5.00	3.00
(4) Harry Malmberg	10.00	5.00	3.00
(5) Dave Mann	10.00	5.00	3.00
(6) Derrell Martin	10.00	5.00	3.00
(7) Erv Palica	10.00	5.00	3.00
(8) John Pesky	15.00	7.50	4.50
(9) Bob Tillman	10.00	5.00	3.00
(10) Marv Toft	10.00	5.00	3.00
(11) Tom Umphlett	10.00	5.00	3.00

1961 Union Oil Spokane Indians

	NM	EX	VG
Complete Set (11):	450.00	225.00	135.00
Common Player:	35.00	17.50	10.00
(1) Doug Camilli	35.00	17.50	10.00
(2) Ramon Conde	35.00	17.50	10.00
(3) Bob Giallombardo	35.00	17.50	10.00
(4) Mike Goliat	35.00	17.50	10.00
(5) Preston Gomez (SP)	135.00	67.00	40.00
(6) Rod Graber	35.00	17.50	10.00
(7) Tim Harkness	35.00	17.50	10.00
(8) Jim Harwell	35.00	17.50	10.00
(9) Howie Reed	35.00	17.50	10.00
(10) Curt Roberts	35.00	17.50	10.00
(11) Rene Valdes (Valdez)	35.00	17.50	10.00

1961 Union Oil Tacoma Giants

	NM	EX	VG
Complete Set (10):	200.00	100.00	60.00
Common Player:	15.00	7.50	4.50
10 Red Davis	15.00	7.50	4.50
12 Dick Phillips	15.00	7.50	4.50
17 Gil Garrido	15.00	7.50	4.50
20 Georges Maranda	15.00	7.50	4.50
25 John Orsino	15.00	7.50	4.50
26 Dusty Rhodes	20.00	10.00	6.00
28 Ron Herbel	15.00	7.50	4.50
29 Gaylord Perry	60.00	30.00	18.00
30 Rafael Alomar	20.00	10.00	6.00
34 Bob Farley	15.00	7.50	4.50

1961 Union Oil Taiyo Whales

This three-card set was produced in conjunction with an exhibition series played in October 1961, between the Taiyo Whales of Japan's Central League, and the Hawaii Islanders, a Class AAA Pacific Cost League farm club of the K.C. Athletics. The player cards measure just over 3" x 4", while the team photo card is 5" x 3-3/4". Cards are black-and-white and have some player biography and ads for Union Oil Co., and the English - and Japanese - language radio stations that carried the games.

	NM	EX	VG
Complete Set (3):	175.00	87.00	52.00
(1) Akihito Kondo	50.00	25.00	15.00
(2) Gentaro Shimada	50.00	25.00	15.00
(3) Taiyo Whales Team	90.00	45.00	27.00

V

1951 Vancouver Capilanos Popcorn Issue

These cards measure 1-7/8" x 2-7/8", are printed in black-and-white and have 1950 stats on back. Names may appear in slightly different form than checklisted here. The Caps played in the Class B Western International League and were not affiliated with any major league club.

	NM	EX	VG
Complete Set (24):	4,000	2,000	1,200
Common Player:	200.00	100.00	60.00
(1) Chuck Abernathy	200.00	100.00	60.00
(2) Jerry Barta	200.00	100.00	60.00
(3) Bud Beasley	200.00	100.00	60.00
(4) Gordy Brunswick	200.00	100.00	60.00
(5) Reno Cheso	200.00	100.00	60.00
(6) Ken Chorlton	200.00	100.00	60.00
(7) Carl Gunnarson	200.00	100.00	60.00
(8) Pete Hernandez	200.00	100.00	60.00
(9) Vern Kindsfather	200.00	100.00	60.00
(10) Bobby McGuire	200.00	100.00	60.00
(11) Bob McLean	200.00	100.00	60.00
(12) Charlie Mead	200.00	100.00	60.00
(13) Jimmy Moore	200.00	100.00	60.00
(14) George Nicholas	200.00	100.00	60.00
(15) John Ritchey	200.00	100.00	60.00
(16) Sandy Robertson	200.00	100.00	60.00
(17) Bill Schuster	200.00	100.00	60.00
(18) Dick Sinovic	200.00	100.00	60.00
(19) Ron Smith	200.00	100.00	60.00
(20) Bob Snyder	200.00	100.00	60.00
(21) Don Tisnerat	200.00	100.00	60.00
(22) Ray Tran	200.00	100.00	60.00
(23) Reg Wallis (Trainer)	200.00	100.00	60.00
(24) Bill Whyte	200.00	100.00	60.00

1952 Vancouver Capilanos Popcorn Issue

These cards measure 2" x 3-1/8", are printed in black-and-white and have 1951 stats on back. Names may appear in slightly different form than checklisted here. The Caps played in the Class A Western International League and were not affiliated with any major league club.

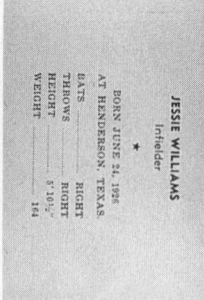

JESSIE WILLIAMS
Infielder

★

BORN JUNE 24, 1926
AT HENDERSON, TEXAS.

BATS   RIGHT
THROWS   RIGHT
HEIGHT   5' 10½"
WEIGHT   164

		NM	EX	VG
Complete Set (20):		3,500	1,750	1,000
Common Player:		200.00	100.00	60.00
(1)	Gordie Brunswick	200.00	100.00	60.00
(2)	Bob Duretto	200.00	100.00	60.00
(3)	Van Fletcher	200.00	100.00	60.00
(4)	John Guldborg	200.00	100.00	60.00
(5)	Paul Jones	200.00	100.00	60.00
(6)	Eddie Locke	200.00	100.00	60.00
(7)	Tom Lovrich	200.00	100.00	60.00
(8)	Jimmy Moore	200.00	100.00	60.00
(9)	George Nicholas	200.00	100.00	60.00
(10a)	John Ritchey	200.00	100.00	60.00
(10b)	Johnny Ritchie	200.00	100.00	60.00
(11)	Bill Schuster	200.00	100.00	60.00
(12)	Bob Snyder	200.00	100.00	60.00
(13)	Len Tran	200.00	100.00	60.00
(14)	Ray Tran	200.00	100.00	60.00
(15)	Edo Vanni	200.00	100.00	60.00
(16)	Jim Wert	200.00	100.00	60.00
(17)	Bill Whyte	200.00	100.00	60.00
(18)	Jessie Williams (Batting)	200.00	100.00	60.00
(19)	Jesse Williams (Fielding)	200.00	100.00	60.00

1953 Vancouver Capilanos Popcorn Issue

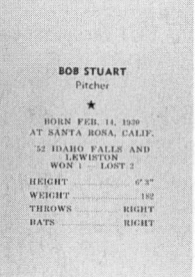

BOB STUART
Pitcher

★

BORN FEB. 14, 1930
AT SANTA ROSA, CALIF.

'52 IDAHO FALLS AND
LEWISTON
WON 1 - LOST 2

HEIGHT   6' 3"
WEIGHT   192
THROWS   RIGHT
BATS   RIGHT

These cards measure 2-3/16" x 3-3/16", are printed in black-and-white and have 1952 stats on back. Names may appear in slightly different form than checklisted here. The Caps played in the Class A Western International League and were not affiliated with any major league club.

		NM	EX	VG
Complete Set (18):		3,000	1,500	900.00
Common Player:		200.00	100.00	60.00
(1)	Dick Briskey	200.00	100.00	60.00
(2)	Jack Bukowatz	200.00	100.00	60.00
(3)	Ken Chorlton	200.00	100.00	60.00
(4)	Van Fletcher	200.00	100.00	60.00
(5)	John Guldborg	200.00	100.00	60.00
(6)	Carl Gunnerson	200.00	100.00	60.00
(7)	Jim Hedgecock	200.00	100.00	60.00
(8)	Gordon Hernandez	200.00	100.00	60.00
(9)	Pete Hernandez	200.00	100.00	60.00
(10)	Jim Leavitt	200.00	100.00	60.00
(11)	Rod MacKay	200.00	100.00	60.00
(12)	Paul Mascaro	200.00	100.00	60.00
(13)	Lonnie Myers	200.00	100.00	60.00
(14)	Rod Owen	200.00	100.00	60.00
(15)	Harvey Storey	200.00	100.00	60.00
(16)	Bob Stuart	200.00	100.00	60.00
(17)	Dale Thomason	200.00	100.00	60.00
(18)	Jim Wert	200.00	100.00	60.00

1954 Vancouver Capilanos Popcorn Issue

K. CHORLTON

These cards measure 2-3/16" x 3-5/16" and are printed in black-and-white. Names may appear in slightly different form than checklisted here. The Caps were the 1954 champs of the Class A Western International League and were not affiliated with any major league club.

		NM	EX	VG
Complete Set (15):		2,500	1,250	750.00
Common Player:		200.00	100.00	60.00
(1)	Bill Brenner	200.00	100.00	60.00
(2)	Ken Chorlton	200.00	100.00	60.00
(3)	Jim Clarke (Clark)	200.00	100.00	60.00
(4)	John Cordell	200.00	100.00	60.00
(5)	Bob Duretto	200.00	100.00	60.00
(6)	Dick Greco	200.00	100.00	60.00
(7)	Arnie Hallgren	200.00	100.00	60.00
(8)	Danny Holden	200.00	100.00	60.00
(9)	Rod McKay	200.00	100.00	60.00
(10)	George Nicholas	200.00	100.00	60.00
(11)	Nick Pesut	200.00	100.00	60.00
(12)	Ken Richardson	200.00	100.00	60.00
(13)	Bob Roberts	200.00	100.00	60.00
(14)	Bob Wellman	200.00	100.00	60.00
(15)	Marvin Williams	200.00	100.00	60.00

1954 Veltex Lewiston Broncs

LARRY BARTON

Compliments of your
VELTEX DEALER

It is evident from the format of the card and of the accompanying album that this is a product of Globe Printing, which produced many minor league sets in the early 1950s. What makes this set of the 1954 Class A (Western International League) affiliate of the Baltimore Orioles unusual among Globe issues is the mention of a sponsor. The blank-back, black-and-white cards measure 2-3/16" x 3-3/8". The checklist below is obviously incomplete.

		NM	EX	VG
Common player:		60.00	30.00	18.00
Album:		150.00	75.00	45.00
(1)	Larry Barton	60.00	30.00	18.00

1952 Ventura Braves Team Issue

These 2-1/4" x 3-3/8" black-and-white, unnumbered, blank-backed cards were one of many minor league team sets issued by Globe Printing of San Jose, Calif., in the early 1950s. Cards were usually given away at the ballpark on a one-per-week or one-per-homestand basis, accounting for the rarity of surviving complete sets. It is known that 18 V-Braves were issued in this set, though only 14 have been checklisted to date. The team was a Class C California League farm club of the Boston Braves.

		NM	EX	VG
Common Player:		60.00	30.00	18.00
Album:		100.00	50.00	30.00
(1)	Al Aguilar	60.00	30.00	18.00
(2)	Bud Belardi	60.00	30.00	18.00
(3)	Frank Followell	60.00	30.00	18.00
(4)	Glenn Hittner	60.00	30.00	18.00
(5)	Lee Kast	60.00	30.00	18.00
(6)	Richie Morse	60.00	30.00	18.00
(7)	Frank Nubin	60.00	30.00	18.00
(8)	George Owen	60.00	30.00	18.00
(9)	Manny Perez	60.00	30.00	18.00
(10)	Jose Perez	60.00	30.00	18.00
(11)	Harley Resh	60.00	30.00	18.00
(12)	Jack Schlarb	60.00	30.00	18.00
(13)	Bob Sturgeon	60.00	30.00	18.00
(14)	Billy Wells	60.00	30.00	18.00

1911 Western Playground Association

Stars from around the Pacific Coast League are featured on this rare and unusual issue. The 2-1/4" x 3-1/2" cards have a front design similar to contemporary Zeenuts cards: A dark brown border surrounding a sepia posed action picture (which appears to be a heavily retouched photo). Printed in white at left or right are "WESTERN PLAYGROUND ASSOCIATION / P.C. (or sometimes 'P.S.') LEAGUE" and the player's last name. Backs are a "Membership Certificate" indicating the cards could be redeemed for five percent of their seven-cent

---

"face value" toward the purchase of school playground apparatus or supplies. The cards were received with the purchase of "Bank Stock" brand composition books.

		NM	EX	VG
Common Player:		6,000	3,000	1,800
(1)	Claude Berry	6,000	3,000	1,800
(2)	Roy Brashear	6,000	3,000	1,800
(3)	Herb Byram	6,000	3,000	1,800
(4)	Walt Carlisle	6,000	3,000	1,800
(5)	Roy Caslleton (Castleton)	6,000	3,000	1,800
(6)	Chet Chadborne (Chadbourne)	6,000	3,000	1,800
(7)	Tyler Christian	6,000	3,000	1,800
(8)	Bert Coy	6,000	3,000	1,800
(9)	Pete Daley	6,000	3,000	1,800
(10)	Pop Dillon	6,000	3,000	1,800
(11)	Joe French	6,000	3,000	1,800
(12)	Howie Gregory	6,000	3,000	1,800
(13)	Spec Harkness	6,000	3,000	1,800
(14)	Heinie Heitmuller	6,000	3,000	1,800
(15)	Ben Henderson	6,000	3,000	1,800
(16)	Cack Henley	6,000	3,000	1,800
(17)	Izzy Hoffman	6,000	3,000	1,800
(18)	Happy Hogan	6,000	3,000	1,800
(19)	Johnny Kane	6,000	3,000	1,800
(20)	Jimmy Lewis	6,000	3,000	1,800
(21)	Tom Madden	6,000	3,000	1,800
(22)	Chris Mahoney	6,000	3,000	1,800
(23)	George Metzger	6,000	3,000	1,800
(24)	Fred Miller	6,000	3,000	1,800
(25)	Kid Mohler	6,000	3,000	1,800
(26)	Walter Nagle	6,000	3,000	1,800
(27)	Patsy O'Rourke	6,000	3,000	1,800
(28)	Ham Patterson	6,000	3,000	1,800
(29)	Roger Peckinpaugh	6,000	3,000	1,800
(30)	Bill Rapps	6,000	3,000	1,800
(31)	Bill Rogers (Rodgers)	6,000	3,000	1,800
(32)	Buddy Ryan	6,000	3,000	1,800
(33)	Walter Schmitt (Schmidt)	6,000	3,000	1,800
(34)	Tom Seaton	6,000	3,000	1,800
(35)	Jerry Sheehan	6,000	3,000	1,800
(36)	Harry Stewart	6,000	3,000	1,800
(37)	George Stinson	6,000	3,000	1,800
(38)	Harry Suter (Sutor)	6,000	3,000	1,800
(39)	Harry Wolverton	6,000	3,000	1,800
(40)	Elmer Zacher	6,000	3,000	1,800

1932 Wheaties Minneapolis Millers

Because of their similarity to the 1933 issue which carried Wheaties advertising on the back, these postcard-size photos of the 1932 Millers are believed to also have been issued by the Minneapolis-based cereal company. The 3-7/16" x 5-7/16" cards have black-and-white portraits or posed action photos on front, along with a facsimile autograph. Backs are blank.

		NM	EX	VG
Complete Set (24):		900.00	450.00	275.00
Common Player:		40.00	20.00	12.00
(1)	J.C. "Rube" Benton	40.00	20.00	12.00
(2)	Donie Bush	40.00	20.00	12.00
(3)	Andy Cohen	45.00	22.00	13.50
(4)	"Pea Ridge" Day	40.00	20.00	12.00
(5)	Ray Fitzgerald	40.00	20.00	12.00
(6)	F.P. "Babe" Ganzel	40.00	20.00	12.00
(7)	Wes Griffin	40.00	20.00	12.00
(8)	Spencer Harris	40.00	20.00	12.00
(9)	Joe Hauser	75.00	37.00	22.00
(10)	Frank J. "Dutch" Henry	40.00	20.00	12.00
(11)	Phil Hensick	40.00	20.00	12.00
(12)	Bunker Hill	40.00	20.00	12.00

		NM	EX	VG
(13)	Joe Mowry	40.00	20.00	12.00
(14)	Jess Petty	40.00	20.00	12.00
(15)	Paul Richards	45.00	22.00	13.50
(16)	Bill Rodda	40.00	20.00	12.00
(17)	Harry Rose	40.00	20.00	12.00
(18)	Art Ruble	40.00	20.00	12.00
(19)	"Rosy" Ryan	40.00	20.00	12.00
(20)	Al Sheehan	40.00	20.00	12.00
(21)	Ed Sicking	40.00	20.00	12.00
(22)	Ernie Smith	40.00	20.00	12.00
(23)	Hy Van Denberg	40.00	20.00	12.00
(24)	E.R. Vangilder	40.00	20.00	12.00

1933 Wheaties Minneapolis Millers

Prior to printing their first major league baseball cards on the backs of cereal boxes in 1935, Wheaties sponsored a minor league set for the hometown Minneapolis Millers in 1933. The 4" x 5-3/4" cards have a sepia-toned posed action photo on front, along with a facsimile autograph. The player's name, position, team and year are printed in the bottom border. The postcard back, printed in black-and-white, has a drawing of a Wheaties box and an ad for the cereal. All unmailed examples seen to date have a purple rubber-stamped "VOID" in the postage box at top. The unnumbered cards are checklisted here alphabetically.

		NM	EX	VG
Complete Set (24):		2,250	1,125	650.00
Common Player:		90.00	45.00	27.00
(1)	Dave Bancroft	150.00	75.00	45.00
(2)	Rube Benton	90.00	45.00	27.00
(3)	Andy Cohen	150.00	75.00	45.00
(4)	Bob Fothergill	90.00	45.00	27.00
(5)	"Babe" Ganzel	90.00	45.00	27.00
(6)	Joe Glenn	90.00	45.00	27.00
(7)	Wes Griffin	90.00	45.00	27.00
(8)	Jack Hallet	90.00	45.00	27.00
(9)	Jerry Harrington (Announcer)	90.00	45.00	27.00
(10)	Spencer Harris	100.00	50.00	30.00
(11)	Joe Hauser	200.00	100.00	60.00
(12)	Butch Henline	90.00	45.00	27.00
(13)	Walter Hilcher	90.00	45.00	27.00
(14)	Dutch Holland	90.00	45.00	27.00
(15)	Harry Holsclaw	90.00	45.00	27.00
(16)	Wes Kingdon	90.00	45.00	27.00
(17)	George Murray	90.00	45.00	27.00
(18)	Leo Norris	90.00	45.00	27.00
(19)	Jess Petty	90.00	45.00	27.00
(20)	Art Ruble	90.00	45.00	27.00
(21)	Al Sheehan (Announcer)	90.00	45.00	27.00
(22)	Ernie Smith	90.00	45.00	27.00
(23)	Wally Tauscher	90.00	45.00	27.00
(24)	Hy VanDenburg	90.00	45.00	27.00

1933 Wheaties Seattle Indians

Prior to printing their first major league baseball cards on the backs of cereal boxes in 1935, Wheaties sponsored a minor league set for the Seattle Indians in 1933. The 4-1/8" x 7" cards have a sepia-toned posed portrait or action photo on front, along with a facsimile autograph. The player's name, position, team and year are printed in the bottom border. The postcard back, printed in black-and-white, has a drawing of a Wheaties box and an ad for the cereal. The unnumbered cards are checklisted here alphabetically; it is likely this list is incomplete.

		NM	EX	VG
Common Player:		450.00	225.00	135.00
(1)	George Burns	600.00	300.00	180.00
(2)	Joe Coscarart	450.00	225.00	135.00
(3)	Leo Lassen (Broadcaster)	450.00	225.00	135.00

		NM	EX	VG
(4)	Bill Radonits	450.00	225.00	135.00
(5)	"Junk" Walters	450.00	225.00	135.00

1912 Whitehead & Hoag P.C.L. Pins

A paper insert originally in the back of these pins identifies the maker as Whitehead & Hoag of San Francisco. The 7/8" diameter celluloid pins are printed in either black or blue on a white background. A player portrait photo is at center, with his last name below. Above is the city of his team and the Pacific Coast League initials. Listed in the "American Card Catalog" as PM5, the unnumbered pins are checklisted here alphabetically; it's possible additional pins in the issue remain to be reported. All pins seen are Oakland players except McCredie, Shehann, Rapp, and Seaton (Portland) as well as Berry (San Fransisco).

		NM	EX	VG
Complete Set (26):		5,000	2,500	1,500
Common Player:		275.00	135.00	85.00
(1)	Harry Ables	275.00	135.00	85.00
(2)	Claude Berry	275.00	135.00	85.00
(3)	Tyler Christian	275.00	135.00	85.00
(4)	Al Cook	275.00	135.00	85.00
(5)	Bert Coy	275.00	135.00	85.00
(6)	Jack Flater	275.00	135.00	85.00
(7)	Howie Gregory	275.00	135.00	85.00
(8)	Joe Hamilton	275.00	135.00	85.00
(9)	Gus Hetling	275.00	135.00	85.00
(10a)	Hille	275.00	135.00	85.00
(10b)	Mgr. Hille	275.00	135.00	85.00
(11)	Izzy Hoffman	275.00	135.00	85.00
(12)	Bill Leard	275.00	135.00	85.00
(13)	Bill Malarkey	275.00	135.00	85.00
(14)	Elmer Martinoni	275.00	135.00	85.00
(15)	Walter McCredie	275.00	135.00	85.00
(16)	Honus Mitze	275.00	135.00	85.00
(17)	Cy Parkins	275.00	135.00	85.00
(18)	Ashley Pope	275.00	135.00	85.00
(19)	Bill Rapp (Rapps)	275.00	135.00	85.00
(20)	Tom Seaton	275.00	135.00	85.00
(21a)	Bud Sharpe	275.00	135.00	85.00
(21b)	Mgr. Sharpe	275.00	135.00	85.00
(22)	Tommy Sheehan	275.00	135.00	85.00
(23)	Smith	275.00	135.00	85.00
(24)	John Tiedeman (Tiedemann)	275.00	135.00	85.00
(25)	Eddie Wilkinson	275.00	135.00	85.00
(26)	Elmer Zacher	275.00	135.00	85.00

1919 Winkelman's Quaker Bread Pins

This issue of 1-1/4" diameter celluloid pinback buttons features members of the Memphis Chickasaws in black-and-white portraits on a pale yellow background, surrounded by an orange border with the sponsor's advertising. A large turtle is pictured at bottom. Currently only three players are known, though it is likely more were issued.

		NM	EX	VG
Common Player:		1,300	650.00	400.00
(1)	Baerwald	1,300	650.00	400.00
(2)	Carey	1,300	650.00	400.00
(3)	Bob Coulson	1,300	650.00	400.00

1933-34 Worch Cigar American Association

Though the issuer is not identified anywhere on these blank-backed, 3-7/16" x 5-7/16" black-and-white cards (though some are found with a box on front crediting the photo to the St. Paul Daily News), the individual player photos were available as premiums for redemption of cigar bands by the Worch Cigar Co., of St. Paul, Minn. The issue is similar in format to the major league cards of the same era, and indeed the cards were offered together. Most collectors prefer to chase either the major leaguers or the minor leaguers independently, so they are cataloged in that fashion. The set encompasses players from the 1932-35 Minneapolis Millers, the 1933 St. Paul Saints and a handful from the Columbus Redbirds, Kan-

Phil Todt

sas City Blues and a few other teams. The unnumbered cards are checklisted below alphabetically. Player identification is presented in several different styles and may include just the last name or also the first name. Several players are known in more than one pose. The checklist here is likely incomplete.

		NM	EX	VG
Common Player:		45.00	22.50	13.50
(1)	Dave Bancroft	100.00	50.00	30.00
(2)	Clyde Beck	45.00	22.50	13.50
(3)	Rube Benton	45.00	22.50	13.50
(4)	W. Berger	45.00	22.50	13.50
(5)	Brannon	45.00	22.50	13.50
(6)	Spurgeon Chandler	45.00	22.50	13.50
(7)	Tiny Chaplin	45.00	22.50	13.50
(8)	Andy Cohen	45.00	22.50	13.50
(9)	Nick Cullop	45.00	22.50	13.50
(10)*	Bob Fenner	45.00	22.50	13.50
(11)	Fischall	45.00	22.50	13.50
(12)	Gaffke	45.00	22.50	13.50
(13a)	Foster Ganzel	45.00	22.50	13.50
(13b)	Foster Ganzel	45.00	22.50	13.50
(14)	Louis Garland	45.00	22.50	13.50
(15)	Joe Glenn	45.00	22.50	13.50
(16)	Angelo Guiliani	45.00	22.50	13.50
(17)	Pinky Hargrave	45.00	22.50	13.50
(18)	Slim Harriss	45.00	22.50	13.50
(19)	Spencer Harris	45.00	22.50	13.50
(20)	Joe Hauser	75.00	37.50	22.50
(21)	Walter Henline	45.00	22.50	13.50
(22)	Phil Hensick	45.00	22.50	13.50
(23)	Walter Hilcher	45.00	22.50	13.50
(24)	Jesse Hill	45.00	22.50	13.50
(25)	Bob Holand	45.00	22.50	13.50
(26)	Harry Holsclaw	45.00	22.50	13.50
(27)	Meredith Hopkins	45.00	22.50	13.50
(28)	Irvine Jeffries	45.00	22.50	13.50
(29)	Monk Joyner	45.00	22.50	13.50
(30)	Fred Koster	45.00	22.50	13.50
(31)	Walter Mails	45.00	22.50	13.50
(32)	Chuck Marrow	45.00	22.50	13.50
(33)	Emmett McCann	45.00	22.50	13.50
(34)	Joe Mowry	45.00	22.50	13.50
(35)	Les Munns	45.00	22.50	13.50
(36)	George Murray	45.00	22.50	13.50
(37)	Floyd Newkirk	45.00	22.50	13.50
(38)	Leo Norris	45.00	22.50	13.50
(39)	Frank Packard	45.00	22.50	13.50
(40)	Ben Paschal	45.00	22.50	13.50
(41a)	Jess Petty (Throwing, right foot off ground.)	45.00	22.50	13.50
(41b)	Jess Petty	45.00	22.50	13.50
(42)	Ray Radcliff	45.00	22.50	13.50
(43)	Larry Rosenthal	45.00	22.50	13.50
(44a)	Art Ruble	45.00	22.50	13.50
(44b)	Art Ruble	45.00	22.50	13.50
(45)	Art Shires	45.00	22.50	13.50
(46a)	Ernest Smith	45.00	22.50	13.50
(46b)	Ernest Smith	45.00	22.50	13.50
(47)	Ray Starr	45.00	22.50	13.50
(48)	Walter Tauscher	45.00	22.50	13.50
(49)	Myles Thomas	45.00	22.50	13.50
(50)	Phil Todt	45.00	22.50	13.50
(51)	Gene Trow	45.00	22.50	13.50
(52)	Hy Van Denburg	45.00	22.50	13.50
(53)	Elam Van Gilder	45.00	22.50	13.50
(54)	Charles Wilson	45.00	22.50	13.50
(55)	Ab. Wright	45.00	22.50	13.50
(56)	Emil Yde	45.00	22.50	13.50
(57)	Russ Young	45.00	22.50	13.50

Z

1911 Zeenut Pacific Coast League

Produced annually for 28 years, these Pacific Coast League cards were the longest-running and most popular baseball issues ever to appear on the West Coast. Issued by the Collins-McCarthy Candy Co. (later known as the Collins-Hencke Candy Co. and then simply the Collins Candy Co.) of San Francisco, Zeenut cards were inserted in boxes of the company's products: Zeenuts, Ruf-Neks and Home Run Kisses. All Zeenut cards issued from 1913 through 1937 had an approximately half-inch coupon at the bottom that could be redeemed for various prizes. Since most of these coupons were removed (and many not too carefully) Zeenuts are difficult to find in top condition today, and only a very small percentage survived with the coupon intact. (The sizes listed in the following descriptions are for cards without coupons.) Over the 28-year span, it is estimated that nearly 3,700 different cards were issued as part of the Zeenuts series, but new discoveries are still being made, and the checklist continues to grow. It is sometimes difficult to differentiate one year from another after 1930. Because it is so rare to find Zeenuts cards with the coupon still attached, values listed are for cards without the coupon. Cards with the coupon still intact will generally command a significant premium. The first Zeenut cards measure about 2-1/8" x 4" and feature a sepia-toned photo on a brown background surrounded by an off-white border. The backs of the cards are blank. Although the 1911 cards did not include the coupon bottom, some cards have been found with punch holes, indicating they may have also been used for redemptions. A total of 122 different players have been found.

		NM	EX	VG
	Common Player:	200.00	85.00	50.00
(1)	Abbott	200.00	85.00	50.00
(2)	Ables	200.00	85.00	50.00
(3a)	Agnew (Large pose.)	200.00	85.00	50.00
(3b)	Agnew (Small pose.)	200.00	85.00	50.00
(4a)	Akin (Large pose.)	200.00	85.00	50.00
(4b)	Akin (Small pose.)	200.00	85.00	50.00
(5)	Frank Arellanes	200.00	85.00	50.00
(6a)	Arlett (Large pose.)	200.00	85.00	50.00
(6b)	Arlett (Middle size pose.)	200.00	85.00	50.00
(6c)	Arlett (Small pose.)	200.00	85.00	50.00
(7)	Barry	200.00	85.00	50.00
(8)	Baum	200.00	85.00	50.00
(9)	Bernard	200.00	85.00	50.00
(10)	Berry	200.00	85.00	50.00
(11)	Bohen (Card is not know in high grade.)	.00	5,000	2,500
(12)	Brackenridge	200.00	85.00	50.00
(13)	Brashear	200.00	85.00	50.00
(14a)	Brown (Large pose.)	200.00	85.00	50.00
(14b)	Brown (Small pose.)	200.00	85.00	50.00
(15)	Browning	200.00	85.00	50.00
(16a)	Burrell (Large pose.)	200.00	85.00	50.00
(16b)	Burrell (Small pose.)	200.00	85.00	50.00
(17)	Byram	200.00	85.00	50.00
(18)	Carlisle	200.00	85.00	50.00
(19)	Carman	200.00	85.00	50.00
(20a)	Carson (Large pose.)	200.00	85.00	50.00
(20b)	Carson (Middle size pose.)	200.00	85.00	50.00
(20c)	Carson (Small pose.)	200.00	85.00	50.00
(21)	Castleton	200.00	85.00	50.00
(22)	Chadbourne	200.00	85.00	50.00
(23)	Christian	200.00	85.00	50.00
(24)	Couchman	200.00	85.00	50.00
(25)	Coy	200.00	85.00	50.00
(26)	Criger	200.00	85.00	50.00
(27)	Cutshaw	200.00	85.00	50.00
(28)	Daley	200.00	85.00	50.00
(29)	Danzig	200.00	85.00	50.00
(30)	Delhi	200.00	85.00	50.00
(31a)	Delmas (Large pose.)	200.00	85.00	50.00
(31b)	Delmas (Small pose.)	200.00	85.00	50.00
(32)	Dillon	200.00	85.00	50.00
(33a)	Discoll (Name incorrect.)	200.00	85.00	50.00
(33b)	Driscoll (Name correct.)	200.00	85.00	50.00
(34)	Dulin	200.00	85.00	50.00
(35)	Fanning	200.00	85.00	50.00
(36)	Fitzgerald	200.00	85.00	50.00
(37)	Flater	200.00	85.00	50.00
(38)	French	200.00	85.00	50.00
(39)	Fullerton	200.00	85.00	50.00
(40)	Gleason	200.00	85.00	50.00
(41)	Gregory	200.00	85.00	50.00
(42)	Halla	350.00	200.00	100.00
(43)	Harkness	200.00	85.00	50.00
(44a)	Heitmuller (Large pose.)	200.00	85.00	50.00
(44b)	Heitmuller (Small pose.)	200.00	85.00	50.00
(45)	Henley	200.00	85.00	50.00
(46)	Hetling	200.00	85.00	50.00
(47)	Hiester	200.00	85.00	50.00
(48a)	Hitt (Large pose.)	200.00	85.00	50.00
(48b)	Hitt (Small pose.)	200.00	85.00	50.00
(50)	Hoffman	200.00	85.00	50.00
(51)	Hogan	200.00	85.00	50.00
(52a)	Holland (Large pose.)	200.00	85.00	50.00
(52b)	Holland (Small pose.)	200.00	85.00	50.00
(53)	Hosp	200.00	85.00	50.00
(54a)	Howard (Large pose.)	200.00	85.00	50.00

		NM	EX	VG
(54b)	Howard (Small pose.)	200.00	85.00	50.00
(55)	Kane	200.00	85.00	50.00
(56)	Kerns	200.00	85.00	50.00
(57)	Kilroy	200.00	85.00	50.00
(58)	Knight	200.00	85.00	50.00
(59)	Koestner	200.00	85.00	50.00
(60)	Krueger	200.00	85.00	50.00
(61)	Kuhn	200.00	85.00	50.00
(62)	LaLonge	200.00	85.00	50.00
(63)	Lerchen	200.00	85.00	50.00
(64)	Leverenz	200.00	85.00	50.00
(65)	Lewis	200.00	85.00	50.00
(66)	Bill Lindsay	200.00	85.00	50.00
(67)	Lober	200.00	85.00	50.00
(68)	Madden	200.00	85.00	50.00
(69)	Maggert	200.00	85.00	50.00
(70)	Mahoney	200.00	85.00	50.00
(71)	Martinoni	200.00	85.00	50.00
(72)	McArdle	200.00	85.00	50.00
(73)	McCredie	200.00	85.00	50.00
(74)	McDonnell	200.00	85.00	50.00
(75a)	McKune (Large pose.)	200.00	85.00	50.00
(75b)	McKune (Middle size pose.)	200.00	85.00	50.00
(75c)	McKune (Small pose.)	200.00	85.00	50.00
(76)	Meikle	200.00	85.00	50.00
(77)	Melchior	200.00	85.00	50.00
(78)	Metzger	200.00	85.00	50.00
(79)	Miller	200.00	85.00	50.00
(80)	Mitze	200.00	85.00	50.00
(81)	Mohler	200.00	85.00	50.00
(82a)	Moore (Large pose.)	200.00	85.00	50.00
(82b)	Moore (Small pose.)	200.00	85.00	50.00
(83a)	Moskiman (Lettering size large.)	200.00	85.00	50.00
(83b)	Moskiman (Lettering size small.)	200.00	85.00	50.00
(84)	Murray	200.00	85.00	50.00
(85)	Naylor	200.00	85.00	50.00
(86)	Nebinger	200.00	85.00	50.00
(87)	Nourse	200.00	85.00	50.00
(88a)	Noyes (Large pose.)	200.00	85.00	50.00
(88b)	Noyes (Small pose.)	200.00	85.00	50.00
(89)	O'Rourke	200.00	85.00	50.00
(90)	Patterson (Oakland)	200.00	85.00	50.00
(91)	Patterson (Vernon)	200.00	85.00	50.00
(92)	Pearce	200.00	85.00	50.00
(93)	Peckinpaugh	250.00	100.00	60.00
(94)	Pernoll	200.00	85.00	50.00
(95)	Pfyl	200.00	85.00	50.00
(96)	Powell	200.00	85.00	50.00
(97a)	Raleigh (Large pose.)	200.00	85.00	50.00
(97b)	Raleigh (Small pose.)	200.00	85.00	50.00
(98)	Rapps	200.00	85.00	50.00
(99)	Rodgers	200.00	85.00	50.00
(100a)	Ryan (Portland, box around name and team.)	300.00	125.00	75.00
(100b)	Ryan (Portland, no box around name and team.)	200.00	85.00	50.00
(101)	Ryan (San Francisco)	200.00	85.00	50.00
(102)	Seaton	200.00	85.00	50.00
(103)	Shaw	200.00	85.00	50.00
(104)	Sheehan	200.00	85.00	50.00
(105)	Shinn	200.00	85.00	50.00
106a	Smith (Los Angeles, large pose.)	200.00	85.00	50.00
(106b)	Smith (Los Angeles, small pose.)	200.00	85.00	50.00
(107a)	Smith (San Francisco, large pose.)	200.00	85.00	50.00
(107b)	Smith (San Francisco, small pose.)	200.00	85.00	50.00
(108)	Steen	200.00	85.00	50.00
(109)	Stewart	200.00	85.00	50.00
(110a)	Stinson (Large pose.)	200.00	85.00	50.00
(110b)	Stinson (Small pose.)	200.00	85.00	50.00
(111)	Sutor	200.00	85.00	50.00
(112)	Tennant	200.00	85.00	50.00
(113)	Thomas	200.00	85.00	50.00
(114)	Thompson	200.00	85.00	50.00
(115)	Thornton	200.00	85.00	50.00
(116)	Tiedeman	200.00	85.00	50.00
(117)	Van Buren	200.00	85.00	50.00
(118)	Vitt	200.00	85.00	50.00
(119)	Wares	200.00	85.00	50.00
(120)	Buck Weaver	14,000	5,500	3,500
(121)	Wolverton	200.00	85.00	50.00
(122)	Zacher	200.00	85.00	50.00
(123)	Zamloch	200.00	85.00	50.00

1912 Zeenut Pacific Coast League

The second series of Zeenut cards measure about 2-1/8" x 4-1/16" and featured sepia-toned photographs on a brown background with no border. Most cards have blank backs, but some have been found with printing advising collectors to "Save Zeenut pictures for valuable premiums," or with one of two sizes of a Bardell logo. The checklist consists of 158 subjects, but more cards are still being discovered. Zeenut cards which were redeemed for prizes will exhibit a hole-punch cancellation, often heart-shaped.

		NM	EX	VG
	Common Player:	120.00	60.00	45.00
(1)	Abbott	120.00	60.00	45.00
(2)	Ables	120.00	60.00	45.00
(3)	Agnew	120.00	60.00	45.00
(4)	Altman	120.00	60.00	45.00
(5)	Frank Arellanes	120.00	60.00	45.00
(6)	Auer	120.00	60.00	45.00
(7)	Baker (Horizontal pose.)	120.00	60.00	45.00
(8)	Baker (Vertical pose.)	120.00	60.00	45.00
(9)	Bancroft	2,000	1,200	600.00
(10)	Baum	120.00	60.00	45.00
(11)	Bayless	120.00	60.00	45.00
(12)	Berger	120.00	60.00	45.00
(13)	Berry	120.00	60.00	45.00
(14)	Bohen	120.00	60.00	45.00
(15)	Boles	120.00	60.00	45.00
(16)	Bonner	120.00	60.00	45.00
(17)	Boone	120.00	60.00	45.00
(18)	Brackenridge	120.00	60.00	45.00
(19)	Brashear	120.00	60.00	45.00
(20)	Breen	120.00	60.00	45.00
(21)	Brooks (Los Angeles)	120.00	60.00	45.00
(22)	Brooks (Oakland)	120.00	60.00	45.00
(23)	Brown	120.00	60.00	45.00
(24)	Burch	120.00	60.00	45.00
(25)	Burrell	120.00	60.00	45.00
(26)	Butcher	120.00	60.00	45.00
(27)	Butler	120.00	60.00	45.00
(28)	Byram	120.00	60.00	45.00
(29)	Carlisle	120.00	60.00	45.00
(30)	Carson	120.00	60.00	45.00
(31)	Castleton	120.00	60.00	45.00
(32)	Chadbourne	120.00	60.00	45.00
(33)	Chech	120.00	60.00	45.00
(34)	Cheek	120.00	60.00	45.00
(35)	Christian	120.00	60.00	45.00
(36)	Cook	120.00	60.00	45.00
(37)	Core	120.00	60.00	45.00
(38)	Corhan	120.00	60.00	45.00
(39)	Coy	120.00	60.00	45.00
(40)	Daley	120.00	60.00	45.00
(41)	Delhi	120.00	60.00	45.00
(42)	Dillon	120.00	60.00	45.00
(43)	Doane	120.00	60.00	45.00
(44)	Driscoll	120.00	60.00	45.00
(45)	Durbin	120.00	60.00	45.00
(46)	Fanning	120.00	60.00	45.00
(47)	Felts	120.00	60.00	45.00
(48)	Fisher	120.00	60.00	45.00
(49)	Fitzgerald	120.00	60.00	45.00
(50)	Flater	120.00	60.00	45.00
(51)	Frick	120.00	60.00	45.00
(52)	Gaddy	120.00	60.00	45.00
(53)	Gedeon	120.00	60.00	45.00
(54)	Gilligan	120.00	60.00	45.00
(55)	Girot	120.00	60.00	45.00
(56)	Gray	120.00	60.00	45.00
(57)	Gregg	120.00	60.00	45.00
(58)	Gregory	120.00	60.00	45.00
(59)	Halla	120.00	60.00	45.00
(60)	Hamilton (Oakland)	120.00	60.00	45.00
(61)	Hamilton (San Francisco)	120.00	60.00	45.00
(62)	Harkness	120.00	60.00	45.00
(63)	Hartley	120.00	60.00	45.00
(64)	Heitmuller	120.00	60.00	45.00
(65)	Henley	120.00	60.00	45.00
(66)	Hetling (Glove open.)	120.00	60.00	45.00
(67)	Hetling (Glove closed.)	120.00	60.00	45.00
(68)	Hiester	120.00	60.00	45.00
(69)	Higginbottom	120.00	60.00	45.00
(70)	Hitt	120.00	60.00	45.00
(71)	Hoffman	120.00	60.00	45.00
(72)	Hogan	120.00	60.00	45.00
(73)	Hosp	120.00	60.00	45.00
(74)	Howard	120.00	60.00	45.00
(75)	Howley	120.00	60.00	45.00
(76)	Ireland	120.00	60.00	45.00
(77)	Jackson	120.00	60.00	45.00
(78)	Johnson	120.00	60.00	45.00
(79)	Kane	120.00	60.00	45.00
(80)	Killilay	120.00	60.00	45.00
(81)	Klawitter	120.00	60.00	45.00
(82)	Knight	120.00	60.00	45.00
(83)	Koestner ("P" visible.)	120.00	60.00	45.00
(84)	Koestner (No "P" visible.)	120.00	60.00	45.00
(85)	Kreitz	120.00	60.00	45.00
(86)	Krueger	120.00	60.00	45.00
(87)	LaLonge	120.00	60.00	45.00
(88)	Leard	120.00	60.00	45.00
(89)	Leverenz	120.00	60.00	45.00
(90)	Lewis	120.00	60.00	45.00
(91)	Bill Lindsay	120.00	60.00	45.00
(92)	Litschi	120.00	60.00	45.00
(93)	Lober	120.00	60.00	45.00
(94)	Madden	120.00	60.00	45.00
(95)	Mahoney	120.00	60.00	45.00
(96)	Malarkey	120.00	60.00	45.00
(97)	Martinoni	120.00	60.00	45.00
(98)	McArdle	120.00	60.00	45.00
(99)	McAvoy	120.00	60.00	45.00
(100)	McCorrey	120.00	60.00	45.00
(101)	McCredie	120.00	60.00	45.00
(102)	McDonald	120.00	60.00	45.00
(103)	McDowell	120.00	60.00	45.00
(104)	McIver	120.00	60.00	45.00
(105)	Meikle	120.00	60.00	45.00
(106)	Metzger	120.00	60.00	45.00
(107)	Miller (Sacramento)	120.00	60.00	45.00
(108)	Miller (San Francisco)	120.00	60.00	45.00

(109)	Mitze	120.00	60.00	45.00
(110)	Mohler	120.00	60.00	45.00
(111)	Moore	120.00	60.00	45.00
(112)	Mundorf (Batting)	120.00	60.00	45.00
(113)	Mundorf (Fielding)	120.00	60.00	45.00
(114)	Nagle	120.00	60.00	45.00
(115)	Noyes	120.00	60.00	45.00
(116)	O'Rourke	120.00	60.00	45.00
(117)	Olmstead	120.00	60.00	45.00
(118)	Orr	120.00	60.00	45.00
(119)	Page	120.00	60.00	45.00
(120)	Parkins	120.00	60.00	45.00
(121)	Patterson (Oakland)	120.00	60.00	45.00
(122)	Patterson (Vernon)	120.00	60.00	45.00
(123)	Pernol	120.00	60.00	45.00
(124)	Pope	120.00	60.00	45.00
(125)	Powell	120.00	60.00	45.00
(126)	Price	120.00	60.00	45.00
(127)	Raftery	120.00	60.00	45.00
(128)	Raleigh	120.00	60.00	45.00
(129)	Rapps ("P" visible.)	120.00	60.00	45.00
(130)	Rapps (No "P" visible.)	120.00	60.00	45.00
(131)	Reidy	120.00	60.00	45.00
(132)	Rodgers	120.00	60.00	45.00
(133)	Rohrer	120.00	60.00	45.00
(134)	Schmidt	120.00	60.00	45.00
(135)	Schwenk	120.00	60.00	45.00
(136)	Sharpe	120.00	60.00	45.00
(137)	Sheehan	120.00	60.00	45.00
(138)	Shinn	120.00	60.00	45.00
(139)	Slagle	120.00	60.00	45.00
(140)	Smith	120.00	60.00	45.00
(141)	Stewart	120.00	60.00	45.00
(142)	Stinson	120.00	60.00	45.00
(143)	Stone	120.00	60.00	45.00
(144)	Sullivan	120.00	60.00	45.00
(145)	Swain	120.00	60.00	45.00
(146)	Taylor	120.00	60.00	45.00
(147)	Temple	120.00	60.00	45.00
(148)	Tiedeman	120.00	60.00	45.00
(149)	Toner	120.00	60.00	45.00
(150)	Tozer	120.00	60.00	45.00
(151)	Van Buren	120.00	60.00	45.00
(152)	Wagner	120.00	60.00	45.00
(153)	Whalen	120.00	60.00	45.00
(154)	Williams (Sacramento)	120.00	60.00	45.00
(155)	Williams (San Francisco)	120.00	60.00	45.00
(156)	Joe Williams	120.00	60.00	45.00
(157)	Wuffli	120.00	60.00	45.00
(158)	Zacher	120.00	60.00	45.00
(159)	Zimmerman	120.00	60.00	45.00

1913 Zeenut Pacific Coast League

The 1913 Zeenut cards measure about 2" x 3-3/4" without the coupon, and feature black-and-white photos on a white, borderless background. To date, 146 different poses have been found. The backs are blank.

		NM	EX	VG
Common Player:		100.00	45.00	25.00
(1)	Abbott	100.00	45.00	25.00
(2)	Ables	100.00	45.00	25.00
(3)	Frank Arelanes (Arellanes)	100.00	45.00	25.00
(4)	Arlett	100.00	45.00	25.00
(5)	Baker	100.00	45.00	25.00
(6)	Baum	100.00	45.00	25.00
(7)	Bayless	100.00	45.00	25.00
(8)	Becker	100.00	45.00	25.00
(9)	Berry	100.00	45.00	25.00
(10)	Bliss	100.00	45.00	25.00
(11)	Boles	100.00	45.00	25.00
(12)	Brackenridge	100.00	45.00	25.00
(13)	Brashear	100.00	45.00	25.00
(14)	Brooks	100.00	45.00	25.00
(15)	Byrnes	100.00	45.00	25.00
(16)	Cadreau	100.00	45.00	25.00
(17)	Carlisle	100.00	45.00	25.00
(18)	Carson	100.00	45.00	25.00
(19)	Cartwright	100.00	45.00	25.00
(20)	Chadbourne	100.00	45.00	25.00
(21)	Charles	100.00	45.00	25.00
(22)	Cheek	100.00	45.00	25.00
(23)	Christian	100.00	45.00	25.00
(24)	Clarke	100.00	45.00	25.00
(25)	Clemons	100.00	45.00	25.00
(26)	Cook	100.00	45.00	25.00
(27)	Corhan	100.00	45.00	25.00
(28)	Coy	100.00	45.00	25.00
(29)	Crabb	100.00	45.00	25.00
(30)	Crisp	100.00	45.00	25.00
(31)	Derrick	100.00	45.00	25.00

(32)	DeCanniere	100.00	45.00	25.00
(33)	Dillon	100.00	45.00	25.00
(34)	Doane	100.00	45.00	25.00
(35)	Douglass	100.00	45.00	25.00
(36)	Downs	100.00	45.00	25.00
(37)	Driscoll	100.00	45.00	25.00
(38)	Drucke	100.00	45.00	25.00
(39)	Elliott	100.00	45.00	25.00
(40)	Ellis	100.00	45.00	25.00
(41)	Fanning	100.00	45.00	25.00
(42)	Fisher	100.00	45.00	25.00
(43)	Fitzgerald	100.00	45.00	25.00
(44)	Gardner	100.00	45.00	25.00
(45)	Gill	100.00	45.00	25.00
(46)	Goodwin	100.00	45.00	25.00
(47a)	Gregory (Large pose.)	100.00	45.00	25.00
(47b)	Gregory (Small pose.)	100.00	45.00	25.00
(48)	Grey	100.00	45.00	25.00
(49)	Guest	100.00	45.00	25.00
(50)	Hagerman	100.00	45.00	25.00
(51)	Halla	100.00	45.00	25.00
(52)	Hallinan	100.00	45.00	25.00
(53)	Harry Heilmann	6,000	4,000	2,000
(54)	Henley	100.00	45.00	25.00
(55)	Hetling	100.00	45.00	25.00
(56)	Higginbotham	100.00	45.00	25.00
(57)	Hitt	100.00	45.00	25.00
(58)	Hoffman	100.00	45.00	25.00
(59)	Hogan (San Francisco)	100.00	45.00	25.00
(60)	Hogan (Vernon)	100.00	45.00	25.00
(61)	Hosp	100.00	45.00	25.00
(62)	Howard (Los Angeles)	100.00	45.00	25.00
(63)	Howard (San Francisco)	100.00	45.00	25.00
(64)	Hughes	100.00	45.00	25.00
(65)	Jackson	100.00	45.00	25.00
(66)	James	100.00	45.00	25.00
(67)	Johnson	100.00	45.00	25.00
(68)	Johnston	100.00	45.00	25.00
(69)	Kane	100.00	45.00	25.00
(70)	Kaylor	100.00	45.00	25.00
(71)	Kenworthy	100.00	45.00	25.00
(72)	Killilay	100.00	45.00	25.00
(73)	Klawitter	100.00	45.00	25.00
(74)	Koestner	100.00	45.00	25.00
(75)	Kores	100.00	45.00	25.00
(76)	Krapp	100.00	45.00	25.00
(77)	Kreitz	100.00	45.00	25.00
(78)	Krause	100.00	45.00	25.00
(79)	Krueger	100.00	45.00	25.00
(80)	Leard	100.00	45.00	25.00
(81)	Leifield	100.00	45.00	25.00
(82)	Lewis	100.00	45.00	25.00
(83)	Bill Lindsay	100.00	45.00	25.00
(84)	Litschi	100.00	45.00	25.00
(85)	Lively	100.00	45.00	25.00
(86)	Lober	100.00	45.00	25.00
(87)	Lohman	100.00	45.00	25.00
(88)	Maggart	100.00	45.00	25.00
(89)	Malarky	100.00	45.00	25.00
(90)	McArdle	100.00	45.00	25.00
(91)	McCarl	100.00	45.00	25.00
(92)	McCormick	100.00	45.00	25.00
(93)	McCorry	100.00	45.00	25.00
(94)	McCredie	100.00	45.00	25.00
(95)	McDonnell	100.00	45.00	25.00
(96)	Meloan	100.00	45.00	25.00
(97)	Metzger	100.00	45.00	25.00
(98)	Miller	100.00	45.00	25.00
(99)	Mitze	100.00	45.00	25.00
(100)	Moore	100.00	45.00	25.00
(101)	Moran	100.00	45.00	25.00
(102)	Mundorf	100.00	45.00	25.00
(103)	Munsell	100.00	45.00	25.00
(104)	Ness	100.00	45.00	25.00
(105)	O'Rourke	100.00	45.00	25.00
(106)	Overall	100.00	45.00	25.00
(107)	Page	100.00	45.00	25.00
(108)	Parkin	100.00	45.00	25.00
(109)	Patterson	100.00	45.00	25.00
(110)	Pearce	100.00	45.00	25.00
(111)	Pernoll	100.00	45.00	25.00
(112)	Perritt	100.00	45.00	25.00
(113)	Pope	100.00	45.00	25.00
(114)	Pruitt	100.00	45.00	25.00
(115)	Raleigh	100.00	45.00	25.00
(116)	Reitmyer	100.00	45.00	25.00
(117)	Riordan	100.00	45.00	25.00
(118)	Rodgers	100.00	45.00	25.00
(119)	Rogers	100.00	45.00	25.00
(120)	Rohrer	100.00	45.00	25.00
(121)	Ryan	100.00	45.00	25.00
(122)	Schaller	100.00	45.00	25.00
(123)	Schirm	100.00	45.00	25.00
(124)	Schmidt	100.00	45.00	25.00
(125)	Schulz	100.00	45.00	25.00
(126)	Sepulveda	100.00	45.00	25.00
(127)	Shinn	100.00	45.00	25.00
(128)	Spenger	100.00	45.00	25.00
(129)	Stanley	100.00	45.00	25.00
(130)	Stanridge	100.00	45.00	25.00
(131)	Stark	100.00	45.00	25.00
(132)	Sterritt	100.00	45.00	25.00
(133)	Stroud	100.00	45.00	25.00
(134)	Tennant	100.00	45.00	25.00
(135)	Thomas	100.00	45.00	25.00
(136)	Todd	100.00	45.00	25.00
(137)	Tonneman	100.00	45.00	25.00
(138)	Tozer	100.00	45.00	25.00
(139)	Van Buren	100.00	45.00	25.00
(140)	Wagner	100.00	45.00	25.00
(141)	West	100.00	45.00	25.00
(142)	Williams	100.00	45.00	25.00
(143)	Wolverton	100.00	45.00	25.00
(144)	Wotell	100.00	45.00	25.00
(145)	Wuffli	100.00	45.00	25.00
(146)	Young	100.00	45.00	25.00
(147)	Zacher	100.00	45.00	25.00
(148)	Zimmerman	100.00	45.00	25.00

1914 Zeenut Pacific Coast League

The 1914 Zeenut cards measure about 2" x 4-1/16" without the coupon, and feature black-and-white photos on a gray, borderless background. To date, 146 different poses have been found. The backs are blank.

		NM	EX	VG
Common Player:		75.00	35.00	17.00
(1)	Ables	75.00	35.00	17.00
(2)	Abstein	75.00	35.00	17.00
(3)	Alexander	75.00	35.00	17.00
(4)	Arbogast	75.00	35.00	17.00
(5)	Arlett	75.00	35.00	17.00
(6)	Frank Arrelanes (Arellanes)	75.00	35.00	17.00
(7)	Bancroft	1,000	700.00	300.00
(8)	Barham	75.00	35.00	17.00
(9)	Barrenkamp	75.00	35.00	17.00
(10)	Barton	75.00	35.00	17.00
(11)	Baum	75.00	35.00	17.00
(12)	Bayless	75.00	35.00	17.00
(13a)	Bliss (Large pose.)	75.00	35.00	17.00
(13b)	Bliss (Small pose.)	75.00	35.00	17.00
(14)	Boles	75.00	35.00	17.00
(15)	Borton	75.00	35.00	17.00
(16)	Brashear	75.00	35.00	17.00
(17)	Brenegan	75.00	35.00	17.00
(18)	Brooks	75.00	35.00	17.00
(19)	Brown	75.00	35.00	17.00
(20)	Butler	75.00	35.00	17.00
(21)	Jacinto Calvo	900.00	600.00	250.00
(22)	Carlisle	75.00	35.00	17.00
(23)	Cartwright	75.00	35.00	17.00
(24)	Charles	75.00	35.00	17.00
(25)	Chech	75.00	35.00	17.00
(26)	Christian	75.00	35.00	17.00
(27)	Clarke	75.00	35.00	17.00
(28)	Colligan	75.00	35.00	17.00
(29)	Cook	75.00	35.00	17.00
(31)	Coy	75.00	35.00	17.00
(32)	Crabb	75.00	35.00	17.00
(33)	Davis	75.00	35.00	17.00
(34)	Derrick	75.00	35.00	17.00
(35)	Devlin	75.00	35.00	17.00
(36)	DeCannier	75.00	35.00	17.00
(37)	Dillon	75.00	35.00	17.00
(38)	Doane	75.00	35.00	17.00
(39)	Downs	75.00	35.00	17.00
(40)	Ehmke	75.00	35.00	17.00
(41)	Ellis	75.00	35.00	17.00
(42)	Evans	75.00	35.00	17.00
(43)	Fanning	75.00	35.00	17.00
(44)	Fisher	75.00	35.00	17.00
(45)	Fitzgerald	75.00	35.00	17.00
(46)	Fleharty	75.00	35.00	17.00
(47)	Frambach	75.00	35.00	17.00
(48)	Gardner	75.00	35.00	17.00
(49)	Gedeon	75.00	35.00	17.00
(50)	Geyer	75.00	35.00	17.00
(51)	Gianini	75.00	35.00	17.00
(52)	Gregory	75.00	35.00	17.00
(53)	Guest	75.00	35.00	17.00
(54)	Hallinan	75.00	35.00	17.00
(55)	Hannah	75.00	35.00	17.00
(56)	Harkness (Batting)	75.00	35.00	17.00
(57)	Haworth (Batting)	75.00	35.00	17.00
(58)	Haworth (Catching)	75.00	35.00	17.00
(59)	Henderson	75.00	35.00	17.00
(60)	Henley	75.00	35.00	17.00
(61)	Hern	75.00	35.00	17.00
(62)	Hettling	75.00	35.00	17.00
(63)	Higginbotham	75.00	35.00	17.00
(64)	Hitt	75.00	35.00	17.00
(65)	Hogan	75.00	35.00	17.00
(66a)	Hosp (Large pose.)	75.00	35.00	17.00
(66b)	Hosp (Small pose.)	75.00	35.00	17.00
(67)	Howard	75.00	35.00	17.00
(68)	Hughes (Los Angeles)	75.00	35.00	17.00
(69)	Hughes (San Francisco)	75.00	35.00	17.00
(70)	Johnson	75.00	35.00	17.00
(71)	Kane	75.00	35.00	17.00
(72)	Kaylor	75.00	35.00	17.00
(73)	Killilay	75.00	35.00	17.00
(74)	Klawitter	75.00	35.00	17.00
(75)	Klepfler	75.00	35.00	17.00
(76)	Kores	75.00	35.00	17.00
(77)	Kramer	75.00	35.00	17.00
(78)	Krause	75.00	35.00	17.00
(79a)	Leard (Large pose.)	75.00	35.00	17.00
(79b)	Leard (Small pose.)	75.00	35.00	17.00
(80)	Liefeld	75.00	35.00	17.00
(81)	Litschi	75.00	35.00	17.00

		NM	EX	VG
(82)	Lober	75.00	35.00	17.00
(83)	Loomis	75.00	35.00	17.00
(84)	Love	75.00	35.00	17.00
(85)	Lynn	75.00	35.00	17.00
(86)	Maggart	75.00	35.00	17.00
(87)	Malarkey	75.00	35.00	17.00
(88)	Martinoni	75.00	35.00	17.00
(89)	McArdle	75.00	35.00	17.00
(90)	McCredie	75.00	35.00	17.00
(91)	McDonald	75.00	35.00	17.00
(92)	Meek	75.00	35.00	17.00
(93)	Meloan	75.00	35.00	17.00
(94)	Menges	75.00	35.00	17.00
(95)	Metzger	75.00	35.00	17.00
(96)	Middleton	75.00	35.00	17.00
(97)	Mitze	75.00	35.00	17.00
(98)	Mohler	75.00	35.00	17.00
(99)	Moore	75.00	35.00	17.00
(100)	Moran	75.00	35.00	17.00
(101)	Mundorf	75.00	35.00	17.00
(102)	Murphy	75.00	35.00	17.00
(103)	Musser	75.00	35.00	17.00
(104)	Ness	75.00	35.00	17.00
(105)	O'Leary	75.00	35.00	17.00
(106)	Orr	75.00	35.00	17.00
(107)	Page	75.00	35.00	17.00
(108)	Pape	75.00	35.00	17.00
(109)	Parkin	75.00	35.00	17.00
(110a)	Peet (Large pose.)	75.00	35.00	17.00
(110b)	Peet (Small pose.)	75.00	35.00	17.00
(111)	Perkins	75.00	35.00	17.00
(112)	Pernoll	75.00	35.00	17.00
(113)	Perritt	75.00	35.00	17.00
(114)	Powell	75.00	35.00	17.00
(115)	Prough	75.00	35.00	17.00
(116)	Pruiett	75.00	35.00	17.00
(117)	Quinlan	75.00	35.00	17.00
(118a)	Raney (Incorrect spelling.)	75.00	35.00	17.00
(118b)	Ramey (Correct spelling.)	75.00	35.00	17.00
(119)	Rieger	75.00	35.00	17.00
(120)	Rodgers	75.00	35.00	17.00
(121)	Rogers	75.00	35.00	17.00
(122)	Rohrer	75.00	35.00	17.00
(123)	Ryan	75.00	35.00	17.00
(124)	Ryan	75.00	35.00	17.00
(125)	Sawyer	75.00	35.00	17.00
(126)	Schaller	75.00	35.00	17.00
(127)	Schmidt	75.00	35.00	17.00
(128)	Sepulveda	75.00	35.00	17.00
(129)	Shinn	75.00	35.00	17.00
(130)	Slagle	75.00	35.00	17.00
(131)	Speas	75.00	35.00	17.00
(132)	Stanridge	75.00	35.00	17.00
(133)	Stroud	75.00	35.00	17.00
(134)	Tennant	75.00	35.00	17.00
(135)	Tobin	75.00	35.00	17.00
(136)	Tozer	75.00	35.00	17.00
(137)	Van Buren	75.00	35.00	17.00
(138)	West	75.00	35.00	17.00
(139)	White	75.00	35.00	17.00
(140)	Wolter	75.00	35.00	17.00
(141)	Wolverton	75.00	35.00	17.00
(142)	Yantz	75.00	35.00	17.00
(143)	Young	75.00	35.00	17.00
(144)	Zacher	75.00	35.00	17.00
(145)	Zumwalt	75.00	35.00	17.00

1915 Zeenut Pacific Coast League

The 1915 Zeenut cards are dated on the front, making identification very easy. They measure about 2" x 3-3/4" without the coupon and feature a black-and-white photo on a light background. To date 141 different cards are known to exist. This year is among the toughest of all Zeenuts to find.

		NM	EX	VG
Common Player:		100.00	45.00	25.00
With Coupon:		900.00	400.00	240.00
(1)	Ables	100.00	45.00	25.00
(2)	Abstein	100.00	45.00	25.00
(3)	Alcock	100.00	45.00	25.00
(4)	Arbogast	100.00	45.00	25.00
(5)	Baerwald	100.00	45.00	25.00
(6)	Barbour	100.00	45.00	25.00
(7)	Bates	100.00	45.00	25.00
(8)	Baum	100.00	45.00	25.00
(9)	Bayless	100.00	45.00	25.00
(10)	Beatty	100.00	45.00	25.00
(11)	Beer	100.00	45.00	25.00
(12)	Benham	100.00	45.00	25.00
(13)	Berger	100.00	45.00	25.00
(14)	Beumiller	100.00	45.00	25.00
(15)	Blankenship	100.00	45.00	25.00
(16)	Block	100.00	45.00	25.00
(17)	Bodie	100.00	45.00	25.00
(18)	Boles	100.00	45.00	25.00
(19)	Boyd	100.00	45.00	25.00
(20)	Bromley	100.00	45.00	25.00
(21)	Brown	100.00	45.00	25.00
(22)	Burns	300.00	135.00	75.00
(23)	Carlisle	100.00	45.00	25.00
(24)	Carrisch	100.00	45.00	25.00
(25)	Charles	100.00	45.00	25.00
(26)	Chech	100.00	45.00	25.00
(27)	Christian	100.00	45.00	25.00
(28)	Clarke	100.00	45.00	25.00
(29)	Couch	100.00	45.00	25.00
(30)	Stan Covaleski (Coveleski)	2,000	1,200	600.00
(31)	Daniels	100.00	45.00	25.00
(32)	Davis	100.00	45.00	25.00
(33)	DeCanniere	100.00	45.00	25.00
(34)	Dent	100.00	45.00	25.00
(35)	Derrick	100.00	45.00	25.00
(36)	Dillon	100.00	45.00	25.00
(37)	Doane	100.00	45.00	25.00
(38)	Downs	100.00	45.00	25.00
(39)	Elliott	100.00	45.00	25.00
(40)	F. Elliott	100.00	45.00	25.00
(41)	Ellis	100.00	45.00	25.00
(42)	Evans	100.00	45.00	25.00
(43)	Fanning	100.00	45.00	25.00
(44)	Faye	100.00	45.00	25.00
(45)	Fisher	100.00	45.00	25.00
(46)	Fittery	100.00	45.00	25.00
(47)	Fitzgerald	100.00	45.00	25.00
(48)	Fromme	100.00	45.00	25.00
(49)	Gardiner	100.00	45.00	25.00
(50)	Gedeon	100.00	45.00	25.00
(51)	Gleischmann	100.00	45.00	25.00
(52)	Gregory	100.00	45.00	25.00
(53)	Guest	100.00	45.00	25.00
(54)	Hall	100.00	45.00	25.00
(55)	Halla	100.00	45.00	25.00
(56)	Hallinan	100.00	45.00	25.00
(57)	Hannah	100.00	45.00	25.00
(58)	Harper	100.00	45.00	25.00
(59)	Harry Heilmann	1,500	800.00	400.00
(60)	Henley	100.00	45.00	25.00
(61)	Hetling	100.00	45.00	25.00
(62)	Higginbotham	100.00	45.00	25.00
(63)	Hilliard	100.00	45.00	25.00
(64)	Hitt (Winding up.)	100.00	45.00	25.00
(65)	Hitt (Throwing)	100.00	45.00	25.00
(66)	Hogan	100.00	45.00	25.00
(67)	Hosp	100.00	45.00	25.00
(68)	Howard	100.00	45.00	25.00
(69)	Hughes	100.00	45.00	25.00
(70)	Johnson	100.00	45.00	25.00
(71)	Jones	100.00	45.00	25.00
(72)	Kahler	100.00	45.00	25.00
(73)	Kane	100.00	45.00	25.00
(74)	Karr	100.00	45.00	25.00
(75)	Killilay	100.00	45.00	25.00
(76)	Klawitter	100.00	45.00	25.00
(77)	Koerner	100.00	45.00	25.00
(78)	Krause	100.00	45.00	25.00
(79)	Kuhn	100.00	45.00	25.00
(80)	LaRoy	100.00	45.00	25.00
(81)	Leard	100.00	45.00	25.00
(82)	Bill Lindsay	100.00	45.00	25.00
(83)	Litschi	100.00	45.00	25.00
(84)	Lober	100.00	45.00	25.00
(85)	Love	100.00	45.00	25.00
(86)	Lush	100.00	45.00	25.00
(87)	Maggart	100.00	45.00	25.00
(88)	Malarkey	100.00	45.00	25.00
(89)	Manda	100.00	45.00	25.00
(90)	Marcan	100.00	45.00	25.00
(91)	Martinoni	100.00	45.00	25.00
(92)	McAvoy	100.00	45.00	25.00
(93)	McCredie	100.00	45.00	25.00
(94)	McDonell	100.00	45.00	25.00
(95)	Fred McMullen (McMullin)	7,500	3,500	2,000
(96)	Meek	100.00	45.00	25.00
(97)	Meloan	100.00	45.00	25.00
(98)	Metzger	100.00	45.00	25.00
(99)	Middleton	100.00	45.00	25.00
(100)	Mitchell	100.00	45.00	25.00
(101)	Mitze	100.00	45.00	25.00
(102)	Morgan	100.00	45.00	25.00
(103)	Mundorff	100.00	45.00	25.00
(104)	Murphy	100.00	45.00	25.00
(105)	Ness	100.00	45.00	25.00
(106)	Nutt	100.00	45.00	25.00
(107)	Orr	100.00	45.00	25.00
(108)	Pernoll	100.00	45.00	25.00
(109)	Perritt	100.00	45.00	25.00
(110)	Piercey	100.00	45.00	25.00
(111)	Price	100.00	45.00	25.00
(112)	Prough	100.00	45.00	25.00
(113)	Pruitt	100.00	45.00	25.00
(114)	Purtell	100.00	45.00	25.00
(115)	Reed	100.00	45.00	25.00
(116)	Reisigl	100.00	45.00	25.00
(117)	Remneas	100.00	45.00	25.00
(118)	Swede Risberg	5,500	2,500	1,500
(119)	Rohrer	100.00	45.00	25.00
(120)	Russell	100.00	45.00	25.00
(121)	Ryan (Los Angeles)	100.00	45.00	25.00
(122)	Ryan	100.00	45.00	25.00
(123)	Schaller	100.00	45.00	25.00
(124)	Schmidt	100.00	45.00	25.00
(125)	Scoggins	100.00	45.00	25.00
(126)	Sepulveda	100.00	45.00	25.00
(127)	Shinn	100.00	45.00	25.00
(128)	Smith	100.00	45.00	25.00
(129)	Speas	100.00	45.00	25.00
(130)	Spencer	100.00	45.00	25.00
(132)	Tennant	100.00	45.00	25.00
(133)	Terry	100.00	45.00	25.00
(134)	Tobin	100.00	45.00	25.00
(135)	West	100.00	45.00	25.00
(136)	White	100.00	45.00	25.00
(137)	Claude Williams	5,500	2,500	1,500
(138)	Johnny Williams	250.00	110.00	65.00
(139)	Wolter	100.00	45.00	25.00
(140)	Wolverton	100.00	45.00	25.00
(141)	Zacher	100.00	45.00	25.00

1916 Zeenut Pacific Coast League

The 1916 Zeenuts measure about 2" x 3-3/4" without the coupon and are dated on the front (some cards were misdated 1915 however). The card fronts feature black-and-white photos on a blue background. There are 144 known subjects. The 1916 series is among the more difficult.

		NM	EX	VG
Common Player:		75.00	30.00	17.50
(1)	Autrey	75.00	30.00	17.50
(2)	Barbeau	75.00	30.00	17.50
(3)	Barry	75.00	30.00	17.50
(4)	Bassler	75.00	30.00	17.50
(5)	Bates	75.00	30.00	17.50
(6)	Baum	75.00	30.00	17.50
(7)	Bayless	75.00	30.00	17.50
(8)	Beer	75.00	30.00	17.50
(9)	Berg	75.00	30.00	17.50
(10)	Berger	75.00	30.00	17.50
(11)	Blankenship	75.00	30.00	17.50
(12)	Block	75.00	30.00	17.50
(13)	Bodie	150.00	80.00	40.00
(14)	Bohne	350.00	200.00	150.00
(15)	Boles	75.00	30.00	17.50
(16)	Boyd	75.00	30.00	17.50
(17)	Brief	75.00	30.00	17.50
(18)	Brooks	75.00	30.00	17.50
(19)	Brown	75.00	30.00	17.50
(20)	Butler	75.00	30.00	17.50
(21)	Callahan	75.00	30.00	17.50
(22)	Carrisch	75.00	30.00	17.50
(23)	Frank Chance	2,000	1,200	600.00
(24)	Jimmy Claxton	15,000	9,500	7,000
(25)	Coffey	75.00	30.00	17.50
(26)	Cook	75.00	30.00	17.50
(27)	Corbett	75.00	30.00	17.50
(28)	Couch	75.00	30.00	17.50
(29)	Crandall	75.00	30.00	17.50
(30)	Dalton	75.00	30.00	17.50
(31)	Davis	75.00	30.00	17.50
(32)	Derrick	75.00	30.00	17.50
(33)	Doane	75.00	30.00	17.50
(34)	Downs	75.00	30.00	17.50
(35)	Dugan	75.00	30.00	17.50
(36)	Eldred	75.00	30.00	17.50
(37)	F. Elliott	75.00	30.00	17.50
(38)	H. Elliott	75.00	30.00	17.50
(39)	Ellis	75.00	30.00	17.50
(40)	Erickson	75.00	30.00	17.50
(41)	Fanning	75.00	30.00	17.50
(42)	Fisher	75.00	30.00	17.50
(43)	Fittery	75.00	30.00	17.50
(44)	Fitzgerald	75.00	30.00	17.50
(45)	Fromme	75.00	30.00	17.50
(46)	Galloway	75.00	30.00	17.50
(47)	Gardner	75.00	30.00	17.50
(48)	Gay	75.00	30.00	17.50
(49)	Gleischmann	75.00	30.00	17.50
(50)	Griffith	75.00	30.00	17.50
(51)	Griggs	75.00	30.00	17.50
(52)	Guisto	75.00	30.00	17.50
(53)	Hagerman	75.00	30.00	17.50
(54)	Hall	75.00	30.00	17.50
(55)	Hallinan	75.00	30.00	17.50
(56)	Hannah	75.00	30.00	17.50
(57)	Harstadt	75.00	30.00	17.50
(58)	Haworth	75.00	30.00	17.50
(59)	Hess	75.00	30.00	17.50
(60)	Higginbotham	75.00	30.00	17.50
(61)	Hitt	75.00	30.00	17.50
(62)	Hogg	75.00	30.00	17.50
(63)	Hollocher	75.00	30.00	17.50
(64)	Horstman	75.00	30.00	17.50
(65)	Houck	75.00	30.00	17.50
(66)	Howard	75.00	30.00	17.50
(67)	Hughes	75.00	30.00	17.50
(68)	E. Johnston	75.00	30.00	17.50
(69)	G. Johnston	75.00	30.00	17.50
(70)	Jones	75.00	30.00	17.50
(71)	Kahler	75.00	30.00	17.50
(72)	Kane	75.00	30.00	17.50
(73)	Kelly	75.00	30.00	17.50

		NM	EX	VG
(74)	Kenworthy	75.00	30.00	17.50
(75)	Klawitter	75.00	30.00	17.50
(76)	Klein	75.00	30.00	17.50
(77)	Koerner	75.00	30.00	17.50
(78)	Krause	75.00	30.00	17.50
(79)	Kuhn	75.00	30.00	17.50
(80)	Lane	75.00	30.00	17.50
(81)	Larsen	75.00	30.00	17.50
(82)	Lush	75.00	30.00	17.50
(83)	Machold	75.00	30.00	17.50
(84)	Maggert	75.00	30.00	17.50
(85)	Manser	75.00	30.00	17.50
(86)	Martin	75.00	30.00	17.50
(87)	Mattick	75.00	30.00	17.50
(88)	McCredie	75.00	30.00	17.50
(89)	McGaffigan	75.00	30.00	17.50
(90)	McLarry	75.00	30.00	17.50
(91)	Menges	75.00	30.00	17.50
(92)	Middleton	75.00	30.00	17.50
(93)	Mitchell	75.00	30.00	17.50
(94)	Mitze	75.00	30.00	17.50
(95)	Munsell	75.00	30.00	17.50
(96)	Murphy	75.00	30.00	17.50
(97)	Nixon	75.00	30.00	17.50
(98)	Noyes	75.00	30.00	17.50
(99)	Nutt	75.00	30.00	17.50
(100)	O'Brien	75.00	30.00	17.50
(101)	Oldham	75.00	30.00	17.50
(102)	Orr	75.00	30.00	17.50
(103)	Patterson	75.00	30.00	17.50
(104)	Perritt	75.00	30.00	17.50
(105)	Prough	75.00	30.00	17.50
(106)	Prueitt	75.00	30.00	17.50
(107)	Quinlan	75.00	30.00	17.50
(108)	Quinn (Portland)	75.00	30.00	17.50
(109)	Quinn (Vernon)	75.00	30.00	17.50
(110)	Rader	75.00	30.00	17.50
(111)	Randall	75.00	30.00	17.50
(112)	Rath	75.00	30.00	17.50
(113)	Reisegl	75.00	30.00	17.50
(114)	Reuther (Ruether)	75.00	30.00	17.50
(115)	Swede Risberg	5,000	2,000	1,250
(116)	Roche	75.00	30.00	17.50
(117)	Ryan	75.00	30.00	17.50
(118)	Ryan	75.00	30.00	17.50
(119)	Scoggins	75.00	30.00	17.50
(120)	Sepulveda	75.00	30.00	17.50
(121)	Schaller	75.00	30.00	17.50
(122)	Sheehan	75.00	30.00	17.50
(123)	Shinn	75.00	30.00	17.50
(124)	Smith	75.00	30.00	17.50
(125)	Sothoron	75.00	30.00	17.50
(126)	Southworth	75.00	30.00	17.50
(127)	Speas	75.00	30.00	17.50
(128)	Spencer	75.00	30.00	17.50
(129)	Standridge	75.00	30.00	17.50
(130)	Steen	75.00	30.00	17.50
(131)	Stumpf	75.00	30.00	17.50
(132)	Vann	75.00	30.00	17.50
(133)	Vaughn	75.00	30.00	17.50
(134)	Ward	75.00	30.00	17.50
(135)	Whalling	75.00	30.00	17.50
(136)	Wilie	75.00	30.00	17.50
(137)	Williams	75.00	30.00	17.50
(138)	Wolverton	75.00	30.00	17.50
(139)	Wuffli	75.00	30.00	17.50
(140)	Zabel	75.00	30.00	17.50
(141)	Zacher	75.00	30.00	17.50
(142)	Zimmerman	75.00	30.00	17.50

1917 Zeenut Pacific Coast League

The 1917 Zeenuts measure about 1-3/4" x 3-3/4" and feature black-and-white photos on a light background. They are dated on the front and have blank backs. An advertising poster has been found listing 119 players (two pose variations brings the total to 121), but to date, six players on the list have not been found.

		NM	EX	VG
Common Player:		70.00	35.00	20.00
(1)	Arlett	70.00	35.00	20.00
(2)	Frank Arrelanes (Arellanes)	70.00	35.00	20.00
(3)	Baker (Catching)	70.00	35.00	20.00
(4)	Baker (Throwing)	70.00	35.00	20.00
(5)	Baldwin	70.00	35.00	20.00
(6)	Bassler	70.00	35.00	20.00
(7)	Baum	70.00	35.00	20.00
(8)	Beer	70.00	35.00	20.00
(9)	Bernhard	70.00	35.00	20.00
(10)	Bliss	70.00	35.00	20.00

		NM	EX	VG
(11)	Boles	70.00	35.00	20.00
(12)	Brenton	70.00	35.00	20.00
(13)	Brief	70.00	35.00	20.00
(14)	Brown	70.00	35.00	20.00
(15)	Burns	200.00	150.00	75.00
(16)	Callahan	70.00	35.00	20.00
(17)	Callan	70.00	35.00	20.00
(18)	Jacinto Calvo	700.00	400.00	200.00
(19)	Chadbourne	70.00	35.00	20.00
(20)	Frank Chance	1,800	1,000	500.00
(21)	Coltrin	70.00	35.00	20.00
(22)	Connifer	70.00	35.00	20.00
(23)	Corhan	70.00	35.00	20.00
(24)	Crandall (Los Angeles)	70.00	35.00	20.00
(25)	Crandall (Salt Lake)	70.00	35.00	20.00
(26)	Cress	70.00	35.00	20.00
(27)	Davis	70.00	35.00	20.00
(28)	DeCanniere	70.00	35.00	20.00
(29)	Doane	70.00	35.00	20.00
(30)	Dougan	70.00	35.00	20.00
(31)	Dougherty	70.00	35.00	20.00
(32)	Downs	70.00	35.00	20.00
(33)	Dubuc	70.00	35.00	20.00
(34)	Ellis	70.00	35.00	20.00
(35)	Erickson	70.00	35.00	20.00
(36)	Evans	70.00	35.00	20.00
(37)	Farmer	70.00	35.00	20.00
(38)	Fincher	70.00	35.00	20.00
(39)	Fisher	70.00	35.00	20.00
(40)	Fitzgerald	70.00	35.00	20.00
(41)	Fournier	70.00	35.00	20.00
(42)	Fromme	70.00	35.00	20.00
(43)	Galloway	70.00	35.00	20.00
(44)	Gislason	70.00	35.00	20.00
(45)	Goodbred	70.00	35.00	20.00
(46)	Griggs	70.00	35.00	20.00
(47)	Groehling	70.00	35.00	20.00
(48)	Hall (Los Angeles)	70.00	35.00	20.00
(49)	Hall (San Francisco)	70.00	35.00	20.00
(50)	Hannah	70.00	35.00	20.00
(51)	Harstad	70.00	35.00	20.00
(52)	Helfrich	70.00	35.00	20.00
(53)	Hess	70.00	35.00	20.00
(54)	Hitt	70.00	35.00	20.00
(55)	Hoff	70.00	35.00	20.00
(56)	Hollacher	70.00	35.00	20.00
(57)	Hollywood	70.00	35.00	20.00
(58)	Houck	70.00	35.00	20.00
(59)	Howard	70.00	35.00	20.00
(60)	Hughes	70.00	35.00	20.00
(61)	Johnson	70.00	35.00	20.00
(62)	Kilhullen	70.00	35.00	20.00
(63)	Killiffer (Killefer)	70.00	35.00	20.00
(64)	Koerner	70.00	35.00	20.00
(65)	Krause	70.00	35.00	20.00
(66)	Lane	70.00	35.00	20.00
(67)	Lapan	70.00	35.00	20.00
(68)	Leake	70.00	35.00	20.00
(69)	Lee	70.00	35.00	20.00
(70)	Leverenz	70.00	35.00	20.00
(71)	Maggert	70.00	35.00	20.00
(72)	Maisel	70.00	35.00	20.00
(73)	Mattick	70.00	35.00	20.00
(74)	McCreedie	70.00	35.00	20.00
(75)	McLarry	70.00	35.00	20.00
(76)	Mensor	500.00	250.00	150.00
(77)	Emil "Irish" Meusel	200.00	100.00	70.00
(78)	Middleton	70.00	35.00	20.00
(79)	Miller (Batting)	70.00	35.00	20.00
(80)	Miller (Throwing)	70.00	35.00	20.00
(81)	Mitchell	70.00	35.00	20.00
(82)	Mitze	70.00	35.00	20.00
(83)	Murphy	70.00	35.00	20.00
(84)	Murray	70.00	35.00	20.00
(85)	O'Brien	70.00	35.00	20.00
(86)	O'Mara	70.00	35.00	20.00
(87)	Oldham	70.00	35.00	20.00
(88)	Orr	70.00	35.00	20.00
(89)	Penelli	70.00	35.00	20.00
(90)	Penner	70.00	35.00	20.00
(91)	Pick	70.00	35.00	20.00
(92)	Prough	70.00	35.00	20.00
(93)	Pruiett	70.00	35.00	20.00
(94)	Quinlan	70.00	35.00	20.00
(95)	Quinn	70.00	35.00	20.00
(96)	Rath	70.00	35.00	20.00
(97)	Roche	70.00	35.00	20.00
(98)	Ryan (Los Angeles)	70.00	35.00	20.00
(99)	Ryan (Salt Lake)	70.00	35.00	20.00
(100)	Schaller	70.00	35.00	20.00
(101)	Schinkle	70.00	35.00	20.00
(102)	Schultz	70.00	35.00	20.00
(103)	Sheehan	70.00	35.00	20.00
(104)	Sheeley	70.00	35.00	20.00
(105)	Shinn	70.00	35.00	20.00
(106)	Siglin	70.00	35.00	20.00
(107)	Simon	70.00	35.00	20.00
(108)	Smith	70.00	35.00	20.00
(109)	Snyder	70.00	35.00	20.00
(110)	Stanridge	70.00	35.00	20.00
(111)	Steen	70.00	35.00	20.00
(112)	Stovall	70.00	35.00	20.00
(113)	Stumpf	70.00	35.00	20.00
(114)	Sullivan	70.00	35.00	20.00
(115)	Terry	70.00	35.00	20.00
(116)	Tobin	70.00	35.00	20.00
(117)	Valencia	70.00	35.00	20.00
(118)	Vaughn	70.00	35.00	20.00
(119)	Whalling	70.00	35.00	20.00
(120)	Wilie	70.00	35.00	20.00
(121)	Wolverton	70.00	35.00	20.00

1918 Zeenut Pacific Coast League

The 1918 Zeenuts are among the most distinctive because of the red borders surrounding the photos. They measure about 1-13/16" x 3-5/8" and are among the more difficult years to find.

		NM	EX	VG
Common Player:		250.00	120.00	60.00
With Coupon:		800.00	400.00	240.00
(1)	Alcock	250.00	120.00	60.00
(2)	Arkenburg	250.00	120.00	60.00
(3)	A. Arlett	250.00	120.00	60.00
(4)	Baum	250.00	120.00	60.00
(5)	Boles	250.00	120.00	60.00
(6)	Borton	250.00	120.00	60.00
(7)	Brenton	250.00	120.00	60.00
(8)	Bromley	250.00	120.00	60.00
(9)	Brooks	250.00	120.00	60.00
(10)	Brown	250.00	120.00	60.00
(11)	Caldera	250.00	120.00	60.00
(12)	Camm (Kamm)	250.00	120.00	60.00
(13)	Chadbourne	250.00	120.00	60.00
(14)	Chappell	250.00	120.00	60.00
(15)	Codington	250.00	120.00	60.00
(16)	Conwright	250.00	120.00	60.00
(17)	Cooper	250.00	120.00	60.00
(18)	Cox	250.00	120.00	60.00
(19)	Crandall (Los Angeles)	250.00	120.00	60.00
(20)	Crandall (Salt Lake)	250.00	120.00	60.00
(21)	Crawford	4,000	3,000	2,000
(22)	Croll	250.00	120.00	60.00
(23)	Davis	250.00	120.00	60.00
(24)	DeVormer	250.00	120.00	60.00
(25)	Dobbs	250.00	120.00	60.00
(26)	Downs	250.00	120.00	60.00
(27)	Dubuc	250.00	120.00	60.00
(28)	Dunn	250.00	120.00	60.00
(29)	Easterly	250.00	120.00	60.00
(30)	Eldred	250.00	120.00	60.00
(31)	Elliot	250.00	120.00	60.00
(32)	Ellis	250.00	120.00	60.00
(33)	Essick	250.00	120.00	60.00
(34)	Farmer	250.00	120.00	60.00
(35)	Fisher	250.00	120.00	60.00
(36)	Fittery	250.00	120.00	60.00
(37)	Forsythe	250.00	120.00	60.00
(38)	Fournier	250.00	120.00	60.00
(39)	Fromme	250.00	120.00	60.00
(40)	Gardner (Oakland)	250.00	120.00	60.00
(41)	Gardner (Sacramento)	250.00	120.00	60.00
(42)	Goldie	250.00	120.00	60.00
(43)	Griggs	250.00	120.00	60.00
(44)	Hawkes	250.00	120.00	60.00
(45)	Hollander	250.00	120.00	60.00
(46)	Hosp	250.00	120.00	60.00
(47)	Howard	250.00	120.00	60.00
(48)	Hummel	250.00	120.00	60.00
(49)	Hunter	250.00	120.00	60.00
(50)	Johnson	250.00	120.00	60.00
(51)	G. Johnson	250.00	120.00	60.00
(52)	Kantlehner	250.00	120.00	60.00
(53)	Killefer	250.00	120.00	60.00
(54)	Koerner	250.00	120.00	60.00
(55)	Konnick	250.00	120.00	60.00
(56)	Kremer	250.00	120.00	60.00
(57)	Lapan	250.00	120.00	60.00
(58)	Leake	250.00	120.00	60.00
(59)	Leathers	250.00	120.00	60.00
(60)	Leifer	250.00	120.00	60.00
(61)	Leverenz	250.00	120.00	60.00
(62)	Llewlyn	250.00	120.00	60.00
(63)	Martin	250.00	120.00	60.00
(64)	McCabe	250.00	120.00	60.00
(65)	McCredie	250.00	120.00	60.00
(66)	McKee	250.00	120.00	60.00
(67)	McNulty	250.00	120.00	60.00
(68)	Mensor	700.00	400.00	200.00
(69)	Middleton	250.00	120.00	60.00
(70)	Miller (Oakland)	250.00	120.00	60.00
(71)	Miller (Salt Lake)	250.00	120.00	60.00
(72)	J. Mitchell	250.00	120.00	60.00
(73)	R. Mitchell	250.00	120.00	60.00
(74)	Mitze	250.00	120.00	60.00
(75)	Moore	250.00	120.00	60.00
(76)	Morton	250.00	120.00	60.00
(77)	Murray	250.00	120.00	60.00
(78)	O'Doul	3,000	2,000	1,000
(79)	Orr	250.00	120.00	60.00
(80)	Pepe	250.00	120.00	60.00
(81)	Pertica	250.00	120.00	60.00
(82)	Phillips	250.00	120.00	60.00
(83)	Pick	250.00	120.00	60.00
(84)	Pinelli	250.00	120.00	60.00
(85)	Prentice	250.00	120.00	60.00
(86)	Prough	250.00	120.00	60.00
(87)	Quinlan	250.00	120.00	60.00

		NM	EX	VG
(88)	Ritchie	250.00	120.00	60.00
(89)	Rogers	250.00	120.00	60.00
(90)	Ryan	250.00	120.00	60.00
(91)	Sand	250.00	120.00	60.00
(92)	Shader	250.00	120.00	60.00
(93)	Sheely	250.00	120.00	60.00
(94)	Siglin	250.00	120.00	60.00
(95)	Smale	250.00	120.00	60.00
(96)	Smith (Salt Lake City)	250.00	120.00	60.00
(97)	Smith (San Francisco)	250.00	120.00	60.00
(98)	Stanbridge	250.00	120.00	60.00
(99)	Terry	250.00	120.00	60.00
(100)	Valencia	250.00	120.00	60.00
(101)	West	250.00	120.00	60.00
(102)	Wilie	250.00	120.00	60.00
(103)	Williams	250.00	120.00	60.00
(104)	Wisterzill	250.00	120.00	60.00

1919 Zeenut Pacific Coast League

The 1919 Zeenuts cards are dated on the front and measure about 1-3/4" x 3-5/8". They featured borderless, sepia-toned photos. To date, 144 subjects exist in the series.

		NM	EX	VG
	Common Player:	80.00	35.00	20.00
(1)	Ally	80.00	35.00	20.00
(2)	Fatty Arbuckle	6,000	4,000	2,000
(3)	A. Arlett	80.00	35.00	20.00
(4)	R. Arlett	80.00	35.00	20.00
(5)	Baker	80.00	35.00	20.00
(6)	Baldwin	80.00	35.00	20.00
(7)	Baum	80.00	35.00	20.00
(8)	Beck	80.00	35.00	20.00
(9)	Bigbee	80.00	35.00	20.00
(10)	Blue	80.00	35.00	20.00
(11)	Bohne	300.00	200.00	100.00
(12)	Boles	80.00	35.00	20.00
(13)	Borton	80.00	35.00	20.00
(14)	Bowman	80.00	35.00	20.00
(15)	Brooks	80.00	35.00	20.00
(16)	Brown	80.00	35.00	20.00
(17)	Byler	80.00	35.00	20.00
(18)	Caldera	80.00	35.00	20.00
(19)	Cavaney	80.00	35.00	20.00
(20)	Chadbourne	80.00	35.00	20.00
(21)	Chech	80.00	35.00	20.00
(22)	Church	80.00	35.00	20.00
(23)	Clymer	80.00	35.00	20.00
(24)	Coleman	80.00	35.00	20.00
(25)	Compton	80.00	35.00	20.00
(26)	Conkwright	80.00	35.00	20.00
(27)	Connolly	80.00	35.00	20.00
(28)	Cook	80.00	35.00	20.00
(29)	Cooper (Los Angeles)	80.00	35.00	20.00
(30)	Cooper (Oakland)	80.00	35.00	20.00
(31)	Cooper (Portland)	80.00	35.00	20.00
(32)	Corhan	80.00	35.00	20.00
(33)	Couch	80.00	35.00	20.00
(34)	Cox	80.00	35.00	20.00
(35)	Crandall (Los Angeles)	80.00	35.00	20.00
(36)	Crandall (San Francisco)	80.00	35.00	20.00
(37)	Crespi	80.00	35.00	20.00
(38)	Croll	80.00	35.00	20.00
(39)	Cunningham	80.00	35.00	20.00
(40)	Dawson	80.00	35.00	20.00
(41)	Dell	80.00	35.00	20.00
(42)	DeVormer	80.00	35.00	20.00
(43)	Driscoll	80.00	35.00	20.00
(44)	Eastley	80.00	35.00	20.00
(45)	Edington	80.00	35.00	20.00
(46)	Eldred	80.00	35.00	20.00
(47)	Elliott	80.00	35.00	20.00
(48)	Ellis	80.00	35.00	20.00
(49)	Essick	80.00	35.00	20.00
(50)	Fabrique	80.00	35.00	20.00
(51)	Falkenberg	80.00	35.00	20.00
(52)	Fallentine	80.00	35.00	20.00
(53)	Finneran	80.00	35.00	20.00
(54)	Fisher (Sacramento)	80.00	35.00	20.00
(55)	Fisher (Vernon)	80.00	35.00	20.00
(56)	Fitzgerald	80.00	35.00	20.00
(57)	Flannigan	80.00	35.00	20.00
(58)	Fournier	80.00	35.00	20.00
(59)	French	80.00	35.00	20.00
(60)	Fromme	80.00	35.00	20.00
(61)	Gibson	80.00	35.00	20.00
(62)	Griggs	80.00	35.00	20.00
(63)	Haney	80.00	35.00	20.00
(64)	Harper	80.00	35.00	20.00
(65)	Henkle	80.00	35.00	20.00
(66)	Herr	80.00	35.00	20.00

		NM	EX	VG
(67)	Hickey	80.00	35.00	20.00
(68)	High	80.00	35.00	20.00
(69)	Holling	80.00	35.00	20.00
(70)	Hosp	80.00	35.00	20.00
(71)	Houck	80.00	35.00	20.00
(72)	Howard	80.00	35.00	20.00
(73)	Kamm	80.00	35.00	20.00
(74)	Kenworthy	80.00	35.00	20.00
(75)	Killefer	80.00	35.00	20.00
(76)	King	80.00	35.00	20.00
(77)	Koehler	80.00	35.00	20.00
(78)	Koerner	80.00	35.00	20.00
(79)	Kramer (Oakland)	80.00	35.00	20.00
(80)	Kramer (San Francisco)	80.00	35.00	20.00
(81)	Land	80.00	35.00	20.00
(82)	Lane	80.00	35.00	20.00
(83)	Lapan	80.00	35.00	20.00
(84)	Larkin	80.00	35.00	20.00
(85)	Lee	80.00	35.00	20.00
(86)	Long	80.00	35.00	20.00
(87)	Mails	80.00	35.00	20.00
(88)	Mains	80.00	35.00	20.00
(89)	Maisel	80.00	35.00	20.00
(90)	Mathes	80.00	35.00	20.00
(91)	McCredie	80.00	35.00	20.00
(92)	McGaffigan	80.00	35.00	20.00
(93)	McHenry	80.00	35.00	20.00
(94)	McNulty	80.00	35.00	20.00
(95)	Meusel	80.00	35.00	20.00
(96)	Middleton	80.00	35.00	20.00
(97)	Mitchell	80.00	35.00	20.00
(98)	Mitze	80.00	35.00	20.00
(99)	Mulory	80.00	35.00	20.00
(100)	Murphy	80.00	35.00	20.00
(101)	Murray	80.00	35.00	20.00
(102)	Niehoff (Los Angeles)	80.00	35.00	20.00
(103)	Niehoff (Seattle)	80.00	35.00	20.00
(104)	Norse	80.00	35.00	20.00
(105)	Oldham	80.00	35.00	20.00
(106)	Orr	80.00	35.00	20.00
(107)	Penner	80.00	35.00	20.00
(108)	Pennington	80.00	35.00	20.00
(109)	Piercy	80.00	35.00	20.00
(110)	Pinelli	150.00	75.00	45.00
(111)	C. Prough	80.00	35.00	20.00
(112)	Rader	80.00	35.00	20.00
(113)	Reiger	80.00	35.00	20.00
(114)	Ritchie	80.00	35.00	20.00
(115)	Roach	80.00	35.00	20.00
(116)	Rodgers	80.00	35.00	20.00
(117)	Rumler	80.00	35.00	20.00
(118)	Sands	80.00	35.00	20.00
(119)	Schick	80.00	35.00	20.00
(120)	Schultz	80.00	35.00	20.00
(121)	Scott	80.00	35.00	20.00
(122)	Seaton	80.00	35.00	20.00
(123)	Sheely	80.00	35.00	20.00
(124)	Siglin	80.00	35.00	20.00
(125)	Smith	80.00	35.00	20.00
(126)	Bill Smith	80.00	35.00	20.00
(127)	Snell	80.00	35.00	20.00
(128)	Spangler	80.00	35.00	20.00
(129)	Speas	80.00	35.00	20.00
(130)	Spencer	80.00	35.00	20.00
(131)	Starasenich	80.00	35.00	20.00
(132)	Stumpf	80.00	35.00	20.00
(133)	Sutherland	80.00	35.00	20.00
(134)	Dazzy Vance	800.00	600.00	400.00
(135)	Walker	80.00	35.00	20.00
(136)	Walsh	80.00	35.00	20.00
(137)	Ware	80.00	35.00	20.00
(138)	Weaver	80.00	35.00	20.00
(139)	Westerzil	80.00	35.00	20.00
(140)	Wilhoit	80.00	35.00	20.00
(141)	Wilie	80.00	35.00	20.00
(142)	Willets	80.00	35.00	20.00
(143)	Zamloch	80.00	35.00	20.00
(144)	Zweifel	80.00	35.00	20.00

1920 Zeenut Pacific Coast League

The 1920 Zeenuts cards were dated on the front and measure about 1-3/4" x 3-5/8". They featured borderless, sepia-toned photos. To date, 151 have been found for 1920.

		NM	EX	VG
	Common Player:	80.00	35.00	20.00
(1)	Adams	80.00	35.00	20.00
(2)	Agnew	80.00	35.00	20.00
(3)	Alcock	80.00	35.00	20.00

		NM	EX	VG
(4)	Aldrige	80.00	35.00	20.00
(5)	Andrews	80.00	35.00	20.00
(6)	Anfinson	80.00	35.00	20.00
(7)	A. Arlett	80.00	35.00	20.00
(8)	R. Arlett	80.00	35.00	20.00
(9)	Baker	80.00	35.00	20.00
(10)	Baldwin	80.00	35.00	20.00
(11)	Bassler	80.00	35.00	20.00
(12)	Baum	80.00	35.00	20.00
(13)	Blue	80.00	35.00	20.00
(14)	Bohne	300.00	200.00	100.00
(15)	Brenton	80.00	35.00	20.00
(16)	Bromley (Dark hat.)	80.00	35.00	20.00
(17)	Bromley (Light hat.)	80.00	35.00	20.00
(18)	Brown	80.00	35.00	20.00
(19)	Butler	80.00	35.00	20.00
(20)	Caveney	80.00	35.00	20.00
(21)	Chadbourne	80.00	35.00	20.00
(22)	Compton	80.00	35.00	20.00
(23)	Connolly	80.00	35.00	20.00
(24)	Cook	80.00	35.00	20.00
(25)	Corhan	80.00	35.00	20.00
(26)	Cox	80.00	35.00	20.00
(27)	K. Crandall	80.00	35.00	20.00
(28)	O. Crandall	80.00	35.00	20.00
(29)	Crawford	2,000	1,200	600.00
(30)	Cullop	80.00	35.00	20.00
(31)	Cunningham	80.00	35.00	20.00
(32)	DeVitalis	80.00	35.00	20.00
(33)	DeVormer	80.00	35.00	20.00
(34)	Dooley	80.00	35.00	20.00
(35)	Dorman	80.00	35.00	20.00
(36)	Dumovich	80.00	35.00	20.00
(37)	Dylar	80.00	35.00	20.00
(38)	Edington	80.00	35.00	20.00
(39)	Eldred	80.00	35.00	20.00
(40)	Ellis	80.00	35.00	20.00
(41)	Essick	80.00	35.00	20.00
(42)	Fisher	80.00	35.00	20.00
(43)	Fitzgerald	80.00	35.00	20.00
(44)	Fromme	80.00	35.00	20.00
(45)	Gardner	80.00	35.00	20.00
(46)	Ginglardi	80.00	35.00	20.00
(47)	Gough	80.00	35.00	20.00
(48)	Griggs	80.00	35.00	20.00
(49)	Guisto	80.00	35.00	20.00
(50)	Hamilton	80.00	35.00	20.00
(51)	Hanicy	80.00	35.00	20.00
(52)	Hartford	80.00	35.00	20.00
(53)	High	80.00	35.00	20.00
(54)	Hill	80.00	35.00	20.00
(55)	Hodges	80.00	35.00	20.00
(56)	Howard	80.00	35.00	20.00
(57)	James	80.00	35.00	20.00
(58)	Jenkins	80.00	35.00	20.00
(59)	Johnson (Portland)	80.00	35.00	20.00
(60)	Johnson (Salt Lake)	80.00	35.00	20.00
(61)	Jones	80.00	35.00	20.00
(62)	Juney	80.00	35.00	20.00
(63)	Kallio	80.00	35.00	20.00
(64)	Kamm	80.00	35.00	20.00
(65)	Keating	80.00	35.00	20.00
(66)	Kenworthy	80.00	35.00	20.00
(67)	Killeen	80.00	35.00	20.00
(68)	Killefer	80.00	35.00	20.00
(69)	Kingdon	80.00	35.00	20.00
(70)	Knight	80.00	35.00	20.00
(71)	Koehler	80.00	35.00	20.00
(72)	Koerner	80.00	35.00	20.00
(73)	Kopp	80.00	35.00	20.00
(74)	Kremer	80.00	35.00	20.00
(75)	Krug	80.00	35.00	20.00
(76)	Kunz	80.00	35.00	20.00
(77)	Lambert	80.00	35.00	20.00
(78)	Lane	80.00	35.00	20.00
(79)	Larkin	80.00	35.00	20.00
(80)	Leverenz	80.00	35.00	20.00
(81)	Long	80.00	35.00	20.00
(82)	Love	80.00	35.00	20.00
(83)	Maggart	80.00	35.00	20.00
(84)	Mails	80.00	35.00	20.00
(85)	Maisel	80.00	35.00	20.00
(86)	Matterson	80.00	35.00	20.00
(87)	Matteson	80.00	35.00	20.00
(88)	McAuley	80.00	35.00	20.00
(89)	McCredie	80.00	35.00	20.00
(90)	McGaffigan	80.00	35.00	20.00
(91)	McHenry	80.00	35.00	20.00
(92)	McQuaid	80.00	35.00	20.00
(93)	Miller	80.00	35.00	20.00
(94)	Mitchell	80.00	35.00	20.00
(95)	J. Mitchell	80.00	35.00	20.00
(96)	Mitchell	80.00	35.00	20.00
(97)	Mitze	80.00	35.00	20.00
(98)	Moffitt	80.00	35.00	20.00
(99)	Mollwitz	80.00	35.00	20.00
(100)	Morse	80.00	35.00	20.00
(101)	Mulligan	80.00	35.00	20.00
(102)	Murphy	80.00	35.00	20.00
(103)	Niehoff	80.00	35.00	20.00
(104)	Nixon	80.00	35.00	20.00
(105)	O'Shaughnessy	80.00	35.00	20.00
(106)	Orr	80.00	35.00	20.00
(107)	Paull	80.00	35.00	20.00
(108)	Penner	80.00	35.00	20.00
(109)	Pertica	80.00	35.00	20.00
(110)	Peterson	80.00	35.00	20.00
(111)	Polson	80.00	35.00	20.00
(112)	Prough	80.00	35.00	20.00
(113)	Reagan	80.00	35.00	20.00
(114)	Reiger	80.00	35.00	20.00
(115)	Reilly	80.00	35.00	20.00
(116)	Rheinhart	80.00	35.00	20.00
(117)	Rodgers	80.00	35.00	20.00
(118)	Ross	80.00	35.00	20.00
(119)	Rumler	80.00	35.00	20.00
(120)	Russell	80.00	35.00	20.00
(121)	Sands	80.00	35.00	20.00

		NM	EX	VG
(122)	Schaller	80.00	35.00	20.00
(123)	Schang	80.00	35.00	20.00
(124)	Schellenback	80.00	35.00	20.00
(125)	Schick	80.00	35.00	20.00
(126)	Schorr	80.00	35.00	20.00
(127)	Schroeder	80.00	35.00	20.00
(128)	Scott	80.00	35.00	20.00
(129)	Seaton	80.00	35.00	20.00
(130)	Sheely	80.00	35.00	20.00
(131)	Siebold	80.00	35.00	20.00
(132)	Siglin	80.00	35.00	20.00
(133)	Smith	80.00	35.00	20.00
(134)	G. Smith	80.00	35.00	20.00
(135)	Spellman	80.00	35.00	20.00
(136)	Spranger	80.00	35.00	20.00
(137)	Stroud	80.00	35.00	20.00
(138)	Stumpf	80.00	35.00	20.00
(139)	Sullivan	80.00	35.00	20.00
(140)	Sutherland	80.00	35.00	20.00
(141)	Thurston (Dark hat.)	80.00	35.00	20.00
(142)	Thurston (Light hat.)	80.00	35.00	20.00
(143)	Walsh	80.00	35.00	20.00
(144)	Wares	80.00	35.00	20.00
(145)	Weaver	80.00	35.00	20.00
(146)	Willie	80.00	35.00	20.00
(147)	Winn	80.00	35.00	20.00
(148)	Wisterzill	80.00	35.00	20.00
(149)	Worth	80.00	35.00	20.00
(150)	Yelle	80.00	35.00	20.00
(151)	Zamlock	80.00	35.00	20.00
(152)	Zeider	80.00	35.00	20.00

1921 Zeenut Pacific Coast League

The 1921 Zeenuts cards were dated on the front and measure about 1-3/4" x 3-11/16". They featured borderless, sepia-toned photos. To date, 168 different subjects have been discovered for 1921 (even though a promotional flier indicates 180 players).

		NM	EX	VG
Common Player:		60.00	25.00	15.00
With Coupon:		1,200	500.00	300.00
(1)	Adams	60.00	25.00	15.00
(2)	Alcock	60.00	25.00	15.00
(3)	Aldridge	60.00	25.00	15.00
(4)	Alton	60.00	25.00	15.00
(5)	Anfinson	60.00	25.00	15.00
(6)	Arlett	60.00	25.00	15.00
(7)	Baker	60.00	25.00	15.00
(8)	Baldwin	60.00	25.00	15.00
(9)	Bates	60.00	25.00	15.00
(10)	Berry	60.00	25.00	15.00
(11)	Blacholder	60.00	25.00	15.00
(12)	Blossom	60.00	25.00	15.00
(13)	Bourg	60.00	25.00	15.00
(14)	Brinley	60.00	25.00	15.00
(15)	Bromley	60.00	25.00	15.00
(16)	Brown	60.00	25.00	15.00
(17)	Brubaker	60.00	25.00	15.00
(18)	Butler	60.00	25.00	15.00
(19)	Byler	60.00	25.00	15.00
(20)	Carroll	60.00	25.00	15.00
(21)	Casey	60.00	25.00	15.00
(22)	Cather	60.00	25.00	15.00
(23)	Caveney	60.00	25.00	15.00
(24)	Chadbourne	60.00	25.00	15.00
(25)	Compton	60.00	25.00	15.00
(26)	Connel	60.00	25.00	15.00
(27)	Cook	60.00	25.00	15.00
(28)	Cooper	60.00	25.00	15.00
(29)	Couch	60.00	25.00	15.00
(30)	Cox	60.00	25.00	15.00
(31)	Crandall	60.00	25.00	15.00
(32)	Cravath	60.00	25.00	15.00
(33)	Crawford	2,000	1,200	600.00
(34)	Crumpler	60.00	25.00	15.00
(35)	Cunningham	60.00	25.00	15.00
(36)	Daley	60.00	25.00	15.00
(37)	Dell	60.00	25.00	15.00
(38)	Demaree	60.00	25.00	15.00
(39)	Douglas	60.00	25.00	15.00
(40)	Dumovich	60.00	25.00	15.00
(41)	Elliott	60.00	25.00	15.00
(42)	Ellis	60.00	25.00	15.00
(43)	Ellison	60.00	25.00	15.00
(44)	Essick	60.00	25.00	15.00
(45)	Faeth	60.00	25.00	15.00
(46)	Fisher	60.00	25.00	15.00
(47)	Fittery	60.00	25.00	15.00
(48)	Fitzgerald	60.00	25.00	15.00
(49)	Flaherty	60.00	25.00	15.00
(50)	Francis	60.00	25.00	15.00
(51)	French	60.00	25.00	15.00
(52)	Fromme	60.00	25.00	15.00
(53)	Gardner	60.00	25.00	15.00
(54)	Geary	60.00	25.00	15.00
(55)	Gennin	60.00	25.00	15.00
(56)	Gorman	60.00	25.00	15.00
(57)	Gould	60.00	25.00	15.00
(58)	Griggs	60.00	25.00	15.00
(59)	Hale	60.00	25.00	15.00
(60)	Hannah	60.00	25.00	15.00
(61)	Hansen	60.00	25.00	15.00
(62)	Hesse	60.00	25.00	15.00
(63)	High	60.00	25.00	15.00
(64)	Hughes	60.00	25.00	15.00
(65)	Hyatt	60.00	25.00	15.00
(66)	Jackson	60.00	25.00	15.00
(67)	Jacobs	60.00	25.00	15.00
(68)	Jacobs	60.00	25.00	15.00
(69)	Jenkins	60.00	25.00	15.00
(70)	Johnson	60.00	25.00	15.00
(71)	Jones	60.00	25.00	15.00
(72)	Jourden	60.00	25.00	15.00
(73)	Kallio	60.00	25.00	15.00
(74)	Kamm	60.00	25.00	15.00
(75)	Kearns	60.00	25.00	15.00
(76)	Kelly	60.00	25.00	15.00
(77)	Kersten	60.00	25.00	15.00
(78)	Kifer	60.00	25.00	15.00
(79)	Killefer	60.00	25.00	15.00
(80)	King	60.00	25.00	15.00
(81)	Kingdon	60.00	25.00	15.00
(82)	Knight	60.00	25.00	15.00
(83)	Koehler	60.00	25.00	15.00
(84)	Kopp	60.00	25.00	15.00
(85)	Krause	60.00	25.00	15.00
(86)	Kremer	60.00	25.00	15.00
(87)	Krug	60.00	25.00	15.00
(88)	Kunz	60.00	25.00	15.00
(89)	Lane	60.00	25.00	15.00
(90)	Leverenz	60.00	25.00	15.00
(91)	Lewis	60.00	25.00	15.00
(92)	Lindimore	60.00	25.00	15.00
(93)	Love	60.00	25.00	15.00
(94)	Ludolph	60.00	25.00	15.00
(95)	Lynn	60.00	25.00	15.00
(96)	Lyons	60.00	25.00	15.00
(97)	McAuley	60.00	25.00	15.00
(98)	McCredie	60.00	25.00	15.00
(99)	McGaffigan	60.00	25.00	15.00
(100)	McGraw	60.00	25.00	15.00
(101)	McQuaid	60.00	25.00	15.00
(102)	Merritt	60.00	25.00	15.00
(103)	Middleton	60.00	25.00	15.00
(104)	Miller	60.00	25.00	15.00
(105)	Mitchell	60.00	25.00	15.00
(106)	Mitze	60.00	25.00	15.00
(107)	Mollwitz	60.00	25.00	15.00
(108)	Morse	60.00	25.00	15.00
(109)	Murphy (Seattle)	60.00	25.00	15.00
(110)	Murphy (Vernon)	60.00	25.00	15.00
(111)	Mustain	60.00	25.00	15.00
(112)	Nickels	60.00	25.00	15.00
(113)	Niehaus	60.00	25.00	15.00
(114)	Niehoff	60.00	25.00	15.00
(115)	Nofziger	60.00	25.00	15.00
(116)	O'Connell	60.00	25.00	15.00
(117)	O'Doul	800.00	600.00	400.00
(118)	O'Malia	60.00	25.00	15.00
(119)	Oldring	60.00	25.00	15.00
(120)	Oliver	60.00	25.00	15.00
(121)	Orr	60.00	25.00	15.00
(122)	Paton	60.00	25.00	15.00
(123)	Penner	60.00	25.00	15.00
(124)	Pick	60.00	25.00	15.00
(125)	Pillette	60.00	25.00	15.00
(126)	Pinelli	60.00	25.00	15.00
(127)	Polson	60.00	25.00	15.00
(128)	Poole	60.00	25.00	15.00
(129)	Prough	60.00	25.00	15.00
(130)	Rath	60.00	25.00	15.00
(131)	Read	60.00	25.00	15.00
(132)	Reinhardt	60.00	25.00	15.00
(133)	Rieger	60.00	25.00	15.00
(134)	Rogers	60.00	25.00	15.00
(135)	Rose (Sacramento)	60.00	25.00	15.00
(136)	Rose (Salt Lake)	60.00	25.00	15.00
(137)	Ross (Portland)	60.00	25.00	15.00
(138)	Ross (Sacramento)	60.00	25.00	15.00
(139)	Ryan	60.00	25.00	15.00
(140)	Sand	60.00	25.00	15.00
(141)	Schick	60.00	25.00	15.00
(142)	Schneider	60.00	25.00	15.00
(143)	Scott	60.00	25.00	15.00
(144)	Shang	60.00	25.00	15.00
(145)	Sheehan	60.00	25.00	15.00
(146)	Shore	60.00	25.00	15.00
(147)	Shorr	60.00	25.00	15.00
(148)	Shultis	60.00	25.00	15.00
(149)	Siebold	60.00	25.00	15.00
(150)	Siglin	60.00	25.00	15.00
(151)	Smallwood	60.00	25.00	15.00
(152)	Smith	60.00	25.00	15.00
(153)	Spencer	60.00	25.00	15.00
(154)	Stanage	60.00	25.00	15.00
(155)	Statz	60.00	25.00	15.00
(156)	Stumph	60.00	25.00	15.00
(157)	Thomas	60.00	25.00	15.00
(158)	Thurston	60.00	25.00	15.00
(159)	Tyrrell	60.00	25.00	15.00
(160)	Van Osdoll	60.00	25.00	15.00
(161)	Walsh	60.00	25.00	15.00
(162)	White	60.00	25.00	15.00
(163)	Wilhoit	60.00	25.00	15.00
(164)	Wilie	60.00	25.00	15.00
(165)	Winn	60.00	25.00	15.00
(166)	Wolfer	60.00	25.00	15.00
(167)	Yelle	60.00	25.00	15.00
(168)	Young	60.00	25.00	15.00
(169)	Zeider	60.00	25.00	15.00

1922 Zeenut Pacific Coast League

The 1922 Zeenuts are dated on the front, measure about 1-13/16" x 3-9/16" and feature black-and-white photos with sepia highlights. There are 162 subjects, and four of them (Koehler, Williams, Gregg and Schneider) have been found with variations in color tones.

		NM	EX	VG
Common Player:		60.00	25.00	15.00
(1)	J. Adams	60.00	25.00	15.00
(2)	S. Adams	60.00	25.00	15.00
(3)	Agnew	60.00	25.00	15.00
(4)	Anfinson	60.00	25.00	15.00
(5)	Arlett	60.00	25.00	15.00
(6)	Baldwin	60.00	25.00	15.00
(7)	Barney	60.00	25.00	15.00
(8)	Bell	60.00	25.00	15.00
(9)	Blaeholder	60.00	25.00	15.00
(10)	Bodie	60.00	25.00	15.00
(11)	Brenton	60.00	25.00	15.00
(12)	Bromley	60.00	25.00	15.00
(13)	Brovold	60.00	25.00	15.00
(14)	Brown	60.00	25.00	15.00
(15)	Brubaker	60.00	25.00	15.00
(16)	Burger	60.00	25.00	15.00
(17)	Byler	60.00	25.00	15.00
(18)	Canfield	60.00	25.00	15.00
(19)	Carroll	60.00	25.00	15.00
(20)	Cartwright	60.00	25.00	15.00
(21)	Chadbourne	60.00	25.00	15.00
(22)	Compton	60.00	25.00	15.00
(23)	Connolly	60.00	25.00	15.00
(24)	Cook	60.00	25.00	15.00
(25)	Cooper	60.00	25.00	15.00
(26)	Coumbe	60.00	25.00	15.00
(27)	Cox	60.00	25.00	15.00
(28)	Crandall	60.00	25.00	15.00
(29)	Crumpler	60.00	25.00	15.00
(30)	Cueto	600.00	400.00	200.00
(31)	Dailey	60.00	25.00	15.00
(32)	Daly	60.00	25.00	15.00
(33)	Deal	60.00	25.00	15.00
(34)	Dell	60.00	25.00	15.00
(35)	Doyle	60.00	25.00	15.00
(36)	Dumovich	60.00	25.00	15.00
(37)	Eldred	60.00	25.00	15.00
(38)	Eller	60.00	25.00	15.00
(39)	Elliott	60.00	25.00	15.00
(40)	Ellison	60.00	25.00	15.00
(41)	Essick	60.00	25.00	15.00
(42)	Finneran	60.00	25.00	15.00
(43)	Fittery	60.00	25.00	15.00
(44)	Fitzgerald	60.00	25.00	15.00
(45)	Freeman	60.00	25.00	15.00
(46)	French	60.00	25.00	15.00
(47)	Gardner	60.00	25.00	15.00
(48)	Geary	60.00	25.00	15.00
(49)	Gibson	60.00	25.00	15.00
(50)	Gilder	60.00	25.00	15.00
(51)	Gould	60.00	25.00	15.00
(52)	Gregg	60.00	25.00	15.00
(53)	Gressett	60.00	25.00	15.00
(54)	Griggs	60.00	25.00	15.00
(55)	Hampton	60.00	25.00	15.00
(56)	Hannah	60.00	25.00	15.00
(57)	Hawks	60.00	25.00	15.00
(58)	Henke	60.00	25.00	15.00
(59)	High (Portland)	60.00	25.00	15.00
(60)	High (Vernon)	60.00	25.00	15.00
(61)	Houck	60.00	25.00	15.00
(62)	Howard	60.00	25.00	15.00
(63)	Hughes	60.00	25.00	15.00
(64)	Hyatt	60.00	25.00	15.00
(65)	Jacobs	60.00	25.00	15.00
(66)	James	60.00	25.00	15.00
(67)	Jenkins	60.00	25.00	15.00
(68)	Jones	60.00	25.00	15.00
(69)	Kallio	60.00	25.00	15.00
(70)	Kamm	60.00	25.00	15.00
(71)	Keiser	60.00	25.00	15.00
(72)	Kelly	60.00	25.00	15.00
(73)	Kenworthy	60.00	25.00	15.00
(74)	Kilduff	60.00	25.00	15.00
(75)	Killefer	60.00	25.00	15.00

No.	Player	NM	EX	VG
(76)	Killhullen	60.00	25.00	15.00
(77)	King	60.00	25.00	15.00
(78)	Knight	60.00	25.00	15.00
(79)	Koehler	60.00	25.00	15.00
(80)	Kremer	60.00	25.00	15.00
(81)	Kunz	60.00	25.00	15.00
(82)	Lafayette	60.00	25.00	15.00
(83)	Lane	60.00	25.00	15.00
(84)	Tony Lazzeri	1,200	600.00	360.00
(85)	Lefevre	60.00	25.00	15.00
(86)	D. Lewis	60.00	25.00	15.00
(87)	S. Lewis	60.00	25.00	15.00
(88)	Lindimore	60.00	25.00	15.00
(89)	Locker	60.00	25.00	15.00
(90)	Lyons	60.00	25.00	15.00
(91)	Mack	60.00	25.00	15.00
(92)	Marriott	60.00	25.00	15.00
(93)	May	60.00	25.00	15.00
(94)	McAuley	60.00	25.00	15.00
(95)	McCabe	60.00	25.00	15.00
(96)	McCann	60.00	25.00	15.00
(97)	McCredie	60.00	25.00	15.00
(98)	McNeely	60.00	25.00	15.00
(99)	McQuaid	60.00	25.00	15.00
(100)	Miller	60.00	25.00	15.00
(101)	Mitchell	60.00	25.00	15.00
(102)	Mitze	60.00	25.00	15.00
(103)	Mollwitz	60.00	25.00	15.00
(104)	Monahan	60.00	25.00	15.00
(105)	Murphy (Seattle)	60.00	25.00	15.00
(106)	Murphy (Vernon)	60.00	25.00	15.00
(107)	Niehaus	60.00	25.00	15.00
(108)	O'Connell	60.00	25.00	15.00
(109)	Orr	60.00	25.00	15.00
(110)	Owen	60.00	25.00	15.00
(111)	Pearce	60.00	25.00	15.00
(112)	Pick	60.00	25.00	15.00
(113)	Ponder	60.00	25.00	15.00
(114)	Poole	60.00	25.00	15.00
(115)	Prough	60.00	25.00	15.00
(116)	Read	60.00	25.00	15.00
(117)	Richardson	60.00	25.00	15.00
(118)	Rieger	60.00	25.00	15.00
(119)	Ritchie	60.00	25.00	15.00
(120)	Ross	60.00	25.00	15.00
(121)	Ryan	60.00	25.00	15.00
(122)	Sand	60.00	25.00	15.00
(123)	Sargent	60.00	25.00	15.00
(124)	Sawyer	60.00	25.00	15.00
(125)	Schang	60.00	25.00	15.00
(126)	Schick	60.00	25.00	15.00
(127)	Schneider	60.00	25.00	15.00
(128)	Schorr	60.00	25.00	15.00
(129)	Schulte (Oakland)	60.00	25.00	15.00
(130)	Schulte (Seattle)	60.00	25.00	15.00
(131)	Scott	60.00	25.00	15.00
(132)	See	60.00	25.00	15.00
(133)	Shea	60.00	25.00	15.00
(134)	Sheehan	60.00	25.00	15.00
(135)	Siglin	60.00	25.00	15.00
(136)	Smith	60.00	25.00	15.00
(137)	Soria	60.00	25.00	15.00
(138)	Spencer	60.00	25.00	15.00
(139)	Stanage	60.00	25.00	15.00
(140)	Strand	60.00	25.00	15.00
(141)	Stumpf	60.00	25.00	15.00
(142)	Sullivan	60.00	25.00	15.00
(143)	Sutherland	60.00	25.00	15.00
(144)	Thomas	60.00	25.00	15.00
(145)	Jim Thorpe	30,000	20,000	10,000
(146)	Thurston	60.00	25.00	15.00
(147)	Tobin	60.00	25.00	15.00
(148)	Turner	60.00	25.00	15.00
(149)	Twombly	60.00	25.00	15.00
(150)	Valla	60.00	25.00	15.00
(151)	Vargas	60.00	25.00	15.00
(152)	Viveros	60.00	25.00	15.00
(153)	Wallace	60.00	25.00	15.00
(154)	Walsh	60.00	25.00	15.00
(155)	Wells	60.00	25.00	15.00
(156)	Westersil	60.00	25.00	15.00
(157)	Wheat	60.00	25.00	15.00
(158)	Wilhoit	60.00	25.00	15.00
(159)	Wilie	60.00	25.00	15.00
(160)	Williams	60.00	25.00	15.00
(161)	Yelle	60.00	25.00	15.00
(162)	Zeider	60.00	25.00	15.00

1923 Zeenut Pacific Coast League

This is the only year that Zeenuts cards were issued in two different sizes. Cards in the "regular" series measure about 1-7/8" x 3-1/2", feature black-and-white photos and are dated 1923. A second series, containing just 24 cards (all San

Francisco and Oakland players), are sepia-toned re-issues of the 1922 series with a "1923" date and measure about 1/16" longer. The re-issued cards have coupons with an expiration date of April 1, 1923. The dated cards have coupons with an expiration date of April 1, 1924.

		NM	EX	VG
Common Player:		60.00	25.00	15.00
With Coupon:		1,000	500.00	300.00
(1)	Agnew (1923 photo)	60.00	25.00	15.00
(2)	Agnew (1922 photo re-dated)	60.00	25.00	15.00
(3)	Alten	60.00	25.00	15.00
(4)	Anderson	60.00	25.00	15.00
(5)	Anfinson	60.00	25.00	15.00
(6)	Arlett	60.00	25.00	15.00
(7)	Baker	60.00	25.00	15.00
(8)	Baldwin	60.00	25.00	15.00
(9)	Barney	60.00	25.00	15.00
(10)	Blake	60.00	25.00	15.00
(11)	Bodie	60.00	25.00	15.00
(12)	Brazil	60.00	25.00	15.00
(13)	Brenton	60.00	25.00	15.00
(14)	Brown (Oakland)	60.00	25.00	15.00
(15)	Brown (Sacramento)	60.00	25.00	15.00
(16)	Brubaker	60.00	25.00	15.00
(17)	Buckley	60.00	25.00	15.00
(18)	Canfield	60.00	25.00	15.00
(19)	Carroll	60.00	25.00	15.00
(20)	Cather	60.00	25.00	15.00
(21)	Chadbourne	60.00	25.00	15.00
(22)	Charvez	60.00	25.00	15.00
(23)	Cochrane	60.00	25.00	15.00
(24)	Colwell	60.00	25.00	15.00
(25)	Compton	60.00	25.00	15.00
(26)	Cook	60.00	25.00	15.00
(27)	Cooper (1923 photo)	60.00	25.00	15.00
(28)	Cooper (1922 photo re-date)	60.00	25.00	15.00
(29)	Coumbe	60.00	25.00	15.00
(30)	Courtney	60.00	25.00	15.00
(31)	Crandall	60.00	25.00	15.00
(32)	Crane	60.00	25.00	15.00
(33)	Crowder	60.00	25.00	15.00
(34)	Crumpler	60.00	25.00	15.00
(35)	Daly (Los Angeles)	60.00	25.00	15.00
(36)	Daly (Portland)	60.00	25.00	15.00
(37)	Deal	60.00	25.00	15.00
(38)	Doyle	60.00	25.00	15.00
(39)	Duchalsky	60.00	25.00	15.00
(40)	Eckert	60.00	25.00	15.00
(41)	Eldred	60.00	25.00	15.00
(42)	Eley	60.00	25.00	15.00
(43)	Eller	60.00	25.00	15.00
(44)	Ellison (1923 photo)	60.00	25.00	15.00
(45)	Ellison (1922 photo re-dated)	60.00	25.00	15.00
(46)	Essick	60.00	25.00	15.00
(47)	Fittery	60.00	25.00	15.00
(48)	Flashkamper	60.00	25.00	15.00
(49)	Frederick	60.00	25.00	15.00
(50)	French	60.00	25.00	15.00
(51)	Geary (1923 photo)	60.00	25.00	15.00
(52)	Geary (1922 photo re-dated)	60.00	25.00	15.00
(53)	Gilder	60.00	25.00	15.00
(54)	Golvin	60.00	25.00	15.00
(55)	Gorman	60.00	25.00	15.00
(56)	Gould	60.00	25.00	15.00
(57)	Gressett	60.00	25.00	15.00
(58)	Griggs	60.00	25.00	15.00
(59)	Hannah (Los Angeles)	60.00	25.00	15.00
(60)	Hannah (Vernon)	60.00	25.00	15.00
(61)	Hemingway	60.00	25.00	15.00
(62)	Hendryx	60.00	25.00	15.00
(63)	High	60.00	25.00	15.00
(64)	H. High	60.00	25.00	15.00
(65)	Hodge	60.00	25.00	15.00
(66)	Hood	60.00	25.00	15.00
(67)	Houghs	60.00	25.00	15.00
(68)	Howard (1923 photo)	60.00	25.00	15.00
(69)	Howard (1922 photo re-date)	60.00	25.00	15.00
(70)	Del Howard	60.00	25.00	15.00
(71)	Jacobs	60.00	25.00	15.00
(72)	James	60.00	25.00	15.00
(73)	Johnson	60.00	25.00	15.00
(74)	Johnston	60.00	25.00	15.00
(75)	Jolly (Jolley)	60.00	25.00	15.00
(76)	Jones (Los Angeles)	60.00	25.00	15.00
(77)	Jones (Oakland)	60.00	25.00	15.00
(78)	Jones (Portland)	60.00	25.00	15.00
(79)	Kallio	60.00	25.00	15.00
(80)	Kearns	60.00	25.00	15.00
(81)	Keiser	60.00	25.00	15.00
(82)	Keller	60.00	25.00	15.00
(83)	Kelly (San Francisco)	60.00	25.00	15.00
(84)	Kelly (Seattle)	60.00	25.00	15.00
(85)	Kenna	60.00	25.00	15.00
(86)	Kilduff	60.00	25.00	15.00
(87)	Killifer	60.00	25.00	15.00
(88)	King	60.00	25.00	15.00
(89)	Knight (1923 photo)	60.00	25.00	15.00
(90)	Knight (1922 photo re-dated)	60.00	25.00	15.00
(91)	Koehler	60.00	25.00	15.00
(92)	Kopp	60.00	25.00	15.00
(93)	Krause	60.00	25.00	15.00
(94)	Kremer	60.00	25.00	15.00
(95)	Krug	60.00	25.00	15.00
(96)	Lafayette (1923 photo)	60.00	25.00	15.00
(97)	Lafayette (1922 photo re-dated)	60.00	25.00	15.00
(98)	Lane	60.00	25.00	15.00
(99)	Lefevre	60.00	25.00	15.00
(100)	Leslie	60.00	25.00	15.00
(101)	Levere	60.00	25.00	15.00
(102)	Leverenz	60.00	25.00	15.00
(103)	Lewis	60.00	25.00	15.00
(104)	Lindimore	60.00	25.00	15.00
(105)	Locker	60.00	25.00	15.00
(106)	Lyons	60.00	25.00	15.00
(107)	Maderas	60.00	25.00	15.00
(108)	Mails	60.00	25.00	15.00
(109)	Marriott	60.00	25.00	15.00
(110)	Matzen	60.00	25.00	15.00
(111)	McAuley	60.00	25.00	15.00
(112)	McAuliffe	60.00	25.00	15.00
(113)	McCabe (Los Angeles)	60.00	25.00	15.00
(114)	McCabe (Salt Lake)	60.00	25.00	15.00
(115)	McCann	60.00	25.00	15.00
(116)	McGaffigan	60.00	25.00	15.00
(117)	McGinnis	60.00	25.00	15.00
(118)	McNeilly	60.00	25.00	15.00
(119)	McWeeney	60.00	25.00	15.00
(120)	Middleton	60.00	25.00	15.00
(121)	Miller	60.00	25.00	15.00
(122)	Mitchell (1923 photo)	60.00	25.00	15.00
(123)	Mitchell (1922 photo re-date)	60.00	25.00	15.00
(124)	Mitze	60.00	25.00	15.00
(125)	Mulligan	60.00	25.00	15.00
(126)	Murchio	60.00	25.00	15.00
(127)	D. Murphy	60.00	25.00	15.00
(128)	R. Murphy	60.00	25.00	15.00
(129)	Noack	60.00	25.00	15.00
(130)	O'Brien	60.00	25.00	15.00
(131)	Onslow	60.00	25.00	15.00
(132)	Orr	60.00	25.00	15.00
(133)	Pearce	60.00	25.00	15.00
(134)	Penner	60.00	25.00	15.00
(135)	Peters	60.00	25.00	15.00
(136)	Pick	60.00	25.00	15.00
(137)	Pigg	60.00	25.00	15.00
(138)	Plummer	60.00	25.00	15.00
(139)	Ponder	60.00	25.00	15.00
(140)	Poole	60.00	25.00	15.00
(141)	Ramage	60.00	25.00	15.00
(142)	Read (1923 photo)	60.00	25.00	15.00
(143)	Read (1922 photo re-dated)	60.00	25.00	15.00
(144)	Rhyne	60.00	25.00	15.00
(145)	Ritchie	60.00	25.00	15.00
(146)	Robertson	60.00	25.00	15.00
(147)	Rohwer (Sacramento)	60.00	25.00	15.00
(148)	Rohwer (Seattle)	60.00	25.00	15.00
(149)	Ryan	60.00	25.00	15.00
(150)	Sawyer	60.00	25.00	15.00
(151)	Schang	60.00	25.00	15.00
(152)	Schneider	60.00	25.00	15.00
(153)	Schroeder	60.00	25.00	15.00
(154)	Scott	60.00	25.00	15.00
(155)	See	60.00	25.00	15.00
(156)	Shea	60.00	25.00	15.00
(157)	M. Shea	60.00	25.00	15.00
(158)	Spec Shea	60.00	25.00	15.00
(159)	Sheehan	60.00	25.00	15.00
(160)	Shellenback	60.00	25.00	15.00
(161)	Siglin	60.00	25.00	15.00
(162)	Singleton	60.00	25.00	15.00
(163)	Smith	60.00	25.00	15.00
(164)	M.H. Smith	60.00	25.00	15.00
(165)	Stanton	60.00	25.00	15.00
(166)	Strand	60.00	25.00	15.00
(167)	Stumpf	60.00	25.00	15.00
(168)	Sutherland	60.00	25.00	15.00
(169)	Tesar	60.00	25.00	15.00
(170)	Thomas (Los Angeles)	60.00	25.00	15.00
(171)	Thomas (Oakland)	60.00	25.00	15.00
(172)	Tobin	60.00	25.00	15.00
(173)	Twombly	60.00	25.00	15.00
(174)	Valla	60.00	25.00	15.00
(175)	Vargas	60.00	25.00	15.00
(176)	Vitt	60.00	25.00	15.00
(177)	Wallace	60.00	25.00	15.00
(178)	Walsh (San Francisco)	60.00	25.00	15.00
(179)	Walsh (Seattle)	60.00	25.00	15.00
(180)	Paul Waner	1,500	800.00	500.00
(181)	Wells (Oakland)	60.00	25.00	15.00
(182)	Wells (San Francisco)	60.00	25.00	15.00
(183)	Welsh	60.00	25.00	15.00
(184)	Wilhoit	60.00	25.00	15.00
(185)	Wilie (1923 photo)	60.00	25.00	15.00
(186)	Wilie (1922 photo re-dated)	60.00	25.00	15.00
(187)	Williams	60.00	25.00	15.00
(188)	Witzel	60.00	25.00	15.00
(189)	Wolfer	60.00	25.00	15.00
(190)	Wolverton	60.00	25.00	15.00
(191)	Yarrison	60.00	25.00	15.00
(192)	Yaryan	60.00	25.00	15.00
(193)	Yelle (1923 photo)	60.00	25.00	15.00
(194)	Yelle (1922 photo re-dated)	60.00	25.00	15.00
(195)	Moses Yellowhorse	600.00	300.00	180.00
(196)	Zeider	60.00	25.00	15.00

1924 Zeenut Pacific Coast League

Zeenut cards in 1924 measure about 1-3/4" x 3-7/16" and display the date on the front. The cards include a full photographic background. There are 144 subjects known.

	NM	EX	VG
Common Player:	60.00	25.00	15.00
(1) Adams	125.00	65.00	40.00
(2) Agnew	60.00	25.00	15.00
(3) Arlett	60.00	25.00	15.00
(4) Baker	60.00	25.00	15.00
(5) E. Baldwin	60.00	25.00	15.00
(6) T. Baldwin	60.00	25.00	15.00
(7) Beck	60.00	25.00	15.00
(8) Benton	60.00	25.00	15.00
(9) Bernard	60.00	25.00	15.00
(10) Bigbee	60.00	25.00	15.00
(11) Billings	60.00	25.00	15.00
(12) Blakesly	60.00	25.00	15.00
(13) Brady	60.00	25.00	15.00
(14) Brazil	60.00	25.00	15.00
(15) Brown	60.00	25.00	15.00
(16) Brubaker	60.00	25.00	15.00
(17) Buckley	60.00	25.00	15.00
(18) Burger	60.00	25.00	15.00
(19) Byler	60.00	25.00	15.00
(20) Cadore	60.00	25.00	15.00
(21) Cather	60.00	25.00	15.00
(22) Chadbourne	60.00	25.00	15.00
(23) Christian	60.00	25.00	15.00
(24) Mickey Cochrane (Portland)	1,200	600.00	360.00
(25) Cochrane (Sacramento)	60.00	25.00	15.00
(26) Cooper	60.00	25.00	15.00
(27) Coumbe	60.00	25.00	15.00
(28) Cox	60.00	25.00	15.00
(29) Crandall	60.00	25.00	15.00
(30) Daly	60.00	25.00	15.00
(31) Deal	60.00	25.00	15.00
(32) Distel	60.00	25.00	15.00
(33) Durst	60.00	25.00	15.00
(34) Eckert	60.00	25.00	15.00
(35) Eldred	60.00	25.00	15.00
(36) Ellison	60.00	25.00	15.00
(37) Essick	60.00	25.00	15.00
(38) Flashkamper	60.00	25.00	15.00
(39) Foster	60.00	25.00	15.00
(40) Fredericks	60.00	25.00	15.00
(41) Geary	60.00	25.00	15.00
(42) Goebel	60.00	25.00	15.00
(43) Golvin	60.00	25.00	15.00
(44) Gorman	60.00	25.00	15.00
(45) Gould	60.00	25.00	15.00
(46) Gressett	60.00	25.00	15.00
(47) Griffin (San Francisco)	60.00	25.00	15.00
(48) Griffin (Vernon)	60.00	25.00	15.00
(49) Guisto	60.00	25.00	15.00
(50) Gunther	60.00	25.00	15.00
(51) Hall	60.00	25.00	15.00
(52) Hannah	60.00	25.00	15.00
(53) Hendryx	60.00	25.00	15.00
(54) High	60.00	25.00	15.00
(55) Hodge	60.00	25.00	15.00
(56) Hood	60.00	25.00	15.00
(57) Ivan Howard	60.00	25.00	15.00
(58) Hughes (Los Angeles)	60.00	25.00	15.00
(59) Hughes (Sacramento)	60.00	25.00	15.00
(60) Jacobs	60.00	25.00	15.00
(61) James	60.00	25.00	15.00
(62) Jenkins	60.00	25.00	15.00
(63) Johnson	60.00	25.00	15.00
(64) Jones	60.00	25.00	15.00
(65) Keck	60.00	25.00	15.00
(66) Kelley	60.00	25.00	15.00
(67) Kenworthy	60.00	25.00	15.00
(68) Kilduff	60.00	25.00	15.00
(69) Killifer	60.00	25.00	15.00
(70) Kimmick	60.00	25.00	15.00
(71) Kopp	60.00	25.00	15.00
(72) Krause	60.00	25.00	15.00
(73) Krug	60.00	25.00	15.00
(74) Kunz	60.00	25.00	15.00
(75) Lafayette	60.00	25.00	15.00
(76) Lennon	60.00	25.00	15.00
(77) Leptich	60.00	25.00	15.00
(78) Leslie	60.00	25.00	15.00
(79) Leverenz	60.00	25.00	15.00
(80) Lewis	60.00	25.00	15.00
(81) Maderas	60.00	25.00	15.00
(82) Mails	60.00	25.00	15.00
(83) McAuley	60.00	25.00	15.00
(84) McCann	60.00	25.00	15.00
(85) McDowell	60.00	25.00	15.00
(86) McNeely	60.00	25.00	15.00
(87) Menosky	60.00	25.00	15.00
(88) Meyers	60.00	25.00	15.00
(89) Miller	60.00	25.00	15.00
(90) Mitchell	60.00	25.00	15.00
(91) Mulligan	60.00	25.00	15.00
(92) D. Murphy	60.00	25.00	15.00
(93) R. Murphy	60.00	25.00	15.00
(94) Osborne	60.00	25.00	15.00
(95) Paynter	60.00	25.00	15.00
(96) Penner	60.00	25.00	15.00
(97) Peters (Sacramento)	60.00	25.00	15.00
(98) Peters (Salt Lake)	60.00	25.00	15.00
(99) Pick	60.00	25.00	15.00
(100) Pillette	60.00	25.00	15.00
(101) Poole	60.00	25.00	15.00
(102) Prough	60.00	25.00	15.00
(103) Querry	60.00	25.00	15.00
(104) Read	60.00	25.00	15.00
(105) Rhyne	60.00	25.00	15.00
(106) Ritchie	60.00	25.00	15.00
(107) Root	60.00	25.00	15.00
(108) Rowher	60.00	25.00	15.00
(109) Schang	60.00	25.00	15.00
(110) Schneider	60.00	25.00	15.00
(111) Schorr	60.00	25.00	15.00
(112) Schroeder	60.00	25.00	15.00
(113) Scott	60.00	25.00	15.00
(114) Sellers	60.00	25.00	15.00
(115) "Speck" Shay	60.00	25.00	15.00

		NM	EX	VG
(116)	Shea (Sacramento)	60.00	25.00	15.00
(117)	Shea (San Francisco)	60.00	25.00	15.00
(118)	Shellenback	60.00	25.00	15.00
(119)	Siebold	60.00	25.00	15.00
(120)	Siglin	60.00	25.00	15.00
(121)	Slade	60.00	25.00	15.00
(122)	Smith (Sacramento)	60.00	25.00	15.00
(123)	Smith (San Francisco)	60.00	25.00	15.00
(124)	Stanton	60.00	25.00	15.00
(125)	Tanner	60.00	25.00	15.00
(126)	Twomley	60.00	25.00	15.00
(127)	Valla	60.00	25.00	15.00
(128)	Vargas	60.00	25.00	15.00
(129)	Vines	60.00	25.00	15.00
(130)	Vitt	60.00	25.00	15.00
(131)	Wallace	60.00	25.00	15.00
(132)	Walsh	60.00	25.00	15.00
(133)	Paul Waner	1,200	600.00	350.00
(134)	Warner (Fielding)	60.00	25.00	15.00
(135)	Warner (Throwing)	60.00	25.00	15.00
(136)	Welsh	60.00	25.00	15.00
(137)	Wetzel	60.00	25.00	15.00
(138)	Whalen	60.00	25.00	15.00
(139)	Wilhoit	60.00	25.00	15.00
(140)	Williams (San Francisco)	60.00	25.00	15.00
(141)	Williams (Seattle)	60.00	25.00	15.00
(142)	Wolfer	60.00	25.00	15.00
(143)	Yelle	60.00	25.00	15.00
(144)	Moses Yellowhorse	350.00	175.00	100.00

1925 Zeenut Pacific Coast League

Zeenut cards in 1925 measure about 1-3/4" x 3-7/16" and display the date on the front. The cards include a full photo-graphic background. There are 162 subjects known for 1925.

		NM	EX	VG
Common Player:		60.00	25.00	15.00
With Coupon:		300.00	150.00	90.00
(1)	Adeylatte	60.00	25.00	15.00
(2)	Agnew	60.00	25.00	15.00
(3)	Arlett	60.00	25.00	15.00
(4)	Bagby	60.00	25.00	15.00
(5)	Bahr	60.00	25.00	15.00
(6)	Baker	60.00	25.00	15.00
(7)	E. Baldwin	60.00	25.00	15.00
(8)	Barfoot	60.00	25.00	15.00
(9)	Beck	60.00	25.00	15.00
(10)	Becker	60.00	25.00	15.00
(11)	Blakesley	60.00	25.00	15.00
(12)	Boehler	60.00	25.00	15.00
(13)	Brady	60.00	25.00	15.00
(14)	Brandt	60.00	25.00	15.00
(15)	Bratcher	60.00	25.00	15.00
(16)	Brazil	60.00	25.00	15.00
(17)	Brower	60.00	25.00	15.00
(18)	Brown	60.00	25.00	15.00
(19)	Brubaker	60.00	25.00	15.00
(20)	Bryan	60.00	25.00	15.00
(21)	Canfield	60.00	25.00	15.00
(22)	W. Canfield	60.00	25.00	15.00
(23)	Cather	60.00	25.00	15.00
(24)	Chavez	60.00	25.00	15.00
(25)	Christain	60.00	25.00	15.00
(26)	Cochrane	60.00	25.00	15.00
(27)	Connolly	60.00	25.00	15.00
(28)	Cook	60.00	25.00	15.00
(29)	Cooper	60.00	25.00	15.00
(30)	Coumbe	60.00	25.00	15.00
(31)	Crandall	60.00	25.00	15.00
(32)	Crane	60.00	25.00	15.00
(33)	Crockett	60.00	25.00	15.00
(34)	Crosby	60.00	25.00	15.00
(35)	Cutshaw	60.00	25.00	15.00
(36)	Daly	60.00	25.00	15.00
(37)	Davis	60.00	25.00	15.00
(38)	Deal	60.00	25.00	15.00
(39)	Delaney	60.00	25.00	15.00
(40)	Dempsey	60.00	25.00	15.00
(41)	Dumovich	60.00	25.00	15.00
(42)	Eckert	60.00	25.00	15.00
(43)	Eldred	60.00	25.00	15.00
(44)	Elliott	60.00	25.00	15.00
(45)	Ellison	60.00	25.00	15.00
(46)	Emmer	60.00	25.00	15.00
(47)	Ennis	60.00	25.00	15.00
(48)	Essick	60.00	25.00	15.00
(49)	Finn	60.00	25.00	15.00
(50)	Flowers	60.00	25.00	15.00
(51)	Frederick	60.00	25.00	15.00
(52)	Fussell	60.00	25.00	15.00
(53)	Geary	60.00	25.00	15.00
(54)	Gorman	60.00	25.00	15.00
(55)	Griffin (San Francisco)	60.00	25.00	15.00

		NM	EX	VG
(56)	Griffin (Vernon)	60.00	25.00	15.00
(57)	Grimes	60.00	25.00	15.00
(58)	Guisto	60.00	25.00	15.00
(59)	Hannah	60.00	25.00	15.00
(60)	Haughy	60.00	25.00	15.00
(61)	Hemingway	60.00	25.00	15.00
(62)	Hendryx	60.00	25.00	15.00
(63)	Herman	200.00	100.00	50.00
(64)	High	60.00	25.00	15.00
(65)	Hoffman	60.00	25.00	15.00
(66)	Hood	60.00	25.00	15.00
(67)	Horan	60.00	25.00	15.00
(68)	Horton	60.00	25.00	15.00
(69)	Howard	60.00	25.00	15.00
(70)	Hughes	60.00	25.00	15.00
(71)	Hulvey	60.00	25.00	15.00
(72)	Hunnefield	60.00	25.00	15.00
(73)	Jacobs	60.00	25.00	15.00
(74)	James	60.00	25.00	15.00
(75)	Keating	60.00	25.00	15.00
(76)	Keefe	60.00	25.00	15.00
(77)	Kelly	60.00	25.00	15.00
(78)	Kilduff	60.00	25.00	15.00
(79)	Kohler	60.00	25.00	15.00
(80)	Kopp	60.00	25.00	15.00
(81)	Krause	60.00	25.00	15.00
(82)	Krug	60.00	25.00	15.00
(83)	Kunz	60.00	25.00	15.00
(84)	Lafayette	60.00	25.00	15.00
(85)	Tony Lazzeri	450.00	250.00	175.00
(86)	Leslie	60.00	25.00	15.00
(87)	Leverenz	60.00	25.00	15.00
(88)	Duffy Lewis	60.00	30.00	20.00
(89)	Lindemore	60.00	25.00	15.00
(90)	Ludolph	60.00	25.00	15.00
(91)	Makin	60.00	25.00	15.00
(92)	Martin (Sacramento)	60.00	25.00	15.00
(93)	Martin (Portland)	60.00	25.00	15.00
(94)	McCabe	60.00	25.00	15.00
(95)	McCann	60.00	25.00	15.00
(96)	McCarren	60.00	25.00	15.00
(97)	McDonald	60.00	25.00	15.00
(98)	McGinnis (Portland)	60.00	25.00	15.00
(99)	McGinnis (Sacramento)	60.00	25.00	15.00
(100)	McLaughlin	60.00	25.00	15.00
(101)	Milstead	60.00	25.00	15.00
(102)	Mitchell	60.00	25.00	15.00
(103)	Moudy	60.00	25.00	15.00
(104)	Mulcahy	60.00	25.00	15.00
(105)	Mulligan	60.00	25.00	15.00
(106)	Lefty O'Doul	450.00	250.00	175.00
(107)	O'Neil	60.00	25.00	15.00
(108)	Ortman	60.00	25.00	15.00
(109)	Pailey	60.00	25.00	15.00
(110)	Paynter	60.00	25.00	15.00
(111)	Peery	60.00	25.00	15.00
(112)	Penner	60.00	25.00	15.00
(113)	Pfeffer	60.00	25.00	15.00
(114)	Phillips	60.00	25.00	15.00
(115)	Pickering	60.00	25.00	15.00
(116)	Piercy	60.00	25.00	15.00
(117)	Pillette	60.00	25.00	15.00
(118)	Plummer	60.00	25.00	15.00
(119)	Ponder	60.00	25.00	15.00
(120)	Pruett	60.00	25.00	15.00
(121)	Rawlings	60.00	25.00	15.00
(122)	Read	60.00	25.00	15.00
(123)	Jimmy Reese	300.00	200.00	100.00
(124)	Rhyne	60.00	25.00	15.00
(125)	Riconda	60.00	25.00	15.00
(126)	Ritchie	60.00	25.00	15.00
(127)	Rohwer	60.00	25.00	15.00
(128)	Rowland	60.00	25.00	15.00
(129)	Ryan	60.00	25.00	15.00
(130)	Sandberg	60.00	25.00	15.00
(131)	Schang	60.00	25.00	15.00
(132)	Shea	60.00	25.00	15.00
(133)	M. Shea	60.00	25.00	15.00
(134)	Shellenback	60.00	25.00	15.00
(135)	Sherling	60.00	25.00	15.00
(136)	Siglin	60.00	25.00	15.00
(137)	Slade	60.00	25.00	15.00
(138)	Spencer	60.00	25.00	15.00
(139)	Steward	60.00	25.00	15.00
(140)	Stivers	60.00	25.00	15.00
(141)	Suhr	60.00	25.00	15.00
(142)	Sutherland	60.00	25.00	15.00
(143)	Thomas (Portland)	60.00	25.00	15.00
(144)	Thomas (Vernon)	60.00	25.00	15.00
(145)	Thompson	60.00	25.00	15.00
(146)	Tobin	60.00	25.00	15.00
(147)	Twombly	60.00	25.00	15.00
(148)	Valla	60.00	25.00	15.00
(149)	Vinci	60.00	25.00	15.00
(150)	O. Vitt	60.00	25.00	15.00
(151)	Wachenfeld	60.00	25.00	15.00
(152)	Paul Waner	1,200	600.00	350.00
(153)	Lloyd Waner	1,200	600.00	360.00
(154)	Warner	60.00	25.00	15.00
(155)	Watson	60.00	25.00	15.00
(156)	Weinert	60.00	25.00	15.00
(157)	Whaley	60.00	25.00	15.00
(158)	Whitney	60.00	25.00	15.00
(159)	Williams	60.00	25.00	15.00
(160)	Winters	60.00	25.00	15.00
(161)	Wolfer	60.00	25.00	15.00
(162)	Woodring	60.00	25.00	15.00
(163)	Yeargin	60.00	25.00	15.00
(164)	Yelle	60.00	25.00	15.00

1926 Zeenut Pacific Coast League

Except for their slightly smaller size (1-3/4" x 3-7/16"), the 1926 Zeenut cards are nearly identical to the previous two years. Considered more difficult than other Zeenuts series of this era, the 1926 set consists of more than 170 known subjects.

1926 Zeenut Pacific Coast League

		NM	EX	VG
	Common Player:	40.00	20.00	12.00
(1)	Agnew	40.00	20.00	12.00
(2)	Allen	40.00	20.00	12.00
(3)	Alley	40.00	20.00	12.00
(4)	Averill	600.00	400.00	200.00
(5)	Bagwell	40.00	20.00	12.00
(6)	Baker	40.00	20.00	12.00
(7)	T. Baldwin	40.00	20.00	12.00
(8)	Berry	40.00	20.00	12.00
(9)	Bool	40.00	20.00	12.00
(10)	Boone	40.00	20.00	12.00
(11)	Boyd	40.00	20.00	12.00
(12)	Brady	40.00	20.00	12.00
(13)	Brazil	40.00	20.00	12.00
(14)	Brower	40.00	20.00	12.00
(15)	Brubaker	40.00	20.00	12.00
(16)	Bryan	40.00	20.00	12.00
(17)	Burns	40.00	20.00	12.00
(18)	C. Canfield	40.00	20.00	12.00
(19)	W. Canfield	40.00	20.00	12.00
(20)	Carson	40.00	20.00	12.00
(21)	Christian	40.00	20.00	12.00
(22)	Cole	40.00	20.00	12.00
(23)	Connolly	40.00	20.00	12.00
(24)	Cook	40.00	20.00	12.00
(25)	Couch	40.00	20.00	12.00
(26)	Coumbe	40.00	20.00	12.00
(27)	Crockett	40.00	20.00	12.00
(28)	Cunningham	40.00	20.00	12.00
(29)	Cutshaw	40.00	20.00	12.00
(30)	Daglia	40.00	20.00	12.00
(31)	Danning	40.00	20.00	12.00
(32)	Davis	40.00	20.00	12.00
(33)	Delaney	40.00	20.00	12.00
(34)	Eckert	40.00	20.00	12.00
(35)	Eldred	40.00	20.00	12.00
(36)	Elliott	40.00	20.00	12.00
(37)	Ellison	40.00	20.00	12.00
(38)	Ellsworth	40.00	20.00	12.00
(39)	Elsh	40.00	20.00	12.00
(40)	Fenton	40.00	20.00	12.00
(41)	Finn	40.00	20.00	12.00
(42)	Flashkamper	40.00	20.00	12.00
(43)	Fowler	40.00	20.00	12.00
(44)	Frederick	40.00	20.00	12.00
(45)	Freeman	40.00	20.00	12.00
(46)	French	40.00	20.00	12.00
(47)	Garrison	40.00	20.00	12.00
(48)	Geary	40.00	20.00	12.00
(49)	Gillespie	40.00	20.00	12.00
(50)	Glazner	40.00	20.00	12.00
(51)	Gould	40.00	20.00	12.00
(52)	Governor	40.00	20.00	12.00
(53)	Griffin (Missions)	40.00	20.00	12.00
(54)	Griffin (San Francisco)	40.00	20.00	12.00
(55)	Guisto	40.00	20.00	12.00
(56)	Hamilton	40.00	20.00	12.00
(57)	Hannah	40.00	20.00	12.00
(58)	Hansen	40.00	20.00	12.00
(59)	Hasty	40.00	20.00	12.00
(60)	Hemingway	40.00	20.00	12.00
(61)	Hendryx	40.00	20.00	12.00
(62)	Hickok	40.00	20.00	12.00
(63)	Hillis	40.00	20.00	12.00
(64)	Hoffman	40.00	20.00	12.00
(65)	Hollerson	40.00	20.00	12.00
(66)	Holmes	40.00	20.00	12.00
(67)	Hood	40.00	20.00	12.00
(68)	Howard	40.00	20.00	12.00
(69)	Hufft	40.00	20.00	12.00
(70)	Hughes	40.00	20.00	12.00
(71)	Hulvey	40.00	20.00	12.00
(72)	Hurst	40.00	20.00	12.00
(73)	R. Jacobs	40.00	20.00	12.00
(74)	Jahn	40.00	20.00	12.00
(75)	Jenkins	40.00	20.00	12.00
(76)	Johnson	40.00	20.00	12.00
(77)	Jolly (Jolley)	65.00	32.50	20.00
(78)	Jones	40.00	20.00	12.00
(79)	Kallio	40.00	20.00	12.00
(80)	Keating	40.00	20.00	12.00
(81)	Kerr (Hollywood)	40.00	20.00	12.00
(82)	Kerr (San Francisco)	40.00	20.00	12.00
(83)	Kilduff	40.00	20.00	12.00
(84)	Killifer	40.00	20.00	12.00
(85)	Knight	40.00	20.00	12.00
(86)	Koehler	40.00	20.00	12.00
(87)	Kopp	40.00	20.00	12.00
(88)	Krause	40.00	20.00	12.00
(89)	Krug	40.00	20.00	12.00
(90)	Kunz	40.00	20.00	12.00
(91)	Lafayette	40.00	20.00	12.00
(92)	Lane	40.00	20.00	12.00
(93)	Lang	40.00	20.00	12.00
(94)	Lary	40.00	20.00	12.00
(95)	Leslie	40.00	20.00	12.00
(96)	Lindemore	40.00	20.00	12.00
(97)	Ludolph	40.00	20.00	12.00
(98)	Makin	40.00	20.00	12.00
(99)	Mangum	40.00	20.00	12.00
(100)	Martin	40.00	20.00	12.00
(101)	McCredie	40.00	20.00	12.00
(102)	McDowell	40.00	20.00	12.00
(103)	McKenry	40.00	20.00	12.00
(104)	McLoughlin	40.00	20.00	12.00
(105)	McNally	40.00	20.00	12.00
(106)	McPhee	40.00	20.00	12.00
(107)	Meeker	40.00	20.00	12.00
(108)	Metz	40.00	20.00	12.00
(109)	Miller	40.00	20.00	12.00
(110)	Mitchell (Los Angeles)	40.00	20.00	12.00
(111)	Mitchell (San Francisco)	40.00	20.00	12.00
(112)	Monroe	40.00	20.00	12.00
(113)	Moudy	40.00	20.00	12.00
(114)	Mulcahy	40.00	20.00	12.00
(115)	Mulligan	40.00	20.00	12.00
(116)	Murphy	40.00	20.00	12.00
(117)	Lefty O'Doul	400.00	300.00	175.00
(118)	O'Neill	40.00	20.00	12.00
(119)	Oeschger	40.00	20.00	12.00
(120)	Oliver	40.00	20.00	12.00
(121)	Ortman	40.00	20.00	12.00
(122)	Osborn	40.00	20.00	12.00
(123)	Paynter	40.00	20.00	12.00
(124)	Peters	40.00	20.00	12.00
(125)	Pfahler	40.00	20.00	12.00
(126)	Pillette	40.00	20.00	12.00
(127)	Plummer	40.00	20.00	12.00
(128)	Prothro	40.00	20.00	12.00
(129)	Pruett	40.00	20.00	12.00
(130)	Rachac	40.00	20.00	12.00
(131)	Ramsey	40.00	20.00	12.00
(132)	Rathjen	40.00	20.00	12.00
(133)	Read	40.00	20.00	12.00
(134)	Redman	40.00	20.00	12.00
(135)	Jimmy Reese	40.00	20.00	12.00
(136)	Rodda	40.00	20.00	12.00
(137)	Rohwer	40.00	20.00	12.00
(138)	Ryan	40.00	20.00	12.00
(139)	Sandberg	40.00	20.00	12.00
(140)	Sanders	40.00	20.00	12.00
(141)	E. Shea	40.00	20.00	12.00
(142)	M. Shea	40.00	20.00	12.00
(143)	Sheehan	40.00	20.00	12.00
(144)	Shellenbach	40.00	20.00	12.00
(145)	Sherlock	40.00	20.00	12.00
(146)	Siglin	40.00	20.00	12.00
(147)	Slade	40.00	20.00	12.00
(148)	E. Smith	40.00	20.00	12.00
(149)	M. Smith	40.00	20.00	12.00
(150)	Staley	40.00	20.00	12.00
(151)	Statz	75.00	37.50	22.50
(152)	Stroud	40.00	20.00	12.00
(153)	Stuart	40.00	20.00	12.00
(154)	Suhr	40.00	20.00	12.00
(155)	Swanson	40.00	20.00	12.00
(156)	Sweeney	40.00	20.00	12.00
(157)	Tadevich	40.00	20.00	12.00
(158)	Thomas	40.00	20.00	12.00
(159)	Thompson	40.00	20.00	12.00
(160)	Tobin	40.00	20.00	12.00
(161)	Valla	40.00	20.00	12.00
(162)	Vargas	40.00	20.00	12.00
(163)	Vinci	40.00	20.00	12.00
(164)	Walters	40.00	20.00	12.00
(165)	Lloyd Waner	600.00	400.00	200.00
(166)	Weis	40.00	20.00	12.00
(167)	Whitney	40.00	20.00	12.00
(168)	Williams	40.00	20.00	12.00
(169)	Wright	40.00	20.00	12.00
(170)	Yelle	40.00	20.00	12.00
(171)	Zaeffel	40.00	20.00	12.00
(172)	Zoellers	40.00	20.00	12.00

1927 Zeenut Pacific Coast League

The 1927 Zeenuts are about the same size (1-3/4" x 3-3/8") and color as the 1926 issue, except the year is expressed in just two digits (27), a practice that continued through 1930. There are 144 subjects known.

		NM	EX	VG
	Common Player:	40.00	20.00	12.00
	With Coupon:	275.00	135.00	85.00
(1)	Agnew	40.00	20.00	12.00
(2)	Arlett	40.00	20.00	12.00
(3)	Averill	600.00	300.00	180.00
(4)	Backer	40.00	20.00	12.00
(5)	Bagwell	40.00	20.00	12.00
(6)	Baker	40.00	20.00	12.00
(7)	D. Baker	40.00	20.00	12.00
(8)	Ballenger	40.00	20.00	12.00
(9)	Baumgartner	40.00	20.00	12.00
(10)	Bigbee	40.00	20.00	12.00
(11)	Boehler	40.00	20.00	12.00
(12)	Bool	40.00	20.00	12.00
(13)	Borreani	40.00	20.00	12.00
(14)	Brady	40.00	20.00	12.00
(15)	Bratcher	40.00	20.00	12.00
(16)	Brett	40.00	20.00	12.00
(17)	Brown	40.00	20.00	12.00
(18)	Brubaker	40.00	20.00	12.00
(19)	Bryan	40.00	20.00	12.00
(20)	Callaghan	40.00	20.00	12.00
(21)	Caveney	40.00	20.00	12.00
(22)	Christian	40.00	20.00	12.00
(23)	Cissell	40.00	20.00	12.00
(24)	Cook	40.00	20.00	12.00
(25)	Cooper (Oakland)	40.00	20.00	12.00
(26)	Cooper (Sacramento)	40.00	20.00	12.00
(27)	Cox	40.00	20.00	12.00
(28)	Cunningham	40.00	20.00	12.00
(29)	Daglia	40.00	20.00	12.00
(30)	Dickerman	40.00	20.00	12.00
(31)	Dumovitch	40.00	20.00	12.00
(32)	Eckert	40.00	20.00	12.00
(33)	Eldred	40.00	20.00	12.00
(34)	Ellison	40.00	20.00	12.00
(35)	Fenton	40.00	20.00	12.00
(36)	Finn	40.00	20.00	12.00
(37)	Fischer	40.00	20.00	12.00
(38)	Frederick	40.00	20.00	12.00
(39)	French	40.00	20.00	12.00
(40)	Fullerton	40.00	20.00	12.00
(41)	Geary	40.00	20.00	12.00
(42)	Gillespie	40.00	20.00	12.00
(43)	Gooch	40.00	20.00	12.00
(44)	Gould	40.00	20.00	12.00
(45)	Governor	40.00	20.00	12.00
(46)	Guisto	40.00	20.00	12.00
(47)	Hannah	40.00	20.00	12.00
(48)	Hasty	40.00	20.00	12.00
(49)	Hemingway	40.00	20.00	12.00
(50)	Hoffman	40.00	20.00	12.00
(51)	Hood	40.00	20.00	12.00
(52)	Hooper	600.00	300.00	180.00
(53)	Hudgens	40.00	20.00	12.00
(54)	Hufft	40.00	20.00	12.00
(55)	Hughes	40.00	20.00	12.00
(56)	Jahn	40.00	20.00	12.00
(57)	Johnson (Portland)	40.00	20.00	12.00
(58)	Johnson (Seals)	40.00	20.00	12.00
(59)	Jolly (Jolley)	60.00	30.00	18.00
(60)	Jones	40.00	20.00	12.00
(61)	Kallio	40.00	20.00	12.00
(62)	Keating	40.00	20.00	12.00
(63)	Keefe	40.00	20.00	12.00
(64)	Killifer	40.00	20.00	12.00
(65)	Kimmick	40.00	20.00	12.00
(66)	Kinney	40.00	20.00	12.00
(67)	Knight	40.00	20.00	12.00
(68)	Koehler	40.00	20.00	12.00
(69)	Kopp	40.00	20.00	12.00
(70)	Krause	40.00	20.00	12.00
(71)	Krug	40.00	20.00	12.00
(72)	Kunz	40.00	20.00	12.00
(73)	Lary	40.00	20.00	12.00
(74)	Leard	40.00	20.00	12.00
(75)	Lingrel	40.00	20.00	12.00
(76)	Ludolph	40.00	20.00	12.00
(77)	Mails	40.00	20.00	12.00
(78)	Makin	40.00	20.00	12.00
(79)	Martin	40.00	20.00	12.00
(80)	May	40.00	20.00	12.00
(81)	McCabe	40.00	20.00	12.00
(82)	McCurdy	40.00	20.00	12.00
(83)	McDaniel	40.00	20.00	12.00
(84)	McGee	40.00	20.00	12.00
(85)	McLaughlin	40.00	20.00	12.00
(86)	McMurtry	40.00	20.00	12.00
(87)	Metz	40.00	20.00	12.00
(88)	Miljus	40.00	20.00	12.00
(89)	Mitchell	40.00	20.00	12.00
(90)	Monroe	40.00	20.00	12.00
(91)	Moudy	40.00	20.00	12.00
(92)	Mulligan	40.00	20.00	12.00
(93)	Murphy	40.00	20.00	12.00
(94)	O'Brien	40.00	20.00	12.00
(95)	Lefty O'Doul	400.00	300.00	175.00
(96)	Oliver	40.00	20.00	12.00
(97)	Osborn	40.00	20.00	12.00
(98)	Parker (Missions, batting.)	40.00	20.00	12.00
(99)	Parker (Missions, throwing.)	40.00	20.00	12.00
(100)	Parker (Portland)	40.00	20.00	12.00
(101)	Peters	40.00	20.00	12.00
(102)	Pillette	40.00	20.00	12.00
(103)	Ponder	40.00	20.00	12.00
(104)	Prothro	80.00	40.00	25.00
(105)	Rachac	40.00	20.00	12.00
(106)	Ramsey	40.00	20.00	12.00
(107)	Read	40.00	20.00	12.00
(108)	Jimmy Reese	250.00	125.00	75.00
(109)	Rodda	40.00	20.00	12.00
(110)	Rohwer	40.00	20.00	12.00
(111)	Rose	40.00	20.00	12.00
(112)	Ryan	40.00	20.00	12.00
(113)	Sandberg	40.00	20.00	12.00
(114)	Sanders	40.00	20.00	12.00
(115)	Severeid	40.00	20.00	12.00
(116)	Shea	40.00	20.00	12.00
(117)	Sheehan (Hollywood)	40.00	20.00	12.00
(118)	Sheehan (Seals)	40.00	20.00	12.00
(119)	Sherlock	40.00	20.00	12.00
(120a)	Shinners (Date is "1927.")	40.00	20.00	12.00
(120b)	Shinners (Date is "27.")	40.00	20.00	12.00

		NM	EX	VG
(121)	Singleton	40.00	20.00	12.00
(122)	Slade	40.00	20.00	12.00
(123)	E. Smith	40.00	20.00	12.00
(124)	Sparks	40.00	20.00	12.00
(125)	Stokes	40.00	20.00	12.00
(126)	J. Storti	40.00	20.00	12.00
(127)	L. Storti	40.00	20.00	12.00
(128)	Strand	40.00	20.00	12.00
(129)	Suhr	40.00	20.00	12.00
(130)	Sunseri	40.00	20.00	12.00
(131)	Swanson	40.00	20.00	12.00
(132)	Tierney	40.00	20.00	12.00
(133)	Valla	40.00	20.00	12.00
(134)	Vargas	40.00	20.00	12.00
(135)	Vitt	40.00	20.00	12.00
(136)	Weinert	40.00	20.00	12.00
(137)	Weis	40.00	20.00	12.00
(138)	Wendell	40.00	20.00	12.00
(139)	Whitney	40.00	20.00	12.00
(140)	Williams	40.00	20.00	12.00
(141)	Guy Williams	40.00	20.00	12.00
(142)	Woodson	40.00	20.00	12.00
(143)	Wright	40.00	20.00	12.00
(144)	Yelle	40.00	20.00	12.00

1928 Zeenut Pacific Coast League

Zeenut cards from 1928 through 1930 maintain the same format as the 1927 series. Measuring about 1-3/4" x 3-3/8", the 1928 series consists of 168 known subjects.

		NM	EX	VG
Common Player:		40.00	20.00	12.00
(1)	Agnew	40.00	20.00	12.00
(2)	Earl Averill	600.00	300.00	180.00
(3)	Backer	40.00	20.00	12.00
(4)	Baker	40.00	20.00	12.00
(5)	Baldwin	40.00	20.00	12.00
(6)	Barfoot	40.00	20.00	12.00
(7)	Bassler	40.00	20.00	12.00
(8)	Berger	40.00	20.00	12.00
(9)	Bigbee (Los Angeles)	40.00	20.00	12.00
(10)	Bigbee (Portland)	40.00	20.00	12.00
(11)	Bodie	40.00	20.00	12.00
(12)	Boehler	40.00	20.00	12.00
(13)	Bool	40.00	20.00	12.00
(14)	Boone	40.00	20.00	12.00
(15)	Borreani	40.00	20.00	12.00
(16)	Bratcher	40.00	20.00	12.00
(17)	Brenzel	40.00	20.00	12.00
(18)	Brubaker	40.00	20.00	12.00
(19)	Bryan	40.00	20.00	12.00
(20)	Burkett	40.00	20.00	12.00
(21)	Camilli	40.00	20.00	12.00
(22)	W. Canfield	40.00	20.00	12.00
(23)	Caveney	40.00	20.00	12.00
(24)	Cohen	100.00	50.00	30.00
(25)	Cook	40.00	20.00	12.00
(26)	Cooper	40.00	20.00	12.00
(27)	Craghead	40.00	20.00	12.00
(28)	Crosetti	200.00	100.00	60.00
(29)	Cunningham	40.00	20.00	12.00
(30)	Daglia	40.00	20.00	12.00
(31)	Davis	40.00	20.00	12.00
(32)	Dean	40.00	20.00	12.00
(33)	Dittmar	40.00	20.00	12.00
(34)	Donovan	40.00	20.00	12.00
(35)	Downs	40.00	20.00	12.00
(36)	Duff	40.00	20.00	12.00
(37)	Eckert	40.00	20.00	12.00
(38)	Eldred	40.00	20.00	12.00
(39)	Ellsworth	40.00	20.00	12.00
(40)	Fenton	40.00	20.00	12.00
(41)	Finn	40.00	20.00	12.00
(42)	Fitterer	40.00	20.00	12.00
(43)	Flynn	40.00	20.00	12.00
(44)	Frazier	40.00	20.00	12.00
(45)	French (Portland)	40.00	20.00	12.00
(46)	French (Sacramento)	40.00	20.00	12.00
(47)	Fullerton	40.00	20.00	12.00
(48)	Gabler	40.00	20.00	12.00
(49)	Gomes	40.00	20.00	12.00
(50)	Gooch	40.00	20.00	12.00
(51)	Gould	40.00	20.00	12.00
(52)	Governor	40.00	20.00	12.00
(53)	Graham ("S" on uniform.)	40.00	20.00	12.00
(54)	Graham (No "S" on uniform.)	40.00	20.00	12.00
(55)	Guisto	40.00	20.00	12.00
(56)	Hannah	40.00	20.00	12.00
(57)	Hansen	40.00	20.00	12.00
(58)	Harris	40.00	20.00	12.00

		NM	EX	VG
(59)	Hasty	40.00	20.00	12.00
(60)	Heath	40.00	20.00	12.00
(61)	Hoffman	40.00	20.00	12.00
(62)	Holling	40.00	20.00	12.00
(63)	Hood	40.00	20.00	12.00
(64)	House	40.00	20.00	12.00
(65)	Howard	40.00	20.00	12.00
(66)	Hudgens	40.00	20.00	12.00
(67)	Hufft	40.00	20.00	12.00
(68)	Hughes	40.00	20.00	12.00
(69)	Hulvey	40.00	20.00	12.00
(70)	Jacobs	40.00	20.00	12.00
(71)	Johnson (Portland)	40.00	20.00	12.00
(72)	Johnson (San Francisco)	40.00	20.00	12.00
(73)	Jolley	60.00	30.00	18.00
(74)	Jones (Batting)	40.00	20.00	12.00
(75)	Jones (Throwing)	40.00	20.00	12.00
(76)	Kallio	40.00	20.00	12.00
(77)	Keating	40.00	20.00	12.00
(78)	Keefe	40.00	20.00	12.00
(79)	Keesey	40.00	20.00	12.00
(80)	Kerr	40.00	20.00	12.00
(81)	Killifer	40.00	20.00	12.00
(82)	Kinney	40.00	20.00	12.00
(83)	Knight	40.00	20.00	12.00
(84)	Knothe	40.00	20.00	12.00
(85)	Koehler	40.00	20.00	12.00
(86)	Kopp	40.00	20.00	12.00
(87)	Krause	40.00	20.00	12.00
(88)	Krug	40.00	20.00	12.00
(89)	Lary	40.00	20.00	12.00
(90)	LeBourveau	40.00	20.00	12.00
(91)	Lee	40.00	20.00	12.00
(92)	Ernie Lombardi	900.00	450.00	275.00
(93)	Mails	40.00	20.00	12.00
(94)	Martin (Missions)	40.00	20.00	12.00
(95)	Martin (Seattle)	40.00	20.00	12.00
(96)	May	40.00	20.00	12.00
(97)	McCabe	40.00	20.00	12.00
(98)	McCrea	40.00	20.00	12.00
(99)	McDaniel	40.00	20.00	12.00
(100)	McLaughlin	40.00	20.00	12.00
(101)	McNulty	40.00	20.00	12.00
(102)	Mellano	40.00	20.00	12.00
(103)	Irish Muesel (Meusel)	40.00	20.00	12.00
(104)	Middleton	40.00	20.00	12.00
(105)	Mishkin	40.00	20.00	12.00
(106)	Mitchell	40.00	20.00	12.00
(107)	Monroe	40.00	20.00	12.00
(108)	Moudy	40.00	20.00	12.00
(109)	Mulcahy	40.00	20.00	12.00
(110)	Muller	40.00	20.00	12.00
(111)	Mulligan	40.00	20.00	12.00
(112)	W. Murphy	40.00	20.00	12.00
(113)	Nance	40.00	20.00	12.00
(114)	Nelson	40.00	20.00	12.00
(115)	Osborn	40.00	20.00	12.00
(116)	Osborne	40.00	20.00	12.00
(117)	Parker	40.00	20.00	12.00
(118)	Peters	40.00	20.00	12.00
(119)	Pillette	40.00	20.00	12.00
(120)	Pinelli	40.00	20.00	12.00
(121)	Plitt	40.00	20.00	12.00
(122)	Ponder	40.00	20.00	12.00
(123)	Rachac	40.00	20.00	12.00
(124)	Read	40.00	20.00	12.00
(125)	Reed	40.00	20.00	12.00
(126)	Jimmy Reese	250.00	125.00	75.00
(127)	Rego	40.00	20.00	12.00
(128)	Rhodes	40.00	20.00	12.00
(129)	Rhyne	40.00	20.00	12.00
(130)	Rodda	40.00	20.00	12.00
(131)	Rohwer	40.00	20.00	12.00
(132)	Rose	40.00	20.00	12.00
(133)	Roth	40.00	20.00	12.00
(134)	Ruble	40.00	20.00	12.00
(135)	Ryan	40.00	20.00	12.00
(136)	Sandberg	40.00	20.00	12.00
(137)	Schulmerich	40.00	20.00	12.00
(138)	Severeid	40.00	20.00	12.00
(139)	Shea	40.00	20.00	12.00
(140)	Sheely	40.00	20.00	12.00
(141)	Shellenback	40.00	20.00	12.00
(142)	Sherlock	40.00	20.00	12.00
(143)	Sigafoos	40.00	20.00	12.00
(144)	Singleton	40.00	20.00	12.00
(145)	Slade	40.00	20.00	12.00
(146)	Smith	40.00	20.00	12.00
(147)	Sprinz	40.00	20.00	12.00
(148)	Staley	40.00	20.00	12.00
(149)	Suhr	40.00	20.00	12.00
(150)	Sunseri	40.00	20.00	12.00
(151)	Swanson	40.00	20.00	12.00
(152)	Sweeney	40.00	20.00	12.00
(153)	Teachout	40.00	20.00	12.00
(154)	Twombly	40.00	20.00	12.00
(155)	Vargas	40.00	20.00	12.00
(156)	Vinci	40.00	20.00	12.00
(157)	Vitt	40.00	20.00	12.00
(158)	Warhop	40.00	20.00	12.00
(159)	Weathersby	40.00	20.00	12.00
(160)	Weiss	40.00	20.00	12.00
(161)	Welch	40.00	20.00	12.00
(162)	Wera	40.00	20.00	12.00
(163)	Wetzel	40.00	20.00	12.00
(164)	Whitney	40.00	20.00	12.00
(165)	Williams	40.00	20.00	12.00
(166)	Wilson	40.00	20.00	12.00
(167)	Wolfer	40.00	20.00	12.00
(168)	Yerkes	40.00	20.00	12.00

1929 Zeenut Pacific Coast League

Zeenut cards from 1928 through 1930 maintain the same format as the 1927 series. Measuring about 1-3/4" x 3-1/2", the 1929 series consists of 168 known subjects.

		NM	EX	VG
Common Player:		40.00	20.00	12.00
With Coupon:		400.00	200.00	120.00
(1)	Albert	40.00	20.00	12.00
(2)	Almada	100.00	50.00	30.00
(3)	Anderson	40.00	20.00	12.00
(4)	Anton	40.00	20.00	12.00
(5)	Backer	40.00	20.00	12.00
(6)	Baker	40.00	20.00	12.00
(7)	Baldwin	40.00	20.00	12.00
(8)	Barbee	40.00	20.00	12.00
(9)	Barfoot	40.00	20.00	12.00
(10)	Bassler	40.00	20.00	12.00
(11)	Bates	40.00	20.00	12.00
(12)	Berger	40.00	20.00	12.00
(13)	Boehler	40.00	20.00	12.00
(14)	Boone	40.00	20.00	12.00
(15)	Borreani	40.00	20.00	12.00
(16)	Brenzel	40.00	20.00	12.00
(17)	Brooks	40.00	20.00	12.00
(18)	Brubaker	40.00	20.00	12.00
(19)	Bryan	40.00	20.00	12.00
(20)	Burke	40.00	20.00	12.00
(21)	Burkett	40.00	20.00	12.00
(22)	Burns	40.00	20.00	12.00
(23)	Bush	40.00	20.00	12.00
(24)	Butler	40.00	20.00	12.00
(25)	Camilli	40.00	20.00	12.00
(26)	Carlyle (Hollywood)	40.00	20.00	12.00
(27)	Carlyle	40.00	20.00	12.00
(28)	Cascarella	40.00	20.00	12.00
(29)	Caveney	40.00	20.00	12.00
(30)	Childs	40.00	20.00	12.00
(31)	Christensen	40.00	20.00	12.00
(32)	Cole	40.00	20.00	12.00
(33)	Collard	40.00	20.00	12.00
(34)	Cooper	40.00	20.00	12.00
(35)	Couch	40.00	20.00	12.00
(36)	Cox	40.00	20.00	12.00
(37)	Craghead	40.00	20.00	12.00
(38)	Crandall	40.00	20.00	12.00
(39)	Cronin	40.00	20.00	12.00
(40)	Crosetti	100.00	50.00	30.00
(41)	Daglia	40.00	20.00	12.00
(42)	Davis	40.00	20.00	12.00
(43)	Dean	40.00	20.00	12.00
(44)	Dittmar	40.00	20.00	12.00
(45)	Donovan	40.00	20.00	12.00
(46)	Dumovich	40.00	20.00	12.00
(47)	Eckardt	40.00	20.00	12.00
(48)	Ellsworth	40.00	20.00	12.00
(49)	Fenton	40.00	20.00	12.00
(50)	Finn	40.00	20.00	12.00
(51)	Fisch	40.00	20.00	12.00
(52)	Flynn	40.00	20.00	12.00
(53)	Frazier	40.00	20.00	12.00
(54)	Freitas	40.00	20.00	12.00
(55)	French	40.00	20.00	12.00
(56)	Gabler	40.00	20.00	12.00
(57)	Glynn	40.00	20.00	12.00
(58)	Lefty Gomez	1,200	600.00	360.00
(59)	Gould	40.00	20.00	12.00
(60)	Governor	40.00	20.00	12.00
(61)	Graham	40.00	20.00	12.00
(62)	Hand	40.00	20.00	12.00
(63)	Hannah	40.00	20.00	12.00
(64)	Harris	40.00	20.00	12.00
(65)	Heath	40.00	20.00	12.00
(66)	Heatherly	40.00	20.00	12.00
(67)	Hepting	40.00	20.00	12.00
(68)	Hillis	40.00	20.00	12.00
(69)	Hoffman	40.00	20.00	12.00
(70)	Holling	40.00	20.00	12.00
(71)	Hood	40.00	20.00	12.00
(72)	House	40.00	20.00	12.00
(73)	Howard	40.00	20.00	12.00
(74)	Hubbell	40.00	20.00	12.00
(75)	Hufft	40.00	20.00	12.00
(76)	Hurst	40.00	20.00	12.00
(77)	Jacobs (Los Angeles)	40.00	20.00	12.00
(78)	Jacobs (San Francisco)	40.00	20.00	12.00
(79)	Jahn	40.00	20.00	12.00
(80)	Jeffcoat	40.00	20.00	12.00
(81)	Johnson	40.00	20.00	12.00
(82)	Jolley	60.00	30.00	18.00
(83)	Jones	40.00	20.00	12.00
(84)	Jones	40.00	20.00	12.00
(85)	Kallio	40.00	20.00	12.00
(86)	Kasich	40.00	20.00	12.00
(87)	Keane	40.00	20.00	12.00
(88)	Keating	40.00	20.00	12.00
(89)	Keesey	40.00	20.00	12.00
(90)	Killifer	40.00	20.00	12.00
(91)	Knight	40.00	20.00	12.00

#	Player	NM	EX	VG
(92)	Knothe	40.00	20.00	12.00
(93)	Knott	40.00	20.00	12.00
(94)	Koehler	40.00	20.00	12.00
(95)	Krasovich	40.00	20.00	12.00
(96)	Krause	40.00	20.00	12.00
(97)	Krug (Hollywood)	40.00	20.00	12.00
(98)	Krug (Los Angeles)	40.00	20.00	12.00
(99)	Kunz	40.00	20.00	12.00
(100)	Langford	40.00	20.00	12.00
(101)	Lee	40.00	20.00	12.00
(102)	Ernie Lombardi	600.00	350.00	175.00
(103)	Mahaffey	40.00	20.00	12.00
(104)	Mails	40.00	20.00	12.00
(105)	Maloney	40.00	20.00	12.00
(106)	McCabe	40.00	20.00	12.00
(107)	McDaniel	40.00	20.00	12.00
(108)	McEvoy	40.00	20.00	12.00
(109)	McIssacs	40.00	20.00	12.00
(110)	McQuaid	40.00	20.00	12.00
(111)	Miller	40.00	20.00	12.00
(112)	Monroe	40.00	20.00	12.00
(113)	Muller	40.00	20.00	12.00
(114)	Mulligan	40.00	20.00	12.00
(115)	Nance	40.00	20.00	12.00
(116)	Nelson	40.00	20.00	12.00
(117)	Nevers	40.00	20.00	12.00
(118)	Oana	450.00	225.00	135.00
(119)	Olney	40.00	20.00	12.00
(120)	Ortman	40.00	20.00	12.00
(121)	Osborne	40.00	20.00	12.00
(122)	Ostenberg	40.00	20.00	12.00
(123)	Peters	40.00	20.00	12.00
(124)	Pillette	40.00	20.00	12.00
(125)	Pinelli	40.00	20.00	12.00
(126)	Pipgras	40.00	20.00	12.00
(127)	Plitt	40.00	20.00	12.00
(128)	Polvogt	40.00	20.00	12.00
(129)	Rachac	40.00	20.00	12.00
(130)	Read	40.00	20.00	12.00
(131)	Reed	40.00	20.00	12.00
(132)	Jimmy Reese	200.00	125.00	75.00
(133)	Rego	40.00	20.00	12.00
(134)	Ritter	40.00	20.00	12.00
(135)	Roberts	40.00	20.00	12.00
(136)	Rodda	40.00	20.00	12.00
(137)	Rodgers	40.00	20.00	12.00
(138)	Rohwer	40.00	20.00	12.00
(139)	Rollings	40.00	20.00	12.00
(140)	Rumler	40.00	20.00	12.00
(141)	Ryan	40.00	20.00	12.00
(142)	Sandberg	40.00	20.00	12.00
(143)	Schino	40.00	20.00	12.00
(144)	Schmidt	40.00	20.00	12.00
(145)	Schulmerich	40.00	20.00	12.00
(146)	Scott	40.00	20.00	12.00
(147)	Severeid	40.00	20.00	12.00
(148)	Shanklin	40.00	20.00	12.00
(149)	Sherlock	40.00	20.00	12.00
(150)	Slade	40.00	20.00	12.00
(151)	Staley	40.00	20.00	12.00
(152)	Statz	60.00	30.00	18.00
(153)	Steinecke	40.00	20.00	12.00
(154)	Suhr	40.00	20.00	12.00
(155)	Taylor	40.00	20.00	12.00
(156)	Thurston	40.00	20.00	12.00
(157)	Tierney	40.00	20.00	12.00
(158)	Tolson	40.00	20.00	12.00
(159)	Tomlin	40.00	20.00	12.00
(160)	Vergez	40.00	20.00	12.00
(161)	Vinci	40.00	20.00	12.00
(162)	Volkman	40.00	20.00	12.00
(163)	Walsh	40.00	20.00	12.00
(164)	Warren	40.00	20.00	12.00
(165)	Webb	40.00	20.00	12.00
(166)	Weustling	40.00	20.00	12.00
(167)	Williams	40.00	20.00	12.00
(168)	Wingo	40.00	20.00	12.00

1930 Zeenut Pacific Coast League

Zeenut cards from 1928 through 1930 maintain the same format as the 1927 series. Measuring about 1-13/16" x 3-1/2", the 1930 series consists of 186 known subjects. There are some lettering variations in the series. Most coupons carry an expiration date of April 1, 1931, but some coupons have no expiration date stated.

		NM	EX	VG
	Common Player:	40.00	20.00	12.00
(1)	Allington	40.00	20.00	12.00
(2)	Almada	50.00	25.00	15.00
(3)	Andrews	40.00	20.00	12.00
(4)	Anton	40.00	20.00	12.00

#	Player	NM	EX	VG
(5)	Arlett	40.00	20.00	12.00
(6)	Backer	40.00	20.00	12.00
(7)	Baecht	40.00	20.00	12.00
(8)	Baker	40.00	20.00	12.00
(9)	Baldwin	40.00	20.00	12.00
(10)	Ballou	40.00	20.00	12.00
(11)	Barbee	40.00	20.00	12.00
(12)	Barfoot	40.00	20.00	12.00
(13)	Bassler	40.00	20.00	12.00
(14)	Bates	40.00	20.00	12.00
(15)	Beck	40.00	20.00	12.00
(16)	Boone	40.00	20.00	12.00
(17)	Bowman	40.00	20.00	12.00
(18)	Brannon	40.00	20.00	12.00
(19)	Brenzel	40.00	20.00	12.00
(20)	Brown	40.00	20.00	12.00
(21)	Brubaker	40.00	20.00	12.00
(22)	Brucker	40.00	20.00	12.00
(23)	Bryan	40.00	20.00	12.00
(24)	Burkett	40.00	20.00	12.00
(25)	Burns	40.00	20.00	12.00
(26)	Butler	40.00	20.00	12.00
(27)	Camilli	40.00	20.00	12.00
(28)	Carlyle	40.00	20.00	12.00
(29)	Caster	40.00	20.00	12.00
(30)	Caveney	40.00	20.00	12.00
(31)	Chamberlain	40.00	20.00	12.00
(32)	Chatham	40.00	20.00	12.00
(33)	Childs	40.00	20.00	12.00
(34)	Christensen	40.00	20.00	12.00
(35)	Church	40.00	20.00	12.00
(36)	Cole	40.00	20.00	12.00
(37)	Coleman	40.00	20.00	12.00
(38)	Collins	40.00	20.00	12.00
(39)	Coscarart	40.00	20.00	12.00
(40)	Cox	40.00	20.00	12.00
(41)	Coyle	40.00	20.00	12.00
(42)	Craghead	40.00	20.00	12.00
(43)	Cronin	40.00	20.00	12.00
(44)	Crosetti	100.00	50.00	30.00
(45)	Daglia	40.00	20.00	12.00
(46)	Davis	40.00	20.00	12.00
(47)	Dean	40.00	20.00	12.00
(48)	DeViveiros	40.00	20.00	12.00
(49)	Dittmar	40.00	20.00	12.00
(50)	Donovan	40.00	20.00	12.00
(51)	Douglas	40.00	20.00	12.00
(52)	Dumovich	40.00	20.00	12.00
(53)	Edwards	40.00	20.00	12.00
(54)	Ellsworth	40.00	20.00	12.00
(55)	Falk	40.00	20.00	12.00
(56)	Fisch	40.00	20.00	12.00
(57)	Flynn	40.00	20.00	12.00
(58)	Freitas	40.00	20.00	12.00
(59)	French (Portland)	40.00	20.00	12.00
(60)	French (Sacramento)	40.00	20.00	12.00
(61)	Gabler	40.00	20.00	12.00
(62)	Gaston	40.00	20.00	12.00
(63)	Gazella	40.00	20.00	12.00
(64)	Gould	40.00	20.00	12.00
(65)	Governor	40.00	20.00	12.00
(66)	Green	40.00	20.00	12.00
(67)	Griffin	40.00	20.00	12.00
(68)	Haney	40.00	20.00	12.00
(69)	Hannah	40.00	20.00	12.00
(70)	Harper	40.00	20.00	12.00
(71)	Heath	40.00	20.00	12.00
(72)	Hillis	40.00	20.00	12.00
(73)	Hoag	40.00	20.00	12.00
(74)	Hoffman	40.00	20.00	12.00
(75)	Holland	40.00	20.00	12.00
(76)	Hollerson	40.00	20.00	12.00
(77)	Holling	40.00	20.00	12.00
(78)	Hood	40.00	20.00	12.00
(79)	Horn	40.00	20.00	12.00
(80)	House	40.00	20.00	12.00
(81)	Hubbell	40.00	20.00	12.00
(82)	Hufft	40.00	20.00	12.00
(83)	Hurst	40.00	20.00	12.00
(84)	Jacobs (Los Angeles)	40.00	20.00	12.00
(85)	Jacobs (Oakland)	40.00	20.00	12.00
(86)	Jacobs	40.00	20.00	12.00
(87)	Jahn	40.00	20.00	12.00
(88)	Jeffcoat	40.00	20.00	12.00
(89)	Johns	40.00	20.00	12.00
(90)	Johnson (Portland)	40.00	20.00	12.00
(91)	Johnson (Seattle)	40.00	20.00	12.00
(92)	Joiner	40.00	20.00	12.00
(93)	Kallio	40.00	20.00	12.00
(94)	Kasich	40.00	20.00	12.00
(95)	Keating	40.00	20.00	12.00
(96)	Kelly	40.00	20.00	12.00
(97)	Killifer	40.00	20.00	12.00
(98)	Knight	40.00	20.00	12.00
(99)	Knothe	40.00	20.00	12.00
(100)	Koehler	40.00	20.00	12.00
(101)	Kunz	40.00	20.00	12.00
(102)	Lamanski	40.00	20.00	12.00
(103)	Lawrence	40.00	20.00	12.00
(104)	Lee	40.00	20.00	12.00
(105)	Leishman	40.00	20.00	12.00
(106)	Lelivelt	40.00	20.00	12.00
(107)	Lieber	40.00	20.00	12.00
(108)	Ernie Lombardi	450.00	300.00	175.00
(109)	Mails	40.00	20.00	12.00
(110)	Maloney	40.00	20.00	12.00
(111)	Martin	40.00	20.00	12.00
(112)	McDougal	40.00	20.00	12.00
(113)	McLaughlin	40.00	20.00	12.00
(114)	McQuaide	40.00	20.00	12.00
(115)	Mellana	40.00	20.00	12.00
(116)	Miljus ("S" on uniform.)	40.00	20.00	12.00
(117)	Miljus ("Seals" on uniform.)	40.00	20.00	12.00
(118)	Monroe	40.00	20.00	12.00
(119)	Montgomery	40.00	20.00	12.00
(120)	Moore	40.00	20.00	12.00
(121)	Mulana	40.00	20.00	12.00
(122)	Muller	40.00	20.00	12.00

#	Player	NM	EX	VG
(123)	Mulligan	40.00	20.00	12.00
(124)	Nelson	40.00	20.00	12.00
(125)	Nevers	300.00	200.00	100.00
(126)	Odell	40.00	20.00	12.00
(127)	Olney	40.00	20.00	12.00
(128)	Osborne	40.00	20.00	12.00
(129)	Page	40.00	20.00	12.00
(130)	Palmisano	40.00	20.00	12.00
(131)	Parker	40.00	20.00	12.00
(132)	Pasedel	40.00	20.00	12.00
(133)	Pearson	40.00	20.00	12.00
(134)	Penebskey	40.00	20.00	12.00
(135)	Perry	40.00	20.00	12.00
(136)	Peters	40.00	20.00	12.00
(137)	Petterson	40.00	20.00	12.00
(138)	H. Pillette	40.00	20.00	12.00
(139)	T. Pillette	40.00	20.00	12.00
(140)	Pinelli	40.00	20.00	12.00
(141)	Pipgrass	40.00	20.00	12.00
(142)	Porter	40.00	20.00	12.00
(143)	Powles	40.00	20.00	12.00
(144)	Read	40.00	20.00	12.00
(145)	Reed	40.00	20.00	12.00
(146)	Rehg	40.00	20.00	12.00
(147)	Ricci	40.00	20.00	12.00
(148)	Roberts	40.00	20.00	12.00
(149)	Rodda	40.00	20.00	12.00
(150)	Rohwer	40.00	20.00	12.00
(151)	Rosenberg	1,500	1,000	500.00
(152)	Rumler	40.00	20.00	12.00
(153)	Ryan	40.00	20.00	12.00
(154)	Schino	40.00	20.00	12.00
(155)	Severeid	40.00	20.00	12.00
(156)	Shanklin	40.00	20.00	12.00
(157)	Sheely	40.00	20.00	12.00
(158)	Sigafoos	40.00	20.00	12.00
(159)	Statz	60.00	30.00	18.00
(160)	Steinbacker	40.00	20.00	12.00
(161)	Stevenson	40.00	20.00	12.00
(162)	Sulik	40.00	20.00	12.00
(163)	Taylor	40.00	20.00	12.00
(164)	Thomas (Sacramento)	40.00	20.00	12.00
(165)	Thomas (San Francisco)	40.00	20.00	12.00
(166)	Trembly	40.00	20.00	12.00
(167)	Turner	40.00	20.00	12.00
(168)	Turpin	40.00	20.00	12.00
(169)	Uhalt	40.00	20.00	12.00
(170)	Vergez	40.00	20.00	12.00
(171)	Vinci	40.00	20.00	12.00
(172)	Vitt	40.00	20.00	12.00
(173)	Wallgren	40.00	20.00	12.00
(174)	Walsh	40.00	20.00	12.00
(175)	Ward	40.00	20.00	12.00
(176)	Warren	40.00	20.00	12.00
(177)	Webb	40.00	20.00	12.00
(178)	Wetzell	40.00	20.00	12.00
(179)	F. Wetzel	40.00	20.00	12.00
(180)	Williams	40.00	20.00	12.00
(181)	Wilson	40.00	20.00	12.00
(182)	Wingo	40.00	20.00	12.00
(183)	Wirts	40.00	20.00	12.00
(184)	Woodall	40.00	20.00	12.00
(185)	Zamlack	40.00	20.00	12.00
(186)	Zinn	40.00	20.00	12.00

1931 Zeenut Pacific Coast League

Beginning in 1931, Zeenuts cards were no longer dated on the front, and cards without the coupon are very difficult to date. The words "Zeenuts Series" were also dropped from the front and replaced with the words "Coast League." Zeenut cards in 1931 measure 1-3/4" x 3-1/2".

		NM	EX	VG
	Common Player:	40.00	20.00	12.00
	With Coupon:	800.00	400.00	240.00
(1)	Abbott	40.00	20.00	12.00
(2)	Andrews	40.00	20.00	12.00
(3)	Anton	40.00	20.00	12.00
(4)	Backer	40.00	20.00	12.00
(5)	Baker	40.00	20.00	12.00
(6)	Baldwin	40.00	20.00	12.00
(7)	Barbee	40.00	20.00	12.00
(8)	Barton	40.00	20.00	12.00
(9)	Bassler	40.00	20.00	12.00
(10)	Berger (Missions)	40.00	20.00	12.00

		NM	EX	VG
(11)	Berger (Portland)	40.00	20.00	12.00
(12)	Biggs	40.00	20.00	12.00
(13)	Bowman	40.00	20.00	12.00
(14)	Brenzel	40.00	20.00	12.00
(15)	Bryan	40.00	20.00	12.00
(16)	Burns	40.00	20.00	12.00
(17)	Camilli	40.00	20.00	12.00
(18)	Campbell	40.00	20.00	12.00
(19)	Carlyle	40.00	20.00	12.00
(20)	Caveney	40.00	20.00	12.00
(21)	Chesterfield	40.00	20.00	12.00
(22)	Cole	40.00	20.00	12.00
(23)	Coleman	40.00	20.00	12.00
(24)	Coscarart	40.00	20.00	12.00
(25)	Crosetti	200.00	100.00	60.00
(26)	Davis	40.00	20.00	12.00
(27)	DeBerry	40.00	20.00	12.00
(28)	Demaree	40.00	20.00	12.00
(29)	Dean	40.00	20.00	12.00
(30)	Delaney	40.00	20.00	12.00
(31)	Dondero	40.00	20.00	12.00
(32)	Donovan	40.00	20.00	12.00
(33)	Douglas	40.00	20.00	12.00
(34)	Ellsworth	40.00	20.00	12.00
(35)	Farrell	40.00	20.00	12.00
(36)	Fenton	40.00	20.00	12.00
(37)	Fitzpatrick	40.00	20.00	12.00
(38)	Flagstead	40.00	20.00	12.00
(39)	Flynn	40.00	20.00	12.00
(40)	Frazier	40.00	20.00	12.00
(41)	Freitas	40.00	20.00	12.00
(42)	French	40.00	20.00	12.00
(43)	Fullerton	40.00	20.00	12.00
(44)	Gabler	40.00	20.00	12.00
(45)	Gazella	40.00	20.00	12.00
(46)	Hale	40.00	20.00	12.00
(47)	Hamilton	40.00	20.00	12.00
(48)	Haney	40.00	20.00	12.00
(49)	Hannah	40.00	20.00	12.00
(50)	Harper	40.00	20.00	12.00
(51)	Henderson	40.00	20.00	12.00
(52)	Herrmann	40.00	20.00	12.00
(53)	Hoffman	40.00	20.00	12.00
(54)	Holland	40.00	20.00	12.00
(55)	Holling	40.00	20.00	12.00
(56)	Hubbell	40.00	20.00	12.00
(57)	Hufft	40.00	20.00	12.00
(58)	Hurst	40.00	20.00	12.00
(59)	Jacobs	40.00	20.00	12.00
(60)	Kallio	40.00	20.00	12.00
(61)	Keating	40.00	20.00	12.00
(62)	Keesey	40.00	20.00	12.00
(63)	Knothe	40.00	20.00	12.00
(64)	Knott	40.00	20.00	12.00
(65)	Kohler	40.00	20.00	12.00
(66)	Lamanski	40.00	20.00	12.00
(67)	Lee	40.00	20.00	12.00
(68)	Lelivelt	40.00	20.00	12.00
(69)	Lieber	40.00	20.00	12.00
(70)	Lipanovic	40.00	20.00	12.00
(71)	McDonald	40.00	20.00	12.00
(72)	McDougall	40.00	20.00	12.00
(73)	McLaughlin	40.00	20.00	12.00
(74)	Monroe	40.00	20.00	12.00
(75)	Moss	40.00	20.00	12.00
(76)	Mulligan	40.00	20.00	12.00
(77)	Ortman	40.00	20.00	12.00
(78)	Orwoll	40.00	20.00	12.00
(79)	Parker	40.00	20.00	12.00
(80)	Penebskey	40.00	20.00	12.00
(81)	H. Pillette	40.00	20.00	12.00
(82)	T. Pillette	40.00	20.00	12.00
(83)	Pinelli	40.00	20.00	12.00
(84)	Pool	40.00	20.00	12.00
(85)	Posedel	40.00	20.00	12.00
(86)	Powers	40.00	20.00	12.00
(87)	Read	40.00	20.00	12.00
(88)	Andy Reese	40.00	20.00	12.00
(89)	Rhiel	40.00	20.00	12.00
(90)	Ricci	40.00	20.00	12.00
(91)	Rohwer	40.00	20.00	12.00
(92)	Ryan	40.00	20.00	12.00
(93)	Schino	40.00	20.00	12.00
(94)	Schulte	40.00	20.00	12.00
(95)	Severeid	40.00	20.00	12.00
(96)	Sharpe	40.00	20.00	12.00
(97)	Shellenback	40.00	20.00	12.00
(98)	Simas	40.00	20.00	12.00
(99)	Steinbacker	40.00	20.00	12.00
(100)	Summa	40.00	20.00	12.00
(101)	Tubbs	40.00	20.00	12.00
(102)	Turner	40.00	20.00	12.00
(103)	Turpin	40.00	20.00	12.00
(104)	Uhalt	40.00	20.00	12.00
(105)	Vinci	40.00	20.00	12.00
(106)	Vitt	40.00	20.00	12.00
(107)	Wade	40.00	20.00	12.00
(108)	Walsh	40.00	20.00	12.00
(109)	Walters	40.00	20.00	12.00
(110)	Wera	40.00	20.00	12.00
(111)	Wetzel	40.00	20.00	12.00
(112)	Williams (Portland)	40.00	20.00	12.00
(113)	Williams (San Francisco)	40.00	20.00	12.00
(114)	Wingo	40.00	20.00	12.00
(115)	Wirts	40.00	20.00	12.00
(116)	Wise	40.00	20.00	12.00
(117)	Woodall	40.00	20.00	12.00
(118)	Yerkes	40.00	20.00	12.00
(119)	Zamlock	40.00	20.00	12.00
(120)	Zinn	40.00	20.00	12.00

1932 Zeenut Pacific Coast League

Beginning in 1931, Zeenuts cards were no longer dated on the front, and cards without the coupon are very difficult to date. The words "Zeenuts Series" were dropped from the front and replaced with "Coast League." Zeenut cards in 1932 measure 1-3/4" x 3-1/2".

		NM	EX	VG
	Common Player:	40.00	20.00	12.00
	With Coupon:	600.00	300.00	180.00
(1)	Abbott	40.00	20.00	12.00
(2)	Almada	50.00	25.00	15.00
(3)	Anton	40.00	20.00	12.00
(4)	Babich	40.00	20.00	12.00
(5)	Backer	40.00	20.00	12.00
(6)	Baker	40.00	20.00	12.00
(7)	Ballou	40.00	20.00	12.00
(8)	Bassler	40.00	20.00	12.00
(9)	Berger	40.00	20.00	12.00
(10)	Blackerby	40.00	20.00	12.00
(11)	Bordagaray	40.00	20.00	12.00
(12)	Brannon	40.00	20.00	12.00
(13)	Briggs	40.00	20.00	12.00
(14)	Brubaker	40.00	20.00	12.00
(15)	Callaghan	40.00	20.00	12.00
(16)	Camilli	40.00	20.00	12.00
(17)	Campbell	40.00	20.00	12.00
(18)	Carlyle	40.00	20.00	12.00
(19)	Caster	40.00	20.00	12.00
(20)	Caveney	40.00	20.00	12.00
(21)	Chamberlain	40.00	20.00	12.00
(22)	Cole	40.00	20.00	12.00
(23)	Collard	40.00	20.00	12.00
(24)	Cook	40.00	20.00	12.00
(25)	Coscarart	40.00	20.00	12.00
(26)	Cox	40.00	20.00	12.00
(27)	Cronin	40.00	20.00	12.00
(28)	Daglia	40.00	20.00	12.00
(29)	Dahlgren	45.00	22.00	13.50
(30)	Davis	40.00	20.00	12.00
(31)	Dean	40.00	20.00	12.00
(32)	Delaney	40.00	20.00	12.00
(33)	Demaree	40.00	20.00	12.00
(34)	Devine	40.00	20.00	12.00
(35)	DeViveiros	40.00	20.00	12.00
(36)	Dittmar	40.00	20.00	12.00
(37)	Donovan	40.00	20.00	12.00
(38)	Ellsworth	40.00	20.00	12.00
(39)	Fitzpatrick	40.00	20.00	12.00
(40)	Frazier	40.00	20.00	12.00
(41)	Freitas	40.00	20.00	12.00
(42)	Garibaldi	40.00	20.00	12.00
(43)	Gaston	40.00	20.00	12.00
(44)	Gazella	40.00	20.00	12.00
(45)	Gillick	40.00	20.00	12.00
(46)	Hafey	40.00	20.00	12.00
(47)	Haney	40.00	20.00	12.00
(48)	Hannah	40.00	20.00	12.00
(49)	Henderson	40.00	20.00	12.00
(50)	Herrmann	40.00	20.00	12.00
(51)	Hipps	40.00	20.00	12.00
(52)	Hofman	40.00	20.00	12.00
(53)	Holland	40.00	20.00	12.00
(54)	House	40.00	20.00	12.00
(55)	Hufft	40.00	20.00	12.00
(56)	Hunt	40.00	20.00	12.00
(57)	Hurst	40.00	20.00	12.00
(58)	Jacobs	40.00	20.00	12.00
(59)	Johns	40.00	20.00	12.00
(60)	Johnson (Missions)	40.00	20.00	12.00
(61)	Johnson (Portland)	40.00	20.00	12.00
(62)	Johnson (Seattle)	40.00	20.00	12.00
(63)	Joiner	40.00	20.00	12.00
(64)	Kallio	40.00	20.00	12.00
(65)	Kasich	40.00	20.00	12.00
(66)	Keesey	40.00	20.00	12.00
(67)	Kelly	40.00	20.00	12.00
(68)	Koehler	40.00	20.00	12.00
(69)	Lee	40.00	20.00	12.00
(70)	Lieber	40.00	20.00	12.00
(71)	Mailho	40.00	20.00	12.00
(72)	Martin (Oakland)	40.00	20.00	12.00
(73)	Martin (San Francisco)	40.00	20.00	12.00
(74)	McNeely	40.00	20.00	12.00
(75)	Miljus	40.00	20.00	12.00
(76)	Monroe	40.00	20.00	12.00
(77)	Mosolf	40.00	20.00	12.00
(78)	Moss	40.00	20.00	12.00
(79)	Muller	40.00	20.00	12.00
(80)	Mulligan	40.00	20.00	12.00
(81)	Oana	350.00	200.00	125.00
(82)	Osborn	40.00	20.00	12.00
(83)	Page	40.00	20.00	12.00
(84)	Penebsky	40.00	20.00	12.00
(85)	H. Pillette	40.00	20.00	12.00
(86)	Pinelli	50.00	25.00	15.00
(87)	Poole	40.00	20.00	12.00
(88)	Quellich	40.00	20.00	12.00
(89)	Read	40.00	20.00	12.00

		NM	EX	VG
(90)	Ricci	40.00	20.00	12.00
(91)	Salvo	40.00	20.00	12.00
(92)	Sankey	40.00	20.00	12.00
(93)	Sheehan	40.00	20.00	12.00
(94)	Shellenback	40.00	20.00	12.00
(95)	Sherlock (Hollywood)	40.00	20.00	12.00
(96)	Sherlock (Missions)	40.00	20.00	12.00
(97)	Shores	40.00	20.00	12.00
(98)	Simas	40.00	20.00	12.00
(99)	Statz	60.00	30.00	18.00
(100)	Steinbacker	40.00	20.00	12.00
(101)	Sulik	40.00	20.00	12.00
(102)	Summa	40.00	20.00	12.00
(103)	Thomas	40.00	20.00	12.00
(104)	Uhalt	40.00	20.00	12.00
(105)	Vinci	40.00	20.00	12.00
(106)	Vitt	40.00	20.00	12.00
(107)	Walsh (Missions)	40.00	20.00	12.00
(108)	Walsh (Oakland)	40.00	20.00	12.00
(109)	Walters	40.00	20.00	12.00
(110)	Ward	40.00	20.00	12.00
(111)	Welsh	40.00	20.00	12.00
(112)	Wera	40.00	20.00	12.00
(113)	Williams	40.00	20.00	12.00
(114)	Willoughby	40.00	20.00	12.00
(115)	Wirts	40.00	20.00	12.00
(116)	Wise	40.00	20.00	12.00
(117)	Woodall	40.00	20.00	12.00
(118)	Yde	40.00	20.00	12.00
(119)	Zahniser	40.00	20.00	12.00
(120)	Zamloch	40.00	20.00	12.00

1933 Zeenut Pacific Coast League (Sepia)

This is the most confusing era for Zeenut cards. The cards of 1933-36 are nearly identical, displaying the words, "Coast League" in a small rectangle with rounded corners, along with the player's name and team. The photos are black-and-white (except 1933 Zeenuts have also been found with sepia photos). Because no date appears on the photos, cards from these years are impossible to tell apart without the coupon bottom that lists an expiration date. To date over 161 subjects have been found, with some known to exist in all four years. There are cases where the exact same photo was used from one year to the next (sometimes with minor cropping differences). All cards of Joe and Vince DiMaggio have their last name misspelled "DeMaggio." Cards of all years measure about 1-3/4" x 3-1/2" with coupon.

		NM	EX	VG
	Common Player:	40.00	20.00	12.00
	With Coupon:	400.00	200.00	120.00
(1)	L. Almada	50.00	25.00	15.00
(2)	Anton	40.00	20.00	12.00
(3)	Bassler	40.00	20.00	12.00
(4)	Bonnelly	40.00	20.00	12.00
(5)	Bordagary	40.00	20.00	12.00
(6)	Bottarini	40.00	20.00	12.00
(7)	Brannan	40.00	20.00	12.00
(8)	Brubaker	40.00	20.00	12.00
(9)	Bryan	40.00	20.00	12.00
(10)	Burns	40.00	20.00	12.00
(11)	Camilli	40.00	20.00	12.00
(12)	Chozen	40.00	20.00	12.00
(13)	Cole	40.00	20.00	12.00
(14)	Cronin	40.00	20.00	12.00
(15)	Dahlgren	40.00	20.00	12.00
(16)	Donovan	40.00	20.00	12.00
(17)	Douglas	40.00	20.00	12.00
(18)	Flynn	40.00	20.00	12.00
(19)	French	40.00	20.00	12.00
(20)	Frietas	40.00	20.00	12.00
(21)	Galan	40.00	20.00	12.00
(22)	Hofmann	40.00	20.00	12.00
(23)	Kelman	40.00	20.00	12.00
(24)	Lelivelt	40.00	20.00	12.00
(25)	Ludolph	40.00	20.00	12.00
(26)	McDonald	40.00	20.00	12.00
(27)	McNeely	40.00	20.00	12.00
(28)	McQuaid	40.00	20.00	12.00
(29)	Moncrief	40.00	20.00	12.00
(30)	Nelson	40.00	20.00	12.00
(31)	Osborne	40.00	20.00	12.00
(32)	Petersen	40.00	20.00	12.00
(33)	Reeves	40.00	20.00	12.00
(34)	Scott	40.00	20.00	12.00
(35)	Shellenback	40.00	20.00	12.00
(36)	J. Sherlock	40.00	20.00	12.00
(37)	V. Sherlock	40.00	20.00	12.00
(38)	Steinbacker	40.00	20.00	12.00
(39)	Stine	40.00	20.00	12.00

		NM	EX	VG
(40)	Strange	40.00	20.00	12.00
(41)	Sulik	40.00	20.00	12.00
(42)	Sweetland	40.00	20.00	12.00
(43)	Uhalt	40.00	20.00	12.00
(44)	Vinci	40.00	20.00	12.00
(45)	Vitt	40.00	20.00	12.00
(46)	Wetzel	40.00	20.00	12.00
(47)	Woodall	40.00	20.00	12.00
(48)	Zinn	40.00	20.00	12.00

1933-36 Zeenut Pacific Coast League (Black-and-White)

CUT **COUPON** HERE
GOOD FOR VALUABLE PREMIUMS
ASK YOUR DEALER FOR LIST
This offer expires April 1st, 1936

		NM	EX	VG
Common Player:		40.00	20.00	12.00
With Coupon:		400.00	200.00	120.00
(1a)	Almada (Large pose.)	50.00	25.00	15.00
(1b)	Almada (Small pose.)	50.00	25.00	15.00
(2a)	Anton (Large pose.)	40.00	20.00	12.00
(2b)	Anton (Small pose.)	40.00	20.00	12.00
(3)	Babich	40.00	20.00	12.00
(4)	Backer	40.00	20.00	12.00
(5)	Ballou (Black stockings.)	40.00	20.00	12.00
(6a)	Ballou (Stockings with band, large pose.)	40.00	20.00	12.00
(6b)	Ballou (Stockings with band, small pose.)	40.00	20.00	12.00
(7)	Barath	40.00	20.00	12.00
(8)	Beck	40.00	20.00	12.00
(9)	C. Beck	40.00	20.00	12.00
(10)	W. Beck	40.00	20.00	12.00
(11)	Becker	40.00	20.00	12.00
(12)	Biongovanni	40.00	20.00	12.00
(13)	Blackerby	40.00	20.00	12.00
(14)	Blakely	40.00	20.00	12.00
(15)	Borja (Sacramento)	40.00	20.00	12.00
(16)	Borja (Seals)	40.00	20.00	12.00
(17)	Brundin	40.00	20.00	12.00
(18)	Carlyle	40.00	20.00	12.00
(19a)	Caveney (Name incorrect.)	40.00	20.00	12.00
(19b)	Cavaney (Name correct.)	40.00	20.00	12.00
(20)	Chelini	40.00	20.00	12.00
(21)	Cole (With glove.)	40.00	20.00	12.00
(22)	Cole (No glove.)	40.00	20.00	12.00
(23)	Connors	40.00	20.00	12.00
(24)	Coscarart (Missions)	40.00	20.00	12.00
(25)	Coscarart (Seattle)	40.00	20.00	12.00
(26)	Cox	40.00	20.00	12.00
(27)	Davis	40.00	20.00	12.00
(28)	J. DeMaggio (DiMaggio) (Batting)	15,000	8,000	4,000
(29)	J. DeMaggio (DiMaggio) (Throwing)	15,000	8,000	4,000
(30)	V. DeMaggio (DiMaggio)	1,200	600.00	360.00
(31)	DeViveiros	40.00	20.00	12.00
(32)	Densmore	40.00	20.00	12.00
(33)	Dittmar	40.00	20.00	12.00
(34)	Donovan	40.00	20.00	12.00
(35)	Douglas (Oakland)	40.00	20.00	12.00
(36)	Douglas (Seals)	40.00	20.00	12.00
(37a)	Duggan (Large pose.)	40.00	20.00	12.00
(37b)	Duggan (Small pose.)	40.00	20.00	12.00
(38)	Durst	40.00	20.00	12.00
(39a)	Eckhardt (Large pose.)	40.00	20.00	12.00
(39b)	Eckhardt (Small pose.)	40.00	20.00	12.00
(40)	Ellsworth	40.00	20.00	12.00
(41)	Fenton	40.00	20.00	12.00
(42)	Fitzpatrick	40.00	20.00	12.00
(43)	Francovich	40.00	20.00	12.00
(44)	Funk	40.00	20.00	12.00
(45a)	Garibaldi (Large pose.)	40.00	20.00	12.00
(45b)	Garibaldi (Small pose.)	40.00	20.00	12.00
(46)	Gibson (Black sleeves.)	40.00	20.00	12.00
(47)	Gibson (White sleeves.)	40.00	20.00	12.00
(48)	Gira	40.00	20.00	12.00
(49)	Glaister	40.00	20.00	12.00
(50)	Graves	40.00	20.00	12.00
(51a)	Hafey (Missions, large pose.)	40.00	20.00	12.00
(51b)	Hafey (Missions, middle-size pose.)	40.00	20.00	12.00
(51c)	Hafey (Missions, small pose.)	40.00	20.00	12.00
(52)	Hafey (Sacramento)	40.00	20.00	12.00
(53)	Haid (Oakland)	40.00	20.00	12.00
(54)	Haid (Seattle)	40.00	20.00	12.00
(55)	Haney	40.00	20.00	12.00
(56a)	Hartwig (Sacramento, large pose.)	40.00	20.00	12.00

		NM	EX	VG
(56b)	Hartwig (Sacramento, small pose.)	40.00	20.00	12.00
(57)	Hartwig (Seals)	40.00	20.00	12.00
(58)	Henderson	40.00	20.00	12.00
(59)	Herrmann	40.00	20.00	12.00
(60)	B. Holder	40.00	20.00	12.00
(61)	Holland	40.00	20.00	12.00
(62)	Horne	40.00	20.00	12.00
(63)	House	40.00	20.00	12.00
(64)	Hunt	40.00	20.00	12.00
(65)	A.E. Jacobs	40.00	20.00	12.00
(66)	Johns	40.00	20.00	12.00
(67)	D. Johnson	40.00	20.00	12.00
(68)	L. Johnson	40.00	20.00	12.00
(69)	Joiner	40.00	20.00	12.00
(70)	Jolley	60.00	30.00	18.00
(71)	Joost	40.00	20.00	12.00
(72)	Jorgensen	40.00	20.00	12.00
(73)	Kallio	40.00	20.00	12.00
(74)	Kamm	40.00	20.00	12.00
(75)	Kampouris	40.00	20.00	12.00
(76)	E. Kelly (Oakland)	40.00	20.00	12.00
(77)	E. Kelly (Seattle)	40.00	20.00	12.00
(78)	Kenna	40.00	20.00	12.00
(79)	Kintana	40.00	20.00	12.00
(80)	Lahman	40.00	20.00	12.00
(81)	Lieber	40.00	20.00	12.00
(82)	Ludolph	40.00	20.00	12.00
(83)	Mailho	40.00	20.00	12.00
(84a)	Mails (Large pose.)	40.00	20.00	12.00
(84b)	Mails (Small pose.)	40.00	20.00	12.00
(85)	Marty (Black sleeves.)	40.00	20.00	12.00
(86)	Marty (White sleeves.)	40.00	20.00	12.00
(87)	Massuci (Batting follow-through.)	40.00	20.00	12.00
(88)	Masucci (Different pose.)	40.00	20.00	12.00
(89a)	McEvoy (Large pose.)	40.00	20.00	12.00
(89b)	McEvoy (Small pose.)	40.00	20.00	12.00
(90)	McIsaacs	40.00	20.00	12.00
(91)	McMullen (Oakland)	40.00	20.00	12.00
(92)	McMullen (Seals)	40.00	20.00	12.00
(93)	Mitchell	40.00	20.00	12.00
(94a)	Monzo (Large pose.)	40.00	20.00	12.00
(94b)	Monzo (Small pose.)	40.00	20.00	12.00
(95)	Mort (Throwing)	40.00	20.00	12.00
(96)	Mort (Batting)	40.00	20.00	12.00
(97a)	Muller (Oakland, large pose.)	40.00	20.00	12.00
(97b)	Muller (Oakland, small pose.)	40.00	20.00	12.00
(98)	Muller (Seattle)	40.00	20.00	12.00
(99)	Mulligan (Hands showing.)	40.00	20.00	12.00
(100)	Mulligan (Hands not showing.)	40.00	20.00	12.00
(101)	Newkirk	40.00	20.00	12.00
(102)	Nicholas	40.00	20.00	12.00
(103)	Nitcholas	40.00	20.00	12.00
(103a)	Norbert (Large pose.)	40.00	20.00	12.00
(103b)	Norbert (Small pose.)	40.00	20.00	12.00
(105)	O'Doul (Black sleeves.)	450.00	325.00	200.00
(106)	O'Doul (White sleeves.)	450.00	325.00	200.00
(107)	Oglesby	40.00	20.00	12.00
(108)	Ostenberg	40.00	20.00	12.00
(109)	Outen (Throwing)	40.00	20.00	12.00
(110)	Outen (Batting)	40.00	20.00	12.00
(111)	Page (Hollywood)	40.00	20.00	12.00
(112)	Page (Seattle)	40.00	20.00	12.00
(113)	Palmisano	40.00	20.00	12.00
(114)	Parker	40.00	20.00	12.00
(115)	Phebus	40.00	20.00	12.00
(116)	T. Pillette	40.00	20.00	12.00
(117)	Pool	40.00	20.00	12.00
(118)	Powers	40.00	20.00	12.00
(119)	Quellich	40.00	20.00	12.00
(120)	Radonitz	40.00	20.00	12.00
(121a)	Raimondi (Large pose.)	40.00	20.00	12.00
(121b)	Raimondi (Small pose.)	40.00	20.00	12.00
(122a)	Jimmy Reese (Large pose.)	300.00	200.00	100.00
(122b)	Jimmy Reese (Small pose.)	300.00	200.00	100.00
(123)	Rego	40.00	20.00	12.00
(124)	Rhyne (Front)	40.00	20.00	12.00
(125)	Rosenberg	40.00	20.00	12.00
(126)	Salinsen	40.00	20.00	12.00
(127)	Salkeld	40.00	20.00	12.00
(128)	Salvo	40.00	20.00	12.00
(129)	Sever	40.00	20.00	12.00
(130)	Sheehan (Black sleeves.)	40.00	20.00	12.00
(131)	Sheehan (White sleeves.)	40.00	20.00	12.00
(132a)	Sheely (Large pose.)	40.00	20.00	12.00
(132b)	Sheely (Small pose.)	40.00	20.00	12.00
(134)	Sprinz	40.00	20.00	12.00
(135)	Starritt	40.00	20.00	12.00
(136)	Statz	60.00	30.00	18.00
(137a)	Steinbacker (Large pose.)	40.00	20.00	12.00
(137b)	Steinbacker (Small pose.)	40.00	20.00	12.00
(138)	Stewart	40.00	20.00	12.00
(139)	Stitzel (Los Angeles)	40.00	20.00	12.00
(140)	Stitzel (Missions)	40.00	20.00	12.00
(141)	Stitzel (Seals)	40.00	20.00	12.00
(142)	Stoneham	40.00	20.00	12.00
(143)	Street	40.00	20.00	12.00
(144)	Stroner	40.00	20.00	12.00
(145)	Stutz	40.00	20.00	12.00
(146)	Sulik	40.00	20.00	12.00
(147a)	Thurston (Mission)	40.00	20.00	12.00
(147b)	Thurston (Missions)	40.00	20.00	12.00
(148)	Vitt (Hollywood)	40.00	20.00	12.00
(149)	Vitt (Oakland)	40.00	20.00	12.00
(150)	Wallgren	40.00	20.00	12.00
(151)	Walsh	40.00	20.00	12.00
(152)	Walters	40.00	20.00	12.00
(153)	West	40.00	20.00	12.00
(154a)	Wirts (Large pose.)	40.00	20.00	12.00
(154b)	Wirts (Small pose.)	40.00	20.00	12.00
(155)	Woodall (Batting)	40.00	20.00	12.00
(156)	Woodall (Throwing)	40.00	20.00	12.00
(157)	Wright (Facing to front.)	40.00	20.00	12.00
(158)	Wright (Facing to left.)	40.00	20.00	12.00
(159)	Zinn	40.00	20.00	12.00

1937-38 Zeenut Pacific Coast League

The 1937 and 1938 Zeenuts are similar to the 1933-1936 issues, except the black rectangle containing the player's name and team has square (rather than rounded) corners. Again, it is difficult to distinguish between the two years. In 1938, Zeenuts eliminated the coupon bottom and began including a separate coupon in the candy package along with the baseball card. The final two years of the Zeenuts issues, the 1937 and 1938 cards, are among the more difficult to find. With coupon, the 1937 cards measure about 1-5/8" x 3-7/16". The coupon-less 1938 cards measure about 1-3/4" x 2-13/16".

		NM	EX	VG
Common Player:		60.00	25.00	15.00
With Coupon:		400.00	200.00	120.00
(1)	Annunzio	60.00	25.00	15.00
(2)	Baker	60.00	25.00	15.00
(3)	Ballou	60.00	25.00	15.00
(4)	C. Beck	60.00	25.00	15.00
(5)	W. Beck	60.00	25.00	15.00
(6)	Bolin	60.00	25.00	15.00
(7)	Bongiavanni	60.00	25.00	15.00
(8)	Boss	60.00	25.00	15.00
(9)	Carson	60.00	25.00	15.00
(10)	Clabaugh	60.00	25.00	15.00
(11)	Clifford	60.00	25.00	15.00
(12)	B. Cole	60.00	25.00	15.00
(13)	Coscarart	60.00	25.00	15.00
(14)	Cronin	60.00	25.00	15.00
(15)	Cullop	60.00	25.00	15.00
(16)	Daglia	60.00	25.00	15.00
(17)	D. DeMaggio (DiMaggio)	1,200	600.00	360.00
(18)	Douglas	60.00	25.00	15.00
(19)	Frankovich	60.00	25.00	15.00
(20)	Frazier	60.00	25.00	15.00
(21)	Fredericks	60.00	25.00	15.00
(22)	Freitas	60.00	25.00	15.00
(23)	Gabrielson (Oakland)	60.00	25.00	15.00
(24)	Gabrielson (Seattle)	60.00	25.00	15.00
(25)	Garibaldi	60.00	25.00	15.00
(26)	Gibson	60.00	25.00	15.00
(27)	Gill	60.00	25.00	15.00
(28)	Graves	60.00	25.00	15.00
(29)	Guay	60.00	25.00	15.00
(30)	Gudat	60.00	25.00	15.00
(31)	Haid	60.00	25.00	15.00
(32)	Hannah	60.00	25.00	15.00
(33)	Hawkins	60.00	25.00	15.00
(34)	Herrmann	60.00	25.00	15.00
(35)	Holder	60.00	25.00	15.00
(36)	Jennings	60.00	25.00	15.00
(37)	Judnich	60.00	25.00	15.00
(38)	Klinger	60.00	25.00	15.00
(39)	Koenig	60.00	25.00	15.00
(40)	Koupal	60.00	25.00	15.00
(41)	Koy	60.00	25.00	15.00
(42)	Lamanski	60.00	25.00	15.00
(43)	Leishman (Oakland)	60.00	25.00	15.00
(44)	Leishman (Seattle)	60.00	25.00	15.00
(45)	G. Lillard	60.00	25.00	15.00
(46)	Mann	60.00	25.00	15.00
(47)	Marble (Hollywood)	60.00	25.00	15.00
(49)	Miller	60.00	25.00	15.00
(50)	Mills	60.00	25.00	15.00
(51)	Monzo	60.00	25.00	15.00
(52)	B. Mort (Hollywood)	60.00	25.00	15.00
(53)	B. Mort (Missions)	60.00	25.00	15.00
(54)	Muller	60.00	25.00	15.00
(55)	Murray	60.00	25.00	15.00
(56)	Newsome	60.00	25.00	15.00
(57)	Nitcholas	60.00	25.00	15.00
(58)	Olds	60.00	25.00	15.00
(59)	Orengo	60.00	25.00	15.00
(60)	Osborne	60.00	25.00	15.00
(61)	Outen	60.00	25.00	15.00
(62)	C. Outen (Hollywood)	60.00	25.00	15.00
(63)	C. Outen (Missions)	60.00	25.00	15.00
(64)	Pippin	60.00	25.00	15.00
(65)	Powell	60.00	25.00	15.00
(66)	Radonitz	60.00	25.00	15.00
(67)	Raimondi (Oakland)	60.00	25.00	15.00
(68)	Raimondi (San Francisco)	60.00	25.00	15.00
(69)	A. Raimondi	60.00	25.00	15.00
(70)	W. Raimondi	60.00	25.00	15.00
(71)	Rhyne	60.00	25.00	15.00
(72)	Rosenberg (Missions)	1,200	600.00	360.00
(73)	Rosenberg (Portland)	1,200	600.00	360.00
(74)	Sawyer	60.00	25.00	15.00
(75)	Seats	60.00	25.00	15.00
(76)	Sheehan (Oakland)	60.00	25.00	15.00
(77)	Sheehan (San Francisco)	60.00	25.00	15.00
(78)	Shores	60.00	25.00	15.00
(79)	Slade (Hollywood)	60.00	25.00	15.00
(80)	Slade (Missions)	60.00	25.00	15.00
(81)	Sprinz (Missions)	60.00	25.00	15.00
(82)	Sprinz (San Francisco)	60.00	25.00	15.00
(83)	Statz	75.00	37.50	22.50
(84)	Storey	60.00	25.00	15.00
(85)	Stringfellow	60.00	25.00	15.00
(86)	Stutz	60.00	25.00	15.00
(87)	Sweeney	60.00	25.00	15.00
(88)	Thomson	60.00	25.00	15.00
(89)	Tost (Hollywood)	60.00	25.00	15.00
(90)	Tost (Missions)	60.00	25.00	15.00
(91)	Ulrich	60.00	25.00	15.00
(92)	Vergez	60.00	25.00	15.00
(93)	Vezelich	60.00	25.00	15.00
(94)	Vitter (Hollywood)	60.00	25.00	15.00
(95)	Vitter (San Francisco)	60.00	25.00	15.00
(96)	West	60.00	25.00	15.00
(97)	Wilson	60.00	25.00	15.00
(98)	Woodall	60.00	25.00	15.00
(99)	Wright	60.00	25.00	15.00

Minor League Team Sets and Singles (1970-2004)

By 1970, the issue of minor league baseball cards as premiums with another product had virtually ceased. Since that time, the vast majority of cards issued each year have been in the form of team sets and, since 1989, wax- or foil-packed singles.

In exchange for the rights to sell card sets within the hobby, various card manufacturers and other sponsors have printed sets for the teams to sell at their concession stand, or give away at promotional games.

Also listed in this section are miscellaneous sets of draft picks, pre-professional summer amateur leagues and Team USA, along with independent professional teams which are not part of Organized Baseball's National Association of Professional Baseball Leagues.

Since minor league teams sets are not usually broken up, and since the presence of a superstar player can represent virtually all of a set's value, only complete set prices are listed.

1970-73 Minor League Team Sets

The mid-1960s brought an end to minor league team set issues intended mainly for fan consumption. In 1970, a new era began with the issue of team sets aimed. primarily at card collectors, and often produced by collectors or dealers with team connections. Compared to major league cards of the era, production values of minor league sets were low, with black-and-white printing the norm and little graphic embellishment. Future minor league team-set giant TCMA issued its first such cards in 1974 (though they included 1972 and 1973 team sets), while Frank Caruso, who issued many Pacific Coast League sets over the years, began in 1973.

18 Team Sets and Variations

		NM
1970	McDonald's Wichita Aeros (18)	300.00
1971	Currie Richmond Braves (18)	100.00
1971	Morey Syracuse Chiefs (18)	115.00
1972	Carl Aldana 1950s S.F. Seals (18)	45.00
"1972"	TCMA Cedar Rapids Cardinals (1974)(29)	30.00
"1972"	TCMA Cedar Rapids Cardinals (1974)(30)	90.00
1972	Fast Service Salem Pirates (4)	125.00
1972	Team Seattle Rainiers (24)	45.00
1972	Team Tacoma Twins (16)	17.50
1972	Virginian-Pilot Tidewater Tides (22)	150.00
"1973"	TCMA Cedar Rapids Astros (1974)(27)	25.00
"1973"	TCMA Cedar Rapids Astros (1974)(28)	30.00
1973	Team Sherbrooke Pirates (18)	200.00
1973	Team Syracuse Chiefs (30)	200.00
1973	Caruso Tacoma Twins (21)	16.00
1973	Click-Click Three Rivers Eagles (18)	150.00
1973	KSB Wichita Aeros (19)	55.00
1973	KSB Wichita Aeros (21)	100.00

1974 Minor League Team Sets

LUIS PUJALS

The number of minor league card sets issued either by the teams themselves or card hobbyists nearly tripled in 1974, to 14. A wide range of formats was seen, with black-and-white photos still the rule.

16 Team Sets and Variations

		NM
1974	Caruso Albuquerque Dukes (16)	15.00
1974	Team Albuquerque Dukes (23)	200.00
1974	TCMA Cedar Rapids Astros (28)	25.00
1974	TCMA Gastonia Rangers (24)	17.50
1974	Caruso Hawaii Islanders (8)	10.00
1974	Falstaff Omaha Royals (10)	125.00
1974	Broder P.C.L. "Popcorn" Cards (235)	325.00
1974	Caruso Phoenix Giants (11)	8.00
1974	Caruso Sacramento Solons (18)	15.00
1974	Caruso Salt Lake City Angels (10)	10.00
1974	Team Seattle Rainiers (20)	45.00
1974	Caruso Spokane Indians (18)	20.00
1974	Team Syracuse Chiefs (30)	400.00
1974	Team Syracuse Chiefs (27)	325.00
1974	Caruso Tacoma Twins (27)	16.00
1974	One Day Wichita Aeros (29)	95.00

1975 Minor League Team Sets

BILL ALMON
infielder - Hawaii
1975 P.C.L.   11

In 1975, the number of teams issuing card sets again doubled to over 35. Among the hobby dealers and collectors who dominated the sponsorship of such sets, TCMA was the unquestioned leader, with nearly half the cards under its banner, originally selling for $3-4 per set.

42 Team Sets and Variations

		NM
1975	Caruso Albuquerque Dukes (21)	12.00
1975	TCMA Anderson Rangers (25)	11.00
1975	TCMA Appleton Foxes (29)	10.00
1975	TCMA Burlington Bees (29)	7.50
1975	Broder California League (30)	40.00
1975	TCMA Cedar Rapids Giants (32)	16.00
1975	TCMA Clinton Pilots (32)	25.00
1975	TCMA Dubuque Packers (32)	22.50
1975	Sussman Ft. Lauderdale Yankees (30)	50.00
1975	Sussman Ft. Lauderdale Yankees (29)	12.50
1975	Caruso Hawaii Islanders (21)	20.00
1975	TCMA International League (31)	13.50
1975	TCMA Iowa Oaks (21)	40.00
1975	TCMA Lafayette Drillers (32)	27.50
1975	TCMA Lynchburg Rangers (26)	12.50
1975	McWilliams 1955 Oakland Oaks (36)	60.00
1975	Team Oklahoma City 89ers (24)	15.00
1975	Top Trophies Omaha Royals (18)	95.00
1975	Broder 1960s Pacific Coast League	100.00
1975	Dobbins PCL All-Stars (37)	80.00
1975	TCMA 1950s PCL (18)	200.00
1975	Caruso Phoenix Giants (21)	10.00
1975	Circle K Phoenix Giants (26)	6.00
1975	TCMA Quad City Angels (34)	40.00
1975	TCMA 1961 Rochester Red Wings (11)	150.00
1975	Caruso Sacramento Solons (22)	16.00
1975	Caruso Salt Lake City Gulls (20)	9.00
1975	TCMA San Antonio Brewers (22)	12.00
1975	TCMA Shreveport Captains (23)	15.00
1975	Caruso Spokane Indians (21)	8.00
1975	Team Syracuse Chiefs (25)	225.00
1975	KMO Tacoma Twins (21)	12.00
1975	Stewart Tidewater Tides (24)	30.00
1975	TCMA Tri-Valley Highlanders (25)	75.00
1975	Caruso Tucson Toros (21)	9.00
1975	Team Tucson Toros (24)	11.00
1975	7-11 Tulsa Oilers (24)	30.00
1975	TCMA Waterbury Dodgers (22)	20.00

		NM
1975	TCMA Waterloo Royals (34)	20.00
1975	TCMA Waterloo Royals (35)	80.00
1975	Sussman West Palm Beach Expos (32)	30.00
1975	Sussman West Palm Beach Expos (29)	11.00

1976 Minor League Team Sets

JACK CLARK
Outfielder

While the number of team-issued minor sets leveled off at around 35 in 1976, the quality standard was raised with the first use of full-color printing. The innovator was Mike Cramer who went on to found Pacific Trading Cards.

35 Team Sets and Variations

		NM
1976	TCMA Appleton Foxes (29)	11.00
1976	TCMA Arkansas Travelers (12)	50.00
1976	TCMA Asheville Tourists (25)	15.00
1976	Team Batavia Trojans (29)	30.00
1976	TCMA Baton Rouge Cougars (22)	30.00
1976	TCMA Burlington Bees (33)	8.00
1976	TCMA Cedar Rapids Giants (39)	20.00
1976	TCMA Clinton Pilots (37)	40.00
1976	TCMA Dubuque Packers (40)	12.00
1976	Sussman Ft. Lauderdale Yankees (30)	35.00
1976	Caruso Hawaii Islanders (21)	25.00
1976	Team Indianapolis Indians (26)	25.00
1976	Team Oklahoma City 89ers (24)	22.50
1976	Top Trophies Omaha Royals (27)	125.00
1976	Caruso Phoenix Giants (22)	9.00
1976	Coke Premiums Phoenix Giants (24)	15.00
1976	Cramer Phoenix Giants (24)	6.00
1976	VNB Phoenix Giants (26)	20.00
1976	TCMA Quad City Angels (39)	20.00
1976	TCMA Quad City Angels (40)	24.00
1976	Caruso Sacramento Solons (23)	15.00

		NM
1976	Caruso Salt Lake City Gulls (22)	9.00
1976	Knowlton's San Antonio Brewers (26)	35.00
1976	Cramer Seattle Rainiers (20)	24.00
1976	TCMA Shreveport Captains (23)	40.00
1976	TCMA Shreveport Captains (23)	95.00
1976	Caruso Spokane Indians (21)	12.00
1976	DQ Tacoma Twins (24)	15.00
1976	Caruso Tucson Toros (19)	10.00
1976	Cramer Tucson Toros (24)	10.00
1976	Goof's Tulsa Oilers (26)	150.00
1976	Goof's Tulsa Oilers w/autographs (26)	350.00
1976	TCMA Waterloo Royals (33)	37.50
1976	TCMA Wausau Mets (25)	30.00
1976	TCMA Williamsport Tomahawks (23)	12.50

1977 Minor League Team Sets

Scott Boras
Infielder

More than 50 minor league team sets were issued in 1977, including a collector-issued black-and-white set of the Modesto A's featuring future Hall of Famer Rickey Henderson. Crudely executed, the Frank Chong set was the first minor league set of the 1970s to (briefly) attain a retail value in excess of $1,000. It was also in 1977 that TCMA began widespread use of updated sets with cards of players who joined teams after the initial card photos had been taken. This created variations which can carry widely diverse pricing.

57 Team Sets and Variations

		NM
1977	TCMA Appleton Foxes (29)	12.50
1977	TCMA Appleton Foxes (30)	75.00
1977	TCMA Arkansas Travelers (12)	30.00
1977	TCMA Arkansas Travelers (21)	75.00
1977	TCMA Asheville Tourists (29)	17.50
1977	TCMA Bristol Red Sox (20)	50.00
1977	TCMA Burlington Bees (25)	30.00

		NM
1977	TCMA Burlington Bees (27)	32.50
1977	TCMA Cedar Rapids Giants (24)	30.00
1977	TCMA Cedar Rapids Giants (25)	65.00
1977	TCMA Charleston Patriots (25)	25.00
1977	TCMA Clinton Dodgers (29)	55.00
1977	TCMA Cocoa Astros (25)	12.50
1977	TCMA Columbus Clippers (22)	100.00
1977	TCMA Columbus Clippers (24)	175.00
1977	LICS 1960s Dallas Rangers (9)	15.00
1977	TCMA Daytona Beach Islanders (27)	20.00
1977	TCMA Evansville Triplets (25)	150.00
1977	Sussman Ft. Lauderdale Yankees (31)	75.00
1977	Caruso Hawaii Islanders (24)	12.50
1977	TCMA Holyoke Millers (28)	10.00
1977	Team Indianapolis Indians (27)	10.00
1977	TCMA Jacksonville Suns (22)	20.00
1977	TCMA Lodi Dodgers (25)	20.00
1977	TCMA Lynchburg Mets (a)(30)	25.00
1977	TCMA Lynchburg Mets (b)(30)	75.00
1977	TCMA Lynchburg Mets (31)	190.00
1977	TCMA Lynchburg Mets (36)	575.00
1977	Chong Modesto A's (23)	700.00
1977	TCMA Newark Co-Pilots (29)	30.00
1977	Top Trophies Omaha Royals (19)	90.00
1977	TCMA Orlando Twins (22)	65.00
1977	TCMA Orlando Twins (23)	75.00
1977	Coke Premiums Phoenix Giants (24)	20.00
1977	Cramer Phoenix Giants (24)	9.00
1977	VNB Phoenix Giants (24)	12.00
1977	TCMA Quad City Angels (29)	22.50
1977	TCMA Reading Phillies (23)	100.00
1977	McCurdy Rochester Red Wings (24)	95.00
1977	McCurdy Rochester Red Wings (Sheets)	100.00
1977	TCMA Salem Pirates (24)	25.00
1977	TCMA Salem Pirates (35)	160.00
1977	Cramer Salt Lake City Gulls (24)	7.50
1977	Mr. Chef San Jose Missions (24)	10.00
1977	TCMA Shreveport Captains (23)	30.00
1977	TCMA Spartanburg Phillies (24)	30.00
1977	Cramer Spokane Indians (24)	6.00
1977	TCMA St. Petersburg Cardinals (25)	17.50
1977	TCMA St. Petersburg Cardinals (26)	60.00
1977	DQ Tacoma Twins (30)	25.00

1977	Cramer Tucson Toros (24)	6.00
1977	TCMA Visalia Oaks (17)	22.50
1977	TCMA Waterloo Indians (29)	25.00
1977	TCMA Waterloo Indians (error)(31):	45.00
1977	TCMA Waterloo Indians (correct)(31)	70.00
1977	TCMA Wausau Mets (24)	30.00
1977	TCMA West Haven Yankees (25)	35.00

1978 Minor League Team Sets

Chicks Chicks
Felipe Alou

Full-color cards became more prevalent in 1978 as TCMA, the market leader, began to offer its client teams the choice between black-and-white or color cards.

NM

45 Team Sets and Variations

1978	Cramer Albuquerque Dukes (20)	17.50
1978	TCMA Appleton Foxes (25)	25.00
1978	TCMA Arkansas Travelers (23)	40.00
1978	TCMA Asheville Tourists (29)	27.50
1978	TCMA Burlington Bees (28)	30.00
1978	TCMA Cedar Rapids Giants (29)	45.00
1978	TCMA Charleston Charlies (20)	20.00
1978	TCMA Charleston Pirates (24)	25.00
1978	TCMA Clinton Dodgers (34)	25.00
1978	TCMA Columbus Clippers (27)	12.00
1978	TCMA Daytona Beach Astros (26)	15.00
1978	Tiefel Denver Bears (25)	10.00
1978	TCMA Dunedin Blue Jays (27)	32.50
1978	Team Geneva Cubs (24)	165.00
1978	TCMA Greenwood Braves (29)	25.00
1978	TCMA Holyoke Millers (24)	12.00
1978	Sertoma 1950 Indianapolis Indians (31)	22.50
1978	Team Indianapolis Indians (27)	9.00
1978	TCMA Knoxville Knox Sox (27)	100.00
1978	TCMA Lodi Dodgers (25)	35.00
1978	TCMA Lodi Dodgers (26)	60.00
1978	Brittling Memphis Chicks (10)	16.00
1978	OLDE Minneapolis/St. Paul (21)	20.00
1978	Chong Modesto A's (26)	35.00
1978	TCMA Newark-Wayne Co-Pilots (45)	27.50
1978	Team Oklahoma City 89ers (26)	55.00
1978	Team Oklahoma City 89ers (27)	150.00
1978	TCMA Orlando Twins (23)	15.00
1978	Cramer Phoenix Giants (25)	15.00
1978	TCMA Quad City Angels (30)	20.00
1978	TCMA Richmond Braves (24)	11.00
1978	TCMA Rochester Red Wings (17)	17.50
1978	TCMA Salem Pirates (18)	20.00
1978	Cramer Salt Lake City Gulls (24)	8.00
1978	Mr. Chef San Jose Missions (24)	12.50
1978	Cramer Spokane Indians (24)	7.50
1978	Weiner King Springfield Redbirds (24)	35.00

1978	TCMA St. Petersburg Cardinals (29)	30.00
1978	TCMA Syracuse Chiefs (22)	25.00
1978	Cramer Tacoma Yankees (25)	13.50
1978	TCMA Tidewater Tides (21)	21.00
1978	Cramer Tucson Toros (25)	10.00
1978	TCMA Waterloo Indians (26)	11.00
1978	TCMA Wausau Mets (25)	20.00
1978	TCMA Wisconsin Rapids Twins (18)	20.00

"1979" Reitz Memorial High School Don Mattingly

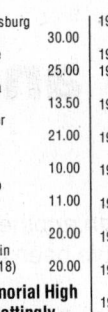

REITZ MEMORIAL TIGERS

DON MATTINGLY OF - P

This 2-1/2" x 3-1/2" black-and-white card is a collectors' issue fantasy created in the late 1980s using a photo of Mattingly which appeared in Sports Illustrated. The back has biographical data and high school stats. As an unauthorized issue, it has no collectible value.

Don Mattingly

1979 Minor League Team Sets

OUTFIELD
PAT ROONEY

TCMA's dominance in the minor league team set market reached new levels in 1979, with the company responsible for 80 percent of the 50+ sets issued. The Iowa Oaks became the first minor league team to issue a set of police-sponsored safety tip player cards.

NM

52 Team Sets and Variations

1979	TCMA Albuquerque Dukes (23)	22.50
1979	University Albuquerque Dukes (23)	180.00
1979	TCMA Appleton Foxes (25)	17.50
1979	TCMA Arkansas Travelers (23)	35.00
1979	TCMA Asheville Tourists (23)	17.50
1979	TCMA Buffalo Bisons (21)	27.50
1979	TCMA Burlington Bees (25)	16.00
1979	TCMA Cedar Rapids Giants (32)	30.00
1979	TCMA Charleston Charlies (19)	15.00
1979	TCMA Charleston Charlies (20)	40.00
1979	TCMA Clinton Dodgers (29)	45.00
1979	TCMA Columbus Clippers (29)	12.00
1979	TCMA Elmira Pioneers (28)	17.50
1979	Cramer Hawaii Islanders (24)	7.50
1979	TCMA Hawaii Islanders (24)	15.00
1979	TCMA Holyoke Millers (30)	12.00

1979	Team Indianapolis Indians (32)	7.50
1979	Police Indianapolis Indians (14)	60.00
1979	TCMA Jackson Mets (24)	10.00
1979	TCMA Jackson Mets (24)	12.00
1979	TCMA Knoxville White Sox (26)	25.00
1979	TCMA Lodi Dodgers (21)	25.00
1979	TCMA Memphis Chicks (24)	75.00
1979	Chong Modesto A's (24)	30.00
1979	Team Nashville Sounds (25)	11.00
1979	TCMA Newark Co-Pilots (24)	22.00
1979	TCMA Ogden A's (26)	50.00
	(counterfeited)	.00
1979	Team Oklahoma City 89ers (27)	185.00
1979	Cramer 1970's P.C.L. Stars (160)	70.00
1979	Cramer Phoenix Giants (24)	10.00
1979	TCMA Portland Beavers (24)	17.50
1979	TCMA Quad City Cubs (27)	35.00
1979	TCMA Richmond Braves (24)	7.50
1979	TCMA Rochester Red Wings (20)	5.00
1979	TCMA Salt Lake City Gulls (23)	7.50
1979	TCMA Savannah Braves (26)	15.00
1979	TCMA Spokane Indians (25)	5.00
1979	TCMA Syracuse Chiefs (20)	20.00
1979	Team Syracuse Chiefs (24)	75.00
1979	TCMA Tacoma Tugs (24)	17.50
1979	Team Tampico Alijadores (27)	100.00
1979	TCMA Tidewater Tides (25)	22.50
1979	TCMA Toledo Mud Hens (22)	20.00
1979	TCMA Tucson Toros (24)	10.00
1979	TCMA Tulsa Drillers (24)	7.50
1979	TCMA Vancouver Canadians (25)	9.00
1979	TCMA Waterbury A's (24)	45.00
1979	TCMA Waterloo Indians (24)	37.50
1979	TCMA Wausau Timbers (25)	12.50
1979	TCMA West Haven Yankees (30)	20.00
1979	TCMA Wisconsin Rapids Twins (23)	35.00

"1980" Greensboro Hornets Don Mattingly

GREENSBORO
1B - OF
1980 SOUTH ATLANTIC LEAGUE
DON MATTINGLY

Don Mattingly (Unauthorized issue produced in late 1980s; no collector value.)

1980 Minor League Team Sets

Charlotte
CAL RIPKEN JR. Infielder

The number of minor league team sets exceeded 60 for the first time in 1980. TCMA issues continued to proliferate, but the sets in greatest demand are two versions of a Charlotte O's set featuring Cal Ripken Jr. as a young infielder. Also making his baseball card debut in 1980, in TCMA's Reading Phillies set, was Ryne Sandberg.

NM

63 Team Sets and Variations

1980	TCMA Albuquerque Dukes (27)	12.50
1980	TCMA Anderson Braves (29)	12.00
1980	TCMA Appleton Foxes (30)	27.50
1980	TCMA Arkansas Travelers (25)	10.00
1980	TCMA Asheville Tourists (28)	8.00
1980	TCMA Batavia Trojans (30)	15.00
1980	TCMA Buffalo Bisons (16)	16.00
1980	TCMA Burlington Bees (29)	20.00
1980	TCMA Cedar Rapids Reds (24)	10.00
1980	TCMA Charleston Charlies (17)	12.50
1980	Team Charlotte O's - Orange (24)	2,750
	(Cal Ripken card widely counterfeited.)	.00
1980	WBTV Charlotte O's - Blue (28)	800.00
1980	TCMA Clinton Giants (27)	30.00
1980	TCMA Columbus Astros (22)	20.00
1980	Police Columbus Clippers (25)	15.00
1980	TCMA Columbus Clippers (28)	12.50
1980	Team Columbus Clippers (25)	15.00
1980	TCMA Elmira Pioneers (44)	35.00
1980	TCMA El Paso Diablos (24)	8.00
1980	TCMA Evansville Triplets (24)	11.00
1980	TCMA Glens Falls White Sox - B/W (29)	45.00
1980	TCMA Glens Falls White Sox - Color (30)	17.50
1980	TCMA Hawaii Islanders (25)	8.00
1980	TCMA Holyoke Millers (25)	15.00
1980	Team Indianapolis Indians (32)	12.00
1980	Police Iowa Oaks (14)	60.00
1980	Police Iowa Oaks (16)	65.00
1980	TCMA Knoxville Blue Jays (30)	30.00
1980	TCMA Lynn Sailors (23)	12.00
1980	TCMA Memphis Chicks (25)	25.00
1980	Chong Modesto A's (29)	30.00
1980	Team Nashville Sounds (25)	10.00
1980	TCMA Ogden A's (23)	15.00
1980	Team Oklahoma City 89ers (24)	17.50
1980	Police Omaha Royals (24)	60.00
1980	TCMA Orlando Twins (22)	30.00
1980	TCMA Peninsula Pilots - B/W (27)	35.00
1980	TCMA Peninsula Pilots - Color (27)	30.00
1980	VNB Phoenix Giants (26)	6.00
1980	TCMA Portland Beavers (27)	11.00
1980	TCMA Quad City Cubs (32)	30.00
1980	TCMA Reading Phillies (24)	500.00
1980	TCMA Richmond Braves (23)	11.00
1980	TCMA Rochester Red Wings (21)	8.00
1980	TCMA Salt Lake City Gulls (26)	12.00
1980	JITB San Jose Missions (21)	15.00
1980	TCMA Spokane Indians (24)	12.50
1980	TCMA Syracuse Chiefs (23)	15.00
1980	Team Syracuse Chiefs (24)	75.00
1980	TCMA Tacoma Tigers (24)	15.00
1980	TCMA Tidewater Tides (24)	10.00
1980	TCMA Toledo Mud Hens (20)	16.00
1980	TCMA Tucson Toros (24)	

1980	TCMA Tulsa Drillers (26)	16.00
1980	TCMA Utica Blue Jays (33)	35.00
1980	TCMA Vancouver Canadians (22)	8.00
1980	TCMA Waterbury Reds (22)	35.00
1980	TCMA Waterloo Indians (35)	40.00
1980	TCMA Wausau Timbers (23)	25.00
1980	TCMA West Haven White Caps (31)	7.50
1980	TCMA Wichita Aeros (22)	17.50
1980	TCMA Wisconsin Rapids Twins (27)	45.00

1981 Minor League Team Sets

DON MATTINGLY First Base

Once again in 1981, TCMA enjoyed an 80 percent share of the minor league team-set market. Two of the American League's most dominant hitters of the 1980s and early 1990s, Don Mattingly and Wade Boggs, made their baseball card debuts in the Arby's Nashville Sounds and TCMA Pawtucket Red Sox sets, respectively. The Nashville set was reprinted by the team in later years, wiping out most of the market value of what should have been 1981's most valuable minor league set.

MT

61 Team Sets and Variations

1981	TCMA Albuquerque Dukes (No Koufax.) (25)	10.00
1981	TCMA Albuquerque Dukes (W/Koufax.) (26)	25.00
1981	Team Albuquerque Dukes (20)	80.00
1981	TCMA Appleton Foxes (29)	12.00
1981	TCMA Arkansas Travelers (23)	15.00
1981	TCMA Batavia Trojans (30)	10.00
1981	TCMA Birmingham Barons (25)	20.00
1981	TCMA Bristol Red Sox (22)	15.00
1981	TCMA Buffalo Bisons (25)	15.00
1981	TCMA Burlington Bees (20)	20.00
1981	TCMA Cedar Rapids Reds (26)	22.50
1981	TCMA Charleston Charlies (24)	12.50
1981	TCMA Charleston Royals (26)	10.00
1981	Team Charlotte O's (25)	75.00
1981	TCMA Chattanooga Lookouts (25)	12.00
1981	TCMA Clinton Giants (27)	12.50
1981	Police Columbus Clippers (25)	11.00
1981	TCMA Columbus Clippers (28)	13.50
1981	TCMA Durham Bulls (27)	11.00
1981	Red Rooster Edmonton Trappers (24)	12.50
1981	TCMA El Paso Diablos (24)	15.00
1981	TCMA Evansville Triplets (22)	10.00
1981	TCMA Glens Falls White Sox (24)	15.00
1981	TCMA Hawaii Islanders (23)	16.00
1981	TCMA Holyoke Millers (26)	14.00
1981	Team Holyoke Millers (23)	40.00
1981	Team Indianapolis Indians (23)	6.00
1981	TCMA Lynn Sailors (29)	10.00
1981	TCMA Miami Orioles (21)	16.00

1981	TCMA Miami Orioles (23)	60.00
1981	Chong Modesto A's (30)	20.00
1981	Arby's Nashville Sounds (25)	11.00
1981	TCMA Oklahoma City 89ers (26)	50.00
1981	TCMA Omaha Royals (24)	15.00
1981	TCMA Pawtucket Red Sox (24)	30.00
1981	VNB Phoenix Giants (27)	12.00
1981	TCMA Portland Beavers (27)	13.50
1981	TCMA Quad City Cubs (33)	15.00
1981	TCMA Reading Phillies (24)	60.00
1981	TCMA Redwood Pioneers (30)	15.00
1981	TCMA Richmond Braves (25)	7.50
1981	TCMA Rochester Red Wings (23)	215.00
	(Cal Ripken card widely counterfeited.)	
1981	WTF Rochester Red Wings (25)	325.00
1981	TCMA Salt Lake City Gulls (26)	12.00
1981	TCMA Shreveport Captains (27)	9.00
1981	TCMA Spokane Indians (32)	10.00
1981	TCMA Syracuse Chiefs (24)	12.00
1981	Team Syracuse Chiefs (24)	75.00
1981	TCMA Tacoma Tigers (32)	6.00
1981	TCMA Tidewater Tides (24)	13.50
1981	TCMA Toledo Mud Hens (22)	20.00
1981	TCMA Tucson Toros (26)	10.00
1981	TCMA Tulsa Drillers (30)	10.00
1981	TCMA Vancouver Canadians (23)	9.00
1981	TCMA Vero Beach Dodgers (27)	15.00
1981	TCMA Waterbury Reds (23)	20.00
1981	TCMA Waterloo Indians (34)	7.00
1981	TCMA Wausau Timbers (23)	40.00
1981	TCMA West Haven A's (23)	20.00
1981	TCMA Wisconsin Rapids Twins (23)	15.00

1982 Minor League Team Sets

NEW YORK
JOHN ELWAY OF

A new hobby player entered the minor league team-set market in 1982. Larry Fritsch Cards of Wisconsin raised the quality bar a bit with its issue for most of the Midwest League teams. The number of sets, including late-issue variations, rose to 90 in 1982. Two of the era's most popularly collected athletes appeared on a baseball card for the first time in TCMA issues that year: Tony Gwynn with the Hawaii Islanders and John Elway with the Oneonta Yankees.

MT

92 Team Sets and Variations

1982	TCMA Albuquerque Dukes (27)	15.00
1982	Team Albuquerque Dukes Photos (28)	100.00
1982	TCMA Alexandria Dukes (27)	15.00
1982	TCMA Amarillo Gold Sox (29)	12.00
1982	Fritsch Appleton Foxes (31)	10.00
1982	Fritsch Appleton Foxes (33)	12.00
1982	TCMA Arkansas Travelers (24)	17.50

1982 TCMA Auburn Astros (19) 15.00
1982 Fritsch Beloit Brewers (27) 12.00
1982 TCMA Birmingham Barons (24) 10.00
1982 TCMA Buffalo Bisons (18) 17.50
1982 Fritsch Burlington Rangers (30) 9.00
1982 Fritsch Burlington Rangers (32) 11.00
1982 TCMA Burlington Rangers (26) 15.00
1982 TCMA Burlington Rangers (27) 25.00
1982 TCMA Cedar Rapids Reds (27) 25.00
1982 TCMA Charleston Charlies (24) 12.00
1982 TCMA Charleston Royals (24) 25.00
1982 Team Charlotte O's (31) 45.00
1982 TCMA Chattanooga Lookouts (25) 20.00
1982 Fritsch Clinton Giants (32) 12.00
1982 Police Columbus Clippers (25) 15.00
1982 TCMA Columbus Clippers (26) 75.00
1982 Fritsch Danville Suns (28) 15.00
1982 TCMA Daytona Beach Astros (25) 16.00
1982 TCMA Durham Bulls (25) 16.00
1982 TCMA Edmonton Trappers (25) 7.00
1982 TCMA El Paso Diablos (24) 9.00
1982 TCMA Evansville Triplets (25) 12.50
1982 TCMA Ft. Myers Royals (23) 15.00
1982 TCMA Glens Falls White Sox (23) 40.00
1982 TCMA Hawaii Islanders (25) 125.00

Tony Gwynn card widely counterfeited.

1982 TCMA Holyoke Millers (26) 15.00
1982 Team Holyoke Millers (29) 45.00
1982 TCMA Idaho Falls Athletics (33) 20.00
1982 Team Indianapolis Indians (32) 11.00
1982 TCMA Iowa Cubs (32) 8.00
1982 TCMA Jackson Mets (25) 25.00
1982 TCMA Knoxville Blue Jays (23) 15.00
1982 Ehrler's Louisville Redbirds (30) 10.00
1982 TCMA Lynchburg Mets (20) 35.00
1982 TCMA Lynchburg Mets (23) 45.00
1982 TCMA Lynn Sailors (18) 6.00
1982 Fritsch Madison Muskies (34) 9.00
1982 TCMA Miami Marlins (22) 12.50
1982 Chong Modesto A's (27) 17.50
1982 Arby's Nashville Sounds (28) 10.00
1982 TCMA Oklahoma City 89ers (27) 10.00
1982 TCMA Omaha Royals (27) 15.00
1982 TCMA Omaha Royals (29) 45.00
1982 TCMA Oneonta Yankees (17) 450.00

John Elway card widely counterfeited.

1982 TCMA Orlando Twins (24) 10.00
1982 TCMA Orlando Twins S.L. Champions (24) 17.50
1982 VNB Phoenix Giants (27) 17.50
1982 TCMA Portland Beavers (25) 17.50
1982 TCMA Quad City Cubs (28) 15.00
1982 TCMA Reading Phillies (22) 30.00
1982 TCMA Redwood Pioneers (27) 15.00
1982 TCMA Richmond Braves (31) 15.00
1982 TCMA Richmond Braves (23) 45.00
1982 TCMA Rochester Red Wings (22) 15.00
1982 TCMA Salt Lake City Gulls (25) 15.00
1982 TCMA Spokane Indians (24) 9.00
1982 Fritsch Springfield Cardinals (24) 12.50
1982 Fritsch Springfield Cardinals (27) 15.00

1982 TCMA Syracuse Chiefs (26) 12.50
1982 TCMA Syracuse Chiefs (29) 25.00
1982 Team Syracuse Chiefs (24) 75.00
1982 TCMA Tacoma Tigers (37) 12.00
1982 TCMA Tacoma Tigers (29) 45.00
1982 TCMA Tidewater Tides (25) 25.00
1982 TCMA Tidewater Tides (26) 50.00
1982 TCMA Toledo Mud Hens (24) 15.00
1982 TCMA Toledo Mud Hens (27) 45.00
1982 TCMA Tucson Toros (28) 11.00
1982 TCMA Tulsa Drillers (25) 15.00
1982 TCMA Tulsa Drillers (28) 45.00
1982 TCMA Vancouver Canadians (24) 16.00
1982 TCMA Vero Beach Dodgers (29) 17.50
1982 TCMA Waterbury Reds (23) 9.00
1982 Fritsch Waterloo Indians (28) 8.00
1982 Fritsch Waterloo Indians (31) 11.00
1982 TCMA Waterloo Indians (25) 15.00
1982 TCMA Waterloo Indians (28) 40.00
1982 Fritsch Wausau Timbers (31) 10.00
1982 Fritsch Wausau Timbers (33) 12.00
1982 TCMA West Haven A's (29) 20.00
1982 Team Wichita Aeros (20) 12.50
1982 Fritsch Wisconsin Rapids Twins (27) 12.00
1982 Fritsch Wisconsin Rapids Twins (28) 12.50

1983 Minor League Team Sets

KIRBY PUCKETT
Visalia Oaks

In his second and final year of minor league team set production, Larry Fritsch scored a coup in issuing the first baseball cards of Jose Canseco (Madison Muskies) and Kirby Puckett (Visalia Oaks). With Fritsch and several other entities, including the newspaper Baseball Hobby News, sponsoring team sets, TCMA's share of the 80-set market in 1983 declined to about 70 percent.

MT

83 Team Sets and Variations
1983 TCMA Albany-Colonie A's (20) 20.00
1983 TCMA Albuquerque Dukes (26) 16.00
1983 Team Albuquerque Dukes Photos (16) 65.00
1983 TCMA Alexandria Dukes (31) 20.00
1983 TCMA Anderson Braves (33) 10.00
1983 TCMA Appleton Foxes (30) 10.00
1983 TCMA Arkansas Travelers (25) 16.00
1983 TCMA Beaumont Golden Gators (23) 35.00
1983 Fritsch Beloit Brewers (30) 10.00
1983 TCMA Birmingham Barons (26) 12.50
1983 TCMA Buffalo Bisons (25) 25.00
1983 Fritsch Burlington Rangers (30) 7.50
1983 TCMA Burlington Rangers (28) 15.00
1983 TCMA Butte Copper Kings (33) 22.50

1983 Fritsch Cedar Rapids Reds (26) 10.00
1983 Fritsch Cedar Rapids Reds (28) 16.00
1983 TCMA Charleston Charlies (29) 9.00
1983 TCMA Charleston Royals (26) 15.00
1983 TCMA Chattanooga Lookouts (28) 65.00
1983 Fritsch Clinton Giants (30) 8.00
1983 TCMA Columbus Astros (24) 10.00
1983 TCMA Columbus Clippers (27) 15.00
1983 TCMA Daytona Beach Astros (24) 10.00
1983 TCMA Durham Bulls (29) 7.50
1983 TCMA El Paso Diablos (25) 10.00
1983 TCMA Erie Cardinals (25) 10.00
1983 TCMA Evansville Triplets (25) 10.00
1983 TCMA Glens Falls White Sox (24) 6.00
1983 TCMA Greensboro Hornets (35) 20.00
1983 TCMA Idaho Falls Athletics (34) 22.50
1983 Team Indianapolis Indians (32) 15.00
1983 TCMA Iowa Cubs (30) 30.00
1983 TCMA Iowa Cubs (31) 60.00
1983 Kelly Kinston Blue Jays (29) 65.00
1983 TCMA Knoxville Blue Jays (22) 7.50
1983 BHN Las Vegas Stars (29) 11.00
1983 Riley Louisville Redbirds (31) 11.00
1983 TCMA Lynchburg Mets (31) 15.00
1983 TCMA Lynn Pirates (27) 20.00
1983 Fritsch Madison Muskies (32) 12.00
1983 TCMA Memphis Chicks (24) 12.00
1983 TCMA Miami Marlins (28) 20.00
1983 TCMA Midland Cubs (26) 15.00
1983 Chong Modesto A's (30) 15.00
1983 TCMA Nashua Angels (27) 9.00
1983 Hill's Nashville Sounds (25) 7.00
1983 TCMA Oklahoma City 89ers (27) 15.00
1983 TCMA Omaha Royals (24) 10.00
1983 TCMA Orlando Twins (22) 12.00
1983 TCMA Orlando Twins (23) 35.00
1983 TCMA Pawtucket Red Sox (26) 25.00
1983 Fritsch Peoria Suns (30) 5.00
1983 BHN Phoenix Giants (28) 20.00
1983 TCMA Portland Beavers (22) 30.00
1983 TCMA Portland Beavers (25) 60.00
1983 TCMA Quad City Cubs (27) 15.00
1983 TCMA Reading Phillies (24) 40.00
1983 TCMA Redwood Pioneers (32) 15.00
1983 TCMA Richmond Braves (25) 20.00
1983 TCMA Rochester Red Wings (25) 7.50
1983 TCMA Salt Lake City Gulls (26) 9.00
1983 Colla San Jose Bees (26) 15.00
1983 Fritsch Springfield Cardinals (26) 7.00
1983 TCMA St. Petersburg Cardinals (30) 10.00
1983 TCMA Syracuse Chiefs (26) 25.00
1983 Team Syracuse Chiefs (25) 75.00
1983 TCMA Tacoma Tigers (31) 12.00
1983 TCMA Tacoma Tigers (36) 55.00
1983 TCMA Tampa Tarpons (29) 30.00
1983 TCMA Tidewater Tides (29) 20.00
1983 TCMA Toledo Mud Hens (25) 10.00
1983 TCMA Toledo Mud Hens (29) 60.00
1983 TCMA Tri-Cities Triplets (30) 10.00
1983 TCMA Tucson Toros (25) 12.50
1983 TCMA Tucson Toros (26) 25.00
1983 TCMA Tulsa Drillers (25) 9.00

1983 TCMA Vero Beach Dodgers (29) 16.00
1983 Fritsch Visalia Oaks (29) 125.00
1983 TCMA Waterbury Reds (19) 22.50
1983 Fritsch Waterloo Indians (29) 8.00
1983 Fritsch Wausau Timbers (31) 8.00
1983 Dog-n-Shake Wichita Aeroes (24) 15.00
1983 Fritsch Wisconsin Rapids Twins (28) 12.50

1984 TCMA Tidewater Tides Darryl Strawberry

OF
Darryl Strawberry
TIDEWATER TIDES

(N.Y. Mets, AAA)

MT

Darryl Strawberry (Reportedly issued by TCMA as a promotion for its 1984 team-set line-up. Blank backed.) 20.00

1984 Minor League Team Sets

P
Roger Clemens
PAWTUCKET RED SOX

A trend toward more baseball card shop sponsorships of minor league team sets is noted with the 1984 issues. Another Mike Cramer innovation that year was the introduction of special high-end ultraviolet-coated glossy versions of his Pacific Coast League sets. The major debut among '84 minor league cards was Roger Clemens' appearance in TCMA's Pawtucket Red Sox set.

MT

72 Team Sets and Variations
1984 TCMA Albany-Colonie A's (26) 15.00
1984 Cramer Albuquerque Dukes (26) 4.00
1984 Cramer Albuquerque Dukes Glossy (26) 15.00
1984 Team Albuquerque Dukes Photos (27) 65.00
1984 TCMA Arkansas Travelers (26) 8.00
1984 TCMA Beaumont Golden Gators (25) 10.00
1984 TCMA Buffalo Bisons (25) 13.50
1984 TCMA Butte Copper Kings (27) 12.50
1984 TCMA Cedar Rapids Reds (28) 11.00
1984 TCMA Charlotte O's (27) 12.50
1984 TCMA Chattanooga Lookouts (29) 6.00
1984 Police Columbus Clippers (25) 10.00
1984 TCMA Columbus Clippers (27) 9.00
1984 Team Daytona Beach Astros (25) 25.00
1984 TCMA Durham Bulls (30) 10.00
1984 Cramer Edmonton Trappers (25) 6.00
1984 Cramer Edmonton Trappers - Glossy (26) 10.00
1984 TCMA El Paso Diablos (25) 9.00

1984 TCMA Evansville Triplets (22) 16.00
1984 Cramer Everett Giants (35) 10.00
1984 Cramer Everett Giants (42) 20.00
1984 TCMA Greensboro Hornets (29) 15.00
1984 Pizza Hut Greenville Braves (25) 40.00
1984 Cramer Hawaii Islanders (25) 7.50
1984 Cramer Hawaii Islanders - Glossy (25) 12.00
1984 Team Idaho Falls A's (30) 25.00
1984 Team Indianapolis Indians (30) 10.00
1984 TCMA Iowa Cubs (31) 15.00
1984 TCMA Jackson Mets (25) 20.00
1984 Smokey Jackson Mets Alumni (15) 35.00
1984 Cramer Las Vegas Stars (25) 12.00
1984 Cramer Las Vegas Stars - Glossy (25) 17.50
1984 TCMA Little Falls Mets (26) 20.00
1984 Riley Louisville Redbirds (30) 6.00
1984 T&J Madison Muskies (25) 9.00
1984 TCMA Maine Guides (23) 12.50
1984 TCMA Memphis Chicks (25) 15.00
1984 TCMA Midland Cubs (24) 8.00
1984 Chong Modesto A's (28) 75.00
1984 Hill's Nashville Sounds (25) 15.00
1984 TCMA Newark Orioles (24) 10.00
1984 TCMA Newark Orioles (25) 30.00
1984 TCMA Oklahoma City 89ers (24) 10.00
1984 TCMA Omaha Royals (30) 10.00
1984 TCMA Pawtucket Red Sox Error Set (25) 125.00
1984 TCMA Pawtucket Red Sox Corrected Set(29) 155.00

Roger Clemens card widely counterfeited.

1984 Cramer Phoenix Giants (25) 9.00
1984 Cramer Phoenix Giants - Glossy (25) 15.00
1984 Cramer Portland Beavers (22) 7.00
1984 Cramer Portland Beavers - Glossy (22) 20.00
1984 TCMA Prince William Pirates (34) 7.00
1984 TCMA Richmond Braves (27) 9.00
1984 TCMA Rochester Red Wings (19) 10.00
1984 Cramer Salt Lake City Gulls (24) 6.00
1984 Cramer SLC Gulls - Glossy (24) 15.00
1984 TCMA Savannah Cardinals (26) 10.00
1984 1stB Shreveport Captains (24) 20.00
1984 Team Spokane Indians (24) 15.00
1984 TCMA Syracuse Chiefs (32) 10.00
1984 Cramer Tacoma Tigers (25) 7.50
1984 Cramer Tacoma Tigers - Glossy (25) 12.00
1984 TCMA Tidewater Tides (28) 6.00
1984 TCMA Toledo Mud Hens (24) 15.00
1984 Cramer Tucson Toros (25) 8.00
1984 Cramer Tucson Toros - Glossy (25) 15.00
1984 Team Tulsa Drillers (22) 7.50
1984 Cramer Vancouver Canadians (25) 10.00
1984 Cramer Vancouver Canadians - Glossy (25) 15.00
1984 TCMA Visalia Oaks (25) 12.50
1984 Rock's Wichita Aeros (23) 16.00
1984 Rock's Wichita Aeros Posters (3) 35.00

1985 Chong Mark McGuire/McGwire Reprints
During the height of Big Mac mania in 1998-1999, the slugger's card from the 1985 Modesto A's team set was reprinted and/or counterfeited in vast quantities. Most of the latter-day printings are of the correct-spelling version, though the "McGuire" type was also reproduced. Collectors who desire an ex-

MARK McGWIRE
Infielder

ample of McGwire's first minor league card should buy it only as part of an unopened Modesto team set. Because of the impossibility of differentiating reprints/counterfeits from originals, singles of the '85 McGwire have only nominal collector value, even when "authenticated" by major grading services.

MT

Mark McGwire 6.00

1985 Columbus Clippers Don Mattingly B/W

COLUMBUS CLIPPERS
DON MATTINGLY 1B

This fantasy issue was designed in rough similitude of the 1985 TCMA minor league cards. Black-and-white, with minimal data on back, it shows Mattingly in action during a game in which the team wore circa 1884 uniforms.

(No collector value.)

1985 Minor League Team Sets

MARVIN FREEMAN
READING Phillies

ProCards, which once dominated the minor league card new-issues market, made its debut in 1985 with a single set for the Reading Phillies. Mark McGwire made his minor league card debut in a Chong team set of the Modesto A's, initially suffering the indignity of having his name misspelled. Latter-day reprinting and/or counterfeiting of the McGwire (and McGuire) cards sapped much for the market strength from what should have been the 1980s' most desirable minor league issue.

MT

79 Team Sets and Variations
1985 TCMA Albany-Colonie Yankees (33) 25.00
1985 TCMA Albany-Colonie Yankees (35) 27.50
1985 Cramer Albuquerque Dukes (25) 6.00
1985 Team Anchorage Glacier Pilots (44) 7.50
1985 TCMA Beaumont Golden Gators (25) 12.00
1985 TCMA Beloit Brewers (26) 10.00

1985 Cramer Bend Phillies (24) 9.00
1985 Team Birmingham Barons (25) 55.00
1985 TCMA Buffalo Bisons (26) 8.00
1985 TCMA Burlington Rangers (28) 10.00
1985 Cramer Calgary Cannons (25) 9.00
1985 TCMA Cedar Rapids Reds (32) 15.00
1985 TCMA Charlotte O's (29) 10.00
1985 TCMA Charlotte O's (31) 17.50
1985 Team Chattanooga Lookouts (26) 50.00
1985 Police Columbus Clippers (25) 4.00
1985 TCMA Columbus Clippers (28) 12.00
1985 Team Daytona Beach Islanders (30) 30.00
1985 TCMA Durham Bulls (32) 12.00
1985 Cramer Edmonton Trappers (25) 7.00
1985 TCMA Elmira Pioneers (25) 13.50
1985 Pacific Everett Giants Series 1 (24) 7.50
1985 Pacific Everett Giants Series 2 (24) 15.00
1985 Smokey Fresno Giants (32) 60.00
1985 TCMA Ft. Myers Royals (30) 8.00
1985 TCMA Greensboro Hornets (28) 12.50
1985 Pizza Hut Greenville Braves (26) 45.00
1985 Team Greenville Braves (26) 35.00
1985 Cramer Hawaii Islanders (25) 7.00
1985 BK Huntsville Stars (25) 9.00
1985 BK Huntsville Stars Uncut Sheet 9.00
1985 Team Indianapolis Indians (36) 24.00
1985 TCMA International League All-Stars (42) 12.50
1985 TCMA International League All-Stars (45) 45.00
1985 TCMA Iowa Cubs (34) 13.50
1985 TCMA Kinston Blue Jays (26) 12.50
1985 Cramer Las Vegas Stars (27) 9.00
1985 TCMA Little Falls Mets (27) 7.00
1985 Riley Louisville Redbirds (30) 5.00
1985 TCMA Lynchburg Mets (27) 10.00
1985 TCMA Madison Muskies (25) 7.00
1985 T&J Madison Muskies (25) 10.00
1985 TCMA Maine Guides (30) 12.50
1985 TCMA Mexico City Tigers (29) 10.00
1985 TCMA Midland Angels (25) 15.00
1985 Chong Modesto A's - Errors (28) 300.00
1985 Chong Modesto A's - Corrected (28) 75.00
1985 TCMA Nashua Pirates (29) 10.00
1985 Hill's Nashville Sounds (25) 4.00
1985 TCMA Newark Orioles (25) 10.00
1985 TCMA Oklahoma City 89ers (30) 15.00
1985 TCMA Omaha Royals (31) 20.00
1985 TCMA Orlando Twins (29) 11.00
1985 Team Osceola Astros (30) 50.00
1985 TCMA Pawtucket Red Sox (20) 20.00
1985 Cramer Phoenix Giants (25) 7.00
1985 Cramer Portland Beavers (25) 11.00
1985 TCMA Prince Williams Pirates (31) 7.50
1985 ProCards Reading Phillies (25) 4.00
1985 TCMA Richmond Braves (26) 5.00
1985 TCMA Rochester Red Wings (31) 10.00
1985 Rochester Red Wings Ripken Ticket 6.00
1985 Cramer Spokane Indians (24) 8.00
1985 Cramer Spokane All-Time Greats (24) 12.50
1985 TCMA Springfield Cardinals (24) 6.00
1985 TCMA Syracuse Chiefs (31) 30.00

1985 Cramer Tacoma Tigers (25) 9.00
1985 TCMA Tidewater Tides (25) 8.00
1985 TCMA Tidewater Tides (28) 30.00
1985 TCMA Toledo Mud Hens (25) 7.00
1985 TCMA Toldeo Mud Hens (26) 11.00
1985 Cramer Tucson Toros (25) 6.00
1985 Team Tulsa Drillers (27) 20.00
1985 Team Tulsa Drillers (28) 30.00
1985 TCMA Utica Blue Sox (26) 40.00
1985 Cramer Vancouver Canadians (25) 9.00
1985 TCMA Vero Beach Dodgers (27) 7.50
1985 TCMA Visalia Oaks (25) 10.00
1985 TCMA Waterbury Indians (25) 9.00

1986 Memphis Chicks Bo Jackson "Blue Jersey"

Bo Jackson
Outfielder

Made to resemble the legitimate Time Out Sports Memphis Chicks team set with a silver border, this unauthorized collector's issue pictures Jackson in a blue away jersey rather than the white home uniform.

Bo Jackson (No collectible value.)

1986 Minor League Team Sets

SANTOS ALOMAR
Beaumont C

After its one-team effort in 1985, ProCards burst onto the team-set minor league market in a major way in 1986, driving the market to a record of more than 130 sets (including variations), for which PC claimed nearly a 75 percent market share. Notable debuts were Greg Maddux in the Pittsfield Cubs set and Randy Johnson in the West Palm Beach Expos issue, both sets a product of ProCards.

MT
133 Team Sets and Variations
1986 TCMA Albany-Colonie Yankees (32) 5.00
1986 PC Albuquerque Dukes (28) 4.00
1986 Team Albuquerque Dukes Photos (28) 75.00
1986 Team Anchorage Glacier Pilots (42) 15.00
1986 PC Appleton Foxes (30) 6.00
1986 PC Arkansas Travelers (24) 10.00
1986 PC Asheville Tourists (29) 5.00
1986 PC Auburn Astros (27) 5.00
1986 PC Bakersfield Dodgers (29) 6.00
1986 PC Beaumont Golden Gators (28) 12.50
1986 Pacific Bellingham Mariners (29) 5.00
1986 PC Beloit Brewers (26) 5.00
1986 Pacific Bend Phillies (25) 10.00

1986 Team Birmingham Barons (28) 55.00
1986 PC Buffalo Bisons (26) 4.00
1986 PC Burlington Expos (28) 8.00
1986 PC Calgary Cannons (26) 4.00
1986 TCMA Cedar Rapids Reds (28) 6.00
1986 PC Charleston Rainbows (29) 20.00
1986 WBTV Charlotte O's (29) 17.50
1986 PC Chattanooga Lookouts (25) 11.00
1986 PC Clearwater Phillies (26) 5.00
1986 PC Clinton Giants (30) 3.00
1986 PC Columbia Mets (28) 11.00
1986 PC Columbus Astros (29) 4.00
1986 Police Columbus Clippers (25) 5.00
1986 PC Columbus Clippers (26) 9.00
1986 PC Daytona Beach Astros (29) 5.00
1986 PC Durham Bulls (27) 5.00
1986 PC Edmonton Trappers (27) 9.00
1986 PC Elmira Pioneers (30) 45.00
1986 PC El Paso Diablos (23) 7.00
1986 PC Erie Cardinals (30) 9.00
1986 PC Erie Cardinals (31) 25.00
1986 Pacific Eugene Emeralds (25) 7.00
1986 Pacific Everett Giants - B/W (36) 7.00
1986 Pacific Everett Giants - Color (32) 16.00
1986 PC Florida State League All-Stars (50) 60.00
1986 Smokey Bear Fresno Giants (32) 25.00
1986 PC Ft. Lauderdale Yankees (29) 5.00
1986 PC Ft. Myers Royals (29) 5.00
1986 PC Geneva Cubs (27) 5.00
1986 PC Glens Falls Tigers (24) 5.00
1986 PC Greensboro Hornets (27) 8.00
1986 PC Greenville Braves (24) 20.00
1986 PC Hagerstown Suns (29) 5.00
1986 PC Hawaii Islanders (23) 5.00
1986 BK Huntsville Stars (25) 16.00
1986 BK Huntsville Stars Uncut Sheet 30.00
1986 Team Indianapolis Indians (36) 10.00
1986 PC Iowa Cubs (26) 4.00
1986 TCMA Jackson Mets (27) 6.00
1986 TCMA Jacksonville Expos (25) 5.00
1986 PC Jamestown Expos (30) 5.00
1986 PC Kenosha Twins (25) 7.00
1986 PC Kinston Eagles (25) 5.00
1986 PC Knoxville Blue Jays (27) 7.00
1986 PC Lakeland Tigers (25) 7.00
1986 PC Las Vegas Stars (24) 4.00
1986 PC Las Vegas Stars (25) 5.00
1986 PC Las Vegas Stars (26) 12.00
1986 PC Little Falls Mets (29) 5.00
1986 Team Louisville Redbirds (30) 7.50
1986 PC Lynchburg Mets (28) 5.00
1986 PC Macon Pirates (25) 12.50
1986 PC Madison Muskies (28) 9.00
1986 T&J Madison Muskies (27) 8.00
1986 Pacific Maine Guides (26) 9.00
1986 Pacific Medford A's (25) 7.00
1986 Time Out Memphis Chicks - Gold (26) 10.00
1986 Time Out Memphis Chicks - Silver (26) 12.00
1986 PC Miami Marlins (29) 5.00
1986 PC Midland Angels (26) 6.00
1986 Chong Modesto A's (27) 9.00
1986 PC Modesto A's (26) 5.00
1986 PC Modesto A's (27) 10.00
1986 PC Nashua Pirates (28) 4.00
1986 Hill's Nashville Sounds (24) 8.00
1986 PC New Britain Red Sox (25) 10.00
1986 PC Oklahoma City 89ers (29) 5.00
1986 PC Omaha Royals (29) 7.50
1986 TCMA Omaha Royals (29) 7.50
1986 PC Orlando Twins (24) 5.00
1986 PC Osceola Astros (29) 5.00
1986 PC Palm Springs Angels (29) 15.00
1986 Smokey Bear Palm Springs Angels (28) 25.00
1986 PC Pawtucket Red Sox (28) 6.00
1986 PC Peninsula White Sox (28) 10.00

1986 PC Peoria Chiefs (27) 25.00
1986 PC Phoenix Firebirds (26) 4.00
1986 PC Pittsfield Cubs (25) 110.00
1986 Team Pittsfield Cubs poster - B/W 75.00
1986 Team Pittsfield Cubs Poster - Color 75.00
1986 PC Portland Beavers (22) 5.00
1986 PC Portland Beavers (23) 10.00
1986 PC Prince William Pirates (27) 4.00
1986 PC Quad Cities Angels (33) 9.00
1986 PC Reading Phillies (26) 4.00
1986 PC Richmond Braves (26) 4.00
1986 PC Rochester Red Wings (26) 5.00
1986 Pacific Salem Angels (25) 6.00
1986 PC Salem Red Birds (29) 7.00
1986 PC San Jose Bees (25) 5.00
1986 PC Shreveport Captains (28) 6.00
1986 DJ Southern League All-Stars (27) 9.00
1986 Pacific Spokane Indians (25) 25.00
1986 University City Spokane Indians (24) 45.00
1986 TCMA Stars of the Future (40) 25.00
1986 PC St. Petersburg Cardinals (29) 5.00
1986 PC Stockton Ports (26) 5.00
1986 PC Sumter Braves (30) 20.00
1986 PC Syracuse Chiefs (27) 10.00
1986 PC Tacoma Tigers (25) 10.00
1986 PC Tampa Tarpons (27) 5.00
1986 PC Tidewater Tides - Mets Logo (29) 4.00
1986 PC Tidewater Tides - Tides Logo (29) 7.00
1986 PC Toledo Mud Hens (24) 4.00
1986 Pacific Tri-Cities Triplets (14) 6.00
1986 PC Tucson Toros (26) 6.00
1986 Team Tulsa Drillers (27) 20.00
1986 PC Vancouver Canadians (27) 5.00
1986 PC Ventura Gulls (28) 8.00
1986 PC Vermont Reds (24) 7.00
1986 PC Vero Beach Dodgers (27) 9.00
1986 PC Visalia Oaks (24) 5.00
1986 PC Waterbury Indians (26) 5.00
1986 PC Waterloo Indians (32) 5.00
1986 PC Watertown Pirates (27) 20.00
1986 PC Watertown Pirates (29) 25.00
1986 PC Wausau Timbers (29) 9.00
1986 PC West Palm Beach Expos (45) 45.00
1986 PC Winston-Salem Spirits (29) 10.00
1986 PC Winter Haven Red Sox (27) 8.00

"1987" Moeller High School Ken Griffey Jr.

KEN GRIFFEY, JR.
Outfielder

These cards are unauthorized collectors' issues purporting to date from 1987, when Junior was a student at Moeller High School in Cincinnati. In reality, the cards were not seen until years later. Fronts have a color photo with a blue border. The back of the "regular" card has biographical data and (incorrect) information and may be found with or without yellow and blue vertical colored stripes. The back of the "All-American" bannered card has a photo of Griffey in Seattle uniform. Because the cards are unauthorized, they have no collector value.

MT
--- Ken Griffey, Jr. (Black-and-white back.)
--- Ken Griffey Jr. (Blue and yellow stripes on back.)
--- Ken Griffey, Jr. (High School All-American banner.)

1987 Minor League Team Sets

KEN GRIFFEY, JR.
OUTFIELD
Bellingham MARINERS

Best, which under new ownership a decade later would become a powerhouse in the minor league team-set field, made its first cards in 1987. The hobby was abuzz about the several Gregg Jefferies cards available, but the year will always be remembered as the baseball card debut of Ken Griffey Jr., in a team-issued set of the Bellingham Mariners. The number of team sets and related collectibles exceeded 150 in 1987.

MT
159 Team Sets and Variations
1987 PC Albany-Colonie Yankees (23) 6.00
1987 Team Albuquerque Dukes (30) 7.00
1987 Team Albuquerque Dukes (Photos)(35) 110.00
1987 Team Anchorage Glacier Pilots (41) 20.00
1987 PC Appleton Foxes (30) 5.00
1987 PC Arkansas Travelers (24) 6.00
1987 PC Asheville Tourists (28) 6.00
1987 PC Auburn Astros (25) 5.00
1987 PC Bakersfield Dodgers (29) 5.00
1987 Baseball USA Pan-Am Games - Blue (34) 40.00
1987 Baseball USA Pan-Am Games - Blue (35) 45.00
1987 Team Bellingham Mariners (34) 35.00
1987 PC Beloit Brewers (26) 8.00
1987 Best Birmingham Barons (28) 6.00
1987 Team Buffalo Bisons (29) 7.00
1987 PC Burlington Expos (29) 5.00
1987 PC Calgary Cannons (24) 12.00
1987 PC Cedar Rapids Reds (28) 5.00
1987 PC Charleston Rainbows (23) 10.00
1987 PC Charleston Wheelers (28) 4.00
1987 Team Charlotte O's (30) 8.00
1987 Best Chattanooga Lookouts (26) 5.00
1987 Best Chattanooga Lookouts (26) (W/Coke logo.) 10.00
1987 PC Clearwater Phillies (27) 5.00
1987 PC Clearwater Phillies (35) 8.00
1987 PC Clinton Giants (29) 5.00
1987 PC Columbia Mets (29) 4.00
1987 PC Columbus Astros (25) 7.00
1987 PC Columbus Clippers (27) 9.00
1987 PC Columbus Clippers (24) 5.00
1987 Police Columbus Clippers (29) 9.00
1987 TCMA Columbus Clippers (25) 7.00
1987 PC Daytona Beach Admirals (26) 5.00
1987 PC Denver Zephyrs (29) 5.00
1987 PC Dunedin Blue Jays (29) 4.00
1987 PC Durham Bulls (28) 5.00
1987 PC Edmonton Trappers (23) 5.00
1987 Team Elmira Pioneers - Black (31) 6.00
1987 Team Elmira Pioneers - Red (36) 35.00
1987 PC El Paso Diablos (27) 5.00
1987 PC El Paso Diablos (30) 7.00
1987 PC Erie Cardinals (29) 5.00

1987 PC Eugene Emeralds (30) 9.00
1987 Pacific Everett Giants (34) 6.00
1987 PC Fayetteville Generals (27) 5.00
1987 PC Ft. Lauderdale Yankees (30) 7.00
1987 PC Ft. Myers Royals (34) 6.00
1987 PC Gastonia Rangers (29) 70.00
1987 PC Geneva Cubs (26) 4.00
1987 PC Glens Falls Tigers (25) 10.00
1987 PC Greensboro Hornets (26) 17.50
1987 Best Greenville Braves (28) 10.00
1987 PC Hagerstown Suns (29) 5.00
1987 PC Harrisburg Senators (29) 4.00
1987 PC Hawaii Islanders (27) 3.00
1987 BK Huntsville Stars (25) 6.00
1987 PC Idaho Falls Braves (27) 5.00
1987 Team Indianapolis Indians (36) 10.00
1987 TCMA International League All-Stars (45) 8.00
1987 Team Iowa Cubs (25) 17.50
1987 Team Jackson Mets (25) 5.00
1987 PC Jacksonville Expos (29) 15.00
1987 PC Jamestown Expos (30) 5.00
1987 PC Kenosha Twins (29) 5.00
1987 PC Kinston Indians (24) 5.00
1987 PC Knoxville Blue Jays (27) 5.00
1987 PC Knoxville Blue Jays (30) 9.00
1987 PC Lakeland Tigers (26) 5.00
1987 PC Las Vegas Stars (27) 4.00
1987 PC Little Falls Mets (27) 6.00
1987 PC Little Falls Mets, W/Variations (31) 8.00
1987 Team Louisville Redbirds (30) 8.00
1987 PC Lynchburg Mets (28) 4.00
1987 PC Macon Pirates (25) 5.00
1987 PC Madison Muskies (29) 4.00
1987 T&J Madison Muskies (29) 7.00
1987 PC Maine Guides (23) 4.00
1987 TCMA Maine Guides (25) 5.00
1987 TCMA Maine Guides (27) 12.00
1987 Best Memphis Chicks (27) 6.00
1987 PC Memphis Chicks (27) 5.00
1987 PC Miami Marlins (25) 5.00
1987 PC Midland Angels (29) 5.00
1987 Chong Modesto A's (32) 5.00
1987 PC Modesto A's (25) 6.00
1987 PC Myrtle Beach Blue Jays (30) 4.00
1987 Hill's Nashville Sounds (26) 5.00
1987 Nashville Sounds Don Mattingly Ticket 5.00
1987 PC Newark Orioles (29) 5.00
1987 PC New Britain Red Sox (29) 5.00
1987 PC Oklahoma City 89ers (27) 6.00
1987 PC Omaha Royals (26) 6.00
1987 PC Oneonta Yankees (33) 12.50
1987 PC Orlando Twins (26) 8.00
1987 PC Osceola Astros (29) 5.00
1987 PC Palm Springs Angels (25) 5.00
1987 PC Pawtucket Red Sox (27) 3.00
1987 TCMA Pawtucket Red Sox (28) 4.00
1987 PC Peninsula White Sox (29) 4.00
1987 Pizza World Peoria Chiefs (28) 60.00
1987 PC Peoria Chiefs (29) 6.00
1987 PC Phoenix Firebirds (28) 6.00
1987 PC Pittsfield Cubs (25) 15.00
1987 Team Pittsfield Cubs Poster 30.00
1987 Bon Pocatello Giants (32) 45.00
1987 PC Port Charlotte Rangers (27) 5.00
1987 PC Portland Beavers (25) 4.00
1987 PC Prince William Yankees (29) 5.00
1987 PC Quad City Angels (31) 6.00
1987 PC Reading Phillies (26) 4.00
1987 Bob's Richmond Braves (23) 75.00
1987 Crown Richmond Braves (30) 17.50
1987 TCMA Richmond Braves (29) 12.00
1987 PC Rochester Red Wings (27) 3.00
1987 TCMA Rochester Red Wings (29) 4.00
1987 PC Salem Angels (34) 4.00

Year	Item	Price
1987	PC Salem Buccaneers (30)	6.00
1987	Smokey Salinas Spurs (32)	40.00
1987	Team Salt Lake City Trappers (30)	6.00
1987	Team San Antonio Dodgers (24)	7.00
1987	Team San Antonio Dodgers (25)	9.00
1987	PC San Bernardino Spirit (23)	5.00
1987	PC San Jose Bees (30)	5.00
1987	PC Savannah Cardinals (26)	5.00
1987	PC Shreveport Captains (25)	
1987	DJ Southern League All-Stars (25)	9.00
1987	PC Spartanburg Phillies (28)	4.00
1987	PC Spokane Indians (25)	5.00
1987	Best Springfield Cardinals (28)	5.00
1987	PC St. Petersburg Cardinals (27)	
1987	PC Stockton Ports (26)	9.00
1987	PC Sumter Braves (30)	4.00
1987	PC Syracuse Chiefs (23)	4.00
1987	TCMA Syracuse Chiefs (33)	11.00
1987	Team Syracuse Chiefs Tickets (12)	25.00
1987	PC Tacoma Tigers (23)	4.00
1987	PC Tampa Tarpons (30)	5.00
1987	Texas League All-Stars (36)	4.00
1987	PC Tidewater Tides (33)	4.00
1987	TCMA Tidewater Tides (30)	4.00
1987	PC Toledo Mud Hens (24)	4.00
1987	TCMA Toledo Mud Hens (25)	4.00
1987	Jones Tucson Toros (24)	45.00
1987	PC Tucson Toros (25)	5.00
1987	Team Tulsa Drillers (28)	6.00
1987	PC Utica Blue Sox (33)	4.00
1987	PC Vancouver Canadians (25)	5.00
1987	PC Vermont Reds (26)	5.00
1987	PC Vero Beach Dodgers (31)	7.00
1987	PC Visalia Oaks (27)	5.00
1987	PC Waterloo Indians (29)	7.00
1987	PC Watertown Pirates (31)	8.00
1987	PC Wausau Timbers (28)	5.00
1987	PC West Palm Beach Expos (28)	5.00
1987	Rock's Wichita Pilots (25)	17.50
1987	PC Williamsport Bills (27)	5.00
1987	PC Winston-Salem Spirits (27)	5.00
1987	PC Winter Haven Red Sox (30)	5.00
1987	PC Wytheville Cubs (31)	5.00

1988 "1982" Anchorage Glacier Pilots

Mark McGwire

While carrying a 1982 date on front, this card was actually issued in 1988, after McGwire had established himself as a slugging major league star. While he had played in the Alaskan summer league in 1982 - as a pitcher and first baseman - the team had issued no contemporary cards. This one-card set was issued in an edition of 10,000 with an original selling price of $5.95. Front of the standard size card has a blue frame around a black-and-white photo of McGwire on the mound. Back has biographical and college ball data, along with the logo of the team. A similar card exists of Casey Candaele.

		MT
---	Mark McGwire	55.00
---	Casey Candaele	2.00

1988 Cal Cards S.B. Spirit Griffey "White Jersey"

KEN GRIFFEY JR.
Outfield

This unauthorized collectors' issue was first seen in the early 1990s using the same format as the Cal Cards San Bernardino Spirit team issue. Because of its illegitimate status, it has no collectible value.

34   Ken Griffey Jr.

1988 Minor League Team Sets

JUAN GONZALEZ
Outfield   CHARLOTTE

Major changes in the minor league team set market were seen in 1988. TCMA, which had pioneered the concept in the early 1970s, merged with Collectors Marketing Corp. (CMC). The new venture nearly tripled the number of team sets issued under the CMC label. Star Co. also joined the market in a major way, producing more than 25 team and all-star sets. Other companies entering the market in 1988 included Grand Slam, Legoe, Sport Pro and Cal Cards. An Anchorage Glacier Pilots card of Mark McGwire purporting to date from 1982 was actually produced in 1988.

		MT
225 Team Sets and Variations		
1988	CMC AAA All-Stars (45)	17.50
1988	PC AAA All-Stars (55)	6.00
1988	Alaska Goldpanners 1960s All Stars (12)	25.00
1988	Alaska Goldpanners 1970s All-Stars (12)	22.50
1988	Team Alaska Goldpanners (20)	15.00
1988	PC Albany-Colonie Yankees (27)	5.00
1988	CMC Albuquerque Dukes (25)	5.00
1988	PC Albuquerque Dukes (29)	4.00
1988	Team Albuquerque Dukes Photos (35)	110.00
1988	"1982" Anchorage Glacier Pilots McGwire	55.00
1988	PC Appleton Foxes (30)	5.00
1988	GS Arkansas Travelers (25)	5.00
1988	PC Asheville Tourists (31)	5.00
1988	PC Auburn Astros (29)	12.00
1988	PC Augusta Pirates (33)	8.00
1988	Cal Bakersfield Dodgers (34)	5.00
1988	Baseball America AA Top Prospects (30)	7.50
1988	Star Baseball City Royals (24)	10.00
1988	Star Baseball City Royals (27)	15.00
1988	PC Batavia Clippers (31)	4.00
1988	Legoe Bellingham Mariners (32)	
1988	GS Beloit Brewers (25)	4.00
1988	Legoe Bend Bucks (36)	15.00
1988	PC Billings Mustangs (31)	
1988	Best Birmingham Barons (29)	5.00
1988	PC Boise Hawks (29)	5.00

Year	Item	Price
1988	PC Bristol Tigers (32)	5.00
1988	CMC Buffalo Bisons (25)	5.00
1988	PC Buffalo Bisons (31)	4.00
1988	Team Buffalo Bisons (8)	15.00
1988	PC Burlington Braves (31)	5.00
1988	PC Burlington Indians (31)	5.00
1988	SP Butte Copper Kings (24)	8.00
1988	CMC Calgary Cannons (25)	5.00
1988	PC Calgary Cannons (28)	6.00
1988	Cal Cards California League A-S (50)	20.00
1988	P&L Cape Cod League (186)	45.00
1988	Ballpark Cape Cod Prospects (30)	30.00
1988	Star Carolina League A-S (40)	12.00
1988	PC Cedar Rapids Reds (31)	4.00
1988	PC Charleston Rainbows (30)	5.00
1988	Best Charleston Wheelers (28)	5.00
1988	Team Charlotte Knights (28)	12.00
1988	Star Charlotte Rangers (23)	40.00
1988	Star Charlotte Rangers (24)	35.00
1988	Best Chattanooga Lookouts (26)	5.00
1988	Team Chattanooga Lookouts Legends (32)	30.00
1988	Star Clearwater Phillies (26)	4.00
1988	PC Clinton Giants (29)	5.00
1988	CMC Colorado Spring Sky Sox (25)	5.00
1988	PC Colorado Springs Sky Sox (29)	5.00
1988	GS Columbia Mets (27)	4.00
1988	Best Columbus Astros (28)	5.00
1988	CMC Columbus Clippers (26)	6.00
1988	PC Columbus Clippers (29)	4.00
1988	Police Columbus Clippers (25)	5.00
1988	CMC Denver Zyphers (29)	6.00
1988	PC Denver Zephyrs (30)	5.00
1988	Star Dunedin Blue Jays (24)	10.00
1988	Star Durham Bulls - Blue (24)	5.00
1988	Star Durham Bulls - Blue (25)	7.00
1988	Star Durham Bulls - Orange (26)	6.00
1988	PC Eastern League A-S (52)	6.00
1988	CMC Edmonton Trappers (25)	5.00
1988	PC Edmonton Trappers (31)	7.00
1988	Team Elmira Pioneers - Blue (12)	75.00
1988	Team Elmira Pioneers - Red (30)	5.00
1988	Best El Paso Diablos (30)	6.00
1988	Best El Paso Diablos - Platinum (30)	25.00
1988	Best Eugene Emeralds (30)	5.00
1988	PC Fayetteville Generals (28)	8.00
1988	Star Florida State League A-S (52)	10.00
1988	Cal Fresno Suns (27)	5.00
1988	PC Fresno Suns (29)	5.00
1988	Star Ft. Lauderdale Yankees (24)	5.00
1988	PC Gastonia Rangers (30)	4.00
1988	PC Geneva Cubs (30)	3.00
1988	PC Glens Falls Tigers (29)	4.00
1988	SP Great Falls Dodgers (27)	20.00
1988	PC Greensboro Hornets (26)	5.00
1988	Best Greenville Braves (24)	5.00
1988	Star Hagerstown Suns (25)	5.00
1988	Star Hagerstown Suns (27)	7.00
1988	PC Hamilton Redbirds (30)	5.00
1988	PC Harrisburg Senators (30)	3.00
1988	BK Huntsville Stars (25)	6.00
1988	PC Idaho Falls Braves (31)	5.00
1988	CMC Indianapolis Indians (25)	20.00
1988	PC Indianapolis Indians (31)	16.00
1988	CMC Iowa Cubs (25)	5.00
1988	PC Iowa Cubs (30)	7.00
1988	GS Jackson Mets (25)	5.00

Year	Item	Price
1988	Best Jacksonville Expos (29)	5.00
1988	PC Jacksonville Expos (32)	4.00
1988	PC Jamestown Expos (31)	10.00
1988	PC Kenosha Twins (29)	5.00
1988	Star Kinston Indians (24)	12.50
1988	Best Knoxville Blue Jays (26)	5.00
1988	Star Lakeland Tigers (25)	4.00
1988	CMC Las Vegas Stars (25)	9.00
1988	PC Las Vegas Stars (28)	4.00
1988	Pucko Little Falls Mets (29)	6.00
1988	Little Sun Legends/ Minor League BB (11)	9.00
1988	CMC Louisville Redbirds (25)	5.00
1988	PC Louisville Redbirds (26)	5.00
1988	Team Louisville Redbirds (25)	9.00
1988	Star Lynchburg Red Sox (28)	5.00
1988	T&J Madison Muskies (25)	5.00
1988	CMC Maine Phillies (25)	5.00
1988	PC Maine Phillies (27)	4.00
1988	Star Managers/Costner Gold Set (21) (Dealer incentive issue.)	12.00
1988	Star Martinsville Phillies - Blue (32)	5.00
1988	Star Martinsville Phillies - Red (32)	6.00
1988	Best Memphis Chicks (27)	5.00
1988	Star Miami Marlins (24)	5.00
1988	GS Midland Angels (25)	5.00
1988	GS Midwest League A-S (59)	8.00
1988	Cal Modesto A's (28)	5.00
1988	Chong Modesto A's (36)	5.00
1988	PC Myrtle Beach Blue Jays (28)	7.50
1988	CMC Nashville Sounds (25)	4.00
1988	Hill's Nashville Sounds (25)	4.00
1988	PC Nashville Sounds (26)	5.00
1988	PC New Britain Red Sox (25)	16.00
1988	CMC Oklahoma City 89ers (25)	4.00
1988	PC Oklahoma City 89ers (27)	4.00
1988	CMC Omaha Royals (25)	5.00
1988	PC Omaha Royals (29)	5.00
1988	PC Oneonta Yankees (34)	4.00
1988	Best Orlando Twins (29)	5.00
1988	Star Osceola Astros (25)	5.00
1988	Cal Palm Springs Angels (31)	5.00
1988	PC Palm Springs Angels (32)	5.00
1988	CMC Pawtucket Red Sox (25)	4.00
1988	PC Pawtucket Red Sox (26)	4.00
1988	Team Peninsula Oilers (31)	35.00
1988	Team Peoria Chiefs (35)	30.00
1988	CMC Phoenix Firebirds (25)	5.00
1988	PC Phoenix Firebirds (29)	8.00
1988	PC Pittsfield Cubs (25)	5.00
1988	Team Pittsfield Cubs Poster	20.00
1988	PC Pocatello Giants (31)	5.00
1988	CMC Portland Beavers (25)	5.00
1988	PC Portland Beavers (27)	4.00
1988	Star Prince Williams Yankees (25)	15.00
1988	PC Pulaski Braves (25)	7.00
1988	GS Quad City Angels (30)	4.00
1988	PC Reading Phillies (27)	4.00
1988	Cal Reno Silver Sox (24)	5.00
1988	Bob's Richmond Braves (25)	75.00
1988	CMC Richmond Braves (25)	7.50
1988	PC Richmond Braves (27)	15.00
1988	Team Richmond Braves (26)	25.00
1988	Cal Riverside Red Wave (28)	5.00
1988	PC Riverside Red Wave (27)	5.00
1988	CMC Rochester Red Wings (25)	5.00
1988	PC Rochester Red Wings (30)	5.00
1988	Pucko Rochester Red Wings (26)	10.00
1988	Team Rochester Red Wings (26)	10.00
1988	Team Rockford Expos (34)	5.00

Year	Item	Price
1988	Star Salem Buccaneers (25)	5.00
1988	Team Salt Lake City Trappers (31)	9.00
1988	Best San Antonio Missions (28)	8.00
1988	Best S.A. Missions - Platinum (28)	12.00
1988	Best San Bernardino Spirit (28)	55.00
1988	Best S.B. Spirit - Platinum (28)	350.00
1988	Best S.B. Spirit Platinum (White "Spirit.")	2,500
1988	Cal San Bernardino Spirit (28)	20.00
1988	Cal San Jose Giants (29)	5.00
1988	PC San Jose Giants (30)	5.00
1988	PC Savannah Cardinals (29)	5.00
1988	PC Shreveport Captains (25)	5.00
1988	PC Shreveport Captains - Taco Bell (25)	30.00
1988	GS South Atlantic League A-S (28)	7.00
1988	GS South Bend White Sox (28)	5.00
1988	DJ Southern League A-S (40)	5.00
1988	PC Southern Oregon A's (28)	4.00
1988	PC Spartanburg Phillies (26)	4.00
1988	Star Spartanburg Phillies - Blue (25)	10.00
1988	Star Spartanburg Phillies - Red (25)	5.00
1988	PC Spokane Indians (26)	5.00
1988	Best Springfield Cardinals (28)	9.00
1988	PC St. Catharines Blue Jays (35)	5.00
1988	Star St. Luice Mets (25)	5.00
1988	Star St. Petersburg Cardinals (25)	5.00
1988	Star St. Petersburg Cardinals (27)	15.00
1988	PC Stockton Ports (33)	5.00
1988	Cal Stockton Ports (31)	5.00
1988	PC Sumter Braves (32)	4.00
1988	CMC Syracuse Chiefs (25)	5.00
1988	PC Syracuse Chiefs (30)	3.00
1988	Team Syracuse Chiefs Tickets (12)	8.00
1988	CMC Tacoma Tigers (25)	5.00
1988	PC Tacoma Tigers (28)	5.00
1988	Star Tampa Tarpons (25)	5.00
1988	GS Texas League A-S (39)	9.00
1988	CMC Tidewater Tides - Jeffries (26)	9.00
1988	CMC Tidewater Tides - Jefferies (26)	5.00
1988	PC Tidewater Tides (29)	4.00
1988	Team Tidewater Tides (31)	15.00
1988	CMC Toledo Mud Hens (25)	5.00
1988	PC Toledo Mud Hens (28)	4.00
1988	CMC Tucson Toros (25)	9.00
1988	Jones Tucson Toros (24)	150.00
1988	PC Tucson Toros (25)	11.00
1988	Team Tulsa Drillers (28)	16.00
1988	Pucko Utica Blue Sox (29)	5.00
1988	CMC Vancouver Canadians (25)	5.00
1988	PC Vancouver Canadians (27)	5.00
1988	PC Vermont Mariners (26)	7.00
1988	PC Vermont Mariners Ken Griffey Jr. (Widely counterfeited.)	12.00
1988	Star Vero Beach Dodgers (26)	5.00
1988	Star Virginia Generals (23)	5.00
1988	Star Virginia Generals (26)	8.00
1988	Cal Visalia Oaks (30)	5.00
1988	PC Visalia Oaks (28)	5.00
1988	PC Waterloo Indians (29)	6.00
1988	Pucko Watertown Pirates (35)	7.00
1988	GS Wausau Timbers (28)	4.00
1988	Star West Palm Beach Astros (26)	5.00
1988	Rock's Wichita Pilots (32)	12.00
1988	PC Williamsport Bills (27)	5.00
1988	Star Winston-Salem Spirits (27)	4.00
1988	Star Winter Haven Red Sox (27)	5.00
1988	PC Wytheville Cubs (31)	4.00

1989 Star Minor League Baseball

DAN WILLIAMS   WATERTOWN
Catcher

In 1989, Star became the first minor league card producer to venture into the wax pack market when it issued a 100-card set. A second series was issued later, numbered 101-200. There were no factory sets issued, nor was there a checklist available to the collector. Unlike its predecessor, which had borders of various colors, the second series all sport red borders. A total of 10,000 cases of 288 packs each was issued for Series 1.

		MT
	Complete Set (200):	10.00
	Common Player:	.05
	Wax Pack (10):	.35
	Wax Box (48):	7.50
1	Eric Anthony	.05
2	David Rohde (Photo of Karl Rhodes.)	.05
3	Mike Simms	.05
4	John Faccio	.05
5	Oreste Marrero	.05
6	Troy O'Leary	.05
7	Rob Maurer	.05
8	Rod Morris	.05
9	Ed Ohman	.05
10	Jim Byrd	.05
11	Mark Cobb	.05
12	Pat Combs	.05
13	Tim Mauser	.05
14	Jim Vatcher	.05
15	Luis Gonzalez	.50
16	Andres Mota	.05
17	Scott Servais	.05
18	David Silvestri	.05
19	Kevin Burdick	.05
20	Tommy Shields	.05
21	Mike York	.05
22	Mike Anaya	.05
23	Dale Plummer	.05
24	Titi Roche	.05
25	Vincent Zawaski	.05
26	Anthony Barron	.05
27	Rafael Bournigal	.05
28	Albert Bustillos	.05
29	Mark Griffin	.05
30	Brett Magnusson	.05
31	Mike Jones	.05
32	Bret Barberie	.05
33	Bert Echemendia	.05
34	Mike Bell	.05
35	Brian Hunter	.05
36	Jim LeMasters	.05
37	Rick Morris	.05
38	Dominic Pierce	.05
39	Joey Wardlow	.05
40	Dera Clark	.05
41	Stu Cole	.05
42	Bob Hamelin	.05
43	Deric Ladnier	.05
44	Brian McRae	.05
45	Mike Tresemer	.05
46	Steve Walker	.05
47	Greg Becker	.05
48	Art Calvert	.05
49	Todd Crosby	.05
50	Shawn Hathaway	.05
51	Rich Garces	.05
52	Todd McClure	.05
53	Steve Morris	.05
54	Tim Dell	.05
55	Antonio Linares	.05
56	John Marshall	.05
57	Mike Morandini	.05
58	Paul Fuller	.05
59	John Hudek	.05
60	Ron Stephens	.05
61	Scott Tedder	.05
62	Pete Alborano	.05
63	Kevin Shaw	.05
64	Anthony Ariola	.05
65	James Buccheri	.05
66	William Love	.05
67	Steve Avery	.05
68	Rich Casarotti	.05
69	Brian Champion	.05
70	Wes Currin	.05
71	Brian Deak	.05
72	Ken Pennington	.05
73	Theron Todd	.05
74	Andy Tomberlin	.05

75	Richard Falkner	.05
76	Tommy Kramer	.05
77	Charles Nagy	.05
78	Chris Howard	.05
79	Mike Rhodes	.05
80	Gabriel Rodriguez	.05
81	Bob Zeihen	.05
82	Rod Beck	.05
83	Jamie Cooper	.05
84	Steve Decker	.05
85	Mark Dewey	.05
86	Juan Guerrero	.05
87	Andres Santana	.05
88	Pedro DeLeon	.05
89	Pat Kelly	.05
90	Bill Masse	.05
91	Jerry Nielson	.05
92	Mark Ohims	.05
93	Moises Alou	.50
94	Ed Hartman	.05
95	Keith Richardson	.05
96	Royal Clayton	.05
97	Bobby Davidson	.05
98	Mitch Lyden	.05
99a	Hensley Meulens, Hensley Meulens (Error - St. Petersburg.)	.75
99b	Hensley Meulens (Correct - Albany.)	.10
100	John Ramos	.05
101	Robin Ventura	.50
102	Luis Mercedes	.05
103	Dave Miller	.05
104	Randy Berlin	.05
105	Mike Campas	.05
106	Jose Trujillo	.05
107	Lem Pikenton	.05
108	Frank Bolick	.05
109	Bert Heffernan	.05
110	Chris Czarnik	.05
111	Andy Benes	.05
112	Skipper Wright	.05
113	Eric Alexander	.05
114	Manny Alexander	.05
115	Jimmy Roso	.05
116	Chris Donnels	.05
117	Jaime Roseboro	.05
118	Julian Yan	.05
119	Vincent Degifico	.05
120	Mike Morandini	.05
121	Goose Gozzo	.05
122	Pedro Munoz	.05
123	Keith Helton	.05
124	Tino Martinez	.50
125	Sandy Alomar	.25
126	Scott Cooper	.05
127	Daryl Irvine	.05
128	Jim Orsag	.05
129	Mickey Pina	.05
130	Scott Sommers	.05
131	Ed Zambrano	.05
132	Dave Bettendorf	.05
133	Steve Allen	.05
134	Kevin Belcher	.05
135	Doug Cronk	.05
136	Tito Stewart	.05
137	Jeff Frye	.05
138	Trey McCoy	.05
139	Robb Nen	.05
140	Jim Hvizda	.05
141	Tommy Boyce	.05
142	Michael Maksudian	.05
143	Matt Current	.05
144	Tom Hardgrove	.05
145	Julio Vargas	.05
146	Dan Welch	.05
147	Steve Dunn	.05
148	Mike Musuraca	.05
149	Mike House	.05
150	Deion Sanders	.35
151	Willie Mota	.05
152	Tim Nedin	.05
153	Kerry Taylor	.05
154	Beau Alred	.05
155	Troy Neel	.05
156	Shawn Hare	.05
157	Chris Butterfield	.05
158	Tim Hines	.05
159	Pat Howell	.05
160	Paul Johnson	.05
161	Ryan Richmond	.05
162	Ernie Baker	.05
163	Pedro Castellano	.05
164	Eric Jaques	.05
165	Mark Willoughby	.05
166	Dan Segui	.05
167	Richard Skackle	.05
168	Mark Lewis	.05
169	John Johnstone	.05
170	Phil Plantier	.05
171	Wes Chamberlain	.05
172	James Harris	.05
173	Felix Antigua	.05
174	Bruce Schreiber	.05
175	Pete Rose Jr.	.25
176	Kelly Woods	.05
177	Anthony DeLaCruz	.05
178	Charles Nagy	.05
179	Nolan Lane	.05
180	Fabio Gomez	.05
181	Chris Butler	.05
182	Brett Merriman	.05
183	Carlos Mota	.05
184	Doug Piatt	.05
185	Marc Tepper	.05
186	Dan Williams	.05
187	Maximo Aleys	.05
188	Ken Lewis	.05
189	Joey Vierra	.05
190	Ron Morton	.05
191	Brook Fordyce	.05
192	Steve McCarthy	.05
193	Steve Hosey	.05
194	Steve Foster	.05
195	Ron Crowe	.05
196	Steve Callahan	.05
197	Benny Colvard	.05
198	Adam Casillas	.05
199	Joey Belle	1.00
200	Ben McDonald	.05

1989 Minor League Team Sets

SAMMY SOSA
Tulsa Drillers • Outfield

For the first time in several years, no major new producers entered the minor league team-set market in 1989. That didn't diminish the number of sets, however, as more than 350 basic sets and variations were issued; the largest number to that date. Some teams had as many as three different sets, not counting variations. Most of the variations were again the result of Star adding late cards to previously issued sets.

MT

354 Team Sets and Variations

1989 CMC AAA All-Stars (45) 6.00
1989 PC AAA All-Stars (55) 9.00
1989 Best Albany Yankees (30) 6.00
1989 Best Albany Yankees - Platinum (30) 17.50
1989 PC Albany Yankees (29) 9.00
1989 Star Albany-Colonie Yankees (22) 4.00
1989 Star Albany-Colonie Yankees (23) 10.00
1989 CMC Albuquerque Dukes (25) 3.00
1989 PC Albuquerque Dukes (30) 4.00
1989 Team Albuquerque Dukes (25)
1989 Dukes Photos (45) 125.00
1989 Tribune Albuquerque Dukes (29) 25.00
1989 Team Anchorage Bucs (29) 8.00
1989 Team Anchorage Glacier Pilots (35) 10.00
1989 PC Appleton Foxes (31) 5.00
1989 GS Arkansas Travelers (25) 7.00
1989 PC Asheville Tourists (25) 4.00
1989 PC Auburn Astros (31) 9.00
1989 PC Auburn Astros Poster 12.50
1989 PC Augusta Pirates (32) 4.00
1989 Cal Bakersfield Dodgers (29) 7.00
1989 Baseball America AA Top Prospects (31) 13.50
1989 Star Baseball City Royals (24) 4.00
1989 Star Baseball City Royals - Glossy (24) 12.00
1989 Star Baseball City Royals (28) 9.00
1989 PC Batavia Clippers (31) 4.00
1989 Legoe Bellingham Mariners (37) 5.00
1989 Star Beloit Brewers 1 (26) 4.00
1989 Star Beloit Brewers 1 - Glossy (26) 15.00
1989 Star Beloit Brewers 2 (29) 5.00
1989 Legoe Bend Bucks (30) 15.00
1989 PC Billings Mustangs (31) 13.00
1989 Best Birmingham Barons (30) 7.00
1989 Best Birmingham Barons - Platinum (30) 20.00
1989 PC Birmingham Barons (31) 6.00
1989 Star Bluefield Orioles (26) 4.00
1989 Star Bluefield Orioles - Glossy (26) 15.00
1989 Star Bluefield Orioles (30) 8.00
1989 PC Boise Hawks (31) 4.00
1989 Star Bristol Tigers (27) 4.00
1989 Star Bristol Tigers (31) 7.00
1989 CMC Buffalo Bisons (25) 5.00
1989 PC Buffalo Bisons (27) 5.00
1989 PC Burlington Braves (32) 4.00
1989 Star Burlington Braves (25) 4.00
1989 Star Burlington Braves - Glossy (25) 10.00
1989 Star Burlington Braves (29) 8.00
1989 Star Burlington Indians (25) 3.00
1989 Star Burlington Indians - Glossy (25) 9.00
1989 Star Burlington Indians (28) 8.00
1989 SP Butte Copper Kings (30) 6.00
1989 CMC Calgary Cannons (25) 7.00
1989 PC Calgary Cannons (24) 7.00
1989 Cal League All-Stars (56) 5.00
1989 Best Canton-Akron Indians (28) 4.00
1989 PC Canton-Akron Indians (28) 4.00
1989 Star Canton-Akron Indians (25) 10.00
1989 Star Canton-Akron Indians - Glossy (25) 35.00
1989 Best Cedar Rapids Reds (28) 4.00
1989 PC Cedar Rapids Reds (29) 4.00
1989 Star Cedar Rapids Reds (29) 4.00
1989 Star Cedar Rapids Reds - Glossy (29) 10.00
1989 Star Cedar Rapids Reds (33) 8.00
1989 PC Charleston Rainbows (29)
1989 Best Charleston Wheelers (27)
1989 PC Charleston Wheelers (28) 4.00
1989 Team Charlotte Knights (25) 5.00
1989 Star Charlotte Rangers (28) 4.00
1989 Star Charlotte Rangers - Glossy (28) 15.00
1989 Star Charlotte Rangers (31) 8.00
1989 Best Chattanooga Lookouts (25) 4.00
1989 GS Chattanooga Lookouts (25) 4.00
1989 Team Chattanooga Lookouts Legends (33) 20.00
1989 Star Clearwater Phillies (25) 4.00
1989 Star Clearwater Phillies - Glossy (25) 10.00
1989 Star Clearwater Phillies (28) 8.00
1989 PC Clinton Giants (31) 6.00
1989 CMC Colorado Spring Sky Sox (25) 4.00
1989 PC Colorado Springs Sky Sox (28) 4.00
1989 Best Columbia Mets (30) 6.00
1989 GS Columbia Mets (30) 6.00
1989 CMC Columbus Clippers (30) 6.00
1989 PC Columbus Clippers (28) 6.00
1989 Police Columbus Clippers (25) 5.00
1989 Best Columbus Mudcats (29)
1989 Best Columbus Mudcats - Platinum (28) 7.00
1989 PC Columbus Mudcats (31) 6.00
1989 Star Columbus Mudcats (23) 6.00
1989 Star Columbus Mudcats - Glossy (23) 15.00
1989 Star Columbus Mudcats (24)
1989 CMC Denver Zyphers (29)
1989 PC Denver Zephyrs (28) 4.00
1989 Star Dunedin Blue Jays (25) 5.00
1989 Star Dunedin Blue Jays - Glossy (25) 20.00
1989 Star Dunedin Blue Jays (26) 7.00
1989 Star Durham Bulls (25) 8.00
1989 Star Durham Bulls Orange/Blue (29) 7.50
1989 Star Durham Bulls Blue/Orange (29) 7.50
1989 Star Durham Bulls - Glossy (28) 20.00
1989 Team Durham Bulls (29) 15.00
1989 PC Eastern League All-Stars (26) 8.00
1989 PC Eastern League Diamond Diplomacy (50) 6.00
1989 CMC Edmonton Trappers (25) 4.00
1989 PC Edmonton Trappers (25) 4.00
1989 Star Elizabethton Twins (31) 8.00
1989 Star Elizabethtown Twins - Glossy (31) 40.00
1989 Pucko Elmira Pioneers (32) 5.00
1989 GS El Paso Diablos (30) 5.00
1989 Star Erie Orioles (25) 5.00
1989 Star Erie Orioles - Glossy (25) 12.50
1989 Star Erie Orioles (29) 9.00
1989 Best Eugene Emeralds (25) 4.00
1989 Star Everett Giants (32) 4.00
1989 Star Everett Giants - Glossy (32) 20.00
1989 PC Fayetteville Generals (29) 4.00
1989 Team Fayetteville Generals (10) 5.00
1989 Star Frederick Keys (24) 5.00
1989 Star Frederick Keys - Glossy (24) 20.00
1989 Star Frederick Keys (28) 10.00
1989 Star Ft. Lauderdale Yankees (25) 5.00
1989 Star Ft. Lauderdale Yankees (29) 9.00
1989 PC Gastonia Rangers (30) 20.00
1989 Star Gastonia Rangers (26) 15.00
1989 Star Gastonia Rangers - Glossy (26) 75.00
1989 PC Geneva Cubs (31) 3.00
1989 SP Great Falls Dodgers (33) 6.00
1989 PC Greensboro Hornets (29) 4.00
1989 Best Greenville Braves (29) 5.00
1989 Best Greenville Braves - Platinum (29) 12.00
1989 PC Greenville Braves (30)
1989 Star Greenville Braves (25) 8.00
1989 Star Greenville Braves - Glossy (25) 15.00
1989 Best Hagerstown Suns (29) 6.00
1989 PC Hagerstown Suns (26) 5.00
1989 Star Hagerstown Suns (22) 4.00
1989 Star Hagerstown Suns - Glossy (22) 10.00
1989 Star Hamilton Redbirds (23) 4.00
1989 Star Hamilton Redbirds - Glossy (23) 15.00
1989 Star Hamilton Redbirds (29) 10.00
1989 PC Harrisburg Senators (26) 5.00
1989 Star Harrisburg Senators (23) 4.00
1989 Star Harrisburg Senators - Glossy (23) 12.00
1989 SP Helena Brewers (27) 6.00
1989 Little Sun High School Prospects (23) 12.50
1989 Best Huntsville Stars (29) 4.00
1989 PC Idaho Falls Braves (31) 5.00
1989 CMC Indianapolis Indians (25) 7.50
1989 PC Indianapolis Indians (32) 7.50
1989 CMC Iowa Cubs (30) 4.00
1989 PC Iowa Cubs (28) 3.00
1989 GS Jackson Mets (30) 4.00
1989 Best Jacksonville Expos (29) 10.00
1989 Best Jacksonville Expos - Platinum (29) 15.00
1989 PC Jacksonville Expos (29) 10.00
1989 PC Jamestown Expos (29) 4.00
1989 Star Johnson City Cardinals (26) 4.00
1989 Star Johnson City Cards - Glossy (26) 10.00
1989 PC Kenosha Twins (29) 4.00
1989 Star Kenosha Twins (25) 4.00
1989 Star Kenosha Twins (27) 8.00
1989 Star Kingsport Mets (25) 5.00
1989 Star Kingsport Mets - Glossy (25) 15.00
1989 Star Kingsport Mets (30) 8.00
1989 Star Kinston Indians (25) 8.00
1989 Star Kinston Indians - Glossy (25) 25.00
1989 Star Kinston Indians (29) 12.00
1989 Best Knoxville Blue Jays (25) 5.00
1989 Best Knoxville Blue Jays (33) 9.00
1989 PC Knoxville Blue Jays (31) 6.00
1989 Star Knoxville Blue Jays (25) 5.00
1989 Star Knoxville Blue Jays - Glossy (25) 15.00
1989 Star Lakeland Tigers (25) 4.00
1989 Star Lakeland Tigers - Glossy (25) 15.00
1989 Star Lakeland Tigers (25) 10.00
1989 CMC Las Vegas Stars (25) 6.00
1989 PC Las Vegas Stars (29) 8.00
1989 PC London Tigers (32) 9.00
1989 CMC Louisville Red Birds (25) 5.00
1989 PC Louisville Redbirds (28) 3.00
1989 Team Louisville Redbirds (38) 7.00
1989 Team Louisville Redbirds - Glossy (38) 15.00
1989 Star Lynchburg Red Sox (25) 4.00
1989 Star Lynchburg Red Sox (29) 8.00
1989 Star Madison Muskies (22) 4.00
1989 Star Madison Muskies - Glossy (22) 15.00
1989 Star Madison Muskies (26) 9.00
1989 Star Martinsville Phillies (35) 4.00
1989 Star Martinsville Phillies - Glossy (35) 15.00
1989 Best Medford A's (31) 4.00
1989 Best Memphis Chicks (28) 5.00
1989 PC Memphis Chicks (28) 4.00
1989 Star Memphis Chicks (24) 5.00
1989 Star Memphis Chicks - Glossy (24) 20.00
1989 Star Miami Miracle 1 (25) 4.00
1989 Star Miami Miracle 1 - Glossy (25) 15.00
1989 Star Miami Miracle 2 (22) 4.00
1989 GS Midland Angels (30) 5.00
1989 Cal Modesto A's (25) 6.00
1989 Chong Modesto A's (36) 20.00
1989 PC Myrtle Beach Blue Jays (30) 4.00
1989 CMC Nashville Sounds (25) 5.00
1989 PC Nashville Sounds (28) 3.00
1989 Team Nashville Sounds (30) 10.00
1989 PC New Britain Red Sox (27) 5.00
1989 Star New Britain Red Sox (25) 5.00
1989 Star New Britain Red Sox - Glossy (25) 15.00
1989 Pucko Niagara Falls Rapids (31) 4.00
1989 CMC Oklahoma City 89ers (29) 6.00
1989 PC Oklahoma City 89ers (29) 4.00
1989 CMC Omaha Royals (25) 5.00
1989 CMC Omaha Royals (27) 4.00
1989 PC Oneonta Yankees (32) 4.00
1989 Best Orlando Twins (31) 4.00
1989 PC Orlando Twins (30) 4.00
1989 Star Osceola Astros (25) 7.00
1989 Star Osceola Astros - Glossy (25) 15.00
1989 Star Osceola Astros (27) 12.00
1989 Cal Palm Springs Angels (32) 4.00
1989 PC Palm Springs Angels (28) 4.00
1989 CMC Pawtucket Red Sox (25) 3.00
1989 DD Pawtucket Red Sox Foldout 40.00
1989 PC Pawtucket Red Sox (24) 3.00
1989 Team Peninsula Oilers (29) 7.00
1989 Star Peninsula Pilots (27) 4.00
1989 Star Peninsula Pilots - Glossy (25) 10.00
1989 Star Peninsula Pilots (26) 6.00
1989 Team Peoria Chiefs (35) 7.00
1989 CMC Phoenix Firebirds (28) 8.00
1989 PC Phoenix Firebirds (29) 8.00
1989 Star Pittsfield Mets (25) 4.00
1989 Star Pittsfield Mets - Glossy (25) 15.00
1989 Star Pittsfield Mets (29) 8.00
1989 CMC Portland Beavers (25) 4.00
1989 PC Portland Beavers (26) 4.00
1989 Star Princeton Pirates (25) 4.00
1989 Star Princeton Pirates - Glossy (25) 10.00
1989 Star Princeton Pirates (28) 7.00
1989 Star Prince William Cannons (25)
1989 Star Prince William Cannons (29) 9.00
1989 PC Pulaski Braves (28) 12.50
1989 Best Quad City Angels (31) 7.00
1989 GS Quad City Angels (30) 7.00
1989 Best Reading Phillies (27) 5.00
1989 PC Reading Phillies (27) 4.00
1989 Star Reading Phillies (26) 4.00
1989 Star Reading Phillies - Glossy (26) 15.00
1989 Star Reading Phillies (28) 8.00
1989 Cal Reno Silver Sox (27) 6.00
1989 Bob's Richmond Braves (29) 30.00
1989 CMC Richmond Braves (25) 10.00
1989 PC Richmond Braves (31) 7.00
1989 Team Richmond Braves Foldout 15.00
1989 Best Riverside Red Wave (30) 4.00
1989 Cal Riverside Red Wave (31) 4.00
1989 PC Riverside Red Wave (31) 4.00
1989 CMC Rochester Red Wings (25) 10.00
1989 PC Rochester Red Wings (30) 9.00
1989 Team Rockford Expos (31) 4.00
1989 Star Salem Buccaneers (25) 7.00
1989 Star Salem Buccaneers - Glossy (25) 20.00
1989 Star Salem Buccaneers (29) 10.00
1989 Team Salem Dodgers (30) 45.00
1989 Cal Salinas Spurs (27) 4.00
1989 PC Salinas Spurs (30) 4.00
1989 Team Salt Lake City Trappers (30) 8.00
1989 Best San Antonio Missions (29) 6.00
1989 Best S.A. Missions - Platinum (29) 9.50
1989 Best San Bernadino Spirit (29) 4.00
1989 Cal San Bernadino Spirit (31) 4.00
1989 Best San Jose Giants (31) 5.00
1989 Cal San Jose Giants (30) 6.00
1989 PC San Jose Giants (30) 5.00
1989 Star San Jose Giants (25) 5.00
1989 Star San Jose Giants - Glossy (25) 15.00
1989 Star San Jose Giants (28) 8.00
1989 Star Sarasota White Sox (25) 5.00
1989 Star Sarasota White Sox - Glossy (25) 15.00
1989 PC Savannah Cardinals (29) 4.00
1989 CMC Scranton Red Barons (25) 4.00
1989 PC Scranton Red Barons (28) 4.00
1989 PC Shreveport Captains (27) 4.00
1989 GS South Atlantic League A-S (46) 15.00
1989 GS South Bend White Sox (30) 5.00
1989 DJ Southern League All-Stars (25) 4.00
1989 PC Spartanburg Phillies (30) 4.00
1989 PC Spartanburg Phillies (27) 4.00
1989 PC Spartanburg Phillies (26) 8.00
1989 SP Spokane Indians (26) 5.00
1989 Best Springfield Cardinals (30) 4.00
1989 PC St. Catharines Blue Jays (28) 20.00
1989 Star St. Lucie Mets (25) 3.00
1989 Star St. Lucie Mets - Glossy (25) 9.00
1989 Star St. Lucie Mets (27) 7.00
1989 Star St. Petersburg Cardinals (25) 4.00
1989 Star St. Pete Cardinals - Glossy (25) 15.00
1989 Star St. Petersburg Cardinals (29) 8.00
1989 Best Stockton Ports (32) 5.00
1989 Cal Stockton Ports (30) 5.00
1989 PC Stockton Ports (31) 5.00
1989 PC Stockton Ports (28) 6.00
1989 PC Stockton Ports - Glossy (25) 15.00
1989 PC Sumter Braves (33) 5.00
1989 CMC Syracuse Chiefs (25) 5.00
1989 PC Syracuse Chiefs (27) 5.00
1989 Team Syracuse Chiefs Foldout 17.50

1989 CMC Tacoma Tigers (25) 4.00
1989 PC Tacoma Tigers (32) 25.00
1989 GS Texas League All-Stars (40) 8.00
1989 Candl Tidewater Tides Foldout (18) 10.00
1989 CMC Tidewater Tides (29) 5.00
1989 PC Tidewater Tides (30) 4.00
1989 CMC Toledo Mud Hens (25) 3.00
1989 PC Toledo Mud Hens (30) 4.00
1989 CMC Tucson Toros (25) 4.00
1989 Jones Tucson Toros (26) 70.00
1989 PC Tucson Toros (28) 3.00
1989 GS Tulsa Drillers (26) 12.50
1989 GS Tulsa Drillers Uncut Sheet 20.00
1989 Team Tulsa Drillers (27) 45.00
1989 Pucko Utice Blue Sox (34) 4.00
1989 CMC Vancouver Canadians (25) 5.00
1989 PC Vancouver Canadians (27) 7.00
1989 Star Vero Beach Dodgers (25) 6.00
1989 Star Vero Beach Dodgers -Glossy (25) 20.00
1989 Star Vero Beach Dodgers (39) 15.00
1989 Cal Visalia Oaks (29) 4.00
1989 PC Visalia Oaks (31) 3.00
1989 PC Waterloo Diamonds (28) 4.00
1989 Star Waterloo Diamonds (32) 4.00
1989 Star Waterloo Diamonds - Glossy (32) 10.00
1989 Star Watertown Indians (25) 4.00
1989 Star Watertown Indians - Glossy (25) 15.00
1989 Star Watertown Indians (29) 8.00
1989 GS Wausau Timbers (28) 4.00
1989 Pucko Welland Pirates (35) 5.00
1989 Star West Palm Beach Expos (24) 6.00
1989 Star West Palm Beach Expos - Glossy (24) 20.00
1989 Star West Palm Beach Expos (31) 10.00
1989 Rock's Wichita Wranglers (30) 8.00
1989 Rock's Wichita Wrangers - Bonus Set (2) 4.00
1989 Rock's Wichita Wranglers - Stadium (30) 6.00
1989 Rock's Wranglers - Highlight (20) 5.00
1989 Rock's Wichita Wranglers - Update (20) 6.00
1989 PC Williamsport Bills (25) 6.00
1989 Star Williamsport Bills (24) 6.00
1989 Star Williamsport Bills - Glossy (24) 20.00
1989 Star Williamsport Bills (25) 12.00
1989 Star Winston-Salem Spirits (22) 4.00
1989 Star Winston-Salem Spirits (26) 8.00
1989 Star Winter Haven Red Sox (25) 7.00
1989 Star Winter Haven Red Sox - Glossy (25) 25.00
1989 Star Winter Haven Red Sox (29) 12.00
1989 Star Wytheville Cubs (25) 4.00
1989 Star Wytheville Cubs - Glossy (25) 10.00
1989 Star Wytheville Cubs (30) 8.00

1990 Best

PAT HENTGEN
Knoxville Blue Jays
Pitcher

Best made its debut in the single-card minor league market in 1990 with a 324-card set. The cards were issued in 12-card foil packs and were not available as a complete set.

		MT
Complete Set (324):		12.00
Common Player:		.05
Foil Pack (12):		.70
Foil Box (36):		17.50
1	Frank Thomas	3.00
2	Eric Wedge	.05
3	Willie Ansley	.05
4	Mark Lewis	.05
5	Greg Colbrunn	.05
6	David Staton	.05
7	Ben McDonald	.05
8	Brent Mayne	.05
9	Ray Holbert	.05
10	T.R. Lewis	.05
11	Willie Banks	.05
12	Steve Dunn	.05
13	Juan Andujar	.05
14	Roger Salkeld	.05
15	Steve Hosey	.05
16	Tyler Houston	.05
17	David Holdridge	.05
18	Todd Malone	.05
19	Tony Scruggs	.05
20	Darron Cox	.05
21	Mike Linskey	.05
22	Darren Lewis	.05
23	Eddie Zosky	.05
24	Ramser Correa	.05
25	Lee Upshaw	.05
26	Bernie Williams	.50
27	Brian Harrison	.05
28	Len Brutcher	.05
29	Scott Centala	.05
30	Kenny Morgan	.05
31	Pedro Borbon	.05
32	Lee Hancock	.05
33	Clay Bellinger	.05
34	Chris Meyers	.05
35	Russ Garside	.05
36	Ron Plemmons	.05
37	Jose LeBron	.05
38	Tom Hardgrove	.05
39	Alan Newman	.05
40	Ramon Jimenez	.05
41	Ezequiel Herrera	.05
42	Jason Satre	.05
43	Bob Malloy	.05
44	William Suero	.05
45	Lenny Webster	.05
46	Andy Ashby	.05
47	Darren Ritter	.05
48	Andy Mota	.05
49	Pat Gomez	.05
50	Ron Stephens	.05
51	Daniel Eskew	.05
52	Joe Andrzejewski	.05
53	Doug Robbins	.05
54	Noel Velez	.05
55	Dana Ridenour	.05
56	Luis Martinez	.05
57	Dave Fleming	.05
58	Adell Davenport	.05
59	Brent McCoy	.05
60	Johnny Ard	.05
61	Cal Eldred	.05
62	Tab Brown	.05
63	Scott Kamieniecki	.05
64	Scott Bryant	.05
65	Brad Pennington	.05
66	Bernie Jenkins	.05
67	Frank Carey	.05
68	Matt Witkowski	.05
69	Checklist 1-48	.05
70	Josias Manzanillo	.05
71	Checklist 49-96	.05
72	Andujar Cedeno	.05
73	Rick Rojas	.05
74	Scott Brosius	.05
75	Tom Redington	.05
76	Kevin Rogers	.05
77	Jerry Wolak	.05
78	Rick Davis	.05
79	Juan Guzman	.05
80	Cesar Bernhardt	.05
81	Randy Simmons	.05
82	Clyde Keller	.05
83	Anthony Manahan	.05
84	Tom Maynard	.05
86	Sean Berry	.05
87	Brian Boltz	.05
88	Shawn Gilbert	.05
89	Rafael Novoa	.05
90	John Vander Wal	.05
91	Scott Pose	.05
92	Don Stanford	.05
93	Joe Federico	.05
94	Todd Watson	.05
95	Luis Gonzalez	.25
96	Pat Leinen	.05
97	Joel Estes	.05
98	Troy O'Leary	.05
99	Matt Stark	.05
100	Tony Tarasco	.05
101	Marc Lipson	.05
102	Kevin Higgins	.05
103	Jack Voight	.05
104	Steve Schrenk	.05
105	Jonathan Hurst	.05
106	Scott Erickson	.05
107	Javier Lopez	.10
108	Bob Zupcic	.05
109	Edwin Marquez	.05
110	Shawn Heiden	.05
111	Mike Maksudian	.05
112	Tony Eusebio	.05
113	Chris Hancock	.05
114	Royce Clayton	.05
115	Tim Mauser	.05
116	Checklist 97-144	.05
117	Carlos Maldonado	.05
118	Rex Da Nuez	.05
119	Mike Curtis	.05
120	Roger Miller	.05
121	Daryl Moore	.05
122	Turk Wendell	.05
123	Dan Rambo	.05
124	Scott Kimball	.05
125	Willie Magallanes	.05
126	Dannie Harris	.05
127	Joey James	.05
128	Wil Cordero	.05
129	Rob Taylor	.05
130	Bryce Florie	.05
131	Mike Mitchner	.05
132	Jeff Bagwell	3.00
133	Caesar Devares	.05
134	Tim Gillis	.05
135	Victor Hithe	.05
136	Earl Steinmetz	.05
137	Carl Keliipuleole	.05
138	Ted Williams	.05
139	Jorge Pedre	.05
140	Amalio Carreno	.05
141	Chris Gill	.05
142	Dennis Wiseman	.05
143	Checklist 145-192	.05
144	Derek Lee	.05
145	Brett Snyder	.05
146	Chuck Knoblauch	.05
147	Rafael Quirico	.05
148	Julian Yan	.05
149	John Thelen	.05
150	Checklist 193-240	.05
151	Darrin Reichle	.05
152	John Ramos	.05
153	Patrick Lennon	.05
154	Wade Taylor	.05
155	Mike Twardoski	.05
156	Jeff Conine	.05
157	Kelly Mann	.05
158	Gary Wilson	.05
159	Chris Frye	.05
160	Roger Hailey	.05
161	Harold Allen	.05
162	Ozzie Canseco	.05
163	Checklist 241-288	.05
164	Rudy Seanez	.05
165	John Zaksek	.05
166	Roberto DeLeon	.05
167	Matt Merullo	.05
168	Checklist 289-324 (Wrong numbers listed on checklist.)	.05
169	Terrell Hansen	.05
170	Ron Crowe	.05
171	Luis Galindez	.05
172	Vilato Marrero	.05
173	Scott Cepicky	.05
174	Gary Resetar	.05
175	Rich Scheid	.05
176	Jimmy Rogers	.05
177	Ken Pennington	.05
178	Tom Martin	.05
179	Mitch Lyden	.05
180	Jorge Brito	.05
181	Chris Gorton	.05
182	Mark Sims	.05
183	Jose Olmeda	.05
184	Ed Taubensee	.05
185	Steve Morris	.05
186	Tim Pugh	.05
187	Barry Winford	.05
188	Allen Leibert	.05
189	Kurt Brown	.05
190	Kelly Lifgren	.05
191	Mike Kelly	.05
192	Robert Munoz	.05
193	Judd Johnson	.05
194	Hector Wagner	.05
195	Dave Reis	.05
196	Isaiah Clark	.05
197	William Schock	.05
198	Ruben Gonzalez	.05
199	Mike Eberle	.05
200	Michael Arner	.05
201	Raphael Bustamante	.05
202	John Patterson	.05
203	Joe Slusarski	.05
204	Rodney McCray	.05
205	Wally Trice	.05
206	Edgar Caceres	.05
207	Eugene Jones	.05
208	Joey Wardlow	.05
209	Steven Martin	.05
210	Woody Williams	.05
211	Kevin Morton	.05
212	Bobby DeJardin	.05
213	Chris Bennett	.05
214	Brian Johnson	.05
215	Randy Snyder	.05
216	Roberto Hernandez	.05
217	Glen Gardner	.05
218	Fred Costello	.05
219	Melvin Nieves	.05
220	Al Martin	.05
221	Kerry Knox	.05
222	Mike Eatinger	.05
223	Jim Myers	.05
224	Jay Owens	.05
225	Jayson Best	.05
226	Mike McDonald	.05
227	Kim Batiste	.05
228	Rich Delucia	.05
229	Chris Delarwelle	.05
230	Jeff Hoffman	.05
231	Bobby Moore	.05
232	Dan Wilson	.05
233	Greg Pirkl	.05
234	Craig Newkirk	.05
235	Mike Hensley	.05
236	Ryan Klesko	.10
237	Donald Sparks	.05
238	J.D. Noland	.05
239	Chris Howard	.05
240	Stan Royer	.05
241	Manuel Alexander	.05
242	Jeff Plympton	.05
243	Jeff Juden	.05
244	Charles Nagy	.05
245	Ryan Bowen	.05
246	Scott Taylor	.05
247	Tom Quinlan	.05
248	Royal Thomas	.05
249	Ricky Rhodes	.05
250	Alex Fernandez	.05
251	Bruce Egloff	.05
252	Greg Sparks	.05
253	Brian Dour	.05
254	John Byington	.05
255	Stacey Burdick	.05
256	Danny Matznick	.05
257	Reed Olmstead	.05
258	Jim Bowie	.05
259	Jim Newlan	.05
260	Ramon Caraballo	.05
261	Brian Barnes	.05
262	Mike Gardiner	.05
263	Andy Fox	.05
264	Brian McKeon	.05
265	Andy Tomberlin	.05
266	Frank Bellino	.05
267	Tim Lata	.05
268	Mike Burton	.05
269	Jim Orsag	.05
270	Scott Romano	.05
271	Leon Glenn	.05
272	Mike Misuraca	.05
273	Randy Knorr	.05
274	Eddie Tucker	.05
275	Ken Powell	.05
276	Brian McRae	.05
277	Mark Merchant	.05
278	Vinny Castilla	.10
279	Stephen Chitren	.05
280	Marteese Robinson	.05
281	Osvaldo Sanchez	.05
282	Mike Mongiello	.05
283	John Valentin	.05
284	Timmie Morrow	.05
285	Matt Murray	.05
286	Darrell Sherman	.05
287	Royal Clayton	.05
288	Jason Robertson	.05
289	John Kilner	.05
290	Jeff Mutis	.05
291	Gary Alexander	.05
292	Oreste Marrero	.05
293	Melvin Wearing	.05
294	Scott Meadows	.05
295	Pat Hentgen	.05
296	John Hudek	.05
297	Tim Stargell	.05
298	Tony Brown	.05
299	Scott Plemmons	.05
300	Chris Nabholz	.05
301	Brian Romero	.05
302	Vince Kindred	.05
303	Robert Ayrault	.05
304	Steve Stowell	.05
305	Don Strange	.05
306	Tim Nedin	.05
307	Derek Livernois	.05
308	Kerry Woodson	.05
309	Sam Ferretti	.05
310	Reuben Smiley	.05
311	Jim Campbell	.05
312	Al Osuna	.05
313	Luis Mercedes	.05
314	Billy Reed	.05
315	Vince Harris	.05
316	Jeff Carter	.05
317	Dave Riddle	.05
318	Frank Thomas (Bonus Card)	2.00
319	Eric Wedge (Bonus Card)	.05
320	Mark Lewis (Bonus Card)	.05
321	Alex Fernandez (Bonus Card)	.05
322	Chuck Knoblauch (Bonus Card)	.15
323	Charles Nagy (Bonus Card)	.10
324	Tyler Houston (Bonus Card)	.05

1990 Classic #1 Draft Picks

#1 Chipper Jones

1990 Collectors Marketing Corp. Pre-Rookie

The first-round draft picks of each team are featured in this issue. Reported production was 150,000 sets, including 2,500 uncut 100-card (four sets) sheets originally retailed within the hobby for $59. A certificate of authenticity accompanies each individually numbered set or sheet. Unlike other Classic issues, this set is not designed for use with the trivia board game. Cards #2 and 22 were not issued.

		MT
Complete Set (27):		2.00
Common Player:		.05
Uncut Set:		5.00
1	Chipper Jones	1.00
2	Not Issued	.00
3	Mike Lieberthal	.15
4	Alex Fernandez	.05
4P	Alex Fernandez (Promo Card)	.25
5	Kurt Miller	.05
6	Marc Newfield	.05
7	Dan Wilson	.05
8	Tim Costo	.05
9	Ron Walden	.05
10	Carl Everett	.25
11	Shane Andrews	.05
12	Todd Ritchie	.05
13	Donovan Osborne	.05
14	Todd Van Poppel	.05
14P	Todd Van Poppel (Promo Card)	.25
15	Adam Hyzdu	.05
16	Dan Smith	.05
17	Jeromy Burnitz	.15
18	Aaron Holbert	.05
19	Eric Christopherson	.05
20	Mike Mussina	.75
21	Tom Nevers	.05
22	Not Issued	.00
23	Lance Dickson	.05
24	Rondell White	.05
25	Robbie Beckett	.05
26	Don Peters	.05
—	Chipper Jones, Rondell White Future Stars-Checklist	.50

1990 Collectors Marketing Corp. Pre-Rookie

RYAN KLESKO
Infield
Sumter Braves

This set combines CMC team sets with cards produced by Pro-Cards and purchased by CMC. The ProCards were given a glossy facing and randomly inserted in wax packs along with CMC cards. The cards are numbered at bottom-right on back. These numbers were not coordinated with the original CMC team sets, and therefore many team sets were separated with ProCards cards between them. The CMC cards in this set differ from the original CMC team sets by the color of their backs (yellow in lieu of green) and the players are pictured in place of the team logos. A checklist was available through the company. Shortly after the cards hit the market, the CMC company was sold to Impel Marketing. Since the original CMC team sets were issued as one complete AAA set in a special wooden box, there were packaging problems with duplicates and/or missing cards.

		MT
Complete Set (880):		17.50
Common Player:		.05
Wax Pack (12):		.50
Wax Box (36):		10.00
1	Stan Belinda	.05
2	Gordon Dillard	.05
3	Terry Collins	.05
4	Mark Huisman	.05
5	Hugh Kemp	.05
6	Scott Medvin	.05
7	Vincente Palacios	.05
8	Rick Reed	.05
9	Mark Ross	.05
10	Dorn Taylor	.05
11	Mike York	.05
12	Jeff Richardson	.05
13	Dann Bilardello	.05
14	Tom Prince	.05
15	Danny Sheaffer	.05
16	Kevin Burdick	.05
17	Steve Kiefer	.05
18	Orlando Merced	.05
19	Armando Moreno	.05
20	Mark Ryal	.05
21	Tommy Shields	.05
22	Steve Carter	.05
23	Wes Chamberlain	.05
24	Jeff Cook	.05
25	Scott Little	.05
26	Jeff Peterek	.05
27	Ed Puig	.05
28	Tim Watkins	.05
29	Tom Edens	.05
30	Mike Capel	.05
31	Darryel Walters	.05
32	Joe Xavier	.05
33	Tim Torricelli	.05
34	Joe Redfield	.05
35	D.L. Smith	.05
36	Billy Moore	.05
37	Joe Mitchell	.05
38	Mario Monico	.05
39	Frank Mattox	.05
40	Tim McIntosh	.05
41	Mark Higgins	.05
42	George Canale	.05
43	Don Grodon	.05
44	Al Sadler	.05
45	Don August	.05
46	Mike Birkbeck	.05
47	Dennis Powell	.05
48	Chuck McGrath	.05
49	Ruben Escalera	.05
50	Dave Machemer	.05
51	Steve Firevoid	.05
52	Danny Clay	.05
53	Howard Farmer	.05
54	Travis Chambers	.05
55	Chris Marchok	.05
56	Dan Gakeler	.05
57	Scott Anderson	.05
58	Dale Mohorcic	.05
59	Richard Thompson	.05
60	Eddie Dixon	.05
61	Jim Davins	.05
62	Edwin Marquez	.05
63	Jerry Goff	.05
64	Dwight Lowery	.05
65	Jim Steels	.05
66	Quinn Mack	.05
67	Eric Bullock	.05
68	Otis Green	.05
69	Randy Braun	.05
70	Mel Houston	.05
71	Johnny Paredes	.05
72	Romy Cucjen	.05
73	Jose Castro	.05
74	Esteban Beltre	.05
75	Tim Johnson	.05
76	Shawn Boskie	.05
77	Dave Masters	.05
78	Kevin Blankenship	.05
79	Greg Kallevig	.05
80	Steve Parker	.05
81	David Pavlas	.05
82	Jeff Pico	.05
83	Laddie Renfroe	.05
84	Dean Wilkins	.05
85	Paul Wilmet	.05
86	Bob Bafia	.05
87	Brian Guinn	.05
88	Greg Smith	.05
89	Derrick May	.05
90	Glenn Sullivan	.05
91	Bill Wrona	.05
92	Eric Pappas	.05
93	Hector Villanueva	.05
94	Ced Landrum	.05
95	Jeff Small	.05
96	Gary Varsho	.05
97	Brad Bierly	.05
98	Jeff Hearron	.05
99	Jim Essian	.05
100	Brian McCann	.05
101	Scott Arnold	.05
102	Gibson Alba	.05
103	Cris Carpenter	.05
104	Stan Clarke	.05
105	Mike Hinkle	.05
106	Howard Hilton	.05
107	Dave Osteen	.05
108	Mike Perez	.05
109	Bernard Gilkey	.05
110	Dennis Carter	.05
111	Julian Martinez	.05
112	Rod Brewer	.05
113	Ray Stephens	.05
114	Ray Lankford	.10
115	Craig Wilson	.05
116	Roy Silver	.05
117	Bien Figueroa	.05
118	Jesus Mendez	.05
119	Geronimo Pena	.05
120	Omar Olivares	.05
121	Mark Grater	.05
122	Tim Sherrill	.05
123	Pat Austin	.05
124	Todd Crosby	.05
125	Scott Nichols	.05
126	Milt Hill	.05
127	Robert Moore	.05
128	Joey Vierra	.05

#	Name	Price	#	Name	Price	#	Name	Price	#	Name	Price	#	Name	Price	#	Name	Price
129	Terry McGriff	.05	246	Chris Knabenshue	.05	364	Julio Valera	.05	481	Timothy Burcham	.05	599	Troy Afenir	.05	714	Jose Garcia	.05
130	Chris Hammond	.05	247	Keith Miller	.05	365	Tim Bogar	.05	482	Sherman Corbett	.05	600	Larry Arndt	.05	715	Adell Davenport	.05
131	Charlie Mitchell	.05	248	Floyd Rayford	.05	366	Mike DeButch	.05	483	Mike Erb	.05	601	Dickie Scott	.05	716	Kevin Rogers	.05
132	Rodney Imes	.05	249	Jim Wright	.05	367	Jeff Gardner	.05	484	Mike Fetters	.05	602	Kevin Ward	.05	717	Dan Rambo	.05
133	Rob Lopez	.05	250	Todd Frohwirth	.05	368	Denny Gonzalez	.05	485	Chuck Hernandez	.05	603	Ryan Bowen	.05	718	Vince Harris	.05
134	Keith Brown	.05	251	Barney Nugent	.05	369	Chris Jelic	.05	486	Jeff Heathcock	.05	604	Brian Meyer	.05	719	Darrell Sherman	.05
135	Scott Scudder	.05	252	Tito Stewart	.05	370	Roger Samuels	.05	487	Scott Lewis	.05	605	Terry Clark	.05	720	Isaiah Clark	.05
136	Bob Sebra	.05	253	John Trautwein	.05	371	Dave Liddell	.05	488	Rafael Montalvo	.05	606	Darryl Kile	.05	721	Miguel Sabino	.05
137	Donnie Scott	.05	254	Mike Rochford	.05	372	Orlando Mercado	.05	489	John Skuria	.05	607	Randy St. Claire	.05	722	Frank Valdez	.05
138	Skeeter Barnes	.05	255	Larry Shikles	.05	373	Kelvin Torva	.05	490	Lee Stevens	.05	608	Randy Hennis	.05	723	Giovanni Miranda	.05
139	Paul Noce	.05	256	Daryl Irvine	.05	374	Alex Diaz	.05	491	Nelson Rood	.05	609	Lee Tunnell	.05	724	Daryl Ratliff	.05
140	Leo Garcia	.05	257	John Leister	.05	375	Keith Hughes	.05	492	Bobby Rose	.05	610	Bill Brennan	.05	725	Mike Brewinton	.05
141	Chris Jones	.05	258	Joe Johnson	.05	376	Darren Reed	.05	493	Dan Grunhard	.05	611	Craig Smajstrla	.05	726	Eric Parkinson	.05
142	Kevin Pearson	.05	259	Mark Meleski	.05	377	Zolio Sanchez	.05	494	Reed Peters	.05	612	Gary Cooper	.05	727	Vin Castilla	.10
143	Darryl Motley	.05	260	Steven Bast	.05	378	Do Vesling	.05	495	Doug Davis	.05	613	Carl Nichols	.05	728	Roger Hailey	.05
144	Keith Lockhart	.05	261	Ed Nottle	.05	379	Scott Aldred	.05	496	Gary DiSarcina	.05	614	Louie Meadows	.05	729	Earl Steinmetz	.05
145	Brian Lane	.05	262	John Flaherty	.05	380	Dennis Burtt	.05	497	Pete Coachman	.05	615	Jose Tolentino	.05	730	Doug Gogolewski	.05
146	Eddie Tanner	.05	263	John Marzano	.05	381	Shawn Holman	.05	498	Chris Cron	.05	616	Harry Spillman	.05	731	Andy Cook	.05
147	Reggie Jefferson	.05	264	Gary Tremblay	.05	382	Matt Kinzer	.05	499	Karl Allaire	.05	617	Javier Ortiz	.05	732	John Toale	.05
148	Neil Allen	.05	265	Scott Cooper	.05	383	Randy Mosek	.05	500	Ron Tingley	.05	618	Doug Strange	.05	733	Mike Curtis	.05
149	Pete Mackanin	.05	266	Angel Gonzalez	.05	384	Jose Ramos	.05	501	Chris Beasley	.05	619	Jim Olander	.05	734	Delwyn Young	.05
150	Ray Ripplemeyer	.05	267	Julius McDougal	.05	385	Kevin Ritz	.05	502	Max Oliveras	.05	620	Karl Rhodes	.05	735	Scott Meadows	.05
151	Jack Hardy	.05	268	Tim Naehring	.05	386	Mike Schwabe	.05	503	Roger Smithberg	.05	621	David Rohde	.05	736	Don Sparks	.05
152	Steve Lankard	.05	269	Jim Pankovits	.05	387	Steve Searcy	.05	504	Steve Peters	.05	622	Mike Simms	.05	737	Gary Wilson	.05
153	John Hoover	.05	270	Rick Lancelotti	.05	388	Eric Stone	.05	505	Matt Maysey	.05	623	Scott Servais	.05	738	Blas Minor	.05
154	David Lynch	.05	271	Mickey Pina	.05	389	Domingo Michel	.05	506	Terry Gilmore	.05	624	Pedro Sanchez	.05	739	Jeff Bagwell	4.00
155	Mark Petkovsek	.05	272	Phil Plantier	.05	390	Phil Ouellette	.05	507	Jeff Datz	.05	625	Kevin Dean	.05	740	Phil Bryant	.05
156	David Miller	.05	273	Jeff Stone	.05	391	Shawn Hare	.05	508	Eric Nolte	.05	626	Brian Fisher	.05	741	Felipe Castillo	.05
157	Brad Arnsberg	.05	274	Scott Wade	.05	392	Jim Lindeman	.05	509	Jim Lewis	.05	627	Bob Skinner	.05	742	Craig Faulkner	.05
158	Jeff Satzinger	.05	275	Mike Dalton	.05	393	Scott Livingstone	.05	510	Pete Roberts	.05	628	Wilson Alvarez	.05	743	Jeff Conine	.05
159	John Barfield	.05	276	Jeff Gray	.05	394	Lavel Freeman	.05	511	Dan Murphy	.05	629	Adam Peterson	.05	744	Kevin Belcher	.05
160	Mike Berger	.05	277	Steve Avery	.05	395	Travis Fryman	.05	512	Rich Rodriguez	.05	630	Tom Drees	.05	745	Bill Haselman	.05
161	John Russell	.05	278	Braves Coaches	.05	396	Scott Lusader	.05	513	Joe Lynch	.05	631	Ravelo Manzanillo	.05	746	Matt Stark	.05
162	Pat Garman	.05	279	Dale Polley	.05	397	Dean Decillis	.05	514	Mike Basso	.05	632	Marv Foley	.05	747	Todd Hall	.05
163	Gary Green	.05	280	Rusty Richards	.05	398	Milt Cuyler	.05	515	Ronn Reynolds	.05	633	Grady Hall	.05	748	Scott Centala	.05
164	Bryan House	.05	281	Andy Nezelek	.05	399	Not issued	.00	516	Jose Mota	.05	634	Mike Campbell	.05	749	Doug Simons	.05
165	Ron Washington	.05	282	Ed Olwine	.05	400	Phil Clark	.05	517	Paul Faries	.05	635	Shawn Hillegas	.05	750	Shawn Gilbert	.05
166	Nick Capra	.05	283	Jim Beauchamp	.05	401	Torey Lovullo	.05	518	Warren Newson	.05	636	C.L. Penigar	.05	751	Kenny Morgan	.05
167	Juan Gonzalez	2.00	284	Paul Marak	.05	402	Aurelio Rodriguez	.05	519	Alex Cole	.05	637	John Pawlowski	.05	752	Andy Mota	.05
168	Gar Millay	.05	285	Dave Justice	.50	403	Mike Christopher	.05	520	Tom Levasseur	.05	638	Steve Rosenberg	.05	753	Jeff Baldwin	.05
169	Kevin Reimer	.05	286	Jimmy Kremers	.05	404	Jeff Bittiger	.05	521	Charles Hillemann	.05	639	Jose Segura	.05	754	Reed Olmstead	.05
170	Bernie Tatis	.05	287	Drew Denson	.05	405	Jeff Fischer	.05	522	Jeff Yurtin	.05	640	Rich Amaral	.05	755	Basil Meyer	.05
171	Steve Smith	.05	288	Barry Jones	.05	406	Steve Davis	.05	523	Rafael Valdez	.05	641	Pete Dalena	.05	756	Mark Razook	.05
172	Dick Egan	.05	289	Francisco Cabrera	.05	407	Morris Madden	.05	524	Brian Ohnoutka	.05	642	Ramon Sambo	.05	757	Ken Pennington	.05
173	Stan Hough	.05	290	Bruce Crabbe	.05	408	Darren Holmes	.05	525	Pat Kelley	.05	643	Marcus Lawton	.05	758	Shane Letterio	.05
174	Ray Ramirez	.05	291	Dennis Hood	.05	409	Greg Mayberry	.05	526	Gary Lance	.05	644	Orsino Hill	.05	759	Ted Williams	.05
175	Moe Drabowsky	.10	292	Geronimo Berroa	.05	410	Mike Maddux	.05	527	Tony Torchia	.05	645	Marlin McPhail	.05	760	Luis Gonzalez	.25
176	Jay Baller	.05	293	Ed Whited	.05	411	Tim Scott	.05	528	Paul McClellan	.05	646	Keith Smith	.05	761	Carlos Garcia	.05
177	Ray Chadwick	.05	294	Sam Ayoub	.05	412	Jim Neidlinger	.05	529	Randy McCament	.05	647	Todd Trafton	.05	762	Terry Crowley	.05
178	Dera Clark	.05	295	Brian Hunter	.05	413	Dave Walsh	.05	530	Gil Heredia	.05	648	Norberto Martin	.05	763	Julio Peguero	.05
179	Luis Encarnacion	.05	296	Tommy Green	.05	414	Dennis Springer	.05	531	George Bonilla	.05	649	Don Wakamatsu	.05	764	Francisco Delarosa	.05
180	Jim LeMasters	.05	297	John Mizerock	.05	415	Terry Wells	.05	532	Russ Swan	.05	650	Jerry Willard	.05	765	Rodney Lofton	.05
181	Mike Magnante	.05	298	Ken Dowell	.05	416	Adam Brown	.05	533	Ed Vosberg	.05	651	Dana Williams	.05	766	Eric McCray	.05
182	Mel Stottlemyre	.05	299	John Alva	.05	417	Darrin Fletcher	.05	534	Eric Gunderson	.05	652	Tracy Woodson	.05	767	Mike Wilkins	.05
183	Tony Ferreira	.05	300	Bill Lasky	.05	418	Carlos Hernandez	.05	535	Trevor Wilson	.05	653	Glenn Hoffman	.05	768	John Kiely	.05
184	Pete Filson	.05	301	Brian Snyder	.05	419	Dave Hansen	.05	536	Greg Booker	.05	654	Anthony Scruggs	.05	769	Derek Lee	.05
185	Andy McGaffigan	.05	302	Ben McDonald	.05	420	Dan Henley	.05	537	Kirt Manwaring	.05	655	Reggie Sanders	.05	770	Bo Kennedy	.05
186	Luis DeLos Santos	.05	303	Rob Woodward	.05	421	Jose Offerman	.05	538	Mike Kingery	.05	656	Rick Lueken	.05	771	John Hudek	.05
187	Mike Loggins	.05	304	Mickey Weston	.05	422	Jose Vizcaino	.05	539	Brian Brady	.05	657	Kent Mercker	.05	772	Bernie Nunez	.05
188	Chito Martinez	.05	305	Mike Jones	.05	423	Luis Lopez	.05	540	Mark Bailey	.05	658	Dukes Coaches	.05	773	Tom Quinlan	.05
189	Bobby Meacham	.05	306	Curtis Schilling	3.00	424	Butch Davis	.05	541	Gregg Ritchie	.05	659	Richard Shockey		774	Jim Tatum	.05
190	Russ Morman	.05	307	Jay Aldrich	.05	425	Wayne Kirby	.05	542	George Hinshaw			(Photo is Mo Sanford.)		775	Casey Waller	.05
191	Bill Pecota	.05	308	Paul Blair	.05	426	Mike Huff	.05	543	Craig Colbert	.05	660a	Brian Barnes	.05	776	Doug Lindsey	.05
192	Harvey Pulliam	.05	309	Mike Smith	.05	427	Billy Bean	.05	544	Kash Beauchamp	.05	660b	Mario Brito	.05	777	Roberto Zambrano	.05
193	Jeff Schulz	.05	310	Jeff Tackett	.05	428	Pat Pacillo	.05	545	Jeff Carter	.05	661	Not issued	.00	778	Wade Taylor	.05
194	Gary Thurman	.05	311	Leo Gomez	.05	429	Tony Blasucci	.05	546	Mark Leonard	.05	662	Ed Quijada	.05	779	Carlos Maldonado	.05
195	Thad Reece	.05	312	Juan Bell	.05	430	Mike Walker	.05	547	Tony Perezchica	.05	663	Steve Wapnick	.05	780	Brent Mayne	.05
196	Tim Spehr	.05	313	Chris Hoiles	.05	431	Pat Rice	.05	548	Mike Laga	.05	664	Kevin Tahan	.05	781	Jerry Rub	.05
197	Paul Zuvella	.05	314	Donell Nixon	.05	432	Terry Taylor	.05	549	Mike Benjamin	.05	665	Johnny Guzman	.05	782	Vincent Phillips	.05
198	Not issued	.00	315	Steve Stanicek	.05	433	David Burba	.05	550	Timber Mead	.05	666	Bronswell Patrick	.05	783	Eric Wedge	.05
199a	Tom Poquette, Rich Dubee	.05	316	Tim Dulin	.05	434	Vance Lovelace	.05	551	Duane Espy	.05	667	Kevin Kennedy	.05	784	Andrew Ashby	.05
199b	Bob Hamelin	.05	317	Chris Padget	.05	435	Ed Vande Berg	.05	552	Tim Ireland	.05	668	Orlando Miller	.05	785	Royal Clayton	.05
200	Sal Rende	.05	318	Greg Walker	.05	436	Greg Fulton	.05	553	Paul Abbott	.05	669	Mauricio Nunez	.05	786	Jeffrey Osbourne	.05
201	Steve Adkins	.05	319	Tony Chance	.05	437	Ed Jurak	.05	554	Pat Bangston	.05	670	Hector Rivera	.05	787	Pat Kelly	.05
202	Dave Eiland	.05	320	Jeff McKnight	.05	438	Dave Cochrane	.05	555	Larry Casian	.05	671	Roger LaFrancois	.05	788	John Wehner	.05
203	John Habyan	.05	321	J.J. Bautista	.05	439	Edgar Martinez	.50	556	Mike Cook	.05	672	Jackson Todd	.05	789	Bernie Williams	.50
204	Mark Leiter	.05	322	John Mitchell	.05	440	Matt Sinatro	.05	557	Pete Delkus	.05	673	John Young	.05	790	Moises Alou	.35
205	Kevin Mmahat	.05	323	Vic Hithe	.05	441	Bill McGuire	.05	558	Mike Dyer	.05	674	Bob Bailor	.05	791	Mark Merchant	.05
206	Hipolito Pena	.05	324	Darrell Miller	.05	442	Mickey Brantley	.05	559	Charlie Scott	.05	675	David Hajeck	.05	792	Chris Myers	.05
207	Willie Smith	.05	325	Shane Turner	.05	443	Tom Dodd	.05	560	Francisco Oliveras	.05	676	Ralph Wheeler	.05	793	Donald Harris	.05
208	Rich Monteleone	.05	326	Greg Biagini	.05	444	Jim Weaver	.05	561	Park Pittman	.05	677	Anthony Gutierrez	.05	794	Michael McDonald	.05
209	Hensley Meulens	.05	327	Alex Sanchez	.05	445	Todd Haney	.05	562	Jimmy Williams	.05	678	Gaylen Pitts	.05	795	Jim Blueberg	.05
210	Andy Stankiewicz	.05	328	Mauro Gozzo	.05	446	Casey Close	.05	563	Rich Yett	.05	679	Mark Riggins	.05	796	James Bowie	.05
211	Jim Leyritz	.10	329	Steven Cummings	.05	447	Theo Shaw	.05	564	Vic Rodriguez	.05	680	Brad Bluestone	.05	797	Ruben Gonzalez	.05
212	Jim Walewander	.05	330	Tom Gilles	.05	448	Keith Helton	.05	565	Jamie Nelson	.05	681	Dick Bosman	.05	798	Rob Maurer	.05
213	Oscar Azocar	.05	331	Douglas Linton	.05	449	Jose Melendez	.05	566	Derek Parks	.05	682	Wil Cordero	.05	799	Monty Farris	.05
214	John Fishel	.05	332	Mike Loynd	.05	450	Tom Jones	.05	567	Ed Naveda	.05	683	Todd Hutcheson	.05	800	Bob Ayrault	.05
215	Jason Maas	.05	333	Bob Shirley	.05	451	Dan Warthen	.05	568	Scott Leius	.05	684	Steve Swisher	.05	801	Tim Mauser	.05
216	Van Snider	.05	334	John Shea	.05	452	Randy Roetter	.05	569	Terry Jorgensen	.05	685	John Cumberland	.05	802	David Holdridge	.05
217	Kevin Maas	.05	335	Paul Kilgus	.05	453	Mike Walker	.05	570	Doug Baker	.05	686	Rich Miller	.05	803	Kim Batiste	.05
218	Ricky Torres	.05	336	Carlos Diaz	.05	454	Colby Ward	.05	571	Chip Hale	.05	687	Scott Lawrenson	.05	804	Dan Peltier	.05
219	Dave Sax	.05	337	Joe Szekely	.05	455	Joe Skalski	.05	572	Dave Jacas	.05	688	Larry Hardy	.05	805	Derek Livernois	.05
220	Darrin Chapin	.05	338	Rick Lysander	.05	456	Efrain Valdez	.05	573	Jim Shellenback	.05	689	Danny Boone	.05	806	Thomas Fischer	.05
221	Rob Sepanek	.05	339	Jim Eppard	.05	457	Doug Robertson	.05	574	Rafael DeLima	.05	690	Terrel Hansen	.05	807	Chuck Knoblauch	.05
222	Mark Wasinger	.05	340	Derek Bell	.05	458	Jeff Edwards	.05	575	Bernardo Brito	.05	691a	Tom Gamboa	.05	808	Willie Banks	.05
223	Jimmy Jones	.05	341	Jose Escobar	.05	459	Greg McMichael	.05	576	J.T. Bruett	.05	691b	Jeff Jones	.05	809	Johnny Ard	.05
224	Clippers Coaches	.05	342	Webster Garrison	.05	460	Carl Willis	.05	577	Paul Sorrento	.05	692	Gavin Osteen	.05	810	Willie Ansley	.05
225	Stump Merrill	.05	343	Paul Runge	.05	461	Beau Allred	.05	578	Ray Young	.05	693	Dave Riddle	.05	811	Andujar Cedeno	.05
226	Bob Davidson	.05	344	Luis Sojo	.05	462	Jeff Kaiser	.05	579	Dave Veres	.05	694	Tim Pugh	.05	812	Eddie Zosky	.05
227	Eric Boudreaux	.05	345	Ed Sprague	.05	463	Ty Gainey	.05	580	Scott Chiamparino	.05	695	Eugene Jones	.05	813	Randy Knorr	.05
228	Marvin Freeman	.05	346	Hector Delacruz	.05	464	Tom Lampkin	.05	581	Tony Ariola	.05	696	Scott Pose	.05	814	Juan Guzman	.05
229	Jason Grimsley	.05	347	Rob Ducey	.05	465	Ever Magallanes	.05	582	Weston Weber	.05	697	Ramon Jimenez	.05	815	Jimmy Rogers	.05
230	Chuck Malone	.05	348	Ozzie Virgil	.05	466	Tom Magrann	.05	583	Bruce Walton	.05	698	Fred Russell	.05	816	Nate Cromwell	.05
231	Dickie Moles	.05	349	Stu Pederson	.05	467	Jeff Manto	.05	584	Dave Otto	.05	699	Louis Talbert	.05	817	Aubrey Waggoner	.05
232	Wally Ritchie	.05	350	Mark Whiten	.05	468	Luis Medina	.05	585	Reese Lambert	.05	700	J.D. Noland	.05	818	Frank Thomas	4.00
233	Bob Scanlan	.05	351	Andy Dziadkowiec	.05	469	Troy Neel	.05	586	Joe Bitker	.05	701	Osvaldo Sanchez	.05	819	Matt Merullo	.05
234	Scott Service	.05	352	Shawn Barton	.05	470	Steve Springer	.05	587	Joe Law	.05	702	David Colon	.05	820	Roberto Hernandez	.05
235	Steve Sharts	.05	353	Kevin Brown	.05	471	Not issued	.05	588	Ed Wojna	.05	703	Jeff Hart	.05	821	Cesar Bernhardt	.05
236	John Gibbons	.05	354	Rocky Childress	.05	472	Turner Ward	.05	589	Timothy Casey	.05	704	Jeff Hoffman	.05	822	Sterling Hitchcock	.05
237	Sal Agostinelli	.05	355	Brian Givens	.05	473	Casey Webster	.05	590	Patrick Dietrick	.05	705	Sean Gilliam	.05	823	Ricky Rhodes	.05
238	Jim Adduci	.05	356	Manny Hernandez	.05	474	Jeff Weatherly	.05	591	Bruce Fields	.05	706	Al Pacheco	.05	824	Todd Malone	.05
239	Kelly Heath	.05	357	Jeff Innis	.05	475	Alan Cockrell	.05	592	Eric Fox	.05	707	Jason Satre	.05	825	Andy Fox	.05
240	Mickey Morandini	.05	358	Cesar Mejia	.05	476a	Rick Adair	.05	593	Scott Hemond	.05	708	Tim Cecil	.05	826	Ryan Klesko	.10
241	Victor Rosario	.05	359	Scott Nielson	.05	476b	Steve McInerney (Trainer)	.05	594	Steve Howard	.05	709	Phil Wiese	.05	827	Tyler Houston	.05
242	Steve Stanicek	.05	360	Dale Plummer	.05	477	Bobby Molinaro	.05	595	Doug Jennings	.05	710	Larry Pardo	.05	828	Tab Brown	.05
243	Jim Vatcher	.05	361	Ray Soff	.05	478	Cliff Young	.05	596	Al Pedrique	.05	711	Clemente Acosta	.05	829	Brian McRae	.05
244	Bill Dancy	.05	362	Lou Thornton	.05	479	Michael Arner	.05	597	Dann Howitt	.05	712	Chris Johnson	.05	830	Victor Cole	.05
245	Ron Jones	.05	363	Dave Trautwein	.05	480	Gary Buckels	.05	598	Russ McGinnis	.05	713	Frank Bolick	.05	831	Mark Lewis	.05

No.	Player	Price
832	Rudy Seanez	.05
833	Charles Nagy	.05
834	Jeff Mutis	.05
835	Carl Keliipuleole	.05
836	Steve Pegues	.05
837	Mike Lumley	.05
838	Tim Leiner	.05
839	Dave Evans	.05
840	Darron Cox	.05
841	Tony Ochs	.05
842	Paul Coleman	.05
843	Rafael Novoa	.05
844	Clay Bellinger	.05
845	Jason McFarlin	.05
846	Craig Paquette	.05
847	Timmie Morrow	.05
848	Brian Hunter	.05
849	Willie Greene	.05
850	Austin Manahan	.05
851	Rich Aude	.05
852	Luis Lopez	.05
853	Darrin Reichle	.05
854	Tim Salmon	1.00
855	Royce Clayton	.05
856	Steve Hosey	.05
857	Kerry Woodson	.05
858	Roger Salkeld	.05
859	Tim Stargell	.05
860	Greg Pirkl	.05
861	Pat Mahomes	.05
862	Denny Naegle	.05
863	Troy Buckley	.05
864	Ray Ortiz	.05
865	Leo Perez	.05
866	Cal Eldred	.50
867	Darin Kracl	.05
868	Lee Tinsley	.05
869	T.R. Lewis	.05
870	Jim Roso	.05
871	Tom Taylor	.05
872	Matt Anderson	.05
873	Kerwin Moore	.05
874	Rich Tunison	.05
875	Brian Ahern	.05
876	Eddie Taubensee	.05
877	Scott Bryant	.05
878	Steve Martin	.05
879	Josias Mazanillo	.05
880	Bob Zupcic	.05

1990 ProCards A & AA Minor League Stars

JIM THOME
Infield
Burlington Indians

This set was originally marketed for ProCards in wax packs by Progressive Sports Images in 1991 and, later, was distributed as a complete set.

	MT
Complete Set (200):	12.50
Common Player:	.05
Wax Box (48):	20.00

No.	Player	Price
1	Mike Linskey	.05
2	Ben McDonald	.05
3	Francisco DeLaRosa	.05
4	Jose Mesa	.05
5	Kevin Morton	.05
6	Dan O'Neill	.05
7	Dave Owen	.05
8	Jeff Plympton	.05
9	Charles Nagy	.05
10	Rudy Seanez	.05
11	Bruce Egloff	.05
12	Joe Ausanio	.05
13	Jim Tracy	.05
14	Randy Tomlin	.05
15	Jim Campbell	.05
16	Mike Gardiner	.05
17	Rusty Meacham	.05
18	John Kiely	.05
19	Darrin Chapin	.05
20	Wade Taylor	.05
21	Don Stanford	.05
22	Andy Ashby	.05
23	Bob Ayrault	.05
24	Luis Mercedes	.05
25	Scott Meadows	.05
26	Jeff Bagwell	3.00
27	Mark Lewis	.05
28	Carlos Garcia	.05
29	Moises Alou	.50
30	Rico Brogna	.05
31	Bernie Williams	.50
32	Pat Kelly	.05
33	Mitch Lyden	.05
34	Hector Wagner	.05
35	Carlos Maldonado	.05
36	Brian Barnes	.05
37	Chris Nabholz	.05
38	Jeff Carter	.05
39	Johnny Ard	.05
40	Willie Banks	.05
41	Scott Erickson	.05
42	Greg Johnson	.05
43	Al Osuna	.05
44	Bob MacDonald	.05
45	Pat Hentgen	.05
46	Frank Thomas	3.00
47	Matt Stark	.05
48	Jeff Conine	.05
49	Sean Berry	.05
50	Brian McRae	.05
51	Bobby Moore	.05
52	Brent Mayne	.05
53	Greg Colbrunn	.05
54	Terrel Hansen	.05
55	Lenny Webster	.05
56	Chuck Knoblauch	.05
57	Willie Ansley	.05
58	Andujar Cedeno	.05
59	Luis Gonzalez	1.00
60	Eddie Zosky	.05
61	William Suero	.05
62	Tom Quinlan	.05
63	Kelly Mann	.05
64	Mike Bell	.05
65	Mark Dewey	.05
66	Tom Hostetler	.05
67	Kevin Belcher	.05
68	Bill Haselman	.05
69	Bob Maurer	.05
70	Dan Rohrmeier	.05
71	Dan Peltier	.05
72	Steven Decker	.05
73	Dave Patterson	.05
74	Ed Zinter	.05
75	David Bird	.05
76	Willie Espinal	.05
77	Dennis Fletcher	.05
78	Travis Buckley	.05
79	Brian Romero	.05
80	Mike Arner	.05
81	Brian Evans	.05
82	John Graves	.05
83	Randy Marshall	.05
84	Mike Garcia	.05
85	Jeff Braley	.05
86	Ricky Rhodes	.05
87	Jim Haller	.05
88	Sterling Hitchcock	.05
89	Rob Blumberg	.05
90	Mike Ogliaruso	.05
91	Gregg Martin	.05
92	Tim Pugh	.05
93	Roger Hailey	.05
94	Don Strange	.05
95	Robert Gaddy	.05
96	Willie Greene	.05
97	Austin Manahan	.05
98	Tony Scruggs	.05
99	Mike Burton	.05
100	Shawn Holtzclaw	.05
101	Orlando Miller	.05
102	David Hajek	.05
103	Scott Pose	.05
104	Tyler Houston	.05
105	Melvin Nieves	.05
106	Ryan Klesko	.10
107	Daryl Moore	.05
108	Skip Wiley	.05
109	Brian McKeon	.05
110	Rusty Kilgo	.05
111	Chris Bushing	.05
112	Alan Newman	.05
113	Marc Lipson	.05
114	Darin Kracl	.05
115	Matt Grott	.05
116	Rafael Novoa	.05
117	Pat Rapp	.05
118	Ed Gustafson	.05
119	Chris Hancock	.05
120	Mo Sanford	.05
121	Bill Risley	.05
122	Victor Garcia	.05
123	Dave McAuliffe	.05
124	Pedro Borbon	.05
125	Rich Tunlson	.05
126	Fred Cooley	.05
127	Joey James	.05
128	Reggie Sanders	.05
129	Scott Bryant	.05
130	Brent McCoy	.05
131	Ramon Caraballo	.05
132	Javier Lopez	.10
133	Brian Harrison	.05
134	Rich DeLucia	.05
135	Roger Salkeld	.05
136	Kerry Woodson	.05
137	Chris Johnson	.05
138	Cal Eldred	.05
139	Angel Miranda	.05
140	Richard Garces	.05
141	Pat Mahomes	.05
142	Denny Neagle	.05
143	George Tsamis	.05
144	Johnny Guzman	.05
145	Dan Rambo	.05
146	Jim Myers	.05
147	Darrell Sherman	.05
148	Dave Staton	.05
149	Brian Turang	.05
150	Bo Dodson	.05
151	Dave Nilsson	.05
152	Frank Bolick	.05
153	Ray Ortiz	.05
154	J.T. Bruett	.05
155	John Patterson	.05
156	Royce Clayton	.05
157	Hilly Hathaway	.05
158	Phil Leftwich	.05
159	Randy Powers	.05
160	Todd Van Poppel	.05
161	Don Peters	.05
162	Dave Zancanaro	.05
163	Kirk Dressendorfer	.05
164	Curtis Shaw	.05
165	Joe Rosselli	.05
166	Mark Dalesandro	.05
167	Eric Helfand	.05
168	Eric Booker	.05
169	Adam Hyzdu	.05
170	Eric Christopherson	.05
171	Marcus Jensen	.05
172	Derek Reid	.05
173	Lance Dickson	.05
174	Tim Parker	.05
175	Jessie Hollins	.05
176	Sam Militello	.05
177	Darren Hodges	.05
178	Kirt Ojala	.05
179	Steve Karsay	.05
180	Andrew Hartung	.05
181	Kevin Jordan	.05
182	Robert Eenhoorn	.05
183	Jalal Leach	.05
184	Carlos Delgado	2.00
185	Sean Cheetham	.05
186	J.J. Munoz	.05
187	Jim Thome	2.50
188	Tracy Sanders	.05
189	Tony Clark	.10
190	Jose Viera	.05
191	Pat Dando	.05
192	Brian Kowitz	.05
193	Mike Lieberthal	.10
194	Jeff Borgese	.05
195	Mike Ferry	.05
196	K.C. Gillum	.05
197	Elliott Quinones	.05
198	Grant Brittain	.05
199	Checklist 1-100	.05
200	Checklist 101-200	.05

1990 ProCards Future Stars AAA Baseball

DAVE JUSTICE
Outfield
Richmond Braves

This series was the second produced for ProCards by Progressive Sports Images. The 1989 issue had simply been AAA players from the regular ProCards team sets with 1989 stats added. The 1990 series, complete with 1990 stats, features cards from all AAA teams in a completely different format from the '90 team sets. Cards were numbered consecutively 1-700, and an attempt was made to maintain team integrity. The series was later issued in an edition of 3,000 factory sets.

	MT
Factory Set (700):	15.00
Complete Set (700):	9.00
Common Player:	.05
Wax Pack (10):	.50
Ser. 1 or 2 Wax Box (48):	10.00

No.	Player	Price
1	Terry Gilmore	.05
2	Jim Lewis	.05
3	Joe Lynch	.05
4	Matt Maysey	.05
5	Dan Murphy	.05
6	Eric Nolte	.05
7	Brian Ohnoutka	.05
8	Steve Peters	.05
9	Paul Quinzer	.05
10	Pete Roberts	.05
11	Rich Rodriguez	.05
12	Roger Smithberg	.05
13	Rafael Valdez	.05
14	Mike Basso	.05
15	Ronn Reynolds	.05
16	Paul Faries	.05
17	Tom LeVasseur	.05
18	Jose Mota	.05
19	Eddie Williams	.05
20	Jeff Yurtin	.05
21	Alex Cole	.05
22	Charles Hillemann	.05
23	Thomas Howard	.05
24	Warren Newson	.05
25	Pat Kelly	.05
26	Gary Lance	.05
27	Tony Torchia	.05
28	George Bonilla	.05
29	Greg Booker	.05
30	Rich Bordi	.05
31	John Burkett	.05
32	Gil Heredia	.05
33	Bob Knepper	.05
34	Randy McCament	.05
35	Paul McClellan	.05
36	Timber Mead	.05
37	Ed Vosberg	.05
38	Trevor Wilson	.05
39	Mark Bailey	.05
40	Kirt Manwaring	.05
41	Mike Benjamin	.05
42	Brian Brady	.05
43	Jeff Carter	.05
44	Craig Colbert	.05
45	Erik Johnson	.05
46	Greg Litton	.05
47	Kash Beauchamp	.05
48	George Hinshaw	.05
49	Mike Kingery	.05
50	Mark Leonard	.05
51	Gregg Ritchie	.05
52	Rick Parker	.05
53	Duane Espy	.05
54	Tim Ireland	.05
55	Larry Hardy	.05
56	Jeff Bittiger	.05
57	Mike Christopher	.05
58	Steve Davis	.05
59	Jeff Fischer	.05
60	Darren Holmes	.05
61	Morris Madden	.05
62	Mike Maddux	.05
63	Greg Mayberry	.05
64	Jim Neidlinger	.05
65	Tim Scott	.05
66	Dave Walsh	.05
67	Terry Wells	.05
68	Adam Brown	.05
69	Darrin Fletcher	.05
70	Carlos Hernandez	.05
71	Dave Hansen	.05
72	Dan Henley	.05
73	Glenn Hoffman	.05
74	Walt McConnell	.05
75	Jose Offerman	.05
76	Jose Vizcaino	.05
77	Billy Bean	.05
78	Butch Davis	.05
79	Mike Huff	.05
80	Wayne Kirby	.05
81	Luis Lopez	.05
82	Kevin Kennedy	.05
83	Claude Osteen	.05
84	Von Joshua	.05
85	Chris Beasley	.05
86	Gary Buckels	.05
87	Tim Burcham	.05
88	Sherman Corbett	.05
89	Mike Erb	.05
90	Mike Fetters	.05
91	Jeff Heathcock	.05
92	Scott Lewis	.05
93	Rafael Montalvo	.05
94	Cliff Young	.05
95	Doug Davis	.05
96	Ron Tingley	.05
97	Karl Allaire	.05
98	Pete Coachman	.05
99	Chris Cron	.05
100	Gary DiSarcina	.05
101	Nelson Rood	.05
102	Bobby Rose	.05
103	Lee Stevens	.05
104	Dan Grunhard	.05
105	Reed Peters	.05
106	John Skurla	.05
107	Max Oliveras	.05
108	Chuck Hernandez	.05
109	Tony Blasucci	.05
110	Dave Burba	.05
111	Keith Helton	.05
112	Vance Lovelace	.05
113	Jose Melendez	.05
114	Pat Pacillo	.05
115	Pat Rice	.05
116	Terry Taylor	.05
117	Mike Walker	.05
118	Bill McGuire	.05
119	Matt Sinatro	.05
120	Mario Diaz	.05
121	Greg Fulton	.05
122	Todd Haney	.05
123	Ed Jurak	.05
124	Tino Martinez	.50
125	Jeff Schaefer	.05
126	Casey Close	.05
127	Tom Dodd	.05
128	Jim Weaver	.05
129	Tommy Jones	.05
130	Dan Warthen	.05
131	Tony Ariola	.05
132	Joe Bitker	.05
133	Scott Chiamparino	.05
134	Reese Lambert	.05
135	Joe Law	.05
136	Dave Otto	.05
137	Dave Veres	.05
138	Bruce Walton	.05
139	Weston Weber	.05
140	Ed Wojna	.05
141	Ray Young	.05
142	Troy Afenir	.05
143	Russ McGinnis	.05
144	Larry Arndt	.05
145	Mike Bordick	.05
146	Scott Hemond	.05
147	Dann Howitt	.05
148	Doug Jennings	.05
149	Al Pedrique	.05
150	Dick Scott	.05
151	Tim Casey	.05
152	Pat Dietrick	.05
153	Bruce Fields	.05
154	Eric Fox	.05
155	Steve Howard	.05
156	Kevin Ward	.05
157	Brad Fischer	.05
158	Chuck Estrada	.05
159	Wilson Alvarez	.05
160	Mike Campbell	.05
161	Tom Drees	.05
162	Grady Hall	.05
163	Shawn Hillegas	.05
164	Ravelo Manzanillo	.05
165	John Pawlowski	.05
166	Adam Peterson	.05
167	Steve Rosenberg	.05
168	Jose Segura	.05
169	Don Wakamatsu	.05
170	Jerry Willard	.05
171	Rich Amaral	.05
172	Pete Dalena	.05
173	Norberto Martin	.05
174	Keith Smith	.05
175	Todd Trafton	.05
176	Tracy Woodson	.05
177	Orsino Hill	.05
178	Marcus Lawton	.05
179	Marlin McPhail	.05
180	C.L. Penigar	.05
181	Ramon Sambo	.05
182	Dana Williams	.05
183	Marv Foley	.05
184	Moe Drabowsky	.10
185	Roger LaFrancois	.05
186	Ryan Bowen	.05
187	William Brennan	.05
188	Terry Clark	.05
189	Brian Fisher	.05
190	Randy Hennis	.05
191	Darryl Kile	.05
192	Brian Meyer	.05
193	Randy St. Claire	.05
194	Lee Tunnell	.05
195	Carl Nichols	.05
196	Scott Servais	.05
197	Pedro Sanchez	.05
198	Mike Simms	.05
199	Craig Smajstria	.05
200	Harry Spilman	.05
201	Doug Strange	.05
202	Jose Tolentino	.05
203	Gary Cooper	.05
204	Kevin Dean	.05
205	Louie Meadows	.05
206	Jim Olander	.05
207	Javier Ortiz	.05
208	Karl Rhodes	.05
209	Bob Skinner	.05
210	Brent Strom	.05
211	Tim Tolman	.05
212	Greg McMichael	.05
213	Doug Robertson	.05
214	Jeff Shaw	.05
215	Joe Skalski	.05
216	Efrain Valdez	.05
217	Mike Walker	.05
218	Colby Ward	.05
219	Carl Willis	.05
220	Tom Lampkin	.05
221	Tom Magrann	.05
222	Juan Castillo	.05
223	Ever Magallanes	.05
224	Jeff Manto	.05
225	Luis Medina	.05
226	Troy Neel	.05
227	Steve Springer	.05
228	Casey Webster	.05
229	Beau Allred	.05
230	Alan Cockrell	.05
231	Ty Gainey	.05
232	Dwight Taylor	.05
233	Turner Ward	.05
234	Jeff Wetherby	.05
235	Bobby Molinaro	.05
236	Buddy Bell	.10
237	Rick Adair	.05
238	Paul Abbott	.05
239	Pat Bangston	.05
240	Larry Casian	.05
241	Mike Cook	.05
242	Pete Delkus	.05
243	Mike Dyer	.05
244	Mark Guthrie	.05
245	Orlando Lind	.05
246	Francisco Oliveras	.05
247	Park Pittman	.05
248	Charles Scott	.05
249	Jimmy Williams	.05
250	Jamie Nelson	.05
251	Derek Parks	.05
252	Doug Baker	.05
253	Chip Hale	.05
254	Jerry Jorgensen	.05
255	Scott Leius	.05
256	Marty Lanoux	.05
257	Ed Naveda	.05
258	Victor Rodriguez	.05
259	Paul Sorrento	.05
260	Bernardo Brito	.05
261	Rafael Delima	.05
262	David Jacas	.05
263	Alonzo Powell	.05
264	Jim Shellenback	.05
265	Shawn Barton	.05
266	Kevin Brown	.05
267	Rocky Childress	.05
268	Brian Givens	.05
269	Manny Hernandez	.05
270	Jeff Innis	.05
271	Cesar Mejia	.05
272	Scott Nielsen	.05
273	Dale Plummer	.05
274	Rogre Samuels	.05
275	Ray Soff	.05
276	Dave Trautwein	.05
277	Julio Valera	.05
278	Dave Liddell	.05
279	Orlando Mercado	.05
280	Tim Bogar	.05
281	Mike DeButch	.05
282	Jeff Gardner	.05
283	Denny Gonzalez	.05
284	Chris Jelic	.05
285	Kelvin Torve	.05
286	Alex Diaz	.05
287	Keith Hughes	.05
288	Darren Reed	.05
289	Zollo Sanchez	.05
290	Lou Thornton	.05
291	Steve Swisher	.05
292	John Cumberland	.05
293	Rich Miller	.05
294	Jose DeJesus	.05
295	Marvin Freeman	.05
296	Todd Frohwirth	.05
297	Jason Grimsley	.05
298	Chuck Malone	.05
299	Brad Moore	.05
300	Wally Ritchie	.05
301	Bob Scanlan	.05
302	Scott Service	.05
303	Steve Sharts	.05
304	John Gibbons	.05
305	Tom Nieto	.05
306	Jim Adduci	.05
307	Kelly Heath	.05
308	Mickey Morandini	.05
309	Victor Rosario	.05
310	Steve Stanicek	.05
311	Greg Legg	.05
312	Ron Jones	.05
313	Chris Knabenshue	.05
314	Keith Miller	.05
315	Jim Vatcher	.05
316	Jim Wright	.05
317	Steve Adkins	.05
318	Darrin Chapin	.05
319	Bob Davidson	.05
320	Dave Eiland	.05
321	John Habyan	.05
322	Jimmy Jones	.05
323	Mark Leiter	.05
324	Kevin Mmahat	.05
325	Rich Monteleone	.05
326	Willie Smith	.05
327	Ricky Torres	.05
328	Jeff Datz	.05
329	Brian Dorsett	.05
330	Dave Sax	.05
331	Jim Leyritz	.10
332	Hensley Meulens	.05
333	Carlos Rodriguez	.05
334	Rob Sepanek	.05
335	Andy Stankiewicz	.05
336	Jim Walewander	.05
337	Mark Wasinger	.05
338	Oscar Azocar	.05
339	John Fishel	.05
340	Jason Maas	.05
341	Kevin Maas	.05
342	Van Snider	.05
343	Field Staff	.05
344	Tom Gilles	.05
345	Mauro Gozzo	.05
346	Paul Kilgus	.05
347	Doug Linton	.05
348	Mike Loynd	.05
349	Rick Lysander	.05
350	Alex Sanchez	.05
351	John Shea	.05
352	Steve Wapnick	.05
353	Andy Dziadkowiec	.05
354	Joe Szekely	.05
355	Ozzie Virgil	.05
356	Jim Eppard	.05
357	Jose Escobar	.05
358	Webster Garrison	.05
359	Paul Runge	.05
360	Luis Sojo	.05
361	Ed Sprague	.05
362	Derek Bell	.05
363	Hector DeLaCruz	.05
364	Rob Ducey	.05
365	Pedro Munoz	.05
366	Stu Pederson	.05
367	Mark Whiten	.05
368	Bob Bailor	.05
369	Bob Shirley	.05
370	Rocket Wheeler	.05
371	Scott Aldred	.05
372	Dennis Burtt	.05
373	Shawn Holman	.05
374	Matt Kinzer	.05
375	Randy Nosek	.05
376	Jose Ramos	.05
377	Kevin Ritz	.05
378	Mike Schwabe	.05
379	Steve Searcy	.05

#	Player	Price
380	Eric Stone	.05
381	Don Vesling	.05
382	Phil Clark	.05
383	Phil Ouellette	.05
384	Dean DeCillis	.05
385	Travis Fryman	.05
386	Jim Lindeman	.05
387	Scott Livingstone	.05
388	Torey Lovullo	.05
389	Domingo Michel	.05
390	Milt Cuyler	.05
391	Lavell Freeman	.05
392	Shawn Hare	.05
393	Scott Lusader	.05
394	Tom Gamboa	.05
395	Jeff Jones	.05
396	Aurelio Rodriguez	.05
397	Steve Avery	.05
398	Tommy Greene	.05
399	Bill Laskey	.05
400	Paul Marak	.05
401	Andy Nezelek	.05
402	Ed Olwine	.05
403	Dale Polley	.05
404	Rusty Richards	.05
405	Brian Snyder	.05
406	Jimmy Kremers	.05
407	John Mizerock	.05
408	John Alva	.05
409	Francisco Cabrera	.05
410	Bruce Crabbe	.05
411	Drew Denson	.05
412	Ken Dowell	.05
413	Ed Whited	.05
414	Geronimo Berroa	.05
415	Dennis Hood	.05
416	Brian Hunter	.05
417	Barry Jones	.05
418	Dave Justice	.50
419	Jim Beauchamp	.05
420	John Grubb	.05
421	Leo Mazzone	.05
422	Sonny Jackson	.05
423	Rick Berg	.05
424	Steve Bast	.05
425	Tom Bolton	.05
426	Steve Curry	.05
427	Mike Dalton	.05
428	Jeff Gray	.05
429	Daryl Irvine	.05
430	Joe Johnson	.05
431	John Leister	.05
432	Mike Rochford	.05
433	Larry Shikles	.05
434	Tito Stewart	.05
435	John Trautwein	.05
436	John Flaherty	.05
437	John Marzano	.05
438	Gary Tremblay	.05
439	Scott Cooper	.05
440	Angel Gonzalez	.05
441	Tim Naehring	.05
442	Jim Pankovits	.05
443	Mo Vaughn	.50
444	Rick Lancellotti	.05
445	Mickey Pina	.05
446	Phil Plantier	.05
447	Jeff Stone	.05
448	Scott Wade	.05
449	Ed Nottle	.05
450	Mark Meleski	.05
451	Lee Stange	.05
452	Jay Aldrich	.05
453	Jose Bautista	.05
454	Eric Bell	.05
455	Dan Boone	.05
456	Ben McDonald	.05
457	John Mitchell	.05
458	Curt Schilling	2.50
459	Mike Smith	.05
460	Rob Woodward	.05
461	Chris Hoiles	.05
462	Darrell Miller	.05
463	Jeff Tackett	.05
464	Juan Bell	.05
465	Tim Dullin	.05
466	Leo Gomez	.05
467	Jeff McKnight	.05
468	Shane Turner	.05
469	Greg Walker	.05
470	Tony Chance	.05
471	Victor Hithe	.05
472	Donnell Nixon	.05
473	Chris Padget	.05
474	Pete Stanicek	.05
475	Mike Linskey	.05
476	Joaquin Contreras	.05
477	Greg Biagini	.05
478	Dick Bosman	.05
479	Paul Blair	.05
480	Stan Belinda	.05
481	Gordon Dillard	.05
482	Mark Huismann	.05
483	Hugh Kemp	.05
484	Scott Medvin	.05
485	Vincente Palacios	.05
486	Rick Reed	.05
487	Mark Ross	.05
488	Dorn Taylor	.05
489	Mike York	.05
490	Dann Bilardello	.05
491	Tom Prince	.05
492	Danny Sheaffer	.05
493	Kevin Burdick	.05
494	Steve Kiefer	.05
495	Orlando Merced	.05
496	Armando Moreno	.05
497	Jeff Richardson	.05
498	Mark Ryal	.05
499	Tommy Shields	.05
500	Steve Carter	.05
501	Wes Chamberlain	.05
502	Jeff Cook	.05
503	Scott Little	.05
504	Terry Collins	.05
505	Jackie Brown	.05
506	Steve Henderson	.05
507	Gibson Alba	.05
508	Scott Arnold	.05
509	Cris Carpenter	.05
510	Stan Clarke	.05
511	Mark Grater	.05
512	Howard Hilton	.05
513	Mike Hinkle	.05
514	Omar Olivares	.05
515	Dave Osteen	.05
516	Mike Perez	.05
517	Tim Sherrill	.05
518	Scott Nichols	.05
519	Ray Stephens	.05
520	Pat Austin	.05
521	Rod Brewer	.05
522	Todd Crosby	.05
523	Bien Figueroa	.05
524	Julian Martinez	.05
525	Jesus Mendez	.05
526	Geronimo Pena	.05
527	Craig Wilson	.05
528	Dennis Carter	.05
529	Bernard Gilkey	.05
530	Ray Lankford	.10
531	Mauricio Nunez	.05
532	Roy Silver	.05
533	Gaylen Pitts	.05
534	Mark Riggins	.05
535	Neil Allen	.05
536	Keith Brown	.05
537	Chris Hammond	.05
538	Milton Hill	.05
539	Rodney Imes	.05
540	Rob Lopez	.05
541	Charlie Mitchell	.05
542	Bobby Moore	.05
543	Rosario Rodriguez	.05
544	Scott Scudder	.05
545	Bob Sebra	.05
546	Joey Vierra	.05
547	Tony DeFrancesco	.05
548	Terry McGriff	.05
549	Donnie Scott	.05
550	Reggie Jefferson	.05
551	Brian Lane	.05
552	Chris Lombardozzi	.05
553	Paul Noce	.05
554	Kevin Pearson	.05
555	Eddie Tanner	.05
556	Skeeter Barnes	.05
557	Leo Garcia	.05
558	Chris Jones	.05
559	Keith Lockhart	.05
560	Darryl Motley	.05
561	Pete Mackanin	.05
562	Ray Ripplemeyer	.05
563	Scott Anderson	.05
564	Esteban Beltre	.05
565	Travis Chambers	.05
566	Randy Braun	.05
567	Danny Clay	.05
568	Eric Bullock	.05
569	Jim Davins	.05
570	Jose Castro	.05
571	Eddie Dixon	.05
572	Romy Cucjen	.05
573	Howard Farmer	.05
574	Jerry Goff	.05
575	Steve Fireovid	.05
576	Otis Green	.05
577	Dan Gakeler	.05
578	Mel Houston	.05
579	Balvino Galvez	.05
580	Dwight Lowery	.05
581	Dale Mohorcic	.05
582	Quinn Mack	.05
583	Chris Marchok	.05
584	Edwin Marquez	.05
585	Mel Rojas	.05
586	Johnny Paredes	.05
587	Rich Thompson	.05
588	German Rivera	.05
589	James Steels	.05
590	Tim Johnson	.05
591	Gomer Hodge	.05
592	Joe Kerrigan	.05
593	Ray Chadwick	.05
594	Dera Clark	.05
595	Luis Encarnacion	.05
596	Tony Ferreira	.05
597	Pete Filson	.05
598	Jim LeMasters	.05
599	Mike Magnante	.05
600	Mike Tresemer	.05
601	Mel Stottlemyre	.05
602	Bill Wilkinson	.05
603	Kevin Burrell	.05
604	Tim Spehr	.05
605	Luis De Los Santos	.05
606	Bob Hamelin	.05
607	Bobby Meacham	.05
608	Russ Morman	.05
609	Thad Reece	.05
610	Paul Zuvella	.05
611	Mike Loggins	.05
612	Chito Martinez	.05
613	Harvey Pulliam	.05
614	Jeff Schulz	.05
615	Sal Rende	.05
616	Tom Poquette	.05
617	Rich Dubee	.05
618	Kevin Blankenship	.05
619	Shawn Boskie	.05
620	Mark Bowden	.05
621	Greg Kallevig	.05
622	Dave Masters	.05
623	Steve Parker	.05
624	Dave Pavlas	.05
625	Laddie Renfroe	.05
626	Paul Wilmet	.05
627	Jeff Hearron	.05
628	Erik Pappas	.05
629	Hector Villanueva	.05
630	Bob Bafia	.05
631	Brian Guinn	.05
632	Jeff Small	.05
633	Greg Smith	.05
634	Glenn Sullivan	.05
635	Bill Wrona	.05
636	Brad Bierley	.05
637	Cedric Landrum	.05
638	Derrick May	.25
639	Gary Varsho	.05
640	Jim Essian	.05
641	Don August	.05
642	Mike Birkbeck	.05
643	Mike Capel	.05
644	Logan Easley	.05
645	Tom Edens	.05
646	Don Gordon	.05
647	Chuck McGrath	.05
648	Jeff Peterek	.05
649	Dennis Powell	.05
650	Ed Puig	.05
651	Alan Sadler	.05
652	Tim Watkins	.05
653	Tim McIntosh	.05
654	Tim Torricelli	.05
655	George Canale	.05
656	Mark Higgins	.05
657	Joe Mitchell	.05
658	Joe Redfield	.05
659	D.L. Smith	.05
660	Joe Xavier	.05
661	Ruben Escalera	.05
662	Mario Monico	.05
663	Billy Moore	.05
664	Darryel Walters	.05
665	Dave Machemer	.05
666	Jackson Todd	.05
667	Gerald Alexander	.05
668	Brad Arnsberg	.05
669	John Barfield	.05
670	Jack Hardy	.05
671	Ray Hayward	.05
672	John Hoover	.05
673	Steve Lankard	.05
674	David Lynch	.05
675	Craig McMurtry	.05
676	David Miller	.05
677	Mark Petkovsek	.05
678	Jeff Satzinger	.05
679	Mike Berger	.05
680	Dave Engle	.05
681	John Russell	.05
682	Pat Dodson	.05
683	Pat Garman	.05
684	Gary Green	.05
685	Bryan House	.05
686	Dean Palmer	.25
687	Ron Washington	.05
688	Nick Capra	.05
689	Juan Gonzalez	1.50
690	Gar Millay	.05
691	Kevin Reimer	.05
692	Bernie Tatis	.05
693	Checklist 1-100	.05
694	Checklist 101-200	.05
695	Checklist 201-300	.05
696	Checklist 301-400	.05
697	Checklist 401-500	.05
698	Checklist 501-600	.05
699	Checklist 601-700	.05

1990 Star Minor League Baseball Wax

JORGE PEDRE — MEMPHIS — Catcher — STAR

Star finished the 1990 season with another 100-card wax series. This series was closely akin in make-up to its 1989 predecessor. The set features yellow borders around color photos. There was no checklist and the cards were not available as a complete set. A second series was planned, but never materialized.

MIKE PIAZZA — VERO BEACH — Catcher — STAR

	MT
Complete Set (100):	9.00
Common Player:	.05
Wax Pack (10):	.50
Wax Box (48):	15.00

#	Player	Price
1	Bruce Schreiber	.05
2	Jeff Juden	.05
3	Kenny Lofton	.25
4	Scott Makarewicz	.05
5	Al Sanders	.05
6	Rod Boddie	.05
7	Jim Faulk	.05
8	Dan Freed	.05
9	D.J. Dozier	.05
10	Nicko Riesgo	.05
11	Alan Zinter	.05
12	Jim Bruske	.05
13	Mark Lewis	.05
14	Willie Ansley	.05
15	Tony Eusebio	.05
16	Luis Gonzalez	.25
17	Andy Mota	.05
18	Tony Barron	.05
19	Kevin Maas	.05
20	Anthony Collier	.05
21	Ramon Taveras	.05
22	Eric Young	.05
23	Everett Cunningham	.05
24	Barry Manuel	.05
25	David Perez	.05
26	Ivan Rodriguez	2.00
27	Fred Samson	.05
28	Ben McDonald	.05
29	Blas Minor	.05
30	Jeff Bagwell	2.50
31	Mike Twardoski	.05
32	T.R. Lewis	.05
33	Ron Cook	.05
34	Ivan Cruz	.05
35	Jody Hurst	.05
36	Keith Kimberlin	.05
37	Lino Rivera	.05
38	Mike Tresh	.05
39	Hernan Cortes	.05
40	Jay Knoblauch	.05
41	Larry Stanford	.05
42	Hector Vargas	.05
43	Jacob Brumfield	.05
44	Mark Parnell	.05
45	Willie Banks	.05
46	Reed Olmstead	.05
47	Mike Redding	.05
48	Rich DeLucia	.05
49	Mike Gardiner	.05
50	Royal Clayton	.05
51	Darrin Chapin	.05
52	Mitch Lyden	.05
53	Don Sparks	.05
54	Bernie Williams	.50
55	Steve Dunn	.05
56	Alan Newman	.05
57	Brent McCoy	.05
58	Mike Galvan	.05
59	Greg Perschke	.05
60	Rob Resnikoff	.05
61	Sammy Sosa	3.00
62	Bobby DeLoach	.05
63	Jesse Cross	.05
64	Ray Giannelli	.05
65	Jeff Kent	.25
66	Greg O'Halloran	.05
67	Mike Timlin	.05
68	Brian McRae	.25
69	Anthony Ward	.05
70	Toby Borland	.05
71	Joe Millette	.05
72	Tony Trevino	.05
73	Anthony Kelley	.05
74	George Kerfut	.05
75	Scott Meadows	.05
76	Luis Mercedes	.05
77	Dan Barbara	.05
78	Rod Poissant	.05
79	Gary Alexander	.05
80	Bob Ayrault	.05
81	Kim Batiste	.05
82	Pete Alborano	.05
83	Scott Centala	.05
84	Stu Cole	.05
85	Jeff Conine	.05
86	Bobby Moore	.05
87	Jorge Pedre	.05
88	Mike Maksudian	.05
89	Jerry Schunk	.05
90	William Suero	.05
91	Eddie Zosky	.05
92	Jeff Hoffman	.05
93	Ramon Jimenez	.05
94	Michael Bell	.05
95	Thomas Redington	.05
96	Michael Arner	.05
97	Brian Romero	.05
98	Tony Scruggs	.05
99	James Harris	.05
100	Tito Navarro	.05

1990 Minor League Team Sets

The number of minor league team sets and variations declined a bit from the peak year of 1989. Sportsprint entered the field with eight sets, while CMC-TCMA issued its final minor league team sets.

304 Team Sets and Variations

Set		MT
1990 PC AAA All-Stars (54)		8.00
1990 Alaska Goldpanners (16)		30.00
1990 Best Albany-Colonie Yankees (26)		6.00
1990 Best Albany Yankees All-Decade (36)		12.00
1990 PC Albany-Colonie Yankees (29)		6.00
1990 Star Albany-Colonie Yankees (28)		6.00
1990 CMC Albuquerque Dukes (28)		5.00
1990 PC Albuquerque Dukes (30)		5.00
1990 Team Albuquerque Dukes Photos (33)		110.00
1990 Box Appleton Foxes (30)		3.00
1990 Diamond Appleton Foxes (30)		3.00
1990 PC Appleton Foxes (29)		3.00
1990 GS Arkansas Travelers (30)		6.00
1990 PC Asheville Tourists (28)		7.00
1990 Best Auburn Astros (25)		4.00
1990 PC Auburn Astros (26)		3.00
1990 PC Augusta Pirates (27)		4.00
1990 Cal Bakersfield Dodgers (32)		4.00
1990 Star Baseball City Royals (31)		3.00
1990 PC Batavia Clippers (31)		3.00
1990 Legoe Bellingham Mariners (38)		4.00
1990 Best Beloit Brewers (27)		4.00
1990 Star Beloit Brewers (27)		4.00
1990 Legoe Bend Bucks (32)		3.00
1990 PC Billings Mustangs (30)		3.00
1990 Best Birmingham Barons (30)		20.00
1990 Best Birmingham Barons All-Decade (34)		7.00
1990 PC Birmingham Barons (28)		9.00
1990 Star Bluefield Orioles (22)		5.00
1990 PC Boise Hawks (33)		4.00
1990 PC Bristol Tigers (29)		8.00
1990 Star Bristol Tigers (30)		8.00
1990 CMC Buffalo Bisons (25)		4.00
1990 PC Buffalo Bisons (28)		4.00
1990 Team Buffalo Bisons (30)		12.50
1990 Best Burlington Braves (30)		5.00
1990 PC Burlington Braves (30)		10.00
1990 Star Burlington Braves (31)		7.00
1990 PC Burlington Indians (29)		17.50
1990 SP Butte Copper Kings (30)		8.00
1990 CMC Calgary Cannons (25)		8.00
1990 PC Calgary Cannons (23)		8.00
1990 Cal League All-Stars (56)		6.00
1990 Best Canton-Akron Indians (28)		6.00
1990 PC Canton-Akron Indians (27)		5.00
1990 Star Canton-Akron Indians (21)		5.00
1990 Sportsprint Carolina League A-S (52)		5.00
1990 Best Cedar Rapids Reds (27)		5.00
1990 Best Cedar Rapids Reds All-Decade (36)		15.00
1990 PC Cedar Rapids Reds (27)		6.00
1990 Best Charleston Rainbows (28)		4.00
1990 PC Charleston Rainbows (28)		3.00
1990 Best Charleston Wheelers (29)		6.00
1990 PC Charleston Wheelers (28)		9.00
1990 Team Charlotte Knights (25)		6.00
1990 Star Charlotte Rangers (30)		15.00
1990 GS Chattanooga Lookouts (27)		4.00
1990 Diamond Clearwater Phillies (9)		5.00
1990 Star Clearwater Phillies (27)		3.00
1990 Best Clinton Giants (29)		4.00
1990 PC Clinton Giants (29)		3.00
1990 Team Clinton Giants Update (12)		3.00
1990 CMC Colorado Springs Sky Sox (24)		4.00
1990 PC Colorado Springs Sky Sox (27)		4.00
1990 GS Columbia Mets (30)		3.00
1990 Play II Columbia Mets (27)		3.00
1990 Play II Columbia Mets Postcards (27)		9.00
1990 CMC Columbus Clippers (27)		7.50
1990 Police Columbus Clippers (25) (Mass)		10.00
1990 Police Columbus Clippers (25) (Maas)		5.00
1990 PC Columbus Clippers (28)		4.00
1990 Team Columbus Clippers Foldout		25.00
1990 Best Columbus Mudcats (26)		6.00
1990 PC Columbus Mudcats (27)		9.00
1990 Star Columbus Mudcats (29)		9.00
1990 CMC Denver Zephyrs (26)		3.00
1990 PC Denver Zephyrs (28)		3.00
1990 Star Dunedin Blue Jays (28)		3.00
1990 Sportsprint Durham Bulls (29)		4.00
1990 Sportsprint Durham Bulls Update (8)		15.00
1990 PC Eastern League All-Stars (48)		7.00
1990 CMC Edmonton Trappers (24)		3.00
1990 PC Edmonton Trappers (25)		3.00
1990 Star Elizabethton Twins (26)		4.00
1990 Pucko Elmira Pioneers (27)		3.00
1990 GS El Paso Diablos (25)		4.00
1990 Team El Paso Diablos All-Time (45)		25.00
1990 Star Erie Sailors (31)		3.00
1990 GS Eugene Emeralds (30)		3.00
1990 Best Everett Giants (28)		4.00
1990 PC Everett Giants (32)		4.00
1990 PC Fayetteville Generals (28)		3.00
1990 Star Florida State League All-Stars (50)		20.00
1990 Sportsprint Frederick Keys (30)		6.00
1990 Star Ft. Lauderdale Yankees (29)		4.00
1990 Best Gastonia Rangers (30)		4.00
1990 PC Gastonia Rangers (29)		3.00
1990 Star Gastonia Rangers (29)		3.00
1990 PC Gate City Pioneers (27)		4.00
1990 SP Gate City Pioneers (24)		4.00
1990 PC Geneva Cubs (27)		4.00
1990 Star Geneva Cubs (32)		3.00
1990 SP Great Falls Dodgers (30)		40.00
1990 Best Greensboro Hornets (30)		4.00
1990 PC Greensboro Hornets (31)		4.00
1990 Star Greensboro Hornets (26)		4.00
1990 Best Greenville Braves (22)		4.00
1990 PC Greenville Braves (26)		4.00
1990 Star Greenville Braves (24)		3.00
1990 Best Hagerstown Suns (30)		4.50
1990 Best Hagerstown Suns All-Decade (36)		10.00
1990 PC Hagerstown Suns (33)		5.00
1990 Star Hagerstown Suns (28)		5.00
1990 Best Hamilton Redbirds (28)		4.00
1990 Star Hamilton Redbirds (29)		4.00
1990 PC Harrisburg Senators (26)		7.00
1990 Star Harrisburg Senators (25)		7.00
1990 SP Helena Brewers (29)		4.00
1990 Little Sun High School Prospects (24)		6.00
1990 PC Huntington Cubs (32)		4.00

Year	Item	Price
1990	Best Huntsville Stars (27)	4.00
1990	PC Idaho Falls Braves (31)	3.00
1990	CMC Indianapolis Indians (25)	3.00
1990	PC Indianapolis Indians (31)	3.00
1990	CMC Iowa Cubs (25)	4.00
1990	PC Iowa Cubs (24)	4.00
1990	GS Jackson Mets (30)	4.00
1990	Best Jacksonville Expos (29)	4.00
1990	PC Jacksonville Expos (29)	5.00
1990	Pucko Jamestown Expos (34)	4.00
1990	Star Johnson City Cardinals (30)	4.00
1990	Best Kenosha Twins (30)	4.00
1990	PC Kenosha Twins (27)	4.00
1990	Star Kenosha Twins (29)	3.00
1990	Best Kingsport Mets (28)	4.00
1990	Star Kingsport Mets (30)	3.00
1990	Sportsprint Kinston Indians (31)	3.00
1990	Diamond Kissimmee Dodgers (29)	3.00
1990	Best Knoxville Blue Jays (28)	4.00
1990	PC Knoxville Blue Jays (25)	4.00
1990	Star Knoxville Blue Jays (26)	4.00
1990	Star Lakeland Tigers (28)	3.00
1990	Star Lakeland Tigers (31)	10.00
1990	CMC Las Vegas Stars (25)	4.00
1990	PC Las Vegas Stars (28)	4.00
1990	PC London Tigers (22)	4.00
1990	CMC Louisville Redbirds (29)	4.00
1990	PC Louisville Redbirds (29)	4.00
1990	Team Louisville Redbirds (42)	9.00
1990	Sportsprint Lynchburg Red Sox (27)	4.00
1990	Best Madison Muskies (29)	4.00
1990	PC Madison Muskies (26)	4.00
1990	PC Martinsville Phillies (34)	4.00
1990	Best Medicine Hat Blue Jays (28)	4.00
1990	Best Memphis Chicks (29)	5.00
1990	PC Memphis Chicks (28)	5.00
1990	Star Memphis Chicks (27)	5.00
1990	Star Miami Miracle I (31)	3.00
1990	Star Miami Miracle II (31)	3.00
1990	GS Midland Angels (28)	4.00
1990	GS Midland Angels (32)	6.00
1990	1 Hour Midland Angels (35)	40.00
1990	GS Midwest League All-Stars (58)	9.00
1990	Star 1989 Midwest League All-Stars (56)	8.00
1990	Cal Modesto A's (25)	3.00
1990	Chong Modesto A's (36)	4.00
1990	PC Modesto A's (29)	3.00
1990	PC Myrtle Beach Blue Jays (29)	7.00
1990	CMC Nashville Sounds (28)	4.00
1990	PC Nashville Sounds (29)	4.00
1990	Team Nashville Sounds (30)	5.00
1990	Best New Britain Red Sox (29)	12.00
1990	PC New Britain Red Sox (26)	12.00
1990	Star New Britain Red Sox (27)	15.00
1990	Pucko Niagara Falls Rapids (33)	5.00
1990	CMC Oklahoma City 89ers (24)	15.00
1990	PC Oklahoma City 89ers (30)	12.50
1990	CMC Omaha Royals (25)	4.00
1990	PC Omaha Royals (26)	4.00
1990	PC Oneonta Yankees (29)	4.00
1990	Best Orlando Sun Rays (30)	7.50
1990	PC Orlando Sun Rays (27)	12.00
1990	Star Orlando Sun Rays (28)	12.00
1990	Star Osceola Astros (30)	6.00
1990	Cal Palm Springs Angels (29)	5.00
1990	PC Palm Springs Angels (28)	7.00
1990	BDK Pan-Am Team USA (Red)(26)	6.00
1990	CMC Pawtucket Red Sox (25)	4.00
1990	DD Pawtucket Red Sox Foldout	30.00

Year	Item	Price
1990	PC Pawtucket Red Sox (29)	9.00
1990	Team Peninsula Oilers (24)	6.00
1990	Star Peninsula Pilots (27)	3.00
1990	Team Peoria Chiefs (38)	10.00
1990	Team Peoria Chiefs Sheet (30)	7.50
1990	Team Peoria Chiefs Update (7)	4.00
1990	Team Peoria Chiefs Earl Cunningham (4)	4.00
1990	CMC Phoenix Firebirds (26)	5.00
1990	PC Phoenix Firebirds (29)	5.00
1990	Pucko Pittsfield Mets (32)	6.00
1990	CMC Portland Beavers (25)	4.00
1990	PC Portland Beavers (28)	4.00
1990	Diamond Princeton Patriots (30)	3.00
1990	Sportsprint Prince William Cannons (30)	3.00
1990	Best Pulaski Braves (29)	3.00
1990	PC Pulaski Braves (31)	4.00
1990	GS Quad City Angels (30)	5.00
1990	Best Reading Phillies (26)	4.00
1990	PC Reading Phillies (27)	6.00
1990	Star Reading Phillies (28)	4.00
1990	Cal Reno Silver Sox (31)	3.00
1990	Bob's Richmond Braves (21)	45.00
1990	Bob's Richmond Braves (22)	50.00
1990	CMC Richmond Braves (27)	7.00
1990	PC Richmond Braves (28)	6.00
1990	Team Richmond Braves Foldout	15.00
1990	Team Richmond 25th Anniversary (23)	25.00
1990	Best Riverside Red Wave (27)	3.00
1990	Cal Riverside Red Wave (27)	3.00
1990	PC Riverside Red Wave (28)	3.00
1990	CMC Rochester Red Wings (27)	6.00
1990	PC Rochester Red Wings (29)	5.00
1990	Team Rochester Red Wings (36)	30.00
1990	PC Rockford Expos (29)	3.00
1990	Team Rockford Expos (30)	4.00
1990	Star Salem Buccaneers (27)	3.50
1990	Cal Salinas Spurs (32)	4.00
1990	PC Salinas Spurs (26)	3.00
1990	GS San Antonio Missions (29)	9.00
1990	Best San Bernardino Spirit (28)	4.00
1990	Cal San Bernardino Spirit (32)	5.00
1990	PC San Bernardino Spirit (28)	4.00
1990	Best San Jose Giants (30)	4.00
1990	Cal San Jose Giants (28)	4.00
1990	PC San Jose Giants (30)	4.00
1990	Star San Jose Giants (30)	4.00
1990	Star Sarasota White Sox (30)	3.00
1990	PC Savannah Cardinals (28)	3.00
1990	CMC Scranton Red Barons (25)	3.00
1990	PC Scranton Red Barons (24)	3.00
1990	PC Shreveport Captains (27)	4.00
1990	Star Shreveport Captains (27)	3.00
1990	Star South Atlantic League A-S (48)	6.00
1990	Best South Bend White Sox (24)	4.00
1990	GS South Bend White Sox (30)	3.00
1990	DJ Southern League A-S (50)	8.00
1990	Best Southern Oregon Athletics (30)	4.00
1990	PC Southern Oregon Athletics (30)	4.00
1990	Best Spartanburg Phillies (30)	3.00
1990	PC Spartanburg Phillies (29)	4.00
1990	Star Spartanburg Phillies (29)	3.00
1990	SP Spokane Indians (28)	5.00
1990	Best Springfield Cardinals (29)	3.00
1990	Best Springfield Cards All-Decade (36)	9.00

Year	Item	Price
1990	PC St. Catharines Blue Jays (34)	10.00
1990	Stearns St. Cloud Rox (9)	25.00
1990	Star St. Lucie Mets (31)	4.00
1990	Star St. Lucie Mets (33)	6.00
1990	Star St. Petersburg Cardinals (26)	3.00
1990	Best Stockton Ports (29)	4.00
1990	Cal Stockton Ports (29)	5.00
1990	PC Stockton Ports (29)	4.00
1990	Best Sumter Braves (30)	10.00
1990	PC Sumter Braves (30)	12.00
1990	CMC Syracuse Chiefs (28)	5.00
1990	PC Syracuse Chiefs (28)	5.00
1990	Team Syracuse Chiefs (28)	20.00
1990	CMC Tacoma Tigers (25)	4.00
1990	PC Tacoma Tigers (29)	4.00
1990	Diamond Tampa Yankees (28)	20.00
1990	GS Texas League A-S (38)	8.00
1990	CMC Tidewater Tides (30)	5.00
1990	PC Tidewater Tides (30)	5.00
1990	Team Tidewater Tides Foldout	5.00
1990	CMC Toledo Mud Hens (27)	8.00
1990	PC Toledo Mud Hens (27)	6.00
1990	CMC Tucson Toros (25)	5.00
1990	PC Tucson Toros (27)	5.00
1990	Best Tulsa Drillers All-Decade (36)	30.00
1990	PC Tulsa Drillers (28)	6.00
1990	Team Tulsa Drillers (28)	12.00
1990	Smokey USC Alumni (12)	40.00
1990	Pucko Utica Blue Sox (30)	4.00
1990	CMC Vancouver Canadians (28)	4.00
1990	PC Vancouver Canadians (28)	4.00
1990	Star Vero Beach Dodgers (32)	30.00
1990	Cal Visalia Oaks (31)	4.00
1990	PC Visalia Oaks (26)	4.00
1990	Best Waterloo Diamonds (28)	4.00
1990	PC Waterloo Diamonds (27)	3.00
1990	Star Watertown Indians (28)	3.00
1990	Best Wausau Timbers (28)	4.00
1990	PC Wausau Timbers (32)	3.00
1990	Star Wausau Timbers (29)	3.00
1990	Pucko Welland Pirates (36)	4.00
1990	Star West Palm Beach Expos (31)	4.00
1990	Star West Palm Beach Expos (34)	6.00
1990	Rock's Wichita Wranglers (29)	8.00
1990	Best Williamsport Bills (27)	4.00
1990	PC Williamsport Bills (26)	3.00
1990	Star Williamsport Bills (27)	3.00
1990	Sportsprint Winston-Salem Spirits (30)	3.00
1990	Star Winter Haven Red Sox (28)	3.00
1990	Star Winter Haven Red Sox (29)	5.00
1990	Golden Yakima Bears (37)	6.00

1991 Classic Best Promo Sheet

Four of the year's brightest minor league stars, along with spokesman Mike Schmidt, are featured on this promo sheet for Classic Best's minor league singles set. The sheet measures 7-1/2" x 7-1/8". The back is printed in black-and-white.

	MT
Uncut Sheet:	7.50

Todd Van Poppel,
Ryan Klesko, Tim Costo,
Mike Schmidt, D.J. Dozier

1991 Classic Best

Classic Best entered the single-card minor league market in 1991 with a 450-card set. The first 396 cards were issued in poly packs and later available in factory sets. Cards numbered 397-450 were only available in the factory sets. Hall of Famer Mike Schmidt, who is card #1 in the set, personally autographed 2,100 of his cards, which were inserted at the rate of one per 8,000 packs.

	MT
Complete Factory Set (450):	12.00
Complete Wax Set (396):	6.00
Common Player:	.05
Wax Pack (12):	.75
Wax Box (36):	17.50
Jumbo Pack (23):	1.00
Jumbo Box (20):	17.50

#	Player	Price
1	Mike Schmidt	.50
1a	Mike Schmidt (Autographed edition of 2,100.)	30.00
2	Kevin Roberson	.05
3	Paul Rodgers	.05
4	Marc Newfield	.05
5	Marc Ronan	.05
6	Marty Willis	.05
7	Jason Hardtke	.05
8	Matt Mieske	.05
9	Brian Johnson	.05
10	Alex Arias	.05
11	Eric Young	.05
12	Donald Harris	.05
13	Bruce Chick	.05
14	Brian Williams	.05
15	Briarl Cornelius	.05
16	Brian Giles	.10
17	Brad Ausmus	.05
18	Ivan Cruz	.05
19	Keven Flora	.05
20	Robbie Katzaroff	.05
21	Randy Knorr	.05
22	Micky Henson	.05
23	Chris Haney	.05
24	Jeff Mutis	.05
25	Barry Winford	.05
26	Ray Giannelli	.05
27	Donovan Osborne	.05
28	Ruben Gonzalez	.05
29	Howard Battle	.05
30	Greg O'Halloran	.05
31	Ben Van Ryn	.05
32	Rick Hulsman	.05
33	Jose Valentin	.05
34	Jose Zambrano	.05
35	John Gross	.05
36	Jessie Hollins	.05
37	Kevin Scott	.05
38	Kerwin Moore	.05
39	Eric Albright	.05
40	Ernesto Rodriguez	.05
41	Reggie Sanders	.05
42	Henry Werland	.05
43	Boo Moore	.05
44	Mike Messerly	.05
45	Mike Lansing	.05
46	Mike Gardella	.05
47	Mo Sanford	.05
48	Tavo Alvarez	.05
49	Nick Davis	.05
50	Charlie Hillemann	.05
51	Jeff Darwin	.05
52	Reid Cornelius	.05
53	Matt Rambo	.05
54	Rich Batchelor	.05
55	Ricky Gutierrez	.05
56	Rod Bolton	.05
57	Pat Bryant	.05
58	Hugh Walker	.05
59	Keith Schmidt	.05
60	Ceasar Morillo	.05
61	Gabe White	.05
62	Davy (Javy) Lopez	.05
63	Carlos Delgado	1.00
64	John Johnstone	.05
65	Andres Berumen	.05
66	Brian Kowitz	.05
67	Shane Reynolds (Photo actually Orlando Miller.)	.10
68	Jeromy Burnitz	.05
69	Scott Bryant	.05
70	Jason McFarlin	.05
71	John Conner	.05

#	Player	Price
72	Garrett Jenkins	.05
73	Greg Kobza	.05
74	Mark Swope	.05
75	Jerome Williams	.05
76	Jeff Bonner	.05
77	Jermaine Swinton	.05
78	John Cohen	.05
79	Johnny Calzado	.05
80	Juan Andujar	.05
81	Paul Ellis	.05
82	Paul Gonzalez	.05
83	Scott Taylor	.05
84	Stan Spencer	.05
85	Steve Martin	.05
86	Scott Cepicky	.05
87	Max Aleys	.05
88	Michael Brown (Photo actually Matt Brown.)	
89	Jim Waggoner	.05
90	Mickey Rivers Jr.	.05
91	Nate Crowmwell	.05
92	Carlos Perez	.05
93	Matt Brown (Photo actually Michael Brown.)	.05
94	Jose Hernandez	.05
95	Johnny Ruffin	.05
96	Kevin Jordan	.05
97	Manny Alexander	.05
98	Tony Longmire	.05
99	Lonell Roberts	.05
100	Doug Lindsey	.05
101	Al Harley	.05
102	Jerry Thurston	.05
103	Mike Williams	.05
104	David Bell	.05
105	Greg Johnson	.05
106	Roger Salkeld	.05
107	Mike Milchin	.05
108	Jeff Kent	.50
109	Tim Stargell	.05
110	Miah Bradbury	.05
111	Paul Fletcher	.05
112	Steven Rolen	.05
113	Tony Spires	.05
114	Kevin Tolar	.05
115	Kevin Dattola	.05
116	Sherman Obando	.05
117	Sean Ryan	.05
118	Carlos Mota	.05
119	Steve Karsay	.05
120	Kelly Lifgren	.05
121	Damion Easley	.05
122	Fred Russell	.05
123	Freddie Davis Jr.	.05
124	Dave Zancanaro	.05
125	Jeff Jackson	.05
126	Steve Pegues	.05
127	Gerald Williams	.05
128	Eric Helfand	.05
129	Gary Painter	.05
130	Colin Ryan	.05
131	Randy Brown	.05
132	Andy Fox	.05
133	Mike Ogliaruso	.05
134	Matt Franco	.05
135	Willie Ansley	.05
136	Ivan Rodriguez	1.00
137	Anthony Lewis	.05
138	Bill Wertz	.05
139	Tom Kinney	.05
140	Brad Hassinger	.05
141	Elliot Gray	.05
142	Clemente Alvarez	.05
143	Mike Hankins	.05
144	Jim Haller	.05
145	Manuel Martinez	.05
146	Nilson Robledo	.05
147	Rex DeLa Nuez	.05
148	Steve Bethea	.05
149	Oscar Munoz	.05
150	Sam Militello	.05
151	Phil Hiatt	.05
152	Alberto de los Santos	.05
153	Darrell Sherman	.05
154	Henry Mercedes	.05
155	David Holdridge	.05
156	Sean Ross	.05
157	Brandon Wilson	.05
158	William Pennyfeather	.05
159	Derek Parks	.05
160	Troy O'Leary	.05
161	Genaro Campusano	.05
162	Robbie Beckett	.05
163	Chris Burton	.05
164	Jeff Williams	.05
165	John Massarelli	.05
166	John Kelly	.05
167	Jim Wiley	.05
168	Mark Mitchelson	.05
169	Jeff McNeely	.05
170	Keith Kimberlin	.05
171	Mike DeKneef	.05
172	Rusty Greer	.05
173	Pete Castellano	.05
174	Paul Torres	.05
175	Rod McCall	.05
176	Jim Bullinger	.05
177	Brian Champion	.05
178	Greg Hunter	.05
179	Luis Galindez	.05
180	Rodney Eldridge	.05
181	Rudy Pemberton	.05
182	Russ Davis	.05
183	Cristobal Colon	.05
184	Scott Bream	.05
185	Tim Nedin	.05
186	Joe Ausanlo	.05
187	Shanhon Withem	.05

#	Player	Price
188	Mike Oquist	.05
189	Pete Young	.05
190	Paul Carey	.05
191	Chris Gies	.05
192	Gar Finnvold	.05
193	Greg Martin	.05
194	Oreste Marrero	.05
195	Jim Thome	1.00
196	Bill Ostermeyer	.05
197	David Hulse	.05
198	Damon Buford	.05
199	Jonathan Hurst	.05
200	Rich Tunison	.05
201	Tom Nevers	.05
202	Tracy Sanders	.05
203	Troy Buckley	.05
204	Todd Guglanna	.05
205	Tim Laker	.05
206	Dean Locklear (Photo actually Jon Jenkins.)	.05
207	Lee Tinsley	.05
208	Jose Velez	.05
209	Gregg Zaun	.05
210	Bill Ashley	.05
211	Gary Caraballo	.05
212	Kiki Jones	.05
213	Dave Wrona	.05
214	Michael Carter	.05
215	Leon Glenn Jr.	.05
216	Glenn Sutko	.05
217	Pat Howell	.05
218	Austin Manahan	.05
219	Jon Jenkins	.05
220	Brook Fordyce	.05
221	Kevin Rodgers	.05
222	David Allen	.05
223	Kurt Archer	.05
224	Keith Mitchell	.05
225	Bruce Schreiber	.05
226	Greg Blosser	.05
227	Dave Nillsson	.05
228	Fred Colley	.05
229	Marc Lipson	.05
230	Jay Gainer	.05
231	Sean Cheetham	.05
232	Tim Howard	.05
233	Steve Hosey	.05
234	Javier Ocasio	.05
235	Ricky Rhodes	.05
236	Mark Griffin	.05
237	Scott Shockey	.05
238	T.R. Lewis	.05
239	Kevin Young	.05
240	Robb Nen	.05
241	Steve Dunn	.05
242	Tommy Taylor	.05
243	Keith Valrie	.05
244	Mateo Ozuna	.05
245	Scott Bullett	.05
246	Anthony Brown	.05
247	Phil Leftwich	.05
248	Cliff Garrett	.05
249	Wade Fyock	.05
250	Shayne Rea	.05
251	Royce Clayton	.05
252	Martin Martinez	.05
253	Dave Patterson	.05
254	Robert Fitzpatrick	.05
255	John Jackson	.05
256	Enoch Simmons	.05
257	Dave Proctor	.05
258	Garret Anderson	.15
259	Mark Delesandro	.05
260	Ken Edenfield	.05
261	Tom Raffo	.05
262	Tim Cecil	.05
263	Bobby Magallanes	.05
264	Vince Castaldo	.05
265	Terry Burrows	.05
266	Victor Madrigal	.05
267	Tyler Houston	.05
268	Chipper Jones	1.50
269	Terry Bradshaw	.05
270	Jalal Leach	.05
271	Jose Ventura	.05
272	Derek Lee	.05
273	Derek Reld	.05
274	David Wilson	.05
275	Patrick Rapp	.05
276	John Roper	.05
277	Rogello Nunez	.05
278	Fred White	.05
279	J.T. Snow	.10
280	Pedro Astacio	.05
281	Corey Thomas	.05
282	Chris Johnson	.05
283	Ignacio Duran	.05
284	Dave Fleming	.05
285	Wilson Alvarez	.05
286	Eric Booker	.05
287	John Ericks	.05
288	Don Peters	.05
289	Ed Ferm	.05
290	Mike Lieberthal	.10
291	John Jaha	.05
292	Bryan Baar	.05
293	Archie Corbin	.05
294	Kevin Tatar	.05
295	Shea Wardwell	.05
296	Hipilito Pichardo	.05
297	Curtis Leskanic	.05
298	Sam August (Photo actually Jeff Juden.)	.05
299	Tim Pugh	.05
300	Mike Huyler	.05
301	Mark Parnell	.05
302	Jeff Juden (Photo actually Shane Reynolds.)	.10

303	Carl Sullivan	.05
304	Tyrone Kingwood	.05
305	Glenn Carter	.05
306	Tom Fischer	.05
307	Braulio Castillo	.05
308	Bob McCreary	.05
309	Ty Kovach	.05
310	Troy Salvior	.05
311	Mike Weimerskirch	.05
312	Chistopher Hatcher	.05
313	Bryan Smith	.05
314	John Patterson	.05
315	Scooter Tucker	.05
316	Ray Callari	.05
317	Mike Moberg	.05
318	Midre Cummings	.05
319	Todd Ritchie	.05
320	Eric Christopherson	.05
321	Adam Hyzdu	.05
322	Andres Duncan	.05
323	Mike Myers	.05
324	Salomon Torres	.05
325	Tony Gilmore	.05
326	Walter Trice	.05
327	Tom Redington	.05
328	Terry Taylor	.05
329	Tim Salmon	.25
330	Dan Masteller	.05
331	Mark Wohlers	.05
332	Willie Smith	.05
333	Todd Jones	.05
334	Alan Zinter	.05
335	Arthur Rhodes	.05
336	Toby Borland	.05
337	Shawn Whalen	.05
338	Scott Sanders	.05
339	Bill Meury	.05
340	Amadoz Arias	.05
341	Denny Hoppe	.05
342	Dave Telgheder	.05
343	Paul Bruno	.05
344	Paul Russo	.05
345	Rich Becker (Photo actually Tim Persing.)	.10
346	Steve Vondran	.05
347	Rich Langford	.05
348	Ron Lockett	.05
349	Sam Taylor	.05
350	Willie Greene	.05
351	Tom Houk	.05
352	Lance Painter	.05
353	Dan Wilson	.05
354	John Kuehl	.05
355	Pedro Martinez	1.50
356	John Byington	.05
357	Scott Freeman	.05
358	Bo Dodson	.05
359	Julian Vasquez	.05
360	Rondell White	.10
361	Aaron Small	.05
362	Doug Fitzer	.05
363	Billy White	.05
364	Jeff Tuss	.05
365	Jeff Barry	.05
366	Craig Pueschner	.05
367	Julio Bruno	.05
368	Jamie Dismuke	.05
369	K.C. Gillium	.05
370	Jason Klonoski	.05
371	Tim Persing (Photo actually Rich Becker.)	.05
372	Mark Borcherding	.05
373	Larry Luebbers	.05
374	Carlos Fermin	.05
375	Charlie Rogers	.05
376	Ramon Caraballo	.05
377	Orlando Miller (Photo actually Sam August.)	.05
378	Joey James	.05
379	Dan Rogers	.05
380	Jon Shave	.05
381	Frank Bolick	.05
382	Frank Seminara	.05
383	Mel Wearing Jr.	.05
384	Zak Shinall	.05
385	Sterling Hitchcock	.05
386	Todd Van Poppel	.05
387	D.J. Dozier	.05
388	Ryan Klesko	.10
389	Tim Costo	.05
390	Brad Pennington	.05
391	Checklist 1-66	.05
392	Checklist 67-132	.05
393	Checklist 133-198	.05
394	Checklist 199-264	.05
395	Checklist 265-330	.05
396	Checklist 331-396	.05
397	Frank Rodriguez	.05
398	Frank Jacons	.05
399	Mike Kelly	.05
400	David McCarty	.05
401	Scott Stahoviak	.05
402	Doug Glanville	.05
403	Curt Krippner	.05
404	Joe Vitiello	.05
405	Justin Thompson	.05
406	Trever Miller	.05
407	Tarrick Brock	.05
408	Eddie Williams	.05
409	Scott Ruffcorn	.05
410	Chris Durkin	.05
411	Jim Kewis	.05
412	Calvin Reese	.05
413	Toby Rumfield	.05
414	Brent Gates	.05
415	Mike Neill	.05
416	Tyler Green	.05
417	Ron Allen	.05

418	Larry Thomas Jr.	.05
419	Chris Weinke	.25
420	Matt Brewer	.05
421	Dax Jones	.05
422	Jon Farrell	.05
423	Dan Jones	.05
424	Eduardo Perez	.05
425	Rodney Pedraza	.05
426	Tom McKinnon	.05
427	Al Watson	.05
428	Herbert Perry	.05
429	Shawn Estes	.05
430	Tommy Adams	.05
431	Mike Grace	.05
432	Tyson Godfrey	.05
433	Andy Hartung	.05
434	Shawn Livsey	.05
435	Earl Cunningham	.05
436	Scott Lydy	.05
437	Aaron Sele	.05
438	Tim Costo	.05
439	Tanyon Sturtze	.05
440	Ed Ramos	.05
441	Buck McNabb	.05
442	Scott Hatteberg	.05
443	Brian Barber	.05
444	Julian Heredia	.05
445	Chris Pritchett	.05
446	Bubba Smith	.05
447	Shawn Purdy	.05
448	Jeff Borski	.05
449	Jamie Gonzalez	.05
450	Checklist 397-450	.05

1991 Classic Best Gold Bonus

Each jumbo pack of Classic Best cards contains one Gold Bonus card of a top prospect. The cards are virtually identical to the regular-issue version except for the use of a gold-foil oval for the player's name. Backs have a "BC" prefix to the card number.

		MT
Complete Set (20):		4.00
Common Player:		.10
1	Mike Schmidt	1.00
2	Marc Newfield	.10
3	Matt Mieske	.10
4	Reggie Sanders	.10
5	Jeromy Burnitz	.15
6	Todd Van Poppel	.10
7	Ivan Rodriguez	2.00
8	Sam Militello	.10
9	Jim Thome	2.00
10	Brook Fordyce	.10
11	Dave Nilsson	.10
12	Royce Clayton	.10
13	Mark Wohlers	.10
14	Arthur Rhodes	.10
15	Ryan Klesko	.10
16	Mike Kelly	.10
17	Frankie Rodriguez	.10
18	David McCarty	.10
19	Tyler Green	.10
20	Eduardo Perez	.10

1991 Classic Draft Picks Promos

Multi-colored backs marked "For Promotional Purposes Only" differentiate the promos for Classic's second annual baseball draft picks set from the regularly issued cards.

1991 Classic Draft Picks

After releasing a 26-card draft pick set in 1990, Classic returned with a 50-card issue for 1991. A reported 330,000 hobby sets were produced, along with 165,000 sets for the retail market. Card fronts feature gray and maroon borders surrounding full-color photos and the Classic logo in the upper-left corner. A special bonus card of Frankie Rodriguez is also included with the set. Each set includes a certificate of authenticity.

		MT
Complete Set (50):		4.00
Common Player:		.05
Wax Box (36):		3.00
1	Brien Taylor	.05
2	Mike Kelly	.05
3	David McCarty	.05
4	Dmitri Young	.05
5	Joe Vitiello	.05
6	Mark Smith	.05
7	Tyler Green	.05
8	Shawn Estes	.05
9	Doug Glanville	.05
10	Manny Ramirez	3.00
11	Cliff Floyd	.05
12	Tyrone Hill	.05
13	Eduardo Perez	.05
14	Al Shirley	.05
15	Benji Gil	.05
16	Calvin Reese	.05
17	Allen Watson	.05
18	Brian Barber	.05
19	Aaron Sele	.05
20	Jon Farrell	.05
21	Scott Ruffcorn	.05
22	Brent Gates	.05
23	Scott Stahoviak	.05
24	Tom McKinnon	.05
25	Shawn Livsey	.05
26	Jason Pruitt	.05
27	Greg Anthony	.05
28	Justin Thompson	.05
29	Steve Whitaker	.05
30	Jorge Fabregas	.05
31	Jeff Ware	.05
32	Bobby Jones	.05
33	J.J. Johnson	.05
34	Mike Rossiter	.05
35	Dan Chowlowsky	.05
36	Jimmy Gonzalez	.05
37	Trever Miller	.05
38	Scott Hatteberg	.05
39	Mike Groppuso	.05
40	Ryan Long	.05
41	Eddie Williams	.05
42	Mike Durant	.05
43	Buck McNabb	.05
44	Jimmy Lewis	.05
45	Eddie Ramos	.05
46	Terry Horn	.05
47	Jon Barnes	.05
48	Shawn Curran	.05
49	Tommy Adams	.05
50	Trevor Mallory	.05
---	Frankie Rodriguez (Bonus card)	.05

1991 Classic Four Sport (Baseball)

Late in 1991, Classic released a four-sport draft picks set of 230 base cards, 10 foil "Limited Print" cards and more than 60,000 autographed cards seeded one per 260 packs. Cards have color photos on front with wide mottled blue-gray borders. A "wax seal" in red at upper-left carries the set's logo. Player name and position are in black at the bottom. Backs are printed in color with biographical

data, high school or college stats and career highlights. Twenty percent of the 25,000 cases printed were an English-French version, which carries a premium of about a 50 percent premium. Only the cards featuring baseball players are checklisted here.

		MT
Common Card:		.05
Wax Box (36):		15.00
1	Russell Maryland, Brien Taylor, Larry Johnson, Eric Lindros Future Stars	.05
51	Brien Taylor	.05
52	Mike Kelly	.05
53	David McCarty	.05
54	Dmitri Young	.05
55	Joe Vitiello	.05
56	Mark Smith	.05
57	Tyler Green	.05
58	Shawn Estes (Photo reversed.)	.15
59	Doug Glanville	.05
60	Manny Ramirez	3.00
61	Cliff Floyd	.10
62	Tyrone Hill	.05
63	Eduardo Perez	.05
64	Al Shirley	.05
65	Benji Gil	.05
66	Calvin Reese	.10
67	Allen Watson	.05
68	Brian Barber	.05
69	Aaron Sele	.05
70	John Farrell	.05
71	Scott Ruffcorn	.05
72	Brent Gates	.05
73	Scott Stahoviak	.05
74	Tom McKinnon	.05
75	Shawn Livsey	.05
76	Jason Pruitt	.05
77	Greg Anthony	.05
78	Justin Thompson	.05
79	Steve Whitaker	.05
80	Jorge Fabregas	.05
81	Jeff Ware	.05
82	Bobby Jones	.05
83	J.J. Johnson	.05
84	Mike Rossiter	.05
85	Dan Chowlowsky	.05
86	Jimmy Gonzalez	.05
87	Trever Miller	.05
88	Scott Hatteberg	.05
89	Mike Groppuso	.05
90	Ryan Long	.05
91	Eddie Williams	.05
92	Mike Durant	.05
93	Buck McNabb	.05
94	Jimmy Lewis	.05
95	Eddie Ramos	.05
96	Terry Horn	.05
97	John Barnes	.05
98	Shawn Curran	.05
99	Tommy Adams	.05
100	Trevor Mallory	.05
101	Frankie Rodriguez	.05
218	Joe Hamilton	.05
219	Marc Kroon	.05
225	Shawn Green	1.50
---	Shawn Green (Promo)	5.00
LP7	Brien Taylor (Limited Print silver foil.)	.25

1991 Classic Four Sport (Baseball) Autographed

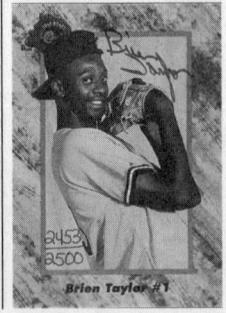

Approximately 60 of the more than 200 players in the 1991 Classic Four Sport draft picks issue autographed as many as 2,600 cards apiece for insertion as random foil-pack inserts; in all more than 60,000 autographed cards were distributed. The number in parentheses in the listings here indicates the number of cards reportedly signed by each player. Only the baseball players are listed here.

		MT
Common Player:		3.00
51	Brien Taylor (2,600)	4.50
52	Mike Kelly (2,600)	3.00
53	David McCarty (2,450)	3.00
54	Dmitri Young (2,600)	5.00
55	Joe Vitiello (1,900)	3.00
56	Mark Smith (1,700)	3.00
58	Shawn Estes (2,000) (Photo reversed.))	5.00
59	Doug Glanville (2,000)	3.00
61	Cliff Floyd (2,000)	5.00
62	Tyrone Hill (1,000)	3.00
63	Eduardo Perez (950)	3.00
101	Frankie Rodriguez	4.00
218	Joe Hamilton (2,000)	3.00

1991 Front Row Draft Picks Promos

These cards were issued to introduce and advertise the premier edition of Front Row draft picks. They are similar in format to the regular-issue cards except for the promo notice/ad on back.

		MT
Complete Set (10):		2.00
Common Player:		.25
(1)	Chris Durkin	.25
(2)	John Farrell	.25
(3)	Scott Hatteberg	.25
(4)	Mike Neill	.25
(5)	Frankie Rodriguez	.25
(6)	Mike Rossiter	.25
(7)	Scott Ruffcorn	.25
(8)	Chad Schoenvogel	.25
(9)	Aaron Sele	.25
(10)	Kevin Stocker	.25

1991 Front Row Draft Picks

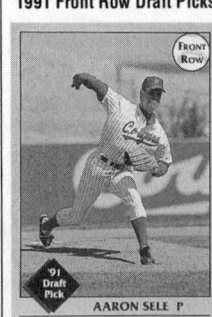

A total of 240,000 of these sets were produced. The bonus card in the set was redeemable by Front Row for a special Frankie Rodriguez card. The first 120,000 collectors returning bonus cards also received Front Row's mini-update set. The cards feature full-color photos on both sides. Each set includes a numbered certificate of authenticity. A silver edition of 7,500 sets and a gold edition of 2,500 sets were also produced.

		MT
Complete Set (50):		1.00
Common Player:		.05
Silver:		3X
Gold:		20X
1	Frankie Rodriguez	.05

2	Aaron Sele	.05
3	Chad Schoenvogel	.05
4	Scott Ruffcorn	.05
5	Dan Chowlowski	.05
6	Gene Schall	.05
7	Trever Miller	.05
8	Chris Durkin	.05
9	Mike Neill	.05
10	Kevin Stocker	.05
11	Bobby Jones	.05
12	Jon Farrell	.05
13	Ronnie Allen	.05
14	Mike Rossiter	.05
15	Scott Hatteberg	.05
16	Rodney Pedraza	.05
17	Mike Durant	.05
18	Ryan Long	.05
19	Greg Anthony	.05
20	Jon Barnes	.05
21	Brian Barber	.05
22	Brent Gates	.05
23	Calvin Reese	.05
24	Terry Horn	.05
25	Scott Stahoviak	.05
26	Jason Pruitt	.05
27	Shawn Curran	.05
28	Jimmy Lewis	.05
29	Alex Ochoa	.05
30	Joe Deberry	.05
31	Justin Thompson	.05
32	Jimmy Gonzalez	.05
33	Eddie Ramos	.05
34	Tyler Green	.05
35	Toby Rumfield	.05
36	Dave Doorneweerd	.05
37	Jeff Hostetler	.05
38	Shawn Livsey	.05
39	Mike Groppuso	.05
40	Steve Whitaker	.05
41	Tom McKinnon	.05
42	Buck McNabb	.05
43	Al Shirley	.05
44	Allan Watson	.05
45	Bill Bliss	.05
46	Todd Hollandsworth	.05
47	Manny Ramirez	1.50
48	J.J. Johnson	.05
49	Cliff Floyd	.10
50a	Bonus card	.05
50(b)	Benji Gil	.05
51	Herb Perry	.05
52	Terrik Brock	.05
53	Trevor Mallory	.05
54	Chris Pritchett	.05
FR1	Frank Rodriguez (Pitching)	.05
FR2	Frank Rodriguez (Pitching)	.05
FR3	Frank Rodriguez (Batting)	.05
FR4	Frank Rodriguez (Pitching)	.05
FR5	Frank Rodriguez (Batting)	.05

1991 Front Row Draft Picks Autographs

The exact scope of the autographed version of player cards from this set is not known including the number of players whose cards be found signed and their specific manner of distribution.

		MT
47	Manny Ramirez (1,900)	20.00
49	Cliff Floyd (1,500)	3.00

1991 Front Row Draft Picks Update

These five cards were distributed to the first 120,000 collectors redeeming a bonus card from the 1991 draft picks set. Fronts have color photos with metallic silver-foil borders. Backs have a color photo of the player as a boy, plus personal data, high school and/or college stats and career achievements.

	MT
Complete Set (5):	.50
Common Player:	.10
50 Benji Gil	.10
51 Herb Perry	.10
52 Terrik Brock	.10
53 Trevor Mallory	.10
54 Chris Pritchett	.10

1991 Front Row Frankie Rodriguez Signature Cards

FRANKIE RODRIGUEZ

This series of five cards was sold in both autographed and unautographed sets, complete with certificates of authenticity, each with an individual serial number from within an edition of 10,000. The 2-1/2" x 3-1/2" cards are UV coated front and back. Fronts have color pitching and batting game-action photos. Backs of cards #1-4 have information on Rodriguez' junior college career, the back of card #5 has another action photo.

	MT
Complete Set (5):	1.00
Complete Set, W/Auto. (5):	3.00
1-5 Frankie Rodriguez	.25

1991 Impel/Line Drive Previews

To introduce its forthcoming series of Class AA and Class AAA minor league wax product, Impel sent dealers this six-card set. Numbered the same as the player's cards in either the AA or AAA issue, the previews differ from the issued versions only in slight variations in photo cropping.

	MT
Complete Set (6):	2.00
Common Player:	.25
47 Greg Tubbs (AAA)	.25
79 Tim Costo (AA)	.25
167 Reggie Sanders (AA)	.25
221 Rick Wilkins (AAA)	.25
422 Hugh Walker (AA)	.25
573 Anthony Young (AAA)	.25

1991 Impel/Line Drive Pre-Rookie AA

RYAN KLESKO

Impel followed its successful AAA wax series with a 650-card AA wax series consisting of 25 players from each team. Like the AAA series, a checklist for the AA series was available from the company. Due to a scarcity of certain cards in inventory and additional labor costs to dealers, consumers can be

expected to pay a minimum of $4-6 for team sets made from this product. Line Drive team sets sold at the stadiums included team checklist cards.

	MT
Complete Set (650):	7.00
Common Player:	.05
Wax Box (36):	15.00

1	Andy Cook	.05
2	Russell Davis	.05
3	Bobby DeJardin	.05
4	Mike Draper	.05
5	Victor Garcia	.05
6	Mike Gardella	.05
7	Cullen Hartzog	.05
8	Jay Knoblauh	.05
9	Billy Masse	.05
10	Jeff Livesey	.05
11	Edward Martel	.05
12	Vince Phillips	.05
13	Tom Popplewell	.05
14	Jerry Rub	.05
15	Dave Silvestri	.05
16	Tom Newell	.05
17	Willie Smith	.05
18	J.T. Snow	.10
19	Don Stanford	.05
20	Larry Stanford	.05
21	John Toale	.05
22	Hector Vargas	.05
23	Gerald Williams	.05
24	Dan Radison	.05
25	Dave Jorn, Bob Mariano (Coaches)	.05
26	Frank Abreu	.05
27	Cliff Brannon	.05
28	Greg Carmona	.05
29	Ric Christian	.05
30	John Ericks	.05
31	Steve Fanning	.05
32	Joey Fernandez	.05
33	Jose Fernandez	.05
34	Mike Flore	.05
35	David Grimes	.05
36	Dale Kisten	.05
37	John Lepley	.05
38	Luis Martinez	.05
39	Mike Milchin	.05
40	Donovan Osborne	.05
41	Gabriel Ozuna	.05
42	Lee Plemel	.05
43	Don Prybylinski	.05
44	John Sellick	.05
45	Jeff Shireman	.05
46	Brian Stone	.05
47	Charlie White	.05
48	Dennis Wiseman	.05
49	Joe Pettini	.05
50	Scott Melvin, Marty Mason	.05
51	Wilson Alvarez	.05
52	Wayne Busby	.05
53	Darrin Campbell	.05
54	Mark Chasey	.05
55	Ron Coomer	.05
56	Argenis Cortez	.05
57	Mike Davino	.05
58	Lindsay Foster	.05
59	Ramon Garcia	.05
60	Kevin Garner	.05
61	Jeff Gay	.05
62	Chris Howard	.05
63	John Hudek	.05
64	Scott Jaster	.05
65	Bo Kennedy	.05
66	Derek Lee	.05
67	Frank Merigliano	.05
68	Scott Middaugh	.05
69	Javier Ocasio	.05
70	Kinnis Pledger	.05
71	Greg Roth	.05
72	Aubrey Waggoner	.05
73	Jose Ventura	.05
74	Tony Franklin	.05
75	Rick Peterson, Pat Roessler, Sam Hairston	.05
76	Ramon Bautista	.05
77	Eric Bell	.05
78	Jim Bruske	.05
79	Tim Costo	.05
80	Mike Curtis	.05
81	Jerry DiPoto	.05
82	Daren Epley	.05
83	Sam Ferrelli	.05
84	Garland Kiser	.05
85	Ty Kovach	.05
86	Tom Kramer	.05
87	Molan Lane	.05
88	Jesse Levis	.05
89	Carlos Martinez	.05
90	Jeff Mutis	.05
91	Rouglas Odor	.05
92	Gary Resetar	.05
93	Greg Roscoe	.05
94	Miguel Sabino	.05
95	Bernie Tatis	.05
96	Jim Thome	3.00
97	Ken Ramos	.05
98	Ken Whitfield	.05
99	Ken Bolek	.05
100	Dave Keller	.05
101	Steve Adams	.05
102	Stan Fansler	.05
103	Mandy Romero	.05
104	Terry Crowley Jr.	.05

105	Chip Duncan	.05
106	Greg Edge	.05
107	Chris Estep	.05
108	Carl Hamilton	.05
109	Lee Hancock	.05
110	Tim Hines	.05
111	Mike Huyler	.05
112	Paul Miller	.05
113	Pete Murphy	.05
114	Darwin Pennye	.05
115	Mike Roesler	.05
116	Bruce Schreiber	.05
117	Greg Sparks	.05
118	Dennis Tafoya	.05
119	Tim Wakefield	.05
120	Ben Webb	.05
121	John Wehner	.05
122	Ed Yacopino	.05
123	Eddie Zambrano	.05
124	Marc Bombard	.05
125	Trent Jewett, Spin Williams	.05
126	Alex Arias	.05
127	Paul Blair	.05
128	Jim Bullinger	.05
129	Dick Canan	.05
130	Rusty Crockett	.05
131	Steve DiBartolomeo	.05
132	John Gardner	.05
133	Henry Gomez	.05
134	Ty Griffin	.05
135	Shannon Jones	.05
136	Mike Knapp	.05
137	Tim Parker	.05
138	Elvin Paulino	.05
139	Fernando Ramsey	.05
140	Kevin Roberson	.05
141	John Salles	.05
142	Mike Sodders	.05
143	Bill St. Peter	.05
144	Julio Strauss	.05
145	Scott Taylor	.05
146	Tim Watkins	.05
147	Doug Welch	.05
148	Billy White	.05
149	Jay Loviglio	.05
150	Rick Kranitz	.05
151	Rick Allen	.05
152	Mike Anderson	.05
153	Bobby Ayala	.05
154	Pete Beeler	.05
155	Jeff Branson	.05
156	Scott Bryant	.05
157	Bill Dodd	.05
158	Steve Foster	.05
159	Victor Garcia	.05
160	Frank Kremblas	.05
161	Greg Lonigro	.05
162	Dave McAuliffe	.05
163	Steve McCarthy	.05
164	Scott Pose	.05
165	Tim Pugh	.05
166	Bill Risley	.05
167	Reggie Sanders	.05
168	Mo Sanford	.05
169	Scott Sellner	.05
170	Jerry Spradlin	.05
171	Glenn Sutko	.05
172	Todd Trafton	.05
173	Bernie Walker	.05
174	Jim Tracy	.05
175	Mike Griffin	.05
176	Shon Ashley	.05
177	John Byington	.05
178	Mark Chapman	.05
179	Jim Czajkowski	.05
180	Ruben Escalera	.05
181	Craig Faulkner	.05
182	Tim Fortugno	.05
183	Don Gordon	.05
184	Mitch Hannahs	.05
185	Steve Lienhard	.05
186	Dave Jacas	.05
187	Kenny Jackson	.05
188	John Jaha	.05
189	Chris Johnson	.05
190	Mark Kiefer	.05
191	Pat Listach	.05
192	Tom McGraw	.05
193	Angel Miranda	.05
194	Dave Nilsson	.05
195	Jeff Schwarz	.05
196	Steve Sparks	.05
197	Jim Tatum	.05
198	Brandy Vann	.05
199	Dave Huppert	.05
200	Paul Lindblad	.05
201	Rich Casarotti	.05
202	Vinnie Castilla	.10
203	Brian Champion	.05
204	Popeye Cole	.05
205	Johnny Cuevas	.05
206	Brian Deak	.05
207	Pat Gomez	.05
208	Judd Johnson	.05
209	Ryan Klesko	.10
210	Rich Maloney	.05
211	Al Martin	.05
212	Keith Mitchell	.05
213	Rick Morris	.05
214	Ben Rivera	.05
215	Napoleon Robinson	.05
216	Boi Rodriguez	.05
217	Sean Ross	.05
218	Earl Sanders	.05
219	Scott Taylor	.05
220	Lee Upshaw	.05
221	Preston Watson	.05

222	Turk Wendell	.05
223	Mark Wohlers	.05
224	Chris Chamblis	.05
225	Terry Harper, Bill Slack, Randy Ingle	.05
226	Jeff Bumgarner	.05
227	Stacey Burdick	.05
228	Paul Carey	.05
229	Bobby Dickerson	.05
230	Roy Gilbert	.05
231	Ricky Gutierrez	.05
232	Tim Holland	.05
233	Stacy Jones	.05
234	Tyrone Kingwood	.05
235	Mike Lehman	.05
236	Rod Lofton	.05
237	Kevin Hickey	.05
238	Joel McKeon	.05
239	Scott Meadows	.05
240	Steve Luebber	.05
241	Mike Oquist	.05
242	Ozzie Peraza	.05
243	Tim Raley	.05
244	Arthur Rhodes	.25
245	Doug Robbins	.05
246	Ken Shamburg	.05
247	Todd Stephan	.05
248	Jack Voight	.05
249	Jerry Narron	.05
250	Joe Durham	.05
251	Chris Cassels	.05
252	Archie Clanfrocco (Archi)	.05
253	Dan Freed	.05
254	Greg Fulton	.05
255	Chris Haney	.05
256	Cesar Hernandez	.05
257	Richard Holsman	.05
258	Rob Katzaroff	.05
259	Bryan Kosco	.05
260	Ken Lake	.05
261	Hector Rivera	.05
262	Chris Marchok	.05
263	Chris Martin	.05
264	Matt Maysey	.05
265	Omer Munoz	.05
266	Bob Natal	.05
267	Chris Pollack	.05
268	F.P. Santangelo	.05
269	Joe Siddall	.05
270	Stan Spencer	.05
271	Matt Stairs	.05
272	David Wainhouse	.05
273	Pete Young	.05
274	Mike Quade	.05
275	Joe Kerrigan, Pete Dalena	.05
276	Marco Armas	.05
277	Bob Bafia	.05
278	Dean Borrelli	.05
279	John Briscoe	.05
280	James Buccheri	.05
281	Tom Carcione	.05
282	Joel Chimelis	.05
283	Fred Cooley	.05
284	Russ Cormier	.05
285	Matt Grott	.05
286	Dwayne Hosey	.05
287	Chad Kuhn	.05
288	Dave Latter	.05
289	Francisco Matos	.05
290	Gavin Osteen	.05
291	Tim Peek	.05
292	Don Peters	.05
293	Scott Shockey	.05
294	Will Tejada	.05
295	Lee Tinsley	.05
296	Todd Van Poppel	.05
297	Darryl Vice	.05
298	Dave Zancanaro	.05
299	Casey Parsons	.05
300	Bert Bradley	.05
301	Frank Carey	.05
302	Larry Carter	.05
303	Royce Clayton	.05
304	Tom Ealy	.05
305	Juan Guerrero	.05
306	Bryan Hickerson	.05
307	Steve Hosey	.05
308	Tom Hostetler	.05
309	Erik Johnson	.05
310	Dan Lewis	.05
311	Paul McClellan	.05
312	Jim McNamara	.05
313	Kevin Meier	.05
314	Jim Myers	.05
315	Dave Patterson	.05
316	John Patterson	.05
317	Jim Pena	.05
318	Dan Rambo	.05
319	Steve Reed	.05
320	Kevin Rogers	.05
321	Reuben Smiley	.05
322	Scooter Tucker	.05
323	Pete Weber	.05
324	Bill Evers	.05
325	Tony Taylor, Todd Oakes	.05
326	Fernando Arguelles	.05
327	Shawn Barton	.05
328	Jim Blueberg	.05
329	Frank Bolick	.05
330	Bret Boone	1.00
331	Jim Bowie	.05
332	Jim Campanis	.05
333	Gary Eave	.05
334	David Evans	.05
335	Fernando Figueroa	.05
336	Dave Fleming	.05
337	Ruben Gonzalez	.05
338	Mike McDonald	.05

339	Jeff Nelson	.05
340	Jim Newlin	.05
341	Ken Pennington	.05
342	Mike Pitz	.05
343	Dave Richards	.05
344	Roger Salkeld	.05
345	Jack Smith	.05
346	Tim Stargell	.05
347	Brian Turang	.05
348	Ted Williams	.05
349	Jim Nettles	.05
350	Bobby Cuellar, Lem Pilkinton	.05
351	Pete Blohm	.05
352	Domingo Cedeno	.05
353	Nate Cromwell	.05
354	Jesse Cross	.05
355	Juan De La Rosa	.05
356	Bobby LeLoach	.05
357	Ray Giannelli	.05
358	Darren Hall	.05
359	Mark Young	.05
360	Jeff Kent	.25
361	Randy Knorr	.05
362	Jose Monzon	.05
363	Bernie Nunez	.05
364	Paul Rodgers	.05
365	Jimmy Rogers	.05
366	Mike Taylor	.05
367	Ryan Thompson	.05
368	Jason Townley	.05
369	Rick Trlicek	.05
370	Anthony Ward	.05
371	Dave Weathers	.05
372	Woody Williams	.05
373	Julian Yan	.05
374	John Stearns	.05
375	Mike McAlpin, Steve Mingori	.05
376	Doyle Balthazar	.05
377	Basilio Cabrera	.05
378	Ron Cook	.05
379	Ivan Cruz	.05
380	Dean Decillis	.05
381	John DeSilva	.05
382	John Doherty	.05
383	Lou Frazier	.05
384	Luis Galindo	.05
385	Greg Gohr	.05
386	Bud Groom	.05
387	Darren Hursey	.05
388	Ricardo Ingram	.05
389	Keith Kimberlin	.05
390	Todd Krumm	.05
391	Randy Marshall	.05
392	Domingo Michel	.05
393	Steve Pegues	.05
394	Jose Ramos	.05
395	Bob Reimink	.05
396	Ruben Rodriguez	.05
397	Eric Stone	.05
398	Marty Willis	.05
399	Gene Roof	.05
400	Jeff Jones, Dan Raley	.05
401	Pete Alborano	.05
402	Jim Baxter	.05
403	Tony Clements	.05
404	Archie Corbin	.05
405	Andres Cruz	.05
406	Jeff Garber	.05
407	David Gonzalez	.05
408	Kevin Koslofski	.05
409	Deric Ladnier	.05
410	Mark Parnell	.05
411	Jorge Pedre	.05
412	Doug Peters	.05
413	Hipolito Pichardo	.05
414	Eddie Pierce	.05
415	Mike Poehl	.05
416	Darryl Robinson	.05
417	Steve Shifflett	.05
418	Jim Smith	.05
419	Lou Talbert	.05
420	Terry Taylor	.05
421	Rich Tunison	.05
422	Hugh Walker	.05
423	Darren Watkins	.05
424	Jeff Cox	.05
425	Brian Peterson, Mike Alvarez	.05
426	Clemente Acosta	.05
427	Jeff Barns	.05
428	Mike Butcher	.05
429	Glenn Carter	.05
430	Marvin Cobb	.05
431	Sherman Corbett	.05
432	Kevin Davis	.05
433	Damion Easley	.05
434	Kevin Flora	.05
435	Larry Gonzales	.05
436	Mark Howie	.05
437	Todd James	.05
438	Bobby Jones	.05
439	Steve King	.05
440	Marcus Lawton	.05
441	Ken Rivers	.05
442	Doug Robertson	.05
443	Tim Salmon	.75
444	Ramon Sambo	.05
445	Daryl Sconiers	.05
446	Dave Shotkoski	.05
447	Terry Taylor	.05
448	Mark Zappelli	.05
449	Don Long	.05
450	Kernan Ronan, Gene Richards	.05
451	Michael Beams	.05
452	Greg Blosser	.05

453	Brian Conroy	.05
454	Freddie Davis	.05
455	Colin Dixon	.05
456	Peter Estrada	.05
457	Ray Fagnant	.05
458	Tom Fischer	.05
459	John Flaherty	.05
460	Donald Florence	.05
461	Blane Fox	.05
462	Steve Hendricks	.05
463	Wayne Housie	.05
464	Peter Hoy	.05
465	Thomas Kane	.05
466	David Milstien	.05
467	Juan Paris	.05
468	Scott Powers	.05
469	Paul Quantrill	.05
470	Randy Randle	.05
471	Al Sanders	.05
472	Scott Taylor	.05
473	John Valentin	.05
474	Gary Allenson	.05
475	Rick Wise	.05
476	Pat Bangtson	.05
477	Carlos Capellan	.05
478	Rafael DeLima	.05
479	Frank Valdez	.05
480	Cheo Garcia	.05
481	Shawn Gilbert	.05
482	Greg Johnson	.05
483	Jay Kvasnicka	.05
484	Orlando Lind	.05
485	Pat Mahomes	.05
486	Jose Marzan	.05
487	Dan Masteller	.05
488	Bob McCreary	.05
489	Steve Muh	.05
490	Reed Olmstead	.05
491	Ray Ortiz	.05
492	Derek Parks	.05
493	Joe Siwa	.05
494	Steve Stowell	.05
495	Mike Trombley	.05
496	Jim Shellenback	.05
497	Rob Wassenaar	.05
498	Phil Wiese	.05
499	Scott Ullger	.05
500	Mark Funderbuck	.05
501	Jason Backs	.05
502	Toby Borland	.05
503	Cliff Brantley	.05
504	Dana Brown	.05
505	John Burgos	.05
506	Andy Carter	.05
507	Bruce Dostal	.05
508	Rick Dunnum	.05
509	John Martin	.05
510	David Holdridge	.05
511	Darrell Lindsey	.05
512	Doug Lindsey	.05
513	Tony Longmire	.05
514	Tom Marsh	.05
515	Rod Robertson	.05
516	Edwin Rosado	.05
517	Sean Ryan	.05
518	Steve Scarsone	.05
519	Mark Sims	.05
520	Jeff Tabaka	.05
521	Tony Trevino	.05
522	Casey Waller	.05
523	Cary Williams	.05
524	Don McCormack	.05
525	Al LeBoeuf	.05
526	Steve Allen	.05
527	Jorge Alvarez	.05
528	Bryan Baar	.05
529	Tim Barker	.05
530	Tony Barron	.05
531	Cam Biberdorf	.05
532	Jason Brosnan	.05
533	Braulio Castillo	.05
534	Steve Finken	.05
535	Freddy Gonzalez	.05
536	Mike James	.05
537	Brett Magnusson	.05
538	Jose Munoz	.05
539	Lance Rice	.05
540	Zak Shinall	.05
541	Dennis Springer	.05
542	Ramon Taveras	.05
543	Jimmy Terrill	.05
544	Brian Traxler	.05
545	Jody Treadwell	.05
546	Mike White	.05
547	Mike Wilkins	.05
548	Eric Young	.05
549	John Shoemaker	.05
550	James Wray	.05
551	Willie Ansley	.05
552	Sam August	.05
553	Jeff Baldwin	.05
554	Pete Bauer	.05
555	Kevin Coffman	.05
556	Kevin Dean	.05
557	Tony Eusebio	.05
558	Dean Freeland	.05
559	Rusty Harris	.05
560	Dean Hartgraves	.05
561	Trent Hubbard	.05
562	Bert Hunter	.05
563	Bernie Jenkins	.05
564	Jeff Juden	.05
565	Keith Kalser	.05
566	Steve Larose	.05
567	Lance Madsen	.05
568	Scott Makarewicz	.05
569	Rob Mallicoat	.05
570	Joe Mikulik	.05

No.	Player	Price
571	Orlando Miller	.05
572	Shane Reynolds	.05
573	Richie Simon	.05
574	Rick Sweet	.05
575	Don Reynolds, Charlie Taylor	.05
576	Rob Brown	.05
577	Mike Burton	.05
578	Evertt Cunningham	.05
579	Jeff Frye	.05
580	Pat Garman	.05
581	Bryan Gore	.05
582	David Green	.05
583	Donald Harris	.05
584	Jose Hernandez	.05
585	Greg Iavarone	.05
586	Barry Manuel	.05
587	Trey McCoy	.05
588	Rod Morris	.05
589	Robb Nen	.05
590	David Perez	.05
591	Bobby Reed	.05
592	Ivan Rodriguez	3.00
593	Dan Rohrmeier	.05
594	Brian Romero	.05
595	Luke Sable	.05
596	Frederic Samson	.05
597	Cedric Shaw	.05
598	Chris Shiflett	.05
599	Bobby Jones	.05
600	Oscar Acosta, Jeff Hubbard	.05
601	Mike Basso	.05
602	Doug Brocail	.05
603	Rafael Chavez	.05
604	Brian Cisarik	.05
605	Greg David	.05
606	Rick Davis	.05
607	Vince Harris	.05
608	Charles Hillemann	.05
609	Kerry Knox	.05
610	Pete Kuid	.05
611	Jim Lewis	.05
612	Luis Lopez	.05
613	Pedro Martinez	.05
614	Tim McWilliam	.05
615	Tom Redington	.05
616	Darrin Reichle	.05
617	A.J. Sager	.05
618	Frank Seminara	.05
619	Darrell Sherman	.05
620	Jose Valentin	.05
621	Guillermo Velasquez	.05
622	Tim Wallace	.05
623	Brian Wood	.05
624	Steve Lubratich	.05
625	John Cumberland, Jack Maloof	.05
626	Tim Bogar	.05
627	Jeromy Burnitz	.15
628	Hernan Cortez	.05
629	Steve Davis	.05
630	Joe Delli Carri	.05
631	D.J. Dozier	.05
632	Javier Gonzalez	.03
633	Rudy Hernandez	.05
634	Chris Hill	.05
635	John Johnstone	.05
636	Doug Kline	.05
637	Loy McBride	.05
638	Joel Horlen	.05
639	Tito Navarro	.05
640	Toby Nivens	.05
641	Bryan Rogers	.05
642	David Sommer	.05
643	Greg Talamantez	.05
644	Dave Telgheder	.05
645	Jose Vargas	.05
646	Agueda Vasquez	.05
647	Paul Williams	.05
648	Alan Zinter	.05
649	Clint Hurdle	.05
650	Jim Eschen	.05

a particular team kept together. The cards were issued only in poly packs and not as a complete set. A checklist was available from the company. Impel is the third company to handle this line. It all started with TCMA in 1972; CMC took over in 1988 and Impel bought out CMC in 1990. Due to a scarcity of certain cards in inventory and additional labor costs to dealers, the consumer can be expected to pay a minimum of $3-6 for team sets from this product. Line Drive team sets sold at the stadiums included team checklist cards.

	MT
Complete Set (650):	6.00
Common Player:	.05
Wax Box (36):	10.00

No.	Player	Price
1	Billy Bean	.05
2	Jerry Brooks	.05
3	Mike Christopher	.05
4	Dennis Cook	.05
5	Butch Davis	.05
6	Tom Goodwin	.05
7	Dave Hansen	.05
8	Jeff Hartsock	.05
9	Bert Heffernan	.05
10	Carlos Hernandez	.05
11	Chris Jones	.05
12	Eric Karros	.15
13	Dave Lynch	.05
14	Luis Martinez	.05
15	Jamie McAndrew	.05
16	Jim Neidlinger	.05
17	Jose Offerman	.05
18	Eddie Pye	.05
19	Henry Rodriguez	.05
20	Greg Smith	.05
21	Dave Veres	.05
22	Dave Walsh	.05
23	John Wetteland	.05
24	Kevin Kennedy	.05
25	Von Joshua, Claude Osteen	.05
26	Jeff Banister	.05
27	Cecil Espy	.05
28	Steve Fireovid	.05
29	Carlos Garcia	.05
30	Mark Huismann	.05
31	Scott Little	.05
32	Tom Magrann	.05
33	Roger Mason	.05
34	Tim Meeks	.05
35	Orlando Merced	.05
36	Joey Meyer	.05
37	Keith Miller	.05
38	Blas Minor	.05
39	Armando Moreno	.05
40	Jeff Neely	.05
41	Joe Redfield	.05
42	Rick Reed	.05
43	Jeff Richardson	.05
44	Rosario Rodriguez	.05
45	Jeff Schulz	.05
46	Jim Tracy	.05
47	Greg Tubbs	.05
48	Mike York	.05
49	Terry Collins	.05
50	Jackie Brown	.05
51	Rich Amaral	.05
52	Rick Balabon	.05
53	Dave Brundage	.05
54	Dave Burba	.05
55	Dave Cochrane	.05
56	Alan Cockrell	.05
57	Mike Cook	.05
58	Keith Helton	.05
59	Dennis Hood	.05
60	Chris Howard	.05
61	Chuck Jackson	.05
62	Calvin Jones	.05
63	Pat Lennon	.05
64	Shane Letterio	.05
65	Vance Lovelace	.05
66	Tino Martinez	.40
67	John Mitchell	.05
68	Dennis Powell	.05
69	Alonzo Powell	.05
70	Pat Rice	.05
71	Ricky Rojas	.05
72	Steve Springer	.05
73	Ed VandeBerg	.05
74	Keith Bodie	.05
75	Ross Grimsley	.05
76	Eddie Taubensee	.05
77	Jeff Bittiger	.05
78	Willie Blair	.05
79	Marty Brown	.05
80	Kevin Burdick	.05
81	Steve Cummings	.05
82	Mauro Gozzo	.05
83	Ricky Horton	.05
84	Stan Jefferson	.05
85	Brian Johnson	.05
86	Barry Jones	.05
87	Wayne Kirby	.05
88	Mark Lewis	.05
89	Rudy Seanez	.05
90	Luis Lopez	.05
91	Ecer Magallanes	.05
92	Luis Medina	.05
93	Dave Otto	.05
94	Roberto Zambrano	.05
95	Jeff Shaw	.05
96	Efrain Valdez	.05
97	Sergio Valdez	.05
98	Kevin Wickander	.05
99	Charlie Manuel	.05
100	Rick Adair, Jim Gabella	.05
101	Steve Adkins	.05
102	Daven Bond	.05
103	Darrin Chapin	.05
104	Royal Clayton	.05
105	Steve Howe	.10
106	Keith Hughes	.05
107	Mike Humphreys	.05
108	Jeff Johnson	.05
109	Scott Kamieniecki	.05
110	Pat Kelly	.05
111	Jason Maas	.05
112	Alan Mills	.05
113	Rich Monteleone	.05
114	Hipolito Pena	.05
115	John Ramos	.05
116	Carlos Rodriguez	.05
117	Dave Sax	.05
118	Van Snider	.05
119	Don Sparks	.05
120	Andy Stankiewicz	.05
121	Wade Taylor	.05
122	Jim Walewander	.05
123	Bernie Williams	1.00
124	Rick Down	.05
125	Denbo, Boyer, Meyer	.05
126	D.L. Smith	.05
127	James Austin	.05
128	Esteban Beltre	.05
129	Mickey Brantley	.05
130	George Canale	.05
131	Matias Carrillo	.05
132	Juan Castillo	.05
133	Jim Davins	.05
134	Carlos Diaz	.05
135	Cal Eldred	.05
136	Narciso Elvira	.05
137	Brian Fisher	.05
138	Chris George	.05
139	Sandy Guerrero	.05
140	Doug Henry	.05
141	Darren Holmes	.05
142	Mike Ignasiak	.05
143	Jeff Kaiser	.05
144	Joe Kmak	.05
145	Tim McIntosh	.05
146	Charlie Montoyo	.05
147	Jim Olander	.05
148	Ed Puig	.05
149	Tony Muser	.05
150	Lamar Johnson, Don Rowe	.05
151	Kyle Abbott	.05
152	Ruben Amaro	.05
153	Kent Anderson	.05
154	Mike Erb	.05
155	Randy Bockus	.05
156	Gary Buckels	.05
157	Tim Burcham	.05
158	Chris Cron	.05
159	Chad Curtis	.05
160	Doug Davis	.05
161	Mark Davis	.05
162	Gary DiSarcina	.05
163	Mike Fetters	.05
164	Joe Grahe	.05
165	Dan Grunhard	.05
166	Dave Leiper	.05
167	Rafael Montalvo	.05
168	Reed Peters	.05
169	Bobby Rose	.05
170	Lee Stevens	.05
171	Ron Tingley	.05
172	Ed Vosberg	.05
173	Mark Wasinger	.05
174	Max Oliveras	.05
175	Lenn Sakata, Gary Ruby	.05
176	Bret Barbarie	.05
177	Kevin Bearse	.05
178	Kent Bottenfield	.05
179	Wil Cordero	.05
180	Mike Davis	.05
181	Alex Diaz	.05
182	Eddie Dixon	.05
183	Jeff Fassero	.05
184	Jerry Goff	.05
185	Todd Haney	.05
186	Steve Hecht	.05
187	Jimmy Kremers	.05
188	Quinn Mack	.05
189	David Masters	.05
190	Marlin McPhail	.05
191	Doug Piatt	.05
192	Dana Ridenour	.05
193	Scott Service	.05
194	Razor Shines	.05
195	Tito Stewart	.05
196	Mel Houston	.05
197	John Vander Wal	.05
198	Darrin Winston	.05
199	Jerry Manuel	.05
200	Gomer Hodge, Nardi Contreras	.05
201	Brad Bierley	.05
202	Steve Carter	.05
203	Frank Castillo	.05
204	Lance Dickson	.05
205	Craig Smajstrla	.05
206	Brian Guinn	.05
207	Joe Kraemer	.05
208	Cedric Landrum	.05
209	Derrick May	.05
210	Scott May	.05
211	Ryss McGinnis	.05
212	Chuck Mount	.05
213	Dave Pavlas	.05
214	Laddie Renfroe	.05
215	David Rosario	.05
216	Rey Sanchez	.05
217	Dan Simonds	.05
218	Jeff Small	.05
219	Doug Strange	.05
220	Glenn Sullivan	.05
221	Rick Wilkins	.05
222	Steve Wilson	.05
223	Bob Scanlan	.05
224	Jim Essian	.05
225	Grant Jackson	.05
226	Luis Alicea	.05
227	Rod Brewer	.05
228	Nick Castaneda	.05
229	Stan Clarke	.05
230	Marty Clary	.05
231	Fidel Compres	.05
232	Todd Crosby	.05
233	Bob Davidson	.05
234	Bien Figueroa	.05
235	Ed Fulton	.05
236	Mark Grater	.05
237	Omar Olivares	.05
238	Brian Jordan	.25
239	Lonnie Maclin	.05
240	Julian Martinez	.05
241	Al Nipper	.05
242	Dave Osteen	.05
243	Leny Picota	.05
244	Dave Richardson	.05
245	Mike Ross	.05
246	Stan Royer	.05
247	Tim Sherrill	.05
248	Carl Ray Stephens	.05
249	Mark DeJohn	.05
250	Mark Riggins	.05
251	Billy Bates	.05
252	Freddie Benavides	.05
253	Keith Brown	.05
254	Adam Casillas	.05
255	Tony DeFrancesco	.05
256	Leo Garcia	.05
257	Angel Gonzalez	.05
258	Denny Gonzalez	.05
259	Kip Gross	.05
260	Charlie Mitchell	.05
261	Milton Hill	.05
262	Rodney Imes	.05
263	Reggie Jefferson	.05
264	Keith Lockhart	.05
265	Manny Jose	.05
266	Terry Lee	.05
267	Rob Lopez	.05
268	Gino Minutelli	.05
269	Kevin Pearson	.05
270	Ross Powell	.05
271	Donnie Scott	.05
272	Luis Vasquez	.05
273	Joey Vierra	.05
274	Pete Mackanin	.05
275	Don Gullett, Jim Lett	.05
276	Oscar Azocar	.05
277	Dann Bilardello	.05
278	Ricky Bones	.05
279	Brian Dorsett	.05
280	Scott Coolbaugh	.05
281	John Costello	.05
282	Terry Gilmore	.05
283	Jeremy Hernandez	.05
284	Kevin Higgins	.05
285	Chris Jelic	.05
286	Dean Kelley	.05
287	Derek Lilliquist	.05
288	Jose Meledez	.05
289	Jose Mota	.05
290	Adam Peterson	.05
291	Ed Romero	.05
292	Steven Rosenberg	.05
293	Tim Scott	.05
294	Dave Staton	.05
295	Will Taylor	.05
296	Jim Vatcher	.05
297	Dan Walters	.05
298	Kevin Ward	.05
299	Jim Riggleman	.05
300	Jon Matlack, Tony Torchia	.05
301	Gerald Alexander	.05
302	Kevin Belcher	.05
303	Jeff Andrews	.05
304	Tony Scruggs	.05
305	Jeff Bronkey	.05
306	Paco Burgos	.05
307	Nick Capra	.05
308	Monty Fariss	.05
309	Darrin Garner	.05
310	Bill Haselman	.05
311	Terry Mathews	.05
312	Rob Maurer	.05
313	Gar Millay	.05
314	Dean Palmer	.05
315	Roger Pavlik	.05
316	Dan Peltier	.05
317	Steve Peters	.05
318	Mark Petkovsek	.05
319	Jim Poole	.05
320	Paul Postier	.05
321	Wayne Rosenthal	.05
322	Dan Smith	.05
323	Terry Wells	.05
324	Tommy Thompson	.05
325	Stan Hough	.05
326	Sean Berry	.05
327	Jacob Brumfield	.05
328	Bob Buchanan	.05
329	Kevin Burrell	.05
330	Stu Cole	.05
331	Victor Cole	.05
332	Jeff Conine	.05
333	Tommy Dunbar	.05
334	Luis Encarnacion	.05
335	Greg Everson	.05
336	Bob Hamelin	.05
337	Joel Johnston	.05
338	Frank Laureano	.05
339	Jim LeMasters	.05
340	Mike Magnante	.05
341	Carlos Maldonado	.05
342	Andy McGaffigan	.05
343	Bobby Moore	.05
344	Harvey Pulliam	.05
345	Daryl Smith	.05
346	Tim Spehr	.05
347	Hector Wagner	.05
348	Paul Zuvella	.05
349	Sal Rende	.05
350	Brian Poldberg, Guy Hansen	.05
351	Luis Aguayo	.05
352	Tom Barrett	.05
353	Mike Brumley	.05
354	Scott Cooper	.05
355	Mike Gardiner	.05
356	Eric Hetzel	.05
357	Mike Twardoski	.05
358	Rick Lancellotti	.05
359	Derek Livernois	.05
360	Mark Meleski	.05
361	Kevin Morton	.05
362	Dan O'Neill	.05
363	Jim Pankovits	.05
364	Mickey Pina	.05
365	Phil Plantier	.05
366	Jeff Plympton	.05
367	Todd Pratt	.05
368	Larry Shikles	.05
369	Jeff Stone	.05
370	Mo Vaughn	.40
371	David Walters	.05
372	Eric Wedge	.05
373	Bob Zupcic	.05
374	Butch Hobson	.05
375	Rich Gale	.05
376	Rich Aldrete	.05
377	Mark Bailey	.05
378	Rod Beck	.05
379	Jeff Carter	.05
380	Craig Colbert	.05
381	Darnell Coles	.05
382	Mark Dewey	.05
383	Gil Heredia	.05
384	Darren Lewis	.05
385	Johnny Ard	.05
386	Rafael Novoa	.05
387	Francisco Oliveras	.05
388	Tony Perezchica	.05
389	Mark Thurmond	.05
390	Mike Remlinger	.05
391	Greg Ritchie	.05
392	Rick Rodriguez	.05
393	Andres Santana	.05
394	Jose Segura	.05
395	Stuart Tate	.05
396	Jimmy Williams	.05
397	Jim Wilson	.05
398	Ted Wood	.05
399	Duane Espy	.05
400	Alan Bannister, Larry Hardy	.05
401	Paul Abbott	.05
402	Willie Banks	.05
403	Bernardo Brito	.05
404	Jarvis Brown	.05
405	J.T. Bruett	.05
406	Tim Drummond	.05
407	Tom Edens	.05
408	Rich Garces	.05
409	Chip Hale	.05
410	Terry Jorgensen	.05
411	Kenny Morgan	.05
412	Pedro Munoz	.05
413	Edgar Naveda	.05
414	Denny Naegle	.05
415	Jeff Reboulet	.05
416	Victor Rodriguez	.05
417	Jack Savage	.05
418	Dan Sheaffer	.05
419	Charles Scott	.05
420	Paul Sorrento	.05
421	George Tsamis	.05
422	Lenny Webster	.05
423	Carl Willis	.05
424	Russ Nixon	.05
425	Jim Dwyer, Gordon Heimueller, Paul Kirsch	.05
426	John Alva	.05
427	Mike Bell	.05
428	Tony Castillo	.05
429	Bruce Crabbe	.05
430	John Davis	.05
431	Brian Hunter	.05
432	Randy Kramer	.05
433	Mike Loggins	.05
434	Kelly Mann	.05
435	Tom McCarthy	.05
436	Yorkis Perez	.05
437	Dale Polley	.05
438	Armando Reynoso	.05
439	Rusty Richards	.05
440	Victor Rosario	.05
441	Mark Ross	.05
442	Rico Rossy	.05
443	Randy St. Claire	.05
444	Joe Szekely	.05
445	Andy Tomberlin	.05
446	Matt Turner	.05
447	Glenn Wilson	.05
448	Tracy Woodson	.05
449	Phil Niekro	.50
450	Bruce Del Canton, Sonny Jackson	.05
451	Tony Chance	.05
452	Joaquin Contreras	.05
453	Francisco DeLaRosa	.05
454	Benny Distefano	.05
455	Mike Eberle	.05
456	Todd Frohwirth	.05
457	Steve Jeltz	.05
458	Chito Martinez	.05
459	Dave Martinez	.05
460	Jeff McKnight	.05
461	Luis Mercedes	.05
462	Mike Mussina	2.00
463	Chris Myers	.05
464	Joe Price	.05
465	Israel Sanchez	.05
466	David Segui	.05
467	Tommy Shields	.05
468	Mike Linskey	.05
469	Jeff Tackett	.05
470	Anthony Telford	.05
471	Shane Turner	.05
472	Jeff Wetherby	.05
473	Rob Woodward	.05
474	Greg Biagini	.05
475	Mike Young, Dick Bosman	.05
476	Sal Agostinelli	.05
477	Gary Alexander	.05
478	Andy Ashby	.05
479	Bob Ayrault	.05
480	Kim Batiste	.05
481	Amalio Carreno	.05
482	Rocky Elli	.05
483	Darrin Fletcher	.05
484	Jeff Grotewold	.05
485	Chris Knabenshue	.05
486	Greg Legg	.05
487	Jim Lindeman	.05
488	Chuck Malone	.05
489	Tim Mauser	.05
490	Louie Meadows	.05
491	Mickey Morandini	.05
492	Julio Peguero	.05
493	Wally Ritchie	.05
494	Bruce Ruffin	.05
495	Rick Schu	.05
496	Ray Searage	.05
497	Scott Wade	.05
498	Gary Wilson	.05
499	Bill Dancy	.05
500	Floyd Rayford, Jim Wright	.05
501	Derek Bell	.05
502	Rob Ducey	.05
503	Julius McDougal	.05
504	Juan Guzman	.05
505	Pat Hentgen	.05
506	Shawn Jeter	.05
507	Doug Linton	.05
508	Bob MacDonald	.05
509	Mike Maksudian	.05
510	Ravelo Manzanillo	.05
511	Domingo Martinez	.05
512	Stu Pederson	.05
513	Marty Pevey	.05
514	Tom Quinlan	.05
515	Alex Sanchez	.05
516	Jerry Schunk	.05
517	John Shea	.05
518	Ed Sprague	.05
519	William Suero	.05
520	Steve Wapnick	.05
521	Mickey Weston	.05
522	John Poloni	.05
523	Eddie Zosky	.05
524	Bob Bailor	.05
525	Rocket Wheeler	.05
526	Troy Afenir	.05
527	Mike Bordick	.05
528	Jorge Brito	.05
529	Scott Brosius	.05
530	Kevin Campbell	.05
531	Pete Coachman	.05
532	Dan Eskew	.05
533	Eric Fox	.05
534	Apolinar Garcia	.05
535	Webster Garrison	.05
536	Johnny Guzman	.05
537	Jeff Pico	.05
538	Dann Howitt	.05
539	Doug Jennings	.05
540	Brad Komminsk	.05
541	Tim McCoy	.05
542	Jeff Musselman	.05
543	Troy Neel	.05
544	Will Schock	.05
545	Nelson Simmons	.05
546	Bruce Walton	.05
547	Pat Wernig	.05
548	Ron Witmeyer	.05
549	Jeff Newman	.05
550	Glenn Abbott	.05
551	Kevin Baez	.05
552	Blaine Beatty	.05
553	Doug Cinnella	.05
554	Chris Donnels	.05
555	Jeff Gardner	.05
556	Terrel Hansen	.05
557	Manny Hernandez	.05
558	Eric Hillman	.05
559	Todd Hundley	.05
560	Alex Jimenez	.05

1991 Impel/Line Drive Pre-Rookie AAA

GREG TUBBS

Impel made its maiden voyage into the minor league market in 1991 with this set of AAA cards issued in poly packs. Unlike its predecessor (see CMC 1990 Pre-Rookie) of 1990, this set featured complete team sets of 25 cards each within the overall issue, with no other company's product mixed in. Cards were numbered consecutively with all cards of

#	Player	MT
561	Tim Leiper	.05
562	Lee May	.05
563	Orlando Mercado	.05
564	Brad Moore	.05
565	Al Pedrique	.05
566	Dale Plummer	.05
567	Rich Saveur	.05
568	Ray Soff	.05
569	Kelvin Torve	.05
570	Dave Trautwein	.05
571	Julio Valera	.05
572	Robbie Wine	.05
573	Anthony Young	.05
574	Steve Swisher	.05
575	Ron Washington, Bob Apodaca	.05
576	Scott Aldred	.05
577	Karl Allaire	.05
578	Skeeter Barnes	.05
579	Arnie Beyeler	.05
580	Rico Brogna	.05
581	Phil Clark	.05
582	Mike Dalton	.05
583	Curt Ford	.05
584	Dan Gakeler	.05
585	David Haas	.05
586	Shawn Hare	.05
587	John Kiely	.05
588	Mark Leiter	.05
589	Scott Livingstone	.05
590	Mitch Lyden	.05
591	Eric Mangham	.05
592	Rusty Meacham	.05
593	Mike Munoz	.05
594	Randy Nosek	.05
595	Johnny Paredes	.05
596	Kevin Ritz	.05
597	Rich Rowland	.05
598	Don Vesling	.05
599	Joe Sparks	.05
600	Mark Wagner, Ralph Treuel	.05
601	Harold Allen	.05
602	Eric Anthony	.05
603	Doug Baker	.05
604	Ryan Bowen	.05
605	Mike Capel	.05
606	Andujar Cedeno	.05
607	Terry Clark	.05
608	Carlo Colombino	.05
609	Gary Cooper	.05
610	Calvin Schiraldi	.05
611	Randy Hennis	.05
612	Butch Henry	.05
613	Blaise Isley	.05
614	Kenny Lofton	.25
615	Terry McGriff	.05
616	Andy Mota	.05
617	Javier Ortiz	.05
618	Scott Servais	.05
619	Mike Simms	.05
620	Jose Tolentino	.05
621	Lee Tunnell	.05
622	Brent Strom	.05
623	Gerald Young	.05
624	Bob Skinner	.05
625	Dave Engle	.05
626	Cesar Bernhardt	.05
627	Mario Brito	.05
628	Kurt Brown	.05
629	John Cangelosi	.05
630	Jeff Carter	.05
631	Tom Drees	.05
632	Grady Hall	.05
633	Joe Hall	.05
634	Curt Hasler	.05
635	Danny Heep	.05
636	Dan Henley	.05
637	Roberto Hernandez	.05
638	Orsino Hill	.05
639	Jerry Kutzler	.05
640	Noberto Martin	.05
641	Rod McCray	.05
642	Bob Nelson	.05
643	Warren Newson	.05
644	Greg Perschke	.05
645	Rich Scheid	.05
646	Matt Stark	.05
647	Ron Stephens	.05
648	Don Wakamatsu	.05
649	Marv Foley	.05
650	Roger LaFrancois, Moe Drabowsky	.05

1991 ProCards Tomorrow's Heroes

This Procards issue is comprised of an assortment of AAA, AA and A classification players representing all 26 contemporary Major League organizations. Cards are numbered beginning with Baltimore of the American League and concluding with San Francisco of the National League. Each of the Major League segments then has representation of the best players within their minor league organization; example: BALTIMORE ORIOLES AAA - Mussina, Mercedes, Frowirth, Martinez, Sequi AA - Rhodes, Jones A - Moore, Alexander, Williams, Anderson, Lemp, Krivda. "Tomorrow's Heroes" is a great title since there are dozens of prospects in the set; many of whom would soon be mainstays on big league rosters. Cards were only available in foil packs. Cards are bordered in white with a prominent pink and gray checkered interior pattern. Card manufacturer, player's name, position, and team are lettered in white and bordered in red. Original plans reportedly called for production of 10,000 cases, but those plans were changed dramatically to a limited production run of 1,007 cases upon the acquisition of ProCards by Fleer; thereby resulting in this product becoming a scarce commodity.

		MT
Complete Set (360):		15.00
Common Player:		.05
Wax Pack (12):		.75
Wax Box (36):		15.00
1	Mike Mussina	2.00
2	Luis Mercedes	.05
3	Todd Frohwirth	.05
4	Chito Martinez	.05
5	David Sequi	.05
6	Arthur Rhodes	.05
7	Stacy Jones	.05
8	Daryl Moore	.05
9	Manny Alexander	.05
10	Jeff Williams	.05
11	Matt Anderson	.05
12	Chris Lemp	.05
13	Rick Krivda	.05
14	Phil Plantier	.05
15	Mo Vaughn	.40
16	Scott Cooper	.05
17	Mike Gardiner	.05
18	Kevin Morton	.05
19	Jeff Plympton	.05
20	Jeff McNeely	.05
21	Willie Tatum	.05
22	Tim Smith	.05
23	Frank Rodriguez	.05
24	Chris Davis	.05
25	Cory Bailey	.05
26	Rob Henkel	.05
27	Kyle Abbott	.05
28	Lee Stevens	.05
29	Chad Curtis	.05
30	Ruben Amaro	.05
31	Mark Howie	.05
32	Tim Salmon	.75
33	Kevin Flora	.05
34	Garret Anderson	.15
35	Darryl Scott	.05
36	Don Vidmar	.05
37	Korey Keling	.05
38	Troy Percival	.05
39	Eduardo Perez	.05
40	Julian Heredia	.05
41	Wilson Alvarez	.05
42	Ramon Garcia	.05
43	Johnny Ruffin	.05
44	Scott Cepicky	.05
45	Rod Bolton	.05
46	Rogelio Nunez	.05
47	Brandon Wilson	.05
48	Marc Kubicki	.05
49	Mark Lewis	.05
50	Jim Thome	2.50
51	Tim Costo	.05
52	Jeff Mutis	.05
53	Tracy Sanders	.05
54	Mike Soper	.05
55	Miguel Flores	.05
56	Brian Giles	.25
57	Curtis Leskanic	.05
58	Kyle Washington	.05
59	Jason Hardtke	.05
60	Albie Lopez	.05
61	Oscar Resendez	.05
62	Manny Ramirez	3.00
63	Rico Brogna	.05
64	Scott Livingstone	.05
65	Greg Gohr	.05
66	Scott Aldred	.05
67	Brian Warren	.05
68	Bob Undorf	.05
69	Rob Grable	.05
70	Tom Mezzanotte	.05

#	Player	MT
71	Justin Thompson	.05
72	Trever Miller	.05
73	Joel Johnston	.05
74	Kevin Koslofski	.05
75	Archie Corbin	.05
76	Phil Hiatt	.05
77	Danny Miceli	.05
78	Joe Randa	.05
79	Mark Johnson	.05
80	Joe Vitiello	.05
81	Cal Eldred	.05
82	Doug Henry	.05
83	Dave Nilsson	.05
84	John Jaha	.05
85	Shon Ashley	.05
86	Jim Tatum	.05
87	Bo Dodson	.05
88	Otis Green	.05
89	Denny Neagle	.05
90	Checklist 1-90	.05
91	Pedro Munoz	.05
92	Jarvis Brown	.05
93	Pat Mahomes	.05
94	Cheo Garcia	.05
95	David McCarty	.05
96	Chris Delarwelle	.05
97	Scott Stahoviak	.05
98	Midre Cummings	.05
99	Todd Ritchie	.05
100	Dave Sartain	.05
101	Pedro Grifol	.05
102	Eddie Guardado	.05
103	Bob Carlson	.05
104	Sandy Diaz	.05
105	John Ramos	.05
106	Bernie Williams	1.00
107	Wade Taylor	.05
108	Pat Kelly	.05
109	Jeff Johnson	.05
110	Scott Kamieniecki	.05
111	Dave Silvestri	.05
112	Ed Maritel	.05
113	Willie Smith	.05
114	J.T. Snow	.10
115	Gerald Williams	.05
116	Larry Stanford	.05
117	Bruce Prybylinski	.05
118	Rey Noriega	.05
119	Rich Batchelor	.05
120	Brad Ausmus	.05
121	Robert Eenhoorn	.05
122	Sam Militello	.05
123	Jason Robertson	.05
124	Carl Everett	.25
125	Kiki Hernandez	.05
126	Rafael Quirico	.05
127	Lyle Mouton	.05
128	Tim Flannelly	.05
129	Todd Van Poppel	.05
130	Tim Peek	.05
131	Henry Mercedes	.05
132	Todd Smith	.05
133	Brent Gates	.05
134	Gary Hust	.05
135	Mike Neill	.05
136	Russ Brock	.05
137	Ricky Kimball	.05
138	Tino Martinez	.40
139	Calvin Jones	.05
140	Roger Salkeld	.05
141	Dave Fleming	.05
142	Bret Boone	1.00
143	Jim Campanis	.05
144	Marc Newfield	.05
145	Mike Hampton	.05
146	Shawn Estes	.05
147	David Lisiecki	.05
148	Dean Palmer	.05
149	Rob Maurer	.05
150	Jim Poole	.05
151	Terry Mathews	.05
152	Monty Fariss	.05
153	Ivan Rodriguez	2.50
154	Barry Manuel	.05
155	Donald Harris	.05
156	Rusty Greer	.05
157	Matt Whiteside	.05
158	Derek Bell	.05
159	Eddie Zosky	.05
160	Domingo Martinez	.05
161	Juan Guzman	.05
162	Ed Sprague	.05
163	Rob Ducey	.05
164	Vince Horsman	.05
165	Darren Hall	.05
166	Rick Trlicek	.05
167	Dave Weathers	.05
168	Robert Perez	.05
169	Nigel Wilson	.05
170	Carlos Delgado	2.50
171	Steve Karsay	.05
172	Howard Battle	.05
173	Huck Fiener	.05
174	Robert Butler	.05
175	Giovanni Carrara	.05
176	Michael Taylor	.05
177	Brian Hunter	.05
178	Turk Wendell	.05
179	Mark Wohlers	.05
180	Checklist 91-180	.05
181	Ryan Klesko	.10
182	Keith Mitchell	.05
183	Vinny Castilla	.10
184	Napoleon Robinson	.05
185	Mike Kelly	.05
186	Javy Lopez	.10
187	Ramon Caraballo	.05
188	David Nied	.05

#	Player	MT
189	Don Strange	.05
190	Chipper Jones	3.00
191	Troy Hughes	.05
192	Don Robinson	.05
193	Lance Marks	.05
194	Manuel Jimenez	.05
195	Tony Graffagnino (Graffanino)	.05
196	Brad Woodall	.05
197	Kevin Grijak	.05
198	Darin Paulino	.05
199	Lance Dickson	.05
200	Rey Sanchez	.05
201	Elvin Paulino	.05
202	Alex Arias	.05
203	Fernando Ramsey	.05
204	Pete Castellano	.05
205	Ryan Hawblitzel	.05
206	John Jensen	.05
207	Jerrone Williams	.05
208	Earl Cunningham	.05
209	Phil Dauphin	.05
210	Doug Glanville	.05
211	Jim Robinson	.05
212	Ken Arnold	.05
213	Reggie Jefferson	.05
214	Reggie Sanders	.05
215	Mo Sanford	.05
216	Steve Foster	.05
217	Dan Wilson	.05
218	John Roper	.05
219	Trevor Hoffman	.05
220	Calvin Reese	.10
221	John Hrusovsky	.05
222	Andy Mota	.05
223	Kenny Lofton	.25
224	Andujar Cedeno	.05
225	Ryan Bowen	.05
226	Jeff Juden	.05
227	Chris Gardner	.05
228	Brian Williams	.05
229	Ed Ponte	.05
230	Chris Hatcher	.05
231	Fletcher Thompson	.05
232	Wally Trice	.05
233	Donne Wall	.05
234	Tom Nevers	.05
235	Jim Daugherty	.05
236	Mark Loughlin	.05
237	Jose Offerman	.05
238	Dave Hansen	.05
239	Carlos Hernandez	.05
240	Eric Karros	.10
241	Henry Rodriguez	.05
242	Jamie McAndrew	.05
243	Tom Goodwin	.05
244	Pedro Martinez	3.00
245	Braulio Castillo	.05
246	Matt Howard	.05
247	Michael Mimbs	.05
248	Murph Proctor	.05
249	Vernon Spearman	.05
250	Jason Kerr	.05
251	Mike Sharp	.05
252	Pedro Osuna	.05
253	Doug Piatt	.05
254	Wil Cordero	.05
255	John VanderWal	.05
256	Bret Barberie	.05
257	Todd Haney	.05
258	Chris Haney	.05
259	Matt Stairs	.05
260	David Wainhouse	.05
261	Bob Natal	.05
262	Rob Katzaroff	.05
263	Willie Greene	.05
264	Reid Cornelius	.05
265	Glenn Murray	.05
266	Rondell White	.05
267	Tavo Alvarez	.05
268	Gabe White	.05
269	Brian Looney	.05
270	Checklist 181-270	.05
271	Derrick White	.05
272	Heath Haynes	.05
273	Mike Daniel	.05
274	Jim Austin	.05
275	Chris Donnels	.05
276	Julio Valera	.05
277	Todd Hundley	.05
278	Anthony Young	.05
279	Jeff Gardner	.05
280	Jeromy Burnitz	.10
281	Tito Navarro	.05
282	D.J. Dozier	.05
283	Julian Vasquez	.05
284	Pat Howell	.05
285	Brook Fordyce	.05
286	Todd Douma	.05
287	Jose Martinez	.05
288	Ricky Otero	.05
289	Quilvio Veras	.05
290	Joe Crawford	.05
291	Todd Fiegel	.05
292	Jason Jacome	.05
293	Kim Batiste	.05
294	Andy Ashby	.05
295	Wes Chamberlain	.05
296	Dave Hollins	.05
297	Tony Longmire	.05
298	Nikco Riesgo	.05
299	Cliff Brantley	.05
300	Troy Paulsen	.05
301	Elliott Gray	.05
302	Mike Lieberthal	.05
303	Tyler Green	.05
304	Dan Brown	.05
305	Carlos Garcia	.05

#	Player	MT
306	John Wehner	.05
307	Paul Miller	.05
308	Tim Wakefield	.05
309	Kurt Miller	.05
310	Joe Sondrini	.05
311	Hector Fajardo	.05
312	Scott Bullett	.05
313	Jon Farrell	.05
314	Marc Pisciotta	.05
315	Rheal Cormier	.05
316	Omar Olivares	.05
317	Donovan Osborne	.05
318	Clyde Keller	.05
319	John Kelly	.05
320	Terry Bradshaw	.05
321	Brian Eversgerd	.05
322	Dmitri Young	.05
323	Eddie Williams	.05
324	Brian Barber	.05
325	Andy Bruce	.05
326	Tom McKinnon	.05
327	Jamie Cochran	.05
328	Steve Jones	.05
329	Jerry Santos	.05
330	Allen Watson	.05
331	John Mabry	.05
332	Jose Melendez	.05
333	Dave Staton	.05
334	Frank Seminara	.05
335	Matt Mieske	.05
336	Jay Gaines	.05
337	J.D. Noland	.05
338	Roberto Arredondo	.05
339	Lance Painter	.05
340	Darren Lewis	.05
341	Ted Wood	.05
342	Johnny Ard	.05
343	Royce Clayton	.05
344	Paul McClellan	.05
345	John Patterson	.05
346	Steve Hosey	.05
347	Larry Carter	.05
348	Juan Guerrero	.05
349	Bryan Hickerson	.05
350	Rich Huisman	.05
351	Kevin McGehee	.05
352	Gary Sharko	.05
353	Salomon Torres	.05
354	Eric Christopherson	.05
355	Rod Huffman	.05
356	Bill VanLandingham	.05
357	Frank Charles	.05
358	Ken Grundt	.05
359	Matt Brewer	.05
360	Checklist 271-360	.05

1991 Minor League Team Sets

The number of independently (team, or card dealer) sponsored team sets continued to decline in 1991, leaving ProCards to slug it out with Classic Best, the new kid on the block created when Best sold out to Classic Games.

Set		MT
285 Team Sets and Variations		
1991 PC AAA All-Stars (55)		6.00
1991 Kraft Albany Yankees (6)		20.00
1991 PC Albany Yankees (28)		5.00
1991 PC Albuquerque Dukes (27)		7.00
1991 Team Albuquerque Dukes Photos (41)		125.00
1991 Team Anchorage Bucs (36)		16.00
1991 CB Appleton Foxes (30)		4.00
1991 PC Appleton Foxes (28)		3.00
1991 PC Arkansas Travelers (30)		3.00
1991 CB Asheville Tourists (30)		4.00
1991 PC Asheville Tourists (29)		3.00
1991 CB Auburn Astros (30)		4.00
1991 PC Auburn Astros (26)		3.00
1991 CB Augusta Pirates (30)		4.00
1991 PC Augusta Pirates (31)		3.00
1991 Cal Bakersfield Dodgers (32)		17.50
1991 CB Baseball City Royals (32)		4.00
1991 PC Baseball City Royals (29)		3.00
1991 CB Batavia Clippers (30)		4.00
1991 PC Batavia Clippers (30)		3.00
1991 CB Bellingham Mariners (30)		
1991 PC Bellingham Mariners (32)		4.00
1991 CB Beloit Brewers (30)		3.00
1991 PC Beloit Brewers (30)		3.00
1991 CB Bend Bucks (29)		4.00
1991 PC Bend Bucks (29)		3.00
1991 PC Billings Mustangs (28)		
1991 SP Billings Mustangs (30)		3.00
1991 PC Birmingham Barons (28)		5.00
1991 CB Bluefield Orioles (30)		4.00
1991 PC Bluefield Orioles (26)		4.00
1991 CB Boise Hawks (30)		3.00
1991 PC Boise Hawks (35)		4.00
1991 CB Bristol Tigers (30)		3.00
1991 PC Bristol Tigers (30)		3.00
1991 Team Buffalo Bisons (27)		3.00
1991 CB Burlington Astros (30)		12.00
1991 PC Burlington Astros (28)		4.00
1991 PC Burlington Indians (34)		3.00
1991 SP Butte Copper Kings (30)		40.00
1991 SP Butte Copper Kings Update (2)		5.00
1991 PC Calgary Cannons (25)		2.00
1991 Cal League All-Stars (56)		4.00
1991 PC Canton-Akron Indians (28)		20.00
1991 PC Carolina League A-S (47)		7.00
1991 PC Carolina Mudcats (26)		8.00
1991 CB Cedar Rapids Reds (30)		3.00
1991 PC Cedar Rapids Reds (30)		5.00
1991 CB Charleston Rainbows (30)		6.00
1991 PC Charleston Rainbows (27)		4.00
1991 CB Charleston Wheelers (30)		3.00
1991 PC Charleston Wheelers (27)		4.00
1991 PC Charlotte Knights (26)		3.00
1991 CB Charlotte Rangers (30)		3.00
1991 PC Charlotte Rangers (28)		3.00
1991 PC Chattanooga Lookouts (27)		4.00
1991 CB Clearwater Phillies (30)		4.00
1991 PC Clearwater Phillies (29)		4.00
1991 PC Clearwater Phillies (29)		3.00
1991 PC Clinton Giants (30)		4.00
1991 PC Clinton Giants (29)		3.00
1991 PC Colorado Springs Sky Sox (30)		4.00
1991 Play II Columbia Mets (30)		7.00
1991 Play II Columbia Mets Postcards (28)		15.00
1991 PC Columbus Clippers (29)		6.00
1991 PC Columbus Clippers (24)		6.50
1991 Police Columbus Clippers		
1991 CB Columbus Indians (30)		4.00
1991 PC Columbus Indians (32)		3.00
1991 PC Denver Zephyrs (27)		3.00
1991 CB Dunedin Blue Jays (30)		4.00
1991 PC Dunedin Blue Jays (29)		3.00
1991 CB Durham Bulls (30)		6.00
1991 PC Durham Bulls (33)		10.00
1991 PC Durham Bulls Update (9)		6.00
1991 PC Edmonton Trappers (29)		6.00
1991 PC Elizabethton Twins (29)		6.00
1991 CB Elmira Pioneers (30)		4.00
1991 PC Elmira Pioneers (29)		3.00
1991 PC El Paso Diablos (26)		3.00
1991 Team El Paso Diablos All-Time (35)		35.00
1991 CB Erie Sailors (30)		4.00
1991 PC Erie Sailors (29)		3.00
1991 CB Eugene Emeralds (30)		4.00
1991 PC Eugene Emeralds (30)		3.00
1991 CB Everett Giants (30)		4.00
1991 PC Everett Giants (33)		3.00
1991 CB Fayetteville Generals (30)		3.00
1991 PC Fayetteville Generals (29)		3.00
1991 PC Florida State League A-S (46)		12.00
1991 CB Frederick Keys (30)		4.00
1991 PC Frederick Keys (29)		4.00
1991 CB Ft. Lauderdale Yankees (30)		4.00

1991 PC Ft. Lauderdale Yankees (31) 3.00
1991 CB Gastonia Rangers (30) 6.00
1991 PC Gastonia Rangers (31) 6.00
1991 CB Geneva Cubs (30) 5.00
1991 PC Geneva Cubs (30) 5.00
1991 SP Great Falls Dodgers (30) 7.00
1991 PC Greensboro Hornets (29) 7.50
1991 CB Greenville Braves (30) 8.00
1991 PC Greenville Braves (27) 4.00
1991 SP Gulf Coast Rangers (30) 4.00
1991 PC Hagerstown Suns (28) 5.00
1991 CB Hamilton Redbirds (30) 5.00
1991 PC Hamilton Redbirds (33) 4.00
1991 PC Harrisburg Senators (29) 5.00
1991 SP Helena Brewers (30) 12.00
1991 CB High Desert Mavericks (30) 4.00
1991 PC High Desert Mavericks (32) 3.00
1991 Little Sun High School Prospects (36) 10.00
1991 LS High School Prospects - Gold (36) 17.50
1991 CB Huntington Cubs (30) 4.00
1991 PC Huntington Cubs (32) 4.00
1991 BK Huntsville Stars (26) 5.00
1991 CB Huntsville Stars (30) 4.00
1991 PC Huntsville Stars (26) 3.00
1991 PC Idaho Falls Braves (29) 3.00
1991 SP Idaho Falls Braves (30) 4.00
1991 PC Indianapolis Indians (28) 6.00
1991 PC Iowa Cubs (26) 4.00
1991 PC Jackson Generals (28) 5.00
1991 PC Jacksonville Suns (29) 8.00
1991 CB Jamestown Expos (30) 5.00
1991 PC Jamestown Expos (29) 6.00
1991 CB Johnson City Cardinals (30) 4.00
1991 PC Johnson City Cardinals (29) 3.00
1991 CB Kane County Cougars (30) 4.00
1991 PC Kane County Cougars (28) 4.00
1991 Team Kane County Cougars (27) 5.00
1991 CB Kenosha Twins (30) 5.00
1991 PC Kenosha Twins (28) 4.00
1991 CB Kingsport Mets (30) 4.00
1991 PC Kingsport Mets (28) 3.00
1991 CB Kinston Indians (31) 9.00
1991 PC Kinston Indians (31) 6.00
1991 PC Kissimmee Dodgers (32) 5.00
1991 PC Knoxville Blue Jays (28) 9.00
1991 CB Lakeland Tigers (30) 3.00
1991 PC Lakeland Tigers (29) 4.00
1991 PC Las Vegas Stars (31) 3.00
1991 PC London Tigers (26) 3.00
1991 PC Louisville Redbirds (29) 6.00
1991 Team Louisville Redbirds (34) 9.00
1991 CB Lynchburg Red Sox (30) 4.00
1991 PC Lynchburg Red Sox (28) 3.00
1991 CB Macon Braves (30) 15.00
1991 PC Macon Braves (31) 24.00
1991 CB Madison Muskies (30) 4.00
1991 PC Madison Muskies (27) 3.00
1991 CB Martinsville Phillies (30) 4.00
1991 PC Martinsville Phillies (31) 3.00
1991 PC Medicine Hat Blue Jays (31) 3.00
1991 SP Medicine Hat Blue Jays (30) 6.00
1991 PC Memphis Chicks (27) 3.00
1991 CB Miami Miracle (30) 4.00
1991 PC Miami Miracle (30) 3.00
1991 GS Midland Angels (1) 3.00
1991 1 Hour Midland Angels (32) 50.00
1991 PC Midland Angels (27) 7.00
1991 PC Midwest League A-S (51) 3.00
1991 CB Modesto A's (28) 4.00
1991 Chong Modesto A's (35) 3.00
1991 PC Modesto A's (31) 3.00
1991 CB Myrtle Beach Hurricanes (30) 7.50
1991 PC Myrtle Beach Hurricanes (30) 6.00

1991 PC Nashville Sounds (27) 6.00
1991 Team Nashville Sounds (34) 6.00
1991 PC New Britain Red Sox (26) 6.00
1991 CB Niagara Falls Rapids (30) 5.00
1991 PC Niagara Falls Rapids (30) 6.00
1991 PC Oklahoma City 89ers (27) 4.00
1991 PC Omaha Royals (26) 5.00
1991 PC Oneonta Yankees (27) 3.00
1991 PC Orlando Sun Rays (28) 3.00
1991 CB Osceola Astros (30) 5.00
1991 PC Osceola Astros (29) 4.00
1991 PC Palm Springs Angels (30) 5.00
1991 DD Pawtucket Red Sox Foldout 50.00
1991 PC Pawtucket Red Sox (27) 5.00
1991 Team Peninsula Oilers (30) 6.00
1991 CB Peninsula Pilots (29) 4.00
1991 CB Peninsula Pilots (28) 3.00
1991 PC Peoria Chiefs (29) 4.00
1991 Team Peoria Chiefs (34) 6.00
1991 PC Phoenix Firebirds (29) 4.50
1991 CB Pittsfield Mets (29) 3.00
1991 PC Pittsfield Mets (28) 3.00
1991 CB Pocatello Pioneers (31) 3.00
1991 SP Pocatello Pioneers (30) 5.00
1991 PC Portland Beavers (28) 4.00
1991 CB Princeton Reds (30) 3.00
1991 PC Princeton Reds (30) 3.00
1991 CB Prince William Cannons (30) 4.00
1991 PC Prince William Cannons (29) 3.00
1991 CB Pulaski Braves (30) 3.00
1991 PC Pulaski Braves (31) 3.00
1991 CB Quad City Angels (30) 5.00
1991 PC Quad City Angels (31) 4.00
1991 PC Reading Phillies (27) 3.00
1991 Penn-Lyn Studio Reading Phillies (24) 75.00
1991 Cal Reno Silver Sox (29) 3.00
1991 Bob's Richmond Braves (42) 115.00
1991 PC Richmond Braves (30) 4.00
1991 Ukrop's Richmond Braves (28) 20.00
1991 PC Rochester Red Wings (27) 6.00
1991 Team Rochester Red Wings Foldout 50.00
1991 CB Rockford Expos (30) 4.00
1991 PC Rockford Expos (29) 3.00
1991 CB Salem Buccaneers (27) 4.00
1991 PC Salem Buccaneers (27) 3.00
1991 CB Salinas Spurs (30) 4.00
1991 PC Salinas Spurs (31) 3.00
1991 PC Salt Lake City Trappers (30) 3.00
1991 SP Salt Lake City Trappers (30) 5.00
1991 HEB San Antonio Missions (32) 65.00
1991 PC San Antonio Missions (30) 15.00
1991 Team San Antonio Missions (30) 12.00
1991 CB San Bernardino Spirit (29) 4.00
1991 PC San Bernardino Spirit (30) 3.00
1991 CB San Jose Giants (30) 4.00
1991 PC San Jose Giants (30) 4.00
1991 CB Sarasota White Sox (30) 5.00
1991 PC Sarasota White Sox (30) 6.00
1991 CB Savannah Cardinals (30) 4.00
1991 PC Savannah Cardinals (29) 3.00
1991 PC Scranton Red Barons (29) 5.00
1991 PC Shreveport Captains (28) 4.00
1991 PC South Atlantic League A-S (48) 12.50
1991 CB South Bend White Sox (30) 5.00
1991 PC South Bend White Sox (30) 3.00
1991 CB Southern Oregon A's (37) 3.00
1991 PC Southern Oregon A's (37) 3.00
1991 PC Southern Oregon's A's Alumni (36) 7.00
1991 CB Spartanburg Phillies (30) 4.00
1991 PC Spartanburg Phillies (30) 3.00
1991 CB Spokane Indians (30) 4.00

1991 PC Spokane Indians (31) 3.00
1991 CB Springfield Cardinals (30) 3.00
1991 PC Springfield Cardinals (31) 3.00
1991 CB St. Catherines Blue Jays (30) 6.00
1991 PC St. Catherines Blue Jays (28) 4.00
1991 CB St. Lucie Mets (30) 4.00
1991 PC St. Lucie Mets (28) 3.00
1991 CB St. Petersburg Cardinals (30) 3.00
1991 PC St. Petersburg Cardinals (30) 3.00
1991 CB Stockton Ports (30) 4.00
1991 PC Stockton Ports (27) 3.00
1991 CB Sumter Flyers (30) 9.00
1991 PC Sumter Flyers (31) 8.00
1991 Kraft Syracuse Chiefs (5) 15.00
1991 MB Syracuse Chiefs Foldout 20.00
1991 PC Syracuse Chiefs (25) 5.00
1991 PC Tacoma Tigers (29) 5.00
1991 Team Tampa Yankees (33) 5.00
1991 PC Tidewater Tides (30) 3.00
1991 PC Toledo Mudhens (28) 3.00
1991 PC Tucson Toros (28) 4.00
1991 PC Tulsa Drillers (27) 10.00
1991 Team Tulsa Drillers (30) 15.00
1991 CB Utica Blue Sox (30) 4.00
1991 PC Utica Blue Sox (29) 3.00
1991 PC Vancouver Canadians (27) 6.00
1991 CB Vero Beach Dodgers (30) 5.00
1991 PC Vero Beach Dodgers (33) 4.00
1991 CB Visalia Oaks (28) 4.00
1991 PC Visalia Oaks (25) 3.00
1991 CB Waterloo Diamonds (30) 4.00
1991 PC Waterloo Diamonds (29) 3.00
1991 CB Watertown Indians (30) 4.00
1991 PC Watertown Indians (31) 3.00
1991 CB Welland Pirates (30) 3.00
1991 PC Welland Pirates (31) 3.00
1991 CB West Palm Beach Expos (31) 4.00
1991 PC West Palm Beach Expos (30) 3.00
1991 PC Wichita Wranglers (28) 3.00
1991 Rock's Wichita Wranglers - Hor. (27) 6.00
1991 Rock's Wichita Wranglers - Vert. (29) 6.00
1991 PC Williamsport Bills (27) 5.00
1991 CB Winston-Salem Spirits (30) 5.00
1991 PC Winston-Salem Spirits (28) 6.00
1991 CB Winter Haven Red Sox (30) 4.00
1991 PC Winter Haven Red Sox (27) 3.00
1991 CB Yakima Bears (30) 4.00
1991 PC Yakima Bears (30) 3.00

1992 Classic Best Promos

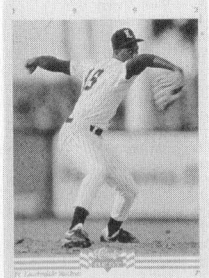

At least three promo cards were issued prior to the release of the 1992 Classic Best minor league card set. There may be others.

	MT
PR1 Nolan Ryan	2.50
PR2 Brien Taylor	1.00
PR3 Ken Griffey Jr.	1.00

1992 Classic Best Nolan Ryan Promo Autograph

This authentically auto-graphed card was not intended or used as a pack insert, but was sold exclusively as a retail item. It is an example of the '92 Classic Best Nolan Ryan promo card which has been signed and numbered within an edition of 1,967. The card was

sold with a certificate of authenticity from Score Board, which produced the Classic Best issues.

	MT
PR1 Nolan Ryan/Auto.	75.00

1992 Classic Best

This 400-card wax-pack set has an All-American look, with a red, white and blue card design. A banner beneath the photo has the player's name, team and position. On back the player's name is stretched horizontally near the top, and there is a portrait photo. A factory set was issued which includes 50 cards not found in wax packs. The same 50 cards were available as a boxed Update set. Autographed cards of five stars and prospects were included as random wax pack inserts, while the Clayton autograph card was found exclusively in jumbo packs.

	MT
Complete Factory Set (450):	7.50
Complete Set (400):	6.00
Factory Update Set (50):	3.00
Common Player:	.05
Wax Pack (12):	.50
Jumbo Pack (23):	.65
Wax Box (36):	12.00

1 Nolan Ryan 2.00
2 Darius Gash .05
3 Brad Ausmus .05
4 Mike Gardella .05
5 Mark Hutton .05
6 Bobby Munoz .05
7 Don Sparks .05
8 Shane Andrews .05
9 Gary Hymel .05
10 Roberto Arredondo .05
11 Joe Randa .05
12 Pedro Grifol .05
13 Steve Dixon .05
14 John Thomas .05
15 Chris Durkin .05
16 Jeff Conger .05
17 Jon Farrell .05
18 Antonio Mitchell .05
19 Matt Ruebel .05
20 Darren Burton .05
21 Lance Jennings .05
22 Kerwin Moore .05
23 Julio Bruno .05
24 Joe Vitiello .05
25 Brook Fordyce .05
26 Rob Katzaroff .05
27 Julian Vasquez .05
28 Alan Zinter .05
29 Clemente Alvarez .05
30 Scott Cepicky .05
31 Mike Mongiello .05
32 Tom Redington .05
33 Johnny Ruffin .05
34 Eric Booker .05
35 Manny Martinez .05
36 Mike Grimes .05
37 Paul Byrd .05
38 Brian Giles .25
39 David Mlicki .05
40 Tracy Sanders .05
41 Kyle Washington .05
42 Scott Bullett .05

43 Steve Cooke .05
44 Austin Manahan .05
45 Ben Shelton .05
46 Joe DeBerry .05
47 Steve Gibralter .05
48 Willie Greene .05
49 Brian Koelling .05
50 Larry Luebbers .05
51 Greg "Pepper" Anthony .05
52 Homer Bush .05
53 Manny Cora .05
54 Joey Hamilton .05
55 David Mowry .05
56 Bobby Perna .05
57 Jamie Dismuke .05
58 Kenneth Gillum .05
59 Calvin Reese .10
60 Phil Dauphin .05
61 Ryan Hawblitzel .05
62 Tim Parker .05
63 Dave Swartzbaugh .05
64 Billy White .05
65 Terry Burrows .05
66 Chris Gies .05
67 Kurt Miller .05
68 Timmie Morrow .05
69 Benny Colvard .05
70 Tim Costo .05
71 Mica Lewis .05
72 John Roper .05
73 Kevin Tatar .05
74 Joel Adamson .05
75 Mike Farmer .05
76 Kevin Stocker .05
77 David Tokheim .05
78 Ray Jackson .05
79 Dax Jones .05
80 Randy Curtis .05
81 Eric Reichenbach .05
82 Jerome Tolliver .05
83 Quilvio Veras .05
84 George Evangelista .05
85 Pat Bryant .05
86 Willie Canate .05
87 Brian Lane .05
88 Howard Battle .05
89 Rob Butler .05
90 Carlos Delgado 1.00
91 Tyler Houston .05
92 Troy Hughes .05
93 Chipper Jones 1.00
94 Mel Nieves .05
95 Jose Olmeda .05
96 John Finn .05
97 Mike Guerrero .05
98 Troy O'Leary .05
99 Ben Blomdahl .05
100 Mike Schmidt .75
101 Carlos Burguillos .05
102 Kiki Hernandez .05
103 Brian Dubose .05
104 Kevin Morgan .05
105 Justin Thompson .05
106 Jason Alstead .05
107 Matt Anderson .05
108 Brad Pennington .05
109 Brad Tyler .05
110 Jovino Carvajal .05
111 Roger Luce .05
112 Ken Powell .05
113 Steve Sadecki .05
114 Craig Clayton .05
115 Russell Davis .05
116 Mike Kelly .15
117 Javier Lopez .15
118 Doug Piatt .05
119 Manny Alexander .05
120 Damon Buford .05
121 Erik Schullstrom .05
122 Mark Smith .05
123 Jeff Williams .05
124 Reid Cornelius .05
125 Tim Laker .05
126 Chris Martin .05
127 Mike Mathile .05
128 Derrick White .05
129 Luis Galindez .05
130 John Kuehl .05
131 Ray McDavid .05
132 Sean Mulligan .05
133 Tookie Spann .05
134 Marcos Armas .05
135 Scott Erwin .05
136 Johnny Guzman .05
137 Mike Mohler .05
138 Craig Paquette .05
139 Dean Tatarian .05
140 Orlando Miller .05
141 Tow Maynard .05
142 Marc Newfield .05
143 Greg Pirkl .05
144 Jesus Tavarez .05
145 Tom Smith .05
146 Brad Seltzer .05
147 Brent Brede .05
148 Elston Hansen .05
149 Jamie Ogden .05
150 Rogelio Nunez .05
151 Manny Cervantes .05
152 David Sartain .05
153 Shawn Bryant .05
154 Chad Ogea .05
155 Manny Ramirez 1.00
156 Darrell Whitmore .05
157 Greg O'Halloran .05
158 Tim Brown .05
159 Curtis Pride .05
160 Marcus Moore .05

161 Robert Perez .05
162 Aaron Small .05
163 David Tollison .05
164 Nigel Wilson .05
165 Jim Givens .05
166 Dennis McNamara .05
167 Kelley O'Neal .05
168 Rudy Pemberton .05
169 Joe Perona .05
170 Brian Cornelius .05
171 Ivan Cruz .05
172 Frank Gonzales .05
173 Mike Lumley .05
174 Brian Warren .05
175 Aaron Sele .05
176 Gary Caraballo .05
177 Creighton Gubanich .05
178 Brad Parker .05
179 Scott Sheldon .05
180 Archie Corbin .05
181 Phil Hiatt .05
182 Domingo Mota .05
183 Dan Carlson .05
184 Hugh Walker .05
185 Joe Ciccarella .05
186 John Jackson .05
187 Brent Gates .05
188 Eric Helfand .05
189 Damon Mashore .05
190 Malcolm (Curtis) Shaw .05
191 Jason Wood .05
192 Terry Powers .05
193 Steve Karsay .05
194 Greg Blosser .05
195 Gar Finnvold .05
196 Scott Hatteberg .05
197 Derek Livernois .05
198 Jeff McNeely .05
199 Rex DeLaNuez .05
200 Ken Griffey Jr. 1.00
201 Pat Meares .05
202 Alan Newman .05
203 Paul Russo .05
204 Anthony Collier .05
205 Roberto Petagine .05
206 Brian Hunter .05
207 James Mouton .05
208 Tom Nevers .05
209 Garret Anderson .15
210 Clifton Garrett .05
211 Eduardo Perez .05
212 Shawn Purdy .05
213 Darren Bragg .05
214 Glenn Murray .05
215 Ruben Santana .05
216 Bubba Smith .05
217 Terry Adams .05
218 William (Bill) Bliss .05
219 German Diaz .05
220 Willie Gardner .05
221 Ed Larregui .05
222 Tim Garland .05
223 Kevin Jordan .05
224 Tim Rumer .05
225 Jason Robertson .05
226 Todd Claus .05
227 Julian Heredia .05
228 Mark Sweeney .05
229 Robert Eenhoorn .05
230 Tyler Green .05
231 Mike Lieberthal .10
232 Ron Lockett .05
233 Tom Nuneviller .05
234 Sean Ryan .05
235 Alvaro Benavides .05
236 Kevin Bellomo .05
237 Tony Bridges .05
238 Eric Whitford .05
239 James Bishop .05
240 Midre Cummings .05
241 Tom Green .05
242 Marcus Hanel .05
243 Billy Ashley .05
244 Matt Howard .05
245 Tommy Adams .05
246 Craig Bryant .05
247 Ron Pezzoni .05
248 Barry Miller .05
249 Jason McFarlin .05
250 Joe Rosselli .05
251 Billy Van Landingham .05
252 Chris Seelbach .05
253 Jason Bere .05
254 Eric Christopherson .05
255 Rick Huisman .05
256 Kevin McGehee .05
257 Salomon Torres .05
258 Brian Boehringer .05
259 Glenn DiSarcina .05
260 Jason Schmidt .05
261 Charles Poe .05
262 Ricky Bottalico .05
263 Tommy Eason .05
264 Joel Gilmore .05
265 Pat Ruth .05
266 Gene Schall .05
267 Jim Campbell .05
268 Brian Barber .05
269 Allen Battle .05
270 Marc Ronan .05
271 Scott Simmons .05
272 Dmitri Young .05
273 Butch Huskey .05
274 Frank Jacobs .05
275 Aaron Ledesma .05
276 Jose Martinez .05
277 Andy Beasley .05
278 Paul Ellis .05

279	John Kelly	.05
280	Jeremy McGarity	.05
281	Mateo Ozuna	.05
282	Allen Watson	.05
283	Francisco Gamez	.05
284	Leon Glenn	.05
285	Duane Singleton	.05
286	Andy Pettitte	.50
287	Donald Harris	.05
288	Robb Nen	.05
289	Jose Oliva	.05
290	Keith Garagozzo	.05
291	Dan Smith	.05
292	Kiki Jones	.05
293	Rich Becker	.05
294	Mike Durant	.05
295	Denny Hocking	.05
296	Mike Lewis	.05
297	Troy Ricker	.05
298	Todd Ritchie	.05
299	Scott Stahoviak	.05
300	Brien Taylor	.05
301	Jim Austin	.05
302	Mike Daniel	.05
303	Joseph Eischen	.05
304	Ranbir Grewal	.05
305	Rondell White (Photo actually Glenn Murray.)	.15
306	Mark Hubbard	.05
307	Tate Seefried	.05
308	Tom Wilson	.05
309	Benji Gil	.05
310	Mike Edwards	.05
311	J.D. Noland	.05
312	Jay Gainer	.05
313	Lance Painter	.05
314	Tim Worell	.05
315	Sean Cheetham	.05
316	Earl Cunningham	.05
317	Brad Erdman	.05
318	Paul Torres	.05
319	Jose Vierra	.05
320	Chris Gambs	.05
321	Brandon Wilson	.05
322	Brett Donovan	.05
323	Larry Thomas	.05
324	Brian Griffiths	.05
325	Chad Schoenvogel	.05
326	Mandy Romero	.05
327	Chris Curtis	.05
328	Jim Campanis	.05
329	Anthony Manahan	.05
330	Jason Townley	.05
331	Fidel Compres	.05
332	John Ericks	.05
333	Don Prybylinski	.05
334	Jason Best	.05
335	Rob Wishnevski	.05
336	John Byington	.05
337	Omar Garcia	.05
338	Tony Eusebio	.05
339	Paul Swingle	.05
340	Mark Zappelli	.05
341	Bobby Jones	.05
342	J.R. Phillips	.05
343	Jim Edmonds	.50
344	Greg Hansell	.05
345	Mike Piazza	1.50
346	Mike Busch	.05
347	Darrell Sherman	.05
348	Shawn Green	.75
349	Willie Mota	.05
350	David McCarty	.05
351	James Dougherty	.05
352	Fernando Vina	.05
353	Ken Huckaby	.05
354	Joe Vitko	.05
355	Roberto (Diaz) Mejia	.05
356	Willis Otanez	.05
357	Billy Lott	.05
358	Jason Pruitt	.05
359	Jorge Fabregas	.05
360	Mike Stefanski	.05
361	Robert Saitz	.05
362	Scott Talanoa	.05
363	LaRue Baber	.05
364	Tyrone Hill	.05
365	Rick Mediavilla	.05
366	Eddie Williams	.05
367	Rigo Beltran	.05
368	Doug VanderWeele	.05
369	Donnie Elliott	.05
370	Dan Cholowsky	.05
371	Derrell Rumsey	.05
372	Anthony Graffagnino (Graffanino)	.05
373	Scott Ruffcorn	.05
374	Mike Rossiter	.05
375	Mike Robertson	.05
376	P.J. Forbes	.05
377	Doug Brady	.05
378	Rick Clelland	.05
379	Ugueth Urbina	.05
380	Cliff Floyd	.10
381	Danny Young	.05
382	Eddie Ramos	.05
383	Bob Abreu	.15
384	Gary Mota	.05
385	Tony Womack	.05
386	Jeff Motuzas	.05
387	Desi Relaford	.05
388	John Elerman	.05
389	Walt McKeel	.05
390	Tim VanEgmond	.05
391	Frank Rodriguez	.05
392	Paul Carey	.05
393	Michael Matheny	.05
394	George Glinatsis	.05

395	Checklist (1-69)	.05
396	Checklist (70-138)	.05
397	Checklist (139-207)	.05
398	Checklist (208-276)	.05
399	Checklist (277-345)	.05
400	Checklist (346-400)	.05
401	Paul Shuey	.05
402	Derek Jeter	2.00
403	Derek Wallace	.05
404	Sean Lowe	.05
405	Jim Pittsley	.05
406	Shannon Stewart	.25
407	Jamie Arnold	.05
408	Jason Kendall	.25
409	Eddie Pearson	.05
410	Todd Steverson	.05
411	Dan Serafini	.05
412	John Burke	.05
413	Jeff Schmidt	.05
414	Sherard Clinkscales	.05
415	Shon Walker	.05
416	Brandon Cromer	.05
417	Johnny Damon	1.00
418	Michael Moore	.05
419	Michael Matthews	.05
420	Brian Sackinsky	.05
421	Jon Lieber	.05
422	Danny Clyburn	.05
423	Chris Smith	.05
424	Dwain Bostic	.05
425	Bob Wolcott	.05
426	Mike Gulan	.05
427	Yuri Sanchez	.05
428	Tony Sheffield	.05
429	Ritchie Moody	.05
430	Andy Hartung	.05
431	Trey Beamon	.05
432	Tim Crabtree	.05
433	Mark Thompson	.05
434	John Lynch	.05
439	Tavo Alvarez	.05
441	Troy Penix	.05
442	Scott Pose	.05
447	Jesus Martinez	.05
449	Chad Fonville	.05
450	Checklist (401-450)	.05

1992 Classic Best Red Bonus

Lenenthtering Reck Size:
Aaron Sele

The red bonus cards were randomly inserted in 1992 Classic Best black jumbo packs, one per pack. Cards are numbered with a BC prefix, and feature red-foil graphic highlights on front.

		MT
Complete Set (20):		5.00
Common Player:		.10
1	Nolan Ryan	2.00
2	Mark Hutton	.10
3	Shane Andrews	.10
4	Scott Bullett	.10
5	Kurt Miller	.10
6	Carlos Delgado	.75
7	Chipper Jones	1.00
8	Dmitri Young	.10
9	Mike Kelly	.10
10	Javy Lopez	.25
11	Aaron Sele	.10
12	Ken Griffey, Jr.	1.50
13	Midre Cummings	.10
14	Salomon Torres	.10
15	Brien Taylor	.10
16	Mike Piazza	2.00
17	David McCarty	.10
18	Scott Ruffcorn	.10
19	Cliff Floyd	.10
20	Frankie Rodriguez	.10

1992 Classic Best Autographs

Autographed cards of five stars and prospects were included as random wax pack inserts, while the Clayton autograph card was found exclusively in jumbo packs. Colorful backs have a statement of authenticity. The announced production number is shown in parentheses.

		MT
Complete Set (6):		125.00
Common Player:		3.00
(1)	Royce Clayton (2,000)	2.00
(2)	Ken Griffey Jr. (3,100)	55.00
(3)	David McCarty (1,000)	2.00
(4)	Nolan Ryan (3,100)	60.00
(5)	Mike Piazza (4,100)	30.00
(6)	Brien Taylor (3,100)	3.00

1992 Classic Draft Picks Previews

To introduce its coming baseball draft picks set, Classic inserted a series of preview cards in foil packs of its basketball draft picks product. Preview card fronts are similar to the issued version, with a large "PREVIEW" over the Classic logo at lower-left. Backs have a cartoon picture of a batter and an announcement that only 11,200 of each of the five preview cards were produced.

		MT
Complete Set (5):		2.50
Common Player:		.50
BB1	Phil Nevin	.75
BB2	Paul Shuey	.50
BB3	B.J. Wallace	.50
BB4	Jeffrey Hammonds	.50
BB5	Chad Mottola	.50

1992 Classic Best Blue Bonus

These bonus cards were randomly inserted into 1992 Classic Best white jumbo packs, one per pack. Cards are numbered with a BC prefix. Format is similar to the regular cards, with the presence of front of blue foil.

		MT
Complete Set (30):		17.50
Common Player:		.25
1	Nolan Ryan	3.00
2	Mark Hutton	.25
3	Shane Andrews	.25
4	Scott Bullett	.25
5	Kurt Miller	.25
6	Carlos Delgado	1.50
7	Chipper Jones	2.00
8	Dmitri Young	.25
9	Mike Kelly	.25
10	Javy Lopez	.35
11	Aaron Sele	.25
12	Ken Griffey Jr.	2.50
13	Midre Cummings	.25
14	Salomon Torres	.25
15	Brien Taylor	.25
16	Mike Piazza	2.50
17	David McCarty	.25
18	Scott Ruffcorn	.25
19	Cliff Floyd	.25
20	Frankie Rodriguez	.25
21	Paul Shuey	.25
22	Derek Jeter	3.00
23	Derek Wallace	.25
24	Shannon Stewart	.50
25	Jamie Arnold	.25
26	Jason Kendall	.35
27	Todd Steverson	.25
28	Dan Serafini	.25
29	John Burke	.25
30	Michael Moore	.50

1992 Classic Draft Picks Promos

These promo cards were released in cello packs to premiere the '92 Classic Draft Picks issue. Cards are similar in design to the issued versions, with color photos front and back. Backs are marked "For Promotional Purposes Only."

		MT
Complete Set (3):		2.00
Common Player:		.75
1	Jeffery Hammonds (Jeffrey)	.75
2	Phil Nevin	1.00
3	Brien Taylor	.75

1992 Classic Draft Picks

Bobby Bonds, Jr. OF

The top draft picks of 1992 are featured in this set, along with a Flashback subset (#86-95) of rising stars from the 1990-91 drafts. Cards were sold in 16-card foil packs including one foil bonus card. Fronts have a color action photo bordered in white with a dark green name stripe at bottom and the set logo at lower-left. Backs are in dark green with another photo and 1991-92 high school or college stats. Production was reported at 5,000 numbered cases.

		MT
Complete Set (125):		6.00
Common Player:		.05
Jumbo Pack (16):		.50
Jumbo Box (24):		9.00
1	Phil Nevin	.05
2	Paul Shuey	.05
3	B.J. Wallace	.05
4	Jeffrey Hammonds	.05
5	Chad Mottola	.05
6	Derek Jeter	3.00
7	Michael Tucker	.05
8	Derek Wallace	.05
9	Kenny Felder	.05
10	Chad McConnell	.05
11	Sean Lowe	.05
12	Ricky Greene	.05
13	Chris Roberts	.05
14	Shannon Stewart	.50
15	Benji Grigsby	.05
16	Jamie Arnold	.05
17	Rick Helling	.05
18	Jason Kendall	.25
19	Todd Steverson	.05
20	Dan Serafini	.05
21	Jeff Schmidt	.05
22	Sherard Clinkscales	.05
23	Ryan Luzinski	.05
24	Shon Walker	.05
25	Brandon Cromer	.05
26	Dave Landaker	.05
27	Michael Mathews	.05
28	Brian Sackinsky	.05
29	Jon Lieber	.05
30	Jim Rosenbohm	.05
31	De Shawn Warren	.05
32	Danny Clyburn	.05
33	Chris Smith	.05
34	Dwain Bostic	.05
35	Bobby Hughes	.05
36	Rick Magdellano	.05
37	Bob Wolcott	.05
38	Mike Gulan	.05
39	Yuri Sanchez	.05
40	Tony Sheffield	.05
41	Dan Melendez	.05
42	Jason Giambi	.75
43	Ritchie Moody	.05
44	Trey Beamon	.05
45	Tim Crabtree	.05
46	Chad Roper	.05
47	Mark Thompson	.05
48	Marquis Riley	.05
49	Tom Knauss	.05
50	Chris Holt	.05
51	Jonathan Nunnally	.05
52	Everett Stull	.05
53	Billy Owens	.05
54	Todd Etler	.05
55	Benji Simonton	.05
56	Dwight Maness	.05
57	Chris Eddy	.05
58	Brant Brown	.05
59	Trevor Humphrey	.05
60	Chris Widger	.05
61	Steve Montgomery	.05
62	Chris Gomez	.05
63	Jared Baker	.05
64	Doug Hecker	.05
65	David Spykstra	.05
66	Scott Miller	.05
67	Carey Paige	.05
68	Dave Manning	.05
69	James Keefe	.05
70	Levon Largusa	.05
71	Roger Bailey	.05
72	Rich Ireland	.05
73	Matt Williams	.05
74	Scott Gentile	.05
75	Hut Smith	.05
76	Rodney Henderson	.05
77	Mike Buddie	.05
78	Stephen Lyons	.05
79	John Burke	.05
80	Jim Pittsley	.05
81	Donnie Leshnock	.05
82	Cory Pearson	.05
83	Kurt Ehmann	.05
84	Bobby Bonds Jr.	.05
85	Steven Cox	.05
86	Brien Taylor (Flashback)	.05
87	Mike Kelly (Flashback)	.05
88	David McCarty (Flashback)	.05
89	Dmitri Young (Flashback)	.05
90	Joe Hamilton (Flashback)	.05
91	Mark Smith (Flashback)	.05
92	Doug Glanville (Flashback)	.05
93	Mike Lieberthal (Flashback)	.15
94	Joe Vitiello (Flashback)	.05
95	Mike Mussina (Flashback)	.75
96	Derek Hacopian	.05
97	Ted Corbin	.05
98	Carlton Fleming	.05
99	Aaron Rounsifer	.05
100	Chad Fox	.05
101	Chris Sheff	.05
102	Ben Jones	.05
103	David Post	.05
104	Jonnie Gendron	.05
105	Bob Juday	.05
106	David Becker	.05
107	Brandon Pico	.05
108	Tom Evans	.05
109	Jeff Faino	.05
110	Shawn Wills	.05
111	Derrick Cantrell	.05
112	Steve Rodriguez	.05
113	Ray Suplee	.05
114	Pat Leahy	.05
115	Matt Luke	.05
116	Jon McMullen	.05
117	Preston Wilson	.15
118	Gus Gandarillas	.05
119	Pete Janicki	.05
120	Byron Mathews	.05
121	Eric Owens	.05
122	John Lynch	.05
123	Mike Hickey	.05
124	Checklist 1	.05
125	Checklist 2	.05

1992 Classic Draft Picks Foil Bonus

Mike Kelly OF

Other than having their fronts printed on metallic foil and card numbers which are preceded by a "BC" prefix, these inserts are identical to the same players' cards in the regular Classic 1992 Draft Picks issue. One foil bonus card was included in each 16-card foil pack.

		MT
Complete Set (20):		5.00
Common Player:		.25
1	Phil Nevin	.25
2	Paul Shuey	.25
3	B.J. Wallace	.25
4	Jeffrey Hammonds	.25
5	Chad Mottola	.25
6	Derek Jeter	3.00
7	Michael Tucker	.25
8	Derek Wallace	.25
9	Kenny Felder	.25
10	Chad McConnell	.25
11	Sean Lowe	.25
12	Chris Roberts	.25

13	Shannon Stewart	.25
14	Benji Grigsby	.25
15	Jamie Arnold	.25
16	Ryan Luzinski	.25
17	Bobby Bonds Jr.	.25
18	Brien Taylor	.25
19	Mike Kelly	.25
20	Mike Mussina	1.00

1992 Classic Four Sport Previews

Foil packs of Classic's baseball and hockey draft picks issues included randomly inserted previews of the Four Sport issue. Fronts of the promos are similar to the issued cards with full-bleed action photos and a vertical player identification strip at right. On these cards, a "PREVIEW" banner is printed above the Classic logo. Backs announce the debut of the Four Sport set and indicate the Preview card is one of an edition of 10,000 of each player. Only the single baseball player among the Preview cards is listed here.

		MT
4	Phil Nevin	1.00

1992 Classic Four Sport

The top draft picks of 1992 are featured in this set, along with a Flashback subset of rising stars. Fronts have a borderless color action photo with a vertical strip at left featuring the player's name and position, with the Four Sport logo at top. Backs have another photo and 1991-92 high school or college stats. Production was reported at 40,000 cases. Only the baseball players are listed here. A gold-foil highlighted factory set version was also produced including a Future Superstars autographed card in an edition of 9,500.

		MT
Common Baseball Player:		.05
Gold:		3X
Gold Factory Set:		45.00
226	Phil Nevin	.05
227	Paul Shuey	.05
228	B.J. Wallace	.05
229	Jeffrey Hammonds	.05
230	Chad Mottola	.05
231	Derek Jeter	3.00
232	Michael Tucker	.05
233	Derek Wallace	.05
234	Kenny Felder	.05
235	Chad McConnell	.05
236	Sean Lowe	.05
237	Ricky Greene	.05
238	Chris Roberts	.05
239	Shannon Stewart	.35
240	Benji Grigsby	.05
241	Jamie Arnold	.05
242	Rick Helling	.05
243	Jason Kendall	.25
244	Todd Steverson	.05
245	Dan Serafini	.05
246	Jeff Schmidt	.05
247	Sherard Clinkscales	.05
248	Ryan Luzinski	.05
249	Shon Walker	.05
250	Brandon Cromer	.05
251	Dave Landaker	.05
252	Michael Mathews	.05
253	Brian Sackinsky	.05
254	Jon Lieber	.05
255	Jim Rosenbohm	.05
256	De Shawn Warren	.05
257	Danny Clyburn	.05
258	Chris Smith	.05
259	Dwain Bostic	.05
260	Bobby Hughes	.05
261	Rick Magdellano	.05
262	Bob Wolcott	.05
263	Mike Gulan	.05
264	Yuri Sanchez	.05
265	Tony Sheffield	.05

266	Dan Melendez	.05
267	Jason Giambi	.50
268	Ritchie Moody	.05
269	Trey Beamon	.05
270	Tim Crabtree	.05
271	Chad Roper	.05
272	Mark Thompson	.05
273	Marquis Riley	.05
274	Tom Knauss	.05
275	Chris Holt	.05
276	Jonathan Nunnally	.05
277	Everett Stull	.05
278	Billy Owens	.05
279	Todd Etler	.05
280	Benji Simonton	.05
281	Dwight Maness	.05
282	Chris Eddy	.05
283	Brant Brown	.05
284	Trevor Humphrey	.05
285	Chris Widger	.05
286	Steve Montgomery	.05
287	Chris Gomez	.05
288	Jared Baker	.05
289	Doug Hecker	.05
290	David Spykstra	.05
291	Scott Miller	.05
292	Carey Paige	.05
293	Dave Manning	.05
294	James Keefe	.05
295	Levon Largusa	.05
296	Roger Bailey	.05
297	Rich Ireland	.05
298	Matt Williams	.05
299	Scott Gentile	.05
300	Hut Smith	.05
301	Dave Brown	.05
302	Bobby Bonds Jr.	.05
303	Reggie Smith	.05
304	Preston Wilson	.15
305	John Burke	.05
306	Rodney Henderson	.05
307	Pete Janicki	.05
308	Brien Taylor (Flashback)	.05
309	Mike Kelly (Flashback)	.05
314	Jim Pittsley	.05

1992 Classic Four Sport Autographs

More than 50 of the draft picks from the four major team sports which appear in Classic's Four Sport issue can also be found among randomly inserted autographed cards. Fronts are formatted like the base set, with full-bleed action photos and include a serial number from within the edition limit specified for each player. Backs have a congratulatory message for finding an autographed card. Only the baseball players from the issue are listed here, arranged by the numerical order of their cards in the base set; the autographed cards are not numbered.

		MT
Common Player:		4.00
(226)	Phil Nevin (1,475)	6.00
(227)	Paul Shuey (4,050)	4.00
(229)	Jeffrey Hammonds (2,950)	4.00
(231)	Derek Jeter (1,125)	150.00
(233)	Derek Wallace (1,475)	4.00
(241)	Jamie Arnold (1,575)	4.00
(242)	Rick Helling (2,875)	4.00
(245)	Dan Serafini (1,475)	4.00
(248)	Ryan Luzinski (1,575)	4.00
(253)	Brian Sackinsky (1,575)	4.00
(259)	Dwain Bostic (2,075)	4.00
(290)	David Spykstra (1,575)	4.00
(307)	Pete Janicki (1,875)	4.00

1992 Classic Four Sport Bonus Cards

These bonus cards were issued one per jumbo pack. In format similar to the base set, they have a silver metallic foil strip vertically on front with player identification. Backs are numbered with a BC prefix. Only the baseball players among the 20 draft picks are listed here,

along with a special Future Superstars multi-player card which was produced in an edition of 10,000.

		MT
Common Player:		.25
BC18	Phil Nevin	.25
BC19	Jeffrey Hammonds	.25
BC20	Michael Tucker	.25
FS1	Phil Nevin, Shaquille O'Neal, Desmond Howard, Roman Hamrlik	2.00

1992 Classic Four Sport LP

These "Limited Print" (46,080 of each) foil cards were random inserts in packs of '92 Classic Four Sport. Only the baseball players are listed here.

		MT
Common Player:		1.00
LP17	Phil Nevin	2.00
LP18	Jeffrey Hammonds	1.00
LP19	Paul Shuey	1.00
LP20	Ryan Luzinsky (Luzinski)	1.00
LP21	Brien Taylor	1.00

1992-93 Fleer Excel

Excel was Fleer's 1992 entry into minor league cards. The 250-card set features full-color photos inside a white border with the player's name, team, logo and Excel logo in gold-foil stamping. Backs have large photos, career statistics, team logos and biographical information. Cards are UV coated. Cards were intended to be sold in 14-card packs for a suggested retail price of $1.49 each. The Excel All-Stars are listed at the end of the 250-card checklist. Cards for these 10 players were randomly inserted into the foil packs.

	MT
Complete Set (250):	12.00
Common Player:	.05
Jumbo Pack (23):	1.25
Wax Box (36):	17.50
Jumbo Box (24):	20.00

1	Mike D'Andrea	.05
2	Chipper Jones	2.00
3	Mike Kelly	.05
4	Brian Kowitz	.05
5	Napoleon Robinson	.05
6	Tony Tarasco	.05
7	Pedro Castellano	.05
8	Doug Glanville	.05
9	Andy Hartung	.05
10	Jay Hassel	.05
11	Ryan Hawblitzel	.05
12	Kevin Roberson	.05
13	Chad Tredaway	.05
14	Jose Vierra	.05
15	Matt Walbeck	.05
16	Tim Belk	.05
17	Jamie Dismuke	.05
18	Chad Fox	.05
19	Micah Franklin	.05
20	Dan Frye	.05
21	Steve Gibralter	.05
22	Demetrish Jenkins	.05
23	Jason Kummerfeidt	.05
24	Bob Loftin	.05
25	Chad Mottola	.05
26	Bobby Perna	.05
27	Scott Pose	.05
28	Calvin Reese	.10
29	John Roper	.05
30	Jerry Spradlin	.05
31	Roger Bailey	.05
32	Jason Bates	.05
33	John Burke	.05
34	Jason Hutchins	.05
35	Troy Ricker	.05
36	Mark Thompson	.05
37	Lou Lucca	.05
38	John Lynch	.05
39	Todd Pridy	.05
40	Gary Cooper	.05
41	Jim Dougherty	.05
42	Tony Eusebio	.05
43	Chris Hatcher	.05
44	Chris Hill	.05
45	Trent Hubbard	.05
46	Todd Jones	.05
47	Jeff Juden	.05
48	James Mouton	.05
49	Tom Nevers	.05
50	Jim Waring	.05
51	Chris Abbe	.05
52	Jay Kirkpatrick	.05
53	Raul Mondesi	.10
54	Vernon Spearman	.05
55	Tavo Alvarez	.05
56	Shane Andrews	.05
57	Yamil Benitez	.05
58	Cliff Floyd	.10
59	Antonio Grissom	.05
60	Tyrone Horne	.05
61	Mike Lansing	.05
62	Edgar Tovar	.05
63	Ugueth Urbina	.05
64	David Wainhouse	.05
65	Derrick White	.05
66	Gabe White	.05
67	Rondell White	.10
68	Edgar Alfonzo	.05
69	Jeromy Burnitz	.10
70	Jay Davis	.05
71	Cesar Diaz	.05
72	Todd Douma	.05
73	Brook Fordyce	.05
74	Butch Huskey	.05
75	Bobby Jones	.05
76	Jose Martinez	.05
77	Ricky Otero	.05
78	Jim Popoff	.05
79	Al Shirley	.05
80	Julian Vasquez	.05
81	Quilvio Veras	.05
82	Fernando Vina	.05
83	Ron Blazier	.05
84	Tommy Eason	.05
85	Tyler Green	.05
86	Mike Lieberthal	.10
87	Tom Nuneviller	.05
88	Matt Whisenant	.05
89	Jon Zuber	.05
90	Midre Cummings	.05
91	Jon Farrell	.05
92	Ramon Martinez	.05
93	Antonio Mitchell	.05
94	Keith Thomas	.05
95	Rene Arocha	.05
96	Brian Barber	.05
97	Jamie Cochran	.05
98	Mike Gulan	.05
99	Keith Johns	.05
100	John Kelly	.05
101	Anthony Lewis	.05
102	T.J. Mathews	.05
103	Kevin Meier	.05
104	David Oehrlein	.05
105	Gerry Santos	.05
106	Basil Shabazz	.05
107	Eddie Williams	.05
108	Dmitri Young	.05
109	Jay Gainer	.05
110	Pedro Martinez	2.00
111	Dave Staton	.05
112	Tim Worrell	.05
113	Dan Carlson	.05
114	Joel Chimelis	.05
115	Eric Christopherson	.05
116	Adell Davenport	.05
117	Ken Grundt	.05
118	Rick Huisman	.05
119	Andre Keene	.05
120	Kevin McGehee	.05
121	Salomon Torres	.05
122	Damon Buford	.05
123	Stanton Cameron	.05
124	Rick Krivda	.05
125	Alex Ochoa	.05
126	Brad Penington	.05
127	Mark Smith	.05
128	Mel Wearing	.05
129	Cory Bailey	.05
130	Greg Blosser	.05
131	Joe Caruso	.05
132	Jason Friedman	.05
133	Jose Malave	.05
134	Jeff McNeely	.05
135	Luis Ortiz	.05
136	Ed Riley	.05
137	Frank Rodriguez	.10
138	Aaron Sele	.15
139	Garret Anderson	.50
140	Ron Correia	.05
141	Jim Edmonds	.50
142	John Fritz	.05
143	Brian Grebeck	.05
144	Jeff Kipila	.05
145	Orlando Palmeiro	.05
146	Eduardo Perez	.05
147	John Pricher	.05
148	Chris Pritchett	.05
149	James Baldwin	.05
150	Rodney Bolton	.05
151	Essex Burton	.05
152	Scott Cepicky	.05
153	Steve Olsen	.05
154	Scott Ruffcorn	.05
155	Scott Schrenk	.05
156	Larry Thomas	.05
157	Brandon Wilson	.05
158	Paul Byrd	.05
159	Willie Canate	.05
160	Marc Marini	.05
161	Jonathan Nunnally	.05
162	Chad Ogea	.05
163	Herb Perry	.05
164	Manny Ramirez	2.00
165	Omar Ramirez	.05
166	Ken Ramos	.05
167	Tracy Sanders	.05
168	Paul Shuey	.05
169	Kyle Washington	.05
170	Ivan Cruz	.05
171	Lou Frazier	.05
172	Brian Bevil	.05
173	Shane Halter	.05
174	Phil Hiatt	.05
175	Lance Jennings	.05
176	Les Norman	.05
177	Joe Randa	.05
178	Dan Rohrmeier	.05
179	Larry Sutton	.05
180	Joe Vitiello	.05
181	John Byington	.05
182	Edgar Caceres	.05
183	Jeff Cirillo	.05
184	Mike Farrell	.05
185	Kenny Felder	.05
186	Tyrone Hill	.05
187	Brian Hostetler	.05
188	Danan Hughes	.05
189	Scott Karl	.05
190	Joe Kmak	.05
191	Rob Lakachyk	.05
192	Matt Mieske	.05
193	Troy O'Leary	.05
194	Cecil Rodriques	.05
195	Tim Unroe	.05
196	Wes Weger	.05
197	Rich Becker	.05
198	Marty Cordova	.05
199	Steve Dunn	.05
200	Mike Durant	.05
201	Denny Hocking	.05
202	David McCarty	.05
203	Damian Miller	.05
204	Scott Stahoviak	.05
205	Russ Davis	.05
206	Mike Draper	.05
207	Carl Everett	.10
208	Lew Hill	.05
209	Mark Hutton	.05
210	Derek Jeter	4.00
211	Kevin Jordan	.05
212	Lyle Mouton	.05
213	Bobby Munoz	.05
214	Andy Pettitte	1.00
215	Brien Taylor	.05
216	Brent Gates	.05
217	Eric Helfand	.05
218	Curtis Shaw	.05
219	Todd Van Poppel	.05
220	Miah Bradbury	.05
221	Darren Bragg	.05
222	Jim Converse	.05
223	John Cummings	.05
224	Shawn Estes	.05
225	Mike Hampton	.05
226	Derek Lowe	.05
227	Ellerton Maynard	.05
228	Fred McNair	.05
229	Marc Newfield	.05
230	Desi Relaford	.05
231	Ruben Santana	.05
232	Bubba Smith	.05
233	Brian Turang	.05
234	Benji Gil	.05
235	Jose Oliva	.05
236	Jon Shave	.05
237	Travis Baptist	.05
238	Howard Battle	.05
239	Rob Butler	.05
240	Tim Crabtree	.05
241	Juan DeLaRosa	.05
242	Carlos Delgado	1.50
243	Alex Gonzalez	.05
244	Steve Karsay	.05
245	Paul Spoljaric	.05
246	Todd Steverson	.05
247	Nigel Wilson	.05
248	Checklist	.05
249	Checklist	.05
250	Checklist	.05

1992-93 Fleer Excel All-Stars

These 10 All-Star cards were randomly inserted in Fleer Excel's 1992-93 foil packs. Cards are UV coated and feature the Excel logo on the front, along with the player's name and All-Star status, stamped in gold foil.

		MT
Complete Set (10):		5.00
Common Player:		.25
1	Brien Taylor	.25
2	Chipper Jones	2.50
3	Rondell White	.25
4	Mike Lieberthal	.40
5	Bobby Jones	.25
6	Carlos Delgado	1.50
7	Aaron Sele	.25
8	Brent Gates	.25
9	Phil Hiatt	.25
10	Brandon Wilson	.25

1992-93 Fleer Excel League Leaders

These randomly inserted cards feature 20 different Minor League league leaders. "League Leaders" and the player's name are stamped in gold foil on the front, which also has an Excel logo. The cards were random inserts in 1992-93 Fleer Excel jumbo packs.

		MT
Complete Set (20):		3.00
Common Player:		.25
1	Travis Baptist	.25
2	Bubba Smith	.25
3	Rob Butler	.25
4	Marty Cordova	.25
5	John Fritz	.25
6	Quilvio Veras	.25
7	Cliff Floyd	.25
8	Denny Hocking	.25
9	Rich Becker	.25
10	Jim Popoff	.25
11	John Kelly	.25
12	Tavo Alvarez	.25
13	Scott Pose	.25
14	Steve Gibralter	.25
15	Joe Caruso	.25
16	Chad Ogea	.25
17	Troy O'Leary	.25
18	Russ Davis	.25
19	John Cummings	.25
20	Ken Ramos	.25

1992 Front Row Draft Picks Promo

These cards were issued to introduce and advertise the second edition of Front Row draft picks.

They are similar in format to the regular-issue cards except for the promo notice/ad on back.

	MT
(1) Derek Jeter	2.00

1992 Front Row Draft Picks

JASON KENDALL

One hundred of the top players in the 1992 amateur draft are featured in this set. Sold in both wax packs and factory sets, the issue included a number of foil-stamped parallel cards, plus gold Frank Thomas and Ken Griffey, Jr. cards. The basic cards are UV-coated front and back and feature posed or game-action color photos of the players in their high school or college uniforms with borders in graduated shades of blue. Backs have biographical data, stats and career highlights, plus another picture - generally a boyhood photo. According to released production figures, about 330,000 sets are possible.

	MT
Complete Set (100):	6.00
Common Player:	.05
Silver:	1.5X
Gold:	2.5X
Wax Pack (10):	1.00
Wax Box (36):	30.00

1	Dan Melendez	.05
2	Billy Owens	.05
3	Sherard Clinkscales	.05
4	Tim Moore	.05
5	Michael Hickey	.05
6	Kenny Carlyle	.05
7	Todd Steverson	.05
8	Ted Corbin	.05
9	Tim Crabtree	.05
10	Jason Angel	.05
11	Mike Gulan	.05
12	Jared Baker	.05
13	Mike Buddie	.05
14	Brandon Pico	.05
15	Jonathan Nunnally	.05
16	Scott Patton	.05
17	Tony Sheffield	.05
18	Danny Clyburn	.05
19	Tom Knauss	.05
20	Carey Paige	.05
21	Keith Johnson	.05
22	Larry Mitchell	.05
23	Tim Leger	.05
24	Doug Hecker	.05
25	Aaron Thatcher	.05
26	Marquis Riley	.05
27	Jamie Taylor	.05
28	Don Wengert	.05
29	Jason Moler	.05
30	Kevin Kloek	.05
31	Kevin Pearson	.05
32	David Mysel	.05
33	Chris Holt	.05
34	Chris Gomez	.05
35	Joe Hamilton	.05
36	Brandon Cromer	.05
37	Lloyd Peever	.05
38	Gordon Sanchez	.05
39	Bonus Card	
40	Jason Giambi	1.00
41	Sean Runyan	.05
42	Jamie Keefe	.05
43	Scott Gentile	.05
44	Michael Tucker	.05
45	Scott Klingenbeck	.05
46	Ed Christian	.05
47	Scott Miller	.05
48	Rick Navarro	.05
49	Bill Selby	.05
50	Chris Roberts	.05
51	John Dillinger	.05
52	Keith Johns	.05
53	Matthew Williams	.05
54	Garvin Alston	.05
55	Derek Jeter	4.00
56	Chris Eddy	.05
57	Jeff Schmidt	.05
58	Chris Petersen	.05
59	Chris Sheff	.05
60	Chad Roper	.05
61	Rich Ireland	.05

62 Tibor Brown .05
63 Todd Etler .05
64 John Turlais .05
65 Shawn Holcomb .05
66 Ben Jones .05
67 Marcel Galligani .05
68 Troy Penix .05
69 Matt Luke .05
70 David Post .05
71 Michael Warner .05
72 Alexis Aranzamendi .05
73 Larry Hingle .05
74 Shon Walker .05
75 Mark Thompson .05
76 Jon Lieber .05
77 Wes Weger .05
78 Mike Smith .05
79 Ritchie Moody .05
80 B.J. Wallace .05
81 Rick Helling .05
82 Chad Mottola .05
83 Brant Brown .05
84 Steve Rodriguez .05
85 John Vanhof .05
86 Brian Wolf .05
87 Steve Montgomery .05
88 Eric Owens .05
89 Jason Kendall .25
90 Bob Bennett .05
91 Joe Petcka .05
92 Jim Rosenbohm .05
93 David Manning .05
94 Dave Landaker .05
95 Dan Kyslinger .05
96 Roger Bailey .05
97 Jon Zuber .05
98 Steve Cox .05
99 Chris Widger .05
100 Checklist .05
--- Ken Griffey Jr. (Gold Card) 6.00
--- Frank Thomas (Gold Card) 5.00

1992 Front Row Draft Picks Autographs

Two types of authentically autographed cards were produced in conjunction with 1992 FR Draft Picks. Unnumbered cards of three Hall of Famers were included in packs as random inserts, while cards of several projected future stars were given to dealers as sales incentives. The autograph cards have a round "AUTHENTIC Signature Card" seal on back.

MT
--- Yogi Berra 25.00
--- Whitey Ford 25.00
--- Brooks Robinson 15.00

14 Brandon Pico 1.00
55 Derek Jeter 125.00
58 Chris Peterson 1.00
81 Rick Helling 1.00
89 Jason Kendall 6.00
92 Jim Rosenbohm 1.00

1992 Front Row Tyler Green Signature Cards

This seven-card series was sold in both autographed and unautographed sets, complete with certificates of authenticity, each with an individual serial number from within an edition of 10,000. The 2-1/2" x 3-1/2" cards are UV coated on fronts, which feature color pitching or portrait poses. Backs have another color photo, high school and college information and stats.

MT
Complete Set (7): .50
Complete Set W/Auto. (7): 3.00
1-7 Tyler Green .10

1992 SkyBox AA

BOBBY JONES AA
Binghamton Mets / Pitcher

SkyBox Pre-Rookie 1992 baseball cards were released in two 310-card sets; one for Triple A and one for Double A. Each set includes 289 top prospects, plus subsets (1991 statistical leaders, players of the year and minor league stadiums) and checklist cards. Cards were intended to be sold in 15-card packs for a suggested retail price of 95 cents each. SkyBox also offered 25-card Pre-Rookie team sets which include all players and coaches on the opening day roster of each of the 52 AA and AAA teams, plus a team checklist. Sets were to be available at most of the teams' stadiums. The top prospects which appear in the 15-card packs are also depicted in the team sets, but the team cards use a different numbering system and delete the card back copy except for statistics.

MT
Complete Set (310): 5.00
Common Player: .05
Wax Pack (15): .50
Wax Box (36): 8.00
1 Rich Batchelor .05
2 Russ Davis .05
3 Kiki Hernandez .05
4 Sterling Hitchcock .05
5 Darren Hodges .05
6 Jeff Hoffman .05
7 Mark Hulton .05
8 Bobby Munoz .05
9 Roy Noriega .05
10 Sherman Obando .05
11 John Viera .05
12 Cliff Brannon .05
13 Chuck Carr .05
14 Fidel Compres .05
15 Tripp Cromer .05
16 John Ericks .05
17 Gabby Ozuna .05
18 Don Prybylinski .05
19 John Sellick .05
20 John Thomas .05
21 Tom Urbani .05
22 Chris Butterfield .05
23 Todd Douma .05
24 Brook Fordyce .05
25 Tim Howard .05
26 John Johnstone .05
27 Bobby Jones .05
28 Rob Katzaroff .05
29 Gregg Langbehn .05
30 Curtis Pride .05
31 Julian Vasquez .05
32 Joe Vitko .05
33 Tom Wegmann .05
34 Mike White .05
35 Alan Zinter .05
36 Clemente Alvarez .05
37 Cesar Bernhardt .05
38 Wayne Busby .05
39 Scott Cepicky .05
40 John Hudek .05
41 Scott Jaster .05
42 Bo Kennedy .05
43 Mike Mongiello .05
44 Kinnis Pledger .05
45 Johnny Ruffin .05
46 Jose Ventura .05
47 Paul Byrd .05
48 Colin Charland .05
49 Miguel Flores .05
50 Brian Giles .25
51 Jose Hernandez .05
52 Nolan Lene .05
53 David Mlicki .05
54 Tracy Sanders .05
55 Mike Soper .05
56 Kelly Stinnett .05
57 Joe Turek .05
58 Kyle Washington .05
59 Dave Bird .05
60 Scott Bullett .05
61 Steve Cooke .05
62 Alberto De Los Santos .05
63 Stan Fansier .05
64 Austin Manahan .05
65 Daryl Ratliff .05
66 Mandy Romero .05
67 Ben Shelton .05
68 Paul Wagner .05
69 Mike Zimmerman .05
70 Phil Dauphin .05
71 Chris Ebright .05
72 Mike Grace .05
73 Ryan Hawblitzel .05
74 Jessie Hollins .05
75 Tim Parker .05
76 Dave Swartzbaugh .05
77 Steve Trachsel .05
78 Billy White .05
79 Bobby Ayala .05
80 Tim Costa .05
81 Ty Griffin .05
82 Cesar Hernandez .05
83 Trevor Hoffman .15
84 Brian Lane .05
85 Scott Pose .05
86 Johnny Ray .05
87 John Roper .05
88 Glenn Sutko .05
89 Kevin Tatar .05
90 John Byington .05
91 Tony Diggs .05
92 Bo Dodson .05
93 Craig Faulkner .05
94 Jim Hunter .05
95 Oreste Marrero .05
96 Troy O'Leary .05
97 Brian Bark .05
98 Dennis Burlingame .05
99 Ramon Carabello .05
100 Mike Kelly .05
101 Javier Lopez .10
102 Don Strange .05
103 Tony Tarasco .05
104 Manny Alexander .05
105 Damon Buford .05
106 Cesar Devares .05
107 Rodney Lofton .05
108 Brent Miller .05
109 David Miller .05
110 Daryl Moore .05
111 John O'Donoghue .05
112 Erik Schulstrom .05
113 Mark Smith .05
114 Mel Wearing .05
115 Jeff Williams .05
116 Kip Yaughn .05
117 Doug Bochler .05
118 Travis Buckley .05
119 Reid Cornelius .05
120 Chris Johnson .05
121 Tim Laker .05
122 Chris Martin .05
123 Mike Mathile .05
124 Darwin Pennye .05
125 Doug Platt .05
126 Kurt Abbott .05
127 Marcos Amas .05
128 James Buccheri .05
129 Kevin Dettola .05
130 Scott Erwin .05
131 Johnny Guzman .05
132 David Jacas .05
133 Francisco Matos .05
134 Mike Mohler .05
135 Craig Paquette .05
136 Todd Revenig .05
137 Todd Smith .05
138 Ricky Strebeck .05
139 Sam August .05
140 Tony Eusebio .05
141 Brian Griffiths .05
142 Todd Jones .05
143 Orlando Miller .05
144 Howard Prager .05
145 Matt Rambo .05
146 Lee Sammons .05
147 Richie Simon .05
148 Frank Bolick .05
149 Jim Campanis .05
150 Jim Converse .05
151 Bobby Holley .05
152 Troy Kent .05
153 Brent Knackert .05
154 Anthony Manahan .05
155 Tow Maynard .05
156 Mike McDonald .05
157 Marc Newfield .05
158 Greg Pirkl .05
159 Jesus Tavarez .05
160 Kerry Woodson .05
161 Graeme Lloyd .05
162 Paul Menhart .05
163 Marcus Moore .05
164 Greg O'Halloran .05
165 Mark Ohlms .05
166 Robert Perez .05
167 Aaron Small .05
168 Nigel Wilson .05
169 Julian Yan .05
170 Jeff Braley .05
171 Brian Cornelius .05
172 Ivan Cruz .05
173 Lou Frazier .05
174 Frank Gonzales .05
175 Tyrone Kingwood .05
176 Leo Torres .05
177 Brien Warren .05
178 Brian Ahern .05
179 Tony Bridges .05
180 Paco Burgos .05
181 Adam Casillas .05
182 Archie Corbin .05
183 Phil Hiatt .05
184 Marcus Lawton .05
185 Domingo Mota .05
186 Mark Pamell .05
187 Ed Pierce .05
188 Rich Tunison .05
189 Hugh Walker .05
190 Skip Wiley .05
191 Dave Adams .05
192 Mick Billmeyer .05
193 Marvin Cobb .05
194 Jim Edmonds 1.00
195 Corey Kapano .05
196 Jeff Kiplia .05
197 Joe Kraemer .05
198 Ray Martinez .05
199 J.R. Phillips .05
200 Darryl Scott .05
201 Paul Swingle .05
202 Mark Zappelli .05
203 Greg Blosser .05
204 Bruce Chick .05
205 Colin Dixon .05
206 Gar Finnvold .05
207 Scott Hatteberg .05
208 Derek Livernois .05
209 Jeff McNeely .05
210 Tony Mosley .05
211 Bill Norris .05
212 Ed Riley .05
213 Ken Ryan .05
214 Tim Smith .05
215 Willie Tatum .05
216 Rex De La Nuez .05
217 Rich Garces .05
218 Curtis Leskanic .05
219 Mica Lewis .05
220 David McCarty .05
221 Pat Meares .05
222 Alan Newman .05
223 Jay Owens .05
224 Carlos Pulido .05
225 Rusty Richards .05
226 Paul Russo .05
227 Brad Brink .05
228 Andy Carter .05
229 Tyler Green .05
230 Mike Lieberthal .10
231 Chris Limbach .05
232 Tom Nuneviller .05
233 Troy Paulsen .05
234 Todd Pratt .05
235 Sean Ryan .05
236 Matt Stevens .05
237 Sam Taylor .05
238 Casey Waller .05
239 Mike Williams .05
240 Jorge Alvarez .05
241 Billy Ashley .05
242 Tim Barker .05
243 Bill Bene .05
244 John Deutsch .05
245 Greg Hansell .05
246 Matt Howard .05
247 Ron Maurer .05
248 Mike Mimbs .05
249 Chris Morrow .05
250 Jose Munoz .05
251 Mike Piazza 3.00
252 Dennis Springer .05
253 Clay Bellinger .05
254 Dan Carlson .05
255 Eric Christopherson .05
256 Adell Davenport .05
257 Steve Finken .05
258 Rick Huisman .05
259 Kevin McGehee .05
260 Don Rambo .05
261 Steve Reed .05
262 Kevin Rogers .05
263 Salomon Torres .05
264 Pete Weber .05
265 Brian Romero .05
266 Cris Colon .05
267 Rusty Greer .05
268 Donald Harris .05
269 David Hulse .05
270 Pete Kuld .05
271 Robb Nen .05
272 Jose Oliva .05
273 Steve Rowley .05
274 Jon Shave .05
275 Cedric Shaw .05
276 Dan Smith .05
277 Matt Whiteside .05
278 Scott Frederickson .05
279 Jay Gainer .05
280 Paul Gonzalez .05
281 Vince Harris .05
282 Ray Holbert .05
283 Dwayne Hosey .05
284 J.D. Noland .05
285 Lance Painter .05
286 Scott Sanders .05
287 Darrell Sherman .05
288 Brian Wood .05
289 Tim Worrell .05
290 John Jaha .05
291 Jim Bowie .05
292 Mark Howie .05
293 Matt Stairs .05
294 Larry Carter .05
295 Pat Mahomes .05
296 Jeff Mutis .05
297 Municipal Stadium .05
298 Knights Castle .05
299 Engel Stadium .05
300 Tim McCarver Stadium .05
301 Beehive Field .05
302 Tinker Field .05
303 Checklist Alpha 1 .05
304 Checklist Alpha 2 .05
305 Checklist Alpha 3 .05
306 Checklist Alpha 4 .05
307 Checklist Numeric 1 .05
308 Checklist Numeric 2 .05
309 Checklist Numeric 3 .05
310 Checklist Numeric 4 .05

1992 SkyBox AAA

JIM BOWIE AAA
Calgary Cannons / Infield

MT
Complete Set (310): 5.00
Common Player: .05
Wax Pack (15): .50
Wax Box (36): 8.00
1 Pedro Astacio .05
2 Bryan Baar .05
3 Tom Goodwin .05
4 Jeff Hamilton .05
5 Pedro Martinez 3.00
6 Jamie McAndrew .05
7 Mark Mimbs .05
8 Raul Mondesi .10
9 Jose Munoz .05
10 Henry Rodriguez .05
11 Eric Young .05
12 Joe Ausanio .05
13 Victor Cole .05
14 Carlos Garcia .05
15 Blas Minor .05
16 William Pennyfeather .05
17 Mark Petkovsek .05
18 Jeff Richardson .05
19 Rosario Rodriguez .05
20 Tim Wakefield .05
21 John Wehner .05
22 Kevin Young .05
23 Mike Blowers .05
24 Bret Boone .50
25 Jim Bowie .05
26 Dave Brundage .05
27 Randy Kramer .05
28 Patrick Lennon .05
29 Jim Newlin .05
30 Jose Nunez .05
31 Mike Remlinger .05
32 Pat Rice .05
33 Roger Salkeld .05
34 Beau Allred .05
35 Denis Boucher .05
36 Mike Christopher .05
37 Daren Epley .05
38 Tom Kramer .05
39 Jerry DiPoto .05
40 Jeff Mutis .05
41 Jeff Shaw .05
42 Lee Tinsley .05
43 Kevin Wickander .05
44 Royal Clayton .05
45 Bobby Dejardin .05
46 Mike Draper .05
47 Mike Humphreys .05
48 Torey Lovullo .05
49 Ed Martel .05
50 Billy Masse .05
51 Hensley Meulens .05
52 Sam Militello .05
53 John Ramos .05
54 David Rosario .05
55 David Silvestri .05
56 J.T. Snow .15
57 Russ Springer .05
58 Jerry Stanford .05
59 Wade Taylor .05
60 Gerald Williams .05
61 Cal Eldred .05
62 Chris George .05
63 Otis Green .05
64 Mike Ignasiak .05
65 John Jaha .05
66 Mark Kiefer .05
67 Matt Mieske .05
68 Angel Miranda .05
69 Dave Nilsson .05
70 Jim Olander .05
71 Jim Tatum .05
72 Jose Valentin .05
73 Don Barbara .05
74 Chris Beasley .05
75 Mike Butcher .05
76 Damion Easley .05
77 Kevin Flora .05
78 Tim Fortugno .05
79 Larry Gonzales .05
80 Todd James .05
81 Tim Salmon .50
82 Don Vidmar .05
83 Cliff Young .05
84 Shon Ashley .05
85 Brian Barnes .05
86 Blaine Beatty .05
87 Kent Bottenfield .05
88 Wil Cordero .05
89 Jerry Goff .05
90 Jon Hurst .05
91 Jim Kremers .05
92 Matt Maysey .05
93 Rob Natal .05
94 Matt Stairs .05
95 David Wainhouse .05
96 Alex Arias .05
97 Scott Bryant .05
98 Jim Bullinger .05
99 Pedro Castellano .05
100 Lance Dickson .05
101 John Gardner .05
102 Jeff Hartsock .05
103 Elvin Paulino .05
104 Fernando Ramsey .05
105 Laddie Renfroe .05
106 Kevin Roberson .05
107 John Salles .05
108 Derrick May .05
109 Turk Wendell .05
110 Doug Brocail .05
111 Terry Bross .05
112 Scott Coolbaugh .05
113 Rick Davis .05
114 Jeff Gardner .05
115 Steve Pegues .05
116 Frank Seminara .05
117 Dave Staton .05
118 Will Taylor .05
119 Jim Vatcher .05
120 Guillermo Velasquez .05
121 Dan Walters .05
122 Rene Arocha .05
123 Rod Brewer .05
124 Ozzie Canseco .05
125 Mark Clark .05
126 Joey Fernandez .05
127 Lonnie Maclin .05
128 Mike Milchin .05
129 Stan Royer .05
130 Tracy Woodson .05
131 Bob Buchanan .05
132 Mark Howie .05
133 Tony Menendez .05
134 Gino Minutelli .05
135 Tim Pugh .05
136 Mo Sanford .05
137 Joey Vierra .05
138 Dan Wilson .05
139 Kevin Blankenship .05
140 Todd Burns .05
141 Tom Drees .05
142 Jeff Frye .05
143 Chuck Jackson .05
144 Rob Maurer .05
145 Russ McGinnis .05
146 Dan Peltier .05
147 Wayne Rosenthal .05
148 Bob Sebra .05
149 Sean Berry .05
150 Stu Cole .05
151 Jeff Conine .05
152 Kevin Koslovski .05
153 Kevin Long .05
154 Carlos Maldonado .05
155 Dennis Moeller .05
156 Harvey Pulliam .05
157 Luis Medina .05
158 Steve Shifflett .05
159 Tim Spehr .05
160 Brian Conroy .05
161 Wayne Housie .05
162 Daryl Irvine .05
163 Dave Milstien .05
164 Jeff Plympton .05
165 Paul Quantrill .05
166 Larry Shikles .05
167 Scott Taylor .05
168 Mike Twardoski .05
169 John Valentin .05
170 David Walters .05
171 Eric Wedge .05
172 Bob Zupcic .05
173 Johnny Ard .05
174 Larry Carter .05
175 Steve Decker .05
176 Steve Hosey .05
177 Paul McClellan .05
178 Jim Myers .05
179 Jamie Cooper .05
180 Pat Rapp .05
181 Ted Wood .05
182 Willie Banks .05
183 Bernardo Brito .05
184 J.T. Bruett .05
185 Larry Casian .05

186	Shawn Gilbert	.05
187	Greg Johnson	.05
188	Terry Jorgensen	.05
189	Edgar Naveda	.05
190	Derek Parks	.05
191	Danny Sheaffer	.05
192	Mike Trombley	.05
193	George Tsamis	.05
194	Rob Waseenaar	.05
195	Vinny Castilla	.10
196	Pat Gomez	.05
197	Ryan Klesko	.10
198	Keith Mitchell	.05
199	Bobby Moore	.05
200	David Nied	.05
201	Amando Reynoso	.05
202	Napoleon Robinson	.05
203	Boi Rodriguez	.05
204	Randy St. Claire	.05
205	Mark Wohlers	.05
206	Ricky Gutierrez	.05
207	Mike Lehman	.05
208	Richie Lewis	.05
209	Scott Meadows	.05
210	Mike Oquist	.05
211	Arthur Rhodes	.05
212	Ken Shamburg	.05
213	Todd Stephan	.05
214	Anthony Telford	.05
215	Jack Voight	.05
216	Bob Ayrault	.05
217	Toby Borland	.05
218	Braulio Castillo	.05
219	Darrin Chapin	.05
220	Bruce Dostal	.05
221	Tim Mauser	.05
222	Steve Scarsone	.05
223	Rick Schu	.05
224	Butch Davis	.05
225	Ray Giannelli	.05
226	Randy Knorr	.05
227	Al Leiter	.05
228	Doug Linton	.05
229	Domingo Martinez	.05
230	Tom Quinlan	.05
231	Jerry Schunk	.05
232	Ed Sprague	.05
233	David Weathers	.05
234	Eddie Zosky	.05
235	John Briscoe	.05
236	Kevin Campbell	.05
237	Jeff Carter	.05
238	Steve Chitren	.05
239	Reggie Harris	.05
240	Dann Howitt	.05
241	Troy Neel	.05
242	Gavin Osteen	.05
243	Tim Peek	.05
244	Todd Van Poppel	.05
245	Ron Witmeyer	.05
246	David Zancanaro	.05
247	Kevin Baez	.05
248	Jeromy Burnitz	.15
249	Chris Donnels	.05
250	D.J. Dozier	.05
251	Terrel Hansen	.05
252	Eric Hillman	.05
253	Pat Howell	.05
254	Lee May	.05
255	Pete Schourek	.05
256	David Telgheder	.05
257	Julio Valera	.05
258	Rico Brogna	.05
259	Steve Carter	.05
260	Steve Cummings	.05
261	Greg Gohr	.05
262	David Haas	.05
263	Shawn Hare	.05
264	Riccardo Ingram	.05
265	John Kiely	.05
266	Kurt Knudsen	.05
267	Victor Rosario	.05
268	Rich Rowland	.05
269	John DeSilva	.05
270	Gary Cooper	.05
271	Chris Gardner	.05
272	Jeff Juden	.05
273	Rob Mallicoat	.05
274	Andy Mota	.05
275	Shane Reynolds	.05
276	Mike Simms	.05
277	Scooter Tucker	.05
278	Brian Williams	.05
279	Rod Bolton	.05
280	Ron Coomer	.05
281	Chris Cron	.05
282	Ramon Garcia	.05
283	Chris Howard	.05
284	Roberto Hernandez	.05
285	Derek Lee	.05
286	Ever Magallanes	.05
287	Norberto Martin	.05
288	Greg Perechke	.05
289	Ron Stephens	.05
290	Derek Bell	.05
291	Rich Amaral	.05
292	Derek Bell	.05
293	Jim Olander	.05
294	Gil Heredia	.05
295	Rick Reed	.05
296	Amando Reynoso	.05
297	Charlotte, N.C.	.05
298	Ottawa, Ontario	.05
299	Pilot Field	.05
300	Harold Cooper Stadium	.05
301	Bush Stadium	.05
302	Silver Stadium	.05
303	Checklist Alpha 1	.05

304	Checklist Alpha 2	.05
305	Checklist Alpha 3	.05
306	Checklist Alpha 4	.05
307	Checklist Numeric 1	.05
308	Checklist Numeric 2	.05
309	Checklist Numeric 3	.05
310	Checklist Numeric 4	.05

1992 Upper Deck Minor League Promos

This two-card promo set was distributed at FanFest, the National Sports Collectors Convention and a number of minor league ballgames. Similar in format to Upper Deck's regular minor league issue, the promos feature a star-shaped hologram on back.

		MT
Complete Set (2):		2.00
1	Brien Taylor	1.00
350	Frank Rodriguez	1.00

1992 Upper Deck Minor League

For the first time in 1992, Upper Deck entered the minor league card market with a set of 330 base cards plus several inserts. The UD minor league cards are very similar in format to the company's 1992 major league issue, including UV-coating front and back and the use of color player photos on both sides. UD adopted a star-shaped foil hologram on back as an anti-counterfeiting device for its minor league issues.

		MT
Complete Set (330):		17.50
Common Player:		.05
Wax Pack (12):		1.00
Wax Box (36):		25.00
1	Johnny Damon, Michael Tucker Draft Pick Checklist	.25
2	B.J. Wallace (Draft Pick)	.05
3	Jeffrey Hammonds (Draft Pick)	.05
4	Chad Mottola (Draft Pick)	.05
5	Derek Jeter (Draft Pick)	5.00
6	Michael Tucker (Draft Pick)	.05
7	Derek Wallace (Draft Pick)	.05
8	Chad McConnell (Draft Pick)	.05
9	Rick Greene (Draft Pick)	.05
10	Shannon Stewart (Draft Pick)	.40
11	Benji Grigsby (Draft Pick)	.05
12	Jamie Arnold (Draft Pick)	.05
13	Rick Helling (Draft Pick)	.05
14	Jason Kendall (Draft Pick)	.25
15	Eddie Pearson (Draft Pick)	.05
16	Todd Steverson (Draft Pick)	.05
17	John Burke (Draft Pick)	.05
18	Brandon Cromer (Draft Pick)	.05
19	Johnny Damon (Draft Pick)	.75
20	Jason Giambi (Draft Pick)	1.50

21	John Lynch (Draft Pick)	.05
22	Jared Baker (Draft Pick)	.05
23	Roger Bailey (Draft Pick)	.05
24	Eduardo Perez Angels Checklist	.05
25	Gary Mota Astros Checklist	.05
26	Mike Neill Athletics Checklist	.05
27	Howard Battle Blue Jays Checklist	.05
28	Mike Kelly Braves Checklist	.05
29	Tyrone Hill Brewers Checklist	.05
30	Dmitri Young Cardinals Checklist	.05
31	Ryan Hawblitzel Cubs Checklist	.05
32	Raul Mondesi Dodgers Checklist	.05
33	Rondell White Expos Checklist	.05
34	Salomon Torres Giants Checklist	.05
35	Manny Ramirez Indians Checklist	.50
36	Marc Newfield Mariners Checklist	.05
37	Butch Huskey Mets Checklist	.05
38	Mark Smith Orioles Checklist	.05
39	Joey Hamilton Padres Checklist	.05
40	Tyler Green Phillies Checklist	.05
41	Midre Cummings Pirates Checklist	.05
42	Kurt Miller Rangers Checklist	.05
43	Frank Rodriguez Red Sox Checklist	.05
44	John Roper Reds Checklist	.05
45	Phil Hiatt Royals Checklist	.05
46	Justin Thompson Tigers Checklist	.05
47	David McCarty Twins Checklist	.05
48	Mike Robertson White Sox Checklist	.05
49	Brien Taylor Yankees Checklist	.05
50	Carlos Delgado, Rondell White Diamond Skills Checklist	.15
51	Damon Buford (Diamond Skills)	.05
52	Mike Nell (Diamond Skills)	.05
53	Carlos Delgado (Diamond Skills)	.50
54	Frank Rodriguez (Diamond Skills)	.05
55	Manny Ramirez (Diamond Skills)	.75
56	Carl Everett (Diamond Skills)	.05
57	Brien Taylor (Diamond Skills)	.05
58	Kurt Miller (Diamond Skills)	.05
59	Alex Ochoa (Diamond Skills)	.05
60	Alex Gonzalez (Diamond Skills)	.05
61	Darrell Sherman (Diamond Skills)	.05
62	Dmitri Young (Diamond Skills)	.05
63	Cliff Floyd (Diamond Skills)	.05
64	Ray McDavid (Diamond Skills)	.05
65	Rondell White (Diamond Skills)	.05
66	Chipper Jones (Diamond Skills)	1.00
67	Allen Watson (Diamond Skills)	.05
68	Tyler Green (Diamond Skills)	.05
69	Steve Gibralter (Diamond Skills)	.05
70	Calvin Reese (Diamond Skills)	.05
71	Scott Burrell	.05
72	Julian Vasquez	.05
73	Juan Delarosa	.05
74	Lance Dickson	.05
75	Todd Van Poppel	.05
76	Joey Hamilton	.05
77	Mark Mimbs	.05
78	Austin Manahan	.05
79	Mike Milchin	.05
80	David Bell	.05
81	Terrell Lowery	.05
82	Tony Tarasco	.05
83	Shon Walker	.05
84	Robb Nen	.05
85	Turk Wendell	.05
86	John Byington	.05
87	Derek Reid	.05
88	Lee Heath	.05
89	Matt Anderson	.05
90	Joe Perona	.05
91	Tito Navarro	.05
92	Scott Erwin	.05

93	Jim Pittsley	.05
94	Chris Seelbach	.05
95	Skeets Thomas	.05
96	Kevin Flora	.05
97	Scott Pose	.05
98	Jason Hardtke	.05
99	Joe Ciccarella	.05
100	Les Norman	.05
101	Joe Calder	.05
102	Willie Otanez	.05
103	Ray Holbert	.05
104	Dan Serafini	.05
105	Trevor Hoffman	.15
106	Todd Ritchie	.05
107	Lance Jennings	.05
108	Jon Farrell	.05
109	Rick Gorecki	.05
110	Kevin Stocker	.05
111	Joe Caruso	.05
112	Tom Nuneviller	.05
113	Matt Mieske	.05
114	Luis Ortiz	.05
115	Marty Cordova	.05
116	Rikkert Faneyte	.05
117	Rodney Bolton	.05
118	Steve Trachsel	.05
119	Sean Lowe	.05
120	Sean Ryan	.05
121	Tim Vanegmond	.05
122	Craig Paquette	.05
123	Andre Keene	.05
124	Kevin Roberson	.05
125	Mark Anthony	.05
126	Joe DeBerry	.05
127	Tracy Sanders	.05
128	Eric Christopherson	.05
129	Steve Dreyer	.05
130	Jeromy Burnitz	.15
131	Mike Lansing	.05
132	Russ Davis	.05
133	Pedro Castellano	.05
134	Troy Percival	.05
135	Tyrone Hill	.05
136	Rene Arocha	.05
137	John DeSilva	.05
138	Donnie Wall	.05
139	Justin Mashore	.05
140	Miguel Flores	.05
141	John Finn	.05
142	Paul Shuey	.05
143	Gabby Martinez	.05
144	Ryan Luzinski	.05
145	Brent Gates	.05
146	Manny Ramirez	.75
147	Mark Hutton	.05
148	Derek Lee	.05
149	Marc Pisciotta	.05
150	Greg Hansell	.05
151	Tyler Houston	.05
152	Chris Pritchett	.05
153	Allen Watson	.05
154	Steve Karsay	.05
155	Carl Everett	.15
156	Mike Robertson	.05
157	Fausto Cruz	.05
158	Kiki Hernandez	.05
159	Bill Bliss	.05
160	Todd Hollandsworth	.05
161	Justin Thompson	.05
162	Ozzie Timmons	.05
163	Raul Mondesi	.10
164	Shawn Estes	.05
165	Chipper Jones	1.00
166	Kurt Miller	.05
167	Tyler Green	.05
168	Jimmy Haynes	.05
169	David Doorneweerd	.05
170	Bubba Smith	.05
171	Scott Lydy	.05
172	Aaron Holbert	.05
173	Doug Glanville	.05
174	Benji Gil	.05
175	Eddie Williams	.05
176	Phil Hiatt	.05
177	Chris Durkin	.05
178	Brian Barber	.05
179	John Cummings	.05
180	Frank Campos	.05
181	Tim Worrell	.05
182	Tony Clark	.05
183	T.R. Lewis	.05
184	Mike Lieberthal	.10
185	Keith Mitchell	.05
186	Rick Huisman	.05
187	Quilvio Veras	.05
188	Brian Hancock	.05
189	Tarrik Brock	.05
190	Herbert Perry	.05
191	Dave Staton	.05
192	Derek Lowe	.10
193	Joel Wolfe	.05
194	Lyle Mouton	.05
195	Greg Gohr	.05
196	Duane Singleton	.05
197	Jamie McAndrew	.05
198	Brad Pennington	.05
199	Pork Chop Pough	.05
200	Boo Moore	.05
201	Henry Blanco	.05
202	Gabe White	.05
203	Manny Cora	.05
204	Keith Gordon	.05
205	John Jackson	.05
206	Mike Hostetler	.05
207	Jeff McCurry	.05
208	Steve Olsen	.05
209	Roberto Mejia	.05
210	Ramon Caraballo	.05

211	Matt Whisenant	.05
212	Mike Bovee	.05
213	Riccardo Ingram	.05
214	Mike Rossiter	.05
215	Andres Duncan	.05
216	Steve Dunn	.05
217	Mike Grace	.05
218	Tim Howard	.05
219	Todd Jones	.05
220	Tyrone Kingwood	.05
221	Damon Buford	.05
222	Bobby Munoz	.05
223	Jim Campanis	.05
224	Johnny Ruffin	.05
225	Shawn Green	.50
226	Calvin Reese	.10
227	Kevin McGehee	.05
228	J.R. Phillips	.05
229	Rafael Quirico	.05
230	Mike Zimmerman	.05
231	Ron Lockett	.05
232	Bobby Reed	.05
233	John Roper	.05
234	John Mabry	.05
235	Chris Martin	.05
236	Ricky Otero	.05
237	Orlando Miller	.05
238	Scott Hatteberg	.05
239	Toby Borland	.05
240	Alan Newman	.05
241	Ivan Cruz	.05
242	Paul Byrd	.05
243	Daryl Henderson	.05
244	Adam Hyzdu	.05
245	Rich Becker	.05
246	Scott Ruffcorn	.05
247	Tommy Adams	.05
248	Jose Martinez	.05
249	Darrell Sherman	.05
250	Tom Nevers	.05
251	Brandon Wilson	.05
252	Mike Hampton	.05
253	Mo Sanford	.05
254	Alex Ochoa	.05
255	David McCarty	.05
256	Ray McDavid	.05
257	Roger Salkeld	.05
258	Jeff McNeely	.05
259	Jim Converse	.05
260	Greg Blosser	.05
261	Salomon Torres	.05
262	Tavo Alvarez	.05
263	Marc Newfield	.05
264	Carlos Delgado	.50
265	Brien Taylor	.05
266	Frank Rodriguez	.05
267	Cliff Floyd	.05
268	Troy O'Leary	.05
269	Butch Huskey	.05
270	Michael Carter	.05
271	Eduardo Perez	.05
272	Gary Mota	.05
273	Mike Neill	.05
274	Dmitri Young	.05
275	Mike Kelly	.05
276	Rondell White	.05
277	Midre Cummings	.05
278	Kerwin Moore	.05
279	Derrick White	.05
280	Howard Battle	.05
281	Mark Smith	.05
282	Ben Shelton	.05
283	Jose Oliva	.05
284	Steve Gibralter	.05
285	Billy Hall	.05
286	Nigel Wilson	.05
287	Brook Fordyce	.05
288	Mike Durrant	.05
289	Gary Caraballo	.05
290	Shane Andrews	.05
291	Aaron Sele	.10
292	Garret Anderson	.10
293	Oscar Munoz	.05
294	Bobby Jones	.05
295	Joe Rosselli	.05
296	Chad Ogea	.05
297	Ugueth Urbina	.05
298	Ryan Hawblitzel	.05
299	Dennis Burlingame	.05
300	Damon Mashore	.05
301	Jeff Jackson	.05
302	Glenn Murray	.05
303	Scott Cepicky	.05
304	Phil Dauphin	.05
305	Kevin Tatar	.05
306	Domingo Jean	.05
307	Darren Oliver	.05
308	Joe Vitiello	.05
309	John Johnstone	.05
310	Bo Dodson	.05
311	Jon Shave	.05
312	Roberto Petagine	.05
313	Clifton Garrett	.05
314	Rob Butler	.05
315	Jermaine Swinton	.05
316	Alex Gonzalez	.05
317	Jeff Williams	.05
318	James Baldwin	.05
319	Scott Stahoviak	.05
320	John Cotton	.05
321	Jim Wawruck	.05
323	Brian Hunter	.05
324	Joe Randa	.05
325	Robert Eenhoorn	.05
326	Rod Lofton	.05
327	Buck McNabb	.05
328	Jorge Fabregas	.05
329	Brian Koelling	.05
330		.05

1992 Upper Deck Minor League Player of the Year

This 26-card insert set features players who are considered as the top minor league player for each major league team. Cards, which are numbered with a PY prefix, have full-bleed photos and gold foil stamping on the fronts.

		MT
Complete Set (26):		7.50
Common Player:		.25
1	Garret Anderson	.25
2	Gary Mota	.25
3	Scott Lydy	.25
4	Carlos Delgado	2.50
5	Chipper Jones	4.00
6	Troy O'Leary	.25
7	Dmitri Young	.25
8	Ozzie Timmons	.25
9	Todd Hollandsworth	.25
10	Cliff Floyd	.25
11	Joe Rosselli	.25
12	Chad Ogea	.25
13	Tommy Adams	.25
14	Bobby Jones	.25
15	Mark Smith	.25
16	Ray McDavid	.25
17	Mike Lieberthal	.35
18	Midre Cummings	.25
19	Kurt Miller	.25
20	Aaron Sele	.25
21	Steve Gibralter	.25
22	Phil Hiatt	.25
23	Ivan Cruz	.25
24	Marty Cordova	.25
25	Brandon Taylor	.25
26	Brien Taylor	.25

1992 Upper Deck Minor League Top Prospect Holograms

These nine holograms were random inserts in Upper Deck's 1992 minor league packs. Cards, numbered with a TP prefix, feature nine of the top minor league prospects.

		MT
Complete Set (9):		4.00
Common Player:		.50
(1)	Midre Cummings	.50
(2)	Cliff Floyd	.75
(3)	Chipper Jones	3.00
(4)	Mike Kelly	.50
(5)	David McCarty	.50
(6)	Frank Rodriguez	.50
(7)	Rondell White	.50
(8)	Dmitri Young	.50
(9)	Brien Taylor	.50

1992 Minor League Team Sets

While the number of minor league team sets issued in 1992 was much greater than the previous year, many of the small set makers left the field in favor of the Classic Best and Fleer/ProCards combines. New to the team set market was Skybox (tracing its roots back to TCMA) which issued team-set versions of its foil-pack AA and AAA cards.

334 Team Sets and Variations

		MT
1992	SB AAA All-Stars (38)	12.00
1992	CB Albany Polecats (29)	6.00
1992	FPC Albany Polecats (27)	6.00
1992	FPC Albany Yankees (28)	4.00
1992	SB Albany Yankees (26)	7.00
1992	FPC Albuquerque Dukes (32)	20.00
1992	SB Albuquerque Dukes (26)	7.50
1992	Team Albuquerque Dukes Photos (49)	150.00
1992	CB Appleton Foxes (30)	4.00
1992	FPC Appleton Foxes (32)	3.00
1992	FPC Arkansas Travelers (27)	3.00
1992	FPC Arkansas Travelers W/Wendy's Ad (28)	6.00
1992	SB Arkansas Travelers (26)	4.00
1992	CB Asheville Tourists (30)	6.00
1992	CB Auburn Astros (30)	4.00
1992	FPC Auburn Astros (31)	4.00
1992	CB Augusta Pirates (27)	4.00
1992	FPC Augusta Pirates (29)	4.00
1992	Cal Bakersfield Dodgers (33)	35.00
1992	CB Baseball City Royals (27)	4.00
1992	FPC Baseball City Royals (27)	3.00
1992	CB Batavia Clippers (29)	4.00
1992	FPC Batavia Clippers (32)	3.00
1992	CB Bellingham Mariners (29)	8.00
1992	FPC Bellingham Mariners (33)	5.00
1992	CB Beloit Brewers (30)	5.00
1992	FPC Beloit Brewers (29)	4.00
1992	CB Bend Rockies (28)	5.00
1992	FPC Bend Rockies (27)	6.00
1992	FPC Billings Mustangs (30)	4.00
1992	SP Billings Mustangs (30)	5.00
1992	SB Binghamton Mets (29)	8.00
1992	FPC Binghamton Mets (28)	4.00
1992	SB Birmingham Barons (29)	4.00
1992	FPC Birmingham Barons (28)	3.00
1992	CB Bluefield Orioles (25)	3.00
1992	FPC Bluefield Orioles (26)	3.00
1992	CB Boise Hawks (30)	4.00
1992	FPC Boise Hawks (33)	4.00
1992	CB Bristol Tigers (29)	4.00
1992	FPC Bristol Tigers (33)	3.00
1992	FPC Buffalo Bisons (27)	5.00
1992	SB Buffalo Bisons (26)	6.00
1992	CB Burlington Astros (29)	4.00
1992	FPC Burlington Astros (30)	3.00
1992	CB Burlington Indians (30)	4.00
1992	FPC Burlington Indians (32)	3.00
1992	SP Butte Copper Kings (30)	6.00
1992	FPC Calgary Cannons (22)	5.00
1992	SB Calgary Cannons (26)	7.00
1992	Cal League All-Stars (53)	5.00
1992	FPC Canton-Akron Indians (28)	6.00
1992	SB Canton-Akron Indians (26)	7.00
1992	FPC Carolina Mudcats (28)	3.00
1992	SB Carolina Mud Cats (26)	4.00
1992	CB Cedar Rapids Reds (30)	3.00
1992	FPC Cedar Rapids Reds (30)	3.00
1992	CB Charleston Rainbows (24)	5.00
1992	FPC Charleston Rainbows (28)	4.00

1992	CB Charleston Wheelers (24)	5.00
1992	FPC Charleston Wheelers (25)	4.00
1992	FPC Charlotte Knights (25)	6.00
1992	SB Charlotte Knights (26)	6.00
1992	CB Charlotte Rangers (29)	3.00
1992	FPC Charlotte Rangers (27)	3.00
1992	FPC Chattanooga Lookouts (27)	3.00
1992	SB Chattanooga Lookouts (26)	4.00
1992	CB Clearwater Phillies (31)	3.00
1992	FPC Clearwater Phillies (32)	3.00
1992	CB Clinton Giants (30)	4.00
1992	FPC Clinton Giants (29)	3.00
1992	FPC Colorado Springs Sky Sox (28)	3.00
1992	SB Colorado Springs Sky Sox (26)	4.00
1992	CB Columbia Mets (29)	4.00
1992	FPC Columbia Mets (26)	4.00
1992	Play II Columbia Mets (42)	20.00
1992	Play II Columbia Mets Inserts (9)	50.00
1992	FPC Columbus Clippers (28)	6.00
1992	Police Columbus Clippers (25)	7.50
1992	SB Columbus Clippers (26)	7.00
1992	CB Columbus Redstixx (29)	4.00
1992	FPC Columbus RedStixx (32)	4.00
1992	Team Columbus RedStixx (7)	6.00
1992	FPC Denver Zephyrs (29)	5.00
1992	Re/Max Denver Record Holders (20)	5.00
1992	SB Denver Zephyrs (26)	6.00
1992	CB Dunedin Blue Jays (30)	25.00
1992	FPC Dunedin Blue Jays (27)	8.00
1992	CB Durham Bulls (27)	20.00
1992	FPC Durham Bulls (35)	15.00
1992	Team Durham Bulls (29)	17.50
1992	FPC Edmonton Trappers (24)	7.00
1992	SB Edmonton Trappers (26)	6.00
1992	FPC Elizabethton Twins (25)	4.00
1992	CB Elizabethton Twins (28)	3.00
1992	FPC Elmira Pioneers (26)	4.00
1992	FPC Elmira Pioneers (25)	3.00
1992	FPC El Paso Diablos (27)	3.00
1992	SB El Paso Diablos (26)	4.00
1992	CB Erie Sailors (30)	4.00
1992	FPC Erie Sailors (33)	4.00
1992	CB Eugene Emeralds (27)	5.00
1992	FPC Eugene Emeralds (30)	5.00
1992	CB Everett Giants (30)	4.00
1992	FPC Everett Giants (32)	4.00
1992	CB Fayetteville Generals (30)	4.00
1992	FPC Fayetteville Generals (29)	3.00
1992	CB Frederick Keys (28)	4.00
1992	FPC Frederick Keys (28)	3.00
1992	CB Ft. Lauderdale Yankees (30)	4.00
1992	FPC Ft. Lauderdale Yankees (31)	10.00
1992	Team Ft. Lauderdale Yankees (33)	7.00
1992	CB Ft. Myers Miracle (28)	4.00
1992	FPC Ft. Myers Miracle (27)	4.00
1992	CB Gastonia Rangers (27)	4.00
1992	FPC Gastonia Rangers (29)	3.00
1992	CB Geneva Cubs (29)	4.00
1992	FPC Geneva Cubs (28)	3.00
1992	SP Great Falls Dodgers (30)	5.00
1992	CB Greensboro Hornets (29)	10.00
1992	FPC Greensboro Hornets (30)	12.00
1992	FPC Greenville Braves (25)	6.00
1992	SB Greenville Braves (26)	7.00
1992	FPC Gulf Coast Dodgers (31)	3.00
1992	FPC Gulf Coast Mets (31)	5.00
1992	SP Gulf Coast Rangers (29)	5.00
1992	FPC Gulf Coast Yankees (30)	75.00
1992	FPC Hagerstown Suns (25)	4.00

1992	SB Hagerstown Suns (26)	5.00
1992	CB Hamilton Redbirds (30)	4.00
1992	FPC Hamilton Redbirds (30)	3.00
1992	FPC Harrisburg Senators (27)	4.00
1992	SB Harrisburg Senators (26)	5.00
1992	FPC Helena Brewers (27)	3.00
1992	SP Helena Brewers (27)	5.00
1992	CB High Desert Mavericks (30)	4.00
1992	Little Sun High School Prospects (30)	75.00
1992	CB Huntington Cubs (30)	4.00
1992	FPC Huntington Cubs (32)	3.00
1992	BK Huntsville Stars (26)	5.00
1992	SB Huntsville Stars (26)	5.00
1992	FPC Huntsville Stars (27)	6.00
1992	FPC Idaho Falls Gems (32)	3.00
1992	SP Idaho Falls Gems (29)	5.00
1992	FPC Indianapolis Indians (27)	5.00
1992	SB Indianapolis Indians (26)	5.00
1992	FPC Iowa Cubs (24)	3.00
1992	SB Iowa Cubs (26)	5.00
1992	FPC Jackson Generals (27)	3.00
1992	SB Jackson Generals (26)	4.00
1992	FPC Jacksonville Suns (29)	3.00
1992	SB Jacksonville Suns (26)	4.00
1992	CB Jamestown Expos (29)	4.00
1992	FPC Jamestown Expos (28)	3.00
1992	CB Johnson City Cardinals (28)	4.00
1992	FPC Johnson City Cardinals (31)	3.00
1992	CB Kane County Cougars (28)	5.00
1992	FPC Kane Couty Cougars (29)	3.00
1992	Team Kane County Cougars (30)	6.00
1992	CB Kenosha Twins (27)	7.50
1992	FPC Kenosha Twins (28)	5.00
1992	CB Kingsport Mets (29)	3.00
1992	FPC Kingsport Mets (31)	3.00
1992	CB Kinston Indians (29)	4.00
1992	FPC Kinston Indians (29)	20.00
1992	FPC Knoxville Blue Jays (29)	4.00
1992	SB Knoxville Blue Jays (26)	4.00
1992	CB Lakeland Tigers (30)	4.00
1992	FPC Lakeland Tigers (26)	3.00
1992	FPC Las Vegas Stars (24)	3.00
1992	SB Las Vegas Stars (26)	4.00
1992	SP Lethbridge Mounties (26)	5.00
1992	FPC London Tigers (29)	3.00
1992	SB London Tigers (26)	4.00
1992	FPC Louisville Redbirds (26)	3.00
1992	SB Louisville Redbirds (26)	4.00
1992	Team Louisville Redbirds (30)	8.00
1992	CB Lynchburg Red Sox (27)	5.00
1992	FPC Lynchburg Red Sox (26)	3.00
1992	CB Macon Braves (28)	4.00
1992	FPC Macon Braves (30)	3.00
1992	CB Madison Muskies (28)	4.00
1992	FPC Madison Muskies (29)	3.00
1992	CB Martinsville Phillies (30)	4.00
1992	FPC Martinsville Phillies (32)	3.00
1992	FPC Medicine Hat Blue Jays (24)	3.00
1992	SP Medicine Hat Blue Jays (30)	5.00
1992	FPC Memphis Chicks (29)	3.00
1992	SB Memphis Chicks (26)	4.00
1992	CB Miami Miracle (30)	4.00
1992	FPC Midland Angels (26)	6.00
1992	SB Midland Angels (26)	6.00
1992	1 Hour Midland Angels (28)	60.00
1992	Midwest League All-Stars (54)	7.50
1992	CB Modesto A's (27)	6.00
1992	Chong Modesto A's (26)	3.00
1992	FPC Modesto A's (22)	3.00
1992	CB Myrtle Beach Hurricanes (30)	4.00
1992	FPC Myrtle Beach Hurricanes (30)	7.00
1992	FPC Nashville Sounds (26)	4.00
1992	SB Nashville Sounds (26)	5.00

1992	Team Nashville Sounds (33)	7.00
1992	FPC New Britain Red Sox (27)	3.00
1992	SB New Britain Red Sox (26)	6.00
1992	CB Niagara Falls Rapids (29)	12.00
1992	FPC Niagara Falls Rapids (32)	10.00
1992	FPC Oklahoma City 89ers (28)	3.00
1992	SB Oklahoma City 89ers (26)	4.00
1992	FPC Omaha Royals (29)	4.00
1992	SB Omaha Royals (26)	5.00
1992	CB Oneonta Yankees (30)	4.00
1992	FPC Orlando Sunrays (29)	4.00
1992	SB Orlando Sunrays (26)	4.00
1992	CB Osceola Astros (29)	5.00
1992	FPC Osceola Astros (28)	4.00
1992	CB Palm Springs Angels (30)	4.00
1992	FPC Palm Springs Angels (29)	5.00
1992	DD Pawtucket Red Sox Foldout	50.00
1992	FPC Pawtucket Red Sox (28)	10.00
1992	Fram Pawtucket Red Sox Poster	35.00
1992	SB Pawtucket Red Sox (26)	5.00
1992	Team Peninsula Oilers (29)	6.00
1992	CB Peninsula Pilots (30)	5.00
1992	FPC Peninsula Pilots (30)	4.00
1992	CB Peoria Chiefs (30)	4.00
1992	Team Peoria Chiefs (31)	5.00
1992	FPC Phoenix Firebirds (26)	3.00
1992	SB Phoenix Firebirds (26)	6.00
1992	CB Pittsfield Mets (21)	9.00
1992	FPC Pittsfield Mets (28)	5.00
1992	FPC Portland Beavers (26)	3.00
1992	SB Portland Beavers (26)	4.00
1992	CB Princeton Reds (29)	4.00
1992	FPC Princeton Reds (29)	3.00
1992	CB Prince William Cannons (29)	4.00
1992	FPC Prince William Cannons (29)	3.00
1992	CB Pulaski Braves (29)	4.00
1992	FPC Pulaski Braves (32)	3.00
1992	CB Quad City Bandits (30)	4.00
1992	FPC Quad City Bandits (30)	3.00
1992	FPC Reading Phillies (29)	4.00
1992	FPC Reading Phillies Police (29)	7.50
1992	Penn-Lyn Studio Reading Phillies (24)	75.00
1992	SB Reading Phillies (26)	15.00
1992	Cal Reno Silver Sox (29)	3.00
1992	Bleacher Bums Richmond Braves (25)	10.00
1992	Bob's Richmond Braves (26)	60.00
1992	FPC Richmond Braves (28)	6.00
1992	Richmond Comix Richmond Braves (26)	15.00
1992	SB Richmond Braves (26)	6.00
1992	Ukrop's Richmond Braves (50)	25.00
1992	FPC Rochester Red Wings (26)	4.00
1992	SB Rochester Red Wings (26)	5.00
1992	CB Rockford Expos (30)	4.00
1992	FPC Rockford Expos (28)	4.00
1992	CB Salem Buccaneers (28)	4.00
1992	FPC Salem Buccaneers (28)	3.00
1992	CB Salinas Spurs (30)	4.00
1992	FPC Salinas Spurs (31)	3.00
1992	SP Salt Lake City Trappers (29)	5.00
1992	FPC San Antonio Missions (24)	8.00
1992	HEB San Antonio Missions (44)	60.00
1992	SB San Antonio Missions (26)	11.00
1992	CB San Bernardino Spirit (30)	4.00
1992	FPC San Bernardino Spirit (33)	3.00
1992	CB San Jose Giants (30)	5.00
1992	CB Sarasota White Sox (30)	6.00
1992	FPC Sarasota White Sox (30)	5.00
1992	CB Savannah Cardinals (25)	4.00
1992	FPC Savannah Cardinals (30)	3.00

1992	FPC Scranton Red Barons (27)	5.00
1992	SB Scranton Red Barons (26)	5.00
1992	Team Scranton Red Barons (33)	10.00
1992	FPC Shreveport Captains (27)	3.00
1992	SB Shreveport Captains (26)	4.00
1992	Play II South Atlantic League A-S (42)	15.00
1992	CB South Bend White Sox (27)	4.00
1992	FPC South Bend White Sox (30)	4.00
1992	CB Southern Oregon A's (30)	4.00
1992	FPC Southern Oregon A's (33)	6.00
1992	CB Spartanburg Phillies (25)	3.00
1992	FPC Spartanburg Phillies (29)	3.00
1992	CB Spokane Indians (30)	4.00
1992	FPC Spokane Indians (30)	4.00
1992	CB Springfield Cardinals (29)	4.00
1992	FPC Springfield Cardinals (29)	3.00
1992	CB St. Catharines Blue Jays (30)	4.00
1992	FPC St. Catharines Blue Jays (29)	5.00
1992	CB St. Lucie Mets (29)	5.00
1992	FPC St. Lucie Mets (30)	4.00
1992	CB St. Petersburg Cardinals (29)	4.00
1992	FPC St. Petersburg Cardinals (26)	4.00
1992	CB Stockton Ports (25)	4.00
1992	FPC Stockton Ports (28)	3.00
1992	FPC Syracuse Chiefs (31)	5.00
1992	MB Syracuse Chiefs Foldout	16.00
1992	SB Syracuse Chiefs (26)	8.00
1992	Tallmadge Syracuse Chiefs Foldout	15.00
1992	FPC Tacoma Tigers (26)	4.00
1992	SB Tacoma Tigers (26)	4.00
1992	FPC Tidewater Tides (28)	5.00
1992	SB Tidewater Tides (26)	6.00
1992	FPC Toledo Mud Hens (29)	4.00
1992	SB Toledo Mud Hens (26)	5.00
1992	FPC Tucson Toros (26)	4.00
1992	SB Tucson Toros (26)	5.00
1992	FPC Tulsa Drillers (27)	4.00
1992	FPC Tulsa Drillers W/BBC Stores Ad (28)	8.00
1992	SB Tulsa Drillers (26)	5.00
1992	Team Tulsa Drillers (30)	8.00
1992	CB Utica Blue Sox (26)	10.00
1992	FPC Vancouver Canadians (24)	3.00
1992	SB Vancouver Canadians (26)	4.00
1992	CB Vero Beach Dodgers (30)	4.00
1992	FPC Vero Beach Dodgers (30)	3.00
1992	CB Visalia Oaks (30)	5.00
1992	FPC Visalia Oaks (28)	6.00
1992	CB Waterloo Diamonds (30)	4.00
1992	FPC Waterloo Diamonds (27)	3.00
1992	CB Watertown Indians (29)	4.00
1992	FPC Watertown Indians (29)	3.00
1992	CB Welland Pirates (29)	4.00
1992	FPC Welland Pirates (30)	3.00
1992	CB West Palm Beach Expos (30)	7.00
1992	FPC West Palm Beach Expos (29)	6.00
1992	FPC Wichita Wranglers (21)	4.00
1992	SB Wichita Wranglers (26)	5.00
1992	CB Winston-Salem Spirits (28)	4.00
1992	FPC Winston-Salem Spirits (28)	6.00
1992	Team Winston-Salem Spirits (27)	4.00
1992	CB Winter Haven Red Sox (30)	4.00
1992	FPC Winter Haven Red Sox (30)	3.00
1992	CB Yakima Bears (26)	4.00
1992	FPC Yakima Bears (32)	3.00

		MT
PR1	Derek Jeter	2.50
PR2	Carlos Delgado (MVP)	1.00
PR3	Rick Helling	.50
PR4	Derek Wallace	.50

1993 Classic Best

Classic Best's 1993 Minor League series is 300 cards, plus four insert sets, a puzzle set and autographed cards from eight players. The set includes players from A, AA and AAA classifications. Autographed Carlos Delgado, Cliff Floyd, Jeffrey Hammonds, Derek Jeter, Mike Kelly, Phil Nevin, Paul Shuey and Dmitri Young cards (1,200 each) were randomly inserted into packs, as were puzzle contest pieces. By completing a nine-card puzzle, 500 collectors could win a plaque of the eight autographed cards featured in the series. The set's inserts are: Young Guns, Expansion #1 Picks, MVPs and Player and Manager of the Year.

		MT
Complete Set (300):		9.00
Common Player:		.05
Wax Pack (12):		.60
Wax Box (36):		12.50
1	Paul Shuey	.05
2	Brad Clontz	.05
3	Phil Dauphin	.05
4	Kevin Flora	.05
5	Doug Glanville	.05
6	Hilly Hathaway	.05
7	Scott Hatteberg	.05
8	Ryan Hawblitzel	.05
9	Bob Henkel	.05
10	Mike Kelly	.05
11	Jose Malave	.05
12	Jeff McNeely	.05
13	Roberto Mejia	.05
14	Kevin Roberson	.05
15	Chad Roper	.05
16	John Roper	.05
17	Pete Rose Jr.	.25
18	Paul Russo	.05
19	John Salles	.05
20	Tracy Sanders	.05
21	Chris Saunders	.05
22	Jason Schmidt	.05
23	Aaron Sele	.10
24	Bob Abreu	.25
25	Don Sparks	.05
26	Scott Stahoviak	.05
27	Matt Stairs	.05
28	Todd Steverson	.05
29	Ozzie Timmons	.05
30	Michael Tucker	.05
31	Jose Viera	.05
32	B.J. Wallace	.05
33	Mark Wohlers	.05
34	Gabe White	.05
35	Rick White	.05
36	Rondell White	.05
37	Gerald Williams	.05
38	Mike Williams	.05
39	Todd Williams	.05
40	Desi Wilson	.05
41	Johnny Ard	.05
42	Jamie Arnold	.05
43	Howard Battle	.05
44	Greg Blosser	.05
45	Rob Butler	.05

1993 Classic Best Promos

These cards were distributed to dealers to preview the forthcoming Classic Best set.

		MT
Complete Set (4):		4.00
Common Player:		.50

46	Dan Carlson	.05
47	Joe Caruso	.05
48	Bobby Chouinard	.05
49	Adell Davenport	.05
50	Juan De La Rosa	.05
51	Alex Gonzalez	.05
52	Steve Hosey	.05
53	Rick Krivda	.05
54	T.R. Lewis	.05
55	Jose Mercedes	.05
56	Melvin Nieves	.05
57	Luis Ortiz	.05
58	Joe Rosselli	.05
59	Brian Sackinsky	.05
60	Salomon Torres	.05
61	James Baldwin	.05
62	Travis Baptist	.05
63	Bret Boone	.50
64	Mike Buddie	.05
65	Paul Carey	.05
66	Tim Crabtree	.05
67	Tony Longmire	.05
68	Robert Eenhoorn	.05
69	Paul Ellis	.05
70	Shawn Estes	.05
71	Andy Fox	.05
72	Shawn Green (Photo actually Alex Gonzalez.)	.50
73	Jimmy Haynes	.05
74	Sterling Hitchcock	.05
75	Mark Hutton	.05
76	Domingo Jean	.05
77	Kevin Jordan	.05
78	Steve Karsay	.05
79	Paul Fletcher	.05
80	Mike Milchin	.05
81	Lyle Mouton	.05
82	Bobby Munoz	.05
83	Alex Ochoa	.05
84	Steve Olsen	.05
85	Billy Owens	.05
86	Eddie Pearson	.05
87	Mike Robertson	.05
88	Johnny Ruffin	.05
89	Mark Smith	.05
90	Brandon Wilson	.05
91	Derek Jeter	3.00
92	Edgardo Alfonzo	.05
93	Jeff Alkire	.05
94	Roger Bailey	.05
95	Jeff Barry	.05
96	Terrell Buckley	.05
97	Hector Carrasco	.05
98	Danny Clyburn	.05
99	Darren Burton	.05
100	Scott Eyre	.05
101	Chad Fox	.05
102	Joe Hudson	.05
103	Jason Hutchins	.05
104	Bobby Jones	.05
105	Jason Kendall	.25
106	Rickey Magdaleno	.05
107	Buck McNabb	.05
108	Doug Mlicki	.05
109	Chris Eddy	.05
110	Jon Lieber	.05
111	Ken Powell	.05
112	Todd Pridy	.05
113	Marquis Riley	.05
114	Steve Rodriguez	.05
115	Brian Rupp	.05
116	Yuri Sanchez	.05
117	Al Shirley	.05
118	Paul Spoljaric	.05
119	Amaury Telemaco	.05
120	Shon Walker	.05
121	Tavo Alvarez	.05
122	Shane Andrews	.05
123	Billy Ashley	.05
124	Brian Barber	.05
125	Trey Beamon	.05
126	Scott Bryant	.05
127	Scott Bullett	.05
128	Ozzie Canseco	.05
129	Brian Carpenter	.05
130	Roger Cedeno (Photos actually Dan Melendez.)	.05
131	Randy Curtis	.05
132	Alberto De Los Santos	.05
133	Steve Dixon	.05
134	Joey Eischen	.05
135	Brook Fordyce	.05
136	Rick Gorecki	.05
137	Lee Hancock	.05
138	Todd Hollandsworth	.05
139	Frank Jacobs	.05
140	Mark Johnson	.05
141	Albie Lopez	.05
142	Dan Malendez	.05
143	William Pennyfeather	.05
144	Scott Lydy	.05
145	Chris Snopek	.05
146	Quilvio Veras	.05
147	Jose Vidro	.10
148	Allen Watson	.05
149	Matt Whisenant	.05
150	Craig Wilson	.05
151	Rich Becker	.05
152	Mike Durant	.05
153	Brad Ausmus	.05
154	Robbie Beckett	.05
155	Steve Dunn	.05
156	Paul Byrd	.05
157	Jason Bere	.05
158	Ben Blomdahl	.05
159	John Brothers	.05
160	Tim Costo	.05
161	Joel Chimelis	.05

162	Kenny Carlyle	.05
163	Garvin Alston	.05
'164	Sean Bergman	.05
165	Marshall Boze	.05
166	Terry Burrows	.05
167	Danny Bautista	.05
168	Jason Bates	.05
169	Brent Bowers	.05
170	Rico Brogna	.05
171	Armann Brown	.05
172	Brant Brown	.05
173	Julio Bruno	.05
174	Mike DeJean	.05
175	Nick Delvecchio	.05
176	Bobby Bonds Jr.	.05
177	Miguel Castellano	.05
178	Tommy Adams	.05
179	Alan Burke	.05
180	John Burke	.05
181	Ivan Cruz	.05
182	Johnny Damon	1.00
183	Carl Everett	.10
184	Jorge Fabregas	.05
185	John Fantauzzi	.05
186	Mike Farmer	.05
187	Mike Farrell	.05
188	Omar Garcia	.05
189	Brent Gates	.05
190	Jason Giambi	1.00
191	K.C. Gullum	.05
192	Chris Gomez	.05
193	Ricky Greene	.05
194	Willie Greene	.05
195	Benji Grigsby	.05
196	Mike Groppuso	.05
197	Johnny Guzman	.05
198	Bob Hamelin	.05
199	Joey Hamilton	.05
200	Chris Haney	.05
201	Donald Harris	.05
202	Andy Hartung	.05
203	Chris Hatcher	.05
204	Rick Helling	.05
205	Edgar Herrera	.05
206	Aaron Holbert	.05
207	Ray Holbert	.05
208	Tyler Houston	.05
209	Brian Hunter	.05
210	Miguel Jiminez	.05
211	Charles Johnson	.05
212	Corey Kapano	.05
213	Tom Knauss	.05
214	Brian Koelling	.05
215	Brian Lane	.05
216	Kevin Legault	.05
217	Mark Lewis	.05
218	Luis Lopez	.05
219	Jose Martinez	.05
220	Mitch Meluskey	.05
221	Casey Mendenhall	.05
222	Danny Mitchell	.05
223	Tony Mitchell	.05
224	Ritchie Moody	.05
225	James Mouton	.05
226	Steve Murphy	.05
227	Mike Neill	.05
228	Tom Nevers	.05
229	Alan Newman	.05
230	Tom Nuneviller	.05
231	Jonathan Nunnally	.05
232	Chad Ogea	.05
233	Ray Ortiz	.05
234	Orlando Palmeiro	.05
235	Craig Paquette	.05
236	Troy Percival	.05
237	Bobby Perna	.05
238	John Pricher	.05
239	Ken Ramos	.05
240	Joe Randa	.05
241	Ron Blazier	.05
242	Terry Bradshaw	.05
243	Jason Hisey	.05
244	Sean Lowe	.05
245	Chad McConnell	.05
246	Jackie Nickell	.05
247	Pat Rapp	.05
248	Calvin Reese	.10
249	Desi Relaford	.05
250	Troy Ricker	.05
251	Todd Ritchie	.05
252	Chris Roberts	.05
253	Scott Sanders	.05
254	Ruben Santana	.05
255	Chris Seelbach	.05
256	Dan Serafini	.05
257	Curtis Shaw	.05
258	Kennie Steenstra	.05
259	Kevin Stocker	.05
260	Tanyon Sturtze	.05
261	Tim Stutheit	.05
262	Jamie Taylor	.05
263	Chad Townsend	.05
264	Steve Trachsel	.05
265	Jose Valentin	.05
266	K.C. Waller	.05
267	Chris Weinke	.25
268	Darrell Whitmore	.05
269	Juan Williams	.05
270	Tim Worrell	.05
271	Tim Belk	.05
272	London Bradley	.05
273	Tilson Brito	.05
274	Felipe Crespo	.05
275	Kenny Felder	.05
276	Billy Hall	.05
277	Terrell Hansen	.05
278	Rod Henderson	.05
279	Bobby Holley	.05

280	Bobby Hughes	.05
281	Rick Huisman	.05
282	Jack Johnson	.05
283	Gabby Martinez	.05
284	Jose Millares	.05
285	Jason Moler	.05
286	Willie Mota	.05
287	Marty Neff	.05
288	Eric Owens	.05
289	Daryl Ratliff	.05
290	Ozzie Sanchez	.05
291	Dave Silvestri	.05
292	Chris Stynes	.05
293	Aubrey Waggoner	.05
294	Jimmy White	.05
295	Jim Campanis	.05
296	Tony Womack	.05
297	Checklist 1	.05
298	Checklist 2	.05
299	Checklist 3	.05
300	Checklist 4	.05

1993 Classic Best Autographs

In its 1993 foil packs, Classic Best randomly included autographed cards of eight top prospects. Each player signed 1,200 cards.

		MT
Complete Set (8):		75.00
Common Player:		3.00
(1)	Carlos Delgado	12.00
(2)	Cliff Floyd	3.00
(3)	Jeffrey Hammonds	3.00
(4)	Derek Jeter	80.00
(5)	Mike Kelly	3.00
(6)	Phil Nevin	3.00
(7)	Paul Shuey	3.00
(8)	Dmitri Young	3.00

1993 Classic Best Expansion #1 Picks

These two cards, featuring the top picks by the Major League's two new expansion clubs (Colorado Rockies and Florida Marlins), were randomly inserted in 1993 Classic Best foil packs. The cards are numbered with an EP prefix.

		MT
1	John Burke	.10
2	Charles Johnson	.10

1993 Classic Best MVPs

These 10 cards, numbered with an MVP prefix, were randomly inserted into 1993 Classic Best foil packs. The cards feature MVP-caliber prospects from the minors.

		MT
Complete Set (10):		3.00
Common Player:		.10
1	Bubba Smith	.10
2	Javy Lopez	.25
3	Marty Cordova	.15
4	Troy O'Leary	.10
5	Steve Gibralter	.10
6	Gary Mota	.10
7	Larry Sutton	.10
8	Dan Frye	.10
9	Russ Davis	.10
10	Carlos Delgado	2.50

1993 Classic Best Player & Manager of the Year

This two-card set features Carlos Delgado as the player of the year and Marc Hill as the manager of the year. Cards, numbered with a PM prefix, were random inserts in 1993 Classic Best foil packs.

		MT
1	Carlos Delgado	3.00
2	Marc Hill	.25

1993 Classic Best Young Guns

These 28 foil-printed cards were randomly inserted into Classic Best's 1993 foil packs. The cards are numbered with a YG prefix.

		MT
Complete Set (28):		7.50
Common Player:		.10
1	Midre Cummings	.10
2	Carlos Delgado	1.50
3	Cliff Floyd	.25
4	Jeffrey Hammonds	.10
5	Tyrone Hill	.10
6	Butch Huskey	.10
7	Chipper Jones	3.00
8	Mike Lieberthal	.25
9	David McCarty	.10
10	Ray McDavid	.10
11	Kurt Miller	.10
12	Raul Mondesi	.15
13	Chad Mottola	.10
14	Calvin Murray	.10
15	Phil Nevin	.15
16	Marc Newfield	.10
17	Eduardo Perez	.10
18	Manny Ramirez	2.00
19	Edgar Renteria	.25
20	Frank Rodriguez	.10
21	Scott Ruffcorn	.10
22	Brien Taylor	.10
23	Justin Thompson	.10
24	Mark Thompson	.10
25	Todd Van Poppel	.10
26	Joe Vitiello	.10
27	Derek Wallace	.10
28	Dmitri Young	.10

1993 Classic Best Gold Promos

This three card set was distributed at Tri-Star Sports' 1993 spring training card show in Phoe-

nix. Cards are virtually identical to the regular-issue Classic Best Gold except for a gold-foil Tri-Star show logo on front and numbering "X of 3" on back.

		MT
Complete Set (3):		5.00
Common Player:		1.00
1	David McCarty	1.00
2	Mike Kelly	1.00
3	Barry Bonds	5.00

1993 Classic Best Gold

The 1993 Classic Best Minor League Baseball Gold Premiere Edition cards feature three color photos of each player and are foil-stamped on both sides. Each card is color-coded using team colors and includes statistics through the 1992 season. The set includes 216 players from Double A, Single A and Rookie leagues, plus randomly inserted autographed cards of Barry Bonds and Gary Sheffield. No factory sets or jumbo packs were produced; cards are limited to 6,000 sequentially-numbered 10-box cases.

		MT
Complete Set (220):		10.00
Common Player:		.05
Wax Pack (10):		.50
Wax Box (36):		9.00
Barry Bonds Autograph:		75.00
Gary Sheffield Autograph:		10.00
1	Barry Bonds	4.00
2	Mark Hutton	.05
3	Lyle Mouton	.05
4	Don Sparks	.05
5	Joe Randa	.05
6	Dave Mlicki	.05
7	Ken Ramos	.05
8	Bill Wertz	.05
9	Jon Shave	.05
10	Dan Smith	.05
11	William Canate	.05
12	Albie Lopez	.05
13	Rod McCall	.05
14	Paul Shuey	.05
15	Ian Doyle	.05
16	Marc Marini	.05
17	Brien Taylor	.05
18	Mike Kelly	.05
19	Andy Nezelek	.05
20	Marcos Armas	.05
21	Chad Ogea	.05
22	Frank Rodriguez	.05
23	Aaron Sele	.10
24	Tim Vanegmond	.05
25	Phil Hiatt	.05
26	Dan Rohrmeir (Rohrmeier)	.05
27	Greg Blosser	.05
28	Scott Hatteberg	.05
29	Ed Riley	.05
30	Edgar Alfonzo	.05
31	Jorge Fabregas	.05
32	Eduardo Perez	.05
33	John Cummings	.05
34	Bubba Smith	.05
35	Kevin Jordan	.05
36	Tyler Green	.05
37	Heath Haynes	.05
38	Gabe White	.05

39	Doug Glanville	.05
40	Jose Viera	.05
41	Richie Becker	.05
42	Marty Cordova	.05
43	Mike Durant	.05
44	Todd Ritchie	.05
45	Scott Stahoviak	.05
46	Tavo Alvarez	.05
47	Chris Malinoski	.05
48	Rondell White	.05
49	Tim Worrell	.05
50	Benji Gil	.05
51	Ben Blomdahl	.05
52	Rich Kelley	.05
53	Justin Thompson	.05
54	Scott Pose	.05
55	John Roper	.05
56	Rafael Chaves	.05
57	Billy Hall	.05
58	Ray McDavid	.05
59	Mark Smith	.05
60	Jeff Williams	.05
61	Bobby Jones	.05
62	Stanton Cameron	.05
63	Mike Lumley	.05
64	Troy Buckley	.05
65	James Dougherty	.05
66	Chris Hill	.05
67	Tom Nevers	.05
68	Joe Rosselli	.05
69	Steve Whitaker	.05
70	Butch Huskey	.05
71	Shane Andrews	.05
72	Cliff Floyd	.05
73	Alex Ochoa	.05
74	Brent Gates	.05
75	Curtis Shaw	.05
76	Midre Cummings	.05
77	Steve Olsen	.05
78	Mike Robertson	.05
79	Scott Ruffcorn	.05
80	Brandon Wilson	.05
81	Darren Burton	.05
82	Kerwin Moore	.05
83	Joe Vitiello	.05
84	Hugh Walker	.05
85	Howard Battle	.05
86	Rob Butler	.05
87	Carlos Delgado	1.50
88	Jeff Ware	.05
89	Mike Hostetler	.05
90	Brian Kowitz	.05
91	Ryan Hawblitzel	.05
92	Juan De La Rosa	.05
93	David McCarty	.05
94	Paul Russo	.05
95	Dan Cholowsky	.05
96	Dmitri Young	.05
97	Paul Ellis	.05
98	Jay Kirkpatrick	.05
99	Jeff Jackson	.05
100	Duane Singleton	.05
101	Kiki Hernandez	.05
102	Raul Hernandez	.05
103	Brian Bevil	.05
104	Mark Johnson	.05
105	Bob Abreu	.25
106	Gary Mota	.05
107	Jose Cabrera	.05
108	Jeff Runion	.05
109	B.J. Wallace	.05
110	Jim Arnold	.05
111	Dwight Maness	.05
112	Fernando DaSilva	.05
113	Chris Burr	.05
114	Dan Serafini	.05
115	Derek Jeter	4.00
116	Lew Hill	.05
117	Andy Pettitte	1.00
118	Keith John	.05
119	Sean Lowe	.05
120	T.J. Mathews	.05
121	Ricardo Medina	.05
122	Scott Gentile	.05
123	Everett Stull	.05
124	Manny Ramirez	2.00
125	Archie Corbin	.05
126	Matt Karchner	.05
127	Domingo Mota	.05
128	Alex Gonzalez	.05
129	Joe Lis	.05
130	Paul Spoljaric	.05
131	Clifton Garrett	.05
132	Marc Hill	.05
133	Jesus Martinez	.05
134	Salomon Torres	.05
135	Tommy Eason	.05
136	Matt Whisenant	.05
137	Jon Zuber	.05
138	Luis Martinez	.05
139	Glenn Murray	.05
140	John Saffer	.05
141	Tommy Adams	.05
142	Manny Cervantes	.05
143	George Glinatsis	.05
144	Chris Dessellier	.05
145	Joe Pomierski	.05
146	John Vanhof	.05
147	Matt Williams	.05
148	Maurice Christman	.05
149	Damon Hollins	.05
150	Sean Smith	.05
151	Doug Hecker	.05
152	Jamie Sepeda	.05
153	Steve Solomon	.05
154	Jeff Tabaka	.05
155	Greg Elliott	.05
156	Jim Waring	.05

157	Omar Garcia	.05
158	Ricky Otero	.05
159	Jami Brewington	.05
160	Chad Fonville	.05
161	Sean Runyan	.05
162	Jim Givens	.05
163	Dennis McNamara	.05
164	Rudy Pemberton	.05
165	Brian Raabe	.05
166	Jeffrey Hammonds	.05
167	Chris Hatcher	.05
168	Chris Saunders	.05
169	Aaron Fultz	.05
170	Mike Freitas	.05
171	Tim Adkins	.05
172	Chipper Jones	2.50
173	Brandon Cromer	.05
174	Shannon Stewart	.25
175	David Tollison	.05
176	Rob Adkins	.05
177	Todd Steverson	.05
178	Dennis Konuszewski	.05
179	Marty Neff	.05
180	Vernon Spearman	.05
181	Don Wengert	.05
182	Alan Battle	.05
183	Michael Moore	.05
184	Sherard Clinkscales	.05
185	Jamie Dismuke	.05
186	Tucker Hammargren	.05
187	John Hrusovsky	.05
188	Elliott Quinones	.05
189	Calvin Reese	.10
190	Rich Ireland	.05
191	Shawn Estes	.05
192	Greg Shockey	.05
193	Mike Zimmerman	.05
194	Danny Clyburn	.05
195	Jason Kendall	.25
196	Shon Walker	.05
197	Gary Wilson	.05
198	John Dillinger	.05
199	Jim Keefe	.05
200	Eddie Pearson	.05
201	Johnny Damon	1.00
202	Jim Pittsley	.05
203	Jason Bere	.05
204	James Baldwin	.05
205	John Burke	.05
206	Scot Sealy	.05
207	Ken Carlyle	.05
208	Tim Crabtree	.05
209	Quilvio Veras	.05
210	Edgardo Alfonzo	.05
211	Adell Davenport	.05
212	Dan Frye	.05
213	Derek Lowe	.10
214	Steve Gibralter	.05
215	Troy O'Leary	.05
216	Gary Sheffield	.50
217	Checklist 1-55	.05
218	Checklist 56-110	.05
219	Checklist 111-165	.05
220	Checklist 166-220	.05

1993 Classic Best Gold LPs

These Limited Print (LP) cards were random inserts in white jumbo packs of Classic Best, seeded on average about two per box. The LPs share the basic design of the Classic Best Gold set, but have on back a congratulatory message on receiving the LP insert.

		MT
Complete Set (5):		4.00
Common Player:		.50
1	David McCarthy	.25
2	Brien Taylor	.25
3	Joe Vitiello	.25
4	Mike Kelly	.25
5	Carlos Delgado	3.00

1993 Classic Best/Fisher Nuts Stars of the Future

Nineteen projected stars of the future were included in this set produced by Classic Best as a promotion for Fisher Nuts. Cards are similar in format to regular-issue Classic Best cards of 1992, but feature Fisher Nuts advertising on front and back.

	MT
Complete Set (20):	4.00

Common Player:		.10
1	Joe Vitiello *	.10
2	Steve Gibralter	.10
3	Rob Butler	.10
4	Carlos Delgado	1.00
5	Chipper Jones	2.00
6	Mike Kelly	.10
7	Marc Newfield	.10
8	Aaron Sele	.15
9	Brent Gates	.10
10	Eduardo Perez	.10
11	Mike Lieberthal	.15
12	Midre Cummings	.10
13	Dmitri Young	.10
14	Brien Taylor	.10
15	David McCarty	.10
16	Scott Ruffcorn	.10
17	Cliff Floyd	.10
18	Rondell White	.10
19	Paul Shuey	.10
---	Checklist	.03

1993 Classic 4 Sport

Fifty top players from the 1993 draft are featured among their counterparts in the other team sports in the base set, parallels and inserts of the '93 4 Sport issue. Only the baseball players are listed here.

		MT
Complete (Baseball) Set (50):		3.00
Common Player:		.05
Wax Pack (12):		.60
Wax Box (36):		15.00
260	Alex Rodriguez	3.00
PR4	Alex Rodriguez (promo card)	3.00
261	Darren Dreifort	.05
262	Matt Brunson	.05
263	Matt Drews	.05
264	Wayne Gomes	.05
265	Jeff Granger	.05
266	Steve Soderstrom	.05
267	Brooks Kieschnick	.05
268	Daron Kirkreit	.05
269	Billy Wagner	.25
270	Alan Benes	.05
271	Scott Christman	.05
272	Willie Adams	.05
273	Jermaine Allensworth	.05
274	Jason Baker	.05
275	Brian Banks	.05
276	Marc Barcelo	.05
277	Jeff D'Amico	.05
278	Todd Dunn	.05
279	Dan Ehler	.05
280	Tony Fuduric	.05
281	Ryan Hancock	.05
282	Vee Hightower	.05
283	Andre King	.05
284	Brett King	.05
285	Derrek Lee	2.00
286	Andrew Lorraine	.05
287	Eric Ludwick	.05
288	Ryan McGuire	.05
289	Anthony Medrano	.05
290	Joel Moore	.05
291	Dan Perkins	.05
292	Kevin Pickford	.05
293	Jon Ratliff	.05
294	Bryan Rekar	.05
295	Andy Rice	.05
296	Carl Schulz	.05
297	Chris Singleton	.05
298	Cameron Smith	.05
299	Marc Valdes	.05
300	Joe Wagner	.05
301	John Wasdin	.05
302	Pat Watkins	.05
303	Dax Winslett	.05
304	Jamey Wright	.05
305	Kelly Wunsch	.05
306	Jeff D'Amico	.05
307	Brian Anderson	.05
308	Trot Nixon	.45
309	Kirk Presley	.05

1993 Classic 4 Sport Gold

Fifty top baseball players from the 1993 draft are featured among their counterparts in the other major team sports in this factory set of gold edition parallel cards. Each set contains autographed cards of Alex Rodriguez, Jerome Bettis, Chris Gratton and Alonzo Mourning. Only the baseball players are listed here.

	MT
Complete Boxed Set (329):	150.00
Baseball Set (50):	15.00
Common Player:	.25
Gold Stars:	5X
Alex Rodriguez (Autographed edition of 3,900.)	110.00

1993 Classic 4 Sport Alex Rodriguez Jumbo

This 3-1/2" x 5" version of A-Rod's card from the Classic 4 Sport set was issued in two versions. One version (#260) was issued in a special boxed set of jumbo cards. The other (#3 of 5) was issued in a serially numbered edition of 8,000, though the manner of distribution is unclear.

		MT
260	Alex Rodriguez	6.00
3 of 5	Alex Rodriguez	6.00

1993 Classic 4 Sport Autographs

Authentically autographed versions of 26 of the players in the Classic 4 Sport set were produced as random pack inserts. Card fronts share the basic format of the regu-

lar version, but have the player signature as well as a serial number from within the edition stated parenthetically in the checklist here. Backs have a congratulatory message. Only the five baseball players from the set are listed here, arranged according to their numbers in the regular set.

		MT
Common Player:		4.00
(260)	Alex Rodriguez (4,300)	90.00
(261)	Darren Dreifort (3,875)	4.00
(265)	Jeff Granger (150)	4.00
(267)	Brooks Kieschnick (450)	4.00
(268)	Daron Kirkreit (275)	4.00

1993 Classic 4 Sport Draft Stars

Top draft picks in all four major team sports are featured in this chrome-technology insert set, found one per jumbo pack of Classic 4 Sport. The cards feature action photos on a silver-metallic background with gold-foil graphics. At lower-left on each card is a notice that it is one of 80,000. Conventionally printed backs have another photo, personal data and career highlight. Only the baseball players are listed here.

		MT
Common Player:		.50
DS55	Alex Rodriguez	3.50
DS56	Brooks Kieschnick	.50
DS57	Jeff Granger	.50

1993 Classic 4 Sport Inserts

A number of baseball players were featured among the draft picks of the major team sports in the many insert series of the '93 Classic 4 Sport issue. Only the baseball players are listed here.

		MT
TRI-CARDS		
3/8/13	Jeff Granger, Brooks Kieschnick, Alex Rodriguez	6.00
5/10/15	Drew Bledsoe, Chris Webber, Alex Rodriguez	4.00
LIMITED PRINT		
LP18	Alex Rodriguez	4.00
LP19	Darren Dreifort	1.00
LP20	Jeff Granger	1.00
LP21	Brooks Kieschnick	1.00
ACETATES		
9	Alex Rodriguez	6.00
10	Jeff Granger	1.00

1993 Classic 4 Sport McDonald's

These 4 Sport "Exclusive Collection" cards were distributed in portions of the Mid-Atlantic states and central Florida at McDonald's. Besides established stars and prospects in each of the major team

sports, the five-card packs contained random LP (Limited Production) inserts, autographs and redemption cards for autographed memorabilia. Cards have action photos bordered at right by a forest green strip with the player name and position in gold-foil. A special logo is at upper-right. Backs repeat a portion of the photo along with personal data, stats and career highlights. A gold-foil McDonald's arches logo is at bottom. Only the baseball players among the 35 cards are listed here.

		MT
Common Player:		.25
11	Darren Daulton	.45
26	Greg Luzinski, Ryan Luzinski Bull and Baby Bull	.45
31	Chad McConnell	.25
32	Phil Nevin	.25
33	Paul Shuey	.25
34	Derek Wallace	.25

1993 Classic Collectors Club (C3)

This multi-sport set was available as part of a benefits package to members of the Classic Collectors Club. Regular charter memberships were limited to 20,000 with presidential charter memberships limited to 5,000. Regular-version cards have action photos on front with dark blue borders and a gold-foil "C3" logo. Horizontal backs have a portrait photo, stats and biography. Only the baseball players from the set are listed here.

		MT
Complete Set (30):		5.00
Common Player:		.25
1	Phil Nevin	.25
2	Jeffrey Hammonds	.25
3	Paul Shuey	.25
4	Derek Jeter	4.50
5	B.J. Wallace	.25
6	Ryan Luzinski	.25
7	Brien Taylor	.25
25	David McCarty	.25
26	Mike Kelly	.25
27	Dmitri Young	.25

1993 Classic Collectors Club (C3) Presidential

As part of the Presidential level membership in the Classic Collectors Club, these cards were distributed in an edition of 5,000 each. Fronts have an action photo with a gold-foil "C3 Presidential" logo at top and player identification in the wide white border at right. Backs have another photo and a few sentences about the player.

		MT
3	Alex Rodriguez	12.00

1993-94 Fleer Excel

Fleer's 1993-94 minor league set features players who have never appeared in a Major League game. The set of 300, up from 250 cards the previous year, uses UV coating for card fronts and backs, plus gold-foil stamping on the fronts. There are 297 players included in the regular issue, plus three checklists. Players are arranged alphabetically within their major league organization and league. Three insert sets were also available: Minor League All-Stars, League Leaders and "First Year Phenoms." Cards from the three insert sets were randomly included in foil packs.

		MT
Complete Set (300):		12.50
Common Player:		.05
Wax Box (36):		20.00
Jumbo Pack (17):		1.50
Jumbo Box (20):		20.00
1	Armando Benitez	.05
2	Stanton Cameron	.05
3	Eric Chavez	1.00
4	Rick Forney	.05
5	Jim Foster	.05
6	Curtis Goodwin	.05
7	Jimmy Haynes	.05
8	Scott Klingenbeck	.05
9	Rick Krivda	.05
10	T.R. Lewis	.05
11	Brian Link	.05
12	Scott McClain	.05
13	Alex Ochoa	.05
14	Jay Powell	.05
15	Brian Sackinsky	.05
16	Brad Tyler	.05
17	Gregg Zaun	.05
18	Joel Bennett	.05
19	Felix Colon	.05
20	Ryan McGuire	.05
21	Frank Rodriguez	.05
22	Tim Vanegmond	.05
23	Garret Anderson	.10
24	Jorge Fabregas	.05
25	P.J. Forbes	.05
26	John Fritz	.05
27	Todd Greene	.05
28	Jose Musset	.05
29	Orlando Palmeiro	.05
30	John Pricher	.05
31	Chris Pritchett	.05
32	Marquis Riley	.05
33	Luis Andujar	.05
34	James Baldwin	.05
35	Brian Boehringer	.05
36	Ron Coomer	.05
37	Ray Durham	.05
38	Robert Ellis	.05
39	Jeff Pierce	.05
40	Olmedo Saenz	.05
41	Brandon Wilson	.05
42	Ian Doyle	.05
43	Jason Fronio	.05
44	Derek Hacopian	.05
45	Daron Kirkreit	.05
46	Mike Neal	.05
47	Chad Ogea	.05
48	Cesar Perez	.05

#	Player	Price
49	Omar Ramirez	.05
50	J.J. Thobe	.05
51	Casey Whitten	.05
52	Eric Danapilis	.05
53	Brian Edmondson	.05
54	Tony Fuduric	.05
55	Rick Greene	.05
56	Bob Higginson	.05
57	Felipe Lira	.05
58	Joshua Neese	.05
59	Shannon Penn	.05
60	John Rosengren	.05
61	Phil Stidham	.05
62	Justin Thompson	.05
63	Shawn Wooten	.05
64	Brian Bevil	.05
65	Mel Bunch	.05
66	Johnny Damon	1.00
67	Chris Eddy	.05
68	Jon Lieber	.05
69	Les Norman	.05
70	Jim Pittsley	.05
71	Kris Ralston	.05
72	Joe Randa	.05
73	Kevin Rawitzer	.05
74	Chris Sheehan	.05
75	Robert Toth	.05
76	Michael Tucker	.05
77	Brian Banks	.05
78	Marshall Boze	.05
79	Jeff Cirillo	.05
80	Bo Dodson	.05
81	Bobby Hughes	.05
82	Scott Karl	.05
83	Mike Matheny	.05
84	Kevin Riggs	.05
85	Sid Roberson	.05
86	Charlie Rogers	.05
87	Mike Stefanski	.05
88	Scott Talanoa	.05
89	Derek Wachter	.05
90	Wes Weger	.05
91	Anthony Byrd	.05
92	Marty Cordova	.05
93	Steve Dunn	.05
94	Gus Gandarillos	.05
95	LaTroy Hawkins	.05
96	Oscar Munoz	.05
97	Dan Perkins	.05
98	Ken Serafini	.05
99	Ken Tirpack	.05
100	Russ Davis	.05
101	Nick Delvecchio	.05
102	Robert Eenhoorn	.05
103	Ron Frazier	.05
104	Kraig Hawkins	.05
105	Keith Heberling	.05
106	Derek Jeter	3.00
107	Kevin Jordan	.05
108	Ryan Karp	.05
109	Matt Luke	.05
110	Lyle Mouton	.05
111	Andy Pettitte	1.00
112	Jorge Posada	.25
113	Ruben Rivera	.05
114	Tate Seefried	.05
115	Brien Taylor	.05
116	Mark Acre	.05
117	Jim Bowie	.05
118	Russ Brock	.05
119	Fausto Cruz	.05
120	Jason Giambi	1.50
121	Izzy Molina	.05
122	George Williams	.05
123	Joel Wolfe	.05
124	Ernie Young	.05
125	Tim Davis	.05
126	Jackie Nickell	.05
127	Ruben Santana	.05
128	Makoto Suzuki (Makoto)	.05
129	Ron Villone	.05
130	Rich Aurilia	.05
131	John Detmer	.05
132	Scott Eyre	.05
133	Dave Geeve	.05
134	Rick Helling	.05
135	Kerry Lacy	.05
136	Trey McCoy	.05
137	Wes Shook	.05
138	Howard Battle	.05
139	D.J. Boston	.05
140	Rich Butler	.05
141	Brad Cornett	.05
142	Jesse Cross	.05
143	Alex Gonzalez	.05
144	Kurt Heble	.05
145	Jose Herrera	.05
146	Ryan Jones	.05
147	Robert Perez	.05
148	Jose Silva	.05
149	Shannon Stewart	.25
150	Chris Weinke	.25
151	Jamie Arnold	.05
152	Chris Brock	.05
153	Tony Graffagnino (Graffanino)	.05
154	Damon Hollins	.05
155	Mike Hostetler	.05
156	Mike Kelly	.05
157	Andre King	.05
158	Darrell May	.05
159	Vince Moore	.05
160	Don Strange	.05
161	Dominic Therrien	.05
162	Terrell Wade	.05
163	Brant Brown	.05
164	Matt Franco	.05
165	Brooks Kieschnick	.05

#	Player	Price
166	Jon Ratliff	.05
167	Kennie Steenstra	.05
168	Amaury Talemaco	.05
169	Ozzie Timmons	.05
170	Hector Trinidad	.05
171	Travis Willis	.05
172	Tim Belk	.05
173	Jamie Dismuke	.05
174	Mike Ferry	.05
175	Chris Hook	.05
176	John Hrusovsky	.05
177	Cleveland Ladell	.05
178	Martin Lister	.05
179	Chad Mottola	.05
180	Eric Owens	.05
181	Scott Sullivan	.05
182	Pat Watkins	.05
183	Jason Bates	.05
184	John Burke	.05
185	Quinton McCracken	.05
186	Neifi Perez	.05
187	Bryan Rekar	.05
188	Mark Thompson	.05
189	Tim Clark	.05
190	Vic Darensbourg	.05
191	Charles Johnson	.05
192	Bryn Kosco	.05
193	Reynol Mendoza	.05
194	Kerwin Moore	.05
195	John Toale	.05
196	Bob Abreu	.05
197	Jim Bruske	.05
198	Jim Dougherty	.05
199	Tony Eusebio	.05
200	Kevin Gallaher	.05
201	Chris Holt	.05
202	Brian Hunter	.05
203	Orlando Miller	.05
204	Donovan Mitchell	.05
205	Alvin Morman	.05
206	James Mouton	.05
207	Phil Nevin	.05
208	Roberto Petagine	.05
209	Billy Wagner	.05
210	Mike Busch	.05
211	Roger Cedeno	.05
212	Chris Demetral	.05
213	Rick Gorecki	.05
214	Ryan Henderson	.05
215	Todd Hollandsworth	.05
216	Ken Huckaby	.05
217	Rich Linares	.05
218	Ryan Luzinski	.05
219	Doug Newstrom	.05
220	Ben Van Ryn	.05
221	Todd Williams	.05
222	Shane Andrews	.05
223	Reid Cornelius	.05
224	Joey Eischen	.05
225	Heath Haynes	.05
226	Rod Henderson	.05
227	Mark LaRosa	.05
228	Glenn Murray	.05
229	Ugueth Urbina	.05
230	B.J. Wallace	.05
231	Gabe White	.05
232	Edgardo Alfonzo	.05
233	Randy Curtis	.05
234	Omar Garcia	.05
235	Jason Isringhausen	.05
236	Eric Ludwick	.05
237	Bill Pulsipher	.05
238	Chris Roberts	.05
239	Quilvio Veras	.05
240	Pete Walker	.05
241	Mike Welch	.05
242	Preston Wilson	.15
243	Ricky Bottalico	.05
244	Alan Burke	.05
245	Phil Geisler	.05
246	Mike Lieberthal	.10
247	Jason Moler	.05
248	Gene Schall	.05
249	Mark Tranberg	.05
250	Jermaine Allensworth	.05
251	Michael Brown	.05
252	Jason Kendall	.25
253	Jeff McCurry	.05
254	Jeff Alkire	.05
255	Mike Badorek	.05
256	Brian Barber	.05
257	Alan Benes	.05
258	Jeff Berblinger	.05
259	Joe Biasucci	.05
260	Terry Bradshaw	.05
261	Duff Brumley	.05
262	Kirk Bullinger	.05
263	Mike Busby	.05
264	Jamie Cochran	.05
265	Clint Davis	.05
266	Mike Gulan	.05
267	Aaron Holbert	.05
268	John Kelly	.05
269	John Mabry	.05
270	Frankie Martinez	.05
271	T.J. Mathews	.05
272	Aldo Pecorilli	.05
273	Doug Radziewicz	.05
274	Brian Rupp	.05
275	Gerald Witasick Jr.	.05
276	Dmitri Young	.05
277	Homer Bush	.05
278	Glenn Dishman	.05
279	Sean Drinkwater	.05
280	Bryce Florie	.05
281	Billy Hall	.05
282	Jason Hardtke	.05
283	Ray Holbert	.05

#	Player	Price
284	Brian Johnson	.05
285	Ray McDavid	.05
286	Ira Smith	.05
287	Steve Day	.05
288	Kurt Ehmann	.05
289	Chad Fonville	.05
290	Kris Franko	.05
291	Aaron Fultz	.05
292	Marcus Jensen	.05
293	Calvin Murray	.05
294	Jeff Richey	.05
295	Bill Van Landingham	.05
296	Keith Williams	.05
297	Chris Wimmer	.05
298	Checklist	.05
299	Checklist	.05
300	Checklist	.05

1993-94 Fleer Excel All-Stars

Fleer Excel All-Star cards, random inserts in foil packs, feature 10 Minor League All-Stars. A crown with the player's name and "All-Star" in gold foil on the front indicates the player's status. Backs, numbered 1 of 10, etc., give a career summary.

		MT
Complete Set (10):		4.00
Common Player:		.25
1	Charles Johnson	.25
2	Roberto Petagine	.25
3	James Mouton	.25
4	Russ Davis	.25
5	Alex Gonzalez	.25
6	Johnny Damon	2.00
7	Garret Anderson	.50
8	Brian Hunter	.25
9	D.J. Boston	.25
10	Terrell Wade	.25

1993-94 Fleer Excel League Leaders

Fleer Excel's League Leader cards feature 10 players who have compiled league-best statistics. The player's name and "League Leader" are stamped in gold foil on the front; the back has a career summary. Cards, numbered 1 of 10, etc., were random inserts in foil packs.

		MT
Complete Set (20):		5.00
Common Player:		.25
1	James Baldwin	.25
2	Joel Bennett	.25
3	Ricky Bottalico	.25
4	Mike Busch	.25
5	Duff Brumley	.25
6	Jamie Cochran	.25
7	John Dettmer	.25
8	Joey Eischen	.25
9	LaTroy Hawkins	.25
10	Derek Jeter	4.50
11	Ryan Karp	.25
12	Rick Krivda	.25
13	Trey McCoy	.25
14	Jason Moler	.25
15	Jose Silva	.25
16	Brien Taylor	.25
17	Michael Tucker	.25
18	Ugueth Urbina	.25
19	Ben Van Ryn	.25

1993-94 Fleer Excel 1st Year Phenoms

"1st Year Phenoms" is stamped in gold foil on the front of each of the 10 different cards representing players who have made their minor league debuts in a grand fashion. The cards, random inserts in foil packs, are numbered 1 of 10, etc., and feature a summary of the player's minor league accomplishments.

		MT
Complete Set (10):		2.00
Common Player:		.25
1	Jim Foster	.25
2	Brian Link	.25
3	Jeff Berblinger	.25
4	Doug Newstrom	.25
5	Mike Neal	.25
6	Jermaine Allensworth	.25
7	Todd Greene	.25
8	Keith Williams	.25
9	Shawn Wooten	.25
10	Joshua Neese	.25

1993 Front Row Draft Picks '93 Update Promo

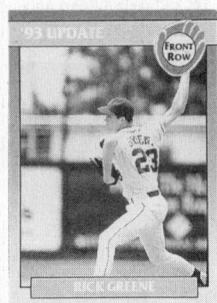

Front Row apparently had thoughts of continuing its draft picks issues in 1993 and issued some promo cards. The set never materialized. Card backs have a large baseball at center with "Front / Row." "PROMO CARD" is above, "1993" is below. Others may exist.

		MT
(1)	Rick Greene	.05
(2)	Sean Lowe	.05

1993 Minor League Team Sets

While the number of team sets grew slightly in 1993, the number of issuers again declined. The market's two giants, Classic Best and Fleer/ProCards had the lion's share of production. Of the team sets issued, Classic Best had 33 percent and Fleer/ProCards 58 percent (with considerable duplication).

287 Team Sets and Variations

Year	Set	MT
1993	FPC AAA All-Stars (55)	10.00
1993	CB Albany Polecats (30)	6.00
1993	FPC Albany Polecats (28)	5.00
1993	FPC Albany-Colonie Yankees (29)	5.00
1993	FPC Albuquerque Dukes (31)	9.00
1993	Team Albuquerque Dukes Photos (40)	125.00
1993	CB Appleton Foxes (30)	4.00
1993	FPC Appleton Foxes (29)	5.00
1993	FPC Arkansas Travelers (27)	4.00
1993	CB Asheville Tourists (28)	10.00
1993	FPC Asheville Tourists (30)	8.00
1993	CB Auburn Astros (30)	6.00
1993	FPC Auburn Astros (30)	5.00
1993	CB Augusta Priates (28)	10.00
1993	FPC Augusta Pirates (27)	8.00
1993	Cal Bakersfield Dodgers (32)	6.00
1993	CB Batavia Clippers (30)	5.00
1993	FPC Batavia Clippers (30)	4.00
1993	CB Bellingham Mariners (30)	4.00
1993	FPC Bellingham Mariners (31)	4.00
1993	CB Beloit Brewers (29)	4.00
1993	FPC Beloit Brewers (30)	5.00
1993	CB Bend Rockies (30)	4.00
1993	FPC Bend Rockies (30)	5.00
1993	FPC Billings Mustangs (30)	5.00
1993	SP Billings Mustangs (28)	7.00
1993	FPC Binghamton Mets (26)	6.00
1993	FPC Birmingham Barons (27)	8.00
1993	CB Bluefield Orioles (30)	4.00
1993	FPC Bluefield Orioles (30)	4.00
1993	CB Boise Hawks (30)	6.00
1993	FPC Boise Hawks (30)	5.00
1993	FPC Bowie Bay Sox (24)	8.00
1993	CB Bristol Tigers (30)	6.00
1993	FPC Bristol Tigers (30)	5.00
1993	FPC Buffalo Bisons (27)	5.00
1993	CB Burlington Bees (29)	10.00
1993	FPC Burlington Bees (28)	8.00
1993	CB Burlington Indians (30)	6.00
1993	FPC Burlington Indians (31)	7.00
1993	SP Butte Copper Kings (24)	6.00
1993	FPC Calgary Cannons (29)	5.00
1993	FPC Canton-Akron Indians (26)	12.00
1993	CB Capital City Bombers (27)	6.00
1993	FPC Capital City Bombers (28)	4.00
1993	FPC Carolina League A-S (52)	9.00
1993	FPC Carolina Mudcats (29)	5.00
1993	Team Carolina Mudcats (24)	7.00
1993	CB Cedar Rapids Kernels (30)	4.00
1993	FPC Cedar Rapids Kernels (28)	4.00
1993	CB Central Valley Rockies (28)	6.00
1993	FPC Central Valley Rockies (29)	4.00
1993	CB Charleston Rainbows (30)	5.00
1993	FPC Charleston Rainbows (31)	4.00
1993	FPC Charlotte Knights (28)	6.00
1993	CB Charlotte Rangers (30)	4.00
1993	FPC Charlotte Rangers (28)	5.00
1993	FPC Chattanooga Lookouts (26)	5.00
1993	CB Clearwater Phillies (30)	6.00
1993	FPC Clearwater Phillies (27)	5.00
1993	CB Clinton Giants (29)	4.00
1993	FPC Clinton Giants (28)	5.00
1993	FPC Colorado Springs Sky Sox (25)	5.00
1993	FPC Columbus Clippers (27)	6.00
1993	Police Columbus Clippers (25)	12.00
1993	Team Columbus Clippers (28)	6.00
1993	CB Columbus RedStixx (30)	7.00
1993	FPC Columbus RedStixx (30)	6.00
1993	CB Danville Braves (30)	6.00
1993	FPC Danville Braves (31)	5.00
1993	CB Daytona Cubs (27)	5.00
1993	FPC Daytona Cubs (26)	4.00
1993	Team Duluth-Superior Dukes (31)	6.00
1993	CB Dunedin Blue Jays (30)	7.00
1993	FPC Dunedin Blue Jays (27)	5.00
1993	Team Dunedin Blue Jays (30)	12.00
1993	CB Durham Bulls (30)	5.00
1993	FPC Durham Bulls (31)	4.00
1993	Team Durham Bulls (31)	7.00
1993	FPC Edmonton Trappers (27)	5.00
1993	CB Elizabethton Twins (30)	6.00
1993	FPC Elizabethton Twins (25)	4.00
1993	CB Elmira Pioneers (30)	5.00
1993	FPC Elmira Pioneers (29)	4.00
1993	FPC El Paso Diablos (28)	5.00
1993	CB Erie Sailors (30)	4.00
1993	FPC Erie Sailors (30)	4.00
1993	CB Eugene Emeralds (30)	4.00
1993	FPC Eugene Emeralds (30)	6.00
1993	CB Everett Giants (30)	6.00
1993	FPC Everett Giants (31)	5.00
1993	CB Fayetteville Generals (30)	5.00
1993	FPC Fayetteville Generals (29)	4.00
1993	FPC Florida State League A-S (51)	7.50
1993	CB Frederick Keys (30)	5.00
1993	FPC Frederick Keys (30)	6.00
1993	CB Ft. Lauderdale Red Sox (30)	5.00
1993	FPC Ft. Lauderdale Red Sox (30)	4.00
1993	CB Ft. Myers Miracle (29)	7.00
1993	FPC Ft. Myers Miracle (29)	5.00
1993	CB Ft. Wayne Wizards (30)	6.00
1993	FPC Ft. Wayne Wizards (30)	5.00
1993	CB Geneva Cubs (30)	5.00
1993	FPC Geneva Cubs (31)	6.00
1993	CB Glens Falls Redbirds (30)	5.00
1993	FPC Glens Falls Redbirds (31)	4.00
1993	SP Great Falls Dodgers (29)	10.00
1993	CB Greensboro Hornets (28)	70.00
1993	FPC Greensboro Hornets (31)	45.00
1993	FPC Greenville Braves (28)	5.00
1993	Team Greenville Braves Foldout	12.50
1993	CB Hagerstown Suns (28)	5.00
1993	FPC Hagerstown Suns (28)	4.00
1993	FPC Harrisburg Senators (28)	9.00
1993	FPC Helena Brewers (31)	5.00
1993	SP Helena Brewers (28)	7.00
1993	CB Hickory Crawdads (30)	16.00
1993	FPC Hickory Crawdads (30)	15.00
1993	CB High Desert Mavericks (29)	8.00
1993	FPC High Desert Mavericks (30)	5.00
1993	CB Huntington Cubs (30)	6.00
1993	FPC Huntington Cubs (30)	5.00
1993	FPC Huntsville Stars (26)	5.00
1993	CB Idaho Falls Braves (31)	5.00
1993	SP Idaho Falls Braves (30)	7.00
1993	FPC Indianapolis Indians (25)	5.00
1993	FPC Iowa Cubs (24)	5.00
1993	FPC Jackson Generals (27)	6.00
1993	FPC Jacksonville Suns (22)	6.00
1993	CB Jamestown Expos (30)	6.00
1993	FPC Jamestown Expos (28)	5.00
1993	CB Johnson City Cardinals (30)	6.00
1993	FPC Johnson City Cardinals (31)	5.00
1993	CB Kane County Cougars (30)	12.00
1993	FPC Kane County Cougars (28)	10.00
1993	Team Kane County Cougars (30)	10.00
1993	CB Kingsport Mets (31)	6.00
1993	FPC Kingsport Mets (27)	5.00
1993	CB Kinston Indians (30)	6.00
1993	FPC Kinston Indians (30)	6.00
1993	Team Kinston Indians (30)	12.00
1993	FPC Knoxville Smokies (29)	10.00
1993	CB Lakeland Tigers (29)	7.00

Year	Card	Price
1993	FPC Lakeland Tigers (31)	6.00
1993	FPC Las Vegas Stars (29)	5.00
1993	FPC Lethbridge Mounties (26)	5.00
1993	SP Lethbridge Mounties (26)	6.00
1993	FPC London Tigers (29)	4.00
1993	FPC Louisville Redbirds (26)	6.00
1993	CB Lynchburg Red Sox (28)	6.00
1993	FPC Lynchburg Red Sox (29)	5.00
1993	CB Macon Braves (30)	5.00
1993	FPC Macon Braves (30)	4.00
1993	CB Madison Muskies (28)	5.00
1993	FPC Madison Muskies (27)	4.00
1993	CB Martinsville Phillies (30)	6.00
1993	FPC Martinsville Phillies (31)	4.00
1993	FPC Medicine Hat Blue Jays (27)	5.00
1993	SP Medicine Hat Blue Jays (25)	6.00
1993	FPC Memphis Chicks (29)	6.00
1993	Team Memphis Chicks All-Stars (36)	10.00
1993	FPC Midland Angels (27)	6.00
1993	FPC Midland W/Bank, Chemical Ads (29)	8.00
1993	OHP Midland Angels (33)	40.00
1993	FPC Midwest League A-S (56)	6.00
1993	CB Modesto A's (28)	15.00
1993	FPC Modesto A's (28)	15.00
1993	FPC Nashville Sounds (25)	6.00
1993	FPC Nashville Xpress (25)	5.00
1993	FPC New Britain Red Sox (28)	5.00
1993	FPC New Orleans Zephyrs (26)	6.00
1993	CB Niagara Falls Rapids (30)	4.00
1993	FPC Niagara Fllas Rapids (31)	4.00
1993	FPC Norfolk Tides (27)	7.00
1993	FPC Oklahoma City 89ers (26)	5.00
1993	FPC Omaha Royals (29)	5.00
1993	TM Omaha Royals 25th Anniversary (18)	30.00
1993	CB Oneonta Yankees (30)	8.00
1993	FPC Oneonta Yankees (31)	7.00
1993	FPC Orlando Cubs (26)	5.00
1993	CB Osceola Astros (29)	8.00
1993	FPC Osceola Astros (27)	7.00
1993	FPC Ottawa Lynx (24)	6.00
1993	CB Palm Springs Angels (29)	4.00
1993	FPC Palm Springs Angels (29)	4.00
1993	DD Pawtucket Red Sox Foldout	45.00
1993	FPC Pawtucket Red Sox (29)	4.00
1993	Team Pawtucket Red Sox (25)	8.00
1993	Team Peninsula Oilers (32)	15.00
1993	CB Peoria Chiefs (27)	4.00
1993	FPC Peoria Chiefs (27)	4.00
1993	Team Peoria Chiefs (30)	12.00
1993	FPC Phoenix Firebirds (29)	5.00
1993	CB Pittsfield Mets (30)	4.00
1993	FPC Pittsfield Mets (30)	7.00
1993	FPC Pocatello Posse (25)	4.00
1993	SP Pocatello Posse (26)	6.00
1993	FPC Portland Beavers (21)	6.00
1993	CB Princeton Reds (30)	4.00
1993	FPC Princeton Reds (31)	4.00
1993	CB Prince Williams Cannons (30)	10.00
1993	FPC Prince Williams Cannons (30)	4.00
1993	CB Quad City Bandits (27)	5.00
1993	FPC Quad City Bandits (29)	4.00
1993	CB Rancho Cucamonga Quakes (30)	4.00
1993	FPC Rancho Cucamonga Quakes (32)	4.00
1993	FPC Reading Phillies (26)	5.00
1993	FPC Reading Phillies Police (26)	7.50
1993	Penn-Lyn Photo Reading Phillies (24)	75.00
1993	Bleacher Bums Richmond Braves Foldout	20.00
1993	Bleacher Bums Richmond Foldout - Gold	60.00
1993	FPC Richmond Braves (30)	7.00
1993	Pepsi Richmond Braves (25)	10.00

Year	Card	Price
1993	Richmond Camera Richmond Braves (25)	75.00
1993	Richmond Comix Richmond Braves (30)	35.00
1993	Cal Riverside Pilots (31)	6.00
1993	FPC Rochester Red Wings (29)	7.00
1993	Rochester Red Wings Foldout	20.00
1993	CB Rockford Royals (30)	12.00
1993	FPC Rockford Royals (31)	10.00
1993	CB Salem Buccaneers (30)	5.00
1993	FPC Salem Buccaneers (29)	4.00
1993	FPC San Antonio Missions (28)	6.00
1993	HEB San Antonio Missions (32)	50.00
1993	CB San Bernardino Spirit (26)	4.00
1993	FPC San Bernardino Spirit (26)	4.00
1993	CB San Jose Giants (30)	5.00
1993	FPC San Jose Giants (29)	4.00
1993	CB Sarasota White Sox (29)	5.00
1993	FPC Sarasota White Sox (30)	4.00
1993	CB Savannah Cardinals (29)	4.00
1993	FPC Savannah Cardinals (27)	4.00
1993	FPC Scranton Red Barons (25)	7.00
1993	Team Scranton Red Barons (30)	8.00
1993	FPC Shreveport Captains (27)	5.00
1993	Team Sioux Falls Canaries (28)	6.00
1993	FPC South Atlantic League A-S (57)	20.00
1993	Play II South Atlantic League A-S (42)	20.00
1993	Play II SAL All-Stars inserts (18)	60.00
1993	CB South Bend White Sox (29)	7.00
1993	FPC South Bend White Sox (30)	6.00
1993	CB Southern Oregon A's (30)	4.00
1993	FPC Southern Oregon A's (30)	4.00
1993	CB Spartanburg Phillies (28)	4.00
1993	FPC Spartanburg Phillies (29)	4.00
1993	CB Spokane Indians (30)	4.00
1993	FPC Spokane Indians (27)	4.00
1993	CB Springfield Cardinals (29)	5.00
1993	FPC Springfield Cardinals (29)	4.00
1993	CB St. Catherines Blue Jays (30)	8.00
1993	FPC St. Catherines Blue Jays (27)	5.00
1993	CB St. Lucie Mets (28)	7.00
1993	FPC St. Lucie Mets (28)	5.00
1993	Team St. Paul Saints (26)	6.00
1993	CB St. Petersburg Cardinals (30)	7.00
1993	FPC St. Petersburg Cardinals (30)	5.00
1993	CB Stockton Ports (30)	5.00
1993	FPC Stockton Ports (29)	4.00
1993	FPC Syracuse Chiefs (27)	6.00
1993	FPC Tacoma Tigers (27)	6.00
1993	FPC Toledo Mud Hens (28)	5.00
1993	FPC Tucson Toros (29)	5.00
1993	FPC Tulsa Drillers (27)	6.00
1993	FPC Tulsa Drillers W/BBC Stores Ad (27)	9.00
1993	Team Tulsa Drillers (30)	17.50
1993	CB Utica Blue Sox (30)	4.00
1993	FPC Utica Blue Sox (26)	4.00
1993	FPC Vancouver Canadians (28)	7.00
1993	CB Vero Beach Dodgers (30)	4.00
1993	FPC Vero Beach Dodgers (30)	4.00
1993	CB Waterloo Diamonds (30)	6.00
1993	FPC Waterloo Diamonds (29)	4.00
1993	CB Watertown Indians (30)	6.00
1993	FPC Watertown Indians (30)	4.00
1993	CB Welland Pirates (30)	5.00
1993	FPC Welland Pirates (31)	4.00
1993	CB West Palm Beach Expos (30)	6.00
1993	FPC West Palm Beach Expos (30)	5.00
1993	CB West Virginia Wheelers (27)	5.00
1993	FPC West Virginia Wheelers (27)	5.00

Year	Card	Price
1993	FPC Wichita Wranglers (26)	4.00
1993	CB Wilmington Blue Rocks (30)	9.00
1993	FPC Wilmington Blue Rocks (30)	7.00
1993	CB Winston-Salem Spirits (27)	5.00
1993	FPC Winston-Salem Spirits (25)	4.00
1993	CB Yakima Bears (30)	6.00
1993	FPC Yakima Bears (31)	5.00

1994 Action Packed Scouting Report Prototype

Though he does not appear in the issued set, Blue Jays prospect Alex Gonzalez was pictured on a prototype card for Action Packed's first foray into the minor league card market. Two other cards, similar in format to the regularly issued version, were also issued. Each of the sample cards has a small gray "PROTOTYPE" on back, above the card number.

		MT
Complete Set (3):		2.50
Common Player:		1.00
1	Trot Nixon	1.50
2	Alex Gonzalez (Franchise Gem)	1.00
3	Russ Davis (Franchise Gem)	1.00

1994 Action Packed Scouting Report

Action Packed Scouting Report features a mix of top prospects from the Class A-AAA minor leagues. Cards feature the hallmark Action Packed technology of embossed, heavily lacquered player photos on front. Backs have the player name in a vertical gold-foil strip at top, and a "scouting report" and minor league stats beneath. A subset of 12 "Franchise Gem" players features a second player photo on back, along with a black diamond, which when activated by finger heat, reveals the players projected Major League debut season. A second subset of five cards honors the 40th anniversary of Roberto Clemente's debut in U.S. professional baseball. The final card in the set is a gold-foil version of MLB's 125th anniversary logo, which is also the set checklist card. Inserts offered 24-karat gold versions of the 12 "Franchise Gem" cards in the set, along with the MLB logo card, plus randomly packaged Franchise Gem cards which have a heat-and-reveal spot on the back with an "Exchange" notation. Those cards could be redeemed for diamond-studded versions of the Franchise Gem cards.

	MT
Complete Set (72):	10.00

Common Player:		.10
Wax Pack (6):		.75
Wax Box (24):		15.00
1	Alex Rodriguez	3.00
2	Trot Nixon	.50
3	Chan Ho Park	.25
4	Brooks Kieshnick	.10
5	Matt Brunson	.10
6	Wayne Gomes	.10
7	Charles Johnson	.10
8	Kirk Presley	.10
9	Daron Kirkriet	.10
10	Curtis Goodwin	.10
11	Alex Ochoa	.10
12	Midre Cummings	.10
13	Russ Davis	.10
14	Phil Nevin	.10
15	J.R. Phillips	.10
16	Jeff Granger	.10
17	Makoto Suzuki (Makoto)	.10
18	Johnny Damon	.75
19	Chad Mottola	.10
20	Scott Ruffcorn	.10
21	Brian Barber	.10
22	Frank Rodriguez	.10
22a	Frank Rodriguez (Autographed edition of 2,500 foil-pack redemptions.)	3.00
23	Michael Jordan	2.00
24	Michael Tucker	.10
25	Rondell White	.10
26	Ugueth Urbina	.10
27	Tyrone Hill	.10
28	Dmitri Young	.10
29	Marshall Boze	.10
30	Marc Newfield	.10
31	James Baldwin	.10
32	Terrell Wade	.10
33	Curtis Pride	.10
34	Gabe White	.10
35	Derrek Lee	.75
36	Bill Pulsipher	.10
37	Butch Huskey	.10
38	Nigel Wilson	.10
39	Tim Clark	.10
40	Ozzie Timmons	.10
41	Brien Taylor	.10
42	J.T. Snow	.15
43	Derek Jeter	3.00
44	Rick Krivda	.10
45	Kevin Millar	.15
46	Matt Franco	.10
47	Jose Silva	.10
48	Benji Gil	.10
49	Pokey Reese	.15
50	Todd Hollandsworth	.10
51	Robert Ellis	.10
52	Brian L. Hunter	.10
53	Todd Ritchie	.10
54	Kurt Miller	.10
55	Alex Rodriguez (Franchise Gem)	2.00
56	Chan Ho Park (FG)	.15
57	Brooks Kieshnick (FG)	.10
58	Charles Johnson (FG)	.10
59	Alex Ochoa (FG)	.10
60	Midre Cummings (FG)	.10
61	Phil Nevin (FG)	.10
62	Jose Silva (FG)	.10
63	James Baldwin (FG)	.10
64	Rondell White (FG)	.10
65	Trot Nixon (FG)	.25
66	Todd Hollandsworth (FG)	.10
67	Roberto Clemente Hidden Talent	.10
68	Roberto Clemente Four-Time Batting Champ	1.00
69	Roberto Clemente 1966 NL MVP	1.00
70	Roberto Clemente 3,000-Hit Club	1.00
71	Roberto Clemente 1973 Hall of Fame	1.00
72	checklist	.10

1994 Action Packed SR Gold Franchise Gems

The 12 24-karat cards in this Action Packed insert set were randomly inserted in foil packs at an average rate of one per 96 packs. This roughly translates to a production figure of 1,850 each of the gold cards. Gold cards have a "24 KT Gold" notation above the Action Packed logo

on front, have the player's name in gold on the back and are specially numbered with a "G" suffix.

		MT
Complete Set (12):		60.00
Common Player:		2.00
1G	Alex Rodriguez	45.00
2G	Chan Ho Park	3.00
3G	Brooks Kieshnick	2.00
4G	Charles Johnson	2.00
5G	Alex Ochoa	2.00
6G	Midre Cummings	2.00
7G	Phil Nevin	3.00
8G	Jose Silva	2.00
9G	James Baldwin	2.00
10G	Rondell White	3.00
11G	Trot Nixon	7.50
12G	Todd Hollandsworth	2.00

1994 Action Packed SR Diamond Franchise Gems

This parallel of the Gold Franchise Gems insert set has a real diamond embedded in each card. Cards are serial numbered within an edition of 100 each and were available by mailing in a redemption card found in packs at a rate of about one per 1,920.

		MT
Complete Set (12):		175.00
Common Player:		12.00
1G	Alex Rodriguez	100.00
2G	Chan Ho Park	12.50
3G	Brooks Kieshnick	12.00
4G	Charles Johnson	12.00
5G	Alex Ochoa	12.00
6G	Midre Cummings	12.00
7G	Phil Nevin	12.00
8G	Jose Silva	12.00
9G	James Baldwin	12.00
10G	Rondell White	12.00
11G	Trot Nixon	20.00
12G	Todd Hollandsworth	12.00

1994 Classic All-Star Minor League Promo

As part of its marketing plan for the 200-card All-Star Minor League set released in mid-summer 1994, Classic produced this promotional card. In the same format as the regular-issue cards, there are action photos on front and back, and each side is UV coated. Back has information on the forthcoming issue.

		MT
CB1	Alex Rodriguez	4.00
CB1	Alex Rodriguez (Scoreboard-certified autographed, numbered edition of 1,994.)	200.00

1994 Classic All-Star Minor League

Classic's minor league wax issue for '94 features a 200-card base set with several chase sets and autograph inserts. Cards feature borderless action phtos on front. Graphics include the Classic

logo (upper-left), MLB team logo (lower-right), and minor league team logo (lower-left). Backs have a large portrait photo with the bottom half "ghosted" to allow overprinting of stats and career data.

	MT
Complete Set (200):	9.00
Common Player:	.05
Wax Pack (10):	.75
Wax Box (36):	20.00
1 Michael Jordan	2.00
2 Felipe Lira	.05
3 Jose Silva	.05
4 Yuri Sanchez	.05
5 Marcus Jensen	.05
6 Julio Santana	.05
7 Angel Martinez	.05
8 Jose Herrera	.05
9 D.J. Boston	.05
10 Trot Nixon	.50
11 Trey Beamon	.05
12 Danny Clyburn	.05
13 John Wasdin	.05
14 Vince Moore	.05
15 Vic Darensbourg	.05
16 Kevin Gallaher	.05
17 Julio Bruno	.05
18 Terrell Lowery	.05
19 Phil Geisler	.05
20 Chan Ho Park	.15
21 Chad McConnell	.05
22 Ricky Bottalico	.05
23 Jim Pittsley	.05
24 Gabe Martinez	.05
25 Johnny Damon	1.00
26 Basil Shabazz	.05
27 Billy Ashley	.05
28 Andy Pettitte	1.00
29 Robert Ellis	.05
30 Mike Zolecki	.05
31 League All-Star #1	.05
32 John Burke	.05
33 Chris Snopek	.05
34 Mark Thompson	.05
35 Jimmy Haynes	.05
36 Ron Villone	.05
37 Curtis Goodwin	.05
38 Tim Belk	.05
39 Rod Henderson	.05
40 Butch Huskey	.05
41 Chris Smith	.05
42 B.J. Wallace	.05
43 Guillermo Mercedes	.05
44 Ugueth Urbina	.05
45 Fausto Cruz	.05
46 Julian Tavarez	.05
47 Scott Lydy	.05
48 Darren Burton	.05
49 Mac Suzuki	.05
50 Kirk Presley	.05
51 Alex Rodriguez Checklist	.50
52 Armando Benitez	.05
53 Rodney Pedraza	.05
54 LaTroy Hawkins	.05
55 Rick Forney	.05
56 Tripp Cromer	.05
57 Andres Berumen	.05
58 Terry Bradshaw	.05
59 Omar Ramirez	.05
60 Derek Jeter	4.00
61 Kerwin Moore	.05
62 Andy Larkin	.05
63 Neifi Perez	.05
64 Casey Whitten	.05
65 Jon Ratliff	.05
66 J.J. Johnson	.05
67 Preston Wilson	.15
68 Jason Isringhausen	.05
69 Adam Meinershagen	.05
70 Rondell White	.05
71 Shannon Stewart	.15
72 Keith Heberling	.05
73 Ruben Rivera	.05
74 Mike Lieberthal	.15
75 Damon Hollins	.05
76 Jason Jacome	.05
77 Amaury Telemaco	.05
78 Scott Talanoa	.05
79 Dave Stevens	.05
80 Brien Taylor	.05
81 League All-Stars #2	.05
82 Brian Barber	.05
83 Ray Durham	.05
84 Brent Bowers	.05
85 Shane Andrews	.05
86 Gabe White	.05
87 Midre Cummings	.05
88 Brad Radke	.15
89 Joe Randa	.05
90 Phil Nevin	.05
91 Joe Vitiello	.05
92 Ray McDavid	.05
93 Robbie Beckett	.05
94 Frank Rodriguez	.05
95 Marc Newfield	.05
96 Joey Eischen	.05
97 Manny Alexander	.05
98 Jeff McNeely	.05
99 Mark Smith	.05
100 Alex Rodriguez	2.50
101 Todd Hollandsworth	.05
102 Scott Ruffcorn	.05
103 Kurt Miller	.05
104 Justin Mashore	.05
105 Garret Anderson	.15

106	Nigel Wilson	.05
107	Howard Battle	.05
108	Calvin Reese	.15
109	Orlando Miller	.05
110	Bill Pulsipher	.05
111	Edgar Renteria	.15
112	Steve Gibralter	.05
113	Gene Schall	.05
114	John Roper	.05
115	Alvin Morman	.05
116	Doug Glanville	.05
117	Mark Hutton	.05
118	Glenn Murray	.05
119	Curtis Shaw	.05
120	Alex Ochoa	.05
121	Michael Moore	.05
122	Joey Hamilton	.05
123	James Baldwin	.05
124	Chad Ogea	.05
125	Rikkert Faneyte	.05
126	Benji Gil	.05
127	Kenny Felder	.05
128	Brant Brown	.05
129	Eddie Pearson	.05
130	Derrek Lee	1.00
131	League All-Stars #3	.05
132	Dan Serafini	.05
133	Ramon Caraballo	.05
134	Derek Wallace	.05
135	Jamie Arnold	.05
136	Domingo Jean	.05
137	Jose Malave	.05
138	Derek Lowe	.10
139	Marshall Boze	.05
140	Billy Wagner	.15
141	Matt Franco	.05
142	Roger Cedeno	.05
143	Russ Davis	.05
144	Kevin Flora	.05
145	Rick Gorecki	.05
146	Rick Greene	.05
147	Brian Hunter	.05
148	Rich Aurilia	.05
149	Jason Moller	.05
150	Michael Tucker	.05
151	Alex Rodriguez Checklist	.50
152	Chad Mottola	.05
153	Calvin Murray	.05
154	Melvin Nieves	.05
155	Luis Ortiz	.05
156	Chris Roberts	.05
157	Todd Williams	.05
158	Tony Phillips	.05
159	DeShawn Warren	.05
160	Paul Shuey	.05
161	Dmitri Young	.05
162	Jermaine Allensworth	.05
163	Daron Kirkreit	.05
164	Scott Christman	.05
165	Steve Soderstrom	.05
166	J.R. Phillips	.05
167	Karim Garcia	.25
168	Mark Acre	.05
169	Jose Paniagua	.05
170	Terrell Wade	.05
171	Mike Bell	.05
172	Alan Benes	.05
173	Jeff D'Amico	.05
174	Tate Seefried	.05
175	Wayne Gomes	.05
176	Chris Singleton	.05
177	Marc Valdes	.05
178	Jamey Wright	.05
179	Jay Powell	.05
180	Charles Johnson	.05
181	Mitch House	.05
182	Torii Hunter	.50
183	Jeff Suppan	.05
184	Roberto Petagine	.05
185	Ryan McGuire	.05
186	Andrew Lorraine	.05
187	Matt Brunson	.05
188	Eduardo Perez	.05
189	Jay Witasick	.05
190	Shawn Green	.50
191	Cleveland Ladell	.05
192	Paul Bako	.05
193	Brook Fordyce	.05
194	Kym Ashworth	.05
195	Tony Mitchell	.05
196	Tony Clark	.05
197	Curtis Pride	.05
198	Arquimedez Pozo	.05
199	Rey Ordonez	.05
200	Brooks Kieschnick	.05

1994 Classic All-Star Minor League Autographs

Randomly inserted into foil packs of Classic All-Star Minor League baseball was this series of seven minor league autographs cards. Fronts have the same format as the regular-issue cards, along with the player signature and serial number from within the edition as specified for each card in this checklist. Backs have a congratulatory message.

		MT
Complete Set (7):		85.00
Common Player:		3.00
AU1	Alex Rodriguez (2,100)	110.00
AU2	Terrell Wade (2,080)	3.00
AU3	Brooks Kieschnick (3,400)	3.00
AU4	Rondell White (2,880)	3.00
AU5	Michael Tucker (2,400)	3.00
AU6	Kirk Presley (1,300)	3.00
AU7	Trot Nixon (1,700)	10.00

1994 Classic Bonus Baby

Five of the hottest prospects of the day are featured in this insert set. Fronts feature action photos which have been graphically enhanced to convey the image of speed. In the lower-right corner is a gold-foil box with "BONUS BABY," the Classic logotype and player name. Backs have another photo, career highlights, appropriate logos and a serial number from within an edition of 9,994 of each card.

		MT
Complete Set (5):		7.00
Common Player:		.50
BB1	Trot Nixon	.75
BB2	Kirk Presley	.50
BB3	Alex Rodriguez	6.00
BB3a	Alex Rodriguez (Autographed edition of 450.)	400.00
BB4	Brooks Kieschnick	.50
BB5	Michael Tucker	.50

1994 Classic Cream of the Crop

These premium cards are a one-per-pack insert in Classic's All-Star minor league issue. Cards have player photos on a borderless "metallized" background. The player and insert set name are printed on black or orange blocks at bottom. Horizontally formatted backs are conventionally printed and include a large photo and career summary.

		MT
Complete Set (25):		5.00
Common Player:		.15
CC1	Trot Nixon	.50
CC2	Kirk Presley	.15
CC3	Mac Suzuki	.15
CC4	Brooks Kieschnick	.15
CC5	Johnny Damon	.75
CC6	Howard Battle	.15
CC7	Michael Tucker	.15
CC8	Todd Hollandsworth	.15

CC9	J.R. Phillips	.15
CC10	Shannon Stewart	.25
CC11	Alex Rodriguez	1.00
CC12	Terrell Wade	.15
CC13	Rondell White	.15
CC14	James Baldwin	.15
CC15	Shane Andrews	.15
CC16	Chan Ho Park	.15
CC17	Derek Jeter	3.00
CC18	Charles Johnson	.15
CC19	Bill Pulsipher	.15
CC20	Phil Nevin	.15
CC21	Scott Ruffcorn	.15
CC22	Midre Cummings	.15
CC23	Frank Rodriguez	.15
CC24	Dmitri Young	.15
CC25	Shawn Green	.75

1994 Classic Cream of the Crop Update

Each pack of Classic Update contains one of these premium inserts. Cards have player photos set against a refractive foil background. The player's name and set logo are printed in white on dark blue panels at bottom. Backs are formatted horizontally, conventionally printed and include another photo, career highlights and appropriate team, licensor and licensee logos.

		MT
Complete Set (20):		5.00
Common Player:		.25
CC1	Paul Wilson	.25
CC2	Ben Grieve	.35
CC3	Dustin Hermanson	.25
CC4	Antone Williamson	.25
CC5	Josh Booty	.25
CC6	Doug Million	.25
CC7	Todd Walker	.35
CC8	C.J. Nitkowski	.25
CC9	Jaret Wright	.25
CC10	Mark Farris	.25
CC11	Nomar Garciaparra	4.00
CC12	Paul Konerko	.50
CC13	Jayson Peterson	.25
CC14	Matt Smith	.25
CC15	Ramon Castro	.25
CC16	Cade Gaspar	.25
CC17	Terrence Long	.25
CC18	Hiram Bocachica	.25
CC19	Dante Powell	.25
CC20	Brian Buchanan	.25

1994 Classic Update Cal Ripken Tribute

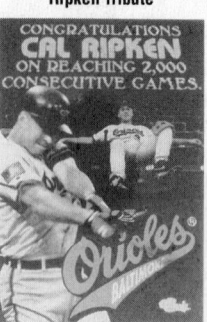

This special insert was issued with the Update series of Classic Minor League Baseball All-Star edition. The front pictures Ripken in a batting swing with another picture of him seated in the box seats in the background. Typography at top congratulates the iron man for reaching his 2,000th consecutive game. On back are photos of Ripken as an Oriole and as a minor leaguer in the uniform of the Rochester Red Wings. Text on back traces his career to that point. An autographed edition of 2,000 of the cards was also produced.

	MT
	MT
CR1	Cal Ripken Jr.	6.00
CR1	Cal Ripken Jr./Auto.	110.00

1994 Classic Assets (Baseball)

A number of baseball players are featured in the five-sport lineup of the base set, inserts and phonecards in Assets' debut year. Parallel cards bearing a silver facsimile autograph on front are worth 4X-6X the values quoted.

		MT
Base Set/Inserts		
4	Nolan Ryan	1.00
4	Nolan Ryan (Silver-foil signature.)	2.00
13	Paul Wilson	.25
13	Paul Wilson (Silver-foil signature.)	.50
18	Ben Grieve	.25
18	Ben Grieve (Silver-foil signature.)	.50
29	Nolan Ryan	1.00
38	Paul Wilson	.25
43	Ben Grieve	.25
64	Doug Million	.25
65	Barry Bonds	1.00
89	Doug Million	.25
90	Barry Bonds	1.00
DC4	Nolan Ryan (Die-Cut)	4.00
DC15	Nomar Garciaparra (Die-Cut)	2.00
DC17	Barry Bonds (Die-Cut)	4.00
DC18	Paul Wilson (Die-Cut)	.50

1994 Classic Assets Chrome

Technology similar to Topps "Finest" was used for the fronts of this four-sport 20-card insert series found in Classic Assets. The final four cards in the set are baseball players and are checklisted here. Fronts have gold-foil graphic highlights and a "1 of 9,750" notation. Backs are conventionally printed with a player portrait photo and career details. Cards are numbered with a "CC" prefix.

		MT
Baseball Set (4):		17.50
Common Player:		1.00
CC17	Alex Rodriguez	15.00
CC18	Kirk Presley	1.00
CC19	Trot Nixon	5.00
CC20	Brooks Kieschnick	1.00

1994 Classic Best Gold

This 200-card set features UV coating on both sides of the cards and foil stamping on the fronts. Virtually every level of minor league baseball is represented in this set. Insert sets highlight first-round draft picks and glow-in-the-dark illustrated acetate cards.

		MT
Complete Set (200):		10.00
Wax Box:		20.00
1	Brien Taylor	.05
2	Jeff D'Amico	.05

3	Trot Nixon	.50
4	Clayton Byrne	.05
5	Eric Chavez	.50
6	Matt Jarvis	.05
7	Billy Owens	.05
8	Jay Powell	.05
9	Robert Eenhoorn	.05
10	Trey Beamon	.05
11	Todd Williams	.05
12	Tim Davis	.05
13	Brian Barber	.05
14	Jeff Shireman	.05
15	Melvin Mora	.05
16	Phil Nevin	.10
17	Kendall Rhine	.05
18	Billy Wagner	.25
19	Jason Kendall	.25
20	Kelly Wunsch	.05
21	D.J. Boston	.05
22	Shannon Stewart	.25
23	Anthony Manahan	.05
24	Dwight Robinson	.05
25	Alan Benes	.05
26	Dennis Slininger	.05
27	John Burke	.05
28	Jamey Wright	.05
29	Scott Eyre	.05
30	Jack Kimel	.05
31	Kerry Lacy	.05
32	Rich Aurilia	.05
33	Dave Giberti	.05
34	Daryl Henderson	.05
35	Stanley Evans	.05
36	Wayne Gomes	.05
37	Rob Grable	.05
38	Mike Juhl	.05
39	Jason Moler	.05
40	Jon Zuber	.05
41	Chad Fonville	.05
42	Mark Thompson	.05
43	Billy Masse	.05
44	Derek Hacopian	.05
45	J.J. Thobe	.05
46	Charles York	.05
47	Jamie Howard	.05
48	Andre King	.05
49	Tim Delgado	.05
50	Mike Hubbard	.05
51	Bernie Nunez	.05
52	Jon Ratliff	.05
53	Pedro Valdez	.05
54	Rich Butler	.05
55	Felipe Crespo	.05
56	Randy Phillips	.05
57	Todd Steverson	.05
58	Chris Stynes	.05
59	Ben Weber	.05
60	Chris Weinke	.15
61	Rob Lukachyk	.05
62	Brett King	.05
63	Chris Singleton	.05
64	Brian Bright	.05
65	Brent Brede	.05
66	Steve Hazlett	.05
67	Dan Serafini	.05
68	Matt Farner	.05
69	Jeremy Lee	.05
70	Anthony Medrano	.05
71	Josue Estrada	.05
72	Martin Mainville	.05
73	Chris Schwab	.05
74	John Roskos	.05
75	Charles Peterson	.05
76	Kevin Pickford	.05
77	Charles Rice	.05
78	Mike Bell	.05
79	Ed Diaz	.05
80	Torii Hunter	.50
81	Kelcey Mucker	.05
82	Nick Delvecchio	.05
83	Derek Jeter	4.00
84	Ryan Karp	.05
85	Matt Luke	.05
86	Ray Suplee	.05
87	Tyler Houston	.05
88	Brad Cornett	.05
89	Kris Harmes	.05
90	Shane Andrews	.05
91	Ugueth Urbina	.05
92	Chris Mader	.05
93	Eddie Pearson	.05
94	Tim Clark	.05
95	Chris Malinoski	.05
96	John Toale	.05
97	Mark Acre	.05
98	Ernie Young	.05
99	Jeff Schmidt	.05
100	Roberto Petagine	.05

101	Eddy Diaz	.05
102	Ruben Santana	.05
103	Ron Villone	.05
104	Nate Dishington	.05
105	Charles Johnson	.05
106	Preston Wilson	.15
107	Paul Shuey	.05
108	Howard Battle	.05
109	Tim Hyers	.05
110	Rick Greene	.05
111	Justin Thompson	.05
112	Frank Rodriguez	.05
113	Jamie Arnold	.05
114	Marty Malloy	.05
115	Darrell May	.05
116	Leo Ramirez	.05
117	Tom Thobe	.05
118	Terrell Wade	.05
119	Marc Valdes	.05
120	Scott Rolen	1.50
121	Les Norman	.05
122	Michael Tucker	.05
123	Joe Vitiello	.05
124	Chris Roberts	.05
125	Jason Giambi	1.50
126	Izzy Molina	.05
127	Scott Shockey	.05
128	John Wasdin	.05
129	Joel Wolfe	.05
130	Brooks Kieschnick	.05
131	Kennie Steenstra	.05
132	Hector Trinidad	.05
133	Derek Wallace	.05
134	Kevin Lane	.05
135	Buck McNabb	.05
136	James Mouton	.05
137	Joey Eischen	.05
138	Todd Haney	.05
139	John Pricher	.05
140	Jeff Brown	.05
141	Jason Hardtke	.05
142	Derek Lee	1.50
143	Ira Smith	.05
144	Mike Kelly	.05
145	Mark Smith	.05
146	Sherard Clinkscales	.05
147	Ben VanRyn	.05
148	Tim Cooper	.05
149	Manny Martinez	.05
150	Kurt Ehmann	.05
151	Doug Mirabelli	.05
152	Chris Wimmer	.05
153	Scott Christman	.05
154	Kevin Coughlin	.05
155	Troy Fryman	.05
156	Sean Johnston	.05
157	Jeff Alkire	.05
158	Mike Busby	.05
159	John O'Brien	.05
160	Brian Rupp	.05
161	Steve Soderstrom	.05
162	Craig Wilson	.05
163	Alan Burke	.05
164	Mike Murphy	.05
165	T.J. Mathews	.05
166	Edgardo Alfonzo	.05
167	Randy Curtis	.05
168	Bernie Millan	.05
169	Mike Cantu	.05
170	Clint Davis	.05
171	Jason Kisey	.05
172	Aldo Pecorilli	.05
173	Dmitri Young	.05
174	Marshall Boze	.05
175	Bill Hardwick	.05
176	Kevin Riggs	.05
177	Lee Stevens	.05
178	Webster Garrison	.05
179	Wally Ritchie	.05
180	Cris Colon	.05
181	Rick Helling	.05
182	Trey McCoy	.05
183	Marc Barcelo	.05
184	Chris Demetral	.05
185	Rick Linares	.05
186	Daron Kirkreit	.05
187	Casey Whitten	.05
188	Shon Walker	.05
189	Rod Henderson	.05
190	Tyrone Horne	.05
191	B.J. Wallace	.05
192	Louis Maberry	.05
193	Brian Boehringer	.05
194	Glenn DiSarcina	.05
195	Melvin Bunch	.05
196	Chad Mottola	.05
197	Ryan Luzinski	.05
198	Tom Wilson	.05
199	Checklist 1	.05
200	Checklist 2	.05

1994 Classic Best Gold #1 Picks

Classic Best's #1 Draft Pick insert cards feature 19 top picks. The cards, numbered with an LP prefix, utilize a chromium effect printing process that gives the cards a reflective textured effect. They are randomly inserted at an average rate of one per 12 foil packs.

		MT
Complete Set (19):		6.00
Common Player:		.25
1	Alan Benes	.25
2	Scott Christman	.25

3	Jeff D'Amico	.25
4	Wayne Gomes	.25
5	Torii Hunter	1.50
6	Brooks Kieschnick	.25
7	Daron Kirkreit	.25
8	Derrek Lee	3.00
9	Trot Nixon	2.00
10	Charles Peterson	.25
11	Jay Powell	.25
12	Jon Ratliff	.25
13	Chris Schwabb	.25
14	Steve Soderstrom	.25
15	Marc Valdes	.25
16	Billy Wagner	1.00
17	John Wasdin	.25
18	Jamey Wright	.25
19	Kelly Wunsch	.25

1994 Classic Best Gold Rookie Express

These chase cards are found only in Classic Best Gold jumbo packs at the rate of one per pack. The cards use the same chromium layered technology as the #1 draft pick inserts and share an identical checklist. Card #20 is printed with glow in the dark ink.

		MT
Complete Set (20):		3.00
Common Player:		.25
1	Alan Benes	.25
2	Scott Christman	.25
3	Jeff D'Amico	.25
4	Wayne Gomes	.25
5	Torii Hunter	.75
6	Brooks Kieschnick	.25
7	Daron Kirkreit	.25
8	Derrek Lee	.25
9	Trot Nixon	1.50
10	Charles Peterson	.25
11	Jay Powell	.25
12	Jon Ratliff	.25
13	Chris Schwab	.25
14	Steve Soderstrom	.25
15	Marc Valdes	.25
16	Billy Wagner	.75
17	John Wasdin	.25
18	Jamey Wright	.25
19	Kelly Wunsch	.25
20	Brooks Kieschnick	.25

1994 Classic Best Gold David Justice Autograph

An authentically autographed card of David Justice was issued as an insert in 1994 Classic Best Gold. The gold-foil highlighted cards were inserted at the rate of about one per case (360 foil packs). Each card is serially numbered within an edition of 4,000.

	MT
David Justice	45.00

1994 Classic Best Illustrated Acetate

Classic Best Gold's acetate insert cards feature illustrations of minor league stars by comic artist Neal Adams, printed on plastic. The glow-in-the-dark cards, are inserted at a rate of one per 90 packs. The unnumbered cards when laid in proper order from left to right share a contiguous background design and have typography which reads "1994 Minor League Gold" across the tops of the cards and "Superstars" in clear letters across the bottoms. Backs also share a cosmic art background, and include a small color player photo and career highlights.

		MT
Complete Set (5):		7.50
Common Player:		1.00
1	Brien Taylor	1.00
2	Dmitri Young	1.00
3	Derek Jeter	6.00
4	Phil Nevin	1.00
5	Frank Rodriguez	1.00

1994 Classic 4 Sport (Baseball)

A number of baseball players are included in the base-card set, parallels and chase cards in this issue.

		MT
Base Set/Inserts		
Printer's Proofs #161-188:		10X
Gold Card #161-188:		2X
Wax Pack (16):		.65
Wax Box (36):		15.00
161	Paul Wilson	.10
162	Ben Grieve	.25
163	Doug Million	.05
164	C.J. Nitkowski	.05
165	Tommy Davis	.05
166	Dustin Hermanson	.10
167	Travis Miller	.05
168	McKay Christiansen	.05
169	Victor Rodriguez	.05
170	Jacob Cruz	.05
171	Rick Heiserman	.05
172	Mark Farris	.05
173	Nomar Garciaparra	3.00
174	Paul Konerko	.40
175	Trey Moore	.05
176	Brian Stephenson	.05
177	Matt Smith	.05
178	Kevin Brown	.05
179	Cade Gaspar	.05
180	Bret Wagner	.05
181	Mike Thurman	.05
182	Doug Webb	.05
183	Ryan Nye	.05
184	Brian Buchanan	.05
185	Scott Elarton	.05
186	Mark Johnson	.05
187	Jacob Shumate	.05
188	Kevin Witt	.05
HV3	Paul Wilson (High Voltage)	.50
HV7	Ben Grieve (High Voltage)	.50
HV11	Dustin Hermanson (High Voltage)	.50
HV15	Doug Million (High Voltage)	.50
HV20	Nomar Garciaparra (High Voltage)	10.00
TC5	Paul Wilson, Doug Million, Cade Gaspar (Tricard)	.50
16/25	Paul Wilson (Classic Picks)	.50
17/25	Ben Grieve (Classic Picks)	.50
18/25	Trey Moore (Classic Picks)	.25
19/25	Nomar Garciaparra (Classic Picks)	7.50
20/25	Doug Million (Classic Picks)	.25

1994 Classic 4 Sport Autographs (Baseball)

Authentically autographed versions of most players in the 4 Sport issue were produced as random pack inserts. Fronts share the basic format with the regular version but include the signature and a serial number from within the edition specified in parentheses (where known). Backs have a congratulatory message. Cards marked with an asterisk are not confirmed to exist.

		MT
Common Player:		3.00
(161)	Paul Wilson (2,400)	3.00
(162)	Ben Grieve (2,500)	3.00
(163)	Doug Million (1,020)	6.00
(164)	C.J. Nitkowski (970)	3.00
(165)	Tommy Davis (?)	3.00
(166)	Dustin Hermanson (1,020)	3.00
(167)	Travis Miller (760)	3.00
(168)	McKay Christensen (*)	3.00
(169)	Victor Rodriguez (1,000)	3.00
(170)	Jacob Cruz (?)	3.00
(171)	Rick Heiserman (?)	3.00
(172)	Mark Farris (1,090)	3.00
(173)	Nomar Garciaparra (1,020)	45.00
(174)	Paul Konerko (970)	4.00
(175)	Trey Moore (*)	3.00
(176)	Brian Stephenson (1,100)	3.00
(177)	Matt Smith (1,090)	3.00
(178)	Kevin Brown (1,090)	3.00
(179)	Cade Gaspar (1,090)	3.00
(180)	Bret Wagner (970)	3.00
(181)	Mike Thurman (990)	3.00
(182)	Doug Webb (1,000)	3.00
(183)	Ryan Nye (1,015)	3.00
(184)	Brian Buchanan (950)	3.00
(185)	Scott Elarton (*)	3.00
(186)	Mark Johnson (1,000)	3.00
(187)	Jacob Shumate (980)	3.00
(188)	Kevin Witt (970)	3.00

1994 Classic 4 Sport Bonus Cards (Baseball)

These were inserts found in each jumbo pack. Fronts differ from the regular 4 Sport cards in the use of silver, rather than gold foil highlights. Backs have a black-and-white ghosted photo of the player overprinted with career highlights and prospects. Cards are num-bered with a "BC" prefix. Only the baseball players from the 20-card set are listed here.

		MT
BC13	Paul Wilson	.25
BC14	Ben Grieve	.35
BC15	Doug Million	.25
BC16	Nomar Garciaparra	8.00

1994 Classic Images (Baseball)

Young players from the four major team sports are featured in the 1994 debut edition of Images. Only the baseball players are listed here.

		MT
Baseball Set (26):		5.00
Common Player:		.05
Wax Pack (10):		.50
Wax Box (36):		10.00
3	Alex Rodriguez	2.50
4	Alex Rodriguez (Promo)	3.00
7	Jeff D'Amico	.05
11	Alan Benes	.05
15	Jeff Granger	.05
19	Daron Kirkreit	.05
23	Billy Wagner	.05
31	Brian Anderson	.05
37	Matt Brunson	.05
42	Kirk Presley	.05
47	Chris Carpenter	.05
49	Kelly Wunsch	.05
51	Jon Ratliff	.05
52	Wayne Gomes	.05
54	Trot Nixon	.50
55	Andre King	.05
63	Darren Dreifort	.05
69	Brooks Kieschnick	.05
72	Torii Hunter	.50
80	Steve Soderstrom	.05
85	Derrek Lee	1.00
93	Jay Powell	.05
105	Matt Drews	.05
115	Scott Christman	.05
131	Kirk Presley (B/W)	.05
139	Trot Nixon (B/W)	.50
143	Alex Rodriguez (B/W)	2.50

1994 Classic Images (Baseball) Sudden Impact

The young professionals who were believed to have the greatest chance for early stardom in the four major team sports were chosen for a one-per-pack insert set called "Sudden Impact." The cards have fronts printed on gold foil. Only the baseball players are listed here.

		MT
Baseball Set (3):		4.00
SI1	Carlos Delgado	1.00
SI3	Derek Jeter	3.00
SI4	Alex Rodriguez	2.00

1994 Classic Tri-Cards

An innovative concept which never caught on with collectors, these minor league "tri-cards" feature three different players in the standard 3-1/2" x 2-1/2" format. The complete set consists of 84 cards on 28 three-player panels.

The panels are perforated to allow separation into three individual cards of about 1-1/8" x 2-1/2". Each panel features one prospect from the Class A, AA and AAA farm clubs of a major league team. Values shown are for complete three-player panels. Individual player cards have little or no collector value. Fronts feature action photos with a minor league team logo at lower-right. Backs have some career data, the major league team logo and a "1 of 8,000" notice.

	MT
Complete Panel Set (28):	20.00
Common Panel:	.50
ATLANTA BRAVES	.50
T1 Jamie Arnold	
T2 Terrell Wade	
T3 Ramon Caraballo	
BALTIMORE ORIOLES	.50
T4 Jay Powell	
T5 Alex Ochoa	
T6 Manny Alexander	
BOSTON RED SOX	.75
T7 Trot Nixon	
T8 Jose Malave	
T9 Frank Rodriguez	
CALIFORNIA ANGELS	.50
T10 De Shawn Warren	
T11 Chris Smith	
T12 Andrew Lorraine	
CHICAGO CUBS	.50
T13 Jon Ratliff	
T14 Brooks Kieschnick	
T15 Matt Franco	
CHICAGO WHITE SOX	.50
T16 Eddie Pearson	
T17 Chris Snopek	
T18 James Baldwin	
CINCINNATI REDS	.50
T19 Paul Bako	
T20 Chad Mottola	
T21 John Roper	
CLEVELAND INDIANS	.50
T22 Daron Kirkreit	
T23 Tony Mitchell	
T24 Chad Ogea	
COLORADO ROCKIES	.50
T25 Mike Zolecki	
T26 Rodney Pedraza	
T27 Mark Thompson	
DETROIT TIGERS	.50
T28 Matt Brunson	
T29 Tony Clark	.00
T30 Felipe Lira	.00
FLORIDA MARLINS	.65
T31 Edgar Renteria	.00
T32 Charles Johnson	.00
T33 Kurt Miller	.00
HOUSTON ASTROS	.75
T34 Billy Wagner	.00
T35 Kevin Gallaher	.00
T36 Phil Nevin	.00
KANSAS CITY ROYALS	1.50
T37 Johnny Damon	
T38 Darren Burton	
T39 Michael Tucker	
LOS ANGELES DODGERS	.75
T40 Kym Ashworth	.00
T41 Chan Ho Park	.00
T42 Todd Hollandsworth	.00
MILWAUKEE BREWERS	.50
T43 Antone Williamson	.00
T44 Scott Talanoa	.00
T45 Marshall Boze	.00
MINNESOTA TWINS	.60
T46 LaTroy Hawkins	.00
T47 Brad Radke	.00
T48 Dave Stevens	.00
MONTREAL EXPOS	.50
T49 Jose Paniagua	.00
T50 Ugueth Urbina	.00
T51 Rondell White	.00
NEW YORK METS	.50
T52 Kirk Presley	.00
T53 Bill Pulsipher	.00
T54 Butch Huskey	.00
NEW YORK YANKEES	6.00
T55 Derek Jeter	.00
T56 Brian Taylor	.00
T57 Russ Davis	.00
OAKLAND A'S	.50
T58 Jose Herrera	.00
T59 Curtis Shaw	.00
T60 Mark Acre	.00
PHILADELPHIA PHILLIES	.50
T61 Wayne Gomes	.00
T62 Jason Moler	.00
T63 Phil Geisler	.00
PITTSBURGH PIRATES	.50
T64 Mitch House	.00
T65 Jermaine Allensworth	.00
T66 Midre Cummings	
SAN DIEGO PADRES	2.00
T67 Derrek Lee	
T68 Robbie Beckett	
T69 Ray McDavid	
SAN FRANCISCO GIANTS	.50
T70 Chris Singleton	
T71 Calvin Murray	
T72 J.R. Phillips	
SEATTLE MARINERS	5.00
T73 Alex Rodriguez	
T74 Mac Suzuki	
T75 Marc Newfield	
ST. LOUIS CARDINALS	.50
T76 Basil Shabazz	
T77 Dmitri Young	
T78 Brian Barber	
TEXAS RANGERS	.50
T79 Mike Bell	
T80 Terrell Lowery	
T81 Benji Gil	
TORONTO BLUE JAYS	1.00
T82 Jose Silva	
T83 Brent Bowers	
T84 Shawn Green	

1994 Classic Collectors Club (C3)

This multi-sport set was part of the membership benefits package in the Classic Collectors Club (C3). Cards have action photos bordered at right and bottom in white, with die-cut play diagram devices. Backs have another photo, along with stats, highlights and biography. Sets were produced in an edition of 10,000. Only the baseball players are listed here.

		MT
Common Player:		.25
14	Jeff Granger	.25
15	Brooks Kieschnick	.25
16	Alex Rodriguez	6.00
17	Darren Dreifort	.25

1994 Classic Collectors Club (C3) Gold Crown

This multi-sport set was part of the membership benefit in the Classic Collectors Club. The cards have action photos bordered only at bottom, where the player name appears. Backs have a vertically "squeezed" photo along with stats and biography. Only one baseball player is included in the set.

		MT
CC2	Brooks Kieschnick	.50

1994-95 Fleer Excel

Color-enhanced photos on both sides, gold-foil highlights and UV coating give a major league look to Fleer's set of prospects. Players are arranged alphabetically within the parent team and are chosen from all rungs of the minor league ladder from Short Season A clubs to AAA. Backs feature a second version of the front photo and complete career stats, along with the minor league team logo. Excel was sold in 14-card packs with a $1.49 retail price. Three insert sets included at random in packs were All-Stars, League Leaders and 1st Year Phenoms.

		MT
Complete Set (300):		13.50
Common Player:		.05
Wax Pack (14):		.75
Wax Box (36):		17.50
1	Kimera Bartee	.05
2	Harry Berrios	.05
3	Tommy Davis	.05
4	Cesar Devarez	.05
5	Curtis Goodwin	.05
6	Jimmy Haynes	.05
7	Chris Lemp	.05
8	Alex Ochoa	.05

9	B.J. Waszgis	.05
10	Nomar Garciaparra	2.00
11	Jose Malave	.05
12	Glenn Murray	.05
13	Trot Nixon	.65
14	Frank Rodriguez	.05
15	Bill Selby	.05
16	Jeff Suppan	.05
17	George Arias	.05
18	Todd Blyleven	.05
19	John Donati	.05
20	Todd Greene	.05
21	Bret Hemphill	.05
22	Michael Holtz	.05
23	Troy Percival	.05
24	Luis Raven	.05
25	James Baldwin	.05
26	Mike Bertotti	.05
27	Ben Boulware	.05
28	Ray Durham	.05
29	Jimmy Hurst	.05
30	Rich Pratt	.05
31	Mike Sirotka	.05
32	Archie Vazquez	.05
33	Harold Williams	.05
34	Chris Woodfin	.05
35	David Bell	.05
36	Todd Betts	.05
37	Jim Betzsold	.05
38	Einar Diaz	.05
39	Travis Driskill	.05
40	Damian Jackson	.05
41	Daron Kirkreit	.05
42	Steve Kline	.05
43	Tony Mitchell	.05
44	Enrique Wilson	.05
45	Jaret Wright	.05
46	Matt Brunson	.05
47	Tony Clark	.05
48	Cade Gaspar	.05
49	John Grimm	.05
50	Bob Higginson	.05
51	Shannon Penn	.05
52	John Rosengren	.05
53	Jaime Bluma	.05
54	Mike Bovee	.05
55	Nevin Brewer	.05
56	Johnny Damon	1.00
57	Lino Diaz	.05
58	Bart Evans	.05
59	Sal Fasano	.05
60	Tim Grieve	.05
61	Jim Pittsley	.05
62	Joe Randa	.05
63	Ken Ray	.05
64	Glendon Rusch	.05
65	Larry Sutton	.05
66	Dilson Torres	.05
67	Michael Tucker	.05
68	Joe Vitiello	.05
69	James Cole	.05
70	Danny Klassen	.05
71	Jeff Kramer	.05
72	Mark Loretta	.05
73	Danny Perez	.05
74	Sid Roberson	.05
75	Scott Talanoa	.05
76	Tim Unroe	.05
77	Antone Williamson	.05
78	Marc Barcelo	.05
79	Trevor Cobb	.05
80	Marty Cordova	.05
81	Darren Fidge	.05
82	Troy Fortin	.05
83	Gus Gandarillas	.05
84	Adrian Gordon	.05
85	LaTroy Hawkins	.05
86	Matt Lawton	.05
87	Jake Patterson	.05
88	Brad Radke	.15
89	Todd Walker	.05
90	Brian Boehringer	.05
91	Brian Buchanan	.05
92	Andy Croghan	.05
93	Chris Cumberland	.05
94	Matt Drews	.05
95	Keith Heberling	.05
96	Jason Jarvis	.05
97	Derek Jeter	4.00
98	Ricky Ledee	.05
99	Matt Luke	.05
100	James Musselwhite	.05
101	Andy Pettitte	1.00
102	Mariano Rivera	.50
103	Ruben Rivera	.20
104	Tate Seefried	.05
105	Scott Standish	.05
106	Jim Banks	.05
107	Tony Batista	.05
108	Ben Grieve	.15
109	Jose Herrera	.05
110	Steve Lemke	.05
111	Eric Martins	.05
112	Scott Spiezio	.05
113	John Wasdin	.05
114	Scott Davison	.05
115	Chris Dean	.05
116	Giomar Guevara	.05
117	Tim Harikkala	.05
118	Brett Hinchliffe	.05
119	Matt Mantei	.05
120	Arquimedez Pozo	.05
121	Marino Santana	.05
122	John Vanhof	.05
123	Chris Widger	.05
124	Mike Bell	.05
125	Mark Brandenburg	.05
126	Kevin Brown	.05
127	Bucky Buckles	.05
128	Jaime Escamilla	.05
129	Terrell Lowery	.05
130	Jerry Martin	.05
131	Reid Ryan	.10
132	Julio Santana	.05
133	Howard Battle	.05
134	D.J. Boston	.05
135	Chris Carpenter	.75
136	Freddy Garcia	.05
137	Aaron Jersild	.05
138	Ricardo Jordan	.05
139	Angel Martinez	.05
140	Jose Pett	.05
141	Jose Silva	.05
142	David Sinnes	.05
143	Rob Steinert	.05
144	Chris Stynes	.05
145	Mike Toney	.05
146	Chris Weinke	.25
147	Kevin Witt	.05
148	Brad Clontz	.05
149	Jermaine Dye	.05
150	Tony Graffanino	.05
151	Kevin Grijak	.05
152	Damon Hollins	.05
153	Marcus Hostetler	.05
154	Darrell May	.05
155	Wonderful Monds	.05
156	Carl Schulz	.05
157	Chris Seelbach	.05
158	Jacob Shumate	.05
159	Terrell Wade	.05
160	Glenn Williams	.05
161	Alex Cabrera	.05
162	Gabe Duross	.05
163	Shawn Hill	.05
164	Mike Hubbard	.05
165	Dave Hutcheson	.05
166	Brooks Kieschnick	.05
167	Bobby Morris	.05
168	Jayson Peterson	.05
169	Jason Ryan	.05
170	Ozzie Timmons	.05
171	Cedric Allen	.05
172	Aaron Boone	.15
173	Ray Brown	.05
174	Damon Callahan	.05
175	Decomba Conner	.05
176	Emiliano Giron	.05
177	James Lofton	.05
178	Nick Morrow	.05
179	C.J. Nitkowski	.05
180	Eddie Priest	.05
181	Pokey Reese	.10
182	Jason Robbins	.05
183	Scott Sullivan	.05
184	Pat Watkins	.05
185	Juan Acevedo	.05
186	Derrick Gibson	.05
187	Pookie Jones	.05
188	Terry Jones	.05
189	Doug Million	.05
190	Lloyd Peever	.05
191	Jacob Viano	.05
192	Mark Voisard	.05
193	Josh Booty	.05
194	Will Cunnane	.05
195	Andy Larkin	.05
196	Billy McMillon	.05
197	Kevin Millar	.05
198	Marc Valdes	.05
199	Bob Abreu	.05
200	Jamie Daspit	.05
201	Scott Elarton	.05
202	Kevin Gallaher	.05
203	Richard Hidalgo	.05
204	Chris Holt	.05
205	Rick Huisman	.05
206	Doug Mlicki	.05
207	Julien Tucker	.05
208	Billy Wagner	.15
209	Juan Castro	.05
210	Roger Cedeno	.05
211	Ron Coomer	.05
212	Karim Garcia	.25
213	Todd Hollandsworth	.05
214	Paul Konerko	.45
215	Antonio Osuna	.05
216	Willis Otanez	.05
217	Dan Ricabal	.05
218	Ken Sikes	.05
219	Yamil Benitez	.05
220	Geoff Blum	.05
221	Scott Gentile	.05
222	Mark Grudzielanek	.05
223	Kevin Northrup	.05
224	Carlos Perez	.05
225	Matt Raleigh	.05
226	Al Reyes	.05
227	Everett Stull	.05
228	Ugueth Urbina	.05
229	Neil Weber	.05
230	Edgardo Alfonzo	.05
231	Jason Isringhausen	.05
232	Terrence Long	.05
233	Rey Ordonez	.05
234	Ricky Otero	.05
235	Jay Payton	.05
236	Kirk Presley	.05
237	Bill Pulsipher	.05
238	Chris Roberts	.05
239	Jeff Tam	.05
240	Paul Wilson	.10
241	David Doster	.05
242	Wayne Gomes	.05
243	Jeremy Kendall	.05
244	Ryan Nye	.05
245	Shane Pullen	.05
246	Scott Rolen	1.50
247	Gene Schall	.05
248	Brian Stumpf	.05
249	Jake Austin	.05
250	Trey Beamon	.05
251	Danny Clyburn	.05
252	Louis Collier	.05
253	Mark Farris	.05
254	Mark Johnson	.05
255	Jason Kendall	.25
256	Esteban Loaiza	.05
257	Joe Maskivish	.05
258	Ramon Morel	.05
259	Gary Wilson	.05
260	Matt Arrandale	.05
261	Allen Battle	.05
262	Alan Benes	.05
263	Jeff Berblinger	.05
264	Terry Bradshaw	.05
265	Darrell Deak	.05
266	Craig Grasser	.05
267	Yates Hall	.05
268	Kevin Lovingier	.05
269	Elieser Marrero	.05
270	Jeff Matulevich	.05
271	Joe McEwing	.05
272	Eric Miller	.05
273	Tom Minor	.05
274	Scott Simmons	.05
275	Chris Stewart	.05
276	Bret Wagner	.05
277	Travis Welch	.05
278	Jay Witasick	.05
279	Homer Bush	.05
280	Raul Casanova	.05
281	Glenn Dishman	.05
282	Gary Dixon	.05
283	Devohn Duncan	.05
284	Dustin Hermanson	.10
285	Earl Johnson	.05
286	Derrek Lee	1.50
287	Todd Schmitt	.05
288	Ira Smith	.05
289	Jason Thompson	.05
290	Bryan Wolff	.05
291	Jeff Martin	.05
292	Dante Powell	.05
293	Jeff Richey	.05
294	Joe Rosselli	.05
295	Benji Simonton	.05
296	Steve Whitaker	.05
297	Keith Williams	.05
298	Checklist	.05
299	Checklist	.05
300	Checklist	.05

1994-95 Fleer Excel All-Stars

An all-star team of minor league prospects is presented in this chase set. Borderless color action photos of the players are surrounded with a colorful graphic "aura", while the player name is given in bold angled type. Fronts are gold-foil enhanced with the Excel and All-Star logos. Backs repeat the front photo in slightly larger size and include career highlights. All-Star inserts are found on an average of one per four packs.

		MT
Complete Set (10):		5.00
Common Player:		.25
1	Raul Casanova	.25
2	Tony Clark	.25
3	Ray Durham	.25
4	Ron Coomer	.25
5	Derek Jeter	4.00
6	Trey Beamon	.25
7	Johnny Damon	1.00
8	Ruben Rivera	.25
9	Todd Greene	.25
10	Alan Benes	.25

1994-95 Fleer Excel League Leaders

Statistical leaders from all levels of minor league play are featured in this insert set. Front action photos are placed against a graphically enhanced background, with the player's name in gold foil at the bottom. Backs feature career summaries. League Leader inserts are found on an average of more than one per two packs.

		MT
Complete Set (20):		2.00
Common Player:		.25
1	Juan Acevedo	.25
2	James Baldwin	.25
3	Allen Battle	.25
4	Harry Berrios	.25
5	Brad Clontz	.25
6	Will Cunnane	.25
7	Glenn Dishman	.25
8	LaTroy Hawkins	.25
9	Jimmy Haynes	.25
10	Richard Hidalgo	.25
11	Earl Johnson	.25
12	Jim Pittsley	.25
13	Bill Pulsipher	.25
14	Benji Simonton	.25
15	Larry Sutton	.25
16	Michael Tucker	.25
17	Tim Unroe	.25
18	Joe Vitiello	.25
19	Billy Wagner	.50
20	Harold Williams	.25

1994-95 Fleer Excel 1st Year Phenoms

Ten players who made an impact in their debut season of pro ball are highlighted in this chase set. Color action photos are set against a background that has been divided into colorized zones. The player's name and team are at bottom, with the card title and Excel logo enhanced in gold foil. Backs have a close-up version of the front photo and a career summary. The First Year Phenom cards are inserted at an average rate of one per 12 packs.

		MT
Complete Set (10):		2.00
Common Player:		.25
1	Paul Konerko	.75
2	Ray Brown	.25
3	Chris Dean	.25
4	Aaron Boone	.25
5	Rey Ordonez	.25
6	Decomba Conner	.25
7	Ben Grieve	.35
8	Jay Payton	.25
9	Dante Powell	.25
10	Dustin Hermanson	.25

1994 Signature Rookies

This 50-card set features top prospects from the minor leagues. Cards are UV coated with gold foil highlights and full color backs and fronts with a borderless design. The issue was sold in packs of seven only through hobby dealers. The print run was limited to 45,000 of each card, as indicated on the fronts. Each pack includes an autographed card or certificate redeemable for an autograph. In addition to the autographed cards, Signature Rookies has a Hottest Prospects insert set, a five-card Bonus Signature insert set, and a five-card Cliff Floyd insert set. Because cards are licensed only by the individual players and not Major League Baseball, minor league uniform logos have been removed from the photos.

		MT
Complete Set (50):		4.00
Common Player:		.25
1	Russell Davis	.05
2	Brant Brown	.05
3a	Ricky Bottalico (Photo actually Jamie Sepeda.)	.10
3b	Ricky Bottalico (Correct photo.)	.50
4	Brian Bevil	.05
5	Garret Anderson	.10
6	Rod Henderson	.05
7	Keith Heberling	.05
8	Scott Hatteberg	.05
9	Brook Fordyce	.05
10	Joey Eischen	.05
11	Orlando Miller	.05
12	Ray McDavid	.05
13	Andre King	.05
14	Todd Hollandsworth	.05
15	Tyrone Hill	.05
16	Paul Spoljaric	.05
17	Todd Ritchie	.05
18	Herbert Perry	.05
19	Alex Ochoa	.05
20	Mike Neill	.05
21	John Burke	.05
22	Alan Benes	.05
23	Robbie Beckett	.05
24	Brian Barber	.05
25	Justin Thompson	.05
26	Joey Hamilton	.05
27	Rick Greene	.05
28	Wayne Gomes	.05
29	Matthew "Big Bird" Drews	.05
30	Jeff D'Amico	.05
31	Bryn Kosco	.05
32	Brooks Kieschnick	.05
33	Jason Kendall	.25
34	Mike Kelly	.05
35	Derek Jeter	3.00
36	Jay Powell	.05
37	Phil Nevin	.10
38	Kurt Miller	.05
39	Chad McConnell	.05
40	Sean Lowe	.05
41	Michael Tucker	.05
42	Paul Shuey	.05
43	Dan Smith	.05
44	Calvin Reese	.10
45	Kirk Presley	.05
46	Jamey "Jamo" Wright	.05
47	Gabe White	.05
48	John Wasdin	.05
49	Billy Wagner	.15
50	Joe "Vit" Vitiello	.05

1994 Signature Rookies - Autographed

The autographed versions of the 1994 Signature Rookies set was a one-pack insert. Basically the same as the regular issue, each card is authentically autographed and numbered from within an edition of 8,650.

		MT
Complete Set (50):		65.00
Common Player:		1.00
1	Russell Davis	2.00
2	Brant Brown	2.00
3	Ricky Bottalico	2.00
4	Brian Bevil	1.00
5	Garret Anderson	5.00
6	Rod Henderson	1.00
7	Keith Heberling	2.00
8	Scott Hatteberg	2.00
9	Brook Fordyce	2.00
10	Joey Eischen	2.00
11	Orlando Miller	1.00
12	Ray McDavid	1.00
13	Andre King	1.00
14	Todd Hollandsworth	1.00
15	Tyrone Hill	1.00
16	Paul Spoljaric	1.00
17	Todd Ritchie	2.00
18	Herbert Perry	1.00
19	Alex Ochoa	2.00
20	Mike Neill	1.00
21	John Burke	1.00
22	Alan Benes	2.00
23	Robbie Beckett	1.00
24	Brian Barber	1.00
25	Justin "J.T." Thompson	1.00
26	Joey Hamilton	2.00
27	Rick Greene	1.00
28	Wayne Gomes	2.00
29	Matthew "Big Bird" Drews	2.00
30	Jeff D'Amico	2.00
31	Bryn Kosco	1.00
32	Brooks Kieschnick	2.00
33	Jason Kendall	5.00
34	Mike Kelly	2.00
35	Derek Jeter	50.00
36	Jay Powell	2.00
37	Phil Nevin	3.00
38	Kurt Miller	2.00
39	Chad McConnell	1.00
40	Sean Lowe	1.00
41	Michael Tucker	2.00
42	Paul Shuey	2.00
43	Dan Smith	1.00
44	Calvin Reese	2.00
45	Kirk Presley	2.00
46	Jamey "Jamo" Wright	2.00
47	Gabe White	2.00
48	John Wasdin	2.00
49	Billy Wagner	2.00
50	Joe "Vit" Vitiello	2.00

1994 Signature Rookies Bonus Signature Autographs

Signature Rookies packs had Bonus cards randomly inserted in them; there were 1,000 sets of the five-card set made. The cards are numbered with a P prefix. Each card is authentically autographed and numbered.

		MT
Complete Set (5):		12.00
Common Player:		3.00
P1	Rick Helling	3.00
P2	Charles Johnson	4.50
P3	Chad Mottola	3.00
P4	J.R. Phillips	3.00
P5	Glen (Glenn) Williams	3.00

1994 Signature Rookies Cliff Floyd Set

Montreal Expos' top prospect Cliff Floyd is featured on this five-card Signature Rookies insert set. The cards, numbered with a B prefix, were limited to 10,000 complete sets. Cards were random inserts inside packs.

		MT
Complete Set (5):		2.00
Common Card:		.50
B1	Cliff Floyd	.50
B1a	Cliff Floyd/Auto.	5.00
B2	Cliff Floyd	.50
B2a	Cliff Floyd/Auto.	5.00
B3	Cliff Floyd	.50
B3a	Cliff Floyd/Auto.	5.00
B4	Cliff Floyd	.50
B4a	Cliff Floyd/Auto.	5.00
B5	Cliff Floyd	.50
B5a	Cliff Floyd/Auto.	5.00

1994 Signature Rookies Hottest Prospects

Signature Rookies' 12-card Hottest Prospects insert set cards are numbered with an S prefix. There were 5,000 complete sets made, with 1,000 of each card hand-signed and numbered.

		MT
Complete Set (12):		3.50
Complete Set, Autographed (12):		75.00
Common Player:		.10
Common Player, Autographed:		1.00
1	John Burke	.10
1	John Burke/Auto.	1.00
2	Russ Davis	.10
2	Russ Davis/Auto.	1.00
3	Todd Hollandsworth	.10
3	Todd Hollandsworth/Auto.	2.00
4	Derek Jeter	3.00
4	Derek Jeter/Auto.	60.00
5	Mike Kelly	.10
5	Mike Kelly/Auto.	1.00
6	Ray McDavid	.10
6	Ray McDavid/Auto.	1.00
7	Kurt Miller	.10
7	Kurt Miller/Auto.	1.00
8	Phil Nevin	.10
8	Phil Nevin/Auto.	3.00
9	Alex Ochoa	.10
9	Alex Ochoa/Auto.	1.00
10	Justin "J.T." Thompson	.10
10	Justin "J.T." Thompson/Auto.	1.00
11	Michael Tucker	.10
11	Michael Tucker/Auto.	1.00
12	Gabe White	.10
12	Gabe White/Auto.	1.00

1994 Signature Rookies Mail In Promos

This set parallels the Hottest Prospects inserts but was only available via a mail-in promotion. Where the pack-insert version has printed down the left side in gold foil, "1 of 5,000," the mail-in cards read, "Mail In Promo / 1 of 3,000." Cards are numbered with an "S" prefix.

		MT
Complete Set (12):		6.00
Common Player:		.15
S1	John Burke	.15
S2	Russ Davis	.15
S3	Todd Hollandsworth	.15
S4	Derek Jeter	5.00
S5	Mike Kelly	.15
S6	Ray McDavid	.15
S7	Kurt Miller	.15
S9	Phil Nevin	.25
S9	Alex Ochoa	.15
S10	Justin "J.T." Thompson	.15
S11	Michael Tucker	.15
S12	Gabe White	.15

1994 Signature Rookies Mail In Promos - Autographed

This set parallels the Mail In Promos set with an issue of 1,000 numbered autographed cards of

each player. They were made abavailable to dealers as an incentive to place advance orders.

		MT
Complete Set (,12):		50.00
Common Player:		3.00
S1	John Burke	3.00
S2	Russ Davis	3.00
S3	Todd Hollandsworth	3.00
S4	Derek Jeter	45.00
S5	Mike Kelly	3.00
S6	Ray McDavid	3.00
S7	Kurt Miller	3.00
S8	Phil Nevin	4.00
S9	Alex Ochoa	3.00
S10	Justin "J.T." Thompson	3.00
S11	Michael Tucker	3.00
S12	Gabe White	3.00

1994 Signature Rookies Draft Picks

One hundred top players from the 1994 amateur draft are featured in this set. Most cards feature game-action, borderless color photos of the players in their college uniforms. At left is a vertical marbled panel with the SR Draft Picks logo on top and the edition number (45,000 for regular, 7,750 for parallel autographs) in gold foil. At bottom the player name is also in gold foil on a marbled panel. Backs have a small portrait photo, college stats and career notes, draft status and appropriate licensors' logos and copyright data.

		MT
Complete Set (101):		4.00
Common Player:		.05
Wax Pack (6):		2.00
Wax Box (18):		24.00
1	Josh Booty	.05
2	Paul Wilson	.10
3	Ben Grieve	.15
4	Dustin Hermanson	.05
5	Antone Williamson	.05
6	McKay Christiansen	.05
7	Doug Million	.05
8	Todd Walker	.10
9	C.J. Nitkowski	.05
10	Jaret Wright	.10
11	Mark Farris	.05
12	Nomar Garciaparra	3.00
13	Paul Konerko	.50
14	Jason Varitek	.50
15	Jayson Peterson	.05
16	Matt Smith	.05
17	Ramon Castro	.05
18	Cade Gaspar	.05
19	Bret Wagner	.05
20	Terrence Long	.05
21	Hiram Bocachica	.05
22	Dante Powell	.05
23	Brian Buchanan	.05
24	Scott Elarton	.05
25	Mark Johnson	.05
26	Jacob Shumate	.05
27	Kevin Witt	.05
28	Jay Payton	.05
29	Mike Thurman	.05
30	Jacob Cruz	.05
31	Chris Clemons	.05
32	Travis Miller	.05
33	Shawn Johnston	.05
34	Brad Rigby	.05
35	Doug Webb	.05
36	John Ambrose	.05
37	Cleatus Davidson	.05
38	Tony Terry	.05
39	Jason Camilli	.05
40	Roger Goedde	.05
41	Corey Pointer	.05
42	Trey Moore	.05
43	Brian Stephenson	.05
44	Dan Lock	.05
45	Mike Darr	.05
46	Carl Dale	.05
47	Tommy Davis	.05
48	Kevin Brown	.05
49	Ryan Nye	.05
50	Rod Smith	.05
51	Andy Taulbee	.05
52	Jerry Whittaker	.05
53	John Crowther	.05
54	Bryon Gainey	.05
55	Bill King	.05
56	Heath Murray	.05
57	Larry Barnes	.05
58	Todd Cady	.05
59	Paul Failla	.05
60	Brian Meadows	.05
61	A.J. Pierzynski	.25
62	Aaron Boone	.05
63	Mike Metcalfe	.05
64	Matt Wagner	.05
65	Jaime Bluma	.05
66	Oscar Robles	.05
67	Greg Whiteman	.05
68	Roger Worley	.05
69	Paul Ottavinia	.05
70	Joe Giuliano	.05
71	Chris McBride	.05
72	Jason Beverlin	.05
73	Gordon Amerson	.05
74	Tom Mott	.05
75	Rob Welch	.05
76	Jason Kelley	.05
77	Matt Treanor	.05
78	Jason Sikes	.05
79	Steve Shoemaker	.05
80	Troy Brohawn	.05
81	Jeff Abbott	.05
82	Steve Woodard	.05
83	Greg Morris	.05
84	John Slamka	.05
85	John Schroeder	.05
86	Clay Carruthers	.05
87	Eddie Brooks	.05
88	Tim Byrdak	.05
89	Bobby Howry	.05
90	Vic Darensbourg	.05
91	Midre Cummings	.05
92	John Dettman	.05
93	Gar Finnvold	.05
94	Dwayne Hosey	.05
95	Jason Jacome	.05
96	Doug Jennings	.05
97	Luis A. Lopez	.05
98	John Mabry	.05
99	Rondell White	.05
100	J.T. Snow	.15
101	Checklist	

1994 Signature Rookies Draft Picks - Autographed

A parallel set featuring the 100 players in the Signature Rookies Draft Pick set has each card authentically autographed. The only differences between the autographed cards and the regular version are the hand-numbered "X of 7,750" notation on the vertical marbled column at left, and the gold-foil "Authentic Signature" logo above that. Autographed cards were inserted on a one-per-pack basis.

		MT
Complete Set (100):		75.00
Common Player:		2.00
1	Josh Booty	4.00
2	Paul Wilson	3.00
3	Ben Grieve	3.00
4	Dustin Hermanson	3.00
5	Antone Williamson	2.00
6	McKay Christiansen	2.00
7	Doug Million	6.00
8	Todd Walker	3.00
9	C.J. Nitkowski	2.00
10	Jaret Wright	4.00
11	Mark Farris	2.00
12	Nomar Garciaparra	25.00
13	Paul Konerko	4.00
14	Jason Varitek	12.50
15	Jayson Peterson	2.00
16	Matt Smith	2.00
17	Ramon Castro	2.00
18	Cade Gaspar	2.00
19	Bret Wagner	2.00
20	Terrence Long	2.00
21	Hiram Bocachica	2.00
22	Dante Powell	2.00
23	Brian Buchanan	2.00
24	Scott Elarton	2.00
25	Mark Johnson	2.00
26	Jacob Shumate	2.00
27	Kevin Witt	2.00
28	Jay Payton	2.00
29	Mike Thurman	2.00
30	Jacob Cruz	2.00
31	Chris Clemons	2.00
32	Travis Miller	2.00
33	Shawn Johnston	2.00
34	Brad Rigby	2.00
35	Doug Webb	2.00
36	John Ambrose	2.00
37	Cleatus Davidson	2.00
38	Tony Terry	2.00
39	Jason Camilli	2.00
40	Roger Goedde	2.00
41	Corey Pointer	2.00
42	Trey Moore	2.00
43	Brian Stephenson	2.00
44	Dan Lock	2.00
45	Mike Darr	6.00
46	Carl Dale	2.00
47	Tommy Davis	2.00
48	Kevin Brown	2.00
49	Ryan Nye	2.00
50	Rod Smith	2.00
51	Andy Taulbee	2.00
52	Jerry Whittaker	2.00
53	John Crowther	2.00
54	Bryon Gainey	2.00
55	Bill King	2.00
56	Heath Murray	2.00
57	Larry Barnes	2.00
58	Todd Cady	2.00
59	Paul Failla	2.00
60	Brian Meadows	2.00
61	A.J. Pierzynski	4.00
62	Aaron Boone	2.00
63	Mike Metcalfe	2.00
64	Matt Wagner	2.00
65	Jaime Bluma	2.00
66	Oscar Robles	2.00
67	Greg Whiteman	2.00
68	Roger Worley	2.00
69	Paul Ottavinia	2.00
70	Joe Giuliano	2.00
71	Chris McBride	2.00
72	Jason Beverlin	2.00
73	Gordon Amerson	2.00
74	Tom Mott	2.00
75	Rob Welch	2.00
76	Jason Kelley	2.00
77	Matt Treanor	2.00
78	Jason Sikes	2.00
79	Steve Shoemaker	2.00
80	Troy Brohawn	2.00
81	Jeff Abbott	2.00
82	Steve Woodard	2.00
83	Greg Morris	2.00
84	John Slamka	2.00
85	John Schroeder	2.00
86	Clay Carruthers	2.00
87	Eddie Brooks	2.00
88	Tim Byrdak	2.00
89	Bobby Howry	2.00
90	Vic Darensbourg	2.00
91	Midre Cummings	2.00
92	John Dettman	2.00
93	Gar Finnvold	2.00
94	Dwayne Hosey	2.00
95	Jason Jacome	2.00
96	Doug Jennings	2.00
97	Luis A. Lopez	2.00
98	John Mabry	2.00
99	Rondell White	3.00
100	J.T. Snow	4.00

1994 Signature Rookies Draft Picks Bonus Signatures

Ten players who do not otherwise appear in the Draft Picks set or inserts are featured in this special autographed chase card set. Between 3,250 and 3,350 of each card were signed by the respective player.

		MT
Complete Set (10):		10.00
Common Player:		2.00
1	Russ Johnson	2.00
2	Carlton Loewer	2.00
3	Matt Beaumont	2.00
4	Yates Hall	2.00
5	Jeremy Powell	2.00
6	Paul O'Malley	2.00
7	Scott Shores	2.00
8	Jed Hansen	2.00
9	Ryan Helms	2.00
10	Darrell Nicholas	2.00

1994 Signature Rookies Draft Picks Flip Cards

These "two-headed" cards have virtually identical fronts and backs with different player photos on each side. According to information provided at the time of issue, each of the featured players autographed 1,000 of the cards, with 250 of each side bearing autographs on each side. Each side is highlighted with gold foil and features a notation that it is "1 of 15,000."

		MT
Complete Set (5):		2.50
Common Player:		.25
1	Ken Griffey Jr., Craig Griffey	1.00
1	Ken Griffey Jr., Craig Griffey (Ken autograph)	50.00
1	Ken Griffey Jr., Craig Griffey (Craig autograph.)	3.00
1	Ken Griffey Jr., Craig Griffey (Both autographs.)	60.00
2	Craig Griffey, Ken Griffey Sr.	.25
2	Craig Griffey, Ken Griffey Sr. (Craig autograph.)	1.00
2	Craig Griffey, Ken Griffey Sr. (Ken autograph.)	5.00
2	Craig Griffey, Ken Griffey Sr. (Both autographs.)	7.50
3	Ken Griffey Jr., Ken Griffey Sr.	1.00
3	Ken Griffey Jr., Ken Griffey Sr. (Junior autograph.)	50.00
3	Ken Griffey Jr., Ken Griffey Sr. (Senior autograph.)	5.00
3	Ken Griffey Jr., Ken Griffey Sr. (Both autographs.)	60.00
4	Nolan Ryan, Reid Ryan	1.00
4	Nolan Ryan, Reid Ryan (Nolan autograph.)	60.00
4	Nolan Ryan, Reid Ryan (Reid autograph.)	5.00
4	Nolan Ryan, Reid Ryan (Both autographs.)	75.00
5	Paul Wilson, Phil Nevin	.50
5	Paul Wilson, Phil Nevin (Wilson autograph.)	5.00
5	Paul Wilson, Phil Nevin (Nevin autograph.)	5.00
5	Paul Wilson, Phil Nevin (Both autographs.)	10.00

1994 Signature Rookies Draft Picks Top Prospects

Five top young pitching prospects are featured in this insert set. Both regular and a parallel autographed edition (2,100 each) were found as pack inserts. Standard 2-1/2" x 3-1/2" cards are UV coated on both sides and gold-foil enhanced on front, including a notice the card is "1 of 20,000." Backs have a ghosted image of the front photo in the background, along with an enlargement of the player's portrait from that photo. Biological data, career highlights and professional career stats are overprinted.

		MT
Complete Set (5):		1.00
Common Player:		.50
T6	Scott Ruffcorn	.25
T6	Scott Ruffcorn/Auto.	3.00
T7	Brad Woodall	.50
T7	Brad Woodall/Auto.	4.50
T8	Andrew Lorraine	.25
T8	Andrew Lorraine/Auto.	3.00
T9	LaTroy Hawkins	.25
T9	LaTroy Hawkins/Auto.	3.00
T10	Alan Benes	.25
T10	Alan Benes/Auto.	3.00

1994 Signature Rookies Gold Standard (Baseball)

Twenty-five young players from each of the four major team sports were featured in the base set

of Gold Standard. In addition, insert sets offered cards of "Legends," Hall of Famers (signed and unsigned) and a partial parallel set featuring gold facsimile autographs. Basic cards have an action photo on front and portrait photo with personal data and stats on back. There is a gold-foil Gold Standard logo on both front and back. Minor and major league uniform logos have been removed from the photos because the cards were only licensed by individual players and collegiate licensing authorities.

		MT
Common Player:		.10
51	Josh Booty	.10
52	Roger Cedeno	.10
53	Cliff Floyd	.10
53(p)	Cliff Floyd (Promo, edition of 10,000.)	1.00
54	Ben Grieve	.15
55	Joey Hamilton	.10
56	Todd Hollandsworth	.10
57	Brian Hunter	.10
58	Charles Johnson	.10
59	Brooks Kieschnick	.10
60	Mike Kelly	.10
61	Ray McDavid	.10
62	Kurt Miller	.10
63	James Mouton	.10
63(p)	James Mouton (Promo, edition of 10,000.)	1.00
64	Phil Nevin	.10
65	Alex Ochoa	.10
66	Herbert Perry	.10
67	Kirk Presley	.10
68	Bill Pulsipher	.10
69	Scott Ruffcorn	.10
70	Paul Shuey	.10
71	Michael Tucker	.10
72	Terrell Wade	.10
73	Gabe White	.10
74	Paul Wilson	.10
75	Dmitri Young	.10
HOF15	Catfish Hunter	.25
HOF15	Catfish Hunter/Auto.	15.00
HOF20	Willie Stargell	.25
HOF20	Willie Stargell/Auto.	20.00
L3	"Pee Wee" Reese (Legends)	.50
L4	Nolan Ryan (Legends)	3.00
GS4	Josh Booty (Gold Signature)	.50
GS6	Brooks Kieschnick (Gold Signature)	.25
GS8	Charles Johnson (Gold Signature)	.50
GS10	Cliff Floyd (Gold Signature)	.50
GS15	James Mouton (Gold Signature)	.25

1994 Signature Rookies Tetrad (Baseball)

Twenty of the 120 cards in the four-sport Tetrad issue, plus several of the inserts, feature baseball players. Fronts have a borderless color action photo with a classic marble column at left bearing the Signature Rookies and Tetrad logos. The player name and "1 of

45,000" notation on front are in gold foil. Backs have an ancient temple background design with player data, stats and career summary. Cards are numbered in Roman numerals at top. All but one of the baseball players' cards was also issued in an edition of 7,500 authentically autographed cards.

		MT
	Common Player:	.20
	Common Player, Autographed:	2.00
84	Edgardo Alfonzo	.10
84a	Edgardo Alfonzo/Auto.	4.00
85	David Bell	.10
85a	David Bell/Auto.	2.00
86	Christopher Carpenter	.10
86a	Christopher Carpenter/Auto.	2.00
87	Roger Cedeno	.10
87a	Roger Cedeno/Auto.	2.00
88	Phil Geisler	.10
88a	Phil Geisler/Auto.	2.00
89	Curtis Goodwin	.10
89a	Curtis Goodwin/Auto.	2.00
90	Jeff Granger	.10
90a	Jeff Granger/Auto.	2.00
91	Brian Hunter	.10
91a	Brian Hunter/Auto.	2.00
92	Adam Hyzdu	.10
92a	Adam Hyzdu/Auto.	2.00
93	Scott Klingenbeck	.10
93a	Scott Klingenbeck (Autographed)	2.00
94	Derrek Lee	2.00
94a	Derrek Lee/Auto.	20.00
95	Calvin Murray	.10
95a	Calvin Murray/Auto.	2.00
96	Roberto Petagine	.10
96a	Roberto Petagine/Auto.	2.00
97	Bill Pulsipher	.10
97a	Bill Pulsipher/Auto.	2.00
98	Marquis Riley	.10
98a	Marquis Riley/Auto.	2.00
99	Frankie Rodriguez	.10
99a	Frank Rodriguez/Auto.	2.00
100	Scott Ruffcorn	.10
100a	Scott Ruffcorn/Auto.	2.00
101	Roger Salkeld	.10
101a	Roger Salkeld/Auto.	2.00
102	Marc Valdes	.10
102a	Marc Valdes/Auto.	2.00
103	Ernie Young	.10
103a	Ernie Young/Auto.	2.00
134	Paul Wilson (Top Prospects)	.25
134a	Paul Wilson (Top Prospects) (Autographed edition of 2,000.)	3.00
FLIP1	Charles Johnson, Charles Johnson (Edition of 7,500.)	.25
FLIP1a	Charles Johnson, Charles Johnson/Auto. (Edition of 275.))	5.00
FLIP5	Glen Williams, Monty Williams (Glenn) (Edition of 7,500.)	.25
FLIP5a	Glen Williams, Monty Williams (Glenn) (Autographed edition of 275.)	5.00
PROMO 1	Paul Wilson (1 of 10,000)	.50

1994 Stadium Club Draft Picks

Produced well after the strike-truncated 1994 baseball season, this set was largely ignored by the hobby at the time of issue. Full-bleed card fronts feature poses of 1994's top draft picks in major league uniforms, giving the hobby a good first look at its future stars. Typography is in gold foil. Horizontal backs have a parti-colored background with another portrait photo, a scouting report, biographical data, amateur and pro career highlights and a box detailing how the team's other recent draft picks at the position have fared. A "Mem-

bers Only" version of the set was also produced, with each card bearing a round gold-foil MO seal. Though much scarcer than the regular cards, they have attained little or no premium value.

		MT
	Complete Set (90):	4.00
	Common Player:	.05
	Wax Box (24):	15.00
1	Jacob Shumate	.05
2	C.J. Nitkowski	.05
3	Doug Million	.05
4	Matt Smith	.05
5	Kevin Lovinger	.05
6	Alberto Castillo	.05
7	Mike Russell	.05
8	Dan Lock	.05
9	Tom Szimanski	.05
10	Aaron Boone	.10
11	Jayson Peterson	.05
12	Mark Johnson	.05
13	Cade Gaspar	.05
14	George Lombard	.05
15	Russ Johnson	.05
16	Travis Miller	.05
17	Jay Payton	.05
18	Brian Buchanan	.05
19	Jacob Cruz	.05
20	Gary Rath	.05
21	Ramon Castro	.05
22	Tommy Davis	.05
23	Tony Terry	.05
24	Jerry Whittaker	.05
25	Mike Darr	.05
26	Doug Webb	.05
27	Jason Camilli	.05
28	Brad Rigby	.05
29	Ryan Nye	.05
30	Carl Dale	.05
31	Andy Taulbee	.05
32	Trey Moore	.05
33	John Crowther	.05
34	Joe Giuliano	.05
35	Brian Rose	.05
36	Paul Failla	.05
37	Brian Meadows	.05
38	Oscar Robles	.05
39	Mike Metcalfe	.05
40	Larry Barnes	.05
41	Paul Ottavinia	.05
42	Chris McBride	.05
43	Ricky Stone	.05
44	Billy Blythe	.05
45	Eddie Priest	.05
46	Scott Forster	.05
47	Eric Pickett	.05
48	Matt Beaumont	.05
49	Darrell Nicolas	.05
50	Mike Hampton	.05
51	Paul O'Malley	.05
52	Steve Shoemaker	.05
53	Jason Sikes	.05
54	Bryan Farson	.05
55	Yates Hall	.05
56	Troy Brohawn	.05
57	Dan Hower	.05
58	Clay Caruthers	.05
59	Pepe McNeal	.05
60	Ray Ricken	.05
61	Scott Shores	.05
62	Eddie Brooks	.05
63	Dave Kauflin	.05
64	David Meyer	.05
65	Geoff Blum	.05
66	Roy Marsh	.05
67	Ryan Beeney	.05
68	Derek Dukart	.05
69	Nomar Garciaparra	3.00
70	Jason Kelley	.05
71	Jesse Ibarra	.05
72	Bucky Buckles	.05
73	Mark Little	.05
74	Heath Murray	.05
75	Greg Morris	.05
76	Mike Halperin	.05
77	Wes Helms	.05
78	Ray Brown	.05
79	Kevin Brown	.05
80	Paul Konerko	.50
81	Mike Thurman	.05
82	Paul Wilson	.10
83	Terrence Long	.05
84	Ben Grieve	.10
85	Mark Farris	.05
86	Bret Wagner	.05
87	Dustin Hermanson	.05
88	Kevin Witt	.05
89	Corey Pointer	.05
90	Tim Grieve	.05

1994 Stadium Club Draft Picks 1st Day Issue

Identical to the regular-issue TSC Draft Picks cards except for a silver-foil 1st Day Issue logo on front, this parallel set was found on average of once per six packs.

		MT
	Complete Set (90):	75.00
	Common Player	.50
	Stars:	8X

(See 1994 Stadium Club Draft Picks for checklist and base card values.)

1994 Upper Deck Minor League

Upper Deck's 1994 minor league cards are similar in format to their major league counterparts. The super-premium set of 270 cards features the top professional players who had yet to appear in a Major League game. Cards have UV coating and foil accents, along with color photography on both sides of the card. The player's name is printed in silver foil, as is his Major League team affiliation. The regular player cards (225) have ratings by Baseball America on the back. Subsets include: Major League Evaluations (15), with backs done by noted statistical innovator Bill James; Star Potential (20), showcasing top young players; and Upper Deck All-Stars, one per position, as selected by experts at Baseball America. Insert series include Organizational Players of the Year (28); Trade Cards redeemable by mail for two top picks in the 1994 draft; and Top 10 Prospects (oversized cards), inserted in each box. These were also available as regular-sized cards through an on-pack offer.

		MT
	Complete Set (270):	10.00
	Common Player:	.05
	Wax Pack (12):	1.00
	Wax Box (36):	22.50
1	Alex Gonzalez	.05
2	Brooks Kieschnick	.05
3	Michael Tucker	.05
4	Trot Nixon	.75
5	Brien Taylor	.05
6	Quinton McCracken	.05
7	Terrell Wade	.05
8	Brandon Wilson	.05
9	Roberto Petagine	.05
10	Chad Mottola	.05
11	T.R. Lewis	.05
12	Herbert Perry	.05
13	Bob Abreu	.25
14	Jorge Fabregas	.05
15	Ryan McGuire	.05
16	Mike Kelly	.05
17	Alan Zinter	.05
18	Troy Hughes	.05
19	Brook Fordyce	.05
20	Alex Ochoa	.05
21	Chris Wimmer	.05
22	Jason Hardtke	.05
23	Ricardo Hildago	.10
24	Gregg Zaun	.05
25	Roger Cedeno	.05
26	Curtis Shaw	.05
27	Brian Giles	.25
28	Felix Rodriguez	.05
29	Motor-Boat Jones	.05
30	Dmitri Young	.05
31	Justin Mashore	.05
32	Curtis Goodwin	.05
33	Marquis Riley	.05
34	Les Norman	.05
35	Billy Hall	.05
36	Jamie Arnold	.05
37	Mike Farmer	.05
38	Brent Bowers	.05
39	Chad McConnell	.05
40	Mike Robertson	.05
41	Brent Cookson	.05
42	Dan Cholowsky	.05
43	Justin Thompson	.05
44	Joe Vitiello	.05
45	Todd Steverson	.05
46	Brian Bevil	.05
47	Paul Shuey	.05
48	Scott Eyre	.05
49	Rick Greene	.05
50	Jose Silva	.05
51	Kurt Miller	.05
52	Ron Villone	.05
53	Darren Bragg	.05
54	Mike Lieberthal	.15
55	Gabe White	.05
56	Vince Moore	.05
57	Tony Clark	.10
58	Chris Eddy	.05
59	Ray Durham	.05
60	Todd Hollandsworth	.05
61	Andres Berumen	.05
62	Quilvio Veras	.05
63	Wayne Gomes	.05
64	Ryan Karp	.05
65	Randy Curtis	.05
66	Steve Rodriguez	.05
67	Jason Schmidt	.25
68	Mark Acre	.05
69	B.J. Wallace	.05
70	Alvin Morman	.05
71	Travis Baptist	.05
72	Jim Wawruck	.05
73	Marty Cordova	.05
74	Jamie Dismuke	.05
75	Joe Randa	.05
76	Danny Clyburn	.05
77	Joey Eischen	.05
78	Chris Seelbach	.05
79	Izzy Molina	.05
80	Chris Roberts	.05
81	Rod Henderson	.05
82	Kennie Steenstra	.05
83	Ugueth Urbina	.05
84	Stanton Cameron	.05
85	Doug Glanville	.05
86	Billy Wagner	.25
87	Tate Seefried	.05
88	Tyler Houston	.05
89	Derek Lowe	.15
90	Alan Benes	.05
91	Terrell Wade	.05
92	Rod Henderson/AS	.05
93	Charles Johnson/AS	.05
94	D.J. Boston/AS	.05
95	Ruben Santana/AS	.05
96	Joe Randa/AS	.05
97	Alex Gonzalez/AS	.05
98	Tim Clark/AS	.05
99	Randy Curtis/AS	.05
100	Brian Hunter/AS	.05
101	Jose Lima	.05
102	Ray Holbert	.05
103	Karim Garcia	.50
104	Chris Martin	.05
105	David Bell	.05
106	Tim Clark	.05
107	Matt Drews	.05
108	Dan Serafini	.05
109	Demetrish Jenkins	.05
110	Charles Johnson	.05
111	Jason Moler	.05
112	Brett Backlund	.05
113	Kevin Jordan	.05
114	Jesus Tavarez	.05
115	Frank Rodriguez	.05
116	Derrek Lee	1.00
117	Pokey Reese	.10
118	Dave Stevens	.05
119	Julio Bruno	.05
120	D.J. Boston	.05
121	Jim Dougherty	.05
122	Daron Kirkreit	.05
123	Kerwin Moore	.05
124	Jason Kendall	.50
125	Johnny Damon	1.00
126	Andre King	.05
127	Raul Gonzalez	.05
128	Eddie Pearson	.05
129	Yuri Sanchez	.05
130	Russ Davis	.05
131	Arquimedez Pozo	.05
132	Jon Lieber	.10
133	Glenn Murray	.05
134	Brant Brown	.05
135	Brian Hunter	.05
136	Mike Gulan	.05
137	Tim Vanegmond	.05
138	Billy Vanlandingham	.05
139	Robert Ellis	.05
140	Calvin Murray	.05
141	Kurt Ehmann	.05
142	Brian DuBose	.05
143	Robert Eenhoorn	.05
144	Howard Battle	.05
145	Jason Giambi	1.00
146	James Baldwin (Major League Evaluation)	.05
147	Rick Helling (MLE)	.05
148	Ricky Bottalico (MLE)	.05
149	Paul Spoljaric (Spoljaric)(MLE)	.05
150	Alex Gonzalez (MLE)	.05
151	Tavo Alvarez (MLE)	.05
152	Joey Eischen (MLE)	.05
153	Shane Andrews (MLE)	.05
154	James Mouton (MLE)	.05
155	Russ Davis (MLE)	.05
156	Phil Nevin (MLE)	.05
157	Garret Anderson (MLE)	.05
158	Gabe White (MLE)	.05
159	Brian Hunter (MLE)	.05
160	Ray McDavid (MLE)	.05
161	Mike Durrant (MLE)	.05
162	Eric Owens	.05
163	Rick Gorecki	.05
164	Lyle Mouton	.05
165	Ray McDavid	.05
166	Tony Graffagnino (Graffanino)	.05
167	Todd Ritchie	.05
168	Jose Herrera	.05
169	Steve Dunn	.05
170	Tavo Alvarez	.05
171	Jon Farrell	.05
172	Omar Ramirez	.05
173	Ruben Santana	.05
174	Tracy Sanders	.05
175	Shane Andrews	.05
176	Rob Henkel	.05
177	Joel Wolfe	.05
178	Chris Schwab	.05
179	Chris Weinke	.25
180	Ozzie Timmons	.05
181	Jason Bates	.05
182	Matt Brunson	.05
183	Garret Anderson	.15
184	Brian Rupp	.05
185	Derek Jeter	3.00
186	Desi Relaford	.05
187	Darren Burton	.05
188	David Mysel	.05
189	Steve Soderstrom	.05
190	Steve Gibralter	.05
191	Brian Sackinsky	.05
192	Marc Pisciotta	.05
193	Gene Schall	.05
194	Jimmy Haynes	.05
195	Shannon Stewart	.25
196	Neifi Perez	.05
197	Cris Colon	.05
198	Trey Beamon	.05
199	Jon Zuber	.05
200	John Burke	.05
201	Derek Wallace	.05
202	Chad Ogea	.05
203	Ernie Young	.05
204	Jose Malave	.05
205	Bill Pulsipher	.05
206	Leon Glenn	.05
207	Scott Sullivan	.05
208	Orlando Miller	.05
209	John Wasdin	.05
210	Paul Spoljaric	.05
211	Charles Peterson	.05
212	Ben Van Ryn	.05
213	Chris Sexton	.05
214	Bobby Bonds Jr.	.05
215	James Mouton	.05
216	Terrell Lowery	.05
217	Oscar Munoz	.05
218	Mike Bell	.05
219	Preston Wilson	.25
220	Mark Thompson	.05
221	Aaron Holbert	.05
222	Tommy Adams	.05
223	Ramon D. Martinez	.05
224	Tim Davis	.05
225	Ricky Bottalico	.05
226	Rick Krivda	.05
227	Troy Percival	.05
228	Mark Sweeney	.05
229	Joey Hamilton	.05
230	Phil Nevin	.05
231	John Ratliff	.05
232	Mark Smith	.05
233	Tyrone Hill	.05
234	Kevin Riggs	.05
235	John Dettmer	.05
236	Brian Barber	.05
237	Hector Trinidad	.05
238	Jeff Alkire	.05
239	Phil Geisler	.05
240	Rick Helling	.05
241	Edgardo Alfonzo	.05
242	Matt Franco	.05
243	Chad Roper	.05
244	Basil Shabazz	.05
245	James Baldwin	.05
246	Scott Hatteberg	.05
247	Glenn DiSarcina	.05
248	LaTroy Hawkins	.05
249	Marshall Boze	.05
250	Michael Moore	.05
251	Brien Taylor/SP	.05
252	Johnny Damon/SP	.65
253	Curtis Goodwin/SP	.05
254	Jose Silva/SP	.05
255	Terrell Wade/SP	.05
256	Dmitri Young/SP	.05
257	Roger Cedeno/SP	.05
258	Alex Ochoa/SP	.05
259	D.J. Boston/SP	.05
260	Michael Tucker/SP	.05
261	Calvin Murray/SP	.05
262	Frank Rodriguez/SP	.05
263	Michael Moore/SP	.05
264	Ugueth Urbina/SP	.05
265	Chad Mottola/SP	.05
266	Todd Hollandsworth/SP	.05
267	Rod Henderson/SP	.05
268	Roberto Petagine/SP	.05
269	Charles Johnson/SP	.05
270	Trot Nixon/SP	.05
MJ23	Michael Jordan/Silver	7.50
MJ23	Michael Jordan/Gold	15.00
TC1	Alex Rodriguez (Trade card.)	30.00
TC2	Kirk Presley (Trade card.)	.50
----	Redemption Card #1, Expired 12/31/94	.50
----	Redemption Card #2, Expired 12/31/94	.50

1994 Upper Deck Michael Jordan Scouting Report Supers

Though all six of the cards in this set show Jordan in the uniform of the Chicago White Sox, the cards were available only in a combination buy with a pack of Upper Deck's 1994 minor league cards at Wal-Mart stores. Each of the cards measures 3-1/2" x 5" and features full-color photos on front and back. Five of the cards have a large "Scouting Report" logo vertically at left and the backs discuss Jordan's baseball tools. The sixth card is a super-size version of his '94 UD minor league card.

		MT
	Complete Set (6):	10.00
	Common Card:	2.00
SR1	Michael Jordan/Htg	2.00
SR2	Michael Jordan/Fldg	2.00
SR3	Michael Jordan/Throwing	2.00
SR4	Michael Jordan (Speed)	2.00
SR5	Michael Jordan (Summary)	2.00
MJ23	Michael Jordan (White Sox Top Prospects)	4.00

1994 Upper Deck Minor League Player of the Year

This 28-card insert set features one top prospect from each Major League organization. The cards, numbered with a PY prefix, were random inserts in 1994 Upper Deck Minor League foil packs.

		MT
	Complete Set (28):	4.00
	Common Player:	.25
1	Marquis Riley	.25
2	Roberto Petagine	.25
3	Ernie Young	.25
4	Alex Gonzalez	.25
5	Hiawatha Wade	.25
6	Marshall Boze	.25
7	Mike Gulan	.25
8	Brant Brown	.25
9	Roger Cedeno	.25
10	Rod Henderson	.25
11	Calvin Murray	.25
12	Omar Ramirez	.25
13	Ruben Santana	.25
14	Charles Johnson	.25
15	Bill Pulsipher	.25
16	Alex Ochoa	.25
17	Ray McDavid	.25
18	Jason Moler	.25
19	Danny Clyburn	.25
20	Rick Helling	.25
21	Frank Rodriguez	.25
22	Chad Mottola	.25
23	John Burke	.25
24	Michael Tucker	.25
25	Brian DuBose	.25
26	LaTroy Hawkins	.25
27	James Baldwin	.25
28	Ryan Karp	.25

1994 Upper Deck Minor League Top 10 Prospects

Alex Rodriguez
SHORTSTOP • APPLETON FOXES

Ten top Major League prospects are featured in two different size versions. A jumbo version of 5-1/4" x 8-1/2" cards was inserted one per foil box of 1994 Upper Deck Minor League baseball cards. The cards are numbered with a TP prefix. The Top 10 Prospects were also available in a standard-size version (2-1/2" x 3-1/2") available through an on-pack offer; collectors could receive a 10-card set by sending in 15 foil pack wrappers, plus $2 for shipping costs. Box-topper card #8 features only a game-action silhouettes; the mail-in offer card pictures Alex Rodriguez.

		MT
Complete Set (10):		15.00
Common Player:		2.00

Jumbo cards worth 50 percent.
Jumbo cards worth 50 percent.

1	Roger Cedeno	2.00
2	Johnny Damon	5.00
3	Alex Gonzalez	2.00
4	Charles Johnson	2.00
5	Chad Mottola	2.00
6	Phil Nevin	2.00
7	Alex Ochoa	2.00
8a	1993 No. 1 Draft Pick (Silhouettes, jumbo.)	1.00
8b	Alex Rodriguez (Mail-in card, standard.)	10.00
9	Jose Silva	2.00
10	Michael Tucker	2.00

1994 Fleer/ProCards Birmingham Barons Jordan Proof

Michael Jordan
Birmingham Barons • OF

Because the printing on Jordan's face was too dark, this card was never officially released. The back is identical to the regularly issued card. Only a handful of examples were known in the hobby prior to 2002 when a former Fleer executive sold several hundred into the market.

		MT
633	Michael Jordan	300.00

1994 Minor League Team Sets

Largely through issues by teams in independent leagues, the number of minor league teams issuing sets and the number of sets issued climbed a bit in 1994 as Classic and Fleer/ProCards retained their grip on the marketplace for a final year, with shares of 33% and 57%, respectively.

MT

299 Team Sets and Variations

1994	FPC AAA All-Stars (47)	10.00

1994	Classic Albany Polecats (30)	5.00
1994	FPC Albany Polecats (30)	4.00
1994	FPC Albany-Colonie Yankees (31)	7.00
1994	Team Albany-Colonie Yearbook W/Cards (3)	65.00
1994	FPC Albuquerque Dukes (27)	6.00
1994	Team Albuquerque Dukes Photos (28)	100.00
1994	Team Amarillo Dillas (30)	5.00
1994	Team Amarillo Aces (26)	5.00
1994	Classic Appleton Foxes (30)	150.00
1994	FPC Appleton Foxes (28)	30.00
1994	Arizona Fall League (21)	15.00
1994	FPC Arkansas Travelers (26)	5.00
1994	Classic Asheville Tourists (30)	6.00
1994	FPC Asheville Tourists (30)	5.00
1994	Classic Auburn Astros (30)	4.00
1994	FPC Auburn Astros (29)	4.00
1994	Classic Augusta Greenjackets (30)	5.00
1994	FPC Augusta Greenjackets (28)	4.00
1994	Classic Bakersfield Dodgers (30)	5.00
1994	Classic Batavia Clippers (30)	5.00
1994	FPC Batavia Clippers (31)	4.00
1994	Team Beaumont Bullfrogs (23)	5.00
1994	Classic Bellingham Mariners (30)	5.00
1994	FPC Bellingham Mariners (31)	4.00
1994	Classic Beloit Brewers (30)	5.00
1994	FPC Beloit Brewers (30)	4.00
1994	Classic Bend Rockies (30)	4.00
1994	FPC Bend Rockies (31)	5.00
1994	FPC Billings Mustangs (27)	12.00
1994	SP Billings Mustangs (30)	12.00
1994	FPC Binghamton Mets (28)	7.50
1994	Classic Birmingham Barons (30)	9.00
1994	FPC Birmingham Barons (30)	6.00
1994	Classic Bluefield Orioles (30)	5.00
1994	FPC Bluefield Orioles (30)	4.00
1994	Classic Boise Hawks (30)	5.00
1994	FPC Boise Hawks (31)	4.00
1994	FPC Bowie Baysox (27)	5.00
1994	Classic Brevard County Manatees (30)	7.00
1994	FPC Brevard County Manatees (30)	6.00
1994	Classic Bristol Tigers (30)	7.00
1994	FPC Bristol Tigers (30)	7.00
1994	FPC Buffalo Bisons (28)	6.00
1994	Classic Burlington Bees (30)	5.00
1994	FPC Burlington Bees (29)	4.00
1994	Classic Burlington Indians (30)	8.00
1994	FPC Burlington Indians (31)	6.00
1994	SP Butte Copper Kings (30)	6.00
1994	FPC Calgary Cannons (24)	5.00
1994	FPC Canton-Akron Indians (30)	5.00
1994	Classic Capital City Bombers (30)	8.00
1994	FPC Capital City Bombers (29)	7.00
1994	FPC Carolina League All-Stars (53)	7.50
1994	FPC Carolina Mudcats (28)	5.00
1994	Classic Cedar Rapids Kernels (30)	—

1994	FPC Cedar Rapids Kernels (27)	4.00
1994	Classic Central Valley Rockies (30)	6.00
1994	FPC Central Valley Rockies (30)	5.00
1994	Classic Charleston River Dogs (30)	6.00
1994	FPC Charleston Riverdogs (29)	5.00
1994	Classic Charleston Wheelers (30)	5.00
1994	FPC Charleston Wheelers (28)	4.00
1994	FPC Charlotte Knights (26)	5.00
1994	Classic Charlotte Rangers (30)	5.00
1994	FPC Charlotte Rangers (27)	4.00
1994	FPC Chattanooga Lookouts (27)	5.00
1994	Team Chillicothe Paints (22)	6.00
1994	Classic Clearwater Phillies (30)	4.00
1994	FPC Clearwater Phillies (30)	4.00
1994	Classic Clinton Lumberkings (30)	5.00
1994	FPC Clinton Lumberkings (30)	4.00
1994	FPC Colorado Springs Sky Sox (28)	5.00
1994	FPC Columbus Clippers (30)	6.00
1994	Police Columbus Clippers (25)	7.00
1994	Team Columbus Clippers (28)	7.00
1994	Classic Columbus RedStixx (30)	7.00
1994	FPC Columbus RedStixx (31)	6.00
1994	Team Corpus Christi Barracudas (28)	5.00
1994	Classic Danville Braves (30)	12.00
1994	FPC Danville Braves (30)	10.00
1994	Classic Daytona Cubs (30)	12.00
1994	FPC Daytona Cubs (29)	6.00
1994	Team Duluth-Superior Dukes (27)	5.00
1994	Classic Dunedin Blue Jays (30)	4.00
1994	FPC Dunedin Blue Jays (30)	4.00
1994	Team Dunedin Blue Jays (29)	45.00
1994	Classic Durham Bulls (30)	5.00
1994	FPC Durham Bulls (30)	4.00
1994	Team Durham Bulls (32)	7.00
1994	FPC Edmonton Trappers (27)	5.00
1994	Classic Elizabethton Twins (30)	5.00
1994	FPC Elizabethton Twins (29)	5.00
1994	Classic Elmira Pioneers (30)	4.00
1994	FPC Elmira Pioneers (27)	7.00
1994	FPC El Paso Diablos (28)	4.00
1994	Classic Eugene Emeralds (30)	4.00
1994	FPC Eugene Emeralds (28)	5.00
1994	Classic Everett Giants (30)	4.00
1994	FPC Everett Giants (31)	5.00
1994	Classic Fayetteville Generals (30)	6.00
1994	FPC Faytetteville Generals (29)	5.00
1994	FPC Florida State League A-S (52)	24.00
1994	Classic Frederick Keys (30)	5.00
1994	FPC Frederick Keys (29)	4.00
1994	Classic Ft. Myers Miracle (30)	6.00
1994	FPC Ft. Myers Miracle (28)	5.00
1994	FPC Ft. Myers Diamond Girls (13)	4.00
1994	Classic Ft. Wayne Wizards (30)	5.00
1994	FPC Ft. Wayne Wizards (28)	5.00
1994	SP Great Falls Dodgers (30)	8.00
1994	Classic Greensboro Bats (30)	5.00
1994	FPC Greensboro Bats (31)	5.00
1994	FPC Greenville Braves (28)	4.00
1994	Team Greenville Braves Foldout (30)	20.00
1994	Classic Hagerstown Suns (30)	6.00
1994	FPC Hagerstown Suns (29)	5.00
1994	FPC Harrisburg Senators (29)	6.00
1994	Classic Helena Brewers (30)	—
1994	FPC Helena Brewers (27)	4.00

1994	SP Helena Brewers (30)	6.00
1994	Classic Hickory Crawdads (30)	8.00
1994	FPC Hickory Crawdads (30)	9.00
1994	Classic High Desert Mavericks (30)	5.00
1994	FPC High Desert Mavericks (30)	4.00
1994	Classic Hudson Valley Renegades (30)	6.00
1994	FPC Hudson Valley Renegades (30)	5.00
1994	Classic Huntington Cubs (30)	5.00
1994	FPC Huntington Cubs (31)	4.00
1994	FPC Huntsville Stars (30)	11.00
1994	Team Huntsville Stars (27)	25.00
1994	FPC Idaho Falls Braves (31)	6.00
1994	SP Idaho Falls Braves (30)	6.00
1994	FPC Indianapolis Indians (27)	7.00
1994	FPC Iowa Cubs (26)	5.00
1994	Team Iowa Cubs (9)	6.00
1994	FPC Jackson Generals (27)	8.00
1994	Smokey Bear Jackson Generals (27)	20.00
1994	FPC Jacksonville Suns (27)	7.00
1994	Classic Jamestown Jammers (30)	6.00
1994	FPC Jamestown Jammers (27)	7.00
1994	Classic Johnson City Cardinals (30)	5.00
1994	FPC Johnson City Cardinals (31)	4.00
1994	Classic Kane County Cougars (30)	4.00
1994	FPC Kane County Cougars (30)	5.00
1994	Team Kane County Cougars (30)	7.00
1994	Classic Kingsport Mets (30)	9.00
1994	FPC Kingsport Mets (29)	7.00
1994	Classic Kinston Indians (30)	8.00
1994	FPC Kinston Indians (29)	7.00
1994	FPC Knoxville Smokies (28)	6.00
1994	Classic Lake Elsinore Storm (30)	6.00
1994	FPC Lake Elsinore Storm (28)	5.00
1994	Classic Lakeland Tigers (30)	4.00
1994	FPC Lakeland Tigers (28)	4.00
1994	FPC Las Vegas Stars (25)	5.00
1994	FPC Lethbridge Mounties (30)	4.00
1994	SP Lethbridge Mounties (30)	6.00
1994	FPC Louisville Redbirds (29)	6.00
1994	Classic Lynchburg Red Sox (30)	7.00
1994	FPC Lynchburg Red Sox (29)	6.00
1994	Classic Macon Braves (30)	9.00
1994	FPC Macon Braves (31)	7.00
1994	Classic Madison Hatters (30)	6.00
1994	FPC Madison Hatters (30)	5.00
1994	Classic Martinsville Phillies (30)	4.00
1994	FPC Martinsville Phillies (31)	4.00
1994	FPC Medicine Hat Blue Jays (29)	4.00
1994	SP Medicine Hat Blue Jays (30)	7.00
1994	FPC Memphis Chicks (28)	5.00
1994	FPC Midland Angels (27)	5.00
1994	OHP Midland Angels (33)	40.00
1994	FPC Midwest League All-Stars (59)	40.00
1994	Team Minneapolis Loons (23)	5.00
1994	Team Mobile Bay Sharks (30)	6.00
1994	Classic Modesto A's (30)	6.00
1994	FPC Modesto A's (26)	5.00
1994	FPC Nashville Sounds (27)	6.00
1994	FPC Nashville Xpress (28)	6.00
1994	FPC New Britain Red Sox (27)	5.00
1994	FPC New Haven Ravens (29)	5.00
1994	Classic New Jersey Cardinals (30)	4.00
1994	FPC New Jersey Cardinals (31)	4.00
1994	FPC New Orleans Zephyrs (27)	5.00
1994	FPC Norfolk Tides (27)	6.00

1994	FPC Ogden Raptors (24)	4.00
1994	SP Ogden Raptors (30)	6.00
1994	FPC Oklahoma City 89ers (25)	6.00
1994	FPC Omaha Royals (27)	6.00
1994	Classic Oneonta Yankees (30)	6.00
1994	FPC Oneonta Yankees (31)	6.00
1994	FPC Orlando Cubs (26)	5.00
1994	Classic Osceola Astros (30)	6.00
1994	Team Osceola Astros All-Time Team (30)	75.00
1994	FPC Osceola Astros (30)	4.00
1994	FPC Ottawa Lynx (19)	7.00
1994	DD Pawtucket Red Sox Foldout	20.00
1994	FPC Pawtucket Red Sox (25)	5.00
1994	Classic Peoria Chiefs (30)	5.00
1994	FPC Peoria Chiefs (29)	4.00
1994	Team Peoria Chiefs (30)	12.00
1994	FPC Phoenix Firebirds (27)	5.00
1994	Classic Pittsfield Mets (30)	6.00
1994	FPC Pittsfield Mets (27)	7.00
1994	FPC Portland Sea Dogs (27)	7.00
1994	Team Portland Sea Dogs (31)	10.00
1994	Classic Princeton Reds (30)	5.00
1994	FPC Princeton Reds (29)	4.00
1994	Classic Prince William Cannons (30)	6.00
1994	FPC Prince William Cannons (28)	7.00
1994	Classic Quad City River Bandits (30)	8.00
1994	FPC Quad City River Bandits (29)	7.00
1994	Classic Rancho Cucamonga Quakes (30)	9.00
1994	FPC Rancho Cucamonga Quakes (29)	9.00
1994	FPC Reading Phillies (27)	4.00
1994	FPC Reading Phils Campbell's Soups (27)	7.50
1994	FPC Richmond Braves (30)	5.00
1994	Richmond Camera Richmond Braves (28)	45.00
1994	Team Richmond Braves Foldout	30.00
1994	Team Rio Grande White Wings (25)	5.00
1994	FPC Rochester Red Wings (27)	5.00
1994	Classic Rockford Royals (30)	8.00
1994	FPC Rockford Royals (31)	7.00
1994	Classic Salem Buccaneers (30)	8.00
1994	FPC Salem Buccaneers (28)	6.00
1994	FPC Salt Lake City Buzz (27)	4.00
1994	FPC San Antonio Missions (31)	9.00
1994	HEB San Antonio Missions (36)	55.00
1994	Team San Antonio Tejanos (28)	5.00
1994	Classic San Bernardino Spirit (30)	5.00
1994	FPC San Bernardino Spirit (28)	4.00
1994	Classic San Jose Giants (30)	6.00
1994	FPC San Jose Giants (29)	5.00
1994	Classic Sarasota Red Sox (30)	8.00
1994	FPC Sarasota Red Sox (30)	7.00
1994	Classic Savannah Cardinals (30)	6.00
1994	FPC Savannah Cardinals (31)	5.00
1994	FPC Scranton Red Barons (28)	5.00
1994	Team Scranton Red Barons (30)	5.00
1994	FPC Shreveport Captains (29)	5.00
1994	Team Sioux City Explorers (26)	6.00
1994	Team Sioux Falls Canaries (28)	6.00
1994	FPC South Atlantic League A-S (57)	20.00
1994	Classic South Bend Silver Hawks (30)	5.00
1994	FPC South Bend Silver Hawks (27)	4.00
1994	Classic Southern Oregon Athletics (30)	15.00
1994	FPC Southern Oregon Athletics (29)	12.00
1994	Classic Spartanburg Phillies (30)	20.00
1994	FPC Spartanburg Phillies (30)	10.00
1994	Classic Spokane Indians (30)	—

1994	FPC Spokane Indians (30)	4.00
1994	Classic Sultans of Springfield (30)	5.00
1994	FPC Springfield Sultans (27)	4.00
1994	Classic St. Catherines Blue Jays (30)	8.00
1994	FPC St. Catherines Blue Jays (30)	4.00
1994	Classic St. Lucie Mets (30)	10.00
1994	FPC St. Lucie Mets (29)	8.00
1994	Team St. Paul Saints (30)	24.00
1994	Classic St. Petersburg Cardinals (30)	5.00
1994	FPC St. Petersburg Cardinals (30)	4.00
1994	Classic Stockton Ports (30)	5.00
1994	FPC Stockton Ports (28)	4.00
1994	FPC Syracuse Chiefs (26)	8.00
1994	FPC Tacoma Tigers (28)	5.00
1994	Classic Tampa Yankees (30)	30.00
1994	FPC Tampa Yankees (32)	25.00
1994	Team Thunder Bay Whiskey Jacks (25)	5.00
1994	FPC Toledo Mud Hens (27)	5.00
1994	FPC Trenton Thunder (27)	5.00
1994	FPC Tucson Toros (29)	5.00
1994	FPC Tulsa Drillers (27)	5.00
1994	Team Tulsa Drillers (30)	8.00
1994	Team Tyler Wildcatters (25)	5.00
1994	Classic Utica Blue Sox (30)	7.00
1994	FPC Utica Blue Sox (29)	4.00
1994	FPC Vancouver Canadians (26)	9.00
1994	Classic Vermont Expos (30)	4.00
1994	FPC Vermont Expos (28)	4.00
1994	Classic Vero Beach Dodgers (30)	11.00
1994	FPC Vero Beach Dodgers (31)	8.00
1994	Classic Watertown Indians (30)	5.00
1994	FPC Watertown Indians (30)	4.00
1994	Classic Welland Pirates (30)	5.00
1994	FPC Welland Pirates (31)	4.00
1994	Classic West Michigan Whitecaps (30)	5.00
1994	FPC West Michigan Whitecaps (28)	4.00
1994	Classic West Palm Beach Expos (30)	8.00
1994	FPC West Palm Beach Expos (30)	7.00
1994	FPC Wichita Wranglers (26)	5.00
1994	Classic Williamsport Cubs (30)	6.00
1994	FPC Williamsport Cubs (30)	5.00
1994	Classic Wilmington Blue Rocks (30)	9.00
1994	FPC Wilmington Blue Rocks (29)	7.00
1994	Team Wilmington Blue Rocks	35.00
1994	Team Winnipeg Goldeyes (30)	6.00
1994	Classic Winston-Salem Spirits (30)	4.00
1994	FPC Winston-Salem Spirits (28)	4.00
1994	Classic Yakima Bears (30)	10.00
1994	FPC Yakima Bears (30)	8.00
1994	Team Zanesville Greys (30)	10.00

1995 Action Packed Scouting Report

RAY DURHAM

Action Packed's final minor league issue combines cards of baseball's best young prospects with cards honoring its oldest performer (#80-82 feature ballpark clown Max Patkin). The basic set features large player photos on front on which the player figure has been embossed. Cards #52-61 have a "#1 Draft Pick" logo in an upper corner. Cards #62-79 are "Franchise Gems" with an appropriate logo in an upper corner. Each of the "Franchise Gem" cards can also be found in a 24-karat gold stamped parallel edition, while card #1, Jeter's "Player of the Year" card can be found once every 480 packs in a diamond-chip encrusted, autographed version.

		MT
Complete Set (83):		10.00
Common Player:		.10
Wax Box:		10.00
1	Derek Jeter	
	(Player of the Year)	4.00
1A	Derek Jeter/Auto.	45.00
1D	Derek Jeter/Auto.	
	(Diamond version.)	50.00
2	Trot Nixon	.50
3	Charles Johnson	.10
4	Chan Ho Park	.25
5	Terrell Wade	.10
6	Carlos Delgado	1.00
7	Brian Hunter	.10
8	Tony Clark	.10
9	Russ Davis	.10
10	Derek Jeter	2.00
11	Alex Gonzalez	.10
12	Scott Ruffcorn	.10
13	Todd Hollandsworth	.10
14	Phil Nevin	.10
15	Marc Newfield	.10
16	Jose Silva	.10
17	Willie Greene	.10
18	Billy Ashley	.10
19	James Baldwin	.10
20	Jeff Granger	.10
21	Michael Tucker	.10
22	Johnny Damon	1.00
23	Roger Cedeno	.10
24	Makoto Suzuki	.10
25	Curtis Goodwin	.10
26	Frankie Rodriguez	.10
27	Roberto Mejia	.10
28	LaTroy Hawkins	.10
29	Alex Ochoa	.10
30	Jose Oliva	.10
31	Ruben Rivera	.10
32	Ray Durham	.10
33	Eduardo Perez	.10
34	Jose Malave	.10
35	Jeromy Burnitz	.25
36	Brad Woodall	.10
37	Joe Vitiello	.10
38	Daron Kirkreit	.10
39	Jimmy Haynes	.10
40	Andrew Lorraine	.10
41	Arquimedez Pozo	.10
42	Armando Benitez	.10
43	Alan Benes	.10
44	Julian Tavarez	.10
45	Curtis Pride	.10
46	Homer Bush	.10
47	Pokey Reese	.25
48	Billy Wagner	.25
49	Richard Hidalgo	.10
50	Allen Battle	.10
51	Kevin Millar	.15
52	Paul Wilson	
	(#1 Draft Pick)	.15
53	Ben Grieve (#1 Draft Pick)	.15
54	Dustin Hermanson	
	(#1 Draft Pick)	.15
55	Antone Williamson	
	(#1 Draft Pick)	.10
56	Josh Booty (#1 Draft Pick)	.10
57	Doug Million	
	(#1 Draft Pick)	.10
58	Jaret Wright	
	(#1 Draft Pick)	.25
59	Todd Walker	
	(#1 Draft Pick)	.10
60	Nomar Garciaparra	
	(#1 Draft Pick)	2.00
61	C.J. Nitkowski	
	(#1 Draft Pick)	.10
62	Charles Johnson	
	(Franchise Gem)	.10
63	Marc Newfield	
	(Franchise Gem)	.10
64	Ray Durham	
	(Franchise Gem)	.10
65	Carlos Delgado	
	(Franchise Gem)	.75
66	Alex Gonzalez	
	(Franchise Gem)	.10
67	Derek Jeter	
	(Franchise Gem)	2.00
68	Jose Oliva	
	(Franchise Gem)	.10
69	Billy Ashley	
	(Franchise Gem)	.10
70	Brian Hunter	
	(Franchise Gem)	.10
71	Ruben Rivera	
	(Franchise Gem)	.10

72	Alan Benes	
	(Franchise Gem)	.10
73	Willie Greene	
	(Franchise Gem)	.10
74	Russ Davis	
	(Franchise Gem)	.10
75	Jose Malave	
	(Franchise Gem)	.10
76	LaTroy Hawkins	
	(Franchise Gem)	.10
77	Frankie Rodriguez	
	(Franchise Gem)	.10
78	Scott Ruffcorn	
	(Franchise Gem)	.10
79	Ben Grieve	
	(Franchise Gem)	.15
80	Max Patkin	.10
81	Max Patkin	.10
82	Max Patkin	.10
83	Derek Jeter Checklist	.75

1995 Action Packed 24KT Gold

Eighteen better-than-average prospects were selected for this random insert series. 24KT Gold Franchise Gem cards are die-cut in a tombstone shape with a large baseball at top on front. The front is highlighted with gold-foil graphics. Backs have a few stats and are numbered with a "G" suffix.

		MT
Complete Set (18):		20.00
Common Player:		1.00
1G	Charles Johnson	1.00
2G	Marc Newfield	1.00
3G	Ray Durham	1.00
4G	Carlos Delgado	4.00
5G	Alex Gonzalez	1.00
6G	Derek Jeter	7.50
	Derek Jeter	
	(24K Gold Autograph)	60.00
	Derek Jeter	
	(Diamond Autograph)	65.00
7G	Jose Oliva	1.00
8G	Billy Ashley	1.00
9G	Brian L. Hunter	1.00
10G	Ruben Rivera	1.00
11G	Alan Benes	1.00
12G	Willie Greene	1.00
13G	Russ Davis	1.00
14G	Jose Malave	1.00
15G	LaTroy Hawkins	1.00
16G	Frank Rodriguez	1.00
17G	Scott Ruffcorn	1.00
18G	Ben Grieve	1.50

1995 Best Top 100

In mid-1995, some of the founding principals of Best re-acquired the brand name from Classic and began production of a new generation of minor league cards. Following the 1995 season, the company released a set of 100 top minor league players. White bordered card fronts feature team logos at upper-right. Backs have a portrait photo, 1995 stats and a scouting report on the player. The issue was sold in 12-card hobby foil packs and 16-card retail packs. Hobby packs included a special au-

tographed edition card of four top prospects randomly inserted at an average rate of one per 18 packs. The retail packs had inserts of 23 First Round Draft Picks and 10 "Best of the Best" cards.

		MT
Complete Set (101):		7.50
Common Player:		.05
Wax Pack (15):		1.50
Wax Box (36):		35.00
1	Rocky Coppinger	.05
2	Rafael Orellano	.05
3	Nomar Garciaparra	2.00
4	Ryan McGuire	.05
5	Pork Chop Pough	.05
6	Trot Nixon	.50
7	Donnie Sadler	.05
8	Chris Allison	.05
9	Todd Greene	.05
10	George Arias	.05
11	Matt Beaumont	.05
12	Jeff Abbott	.05
13	Tom Fordham	.05
14	Damian Jackson	.05
15	Richie Sexson	.25
16	Bartolo Colon	.05
17	David Roberts	.05
18	Daryle Ward	.05
19	Brandon Reed	.05
20	Juan Encarnacion	.10
21	Eddy Gaillard	.05
22	Derek Hacopian	.05
23	Glendon Rusch	.05
24	Lino Diaz	.05
25	Tim Byrdak	.05
26	Antone Williamson	.05
27	Jonas Hamlin	.05
28	Todd Walker	.10
29	Dan Serafini	.05
30	Kimera Bartee	.05
31	Shane Bowers	.05
32	Tyrone Horne	.05
33	Nick Del Vecchio	.05
34	Mike Figga	.05
35	Matt Drews	.05
36	Ray Ricken	.05
37	Ben Grieve	.15
38	Steve Cox	.05
39	Scott Spiezio	.05
40	Desi Relaford	.05
41	Matt Wagner	.05
42	James Bonnici	.05
43	Osvaldo Fernandez	.05
44	Marino Santana	.05
45	Julio Santana	.05
46	Jeff Davis	.05
47	Trey Beamon	.05
48	Jose Pett	.05
49	Chris Carpenter	.05
50	Andruw Jones	1.00
51	Damon Hollins	.05
52	Jermaine Dye	.15
53	Aldo Pecorilli	.05
54	Carey Paige	.05
55	Damian Moss	.05
56	Ron Wright	.05
57	Brooks Kieschnick	.05
58	Pedro Valdes	.05
59	Scott Samuels	.05
60	Bobby Morris	.05
61	Amaury Telemaco	.05
62	Steve Gibraltar	.05
63	Pokey Reese	.15
64	Pat Watkins	.05
65	Aaron Boone	.10
66	Jamey Wright	.05
67	Derrick Gibson	.05
68	Brent Crowther	.05
69	Ralph Milliard	.05
70	Edgar Renteria	.15
71	Billy McMillon	.05
72	Clemente Nunez	.05
73	Bob Abreu	.05
74	Eric Ludwick	.05
75	Tony Mounce	.05
76	Chris Latham	.05
77	Wilton Guerrero	.05
78	Adam Riggs	.05
79	Paul Konerko	.50
80	Vladimir Guerrero	1.00
81	Brad Fullmer	.05
82	Hiram Bocachica	.05
83	Paul Wilson	.10
84	Jay Payton	.10
85	Rey Ordonez	.05
86	Wendell Magee	.05
87	Wayne Gomes	.05
88	Carlton Loewer	.05
89	Scott Rolen	.75
90	Rich Hunter	.05
91	Jason Kendall	.40
92	Micah Franklin	.05
93	Elmer Dessens	.05
94	Matt Ruebel	.05
95	Mike Gulan	.05
96	Jay Witasick	.05
97	Bret Wagner	.05
98	Greg LaRocca	.05
99	Jason Thompson	.05
100	Derrek Lee	.50
---	Checklist	.05

1995 Best Top 100 Autographed

A special autographed edition of four of the top prospects from Best's Top 100 set was produced as a random insert. The autographed cards were inserted only in the 12-card hobby version foil packs, at an average rate of one per 18 packs (two per box). The autograph cards feature a vignetted photo of the player on front with his name printed in silver at lower-right and an authentic autograph on front. Backs have a ghost image of the front photo and a congratulatory message, along with appropriate logos and copyright notices.

		MT
Complete Set (4):		20.00
Common Player:		2.00
(1)	Todd Greene	2.00
(2)	Andruw Jones	15.00
(3)	Jay Payton	2.00
(4)	Paul Wilson	2.00

1995 Best Top 100 Best of the Best

Numbered contiguously from the regular set, but found only as one-per-pack inserts in 16-card retail foil packs, this chase set features 10 of the brightest minor league stars of 1995. Fronts are in horizontal format with a color photo superimposed on a green background photo. Backs have 1995 and career stats along with career highlights.

		MT
Complete Set (10):		6.00
Common Card:		.25
101	Jason Kendall	.50
102	Derrek Lee	1.50
103	Todd Walker	.25
104	Edgar Renteria	.25
105	Scott Rolen	2.00
106	Andruw Jones	3.00
107	Jay Payton	.25
108	Derrick Gibson	.25
109	Paul Wilson	.25
110	Brandon Reed	.25

1995 Best Top 100 First Round Draft Picks

Another one-per-pack insert exclusive to 16-card retail foil packs of Best Top 100 is this set of first round picks from the June 1995 amateur draft. Cards are similar in format to the regular-issue Top 100

but have the front photo background posterized. Backs have a short biography.

		MT
Complete Set (23):		5.00
Common Player:		.10
111	Ben Davis	.10
112	Chad Hermansen	.10
113	Corey Jenkins	.10
114	Geoff Jenkins	.25
115	Ryan Jaroncyk	.10
116	Andy Yount	.10
117	Reggie Taylor	.10
118	Joe Fontenot	.10
119	Mike Drumright	.10
120	David Yokum	.10
121	Jonathan Johnson	.10
122	Jaime Jones	.10
123	Tony McKnight	.10
124	Michael Barrett	.15
125	Roy Halladay	.50
126	Todd Helton	2.00
127	Juan LeBron	.10
128	Darin Erstad	.50
129	Jose Cruz, Jr.	.10
130	Kerry Wood	2.00
131	Shea Morenz	.10
132	Mark Redman	.10
133	Matt Morris	.25

1995 Best Top 100 Franchise

A dozen projected franchise players of the future are included in this insert set. Cards F1-F6 are retail pack inserts, cards F7-F12 are hobby pack inserts. All cards have gold-foil highlights on front. Franchise inserts are found on average of one per three foil boxes.

		MT
Complete Set (12):		15.00
Common Player:		.50
F1	Darin Erstad	1.50
F2	Nomar Garciaparra	6.00
F3	Rocky Coppinger	.50
F4	Matt Drews	.50
F5	Ben Grieve	.65
F6	Todd Walker	.50
F7	Edgar Renteria	.75
F8	Derrick Gibson	.50
F9	Andruw Jones	4.50
F10	Derrek Lee	2.00
F11	Jason Kendall	1.50
F12	Paul Wilson	.50

1995 Classic Assets Gold (Baseball)

This super-premium five-sport set offers 50 base cards and a wide range of inserts with extremely limited production on some. The baseball players from the issue are listed here. Only 500 of each gold diecut were produced and 349 of each gold signature.

Base Set/Inserts		MT
11	Nolan Ryan	1.00
11	Nolan Ryan	
	(Silver signature.)	5.00
11	Nolan Ryan	
	(Gold signature.)	15.00
SDC18	Nolan Ryan	
	(Silver die-cut.)	5.00
GDC18	Nolan Ryan	
	(Gold die-cut.)	15.00
12	Barry Bonds	2.00
12	Barry Bonds	
	(Silver signature.)	5.00
12	Barry Bonds	
	(Gold signature.)	15.00
SDC9	Barry Bonds	
	(Silver die-cut.)	5.00
GDC9	Barry Bonds	
	(Gold die-cut.)	15.00
13	Ben Grieve	.25
13	Ben Grieve	
	(Silver signature.)	1.00
13	Ben Grieve	
	(Gold signature.)	2.50
SDC1	Ben Grieve	
	(Silver die-cut.)	1.00

GDC1	Ben Grieve	
	(Gold die-cut.)	2.50
14	Dustin Hermanson	.15
14	Dustin Hermanson	
	(Silver signature.)	1.00
14	Dustin Hermanson	
	(Gold signature.)	3.00

1995 Classic 5 Sport (Baseball)

Thirty-one baseball players are included in the 200 cards of this issue which covers the four major team sports plus auto racing, with the emphasis on up-and-coming youngsters. Fronts have color poses or action photos at left. Minor or major league uniform logos have been removed because the cards are licensed only by the individual players. At right is a stack of baseballs with the player's name in gold vertically and the city in which he plays and his position in white. Backs have another color photo at right with personal data and a career summary in a gold marbled panel at left. Professional stats are in a black box at bottom. Besides the standard format, each card can also be found in a die-cut and a printer's proof version as random pack inserts, as well as an autographed version.

		MT
Baseball Set (33):		5.00
Common Player:		.10
93	Ben Grieve	.15
94	Roger Cedeno	.10
95	Michael Barrett	.10
96	Ben Davis	.10
97	Paul Wilson	.15
98	Calvin Reese	.10
99	Jermaine Dye	.15
100	Alvie Shepherd	.10
101	Ryan Jaroncyk	.10
102	Mark Farris	.10
103	Karim Garcia	.30
104	Rey Ordonez	.10
105	Jay Payton	.10
106	Dustin Hermanson	.10
107	Tommy Davis	.10
108	C.J. Nitkowski	.10
109	Todd Greene	.10
110	Billy Wagner	.10
111	Mark Redman	.10
112	Brooks Kieschnick	.10
113	Paul Konerko	.50
114	Brad Fullmer	.10
115	Vladimir Guerrero	2.00
116	Bartolo Colon	.35
117	Doug Million	.10
118	Steve Gibraltar	.10
119	Tony McKnight	.10
120	Derrek Lee	1.00
121	Nomar Garciaparra	2.50
122	Chad Hermansen	.10
183	Nomar Garciaparra,	
	W/Travis Best	
	(Alma Mater)	1.50
188	Paul Wilson,	
	W/Derrick Brooks	
	(Alma Mater)	.10
193	Barry Bonds	
	(Picture Perfect)	3.00

1995 Classic 5 Sport (Baseball) Autographed

Authentically autographed versions of each of the base cards in the 5 sport set were available as random pack inserts. Backs have a message of congratulations and authenticity. Some cards are seen with an embossed "Classic Certified" logo and with numbered signatures.

		MT
Baseball Set (31):		165.00
Common Player:		1.00
93	Ben Grieve	2.00
94	Roger Cedeno	2.00

95	Michael Barrett	2.00
96	Ben Davis	1.00
97	Paul Wilson	2.00
98a	Calvin Reese ("Calvin Reese" autograph.)	4.00
98b	Pokey Reese ("Pokey Reese" autograph.)	4.00
99	Jermaine Dye	4.00
100	Alvie Shepherd	1.00
101	Ryan Jaroncyk	1.00
102	Mark Farris	1.00
103	Karim Garcia	3.00
104	Rey Ordonez	1.00
105	Jay Payton	2.00
106	Dustin Hermanson	1.00
107	Tommy Davis	1.00
108	C.J. Nitkowski	1.00
109	Todd Greene	1.00
110	Billy Wagner	3.00
111	Mark Redman	1.00
112	Brooks Kieschnick	1.00
113	Paul Konerko	3.00
114	Brad Fullmer	1.00
115	Vladimir Guerrero	20.00
116	Bartolo Colon	4.00
117	Doug Million	3.00
118	Steve Gibralter	1.00
119	Tony McKnight	1.00
120	Derrek Lee	15.00
121	Nomar Garciaparra	25.00
122	Chad Hermansen	1.00
193	Barry Bonds (Picture Perfect)	100.00

1995 Classic 5 Sport (Baseball) Autograph Edition

"Autograph Edition" versions bearing facsimile signatures on each of the base cards in the 5 Sport set were available as random pack inserts. Variations in the color of the facsimile signature are known as is a die-cut version.

		MT
Baseball Set (31):		10.00
Common Player:		.20
93	Ben Grieve	.30
94	Roger Cedeno	.20
95	Michael Barrett	.20
96	Ben Davis	.20
97	Paul Wilson	.20
98	Calvin Reese	.30
99	Jermaine Dye	.25
100	Alvie Shepherd	.20
101	Ryan Jaroncyk	.20
102	Mark Farris	.20
103	Karim Garcia	.40
104	Rey Ordonez	.20
105	Jay Payton	.20
106	Dustin Hermanson	.20
107	Tommy Davis	.20
108	C.J. Nitkowski	.20
109	Todd Greene	.20
110	Billy Wagner	.30
111	Mark Redman	.20
112	Brooks Kieschnick	.20
113	Paul Konerko	.60
114	Brad Fullmer	.20
115	Vladimir Guerrero	3.00
116	Bartolo Colon	.40
117	Doug Million	.20
118	Steve Gibralter	.20
119	Tony McKnight	.20
120	Derrek Lee	1.50
121	Nomar Garciaparra	4.00
122	Chad Hermansen	.20
193	Barry Bonds (Picture Perfect)	5.00

1995 Classic 5 Sport (Baseball) Die-Cuts

Each of the 200 players in the 5 Sport set can also be found in a die-cut parallel version which was inserted at the rate of one per pack. Other than the die-cutting around the baseball at the right edge, and the player's name being printed in silver, rather than gold, ink the die-cuts are identical to the standard format.

	MT
Baseball Set (31):	20.00
Common Player:	.25
(Stars valued 3X base cards.)	

1995 Classic 5 Sport (Baseball) Inserts

A number of the insert sets found with 5 Sports include baseball players.

		MT
Baseball Set (4):		60.00
SP5	Paul Wilson (5 Sport Preview, Hockey Pack Insert)	1.00
RS7	Paul Wilson (Record Setters)	1.00
FT13	Ben Grieve (Fast Track)	1.00
1	Barry Bonds (Hot Box Autographs) (Edition of 630.))	100.00

1995 Classic 5 Sport (Baseball) Printers Proofs

A random pack insert, this parallel set of all 200 cards in the 5 Sport set is printed in an edition of just 795 cards each. Identical in format to the standard issue, the cards feature a purple-foil notation on front.

	MT
Baseball Set (31):	50.00
Common Player:	.50
(Stars valued 150X base cards.)	

1995 Classic 5 Sport (Baseball) Strive For Five

These interactive game cards were inserted approximately one per 10 packs by number and/or suit

(sport) and redeemed for prizes ranging from autographed cards to $5,000 cash. The standard size cards have silver metallic foil borders and numbers on front. Player action photos are separated from the background by a large 5 Sport logo. Printed in fine white type on the green back are game rules and prize details. Only the baseball players among the issue's 65 cards are listed here.

		MT
Complete Set (13):		5.00
Common Player:		.25
1	Paul Wilson	.40
2	Billy Wagner	.40
3	Ben Grieve	.25
4	Bartolo Colon	.60
5	Tommy Davis	.25
6	C.J. Nitkowski	.25
7	Mark Redman	.25
8	Todd Greene	.25
9	Jay Payton	.25
10	Nomar Garciaparra	4.00
J	Ben Davis	.25
Q	Doug Million	.25
K	Dustin Hermanson	.25

1995 Classic Images '95 (Baseball)

Eighteen of the 120 regular cards in this four-sport prospects collection feature baseball players. Cards feature a color action photo on an etched metallic foil background. Backs have another player photo, personal data, stats and a career summary.

		MT
Baseball Set (18):		5.00
Common Player:		.10
76	Paul Wilson	.10
77	Ben Grieve	.10
78	Doug Million	.10
79	Bret Wagner	.10
80	Dustin Hermanson	.10
81	Doug Webb	.10
82	Brian Stephenson	.10
83	Jacob Cruz	.10
84	Cade Gaspar	.10
85	Nomar Garciaparra	2.00
86	Mike Thurman	.10
87	Brian Buchanan	.10
88	Mark Johnson	.10
89	Jacob Shumate	.10
90	Kevin Witt	.10
91	Victor Rodriguez	.10
92	Trey Moore	.10
93	Barry Bonds	4.00

1995 Classic Images '95 Classic Performances

This is the only one of the several Images '95 insert sets to include baseball players. Horizontal format cards feature color player photos on a background of etched gold metallic foil. Backs have another color photo and a description of the career highlight, along with a serial number from within an edition of 4,495. Stated odds of picking a Classic Performances card were one per 12 packs.

		MT
Baseball Set (3):		10.00
CP16	Paul Wilson	1.00
CP17	Barry Bonds	7.50
CP18	Nolan Ryan	7.50

1995 Signature Rookies

Fifty top prospects are featured in the 1995 Signature Rookies base set, along with many types of insert cards at varying levels of scarcity. The 2-1/2" x 3-1/2" cards have the player's last name in gold-foil on a marble-look panel at top (first name in red), and at bottom have a gold-foil notation "1 of 25,000." Backs repeat a detail of the front photo, add a second photo and provide stats, personal data and career highlights.

		MT
Complete Set (50):		1.00
Common Player:		.05
1	Mark Acre	.05
2	Edgar Alfonzo	.05
3	Ivan Arteaga	.05
4	Rich Aude	.05
5	Joe Ausanio	.05
6	Marc Barcelo	.05
7	Allen Battle	.05
8	Rigo Beltran	.05
9	Darren Bragg	.05
10	Rico Brogna	.05
11	Mike Busch	.05
12	Juan F. Castillo	.05
13	Joe Ciccarella	.05
14	Darrel Deak	.05
15	Steve Dunn	.05
16	Vaughn Eshelman	.05
17	Bart Evans	.05
18	Rikkert Faneyte	.05
19	Kenny Felder	.05
20	Micah Franklin	.05
21	Brad Fullmer	.05
22	Willie Greene	.05
23	Greg Hansell	.05
24	Phil Hiatt	.05
25	Todd Hollandsworth	.05
26	Damon Hollins	.05
27	Chris Hook	.05
28	Kerry Lacy	.05
29	Todd LaRocca	.05
30	Sean Lawrence	.05
31	Aaron Ledesma	.05
32	Esteban Loaiza	.05
33	Albie Lopez	.05
34	Luis Lopez	.05
35	Marc Marini	.05
36	Nate Minchey	.05
37	Doug Mlicki	.05
38	Glenn Murray	.05
39	Troy O'Leary	.05
40	Eric Owens	.05
41	Orlando Palmeiro	.05
42	Todd Pridy	.05
43	Joe Randa	.05
44	Jason Schmidt	.25
45	Basil Shabazz	.05
46	Paul Spoljaric	.05
47	J.J. Thobe	.05
48	Sean Whiteside	.05
49	Gary Wilson	.05
50	Shannon Withem	.05
JD 2	Joe DiMaggio	3.00

1995 Signature Rookies - Autographed

Each of the cards in the Signature Rookies set was also issued in an authentically-autographed edition of 5,750 as random pack inserts. Some cards were represented in packs by coupons redeemable for the cards. Cards of Kerry Lacy and Basil Shabazz were never autographed.

		MT
Complete Set (48/50):		40.00
Common Player:		1.00
1	Mark Acre	1.00
2	Edgar Alfonzo	1.00
3	Ivan Arteaga	1.00
4	Rich Aude	1.00
5	Joe Ausanio	1.00
6	Marc Barcelo	1.00
7	Allen Battle	1.00
8	Rigo Beltran	1.00
9	Darren Bragg	1.00
10	Rico Brogna	1.00
11	Mike Busch	1.00
12	Juan F. Castillo	1.00
13	Joe Ciccarella	1.00
14	Darrel Deak	1.00
15	Steve Dunn	1.00
16	Vaughn Eshelman	1.00
17	Bart Evans	1.00
18	Rikkert Faneyte	1.00
19	Kenny Felder	1.00
20	Micah Franklin	1.00
21	Brad Fullmer	1.00
22	Willie Greene	1.00
23	Greg Hansell	1.00
24	Phil Hiatt	1.00
25	Todd Hollandsworth	1.50
26	Damon Hollins	1.00
27	Chris Hook	1.00
28	Kerry Lacy (Not signed.)	.25
29	Todd LaRocca	1.00
30	Sean Lawrence	1.00
31	Aaron Ledesma	1.00
32	Esteban Loaiza	2.00
33	Albie Lopez	1.00
34	Luis Lopez	1.00
35	Marc Marini	1.00
36	Nate Minchey	1.00
37	Doug Mlicki	1.00
38	Glenn Murray	1.00
39	Troy O'Leary	1.00
40	Eric Owens	1.00
41	Orlando Palmeiro	1.00
42	Todd Pridy	1.00
43	Joe Randa	1.00
44	Jason Schmidt	6.00
45	Basil Shabazz (Not signed.)	.25
46	Paul Spoljaric	1.00
47	J.J. Thobe	1.00
48	Sean Whiteside	1.00
49	Gary Wilson	1.00
50	Shannon Withem	1.00

1995 Signature Rookies Draft Day Stars

Five hot picks from the 1994 amateur draft are featured in this insert set on both unsigned and authentically autographed cards. Fronts have a pair of photos on a background of bright colors. The player name, Draft Day Star logo and edition number (10,000 each plain, 2,000 autographed) are in gold foil. Backs repeat one of the front photos and have a few career notes and stats along with personal data.

		MT
Complete Set (5):		1.00
Complete Set, Autographed (5):		9.00
Common Player:		.25
Common Autograph:		2.00
DD1	Matt Beaumont	.25
DD1a	Matt Beaumont/Auto.	2.00
DD2	Josh Booty	.25
DD2a	Josh Booty/Auto.	3.00
DD3	Russ Johnson	.25
DD3a	Russ Johnson/Auto.	2.00
DD4	Todd Walker	.25
DD4a	Todd Walker/Auto.	3.00
DD5	Jaret Wright	.25
DD5a	Jaret Wright/Auto.	3.00

1995 Signature Rookies Fame & Fortune Erstad!

This insert issue to the Fame & Fortune football/ basketball set features University of Nebraska football/ baseball star and 1995 #1 overall draft pick Darin Erstad. The cards have borderless color game-action (either baseball or football) photos of the player with his name repeated in varying sizes of gray letters in the background. Down one side in gold foil is "ERSTAD!," shadowed in red. The Fame & Fortune logo is in gold in a lower corner. Backs have a white background, another color photo, his college baseball stats and a few sentences about his career to date.

		MT
Complete Set (5):		5.00
Common Player:		1.00
E1	Darin Erstad/Btg	1.00
E2	Darin Erstad/Btg	1.00
E3	Darin Erstad/Punting	1.00
E4	Darin Erstad/Btg	1.00
E5	Darin Erstad/Fldg	1.00

1995 Signature Rookies Future Dynasty

A player action photo is set in a homeplate design on a garish background of tan, burgundy, blue and green waves on this insert series. The player name, edition limit (5,000 of each regular card, 1,000 of each autographed, 30,000 of each promo) and other graphic highlights are in gold foil. Backs have two more player photos, stats, personal data and career summary.

		MT
Complete Set (5):		2.00
Complete Set, Autographed (5):		65.00
Common Player:		.25
Common Autograph:		2.00
Promos: 50 Percent		
FD1	Billy Ashley	.25

FD1a	Billy Ashley/Auto.	2.00
FD2	Ben Grieve	.50
FD2a	Ben Grievey/Auto.	3.00
FD3	Derek Jeter	1.50
FD3a	Derek Jetery/Auto.	60.00
FD4	Ruben Rivera	.25
FD4a	Ruben Riveray/Auto.	3.00
FD5	Antone Williamson	.25
FD5a	Antone Williamsony/ Auto.	2.00

1995 Signature Rookies Major Rookies

Five of 1995's top rookies are featured in this insert set. Cards come in both unsigned (edition of 10,000 each) and genuinely autographed (edition of 750 each). Fronts have player action photos with a huge green and orange "MAJOR ROOKIES" logo behind. The player name and edition number are in gold foil. Backs also feature the green and orange color scheme and have another color photo, stats and personal data, and a paragraph about the player.

		MT
Complete Set (5):		5.00
Complete Set,		
Autographed (5):		100.00
Common Player:		.50
Common Autograph:		2.00
MR1	Marty Cordova	.75
MR1a	Marty Cordovay/Auto.	3.00
MR2	Benji Gil	.50
MR2a	Benji Gily/Auto.	2.00
MR3	Charles Johnson	.75
MR3a	Charles Johnsony/Auto.	3.00
MR4	Manny Ramirez	2.00
MR4a	Manny Ramirezy/Auto.	45.00
MR5	Alex Rodriguez	3.00
MR5a	Alex Rodriguezy/Auto.	60.00

1995 Signature Rookies Organizational Player/Year

These inserts are found in both autographed (edition of 1,000) and unsigned (7,500) form. The design emphasizes the foundation nature of the players chosen, with a red brick wall at one side and an action photo at the other. The card title and player name are in gold foil. Backs repeat the brick wall background, have another color photo and the usual personal data, stats and career summary.

		MT
Complete Set (5):		1.00
Complete Set, Autographed (5):		15.00
Common Player:		.25
Common Autograph:		2.00
OP1	Juan Acevedo	.25
OP1a	Juan Acevedoy/Auto.	1.00
OP2	Johnny Damon	.75
OP2a	Johnny Damony/Auto.	2.00
OP3	Ray Durham	.25
OP3a	Ray Durhamy/Auto.	3.00
OP4	LaTroy Hawkins	.25
OP4a	LaTroy Hawkinsy/Auto.	1.00
OP5	Brad Woodall	.25
OP5a	Brad Woodally/Auto.	3.00

1995 Signature Rookies Preview

Players who looked to be ready for the major leagues are the focus of this set. Large color action photos on front are surmounted by a red strip bearing the player's name in gold foil. Gold highlights at bottom have the SR Preview logo at lower-left and "1 of 25,000" at center. Backs have two more color photos of the player, with one of them ghosted in muted shades. The player's complete minor league record is included. Each of the cards in the set can also be found in an autographed version of 6,000. Minor and major league team logos have been removed from the player photos and, in some cases, replaced with unofficial logos to avoid licensing problems.

		MT
Complete Set (38):		1.00
Common Player:		.05
1	Tavo Alvarez	.05
2	Rich Batchelor	.05
3	Doug Bochtler	.05
4	Jerry Brooks	.05
5	Scott Bryant	.05
6	Mike Busby	.05
7	Fred Costello	.05
8	Glenn Dishman	.05
9	James Foster	.05
10	Webster Garrison	.05
11	Tony Graffanino	.05
12	Billy Hall	.05
13	Mike Hubbard	.05
14	Jason Hutchins	.05
15	Rick Kelley	.05
16	Jerry Koller	.05
17	Ryan Luzinski	.05
18	Anthony Manahan	.05
19	Mike Matthews	.05
20	Greg McCarty	.05
21	Jeff McCurry	.05
22	Gino Minutelli	.05
23	Izzy Molina	.05
24	Scott Moten	.05
25	Peter Munro	.05
26	Willis Otanez	.05
27	Rodney Pedraza	.05
28	Brandon Pico	.05
29	Brian Raabe	.05
30	Eddie Rios	.05
31	Toby Rumfield	.05
32	Andy Sheets	.05
33	Larry Sutton	.05
34	Brian Thomas	.05
35	Hector Trinidad	.05
36	Jim Waring	.05
37	Mike Welch	.05
38	Steve Wojciechowski	.05

1995 Signature Rookies Star Squad

Ten players who were already making their marks in the Major Leagues were featured in this insert set. The cards have player action photos on front with large red areas above and below containing a star and "STAR SQUAD" designation and the player's name and manufacturer's logo. A vertical gold-foil stamping notes, "1 of 10,000." Backs have another player photo along with a few stats, biographical bits and career summary. Uniform logos have been airbrushed away or replaced with unofficial logos since the cards are licensed only by the individual players and not Major League Baseball. An autographed edition of each player was also randomly inserted.

		MT
Complete Set (10):		6.00
Complete Autographed		
Set (10):		110.00
Common Player:		.25
Common Autograph:		2.00
1	Ruben Rivera	.25
1a	Ruben Riveray/Auto.	2.00
2	Charles Johnson	.25
2a	Charles Johnson/Auto.	2.00
3	Derek Jeter	4.00
3a	Derek Jetery/Auto. (Edition of 250.)	75.00
4	Todd Hollandsworth	.25
4a	Todd Hollandsworthy/ Auto.	3.00
5	Billy Ashley	.25
5a	Billy Ashleyy/Auto.	2.00
6	Benji Gil	.25
6a	Benji Gily/Auto.	2.00
7	Vaughn Eshelman	.25
7a	Vaughn Eshelmany/ Auto.	2.00
8	Ray Durham	.25
8a	Ray Durhamy/Auto.	3.00
9	Marty Cordova	.25

1995 Signature Rookies Preview - Autographed

Each of the cards in the 1995 Signature Rookies Preview set can be found in an autographed edition. The cards are hand-signed and numbered within an edition of 6,000. The autographed cards have a gold-foil "1 of 6,000" notation at bottom-center on front.

		MT
Complete Set (38):		35.00
Common Player:		1.00
1	Tavo Alvarez	1.00
2	Rich Batchelor	1.00
3	Doug Bochtler	1.00
4	Jerry Brooks	1.00
5	Scott Bryant	1.00
6	Mike Busby	1.00
7	Fred Costello	1.00
8	Glenn Dishman	1.00
9	James Foster	1.00
10	Webster Garrison	1.00
11	Tony Graffanino	1.00
12	Billy Hall	1.00
13	Mike Hubbard	1.00
14	Jason Hutchins	1.00
15	Rick Kelley	1.00
16	Jerry Koller	1.00
17	Ryan Luzinski	1.50
18	Anthony Manahan	1.00
19	Mike Matthews	1.00
20	Greg McCarty	1.00
21	Jeff McCurry	1.00
22	Gino Minutelli	1.00
23	Izzy Molina	1.00
24	Scott Moten	1.00
25	Peter Munro	1.00
26	Willis Otanez	1.00
27	Rodney Pedraza	1.00
28	Brandon Pico	1.00
29	Brian Raabe	1.00
30	Eddie Rios	1.00
31	Toby Rumfield	1.00
32	Andy Sheets	1.00
33	Larry Sutton	1.00
34	Brian Thomas	1.00
35	Hector Trinidad	1.00
36	Jim Waring	1.00
37	Mike Welch	1.00
38	Steve Wojciechowski	1.00

9a	Marty Cordovay/Auto.	3.00
10	Manny Ramirez	2.00
10a	Manny Ramirezy/Auto.	35.00

1995 Signature Rookies Tetrad (Baseball)

Thirty-one baseball players are featured among the young stars of the four major team sports in this issue. Fronts have a color action photo with the background muted in black-and-white. The player's name is in gold foil in a green marbled panel at bottom. Tetrad's "You Make the Call" logo is also in gold foil. Backs have two more photos, personal data and stats and repeated the green marbled motif.

		MT
Complete (Baseball) Set (31):		3.00
Common Player:		.05
31	Andy Yount	.05
32	Jose Cruz, Jr.	.10
33	Dustin Hermanson	.10
34	David Yocum	.05
35	Dmitri Young	.10
36	Kerry Wood	1.00
37	Jonathan Johnson	.05
38	Shea Morenz	.10
39	Matt Morris	.10
40	Reggie Taylor	.10
41	Antone Williamson	.05
42	Derek Wallace	.05
43	Ben Grieve	.10
44	Benji Gil	.05
45	Todd Walker	.10
46	Jason Thompson	.05
47	Scott Stahoviak	.05
48	Chris Roberts	.05
49	Dante Powell	.05
50	Torii Hunter	.50
56	Bryan Rekar	.05
57	Jaime Jones	.05
58	Todd Helton	1.00
59	Joe Fontenot	.05
60	Tony Clark	.10
72	Tony McKnight	.05
73	Roy Halladay	.25
74	Mike Drumright	.05
74	Ben Davis	.05
75	Michael Barrett	.10
76	Sid Roberson	.05

1995 Signature Rookies Tetrad (Baseball) Autographs

Each of the cards in SR Tetrad was also issued in an authentically autographed version, numbered to 5,000 each.

		MT
Baseball Set (31):		60.00
Common Player:		1.00
31	Andy Yount	1.00
32	Jose Cruz, Jr.	3.00
33	Dustin Hermanson	1.00
34	David Yocum	1.00
35	Dmitri Young	1.00
36	Kerry Wood	20.00
37	Jonathan Johnson	1.00
38	Shea Morenz	1.00
39	Matt Morris	1.00
40	Reggie Taylor	1.00
41	Antone Williamson	1.00
42	Derek Wallace	1.00
43	Ben Grieve	2.00
44	Benji Gil	1.00
45	Todd Walker	3.00
46	Jason Thompson	1.00
47	Scott Stahoviak	1.00
48	Chris Roberts	1.00
49	Dante Powell	1.00
50	Torii Hunter	17.50
56	Bryan Rekar	1.00
57	Jaime Jones	1.00
q8	Todd Helton	12.50
59	Joe Fontenot	1.00
60	Tony Clark	2.00
71	Tony McKnight	1.00
72	Roy Halladay	6.00
73	Mike Drumright	1.00
74	Ben Davis	1.50
75	Michael Barrett	2.00
76	Sid Roberson	1.00

1995 Signature Rookies Tetrad Autobilia (Baseball)

Thirty baseball players are included among the young stars of the four major team sports in this 100-card issue. Fronts have a background of greens and purples with three sizes of a player action photo muted in the background. In the foreground is a large color action photo. Graphic highlights are in gold foil, including a bar at bottom with the player name. Backs have a couple more color player photos on a yellow and magenta background. Stats, draft status and a few words about the player are included. Each of the cards could also be found in an autographed version as a random pack insert, and in a "CLUB SET" version so designated by vertical gold-foil typography on front.

		MT
Baseball Set (30):		7.50
Common Player:		.05
18	Juan Acevedo	.05
19	Trey Beamon	.05
20	Tim Belk	.05
21	Mike Bovee	.05
22	Brad Clontz	.05
23	Marty Cordova	.10
24	Johnny Damon	1.00
25	Jeff Darwin	.05
26	Nick Delvecchio	.05
27	Ray Durham	.05
28	Jermaine Dye	.15
29	Jimmy Haynes	.05
30	Mark Hubbard	.05
31	Russ Johnson	.05
33	Andy Larkin	.05
33	Kris Ralston	.05
34	Luis Raven	.05
35	Desi Relaford	.05
36	Jeff Suppan	.05
37	Brad Woodall	.15
72	Ruben Rivera	.05
85	Jose Cruz, Jr.	.10
86	Darin Erstad	.35
87	Todd Helton	2.00
88	Chad Hermansen	.05
89	Jonathan Johnson	.05
90	Manny Ramirez	3.00
91	Kerry Wood	2.00
92	Ben Davis	.05
93	Jaime Jones	.05

1995 Signature Rookies Tetrad Autobilia Autographs

Each card in Tetrad Autobilia was also released in an authentically autographed edition.

		MT
Baseball Set (30):		75.00
Common Player:		1.00
18	Juan Acevedo	1.00
19	Trey Beamon	1.00
20	Tim Belk	1.00
21	Mike Bovee	1.00
22	Brad Clontz	1.00
23	Marty Cordova	3.00
24	Johnny Damon	12.50
25	Jeff Darwin	1.00
26	Nick Delvecchio	1.00

27	Ray Durham	3.00
28	Jermaine Dye	2.00
29	Jimmy Haynes	1.00
30	Mark Hubbard	1.00
31	Russ Johnson	1.00
32	Andy Larkin	1.00
33	Kris Ralston	1.00
34	Luis Raven	1.00
35	Desi Relaford	1.00
36	Jeff Suppan	2.00
37	Brad Woodall	2.00
72	Ruben Rivera	1.00
85	Jose Cruz, Jr.	2.00
86	Darin Erstad	4.50
87	Todd Helton	12.50
88	Chad Hermansen	1.00
89	Jonathan Johnson	1.00
90	Manny Ramirez	50.00
91	Kerry Wood	20.00
92	Ben Davis	2.00
93	Jaime Jones	1.00

1995 Signature Rookies Tetrad Auto-Phonex Test Issue

One baseball player was included in this promo set for an SR Tetrad product. Standard-size cards are highlighted on front with gold foil. Backs have color portrait and action photos, player data and stats.

		MT
T4	Ruben Rivera	.50

1995 Signature Rookies Tetrad B-1 Bomber

The #1 overall pick in the 1995 amateur draft is honored on this five-card insert set recalling the college career of Darin Erstad. Fronts have various action photos of Erstad in his college uniform. Half of the background has been replaced with a vertical green area featuring a large purple "B-1 BOMBER" logo and a gold-foil notation that the card is "1 of 30,000." Erstad's name also appears in gold foil, along with Tetrad's "You Make the Call" logo. Backs have more photos of Erstad, some in his uniform as Big Red's punter/field goal specialist, along with biographical data, college stats and highlights. Cards are numbered B1-B5.

		MT
Complete Set (5):		5.00
Complete Set, Autographed (5):		50.00
Common Card:		1.00
Common Card, Autographed:		10.00
B1	Darin Erstad/Btg	1.00
B1a	Darin Erstady/Auto./Btg	10.00
B2	Darin Erstad/Fldg	1.00
B2a	Darin Erstad/ Auto./Fldg	10.00
B3	Darin Erstad/Btg	1.00
B3a	Darin Erstad/Auto./Btg	10.00
B4	Darin Erstad/Running	1.00
B4a	Darin Erstad/ Auto./Running	10.00
B5	Darin Erstad/Btg	1.00
B5a	Darin Erstad/Auto./Btg	10.00

1995 Signature Rookies Tetrad SR Force (Baseball)

Ten of the top young players in each of the four major team sports were included in an SR Force insert set with Signature Rookies Tetrad. A color action photo on the white front background has had team logos removed to avoid licensing problems. Three inset photos repeat details from the large picture. "SR FORCE" is printed in purples and greens at top. Gold-foil highlights include the player name and "1 of 6,000" notation. Backs have a large ghosted photo in the background and three detail photos at left, along with personal data, stats and a few words about the player.

	MT
Complete Set (10):	6.00
Autographed Set (10):	175.00
Common Player:	.25
Common Autograph (10):	2.00
F11 Manny Ramirez	1.50
F11a Manny Ramirez/Auto.	50.00
F12 Jaret Wright	.25
F12a Jaret Wright/Auto.	3.00
F13 Ruben Rivera	.25
F13a Ruben Rivera/Auto.	2.00
F14 Derek Jeter	3.00
F14a Derek Jeter/Auto.	75.00
F15 Monty Fariss	.25
F15a Monty Fariss/Auto.	2.00
F16 Jason Isringhausen	.25
F16a Jason Isringhausen/Auto.	2.00
F17 Marty Cordova	.25
F17a Marty Cordova/Auto.	3.00
F18 Garret Anderson	.25
F18a Garrett Anderson/Auto.	3.00
F19 Alex Rodriguez	2.00
F19a Alex Rodriguez/Auto.	60.00
F20 Carlton Loewer	.25
F20a Carlton Loewer/Auto.	2.00

1995 Signature Rookies Tetrad You Make the Call

Details of this issue, including the scope of players and/or cards involved and the manner of distribution, are unknown. Each card has a gold-foil "You Make the Call" logo on front, a hand-numbered serial number and an autograph. Backs are identical to the regularly issued versions except for the application of a silver-foil Signature Rookies hologram.

	MT
58 Todd Helton (SR Tetrad, edition of 5,000.)	10.00
B5 Darin Erstad (B-1 Bomber, edition of 2,500.)	10.00

1995 Signature Rookies T-95 Old Judge Series

In an unusual size (2-1/16" x 3-1/16") and in a format more reminiscent of the 1914-15 Cracker Jack cards than the original Old Judge issue of the 1880s, Signature Rookies produced a minor

league issue for 1995. Cards have player photos set against bright solid-colored backgrounds. The player's last name and city of major league affiliation are printed in the white border at bottom. Backs have a few biographical details, 1994 stats and a paragraph about the prospect. Because the cards are licensed only by the individual players, and not Major League Baseball, uniform logos have been airbrushed off and unofficial cap logos and, in some cases, team names have been added. Each of the 35 regular cards in the set can also be found in an autographed version of 5,750. In addition 250 autographed cards of Joe DiMaggio were also randomly inserted. One autographed card or trade-in coupon was included in each pack. Several series of insert cards were issued, besides the autographs.

	MT
Complete Set (36):	2.00
Autographed Set (35):	30.00
Common Player:	.05
Common Autograph:	1.00
1 Bob Abreu	.25
1a Bob Abreu/Auto.	5.00
2 Kym Ashworth	.05
2a Kym Ashworth/Auto.	1.00
3 Jared Baker	.05
3a Jared Baker/Auto.	1.00
4 Paul Bako	.05
4a Paul Bako/Auto.	1.00
5 Jason Bates	.05
5a Jason Bates/Auto.	1.00
6 Yamil Benitez	.05
6a Yamil Benitez/Auto.	1.00
7 Marshall Boze	.05
7a Marshall Boze/Auto.	1.00
8 Rich Butler	.05
8a Rich Butler/Auto.	1.00
9 John Carter	.05
9a John Carter/Auto.	1.00
10 Jeff Cirillo	.15
10a Jeff Cirillo/Auto.	2.50
11 Randy Curtis	.05
11a Randy Curtis/Auto.	1.00
12 Sal Fasano	.05
12a Sal Fasano/Auto.	1.00
13 Aaron Fultz	.05
13a Aaron Fultz/Auto.	1.00
14 Karim Garcia	.35
14a Karim Garcia/Auto.	3.00
15 Kevin Grijak	.05
15a Kevin Grijak/Auto.	1.00
16 Wilton Guerrero	.05
16a Wilton Guerrero/Auto.	1.00
17 Stacy Hollins	.05
17a Stacy Hollins/Auto.	1.00
18 Bobby Hughes	.05
18a Bobby Hughes/Auto.	1.00
19 Jimmy Hurst	.05
19a Jimmy Hurst/Auto.	1.00
20 Jason Isringhausen	.15
20a Jason Isringhausen/Auto.	3.00
21 Ryan Karp	.05
21a Ryan Karp/Auto.	1.00
22 Derek Lowe	.05
22a Derek Lowe/Auto.	15.00
23 Matt Luke	.05
23a Matt Luke/Auto.	1.00
24 Lyle Mouton	.05
24a Lyle Mouton/Auto.	1.00
25 Dave Mysel	.05
25a Dave Mysel/Auto.	1.00
26 Marc Newfield	.05
26a Marc Newfield/Auto.	1.00
27 Jim Pittsley	.05
27a Jim Pittsley/Auto.	1.00
28 Chris Sheff	.05
28a Chris Sheff/Auto.	1.00
29 Tate Seefried	.05
29a Tate Seefried/Auto.	1.00
30 Shawn Senior	.05
30a Shawn Senior/Auto.	1.00
31 Andy Stewart	.05
31a Andy Stewart/Auto.	1.00
32 Ozzie Timmons	.05
32a Ozzie Timmons/Auto.	1.00
33 Quilvio Veras	.05
33a Quilvio Veras/Auto.	1.00
34 Donnie White	.05
34a Donnie White/Auto.	1.00
35 Mike Zimmerman	.05
35a Mike Zimmerman/Auto.	1.00
36 Ruben Rivera Checklist	.05

1995 Signature Rookies T-95 Joe DiMaggio Bonus Cards

DiMAGGIO, New York (AL)

A classic photo of Joe DiMaggio, minus uniform logos, is featured in this, the scarcest of the T-95 inserts. There are 5,000 unsigned cards, inserted at the rate of one per 43 packs (about three boxes), and 250 autographed cards (one per three cases or 864 packs).

	MT
JD1 Joe DiMaggio	2.00
JD1a Joe DiMaggio/Auto.	250.00
PROMO Joe DiMaggio (Marked PROMO on back.)	2.00

1995 Signature Rookies T-95 Hot Prospects

Brad CLONTZ

Five players judged destined for big league fame are featured in this insert set. Cards measure 2-1/16" x 3-1/16". Action photos on front have a large black vertical strip down one side with the player's name in red and gold. A gold-foil notation at bottom says each card is "1 of 7,500." Backs have another color photo and a vertically compressed black-and-white version of the front photo, along with a paragraph about the prospect and his '94 stats. Cards are licensed only by the individual players, so uniform logos have been replaced with unofficial lettering, or airbrushed completely away. Each of the Hot Prospects inserts can also be found in an autographed edition of 1,550. Insertion rates are one per 16 packs for the regular cards, one per 45 packs for the autographed cards.

	MT
Complete Set (5):	1.00
Autographed Set (5):	10.00
Common Player:	.25
Common Autograph:	2.00
HP1 Billy Ashley	.25
HP1a Billy Ashley/Auto.	2.00
HP2 Brad Clontz	.25
HP2a Brad Clontz/Auto.	2.00
HP3 Andrew Lorraine	.25
HP3a Andrew Lorraine/Auto.	2.00
HP4 Ruben Rivera	.25
HP4a Ruben Rivera/Auto.	2.00
HP5 Jason Thompson	.25
HP5a Jason Thompson/Auto.	2.00

1995 Signature Rookies T-95 Minor League All Stars

In the same 2-1/16" x 3-1/16" size as the regular-issue Old Judge T-95 cards and other inserts for

JOHNSON

1995, this All-Star insert set was printed in an edition of 7,500 cards of each player (one per 20 packs, on average). Fronts have a borderless negative black-and-white player photo of which a 1" x 1-1/2" portion has been rendered in color. The player name is in gold foil in a black marbled panel at lower-right. Backs have a color dual-image player photo, a paragraph about his prospects and his 1994 stats. Uniform and cap logos have been removed and replaced with unofficial lettering because the cards are licensed only by the players and not by Major League Baseball. Each All-Star card can also be found in an autographed edition of 2,100 (one per 30 packs).

	MT
Complete Set (5):	1.00
Autographed Set (5):	10.00
Common Player:	.25
Common Autograph:	2.00
AS1 Trey Beamon	.25
AS1a Trey Beamon/Auto.	2.00
AS2 Tim Belk	.25
AS2a Tim Belk/Auto.	2.00
AS3 Jimmy Haynes	.25
AS3a Jimmy Haynes/Auto.	2.00
AS4 Mark Johnson	.25
AS4a Mark Johnson/Auto.	2.00
AS5 Chris Stynes	.25
AS5a Chris Stynes/Auto.	2.00

1995 Signature Rookies T-95 Preview '95

GUERRERO 55

In the same size (2-1/16" x 3-1/16") as the Signature Rookies Old Judge T-95 Series with which they were issued as inserts (one per two packs, average), the Preview '95 cards offer action photos with gold-foil highlights set against black marbled panels at top-right and lower-left. A gold-foil notation at bottom indicates each card is "1 of 5,750." Backs have a close-up repeat of the front photo, a second photo, biographical notes, career summary and 1994 stats. Because the cards are licensed only by the individual players, and not Major League Baseball, uniform logos have been airbrushed off and unofficial cap logos and, in some cases, team names have been added. Each of the 35 regular cards in the set can also be found in an autographed version of 500, about once every 14 packs.

	MT
Complete Set (35):	2.00
Autographed Set (35):	40.00
Common Player:	.10
Common Autograph:	1.00
1 Bob Abreu	.35
1a Bob Abreu/Auto.	5.00
2 Kym Ashworth	.10
2a Kym Ashworth/Auto.	1.00
3 Jared Baker	.10
3a Jared Baker/Auto.	1.00
4 Paul Bako	.10
4a Paul Bako/Auto.	1.00
5 Jason Bates	.10
5a Jason Bates/Auto.	1.00
6 Yamil Benitez	.10
6a Yamil Benitez/Auto.	1.00
7 Marshall Boze	.10
7a Marshall Boze/Auto.	1.00
8 Rich Butler	.10
8a Rich Butler/Auto.	1.00
9 John Carter	.10
9a John Carter/Auto.	1.00
10 Jeff Cirillo	.35
10a Jeff Cirillo/Auto.	2.50
11 Randy Curtis	.10
11a Randy Curtis/Auto.	1.00
12 Sal Fasano	.10
12a Sal Fasano/Auto.	1.00
13 Aaron Fultz	.10
13a Aaron Fultz/Auto.	1.00
14 Karim Garcia	.50
14a Karim Garcia/Auto.	3.00
15 Kevin Grijak	.10
15a Kevin Grijak/Auto.	1.00
16 Wilton Guerrero	.10
16a Wilton Guerrero/Auto.	1.00
17 Stacy Hollins	.10
17a Stacy Hollins/Auto.	1.00
18 Bobby Hughes	.10
18a Bobby Hughes/Auto.	1.00
19 Jimmy Hurst	.10
19a Jimmy Hurst/Auto.	1.00
20 Jason Isringhausen	.25
20a Jason Isringhausen/Auto.	2.50
21 Ryan Karp	.10
21a Ryan Karp/Auto.	1.00
22 Derek Lowe	.25
22a Derek Lowe/Auto.	15.00
23 Matt Luke	.10
23a Matt Luke/Auto.	1.00
24 Lyle Mouton	.10
24a Lyle Mouton/Auto.	1.00
25 Dave Mysel	.10
25a Dave Mysel/Auto.	1.00
26 Marc Newfield	.10
26a Marc Newfield/Auto.	1.00
27 Jim Pittsley	.10
27a Jim Pittsley/Auto.	1.00
28 Chris Sheff	.10
28a Chris Sheff/Auto.	1.00
29 Tate Seefried	.10
29a Tate Seefried/Auto.	1.00
30 Shawn Senior	.10
30a Shawn Senior/Auto.	1.00
31 Andy Stewart	.10
31a Andy Stewart/Auto.	1.00
32 Ozzie Timmons	.10
32a Ozzie Timmons/Auto.	1.00
33 Quilvio Veras	.10
33a Quilvio Veras/Auto.	1.00
34 Donnie White	.10
34a Donnie White/Auto.	1.00
35 Mike Zimmerman	.10
35a Mike Zimmerman/Auto.	1.00

1995 Upper Deck Minor League

RICK WILSON
Mets Top Prospect - P

Superb borderless color photos front and back are featured in UD's 1995 minor league base set. A number of subsets within the 225-card issue allow the showcasing of top prospects on multiple cards. Still more cards of the same players are featured in the various chase sets randomly found in the foil packs. The player's name and UD logo are stamped in silver-foil on card fronts, while a star-shaped hologram is on back. As a dealer incentive for early orders, 10 players signed 1,000 cards each.

	MT
Complete Set (225):	10.00
Common Player:	.05
Wax Pack (12):	1.00
Wax Box (25):	25.00
1 Derek Jeter	3.00
1a Derek Jeter/Auto.	80.00
2 Michael Tucker	.05
3 Alex Ochoa	.05
3a Alex Ochoa/Auto.	1.00
4 Bill Pulsipher	.05
5 Terrell Wade	.05
5a Terrell Wade/Auto.	2.00
6 Johnny Damon	1.00
6a Johnny Damon (Autographed)	20.00
7 LaTroy Hawkins	.05
7a LaTroy Hawkins/Auto.	2.00
8 Ruben Rivera	.05
9 Jason Giambi	.05
9a Jason Giambi/Auto.	15.00
10 Todd Hollandsworth	.05
10a Todd Hollandsworth/Auto.	3.00
11 Alan Benes	.05
11a Alan Benes/Auto.	3.00
12 John Wasdin	.05
13 Roger Cedeno	.05
14 Karim Garcia	.40
15 Brooks Kieschnick	.05
16 David Bell	.05
17 Trot Nixon	.50
18 Jose Malave	.05
19 Rey Ordonez	.05
20 Raul Casanova	.05
21 Chad Mottola	.05
22 Phil Nevin	.05
23 Jim Pittsley	.05
24 Frank Rodriguez	.05
25 Todd Greene	.05
26 Mike Bell	.05
26a Mike Bell/Auto.	2.00
27 Jason Kendall	.35
28 Pokey Reese	.05
29 Jose Silva	.05
30 Kirk Presley	.05
31 Joe Randa	.05
32 Shannon Stewart	.15
33 Danny Clyburn	.05
34 Glenn Williams	.05
35 Terry Bradshaw	.05
36 Jimmy Hurst	.05
37 Scott Spiezio	.05
38 Richard Hidalgo	.05
39 Matt Brunson	.05
40 Juan Acevedo	.05
41 Trey Beamon	.05
42 Kimera Bartee	.05
43 James Baldwin	.05
44 Matt Arrandale	.05
45 Michael Jordan	2.00
46 Wonderful Terrific Monds	.05
47 Bob Abreu	.25
48 Edgardo Alfonzo	.05
49 Damon Hollins	.05
50 Marc Barcelo	.05
51 D.J. Boston	.05
52 Einar Diaz	.05
53 Matt Drews	.05
54 Benji Simonson	.05
55 Bart Evans	.05
56 Micah Franklin	.05
57 Curtis Goodwin	.05
58 Craig Griffey	.10
59 Billy Wagner	.15
60 Jimmy Haynes	.05
61 Jose Herrera	.05
62 Greg Keagle	.05
63 Andy Larkin	.05
64 Jason Isringhausen	.10
65 Derek Lee	1.00
66 Terrell Lowery	.05
67 Ryan Luzinski	.05
68 Angel Martinez	.05
69 Tony Clark	.05
70 Ryan McGuire	.05
71 Damian Moss	.05
72 Hugo Pivaral	.05
73 Arquimedez Pozo	.05
74 Daron Kirkreit	.05
75 Luis Raven	.05
76 Desi Relaford	.05
77 Scott Rolen	1.25
78 Joe Rosselli	.05
79 Chris Roberts	.05
80 Giomar Guevara	.05
81 Gene Schall	.05
82 Jeff Suppan	.10
83 Makoto Suzuki (Makoto)	.05
84 Jason Thompson	.05
85 Marc Valdes	.05
86 Pat Watkins	.05
87 Jay Witasick	.05
88 Ray Durham	.05
89 Brad Fullmer	.05
90 Roger Bailey	.05
91 DeShawn Warren	.05
92 Jermaine Dye	.15
93 Scott Romano	.05
94 Aaron Boone	.10
95 Tate Seefried	.05
96 Chris Stynes	.05
97 Chris Widger	.05
98 Desi Wilson	.05
99 Dante Powell	.05
100 Neifi Perez (Season Highlights)	.05
101 Alex Ochoa (SH)	.05
102 Kelly Wunsch (SH)	.05
103 Jason Robbins (SH)	.05
104 Kevin Coughlin (SH)	.05
105 Bill Pulsipher (SH)	.05
106 Roger Cedeno (International Flavor)	.05
107 Jose Herrera (IF)	.05
108 Andre King (IF)	.05
109 Rey Ordonez (IF)	.10
110 Jose Pett (IF)	.05

112	Ruben Rivera (IF)	.05
113	Jose Silva (IF)	.05
114	Makato Suzuki	
	(Makoto)(IF)	.05
115	Glenn Williams (IF)	.05
116	Wil Cunnane	.05
117	Neifi Perez	.05
118	Andre King	.05
119	Quinton McCracken	.05
120	Brian Giles	.25
121	Kenny Felder	.05
122	Jermaine Allensworth	.05
123	Allen Battle	.05
124	Howard Battle	.05
125	Doug Million	.05
126	Geoff Blum	.05
127	Vladimir Guerrero	1.50
128	Torii Hunter	1.00
129	Doug Glanville	.05
130	Dustin Hermanson	.05
131	Mark Grudzielanek	.15
132	Phil Geisler	.05
133	Chris Carpenter	.05
134	Brian Seckinsky	.05
135	Josh Booty	.05
136	Shane Andrews	.05
137	Scott Eyre	.05
138	Chad Fox	.05
139	George Arias	.05
140	Scott Sullivan	.05
141	Todd Dunn	.05
142	Nate Holdren	.05
143	Gus Gandarillas	.05
144	Scott Talanoa	.05
145	Sal Fasano	.05
146	Stoney Briggs	.05
147	Yamil Benitez	.05
148	Chris Wimmer	.05
149	Mariano De Los Santos	.05
150	Ben Grieve	.10
151	Homer Bush	.05
152	Wilton Guerrero	.05
153	Benji Grigsby	.05
154	Cade Caspar	.05
155	Hiram Bocachica	.05
156	Dave Vanhof	.05
157	Frank Catalanotto	.15
158	Marcus Jensen	.05
159	Jamie Arnold	.05
160	Cesar Devarez	.05
161	Alan Benes	
	(Road to the Show)	.05
162	Johnny Damon (RS)	.50
163	LaTroy Hawkins (RS)	.05
164	Dustin Hermanson (RS)	.05
165	Derek Jeter (RS)	1.50
166	Terrell Wade (RS)	.05
167	Todd Walker (RS)	.10
168	John Wasdin (RS)	.05
169	Paul Wilson (RS)	.05
170	Todd Walker	.10
171	Danny Klassen	.05
172	Bobby Morris	.05
173	Kelly Wunsch	.05
174	Fletcher Thompson	.05
175	Terrence Long	.05
176	Andy Petitte	1.00
177	Lou Pote	.05
178	Steve Kline	.05
179	Damian Jackson	.05
180	Matt Smith	.05
181	Tim Unroe	.05
182	Jim Cole	.05
183	Bill McMillon	.05
184	Matt Luke	.05
185	Sergio Nunez	.05
186	Edgar Renteria	.10
187	Bill Selby	.05
188	Jamey Wright	.05
189	Steve Whitaker	.05
190	Joe Vitiello	.05
191	Jacob Shumate	.05
192	C.J. Nitkowski	.05
193	Mark Johnson	.05
194	Paul Konerko	.50
195	Jay Payton	.10
196	Jayson Peterson	.05
197	Brian Buchanan	.05
198	Ramon Castro	.05
199	Antone Williamson	.05
200	Paul Wilson	.10
200a	Paul Wilson/Auto.	3.00
201	Jaret Wright	.05
202	Carlton Loewer	.05
203	Jon Zuber	.05
204	Ugueth Urbina	.05
205	Nomar Garciaparra	2.00
206	Yuri Sanchez	.05
207	Jason Moler	.05
208	Lyle Mouton	.05
209	Mark Johnson	.05
210	Matt Raleigh	.05
211	Julio Santana	.05
212	Willie Ontafez	.05
213	Ozzie Timmons	.05
214	Victor Rodriguez	.05
215	Paul Wilson	
	(1994 Draft Class)	.05
216	Ben Grieve (DC)	.10
217	Dustin Hermanson (DC)	.05
218	Antone Williamson (DC)	.05
219	Josh Booty (DC)	.05
220	Todd Walker (DC)	.05
221	Jason Varitek (DC)	.50
222	Paul Konerko (DC)	.35
223	Doug Million (DC)	.05
224	Hiram Bocachica (DC)	.05
225	Durham Athletic Park	.10

1995 Upper Deck Minor League Future Stock

Each card in the base set of 1995 Upper Deck minor league can also be found in a "Future Stock" parallel issue. The cards are identical except for the appearance of an FS shield in silver-foil in an upper corner of the card front.

	MT
Complete Set (225):	25.00
Common Player:	.15

(Star players valued at 2X the same card in the regular issue.)

1995 Upper Deck Minor League Michael Jordan Highlights

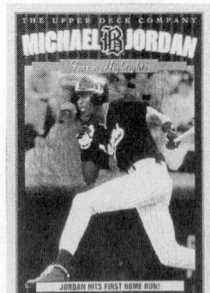

This set of 3-1/2" x 5" cards was available only via a mail-in offer for $3 and 15 UD Minor League foil wrappers. Card fronts are printed on foil and feature highlights from Jordan's only season of professional baseball. Backs have a graduated yellow background with a color photo of Jordan and a few words about the highlight, along with the logos of the Birmingham Barons, UD and the minor league licensing authority.

	MT
Complete Set (5):	15.00
Common Card:	3.00
MJ-1	Michael Jordan	
	(White Sox Welcome)	3.00
MJ-2	Michael Jordan	
	(Jordan Supplies Offense	
	at Classic)	3.00
MJ-3	Michael Jordan	
	(13-Game Hitting Streak)	3.00
MJ-4	Michael Jordan (Jordan Hits	
	First Home Run!)	3.00
MJ-5	Michael Jordan (Jordan Does	
	Extracurricular Baseball)	3.00

1995 Upper Deck Minor League Michael Jordan One-On-One

This 10-card set was produced for inclusion exclusively in mini-packs of Upper Deck Minor League baseball cards sold in Wal-Mart stores. The packs had three cards from the regular set plus one of the 10 One-On-One Jordan cards. Card fronts are in horizontal format and include a silver-foil

"Michael Jordan / 95 / Retires" stamp on front. Backs have a color photo of Jordan and short text.

	MT
Complete Set (10):	4.00
Common Card:	.50
1	Michael Jordan	
	(Throwing)	.50
2	Michael Jordan/Fldg	.50
3	Michael Jordan (Hitting)	.50
4	Michael Jordan (Speed)	.50
5	Michael Jordan	
	(Overall Report)	.50
6	Michael Jordan	
	('94 Spring Training)	.50
7	Michael Jordan	
	('94 Regular Season)	.50
8	Michael Jordan	
	(1st Home Run)	.50
9	Michael Jordan	
	('94 Autumn)	.50
10	Michael Jordan	
	(The Future)	.50

1995 Upper Deck Minor League Michael Jordan's Scrapbook

Printed on metallic-foil fronts, this 10-card chase series chronicles Michael Jordan's season of minor league baseball with the Birmingham Barons. Backs feature a continuing narrative.

	MT
Complete Set (10):	25.00
Common Card:	3.00
1	Michael Jordan	
	Decisions	3.00
2	Michael Jordan Practice	3.00
3	Michael Jordan Spring	
	Training and Assignment	3.00
4	Michael Jordan	
	Windy City Classic	3.00
5	Michael Jordan Firsts	3.00
6	Michael Jordan	
	The Hitting Streak	3.00
7	Michael Jordan Struggles	3.00
8	Michael Jordan	
	Life on the Road	3.00
9	Michael Jordan	
	First Home Run	3.00
10	Michael Jordan	
	Arizona Fall League	3.00

1995 Upper Deck Minor League Organizational Pro-Files

Each team's top prospect is featured in this chase card set. Fronts are in horizontal format, printed on metallic foil. Backs have a checklist of that team's minor leaguers found in the regular UD minor league set.

	MT
Complete Set (28):	12.50
Common Player:	.50
OP1	Terrell Wade	.50
OP2	Alex Ochoa	.50
OP3	Nomar Garciaparra	3.00
OP4	Todd Greene	.50
OP5	Brooks Kieschnick	.50
OP6	Michael Jordan	3.00
OP7	C.J. Nitkowski	.50
OP8	Daron Kickreit	.50
OP9	Juan Acevedo	.50
OP10	Tony Clark	.70
OP11	Josh Booty	.50
OP12	Billy Wagner	1.00
OP13	Johnny Damon	2.00
OP14	Paul Konerko	1.25
OP15	Antone Williamson	.50
OP16	Todd Walker	.75
OP17	Ugueth Urbina	.50
OP18	Bill Pulsipher	.50
OP19	Ruben Rivera	.50
OP20	John Wasdin	.50
OP21	Scott Rolen	2.00
OP22	Trey Beamon	.50
OP23	Alan Benes	.50
OP24	Raul Casanova	.50
OP25	Dante Powell	.50
OP26	Arquimedez Pozo	.50
OP27	Julio Santana	.50
OP28	Jose Silva	.50

1995 Upper Deck Minor League Top 10 Prospects

A copper "10" on a background of silver and purple metallic foil is featured on the front of these insert cards. Backs serve as a checklist for the regular UD minor league cards. Unlike the previous year, the Top 10 Prospects cards were issued only in 2-1/2" x 3-1/2" format in 1995.

	MT
Complete Set (10):	5.00
Common Card:	.50
1	Derek Jeter	3.00
2	James Baldwin	.50
3	Johnny Damon	1.50
4	Ruben Rivera	.50
5	Bill Pulsipher	.50
6	Jose Silva	.50
7	Roger Cedeno	.50
8	Alan Benes	.50
9	Michael Tucker	.50
10	Todd Hollandsworth	.50

1995 Upper Deck/SP Top Prospects

Upper Deck brought its premium SP brand name to minor league cards in late 1995 with the issue of Top Prospects. Base cards all feature die-cut tops and have fronts with color player action photos printed on metallic foil backgrounds. Backs have another photo along with a few stats, personal data and career highlights. The set's first 10 cards are a Top 10 Prospects subset which have checklists on back and feature a different front design showing the player in a golden oval against a mauve textured background. Cards #100-115 are a subset titled "1995 Draft Class" and feature the player photos against a golden sunrise design. Insert cards found in foil packs include autographed cards of 26 players, "Destination the Show" cards of fast-track minor leaguers and Jordan Time Capsule cards. SP Top Prospects was sold in eight-card foil packs with a $4.19 suggested retail.

	MT
Complete Set (165):	35.00
Common Player:	.05

Wax Pack (8):		7.50
Wax Box:		215.00
1	Andruw Jones	
	(Top 10 Prospect)	6.00
2	Brooks Kieschnick	
	(Top 10 Prospect)	.05
3	Nomar Garciaparra	
	(Top 10 Prospect)	6.00
4	Adam Riggs	
	(Top 10 Prospect)	.05
5	Paul Wilson	
	(Top 10 Prospect)	.10
6	Trey Beamon	
	(Top 10 Prospect)	.05
7	Vladimir Guerrero	
	(Top 10 Prospect)	4.00
8	Ben Grieve	
	(Top 10 Prospect)	.15
9	Jay Payton	
	(Top 10 Prospect)	.10
10	Todd Walker	
	(Top 10 Prospect)	.10
11	Jermaine Dye	.15
12	Damon Hollins	.05
13	Wonderful Monds	.05
14	Damian Moss	.05
15	Andruw Jones	4.00
16	Danny Clyburn	.05
17	Billy Percibal	.05
18	Rocky Coppinger	.05
19	Tommy Davis	.05
20	Nomar Garciaparra	4.50
21	Trot Nixon	.50
22	Jose Malave	.05
23	Ryan McGuire	.05
24	Rafael Orellano	.05
25	Darin Erstad	.25
26	George Arias	.05
27	Matt Beaumont	.05
28	Jason Dickson	.05
29	Greg Shockey	.05
30	Brooks Kieschnick	.05
31	Jon Ratliff	.05
32	Amaury Telemaco	.05
33	Bob Morris	.05
34	Charles Poe	.05
35	Harold Williams	.05
36	Jeff Abbott	.05
37	Tom Fordham	.05
38	Pokey Reese	.10
39	Pat Watkins	.05
40	Aaron Boone	.10
41	Chad Mottola	.05
42	Jason Robbins	.05
43	Jaret Wright	.10
44	Casey Whitten	.05
45	Bartolo Colon	.45
46	Richie Sexson	.25
47	Enrique Wilson	.10
48	Doug Million	.05
49	Joel Moore	.05
50	Derrick Gibson	.05
51	Neifi Perez	.05
52	Jamey Wright	.05
53	Juan Encarnacion	.10
54	Cade Gaspar	.05
55	Justin Thompson	.05
56	Bubba Trammell	.05
57	Daryle Ward	.05
58	Clemente Nunez	.05
59	Will Cunnane	.05
60	Billy McMillon	.05
61	Matt Whisenant	.05
62	Edgar Renteria	.10
63	Josh Booty	.05
64	Bob Abreu	.25
65	Richard Hidalgo	.05
66	Ramon Castro	.05
67	Scott Elarton	.05
68	Jhonny Perez	.05
69	Mendy Lopez	.05
70	Glendon Rusch	.05
71	Sal Fasano	.05
72	Sergio Nunez	.05
73	Matt Smith	.05
74	Chris Latham	.05
75	Adam Riggs	.05
76	Wilton Guerrero	.05
77	Paul Konerko	.50
78	Gary Rath	.05
79	Jim Cole	.05
80	Jeff D'Amico	.05
81	Antone Williamson	.05
82	Todd Dunn	.05
83	Brian Banks	.05
84	Shane Bowers	.05
85	Todd Walker	.10
86	Troy Carrasco	.05
87	Travis Miller	.05
88	Kimera Bartee	.05
89	Dan Serafini	.05
90	Vladimir Guerrero	3.00
91	Hiram Bocachica	.05
92	Brad Fullmer	.05
93	Geoff Blum	.05
94	Israel Alcantara	.05
95	Jay Payton	.10
96	Rey Ordonez	.05
97	Paul Wilson	.15
98	Preston Wilson	.35
99	Terrence Long	.05
100	Darin Erstad (Draft Class)	.25
101	Gabe Alvarez (DC)	.05
102	Jonathan Johnson (DC)	.05
103	Adam Barnes (DC)	.05
104	Dennis Martinez, Jr. (DC)	.05
105	Jaime Jones (DC)	.05
106	Chad Hermansen (DC)	.05
107	Geoff Jenkins (DC)	.15
108	Juan LeBron (DC)	.05
109	Mark Redman (DC)	.05
110	Jose Cruz Jr. (DC)	.10
111	Carlos Beltran (DC)	12.00
112	Todd Helton (DC)	3.00
113	Andy Yount (DC)	.05
114	Ryan Jaroncyk (DC)	.05
115	Sean Johnston	.05
116	Scott Romano	.05
117	Brian Buchanan	.05
118	Nick Delvecchio	.05
119	Ramiro Mendoza	.05
120	Matt Drews	.05
121	Shane Spencer	.05
122	Jason McDonald	.05
123	Scott Spiezio	.05
124	Brad Rigby	.05
125	Ben Grieve	.10
126	Steve Cox	.05
127	Willie Morales	.05
128	Wayne Gomes	.05
129	Larry Wimberly	.05
130	Scott Rolen	1.50
131	Carlton Loewer	.05
132	Wendell Magee	.05
133	Charles Peterson	.05
134	Lou Collier	.05
135	Trey Beamon	.05
136	Micah Franklin	.05
137	Jason Kendall	.35
138	Homer Bush	.05
139	Dickie Woodridge	.05
140	Derrek Lee	2.00
141	Raul Casanova	.05
142	Greg LaRocca	.05
143	Jason Thompson	.05
144	Jacob Cruz	.05
145	Jesse Ibarra	.05
146	Jay Canizaro	.05
147	Steve Soderstrom	.05
148	Dante Powell	.05
149	James Bonnici	.05
150	Raul Ibanez	.05
151	Trey Moore	.05
152	Desi Relaford	.05
153	Jason Varitek	.45
154	Jay Witasick	.05
155	Bret Wagner	.05
156	Aaron Holbert	.05
157	Fernando Tatis	.05
158	Mike Bell	.05
159	Jeff Davis	.05
160	Julio Santana	.05
161	Kevin Brown	.05
162	Felipe Crespo	.05
163	Kevin Witt	.05
164	Mark Sievert	.05
165	Jose Pett	.05

1995 Upper Deck/SP Top Prospects Autographs

Similar in format to the rest of the SP Top Propects set, including the die-cut tops, the autograph insert cards have standard (non-metallized) printing on front and no UV coat, allowing the autograph to be more efficiently signed. Each card has a uniquely numbered hologram serial number attached and the back is a certificate of authenticity. Autograph cards were inserted at an average rate of once per 31 foil packs; about one per box. It is believed only about 20 of the Michael Jordan cards were printed.

		MT
Common Player:		3.00
(1)	Bob Abreu	50.00
(2)	Gabe Alvarez	3.00
(3)	George Arias	3.00
(4)	Trey Beamon	3.00
(5)	Aaron Boone	3.00
(6)	Raul Casanova	3.00
(7)	Bartolo Colon	7.50
(8)	Jermaine Dye	5.00
(9)	Nomar Garciaparra	95.00
(10)	Todd Greene	3.00
(11)	Ben Grieve	4.50
(12)	Vladimir Guerrero	45.00
(13)	Richard Hidalgo	3.00
(14)	Andruw Jones	45.00
(15)	Michael Jordan	1,725
(16)	Jason Kendall	5.00

(17) Brooks Kieschnick 3.00
(18) Derrek Lee 25.00
(19) Wonderful Monds 3.00
(20) Rey Ordonez 3.00
(21) Jay Payton 3.00
(22) Adam Riggs 3.00
(23) Scott Rolen 30.00
(24) Jason Thompson 3.00
(25) Paul Wilson 3.00
(26) Jaret Wright 3.00

1995 Upper Deck/SP Top Prospects Promos

Paralleling the Top Prospects Autographs inserts (plus a Todd Helton card which was never issued in autographed form) these cards are unsigned and lack the serial number hologram on front. Printed on back is "For Promotional Use Only / This is Not a Signature Card."

MT
Common Player: 10.00
(1) Bob Abreu 15.00
(2) Gabe Alvarez 10.00
(3) George Arias 10.00
(4) Trey Beamon 10.00
(5) Aaron Boone 12.50
(6) Raul Casanova 10.00
(7) Bartolo Colon 10.00
(8) Jermaine Dye 12.50
(9) Nomar Garciaparra 100.00
(10) Todd Greene 10.00
(11) Ben Grieve 10.00
(12) Vladimir Guerrero 90.00
(13) Todd Helton 75.00
(14) Richard Hidalgo 10.00
(15) Andruw Jones 90.00
(16) Michael Jordan 250.00
(17) Jason Kendall 15.00
(18) Brooks Kieschnick 10.00
(19) Derrek Lee 65.00
(20) Wonderful Monds 10.00
(21) Rey Ordonez 10.00
(22) Jay Payton 10.00
(23) Adam Riggs 10.00
(24) Scott Rolen 60.00
(25) Jason Thompson 10.00
(26) Paul Wilson 10.00
(27) Jaret Wright 10.00

1995 Upper Deck/SP Top Prospects Destination the Show

Players deemed to be on the fast track to the majors are featured in this insert set. Like the rest of the SP Top Prospect cards, the tops are die-cut and the player photo is set against a metallic foil background. Tan borders and gold-foil graphic highlights complete the front design. Backs have another player photo and career highlights.

MT
Complete Set (20): 175.00
Common Player: 5.00
DS1 Andruw Jones 35.00
DS2 Richard Hidalgo 5.00
DS3 Paul Wilson 5.00
DS4 Brooks Kieschnick 5.00
DS5 Ben Grieve 6.00
DS6 Adam Riggs 5.00
DS7 Vladimir Guerrero 40.00

DS8 Paul Konerko 7.50
DS9 Jose Cruz Jr. 5.00
DS10 Todd Walker 5.00
DS11 Darin Erstad 7.50
DS12 Derrek Lee 30.00
DS13 Scott Rolen 30.00
DS14 Trey Beamon 5.00
DS15 Nomar Garciaparra 50.00
DS16 Jason Kendall 7.50
DS17 Aaron Boone 5.00
DS18 Matt Drews 5.00
DS19 Derrick Gibson 5.00
DS20 Jay Payton 5.00

1995 Upper Deck/SP Top Prospects Jordan Time Capsule

Taking full advantage of its license to produce Michael Jordan baseball cards, Upper Deck included a four-card Time Capsule chase set in its SP Top Prospects minor league set. Cards feature photos of Jordan in his minor league days, vignetted with a silver-foil effect around the borders. The Jordan cards are inserted at an average rate of about one per 19 packs.

MT
Complete Set (4): 12.00
Common Card: 3.00
TC1-4 Michael Jordan 3.00

1995 Minor League Team Sets

A major change in the market for minor league team sets came in 1995 when the field's top two players, Classic and Fleer/Pro Cards dropped out. Classic was gone entirely in 1995 and Fleer was down to a handful of sets. Both of the major card companies had discovered the short press runs and high costs of production could not be recouped in a thin market. Teams desiring card sets were left to produce their own. A small group of regional graphics firms was able to sign a few teams each. One such company, Grandstand (GS) remains active. For collectors, the big boys dropping out meant an end to easy availability of the annual issues. Some teams sold or gave away their entire production and a strong market arose of dealers who scoured the nation to pick up sets to serve the hobby market. Player selection no longer was the sole basis of value beginning in 1995; market availability became critical to price. When all was said and done, over 140 team sets were issued in 1995, compared to the 275 of the previous year.

MT
146 Team Sets and Variations

1995 Team Abilene Prairie Dogs (30) 5.00
1995 Team Albany Diamond Dogs (26) 5.00
1995 Team Alexandria Aces (24) 5.00
1995 Team Amarillo Dillas (25) 5.00
1995 Arizona Fall League (22) 20.00
1995 Team Arkansas Travelers (30) 12.00
1995 Team Asheville Tourists (30) 20.00
1995 Team Asheville Tourists Update (14) 30.00
1995 Team Auburn Astros (30) 8.00
1995 Team Bakersfield Blaze (30) 11.00
1995 Team Batavia Clippers (33) 10.00
1995 Team Bellingham Giants (36) 8.00
1995 Team Beloit Snappers (31) 12.00
1995 Team Billings Mustangs (29) 75.00
1995 Team Binghamton Mets (28) 10.00
1995 Team Boise Hawks (35) 9.00
1995 Team Bowie Baysox (31) 7.00
1995 Fleer/PC Brevard County Manatees (30) 8.00
1995 Team Burlington Bees (36) 15.00
1995 Team Butte Copper Kings (32) 7.00
1995 Fleer/PC Carolina Mudcats (30) 9.00
1995 Carolina League 50th Anniversary (35) 17.50
1995 Team Cedar Rapids Kernels (32) 8.00
1995 Team Charleston RiverDogs (30) 10.00
1995 Team Charleston RiverDogs Update (9) 10.00
1995 Team Charlotte Knights (30) 8.00
1995 Team Chattanooga Lookouts (32) 8.00
1995 Fleer/PC Clearwater Phillies (30) 7.00
1995 Team Colorado Springs Sky Sox (34) 10.00
1995 Kroger Columbus Clippers Panels (8) 30.00
1995 Police Columbus Clippers (32) 30.00
1995 Team Columbus Clippers (32) 35.00
1995 Team Corpus Christi Barracudas (24) 5.00
1995 Team Danville Braves (Six panels.) 20.00
1995 Photostars USA Ben Davis (2) 4.00
1995 Team Dunedin Blue Jays (3) 60.00
1995 Team Durham Bulls (40) 7.00
1995 Team Edmonton Trappers (30) 22.50
1995 Team Elmira Pioneers (30) 10.00
1995 Team Elmira Pioneers Update (31) 12.00
1995 Team El Paso Diablos (24) 7.00
1995 Team Eugene Emeralds (24) 15.00
1995 Team Evansville Otters (26) 5.00
1995 Team Evansville Otters Update (26) 5.00
1995 Team Everett Aquasox (30) 10.00
1995 Team Fayetteville Generals (30) 15.00
1995 Team Ft. Myers Miracle (32) 15.00
1995 Team Ft. Wayne Wizards (32) 8.00
1995 GS Grays Harbor Gulls (31) 5.00
1995 Team Great Falls Dodgers (40) 45.00
1995 Team Greensboro Bats (33) 8.00
1995 Team Greensboro Bats POGs (6) 10.00
1995 Team Greenville Braves (30) 9.00
1995 Fleer/PC Hagerstown Suns (30) 7.00
1995 Team Hardware City Rock Cats (29) 15.00
1995 Team Harrisburg Senators (28) 20.00
1995 Team Helena Brewers (32) 7.00
1995 Team Hudson Valley Renegades (30) 7.00
1995 Team Huntsville Stars (29) 11.00
1995 Team Idaho Falls Braves (27) 10.00
1995 Fleer/PC Indianapolis Indians (30) 7.00
1995 Team Iowa Cubs (25) 10.00
1995 Smokey Bear Jackson Generals (26) 15.00

1995 Team Jackson Generals (27) 12.50
1995 Team Jacksonville Suns (28) 9.00
1995 Team Kane County Cougars (32) 8.00
1995 Team Kane County Cougars - Eckrich (31) 15.00
1995 Team Kane Co. Cougars Legends (15) 10.00
1995 Team Kinston Indians (30) 10.00
1995 Fleer/PC Knoxville Smokies (30) 8.00
1995 Team Lake Elsinore Storm (30) 10.00
1995 Team Laredo Apaches (25) 5.00
1995 FPC Louisville Redbirds (25) 25.00
1995 Team Lubbock Crickets (25) 5.00
1995 Team Lynchburg Hillcats (30) 7.00
1995 Team Macon Braves (30) 75.00
1995 Team Macon Braves Update (6) 45.00
1995 Team Martinsville Phillies (Six panels.) 125.00
1995 Team Memphis Chicks (27) 8.00
1995 Team Michigan Battle Cats (30) 8.00
1995 1 Hour Midland Angels (36) 60.00
1995 Team Midland Angels (30) 6.00
1995 Midwest League All-Stars (58) 12.50
1995 Team Minneapolis Loons (30) 15.00
1995 Team Mobile BaySharks (25) 5.00
1995 Team Modesto A's (32) 12.00
1995 Team Nashville Sounds Foldout 25.00
1995 Team New Haven Ravens (33) 9.00
1995 Team New Jersey Cardinals (30) 5.00
1995 Team Norfolk Tides (30) 10.00
1995 Team Norwich Navigators (42) 8.00
1995 Team Norwich Navigators Update (11) 6.00
1995 Team Ogden Raptors (30) 8.00
1995 Team Ogden Raptors Poster 12.00
1995 Team Oklahoma City 89ers (27) 9.00
1995 Team Omaha Royals (29) 10.00
1995 Fleer/PC Orlando Cubs (30) 7.00
1995 DD Pawtucket Red Sox Foldout 25.00
1995 Team Pawtucket Red Sox (30) 7.00
1995 Team Peoria Chiefs (31) 7.00
1995 Team Phoenix Firebirds (30) 8.00
1995 Fleer/PC Piedmont Phillies (30) 6.00
1995 Team Pittsfield Mets (32) 9.00
1995 Team Port City Roosters (29) 8.00
1995 Team Portland Sea Dogs (30) 9.00
1995 Team Prince William Cannons (30) 11.00
1995 Team Quad Cities River Bandits (30) 10.00
1995 Team Rancho Cucamonga Quakes (30) 20.00
1995 Ritz Camera Reading Phillies Sheet (25) 30.00
1995 Team Reading Phillies (28) 10.00
1998 Team Reading Phils Fairground Sq. (28) 12.50
1995 Team Reading Phillies E.L. Champs (36) 10.00
1995 Pepsi Richmond Braves POGs (27) 25.00
1995 Richmond Camera Richmond Braves (29) 50.00
1995 Team Richmond Braves (30) 7.00
1995 Team Rio Grande Valley White Wings (26) 5.00
1995 Team Rochester Red Wings (48) 8.00
1995 Team Rockford Cubbies (32) 9.00
1995 Team Salem Avalanche (28) 8.00
1995 HEB San Antonio Missions (32) 50.00
1995 Team San Antonio Missions (32) 11.00
1995 Team San Bernardino Spirit (32) 15.00
1995 Team Scranton Red Barons (30) 15.00

1995 Team Spokane Indians (32) 8.00
1995 Team Sultans of Springfield (30) 8.00
1995 Team St. Catherines Stompers (36) 30.00
1995 Team St. Lucie Mets (37) 7.00
1995 Team St. Paul Saints (29) 6.00
1995 Team Syracuse Chiefs (30) 10.00
1995 Team All-Time Syracuse Chiefs (72) 60.00
1995 Team Tacoma Rainiers (30) 20.00
1995 Team Tampa Yankees (30) 9.00
1995 Team Thunder Bay Whiskey Jacks (25) 5.00
1995 Team Toledo Mud Hens (30) 8.00
1995 Team Trenton Thunder (31) 90.00
1995 Team Trenton Thunder Foldout 125.00
1995 Team Tucson Toros (29) 8.00
1995 Team Tulsa Drillers (30) 8.00
1995 Team Tyler Wildcatters (30) 5.00
1995 Team Vero Beach Dodgers (30) 10.00
1995 Team Watertown Indians (30) 30.00
1995 Team West Michigan Whitecaps (30) 8.00
1995 Team Wichita Wranglers (30) 7.50
1995 Team Wilmington Blue Rocks (30) 12.50
1995 Team Yakima Bears (36) 6.00
1995 Team Zansville Greys (25) 5.00

1996 Best Autograph Series

The basic set for this premiere edition consists of 99 of the top prospects from all levels of minor league baseball from Instructional League through Class AAA. Released at the end of October, cards picture players with their 1996 teams, mostly in game-action photos on the fronts. The player's minor league team logo, name and position are at bottom. Backs have a portrait photo in an oval at top-right, with a career summary in the black box at left and 1995 stats at bottom. The cards were issued in foil packs of six, with one card being of the special autographed type. An insert set features 1996 first-round draft picks.

MT
Complete Set (99): 4.00
Common Player: .05
Wax Pack (6): 2.50
Wax Box: 35.00
1 Winston Abreu .05
2 Antonio Alfonseca .10
3 Richard Almanzar .05
4 Gabe Alvarez .05
5 Marlon Anderson .15
6 Kym Ashworth .05
7 Marc Barcelo .05
8 Brian Barkley .05
9 Mike Bell .05
10 Carlos Beltran .50
11 Shayne Bennett .05
12 Jeremy Blevins .05
13 Kevin Brown .05
14 Ray Brown .05
15 Homer Bush .05
16 Jay Canizaro .05
17 Troy Carrasco .05
18 Raul Casanova .05
19 Luis Castillo .10
20 Ramon Castro .05
21 Gary Coffee .05
22 Decomba Conner .05
23 Kevin Coughlin .05
24 Jacob Cruz .05
25 Jeff D'Amico .10
26 Tommy Davis .05

27 Edwin Diaz .05
28 Einar Diaz .05
29 David Doster .05
30 Derrin Ebert .05
31 Bobby Estalella .15
32 Alex Gonzalez .05
33 Kevin Grijak .05
34 Jose Guillen .25
35 Tim Harkrider .05
36 Dan Held .05
37 Wes Helms .05
38 Erik Hiljus .05
39 Aaron Holbert .05
40 Raul Ibanez .05
41 Jesse Ibarra .05
42 Marty Janzen .05
43 Robin Jennings .05
44 Shawn Johnston .05
45 Randy Jorgensen .05
46 Marc Kroon .05
47 Mike Kusiewicz .05
48 Carlos Lee .25
49 Brian Lesher .05
50 George Lombard .05
51 Roberto Lopez .05
52 Fernando Lunar .05
53 Len Manning .05
54 Eddy Martinez .05
55 Jesus Martinez .05
56 Onan Masaoka .05
57 Joe Maskivish .05
58 Jeff Matulevich .05
59 Brian Meadows .05
60 Mike Metcalfe .05
61 Doug Mlicki .05
62 Steve Montgomery .05
63 Trey Moore .05
64 Nick Morrow .05
65 Bryant Nelson .05
66 Sergio Nunez .05
67 Hector Ortega .05
68 Russell Ortiz .10
69 Eric Owens .05
70 Billy Percibal .05
71 Charles Peterson .05
72 A.J. Pierzynski .25
73 Charles Poe .05
74 Dante Powell .05
75 Kenny Pumphrey .05
76 Angel Ramirez .05
77 Julio Ramirez .05
78 Gary Rath .05
79 Jon Ratliff .05
80 Brad Rigby .05
81 Benj Sampson .05
82 Greg Shockey .05
83 Steve Shoemaker .05
84 Demond Smith .05
85 Robert Smith .05
86 Steve Soderstrom .05
87 Fernando Tatis .10
88 Jose Teixidor .05
89 Brett Tomko .05
90 Jose Valentin .05
91 Jason Varitek .35
92 Andrew Vessel .05
93 Casey Whitten .05
94 Enrique Wilson .15
95 Preston Wilson .25
96 Larry Wimberly .05
97 Jaret Wright .10
98 Dmitri Young .10
99 Joe Young .05

1996 Best Autograph Series Autographs

The top prospects in Class A, AA and AAA are featured on the autographed cards which are the heart of Best's premiere Autograph Series issue. One genuinely autographed card is included in each six-card foil pack. Autographed cards differ in design from the base set in that action photos on front are vignetted in an oval against a white background. The player name and minor league team logo are at bottom. Backs carry a congratulatory message over a large issuer logo. The unnumbered autographed cards are checklisted here in alphabetical order.

MT
Common Player: 1.00

1996 Best Autograph Series Autographs

(1)	Israel Alcantera	1.00
(2)	Richard Almanzar	1.00
(3)	Brian Banks	1.00
(4)	Marc Barcelo	1.00
(5)	Kimera Bartee	1.00
(6)	Jeremy Blevins	1.00
(7)	Jaime Bluma	1.00
(8)	D.J. Boston	1.00
(9)	Kevin Brown	1.00
(10)	Homer Bush	1.00
(11)	Jay Canizaro	1.00
(12)	Luis Castillo	2.00
(13)	Davey Coggin	1.00
(14)	Bartolo Colon	6.00
(15)	Jacob Cruz	1.00
(16)	Lino Diaz	1.00
(17)	Todd Dunn	1.00
(18)	Jermaine Dye	6.00
(19)	Bobby Estalella	2.00
(20)	Tom Fordham	1.00
(21)	Karim Garcia	4.00
(22)	Todd Greene	1.00
(23)	Ben Grieve	2.00
(24)	Mike Gulan	1.00
(25)	Derek Hacopian	1.00
(26)	Wes Helms	1.00
(27)	Brett Herbison	1.00
(28)	Chad Hermansen	1.00
(29)	Aaron Holbert	1.00
(30)	Damon Hollins	1.00
(31)	Ryan Jaroncyk	1.00
(32)	Geoff Jenkins	2.50
(33)	Earl Johnson	1.00
(34)	Andruw Jones	12.00
(35)	Jason Kendall	4.00
(36)	Brooks Kieschnick	1.00
(37)	Andre King	1.00
(38)	Paul Konerko	4.00
(39)	Todd Landry	1.00
(40)	Mendy Lopez	1.00
(41)	Roberto Lopez	1.00
(42)	Eric Ludwick	1.00
(43)	Mike Maurer	1.00
(44)	Brian Meadows	1.00
(45)	Ralph Milliard	1.00
(46)	Doug Mlicki	1.00
(47)	Julio Mosquera	1.00
(48)	Tony Mounce	1.00
(49)	Sergio Nunez	1.00
(50)	Russell Ortiz	3.00
(51)	Carey Paige	1.00
(52)	Jay Payton	3.00
(53)	Charles Peterson	1.00
(54)	Tommy Phelps	1.00
(55)	Hugo Pivaral	1.00
(56)	Dante Powell	1.00
(57)	Angel Ramirez	1.00
(58)	Gary Rath	1.00
(59)	Mark Redman	1.00
(60)	Adam Riggs	1.00
(61)	Lonell Roberts	1.00
(62)	Scott Rolen	9.00
(63)	Glendon Rusch	1.00
(64)	Matt Sachse	1.00
(65)	Donnie Sadler	1.50
(66)	William Santamaria	1.00
(67)	Todd Schmitt	1.00
(68)	Richie Sexson	4.00
(69)	Alvie Shepherd	1.00
(70)	Steve Shoemaker	1.00
(71)	Brian Sikorski	1.00
(72)	Randall Simon	2.00
(73)	Matt Smith	1.00
(74)	Scott Spiezio	1.00
(75)	Everett Stull, II	1.00
(76)	Jose Texidor	1.00
(77)	Mike Thurman	1.00
(78)	Brett Tomko	1.00
(79)	Bubba Trammell (Issued in 1998.)	2.00
(80)	Hector Trinidad	1.00
(81)	Pedro Valdes	1.00
(82)	Andrew Vessel	1.00
(83)	Jacob Viano	1.00
(84)	Terrell Wade	1.00
(85)	Bret Wagner	1.00
(86)	Todd Walker	1.50
(87)	Travis Welch	1.00
(88)	Casey Whitten	1.00
(89)	Paul Wilson	1.50
(90)	Preston Wilson	3.50
(91)	Kevin Witt	1.00
(92)	Jamey Wright	1.00

1996 Best Autograph Series First Round Draft Picks

Issued in two series this five-sport card set provides the base set for a phone card chase program. Only the baseball players from the base set, inserts and phone cards are listed here.

		MT
Base Set/Inserts:		
4	Barry Bonds	.75
18	Jason Kendall	.40
33	Jay Payton	.25
39	Nolan Ryan	.75
48	Paul Wilson	.25
64	Doug Million	.25
64	Doug Million (Silver signature.)	.50
65	Barry Bonds	.75

Besides the autographed cards, the only other inserts found in Best's '96 Autograph Series is this run of 16 first-round draft picks who made their pro debut in 1996. For some of the players it is their first baseball card. Fronts have player poses against large minor league team logos. Backs repeat the front player photo in a subdued sepia image over which is printed the player biography. Cards are numbered with a "FR" prefix.

		MT
Complete Set (16):		5.00
Common Player:		.50
1	Chad Green	.50
2	Mark Kotsay	1.00
3	Robert Stratton	.50
4	Dermal Brown	.50
5	Matt Halloran	.50
6	Joe Lawrence	.50
7	Todd Noel	.50
8	Jake Westbrook	.50
9	Gil Meche	1.00
10	Damian Rolls	.50
11	John Oliver	.50
12	Josh Garrett	.50
13	A.J. Zapp	.50
14	Danny Peoples	.50
15	Paul Wilder	.50
16	Nick Bierbrodt	.50

1996 Best Player of the Year

Budding Braves superstar Andruw Jones is featured in this late-season insert issue. Five hundred of each card were autographed and have a certificate of authenticity on back.

		MT
Complete Set (5):		15.00
Autographed Set (5):		90.00
Common Card:		3.00
Autographed Card:		20.00
(1)	Andruw Jones/Btg	.00
(2)	Andruw Jones (Running)	.00
(3)	Andruw Jones (Seated w/bat.)	.00
(4)	Andruw Jones (Seated w/glove.)	.00
(5)	Andruw Jones (In minors uniforms.)	.00

1996 Classic Assets (Baseball)

		MT
Base Set/Inserts:		
4	Barry Bonds	.75
18	Jason Kendall	.40
33	Jay Payton	.25
39	Nolan Ryan	.75
48	Paul Wilson	.25
64	Doug Million	.25
64	Doug Million (Silver signature.)	.50
65	Barry Bonds	.75

65	Barry Bonds (Silver signature.)	6.00
DC15	Nomar Garciaparra (Die-Cut)	3.00
DC17	Barry Bonds (Die-Cut)	6.00
DC18	Paul Wilson (Die-Cut)	.25
CA7	Cal Ripken Jr. (Above)	6.00
CA10	Barry Bonds (Cut Above)	6.00
S1	Barry Bonds (Silksations)	6.00

1996 Classic Clear Assets (Baseball)

A number of baseball players are featured in the base set, inserts and phone cards which make up the all-acetate Clear Assets set.

		MT
Base Set/Inserts		
52	Barry Bonds	2.00
53	Chad Hermansen	.50
54	Ben Davis	.50
55	Jay Payton	.50
X4	Barry Bonds (3X)	20.00

1996 Classic Signings (Baseball)

Another five-sport card set with the lure of an autographed card in every pack and a chance to win autographed memorabilia, Signings includes the usual line-up of Classic spokesmen and baseball prospects among the 100-card base set, parallel editions and chase sets.

		MT
Base Set/Inserts		
60	Ben Grieve	.35
60	Ben Grieve (Die-Cut)	.50
60	Ben Grieve/Auto.	3.00
61	Paul Wilson	.35
61	Paul Wilson (Die-Cut)	.50
61	Paul Wilson/Auto.	3.00
62	Calvin Reese	.35
62	Calvin Reese (Die-Cut)	.50
62	Calvin Reese/Auto.	3.00
63	Karim Garcia	.75
63	Karim Garcia (Die-Cut)	1.00
63	Karim Garcia/Auto.	4.50
64	Mark Farris	.25
64	Mark Farris (Die-Cut)	.50
64	Mark Farris/Auto.	2.00
65	Jay Payton	.35
65	Jay Payton (Die-Cut)	.50
65	Jay Payton/Auto.	3.00
66	Dustin Hermanson	.25
66	Dustin Hermanson (Die-Cut)	.50
66	Dustin Hermanson/Auto.	2.00
67	Michael Barrett	.35
67	Michael Barrett (Die-Cut)	.50
67	Michael Barrett (Autographed)	3.00
68	Ryan Jaroncyk	.25
68	Ryan Jaroncyk (Die-Cut)	.50
68	Ryan Jaroncyk/Auto.	2.00
69	Ben Davis	.25
69	Ben Davis (Die-Cut)	.50
69	Ben Davis/Auto.	3.00
93	Barry Bonds	2.00
93	Barry Bonds (Die-Cut)	6.00
93	Barry Bonds/Auto.	90.00
21	Paul Wilson (Freshly Inked)	2.00
22	Nomar Garciaparra (Freshly Inked)	2.00
8	Barry Bonds (Etched in Stone)	7.50

1996 Classic Visions (Baseball)

The usual prospects and Classic spokesmen are included in this five-sports issue printed on extra-thick card stock and highlighted with both silver- and gold-foil stamping.

		MT
Complete (Baseball) Set (14):		3.00
Common Player:		.10
95	Barry Bonds	1.00
96	Nolan Ryan	1.50
97	Ben Grieve	.25
98	Ben Davis	.15

99	Paul Wilson	.25
100	C.J. Nitkowski	.15
101	Chad Hermansen	.15
102	Jason Kendall	.35
103	Todd Greene	.15
104	Dustin Hermanson	.15
105	Karim Garcia	.35
106	Doug Million	.15
107	Jay Payton	.25
130	Nolan Ryan (Legendary Futures)	.50

1996 Classic Visions Signings (Baseball)

A handful of baseball players is included among the five sports represented in this set.

		MT
Complete (Baseball) Set (8):		3.00
Common Player:		.25
80	Barry Bonds	1.00
81	Nolan Ryan	1.00
82	Ben Davis	.25
83	Chad Hermansen	.25
84	Jason Kendall	.50
85	Todd Greene	.25
86	Karim Garcia	.50
87	Jay Payton	.35

1996 Classic Visions Signings (Baseball) Autographs

In roughly the same format as the base cards, except for the congratulatory message on the cards' backs, authentically autographed cards of some of the players in this five-sport set were included as 1:12 pack inserts. Some players signed numbered silver autograph versions while others signed both the silver and an unnumbered gold version. Because they are not numbered, the gold version is perceived as being more common.

		MT
Common Player:		3.00
(80)	Barry Bonds/Silver (240)	125.00
(82)	Ben Davis/Silver (360)	6.00
(85)	Todd Greene/Silver (385)	6.00
(85)	Todd Greene/Gold	3.00
(86)	Karim Garcia/Silver (370)	7.50

---

(86)	Karim Garcia/Gold	4.00
(87)	Jay Payton/Silver (365)	6.00
(87)	Jay Payton/Gold	3.00

1996 Classic 4 Sports McDonald's LP

Randomly inserted in the five-card packs of a special 4 Sport version issued regionally by McDonald's are these premium LP (Limited Production) cards. Format is similar to the base cards except for a gold-foil notation on front that the card is "1 of 16,750." Darren Daulton is the only baseball player among the LPs.

		MT
LP1	Darren Daulton	.50

1996 Fleer Excel

Major league quality in a minor league set was touted by Fleer for its 1996 Excel issue. Cards were printed on cardboard described as 40% thicker than typical minor league cards, with each card having copper-foil highlights on front. Each of the players in the basic 250-card set is depicted on front in a posed or game-action borderless photo. Backs have two more photos of the player, generally close-up action and portraits. Backs also provide full pro stats. The set is arranged alphabetically by player within organization and league. Each foil pack includes one card from among the five insert sets produced in conjunction with the Excel set.

		MT
Complete Set (250):		15.00
Common Player:		.05
Wax Pack (12):		1.50
Wax Box (36):		35.00
1	Kimera Bartee	.05
2	Carlos Chavez	.05
3	Rocky Coppinger	.05
4	Tommy Davis	.05
5	Eddy Martinez	.05
6	Billy Owens	.05
7	Billy Percibal	.05
8	Garrett Stephenson	.05
9	Rachaad Stewart	.05
10	Chris Allison	.05
11	Virgil Chevalier	.05
12	Nomar Garciaparra	3.00
13	Jose Malave	.05
14	Ryan McGuire	.05
15	Trot Nixon	.50
16	Rafael Orellano	.05
17	Pork Chop Pough	.05
18	Donnie Sadler	.10
19	Bill Selby	.05
20	Nathan Tebbs	.05
21	George Arias	.05
22	Matt Beaumont	.05
23	Danny Buxbaum	.05
24	Jovino Carvajal	.05
25	Geoff Edsell	.05
26	Darin Erstad	.50
27	Aaron Guiel	.05
28	Mike Holtz	.05
29	Ryan Kane	.05
30	Jeff Abbott	.05
31	Kevin Coughlin	.05
32	Tom Fordham	.05
33	Carlos Lee	.25
34	Frank Menechino	.05
35	Charles Poe	.05
36	Nilson Robledo	.05
37	Juan Thomas	.05
38	Archie Vazquez (Vazquez)	.05
39	Bruce Aven	.05
40	Russ Branyan	.05
41	Bartolo Colon	.35
42	Einar Diaz	.05
43	Mike Glavine	.05
44	Ricky Gutierrez	.05
45	Rick Heiserman	.05
46	Richie Sexson	.35
47	Enrique Wilson	.15

48	Jaret Wright	.10
49	Bryan Corey	.05
50	Mike Drumright	.05
51	Juan Encarnacion	.10
52	Brandon Reed	.05
53	Bubba Trammell	.05
54	Daryle Ward	.05
55	Jaime Bluma	.05
56	Tim Byrdak	.05
57	Gary Coffee	.05
58	Lino Diaz	.05
59	Sal Fasano	.05
60	Jed Hansen	.05
61	Juan LeBron	.05
62	Sean McNally	.05
63	Anthony Medrano	.05
64	Rodolfo Mendez	.05
65	Sergio Nunez	.05
66	Mandy Romero	.05
67	Glendon Rusch	.10
68	Brian Banks	.05
69	Jeff D'Amico	.10
70	Jonas Hamlin	.05
71	Geoff Jenkins	.15
72	Roberto Lopez	.05
73	Gerald Parent	.05
74	Doug Webb	.05
75	Antone Williamson	.05
76	Shane Bowers	.05
77	Shane Gunderson	.05
78	Corey Koskie	.25
79	Jake Patterson	.05
80	A.J. Pierzynski	.05
81	Mark Redman	.05
82	Dan Serafini	.05
83	Todd Walker	.10
84	Chris Corn	.05
85	Nick Delvecchio	.05
86	Dan Donato	.05
87	Matt Drews	.05
88	Mike Figga	.05
89	Ben Ford	.05
90	Marty Janzen	.05
91	Shea Morenz	.10
92	Ray Ricken	.05
93	Shane Spencer	.05
94	Bob St. Pierre	.05
95	Jay Tessmer	.05
96	Chris Wilcox	.05
97	Steve Cox	.05
98	Ben Grieve	.10
99	Jason McDonald	.05
100	Brad Rigby	.05
101	Demond Smith	.05
102	Jim Bonnici	.05
103	Jose Cruz Jr.	.10
104	Osvaldo Fernandez	.05
105	Raul Ibanez	.05
106	Desi Relaford	.10
107	Marino Santana	.05
108	Kevin Brown	.05
109	Jeff Davis	.05
110	Edwin Diaz	.05
111	Jonathan Johnson	.05
112	Fernando Tatis	.10
113	Andrew Vessel	.05
114	John Curl	.05
115	Ryan Jones	.05
116	Julio Mosquera	.05
117	Jeff Patzke	.05
118	Mike Peeples	.05
119	Mark Sievert	.05
120	Joe Young	.05
121	Winston Abreu	.05
122	Anthony Briggs	.05
123	Matt Byrd	.05
124	Jermaine Dye	.15
125	Derrin Ebert	.05
126	Wes Helms	.05
127	Damon Hollins	.05
128	Ryan Jacobs	.05
129	Andruw Jones	2.00
130	Gus Kennedy	.05
131	George Lombard	.05
132	Damian Moss	.05
133	Robert Smith	.05
134	Pedro Swann	.05
135	Ron Wright	.05
136	Pat Cline	.05
137	Robin Jennings	.05
138	Brooks Kieschnick	.05
139	Ed Larregui	.05
140	Jason Maxwell	.05
141	Bobby Morris	.05
142	Amaury Telemaco	.05
143	Pedro Valdes	.05
144	Cedric Allen	.05
145	Justin Atchley	.05
146	Aaron Boone	.10
147	Steve Goodhart	.05
148	Chris Murphy	.05
149	Christian Rojas	.05
150	Terry Wright	.05
151	Brent Crowther	.05
152	Angel Echevarria	.05
153	Derrick Gibson	.05
154	Todd Helton	2.00
155	Terry Jones	.05
156	David Kennedy	.05
157	Mike Kusiewicz	.05
158	Joel Moore	.05
159	Jacob Viano	.05
160	Jamey Wright	.05
161	Todd Dunwoody	.05
162	Ryan Jackson	.05
163	Billy McMillon	.05
164	Ralph Milliard	.05
165	Clemente Nunez	.05

166	Edgar Renteria	.15
167	Chris Sheff	.05
168	Matt Whisenant	.05
169	Bob Abreu	.25
170	Ramon Castro	.05
171	Richard Hidalgo	.10
172	Tony McKnight	.05
173	Tony Mounce	.05
174	Roberto Duran	.05
175	Wilton Guerrero	.05
176	Joe Jacobsen	.05
177	Paul Konerko	.50
178	Chris Latham	.05
179	Onan Masaoka	.05
180	Mike Metcalfe	.05
181	Kevin Pincavitch	.05
182	Adam Riggs	.05
183	David Yocum	.05
184	Jake Benz	.05
185	Hiram Bocachica	.05
186	Brad Fullmer	.10
187	Vladimir Guerrero	2.00
188	Eric Ludwick	.05
189	Carlos Mendoza	.05
190	Jarrod Patterson	.05
191	Jay Payton	.10
192	Paul Wilson	.05
193	Julio Zorrilla	.05
194	Marlon Anderson	.10
195	Ron Blazier	.05
196	Steve Carver	.05
197	Blake Doolan	.05
198	David Doster	.05
199	Tommy Eason	.05
200	Zach Elliott	.05
201	Bobby Estalella	.10
202	Rob Grable	.05
203	Bronson Heflin	.05
204	Dan Held	.05
205	Kevin Hooker	.05
206	Rich Hunter	.05
207	Carlton Loewer	.05
208	Wendell Magee	.05
SAMPLE	Wendell Magee (Different back design.)	1.00
209	Len Manning	.05
210	Fred McNair	.05
211	Ryan Nye	.05
212	Scott Rolen	1.50
213	Brian Stumpf	.05
214	Reggie Taylor	.05
215	Larry Wimberly	.05
216	Micah Franklin	.05
217	Chad Hermansen	.35
218	Jason Kendall	.35
219	Garrett Long	.05
220	Joe Maskivish	.05
221	Chris Peters	.05
222	Charles Peterson	.05
223	Charles Rice	.05
224	Reed Secrist	.05
225	Derek Swafford	.05
226	Mike Busby	.05
227	Mike Gulan	.05
228	Chris Haas	.05
229	Jeff Matulevich	.05
230	Steve Montgomery	.05
231	Matt Morris	.15
232	Bret Wagner	.05
233	Gabe Alvarez	.05
234	Raul Casanova	.05
235	Ben Davis	.05
236	Bubba Dixon	.05
237	Greg LaRocca	.05
238	Derrek Lee	.05
239	Jason Thompson	.05
240	Darin Blood	.05
241	Jay Canizaro	.05
242	Edwin Corps	.05
243	Jacob Cruz	.05
244	Joe Fontenot	.05
245	Jesse Ibarra	.05
246	Dante Powell	.05
247	Keith Williams	.05
248	Checklist 1-103	.05
249	Checklist 104-213	.05
250	Checklist 214-250, Inserts	.05

1996 Fleer Excel All-Stars

Labeled "can't miss" stars from all minor league levels, the players in this insert set are "up in lights" as the color action photo on front is repeated in the background as if being projected on a scoreboard. The player's name, team and

the Fleer Excel All-Star logo are printed in silver holographic foil. Backs have a portrait photo at one side with career highlights on the other. All-Star cards are found, on average, once per 13 packs of Excel.

		MT
Complete Set (10):		8.00
Common Player:		.25
1	Jason Kendall	.50
2	Steve Cox	.25
3	Adam Riggs	.25
4	George Arias	.25
5	Wilton Guerrero	.25
6	Vladimir Guerrero	4.00
7	Andruw Jones	4.00
8	Jay Payton	.35
9	Raul Ibanez	.25
10	Paul Wilson	.35

1996 Fleer Excel Climbing

Players who are "Climbing" their organization's minor league ladder at a faster than usual pace are featured in this insert set. Against a background of colorful, out-of-focus A's (Fleer calls the background "pearlized") is a player action photo. The name and Excel Climbing logo are in gold-foil. On back is a large portrait photo and details of the player's rise through the classifications, printed on a background of green, blue and purple. Climbing inserts are found at an average rate of one per six packs.

		MT
Complete Set (10):		3.50
Common Player:		.25
1	Jeff Abbott	.25
2	Rocky Coppinger	.25
3	Brent Crowther	.25
4	Rich Hunter	.25
5	Chris Latham	.25
6	Wendell Magee	.25
7	Jay Payton	.50
8	Ray Ricken	.25
9	Scott Rolen	3.00
10	Paul Wilson	.50

1996 Fleer Excel First Year Phenoms

Potential future superstars in their first year of pro ball are featured in this chase set. Cards feature action photos on a background of garishly colored baseball equipment and silver-foil graphic highlights. Backs have subdued earth tones as a background with a haloed player portrait on one end and a necessarily short career summary at the other end. The First Year Phemons cards are found, on average, once per three foil packs.

		MT
Complete Set (10):		5.00
Common Player:		.25
1	Gabe Alvarez	.25
2	Jose Cruz Jr.	.25
3	Ben Davis	.25

4	Darin Erstad	.75
5	Todd Helton	4.50
6	Chad Hermansen	.25
7	Geoff Jenkins	.50
8	Carlton Loewer	.25
9	Shea Morenz	.25
10	Matt Morris	.25

1996 Fleer Excel Season Crowns

Statistical leaders and award winners from various minor leagues are featured in this chase set. Fronts feature a rich brown tapestry background, with player action photo superimposed. The player's name, Excel logo and large Season Crown title and crown are in silver-foil. Backs have a white version of the tapestry background over which are printed the details of the player's performance. A large color portrait photo on one end completes the design. Season Crown inserts are found at an average rate of one per four packs.

		MT
Complete Set (10):		8.00
Common Player:		.25
1	Matt Beaumont	.25
2	Bartolo Colon	1.00
3	Matt Drews	.25
4	Derrick Gibson	.25
5	Vladimir Guerrero	4.00
6	Andruw Jones	4.00
7	Brandon Reed	.25
8	Glendon Rusch	.25
9	Richie Sexson	.50
10	Shane Spencer	.25

1996 Fleer Excel Team Leaders

Team offensive statistical leaders are featured on this, the scarcest of the Excel chase sets. Printed on plastic, the cards feature player action poses on a background which includes portions of the team logo. Backs have a portrait photo and information the player's statistical feat. The plastic Team Leaders cards are seeded one per 35 packs, on average.

		MT
Complete Set (10):		8.00
Common Player:		1.00
1	George Arias	1.00
2	Kevin Coughlin	1.00
3	Wilton Guerrero	1.00
4	Dan Held	1.00
5	Brooks Kieschnick	1.00
6	Wendell Magee	1.00
7	Jason McDonald	1.00
8	Adam Riggs	1.00
9	Juan Thomas	1.00
10	Ron Wright	1.00

1996 Signature Rookies Old Judge T-96

Signature Rookies returned for a second year with a smaller than standard size minor league issue; all cards except the checklist are in 2" x 3" format. Because SR contracted with individual players and did not seek Major League Baseball licensing, neither team names nor logos appear on the cards. Most cards have had the

BUTCH HUSKEY
NEW YORK (NL)

major or minor league uniform logos airbrushed off, while some have a fantasy logo added in their place. The set was issued in seven-card foil packs which contain five regular cards, one autographed card and one card from the six insert series. Given the advertised print run, and equal production of each card, about 16,000 of each were available. Fronts of the regular issue cards have a player portrait against a solid color background. Stats on back are complete only through 1994, though some of the career highlights refer to the 1995 season. Fronts of the autographed cards have a line of print added in the top border: "Authentic Signature," and are UV coated. Besides the player autograph on those cards, there is a serial number from within an edition of 6,000.

		MT
Complete Set (38):		2.00
Common Player:		.05
1	Tommy Adams	.05
2	Travis Baptist	.05
3	Mike Birkbeck	.05
4	Jim Bowie	.05
5	Duff Brumley	.05
6	Scott Bullett	.05
7	Frank Catalanotto	.10
8	Chris Cumberland	.05
9	Travis Driskill	.05
10	John Frascatore	.05
11	Brian Giles	.25
12	Vladimir Guerrero	1.00
13	Butch Huskey	.05
14	Greg Keagle	.05
15	Jay Kirkpatrick	.05
16	Ed Larregui	.05
17	Mitch Lyden	.05
18	T.J. Mathews	.05
19	Brian Maxcy	.05
20	Jeff McNeely	.05
21	Tony Mitchell	.05
22	Kerwin Moore	.05
23	Oscar Munoz	.05
24	Les Norman	.05
25	Jayhawk Owens	.05
26	Mark Petkovsek	.05
27	Hugo Pivaral	.05
28	Chad Renfroe	.05
29	Victor Rodriguez	.05
30	Matt Rundels	.05
31	Willie Smith	.05
32	Amaury Telemaco	.05
33	Robert Toth	.05
34	Ben Van Ryn	.05
35	Wes Weger	.05
36	Don Wengert	.05
37	Kelly Wunsch	.05
	Checklist	

1996 Signature Rookies Old Judge T-96 - Autographed

GREG KEAGLE
SAN DIEGO
1356/6000

Each pack of SR's Old Judge T-96 Series includes an authentically autographed card. Almost

identical to the regular-issue cards, fronts of the autographed cards have a line of print added in the top border: "Authentic Signature," and are UV coated. Besides the player autograph on those cards, there is a serial number from within an edition of 6,000.

		MT
Complete Set, Autographs (37):		30.00
Common Autograph:		1.00
1	Tommy Adams	1.00
2	Travis Baptist	1.00
3	Mike Birkbeck	1.00
4	Jim Bowie	1.00
5	Duff Brumley	1.00
6	Scott Bullett	1.00
7	Frank Catalanotto	2.00
8	Chris Cumberland	1.00
9	Travis Driskill	1.00
10	John Frascatore	1.00
11	Brian Giles	4.00
12	Vladimir Guerrero	25.00
13	Butch Huskey	1.00
14	Greg Keagle	1.00
15	Jay Kirkpatrick	1.00
16	Ed Larregui	1.00
17	Mitch Lyden	1.00
18	T.J. Mathews	1.00
19	Brian Maxcy	1.00
20	Jeff McNeely	1.00
21	Tony Mitchell	1.00
22	Kerwin Moore	1.00
23	Oscar Munoz	1.00
24	Les Norman	1.00
25	Jayhawk Owens	1.00
26	Mark Petkovsek	1.00
27	Hugo Pivaral	1.00
28	Chad Renfroe	1.00
29	Victor Rodriguez	1.00
30	Matt Rundels	1.00
31	Willie Smith	1.00
32	Amaury Telemaco	1.00
33	Robert Toth	1.00
34	Ben Van Ryn	1.00
35	Wes Weger	1.00
36	Don Wengert	1.00
37	Kelly Wunsch	1.00

1996 Signature Rookies Old Judge T-96 Junior Hit Man

Ken Griffey, Jr., is the featured player in this insert set. Each card pictures him in action on the UV-coated borderless front photo. His name and the set logo are in gold foil. Backs, also UV coated, have a portrait photo, stats and a few words about Junior, all on a red and white bull's eye background. Cards are numbered with a "J" prefix. Each card can be found in a regular and an autographed (250 each) version.

		MT
Complete Set (5):		15.00
Complete Set, Autographed (5):		200.00
Common Card:		1.50
Autographed Card:		40.00
1	Ken Griffey Jr.	1.50
1a	Ken Griffey Jr./Auto.	40.00
2	Ken Griffey Jr.	1.50
2a	Ken Griffey Jr./Auto.	40.00
3	Ken Griffey Jr.	1.50
3a	Ken Griffey Jr./Auto.	40.00
4	Ken Griffey Jr.	1.50
4a	Ken Griffey Jr./Auto.	40.00
5	Ken Griffey Jr.	1.50
5a	Ken Griffey Jr./Auto.	40.00

1996 Signature Rookies Old Judge T-96 Major Respect

Five players whose major league careers began with a bang are the subject of this insert set. UV-coated cards have player action photos on a background of red rays with a purple "MAJOR RESPECT" logo at bottom. The player's name is in gold foil down the side. Backs

have the standard stats, player data and career notes along with a portrait photo. All uniform logos have been airbrushed off since the cards are not licensed by Major League Baseball. Card numbers have an "M" prefix. Each card can be found in both an unautographed form and authentically signed.

		MT
Complete Set (5):		2.00
Complete Set, Autographed (5):		75.00
Common Player:		.25
Common Autograph:		3.00
1	Alex Rodriguez	1.50
1a	Alex Rodriguez/Auto.	60.00
2	Johnny Damon	.75
2a	Johnny Damon/Auto.	10.00
3	Karim Garcia	.50
3a	Karim Garcia/Auto.	5.00
4	Garrett Anderson	.75
4a	Garrett Anderson/Auto.	4.50
5	Bill Pulsipher	.25
5a	Bill Pulsipher/Auto.	3.00

1996 Signature Rookies Old Judge T-96 Peak Picks

Some of the top picks of the 1995 draft are shown in this insert issue. Fronts have borderless action photos of the players in their college uniforms. "PEAK PICKS" and their names are in gold foil. Backs have a close-up picture, vital data, college and 1995 minor league stats and a few words about the player's college career. Cards are UV coated both front and back and carry a "P" prefix to the number. Each card can be found in an authentically autographed version, as well as unsigned.

		MT
Complete Set (10):		3.00
Complete Set, Autographed (10):		25.00
Common Player:		.25
Common Autograph:		2.00
1	Darin Erstad	.50
1a	Darin Erstad/Auto.	7.50
2	Jose Cruz, Jr.	.25
2a	Jose Cruz, Jr./Auto.	4.00
3	Jonathan Johnson	.25
3a	Jonathan Johnson/Auto.	1.00
4	Todd Helton	1.50
4a	Todd Helton/Auto.	17.50
5	Matt Morris	.25
5a	Matt Morris/Auto.	2.00
6	Tony McKnight	.25
6a	Tony McKnight/Auto.	1.00
7	Reggie Taylor	.25
7a	Reggie Taylor/Auto.	1.00
8	David Yocum	.25
8a	David Yocum/Auto.	1.00
9	Shea Morenz	.25
9a	Shea Morenz/Auto.	2.00
10	Ben Davis	.25
10a	Ben Davis/Auto.	2.00

1996 Signature Rookies Old Judge T-96 Rising Stars

Five players projected to be major league stars are the focus of this insert set. Cards are UV-coated on each side. Fronts have borderless color action photos with the player name and "Rising Stars" logo in gold foil. Backs have a portrait photo, biographical details and complete minor league stats through 1995. Because the cards are licensed only with individual players and collegiate authorities, minor and major league uniform logos have been removed from the photos. Each card can be found in both an autographed and unautographed version. Cards are numbered with a "R" prefix.

		MT
Complete Set (5):		1.00
Complete Set, Autographed (5):		5.00
Common Player:		.25
Common Autograph:		2.00
1	Jermaine Dye	.50
1a	Jermaine Dye/Auto.	4.50
2	Ben Grieve	.50
2a	Ben Grieve/Auto.	2.00
3	Ryan Helms	.25
3a	Ryan Helms/Auto.	1.00
4	Jeff Darwin	.25
4a	Jeff Darwin/Auto.	1.00
5	Alan Benes	.25
5a	Alan Benes/Auto.	1.00

1996 Signature Rookies Old Judge T-96 Rookie/Year

American League Rookie of the Year Marty Cordova is the focus of this insert set. Each card pictures him in a borderless game-action photo. His name and the set logo are in gold foil. Backs have another photo, full stats, vital data and a few words about the player. The card number is preceded by a "RY" prefix. Twins logos have been airbrushed off the photos. Besides the regular version, each card can be found authentically autographed.

		MT
Complete Set (5):		1.00
Complete Set, Autographed (5):		20.00
Common Card:		.25
Autographed Card:		5.00
1	Marty Cordova	.25
1a	Marty Cordova/Auto.	5.00
2	Marty Cordova	.25
2a	Marty Cordova/Auto.	5.00
3	Marty Cordova	.25
3a	Marty Cordova/Auto.	5.00
4	Marty Cordova	.25
4a	Marty Cordova/Auto.	5.00
5	Marty Cordova	.25
5a	Marty Cordova/Auto.	5.00

1996 Signature Rookies Old Judge T-96 Top Prospect

Ten of the minor leagues' best players are featured in this insert set. UV-coated on both sides, fronts have an action photo on a white background with the player's name in gold foil. Backs have a portrait photo, complete pro stats through the 1995 season and a few personal details. Cards are numbered with a "T" prefix.

		MT
Complete Set (10):		1.00
Complete Autographed Set (10):		10.00
Common Player:		.10
Common Autograph:		1.00
1	Juan Acevedo	.25
1a	Juan Acevedo/Auto.	2.00
2	Mike Bovee	.10
2a	Mike Bovee/Auto.	1.00
3	Mark Hubbard	.10
3a	Mark Hubbard/Auto.	1.00
4	Luis Raven	.10
4a	Luis Raven/Auto.	1.00
5	Desi Relaford	.25
5a	Desi Relaford/Auto.	2.00
6	Antone Williamson	.10
6a	Antone Williamson/Auto.	1.00
7	Nick Delvecchio	.10
7a	Nick Delvecchio/Auto.	1.00
8	Andy Larkin	.10
8a	Andy Larkin/Auto.	1.00
9	Kris Ralston	.10
9a	Kris Ralston/Auto.	1.00
10	Jeff Suppan	.35
10a	Jeff Suppan/Auto.	3.00

1996 Signature Rookies Ken Griffey Jr.

This five-card set features logoless front and back photos of Ken Griffey Jr. Fronts have his name in both red ink and gold foil. Backs have personal data, stats and a few kind words.

		MT
Complete Set (5):		5.00
G1-G5 Ken Griffey Jr.		1.00

1996 Signature Rookies Rookie of the Year

The American League Rookie of the Year (Cordova) and runner-up (Anderson) are featured in this five-card insert set. Color action photos and gold-foil highlights are featured on front; portrait photos, biographical notes and pro stats are on back.

		MT
Complete Set (5):		1.00
Common Card:		.25
R1	Garret Anderson	.25
R2	Garret Anderson	.25
R3	Marty Cordova	.25
R4	Marty Cordova	.25
R5	Garret Anderson, Marty Cordova	.25

1996 Minor League Team Sets

Heisman Hopeful?

Ricky Williams

For 1996, Best leapt into the void created by the pullback of Classic and Fleer from the minor league team set market, claiming a 75 percent share of the approximately 175 team sets issued. Many other teams issued their sets independently or with small regional graphic firms such as Grand Stand (GS). Availability of many teams sets continued to outstrip player popularity as a factor in determining prices in the hobby market.

		MT
188 Team Sets and Variations		
1996	Best AA All-Stars (56)	11.00
1996	Best Reading School AA All-Stars (56)	20.00
1996	Aberdeen Pheasants Team Issue (25)	4.00
1996	GS Abilene Prairie Dogs (28)	4.00
1996	GS Alexandria Aces (26)	4.00
1996	GS Amarillo Dillas (19)	4.00
1996	Best Appalachian League Prospects (30)	8.00
1996	Best Arkansas Travelers (29)	10.00
1996	Best Asheville Tourists (30)	6.00
1996	Best Auburn Doubledays (30)	5.00
1996	Best Augusta Greenjackets (29)	20.00
1996	Team Batavia Clippers (34)	6.00
1996	Team Bellingham Giants (36)	6.00
1996	Team Beloit Snappers (36)	10.00
1996	Team Billings Mustangs (31)	40.00
1996	Best Binghamton Mets (30)	7.00
1996	Best Birmingham Barons (30)	8.00
1996	Best Bluefield Orioles (30)	8.00
1996	Best Boise Hawks (30)	6.00
1996	Best Bowie Baysox (27)	6.00
1996	Best Brevard County Manatees (30)	7.00
1996	Best Bristol White Sox (30)	5.00
1996	Best Buffalo Bisons (24)	11.00
1996	Team Burlington Bees (33)	15.00
1996	Best Burlington Indians (30)	6.00
1996	Best Butte Copper Kings (30)	6.00
1996	Best Canton-Akron Indians (30)	12.00
1996	Best Carolina Mudcats (30)	5.00
1996	Best Carolina League/ Modesto A-S (26)	40.00
1996	Best Carolina/Modesto Sponsor's Set (28)	40.00
1996	Best Carolina/Modesto Insert Set (10)	50.00
1996	Team Cedar Rapids Kernels (34)	6.00

		MT
1996	Team Charleston RiverDogs (32)	25.00
1996	Best Charlotte Knights (29)	8.00
1996	Best Chattanooga Lookouts (30)	6.00
1996	Team Clinton Lumberkings (30)	20.00
1996	Team Colorado Springs Sky Sox (34)	8.00
1996	Best Columbus Clippers (30)	7.00
1996	Police Columbus Clippers (25)	9.00
1996	Team Columbus Clippers POGs (24)	35.00
1996	Best Danville Braves (30)	12.00
1996	Best Daytona Cubs (30)	20.00
1996	Best Delmarva Shorebirds (30)	35.00
1996	Best Dunedin Blue Jays (30)	10.00
1996	Team Dunedin Blue Jays (30)	20.00
1996	Team Dunedin Blue Jays Update (18)	10.00
1996	Best Durham Bulls, Blue (30)	40.00
1996	Best Durham Bulls Update, Brown (30)	30.00
1996	Team Edmonton Trappers (xx)	30.00
1996	Best El Paso Diablos (30)	9.00
1996	Best Erie Sea Wolves (30)	7.00
1996	Best Eugene Emeralds (27)	5.00
1996	Best Everett Aquasox (30)	7.00
1996	Best Fayetteville Generals (30)	20.00
1996	Best Frederick Keys (30)	5.00
1996	Best Ft. Myers Miracle (30)	12.00
1996	Best Ft. Wayne Wizards (31)	9.00
1996	Team Grays Harbor Gulls (26)	4.00
1996	Best Great Falls Dodgers (30)	7.00
1996	Team Great Falls Dodgers (35)	9.00
1996	Best Greensboro Bats (30)	12.00
1996	Best Greenville Braves (30)	11.00
1996	Team/Coke Greenville Braves (30)	17.50
1996	Best Hagerstown Suns (30)	7.00
1996	Best Hardware City Rock Cats (30)	8.00
1996	Best Harrisburg Senators (29)	17.50
1996	Team Helena Brewers (34)	15.00
1996	Best Hickory Crawdads (30)	8.00
1996	Best High Desert Mavericks (30)	6.00
1996	Police High Desert Mavericks (24)	12.00
1996	Team Hilo Stars (36)	12.50
1996	Team Honolulu Sharks (35)	15.00
1996	Best Hudson Valley Renegades (30)	6.00
1996	Burger King Huntsville Stars (28)	35.00
1996	BK Huntsville Stars Uncut Sheet	65.00
1996	Team Idaho Falls Braves (32)	8.00
1996	Best Indianapolis Indians (30)	7.50
1996	Best Iowa Cubs (30)	9.00
1996	Best Jackson Generals (27)	8.00
1996	Smokey Bear Jackson Generals (27)	12.00
1996	Best Jacksonville Suns (30)	12.00
1996	Best Johnson City Cardinals (30)	7.00
1996	Johnson City Cardinals Team Issue (35)	10.00
1996	Team Kane County Cougars (31)	5.00
1996	Team Kane Co. Cougars - Connie's (30)	9.00
1996	Team Kane County Cougars - Gold (30)	9.00
1996	Team Kane County Cougars Update (13)	20.00
1996	Best Kinston Indians (30)	11.00
1996	Best Kissimmee Cobras (30)	5.00
1996	Best Knoxville Smokies (25)	7.00
1996	Best Lake Elsinore Storm (30)	7.00
1996	Best Lakeland Tigers (30)	9.00
1996	Best Lancaster Jethawks (30)	10.00

		MT
1996	Best Lansing Lugnuts (30)	40.00
1996	Best Las Vegas Stars (30)	8.00
1996	Best Lethbridge Black Diamonds (33)	8.00
1996	Best Louisville Redbirds (29)	6.00
1996	Best Lowell Spinners (30)	12.00
1996	GS Lubbock Crickets (24)	4.00
1996	Best Lynchburg Hillcats (30)	15.00
1996	Best Lynchburg Hillcats Update (1)	6.00
1996	Best Macon Braves (30)	7.00
1996	Best Martinsville Phillies (30)	10.00
1996	Mascots of the Midwest League (12)	4.00
1996	Team Maui Stingrays (36)	25.00
1996	Team Medicine Hat Blue Jays (33)	35.00
1996	Best Memphis Chicks (30)	6.00
1996	Team Meridian Brakemen (24)	4.00
1996	Best Michigan Battle Cats (30)	6.00
1996	Best Midland Angels (29)	6.00
1996	Team Midland Angels (24)	50.00
1996	Best Midwest League A-S (58)	9.00
1996	Best Modesto A's (30)	18.00
1996	Best Nashville Sounds (30)	7.00
1996	Team Nashville Sounds Foldout	20.00
1996	Best New Haven Ravens (30)	9.00
1996	Best New Haven Ravens (30)	16.00
1996	Team New Haven Ravens Raffle Sheet	10.00
1996	Best New Jersey Cardinals (30)	6.00
1996	Best Norfolk Tides (30)	7.50
1996	Best Norwich Navigators (28)	8.00
1996	Team Norwich Navigators Update (12)	12.00
1996	Team Ogden Raptors (39)	8.00
1996	Best Oklahoma City 89ers (28)	8.00
1996	Best Omaha Royals (30)	9.00
1996	Best Orlando Cubs (30)	6.00
1996	DD Pawtucket Red Sox Foldout	35.00
1996	Best Peoria Chiefs (30)	6.00
1996	Best Phoenix Firebirds (30)	9.00
1996	Team Phoenix Firebirds (30)	9.00
1996	Best Piedmont Boll Weevils (30)	75.00
1996	Best Pittsfield Mets (30)	6.00
1996	Best Port City Roosters (29)	10.00
1996	Best Portland Rockies (30)	5.00
1996	Best Portland Sea Dogs (29)	35.00
1996	Best Prince William Cannons (30)	5.00
1996	Best Quad City River Bandits (29)	7.00
1996	Best Rancho Cucamonga Quakes (30)	7.00
1996	Best Reading Phillies (29)	12.00
1996	Best Reading Phils Fairground Sq. (29)	25.00
1996	Best Reading Phillies Boy Scouts (1)	25.00
1996	Best Richmond Braves (30)	7.00
1996	Best Richmond Braves Update (30)	20.00
1996	Richmond Camera Richmond Braves (25)	75.00
1996	Team Richmond Braves Alumni (6)	25.00
1996	GS Rio Grande Valley White Wings (23)	4.00
1996	Best Rochester Red Wings (30)	7.00
1996	Team Rockford Cubbies (32)	6.00
1996	Best Salem Avalanche (30)	5.00
1996	Best San Antonio Missions (30)	7.00
1996	HEB San Antonio Missions (30)	50.00
1996	Best San Bernardino Stampede (30)	7.00
1996	Best San Jose Giants (30)	6.00
1996	Best Sarasota Red Sox (30)	5.00
1996	Best Savannah Sandgnats (30)	50.00
1996	Best Scranton/W-B Red Barons (30)	6.00

		MT
1996	Team Sioux City Explorers (30)	4.00
1996	Best South Bend Silver Hawks (28)	5.00
1996	Team Southern Oregon Timberjacks (28)	42.50
1996	Best Spokane Indians (30)	20.00
1996	Best St. Catherines Stompers (30)	9.00
1996	Team St. Lucie Mets (36)	12.00
1996	Best St. Petersburg Cardinals (30)	5.00
1996	Best Stockton Ports (30)	5.00
1996	Team Syracuse Chiefs (30)	11.00
1996	Best Tacoma Rainiers (30)	7.00
1996	Best Tampa Yankees (29)	6.00
1996	Best Texas League All-Stars (36)	11.00
1996	Team Thunder Bay Whiskey Jacks (25)	5.00
1996	Best Toledo Mud Hens (30)	8.00
1996	Best Trenton Thunder (30)	7.50
1996	Best Tucson Toros (29)	8.00
1996	Best Tulsa Drillers (30)	8.00
1996	Team Tulsa 20th Anniversary (32)	25.00
1996	GS Tyler Wildcatters (25)	4.00
1996	Best Vancouver Canadians (30)	15.00
1996	Best Vermont Expos (30)	6.00
1996	Best Vero Beach Dodgers (30)	35.00
1996	Team Watertown Indians (36)	9.00
1996	Best West Michigan Whitecaps (30)	10.00
1996	Team West Oahu Canefires (35)	12.50
1996	Best West Palm Beach Expos (31)	80.00
1996	Best Wichita Wranglers (30)	12.00
1996	Team Wichita Wranglers (18)	8.00
1996	Best Wilmington Blue Rocks (30)	6.00
1996	Best Wisconsin Timber Rattlers (30)	15.00
1996	Team Yakima Bears (35)	6.00
1996	Team Zanesville Greys (23)	4.00

1997 Best Prospects Promos

Kerry Wood

Some of the hottest players in the minor leagues at the start of 1997 were chosen by Best to showcase its 1997 "Prospects" issue. Fronts are virtually identical to the regular-issue cards, with action photos and team and Best logos. Backs of the 2-1/2" x 3-1/2" cards are in full color and include the issue's logo and a large team logo. A green strip at top center reads "FOR PROMOTIONAL PURPOSES ONLY." The unnumbered promo cards are checklisted here in alphabetical order.

		MT
Complete Set (5):		3.00
Common Player:		.50
(1)	Kris Benson	.50
(2)	Hideki Irabu	.50
(3)	Travis Lee	1.00
(4)	Matt White	.50
(5)	Kerry Wood	1.50

1997 Best Prospects

The basic set of minor league player cards from Best in 1997 includes 50 top prospects. Fronts of the 2-1/2" x 3-1/2" cards have action photos with Best and team logos superimposed. Player name is in typewriter style at bottom, with his position abbreviated in a red home plate. Backs have a close-up version of the front photo, a black

Jose Cruz, Jr.

box at top with personal data, an overall purple background and 1996 stats at bottom.

	MT
Complete Set (50):	5.00
Common Player:	.05
Wax Pack (6):	1.50
Wax Box (18):	20.00
1 Kerry Wood	1.00
2 Matt White	.05
3 Travis Lee	.50
4 Miguel Tejada	.60
5 Kris Benson	.15
6 Paul Konerko	.60
7 Jose Cruz, Jr.	.15
8 Derrek Lee	.60
9 Todd Helton	1.00
10 Carl Pavano	.25
11 Ben Grieve	.10
12 Richard Hidalgo	.10
13 Chad Hermansen	.05
14 Jaret Wright	.05
15 Roy Halladay	.25
16 Hideki Irabu	.05
17 Matt Morris	.10
18 Aramis Ramirez	.35
19 Robinson Checo	.05
20 Chris Carpenter	.05
21 Adrian Beltre	.60
22 Braden Looper	.05
23 Luis Rolando Arrojo	.10
24 Juan Melo	.05
25 Elieser Marrero	.10
26 Kevin McGlinchy	.10
27 Sidney Ponson	.15
28 John Patterson	.05
29 Brian Rose	.05
30 Joe Fontonot	.05
31 Chris Reitsma	.05
32 Paul Wilder	.05
33 Ron Wright	.05
34 A.J. Zapp	.05
35 Donnie Sadler	.10
36 Valerio De Los Santos	.05
37 Eric Chavez	.60
38 Jake Westbrook	.05
39 Seth Greisinger	.05
40 Derrick Gibson	.05
41 Ben Davis	.05
42 Rafael Medina	.05
43 Britt Reames	.05
44 Ben Petrick	.05
45 Josh Paul	.05
46 Brad Fullmer	.10
47 Jarrod Washburn	.15
48 Kevin Escobar	.05
49 Manuel Aybar	.05
50 Wes Helms	.05

1997 Best Prospects All Stars

Players who made their league all-star teams are featured in this insert set which was a 1:6 pack pick.

	MT
Complete Set (15):	7.50
Common Player:	.25
1 Seth Greisinger	.25
2 Hideki Irabu	.25
3 Josh Paul	.25
4 Jaret Wright	.25
5 Norm Hutchins	.25
6 Miguel Tejada	3.00
7 Ruben Mateo	.25
8 Matt White	.25
9 Marc Lewis	.25
10 Jose Cruz	.25
11 Quincy Carter	.25
12 Kris Benson	.35
13 Ben Petrick	.35
14 Adrian Beltre	2.00
15 Travis Lee	2.00

1997 Best Prospects Autographs

Ten of the best prospects in the minor leagues are featured in this insert set. Fronts feature action photos vignetted against a white background. The Best logo is printed at top-left, while a holographic-foil "Best Prospects" logo is at upper-right. The player name and team logo are at bottom. Backs have a Best Autograph Series logo ghosted on a white background, and a congratulatory message in orange and black. Stated rate of insertion for the autographed cards is one per box (18 packs). The autographed cards are not numbered. An announced Jeff Liefer card was replaced by Wes Helms.

	MT
Complete Set (10):	15.00
Common Autograph:	2.00
(1) Ben Grieve	3.00
(2) Wes Helms	2.00
(3) Brett Herbison	2.00
(4) Chad Hermansen	2.00
(5) Geoff Jenkins	3.00
(6) Paul Konerko	6.00
(7) Ben Petrick	2.00
(8) Donnie Sadler	2.00
(9) Randall Simon	2.00
(10) Brett Tomko	2.00

1997 Best Prospects Best Bets Preview

Kris Benson

With only 200 hand-numbered cards of each player issued, these are the toughest pull among the Best Prospects inserts, being found on average only one per 90 packs. Fronts have an action photo against a background of red bricks and green stripes. Team and manufacturer logos are also featured on front. Backs have a close-up version of the front photo on a background of green stripes and a black polygon. Cards are individually numbered at top-right.

	MT
Complete Set (10):	15.00
Common Player:	1.00
1 Miguel Tejada	5.00
2 Adrian Beltre	5.00
3 Hideki Irabu	1.00
4 Kris Benson	1.50
5 Matt White	1.00
6 Travis Lee	5.00
7 Corey Erickson	1.00
8 Jose Cruz	1.50
9 Marc Lewis	1.00
10 Luis Rolando Arrojo	2.00

1997 Best Prospects Best Five

Matt White

The field of best minor leaguers is whittled to five for this insert set. Rather than being issued inside the foil packs, these cards are placed one per box as a dealer pre-

mium. A close-up baseball design is used for a background on both front and back. An action photo dominates the front with a "Best 5" logo at top and player ID at bottom, along with his team logo. Backs have personal data, career highlights and stats, along with a small detail of the front photo.

	MT
Complete Set (5):	10.00
Common Player:	1.00
1 Kris Benson	1.00
2 Kerry Wood	6.00
3 Travis Lee	4.00
4 Hideki Irabu	1.00
5 Matt White	1.00

1997 Best Prospects Best Guns

Kris Benson

Top minor league pitchers are featured in this retail-only insert. One card was inserted atop the packs in each box.

	MT
Complete Set (10):	10.00
Common Player:	.70
1 Robinson Checo	.75
2 Rolando Arrojo	1.00
3 Clayton Bruner	.75
4 Grant Roberts	.75
5 Brian Rose	.75
6 Carl Pavano	2.00
7 Kerry Wood	6.00
8 Kris Benson	1.00
9 Jaret Wright	.75
10 Cliff Politte	.75

1997 Best Prospects Best Lumber

Paul Konerko

The scarcest of three retail-only inserts in Best Prospects issue is this run of potentially big hitters. The Best Lumber cards are found only on average of one per five boxes.

	MT
Complete Set (10):	50.00
Common Player:	4.00
1 Paul Konerko	7.50
2 Derrek Lee	7.50
3 Ricky Ledee	4.00
4 Brad Fullmer	4.00
5 Ben Grieve	4.00
6 Russ Branyon	4.00
7 A.J. Hinch	4.00
8 Adrian Beltre	7.50
9 Mike Stoner	4.00
10 Travis Lee	7.50

1997 Best Prospects Best Wheels

The speed merchants of the minor leagues are featured in this retail-only Best Propsects insert. Cards are random pack inserts at a rate of one per box.

	MT
Complete Set (5):	10.00
Common Player:	2.00
1 Donnie Sadler	2.00
2 Juan Encarnacion	3.00
3 Damian Jackson	2.00
4 Chad Green	2.00
5 Mark Kotsay	3.00

1997 Best Prospects Diamond Best

Seeded at a rate of fewer than one per box (about every 19 packs), this insert set features arguably the top 10 minor league players of 1996.

WHITE

Fronts of the 2-1/2" x 3-1/2" cards have a white background surrounded by a blue border. An action photo is superimposed on a large team logo. The "Diamond Best" logo, player name and position are in red, white and blue at bottom. Backs have a second version of the player photo on a white background streaked with gray. A red box has career highlights; personal data is at right.

	MT
Complete Set (10):	25.00
Common Player:	1.00
1 Hideki Irabu	1.00
2 Kerry Wood	6.00
3 Matt White	1.00
4 Travis Lee	3.00
5 Miguel Tejada	4.00
6 Kris Benson	1.00
7 Paul Konerko	4.00
8 Jose Cruz	1.00
9 Derrek Lee	4.00
10 Todd Helton	4.00

1997 Best International Best

These late-season hobby-only inserts feature top prospects who were born outside the U.S. The cards share a basic design with Best Prospects base cards, but feature a national flag logo at top-right and minor modifications to the back.

	MT
Complete Set (5):	3.00
Common Player:	.50
IB1 Miguel Tejada	1.50
IB2 Hideki Irabu	.50
IB3 Adrian Beltre	1.50
IB4 Rolando Arrojo	.75
IB5 Robinson Checo	.50

1997 Best Autograph Series

Ted Lilly

This end-of-year product showcases minor league talent which developed during the season including cards of 1997 draft picks and players who climbed their organizational ladder. The series is numbered 51-100 in continuation of the early-season Best Prospects issue. Cards were sold in foil packs with four regular cards and an autographed card. Fronts have action photos on a ragged-edged background with Best and team logos. Backs have a portrait photo, player data, highlights and stats.

	MT
Complete Set (50):	6.00
Common Player:	.05
51 Mike Stoner	.05
52 George Lombard	.05
53 Calvin Pickering	.05
54 Antonio Armas	.10
55 John Barnes	.05
56 Russell Branyan	.10
57 Sean Casey	.60
58 Edgard Velasquez	.05
59 Mike Vavrek	.05
60 Magglio Ordonez	1.00
61 Mike Caruso	.05
62 Pat Cline	.05
63 Courtney Duncan	.05
64 Juan Encarnacion	.10
65 Jason Varitek	.50
66 Alex Gonzalez	.05
67 Ryan Jackson	.05
68 Kevin Millar	.10
69 John Roskos	.05
70 Daryle Ward	.05
71 Dermal Brown	.05
72 Ted Lilly	.05
73 Chad Green	.05
74 David Ortiz	1.00
75 Jacque Jones	.50
76 Luis Rivas	.05
77 Orlando Cabrera	.25
78 Javier Vazquez	.45
79 Jesus Sanchez	.05
80 Eric Milton	.10
81 Ricky Ledee	.05
82 Ramon Hernandez	.05
83 A.J. Hinch	.05
84 Marlon Anderson	.25
85 Ryan Brannan	.05
86 Abraham Nunez	.15
87 Matt Clement	.25
88 Kerry Robinson	.05
89 Cliff Politte	.05
90 Pablo Ortega	.05
91 Aramis Ramirez	.25
92 Eric Chavez	.75
93 Brent Butler	.05
94 Cole Liniak	.05
95 Travis Lee	.60
96 Adrian Beltre	.50
97 Paul Konerko	.50
98 Brad Fullmer	.15
99 Jeremy Giambi	.15
100 Gil Meche	.10

1997 Best Autograph Series Autographs

Russell Ortiz — GIANTS

Dozens of top prospects are featured on the autographed cards which are the heart of Best's Autograph Series issue. One genuinely autographed card is included in each six-card foil pack. Autographed cards differ in design from the base set in that action photos on front are vignetted in an oval against a white background. The player name and minor league team logo are at bottom. Backs carry a congratulatory message over a large issuer logo. The unnumbered autographed cards are checklisted here in alphabetical order.

		MT
Common Player:		1.00
(1)	Israel Alcantera	1.00
(2)	Richard Almanzar	1.00
(3)	Marc Barcelo	1.00
(4)	Tim Belk	1.00
(5)	Jeremy Blevins	1.00
(6)	James Bonnici	1.00
(7)	Homer Bush	1.00
(8)	Davey Coggin	1.00
(9)	Bartolo Colon	10.00
(10)	Lee Daniels	1.00
(11)	Ryan Dempster	2.00
(12)	Lino Diaz	1.00
(13)	Tom Fordham	1.00
(14)	Anton French	1.00
(15)	Ben Grieve	2.00
(16)	Mike Gulan	1.00
(17)	Ryan Hancock	1.00
(18)	Wes Helms	1.00
(19)	Brett Herbison	1.00
(20)	Chad Hermansen	1.00
(21)	Damon Hollins	1.00
(22)	Ryan Jaroncyk	1.00
(23)	Geoff Jenkins	5.00
(24)	Earl Johnson	1.00
(25)	Andre King	1.00
(26)	Paul Konerko	4.00
(27)	Todd Landry	1.00
(28)	Jeff Liefer	1.00
(29)	Mendy Lopez	1.00
(30)	Roberto Lopez	1.00
(31)	Johnny Martinez	1.00
(32)	Mike Maurer	1.00
(33)	Brian Meadows	1.00
(34)	Doug Mlicki	1.00
(35)	Tony Mounce	1.00
(36)	Sergio Nunez	1.00
(37)	Russell Ortiz	2.00
(38)	Carey Paige	1.00
(39)	Jay Payton	3.00
(40)	Ben Petrick	1.00
(41)	Tommy Phelps	1.00
(42)	Hugo Pivaral	1.00
(43)	Angel Ramirez	1.00
(44)	Gary Rath	1.00
(45)	Mark Redman	1.00
(46)	Adam Riggs	1.00
(47)	Lonell Roberts	1.00
(48)	Glendon Rusch	1.00
(49)	Matt Ryan	1.00
(50)	Donnie Sadler	1.50
(51)	William Santamaria	1.00
(52)	Todd Schmitt	1.00
(53)	Richie Sexson	5.00
(54)	Alvie Shepherd	1.00
(55)	Steve Shoemaker	1.00
(56)	Brian Sikorski	1.00
(57)	Randall Simon	2.00
(58)	Bobby Smith	1.00
(59)	Matt Smith	1.00
(60)	Jose Texidor	1.00
(61)	Jason Thompson	1.00
(62)	Mike Thurman	1.00
(63)	Brett Tomko	1.00
(64)	Hector Trinidad	1.00
(65)	Andrew Vessel	1.00
(66)	Jacob Viano	1.00
(67)	Jarrod Washburn	5.00
(68)	Travis Welch	1.00
(69)	Casey Whitten	1.00
(70)	Shad Williams	1.00
(71)	Paul Wilson	1.50
(72)	Preston Wilson	6.00
(73)	Randy Winn	1.00
(74)	Kevin Witt	1.00

1997 Best Autograph Series Autographed Edition of 250

Mark Kotsay

The 45 players in this random pack insert series include two dozen of the first round draft picks of 1997. Each player autographed 250 cards, which are serially numbered on back. Autographed cards are listed here in alphabetical order.

		MT
Complete Set (45):		50.00
Common Player:		1.00
(1)	Richard Almanzar	1.00
(2)	Kris Benson	2.00
(3)	Darin Blood	1.00
(4)	Adrian Brown	1.00
(5)	Dermal Brown	1.00
(6)	Kevin Brown	1.00
(7)	Eric Chavez	5.00
(8)	D.T. Cromer	1.00
(9)	Lorenzo de la Cruz	1.00
(10)	Adam Eaton	1.00
(11)	Nelson Figueroa	1.00
(12)	Juan Gonzalez	1.00
(13)	Chad Green	1.00
(14)	Seth Greisinger	1.00
(15)	Ben Grieve	2.00
(16)	Matt Halloran	1.00
(17)	Chad Hermansen	1.00
(18)	Mark Johnson	1.00
(19)	Andruw Jones	15.00
(20)	Billy Koch	1.00
(21)	Paul Konerko	5.00
(22)	Mark Kotsay	3.00
(23)	Joe Lawrence	1.00
(24)	Braden Looper	1.00
(25)	Gil Meche	2.00
(26)	Eric Milton	1.00
(27)	Abraham Nunez	2.00
(28)	John Oliver	1.00
(29)	Russell Ortiz	2.00
(30)	John Patterson	1.00
(31)	Carl Pavano	5.00
(32)	Elvis Pena	1.00
(33)	Danny Peoples	1.00
(34)	Neifi Perez	1.00
(35)	Sidney Ponson	2.00
(36)	Aramis Ramirez	2.00
(37)	Britt Reames	1.00
(38)	Kerry Robinson	1.00
(39)	Bubba Trammell	1.00
(40)	Mike Villano	1.00
(41)	Jake Westbrook	1.00
(42)	Paul Wilder	1.00
(43)	Enrique Wilson	3.00

(44) Kerry Wood 20.00
(45) A.J. Zapp 1.00

1997 Best Autograph Series Cornerstone

A dozen of the biggest names in the minor leagues are featured in this insert set as future cornerstones of Major League teams. Backs have a close-up photo of that on front and typical player data, highlights and stats. Insertion rate was given as one per 49 packs.

		MT
Complete Set (12):		20.00
Common Player:		1.50
1	Travis Lee	4.00
2	Adrian Beltre	5.00
3	Ben Grieve	1.50
4	Paul Konerko	4.00
5	Ricky Ledee	1.50
6	Brad Fullmer	1.50
7	Alex Gonzalez	1.50
8	Russell Branyan	1.50
9	Eric Milton	1.50
10	Jaret Wright	1.50
11	Derrek Lee	4.00
12	Kris Benson	1.50

1997 Best Autograph Series Diamond Best II

Younger minor league stars are featured in this insert set carried over from the Best Prospects issue earlier in the year. Cards have action photos on a white background with a large team logo. Backs repeat the photo and logo in smaller size and provide player data and stats.

		MT
Complete Set (10):		15.00
Common Player:		2.00
11	Dermal Brown	2.00
12	Aramis Ramirez	3.00
13	Ramon Hernandez	2.00
14	Eric Chavez	6.00
15	A.J. Zapp	2.00
16	A.J. Hinch	2.00
17	Juan Melo	2.00
18	Cole Liniak	2.00
19	David Ortiz	6.00
20	Russell Branyan	2.00

1997 Best Autograph Series Premium Preview

These cards were inserted one per box as a box-topper to promote box purchases. Each card is numbered within an edition of 200. Fronts have color action photos against a ghost-image black-and-white photo. Backs repeat the front's background photo and have a small close-up of the color picture. Personal data, stats and highlights are given on back, as well.

		MT
Complete Set (50):		160.00
Common Player:		2.50
1	Jaret Wright	2.50
2	Damian Jackson	2.50

JARET WRIGHT • BUFFALO BISONS • P

3	Kerry Wood	17.50
4	Adrian Beltre	15.00
5	Sean Casey	10.00
6	Paul Konerko	10.00
7	Ben Grieve	5.00
8	Hideki Irabu	3.00
9	Rolando Arrojo	3.50
10	Robinson Checo	2.50
11	Donnie Sadler	3.00
12	Todd Helton	17.50
13	Jose Cruz Jr.	5.00
14	Ricky Ledee	2.50
15	Calvin Pickering	2.50
16	Alex Gonzalez	3.00
17	Alvie Shepherd	2.50
18	Michael Coleman	2.50
19	Derrek Lee	10.00
20	Brad Fullmer	3.00
21	Derrick Gibson	2.50
22	A.J. Hinch	3.50
23	Juan Melo	2.50
24	David Ortiz	15.00
25	Ramon Hernandez	2.50
26	Mike Stoner	2.50
27	George Lombard	2.50
28	Chad Hermansen	2.50
29	Mark Fischer	2.50
30	Trot Nixon	7.50
31	Kevin Nicholson	2.50
32	Kevin Millar	2.50
33	John Roskos	2.50
34	Aramis Ramirez	6.00
35	Randall Simon	2.50
36	Carl Pavano	6.50
37	Brian Rose	2.50
38	Enrique Wilson	3.50
39	Russell Branyan	3.00
40	Chan Perry	2.50
41	Juan Encarnacion	3.50
42	Grant Roberts	2.50
43	Marlon Anderson	2.50
44	Matt White	2.50
45	Jason Varitek	5.00
46	Cole Liniak	2.50
47	Roy Halladay	3.50
48	Magglio Ordonez	12.50
49	Richie Sexson	5.00
50	Travis Lee	7.50

1997 Best Full Count Autographs

Dermal Brown DF

While these authentically autographed cards were packaged with 1998 Team Best Signature Series at the announced rate of one per 19 hobby packs, they share a design and copyright date with the base cards of 1997 Best and were probably originally intended for release in those products. The Full Count autographed cards have a logo to that effect at top-right and on the baseball diamond design on back.

		MT
Complete Set (25):		90.00
Common Player:		2.00
(1)	Kris Benson	3.00
(2)	Dermal Brown	2.00
(3)	Eric Chavez (Both feet on ground.)	9.00
(4)	Eric Chavez (One foot on ground.)	12.00
(5)	Chad Green	2.00
(6)	Ben Grieve	3.00
(7)	Todd Helton	16.00

(8)	Chad Hermansen	2.00
(9)	Paul Konerko	5.00
(10)	Mark Kotsay	3.00
(11)	Braden Looper	2.00
(12)	Gil Meche	2.00
(13)	Juan Melo	2.00
(14)	Eric Milton	2.00
(15)	Abraham Nunez	3.00
(16)	John Patterson	2.00
(17)	Carl Pavano	5.00
(18)	Sidney Ponson	3.00
(19)	Aramis Ramirez	3.00
(20)	Britt Reames	2.00
(21)	Kerry Robinson	2.00
(22)	Jake Westbrook	2.00
(23)	Paul Wilder	2.00
(24)	Kerry Wood	20.00
(25)	A.J. Zapp	2.00

1997 Best Premium Autographs

A completely different selection of players and design was presented in the autographed cards inserted into Team Best retail packs. Fronts have action photos with a large team logo in the background. In the top-right corner "Best Premium" appears in gold-foil script. Backs have a Best Premium logo and are hand-numbered from within an edition of 250 of each player.

		MT
Complete Set (49):		125.00
Common Player:		2.50
(1)	Richard Almanzar	2.50
(2)	Kris Benson	5.00
(3)	Darin Blood	2.50
(4)	Adrian Brown	2.50
(5)	Dermal Brown	2.50
(6)	Kevin Brown	2.50
(7)	Eric Chavez	10.00
(8)	D.T. Cromer	2.50
(9)	Lorenzo de la Cruz	2.50
(10)	Adam Eaton	2.50
(11)	Nelson Figueroa	2.50
(12)	Juan Gonzalez	2.50
(13)	Chad Green	2.50
(14)	Seth Greisinger	2.50
(15)	Ben Grieve	3.00
(16)	Matt Halloran	2.50
(17)	Chad Hermansen	2.50
(18)	Mark Johnson	2.50
(19)	Billy Koch	2.50
(20)	Paul Konerko	7.50
(21)	Mark Kotsay	5.00
(22)	Joe Lawrence	2.50
(23)	Braden Looper	3.00
(24)	Kevin McGlinchy	3.00
(25)	Gil Meche	4.00
(26)	Juan Melo	2.50
(27)	Eric Milton	2.50
(28)	John Nicholson	2.50
(29)	Todd Noel	2.50
(30)	Abraham Nunez	4.00
(31)	Russell Ortiz	2.50
(32)	Yudith Ozario	2.50
(33)	John Patterson	3.00
(34)	Carl Pavano	5.00
(35)	Elvis Pena	2.50
(36)	Danny Peoples	2.50
(37)	Neifi Perez	2.50
(38)	Sidney Ponson	6.00
(39)	Aramis Ramirez	4.00
(40)	Britt Reames	2.50
(41)	Kerry Robinson	2.50
(42)	Jeff Sexton	2.50
(43)	Bubba Trammell	3.00
(44)	Mike Villano	2.50
(45)	Jake Westbrook	2.50
(46)	Paul Wilder	2.50
(47)	Enrique Wilson	2.50
(48)	Kerry Wood	20.00
(49)	A.J. Zapp	2.50

1997 Best Autographed Supers

Each 10-box case of 1998 Team Best Signature Series included one of 10 authentically autographed large-format (4" x 6") case-topper cards. Fronts have Best and team logos at top and a silver-foil Auto Best logo at bottom. Also on

PAUL KONERKO

front is a serial number from within an edition of 500 each. Backs have a large notice of authenticity. Because the cards are dated 1997 and share the basic '97 Best format, they are listed here.

		MT
Complete Set (12):		85.00
Common Player:		6.00
1	Kris Benson	6.00
2	Sean Casey (Akron)	15.00
3	Sean Casey (Buffalo)	15.00
4	Seth Greisinger	6.00
5	Ben Grieve	6.00
6	Chad Hermansen	6.00
7	Paul Konerko	9.00
8	Britt Reames	6.00
9	Jake Westbrook	6.00
10	Paul Wilder	6.00
11	Kerry Wood	20.00
12	A.J. Zapp	6.00

1997 Minor League Team Sets

Frank Kellner

The number of team sets increased a bit for 1997. Market leader Best again produced more than 100 teams' sets. A developing trend in 1997 was the growth of formats other than single cards, such as strips and sheets, and the issue of late-season or post-season update sets.

		MT
198 Team Sets and Variations		
1997	Team Aberdeen Pheasants (28)	4.00
1997	Team Abilene Prairie Dogs (30)	4.00
1997	Best Akron Aeros (31)	10.00
1997	GS Albuquerque Dukes (30)	4.00
1997	GS Albuquerque Dukes Update (5)	5.00
1997	GS Alexandria Aces (26)	4.00
1997	Team Amarillo Dillas (21)	4.00
1997	Best Appalachian League Propsects (30)	10.00
1997	Arizona Fall League (21)	12.50
1997	Best Arkansas Travelers (30)	8.00
1997	Best Asheville Tourists (30)	6.00
1997	Team Auburn Doubledays (30)	45.00
1997	Best Augusta Greenjackets (30)	4.00
1997	Team Bakersfield Blaze (30)	6.00
1997	Team Bakersfield Blaze W/Pepsi Ads (30)	8.00
1997	Team Batavia Clippers (32)	9.00
1997	Best Beloit Snappers (30)	6.00
1997	GS Bend Bandits (27)	4.00
1997	Team Billings Mustangs (36)	60.00
1997	Best Binghamton Mets (32)	5.00
1997	Magic Prints Binghamton Mets (5)	9.00
1997	Best Birmingham Barons (30)	5.00
1997	GS Boise Hawks (32)	7.00

1997	Best Bowie Baysox (29)	15.00
1997	Best Brevard County Manatees (31)	7.00
1997	Best Bristol Sox (30)	7.00
1997	Best Buffalo Bisons (30)	10.00
1997	Best Burlington Bees (31)	7.00
1997	GS Burlington Indians (31)	7.00
1997	Best Butte Copper Kings (30)	7.00
1997	Best Butte C.K. W/Sponsors' Ads (30)	7.00
1997	Best Calgary Cannons (30)	12.00
1997	Team Calgary Cannons (36)	65.00
1997	Best California League Prospects (31)	8.00
1997	Best California-Carolina League A-S (50)	10.00
1997	Best Capital City Bombers (30)	15.00
1997	Best Carolina Legue Prospects (31)	12.00
1997	Best Carolina Mudcats (29)	7.00
1997	GS Cedar Rapids Kernels (30)	9.00
1997	GS Charleston RiverDogs (29)	7.00
1997	Best Charlotte Knights (30)	8.00
1997	Best Chattanooga Lookouts (27)	7.00
1997	GS Chillicothe Paints (28)	4.00
1997	GS Clarksville Coyotes (25)	4.00
1997	Best Clearwater Phillies (30)	6.00
1997	GS Clinton Lumber Kings (30)	6.00
1997	Team Colorado Springs Sky Sox (29)	9.00
1997	Team Colorado Springs All-Time (32)	8.00
1997	Best Columbus Clippers (30)	8.00
1997	Police Columbus Clippers (29)	8.00
1997	Team Columbus Clippers 20th Anniv. (30)	12.00
1997	Best Danville Braves (30)	10.00
1997	Best Delmarva Shorebirds (30)	15.00
1997	GS Duluth-Superior Dukes (26)	4.00
1997	Team Dunedin Blue Jays (34)	7.50
1997	Team Dunedin Blue Jays Family Night (30)	12.00
1997	Team Durham Bulls (30)	15.00
1997	Team Durham Bulls "Bulls to Braves" (10)	12.00
1997	Best Eastern League Prospects (31)	7.00
1997	Team Edmonton Trappers (xx)	30.00
1997	Best El Paso Diablos (30)	5.00
1997	Best Erie Sea Wolves (30)	3.00
1997	Best Eugene Emeralds (30)	5.00
1997	GS Everett Aquasox (30)	6.00
1997	MA Fargo-Moorhead RedHawks (30)	4.00
1997	Best Florida State League Prospects (31)	15.00
1997	Best Florida State League Prospects (33)	18.00
1997	Best Frederick Keys (30)	5.00
1997	Best Ft. Myers Miracle (30)	10.00
1997	Best Ft. Wayne Wizards (29)	8.00
1997	GS Grand Forks Varmints (21)	4.00
1997	GS Grays Harbor Gulls (27)	4.00
1997	Best Great Falls Dodgers (30)	7.00
1997	Best Greensboro Bats (30)	50.00
1997	GS Greenville Braves (28)	10.00
1997	Best Hagerstown Suns (30)	11.00
1997	Best Harrisburg Senators (30)	8.00
1997	Best Harrisburg W/Ad Logos (28)	12.00
1997	Best Helena Brewers (30)	7.00
1997	Best Hickory Crawdads (30)	10.00
1997	Best Hickory Crawdads Update (30)	12.00
1997	GS High Desert Mavericks (30)	35.00
1997	GS High Desert Mavericks Update (18)	12.50
1997	Best Hudson Valley Renegades (30)	6.00
1997	Burger King Huntsville Stars (27)	7.00

1997	Team Idaho Falls Braves (32)	8.00
1997	Best Indianapolis Indians (29)	8.00
1997	Best Iowa Cubs (29)	8.00
1997	Best Jackson Generals (28)	6.00
1997	Smokey Bear Jackson Generals (28)	12.00
1997	Best Jacksonville Suns (27)	8.00
1997	Team Johnson City Cardinals (37)	6.00
1997	Team Kane County Cougars (32)	9.00
1997	Connie's Pizza Kane County Cougars (32)	15.00
1997	Best Kinston Indians (30)	4.00
1997	Best Kissimee Cobras (30)	9.00
1997	Best Knoxville Smokies (28)	6.00
1997	GS Lafayette Leopards (26)	5.00
1997	Horizon Outlet Lake Elsinore Storm (20)	16.00
1997	GS Lake Elsinore Storm (30)	6.00
1997	Best Lakeland Tigers (30)	10.00
1997	Best Lancaster JetHawks (30)	6.00
1997	Team Lansing Lugnuts (30)	12.00
1997	Best Las Vegas Stars (30)	7.00
1997	Best Lethbridge Black Diamonds (30)	6.00
1997	Best Louisville Redbirds (30)	11.00
1997	Best Lowell Spinners (30)	6.00
1997	Best Lynchburg Hillcats (30)	11.00
1997	Best Macon Braves (30)	12.00
1997	Team Madison Black Wolf (?)	17.50
1997	Best Michigan Battle Cats (30)	10.00
1997	Best Midland Angels (29)	6.00
1997	Team Midland Angels (23)	40.00
1997	Best Midwest League Prospects (30)	9.00
1997	Best Mobile BayBears (30)	8.00
1997	GS Modesto A's (30)	8.00
1997	Team Nashville Sounds (32)	12.00
1997	Best New Britain Rock Cats (30)	5.00
1997	Best New Haven Ravens (30)	6.00
1997	Best New Jersey Cardinals (30)	5.00
1997	Best N.J. Cardinals Top Prospects (6)	7.00
1997	Best Norfolk Tides (34)	7.00
1997	Northern League All-Stars (42)	8.00
1997	Best Norwich Navigators (32)	6.00
1997	Team Norwich Navigators (30)	18.00
1997	Team Ogden Raptors (32)	9.00
1997	Best Oklahoma City 89ers (25)	6.00
1997	Best Omaha Royals (26)	4.00
1997	Best Orlando Rays (30)	20.00
1997	Denny's Orlando Rays (25)	40.00
1997	Best Pawtucket Red Sox (30)	7.50
1997	Dunkin' Donuts Pawtucket Red Sox Foldout	24.00
1997	Team Pawtucket 25th Anniversary (31)	17.50
1997	Team Pawtucket 25th Anniversary Foldout	40.00
1997	Best Peoria Chiefs (30)	6.00
1997	Team Phoenix Firebirds (30)	10.00
1997	All-Time Firebirds Dream Team (30)	9.00
1997	Best Piedmont Boll Weevils (30)	9.00
1997	Best Pittsfield Mets (30)	6.00
1997	Best Portland Rockies (30)	5.00
1997	Best Portland Sea Dogs (30)	7.50
1997	Best Prince William Cannons (30)	6.00
1997	Best Princeton Devil Rays (30)	9.00
1997	Best Quad City River Bandits (30)	10.00
1997	GS Rancho Cucamonga Quakes (30)	7.00
1997	GS Rancho Cucamonga Quakes Update (7)	5.00
1997	Best Reading Phillies (27)	6.00
1997	GS Reno Chukars (27)	4.00
1997	Best Richmond Braves (30)	6.00
1997	Richmond Camera Richmond Braves (20)	45.00

		MT
1997	Team Rio Grande Valley White Wings (23)	4.00
1997	Best Rochester Red Wings (30)	4.00
1997	Best Rockford Cubbies (30)	40.00
1997	Team Salem Avalanche (38)	10.00
1997	Team Salem Avalanche Update (10)	5.00
1997	Team Salem-Keizer Volcanoes (42)	6.00
1997	Best Salt Lake City Buzz (30)	6.00
1997	Best San Antonio Missions (30)	7.00
1997	Best San Bernardino Stampede (30)	6.00
1997	Best San Jose Giants (30)	6.00
1997	Best Sarasota Red Sox (30)	20.00
1997	Best Scranton Red Barons (30)	7.00
1997	Best Shreveport Captains (28)	7.00
1997	Best Shreveport W/WK SportsCare Ads (29)	7.00
1997	GS Sioux City Explorers (27)	4.00
1997	GS Sioux Falls Canaries (28)	4.00
1997	Best So. Atlantic League Prospects (31)	12.50
1997	Best South Bend Silver Hawks (30)	5.00
1997	Best Southern League Prospects (32)	11.00
1997	Best Southern Oregon Timberjacks (29)	9.00
1997	GS Spokane Indians (31)	7.00
1997	Best St. Catherines Stompers (30)	9.00
1997	Best St. Lucie Mets (30)	9.00
1997	Team St. Paul Saints (32)	65.00
1997	Best St. Petersburg Devil Rays (30)	4.00
1997	Best St. Pete Devil Rays update (30)	12.00
1997	Best Stockton Ports (30)	6.00
1997	Best Syracuse Chiefs (30)	9.00
1997	Best Tacoma Rainiers (30)	10.00
1997	Best Tampa Yankees (33)	5.00
1997	Best Texas League Prospects (31)	10.00
1997	Best Toledo Mud Hens (36)	7.00
1997	Best Trenton Thunder (30)	6.00
1997	Best Tucson Toros (29)	7.50
1997	Jones Photo Tucson Toros (5)	80.00
1997	Team Tulsa Drillers (30)	8.00
1997	GS Tyler Wildcatters (24)	4.00
1997	Best Vancouver Canadians (30)	8.00
1997	Best Vermont Expos (30)	6.00
1997	Best Vero Beach Dodgers (30)	17.50
1997	GS Visalia Oaks (30)	16.00
1997	Team Watertown Indians (36)	9.00
1997	Best West Michigan Whitecaps (30)	7.00
1997	Best Wichita Wranglers (30)	6.00
1997	Best Williamsport Cubs (29)	6.00
1997	Best Wilmington Blue Rocks (30)	9.00
1997	Best Wisconsin Timber Rattlers (29)	6.00
1997	GS Yakima Bears (36)	7.00

1998 Best Autographs

Brian Rose

The extent of the checklist for this issue, and the manner of its distribution are unknown. Like similar Best autograph cards from 1996-97, they feature game-action photos vignetted in white on front. A minor league team logo is at top-left, and the Best logo is at bottom-right. Backs

have a photo of a Best-logoed glove with a statement of authenticity. Best and Minor League licensing logos are at bottom. The cards carry a 1998 copyright date.

		MT
Common Player:		2.00
(1)	Kris Benson	3.00
(3)	Dermal Brown	2.00
(5)	Lorenzo de la Cruz	2.00
(6)	Adam Eaton	2.00
(7)	Chad Green	2.00
(9)	Chad Hermansen	2.00
(10)	Mark Johnson	2.00
(11)	Billy Koch	3.00
(13)	Joe Lawrence	2.00
(14)	Braden Looper	3.00
(15)	Gil Meche	4.50
(17)	Abraham Nunez	4.50
(18)	Russ Ortiz	4.50
(19)	Carl Pavano	7.00
(21)	Danny Peoples	3.00
(23)	Britt Reames	2.00
(25)	Brian Rose	2.00
(27)	Bubba Trammell	2.00
(29)	Jake Westbrook	2.00
(31)	Enrique Wilson	4.50
(33)	A.J. Zapp	2.00

1998 Best Premium Preview Sean Casey Super

This 5" x 7" version of Casey's 1997 Best Premium Preview card was created as a giveaway for use at January 9-11 Tuff Stuff Classic card show. The front has a large color pose of Casey against a black-and-white ghost-image portrait photo. Tuff Stuff and Best logos are in the upper corners. On back is a large show logo, Casey biographical data and a serial number from within an edition of 1,000.

	MT
Sean Casey	6.00

1998 Team Best Player of the Year Promos

PAUL KONERKO

This promo set was issued to preview Team Best's first 1998 minor league singles issue - Player of the Year. The promos feature the base card and four of the set's inserts. Fronts are nearly identical to the issued versions, except for the use of "Best" rather than "Team Best" logos. Promo card backs have the PoY logo in color at center. The unnumbered promo cards are checklisted here alphabetically.

		MT
Complete Set (5):		10.00
Common Player:		1.00
(1)	Todd Helton (Contender)	3.00
(2)	Paul Konerko (Player of the Year)	2.00
(3)	Mark Kotsay (Diamond Best)	2.00
(4)	Darnell McDonald (Base card.)	1.00
(5)	Kerry Wood (Possibilities)	3.00

1998 Team Best Player of the Year

The first product under the firm's new Team Best logo was this foil-pack series of 50 minor leaguers, many of whom began making their names in the big leagues in 1998. Fronts feature color action photos with tan borders. Manufacturer and minor league team logos appear in the upper corners. On back are a postage-stamp size repeat of the head portion of the player photo at upper-left. To the right are personal data. At lower-left are

1997 season stats, with career highlights to the right. Cards were sold in six-card packs.

		MT
Complete Set (50):		4.00
Common Player:		.05
Wax Pack (6):		1.50
Wax Box (18):		20.00
1	Ryan Anderson	.25
2	Lorenzo Barcelo	.05
3	Hiram Bocachica	.05
4	David Borkowski	.05
5	Russ Branyan	.10
6	Dermal Brown	.05
7	Brent Butler	.05
8	Enrique Calero	.05
9	Bruce Chen	.05
10	Ryan Christenson	.05
11	Pat Cline	.05
12	Scott Elarton	.05
13	Juan Encarnacion	.25
14	Mark Fischer	.05
15	Troy Glaus	2.00
16	Alex Hernandez	.05
17	Norm Hutchins	.05
18	Geoff Jenkins	.25
19	Adam Kennedy	.10
20	Corey Koskie	.05
21	Mark Kotsay	.15
22	Ricky Ledee	.05
23	Carlos Lee	.15
24	Corey Lee	.05
25	Mike Lowell	.50
26	T.R. Marcinczyk	.05
27	Willie Martinez	.05
28	Darnell McDonald	.05
29	Jackson Melian	.05
30	Chad Meyers	.05
31	Ryan Minor	.05
32	Kenderick Moore	.05
33	Julio Moreno	.05
34	Rod Myers	.05
35	Abraham Nunez	.25
36	Vladimir Nunez	.05
37	Ramon Ortiz	.05
38	Chan Perry	.05
39	Ben Petrick	.05
40	Angel Ramirez	.05
41	Grant Roberts	.05
42	Alex Sanchez	.05
43	Jared Sandberg	.05
44	Scott Schoeneweis	.05
45	Steve Shoemaker	.05
46	Matt White	.05
47	Paul Wilder	.05
48	Preston Wilson	.50
49	Kevin Witt	.05
50	Jay Yennaco	.05

1998 Team Best Player of the Year Autographs

Braden Looper

These autographed cards of top prospects were a 1:19 insert in Team Best Player of the Year hobby packs. Fronts have action photos with a ghost-image background. The player name is in a baseball bat at bottom. Backs have a statement of authenticity.

		MT
Complete Set (21):		50.00
Common Player:		3.00
(1)	Kris Benson	4.00
(2)	Dermal Brown	3.00
(3)	Eric Chavez	5.00
(4)	Adam Eaton	3.00
(5)	Chad Green	3.00
(6)	Seth Greisinger	3.00
(7)	Ben Grieve	4.00
(8)	Chad Hermansen	4.50
(9)	Billy Koch	3.00
(10)	Braden Looper	3.00
(11)	Gil Meche	4.50
(12)	Eric Milton	3.00
(13)	John Patterson	3.00
(14)	Carl Pavano	7.00
(15)	Danny Peoples	3.00
(16)	Sidney Ponson	4.50
(17)	Brian Rose	3.00
(18)	Jake Westbrook	3.00
(19)	Paul Wilder	3.00
(20)	Kerry Wood	25.00
(21)	A.J. Zapp	3.00

1998 Team Best Player of the Year Contenders

BEN GRIEVE

Candidates for minor league player of the year are featured in this scarce insert set. Six of the players are pictured in horizontal-format cards which have three photos on front showing the player in different uniforms on his road to the majors. Four of the players also have a vertical-format card with a single photo on front. Each card is serially numbered on the back from within an edition of 400 each. The background on back is a sepia version of the front photo and there is a PoY stamp logo at center. Stated odds of finding a Contender card are one per 90 packs.

		MT
Complete Set (10):		35.00
Common Player:		3.00
1	Derrick Gibson	3.00
2	Ben Grieve	3.00
3	Ben Grieve (Vertical)	3.00
4	Todd Helton	12.50
5	Todd Helton (Vertical)	12.50
6	Mark Kotsay	3.00
7	Mark Kotsay (Vertical)	3.00
8	Carl Pavano	7.50
9	Brian Rose	3.00
10	Brian Rose (Vertical)	3.00

1998 Team Best Player of the Year Young Guns

BEN GRIEVE

3 of 10

This is a retail-only insert, with each card individually serial numbered on back to a limit of 100. Cards share the photos used on the hobby-only Contenders insert set (edition of 400), except the Young Guns cards have a white background instead of the mottled brown of the Contenders. Insert ratio was reported at one per 90 packs on average.

		MT
Complete Set (10):		50.00
Common Player:		4.00
1	Derrick Gibson	4.00
2	Ben Grieve	5.00
3	Ben Grieve (Vertical)	5.00
4	Todd Helton	20.00
5	Todd Helton (Vertical)	20.00
6	Mark Kotsay	4.00
7	Mark Kotsay (Vertical)	4.00
8	Carl Pavano	7.50
9	Brian Rose	4.00
10	Brian Rose (Vertical)	4.00

1998 Team Best Diamond Best

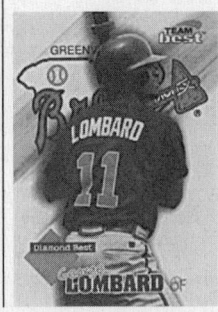

LOMBARD

Designated as Player of the Year, former Dodgers farmhand Paul Konerko was honored with a six-card insert issue. Found at the average rate of just one per two boxes (36 packs), the Konerko cards trace his rise through the minor leagues. Fronts have borderless photos and team logos of his minor league stops. Backs detail each season's stats and highlights on a background of a sepia version of the front photo. Autographed

	MT
Complete Set (20):	12.00
Common Player:	1.00

Red, white and blue typography and a team logo in the background mark this insert series. Backs have a smaller version of the front photo, biographical data, 1997 stats and appropriate logos. Odds of pulling a Diamond Best card are stated as one per 19 packs.

		MT
Complete Set (20):		12.00
Common Player:		1.00
1	Darnell McDonald	1.00
2	Adrian Beltre	2.00
3	Derrick Gibson	1.00
4	Mark Kotsay	1.00
5	Braden Looper	1.00
6	Carl Pavano	1.50
7	Brian Rose	1.00
8	Jared Sandberg	1.00
9	Vernon Wells	2.00
10	Sean Casey	2.50
11	Rick Ankiel	1.00
12	Michael Barrett	1.00
13	Matt Clement	1.50
14	J.D. Drew	2.50
15	Bobby Estalella	1.00
16	Troy Glaus	3.00
17	Alex Gonzalez	1.00
18	George Lombard	1.00
19	Mike Lowell	1.50
20	Dernell Stenson	1.00

1998 Team Best Diamond Best Autographs

BENSON

Autographs of eight top prospects are featured on Diamond Best style inserts in this chase card set. Actual odds of finding one of the autographed cards is one in 180 packs. Konerko's and Patterson's cards were never released. Each card is numbered within an edition of 250.

		MT
Complete Set (8):		45.00
Common Player:		2.00
1	Kris Benson	4.00
2	Dermal Brown	2.00
3	Eric Chavez	4.00
4	Todd Helton	20.00
5	Paul Konerko (Never released.)	.00
6	John Patterson (Never released.)	.00
7	Braden Looper	2.00
8	Juan Melo	2.00
9	Kerry Wood	20.00
10	A.J. Zapp	2.00

1998 Team Best Paul Konerko

PAUL KONERKO

Designated as Player of the Year, former Dodgers farmhand Paul Konerko was honored with a six-card insert issue. Found at the average rate of just one per two boxes (36 packs), the Konerko cards trace his rise through the minor leagues. Fronts have borderless photos and team logos of his minor league stops. Backs detail each season's stats and highlights on a background of a sepia version of the front photo. Autographed

versions of each card, with a statement of authenticity on the back, we released as pack inserts and in a mail-in redemption offer.

		MT
Complete Set (6):		12.00
Common Card:		2.00
Autographed:		4.00
1	Paul Konerko (Three-photo horizontal.)	2.00
2	Paul Konerko (San Bernardino Stampede)	2.00
3	Paul Konerko (San Antonio Missions)	2.00
4	Paul Konerko (Albuquerque Dukes)	2.00
5	Paul Konerko (Yakima Bears)	2.00
6	Paul Konerko (PoY Stamp)	2.00

1998 Team Best Possibilities

Kerry Wood

Two players each are featured in this insert card series. Both fronts and backs have action player photos set against a swirling blue background. Team and licensor logos are part of the design as well. Odds to pull this insert were stated as one per 19 packs.

		MT
Complete Set (5):		5.00
Common Player:		.75
1	Kris Benson, Mark Kotsay	1.00
2	Braden Looper, Sean Casey	1.00
3	Brian Rose, Dermal Brown	.75
4	Matt White, Ben Grieve	.75
5	Kerry Wood, Todd Helton	4.00

1998 Team Best Signature Series Promos

J.D. DREW

To introduce its Signature Series of minor league cards, Team Best created a group of promo cards featuring top players. The promo cards have fronts which are identical to the regular-issue versions. Backs have a blue background with a large Signature Series logo at center and a notice at bottom: "Promotional Purposes Only."

		MT
Complete Set (5):		5.00
Common Player:		.75
(1)	Rich Ankiel (Diamond Best)	.75
(2)	Bruce Chen (Base set.)	.75
(3)	J.D. Drew (#1 Pick)	2.00
(4)	Troy Glaus (#1 Pick)	2.50
(5)	Ryan Minor (Cornerstone)	.75

1998 Team Best Signature Series

In many ways Team Best's Signature Series minor league issue is a continuation of the company's Player of the Year series issued earlier in the year. For exam-

Julio Ramirez

ple, the base cards in the Signature Series retain the design and continue the card numbering of the earlier series. The Signature Series debuted in September, in six-card foil packs. Half a dozen insert sets were included among the base cards.

	MT
Complete Set (50):	5.00
Common Player:	.05
Wax Pack (6):	2.25
Wax Box (18):	30.00
51 Matt Anderson	.10
52 Rich Ankiel	.05
53 Tony Armas	.10
54 John Barnes	.05
55 Robbie Bell	.05
56 Kris Benson	.20
57 Lance Berkman	.50
58 Russell Branyan	.10
59 Brent Butler	.05
60 Troy Cameron	.05
61 Eric Chavez	.50
62 Bruce Chen	.05
63 Matt Clement	.50
64 Ben Davis	.05
65 J.D. Drew	1.00
66 Tim Drew	.05
67 Derrick Gibson	.05
68 Troy Glaus	2.00
69 Chad Hermansen	.05
70 Ramon Hernandez	.05
71 Gabe Kapler	.25
72 Mike Kinkade	.05
73 Scott Krause	.05
74 Mike Lowell	.50
75 Willie Martinez	.05
76 Donzell McDonald	.05
77 Gil Meche	.15
78 Juan Melo	.05
79 Wade Miller	.10
80 Ryan Minor	.05
81 Abraham Nunez	.10
82 Pablo Ozuna	.05
83 John Patterson	.05
84 Josh Paul	.05
85 Ben Petrick	.05
86 Calvin Pickering	.05
87 Placido Polanco	.10
88 Aramis Ramirez	.25
89 Julio Ramirez	.05
90 Luis Rivas	.05
91 Luis Rivera	.05
92 Ruben Rivera	.05
93 Grant Roberts	.05
94 Jimmy Rollins	.50
95 Bobby Seay	.05
96 Jason Standridge	.05
97 Dernell Stenson	.05
98 Vernon Wells	.50
99 Matt White	.10
100 Ed Yarnall	.05
--- Special Offer Card, Kerry Wood Autograph	.05
--- Special Offer Card, Team Best Promos	.05
--- Special Offer Card - Sig. Series Promos	.05

1998 Team Best Signature Series Autographs

Glenn Davis

This series of authentically autographed insert cards was inserted at the rate of about five per box of TB Signature Series. Cards feature

color photos on a beige pinstriped background. Backs repeat the background and have a large baseball with an authenticity notice overprinted. The unnumbered cards are listed here alphabetically. Announced autographed cards of Barrett, Colon, Teut and Westbrook were received too late to be inserted.

	MT
Complete Set (53):	50.00
Common Player:	1.00
(1) John Bale	1.00
(2) Kevin Barker	1.00
(3) Michael Barrett Not Issued	.00
(4) Todd Belitz	1.00
(5) Aaron Bond	1.00
(6) A.J. Burnett	2.00
(7) Brent Butler	1.00
(8) Buddy Carlyle	1.00
(9) Ramon Castro	1.00
(10) Frank Catalanotto	2.00
(11) Giuseppe Chiaramonte	1.00
(12) Bartolo Colon Not Issued	.00
(13) Alex Cora	1.00
(14) Francisco Cordero	1.00
(15) David Cortes	1.00
(16) Dean Crow	1.00
(17) Doug Davis	1.00
(18) Glenn Davis	1.00
(19) Travis Dawkins	3.00
(20) Matt DeWitt	1.00
(21) Octavio Dotel	1.00
(22) Mike Duvall	1.00
(23) Troy Glaus	10.00
(24) Geoff Goetz	1.00
(25) Jason Grilli	1.00
(26) Al Hawkins	1.00
(27) Bryan Hebson	1.00
(28) Alex Hernandez	1.00
(29) Doug Johnston	1.00
(30) Juan LeBron	1.00
(31) John Leroy	1.00
(32) Randi Mallard	1.00
(33) Sam Marsonek	1.00
(34) Ramon Martinez	1.00
(35) Ruben Mateo	2.00
(36) Joe Mays	2.00
(37) David Melendez	1.00
(38) Justin Miller	1.00
(39) Ryan Minor	1.00
(40) Warren Morris	2.00
(41) Pablo Ozuna	1.00
(42) Brian Passini	1.00
(43) Santiago Perez	1.00
(44) Marc Pisciotta	1.00
(45) Rob Ramsey	1.00
(46) Grant Roberts	1.00
(47) John Roskos	1.00
(48) Luis de los Santos	1.00
(49) Brian Simmons	1.00
(50) Reggie Taylor	2.00
(51) Nathan Teut Not Issued	.00
(52) Andy Thompson	1.00
(53) Chris Tynan	1.00
(54) Jose Vidro	4.00
(55) Jayson Werth	1.00
(56) Jake Westbrook Not Issued	.00
(57) Ed Yarnall	1.00

1998 Team Best Signature Series Autographed Super

Each 10-box case of late-season Team Best Signature Series included one of 10 authentically autographed large-format (4" x 6") case-topper cards. Fronts have Best and team logos at top and a silver-foil Auto Best logo at bottom. Also on front is a serial number from within an edition of 500 of each player. Backs have a large notice of authenticity. Because the cards share the 1997 Best format and are dated 1997, the complete listing is found there.

(See 1997 Best Autographed Supers.)

1998 Team Best Signature Series Best Bets

This retail-exclusive insert set features the cream of the 1998 minor league crop. Fronts have player action photos separated from a white background by a colorful aura. A team logo appears at bottom. Backs repeat a close-up of the photo and have 1997 stats, biographical data and a few words about the player. The Best Bet cards use the same photos found on the hobby-only Cornerstone inserts. Best Bets were inserted at an advertised rate of one per 90 packs.

	MT
Complete Set (12):	40.00
Common Player:	2.00
(1) Matt Anderson	2.00
(2) Lance Berkman	4.00
(3) Eric Chavez	6.00
(4) Bruce Chen	2.00
(5) Matt Clement	6.00
(6) J.D. Drew	10.00
(7) Troy Glaus	12.50
(8) George Lombard	2.00
(9) Ryan Minor	2.00
(10) Dernell Stenson	2.00
(11) Jayson Werth	2.00
(12) Ed Yarnall	2.00

1998 Team Best Signature Series Cornerstone

This hobby-exclusive insert set features the cream of the 1998 minor league top and many of tomorrow's big league stars. Fronts have player action photos separated from a checkered background by a colored aura. A team logo also appears. Backs repeat the photo in a close-up format and have 1997 stats, biographical data and a few words about the player. The Best Bet cards use the same photos as those found on the Cornerstone insert issue. Insertion rate was reported as one per 90 packs. The cards are listed here in alphabetical order.

	MT
Complete Set (12):	40.00
Common Player:	2.00
(1) Matt Anderson	2.00
(2) Lance Berkman	4.00
(3) Eric Chavez	6.00
(4) Bruce Chen	2.00
(5) Matt Clement	6.00
(6) J.D. Drew	10.00
(7) Troy Glaus	12.50
(8) George Lombard	2.00
(9) Ryan Minor	2.00
(10) Dernell Stenson	2.00
(11) Jayson Werth	2.00
(12) Ed Yarnall	2.00

1998 Team Best Signature Series Diamond Best

Another insert series which was continued from Team Best's Player of the Year series is Dia-

mond Best. Cards in the Signature Series are numbered contiguously from the earlier series and have the same basic design of an action photo on a white background with a large minor league team logo. Backs have a smaller version of the front photo, a bit of personal data and a few words about the player. Diamond Best inserts are found on average of about one per 19 packs (just under one per box).

	MT
Complete Set (10):	15.00
Common Player:	1.50
11 Rich Ankiel	1.00
12 Michael Barrett	1.00
13 Matt Clement	1.50
14 J.D. Drew	5.00
15 Bobby Estalella	1.00
16 Troy Glaus	7.50
17 Alex Gonzalez	1.00
18 George Lombard	1.00
19 Mike Lowell	2.00
20 Dernell Stenson	1.00

1998 Team Best Signature Series Full Count Autographs

While these authentically autographed cards were packaged with 1998 Team Best Signature Series at the announced rate of one per 19 hobby packs, they share a design and copyright date with the base cards of 1997 Best and were probably originally intended for release in those products.

(See 1997 Best Full Count Autographs.)

1998 Team Best Signature Series Kerry Wood Autograph

A special-offer card found in Signature Series packs allowed collectors to mail in for a Kerry Wood autographed card in a format unique to the series. Front has an action photo on a background of vertically stretched and colorized photos. Back repeats the back-

ground and has a statement of authenticity. Issue price for the card was $49.95.

	MT
Kerry Wood/Auto.	25.00
Kerry Wood (Offer card.)	.50

1998 Team Best Signature Series #1 Pick

This special series of chase cards was issued as a box-topper, one per 18-pack box. Card fronts feature both portrait and action photos. In a baseball at lower-right is a "#1 PICK" gold hologram. Backs have individual silver-foil serial numbers from within an edition of 900 each.

	MT
Complete Set (42):	75.00
Common Player:	1.00
1 Aaron Akin	1.00
2 Matt Anderson	1.50
3 Ryan Anderson	2.00
4 Shane Arthurs	1.00
5 Michael Barrett	1.50
6 Kris Benson	2.00
7 Lance Berkman	3.00
8 Rocky Biddle	1.00
9 Ryan Bradley	1.00
10 Dermal Brown	1.00
11 Troy Cameron	1.00
12 Brett Caradonna	1.00
13 Eric Chavez	3.00
14 Mike Cuddyer	1.50
15 John Curtice	1.00
16 Glenn Davis	1.00
17 J.J. Davis	1.00
18 Jason Dellaero	1.00
19 J.D. Drew	10.00
20 Tim Drew	1.00
21 Brian DuBose	1.00
22 Mark Fischer	1.00
23 Troy Glaus	12.00
24 Geoff Goetz	1.00
25 Jason Grilli	1.00
26 Nathan Haynes	1.00
27 Bryan Hebson	1.00
28 Geoff Jenkins	2.00
29 Adam Kennedy	2.00
30 Billy Koch	1.00
31 Matt LeCroy	1.00
32 Mark Mangum	1.00
33 Darnell McDonald	1.00
34 Kevin Nicholson	1.00
35 John Patterson	1.00
36 Danny Peoples	1.00
37 Dan Reichert	1.00
38 Jason Romano	1.00
39 Jason Standridge	1.00
40 Vernon Wells	4.00
41 Jayson Werth	1.00
42 Matt White	1.00

1998 Upper Deck SP Prospects

The best of the minor league class of 1997 are featured in this issue which marks Upper Deck's return to the minor league card market after a two-year layoff. All players, even the relatively few who have had major league experience,

are featured in their minor league uniforms in the base set of 126 cards. There are three 30-card insert sets: Destination the Show (1:90 packs), Signature Cards (1:16) and Small Town Heroes (1:5). At the high end of the chase spectrum, a President's Edition parallel set of the regular, DS and STH cards was produced in an edition of just 10 cards each. Retail price at issue was $4.39 for an eight-card pack. Fronts are printed on a foiled background with a textured silver-foil border; team and SP logos are in the bottom corners. Backs are conventionally printed with another color photo and up to two years of stats. The first 10 cards in the set are a series of Top 10 prospects which have checklist backs. Production was reported to be 1,000 hobby-only cases.

	MT
Complete Set (126):	7.50
Common Player:	.05
Wax Box:	25.00
1 Travis Lee (Top 10 Prospects)	.50
2 Paul Konerko (Top 10 Prospects)	.50
3 Ben Grieve (Top 10 Prospects)	.25
4 Kerry Wood (Top 10 Prospects)	1.00
5 Miguel Tejada (Top 10 Prospects)	.50
6 Juan Encarnacion (Top 10 Prospects)	.10
7 Jackson Melian (Top 10 Prospects)	.05
8 Chad Hermansen (Top 10 Prospects)	.05
9 Aramis Ramirez (Top 10 Prospects)	.10
10 Russell Branyan (Top 10 Prospects)	.05
11 Norm Hutchins	.05
12 Jarrod Washburn	.15
13 Larry Barnes	.05
14 Scott Schoeneweis	.05
15 Travis Lee	1.00
16 Mike Stoner	.05
17 Nick Bierbrodt	.05
18 Vladimir Nunez	.05
19 Wes Helms	.05
20 Jason Marquis	.15
21 George Lombard	.05
22 Bruce Chen	.05
23 Rob Bell	.05
24 Adam Johnson	.05
25 Ryan Minor	.05
26 Sidney Ponson	.10
27 Calvin Pickering	.05
28 Donnie Sadler	.15
29 Cole Liniak	.05
30 Carl Pavano	.25
31 Kerry Wood	2.00
32 Pat Cline	.05
33 Jason Maxwell	.05
34 Jason Dellaero	.05
35 Mike Caruso	.05
36 Jeff Liefer	.05
37 Brian Simmons	.05
38 Carlos Lee	.25
39 Jeff Inglin	.05
40 Darron Ingram	.05
41 Justin Towle	.05
42 Pat Watkins	.05
43 Richie Sexson	.25
44 Danny Peoples	.05
45 Russell Branyan	.10
46 Scott Morgan	.05
47 Mike Glavine	.05
48 Willie Martinez	.05
49 Jake Westbrook	.05
50 Derrick Gibson	.05
51 Ben Petrick	.05
52 Juan Encarnacion	.45
53 Seth Greisinger	.05
54 Robert Fick	.05
55 Dave Borkowski	.05
56 Jesse Ibarra	.05
57 Nate Rolison	.05
58 Jaime Jones	.05
59 Aaron Akin	.05
60 Alex Gonzalez	.05
61 Richard Hidalgo	.25
62 Scott Elarton	.05
63 Daryle Ward	.05
64 Jeremy Giambi	.25
65 Dermal Brown	.05
66 Enrique Calero	.05
67 Glenn Davis	.05
68 Adrian Beltre	.75
69 Alex Cora	.05
70 Paul Konerko	.50
71 Mike Kincade	.05
72 Danny Klassen	.05
73 Chad Green	.05
74 Kevin Barker	.05
75 David Ortiz	1.00
76 Jacque Jones	.50

#	Player	
77	Luis Rivas	.05
78	Hiram Bocachica	.05
79	Javier Vazquez	.50
80	Brad Fullmer	.10
81	Preston Wilson	.60
82	Octavio Dotel	.05
83	Fletcher Bates	.05
84	Grant Roberts	.05
85	Jackson Melian	.05
86	Katsuhiro Maeda	.05
87	Ricky Ledee	.05
88	Eric Milton	.15
89	Eric Chavez	.50
90	Ben Grieve	.25
91	Miguel Tejada	.50
92	A.J. Hinch	.05
93	Ramon Hernandez	.10
94	Chris Enochs	.05
95	Marlon Anderson	.30
96	Reggie Taylor	.05
97	Steve Carver	.05
98	Ron Wright	.05
99	Kris Benson	.15
100	Chad Hermansen	.05
101	Aramis Ramirez	.25
102	Adam Kennedy	.20
103	Braden Looper	.05
104	Cliff Politte	.05
105	Brent Butler	.05
106	Juan Melo	.05
107	Ben Davis	.05
108	Kevin Nicholson	.05
109	Gary Matthews Jr.	.05
110	Matt Clement	.50
111	Jason Brester	.05
112	Joe Fontenot	.05
113	Darin Blood	.05
114	Greg Wooten	.05
115	Jeff Farnsworth	.05
116	Robert Luce	.05
117	Rolando Arrojo	.20
118	Doug Johnson	.05
119	James Manias	.05
120	Alex Sanchez	.05
121	Warren Morris	.05
122	Ruben Mateo	.25
123	Corey Lee	.05
124	Roy Halladay	.75
125	Kevin Witt	.05
126	Tom Evans	.05

1998 Upper Deck SP Prospects President's Edition

Among the rarest minor league cards of the modern era are the foiled and die-cut version of SP Top Prospects known as the President's Edition. The set parallels the 126 cards of the base issue, plus the 30-card Destination the Show and Small Town Heroes inserts. Only 10 cards each exist in the parallel version.

	MT
Common Player:	10.00

(President's Edition cards valued at 10X regular versions.)

1998 Upper Deck SP Prospects Autographs

Authentically autographed cards of some of the minor leagues' top prospects are featured in this insert set found on average of once per 16 packs. The autograph cards have a player photo vignetted in a white panel at center, with his signature below. Backs have a printed certificate of authenticity. Cards of Wes Helms, Jackson Melian and David Ortiz, originally announced on UD's checklist, were never issued.

		MT
	Complete Set (26):	50.00
	Common Player:	2.00
AB	Adrian Beltre	15.00
KB	Kris Benson	3.00
RB	Russell Branyan	2.00
BB	Brent Butler	2.00
EC	Eric Chavez	6.00
RF	Robert Fick	2.00
DG	Derrick Gibson	2.00
BG	Ben Grieve	2.00
CH	Chad Hermansen	2.00
RH	Ramon Hernandez	2.00
JJ	Jacque Jones	6.00
PK	Paul Konerko	6.00
RL	Ricky Ledee	2.00
CL	Corey Lee	2.00
TL	Travis Lee	6.00
KM	Katsuhiro Maeda	2.00
GM	Gary Matthews Jr.	2.00
JMO	Juan Melo	2.00
SM	Scott Morgan	2.00
WM	Warren Morris	2.00
DP	Danny Peoples	2.00
GR	Grant Roberts	2.00
MT	Miguel Tejada	25.00
JT	Justin Towle	2.00
DW	Daryle Ward	2.00
KW	Kerry Wood	30.00

1998 Upper Deck SP Prospects Destination The Show

Thirty top minor leaguers who are likely to begin major leagues careers in 1998 are featured in this insert set. The chase cards are seeded on average of one per 90 packs.

		MT
	Complete Set (30):	75.00
	Common Player:	3.00
DS1	Travis Lee	6.00
DS2	Eric Chavez	4.50
DS3	Ramon Hernandez	3.00
DS4	Daryle Ward	3.00
DS5	Jackson Melian	3.00
DS6	Ben Grieve	3.50
DS7	Brent Butler	3.00
DS8	Rolando Arrojo	4.50
DS9	Ryan Minor	3.00
DS10	Adrian Beltre	7.50
DS11	Sidney Ponson	4.50
DS12	Gary Matthews Jr.	3.00
DS13	Ron Wright	3.00
DS14	Warren Morris	3.00
DS15	Russell Branyan	3.00
DS16	Paul Konerko	6.00
DS17	Mike Caruso	3.00
DS18	Jacque Jones	6.00
DS19	Preston Wilson	4.50
DS20	Chad Hermansen	3.00
DS21	Aramis Ramirez	3.00
DS22	Kerry Wood	10.00
DS23	Corey Lee	3.00
DS24	Carl Pavano	3.00
DS25	Kris Benson	3.00
DS26	Derrick Gibson	3.00
DS27	Mike Stoner	3.00
DS28	Juan Melo	3.00
DS29	Mike Kinkade	3.00
DS30	Alex Gonzalez	3.00

1998 Upper Deck SP Prospects Small Town Heroes

The small towns across America which are the roots of many pro ballplayers are featured in this chase set from Upper Deck's 1998 SP Top Prospects issue. The series focuses for the most part on players who are early in their minor league careers. These cards are inserted at an average rate of one per five packs.

		MT
	Complete Set (30):	35.00
	Common Player:	1.00
H1	Travis Lee	4.00
H2	Eric Chavez	2.50
H3	Mike Caruso	1.00
H4	Adrian Beltre	4.00
H5	Jackson Melian	1.00
H6	Adam Johnson	1.00
H7	Carlos Lee	2.00
H8	Kris Benson	1.50
H9	Jacque Jones	3.00
H10	Russell Branyan	1.00
H11	John Patterson	1.00
H12	Ryan Minor	1.00
H13	Dermal Brown	1.00
H14	Mike Stoner	1.00
H15	Derrick Gibson	1.00
H16	Ben Davis	1.00
H17	Kevin Witt	1.00
H18	Justin Towle	1.00
H19	Doug Johnson	1.00
H20	Chad Hermansen	1.00
H21	Sidney Ponson	2.00
H22	Marlon Anderson	1.50
H23	Kerry Wood	5.00
H24	Alex Gonzalez	1.00
H25	Carl Pavano	2.50
H26	A.J. Hinch	1.00
H27	Juan Melo	1.00
H28	Dave Borkowski	1.00
H29	Jake Westbrook	1.00
H30	Daryle Ward	1.00

1998 Minor League Team Sets

Besides Best (under the Multi-Ad Sports logo), which maintained the lion's share of the team-set market, several other companies - notably Grandstand (GS), Choice Marketing, Blueline Communications (BL) and Warning Track Cards (WTC) - also produced sets for more than one team.

	MT
217 Team Sets and Variations	8.00
1998 MA AA All-Star Game (60)	9.00
1998 MA AA All-Star Berks Packing (56)	12.00
1998 Team Aberdeen Pheasants (25)	4.00
1998 WTC Adirondack Lumberjacks (25)	4.00
1998 MA Akron Aeros (30)	7.00
1998 WTC Albany-Colonie Diamond Dogs (25)	4.00
1998 GS Albuquerque Dukes (30)	7.00
1998 WTC Allentown (25)	4.00
1998 BL Appalachian League Top Prospects (31)	11.00
1998 Arizona Fall League (25)	15.00
1998 Arizona Fall League - Gold (25)	35.00
1998 MA Arkansas Travelers (30)	8.00
1998 Team Arkansas Travelers Highlights (10)	25.00
1998 Team Arkansas Travelers Update (1)	12.00
1998 MA Asheville Tourists (30)	6.00
1998 Team Atlantic City Surf (31)	4.00
1998 Team Auburn Doubledays (34)	50.00
1998 MA Augusta Greenjackets (30)	6.00
1998 MA Beloit Snappers (30)	11.00
1998 Team Billings Mustangs (38)	95.00
1998 BL Binghamton Mets (30)	8.00
1998 TM Binghamton Mets "Jumbo" (12)	20.00
1998 GS Birmingham Barons (30)	7.00
1998 BL Bluefield Orioles (32)	6.00
1998 GS Boise Hawks (34)	6.00
1998 MA Bowie Baysox (30)	10.00
1998 Team Bowie Nationals (31)	7.00
1998 MA Bridgeport Bluefish (30)	4.00
1998 BL Bristol White Sox (30)	7.00
1998 GS Buffalo Bisons (30)	8.00
1998 MA Burlington Bees (30)	9.00
1998 GS Butte Copper Kings (34)	7.00
1998 MA Cape Fear Crocs (30)	7.00
1998 MA Capital City Bombers (30)	20.00
1998 MA C.C. Bombers W/Fox 57 Ads (30)	22.00
1998 Choice Carolina League All-Stars (42)	12.00
1998 BL Carolina League Top Prospects (33)	10.00
1998 MA Carolina Mudcats (30)	6.00
1998 Team Cedar Rapids Kernels (31)	6.00
1998 MA Charleston Alley Cats (31)	6.00
1998 GS Charleston RiverDogs (30)	7.00
1998 BL Charlotte Knights (30)	7.00
1998 MA Charlotte Rangers (30)	15.00
1998 GS Chattanooga Lookouts (30)	7.00
1998 GS Chattanooga W/Slush Puppy Ads (31)	30.00
1998 MA Clearwater Phillies (30)	7.00
1998 MA Clearwater Phillies Update (30)	15.00
1998 GS Clinton LumberKings (30)	6.00
1998 Team Colorado Springs Sky Sox (31)	7.00
1998 MA Columbus Clippers (30)	8.00
1998 Police Columbus Clippers (25)	8.00
1998 MA Columbus RedStixx (30)	12.00
1998 BL Danville Braves (31)	24.00
1998 BL Danville 97s (31)	9.00
1998 GS Daytona Cubs (21)	9.00
1998 Team Delaware Stars (30)	12.00
1998 Team Delmarva Rockfish (32)	7.00
1998 MA Delmarva Shorebirds (30)	10.00
1998 GS Duluth-Superior Dukes (27)	5.00
1998 Team Dunedin Blue Jays (33)	8.00
1998 Team Dunedin Blue Jays stickers (24)	12.00
1998 Team Durham Bulls (30)	8.00
1998 MA Eastern League Top Prospects (30)	12.00
1998 Edmonton Trappers (XX)	45.00
1998 GS El Paso Diablos (29)	6.00
1998 MA Erie Seawolves (30)	6.00
1998 GS Eugene Emeralds (32)	12.50
1998 GS Everett Aquasox (30)	6.00
1998 MA Fargo-Moorhead RedHawks (30)	4.00
1998 MA Frederick Keys (30)	7.00
1998 Team Frederick Regiment (32)	7.00
1998 GS Fresno Grizzlies (30)	9.00
1998 Team Ft. Myers Miracle (32)	7.00
1998 BL Ft. Wayne Wizards (30)	7.00
1998 GS Grays Harbor Gulls (30)	4.00
1998 GS Great Falls Dodgers (31)	8.00
1998 MA Greensboro Bats (30)	7.00
1998 GS Greenville Braves (28)	10.00
1998 MA Hagerstown Suns (30)	11.00
1998 MA Harrisburg Senators (30)	9.00
1998 MA Harris. Senators W/WINK 104 Ad (30)	12.00
1998 MA Helena Brewers (33)	8.00
1998 MA Hickory Crawdads (30)	7.00
1998 Team Hickory Crawdads Update (30)	8.00
1998 GS High Desert Mavericks (30)	11.00
1998 Team Hudson Valley Renegades (30)	11.00
1998 Team Huntsville Stars (26)	9.00
1998 Team Huntsville Stars Uncut Sheet	12.00
1998 BL Indianapolis Indians (36)	6.00
1998 BL Iowa Cubs (30)	12.00
1998 MA Jackson Generals (28)	7.00
1998 MA Jacksonville Suns (28)	7.00
1998 Team Johnson City Cardinals (36)	8.00
1998 WTC Johnstown Johnnies (25)	4.00
1998 BL Jupiter Hammerheads (30)	8.00
1998 Team Kane County Cougars (32)	8.00
1998 Team Kane County Cougars, Connie's (32)	12.00
1998 BL Kinston Indians (30)	6.00
1998 BL Kissimmee Cobras (30)	7.00
1998 GS Knoxville Smokies (27)	6.00
1998 GS Lafayette Leopards (30)	4.00
1998 GS Lake Elsinore Storm (30)	7.00
1998 MA Lakeland Tigers (30)	9.00
1998 GS Lancaster JetHawks (30)	7.00
1998 BL Lansing Lugnuts (31)	7.00
1998 MA Las Vegas Stars (28)	7.00
1998 GS Lethbridge Black Diamonds (30)	6.00
1998 BL Louisville Redbirds (36)	7.00
1998 MA Lowell Spinners (31)	7.00
1998 BL Lynchburg HillCats (29)	7.00
1998 BL Macon Braves (29)	12.50
1998 MA Madison Black Wolf (25)	4.00
1998 GS Martinsville Phillies (29)	7.00
1998 GS Memphis Redbirds (25)	7.00
1998 Team Memphis Redbirds Update (1)	20.00
1998 MA Michigan Battle Cats (30)	11.00
1998 GS Midland Angels (28)	22.50
1998 GS Midland Angels Sponsor's Set (30)	25.00
1998 Team Midland Angels, "Claus" (28)	60.00
1998 Team Midland Angels, "Glaus" (28)	60.00
1998 GS Midwest League Top Prospects (28)	9.00
1998 GS Mobile BayBears S.L. Champs (25)	12.00
1998 Team Mobile Bay Bears (31)	4.00
1998 GS Modesto A's (30)	12.00
1998 Team Nashville Sounds - Numbered (31)	14.00
1998 Team Nashville Sounds - Unnumbered (31)	14.00
1998 MA New Britain Rock Cats (27)	8.00
1998 MA New Haven Ravens (31)	7.00
1998 MA N.H. Ravens W/Maritime Ads (31)	8.00
1998 MA New Jersey Cardinals (33)	7.00
1998 WTC New Jersey Jackals (28)	4.00
1998 MA New Orleans Zephyrs (28)	8.00
1998 BL Norfolk Tides (36)	7.00
1998 BL Norfolk Tides W/Fox 33 Ads (30)	8.00
1998 BL Norwich Navigators (26)	6.00
1998 Team Ogden Raptors (36)	8.00
1998 MA Oklahoma City Redhawks (30)	7.00
1998 MA Omaha Royals (30)	7.00
1998 GS Oneonta Yankees (32)	7.00
1998 MA Orlando Rays (29)	6.00
1998 Ottawa Lynx (xx)	45.00
1998 BL Pawtucket Red Sox (30)	7.00
1998 DD Pawtucket Red Sox Foldout	25.00
1998 MA Peoria Chiefs (30)	30.00
1998 MA Piedmont Boll Weevils (29)	7.00
1998 MA Pittsfield Mets (34)	7.00
1998 GS Portland Rockies (30)	7.00
1998 BL Portland Sea Dogs (30)	6.00
1998 BL Portland Sea Dogs 5th Anniv. (36)	9.00
1998 BL Princeton Devil Rays (30)	8.00
1998 BL Prince William Cannons (30)	10.00
1998 MA Prince William Decade Greats (30)	10.00
1998 GS Quad City River Bandits (30)	7.00
1998 GS Rancho Cucamonga Quakes (31)	25.00
1998 GS R.C. Quakes W/GTE Ads (31)	30.00
1998 MA Reading Phillies (28)	6.00
1998 MA Reading Phillies Update (30)	7.00
1998 MA Reading Phillies Boy Scouts (1)	6.00
1998 Berks County News Reading Phillies (5)	40.00
1998 BL Richmond Braves (30)	
1998 Richmond Camera Richmond Braves (20)	45.00
1998 BL Rochester Red Wings (30)	7.00
1998 MA Rockford Cubbies (30)	9.00
1998 Team Rockford Cubbies (30)	11.00
1998 Choice Salem Avalanche (30)	6.00
1998 GS Salem-Keizer Volcanoes (36)	7.00
1998 Team Salt Lake City Buzz (30)	8.00
1998 GS San Antonio Missions (30)	7.00
1998 GS San Bernardino Stampede (32)	8.00
1998 San Bernardino Stampede Team Issue (28)	20.00
1998 BL San Jose Giants (30)	7.00
1998 MA Savannah Sand Gnats (30)	7.00
1998 BL Scranton/Wilkes-Barre Red Barons (30)	8.00
1998 Team S/W-B Red Barons 10th Anniver. (20)	9.00
1998 MA Shreveport Captains (29)	7.00
1998 MA Shreveport W/WK SportsCare Ads (30)	7.00
1998 GS Sioux City Explorers (29)	4.00
1998 Team Sonoma County Crushers (28)	4.00
1998 MA South Atlantic League Prospects (30)	10.00
1998 MA South Bend Silver Hawks (27)	6.00
1998 GS Southern League Top Prosepcts (32)	7.00
1998 GS Southern Oregon Timberjacks (33)	8.00
1998 GS Spokane Indians (33)	7.00
1998 MA St. Catherines Stompers	7.00
1998 MA St. Luice Mets (30)	8.00
1998 Team St. Paul Saints, Wheaties logo (32)	35.00
1998 Team St. Paul Saints, No Logo (32)	20.00
1998 MA St. Petersburg Devil Rays (30)	8.00
1998 GS Stockton Ports (30)	7.00
1998 GS Stockton Ports Update (6)	6.00
1998 GS Syracuse SkyChiefs (31)	8.00
1998 BL Tacoma Rainiers (30)	7.00
1998 MA Tampa Yankees (30)	11.00
1998 GS Texas League Top Prospects (30)	10.00
1998 BL Toledo Mud Hens (33)	7.00
1998 MA Trenton Thunder (30)	7.00
1998 MA Tucson Sidewinders (29)	7.00
1998 Team Tulsa Drillers (27)	8.00
1998 Team Tulsa Texas League Champs (32)	10.00
1998 Vancouver Canadians (30)	37.50
1998 Team Vermont Expos (35)	7.00
1998 MA Vero Beach Dodgers (31)	15.00
1998 GS Visalia Oaks (31)	11.00
1998 WTC Waterbury Spirit (25)	4.00
1998 Team Watertown Indians (35)	8.00
1998 MA West Michigan Whitecaps (30)	6.00
1998 MA West Tennessee Diamond Jaxx (30)	8.00
1998 MA Wichita Wranglers (30)	8.00
1998 MA Williamsport Cubs (30)	15.00
1998 Team Williamsport Cubs Jeremy Gonzalez	5.00
1998 Team Williamsport Cubs Kerry Wood	9.00
1998 Team W. Cubs Kerry Wood Phone Card	9.00
1998 Choice Wilmington Blue Rocks (30)	8.00
1998 BL Winston-Salem Warthogs (30)	10.00
1998 MA Wisconsin Timber Rattlers (30)	8.00
1998 GS Yakima Bears (34)	7.00

1999 Diamond Authentics Signature Series

Production of each card in this minor-league issue was limited to 3,250 signed and numbered autographed versions and 10,000 unautographed cards. The autographed cards were sold three per pack. Unautographed cards were sold via a mail-in offer. Card fronts feature color photos which are borderless

JULIO LUGO, JR.
Signature Series

on two or three sides. Backs have a few words about the player and a gold-foil autograph guarantee along with the serial number. Values shown are for autographed cards.

		MT
Complete Set, Autographed (30):		25.00
Common Player, Autographed:		1.00
Complete Set, Unautographed (30):		1.00
Common Player, Unautographed:		.05
Wax Pack (6):		2.00
Wax Box (6):		12.50
1	Fletcher Bates	1.00
2	Mark Harriger	1.00
3	Jesse Ibarra	1.00
4	Keith Glauber	1.00
5	Melvin Rosario	1.00
6	Mike Rodriguez	1.00
7	Paul Avery	1.00
8	Larry Barnes	1.00
9	Eric Gillespie	1.00
10	Mike Glendenning	1.00
11	Josh Goldfield	1.00
12	Dan Phillips	1.00
13	Josh Reding	1.00
14	Jon Schaeffer	1.00
15	Kevin Sheredy	1.00
16	Julio Lugo, Jr.	1.00
17	Tonayne Brown	1.00
18	Jon Hamilton	1.00
19	Vince LaCorte	1.00
20	Ruddy Lugo	1.00
21	Danny Ardoin	1.00
22	Jermaine Clark	1.00
23	Jason Sekany	1.00
24	Mike Villano	1.00
25	Justin Albertson	1.00
26	Jesse Garcia	1.00
27	Rikki Johnston	1.00
28	Roosevelt Brown	1.00
29	Rickey Cradle	1.00
30	Shea Hillenbrand	6.00

1999 Diamond Authentics Signature Series Magnificent 7

LUIS RIVERA
Signature Series

Seven top prospects are featured in this insert series which has the same basic format at the base set except that autographed cards are serially numbered within editions of 1,250 each and card numbers carry an "MS" prefix. Unsigned versions of the cards were available via a mail-in offer. Values shown are for signed versions.

		MT
Complete Set, Autographed (7):		25.00
Common Player, Autographed:		2.00
Complete Set, Unautographed (7):		1.00
Common Player, Unautographed:		.10
MS1	Eric Gagne	12.00
MS2	Luis Rivera	2.00
MS3	D'Angelo Jimenez	2.00
MS4	Jackson Melian	2.00
MS5	Barry Zito	12.00
MS6	Scott Comer	2.00
MS7	Jeff DeVanon	2.00

1999 Diamond Authentics Signature Series Triple Crown

Super prospect Adam Piatt is featured in this insert set. Autographed versions of the cards were random pack inserts, unsigned versions were available via a mail-in offer.

		MT
Complete Set, Autographed (3):		6.00
Common Card, Autographed:		2.00
Complete Set, Unautographed (3):		1.00
Common Card, Unautographed:		.50
1	Adam Piatt	2.00
2	Adam Piatt	2.00
3	Adam Piatt	2.00

1999 Huntsville Stars 1986 Mark McGwire Reprint

33 MARK McGWIRE
Third Base

A virtual reprint of the 1986 team-issue Burger King-sponsored Mark McGwire card, this "1999 SPECIAL EDITION" is clearly marked with a red banner in the upper-left corner. Typography on front and back also differs from the original. The reprint card was given away at a promotional game in Huntsville during the 1999 season.

		MT
33	Mark McGwire	3.00

1999 Just Imagine Promos

These 10-card promo packs were issued to preview Just Minors second card issue of the season. All of the promo cards share a common back advertising the set and its inserts.

		MT
Complete Set (10):		12.50
Common Player:		1.00
(1)	Jeff Austin (Just Debuts)	.50
(2)	Pat Burrell (Just 9)	2.50
(3)	Sean Casey (Just Longshots)	1.50
(4)	Sean Casey (Just Stars)	1.50
(5)	John Elway (vertical art)	2.00
(6)	John Elway (horizontal art)	2.00
(7)	Jody Gerut (Just Debuts)	.50
(8)	Nick Johnson (Just Longshots)	1.50
(9)	Aramis Ramirez (Just 9)	1.00
(10)	Alfonso Soriano (Just Stars)	4.00

1999 Just Imagine

ROBERT STRATTON 1B
CAPITAL CITY BOMBERS

Contiguously numbered (#51-150) from where the company's earlier Just 99 series left off (#1-50), Just Imagine presents an almost entirely new checklist while retaining many of the design elements and insert series from the Just 99 issue. The main difference in the base cards is that the colored stripe presenting the player name is horizontal on Just

Imagine, where it was vertical on Just 99 cards. Backs of the JI repeat a vertical slice of the front photo and offer previous year and career professional stats. Just Imagine was issued in six-card foil packs in which were seeded several insert series, including autographed cards.

		MT
Complete Set (100):		9.00
Common Player:		.05
Wax Pack (6):		1.50
Wax Box:		25.00
51	Paul Ah Yat	.05
52	Israel Alcantara (Team name in stripe.)	.05
53	Erick Almonte	.05
54	Gabe Alvarez	.15
55	Tony Armas Jr.	.15
56	Jeff Austin	.10
57	Benito Baez	.05
58	Kevin Beirne	.05
59	Ron Belliard	.05
60	Micah Bowie	.05
61	Russell Branyan	.10
62	Antone Brooks	.05
63	A.J. Burnett	.20
64	Pat Burrell	.75
65	Brent Butler	.05
66	Troy Cameron	.05
67	Sean Casey	.45
68	Bruce Chen	.05
69	Chin-Feng Chen	.15
70	Jin Ho Cho	.10
71	Jesus Colome	.05
72	Carl Crawford	.25
73	Bubba Crosby	.05
74	Jack Cust	.10
75	Mike Darr	.05
76	Ben Davis	.05
77	Octavio Dotel	.05
78	Kelly Dransfeldt	.05
79	Adam Dunn	.75
80	Erubiel Durazo	.10
81	John Elway (Oneonta Yankees)	1.00
81a	John Elway (Autographed edition of 100.)	140.00
82	John Elway (Denver Broncos)	.75
83	Mario Encarnacion	.05
84	Seth Etherton	.05
85	Adam Everett	.15
86	Franky Figueroa	.05
87	Mike Frank	.05
88	Jon Garland	.15
89	Chris George	.05
90	Jody Gerut	.05
91	Derrick Gibson	.05
92	Jerry Hairston Jr.	.05
93	Josh Hamilton	.10
94	Jason Hart	.05
95	Chad Harville	.05
96	Nathan Haynes	.05
97	Junior Herndon	.05
98	Shea Hillenbrand	.25
99	Matt Holliday	.25
100	Brandon Inge	.05
101	Jacque Jones	.45
102	Gabe Kapler	.15
103	Austin Kearns	.65
104	Brandon Larson	.05
105	Jason LaRue	.05
106	Carlos Lee	.25
107	Corey Lee	.05
108	Donny Leon	.05
109	George Lombard	.05
110	Julio Lugo, Jr.	.05
111	Chris Magruder	.05
112	Mark Mangum	.05
113	Jason Marquis	.10
114	Ruben Mateo	.05
115	Luis Matos	.05
116	Gary Matthews Jr.	.05
117	Juan Melo	.05
118	Orber Moreno	.05
119	Mark Mulder	.25
120	Corey Patterson	.50
121	Angel Pena	.05
122	Elvis Pena	.05
123	Kyle Peterson	.05
124	Adam Piatt	.05
125	Calvin Pickering	.05
126	Jeremy Powell	.05
127	Luke Prokopec	.05
128	Aramis Ramirez	.05
129	Julio Ramirez	.05
130	Matt Riley	.05
131	Luis Rivera	.05
132	Grant Roberts	.10
133	Ryan Rupe	.05
134	C.C. Sabathia	.25
135	Luis Saturria	.05
136	Fernando Seguignol	.05
137	Alfonso Soriano	1.00
138	Patrick Strange	.05
139	Robert Stratton	.05
140	Reggie Taylor	.10
141	Jorge Toca	.05
142	Tony Torcato	.05
143	Bubba Trammell	.10
144	T.J. Tucker	.05
145	Juan Uribe	.05
146	Kip Wells	.25
147	Ricky Williams (Piedmont Boll Weevils)	.75
148	Ricky Williams (Texas Longhorns)	.75
149	Kevin Witt	.05
150	Ed Yarnall	.05

1999 Just Imagine Just Black

Issued at the rate of just one per case (240 packs), this set parallels the base issue, except for the presence of black borders on front and individual serial numbers within an edition of 50 cards each.

		MT
Common Player:		3.00
High-Demand Players:		15X
(See 1999 Just Imagine for checklist and base card values.)		

1999 Just Imagine Autographs - Base Set

Authentically autographed cards from Just Minors' Imagine issue were seeded at the average rate of two per 24-pack box. Autographed cards repeat the photo used in the base set but have the bottom portion ghosted to allow the autograph to appear more prominently. Backs have a congratulatory message.

		MT
Complete Set (46):		45.00
Common Player:		1.00
(1)	Israel Alcantara	1.00
(2)	Hector Almonte	1.00
(3)	Rick Ankiel	2.00
(4)	Jeff Austin	1.50
(5)	Benito Baez	1.00
(6)	Kevin Barker	1.00
(7)	Kevin Beirne	1.00
(8)	Micah Bowie	1.00
(9)	Antone Brooks	1.00
(10)	Sean Casey	6.00
(11)	Jesus Colome	1.00
(12)	Bubba Crosby	1.00
(13)	Jack Cust	1.00
(14)	Ben Davis	1.00
(15)	Seth Etherton	1.50
(16)	Mike Frank	1.00
(17)	Jon Garland	2.00
(18)	Chris George	1.00
(19)	Jason Grilli	1.00
(20)	Junior Herndon	1.00
(21)	Gabe Kapler	2.00
(22)	Corey Lee	1.00
(24)	Danny Leon	1.00
(25)	George Lombard	1.00
(26)	Julio Lugo, Jr.	1.00
(27)	Chris Magruder	1.00
(28)	Mark Mangum	1.00
(29)	Jason Marquis	2.00
(30)	Luis Matos	1.00
(31)	Juan Melo	1.00
(31)	Orber Moreno	1.00
(32)	Pablo Ozuna	1.00
(33)	Kyle Peterson	1.00
(34)	Ben Petrick	1.00
(35)	Calvin Pickering	1.00
(36)	Aramis Ramirez	3.00
(37)	Zach Sorensen	1.00
(38)	Alfonso Soriano	15.00
(39)	Patrick Strange	1.00
(40)	Reggie Taylor	1.50
(41)	Jorge Toca	1.00
(42)	Bubba Trammell	2.00
(43)	T.J. Tucker	1.00
(44)	Juan Uribe	1.00
(45)	Kip Wells	3.00
(46)	Randy Wolf	3.00

1999 Just Imagine Autographs - Die-Cut

Some of the players who appear in the autographed card series (and a few who don't) can also be found in a much more limited autographed insert. Called die-cut autographs, these cards repeat in a circle at center the photo found on the base card. The background is white with the autograph at top; corners are rounded. On back, each die-cut autograph card is serially numbered from within an edition of 200.

		MT
Complete Set (17):		20.00
Common Player:		2.00
(1)	Rick Ankiel	2.00
(2)	Jeff Austin	2.00
(3)	Kevin Beirne	2.00
(4)	Micah Bowie	2.00
(5)	Troy Cameron	2.00
(6)	Seth Etherton	2.00
(7)	Mike Frank	2.00
(8)	Chris George	2.00
(9)	Gabe Kapler	2.00
(10)	George Lombard	2.00
(11)	Jason Marquis	3.00
(12)	Pablo Ozuna	2.00
(13)	Calvin Pickering	2.00
(14)	Zach Sorensen	2.00
(15)	Jorge Toca	2.00
(16)	T.J. Tucker	2.00
(17)	Randy Wolf	3.00

1999 Just Imagine Autographs - Just Imagine

Some of the players who appear in the base autographed card series (and a few who don't) can also be found in a much more limited insert, called Just Imagine Autographs. On back, each Just Imagine autograph card is serially numbered from within an edition of 200.

		MT
Complete Set (23):		250.00
Common Player:		2.00
(1)	Israel Alcantara	2.00
(2)	Rick Ankiel	3.00
(3)	Jeff Austin	2.00
(4)	Micah Bowie	2.00
(5)	Sean Casey	6.00
(6)	Jack Cust	2.00
(7)	John Elway	140.00
(8)	Mike Frank	2.00
(9)	Rafael Furcal	4.00
(10)	Jon Garland	2.00
(11)	Gabe Kapler	2.00
(12)	Julio Lugo, Jr.	2.00
(13)	Jason Marquis	4.00
(14)	Pablo Ozuna	2.00
(15)	Kyle Peterson	2.00
(16)	Julio Ramirez	2.00
(17)	Alfonso Soriano	25.00
(18)	Jorge Toca	2.00
(19)	T.J. Tucker	2.00
(20)	Kip Wells	3.00
(22)	Ricky Williams (Texas Longhorns)	75.00
(23)	Ricky Williams (Heisman Trophy)	75.00

1999 Just Imagine Just Debut

Inserted one per box as a box-topper and sealed inside a paper envelope, this insert set chronicles the professional debut of 10 top minor league prospects. Fronts have a color photo at center with a ticket design at bottom. Backs have two small black-and-white copies of the front photo, statistics from the debut game and career highlights. Numbered on front, cards have a "JD-0999-" prefix.

		MT
Complete Set (10):		10.00

1999 Just Imagine Debuts

CHIN FENG CHEN OF

		MT
Common Player:		1.00
01	Jeff Austin	1.00
02	Chin-Feng Chen	1.50
03	Erubiel Durazo	1.00
04	Jody Gerut	1.00
05	Josh Hamilton	1.50
06	Corey Patterson	2.50
07	Alfonso Soriano	7.50
08	Jorge Toca	1.00
09	Kip Wells	1.50
10	Brad Wilkerson	1.00

1999 Just Imagine Just Longshots

JUST LONGSHOTS
MARCUS GILES 2B
ROUND 53 - PICK 1512
MYRTLE BEACH PELICANS

Seeded at the rate of about one per eight foil packs (three per box) these insert cards feature players who have overcome long odds as low picks in the amateur draft to arrive on the brink of major league stardom. Fronts have action photos on a white background. In the black data box at bottom along with player identification is information on the round in which he was drafted and his overall rank in the draft. Backs have a monocolor version of the photo in the background and a few words about the player and his career to date. Card numbers on back have an "LS" prefix and the player's initials as a suffix.

		MT
Complete Set (10):		3.00
Common Player:		.50
001	Wes Anderson	.50
002	David Eckstein	.75
003	Marcus Giles	1.50
004	Kevin Haverbusch	.50
005	Gabe Kapler	.50
006	Julio Lugo, Jr.	.50
007	Gary Matthews Jr.	.50
008	Ryan Minor	.50
009	Jason Regan	.50
010	Daryle Ward	.50

1999 Just Imagine Just Nine

JUST 9
COREY PATTERSON

Top Prospects at each position are featured in this insert set. Fronts have a small player photo at top-center, which is repeated larger in the background in a single color. Backs repeat the front photo and have a few career highlights. Cards are inserted one per case (240 packs).

	MT
Complete Set (9):	45.00
Common Player:	5.00
JN-01 Rick Ankiel	5.00
JN-02 Ron Belliard	5.00
JN-03 Pat Burrell	12.00
JN-04 Lance Berkman	6.00
JN-05 Ben Davis	5.00
JN-06 Ruben Mateo	5.00
JN-07 Corey Patterson	6.00
JN-08 Aramis Ramirez	6.00
JN-09 Alfonso Soriano	15.00

1999 Just Imagine Just Stars

Ten of the biggest names on 1999 minor league rosters are presented in this insert series which was seeded on the average of one per box (24 packs) in Just Imagine. Only the star-shaped central portion of the front photo is printed in color, the rest is black-and-white. Backs repeat a portion of the front photo in a colored star on a white background. A few career highlights and predictions are also included.

	MT
Complete Set (10):	12.00
Common Player:	1.00
JS-01 Rick Ankiel	1.00
JS-02 Pat Burrell	2.50
JS-03 Sean Casey	2.00
JS-04 Erubiel Durazo	1.00
JS-05 Ben Davis	1.00
JS-06 Jacque Jones	1.50
JS-07 Ruben Mateo	1.00
JS-08 Gary Matthews Jr.	1.00
JS-09 Adam Piatt	1.00
JS-10 Alfonso Soriano	15.00

1999 Just Justifiable '99 Promos

Top minor league stars are featured on the sample cards issued to promote Just's third issue of 1999. As was the case with the company's other promo cards, not all of the players seen on the samples were issued in the set. Backs of all the sample cards are identical, detailing the forthcoming Justifiable '99 issue.

		MT
Complete Set (5):		6.00
Common Player:		1.00
(1)	Pat Burrell (Just the Facts)	3.00
(2)	Sean Burroughs (Base card.)	1.50
(3)	Josh Hamilton (Just Debuts)	1.00
(4)	Adam Piatt (Just Spotlights)	1.00
(5)	Ben Sheets (Just Drafted)	1.50

1999 Just Justifiable

Numbered from 151-250, this minor league singles issue continues where Just's The Start (#1-50)

and Imagine (#51-150) left off earlier in the year. Justifiable was sold in a 24-pack box (six cards per pack) which included one of five 6" player action figures. The Justifiable base cards are in the same basic format as the earlier issues, except the color strip which contains the player name is vertically on the right side of the card. Backs repeat a vertical slice of the front photo and include 1998 and career stats, along with a team logo.

	MT
Complete Set (100):	6.00
Common Player:	.05
Hobby Wax Box (24+1):	25.00
Retail Wax Box (10+1):	12.00
151 Winston Abreu	.05
152 Chris Aguila	.05
153 Bronson Arroyo	.05
154 Robert Averette	.05
155 Mike Bacsik	.05
156 Andrew Beinbrink	.05
157 Matt Belisle	.05
158 Matt Blank	.05
159 Jung Bong	.10
160 Milton Bradley	.25
161 Ryan Bradley	.05
162 Dee Brown	.05
163 Sean Burroughs	.50
164 Chance Caple	.05
165 Hee Choi	.50
166 Mike Christensen	.05
167 Doug Clark	.05
168 Javier Colina	.05
169 Brian Cooper	.05
170 Pat Daneker	.05
171 Randey Dorame	.05
172 Ryan Drese	.05
173 Chris Duncan	.05
174 Adam Dunn	2.00
175 David Eckstein	.25
176 Alex Fernandez	.05
177 Choo Freeman	.10
178 Neil Friendling	.05
179 Eddy Furniss	.05
180 B.J. Garbe	.05
181 Yon German	.05
182 Esteban German	.05
183 Dan Gummitt	.05
184 Will Hartley	.05
185 Jesus Hernandez	.05
186 Alex Hernandez	.05
187 Jay Hood	.05
188 Aubrey Huff	.10
189 Chad Hutchinson	.05
190 Jason Jennings	.05
191 Jaime Jones	.05
192 David Kelton	.05
193 Michael Lamb	.05
194 Jacques Landry	.05
195 Ryan Langerhans	.10
196 Nelson Lara	.05
197 Nick Leach	.05
198 Steve Lomasney	.05
199 Felipe Lopez	.05
200 Ryan Ludwick	.05
201 Pat Manning	.05
202 T.R. Marcinczyk	.05
203 Hipolito Martinez	.05
204 Tony McKnight	.05
205 Tydus Meadows	.05
206 Corky Miller	.05
207 Frank Moore	.05
208 Scott Morgan	.05
209 Tony Mota	.05
210 Ntema Ndungidi	.05
211 David Noyce	.05
212 Franklin Nunez	.05
213 Jose Ortiz	.05
214 Jimmy Osting	.05
215 Jorge Padilla	.05
216 Mike Paradis	.05
217 Brandon Parker	.05
218 Jarrod Patterson	.05
219 John Patterson	.05
220 Jay Payton	.15
221 Juan Pena	.10
222 Brad Penny	.05
223 Danny Peoples	.05
224 Paul Phillips	.05
225 Josh Pressley	.05
226 Tim Raines Jr.	.05
227 Paul Rigdon	.05
228 Jimmy Rollins	1.00
229 J.C. Romero	.05
230 Marcos Scutaro	.05
231 Sammy Serrano	.05
232 Wascar Serrano	.05
233 Ben Sheets	.50
234 Carlos Silva	.05
235 Scott Sobkowiak	.05
236 Ramon Soler	.05
237 Shawn Sonnier	.05
238 Jovanny Sosa	.05
239 Jason Standridge	.05
240 Brent Stentz	.05
241 Seth Taylor	.05
242 Jason Tyner	.05
243 Brant Ust	.05
244 Eric Valent	.10
245 Ismael Villegas	.05
246 David Walling	.05
247 Rico Washington	.05
248 Brad Wilkerson	.10
249 Patrick Williams	.05
250 Barry Zito	1.00

1999 Just Justifiable Just Black

Issued at the rate of just one per case (240 packs), this set parallels the base issue, except the presence of black borders on front and individual serial numbers within an edition of 50 cards each.

	MT
Common Player:	3.00
High-demand Players:	15X
(See 1999 Just Justifiable for checklist and base card values.)	

1999 Just Justifiable Autographs - Base Set

Base-set autographed cards from Just Minors' Justifiable issue were seeded at the average rate of two per 24-pack box. Autographed cards repeat the photo used in the base set but have the bottom portion ghosted to allow the autograph to appear more prominently. Backs have a congratulatory message.

		MT
Complete Set (18):		35.00
Common Player:		1.00
(1)	Rick Ankiel	2.00
(2)	Sean Burroughs	4.00
(3)	Eric Byrnes	1.00
(4)	Troy Cameron	1.00
(5)	Juan Dilone	1.00
(6)	Rafael Furcal	4.00
(7)	Jason Hart	1.00
(8)	Shea Hillenbrand	5.00
(9)	Nick Johnson	5.00
(10)	Adam Kennedy	4.00
(11)	Mark Mulder	5.00
(12)	Pablo Ozuna	1.00
(13)	Corey Patterson	5.00
(14)	Angel Pena	1.00
(15)	Julio Ramirez	1.00
(16)	Matt Riley	1.50
(17)	Grant Roberts	1.00
(18)	Tony Torcato	1.00

1999 Just Justifiable Autographs - Die-Cut

Some of the players who appear in the autographed card base set (and a few who don't) can also be found in a much more limited autographed insert. Called die-cut autographs, these cards repeat the photo found on the base card in a circle at center. The background is white with the autograph at top; corners are rounded. On back, each die-cut autograph card is serially numbered from within an edition of 200.

		MT
Complete Set (7):		20.00
Common Player:		2.00
(1)	Rick Ankiel	3.00
(2)	Matt Belisle	2.00
(3)	Sean Burroughs	4.00
(4)	Gil Meche	4.00
(5)	Mark Mulder	6.00
(6)	Corey Patterson	6.00
(7)	Matt Riley	2.00

1999 Just Justifiable Autographs - Just Diamonds

Some of the players who appear in the base autographed card series (and a few who don't) can also be found in a much more limited insert, called Just Diamonds Autographs. The cards have player pictures in a diamond frame at the center of a white background. A trapazoid at bottom has the signature. On back, each Just Diamonds autograph card is serially numbered from within an edition of 100.

		MT
Complete Set (11):		40.00
Common Player:		2.00
(1)	Rick Ankiel	3.00
(2)	Matt Belisle	2.00
(3)	Sean Burroughs	4.00
(4)	Troy Cameron	2.00
(5)	Dionys Cesar	2.00
(6)	Rafael Furcal	4.00
(7)	Nick Johnson	5.00
(8)	Pablo Ozuna	2.00
(9)	Corey Patterson	6.00
(10)	Aramis Ramirez	4.00
(11)	Kip Wells	6.00

1999 Just Justifiable Just Debut

These are the rarest inserts in Justifiable, found only one per 240 packs. There is a horizontal color photo at center with black borders at top and bottom. Details of the player's first professional game are in the bottom border. Card numbers are prefixed with "JD".

		MT
Complete Set (10):		25.00
Common Player:		4.00
01	B.J. Garbe	4.00
02	Ben Sheets	6.00
03	Jeff Austin	6.00
04	Chin-Feng Chen	5.00

05	Jody Gerut	4.00
06	Josh Hamilton	4.00
07	Corey Patterson	7.50
08	Alfonso Soriano	10.00
09	Jorge Luis Toca	4.00
10	Kip Wells	4.00

1999 Just Justifiable Just Drafted

This insert of 1999 draftees was issued one per box sealed in a black paper envelope. Fronts have a horizontal color photo at center with draft details below. Backs have a few career numbers and a team logo. Cards are numbered with a "JD" prefix.

		MT
Complete Set (10):		12.00
Common Player:		2.00
01	Larry Bigbie	2.00
02	Chance Caple	2.00
03	Chris Duncan	2.00
04	B.J. Garbe	2.00
05	Josh Hamilton	2.00
06	Will Hartley	2.00
07	Mike Paradis	2.00
08	Ben Sheets	3.00
09	David Walling	2.00
10	Barry Zito	7.50

1999 Just Justifiable Just Figures

Michael Barrett
Harrisburg Senators '98

In the first-ever random pairing of baseball cards and action figures, each box of Just Justifiable included one of five action player figures along with 24 foil packs of minor league cards. About 6" tall, each figure has poseable arms and legs. Each player was issued in both fielding and batting versions. Certain figures, details of which were not released, were issued in more limited numbers in one or the other of their poses. Until that situation is clarified, only a common figure value will be shown in these listings. Besides the five players issued in boxes, a Rick Ankiel figure was available exclusive via mail-in offer for $13.

		MT
Common Figure:		6.00
(1a)	Hank Aaron/Btg (1974 Atlanta Braves)	12.50
(1b)	Hank Aaron/Fldg (1974 Atlanta Braves)	6.00
(2a)	Michael Barrett/Btg (1998 Harrisburg Senators)	6.00
(2b)	Michael Barrett/Fldg (1998 Harrisburg Senators)	6.00
(3a)	John Elway/Btg (1982 Oneonta Yankees)	9.00
(3b)	John Elway/Fldg (1982 Oneonta Yankees)	10.00
(4a)	Gabe Kapler/Btg (1998 Jacksonville Suns)	6.00
(4b)	Gabe Kapler/Fldg (1998 Jacksonville Suns)	6.00

(5a)	Ricky Williams/Btg (1996 Piedmont Boll Weevils)	7.50
(5b)	Ricky Williams/Fldg (1996 Piedmont Boll Weevils)	7.50
(6a)	Rick Ankiel (1999 Arkansas Travelers - Home)	7.50
(6b)	Rick Ankiel (1999 Arkansas Travelers - Away)	7.50

1999 Just Justifiable Just Spotlights

Seeded one per 24-pack box, these inserts feature top minor league stars. Fronts have a white background with spotlight beams and a color player photo in the center circle. Backs repeat the front photo in full-size format and have career highlights and biographical data. Cards numbers are prefixed with "JS."

		MT
Complete Set (10):		35.00
Common Player:		2.00
01	Dee Brown	2.00
02	Pat Burrell	10.00
03	Josh Hamilton	2.00
04	Nick Johnson	6.00
05	Jason Marquis	4.00
06	Pablo Ozuna	2.00
07	John Patterson	2.00
08	Adam Piatt	2.00
09	Matt Riley	2.00
10	Alfonso Soriano	15.00

1999 Just Justifiable Just the Facts

Top talent in the minor leagues is featured in this insert set found on average of one per 24 packs. Cards have monochromatic versions of the same photo on front, along with a few player details and career highlights. Backs have the full-color version of the photo vertically and a bit more personal detail. Card numbers have a "JTF" prefix.

		MT
Complete Set (10):		40.00
Common Player:		2.00
01	Pat Burrell	10.00
02	Sean Burroughs	4.00
03	Adam Eaton	2.50
04	Marcus Giles	2.50
05	Josh Hamilton	2.00
06	Nick Johnson	6.00
07	Corey Patterson	6.00
08	Jason Standridge	2.00
09	Jorge Luis Toca	2.00
10	Eric Valent	2.00

1999 Just The Start Promos

To introduce its premiere minor league issue, Just Minors produced a set of five promotional cards typifying its base set and four inserts. Fronts are virtually identical to the issued versions. Backs are generic with manufacturer and minor league association logo, copyright information, promotional notice and "1 of 5."

STAFF AND NEWS SERVICES

	MT
Complete Set (5):	9.00
Common Player:	1.00
(1) Ryan Anderson (Base set.)	1.00
(2) Lance Berkman (Just Nine)	3.00
(3) Pat Burrell (Just News)	5.00
(4) Gabe Kapler (Just Power)	2.00
(5) Ruben Mateo (Just Due)	1.00

1999 Just The Start

The Just 99 base set features a large color photo on front with white borders at top, bottom and right. At left is a 1/2" vertical color strip in which the player's name and position appears; his team name is vertically to the right of that strip. The Just 99 logo is at bottom. Backs repeat a portion of the front photo on the right. Horizontally at left are personal data, 1998 and pro career stats. A team logo and card number are at top center. The issue was sold in six-card foil packs and 24-pack boxes.

	MT
Complete Set (50):	4.00
Common Player:	.05
Wax Pack (6):	1.00
Wax Box (24):	16.00
1 Hector Almonte	.05
2 Wes Anderson	.05
3 Ryan Anderson	.20
4 Clayton Andrews	.05
5 Rick Ankiel	.10
6 Brad Baisley	.05
7 Kevin Barker	.05
8 Michael Barrett	.15
9 Kris Benson	.10
10 Peter Bergeron	.05
11 Lance Berkman	.35
12 Nate Bump	.05
13 Eric Byrnes	.05
14 Giuseppe Chiaramonte	.05
15 Glenn Davis	.05
16 Juan Dilone	.05
17 Eric DuBose	.05
18 Rick Elder	.05
19 Alex Escobar	.15
20 Rafael Furcal	.25
21 Shawn Gallagher	.05
22 Marcus Giles	.35
23 Geoff Goetz	.05
24 Jason Grilli	.05
25 Cristian Guzman	.25
26 Mark Harriger	.05
27 Nick Johnson	.40
28 Gabe Kapler	.15
29 Kenny Kelly	.05
30 Adam Kennedy	.20
31 Corey Lee	.05
32 Kevin McGlinchy	.10
33 Gil Meche	.15
34 Jackson Melian	.05
35 Warren Morris	.10
36 Ricky Williams (Baseball)	1.50
37 Pablo Ozuna	.05
38 Ben Petrick	.05
39 Scott Pratt	.05
40 Chris Reinike	.05
41 Zach Sorenson	.05
42 Dernell Stenson	.05

43 Andy Thompson	.05
44 Luis Vizcaino	.05
45 Daryle Ward	.05
46 Vernon Wells	.50
47 Jayson Werth	.05
48 Jake Westbrook	.05
49 Ricky Williams (Football)	1.50
50 Randy Wolf	.10

1999 Just The Start Just Black

Issued at the rate of just one per case (240 packs), this set parallels the base issue, except for the presence of black borders on front and individual serial numbers within an edition of 50 cards each.

	MT
Common Player:	3.00
High-Demand Players:	15X

(See 1999 Just the Start for checklist and base card values.)

1999 Just The Start Autographs

Authentically autographed cards from Just Minors debut issue were seeded at the average rate of two per 24-pack box. Autographed cards repeat the photo used in the base set but have the bottom portion ghosted to allow the autograph to appear more prominently. Backs have a congratulatory message.

	MT
Complete Set (25):	65.00
Common Player:	1.00
(1) Hector Almonte	1.00
(2) Brad Baisley	1.00
(3) Michael Barrett	3.00
(4) Kris Benson	3.00
(5) Brent Billingsley	1.00
(6) Casey Blake	1.00
(7) Glenn Davis	1.00
(8) Juan Dilone	1.00
(9) Rick Elder	1.00
(10) Mark Fischer	1.00
(11) Rafael Furcal	3.00
(12) Geoff Goetz	1.00
(13) Jason Grilli	1.00
(14) Mark Harriger	1.00
(15) Heath Honeycutt	1.00
(16) Gabe Kapler	2.00
(17) Adam Kennedy	3.00
(18) Juan Melo	1.00
(19) Mark Mulder	6.00
(20) Andy Thompson	1.00
(21) Peter Tucci	1.00
(22) Luis Vizcaino	1.00
(23) Jayson Werth	1.00
(24) Jake Westbrook	1.00
(25) Ricky Williams	60.00

1999 Just The Start Autographs - Die-Cut

Some of the players who appear in the autographed card series can also be found in a much more limited autographed insert. Called die-cut autographs, these cards repeat in a circle at center the photo found on the base card. The background is white with the autograph

at top; corners are rounded. On back, each die-cut autograph card is serially numbered from within an edition of 200.

	MT
Complete Set (15):	65.00
Common Player:	2.00
(1) Hector Almonte	2.00
(2) Brad Baisley	2.00
(3) Michael Barrett	3.00
(4) Kris Benson	3.00
(5) Casey Blake	2.00
(6) Glenn Davis	2.00
(7) Rick Elder	2.00
(8) Geoff Goetz	2.00
(9) Jason Grilli	2.00
(10) Mark Harriger	2.00
(11) Gabe Kapler	3.00
(12) Mark Mulder	6.00
(13) Jayson Werth	2.00
(14) Jake Westbrook	2.00
(15) Ricky Williams	75.00

1999 Just The Start Just Due

Players on the brink of their major league careers and projected stardom are featured in this insert series. Cards have large color action photos on front and a tiny map at left specifying the city where their parent major league team plays. Backs have a repeat of the front elements, with a small photo and larger map photo, along with personal data and career highlights. Stated odds of insertion are one per six packs.

	MT
Complete Set (10):	4.00
Common Player:	.35
Jd-01 Michael Barrett	.50
Jd-02 Kris Benson	.50
Jd-03 Peter Bergeron	.35
Jd-04 Lance Berkman	.50
Jd-05 Nick Johnson	1.00
Jd-06 Gabe Kapler	.50
Jd-07 Corey Lee	.35
Jd-08 Jackson Melian	.35
Jd-09 Dernell Stenson	.35
Jd-10 Randy Wolf	.50

1999 Just The Start Just News

The scarcest of the Just 99 inserts, found at the rate of just one per 240 packs.

	MT
Complete Set (6):	30.00
Common Player:	5.00
Jn-01 Rick Ankiel, Alex Escobar	5.00
Jn-02 Marcus Giles, Mark Harriger	6.00
Jn-03 Gabe Kapler, Kevin McGlinchy	6.00
Jn-04 Jackson Melian, Warren Morris	5.00
Jn-05 Dernell Stenson, Vernon Wells	5.00
Jn-06 Ricky Williams, Ricky Williams	10.00

1999 Just The Start Just Nine

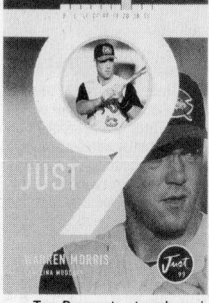

Top Prospects at each position are featured in this insert set. Fronts have a small player photo at

top-center, which is repeated larger in the background in a single color. Backs repeat the front photo and have a few career highlights. Cards are inserted one per box as a box-topper in a sealed paper envelope.

	MT
Complete Set (9):	7.50
Common Player:	1.00
J9-01 Rick Ankiel	1.00
J9-02 Michael Barrett	1.00
J9-03 Lance Berkman	2.00
J9-04 Alex Escobar	1.00
J9-05 Nick Johnson	3.00
J9-06 Gabe Kapler	1.00
J9-07 Warren Morris	1.00
J9-08 Pablo Ozuna	1.00
J9-09 Ben Petrick	1.00

1999 Just The Start Just Power

Some of the hardest hitters and throwers in the minor leagues are included in this chase set. Seeded one per 24-pack box, the cards have player action photos on front on a white background. The photo is repeated on back, but only in one color. A few career highlights also appear on back.

	MT
Complete Set (10):	12.00
Common Player:	1.00
Jp-01 Ryan Anderson	1.50
Jp-02 Wes Anderson	1.00
Jp-03 Lance Berkman	2.00
Jp-04 Juan Dilone	1.00
Jp-05 Marcus Giles	2.00
Jp-06 Gabe Kapler	2.00
Jp-07 Kevin McGlinchy	1.50
Jp-08 Gil Meche	1.50
Jp-09 Dernell Stenson	1.00
Jp-10 Ricky Williams	5.00

1999 Just Autographs Black

These authentically autographed black-bordered cards were random inserts in the 2000 Just Gold 2k factory sets. Each card was produced in a numbered edition of 50 each. Some players appear in more than one pose. The unnumbered cards are checklisted here in alphabetical order.

	MT
Common Player:	5.00
(1) Rick Ankiel	5.00
(2) Tony Armas Jr.	7.50
(3) Matt Belisle	5.00
(4) Jacob Cruz	5.00
(5) Jack Cust	6.00
(6) Pat Daneker	5.00
(7) Mario Encarnacion	5.00
(8) Robert Fick	5.00
(9) Nick Johnson	10.00
(10) Jaime Jones	5.00
(11) Austin Kearns	12.00
(12) David Kelton	5.00
(13) Nelson Lara	5.00
(14) Brandon Larson	5.00
(15) Steve Lomasney	5.00
(16) Gil Meche	5.00

(17) Guillermo Mota	5.00
(18) Tony Mota	5.00
(19) Pablo Ozuna	5.00
(20) Pablo Ozuna	5.00
(21) Corey Patterson	20.00
(22) Corey Patterson	20.00
(23) Corey Patterson	20.00
(24) Jay Payton	5.00
(25) Aramis Ramirez	7.50
(26) Ryan Rupe	5.00
(27) Alfonso Soriano	75.00
(28) Jovanny Sosa	5.00
(29) Jorge Toca	5.00
(30) Jorge Toca	5.00
(31) Enrique Wilson	7.50
(32) Barry Zito	55.00
(33) Barry Zito	55.00

1999 SP Top Prospects

The projected stars of the new millenium were previewed in Upper Deck's SP Top Prospects minor league set issued in the 1999 pre-season. The 126 cards in the base set have player photos surrounded by gold refractive-foil borders. The player's major league parent team is named at top and the logo of his 1998 minor league team is at lower-right. Backs have another color photo, a few words about the player and his minor league career stats. A parallel President's Edition set, with only 10 numbered cards of each player, was also released. The President's Edition cards replace the gold front borders with silver. The issue was sold in eight-card packs with a suggested retail price of $4.99.

	MT
Complete Set (126):	10.00
Common Player:	.05
Wax Pack (8):	1.50
Wax Box (24):	25.00
1 J.D. Drew (Top Ten Prospects)	.50
2 Matt Clement (Top Ten Prospects)	.15
3 Alex Gonzalez (Top Ten Prospects)	.10
4 Rich Ankiel (Top Ten Prospects)	.50
5 Alex Escobar (Top Ten Prospects)	.10
6 Eric Chavez (Top Ten Prospects)	.25
7 Lance Berkman (Top Ten Prospects)	.25
8 Russell Branyan (Top Ten Prospects)	.05
9 Gabe Kapler (Top Ten Prospects)	.10
10 Bruce Chen (Top Ten Prospects)	.05
11 Chuck Abbott	.05
12 Ryan Anderson	.15
13 Rick Ankiel	1.00
14 Michael Barrett	.25
15 Carlos Beltran	2.00
16 Buck Jacobsen	.05
17 Kris Benson	.25
18 Lance Berkman	.50
19 Ryan Brannan	.05
20 Russell Branyan	.10
21 Dermal Brown	.05
22 Roosevelt Brown	.05
23 Juan LeBron	.05
24 Brent Butler	.05
25 Ross Gload	.05
26 Eric Chavez	.50
27 Bruce Chen	.05
28 Matt Clement	.25
29 Adonis Harrison	.05
30 Francisco Cordero	.05
31 David Cortes	.05
32 Paxton Crawford	.05
33 Joe Crede	.50
34 Bobby Cripps	.05
35 Mike Cuddyer	.10
36 John Curtice	.05
37 Mike Darr	.05
38 Ben Davis	.05
39 Glenn Davis	.05
40 Matt DeWitt	.05

41 Shea Hillenbrand	.50
42 Adam Eaton	.20
43 Mario Encarnacion	.05
44 Chris Enochs	.05
45 Pat Burrell	1.50
46 Kyle Farnsworth	.05
47 Nelson Figueroa	.05
48 Shawn Gallagher	.05
49 Chad Hutchinson	.05
50 Marcus Giles	.25
51 J.D. Drew	1.50
52 Alex Gonzalez	.10
53 Chad Green	.05
54 Jason Grilli	.05
55 Seth Etherton	.10
56 Roy Halladay	.50
57 Tyson Hartshorn	.05
58 Al Hawkins	.05
59 Chad Hermansen	.10
60 Ramon Hernandez	.15
61 Mark Johnson	.05
62 Doug Johnston	.05
63 Jacque Jones	.40
64 Adam Kennedy	.25
65 Cesar King	.05
66 Brendan Kingman	.05
67 Mike Kinkade	.15
68 Corey Koskie	.50
69 Mike Kusiewicz	.05
70 Mike Colangelo	.05
71 Jason LaRue	.05
72 Joe Lawrence	.05
73 Carlos Lee	.25
74 Jeff Liefer	.05
75 Mike Lincoln	.05
76 George Lombard	.05
77 Mike Lowell	.50
78 Alex Escobar	.15
79 Sam Marsonek	.05
80 Ruben Mateo	.05
81 Brian Benefield	.05
82 Gary Matthews Jr.	.05
83 Joe Mays	.35
84 Jackson Melian	.05
85 Juan Melo	.05
86 Chad Meyers	.05
87 Matt Miller	.05
88 Damon Minor	.05
89 Ryan Minor	.05
90 Mike Mitchell	.05
91 Shea Morenz	.10
92 Warren Morris	.05
93 Drew Henson	2.00
94 Todd Noel	.05
95 Pablo Ozuna	.05
96 John Patterson	.05
97 Josh Paul	.05
98 Angel Pena	.05
99 Juan Pena	.05
100 Danny Peoples	.05
101 Santiago Perez	.05
102 Tommy Peterman	.05
103 Ben Petrick	.05
104 Calvin Pickering	.05
105 John Powers	.05
106 Gabe Kapler	.15
107 Rob Ramsey	.05
108 Luis Figueroa	.05
109 Grant Roberts	.05
110 Fernando Seguignol	.05
111 Juan Sosa	.05
112 Dernell Stenson	.05
113 John Stephens	.05
114 Mike Stoner	.05
115 Reggie Taylor	.10
116 Justin Towle	.05
117 Carlos Villalobos	.05
118 Vernon Wells	.45
119 Jason Werth	.05
120 Jake Westbrook	.05
121 Matt White	.05
122 Ricky Williams	2.00
123 Kevin Witt	.05
124 Dewayne Wise	.05
125 Ed Yarnall	.05
126 Mike Zywica	.05

1999 SP Top Prospects President's Edition

The use of silver prismatic foil borders on front is the key visual difference on this parallel issue. Also on the front, the notation "President's Edition" is printed at top. On back the cards have a silver-foil serial number from within an edition of just 10 pieces each.

	MT
Common Player:	10.00
Stars:	60X

(See 1999 SP Top Prospects for checklist and base card values.)

1999 SP Top Prospects Chirography

Top draft picks are featured in this set of autographed insert cards. Fronts have player photos framed in gold foil on a white border. At bottom is the player's authentic autograph. Backs have a congratulatory notice from Upper Deck CEO Richard McWilliam. Cards are "numbered" with player initials. Insertion rate is one per 10 packs.

		MT
Complete Set (30):		75.00
Common Player:		3.00
RA	Ryan Anderson	6.00
RiA	Rick Ankiel	15.00
LB	Lance Berkman	9.00
DB	Dermal Brown	3.00
BB	Brent Butler	3.00
EC	Eric Chavez	6.00
BC	Bruce Chen	3.00
MC	Matt Clement	4.50
FC	Francisco Cordero	3.00
DC	David Cortes	3.00
MD	Mike Darr	9.00
CE	Chris Enochs	3.00
CH	Chad Hermansen	3.00
RH	Ramon Hernandez	3.00
CK	Cesar, King	3.00
MK	Mike Kinkade	3.00
CL	Carlos Lee	4.50
GL	George Lombard	3.00
ML	Mike Lowell	6.00
RM	Ruben Mateo	3.00
GM	Gary Matthews Jr.	3.00
JaM	Jackson Melian	3.00
JM	Juan Melo	3.00
RyM	Ryan Minor	3.00
WM	Warren Morris	4.50
JP	John Patterson	3.00
BP	Ben Petrick	3.00
JW	Jayson Werth	3.00
MW	Matt White	3.00
EY	Eddie Yarnell	3.00

1999 SP Top Prospects Chirography Gold

This parallel of the 30-player Chirography insert series is highlighted on front with gold graphics. Each card is hand serially numbered within an edition of 25.

	MT
Common Player:	7.50
Stars:	4X

(See 1999 SP Top Prospects Chirography for checklist and base card values.)

1999 SP Top Prospects Destination the Show

The top names in minor league baseball are found in the checklist of this insert set. Cards have player photos on a silver-foil background. On the back the player

---

photo is repeated and there is a silver-foil serial number from within an edition of 100 of each card.

		MT
Complete Set (30):		50.00
Common Player:		2.00
D1	Ryan Anderson	3.00
D2	Rick Ankiel	8.00
D3	Lance Berkman	6.00
D4	Russell Branyan	2.00
D5	Juan Melo	2.00
D6	Alex Gonzalez	2.00
D7	Eric Chavez	6.00
D8	Bruce Chen	2.00
D9	Matt Clement	3.00
D10	Eddie Yarnell	2.00
D11	Dernell Stenson	2.00
D12	Corey Koskie	6.00
D13	J.D. Drew	12.50
D14	Chad Hermansen	2.00
D15	Ramon Hernandez	2.00
D16	Cesar King	2.00
D17	Mike Kinkade	3.00
D18	Carlos Lee	3.00
D19	George Lombard	2.00
D20	Ruben Mateo	2.00
D21	Gary Matthews Jr.	2.00
D22	Pat Burrell	10.00
D23	Ryan Minor	2.00
D24	Warren Morris	2.00
D25	Gabe Kapler	3.00
D26	Mike Lowell	6.00
D27	Jason Werth	2.00
D28	Matt White	2.00
D29	Pablo Ozuna	2.00
D30	Mike Stoner	2.00

1999 SP Top Prospects Great Futures

Minor league players deemed to have especially "Great Futures" are featured in this insert set. Fronts have action photos on gold refractive-foil backgrounds. Backs repeat a detail of the front photo and offer a few career highlights and stats. Cards are numbered with a "GF" prefix. Stated rate of insertion was one per five packs.

		MT
Complete Set (30):		45.00
Common Player:		1.50
GF1	Ryan Anderson	2.00
GF2	Rick Ankiel	2.00
GF3	Lance Berkman	2.50
GF4	Russell Branyan	1.50
GF5	Dermal Brown	1.50
GF6	Brent Butler	1.50
GF7	Eric Chavez	3.00
GF8	Bruce Chen	1.50
GF9	Matt Clement	2.50
GF10	Eddie Yarnell	1.50
GF11	Mike Darr	1.50
GF12	Chris Enochs	1.50
GF13	J.D. Drew	6.00
GF14	Chad Hermansen	1.50
GF15	Ramon Hernandez	1.50
GF16	Cesar King	1.50
GF17	Mike Kinkade	2.00
GF18	Carlos Lee	2.50
GF19	George Lombard	1.50
GF20	Ruben Mateo	1.50
GF21	Gary Matthews Jr.	1.50
GF22	Jackson Melian	1.50

GF23	Ryan Minor	1.50
GF24	Warren Morris	1.50
GF25	John Patterson	1.50
GF26	Ben Petrick	1.50
GF27	Jason Werth	1.50
GF28	Matt White	1.50
GF29	Francisco Cordero	1.50
GF30	Mike Stoner	1.50

1999 SP Top Prospects Retrospectives

The minor league careers of two of the 20th Century's greatest athletes are recalled in this insert set. Fronts have player photos with a gold-foil frame on a white background. The regular inserts are inserted at an announced rate of one per 13 packs. Additionally, each player autographed 10 of the his cards.

	MT
Complete Set (10):	10.00
Common Griffey (R1-R5):	1.50
Common Jordan (R6-R10):	1.50
Griffey Autographed Card:	200.00
Jordan Autographed Card:	325.00
(Random Inserts)	.00

1999 Starting Lineup Classic Doubles

"From the Minors to the Majors" was the theme chosen by Hasbro for its '99 Classic Doubles series. Each colorful 10" x 12" blister pack contains a pair of baseball cards and a pair of plastic action figures. One card/figure pair depicts the player in the uniform of one of his minor league teams. The other pair depicts him as a major leaguer. Values shown are for complete, unopened packages.

		MT
Complete Set (10):		75.00
Common Player:		7.00
(1)	Sandy Alomar Jr.	7.00
(2)	Darin Erstad	7.00
(3)	Nomar Garciaparra	8.00
(4)	Ken Griffey Jr.	11.00
(5)	Derek Jeter	12.00
(6)	Javy Lopez	7.00
(7)	Greg Maddux	8.00
(8)	Mark McGwire	11.00
(9)	Raul Mondesi	7.00
(10)	Alex Rodriguez	9.00

1999 Team Best Baseball America's Diamond Best Edition

The use on front of a gold- or silver-foil (each card can be found both ways) Team Best logo surmounted by a quartet of diamonds is all that differentiates the base cards in this issue from TB's earlier Baseball America Top Prospects issue. Diamond Best cards were issued six cards per pack, six packs per box along with a Team Best/Salvino Rookie Bammer stuffed bear representing one of five top minor league stars. Each bear is

---

accompanied by a special "Card of Authenticity" serially numbered within an edition of 10,000 each.

		MT
Complete Set (100):		5.00
Common Player:		.05
Wax Box (6+Bear):		
1	Paul Ah Yat	.05
2	Efrain Alamo	.05
3	Chip Alley	.05
4	Ryan Anderson	.25
5	Rick Ankiel	.10
6	Tony Armas Jr.	.10
7	Bronson Arroyo	.05
8	Mike Bacsik	.05
9	Kevin Barker	.05
10	Fletcher Bates	.05
11	Rob Bell	.05
12	Ron Belliard	.10
13	Peter Bergeron	.10
14	Lance Berkman	.25
15	Nick Bierbrodt	.05
16	Milton Bradley	.25
17	Russell Branyan	.10
18	Pat Burrell	2.00
19	Sean Burroughs	.50
20	Brent Butler	.05
21	Bruce Chen	.05
22	Chin-Feng Chen	.50
23	Giuseppe Chiaramonte	.05
24	Jin Ho Cho	.10
25	Francis Collins	.05
26	Joe Crede	.50
27	Cesar Crespo	.05
28	Bubba Crosby	.05
29	Michael Cuddyer	.15
30	Ben Davis	.05
31	Tim DeCinces	.05
32	Tomas de la Rosa	.05
33	Octavio Dotel	.05
34	Kelly Dransfeldt	.05
35	Tim Drew	.05
36	Matt Drews	.05
37	Mike Drumright	.05
38	Todd Dunn	.05
39	Chad Durham	.05
40	Alex Eckelman	.05
41	Chris Enochs	.05
42	Cordell Farley	.05
43	Frankie Figueroa	.05
44	Joe Fontenot	.05
45	Eric Gillespie	.05
46	Mike Glavine	.05
47	Jason Grote	.05
48	Jerry Hairston Jr.	.10
49	Toby Hall	.05
50	Chad Harville	.05
51	Alex Hernandez	.05
52	Junior Herndon	.05
53	Mike Huelsmann	.05
54	Aubrey Huff	.10
55	Chad Hutchinson	.05
56	Jamie Jones	.05
57	Kenny Kelly	.05
58	Scott Krause	.05
59	Jason LaRue	.05
60	Carlos Lee	.25
61	Corey Lee	.05
62	Willie Martinez	.05
63	Ruben Mateo	.10
64	Darnell McDonald	.05
65	Cody McKay	.05
66	Dan McKinley	.05
67	Jackson Melian	.05
68	Jason Middlebrook	.05
69	Ryan Minor	.05
70	Mark Mulder	.50
71	Vladimir Nunez	.05
72	Pablo Ozuna	.05
73	Corey Patterson	.50
74	John Patterson	.05
75	Josh Paul	.05
76	Angel Pena	.05
77	Carlos Pena	.05
78	Juan Pena	.05
79	Brad Penny	.10
80	Kyle Peterson	.05
81	Ben Petrick	.05
82	Calvin Pickering	.05
83	Arquimedez Pozo	.05
84	Paul Rigdon	.05
85	Grant Roberts	.05
86	Nate Rolison	.05
87	Damian Rolls	.05
88	Ryan Rupe	.05
89	Jose Santos	.05
90	Todd Sears	.05

91	Fernando Seguignol	.05
92	Brett Taft	.05
93	Chris Truby	.05
94	Jayson Werth	.05
95	Matt White	.05
96	Todd Williams	.05
97	Cliff Wilson	.05
98	Randy Wolf	.10
99	Kelly Wunsch	.05
100	Mike Zwicka	.05

1999 Team Best BA's Diamond Best Inserts

Player action photos and team logos on a white background are the front design for this insert set. Backs have a small copy of the front photo, a few biographical notes and career highlights. Cards are found on an average of one per 30 packs of Team Best Baseball America's Diamond Best Edition.

		MT
Complete Set (10):		20.00
Common Player:		2.00
1	Ryan Anderson	3.00
2	Pat Burrell	9.00
3	Bruce Chen	2.00
4	Mike Darr	2.00
5	Octavio Dotel	2.00
6	Jason LaRue	2.00
7	Damon Minor	2.00
8	Kyle Peterson	2.00
9	Fernando Seguignol	2.00
10	Alfonso Soriano	12.00

1999 Team Best Baseball America's Top Prospects Promos

Team Best partnered with baseball's best publication for minor league coverage to create a top prospects' card set. To debut the concept, this series of promo cards was issued. Fronts are virtually identical to the later-issued versions while all of the sample cards have an identical back. The back has a green baseball background with Team Best, Baseball America's Top Prospects, and National Association of Professional Baseball League's logos. A red strip at bottom has "Promotional Purposes Only" printed in white.

		MT
Complete Set (5):		5.00
Common Player:		1.00
(1)	Rick Ankiel (Regular)	1.00
(2)	Lance Berkman (Regular)	1.00
(3)	Pat Burrell (Possibilities)	2.50
(4)	Marcus Giles (MVP)	1.00
(5)	Ryan Minor (Scout's Choice)	1.00

1999 Team Best Baseball America's Top Prospects

The editors of "Baseball America" selected 100 top prospects for inclusion in this Team Best minor league issue which debuted in June. Cards have action photos on front

---

which are bordered at top and right in red. BA's logotype appears at top. The player's minor league team logo is at bottom-right. Backs have biographical data, draft details and career highlights along with appropriate logos. Cards were sold in six-card foil packs.

		MT
Complete Set (100):		5.00
Common Player:		.05
Wax Box (18):		15.00
1	Paul Ah Yat	.05
2	Efrain Alamo	.05
3	Chip Alley	.05
4	Ryan Anderson	.15
5	Rick Ankiel	.10
6	Tony Armas Jr.	.10
7	Bronson Arroyo	.05
8	Mike Bacsik	.05
9	Kevin Barker	.05
10	Fletcher Bates	.05
11	Rob Bell	.05
12	Ron Belliard	.10
13	Peter Bergeron	.10
14	Lance Berkman	.25
15	Nick Bierbrodt	.05
16	Milton Bradley	.25
17	Russell Branyan	.05
18	Pat Burrell	1.00
19	Sean Burroughs	.50
20	Brent Butler	.05
21	Bruce Chen	.05
22	Chin-Feng Chen	.50
23	Giuseppe Chiaramonte	.05
24	Jin Ho Cho	.10
25	Francis Collins	.05
26	Joe Crede	.50
27	Cesar Crespo	.05
28	Bubba Crosby	.05
29	Michael Cuddyer	.10
30	Ben Davis	.05
31	Tim DeCinces	.05
32	Tomas de la Rosa	.05
33	Octavio Dotel	.05
34	Kelly Dransfeldt	.05
35	Tim Drew	.05
36	Matt Drews	.05
37	Mike Drumright	.05
38	Todd Dunn	.05
39	Chad Durham	.05
40	Alex Eckelman	.05
41	Chris Enochs	.05
42	Cordell Farley	.05
43	Frankie Figueroa	.05
44	Joe Fontenot	.05
45	Eric Gillespie	.05
46	Mike Glavine	.05
47	Jason Grote	.05
48	Jerry Hairston Jr.	.10
49	Toby Hall	.05
50	Chad Harville	.05
51	Alex Hernandez	.05
52	Junior Herndon	.05
53	Mike Huelsmann	.05
54	Aubrey Huff	.10
55	Chad Hutchinson	.05
56	Jamie Jones	.05
57	Kenny Kelly	.05
58	Scott Krause	.05
59	Jason LaRue	.05
60	Carlos Lee	.25
61	Corey Lee	.05
62	Willie Martinez	.05
63	Ruben Mateo	.05
64	Darnell McDonald	.05
65	Cody McKay	.05
66	Dan McKinley	.05
67	Jackson Melian	.05
68	Jason Middlebrook	.05
69	Ryan Minor	.05
70	Mark Mulder	.45
71	Vladimir Nunez	.05
72	Pablo Ozuna	.05
73	Corey Patterson	.50
74	John Patterson	.05
75	Josh Paul	.05
76	Angel Pena	.05
77	Carlos Pena	.05
78	Juan Pena	.05
79	Brad Penny	.05
80	Kyle Peterson	.05
81	Ben Petrick	.05
82	Calvin Pickering	.05
83	Arquimedez Pozo	.05
84	Paul Rigdon	.05

85	Grant Roberts	.05
86	Nate Rolison	.05
87	Damian Rolls	.05
88	Ryan Rupe	.05
89	Jose Santos	.05
90	Todd Sears	.05
91	Fernando Seguignol	.05
92	Brett Taft	.05
93	Chris Truby	.05
94	Jayson Werth	.05
95	Matt White	.05
96	Todd Williams	.05
97	Cliff Wilson	.05
98	Randy Wolf	.05
99	Kelly Wunsch	.05
100	Mike Zwicka	.05
---	Promo Set/ Autograph Card Offer	
---	Promo Set/ 1996-1997 Pack Offer	
---	Promo Set Offer	

1999 Team Best BA's Top Prospects Box-Toppers

Each 18-pack box of Team Best Baseball America's Top Prospects includes one individually sleeved parallel card of the base set. Silver parallels are individually serial numbered to 150; gold parallels to 50.

	MT
Common Player, Silver:	1.00
Common Player, Gold:	3.00

(See checklist for base values; silvers valued at 7X, golds at 25X.)

1999 Team Best BA's Top Prospects Autographs

Sharing the format used in Team Best's earlier 1999 issue, the two-per-box autograph inserts in Baseball America's Top Prospects issue features virtually an entirely new line-up. Fronts have color photos with a diffused green background and the player's name in green. The Team Best logo is at top-left, the minor league team logo at bottom-left. Backs have an authentication statement overprinted on a baseball diamond photo. The autograph cards are not numbered and are listed here alphabetically. Insert signature cards of Mike Darr, Kevin McGlinchy and Tony Torcato which had been announced for this product were late in being returned to Team Best and were inserted into Player of the Year packs in the post-season.

		MT
Complete Set (47):		60.00
Common Player:		1.00
(1)	Rick Ankiel	2.50
(2)	Michael Barrett	2.50
(3)	Lance Berkman	3.00
(4)	A.J. Burnett	4.00
(5)	Steve Carver	1.00
(6)	Bruce Chen	1.00
(7)	Michael Cuddyer	3.00
(8)	Mike Darr	4.00
(9)	J.D. Drew	12.00

(10)	Tim Drew	1.00
(11)	Alex Escobar	2.00
(12)	Seth Etherton	1.50
(13)	Brian Falkenborg	1.00
(14)	Robert Fick	1.00
(15)	Mark Fischer	1.00
(16)	Eddy Furniss	1.00
(17)	Troy Glaus	15.00
(18)	Nathan Haynes	1.00
(19)	Chad Hermansen	2.00
(20)	Shea Hillenbrand	6.00
(21)	Mark Johnson	1.00
(22)	Adam Kennedy	2.00
(23)	Jason LaRue	1.50
(24)	Matt LeCroy	1.50
(25)	Carlos Lee	4.00
(26)	Corey Lee	1.00
(27)	Felipe Lopez	1.00
(28)	Darnell McDonald	1.00
(29)	Kevin McGlinchy	2.00
(30)	Mark Mulder	6.00
(31)	Trot Nixon	4.00
(32)	Todd Noel	1.00
(33)	Pablo Ozuna	1.00
(34)	Brad Penny	1.50
(35)	Calvin Pickering	1.00
(36)	Matt Riley	1.00
(37)	Jason Romano	1.00
(38)	Ryan Rupe	1.00
(39)	Randall Simon	1.00
(40)	Jason Standridge	1.00
(41)	Nathan Teut	1.00
(42)	Tony Torcato	1.00
(43)	Pete Tucci	1.00
(44)	Eric Valent	1.00
(45)	Vernon Wells	4.00
(46)	Jake Westbrook	1.00
(47)	Randy Wolf	2.00

1999 Team Best BA's Top Prospects Best Possibilities

Two players each are featured on these double-front cards. Inserted at the rate of about one per 18-pack box, the inserts feature action photos against a pastel swirling background.

		MT
Complete Set (5):		5.00
Common Player:		.75
1	Ryan Anderson, Calvin Pickering	1.00
2	Rick Ankiel, Chad Hermansen	1.00
3	Ryan Bradley, Ryan Minor	.75
4	John Patterson, Lance Berkman	1.00
5	Brad Penny, Pat Burrell	2.00

1999 Team Best BA's Top Prospects League MVP

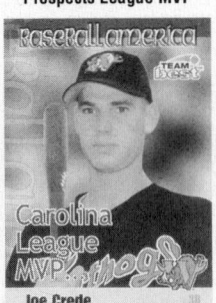

MVPs of various minor leagues are featured in this one-per-box insert set. Fronts have portrait photos on a blurred background. BA's logotype is in a blue stripe at top, player name and position are in an orange stripe at bottom. Team logos appear at lower-right. On back is a large Baseball America Top Prospects logo and a summary of the player's MVP season. The same cards were inserted

into TB's Baseball America's Diamond Best edition at the rate of one per 19 packs.

		MT
Complete Set (10):		15.00
Common Player:		2.00
1	Brian August	2.00
2	Joe Crede	4.00
3	Shawn Gallagher	2.00
4	Jay Gibbons	4.00
5	Marcus Giles	4.00
6	Jason Hart	2.00
7	Tyrone Horne	2.00
8	Pablo Ozuna	2.00
9	Brad Penny	2.50
10	Calvin Pickering	2.00

1999 Team Best BA's Top Prospects Scout's Choice

The "Scout's Choice" for major league stardom are presented in the scarcest (one per 90 packs) of the BA's Top Prospects insert sets. Cards have a simulated Polaroid photo of the player on a woodlook background with a paperclip and team logo at upper-right and a gold seal at lower-right. Backs repeat some of the front details and have a scouting report and previous season stats.

		MT
Complete Set (10):		12.00
Common Player:		1.50
1	Rick Ankiel	1.50
2	Lance Berkman	2.00
3	Pat Burrell	5.00
4	Octavio Dotel	1.50
5	Alex Escobar	1.50
6	George Lombard	1.50
7	Ruben Mateo	1.50
8	Ryan Minor	1.50
9	Pablo Ozuna	1.50
10	Dernell Stenson	1.50

1999 Team Best Player of the Year

Team Best's post-season card set features top stars at all stops on road to the big leagues. The 50-card base set offers color action photos on which the background has been muted in shades of blue. Backs have season stats, a few biographical data, a career highlight or two and a color team logo. Player of the Year was sold in six-card foil packs.

		MT
Complete Set (50):		5.00
Common Player:		.05
Wax Box (18):		24.00
1	Ryan Anderson	.10
2	Rick Ankiel	.10
3	Jeff Austin	.05
4	Kurt Bierek	.05
5	Jung Bong	.10
6	Dee Brown	.05
7	Nate Bump	.05
8	Pat Burrell	1.00
9	Sean Burroughs	.35
10	Brent Butler	.05
11	Chin-Feng Chen	.50

12	Hee Seop Choi	.50
13	Joe Crede	.50
14	Jack Cust	.20
15	Travis Dawkins	.25
16	Trent Durrington	.05
17	Seth Etherton	.10
18	Vince Faison	.05
19	Choo Freeman	.10
20	Rafael Furcal	.25
21	Jay Gibbons	.15
22	Marcus Giles	.25
23	J.M. Gold	.05
24	Jeff Goldbach	.05
25	Josh Hamilton	.10
26	Kevin Haverbusch	.05
27	D'Angelo Jimenez	.05
28	Nick Johnson	.75
29	Adam Kennedy	.15
30	Steve Lomasney	.05
31	George Lombard	.05
32	Felipe Lopez	.05
33	Jason Marquis	.25
34	Tydus Meadows	.05
35	Aaron Myette	.05
36	Corey Patterson	.40
37	Carlos Pena	.10
38	Adam Piatt	.15
39	Julio Ramirez	.05
40	Matt Riley	.05
41	Juan Rivera	.15
42	Jason Romano	.05
43	Aaron Rowand	.05
44	C.C. Sabathia	.25
45	Alfonso Soriano	2.00
46	Jason Standridge	.05
47	Dernell Stenson	.05
48	Jorge Toca	.05
49	Eric Valent	.05
50	Jayson Werth	.05

1999 Team Best Player of the Year Silver/Gold

Each of the 50 base cards in Player of the Year was paralleled in silver- and gold-foil enhanced editions. Fronts have a foil company logo at upper-right, while each card is serially numbered on back; the silvers to 150, the golds to 50.

	MT
Common Silver:	1.50
Silver Stars:	7X
Common Gold:	3.00
Gold Stars:	25X

(See 1999 Team Best Player of the Year for checklist and base card values.)

1999 Team Best Player of the Year Ankiel/Piatt

Two top candidates for Player of the Year honors, pitcher Rick Ankiel and third baseman Adam Piatt are featured in this insert set. Cards have player photos on a sepia background with a pair of TB POY logos. Backs repeat the front photo in a muted image and have stats, biographical data and career highlights.

		MT
Complete Set (10):		5.00
Common Card:		.50
1-6	Rick Ankiel	.50
7-10	Adam Piatt	.50

1999 Team Best Player of the Year Autographs

The authentically autographed cards which drive the sale of most minor league singles products were inserted about one per three packs of Player of the Year. Besides 19 autograph cards specifically designated for the POY issue, cards of Mike Darr, Kevin McGlinchy and Tony Torcato which were received too late for inclusion in TB's Baseball America's Top Prospects issue were also inserted. (They are cataloged with the BATP issue.) The POY autographs have player photos on a linen-look background with the name in purple and a graduated purple band vertically at left. Backs have a congratulatory message of appreciation from TB's chairman. The unnumbered cards are checklisted here alphabetically.

		MT
Complete Set (19):		25.00
Common Player:		2.00
(1)	Tony Armas Jr.	2.00
(2)	Nick Bierbrodt	1.00
(3)	Jamie Brown	1.00
(4)	Jesus Colome	1.00
(5)	Kelly Dransfeldt	1.00
(6)	Adam Everett	2.00
(7)	Vince Faison	1.00
(8)	Junior Herndon	1.00
(9)	Aubrey Huff	2.00
(10)	Corey Lee	1.00
(11)	Jason Marquis	2.00
(12)	Willie Martinez	1.00
(13)	Corey Patterson	6.00
(14)	Carlos Pena	2.00
(15)	Ben Petrick	2.00
(16)	Paul Rigdon	1.00
(17)	Grant Roberts	1.00
(18)	C.C. Sabathia	6.00
(19)	Jason Tyner	1.00

1999 Team Best Player of the Year Contenders

The scarcest inserts in the set are these top candidates for Minor League Player of the Year honors. Fronts have action photos set on a silver foil-look background with a large POY logo. Backs have a smaller version of the front photo, personal data, season stats and the players credentials for the honor. Contenders were seeded on average of one per 90 packs.

		MT
Complete Set (10):		35.00
Common Player:		2.00
1	Dee Brown	2.00
2	Pat Burrell	9.00
3	Chin-Feng Chen	3.00
4	Rafael Furcal	3.00
5	Nick Johnson	7.50
6	Ramon Ortiz	2.00
7	Aramis Ramirez	3.00
8	Matt Riley	2.00
9	Jason Standridge	2.00
10	Vernon Wells	2.00

1999 Team Best Player of the Year Past POY Autographs

Autographed cards of past Team Best Players of the Year were a special insert in the '99 issue. No average insertion rate was given.

		MT
Complete Set (3):		15.00
(1)	Andruw Jones	10.00
(2)	Paul Konerko	5.00
(3)	Eric Chavez	5.00

1999 Team Best Rookie Promos

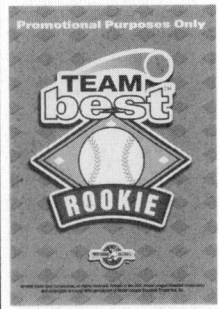

This quartet of sample cards was issued to introduce Team Best's 1999 Rookie edition. Fronts of the cards are identical to the issued versions. Backs have a red background with large Team Best Rookie logo and promo notice.

		MT
Complete Set (5):		5.00
Common Player:		1.00
(1)	Ryan Bradley (Best Guns)	1.00
(2)	Alex Escobar (Best Wheels)	1.00
(3)	Adam Everett (Best Lumber)	1.00
(4)	Marcus Giles (Best Lumber)	2.00
(5)	Pablo Ozuna, J.D. Drew (1999 Future Stars)	2.00

1999 Team Best Rookie

J.D. Drew • OF

Top prospects at all levels of the minor leagues going into the 1999 season are featured in the base set and insert series of Team Best Rookie. Regular cards have action photos set against a woven-look background with a large baseball, diamond diagram and "ROOKIE" banner. The issuer's logo is at upper-left, the player's minor league team logo from the previous season is at upper-right. Backs have a large team logo at center and 1998 stats. Each box of 18 foil packs included one individually sleeved gold (edition of 50) or silver (edition of 125) parallel of a base-set card.

		MT
Complete Set (100):		5.00
Common Player:		.05
Wax Box (18):		15.00
1	Chip Ambres	.05
2	Scott Barrett	.05
3	Todd Bellhorn	.05
4	Darren Blakely	.05
5	Matt Borne	.05
6	Nate Bump	.05
7	Ryan Bundy	.05
8	Eric Byrnes	.05
9	David Callahan	.05
10	Rob Castelli	.05
11	Doug Clark	.05
12	Greg Clark	.05
13	Darryl Conyer	.05
14	Jeremy Cotten	.05
15	Bubba Crosby	.05

16	Mike Curry	.05
17	Mike Dean	.05
18	David Diaz	.05
19	Jeremy Dodson	.05
20	Ryan Drese	.05
21	J.D. Drew	1.00
22	Morgan Ensberg	.10
23	Adam Everett	.10
24	Mike Fischer	.05
25	Pete Fisher	.05
26	Josh Fogg	.05
27	Brad Freeman	.05
28	Nate Frese	.05
29	Eddy Furniss	.05
30	Keith Ginter	.05
31	Eric Good	.05
32	Josh Hancock (Error, blue cap.)	.25
32	Josh Hancock (Correct, red cap.)	.25
33	Ryan Harber	.05
34	Jason Hart	.05
35	Jason Hill	.05
36	Heath Honeycutt	.05
37	Aubrey Huff	.10
38	Chad Hutchinson	.05
39	Brandon Inge	.05
40	Brett Jodie	.05
41	Gabe Johnson	.05
42	Clint Johnston	.05
43	Jesse Joyce	.05
44	Randy Keisler	.05
45	Jarrod Kingrey	.05
46	Craig Kuzmic	.05
47	Tim Lemon	.05
48	Ryan Lentz	.05
49	Neil Longo	.05
50	Felipe Lopez	.05
51	Javier Lopez	.05
52	Phil Lowery	.05
53	Chris Magruder	.05
54	Mike Maroth	.05
55	Kennon McArthur	.05
56	Shawn McCorkle	.05
57	Arturo McDowell	.05
58	Josh McKinley	.05
59	Jason Michaels	.05
60	Ryan Moskau	.05
61	Mark Mulder	.65
62	Will Ohman	.05
63	Todd Ozias	.05
64	Matt Padgett	.05
65	Corey Patterson	.50
66	Adam Pettyjohn	.05
67	Brad Piercy	.05
68	Scott Pratt	.05
69	Kris Rayborn	.05
70	Chris Reinike	.05
71	Billy Rich	.05
72	Ryan Ridenour	.05
73	Brian Rogers	.05
74	Aaron Rowand	.10
75	Ryan Rupe	.05
76	C.C. Sabathia	.50
77	Jason Saenz	.05
78	Aaron Sams	.05
79	Sammy Serrano	.05
80	Clint Smith	.05
81	Pat Burrell	1.00
82	Zach Sorensen	.05
83	Steve Stemle	.05
84	John Stewart	.05
85	Tyler Thompson	.05
86	Matt Thornton	.05
87	Tony Torcato	.05
88	Keola de la Tori	.05
89	Andres Torres	.05
90	Jason Tyner	.05
91	Jeff Urban	.05
92	Eric Valent	.05
93	Derek Wathan	.05
94	Jeff Weaver	.05
95	Jake Weber	.05
96	Ken Westmoreland	.05
97	Brad Wilkerson	.10
98	Clyde Williams	.05
99	Jeff Winchester	.05
100	Mitch Wylie	.05

INSERTED OFFER CARDS

	'95 First Round Picks Set	.05
	Baseball America Subscription	.05
	Promo Card Set	
	Promo Card Set Plus Packs and Autograph	.05

1999 Team Best Rookie Gold/Silver Parallels

Eric Valent • OF

Each 18-pack box of Team Best Rookie includes as a box-topper an individually sleeved silver- or gold-foil parallel to one of the base cards. Except for the metallic foil on front and the serial number on back, the parallels are identical to the issued cards. Silver parallels are numbered within an edition of 125; golds in an edition of 50.

	MT
Common Silver:	1.50
Common Gold:	3.00

(High-demand cards valued at multipliers of base cards: Silver - 7X; Gold - 25X.)

1999 Team Best Rookie Autographs

The best of the Best Rookie series is featured in this insert set. Cards have authentic autographs across the front and have an authenticity notice on back. Two dozen of the featured players were inserted at the average rate of two per box (about one per nine packs) while autographed cards of J.D. Drew were seeded at one per case (180 packs).

		MT
Complete Set (25):		35.00
Common Player:		1.00
1	Rick Ankiel	2.00
2	Michael Barrett	3.00
3	Lance Berkman	3.00
4	A.J. Burnett	3.00
5	Bruce Chen	1.00
6	Michael Cuddyer	1.50
7	J.D. Drew	6.00
8	Alex Escobar	2.00
9	Seth Etherton	1.50
10	Mark Fischer	1.00
11	Troy Glaus	12.00
12	Nathan Haynes	1.00
13	Shea Hillenbrand	4.00
14	Matt LeCroy	1.00
15	Corey Lee	1.00
16	Trot Nixon	4.00
17	Todd Noel	1.00
18	Pablo Ozuna	1.00
19	Brad Penny	1.50
20	Calvin Pickering	1.00
21	Matt Riley	1.00
22	Jason Romano	1.00
23	Pete Tucci	1.00
24	Eric Valent	1.00
25	Jake Westbrook	1.00

1999 Team Best Rookie Best Guns

Inserted at an announced rate of about one per box, this chase set features the hardest-throwing prospects in the minor leagues. Fronts have photos showing the awesome arms in action. A baseball trailing flames appears at lower-left, the player's minor league team logo at upper-right. Backs repeat part of the front photo within the

flaming fastball motif and offer previous season's stats and a few words about the pitcher.

		MT
Complete Set (10):		7.50
Common Player:		1.00
1	Ryan Anderson	1.50
2	Rick Ankiel	1.00
3	Ryan Bradley	1.00
4	Bruce Chen	1.00
5	Matt Clement	2.00
6	Octavio Dotel	1.00
7	John Patterson	1.00
8	Matt Riley	1.00
9	Brent Stentz	1.00
10	Ed Yarnall	1.00

1999 Team Best Rookie Best Lumber

Projected heavy hitters on their way to the major leagues are featured in this hobby-only chase set. The players' power swings are shown on front photos superimposed over a bat knob and overprinted with a "best LUMBER" logo in the style of a bat's label. Average rate of insertion was announced as one per 90 packs. Backs repeat the front motif and part of the front photo, adding some biographical and career details, along with 1998 stats.

		MT
Complete Set (10):		45.00
Common Player:		2.00
1	Michael Barrett	4.00
2	Lance Berkman	4.00
3	J.D. Drew	10.00
4	Marcus Giles	6.00
5	Troy Glaus	15.00
6	George Lombard	2.00
7	Doug Mientkiewicz	6.00
8	Trot Nixon	4.00
9	Calvin Pickering	2.00
10	Pete Tucci	2.00

1999 Team Best Rookie Best Wheels

Carlos Febles

The projected base-stealing and ball-hawking kings of the future are presented in this insert set. Stated insertion rate is one per 19 packs. Fronts have a portrait photo. Backs repeat part of the photo and offer biographical data, 1998 stats and a few words about the player.

		MT
Complete Set (5):		3.00
Common Player:		.50
1	Alex Escobar	2.50
2	Cordell Farley	.50
3	Carlos Febles	1.00
4	Nathan Haynes	.50
5	Pablo Ozuna	.50

1999 Team Best Rookie Future Stars

With two players per card, the odds are doubled that one will be a major league superstar of the future. Fronts have a pair of portrait

1999 FUTURE STARS

Rick Ankiel - P   Chad Hutchinson - P

photos. Backs have a large Team Best Rookie logo and a serial number from within an edition of 900 per card. Stated odds of finding a Future Stars card are one per box.

		MT
Complete Set (25):		35.00
Common Player:		1.00
1	Darryl Conyer, Javier Lopez	1.00
2	Troy Cameron, Luis Rivera	1.00
3	Troy Glaus, Darren Blakely	5.00
4	Jayson Werth, Darnell McDonald	1.00
5	Adam Everett, Mike Maroth	1.00
6	Aaron Rowand, Josh Fogg	1.00
7	Corey Patterson, Aaron Sams	3.00
8	C.C. Sabathia, Zach Sorensen	2.00
9	Jeff Weaver, Brandon Inge	1.50
10	Chip Ambres, Derek Wathan	1.00
11	Bubba Crosby, Ryan Moskau	1.00
12	Josh McKinley, Brad Wilkerson	1.00
13	Randy Keisler, Ryan Bradley	1.00
14	Jason Tyner, Jason Saenz	1.00
15	Mark Mulder, Jason Hart	3.00
16	Eric Valent, Jason Michaels	1.00
17	Clint Johnston, Eddy Furniss	1.00
18	Pablo Ozuna, J.D. Drew	4.00
19	Rick Ankiel, Chad Hutchinson	1.50
20	J.D. Drew, Tim Drew	4.00
21	Darnell McDonald, Donzell McDonald	1.00
22	Tony Torcato, Nate Bump	1.00
23	Matt Thornton, Ryan Anderson	1.50
24	Felipe Lopez, Vernon Wells	1.50
25	Ryan Bundy, Jarrod Kingrey	1.00

1999 Team Best Rookie League Leaders

Projected league leaders on their way to the major leagues are featured in this retail-only chase set which is virtually identical to the Best Lumber hobby insert. The players' power swings are shown on front photos superimposed on a plain blue background with a "League Leaders" logo in the style of a bat's label. Backs repeat the front motif and part of the front photo, adding some biographical and career details, along with 1998 stats.

		MT
Complete Set (10):		45.00
Common Player:		2.00
1	Michael Barrett	4.00
2	Lance Berkman	4.00
3	J.D. Drew	7.50
4	Marcus Giles	6.00
5	Troy Glaus	15.00
6	George Lombard	2.00
7	Doug Mientkiewicz	6.00
8	Trot Nixon	6.00
9	Calvin Pickering	2.00
10	Pete Tucci	2.00

1999 Team Best Salvino Rookie Bammers Card/Authenticity

Each of the "Rookie Bammer" stuffed bears issued with the Baseball America's Diamond Best Edition card set was accompanied by a "Card of Authenticity." Fronts have action photos with three stars in the background and a minor league team logo at lower-right. Backs repeat the front photo in a ghosted image and have a notice of authenticity from Team Best CEO Don White. Each card is serially numbered from within an edition of 10,000 each. Sample versions of each card were also produced, marked with a strip on back, "Promotional Purposes Only" and numbered "10000/10000." they are valued at $1-2 apiece.

		MT
Complete Set (6):		15.00
Common Player:		2.50
(1)	Ryan Anderson	2.50
(2)	Rick Ankiel	2.50
(3)	Lance Berkman	3.00
(4)	Pat Burrell	5.00
(5)	J.D. Drew (Arkansas Travelers)	4.00
(6)	J.D. Drew (Memphis Redbirds)	4.00

1999 Minor League Team Sets

Manufacturers abbreviations used include: BL - Blueline Communications; GS - Grandstand; MA - Multi-Ad Services; TM - team issued; CH - Choice Marketing.

		MT
200 Team Sets and Variations		8.50
1999	WT Adirondack Lumberjacks (26)	4.00
1999	MA Akron Aeros (30)	6.00
1999	WT Albany-Colonie Diamond Dogs (26)	4.00
1999	GS Albuquerque Dukes (30)	12.00
1999	GS Albuquerque Dukes Sponsor's Set (31)	6.00
1999	GS Altoona Curve (31)	8.00
1999	MA Appalachian League Top Prospects (30)	12.00
1999	Arizona Fall League (30)	15.00
1999	MA Arkansas Travelers (30)	16.00
1999	MA Asheville Tourists (30)	12.00
1999	GS Asheville Tourists Update (10)	12.00
1999	GS Auburn Doubledays (33)	7.00
1999	MA Augusta GreenJackets (30)	7.00
1999	TM Bakersfield Blaze (30)	8.00
1999	TM Batavia Muckdogs (41)	17.50
1999	MA Beloit Snappers (29)	7.00

		MT
1999	GS Billings Mustangs (32)	11.00
1999	BL Binghamton Mets (30)	8.00
1999	TM Binghamton Mets "Jumbo" (12)	20.00
1999	GS Birmingham Barons (30)	8.00
1999	GS Bluefield Orioles (32)	7.00
1999	GS Boise Hawks (34)	7.00
1999	MA Bowie Baysox (30)	7.00
1999	MA Brevard County Manatees (30)	7.00
1999	GS Bristol Sox (30)	7.00
1999	GS Bristol Sox Update (6)	4.00
1999	BL Buffalo Bisons (32)	7.00
1999	MA Burlington Bees (33)	7.00
1999	GS Burlington Indians (32)	8.00
1999	GS Butte Copper Kings (33)	8.00
1999	TM Cape Fear Crocs (30)	9.00
1999	MA Capital City Bombers (30)	8.00
1999	MA Capital City '98 SAL Champs (31)	20.00
1999	CH Carolina League Prospects (30)	10.00
1999	TM Carolina Mudcats (31)	9.00
1999	MA Cedar Rapids Kernels (34)	5.00
1999	MA Charleston Alley Cats (30)	7.00
1999	TM Charleston River Dogs (32)	8.00
1999	BL Charlotte Knights (30)	7.00
1999	GS Chattanooga Lookouts (30)	7.00
1999	GS Chico Heat (27)	4.00
1999	GS Chillicothe Paints (26)	4.00
1999	MA Clearwater Phillies (30)	8.00
1999	GS Clinton LumberKings (32)	7.00
1999	TM Colorado Springs Sky Sox (30)	8.00
1999	BL Columbus Clippers (31)	8.00
1999	MA Columbus RedStixx (30)	8.00
1999	TM Columbus RedStixx (30)	45.00
1999	GS Danville Braves (30)	25.00
1999	Roox Daytona Cubs (30)	10.00
1999	MA Delmarva Shorebirds (29)	9.00
1999	MA Dunedin Blue Jays (30)	6.00
1999	BL Durham Bulls (30)	7.00
1999	TM Edmonton Trappers (25)	10.00
1999	TM Edmonton Trappers W/QCP Logos (25)	15.00
1999	TM Elizabethton Twins (32)	12.00
1999	GS El Paso Diablos (30)	5.00
1999	MA Erie Seawolves (28)	7.00
1999	GS Eugene Emeralds (30)	6.00
1999	GS Everett Aqua Sox (31)	6.00
1999	TM Fargo-Moorhead RedHawks (29)	4.00
1999	GS Frederick Keys (28)	5.00
1999	GS Fresno Grizzlies (30)	8.00
1999	TM Ft. Myers Miracle (31)	7.00
1999	MA Ft. Wayne Wizards (30)	10.00
1999	MA Great Falls Dodgers (30)	7.00
1999	MA Greensboro Bats (30)	7.00
1999	GS Greenville Braves (28)	7.00
1999	MA Hagerstown Suns (30)	7.00
1999	MA Harrisburg Senators (30)	9.00
1999	MA Helena Brewers (30)	8.00
1999	MA Hickory Crawdads (30)	6.50
1999	MA Hickory Crawdads Update (30)	6.50
1999	GS High Desert Mavericks (30)	7.00
1999	GS H.D. Mavericks Sponsor's Set (27)	9.00
1999	GS Hudson Valley Renegades (32)	11.00
1999	GS Hudson Valley Renegades Update (1)	6.00
1999	GS H.V. Renegades Update, Autographed	20.00
1999	TM Huntsville Stars (30)	10.00
1999	BL Indianapolis Indians (31)	8.00
1999	International League Top Prospects (30)	10.00
1999	MA Iowa Cubs (30)	7.00
1999	MA Jackson Generals (30)	7.00
1999	GS Jacksonville Suns (28)	7.00

1999	GS Jacksonville Suns Update (5)	15.00
1999	TM Johnson City Cardinals (36)	6.50
1999	TM Kane County Cougars (31)	8.00
1999	CH Kinston Indians (30)	8.00
1999	MA Kissimmee Cobras (30)	15.00
1999	GS Knoxville Smokies (27)	7.00
1999	GS Lake Elsinore Land Sharks (33)	9.00
1999	GS Lake Elsinore Storm (30)	7.00
1999	MA Lakeland Tigers (30)	6.00
1999	GS Lancaster JetHawks (30)	6.00
1999	GS Lancaster JetHawks (Valley Press)(30)	9.00
1999	GS Lancaster Stealth (34)	9.00
1999	GS Lansing Lugnuts (29)	10.00
1999	MA Las Vegas Stars (30)	8.00
1999	BL Louisville RiverBats (34)	10.00
1999	MA Lowell Spinners (32)	8.00
1999	CH Lynchburg Hillcats (30)	8.00
1999	MA Macon Braves (30)	10.00
1999	MA Mahoning Valley Scrappers (30)	12.50
1999	GS Martinsville Astros (30)	8.00
1999	TM Memphis Redbirds (30)	12.00
1999	MA Michigan Battle Cats (30)	12.00
1999	GS Midland Rockhounds (30)	10.00
1999	TM Midland Rockhounds (25)	55.00
1999	MA Midwest League Prospects (29)	12.00
1999	GS Missoula Osprey (31)	15.00
1999	TM Mobile Baybears (32)	10.00
1999	GS Modesto A's (30)	6.00
1999	GS Modesto Sponsor's Set - Krier's (30)	9.00
1999	MA Myrtle Beach Pelicans (30)	9.00
1999	TM Nashville Sounds (30)	8.00
1999	MA New Britain Rock Cats (30)	8.00
1999	BL New Haven Ravens (30)	8.00
1999	MA New Jersey Cardinals (32)	8.00
1999	TM N.J. Cardinals Top Prospects (6)	9.00
1999	WT New Jersey Jackals (27)	7.00
1999	MA New Orleans Zephyrs (28)	11.00
1999	BL Norfolk Tides (36)	9.00
1999	BL Norwich Navigators (30)	11.00
1999	TM Ogden Raptors (37)	15.00
1999	MA Oklahoma Redhawks (30)	7.00
1999	MA Omaha Golden Spikes (30)	8.00
1999	MA Orlando Rays (30)	9.00
1999	BL Pawtucket Red Sox (30)	9.00
1999	DD Pawtucket Red Sox Foldout	30.00
1999	MA Peoria Chiefs (30)	7.00
1999	MA Piedmont Boll Weevils (30)	8.00
1999	MA Pittsfield Mets (30)	7.00
1999	GS Portland Sea Dogs (30)	9.00
1999	CH Potomac Cannons (30)	7.00
1999	CH Potomac Cannons Update (7)	6.50
1999	GS Princeton Devil Rays (30)	25.00
1999	GS Princeton Devil Rays Update (30)	5.00
1999	GS Pulaski Rangers (30)	6.00
1999	TM Quad City River Bandits (31)	8.00
1999	GS Rancho Cucamonga Surfers (31)	8.00
1999	GS Rancho Cucamonga Quakes (30)	8.00
1999	GS Rancho Cucamonga Quakes Update (1)	12.00
1999	MA Reading Phillies (28)	9.00
1999	MA Reading Phils Alvernia College (28)	35.00
1999	MA Reading Phillies Update (30)	15.00
1999	MA Reading Phillies Stadium Cards (3)	24.00
1999	BL Richmond Braves (30)	8.00
1999	Richmond Camera Richmond Braves (20)	40.00
1999	GS Rio Grand Valley WhiteWings (25)	4.00

1999	BL Rochester Red Wings (30)	7.00
1999	TM Rockford Reds (28)	10.00
1999	CH Salem Avalanche (30)	7.00
1999	GS Salem-Keizer Volcanoes (36)	7.00
1999	GS San Antonio Missions (31)	10.00
1999	GS San Bernardino Stampede (31)	8.00
1999	BL San Jose Giants (30)	8.00
1999	TM Sarasota Red Sox (29)	8.00
1999	MA Savannah Sand Gnats (29)	8.00
1999	BL Scranton/Wilkes-Barre Red Barons (32)	8.00
1999	MA Shreveport Captains (28)	9.00
1999	GS Sioux City X's (30)	4.00
1999	TM Sonoma County Crushers (24)	8.00
1999	MA South Atlantic League Prospects (30)	15.00
1999	MA South Bend Silver Hawks (31)	7.00
1999	GS Southern League Top Prospects (31)	9.00
1999	GS Southern Oregon Timberjacks (29)	8.00
1999	Wonder Bread So. Oregon Timberjacks (10)	20.00
1999	GS So. Oregon Timberjacks Update (8)	5.00
1999	GS Spokane Indians (35)	9.00
1999	MA Staten Island Yankees (33)	10.00
1999	GS Stockton Ports (30)	7.00
1999	MA St. Catherines Stompers (30)	8.00
1999	GS St. Lucie Mets (31)	9.00
1999	TM St. Paul Saints (32)	5.00
1999	MA St. Petersburg Devil Rays (29)	10.00
1999	TM Syracuse SkyChiefs (28)	8.00
1999	BL Tacoma Rainiers (30)	8.00
1999	MA Tampa Yankees (28)	15.00
1999	MA Tampa Yankees Update (30)	17.50
1999	GS Texas League Top Prospects (32)	12.00
1999	BL Toledo Mud Hens (32)	8.00
1999	MA Trenton Thunder (30)	10.00
1999	MA Tucson Sidewinders (29)	7.00
1999	TM Tulsa Drillers (30)	9.00
1999	GS Vancouver Canadians (30)	24.00
1999	GS Vermont Expos (35)	8.00
1999	MA Vero Beach Dodgers (30)	8.00
1999	GS Visalia Oaks (27)	10.00
1999	WT Waterbury Spirit (25)	4.00
1999	MA West Michigan Whitecaps (30)	7.00
1999	MA West Michigan Whitecaps Update (12)	12.00
1999	MA W. Mich. Whitecaps '94-'98 Stars (30)	9.00
1999	GS West Tennessee Diamond Jaxx (30)	8.00
1999	CH Wichita Wranglers (30)	8.00
1999	CH Wichita Wranglers/ Sedgwick Zoo (30)	12.00
1999	MA Williamsport Crosscutters (34)	8.00
1999	CH Wilmington Blue Rocks (30)	9.00
1999	CH Winston- Salem Warthogs (30)	9.00
1999	MA Wisconsin Timber Rattlers (35)	8.00
1999	GS Yakima Bears (31)	9.00

2000 High School All-Americans

JUSTIN HILEMAN
PALMYRA HIGH SCHOOL

(Production reported as 10,000 regular sets, 1,000 foil sets; 1,000 autographed Espinosa and Stokes cards randomly inserted.)

	MT
Complete Set (10):	12.50

Complete Set, Foil (10):		40.00
Autographed Stokes:		25.00
Autographed Espinosa:		10.00
1	Jason Stokes	.00
2	Laynce Nix	.00
3	Rocco Baldelli	.00
4	Justin Hileman	.00
5	Jason Kaanoi	.00
6	Derek Thompson	.00
7	David Espinosa	.00
8	Dustin McGowan	.00
9	Rocco Baldelli (Player/Year)	.00
10	Checklist	.00

2000 Huntsville Stars 1986 Mark McGwire Reprint

This unmarked reprint of the 1986 team-issued, Burger King-sponsored McGwire minor league card was produced by the team in 2000 and sold in its concession stands. Identical in format and size (2-3/8" x 3-1/2") to the original, the reprint has different typography on front and back and is easily differentiated by the lack of a registration symbol at the bottom-right of the BK logo. Production was reported as at least 10,000.

		MT
33	Mark McGwire	6.00

2000 Just Imagine 2k

BOBBY SEAY P
ST. PETERSBURG DEVIL RAYS

The use of third-party certified autograph cards on a two-per-box basis, along with randomly inserted game-used equipment cards was featured in this mid-season minor league foil-pack product. Cards in the six-card foil packs are numbered contiguously from the company's Just the Preview 2k product, from #101-199. Fronts of the base cards have white-bordered photos with a large color band horizontally at center, which carries the product logo, player name, position abbreviation and team. On back is the same photo with a white band at center carrying vital data and 1999 stats. A large color block at bottom has a small team logo and copyright notice. A gold-bordered factory set version was issued in an edition of 5,000.

	MT
Complete Set (100):	5.00
Common Player:	.05
Gold:	1X
Wax Box (24+2):	20.00

101	Rick Ankiel	.10
102	Ricardo Aramboles	.05
103	Rick Asadoorian	.05
104	Jeff Austin	.05
105	Danys Baez	.05
106	Brad Baisley	.05
107	Matt Belisle	.05
108	Lance Berkman	.25
109	Wilson Betemit	.10
110	Nick Bierbrodt	.05
111	Casey Blake	.05
112	Josh Bonifay	.05
113	Bobby Bradley	.05
114	Milton Bradley	.25
115	Junior Brignac	.05
116	Roosevelt Brown	.05
117	Pat Burrell	.50
118	Sean Burroughs	.50
119	Ben Christiansen	.35
120	Ryan Christenson	.05
121	Michael Coleman	.05
122	Jesus Colome	.05
123	Jesus Cordero	.05
124	Nate Cornejo	.05
125	Robbie Crabtree	.05
126	Jack Cust	.05
127	Casey Daigle	.05
128	Ben Davis	.05
129	Travis Dawkins	.25
130	Choo Freeman	.10

131	Chris George	.05
132	Gary Glover	.05
133	Jerry Hairston Jr.	.10
134	Ken Harvey	.05
135	Jeff Heaverlo	.05
136	Elvin Hernandez	.05
137	J.R. House	.05
138	Ty Howington	.05
139	Aubrey Huff	.10
140	Norm Hutchins	.05
141	Chad Hutchinson	.05
142	Brandon Inge	.05
143	Jason Jennings	.05
144	Ben Johnson	.05
145	Jaime Jones	.05
146	Jason Jones	.05
147	Ryan Kibler	.05
148	Bobby Kielty	.15
149	Hong-Chih Kuo	.05
150	John Lackey	.10
151	Gerald Laird	.05
152	Allen Levrault	.10
153	Steve Lomasney	.20
154	George Lombard	.05
155	Felipe Lopez	.05
156	Pat Manning	.05
157	Luis Matos	.05
158	Matt McClendon	.05
159	Brian McNichol	.05
160	Chris Mears	.05
161	Jackson Melian	.05
162	Ryan Minor	.05
163	Chad Moeller	.10
164	Scott Morgan	.05
165	Tony Mota	.05
166	Eric Munson	.10
167	Greg Myers	.05
168	Miguel Olivo	.05
169	Ramon Ortiz	.05
170	Jarrod Patterson	.05
171	Alex Pena	.05
172	Wily Mo Pena	.20
173	Ben Petrick	.05
174	Paul Phillips	.05
175	Calvin Pickering	.05
176	Guillermo Quiroz	.05
177	Tim Raines Jr.	.05
178	Aramis Ramirez	.25
179	Julio Ramirez	.05
180	Matt Riley	.05
181	David Riske	.05
182	Juan Rivera	.05
183	Luis Rivera	.05
184	J.P. Roberge	.05
185	Grant Roberts	.05
186	C.C. Sabathia	.25
187	Brian Sanches	.05
188	Bobby Seay	.05
189	Wascar Serrano	.05
190	Juan Silvestre	.05
191	Chris Snelling	.05
192	Kyle Snyder	.05
193	Alfonso Soriano	1.00
194	Jason Standridge	.05
195	Andy Thompson	.05
196	Luis Torres	.05
197	Roberto Vaz	.05
198	Rico Washington	.05
199	Peanut Williams	.05
200	Kevin Witt	.05

2000 Just Imagine 2k Just Black

Issued at the rate of just one per case (240 packs), this set parallels the base issue, except for the presence of black borders on front and individual serial numbers within an edition of 50 cards each.

	MT
Common Player:	5.00
High-Demand Players:	25X

(See 2000 Just Imagine 2k for checklist and base card values.)

2000 Just Imagine 2k Autographs - Base

All autographed cards in Just Imagine 2k were inserted as box-toppers at the rate of two per box. By arrangement with USA certifica-

tion service, all autographed cards were graded and slabbed. Values shown are for cards graded 8 or 9.

	MT
Common Player:	2.00
BA-01	Brent Abernathy	3.00
	Tony Armas Jr.	4.00
BA-02	Roosevelt Brown	3.00
BA-05	Joe Crede	6.00
BA-08	Alex Escobar	3.00
BA-09	Rafael Furcal	6.00
BA-12	Aubrey Huff	2.00
BA-15	Josh Kalinowski	2.00
	Jackson Melian	2.00
BA-17	Mike Meyers	2.00
BA-18	Talmadge Nunnari	2.00
BA-19	Jose Ortiz	2.00
	Pablo Ozuna	2.00
BA-23	Julio Ramirez	2.00
BA-26	Ruben Salazar	2.00
	Jovanny Sosa	2.00
	Jorge Luis Toca	2.00
BA-27	T.J. Tucker	2.00
BA-30	Kevin Witt	2.00
	Barry Zito	15.00

2000 Just Imagine 2k Autographs - Die-Cut

NICK JOHNSON
SIGN HERE

All autographed cards in Just Imagine 2k were inserted as box-toppers at the rate of two per box. By arrangement with USA certification service, all autographed cards were graded and slabbed. Values shown are for cards graded 8 or 9. Die-cut autographs are serially numbered to 200 each.

	MT
Common Player:	4.00
	Tony Armas Jr.	6.00
DC-01	Roosevelt Brown	4.00
DC-08	Rafael Furcal	5.00
DC-10	Nick Johnson	6.00
DC-12	Steve Lomasney	4.00
DC-12	Mike Meyers	4.00
DC-13	Talmadge Nunnari	4.00
DC-15	Pablo Ozuna	4.00
DC-17	Julio Ramirez	4.00
DC-19	Ruben Salazar	4.00

2000 Just Imagine 2k Autographs - Gold

All autographed cards in Just Imagine 2k were inserted as box-toppers at the rate of two per box. By arrangement with USA certification service, all autographed cards were graded and slabbed. Values shown are for cards graded 8 or 9. Gold autographs are serially numbered 1 of 1.

	MT
Common Player:	50.00
	Brent Abernathy	50.00
	Joe Crede	50.00
	Alex Escobar	5.00
	Rafael Furcal	50.00
	Aubrey Huff	50.00
	Nick Johnson	50.00
	Steve Lomasney	50.00
	Mike Meyers	50.00
	Talmadge Nunnari	50.00
	Jose Ortiz	50.00
	Pablo Ozuna	50.00
	Julio Ramirez	50.00
	T.J. Tucker	50.00
	Kevin Witt	50.00

2000 Just Imagine 2k Autographs - Justinkt

All autographed cards in Just Imagine 2k were inserted as box-toppers at the rate of two per box. By arrangement with USA certification service, all autographed cards were graded and slabbed. Values shown are for cards graded 8 or 9. Justinkt autographs are serially numbered to 100 each.

	MT
Common Player:	4.00
JK.01	Tony Armas Jr.	6.00
JK.02	Jeff Austin	4.00
JK.08	Rafael Furcal	4.00
JK.09	Jon Garland	6.00
JK.10	Aubrey Huff	4.00
JK.11	Nick Johnson	7.50
JK.12	Steve Lomasney	4.00
JK.14	Talmadge Nunnari	4.00
JK.15	Pablo Ozuna	4.00
JK.18	Julio Ramirez	4.00

2000 Just Imagine 2k Just Debuts

OPENING DAY 99
AISLE ROW SEAT
MARK MULDER

These cards, which are made to resemble game tickets, herald the professional debuts of 10 minor leaguers who may one day find fame in the big leagues. Card numbers, at lower-left on front, have a JD prefix. Backs repeat the front photo and have a career highlight or two along with the player's debut day stats. Insertion rate is 1:24 packs.

	MT
Complete Set (10):	10.00
Common Player:	1.50
11	Casey Burns	1.50
12	Donovan Graves	1.50
13	Ty Howington	1.50
14	Ben Johnson	1.50
15	Bobby Kielty	2.00
16	Hong-Chih Kuo	1.50
17	Sean McGowan	1.50
18	Mark Mulder	4.00
19	Eric Munson	1.50
20	Chin-Hui Tsao	1.50

2000 Just Imagine 2k Just Dominant

Seeded one per 24 packs, on average, this insert series offers some of the top names in minor league baseball from the previous season. Fronts have a monochromatic action shot with the same photo repeated on back in color. Card numbers in the upper-left corner on front are prefixed with "JI0.JD."

		MT
Complete Set (10):		15.00
Common Player:		1.50
1	Rick Ankiel	1.50
2	Lance Berkman	2.50
3	Ben Broussard	1.50
4	Pat Burrell	4.00
5	Chin-Feng Chen	2.00
6	Carl Crawford	2.50
7	Josh Hamilton	1.50
8	Eric Munson	1.50
9	Corey Patterson	3.00
10	Vernon Wells	2.50

2000 Just Imagine 2k Just Gamers

Game-used equipment cards in a variety of die-cut/autograph combinations were seeded one per 275 packs.

	MT
Rick Ankiel (Base jersey.)	6.00
Rick Ankiel/Auto. (Base jersey.) (24)	20.00
Rick Ankiel (Die-cut jersey.) (100)	9.00
Rick Ankiel/Auto. (Die-cut jersey.) (10)	35.00
Rafael Furcal (Base bat.)	6.00
Rafael Furcal/Auto. (Base bat.) (24)	20.00
Rafael Furcal (Die-cut bat.) (100)	9.00
Rafael Furcal/Auto. (Die-cut bat.) (10)	35.00
Ken Griffey, Jr. Mystery Gamers (Die-cut bat.) (100))	15.00
Ken Griffey Jr. Mystery Gamers (Bat)(100)	15.00

2000 Just Imagine 2k Just Gems

Yet another showcase for the top-name stars of the 1999 minor league season, this insert set is a 1:24 pick. Fronts are largely bordered in black, with a color photo set within a gem-shaped figure. On back the motif is repeated with a much smaller version of the same photo. Career highlights are presented. Card numbers are prefixed with "JI0.JG."

		MT
Complete Set (10):		12.00
Common Player:		1.50
1	Ryan Anderson	1.50
2	Pat Burrell	3.00
3	Sean Burroughs	2.00
4	Chin-Feng Chen	2.00
5	Gookie Dawkins	1.50
6	Marcus Giles	2.00
7	Josh Hamilton	1.50
8	Corey Patterson	3.00
9	Adam Piatt	1.50
10	Nick Johnson, Alfonso Soriano	2.50

2000 Just Imagine 2k Just Tools

The most difficult of the insert sets at a 1:240 pack ratio, this series features the players with the best physical talent destined to translate to big-league success. Fronts and backs share the same photos with various size and color combinations.

		MT
Complete Set (10):		50.00
Common Player:		5.00
1	Ryan Anderson	5.00
2	Rick Ankiel	5.00
3	Pat Burrell	9.00
4	Chin-Feng Chen	7.50
5	Rafael Furcal	6.00
6	B.J. Garbe	5.00
7	Josh Hamilton	5.00
8	Nick Johnson	6.00
9	Pablo Ozuna	5.00
10	Corey Patterson	7.50

2000 Just the Preview 2k

The use of third-party certified autograph cards on a one-per-box basis was featured in this early-season minor league foil-pack product. Fronts of the base cards have white-bordered photos with a large color band horizontally at center, which carries the product logo, player name, position abbreviation and team. On back is the same photo with a white band at center carrying vital data and 1999 stats. A large color block at bottom has a small team logo and copyright notice. A factory-set version of the issue was produced in an edition of 5,000 with each card featuring gold borders rather than the standard white.

		MT
Complete Set (100):		3.00
Common Player:		.05
Wax Pack (6):		1.00
Wax Box (24):		20.00
Gold:		1X
1	Andy Abad	.05
2	Brent Abernathy	.10
3	Luke Allen	.05
4	Ryan Anderson	.15
5	Wes Anderson	.05
6	Rod Bair	.05
7	Larry Barnes	.05
8	Rob Bell	.05
9	Darren Blakely	.05
10	Lesli Brea	.05
11	Ben Broussard	.10
12	Nate Bump	.05
13	Morgan Burkhart	.15
14	Brent Butler	.05
15	Eric Byrnes	.05
16	Eric Cammack	.05
17	Marcos Castillo	.05
18	Jim Chamblee	.05
19	Carlos Chantres	.05
20	Chin-Feng Chen	.50
21	Jermaine Clark	.05
22	Pasqual Coco	.05
23	Eric Cole	.05
24	Steve Colyer	.05

25	Joe Crede	.75
26	Cesar Crespo	.05
27	Michael Cuddyer	.15
28	John Curl	.05
29	Brian Daubach	.25
30	Luis de los Santos	.05
31	Jason Dewey	.05
32	Alejandro Diaz	.05
33	R.A. Dickey	.05
34	Tim Drew	.05
35	Trent Durrington	.05
36	Josue Espada	.05
37	Ben Ford	.05
38	Rafael Furcal	.25
39	Jay Gibbons	.25
40	Marcus Giles	.30
41	Jeff Goldbach	.10
42	Jimmy Gonzalez	.05
43	Jason Grabowski	.05
44	Junior Guerrero	.05
45	Rickey Guttormson	.05
46	Josh Hamilton	.10
47	Chad Harville	.05
48	Kevin Haverbusch	.05
49	Eric Ireland	.05
50	Cesar Izturiz	.05
51	Nick Johnson	.50
52	Josh Kalinowski	.05
53	Michael Lamb	.10
54	Matthew LeCroy	.05
55	Garry Maddox II	.10
56	Willie Martinez	.05
57	Shawn McCorkle	.05
58	Darnell McDonald	.05
59	Donzell McDonald	.05
60	Sean McGowan	.05
61	Aaron McNeal	.05
62	Steve Medrano	.05
63	Todd Mensik	.05
64	Phil Merrell	.05
65	Mike Meyers	.05
66	Ryan Mills	.05
67	Ryan Moskau	.05
68	Abraham Nunez	.25
69	Jorge Nunez	.05
70	Talmadge Nunnari	.05
71	Jeremy Owens	.05
72	Pablo Ozuna	.05
73	Corey Patterson	.75
74	Kit Pellow	.15
75	Carlos Pena	.15
76	Wynter Phoenix	.05
77	Adam Piatt	.60
78	Juan Pierre	.05
79	Rob Pugmire	.05
80	Tim Redding	.10
81	Brian Reith	.05
82	Michael Restovich	.05
83	Damian Rolls	.05
84	Aaron Rowand	.15
85	Ruben Salazar	.05
86	Alex Sanchez	.05
87	Jared Sandberg	.05
88	Jason Sekany	.05
89	Pat Strange	.05
90	David Therneau	.05
91	Chris Truby	.05
92	T.J. Tucker	.10
93	Jeff Urban	.05
94	Scott Vieira	.05
95	Matt Wade	.05
96	Jake Weber	.05
97	Jayson Werth	.05
98	Matt White	.05
99	Jack Wilson	.05
100	Mike Zywica	.05

2000 Just the Preview 2k Just Black

Issued at the rate of just one per case (240 packs), this set parallels the base issue, except for the presence of black borders on front and individual serial numbers within an edition of 50 cards each.

	MT
Common Player:	5.00
High-Demand Players:	20X

(See 2000 Just the Preview 2k for checklist and base card values.)

2000 Just the Preview 2k Autographs - Base

All autographed cards in Just the Preiew 2k were inserted as box-toppers at the rate of one per box. By arrangement with USA certification service, all autographed cards were graded and slabbed. Values shown are for cards graded 8 or 9.

		MT
Common Player:		2.00
(1)	Erick Almonte	2.00
(2)	Wes Anderson	2.00
(3)	Kevin Barker	2.00
(4)	Matt Belisle	2.00
(5)	A.J. Burnett	3.00
(6)	Jack Cust	6.00
(7)	Pat Daneker	2.00
(8)	Mike Darr	2.50
(9)	Glenn Davis	2.00
(10)	Mario Encarnacion	2.00
(11)	Francisco Figueroa	2.00
(12)	Jody Gerut	2.00
(13)	Nathan Haynes	2.00
(14)	Jay Hood	2.00
(15)	Jaime Jones	2.00
(16)	Gabe Kapler	4.00
(17)	Austin Kearns	10.00
(18)	David Kelton	2.00
(19)	Nelson Lara	2.00
(20)	Jason LaRue	2.00
(21)	Steve Lomasney	2.00
(22)	Gil Meche	2.50
(23)	Guillermo Mota	2.00
(24)	Tony Mota	2.00
(25)	Corey Patterson	6.00
(26)	Jay Payton	4.00
(27)	Aramis Ramirez	3.00
(28)	Luis Rivera	2.00
(29)	Luis Saturria	2.00
(30)	Ismael Villegas	2.00
(31)	Jayson Werth	2.00
(32)	Jake Westbrook	2.50
(33)	Enrique Wilson	3.00
(34)	Barry Zito	10.00

2000 Just the Preview 2k Autographs - Die-cut

All autographed cards in Just the Preiew 2k were inserted as box-toppers at the rate of one per box. By arrangement with USA certification service, all autographed cards were graded and slabbed. Values shown are for cards graded 8 or 9. Die-cuts are serially numbered to 200 each.

		MT
Common Player:		2.00
(1)	Rick Ankiel	3.00
(2)	Kevin Barker	2.00
(3)	Jacob Cruz	2.00
(4)	Jack Cust	6.00
(5)	Robert Fick	2.00
(6)	Gabe Kapler	4.00
(7)	Austin Kearns	10.00
(8)	Tony Mota	2.00
(9)	Corey Patterson	9.00
(10)	Elvis Pena	2.00
(11)	Ryan Rupe	2.00
(12)	Barry Zito	9.00

2000 Just the Preview 2k Autographs - Just Diamonds

All autographed cards in Just the Preview 2k were inserted as box-toppers at the rate of one per box. By arrangement with USA certification service, all autographed cards were graded and slabbed. Values shown are for cards graded 8 or 9. Diamond autographs are serially numbered to 100 each.

		MT
Common Player:		5.00
(1)	Sean Casey	7.50
(2)	Jacob Cruz	5.00
(3)	Jack Cust	6.00
(4)	David Kelton	5.00
(5)	Jay Payton	5.00
(6)	Alfonso Soriano	25.00
(7)	Enrique Wilson	6.00

2000 Just the Preview 2k Just Debuts

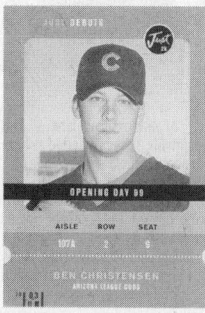

These cards, which are made to resemble game tickets, herald the professional debuts of 10 minor leaguers who may one day find fame in the big leagues. Card numbers, at lower-left on front, have a JD- prefix. Backs repeat the front photo and have a career highlight or two along with the player's debut day stats. Insertion rate is 1:24 packs.

		MT
Complete Set (10):		10.00
Common Player:		1.50
01	Kurt Ainsworth	1.50
02	Ben Broussard	1.50
03	Ben Christensen	2.00
04	Alejandro Diaz	1.50
05	Corey Myers	1.50
06	Omar Ortiz	1.50
07	Lyle Overbay	2.00
08	Brian Roberts	2.00
09	Jerome Williams	1.50
10	Barry Zito	5.00

2000 Just the Preview 2k Just Drafted

The players' overall position in the 1999 amateur draft is used as their card number on this insert series. The cards are inserted at an advertised rate of one per 240 packs. Fronts have black borders at top and bottom. The player photo at center is monochrome and repeated in color on back in a smaller version.

		MT
Complete Set (10):		25.00
Common Player:		3.00
01	Josh Hamilton	4.00
05	B.J. Garbe	3.00
09	Barry Zito	9.00
10	Ben Sheets	5.00
13	Mike Paradis	3.00
21	Larry Bigbie	3.00
27	David Walling	3.00
30	Chance Caple	4.00
46	Chris Duncan	3.00
74	Will Hartley	3.00

2000 Just the Preview 2k Just the One

Inserted one per 24 packs, this series features minor league player of the year in 1999, Rick Ankiel.

		MT
Complete Set (5):		5.00
Common Card:		1.00
01	Rick Ankiel (Peoria)	1.00
02	Rick Ankiel (Arkansas)	1.00
03	Rick Ankiel (Potomac)	1.00
04	Rick Ankiel (Memphis)	1.00
05	Rick Ankiel (Collage)	1.00

2000 Just the Preview 2k Just Tools

Inserted at a 1:24 pack ratio as a box-topper in a sealed paper envelope, this series features the players with the best physical talent destined to translate to big-league success. Fronts and backs share the same photos with various size and color combinations.

		MT
Complete Set (10):		15.00
Common Player:		1.50
1	Ryan Anderson	1.50
2	Rick Ankiel	1.00
3	Pat Burrell	3.50
4	Chin-Feng Chen	2.00
5	Rafael Furcal	1.50
6	B.J. Garbe	1.00
7	Josh Hamilton	1.50
8	Nick Johnson	2.00
9	Pablo Ozuna	1.00
10	Corey Patterson	2.50

2000 Just Justifiable 2k

The debut cards of some of the 2000 amateur draft's top picks, along with two graded autograph cards per box were features of Just Minors' final card issue of 2000. The 100-card base set retains the same basic format seen on the company's earlier releases. Several insert sets, including those featuring game-used equipment cards and autographs, were also found in the six-card foil packs. A gold-bordered factory set edition was produced in an issue of 5,000 sets.

		MT
Complete Set (100):		6.00
Common Player:		.05
Wax Box (24+2):		20.00
Gold:		1.5X
201	Kurt Ainsworth	.10
202	Tony Alvarez	.05
203	Craig Anderson	.05
204	Robert Averette	.05
205	Josh Beckett	.75
206	Adam Bernero	.05
207	Tony Blanco	.05
208	Willie Bloomquist	.10
209	Joe Borchard	.75
210	Danny Borrell	.05
211	Shaun Boyd	.05
212	Donnie Bridges	.05
213	Dee Brown	.05

214	Eric Bruntlett	.05
215	A.J. Burnett	.25
216	Sean Burnett	.35
217	Matt Butler	.05
218	Marlon Byrd	.15
219	Alex Cabrera	.05
220	Hee Seop Choi	.75
221	Alex Cintron	.05
222	Brian Cole	.05
223	Carl Crawford	.05
224	Brad Cresse	.05
225	Chuck Crowder	.05
226	Daniel Curtis	.05
227	Zach Day	.05
228	Mario Encarnacion	.05
229	Alex Escobar	.10
230	Eric Gagne	.40
231	Jon Garland	.15
232	Jay Gehrke	.05
233	David Gil	.05
234	Keith Ginter	.05
235	Matt Ginter	.05
236	Josh Girdley	.05
237	Adrian Gonzalez	.25
238	Ryan Gripp	.05
239	Matt Guerrier	.05
240	Elpidio Guzman	.05
241	Geraldo Guzman	.05
242	Toby Hall	.05
243	Jason Hart	.05
244	Shane Heams	.05
245	Adrian Hernandez	.05
246	Aaron Herr	.05
247	Bobby Hill	.50
248	Eric Johnson	.05
249	Gary Johnson	.05
250	Kelly Johnson	.05
251	Tripper Johnson	.05
252	Austin Kearns	.50
253	Randy Keisler	.05
254	David Kelton	.05
255	Bob Keppel	.05
256	Mike Kinney	.05
257	Brandon Larson	.05
258	Gary Majewski	.05
259	Kevin Mench	.05
260	Luis Montanez	.05
261	Brett Myers	.05
262	Tomo Ohka	.10
263	Bill Ortega	.05
264	Omar Ortiz	.05
265	Christian Parra	.05
266	David Parrish	.05
267	Chad Petty	.05
268	Jon Rauch	.25
269	Keith Reed	.05
270	Dominic Rich	.05
271	Frank Rodriguez	.05
272	Nate Rolison	.10
273	Vince Rooi	.05
274	B.J. Ryan	.05
275	Mike Schultz	.05
276	Jacobo Sequea	.05
277	Bud Smith	.15
278	Corey Smith	.05
279	S.J. Song	.25
280	John Stephens	.05
281	Mike Stodolka	.05
282	Robert Stratton	.05
283	Jason Stumm	.05
284	Brian Tallet	.05
285	Derek Thompson	.05
286	Scott Thorman	.05
287	Tony Torcato	.05
288	Torre Tyson	.05
289	Eric Valent	.05
290	Luis Vizcaino	.05
291	Adam Wainright	.25
292	Chris Wakeland	.05
293	Tiger Wang	.25
294	David Watkins	.05
295	Brian West	.05
296	Jake Westbrook	.05
297	Dan Wheeler	.05
298	Brad Wilkerson	.10
299	Blake Williams	.05
300	Carlos Zambrano	.05

2000 Just Justifiable 2k Just Black

Issued at the rate of just one per case (240 packs), this set parallels the base issue, except for the presence of black borders on front and individual serial numbers within an edition of 50 cards each.

		MT
Common Player:		5.00
High-Demand Players:		25X

(See 2000 Just Justifiable 2k for checklist and base card values.)

2000 Just Justifiable 2k Autographs - Base

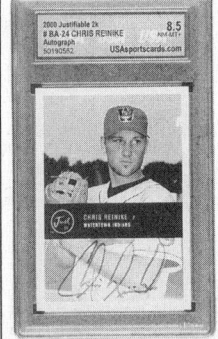

All autographed cards in Just Justifiable 2k were inserted as box-toppers at the rate of two per box. By arrangement with USA certification service, all autographed cards were graded and slabbed. Values shown are for cards graded 8, 8.5 or 9. The base autographed cards of Larson, Patterson and Soriano are from Just's 1999 issue.

		MT
Common Player:		3.00
BA-03	A.J. Burnett	6.00
BA-06	Brian Daubach	4.50
BA-46	Tim Drew	3.00
BA-10	Eric Gagne	15.00
BA-49	Aubrey Huff	3.00
BA-13	Brandon Inge	3.00
BA-56	Bobby Kielty	3.00
	Brandon Larson	3.00
BA-60	Allen Levrault	3.00
BA-16	Steve Lomasney	3.00
BA-66	Mike Meyers	3.00
BA-21	Pablo Ozuna	3.00
	Corey Patterson	10.00
BA-70	Alex Pena	3.00
BA-24	Chris Reinike	3.00
BA-75	Luis Rivera	3.00
BA-80	Juan Silvestre	3.00
	Alfonso Soriano	25.00
BA-85	Matt White	3.00
BA-87	Jack Wilson	3.00

2000 Just Justifiable 2k Autographs - Justinkt

All autographed cards in Just Justifiable 2k were inserted as box-toppers at the rate of two per box. By arrangement with USA certification service, all autographed cards were graded and slabbed. Values shown are for cards graded 8, 8.5 or 9. Justinkt autographs are serially numbered to 100 each.

		MT
Common Player:		5.00
JK.03	A.J. Burnett	6.00
JK.05	Jack Cust	5.00
JK.06	Brian Daubach	5.00
JK.16	Corey Patterson	10.00
JK.17	Adam Piatt	6.00
JK.19	Matt Riley	5.00
JK.21	T.J. Tucker	5.00

2000 Just Justifiable 2k Autographs - Die-Cut

All autographed cards in Just Justifiable 2k were inserted as box-toppers at the rate of two per box. By arrangement with USA certification service, all autographed cards were graded and slabbed. Values shown are for cards graded 8, 8.5 or 9. Die-cut autograph cards are serially numbered to 200.

		MT
Common Player:		4.00
DC-22	Wes Anderson	4.00
DC-23	Tony Armas Jr.	4.00
DC-24	Brad Baisley	4.00
DC-33	Tim Drew	4.00
DC-38	Darnell McDonald	4.00
DC-40	Mike Meyers	4.00
DC-16	Adam Piatt	7.50
DC-45	Aramis Ramirez	6.00
DC-46	Luis Rivera	4.00
DC-51	Chris Snelling	4.00
DC-20	T.J. Tucker	4.00
DC-54	Matt White	4.00

2000 Just Justifiable 2k Autographs - Gold

All autographed cards in Just Justifiable 2k were inserted as box-toppers at the rate of two per box. By arrangement with USA certification service, all autographed cards were graded and slabbed. Values shown are for cards graded 8 or 9. Gold autograph cards are serially numbered 1 of 1.

		MT
Common Player:		50.00
	Wes Anderson	50.00
	Tony Armas Jr.	50.00
	Brad Baisley	50.00
	Bobby Bradley	50.00
	A.J. Burnett	75.00
	Sean Burroughs	75.00
	Eric Gagne	100.00
	Elvin Hernandez	50.00
	Aubrey Huff	50.00
	Josh Kalinowski	50.00
	Pat Manning	50.00
	Darnell McDonald	50.00
	Mark Mulder	50.00
	Juan Pierre	50.00
	Chris Reinike	50.00
	J.P. Roberge	50.00
	Juan Silvestre	50.00
	Chris Snelling	50.00
	Peanut Williams	50.00
	Jack Wilson	50.00

2000 Just Justifiable 2k Just Candidates

Potential big-league superstars are featured in this insert set. Cards are a 1:24 pick and have a JC- prefix to the card number on front. The player photo on front is in a vertical oval with black at bottom and a bright color at top. Backs have a gold border with the same photo repeated in black-and-white in a circle, along with a few words about the player.

		MT
Complete Set (10):		10.00
Common Player:		1.50

01	Ryan Anderson	1.50
02	Bobby Bradley	1.50
03	Pat Burrell	3.50
04	Alex Cabrera	1.50
05	Keith Ginter	1.50
06	Josh Hamilton	1.50
07	Jason Hart	1.50
08	Adam Piatt	1.50
09	Juan Silvestre	1.50
10	Chin-Hui Tsao	2.50

2000 Just Justifiable 2k Just Debuts

These cards, which are made to resemble game tickets, herald the professional debuts of 10 minor leaguers who may one day find fame in the big leagues. Card numbers, at lower-left on front, have a JD prefix. Backs repeat the front photo and have a career highlight or two along with the player's debut day stats. Insertion rate is 1:24 packs.

		MT
Complete Set (10):		12.50
Common Player:		1.50
21	Rick Asadoorian	1.50
22	Danys Baez	1.50
23	Josh Beckett	6.00
24	Shaun Boyd	1.50
25	Bobby Bradley	1.50
26	Jace Brewer	1.50
27	Brad Cresse	1.50
28	Adrian Gonzalez	1.50
29	Adrian Hernandez	1.50
30	Corey Smith	1.50

2000 Just Justifiable 2k Just Gems

The most difficult of the insert sets at a 1:240 pack ratio, this series features the players with the best chance at quick big-league success. Each card has a 'JO.JG.' prefix to the card number. The checklist and the format are the same as the Just Gems inserts in the Just Imagine 2k issue, though gold predominates on the Justifiable version.

		MT
Complete Set (10):		100.00
Common Player:		10.00
11	Ryan Anderson	10.00
12	Pat Burrell	20.00
13	Sean Burroughs	15.00
14	Chin-Feng Chen	15.00
15	Gookie Dawkins	12.50
16	Marcus Giles	10.00
17	Josh Hamilton	15.00
18	Corey Patterson	20.00
19	Adam Piatt	10.00
20	Nick Johnson,	
	Alfonso Soriano	15.00

2000 Just Justifiable 2k Just Gamers

Game-used equipment cards in a variety of die-cut/autograph combinations were seeded one per 275 packs.

		MT
Pat Burrell (Base jersey.)		7.50

Pat Burrell (Base jersey die-cut, numbered to 100.)	10.00
Sean Burroughs (Base bat.)	7.50
Sean Burroughs (Base bat autographed, numbered to 24.)	35.00
Sean Burroughs (Die-cut bat, numbered to 100.)	10.00
Sean Burroughs (Die-cut autographed bat, numbered to 10.)	50.00
Corey Patterson (Base bat.)	7.50
Corey Patterson (Base bat autographed, numbered to 24.)	50.00
Corey Patterson (Die-cut bat, numbered to 100.)	10.00
Corey Patterson (Die-cut autographed bat, numbered to 10.)	65.00
Chipper Jones Mystery Gamers (Base bat.)	15.00
Chipper Jones Mystery Gamers (Die-cut bat, numbered to 100.)	15.00

2000 Just Justifiable 2k Just Nine

Players on the verge of making their mark in the majors are featured in this insert set. Seeded one per 24 packs (about one per box), the set has one player for each position.

		MT
Complete Set (9):		12.50
Common Player:		1.50
J9-1	Josh Beckett	4.00
J9-2	Sean Burroughs	2.50
J9-3	Jack Cust	1.50
J9-4	Marcus Giles	2.00
J9-5	Josh Hamilton	1.50
J9-6	J.R. House	1.50
J9-7	Nick Johnson	2.50
J9-8	Corey Patterson	3.00
J9-9	Alfonso Soriano	4.00

2000 Just Gold

Special gold-bordered parallel versions of the 300 base cards in Just Minors debut year sets were assembled into a limited edition (5,000) run of factory sets with a suggested retail price at issue of $49.95. Each set includes eight Just Black autographed cards numbered from within editions of 50 each in either the 1999 or 2000 format.

		MT
Complete Set (308):		35.00
Gold Commons and Stars:		1X

(See 2000 Just the Preview, Just Imagine and Just Justifiable for checklists.)

2000 Just Graded 2k

With a suggested retail price of $14.99 per single-card pack at issue Just Graded 2k offers three versions of each card. White-bordered base cards are limited to 500 each. Black-bordered parallels (1:16) were issued in editions of 50 and gold-bordered

---

(1:640) parallels are each unique. Autographed inserts were found at the rate of 1:9 for base-design autographs, 1:13 for die-cut design autographs and 1:20 for Just 'Graphs autographs. Each card was graded and slabbed by USA, though in the aftermarket the assigned grade has little effect on value. While every foil wrapper says "Each pack contains 1 graded autograph card and nothing else!," not every pack in fact has an autographed card.

		MT
Common Player:		1.00
Box (8):		24.00
Pack (1):		3.00
Black:		4X
Gold: Values Undetermined		
001	Ryan Anderson	3.00
002	Rick Asadoorian	1.00
003	Danys Baez	1.00
004	Josh Beckett	20.00
005	Boof Bonser	1.00
006	Chris Bootcheck	1.00
007	Joe Borchard	6.00
008	Shaun Boyd	1.00
009	Bobby Bradley	2.00
010	Sean Burroughs	6.00
011	Hee Seop Choi	6.00
012	Joe Crede	6.00
013	Brad Cresse	2.00
014	Ben Diggins	1.00
015	Adrian Gonzalez	1.00
016	Cristian Guerrero	1.00
017	Josh Hamilton	2.00
018	Adrian Hernandez	1.00
019	Aaron Herr	1.00
020	J.R. House	2.00
021	Adam Johnson	1.00
022	Kelly Johnson	1.00
023	Tripper Johnson	1.00
024	Deivi Mendez	1.00
025	Luis Montanez	1.00
026	Eric Munson	2.00
027	Xavier Nady	1.00
028	Lance Niekro	1.00
029	David Parrish	1.00
030	Corey Patterson	4.00
031	Carlos Pena	3.00
032	Jon Rauch	2.00
033	C.C. Sabathia	3.00
034	Mike Schultz	1.00
035	Ben Sheets	2.00
036	Corey Smith	1.00
037	Seung Song	2.00
038	Alfonso Soriano	20.00
039	Robert Stiehl	1.00
040	Mike Stodolka	1.00
041	Derek Thompson	1.00
042	Joe Torres	1.00
043	Chin-Hui Tsao	3.00
044	Chase Utley	6.00
045	Adam Wainright	2.00
046	Tiger Wang	6.00
047	Vernon Wells	3.00
048	Matt Wheatland	1.00
049	Blake Williams	1.00
050	Barry Zito	7.50

2000 Just Graded 2k Autographs

Autographed cards were found in three styles as random pack inserts in Just Graded 2k. Base-design autographed cards are a 1:9 find; die-cuts are found on average at 1:13 and Just 'Graphs cards are a 1:20 pick.

		MT
BASE AUTOGRAPHS (1:9)		
BA14	Nick Johnson	7.50
BA22	Adam Piatt	3.00
BA36	Bobby Bradley	3.00
DIE-CUT AUTOGRAPHS (1:13)		
DC2	A.J. Burnett	5.00
DC9	Eric Gagne	6.00
DC18	Matt Riley	3.00
DC26	Bobby Bradley	6.00

DC27	Ben Broussard	6.00
DC28	Jesus Colome	3.00
DC32	Brian Daubach	4.00
DC34	Aubrey Huff	5.00
DC44	Juan Pierre	6.00
DC47	Grant Roberts	4.00
DC50	Juan Silvestre	3.00
DC55	Matt White	4.00
DC56	Jack Wilson	3.00

JUST 'GRAPHS (1:20)

JG2	Wes Anderson	4.00
JG3	Rick Ankiel	4.00
JG4	Tony Armas Jr.	6.00
JG6	Ben Broussard	7.50
JG7	Sean Burroughs	7.50
JG8	Jesus Colome	3.00
JG12	Rafael Furcal	7.50
JG14	Aubrey Huff	4.00
JG17	Mike Meyers	6.00
JG18	Mark Mulder	7.50
JG21	Adam Piatt	4.00
JG22	Juan Pierre	6.00
JG23	Julio Ramirez	4.00
JG24	Luis Rivera	4.00
JG25	Juan Silvestre	4.00
JG28	Matt White	5.00
JG29	Peanut Williams	4.00

2000 Just Autographs Black

These authentically autographed black-bordered cards were random inserts in Just Gold factory sets. Each card was produced in a numbered edition of 50 each.

		MT
Common Player:		5.00
BA1	Brent Abernathy	6.00
BA3	A.J. Burnett	7.50
BA4	Sean Burroughs	10.00
BA5	Joe Crede	20.00
BA6	Brian Daubach	7.50
BA8	Alex Escobar	6.00
BA9	Rafael Furcal	6.00
BA10	Eric Gagne	12.50
BA12	Aubrey Huff	5.00
BA13	Brandon Inge	5.00
BA14	Nick Johnson	10.00
BA15	Josh Kalinowski	5.00
BA16	Steve Lomasney	5.00
BA17	Mike Meyers	5.00
BA18	Talmadge Nunnari	5.00
BA19	Jose Ortiz	5.00
BA20	Ramon Ortiz	5.00
BA21	Pablo Ozuna	5.00
BA22	Adam Piatt	7.50
BA23	Julio Ramirez	5.00
BA24	Chris Reinike	5.00
BA27	T.J. Tucker	5.00
BA29	Rico Washington	5.00
BA30	Kevin Witt	5.00
BA31	Wes Anderson	5.00
BA32	Tony Armas Jr.	5.00
BA33	Brad Baisley	5.00
BA34	Matt Belisle	5.00
BA35	Casey Blake	5.00
BA36	Bobby Bradley	6.00
BA37	Ben Broussard	7.50
BA38	Jesus Colome	5.00
BA40	Nate Cornejo	5.00
BA41	Robbie Crabtree	5.00
BA47	Chad Harville	5.00
BA48	Elvin Hernandez	5.00
BA49	Aubrey Huff	5.00
BA50	Norm Hutchins	5.00

BA51	Brandon Inge	5.00
BA61	Pat Manning	5.00
BA62	Hipolito Martinez	5.00
BA63	Darnell McDonald	5.00
BA64	Brian McNichol	5.00
BA66	Mike Meyers	5.00
BA67	Mark Mulder	7.50
BA69	Pablo Ozuna	5.00
BA72	Juan Pierre	7.50
BA73	Aramis Ramirez	6.00
BA74	Juan Rivera	7.50
BA75	Luis Rivera	5.00
BA76	J.P. Roberge	5.00
BA77	Grant Roberts	5.00
BA78	C.C. Sabathia	7.50
BA80	Juan Silvestre	5.00
BA81	Chris Snelling	5.00
BA83	Jayson Werth	6.00
BA86	Peanut Williams	5.00
BA87	Jack Wilson	5.00

2000 Just Minors Mystery Signatures

These unusual autograph cards neither picture nor name the player who signed them. Biographical data, stats and career highlights on back provide clues. The cards, bearing an "MS-" prefix to the number, were included in various Just Minors products and, like the other autograph cards, were issued as boxtoppers in the slabs of USA certification services. Assigned grade has no effect on value.

		MT
Complete Set (10):		35.00
Common Player:		3.00
01	Miguel Cabrera (Imagine 2K)	15.00
02	Guillermo Quiroz (Imagine 2K)	3.00
04	Ramon Ortiz (Factory set.)	3.00
06	Nick Johnson (Imagine 2k)	7.50
07	Placido Polanco (Imagine 2k)	3.00
08	Wily Mo Pena (Factory set.)	4.50
09	Jim Parque (Stuff 2k1.3)	3.00
10	Odalis Perez (Factory set.)	3.00
12	Gabe Kapler (Graded 2k)	4.50
13	Wilfredo Rodriguez (Distribution not specified.)	3.00

2000 Just Stuff

Just Stuff packages were marketed to consumers directly from Just Minors, offering a variety of new and remainder products including autographed photos and mini-helmets along with unopened packs and autographed cards not found in other Just Minors products or originally issued only in unautographed form. Some cards are numbered contiguously with contemporary regular-issue Just Minors products, others carry a JS card number prefix and some cards are unnumbered. Because of the constant addition of items, no attempt is being made to checklist specific cards from this program. Market values can be approximated by comparison with similar regular-issue cards.

(See contemporary Just Minors issues for value guidelines.)

2000 Minor League Legends

These are unauthorized collectors' issues, apparently created by someone with a cut-and-paste computer program who took the color photos from genuine minor league cards and mated them with a red-and-white striped border and design reminiscent of 1986 Don-

russ. Backs are in black-and-white with a photo, minimal personal data and career highlights. Because they are not a legitimate issue, no value is assigned.

(1)	Jose Canseco	
(2)	Ken Griffey Jr.	

2000 Royal Rookies Signature Series

This minor-league issue features a 40-card base set and several inserts, sold in six-card foil packs with one authentically autographed card in every pack. Fronts have a rather small player picture on a graduated violet-to-white background. Because the set was not licensed by Major League Baseball, only the individual players, most cap and uniform logos have been removed from the photos. Backs repeat the front photo and have a few words about the player along with his 1999 stats.

		MT
Complete Set (40):		1.50
Common Player:		.05
Wax Pack (7):		1.50
Wax Box (12):		16.00
1	Eddy Garabito	.05
2	Fletcher Bates	.05
3	Juan Aracena	.05
4	Andrew Beinbrink	.10
5	Edward Rogers	.05
6	Jason Sekany	.05
7	Juan Guzman	.05
8	Howie Clark	.05
9	Jody Gerut	.10
10	Chris Snelling	.25
11	Nick Theodorou	.05
12	Jermaine Clark	.10
13	Chris Richard	.05
14	Brent Hoard	.05
15	Josh Reding	.05
16	Mike Glendenning	.05
17	Dan Phillips	.05
18	Eric Gillespie	.05
19	Larry Barnes	.05
20	Chris Barski	.05
21	Julio Zuleta	.10
22	Damon Minor	.10
23	Brian Cooper	.05
24	Adam Eaton	.10
25	Carlos Casamiro (Casamiro)	.05
26	Jeremy Blevins	.05
27	Jon Schaeffer	.05
28	Mark Lukasiewicz	.05
29	Norm Hutchinson (Hutchins)	.05
30	Mark Harriger	.05
31	Rikki Johnston	.05
32	Jon Tucker	.05
33	Brett Caradonna	.05
34	Adam Piatt, Rick Ankiel	.25
35	Mark Seaver	.05
36	Mike Villano	.05
37	Danny Ardoin	.05
38	J.J. Sherill	.05
39	Ryan Drese	.10
40	Checklist	.05

2000 Royal Rookies Signature Series Autographs

Each six-card foil pack of Royal Rookies contains one authentically autographed card. The autograph cards are in the same format as the base set, except have a gold-foil logo on front and a serial number from within an edition of 4,950.

		MT
Complete Set (39):		35.00
1	Eddy Garabito	1.00
2	Fletcher Bates	1.00
3	Juan Aracena	1.00
4	Andrew Beinbrink	1.00
5	Edward Rogers	1.00
6	Jason Sekany	1.00
7	Juan Guzman	1.00
8	Howie Clark	1.00
9	Jody Gerut	2.00
10	Chris Snelling	1.00
11	Nick Theodorou	1.00
12	Jermaine Clark	1.50
13	Chris Richard	1.00
14	Brent Hoard	1.00
15	Josh Reding	1.00
16	Mike Glendenning	1.00
17	Dan Phillips	1.00
18	Eric Gillespie	1.00
19	Larry Barnes	1.00
20	Chris Barski	1.00
21	Julio Zuleta	1.00
22	Damon Minor	1.00
23	Brian Cooper	1.00
24	Adam Eaton	1.50
25	Carlos Casamiro (Casamiro)	1.00
26	Jeremy Blevins	1.00
27	Jon Schaeffer	1.00
28	Mark Lukasiewicz	1.00
29	Norm Hutchinson (Hutchins)	1.00
30	Mark Harriger	1.00
31	Rikki Johnston	1.00
32	Jon Tucker	1.00
33	Brett Caradonna	1.00
34	Adam Piatt, Rick Ankiel	6.00
35	Mark Seaver	1.00
36	Mike Villano	1.00
37	Danny Ardoin	1.00
38	J.J. Sherill	1.00
39	Ryan Drese	1.00

2000 Royal Rookies Elite Eight

This insert set features top prospects in a format similar to the base cards except for the use of an orange-to-white background and the appearance on front of an "Elite 8" logo. Autographed versions, numbered from an edition of 2,500 each were issued as random pack inserts and are valued at 10 times the regular-issue card.

		MT
Complete Set (8):		1.00
Common Player:		.25
1	Roosevelt Brown	.25
2	Travis Dawkins	.35
3	Barry Zito	.50
4	Eric Gagne	.40
5	Jeff DaVanon	.25
6	Brett Myers	.25
7	Julio Lugo, Jr.	.25
8	Shea Hillenbrand	.35

2000 Royal Rookies Elite Eight Autographs

Autographed versions, numbered from editions of up to 2,500 each were issued as random pack inserts.

		MT
Complete Set (8):		30.00
Common Player:		1.00
1	Roosevelt Brown	1.00
2	Travis Dawkins	3.00

3	Barry Zito (Edition of 25.)	15.00
4	Eric Gagne	9.00
5	Jeff DaVanon	1.00
6	Brett Myers	2.00
7	Julio Lugo, Jr.	3.00
8	Shea Hillenbrand	6.00

2000 Royal Rookies Ken Griffey Jr.

Five cards of Ken Griffey Jr. were issued as inserts in an unnumbered edition of 10,000 each. Large photos on front and smaller back photos have had uniform logos removed. A second version, featuring gold-foil logo on front and serially numbered within an edition of 2,500 each was also issued, though the details of distribution are unclear.

		MT
Complete Set (5):		2.00
Common Card:		.50
Gold-Foil:		2X
1-5	Ken Griffey Jr.	.50

2000 Royal Rookies Pitcher of the Year

Three cards of Rick Ankiel were issued as inserts, maintaining the same basic format as the set's regular cards.

		MT
Complete Set (3):		1.50
Common Card:		.50
1-3	Rick Ankiel	.50

2000 Royal Rookies Player of the Year

Three cards of Adam Piatt were issued as inserts, maintaining the same basic format as the set's regular cards.

		MT
Complete Set (3):		.75
Common Card:		.25
1-3	Adam Piatt	.25

2000 SP Top Prospects

As the brand name implies, only the minor leaguers with the brightest futures are featured in the

135-card base set of this Upper Deck specialty issue. The first 10 cards in the set are checklists featuring the biggest names. Nearly a dozen parallel and insert sets are found in the eight-card, $4.99 foil packs. Besides the "regular" version, the base set can be found in a Premium Edition parallel of 175 each and a President's Edition of just 10 each, utilizing holo-patterned foil technology.

		MT
Complete Set (135):		7.50
Common Player:		.05
Wax Pack (8):		1.50
Wax Box (24):		17.50
1	Rick Ankiel (Top 10 Checklist)	.50
2	Brad Penny (Top 10 Checklist)	.05
3	Ryan Anderson (Top 10 Checklist)	.10
4	Pablo Ozuna (Top 10 Checklist)	.05
5	Alex Escobar (Top 10 Checklist)	.05
6	John Patterson (Top 10 Checklist)	.05
7	Corey Patterson (Top 10 Checklist)	.05
8	Nick Johnson (Top 10 Checklist)	.20
9	Pat Burrell (Top 10 Checklist)	.75
10	Matt Riley (Top 10 Checklist)	.05
11	Larry Barnes	.05
12	Brian Cooper	.05
13	E.J. t'Hoen	.05
14	Oscar Salazar	.05
15	Mark Mulder	.50
16	Roberto Vaz	.05
17	Eric DuBose	.05
18	Jacques Landry	.05
19	Adam Piatt	.25
20	Josue Espada	.05
21	Jesus Colome	.05
22	Barry Zito	1.50
23	Eric Byrnes	.05
24	Jason Hart	.05
25	Felipe Lopez	.05
26	Pascual Coco	.05
27	Vernon Wells	.45
28	John Sneed	.05
29	Jorge Nunez	.05
30	Cameron Reimers	.05
31	Jung Bong	.05
32	Rafael Furcal	.25
33	Jason Marquis	.15
34	Derrin Ebert	.05
35	Troy Cameron	.05
36	Chad Green	.05
37	Rick Ankiel	.25
38	Chad Hutchinson	.05
39	Chris Haas	.05
40	Brent Butler	.05
41	Adam Kennedy	.15
42	Donovan Graves	.05
43	Ben Christiansen	.05
44	Corey Patterson	1.00
45	Eric Hinske	.50
46	Tydus Meadows	.10
47	Micah Bowie	.05
48	Todd Belitz	.05
49	Matt White	.05
50	Kenny Kelly	.10
51	Josh Hamilton	4.00
52	Aubrey Huff	.15
53	Abraham Nunez	.15
54	John Patterson	.05
55	Bubba Crosby	.05
56	Chin-Feng Chen	.50
57	David Ross	.05
58	Guillermo Mota	.05
59	Milton Bradley	.25
60	Peter Bergeron	.10
61	Josh McKinley	.05
62	Tony Armas Jr.	.25
63	Josh Reding	.05
64	Tony Torcato	.05
65	Mike Glendenning	.05
66	Jesus Hernandez	.05
67	C.C. Sabathia	.25
68	Mike Edwards	.05
69	Kevin Gryboski	.05

70	Harvey Hargrove	.05
71	Ryan Anderson	.25
72	Peanut Williams	.05
73	Brad Penny	.10
74	Pablo Ozuna	.05
75	Jason Grilli	.10
76	Julio Ramirez	.05
77	A.J. Burnett	.25
78	Nate Bump	.05
79	Wes Anderson	.05
80	Grant Roberts	.05
81	Alex Escobar	.10
82	Jason Tyner	.05
83	Jorge Toca	.05
84	Robert Stratton	.05
85	Rick Elder	.05
86	Keith Reed	.05
87	Darnell McDonald	.05
88	Jayson Werth	.05
89	Matt Riley	.10
90	Wascar Serrano	.05
91	Vince Faison	.05
92	Omar Ortiz	.05
93	Junior Herndon	.05
94	Sean Burroughs	.50
95	Eric Valent	.05
96	Pat Burrell	2.00
97	Reggie Taylor	.05
98	Eddy Furniss	.05
99	Chad Hermansen	.05
100	Kevin Haverbusch	.05
101	Carlos Pena	.50
102	Adam Everett	.05
103	Dernell Stenson	.05
104	David Eckstein	.30
105	John Curtice	.05
106	Travis Dawkins	.35
107	Jacobo Sequea	.05
108	Eric LeBlanc	.05
109	Rob Bell	.05
110	Austin Kearns	.75
111	Jeff Winchester	.05
112	Choo Freeman	.10
113	Ben Petrick	.05
114	Jody Gerut	.10
115	Josh Kalinowski	.05
116	Travis Thompson	.05
117	Jeff Austin	.05
118	Junior Guerrero	.05
119	Eric Munson	.10
120	Eric Gillespie	.05
121	Michael Cuddyer	.15
122	Jason Ryan	.05
123	Luis Rivas	.05
124	Ryan Mills	.05
125	Michael Restovich	.10
126	Josh Fogg	.05
127	Luis Raven	.05
128	Joe Crede	.50
129	Aaron Rowand	.15
130	Kip Wells	.15
131	Nick Johnson	.75
132	Ryan Bradley	.05
133	Andy Brown	.05
134	Donny Leon	.05
135	Jackson Melian	.05

2000 SP Top Prospects Premium Edition

Each of the 135 cards in the base set were also issued in this parallel edition numbered on front to just 175 each. Cards fronts have a metallic-foil background.

	MT
Common Player:	3.00
Stars:	5X

(See 2000 SP Top Prospects for checklist and base card values.)

2000 SP Top Prospects President's Edition

Utilizing holo-patterned foil technology, each of the 135 base cards in SP Top Prospects was also issued in this numbered edition of just 10 pieces each.

	MT
Common Player:	25.00
Stars:	75-150X

(See 2000 SP Top Prospects for checklist and base card values.)

2000 SP Top Prospects Big Town Dreams

Premium holo-foil technology is showcased in the background to the player photo insert. Backs repeat the stylized skyscraper motif and have a few words about the player. They are inserted at an average rate of one per 11 packs.

		MT
Complete Set (10):		17.50
Common Player:		1.50
1	Jorge Toca	1.50
2	Josh Hamilton	3.00
3	Alex Escobar	1.50
4	Joe Crede	3.00
5	Eric Munson	2.00
6	Chin-Feng Chen	2.50
7	Dernell Stenson	1.50
8	Pat Burrell	4.50
9	Corey Patterson	3.50
10	Donny Leon	1.50

2000 SP Top Prospects Chirography

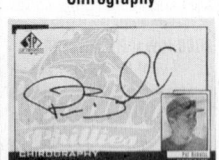

For 2000, Upper Deck improved the odds of finding an autographed card to one per eight packs. Cards feature 34 top prospects in a horizontal format which uses a ghosted minor league logo on a white background to host the signature. A gold version parallels the Chirography inserts, with cards numbered to 25 apiece.

		MT
Complete Set (45):		100.00
Common Player:		1.50
RA	Rick Ankiel	10.00
TA	Tony Armas Jr.	2.00
Rob	Rob Bell	1.50
PBe	Peter Bergeron	1.50
RB	Ryan Bradley	1.50
AJ	A.J. Burnett	3.00
PB	Pat Burrell	10.00
SB	Sean Burroughs	4.00
Ben	Ben Christiansen	2.00
PC	Pascual Coco	1.50
JC	Joe Crede	5.00
BC	Bubba Crosby	1.50
MC	Michael Cuddyer	2.00
ED	Eric DuBose	1.50
AE	Alex Escobar	1.50
AEv	Adam Everett	2.00
JG	Jody Gerut	1.50
JGr	Jason Grilli	2.00
JH	Josh Hamilton	35.00
CH	Chad Hermansen	1.50
JHe	Junior Herndon	1.50
AH	Aubrey Huff	2.00
CHu	Chad Hutchinson	1.50
NJ	Nick Johnson	12.50
AK	Austin Kearns	10.00
FL	Felipe Lopez	1.50
JMA	Jason Marquis	3.00
JM	Josh McKinley	1.50
RM	Ryan Mills	1.50
MM	Mark Mulder	6.00
EM	Eric Munson	2.00
PO	Pablo Ozuna	1.50
Cpa	Corey Patterson	6.00
CP	Carlos Pena	10.00
BP	Brad Penny	2.00
JR	Julio Ramirez	1.50
MR	Matt Riley	2.00
GR	Grant Roberts	1.50
AS	Alfonso Soriano	20.00
DS	Dernell Stenson	1.50
RT	Reggie Taylor	2.00
Jto	Jorge Toca	1.50
TT	Tony Torcato	1.50
JT	Jason Tyner	1.50
JW	Jayson Werth	1.50

2000 SP Top Prospects Chirography Gold

This parallel of the 34-player Chirography insert series is highlighted on front with gold graphics. Each card is serially numbered within an edition of 25.

	MT
Common Player:	10.00
Stars:	4X

(See 2000 SP Top Prospects Chirography for checklist and base card values.)

2000 SP Top Prospects Destination the Show

A horizontal format with a black-and-white backdrop to the color action photo is found on this top of the line insert series featuring 20 players who are most likely to be seen in the major leagues. Stated insertion rate was one per 92 packs.

		MT
Complete Set (20):		125.00
Common Player:		5.00
1	Rick Ankiel	5.00
2	Brad Penny	5.00
3	John Patterson	5.00
4	Rob Bell	5.00
5	Mark Mulder	10.00
6	Corey Patterson	15.00
7	Eric Munson	5.00
8	Nick Johnson	20.00
9	Dernell Stenson	5.00
10	Ryan Bradley	5.00
11	Alex Escobar	5.00
12	Matt White	5.00
13	Michael Cuddyer	6.00
14	Ryan Anderson	6.00
15	Pablo Ozuna	5.00
16	Pat Burrell	25.00
17	A.J. Burnett	9.00
18	Josh Hamilton	15.00
19	Jason Grilli	5.00
20	Matt Riley	5.00

2000 SP Top Prospects Game-Used Bat Cards

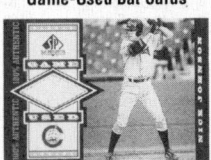

Slices of minor-league lumber wielded by top minor league stars of 1999, plus Ken Griffey Jr. and Michael Jordan are the "holy grail" for pack busters of SP Top Prospects. The horizontal-format cards have a diamond-shaped piece of game-used bat along with a color photo. Besides the regular version, Junior and Jordan also autographed a limited number of the cards, 24 and 45, respectively. The stated overall insertion rate for the bat cards is one per 288 packs (about one per 12 boxes).

		MT
Complete Set (13):		150.00
Common Player:		10.00
Pbe	Peter Bergeron	10.00
PB	Pat Burrell	15.00
RF	Rafael Furcal	10.00
JR	Ken Griffey Jr.	20.00
JR	Ken Griffey Jr. (Autographed edition of 24.)	400.00
JH	Josh Hamilton	15.00
NJ	Nick Johnson	12.50
MJ	Michael Jordan	25.00
A-MJ	Michael Jordan (Autographed edition of 45.)	1,250.
EM	Eric Munson	10.00
PO	Pablo Ozuna	10.00
CP	Corey Patterson	12.50
AS	Alfonso Soriano	30.00
JT	Jorge Toca	10.00
JW	Jayson Werth	10.00

2000 SP Top Prospects Great Futures

Twenty top minor league stars destined for big-league futures are the content of this insert set, found on average of one per four packs.

		MT
Complete Set (20):		30.00
Common Player:		.75
1	Jorge Toca	.75
2	Ryan Anderson	1.50
3	Eric Munson	.75
4	Rick Ankiel	1.00
5	Rob Bell	.75
6	Matt Riley	.75
7	Pat Burrell	6.00
8	Nick Johnson	2.50
9	Jody Gerut	1.00
10	Sean Burroughs	3.00
11	Austin Kearns	2.50
12	Corey Patterson	3.00
13	Josh Hamilton	3.00
14	Rafael Furcal	1.50
15	Donny Leon	.75
16	Peter Bergeron	1.50
17	A.J. Burnett	1.50
18	Alex Escobar	.75
19	Brad Penny	.75
20	Chin-Feng Chen	2.50

2000 SP Top Prospects Minor Memories

The minor league careers of Ken Griffey Jr. and Michael Jordan are traced in this series. Stated odds of pulling one of the inserts are one per 11 packs.

		MT
Complete Set (10):		15.00
Common Player:		1.50
MJ01-5	Michael Jordan	2.50
Jr01-5	Ken Griffey Jr.	1.50

2000 SP Top Prospects Prospective Superstars

Upper Deck labled the dozen players in this insert set as "can't-miss super prospects" and inserted these cards one per 24 packs of SP Top Prospects.

		MT
Complete Set (12):		25.00
Common Player:		2.00
1	Pat Burrell	5.00
2	Eric Munson	2.00
3	Rick Ankiel	2.00
4	Brad Penny	2.00
5	Ben Petrick	2.00
6	Josh Hamilton	4.00
7	Adam Piatt	3.00
8	A.J. Burnett	2.00
9	Rafael Furcal	2.00
10	Sean Burroughs	4.00

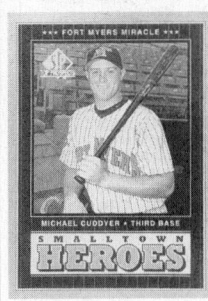

11	Chin-Feng Chen	3.00
12	Nick Johnson	4.00

2000 SP Top Prospects Small Town Heroes

Capturing the feel of minor league baseball across the nation, this insert series showcases players whose 1999 season were spent in places like Princeton and Norwich. Insertion rate was announced as one per 11 packs.

		MT
Complete Set (12):		15.00
Common Player:		2.00
1	Josh Hamilton	4.00
2	Jorge Toca	2.00
3	John Patterson	2.00
4	Jacques Landry	2.00
5	Felipe Lopez	2.00
6	Choo Freeman	2.00
7	Eric Valent	2.00
8	Jody Gerut	2.00
9	Michael Restovich	2.00
10	Pablo Ozuna	2.00
11	Kip Wells	3.00
12	Michael Cuddyer	2.50

2000 Team Best Rookies 2000 Promos

These cards introduced both TB's Rookies 2000 and Baseball Fanatics Trading Card Game issues. Fronts are virtually identical to the issued versions of the cards. Backs have a large Rookies 2000 or Baseball Fanatics logo at center.

		MT
Complete Set (5):		8.00
Common Player:		1.00
(1)	Baseball Fanatics Header Card	.50
(2)	Pat Burrell (Babbitt's Bombers)	4.00
(3)	Sean Burroughs	2.00
(4)	Corey Myers	1.00
(5)	Corey Patterson (#1 Pick)	3.00

2000 Team Best Rookies 2000

Significant problems with numbering of cards in the range #3-99 plagued this otherwise attractive minor league presentation. Cor-

rected versions, which were available only by mail-in-exchange, had to be issued for some 20 cards. They are marked with an SP in the checklist here. All but one (Ben Broussard) of the players in the base set is presented in two different formats. Cards #1-100 have player photos surrounded with a frame resembling cut stone. A Rookies 2000 logo is at upper-right. On most cards, there is a Team Best logo at lower-left and a minor league team logo at lower-right. On some cards, the team logo is replaced with the TB logo. Cards #101-112 are similar in design though the color of stone borders is brown, rather than gray; these player's represent #1 draft picks. Backs repeat a portion of the front photo in tight vertical format at left, and offer personal data and career highlights. Cards #113-213 feature the same line-up as #1-100, and most use the same photo on front, though in a borderless design. Their backs are similar in format to the low-numbers. Cards #214-225 repeat the checklist of #1 picks on a "two-headed" borderless format. All "b" version cards in the checklist represent the originally printed error cards that have the correct photos on front and back, but have the "a" player's biographical data and career highlights. Team Best Rookie 2000 cards were sold in a basic six-card foil pack in several different box compositions.

		MT
Complete Set (225):		9.00
Common Player:		.05
Wax Pack (6):		1.50
1	Kurt Ainsworth	.10
2	Travis Anderson	.05
3a	Ryan Baerlocher	.05
3b	Chris Sampson	.05
4	Andrew Beinbrink/SP	.10
5	Jonathan Berry	.05
6	Larry Bigbie	.05
7	Josh Bonifay	.05
8	Casey Burns	.05
9	Mike Bynum/SP	.10
10	Marlon Byrd	.05
11	Terry Byron/SP	.10
12	Chance Caple	.10
13	Matt Cepicky	.10
14a	Ryan Christianson	.10
14b	Joe Thurston	.10
15	B.R. Cook	.05
16	Carl Crawford	.25
17	Chuck Crowder	.05
18	Jeremy Cunningham	.05
19a	Chris Curry	.05
19b	Mike Bynum	.05
20a	Phil Devey	.05
20b	Andrew Beinbrink	.05
21a	Grant Dorn	.05
21b	Chris Testa	.05
22	Mike Dwyer/SP	.10
23a	Mike Dzurilla	.05
23b	Barry Zito	.50
24	Vince Faison	.05
25	Carlos Figueroa	.05
26	Aaron Franke	.05
27	Charlie Frazier	.05
28	B.J. Garbe	.05
29	Curtis Gay	.05
30	Jay Gehrke	.05
31	Scott Goodman	.05
32	Alex Graman	.05
33a	Ryan Gripp	.05
33b	Robb Quinlan	.05
34	Josh Hamilton/SP	.25
35	Ken Harvey	.05
36	Jeff Heaverlo	.05
37	Ben Hickman	.05
38	Mike Hill/SP	.10
39	Josh Holliday	.05
40	Kevin Hooper	.05
41a	Ryan Jamison	.05
41b	Josh Hamilton	.15
42	Eric Johnson	.05
43	Jake Joseph	.05
44	Ryan Kibler/SP	.05
45	John Lackey	.15
46	Jake Laidlaw	.05
47	Jay Landreth/SP	.10
48	Jason Lane	.15
49	Jay Langston	.05
50	Peyton Lewis	.05
51a	Robert MacDougal	.05
51b	Ben Sheets	.25
52	Mike Mallory	.05
53	Justin Martin	.05
54	Lamont Matthews	.05
55	Matt McClendon	.05
56	Sean McGowan	.05
57a	Todd Mitchell	.05

57b	Terry Byron	.05
58a	Matt Mize	.05
58b	Matt Watson	.05
59	Jason Moore	.05
60	Corey Myers	.05
61	Derrick Nunley	.05
62	Rodney Nye	.05
63a	Mike Paradis	.05
63b	Mike Dwyer	.05
64	Tino Pascucci	.05
65	Dustin Pate	.05
66	Mike Patten	.05
67	Brad Pautz	.05
68a	Josh Pearse	.05
68b	Ryan Kibler	.05
69	Andy Phillips	.10
70	Robb Quinlan/SP	.10
71a	G.J. Raymundo	.05
71b	Dominic Woody	.05
72a	Justin Reid	.05
72b	Mike Rosamond	.05
73	Nate Robertson	.05
74	Mike Rosamond/SP	.10
75	Chris Sampson/SP	.10
76	Matt Schneider	.05
77	Sean Schumacher	.05
78	Ben Sheets/SP	.50
79	Jeremy Sickles	.05
80a	Kyle Snyder	.05
80b	Mike Hill	.05
81	Jack Taschner	.05
82a	Seth Taylor	.05
82b	Charles Williams	.05
83	Chris Testa/SP	.10
84	Mike Thompson/SP	.10
85	Joe Thurston/SP	.25
86a	Jon Topolski	.05
86b	Jerome Williams	.10
87a	Dan Tosca	.05
87b	Jay Landreth	.05
88	Nick Trzeniak	.05
89	Brant Ust	.05
90	Josh Vitek	.05
91	David Walling	.05
92	Jeremy Ward	.05
93	Anthony Ware	.05
94	Matt Watson (SP)	.10
95	Charles Williams (SP)	.10
96	Jerome Williams (SP)	.25
97	Dominic Woody (SP)	.10
98	Shane Wright	.05
99	Barry Zito (SP)	.75
100	Alec Zumwalt	.05
101	Chip Ambres (#1 Pick)	.10
102	Jeff Austin (#1 Pick)	.10
103	Pat Burrell (#1 Pick)	1.00
104	Sean Burroughs (#1 Pick)	.75
105	Bubba Crosby (#1 Pick)	.10
106	Choo Freeman (#1 Pick)	.10
107	Josh Hamilton (#1 Pick)	.25
108	Mark Mulder (#1 Pick)	.50
109	Corey Patterson (#1 Pick)	1.00
110	Carlos Pena (#1 Pick)	.25
111	Eric Valent (#1 Pick)	.10
112	Kip Wells (#1 Pick)	.10
113	Kurt Ainsworth (#1 On Front)	.10
114	Travis Anderson	.05
115	Ryan Baerlocher (#3 On Front)	.05
116	Andrew Beinbrink	.05
117	Jonathan Berry	.05
118	Larry Bigbie	.05
119	Josh Bonifay	.05
120	Ben Broussard	.25
121	Casey Burns (#8 On Front)	.05
122	Mike Bynum	.10
123	Marlon Byrd	.10
124	Terry Byron	.05
125	Chance Caple	.10
126	Matt Cepicky	.05
127	Ryan Christianson	.10
128	B.R. Cook	.05
129	Carl Crawford	.30
130	Chuck Crowder	.05
131	Jeremy Cunningham	.05
132	Chris Curry	.05
133	Phil Devey	.05
134	Grant Dorn	.05
135	Mike Dwyer	.05
136	Mike Dzurilla	.05
137	Vince Faison	.10
138	Carlos Figueroa	.05
139	Aaron Franke	.05
140	Charlie Frazier	.05
141	B.J. Garbe	.05
142	Curtis Gay	.05
143	Jay Gehrke	.05
144	Scott Goodman	.05
145	Alex Graman	.05
146	Ryan Gripp	.05
147	Josh Hamilton	.25
148	Ken Harvey	.10
149	Jeff Heaverlo	.05
150	Ben Hickman	.05
151	Mike Hill	.05
152	Josh Holliday	.05
153	Kevin Hooper	.05
154	Ryan Jamison	.05
155	Eric Johnson	.05
156	Jake Joseph	.05
157	Ryan Kibler	.05
158	John Lackey	.05
159	Jake Laidlaw	.05
160	Jay Landreth	.05
161	Jason Lane	.15
162	Jay Langston	.05
163	Peyton Lewis	.05
164	Robert MacDougal	.05
165	Mike Mallory	.05
166	Justin Martin	.05
167	Lamont Matthews	.05
168	Matt McClendon	.05
169	Sean McGowan	.05
170	Todd Mitchell	.05
171	Matt Mize	.05
172	Jason Moore	.05
173	Corey Myers	.05
174	Derrick Nunley	.05
175	Rodney Nye	.05
176	Mike Paradis	.05
177	Tino Pascucci	.05
178	Dustin Pate	.05
179	Mike Patten	.05
180	Brad Pautz	.05
181	Josh Pearse	.05
182	Andy Phillips	.10
183	Robb Quinlan	.05
184	G.J. Raymundo	.05
185	Justin Reid	.05
186	Nate Robertson	.05
187	Mike Rosamond	.05
188	Chris Sampson	.05
189	Matt Schneider	.05
190	Sean Schumacher	.05
191	Ben Sheets	.25
192	Jeremy Sickles	.05
193	Kyle Snyder	.05
194	Jack Taschner	.05
195	Seth Taylor	.05
196	Chris Testa	.05
197	Mike Thompson	.05
198	Joe Thurston	.10
199	Jon Topolski	.05
200	Dan Tosca	.05
201	Nick Trzeniak	.05
202	Brant Ust	.05
203	Josh Vitek	.05
204	David Walling	.05
205	Jeremy Ward	.05
206	Anthony Ware	.05
207	Matt Watson	.05
208	Charles Williams	.05
209	Jerome Williams	.15
210	Dominic Woody	.05
211	Shane Wright	.05
212	Barry Zito	.50
213	Alec Zumwalt	.05
214	Chip Ambres (#1 Pick)	.10
215	Jeff Austin (#1 Pick)	.10
216	Pat Burrell (#1 Pick)	1.00
217	Sean Burroughs (#1 Pick)	.75
218	Bubba Crosby (#1 Pick)	.10
219	Choo Freeman (#1 Pick)	.10
220	Josh Hamilton (#1 Pick)	.25
221	Mark Mulder (#1 Pick)	.50
222	Corey Patterson (#1 Pick)	1.00
223	Carlos Pena (#1 Pick)	.25
224	Eric Valent (#1 Pick)	.10
225	Kip Wells (#1 Pick)	.10
---	Autograph Contest Card	.05
---	Baseball Fanatics Preview Card	.05
---	Babbitt's Bomber's Offer Card	.05

2000 Team Best Rookies 2000 Autographs

NATE ROLISON

A mixed line-up of first-year pros and established minor league stars is featured in the autographed inserts seeded in TB Rookies 2000 at a rate of about one per three packs. Autograph cards follow the format of the low-number cards in the base set. Backs have a "Declaration of Authenticity" from TB chairman/CEO Dan R. White, Jr. The unnumbered autograph cards are listed here alphabetically.

		MT
Complete Set (25):		30.00
Common Player:		1.00
(1)	Kurt Ainsworth	2.00
(2)	Chad Allen	1.00
(3)	Chip Ambres	2.00
(4)	Ryan Anderson	3.00
(5)	Andy Brown	1.00
(6)	Sean Burroughs	4.00
(7)	Francisco Cordero	1.00
(8)	Bubba Crosby	1.00
(9)	Jack Cust	4.50
(10)	Rick Elder	1.00
(11)	Choo Freeman	1.00
(12)	Jeff Goldbach	1.00
(13)	Josh Hamilton	2.00
(14)	Chad Harville	1.00
(15)	Jeff Heaverlo	1.00
(16)	Cesar Izturis	1.00
(17)	Austin Kearns	10.00
(18)	Mike Lincoln	1.00
(19)	George Lombard	1.00
(20)	Julio Lugo	1.00
(21)	Jim Morris	9.00
(22)	Nate Rolison	1.00
(23)	B.J. Ryan	1.00
(24)	Pat Strange	1.00
(25)	Tyler Walker	1.00

2000 Team Best Rookies 2000 Babbitt's Bombers

CARLOS PENA

While most of the players in the base set were first year pros in 1999, the selection of players in the Rookie 2000 set leans to established minor league (and future Major League) stars. Seeded only one per 72 foil packs, the Bombers cards feature top sluggers in a format similar to the low-number cards in the base set. The silhouette of a four-engine bomber appears at upper-left on front. Backs have multiple copies of the bomber symbol, along with personal data and career highlights. Parallels of the insert are a silver version, numbered to 150, and a gold version, numbered to 100.

		MT
Complete Set (8):		9.00
Common Player:		1.00
Silver:		1.5X
Gold:		2X
1	Russell Branyan	1.00
2	Morgan Burkhart	1.00
3	Pat Burrell	3.00
4	Josh Hamilton	1.00
5	Nick Johnson	3.00
6	George Lombard	1.00
7	Carlos Pena	1.00
8	Dernell Stenson	1.00

2000 Team Best Rookies 2000 Extended

Twenty-five new cards were packaged with 100 of the base cards from the Rookies 2000 issue to provide the basis for this postseason issue. The numbering errors which had plagued the earlier version were corrected this time out, as were eight other base-card errors, the corrected version for which can be found only in the Extended packaging. The six-card packs each contain one autographed card from a new group of 25 players or from one of Team Best's earlier releases. Three "foil" versions of each base card were also produced as random inserts as was a 10-card Diamond Best set.

		MT
Complete Set (150):		6.00
Common Player:		.05
Wax Box:		30.00
1	Kurt Ainsworth	.15
2	Travis Anderson	.05
3	Ryan Baerlocher	.05
4	Andrew Beinbrink	.05
5	Jonathan Berry	.05
6	Larry Bigbie	.05
7	Josh Bonifay	.05
8	Casey Burns	.05
9	Mike Bynum	.10
10	Marlon Byrd	.15
11	Terry Byron	.05
12	Chance Caple	.05
13	Matt Cepicky	.10
14	Ryan Christianson	.10
15	B.R. Cook	.05
16	Carl Crawford	.25
17	Chuck Crowder	.05
18	Jeremy Cunningham	.05
19	Chris Curry	.05
20	Phil Devey	.05
21	Grant Dorn	.05
22	Mike Dwyer	.10
23	Mike Dzurilla	.05
24	Vince Faison	.05
25	Carlos Figueroa	.05
26	Aaron Franke	.05
27	Charlie Frazier	.05
28	B.J. Garbe	.05
29	Curtis Gay	.05
30	Jay Gehrke	.05
31	Scott Goodman	.05
32	Alex Graman	.05
33	Ryan Gripp	.05
34	Josh Hamilton	.25
35	Ken Harvey	.05
36	Jeff Heaverlo	.05
37	Ben Hickman	.05
38	Mike Hill	.05
39	Josh Holliday	.05
40	Kevin Hooper	.05
41	Ryan Jamison	.05
42	Eric Johnson	.05
43	Jake Joseph	.05
44	Ryan Kibler	.15
45	John Lackey	.15
46	Jake Laidlaw	.05
47	Jay Landreth	.05
48	Jason Lane	.15
49	Jay Langston	.05
50	Peyton Lewis	.05
51	Robert MacDougal	.05
52	Mike Mallory	.05
53	Justin Martin	.05
54	Lamont Matthews	.05
55	Matt McClendon	.05
56	Sean McGowan	.05
57	Todd Mitchell	.05
58	Matt Mize	.05
59	Jason Moore	.05
60	Corey Myers	.05
61	Derrick Nunley	.05
62	Rodney Nye	.05
63	Mike Paradis	.05
64	Tino Pascucci	.05
65	Dustin Pate	.05
66	Mike Patten	.05
67	Brad Pautz	.05
68	Josh Pearse	.05
69	Andy Phillips	.10
70	Robb Quinlan	.05
71	G.J. Raymundo	.05
72	Justin Reid	.05
73	Nate Robertson	.05
74	Mike Rosamond	.05
75	Chris Sampson	.05
76	Matt Schneider	.05
77	Sean Schumacher	.05
78	Ben Sheets	.50
79	Jeremy Sickles	.05
80	Kyle Snyder	.05
81	Jack Taschner	.05
82	Seth Taylor	.05
83	Chris Testa	.05
84	Mike Thompson	.05
85	Joe Thurston	.25
86	Jon Topolski	.05
87	Dan Tosca	.05
88a	Nick Trzeniak	.05
88b	Nick Trzesniak (Birthplace corrected, bio text rearranged.)	.10
89	Brant Ust	.05
90	Josh Vitek	.05
91	David Walling	.05
92	Jeremy Ward	.05
93	Anthony Ware	.05
94	Matt Watson	.05
95	Charles Williams	.05
96	Jerome Williams	.10
97	Dominic Woody	.05
98	Shane Wright	.05
99	Barry Zito	1.00
100	Alec Zumwalt	.05
115	Ryan Baerlocher (Card number of front corrected from 3.)	.10
119	Josh Bonifay (Bio corrected.)	.10
121	Casey Burns (Card number on front corrected from 8.)	.10
153	Kevin Hooper (Card number on front corrected from 201.)	.10
193	Kyle Snyder (Size of name on front reduced.)	.05
201	Nick Trzesniak (Birthplace corrected; logo and player ID moved on front.)	.10
210	Dominic Woody (Size of player name reduced.)	.05
226	Danys Baez	.10
227	Josh Beckett	2.00
228	Willie Bloomquist	.05
229	Bobby Bradley	.05
230	Ben Broussard	.25
231	Ben Christensen	.05
232	Brian Cole	.05
233	Enrique Cruz	.05
234	Matt Ginter	.05
235	J.R. House	.05
236	Ty Howington	.10
237	Russ Jacobson	.05
238	Neil Jenkins	.05
239	Jason Jennings	.10
240	Colby Lewis	.20
241	Ryan Ludwick	.05
242	Mike Maroth	.05
243	Eric Munson	.10
244	Neal Musser	.05
245	Brett Myers	.10
246	Wily Mo Pena	.15
247	Brian Sanches	.05
248	Ramon Santiago	.05
249	Jason Stumm	.05
250	Dan Wright	.05

2000 Team Best Rookies 2000 Extended Foil

JOSH HAMILTON

Each base card in Rookies 2000 Extended was also produced in an edition of 2,000 cards with either bronze, silver or gold metallic foil highlights on front. The cards were random pack inserts.

		MT
Common Player:		.50
High-Demand Cards:		3X
(See Team Best Rookies 2000 Extended for checklist and base card values.)		
---	Josh Hamilton (Bronze-foil promo.)	1.50
---	Josh Hamilton (Silver-foil promo.)	1.50
---	Josh Hamilton (Gold-foil promo.)	1.50

2000 Team Best Rookies 2000 Extended Autographs

One of the six cards in each pack of Rookies 2000 Extended was an authentically autographed card produced either specifically for the issue or for one of Team Best's earlier issues (1998 Signature Series, 1999 Rookie, 1999 Baseball America or 1999 Player of the Year). Card #16 Ty Howington was not returned by the player in time for inclusion and was seeded into a later issue.

		MT
Complete Set (24):		30.00
Common Player:		2.00
1	Rick Asadoorian	2.00
2	Jeff Austin	4.00
3	Peter Bergeron	3.00
4	Bobby Bradley	3.00
5	Milton Bradley	3.00
6	Ben Broussard	2.00
7	Roosevelt Brown	3.00
8	Brian Cooper	2.00
9	Ryan Dempster	3.00
10	B.J. Garbe	2.00
11	Jon Garland	3.00
12	Marcus Giles	6.00
13	Keith Ginter	2.00
14	Jason Hart	2.00
15	Shane Heams	2.00
16	Ty Howington (Not Issued)	.00
17	Matt McClendon	2.00
18	Mike Meyers	2.00
19	Brett Myers	2.00
20	Danny Peoples	2.00
21	Luis Rivera	2.00
22	Kyle Snyder	2.00
23	Jason Stumm	2.00
24	Brad Wilkerson	2.00
25	Barry Zito	10.00

2000 Team Best Rookies 2000 Extended Diamond Best

Ten big name minor leaguers were chosen for this 1:90 pack insert series. Cards share the same basic design as the base-card issue, but have a dark blue background and a Diamond Best logo in the upper-left.

		MT
Complete Set (10):		30.00

JOSH BECKETT

Common Player:		3.00
1	Josh Beckett	10.00
2	Russell Branyan	3.00
3	Pat Burrell	7.50
4	Michael Cuddyer	3.00
5	Alex Escobar	3.00
6	Josh Hamilton	3.00
7	Steve Lomasney	3.00
8	Tomokazu Ohka	3.00
9	Adam Piatt	3.00
10	Jimmy Rollins	5.00

2000 Minor League Team Sets

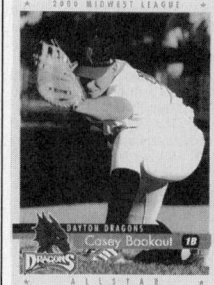
DAYTON DRAGONS — Casey Bookout

Manufacturer abbreviations used are: BL - Blueline, CH - Choice, GS - Grandstand, MA - Multi-Ad, WT - Warning Track.

188 Team Sets and Variations

		MT
2000	WT Adirondack Lumberjacks (30)	6.00
2000	MA Akron Aeros (30)	8.50
2000	GS Akron Aeros (30)	6.00
2000	Team Alaska Goldpanners (18)	22.50
2000	WT Albany-Colonie Diamond Dogs (30)	9.00
2000	GS Albuquerque Dukes (30)	6.00
2000	WT Allentown Ambassadors (26)	9.00
2000	GS Altoona Curve (30)	12.00
2000	GS Appalachian League Top Prospects (30)	16.00
2000	Team Arizona Fall League (30)	11.00
2000	MA Arkansas Travelers (30)	15.00
2000	GS Asheville Tourists (25)	9.00
2000	GS Auburn Doubledays (29)	9.00
2000	MA Augusta Greenjackets (30)	12.00
2000	Team Bakersfield Blaze (31)	9.50
2000	Team Batavia Muckdogs (39)	11.00
2000	Team Beloit Snappers (33)	12.50
2000	GS Billings Mustangs (34)	9.50
2000	BL Binghamton Mets (30)	10.00
2000	GS Birmingham Barons (31)	7.50
2000	GS Birmingham Barons Update (10)	9.00
2000	GS Bluefield Orioles (34)	9.00
2000	GS Boise Hawks (34)	11.50
2000	GS Bowie Baysox (28)	8.00
2000	MA Brevard County Manatees (30)	9.00
2000	GS Bristol Sox (30)	9.50
2000	BL Buffalo Bisons (30)	9.00
2000	MA Burlington Bees (30)	9.00
2000	GS Burlington Indians (30)	9.00
2000	GS Butte Copper Kings (32)	13.00
2000	Team Calgary Cannons (34)	11.00
2000	GS California League Top Prospects (29)	7.00
2000	MA Cape Fear Crocs (30)	9.00

2000 MA Capital City Bombers (30) 7.00
2000 CH Carolina League Prospects (35) 9.00
2000 GS Carolina Mudcats (30) 9.00
2000 MA Cedar Rapids Kernels (30) 12.00
2000 MA Charleston Alley Cats (30) 14.00
2000 MA Charleston RiverDogs (30) 7.00
2000 BL Charlotte Knights (30) 12.00
2000 MA Charlotte Rangers (30) 9.00
2000 GS Chattanooga Lookouts (30) 50.00
2000 GS Chattanooga Lookouts Update (9) 15.00
2000 MA Clearwater Phillies (30) 7.00
2000 GS Clinton LumberKings (30) 9.00
2000 Team Colorado Springs Sky Sox (31) 10.50
2000 BL Columbus Clippers (36) 10.00
2000 MA Columbus RedStixx (32) 12.00
2000 GS Danville Braves (31) 27.50
2000 Team Dayton Dragons (30) 11.00
2000 GS Daytona Cubs (33) 11.00
2000 MA Delmarva Shorebirds (30) 7.00
2000 WT Duluth-Superior Dukes (29) 15.00
2000 GS Dunedin Blue Jays (30) 9.50
2000 GS Durham Bulls (30) 20.00
2000 Team Edmonton Trappers (30) 11.00
2000 GS El Paso Diablos (30) 4.00
2000 MA Erie SeaWolves (30) 9.00
2000 GS Eugene Emeralds (31) 9.00
2000 WT Evansville Otters (25) 9.00
2000 GS Everett Aquasox (31) 9.00
2000 Team Fargo-Moorehead RedHawks (30) 9.00
2000 MA Ft. Myers Miracle (30) 13.00
2000 Team Ft. Wayne Wizards (34) 7.00
2000 GS Frederick Keys (31) 22.50
2000 GS Frederick Keys W/Pepsi Logo (30) 11.00
2000 GS Fresno Grizzlies (26) 11.00
2000 GS Great Falls Dodgers (29) 15.00
2000 MA Greensboro Bats (30) 9.50
2000 Team Greenville Bluesmen (23) 9.50
2000 GS Greenville Braves (29) 10.00
2000 MA Hagerstown Suns (30) 9.00
2000 Common Harrisburg Senators (28) 10.00
2000 MA Helena Brewers (30) 10.00
2000 MA Hickory Crawdads (30) 7.00
2000 MA Hickory Crawdads Update (30) 9.50
2000 GS High Desert Mavericks (30) 10.00
2000 GS Hudson Valley Renegades (33) 13.50
2000 Team Huntsville Stars (29) 10.00
2000 GS Idaho Falls Padres (30) 9.00
2000 BL Indianapolis Indians (30) 9.00
2000 MA Iowa Cubs (30) 9.00
2000 GS Jacksonville Suns (31) 9.00
2000 Team Johnson City Cardinals (40) 27.00
2000 Team Jupiter Hammerheads (40) 20.00
2000 Connie's Kane County Cougars (32) 12.50
2000 Old Navy Kane County Cougars (32) 40.00
2000 Team Kane County Cougars (32) 10.00
2000 CH Kinston Indians (30) 10.00
2000 MA Kissimmee Cobras (30) 9.00
2000 Team Lafayette Bayou Bullfrogs (22) 12.00
2000 GS Lake Elsinore Storm (36) 10.00
2000 MA Lakeland Tigers (30) 13.00
2000 GS Lancaster Jethawks (30) 12.00
2000 GS Lansing Lugnuts (31) 9.00
2000 MA Las Vegas Stars (30) 12.00
2000 BL Louisville RiverBats (36) 9.00
2000 MA Lowell Spinners (30) 9.50

2000 CH Lynchburg Hillcats (32) 12.00
2000 MA Macon Braves (30) 10.00
2000 MA Mahoning Valley Scrappers (30) 10.00
2000 MA Martinsville Astros (30) 65.00
2000 Team Memphis Redbirds (30) 32.00
2000 MA Michigan Battle Cats (30) 10.00
2000 GS Midland RockHounds (28) 12.00
2000 Team Midland RockHounds (26) 12.50
2000 MA 1999 Midwest League Prospects (35) 15.00
2000 MA Midwest League Top Prospects (29) 12.00
2000 Team Midwest League All-Stars (57) 30.00
2000 GS Missoula Osprey (31) 9.00
2000 GS Mobile BayBears (30) 10.00
2000 GS Modesto A's (30) 7.00
2000 GS Mudville Nine (30) 9.50
2000 MA Myrtle Beach Pelicans (30) 9.50
2000 MA Nashville Sounds (30) 9.50
2000 Team Newark Bears (26) 5.00
2000 BL New Britain Rock Cats (30) 8.00
2000 Team New Haven Ravens (31) 6.00
2000 GS New Jersey Cardinals (33) 9.00
2000 GS New Jersey Cardinals Update (3) 10.00
2000 Team New Jersey Cardinals (6) 10.50
2000 WT New Jersey Jackals (31) 14.00
2000 MA New Orleans Zephyrs (29) 9.50
2000 BL Norfolk Tides (36) 9.00
2000 BL Norwich Navigators (30) 15.00
2000 Team Ogden Raptors (40) 20.00
2000 MA Oklahoma City Redhawks (29) 11.00
2000 MA Omaha GoldenSpikes (35) 25.00
2000 MA Orlando Devil Rays Strip Set (29) 60.00
2000 BL Ottawa Lynx (30) 7.00
2000 BL Pawtucket Red Sox (30) 9.50
2000 DD Pawtucket Red Sox (31) 10.00
2000 MA Peoria Chiefs (30) 70.00
2000 MA Piedmont Boll Weevils (30) 6.00
2000 MA Pittsfield Mets (32) 10.00
2000 GS Portland Sea Dogs (33) 7.00
2000 CH Potomac Cannons (30) 10.00
2000 CH Potomac Cannons All-Stars (8) 9.50
2000 GS Princeton Devil Rays (30) 9.50
2000 GS Pulaski Rangers (29) 9.50
2000 Roox Quad City Bandits (30) 50.00
2000 GS Rancho Cucamonga Quakes (30) 9.50
2000 MA Reading Phillies (29) 7.00
2000 MA Reading Phils Avernia College (29) 12.50
2000 BL Richmond Braves (36) 12.00
2000 Richmond Camera Richmond Braves (25) 9.00
2000 GS Rochester Red Wings (25) 9.00
2000 MA Round Rock Express (30) 12.00
2000 GS Sacramento River Cats (30) 9.00
2000 GS Salem Avalanche (31) 9.00
2000 GS Salem-Keizer Volcanoes (36) 7.00
2000 GS San Antonio Missions (30) 9.00
2000 GS San Bernardino Stampede (30) 9.00
2000 GS San Jose Giants (30) 9.00
2000 MA Sarasota Red Sox (30) 13.00
2000 MA Savannah Sand Gnats (29) 12.00
2000 BL Scranton/Wilkes-Barre Red Barons (30) 7.00
2000 GS Shreveport Captains (30) 10.00
2000 GS Sioux Falls Canaries (28) 10.00
2000 MA South Atlantic League Prospects (30) 9.50
2000 MA South Bend Silver Hawks (30) 10.00
2000 GS Southern League Top Prospects (31) 9.50
2000 GS Spokane Indians (37) 9.50
2000 GS St. Lucie Mets (32) 10.00

2000 MA St. Petersburg Devil Rays (30) 9.50
2000 MA Staten Island Yankees (36) 15.00
2000 GS Syracuse SkyChiefs (47) 11.50
2000 BL Tacoma Rainiers (30) 9.50
2000 MA Tampa Yankees (30) 25.00
2000 GS Tennessee Smokies (28) 20.00
2000 GS Toledo Mud Hens (30) 9.00
2000 MA Trenton Thunder (30) 7.00
2000 Team Tulsa Drillers (28) 10.00
2000 MA Utica Blue Sox (40) 20.00
2000 GS Vancouver Canadians (35) 13.00
2000 GS Vermont Expos (34) 9.50
2000 MA Vero Beach Dodgers (30) 9.00
2000 GS Visalia Oaks (30) 9.00
2000 MA West Michigan Whitecaps (30) 9.00
2000 GS West Tennessee Diamond Jaxx (30) 20.00
2000 CH Wichita Wranglers (30) 9.00
2000 MA Williamsport Crosscutters (30) 10.00
2000 CH Wilmington Blue Rocks (30) 10.00
2000 CH Winston-Salem Warthogs (30) 12.00
2000 CH Winston-Salem Warthogs Update (30) 20.00
2000 MA Wisconsin Timber Rattlers (30) 10.00
2000 GS Yakima Bears (31) 10.00

2001 Just 2k1 Top Prospect Promos

Produced as previews for an intended product that was never issued, these promos were available in complete-set form via mail from the manufacturer.

	MT
Complete Set (13):	5.00
Common Player:	.25
TPP.01 Wilson Betemit	.25
TPP.02 Joe Borchard	.50
TPP.03 Cristian Guerrero	.25
TPP.04 J.R. House	.25
TPP.05 Hee Seop Choi	.35
TPP.06 Tiger Wang	.25
TPP.07 Justin Morneau	.50
TPP.08 Tony Blanco	.25
TPP.09 Luis Montanez	.25
TPP.10 Drew Henson	1.00
TPP.11 Adrian Gonzalez	.25
TPP.12 Bobby Hill	.65
BONUS Drew Henson	1.00

2001 Pacific Sports Promotions Reprints

(The first "American" baseball cards of Ichiro Suzuki from the 1993 Hawaii Winter Baseball League Hilo Stars team set were reprinted in 2001. Reprints are marked as such on back.)

	MT
Complete Set (4):	125.00
1 Ichiro Suzuki (Red cap.)	25.00
1 Ichiro Suzuki (Red cap.) (Gold signature.)	40.00
5 Ichiro Suzuki (Blue helmet.)	25.00
5 Ichiro Suzuki (Blue helmet.) (Gold signature.)	40.00

2001 Royal Rookies Futures

This minor-league issue features a 40-card base set and several inserts, sold in six-card foil packs with one authentically autographed card in every pack. Fronts have a borderless player photo. Because the set was not licensed by Major League Baseball, only by the individual players, most cap and uniform logos have been removed from the photos. Backs repeat the front photo and have a few sentences about the player.

	MT
Complete Set (40):	1.00
Common Player:	.05
Wax Pack (5+1):	2.50
Wax Box (12):	20.00
1 Ramon Soler	.05
2 Aron Weston	.05
3 Alex Requena	.05
4 Eric Johnson	.05
5 Tony Mota	.05
6 Miguel Cabrera	.50
7 Jovanny Cedano (Cedeno)	.05
8 Jose Morban	.05
9 Enrique Ramirez	.05
10 Steve Goodson	.05
11 Carlos Silva	.05
12 Jovanny Sosa	.05
13 Jeff Bailey	.05
14 Eric Byrnes	.05
15 Rob Pugmire	.05
16 Frederick Torres	.05
17 Jeff Inglin	.05
18 Jermaine Clark	.10
19 Adam Melhuse	.05
20 Dustin Carr	.05
21 Paul Hoover	.05
22 Christian Parker	.05
23 Paul Ottavinia	.05
24 Maxim St. Pierre	.05
25 Tony Pena Jr.	.05
26 Jay Gehrke	.05
27 Scott Seal	.05
28 J.J. Putz	.05
29 Jesus Medrano	.05
30 Bret Prinz	.05
31 Derrick Cook	.05
32 Mark Roberts	.05
33 Napoleon Calzado	.05
34 Francisco Rodriguez	.05
35 Brant Ust	.05
36 Ken Griffey Jr. (Base Card Checklist)	.10
(37) Rick Ankiel, Alex Escobar	.10
(38) Roosevelt Brown, Julio Lugo, Jr.	.05
(39) Adam Piatt, Travis Dawkins	.10
(40) Alex Rodriguez Chase Card Checklist	.10

2001 Royal Rookies Futures Autographs

2001 Royal Rookies Futures Blue Chips

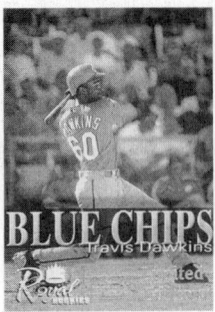

Ten top prospects are included in this insert set. Fronts have game-action photos with the borders and background tinted blue and a large "BLUE CHIPS" banner across the front. A gold-foil "LIMITED EDITION" logo also appears. Backs have a smaller version of the front photo and a few sentences about the player. Although the cards are un-numbered, they are numbered here according to the checklist.

	MT
Complete Set (10):	3.00
Common Player:	.50
(1) Rick Ankiel	.75
(1p) Rick Ankiel (PROMO)	.65
(2) C.C. Sabathia	.65
(3) Jayson Werth	.50
(4) Brad Baisley	.50
(5) Adam Piatt	.60
(6) Travis Dawkins	.60
(7) Jeremy Ward	.50
(8) Luis Rivera	.50
(9) Eric Gagne	1.00
(10) Alex Escobar	.50

2001 Royal Rookies Futures High Yield

Ten prospects with bright futures are featured in this insert set. Fronts have borderless action photos with a large "HIGH YIELD" logo vertically at left. Backs have a smaller version of the front photo, along with a few words about the player and his 1999 stats. The cards have no numbers and are presented here as numbered on the checklist. An autographed version of each card, numbered to 2,500 each, was also produced. They are valued about 10X the unsigned version.

	MT
Complete Set (10):	3.00
Common Player:	.50
(1) Ty Howington	.50
(2) Brennan King	.50
(3) Jason Stumm	.50
(4) Roosevelt Brown	.50
(5) Julio Lugo, Jr.	.50
(6) Colby Lewis	.50
(7) Jamie Brown	.50
(8) Julio Ramirez	.50
(9) Jorge Toca	.50
(10) Nathan Haynes	.50

2001 Royal Rookies Futures Wall Street

Five cards of Alex Rodriguez were issued as inserts bearing a gold-foil "Limited Edition" logo. Large photos on front and smaller back photos have had uniform logos removed. Each card was also released in an autographed version with an authenticity seal and serial number from within an edition of 20 each on back.

	MT
Complete Set (5):	2.00
Common Card:	.50
Autographed Card:	100.00
1-5 Alex Rodriguez	.50

2001 Royal Rookies Throwbacks

This minor-league issue features a 44-card base set and several inserts, sold in six-card foil packs. Two authentically autographed cards were inserted in every 12-pack box. Fronts of the base cards have a borderless player photo on which the colors have been muted. Because the set was not licensed by Major League Baseball, only by the individual players, all cap and uniform logos have been removed from the photos. Backs repeat detail of the front photo and have a few sentences about the player. The two-player Flipcards and the checklists do not have numbers on the cards, but are listed here according to the checklist.

		MT
	Complete Set (44):	1.00
	Common Player:	.05
	Wax Pack (5+1):	2.00
	Wax Box (12):	20.00
	Wax Box (18):	25.00
1	Mark Brownson	.05
2	Jason Woolf	.05
3	Enrique Cruz	.05
4	Jose Mieses	.05
5	Erick Almonte	.05
6	Randey Dorame	.05
7	Alex Hernandez	.05
8	Marlon Byrd	.05
9	Kevin Connacher	.05
10	Asdrubal Orapeza (Oropeza)	.05
11	Seth McClung	.10
12	Delvin James	.05
13	Albenis Machado	.05
14	Jose Leon	.05
15	Randel (Randall) Meadows	.05
16	Luke Allen	.05
17	Hector Almonte	.05
18	Peter Bauer	.05
19	Todd Betts	.05
20	Adrian Burnside	.05
21	Angel Berroa	.50
22	Cesar Saba	.05
23	Luis Garcia	.05
24	Ron Paulino	.05
25	Alex Gomez	.05
26	Ryan Ballard	.05
27	Enemencio Pacheco	.05
28	Michael Napoli	.05
29	Francis Finnerty	.05
30	Javier Calzada	.05
31	Shawn Sonnier	.05
32	Mike Porzio	.05
33	Rafael Pujols	.05
34	Pedro Santana	.05
35	Carlos Urquiola	.05
(36)	Ty Howington, Jason Stumm (Flipcard)	.10
(37)	Brennan King, Jorge Toca (Flipcard)	.05
(38)	Alex Escobar, Jeremy Ward (Flipcard)	.10
(39)	C.C. Sabathia, Brad Baisley (Flipcard)	.15
(40)	Nathan Haynes, Julio Ramirez (Flipcard)	.05
(41)	Colby Lewis, Jamie Brown (Flipcard)	.05
(42)	Roosevelt Brown, Eric Byrnes (Flipcard)	.10
(43)	Todd Helton Checklist - Base Set	.10
(44)	Todd Helton Checklist - Inserts	.10

2001 Royal Rookies Throwbacks Autographs

Two of the 12 six-card foil packs in each box of Royal Rookies Throwbacks contain an authentically autographed card. The autograph cards are in the same format as the base set, except have a gold-foil logo on front and a serial number from within an edition of 5,950.

		MT
	Complete Set (44):	55.00
	Common Player:	1.00
1	Mark Brownson	1.00
2	Jason Woolf	1.00
3	Enrique Cruz	1.00
4	Jose Mieses	1.00
5	Erick Almonte	1.00
6	Randey Dorame	1.00
7	Alex Hernandez	1.00
8	Marlon Byrd	3.00
9	Kevin Connacher	1.00
10	Asdrubal Orapeza (Oropeza)	1.00
11	Seth McClung	2.00
12	Delvin James	1.00
13	Albenis Machado	1.00
14	Jose Leon	1.00
15	Randel (Randall) Meadows	1.00
16	Luke Allen	1.00
17	Hector Almonte	1.00
18	Peter Bauer	1.00
19	Todd Betts	1.00
20	Adrian Burnside	1.00
21	Angel Berroa	7.50
22	Cesar Saba	1.00
23	Luis Garcia	1.00
24	Ron Paulino	1.00
25	Alex Gomez	1.00
26	Ryan Ballard	1.00
27	Enemencio Pacheco	1.00
28	Michael Napoli	1.00
29	Francis Finnerty	1.00
30	Javier Calzada	1.00
31	Shawn Sonnier	1.00
32	Mike Porzio	1.00
33	Rafael Pujols	1.00
34	Pedro Santana	1.00
35	Carlos Urquiola	1.00
(36)	Ty Howington, Jason Stumm (Flipcard)	2.00
(37)	Brennan King, Jorge Toca (Flipcard)	2.00
(38)	Alex Escobar, Jeremy Ward (Flipcard)	5.00
(39)	C.C. Sabathia, Brad Baisley (Flipcard)	5.00
(40)	Nathan Haynes, Julio Ramirez (Flipcard)	2.00
(41)	Colby Lewis, Jamie Brown (Flipcard)	2.00
(42)	Roosevelt Brown, Eric Byrnes (Flipcard)	3.00

2001 Royal Rookies Amazing

Rockies star Todd Helton is featured in this five-card insert set. Fronts have an action photo with a large vertical "AMAZING" at left. Backs of four of the cards have a detail repeated from the front photo and a few sentences about Helton. The fifth card is a "flipcard" with two fronts. One of the five Helton cards was found in every other foil pack, while the other packs contained a "Special Offer" card by which the five-card set could be order by mail for $2 (+43.95 shipping).

		MT
	Complete Set (5):	1.00
	Common Card:	.25
A1	Todd Helton	.25
A2	Todd Helton	.25
(A3)	Todd Helton (Flipcard)	.25
A4	Todd Helton	.25
A5	Todd Helton	.25
	Todd Helton (Special Offer)	.10

2001 Royal Rookies Barnstormers

Each six-card foil pack of Royal Rookies Throwbacks contains one of 10 Barnstormers inserts. The colors on the borderless front photos are not muted as much as on the base cards and there is a vertical Barnstormers logo at left. On back is a background of a wooden fence with a detail from the front photo repeated, along with a few words about the player.

	MT
Complete Set (10):	1.00
Common Player:	.10

B1	Brian Wolfe	.10
B2	Garett Gentry	.10
B3	Cory (Corey) Spencer	.10
B4	Alfredo Amezaga	.10
B5	Vince Faison	.10
B6	Darron Cox	.10
B7	Luis Martinez	.10
B8	Junior Herndon	.10
B9	Kenny Nelson	.25
B10	Jay Sitzman	.10

2001 Royal Rookies Boys of Summer

Each six-card foil pack of Royal Rookies Throwbacks contains one of 10 Boys of Summer inserts. Colors on the borderless front photos are not muted as they are on the base cards and there is a Boys of Summer logo at bottom. On back is a detail from the front photo, along with a few words about the player. Card numbers are preceded by "BOS#."

		MT
	Complete Set (10):	1.00
	Common Player:	.10
1	Luke Prokopec	.15
2	Tim Drew	.10
3	Joe Crede	.50
4	Dan Wheeler	.10
5	Horacio Estrada	.10
6	Andy Beal	.10
7	Ted Rose	.10
8	Bert Snow	.10
9	Kevin Burford	.10
10	Brett Weber	.10

2001 SP Top Prospects

Only the top talent is included in Upper Deck's annual minor league issue. A wood-look design theme is carried throughout the base set and inserts. Fronts have a metallized photo background with the player name in silver foil. Backs have logos of the parent team's minor league clubs, a few words about the player, 2000 season stats and career stats. The set was released in December 2000.

		MT
	Complete Set (90):	10.00
	Common Player:	.05
	Wax Pack (5):	1.00
	Wax Box (24):	15.00
1	Nathan Haynes	.05
2	Francisco Rodriguez	.15
3	Joe Torres	.05
4	Mario Encarnacion	.05
5	Justin Miller	.05
6	Jason Hart	.05
7	Miguel Olivo	.05
8	Felipe Lopez	.05
9	Vernon Wells	.50
10	Cesar Izturis	.25
11	Kenny Kelly	.25
12	Josh Hamilton	.50
13	Jesus Colome	.05
14	Aubrey Huff	.25
15	Toby Hall	.05
16	Danys Baez	.05
17	C.C. Sabathia	.50
18	Ryan Anderson	.25
19	Ryan Christianson	.25
20	Richard Stahl	.05
21	Matt Riley	.05
22	Jayson Werth	.05
23	Tripper Johnson	.05
24	Jason Grabowski	.05
25	Jason Romano	.05
26	Carlos Pena	.25
27	Rick Asadoorian	.05
28	Steve Lomasney	.10
29	Sun-Woo Kim	.15
30	Phillip Dumatrait	.05
31	Chris George	.05
32	Dee Brown	.05
33	Jeff Austin	.05
34	Ramon Santiago	.05
35	Chris Wakeland	.05
36	Brandon Inge	.05
37	Michael Cuddyer	.15
38	Michael Restovich	.10
39	Ruben Salazar	.05
40	Joe Crede	.75
41	Aaron Rowand	.15
42	Wily Mo Pena	.25
43	Nick Johnson	1.00
44	Aaron McNeal	.05
45	Wilfredo Rodriguez	.05
46	Keith Ginter	.05
47	Pat Manning	.05
48	George Lombard	.05
49	Marcus Giles	.25
50	Nick Neugebauer	.10
51	Ben Sheets	.50
52	Ben Johnson	.05
53	Chad Hutchinson	.05
54	Luis Saturria	.05
55	Corey Patterson	.75
56	Hee Seop Choi	.50
57	Ben Christiansen	.25
58	John Patterson	.05
59	Jack Cust	.15
60	Hong-Chih Kuo	.05
61	Chin-Feng Chen	.50
62	Justin Wayne	.05
63	Brad Wilkerson	.10
64	Kurt Ainsworth	.05
65	Tony Torcato	.05
66	Michael Byas	.05
67	Julio Ramirez	.05
68	Josh Beckett	2.00
69	Abraham Nunez	.25
70	Adrian Gonzalez	.50
71	Alex Escobar	.05
72	Pat Strange	.05
73	Brian Cole	.05
74	Sean Burroughs	.60
75	Wascar Serrano	.05
76	Vince Faison	.05
77	Dennis Tankersley	.25
78	Brad Baisley	.05
79	Jimmy Rollins	.75
80	Eric Valent	.10
81	J.J. Davis	.05
82	Bobby Bradley	.20
83	Adam Dunn	.75
84	Drew Henson	1.00
85	Jackson Melian	.05
86	Choo Freeman	.05
87	Jason Jennings	.05
88	Corey Patterson (Checklist)	.25
89	Josh Hamilton (Checklist)	.50
90	Sean Burroughs (Checklist)	.25

2001 SP Top Prospects Big Town Dreams

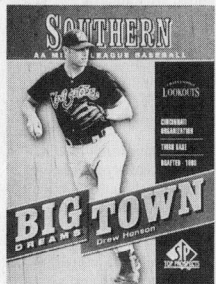

The bright lights of big-league baseball cities are in the sights of this group of hot prospects. On front, action photos are set against a textured woodgrain panel; graphic highlights are silver foil. Backs have basic player information. Advertised insertion rate for this chase series is one per 12 packs.

		MT
	Complete Set (15):	9.00
	Common Player:	.50
BD1	Vernon Wells	1.00
BD2	Corey Patterson	1.00
BD3	Michael Cuddyer	.50
BD4	Aaron McNeal	.50
BD5	Josh Beckett	2.00
BD6	Drew Henson	2.00
BD7	Sean Burroughs	.50
BD8	Alex Escobar	.50
BD9	C.C. Sabathia	.75
BD10	Josh Hamilton	1.00
BD11	John Patterson	.50
BD12	Aaron Rowand	.50
BD13	Dee Brown	.50
BD14	Choo Freeman	.50
BD15	Nick Johnson	1.50

2001 SP Top Prospects Chirography

Inserted at an average rate of 1:11 packs (about two per box), these inserts offer authentic autographs of future stars. Fronts have silver-foil highlights. Backs repeat the front photo and have a statement authenticating the autograph.

		MT
	Complete Set (29):	60.00
	Common Player:	2.00
AG	Adrian Gonzalez	15.00
AH	Aubrey Huff	3.00
AM	Aaron McNeal	2.00
BC	Ben Christensen	3.00
BC	Brian Cole	2.00
BI	Brandon Inge	2.00
CC	Chin-Feng Chen	10.00
CP	Corey Patterson	6.00
CS	C.C. Sabathia	20.00
CW	Chris Wakeland	2.00
DH	Drew Henson	15.00
GR	Keith Ginter	2.00
JB	Josh Beckett	30.00
JCo	Jesus Colome	2.00
JCu	Jack Cust	8.00
JH	Josh Hamilton	25.00
JM	Justin Miller	2.00
JT	Joe Torres	3.00
JWa	Justin Wayne	2.00
KA	Kurt Ainsworth	2.00
MC	Michael Cuddyer	3.00
MR	Matt Riley	2.00
PS	Pat Strange	2.00
RA	Ryan Anderson	4.00
RS	Ramon Santiago	2.00
SB	Sean Burroughs	4.00
TH	Toby Hall	2.00
TJ	Tripper Johnson	2.00
VW	Vernon Wells	5.00

2001 SP Top Prospects Chirography Gold

Each of the players whose cards appear in the Chirography autographed inserts also signed an edition of 25 serially numbered gold version autograph cards.

	MT
Common Player:	6.00
Stars:	4X

(See 2001 SP Top Prospects Chirography for checklist and base card values.)

2001 SP Top Prospects Destination the Show

All the same prospects seen in the other inserts in 2001 SP are found in this 1:18 insert set. These players were deemed the closest to major league stardom prior to the 2001 season. Fronts have a textured wood-look background. Backs repeat the front background design and have a few words about the player.

		MT
	Complete Set (12):	15.00
	Common Player:	1.00
S1	Corey Patterson	2.00
S2	Drew Henson	2.50
S3	Chin-Feng Chen	1.50
S4	Josh Hamilton	2.00
S5	Nick Johnson	2.00
S6	Ben Sheets	1.00
S7	Sean Burroughs	1.00
S8	C.C. Sabathia	1.00
S9	Ryan Anderson	1.00
S10	Michael Cuddyer	1.00
S11	Vernon Wells	1.00
S12	Josh Beckett	2.00

2001 SP Top Prospects Game-Used Bat Cards

Inserted at a rate of about one per box (every 23 packs), these memorabilia cards feature game-used bat pieces from 35 players including Ken Griffey Jr. and Michael Jordan. The dime-sized bat piece has been embossed with baseball-style stitching. The back has a certification of authenticity from Upper Deck's CEO.

		MT
	Complete Set (30):	50.00
	Common Player:	2.00
B-AD	Adam Dunn	4.00
B-AEs	Alex Escobar	2.00
B-AH	Aubrey Huff	2.00
B-AM	Aaron McNeal	2.00
B-AR	Aaron Rowand	3.00
B-BC	Brian Cole	2.00
B-BI	Brandon Inge	2.00
B-CC	Chin-Feng Chen	4.00
B-CP	Corey Patterson	6.00
B-DH	Drew Henson	7.50
B-FL	Felipe Lopez	2.00
B-HC	Hee Seop Choi	6.00
B-JCr	Joe Crede	4.00
B-JCu	Jack Cust	2.00
B-JH	Josh Hamilton	8.00
B-JJ	J.J. Davis	2.00
B-JM	Jackson Melian	2.00
B-JR	Jason Romano	2.00
B-JW	Jayson Werth	2.00
B-KG	Ken Griffey Jr.	7.50
B-KK	Kenny Kelly	3.00
B-MC	Michael Cuddyer	3.00
B-MG	Marcus Giles	3.00
B-MJ	Michael Jordan	7.50
B-MRe	Michael Restovich	2.00
B-MRi	Matt Riley	2.00
B-PM	Pat Manning	2.00
B-RS	Ramon Santiago	2.00
B-SB	Sean Burroughs	3.00
B-VW	Vernon Wells	3.00

2001 SP Top Prospects Game-Used Bat Cards - Autographed

Each of the game-used bat cards in Top Prospects was also found in an autographed edition serially numbered to just 25 pieces each.

		MT
	Common Player:	7.50
B-AD	Adam Dunn	15.00
B-AEs	Alex Escobar	7.50
B-AH	Aubrey Huff	7.50
B-AM	Aaron McNeal	7.50
B-AR	Aaron Rowand	7.50
B-BC	Brian Cole	7.50
B-BI	Brandon Inge	7.50
B-CC	Chin-Feng Chen	15.00
B-CP	Corey Patterson	25.00

B-DH	Drew Henson	25.00
B-FL	Felipe Lopez	7.50
B-HC	Hee Seop Choi	25.00
B-JCr	Joe Crede	15.00
B-JCu	Jack Cust	7.50
B-JH	Josh Hamilton	20.00
B-JJ	J.J. Davis	7.50
B-JM	Jackson Melian	7.50
B-JR	Jason Romano	7.50
B-JW	Jayson Werth	7.50
B-KG	Ken Griffey Jr.	300.00
B-KK	Kenny Kelly	10.00
B-MC	Michael Cuddyer	10.00
B-MG	Marcus Giles	10.00
B-MJ	Michael Jordan	600.00
B-MRe	Michael Restovich	7.50
B-MRi	Matt Riley	7.50
B-PM	Pat Manning	7.50
B-RS	Ramon Santiago	7.50
B-SB	Sean Burroughs	10.00
B-VW	Vernon Wells	10.00

2001 SP Top Prospects Great Futures

Arguably the top players from the SP line-up are featured in this insert set, found about one per 12 packs. The horizontal format has an action photo at left, morphing into a sky-with-clouds at right. A panel at right has player name and team logo. Backs repeat the front design and photo and have a few words about the player.

		MT
Complete Set (15):		10.00
Common Player:		.50
GF1	Josh Beckett	3.00
GF2	Josh Hamilton	1.00
GF3	Bobby Bradley	.50
GF4	Ben Sheets	.75
GF5	Nick Johnson	1.50
GF6	Corey Patterson	1.00
GF7	Sean Burroughs	.75
GF8	Alex Escobar	.75
GF9	Chin-Feng Chen	.75
GF10	Ryan Anderson	.50
GF11	Drew Henson	2.00
GF12	Rick Asadoorian	.50
GF13	Aaron Rowand	.50
GF14	C.C. Sabathia	.50
GF15	John Patterson	.50

2001 Team Best Set Collector Edition

The inclusion of a pair of mail-order-only cards among the 102 cards in the base set is a feature of Team Best's minor league issue. Fronts have game-action or posed photos framed in blue-and-white and bordered in gray. Backs have a close-up of the front photo in an oval at top. Printed below are personal data and career highlights. Vertically at left are the player's 2000 stats. Basic packaging was five player cards per foil pack and 24 packs per box. The two cards of Joe Borchard could only be obtained by sending in 12 foil wrappers and $5.

		MT
Complete Set (102):		15.00
Common Player:		.05
Foil Box (24):		17.50
1	Brent Abernathy	.05
2	Kurt Ainsworth	.05
3	Israel Alcantara	.05
4	Marlon Anderson	.05
5	Ryan Anderson	.10
6	Robert Averette	.05

7	Brad Baisley	.05
8	Lorenzo Barcelo	.05
9	Josh Beckett	2.00
10	Rob Bell	.05
11	Todd Betts	.05
12	Willie Bloomquist	.10
13	Joe Borchard (Winston-Salem)	4.00
14	Joe Borchard (Birmingham)	4.00
15	Bobby Bradley	.10
16	Milton Bradley	.25
17	Ben Broussard	.15
18	Mark Buehrle	.15
19	Pat Burrell	.50
20	Sean Burroughs	.35
21	Mike Bynum	.05
22	Ramon Castro	.05
23	Chin-Feng Chen	.35
24	Hee Seop Choi	1.00
25	Ryan Christenson	.10
26	Brian Cole	.05
27	Jesus Colome	.05
28	Paxton Crawford	.05
29	Joe Crede	.25
30	Brad Cresse	.05
31	Michael Cuddyer	.10
32	Jack Cust	.10
33	Travis Dawkins	.10
34	Zach Day	.05
35	Tim Drew	.05
36	Adam Dunn	.50
37	Alex Escobar	.05
38	Casey Fossum	.05
39	Mike Frank	.05
40	Choo Freeman	.05
41	B.J. Garbe	.05
42	Jon Garland	.10
43	Marcus Giles	.15
44	Keith Ginter	.05
45	Elpidio Guzman	.05
46	Josh Hamilton	.10
47	Jason Hart	.05
48	Jeff Heaverlo	.05
49	Drew Henson	1.00
50	J.R. House	.05
51	Aubrey Huff	.05
52	Brandon Inge	.05
53	Cesar Izturis	.05
54	Jason Jennings	.05
55	Kenny Kelly	.25
56	Sun Woo Kim	.10
57	Mike Kinkade	.05
58	Matt Kinney	.05
59	Jason LaRue	.05
60	Allen Levrault	.05
61	George Lombard	.05
62	Willie Martinez	.05
63	Sam McConnell	.05
64	Eric Munson	.10
65	Kevin Nicholson	.05
66	Tomokazu Ohka	.10
67	Pablo Ozuna	.05
68	Corey Patterson	.50
69	Carlos Pena	.15
70	Adam Piatt	.05
71	Juan Pierre	.45
72	Tim Raines Jr.	.05
73	Aramis Ramirez	.15
74	Julio Ramirez	.05
75	Jon Rauch	.05
76	Michael Restovich	.10
77	Justo Rivas	.05
78	Luis Rivas	.05
79	Luis Rivera	.05
80	Grant Roberts	.05
81	Cesar Saba	.05
82	C.C. Sabathia	.25
83	Bobby Seay	.05
84	Wascar Serrano	.05
85	Ben Sheets	.10
86	Carlos Silva	.05
87	Bud Smith	.15
88	Alfonso Soriano	1.50
89	Richard Stahl	.05
90	Dernell Stenson	.05
91	John Stephens	.05
92	Jay Tessmer	.05
93	Brad Thomas	.05
94	Tony Torcato	.05
95	Chin-Hui Tsao	.15
96	Jason Tyner	.05
97	Vernon Wells	.05
98	Jake Westbrook	.05
99	Brad Wilkerson	.05
100	Jason Williams	.05
101	Ed Yarnall	.05
102	Barry Zito	.45
		.00
---	"Autograph Conest!" Offer	.05
---	"Joe Borchard Cards!" Offer	.05
---	"Rookies 2000 Extended" Offer	.05

2001 Team Best Authentic Autograph Cards

Top names from the checklist of Team Best 2001 are found in the autographed insert cards, along with several players who do not appear in the base set. Inserted at an average rate of one per eight packs, fronts of the autographed cards are similar in format to the base cards,

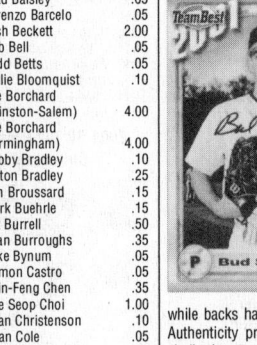

while backs have a Declaration of Authenticity printed over the facsimile signature of the card company's CEO.

		MT
Complete Set (20):		75.00
Common Player:		2.00
1	Andrew Beinbrink	2.00
2	Joe Borchard (Winston-Salem)	6.00
3	Joe Borchard (Birmingham)	6.00
4	Mike Bynum	2.00
5	Ryan Christianson	2.00
6	Adam Dunn	15.00
7	Casey Fossum	3.00
8	Josh Hamilton	3.00
9	J.R. House	3.00
10	Kenny Kelly	6.00
11	Matt Kinney	2.00
12	John Lackey	3.00
13	Kevin Nicholson	2.00
14	Tomokazu Ohka	2.00
15	Juan Pierre	5.00
16	Jon Rauch	3.00
17	Ben Sheets	4.00
18	Bud Smith	4.00
19	Richard Stahl	2.00
20	Barry Zito	8.00
20a	Barry Zito (Edition of 250.)	40.00

2001 Team Best Babbitt's Bombers

Big hitters are posed with an oversized novelty baseball bat in this insert set. Found on average of one per 48 packs, the cards have a monument style frame on front. Backs have an oval close-up from the front photo along with some player data and highlights.

		MT
Complete Set (11):		15.00
Common Player:		2.00
1	Sean Burroughs	3.00
2	Michael Cuddyer	3.00
3	Jack Cust	2.00
4	Choo Freeman	2.00
5	Marcus Giles	2.50
6	Keith Ginter	2.00
7	Jason Hart	2.00
8	Danny Peoples	2.00
9	Keith Reed	2.00
10	Vernon Wells	4.00
11	Brad Wilkerson	2.00

2001 Team Best Best Lumber

Top hitters are featured in this 1:96 pack insert. Fronts have a woodgrain background, backs have a close-up repeat of the front photo and a bit of player information.

		MT
Complete Set (10):		24.00
Common Player:		2.00
1	Russell Branyan	2.00
2	Morgan Burkhart	2.00
3	Pat Burrell	5.00
4	Sean Burroughs	3.00
5	Drew Henson, Sean Burroughs	5.00
6	Josh Hamilton	2.50
7	Nick Johnson	5.00
8	George Lombard	2.00
9	Carlos Pena	3.00
10	Dernell Stenson	2.00

2001 Upper Deck Minor League Baseball Centennial

On the centennial anniversary of the founding of true minor leagues in professional baseball, Upper Deck issued this set which combines cards of contemporary minor leaguers with former stars of the game, most of whom never appeared on a minor league card during their career. The 100-card base set is dominated by current prospects. A 10-card UD Draft Picks subset comprises the first 10 cards, while five dual-player past/present stars checklist cards conclude the base set. Throughout the checklist are cards of former stars depicted in sepia photos on which major league team logos have been removed. A strong line-up of autographed and game-used bat and/or jersey cards was included as inserts.

		MT
Complete Set (100):		10.00
Common Player:		.05
Foil Pack (5):		1.50
Foil Box (24):		25.00
1	Joe Mauer (Draft Picks)	1.50
2	Jake Gautreau (Draft Picks)	.10
3	Mike Jones (Draft Picks)	.10
4	Bobby Crosby (Draft Picks)	.40
5	Chris Smith (Draft Picks)	.10
6	John VanBenschoten (Draft Picks)	.10
7	Colt Griffin (Draft Picks)	.10
8	Chris Burke (Draft Picks)	.25
9	Kenny Baugh (Draft Picks)	.10
10	Casey Kotchman (Draft Picks)	.50
11	Joe Torres	.05
12	Alfredo Amezaga	.05
13	Chris Bootcheck	.05
14	Jason Hart	.05
15	Ryan Ludwick	1.50
16	Mario Ramos	.05
17	Tyrell Godwin	.05
18	Orlando Hudson	.25
19	Josh Hamilton	.50

20	Toe Nash	.05
21	Carl Crawford	.25
22	Roger Maris	.25
23	J.D. Martin	.05
24	Alex Herrera	.05
25	Rafael Soriano	.05
26	Antonio Perez	.05
27	Jamal Strong	.05
28	Eddie Murray	.10
29	Keith Reed	.05
30	John Stephens	.05
31	Hank Blalock	1.50
32	Wade Boggs	.25
33	Freddy Sanchez	.05
34	Seung Song	.05
35	George Brett	.25
36	Corey Thurman	.05
37	Omar Infante	.05
38	Matt Wheatland	.05
39	Justin Morneau	1.50
40	Michael Restovich	.15
41	Joe Borchard	1.00
42	Corwin Malone	.05
43	Jon Rauch	.05
44	Joe DiMaggio	.50
45	Deivi Mendez	.05
46	Drew Henson	1.00
47	Jason Lane	.15
48	Mike Nannini	.05
49	Garett Gentry	.05
50	Trey Hodges	.05
51	Kelly Johnson	.05
52	Dave Krynzel	.10
53	Will Hall	.05
54	Blake Williams	.05
55	John Gall	.05
56	Joe Carter	.05
57	Ryne Sandberg	.25
58	Hee Seop Choi	.50
59	Nick Jackson (Nic)	.10
60	Bobby Hill	.50
61	Brad Cresse	.15
62	Corey Myers	.05
63	Steve Garvey	.05
64	Chin-Feng Chen	.05
65	Ben Diggins	.10
66	Willy Aybar	.10
67	Andre Dawson	.05
68	Brandon Phillips	.15
69	Justin Wayne	.10
70	Brandon Watson	.05
71	Willie McCovey	.05
72	Jerome Williams	.10
73	Boof Bonser	.05
74	Lance Niekro	.05
75	Adrian Gonzalez	.15
76	Will Smith	.05
77	Miguel Cabrera	1.50
78	Nolan Ryan	.25
79	Pat Strange	.05
80	Jae Seo	.05
81	Ozzie Smith	.15
82	Sean Burroughs	.35
83	Dennis Tankersley	.15
84	Jake Peavy	.25
85	Gary Burnham	.05
86	Marlon Byrd	.15
87	Brett Myers	.25
88	Adam Walker	.05
89	Dave Parker	.05
90	J.R. House	.05
91	Bobby Bradley	.05
92	Sean Burnett	.15
93	Austin Kearns	.65
94	Ty Howington	.05
95	Chin-Hui Tsao	.25
96	Joe DiMaggio, Josh Hamilton (Checklist 1-20)	.50
97	Ozzie Smith, Bobby Hill (Checklist 21-40)	.05
98	George Brett, Sean Burroughs (Checklist 41-60)	.15
99	Willie McCovey, Adrian Gonzalez (Checklist 61-80)	.05
100	Nolan Ryan, Dennis Tankersley (Photo Josh Beckett.) (Checklist 81-100)	.25

2001 UD Minor League Centennial Authentic Signatures

Top prospects' autographs are featured in this insert set. Regular versions are serially numbered to 100 each, while Gold cards were issued in an edition of 25 each.

		MT
Common Player:		5.00
Gold Editions:		2.5X
S-AG	Adrian Gonzalez	7.50
S-BBo	Boof Bonser	5.00
S-BBr	Bobby Bradley	7.50
S-BC	Brad Cresse	7.50
S-BH	Bobby Hill	10.00
S-BP	Brandon Phillips	7.50
S-DT	Dennis Tankersley	7.50
S-HB	Hank Blalock	15.00
S-JBo	Joe Borchard	12.50
S-JHa	Josh Hamilton	20.00
S-JHo	J.R. House	5.00
S-JL	Jason Lane	5.00
S-JM	J.D. Martin	5.00
S-JR	Jon Rauch	5.00
S-JT	Joe Torres	5.00
S-JWa	Justin Wayne	5.00
S-JWi	Jerome Williams	7.50
S-KJ	Kelly Johnson	5.00
S-RS	Rafael Soriano	5.00
S-SB	Sean Burroughs	7.50
S-TN	Toe Nash	12.50
S-WA	Willy Aybar	5.00

2001 UD Minor League Centennial Legendary Signatures

Autographs of nine former major league stars whose cards and game-used memorabilia are also found in this set were featured in these inserts. Regular cards are numbered to 50, Gold Edition cards are in an edition of 25 each. Redemption cards were originally issued for Tommy Lasorda autographs.

		MT
Complete Set (9):		250.00
Common Player:		15.00
Gold Editions:		1.5X
L-DP	Dave Parker	10.00
L-JC	Joe Carter	10.00
L-NR	Nolan Ryan	100.00
L-OS	Ozzie Smith	65.00
L-RS	Ryne Sandberg	65.00
L-SG	Steve Garvey	15.00
L-TL	Tommy Lasorda	45.00
L-WB	Wade Boggs	45.00
L-WM	Willie McCovey	15.00

2001 UD Minor League Centennial Combination Signatures

The autographs of one former star major leaguer and one minor league prospect are found in tandem on this insert series. Fifty of each were produced in a standard version, and 25 each in a Gold Edition.

		MT
Common Card:		15.00
Gold Editions:		1.5X
CS-BBl	Wade Boggs, Hank Blalock	100.00
CS-CL	Joe Carter, Jason Lane	15.00
CS-MG	Willie McCovey, Adrian Gonzalez	25.00
CS-PN	Dave Parker, Toe Nash	15.00
CS-SH	Ryne Sandberg, Bobby Hill	100.00

2001 UD Minor League Centennial Game-Used Bat

Game-used bat pieces from nine of the minor leagues' brightest stars are featured in this insert series. Combined with the game-used jersey cards of former major leaguers and combo cards, these are a one per 23 packs insert. A gold parallel of each card, numbered within an edition of 25, was also produced.

	MT
Complete Set (9):	10.00
Common Player:	1.00
Gold Editions:	4X
B-AG Adrian Gonzalez	1.00
B-BC Brad Cresse	1.00
B-BP Brandon Phillips	1.00
B-HB Hank Blalock	2.00
B-JB Joe Borchard	3.00
B-JL Jason Lane	1.00
B-JH Josh Hamilton	15.00
B-JR J.R. House	1.00
B-SB Sean Burroughs	2.00

2001 UD Minor League Centennial Game-Used Jersey

Major league jersey swatches and sepia photos (not necessarily from the players' minor league days) of 14 former stars are featured in this insert series. Combined with the game-used bat cards of current minor leaguers and combo cards, these are a one per 23 packs insert. A gold parallel of each card, numbered within an edition of 25, was also produced.

	MT
Complete Set (14):	175.00
Common Player:	4.00
Gold Editions:	1.5X
J-AD Andre Dawson	4.00
J-DP Dave Parker	4.00
J-EM Eddie Murray	5.00
J-GB George Brett	10.00
J-JD Joe DiMaggio	100.00
J-JC Joe Carter	4.00
J-NR Nolan Ryan	15.00
J-OS Ozzie Smith	6.00
J-RM Roger Maris	45.00
J-RS Ryne Sandberg	10.00
J-SG Steve Garvey	4.00
J-TL Tommy Lasorda	4.00
J-WB Wade Boggs	6.00
J-WM Willie McCovey	4.00

2001 UD Minor League Centennial Jersey & Bat

Major league jersey swatches of former stars and bat pieces from 2001 minor league prospects are combined on these insert cards. With the individual game-used bat and jersey cards, these are a one per 23 packs insert. A gold parallel of each card, numbered within an edition of 25, was also produced.

	MT
Complete Set (4):	75.00
Common Card:	10.00
Gold Editions:	2X
C-BB George Brett, Sean Burroughs	30.00
C-BBl Wade Boggs, Hank Blalock	20.00
C-DH Joe DiMaggio, Josh Hamilton	50.00
C-MG Willie McCovey, Adrian Gonzalez	10.00

2001 UD Minor League Centennial Michael Jordan Salute

Game-used jerseys, bats, pants, batting gloves and cleats from his 1994 minor league season were sliced and diced to provide pieces for inclusion in these Salute inserts. Bat cards are found about one per box (every 24 packs). Jersey inserts are a 1:136 pick. Both the bat and jersey cards were also issued in a Gold Edition numbered to 25 apiece. A bat and jersey combo card (1:336) was also made, as were batting glove and cleat cards (100 of each) and a batting glove/jersey combo (25). All cards are numbered with an "MJ-" prefix.

		MT
Gold Editions:		10X
B1	Michael Jordan/Bat (Birmingham)	10.00
B2	Michael Jordan/Bat (Birmingham)	10.00
B3	Michael Jordan/Bat (Birmingham)	10.00
B4	Michael Jordan/Bat (Birmingham)	10.00
B5	Michael Jordan/Bat (Birmingham)	10.00
B6	Michael Jordan/Bat (Birmingham)	10.00
B7	Michael Jordan/Bat (Birmingham)	10.00
B8	Michael Jordan/Bat (Birmingham)	10.00
B9	Michael Jordan/Bat (Birmingham)	10.00
B10	Michael Jordan/Bat (Birmingham)	10.00
B11	Michael Jordan/Bat (Scottsdale, AFL)	10.00
B12	Michael Jordan/Bat (White Sox, spring.)	12.00
J1	Michael Jordan/Jsy (Birmingham)	20.00
J2	Michael Jordan/Jsy (Birmingham)	20.00
J3	Michael Jordan/Jsy (Scottsdale, AFL)	20.00
P1	Michael Jordan/Pants (White Sox, spring.)	25.00
P2	Michael Jordan/Pants (Arizona League)	25.00
BJ	Michael Jordan/Bat/Jersey (Birmingham)	45.00
BG	Michael Jordan/Btg Glv (Birmingham)	120.00
C	Michael Jordan/Cleats (Birmingham)	125.00
JBG	Michael Jordan/Jsy/Btg Glv (Birmingham)	175.00

2001 Minor League Team Sets

JOHN GRABOW
Altoona Curve
2001

Manufacturer abbreviations used are: CH - Choice, GS - Grandstand, MA - Multi-Ad, WT - Warning Track.

207 Sets and Variations

		MT
2001	MA Akron Aeros (30)	10.00
2001	MA Akron Aeros 5th Anniversary (21)	8.50
2001	Team Alaska Gold Panners (21)	
2001	Team Alaska Goldpanners Bonus Cards (3)	9.00
2001	WT Albany-Colonie Diamond Dogs (26)	7.00
2001	TM Alexandria Aces (25)	9.00
2001	GS Altoona Curve (29)	10.00
2001	GS Appalachian League Top Prospects (30)	12.50
2001	GS Appy League Top Prospects Update (10)	15.00
2001	Team Arizona Fall League (32)	20.00
2001	MA Arkansas Travelers	11.00
2001	GS Asheville Bears (30)	14.50
2001	MA Auburn Doubledays (30)	9.00
2001	MA Augusta Greenjackets (30)	10.00
2001	Team Bakersfield Blaze (33)	10.00
2001	Team Batavia Muckdogs (30)	20.00
2001	Team Batavia 1990s stars (15)	20.00
2001	Team Batavia Muckdogs Magnets (3)	5.00
2001	MA Beloit Snappers (30)	12.50
2001	GS Billings Mustangs (30)	11.50
2001	Choice Binghamton Mets (30)	9.50
2001	GS Birmingham Barons (31)	8.00
2001	GS Bluefield Orioles (30)	11.00
2001	GS Boise Hawks (32)	15.00
2001	GS Bowie Baysox (30)	12.00
2001	MA Brevard County Manatees (30)	8.00
2001	GS Bristol Sox (30)	9.00
2001	MA Brooklyn Cyclones (36)	11.00
2001	Choice Buffalo Bisons (30)	9.50
2001	MA Burlington Bees (31)	10.00
2001	GS Burlington Indians (37)	7.50
2001	Team Calgary Cannons (31)	12.00
2001	GS California League Prospects (30)	14.00
2001	CSC Canadian Junior National Team (10)	15.00
2001	GS Canton Crocodiles (30)	9.00
2001	MA Capital City Bombers (30)	12.00
2001	GS Capital City Bombers Update (1)	10.00
2001	GS Capital City Bombers Update Auto. (1)	45.00
2001	CH Carolina-California League A-S (50)	11.00
2001	Choice Carolina League Prospects (30)	14.00
2001	GS Casper Rockies (31)	10.00
2001	MA Cedar Rapids Kernels (30)	9.00
2001	MA Charleston Aleey Cats (30)	10.00
2001	MA Charleston River Dogs (31)	9.00
2001	CH Charlotte Knights (30)	10.00
2001	MA Charlotte Rangers (31)	20.00
2001	GS Chattanooga Lookouts (30)	12.50
2001	MA Clearwater Phillies (30)	15.00
2001	GS Clinton Lumber Kings (31)	15.00
2001	Team Colorado Springs Sky Sox (31)	8.00
2001	Choice Columbus Clippers (31)	10.00
2001	Team Columbus Mudcats (30)	9.50
2001	MA Columbus RedStixx (30)	12.00
2001	GS Danville Braves (35)	12.00
2001	GS Dayton Dragons (30)	27.50
2001	MA Daytona Cubs (30)	13.00
2001	MA Delmarva Shorebirds (30)	10.00
2001	WT Duluth-Superior Dukes (25)	7.00
2001	GS Dunedin Blue Jays (30)	15.00
2001	Choice Durham Bulls (30)	12.50
2001	GS Edinburg Roadrunners (30)	9.50
2001	Team Edmonton Trappers (30)	11.00
2001	GS Elizabethton Twins (30)	11.00
2001	GS Elizabethton Twins Update (10)	11.00
2001	GS El Paso Diablos (30)	13.50
2001	MA Erie Sea Wolves (30)	10.00
2001	GS Eugene Emeralds (35)	10.00
2001	Team Eugene Emeralds Ems Greats (10)	7.50
2001	GS Everett Aquasox (32)	12.50

		MT
2001	Team Fargo-Moorhead RedHawks (30)	8.00
2001	GS Florida State League Prospects (30)	12.00
2001	GS Florida State Lea. Gold Prospects (9)	20.00
2001	GS Frederick Keys (30)	10.00
2001	GS Frederick Keys W/Pepsi Logo (30)	16.00
2001	GS Fresno Grizzlies (30)	10.00
2001	MA Ft. Myers Miracle (30)	10.00
2001	Team Ft. Wayne Wizards (29)	8.00
2001	GS Future Angels (30)	10.00
2001	MA Great Falls Dodgers (30)	9.00
2001	MA Greensboro Bats (30)	10.00
2001	GS Greenville Braves (39)	9.00
2001	MA Hagerstown Suns (30)	10.00
2001	MA Harrisburg Senators (30)	10.00
2001	MA Hickory Crawdads (30)	7.50
2001	MA Hickory Crawdads Update (30)	9.50
2001	GS High Desert Mavericks (31)	10.00
2001	GS High Desert Mavericks W/Pepsi Ad (31)	20.00
2001	MA Hudson Valley Renegades (33)	12.00
2001	Team Huntsville Stars (29)	10.00
2001	Choice Indianapolis Indians (30)	9.00
2001	CH International League Prospects (30)	10.00
2001	MA Iowa Cubs (30)	12.00
2001	GS Jacksonville Suns (31)	8.50
2001	GS Jacksonville Suns Sponsor's Set (32)	10.00
2001	GS 2000 Jamestown Jammers (28)	20.00
2001	GS Jamestown Jammers (28)	17.50
2001	GS Johnson City Cardinals (31)	7.00
2001	Team Jupiter Hammerheads (36)	9.00
2001	GS Kane County Cougars (31)	15.00
2001	Connie's Kane County Cougars (31)	15.00
2001	MA Kannapolis Intimadators (31)	9.00
2001	CH Kinston Indians (33)	14.00
2001	GS Lake Elsinore Storm (31)	10.00
2001	MA Lakeland Tigers (30)	9.50
2001	MA Lakewood BlueClaws (32)	9.00
2001	GS Lancaster JetHawks (30)	9.00
2001	GS Lansing Lugnuts (30)	7.00
2001	MA Las Vegas 51s (30)	12.00
2001	MA Lexington Legends (30)	9.00
2001	GS Lincoln Saltdogs (26)	10.00
2001	CH Louisville RiverBats (33)	16.50
2001	GS Lowell Spinners 2000 Update (11)	22.00
2001	MA Lowell Spinners (30)	11.00
2001	Choice Lynchburg Hillcats (30)	12.00
2001	MA Macon Braves (30)	12.00
2001	MA Mahoning Valley Scrappers (30)	6.00
2001	GS Martinsville Astros (30)	10.00
2001	Team Memphis Redbirds (30)	32.50
2001	Team Michigan Battle Cats (30)	10.00
2001	GS Midland RockHounds (27)	10.00
2001	Team Midland RockHounds (31)	60.00
2001	GS Midland RockHounds Sponsor's Set (28)	12.50
2001	MA Midwest League Top Prospects (29)	7.00
2001	GS Missoula Osprey (35)	10.00
2001	GS Modesto A's (30)	9.00
2001	GS Mudville Nine (30)	12.00
2001	MA Myrtle Beach Pelicans (30)	12.00
2001	Team Nashua Pride (29)	8.50
2001	GS Nashville Sounds (30)	11.00
2001	MA New Britain Rock Cats (30)	10.00
2001	CH New Haven Ravens (30)	9.50
2001	GS New Jersey Cardinals (30)	9.50
2001	GS New Jersey Cardinals Update (1)	6.00
2001	WT New Jersey Jackals (26)	7.00

		MT
2001	MA New Orleans Zephyrs (30)	9.50
2001	Choice Norfolk Tides (30)	9.00
2001	Choice Norfolk Tides Sheriff's (10)	10.00
2001	GS Norwich Navigators (26)	9.50
2001	Team Ogden Raptors (42)	15.00
2001	MA Oklahoma RedHawks (29)	12.50
2001	GS 2000 Oneonta Tigers (29)	10.00
2001	GS Oneonta Tigers (31)	12.50
2001	Choice Ottawa Lynx (31)	12.00
2001	Choice Pawtucket Red Sox (30)	7.00
2001	DD Pawtucket Red Sox Foldout (30)	25.00
2001	MA Peoria Chiefs (30)	10.00
2001	MA Pittsfield Astros (31)	13.50
2001	GS Portland Sea Dogs (32)	9.00
2001	Choice Potomac Cannons (30)	8.00
2001	GS Princeton Devil Rays (30)	13.00
2001	GS Provo Angels (35)	16.00
2001	GS Pulaski Rangers (31)	10.00
2001	GS Quad City River Bandits (30)	8.00
2001	GS Rancho Cucamonga Quakes (30)	11.50
2001	GS Rancho Cucamonga Quakes Update (17)	14.00
2001	MA Reading Phillies (30)	7.50
2001	MA Reading Phils Alvernia College (30)	12.50
2001	Choice Richmond Braves (32)	15.00
2001	GS Rio Grande Valley White Wings (25)	9.00
2001	Choice Rochester Red Wings (30)	9.50
2001	MA Round Rock Express (30)	10.00
2001	GS Sacramento River Cats (30)	10.00
2001	GS Salem Avalanche (30)	9.00
2001	GS Salem-Keizer Volcanoes (36)	10.00
2001	GS San Antonio Missions (31)	11.00
2001	GS San Bernardino Stampede (29)	11.00
2001	GS San Jose Giants (30)	9.00
2001	MA Sarasota Red Sox (30)	7.50
2001	MA Savannah Sand Gnats (30)	11.00
2001	CH Scranton/Wilkes-Barre Red Barons (30)	9.00
2001	TM Shreveport Swamp Dragons (?)	15.00
2001	GS Sioux Falls Canaries (30)	9.00
2001	MA South Atlantic League Prospects (32)	9.00
2001	MA South Bend Silver Hawks (30)	10.00
2001	GS Southern League Prospects (31)	12.00
2001	GS Spokane Indians (35)	8.00
2001	GS Springfield Capitols (30)	9.00
2001	GS St. Lucie Mets (32)	10.00
2001	GS St. Lucie Mets Update (1)	4.00
2001	MA Staten Island Yankees (36)	10.00
2001	CH Syracuse SkyChiefs (30)	7.00
2001	GS Syracuse SkyChiefs Wall of Fame (28)	10.00
2001	GS Tacoma Rainiers (30)	9.50
2001	MA Tampa Yankees (30)	9.00
2001	GS Tennessee Smokies (28)	9.00
2001	GS Texas League Prospects (30)	8.00
2001	Choice Toledo Mud Hens (30)	9.00
2001	MA Trenton Thunder (30)	11.50
2001	MA Trenton Thunder Road/Majors 1 (25)	20.00
2001	GS Tucson Sidewinders (30)	10.00
2001	Team Tulsa Drillers (31)	10.00
2001	Team Tulsa Drillers Update (11)	12.00
2001	Team Vancouver Canadians (39)	12.00
2001	GS Vermont Expos (34)	10.00
2001	MA Vero Beach Dodgers (30)	12.50
2001	GS Visalia Oaks (30)	9.00
2001	MA West Michigan Whitecaps (30)	9.50
2001	GS West Tenn Diamond Jaxx (30)	11.00
2001	GS West Tenn Diamond Jaxx SL Champs (29)	11.00

		MT
2001	GS Wichita Wranglers (31)	8.50
2001	MA Williamsport Crosscutters (30)	15.00
2001	Choice Wilmington Blue Rocks (30)	9.00
2001	MA Wilmington Waves (30)	12.50
2001	Choice Winston-Salem Warthogs (30)	12.50
2001	MA Wisconsin Timber Rattlers (30)	9.00
2001	GS Yakima Bears (31)	9.00
2001	WT Yuma Bullfrogs (26)	7.00

2002 Just Justifiable Prototypes

White- and gold-bordered versions of the Justifiable promo cards were issued, with no value differential.

		MT
Complete Set (13):		5.00
Common Player:		.50
01	Jose Reyes	.40
02	Jason Stokes	.50
03	Casey Kotchman	.40
04	Jeff Francoeur	.40
05	B.J. Upton	.40
06	Mark Teixeira	.50
07	Andy Marte	.40
08	Felix Pie	.40
09	Gavin Floyd	.50
10	Shin Soo Choo	.50
11	Joel Guzman	.40
12	Khalil Greene	.50
---	Joe Mauer	.50

2002 Just Justifiable

Just Minors' foil-pack product for 2002 was a mid-December release, allowing the appearance of top players from the 2002 draft. Each base card was available in four versions differentiated by their border color, production quantity and manner of distribution. The white-bordered base set was issued in packs in an undisclosed quantity. Black-bordered versions, serially numbered to 50, were random pack inserts. Silver- and gold-bordered cards were sold only in complete set form in editions of 5,000 and 1,000, respectively. White-bordered cards #41-60 were short-printed and only issued in autographed form, serially numbered to either 500 or 1,000. Cards #41-50 were inserted at a rate of two per foil box. Cards #51-60, also numbered to either 500 or 1,000, were found at the same rate in boxes of the Memorabilia Edition only.

		MT
Complete Set, No SPs (39):		7.50
Complete Set, W/SPs (59):		125.00
Common Player, #2-40:		.25
Common Player, #41-60:		4.00
Hobby Box (18):		20.00
1	Russ Adams (Not officially issued.)	.00
2	Travis Blackley	.25
3	Matt Cain	.45
4	Travis Chapman	.35
5	Kyle Davies	.35
6	Carlos Duran	.35
7	Gavin Floyd	.50
8	Jesse Foppert	.45
9	Choo Freeman	.25
10	Jimmy Gobble	.35
11	Jonny Gomes	.45
12	Khalil Greene	.50
13	Joel Guzman	.50
14	Luke Hagerty	.25
15	Jack Hannahan	.25
16	Rich Harden	.65
17	J.J. Hardy	.35
18	Jeremy Hermida	.45
19	Kris Honel	.25
20	Casey Kotchman	.50
21	Cliff Lee	.25
22	Francisco Liriano	.50
23	Jose Lopez	.25
24	Andy Marte	.35
25	Victor Martinez	.25
26	Joe Mauer	.25
27	Drew Meyer	.25
28	Dustin Moseley	.25
29	Clint Nageotte	.35
30	Rhett Parrott	.25
31	Josh Phelps	.25
32	Brandon Phillips	.50
33	Jose Reyes	.50
34	Felix Sanchez	.25
35	Sergio Santos	.60
36	Mark Teixeira	.25
37	Andres Torres	.25
38	B.J. Upton	.50
39	Shane Victorino	.25
40	David Wright	1.00

41 Joseph Blanton
(1,000 Autographed) 4.00
42 Shin Soo Choo
(500 Autographed) 6.00
43 Jason Cooper
(1,000 Autographed) 4.00
44 Jeff Francis
(1,000 Autographed) 4.00
45 Jeff Francoeur
(500 Autographed) 30.00
46 Joey Gomes
(1,000 Autographed) 4.00
47 Corey Hart
(500 Autographed) 6.00
48 Justin Huber (500
Autographed) 6.00
49 Dan Meyer (500
Autographed) 6.00
50 Dontrelle Willis
(500 Autographed) 15.00
51 Scott Hairston
(1,000 Autographed) 5.00
52 Anthony Lerew
(1,000 Autographed) 4.00
53 Jeff Mathis
(1,000 Autographed) 4.00
54 Felix Pie
(500 Autographed) 15.00
55 Jason Pridie
(500 Autographed) 6.00
56 Hanley Ramirez
(500 Autographed) 20.00
57 Joe Saunders
(1,000 Autographed) 4.00
58 Jason Stokes
(500 Autographed) 20.00
59 Brian Tallet
(1,000 Autographed) 4.00
60 Chad Tracy
(1,000 Autographed) 5.00

2002 Just Justifiable Silver

Complete boxed sets of silver-bordered parallel Justifiable 2002 were sold at $9.95. The edition was limited to 5,000 sets. Some of the cards were also produced in an autographed edition of 375, randomly inserted.

	MT
Complete Set (59):	10.00
Common Player:	.25
1 Russ Adams	
(Not officially issued.)	.00
2 Travis Blackley	.25
3 Matt Cain	.45
4 Travis Chapman	.35
5 Kyle Davies	.35
6 Carlos Duran	.35
7 Gavin Floyd	.50
8 Jesse Foppert	.35
9 Choo Freeman	.35
10 Jimmy Gobble	.35
11 Jonny Gomes	.50
12 Khalil Greene	.45
13 Joel Guzman	.45
14 Luke Hagerty	.25
15 Jack Hannahan	.25
16 Rich Harden	.45
17 J.J. Hardy	.45
18 Jeremy Hermida	.45
19 Kris Honel	.25
20 Casey Kotchman	.50
21 Cliff Lee	.25
22 Francisco Liriano	.25
23 Jose Lopez	.25
24 Andy Marte	.35
25 Victor Martinez	.25
26 Joe Mauer	.50
27 Drew Meyer	.25
28 Dustin Moseley	.25
29 Clint Nageotte	.25
30 Rhett Parrott	.25
31 Josh Phelps	.45
32 Brandon Phillips	.45
33 Jose Reyes	.45
34 Felix Sanchez	.25
35 Sergio Santos	.60
36 Mark Teixeira	.50
37 Andres Torres	.25
38 B.J. Upton	.50
39 Shane Victorino	.25
40 David Wright	2.00
41 Joseph Blanton	.50
42 Shin Soo Choo	.35
43 Jason Cooper	.25
44 Jeff Francis	.30
45 Jeff Francoeur	.75
46 Joey Gomes	.25
47 Corey Hart	.25
48 Justin Huber	.25
49 Dan Meyer	.40
50 Dontrelle Willis	.30
51 Scott Hairston	.40
52 Anthony Lerew	.25
53 Jeff Mathis	.25
54 Felix Pie	.35
55 Jason Pridie	.25
56 Hanley Ramirez	.75
57 Joe Saunders	.25
58 Jason Stokes	.50
59 Brian Tallet	.25
60 Chad Tracy	.35

2002 Just Justifiable Gold

Complete boxed sets of gold-bordered parallel Justifiable 2002 were sold to Collector's Club members only at $12.95 per set. The edition was limited to 1,000 sets. Each card was also produced in an autographed edition of 100, randomly inserted.

	MT
Complete Set (59):	15.00
Common Player:	.50
1 Russ Adams	
(Not officially issued.)	.00
2 Travis Blackley	.50
3 Matt Cain	.65
4 Travis Chapman	1.00
5 Kyle Davies	.60
6 Carlos Duran	1.00
7 Gavin Floyd	1.00
8 Jesse Foppert	.75
9 Choo Freeman	1.00
10 Jimmy Gobble	.75
11 Jonny Gomes	1.00
12 Khalil Greene	.75
13 Joel Guzman	.75
14 Luke Hagerty	.50
15 Jack Hannahan	.50
16 Rich Harden	.65
17 J.J. Hardy	.75
18 Jeremy Hermida	.75
19 Kris Honel	.50
20 Casey Kotchman	1.00
21 Cliff Lee	.50
22 Francisco Liriano	.50
23 Jose Lopez	.50
24 Andy Marte	.75
25 Victor Martinez	.50
26 Joe Mauer	1.00
27 Drew Meyer	.50
28 Dustin Moseley	.50
29 Clint Nageotte	.50
30 Rhett Parrott	.50
31 Josh Phelps	1.00
32 Brandon Phillips	1.00
33 Jose Reyes	1.00
34 Felix Sanchez	.50
35 Sergio Santos	.90
36 Mark Teixeira	1.00
37 Andres Torres	.50
38 B.J. Upton	1.50
39 Shane Victorino	.50
40 David Wright	3.00
41 Joseph Blanton	.75
42 Shin Soo Choo	.75
43 Jason Cooper	.50
44 Jeff Francis	.60
45 Jeff Francoeur	1.50
46 Joey Gomes	.50
47 Corey Hart	.50
48 Justin Huber	.50
49 Dan Meyer	.65
50 Dontrelle Willis	.60
51 Scott Hairston	.60
52 Anthony Lerew	.50
53 Jeff Mathis	.50
54 Felix Pie	.75
55 Jason Pridie	.50
56 Hanley Ramirez	1.50
57 Joe Saunders	.50
58 Jason Stokes	1.00
59 Brian Tallet	.50
60 Chad Tracy	.75

2002 Just Justifiable Black

Each card in Justifiable 2002 was issued in a black-bordered version serially numbered to 50 each. An autographed version of each card, numbered to 25, was also produced. The black parallels were random pack inserts.

	MT
Common Player:	5.00
1 Russ Adams	
(Not officially issued.)	.00
2 Travis Blackley	5.00
3 Matt Cain	8.00
4 Travis Chapman	10.00
5 Kyle Davies	5.00
6 Carlos Duran	5.00
7 Gavin Floyd	10.00
8 Jesse Foppert	6.00
9 Choo Freeman	7.50
10 Jimmy Gobble	10.00
11 Jonny Gomes	7.50
12 Khalil Greene	15.00
13 Joel Guzman	7.50
14 Luke Hagerty	5.00
15 Jack Hannahan	5.00
16 Rich Harden	7.50
17 J.J. Hardy	6.00
18 Jeremy Hermida	5.00
19 Kris Honel	5.00
20 Casey Kotchman	16.00
21 Cliff Lee	5.00
22 Francisco Liriano	5.00
23 Jose Lopez	5.00
24 Andy Marte	15.00
25 Victor Martinez	5.00
26 Joe Mauer	25.00
27 Drew Meyer	5.00
28 Dustin Moseley	5.00
29 Clint Nageotte	5.00
30 Rhett Parrott	5.00
31 Josh Phelps	15.00
32 Brandon Phillips	15.00
33 Jose Reyes	15.00
34 Felix Sanchez	5.00
35 Sergio Santos	6.00
36 Mark Teixeira	15.00
37 Andres Torres	5.00
38 B.J. Upton	20.00
39 Shane Victorino	5.00
40 David Wright	20.00
41 Joseph Blanton	5.00
42 Shin Soo Choo	7.50
43 Jason Cooper	5.00
44 Jeff Francis	5.00
45 Jeff Francoeur	25.00
46 Joey Gomes	5.00
47 Corey Hart	5.00
48 Justin Huber	5.00
49 Dan Meyer	5.00
50 Dontrelle Willis	25.00
51 Scott Hairston	5.00
52 Anthony Lerew	7.50
53 Jeff Mathis	7.50
54 Felix Pie	20.00
55 Jason Pridie	5.00
56 Hanley Ramirez	25.00
57 Joe Saunders	5.00
58 Jason Stokes	15.00
59 Brian Tallet	5.00
60 Chad Tracy	6.00

2002 Just Justifiable Autographs - White

Randomly inserted into foil boxes of Justifiable 2002 and Memorabilia Edition at a rate of about two per box were white-bordered autograph cards. Numbers signed ranged from 50 to 1,000 and are indicated parenthetically in the checklist. Values for cards #41-60, which are considered short-printed base cards, are found in the listings under Justifiable 2002.

	MT
Common Player, #1-40:	5.00
(See Justifiable 2002 for #41-60.)	
(See Justifiable 2002 for #41-60.)	.00
1 Russ Adams (400)	5.00
2 Travis Blackley (400)	5.00
3 Matt Cain (400)	6.00
4 Travis Chapman (400)	7.50
5 Kyle Davies (400)	6.00
6 Carlos Duran (50)	10.00
7 Gavin Floyd (50)	20.00
8 Jesse Foppert (400)	6.00
9 Choo Freeman (400)	5.00
10 Jimmy Gobble (50)	10.00
11 Jonny Gomes (50)	15.00
12 Khalil Greene (50)	15.00
13 Joel Guzman (50)	10.00
14 Luke Hagerty (400)	5.00
15 Jack Hannahan (400)	5.00
16 Rich Harden (50)	6.00
17 J.J. Hardy (400)	6.00
18 Jeremy Hermida (50)	5.00
19 Kris Honel (400)	5.00
20 Casey Kotchman (400)	7.50
21 Cliff Lee (400)	5.00
22 Francisco Liriano (400)	5.00
23 Jose Lopez (400)	5.00
24 Andy Marte (50)	30.00
25 Victor Martinez (50)	10.00
26 Joe Mauer (50)	30.00
27 Drew Meyer (400)	5.00
28 Dustin Moseley (400)	5.00
29 Clint Nageotte (50)	10.00
30 Rhett Parrott (400)	5.00
31 Josh Phelps (50)	25.00
32 Brandon Phillips (75)	25.00
33 Jose Reyes (50)	25.00
34 Felix Sanchez (400)	5.00
35 Sergio Santos (400)	5.00
36 Mark Teixeira (50)	25.00
37 Andres Torres (400)	5.00
38 B.J. Upton (50)	25.00
39 Shane Victorino (400)	5.00
40 David Wright (400)	25.00

2002 Just Justifiable Autographs - Silver

Sixteen of the players in Justifiable 2002 appear in a silver-bordered autographed parallel edition, serially numbered to 375 each and randomly inserted in all forms of packaging.

	MT
Common Player:	5.00
7 Gavin Floyd	10.00
12 Khalil Greene	15.00
13 Joel Guzman	7.50
18 Jeremy Hermida	6.00
24 Andy Marte	7.50
33 Jose Reyes	17.50
38 B.J. Upton	7.50
40 David Wright	25.00
42 Shin Soo Choo	7.50
47 Corey Hart	5.00
48 Justin Huber	5.00
54 Felix Pie	12.50
55 Jason Pridie	5.00
56 Hanley Ramirez	15.00
58 Jason Stokes	15.00

2002 Just Justifiable Autographs - Gold

Gold-bordered autographed versions of each card in Justifiable 2002 were produced in an edition of 100 each and randomly inserted into all forms of packaging.

	MT
Common Player:	5.00
1 Russ Adams	5.00
2 Travis Blackley	5.00
3 Matt Cain	7.50
4 Travis Chapman	10.00
5 Kyle Davies	6.00
6 Carlos Duran	7.50
7 Gavin Floyd	15.00
8 Jesse Foppert	7.50
9 Choo Freeman	10.00
10 Jimmy Gobble	6.00
11 Jonny Gomes	10.00
12 Khalil Greene	10.00
13 Joel Guzman	7.50
14 Luke Hagerty	5.00
15 Jack Hannahan	5.00
16 Rich Harden	7.50
17 J.J. Hardy	7.50
18 Jeremy Hermida	8.00
19 Kris Honel	5.00
20 Casey Kotchman	15.00
21 Cliff Lee	5.00
22 Francisco Liriano	5.00
23 Jose Lopez	5.00
24 Andy Marte	7.50
25 Victor Martinez	5.00
26 Joe Mauer	20.00
27 Drew Meyer	5.00
28 Dustin Moseley	5.00
29 Clint Nageotte	5.00
30 Rhett Parrott	5.00
31 Josh Phelps	25.00
32 Brandon Phillips	25.00
33 Jose Reyes	20.00
34 Felix Sanchez	5.00
35 Sergio Santos	7.50
36 Mark Teixeira	20.00
37 Andres Torres	5.00
38 B.J. Upton	20.00
39 Shane Victorino	5.00
40 David Wright	25.00
41 Joseph Blanton	6.00
42 Shin Soo Choo	10.00
43 Jason Cooper	5.00
44 Jeff Francis	5.00
45 Jeff Francoeur	25.00
46 Joey Gomes	5.00
47 Corey Hart	5.00
48 Justin Huber	5.00
49 Dan Meyer	5.00
50 Dontrelle Willis	17.50
51 Scott Hairston	7.50
52 Anthony Lerew	5.00
53 Jeff Mathis	5.00
54 Felix Pie	10.00
55 Jason Pridie	5.00
56 Hanley Ramirez	20.00
57 Joe Saunders	5.00
58 Jason Stokes	20.00
59 Brian Tallet	5.00
60 Chad Tracy	7.50

2002 Just Justifiable Autographs - Black

Each card in Justifiable 2002 was issued in a black-bordered autographed version, randomly inserted. Each black parallel autograph was serially numbered in an edition of 25.

	MT
Common Player:	15.00
1 Russ Adams	15.00
2 Travis Blackley	15.00
3 Matt Cain	25.00
4 Travis Chapman	25.00
5 Kyle Davies	25.00
6 Carlos Duran	25.00
7 Gavin Floyd	40.00
8 Jesse Foppert	25.00
9 Choo Freeman	25.00
10 Jimmy Gobble	25.00
11 Jonny Gomes	25.00
12 Khalil Greene	25.00
13 Joel Guzman	25.00
14 Luke Hagerty	15.00
15 Jack Hannahan	15.00
16 Rich Harden	22.50
17 J.J. Hardy	20.00
18 Jeremy Hermida	15.00
19 Kris Honel	15.00
20 Casey Kotchman	40.00
21 Cliff Lee	15.00
22 Francisco Liriano	15.00
23 Jose Lopez	15.00
24 Andy Marte	25.00
25 Victor Martinez	15.00
26 Joe Mauer	75.00
27 Drew Meyer	15.00
28 Dustin Moseley	15.00
29 Clint Nageotte	15.00
30 Rhett Parrott	15.00
31 Josh Phelps	60.00
32 Brandon Phillips	60.00
33 Jose Reyes	60.00
34 Felix Sanchez	15.00
35 Sergio Santos	15.00
36 Mark Teixeira	45.00
37 Andres Torres	15.00
38 B.J. Upton	40.00
39 Shane Victorino	15.00
40 David Wright	50.00
41 Joseph Blanton	25.00
42 Shin Soo Choo	25.00
43 Jason Cooper	15.00
44 Jeff Francis	15.00
45 Jeff Francoeur	75.00
46 Joey Gomes	15.00
47 Corey Hart	15.00
48 Justin Huber	15.00
49 Dan Meyer	15.00
50 Dontrelle Willis	60.00
51 Scott Hairston	15.00
52 Anthony Lerew	15.00
53 Jeff Mathis	15.00
54 Felix Pie	25.00
55 Jason Pridie	15.00
56 Hanley Ramirez	15.00
57 Joe Saunders	15.00
58 Jason Stokes	60.00
59 Brian Tallet	15.00
60 Chad Tracy	20.00

2002 Just Prospects

After a one-year hiatus, Just Minors returned to the production of cards with a 2002 issue released only in boxed-set form, rather than foil packs. Each box, with a suggested retail price of $19.95, includes the 40-card base set plus one of 10 short-printed autograph cards. Autographed base-set cards were a 1:2 random box insert and Just Black parallels, numbered to 50, were found one per 10 boxes. Rather than photographs, each card features artwork by Noah Stokes. Backs have a ghost image of the front art, along with vital data, a few words about the player and, in the case of autographed cards, a hand-numbered holographic sticker. The SP cards #41-50 are numbered from an edition of 1,200 each.

	MT
Complete Set (50):	25.00
Common Player:	.25
01 Willy Aybar	.25
02 Angel Berroa	.50
03 Wilson Betemit	.50
04 Hank Blalock	.50
05 Tony Blanco	.25
06 Boof Bonser	.50
07 Joe Borchard	.50
08 Carl Crawford	.35
09 Juan Cruz	.25
10 Nelson Cruz	.25
11 Domingo Cuello	.50
12 Gavin Floyd	.25
13 Franklyn German	.25
14 Adrian Gonzalez	.50
15 Danny Gonzalez	.25
16 Gabe Gross	.25
17 Angel Guzman	.35
18 Joel Guzman	.35
19 Josh Karp	.50
20 Austin Kearns	.40
21 Joe Mauer	1.00
22 Yadier Molina	.75
23 Justin Morneau	1.00
24 Xavier Nady	2.00
25 Chris Narveson	.35
26 Miguel Negron	.25
27 Bubba Nelson	.25
28 Nick Neugebauer	.35
29 Jake Peavy	.75
30 Carlos Pena	.40
31 Antonio Perez	.50
32 Jon Rauch	.25
33 Jose Rojas	.25
34 Felix Sanchez	.25
35 Chris Snelling	.25
36 Rafael Soriano	.25
37 Dennis Tankersley	.25
38 Mark Teixeira	1.00
39 Josh Thigpen	.25
40 Billy Traber	.75
41 Taggert Bozied/SP/Auto.	2.50
42 Aaron Cook/SP/Auto.	2.00
43 Carlos Duran/SP/Auto.	2.00
44 Mike Fontenot/SP/Auto.	3.00
45 Jimmy Gobble/SP/Auto.	2.00
46 Jonny Gomes/SP/Auto.	4.00
47 Matt Harrington/SP/Auto.	2.50
48 Bobby Jenks/SP/Auto.	2.00
49 Todd Linden/SP/Auto.	4.00
50 Clint Nageotte/SP/Auto.	2.00

2002 Just Prospects Gold Edition

Packaged with a mini-helmet autographed by a former, current or prospective major league star, this boxed set parallels the Just Prospects issue. Cards #1-40 are virtually identical to the regular issue except for the gold borders on front and a "Gold Edition" logo on back. Cards #41-50 are unautographed short-prints with a hologram on back numbered to 500. Each boxed set with a suggested retail price of $44.95 includes one of the short-print and two autographed cards.

	MT
Factory Set:	25.00
Complete Set (50):	15.00
Common Player:	.50
01 Willy Aybar	.50
02 Angel Berroa	1.00
03 Wilson Betemit	1.00
04 Hank Blalock	1.00
05 Tony Blanco	.50
06 Boof Bonser	.50
07 Joe Borchard	.50
08 Carl Crawford	.75
09 Juan Cruz	.50
10 Nelson Cruz	.50
11 Domingo Cuello	1.00
12 Gavin Floyd	1.50
13 Franklyn German	.50
14 Adrian Gonzalez	1.00
15 Danny Gonzalez	.50
16 Gabe Gross	.50
17 Angel Guzman	.65
18 Joel Guzman	.65
19 Josh Karp	.75
20 Austin Kearns	.75
21 Joe Mauer	2.00
22 Yadier Molina	1.50
23 Justin Morneau	2.00
24 Xavier Nady	2.00

25	Chris Narveson		.60
26	Miguel Negron		.50
27	Bubba Nelson		.50
28	Nick Neugebauer		.75
29	Jake Peavy		1.50
30	Carlos Pena		.75
31	Antonio Perez		1.00
32	Jon Rauch		1.00
33	Jose Rojas		.50
34	Felix Sanchez		.50
35	Chris Snelling		.50
36	Rafael Soriano		.50
37	Dennis Tankersley		.50
38	Mark Teixeira		2.00
39	Josh Thigpen		.50
40	Billy Traber		1.75
41	Taggert Bozied/SP		2.00
42	Aaron Cook/SP		2.00
43	Carlos Duran/SP		2.50
44	Mike Fontenot/SP		1.00
45	Jimmy Gobble/SP		1.00
46	Jonny Gomes/SP		2.00
47	Matt Harrington/SP		3.00
48	Bobby Jenks/SP		2.00
49	Todd Linden/SP		2.00
50	Clint Nageotte/SP		1.00

2002 Just Prospects Just Black

This limited-edition parallel set has black borders. Cards #1-40 are serially numbered to 50 and found at the rate of one per 10 sets. Just Black versions of the autographed cards #41-50 are limited to 25 each.

	MT
Common Player:	3.50
Stars and High-Demand:	2X
Autographs:	2.5X

(See 2002 Just Prospects for base card checklist and values.)

2002 Just Prospects Autographed Base Cards

Inserted at a rate of one per two boxed sets were autographed versions of the base cards #1-40. These white-bordered cards were released in editions of either 50 or 200, with a serially-numbered hologram on back.

		MT
Common Player:		2.00
01	Willy Aybar (200)	2.00
02	Angel Berroa (50)	10.00
03	Wilson Betemit (50)	9.00
04	Hank Blalock (50)	14.00
05	Tony Blanco (50)	11.00
06	Boof Bonser (200)	2.00
07	Joe Borchard (50)	17.50
08	Carl Crawford (50)	10.00
09	Juan Cruz (50)	5.00
10	Nelson Cruz (200)	2.00
11	Domingo Cuello (200)	2.00
12	Gavin Floyd (50)	27.50
13	Franklyn German (200)	5.00
14	Adrian Gonzalez (75)	12.50
15	Danny Gonzalez (200)	5.00
16	Gabe Gross (200)	2.50
17	Angel Guzman (200)	7.00
18	Joel Guzman (200)	8.00
19	Josh Karp (200)	5.00
20	Austin Kearns (50)	15.00
21	Joe Mauer (50)	35.00
22	Yadier Molina (200)	4.00
23	Justin Morneau (50)	15.00
24	Xavier Nady (50)	15.00
25	Chris Narveson (200)	3.00
26	Miguel Negron (200)	2.50
27	Bubba Nelson (200)	6.00
28	Nick Neugebauer (?)	6.00
29	Jake Peavy (200)	8.00
30	Carlos Pena (?)	7.50
31	Antonio Perez (200)	6.00
32	Jon Rauch (200)	4.00
33	Jose Rojas (200)	2.00
34	Felix Sanchez (?)	2.00
35	Chris Snelling (200)	4.00
36	Rafael Soriano (50)	9.00
37	Dennis Tankersley (50)	10.00
38	Mark Teixeira (50)	25.00
39	Josh Thigpen (200)	3.00
40	Billy Traber (200)	12.50

2002 Just Prospects Gold Edition Autographs

At the rate of two per boxed set, autographed versions of each Gold Edition card were randomly inserted. Cards have a serially numbered hologram on back within editions of 300 or fewer per card.

		MT
Common Player:		2.00
01	Willy Aybar	2.50
02	Angel Berroa	7.00
03	Wilson Betemit	5.00
04	Hank Blalock	9.00
05	Tony Blanco	5.00
06	Boof Bonser	2.00
07	Joe Borchard	8.00
08	Carl Crawford	6.00
09	Juan Cruz	6.00
10	Nelson Cruz	2.00
11	Domingo Cuello	4.00
12	Gavin Floyd	6.00
13	Franklyn German	4.00
14	Adrian Gonzalez	6.00
15	Danny Gonzalez	2.00
16	Gabe Gross	2.00
17	Angel Guzman	2.00
18	Joel Guzman	4.00
19	Josh Karp	2.00
20	Austin Kearns	6.00
21	Joe Mauer	10.00
22	Yadier Molina	10.00
23	Justin Morneau	6.00
24	Xavier Nady	10.00
25	Chris Narveson	5.00
26	Miguel Negron	2.00
27	Bubba Nelson	2.00
28	Nick Neugebauer	4.00
29	Jake Peavy	3.00
30	Carlos Pena	3.00
31	Antonio Perez	3.00
32	Jon Rauch	3.00
33	Jose Rojas	3.00
34	Felix Sanchez	2.00
35	Chris Snelling	4.00
36	Rafael Soriano	7.00
37	Dennis Tankersley	3.00
38	Mark Teixeira	8.00
39	Josh Thigpen	7.00
40	Billy Traber	7.00
41	Taggert Bozied	2.00
42	Aaron Cook	2.00
43	Carlos Duran	2.50
44	Mike Fontenot	2.00
45	Jimmy Gobble	2.00
46	Jonny Gomes	3.00
47	Matt Harrington	3.00
48	Bobby Jenks	3.00
49	Todd Linden	4.00
50	Clint Nageotte	2.00

2002 Just The Franchise Rookie Preview Prototypes

This baker's dozen promo cards was produced for a set which was to be known as Just The Franchise Rookie Review, but was never issued. Unlike the Just Prospects issues, these promos have photographic fronts with the same picture ghosted on the back. Cards have a "PROTOTYPE" notice on back at bottom-right and are numbered

with a "JTF." prefix. White- and gold-bordered versions were produced, with no value differential.

		MT
Complete Set (13):		5.00
Common Player:		.25
01	Joe Mauer	1.00
02	Taggert Bozied	.50
03	Corey Hart	.25
04	Jeff Mathis	.25
05	Justin Huber	.25
06	David Wright	1.00
07	Brandon Phillips	.75
08	Todd Linden	.50
09	Jonny Gomes	.35
10	Mark Teixeira	.75
11	Josh Phelps	.75
12	Chad Tracy	.35
---	Shin-Soo Choo	.50

2002 Upper Deck Minor League

A November-released, post-season set, UD Minor League offers a base set of 400 cards. Cards #1-200 are regular player cards. Cards #201-230 are a subset titled "On the Fast Track." Cards #231-240 are "Draft Day Gems" and cards #241-400 are nonplayer "Team Profiles" logo/history cards. All cards are silver-foil highlighted on front and have color backs. Insert sets feature game-used jerseys, player autographs and a group of Michael Jordan memorabilia cards. Cards were sold in six-card foil packs.

		MT
Complete Set (400):		35.00
Common Player:		.05
Wax Pack (6):		1.50
Wax Box (24):		25.00
1	Bobby Jenks	.25
2	Chris Bootcheck	.05
3	Francisco Rodriguez	.25
4	Johan Santana	.60
5	Casey Kotchman	.25
6	Jeff Mathis	.10
7	Joe Torres	.10
8	Anthony Pluta	.05
9	John Buck	.05
10	Chris Burke	.25
11	Rodrigo Rosario	.05
12	Chad Qualls	.15
13	Tommy Whiteman	.05
14	Bobby Crosby	.25
15	Chris Tritle	.05
16	Mike Wood	.05
17	Freddie Bynum	.05
18	John-Ford Griffin	.10
19	Nick Swisher	.10
20	Gabe Gross	.10
21	Tracy Thorpe	.05
22	Alexis Rios	.20
23	Ramon Castro	.05
24	Richard Lewis	.05
25	Brian Digby	.05
26	Brett Evert	.10
27	Matt Belisle	.05
28	Carlos Duran	.05
29	Zach Miner	.05
30	Gonzalo Lopez	.05
31	Adam Wainwright	1.00
32	Kelly Johnson	.10
33	Bubba Nelson	.10
34	Wilson Betemit	.05
35	Mike Jones	.05
36	Ben Hendrickson	.10
37	Corey Hart	.10
38	David Krynzel	.25
39	Cristian Guerrero	.10
40	Matt Yeatman	.10
41	Prince Fielder	3.00
42	Cristobal Correa	.05
43	Jimmy Journell	.05
44	Scotty Layfield	.05
45	Justin Pope	.05
46	B.R. Cook	.05
47	Yadier Molina	.25
48	Dan Haren	.25
49	Chris Duncan	.50
50	Luis Montanez	.05
51	Angel Guzman	.10
52	J.J. Johnson	.05
53	Nic Jackson	.05
54	David Kelton	.10
55	Ben Christensen	.25
56	Felix Sanchez	.05
57	Rocco Baldelli	.50
58	Josh Hamilton	.50
59	Jon Switzer	.05
60	Jace Brewer	.05
61	Jorge Cantu	.05
62	Chad Tracy	.25
63	Luis Terrero	.05
64	Mike Gosling	.05
65	Brad Cresse	.10
66	Jesus Cota	.05
67	Scott Hairston	.05
68	Lino Garcia	.05
69	Jason Bulger	.05
70	Oscar Villarreal	.05
71	Beltran Perez	.05
72	Jose Rojas	.05
73	Brennan King	.05
74	Koyie Hill	.05
75	Hong-Chih Kuo	.15
76	Willy Aybar	.10
77	Joel Guzman	.10
78	Josh Karp	.05
79	Rich Rundles	.05
80	Luke Lockwood	.05
81	Donnie Bridges	.05
82	Eric Good	.05
83	Claudio Vargas	.05
84	Seung Song	.10
85	Jerome Williams	.05
86	Boof Bonser	.05
87	Erick Threets	.05
88	Jesse Foppert	.10
89	Lance Niekro	.10
90	Julian Benavidez	.05
91	Francisco Liriano	2.00
92	Grady Sizemore	.35
93	Ryan Church	.10
94	Travis Foley	.05
95	Brian Tallet	.05
96	Billy Traber	.10
97	Dan Denham	.05
98	J.D. Martin	.05
99	Corey Smith	.05
100	Derek Thompson	.05
101	Michael Garciaparra	.10
102	Ryan Christenson	.10
103	Jamal Strong	.05
104	Matt Thornton	.05
105	Rett Johnson	.05
106	Clint Nageotte	.10
107	Shin-Soo Choo	.25
108	Allen Baxter	.05
109	Adrian Gonzalez	.15
110	Denny Bautista	.10
111	Miguel Cabrera	.45
112	Josh Wilson	.05
113	Rob Henkel	.05
114	Craig Brazell	.10
115	Enrique Cruz	.05
116	Aaron Heilman	.10
117	David Wright	3.00
118	Justin Huber	.20
119	Jose Reyes	.50
120	Neal Musser	.05
121	Keith Reed	.05
122	Richard Stahl	.05
123	Matt Riley	.10
124	Mike Fontenot	.10
125	Tim Raines Jr.	.05
126	Beau Hale	.05
127	Josh Barfield	.15
128	Tagg Bozied	.15
129	Mark Phillips	.10
130	Jake Gautreau	.05
131	Ben Johnson	.05
132	Xavier Nady	.10
133	Taylor Buchholz	.05
134	Gavin Floyd	.25
135	Anderson Machado	.05
136	Jorge Padilla	.05
137	Yoel Hernandez	.05
138	Chase Utley	3.00
139	J.R. House	.05
140	Justin Reid	.05
141	Jon VanBenschoten	.15
142	Chris Young	1.00
143	Sean Burnett	.10
144	Jose Castillo	.05
145	Mario Ramos	.05
146	Patrick Boyd	.05
147	Jason Bourgeois	.05
148	Mark Teixeira	.50
149	Mauricio Lara	.05
150	Manny Delcarmen	.05
151	Phil Dumatrait	.10
152	Josh Thigpen	.05
153	Tony Blanco	.05
154	Rene Miniel	.05
155	Kevin Huang	.05
156	Anastacio Martinez	.05
157	Ty Howington	.10
158	Dane Sardinha	.05
159	Rainier Olmedo	.05
160	Dustin Moseley	.10
161	Ryan Snare	.05
162	Justin Gillman	.05
163	Choo Freeman	.10
164	Jayson Nix	.05
165	Garrett Atkins	.25
166	Javier Colina	.05
167	Rene Reyes	.05
168	Ching-Lung Lo	.05
169	Chin-Hui Tsao	.15
170	Brad Hawpe	.10
171	Jason Young	.05
172	Cory Vance	.05
173	Matt Holliday	1.00
174	Mike Stodolka	.05
175	Colt Griffin	.10
176	Alejandro Machado	.05
177	Kenny Baugh	.10
178	Charley Carter	.05
179	Preston Larrison	.10
180	Cody Ross	.05
181	Nook Logan	.05
182	Jeremy Bonderman	1.50
183	David Espinosa	.05
184	Michael Restovich	.10
185	Rob Bown	.05
186	B.J. Garbe	.05
187	Justin Morneau	.25
188	Joe Mauer	2.00
189	Jon McDonald	.05
190	Franklin Francisco	.05
191	Corwin Malone	.05
192	Felix Diaz	.05
193	Tim Hummel	.05
194	Kris Honel	.05
195	Matt Smith	.05
196	Alex Graman	.05
197	Brandon Claussen	.15
198	Erick Almonte	.05
199	Bronson Sardinha	.05
200	Danny Borrell	.05
201	Casey Kotchman	.15
202	John Buck	.10
203	Bobby Crosby	.05
204	Gabe Gross	.05
205	Wilson Betemit	.10
206	David Krynzel	.05
207	Jimmy Journell	.05
208	David Kelton	.05
209	Josh Hamilton	.50
210	Luis Terrero	.05
211	Joel Guzman	.15
212	Seung Song	.05
213	Jerome Williams	.05
214	J.D. Martin	.05
215	Clint Nageotte	.05
216	Miguel Cabrera	.25
217	Aaron Heilman	.05
218	Richard Stahl	.05
219	Jake Gautreau	.05
220	Taylor Buchholz	.05
221	J.R. House	.05
222	Mark Teixeira	.15
223	Tony Blanco	.05
224	Ty Howington	.05
225	Chin-Hui Tsao	.10
226	Colt Griffin	.05
227	Kenny Baugh	.05
228	Joe Mauer	1.00
229	Corwin Malone	.05
230	Brandon Claussen	.10
231	Scott Kazmir	2.00
232	Zack Greinke	1.00
233	Scott Moore	.25
234	Drew Meyer	.25
235	Khalil Greene	.75
236	Chris Gruler	.25
237	Prince Fielder	2.00
238	Jeff Francis	1.00
239	Jeremy Hermida	.40
240	Nick Swisher	.75
241	Salt Lake Stingers	.05
242	Arkansas Travelers	.05
243	Rancho Cucamonga Quakes	.05
244	Cedar Rapids Kernals	.05
245	Provo Angels	.05
246	New Orleans Zephyrs	.05
247	Round Rock Express	.05
248	Lexington Legends	.05
249	Michigan City Battle Cats	.05
250	Tri-City ValleyCats	.05
251	Sacramento River Cats	.05
252	Midland Rockhounds	.05
253	Modesto A's	.05
254	Visalia Oaks	.05
255	Vancouver Canadians	.05
256	Syracuse Skychiefs	.05
257	Tennessee Smokies	.05
258	Dunedin Blue Jays	.05
259	Charleston Alleycats	.05
260	Auburn Doubledays	.05
261	Richmond Braves	.05
262	Greenville Braves	.05
263	Macon Braves	.05
264	Myrtle Beach Pelicans	.05
265	Danville Braves	.05
266	Gulf Coast Braves	.05
267	Indianapolis Indians	.05
268	Hunstville Stars	.05
269	High Desert Mavericks	.05
270	Beloit Snappers	.05
271	Ogden Raptors	.05
272	Memphis Redbirds	.05
273	New Haven Ravens	.05
274	Potomac Cannons	.05
275	Peoria Chiefs	.05
276	New Jersey Cardinals	.05
277	Johnson City Cardinals	.05
278	Iowa Cubs	.05
279	West Tenn Diamond Jaxx	.05
280	Daytona Cubs	.05
281	Lansing Lugnuts	.05
282	Boise Hawks	.05
283	Mesa Cubs	.05
284	Durham Bulls	.05
285	Orlando Rays	.05
286	Bakersfield Blaze	.05
287	Charleston Riverdogs	.05
288	Hudson Valley Renegades	.05
289	Tucson Sidewinders	.05
290	El Paso Diablos	.05
291	Lancaster JetHawks	.05
292	South Bend Silver Hawks	.05
293	Yakima Bears	.05
294	Missoula Osprey	.05
295	Las Vegas 51s	.05
296	Jacksonville Suns	.05
297	Vero Beach Dodgers	.05
298	South Georgia Waves	.05
299	Great Falls Dodgers	.05
300	Gulf Coast Dodgers	.05
301	Ottawa Lynx	.05
302	Harrisburg Senators	.05
303	Brevard County Manatees	.05
304	Clinton Lumberkings	.05
305	Vermont Expos	.05
306	Fresno Grizzlies	.05
307	Shreveport Swamp Dragons	.05
308	San Jose Giants	.05
309	Hagerstown Suns	.05
310	Salem-Keizer Volcanoes	.05
311	Arizona Giants	.05
312	Buffalo Bisons	.05
313	Akron Aeros	.05
314	Kinston Indians	.05
315	Columbus RedStixx	.05
316	Mahoning Valley Scrappers	.05
317	Burlington Indians	.05
318	Tacoma Rainiers	.05
319	San Antonio Missions	.05
320	San Bernardino Stampede	.05
321	Wisconsin Timber Rattlers	.05
322	Everett Aqua Sox	.05
323	Calgary Cannons	.05
324	Portland Sea Dogs	.05
325	Jupiter Hammerheads	.05
326	Kane County Cougars	.05
327	Jamestown Jammers	.05
328	Norfolk Tides	.05
329	Binghamton Mets	.05
330	St. Lucie Mets	.05
331	Capital City Bombers	.05
332	Brooklyn Cyclones	.05
333	Kingsport Mets	.05
334	Rochester Red Wings	.05
335	Bowie Baysox	.05
336	Frederick Keys	.05
337	Delmarva Shorebirds	.05
338	Bluefield Orioles	.05
339	Portland Beavers	.05
340	Mobile BayBears	.05
341	Lake Elsinore Storm	.05
342	Ft. Wayne Wizards	.05
343	Eugene Emeralds	.05
344	Scranton, Wilkes-Barre Red Barons	.05
345	Reading Phillies	.05
346	Clearwater Phillies	.05
347	Lakewood BlueClaws	.05
348	Batavia Muckdogs	.05
349	Nashville Sounds	.05
350	Altoona Curve	.05
351	Hickory Crawdads	.05
352	Lynchburg Hillcats	.05
353	Williamsport Crosscutters	.05
354	Oklahoma RedHawks	.05
355	Tulsa Drillers	.05
356	Charlotte Rangers	.05
357	Savannah Sand Gnats	.05
358	Pulaski Rangers	.05
359	Pawtucket Red Sox	.05
360	Trenton Thunder	.05
361	Sarasota Red Sox	.05
362	Augusta GreenJackets	.05
363	Lowell Spinners	.05
364	Gulf Coast Red Sox	.05
365	Louisville Bats	.05
366	Chattanooga Lookouts	.05
367	Stockton Ports	.05
368	Dayton Dragons	.05
369	Billings Mustangs	.05
370	Colorado Springs Sky Sox	.05
371	Carolina Mudcats	.05
372	Salem Avalanche	.05
373	Tri City Dust Devils	.05
374	Asheville Tourists	.05
375	Omaha Royals	.05
376	Wichita Wranglers	.05
377	Wilmington Blue Rocks	.05
378	Burlington Bees	.05
379	Spokane Indians	.05
380	Toledo Mud Hens	.05
381	Erie Seawolves	.05
382	Lakeland Tigers	.05

383	West Michigan Whitecaps	.05
384	Oneonta Tigers	.05
385	Edmonton Trappers	.05
386	New Britain Rock Cats	.05
387	Ft. Myers Miracle	.05
388	Quad City River Bandits	.05
389	Elizabethton Twins	.05
390	Charlotte Knights	.05
391	Birmingham Barons	.05
392	Winston-Salem Warthogs	.05
393	Kannapolis Intimidators	.05
394	Bristol White Sox	.05
395	Columbus Clippers	.05
396	Norwich Navigators	.05
397	Tampa Yankees	.05
398	Greensboro Bats	.05
399	Staten Island Yankees	.05
400	Gulf Coast Yankees	.05

2002 Upper Deck Minor League Game Jerseys

Ten players are included in this insert set featuring game-worn jersey pieces framed in a team-related monogram. Each card was produced in an edition of 850 pieces.

		MT
Complete Set (10):		40.00
Common Player:		3.00
J-AH	Aaron Heilman	3.00
J-BU	Chris Burke	5.00
J-CR	Bobby Crosby	7.50
J-CT	Chad Tracy	4.50
J-DK	David Krynzel	5.00
J-JB	Jeremy Bonderman	15.00
J-JH	Josh Hamilton	15.00
J-JJ	Jimmy Journell	3.00
J-MT	Mark Teixeira	6.00
J-RB	Rocco Baldelli	7.50

2002 Upper Deck Minor League Michael Jordan Flashbacks

More than 1,500 memorabilia cards featuring swatches of jerseys worn by Michael Jordan during his brief professional baseball fling were random pack inserts in UD Minor League. Numbers reported produced are indicated parenthetically.

		MT
MJ-SS	Michael Jordan (Scorpions/1,490)	55.00
MS-WS1	Michael Jordan (White Sox black/25.)	115.00
MS-WS2	Michael Jordan (White Sox white/10.)	200.00
MS-WS3	Michael Jordan (White Sox silver/5.)	
MS-WS4	Michael Jordan (White Sox gold/1.)	

2002 Upper Deck Minor League Signature Collection

Nearly three dozen players provided authentically autographed cards for random pack inserts in Upper Deck Minor League. Stated odds of finding a signed card were 1:18 packs. Besides the base autograph cards, four players each signed more limited-edition Silver (numbered to 25) or Gold (10 each) versions.

		MT
Common Player:		3.00
AG	Adrian Gonzalez	5.00
AG	Adrian Gonzalez/Silver/25	25.00
AH	Aaron Heilman	7.50
AH	Aaron Heilman/Silver/25	50.00
BB	Brian Bass	3.00
BC	Brad Cresse	4.00
BT	Billy Traber	7.00
CB	Chris Burke	7.50
CG	Colt Griffin	4.00
CK	Casey Kotchman	12.50
CL	Brandon Claussen	4.00
CM	Corwin Malone	3.00
CT	Chad Tracy	12.00
DK	David Krynzel	4.00
DKe	David Kelton	4.00
GF	Gavin Floyd	8.00
GG	Gabe Gross	4.00
JB	John Buck	4.00
JB	John Buck/Silver/25	20.00
JE	Jerome Williams	7.00
JE	Jérome Williams/Gold/10	50.00
JF	John-Ford Griffin	4.00
JG	Jake Gautreau	4.00
JH	Josh Hamilton	40.00
JJ	Jimmy Journell	3.00
JJ	Jimmy Journell/Gold/10	50.00
JM	J.D. Martin	4.00
JO	Joe Mauer	25.00
JO	Joe Mauer/Gold/10	100.00
JS	Jason Stokes	12.50
JU	Justin Huber	12.00
KB	Kenny Baugh	3.00
MC	Miguel Cabrera	45.00
MG	Michael Garciaparra	16.00
MG	Michael Garciaparra/Silver/25	50.00
MJ	Mike Jones	5.00
MT	Mark Teixeira	15.00
MT	Mark Teixeira/Gold/10	100.00
PF	Prince Fielder	60.00
SB	Sean Burnett	6.00
TH	Ty Howington	3.00
WA	Willy Aybar	3.00

2002 Upper Deck Minor League Star Swatch

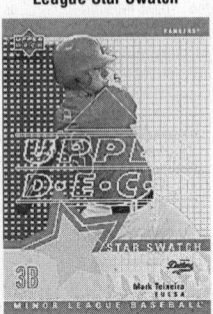

Five of the top prospects in Upper Deck Minor League are featured in this uniform-swatch insert, serially numbered to just 25 pieces each.

		MT
Common Player:		15.00
SS-AH	Aaron Heilman	15.00
SS-JH	Josh Hamilton	25.00
SS-JJ	Jimmy Journell	15.00
SS-MT	Mark Teixeira	35.00
SS-RB	Rocco Baldelli	35.00

2002 Upper Deck USA Baseball

This boxed set commemorating the 2002 U.S. National Team was produced in an edition of 10,000 with a suggested retail price of $19.95. Each set contains 30 gold-foil enhanced player cards, plus one jersey-patch insert serially numbered to 475 each and an alumni autographed card numbered within an edition of 375 each.

		MT
Unopened Boxed Set (32):		30.00
Complete Set (30):		7.00
Common Player:		.10
1	Chad Cordero	.35
2	Philip Humber	.30
3	Grant Johnson	.25
4	Wes Littleton	.25
5	Kyle Sleeth	.60
6	Huston Street	.25
7	Brad Sullivan	.40
8	Bob Zimmerman	.25
9	Abe Alvarez	.30
10	Kyle Bakker	.35
11	Clint Sammons	.25
12	Landon Powell	.55
13	Michael Aubrey	.45
14	Aaron Hill	.35
15	Conor Jackson	.25
16	Eric Patterson	1.00
17	Dustin Pedroia	.75
18	Rickie Weeks	1.50
19	Shane Costa	.20
20	Mark Jurich	.25
21	Sam Fuld	.30
22	Carlos Quentin	1.00
23	Ryan Garko	.40
24	Lelo Prado	.10
25	Terry Alexander	.10
26	Sunny Golloway	.10
27	Terry Rupp	.10
28	Team photo	.10
29	Team photo	.05
30	Checklist	.05

2002 Upper Deck USA Baseball Alumni Signatures

Each 32-card boxed set of USA Baseball includes one of 27 authentically autographed Alumni Signatures card of a former member of the national team. Cards have a vertical white cardboard panel at left with the autograph. At right is a purple duotone photo of the player. A serial number from an edition of 375 each appears at bottom-right. Backs have a statement of authenticity.

		MT
Complete Set (27):		350.00
Common Player:		5.00
JB	Josh Bard	12.00
WB	Willie Bloomquist	20.00
SB	Sean Burnett	8.00
BC	Bobby Crosby	30.00
KD	Keoni DeRenne	7.00
BD	Ben Diggins	12.00
LD	Lenny Dinardo	15.00
CE	Clint Everts	35.00
JF	Jeff Francoeur	250.00
MG	Mike Gosling	7.00
JH	J.J. Hardy	50.00
KH	Koyie Hill	5.00
MH	Matt Holliday	100.00
RH	Ryan Howard	300.00
JJ	Jacque Jones	8.00
JK	Josh Karp	8.00
CK	Casey Kotchman	30.00
DK	David Krynzel	10.00
JL	James Loney	40.00
JM	Joe Mauer	40.00
SN	Shane Nance	5.00
MP	Mark Prior	40.00
ZS	Zach Segovia	9.00
PS	Phil Seibel	5.00
JS	Jason Stanford	10.00
JW	Justin Wayne	10.00
MW	Matt Whitney	10.00

2002 Upper Deck USA Baseball Jerseys

A 7/8" square swatch of National Team jersey fabric is sandwiched on these one-per-box inserts. Each card is numbered from within an edition of 475. A purple duotone photo of the player fills the top-right quadrant of the front. Backs have a statement of authenticity.

		MT
Complete Set (22):		125.00
Common Player:		3.00
AA	Abe Alvarez	4.00
MA	Michael Aubrey	9.00
KB	Kyle Bakker	12.00
CC	Chad Cordero	3.00
SC	Shane Costa	4.00
SF	Sam Fuld	5.00
AH	Aaron Hill	5.00
PH	Philip Humber	5.00
CJ	Conor Jackson	4.00
GJ	Grant Johnson	4.00
MJ	Mark Jurich	3.00
WL	Wes Littleton	4.00
EP	Eric Patterson	3.00
DP	Dustin Pedroia	10.00
LP	Landon Powell	10.00
CQ	Carlos Quentin	10.00
CS	Clint Sammons	5.00
KS	Kyle Sleeth	30.00
HS	Huston Street	5.00
BS	Brad Sullivan	8.00
RW	Rickie Weeks	10.00
BZ	Bob Zimmerman	4.00

2002 Minor League Team Sets

Manufacturer abbreviations used are: CH - Choice, GS - Grandstand, MA - Multi-Ad, WT - Warning Track.

		MT
229 Team Sets and Variations		
2002	GS AA All-Star Game (61)	15.00
2002	GS Aberdeen IronBirds (30)	13.50
2002	MA Akron Aeros (30)	9.50
2002	Team Alaska BB League Prospects (21)	25.00
2002	Team Alaska Goldpanners (20)	22.50
2002	Team Alaska Goldpanners Bonus Cards (3)	9.00
2002	Alaska Goldpanners Decade Greats (11)	15.00
2002	Team 1999 Alaska Goldpanners (11)	15.00
2002	TM Alexandria Aces (24)	9.00
2002	GS Altoona Curve (30)	10.00
2002	GS Appalachian League Top Prospects (30)	11.00
2002	GS Arkansas Travelers (30)	11.00
2002	GS Asheboro Copperheads (25)	8.50
2002	GS Asheville Tourists (30)	14.00
2002	GS Asheville Tourists Update (9)	15.00
2002	Team Auburn Doubledays (35)	12.00
2002	MA Augusta GreenJackets (30)	12.00
2002	Team Bakersfield Blaze (32)	15.00
2002	Team Batavia Muckdogs (40)	12.00
2002	MA Beloit Snappers (31)	11.00
2002	MA Beloit Snappers Update (7)	12.00
2002	MA Beloit Snappers To The Majors (7)	7.00
2002	WTC Berkshire Black Bears (26)	8.50
2002	GS Billings Mustangs (31)	11.00
2002	CH Binghamton Mets (31)	11.00
2002	CH Binghamton Mets Update (1)	7.50
2002	GS Birmingham Barons (30)	12.00
2002	GS Bluefield Orioles (36)	11.00
2002	GS Boise Hawks (30)	7.00
2002	GS Bowie Baysox (29)	11.00
2002	MA Brevard County Manatees (30)	11.00
2002	GS Bristol White Sox (30)	9.50
2002	MA Brockton Rox (30)	9.00
2002	MA Brooklyn Cyclones (34)	11.00
2002	CH Buffalo Bisons (30)	12.00
2002	MA Burlington Bees (30)	11.00
2002	MA Calgary Cannons (27)	15.00
2002	CH California/Carolina Leagues A-S (51)	12.50
2002	GS California League Top Prospects (30)	11.00
2002	CH Camden Riversharks (31)	7.50
2002	GS Canton Coyotes (30)	8.50
2002	MA Capital City Bombers (30)	30.00
2002	CH Carolina League Top Prospects (30)	12.00
2002	Team Carolina Mudcats (30)	16.50
2002	GS Casper Rockies (30)	10.00
2002	Team Cedar Rapids Kernels (33)	8.00
2002	MA Charleston Alley Cats (30)	10.00
2002	MA Charleston R iverDogs (29)	11.00
2002	GS Charlotte Knights (30)	10.00
2002	GS Charlotte Rangers (30)	15.00
2002	GS Chattanooga Lookouts (30)	12.50
2002	GS Clearwater Phillies (30)	11.00
2002	GS Clinton LumberKings (31)	15.00
2002	MA Colorado Springs Sky Sox (30)	9.00
2002	CH Columbus Clippers (30)	12.50
2002	Team Columbus Clippers (25)	25.00
2002	MA Columbus RedStixx (30)	9.00
2002	GS Danville Braves (33)	32.50
2002	MA Dayton Dragons (30)	9.00
2002	CH Daytona Cubs (30)	10.00
2002	MA Delmarva Shorebirds (30)	12.50
2002	WTC Duluth-Superior Dukes (26)	8.00
2002	WTC Duluth-Superior Dukes Update (6)	2.50
2002	GS Dunedin Blue Jays (30)	12.50
2002	CH Durham Bulls (30)	12.00
2002	GS Eastern League Top Prospects (30)	8.00
2002	GS Edinburg Roadrunners (30)	9.00
2002	MA Edmonton Trappers (30)	8.00
2002	GS Elizabethton Twins (30)	9.00
2002	GS El Paso Diablos (30)	15.00
2002	GS Erie SeaWolves (27)	9.50
2002	GS Eugene Emeralds (32)	11.00
2002	GS Everett Aquasox (30)	14.50
2002	Team Fargo-Moorhead RedHawks (30)	9.00
2002	GS Fla. State League Top Prospects (24)	11.00
2002	GS Frederick Keys (30)	11.00
2002	MA Fresno Grizzlies (29)	10.00
2002	MA Ft. Myers Miracle (30)	10.00
2002	GS Ft. Wayne Wizards (32)	9.00
2002	MA Gateway Grizzlies (28)	9.00
2002	MA Great Falls Dodgers (30)	9.00
2002	MA Greensboro Bats (29)	10.00
2002	GS Greenville Braves (34)	9.00
2002	MA Hagerstown Suns (29)	9.00
2002	GS Harrisburg Senators (28)	15.00
2002	MA Hickory Crawdads (30)	12.00
2002	MA Hickory Crawdads Update (30)	12.50
2002	GS High Desert Mavericks (32)	12.00
2002	GS High Desert Mavericks Update (1)	5.00
2002	MA Hudson Valley Renegades (34)	11.00
2002	Hudson Valley Renegades Team Issue (33)	60.00
2002	Team Huntsville Stars (29)	10.00
2002	CH Indianapolis Indians (30)	9.00
2002	CH International League All-Stars (33)	9.00
2002	GS Int'l League Top Prospects (30)	11.00
2002	MA Iowa Cubs (30)	17.50
2002	Des Moines Register Iowa Cubs (5)	50.00
2002	GS Jacksonville Suns (30)	10.00
2002	GS Johnson City Cardinals (36)	7.00
2002	Team Jupiter Hammerheads (40)	13.50
2002	GS Kane County Cougars (30)	10.00
2002	Team Kane County Cougars (30)	25.00
2002	Team Kane Co. Cougars - Old Navy (30)	35.00
2002	TM Kane County Cougars Update Auto. (1)	32.50
2002	MA Kannapolis Intimidators (30)	11.00
2002	Team Keene Swamp Bats (?)	15.00
2002	CH Kinston Indians (32)	14.00
2002	GS Lake Elsinore Storm (31)	13.00
2002	MA Lakewood BlueClaws (30)	8.00
2002	MA Lakewood BlueClaws Update (15)	6.50
2002	GS Lancaster JetHawks (30)	9.00
2002	GS Lansing Lugnuts (30)	7.00
2002	MA Las Vegas 51s (30)	15.00
2002	MA Lexington Legends (30)	11.00
2002	GS Lincoln Saltdogs (25)	8.50
2002	CH Long Island Ducks (29)	7.50
2002	CH Louisville Bats (31)	17.50
2002	CH Lowell Spinners (36)	11.00
2002	CH Lowell Spinners Update (5)	10.00
2002	CH Lowell Spinners Legends (14)	14.00
2002	CH Lynchburg Hillcats (31)	12.00
2002	MA Macon Braves (32)	12.00
2002	MA Mahoning Valley Scrappers (30)	8.00
2002	GS Martinsville Astros (32)	12.00
2002	Team Medicine Hat Blue Jays (35)	15.00
2002	Team Memphis Redbirds (30)	10.00
2002	MA Michigan Battle Cats (30)	16.00
2002	GS Midland RockHounds (30)	9.00
2002	GS Midland RockHounds-Texas Burger (30)	9.50
2002	Team Midland RockHounds (24)	50.00
2002	GS Missoula Osprey (35)	10.00
2002	GS Mobile BayBears (30)	14.00
2002	GS Modesto A's (30)	7.00
2002	MA Myrtle Beach Pelicans (30)	11.00
2002	Team Nashua Pride (28)	8.50
2002	MA Nashville Sounds (30)	9.00
2002	GS New Britain Rock Cats (30)	10.00
2002	GS N.B. Rock Cats 2001 E.L. Champs (9)	10.00
2002	GS N.B. Red Sox/Rock Cats ATG (9)	10.00
2002	GS New Haven Ravens (30)	10.00
2002	GS New Jersey Cardinals (30)	10.00
2002	WTC New Jersey Jackals (27)	8.50
2002	MA New Orleans Zephyrs (30)	10.00
2002	CH Norfolk Tides (37)	9.00
2002	GS Norwich Navigators (30)	10.00
2002	MA Ogden Raptors (36)	20.00
2002	MA Oklahoma City RedHawks (36)	10.00
2002	Team Omaha Royals (30)	10.00
2002	MA Orlando Rays (29)	50.00
2002	CH Ottawa Lynx (30)	10.00
2002	MA Pacific Coast League All-Stars (32)	12.00
2002	MA Pacific Coast Lea. Top Prospects (36)	11.00

2002 CH Pawtucket Red Sox (30) 10.00
2002 MA Peninsula Pilots (31) 7.50
2002 MA Peoria Chiefs (30) 10.00
2002 MA Portland Beavers (29) 10.00
2002 GS Portland Sea Dogs (30) 12.00
2002 CH Potomac Cannons (32) 10.00
2002 GS Princeton Devil Rays (30) 10.00
2002 Team Provo Angels (39) 11.00
2002 GS Pulaski Rangers (33) 10.00
2002 GS Quad City River Bandits (30) 11.00
2002 GS Rancho Cucamonga Quakes (30) 12.00
2002 MA Reading Phillies (30) 12.00
2002 MA Reading Area CC Reading Phillies (30) 12.50
2002 MA Reading Phillies Update (30) 9.50
2002 MA Reading Baseball Town (20) 30.00
2002 MA Reading Baseballtown (18) 25.00
2002 MA Reading Baseballtown Pepsi (18) 25.00
2002 CH Richmond Braves (30) 8.00
2002 CH Rochester Red Wings (29) 9.00
2002 GS Rockford RiverHawks (30) 8.50
2002 Team Round Rock Express (30) 9.00
2002 MA Sacramento River Cats (30) 10.00
2002 GS Salem Avalanche (30) 9.00
2002 GS Salem-Keizer Volcanoes (36) 10.00
2002 MA Salt Lake City Stingers (30) 10.00
2002 Team San Angelo Colts (25) 9.00
2002 GS San Antonio Missions (30) 10.00
2002 GS San Bernardino Stampede (30) 10.00
2002 GS San Jose Giants (30) 9.00
2002 GS Sarasota Red Sox (30) 8.00
2002 MA Savannah Sand Gnats (30) 10.00
2002 Team Schaumburg Flyers (23) 10.00
2002 CH Scranton/Wilkes-Barre Red Barons (30) 10.00
2002 Team Scrantron/WB Red Baron Magnets (4) 8.00
2002 GS Shreveport Swamp Dragons (26) 15.00
2002 GS Shreve. Swamp Dragons Update Auto.(1) 15.00
2002 MA Sioux Falls Canaries (30) 8.00
2002 MA Somerset Patriots (30) 7.50
2002 MA South Atlantic League Prospects (33) 12.50
2002 MA South Bend Silver Hawks (29) 10.00
2002 GS Southern League Top Prospects (30) 14.00
2002 GS South Georgia Waves (30) 12.00
2002 GS Spokane Indians (32) 10.00
2002 MA Staten Island Yankees (35) 10.00
2002 GS St. Lucie Mets (33) 12.00
2002 GS St. Lucie Mets Update (1) 5.00
2002 GS St. Lucie Mets Update Autographed (1) 15.00
2002 GS Stockton Ports (30) 13.00
2002 TM St. Paul Saints (32) 9.00
2002 CH Syracuse SkyChiefs (30) 10.00
2002 MA Tacoma Rainiers (30) 10.00
2002 MA Tampa Yankees (30) 10.00
2002 GS Tennessee Smokies (30) 10.00
2002 GS Texas League Top Prospects (24) 10.00
2002 CH Toledo Mud Hens (31) 10.00
2002 MA Trenton Thunder (30) 11.00
2002 Team Tri-City Dust Devils (36) 12.50
2002 MA Tucson Sidewinders (30) 10.00
2002 Team Tulsa Drillers (29) 13.00
2002 MA Vancouver Canadians (42) 12.50
2002 GS Vermont Expos (36) 10.00
2002 GS Vero Beach Dodgers (31) 12.00
2002 GS Visalia Oaks (30) 13.00

2002 CH Washington Wild Things (30) 8.00
2002 Team Waterloo Bucks (18) 6.00
2002 MA West Michigan Whitecaps (30) 10.00
2002 GS West Tenn Diamond Jaxx (30) 12.50
2002 GS West Tenn Diamond Jaxx Update (6) 12.00
2002 GS Wichita Wranglers (29) 10.00
2002 CH Williamsport Crosscutters (34) 10.00
2002 CH Wilmington Blue Rocks (30) 9.00
2002 CH Wilmington Blue Rocks sheet (9) 10.00
2002 TM Winnipeg Goldeyes (30) 10.00
2002 CH Winston-Salem Warthogs (30) 11.00
2002 CH Winston-Salem Warthogs Update (30) 10.00
2002 MA Wisconsin Timber Rattlers (28) 8.00
2002 GS Yakima Bears (34) 12.00

34 Brian Bruney .25
35 Chris Gruler .25
36 Merkin Valdez-Mateo .25
37 Clint Everts .65
38 Scott Moore .25
39 Bryan Bullington .75
40 Zach Parker .35

2003 Just Rookies 2002 Autographs

JEFF FRANCOEUR of

Autographed cards were made available directly to consumers in four varieties. Base autographs, with player inset portraits framed in white, were produced in editions of 50 to 500, as indicated parenthetically in the checklist. Silver parallels were in an edition of 375 each, golds in a 100-per-card edition and blacks were limited to 25 each.

MT
Common Base (White) Player: 6.00
Silver: 1-2X
Production 375 Each
Gold: 2X
Production 100 Each
Black: 2.5X
Production 25 Each
1 Wes Bankston (200) 8.00
2 Jake Blalock (400) 6.00
3 Gregor Blanco (400) 6.00
4 Taggert Bozied (100) 10.00
5 Brian Bruney (500) 6.00
6 Bryan Bullington (500) 15.00
7 Shin-Soo Choo (50) 10.00
8 Francisco Cruceta (400) 6.00
9 Clint Everts (400) 7.50
10 Jonathan Figueroa (400) 6.00
11 Jeff Francoeur (400) 20.00
12 Khalil Greene (50) 15.00
13 John-Ford Griffin (400) 6.00
14 Chris Gruler (400) 6.00
15 Rudy Guillen (200) 10.00
16 Corey Hart (400) 6.00
17 Jeremy Hermida (400) 8.00
18 Justin Huber (50) 10.00
19 Travis Ishikawa (400) 6.00
20 Todd Linden (50) 10.00
21 James Loney (200) 12.00
22 Andy Marte (50) 12.00
23 Manny Mateo (400) 6.00
24 Dan Meyer (300) 7.50
25 Scott Moore (500) 6.00
26 Laynce Nix (400) 6.00
27 Zach Parker (400) 6.00
28 Kyle Pawelczyk (400) 6.00
29 Felix Pie (200) 10.00
30 Jason Pridie (400) 8.00
31 Hanley Ramirez (200) 20.00
32 Sergio Santos (400) 9.00
33 Micah Schilling (400) 6.00
34 Denard Span (400) 6.00
35 Jason Stokes (100) 10.00
36 Chad Tracy (400) 6.50
37 B.J. Upton (50) 30.00
38 Matt Whitney (200) 8.00
39 Dontrelle Willis (100) 8.00
40 C.J. Wilson (400) 6.00

2003 Just Rookies 2002

LAYNCE NIX of

Many of the top players from the 2002 draft are featured in Just Minors' first issue for 2003. In an innovative marketing move, the company made the cards available directly to consumers as sets, singles or multiple-card lots. There was no retail packaging of the product. Card fronts have borderless player photos on which team logos have been removed. An inset repeat of the player's head is at lower-right, bordered in either white for base cards, or black, gold or silver for limited-edition parallels. Base cards were issued in an edition of 22,000 each. Silver parallels were in an edition of 5,000 each, golds at 1,000 and blacks at 50 serially numbered cards each. The Silver and Gold parallels were sold only as complete sets. The blacks were sold only as singles, with a limit of one card per player.

MT
Complete Base Set (40): 7.00
Common Player: .25
Complete Silver Set (40): 10.00
Silver Singles: 1.5X
Complete Gold Set (40): 15.00
Gold Singles: 2.5X
Blacks: 25X
1 B.J. Upton .50
2 Khalil Greene .50
3 Jeremy Hermida .35
4 Chad Tracy .35
5 Francisco Cruceta .35
6 Hanley Ramirez 1.50
7 Jeff Francoeur 1.50
8 Kyle Pawelczyk .25
9 Justin Huber .40
10 Gregor Blanco .25
11 Andy Marte 1.00
12 Taggert Bozied .50
13 Felix Pie .75
14 Dontrelle Willis 1.00
15 J.J. Stokes .75
16 Corey Hart .50
17 Sergio Santos .35
18 Colt Griffin .25
19 Shin-Soo Choo .35
20 Todd Linden .25
21 Jonathan Figueroa .25
22 James Loney .50
23 Jason Pridie .25
24 Denard Span .25
25 Matt Whitney .25
26 Dan Meyer .50
27 Rudy Guillen .25
28 Micah Schilling .25
29 Wes Bankston .25
30 Travis Ishikawa .25
31 Jake Blalock .25
32 C.J. Wilson .25
33 Laynce Nix .50

2003 Just Prospects Preview

DIONER NAVARRO c
Just Minors.

Ten players expected to make a splash in 2004 were selected for this edition. Unsigned cards were available in complete-set form, either directly from the manufacturer (gold) or through its network of retailers (base, silver and black). Production was announced as 15,000 base sets, 5,000 silver, 1,000 gold and 50 serially-numbered sets in black.

MT
Complete Set (10): 6.00
Common Player: .50
Silver: 1.5X
Gold: 1X
Black: 8X
1 Robinson Cano 1.00
2 Franklin Gutierrez .50
3 Felix Hernandez 1.00
4 Edwin Jackson .50
5 Chris Lubanski .50
6 Lastings Milledge .75
7 Greg Miller .75
8 Dioner Navarro .50
9 Mark Prior 1.00
10 Brad Sullivan .50

2003 Just Prospects Preview - Autographs

Ten elite prospects were selected for this edition. Autographed cards were available directly from the manufacturer. Gold cards, in an edition of 100 each were sold only as complete sets. White and black versions were sold singly in editions of 50 and 25, respectively.

MT
Complete Set, Gold (10): 110.00
Common Player, Gold: 7.50
White: 2X
Black: 3X
1 Robinson Cano 10.00
2 Franklin Gutierrez 9.00
3 Felix Hernandez 12.00
4 Edwin Jackson 9.00
5 Chris Lubanski 9.00
6 Lastings Milledge 10.00
7 Greg Miller 9.00
8 Dioner Navarro 9.00
9 Mark Prior 60.00
10 Brad Sullivan 9.00

2003 Just Rookies Preview

ANTHONY GWYNN
JUST ROOKIES PREVIEW

Ten elite prospects were selected for this edition. Unsigned cards were available in complete-set form either directly from the manufacturer (gold) or through its network of retailers (base, silver and black). Production was announced as 15,000 base sets, 5,000 silver, 1,000 gold and 50 serially-numbered sets in black.

MT
Complete Set (10): 6.50
Common Player: .50
Silver: 1.5X
Gold: 1X
Black: 8X
1 Anderson Amador .50
2 Eric Duncan 1.00
3 Anthony Gwynn .75
4 Cole Hamels 1.00
5 Adam LaRoche 1.00
6 Adam Loewen 1.00
7 David Murphy .50
8 Mark Prior 1.00
9 Alexis Rios .50
10 Delmon Young 1.00

2003 Just Rookies Preview - Autographs

Ten elite prospects were selected for this edition. Autographed cards were available directly from the manufacturer. Gold cards, in an edition of 100 each were sold only as complete sets. White and black versions were sold singly in editions of 50 and 25, respectively.

MT
Complete Set, Gold (10): 100.00
Common Player, Gold: 7.50
White: 2X
Black: 3X
1 Anderson Amador 7.50
2 Eric Duncan 10.00
3 Anthony Gwynn 9.00
4 Cole Hamels 10.00
5 Adam LaRoche 10.00
6 Adam Loewen 10.00
7 David Murphy 7.50
8 Mark Prior 40.00
9 Alexis Rios 7.50
10 Delmon Young 20.00

2003 Just Rookies 2003

ANDY LAROCHE SS
JUST ROOKIES

Many of the top players from the 2003 draft are featured in Just Minors' final issue for 2003. As with Just Rookies 2002, the company made the cards available directly to consumers as sets, singles or multiple-card lots. There was no retail packaging of the product. Base cards were issued in an edition of 15,000 each. Silver parallels were in an edition of 5,000 each, golds at 1,000 and blacks at 50 serially numbered cards each. The Silver and Gold parallels were sold only as complete sets. The blacks were sold only as singles, with a limit of one card per player.

MT
Complete Base Set (80): 13.00
Common Player: .25
Complete Silver Set (80): 16.00
Silver Singles: 1.5X
Complete Gold Set (80): 20.00
Gold Singles: 2.5X
Blacks: 15X
1 Anderson Amador .50
2 Luis Atilano .50
3 Paul Bacot .25
4 Aarom Baldiris .50
5 Jimmy Barthmaier .25
6 Daric Barton .60
7 Chad Billingsley .65
8 Andres Blanco .25
9 Larry Broadway .30
10 Robinson Cano .75
11 Matt Chico .25
12 Hu Chin-Lung .75
13 Jesse Crain .40
14 Juan Dominguez .35
15 Dennis Dove .35
16 Eric Duncan 1.00
17 Jesse English .30
18 Brian Finch .25
19 Enrique Gonzalez .25
20 Tom Gorzelanny .50
21 Franklin Gutierrez .75
22 Anthony Gwynn .75
23 Josh Hall .25
24 Mickey Hall .25
25 Ryan Hannaman .25
26 Matt Harrison .25
27 Felix Hernandez 1.25
28 Shawn Hill .40
29 Jason Hirsh .25
30 James Houser .50
31 Kevin Howard .25
32 Edwin Jackson .50
33 Blair Johnson .50
34 Kody Kirkland .40
35 Jason Kubel .65
36 Andy LaRoche 1.00
37 Donald Levinski .25
38 Kenny Lewis .25
39 Bobby Livingston .25
40 Adam Loewen 1.00
41 Chris Lubanski 1.00
42 Luis Martinez .50
43 Macay McBride .25
44 Brian McCann .25
45 Dallas McPherson .65
46 Lastings Milledge 1.00
47 Greg Miller 1.00
48 Daniel Moore .25
49 Steve Moss .25
50 David Murphy .75
51 Darin Naatjes .25
52 Dioner Navarro .75
53 Ramon Nivar .50
54 David Pauley .25
55 Elizardo Ramirez .25
56 Jeremy Reed .50
57 JoJo Reyes .50
58 Tony Richie .25
59 Alexis Rios .50
60 Arturo Rivas .25
61 Jarrod Saltalamacchia .40
62 Dennis Sarfate .50
63 Chris Seddon .25
64 Alexander Smit .50
65 Sean Smith .25
66 Brad Snyder .40
67 Brian Snyder .35
68 Edgar Soto .25
69 Tim Stauffer .75
70 Jake Stevens .25
71 Brad Sullivan .50
72 Kazuhito Tadano .75
73 Anderson Tavarez .50
74 James Tomlin .50
75 Rusty Tucker .50
76 Doug Waechter .25
77 Ryan Wagner .75
78 Brandon Weeden .25
79 Delmon Young 1.00
80 Joel Zumaya .40

2003 Just Rookies 2003 Autographs - Base

Autographed cards were made available directly to consumers in four varieties. Base autographs were produced in editions of 50 to 875 as indicated parenthetically in the checklist. Silver parallels of only 16 players were produced for retail-only distribution in an edition of 375 each. Gold autographs of all 80 players were in a 100-per-card edition available only as complete sets. Black autographs were limited to 25 for each player.

MT
Complete Set (80): 600.00
Common Player: 6.00
Complete Gold Set (80):
Gold Players: 2X
Blacks: 2-3X
1 Anderson Amador (50) 10.00
2 Luis Atilano (375) 6.00
3 Paul Bacot (375) 6.00
4 Aarom Baldiris (375) 8.00
5 Jimmy Barthmaier (875) 6.00
6 Daric Barton (375) 8.00
7 Chad Billingsley (375) 8.00
8 Andres Blanco (375) 6.00
9 Larry Broadway (875) 6.00
10 Robinson Cano (50) 10.00
11 Matt Chico (375) 6.00
12 Hu Chin-Lung (50) 15.00
13 Jesse Crain (375) 6.00
14 Juan Dominguez (375) 8.00
15 Dennis Dove (375) 8.00
16 Eric Duncan (350) 20.00
17 Jesse English (375) 6.00
18 Brian Finch (375) 6.00
19 Enrique Gonzalez (375) 6.00
20 Tom Gorzelanny (375) 6.00
21 Franklin Gutierrez (50) 20.00
22 Anthony Gwynn (100) 12.00
23 Josh Hall (875) 6.00
24 Mickey Hall (875) 6.00
25 Ryan Hannaman (375) 8.00
26 Matt Harrison (375) 6.00
27 Felix Hernandez (375) 15.00
28 Shawn Hill (375) 8.00
29 Jason Hirsh (875) 6.00
30 James Houser (875) 6.00
31 Kevin Howard (375) 6.00
32 Edwin Jackson (50) 15.00
33 Blair Johnson (375) 8.00
34 Kody Kirkland (375) 8.00
35 Jason Kubel (375) 9.00
36 Andy LaRoche (350) 12.00
37 Donald Levinski (375) 6.00
38 Kenny Lewis (375) 6.00
39 Bobby Livingston (875) 6.00
40 Adam Loewen (50) 20.00
41 Chris Lubanski (375) 10.00
42 Luis Martinez (375) 8.00
43 Macay McBride (375) 8.00
44 Brian McCann (375) 8.00
45 Dallas McPherson (50) 20.00
46 Lastings Milledge (350) 12.00
47 Greg Miller (50) 20.00
48 Daniel Moore (375) 6.00
49 Steve Moss (375) 6.00
50 David Murphy (100) 10.00
51 Darin Naatjes (875) 6.00
52 Dioner Navarro (200) 10.00
53 Ramon Nivar (375) 6.00
54 David Pauley (375) 6.00
55 Elizardo Ramirez (375) 6.00
56 Jeremy Reed (375) 10.00
57 JoJo Reyes (375) 8.00
58 Tony Richie (375) 6.00
59 Alexis Rios (50) 20.00
60 Arturo Rivas (875) 6.00
61 Jarrod Saltalamacchia (375) 7.50
62 Dennis Sarfate (375) 8.00
63 Chris Seddon (375) 6.00
64 Alexander Smit (375) 8.00
65 Sean Smith (375) 6.00
66 Brad Snyder (875) 6.00
67 Brian Snyder (875) 6.00
68 Edgar Soto (375) 6.00
69 Tim Stauffer (875) 6.00
70 Jake Stevens (375) 6.00

71	Brad Sullivan (350)	7.00
72	Kazuhito Tadano (50)	15.00
73	Anderson Tavarez (875)	8.00
74	James Tomlin (375)	8.00
75	Rusty Tucker (375)	8.00
76	Doug Waechter (375)	8.00
77	Ryan Wagner (375)	8.00
78	Brandon Weeden (375)	8.00
79	Delmon Young (50)	40.00
80	Joel Zumaya (375)	8.00

2003 Just Rookies 2003 Autographs - Silver

Autographed cards were made available directly to consumers in four varieties. Silver parallels of only 16 players were produced for retail-only distribution in an edition of 375 each.

		MT
Complete Set (16):		125.00
Common Player:		7.50
1	Anderson Amador	7.50
10	Robinson Cano	9.00
12	Hu Chin-Lung	10.00
16	Eric Duncan	9.00
21	Franklin Gutierrez	7.50
22	Anthony Gwynn	9.00
27	Felix Hernandez	9.00
36	Andy LaRoche	9.00
40	Adam Loewen	12.00
41	Chris Lubanski	7.50
45	Dallas McPherson	10.00
46	Lastings Milledge	7.50
47	Greg Miller	9.00
52	Dioner Navarro	7.50
59	Alexis Rios	9.00
71	Brad Sullivan	7.50

2003 Just Stars 2003 Prototype Gold

		MT
JS03.JF	Jeff Francoeur	2.50

2003 Just Stars

Some of the top players selected in the 2002 and 2003 drafts, as well as key players making some of their earliest baseball card appearances, were featured in this set. As with other recent Just Minors issues, cards were not packaged in traditional wax packs, but were available as singles and/or sets either directly from the manufacturer or through its hobby retailer outlets. The base (white) set was produced in an edition of 10,000. Silver sets were produced in an edition of 5,000; golds to 1,000 and blacks in an edition of 50 serially numbered cards each.

		MT
Complete Set (50):		8.00
Common Player:		.15
Complete Silver Set (50):		10.00
Silver Singles:		1.5X
Complete Gold Set (50):		12.00
Gold Singles:		2.5X
Black:		15X
1	Joaquin Arias	.25
2	Eric Aybar	.25
3	Josh Barfield	.40
4	Bobby Basham	.40
5	Ronald Belisario (Belizario)	.15
6	Bobby Brownlie	.40
7	Miguel Cabrera	.85
8	Alberto Callaspo	.35
9	Jose Capellan	.25
10	Fausto Carmona	.40
11	Jose Castillo	.15
12	Hu Chin-Lung	.40
13	Jose Raphael Diaz	.20
14	Zach Duke	.35
15	Elijah Dukes	.25
16	J.D. Durbin	.35
17	Justin Germano	.15
18	Byron Gettis	.15
19	Alfredo Gonzalez	.15
20	Edgar Gonzalez	.15
21	Derek (Derick) Grigsby	.15
22	Jeremy Guthrie	.40
23	Franklin Gutierrez	.40
24	Cole Hamels	.75
25	Zach Hammes	.15
26	Dan Haren	.40
27	Brendan Harris	.15
28	Blake Hawksworth	.15
29	Trevor Hutchinson	.15
30	Edwin Jackson	.40
31	Kevin Jepsen	.15
32	Adam Loewen	.75
33	John Maine	.50
34	John McCurdy	.15
35	Dustin McGowan	.25
36	Brian Miller	.15
37	Dustin Nippert	.15
38	Leo Nunez	.15
39	Vince Perkins	.40
40	Mark Schramek	.15
41	Kelly Shoppach	.15
42	Andy Sisco	.40
43	Grady Sizemore	.75
44	Chris Snyder	.15
45	Kazuhito Tadano	.75
46	Ferdin Tejeda	.15
47	Jose Valdez	.15
48	Joe Valentine	.15
49	Adam Wainwright	.40
50	Matt Yeatman	.15

2003 Just Stars Autographs - Base

Autographed cards were made available directly to consumers in four varieties. Base autographs were produced in editions of 50 to 875, as indicated parenthetically in the checklist. Silver parallels of only 15 players were produced for retail-only distribution in an edition of 375 each. Gold autographs of all 50 players were in a 100-per-card edition available only as complete sets. Black autographs were limited to 25 for each player.

		MT
Complete Set (50):		365.00
Common Player:		6.00
Complete Gold Set:		300.00
Gold Singles:		1.5X
Blacks:		2-3X
1	Joaquin Arias (375)	8.00
2	Eric Aybar (375)	8.00
3	Josh Barfield (50)	15.00
4	Bobby Basham (375)	8.00
5	Ronald Belisario (Belizario) (875)	6.00
6	Bobby Brownlie (50)	20.00
7	Miguel Cabrera (50)	30.00
8	Alberto Callaspo (375)	10.00
9	Jose Capellan (375)	9.00
10	Fausto Carmona (875)	10.00
11	Jose Castillo (875)	6.00
12	Hu Chin-Lung (50)	20.00
13	Jose Raphael Diaz (375)	7.00
14	Zach Duke (375)	15.00
15	Elijah Dukes (500)	6.00
16	J.D. Durbin (375)	9.00
17	Justin Germano (375)	6.00
18	Byron Gettis (375)	8.00
19	Alfredo Gonzalez (875)	6.00
20	Edgar Gonzalez (375)	8.00
21	Derek (Derick) Grigsby (375)	6.00
22	Jeremy Guthrie (50)	20.00
23	Franklin Gutierrez (500)	9.00
24	Cole Hamels (250)	15.00
25	Zach Hammes (375)	6.00
26	Dan Haren (50)	15.00
27	Brendan Harris (375)	8.00
28	Blake Hawksworth (500)	7.00
29	Trevor Hutchinson (875)	6.00
30	Edwin Jackson (500)	7.00
31	Kevin Jepsen (375)	6.00
32	Adam Loewen (500)	20.00
33	John Maine (500)	15.00
34	John McCurdy (375)	6.00
35	Dustin McGowan (375)	12.00
36	Brian Miller (375)	8.00
37	Dustin Nippert (375)	8.00
38	Leo Nunez (375)	8.00
39	Vince Perkins (50)	8.00
40	Mark Schramek (875)	6.00
41	Kelly Shoppach (375)	8.00
42	Andy Sisco (875)	9.00
43	Grady Sizemore (50)	20.00
44	Chris Snyder (375)	8.00
45	Kazuhito Tadano (875)	20.00
46	Ferdin Tejeda (375)	6.00
47	Jose Valdez (375)	6.00
48	Joe Valentine (375)	8.00
49	Adam Wainwright (400)	15.00
50	Matt Yeatman (375)	8.00

2003 Just Stars Autographs - Silver

Autographed cards were made available directly to consumers in four varieties. Silver parallels of only 15 players were produced for retail-only distribution in an edition of 375 each.

		MT
Complete Set (15):		160.00
Common Player:		7.50
3	Josh Barfield	10.00
6	Bobby Brownlie	10.00
7	Miguel Cabrera	25.00
12	Hu Chin-Lung	15.00
15	Elijah Dukes	7.50
22	Jeremy Guthrie	10.00
23	Franklin Gutierrez	15.00
24	Cole Hamels	15.00
26	Dan Haren	10.00
28	Blake Hawksworth	10.00
30	Edwin Jackson	10.00
32	Adam Loewen	15.00
33	John Maine	12.00
39	Vince Perkins	10.00
43	Grady Sizemore	15.00

2003 Upper Deck USA Baseball

Offered only as a boxed set featuring 27 regular cards, two autographed cards and an autographed jersey card, this issue features a coming generation of major league stars.

		MT
Sealed Factory Set (30):		40.00
Complete Base Set (27):		7.50
Common Player:		.25
1	Justin Orenduff	.25
2	Micah Owings	.25
3	Steven Register	.25
4	Huston Street	.50
5	Justin Verlander	2.00
6	Jered Weaver	4.00
7	Matt Campbell	.25
8	Stephen Head	.50
9	Mark Romanczuk	.50
10	Jeff Clement	.50
11	Mike Nickeas	.25
12	Tyler Greene	.25
13	Paul Janish	.25
14	Jeff Larish	.50
15	Eric Patterson	.25
16	Dustin Pedroia	2.00
17	Michael Griffin	.25
18	Brent Lillibridge	.25
19	Danny Putnam	.50
20	Seth Smith	.25
21	Ray Tanner	.15
22	Dick Cooke	.15
23	Mark Scalf	.15
24	Mike Weathers	.15
25	Team Card	.15
26	Commemorative Card	.10
27	Checklist	.10

2003 Upper Deck USA Baseball Autographs

The Team USA players in the 2003 Upper Deck boxed set each signed 1,000 cards which appeared two per set. Cards signed in red ink are numbered to 750 per player; cards signed in blue are in an edition of 250 each.

		MT
Common Red Autograph:		2.00
Common Blue Autograph:		7.00
Blue Stars:		2.5X
1	Justin Orenduff	3.50
2	Micah Owings	10.00
3	Steven Register	2.00
4	Huston Street	7.50
5	Justin Verlander	40.00
6	Jered Weaver	55.00
7	Matt Campbell	3.00
8	Stephen Head	10.00
9	Mark Romanczuk	4.00
10	Jeff Clement	15.00
11	Mike Nickeas	2.00
12	Tyler Greene	5.00
13	Paul Janish	3.50
14	Jeff Larish	9.00
15	Eric Patterson	10.00
16	Dustin Pedroia	50.00
17	Michael Griffin	2.00
18	Brent Lillibridge	2.00
19	Danny Putnam	7.50
20	Seth Smith	6.00

2003 Upper Deck USA Baseball Autographed Jerseys

The Team USA players in the 2003 Upper Deck boxed set each signed 500 game-used jersey-swatch cards which were randomly inserted one per set. Cards signed in red ink are numbered to 350 per player; cards signed in blue are in an edition of 150 each.

		MT
Common Red Autograph:		5.00
Common Blue Autograph:		12.00
Blue Stars:		2.5X
1	Justin Orenduff	8.00
2	Micah Owings	15.00
3	Steven Register	5.00
4	Huston Street	11.00
5	Justin Verlander	50.00
6	Jered Weaver	80.00
7	Matt Campbell	6.00
8	Stephen Head	13.50
9	Mark Romanczuk	5.00
10	Jeff Clement	20.00
11	Mike Nickeas	5.00
12	Tyler Greene	6.00
13	Paul Janish	5.00
14	Jeff Larish	16.00
15	Eric Patterson	5.00
16	Dustin Pedroia	75.00
17	Michael Griffin	6.00
18	Brent Lillibridge	4.00
19	Danny Putnam	15.00
20	Seth Smith	12.50

2003 Minor League Team Sets

Manufacturer abbreviations used are: GS - Grandstand, MA - Multi-Ad, CH - Choice, TM - Team

221 Sets and Variations — MT

Year	Set	Price
2003	GS Aberdeen IronBirds (30)	14.00
2003	GS Aberdeen IronBirds Update (3)	11.00
2003	MA Akron Aeros (29)	12.00
2003	Team Alaska Goldpanners (24)	20.00
2003	Team Alaska Goldpanners Bonus Cards (3)	9.00
2003	MA Albuquerque Isotopes (32)	12.00
2003	GS Altoona Curve (30)	11.00
2003	GS Altoona Curve Update (6)	12.50
2003	GS Apalachian League Top Prospects (30)	13.50
2003	GS Arkansas Travelers (31)	12.00
2003	GS Asheville Tourists	16.00
2003	GS Asheville Tourists Update (12)	15.00
2003	Team Atlantic League All-Stars (52)	17.50
2003	Team Auburn Doubledays (39)	12.50
2003	MA Augusta Green Jackets (33)	12.50
2003	CH Bangor Lumberjacks (26)	10.00
2003	Team Batavia Muckdogs (39)	13.00
2003	CH Battle Creek Yankees (30)	11.00
2003	MA Beloit Snappers (30)	12.00
2003	MA Beloit Snappers Prospects (6)	14.00
2003	GS Update (9)	12.00
2003	GS Billings Mustangs (30)	10.00
2003	GS Binghamton Mets (30)	11.50
2003	GS Birmingham Barons (29)	11.50
2003	GS Birmingham Barons Update (3)	9.00
2003	GS Bluefield Orioles (34)	12.50
2003	GS Boise Hawks (30)	12.50
2003	GS Bowie Baysox (29)	12.50
2003	MA Brevard County Manatees (30)	11.50
2003	CH Bridgeport Bluefish (30)	9.00
2003	GS Bristol White Sox (31)	12.00
2003	GS Brockton Rox (27)	9.50
2003	CH Brooklyn Cyclones (39)	12.00
2003	CH Buffalo Bisons (30)	12.50
2003	CH Classic Buffalo Bisons (12)	10.00
2003	MA Burlington Bees (30)	11.50
2003	GS California-Carolina Leagues AS (52)	17.50
2003	CH Camden Riversharks (30)	9.50
2003	MA Capital City Bombers (34)	14.00
2003	CH Carolina League Prospects (32)	11.00
2003	Team Carolina Mudcats (31)	12.50
2003	GS Casper Rockies (32)	12.50
2003	TM Cedar Rapids Kernels (31)	11.00
2003	MA Charleston Alley Cats (33)	11.00
2003	MA Charleston RiverDogs (30)	16.00
2003	CH Charlotte Knights (30)	11.50
2003	GS Chattanooga Lookouts (29)	15.00
2003	GS Chillicothe Paints (27)	9.00
2003	GS Clearwater Phillies (30)	13.00
2003	CH Clinton LumberKings (33)	10.00
2003	CH Coastal Bend Aviators (30)	10.00
2003	MA Colorado Springs Sky Sox (30)	11.00
2003	CH Columbus Clippers (30)	15.00
2003	GS Danville Braves (32)	12.50
2003	MA Dayton Dragons (30)	14.50
2003	CH Daytona Cubs (30)	12.00
2003	MA Delmarva Shorebirds (30)	9.00
2003	GS Dunedin Blue Jays (30)	12.00
2003	CH Durham Bulls (30)	14.50
2003	GS Eastern League Top Prospects (31)	11.00
2003	GS Eastern League Greats - Set A (10)	22.50
2003	GS Eastern League Greats - Set B (10)	12.50
2003	GS Edinburg Roadrunners (30)	9.50
2003	MA Edmonton Trappers (30)	12.50
2003	GS Elizabethton Twins (31)	11.00
2003	GS El Paso Diablos (30)	12.50
2003	GS Erie SeaWolves (28)	10.00
2003	GS Eugene Emeralds (32)	13.00
2003	GS Everett Aquasox (30)	14.50
2003	Team Fargo-Moorhead RedHawks (30)	10.00
2003	GS Florida State League Prospects (25)	13.50
2003	GS Frederick Keys (30)	13.00
2003	GS Frederick Keys "No Smoking" (30)	11.00
2003	MA Fresno Grizzlies (30)	11.50
2003	GS Frisco RoughRiders (35)	25.00
2003	Team Frisco RoughRiders (31)	11.00
2003	GS Ft. Myers Miracle (30)	10.00
2003	GS Ft. Wayne Wizards (29)	11.00
2003	TM Ft. Wayne Wizards Strip Set (5)	9.00
2003	Team Gary Southshore RailCats (28)	11.00
2003	MA Great Falls White Sox (30)	11.50
2003	MA Greensboro Bats (30)	13.00
2003	GS Greenville Braves (29)	11.50
2003	MA Hagerstown Suns (36)	12.00
2003	GS Harrisburg Senators (33)	11.00
2003	GS Helena Brewers Top Prospects (4)	5.00
2003	MA Hickory Crawdads (32)	13.00
2003	MA Hickory Crawdads Update (33)	12.50
2003	GS High Desert Mavericks (34)	12.50
2003	GS Hudson Valley Renegades (35)	10.00
2003	TM Huntsville Stars (29)	22.50
2003	CH Indianapolis Indians (30)	11.00
2003	GS Inland Empire 66ers (31)	12.00
2003	CH International League All-Stars (31)	11.00
2003	CH International League Prospects (30)	11.00
2003	GS Iowa Cubs (30)	13.00
2003	GS Jacksonville Suns (30)	10.00
2003	GS Johnson City Cardinals (21)	10.00
2003	Team Jupiter Hammerheads (37)	20.00
2003	GS Kane County Cougars (31)	10.00
2003	TM Kane County Cougars/Sponsor (31)	20.00
2003	GS Kane County Cougars Update (10)	15.00
2003	MA Kannapolis Intimidators (36)	12.00
2003	CH Kingsport Mets (40)	12.50
2003	GS Kingsport Mets Update (2)	12.00
2003	CH Kinston Indians (31)	14.50
2003	CH Lake County Captains (31)	10.00
2003	CH Lake County Captains Update (30)	14.00
2003	GS Lake Elsinore Storm (30)	12.50
2003	GS Lakeland Tigers (29)	11.00
2003	MA Lakewood BlueClaws (35)	11.50
2003	GS Lancaster JetHawks (30)	12.50
2003	GS Lansing Lugnuts (30)	12.50
2003	GS Las Vegas 51s (32)	15.00
2003	MA Lexington Legends (31)	12.00
2003	CH Long Island Ducks (29)	12.00
2003	GS Louisville Bats (38)	22.50
2003	CH Lowell Spinners (39)	50.00
2003	GS Lowell Spinners Update (1)	5.00
2003	CH Lynchburg Hillcats (30)	12.50
2003	TM Lynchburg Hillcats (30)	15.00
2003	CH Martinsville Astros (30)	12.50
2003	MA Memphis Redbirds (30)	12.50
2003	GS Midland RockHounds (26)	10.00
2003	Team Midland RockHounds (30)	60.00
2003	CH Midwest League All-Stars (69)	12.50
2003	GS Midwest League Prospects (29)	11.00
2003	GS Missoula Osprey (36)	11.00
2003	GS Mobile BayBears (29)	16.00
2003	GS Modesto A's (29)	10.00
2003	CH Myrtle Beach Pelicans (30)	12.50
2003	MA Nashville Sounds (30)	13.00
2003	CH Newark Bears (30)	13.00
2003	GS New Britain Rock Cats (32)	10.00
2003	GS New Haven Ravens (29)	12.50
2003	GS New Jersey Cardinals (29)	11.00
2003	GS New Jersey Cardinals 10th Anniv. (15)	12.50
2003	WTC New Jersey Jackals (26)	9.50
2003	MA New Orleans Zephyrs (31)	12.00
2003	CH Norfolk Tides (37)	12.50
2003	GS Norwich Navigators (29)	12.00
2003	MA Ogden Raptors (36)	12.50
2003	MA Oklahoma RedHawks (30)	10.00
2003	Team Omaha Royals (26)	11.00
2003	GS Oneonta Tigers Top Prospects (3)	8.00
2003	CH Ottawa Lynx (30)	12.50
2003	MA Pacific Coast League All-Stars (30)	12.50

2003	MA Pacific Coast League Prospects (36)	13.00
2003	TM Palm Beach Cardinals (36)	25.00
2003	CH Pawtucket Red Sox (30)	12.00
2003	DD Pawtucket Red Sox Foldout (31)	15.00
2003	MA Peoria Chiefs (30)	13.00
2003	MA Peoria Chiefs Update (30)	40.00
2003	MA Portland Beavers (28)	11.50
2003	GS Portland Sea Dogs (35)	11.00
2003	CH Potomac Cannons (30)	10.00
2003	GS Princeton Devil Rays (30)	10.00
2003	TM Princeton Devil Rays (4)	45.00
2003	TM Provo Angels (30)	60.00
2003	CH Pulaski Blue Jays (37)	11.00
2003	GS Quad City River Bandits (36)	12.50
2003	GS Rancho Cucamonga Quakes (30)	12.50
2003	MA Reading Phillies (30)	
2003	MA Reading Area CC Reading Phillies (30)	12.50
2003	CH Richmond Braves (30)	9.00
2003	CH Rochester Red Wings (31)	11.00
2003	GS Rockford RiverHawks (30)	9.50
2003	MA Rome Braves (31)	15.00
2003	Team Round Rock Express (30)	17.50
2003	MA Sacramento River Cats (30)	11.50
2003	GS Salem Avalanche (30)	11.00
2003	GS Salem-Keizer Volcanoes (36)	12.00
2003	MA Salt Lake City Stingers (34)	12.50
2003	Team San Angelo Colts (35)	9.50
2003	CH San Antonio Missions (31)	11.00
2003	CH San Antonio Missions Update (30)	12.00
2003	GS San Jose Giants (30)	10.00
2003	GS San Jose Giants Update (1)	8.00
2003	GS Sarasota Red Sox (30)	10.00
2003	MA Savannah Sand Gnats (30)	12.50
2003	GS Savannah Sand Gnats Greats (17)	11.00
2003	Team Schaumburg Flyers (25)	
2003	CH Scranton/Wilkes-Barre Red Barons (30)	
2003	TM S/W-B Lackawanna Legends Magnets (9)	15.00
2003	MA Sioux Falls Canaries (30)	9.00
2003	MA So. Atlantic League Prospects (36)	10.00
2003	GS South Bend Silver Hawks (31)	11.00
2003	GS Southern League Top Prospects (31)	10.00
2003	GS Spokane Indians (32)	10.00
2003	GS Staten Island Yankees (36)	10.00
2003	GS St. Lucie Mets (35)	12.50
2003	GS St. Lucie Mets Update	15.00
2003	GS St. Lucie Mets Update (1)	30.00
2003	MA Stockton Ports (30)	12.50
2003	CH Syracuse Skychiefs (30)	12.00
2003	MA Tacoma Rainiers (31)	11.50
2003	GS Tampa Yankees (30)	10.00
2003	GS Tennessee Smokies (30)	10.00
2003	CH Toledo Mud Hens (30)	11.00
2003	MA Trenton Thunder (31)	12.50
2003	GS Tri-City Dust Devils (32)	12.50
2003	CH Tri-City Valley Cats (38)	10.00
2003	MA Tucson Sidewinders (36)	13.00
2003	Team Tulsa Drillers (29)	11.00
2003	Team Vancouver Canadians (38)	12.50
2003	GS Vermont Expos (34)	10.00
2003	GS Vero Beach Dodgers (39)	14.50
2003	GS Visalia Oaks (30)	15.00
2003	CH Washington Wild Things (30)	9.50
2003	CH West Michigan Whitecaps (31)	11.00

2003	GS West Tenn Diamond Jaxx (30)	12.50
2003	GS Wichita Wranglers (30)	11.00
2003	CH Williamsport Crosscutters (36)	12.50
2003	CH Williamsport Crosscutters Legends (5)	6.00
2003	CH Wilm. Blue Rocks In the Show 1 (41)	12.50
2003	CH Wilm. Blue Rocks In the Show 2 (24)	12.50
2003	CH Wilmington Blue Rocks (32)	13.00
2003	Team Winnipeg Goldeyes (30)	8.00
2003	CH Winston-Salem Warthogs (30)	12.50
2003	CH Wisconsin Timber Rattlers (31)	12.50
2003	GS Yakima Bears (34)	14.00

2004 Just Justifiable Preview

Ten elite prospects were selected for this edition. Unsigned cards were available in complete-set form either directly from the manufacturer (gold) or through its network of retailers (white, silver and black). Production was announced as 15,000 white sets, 5,000 silver, 100 serially numbered gold and 50 serially numbered sets in black.

		MT
Complete Set (10):		3.00
Common Player:		.50
Silver:		1.5X
Gold:		5X
Black:		8X
1	Bill Bray	.50
2	Mitch Einertson	.75
3	Josh Fields	.75
4	Dexter Fowler	.50
5	Javier Herrera	1.00
6	Chris Lambert	.50
7	Brandon Moss	.50
8	Yusmeiro Petit	.50
9	Taylor Tankersley	.50
10	Jon Zeringue	.50

2004 Just Justifiable Preview Autographs

Ten elite prospects were selected for this edition. Autographed cards were available directly from the manufacturer. Base (white bordered) version were sold individually, serially numbered to 200. Silvers were numbered to 100 each and only available through retail distribution. Gold cards, in an edition of 50 each were sold only as complete sets. Black versions were sold singly in an edition of 25.

		MT
Complete Set (10):		40.00
Common Player:		4.00
Silver:		1.5X
Gold:		2X
Black:		3X
1	Bill Bray	4.00
2	Mitch Einertson	6.00
3	Josh Fields	4.00
4	Dexter Fowler	4.00
5	Javier Herrera	7.50
6	Chris Lambert	4.00
7	Brandon Moss	4.00
8	Yusmeiro Petit	5.00
9	Taylor Tankersley	4.00
10	Jon Zeringue	5.00

2004 Just Justifiable

Some of the top players selected in the 2004 draft, as well as key players making some of their earliest baseball card appearances, are featured in this set. For the first time in several years, cards were packaged in traditional wax packs, as well as being sold as singles and/or sets either directly from the manufacturer or through its hobby retailer outlets. The base (white) set was produced in an edition of 15,000. Silver sets were produced in an edition of 5,000; golds to 100 and blacks in an edition of 50 serially numbered cards each.

		MT
Complete Set (90):		15.00
Common Player:		.25
Silver:		1.5X
Gold:		16X
Black:		16X
Wax Pack (5):		2.50
Wax Box (18):		30.00
1	Brian Anderson	.25
2	Homer Bailey	.50
3	Scott Baker	.25
4	Joseph Bauserman	.25
5	Brian Bixler	.25
6	Ian Bladergroen	.25
7	Bill Bray	.25
8	Reid Brignac	.25
9	Billy Butler	.50
10	Eric Campbell	.25
11	Gustavo Chacin	.45
12	Ryan Church	.25
13	Jamie D'Antona	.25
14	Brad Davis	.25
15	Jorge de la Rosa	.25
16	Thomas Diamond	.35
17	Andrew Dobies	.25
18	Ryan Doumit	.25
19	Jason Dubois	.25
20	Mitch Einertson	.75
21	Josh Fields	.50
22	Dexter Fowler	.25
23	Matt Fox	.25
24	Jairo Garcia	.25
25	Ryan Garko	.25
26	Greg Golson	.25
27	Jared Gothreaux	.25
28	Curtis Granderson	.25
29	Eric Haberer	.25
30	J.A. Happ	.25
31	Lucas Harrell	.25
32	Gaby Hernandez	.25
33	Javier Herrera	.50
34	J.C. Holt	.25
35	Justin Hoyman	.25
36	Zach Jackson	.25
37	Mark Jecmen	.25
38	Rob Johnson	.25
39	Jason Jones	.25
40	Jeff Keppinger	.25
41	Ian Kinsler	.25
42	Josh Kroeger	.25
43	Chris Lambert	.25
44	Richard Lewis	.25
45	Scott Lewis	.25
46	Adam Lind	.25
47	Tyler Lumsden	.25
48	Paul Maholm	.25
49	Collin Mahoney	.25
50	Gabriel Martinez	.25
51	Eddy Martinez-Esteve	.50
52	Brandon McCarthy	.25
53	Garrett Mock	.25
54	Mike Morse	.25
55	Brandon Moss	.50
56	Chris Nelson	.50
57	Dan Ortmeier	.25
58	Chad Orvella	.25
59	Jon Mark Owings	.25
60	Dustin Pedroia	.25
61	Tony Pena	.25
62	Hunter Pence	.25
63	Yusmeiro Petit	.50
64	Eddie Prasch	.25
65	David Purcey	.25
66	Danny Putnam	.25
67	Omar Quintanilla	.25
68	Ryan Raburn	.25
69	Ramon Ramirez	.25
70	Anthony Reyes	.30
71	Richie Robnett	.35
72	Sean Rodriguez	.25
73	Willie Joe Ronda	.25
74	Brendan Ryan	.25
75	Jeff Salazar	.25
76	Ervin Santana	.25
77	Michael Schlact	.25
78	Ryan Schroyer	.25
79	Steven Shell	.25
80	Ian Snell	.25
81	Huston Street	.50
82	Kurt Suzuki	.25
83	Taylor Tankersley	.25
84	Mark Teahen	.25
85	Matt Tuiasosopo	.50
86	Josh Wahpepah	.25
87	Neil Walker	.25
88	Wes Whisler	.25
89	Tommy Whiteman	.25
90	Jon Zeringue	.25

2004 Just Justifiable Autographs

Autographed cards of 60 of the players in Justifiable 2004 were available in four varieties. Base (white) autographs, were generally produced in an edition of 725 (unless otherwise indicated parenthetically in the checklist). Silver parallels were serially numbered to 200 each and were produced for retail-only distribution. Gold autographs were sold only as complete sets in a 50-per-card edition. Black autographs were limited to 25 for each player.

		MT
Common Player:		3.00
Silver:		1.5X
Complete Set, Gold (60):		350.00
Gold:		2X
Black:		3X
2	Homer Bailey (225)	5.00
4	Joseph Bauserman (225)	4.00
5	Brian Bixler	.25
7	Bill Bray (50)	7.50
11	Gustavo Chacin (475)	6.00
12	Ryan Church	3.00
13	Jamie D'Antona	3.00
14	Brad Davis (225)	4.00
16	Thomas Diamond (225)	6.00
17	Andrew Dobies	3.00
20	Mitch Einertson (1,000)	7.50
21	Josh Fields (350)	5.00
22	Dexter Fowler (350)	5.00
23	Matt Fox	4.00
25	Ryan Garko	4.00
26	Greg Golson (225)	4.00
27	Jared Gothreaux (225)	4.00
29	Eric Haberer	4.00
30	J.A. Happ (225)	4.00
31	Lucas Harrell (225)	4.00
33	Javier Herrera (350)	6.00
34	J.C. Holt	3.00
35	Justin Hoyman	4.00
36	Zach Jackson	3.00
37	Mark Jecmen	3.00
38	Rob Johnson	3.00
39	Jason Jones (225)	3.00
42	Josh Kroeger	4.00
43	Chris Lambert (350)	5.00
46	Adam Lind	3.00
48	Paul Maholm	4.00
49	Collin Mahoney (225)	4.00
52	Brandon McCarthy	3.00
53	Garrett Mock	4.00
54	Mike Morse (350)	4.00
55	Brandon Moss	6.00
56	Chris Nelson	3.00
58	Chad Orvella (225)	4.00
59	Jon Mark Owings (225)	4.00
60	Dustin Pedroia	3.00
61	Tony Pena	3.00
62	Hunter Pence (350)	6.00
63	Yusmeiro Petit	4.00
64	Eddie Prasch	4.00
69	Danny Putnam	3.00
72	Ramon Ramirez	3.00
72	Sean Rodriguez	3.00
76	Ervin Santana	3.00
77	Michael Schlact (225)	4.00
78	Ryan Schroyer	4.00
80	Ian Snell (225)	4.00
81	Huston Street	6.00
82	Kurt Suzuki (350)	4.00
84	Mark Teahen	5.00
86	Josh Wahpepah (225)	4.00
87	Neil Walker	5.00
89	Tommy Whiteman (350)	5.00

2004 Just Prospects Preview

Ten elite prospects were selected for this edition. Unsigned cards were available in complete-set form or as singles in multi-card lots either directly from the manufacturer or through its network of retailers. Production was announced as 15,000 white sets, 5,000 silver, 100 serially numbered gold and 50 serially numbered sets in black.

		MT
Complete Set (10):		2.50
Common Player:		.25
Silver:		1X
Gold:		5X
Black:		8X
1	John Danks	.25
2	Prince Fielder	.50
3	Zack Greinke	.35
4	Conor Jackson	.25
5	Scott Kazmir	.25
6	Nick Markakis	.25
7	Xavier Paul	.25
8	Kyle Sleeth	.25
9	Ian Stewart	.35
10	Rickie Weeks	.50

2004 Just Prospects Preview Autographs

Ten elite prospects were selected for this edition. Autographed cards were available directly from the manufacturer. Base (white bordered) version were sold individually in a serially numbered edition of 200 each. Gold cards were numbered to 50 and sold only as complete sets. Black versions were sold singly in an edition of 25.

		MT
Complete Set (10):		45.00
Common Player:		3.00
Gold:		2X
Black:		3X
1	John Danks	5.00
2	Prince Fielder	15.00
3	Zack Greinke	4.00
4	Conor Jackson	5.00
5	Scott Kazmir	4.00
6	Nick Markakis	6.00
7	Xavier Paul	3.00
8	Kyle Sleeth	4.00
9	Ian Stewart	5.00
10	Rickie Weeks	5.00

2004 Just Prospects

Some of the top players selected in the 2003 and 2004 drafts, as well as key players making some of their earliest baseball card appearances, were featured in this set. As with other recent Just Minors issues, cards were not packaged in traditional wax packs, but were available as singles and/or sets either directly from the manufacturer or through its hobby retailer outlets. The base (white) set was produced in an edition of 15,000. Silver sets were produced in an edition of 5,000; golds to 100 and blacks in an edition of 50 serially numbered cards each.

		MT
Complete Set (90):		15.00
Common Player:		.25
Silver:		1.5X
Gold:		8X
Black:		16X
1	Abe Alvarez	.25
2	Josh Anderson	.25
3	Michael Aubrey	.25
4	Cha Baek	.25
5	Jeff Baker	.25
6	Wladimir Balentien	.50
7	Josh Banks	.25
8	Tim Battle Jr.	.25
9	Denny Bautista	.25
10	Michael Bourn	.25
11	Craig Brazell	.25
12	Jonathan Broxton	.25
13	David Bush	.25
14	Daniel Cabrera	.25
15	Melky Cabrera	.50
16	Brent Cleven	.25
17	Tyler Clippard	.25
18	Shane Costa	.25
19	John Danks	.25
20	Jamie D'Antona	.25
21	David DeJesus	.25
22	Matt DeSalvo	.25
23	Victor Diaz	.25
24	Jake Dittler	.25
25	Steve Doetsch	.50
26	Edwin Encarnacion	.25
27	Matt Esquivel	.25
28	Andre Ethier	.25
29	Prince Fielder	1.00
30	Richie Gardner	.25
31	Joey Gathright	.50
32	Tony Giarratano	.50
33	Ryan Goleski	.25
34	Ruben Gotay	.25
35	Zack Greinke	.50
36	Freddy Guzman	.25
37	Estee Harris	.25
38	Sean Henn	.25
39	Aaron Hill	.25
40	Mike Hinckley	.25
41	Ryan Howard	.45
42	Conor Jackson	.50
43	Chuck James	.50
44	Dan Johnson	.50
45	Adam Jones	.35
46	Justin Jones	.25
47	Kennard Jones	.25
48	Mike Jones	.25
49	Scott Kazmir	.60
50	Howie Kendrick	.25
51	Jon Knott	.25
52	David Krynzel	.25
53	Brandon League	.25
54	Fred Lewis	.25
55	Hector Made	.25
56	Mitch Maier	.25
57	Val Majewski	.25
58	Nick Markakis	.50
59	Adam Miller	.50
60	Jai Miller	.50
61	Matt Moses	.30
62	Bill Murphy	.25
63	Matt Murton	.25
64	Brad Nelson	.25
65	Scott Olsen	.25
66	Jerry Owens	.50
67	Lou Palmisano	.25
68	Xavier Paul	.25
69	Carlos Quentin	.25
70	Wilkin Ramirez	.25
71	Eric Reed	.25
72	Bronson Sardinha	.25
73	Jay Sborz	.25
74	Nate Schierholtz	.50
75	Cole Seifrig	.25
76	Kyle Sleeth	.25
77	Ian Stewart	.25
78	Nick Swisher	.50
79	Willy Taveras	.75
80	Luis Terrero	.25
81	Brad Thompson	.25
82	Chuck Tiffany	.25
83	Chin-Hui Tsao	.25
84	John VanBenschoten	.25
85	Joey Votto	.25
86	Brandon Weeden	.25
87	Rickie Weeks	.75
88	Brandon Wood	.40
89	Jake Woods	.25
90	Kevin Youkilis	.25

2004 Just Prospects Autographs

Autographed cards of up to 50 of the players in Just Prospects 2004 were available in four varieties. Base autographs, were generally produced in an edition of 725 (unless otherwise indicated parenthetically in the checklist). Silver parallels were serially numbered to 200 each and were produced for retail-only distribution. Gold autographs were sold only as complete sets in a 50-per-card edition. Black autographs were limited to 25 for each player.

		MT
Common Player, White:		3.00
Silver:		1.5X
Complete Gold Set (50):		325.00
Gold:		2X
Black:		4X
1	Abe Alvarez	3.00
4	Cha Baek (225)	4.00
6	Wladimir Balentien	4.00
7	Josh Banks	3.00
8	Tim Battle Jr.	3.00
11	Craig Brazell	3.00
12	Jonathan Broxton	3.00
13	David Bush	4.00
15	Melky Cabrera	4.00
16	Brent Cleven	3.00
21	David DeJesus	4.00
23	Victor Diaz (225)	3.00
24	Jake Dittler	3.00
25	Steve Doetsch	3.00
26	Edwin Encarnacion	3.00
27	Matt Esquivel	4.00
28	Andre Ethier	3.00
31	Joey Gathright	4.00
32	Tony Giarratano	4.00
33	Ryan Goleski	4.00
34	Ruben Gotay	3.00
35	Zack Greinke (100) (no Silver, two Gold)	15.00
38	Sean Henn	4.00
40	Mike Hinckley	3.00
41	Ryan Howard	6.00
43	Chuck James	6.00
44	Dan Johnson	6.00
46	Justin Jones (225)	4.00
52	David Krynzel	4.00
53	Brandon League	3.00
54	Fred Lewis	3.00
55	Hector Made (225)	3.00
57	Val Majewski	3.00
59	Adam Miller	15.00
60	Jai Miller (225)	4.00
61	Bill Murphy	4.00
63	Matt Murton	6.00
66	Jerry Owens (225)	4.00
67	Lou Palmisano	4.00
71	Eric Reed	3.00
72	Bronson Sardinha	3.00
75	Cole Seifrig (225)	3.00
79	Willy Taveras	6.00
80	Luis Terrero	3.00
81	Brad Thompson	3.00
82	Chuck Tiffany (225)	5.00
85	Joey Votto	5.00
86	Brandon Weeden (225)	4.00
89	Jake Woods	3.00

2004 Just Rookies Preview

Ten top prospects were selected for this edition. Unsigned cards were available in complete-set form or as singles in lots of 10-500 either directly from the manufacturer or through its network of retailers. Production was announced as 15,000 white sets, 5,000 silver, 100 serially numbered gold and 50 serially numbered sets in black.

		MT
Complete Set (10):		3.00
Common Player:		.50
Silver:		1X
Gold:		5X
Black:		8X
1	Thomas Diamond	.50
2	Mitch Einertson	1.00
3	Greg Golson	.50
4	Javier Herrera	.50
5	Chris Nelson	.75
6	Mark Rogers	.50
7	Anibal Sanchez	.50
8	Luis Soto	.50
9	Marcos Vechionacci	.50
10	Neil Walker	.50

2004 Just Rookies Preview Autographs

Ten elite prospects were selected for this edition. Autographed cards were available directly from the manufacturer. Base (white bordered) version were sold individually. Gold cards, in an edition of 50 each were sold only as complete sets. Black versions were sold singly in an edition of 25.

	MT
Complete Set (10):	40.00
Common Player:	4.00
Silver:	1.5X
Gold:	2X
Black:	3X
1 Thomas Diamond	6.00
2 Mitch Einertson	5.00
3 Greg Golson	4.00
4 Javier Herrera	6.00
5 Chris Nelson	6.00
6 Mark Rogers	6.00
7 Anibal Sanchez	5.00
8 Luis Soto	5.00
9 Marcos Vechionacci	4.00
10 Neil Walker	4.00

2004 Just Rookies

Some of the top minor league players of 2004, including some making their earliest baseball card appearance, are featured in this set. For the first time in several years, cards were packaged in traditional wax packs, as well as being sold as singles and/or sets either directly from the manufacturer or through its hobby retailer outlets. The base (white) set was produced in an edition of 15,000. Silver sets were produced in an edition of 5,000; golds to 100 and blacks in an edition of 50 serially numbered cards each.

	MT
Complete Set (90):	15.00
Common Player:	.25
Silver:	1.5X
Gold:	8X
Black:	16X
1 Nick Adenhart	1.00
2 Ezequiel Astacio	.25
3 Homer Bailey	.25
4 Josh Baker	.25
5 Collin Balester	.25
6 Jon Barratt	.25
7 William Bergolla	.25
8 Kyle Bono	.50
9 Bill Bray	.50
10 Billy Buckner	.25
11 Ambiorix Burgos	.25
12 Greg Burns	.25
13 Matt Bush	.75
14 Mike Butia	.25
15 Billy Butler	.75
16 Asdrubal Cabrera	.50
17 Juan Cedeno	.25
18 Ambiorix Concepcion	.50
19 Luis Cota	.50
20 Frank Curreri	.25
21 Blake DeWitt	.50
22 Brian Dopirak	.75
23 Cory Dunlap	.50
24 Scott Elbert	.50
25 Dana Eveland	.25
26 Mike Ferris	.25
27 Jeff Frazier	.25
28 Jonathan Fulton	.50
29 Gio Gonzalez	.50
30 Rafael Gonzalez	.25
31 Javy Guerra	.50
32 David Haehnel	.50
33 Adam Harben	.50
34 Ryan Harvey	.25
35 Danny Hill	.25
36 Jamie Hoffmann	.50
37 Jesse Hoover	.25
38 Tommy Hottovy	.25
39 John Hudgins	.25
40 Hernan Iribarren	.50
41 Jason Jaramillo	.25
42 A.J. Johnson	.25
43 Blake Johnson	.25
44 Jon Lester	.25
45 Jeff Marquez	.25
46 Sean Marshall	.50
47 Louis Marson	.25
48 Eddy Martinez-Esteve	.75
49 Brian McFall	.25
50 Jacob McGee	.35
51 Joey Metropoulos	.25
52 Scott Mitchinson	.25
53 Eduardo Morlan	.25
54 Jake Mullinax	.25
55 Chris Nelson	.75
56 Fernando Nieve	.25
57 Justin Orenduff	.50
58 Jonathan Papelbon	.50
59 Jordan Parraz	.25
60 Dustin Pedroia	.50
61 Hayden Penn	1.00
62 Glen Perkins	.50
63 Trevor Plouffe	.50
64 Van Pope	.25
65 Landon Powell	.50
66 Jay Rainville	.50
67 Chris Ray	.25
68 Argenis Reyes	.25
69 Eric Ridener	.25
70 Mark Rogers	.75
71 Francisco Rosario	.25
72 Vinny Rottino	.25

73 Anibal Sanchez	.50
74 Ryan Shealy	.25
75 Johan Silva	.25
76 Brandon Sing	.25
77 Tony Sipp	.50
78 Luis Soto	.50
79 Huston Street	.50
80 Anthony Swarzak	.25
81 Ryan Sweeney	.35
82 Raul Tablado	.25
83 Curtis Thigpen	.25
84 Jason Vargas	.25
85 Marcos Vechionacci	.50
86 Miguel Vega	.25
87 Mark Worrell	.25
88 Brandon Yarbrough	.25
89 Chris Young	.25
90 Ben Zobrist	.50

2004 Just Rookies Autographs

NICK ADENHART

Autographed cards of 40 of the players in Just Rookies 2004 were available in four varieties. Base autographs were generally produced in an edition of 825 (unless otherwise indicated parenthetically in the checklist). Silver parallels were serially numbered to 100 each and were produced for retail-only distribution. Gold autographs were sold only as complete sets in a 50-per-card edition. Black autographs were limited to 25 for each player.

	MT
Common Player:	3.00
Silver:	1.5X
Complete Gold Set (40):	
Gold:	2X
Black:	4X
1 Nick Adenhart	3.00
3 Homer Bailey (325)	5.00
5 Collin Balester (325)	4.00
8 Kyle Bono (325)	4.00
9 Bill Bray (225)	5.00
10 Billy Buckner	3.00
14 Mike Butia (325)	4.00
20 Frank Curreri (325)	4.00
23 Cory Dunlap	3.00
26 Mike Ferris	3.00
27 Jeff Frazier	3.00
28 Jonathan Fulton (325)	5.00
31 Rafael Gonzalez	4.00
31 Javy Guerra (325)	4.00
33 Adam Harben	4.00
35 Danny Hill	3.00
37 Jesse Hoover (325)	4.00
41 Jason Jaramillo	3.00
44 Jon Lester	4.00
47 Jeff Marquez	4.00
47 Louis Marson (325)	4.00
50 Jacob McGee (325)	4.00
53 Eduardo Morlan	3.00
55 Chris Nelson (275)	7.50
57 Justin Orenduff	4.00
60 Dustin Pedroia (325)	20.00
63 Trevor Plouffe	4.00
66 Jay Rainville	4.00
66 Eric Ridener (325)	4.00
70 Mark Rogers	6.00
72 Vinny Rottino (325)	4.00
73 Anibal Sanchez	6.00
78 Luis Soto	6.00
79 Huston Street (325)	6.00
80 Anthony Swarzak	3.00
83 Curtis Thigpen	5.00
84 Jason Vargas	4.00
85 Marcos Vechionacci (325)	6.00
88 Brandon Yarbrough	3.00
90 Ben Zobrist	6.00

2004 Minor League Team Sets

Manufacturer abbreviations used are: GS - Grandstand, MA - Multi-Ad, CH - Choice, TM - Team

	MT
209 Sets and Variations	.00
2004 GS Aberdeen IronBirds (36)	14.50
2004 MA Akron Aeros (29)	11.00
2004 MA Albuquerque Isotopes (35)	11.00

2004 GS Altoona Curve (30)	11.00
2004 GS Altoona Curve Update (10)	7.50
2004 GS Appalachian League Top Prospects (31)	11.00
2004 GS Arkansas Travelers (30)	11.00
2004 CH Arkansas Travelers Strip (5)	15.00
2004 GS Asheville Tourists (33)	15.00
2004 TM Auburn Doubledays (49)	12.00
2004 MA Augusta Greenjackets (30)	17.50
2004 TM Batavia Muckdogs (45)	11.00
2004 CH Battle Creek Yankees (35)	10.00
2004 MA Beloit Snappers (30)	12.50
2004 GS Billings Mustangs (30)	11.00
2004 GS Binghamton Mets (29)	13.50
2004 GS Birmingham Barons (31)	11.00
2004 GS Bluefield Orioles (40)	11.00
2004 GS Boise Hawks (29)	12.00
2004 GS Bowie Bay Sox (30)	14.00
2004 CH Brevard County Manatees (30)	12.00
2004 CH Bridgeport Bluefish (31)	9.50
2004 GS Bristol White Sox (35)	11.00
2004 GS Brockton Rox (30)	9.50
2004 CH Brooklyn Cyclones (36)	11.00
2004 GS Buffalo Bisons (30)	12.00
2004 MA Burlington Bees (30)	11.00
2004 CH Camden Riversharks (30)	9.00
2004 MA Capital City Bombers (36)	10.00
2004 CH Carolina League Top Prospects (32)	11.00
2004 TM Carolina Mudcats (32)	11.00
2004 MA Casper Rockies (36)	11.00
2004 Team Cedar Rapids Kernels (34)	11.00
2004 MA Charleston Alley Cats (34)	11.00
2004 MA Charleston RiverDogs (33)	13.00
2004 MA Charleston RiverDogs Update (30)	22.50
2004 MA Char'ston RiverDogs Delmon Young (11)	12.50
2004 Team Charlotte Knights (31)	11.00
2004 GS Chattanooga Lookouts (30)	15.00
2004 MA Chillicothe Paints (27)	10.00
2004 GS Clearwater Threshers (30)	14.00
2004 GS Clinton LumberKings (32)	11.00
2004 GS Clinton Lumber Kings Strip Set (32)	25.00
2004 GS Clinton LumberKings Update (5)	5.00
2004 GS Coastal Bend Aviators (29)	9.50
2004 GS Colorado Springs Sky Sox (30)	10.00
2004 CH Columbus Clippers (30)	16.00
2004 GS Danville Braves (37)	11.00
2004 MA Dayton Dragons (30)	12.00
2004 GS Daytona Cubs (30)	20.00
2004 MA Delmarva Shorebirds (33)	11.00
2004 GS Dunedin Blue Jays (33)	13.00
2004 CH Durham Bulls (30)	12.00
2004 GS Eastern League Top Prospects (31)	16.00
2004 GS Edinburg Roadrunners (30)	11.00
2004 MA Edmonton Trappers (30)	14.00

2004 GS Elizabethton Twins (32)	11.00
2004 CH El Paso Diablos (31)	13.00
2004 MA Erie Sea Wolves (30)	11.00
2004 CH Erie Sea Wolves Update (1)	1.50
2004 GS Eugene Emeralds (32)	10.00
2004 GS Everett AquaSox (30)	13.00
2004 TM Fargo-Moorhead Redhawks (30)	10.00
2004 GS Florida State Lea. Top Prospects (25)	10.00
2004 GS Fort Myers Miracle (31)	11.00
2004 GS Fort Wayne Wizards (32)	10.00
2004 TM Fort Wayne Wizards Strip Set (15)	7.50
2004 CH Frederick Keys (30)	10.00
2004 CH Frederick Keys Anti-Smoking (30)	10.00
2004 MA Fresno Grizzlies (36)	11.00
2004 TM Frisco Rough Riders (30)	17.50
2004 TM Gateway Grizzlies (30)	10.00
2004 MA Greensboro Astros (30)	15.00
2004 MA Greensboro Bats (36)	10.00
2004 GS Greenville Braves (31)	11.00
2004 MA Hagerstown Suns (36)	11.00
2004 GS Harrisburg Senators (29)	11.00
2004 MA Hickory Crawdads (34)	10.00
2004 MA Hickory Crawdads Update (30)	10.00
2004 GS High Desert Mavericks (31)	11.00
2004 GS H.D. Mavericks Sponsor's Set (14)	14.00
2004 GS Hudson Valley Renegades (29)	11.00
2004 GS H.V. Renegades 10th Anniversary (32)	15.00
2004 TM Hudson Valley Renegades (29)	25.00
2004 Team Huntsville Stars (30)	22.50
2004 GS Idaho Falls Chukars (20)	12.00
2004 CH Indianapolis Indians (30)	10.00
2004 GS Inland Empire 66ers (31)	12.50
2004 CH International League All-Stars (33)	12.00
2004 CH Int'l League Top Prospects (30)	11.00
2004 MA Iowa Cubs (30)	14.00
2004 GS Jacksonville Suns (31)	11.00
2004 TM Jamestown Jammers (38)	20.00
2004 CH Johnson City Cardinals (35)	11.00
2004 MA Jupiter Hammerheads (36)	14.50
2004 GS Kane County Cougars (30)	16.00
2004 GS Kane Co. Cougars Sponsor's Set (30)	20.00
2004 GS Kane County Cougars Update (11)	12.00
2004 MA Kannapolis Intimidators (35)	11.00
2004 GS Kansas City T-Bones (30)	9.00
2004 GS Kingsport Mets (32)	10.00
2004 GS Kinston Indians (30)	13.00
2004 CH Lake County Captains (30)	12.00
2004 GS Lake Elsinore Storm (30)	13.00
2004 GS Lakeland Tigers (28)	13.50
2004 CH Lakewood BlueClaws (31)	12.50
2004 CH Best of Lakewood Blue Claws (25)	13.50
2004 GS Lancaster JetHawks (30)	10.00
2004 GS Lansing Lugnuts (26)	12.00
2004 MA Las Vegas 51s (33)	11.00
2004 MA Lexington Legends (31)	10.00
2004 CH Louisville Bats (36)	24.00
2004 CH Lowell Spinners (38)	11.00
2004 CH Lynchburg Hillcats (30)	11.00
2004 Team Lynchburg Hillcats (30)	16.00
2004 MA Mahoning Valley Scrappers (30)	10.00
2004 MA Memphis Redbirds (30)	11.00
2004 GS Midland RockHounds (28)	10.00
2004 One Hour Photo Midland RockHounds (21)	62.50

2004 Team Midwest League All-Stars (72)	13.50
2004 GS Midwest League Top Prospects (28)	12.50
2004 GS Missoula Osprey (30)	11.00
2004 GS Modesto A's (28)	11.00
2004 GS Montgomery Biscuits (33)	13.50
2004 CH Myrtle Beach Pelicans (40)	11.00
2004 MA Nashville Sounds (36)	12.00
2004 CH Newark Bears (30)	17.50
2004 GS New Britain Rock Cats (37)	11.00
2004 CH New Hampshire Fisher Cats (31)	12.00
2004 GS New Jersey Cardinals (33)	11.00
2004 CH New Jersey Jackals (30)	9.00
2004 MA New Orleans Zephyrs (30)	10.00
2004 CH NY-Penn League Top Prospects (30)	12.50
2004 CH Norfolk Tides (37)	13.50
2004 GS Northwest League All-Star Game (55)	17.50
2004 GS Norwich Navigators (30)	11.00
2004 TM Ogden Raptors (42)	15.00
2004 MA Oklahoma RedHawks (30)	11.00
2004 MA Omaha Royals (31)	11.00
2004 CH Ottawa Lynx (30)	12.00
2004 MA Pacific Coast League All-Stars (29)	11.00
2004 MA Pacific Coast League Prospects (36)	12.00
2004 MA Palm Beach Cardinals (36)	15.00
2004 CH Pawtucket Red Sox (30)	11.00
2004 DD Pawtucket Red Sox Foldout (30)	15.00
2004 MA Peoria Chiefs (30)	14.50
2004 MA Portland Beavers (32)	12.00
2004 GS Portland Sea Dogs (33)	11.00
2004 CH Potomac Cannons (30)	11.00
2004 GS Princeton Devil Rays (33)	11.00
2004 TM Princeton Devil Rays (30)	45.00
2004 TM Provo Angels (40)	11.00
2004 CH Pulaski Blue Jays (41)	10.00
2004 GS Swing of the Quad Cities (30)	12.50
2004 TM Capitales de Quebec (28)	9.50
2004 GS Rancho Cugamonga Quakes (30)	13.50
2004 MA Reading Phillies (30)	14.00
2004 MA Reading Area CC Reading Phillies (30)	12.50
2004 TM Reading Phillies Magnets (20)	20.00
2004 CH Richmond Braves (30)	10.00
2004 CH Richmond Braves Diamond 20th (22)	20.00
2004 CH Rochester Red Wings (30)	11.00
2004 GS Rockford RiverHawks (32)	9.50
2004 MA Rome Braves (32)	13.50
2004 GS Round Rock Express (30)	11.00
2004 MA Sacramento River Cats (30)	11.00
2004 GS Salem Avalanche (30)	11.00
2004 GS Salem-Keizer Volcanoes (36)	12.00
2004 GS Salem-Keizer Volcanoes Update (6)	8.00
2004 MA Salt Lake Stingers (30)	11.00
2004 CH San Antonio Missions (31)	11.00
2004 GS San Jose Giants (30)	11.00
2004 GS Sarasota Red Sox (30)	10.00
2004 MA Savannah Sand Gnats (36)	11.00
2004 CH Scranton/Wilkes-Barre Red Barons (32)	10.00
2004 TM Sioux City Explolorers (24)	9.50
2004 MA Sioux Falls Canaries (30)	9.50
2004 MA S. Atlantic League Top Prospects (32)	11.00
2004 GS South Bend Silver Hawks (33)	10.00
2004 GS Southern League Top Prospects (31)	12.00
2004 GS Spokane Indians (33)	12.00
2004 CH Staten Islands Yankees (34)	10.00
2004 GS St. Lucie Mets (33)	11.00

2004 CH Stockton Ports (30)	11.00
2004 TM St. Paul Saints (32)	10.00
2004 CH Syracuse SkyChiefs (31)	11.00
2004 MA Tacoma Rainiers (37)	12.50
2004 GS Tampa Yankees (29)	11.00
2004 GS Tennessee Smokies (28)	10.00
2004 GS Texas League Top Prospects (25)	11.00
2004 CH Toledo Mudhens (30)	11.00
2004 MA Trenton Thunder (31)	12.50
2004 GS Tri-City Dust Devils (32)	10.00
2004 CH Tri-City ValleyCats (35)	13.00
2004 MA Tucson Sidewinders (36)	11.00
2004 TM Tulsa Drillers (31)	11.00
2004 TM Vancouver Canadians (45)	11.00
2004 GS Vermont Expos (36)	10.00
2004 GS Vero Beach Dodgers (30)	16.00
2004 GS Visalia Oaks (30)	13.00
2004 CH West Michigan Whitecaps (30)	11.00
2004 GS West Tenn Diamond Jaxx (32)	10.00
2004 GS Wichita Wranglers (28)	11.00
2004 CH Williamsport Crosscutters (38)	13.00
2004 CH Wilmington Blue Rocks (32)	10.00
2004 TM Winnipeg Goldeyes (28)	10.00
2004 CH Winston-Salem Warthogs (30)	11.00
2004 GS Wisconsin Timber Rattlers (30)	10.00
2004 GS Yakima Bears (33)	11.00

Chronological Index

Alphabetical Index